The National Hockey League

Official Guide & Record Book 2011

2 •

THE NATIONAL HOCKEY LEAGUE
Official Guide & Record Book/2011

TERMS & CONDITIONS FOR USING THE DATA CONTAINED IN THIS BOOK

ATTENTION: PLEASE READ THIS DOCUMENT CAREFULLY BEFORE USING THIS BOOK (THE "BOOK") AND/OR THE DATA IT CONTAINS (THE "DATA"). INDIVIDUALS OR ENTITIES USING THE DATA ("END USERS") AGREE TO BE BOUND BY THE TERMS OF THIS LICENSE. IF YOU DO NOT AGREE TO THE TERMS OF THIS LICENSE, DO NOT USE THE DATA AND PROMPTLY RETURN THE UNUSED BOOK AND PROOF OF PAYMENT TO THE FOLLOWING ADDRESS FOR A REFUND:

> Dan Diamond & Associates, Inc.
> 194 Dovercourt Road, Toronto, Ontario, M6J 3C8
> dda.nhl@sympatico.ca.

Dan Diamond & Associates, Inc. (the "Publisher") owns, and retains ownership of, the Data. The Publisher reserves any right not expressly granted to End Users.

1. License. End-Users are granted a limited, non-exclusive license to do only the following, subject to the restrictions set out in Section 2 below:
   (a) End-Users may use the Data for personal, non-commercial purposes.
   (b) End-Users may reproduce individual player records, tables and data panels in connection with bona fide private study and research.
   (c) End-Users who are journalists may reproduce individual player records, tables and data panels for use by the broadcast and print media.

2. Restrictions. End-Users may NOT reproduce the Data, in whole or in part, in any form or by any means, electronic or mechanical, including photocopying, recording, or by any information storage and retrieval system now known or hereafter invented, without written permission from the Publisher. End-Users may NOT sublicense, assign, or distribute (via the World Wide Web or otherwise) copies of the Data, in whole or in part, to others. END-USERS MAY NOT MODIFY, ADAPT, TRANSLATE, RENT, LEASE, LOAN, RESELL FOR PROFIT, DISTRIBUTE, OR OTHERWISE ASSIGN OR TRANSFER THE DATA, OR CREATE DERIVATIVE WORKS BASED UPON THE DATA OR ANY PART THEREOF, EXCEPT AS PROVIDED ABOVE.

3. Commercial Users. Commercial users (such as sports reference and sports gaming websites) may obtain a license to use customized Data upon payment of a reasonable fee. Please contact the Publisher at the address provided above.

4. Termination. This License is effective until terminated. This License will terminate immediately without notice from the Publisher if the End User fails to comply with any of its provisions. Upon termination End Users must destroy the Data and all copies thereof.

5. General. This License will be governed by and construed in accordance with the laws of the province of Ontario and the laws of Canada applicable therein, and shall inure to the benefit of the Publisher and End-Users and their successors, assigns and legal representatives. If any provision of this License is held by a court of competent jurisdiction to be invalid or unenforceable to any extent under applicable law, that provision will be enforced to the maximum extent permissible and the remaining provisions of this License will remain in full force and effect. Any notices or other communications to be sent to the Publishers must be mailed first class, postage prepaid, to the address provided above. This Agreement constitutes the entire agreement between the parties with respect to the subject matter hereof, and all prior proposals, agreements, representations, statements and undertakings are hereby expressly cancelled and superseded. This Agreement may not be changed or amended except by a written instrument executed by a duly authorized officer of the Publisher.

6. Acknowledgment. BY USING THE DATA, THE END-USER ACKNOWLEDGES THAT IT HAS READ THIS LICENSE, UNDERSTANDS IT, AND AGREES TO BE BOUND BY ITS TERMS AND CONDITIONS. Should you have any questions concerning this License, contact the Publisher at the address provided above.

2Copyright © 2010 by the National Hockey League.
Compiled by the NHL Public Relations Department and the 30 NHL Club Public Relations Directors.
Printed in Canada. All rights reserved under the Pan-American and International Copyright Conventions.
Published in Canada by: Dan Diamond and Associates, Inc., 194 Dovercourt Road, Toronto, Ontario M6J 3C8 Canada
ISBN in Canada 978-1-894801-19-5
Published in the United States by: Triumph Books, 542 South Dearborn Street, Chicago, Illinois 60605
ISBN in USA 978-1-60078-422-4

Staff

For the NHL: Dave McCarthy; Supervising Editor: Greg Inglis; Statistician: Benny Ercolani;
Editorial Staff: Dave Baker, John Dellapina, David Keon, Jen Raimondi, Kelley Rosset, Susan Snow, Julie Young.

Senior Managing Editor: Ralph Dinger | **Associate Managing Editor:** Paul Bontje
Production Editors: John Pasternak, Alex Dubiel, Becky Gowing | **Photo Editor:** Eric Zweig
Publisher: Dan Diamond

Data Management and Typesetting: Caledon Data Management, Eden, Ontario
Film Output and Scanning: Embassy Graphics, Toronto, Ontario
Printing: Sunrise Consulting Inc., Port Perry, Ontario; Webcom Limited, Toronto, Ontario
Production Management: Dan Diamond and Associates, Inc., Toronto, Ontario
Contributors and Photo Credits: see page 663

Distribution

Trade sales and distribution in Canada by:
North 49 Books, 35 Prince Andrew Drive, Toronto, Ontario M3C 2H2 416/449-4000; Fax 416/449-9924
Dan Diamond and Associates, Inc., Toronto 416/531-6535; Fax 416/531-3939 dda.nhl@sympatico.ca www.nhlofficialguide.com

Trade sales and distribution in the United States by:
Triumph Books, 542 South Dearborn Street, Chicago, Illinois 60605 312/939-3330; Fax 312/663-3557

International representatives:
Barkers Worldwide Publications, Unit 6/7 The Elms Centre, Glaziers Lane, Normandy, Guildford, Surrey GU3 2DF England
Tel 011/441/483/811-971; Fax 011/441/483/811-972 sales@bwwp.co.uk www.bwwp.co.uk

Licensed by the National Hockey League®
NHL and the NHL Shield are registered trademarks of the National Hockey League.
All NHL logos and marks and team logos and marks depicted herein are the property of the NHL and the respective teams and may not be reproduced without the prior written consent of Enterprises, L.P. © NHL 2010. All Rights Reserved.

The National Hockey League

1185 Avenue of the Americas, 14th Floor, New York, New York 10036
1800 McGill College Ave., Suite 2600, Montreal, Quebec H3A 3J6
50 Bay Street, 11th Floor, Toronto, Ontario M5J 2X8

Table of Contents

Table of Contents *continued*

Introduction

WELCOME TO THE **79**TH EDITION OF *THE NATIONAL HOCKEY LEAGUE OFFICIAL GUIDE & RECORD BOOK*, the definitive statistical record of the NHL. As always, if it has happened in this League, or is about to happen, it's in the *Guide*. The 2010 Stanley Cup champion Chicago Blackhawks are a prime example. Just three years after entering the NHL together and earning All-Rookie Team honors in 2007-08 (page 231), Jonathan Toews and Patrick Kane reached superstar status in 2009-10. Their seasons culminated with Kane scoring the Stanley Cup-winning goal in overtime to give the Blackhawks their first title since 1961 and the glory days of Bobby Hull and Stan Mikita. As captain, Toews was not only the first Chicago player in 49 years to hoist the Stanley Cup, he also won the Conn Smythe Trophy as playoff MVP.

For Toews, the Stanley Cup capped an astonishing 2009-10 that included an Olympic gold medal. Though it was Pittsburgh Penguins superstar Sidney Crosby who scored the "Golden Goal" in overtime to give Team Canada a 3-2 victory over the United States in the final game, Toews tied for the tournament lead with seven assists, was Canada's top scorer with eight points and was named the best forward at the Olympics. Patrick Kane and his American teammates led by New Jersey's Zach Parise and Buffalo goalie Ryan Miller—the Olympic MVP—had to settle for silver, but for Kane, his first appearance among the NHL's top 10 scorers (see page 136 and 157), his selection to the First All-Star Team at right wing (page 227) and, of course, his own overtime heroics in June made his 2009-10 campaign one to remember. A list of every overtime playoff game since 1918 begins on 267. A 2010 Olympic Hockey Review is found on page 13.

All around the NHL in 2009-10, a new wave of young stars continued to make their mark. Steven Stamkos didn't turn 20 until February of 2010 but the second-year player, who was picked first overall by the Tampa Bay Lightning in the 2008 Entry Draft, scored 51 goals and shared the League goal-scoring lead with Sidney Crosby. (A complete Draft history begins on page 212.)

Crosby and Washington's Alex Ovechkin both finished the season tied with 109 points to mark the fourth time in five years that each of them has reached the century mark. Ovechkin's teammate Nicklas Backstrom topped 100 for the first time in 2009-10 and has established himself as an elite player. The League's top scorer in 2009-10 was Vancouver's Henrik Sedin, who set a club record with 112 points and became the ninth different player in the last nine years to win the Art Ross Trophy as the League's scoring leader. He is also the first player in Canucks history to win that award and the Hart Trophy as League MVP. (NHL Awards, page 204.) Henrik was also a First-Team All-Star for the first time, while his twin brother Daniel earned his first selection to the Second Team.

Veterans also made their presence known in 2009-10, and perhaps none more so than New Jersey's Martin Brodeur. A year after breaking Patrick Roy's career record of 551 victories, Brodeur surpassed Terry Sawchuk's long-standing mark of 103 career shutouts. Brodeur got #104 on December 21, 2009 and his league-leading nine shutouts on the season pushed his career total to 110. Brodeur also joined Roy as the only goalies to appear in 1,000 games and became the first to record 600 career victories during the 2009-10 season. (Complete goaltending records can be found beginning on page 176 and 186).

At every turn, the *NHL Official Guide & Record Book* reveals the increasing complexity and intricacy of on-ice play and off-ice team management. The book's Club section, which begins on page 15, offers four densely-packed pages containing 16 separate tables, lists or biographies for each of the League's 30 clubs. These include 2009-10's wins and losses and finish in the standings, Year-by-Year Record, Key Off-Season Signings/Acquisitions, 2010-11 Schedule, 2009-10 Schedule Results, 2010-11 Player Personnel, 2009-10 Regular-Season and Playoff Scoring and Goaltending totals, Club Records, All-Time Record vs. Other Clubs, General Manager's biography, Coach's biography and year-by-year record, G.M., Coach and Captain's history, Entry Draft Selections from 2010 to 1996 and a Front Office Club Directory. This Club Directory, found on the final page of each Club's section, reveals how the game is changing. Compared to the *NHL Guide* of 25 years ago, a typical Club Directory consisted of approximately 50 names; today that same Club Directory would likely include more than 120. In the 1986-87 edition, some teams had goaltending coaches, but none had strength and conditioning coaches, mental skills coaches, social media coordinators, managers of digital media, video scoreboard producers, graphic artists and mascot coordinators, to name just a few of the positions found on a modern NHL club's organizational list.

As always in the *NHL Guide & Record Book*, every one of the more than 6,000 players who have appeared in an NHL game, plus more than 1,000 prospects who have yet to do so, are in this book, either in the Prospect Register (275), Active Player Register (345), Goaltender Register (583), Retired Players Index (610), regular-season or playoff Record Books (166 and 242), Award Winners (204), All-Star Teams (227) or Hockey Hall of Fame sections (235). A special tribute to the 2010 inductees to the Hockey Hall of Fame is found on page 657 and winners of the NHL's Player of the Week and Month Awards for 2009-10 are listed on page 656. A register of free agent signings begins on page 658 and a trade register is found on page 660.

A key to the abbreviations and symbols used in individual player and goaltender data panels, along with useful information on how to use the Registers, is found on page 274. Late additions are found on page 609 and each NHL club's minor-pro affiliates are found on page 14. A list of league abbreviations used in the Prospect, Player and Goaltender Registers is found on page 662 and a useful table on page 216 breaks down U.S. and Canadian-born draftees by state or province of birth. Players from 21 states and nine provinces were drafted in 2010.

As always, our thanks to readers, correspondents and members of the media who take the time to comment on the *Guide & Record Book*. Thanks as well to the people working in the communications departments of the NHL's member clubs and to their counterparts in minor pro, junior, college and European hockey.

Best wishes for an enjoyable 2010-11 season.

ACCURACY REMAINS THE *GUIDE & RECORD BOOK*'S TOP PRIORITY.
We appreciate comments and clarification from our readers. Please direct these to:

- Ralph Dinger   Senior Managing Editor, 194 Dovercourt Road, Toronto, Ontario M6J 3C8. e-mail: ralph.dda@sympatico.ca.
- Greg Inglis   1185 Avenue of the Americas, New York, New York 10036 . . . or . . .
- David Keon   50 Bay Street, 11th Floor, Toronto, Ontario, M5J 2X8

Your involvement makes a better book.

NATIONAL HOCKEY LEAGUE

New York, 1185 Avenue of the Americas, New York, NY 10036,
212/789-2000, Fax: 212/789-2020, PR Fax: 212/789-2070

Montréal, 1800 McGill College Avenue, Suite 2600, Montréal, Québec, H3A 3J6
514/841-9220, Fax: 514/841-1070

Toronto, 50 Bay Street, 11th Floor, Toronto, Ontario, M5J 2X8 • 416/359-7900, Fax: 416/981-2779

League and Club websites: www.nhl.com

Executive
Commissioner ....Gary B. Bettman
Deputy Commissioner ....William Daly
Chief Operating Officer ....John Collins
Senior Executive Vice President of Hockey Operations ....Colin Campbell

NHL Critical Dates 2010-11

September

10	Opening Day of Rookie Camps
14	NHL Board of Governors Meeting
17	Opening Day of NHL Training Camps
21	Pre-season schedule begins
28	Kraft Hockeyville Game – Buffalo Sabres vs. Ottawa Senators (Dundas, ON)

October
1	Hockey Fights Cancer Awareness Month
6	Opening Day Playing Rosters set (3:00 p.m. ET)
7	Opening Night – 93rd NHL Regular Season begins
7	NHL Face-Off (Toronto)
7	2010 Compuware NHL Premiere – Carolina at Minnesota (Helsinki, FIN)
7	Official Opening of CONSOL Energy Center - Philadelphia at Pittsburgh
8	2010 Compuware NHL Premiere – Minnesota at Carolina (Helsinki, FIN)
8	2010 Compuware NHL Premiere – Columbus at San Jose (Stockholm, SWE)
9	2010 Compuware NHL Premiere – San Jose at Columbus (Stockholm, SWE)
9	2010 Compuware NHL Premiere – Phoenix at Boston (Prague, CZE)
9	Stanley Cup Banner Raised – Detroit at Chicago
10	2010 Compuware NHL Premiere – Boston at Phoenix (Prague, CZE)
21	U.S. Hockey Hall of Fame Induction Ceremony (Buffalo, NY)
	Inductees: Art Berglund, Derian Hatcher, Kevin Hatcher,
	Dr. George V. Nagobads, Jeremy Roenick
23	Missouri Hockey Day (USA Hockey and NHL)
27 or 28	A Celebration of Lester Patrick (Boston, MA)
	Recipients: Cam Neely, David Andrews, Jerry York, Jack Parker
30	Texas Hockey Day (USA Hockey and NHL)
30	Busiest Day in NHL season – 28 teams play

November
6	Hockey Hall of Fame Game (Buffalo at Toronto)
6	New England Hockey Day (USA Hockey and NHL)
7	Hockey Hall of Fame Legends Classic (Toronto, ON)
8	Hockey Hall of Fame Induction Ceremony (Toronto, ON)
	Inductees: Dino Ciccarelli, Cammi Granato, Angela James (Player category);
	Jim Devellano, the late Daryl "Doc" Seaman (Builder category)
9	NHL General Managers Meeting (Toronto)

December
1	Signing deadline for Group 2 free agents
6-7	NHL Board of Governors Meeting (Palm Beach, FL)
11	Western New York Hockey Day (USA Hockey and NHL)
19-27	Holiday Roster Freeze in effect. For all players on an NHL active roster, injured reserve, or players with non-roster and injured non-roster status as of midnight, local time, December 19, a roster freeze shall apply through midnight local time December 27, with respect to waivers, trades and loans, subject to the exceptions provided for in CBA Article 16.10.
24-25	No scheduled practices - dressing rooms closed
26 – Jan.5	IIHF World U20 Championship (Buffalo, NY)

January
1	2011 Bridgestone NHL Winter Classic – Washington at Pittsburgh (Heinz Field, PIttsburgh)
27-31	NHL All-Star Break (no games played)
28	NHL Board of Governors Meeting (Raleigh)
29	Honda SuperSkills, 7 p.m., Raleigh, NC (RBC Center)
30	58th NHL All-Star Game, 4 p.m., Raleigh, NC (RBC Center)

February
1	Hockey is for Everyone Month
1	NHL Regular Season Schedule Resumes
12	CBC's Hockey Day in Canada (Host: Whitehorse, YT) Ottawa at Edmonton; Toronto at Montreal; Calgary at Vancouver
18-20	Hockey Weekend Across America (USA Hockey)
20	Hockey Day in America
20	2011 NHL Heritage Classic – Montreal at Calgary (McMahon Stadium, Calgary)
28	Trade deadline (3:00 p.m. ET)
TBA	NHL on NBC (game of the week coverage begins)
TBA	Home Hardware CHL/NHL Top Prospects Game (QMJHL)

March
14-16	NHL General Managers Meeting (Boca Raton, FL)

April
7-9	NCAA Frozen Four (Xcel Energy Center, St. Paul, MN)
10	Last day of 2010-11 regular season
13	Stanley Cup Playoffs begin
14-24	IIHF U18 World Championship (Germany)
29-May 15	IIHF World Championship (Ondrej Nepela Arena in Bratislava and Ladislav Trojak Arena in Kosice, Slovakia)
30	2011 RBC Royal Bank Cup (Edgeworth Centre, Camrose, AB)

May
20-29	2011 Mastercard Memorial Cup (Hershey Centre, Mississauga, ON)
29-June 4	NHL Combine (Location: TBA)

June
17/18	Last possible day for 2011 Stanley Cup Final
TBA	Deadline for first club-elected salary arbitration (later of June 15 or 48 hours after the conclusion of the Stanley Cup Final, 5:00 p.m. ET)
22	2011 NHL Awards (Las Vegas, Nevada)
24-25	NHL Entry Draft (Xcel Energy Center, St. Paul, MN)

July
1	Free Agency period begins
5	Deadline for player-elected salary arbitration notification (5:00 p.m. ET)
6	Deadline for club-elected salary arbitration notification (5:00 p.m. ET)
20 – Aug. 4	Salary arbitration hearings held

August
6	Deadline for salary arbitration decisions to be rendered

BOARD OF GOVERNORS
Chairman of the Board – Jeremy M. Jacobs
Vice Chair – Tom Hicks

Anaheim Ducks
Michael Schulman...................................... Governor
Michael Schulman ....Alternate Governor
Tim Ryan ....Alternate Governor
Bob Murray ....Alternate Governor

Atlanta Thrashers
Bruce Levenson...Governor
Don Waddell ....Alternate Governor
J. Rutherford Seydel, II ....Alternate Governor
Ed Peskowitz ....Alternate Governor

Boston Bruins
Jeremy M. Jacobs.......................................Governor
Charles Jacobs ....Alternate Governor
Jeremy Jacobs, Jr..........................Alternate Governor
Louis Jacobs ....Alternate Governor
Harry J. Sinden ....Alternate Governor
Cam Neely....................................Alternate Governor

Buffalo Sabres
B. Thomas Golisano .... Governor
Lawrence Quinn ....Alternate Governor
Daniel J. DiPofi ....Alternate Governor
Darcy Regier ....Alternate Governor

Calgary Flames
N. Murray Edwards......................................Governor
Harley N. Hotchkiss......................Alternate Governor
Ken King ....Alternate Governor
Alvin Libin ....Alternate Governor
Darryl Sutter ....Alternate Governor

Carolina Hurricanes
Peter Karmanos, Jr. ....Governor
Jim Rutherford..............................Alternate Governor
Michael Amendola ....Alternate Governor
Jason Karmanos ....Alternate Governor

Chicago Blackhawks
W. Rockwell Wirtz ....Governor
Robert J. Pulford...........................Alternate Governor
John A. Ziegler, Jr..........................Alternate Governor
John McDonough..........................Alternate Governor

Colorado Avalanche
Stan Kroenke ....Governor
Pierre Lacroix ....Alternate Governor
Paul Andrews ....Alternate Governor
Mark Waggoner ....Alternate Governor
Greg Sherman ....Alternate Governor

Columbus Blue Jackets
John P. McConnell ....Governor
Mike Priest ....Alternate Governor
Scott Howson...............................Alternate Governor

Dallas Stars
Tom Hicks ....Governor
Jeffrey Cogen ....Alternate Governor
Tom Hicks, Jr................................Alternate Governor
Brett Hull......................................Alternate Governor

Detroit Red Wings
Michael Ilitch...Governor
Jim Devellano ....Alternate Governor
Ken Holland ....Alternate Governor
Christopher Ilitch ....Alternate Governor
Rob Carr ....Alternate Governor
Tom Wilson ....Alternate Governor

Edmonton Oilers
Daryl Katz ....Governor
Patrick LaForge ....Alternate Governor
Kevin Lowe ....Alternate Governor
Bob Black ....Alternate Governor

Florida Panthers
Cliff Viner ....Governor
Bill Torrey ....Alternate Governor
Michael Yormark ....Alternate Governor
Stu Siegel ....Alternate Governor

Los Angeles Kings
Timothy J. Leiweke ....Governor
Philip F. Anschutz.........................Alternate Governor
Luc Robitaille ....Alternate Governor
Dean Lombardi..............................Alternate Governor

Minnesota Wild
Craig Leopold ....Governor
Phil Falcone ....Alternate Governor
Jac Sperling ....Alternate Governor

Montréal Canadiens
Geoff Molson ....Governor
Pierre Boivin.................................Alternate Governor
Fred Steer.....................................Alternate Governor
Michael Andlauer ....Alternate Governor
Andrew T. Molson ....Alternate Governor
Pierre Gauthier ....Alternate Governor

Nashville Predators
Joel Dobberpuhl..Governor
Tom Cigarran ....Alternate Governor
Herbert Fritch ....Alternate Governor
Ed Lang ....Alternate Governor
David Poile ....Alternate Governor

New Jersey Devils
Lou Lamoriello ....Governor
Jeff Vanderbeek............................Alternate Governor
Michael Gilfillan ....Alternate Governor

New York Islanders
Charles Wang..Governor
Roy Reichbach ....Alternate Governor
Arthur J. McCarthy ....Alternate Governor
Michael J. Picker ....Alternate Governor
Garth Snow ....Alternate Governor

New York Rangers
James L. Dolan.. Governor
Glen Sather ....Alternate Governor
Hank Ratner ....Alternate Governor
Scott O'Neil ....Alternate Governor

Ottawa Senators
Eugene Melnyk...Governor
Sheldon Plener ....Alternate Governor
Cyril Leeder ....Alternate Governor
Erin Crowe ....Alternate Governor
Bryan Murray................................Alternate Governor

Philadelphia Flyers
Edward M. Snider ....Governor
Philip I. Weinberg ....Alternate Governor
Peter Luukko ....Alternate Governor
Paul Holmgren..............................Alternate Governor

Phoenix Coyotes
Don Maloney ....Alternate Governor
Mike Nealy ....Alternate Governor

Pittsburgh Penguins
Ronald Burkle ....Alternate Governor
Anthony Liberati............................Alternate Governor
Ray Shero ....Alternate Governor
David Morehouse ....Alternate Governor
Mario Lemieux...............................Alternate Governor

St. Louis Blues
Dave Checketts...Governor
Kenneth Munoz ....Alternate Governor
John Davidson ....Alternate Governor
Michael McCarthy ....Alternate Governor

San Jose Sharks
Greg Jamison...Governor
Kevin Compton ....Alternate Governor
Doug Wilson ....Alternate Governor

Tampa Bay Lightning
Jeff Vinik...Governor
Steve Yzerman ....Alternate Governor
Tod Leiweke ....Alternate Governor

Toronto Maple Leafs
Larry Tanenbaum ....Governor
Richard A. Peddie ....Alternate Governor
Dale Lastman................................Alternate Governor
Erol Uzumeri.................................Alternate Governor
Brian Burke...................................Alternate Governor

Vancouver Canucks
Francesco Aquilini.......................................Governor
Paolo Aquilini ....Alternate Governor
Roberto Aquilini ....Alternate Governor
Michael Gillis ....Alternate Governor
Victor de Boris ....Alternate Governor

Washington Capitals
Ted Leonsis ....Governor
Richard M. Patrick ....Alternate Governor
George McPhee.............................Alternate Governor

Commissioner and League Presidents

Gary B. Bettman

Gary B. Bettman took office as the NHL's first Commissioner on February 1, 1993. Since the League was formed in 1917, there have been five League Presidents.

NHL President	Years in Office
Frank Calder	1917-1943
Mervyn "Red" Dutton	1943-1946
Clarence Campbell	1946-1977
John A. Ziegler, Jr.	1977-1992
Gil Stein	1992-1993

Hockey Hall of Fame

Hockey Hall of Fame

Brookfield Place
30 Yonge Street
Toronto, Ontario M5E 1X8
Phone: 416/360-7735 • Executive Fax: 416/360-1501

William C. Hay – Chairman and Chief Executive Officer
Jeff Denomme – President, C.O.O. and Treasurer
Craig Baines – Vice President, Operations
Peter Jagla – Vice President, Marketing
Ron Ellis – Director, Public Affairs & Asst. to the President
Kelly Massé – Director, Corporate & Media Relations
Steve Ozimec – Manager, Special Events & Hospitality
Jacqueline Schwartz – Manager, Marketing & Promotions
Darren Boyko – Manager, Business Development

D.K. (Doc) Seaman Resource Centre and Archives Images On Ice

400 Kipling Avenue
Toronto, Ontario M8V 3L1
Phone: 416/360-7735 • Fax: 416/251-5770
www.hhof.com, www.imagesonice.net

Phil Pritchard – Vice President and Curator
Craig Campbell – Manager, Resource Centre & Archives
Izak Westgate – Manager, Outreach & Asst. Curator
Steve Poirier – Coord., HHOF Images & Archival Services
Miragh Bitove – Archivist & Collections Registrar
Photographers – Matthew Manor, Jukka Rautio and Dave Sanford

National Hockey League Players' Association

20 Bay Street, Suite 1700
Toronto, Ontario M5J 2N8
Phone: 416/313-2300 • Fax: 416/313-2301
www.nhlpa.com

Mike Ouellet – Chief of Business Affairs
Roman Stoykewych – Associate Counsel, Labour
Matt Nussbaum – Associate Counsel, Labour
Roland Lee – Director, Salary Cap and Marketplace and Associate Counsel
Adam Larry – Director, Licensing and Associate Counsel
Kim Murdoch – Director, Player Insurance & Pensions
Richard Smit – Director, Finance and HRR
Devin Smith – Director, Marketing & Community Relations
Jonathan Weatherdon – Director, Communications
Tyler Currie – Director, International Affairs
Stephen Frank – Director, Information Technology
Casey Rovinelli – Director, Digital Marketing

NHL On-Ice Officials

Total NHL Games and 2009-10 Games columns count regular-season games only.

Referees

#	Name	Birthplace	*Age	First NHL Game	Total NHL Games	2009-10 Games
15	Stephane Auger	Montreal, Que.	40	Apr 1/00	605	76
44	David Banfield	Halifax, N.S.	31	Mar 17/08	43	25
46	Frances Charron	Ottawa, Ont.	27	Apr 5/10	1	1
41	Chris Ciamaga	Buffalo, NY	33	Mar 22/08	39	23
10	Paul Devorski	Guelph, Ont.	52	Oct 14/89	1259	72
19	Gord Dwyer	Halifax, N.S.	33	Nov 19/05	317	76
27	Eric Furlatt	Trois-Rivieres, Que.	39	Oct 8/01	536	77
30	Mike Hasenfratz	Regina, Sask.	44	Oct 21/00	541	0
49	Ghislain Hebert	Bathurst, NB	29	Mar 2/09	11	10
43	Jean Hebert	Moncton, NB	30			
8	Dave Jackson	Montreal, Que.	46	Dec 22/90	1068	22
25	Marc Joannette	Verdun, Que.	42	Oct 1/99	658	76
18	Greg Kimmerly	Toronto, Ont.	46	Nov 30/96	745	76
32	Tom Kowal	Vernon, B.C.	43	Oct 29/99	543	76
40	Steve Kozari	Penticton, B.C.	37	Oct 15/05	269	76
14	Dennis LaRue	Savannah, GA	51	Mar 26/91	935	74
17	Frederick L'Ecuyer	Trois-Rivieres, Que.	33	Oct 11/07	65	36
28	Chris Lee	Saint John, N.B.	40	Apr 2/00	518	76
3	Mike Leggo	North Bay, Ont.	46	Mar 3/98	732	73
26	Rob Martell	Winnipeg, Man.	47	Mar 14/84	[1]628	73
4	Wes McCauley	Georgetown, Ont.	38	Jan 20/03	392	76
7	Bill McCreary	Guelph, Ont.	55	Nov 3/84	1669	72
34	Brad Meier	Dayton, OH	43	Oct 23/99	660	77
36	Dean Morton	Peterborough, Ont.	42	Nov 11/00	220	76
13	Dan O'Halloran	Essex, Ont.	46	Oct 1/95	813	75
9	Dan O'Rourke	Calgary, Alta.	38	Oct 2/99	[2]390	77
20	Tim Peel	Toronto, Ont.	44	Oct 21/99	668	76
16	Brian Pochmara	Detroit, MI	34	Dec 23/05	201	77
33	Kevin Pollock	Kincardine, Ont.	40	Mar 28/00	666	77
37	Kyle Rehman	Stettler, Alta.	32	Jan 22/08	46	29
5	Chris Rooney	Boston, MA	35	Nov 22/00	560	74
38	Francois St. Laurent	Greenfield Park, Que.	33	Nov 10/05	142	76
12	Justin St. Pierre	Dolbeau, Que.	38	Nov 9/05	321	76
11	Kelly Sutherland	Richmond, BC	39	Dec 19/00	602	77
21	Don Van Massenhoven	Parkhill, Ont.	50	Nov 11/93	1016	55
45	Marcus Vinnerborg	Ljungby, Sweden	38			
29	Ian Walsh	Philadelphia, PA	38	Oct 14/00	504	77
23	Brad Watson	Regina, Sask.	49	Mar 7/96	764	76

[1] plus 1 game as a linesman.   [2] plus 120 games as a linesman.

Linesmen

#	Name	Birthplace	*Age	First NHL Game	Total NHL Games	2009-10 Games
75	Derek Amell	Port Colborne, Ont.	42	Oct 11/97	800	76
59	Steve Barton	Vankleek Hill, Ont.	39	Nov 1/00	576	72
96	David Brisebois	Sudbury, Ont.	34	Oct 11/99	533	72
74	Lonnie Cameron	Victoria, B.C.	46	Oct 5/96	911	71
67	Pierre Champoux	Ville St-Pierre, Que.	47	Oct 8/88	1363	72
50	Scott Cherrey	Drayton, Ont.	34	Oct 6/07	193	72
76	Michel Cormier	Trois-Rivieres, Que.	36	Oct 10/03	437	72
88	Mike Cvik	Calgary, Alta.	48	Oct 8/87	1496	71
54	Greg Devorski	Guelph, Ont.	41	Oct 9/93	1076	71
68	Scott Driscoll	Seaforth, Ont.	42	Oct 10/92	1150	73
82	Ryan Galloway	Winnipeg, Man.	38	Oct 17/02	460	72
66	Darren Gibbs	Edmonton, Alta.	44	Oct 1/97	764	70
91	Don Henderson	Calgary, Alta.	42	Mar 11/95	899	71
55	Shane Heyer	Summerland, B.C.	46	Oct 6/88	[3]1075	72
71	Brad Kovachik	Woodstock, Ont.	39	Oct 10/96	879	71
86	Brad Lazarowich	Vancouver, B.C.	48	Oct 9/86	1590	72
78	Brian Mach	Little Falls, MN	36	Oct 7/00	640	72
90	Andy McElman	Chicago Heights, IL	49	Oct 3/93	1081	71
89	Steve Miller	Stratford, Ont.	38	Oct 11/00	628	72
97	Jean Morin	Sorel, Que.	47	Oct 5/91	1190	72
93	Brian Murphy	Dover, NH	46	Oct 7/88	[4]1278	71
95	Jonny Murray	Beauport, Que.	36	Oct 7/00	641	71
70	Derek Nansen	Ottawa, Ont.	39	Oct 11/02	489	62
80	Thor Nelson	Westminister, CA	42	Feb 16/95	795	71
77	Tim Nowak	Buffalo, NY	43	Oct 8/93	1083	72
94	Bryan Pancich	Great Falls, MT	28	Oct 3/09	45	45
65	Pierre Racicot	Verdun, Que.	43	Oct 12/93	1111	71
73	Vaughan Rody	Winnipeg, Man.	42	Oct 8/00	612	72
52	Dan Schachte	Madison, WI	52	Oct 6/82	1893	71
84	Anthony Sericolo	Troy, NY	42	Oct 21/98	733	69
57	Jay Sharrers	New Westminster, B.C.	43	Oct 6/90	[5]997	70
92	Mark Shewchyk	Waterdown, Ont.	35	Oct 9/03	437	73
56	Mark Wheler	North Battleford, Sask.	45	Oct 10/92	1175	71

[3] plus 386 games as a referee.   [4] plus 88 games as a referee.   [5] plus 136 games as a referee.

– Age at start of 2009-10 season

NHL History

1917 — National Hockey League organized November 26 in Montreal following suspension of operations by the National Hockey Association of Canada Limited (NHA). Montreal Canadiens, Montreal Wanderers, Ottawa Senators and Quebec Bulldogs attended founding meeting. Delegates decided to use NHA rules.

Toronto Arenas were later admitted as fifth team; Quebec decided not to operate during the first season. Quebec players allocated to remaining four teams.

Frank Calder elected president and secretary-treasurer.

First NHL games played December 19, with Toronto only arena with artificial ice. Clubs played 22-game split schedule.

1918 — Emergency meeting held January 3 due to destruction by fire of Montreal Arena which was home ice for both Canadiens and Wanderers.

Wanderers withdrew, reducing the NHL to three teams; Canadiens played remaining home games at 3,250-seat Jubilee rink.

Quebec franchise sold to P.J. Quinn of Toronto on October 18 on the condition that the team operate in Quebec City for 1918-19 season. Quinn did not attend the November League meeting and Quebec did not play in 1918-19.

1919-20 — NHL reactivated Quebec Bulldogs franchise. Former Quebec players returned to the club. New Mount Royal Arena became home of Canadiens. Toronto Arenas changed name to St. Patricks. Clubs played 24-game split schedule.

1920-21 — H.P. Thompson of Hamilton, Ontario made application for the purchase of an NHL franchise. Quebec franchise shifted to Hamilton with other NHL teams providing players to strengthen the club.

1921-22 — Split schedule abandoned. First and second place teams at the end of full schedule to play for championship.

1922-23 — Clubs agreed that players could not be sold or traded to clubs in any other league without first being offered to all other clubs in the NHL. Norman Albert made the first broadcast of a hockey game on February 8, 1923. The first NHL game was broadcast on February 14, 1923. Foster Hewitt called his first game on February 16, 1923. All games were broadcast on Toronto radio station CFCA.

1923-24 — Ottawa's new 10,000-seat arena opened. First U.S. franchise granted to Boston for following season.

Dr. Cecil Hart Trophy donated to NHL to be awarded to the player judged most useful to his team.

1924-25 — Canadian Arena Company of Montreal granted a franchise to operate Montreal Maroons. NHL now six team league with two clubs in Montreal. Inaugural game in new Montreal Forum played November 29, 1924 as Canadiens defeated Toronto 7-1.

Hamilton finished first in the standings, receiving a bye into the finals. But Hamilton players, demanding $200 each for additional games in the playoffs, went on strike. The NHL suspended all players, fining them $200 each. Stanley Cup finalist to be the winner of NHL semi-final between Toronto and Canadiens.

Prince of Wales and Lady Byng trophies donated to NHL.

Clubs played 30-game schedule.

1925-26 — Hamilton club dropped from NHL. Players signed by new New York Americans franchise. Pittsburgh Pirates granted franchise.

Clubs played 36-game schedule.

1926-27 — New York Rangers granted franchise May 15, 1926. Chicago Black Hawks and Detroit Cougars granted franchises September 25, 1926. NHL now ten-team league with an American and a Canadian Division.

Stanley Cup came under the control of NHL. In previous seasons, winners of the now-defunct Western or Pacific Coast leagues would play NHL champion in Cup finals.

Toronto franchise sold to a new company controlled by Hugh Aird and Conn Smythe. Name changed from St. Patricks to Maple Leafs.

Clubs played 44-game schedule.

The Montreal Canadiens donated the Vezina Trophy to be awarded to the team allowing the fewest goals-against in regular season play. The winning team would, in turn, present the trophy to the goaltender playing in the greatest number of games during the season.

1930-31 — Detroit franchise changed name from Cougars to Falcons. Pittsburgh transferred to Philadelphia for one season. Pirates changed name to Philadelphia Quakers. Trading deadline for teams set at February 15 of each year. NHL approved operation of farm teams by Rangers, Americans, Falcons and Bruins. Four-sided electric arena clock first demonstrated.

1931-32 — Philadelphia dropped out. Ottawa withdrew for one season. New Maple Leaf Gardens completed. Clubs played 48-game schedule.

1932-33 — Detroit franchise changed name from Falcons to Red Wings. Franchise application received from St. Louis but refused because of additional travel costs. Ottawa team resumed play.

1933-34 — First All-Star Game played as a benefit for injured player Ace Bailey. Leafs defeated All-Stars 7-3 in Toronto.

1934-35 — Ottawa franchise transferred to St. Louis. Team called St. Louis Eagles and consisted largely of Ottawa's players.

1935-36 — Ottawa-St. Louis franchise terminated. Montreal Canadiens finished season with very poor record. To strengthen the club, NHL gave Canadiens first call on the services of all French-Canadian players for three seasons.

1937-38 — Second benefit All-Star game staged November 2 in Montreal in aid of the family of the late Canadiens star Howie Morenz.

Montreal Maroons withdrew from the NHL on June 22, 1938, leaving seven clubs in the League.

1938-39 — Expenses for each club regulated at $5 per man per day for meals and $2.50 per man per day for accommodation.

1939-40 — Benefit All-Star Game played October 29, 1939 in Montreal for the children of the late Albert (Babe) Siebert.

1940-41 — Ross-Tyer puck adopted as the official puck of the NHL. Early in the season it was apparent that this puck was too soft. The Spalding puck was adopted in its place.

On May 16, 1941, Arthur Ross, NHL governor from Boston, donated a perpetual trophy to be awarded annually to the player voted outstanding in the league. Due to wartime restrictions, the trophy was never awarded.

1941-42 — New York Americans changed name to Brooklyn Americans.

1942-43 — Brooklyn Americans withdrew from NHL, leaving six teams: Boston, Chicago, Detroit, Montreal, New York and Toronto. Playoff format saw first-place team play third-place team and second play fourth.

Clubs played 50-game schedule.

Frank Calder, president of the NHL since its inception, died in Montreal. Meryn "Red" Dutton, former manager of the New York Americans, became president. The NHL commissioned the Calder Memorial Trophy to be awarded to the League's outstanding rookie each year.

1945-46 — Philadelphia, Los Angeles and San Francisco applied for NHL franchises.

The Philadelphia Arena Company of the American Hockey League applied for an injunction to prevent the possible operation of an NHL franchise in that city.

1946-47 — Mervyn Dutton retired as president of the NHL prior to the start of the season. He was succeeded by Clarence S. Campbell.

Individual trophy winners and all-star team members to receive $1,000 awards.

Playoff guarantees for players introduced.

Clubs played 60-game schedule.

1947-48 — The first annual All-Star Game for the benefit of the players' pension fund was played when the All-Stars defeated the Stanley Cup Champion Toronto Maple Leafs 4-3 in Toronto on October 13, 1947.

Criteria for awarding Art Ross Trophy changed. Now awarded to top scorer. Elmer Lach was its first winner.

Philadelphia and Los Angeles franchise applications refused.

National Hockey League Pension Society formed.

1949-50 — Clubs played 70-game schedule.

First intra-league draft held April 30, 1950. Clubs allowed to protect 30 players. Remaining players available for $25,000 each.

1951-52 — Referees included in the League's pension plan.

1952-53 — In May of 1952, City of Cleveland applied for NHL franchise. Application denied. In March of 1953, the Cleveland Barons of the AHL challenged the NHL champions for the Stanley Cup. The NHL governors did not accept this challenge.

1953-54 — The James Norris Memorial Trophy presented to the NHL for annual presentation to the League's best defenseman.

Intra-league draft rules amended to allow teams to protect 18 skaters and two goaltenders, claiming price reduced to $15,000.

1954-55 — Each arena to operate an "out-of-town" scoreboard.

1956-57 — Referees and linesmen to wear shirts of black and white vertical stripes. Standardized signals for referees and linesmen introduced.

1960-61 — Canadian National Exhibition, City of Toronto and NHL reach agreement for the construction of a Hockey Hall of Fame on the CNE grounds. Hall opens on August 26, 1961.

1963-64 — Player development league established with clubs operated by NHL franchises located in Minneapolis, St. Paul, Indianapolis, Omaha and, beginning in 1964-65, Tulsa. First universal amateur draft took place. All players of qualifying age (17) unaffected by sponsorship of junior teams available to be drafted.

1964-65 — Conn Smythe Trophy presented to the NHL to be awarded annually to the outstanding player in the Stanley Cup playoffs.

Minimum age of players subject to amateur draft changed to 18.

1965-66 — NHL announced expansion plans for a second six-team division to begin play in 1967-68.

1966-67 — Fourteen applications for NHL franchises received.

Lester Patrick Trophy presented to the NHL to be awarded annually for outstanding service to hockey in the United States.

NHL sponsorship of junior teams ceased, making all players of qualifying age not already on NHL-sponsored lists eligible for the amateur draft.

1967-68 — Six new teams added: California Seals, Los Angeles Kings, Minnesota North Stars, Philadelphia Flyers, Pittsburgh Penguins, St. Louis Blues. New teams to play in West Division. Remaining six teams to play in East Division.

Minimum age of players subject to amateur draft changed to 20.

Clubs played 74-game schedule.

Clarence S. Campbell Trophy awarded to team finishing the regular season in first place in West Division.

California Seals change name to Oakland Seals on December 8, 1967.

1968-69 — Clubs played 76-game schedule.

Amateur draft expanded to cover any amateur player of qualifying age throughout the world.

1970-71 — Two new teams added: Buffalo Sabres and Vancouver Canucks. These teams joined East Division. Chicago switched to West Division. Oakland Seals change name to California Golden Seals prior to season. Clubs played 78-game schedule.

1971-72 — Playoff format amended. In each division, first to play fourth; second to play third.

1972-73 — Soviet Nationals and Canadian NHL stars play eight-game pre-season series. Canadians win 4-3-1.

Two new teams added. Atlanta Flames join West Division; New York Islanders join East Division.

1974-75 — Two new teams added: Kansas City Scouts and Washington Capitals. Teams realigned into two nine-team conferences, the Prince of Wales made up of the Norris and Adams Divisions, and the Clarence Campbell made up of the Smythe and Patrick Divisions.

Clubs played 80-game schedule.

1976-77 — California franchise transferred to Cleveland. Team named Cleveland Barons. Kansas City franchise transferred to Denver. Team named Colorado Rockies.

1977-78 — Clarence S. Campbell retires as NHL president. Succeeded by John A. Ziegler, Jr.

1978-79 — Cleveland and Minnesota franchises merge, leaving NHL with 17 teams. Merged team placed in Adams Division, playing home games in Minnesota.

Minimum age of players subject to amateur draft changed to 19.

1979-80 — Four new teams added: Edmonton Oilers, Hartford Whalers, Quebec Nordiques and Winnipeg Jets.

Minimum age of players subject to entry draft changed to 18.

1980-81 — Atlanta franchise shifted to Calgary, retaining "Flames" name.

1981-82 — Teams realigned within existing divisions. New groupings based on geographical areas. Unbalanced schedule adopted.

1982-83 — Colorado Rockies franchise shifted to East Rutherford, New Jersey. Team named New Jersey Devils. Franchise moved to Patrick Division from Smythe; Winnipeg moved to Smythe Division from Norris.

1991-92 — San Jose Sharks added, making the NHL a 22-team league. NHL celebrates 75th Anniversary Season. The 1991-92 regular season suspended due to a players' strike on April 1, 1992. Play resumed April 12, 1992.

NHL History — *continued*

1992-93 — Gil Stein named NHL president (October, 1992). Gary Bettman named first NHL Commissioner (February, 1993). Ottawa Senators and Tampa Bay Lightning added, making the NHL a 24-team league. NHL celebrates Stanley Cup Centennial. Clubs played 84-game schedule.

1993-94 — Mighty Ducks of Anaheim and Florida Panthers added, making the NHL a 26-team league. Minnesota franchise shifted to Dallas, team named Dallas Stars. Prince of Wales and Clarence Campbell Conferences renamed Eastern and Western. Adams, Patrick, Norris and Smythe Divisions renamed Northeast, Atlantic, Central and Pacific. Winnipeg moved to Central Division from Pacific; Tampa Bay moved to Atlantic Division from Central; Pittsburgh moved to Northeast Division from Atlantic.

1994-95 — A lockout resulted in the cancellation of 468 games from October 1, 1994 to January 19, 1995. Clubs played a 48-game schedule that began January 20, 1995 and ended May 3, 1995. No inter-conference games were played.

1995-96 — Quebec franchise transferred to Denver. Team named Colorado Avalanche and placed in Pacific Division of Western Conference. Clubs to play 82-game schedule.

1996-97 — Winnipeg franchise transferred to Phoenix. Team named Phoenix Coyotes and placed in Central Division of Western Conference.

1997-98 — Hartford franchise transferred to Raleigh. Team named Carolina Hurricanes and remains in Northeast Division of Eastern Conference.

1998-99 — The addition of the Nashville Predators made the NHL a 27-team league and brought about the creation of two new divisions and a League-wide realignment in preparation for further expansion to 30 teams by 2000-2001. Nashville was added to the Central Division of the Western Conference, while Toronto moved into the Northeast Division of the Eastern Conference. Pittsburgh was shifted from the Northeast to the Atlantic, while Carolina left the Northeast for the newly created Southeast Division of the Eastern Conference. Florida, Tampa Bay and Washington also joined the Southeast. In the Western Conference, Calgary, Colorado, Edmonton and Vancouver make up the new Northwest Division. Dallas and Phoenix moved from the Central to the Pacific Division.

The NHL retired uniform number 99 in honor of all-time scoring leader Wayne Gretzky who retired at the end of the season.

1999-2000 — Atlanta Thrashers added, making the NHL a 28-team league.

2000-01 — Columbus Blue Jackets and Minnesota Wild added, making the NHL a 30-team league.

2003-04 — First outdoor NHL game. 57,167 attend Heritage Classic at Edmonton's Commonwealth Stadium. Montreal defeated Edmonton 4-3, November 22, 2003.

2004-05 — A lockout resulted in the cancellation of the season.

2007-08 — NHL-record crowd of 71,217 fills Buffalo's Ralph Wilson Stadium on New Year's Day for the 2008 Winter Classic, the first NHL outdoor game in the United States. Sidney Crosby's shootout goal gives the Pittsburgh Penguins a 2-1 win over the Buffalo Sabres.

Major Rule Changes

1910-11 — Game changed from two 30-minute periods to three 20-minute periods.

1911-12 — National Hockey Association (forerunner of the NHL) originated six-man hockey, replacing seven-man game.

1917-18 — Goalies permitted to fall to the ice to make saves. Previously a goaltender was penalized for dropping to the ice.

1918-19 — Penalty rules amended. For minor fouls, substitutes not allowed until penalized player had served three minutes. For major fouls, no substitutes for five minutes. For match fouls, no substitutes allowed for the remainder of the game.

With the addition of two lines painted on the ice twenty feet from center, three playing zones were created, producing a forty-foot neutral center ice area in which forward passing was permitted. Kicking the puck was permitted in this neutral zone.

Tabulation of assists began.

1921-22 — Goaltenders allowed to pass the puck forward up to their own blue line.

Overtime limited to twenty minutes.

Minor penalties changed from three minutes to two minutes.

1923-24 — Match foul defined as actions deliberately injuring or disabling an opponent. For such actions, a player was fined not less than $50 and ruled off the ice for the balance of the game. A player assessed a match penalty may be replaced by a substitute at the end of 20 minutes. Match penalty recipients must meet with the League president who can assess additional punishment.

1925-26 — Delayed penalty rules introduced. Each team must have a minimum of four players on the ice at all times.

Two rules were amended to encourage offense: No more than two defensemen permitted to remain inside a team's own blue line when the puck has left the defensive zone. A faceoff to be called for ragging the puck unless shorthanded.

Team captains only players allowed to talk to referees.

Goaltender's leg pads limited to 12-inch width.

Timekeeper's gong to mark end of periods rather than referee's whistle. Teams to dress a maximum of 12 players for each game from a roster of no more than 14 players.

1926-27 — Blue lines repositioned to sixty feet from each goal-line, thereby enlarging the neutral zone and standardizing distance from blue line to goal.

Uniform goal nets adopted throughout NHL with goal posts securely fastened to the ice.

1927-28 — To further encourage offense, forward passes allowed in defending and neutral zones and goaltender's pads reduced in width from 12 to 10 inches.

Game standardized at three twenty-minute periods of stop-time separated by ten-minute intermissions.

Teams to change ends after each period.

Ten minutes of sudden-death overtime to be played if the score is tied after regulation time.

Minor penalty to be assessed to any player other than a goaltender for deliberately picking up the puck while it is in play. Minor penalty to be assessed for deliberately shooting the puck out of play.

The Art Ross goal net adopted as the official net of the NHL.

Maximum length of hockey sticks limited to 53 inches measured from heel of blade to end of handle. No minimum length stipulated.

Home teams given choice of end to defend at start of game.

1928-29 — Forward passing permitted in defensive and neutral zones and into attacking zone if pass receiver is in neutral zone when pass is made. No forward passing allowed inside attacking zone.

Minor penalty to be assessed to any player who delays the game by passing the puck back into his defensive zone.

Ten-minute overtime without sudden-death provision to be played in games tied after regulation time. Games tied after this overtime period declared a draw.

Exclusive of goaltenders, team to dress at least 8 and no more than 12 skaters.

NHL Attendance

Season	Games	Regular Season Attendance	Games	Playoffs Attendance	Total Attendance
1967-68	444	4,938,043	40	495,089	5,433,132
1968-69	456	5,550,613	33	431,739	5,982,352
1969-70	456	5,992,065	34	461,694	6,453,759
1970-71	546	7,257,677	43	707,633	7,965,310
1971-72	546	7,609,368	36	582,666	8,192,034
1972-73	624	8,575,651	38	624,637	9,200,288
1973-74	624	8,640,978	38	600,442	9,241,420
1974-75	720	9,521,536	51	784,181	10,305,717
1975-76	720	9,103,761	48	726,279	9,830,040
1976-77	720	8,563,890	44	646,279	9,210,169
1977-78	720	8,526,564	45	686,634	9,213,198
1978-79	680	7,758,053	45	694,521	8,452,574
1979-80	840	10,533,623	63	976,699	11,510,322
1980-81	840	10,726,198	68	966,390	11,692,588
1981-82	840	10,710,894	71	1,058,948	11,769,842
1982-83	840	11,020,610	66	1,088,222	12,028,832
1983-84	840	11,359,386	70	1,107,400	12,466,786
1984-85	840	11,633,730	70	1,107,500	12,741,230
1985-86	840	11,621,000	72	1,152,503	12,773,503
1986-87	840	11,855,880	87	1,383,967	13,239,847
1987-88	840	12,117,512	83	1,336,901	13,454,413
1988-89	840	12,417,969	83	1,327,214	13,745,183
1989-90	840	12,579,651	85	1,355,593	13,935,244
1990-91	840	12,343,897	92	1,442,203	13,786,100
1991-92	880	12,769,676	86	1,327,920	14,097,596
1992-93	1,008	14,158,177 [1]	83	1,346,034	15,504,211
1993-94	1,092	16,105,604 [2]	90	1,440,095	17,545,699
1994-95	624 [3]	9,233,884	81	1,329,130	10,563,014
1995-96	1,066	17,041,614	86	1,540,140	18,581,754
1996-97	1,066	17,640,529	82	1,494,878	19,135,407
1997-98	1,066	17,264,678	82	1,507,416	18,772,094
1998-99	1,107	18,001,741	86	1,509,411	19,511,152
1999-2000	1,148	18,800,139	83	1,524,629	20,324,768
2000-01	1,230	20,373,379	86	1,584,011	21,957,390
2001-02	1,230	20,614,613	90	1,691,174	22,305,787
2002-03	1,230	20,408,704	89	1,636,120	22,044,824
2003-04	1,230	20,356,199	89	1,708,691	22,064,890
2004-05	....	....	....	....	....
2005-06	1,230	20,854,169	83	1,530,405	22,384,574
2006-07	1,230	20,861,787	81	1,496,501	22,358,288
2007-08	1,230	21,236,255	85	1,587,054	22,823,309
2008-09	1,230	21,475,223	87	1,639,602	23,114,825
2009-10	1,230	20,996,455	90	1,702,371	22,698,826

NHL Expansion: the NHL operated as a six-team league from 1942-43 to 1966-67. Six teams were added in 1967-68: California (later to move to Cleveland), Los Angeles, Minnesota (later to move to Dallas), Philadelphia, Pittsburgh and St. Louis. In 1970-71: Buffalo and Vancouver. In 1972-73: Atlanta (later to move to Calgary) and NYIslanders. In 1974-75: Kansas City (later to move to Colorado and then to New Jersey) and Washington. In 1979-80, Hartford (later to move to Carolina), Edmonton, Quebec (later to move to Colorado) and Winnipeg (later to move to Phoenix). In 1991-92, San Jose. In 1992-93, Ottawa and Tampa Bay. In 1993-94, Anaheim and Florida. In 1998-99, Nashville. In 1999-2000, Atlanta. In 2000-01, Columbus and Minnesota.

[1] Includes 24 neutral site games • [2] Includes 26 neutral site games
[3] Lockout resulted in the cancellation of 468 regular-season games.

Major Rule Changes — *continued*

1929-30 — Forward passing permitted inside all three zones but not permitted across either blue line.

Kicking the puck allowed, but a goal cannot be scored by kicking the puck in.

No more than three players including the goaltender may remain in their defensive zone when the puck has gone up ice. Minor penalties to be assessed for the first two violations of this rule in a game; major penalties thereafter.

Goaltenders forbidden to hold the puck. Pucks caught must be cleared immediately. For infringement of this rule, a faceoff to be taken ten feet in front of the goal with no player except the goaltender standing between the faceoff spot and the goal-line.

Highsticking penalties introduced.

Maximum number of players in uniform increased from 12 to 15.

December 21, 1929 — Forward passing rules instituted at the beginning of the 1929-30 season more than doubled number of goals scored. Partway through the season, these rules were further amended to read, "No attacking player allowed to precede the play when entering the opposing defensive zone." This is similar to modern offside rule.

1930-31 — A player without a complete stick ruled out of play and forbidden from taking part in further action until a new stick is obtained. A player who has broken his stick must obtain a replacement at his bench.

A further refinement of the offside rule stated that the puck must first be propelled into the attacking zone before any player of the attacking side can enter that zone; for infringement of this rule a faceoff to take place at the spot where the infraction took place.

1931-32 — Though there is no record of a team attempting to play with two goaltenders on the ice, a rule was instituted which stated that each team was allowed only one goaltender on the ice at one time.

Attacking players forbidden to impede the movement or obstruct the vision of opposing goaltenders.

Defending players with the exception of the goaltender forbidden from falling on the puck within 10 feet of the net.

1932-33 — Each team to have captain on the ice at all times. Maximum number of players in uniform reduced to 14 from 15.

If the goaltender is removed from the ice to serve a penalty, the manager of the club to appoint a substitute.

Match penalty with substitution after five minutes instituted for kicking another player.

1933-34 — Number of players permitted to stand in defensive zone restricted to three including goaltender.

Visible time clocks required in each rink.

Two referees replace one referee and one linesman.

1934-35 — Penalty shot awarded when a player is tripped and thus prevented from having a clear shot on goal, having no player to pass to other than the offending player. Shot taken from inside a 10-foot circle located 38 feet from the goal. The goaltender must not advance more than one foot from his goal-line when the shot is taken.

1937-38 — Rules introduced governing icing the puck.

Penalty shot awarded when a player other than a goaltender falls on the puck within 10 feet of the goal.

1938-39 — Penalty shot modified to allow puck carrier to skate in before shooting.

One referee and one linesman replace two referee system.

Blue line widened to 12 inches.

Maximum number of players in uniform increased from 14 to 15.

1939-40 — A substitute replacing a goaltender removed from ice to serve a penalty may use a goaltender's stick and gloves but no other goaltending equipment.

1940-41 — Flooding ice surface between periods made obligatory.

1941-42 — Penalty shots classified as minor and major. Minor shot to be taken from a line 28 feet from the goal. Major shot, awarded when a player is tripped with only the goaltender to beat, permits the player taking the penalty shot to skate right into the goalkeeper and shoot from point-blank range.

One referee and two linesmen employed to officiate games.

For playoffs, standby minor league goaltenders employed by NHL as emergency substitutes.

1942-43 — Because of wartime restrictions on train scheduling, regular-season overtime was discontinued on November 21, 1942.

Player limit reduced from 15 to 14. Minimum of 12 men in uniform abolished.

1943-44 — Red line at center ice introduced to speed up the game and reduce offside calls. This rule is considered to mark the beginning of the modern era in the NHL.

1945-46 — Goal indicator lights synchronized with official time clock required at all rinks.

1946-47 — System of signals by officials to indicate infractions introduced.

Linesmen from neutral cities employed for all games.

1947-48 — Goal awarded when a player with the puck has an open net to shoot at and a thrown stick prevents the shot on goal. Major penalty to any player who throws his stick in any zone other than defending zone. If a stick is thrown by a player in his defending zone but the thrown stick is not considered to have prevented a goal, a penalty shot is awarded.

All playoff games played until a winner determined, with 20-minute sudden-death overtime periods separated by 10-minute intermissions.

1949-50 — Ice surface painted white.

Clubs allowed to dress 17 players exclusive of goaltenders.

Major penalties incurred by goaltenders served by a member of the goaltender's team instead of resulting in a penalty shot.

1950-51 — Each team required to provide an emergency goaltender in attendance with full equipment at each game for use by either team in the event of illness or injury to a regular goaltender.

1951-52 — Home teams to wear basic white uniforms; visiting teams basic colored uniforms.

Goal crease enlarged from 3 × 7 feet to 4 × 8 feet.

Number of players in uniform reduced to 15 plus goaltenders.

Faceoff circles enlarged from 10-foot to 15-foot radius.

1952-53 — Teams permitted to dress 15 skaters on the road and 16 at home.

1953-54 — Number of players in uniform set at 16 plus goaltenders.

1954-55 — Number of players in uniform set at 18 plus goaltenders up to December 1 and 16 plus goaltenders thereafter. Teams agree to wear colored uniforms at home and white uniforms on the road.

1956-57 — Player serving a minor penalty allowed to return to ice when a goal is scored by opposing team.

1959-60 — Players prevented from leaving their benches to enter into an altercation. Substitutions permitted providing substitutes do not enter into altercation.

1960-61 — Number of players in uniform set at 16 plus goaltenders.

1961-62 — Penalty shots to be taken by the player against whom the foul was committed. In the event of a penalty shot called in a situation where a particular player hasn't been fouled, the penalty shot to be taken by any player on the ice when the foul was committed.

1964-65 — No body contact on faceoffs.

In playoff games, each team to have its substitute goaltender dressed in his regular uniform except for leg pads and body protector. All previous rules governing standby goaltenders terminated.

1965-66 — Teams required to dress two goaltenders for each regular-season game. Maximum stick length increased to 55 inches.

1966-67 — Substitution allowed on coincidental major penalties.

Between-periods intermissions fixed at 15 minutes.

1967-68 — If a penalty incurred by a goaltender is a co-incident major, the penalty to be served by a player of the goaltender's team on the ice at the time the penalty was called. Limit of curvature of hockey stick blade set at 1½ inches.

1969-70 — Limit of curvature of hockey stick blade set at 1 inch.

1970-71 — Home teams to wear basic white uniforms; visiting teams to wear basic colored uniforms.

Limit of curvature of hockey stick blade set at ½ inch.

Minor penalty for deliberately shooting the puck out of the playing area.

1971-72 — Number of players in uniform set at 17 plus 2 goaltenders.

Third man to enter an altercation assessed an automatic game misconduct penalty.

1972-73 — Minimum width of stick blade reduced to 2 inches from 2½ inches.

1974-75 — Bench minor penalty imposed if a penalized player does not proceed directly and immediately to the penalty box.

1976-77 — Rule dealing with fighting amended to provide a major and game misconduct penalty for any player who is clearly the instigator of a fight.

1977-78 — Teams requesting a stick measurement to be assessed a minor penalty in the event that the measured stick does not violate the rules.

1979-80 — Wearing of helmets made mandatory for players entering the NHL.

1980-81 — Maximum stick length increased to 58 inches.

1981-82 — If both of a team's listed goaltenders are incapacitated, the team can dress and play any eligible goaltender who is available.

1982-83 — Number of players in uniform set at 18 plus 2 goaltenders.

1983-84 — Five-minute sudden-death overtime to be played in regular-season games that are tied at the end of regulation time.

1985-86 — Substitutions allowed in the event of co-incidental minor penalties. Maximum stick length increased to 60 inches.

1986-87 — Delayed off-side is no longer in effect once the players of the offending team have cleared the opponents' defensive zone.

1990-91 — The goal lines, blue lines, defensive zone face-off circles and markings all moved one foot out from the end boards, creating 11 feet of room behind the nets and shrinking the neutral zone from 60 to 58 feet.

1991-92 — Video replays employed to assist referees in goal/no goal situations. Size of goal crease increased. Crease changed to semi-circular configuration. Time clock to record tenths of a second in last minute of each period and overtime. Major and game misconduct penalty for checking from behind into boards. Penalties added for crease infringement and unnecessary contact with goaltender. Goal disallowed if puck enters net while a player of the attacking team is standing on the goal crease line, is in the goal crease or places his stick in the goal crease.

1992-93 — No substitutions allowed in the event of coincidental minor penalties called when both teams are at full strength. Minor penalty for attempting to draw a penalty ("diving"). Major and game misconduct penalty for checking from behind into goal frame. Game misconduct penalty for instigating a fight. High sticking redefined to include any use of the stick above waist-height. Previous rule stipulated shoulder-height.

1993-94 — High sticking redefined to allow goals scored with a high stick below the height of the crossbar of the goal frame.

1996-97 — Maximum stick length increased to 63 inches. All players must be clear of the attacking zone prior to the puck being shot into that zone. The opportunity to "tag-up" and return into the zone has been removed.

1998-99 — The league instituted a two-referee system with each team to play 20 regular-season games with two referees and a pair of linesmen. Goal line moved to 13 feet from end boards. Goal crease altered to extend one foot beyond each goal post (eight feet across in total). Sides of crease squared off, extending 4'6". Only the top of the crease remains rounded. Only the top of the crease remains rounded.

1999-2000 — Each team to play 25 home and 25 road games using the two-referee system. Crease rule revised to implement a "no harm, no foul, no video review" standard. Teams to play with four skaters and a goaltender in regular-season overtime. If a goal is scored in regular-season overtime, the winner is awarded two points and the loser one point. In no goal is scored in overtime, both teams are awarded one point.

2000-01 — All games to be played using the two-referee system.

2002-03 — "Hurry-up" faceoff and line-change rules implemented.

2003-04 — Home teams to wear basic colored uniforms; visiting teams to wear basic white uniforms. Maximum length of goaltender's pads set at 38 inches.

2005-06 — The NHL adopted a comprehensive package of rule changes that included the following:

Goal line moved to 11 feet from end boards; blue lines moved to 75 feet from end boards, reducing neutral zone from 54 feet to 50 feet. Center red line eliminated for two-line passes. "Tag-up" off-side rule reinstituted. This rule was previously used from 1986-87 through 1995-96. Goaltender not permitted to play the puck outside a designated trapezoid-shaped area behind the net. A team that ices the puck will not be permitted to make any player substitutions prior to the ensuing faceoff. A player who instigates a fight in the final five minutes of regulation time or at any time of overtime will receive a minor, a major, a misconduct and an automatic one-game suspension. The size of goaltender equipment has been reduced by approximately 11 percent. If a game remains tied after five minutes of overtime, a shootout will be conducted to determine a winner.

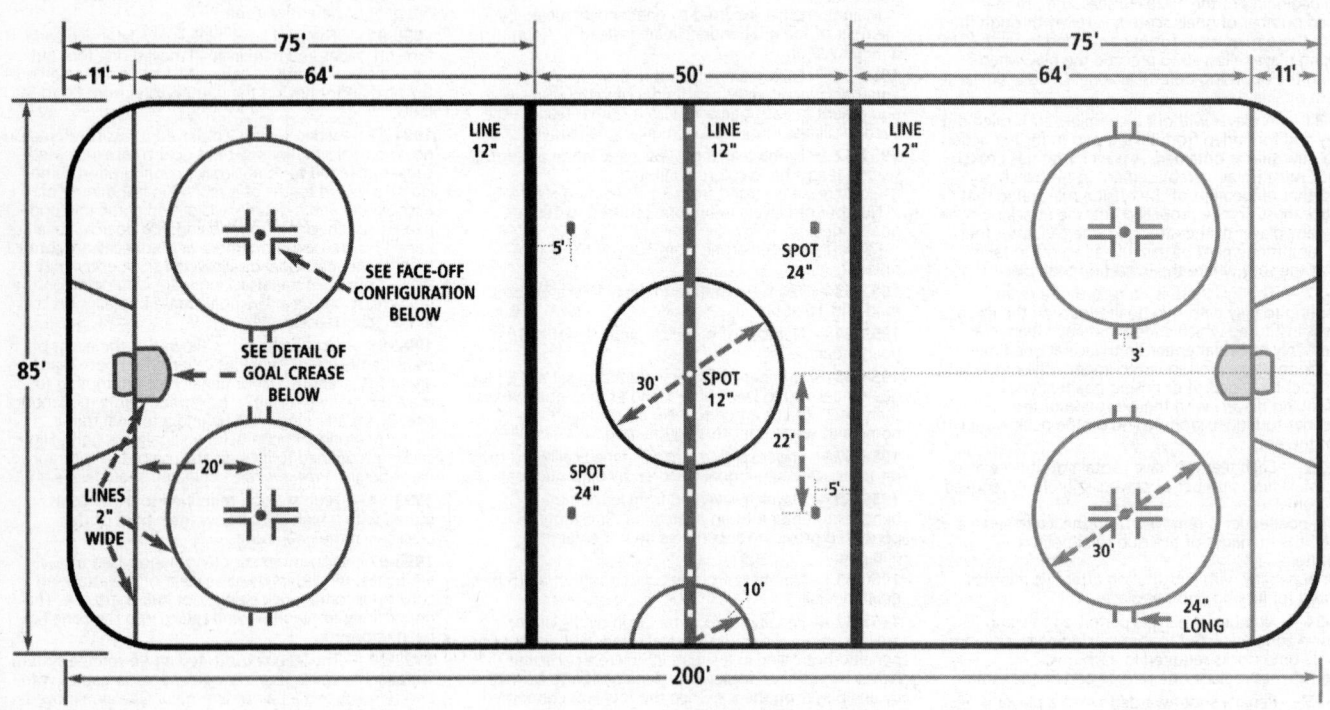

NHL RINK DIMENSIONS

FACEOFF CONFIGURATION

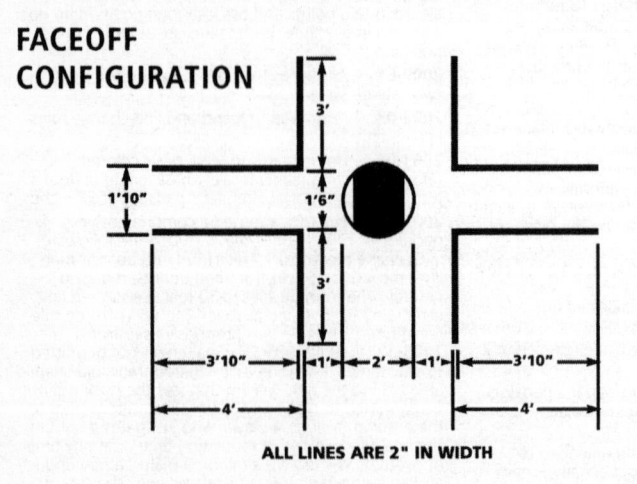

ALL LINES ARE 2" IN WIDTH

CREASE DIMENSIONS

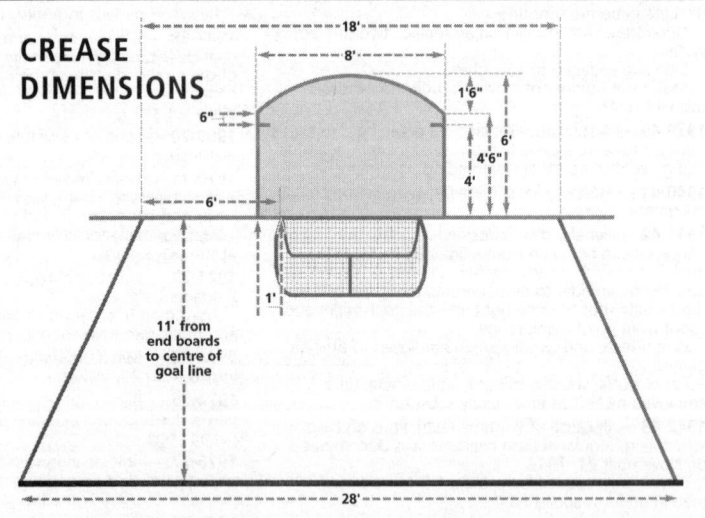

There's No Place Like Home at 2010 Olympic Winter Games

NO ATHLETE FROM CANADA HAD WON A GOLD MEDAL ON HOME SOIL when the country hosted the Summer Olympics in 1976 or the Winter Olympics in 1988, but Canadians were promised they would "Own the Podium" at the Vancouver Games in 2010. After a slow start, Canadians had tied a Winter Games record with 13 gold medals heading into the final event of the Olympics, which was the championship game in Men's Hockey.

Canadian women would win gold for the third straight Games, beating their arch-rivals from the USA in the finals, but the Canadian men's team started slowly. After an 8-0 win over Norway, it took a shootout to defeat Switzerland 3-2 before a 5-3 loss to the United States that resulted in the Americans gaining a bye into the medal round while Canada was forced to play a qualification game which proved to be an easy 8-2 win over Germany. This was followed by a decisive 7-3 win over Russia in the quarterfinals and a much closer 3-2 win over Slovakia in the semifinals.

Though Ryan Miller had been the NHL's hottest goaltender heading into the Olympics, few had given the young American team serious consideration as a gold medal threat. The Americans would go through the tournament undefeated, beating Canada in the preliminary round and crushing Finland 6-1 in the semifinals. (Finland rebounded to defeat Slovakia 5-3 in the bronze medal game.)

Like the Americans, Canada had selected younger players for its 2010 Olympic roster, though some veterans (notably Scott Niedermayer and Chris Pronger) were on hand. In the gold medal game, Jonathan Toews put Canada on the scoreboard first midway through the first period. Corey Perry upped the lead to 2-0 midway through the second, but the Vancouver Canucks' Ryan Kesler beat NHL teammate Roberto Luongo to cut Canada's margin to 2-1 a few minutes later. The score remained that way until late in the third period when Zach Parise tied the game with the American net empty and just 25 seconds to go. In overtime, Sidney Crosby swept in a no-look pass from Jarome Iginla for the "Golden Goal" at 7:40 and Canadians had the gold medal they wanted most.

2010 Men's Olympic Hockey Results

Preliminary Round (round robin)

Feb. 16	United States	3	Switzerland	1
	Canada	8	Norway	0
	Russia	8	Latvia	2
Feb. 17	Finland	5	Belarus	1
	Sweden	2	Germany	0
	Czech Republic	3	Slovakia	1
Feb. 18	United States	6	Norway	1
	Switzerland	2	Canada	3
	Slovakia	2	Russia	1
Feb. 19	Belarus	2	Sweden	4
	Czech Republic	5	Latvia	2
	Finland	5	Germany	0
Feb. 20	Norway	4	Switzerland	5
	Latvia	0	Slovakia	6
	Germany	3	Belarus	5
Feb. 21	Russia	4	Czech Republic	2
	Canada	3	United States	5
	Sweden	3	Finland	0

Playoff Round (single elimination)

Feb. 23	Switzerland	3	Belarus	2
	Czech Republic	3	Latvia	2
	Slovakia	4	Norway	3
	Canada	8	Germany	2
Feb. 24	**Quarterfinals**			
	United States	2	Switzerland	0
	Finland	2	Czech Republic	0
	Sweden	3	Slovakia	4
	Russia	3	Canada	7
Feb. 26	**Semifinals**			
	United States	6	Finland	1
	Canada	3	Slovakia	2
Feb. 27	**Bronze Medal Game**			
	Finland	5	Slovakia	2
Feb. 28	**Gold Medal Game**			
	United States	2	Canada	3

2010 Women's Olympic Hockey Results

Preliminary Round (round robin)

Feb. 13	Sweden	3	Switzerland	0
	Canada	18	Slovakia	0
Feb. 14	United States	12	China	1
	Finland	5	Russia	1
Feb. 15	Switzerland	1	Canada	10
	Sweden	6	Slovakia	2
Feb. 16	Russia	0	United States	13
	Finland	2	China	1
Feb. 17	Canada	13	Sweden	1
	Slovakia	2	Switzerland	5
Feb. 18	United States	6	Finland	0
	China	1	Russia	2

Playoff Round (single elimination)

Feb. 20	**Classification Games**			
	Switzerland	6	China	0
	Russia	4	Slovakia	2
Feb. 22	**Semifinals**			
	United States	9	Sweden	1
	Canada	5	Finland	0
Feb. 22	**7th place game**			
	China	3	Slovakia	1
	5th place game			
	Switzerland	2	Russia	1
Feb. 25	**Bronze Medal Game**			
	Finland	3	Sweden	2
	Gold Medal Game			
	Canada	2	United States	0

Cumulative Medal Standings, Women's Olympic Hockey, 1998-2010

		G	S	B	Total	Last Medal
1.	Canada	3	1	0	4	Gold 10
2.	USA	1	2	1	4	Silver 10
3.	Sweden	0	1	1	2	Silver 06
4.	Finland	0	0	2	2	Bronze 10

Men's Standings • 2010
Preliminary Round
(Note: W = 3 pts; OTW = 2 pts; OTL = 1 pt.)

Group A

Team	GP	W	OTW	OTL	L	GF	GA	Pts
USA	3	3	0	0	0	14	5	9
CAN	3	1	1	0	1	14	7	5
SUI	3	0	1	1	1	8	10	3
NOR	3	0	0	1	2	5	19	1

Group B

Team	GP	W	OTW	OTL	L	GF	GA	Pts
RUS	3	2	0	1	0	13	6	7
CZE	3	2	0	0	1	10	7	6
SVK	3	1	1	0	1	9	4	5
LAT	3	0	0	0	3	4	19	0

Group C

Team	GP	W	OTW	OTL	L	GF	GA	Pts
SWE	3	3	0	0	0	9	2	9
FIN	3	2	0	1	0	10	4	6
BLR	3	1	0	0	2	8	12	3
GER	3	0	0	0	3	3	12	0

2010 Final Rankings

1. Canada
2. United States
3. Finland
4. Slovakia
5. Sweden
6. Russia
7. Czech Republic
8. Switzerland
9. Belarus
10. Norway
11. Germany
12. Latvia

2010 Scoring Leaders

Player	Team	GP	G	A	PTS	PIM
Pavol Demitra	Slovakia	7	3	7	10	2
Marian Hossa	Slovakia	7	3	6	9	6
Zach Parise	USA	6	4	4	8	0
Brian Rafalski	USA	6	4	4	8	2
Jonathan Toews	Canada	7	1	7	8	2
Jarome Iginla	Canada	7	5	2	7	0
Sidney Crosby	Canada	7	4	3	7	4
Dany Heatley	Canada	7	4	3	7	4
Ryan Getzlaf	Canada	7	3	4	7	2
Niklas Hagman	Finland	6	4	2	6	2
Evgeni Malkin	Russia	4	3	3	6	0
Michal Handzus	Slovakia	7	3	3	6	0
Shea Weber	Canada	7	2	4	6	2
Richard Zednik	Slovakia	7	2	4	6	6
Nicklas Backstrom	Sweden	4	1	5	6	0
Dan Boyle	Canada	7	1	5	6	2
Eric Staal	Canada	7	1	5	6	6
Duncan Keith	Canada	7	0	6	6	2
Marian Gaborik	Slovakia	7	4	1	5	6
Corey Perry	Canada	7	4	1	5	2

2010 Goaltending Leaders
(Minimum 150 Mins)

Player	Team	GP	Min	GA	SO	GAA
Henrik Lundqvist	Sweden	3	179	4	2	1.34
Ryan Miller	USA	6	355	8	1	1.35
Roberto Luongo	Canada	5	308	9	1	1.76
Tomas Vokoun	Czech Rep.	5	304	9	0	1.78
Jaroslav Halak	Slovakia	7	423	17	1	2.41
Miikka Kiprusoff	Finland	5	250	11	1	2.64
Thomas Greiss	Germany	3	179	15	0	5.03
Pal Grotnes	Norway	4	226	19	0	5.04
Edgars Masalskis	Latvia	4	244	21	0	5.15

Women's Standings • 2010
Preliminary Round
(Note: W = 3 pts; OTW = 2 pts; OTL = 1 pt.)

Group A

Team	GP	W	OTW	OTL	L	GF	GA	Pts
CAN	3	3	0	0	0	41	2	9
SWE	3	2	0	0	1	10	15	6
SUI	3	1	0	0	2	6	15	3
SVK	3	0	0	0	3	4	29	0

Group B

Team	GP	W	OTW	OTL	L	GF	GA	Pts
USA	3	3	0	0	0	31	1	9
FIN	3	2	0	0	1	7	8	6
RUS	3	1	0	0	2	3	19	3
CHN	3	0	0	0	3	3	16	0

2010 Final Rankings

1. Canada
2. United States
3. Finland
4. Sweden
5. Switzerland
6. Russia
7. China
8. Slovakia

2010 Scoring Leaders

Player	Team	GP	G	A	PTS	PIM
Meghan Agosta	Canada	5	9	6	15	2
Jayna Hefford	Canada	5	5	7	12	8
Stefanie Marty	Switzerland	5	9	2	11	6
Jenny Porty	USA	5	6	5	11	2
Natalie Darwitz	USA	5	4	7	11	0
Caroline Ouellette	Canada	5	2	9	11	2
H. Wickenheiser	Canada	5	2	9	11	0
Cherie Piper	Canada	5	5	5	10	0
M. Lamoureux	USA	5	4	6	10	2
Kelli Stack	USA	5	3	5	8	2
Sarah Vaillancourt	Canada	5	3	5	8	6
Hilary Knight	USA	5	1	7	8	0
Marie-Philip Poulin	Canada	5	5	2	7	2
Gillian Apps	Canada	5	3	4	7	2
Molly Engstrom	USA	5	3	4	7	6
Karen Thatcher	USA	5	3	6	2	2
Julie Chu	USA	5	2	4	6	0
J. Lamoureaux	USA	5	2	4	6	0
Kathrin Lehmann	Switzerland	5	2	4	6	0
Rebecca Johnston	Canada	5	1	5	6	2

2010 Goaltending Leaders
(Minimum 150 Mins)

Player	Team	GP	Min	GA	SO	GAA
Shannon Szabados	Canada	3	180	1	2	0.33
Jessie Vetter	USA	4	240	3	2	0.75
Florence Schelling	Switzerland	5	302	16	1	3.18
Irina Gasennikova	Russia	4	250	10	0	2.40
Yao Shi	China	5	248	19	0	4.60
Noora Raty	Finland	5	303	15	0	2.97
Sara Grahn	Sweden	3	154	8	0	3.12
Zuzana Tomcikova	Slovakia	5	300	36	0	7.20
Kim Martin	Sweden	3	149	19	1	7.66
Kim St-Pierre	Canada	2	100	0	1	0.00

Cumulative Medal Standings, Men's Olympic Hockey, 1924-2010

		G	S	B	Total	Last Medal
1.	USSR/Russia*	8	2	2	12	Bronze 02
2.	Canada	7	4	2	13	Gold 10
3.	USA	2	7	1	10	Silver 10
4.	Sweden	2	2	4	8	Gold 06
5.	Czechoslovakia/Czech Rep.	1	4	4	9	Bronze 06
6.	Great Britain	1	0	1	2	Gold 36
7.	Finland	0	2	3	5	Bronze 10
8.	W. Germany	0	0	2	2	Bronze 76
9.	Switzerland	0	0	2	2	Bronze 48

* Soviet Union/Russia played as the Unified Team in 1992.

NHL Clubs' Minor-League Affiliations, 2010-11

NHL CLUB	MINOR-LEAGUE AFFILIATES
Anaheim	Syracuse Crunch (AHL) Elmira Jackals (ECHL)
Atlanta	Chicago Wolves (AHL) Gwinnett Gladiators (ECHL)
Boston	Providence Bruins (AHL) Reading Royals (ECHL)
Buffalo	Portland Pirates (AHL)
Calgary	Abbotsford Heat (AHL) Utah Grizzlies (ECHL)
Carolina	Charlotte Checkers (AHL) Florida Everblades (ECHL)
Chicago	Rockford IceHogs (AHL) Toledo Walleye (ECHL)
Colorado	Lake Erie Monsters (AHL)
Columbus	Springfield Falcons (AHL)
Dallas	Texas Stars (AHL) Idaho Steelheads (ECHL)
Detroit	Grand Rapids Griffins (AHL) Toledo Walleye (ECHL)
Edmonton	Oklahoma City Barons (AHL) Stockton Thunder (ECHL)
Florida	Rochester Americans (AHL) Cincinnati Cyclones (ECHL)
Los Angeles	Manchester Monarchs (AHL) Ontario (CA) Reign (ECHL)
Minnesota	Houston Aeros (AHL)
Montreal	Hamilton Bulldogs (AHL)

NHL CLUB	MINOR-LEAGUE AFFILIATES
Nashville	Milwaukee Admirals (AHL) Cincinnati Cyclones (ECHL)
New Jersey	Albany Devils (AHL) Trenton Devils (ECHL)
NY Islanders	Bridgeport Sound Tigers (AHL) Kalamazoo Wings (ECHL) Odessa Jackalopes (CHL)
NY Rangers	Hartford Wolf Pack (AHL) Greenville Grrrowl (ECHL)
Ottawa	Binghamton Senators (AHL) Elmira Jackals (ECHL)
Philadelphia	Adirondack Phantoms (AHL) Greenville Road Warriors (ECHL)
Phoenix	San Antonio Rampage (AHL) Las Vegas Wranglers (ECHL)
Pittsburgh	Wilkes-Barre/Scranton Penguins (AHL) Wheeling Nailers (ECHL)
St. Louis	Peoria Rivermen (AHL) Alaska Aces (ECHL)
San Jose	Worcester Sharks (AHL) Stockton Thunder (ECHL)
Tampa Bay	Norfolk Admirals (AHL) Florida Everblades (ECHL)
Toronto	Toronto Marlies (AHL) Reading Royals (ECHL)
Vancouver	Manitoba Moose (AHL) Victoria Salmon Kings (ECHL)
Washington	Hershey Bears (AHL) South Carolina Stingrays (ECHL)

Anaheim Ducks

Key Off-Season Signings/Acquisitions

2010

June   2 • Re-signed D **Sheldon Brookbank**.
       18 • Re-signed C **Kyle Chipchura**.
       24 • Named **Mike Foligno** assistant coach.

July   1 • Signed D **Toni Lydman**.
        1 • Re-signed C **Saku Koivu**.
        9 • Acquired LW **Aaron Voros** and LW **Ryan Hillier** from NY Rangers for D **Steve Eminger**.
       12 • Signed LW **Josh Green**.
       15 • Re-signed D **Brendan Mikkelson**.
       21 • Signed D **Danny Syvret**.

Aug.   2 • Signed D **Andy Sutton**.
        9 • Re-signed RW **Teemu Selanne**.

2009-10 Results: 39W-32L-3OTL-8SOL 89PTS.
Fourth, Pacific Division

Year-by-Year Record

Season	GP	Home W	L	T	OL	Road W	L	T	OL	Overall W	L	T	OL	GF	GA	Pts.	Finished	Playoff Result
2009-10	82	25	11	....	5	14	21	....	6	39	32	....	11	238	251	89	4th, Pacific Div.	Out of Playoffs
2008-09	82	20	18	....	3	22	15	....	4	42	33	....	7	245	238	91	2nd, Pacific Div.	Lost Conf. Semi-Final
2007-08	82	28	9	....	4	19	18	....	4	47	27	....	8	205	191	102	2nd, Pacific Div.	Lost Conf. Quarter-Final
2006-07	**82**	**26**	**6**	....	**9**	**22**	**14**	....	**5**	**48**	**20**	....	**14**	**258**	**208**	**110**	**1st, Pacific Div.**	**Won Stanley Cup**
2005-06*	82	26	10	....	5	17	17	....	7	43	27	....	12	254	229	98	3rd, Pacific Div.	Lost Conf. Championship
2004-05*	....																	
2003-04*	82	19	11	7	4	10	24	3	4	29	35	10	8	184	213	76	4th, Pacific Div.	Out of Playoffs
2002-03*	82	22	10	7	2	18	17	2	4	40	27	9	6	203	193	95	2nd, Pacific Div.	Lost Final
2001-02*	82	15	19	5	2	14	23	3	1	29	42	8	3	175	198	69	5th, Pacific Div.	Out of Playoffs
2000-01*	82	15	20	4	2	10	21	7	3	25	41	11	5	188	245	66	5th, Pacific Div.	Out of Playoffs
1999-2000*	82	19	13	7	2	15	20	5	1	34	33	12	3	217	227	83	5th, Pacific Div.	Out of Playoffs
1998-99*	82	21	14	6	....	14	20	7	....	35	34	13	....	215	206	83	3rd, Pacific Div.	Lost Conf. Quarter-Final
1997-98*	82	12	23	6	....	14	20	7	....	26	43	13	....	205	261	65	6th, Pacific Div.	Out of Playoffs
1996-97*	82	23	12	6	....	13	21	7	....	36	33	13	....	245	233	85	2nd, Pacific Div.	Lost Conf. Semi-Final
1995-96*	82	22	15	4	....	13	24	4	....	35	39	8	....	234	247	78	4th, Pacific Div.	Out of Playoffs
1994-95*	48	11	9	4	....	5	18	1	....	16	27	5	....	125	164	37	6th, Pacific Div.	Out of Playoffs
1993-94*	84	14	26	2	....	19	20	3	....	33	46	5	....	229	251	71	4th, Pacific Div.	Out of Playoffs

* Mighty Ducks of Anaheim

2010-11 Schedule

Oct.					Jan.			
	Fri.	8	at Detroit		Jan.	Sun.	2	Chicago*
	Sat.	9	at Nashville			Wed.	5	Nashville
	Mon.	11	at St. Louis*			Fri.	7	Columbus
	Wed.	13	Vancouver			Sun.	9	San Jose*
	Fri.	15	Atlanta			Wed.	12	St. Louis
	Sun.	17	Phoenix*			Sat.	15	at Phoenix
	Wed.	20	at Columbus			Sun.	16	Edmonton*
	Thu.	21	at Philadelphia			Tue.	18	at Ottawa
	Sat.	23	at Detroit			Thu.	20	at Toronto
	Tue.	26	at Dallas			Sat.	22	at Montreal
	Fri.	29	New Jersey			Tue.	25	at Columbus
	Sat.	30	at San Jose		Feb.	Wed.	2	San Jose
Nov.	Wed.	3	Tampa Bay			Sat.	5	at Colorado*
	Fri.	5	Pittsburgh			Wed.	9	at Vancouver
	Sun.	7	Nashville*			Fri.	11	at Calgary
	Tue.	9	at San Jose			Sun.	13	at Edmonton
	Wed.	10	NY Islanders			Wed.	16	Washington
	Fri.	12	Dallas			Fri.	18	at Minnesota
	Sun.	14	at Chicago			Sat.	19	at St. Louis
	Tue.	16	at Dallas			Wed.	23	Los Angeles
	Wed.	17	at Minnesota			Fri.	25	Minnesota
	Fri.	19	Columbus			Sun.	27	Colorado*
	Sun.	21	Edmonton*		Mar.	Wed.	2	Detroit
	Fri.	26	Chicago*			Fri.	4	Dallas
	Sat.	27	at Phoenix			Sun.	6	Vancouver*
	Mon.	29	Los Angeles			Wed.	9	NY Rangers
Dec.	Wed.	1	Florida			Fri.	11	at Colorado
	Fri.	3	Detroit			Sun.	13	Phoenix*
	Sun.	5	Phoenix*			Wed.	16	St. Louis
	Tue.	7	at Edmonton			Sat.	19	at Los Angeles
	Wed.	8	at Vancouver			Sun.	20	Calgary*
	Fri.	10	Calgary			Wed.	23	at Dallas
	Sun.	12	Minnesota*			Thu.	24	at Nashville
	Wed.	15	at Washington			Sat.	26	at Chicago
	Thu.	16	at NY Islanders			Mon.	28	Colorado
	Sat.	18	at Carolina			Wed.	30	at Calgary
	Mon.	20	at Boston		Apr.	Sat.	2	at San Jose
	Tue.	21	at Buffalo			Sun.	3	Dallas*
	Sun.	26	at Los Angeles			Wed.	6	San Jose
	Tue.	28	at Phoenix			Fri.	8	Los Angeles
	Fri.	31	Philadelphia*			Sat.	9	at Los Angeles

* Denotes afternoon game.

Corey Perry and Ryan Getzlaf celebrate with Joffrey Lupul (number 14) after a goal. Perry led the Ducks with 76 points in 2009-10 while Getzlaf led the team with 50 assists.

PACIFIC DIVISION
18th NHL Season

Franchise date: June 15, 1993

2010-11 Player Personnel

FORWARDS	HT	WT	S	Place of Birth	*Age	2009-10 Club
BELESKEY, Matt	6-0	204	L	Windsor, Ont.	22	Ana-San Antonio-Tor (AHL)
BLAKE, Jason	5-10	186	L	Moorhead, MN	37	Toronto-Anaheim
BODIE, Troy	6-4	214	R	Portage La Prairie, Man.	25	Ana-San Antonio-Tor (AHL)
BONINO, Nick	6-1	190	L	Hartford, CT	22	Boston University-Anaheim
BORDSON, Rob	6-2	190	L	Duluth, MN	22	U. Minn-Duluth
BRITTAIN, Josh	6-5	217	L	Milton, Ont.	20	Barrie-Plymouth
CARTER, Ryan	6-2	200	L	White Bear Lake, MN	27	Anaheim
CHIPCHURA, Kyle	6-2	206	L	Westlock, Alta.	24	Montreal-Anaheim
DESCHAMPS, Nicolas	6-1	189	L	Lasalle, Que.	20	Chicoutimi-Moncton
GETZLAF, Ryan	6-4	220	R	Regina, Sask.	25	Anaheim
GREEN, Josh	6-4	225	L	Camrose, Alta.	32	MODO
HOLLAND, Peter	6-2	187	L	Toronto, Ont.	19	Guelph
JAFFRAY, Jason	6-1	195	L	Rimbey, Alta.	29	Calgary-Abbotsford
KOIVU, Saku	5-10	178	L	Turku, Finland	35	Anaheim
LUPUL, Joffrey	6-1	206	R	Fort Saskatchewan, Alta.	27	Anaheim
MACENAUER, Maxime	6-0	205	L	Laval, Que.	21	Bakersfield
MARCHANT, Todd	5-10	179	L	Buffalo, NY	37	Anaheim
McMILLAN, Brandon	5-11	185	L	Richmond, B.C.	20	Kelowna
PALMIERI, Kyle	5-10	194	R	Smithtown, NY	19	U. of Notre Dame
PARROS, George	6-5	222	R	Washington, PA	30	Anaheim
PERRY, Corey	6-3	206	R	Peterborough, Ont.	25	Anaheim
RYAN, Bobby	6-2	208	R	Cherry Hill, NJ	23	Anaheim
SELANNE, Teemu	6-0	196	R	Helsinki, Finland	40	Anaheim
SEXTON, Dan	5-10	170	R	Apple Valley, MN	23	Ana-Manitoba-Bakersfield
SHARP, MacGregor	6-1	186	L	Vancouver, B.C.	25	Ana-San Antonio-Bakersfield
SMITH, Trevor	6-1	195	L	North Vancouver, B.C.	25	Bridgeport
VOROS, Aaron	6-4	215	L	Vancouver, B.C.	29	NY Rangers

DEFENSEMEN						
BICKEL, Stu	6-4	207	R	Chanhassen, MN	24	San Antonio-Bakersfield
BROOKBANK, Sheldon	6-1	200	R	Lanigan, Sask.	30	Anaheim
CLARK, Mat	6-3	211	R	Lakewood, CO	19	Brampton-Manitoba
de GRAY, John	6-4	215	L	Richmond Hill, Ont.	22	Bakersfield-Rochester
FESTERLING, Brett	6-1	210	R	Quesnel, B.C.	24	Ana-San Antonio-Tor (AHL)
FOWLER, Cam	6-1	190	L	Windsor, Ont.	18	Windsor
LYDMAN, Toni	6-1	210	L	Lahti, Finland	33	Buffalo
MIKKELSON, Brendan	6-3	205	L	Regina, Sask.	23	Anaheim-Toronto (AHL)
MITERA, Mark	6-4	214	L	Royal Oak, MI	22	San Antonio-Abbotsford-Bakersfield
NEWTON, Jake	6-3	205	L	San Jacinto, CA	22	Northeastern
REGAN, Eric	6-2	206	R	Ajax, Ont.	22	San Antonio-Bakersfield
SBISA, Luca	6-2	204	L	Ozieri, Italy	20	Ana-Leth-Port (WHL)
SUTTON, Andy	6-6	245	L	Kingston, Ont.	35	NY Islanders-Ottawa
SYVRET, Danny	5-11	203	L	Millgrove, Ont.	25	Philadelphia-Adirondack
VISNOVSKY, Lubomir	5-10	188	L	Topolcany, Czech.	34	Edmonton-Anaheim

GOALTENDERS	HT	WT	C	Place of Birth	*Age	2009-10 Club
COUSINEAU, Marco	6-0	200	L	St.Lazare, Que.	20	P.E.I.-Saint John
HILLER, Jonas	6-2	190	R	Felben Wellhausen, Switz.	28	Anaheim
LEVASSEUR, Jean-Philippe	6-1	199	R	Victoriaville, Que.	23	Springfield-Laredo-Bakersfield
McELHINNEY, Curtis	6-2	196	L	London, Ont.	27	Calgary-Anaheim
PIELMEIER, Timo	6-0	167	L	Deggendorf, W. Germany	21	Bakersfield

*– Age at start of 2010-11 season

2009-10 Scoring
*– rookie

Regular Season

Pos	#	Player	Team	GP	G	A	Pts	TOI	+/-	PIM	PP	SH	GW	S	%
R	10	Corey Perry	ANA	82	27	49	76	21:03	0	111	6	1	2	270	10.0
C	15	Ryan Getzlaf	ANA	66	19	50	69	21:40	4	79	8	0	5	149	12.8
R	9	Bobby Ryan	ANA	81	35	29	64	18:29	9	81	11	0	3	258	13.6
C	11	Saku Koivu	ANA	71	19	33	52	18:34	14	36	5	1	6	124	15.3
R	8	Teemu Selanne	ANA	54	27	21	48	17:19	3	16	14	0	5	173	15.6
D	27	Scott Niedermayer	ANA	80	10	38	48	26:30	-9	38	5	0	2	168	6.0
D	17	Lubomir Visnovsky	EDM	57	10	22	32	20:45	-4	16	4	0	1	78	12.8
			ANA	16	5	8	13	25:59	-6	4	1	0	1	53	9.4
			Total	73	15	30	45	21:54	-10	20	5	0	2	131	11.5
L	33	Jason Blake	TOR	56	10	16	26	15:50	-4	26	2	0	2	170	5.9
			ANA	26	6	9	15	16:02	-6	10	4	0	0	69	8.7
			Total	82	16	25	41	15:54	-10	36	6	0	2	239	6.7
D	34	James Wisniewski	ANA	69	3	27	30	24:20	-5	56	2	0	0	146	2.1
C	22	Todd Marchant	ANA	78	9	13	22	15:48	-16	32	0	3	1	83	10.8
R	42	* Dan Sexton	ANA	41	9	10	19	13:29	-3	16	2	0	0	93	9.7
L	39	* Matt Beleskey	ANA	60	11	7	18	13:59	-10	35	0	0	3	123	8.9
D	7	Steve Eminger	ANA	63	4	12	16	19:28	1	30	0	0	1	45	8.9
R	14	Joffrey Lupul	ANA	23	10	4	14	15:57	3	18	0	0	0	66	15.2
D	4	Aaron Ward	CAR	60	1	10	11	18:06	-17	54	0	0	0	32	3.1
			ANA	17	0	2	2	14:26	2	8	0	0	0	9	0.0
			Total	77	1	12	13	17:18	-15	62	0	0	0	41	2.4
C	28	Kyle Chipchura	MTL	19	0	0	0	8:37	-10	16	0	0	0	11	0.0
			ANA	55	6	6	12	12:28	-2	56	0	1	1	43	14.0
			Total	74	6	6	12	11:29	-12	72	0	1	1	54	11.1
C	20	Ryan Carter	ANA	38	4	5	9	9:51	0	31	0	0	1	38	10.5
D	21	Sheldon Brookbank	ANA	66	0	9	9	14:57	10	114	0	0	0	60	0.0
R	13	Mike Brown	ANA	75	6	1	7	8:21	1	106	0	1	2	82	7.3
R	50	* Troy Bodie	ANA	44	5	2	7	11:14	-8	80	0	1	1	58	8.6
R	16	George Parros	ANA	57	4	0	4	6:00	4	136	0	0	0	25	16.0
D	53	Brett Festerling	ANA	42	0	3	3	12:30	1	15	0	0	0	25	0.0
C	63	* Nick Bonino	ANA	9	1	1	2	14:13	0	6	1	0	0	14	7.1
C	32	Kyle Calder	ANA	10	0	2	2	14:07	-7	8	0	0	0	20	0.0
D	60	Brendan Mikkelson	ANA	28	0	2	2	14:59	-5	14	0	0	0	21	0.0
D	41	Nathan Oystrick	ANA	3	0	0	0	10:34	-1	2	0	0	0	0	0.0
D	5	Luca Sbisa	ANA	8	0	0	0	12:37	-1	4	0	0	0	3	0.0
C	67	* MacGregor Sharp	ANA	8	0	0	0	4:09	0	0	0	0	0	6	0.0

Goaltending

No.	Goaltender	GPI	Mins	Avg	W	L	OT	EN	SO	GA	SA	S%	G	A	PIM
1	Jonas Hiller	59	3338	2.73	30	23	4	6	2	152	1860	.918	0	2	0
31	Curtis McElhinney	10	521	2.76	5	1	2	0	0	24	288	.917	0	0	0
35	Jean-Sebastien Giguere	20	1108	3.14	4	8	5	3	1	58	580	.900	0	0	2
	Totals	82	4996	2.92	39	32	11	9	3	243	2737	.911			

Randy Carlyle
Head Coach
Born: Sudbury, Ont., April 19, 1956.

Randy Carlyle was hired as the head coach in Anaheim on August 1, 2005. In his first season behind the bench in 2005-06, he led the Ducks to the Western Conference Final. He led Anaheim to its first Stanley Cup championship in 2007.

Prior to joining Anaheim, Carlyle had served as the head coach of the Manitoba Moose, the Vancouver Canucks' primary development team. In all, Carlyle spent six seasons between 1996 and 2005 as head coach in Manitoba (both in the International and American Hockey Leagues) with his team posting an overall record of 222-159-52-7. He had the additional duties of general manager of the Moose from 1996 to 2000, and served as club president for the 2001-02 season. Carlyle helped the Moose to a 47-21-14 record for 108 points in 1998-99, for which he was named the IHL's general manager of the year.

Following the 2001-02 season, Carlyle joined the coaching staff of the Washington Capitals. He served as an assistant coach with Washington for two seasons (2002 to 2004), before rejoining Manitoba in 2004–05.

Carlyle played 17 seasons in the NHL with Toronto, Pittsburgh and Winnipeg. He appeared in 1,055 games and had 148 goals and 499 assists for 647 points. Known as a fiery, tough-nosed defenseman, he was selected to play in four NHL All-Star Games, winning the Norris Trophy as the league's top defenseman in 1981. At the conclusion of his playing career in 1993, Carlyle remained with the Winnipeg organization's hockey operations staff, eventually becoming an assistant coach for the 1995-96 season.

Coaching Record

Season	Team	League	Regular Season GC	W	L	O/T	Playoffs GC	W	L	T
1996-97	Manitoba	IHL	32	16	14	2	....	....	....	....
1997-98	Manitoba	IHL	82	39	36	7	3	0	3	....
1998-99	Manitoba	IHL	82	47	21	14	5	2	3	....
99-2000	Manitoba	IHL	82	37	31	14	2	0	2	....
2000-01	Manitoba	IHL	82	39	31	12	13	6	7	....
2004-05	Manitoba	AHL	80	44	26	10	14	6	8	....
2005-06	**Anaheim**	NHL	82	43	27	12	16	9	7	
2006-07 ♦	**Anaheim**	NHL	82	48	20	14	21	16	5	
2007-08	**Anaheim**	NHL	82	47	27	8	6	2	4	
2008-09	**Anaheim**	NHL	82	42	33	7	13	7	6	
2009-10	**Anaheim**	NHL	82	39	32	11	....	....	....	....
	NHL Totals		410	219	139	52	56	34	22	

♦ Stanley Cup win.

Having established himself as the club's number-one goalie in 2008-09, Jonas Hiller had a heavier workload in 2009-10 and won 30 games.

Club Records

Team

(Figures in brackets for season records are games played; records for fewest points, wins, ties, losses, goals, goals against are for 70 or more games)

Most Points	110	2006-07 (82)
Most Wins	48	2006-07 (82)
Most Ties	13	1996-97 (82), 1997-98 (82), 1998-99 (82)
Most Losses	46	1993-94 (84)
Most Goals	258	2006-07 (82)
Most Goals Against	261	1997-98 (82)
Fewest Points	65	1997-98 (82)
Fewest Wins	25	2000-01 (82)
Fewest Ties	5	1993-94 (84)
Fewest Losses	20	2006-07 (82)
Fewest Goals	175	2001-02 (82)
Fewest Goals Against	191	2007-08 (82)

Longest Winning Streak

Overall	7	Feb. 20-Mar. 7/99
Home	11	Dec. 8/09-Feb. 10/10
Away	7	Nov. 28-Dec. 13/06

Longest Undefeated Streak

Overall	12	Feb. 22-Mar. 19/97 (7 wins, 5 ties)
Home	14	Feb. 12-Apr. 9/97 (10 wins, 4 ties)
Away	7	Nov. 28-Dec. 13/06 (7 wins)

Longest Losing Streak

Overall	8	Oct. 12-30/96, Nov. 3-20/05
Home	8	Jan. 10-Feb. 9/01
Away	9	Oct. 11-Dec. 11/09

Longest Winless Streak

Overall	9	Three times
Home	11	Jan. 5-Feb. 14/01 (8 losses, 3 ties)
Away	13	Nov. 1-Dec. 27/03 (11 losses, 2 ties)

Most Shutouts, Season	9	2002-03 (82)
Most PIM, Season	1,843	1997-98 (82)
Most Goals, Game	8	Jan. 21/98 (Fla. 3 at Ana. 8), Mar. 21/04 (Det. 6 at Ana. 8)

Individual

Most Seasons	11	Teemu Selanne
Most Games	701	Teemu Selanne
Most Goals, Career	379	Teemu Selanne
Most Assists, Career	412	Teemu Selanne
Most Points, Career	791	Teemu Selanne (379G, 412A)
Most PIM, Career	788	Dave Karpa
Most Shutouts, Career	32	Jean-Sebastien Giguere
Longest Consecutive Games Streak	276	Andy McDonald (Oct. 17/03-Dec. 12/07)
Most Goals, Season	52	Teemu Selanne (1997-98)
Most Assists, Season	66	Ryan Getzlaf (2008-09)
Most Points, Season	109	Teemu Selanne (1996-97; 51G, 58A)
Most PIM, Season	285	Todd Ewen (1995-96)
Most Points, Defenseman, Season	69	Scott Niedermayer (2006-07; 15G, 54A)
Most Points, Center, Season	91	Ryan Getzlaf (2008-09; 25G, 66A)
Most Points, Right Wing, Season	109	Teemu Selanne (1996-97; 51G, 58A)
Most Points, Left Wing, Season	108	Paul Kariya (1995-96; 50G, 58A)
Most Points, Rookie, Season	57	Bobby Ryan (2008-09; 31G, 26A)
Most Shutouts, Season	8	Jean-Sebastien Giguere (2002-03)
Most Goals, Game	3	Twenty-seven times
Most Assists, Game	5	Dmitri Mironov (Dec. 12/97) Teemu Selanne (Nov. 19/06) Ryan Getzlaf (Oct. 29/08)
Most Points, Game	5	Thirteen times

General Managers' History

Jack Ferreira, 1993-94 to 1997-98; Pierre Gauthier, 1998-99 to 2001-02; Bryan Murray, 2002-03, 2003-04; Al Coates, 2004-05; Brian Burke, 2005-06 to 2007-08; Brian Burke and Bob Murray, 2008-09; Bob Murray, 2009-10 to date.

Coaching History

Ron Wilson, 1993-94 to 1996-97; Pierre Page, 1997-98; Craig Hartsburg, 1998-99, 1999-2000; Craig Hartsburg and Guy Charron, 2000-01; Bryan Murray, 2001-02; Mike Babcock, 2002-03 to 2004-05; Randy Carlyle, 2005-06 to date.

Captains' History

Troy Loney, 1993-94; Randy Ladouceur, 1994-95, 1995-96; Paul Kariya, 1996-97; Paul Kariya and Teemu Selanne, 1997-98; Paul Kariya, 1998-99 to 2002-03; Steve Rucchin, 2003-04; Scott Niedermayer, 2005-06, 2006-07; Chris Pronger, 2007-08; Scott Niedermayer, 2008-09, 2009-10.

All-time Record vs. Other Clubs

Regular Season

	At Home								On Road								Total							
	GP	W	L	T	OL	GF	GA	PTS	GP	W	L	T	OL	GF	GA	PTS	GP	W	L	T	OL	GF	GA	PTS
Atlanta	6	3	3	0	0	18	18	6	6	4	2	0	0	19	13	8	12	7	5	0	0	37	31	14
Boston	11	4	3	2	2	24	28	12	11	5	5	0	1	33	34	11	22	9	8	2	3	57	62	23
Buffalo	12	5	7	0	0	27	37	10	11	3	4	3	1	25	30	10	23	8	11	3	1	52	67	20
Calgary	36	22	8	6	0	118	90	50	35	11	23	1	0	78	101	23	71	33	31	7	0	196	191	73
Carolina	12	6	5	1	0	35	37	13	11	4	6	1	0	25	28	9	23	10	11	2	0	60	65	22
Chicago	32	20	8	3	1	91	64	44	34	16	15	2	1	85	91	35	66	36	23	5	2	176	155	79
Colorado	31	14	12	3	2	83	77	33	31	11	14	4	2	83	89	28	62	25	26	7	4	166	166	61
Columbus	18	9	6	1	2	52	49	21	18	9	8	0	1	45	47	19	36	18	14	1	3	97	96	40
Dallas	45	20	21	3	1	112	122	44	45	10	28	2	5	87	149	27	90	30	49	5	6	199	271	71
Detroit	32	14	14	4	0	85	86	32	32	3	22	3	4	67	114	13	64	17	36	7	4	152	200	45
Edmonton	36	19	14	1	2	104	96	41	35	14	18	0	3	81	87	31	71	33	32	2	4	185	183	72
Florida	11	4	6	1	0	29	33	9	10	4	3	2	1	25	27	11	21	8	9	3	1	54	60	20
Los Angeles	48	24	10	7	7	163	129	62	48	18	24	4	2	123	144	42	96	42	34	11	9	286	273	104
Minnesota	18	11	5	0	2	46	42	24	18	5	8	2	3	36	47	15	36	16	13	2	5	82	89	39
Montreal	10	4	5	0	1	31	32	9	10	4	4	2	0	30	31	10	20	8	9	2	1	61	63	19
Nashville	22	17	2	0	3	69	37	37	22	9	9	2	2	50	52	22	44	26	11	2	5	119	89	59
New Jersey	12	6	5	1	0	34	31	13	10	2	7	0	1	17	35	5	22	8	12	1	1	51	66	18
NY Islanders	11	3	4	3	1	27	33	10	10	4	5	1	0	27	26	9	21	7	9	4	1	54	59	19
NY Rangers	10	6	2	0	2	36	32	14	12	6	4	1	1	32	31	14	22	12	6	1	3	68	63	28
Ottawa	11	5	3	2	1	27	23	13	10	5	4	3	0	27	27	9	21	7	8	5	1	54	67	20
Philadelphia	11	4	4	2	1	38	40	11	10	3	4	3	0	20	27	9	21	7	8	5	1	58	67	20
Phoenix	45	28	11	3	3	140	110	62	44	22	14	2	6	125	122	52	89	50	25	5	9	265	232	114
Pittsburgh	10	6	4	0	0	35	30	12	12	2	8	2	0	34	42	6	22	8	12	2	0	69	72	18
St. Louis	32	15	15	2	0	90	92	32	32	12	13	3	4	87	101	31	64	27	28	5	4	177	193	63
San Jose	48	19	24	2	3	126	144	43	48	23	22	2	1	126	132	49	96	42	46	4	4	252	276	92
Tampa Bay	11	6	4	1	0	35	29	13	11	7	4	0	0	29	21	14	22	13	8	1	0	64	50	27
Toronto	13	6	6	1	0	42	34	13	17	3	10	4	0	35	55	10	30	9	16	5	0	77	89	23
Vancouver	35	12	12	7	4	100	105	35	36	14	20	2	0	88	116	30	71	26	32	9	4	188	221	65
Washington	11	6	3	1	1	35	31	14	11	6	5	0	0	29	22	12	22	12	8	1	1	64	53	26
Totals	640	318	226	58	38	1852	1711	732	640	239	313	49	39	1568	1844	566	1280	557	539	107	77	3420	3555	1298

Playoffs

	Series	W	L	GP	W	L	T	GF	GA	Last Mtg.	Rnd.	Result
Calgary	1	1	0	7	4	3	0	17	16	2006	CQF	W 4-3
Colorado	1	1	0	4	4	0	0	16	4	2006	CSF	W 4-0
Dallas	2	1	1	12	6	6	0	27	34	2008	CQF	L 2-4
Detroit	5	2	3	25	11	14	0	57	75	2009	CSF	L 3-4
Edmonton	1	0	1	5	1	4	0	13	16	2006	CF	L 1-4
Minnesota	2	2	0	9	8	1	0	21	10	2007	CQF	W 4-1
New Jersey	1	0	1	7	3	4	0	12	19	2003	F	L 3-4
Ottawa	1	1	0	5	4	1	0	16	11	2007	F	W 4-1
Phoenix	1	1	0	7	4	3	0	17	17	1997	CQF	W 4-3
San Jose	1	1	0	4	4	0	0	18	10	2009	CQF	W 4-2
Vancouver	1	1	0	5	4	1	0	14	8	2007	CSF	W 4-1
Totals	17	11	6	92	53	39	0	228	220			

Playoff Results 2010-2006

Year	Round	Opponent	Result	GF	GA
2009	CSF	Detroit	L 3-4	17	22
	CQF	San Jose	W 4-2	18	10
2008	CQF	Dallas	L 2-4	13	20
2007	**F**	**Ottawa**	**W 4-1**	**16**	**11**
	CF	Detroit	W 4-2	16	17
	CSF	Vancouver	W 4-1	14	8
	CQF	Minnesota	W 4-1	12	9
2006	CF	Edmonton	L 1-4	13	16
	CSF	Colorado	W 4-0	16	4
	CQF	Calgary	W 4-3	17	16

Abbreviations: Round: F - Final; **CF** – conference final; **CSF** – conference semi-final; **CQF** – conference quarter-final

Carolina totals include Hartford, 1993-94 to 1996-97.
Colorado totals include Quebec, 1993-94 to 1994-95.
Phoenix totals include Winnipeg, 1993-94 to 1995-96.

2009-10 Results

Date		Opponent	Result		Opponent	Result
Oct.	3	San Jose	1-4	3	at Chicago	2-5
	6	at Minnesota	3-4*	5	Detroit	4-1
	8	at Boston	6-1	7	St. Louis	4-2
	10	at Philadelphia	3-2†	9	at Nashville	3-2
	11	at NY Rangers	0-3	10	at Chicago	3-1
	14	Minnesota	3-2	13	Boston	4-3
	17	St. Louis	0-5	14	at Los Angeles	0-4
	21	Dallas	2-4	17	Calgary	5-4
	24	Columbus	4-6	19	Buffalo	5-4
	26	Toronto	3-6	21	at San Jose	1-3
	30	Vancouver	7-2	23	at St. Louis	4-3†
	31	at Phoenix	2-3†	26	at Atlanta	1-2
Nov.	3	Pittsburgh	3-4	27	at Washington	1-5
	5	Nashville	4-0	29	at Tampa Bay	2-1†
	7	Phoenix	4-3	Feb. 1	at Florida	3-0
	11	at New Jersey	1-3	3	Detroit	3-1
	13	at Columbus	2-3†	4	at Los Angeles	4-6
	14	at Detroit	4-7	8	Los Angeles	4-2
	16	at Pittsburgh	2-5	10	Edmonton	3-2
	19	Tampa Bay	4-3*	13	at Calgary	1-3
	21	San Jose	2-3	14	at Edmonton	7-3
	23	Calgary	3-2†	Mar. 3	Colorado	3-4
	25	Carolina	3-2	5	at Phoenix	0-4
	27	Chicago	3-0	7	Montreal	3-4†
	29	Phoenix	2-3*	9	Columbus	2-5
Dec.	1	Los Angeles	2-3*	12	Nashville	0-1
	3	at Dallas	1-3	14	San Jose	4-2
	4	at Minnesota	4-5†	17	Chicago	4-2
	6	Ottawa	3-4†	19	NY Islanders	5-4*
	8	Dallas	4-3*	21	Colorado	5-2
	11	at Detroit	2-3*	23	at Calgary	1-3
	12	at Columbus	3-1	24	at Vancouver	1-4
	16	at Vancouver	3-2	26	at Edmonton	3-2
	17	at San Jose	1-4	29	Dallas	3-1
	19	Phoenix	4-2	31	at Colorado	0-2
	22	at Colorado	4-2	Apr. 2	Vancouver	4-5†
	23	at Phoenix	0-4	3	at Los Angeles	2-1†
	26	at San Jose	2-5	6	Los Angeles	4-5†
	29	Minnesota	3-5	8	at Dallas	2-3†
	31	at Dallas	3-5	9	at St. Louis	3-6
Jan.	2	at Nashville	1-3	11	Edmonton	7-2

* – Overtime   † – Shootout

Entry Draft Selections 2010-1996

Name in bold denotes played in NHL.

2010
Pick
- 12 Cam Fowler
- 29 Emerson Etem
- 42 Devante Smith-Pelly
- 122 Chris Wagner
- 132 Tim Heed
- 161 Andreas Dahlstrom
- 177 Kevin Lind
- 192 Brett Perlini

2009
Pick
- 15 Peter Holland
- 26 Kyle Palmieri
- 37 Matt Clark
- 76 Igor Bobkov
- 106 Sami Vatanen
- 136 Radoslav Illo
- 166 Scott Valentine

2008
Pick
- 17 Jake Gardiner
- 35 Nicolas Deschamps
- 39 Eric O'Dell
- 43 Justin Schultz
- 71 Josh Brittain
- 83 Marco Cousineau
- 85 Brandon McMillan
- 113 Ryan Hegarty
- 143 Stefan Warg
- 208 Nick Pryor

2007
Pick
- 19 Logan MacMillan
- 42 **Eric Tangradi**
- 63 Maxime Macenauer
- 92 Justin Vaive
- 93 Steven Kampfer
- 98 Sebastian Stefaniszin
- 121 Mattias Modig
- 151 Brett Morrison

2006
Pick
- 19 Mark Mitera
- 38 Bryce Swan
- 83 John Degray
- 112 **Matt Beleskey**
- 172 Petteri Wirtanen

2005
Pick
- 2 **Bobby Ryan**
- 31 **Brendan Mikkelson**
- 63 Jason Bailey
- 127 Bobby Bolt
- 141 Brian Salcido
- 197 Jean-Philippe Levasseur

2004
Pick
- 9 **Ladislav Smid**
- 39 Jordan Smith
- 74 Kyle Klubertanz
- 75 **Tim Brent**
- 172 Matt Auffrey
- 203 Gabriel Bouthillette
- 236 Matt Christie
- 269 **Janne Pesonen**

2003
Pick
- 19 **Ryan Getzlaf**
- 28 **Corey Perry**
- 86 Shane Hynes
- 90 Juha Alen
- 119 Nathan Saunders
- 186 **Drew Miller**
- 218 Dirk Southern
- 250 **Shane O'Brien**
- 280 Ville Mantymaa

2002
Pick
- 7 **Joffrey Lupul**
- 37 **Tim Brent**
- 71 Brian Lee
- 103 Joonas Vihko
- 140 George Davis
- 173 Luke Fritshaw
- 261 Francois Caron
- 267 Chris Petrow

2001
Pick
- 5 **Stanislav Chistov**
- 35 **Mark Popovic**
- 69 Joel Stepp
- 102 **Timo Parssinen**
- 105 Vladimir Korsunov
- 118 Brandon Rogers
- 137 **Joel Perrault**
- 170 Jan Tabacek
- 224 **Tony Martensson**
- 232 **Martin Gerber**
- 264 **P.A. Parenteau**

2000
Pick
- 12 **Alexei Smirnov**
- 44 **Ilya Bryzgalov**
- 98 **Jonas Ronnqvist**
- 134 Peter Podhradsky
- 153 Bill Cass

1999
Pick
- 44 **Jordan Leopold**
- 83 **Niclas Havelid**
- 105 Alexandr Chagodayev
- 141 Maxim Rybin
- 173 Jan Sandstrom
- 230 **Petr Tenkrat**
- 258 Brian Gornick

1998
Pick
- 5 **Vitaly Vishnevski**
- 32 **Stephen Peat**
- 112 Viktor Wallin
- 150 **Trent Hunter**
- 178 Jesse Fibiger
- 205 David Bernier
- 233 Pelle Prestberg
- 245 Andreas Andersson

1997
Pick
- 18 **Michael Holmqvist**
- 45 **Maxim Balmochnykh**
- 72 Jay Legault
- 125 Luc Vaillancourt
- 178 Tony Mohagen
- 181 Mat Snesrud
- 209 Rene Stussi
- 235 Tommi Degerman

1996
Pick
- 9 **Ruslan Salei**
- 35 **Matt Cullen**
- 117 Brendan Buckley
- 149 Blaine Russell
- 172 Timo Ahmaoja
- 198 Kevin Kellett
- 224 Tobias Johwelin

Bob Murray
Executive Vice President and General Manager
Born: Kingston, Ont., November 26, 1954.

Bob Murray was named executive vice president and general manager of the Anaheim Ducks on November 12, 2008 after 3 1/2 years as senior vice president of hockey operations. He was named to that original position on July 14, 2005. Murray's astute judgment of hockey talent and player evaluation were instrumental in several trades and acquisitions the Ducks made over his tenure, highlighted by a Stanley Cup championship in 2007.

Murray's responsibilities include overseeing all aspects of player development, playing a key role in the club's professional scouting efforts, contract negotiations and all matters relating to the National Hockey League. He has been instrumental in the organization's success at both the NHL and AHL level. Both the Ducks and American Hockey League's Portland Pirates made Conference Final appearances in 2006, making Anaheim the only organization to have both their NHL and AHL teams advance to their league's respective Conference Finals.

Prior to joining the Ducks, Murray worked as a professional scout with the Vancouver Canucks from 1999 to 2005 under then-general manager Brian Burke (1998 to 2004). Murray's scouting expertise helped to build teams that recorded 100+ point season two years in a row (2002-03 and 2003-04) and advanced to the Stanley Cup playoffs four seasons in a row (2001 to 2004). Before his stint in Vancouver, he served as a scouting consultant for Anaheim during the 1998-99 season.

Murray was a member of the Chicago Blackhawks organization for 25 years, serving as general manager from 1997 to 1999. He was promoted to the post after serving as assistant general manager under Bob Pulford for two seasons. Before joining upper management, Murray was named the director of player personnel in 1991 and was largely responsible for the club's entry draft selections over eight seasons.

Drafted by the Blackhawks in 1974, Murray spent his entire 1,008-game, 15-year career in a Chicago uniform. He became just the fourth player in Blackhawks history to reach the 1,000-game plateau. In addition, he became the first defenseman in club history to appear in 100 postseason contests, reaching the mark during the 1990 Stanley Cup playoffs. In all, Murray scored had 132 goals and 382 assists for 514 points, and currently ranks second in all-time points among Blackhawk defensemen. He was named to both the 1981 and 1983 NHL All-Star Games. Murray retired at the conclusion of the 1989-90 season. Known for his work ethic, intelligence and determination as a player, Murray remained with the organization as a professional scout following his retirement in 1990.

Club Directory

Honda Center

Anaheim Ducks
Honda Center
2695 E. Katella Ave.
Anaheim, CA 92806
Phone 714/940-2900
FAX 714/940-2953
Ticket Information 877/WILDWING
www.anaheimducks.com
Capacity: 17,174

Executive Management
Owners	Henry and Susan Samueli
Chief Executive Officer	Michael Schulman
Executive Vice President/General Manager	Bob Murray
Executive Vice President/Chief Operating Officer	Tim Ryan
Senior Vice President, Hockey Operations	David McNab
Chief Financial Officer/Vice President of Finance	Doug Heller
Vice President, Human Resources	Jay Scott
Vice President, Operations, Anaheim Arena	Kevin Starkey
Vice President, Multi-Media & Community Devel.	Aaron Teats
Vice President of Sales and Marketing	Bob Wagner
Vice President of Finance, Anaheim Arena	Angela Wergechik
Senior Manager of Hockey Operations	Maureen Nyeholt
Exec. Asst. to the Executive V.P./COO	Cheryl Gorman
Exec. Asst. to the V.P., Sales and Marketing	Janet Conley

Coaching Staff
Head Coach	Randy Carlyle
Assistant Coaches	Dave Farrish, Mike Foligno
Goaltending Consultant	Pete Peeters
Video Coordinator	Joe Trotta
Strength and Conditioning Coach	Sean Skahan

Hockey Operations
Director of Player Personnel	Rick Paterson
Director of Amateur Scouting	Martin Madden
Director of Player Development	Alain Chainey
Scouting Staff	David Baseggio, Glen Cochrane, Jeff Crisp, Jan-Åke Danielson, Casey Hankinson, Konstantin Krylov, Matt Laatsch, Kevin Murray, Jim Pappin, Jim Sandlak
Manager of Hockey Operations	Ryan Lichtenfels
Coordinator of Minor League Hockey Ops	Jillian Samueli
Video Scouting Analyst	Joe Piscotty
Head Athletic Trainer	Tim Clark
Assistant Athletic Trainer	Rick Burrill
Massage Therapist	James Partida
Equipment Manager	Doug Shearer
Assistant Equipment Manager	Chris Aldrich
Equipment Assistant	Chris Kincaid
Team Physicians	Dr. Ronald Glousman, Dr. Craig Milhouse

Broadcasting
TV: FSN Prime Ticket (Cable), KDOC-TV	John Ahlers, Brian Hayward
Radio: KLAA AM 830 & Ducks Radio Network	Steve Carroll, Dan Wood
Host/Producer	Kent French

Communications
Director of Media & Communications	Alex Gilchrist
Media & Communications Managers	Steve Hoem, Lauren O'Gorman
Game Night Communications Staff	Chelsea Lawson, Lisa Parris, Courtney Strayer, Larry Woodard

Community Relations
Director of Community Relations	Wendy Yamagishi
Community Relations Managers	Jesse Bryson, Jennifer Walker

Entertainment
Editor/Producer	Rich Cooley
Entertainment Manager	Chris Brown
Arena Vision Editor/Producer	Davin Maske
Producer / Associate Producer	Peter Uvalle / Gabriel Suarez

Fan Development
Director of Fan Development	Matt Savant
Sr Manager of Fan Development, School and Education Programs	Joseph Hwang
Fan Development Manager / Coordinator	Champ Baginski, Mike Hermosa

Finance, Human Resources, Information Technology and Legall
General Counsel	Bernard Schneider
Controller / IT Manager	Melody Martin / Mike Wing
Human Resources Managers	Wendy Mulhall, Donna Vass

Corporate Partnerships
Director of Corporate Partnerships	Greg Rieber
Director of Corporate Partnership Activation	Alex Anderson
Managers	Greg Geffs, Matt Wiech, Mark Hermanson, Robert Flanigan, Rachel Kaizoji, Erin Ogawa

Marketing
Director of Marketing	Tracie Jones
Sr. Manager of Signature Programs and Events	Kris Loomis
Senior Media and Marketing Manager	Adam Mendelsohn
Marketing Managers	Jesse Chatfield, Ryan Spillers
Signature Programs and Events Manager	Jamie Minkler
Designers, Senior / Junior	Mariana Stoopen / Patrick Boykin

Publications and New Media
Director of Publications and New Media	Adam Brady
Social Media Producer	Neil Horowitz

Premium Sales and Service
Director of Premium Sales & Service	Jim Panetta
Premium Account Executives	Mark Eggering, Geoff Matthews, Timothy Thompson
Premium Services Manager	Jana Cannavo

Ticketing
Manager of Ticket Operations	James Bakken
Assistant Managers	Jonas Calicdan, Gina Bulgheroni

Ticket Sales and Customer Service
Director of Ticket Sales and Service	Lisa Johnson
Sr. Manager of Season and Group Sales	Mike Morrow
Inside Sales Manager	Graham Siderius

Atlanta Thrashers

Key Off-Season Signings/Acquisitions

2010

April 14 • Named **Rick Dudley** general manager.

June 8 • Re-signed C **Jim Slater**.

24 • Acquired RW **Dustin Byfuglien**, LW **Ben Eager**, RW **Akim Aliu** and D **Brent Sopel** from Chicago for C **Marty Reasoner**, RW **Joey Crabb**, LW **Jeremy Morin** and New Jersey's 1st and 2nd round picks in the 2010 Entry Draft (previously acquired).

24 • Named **Craig Ramsay** head coach.

July 1 • Signed G **Chris Mason**.

1 • Acquired LW **Andrew Ladd** from Chicago for D **Ivan Vishnevskiy** and a 2nd round pick in the 2011 Entry Draft.

8 • Named **John Torchetti** associate coach.

12 • Named **Mike Stothers** assistant coach.

22 • Re-signed G **Ondrej Pavelec**.

2009-10 Results: 35w-34L-7OTL-6SOL 83PTS.
Second, Southeast Division

Year-by-Year Record

Season	GP	Home W	Home L	Home T	Home OL	Road W	Road L	Road T	Road OL	Overall W	Overall L	Overall T	Overall OL	GF	GA	Pts.	Finished	Playoff Result
2009-10	82	19	16	....	6	16	18	....	7	35	34	....	13	234	256	83	2nd, Southeast Div.	Out of Playoffs
2008-09	82	18	21	....	2	17	20	....	4	35	41	....	6	257	280	76	4th, Southeast Div.	Out of Playoffs
2007-08	82	19	19	....	3	15	21	....	5	34	40	....	8	216	272	76	4th, Southeast Div.	Out of Playoffs
2006-07	82	23	12	....	6	20	16	....	5	43	28	....	11	246	245	97	1st, Southeast Div.	Lost Conf. Quarter-Final
2005-06	82	24	13	....	4	17	20	....	4	41	33	....	8	281	275	90	3rd, Southeast Div.	Out of Playoffs
2004-05	....	....																
2003-04	82	18	17	4	2	15	20	4	2	33	37	8	4	214	243	78	2nd, Southeast Div.	Out of Playoffs
2002-03	82	15	19	4	3	16	20	3	2	31	39	7	5	226	284	74	3rd, Southeast Div.	Out of Playoffs
2001-02	82	11	21	9	0	8	26	2	5	19	47	11	5	187	288	54	5th, Southeast Div.	Out of Playoffs
2000-01	82	10	23	6	2	13	22	6	0	23	45	12	2	211	289	60	4th, Southeast Div.	Out of Playoffs
1999-2000	82	9	26	3	3	5	31	4	1	14	57	7	4	170	313	39	5th, Southeast Div.	Out of Playoffs

2010-11 Schedule

Oct. Fri. 8 Washington
Sat. 9 at Tampa Bay
Tue. 12 at Los Angeles
Fri. 15 at Anaheim
Sat. 16 at San Jose
Wed. 20 Buffalo
Fri. 22 Tampa Bay
Sat. 23 at Washington
Wed. 27 at NY Rangers
Fri. 29 Buffalo
Sat. 30 at St. Louis

Nov. Wed. 3 at Florida
Thu. 4 Columbus
Sat. 6 Chicago
Tue. 9 at Ottawa
Thu. 11 Minnesota
Sat. 13 Pittsburgh
Sun. 14 at Washington*
Wed. 17 Florida
Fri. 19 Washington
Sun. 21 NY Islanders*
Wed. 24 Detroit
Fri. 26 Montreal
Sun. 28 Boston*
Tue. 30 at Colorado

Dec. Thu. 2 at Pittsburgh
Sat. 4 at Washington
Mon. 6 Nashville
Fri. 10 Colorado
Sat. 11 at NY Islanders
Mon. 13 at Ottawa
Wed. 15 at Tampa Bay
Thu. 16 Carolina
Sat. 18 New Jersey
Mon. 20 at Toronto
Tue. 21 St. Louis
Thu. 23 at Boston
Sun. 26 Tampa Bay
Tue. 28 at Pittsburgh
Thu. 30 Boston
Fri. 31 at New Jersey*

Jan. Sun. 2 at Montreal*
Wed. 5 at Florida
Fri. 7 Toronto
Sun. 9 at Carolina*
Fri. 14 Philadelphia
Sat. 15 at Dallas
Mon. 17 at Florida
Thu. 20 Tampa Bay
Sat. 22 NY Rangers
Sun. 23 at Tampa Bay
Wed. 26 Washington

Feb. Tue. 1 NY Islanders
Thu. 3 Calgary
Sat. 5 at Carolina
Mon. 7 at Toronto
Fri. 11 NY Rangers
Sun. 13 Carolina*
Thu. 17 at Phoenix
Sat. 19 at Edmonton*
Wed. 23 at Buffalo
Fri. 25 Florida
Sun. 27 Toronto*

Mar. Tue. 1 Montreal
Thu. 3 Ottawa
Sat. 5 Florida
Wed. 9 at Carolina
Fri. 11 New Jersey
Sat. 12 at Philadelphia
Tue. 15 at New Jersey
Thu. 17 Philadelphia
Sat. 19 at Buffalo
Thu. 24 at NY Islanders
Fri. 25 Vancouver
Sun. 27 Ottawa*
Tue. 29 at Montreal
Thu. 31 at Philadelphia

Apr. Sat. 2 at Boston*
Tue. 5 at Nashville
Thu. 7 at NY Rangers
Fri. 8 Carolina
Sun. 10 Pittsburgh*

* Denotes afternoon game.

Nik Antropov scored 24 goals during his first season with Atlanta in 2009-10 and established career highs with 43 assists and 67 points. His 67 points led the team.

SOUTHEAST DIVISION
12th NHL Season

Franchise date: June 25, 1997

2010-11 Player Personnel

FORWARDS	HT	WT	S	Place of Birth	*Age	2009-10 Club
ALIU, Akim	6-3	225	R	Okene, Nigeria	21	Rockford-Toledo
ANTROPOV, Nik	6-6	240	L	Ust-Kamenogorsk, USSR	30	Atlanta
BERGFORS, Niclas	5-11	195	R	Sodertalje, Sweden	23	New Jersey-Atlanta
BOULTON, Eric	6-1	225	L	Halifax, N.S.	34	Atlanta
BURMISTROV, Alexander	6-0	175	L	Kazan, USSR	18	Barrie
BYFUGLIEN, Dustin	6-4	255	R	Minneapolis, MN	25	Chicago
CORMIER, Patrice	6-2	210	L	Moncton, N.B.	20	Rimouski-Rou-Nor-Chi (AHL)
EAGER, Ben	6-2	230	L	Ottawa, Ont.	26	Chicago
ESPOSITO, Angelo	6-1	195	L	Montreal, Que.	21	Chicago (AHL)
HOLZAPFEL, Riley	5-11	195	L	Regina, Sask.	22	Chicago (AHL)
KANE, Evander	6-2	190	L	Vancouver, B.C.	19	Atlanta
KROG, Jason	5-11	185	L	Fernie, B.C.	34	Chicago (AHL)
LADD, Andrew	6-2	200	L	Maple Ridge, B.C.	24	Chicago
LITTLE, Bryan	5-11	185	R	Edmonton, Alta.	22	Atlanta
MACHACEK, Spencer	6-1	195	R	Lethbridge, Alta.	21	Chicago (AHL)
PEVERLEY, Rich	6-0	200	R	Guelph, Ont.	28	Atlanta
RISSMILLER, Patrick	6-4	215	L	Belmont, MA	31	Hartford-Grand Rapids
ROSS, Jared	5-9	165	L	Huntsville, AL	28	Philadelphia-Adirondack
SLATER, Jim	6-0	200	L	Lapeer, MI	27	Atlanta
STEWART, Anthony	6-2	235	R	LaSalle, Que.	25	Chicago (AHL)
THORBURN, Chris	6-3	230	R	Sault Ste. Marie, Ont.	27	Atlanta

DEFENSEMEN						
BOGOSIAN, Zach	6-3	205	R	Massena, NY	20	Atlanta
ENSTROM, Tobias	5-10	180	L	Nordingra, Sweden	25	Atlanta
HAINSEY, Ron	6-3	210	L	Bolton, CT	29	Atlanta
KULDA , Arturs	6-2	210	L	Riga, Latvia	22	Atlanta-Chicago (AHL)
LEWIS, Grant	6-3	205	R	Pittsburgh, PA	25	Chicago (AHL)-Hershey
ODUYA, Johnny	6-0	200	L	Stockholm, Sweden	29	New Jersey-Atlanta
POSTMA, Paul	6-3	195	R	Red Deer, Alta.	21	Chicago (AHL)
SIFERS, Jaime	5-11	210	R	Stratford, CT	27	Minnesota-Houston
SOPEL, Brent	6-1	200	R	Calgary, Alta.	33	Chicago
VALABIK, Boris	6-7	245	L	Nitra, Czech.	24	Atlanta-Chicago (AHL)
WELCH, Noah	6-4	220	L	Brighton, MA	28	Chicago (AHL)

GOALTENDERS	HT	WT	C	Place of Birth	*Age	2009-10 Club
MacINTYRE, Drew	6-0	190	L	Charlottetown, P.E.I.	27	Chicago (AHL)
MANNINO, Peter	6-0	190	R	Farmington Hills, MI	26	Chicago (AHL)
MASON, Chris	6-0	200	L	Red Deer, Alta.	34	St. Louis
PAVELEC, Ondrej	6-3	220	L	Kladno, Czech.	23	Atlanta

* – Age at start of 2010-11 season

Rich Peverly played in 82 games for the first time in 2009-10 and reached career highs in goals (22), assists (33) and points (55).

General Managers' History

Don Waddell, 1999-2000 to 2009-10; Rick Dudley, 2010-11.

Captains' History

Kelly Buchberger, 1999-2000; Steve Staios, 2000-01; Ray Ferraro, 2001-02; no captain, 2002-03; Shawn McEachern, 2002-03, 2003-04; Scott Mellanby, 2005-06, 2006-07; Bobby Holik, 2007-08; no captain and Ilya Kovalchuk, 2008-09; Ilya Kovalchuk, 2009-10.

Coaching History

Curt Fraser, 1999-2000 to 2001-02; Curt Fraser, Don Waddell and Bob Hartley, 2002-03; Bob Hartley, 2003-04 to 2006-07; Bob Hartley and Don Waddell, 2007-08; John Anderson, 2008-09, 2009-10; Craig Ramsay, 2010-11.

2009-10 Scoring

* – rookie

Regular Season

Pos	#	Player	Team	GP	G	A	Pts	TOI	+/-	PIM	PP	SH	GW	S	%
R	80	Nik Antropov	ATL	76	24	43	67	18:13	13	44	8	0	4	126	19.0
R	61	Maxim Afinogenov	ATL	82	24	37	61	17:23	-17	46	6	0	3	181	13.3
C	47	Rich Peverley	ATL	82	22	33	55	18:39	-14	36	7	2	7	166	13.3
D	39	Tobias Enstrom	ATL	82	6	44	50	22:26	-5	30	2	0	0	109	5.5
R	18 *	Niclas Bergfors	N.J.	54	13	14	27	14:52	-7	10	8	0	4	134	9.7
			ATL	27	8	9	17	16:29	-3	0	1	0	2	83	9.6
			Total	81	21	23	44	15:25	-10	10	9	0	6	217	9.7
D	77	Pavel Kubina	ATL	76	6	32	38	22:37	0	66	2	0	1	159	3.8
L	41	Clarke MacArthur	BUF	60	13	13	26	14:22	-14	47	3	0	3	99	13.1
			ATL	21	3	6	9	15:36	-2	2	1	1	0	30	10.0
			Total	81	16	19	35	14:41	-16	49	4	1	3	129	12.4
C	10	Bryan Little	ATL	79	13	21	34	15:45	-6	20	3	0	1	165	7.9
R	20	Colby Armstrong	ATL	79	15	14	29	14:47	6	61	0	1	1	101	14.9
C	9 *	Evander Kane	ATL	66	14	12	26	13:59	2	62	0	1	3	127	11.0
L	13	Vyacheslav Kozlov	ATL	55	8	18	26	15:15	-15	33	3	0	1	113	7.1
C	12	Todd White	ATL	65	7	19	26	15:11	-11	24	2	0	3	92	7.6
D	6	Ron Hainsey	ATL	80	5	21	26	22:08	-6	39	0	0	0	121	4.1
D	4	Zach Bogosian	ATL	81	10	13	23	21:24	-18	61	3	1	0	155	6.5
C	23	Jim Slater	ATL	61	11	7	18	12:12	1	61	0	2	2	107	10.3
C	19	Marty Reasoner	ATL	80	4	13	17	12:30	-3	24	0	0	0	86	4.7
R	76	Evgeny Artyukhin	ANA	37	4	5	9	9:04	0	41	0	0	0	21	19.0
			ATL	17	5	2	7	8:38	-4	31	0	0	2	21	23.8
			Total	54	9	7	16	8:56	-4	72	0	0	2	42	21.4
R	27	Chris Thorburn	ATL	76	4	9	13	9:58	6	89	0	3	0	63	6.3
D	29	Johnny Oduya	N.J.	40	2	2	4	21:11	2	18	0	0	0	44	4.5
			ATL	27	1	8	9	21:22	6	12	0	0	0	24	4.2
			Total	67	3	10	13	21:15	8	30	0	0	0	68	4.4
L	36	Eric Boulton	ATL	62	2	6	8	6:50	-1	113	1	0	0	39	5.1
D	16	Christoph Schubert	ATL	47	2	5	7	15:46	-6	69	0	0	0	73	2.7
D	3	Mark Popovic	ATL	37	2	4	6	14:47	0	10	0	0	0	24	8.3
R	42	Tim Stapleton	ATL	6	2	0	2	11:52	1	2	1	0	0	6	33.3
D	44 *	Arturs Kulda	ATL	4	0	2	2	11:59	2	2	0	0	0	5	0.0
D	5	Boris Valabik	ATL	23	0	2	2	13:13	2	36	0	0	0	22	0.0
D	24	Chris Chelios	ATL	7	0	0	0	11:10	-2	0	0	0	0	5	0.0

Goaltending

No.	Goaltender	GPI	Mins	Avg	W	L	OT	EN	SO	GA	SA	S%	G	A	PIM
1	Johan Hedberg	47	2632	2.62	21	16	6	4	3	115	1355	.915	0	1	6
31	Ondrej Pavelec	42	2317	3.29	14	18	7	4	2	127	1353	.906	0	1	0
	Totals	82	4988	3.01	35	34	13	8	5	250	2716	.908			

Rick Dudley

General Manager

Born: Toronto, Ont., January 31, 1949.

Rick Dudley joined the Atlanta Thrashers as the associate general manager in June of 2009 and was promoted to the position of general manager on April 14, 2010. He brings more than 40 years of experience in professional hockey as a player, coach and executive to the organization.

Dudley joined Atlanta after five years with the Chicago Blackhawks, where he served as the team's assistant general manager for the last three seasons. Before joining the Blackhawks in 2004, Dudley served as the general manager of the Florida Panthers for two seasons from 2002-03 to 2003-04. With the Panthers, he guided the team to improved records both seasons while drafting players such as Jay Bouwmeester and Nathan Horton. From 1999-00 to 2001-02, Dudley was the Tampa Bay Lightning's general manager and was responsible for rebuilding a last-place franchise and setting them on a path that culminated in the 2004 Stanley Cup championship. Prior to joining the Lightning, Dudley served as the general manager for the Ottawa Senators for one season in 1998-99.

Dudley was the general manager for the Detroit Vipers of the former International Hockey League for four seasons before joining the Senators. With the Vipers, Dudley led the team to a 200-92-35 record and the 1997 Turner Cup championship. Overall, as a general manager he has led his teams to the league finals eight times and won four championships in the American Hockey League, IHL and ECHL. Dudley also has a lengthy and successful record as a head coach in both the NHL and minor leagues. He spent two-and-a-half seasons as head coach of the Buffalo Sabres from 1989-90 to 1991-92, posting an 85-72-31 record while leading the team to the playoffs twice. During the 2003-04 season, he spent 40 games behind the bench of the Florida Panthers.

The Toronto native played seven NHL seasons with Buffalo and Winnipeg, recording 174 points (75 goals, 99 assists) in 309 games. He also appeared in 270 World Hockey Association games over four seasons with the Cincinnati Stingers, where he earned 277 points (131 goals, 146 assists) and tallied back-to-back 40-goal seasons in 1975-76 and 1976-77. After retiring as a player, Dudley became the owner, general manager and head coach of the ECHL's Carolina Thunderbirds. He also served as the league's president from 1983 to 1986. Prior to retiring, he was part owner and vice president of the Ontario Hockey League's Belleville Bulls.

Coaching Record

			Regular Season					Playoffs			
Season	Team	League	GC	W	L	O/T		GC	W	L	T
1989-90	Buffalo	NHL	80	45	27	8		6	2	4	....
1990-91	Buffalo	NHL	80	31	30	19		6	2	4	....
1991-92	Buffalo	NHL	28	9	15	4		....	....	....	....
2003-04	Florida	NHL	40	13	15	12		....	....	....	....
	NHL Totals		228	98	87	43		12	4	8	....

Club Records

Team

(Figures in brackets for season records are games played.)

Most Points	97	2006-07 (82)
Most Wins	43	2006-07 (82)
Most Ties	12	2000-01 (82)
Most Losses	57	1999-2000 (82)
Most Goals	281	2005-06 (82)
Most Goals Against	313	1999-2000 (82)
Fewest Points	39	1999-2000 (82)
Fewest Wins	14	1999-2000 (82)
Fewest Ties	7	1999-2000 (82), 2002-03 (82)
Fewest Losses	33	2005-06 (82)
Fewest Goals	170	1999-2000 (82)
Fewest Goals Against	243	2003-04 (82)

Longest Winning Streak
- Overall ... 6 ... Mar. 6-16/09
- Home ... 7 ... Mar. 2-18/07
- Away ... 4 ... Jan. 13-Feb. 7/03, Nov. 3-21/07, Feb. 3-16/09, Nov. 12-Dec. 5/09

Longest Undefeated Streak
- Overall ... 6 ... Mar. 6-16/09 (6 wins)
- Home ... 7 ... Mar. 2-18/07 (7 wins)
- Away ... 7 ... Oct. 21-Nov. 13/00 (3 wins, 4 ties)

Longest Losing Streak
- Overall ... 12 ... Jan. 24-Feb. 20/00
- Home ... 11 ... Jan. 24-Mar. 16/00
- Away ... 10 ... Oct. 6-Nov. 18/01, Feb. 16-Mar. 18/08

Longest Winless Streak
- Overall ... 16 ... Jan. 16-Feb. 20/00 (14 losses, 2 ties)
- Home ... *17 ... Jan. 19-Mar. 29/00 (15 losses, 2 ties)
- Away ... 10 ... Oct. 6-Nov. 18/01 (10 losses)

Most Shutouts, Season ... 5 ... 2005-06 (82), 2007-08 (82)
Most PIM, Season ... 1,505 ... 2003-04 (82)
Most Goals, Game ... 9 ... Nov. 12/05 (Atl. 9 at Car. 0)

Individual

Most Seasons	8	Ilya Kovalchuk
Most Games	594	Ilya Kovalchuk
Most Goals, Career	328	Ilya Kovalchuk
Most Assists, Career	287	Ilya Kovalchuk
Most Points, Career	615	Ilya Kovalchuk (328G, 287A)
Most PIM, Career	552	Eric Boulton
Most Shutouts, Career	14	Kari Lehtonen

Longest Consecutive Games Streak ... 252 ... Vyacheslav Kozlov (Jan. 9/07-Jan. 21/10)
Most Goals, Season ... 52 ... Ilya Kovalchuk (2005-06), (2007-08)

Most Assists, Season ... 69 ... Marc Savard (2005-06)
Most Points, Season ... 100 ... Marian Hossa (2006-07; 43G, 57A)
Most PIM, Season ... 226 ... Jeff Odgers (2000-01)
Most Points, Defenseman, Season ... 50 ... Tobias Enstrom (2009-10; 6G, 44A)
Most Points, Center, Season ... 97 ... Marc Savard (2005-06; 28G, 69A)
Most Points, Right Wing, Season ... 100 ... Marian Hossa (2006-07; 43G, 57A)
Most Points, Left Wing, Season ... 98 ... Ilya Kovalchuk (2005-06; 52G, 46A)
Most Points, Rookie, Season ... 67 ... Dany Heatley (2001-02; 26G, 41A)
Most Shutouts, Season ... 4 ... Kari Lehtonen (2006-07), (2007-08)
Most Goals, Game ... 4 ... Pascal Rheaume (Jan. 19/02), Ilya Kovalchuk (Nov. 11/05)
Most Assists, Game ... 4 ... Seven times
Most Points, Game ... 5 ... Seven times

* NHL Record.

Selected fourth overall in the 2009 Entry Draft, Evander Kane's 14 goals as an 18-year-old in 2009-10 ranked him seventh among NHL rookies.

2009-10 Results

Oct.	3	Tampa Bay	6-3		5	at Pittsburgh	2-5
	8	at St. Louis	4-2		7	NY Rangers	2-1†
	10	at Ottawa	2-4		9	Washington	1-8
	16	at New Jersey	4-2		12	Ottawa	6-1
	17	at Buffalo	4-2		14	Buffalo	1-2*
	20	at Montreal	1-2†		16	at Carolina	5-3
	22	Washington	4-5		18	at Florida	0-1
	24	San Jose	3-4		19	Toronto	4-3
	29	Washington	3-4		21	Carolina	3-5
	31	at Ottawa	3-1		23	at Tampa Bay	1-2†
Nov.	3	at Montreal	5-4		26	Anaheim	2-1
	5	Columbus	3-4		28	at Philadelphia	4-3
	7	at NY Islanders	3-6		30	at Nashville	3-4
	8	St. Louis	3-2†	Feb.	2	Tampa Bay	1-2
	12	at NY Rangers	5-3		5	at Washington	2-5
	13	Los Angeles	7-0		6	Florida	4-2
	15	Edmonton	3-2		10	at Colorado	3-4*
	19	Boston	3-4†		12	at Minnesota	3-2
	21	Pittsburgh	2-3		13	at Chicago	4-5†
	22	Tampa Bay	3-4*	Mar.	2	Florida	4-2
	25	at Detroit	2-0		4	NY Islanders	6-3
	27	at Carolina	6-4		6	at Tampa Bay	2-6
	28	Philadelphia	1-0		7	Carolina	0-4
	30	Florida	4-3		9	Nashville	1-2
Dec.	3	NY Islanders	1-4		11	at Columbus	1-2
	5	at Florida	2-1†		12	NY Rangers	2-5
	7	at Toronto	2-5		14	Phoenix	2-3†
	9	at Calgary	1-3		16	Buffalo	4-3
	10	at Vancouver	2-4		18	Ottawa	6-3
	12	Montreal	4-3*		20	Philadelphia	3-5
	14	at NY Rangers	3-2†		21	at Philadelphia	3-1
	16	at Florida	3-4		23	Boston	0-4
	17	Dallas	6-5*		25	Toronto	1-2*
	19	New Jersey	4-5		27	at Carolina	4-0
	21	Montreal	3-4*		29	Carolina	1-4
	23	at Boston	4-6		30	at Toronto	3-2
	26	at Tampa Bay	3-4	Apr.	1	at Washington	1-2
	28	at New Jersey	2-3		3	at Pittsburgh	3-4*
Jan.	1	at Buffalo	3-4*		6	New Jersey	0-3
	2	at NY Islanders	5-6†		9	at Washington	2-5
					10	Pittsburgh	1-0

* – Overtime † – Shootout

All-time Record vs. Other Clubs

Regular Season

	At Home								On Road								Total							
	GP	W	L	T	OL	GF	GA	PTS	GP	W	L	T	OL	GF	GA	PTS	GP	W	L	T	OL	GF	GA	PTS
Anaheim	6	2	4	0	0	13	19	4	6	3	3	0	0	18	18	6	12	5	7	0	0	31	37	10
Boston	20	8	11	0	1	58	62	17	20	6	9	2	3	65	74	17	40	14	20	2	4	123	136	34
Buffalo	20	13	3	1	3	66	58	30	20	9	10	0	1	57	86	19	40	22	13	1	4	123	144	49
Calgary	6	5	0	1	0	19	11	11	5	0	5	0	0	8	21	0	11	5	5	1	0	27	32	11
Carolina	31	7	18	3	3	80	108	20	31	13	14	1	3	97	97	30	62	20	32	4	6	177	205	50
Chicago	6	2	3	1	0	19	18	5	4	1	2	0	1	7	13	3	10	3	5	1	1	26	31	8
Colorado	6	2	2	1	1	13	16	6	7	4	2	0	1	22	24	9	13	6	4	1	2	35	40	15
Columbus	6	3	3	0	0	13	14	6	6	2	3	0	1	12	16	5	12	5	6	0	1	25	30	11
Dallas	6	1	4	0	1	18	26	3	6	1	5	0	0	9	13	2	12	2	9	0	1	27	39	5
Detroit	5	1	4	0	0	17	31	2	7	2	3	0	2	18	23	6	12	3	7	0	2	35	54	8
Edmonton	5	2	3	0	0	8	14	4	6	2	3	1	0	16	22	5	11	4	6	1	0	24	36	9
Florida	31	18	7	4	2	106	86	42	31	15	11	1	4	89	79	35	62	33	18	5	6	195	165	77
Los Angeles	6	3	3	0	0	20	18	6	6	2	4	0	0	22	32	4	12	5	7	0	0	42	50	10
Minnesota	4	1	3	0	0	11	16	2	5	1	3	1	0	16	21	3	9	2	6	1	0	27	37	5
Montreal	20	7	9	2	2	41	53	18	20	6	12	0	2	48	69	14	40	13	21	2	4	89	122	32
Nashville	7	3	1	1	2	20	19	9	6	2	4	0	0	16	21	4	13	5	5	1	2	36	40	13
New Jersey	20	5	13	2	0	43	73	12	20	9	9	1	1	46	57	20	40	14	22	3	1	89	130	32
NY Islanders	20	7	10	2	1	64	78	17	20	9	10	0	1	55	71	19	40	16	20	2	2	119	149	36
NY Rangers	20	9	10	0	1	58	66	19	20	12	6	1	1	59	55	26	40	21	16	1	2	117	121	45
Ottawa	20	9	10	1	0	73	72	19	20	7	12	1	0	55	85	15	40	16	22	2	0	128	157	34
Philadelphia	20	4	13	1	2	43	68	11	20	4	13	2	1	56	81	11	40	8	26	3	3	99	149	22
Phoenix	6	1	3	0	2	12	20	4	7	0	5	1	1	12	25	2	13	1	8	1	3	24	45	6
Pittsburgh	20	7	11	0	0	57	65	16	20	4	13	0	3	49	79	11	40	11	24	0	5	106	144	27
St. Louis	7	3	3	1	0	21	22	7	5	2	3	0	0	8	15	4	12	5	6	1	0	29	37	11
San Jose	6	1	4	1	0	11	20	3	6	0	5	1	0	11	24	1	12	1	9	2	0	22	44	4
Tampa Bay	31	18	7	3	3	103	83	42	31	10	15	1	5	79	112	26	62	28	22	4	8	182	195	68
Toronto	19	7	10	0	2	38	68	16	19	7	10	1	1	50	69	16	38	14	20	1	3	88	137	32
Vancouver	5	2	3	0	0	16	17	4	5	1	3	1	0	3	14	3	10	3	6	1	0	19	31	7
Washington	31	15	12	2	2	92	98	34	31	8	17	3	3	87	113	22	62	23	29	5	5	179	211	56
Totals	**410**	**166**	**187**	**26**	**31**	**1153**	**1319**	**389**	**410**	**142**	**214**	**19**	**35**	**1089**	**1426**	**338**	**820**	**308**	**401**	**45**	**66**	**2242**	**2745**	**727**

Playoffs

	Series	W	L	GP	W	L	T	GF	GA	Last Mtg.	Rnd.	Result
NY Rangers	1	0	1	4	0	4	0	6	17	2007	CQF	L 0-4
Totals	**1**	**0**	**1**	**4**	**0**	**4**	**0**	**6**	**17**			

Playoff Results 2010-2006

Year	Round	Opponent	Result	GF	GA
2007	CQF	NY Rangers	L 0-4	6	17

Abbreviations: Round: CQF – conference quarter-final.

Entry Draft Selections 2010-1999

Name in bold denotes played in NHL.

2010
Pick
- 8 Alexander Burmistrov
- 87 Julian Melchiori
- 101 Ivan Telegin
- 128 Fredrik Pettersson-Wentzel
- 150 Yasin Cisse
- 155 Kendall McFaull
- 160 Tanner Lane
- 169 Sebastian Owuya
- 199 Peter Stoykewych

2009
Pick
- 4 **Evander Kane**
- 34 Carl Klingberg
- 45 Jeremy Morin
- 117 Edward Pasquale
- 120 Ben Chiarot
- 125 Cody Sol
- 155 Jimmy Bubnick
- 185 Levko Koper
- 203 Jordan Samuels-Thomas

2008
Pick
- 3 **Zach Bogosian**
- 29 Daultan Leveille
- 64 Danick Paquette
- 94 Vinny Saponari
- 124 Nicklas Lasu
- 154 Chris Carrozzi
- 184 Zach Redmond

2007
Pick
- 67 **Spencer Machacek**
- 115 Niclas Lucenius
- 175 John Albert
- 205 Paul Postma

2006
Pick
- 12 **Bryan Little**
- 43 Riley Holzapfel
- 80 Michael Forney
- 135 Alex Kangas
- 165 Jonas Enlund
- 195 Jesse Martin
- 200 **Arturs Kulda**
- 210 Will O'Neill

2005
Pick
- 16 Alex Bourret
- 41 **Ondrej Pavelec**
- 49 Chad Denny
- 53 Andrew Kozek
- 116 **Jordan LaVallee**
- 135 Tomas Pospisil
- 187 Andrei Zubarev
- 207 Myles Stoesz

2004
Pick
- 10 **Boris Valabik**
- 40 **Grant Lewis**
- 76 **Scott Lehman**
- 106 Chad Painchaud
- 142 Juraj Gracik
- 186 Dan Turple
- 204 Miikka Tuomainen
- 237 Mitch Carefoot
- 270 Matt Siddall

2003
Pick
- 8 **Braydon Coburn**
- 110 Jim Sharrow
- 116 **Guillaume Desbiens**
- 136 Michael Vannelli
- 145 **Brett Sterling**
- 175 Mike Hamilton
- 203 Denis Loginov
- 239 **Tobias Enstrom**
- 269 Rylan Kaip

2002
Pick
- 2 **Kari Lehtonen**
- 30 **Jim Slater**
- 116 **Patrick Dwyer**
- 124 Lane Manson
- 144 Paul Flache
- 167 Brad Schell
- 198 **Nathan Oystrick**
- 230 Colton Fretter
- 236 Tyler Boldt
- 257 Pauli Levokari

2001
Pick
- 1 **Ilya Kovalchuk**
- 80 **Michael Garnett**
- 100 Brian Sipotz
- 112 Milan Gajic
- 135 **Colin Stuart**
- 189 **Pasi Nurminen**
- 199 Matt Suderman
- 201 Colin FitzRandolph
- 262 Mario Cartelli

2000
Pick
- 2 **Dany Heatley**
- 31 Ilja Nikulin
- 42 Libor Ustrnul
- 107 Carl Mallette
- 108 Blake Robson
- 147 Matt McRae
- 168 Zdenek Smid
- 178 Jeff Dwyer
- 180 **Darcy Hordichuk**
- 230 Samu Isosalo
- 242 Evan Nielsen
- 244 Eric Bowen
- 288 Mark McRae
- 290 **Simon Gamache**

1999
Pick
- 1 **Patrik Stefan**
- 30 **Luke Sellars**
- 68 **Zdenek Blatny**
- 98 David Kaczowka
- 99 Rob Zepp
- 128 **Derek MacKenzie**
- 159 Yuri Dobryshkin
- 188 Stephen Baby
- 217 **Garnet Exelby**
- 245 **Tommi Santala**
- 246 Raymond DiLauro

Club Directory

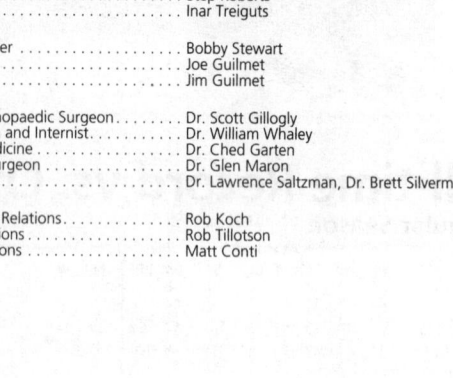

Philips Arena

Atlanta Thrashers
Centennial Tower
101 Marietta St.
Suite 1900
Atlanta, GA 30303
Phone **404/878-3800**
FAX 404/878-3765
www.atlantathrashers.com
Capacity: 18,545

Ownership . . . . Atlanta Spirit, LLC
Owners . . . . Bruce Levenson, Michael Gearon, Steve Belkin, Ed Peskowitz, Rutherford Seydel, Todd Foreman, Felix Riccio, Michael Gearon, Sr., Beau Turner

Executive Management
President, Atlanta Thrashers
and Executive Vice President, Atlanta Spirit LLC . . Don Waddell
President, Philips Arena and Atlanta Hawks
and Exec. Vice President, Atlanta Spirit LLC . . . . . Bob Williams
Exec. Vice President and G.M., Atlanta Hawks. . . . . Rick Sund
Sr. V.P., Sales and Marketing, Chief Sales Officer . . Tracy White
Sr. V.P. and Chief Financial Officer . . . . Phil Ebinger
Sr. V.P., Chief Legal Officer, Atlanta Spirit LLC
and Assistant G.M., Atlanta Hawks . . . . Scott Wilkinson

Hockey Operations
General Manager . . . . Rick Dudley
Vice President and Assistant General Manager . . . . Larry Simmons
Director of Amateur Scouting
and Player Development . . . . Dan Marr
Director of Player Personnel . . . . Mark Dobson
Senior Director of Team Services . . . . Michele Zarzaca
Manager of Player Development
and Hockey Administration . . . . Ryan Bowness
Hockey Operations Office Coordinator . . . . Rachel Stamper

Coaching Staff
Head Coach . . . . Craig Ramsay
Associate Coach . . . . John Torchetti
Assistant Coach . . . . Mike Stothers
Video Coach. . . . . Tony Borgford

Scouting Staff
Head Scout . . . . Marcel Comeau
Full-Time Scouts . . . . Evgeny Bogdanovich, Bernd Freimuller, Mark Hillier, Tavis MacMillan, Bob Owen, John Perpich, Grant Sonier
Part-Time Scouts. . . . . Pat Carmichael, Freddie Jax

Training Staff
Strength and Conditioning Coach. . . . . Barry Brennan
Head Athletic Trainer. . . . . Tommy Alva
Assistant Athletic Trainer. . . . . Step Roberts
Massage Therapist . . . . Inar Treiguts

Equipment Staff
Head Equipment Manager . . . . Bobby Stewart
Equipment Manager . . . . Joe Guilmet
Equipment Assistant . . . . Jim Guilmet

Medical Staff
Team Physician and Orthopaedic Surgeon. . . . . . . Dr. Scott Gillogly
Assistant Team Physician and Internist. . . . . Dr. William Whaley
Primary Care Sports Medicine . . . . Dr. Ched Garten
Oral and Maxillofacial Surgeon . . . . Dr. Glen Maron
Team Dentists . . . . Dr. Lawrence Saltzman, Dr. Brett Silverman

Public Relations
Senior Director of Public Relations. . . . . Rob Koch
Manager of Media Relations . . . . Rob Tillotson
Manager of Public Relations . . . . Matt Conti

Craig Ramsay
Head Coach

Born: Weston, Ont., March 17, 1951.

The Atlanta Thrashers named Craig Ramsay the fifth head coach in franchise history on June 24, 2010. Ramsay brings nearly 40 years of NHL experience as a player, coach and talent evaluator in six different NHL organizations. Most recently Ramsay served as an assistant coach for the Bruins from 2007 to 2010. While in Boston, Ramsay helped the Bruins reach the postseason each year, while capturing the Eastern Conference's best record during the 2008-09 season.

Prior to joining the Bruins, Ramsay served as an associate coach for the Tampa Bay Lightning from 2001 to 2007, earning a Southeast Division title and the Stanley Cup during the 2003-04 campaign. Ramsay also served as an assistant coach with the Philadelphia Flyers from 1998 to 2000. He was named interim head coach in February 2000 while Roger Neilson was being treated for cancer, guiding the team to a 16-8-1 mark while claiming the Atlantic Division title with 105 points. Ramsay led the Flyers to the Eastern Conference Finals where they lost to the eventual Stanley Cup champion New Jersey Devils in seven games. He remained behind the bench to begin the 2000-01 season until being replaced after 28 games.

Before joining Philadelphia, Ramsay worked as an assistant coach for the Ottawa Senators (1996 to 1998) and the Florida Panthers (1993 to 1995). He began his coaching career with the Buffalo Sabres organization where he served as an assistant coach during the 1986-87 season and took over as interim head coach for part of the year. Prior to leaving the Sabres in 1993, Ramsay also served as the team's director of player personnel and assistant general manager.

Ramsay's NHL playing career spanned 14 seasons with the Buffalo Sabres from 1971 to 1985, earning 672 points (252 goals, 420 assists) in 1,070 career games. The Weston, Ontario, native twice reached a career high with 71 points and tallied eight straight 20-goal seasons for the Sabres from 1973 to 1981. He also appeared in 89 Stanley Cup playoff games with the Sabres, posting 48 points (17 goals, 31 assists) in those contests. Ramsay, who was selected by Buffalo in the second round (19th overall) of the 1971 NHL Entry Draft, appeared in 776 consecutive games with the Sabres from 1973 to 1983, which ranks as the fourth longest consecutive games streak in NHL history. He was also named the recipient of the Frank J. Selke Trophy in 1985, given annually to the forward who best excels in the defensive aspects of the game. Ramsay began his professional career with the Cincinnati Swords of the American Hockey League during the 1971-72 season. During his career, Ramsay played alongside Thrashers general manager Rick Dudley for a total of seven seasons with Cincinnati (1971-72) and Buffalo (1972-73 to 1974-95 and 1978-79 to 1980-81). Prior to his professional career, Ramsay played four junior seasons for the Peterborough Petes of the Ontario Hockey Association from 1967 to 1971. His best junior season came in 1970-71, when he earned 106 points (30 goals, 76 assists) in 58 games with Peterborough.

Coaching Record

| Season | Team | League | Regular Season | | | | Playoffs | | | |
			GC	W	L	O/T	GC	W	L	T
1986-87	**Buffalo**	NHL	21	4	15	2	....	....	....	....
2000-01	**Philadelphia**	NHL	28	12	12	4	....	....	....	....
	NHL Totals		49	16	27	6				

Posted a 16-8-1 regular-season record and an 11-7 playoff record as interim coach when Roger Neilson was sidelined for treatment of bone-marrow cancer after February 20, 2000. All games are credited to Neilson's coaching record.

Boston Bruins

Key Off-Season Signings/Acquisitions

2010

June
- 4 • Re-signed LW **Shawn Thornton**.
- 5 • Re-signed D **Dennis Seidenberg**.
- 22 • Acquired RW **Nathan Horton** and C **Gregory Campbell** from Florida for D **Dennis Wideman**, the Bruins' 1st round pick in the 2010 Entry Draft and 3rd round pick in 2011.
- 24 • Re-signed D **Johnny Boychuk**.
- 25 • Selected C **Tyler Seguin** (Plymouth Whalers, OHL) with the 2nd overall pick of the 2010 Entry Draft.
- 28 • Re-signed RW **Mark Recchi**.

July
- 1 • Re-signed LW **Daniel Paille**.
- 9 • Re-signed D **Mark Stuart**.
- 15 • Re-signed C **Gregory Campbell** and D **Adam McQuaid**.
- 30 • LW **Blake Wheeler** awarded one-year contract in arbitration.

Aug.
- 4 • Named **Doug Jarvis** assistant coach.

2009-10 Results: 39W-30L-4OTL-9SOL 91PTS.
Third, Northeast Division

Year-by-Year Record

Season	GP	Home W	Home L	Home T	Home OL	Road W	Road L	Road T	Road OL	Overall W	Overall L	Overall T	Overall OL	GF	GA	Pts.	Finished	Playoff Result
2009-10	82	18	17	....	6	21	13	....	7	39	30	....	13	206	200	91	3rd, Northeast Div.	Lost Conf. Semi-Final
2008-09	82	29	6	....	6	24	13	....	4	53	19	....	10	274	196	116	1st, Northeast Div.	Lost Conf. Semi-Final
2007-08	82	21	16	....	4	20	13	....	8	41	29	....	12	212	222	94	3rd, Northeast Div.	Lost Conf. Quarter-Final
2006-07	82	18	19	....	4	17	22	....	2	35	41	....	6	219	289	76	5th, Northeast Div.	Out of Playoffs
2005-06	82	16	15	....	10	13	22	....	6	29	37	....	16	230	266	74	5th, Northeast Div.	Out of Playoffs
2004-05	....	....	....	....	....	....	....	....	....	....	....	....	....	....	....	....		
2003-04	82	18	12	9	2	23	7	6	5	41	19	15	7	209	188	104	1st, Northeast Div.	Lost Conf. Quarter-Final
2002-03	82	23	11	5	2	13	20	6	2	36	31	11	4	245	237	87	3rd, Northeast Div.	Lost Conf. Quarter-Final
2001-02	82	23	11	2	5	20	13	4	4	43	24	6	9	236	201	101	1st, Northeast Div.	Lost Conf. Quarter-Final
2000-01	82	21	12	5	3	15	18	3	5	36	30	8	8	227	249	88	4th, Northeast Div.	Out of Playoffs
1999-2000	82	12	17	11	1	12	16	8	5	24	33	19	6	210	248	73	5th, Northeast Div.	Out of Playoffs
1998-99	82	22	10	9	....	17	20	4	....	39	30	13	....	214	181	91	3rd, Northeast Div.	Lost Conf. Semi-Final
1997-98	82	19	16	6	....	20	14	7	....	39	30	13	....	221	194	91	2nd, Northeast Div.	Lost Conf. Quarter-Final
1996-97	82	14	20	7	....	12	27	2	....	26	47	9	....	234	300	61	6th, Northeast Div.	Out of Playoffs
1995-96	82	22	14	5	....	18	17	6	....	40	31	11	....	282	269	91	2nd, Northeast Div.	Lost Conf. Quarter-Final
1994-95	48	15	7	2	....	12	11	1	....	27	18	3	....	150	127	57	3rd, Northeast Div.	Lost Conf. Quarter-Final
1993-94	84	20	14	8	....	22	15	5	....	42	29	13	....	289	252	97	2nd, Northeast Div.	Lost Conf. Semi-Final
1992-93	84	29	10	3	....	22	16	4	....	51	26	7	....	332	268	109	1st, Adams Div.	Lost Div. Semi-Final
1991-92	80	23	11	6	....	13	21	6	....	36	32	12	....	270	275	84	2nd, Adams Div.	Lost Conf. Championship
1990-91	80	26	9	5	....	18	15	7	....	44	24	12	....	299	264	100	1st, Adams Div.	Lost Conf. Championship
1989-90	80	23	13	4	....	23	12	5	....	46	25	9	....	289	232	101	1st, Adams Div.	Lost Final
1988-89	80	17	15	8	....	20	14	6	....	37	29	14	....	289	256	88	2nd, Adams Div.	Lost Div. Final
1987-88	80	24	13	3	....	20	17	3	....	44	30	6	....	300	251	94	2nd, Adams Div.	Lost Final
1986-87	80	25	11	4	....	14	23	3	....	39	34	7	....	301	276	85	3rd, Adams Div.	Lost Div. Semi-Final
1985-86	80	24	9	7	....	13	22	5	....	37	31	12	....	311	288	86	3rd, Adams Div.	Lost Div. Semi-Final
1984-85	80	21	15	4	....	15	19	6	....	36	34	10	....	303	287	82	4th, Adams Div.	Lost Div. Semi-Final
1983-84	80	25	12	3	....	24	13	3	....	49	25	6	....	336	261	104	1st, Adams Div.	Lost Div. Semi-Final
1982-83	80	28	6	6	....	22	14	4	....	50	20	10	....	327	228	110	1st, Adams Div.	Lost Conf. Championship
1981-82	80	24	12	4	....	19	15	6	....	43	27	10	....	323	285	96	2nd, Adams Div.	Lost Div. Final
1980-81	80	26	10	4	....	11	20	9	....	37	30	13	....	316	272	87	2nd, Adams Div.	Lost Prelim. Round
1979-80	80	27	9	4	....	19	12	9	....	46	21	13	....	310	234	105	2nd, Adams Div.	Lost Quarter-Final
1978-79	80	25	10	5	....	18	13	9	....	43	23	14	....	316	270	100	1st, Adams Div.	Lost Semi-Final
1977-78	80	29	6	5	....	22	12	6	....	51	18	11	....	333	218	113	1st, Adams Div.	Lost Final
1976-77	80	27	7	6	....	22	16	2	....	49	23	8	....	312	240	106	1st, Adams Div.	Lost Final
1975-76	80	27	5	8	....	21	10	9	....	48	15	17	....	313	237	113	1st, Adams Div.	Lost Semi-Final
1974-75	80	29	5	6	....	11	21	8	....	40	26	14	....	345	245	94	2nd, Adams Div.	Lost Prelim. Round
1973-74	78	33	4	2	....	19	13	7	....	52	17	9	....	349	221	113	1st, East Div.	Lost Final
1972-73	78	27	10	2	....	24	12	3	....	51	22	5	....	330	235	107	2nd, East Div.	Lost Quarter-Final
1971-72	**78**	**28**	**4**	**7**	....	**26**	**9**	**4**	....	**54**	**13**	**11**	....	**330**	**204**	**119**	**1st, East Div.**	**Won Stanley Cup**
1970-71	78	33	4	2	....	24	10	5	....	57	14	7	....	399	207	121	1st, East Div.	Lost Quarter-Final
1969-70	**76**	**27**	**3**	**8**	....	**13**	**14**	**11**	....	**40**	**17**	**19**	....	**277**	**216**	**99**	**2nd, East Div.**	**Won Stanley Cup**
1968-69	76	29	3	6	....	13	15	10	....	42	18	16	....	303	221	100	2nd, East Div.	Lost Semi-Final
1967-68	74	22	9	6	....	15	18	4	....	37	27	10	....	259	216	84	3rd, East Div.	Lost Quarter-Final
1966-67	70	10	21	4	....	7	22	6	....	17	43	10	....	182	253	44	6th,	Out of Playoffs
1965-66	70	15	17	3	....	6	26	3	....	21	43	6	....	174	275	48	5th,	Out of Playoffs
1964-65	70	12	17	6	....	9	26	0	....	21	43	6	....	166	253	48	6th,	Out of Playoffs
1963-64	70	13	15	7	....	5	25	5	....	18	40	12	....	170	212	48	6th,	Out of Playoffs
1962-63	70	7	18	10	....	7	21	7	....	14	39	17	....	198	281	45	6th,	Out of Playoffs
1961-62	70	9	22	4	....	6	25	4	....	15	47	8	....	177	306	38	6th,	Out of Playoffs
1960-61	70	13	17	5	....	2	25	8	....	15	42	13	....	176	254	43	6th,	Out of Playoffs
1959-60	70	21	11	3	....	7	23	5	....	28	34	8	....	220	241	64	5th,	Out of Playoffs
1958-59	70	21	11	3	....	11	18	6	....	32	29	9	....	205	215	73	2nd,	Lost Semi-Final
1957-58	70	15	14	6	....	12	14	9	....	27	28	15	....	199	194	69	4th,	Lost Final
1956-57	70	20	9	6	....	14	15	6	....	34	24	12	....	195	174	80	3rd,	Lost Final
1955-56	70	14	14	7	....	9	20	6	....	23	34	13	....	147	185	59	5th,	Out of Playoffs
1954-55	70	16	10	9	....	7	16	12	....	23	26	21	....	169	188	67	4th,	Lost Semi-Final
1953-54	70	22	8	5	....	10	20	5	....	32	28	10	....	177	181	74	4th,	Lost Semi-Final
1952-53	70	19	10	6	....	9	19	7	....	28	29	13	....	152	172	69	3rd,	Lost Final
1951-52	70	15	12	8	....	10	17	8	....	25	29	16	....	162	176	66	4th,	Lost Semi-Final
1950-51	70	13	12	10	....	9	18	8	....	22	30	18	....	178	197	62	4th,	Lost Semi-Final
1949-50	70	15	12	8	....	7	20	8	....	22	32	16	....	198	228	60	5th,	Out of Playoffs
1948-49	60	18	10	2	....	11	13	6	....	29	23	8	....	178	163	66	2nd,	Lost Semi-Final
1947-48	60	12	8	10	....	11	16	3	....	23	24	13	....	167	168	59	3rd,	Lost Semi-Final
1946-47	60	18	7	5	....	8	16	6	....	26	23	11	....	190	175	63	3rd,	Lost Semi-Final
1945-46	50	11	5	4	....	13	13	4	....	24	18	8	....	167	156	56	2nd,	Lost Final
1944-45	50	11	12	2	....	5	18	2	....	16	30	4	....	179	219	36	4th,	Lost Semi-Final
1943-44	50	15	8	2	....	4	18	3	....	19	26	5	....	223	268	43	5th,	Out of Playoffs
1942-43	50	17	3	5	....	7	14	4	....	24	17	9	....	195	176	57	2nd,	Lost Final
1941-42	48	17	4	3	....	8	13	3	....	25	17	6	....	160	118	56	3rd,	Lost Semi-Final
1940-41	**48**	**15**	**4**	**5**	....	**12**	**4**	**8**	....	**27**	**8**	**13**	....	**168**	**102**	**67**	**1st,**	**Won Stanley Cup**
1939-40	48	20	3	1	....	11	9	4	....	31	12	5	....	170	98	67	1st,	Lost Semi-Final
1938-39	**48**	**20**	**2**	**2**	....	**16**	**8**	**0**	....	**36**	**10**	**2**	....	**156**	**76**	**74**	**1st,**	**Won Stanley Cup**
1937-38	48	18	3	3	....	12	8	4	....	30	11	7	....	142	89	67	1st, Amn. Div.	Lost Semi-Final
1936-37	48	9	11	4	....	14	7	3	....	23	18	7	....	120	110	53	2nd, Amn. Div.	Lost Quarter-Final
1935-36	48	15	8	1	....	7	12	5	....	22	20	6	....	92	83	50	2nd, Amn. Div.	Lost Quarter-Final
1934-35	48	17	7	0	....	9	9	6	....	26	16	6	....	129	112	58	1st, Amn. Div.	Lost Semi-Final
1933-34	48	11	11	2	....	7	14	3	....	18	25	5	....	111	130	41	4th, Amn. Div.	Out of Playoffs
1932-33	48	19	2	3	....	6	13	5	....	25	15	8	....	124	88	58	1st, Amn. Div.	Lost Semi-Final
1931-32	48	11	10	3	....	4	11	9	....	15	21	12	....	122	117	42	4th, Amn. Div.	Out of Playoffs
1930-31	44	16	1	5	....	12	9	1	....	28	10	6	....	143	90	62	1st, Amn. Div.	Lost Semi-Final
1929-30	44	21	1	0	....	17	4	1	....	38	5	1	....	179	98	77	1st, Amn. Div.	Lost Final
1928-29	**44**	**15**	**6**	**1**	....	**11**	**7**	**4**	....	**26**	**13**	**5**	....	**89**	**52**	**57**	**1st, Amn. Div.**	**Won Stanley Cup**
1927-28	44	13	4	5	....	7	9	6	....	20	13	11	....	77	70	51	1st, Amn. Div.	Lost Semi-Final
1926-27	44	15	7	0	....	6	13	3	....	21	20	3	....	97	89	45	2nd, Amn. Div.	Lost Final
1925-26	36	10	7	1	....	7	8	3	....	17	15	4	....	92	85	38	4th,	Out of Playoffs
1924-25	30	3	12	0	....	3	12	0	....	6	24	0	....	49	119	12	6th,	Out of Playoffs

2010-11 Schedule

Month	Day	Date	Opponent	Month	Day	Date	Opponent
Oct.	Sat.	9	Phoenix†		Tue.	11	Ottawa
	Sun.	10	at Phoenix*†		Thu.	13	Philadelphia
	Sat.	16	at New Jersey		Sat.	15	Pittsburgh*
	Tue.	19	at Washington		Mon.	17	Carolina*
	Thu.	21	Washington		Tue.	18	at Carolina
	Sat.	23	NY Rangers		Thu.	20	Buffalo
	Thu.	28	Toronto		Sat.	22	at Colorado*
	Sat.	30	at Ottawa		Mon.	24	at Los Angeles
Nov.	Wed.	3	at Buffalo		Wed.	26	Florida
	Fri.	5	at Washington	Feb.	Tue.	1	at Carolina
	Sat.	6	St. Louis		Thu.	3	Dallas
	Wed.	10	at Pittsburgh		Sat.	5	San Jose*
	Thu.	11	Montreal		Wed.	9	Montreal
	Sat.	13	Ottawa		Fri.	11	Detroit
	Mon.	15	New Jersey		Sun.	13	at Detroit*
	Wed.	17	at NY Rangers		Tue.	15	Toronto
	Thu.	18	Florida		Thu.	17	at NY Islanders
	Sat.	20	Los Angeles		Fri.	18	at Ottawa
	Mon.	22	at Tampa Bay		Wed.	23	at Calgary
	Wed.	24	at Florida		Sat.	26	at Vancouver
	Fri.	26	Carolina*		Sun.	27	at Edmonton
	Sun.	28	at Atlanta*	Mar.	Tue.	1	at Ottawa
Dec.	Wed.	1	at Philadelphia		Thu.	3	Tampa Bay
	Thu.	2	Tampa Bay		Sat.	5	Pittsburgh
	Sat.	4	at Toronto		Tue.	8	at Montreal
	Tue.	7	Buffalo		Thu.	10	Buffalo
	Thu.	9	NY Islanders		Fri.	11	at NY Islanders
	Sat.	11	Philadelphia		Tue.	15	at Columbus
	Wed.	15	at Buffalo		Thu.	17	at Nashville
	Thu.	16	at Montreal		Sat.	19	at Toronto
	Sat.	18	Washington		Tue.	22	New Jersey
	Mon.	20	Anaheim		Thu.	24	Montreal
	Thu.	23	Atlanta		Sat.	26	NY Rangers*
	Mon.	27	at Florida		Sun.	27	at Philadelphia
	Tue.	28	at Tampa Bay		Tue.	29	Chicago
	Thu.	30	at Atlanta		Thu.	31	Toronto
Jan.	Sat.	1	at Buffalo*	Apr.	Sat.	2	Atlanta*
	Mon.	3	at Toronto		Mon.	4	at NY Rangers
	Thu.	6	Minnesota		Wed.	6	NY Islanders
	Sat.	8	at Montreal		Sat.	9	Ottawa*
	Mon.	10	at Pittsburgh		Sun.	10	at New Jersey*

* Denotes afternoon game. † Games played in Prague, CZ.

NORTHEAST DIVISION
87th NHL Season

Franchise date: November 1, 1924

2010-11 Player Personnel

FORWARDS	HT	WT	S	Place of Birth	*Age	2009-10 Club
ARNIEL, Jamie	5-11	191	R	Kingston, Ont.	20	Providence (AHL)
BERGERON, Patrice	6-2	194	R	Ancienne-Lorette, Que.	25	Boston
CAMPBELL, Gregory	6-0	197	L	London, Ont.	26	Florida
CARON, Jordan	6-3	204	L	Sayabec, Que.	19	Rimouski-Rouyn-Noranda
COLBORNE, Joe	6-5	216	L	Calgary, Alta.	20	U. of Denver-Prov (AHL)
HAMILL, Zach	5-11	180	R	Vancouver, B.C.	22	Boston-Providence (AHL)
HORTON, Nathan	6-2	229	R	Welland, Ont.	25	Florida
KNACKSTEDT, Jordan	6-3	195	R	Saskatoon, Sask.	22	Providence (AHL)
KREJCI, David	6-0	177	R	Sternberk, Czech.	24	Boston
LoVECCHIO, Jeff	6-2	198	L	Arlington Heights, IL	25	Providence (AHL)
LUCIC, Milan	6-3	228	L	Vancouver, B.C.	22	Boston
MacDERMID, Lane	6-3	205	L	Hartford, CT	21	Providence (AHL)
MARCHAND, Brad	5-9	183	L	Halifax, N.S.	22	Boston-Providence (AHL)
NELSON, Levi	6-0	187	L	Calgary, Alta.	22	Providence (AHL)
PAILLE, Daniel	6-1	200	L	Welland, Ont.	26	Buffalo-Boston
RECCHI, Mark	5-10	195	L	Kamloops, B.C.	42	Boston
REICH, Jeremy	6-1	203	L	Craik, Sask.	31	Bridgeport
RIENDEAU, Yannick	5-11	187	L	Boucherville, Que.	22	Providence (AHL)-Reading
RYDER, Michael	6-0	192	R	St. John's, Nfld.	30	Boston
SAUVE, Maxime	6-0	185	L	Tours, France	20	Val-d'Or-Providence (AHL)
SAVARD, Marc	5-10	191	L	Ottawa, Ont.	33	Boston
SEGUIN, Tyler	6-1	186	R	Brampton, Ont.	18	Plymouth
STURM, Marco	6-0	194	L	Dingolfing, West Germany	32	Boston
THORNTON, Shawn	6-2	217	R	Oshawa, Ont.	33	Boston
WHEELER, Blake	6-5	208	R	Robbinsdale, MN	24	Boston
WHITFIELD, Trent	5-11	209	L	Estevan, Sask.	33	Boston-Providence (AHL)
DEFENSEMEN						
ALEXANDROV, Yury	6-1	185	L	Cherepovets, USSR	22	Cherepovets-Cherepovets Jr.
BARTKOWSKI, Matt	6-1	196	L	Pittsburgh, PA	22	Ohio State
BODNARCHUK, Andrew	5-11	185	L	Drumheller, Alta.	22	Boston-Providence (AHL)
BOYCHUK, Johnny	6-2	225	R	Edmonton, Alta.	26	Boston-Providence (AHL)
CHARA, Zdeno	6-9	255	L	Trencin, Czechoslovakia	33	Boston
FERENCE, Andrew	5-11	189	L	Edmonton, Alta.	31	Boston
HUNWICK, Matt	5-11	193	L	Warren, MI	25	Boston
KAMPFER, Steven	5-10	188	R	Ann Arbor, MI	22	U. of Michigan-Prov (AHL)
McIVER, Nathan	6-2	211	L	Summerside, P.E.I.	25	Manitoba
McQUAID, Adam	6-5	209	R	Charlottetown, P.E.I.	23	Boston-Providence (AHL)
PENNER, Jeff	5-10	191	L	Winnipeg, Man.	23	Boston-Providence (AHL)
SEIDENBERG, Dennis	6-1	210	L	Schwenningen, W. Ger.	29	Florida-Boston
STUART, Mark	6-2	213	L	Rochester, MN	26	Boston
WILD, Cody	6-1	205	L	Limestone, ME	23	Sprfld-Prov (AHL)-Stockton
GOALTENDERS	**HT**	**WT**	**C**	**Place of Birth**	***Age**	**2009-10 Club**
COURCHAINE, Adam	6-2	191	L	Calgary, Alta.	21	Sarnia-Erie (OHL)
DALTON, Matt	6-1	181	L	Clinton, Ont.	24	Providence (AHL)-Reading
HUTCHINSON, Michael	6-3	192	R	Barrie, Ont.	20	London
RASK, Tuukka	6-2	171	L	Savonlinna, Finland	23	Boston
SCHAEFER, Nolan	6-2	195	R	Regina, Sask.	30	CSKA
THOMAS, Tim	5-11	208	L	Flint, MI	36	Boston

* – Age at start of 2010-11 season

Claude Julien

Head Coach

Born: Orleans, Ont., April 23, 1960.

The Boston Bruins named Claude Julien the 28th head coach in club history on June 21, 2007. In his first season behind the bench in 2007-08, he guided the Bruins back to the playoffs for the first time since 2003-04. In 2008-09, the Bruins posted the best record in the Eastern Conference and were second overall in the NHL, earning Julien the Jack Adams Award for coach of the year. Julien joined the Bruins with four years of NHL head coaching experience. In his lone season with New Jersey, he held a record of 47-24-8 before being replaced on April 2, 2007 with three games remaining in the 2006-07 regular season. At the time he was replaced by the Devils, Julien's club was in first place in the Atlantic Division.

Prior to being named head coach of the Devils, Julien spent three seasons as the head coach of the Montreal Canadiens, serving from January 2003 until January of 2006. During his tenure with Montreal, Julien led the Canadiens to a record of 72-71-16 in 159 games.

Before joining the NHL coaching ranks, Julien spent four seasons with Hull of the Quebec Major Junior Hockey League and three campaigns with Hamilton of the American Hockey League. While with Hamilton, Julien was co-awarded the Louis A. R. Pieri Award as the league's outstanding coach during the 2002-03 season.

Julien has also coached at the international level, having served as an assistant coach to Team Canada at the 2006 World Championship after he led Team Canada to a bronze medal as a head coach at the 2000 World Junior Championship.

A defenseman, Julien's professional playing career spanned 12 seasons from 1981 to 1992, highlighted by stints with the Quebec Nordiques between 1984 and 1986.

Coaching Record

			Regular Season				Playoffs			
Season	Team	League	GC	W	L	O/T	GC	W	L	T
1996-97	Hull	QMJHL	70	48	19	3	14	12	2	....
1996-97	Hull	M-Cup	....	....	....	....	5	3	2	....
1997-98	Hull	QMJHL	70	32	37	1	11	6	5	....
1998-99	Hull	QMJHL	70	23	38	9	23	15	8	....
99-2000	Hull	QMJHL	72	42	24	6	15	9	6	....
2000-01	Hamilton	AHL	80	28	41	11	....	....	....	....
2001-02	Hamilton	AHL	80	37	30	13	15	10	5	....
2002-03	Hamilton	AHL	45	33	9	3	....	....	....	....
2002-03	**Montreal**	**NHL**	**36**	**12**	**16**	**8**	....	....	....	....
2003-04	**Montreal**	**NHL**	**82**	**41**	**30**	**11**	**11**	**4**	**7**	....
2004-05	**Montreal**		SEASON CANCELLED							
2005-06	**Montreal**	**NHL**	**41**	**19**	**16**	**6**	....	....	....	....
2006-07	**New Jersey**	**NHL**	**79**	**47**	**24**	**8**	....	....	....	....
2007-08	**Boston**	**NHL**	**82**	**41**	**29**	**12**	**7**	**3**	**4**	....
2008-09	**Boston**	**NHL**	**82**	**53**	**19**	**19**	**11**	**7**	**4**	....
2009-10	**Boston**	**NHL**	**82**	**39**	**30**	**13**	**13**	**7**	**6**	....
	NHL Totals		**484**	**252**	**164**	**77**	**42**	**21**	**21**	....

Won Jack Adams Award (2009)

2009-10 Scoring

* – rookie

Regular Season

Pos	#	Player	Team	GP	G	A	Pts	TOI	+/–	PIM	PP	SH	GW	S	%
C	37	Patrice Bergeron	BOS	73	19	33	52	18:54	6	28	0	1	4	184	10.3
C	46	David Krejci	BOS	79	17	35	52	18:14	8	26	6	0	3	156	10.9
D	33	Zdeno Chara	BOS	80	7	37	44	25:22	19	87	4	0	1	242	2.9
R	28	Mark Recchi	BOS	81	18	25	43	17:03	4	34	8	0	2	152	11.8
L	26	Blake Wheeler	BOS	82	18	20	38	15:47	–4	53	3	1	2	159	11.3
L	16	Marco Sturm	BOS	76	22	15	37	16:46	14	30	4	1	2	203	10.8
R	73	Michael Ryder	BOS	82	18	15	33	15:17	3	35	7	0	1	191	9.4
C	91	Marc Savard	BOS	41	10	23	33	18:34	2	14	6	0	2	90	11.1
D	44	Dennis Seidenberg	FLA	62	2	21	23	22:54	–3	33	1	0	0	116	1.7
			BOS	17	2	7	9	22:57	9	6	1	0	1	37	5.4
			Total	79	4	28	32	22:55	6	39	2	0	1	153	2.6
D	6	Dennis Wideman	BOS	76	6	24	30	23:33	–14	34	2	0	2	146	4.1
L	20	Daniel Paille	BUF	2	0	1	1	10:22	1	0	0	0	0	2	0.0
			BOS	74	10	9	19	13:48	–4	12	0	1	0	118	8.5
			Total	76	10	10	20	13:43	–3	12	0	1	0	120	8.3
L	17	Milan Lucic	BOS	50	9	11	20	14:21	–7	44	0	0	2	72	12.5
D	55	* Johnny Boychuk	BOS	51	5	10	15	17:39	10	43	0	0	0	96	5.2
R	81	Miroslav Satan	BOS	38	9	5	14	15:45	8	12	0	0	1	59	15.3
D	48	Matt Hunwick	BOS	76	6	8	14	17:57	–16	32	1	1	1	60	10.0
L	27	Steve Begin	BOS	77	5	9	14	12:49	–7	53	0	1	2	110	4.5
C	60	Vladimir Sobotka	BOS	61	4	6	10	11:05	–7	30	0	0	0	67	6.0
L	22	Shawn Thornton	BOS	74	1	9	10	9:02	–9	141	0	0	0	119	0.8
D	21	Andrew Ference	BOS	51	0	8	8	19:42	–7	16	0	0	0	60	0.0
D	45	Mark Stuart	BOS	56	2	5	7	17:01	1	80	0	0	0	53	3.8
D	54	* Adam McQuaid	BOS	19	1	0	1	10:44	–5	21	0	0	1	10	10.0
C	52	* Zach Hamill	BOS	1	0	1	1	12:08	1	0	0	0	0	1	0.0
C	42	Trent Whitfield	BOS	16	0	1	1	11:02	–2	7	0	0	0	15	0.0
C	63	* Brad Marchand	BOS	20	0	1	1	11:57	–3	20	0	0	0	32	0.0
L	92	Guillaume Lefebvre	BOS	1	0	0	0	11:01	0	0	0	0	0	0	0.0
R	68	* Mikko Lehtonen	BOS	1	0	0	0	7:08	–1	0	0	0	0	1	0.0
D	44	Andy Wozniewski	BOS	2	0	0	0	9:17	0	0	0	0	0	1	0.0
D	62	* Jeffrey Penner	BOS	2	0	0	0	14:01	0	0	0	0	0	1	0.0
C	43	Drew Larman	BOS	4	0	0	0	8:05	–1	0	0	0	0	5	0.0
D	65	* Andrew Bodnarchuk	BOS	5	0	0	0	7:19	–2	2	0	0	0	0	0.0

Goaltending

No.	Goaltender	GPI	Mins	Avg	W	L	OT	EN	SO	GA	SA	S%	G	A	PIM
40	* Tuukka Rask	45	2562	1.97	22	12	5	1	5	84	1221	.931	0	3	2
30	Tim Thomas	43	2442	2.56	17	18	8	2	5	104	1221	.915	0	0	8
	Totals	**82**	**5033**	**2.28**	**39**	**30**	**13**	**3**	**10**	**191**	**2445**	**.922**			

Playoffs

Pos	#	Player	Team	GP	G	A	Pts	TOI	+/–	PIM	PP	SH	GW	OT	S	%
D	6	Dennis Wideman	BOS	13	1	11	12	26:02	3	4	0	0	0	0	29	3.4
C	37	Patrice Bergeron	BOS	13	4	7	11	20:22	4	2	0	0	1	0	37	10.8
R	28	Mark Recchi	BOS	13	6	4	10	19:29	0	6	3	0	0	0	26	23.1
R	81	Miroslav Satan	BOS	13	5	5	10	18:31	4	16	2	0	3	1	37	13.5
L	17	Milan Lucic	BOS	13	5	4	9	16:26	1	19	2	0	1	0	24	20.8
C	46	David Krejci	BOS	9	4	4	8	19:06	3	2	2	0	0	0	17	23.5
D	33	Zdeno Chara	BOS	13	2	5	7	28:07	1	29	0	0	1	0	34	5.9
D	55	* Johnny Boychuk	BOS	13	2	4	6	26:10	0	6	1	0	0	0	32	6.3
L	26	Blake Wheeler	BOS	13	1	5	6	14:13	–6	6	0	0	0	0	18	5.6
D	48	Matt Hunwick	BOS	13	0	6	6	21:56	–1	2	0	0	0	0	15	0.0
R	73	Michael Ryder	BOS	13	4	1	5	15:47	–4	2	1	0	0	0	37	10.8
C	91	Marc Savard	BOS	7	1	2	3	17:21	2	12	0	0	1	1	22	4.5
L	20	Daniel Paille	BOS	13	0	2	2	16:01	–2	2	0	0	0	0	21	0.0
C	60	Vladimir Sobotka	BOS	13	0	2	2	13:19	–10	15	0	0	0	0	13	0.0
L	27	Steve Begin	BOS	13	1	0	1	11:57	–7	10	0	0	0	0	12	8.3
D	21	Andrew Ference	BOS	13	0	1	1	14:57	–9	18	0	0	0	0	12	0.0
C	42	Trent Whitfield	BOS	4	0	0	0	8:32	–1	0	0	0	0	0	2	0.0
D	45	Mark Stuart	BOS	4	0	0	0	14:38	–4	6	0	0	0	0	3	0.0
L	16	Marco Sturm	BOS	7	0	0	0	14:14	0	4	0	0	0	0	11	0.0
D	54	* Adam McQuaid	BOS	9	0	0	0	10:11	–4	6	0	0	0	0	3	0.0
L	22	Shawn Thornton	BOS	12	0	0	0	7:08	–4	4	0	0	0	0	9	0.0

Goaltending

No.	Goaltender	GPI	Mins	Avg	W	L	EN	SO	GA	SA	S%	G	A	PIM
40	* Tuukka Rask	13	829	2.61	7	6	1	0	36	409	.912	0	1	0
	Totals	13	836	2.66	7	6	1	0	37	410	.910			

Coaching History

Art Ross, 1924-25 to 1927-28; Cy Denneny, 1928-29; Art Ross, 1929-30 to 1933-34; Frank Patrick, 1934-35, 1935-36; Art Ross, 1936-37 to 1938-39; Cooney Weiland, 1939-40, 1940-41; Art Ross, 1941-42 to 1944-45; Dit Clapper, 1945-46 to 1948-49; Georges Boucher, 1949-50; Lynn Patrick, 1950-51 to 1953-54; Lynn Patrick and Milt Schmidt, 1954-55; Milt Schmidt, 1955-56 to 1960-61; Phil Watson, 1961-62; Phil Watson and Milt Schmidt, 1962-63; Milt Schmidt, 1963-64 to 1965-66; Harry Sinden, 1966-67 to 1969-70; Tom Johnson, 1970-71, 1971-72; Tom Johnson and Bep Guidolin, 1972-73; Bep Guidolin, 1973-74; Don Cherry, 1974-75 to 1978-79; Fred Creighton and Harry Sinden, 1979-80; Gerry Cheevers, 1980-81 to 1983-84; Gerry Cheevers and Harry Sinden, 1984-85; Butch Goring, 1985-86; Butch Goring and Terry O'Reilly, 1986-87; Terry O'Reilly, 1987-88, 1988-89; Mike Milbury, 1989-90, 1990-91; Rick Bowness, 1991-92; Brian Sutter, 1992-93 to 1994-95; Steve Kasper, 1995-96, 1996-97; Pat Burns, 1997-98 to 1999-2000; Pat Burns and Mike Keenan, 2000-01; Robbie Ftorek, 2001-02; Robbie Ftorek and Mike O'Connell, 2002-03; Mike Sullivan, 2003-04 to 2005-06; Dave Lewis, 2006-07; Claude Julien, 2007-08 to date.

Club Records

Team

(Figures in brackets for season records are games played; records for fewest points, wins, ties, losses, goals, goals against are for 70 or more games)

Most Points	121	1970-71 (78)
Most Wins	57	1970-71 (78)
Most Ties	21	1954-55 (70)
Most Losses	47	1961-62 (70), 1996-97 (82)
Most Goals	399	1970-71 (78)
Most Goals Against	306	1961-62 (70)
Fewest Points	38	1961-62 (70)
Fewest Wins	14	1962-63 (70)
Fewest Ties	5	1972-73 (78)
Fewest Losses	13	1971-72 (78)
Fewest Goals	147	1955-56 (70)
Fewest Goals Against	172	1952-53 (70)
Longest Winning Streak		
Overall	14	Dec. 3/29-Jan. 9/30
Home	*20	Dec. 3/29-Mar. 18/30
Away	8	Feb. 17-Mar. 8/72, Mar. 15-Apr. 14/93
Longest Undefeated Streak		
Overall	23	Dec. 22/40-Feb. 23/41 (15 wins, 8 ties)
Home	27	Nov. 22/70-Mar. 20/71 (26 wins, 1 tie)
Away	15	Dec. 22/40-Mar. 16/41 (9 wins, 6 ties)
Longest Losing Streak		
Overall	11	Dec. 3/24-Jan. 5/25
Home	11	Dec. 8/24-Feb. 17/25
Away	14	Dec. 27/64-Feb. 21/65
Longest Winless Streak		
Overall	20	Jan. 28-Mar. 11/62 (16 losses, 4 ties)
Home	11	Dec. 8/24-Feb. 17/25 (11 losses)
Away	14	Three times
Most Shutouts, Season	15	1927-28 (44)
Most PIM, Season	2,443	1987-88 (80)
Most Goals, Game	14	Jan. 21/45 (NYR 3 at Bos. 14)

Individual

Most Seasons	21	John Bucyk, Raymond Bourque
Most Games	1,518	Raymond Bourque
Most Goals, Career	545	John Bucyk
Most Assists, Career	1,111	Raymond Bourque
Most Points, Career	1,506	Raymond Bourque (395G, 1,111A)
Most PIM, Career	2,095	Terry O'Reilly
Most Shutouts, Career	74	Tiny Thompson
Longest Consecutive Games Streak	418	John Bucyk (Jan. 23/69-Mar. 2/75)
Most Goals, Season	76	Phil Esposito (1970-71)
Most Assists, Season	102	Bobby Orr (1970-71)
Most Points, Season	152	Phil Esposito (1970-71; 76G, 76A)
Most PIM, Season	302	Jay Miller (1987-88)
Most Points, Defenseman, Season	*139	Bobby Orr (1970-71; 37G, 102A)
Most Points, Center, Season	152	Phil Esposito (1970-71; 76G, 76A)
Most Points, Right Wing, Season	105	Ken Hodge (1970-71; 43G, 62A), (1973-74; 50G, 55A) Rick Middleton (1983-84; 47G, 58A)
Most Points, Left Wing, Season	116	John Bucyk (1970-71; 51G, 65A)
Most Points, Rookie, Season	102	Joe Juneau (1992-93; 32G, 70A)
Most Shutouts, Season	15	Hal Winkler (1927-28)
Most Goals, Game	4	Twenty one times
Most Assists, Game	6	Ken Hodge (Feb. 9/71) Bobby Orr (Jan. 1/73)
Most Points, Game	7	Bobby Orr (Nov. 15/73; 3G, 4A) Phil Esposito (Dec. 19/74; 3G, 4A) Barry Pederson (Apr. 4/82; 3G, 4A) Cam Neely (Oct. 16/88; 3G, 4A)

* NHL Record.

Retired Numbers

2	Eddie Shore	1926-1940
3	Lionel Hitchman	1925-1934
4	Bobby Orr	1966-1976
5	Dit Clapper	1927-1947
7	Phil Esposito	1967-1975
8	Cam Neely	1986-1996
9	John Bucyk	1957-1978
15	Milt Schmidt	1936-1955
24	Terry O'Reilly	1971-1985
77	Raymond Bourque	1979-2000

All-time Record vs. Other Clubs

Regular Season

	At Home								On Road								Total							
	GP	W	L	T	OL	GF	GA	PTS	GP	W	L	T	OL	GF	GA	PTS	GP	W	L	T	OL	GF	GA	PTS
Anaheim	11	6	5	0	0	34	33	12	11	5	4	2	0	28	24	12	22	11	9	2	0	62	57	24
Atlanta	20	12	4	2	2	74	65	28	20	12	7	0	1	62	58	25	40	24	11	2	3	136	123	53
Buffalo	125	69	41	14	1	451	367	153	126	45	62	15	4	360	447	109	251	114	103	29	5	811	814	262
Calgary	49	30	12	6	1	173	132	67	46	22	20	4	0	156	166	48	95	52	32	10	1	329	298	115
Carolina	88	51	29	7	1	306	234	110	86	41	35	9	1	296	284	92	174	92	64	16	2	602	518	202
Chicago	287	163	90	34	0	1033	817	360	289	96	145	45	3	778	935	240	576	259	235	79	3	1811	1752	600
Colorado	64	31	23	9	1	243	198	72	68	37	25	6	0	277	242	80	132	68	48	15	1	520	440	152
Columbus	4	2	2	0	0	12	10	4	5	2	1	0	2	18	10	6	9	4	3	0	2	30	20	10
Dallas	62	42	9	10	1	264	149	95	63	31	18	13	1	224	179	76	125	73	27	23	2	488	328	171
Detroit	289	155	90	43	1	1012	765	354	287	80	154	52	1	726	957	213	576	235	244	95	2	1738	1722	567
Edmonton	32	23	6	3	0	131	80	49	31	17	11	3	0	103	102	37	63	40	17	6	0	234	182	86
Florida	32	11	14	4	3	81	83	29	31	16	12	2	1	90	92	35	63	27	26	6	4	171	175	64
Los Angeles	64	44	12	6	2	291	181	96	63	34	21	7	1	235	220	76	127	78	33	13	3	526	401	172
Minnesota	5	0	5	0	0	5	16	0	5	2	3	0	0	10	14	4	10	2	8	0	0	15	30	4
Montreal	353	161	132	56	4	1034	956	382	352	102	201	47	2	829	1184	253	705	263	333	103	6	1863	2140	635
Nashville	7	4	2	1	0	20	12	9	8	4	2	0	2	18	21	10	15	8	4	1	2	38	33	19
New Jersey	66	34	18	8	6	244	202	82	63	30	18	11	4	191	161	75	129	64	36	19	10	435	363	157
NY Islanders	69	38	18	11	2	252	191	89	71	31	28	10	2	223	230	74	140	69	46	21	4	475	421	163
NY Rangers	308	165	97	42	4	1093	856	376	312	117	138	55	2	868	952	291	620	282	235	97	6	1961	1808	667
Ottawa	51	30	15	5	1	174	137	66	49	25	15	3	6	146	124	59	100	55	30	8	7	320	261	125
Philadelphia	86	49	23	11	3	305	240	112	83	38	33	10	2	251	269	88	169	87	56	21	5	556	509	200
Phoenix	32	22	5	4	1	138	96	49	32	15	14	3	0	106	106	33	64	37	19	7	1	244	202	82
Pittsburgh	88	62	18	6	2	379	245	132	90	38	35	15	2	319	309	93	178	100	53	21	4	698	554	225
St. Louis	61	35	15	9	2	252	170	81	62	25	24	9	4	210	196	63	123	60	39	18	6	462	366	144
San Jose	12	7	2	3	0	43	37	17	13	7	4	2	0	42	32	16	25	14	6	5	0	85	69	33
Tampa Bay	33	23	4	6	0	125	80	52	33	17	13	3	0	99	95	37	66	40	17	9	0	224	175	89
Toronto	316	173	94	47	2	1031	844	395	317	103	159	51	4	828	1051	261	633	276	253	98	6	1859	1895	656
Vancouver	54	39	7	7	1	221	127	86	53	28	17	8	0	212	171	64	107	67	24	15	1	433	298	150
Washington	66	38	17	9	2	232	175	87	65	31	19	12	3	215	187	77	131	69	36	21	5	447	362	164
Defunct Clubs	164	112	39	13	0	525	306	237	164	79	67	18	0	496	440	176	328	191	106	31	0	1021	746	413
Totals	**2898**	**1631**	**848**	**376**	**43**	**10178**	**7804**	**3681**	**2898**	**1130**	**1305**	**415**	**48**	**8416**	**9258**	**2723**	**5796**	**2761**	**2153**	**791**	**91**	**18594**	**17062**	**6404**

Playoffs

	Series	W	L	GP	W	L	T	GF	GA	Last Mtg.	Rnd.	Result
Buffalo	8	6	2	45	25	20	0	155	145	2010	CQF	W 4-2
Carolina	4	3	1	26	15	11	0	80	64	2009	CSF	L 3-4
Chicago	6	5	1	22	16	5	1	97	63	1978	QF	W 4-0
Colorado	2	1	1	11	6	5	0	37	36	1983	DSF	W 3-1
Dallas	1	0	1	3	0	3	0	13	20	1981	PRE	L 0-3
Detroit	7	4	3	33	19	14	0	96	98	1957	SF	W 4-1
Edmonton	2	0	2	9	1	8	0	20	41	1990	F	L 1-4
Florida	1	0	1	5	1	4	0	16	22	1996	CQF	L 1-4
Los Angeles	2	2	0	13	8	5	0	56	38	1977	QF	W 4-2
Montreal	32	8	24	163	64	99	0	403	494	2009	CQF	W 4-0
New Jersey	4	1	3	23	8	15	0	60	68	2003	CQF	L 1-4
NY Islanders	2	0	2	11	3	8	0	35	49	1983	CF	L 2-4
NY Rangers	9	6	3	42	22	18	2	114	104	1973	QF	L 1-4
Philadelphia	5	2	3	27	14	13	0	80	79	2010	CSF	L 3-4
Pittsburgh	4	2	2	19	9	10	0	62	67	1992	CF	L 0-4
St. Louis	2	2	0	8	8	0	0	48	15	1972	SF	W 4-0
Toronto	13	5	8	62	30	31	1	153	150	1974	QF	W 4-0
Washington	2	1	1	10	6	4	0	28	21	1998	CQF	L 2-4
Defunct Clubs	3	1	2	11	4	5	2	20	20			
Totals	**109**	**49**	**60**	**543**	**259**	**278**	**6**	**1573**	**1594**			

Calgary totals include Atlanta Flames, 1972-73 to 1979-80.
Carolina totals include Hartford, 1979-80 to 1996-97.
Colorado totals include Quebec, 1979-80 to 1994-95.
Dallas totals include Minnesota North Stars, 1967-68 to 1992-93.
New Jersey totals include Kansas City, 1974-75, 1975-76, and Colorado Rockies, 1976-77 to 1981-82.
Phoenix totals include Winnipeg, 1979-80 to 1995-96.

Playoff Results 2010-2006

Year	Round	Opponent	Result	GF	GA
2010	CSF	Philadelphia	L 3-4	20	22
	CQF	Buffalo	W 4-2	16	15
2009	CSF	Carolina	L 3-4	17	16
	CQF	Montreal	W 4-0	17	6
2008	CQF	Montreal	L 3-4	15	19

Abbreviations: Round: F - Final; **CF** - conference final; **CSF** - conference semi-final; **CQF** - conference quarter-final; **DSF** - division semi-final; **SF** - semi-final; **QF** - quarter-final; **PRE** - preliminary round.

2009-10 Results

Oct.	1	Washington	1-4		5	at Ottawa	4-1
	3	Carolina	7-2		7	Chicago	2-5
	8	Anaheim	1-6		9	NY Rangers	1-3
	10	NY Islanders	4-3†		13	at Anaheim	3-4
	12	Colorado	3-4		14	at San Jose	2-1†
	16	at Dallas	3-0		16	at Los Angeles	3-4†
	17	at Phoenix	1-4		18	Ottawa	1-5
	21	Nashville	3-2		21	Columbus	2-3
	22	at Philadelphia	3-4†		23	Ottawa	1-2
	24	at Ottawa	4-3†		24	at Carolina	1-5
	29	New Jersey	1-2		29	at Buffalo	1-2
	31	Edmonton	2-0		30	Los Angeles	2-3†
Nov.	1	at NY Rangers	0-1	**Feb.**	2	Washington	1-4
	3	at Detroit	0-2		4	Montreal	2-3†
	5	Montreal	1-2†		6	Vancouver	2-3†
	7	Buffalo	4-2		7	at Montreal	3-0
	10	Pittsburgh	3-0		9	at Buffalo	3-2†
	12	Florida	0-1†		11	at Tampa Bay	5-4
	14	at Pittsburgh	5-6*		13	at Florida	3-2†
	16	NY Islanders	1-4	**Mar.**	2	Montreal	1-4
	19	at Atlanta	4-3†		4	Toronto	3-2†
	20	at Buffalo	2-1*		6	at NY Islanders	3-2
	23	at St. Louis	4-2		7	at Pittsburgh	1-2
	25	at Minnesota	2-1†		9	at Toronto	3-4*
	27	New Jersey	1-2†		11	at Philadelphia	5-1
	28	Ottawa	4-3†		13	at Montreal	2-3
Dec.	2	Tampa Bay	4-1		15	at New Jersey	2-3
	4	at Montreal	1-5		16	at Carolina	5-2
	5	Toronto	7-2		18	Pittsburgh	0-3
	10	Toronto	5-2		21	NY Rangers	2-1
	12	at NY Islanders	2-3*		23	at Atlanta	4-0
	14	Philadelphia	1-3		25	Tampa Bay	3-5
	18	at Chicago	4-5†		27	Calgary	5-0
	19	at Toronto	0-2		29	Buffalo	2-3
	21	at Ottawa	2-0		30	at New Jersey	1-0*
	23	Atlanta	6-4	**Apr.**	1	Florida	0-1
	27	at Florida	2-1		3	at Toronto	2-1*
	28	at Tampa Bay	1-2		5	at Washington	2-3*
	30	Atlanta	4-0		8	Buffalo	3-1
Jan.	1	Philadelphia	2-1*		10	Carolina	4-2
	4	at NY Rangers	2-3		11	at Washington	4-3†

* – Overtime † – Shootout

Entry Draft Selections 2010-1996

Name in bold denotes played in NHL.

2010

Pick	
2	Tyler Seguin
32	Jared Knight
45	Ryan Spooner
97	Craig Cunningham
135	Justin Florek
165	Zane Gothberg
195	Maxim Chudinov
210	Zach Trotman

2009

Pick	
25	Jordan Caron
86	Ryan Button
112	Lane MacDermid
176	Tyler Randell
206	Ben Sexton

2008

Pick	
16	Joe Colborne
47	Maxime Sauve
77	Michael Hutchinson
97	Jamie Arniel
173	Nick Tremblay
197	Mark Goggin

2007

Pick	
8	**Zach Hamill**
35	Tommy Cross
130	Denis Reul
159	Alain Goulet
169	Radim Ostrcil
189	Jordan Knackstedt

2006

Pick	
5	**Phil Kessel**
37	Yuri Alexandrov
50	**Milan Lucic**
71	**Brad Marchand**
128	**Andrew Bodnarchuk**
158	Levi Nelson

2005

Pick	
22	**Matt Lashoff**
39	**Petr Kalus**
83	**Mikko Lehtonen**
100	**Jonathan Sigalet**
106	**Vladimir Sobotka**
154	Wacey Rabbit
172	Lukas Vantuch
217	Brock Bradford

2004

Pick	
63	**David Krejci**
64	**Martins Karsums**
108	Ashton Rome
134	**Kris Versteeg**
160	**Ben Walter**
224	**Matt Hunwick**
255	Anton Hedman

2003

Pick	
21	**Mark Stuart**
45	**Patrice Bergeron**
66	**Masi Marjamaki**
107	**Byron Bitz**
118	Frank Rediker
129	Patrik Valcak
153	Mike Brown
183	**Nate Thompson**
247	Benoit Mondou
277	Kevin Regan

2002

Pick	
29	**Hannu Toivonen**
56	Vladislav Evseev
130	Jan Kubista
153	Peter Hamerlik
228	Dmitri Utkin
259	**Yan Stastny**
290	Pavel Frolov

2001

Pick	
19	**Shaone Morrisonn**
77	Darren McLachlan
111	Matti Kaltiainen
147	Jiri Jakes
179	**Andrew Alberts**
209	**Jordan Sigalet**
241	**Milan Jurcina**
282	Marcel Rodman

2000

Pick	
7	**Lars Jonsson**
27	**Martin Samuelsson**
37	**Andy Hilbert**
59	**Ivan Huml**
66	Tuukka Makela
73	**Sergei Zinovjev**
103	Brett Nowak
174	**Jarno Kultanen**
204	Chris Berti
237	**Zdenek Kutlak**
268	**Pavel Kolarik**
279	Andreas Lindstrom

1999

Pick	
21	**Nick Boynton**
56	Matt Zultek
89	**Kyle Wanvig**
118	Jaakko Harikkala
147	Seamus Kotyk
179	Donald Choukalos
207	Greg Barber
236	John Cronin
247	**Mikko Eloranta**
264	Georgy Pujacs

1998

Pick	
48	**Jonathan Girard**
52	**Bobby Allen**
78	**Peter Nordstrom**
135	**Andrew Raycroft**
165	Ryan Milanovic

1997

Pick	
1	**Joe Thornton**
8	**Sergei Samsonov**
27	**Ben Clymer**
54	Mattias Karlin
63	**Lee Goren**
81	Karol Bartanus
135	Denis Timofeev
162	Joel Trottier
180	Jim Baxter
191	**Antti Laaksonen**
218	Eric Van Acker
246	**Jay Henderson**

1996

Pick	
8	**Johnathan Aitken**
45	Henry Kuster
53	Eric Naud
80	Jason Doyle
100	**Trent Whitfield**
132	Elias Abrahamsson
155	Chris Lane
182	Thomas Brown
208	Bob Prier
234	Anders Soderberg

Captains' History

No captain, 1924-25 to 1926-27; Lionel Hitchman, 1927-28 to 1930-31; George Owen, 1931-32; Dit Clapper, 1932-33 to 1937-38; Cooney Weiland, 1938-39; Dit Clapper, 1939-40 to 1945-46; Dit Clapper and John Crawford, 1946-47; John Crawford 1947-48 to 1949-50; Milt Schmidt, 1950-51 to 1953-54; Milt Schmidt, Ed Sanford, 1954-55; Fern Flaman, 1955-56 to 1960-61; Don McKenney, 1961-62, 1962-63; Leo Boivin, 1963-64 to 1965-66; John Bucyk, 1966-67; no captain, 1967-68 to 1972-73; John Bucyk, 1973-74 to 1976-77; Wayne Cashman, 1977-78 to 1982-83; Terry O'Reilly, 1983-84, 1984-85; Raymond Bourque, Rick Middleton (co-captains) 1985-86 to 1987-88; Raymond Bourque, 1988-89 to 1999-2000; Jason Allison, 2000-01; no captain, 2001-02; Joe Thornton, 2002-03, 2003-04; Joe Thornton and no captain, 2005-06; Zdeno Chara, 2006-07 to date.

General Managers' History

Art Ross, 1924-25 to 1953-54; Lynn Patrick, 1954-55 to 1964-65; Hap Emms, 1965-66, 1966-67; Milt Schmidt, 1967-68 to 1971-72; Harry Sinden, 1972-73 to 1999-2000; Harry Sinden and Mike O'Connell, 2000-01; Mike O'Connell, 2001-02 to 2005-06; Peter Chiarelli, 2006-07 to date.

Peter Chiarelli

General Manager

Born: Nepean, Ont., August 5, 1964.

Peter Chiarelli became just the seventh man in club history to hold the position of general manager when he was named to the post on May 26, 2006. He is in charge of every aspect of the team's hockey operations. He officially began his position in Boston on July 10, 2006 as a result of a league-arbitrated compensation agreement that saw the Bruins surrender a third-round draft pick in the 2006 NHL Entry Draft (Eric Gryba, 68th overall) to the Ottawa Senators. By his third season in Boston in 2008-09, the Bruins posted the best record in the Eastern Conference and were second overall in the NHL.

Chiarelli came to the Bruins after seven seasons with the Ottawa Senators, five as the director of legal relations and the last two as assistant general manager. He was involved in all aspects of that team's hockey operations, including contract research and negotiations, salary arbitration and all player personnel matters. He was also involved in overseeing Ottawa's top developmental affiliate, the Binghamtom Senators of the American Hockey League. The Senators had four 100+ point seasons during his tenure and never finished below 94 points, finished with the NHL's top record in 2002-03 (113 points) and the best record in the Eastern Conference in 2005-06 (113 points).

A native of the Ottawa area, Chiarelli played four seasons of college hockey at Harvard University where he served the team as captain and was a teammate of former Bruin Don Sweeney. He had 21 goals and 28 assists for 49 points with 70 penalty minutes in 109 career college games and earned his degree in Economics in 1987. He played professionally in Europe for one year before returning to school and obtaining his law degree from the University of Ottawa. He was admitted to the Ontario bar in 1993 and spent six years as a lawyer and player agent prior to joining the Senators front office in 1999.

Club Directory

TD Garden

Boston Bruins
TD Garden
100 Legends Way
Boston, MA 02114
Phone **617/624-BEAR (2327)**
FAX 617/523-7184
www.bostonbruins.com
Capacity: 17,565

Ownership

Owner & Governor, Boston Bruins; Chairman, NHL Board of Governors	Jeremy M. Jacobs
Principal, Boston Bruins	Charlie Jacobs
Alternate Governors	Charlie Jacobs, Jeremy Jacobs, Jr., Louis Jacobs, Harry Sinden, Peter Chiarelli, Cam Neely
Senior Advisor to the Owner	Harry Sinden

Executive

President	Cam Neely
Sr. Vice President, Sales & Marketing	Amy Latimer
Vice President, Finance	Jim Bednarek
Vice President, Marketing	Jen Compton
Vice President, Corporate Partnerships	Chris Johnson
Director of Administration	Dale Hamilton-Powers
Executive Secretary	Rita Brandano
Administrative Assistant	Karen Ondo

Hockey Operations

General Manager	Peter Chiarelli
Assistant General Managers	Jim Benning, Don Sweeney
Director of Player Personnel	Scott Bradley
Director of Amateur Scouting	Wayne Smith
Director of Collegiate Scouting	John Weisbrod
Scouting Staff	Mike Chiarelli, Adam Creighton, Scott Fitzgerald, Jack Higgins, Jukka Holtari, Denis LeBlanc, Dean Malkoc, Mike McGraw, Tom McVie, Svenake Svensson
Manager of Hockey Administration	Ryan Nadeau
Assistant to Hockey Administration	Jeremy Rogalski
Team Road Services Coordinator	John Bucyk

Coaching

Head Coach	Claude Julien
Assistant Coaches	Doug Houda, Geoff Ward, Doug Jarvis
Goaltending Coach	Bob Essensa
Video Coach	Brant Berglund

Medical, Training and Equipment

Strength & Conditioning Coach	John Whitesides
Athletic Trainer	Don DelNegro
Physical Therapist	Scott Waugh
Assistant Athletic Trainer & Massage Therapist	Derek Repucci
Equipment Manager	Keith Robinson
Assistant Equipment Managers	TBA, Matt Falconer
Head Team Physician/Orthopedist	Dr. Peter Asnis
Team Psychologist	Dr. Frank Lodato

Communications and Community Relations

Director of Communications	Matthew Chmura
Director of Publications & Information	Heidi Holland
Director of Community Relations & Promotions	Kerry Collins
Director of Development, Bruins Foundation	Bob Sweeney
Director of Interactive	Darrell Wood
Manager of Media Relations	Eric Tosi
Content Manager, BostonBruins.com	John Bishop
Public Relations Coordinator	Kelly Mohr
Community Relations Coordinator	Cathlin Allen
Coordinators, Boston Bruins Foundation	Erin McEvoy, Zack Fitzgerald
Web Video Producer	Jonathan Gotlib
Administrative Assistant, Alumni Office	Mal Viola

Sales, Marketing and Retail

Senior Director, Premium Sales	Leah Leahy-Williams
Senior Director, The Premium Club	Dana Petrie
Director of Marketing	Chris DiPierro
Director of Ticket Sales & Fan Relations	Leigh Castergine
Retail Director	Lauma Cerlins
Ticket Sales Manager	Mark Rodrigues
Marketing Manager	Liz d'Entremont
Game Presentation & Promotions Manager	Cole Parsons
Youth Hockey Development Manager	Lori DiGiacomo
Fan Relations Manager	Tamala Sweesy
Group Sales Manager	Chris Spano
Graphic Designer	Jason Petrie
Promotions Coordinator	Brett Bovio
Marketing Coordinator	Laura Caso
Fan Relations Representatives	John Cadigan, Nick Camara, Lindsay Corbo, Nikki Gullotti, Courtney McNeice, Kaitlin Rowe
Season Sales Account Executives	Sean Cummings, Adam DiVincenzo, Matt Gulley, Tina Zettel
Group Sales Account Executives	Charlie Karoly, Briana Lynch, Caillin Miller
Ticket Sales Representatives	James Brown, Davienne Dente, Sarah Fucigna, Chris Silvia

Finance, Legal, Human Resources and Box Office

Controller	Rick McGlinchey
Staff Accountant	Linda Bartlett
Payroll & Benefits Manager	Botin Bou
Assistant General Counsel	Matt Reece
Legal Assistant	Binnie Hundley
Director of Human Resources	Joe Lawlor
Human Resources Generalist	Kate Gibbon
Director of Ticket Operations	Matthew Whelan
Assistant Director of Ticket Operations	Jim Foley
Senior Box Office Analyst	Allyson Leonard
Ticket Office Receptionist	Jo-Ann Connolly-White
Business Analyst	Matt Synakowski

Broadcasting

TV Rightsholder	New England Sports Network (NESN)
Radio play-by-play / analyst	Jack Edwards / Andy Brickley
Radio Rightsholder	98.5 The Sports Hub (CBS Radio Boston)
Radio play-by-play / analyst	Dave Goucher / Bob Beers

Buffalo Sabres

2009-10 Results: 45W-27L-4OTL-6SOL 100PTS.
First, Northeast Division

Ryan Miller broke his own franchise record with 41 wins in 2009-10. He ranked second in the NHL with a 2.22 goals-against average and a .929 save percentage.

2010-11 Schedule

Oct. Fri. 8 at Ottawa	Tue. 11 Philadelphia
Sat. 9 NY Rangers	Thu. 13 Carolina
Mon. 11 Chicago	Sat. 15 at NY Islanders
Wed. 13 New Jersey	Tue. 18 Montreal
Fri. 15 Montreal	Thu. 20 at Boston
Sat. 16 at Chicago	Fri. 21 NY Islanders
Wed. 20 at Atlanta	Sun. 23 at NY Islanders*
Fri. 22 Ottawa	Tue. 25 at Ottawa
Sat. 23 at New Jersey	**Feb.** Fri. 4 at Pittsburgh
Tue. 26 at Philadelphia	Sat. 5 Toronto
Fri. 29 at Atlanta	Tue. 8 at Tampa Bay
Sat. 30 at Dallas	Thu. 10 at Florida
Nov. Wed. 3 Boston	Sun. 13 NY Islanders*
Fri. 5 Montreal	Tue. 15 at Montreal
Sat. 6 at Toronto	Wed. 16 Toronto
Wed. 10 at New Jersey	Fri. 18 St. Louis
Thu. 11 at NY Rangers	Sun. 20 Washington*
Sat. 13 Washington	Wed. 23 Atlanta
Mon. 15 Vancouver	Fri. 25 Ottawa
Wed. 17 at Washington	Sat. 26 Detroit
Fri. 19 Los Angeles	**Mar.** Tue. 1 at NY Rangers
Sat. 20 Tampa Bay	Thu. 3 at Carolina
Wed. 24 Pittsburgh	Sat. 5 at Philadelphia*
Fri. 26 Toronto	Sun. 6 at Minnesota*
Sat. 27 at Montreal	Tue. 8 at Pittsburgh
Dec. Fri. 3 Columbus	Thu. 10 at Boston
Sat. 4 at Ottawa	Sat. 12 at Toronto
Tue. 7 at Boston	Sun. 13 Ottawa*
Thu. 9 San Jose	Tue. 15 Carolina
Sat. 11 Pittsburgh	Sat. 19 Atlanta
Wed. 15 Boston	Sun. 20 Nashville*
Fri. 17 at Florida	Tue. 22 at Montreal
Sat. 18 at Tampa Bay	Fri. 25 Florida
Tue. 21 Anaheim	Sat. 26 New Jersey
Thu. 23 Florida	Tue. 29 at Toronto
Mon. 27 at Calgary	Wed. 30 NY Rangers
Tue. 28 at Edmonton	**Apr.** Sat. 2 at Washington
Jan. Sat. 1 Boston*	Sun. 3 at Carolina*
Tue. 4 at Colorado	Tue. 5 Tampa Bay
Thu. 6 at San Jose	Fri. 8 Philadelphia
Sat. 8 at Phoenix	Sat. 9 at Columbus

* Denotes afternoon game.

NORTHEAST DIVISION
41st NHL Season

Franchise date: May 22, 1970

Year-by-Year Record

		Home				Road				Overall							
Season	GP	W	L	T	OL	W	L	T	OL	W	L	T	OL	GF	GA	Pts.	Finished	Playoff Result
2009-10	82	25	10	....	6	20	17	....	4	45	27	....	10	235	207	100	1st, Northeast Div.	Lost Conf. Quarter-Final
2008-09	82	23	15	....	3	18	17	....	6	41	32	....	9	250	234	91	3rd, Northeast Div.	Out of Playoffs
2007-08	82	20	15	....	6	19	16	....	6	39	31	....	12	255	242	90	4th, Northeast Div.	Out of Playoffs
2006-07	82	28	10	....	3	25	12	....	4	53	22	....	7	308	242	113	1st, Northeast Div.	Lost Conf. Championship
2005-06	82	27	11	....	3	25	13	....	3	52	24	....	6	281	239	110	2nd, Northeast Div.	Lost Conf. Championship
2004-05	....																	
2003-04	82	21	13	4	3	16	21	3	1	37	34	7	4	220	221	85	5th, Northeast Div.	Out of Playoffs
2002-03	82	18	16	5	2	9	21	5	6	27	37	10	8	190	219	72	5th, Northeast Div.	Out of Playoffs
2001-02	82	20	16	5	0	15	19	6	1	35	35	11	1	213	200	82	5th, Northeast Div.	Out of Playoffs
2000-01	82	26	12	3	0	20	18	2	1	46	30	5	1	218	184	98	2nd, Northeast Div.	Lost Conf. Semi-Final
1999-2000	82	21	14	5	1	14	18	6	3	35	32	11	4	213	204	85	3rd, Northeast Div.	Lost Conf. Quarter-Final
1998-99	82	23	12	6	....	14	16	11	....	37	28	17	....	207	175	91	4th, Northeast Div.	Lost Final
1997-98	82	20	13	8	....	16	16	9	....	36	29	17	....	211	187	89	3rd, Northeast Div.	Lost Conf. Championship
1996-97	82	24	11	6	....	16	19	6	....	40	30	12	....	237	208	92	1st, Northeast Div.	Lost Conf. Semi-Final
1995-96	82	19	17	5	....	14	25	2	....	33	42	7	....	247	262	73	5th, Northeast Div.	Out of Playoffs
1994-95	48	15	8	1	....	7	11	6	....	22	19	7	....	130	119	51	4th, Northeast Div.	Lost Conf. Quarter-Final
1993-94	84	22	17	3	....	21	15	6	....	43	32	9	....	282	218	95	4th, Northeast Div.	Lost Conf. Quarter-Final
1992-93	84	25	15	2	....	13	21	8	....	38	36	10	....	335	297	86	4th, Adams Div.	Lost Div. Final
1991-92	80	22	13	5	....	9	24	7	....	31	37	12	....	289	299	74	3rd, Adams Div.	Lost Div. Semi-Final
1990-91	80	15	13	12	....	16	17	7	....	31	30	19	....	292	278	81	3rd, Adams Div.	Lost Div. Semi-Final
1989-90	80	27	11	2	....	18	16	6	....	45	27	8	....	286	248	98	2nd, Adams Div.	Lost Div. Semi-Final
1988-89	80	25	12	3	....	13	23	4	....	38	35	7	....	291	299	83	3rd, Adams Div.	Lost Div. Semi-Final
1987-88	80	19	14	7	....	18	18	4	....	37	32	11	....	283	305	85	3rd, Adams Div.	Lost Div. Semi-Final
1986-87	80	18	18	4	....	10	26	4	....	28	44	8	....	280	308	64	5th, Adams Div.	Out of Playoffs
1985-86	80	23	16	1	....	14	21	5	....	37	37	6	....	296	291	80	5th, Adams Div.	Out of Playoffs
1984-85	80	23	10	7	....	15	18	7	....	38	28	14	....	290	237	90	3rd, Adams Div.	Lost Div. Semi-Final
1983-84	80	25	9	6	....	23	16	1	....	48	25	7	....	315	257	103	2nd, Adams Div.	Lost Div. Semi-Final
1982-83	80	25	7	8	....	13	22	5	....	38	29	13	....	318	285	89	3rd, Adams Div.	Lost Div. Final
1981-82	80	23	8	9	....	16	18	6	....	39	26	15	....	307	273	93	3rd, Adams Div.	Lost Div. Semi-Final
1980-81	80	21	7	12	....	18	13	9	....	39	20	21	....	327	250	99	1st, Adams Div.	Lost Quarter-Final
1979-80	80	27	5	8	....	20	12	8	....	47	17	16	....	318	201	110	1st, Adams Div.	Lost Semi-Final
1978-79	80	19	13	8	....	17	15	8	....	36	28	16	....	280	263	88	2nd, Adams Div.	Lost Prelim. Round
1977-78	80	25	7	8	....	19	12	9	....	44	19	17	....	288	215	105	2nd, Adams Div.	Lost Quarter-Final
1976-77	80	27	8	5	....	21	16	3	....	48	24	8	....	301	220	104	2nd, Adams Div.	Lost Quarter-Final
1975-76	80	28	7	5	....	18	14	8	....	46	21	13	....	339	240	105	2nd, Adams Div.	Lost Quarter-Final
1974-75	80	28	6	6	....	21	10	9	....	49	16	15	....	354	240	113	1st, Adams Div.	Lost Final
1973-74	78	24	9	6	....	9	24	6	....	32	34	12	....	242	250	76	5th, East Div.	Out of Playoffs
1972-73	78	30	6	3	....	7	21	11	....	37	27	14	....	257	219	88	4th, East Div.	Lost Quarter-Final
1971-72	78	11	19	9	....	5	24	10	....	16	43	19	....	203	289	51	6th, East Div.	Out of Playoffs
1970-71	78	16	13	10	....	8	26	5	....	24	39	15	....	217	291	63	5th, East Div.	Out of Playoffs

2010-11 Player Personnel

FORWARDS	HT	WT	S	Place of Birth	*Age	2009-10 Club
CONNOLLY, Tim	6-1	191	R	Syracuse, NY	29	Buffalo
ENNIS, Tyler	5-9	163	L	Edmonton, Alta.	21	Buffalo-Portland (AHL)
GAUSTAD, Paul	6-4	224	L	Fargo, ND	28	Buffalo
GERBE, Nathan	5-6	178	L	Oxford, MI	23	Buffalo-Portland (AHL)
GRIER, Mike	6-1	227	R	Detroit, MI	35	Buffalo
HECHT, Jochen	6-1	196	L	Mannheim, W. Germany	33	Buffalo
KALETA, Patrick	5-11	198	R	Buffalo, NY	24	Buffalo
McCORMICK, Cody	6-3	215	R	London, Ont.	27	Portland (AHL)-Buffalo
NIEDERMAYER, Rob	6-2	200	L	Cassiar, B.C.	35	New Jersey
POMINVILLE, Jason	6-0	189	R	Repentigny, Que.	27	Buffalo
ROY, Derek	5-9	188	L	Ottawa, Ont.	27	Buffalo
STAFFORD, Drew	6-1	216	R	Milwaukee, WI	24	Buffalo
VANEK, Thomas	6-2	212	R	Vienna, Austria	26	Buffalo

DEFENSEMEN						
BUTLER, Chris	6-2	205	L	St. Louis, MO	23	Buffalo
LEOPOLD, Jordan	6-1	200	L	Golden Valley, MN	30	Florida-Pittsburgh
MONTADOR, Steve	6-0	207	R	Vancouver, B.C.	30	Buffalo
MORRISONN, Shaone	6-4	217	L	Vancouver, B.C.	27	Washington
MYERS, Tyler	6-8	219	R	Houston, TX	20	Buffalo
RIVET, Craig	6-2	210	R	North Bay, Ont.	36	Buffalo
SEKERA, Andrej	6-0	202	L	Bojnice, Czech.	24	Buffalo
WEBER, Mike	6-2	211	L	Pittsburgh, PA	22	Portland (AHL)

GOALTENDERS	HT	WT	C	Place of Birth	*Age	2009-10 Club
LALIME, Patrick	6-3	198	L	St-Bonaventure, Que.	36	Buffalo-Portland (AHL)
MILLER, Ryan	6-2	175	L	East Lansing, MI	30	Buffalo

* – Age at start of 2010-11 season

Coaching History

Punch Imlach, 1970-71; Punch Imlach, Floyd Smith and Joe Crozier, 1971-72; Joe Crozier, 1972-73, 1973-74; Floyd Smith, 1974-75 to 1976-77; Marcel Pronovost, 1977-78; Marcel Pronovost and Billy Inglis, 1978-79; Scotty Bowman, 1979-80; Roger Neilson, 1980-81; Jim Roberts and Scotty Bowman, 1981-82; Scotty Bowman 1982-83 to 1984-85; Jim Schoenfeld and Scotty Bowman, 1985-86; Scotty Bowman, Craig Ramsay and Ted Sator, 1986-87; Ted Sator, 1987-88, 1988-89; Rick Dudley, 1989-90, 1990-91; Rick Dudley and John Muckler, 1991-92; John Muckler, 1992-93 to 1994-95; Ted Nolan, 1995-96, 1996-97; Lindy Ruff, 1997-98 to date.

Captains' History

Floyd Smith, 1970-71; Gerry Meehan, 1971-72 to 1973-74; Gerry Meehan and Jim Schoenfeld, 1974-75; Jim Schoenfeld, 1975-76, 1976-77; Danny Gare, 1977-78 to 1980-81; Danny Gare and Gilbert Perreault, 1981-82; Gilbert Perreault, 1982-83 to 1985-86; Gilbert Perreault and Lindy Ruff, 1986-87; Lindy Ruff, 1987-88; Lindy Ruff and Mike Foligno, 1988-89; Mike Foligno, 1989-90; Mike Foligno and Mike Ramsey, 1990-91; Mike Ramsey, 1991-92; Mike Ramsey and Pat LaFontaine, 1992-93; Pat LaFontaine and Alexander Mogilny, 1993-94; Pat LaFontaine, 1994-95 to 1996-97; Donald Audette and Michael Peca, 1997-98; Michael Peca, 1998-99, 1999-2000; no captain, 2000-01; Stu Barnes, 2001-02, 2002-03; Miroslav Satan, Chris Drury, James Patrick, J.P. Dumont, Daniel Briere, 2003-04; Daniel Briere and Chris Drury, 2005-06, 2006-07; Jochen Hecht, Toni Lydman, Brian Campbell, Jaroslav Spacek, Jason Pominville, 2007-08; Craig Rivet, 2008-09 to date.

Lindy Ruff
Head Coach
Born: Warburg, Alta., February 17, 1960.

A former captain of the Sabres, Lindy Ruff was appointed as the club's 15th head coach on July 21, 1997. In 1999, he led the Sabres to the Stanley Cup Finals for just the second time in club history and in 2006 he guided the Sabres to the Eastern Conference Final and was rewarded with the Jack Adams Award as coach of the year. The Sabres won the Presidents' Trophy for finishing first overall in the NHL standings in 2006-07, recording 113 points and a franchise-record 53 wins. Ruff is the winningest coach in club history. As a player, Ruff was drafted 32nd overall by the Sabres in the 1979 Entry Draft. He played both defense and left wing in an NHL career that spanned 12 seasons including 608 regular-season games with Buffalo. He became a playing assistant coach with Rochester of the AHL in 1991-92 and San Diego of the IHL in 1992-93. Ruff's San Diego club set a pro hockey record with 62 wins. In 1993-94 he became an NHL assistant coach with the Florida Panthers.

Coaching Record

			Regular Season						Playoffs			
Season	Team	League	GC	W	L	O/T		GC	W	L		T
1997-98	Buffalo	NHL	82	36	29	17		15	10	5		....
1998-99	Buffalo	NHL	82	37	28	17		21	14	7		....
99-2000	Buffalo	NHL	82	35	32	15		5	1	4		....
2000-01	Buffalo	NHL	82	46	30	6		13	7	6		....
2001-02	Buffalo	NHL	82	35	35	12		....	....	....		....
2002-03	Buffalo	NHL	82	27	37	18		....	....	....		....
2003-04	Buffalo	NHL	82	37	34	11		....	....	....		....
2004-05	Buffalo					SEASON CANCELLED						
2005-06	Buffalo	NHL	82	52	24	6		18	11	7		....
2006-07	Buffalo	NHL	82	53	22	7		16	9	7		....
2007-08	Buffalo	NHL	82	39	31	12		....	....	....		....
2008-09	Buffalo	NHL	82	41	32	9		....	....	....		....
2009-10	Buffalo	NHL	82	45	27	10		6	2	4		....
NHL Totals			984	483	361	140		94	54	40		

Won Jack Adams Award (2006)
Assistant coaches Brian McCutheon and Scott Arniel posted an 0-1-0 record as replacement coach when Lindy Ruff was sidelined due to a family medical emergency, March 20, 2006. Game is credited to Ruff's coaching record.

2009-10 Scoring
* - rookie

Regular Season

Pos	#	Player	Team	GP	G	A	Pts	TOI	+/-	PIM	PP	SH	GW	S	%
C	9	Derek Roy	BUF	80	26	43	69	19:22	9	48	10	1	6	215	12.1
C	19	Tim Connolly	BUF	73	17	48	65	18:37	10	28	7	1	5	206	8.3
R	29	Jason Pominville	BUF	82	24	38	62	18:44	13	22	8	0	2	252	9.5
L	26	Thomas Vanek	BUF	71	28	25	53	16:45	9	42	10	0	6	182	15.4
D	57	* Tyler Myers	BUF	82	11	37	48	23:44	13	32	3	0	1	104	10.6
C	55	Jochen Hecht	BUF	79	21	21	42	17:11	14	35	3	0	2	224	9.4
L	17	Raffi Torres	CBJ	60	19	12	31	13:34	-8	32	7	0	3	99	19.2
			BUF	14	0	5	5	13:20	-3	2	0	0	0	21	0.0
			Total	74	19	17	36	13:31	-11	34	7	0	3	120	15.8
R	21	Drew Stafford	BUF	71	14	20	34	14:28	4	35	5	0	1	181	7.7
L	13	* Tim Kennedy	BUF	78	10	16	26	12:57	-3	50	1	0	3	98	10.2
D	4	Steve Montador	BUF	78	5	18	23	17:05	0	75	0	0	2	134	3.7
C	28	Paul Gaustad	BUF	65	12	10	22	15:44	-7	82	3	0	1	111	10.8
R	25	Mike Grier	BUF	73	10	12	22	15:47	-4	14	0	0	2	123	8.1
D	34	Chris Butler	BUF	59	1	20	21	20:01	-15	22	0	0	0	61	1.6
D	5	Toni Lydman	BUF	67	4	16	20	18:51	10	30	0	0	1	77	5.2
D	10	Henrik Tallinder	BUF	82	4	16	20	20:36	13	32	0	0	0	53	7.5
R	36	Patrick Kaleta	BUF	55	10	5	15	10:09	2	89	0	2	4	64	15.6
D	52	Craig Rivet	BUF	78	1	14	15	18:13	-6	100	0	0	0	63	1.6
C	22	Adam Mair	BUF	69	6	8	14	9:14	-2	73	0	0	0	67	9.0
L	37	Matt Ellis	BUF	72	3	10	13	9:03	-1	12	0	0	1	112	2.7
D	44	Andrej Sekera	BUF	49	4	7	11	17:26	-1	6	0	0	0	59	6.8
C	63	* Tyler Ennis	BUF	10	3	6	9	15:20	1	6	0	0	2	23	13.0
C	42	* Nathan Gerbe	BUF	10	2	3	5	14:38	1	4	2	0	1	29	6.9
R	12	* Mark Mancari	BUF	6	1	1	2	14:04	3	4	0	0	0	19	5.3

Goaltending

No.	Goaltender	GPI	Mins	Avg	W	L	OT	EN	SO	GA	SA	S%	G	A	PIM
30	Ryan Miller	69	4047	2.22	41	18	8	7	5	150	2098	.929	0	0	4
40	Patrick Lalime	16	854	2.81	4	8	2	0	0	40	432	.907	0	0	2
1	* Jhonas Enroth	1	58	4.14	0	1	0	0	0	4	37	.892	0	0	0
	Totals	82	4992	2.42	45	27	10	7	5	201	2573	.922			

Playoffs

Pos	#	Player	Team	GP	G	A	Pts	TOI	+/-	PIM	PP	SH	GW	OT	S	%
R	29	Jason Pominville	BUF	6	2	2	4	20:17	-1	2	0	0	1	0	18	11.1
C	63	* Tyler Ennis	BUF	6	1	3	4	17:08	1	0	0	0	0	0	20	5.0
L	26	Thomas Vanek	BUF	6	3	0	3	13:37	1	2	0	0	0	0	10	20.0
L	13	* Tim Kennedy	BUF	6	1	2	3	14:25	3	4	0	0	0	0	7	14.3
R	25	Mike Grier	BUF	6	2	0	2	18:34	0	2	0	0	0	0	19	10.5
C	42	* Nathan Gerbe	BUF	2	1	1	2	14:37	2	0	0	0	0	0	6	16.7
C	22	Adam Mair	BUF	6	1	1	2	12:00	2	4	0	0	0	0	6	16.7
R	36	Patrick Kaleta	BUF	6	1	1	2	10:04	4	22	0	0	0	0	5	20.0
C	8	Cody McCormick	BUF	3	0	2	2	10:41	1	14	0	0	0	0	4	0.0
L	17	Raffi Torres	BUF	4	0	2	2	12:54	1	12	0	0	0	0	7	0.0
D	10	Henrik Tallinder	BUF	6	0	2	2	22:40	2	2	0	0	0	0	6	0.0
C	9	Derek Roy	BUF	6	0	2	2	22:58	2	4	0	0	0	0	13	0.0
L	37	Matt Ellis	BUF	3	1	0	1	9:44	1	0	0	0	0	0	5	20.0
D	52	Craig Rivet	BUF	6	1	0	1	14:34	2	11	0	0	1	0	3	33.3
D	4	Steve Montador	BUF	6	1	0	1	23:54	3	4	0	0	0	0	6	16.7
D	57	* Tyler Myers	BUF	6	1	0	1	25:54	0	4	0	0	0	0	18	5.6
D	5	Toni Lydman	BUF	6	0	1	1	26:14	1	6	0	0	0	0	6	0.0
C	19	Tim Connolly	BUF	6	0	1	1	17:49	-2	2	0	0	0	0	16	0.0
C	28	Paul Gaustad	BUF	6	0	1	1	18:40	1	8	0	0	0	0	7	0.0
R	21	Drew Stafford	BUF	3	0	0	0	14:06	0	0	0	0	0	0	8	0.0
D	44	Andrej Sekera	BUF	6	0	0	0	13:55	2	7	0	0	0	0	4	0.0

Goaltending

No.	Goaltender	GPI	Mins	Avg	W	L	EN	SO	GA	SA	S%	G	A	PIM
30	Ryan Miller	6	384	2.34	2	4	1	0	15	204	.926	0	0	2
	Totals	6	388	2.47	2	4	1	0	16	205	.922			

Club Records

Team

(Figures in brackets for season records are games played; records for fewest points, wins, ties, losses, goals, goals against are for 70 or more games)

Most Points **113** 1974-75 (80), 2006-07 (82)
Most Wins **53** 2006-07 (82)
Most Ties **21** 1980-81 (80)
Most Losses **44** 1986-87 (80)
Most Goals **354** 1974-75 (80)
Most Goals Against **308** 1986-87 (80)
Fewest Points **51** 1971-72 (78)
Fewest Wins **16** 1971-72 (78)
Fewest Ties **5** 2000-01 (82)
Fewest Losses **16** 1974-75 (80)
Fewest Goals **190** 2002-03 (82)
Fewest Goals Against **175** 1998-99 (82)
Longest Winning Streak
Overall .... **10** Jan. 4-23/84, Oct. 4-26/06
Home .... **12** Nov. 12/72-Jan. 7/73, Oct. 13-Dec. 10/89
Away .... **10** Dec. 10/83-Jan. 23/84, Oct. 4-Nov. 13/06
Longest Undefeated Streak
Overall .... **14** Mar. 6-Apr. 6/80 (8 wins, 6 ties)
Home .... **21** Oct. 8/72-Jan. 7/73 (18 wins, 3 ties)
Away .... **10** Dec. 10/83-Jan. 23/84 (10 wins), Oct. 4-Nov. 13/06 (10 wins)
Longest Losing Streak
Overall .... **8** Jan. 25-Feb. 13/03
Home .... **6** Oct. 10-Nov. 10/93, Mar. 3-Apr. 3/96
Away .... **7** Oct. 14-Nov. 7/70, Feb. 6-27/71, Jan. 10-Feb. 3/96, Feb. 19-Mar. 21/09
Longest Winless Streak
Overall .... **12** Nov. 23-Dec. 20/91 (8 losses, 4 ties), Oct. 25-Nov. 19/02 (10 losses, 2 ties)
Home .... **12** Jan. 27-Mar. 10/91 (7 losses, 5 ties)
Away .... **23** Oct. 30/71-Feb. 19/72 (15 losses, 8 ties)
Most Shutouts, Season **13** 1997-98 (82)
Most PIM, Season ***2,713** 1991-92 (80)
Most Goals, Game .... **14** Jan. 21/75 (Wsh. 2 at Buf. 14), Mar. 19/81 (Tor. 4 at Buf. 14)

Individual

Most Seasons .... **17** Gilbert Perreault
Most Games .... **1,191** Gilbert Perreault
Most Goals, Career .... **512** Gilbert Perreault
Most Assists, Career .... **814** Gilbert Perreault
Most Points, Career .... **1,326** Gilbert Perreault (512G, 814A)
Most PIM, Career .... **3,189** Rob Ray
Most Shutouts, Career .... **55** Dominik Hasek
Longest Consecutive Games Streak .... **776** Craig Ramsay (Mar. 27/73-Feb. 10/83)
Most Goals, Season .... **76** Alexander Mogilny (1992-93)
Most Assists, Season .... **95** Pat LaFontaine (1992-93)
Most Points, Season .... **148** Pat LaFontaine (1992-93; 53G, 95A)
Most PIM, Season .... **354** Rob Ray (1991-92)
Most Points, Defenseman, Season .... **81** Phil Housley (1989-90; 21G, 60A)
Most Points, Center, Season .... **148** Pat LaFontaine (1992-93; 53G, 95A)
Most Points, Right Wing, Season .... **127** Alexander Mogilny (1992-93; 76G, 51A)
Most Points, Left Wing, Season .... **95** Rick Martin (1974-75; 52G, 43A)
Most Points, Rookie, Season .... **74** Rick Martin (1971-72; 44G, 30A)
Most Shutouts, Season .... **13** Dominik Hasek (1997-98)
Most Goals, Game .... **5** Dave Andreychuk (Feb. 6/86)
Most Assists, Game .... **5** Gilbert Perreault (Feb. 1/76), (Mar. 9/80), (Jan. 4/84); Dale Hawerchuk (Jan. 15/92); Pat LaFontaine (Mar. 19/92), (Dec. 31/92), (Feb. 10/93)
Most Points, Game .... **7** Gilbert Perreault (Feb. 1/76; 2G, 5A)

* NHL Record.

Retired Numbers

2	Tim Horton	1972-1974
7	Rick Martin	1971-1981
11	Gilbert Perreault	1970-1987
14	Rene Robert	1971-1979
16	Pat Lafontaine	1991-1996
18	Danny Gare	1974-1981

All-time Record vs. Other Clubs

Regular Season

	At Home								On Road								Total							
	GP	W	L	T	OL	GF	GA	PTS	GP	W	L	T	OL	GF	GA	PTS	GP	W	L	T	OL	GF	GA	PTS
Anaheim	11	5	3	3	0	30	25	13	12	7	5	0	0	37	27	14	23	12	8	3	0	67	52	27
Atlanta	20	11	6	0	3	86	57	25	20	6	8	1	5	58	66	18	40	17	14	1	8	144	123	43
Boston	126	66	40	15	5	447	360	152	125	42	66	14	3	367	451	101	251	108	106	29	8	814	811	253
Calgary	47	29	13	5	0	194	134	63	48	18	19	11	0	149	161	47	95	47	32	16	0	343	295	110
Carolina	87	52	27	7	1	350	251	112	88	40	33	11	4	266	257	95	175	92	60	18	5	616	508	207
Chicago	55	34	14	7	0	204	140	75	53	19	28	6	0	142	169	44	108	53	42	13	0	346	309	119
Colorado	65	36	19	9	1	252	211	82	66	23	31	11	1	204	233	58	131	59	50	20	2	456	444	140
Columbus	6	2	4	0	0	14	18	4	4	0	3	1	0	6	12	1	10	2	7	1	0	20	30	5
Dallas	54	30	13	11	0	197	145	71	56	23	27	6	0	163	178	52	110	53	40	17	0	360	323	123
Detroit	55	34	13	8	0	235	163	76	58	19	32	5	2	165	211	45	113	53	45	13	2	400	374	121
Edmonton	32	12	13	7	0	114	114	31	31	7	21	3	0	87	123	17	63	19	34	10	0	201	237	48
Florida	33	22	8	3	0	100	66	47	31	16	14	1	0	89	81	33	64	38	22	4	0	189	147	80
Los Angeles	55	30	16	9	0	232	158	69	56	23	23	9	1	192	197	56	111	53	39	18	1	424	355	125
Minnesota	5	1	4	0	0	10	16	2	5	4	1	0	0	14	9	8	10	5	5	0	0	24	25	10
Montreal	120	65	32	19	4	376	315	153	121	43	65	12	1	351	437	99	241	108	97	31	5	727	752	252
Nashville	6	1	4	1	0	17	22	3	7	5	2	0	0	17	12	10	13	6	6	1	0	34	34	13
New Jersey	64	35	20	8	1	237	192	79	64	30	22	9	3	198	182	72	128	65	42	17	4	435	374	151
NY Islanders	71	40	21	9	1	242	195	90	71	30	30	9	2	195	199	71	142	70	51	18	3	437	394	161
NY Rangers	78	45	21	10	2	312	237	102	76	29	30	15	2	206	241	75	154	74	51	25	4	518	478	177
Ottawa	49	27	18	3	1	149	119	58	51	21	20	7	3	136	144	52	100	48	38	10	4	285	263	110
Philadelphia	73	37	27	8	1	245	208	83	77	22	42	12	1	201	264	57	150	59	69	20	2	446	472	140
Phoenix	34	22	6	5	1	135	84	50	32	16	14	2	0	103	95	34	66	38	20	7	1	238	179	84
Pittsburgh	81	39	20	17	5	301	219	100	81	21	41	18	1	247	302	61	162	60	61	35	6	548	521	161
St. Louis	54	30	18	6	0	207	171	66	52	15	28	7	2	132	186	39	106	45	46	13	2	339	357	105
San Jose	14	13	1	0	0	61	38	26	12	2	5	4	1	42	42	9	26	15	6	4	1	103	80	35
Tampa Bay	33	21	10	2	0	112	92	44	33	23	7	3	0	109	73	49	66	44	17	5	0	221	165	93
Toronto	87	56	24	6	1	343	227	119	85	40	30	12	3	292	248	95	172	96	54	18	4	635	475	214
Vancouver	54	28	18	8	0	195	157	64	54	16	27	11	0	165	200	43	108	44	45	19	0	360	357	107
Washington	66	41	19	6	0	256	172	88	66	38	19	9	0	228	171	85	132	79	38	15	0	484	343	173
Defunct Clubs	23	13	5	5	0	94	63	31	23	12	8	3	0	97	76	27	46	25	13	8	0	191	139	58
Totals	**1558**	**877**	**457**	**197**	**27**	**5747**	**4369**	**1978**	**1558**	**610**	**701**	**212**	**35**	**4658**	**5047**	**1467**	**3116**	**1487**	**1158**	**409**	**62**	**10405**	**9416**	**3445**

Playoffs

	Series	W	L	GP	W	L	T	GF	GA	Last Mtg.	Rnd.	Result
Boston	8	2	6	45	20	25	0	145	155	2010	CQF	L 2-4
Carolina	1	0	1	7	3	4	0	17	22	2006	CF	L 3-4
Chicago	2	2	0	9	8	1	0	36	17	1980	QF	W 4-0
Colorado	2	0	2	8	2	6	0	27	35	1985	DSF	L 2-3
Dallas	3	1	2	13	5	8	0	37	39	1999	F	L 2-4
Montreal	7	3	4	35	17	18	0	111	124	1998	CSF	W 4-0
New Jersey	1	0	1	7	3	4	0	14	14	1994	CQF	L 3-4
NY Islanders	4	1	3	21	8	13	0	62	70	2007	CQF	W 4-1
NY Rangers	2	2	0	9	6	3	0	28	19	2007	CSF	W 4-2
Ottawa	4	3	1	21	13	8	0	52	47	2007	CF	L 1-4
Philadelphia	8	3	5	43	18	25	0	123	124	2006	CQF	W 4-2
Pittsburgh	2	0	2	10	4	6	0	26	26	2001	CSF	L 3-4
St. Louis	1	1	0	3	2	1	0	7	8	1976	PRE	W 2-1
Toronto	1	1	0	5	4	1	0	21	16	1999	CF	W 4-1
Vancouver	2	2	0	7	6	1	0	28	14	1981	PRE	W 3-0
Washington	1	0	1	6	2	4	0	11	13	1998	CF	L 2-4
Totals	**49**	**21**	**28**	**249**	**121**	**128**	**0**	**745**	**743**			

Calgary totals include Atlanta Flames, 1972-73 to 1979-80. Carolina totals include Hartford, 1979-80 to 1996-97.
Colorado totals include Quebec, 1979-80 to 1994-95. Dallas totals include Minnesota North Stars, 1970-71 to 1992-93.
New Jersey totals include Kansas City, 1974-75, 1975-76, and Colorado Rockies, 1976-77 to 1981-82.
Phoenix totals include Winnipeg, 1979-80 to 1995-96.

Playoff Results 2010-2006

Year	Round	Opponent	Result	GF	GA
2010	CQF	Boston	L 2-4	15	16
2007	CF	Ottawa	L 1-4	10	15
	CSF	NY Rangers	W 4-2	17	13
	CQF	NY Islanders	W 4-1	17	11
2006	CF	Carolina	L 3-4	17	22
	CSF	Ottawa	W 4-1	16	13
	CQF	Philadelphia	W 4-2	27	14

Abbreviations: Round: F - Final; **CF** - conference final; **CSF** - conference semi-final; **CQF** - conference quarter-final; **DSF** - division semi-final; **QF** - quarter-final; **PRE** - preliminary round.

2009-10 Results

Oct.	3	Montreal	1-2*		6	Tampa Bay	5-3
	8	Phoenix	2-1		8	Toronto	3-2
	10	at Nashville	1-0		9	Colorado	3-4†
	13	Detroit	6-2		14	at Atlanta	2-1*
	16	NY Islanders	6-3		16	at NY Islanders	2-3†
	17	Atlanta	2-4		18	at Phoenix	7-2
	21	at Florida	5-2		19	at Anaheim	4-5
	24	at Tampa Bay	3-2†		21	at Los Angeles	3-4†
	28	at New Jersey	4-1		23	at San Jose	2-5
	30	Toronto	3-2*		25	at Vancouver	2-3
	31	at NY Islanders	0-5		27	New Jersey	2-1†
Nov.	4	NY Islanders	3-0		29	Boston	2-1
	6	Philadelphia	2-5	Feb.	1	at Pittsburgh	4-5
	7	at Boston	2-4		3	Ottawa	2-4
	11	Edmonton	3-1		5	Carolina	3-4
	13	Calgary	2-1†		6	at Columbus	0-4
	14	at Philadelphia	3-2		9	Boston	2-3†
	18	Florida	2-6		11	at Carolina	3-4*
	20	Boston	1-2*		13	San Jose	3-1
	21	at Ottawa	3-5	Mar.	2	at Pittsburgh	2-3
	25	at Washington	0-2		3	Washington	1-3
	27	at Philadelphia	4-2		5	Philadelphia	3-2*
	28	Carolina	5-1		7	at NY Rangers	2-1*
	30	at Toronto	3-0		10	Dallas	5-3
Dec.	3	Montreal	6-2		12	Minnesota	2-3
	5	NY Rangers	1-2		13	at Detroit	2-3*
	7	New Jersey	0-3		16	at Atlanta	3-4
	9	Washington	3-0		18	at Tampa Bay	6-2
	11	Chicago	2-1		20	at Florida	3-1
	12	at NY Rangers	3-2		21	at Carolina	5-3
	14	at Montreal	4-3		24	Montreal	3-2†
	16	at Ottawa	0-2		26	Ottawa	2-4
	18	Toronto	5-2		27	Tampa Bay	7-1
	19	Pittsburgh	1-2†		29	at Boston	3-2
	21	at Toronto	3-2*		31	Florida	6-2
	23	at Washington	2-5	Apr.	1	at Toronto	2-4
	26	Ottawa	2-3†		3	at Montreal	0-3
	27	at St. Louis	5-3		6	NY Rangers	5-2
	29	Pittsburgh	4-3		8	at Boston	1-3
Jan.	1	Atlanta	4-3*		10	at Ottawa	5-2
	3	at Montreal	1-0		11	at New Jersey	1-2

* – Overtime † – Shootout

Entry Draft Selections 2010-1996

Name in bold denotes played in NHL.

2010 Pick	2006 Pick	2002 Pick	1998 Pick
23 Mark Pysyk	24 Dennis Persson	**11 Keith Ballard**	18 Dmitri Kalinin
68 Jerome Gauthier-Leduc	46 **Jhonas Enroth**	**20 Daniel Paille**	34 Andrew Peters
75 Kevin Sundher	57 **Mike Weber**	76 Michael Tessier	47 Norm Milley
83 Matt MacKenzie	117 Felix Schutz	82 John Adams	50 Jaroslav Kristek
98 Steven Shipley	147 Alex Biega	108 Jakub Hulva	77 **Mike Pandolfo**
143 Gregg Sutch	207 Benjamin Breault	121 Marty Magers	137 Aaron Goldade
173 Cedrick Henley		178 Maxim Sheviev	164 **Ales Kotalik**
203 Christian Isackson	**2005** Pick	208 **Radoslav Hecl**	191 Brad Moran
208 Riley Boychuk	13 Marek Zagrapan	241 Dennis Wideman	218 **David Moravec**
	48 Philip Gogulla	271 Martin Cizek	249 Edo Terglav
2009 Pick	87 **Marc-Andre Gragnani**		
13 Zack Kassian	96 **Chris Butler**	**2001** Pick	**1997** Pick
66 Brayden McNabb	142 **Nathan Gerbe**	22 **Jiri Novotny**	21 **Mika Noronen**
104 Marcus Foligno	182 Adam Dennis	32 **Derek Roy**	48 **Henrik Tallinder**
134 Mark Adams	191 Vyacheslav Buravchikov	50 **Chris Thorburn**	69 **Maxim Afinogenov**
164 Connor Knapp	208 Matt Generous	55 **Jason Pominville**	75 Jeff Martin
194 Maxime Legault	227 Andrew Orpik	155 Michal Vondrka	101 Luc Theoret
		234 Calle Aslund	128 Torrey DiRoberto
2008 Pick	**2004** Pick	247 Marek Dubec	156 Brian Campbell
12 **Tyler Myers**	13 **Drew Stafford**	279 Ryan Jorde	184 Jeremy Adduono
26 **Tyler Ennis**	43 **Michael Funk**		212 **Kamil Piros**
44 Luke Adam	71 **Andrej Sekera**	**2000** Pick	238 Dylan Kemp
81 Corey Fienhage	145 Michal Valent	15 Artem Kryukov	
101 Justin Jokinen	176 **Patrick Kaleta**	48 Gerard Dicaire	**1996** Pick
104 Jordon Southorn	207 **Mark Mancari**	111 Ghyslain Rousseau	7 **Erik Rasmussen**
134 Jacob Lagace	241 **Mike Card**	149 Denis Denisov	27 Cory Sarich
164 Nick Crawford	273 Dylan Hunter	213 Vasily Bizyayev	33 Darren Van Oene
		220 **Paul Gaustad**	54 Francois Methot
2007 Pick	**2003** Pick	258 **Sean McMorrow**	87 Kurt Walsh
31 **T.J. Brennan**	5 **Thomas Vanek**	277 Ryan Courtney	106 Mike Martone
59 Drew Schiestel	65 Branislav Fabry		115 **Alexei Tezikov**
89 Corey Tropp	74 **Clarke MacArthur**	**1999** Pick	142 Ryan Davis
139 Brad Eidsness	106 **Jan Hejda**	20 **Barrett Heisten**	161 Darren Mortier
147 Jean-Simon Allard	114 Denis Ezhov	35 **Milan Bartovic**	222 Scott Buhler
179 Paul Byron	150 Thomas Morrow	55 **Doug Janik**	
187 Nick Eno	172 Pavel Voroshnin	64 **Mike Zigomanis**	
209 Drew Mackenzie	202 **Nathan Paetsch**	73 Tim Preston	
	235 Jeff Weber	117 Karel Mosovsky	
	266 Louis-Philippe Martin	138 **Ryan Miller**	
		146 Matt Kinch	
		178 Seneque Hyacinthe	
		206 Bret DeCecco	
		235 Brad Self	
		263 Craig Brunel	

General Managers' History

Punch Imlach, 1970-71 to 1977-78; John Anderson, 1978-79; Scotty Bowman, 1979-80 to 1985-86; Scotty Bowman and Gerry Meehan, 1986-87; Gerry Meehan, 1987-88 to 1992-93; John Muckler, 1993-94 to 1996-97; Darcy Regier, 1997-98 to date.

Darcy Regier
General Manager

Born: Swift Current, Sask., November 27, 1957.

Darcy Regier became the sixth general manager of the Buffalo Sabres on June 11, 1997 after a lengthy management apprenticeship in the New York Islanders organization. As a player, Regier played eight pro seasons, including part of the 1977-78 season with the Cleveland Barons and parts of the 1982-83 and 1983-84 campaigns with the New York Islanders.

He began his career as an administrator with the Islanders in 1984-85 and went on to serve in a variety of capacities including director of administration, assistant director of hockey operations, assistant coach and assistant general manager. He also served as an assistant coach with Hartford in 1991-92.

While with the Islanders, Regier benefited from working with talented managers and coaches including Bill Torrey and Al Arbour. As a minor pro player with Indianapolis of the CHL he became associated with another important influence on his hockey career, current Detroit Red Wing executive Jim Devellano.

Club Directory

HSBC Arena

Buffalo Sabres
HSBC Arena
One Seymour H. Knox III Plaza
Buffalo, NY 14203
Phone **716/855-4100**
Fax 716/855-4110
Tickets, U.S.: 888/GO-SABRES
Canada: 888/669-GOAL
www.sabres.com
Capacity: 18,690

Executive
Owner . . . . B. Thomas Golisano
Managing Partner/Minority Owner . . . . Lawrence Quinn
Chief Operating Officer/Minority Owner . . . . Daniel DiPofi

Hockey Department
General Manager . . . . Darcy Regier
Director of Amateur Scouting . . . . Kevin Devine
Director of Pro Scouting . . . . Jon Christiano
Pro Scout / Player Development . . . . Dennis Miller
Amateur Scouts . . . . Bo Berglund, Nik Fattey, Iouri Khmylev, Al MacAdam, Paul Merritt, Craig Benning, Kim Gellert, Eric Weissman
Director, Hockey Analytics . . . . Scott Schranz
Asst. Director, Hockey Analytics . . . . Ryan Vinz
Graduate Asst., Hockey Analytics . . . . Graham Beamish
Assistant to the General Manager . . . . Mark Jakubowski
Coordinator of Hockey Operations . . . . Michael Bermingham

Coaching Staff
Head Coach . . . . Lindy Ruff
Associate Coach . . . . Brian McCutcheon
Assistant Coach . . . . James Patrick
Player Development Coach . . . . Kevyn Adams
Strength & Conditioning Coach . . . . Doug McKenney
Goaltender Coach . . . . Jim Corsi
Administrative Assistant Coach . . . . Corey Smith
Athletic Trainer . . . . Tim Macre
Equipment Managers / Asst. Mgr. . . . . Dave Williams, Rip Simonick / George Babcock
Massage Therapist . . . . Chuck Garlow

Medical
Medical Director . . . . Les Bisson, M.D.
Team Physicians . . . . Nicholas Aquino, M.D., William Hartrich, M.D., Mark Feinberg, M.D.
Oral Surgeon / Team Dentist . . . . Steven Jenson, DDS, David Croglio, DDS
Team Doctor Emeritus . . . . John L. Butsch, M.D.

Legal
Director of Legal Affairs & Human Resources . . . . . Dave Zygaj

Finance and Administration
Director of Finance & Administration . . . . Chuck LaMattina
Accounting Manager . . . . Christine Ivansitz
Payroll & Human Resource Manager . . . . Birgid Haensel
Accounts Payable Clerk / Executive Assistant . . . . . Kim Binkley / Nadine Leone
IT Systems Engineer . . . . Matt Kleeh

Broadcast
Director of Broadcasting . . . . Chrisanne Bellas
TV Producer / TV Director . . . . Joe Pinter / Matt Gould
Lead Feature Editor / Photographer/Editor . . . . . . Drew Boeing / Mark Blaszak
Production Assistant . . . . Jason Wiese
Scoreboard Director/Editor . . . . Jeff Hill
Broadcast Team . . . . Rick Jeanneret (Play-by-Play), Harry Neale (Commentator), Kevin Sylvester (Studio Host), Mike Robitaille, Rob Ray (Analysts)

Merchandise
Director of Merchandise . . . . Mike Kaminska
Merchandise Mgrs., Inventory / Event Sales . . . . . . Glenn Barker, Jeff Smith
Store Manager . . . . Alec Moslow

Marketing
Director of Marketing . . . . Rob Kopacz
Director of Game Presentation . . . . Jenifer Dunford
Database Marketing Manager . . . . Tom Matheny
Promotions Coordinator . . . . Jacqueline Tollar
Game Presentation Coordinator . . . . Robert Neumann
Website Manager . . . . Scott Miner
Web Content Coordinator . . . . Erin Pollina
Director of Creative Services . . . . Frank Cravotta
Graphic Artist . . . . Vicki Sitek

Public and Community Relations
Director of Public Relations . . . . Michael Gilbert
Manager of Publications & Hockey Information . . . . Kevin Snow
Manager of Community Development . . . . Rich Jureller
Coordinator of Media Relations . . . . Chris Bandura
Community Relations Coordinator . . . . Teresa Belbas
Mascot Coordinator . . . . Ed Grudzinski
Team Photographer . . . . Bill Wippert
Director of Alumni Relations . . . . Larry Playfair
Corporate & Community Relations Liaison . . . . Gilbert Perreault

Sales and Business Development
VP Sales & Business Development . . . . John Livsey
Director of Corporate Sales / Fulfillment . . . . Joe Foy / Rob Nugent
Director of Sales/Marketing – Rochester . . . . Gary Muxworthy
Corporate Fulfillment Coordinator . . . . Chad Buck

Ticket Sales and Operations
Director of Ticket Operations & Services . . . . John Sinclair
Account Services Manager . . . . Michael Tout
Box Office Manager / Coordinators . . . . Marty Maloney / Gretchen Knott, Paul Barker
Account Services Representatives . . . Roxanne Anderson, Kevin Kennedy, Melissa Rugg
Special Consultant . . . . Joe Crozier
Coordinator of Suite Services . . . . Michelle Mitchell

HSBC Arena
Director of Arena Operations . . . . Stan Makowski, Jr.
Director of Arena Services . . . . Thomas Ahern
Director of Event Booking . . . . Jennifer Van Rysdam
Arena Marketing Manager . . . . Tracey Penner
Director of Amateur Athletics . . . . Kevin Sylvester
Event Managers . . . . Beth Guiliani Gatto
Mgr. of Technical Communications . . . . Mike Queeno, Ray Riel
Chief Engineer . . . . Bruce Johnson
Building Services Manager . . . . Dennis Hooper
Security Manager . . . . Marc Brenner

Calgary Flames

2009-10 Results: 40w-32L-3oTL-7SOL 90PTS.
Third, Northwest Division

Matt Stajan, Rene Bourque and Jarome Iginla celebrate a goal. Iginla led the team with 32 goals and 69 points in 2009-10 while Bourque was second with 27 and 58.

2010-11 Schedule

Oct. Thu.	7 at Edmonton	Fri.	7 Detroit
Sun.	10 Los Angeles	Tue.	11 at Carolina
Thu.	14 Florida	Fri.	14 at Ottawa
Sat.	16 Edmonton	Sat.	15 at Toronto
Tue.	19 at Nashville	Mon.	17 at Montreal
Thu.	21 at Detroit	Wed.	19 Minnesota
Fri.	22 at Columbus	Fri.	21 Dallas
Sun.	24 San Jose	Sat.	22 at Vancouver
Tue.	26 Edmonton	Mon.	24 Nashville
Thu.	28 Colorado	Wed.	26 St. Louis
Sat.	30 Washington	**Feb.** Tue.	1 at Nashville
Nov. Wed.	3 Detroit	Thu.	3 at Atlanta
Fri.	5 at Minnesota	Sat.	5 Los Angeles
Tue.	9 at Colorado	Mon.	7 Chicago
Fri.	12 at Phoenix	Wed.	9 Ottawa
Sat.	13 at San Jose	Fri.	11 Anaheim
Wed.	17 Phoenix	Sat.	12 at Vancouver
Fri.	19 Chicago	Mon.	14 at Colorado
Sun.	21 at Detroit*	Wed.	16 Dallas
Mon.	22 at NY Rangers	Sun.	20 Montreal*
Wed.	24 at New Jersey	Wed.	23 Boston
Fri.	26 at Philadelphia*	Fri.	25 San Jose
Sat.	27 at Pittsburgh*	Sun.	27 St. Louis
Mon.	29 Minnesota	**Mar.** Tue.	1 at St. Louis
Dec. Wed.	1 Vancouver	Wed.	2 at Chicago
Fri.	3 at Minnesota	Fri.	4 Columbus
Sun.	5 at Chicago	Sun.	6 Nashville
Tue.	7 Tampa Bay	Wed.	9 at Dallas
Thu.	9 at Los Angeles	Thu.	10 at Phoenix
Fri.	10 at Anaheim	Sat.	12 Vancouver
Mon.	13 Columbus	Tue.	15 Phoenix
Thu.	16 Toronto	Thu.	17 Colorado
Sat.	18 Minnesota	Sun.	20 at Anaheim*
Mon.	20 at Minnesota	Mon.	21 at Los Angeles
Tue.	21 at Columbus	Wed.	23 at San Jose
Thu.	23 at Dallas	Sat.	26 at Edmonton
Mon.	27 Buffalo	Wed.	30 Anaheim
Fri.	31 Colorado	**Apr.** Fri.	1 at St. Louis
Jan. Sat.	1 at Edmonton	Sun.	3 at Colorado
Mon.	3 NY Islanders	Wed.	6 Edmonton
Wed.	5 at Vancouver	Sat.	9 Vancouver

* Denotes afternoon game.

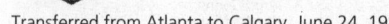

NORTHWEST DIVISION
39th NHL Season

Franchise date: June 6, 1972

Transferred from Atlanta to Calgary, June 24, 1980.

Year-by-Year Record

Season	GP	Home W	L	T	OL	Road W	L	T	OL	Overall W	L	T	OL	GF	GA	Pts.	Finished	Playoff Result
2009-10	82	20	17	....	4	20	15	....	6	40	32	....	10	204	210	90	3rd, Northwest Div.	Out of Playoffs
2008-09	82	27	10	....	4	19	20	....	2	46	30	....	6	254	248	98	2nd, Northwest Div.	Lost Conf. Quarter-Final
2007-08	82	21	11	....	9	21	19	....	1	42	30	....	10	229	227	94	3rd, Northwest Div.	Lost Conf. Quarter-Final
2006-07	82	30	9	....	2	13	20	....	8	43	29	....	10	258	226	96	3rd, Northwest Div.	Lost Conf. Quarter-Final
2005-06	82	30	7	....	4	16	18	....	7	46	25	....	11	218	200	103	1st, Northwest Div.	Lost Conf. Quarter-Final
2004-05																		
2003-04	82	21	14	5	1	21	16	2	2	42	30	7	3	200	176	94	3rd, Northwest Div.	Lost Final
2002-03	82	14	16	10	1	15	20	3	3	29	36	13	4	186	228	75	5th, Northwest Div.	Out of Playoffs
2001-02	82	20	14	5	2	12	21	7	1	32	35	12	3	201	220	79	4th, Northwest Div.	Out of Playoffs
2000-01	82	12	18	9	2	15	18	6	2	27	36	15	4	197	236	73	4th, Northwest Div.	Out of Playoffs
1999-2000	82	20	14	6	1	11	22	4	4	31	36	10	5	211	256	77	4th, Northwest Div.	Out of Playoffs
1998-99	82	15	20	6	....	15	20	6	....	30	40	12	....	211	234	72	3rd, Northwest Div.	Out of Playoffs
1997-98	82	18	17	6	....	8	24	9	....	26	41	15	....	217	252	67	5th, Pacific Div.	Out of Playoffs
1996-97	82	18	17	6	....	11	23	7	....	32	41	9	....	214	239	73	5th, Pacific Div.	Out of Playoffs
1995-96	82	18	18	5	....	16	19	6	....	34	37	11	....	241	240	79	2nd, Pacific Div.	Lost Conf. Quarter-Final
1994-95	48	15	7	2	....	9	10	5	....	24	17	7	....	163	135	55	1st, Pacific Div.	Lost Conf. Quarter-Final
1993-94	84	25	12	5	....	17	17	8	....	42	29	13	....	302	256	97	1st, Pacific Div.	Lost Conf. Quarter-Final
1992-93	84	23	14	5	....	20	16	6	....	43	30	11	....	322	282	97	2nd, Smythe Div.	Lost Div. Semi-Final
1991-92	80	19	14	7	....	12	23	5	....	31	37	12	....	296	305	74	5th, Smythe Div.	Out of Playoffs
1990-91	80	29	8	3	....	17	18	5	....	46	26	8	....	344	263	100	2nd, Smythe Div.	Lost Div. Semi-Final
1989-90	80	28	7	5	....	14	16	10	....	42	23	15	....	348	265	99	1st, Smythe Div.	Lost Div. Semi-Final
1988-89	**80**	**32**	**4**	**4**	**....**	**22**	**13**	**5**	**....**	**54**	**17**	**9**	**....**	**354**	**226**	**117**	**1st, Smythe Div.**	**Won Stanley Cup**
1987-88	80	26	11	3	....	22	12	6	....	48	23	9	....	397	305	105	1st, Smythe Div.	Lost Div. Final
1986-87	80	25	13	2	....	21	18	1	....	46	31	3	....	318	289	95	2nd, Smythe Div.	Lost Div. Semi-Final
1985-86	80	23	11	6	....	17	20	3	....	40	31	9	....	354	315	89	2nd, Smythe Div.	Lost Final
1984-85	80	23	11	6	....	18	16	6	....	41	27	12	....	363	302	94	3rd, Smythe Div.	Lost Div. Semi-Final
1983-84	80	22	11	7	....	12	21	7	....	34	32	14	....	311	314	82	2nd, Smythe Div.	Lost Div. Final
1982-83	80	21	12	7	....	11	22	7	....	32	34	14	....	321	317	78	2nd, Smythe Div.	Lost Div. Final
1981-82	80	20	11	9	....	9	23	8	....	29	34	17	....	334	345	75	3rd, Smythe Div.	Lost Div. Semi-Final
1980-81	80	25	5	10	....	14	22	4	....	39	27	14	....	329	298	92	3rd, Patrick Div.	Lost Semi-Final
1979-80*	80	18	15	7	....	17	17	6	....	35	32	13	....	282	269	83	4th, Patrick Div.	Lost Prelim. Round
1978-79*	80	25	11	4	....	16	20	4	....	41	31	8	....	327	280	90	4th, Patrick Div.	Lost Prelim. Round
1977-78*	80	20	13	7	....	14	14	12	....	34	27	19	....	274	252	87	3rd, Patrick Div.	Lost Prelim. Round
1976-77*	80	22	11	7	....	12	23	5	....	34	34	12	....	264	265	80	3rd, Patrick Div.	Lost Prelim. Round
1975-76*	80	19	14	7	....	16	19	5	....	35	33	12	....	262	237	82	3rd, Patrick Div.	Lost Prelim. Round
1974-75*	80	24	9	7	....	10	22	8	....	34	31	15	....	243	233	83	4th, Patrick Div.	Out of Playoffs
1973-74*	78	17	15	7	....	13	19	7	....	30	34	14	....	214	238	74	4th, West Div.	Lost Quarter-Final
1972-73*	78	16	16	7	....	9	22	8	....	25	38	15	....	191	239	65	7th, West Div.	Out of Playoffs

* Atlanta Flames

2010-11 Player Personnel

FORWARDS	HT	WT	S	Place of Birth	*Age	2009-10 Club
BOURQUE, Rene	6-2	213	L	Lac La Biche, Alta.	28	Calgary
CONROY, Craig	6-2	193	R	Potsdam, NY	39	Calgary
GLENCROSS, Curtis	6-1	195	L	Kindersley, Sask.	27	Calgary
HAGMAN, Niklas	6-0	209	L	Espoo, Finland	30	Toronto-Calgary
IGINLA, Jarome	6-1	207	R	Edmonton, Alta.	33	Calgary
IVANANS, Raitis	6-4	240	L	Riga, Latvia	31	Los Angeles
JACKMAN, Tim	6-4	210	R	Minot, ND	28	NY Islanders
JOKINEN, Olli	6-3	215	L	Kuopio, Finland	31	Calgary-NY Rangers
KOTALIK, Ales	6-1	225	R	Jindrichuv Hradec, Czech.	31	NY Rangers-Calgary
LANGKOW, Daymond	5-10	183	L	Edmonton, Alta.	34	Calgary
MOSS, Dave	6-3	200	L	Livonia, MI	28	Calgary
STAJAN, Matt	6-1	200	L	Mississauga, Ont.	26	Toronto-Calgary
TANGUAY, Alex	6-1	192	L	Ste-Justine, Que.	30	Tampa Bay
DEFENSEMEN	HT	WT	S	Place of Birth	*Age	2009-10 Club
BOUWMEESTER, Jay	6-4	212	L	Edmonton, Alta.	27	Calgary
GIORDANO, Mark	6-0	203	L	Toronto, Ont.	27	Calgary
KRONWALL, Staffan	6-4	209	L	Jarfalla, Sweden	28	Calgary-Abbotsford
PARDY, Adam	6-2	206	L	Bonavista, Nfld.	26	Calgary
REGEHR, Robyn	6-3	225	L	Recife, Brazil	30	Calgary
SARICH, Cory	6-4	207	R	Saskatoon, Sask.	32	Calgary
STAIOS, Steve	6-1	200	R	Hamilton, Ont.	37	Edmonton-Calgary
WHITE, Ian	5-10	191	R	Steinbach, Man.	26	Toronto-Calgary
GOALTENDERS	HT	WT	C	Place of Birth	*Age	2009-10 Club
KARLSSON, Henrik	6-6	215	L	Stockholm, Sweden	26	Farjestad
KIPRUSOFF, Miikka	6-1	184	L	Turku, Finland	33	Calgary

* – Age at start of 2010-11 season

Coaching History

Bernie Geoffrion, 1972-73, 1973-74; Bernie Geoffrion and Fred Creighton, 1974-75; Fred Creighton, 1975-76 to 1978-79; Al MacNeil, 1979-80 to 1981-82; Bob Johnson, 1982-83 to 1986-87; Terry Crisp, 1987-88 to 1989-90; Doug Risebrough, 1990-91; Doug Risebrough and Guy Charron, 1991-92; Dave King, 1992-93 to 1994-95; Pierre Page, 1995-96, 1996-97; Brian Sutter, 1997-98 to 1999-2000; Don Hay and Greg Gilbert, 2000-01; Greg Gilbert, 2001-02; Greg Gilbert, Al MacNeil and Darryl Sutter, 2002-03; Darryl Sutter, 2003-04 to 2005-06; Jim Playfair, 2006-07; Mike Keenan, 2007-08, 2008-09; Brent Sutter, 2009-10 to date.

Brent Sutter

Head Coach

Born: Viking, Alta., June 10, 1962.

General manager Darryl Sutter announced on June 23, 2009 that his brother Brent Sutter had been named head coach of the Calgary Flames. Brent Sutter joined the Flames after two seasons as the bench boss of the New Jersey Devils compiling a 97-56-11 (.625) record during the regular season, and an Atlantic Division title in 2008-09.

Prior to joining the Devils, Sutter spent eight seasons as owner, president, general manager, and head coach of the Red Deer Rebels of the Western Hockey League. During that time, he led the Rebels to a 314-194-68 (.604) record as the team's head coach. Sutter guided the Rebels to a WHL championship and Memorial Cup title in 2001, and three consecutive WHL Eastern Conference championships from 2001 to 2003. He was named the WHL's top coach in 2001.

Internationally, Sutter has represented Canada twice as the head coach guiding the national junior team to consecutive 6-0-0 marks and gold medals at the 2005 and 2006 World Junior Championships. As a player, the Viking, Alberta native helped his country win the 1984, 1987, and 1991 Canada Cup titles. Sutter was also a member of Canada's 1986 bronze medal-winning World Championship team.

Sutter played 18 years in the NHL with the New York Islanders and Chicago Blackhawks. Originally the Islanders' first choice (17th overall) in the 1980 NHL Entry Draft, he recorded 363 goals and 466 assists for 829 points and 1,054 penalty minutes in 1,111 career regular-season games. Sutter scored an additional 30 goals and 44 assists for 74 points and 164 penalty minutes in 144 career playoff games. Along with current Flames director of player personnel and brother Duane Sutter, Brent Sutter was a member of New York Islanders 1982 and 1983 Stanley Cup championship teams, and served as captain from 1987 through 1991. Brent was traded to Chicago on October 25, 1991 and played seven more seasons, including three years under his brother Darryl. Brent retired on April 18, 1998.

Brent Sutter is the third youngest of seven Sutter brothers, six of whom played in the NHL. His son Brandon is a member of the Carolina Hurricanes, and was their first choice (11th overall) in the 2007 NHL Entry Draft.

Coaching Record

Season	Team	League	GC	W	L	O/T	GC	W	L	T
				Regular Season				**Playoffs**		
99-2000	Red Deer	WHL	72	32	31	9	4	0	4	....
2000-01	Red Deer	WHL	72	54	12	6	22	16	6	....
2000-01	Red Deer	M-Cup	....	....	....	....	4	3	1	....
2001-02	Red Deer	WHL	72	46	18	8	23	14	9	....
2002-03	Red Deer	WHL	72	50	17	5	23	14	9	....
2003-04	Red Deer	WHL	72	35	22	15	19	10	9	....
2004-05	Red Deer	WHL	72	36	26	10	7	3	4	....
2005-06	Red Deer	WHL	72	26	40	6	....	....	....	....
2006-07	Red Deer	WHL	72	35	28	9	7	3	4	....
2007-08	New Jersey	NHL	82	46	29	7	5	1	4	....
2008-09	New Jersey	NHL	82	51	27	4	7	3	4	....
2009-10	Calgary	NHL	82	40	32	10	....	....	....	....
	NHL Totals		246	137	88	21	12	4	8	....

2009-10 Scoring

* – rookie

Regular Season

Pos	#	Player	Team	GP	G	A	Pts	TOI	+/–	PIM	PP	SH	GW	S	%
R	12	Jarome Iginla	CGY	82	32	37	69	20:36	-2	58	10	0	5	257	12.5
L	17	Rene Bourque	CGY	73	27	31	58	18:19	7	88	6	4	5	215	12.6
C	18	Matt Stajan	TOR	55	16	41	57	18:47	-3	30	7	0	2	99	16.2
			CGY	27	3	13	16	19:10	-3	2	0	0	2	33	9.1
			Total	82	19	38	57	18:54	-6	32	7	0	4	132	14.4
R	11	Niklas Hagman	TOR	55	20	13	33	16:08	-3	23	4	0	1	148	13.5
			CGY	27	5	6	11	16:04	-1	2	0	0	1	68	7.4
			Total	82	25	19	44	16:07	-4	25	4	0	2	216	11.6
D	3	Ian White	TOR	56	9	17	26	23:47	1	39	2	0	1	130	6.9
			CGY	27	4	8	12	20:42	7	12	1	0	0	43	9.3
			Total	83	13	25	38	22:47	8	51	3	0	1	173	7.5
C	22	Daymond Langkow	CGY	72	14	23	37	18:54	2	30	1	1	2	126	11.1
L	20	Curtis Glencross	CGY	67	15	18	33	15:43	11	58	2	3	2	117	12.8
L	15	Nigel Dawes	CGY	66	14	18	32	14:32	1	16	4	0	2	96	14.6
D	5	Mark Giordano	CGY	82	11	19	30	20:50	17	81	5	0	1	111	9.9
D	4	Jay Bouwmeester	CGY	82	3	26	29	25:55	-4	48	1	0	0	130	2.3
R	26	Ales Kotalik	NYR	45	8	14	22	13:56	-18	38	6	0	3	100	8.0
			CGY	26	3	2	5	14:36	1	29	1	0	1	72	4.2
			Total	71	11	16	27	14:10	-17	67	5	0	4	172	6.4
L	23	Eric Nystrom	CGY	82	11	8	19	13:10	0	54	0	0	2	91	12.1
R	25	David Moss	CGY	64	8	9	17	13:42	-9	20	3	0	2	133	6.0
L	21	Christopher Higgins	NYR	55	6	8	14	17:54	-9	32	0	0	1	137	4.4
			CGY	12	2	1	3	15:51	0	0	0	0	0	28	7.1
			Total	67	8	9	17	17:32	-9	32	0	0	1	165	4.8
D	28	Robyn Regehr	CGY	81	2	15	17	21:38	2	80	0	0	0	78	2.6
C	24	Craig Conroy	CGY	63	3	12	15	13:33	-6	30	0	0	1	52	5.8
R	19	Jamal Mayers	TOR	44	2	6	8	8:54	-5	78	0	0	0	47	4.3
			CGY	27	1	5	6	9:11	2	53	0	0	1	28	3.6
			Total	71	3	11	14	9:00	-3	131	0	0	1	75	4.0
C	60	* Mikael Backlund	CGY	23	1	9	10	12:36	5	6	0	0	0	47	2.1
D	27	Steve Staios	EDM	40	0	7	7	18:50	-19	59	0	0	0	45	0.0
			CGY	18	1	2	3	18:22	-8	16	1	0	0	16	6.3
			Total	58	1	9	10	18:42	-27	75	1	0	0	61	1.6
D	7	Adam Pardy	CGY	57	2	7	9	15:51	-3	48	0	0	0	40	5.0
D	6	Cory Sarich	CGY	57	1	5	6	15:56	4	58	0	0	1	46	2.2
R	10	Brian McGrattan	CGY	34	1	3	4	3:26	3	86	0	0	0	19	5.3
D	8	Staffan Kronwall	CGY	11	1	2	3	9:54	-1	2	0	0	1	6	16.7
R	38	Jason Jaffray	CGY	3	0	0	0	6:39	-1	0	0	0	0	4	0.0
L	42	* Brett Sutter	CGY	10	0	0	0	9:39	-1	5	0	0	0	9	0.0

Goaltending

No.	Goaltender	GPI	Mins	Avg	W	L	OT	EN	SO	GA	SA	S%	G	A	PIM
35	Vesa Toskala	6	212	2.26	2	0	0	0	0	8	97	.918	0	0	0
34	Miikka Kiprusoff	73	4235	2.31	35	28	10	4	4	163	2035	.920	0	0	4
31	Curtis McElhinney	10	502	3.23	3	4	0	1	0	27	235	.885	0	0	0
	Totals	82	4980	2.45	40	32	10	5	4	203	2372	.914			

Defenseman Mark Giordano led the Flames with a +17 rating in 2009-10.

Captains' History

Keith McCreary, 1972-73 to 1974-75; Pat Quinn, 1975-76, 1976-77; Tom Lysiak, 1977-78, 1978-79; Jean Pronovost, 1979-80; Brad Marsh, 1980-81; Phil Russell, 1981-82, 1982-83; Lanny McDonald, Doug Risebrough, 1983-84; Lanny McDonald, Doug Risebrough, Jim Peplinski, 1984-85 to 1986-87; Lanny McDonald, Jim Peplinski, 1987-88; Lanny McDonald, Jim Peplinski, Tim Hunter, 1988-89; Brad McCrimmon, 1989-90; alternating captains, 1990-91; Joe Nieuwendyk, 1991-92 to 1994-95; Theoren Fleury, 1995-96, 1996-97; Todd Simpson, 1997-98, 1998-99; Steve Smith, 1999-2000; Steve Smith and Dave Lowry, 2000-01; Dave Lowry; Bob Boughner and Craig Conroy, 2001-02; Bob Boughner and Craig Conroy, 2002-03; Jarome Iginla, 2003-04 to date.

Club Records

Team

(Figures in brackets for season records are games played; records for fewest points, wins, ties, losses, goals, goals against are for 70 or more games)

Most Points **117** 1988-89 (80)
Most Wins **54** 1988-89 (80)
Most Ties **19** 1977-78 (80)
Most Losses **41** 1996-97 (82), 1997-98 (82), 1999-2000 (82)
Most Goals **397** 1987-88 (80)
Most Goals Against **345** 1981-82 (80)
Fewest Points **65** 1972-73 (78)
Fewest Wins **25** 1972-73 (78)
Fewest Ties **3** 1986-87 (80)
Fewest Losses **17** 1988-89 (80)
Fewest Goals **186** 2002-03 (82)
Fewest Goals Against **176** 2003-04 (82)
Longest Winning Streak
Overall .... **10** Oct. 14-Nov. 3/78
Home .... **10** Nov. 7-Dec. 12/06
Away .... **7** Nov. 10-Dec. 4/88
Longest Undefeated Streak
Overall .... **13** Nov. 10-Dec. 8/88 (12 wins, 1 tie)
Home .... **18** Dec. 29/90-Mar. 14/91 (17 wins, 1 tie)
Away .... **9** Feb. 20-Mar. 21/88 (6 wins, 3 ties), Nov. 11-Dec. 16/90 (6 wins, 3 ties)
Longest Losing Streak
Overall .... **11** Dec. 14/85-Jan. 7/86
Home .... **6** Dec. 5-31/98, Jan. 8-25/10
Away .... **9** Dec. 1/85-Jan. 12/86
Longest Winless Streak
Overall .... **11** Dec. 14/85-Jan. 7/86 (11 losses), Jan. 5-26/93 (9 losses, 2 ties)
Home .... **10** Oct. 21-Dec. 4/00 (6 losses, 4 ties)
Away .... **13** Feb. 3-Mar. 29/73 (10 losses, 3 ties)
Most Shutouts, Season **11** 2003-04 (82)
Most PIM, Season **2,643** 1991-92 (80)
Most Goals, Game .... **13** Feb. 10/93 (S.J. 1 at Cgy. 13)

Individual

Most Seasons .... **13** Al MacInnis, Jarome Iginla
Most Games .... **1,024** Jarome Iginla
Most Goals, Career .... **441** Jarome Iginla
Most Assists, Career .... **609** Al MacInnis
Most Points, Career .... **920** Jarome Iginla (441G, 479A)
Most PIM, Career .... **2,405** Tim Hunter
Most Shutouts, Career .... **31** Miikka Kiprusoff
Longest Consecutive Games Streak .... **257** Brad Marsh (Oct. 11/78-Nov. 10/81)
Most Goals, Season .... **66** Lanny McDonald (1982-83)
Most Assists, Season .... **82** Kent Nilsson (1980-81)
Most Points, Season .... **131** Kent Nilsson (1980-81; 49G, 82A)
Most PIM, Season .... **375** Tim Hunter (1988-89)
Most Points, Defenseman, Season .... **103** Al MacInnis (1990-91; 28G, 75A)
Most Points, Center, Season .... **131** Kent Nilsson (1980-81; 49G, 82A)
Most Points, Right Wing, Season .... **110** Joe Mullen (1988-89; 51G, 59A)
Most Points, Left Wing, Season .... **90** Gary Roberts (1991-92; 53G, 37A)
Most Points, Rookie, Season .... **92** Joe Nieuwendyk (1987-88; 51G, 41A)
Most Shutouts, Season .... **10** Miikka Kiprusoff (2005-06)
Most Goals, Game .... **5** Joe Nieuwendyk (Jan. 11/89)
Most Assists, Game .... **6** Guy Chouinard (Feb. 25/81), Gary Suter (Apr. 4/86)
Most Points, Game .... **7** Sergei Makarov (Feb. 25/90; 2G, 5A)

Records include Atlanta Flames, 1972-73 through 1979-80.

Retired Numbers

9	Lanny McDonald	1981-1989
30	Mike Vernon	1982-1994; 2000-2002

All-time Record vs. Other Clubs

Regular Season

	At Home								On Road								Total							
	GP	W	L	T	OL	GF	GA	PTS	GP	W	L	T	OL	GF	GA	PTS	GP	W	L	T	OL	GF	GA	PTS
Anaheim	35	23	11	1	0	101	78	47	36	8	18	6	4	90	118	26	71	31	29	7	4	191	196	73
Atlanta	5	5	0	0	0	21	8	10	6	0	5	1	0	11	19	1	11	5	5	1	0	32	27	11
Boston	46	20	22	4	0	166	156	44	49	13	30	6	0	132	173	32	95	33	52	10	0	298	329	76
Buffalo	48	19	18	11	0	161	149	49	47	13	26	5	3	134	194	34	95	32	44	16	3	295	343	83
Carolina	31	23	6	2	0	147	93	48	30	14	11	5	0	108	100	33	61	37	17	7	0	255	193	81
Chicago	73	31	27	13	2	220	222	77	71	26	30	13	2	206	232	67	144	57	57	26	4	426	454	144
Colorado	65	31	21	9	4	223	187	75	65	24	28	11	2	202	229	61	130	55	49	20	6	425	416	136
Columbus	18	12	4	0	2	56	39	26	18	5	12	0	1	35	54	11	36	17	16	0	3	91	93	37
Dallas	72	37	19	14	2	227	178	90	72	25	34	11	2	218	255	63	144	62	53	25	4	445	433	153
Detroit	70	39	24	6	1	249	201	85	69	22	36	10	1	207	253	55	139	61	60	16	2	456	454	140
Edmonton	99	56	33	9	1	385	311	122	99	39	48	10	2	313	350	90	198	95	81	19	3	698	661	212
Florida	10	5	3	1	1	28	27	12	11	6	3	2	0	26	23	14	21	11	6	3	1	54	50	26
Los Angeles	104	64	28	12	0	451	330	140	101	42	48	9	2	346	364	95	205	106	76	21	2	797	694	235
Minnesota	28	19	3	3	3	73	55	44	29	14	11	1	3	61	71	32	57	33	14	4	6	134	126	76
Montreal	52	19	26	7	0	159	171	45	49	13	28	8	0	118	172	34	101	32	54	15	0	277	343	79
Nashville	22	10	7	3	2	64	54	25	23	9	13	1	0	58	74	19	45	19	20	4	2	122	128	44
New Jersey	44	29	6	8	1	189	115	67	47	28	16	3	0	168	132	59	91	57	22	11	1	357	247	126
NY Islanders	51	25	14	11	1	181	152	62	53	17	27	9	0	147	197	43	104	42	41	20	1	328	349	105
NY Rangers	51	29	11	10	1	223	152	69	54	24	23	5	2	189	182	55	105	53	34	15	3	412	334	124
Ottawa	14	9	4	1	0	48	29	19	13	4	6	3	0	33	33	11	27	13	10	4	0	81	62	30
Philadelphia	54	25	20	9	0	210	178	59	53	16	33	3	1	142	201	36	107	41	53	12	1	352	379	95
Phoenix	81	45	26	9	1	325	250	100	80	31	35	11	3	273	289	76	161	76	61	20	4	598	539	176
Pittsburgh	48	27	12	8	1	207	146	63	46	11	25	10	0	136	171	32	94	38	37	18	1	343	317	95
St. Louis	72	36	28	5	3	231	199	80	74	31	33	9	1	231	255	72	146	67	61	14	4	462	454	152
San Jose	42	24	14	4	0	146	114	52	44	22	17	4	1	126	137	49	86	46	31	8	1	272	251	101
Tampa Bay	12	6	5	0	1	40	35	13	12	5	5	1	1	42	39	12	24	11	10	1	2	82	74	25
Toronto	64	37	22	5	0	247	199	79	56	19	29	7	1	204	217	46	120	56	51	12	1	451	416	125
Vancouver	116	66	32	15	3	442	334	150	117	52	43	18	4	377	402	126	233	118	75	33	7	819	736	276
Washington	40	25	8	7	0	161	98	57	43	15	22	6	0	146	159	36	83	40	30	13	0	307	257	93
Defunct Clubs	13	8	4	1	0	51	34	17	13	7	3	3	0	43	33	17	26	15	7	4	0	94	67	34
Totals	**1480**	**804**	**458**	**188**	**30**	**5432**	**4294**	**1826**	**1480**	**555**	**698**	**191**	**36**	**4522**	**5128**	**1337**	**2960**	**1359**	**1156**	**379**	**66**	**9954**	**9422**	**3163**

Playoffs

	Series	W	L	GP	W	L	T	GF	GA	Last Mtg.	Rnd.	Result
Anaheim	1	0	1	7	3	4	0	16	17	2006	CQF	L 3-4
Chicago	4	2	2	18	9	9	0	53	54	2009	CQF	L 2-4
Dallas	1	0	1	6	2	4	0	18	25	1981	SF	L 2-4
Detroit	3	1	2	14	6	8	0	26	38	2007	CQF	L 2-4
Edmonton	5	1	4	30	11	19	0	96	132	1991	DSF	L 3-4
Los Angeles	6	2	4	26	13	13	0	112	105	1993	DSF	L 2-4
Montreal	2	1	1	11	5	6	0	32	31	1989	F	W 4-2
NY Rangers	1	0	1	4	1	3	0	8	14	1980	PRE	L 1-3
Philadelphia	2	1	1	11	4	7	0	28	43	1981	QF	W 4-3
Phoenix	3	1	2	13	6	7	0	43	45	1987	DSF	L 2-4
St. Louis	1	1	0	7	4	3	0	28	22	1986	CF	W 4-3
San Jose	3	1	2	20	10	10	0	68	57	2008	CQF	L 3-4
Tampa Bay	1	0	1	7	3	4	0	14	13	2004	F	L 3-4
Toronto	1	0	1	2	0	2	0	5	9	1979	PRE	L 0-2
Vancouver	6	4	2	32	17	15	0	101	96	2004	CQF	W 4-3
Totals	**40**	**15**	**25**	**208**	**94**	**114**	**0**	**648**	**701**			

Carolina totals include Hartford, 1979-80 to 1996-97.
Colorado totals include Quebec, 1979-80 to 1994-95.
Dallas totals include Minnesota North Stars, 1972-73 to 1992-93.
New Jersey totals include Kansas City, 1974-75, 1975-76, and Colorado Rockies, 1976-77 to 1981-82.
Phoenix totals include Winnipeg, 1979-80 to 1995-96.

Playoff Results 2010-2006

Year	Round	Opponent	Result	GF	GA
2009	CQF	Chicago	L 2-4	16	21
2008	CQF	San Jose	L 3-4	17	19
2007	CQF	Detroit	L 2-4	10	18
2006	CQF	Anaheim	L 3-4	16	17

Abbreviations: Round: F - Final; **CF** - conference final; **CSF** - conference semi-final; **CQF** - conference quarter-final; **DSF** - division semi-final; **SF** - semi-final; **QF** - quarter-final; **PRE** - preliminary round.

2009-10 Results

Oct.	1	Vancouver	5-3		5	at Nashville	3-1
	3	at Edmonton	4-3		6	at Minnesota	1-4
	6	Montreal	4-3		8	Columbus	2-3
	8	at Edmonton	4-3†		9	at Vancouver	3-2†
	9	Dallas	2-5		11	Colorado	2-3†
	12	at Chicago	5-6*		13	Pittsburgh	1-3
	13	at Columbus	1-2		15	Nashville	0-1
	16	Vancouver	5-3		17	at Anaheim	4-5
	20	Columbus	6-3		18	at San Jose	1-9
	24	Edmonton	5-2		21	Chicago	1-3
	28	Colorado	2-3		25	St. Louis	0-2
	31	Detroit	1-3		27	at Dallas	3-4†
Nov.	4	at Dallas	3-2*		28	at Phoenix	2-3†
	5	at St. Louis	2-1*		30	Edmonton	6-1
	7	NY Rangers	3-1	**Feb.**	1	Philadelphia	0-3
	10	at Montreal	1-0		3	Carolina	4-1
	13	at Buffalo	1-2†		5	at Florida	2-1
	14	at Toronto	5-2		6	at Tampa Bay	1-2*
	17	Colorado	2-3		9	at Ottawa	2-3
	19	Chicago	1-7		11	Dallas	1-3
	21	at Los Angeles	5-2		13	Anaheim	3-1
	23	at Anaheim	2-3†	**Mar.**	3	Minnesota	0-4
	25	Phoenix	2-1		5	New Jersey	5-3
	27	at Detroit	3-0		7	at Minnesota	5-2
	28	at Columbus	4-3†		9	at Detroit	4-2
	30	at Nashville	5-0		11	Ottawa	2-0
Dec.	3	at Phoenix	1-2		14	at Vancouver	1-3
	5	at San Jose	2-1		15	Detroit	1-2
	7	at Los Angeles	1-2		17	at Colorado	3-2
	9	Atlanta	3-1		19	San Jose	4-3
	11	Minnesota	1-2*		21	at Minnesota	3-4
	13	at Colorado	2-3		23	Anaheim	3-1
	15	at St. Louis	3-4		25	at NY Islanders	2-3
	17	Los Angeles	2-1		27	at Boston	0-5
	19	Nashville	3-5		28	at Washington	5-3
	23	St. Louis	1-2†		31	Phoenix	2-1
	27	Vancouver	1-5	**Apr.**	2	at Colorado	2-1
	28	at Edmonton	4-1		4	at Chicago	1-4
	30	Los Angeles	2-1		6	San Jose	1-2
	31	Edmonton	2-1		8	Minnesota	1-2†
Jan.	2	Toronto	3-1		10	at Vancouver	3-7

* – Overtime † – Shootout

Entry Draft Selections 2010-1996

Name in bold denotes played in NHL.

2010

Pick	
64	Max Reinhart
73	Joey Leach
103	John Ramage
108	Bill Arnold
133	Michael Ferland
193	Patrick Holland

2009

Pick	
23	Tim Erixon
74	Ryan Howse
111	Henrik Bjorklund
141	Spencer Bennett
171	Joni Ortio
201	Gaelan Patterson

2008

Pick	
25	Greg Nemisz
48	Mitch Wahl
78	Lance Bouma
108	Nick Larson
114	T.J. Brodie
168	Ryley Grantham
198	Alexander Deilert

2007

Pick	
24	**Mikael Backlund**
70	**John Negrin**
116	Keith Aulie
143	Mickey Renaud
186	C.J. Severyn

2006

Pick	
26	Leland Irving
87	John Armstrong
89	Aaron Marvin
118	Hugo Carpentier
149	Juuso Puustinen
179	Jordan Fulton
187	Devin Didiomete
209	Per Jonsson

2005

Pick	
26	**Matt Pelech**
69	Gord Baldwin
74	Dan Ryder
111	J.D. Watt
128	Kevin Lalande
158	**Matt Keetley**
179	**Brett Sutter**
221	Myles Rumsey

2004

Pick	
24	**Kris Chucko**
70	**Brandon Prust**
98	**Dustin Boyd**
118	Aki Seitsonen
121	Kris Hogg
173	**Adam Pardy**
182	Fred Wikner
200	Matt Schneider
213	James Spratt
279	Adam Cracknell

2003

Pick	
9	**Dion Phaneuf**
39	**Tim Ramholt**
97	Ryan Donally
112	Jamie Tardif
143	**Greg Moore**
173	Tyler Johnson
206	Thomas Bellemare
240	Cam Cunning
270	Kevin Harvey

2002

Pick	
10	**Eric Nystrom**
39	Brian McConnell
90	**Matthew Lombardi**
112	Yuri Artemenkov
141	Jiri Cetkovsky
142	Emanuel Peter
146	Viktor Bobrov
159	Kristofer Persson
176	**Curtis McElhinney**
206	**David Van Der Gulik**
207	Pierre Johnsson
238	Jyri Marttinen

2001

Pick	
14	**Chuck Kobasew**
41	Andrei Taratukhin
56	Andrei Medvedev
108	**Tomi Maki**
124	Yegor Shastin
145	James Hakewill
164	Yuri Trubachev
207	Garrett Bembridge
220	**Dave Moss**
233	Joe Campbell
251	Ville Hamalainen

2000

Pick	
9	**Brent Krahn**
40	**Kurtis Foster**
46	**Jarret Stoll**
116	Levente Szuper
141	Wade Davis
155	**Travis Moen**
176	**Jukka Hentunen**
239	David Hajek
270	**Micki DuPont**

1999

Pick	
11	**Oleg Saprykin**
38	Dan Cavanaugh
77	**Craig Anderson**
106	Roman Rozakov
135	Matt Doman
153	Jesse Cook
166	Cory Pecker
170	**Matt Underhill**
190	Blair Stayzer
252	Dmitri Kirilenko

1998

Pick	
6	**Rico Fata**
33	**Blair Betts**
62	**Paul Manning**
102	Shaun Sutter
108	**Dany Sabourin**
120	Brent Gauvreau
192	Radek Duda
206	**Jonas Frogren**
234	Kevin Mitchell

1997

Pick	
6	**Daniel Tkaczuk**
32	Evan Lindsay
42	**John Tripp**
51	Dmitri Kokorev
60	Derek Schutz
70	**Erik Andersson**
92	Chris St. Croix
100	**Ryan Ready**
113	Martin Moise
140	Ilja Demidov
167	Jeremy Rondeau
223	Dustin Paul

1996

Pick	
13	**Derek Morris**
39	**Travis Brigley**
40	**Steve Begin**
73	Dmitri Vlasenkov
89	**Toni Lydman**
94	Christian Lefebvre
122	Josef Straka
202	Ryan Wade
228	**Ronald Petrovicky**

Darryl Sutter

General Manager

Born: Viking, Alta., August 19, 1958.

Darryl Sutter was named general manager of the Calgary Flames on April 11, 2003 after having joined the club as coach on December 28, 2002. In 2003-04, he led the team back to the playoffs after a seven-year absence and guided the club on a thrilling run to the seventh game of the Stanley Cup Finals. He stepped down as coach prior to the 2006-07 season.

Before joining the Flames, Sutter was the San Jose Sharks franchise leader in regular-season games coached (434) and wins (192). Prior to San Jose, Sutter coached Chicago for three years (1992 to 1995) and spent two seasons (1995 to 1997) with the Blackhawks as a consultant for special assignments. He spent the 1987-88 campaign as a Blackhawks assistant coach to Bob Murdoch and served as an associate coach for Mike Keenan during the 1990-91 and 1991-92 seasons. During his final season as associate coach, the Blackhawks advanced to the Stanley Cup Finals. Sutter spent two seasons coaching the Blackhawks' top development affiliate in the IHL, which played in Saginaw (1988-89) and in Indianapolis (1989-90). Under his leadership, the Indianapolis Ice won the Turner Cup championship. He was named IHL coach of the year.

As a player, Sutter was selected by Chicago in the ninth round, 179th overall, in the 1978 NHL Entry Draft. During his eight-year career with the Blackhawks from 1979 to 1987, he scored 279 points (161 goals, 118 assists) with 288 penalty minutes in 406 NHL career games. Sutter served as team captain with the Blackhawks for five seasons before he was forced to retire prematurely due to a series of injuries.

Darryl is a member of the famous Sutter hockey family that had six brothers who played in the NHL. Along with his brothers, Darryl is very involved in the Sutter Foundation, which raises money for non-profit organizations in Alberta.

Coaching Record

			Regular Season				Playoffs			
Season	Team	League	GC	W	L	O/T	GC	W	L	T
1992-93	Chicago	NHL	84	47	25	12	4	0	4	....
1993-94	Chicago	NHL	84	39	36	9	6	2	4	....
1994-95	Chicago	NHL	48	24	19	5	16	9	7	....
1997-98	San Jose	NHL	82	34	38	10	6	2	4	....
1998-99	San Jose	NHL	82	31	33	18	6	2	4	....
99-2000	San Jose	NHL	82	35	30	17	12	5	7	....
2000-01	San Jose	NHL	82	40	27	15	6	2	4	....
2001-02	San Jose	NHL	82	44	27	11	12	7	5	....
2002-03	San Jose	NHL	24	8	12	4	....	....	....	....
2002-03	Calgary	NHL	46	19	18	9	....	....	....	....
2003-04	Calgary	NHL	82	42	30	10	26	15	11	....
2004-05	Calgary				SEASON CANCELLED					
2005-06	Calgary	NHL	82	46	25	11	7	3	4	....
	NHL Totals		860	409	320	131	101	47	54	....

Club Directory

Pengrowth Saddledome

Calgary Flames
Pengrowth Saddledome
P.O. Box 1540 Station M
Calgary, Alberta T2P 3B9
Phone **403/777-2177**
FAX 403/777-2195
www.calgaryflames.com
Capacity: 19,289

Owners	N. Murray Edwards (Chairman), Harley N. Hotchkiss, Alvin G. Libin, Allan P. Markin, Jeff McCaig, Clayton H. Riddell

Executive

President & Chief Executive Officer	Ken King
Executive V.P. and General Manager	Darryl Sutter
Assistant General Manager	Jay Feaster
Senior V.P., Assistant General Manager	Michael Holditch
Senior V.P., Finance and Administration	John Bean
V.P., Building Operations	Libby Raines
V.P., Advertising, Sponsorship & Marketing	Jim Bagshaw
V.P., Sales, Customer Service & Ticketing	Rollie Cyr
V.P., Communications	Peter Hanlon
V.P., Business Development	Jim Peplinski
V.P., Food and Beverage	Mark Vaillant

Hockey Club Personnel

Executive V.P., General Manager	Darryl Sutter
Assistant General Manager	Jay Feaster
Senior V.P., Assistant General Manager	Michael Holditch
Director, Hockey Administration	Mike Burke
Director, Player Personnel	Duane Sutter
Director of Scouting	Tod Button
Pro Scout/Player Development	Ron Sutter
Amateur Scout/Player Development	Tom Webster
Head Coach	Brent Sutter
Assistant Coaches	Dave Lowry, Ryan McGill, Jamie McLennan, Rob Cookson
Team Services Manager	Sean O'Brien
Exec. Asst. to GM and Hockey Operations	Brenda Koyich
Scouts	Juha Hautamaa, Steve Leach, Bob MacMillan, Robert Pulford, Greg Rejanen, Blair Reid, Anders Steen, Ritch Thibeau

Medical/Training Staff

Strength & Conditioning Coach	Rich Hesketh
Athletic Therapist	Morris Boyer
Assistant Athletic Therapist	Schad Richea
Equipment Manager	Mark DePasquale
Assistant Equipment Manager	Corey Osmak
Massage Therapist	Bryan Lentz
Head Physician	Dr. Kelly Brett
Team Physician/Sports Medicine	Dr. Jim Thorne
Team Orthopedic Surgeons	Dr. Nicholas Mohtadi, Dr. Richard Boorman
Team Dentist	Dr. Bill Blair
Team Optometrist	Dr. Derek Gaume
Dressing Room Attendant	Jules Carriere

Abbotsford Heat

President	Tom Mauthe
Head Coach	Jim Playfair
Assistant Coaches	Troy Ward, Steve O'Rourke

Communications

Vice-President, Communications	Peter Hanlon
Manager, Media Relations	Sean Kelso
Administrative Assistant, Communications	Bernie Hargrave

Administration

Senior V.P., Finance and Administration	John Bean
Exec. Asst. to President/CEO	Judy O'Brien
Exec. Asst. to V.P. Hockey Admin/CFO	Anita Cranston
Director, Finance	Deniece Kennedy
Manager, Human Resources	Betty Mah

Marketing/Ticketing

V.P. Advertising, Sponsorship & Marketing	Jim Bagshaw
V.P. Sales, Customer Service & Ticketing	Rollie Cyr
V.P. Business Development	Jim Peplinski
Senior Director, Advertising	Pat Halls
Director, Corporate Sponsorship	Kevin Gross
Manager, Key Corporate Accounts	Mark Stiles
Manager, Promotions	Scott Matheson
Executive Assistant Marketing	Suzanna Chapman
Executive Assistant to V.P. of Sales	Vicki Rinke
Director, Executive Suites	Bob White
Director of Sales	Mike Franco
Customer Service Manager	Marc Leost
Director, Broadcast & Production	Carlo Petrini
Manager, Game Entertainment	Geordie Macleod
Director, Retail/FanAttic	Brent Gibbs
Publications Manager	Laurie Wheeler
Content Manager	Mike Board

Pengrowth Saddledome

V.P. Building Operations	Libby Raines
V.P. Food and Beverage	Mark Vaillant
Director, Building Operations	Rob Blanchard
Director, Food Services	Art Hernandez
Operations Manager	George Greenwood
Senior Food Services Manager	Sheila Parisien
Security/Parking/Loss Prevention Manager	Bob Godun

Miscellaneous

Radio Affiliate	The FAN 960 (960 AM)
TV Affiliate	Rogers Sportsnet, CBC-TV, Flames PPV, TSN

General Managers' History

Cliff Fletcher, 1972-73 to 1990-91; Doug Risebrough, 1991-92 to 1994-95; Doug Risebrough and Al Coates, 1995-96; Al Coates, 1996-97 to 1999-2000; Craig Button, 2000-01 to 2002-03; Darryl Sutter, 2003-04 to date.

Key Off-Season Signings/Acquisitions

2010

May 13 • Acquired RW **Jared Staal** from Phoenix for Nashville's 5th round pick (previously acquired) in the 2010 Entry Draft.
28 • Re-signed C **Jiri Tlusty** and D **Jay Harrison**.
July 1 • Signed D **Anton Babchuk**.
5 • Re-signed G **Justin Peters**.
7 • Signed D **Joe Corvo**.
15 • Re-signed G **Justin Pogge** and D **Bryan Rodney**.
20 • Re-signed D **Brett Carson**.

Carolina Hurricanes

2009-10 Results: 35w-37l-5otl-5sol 80pts.
Third, Southeast Division

Eric Staal led the Hurricanes in scoring for the third time in the last five years. After missing only one game in his career, Staal played just 70 games for Carolina in 2009-10 but still collected 70 points.

2010-11 Schedule

Oct.	Thu.	7	at Minnesota†		Tue.	11	Calgary
	Fri.	8	Minnesota†		Thu.	13	at Buffalo
	Thu.	14	at Ottawa		Sat.	15	Tampa Bay
	Sun.	17	at Vancouver		Mon.	17	at Boston*
	Tue.	19	at San Jose		Tue.	18	Boston
	Wed.	20	at Los Angeles		Thu.	20	NY Rangers
	Sat.	23	at Phoenix		Sat.	22	at Pittsburgh
	Wed.	27	Washington		Mon.	24	Toronto
	Fri.	29	at NY Rangers		Wed.	26	at NY Islanders
	Sat.	30	Pittsburgh	Feb.	Tue.	1	Boston
Nov.	Mon.	1	at Philadelphia		Thu.	3	at Toronto
	Wed.	3	NY Islanders		Sat.	5	Atlanta
	Fri.	5	at Florida		Tue.	8	at New Jersey
	Sat.	6	Florida		Thu.	10	at Philadelphia
	Tue.	9	Edmonton		Sat.	12	at Tampa Bay
	Thu.	11	Philadelphia		Sun.	13	at Atlanta*
	Sat.	13	at Montreal		Wed.	16	at New Jersey
	Wed.	17	Ottawa		Fri.	18	Philadelphia
	Fri.	19	at Pittsburgh		Sat.	19	New Jersey
	Sat.	20	Nashville		Tue.	22	NY Rangers
	Wed.	24	Washington		Fri.	25	Pittsburgh
	Fri.	26	at Boston*		Sat.	26	at Montreal
	Sun.	28	at Washington*	Mar.	Tue.	1	Florida
	Mon.	29	Dallas		Thu.	3	Buffalo
Dec.	Fri.	3	Colorado		Fri.	4	at Chicago
	Sat.	4	at Nashville		Wed.	9	Atlanta
	Fri.	10	at Dallas		Fri.	11	at Washington
	Sat.	11	at St. Louis		Sat.	12	Columbus
	Wed.	15	at Florida		Tue.	15	at Buffalo
	Thu.	16	at Atlanta		Wed.	16	Toronto
	Sat.	18	Anaheim		Fri.	18	NY Islanders
	Mon.	20	at Tampa Bay		Tue.	22	Ottawa
	Thu.	23	Montreal		Fri.	25	at Tampa Bay
	Sun.	26	Washington		Sat.	26	Tampa Bay
	Tue.	28	at Toronto		Tue.	29	at Washington
	Wed.	29	at Ottawa		Wed.	30	Montreal
Jan.	Sat.	1	New Jersey	Apr.	Sat.	2	at NY Islanders
	Mon.	3	Florida		Sun.	3	Buffalo*
	Wed.	5	at NY Rangers		Wed.	6	Detroit
	Fri.	7	at Florida		Fri.	8	at Atlanta
	Sun.	9	Atlanta*		Sat.	9	Tampa Bay

* Denotes afternoon game.   † Games played in Helsinki, Fl.

SOUTHEAST DIVISION
32nd NHL Season

Franchise date: June 22, 1979

Transferred from Hartford to Carolina, June 25, 1997.

Year-by-Year Record

Season	GP	Home W	L	T	OL	Road W	L	T	OL	Overall W	L	T	OL	GF	GA	Pts.	Finished	Playoff Result
2009-10	82	21	17	....	3	14	20	....	7	35	37	....	10	230	256	80	3rd, Southeast Div.	Out of Playoffs
2008-09	82	26	14	....	1	19	16	....	6	45	30	....	7	239	226	97	2nd, Southeast Div.	Lost Conf. Championship
2007-08	82	24	13	....	4	19	20	....	2	43	33	....	6	252	249	92	2nd, Southeast Div.	Out of Playoffs
2006-07	82	21	16	....	4	19	18	....	4	40	34	....	8	241	253	88	3rd, Southeast Div.	Out of Playoffs
2005-06	82	31	8	....	2	21	14	....	6	52	22	....	8	294	260	112	1st, Southeast Div.	Won Stanley Cup
2004-05	....	....				....				....								
2003-04	82	13	18	8	2	15	16	4		28	34	14	6	172	209	76	3rd, Southeast Div.	Out of Playoffs
2002-03	82	12	17	9	3	10	26	2	3	22	43	11	6	171	240	61	5th, Southeast Div.	Out of Playoffs
2001-02	82	15	13	11	2	20	13	5	3	35	26	16	5	217	217	91	1st, Southeast Div.	Lost Final
2000-01	82	23	15	3	0	15	17	6	3	38	32	9	3	212	225	88	2nd, Southeast Div.	Lost Conf. Quarter-Final
1999-2000	82	20	16	5	0	17	19	5	0	37	35	10	0	217	216	84	3rd, Southeast Div.	Out of Playoffs
1998-99	82	20	12	9	....	14	18	9	....	34	30	18	....	210	202	86	1st, Southeast Div.	Lost Conf. Quarter-Final
1997-98	82	16	18	7	....	17	23	1	....	33	41	8	....	200	219	74	6th, Northeast Div.	Out of Playoffs
1996-97*	82	23	15	3	....	9	24	8	....	32	39	11	....	226	256	75	5th, Northeast Div.	Out of Playoffs
1995-96*	82	22	15	4	....	12	24	5	....	34	39	9	....	237	259	77	4th, Northeast Div.	Out of Playoffs
1994-95*	48	12	10	2	....	7	14	3	....	19	24	5	....	127	141	43	5th, Northeast Div.	Out of Playoffs
1993-94*	84	14	22	6	....	13	26	3	....	27	48	9	....	227	288	63	6th, Northeast Div.	Out of Playoffs
1992-93*	84	12	25	5	....	14	27	1	....	26	52	6	....	284	369	58	5th, Adams Div.	Out of Playoffs
1991-92*	80	13	17	10	....	13	24	3	....	26	41	13	....	247	283	65	4th, Adams Div.	Lost Div. Semi-Final
1990-91*	80	18	16	6	....	13	22	5	....	31	38	11	....	238	276	73	4th, Adams Div.	Lost Div. Semi-Final
1989-90*	80	17	18	5	....	21	15	4	....	38	33	9	....	275	268	85	4th, Adams Div.	Lost Div. Semi-Final
1988-89*	80	21	17	2	....	16	21	3	....	37	38	5	....	299	290	79	4th, Adams Div.	Lost Div. Semi-Final
1987-88*	80	21	14	5	....	14	24	2	....	35	38	7	....	249	267	77	4th, Adams Div.	Lost Div. Semi-Final
1986-87*	80	26	9	5	....	17	21	2	....	43	30	7	....	287	270	93	1st, Adams Div.	Lost Div. Semi-Final
1985-86*	80	21	17	2	....	19	19	2	....	40	36	4	....	332	302	84	4th, Adams Div.	Lost Div. Final
1984-85*	80	17	18	5	....	13	23	4	....	30	41	9	....	268	318	69	5th, Adams Div.	Out of Playoffs
1983-84*	80	19	16	5	....	9	26	5	....	28	42	10	....	288	320	66	5th, Adams Div.	Out of Playoffs
1982-83*	80	13	22	5	....	6	32	2	....	19	54	7	....	261	403	45	5th, Adams Div.	Out of Playoffs
1981-82*	80	13	17	10	....	8	24	8	....	21	41	18	....	264	351	60	5th, Adams Div.	Out of Playoffs
1980-81*	80	14	17	9	....	7	24	9	....	21	41	18	....	292	372	60	4th, Norris Div.	Out of Playoffs
1979-80*	80	22	12	6	....	5	22	13	....	27	34	19	....	303	312	73	4th, Norris Div.	Lost Prelim. Round

* Hartford Whalers

2010-11 Player Personnel

FORWARDS	HT	WT	S	Place of Birth	*Age	2009-10 Club
BLANCHARD, Nicolas	6-3	200	L	Granby, Que.	23	Albany
BOWMAN, Drayson	6-1	190	L	Grand Rapids, MI	21	Carolina-Albany
BOYCHUK, Zach	5-10	185	L	Airdrie, Alta.	21	Carolina-Albany
COLE, Erik	6-2	205	L	Oswego, NY	31	Carolina
DALPE, Zac	6-1	195	R	Paris, Ont.	20	Ohio State-Albany
DODGE, Nick	5-10	185	R	Oakville, Ont.	24	Albany
DWYER, Patrick	5-11	175	R	Spokane, WA	27	Carolina
JOKINEN, Jussi	5-11	198	L	Kalajoki, Finland	27	Carolina
KOSTOPOULOS, Tom	6-0	200	R	Mississauga, Ont.	31	Carolina
LaROSE, Chad	5-10	181	R	Fraser, MI	28	Carolina
MATSUMOTO, Jonathan	6-0	184	L	Ottawa, Ont.	23	Adirondack
NASH, Riley	6-1	191	R	Consort, Alta.	21	Cornell
OSALA, Oskar	6-4	219	L	Vaasa, Finland	22	Carolina-Hershey-Albany
RUUTU, Tuomo	6-0	205	L	Vantaa, Finland	27	Carolina
SAMSON, Jerome	6-0	195	R	Greenfield Park, Que.	23	Carolina-Albany
SAMSONOV, Sergei	5-8	188	R	Moscow, USSR	31	Carolina
SKINNER, Jeff	5-10	193	L	Markham, Ont.	18	Kitchener
STAAL, Eric	6-4	205	L	Thunder Bay, Ont.	25	Carolina
SUTTER, Brandon	6-3	183	R	Huntington, NY	21	Carolina-Albany
TERRY, Chris	5-10	190	L	Brampton, Ont.	21	Albany
TLUSTY, Jiri	6-0	209	L	Slany, Czech.	22	Tor-Tor (AHL)-Car-Alb

DEFENSEMEN	HT	WT	S	Place of Birth	*Age	2009-10 Club
BABCHUK, Anton	6-5	212	R	Kiev, USSR	26	Omsk
BELLEMORE, Brett	6-4	205	R	Windsor, Ont.	22	Albany
BORER, Casey	6-2	205	L	Minneapolis, MN	25	Carolina-Albany
CARSON, Brett	6-4	210	R	Regina, Sask.	24	Carolina-Albany
CORVO, Joe	6-0	204	R	Oak Park, IL	33	Carolina-Washington
FITZGERALD, Zack	6-2	205	L	Two Harbors, MN	25	Albany
GLEASON, Tim	6-0	217	L	Clawson, MI	27	Carolina
HARRISON, Jay	6-4	211	L	Oshawa, Ont.	27	Carolina-Albany
McBAIN, Jamie	6-2	200	R	Edina, MN	22	Albany-Carolina
PITKANEN, Joni	6-3	210	L	Oulu, Finland	27	Carolina
RODNEY, Bryan	6-0	195	R	London, Ont.	26	Carolina-Albany
SANGUINETTI, Bobby	6-3	190	L	Trenton, NJ	22	NY Rangers-Hartford

GOALTENDERS	HT	WT	C	Place of Birth	*Age	2009-10 Club
MURPHY, Mike	5-11	165	L	Kingston, Ont.	21	Albany
PETERS, Justin	6-1	205	L	Blyth, Ont.	24	Carolina-Albany
POGGE, Justin	6-3	204	L	Ft. McMurray, Alta.	24	Bakersfield-San Antonio-Albany
WARD, Cam	6-1	185	L	Saskatoon, Sask.	26	Carolina

* – Age at start of 2010-11 season

2009-10 Scoring
* – rookie

Regular Season

Pos	#	Player	Team	GP	G	A	Pts	TOI	+/–	PIM	PP	SH	GW	S	%
C	12	Eric Staal	CAR	70	29	41	70	20:42	4	68	13	0	5	277	10.5
L	36	Jussi Jokinen	CAR	81	30	35	65	16:48	3	36	10	0	6	160	18.8
L	13	Ray Whitney	CAR	80	21	37	58	19:08	-6	26	7	0	5	171	12.3
D	25	Joni Pitkanen	CAR	71	6	40	46	27:22	-11	72	1	0	1	161	3.7
C	16	Brandon Sutter	CAR	72	21	19	40	16:32	-1	2	5	0	3	168	12.5
C	15	Tuomo Ruutu	CAR	54	14	21	35	16:23	-4	50	5	0	1	122	11.5
L	14	Sergei Samsonov	CAR	72	14	15	29	13:22	-15	32	2	0	2	104	13.5
C	59	Chad Larose	CAR	56	11	17	28	15:42	-2	24	0	1	0	138	8.0
R	29	Tom Kostopoulos	CAR	82	8	13	21	12:31	4	106	0	2	0	103	7.8
C	17	Rod Brind'Amour	CAR	80	9	10	19	12:42	-29	36	2	0	2	95	9.5
D	6	Tim Gleason	CAR	61	5	14	19	21:12	0	78	1	1	0	76	6.6
L	26	Erik Cole	CAR	40	11	5	16	16:23	-9	29	2	0	1	81	13.6
D	5	Brian Pothier	WSH	41	4	7	11	18:02	12	10	1	0	1	57	7.0
			CAR	20	1	3	4	21:00	-8	11	0	0	0	24	4.2
			Total	61	5	10	15	19:01	4	21	1	0	2	81	6.2
D	45	Alexandre Picard	OTT	45	4	11	15	19:02	-2	20	1	0	1	64	6.3
			CAR	9	0	0	0	15:04	2	6	0	0	0	7	0.0
			Total	54	4	11	15	18:23	0	26	1	0	1	71	5.6
R	39	Patrick Dwyer	CAR	58	7	5	12	12:30	-3	6	0	0	2	80	8.8
D	27	* Brett Carson	CAR	54	2	10	12	17:22	5	12	0	0	0	42	4.8
D	33	* Bryan Rodney	CAR	22	1	10	11	16:43	-4	8	0	0	0	24	4.2
D	28	* Jamie McBain	CAR	14	3	7	10	25:46	6	0	1	0	1	29	10.3
L	11	* Zach Boychuk	CAR	31	3	6	9	10:45	1	2	0	0	0	37	8.1
C	19	Jiri Tlusty	TOR	2	0	0	0	12:13	-2	0	0	0	0	2	0.0
			CAR	18	1	5	6	12:35	2	6	0	0	0	15	6.7
			Total	20	1	5	6	12:33	0	6	0	0	0	17	5.9
D	44	Jay Harrison	CAR	38	1	5	6	14:43	-8	50	0	0	0	30	3.3
L	21	* Drayson Bowman	CAR	9	2	0	2	12:01	-1	4	1	0	0	17	11.8
R	67	* Jerome Samson	CAR	7	0	2	2	8:26	-1	10	0	0	0	17	0.0
L	32	* Oskar Osala	CAR	1	0	0	0	6:46	0	0	0	0	0	1	0.0
D	53	* Casey Borer	CAR	2	0	0	0	10:45	-1	0	0	0	0	1	0.0
R	23	Steven Goertzen	CAR	6	0	0	0	7:44	-2	5	0	0	0	1	0.0
R	38	Tim Conboy	CAR	12	0	0	0	4:18	-5	24	0	0	0	5	0.0

Goaltending

No.	Goaltender	GPI	Mins	Avg	W	L	OT	EN	SO	GA	SA	S%	G	A	PIM
30	Cam Ward	47	2651	2.69	18	23	5	11	0	119	1409	.916	0	3	0
34	Manny Legace	28	1472	2.81	10	7	5	3	1	69	745	.907	0	1	0
60	* Justin Peters	9	488	2.83	6	3	0	1	0	23	241	.905	0	0	0
49	Michael Leighton	7	350	4.29	1	4	0	0	0	25	164	.848	0	0	0
	Totals	82	4992	3.02	35	37	10	15	1	251	2574	.902			

Captains' History
Rick Ley, 1979-80; Rick Ley and Mike Rogers, 1980-81; Dave Keon, 1981-82; Russ Anderson, 1982-83; Mark Johnson, 1983-84; Mark Johnson and Ron Francis, 1984-85; Ron Francis, 1985-86 to 1990-91; Randy Ladouceur, 1991-92; Pat Verbeek, 1992-93 to 1994-95; Brendan Shanahan, 1995-96; Kevin Dineen, 1996-97, 1997-98; Keith Primeau, 1998-99; Keith Primeau and Ron Francis, 1999-2000; Ron Francis, 2000-01 to 2003-04; Rod Brind'Amour, 2005-06 to 2008-09; Rod Brind'Amour and Eric Staal, 2009-10; Eric Staal, 2010-11.

Paul Maurice
Head Coach
Born: Sault Ste. Marie, Ont., January 30, 1967.

Paul Maurice was named head coach of the Carolina Hurricanes on December 3, 2008. After coaching the Toronto Maple Leafs for two seasons, he returned to a franchise where he was the winningest coach in history, having amassed 268 wins in his 674 regular-season games coached during first eight-plus seasons with the team from November 6, 1995, until December 15, 2003. After taking over the Hurricanes midway through the 2008-09 season, he led the team to the Eastern Conference Finals.

Maurice guided the Hurricanes to the 2002 Eastern Conference title and two Southeast Division crowns during his first stint as the team's head coach. He led the team to four consecutive winning seasons from 1999 to 2002. Prior to the 2003-04 season, Maurice was the longest-tenured head coach in the NHL after having originally been promoted from a Hartford Whalers assistant coach's position on November 6, 1995. At only 28 years old when he was first hired, Maurice was the league's youngest head coach, a distinction he maintained until the Boston Bruins hired Mike Sullivan on June 23, 2003.

Prior to joining the Whalers as an assistant coach during the summer of 1995, Maurice spent two seasons as head coach of the Ontario Hockey League's Detroit Jr. Red Wings. He led the team to the 1995 OHL championship and an appearance in the Memorial Cup. That season, he finished second in voting to Guelph's Craig Hartsburg for the Matt Leyden Trophy, which is annually awarded to the OHL's Coach of the Year.

Maurice played his junior hockey with the OHL's Windsor Spitfires (1984 to 1988). He was Philadelphia's 12th choice, 252nd overall, in the 1985 NHL Entry Draft but had his career cut short due to an eye injury and began coaching as an assistant with the Jr. Red Wings shortly thereafter.

Tom Kostopoulos played all 82 games for Carolina in 2009-10, the first time in his career that he saw action in every game.

Coaching Record

			Regular Season				Playoffs			
Season	Team	League	GC	W	L	O/T	GC	W	L	T
1993-94	Detroit	OHL	66	42	20	4	17	11	6	....
1994-95	Detroit	OHL	44	18	4	....	21	16	5	....
1994-95	Detroit	M-Cup	....	....	....	....	5	3	2	....
1995-96	Hartford	NHL	70	29	33	8	....	....	....	....
1996-97	Hartford	NHL	82	32	39	11	....	....	....	....
1997-98	Carolina	NHL	82	33	41	8	....	....	....	....
1998-99	Carolina	NHL	82	34	30	18	6	2	4	....
99-2000	Carolina	NHL	82	37	35	10	....	....	....	....
2000-01	Carolina	NHL	82	38	32	12	6	2	4	....
2001-02	Carolina	NHL	82	35	26	21	23	13	10	....
2002-03	Carolina	NHL	82	22	43	17	....	....	....	....
2003-04	Carolina	NHL	30	8	12	10	....	....	....	....
2005-06	Toronto	AHL	80	41	29	10	5	1	4	....
2006-07	Toronto	NHL	82	40	31	11	....	....	....	....
2007-08	Toronto	NHL	82	36	35	11	....	....	....	....
2008-09	Carolina	NHL	57	33	19	5	18	8	19	....
2009-10	Carolina	NHL	82	35	37	10	....	....	....	....
	NHL Totals		977	412	413	152	53	25	37	

Club Records

Team

(Figures in brackets for season records are games played; records for fewest points, wins, ties, losses, goals, goals against are for 70 or more games)

Most Points **112** 2005-06 (82)
Most Wins **52** 2005-06 (82)
Most Ties **19** 1979-80 (80)
Most Losses **54** 1982-83 (80)
Most Goals **332** 1985-86 (80)
Most Goals Against **403** 1982-83 (80)
Fewest Points **45** 1982-83 (80)
Fewest Wins **19** 1982-83 (80)
Fewest Ties **4** 1985-86 (80)
Fewest Losses **22** 2005-06 (82)
Fewest Goals **171** 2002-03 (82)
Fewest Goals Against **202** 1998-99 (82)

Longest Winning Streak
Overall .... **9** Oct. 22-Nov. 11/05, Dec. 31/05-Jan. 19/06, Mar. 18-Apr. 07/09
Home .... **12** Feb. 20-Apr. 7/09
Away .... **6** Nov. 10-Dec. 7/90

Longest Undefeated Streak
Overall .... **10** Jan. 20-Feb. 10/82 (6 wins, 4 ties)
Home .... **12** Feb. 20-Apr. 7/09 (12 wins)
Away .... **8** Nov. 11-Dec. 5/96 (4 wins, 4 ties)

Longest Losing Streak
Overall .... **14** Oct. 10-Nov. 13/09
Home .... **7** Dec. 27/02-Jan. 20/03
Away .... **13** Dec. 18/82-Feb. 5/83, Oct. 3-Nov. 28/09

Longest Winless Streak
Overall .... **14** Jan. 4-Feb. 9/92 (8 losses, 6 ties), Oct. 10-Nov. 13/09 (10 losses, 4 OT losses)
Home .... **13** Jan. 15-Mar. 10/85 (11 losses, 2 ties)
Away .... **15** Nov. 11/79-Jan. 9/80 (11 losses, 4 ties), Jan. 7-Mar. 2/03 (13 losses, 2 ties)

Most Shutouts, Season **8** 1998-99 (82)
Most PIM, Season **2,354** 1992-93 (84)
Most Goals, Game .... **11** Feb. 12/84 (Edm. 0 at Hfd. 11), Oct. 19/85 (Mtl. 6 at Hfd. 11), Jan. 17/86 (Que. 6 at Hfd. 11), Mar. 15/86 (Chi. 4 at Hfd. 11)

Individual

Most Seasons .... **16** Ron Francis
Most Games .... **1,186** Ron Francis
Most Goals, Career .... **382** Ron Francis
Most Assists, Career .... **793** Ron Francis
Most Points, Career .... **1,175** Ron Francis (382G, 793A)
Most PIM, Career .... **1,439** Kevin Dineen
Most Shutouts, Career .... **20** Arturs Irbe
Longest Consecutive Games Streak .... **419** Dave Tippett (Mar. 3/84-Oct. 7/89)
Most Goals, Season .... **56** Blaine Stoughton (1979-80)
Most Assists, Season .... **69** Ron Francis (1989-90)
Most Points, Season .... **105** Mike Rogers (1979-80; 44G, 61A), (1980-81; 40G, 65A)
Most PIM, Season .... **358** Torrie Robertson (1985-86)
Most Points, Defenseman, Season .... **69** Dave Babych (1985-86; 14G, 55A)
Most Points, Center, Season .... **105** Mike Rogers (1979-80; 44G, 61A), (1980-81; 40G, 65A)
Most Points, Right Wing, Season .... **100** Blaine Stoughton (1979-80; 56G, 44A)
Most Points, Left Wing, Season .... **89** Geoff Sanderson (1992-93; 46G, 43A)
Most Points, Rookie, Season .... **72** Sylvain Turgeon (1983-84; 40G, 32A)
Most Shutouts, Season .... **6** Arturs Irbe (1998-99), (2000-01) Kevin Weekes (2003-04) Cam Ward (2008-09)
Most Goals, Game .... **4** Jordy Douglas (Feb. 3/80) Ron Francis (Feb. 12/84) Eric Staal (Mar. 7/09)
Most Assists, Game .... **6** Ron Francis (Mar. 5/87)
Most Points, Game .... **6** Paul Lawless (Jan. 4/87; 2G, 4A) Ron Francis (Mar. 5/87; 6A), (Oct. 8/89; 3G, 3A) Eric Staal (Mar. 7/09; 4G, 2A)

Records include Hartford Whalers, 1979-80 through 1996-97.

Retired Numbers

2	Glen Wesley	1994-2008
10	Ron Francis	1981-1991; 1998-2004

All-time Record vs. Other Clubs

Regular Season

	At Home								On Road								Total							
	GP	W	L	T	OL	GF	GA	PTS	GP	W	L	T	OL	GF	GA	PTS	GP	W	L	T	OL	GF	GA	PTS
Anaheim	11	6	4	1	0	28	25	13	12	5	6	1	0	37	35	11	23	11	10	2	0	65	60	24
Atlanta	31	17	11	1	2	97	97	37	31	21	6	3	1	108	80	46	62	38	17	4	3	205	177	83
Boston	86	36	39	9	2	284	296	83	88	30	51	7	0	234	306	67	174	66	90	16	2	518	602	150
Buffalo	88	37	39	11	1	257	266	86	87	28	51	7	1	251	350	64	175	65	90	18	2	508	616	150
Calgary	30	11	14	5	0	100	108	27	31	6	23	2	0	93	147	14	61	17	37	7	0	193	255	41
Chicago	32	16	12	4	0	106	98	36	31	11	16	3	1	88	120	26	63	27	28	7	1	194	218	62
Colorado	65	26	26	12	1	214	222	65	67	17	41	9	0	197	284	43	132	43	67	21	1	411	506	108
Columbus	6	4	2	0	0	16	17	8	5	2	3	0	0	12	13	4	11	6	5	0	0	28	30	12
Dallas	34	15	15	4	0	111	117	34	32	10	18	2	2	92	125	24	66	25	33	6	2	203	242	58
Detroit	32	18	13	1	0	108	91	37	33	7	18	7	1	89	127	22	65	25	31	8	1	197	218	59
Edmonton	31	12	12	7	0	120	103	31	33	7	21	5	0	95	128	19	64	19	33	12	0	215	231	50
Florida	43	29	11	3	0	141	107	61	44	15	19	8	2	102	134	40	87	44	30	11	2	243	241	101
Los Angeles	33	16	12	5	0	118	121	37	32	11	17	3	1	119	135	26	65	27	29	8	1	237	256	63
Minnesota	4	4	0	0	0	11	6	8	7	1	3	2	1	20	20	5	11	5	3	2	1	31	26	13
Montreal	88	35	39	13	1	257	300	84	85	26	49	7	3	250	327	62	173	61	88	20	4	507	627	146
Nashville	7	3	2	1	1	21	22	8	6	1	5	0	0	9	14	2	13	4	7	1	1	30	36	10
New Jersey	54	23	22	8	1	161	159	55	55	19	30	4	2	163	188	44	109	42	52	12	3	324	347	99
NY Islanders	55	28	20	5	2	194	174	63	54	26	21	4	3	158	158	59	109	54	41	9	5	352	332	122
NY Rangers	53	30	20	3	0	172	158	63	55	18	31	4	2	138	195	42	108	48	51	7	2	310	353	105
Ottawa	37	22	11	4	0	107	91	48	39	16	18	4	1	99	117	37	76	38	29	8	1	206	208	85
Philadelphia	54	15	26	9	4	165	195	43	53	13	30	5	5	135	200	36	107	28	56	14	9	300	395	79
Phoenix	33	15	12	6	0	108	97	36	33	16	15	2	0	123	120	34	66	31	27	8	0	231	217	70
Pittsburgh	58	29	23	5	1	212	203	64	56	23	25	6	2	200	214	54	114	52	48	11	3	412	417	118
St. Louis	34	14	18	2	0	100	105	30	33	10	19	3	1	95	120	24	67	24	37	5	1	195	225	54
San Jose	13	7	6	0	0	41	32	14	13	5	8	0	0	38	57	10	26	12	14	0	0	79	89	24
Tampa Bay	45	27	9	7	2	142	118	63	44	16	22	3	3	124	134	38	89	43	31	10	5	266	252	101
Toronto	47	24	16	6	1	180	155	55	46	24	16	5	1	164	148	54	93	48	32	11	2	344	303	109
Vancouver	31	14	12	5	0	102	104	33	32	10	14	6	2	87	113	28	63	24	26	11	2	189	217	61
Washington	67	27	28	10	2	194	201	66	65	22	36	4	3	172	220	51	132	49	64	14	5	366	421	117
Totals	**1202**	**560**	**474**	**147**	**21**	**3867**	**3788**	**1288**	**1202**	**416**	**632**	**116**	**38**	**3492**	**4329**	**986**	**2404**	**976**	**1106**	**263**	**59**	**7359**	**8117**	**2274**

Playoffs

	Series	W	L	GP	W	L	T	GF	GA	Last Mtg.	Rnd.	Result
Boston	4	1	3	26	11	15	0	64	80	2009	CSF	W 4-3
Buffalo	1	1	0	7	4	3	0	22	17	2006	CF	W 4-3
Colorado	2	1	1	9	5	4	0	35	34	1987	DSF	L 2-4
Detroit	1	0	1	5	1	4	0	7	14	2002	F	L 1-4
Edmonton	1	1	0	7	4	3	0	19	16	2006	F	W 4-3
Montreal	7	2	5	39	16	23	0	106	125	2006	CQF	W 4-2
New Jersey	4	3	1	24	14	10	0	51	56	2009	CQF	W 4-3
Pittsburgh	1	0	1	4	0	4	0	9	20	2009	CF	L 0-4
Toronto	1	1	0	6	4	2	0	10	6	2002	CF	W 4-2
Totals	**22**	**10**	**12**	**127**	**59**	**68**	**0**	**323**	**368**			

Playoff Results 2010-2006

Year	Round	Opponent	Result	GF	GA
2009	CF	Pittsburgh	L 0-4	9	20
	CSF	Boston	W 4-3	16	17
	CQF	New Jersey	W 4-3	17	15
2006	**F**	**Edmonton**	**W 4-3**	**19**	**16**
	CF	Buffalo	W 4-3	22	17
	CSF	New Jersey	W 4-1	17	10
	CQF	Montreal	W 4-2	15	17

Abbreviations: Round: F - Final; **CF** - conference final; **CSF** - conference semi-final; **CQF** - conference quarter-final; **DSF** - division semi-final.

Calgary totals include Atlanta Flames, 1979-80.
Dallas totals include Minnesota North Stars, 1979-80 to 1992-93.
Phoenix totals include Winnipeg, 1979-80 to 1995-96.
Colorado totals include Quebec, 1979-80 to 1994-95.
New Jersey totals include Colorado Rockies, 1979-80 to 1981-82.

2009-10 Results

Month	Day	Opponent	Score
Oct.	2	Philadelphia	0-2
	3	at Boston	2-7
	6	Tampa Bay	2-1†
	9	Florida	7-2
	10	at Tampa Bay	2-5
	14	Pittsburgh	2-3†
	17	at New Jersey	0-2
	21	at NY Islanders	3-4†
	23	at Colorado	4-5
	24	at Minnesota	2-3*
	28	St. Louis	2-5
	31	at Philadelphia	1-6
Nov.	1	San Jose	1-5
	4	at Florida	0-3
	6	Toronto	2-3
	7	at Columbus	2-3
	11	Los Angeles	2-5
	13	NY Islanders	3-4*
	15	Minnesota	5-4†
	17	at Montreal	2-3†
	19	Toronto	6-5†
	21	Tampa Bay	3-1
	23	at Dallas	0-2
	25	at Anaheim	2-3
	27	Atlanta	4-6
	28	at Buffalo	1-5
	30	Washington	2-3
Dec.	5	Vancouver	5-3
	7	at Pittsburgh	3-2
	9	at New Jersey	2-4
	11	at Washington	3-4*
	12	at Ottawa	2-4
	16	Dallas	5-3
	18	at Florida	3-6
	19	Florida	3-2
	21	NY Rangers	1-3
	23	Montreal	1-5
	26	Philadelphia	3-4†
	28	at Washington	6-3
	31	NY Rangers	1-2
Jan.	2	at NY Rangers	2-1*
	7	at Nashville	2-4
	8	Colorado	2-1
	10	Ottawa	4-1
	12	at Toronto	4-2
	14	at Detroit	1-3
	16	Atlanta	3-5
	18	Tampa Bay	2-3
	21	at Atlanta	5-2
	23	at Philadelphia	2-4
	24	Boston	5-1
	27	at NY Rangers	5-1
	28	NY Islanders	4-1
	30	Chicago	4-2
Feb.	1	at Edmonton	2-4
	3	at Calgary	1-4
	5	at Buffalo	4-3
	6	at NY Islanders	3-1
	9	Florida	4-1
	11	Buffalo	4-3*
	13	New Jersey	5-2
Mar.	2	at Toronto	5-1
	4	Ottawa	4-1
	6	at Florida	1-4
	7	at Atlanta	4-0
	10	at Washington	3-4*
	11	Pittsburgh	4-3*
	13	Phoenix	0-4
	16	Boston	2-5
	18	Washington	4-3*
	20	at Pittsburgh	3-2*
	21	Buffalo	3-5
	23	at Tampa Bay	2-3*
	25	Washington	3-2†
	27	Atlanta	0-4
	29	at Atlanta	4-1
	31	at Montreal	2-1
Apr.	1	at Ottawa	3-4†
	3	New Jersey	0-4
	6	at Tampa Bay	8-5
	8	Montreal	5-2
	10	at Boston	2-4

* – Overtime † – Shootout

Entry Draft Selections 2010-1996

Name in bold denotes played in NHL.

2010 Pick		2006 Pick		2002 Pick		1998 Pick	
7	Jeff Skinner	63	**Jamie McBain**	25	**Cam Ward**	11	**Jeff Heerema**
37	Justin Faulk	93	Harrison Reed	91	Jesse Lane	70	Kevin Holdridge
53	Mark Alt	123	Bobby Hughes	160	Daniel Manzato	71	**Erik Cole**
67	Danny Biega	153	Stefan Chaput	224	Adam Taylor	91	**Josef Vasicek**
85	Austin Levi	183	Nick Dodge			93	**Tommy Westlund**
105	Justin Shugg	213	Justin Krueger	**2001**		97	Chris Madden
167	Tyler Stahl			**Pick**		184	Don Smith
187	Frederik Andersen	**2005**		15	Igor Knyazev	208	**Jaroslav Svoboda**
		Pick		46	**Mike Zigomanis**	211	Mark Kosick
2009		3	**Jack Johnson**	91	Kevin Estrada	239	Brent McDonald
Pick		58	Nate Hagemo	110	Rob Zepp		
27	Philippe Paradis	64	Joe Barnes	181	Daniel Boisclair	**1997**	
51	Brian Dumoulin	94	Jakub Vojta	211	Sean Curry	**Pick**	
88	Mattias Lindstrom	123	Ondrej Otcenas	244	Carter Trevisani	22	**Nikos Tselios**
131	Matt Kennedy	145	Tim Kunes	274	Peter Reynolds	28	**Brad DeFauw**
178	Rasmus Rissanen	159	Risto Korhonen			80	**Francis Lessard**
208	Tommi Kivisto	192	Nicolas Blanchard	**2000**		88	**Shane Willis**
		198	Kyle Lawson	**Pick**		142	Kyle Dafoe
2008				32	**Tomas Kurka**	169	Andrew Merrick
Pick		**2004**		80	**Ryan Bayda**	195	**Niklas Nordgren**
14	**Zach Boychuk**	**Pick**		97	**Niclas Wallin**	199	Randy Fitzgerald
45	Zac Dalpe	4	**Andrew Ladd**	110	Jared Newman	225	**Kent McDonell**
105	Michal Jordan	38	**Justin Peters**	181	J.D. Forrest		
165	Mike Murphy	69	**Casey Borer**	212	Magnus Kahnberg	**1996**	
195	Samuel Morneau	109	**Brett Carson**	235	Craig Kowalski	**Pick**	
		137	Magnus Akerlund	276	Troy Ferguson	34	Trevor Wasyluk
2007		202	Ryan Pottruff			61	Andrei Petrunin
Pick		235	Jonas Fiedler	**1999**		88	**Craig MacDonald**
11	**Brandon Sutter**	268	Martin Vagner	**Pick**		104	Steve Wasylko
72	**Drayson Bowman**			16	**David Tanabe**	116	Mark McMahon
102	Justin McCrae	**2003**		49	**Brett Lysak**	143	Aaron Baker
132	Chris Terry	**Pick**		84	**Brad Fast**	171	**Greg Kuznik**
162	Brett Bellemore	2	**Eric Staal**	113	Ryan Murphy	197	Kevin Marsh
		31	**Danny Richmond**	174	**Damian Surma**	223	**Craig Adams**
		102	Aaron Dawson	202	Jim Baxter	231	Ashkat Rakhmatullin
		126	Kevin Nastiuk	231	David Evans		
		130	Matej Trojovsky	237	Antti Jokela		
		137	**Tyson Strachan**	259	Yevgeny Kurilin		
		198	**Shay Stephenson**				
		230	Jamie Hoffmann				
		262	Ryan Rorabeck				

Coaching History

Don Blackburn, 1979-80; Don Blackburn and Larry Pleau, 1980-81; Larry Pleau, 1981-82; Larry Kish, Larry Pleau and John Cuniff, 1982- 83; Jack Evans, 1983-84 to 1986-87; Jack Evans and Larry Pleau, 1987-88; Larry Pleau, 1988-89; Rick Ley, 1989-90, 1990-91; Jim Roberts, 1991-92; Paul Holmgren, 1992-93; Paul Holmgren and Pierre Maguire, 1993-94; Paul Holmgren, 1994-95; Paul Holmgren and Paul Maurice, 1995-96; Paul Maurice, 1996-97 to 2002-03; Paul Maurice and Peter Laviolette, 2003-04; Peter Laviolette, 2004-05 to 2007-08; Peter Laviolette and Paul Maurice, 2008-09; Paul Maurice, 2009-10 to date.

General Managers' History

Jack Kelley, 1979-80, 1980-81; Larry Pleau, 1981-82, 1982-83; Emile Francis, 1983-84 to 1988-89; Eddie Johnston, 1989-90 to 1991-92; Brian Burke, 1992-93; Paul Holmgren, 1993-94; Jim Rutherford, 1994-95 to date.

Jim Rutherford

President and General Manager

Born: Beeton, Ont., February 17, 1949.

Jim Rutherford, a former NHL goaltender, is the franchise's seventh general manager and the only general manager of the Carolina Hurricanes. Named to his position on June 28, 1994, Rutherford has always taken an aggressive approach towards improving the fortunes of the franchise through trades and the NHL Entry Draft. In 2002, the team reached the Stanley Cup Finals for the first time in history. The Hurricanes won the Stanley Cup in 2006.

A veteran of 13 NHL seasons, Rutherford began his professional goaltending career in 1969 as a first-round selection of the Detroit Red Wings. While playing for Detroit, Pittsburgh, Toronto and Los Angeles, Rutherford collected 14 career shutouts. For five seasons he also served as the Red Wings' player representative. Rutherford also played for Team Canada at the World Championships in Vienna in 1977 and Moscow in 1979.

After his playing days with the Red Wings, Rutherford joined Compuware to serve as the director of hockey operations for Compuware Sports Corporation. Rutherford gained a wealth of experience in youth hockey and junior programs. As a former player, coach, and general manager, his ability to develop players and produce winning programs is widely respected throughout the hockey community.

He started his management career by guiding Compuware Sports Corporation's purchase of the Windsor Spitfires of the Ontario Hockey League in April of 1984. During the next four years, Rutherford acted as general manager of the Spitfires. After the Spitfires advanced to the 1988 Memorial Cup finals, Rutherford led Compuware's efforts to bring the first American-based OHL franchise to Detroit on December 11, 1989. Rutherford was voted the 1987 executive of the year in both the OHL and the Canadian Hockey League and won the OHL executive of the year award again in 1988.

Club Directory

RBC Center

Carolina Hurricanes
1400 Edwards Mill Rd.
Raleigh, NC 27607
Phone **919/467-7825**
FAX 919/462-0123
Tickets 1.866.NHL.CANES
www.carolinahurricanes.com
Capacity: 18,680

Executive Management
Chief Executive Officer/Owner/Governor . . . . Peter Karmanos, Jr.
President/General Manager . . . . Jim Rutherford
Vice President/Assistant General Manager . . . . Jason Karmanos
Chief Financial Officer/Alternate Governor . . . . . . Mike Amendola
Vice President/General Manager, RBC Center . . . . . Davin Olsen

Hockey Operations
Head Coach . . . . Paul Maurice
Associate Head Coach/Dir. of Player Personnel . . . . Ron Francis
Assistant Coaches . . . . Tom Rowe, Tom Barrasso
Dir. of Development, Defensemen / Forwards . . . . . Glen Wesley / Rod Brind'Amour
Video Coach . . . . Chris Huffine
Head Ath. Trainer/Strength Conditioning Coach . . . Peter Friesen
Assistant Athletic Trainer . . . . Doug Bennett
Equipment Managers . . . . Wally Tatomir, Skip Cunningham, Bob Gorman
Senior Director of Team Operations . . . . Brian Tatum
Executive Assistant to the President/G.M. . . . . Mari Jeter
Motivational Consultant/Mgr. Community Dev. . . . . Doris E. Barksdale
Video Scouting Coordinator . . . . Darren Yorke
Director of Amateur Scouting . . . . Tony MacDonald
Amateur Scouts . . . . Sheldon Ferguson, Robert Kron, Bob Luccini, Bert Marshall
Director of Pro Scouting . . . . Marshall Johnston
Pro Scouts . . . . Claude Larose, Ron Smith
Charlotte Checkers Head Coach/G.M. . . . . Jeff Daniels
Charlotte Checkers Assistant Coach . . . . Geordie Kinnear

Administration
Receptionists . . . . Mary Lou Ruetz, Janet Davis

Arena – Operations
Assistant General Manager, RBC Center . . . . Larry Perkins
Marketing Manager . . . . Crystal Pace
Security Manager / Parking Manager . . . . Clinton Peterson / Mike Alexander
Event Services Manager . . . . Steve Congress
Premium Services and Sales Manager . . . . Suzanne Golden
Assistant Operations Manager . . . . Melvin Terrell
Facility Systems Manager . . . . Alan Wobbleton
Director of Ticket Operations . . . . Bill Nowicki
Arena Box Office / Office Manager . . . . Joe Sousa, Hilman Huskey
Assistant Mgr., Box Office / Ticket Ops . . . . Chris Jovino / Erin Wallace

Broadcasters
Television Rightsholder . . . . Fox Sports Carolinas
Radio Flagship . . . . WCMC 99.9 FM The Fan
Television Play-by-Play / Analyst. . . . . John Forslund / Tripp Tracy
Radio Play-by-Play . . . . Chuck Kaiton

Communications
Director of Media Relations . . . . Mike Sundheim
Mgr. of Media Relations/Broadcast Coord. . . . . Kyle Hanlin
Team Photographer . . . . Gregg Forwerck

Finance/Information Technology
General Counsel/Senior Director of Finance . . . . . . William Traurig
Accountant. . . . . David Johnston
Accounts Payable / Receivable. . . . . Michael Arrington / Patty Hilliard, Temika Smith-Harris
Payroll/Human Resources Coordinator . . . . Cyndy Coffey
Payroll Coordinator. . . . . Crystal DeDitius
Assistant to the CFO . . . . Stacey Ustin
Director of Information Technology. . . . . Glenn Johnson
Client/Server Technologists . . . . Dwight Baptist, Alex Byrd, Myatt Williams

Food and Beverage
Director of Food and Beverage . . . . Chris Diamond
Concessions Manager. . . . . Rick Rhodes
Chefs . . . . Dennis Atkinson, Michael Flood, Kevin Heintz
Managers. . . . . Katrina Ryan, Gary Berry,
Assistant Managers. . . . . Jim O'Brien, Skip Roach, Barbara Couch,

Marketing
Sr Director of Marketing/
  Exec. Dir., Kids 'n Community Foundation . . . . . . Doug Warf
Director of Marketing and Brand Development . . . . Ben Aycock
Dir. of Advertising Prod. and In-Game Marketing . . Pete Soto
Dir. of Community Relations and Promotions . . . . . Jon Chase
Website Producer / Graphic Designers. . . . . Paul Branecky / Lauren Baxter, Andrew Roman
Marketing Coordinator . . . . Coop Elias
Producers, Gale Force/CanesVision/Wolfpack TV . . . Charles Graham, Don Sill, Marshall Alderman
Graphics Prod., Gale Force /
  CanesVision/Wolfpack TV . . . . Stephen Rutherford
Youth and Amateur Hockey Coordinator . . . . Paul Strand
Mascot Coordinator . . . . George Brown
Promotions/Fan Development Coordinator . . . . Ryan O'Quinn
Sr. Coordinator, Community Relations/
  Asst. Dir., Kids 'n Community Foundation . . . . . . Katharine Kelley
Community Relations Coordinator . . . . Kristina Boyce

Merchandise
Retail Operations Manager . . . . James Blitch

Sales
Senior Director of Corporate Sponsorships . . . . Jim Ballweg
Senior Corporate Sales Executives . . . . Rick Francis, Julia Zeigler
Corporate Sales Executives . . . . Johnny Gill, Lindsey Moore
Director of Ticket Sales . . . . Kyle Prairie
Manager of Sales and Client Services . . . . Peterson Avetta
Account Executives/Business Development . . . . Rich Davis, Jonathan Feldman, Michael Miller
Client Relations Representative . . . . Matt Horton
Group Sales Mgr., Hurricanes / RBC Center . . . . . . Brian Kapusta / Brian Slais
Group Sales Representative. . . . . TBD
Ticket Sales Asst / Client Services Coord. . . . . Karen Prince / Kaitlyn Szulik
Business Development Exec. Group Sales . . . . Greg Perna

Chicago Blackhawks

2009-10 Results: 52W-22L-2OTL-6SOL 112PTS.
First, Central Division

Key Off-Season Signings/Acquisitions

2010

- **June 24** • Acquired C **Marty Reasoner**, RW **Joey Crabb**, LW **Jeremy Morin** and New Jersey's 1st and 2nd round picks in the 2010 Entry Draft (previously acquired) from Atlanta for RW **Dustin Byfuglien**, LW **Ben Eager**, RW **Akim Aliu** and D **Brent Sopel**.
- **30** • Acquired LW **Viktor Stalberg**, C **Philippe Paradis** and C **Christopher DiDomenico** from Toronto for RW **Kris Versteeg** and LW **Bill Sweatt**.
- **July 1** • Acquired D **Ivan Vishnevskiy** and a 2nd round pick in the 2011 Entry Draft from Atlanta for LW **Andrew Ladd**.
- **2** • Signed D **John Scott**.
- **12** • Named **Mike Kitchen** assistant coach.
- **12** • Re-signed D **Niklas Hjalmarsson**.
- **22** • Acquired C **Jeff Taffe** from Florida for C **Marty Reasoner**.
- **28** • Re-signed LW **Bryan Bickell** and RW **Jack Skille**.
- **Aug. 2** • Signed G **Marty Turco**.

2010-11 Schedule

Oct.	Thu.	7	at Colorado
	Sat.	9	Detroit
	Mon.	11	at Buffalo
	Wed.	13	Nashville
	Fri.	15	at Columbus
	Sat.	16	Buffalo
	Mon.	18	St. Louis
	Wed.	20	Vancouver
	Fri.	22	at St. Louis
	Sat.	23	Columbus
	Wed.	27	Los Angeles
	Fri.	29	Edmonton
	Sat.	30	at Minnesota
Nov.	Mon.	1	at NY Rangers
	Wed.	3	New Jersey
	Sat.	6	at Atlanta
	Sun.	7	Edmonton
	Wed.	10	Phoenix
	Sat.	13	at Nashville
	Sun.	14	Anaheim
	Wed.	17	at Edmonton
	Fri.	19	at Calgary
	Sat.	20	at Vancouver
	Wed.	24	at San Jose
	Fri.	26	at Anaheim*
	Sat.	27	at Los Angeles
	Tue.	30	St. Louis
Dec.	Fri.	3	Vancouver
	Sun.	5	Calgary
	Wed.	8	Dallas
	Sat.	11	at San Jose
	Mon.	13	at Colorado
	Wed.	15	Colorado
	Fri.	17	Detroit
	Sun.	19	Los Angeles
	Wed.	22	Nashville
	Sun.	26	Columbus
	Tue.	28	at St. Louis
	Thu.	30	San Jose
Jan.	Sun.	2	at Anaheim*
	Mon.	3	at Los Angeles
	Wed.	5	Dallas
	Fri.	7	Ottawa
	Sun.	9	NY Islanders
	Wed.	12	Colorado
	Sat.	15	at Nashville
	Sun.	16	Nashville
	Sat.	22	at Detroit*
	Sun.	23	Philadelphia*
	Tue.	25	Minnesota
Feb.	Tue.	1	at Columbus
	Fri.	4	at Vancouver
	Mon.	7	at Calgary
	Wed.	9	at Edmonton
	Fri.	11	at Dallas
	Sat.	12	at Phoenix
	Wed.	16	Minnesota
	Fri.	18	Columbus
	Sun.	20	Pittsburgh*
	Mon.	21	at St. Louis*
	Thu.	24	at Nashville
	Sun.	27	Phoenix
	Mon.	28	at Minnesota
Mar.	Wed.	2	Calgary
	Fri.	4	Carolina
	Sat.	5	at Toronto
	Tue.	8	at Florida
	Wed.	9	at Tampa Bay
	Sun.	13	at Washington*
	Mon.	14	San Jose
	Thu.	17	at Dallas
	Sun.	20	at Phoenix*
	Wed.	23	Florida
	Sat.	26	Anaheim
	Mon.	28	at Detroit
	Tue.	29	at Boston
Apr.	Fri.	1	at Columbus
	Sun.	3	Tampa Bay
	Tue.	5	at Montreal
	Wed.	6	St. Louis
	Fri.	8	at Detroit
	Sun.	10	Detroit*

* Denotes afternoon game.

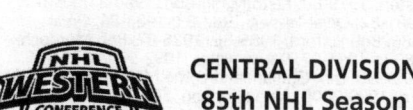

CENTRAL DIVISION
85th NHL Season

Franchise date: September 25, 1926

Year-by-Year Record

		Home				Road				Overall								
Season	GP	W	L	T	OL	W	L	T	OL	W	L	T	OL	GF	GA	Pts.	Finished	Playoff Result
2009-10	**82**	**29**	**8**	....	**4**	**23**	**14**	....	**4**	**52**	**22**	....	**8**	**271**	**209**	**112**	**1st, Central Div.**	**Won Stanley Cup**
2008-09	82	24	9	....	8	22	15	....	4	46	24	....	12	264	216	104	2nd, Central Div.	Lost Conf. Championship
2007-08	82	23	16	....	2	17	18	....	6	40	34	....	8	239	235	88	3rd, Central Div.	Out of Playoffs
2006-07	82	17	20	....	4	14	22	....	5	31	42	....	9	201	258	71	5th, Central Div.	Out of Playoffs
2005-06	82	16	19	....	6	10	24	....	7	26	43	....	13	211	285	65	4th, Central Div.	Out of Playoffs
2004-05	....	....	....	....	....	....	....	....	....	....	....	....	....	....	....	....		
2003-04	82	13	17	6	5	7	26	5	3	20	43	11	8	188	259	59	5th, Central Div.	Out of Playoffs
2002-03	82	17	15	7	2	13	18	6	4	30	33	13	6	207	226	79	3rd, Central Div.	Out of Playoffs
2001-02	82	28	7	5	1	13	20	8	0	41	27	13	1	216	207	96	3rd, Central Div.	Lost Conf. Quarter-Final
2000-01	82	14	21	4	2	15	19	4	3	29	40	8	5	210	246	71	4th, Central Div.	Out of Playoffs
1999-2000	82	16	19	5	1	17	18	5	1	33	37	10	2	242	245	78	3rd, Central Div.	Out of Playoffs
1998-99	82	20	17	4	....	9	24	8	....	29	41	12	....	202	248	70	3rd, Central Div.	Out of Playoffs
1997-98	82	14	19	8	....	16	20	5	....	30	39	13	....	192	199	73	5th, Central Div.	Out of Playoffs
1996-97	82	16	21	4	....	18	14	9	....	34	35	13	....	223	210	81	5th, Central Div.	Lost Conf. Quarter-Final
1995-96	82	22	13	6	....	18	15	8	....	40	28	14	....	273	220	94	2nd, Central Div.	Lost Conf. Semi-Final
1994-95	48	11	10	3	....	13	9	2	....	24	19	5	....	156	115	53	3rd, Central Div.	Lost Conf. Championship
1993-94	84	21	16	5	....	18	20	4	....	39	36	9	....	254	240	87	5th, Central Div.	Lost Conf. Quarter-Final
1992-93	84	25	11	6	....	22	14	6	....	47	25	12	....	279	230	106	1st, Norris Div.	Lost Div. Semi-Final
1991-92	80	23	9	8	....	13	20	7	....	36	29	15	....	257	236	87	2nd, Norris Div.	Lost Final
1990-91	80	28	8	4	....	21	15	4	....	49	23	8	....	284	211	106	1st, Norris Div.	Lost Div. Semi-Final
1989-90	80	25	13	2	....	16	20	4	....	41	33	6	....	316	294	88	1st, Norris Div.	Lost Conf. Championship
1988-89	80	16	14	10	....	11	27	2	....	27	41	12	....	297	335	66	4th, Norris Div.	Lost Conf. Championship
1987-88	80	21	17	2	....	9	24	7	....	30	41	9	....	284	328	69	3rd, Norris Div.	Lost Div. Semi-Final
1986-87	80	18	13	9	....	11	24	5	....	29	37	14	....	290	310	72	3rd, Norris Div.	Lost Div. Semi-Final
1985-86	80	23	12	5	....	16	21	3	....	39	33	8	....	351	349	86	1st, Norris Div.	Lost Div. Semi-Final
1984-85	80	22	16	2	....	16	19	5	....	38	35	7	....	309	299	83	2nd, Norris Div.	Lost Conf. Championship
1983-84	80	25	13	2	....	5	29	6	....	30	42	8	....	277	311	68	4th, Norris Div.	Lost Div. Semi-Final
1982-83	80	29	8	3	....	18	15	7	....	47	23	10	....	338	268	104	1st, Norris Div.	Lost Conf. Championship
1981-82	80	20	13	7	....	10	25	5	....	30	38	12	....	332	363	72	4th, Norris Div.	Lost Conf. Championship
1980-81	80	21	11	8	....	10	22	8	....	31	33	16	....	304	315	78	2nd, Smythe Div.	Lost Prelim. Round
1979-80	80	21	12	7	....	13	15	12	....	34	27	19	....	241	250	87	1st, Smythe Div.	Lost Quarter-Final
1978-79	80	18	12	10	....	11	24	5	....	29	36	15	....	244	277	73	1st, Smythe Div.	Lost Quarter-Final
1977-78	80	20	9	11	....	12	20	8	....	32	29	19	....	230	220	83	1st, Smythe Div.	Lost Quarter-Final
1976-77	80	19	16	5	....	7	27	6	....	26	43	11	....	240	298	63	3rd, Smythe Div.	Lost Prelim. Round
1975-76	80	17	15	8	....	15	15	10	....	32	30	18	....	254	261	82	1st, Smythe Div.	Lost Quarter-Final
1974-75	80	24	12	4	....	13	23	4	....	37	35	8	....	268	241	82	3rd, Smythe Div.	Lost Quarter-Final
1973-74	78	20	6	13	....	21	8	10	....	41	14	23	....	272	164	105	2nd, West Div.	Lost Semi-Final
1972-73	78	26	9	4	....	16	18	5	....	42	27	9	....	284	225	93	1st, West Div.	Lost Final
1971-72	78	28	3	8	....	18	14	7	....	46	17	15	....	256	166	107	1st, West Div.	Lost Semi-Final
1970-71	78	30	6	3	....	19	14	6	....	49	20	9	....	277	184	107	1st, West Div.	Lost Final
1969-70	76	26	7	5	....	19	15	4	....	45	22	9	....	250	170	99	1st, East Div.	Lost Semi-Final
1968-69	76	20	14	4	....	14	19	5	....	34	33	9	....	280	246	77	6th, East Div.	Out of Playoffs
1967-68	74	20	13	4	....	12	13	12	....	32	26	16	....	212	222	80	4th, East Div.	Lost Semi-Final
1966-67	70	24	5	6	....	17	12	6	....	41	17	12	....	264	170	94	1st,	Lost Semi-Final
1965-66	70	21	8	6	....	16	17	2	....	37	25	8	....	240	187	82	2nd,	Lost Semi-Final
1964-65	70	20	13	2	....	14	15	6	....	34	28	8	....	224	176	76	3rd,	Lost Final
1963-64	70	26	4	5	....	10	18	7	....	36	22	12	....	218	169	84	2nd,	Lost Semi-Final
1962-63	70	17	9	9	....	15	12	8	....	32	21	17	....	194	178	81	2nd,	Lost Semi-Final
1961-62	70	20	10	5	....	11	16	8	....	31	26	13	....	217	186	75	3rd,	Lost Final
1960-61	**70**	**20**	**6**	**9**	....	**9**	**18**	**8**	....	**29**	**24**	**17**	....	**198**	**180**	**75**	**3rd,**	**Won Stanley Cup**
1959-60	70	18	11	6	....	10	18	7	....	28	29	13	....	191	180	69	3rd,	Lost Semi-Final
1958-59	70	14	12	9	....	14	17	4	....	28	29	13	....	197	208	69	3rd,	Lost Semi-Final
1957-58	70	15	17	3	....	9	22	4	....	24	39	7	....	163	202	55	5th,	Out of Playoffs
1956-57	70	12	15	8	....	4	24	7	....	16	39	15	....	169	225	47	6th,	Out of Playoffs
1955-56	70	9	19	7	....	10	20	5	....	19	39	12	....	155	216	50	6th,	Out of Playoffs
1954-55	70	6	21	8	....	7	19	9	....	13	40	17	....	161	235	43	6th,	Out of Playoffs
1953-54	70	8	21	6	....	4	30	1	....	12	51	7	....	133	242	31	6th,	Out of Playoffs
1952-53	70	14	11	10	....	13	17	5	....	27	28	15	....	169	175	69	4th,	Lost Semi-Final
1951-52	70	9	19	7	....	8	25	2	....	17	44	9	....	158	241	43	6th,	Out of Playoffs
1950-51	70	8	22	5	....	5	25	5	....	13	47	10	....	171	280	36	6th,	Out of Playoffs
1949-50	70	13	18	4	....	9	20	6	....	22	38	10	....	203	244	54	6th,	Out of Playoffs
1948-49	60	13	12	5	....	8	19	3	....	21	31	8	....	173	211	50	5th,	Out of Playoffs
1947-48	60	10	17	3	....	10	17	3	....	20	34	6	....	195	225	46	6th,	Out of Playoffs
1946-47	60	10	17	3	....	9	20	1	....	19	37	4	....	193	274	42	6th,	Out of Playoffs
1945-46	50	15	5	5	....	8	15	2	....	23	20	7	....	200	178	53	3rd,	Lost Semi-Final
1944-45	50	9	14	2	....	4	16	5	....	13	30	7	....	141	194	33	5th,	Out of Playoffs
1943-44	50	15	6	4	....	7	17	1	....	22	23	5	....	178	187	49	4th,	Lost Final
1942-43	50	14	3	8	....	3	15	7	....	17	18	15	....	179	180	49	5th,	Out of Playoffs
1941-42	48	15	8	1	....	7	15	2	....	22	23	3	....	145	155	47	4th,	Lost Quarter-Final
1940-41	48	11	10	3	....	5	15	4	....	16	25	7	....	112	139	39	5th,	Lost Semi-Final
1939-40	48	15	7	2	....	8	12	4	....	23	19	6	....	112	120	52	4th,	Lost Quarter-Final
1938-39	48	5	13	6	....	7	15	2	....	12	28	8	....	91	132	32	7th,	Out of Playoffs
1937-38	**48**	**10**	**10**	**4**	....	**4**	**15**	**5**	....	**14**	**25**	**9**	....	**97**	**139**	**37**	**3rd, Amn. Div.**	**Won Stanley Cup**
1936-37	48	8	13	3	....	6	14	4	....	14	27	7	....	99	131	35	4th, Amn. Div.	Out of Playoffs
1935-36	48	15	7	2	....	6	12	6	....	21	19	8	....	93	92	50	3rd, Amn. Div.	Lost Quarter-Final
1934-35	48	12	9	3	....	14	8	2	....	26	17	5	....	118	88	57	2nd, Amn. Div.	Lost Quarter-Final
1933-34	**48**	**13**	**4**	**7**	....	**7**	**13**	**4**	....	**20**	**17**	**11**	....	**88**	**83**	**51**	**2nd, Amn. Div.**	**Won Stanley Cup**
1932-33	48	12	7	5	....	4	13	7	....	16	20	12	....	88	101	44	4th, Amn. Div.	Out of Playoffs
1931-32	48	13	5	6	....	5	14	5	....	18	19	11	....	86	101	47	2nd, Amn. Div.	Lost Quarter-Final
1930-31	44	13	8	1	....	11	9	2	....	24	17	3	....	108	78	51	2nd, Amn. Div.	Lost Final
1929-30	44	12	9	1	....	9	9	4	....	21	18	5	....	117	111	47	2nd, Amn. Div.	Lost Quarter-Final
1928-29	44	3	13	6	....	4	16	2	....	7	29	8	....	33	85	22	5th, Amn. Div.	Out of Playoffs
1927-28	44	2	18	2	....	5	16	1	....	7	34	3	....	68	134	17	5th, Amn. Div.	Out of Playoffs
1926-27	44	12	8	2	....	7	14	1	....	19	22	3	....	115	116	41	3rd, Amn. Div.	Lost Quarter-Final

2010-11 Player Personnel

FORWARDS	HT	WT	S	Place of Birth	*Age	2009-10 Club
BEACH, Kyle	6-3	210	R	Vancouver, B.C.	20	Spokane-Rockford
BICKELL, Bryan	6-4	223	L	Bowmanville, Ont.	24	Chicago-Rockford
BOLLAND, Dave	6-0	181	R	Toronto, Ont.	24	Chicago
BOLLIG, Brandon	6-3	215	L	St. Charles, MO	23	St. Lawrence-Rockford
BROPHEY, Evan	6-2	199	L	Kitchener, Ont.	23	Rockford
BROUWER, Troy	6-2	214	R	Vancouver, B.C.	25	Chicago
DAVIS, Nathan	6-1	205	L	Cleveland, OH	24	Rockford
DIDOMENICO, Chris	5-11	165	R	Toronto, Ont.	21	Drummondville
DOWELL, Jake	6-0	199	L	Eau Claire, WI	25	Chicago-Rockford
HOSSA, Marian	6-1	210	L	Stara Lubovna, Czech.	31	Chicago
JESSIMAN, Hugh	6-6	221	R	New York, NY	26	Milwaukee
KANE, Patrick	5-10	178	L	Buffalo, NY	21	Chicago
KLINKHAMMER, Robert	6-3	206	L	Lethbridge, Alta.	24	Rockford
KOPECKY, Tomas	6-3	203	L	Ilava, Czech.	28	Chicago
KRUGER, Marcus	5-11	172	L	Stockholm, Sweden	20	Djurgarden
MAKAROV, Igor	6-1	195	R	Moscow, USSR	23	St. Petersburg-Dyn. Moscow
MORIN, Jeremy	6-1	190	R	Auburn, NY	19	Kitchener
OLIMB, Mathis	5-10	175	L	Oslo, Norway	24	Frolunda
PARADIS, Philippe	6-2	205	L	Dolbeau, Que.	19	Shawinigan-Toronto (AHL)
SHARP, Patrick	6-1	199	R	Winnipeg, Man.	28	Chicago
SKILLE, Jack	6-1	215	R	Madison, WI	23	Chicago-Rockford
SMITH, Ben	5-11	205	R	Winston-Salem, NC	22	Rockford-Boston College
STALBERG, Viktor	6-3	210	L	Stockholm, Sweden	24	Toronto-Toronto (AHL)
TAFFE, Jeff	6-3	207	L	Hastings, MN	29	Florida-Rochester
TOEWS, Jonathan	6-2	210	L	Winnipeg, Man.	22	Chicago
DEFENSEMEN						
BOYNTON, Nick	6-1	218	R	Nobleton, Ont.	31	Ana-Man-Chi-Rockford
CAMPBELL, Brian	6-0	189	L	Strathroy, Ont.	31	Chicago
CARLSSON, Jonathan	6-2	187	R	Uppsala, Sweden	22	Rockford-Toledo
CONNELLY, Brian	5-10	167	L	Bloomington, MN	24	Rockford
CULLIMORE, Jassen	6-5	235	L	Simcoe, Ont.	37	Rockford
DANIS-PEPIN, Simon	6-6	229	R	Gatineau, Que.	22	Rockford-Toledo
HENDRY, Jordan	6-0	197	L	Nokomis, Sask.	26	Chicago
HJALMARSSON, Niklas	6-3	205	L	Eksjo, Sweden	23	Chicago
KEITH, Duncan	6-1	196	L	Winnipeg, Man.	27	Chicago
LALONDE, Shawn	6-1	192	R	Ottawa, Ont.	20	Belleville-Rockford
LEDDY, Nick	5-11	179	L	Eden Prairie, MN	19	U. of Minnesota
SCOTT, John	6-8	258	L	St. Catharines, Ont.	28	Minnesota
SEABROOK, Brent	6-3	218	R	Richmond, B.C.	25	Chicago
STANTON, Ryan	6-2	205	L	St. Albert, Alta.	21	Moose Jaw-Rockford
VISHNEVSKIY, Ivan	6-0	193	L	Barnaul, USSR	22	Dal-Texas-Chi (AHL)

GOALTENDERS	HT	WT	C	Place of Birth	*Age	2009-10 Club
CRAWFORD, Corey	6-2	200	L	Montreal, Que.	25	Chicago-Rockford
HUET, Cristobal	6-1	206	L	St. Martin d'Heres, France	35	Chicago
RICHARDS, Alec	6-4	190	L	Robbinsdale, MN	23	Rockford-Toledo
TOIVONEN, Hannu	6-2	200	L	Kalvola, Finland	26	Peoria-Rockford
TURCO, Marty	5-11	184	L	Sault Ste. Marie, Ont.	35	Dallas

* – Age at start of 2010-11 season

Joel Quenneville

Head Coach

Born: Windsor, Ont., September 15, 1958.

Joel Quenneville was named the 37th head coach in Chicago Blackhawks history on October 16, 2008 and in 2009-10 he guided the team to its first Stanley Cup championship since 1961. Quenneville originally joined the Blackhawks as a pro scout in September 2008. He has been a proven winner throughout his career as a head coach in the NHL, including seven seasons with the St. Louis Blues (1996 to 2004) and three with the Colorado Avalanche (2005 to 2008). In his first season behind the bench in Chicago, he led the Blackhawks to the Western Conference Final in just their second playoff appearance since the 1996-97 season.

One of only three men in the history of the NHL to have played in and coached 800 or more games, Quenneville is the winningest coach in Blues history, having compiled a 307-191-95 record. He was awarded the 2000 Jack Adams Trophy as the league's top coach. Quenneville was drafted by the Toronto Maple Leafs in the first round (21st overall) of the 1978 NHL Entry Draft. He spent 13 seasons as an NHL defenseman, netting 54 goals, 136 assists, 190 points and 705 penalty minutes in 803 career games with the Toronto Maple Leafs, Colorado Rockies, New Jersey Devils, Hartford Whalers and Washington Capitals.

Quenneville retired as an active player after the 1991-92 season, when he served as a player-coach for the American Hockey League's St. John's Maple Leafs. Quenneville broke into coaching with the AHL's Springfield Indians before serving as an assistant coach for the Quebec Nordiques/Colorado Avalanche organization for two and a half seasons. He helped Colorado capture the 1996 Stanley Cup in that position before accepting his first NHL head coaching job with St. Louis for the 1996-97 campaign.

Coaching Record

			Regular Season				Playoffs			
Season	Team	League	GC	W	L	O/T	GC	W	L	T
1993-94	Springfield	AHL	80	29	38	13	6	2	4	....
1996-97	**St. Louis**	**NHL**	**40**	**18**	**15**	**7**	**6**	**2**	**4**	....
1997-98	**St. Louis**	**NHL**	**82**	**45**	**29**	**8**	**10**	**6**	**4**	....
1998-99	**St. Louis**	**NHL**	**82**	**37**	**32**	**13**	**13**	**6**	**7**	....
99-2000	**St. Louis**	**NHL**	**82**	**51**	**19**	**12**	**7**	**3**	**4**	....
2000-01	**St. Louis**	**NHL**	**82**	**43**	**22**	**17**	**15**	**9**	**6**	....
2001-02	**St. Louis**	**NHL**	**82**	**43**	**27**	**12**	**10**	**5**	**5**	....
2002-03	**St. Louis**	**NHL**	**82**	**41**	**24**	**17**	**7**	**3**	**4**	....
2003-04	**St. Louis**	**NHL**	**61**	**29**	**23**	**9**	....	....	....	....
2004-05	**Colorado**				SEASON CANCELLED					
2005-06	**Colorado**	**NHL**	**82**	**43**	**30**	**9**	**9**	**4**	**5**	....
2006-07	**Colorado**	**NHL**	**82**	**44**	**31**	**7**	....	....	....	....
2007-08	**Colorado**	**NHL**	**82**	**44**	**31**	**7**	**10**	**4**	**6**	....
2008-09	**Chicago**	**NHL**	**78**	**45**	**22**	**11**	**17**	**9**	**8**	....
2009-10♦	**Chicago**	**NHL**	**82**	**52**	**22**	**8**	**22**	**16**	**6**	....
	NHL Totals		**999**	**535**	**327**	**137**	**126**	**67**	**59**	....

♦ Stanley Cup win.
Won Jack Adams Award (2000)

2009-10 Scoring

* – rookie

Regular Season

Pos	#	Player	Team	GP	G	A	Pts	TOI	+/–	PIM	PP	SH	GW	S	%
R	88	Patrick Kane	CHI	82	30	58	88	19:11	16	20	9	0	6	261	11.5
D	2	Duncan Keith	CHI	82	14	55	69	26:35	21	51	3	1	1	213	6.6
C	19	Jonathan Toews	CHI	76	25	43	68	20:00	22	47	9	1	3	202	12.4
R	10	Patrick Sharp	CHI	82	25	41	66	18:07	24	28	4	2	4	266	9.4
R	81	Marian Hossa	CHI	57	24	27	51	18:43	24	18	2	5	2	199	12.1
R	32	Kris Versteeg	CHI	79	20	24	44	15:43	8	35	4	3	4	184	10.9
R	22	Troy Brouwer	CHI	78	22	18	40	16:22	9	66	7	1	7	116	19.0
L	16	Andrew Ladd	CHI	82	17	21	38	13:41	2	67	0	0	1	148	11.5
D	51	Brian Campbell	CHI	68	7	31	38	23:12	18	18	3	0	2	131	5.3
R	33	Dustin Byfuglien	CHI	82	17	17	34	16:25	–7	94	6	0	3	211	8.1
D	7	Brent Seabrook	CHI	78	4	26	30	23:13	20	59	0	0	2	129	3.1
C	11	John Madden	CHI	79	10	13	23	15:24	–2	12	0	0	0	127	7.9
C	82	Tomas Kopecky	CHI	74	10	11	21	9:28	0	28	1	0	2	95	10.5
C	46	Colin Fraser	CHI	70	7	12	19	9:35	6	44	0	0	0	92	7.6
D	8	Kim Johnsson	MIN	52	6	8	14	23:46	3	26	3	0	0	84	7.1
			CHI	8	1	2	3	16:24	7	4	0	0	0	10	10.0
			Total	60	7	10	17	22:47	10	30	3	0	0	94	7.4
D	4	Niklas Hjalmarsson	CHI	77	2	15	17	19:39	9	20	0	0	1	62	3.2
L	55	Ben Eager	CHI	60	7	9	16	8:19	9	120	0	0	2	68	10.3
C	36	Dave Bolland	CHI	39	6	10	16	17:21	5	28	1	0	0	52	11.5
D	6	Jordan Hendry	CHI	43	2	6	8	11:51	5	10	0	0	1	42	4.8
D	24	Nick Boynton	ANA	42	1	6	7	16:45	1	59	1	0	0	39	2.6
			CHI	7	0	1	1	15:56	4	12	0	0	0	11	0.0
			Total	49	1	7	8	16:38	5	71	1	0	0	50	2.0
D	5	Brent Sopel	CHI	73	1	7	8	14:51	3	34	0	0	0	48	2.1
L	29	* Bryan Bickell	CHI	16	3	1	4	9:35	4	5	0	0	1	20	15.0
R	37	Adam Burish	CHI	13	1	3	4	8:46	2	14	0	0	0	9	11.1
C	28	* Jacob Dowell	CHI	3	1	1	2	6:56	1	5	0	0	0	4	25.0
R	20	Jack Skille	CHI	6	1	1	2	7:39	–3	0	0	0	0	9	11.1
L	52	* Radek Smolenak	CHI	1	0	0	0	4:41	0	5	0	0	0	1	0.0

Goaltending

No.	Goaltender	GPI	Mins	Avg	W	L	OT	EN	SO	GA	SA	S%	G	A	PIM
31	Antti Niemi	39	2190	2.25	26	7	4	2	7	82	936	.912	0	1	0
39	Cristobal Huet	48	2731	2.50	26	14	4	1	4	114	1083	.895	0	0	4
50	* Corey Crawford	1	59	3.05	0	1	0	1	0	3	35	.914	0	0	0
	Totals	**82**	**5013**	**2.43**	**52**	**22**	**8**	**4**	**11**	**203**	**2058**	**.901**			

Playoffs

Pos	#	Player	Team	GP	G	A	Pts	TOI	+/–	PIM	PP	SH	GW	OT	S	%
C	19	Jonathan Toews	CHI	22	7	22	29	20:58	–1	4	5	0	3	0	58	12.1
R	88	Patrick Kane	CHI	22	10	18	28	18:54	–2	6	1	1	1	1	64	15.6
R	10	Patrick Sharp	CHI	22	11	11	22	17:51	10	16	3	1	1	0	76	14.5
D	2	Duncan Keith	CHI	22	2	15	17	28:11	2	10	0	0	0	0	61	3.3
R	33	Dustin Byfuglien	CHI	22	11	5	16	16:15	–4	20	5	0	5	1	45	24.4
C	36	Dave Bolland	CHI	22	8	8	16	18:39	6	30	2	2	1	0	35	22.9
R	81	Marian Hossa	CHI	22	3	12	15	18:25	7	25	0	0	1	1	73	4.1
R	32	Kris Versteeg	CHI	22	6	8	14	17:12	4	14	0	0	2	0	55	10.9
D	7	Brent Seabrook	CHI	22	4	7	11	24:10	8	14	1	0	0	0	39	10.3
R	22	Troy Brouwer	CHI	19	4	4	8	11:01	–1	8	0	0	0	0	21	19.0
D	4	Niklas Hjalmarsson	CHI	22	1	7	8	21:00	9	6	0	0	0	0	17	5.9
C	82	Tomas Kopecky	CHI	17	4	2	6	13:34	2	8	1	0	1	0	28	14.3
L	16	Andrew Ladd	CHI	19	3	3	6	12:47	4	12	0	0	0	0	23	13.0
D	5	Brent Sopel	CHI	22	1	5	6	18:29	7	8	0	0	0	0	16	6.3
D	51	Brian Campbell	CHI	19	1	4	5	19:34	11	2	0	0	0	0	23	4.3
L	55	Ben Eager	CHI	18	1	2	3	6:02	2	20	0	0	1	0	13	7.7
C	11	John Madden	CHI	22	1	1	2	11:34	–2	2	0	0	0	0	24	4.2
L	29	* Bryan Bickell	CHI	4	0	1	1	13:14	3	2	0	0	0	0	3	0.0
D	24	Nick Boynton	CHI	3	0	0	0	8:22	2	2	0	0	0	0	2	0.0
C	46	Colin Fraser	CHI	3	0	0	0	8:23	0	0	0	0	0	0	1	0.0
R	37	Adam Burish	CHI	15	0	0	0	5:34	–1	2	0	0	0	0	15	0.0
D	6	Jordan Hendry	CHI	15	0	0	0	8:08	–4	2	0	0	0	0	8	0.0

Goaltending

No.	Goaltender	GPI	Mins	Avg	W	L	EN	SO	GA	SA	S%	G	A	PIM
39	Cristobal Huet	1	20	0.00	0	0	0	0	0	3	1.000	0	0	0
31	Antti Niemi	22	1322	2.63	16	6	4	2	58	645	.910	0	0	2
	Totals	**22**	**1347**	**2.76**	**16**	**6**	**4**	**2**	**62**	**652**	**.905**			

Coaching History

Pete Muldoon, 1926-27; Barney Stanley and Hugh Lehman, 1927-28; Herb Gardiner and Dick Irvin, 1928-29; Tom Shaughnessy and Bill Tobin, 1929-30; Dick Irvin, 1930-31; Bill Tobin, 1931-32; Emil Iverson, Godfrey Matheson and Tommy Gorman, 1932-33; Tommy Gorman, 1933-34; Clem Loughlin, 1934-35 to 1936-37; Bill Stewart, 1937-38; Bill Stewart and Paul Thompson, 1938-39; Paul Thompson, 1939-40 to 1943-44; Paul Thompson and Johnny Gottselig, 1944-45; Johnny Gottselig, 1945-46, 1946-47; Johnny Gottselig and Charlie Conacher, 1947-48; Charlie Conacher, 1948-49, 1949-50; Ebbie Goodfellow, 1950-51, 1951-52; Sid Abel, 1952-53, 1953-54; Frank Eddolls, 1954-55; Dick Irvin, 1955-56; Tommy Ivan, 1956-57; Tommy Ivan and Rudy Pilous, 1957-58; Rudy Pilous, 1958-59 to 1962-63; Billy Reay, 1963-64 to 1975-76; Billy Reay and Bill White, 1976-77; Bob Pulford, 1977-78, 1978-79; Eddie Johnston, 1979-80; Keith Magnuson, 1980-81; Keith Magnuson and Bob Pulford, 1981-82; Orval Tessier, 1982-83, 1983-84; Orval Tessier and Bob Pulford, 1984-85; Bob Pulford, 1985-86, 1986-87; Bob Murdoch, 1987-88; Mike Keenan, 1988-89 to 1991-92; Darryl Sutter, 1992-93 to 1994-95; Craig Hartsburg, 1995-96 to 1997-98; Dirk Graham and Lorne Molleken, 1998-99; Lorne Molleken and Bob Pulford, 1999-2000; Alpo Suhonen, 2000-01; Brian Sutter, 2001-02 to 2004-05; Trent Yawney, 2005-06; Trent Yawney and Denis Savard, 2006-07; Denis Savard, 2007-08; Denis Savard and Joel Quenneville, 2008-09; Joel Quenneville, 2009-10 to date.

Club Records

Team

(Figures in brackets for season records are games played; records for fewest points, wins, ties, losses, goals, goals against are for 70 or more games)

Record		
Most Points	112	2009-10 (82)
Most Wins	52	2009-10 (82)
Most Ties	23	1973-74 (78)
Most Losses	56	2005-06 (82)
Most Goals	351	1985-86 (80)
Most Goals Against	363	1981-82 (80)
Fewest Points	31	1953-54 (70)
Fewest Wins	12	1953-54 (70)
Fewest Ties	6	1989-90 (80)
Fewest Losses	14	1973-74 (78)
Fewest Goals	*133	1953-54 (70)
Fewest Goals Against	164	1973-74 (78)
Longest Winning Streak		
Overall	9	Dec. 7-28/08
Home	13	Nov. 11-Dec. 20/70
Away	7	Dec. 9-29/64
Longest Undefeated Streak		
Overall	15	Jan. 14-Feb. 16/67 (12 wins, 3 ties), Oct. 29-Dec. 3/75 (6 wins, 9 ties)
Home	18	Oct. 11-Dec. 20/70 (16 wins, 2 ties)
Away	12	Nov. 2-Dec. 16/67 (6 wins, 6 ties)
Longest Losing Streak		
Overall	12	Feb. 25-Mar. 25/51
Home	10	Jan. 29-Mar. 21/28
Away	19	Nov. 10/03-Jan. 29/04
Longest Winless Streak		
Overall	21	Dec. 17/50-Jan. 28/51 (18 losses, 3 ties)
Home	15	Dec. 16/28-Feb. 28/29 (11 losses, 4 ties)
Away	22	Dec. 19/50-Mar. 25/51 (20 losses, 2 ties)
Most Shutouts, Season	15	1969-70 (76)
Most PIM, Season	2,663	1991-92 (80)
Most Goals, Game	12	Jan. 30/69 (Chi. 12 at Phi. 0)

Individual

Record		
Most Seasons	22	Stan Mikita
Most Games	1,394	Stan Mikita
Most Goals, Career	604	Bobby Hull
Most Assists, Career	926	Stan Mikita
Most Points, Career	1,467	Stan Mikita (541G, 926A)
Most PIM, Career	1,495	Chris Chelios
Most Shutouts, Career	74	Tony Esposito
Longest Consecutive Games Streak	884	Steve Larmer (Oct. 6/82-Apr. 15/93)
Most Goals, Season	58	Bobby Hull (1968-69)
Most Assists, Season	87	Denis Savard (1981-82, 1987-88)
Most Points, Season	131	Denis Savard (1987-88; 44G, 87A)
Most PIM, Season	408	Mike Peluso (1991-92)
Most Points, Defenseman, Season	85	Doug Wilson (1981-82; 39G, 46A)
Most Points, Center, Season	131	Denis Savard (1987-88; 44G, 87A)
Most Points, Right Wing, Season	101	Steve Larmer (1990-91; 44G, 57A)
Most Points, Left Wing, Season	107	Bobby Hull (1968-69; 58G, 49A)
Most Points, Rookie, Season	90	Steve Larmer (1982-83; 43G, 47A)
Most Shutouts, Season	15	Tony Esposito (1969-70)
Most Goals, Game	5	Grant Mulvey (Feb. 3/82)
Most Assists, Game	6	Pat Stapleton (Mar. 30/69)
Most Points, Game	7	Max Bentley (Jan. 28/43; 4G, 3A), Grant Mulvey (Feb. 3/82; 5G, 2A)

* NHL Record.

General Managers' History

Major Frederic McLaughlin, 1926-27 to 1941-42; Bill Tobin, 1942-43 to 1953-54; Tommy Ivan, 1954-55 to 1976-77; Bob Pulford, 1977-78 to 1989-90; Mike Keenan, 1990-91, 1991-92; Mike Keenan and Bob Pulford, 1992-93; Bob Pulford, 1993-94 to 1996-97; Bob Murray, 1997-98, 1998-99; Bob Murray and Bob Pulford, 1999-2000; Mike Smith, 2000-01 to 2002-03; Mike Smith and Bob Pulford, 2003-04; Bob Pulford, 2004-05; Dale Tallon, 2005-06 to 2008-09; Stan Bowman, 2009-10 to date.

Retired Numbers

1	Glenn Hall	1957-1967
3	Pierre Pilote	1955-1968
	Keith Magnuson	1969-1980
9	Bobby Hull	1957-1972
18	Denis Savard	1980-1990, 1995-1997
21	Stan Mikita	1958-1980
35	Tony Esposito	1969-1984

All-time Record vs. Other Clubs

Regular Season

	At Home								On Road								Total							
	GP	W	L	T	OL	GF	GA	PTS	GP	W	L	T	OL	GF	GA	PTS	GP	W	L	T	OL	GF	GA	PTS
Anaheim	34	16	16	2	0	91	85	34	32	9	20	3	0	64	91	21	66	25	36	5	0	155	176	55
Atlanta	4	3	1	0	0	13	7	6	6	4	2	0	0	18	19	8	10	7	3	0	0	31	26	14
Boston	289	148	95	45	1	935	778	342	287	90	163	34	0	817	1033	214	576	238	258	79	1	1752	1811	556
Buffalo	53	28	18	6	1	169	142	63	55	14	34	7	0	140	204	35	108	42	52	13	1	309	346	98
Calgary	71	32	26	13	0	232	206	77	73	29	30	13	1	222	220	72	144	61	56	26	1	454	426	149
Carolina	31	17	10	3	1	120	88	38	32	12	16	4	0	98	106	28	63	29	26	7	1	218	194	66
Colorado	51	28	17	3	3	173	157	62	49	17	25	6	1	155	188	41	100	45	42	9	4	328	345	103
Columbus	28	16	9	1	2	85	68	35	29	13	12	1	3	95	100	30	57	29	21	2	5	180	168	65
Dallas	120	70	35	15	0	442	318	155	122	48	56	16	2	376	419	114	242	118	91	31	2	818	737	269
Detroit	356	161	139	51	5	1067	1011	378	353	105	213	33	2	879	1213	245	709	266	352	84	7	1946	2224	623
Edmonton	54	28	15	7	4	203	177	67	55	23	26	5	1	177	194	52	109	51	41	12	5	380	371	119
Florida	12	5	4	2	1	38	37	13	11	7	2	1	1	41	22	16	23	12	6	3	2	79	59	29
Los Angeles	85	42	33	9	1	293	241	94	84	37	37	8	2	275	284	84	169	79	70	17	3	568	525	178
Minnesota	18	7	9	1	1	40	50	16	18	5	9	0	4	46	55	14	36	12	18	1	5	86	105	30
Montreal	275	95	125	55	0	736	764	245	278	54	174	48	2	657	1075	158	553	149	299	103	2	1393	1839	403
Nashville	35	20	12	1	2	97	90	43	34	14	13	3	4	97	108	35	69	34	25	4	6	194	198	78
New Jersey	49	26	12	10	1	186	133	63	50	17	21	11	1	147	153	46	99	43	33	21	2	333	286	109
NY Islanders	50	26	18	5	1	165	168	58	49	14	20	15	0	146	173	43	99	40	38	20	1	311	341	101
NY Rangers	289	130	115	43	1	876	797	304	287	113	119	55	0	810	847	281	576	243	234	98	1	1686	1644	585
Ottawa	10	6	2	2	0	24	21	14	12	7	5	0	0	35	38	14	22	13	7	2	0	59	59	28
Philadelphia	62	27	16	19	0	212	176	73	64	16	37	11	0	164	210	43	126	43	53	30	0	376	386	116
Phoenix	58	32	14	10	2	212	143	76	60	23	29	5	3	187	192	54	118	55	43	15	5	399	335	130
Pittsburgh	62	40	11	10	1	244	163	91	61	24	29	7	1	196	216	56	123	64	40	17	2	440	379	147
St. Louis	136	77	40	18	1	493	387	173	133	50	63	17	3	406	441	120	269	127	103	35	4	899	828	293
San Jose	35	16	15	2	2	107	113	36	36	13	17	3	3	98	105	32	71	29	32	5	5	205	218	68
Tampa Bay	16	10	4	2	0	54	36	22	13	5	4	3	1	35	32	14	29	15	8	5	1	89	68	36
Toronto	320	158	120	42	0	974	834	358	317	99	164	54	0	832	1079	252	637	257	284	96	0	1806	1913	610
Vancouver	81	50	21	7	3	292	195	110	82	25	40	15	2	227	247	67	163	75	61	22	5	519	442	177
Washington	42	23	12	6	1	159	124	53	43	16	22	5	0	133	152	37	85	39	34	11	1	292	276	90
Defunct Clubs	139	79	40	20	0	408	268	178	140	52	67	21	0	316	346	125	279	131	107	41	0	724	614	303
Totals	**2865**	**1416**	**1004**	**410**	**35**	**9140**	**7777**	**3277**	**2865**	**955**	**1469**	**404**	**37**	**7889**	**9562**	**2351**	**5730**	**2371**	**2473**	**814**	**72**	**17029**	**17339**	**5628**

Playoffs

	Series	W	L	GP	W	L	T	GF	GA	Last Mtg.	Rnd.	Result
Boston	6	1	5	22	5	16	1	63	97	1978	QF	L 0-4
Buffalo	2	0	2	9	1	8	0	17	36	1980	QF	L 0-4
Calgary	4	2	2	18	9	9	0	54	53	2009	CQF	W 4-2
Colorado	2	0	2	12	4	8	0	28	49	1997	CQF	L 2-4
Dallas	6	4	2	33	19	14	0	120	118	1991	DSF	L 2-4
Detroit	15	8	7	74	39	35	0	220	209	2009	CF	L 1-4
Edmonton	4	1	3	20	8	12	0	77	102	1992	CF	W 4-0
Los Angeles	1	1	0	5	4	1	0	10	7	1974	QF	W 4-1
Montreal	17	5	12	81	29	50	2	185	261	1976	QF	L 0-4
Nashville	1	1	0	6	4	2	0	17	15	2010	CQF	W 4-2
NY Islanders	2	0	2	6	0	6	0	6	21	1979	QF	L 0-4
NY Rangers	5	4	1	24	14	10	0	66	54	1973	SF	W 4-1
Philadelphia	2	2	0	10	8	2	0	45	30	2010	F	W 4-2
Pittsburgh	2	1	1	8	4	4	0	24	23	1992	F	L 0-4
St. Louis	10	7	3	50	28	22	0	171	142	2002	CQF	L 1-4
San Jose	1	1	0	4	4	0	0	13	7	2010	CF	W 4-0
Toronto	9	3	6	38	15	22	1	89	111	1995	CQF	W 4-3
Vancouver	4	3	1	21	13	8	0	70	61	2010	CSF	W 4-2
Defunct Clubs	4	2	2	9	5	3	1	16	15			
Totals	**97**	**46**	**51**	**450**	**213**	**232**	**5**	**1291**	**1411**			

Calgary totals include Atlanta Flames, 1972-73 to 1979-80.
Colorado totals include Quebec, 1979-80 to 1994-95.
Carolina totals include Hartford, 1979-80 to 1996-97.
Dallas totals include Minnesota North Stars, 1967-68 to 1992-93.
New Jersey totals include Kansas City, 1974-75, 1975-76, and Colorado Rockies, 1976-77 to 1981-82.
Phoenix totals include Winnipeg, 1979-80 to 1995-96.

Playoff Results 2010-2006

Year	Round	Opponent	Result	GF	GA
2010	**F**	**Philadelphia**	**W 4-2**	**25**	**22**
	CF	San Jose	W 4-0	13	7
	CSF	Vancouver	W 4-2	23	18
	CQF	Nashville	W 4-2	17	15
2009	CF	Detroit	L 1-4	10	19
	CSF	Vancouver	W 4-2	23	19
	CQF	Calgary	W 4-2	21	16

Abbreviations: Round: F - Final; **CF** - conference final; **CSF** - conference semi-final; **CQF** - conference quarter-final; **DSF** - division semi-final; **SF** - semi-final; **QF** - quarter-final.

2009-10 Results

Oct.	2	Florida	3-4†		3	Anaheim	5-2
	3	at Florida	4-0		5	Minnesota	4-1
	8	at Detroit	2-3		7	at Boston	5-2
	10	Colorado	4-3†		9	at Minnesota	5-6†
	12	Calgary	6-5*		10	Anaheim	1-3
	14	Edmonton	4-3		14	Columbus	3-0
	15	at Nashville	3-1		16	at Columbus	6-5
	17	Dallas	3-4		17	at Detroit	4-3†
	21	Vancouver	2-3		19	at Ottawa	1-4
	24	Nashville	2-0		21	at Calgary	3-1
	26	Minnesota	3-1		23	at Vancouver	1-5
	29	at Nashville	0-2		26	at Edmonton	4-2
	30	Montreal	3-2		28	at San Jose	4-3*
Nov.	5	at Phoenix	1-3		30	at Carolina	2-4
	6	at Colorado	3-4†	**Feb.**	3	St. Louis	2-3
	9	Los Angeles	4-1		5	Phoenix	1-2†
	11	Colorado	3-2†		6	at St. Louis	2-1
	13	Toronto	3-2		9	Dallas	4-3†
	15	San Jose	4-3*		13	Atlanta	5-4†
	19	at Calgary	7-1		14	at Columbus	5-4†
	21	at Edmonton	5-2	**Mar.**	2	at NY Islanders	3-5
	22	at Vancouver	1-0		3	Edmonton	5-2
	25	at San Jose	7-2		5	Vancouver	6-3
	27	at Anaheim	0-3		7	Detroit	4-5
	28	at Los Angeles	1-2†		10	Los Angeles	3-2*
Dec.	1	Columbus	4-3†		13	at Philadelphia	2-3
	4	Nashville	1-4		14	Washington	3-4*
	5	at Pittsburgh	2-1*		17	at Anaheim	2-4
	9	NY Rangers	2-1*		18	at Los Angeles	3-0
	11	at Buffalo	1-2		20	at Phoenix	4-5†
	13	Tampa Bay	4-0		23	Phoenix	2-0
	16	St. Louis	3-0		25	at Columbus	3-8
	18	Boston	5-4†		28	Columbus	2-4
	20	Detroit	3-0		30	at St. Louis	2-4
	22	San Jose	2-3		31	at Minnesota	4-0
	23	at Detroit	3-0	**Apr.**	2	at New Jersey	2-1†
	26	at Nashville	4-1		4	Calgary	4-1
	27	Nashville	5-4		6	at Dallas	5-2
	29	at Dallas	4-5		7	St. Louis	6-5
	31	New Jersey	5-1		9	at Colorado	5-2
Jan.	2	at St. Louis	6-3		11	Detroit	2-3*

* – Overtime † – Shootout

Entry Draft Selections 2010-1996

Name in bold denotes played in NHL.

2010
Pick
- 24 Kevin Hayes
- 35 Ludvig Rensfeldt
- 54 Justin Holl
- 58 Kent Simpson
- 60 Stephen Johns
- 90 Joakim Nordstrom
- 120 Rob Flick
- 151 Mirko Hofflin
- 180 Nick Mattson
- 191 Mac Carruth

2009
Pick
- 28 Dylan Olsen
- 59 Brandon Pirri
- 89 Dan Delisle
- 119 Byron Froese
- 149 Marcus Kruger
- 177 David Pacan
- 195 Paul Phillips
- 209 David Gilbert

2008
Pick
- 11 Kyle Beach
- 68 Shawn Lalonde
- 132 Teigan Zahn
- 162 Jonathan Carlsson
- 169 Ben Smith
- 179 Braden Birch
- 192 Joe Gleason

2007
Pick
- 1 **Patrick Kane**
- 38 Bill Sweatt
- 56 Akim Aliu
- 69 Maxime Tanguay
- 86 Josh Unice
- 126 Joseph Lavin
- 156 Richard Greenop

2006
Pick
- 3 **Jonathan Toews**
- 33 Igor Makarov
- 61 Simon Danis-Pepin
- 76 Tony Lagerstrom
- 95 Ben Shutron
- 96 Joe Palmer
- 156 Jan-Mikael Juutilainen
- 169 Chris Auger
- 186 Peter Leblanc

2005
Pick
- 7 **Jack Skille**
- 43 **Michael Blunden**
- 54 Dan Bertram
- 68 Evan Brophey
- 108 **Niklas Hjalmarsson**
- 113 Nathan Davis
- 117 Denis Istomin
- 134 Brennan Turner
- 167 Joe Fallon
- 188 Joe Charlebois
- 202 David Kuchejda
- 203 Adam Hobson

2004
Pick
- 3 **Cam Barker**
- 32 **Dave Bolland**
- 41 **Bryan Bickell**
- 45 Ryan Garlock
- 54 Jakub Sindel
- 68 **Adam Berti**
- 120 Mitch Maunu
- 123 Karel Hromas
- 131 Trevor Kell
- 140 **Jake Dowell**
- 165 Scott McCulloch
- 196 **Petri Kontiola**
- 214 **Troy Brouwer**
- 223 Jared Walker
- 229 Eric Hunter
- 256 Matthew Ford
- 260 Marko Anttila

2003
Pick
- 14 **Brent Seabrook**
- 52 **Corey Crawford**
- 59 **Michal Barinka**
- 151 Lasse Kukkonen
- 156 Alexei Ivanov
- 181 Johan Andersson
- 211 **Mike Brodeur**
- 245 **Dustin Byfuglien**
- 275 Michael Grenzy
- 282 **Chris Porter**

2002
Pick
- 21 **Anton Babchuk**
- 54 **Duncan Keith**
- 93 Alexander Kojevnikov
- 128 **Matt Ellison**
- 156 **James Wisniewski**
- 188 Kevin Kantee
- 219 Tyson Kellerman
- 251 Jason Kostadine
- 282 **Adam Burish**

2001
Pick
- 9 **Tuomo Ruutu**
- 29 **Adam Munro**
- 59 **Matt Keith**
- 73 **Craig Anderson**
- 104 Brent MacLellan
- 115 Vladimir Gusev
- 119 Alexei Zotkin
- 142 Tommi Jaminki
- 174 Alexander Golovin
- 186 Petr Puncochar
- 205 Teemu Jaaskelainen
- 216 Oleg Minakov
- 268 Jeff Miles

2000
Pick
- 10 **Mikhail Yakubov**
- 11 **Pavel Vorobiev**
- 49 **Jonas Nordqvist**
- 74 **Igor Radulov**
- 106 Scott Balan
- 117 **Olli Malmivaara**
- 151 Alexander Barkunov
- 177 Michael Ayers
- 193 Joey Martin
- 207 Cliff Loya
- 225 Vladislav Luchkin
- 240 **Adam Berkhoel**
- 262 Peter Flache
- 271 **Reto Von Arx**
- 291 Arne Ramholt

1999
Pick
- 23 **Steve McCarthy**
- 46 Dimitri Levinski
- 63 Stepan Mokhov
- 134 Michael Jacobsen
- 165 **Michael Leighton**
- 194 Mattias Wennerberg
- 195 Yorick Treille
- 223 Andrew Carver

1998
Pick
- 8 **Mark Bell**
- 94 Matthias Trattnig
- 156 **Kent Huskins**
- 158 Jari Viuhkola
- 166 Jonathan Pelletier
- 183 **Tyler Arnason**
- 210 Sean Griffin
- 238 Alexandre Couture
- 240 Andrei Yershov

1997
Pick
- 13 **Daniel Cleary**
- 16 **Ty Jones**
- 39 **Jeremy Reich**
- 67 Mike Souza
- 110 **Ben Simon**
- 120 Peter Gardiner
- 130 **Kyle Calder**
- 147 Heath Gordon
- 174 Jerad Smith
- 204 Sergei Shikhanov
- 230 Chris Feil

1996
Pick
- 31 **Remi Royer**
- 42 **Jeff Paul**
- 46 Geoff Peters
- 130 Andy Johnson
- 184 Mike Vellinga
- 210 Chris Twerdun
- 236 Andrei Kozyrev

Captains' History

Dick Irvin, 1926-27 to 1928-29; Duke Dukowski, 1929-30; Ty Arbour, 1930-31; Cy Wentworth, 1931-32; Helge Bostrom, 1932-33; Charlie Gardiner, 1933-34; no captain, 1934-35; Johnny Gottselig, 1935-36 to 1939-40; Earl Seibert, 1940-41, 1941-42; Doug Bentley, 1942-43, 1943-44; Clint Smith 1944-45; John Mariucci, 1945-46; Red Hamill, 1946-47; John Mariucci, 1947-48; Gaye Stewart, 1948-49; Doug Bentley, 1949-50; Jack Stewart, 1950-51, 1951-52; Bill Gadsby, 1952-53, 1953-54; Gus Mortson, 1954-55 to 1956-57; no captain, 1957-58; Ed Litzenberger, 1958-59 to 1960-61; Pierre Pilote, 1961-62 to 1967-68, no captain, 1968-69; Pat Stapleton, 1969-70; no captain, 1970-71 to 1974-75; Stan Mikita and Pit Martin, 1975-76; Stan Mikita, Pit Martin and Keith Magnuson, 1976-77; Keith Magnuson, 1977-78, 1978-79; Keith Magnuson and Terry Ruskowski, 1979-80; Terry Ruskowski, 1980-81, 1981-82; Darryl Sutter, 1982-83 to 1984-85; Darryl Sutter and Bob Murray, 1985-86; Darryl Sutter, 1986-87; no captain, 1987-88; Denis Savard and Dirk Graham, 1988-89; Dirk Graham, 1989-90 to 1994-95; Chris Chelios, 1995-96 to 1998-99; Doug Gilmour, 1999-2000; Tony Amonte, 2000-01, 2001-02; Alex Zhamnov, 2002-03, 2003-04; Adrian Aucoin and Martin Lapointe, 2005-06, 2006-07; no captain, 2007-08; Jonathan Toews, 2008-09 to date.

Stan Bowman
General Manager
Born: Montreal, Que., June 28, 1973.

Stan Bowman was named general manager of the Chicago Blackhawks on July 14, 2009. In his first season on the job in 2009-10, the Blackhawks won the Stanley Cup for the first time since 1961. Prior to being named to the position, Bowman had served for eight years in the Blackhawks operations department, including two seasons as assistant general manager from 2007 to 2009.

Bowman originally joined the Blackhawks in 2001, serving for four seasons as special assistant to the general manager before being promoted to director of hockey operations, a role he served in for two years (2005 to 2007). As assistant general manager, Bowman attended to the day-to-day administration of the Blackhawks' hockey operations department with his primary responsibilities including all CBA-related matters such as contract negotiations, free agency, salary arbitration, player movement and player assignment. He also tracked the progress of the Blackhawks prospects by working closely with the staff of the club's minor league affiliate in Rockford, while also assisting with player evaluation, prospect development and professional and amateur scouting.

Bowman played an integral part in the free agent signings of Marian Hossa, Tomas Kopecky and John Madden in 2009 while weighing in on the decision making that brought players such as Patrick Sharp, Kris Versteeg and Andrew Ladd to the club in trades.

Bowman graduated from the University of Notre Dame in 1995 with degrees in Finance and Computer Applications. He was born in Montreal where his father, legendary National Hockey League fixture and current Blackhawks senior advisor Scotty Bowman was coaching at the time.

Club Directory

United Center

Chicago Blackhawks
United Center
1901 W. Madison Street
Chicago, IL 60612
Phone **312/455-7000**
FAX 312/455-7041
www.chicagoblackhawks.com
Capacity: 19,717

Management
Chairman	W. Rockwell "Rocky" Wirtz
President	John F. McDonough
Senior Vice President, Business Operations	Jay Blunk
General Manager	Stan Bowman
Assistant General Manager	Kevin Cheveldayoff
Sr. Director, Hockey Admin/Asst. to the President	Al MacIsaac
Sr. Advisor, Hockey Operations	Scotty Bowman
Sr. Exec. Asst. to GM / Hockey Operations	Julie Kavanaugh
Executive Asst. to the President	Jillian Smith
Exec. Asst. to the Sr. V.P., Business Operations	Kayla Kindred

Coaching Staff
Head Coach	Joel Quenneville
Assistant Coaches	Mike Haviland, Mike Kitchen
Goaltending Coach	Stephane Waite
Strength & Conditioning Coach	Paul Goodman
Skating Coach	Paul Vincent

Training/Equipment Staff
Head Athletic Trainer	Mike Gapski
Assistant Athletic Trainer	Jeff Thomas
Massage Therapist	Pawel Prylinski
Equipment Manager	Troy Parchman
Assistant Equipment Manager	Clint Reif
Equipment Assistant	Jim Heintzelman

Medical
Head Team Physicians	Drs. Michael Terry, William Harper
Team Physicians	Drs. Sherwin Ho, Martin Leland, Ari Levy, Bradley Merk, Todd Stern
Team Dentists	Drs. Russ Baer, Anthony LaVacca, Martin Marcus
Mental Skills Coach	James Gary

Hockey Operations and Scouting
Director, Player Personnel	Marc Bergevin
General Manager of Minor League Affiliations	Mark Bernard
Director, Player Development	Norm MacIver
Director, Amateur Scouting	Mark Kelley
Director, Player Recruitment	Ron Anderson
Developmental Goalie Coach	Wade Flaherty
Senior Director, Team Services	Tony Ommen
Coordinator, Hockey Operations	Ian Gentile
Chief Scout	Bruce Franklin
Amateur Scouts	Gord Donnelly, Mike Doneghy, Michel Dumas, Tim Keon, Darrell May, Peter Nevin, Jad Ramsay
Head European Scout	Niklas Blomgren
European Amateur Scouts	Karel Pavlik, Ruslan Shabanov
Pro Scouts	Dennis Bonvie, Martin Lapointe, Barry Smith, Ryan Stewart
European Pro Scout	Mats Hallin

Media Relations
Directors, Media Relations / Public Relations	Brandon Faber / Adam Rogowin
Coordinator, Media Relations	Paul Kennedy
Coordinator, Team Photography	Chase Agnello-Dean

Broadcasters
Television Play-By-Play / Analyst	Pat Foley / Ed Olczyk
Radio Play-By-Play / Analyst / Host	John Wiedeman / Troy Murray / Judd Sirott

Community Relations
Sr. Director, Market Dev. and Community Affairs	Pete Hassen
Director / Assistant Youth Hockey	Annie Camins / Ashley Hinton
Coordinator, Community Relations	Elizabeth Queen
Mascot Coordinator	Joe Doyle

Corporate Sponsorships
Senior Director, Corporate Sponsorships	Steve Waight
Manager, Client Services	Kelly Smith
Account Execs., Sponsorships	Sara Bailey, Steve McNelley, Rich Sommers, Greg Zinsmeister

Finance
Director, Finance	TJ Skattum
Accounting Mgr. / Payroll Administrator	Michael Dorsch, Patricia Walsh

Human Resources
Director / Assistant, Human Resources	Marie Sutera / Kyleen King
Office Coordinator/Receptionist	Leanne Mayville

Marketing and Business Development
Sr. Exec. Director, Mktg. and Business Dev.	Dave Knickerbocker
Director, Advertising	Patrick Dahl
Graphic Designer	Chris Weibring
Editor/Motion Graphics Designer	Scott Hanson
Coordinator, Event Marketing	Brian Howe
Producer, New Media	Matthew Dominick
Assistants, Marketing	A.J. Dolan / Morgan Sharar-Stoppel

New Media and Publications
Director, New Media and Publications	Adam Kempenaar
Coordinator, Publications	John Sandberg
Assistant, New Media and Publications	Brad Boron
Team Historian	Bob Verdi

Tickets
Sr. Exec. Director, Ticketing & Business Dev.	Chris Werner
Executive Director, Ticket Operations	Jim Bare
Director, Ticket Sales and Service	Dan Rozenblat
Senior Manager, Customer Service	Julie Lovins
Manager, Season Ticket Services	Trisha Ithal
Manager, Group Sales and Special Projects	Steve DiLenardi
Ticket Operations Assistant	Allison Westfall
Customer Service Execs.	Brad Chase, Tracy Cunningham, T.R. Johnson, Janelle Miller, Shilpa Rupani
Sr. Customer Service Execs.	Liz Breuer, Kathie Raimondi, Aaron Salsbury
Senior Account Executive, Ticket Sales	Eric Dumais
Account Execs., Ticket / Group Sales	Andrew Roan, Jake Tuton, Nick Zombolas

Colorado Avalanche

2009-10 Results: 43w-30L-4oTL-5soL 95pts.
Second, Northwest Division

Bouncing back from a short stint in the minors, Chris Stewart would play 77 games for Colorado in 2009-10 and lead the team with 28 goals. His 36 assists and 64 points put him second behind Paul Stastny.

2010-11 Schedule

Oct.	Thu.	7	Chicago	Sat.	8	NY Islanders*
	Mon.	11	at Philadelphia	Mon.	10	Detroit
	Tue.	12	at Detroit	Wed.	12	at Chicago
	Fri.	15	at New Jersey	Fri.	14	at Minnesota
	Sat.	16	at NY Islanders	Tue.	18	Vancouver
	Mon.	18	at NY Rangers	Thu.	20	Nashville
	Thu.	21	San Jose	Sat.	22	Boston*
	Sat.	23	Los Angeles	Mon.	24	St. Louis
	Tue.	26	at Vancouver	Wed.	26	Phoenix
	Thu.	28	at Calgary	**Feb.** Tue.	1	at St. Louis
	Sat.	30	Columbus	Thu.	3	Minnesota
Nov.	Thu.	4	Vancouver	Sat.	5	Anaheim*
	Sat.	6	Dallas	Mon.	7	at Phoenix
	Tue.	9	Calgary	Wed.	9	at Minnesota
	Fri.	12	at Columbus	Fri.	11	at Columbus
	Sat.	13	at Detroit	Sat.	12	at Nashville
	Mon.	15	St. Louis	Mon.	14	Calgary
	Wed.	17	San Jose	Wed.	16	Pittsburgh
	Fri.	19	NY Rangers	Sat.	19	at San Jose
	Sat.	20	at Dallas	Wed.	23	Edmonton
	Wed.	24	at Vancouver	Sat.	26	at Los Angeles*
	Thu.	25	at Edmonton	Sun.	27	at Anaheim*
	Sat.	27	Minnesota	**Mar.** Tue.	1	at San Jose
	Tue.	30	Atlanta	Sat.	5	Edmonton
Dec.	Fri.	3	at Carolina	Tue.	8	at Minnesota
	Sat.	4	at Tampa Bay	Fri.	11	Anaheim
	Tue.	7	at Florida	Sat.	12	at Nashville
	Fri.	10	at Atlanta	Wed.	16	at Vancouver
	Sat.	11	at Washington	Thu.	17	at Calgary
	Mon.	13	Chicago	Sat.	19	at Edmonton
	Wed.	15	at Chicago	Tue.	22	Columbus
	Fri.	17	Ottawa	Thu.	24	Toronto
	Sun.	19	Montreal	Sat.	26	at Los Angeles*
	Tue.	21	Los Angeles	Mon.	28	at Anaheim
	Thu.	23	Minnesota	Thu.	31	Nashville
	Mon.	27	Detroit	**Apr.** Fri.	1	at Phoenix
	Thu.	30	at Edmonton	Sun.	3	Calgary
	Fri.	31	at Calgary	Tue.	5	at St. Louis
Jan.	Sun.	2	Vancouver	Thu.	7	at Dallas
	Tue.	4	Buffalo	Fri.	8	Dallas
	Thu.	6	Phoenix	Sun.	10	Edmonton*

* Denotes afternoon game.

Year-by-Year Record

Season	GP	Home W	L	T	OL	Road W	L	T	OL	Overall W	L	T	OL	GF	GA	Pts.	Finished	Playoff Result
2009-10	82	24	14	....	3	19	16	....	6	43	30	....	9	244	233	95	2nd, Northwest Div.	Lost Conf. Quarter-Final
2008-09	82	18	21	....	2	14	24	....	3	32	45	....	5	199	257	69	5th, Northwest Div.	Out of Playoffs
2007-08	82	27	12	....	2	17	19	....	5	44	31	....	7	231	219	95	2nd, Northwest Div.	Lost Conf. Semi-Final
2006-07	82	22	16	....	3	22	15	....	4	44	31	....	7	272	251	95	4th, Northwest Div.	Out of Playoffs
2005-06	82	25	10	....	6	18	20	....	3	43	30	....	9	283	257	95	2nd, Northwest Div.	Lost Conf. Semi-Final
2004-05	....																	
2003-04	82	19	14	6	2	21	8	7	5	40	22	13	7	236	198	100	2nd, Northwest Div.	Lost Conf. Semi-Final
2002-03	82	21	9	8	3	21	10	5	5	42	19	13	8	251	194	105	1st, Northwest Div.	Lost Conf. Quarter-Final
2001-02	82	24	12	4	1	21	16	4	0	45	28	8	1	212	169	99	1st, Northwest Div.	Lost Conf. Championship
2000-01	**82**	**28**	**6**	**5**	**2**	**24**	**10**	**5**	**2**	**52**	**16**	**10**	**4**	**270**	**192**	**118**	**1st, Northwest Div.**	**Won Stanley Cup**
1999-2000	82	25	12	4	0	17	16	7	1	42	28	11	1	233	201	96	1st, Northwest Div.	Lost Conf. Championship
1998-99	82	21	14	6		23	14	4		44	28	10		239	205	98	1st, Northwest Div.	Lost Conf. Championship
1997-98	82	21	10	10		18	16	7		39	26	17		231	205	95	1st, Pacific Div.	Lost Conf. Quarter-Final
1996-97	82	26	10	5		23	14	4		49	24	9		277	205	107	1st, Pacific Div.	Lost Conf. Championship
1995-96	**82**	**24**	**10**	**7**		**23**	**15**	**3**		**47**	**25**	**10**		**326**	**240**	**104**	**1st, Pacific Div.**	**Won Stanley Cup**
1994-95*	48	19	1	4		11	12	1		30	13	5		185	134	65	1st, Northeast Div.	Lost Conf. Quarter-Final
1993-94*	84	19	17	6		15	25	2		34	42	8		277	292	76	5th, Northeast Div.	Out of Playoffs
1992-93*	84	23	17	2		24	10	8		47	27	10		351	300	104	2nd, Adams Div.	Lost Div. Semi-Final
1991-92*	80	18	19	3		2	29	9		20	48	12		255	318	52	5th, Adams Div.	Out of Playoffs
1990-91*	80	9	23	8		7	27	6		16	50	14		236	354	46	5th, Adams Div.	Out of Playoffs
1989-90*	80	8	26	6		4	35	1		12	61	7		240	407	31	5th, Adams Div.	Out of Playoffs
1988-89*	80	16	20	4		11	26	3		27	46	7		269	342	61	5th, Adams Div.	Out of Playoffs
1987-88*	80	15	23	2		17	20	3		32	43	5		271	306	69	5th, Adams Div.	Out of Playoffs
1986-87*	80	20	13	7		11	26	3		31	39	10		267	276	72	4th, Adams Div.	Lost Div. Final
1985-86*	80	23	13	4		20	18	2		43	31	6		330	289	92	1st, Adams Div.	Lost Div. Semi-Final
1984-85*	80	24	12	4		17	18	5		41	30	9		323	275	91	2nd, Adams Div.	Lost Conf. Championship
1983-84*	80	24	11	5		18	17	5		42	28	10		360	278	94	3rd, Adams Div.	Lost Div. Final
1982-83*	80	23	10	7		11	24	5		34	34	12		343	336	80	4th, Adams Div.	Lost Div. Semi-Final
1981-82*	80	24	13	3		9	18	13		33	31	16		356	345	82	4th, Adams Div.	Lost Conf. Championship
1980-81*	80	18	11	11		12	21	7		30	32	18		314	318	78	4th, Adams Div.	Lost Prelim. Round
1979-80*	80	17	16	7		8	28	4		25	44	11		248	313	61	5th, Adams Div.	Out of Playoffs

* Quebec Nordiques

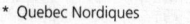

2010-11 Player Personnel

FORWARDS	HT	WT	S	Place of Birth	*Age	2009-10 Club
CARMAN, Michael	6-0	180	L	Augusta, GA	22	U. of Minnesota-Lake Erie
COHEN, Zach	6-3	208	L	Schaumburg, IL	23	Boston University-Lake Erie
DUCHENE, Matt	5-11	200	L	Haliburton, Ont.	19	Colorado
DUPUIS, Philippe	6-0	196	R	Laval, Que.	25	Colorado-Lake Erie
FRITSCHE, Tom	5-11	183	L	Parma, OH	24	Lake Erie
GALIARDI, T.J.	6-2	190	L	Calgary, Alta.	22	Colorado
HEJDUK, Milan	6-0	190	R	Usti nad Labem, Czech.	34	Colorado
JONES, David	6-2	210	R	Guelph, Ont.	26	Colorado
KOCI, David	6-6	238	L	Prague, Czech.	29	Colorado
MAULDIN, Greg	5-11	195	R	Boston, MA	28	NY Islanders-Bridgeport
McLEOD, Cody	6-2	210	L	Binscarth, Man.	26	Colorado
MERCIER, Justin	5-11	190	L	Erie, PA	23	Colorado-Lake Erie
MUELLER, Peter	6-2	205	R	Bloomington, MN	22	Phoenix-Colorado
OLVER, Mark	5-10	155	L	Burnaby, B.C.	22	Northern Mich.-Lake Erie
O'REILLY, Ryan	6-0	200	L	Clinton, Ont.	19	Colorado
PORTER, Kevin	6-0	190	L	Detroit, MI	24	Phx-San Antonio-Col-Lake Erie
REED, Harrison	6-1	185	R	Newmarket, Ont.	22	Alb-Lake Erie-Fla (ECHL)
STASTNY, Paul	6-0	205	L	Quebec City, Que.	24	Colorado
STEWART, Chris	6-2	228	R	Toronto, Ont.	22	Colorado-Lake Erie
STOA, Ryan	6-3	200	L	Bloomington, MN	23	Colorado-Lake Erie
TALBOT, Julian	6-0	185	L	Wahnapitae, Ont.	25	Peoria
VAN DER GULIK, David	5-10	173	L	Abbotsford, B.C.	27	Abbotsford
WALTER, Ben	6-1	195	L	Beaconsfield, Que.	26	New Jersey-Lowell
WINNIK, Daniel	6-2	210	R	Toronto, Ont.	25	Phoenix
YIP, Brandon	6-1	195	R	Vancouver, B.C.	25	Colorado-Lake Erie
DEFENSEMEN						
CHOUINARD, Joel	6-1	186	L	Longueuil, Que.	20	Victoriaville
COHEN, Colby	6-2	200	R	Villanova, PA	21	Boston University-Lake Erie
CUMISKEY, Kyle	5-10	185	L	Abbotsford, B.C.	23	Colorado
FOOTE, Adam	6-2	220	R	Toronto, Ont.	39	Colorado
GAUNCE, Cameron	6-1	203	L	Sudbury, Ont.	20	St. Michael's
HANNAN, Scott	6-1	225	L	Richmond, B.C.	31	Colorado
HOLOS, Jonas	5-11	196	R	Sarpsborg, Norway	23	Farjestad
LIFFITON, David	6-2	210	L	Windsor, Ont.	25	Syracuse
LILES, John-Michael	5-10	185	L	Indianapolis, IN	29	Colorado
MACIAS, Ray	6-2	195	R	Long Beach, CA	24	Lake Erie
MONTGOMERY, Kevin	6-1	185	L	Rochester, NY	22	Lake Erie
QUINCEY, Kyle	6-2	207	L	Kitchener, Ont.	25	Colorado
SHATTENKIRK, Kevin	5-11	193	R	Greenwich, CT	21	Boston University-Lake Erie
WILSON, Ryan	6-1	207	L	Windsor, Ont.	23	Colorado-Lake Erie

GOALTENDERS	HT	WT	C	Place of Birth	*Age	2009-10 Club
ANDERSON, Craig	6-2	180	L	Park Ridge, IL	29	Colorado
BACASHIHUA, Jason	5-11	175	L	Dearborn Heights, MI	28	Hershey
BUDAJ, Peter	6-1	200	L	Banska Bystrica, Czech.	28	Colorado
CANN, Trevor	5-11	199	L	Oakville, Ont.	21	Lake Erie-Tulsa
GRAHAME, John	6-3	220	L	Denver, CO	35	Adirondack-Lake Erie

* – Age at start of 2010-11 season

Joe Sacco

Head Coach

Born: Medford, MA, February 4, 1969.

Joe Sacco, former head coach of Colorado's American Hockey League affiliate, the Lake Erie Monsters, was named the 13th head coach in franchise history on June 4, 2009. In his first season behind the bench in 2009-10, he led the Avalanche back into the playoffs and was rewarded with a nomination for the Jack Adams Award as coach of the year. Sacco moved into the Avalanche head coach position after four seasons with the organization serving both as assistant coach (Lowell 2005-06; Albany 2006-07) and head coach (Lake Erie 2007-08, 2008-09) with the club's American Hockey League affiliates.

Under Sacco's guidance, the Monsters finished with a 34-38-13 record (76 points) in 2008-09, posting eight more wins and 11 more points than they did in their inaugural season of 2007-08. Following the season, Sacco was tabbed as an assistant coach for Team USA at the 2009 Men's World Championship in Switzerland.

Sacco, a native of Medford, Massachusetts, played college hockey at Boston University where he appeared in 111 games over three seasons with the Terriers. He was a fourth-round draft pick (71st overall) by the Toronto Maple Leafs in the 1987 NHL Entry Draft and went on to play in 738 total games over a 13-year NHL career, which included stints with Toronto, Anaheim, the New York Islanders, Washington and Philadelphia. The right winger finished with 94 goals and 119 assists. Sacco also competed internationally with the United States at the 1992 Olympics in Albertville, France, where the team finished fourth. He would go on to play for Team USA in six World Championships, winning a bronze medal in 1996.

Coaching Record

			Regular Season				Playoffs			
Season	Team	League	GC	W	L	O/T	GC	W	L	T
2007-08	Lake Erie	AHL	80	26	41	13	....	....	....	....
2008-09	Lake Erie	AHL	80	34	38	8	....	....	....	....
2009-10	**Colorado**	**NHL**	**82**	**43**	**30**	**9**	**6**	**2**	**4**	....
	NHL Totals		**82**	**43**	**30**	**9**	**6**	**2**	**4**	....

2009-10 Scoring

* – rookie

Regular Season

Pos	#	Player	Team	GP	G	A	Pts	TOI	+/–	PIM	PP	SH	GW	S	%
C	26	Paul Stastny	COL	81	20	59	79	21:23	2	50	9	0	2	199	10.1
R	25	Chris Stewart	COL	77	28	36	64	16:41	4	73	3	0	5	221	12.7
C	9	* Matt Duchene	COL	81	24	31	55	17:43	1	16	10	1	2	180	13.3
R	23	Milan Hejduk	COL	56	23	21	44	19:01	6	10	8	0	4	153	15.0
L	39	* T.J. Galiardi	COL	70	15	24	39	18:10	6	28	2	1	3	120	12.5
R	88	Peter Mueller	PHX	54	4	13	17	12:55	–5	8	1	0	1	89	4.5
			COL	15	9	11	20	17:50	4	8	3	0	1	35	25.7
			Total	69	13	24	37	13:59	–1	16	4	0	2	124	10.5
D	4	John-Michael Liles	COL	59	6	25	31	18:27	–2	30	3	0	2	96	6.3
D	27	Kyle Quincey	COL	79	6	23	29	23:36	9	76	1	0	0	139	4.3
C	37	* Ryan O'Reilly	COL	81	8	18	26	16:45	4	18	0	2	2	135	5.9
R	16	Darcy Tucker	COL	71	10	14	24	12:07	–3	47	3	0	1	73	13.7
D	44	* Ryan Wilson	COL	61	3	18	21	16:16	13	36	0	0	0	46	6.5
D	10	Kyle Cumiskey	COL	61	7	13	20	19:47	0	20	2	0	1	74	9.5
D	5	Brett Clark	COL	64	3	17	20	19:08	6	28	2	0	1	75	4.0
R	59	* Brandon Yip	COL	32	11	8	19	14:41	5	22	4	0	2	65	16.9
L	55	Cody McLeod	COL	74	7	11	18	12:55	–13	138	0	0	1	117	6.0
R	54	David Jones	COL	23	10	6	16	17:55	1	2	1	2	3	39	25.6
C	15	Matt Hendricks	COL	56	9	7	16	9:15	1	74	0	1	1	63	14.3
D	22	Scott Hannan	COL	81	2	14	16	21:55	2	40	0	0	0	53	3.8
R	40	Marek Svatos	COL	54	7	4	11	11:24	–13	35	3	0	1	84	8.3
D	52	Adam Foote	COL	67	0	9	9	19:21	8	64	0	0	0	26	0.0
L	45	Chris Durno	COL	41	4	4	8	7:27	3	47	0	0	0	27	14.8
C	18	Stephane Yelle	CAR	59	4	3	7	9:21	–6	28	0	1	0	34	11.8
			COL	11	0	1	1	9:59	0	4	0	0	0	5	0.0
			Total	70	4	4	8	9:27	–6	32	0	1	0	39	10.3
D	24	Ruslan Salei	COL	14	1	5	6	18:46	–1	10	0	0	0	22	4.5
C	29	* Ryan Stoa	COL	12	2	1	3	11:04	–3	0	0	0	0	26	7.7
C	32	Kevin Porter	PHX	4	0	0	0	7:21	1	0	0	0	0	3	0.0
			COL	16	2	1	3	13:12	–4	0	0	1	0	18	11.1
			Total	20	2	1	3	12:02	–3	0	0	1	0	21	9.5
C	7	T.J. Hensick	COL	7	1	2	3	9:26	0	0	0	0	0	13	7.7
C	43	* Justin Mercier	COL	9	1	1	2	7:11	2	0	0	0	0	5	20.0
L	28	David Koci	COL	43	1	0	1	3:03	–2	84	0	0	0	6	16.7
D	20	Tom Preissing	COL	4	0	1	1	13:04	–6	0	0	0	0	6	0.0
C	11	* Philippe Dupuis	COL	4	0	1	1	8:14	1	2	0	0	0	4	0.0
R	12	Darren Haydar	COL	1	0	0	0	5:22	0	0	0	0	0	2	0.0
D	2	* Wes O'Neill	COL	2	0	0	0	9:43	1	2	0	0	0	1	0.0
D	6	* Derek Peltier	COL	3	0	0	0	9:00	0	0	0	0	0	1	0.0
R	18	Brian Willsie	COL	4	0	0	0	11:05	–1	0	0	0	0	2	0.0

Goaltending

No.	Goaltender	GPI	Mins	Avg	W	L	OT	EN	SO	GA	SA	S%	G	A	PIM
31	Peter Budaj	15	728	2.64	5	5	2	4	1	32	386	.917	0	1	0
41	Craig Anderson	71	4235	2.64	38	25	7	6	7	186	2233	.917	0	3	16
	Totals	**82**	**4995**	**2.74**	**43**	**30**	**9**	**10**	**8**	**228**	**2629**	**.913**			

Playoffs

Pos	#	Player	Team	GP	G	A	Pts	TOI	+/–	PIM	PP	SH	GW	OT	S	%
C	26	Paul Stastny	COL	6	1	4	5	20:22	–2	4	1	0	0	0	13	7.7
R	59	* Brandon Yip	COL	6	2	2	4	17:51	–3	6	0	0	0	0	13	15.4
R	25	Chris Stewart	COL	6	3	0	3	17:59	–1	4	0	0	1	0	20	15.0
C	9	* Matt Duchene	COL	6	0	3	3	19:19	–2	0	0	0	0	0	9	0.0
D	4	John-Michael Liles	COL	6	1	1	2	19:00	–2	4	1	0	0	0	14	7.1
D	10	Kyle Cumiskey	COL	6	1	1	2	22:37	–7	2	0	0	0	0	3	33.3
L	39	* T.J. Galiardi	COL	6	0	2	2	20:49	–1	6	0	0	0	0	8	0.0
R	23	Milan Hejduk	COL	3	1	0	1	12:58	0	0	0	0	0	0	4	25.0
R	40	Marek Svatos	COL	3	1	0	1	13:17	–1	2	0	0	0	0	10	10.0
C	37	* Ryan O'Reilly	COL	6	1	0	1	17:04	0	2	0	0	1	1	7	14.3
D	44	* Ryan Wilson	COL	4	0	1	1	14:39	–1	0	0	0	0	0	2	0.0
D	52	Adam Foote	COL	6	0	1	1	21:22	–4	10	0	0	0	0	6	0.0
D	24	Ruslan Salei	COL	1	0	0	0	21:54	0	0	0	0	0	0	0	0.0
D	5	Brett Clark	COL	1	0	0	0	17:55	0	0	0	0	0	0	3	0.0
C	29	* Ryan Stoa	COL	1	0	0	0	8:45	0	2	0	0	0	0	1	0.0
L	45	Chris Durno	COL	1	0	0	0	6:09	0	0	0	0	0	0	0	0.0
C	32	Kevin Porter	COL	4	0	0	0	10:38	–2	0	0	0	0	0	2	0.0
C	18	Stephane Yelle	COL	6	0	0	0	11:12	–1	2	0	0	0	0	4	0.0
R	16	Darcy Tucker	COL	6	0	0	0	11:59	–1	2	0	0	0	0	4	0.0
D	22	Scott Hannan	COL	6	0	0	0	22:32	3	4	0	0	0	0	3	0.0
C	15	Matt Hendricks	COL	6	0	0	0	9:51	–2	0	0	0	0	0	5	0.0
D	27	Kyle Quincey	COL	6	0	0	0	22:06	2	8	0	0	0	0	14	0.0
L	55	Cody McLeod	COL	6	0	0	0	11:02	–2	5	0	0	0	0	4	0.0

Goaltending

No.	Goaltender	GPI	Mins	Avg	W	L	EN	SO	GA	SA	S%	G	A	PIM
41	Craig Anderson	6	366	2.62	2	4	2	1	16	239	.933	0	1	0
31	Peter Budaj	1	9	6.67	0	0	0	0	1	4	.750	0	0	0
	Totals	**6**	**377**	**3.02**	**2**	**4**	**2**	**1**	**19**	**245**	**.922**			

Coaching History

Jacques Demers, 1979-80; Maurice Filion and Michel Bergeron, 1980-81; Michel Bergeron, 1981-82 to 1986-87; Andre Savard and Ron Lapointe, 1987-88; Ron Lapointe and Jean Perron, 1988-89; Michel Bergeron, 1989-90; Dave Chambers, 1990-91; Dave Chambers and Pierre Page, 1991-92; Pierre Page, 1992-93, 1993-94; Marc Crawford, 1994-95 to 1997-98; Bob Hartley, 1998-99 to 2001-02; Bob Hartley and Tony Granato, 2002-03; Tony Granato, 2003-04; Joel Quenneville, 2004-05 to 2007-08; Tony Granato, 2008-09; Joe Sacco, 2009-10 to date.

Captains' History

Marc Tardif, 1979-80, 1980-81; Robbie Ftorek and Andre Dupont, 1981-82; Mario Marois, 1982-83 to 1984-85; Mario Marois and Peter Stastny, 1985-86; Peter Stastny, 1986-87 to 1989-90; Joe Sakic and Steven Finn, 1990-91; Mike Hough, 1991-92; Joe Sakic, 1992-93 to 2008-09; Adam Foote, 2009-10 to date.

Club Records

Team

(Figures in brackets for season records are games played; records for fewest points, wins, ties, losses, goals, goals against are for 70 or more games)

Most Points	**118**	2000-01 (82)
Most Wins	**52**	2000-01 (82)
Most Ties	**18**	1980-81 (80)
Most Losses	**61**	1989-90 (80)
Most Goals	**360**	1983-84 (80)
Most Goals Against	**407**	1989-90 (80)
Fewest Points	**31**	1989-90 (80)
Fewest Wins	**12**	1989-90 (80)
Fewest Ties	**5**	1987-88 (80)
Fewest Losses	**16**	2000-01 (82)
Fewest Goals	**199**	2008-09 (82)
Fewest Goals Against	**169**	2001-02 (82)
Longest Winning Streak		
Overall	**12**	Jan. 10-Feb. 7/99
Home	**10**	Nov. 26/83-Jan. 10/84, Mar. 6-Apr. 16/95
Away	**7**	Jan. 10-Feb. 7/99
Longest Undefeated Streak		
Overall	**12**	Dec. 23/96-Jan. 20/97 (9 wins, 3 ties), Jan. 10-Feb. 7/99 (12 wins)
Home	**14**	Nov. 19/83-Jan. 21/84 (11 wins, 3 ties)
Away	**10**	Jan. 10-Mar. 3/99 (8 wins, 2 ties)
Longest Losing Streak		
Overall	**14**	Oct. 21-Nov. 19/90
Home	**8**	Oct. 21-Nov. 24/90
Away	**18**	Jan. 18-Apr. 1/90
Longest Winless Streak		
Overall	**17**	Oct. 21-Nov. 25/90 (15 losses, 2 ties)
Home	**11**	Nov. 14-Dec. 26/89 (7 losses, 4 ties)
Away	**33**	Oct. 8/91-Feb. 27/92 (25 losses, 8 ties)
Most Shutouts, Season	**11**	2001-02 (82)
Most PIM, Season	**2,104**	1989-90 (80)
Most Goals, Game	**12**	Feb. 1/83 (Hfd. 3 at Que. 12), Oct. 20/84 (Que. 12 at Tor. 3), Dec. 5/95 (S.J. 2 at Col. 12)

Individual

Most Seasons	**20**	Joe Sakic
Most Games	**1,378**	Joe Sakic
Most Goals, Career	**625**	Joe Sakic
Most Assists, Career	**1,016**	Joe Sakic
Most Points, Career	**1,641**	Joe Sakic (625G, 1,016A)
Most PIM, Career	**1,562**	Dale Hunter
Most Shutouts, Career	**37**	Patrick Roy
Longest Consecutive Games Streak	**312**	Dale Hunter (Oct. 9/80-Mar. 13/84)
Most Goals, Season	**57**	Michel Goulet (1982-83)
Most Assists, Season	**93**	Peter Stastny (1981-82)
Most Points, Season	**139**	Peter Stastny (1981-82; 46G, 93A)
Most PIM, Season	**301**	Gord Donnelly (1987-88)
Most Points, Defenseman, Season	**82**	Steve Duchesne (1992-93; 20G, 62A)
Most Points, Center, Season	**139**	Peter Stastny (1981-82; 46G, 93A)
Most Points, Right Wing, Season	**103**	Jacques Richard (1980-81; 52G, 51A)
Most Points, Left Wing, Season	**121**	Michel Goulet (1983-84; 56G, 65A)
Most Points, Rookie, Season	**109**	Peter Stastny (1980-81; 39G, 70A)
Most Shutouts, Season	**9**	Patrick Roy (2001-02)
Most Goals, Game	**5**	Mats Sundin (Mar. 5/92), Mike Ricci (Feb. 17/94)
Most Assists, Game	**5**	Eight times
Most Points, Game	**8**	Peter Stastny (Feb. 22/81; 4G, 4A), Anton Stastny (Feb. 22/81; 3G, 5A)

Records include Quebec Nordiques, 1979-80 through 1994-95.

Retired Numbers

3	J.C. Tremblay*	1972-1979
8	Marc Tardif*	1979-1983
16	Michel Goulet*	1979-1990
19	Joe Sakic	1988-2009
26	Peter Stastny*	1980-1990
33	Patrick Roy	1995-2003
77	Raymond Bourque	2000-2001

* Quebec Nordiques

All-time Record vs. Other Clubs

Regular Season

	At Home								On Road								Total							
	GP	W	L	T	OL	GF	GA	PTS	GP	W	L	T	OL	GF	GA	PTS	GP	W	L	T	OL	GF	GA	PTS
Anaheim	31	16	10	4	1	89	83	37	31	14	9	3	5	77	83	36	62	30	19	7	6	166	166	73
Atlanta	7	3	3	0	1	24	22	7	6	3	2	1	0	16	13	7	13	6	5	1	1	40	35	14
Boston	68	25	37	6	0	242	277	56	64	24	31	9	0	198	243	57	132	49	68	15	0	440	520	113
Buffalo	66	32	22	11	1	233	204	76	65	20	35	9	1	211	252	50	131	52	57	20	2	444	456	126
Calgary	65	30	23	11	1	229	202	72	65	25	31	9	0	187	223	59	130	55	54	20	1	416	425	131
Carolina	67	41	17	9	0	284	197	91	65	27	26	12	0	222	214	66	132	68	43	21	0	506	411	157
Chicago	49	26	15	6	2	188	155	60	51	20	26	3	2	157	173	45	100	46	41	9	4	345	328	105
Columbus	18	15	3	0	0	66	32	30	18	12	4	1	1	62	37	26	36	27	7	1	1	128	69	56
Dallas	51	28	12	7	4	180	127	67	51	18	26	5	2	144	171	43	102	46	38	12	6	324	298	110
Detroit	52	23	23	4	2	170	172	52	50	19	29	1	1	146	178	40	102	42	52	5	3	316	350	92
Edmonton	65	34	26	4	1	241	220	73	64	27	30	4	3	207	243	61	129	61	56	8	4	448	463	134
Florida	13	6	4	3	0	38	31	15	14	11	2	0	1	57	42	23	27	17	6	3	1	95	73	38
Los Angeles	52	27	21	3	1	209	174	58	53	18	28	5	2	174	208	43	105	45	49	8	3	383	382	101
Minnesota	29	17	9	2	1	79	65	37	28	12	8	1	7	81	77	32	57	29	17	3	8	160	142	69
Montreal	65	33	27	5	0	220	227	71	66	17	39	10	0	206	271	44	131	50	66	15	0	426	498	115
Nashville	22	12	6	2	2	59	47	28	22	9	8	3	2	66	64	23	44	21	14	5	4	125	111	51
New Jersey	37	19	14	4	0	129	103	42	38	14	20	4	0	125	154	32	75	33	34	8	0	254	257	74
NY Islanders	36	21	12	3	0	127	101	45	34	13	20	1	0	115	138	27	70	34	32	4	0	242	239	72
NY Rangers	37	20	14	3	0	148	136	43	36	12	20	4	0	102	141	28	73	32	34	7	0	250	277	71
Ottawa	17	13	3	1	0	75	49	27	20	9	8	3	0	70	57	21	37	22	11	4	0	145	106	48
Philadelphia	38	15	10	12	1	136	129	43	36	11	22	2	1	97	130	25	74	26	32	14	2	233	259	68
Phoenix	51	27	17	5	2	179	167	61	50	22	19	7	2	171	173	53	101	49	36	12	4	350	340	114
Pittsburgh	34	19	13	2	0	150	127	40	39	17	17	5	0	156	153	39	73	36	30	7	0	306	280	79
St. Louis	51	27	16	7	1	179	135	62	50	19	27	4	0	149	177	42	101	46	43	11	1	328	312	104
San Jose	33	19	9	4	1	116	72	43	34	18	14	1	1	112	96	38	67	37	23	5	2	228	168	81
Tampa Bay	16	11	3	2	0	60	34	24	15	6	8	1	0	40	40	13	31	17	11	3	0	100	74	37
Toronto	31	18	8	5	0	120	97	41	37	17	16	4	0	141	120	38	68	35	24	9	0	261	217	79
Vancouver	65	33	22	8	2	215	184	76	65	32	23	7	3	236	208	74	130	65	45	15	5	451	392	150
Washington	36	15	16	5	0	109	127	35	35	12	19	4	0	110	134	28	71	27	35	9	0	219	261	63
Totals	**1202**	**625**	**415**	**138**	**24**	**4294**	**3696**	**1412**	**1202**	**478**	**567**	**123**	**34**	**3835**	**4213**	**1113**	**2404**	**1103**	**982**	**261**	**58**	**8129**	**7909**	**2525**

Playoffs

	Series	W	L	GP	W	L	T	GF	GA	Last Mtg.	Rnd.	Result
Anaheim	1	0	1	4	0	4	0	4	16	2006	CSF	L 0-4
Boston	2	1	1	11	5	6	0	36	37	1983	DSF	L 1-3
Buffalo	2	2	0	8	6	2	0	35	27	1985	DSF	W 3-2
Carolina	2	1	1	9	4	5	0	34	35	1987	DSF	W 4-2
Chicago	2	2	0	12	8	4	0	49	28	1997	CQF	W 4-2
Dallas	4	2	2	24	14	10	0	66	62	2006	CQF	W 4-1
Detroit	6	3	3	34	17	17	0	88	97	2008	CSF	L 0-4
Edmonton	2	1	1	12	7	5	0	35	30	1998	CQF	L 3-4
Florida	1	1	0	4	4	0	0	15	4	1996	F	W 4-0
Los Angeles	2	2	0	14	8	6	0	33	23	2002	CQF	W 4-3
Minnesota	2	1	1	13	7	6	0	34	28	2008	CQF	W 4-2
Montreal	5	2	3	31	14	17	0	85	105	1993	DSF	L 2-4
New Jersey	1	1	0	7	4	3	0	19	11	2001	F	W 4-3
NY Islanders	1	0	1	4	0	4	0	9	18	1982	CF	L 0-4
NY Rangers	1	0	1	6	2	4	0	19	25	1995	CQF	L 2-4
Philadelphia	2	0	2	11	4	7	0	29	39	1985	CF	L 2-4
Phoenix	1	1	0	5	4	1	0	17	10	2000	CQF	W 4-1
St. Louis	1	1	0	5	4	1	0	17	11	2001	CF	W 4-1
San Jose	4	2	2	25	12	13	0	62	71	2010	CQF	L 2-4
Vancouver	2	2	0	10	8	2	0	40	26	2001	CQF	W 4-0
Totals	**44**	**25**	**19**	**249**	**132**	**117**	**0**	**726**	**703**			

Playoff Results 2010-2006

Year	Round	Opponent	Result	GF	GA
2010	CQF	San Jose	L 2-4	11	19
2008	CSF	Detroit	L 0-4	9	21
	CQF	Minnesota	W 4-2	17	12
2006	CSF	Anaheim	L 0-4	4	16
	CQF	Dallas	W 4-1	18	15

Abbreviations: Round: F - Final; **CF** - conference final; **CSF** - conference semi-final; **CQF** - conference quarter-final; **DSF** - division semi-final.

Calgary totals include Atlanta Flames, 1979-80.
Dallas totals include Minnesota North Stars, 1979-80 to 1992-93.
Phoenix totals include Winnipeg, 1979-80 to 1995-96.
Carolina totals include Hartford, 1979-80 to 1996-97.
New Jersey totals include Colorado Rockies, 1979-80 to 1981-82.

2009-10 Results

Oct.	1	San Jose	5-2		31	at Detroit	2-4
	3	Vancouver	3-0	**Jan.**	2	at Columbus	3-2
	8	at Nashville	2-3		6	NY Islanders	2-3
	10	at Chicago	3-4†		8	at Carolina	1-2
	12	at Boston	4-3		9	at Buffalo	4-3†
	13	at Toronto	4-1		11	at Calgary	3-2†
	15	at Montreal	3-2		16	New Jersey	3-1
	17	at Detroit	4-3†		18	Edmonton	6-0
	21	at Minnesota	2-3†		22	Nashville	2-1
	23	Carolina	5-4		24	Dallas	4-0
	24	Detroit	3-1		28	Minnesota	0-1
	27	at Edmonton	3-0		29	at Dallas	2-3
	28	at Calgary	3-2		31	NY Rangers	1-3
	30	at San Jose	1-3	**Feb.**	2	Columbus	5-1
Nov.	1	at Vancouver	0-3		4	at Nashville	3-5
	4	Phoenix	4-1		6	Edmonton	3-0
	6	Chicago	4-3†		8	St. Louis	5-2
	8	Edmonton	3-5		10	Atlanta	4-3*
	11	at Chicago	2-3†		12	Phoenix	2-1
	14	Vancouver	2-8		13	at Los Angeles	0-3
	17	at Calgary	3-2	**Mar.**	1	Detroit	2-3
	18	at Edmonton	4-6		3	at Anaheim	4-3
	20	at Vancouver	2-5		4	at Phoenix	1-3
	23	Philadelphia	5-4		6	St. Louis	7-3
	25	Nashville	3-4*		9	Vancouver	4-6
	27	at Minnesota	3-5		11	Florida	3-0
	28	Minnesota	2-3†		14	at Dallas	5-3
	30	at Tampa Bay	3-0		16	at St. Louis	5-3
Dec.	2	at Florida	5-6†		17	Calgary	2-3
	3	at Pittsburgh	1-4		21	at Anaheim	2-5
	5	at Columbus	3-2		22	at Los Angeles	3-4*
	7	at St. Louis	4-0		24	Los Angeles	4-3†
	9	Minnesota	0-1		27	at Phoenix	2-6
	11	Tampa Bay	2-1†		28	at San Jose	3-4
	13	Calgary	3-2		31	Anaheim	2-5
	15	Washington	1-6	**Apr.**	2	Calgary	1-2
	19	Columbus	5-2		4	San Jose	5-4*
	21	at Minnesota	4-3		6	at Vancouver	4-3†
	22	Anaheim	2-4		7	at Edmonton	4-5*
	26	Dallas	4-1		9	Chicago	2-5
	30	at Ottawa	4-3		11	Los Angeles	1-2*

* – Overtime † – Shootout

Entry Draft Selections 2010-1996

Name in bold denotes played in NHL.

2010
Pick
17	Joey Hishon
49	Calvin Pickard
71	Michael Bournival
95	Stephen Silas
107	Sami Aittokallio
137	Troy Rutkowski
139	Luke Walker
197	Luke Moffatt

2009
Pick
3	**Matt Duchene**
33	**Ryan O'Reilly**
49	Stefan Elliott
64	Tyson Barrie
124	Kieran Millan
154	Brandon Maxwell
184	Gus Young

2008
Pick
50	Cameron Gaunce
61	Peter Delmas
110	Kelsey Tessier
140	Mark Olver
167	Joel Chouinard
170	Jonas Holos
200	Nathan Condon

2007
Pick
14	Kevin Shattenkirk
45	Colby Cohen
49	Trevor Cann
55	**T.J. Galiardi**
105	Brad Malone
113	Kent Patterson
135	Paul Carey
155	Jens Hellgren
195	Johan Alcen

2006
Pick
18	**Chris Stewart**
51	Nigel Williams
59	Codey Burki
81	Michael Carman
110	Kevin Montgomery
201	Billy Sauer

2005
Pick
34	**Ryan Stoa**
44	**Paul Stastny**
47	Tom Fritsche
52	Chris Durand
88	**T.J. Hensick**
124	Ray Macias
166	Jason Lynch
168	**Justin Mercier**
222	Kyle Cumiskey

2004
Pick
21	**Wojtek Wolski**
55	**Victor Oreskovich**
72	Denis Parshin
154	Richard Demen-Willaume
184	**Derek Peltier**
215	Ian Keserich
239	**Brandon Yip**
249	J.D. Corbin
281	Steve McClellan

2003
Pick
63	**David Liffiton**
131	David Svagrovsky
146	Mark McCutcheon
163	**Brad Richardson**
204	Linus Videll
225	Brett Hemingway
257	Darryl Yacboski
288	**David Jones**

2002
Pick
28	**Jonas Johansson**
61	**Johnny Boychuk**
94	Eric Lundberg
107	Mikko Kalteva
129	**Tom Gilbert**
164	**Tyler Weiman**
195	Taylor Christie
227	Ryan Steeves
258	Sergei Shemetov
289	Sean Collins

2001
Pick
63	**Peter Budaj**
97	**Danny Bois**
130	Colt King
143	Frantisek Skladany
144	**Cody McCormick**
149	Mikko Viitanen
165	Pierre-Luc Emond
184	Scott Horvath
196	**Charlie Stephens**
227	**Marek Svatos**

2000
Pick
14	**Vaclav Nedorost**
47	**Jared Aulin**
50	Sergei Soin
63	Agris Saviels
88	**Kurt Sauer**
92	Sergei Klyazmin
119	Brian Fahey
159	**John-Michael Liles**
189	Chris Bahen
221	Aaron Molnar
252	**Darryl Bootland**
266	Sean Kotary
285	Blake Ward

1999
Pick
25	**Mikhail Kuleshov**
45	**Martin Grenier**
93	**Branko Radivojevic**
112	Sanny Lindstrom
122	Kristian Kovac
142	Will Magnuson
152	**Jordan Krestanovich**
158	Anders Lovdahl
183	**Riku Hahl**
212	**Radim Vrbata**
240	Jeff Finger

1998
Pick
12	**Alex Tanguay**
17	**Martin Skoula**
19	**Robyn Regehr**
20	**Scott Parker**
28	**Ramzi Abid**
38	**Philippe Sauve**
53	**Steve Moore**
79	Evgeny Lazarev
141	K.C. Timmons
167	Alexander Ryazantsev

1997
Pick
26	Kevin Grimes
53	Graham Belak
55	**Rick Berry**
78	**Ville Nieminen**
87	**Brad Larsen**
133	Aaron Miskovich
161	**David Aebischer**
217	Doug Schmidt
243	Kyle Kidney
245	Stephen Lafleur

1996
Pick
25	**Peter Ratchuk**
51	**Yuri Babenko**
79	**Mark Parrish**
98	Ben Storey
107	Randy Petruk
134	Luke Curtin
146	**Brian Willsie**
160	Kai Fischer
167	**Dan Hinote**
176	**Samuel Pahlsson**
188	Roman Pylner
214	Matt Scorsune
240	Justin Clark

Club Directory

Pepsi Center

Colorado Avalanche
Pepsi Center
1000 Chopper Circle
Denver, CO 80204
Phone 303/405-1100
FAX 303/893-0614
Press Box 303/575-1926
www.coloradoavalanche.com
Capacity: 18,007

Executive
Owner and Governor	E. Stanley Kroenke
President and Alternate Governor	Pierre Lacroix
G.M., Executive V.P. & Alt. Governor	Greg Sherman
Vice President of Player Development	Craig Billington
Vice President of Hockey Administration	Charlotte Grahame
Director of Hockey Operations	Eric Lacroix
Director of Player Personnel	Brad Smith

Coaching Staff
Head Coach	Joe Sacco
Assistant Coaches	Sylvain Lefebvre, Steve Konowalchuk
Video/Development Coach	Adam Deadmarsh

Training Staff
Head Athletic Trainer	Matthew Sokolowski
Assistant Athletic Trainer/Physical Therapist	Scott Woodward
Head Equipment Manager	Mark Miller
Assistant Equipment Managers	Kurt Harvey, Cliff Halstead
Inventory Manager	Wayne Flemming
Strength & Conditioning Coach	Robert McLean
Massage Therapist	Gregorio Pradera

Scouting
Director of Amateur Scouting	Richard Pracey
Assistant Director of Amateur Scouting	Alan Hepple
Scouts	Anders Carlsson, Rick Lanz, Joni Lehto, Don Paarup, Guy Perron, Neil Shea
Pro Scouts	Garth Joy, Terry Martin

Communications/Team Services
Sr. V.P., Communications & Business Operations	Jean Martineau
Sr. Director of Media Services/Internet	Brendan McNicholas
Manager of Media Relations/Website	Craig Stancher
Team Services Coordinator	Erin DeGraff

Lake Erie Monsters (AHL affiliate)
G.M./Director of Player Development	David Oliver
Head Coach	David Quinn
Assistant Coach	Dan Laperriere
Head Athletic Trainer	Brent Woodside
Head Equipment Manager	Dusty Halstead

Team Information
Practice Facility	South Suburban Family Sports Center
Television Outlet	Altitude Sports & Entertainment Network
Radio	Altitude Radio Network

General Managers' History

Maurice Filion, 1979-80 to 1987-88; Martin Madden, 1988-89; Martin Madden and Maurice Filion, 1989-90; Pierre Page, 1990-91 to 1993-94; Pierre Lacroix, 1994-95 to 2005-06; Francois Giguere, 2006-07 to 2008-09; Greg Sherman, 2009-10 to date.

Greg Sherman
General Manager/Executive V.P. and Alt. Governor
Born: Scranton, PA, March 30, 1970.

Greg Sherman was named general manager of the Colorado Avalanche on June 3, 2009. At the time of his appointment, he had spent the last seven years as the team's assistant general manager and had been associated with the franchise for 13 years. In his first few weeks on the job, Sherman hired Joe Sacco as the Avalanche's head coach and oversaw the selection of Matt Duchene with the third pick in the NHL Entry Draft. The team showed a 26-point improvement in 2009-10 and returned to the playoffs.

In his previous role in Colorado, Sherman worked on contract negotiations, arbitration cases, salary cap management and matters concerning personnel at all levels of the organization. In addition, Sherman also served as a liaison between the Avalanche and its American Hockey League affiliate, the Lake Erie Monsters. He oversaw and coordinated all financial obligations of both clubs.

Born in Scranton, Pennsylvania and raised in Denver, Sherman has spent most of his life in Colorado. He attended the University of San Diego and received his Bachelor in Accountancy in May 1992.

Picked third overall in the 2009 Entry Draft, Matt Duchene paid instant dividends. He played 81 games in 2009-10 and was third in team scoring.

Key Off-Season Signings/Acquisitions

2010

June 8 • Named **Scott Arniel** head coach.
23 • Named **Brad Berry** assistant coach.
30 • Claimed LW **Ethan Moreau** on waivers from Edmonton.
July 1 • Named **Dan Hinote** assistant coach.
5 • Named **Bob Boughner** assistant coach.
13 • Re-signed RW **Jared Boll**.
22 • Re-signed D **Grant Clitsome**.
28 • Re-signed D **Anton Stralman**.

Columbus Blue Jackets

2009-10 Results: 32w-35L-5OTL-10SOL 79PTS.
Fifth, Central Division

Year-by-Year Record

		Home				Road				Overall						
Season	GP	W	L	T	OL	W	L	T	OL	W	L	T	OL	GF	GA	Pts.	Finished	Playoff Result
2009-10	82	20	12	....	9	12	23	....	6	32	35	....	15	216	259	79	5th, Central Div.	Out of Playoffs
2008-09	82	25	13	....	3	16	18	....	7	41	31	....	10	226	230	92	4th, Central Div.	Lost Conf. Quarter-Final
2007-08	82	20	14	....	7	14	22	....	5	34	36	....	12	193	218	80	4th, Central Div.	Out of Playoffs
2006-07	82	18	19	....	4	15	23	....	3	33	42	....	7	201	249	73	4th, Central Div.	Out of Playoffs
2005-06	82	23	18	....	0	12	25	....	4	35	43	....	4	223	279	74	3rd, Central Div.	Out of Playoffs
2004-05																		
2003-04	82	17	18	4	2	8	27	4	2	25	45	8	4	177	238	62	4th, Central Div.	Out of Playoffs
2002-03	82	20	14	5	2	9	28	3	1	29	42	8	3	213	263	69	5th, Central Div.	Out of Playoffs
2001-02	82	14	18	5	4	8	29	3	1	22	47	8	5	164	255	57	5th, Central Div.	Out of Playoffs
2000-01	82	19	15	4	3	9	24	5	3	28	39	9	6	190	233	71	5th, Central Div.	Out of Playoffs

2010-11 Schedule

Oct.	Fri.	8	at San Jose†	Sat.	8	at Los Angeles
	Sat.	9	San Jose†	Tue.	11	Phoenix
	Fri.	15	Chicago	Fri.	14	Detroit
	Sat.	16	at Minnesota	Sat.	15	at Detroit
	Wed.	20	Anaheim	Tue.	18	at Tampa Bay
	Fri.	22	Calgary	Wed.	19	at Florida
	Sat.	23	at Chicago	Sat.	22	at St. Louis
	Mon.	25	Philadelphia	Tue.	25	Anaheim
	Thu.	28	Edmonton	**Feb.** Tue.	1	at Chicago
	Sat.	30	at Colorado	Fri.	4	at Detroit
Nov.	Tue.	2	Montreal	Sat.	5	Edmonton
	Thu.	4	at Atlanta	Tue.	8	at Pittsburgh
	Sat.	6	Minnesota	Wed.	9	San Jose
	Wed.	10	St. Louis	Fri.	11	Colorado
	Fri.	12	Colorado	Sun.	13	at Dallas*
	Wed.	17	at Los Angeles	Wed.	16	Los Angeles
	Fri.	19	at Anaheim	Fri.	18	at Chicago
	Sat.	20	at San Jose	Tue.	22	Nashville
	Mon.	22	Nashville	Fri.	25	Phoenix
	Wed.	24	at NY Islanders	Sun.	27	at Nashville*
	Fri.	26	Detroit	**Mar.** Tue.	1	at Vancouver
	Sun.	28	at Detroit*	Thu.	3	at Edmonton
Dec.	Wed.	1	Nashville	Fri.	4	at Calgary
	Fri.	3	at Buffalo	Mon.	7	at St. Louis
	Sat.	4	Pittsburgh	Wed.	9	St. Louis
	Mon.	6	Dallas	Fri.	11	Los Angeles
	Thu.	9	at St. Louis	Sat.	12	at Carolina
	Sat.	11	NY Rangers	Tue.	15	Boston
	Mon.	13	at Calgary	Thu.	17	Detroit
	Wed.	15	at Vancouver	Sat.	19	at Minnesota*
	Thu.	16	at Edmonton	Sun.	20	New Jersey*
	Sat.	18	Dallas	Tue.	22	at Colorado
	Tue.	21	Calgary	Thu.	24	at Phoenix
	Thu.	23	Vancouver	Sun.	27	Vancouver*
	Sun.	26	at Chicago	Tue.	29	Florida
	Mon.	27	Minnesota	Thu.	31	at Washington
	Thu.	30	at Toronto	**Apr.** Fri.	1	Chicago
	Fri.	31	Ottawa	Sun.	3	St. Louis*
Jan.	Sun.	2	at Nashville*	Tue.	5	at Dallas
	Tue.	4	at Phoenix	Fri.	8	at Nashville
	Fri.	7	at Anaheim	Sat.	9	Buffalo

* Denotes afternoon game. † Games played in Stockholm, SE.

Rick Nash was the Blue Jackets' top scorer for the third year in a row with 33 goals and 34 assists in 2009-10. He has led the team in points four times in his seven-year career and in goals six times.

CENTRAL DIVISION
11th NHL Season

Franchise date: June 25, 1997

2010-11 Player Personnel

FORWARDS	HT	WT	S	Place of Birth	*Age	2009-10 Club
BLUNDEN, Michael	6-4	211	R	Toronto, Ont.	23	Syracuse-Columbus
BOLL, Jared	6-3	210	R	Charlotte, NC	24	Columbus
BRASSARD, Derick	6-1	190	L	Hull, Que.	23	Columbus
CALVERT, Matt	5-11	180	L	Brandon, Man.	20	Brandon
CLARK, Chris	6-0	196	R	South Windsor, CT	34	Washington-Columbus
DORSETT, Derek	5-11	187	R	Kindersley, Sask.	23	Columbus
FILATOV, Nikita	6-0	185	R	Moscow, USSR	20	Columbus-CSKA
FRISCHMON, Trevor	6-0	202	L	Ham Lake, MN	29	Columbus-Syracuse
HUSELIUS, Kristian	6-2	184	L	Osterhaninge, Sweden	31	Columbus
JOHANSEN, Ryan	6-3	192	R	Port Moody, B.C.	18	Portland (WHL)
KANA, Tomas	6-0	208	R	Opava, Czech.	22	Alaska-Columbus-Syracuse
KOLARIK, Chad	5-10	175	R	Abington, PA	24	San Antonio-CBJ-Syr
MacKENZIE, Derek	5-11	182	L	Sudbury, Ont.	29	Columbus-Syracuse
MAYOROV, Maksim	6-2	213	L	Andizhan, USSR	21	Columbus-Syracuse
MOREAU, Ethan	6-2	220	L	Huntsville, Ont.	35	Edmonton
MURRAY, Andrew	6-2	210	L	Selkirk, Man.	28	Columbus
NASH, Rick	6-4	218	L	Brampton, Ont.	26	Columbus
PAHLSSON, Samuel	6-0	203	L	Ange, Sweden	32	Columbus
SESTITO, Tom	6-5	228	L	Rome, NY	23	Columbus-Syracuse
UMBERGER, R.J.	6-2	219	L	Pittsburgh, PA	28	Columbus
VERMETTE, Antoine	6-1	200	L	St-Agapit, Que.	28	Columbus
VORACEK, Jakub	6-2	213	L	Kladno, Czech.	21	Columbus
WILSON, Kyle	6-1	201	R	Oakville, Ont.	25	Washington-Hershey

DEFENSEMEN						
CLITSOME, Grant	6-0	210	L	Gloucester, Ont.	25	Columbus-Syracuse
COMMODORE, Mike	6-5	235	R	Fort Saskatchewan, Alta.	30	Columbus
GUENIN, Nate	6-2	210	R	Sewickley, PA	27	Pit-Wilkes-Barre-Peoria
HEJDA, Jan	6-3	229	L	Prague, Czech.	32	Columbus
KLESLA, Rostislav	6-3	220	L	Novy Jicin, Czech.	28	Columbus
METHOT, Marc	6-3	230	L	Ottawa, Ont.	25	Columbus
MOORE, John	6-3	198	L	Winnetka, IL	19	Kitchener
RUSSELL, Kris	5-10	185	L	Red Deer, Alta.	23	Columbus
SIGALET, Jonathan	6-1	199	L	Vancouver, B.C.	24	Syracuse
STRALMAN, Anton	6-1	193	R	Tibro, Sweden	24	Columbus
TYUTIN, Fedor	6-3	218	L	Izhevsk, USSR	27	Columbus

GOALTENDERS	HT	WT	C	Place of Birth	*Age	2009-10 Club
GARON, Mathieu	6-2	202	R	Chandler, Que.	32	Columbus
LeNEVEU, David	6-1	187	L	Fernie, B.C.	27	Salzburg
MASON, Steve	6-4	220	R	Oakville, Ont.	22	Columbus
WESSLAU, Gustaf	6-4	199	L	Upplands Vasby, Sweden	25	Djurgarden

* – Age at start of 2010-11 season

2009-10 Scoring

* – rookie

Regular Season

Pos		Player	Team	GP	G	A	Pts	TOI	+/-	PIM	PP	SH	GW	S	%
L	61	Rick Nash	CBJ	76	33	34	67	20:56	-2	58	10	2	6	254	13.0
C	50	Antoine Vermette	CBJ	82	27	38	65	20:08	2	32	6	2	1	156	17.3
L	20	Kristian Huselius	CBJ	74	23	40	63	18:23	-4	36	8	1	5	162	14.2
C	18	R.J. Umberger	CBJ	82	23	32	55	19:10	-16	40	8	1	4	221	10.4
R	93	Jakub Voracek	CBJ	81	16	34	50	15:37	-7	26	4	0	1	154	10.4
C	16	Derick Brassard	CBJ	79	9	27	36	14:56	-17	48	4	0	0	125	7.2
D	6	Anton Stralman	CBJ	73	6	28	34	20:29	-17	37	4	0	0	121	5.0
D	51	Fedor Tyutin	CBJ	80	6	26	32	23:31	-7	49	3	0	2	149	4.0
D	10	Kris Russell	CBJ	70	7	15	22	18:35	3	32	0	0	1	108	6.5
R	11	Chris Clark	WSH	38	4	11	15	11:39	-4	27	0	0	1	59	6.8
			CBJ	36	3	2	5	12:06	-8	21	0	0	0	46	6.5
			Total	74	7	13	20	11:52	-12	48	0	0	1	105	6.7
C	26	Samuel Pahlsson	CBJ	79	3	13	16	16:16	-9	32	0	0	0	93	3.2
R	15	Derek Dorsett	CBJ	51	4	10	14	10:53	6	105	0	0	0	57	7.0
D	8	Jan Hejda	CBJ	62	3	10	13	20:38	-14	36	1	0	0	63	4.8
D	22	Mike Commodore	CBJ	57	2	9	11	19:00	-9	62	0	0	1	54	3.7
D	36	Mathieu Roy	CBJ	31	0	10	10	18:19	-2	17	0	0	0	32	0.0
D	97	Rostislav Klesla	CBJ	26	2	6	8	20:06	-7	26	0	0	1	24	8.3
D	3	Marc Methot	CBJ	60	2	6	8	19:31	-8	51	0	0	0	42	4.8
C	17	Andrew Murray	CBJ	46	5	2	7	10:21	-6	6	0	0	0	73	6.8
R	40	Jared Boll	CBJ	68	4	3	7	7:12	-8	149	0	0	0	56	7.1
D	23	Milan Jurcina	WSH	27	0	4	4	17:26	0	14	0	0	0	32	0.0
			CBJ	17	1	2	3	18:01	2	10	0	0	1	17	5.9
			Total	44	1	6	7	17:40	2	24	0	0	1	49	2.0
R	12*	Michael Blunden	CBJ	40	2	2	4	8:06	3	59	0	0	0	40	5.0
C	24*	Derek MacKenzie	CBJ	18	1	3	4	8:41	3	0	0	0	0	14	7.1
D	44*	Grant Clitsome	CBJ	11	1	2	3	14:44	0	6	0	0	0	7	14.3
L	28*	Nikita Filatov	CBJ	13	0	2	2	8:06	0	8	0	0	1	11	18.2
D	4	Nathan Paetsch	BUF	11	1	1	2	9:39	2	6	0	0	0	9	11.1
			CBJ	10	0	0	0	11:14	-5	6	0	0	0	8	0.0
			Total	21	1	1	2	10:24	-3	12	0	0	0	17	5.9
C	46*	Tomas Kana	CBJ	6	0	2	2	8:40	2	2	0	0	0	4	0.0
C	42*	Chad Kolarik	CBJ	2	0	0	0	6:29	-1	0	0	0	0	2	0.0
L	23*	Tom Sestito	CBJ	3	0	0	0	5:33	0	7	0	0	0	0	0.0
C	38	Trevor Frischmon	CBJ	3	0	0	0	6:06	0	4	0	0	0	1	0.0
R	39*	Greg Moore	CBJ	4	0	0	0	5:54	0	0	0	0	0	2	0.0
R	43*	Maksim Mayorov	CBJ	4	0	0	0	7:40	-1	0	0	0	0	4	0.0
L	21	Alexandre Picard	CBJ	9	0	0	0	7:13	-3	0	0	0	0	12	0.0

Goaltending

No.	Goaltender	GPI	Mins	Avg	W	L	OT	EN	SO	GA	SA	S%	G	A	PIM
32	Mathieu Garon	35	1771	2.81	12	9	6	1	2	83	858	.903	0	0	2
1	Steve Mason	58	3201	3.06	20	26	9	2	5	163	1653	.901	0	2	2
	Totals	82	4997	2.99	32	35	15	3	7	249	2514	.901			

Scott Arniel
Head Coach
Born: Kingston, Ont., September 17, 1962.

The Columbus Blue Jackets named Scott Arniel as their new head coach on June 8, 2010. Arniel joined the Blue Jackets after spending four seasons as head coach of the American Hockey League's Manitoba Moose, the top affiliate for the Vancouver Canucks. He led the club to a 181-106-33 record (.617) from 2006 to 2010, including North Division titles during the 2006-07 and 2008-09 seasons, four playoff appearances and a trip to the 2009 Calder Cup Final.

Arniel was named the winner of the 2008-09 A.R. Pieri Memorial Award as the AHL's outstanding coach after guiding the club to a 50-23-7 record, which marked the most successful season in franchise history. The team set franchise records for wins and finished first overall in the AHL for the first time in club history. Prior to his stint in Manitoba, he served as an assistant coach for the Buffalo Sabres for three seasons from 2002 to 2006 and helped the club to a 52-24-6 record and a berth in the Eastern Conference Final in 2005-06. He began his coaching career as an assistant coach with the Moose, serving in that capacity from 1999-2002.

Winnipeg's second pick, 22nd overall, in the 1981 Entry Draft, Arniel spent parts of 11 seasons in the NHL from 1981 to 1992 and registered 149 goals and 189 assists for 338 points and 599 penalty minutes in 730 career games with the Sabres, Winnipeg Jets and Boston Bruins. He helped his teams qualify for the Stanley Cup playoffs in eight of those seasons. Arniel set career highs with 21 goals and 35 assists for 56 points in 80 games with Winnipeg during the 1983-84 season.

The Kingston, Ontario native also played eight seasons in the AHL and former International Hockey League, collecting 201 goals, 273 assists (474 points) and 713 penalty minutes in 555 career games with Maine (AHL), New Haven (AHL), San Diego (IHL), Houston (IHL), Utah (IHL) and Manitoba (IHL). He added 25 goals and 17 assists for 42 and 88 penalty minutes in 55 career playoff games and helped the Utah Grizzlies win the Turner Cup in 1995-96. Arniel retired as a player following the 1998-99 season.

Prior to his professional career, Arniel played three seasons of major junior hockey with the Cornwall Royals and tallied 92 goals and 125 assists for 217 points and 196 penalty minutes in 153 career games. He helped the Royals win the Memorial Cup in 1980 and 1981. He also was a member of Team Canada at the 1982 World Junior Championships and helped the team to its first gold medal at the tournament.

Coaching Record

Season	Team	League	Regular Season				Playoffs			
			GC	W	L	O/T	GC	W	L	T
2006-07	Manitoba	AHL	80	45	23	12	13	6	7	....
2007-08	Manitoba	AHL	80	46	27	7	6	2	4	....
2008-09	Manitoba	AHL	80	50	23	7	22	14	8	....
2009-10	Manitoba	AHL	80	40	33	7	6	2	4	....

Antoine Vermette, Kristian Huselius and Jakub Voracek celebrate a goal.

General Managers' History

Doug MacLean, 2000-01 to 2006-07; Scott Howson, 2007-08 to date.

Coaching History

Dave King, 2000-01, 2001-02; Dave King and Doug MacLean, 2002-03; Doug MacLean and Gerard Gallant, 2003-04; Gerard Gallant, 2004-05, 2005-06; Gerard Gallant, Gary Agnew and Ken Hitchcock, 2006-07; Ken Hitchcock, 2007-08 to 2008-09; Ken Hitchcock and Claude Noel, 2009-10; Scott Arniel, 2010-11.

Club Records

Team

(Figures in brackets for season records are games played.)

Most Points	92	2008-09 (82)
Most Wins	41	2008-09 (82)
Most Ties	9	2000-01 (82)
Most Losses	47	2001-02 (82)
Most Goals	226	2008-09 (82)
Most Goals Against	279	2005-06 (82)
Fewest Points	57	2001-02 (82)
Fewest Wins	22	2001-02 (82)
Fewest Ties	8	2001-02 (82), 2002-03 (82), 2003-04 (82)
Fewest Losses	31	2008-09 (82)
Fewest Goals	164	2001-02 (82)
Fewest Goals Against	218	2007-08 (82)
Longest Winning Streak		
Overall	6	Mar. 24-Apr. 3/06
Home	6	Dec. 26/07-Jan. 15/08
Away	4	Dec. 2-12/06
Longest Undefeated Streak		
Overall	6	Mar. 24-Apr. 3/06 (6 wins)
Home	6	Dec. 26/07-Jan. 15/08 (6 wins)
Away	4	Jan. 3-11/03 (3 wins, 1 tie), Dec. 2-12/06 (4 wins)
Longest Losing Streak		
Overall	9	Dec. 10-26/09
Home	6	Oct. 12-Nov. 9/01
Away	13	Nov. 21/09-Jan. 5/10
Longest Winless Streak		
Overall	9	Dec. 4-23/03 (8 losses, 1 tie), Dec. 10-26/09 (7 losses, 2 ties)
Home	8	Oct. 4-Nov. 9/01 (6 losses, 2 ties), Dec. 4-31/03 (7 losses, 1 tie)
Away	14	Oct. 9-Dec. 23/03 (13 losses, 1 tie)
Most Shutouts, Season	11	2007-08 (82), 2008-09 (82)
Most PIM, Season	1,505	2002-03 (82)
Most Goals, Game	8	Mar. 7/09 (CBJ 8 at Det. 2)

Individual

Most Seasons	9	Rostislav Klesla
Most Games	543	David Vyborny
Most Goals, Career	227	Rick Nash
Most Assists, Career	204	David Vyborny
Most Points, Career	422	Rick Nash (227G, 195A)
Most PIM, Career	1,025	Jody Shelley
Most Shutouts, Career	15	Steve Mason
Longest Consecutive Games Streak	243	Jason Chimera (Oct. 9/05-Apr. 5/08)
Most Goals, Season	41	Rick Nash (2003-04)
Most Assists, Season	52	Ray Whitney (2002-03)
Most Points, Season	79	Rick Nash (2008-09; 40G, 39A)
Most PIM, Season	249	Jody Shelley (2002-03)
Most Points, Defenseman, Season	45	Jaroslav Spacek (2002-03; 9G, 36A)
Most Points, Center, Season	68	Andrew Cassels (2002-03; 20G, 48A)
Most Points, Right Wing, Season	65	David Vyborny (2005-06; 22G, 43A)
Most Points, Left Wing, Season	79	Rick Nash (2008-09; 40G, 39A)
Most Points, Rookie, Season	39	Rick Nash (2002-03; 17G, 22A)
Most Shutouts, Season	10	Steve Mason (2008-09)
Most Goals, Game	4	Geoff Sanderson (Mar. 29/03)
Most Assists, Game	5	Espen Knutsen (Mar. 24/01)
Most Points, Game	5	Espen Knutsen (Mar. 24/01; 5A), Geoff Sanderson (Mar. 29/03; 4G, 1A), Andrew Cassels (Mar. 29/03; 1G, 4A), David Vyborny (Feb. 28/04; 1G, 4A)

Captains' History

Lyle Odelein, 2000-01, 2001-02; Ray Whitney, 2002-03; Luke Richardson, 2003-04; Luke Richardson and Adam Foote, 2005-06; Adam Foote, 2006-07; Adam Foote and Rick Nash, 2007-08; Rick Nash, 2008-09 to date.

All-time Record vs. Other Clubs

Regular Season

	At Home								On Road								Total							
	GP	W	L	T	OL	GF	GA	PTS	GP	W	L	T	OL	GF	GA	PTS	GP	W	L	T	OL	GF	GA	PTS
Anaheim	18	9	8	0	1	47	45	19	18	8	7	1	2	49	52	19	36	17	15	1	3	96	97	38
Atlanta	6	4	2	0	0	16	12	8	6	3	3	0	0	14	13	6	12	7	5	0	0	30	25	14
Boston	5	3	2	0	0	10	18	6	4	2	2	0	0	10	12	4	9	5	4	0	0	20	30	10
Buffalo	4	3	0	1	0	12	6	7	6	4	2	0	0	18	14	8	10	7	2	1	0	30	20	15
Calgary	18	13	3	0	2	54	35	28	18	6	11	0	1	39	56	13	36	19	14	0	3	93	91	41
Carolina	5	3	2	0	0	13	12	6	6	2	4	0	0	17	16	4	11	5	6	0	0	30	28	10
Chicago	29	15	10	1	3	100	95	34	28	11	14	1	2	68	85	25	57	26	24	2	5	168	180	59
Colorado	18	5	12	1	0	37	62	11	18	3	14	0	1	32	66	7	36	8	26	1	1	69	128	18
Dallas	18	6	9	0	3	41	55	15	18	5	11	0	2	40	57	12	36	11	20	0	5	81	112	27
Detroit	29	9	13	1	6	57	93	25	28	6	20	0	2	66	101	14	57	15	33	1	8	123	194	39
Edmonton	18	6	8	3	1	46	61	16	18	5	11	0	2	42	61	12	36	11	19	3	3	88	122	28
Florida	4	2	2	0	0	9	9	4	5	3	2	0	0	15	14	6	9	5	4	0	0	24	23	10
Los Angeles	18	11	6	0	1	49	56	23	18	6	11	1	0	34	51	13	36	17	17	1	1	83	107	36
Minnesota	17	12	4	1	0	48	33	25	18	4	11	0	3	35	53	11	35	16	15	1	3	83	86	36
Montreal	3	1	2	0	0	7	9	2	6	3	2	1	0	12	11	7	9	4	4	1	0	19	20	9
Nashville	28	12	13	0	3	65	81	27	29	4	19	1	5	60	100	14	57	16	32	1	8	125	181	41
New Jersey	6	3	3	0	0	17	17	6	4	0	3	1	0	7	12	1	10	3	6	1	0	24	29	7
NY Islanders	7	5	0	1	1	23	15	12	5	2	1	0	2	15	17	6	12	7	1	1	3	38	32	18
NY Rangers	6	4	2	0	0	21	13	8	4	1	2	1	0	12	16	3	10	5	4	1	0	33	29	11
Ottawa	4	2	1	1	0	14	11	5	5	1	3	1	0	10	16	3	9	3	4	2	0	24	27	8
Philadelphia	5	1	2	2	0	10	10	4	4	0	3	1	0	8	15	1	9	1	5	3	0	18	25	5
Phoenix	18	7	9	1	1	42	45	16	18	5	9	3	1	40	53	14	36	12	18	4	2	82	98	30
Pittsburgh	6	3	0	0	3	23	17	9	5	1	4	0	0	13	21	2	11	4	4	0	3	36	38	11
St. Louis	28	14	9	2	3	76	75	33	29	7	16	1	5	66	103	20	57	21	25	3	8	142	178	53
San Jose	18	10	6	0	2	46	36	22	18	1	15	0	2	29	71	4	36	11	21	0	4	75	107	26
Tampa Bay	5	3	1	1	0	13	9	7	5	1	3	0	1	6	11	3	10	4	4	1	1	19	20	10
Toronto	3	1	2	0	0	9	13	2	5	1	3	1	0	9	16	3	8	2	5	1	0	18	29	5
Vancouver	18	7	7	2	2	47	60	18	18	6	11	0	1	51	71	13	36	13	18	2	3	98	131	31
Washington	7	2	3	0	2	19	22	6	5	2	2	1	0	15	15	5	12	4	5	1	2	34	37	11
Totals	**369**	**176**	**141**	**18**	**34**	**971**	**1025**	**404**	**369**	**103**	**219**	**15**	**32**	**832**	**1199**	**253**	**738**	**279**	**360**	**33**	**66**	**1803**	**2224**	**657**

Playoffs

	Series	W	L	GP	W	L	T	GF	GA	Last Mtg.	Rnd.	Result
Detroit	1	0	1	4	0	4	0	7	18	2009	CQF	L 0-4
Totals	**1**	**0**	**1**	**4**	**0**	**4**	**0**	**7**	**18**			

Playoff Results 2010-2006

Year	Round	Opponent	Result	GF	GA
2009	CQF	Detroit	L 0-4	7	18

Abbreviations: Round: CQF – conference quarter-final.

2009-10 Results

Oct.	3	Minnesota	2-1		31	Nashville	1-2*
	5	at Vancouver	5-3	Jan.	2	Colorado	2-3
	8	at San Jose	3-6		5	at Vancouver	3-7
	10	at Phoenix	2-0		7	at Edmonton	4-2
	13	Calgary	2-1		8	at Calgary	3-2
	17	Los Angeles	4-1		10	Dallas	2-0
	20	at Calgary	3-6		12	at St. Louis	1-4
	22	at Edmonton	4-6		14	at Chicago	0-3
	24	at Anaheim	6-4		16	Chicago	5-6
	25	at Los Angeles	2-6		18	St. Louis	4-2
	28	Phoenix	1-4		19	at Philadelphia	3-5
	30	Pittsburgh	3-4†		21	at Boston	3-2
Nov.	1	at Washington	5-4*		23	at Minnesota	2-4
	4	San Jose	2-3†		26	Nashville	3-2
	5	at Atlanta	4-3		28	Los Angeles	1-4
	7	Carolina	3-2		30	at St. Louis	3-2*
	11	Detroit	1-9	Feb.	2	at Colorado	1-5
	13	Anaheim	3-2†		4	Dallas	2-1
	16	Edmonton	3-2†		6	Buffalo	4-0
	19	at Dallas	4-1		10	San Jose	3-0
	21	at Nashville	3-4†		12	Vancouver	3-4
	23	at NY Rangers	4-7		14	Chicago	4-5†
	24	at Montreal	3-5	Mar.	2	Vancouver	3-4*
	26	at Ottawa	1-2		6	at San Jose	1-2
	28	Calgary	3-4†		8	at Los Angeles	0-6
	30	St. Louis	5-2		9	at Anaheim	5-2
Dec.	1	at Chicago	3-4†		11	Atlanta	2-1
	3	Toronto	3-6		13	St. Louis	1-5
	5	Colorado	2-3		15	Edmonton	5-3
	9	Florida	3-0		19	Minnesota	4-2
	10	at Nashville	3-4†		20	at Nashville	0-1*
	12	Anaheim	1-3		23	at New Jersey	3-6
	14	Nashville	3-5		25	Chicago	8-3
	15	at Minnesota	1-2		27	NY Islanders	3-4*
	17	Phoenix	1-2†		28	at Chicago	4-2
	19	at Colorado	2-5		30	Tampa Bay	3-2
	21	at Phoenix	2-5	Apr.	1	at Detroit	2-3
	23	at Dallas	1-3		3	Washington	2-3
	26	at Detroit	1-2		5	at St. Louis	1-2*
	28	Detroit	1-0*		7	at Detroit	3-4
	29	at NY Islanders	1-2†		9	Detroit	0-1†

* – Overtime † – Shootout

Entry Draft Selections 2010-2000

Name in bold denotes played in NHL.

2010

Pick	
4	Ryan Johansen
34	Dalton Smith
55	Petr Straka
94	Brandon Archibald
102	Mathieu Corbeil
124	Austin Madaisky
154	Dalton Prout
184	Martin Ouellette

2009

Pick	
21	John Moore
56	Kevin Lynch
94	David Savard
137	Thomas Larkin
167	Anton Blomqvist
197	Kyle Neuber

2008

Pick	
6	**Nikita Filatov**
37	Cody Goloubef
107	Steven Delisle
118	Drew Olson
127	Matt Calvert
135	Tomas Kubalik
137	Brent Regner
157	Cam Atkinson
187	Sean Collins

2007

Pick	
7	**Jakub Voracek**
37	Stefan Legein
53	Will Weber
68	Jake Hansen
94	**Maksim Mayorov**
158	Allen York
211	Trent Vogelhuber

2006

Pick	
6	**Derick Brassard**
69	**Steve Mason**
85	**Tom Sestito**
113	Ben Wright
129	Robert Nyholm
136	Nick Sucharski
142	Maxime Frechette
159	Jesse Dudas
189	**Derek Dorsett**
194	Matt Marquardt

2005

Pick	
6	**Gilbert Brule**
55	**Adam McQuaid**
67	**Kris Russell**
101	**Jared Boll**
131	**Tomas Popperle**
177	Derek Reinhart
189	Kirill Starkov
201	Trevor Hendrikx

2004

Pick	
8	**Alexandre Picard**
46	**Adam Pineault**
59	Kyle Wharton
93	**Dan LaCosta**
96	Andrey Plekhanov
133	Petr Pohl
167	Rob Page
190	Lennart Petrell
198	Justin Vienneau
231	Brian McGuirk
233	Matt Greer
271	**Grant Clitsome**

2003

Pick	
4	**Nikolai Zherdev**
46	**Dan Fritsche**
71	Dmitry Kosmachev
103	Kevin Jarman
104	**Philippe Dupuis**
138	Arsi Piispanen
168	**Marc Methot**
200	Alexander Guskov
233	Mathieu Gravel
283	Trevor Hendrikx

2002

Pick	
1	**Rick Nash**
41	**Joakim Lindstrom**
65	**Ole-Kristian Tollefsen**
96	Jeff Genovy
98	Ivan Tkachenko
119	Jekabs Redlihs
133	**Lasse Pirjeta**
168	Tim Konsorada
184	**Jaroslav Balastik**
199	**Greg Mauldin**
225	**Steven Goertzen**
231	Jaroslav Kracik
263	Sergei Mozyakin

2001

Pick	
8	**Pascal Leclaire**
38	**Tim Jackman**
53	Kiel McLeod
85	**Aaron Johnson**
87	Per Mars
141	**Cole Jarrett**
173	Justin Aikins
187	Artem Vostrikov
204	Raffaele Sannitz
236	Ryan Bowness
242	**Andrew Murray**

2000

Pick	
4	**Rostislav Klesla**
69	Ben Knopp
133	**Petteri Nummelin**
138	Scott Heffernan
150	Tyler Kolarik
169	Shane Bendera
200	Janne Jokila
231	Peter Zingoni
278	Martin Paroulek
286	**Andrej Nedorost**
292	Louis Mandeville

Scott Howson

General Manager

Born: Toronto, Ont., April 9, 1960.

The Columbus Blue Jackets announced the signing of Scott Howson as the second general manager in franchise history on June 15, 2007. In 2008-09 he led the Blue Jackets to the playoffs for the first time in franchise history. Howson joined the Blue Jackets after spending seven years with the Edmonton Oilers. He joined the Oilers in June 2000 as assistant to the general manager and was named assistant general manager a year later. In that role, he was responsible for all aspects of the club's hockey administration, including player contracts, personnel decisions, the collective bargaining agreement, its American Hockey League affiliates and the salary cap.

During his six seasons with the Oilers, the club posted five-straight winning campaigns from 2000 to 2006, averaged 37 wins and 89 points per season, topped 90 points four times and advanced to the 2006 Stanley Cup Final, where they were defeated in seven games by the Carolina Hurricanes.

Prior to his arrival in Edmonton, Howson spent six years with the club's AHL affiliates. As general manager of the Cape Breton Oilers from 1994 to 1996, he oversaw the franchise's move to Hamilton in 1996 and was the Bulldogs' general manager from 1996 to 2000. During that time, he led Hamilton to a pair of berths in the Calder Cup Finals (1997, 2003) and a conference semifinals appearance in 2002.

Howson played three seasons in the Ontario Hockey League as a forward with the Kingston Canadiens from 1978 to 1981, serving as team captain and earning OHL All-Star honors. Following his junior career, he signed a free agent contract with the New York Islanders and spent the next five years playing at various levels throughout the organization.

During his rookie season in 1981-82, he was named the International Hockey League's rookie of the year after registering 55 goals and 65 assists for 120 points in 71 games with the Toledo Goaldiggers. He was the league's second-leading scorer that year and helped Toledo capture the league championship. Howson also won a Central Hockey League title with the Indianapolis Checkers in 1982-83. He made his NHL debut with the Islanders during the 1984-85 season and tallied 4 goals and one assist in eight games. He added a goal and two assists in 10 games the following season before retiring as a player at the end of the 1985-86 season. Howson received his bachelor's degree in 1987 from York University in Toronto and is a 1990 graduate of the university's Osgoode Hall Law School.

Club Directory

Nationwide Arena

Columbus Blue Jackets
Nationwide Arena
200 W. Nationwide Blvd.
Columbus, Ohio 43215
Phone **614/246-4625**
FAX 614/246-4007
www.BlueJackets.com
Capacity: 18,144

Ownership

Majority Owner/Governor	John P. McConnell

Executive Staff

President/Alternate Governor	Mike Priest
Executive Vice President of Business Operations	Larry Hoepfner
Sr. Vice President/General Counsel	Greg Kirstein
Sr. Vice President of Corporate Development	Cameron Scholvin
Chief Financial Officer	T.J. LaMendola
Senior Vice President of Sales and Marketing	John Browne
Vice President of Marketing	Marc Gregory
Vice President of Public Relations	Todd Sharrock

Hockey Operations

Exec. V.P. of Hockey Ops/General Manager	Scott Howson
Assistant General Manager	Chris MacFarland
Director of Hockey Operations & Player Personnel	Don Boyd
Director of Pro Scouting	Bob Strumm
Director of Amateur Scouting	Paul Castron
Assistant Director of Amateur Scouting	John Williams
Amateur Scouts	Brian Bates, Andrew Dickson, Sam McMaster, Andrew Shaw
Pro Scout	Peter Dineen
Professional European Scout	Kjell Larsson
Regional Scouts	Artem Telepin, Milan Tichy
Director of Video Scouting	Bryan Stewart
Assistant Video Scout	Scott Harris
Manager of Team Services	Julie Gamble
Manager of Hockey Administration	Josh Flynn

Coaching Staff

Head Coach	Scott Arniel
Assistant Coaches	Brad Berry, Bob Boughner, Dan Hinote
Goaltending Coach	Dave Rook
Development Coach	Tyler Wright
Strength & Conditioning Coach	Kevin Collins
Video Coordinator	Dan Singleton

Training & Equipment Staff

Head Athletic Trainer	Mike Vogt
Assistant Athletic Trainers	Chris Strickland, Mark Teeples
Equipment Manager	Tim LeRoy
Assistant Equipment Manager	Jamie Healy
Equipment Assistant	Jason Stypinski

Business Operations

Director of Business Communications	Karen Davis
Director of Event Presentation/Production	Kimberly Kershaw
Director of Marketing & Fan Development	J.D. Kershaw
Director of Community Development	Wendy Bradshaw
Director of Creative Services	Jason Rothwell
Senior Graphic Designer	Will Bennett
Graphic Designer	Jessica Dusenbery
Manager of Communications	Ryan Holtmann
Manager of Multimedia	Ryan Mulcrone
Manager of Marketing	Jim Riley
Partnership Activation Manager	Mike Kerrigan
Manager of Corporate Development Services	Craig Smith
Partnership Account Specialists	Becky Ackford, Erin Gibbons, Josh Hafer
Partnership Account Executives	Jerry Angel, Ryan Shirk, Matt Tremblay
Premium Seating Account Executive	Evan Bollie
Premium Seating Relationship Manager	Rachel Mayfield
Premium Services Specialist	Amanda Horning
Manager of Production	David Traube
Manager of Event Presentation	Lynn Truitt
Broadcast Engineer	Rick Shepherd
Graphics Coordinator	Andy Hookman
Manager of Fan Development	Joel Siegman
Manager of Community Development	Kate Furman
Community Development & Mascot Coordinator	Jason Zumpano
Office Coordinator/Receptionist	Beth Carlisle

Human Resources and Legal

Director of Human Resources	Kelly Miller
Payroll Manager	Christine Parthemore
Paralegal	Ken Erney
Legal Assistant	Rachel Phillips

Finance and Information Technology

Controller	Jeremy Manly
Assistant Controller	Jason LaPlace
Staff Accountant	Nora Ludwig
Accounts Payable Coordinators	Beth Carpenter, Lindsay Rice
Director of Information Technology	Jim Connolly
Information Technology Manager	John Gruber
Systems Analyst	Matthew DeStephen

Ticket Sales and Operations

Director of Ticket Operations	Mark Morris
Manager of Ticket Sales & Service	Cory Rowe
Group Sales Manager	Luke Burket
Inside Sales Supervisor	Drew Ribarchak
Ticket Operations Manager	Brian Forth

Broadcasting

Director of Broadcasting	Russ Mollohan
FOX Sports Ohio Play-By-Play Announcer / Color	Jeff Rimer / Bill Davidge
Radio Play-By-Play Announcer / Color	George Matthews / Bob McElligott

Nationwide Arena Management

Director of Operations	Scott Lofton
Director of Event Services	Blake Schilling
Assistant Director of Operations	Brad Cleveland
Guest Services Manager	Adam Borland
Ice Technician	Ian Huffman

Dallas Stars

2009-10 Results: 37w-31L-4OTL-10SOL 88PTS.
Fifth, Pacific Division

Key Off-Season Signings/Acquisitions

2010
May 11 • Re-signed G **Kari Lehtonen**.
June 30 • Re-signed RW **Krys Barch**.
July 1 • Signed C **Adam Burish** and G **Andrew Raycroft**.
13 • Named **Willie Desjardins** assistant coach.
16 • Re-signed D **Maxime Fortunus**.
16 • Signed D **Brad Lukowich**.
23 • Re-signed LW **Fabian Brunnstrom**.

2010-11 Schedule

Oct. Fri.	8	at New Jersey	
Sat.	9	at NY Islanders	
Thu.	14	Detroit	
Sat.	16	St. Louis	
Mon.	18	at Tampa Bay	
Thu.	21	at Florida	
Sat.	23	Nashville	
Tue.	26	Anaheim	
Thu.	28	Los Angeles	
Sat.	30	Buffalo	
Nov. Wed.	3	Pittsburgh	
Fri.	5	Phoenix	
Sat.	6	at Colorado	
Thu.	11	at Los Angeles	
Fri.	12	at Anaheim	
Tue.	16	Anaheim	
Thu.	18	San Jose	
Sat.	20	Colorado	
Mon.	22	at Toronto	
Wed.	24	at Ottawa	
Fri.	26	St. Louis	
Sat.	27	at St. Louis	
Mon.	29	at Carolina	
Dec. Thu.	2	Washington	
Sat.	4	Minnesota	
Mon.	6	at Columbus	
Wed.	8	at Chicago	
Fri.	10	Carolina	
Sat.	11	at Phoenix	
Mon.	13	at San Jose	
Thu.	16	San Jose	
Sat.	18	at Columbus	
Sun.	19	at Detroit*	
Tue.	21	Montreal	
Thu.	23	Calgary	
Sun.	26	Phoenix	
Tue.	28	at Nashville	
Wed.	29	Detroit	
Fri.	31	Vancouver	
Jan. Sun.	2	at St. Louis*	
Wed.	5	at Chicago	
Fri.	7	NY Rangers	
Sun.	9	at Minnesota*	
Tue.	11	Edmonton	
Sat.	15	Atlanta	
Mon.	17	Los Angeles	
Thu.	20	at Edmonton	
Fri.	21	at Calgary	
Mon.	24	at Vancouver	
Wed.	26	Edmonton	
Feb. Tue.	1	Vancouver	
Thu.	3	at Boston	
Sat.	5	at Philadelphia	
Wed.	9	Phoenix	
Fri.	11	Chicago	
Sun.	13	Columbus*	
Tue.	15	at Edmonton	
Wed.	16	at Calgary	
Sat.	19	at Vancouver	
Tue.	22	New Jersey	
Thu.	24	at Detroit	
Sat.	26	Nashville*	
Mar. Tue.	1	at Phoenix	
Fri.	4	at Anaheim	
Sat.	5	at San Jose	
Mon.	7	at Los Angeles	
Wed.	9	Calgary	
Fri.	11	Minnesota	
Sun.	13	Los Angeles*	
Tue.	15	San Jose	
Thu.	17	Chicago	
Sat.	19	Philadelphia	
Wed.	23	Anaheim	
Sat.	26	at Nashville	
Tue.	29	at Phoenix	
Thu.	31	at San Jose	
Apr. Sat.	2	at Los Angeles*	
Sun.	3	at Anaheim*	
Tue.	5	Columbus	
Thu.	7	Colorado	
Fri.	8	at Colorado	
Sun.	10	at Minnesota*	

* Denotes afternoon game.

PACIFIC DIVISION
44th NHL Season

Franchise date: June 5, 1967
Transferred from Minnesota to Dallas, June 9, 1993.

After an injury-plagued 2008-09 season, Brad Richards played 80 games in 2009-10 and led the Stars with 67 assists and 91 points. His 24 goals ranked him third, but his 13 power-play goals were tops on the team.

Year-by-Year Record

Season	GP	Home W	L	T	OL	Road W	L	T	OL	Overall W	L	T	OL	GF	GA	Pts.	Finished	Playoff Result
2009-10	82	23	11		7	14	20		7	37	31		14	237	254	88	5th, Pacific Div.	Out of Playoffs
2008-09	82	20	16		5	16	19		6	36	35		11	230	257	83	3rd, Pacific Div.	Out of Playoffs
2007-08	82	23	16		2	22	14		5	45	30		7	242	207	97	3rd, Pacific Div.	Lost Conf. Championship
2006-07	82	28	11		2	22	14		5	50	25		7	226	197	107	3rd, Pacific Div.	Lost Conf. Quarter-Final
2005-06	82	28	11		2	25	12		4	53	23		6	265	218	112	1st, Pacific Div.	Lost Conf. Quarter-Final
2004-05	....																	
2003-04	82	26	7	8	0	15	19	5	2	41	26	13	2	194	175	97	2nd, Pacific Div.	Lost Conf. Quarter-Final
2002-03	82	28	5	6	2	18	12	9	2	46	17	15	4	245	169	111	1st, Pacific Div.	Lost Conf. Semi-Final
2001-02	82	18	13	6	4	18	15	7	1	36	28	13	5	215	213	90	4th, Pacific Div.	Out of Playoffs
2000-01	82	26	10	5	0	22	14	3	2	48	24	8	2	241	187	106	1st, Pacific Div.	Lost Conf. Semi-Final
1999-2000	82	21	11	5	4	22	12	5	2	43	23	10	6	211	184	102	1st, Pacific Div.	Lost Final
1998-99	**82**	**29**	**8**	**4**		**22**	**11**	**8**		**51**	**19**	**12**		**236**	**168**	**114**	**1st, Pacific Div.**	**Won Stanley Cup**
1997-98	82	26	8	7		23	14	4		49	22	11		242	167	109	1st, Central Div.	Lost Conf. Championship
1996-97	82	25	13	3		23	13	5		48	26	8		252	198	104	1st, Central Div.	Lost Conf. Quarter-Final
1995-96	82	14	18	9		12	24	5		26	42	14		227	280	66	6th, Central Div.	Out of Playoffs
1994-95	48	9	10	5		8	13	3		17	23	8		136	135	42	5th, Central Div.	Lost Conf. Quarter-Final
1993-94	84	23	12	7		19	17	6		42	29	13		286	265	97	3rd, Central Div.	Lost Conf. Semi-Final
1992-93*	84	18	17	7		18	21	3		36	38	10		272	293	82	5th, Norris Div.	Out of Playoffs
1991-92*	80	20	16	4		12	26	2		32	42	6		246	278	70	4th, Norris Div.	Lost Div. Semi-Final
1990-91*	80	19	15	6		8	24	8		27	39	14		256	266	68	4th, Norris Div.	Lost Final
1989-90*	80	26	12	2		10	28	2		36	40	4		284	291	76	4th, Norris Div.	Lost Div. Semi-Final
1988-89*	80	17	15	8		10	22	8		27	37	16		258	278	70	3rd, Norris Div.	Lost Div. Semi-Final
1987-88*	80	10	24	6		9	24	7		19	48	13		242	349	51	5th, Norris Div.	Out of Playoffs
1986-87*	80	17	20	3		13	20	7		30	40	10		296	314	70	5th, Norris Div.	Out of Playoffs
1985-86*	80	21	15	4		17	18	5		38	33	9		327	305	85	2nd, Norris Div.	Lost Div. Semi-Final
1984-85*	80	14	19	7		11	24	5		25	43	12		268	321	62	4th, Norris Div.	Lost Div. Final
1983-84*	80	22	14	4		17	17	6		39	31	10		345	344	88	1st, Norris Div.	Lost Conf. Championship
1982-83*	80	23	6	11		17	18	5		40	24	16		321	290	96	2nd, Norris Div.	Lost Div. Final
1981-82*	80	21	7	12		16	16	8		37	23	20		346	288	94	1st, Norris Div.	Lost Div. Semi-Final
1980-81*	80	23	10	7		12	18	10		35	28	17		291	263	87	3rd, Adams Div.	Lost Final
1979-80*	80	25	8	7		11	20	9		36	28	16		311	253	88	3rd, Adams Div.	Lost Semi-Final
1978-79*	80	19	15	6		9	25	6		28	40	12		257	289	68	4th, Adams Div.	Out Of Playoffs
1977-78*	80	12	24	4		6	25	9		18	53	9		218	325	45	5th, Smythe Div.	Out of Playoffs
1976-77*	80	17	14	9		6	25	9		23	39	18		240	310	64	2nd, Smythe Div.	Lost Prelim. Round
1975-76*	80	15	22	3		5	31	4		20	53	7		195	303	47	4th, Smythe Div.	Out of Playoffs
1974-75*	80	17	20	3		6	30	4		23	50	7		221	341	53	4th, Smythe Div.	Out of Playoffs
1973-74*	78	18	15	6		5	23	11		23	38	17		235	275	63	7th, West Div.	Out of Playoffs
1972-73*	78	26	8	5		11	22	6		37	30	11		254	230	85	3rd, West Div.	Lost Quarter-Final
1971-72*	78	22	11	6		15	18	6		37	29	12		212	191	86	2nd, West Div.	Lost Quarter-Final
1970-71*	78	16	15	8		12	19	8		28	34	16		191	223	72	4th, West Div.	Lost Semi-Final
1969-70*	76	11	16	11		8	19	11		19	35	22		224	257	60	3rd, West Div.	Lost Quarter-Final
1968-69*	76	11	21	6		7	22	9		18	43	15		189	270	51	6th, West Div.	Out of Playoffs
1967-68*	74	17	12	8		10	20	7		27	32	15		191	226	69	4th, West Div.	Lost Semi-Final

* Minnesota North Stars

2010-11 Player Personnel

FORWARDS	HT	WT	S	Place of Birth	*Age	2009-10 Club
BARCH, Krys	6-1	222	L	Hamilton, Ont.	30	Dallas
BENN, Jamie	6-2	207	L	Victoria, B.C.	21	Dallas-Texas
BRUNNSTROM, Fabian	6-2	212	L	Jonstorp, Sweden	25	Dallas-Texas
BURISH, Adam	6-0	189	R	Madison, WI	27	Chicago
ERIKSSON, Loui	6-1	189	L	Goteborg, Sweden	25	Dallas
MORROW, Brenden	6-0	205	L	Carlyle, Sask.	31	Dallas
NEAL, James	6-2	208	L	Whitby, Ont.	23	Dallas
OTT, Steve	6-0	194	L	Summerside, P.E.I.	28	Dallas
PETERSEN, Toby	5-10	198	L	Minneapolis, MN	31	Dallas
RIBEIRO, Mike	6-0	173	L	Montreal, Que.	30	Dallas
RICHARDS, Brad	6-0	196	L	Murray Harbour, P.E.I.	30	Dallas
SAWADA, Raymond	6-2	207	R	Richmond, B.C.	25	Dallas-Texas
SEGAL, Brandon	6-2	209	R	Richmond, B.C.	27	L.A.-Manchester-Dal
SUTHERBY, Brian	6-2	204	L	Edmonton, Alta.	28	Dallas
WANDELL, Tom	6-1	195	L	Sodertalje, Sweden	23	Dallas

DEFENSEMEN	HT	WT	S	Place of Birth	*Age	2009-10 Club
DALEY, Trevor	5-11	199	L	Toronto, Ont.	26	Dallas
FISTRIC, Mark	6-3	234	L	Edmonton, Alta.	24	Dallas
GROSSMAN, Nicklas	6-4	226	L	Stockholm, Sweden	25	Dallas
LUKOWICH, Brad	6-1	200	L	Cranbrook, B.C.	34	Texas-Vancouver
NISKANEN, Matt	6-0	204	R	Virginia, MN	23	Dallas
ROBIDAS, Stephane	5-11	193	R	Sherbrooke, Que.	33	Dallas
SKRASTINS, Karlis	6-1	208	L	Riga, Latvia	36	Dallas
WOYWITKA, Jeff	6-2	224	L	Vermilion, Alta.	27	Dallas

GOALTENDERS	HT	WT	C	Place of Birth	*Age	2009-10 Club
KRAHN, Brent	6-4	232	L	Winnipeg, Man.	28	Texas
LEHTONEN, Kari	6-4	215	L	Helsinki, Finland	26	Chicago (AHL)-Dallas
RAYCROFT, Andrew	6-0	173	L	Belleville, Ont.	30	Vancouver

* – Age at start of 2010-11 season

2009-10 Scoring
* – rookie

Regular Season

Pos	#	Player	Team	GP	G	A	Pts	TOI	+/-	PIM	PP	SH	GW	S	%
C	91	Brad Richards	DAL	80	24	67	91	20:51	-12	14	13	0	2	284	8.5
L	21	Loui Eriksson	DAL	82	29	42	71	19:45	-4	26	6	2	4	214	13.6
L	18	James Neal	DAL	78	27	28	55	18:11	-5	64	2	1	4	200	13.5
L	63	Mike Ribeiro	DAL	66	19	34	53	19:32	-5	38	8	2	0	155	12.3
L	10	Brenden Morrow	DAL	76	20	26	46	19:10	-3	69	9	1	2	155	12.9
L	14 *	Jamie Benn	DAL	82	22	19	41	14:42	-1	45	2	0	3	182	12.1
D	3	Stephane Robidas	DAL	82	10	31	41	24:29	-10	70	7	0	1	199	5.0
C	29	Steve Ott	DAL	73	22	14	36	16:28	-14	153	8	1	2	146	15.1
C	9	Mike Modano	DAL	59	14	16	30	14:18	-6	22	3	0	2	115	12.2
D	6	Trevor Daley	DAL	77	6	16	22	22:11	9	25	2	0	2	107	5.6
R	26	Jere Lehtinen	DAL	58	4	13	17	14:44	-8	8	1	1	0	87	4.6
C	17	Toby Petersen	DAL	78	9	6	15	10:55	3	6	0	1	0	110	8.2
C	23 *	Tom Wandell	DAL	50	5	10	15	13:52	2	14	0	0	3	85	5.9
D	5	Matt Niskanen	DAL	74	3	12	15	18:15	-15	18	0	0	2	110	2.7
D	37	Karlis Skrastins	DAL	79	2	11	13	19:34	-4	24	0	0	0	53	3.8
R	24	Brandon Segal	L.A.	25	1	1	2	6:46	0	20	0	0	0	24	4.2
			DAL	19	5	5	10	11:20	3	18	0	0	2	31	16.1
			Total	44	6	6	12	8:44	3	38	0	0	2	55	10.9
L	96	Fabian Brunnstrom	DAL	44	2	9	11	10:40	-3	10	0	0	0	38	5.3
D	28	Mark Fistric	DAL	67	1	9	10	14:55	27	69	0	0	0	46	2.2
D	20	Brian Sutherby	DAL	46	5	4	9	8:36	8	66	0	0	0	49	10.2
D	2	Nicklas Grossman	DAL	71	0	7	7	19:11	-3	32	0	0	0	58	0.0
R	13	Krys Barch	DAL	63	0	6	6	7:02	0	130	0	0	0	29	0.0
D	44	Jeff Woywitka	DAL	36	0	3	3	14:06	-6	11	0	0	0	44	0.0
C	25	Warren Peters	DAL	11	1	0	1	7:13	1	2	0	0	0	8	12.5
D	36 *	Philip Larsen	DAL	2	0	1	1	12:27	1	0	0	0	0	1	0.0
C	15 *	Perttu Lindgren	DAL	1	0	0	0	8:33	0	0	0	0	0	0	0.0
C	11 *	Aaron Gagnon	DAL	2	0	0	0	8:49	0	0	0	0	0	2	0.0
D	59 *	Ivan Vishnevskiy	DAL	2	0	0	0	16:38	-2	0	0	0	0	4	0.0
L	58 *	Francis Wathier	DAL	5	0	0	0	5:17	0	5	0	0	0	1	0.0
R	12 *	Raymond Sawada	DAL	5	0	0	0	8:09	1	4	0	0	0	2	0.0
D	38	Maxime Fortunus	DAL	8	0	0	0	15:08	-6	4	0	0	0	5	0.0

Goaltending

No.	Goaltender	GPI	Mins	Avg	W	L	OT	EN	SO	GA	SA	S%	G	A	PIM
35	Marty Turco	53	3088	2.72	22	20	11	8	4	140	1605	.913	0	4	10
32	Kari Lehtonen	12	663	2.81	6	4	0	0	0	31	350	.911	0	1	0
31	Alex Auld	21	1181	3.00	9	6	3	1	0	59	558	.894	0	2	2
33	Matt Climie	1	60	5.00	0	1	0	0	0	5	38	.868	0	0	0
	Totals	82	5018	2.92	37	31	14	9	4	244	2559	.905			

Marc Crawford
Head Coach

Born: Belleville, Ont., February 13, 1961.

Dallas Stars general manager Joe Nieuwendyk announced on June 11, 2009 that the club had hired Marc Crawford as the 20th head coach in franchise history. Crawford became just the 15th coach in NHL history to serve 1,000 games behind the bench when he reached the milestone with the Stars on October 30, 2009. He became the 15th to win 500 on March 16, 2010. Prior to his arrival in Dallas, Crawford had served behind the bench for Quebec/Colorado, Vancouver and Los Angeles from 1994 to 2008. He won the 1996 Stanley Cup championship with Colorado, as well as five division titles and had six seasons of 40-or-more wins. Crawford was the youngest recipient of the Jack Adams Award as NHL coach of the year, winning at age 34 with the Quebec Nordiques in 1995.

Crawford is the all-time winningest coach in Vancouver Canucks history with 246 wins over seven seasons from 1999 to 2006. The Canucks made the playoffs in four of his last five seasons as head coach. Crawford began his NHL coaching career with Quebec in 1994 and, after the Nordiques relocated to Denver in 1996, became the third-youngest coach in NHL history to win the Stanley Cup.

The native of Belleville, Ontario, served as the head coach for Team Canada at the 1998 Winter Olympic Games in Nagano, Japan, finishing first in its pool and advancing to the semifinals before losing to the eventual champions, Czech Republic. Crawford spent three seasons as the head coach of St. John's in the American Hockey League from 1991 to 1994, where he won the 1993 Louis A.R. Pieri Memorial Award as AHL coach of the year, and two campaigns with the Cornwall Royals of the Ontario Hockey League from 1989 to 1991.

Prior to beginning his coaching career, Crawford was selected in the fourth round (70th overall) of the 1980 Entry Draft by Vancouver, and skated in 176 career NHL games, all with the Canucks, recording 19 goals and 31 assists for 50 points. He made his NHL debut with Vancouver during the 1981-82 season, which he split between the Canucks and the Dallas Black Hawks of the Central Hockey League.

Coaching Record

Season	Team	League	Regular Season GC	W	L	O/T	Playoffs GC	W	L	T
1989-90	Cornwall	OHL	66	24	38	4	6	2	4	....
1990-91	Cornwall	OHL	66	23	42	1	....	....	....	....
1991-92	St. John's	AHL	80	39	29	12	16	11	5	....
1992-93	St. John's	AHL	80	41	26	13	9	4	5	....
1993-94	St. John's	AHL	80	45	23	12	11	6	5	....
1994-95	Quebec	NHL	48	30	13	5	6	2	4	....
1995-96 ♦	Colorado	NHL	82	47	25	10	22	16	6	....
1996-97	Colorado	NHL	82	49	24	9	17	10	7	....
1997-98	Colorado	NHL	82	39	26	17	7	3	4	....
1998-99	Vancouver	NHL	37	8	23	6	....	....	....	....
99-2000	Vancouver	NHL	82	30	29	23	....	....	....	....
2000-01	Vancouver	NHL	82	36	28	18	....	....	....	....
2001-02	Vancouver	NHL	82	42	30	10	6	2	4	....
2002-03	Vancouver	NHL	82	45	23	14	14	7	7	....
2003-04	Vancouver	NHL	82	43	24	15	7	3	4	....
2004-05	Vancouver		SEASON CANCELLED							
2005-06	Vancouver	NHL	82	42	32	8	....	....	....	....
2006-07	Los Angeles	NHL	82	27	41	14	....	....	....	....
2007-08	Los Angeles	NHL	82	32	43	7	....	....	....	....
2009-10	Dallas	NHL	82	37	31	14	....	....	....	....
	NHL Totals		1069	507	392	170	79	43	36	....

♦ Stanley Cup win.
Won Jack Adams Award (1995)

Coaching History

Wren Blair, 1967-68; Wren Blair and John Muckler, 1968-69; Wren Blair and Charlie Burns, 1969-70; Jack Gordon, 1970-71 to 1972-73; Jack Gordon and Parker MacDonald, 1973-74; Jack Gordon and Charlie Burns, 1974-75; Ted Harris, 1975-76, 1976-77; Ted Harris, André Beaulieu and Lou Nanne, 1977-78; Harry Howell and Glen Sonmor, 1978-79; Glen Sonmor, 1979-80 to 1981-82; Glen Sonmor and Murray Oliver, 1982-83; Bill Mahoney, 1983-84, 1984-85; Lorne Henning, 1985-86; Lorne Henning and Glen Sonmor, 1986-87; Herb Brooks, 1987-88; Pierre Page, 1988-89, 1989-90; Bob Gainey, 1990-91 to 1994-95; Bob Gainey and Ken Hitchcock, 1995-96; Ken Hitchcock, 1996-97 to 2000-01; Ken Hitchcock and Rick Wilson, 2001-02; Dave Tippett, 2002-03 to 2008-09; Marc Crawford, 2009-10 to date.

Club Records

Team

(Figures in brackets for season records are games played; records for fewest points, wins, ties, losses, goals, goals against are for 70 or more games)

Most Points **114** 1998-99 (82)
Most Wins **53** 2005-06 (82)
Most Ties **22** 1969-70 (76)
Most Losses **53** 1975-76 (80), 1977-78 (80)
Most Goals **346** 1981-82 (80)
Most Goals Against **349** 1987-88 (80)
Fewest Points **45** 1977-78 (80)
Fewest Wins **18** 1968-69 (76), 1977-78 (80)
Fewest Ties **4** 1989-90 (80)
Fewest Losses **19** 1998-99 (82)
Fewest Goals **189** 1968-69 (76)
Fewest Goals Against **167** 1997-98 (82)
Longest Winning Streak
Overall .... **7** Mar. 16-28/80, Mar. 16-Apr. 2/97, Nov. 22-Dec. 5/97, Jan. 29-Feb. 11/08
Home .... **11** Nov. 4-Dec. 27/72
Away .... **7** Four times
Longest Undefeated Streak
Overall .... **15** Dec. 6/98-Jan. 6/99 (12 wins, 3 ties)
Home .... **17** Jan. 23-Mar. 20/04 (13 wins, 4 ties)
Away .... **10** Jan. 12-Mar. 4/99 (8 wins, 2 ties), Dec. 27/02-Feb. 25/03 (7 wins, 3 ties)
Longest Losing Streak
Overall .... **10** Feb. 1-20/76
Home .... **6** Jan. 17-Feb. 4/70, Feb. 21-Mar. 8/09
Away .... **10** Dec. 12/09-Jan. 21/10
Longest Winless Streak
Overall .... **20** Jan. 15-Feb. 28/70 (15 losses, 5 ties)
Home .... **12** Jan. 17-Feb. 25/70 (8 losses, 4 ties)
Away .... **23** Oct. 25/74-Jan. 28/75 (19 losses, 4 ties)
Most Shutouts, Season **11** 2000-01 (82), 2002-03 (82)
Most PIM, Season **2,313** 1987-88 (80)
Most Goals, Game .... **15** Nov. 11/81 (Wpg. 2 at Min. 15)

Individual

Most Seasons .... **21** Mike Modano
Most Games .... **1,459** Mike Modano
Most Goals, Career .... **557** Mike Modano
Most Assists, Career .... **802** Mike Modano
Most Points, Career .... **1,359** Mike Modano (557G, 802A)
Most PIM, Career .... **1,883** Shane Churla
Most Shutouts, Career .... **40** Marty Turco
Longest Consecutive Games Streak .... **442** Danny Grant (Dec. 4/68-Apr. 7/74)
Most Goals, Season .... **55** Dino Ciccarelli (1981-82), Brian Bellows (1989-90)
Most Assists, Season .... **76** Neal Broten (1985-86)
Most Points, Season .... **114** Bobby Smith (1981-82; 43G, 71A)
Most PIM, Season .... **382** Basil McRae (1987-88)
Most Points, Defenseman, Season .... **77** Craig Hartsburg (1981-82; 17G, 60A)
Most Points, Center, Season .... **114** Bobby Smith (1981-82; 43G, 71A)
Most Points, Right Wing, Season .... **106** Dino Ciccarelli (1981-82; 55G, 51A)
Most Points, Left Wing, Season .... **99** Brian Bellows (1989-90; 55G, 44A)
Most Points, Rookie, Season .... **98** Neal Broten (1981-82; 38G, 60A)
Most Shutouts, Season .... **9** Ed Belfour (1997-98), Marty Turco (2003-04)
Most Goals, Game .... **5** Tim Young (Jan. 15/79)
Most Assists, Game .... **5** Murray Oliver (Oct. 24/71), Larry Murphy (Oct. 17/89), Brad Richards (Feb. 28/08)
Most Points, Game .... **7** Bobby Smith (Nov. 11/81; 4G, 3A)

Records include Minnesota North Stars, 1967-68 through 1992-93.

Retired Numbers

7	Neal Broten	1980-1995, 1996-1997
8	Bill Goldsworthy*	1967-1976
19	Bill Masterton*	1967-1968

* Minnesota North Stars

All-time Record vs. Other Clubs

Regular Season

	At Home								On Road								Total							
	GP	W	L	T	OL	GF	GA	PTS	GP	W	L	T	OL	GF	GA	PTS	GP	W	L	T	OL	GF	GA	PTS
Anaheim	45	33	9	2	1	149	87	69	45	22	15	3	5	122	112	52	90	55	24	5	6	271	199	121
Atlanta	6	5	1	0	0	13	9	10	6	5	0	0	1	26	18	11	12	10	1	0	1	39	27	21
Boston	63	19	31	13	0	179	224	51	62	10	42	10	0	149	264	30	125	29	73	23	0	328	488	81
Buffalo	56	27	22	6	1	178	163	61	54	13	30	11	0	145	197	37	110	40	52	17	1	323	360	98
Calgary	72	36	22	11	3	255	218	86	72	21	35	14	2	178	227	58	144	57	57	25	5	433	445	144
Carolina	32	20	10	2	0	125	92	42	34	15	15	4	0	117	111	34	66	35	25	6	0	242	203	76
Chicago	122	58	47	16	1	419	376	133	120	35	68	15	2	318	442	87	242	93	115	31	3	737	818	220
Colorado	51	28	16	5	2	171	144	63	51	16	27	7	1	127	180	40	102	44	43	12	3	298	324	103
Columbus	18	13	3	0	2	57	40	28	18	12	4	0	2	55	41	26	36	25	7	0	4	112	81	54
Detroit	116	57	40	18	1	393	344	133	116	41	59	16	0	362	439	98	232	98	99	34	1	755	783	231
Edmonton	55	31	16	7	1	199	152	70	54	22	22	8	2	178	207	54	109	53	38	15	3	377	359	124
Florida	11	4	3	2	2	37	37	12	12	6	4	1	1	33	25	14	23	10	7	3	3	70	62	26
Los Angeles	102	61	26	13	2	372	270	137	100	36	38	19	7	296	328	98	202	97	64	32	9	668	598	235
Minnesota	18	14	2	1	1	69	41	30	18	9	8	0	1	40	47	19	36	23	10	1	2	109	88	49
Montreal	61	18	31	12	0	158	207	48	60	12	39	9	0	149	259	33	121	30	70	21	0	307	466	81
Nashville	22	17	4	0	1	66	30	35	22	9	12	1	0	48	58	19	44	26	16	1	1	114	88	54
New Jersey	48	29	13	6	0	176	123	64	46	19	24	3	0	134	159	41	94	48	37	9	0	310	282	105
NY Islanders	49	19	21	8	1	143	176	47	50	16	25	8	1	142	181	41	99	35	46	16	2	285	357	88
NY Rangers	63	21	31	11	0	199	228	53	65	17	37	11	0	172	221	45	128	38	68	22	0	371	449	98
Ottawa	13	8	5	0	0	51	36	16	11	6	3	0	2	30	27	14	24	14	8	0	2	81	63	30
Philadelphia	68	28	24	16	0	221	217	72	70	10	44	16	0	160	266	36	138	38	68	32	0	381	483	108
Phoenix	73	35	28	9	1	243	211	80	72	38	28	4	2	238	220	82	145	73	56	13	3	481	431	162
Pittsburgh	66	37	22	6	1	250	221	81	65	19	40	6	0	182	246	44	131	56	62	12	1	432	467	125
St. Louis	125	59	42	22	2	417	365	142	127	35	69	21	2	355	455	93	252	94	111	43	4	772	820	235
San Jose	47	22	18	4	3	131	115	51	48	29	16	1	2	132	112	61	95	51	34	5	5	263	227	112
Tampa Bay	13	8	4	1	0	46	36	17	15	11	2	2	0	41	25	24	28	19	6	3	0	87	61	41
Toronto	99	52	36	11	0	372	310	115	103	37	49	17	0	329	359	91	202	89	85	28	0	701	669	206
Vancouver	81	44	25	12	0	283	232	100	81	33	35	10	3	241	282	79	162	77	60	22	3	524	514	179
Washington	43	22	11	8	2	161	117	54	42	18	16	8	0	136	127	44	85	40	27	16	2	297	244	98
Defunct Clubs	33	19	8	6	0	123	86	44	32	10	16	6	0	84	105	26	65	29	24	12	0	207	191	70
Totals	**1671**	**844**	**571**	**228**	**28**	**5656**	**4907**	**1944**	**1671**	**582**	**822**	**231**	**36**	**4719**	**5740**	**1431**	**3342**	**1426**	**1393**	**459**	**64**	**10375**	**10647**	**3375**

Playoffs

	Series	W	L	GP	W	L	T	GF	GA	Last Mtg.	Rnd.	Result
Anaheim	2	1	1	12	6	6	0	34	27	2008	CQF	W 4-2
Boston	1	1	0	3	3	0	0	20	13	1981	PRE	W 3-0
Buffalo	3	2	1	13	8	5	0	39	37	1999	F	W 4-2
Calgary	1	1	0	6	4	2	0	25	18	1981	SF	W 4-2
Chicago	6	2	4	33	14	19	0	118	120	1991	DSF	W 4-2
Colorado	4	2	2	24	10	14	0	62	66	2006	CQF	L 1-4
Detroit	4	0	4	24	8	16	0	50	72	2008	CF	L 2-4
Edmonton	8	6	2	42	27	15	0	118	104	2003	CQF	W 4-2
Los Angeles	1	1	0	7	4	3	0	26	21	1968	QF	W 4-3
Montreal	2	1	1	13	6	7	0	37	48	1980	QF	W 4-3
New Jersey	1	0	1	6	2	4	0	9	15	2000	F	L 2-4
NY Islanders	1	0	1	5	1	4	0	16	26	1981	F	L 1-4
Philadelphia	2	0	2	11	3	8	0	26	41	1980	SF	L 1-4
Pittsburgh	1	0	1	6	2	4	0	16	28	1991	F	L 2-4
St. Louis	12	6	6	66	34	32	0	197	187	2001	CSF	L 0-4
San Jose	3	3	0	17	12	5	0	46	30	2008	CSF	W 4-2
Toronto	2	2	0	7	6	1	0	35	26	1983	DSF	W 3-1
Vancouver	2	0	2	12	4	8	0	23	31	2007	CQF	L 3-4
Totals	**56**	**28**	**28**	**307**	**154**	**153**	**0**	**897**	**910**			

Calgary totals include Atlanta Flames, 1972-73 to 1979-80. Carolina totals include Hartford, 1979-80 to 1996-97.
Colorado totals include Quebec, 1979-80 to 1994-95.
New Jersey totals include Kansas City, 1974-75, 1975-76, and Colorado Rockies, 1976-77 to 1981-82.
Phoenix totals include Winnipeg, 1979-80 to 1995-96.

Playoff Results 2010-2006

Year	Round	Opponent	Result	GF	GA
2008	CF	Detroit	L 2-4	10	17
	CSF	San Jose	W 4-2	15	11
	CQF	Anaheim	W 4-2	20	13
2007	CQF	Vancouver	L 3-4	12	13
2006	CQF	Colorado	L 1-4	15	18

Abbreviations: Round: F - Final;
CF - conference final; **CSF** - conference semi-final;
CQF - conference quarter-final;
DSF - division semi-final; **SF** - semi-final;
QF - quarter-final; **PRE** - preliminary round.

2009-10 Results

Month	Date	Opponent	Score	Month	Date	Opponent	Score
Oct.	3	Nashville	2-3†		5	at New Jersey	0-4
	6	at Edmonton	4-5†		6	at NY Rangers	2-5
	9	at Calgary	5-2		8	NY Islanders	4-3
	11	at Vancouver	3-4†		10	at Columbus	0-2
	14	Nashville	6-0		12	at Philadelphia	3-6
	16	Boston	0-3		14	at Montreal	3-5
	17	at Chicago	4-3		16	Detroit	3-2†
	19	Los Angeles	1-4		18	Minnesota	4-3
	21	at Anaheim	4-2		21	at Vancouver	3-4
	22	at Los Angeles	4-5*		22	at Edmonton	4-3
	24	at St. Louis	4-1		24	at Colorado	0-4
	28	Toronto	4-3*		27	Calgary	4-3†
	30	Florida	5-6†		29	Colorado	3-2
	31	at Nashville	2-4		31	Phoenix	2-4
Nov.	4	Calgary	2-3*	**Feb.**	2	Minnesota	4-2
	6	Vancouver	2-1		4	at Columbus	1-2
	7	at Minnesota	2-3		6	Phoenix	4-0
	12	at San Jose	3-2†		9	at Chicago	3-4†
	14	at Phoenix	2-3		11	at Calgary	3-1
	18	at Detroit	3-1		13	at Phoenix	3-0
	19	Columbus	1-4	**Mar.**	2	Los Angeles	1-5
	21	New Jersey	5-3		4	St. Louis	1-6
	23	Carolina	2-0		6	at Pittsburgh	3-6
	25	St. Louis	3-4†		8	at Washington	4-3†
	27	at Phoenix	2-5		10	at Buffalo	3-5
	28	Tampa Bay	4-3*		12	Los Angeles	1-2†
	30	at Detroit	1-4		14	Colorado	3-5
Dec.	3	Anaheim	3-1		16	San Jose	8-2
	5	Edmonton	2-3†		18	Philadelphia	2-3
	8	at Anaheim	3-4*		20	Ottawa	5-4
	11	at San Jose	3-2†		21	Phoenix	2-3†
	12	at Los Angeles	2-3†		23	at Nashville	3-1
	16	at Carolina	3-5		25	at San Jose	0-3
	17	at Atlanta	5-6*		27	at Los Angeles	4-1
	19	Detroit	4-3		29	at Anaheim	1-3
	21	San Jose	2-4		31	San Jose	5-1
	23	Columbus	3-1	**Apr.**	2	Edmonton	6-3
	26	at Colorado	1-4		3	at St. Louis	1-2
	29	Chicago	5-4		6	Chicago	2-5
	31	Anaheim	5-3		8	Anaheim	3-2†
Jan.	2	Vancouver	1-3		10	at Minnesota	4-3†

* – Overtime † – Shootout

Entry Draft Selections 2010-1996

Name in bold denotes played in NHL.

2010
Pick
11	Jack Campbell
41	Patrik Nemeth
77	Alexander Guptill
109	Alex Theriau
131	John Klingberg

2009
Pick
8	Scott Glennie
38	Alex Chiasson
69	Reilly Smith
129	Tomas Vincour
159	Curtis McKenzie

2008
Pick
59	Tyler Beskorowany
89	Scott Winkler
149	**Philip Larsen**
176	Matthew Tassone
209	Mike Bergin

2007
Pick
50	Nico Sacchetti
64	Sergei Korostin
112	Colton Sceviour
128	Austin Smith
129	**Jamie Benn**
136	Ondrej Roman
149	Michael Neal
172	Luke Gazdic

2006
Pick
27	Ivan Vishnevskiy
90	Aaron Snow
120	Richard Bachman
138	David McIntyre
150	Max Warn

2005
Pick
28	**Matt Niskanen**
33	**James Neal**
71	**Rich Clune**
75	**Perttu Lindgren**
146	**Tom Wandell**
160	Matt Watkins
223	Pat McGann

2004
Pick
28	**Mark Fistric**
34	Johan Fransson
52	**Raymond Sawada**
56	**Nicklas Grossman**
86	John Lammers
104	Fredrik Naslund
183	Trevor Ludwig
218	Sergei Kukushkin
248	Lukas Vomela
280	Matt McKnight

2003
Pick
33	**Loui Eriksson**
36	**Vojtech Polak**
54	**B.J. Crombeen**
99	Matt Nickerson
134	Alexander Naurov
144	Eero Kilpelainen
165	Gino Guyer
185	**Francis Wathier**
195	Drew Bagnall
196	Elias Granath
259	Niko Vainio

2002
Pick
26	Martin Vagner
32	Janos Vas
34	**Tobias Stephan**
42	Marius Holtet
43	**Trevor Daley**
78	Geoff Waugh
110	Jarkko A. Immonen
147	David Bararuk
180	Kirill Sidorenko
210	Bryan Hamm
243	Tuomas Mikkonen
273	Ned Havern

2001
Pick
26	**Jason Bacashihua**
70	Yared Hagos
92	Anthony Aquino
126	Daniel Volrab
161	**Mike Smith**
167	Michal Blazek
192	**Jussi Jokinen**
255	Marco Rosa
265	Dale Sullivan
285	Marek Tomica

2000
Pick
25	**Steve Ott**
60	**Dan Ellis**
68	**Joel Lundqvist**
91	Alexei Tereschenko
123	Vadim Khomitski
139	Ruslan Bernikov
162	Artem Chernov
192	Ladislav Vlcek
219	Marco Tuokko
224	**Antti Miettinen**

1999
Pick
32	**Michael Ryan**
66	**Dan Jancevski**
96	**Mathias Tjarnqvist**
126	Jeff Bateman
156	Gregor Baumgartner
184	Justin Cox
186	Brett Draney
215	**Jeff MacMillan**
243	Brian Sullivan
265	Jamie Chamberlain
272	Mikhail Donika

1998
Pick
39	**John Erskine**
57	**Tyler Bouck**
86	Gabriel Karlsson
153	**Pavel Patera**
173	**Niko Kapanen**
200	Scott Perry

1997
Pick
25	**Brenden Morrow**
52	**Roman Lyashenko**
77	**Steve Gainey**
105	Marcus Kristoffersson
132	Teemu Elomo
160	Alexei Timkin
189	Jeff McKercher
216	Alexei Komarov
242	**Brett McLean**

1996
Pick
5	**Ric Jackman**
70	**Jon Sim**
90	Mike Hurley
112	**Ryan Christie**
113	Yevgeny Tsybuk
166	Eoin McInerney
194	**Joel Kwiatkowski**
220	Nick Bootland

Club Directory

American Airlines Center

Dallas Stars
Office Address:
2601 Ave. of the Stars
Frisco, TX 75034
Phone **214/387-5500**
FAX 214/387-5564
Ticket Information 214/GO STARS
www.dallasstars.com
Capacity: 18,532

General Manager	Joe Nieuwendyk
Director, Scouting & Player Development	Les Jackson
Assistant General Manager	Frank Provenzano
General Manager, Texas Stars	Scott White
Head Coach	Marc Crawford
Associate Coach	Willie Desjardins
Assistant Coaches	Charlie Huddy, Stu Barnes
Goaltending Coach	Mike Valley
Strength and Conditioning Coach	J.J. McQueen
Video Coordinator	Kelly Forbes
Director, Amateur Scouting	Tim Bernhardt
Director, European Scouting	Kari Takko
Director, Professional Scouting	Doug Overton
Regional Scouts	Shane Churla, Jack Foley, Bob Gernander, Dennis Holland, Jiri Hrdina, Jimmy Johnston, Alex LePore, Paul McIntosh, Rickard Oquist, Butch Ott, Jim Pedersen, Borys Protsenko, Shane Turner
Head Athletic Trainer	Dave Zeis
Associate Athletic Trainer	Craig Lowry
Head Equipment Manager	Steve Sumner
Assistant Equipment Manager	Dennis Soetaert
Assistant Equipment Manager	Donny White
Massage Therapist	Cleo Bates
Manager, Hockey Administration	Mark Janko
Director, Team Services	Jason Rademan
Executive Assistant, Hockey Operations	Pam Wenzel

Selected 129th overall back in 2007, Jamie Benn's 22 goals trailed only John Tavares and Matt Duchene among NHL rookies in 2009-10.

General Managers' History

Wren Blair, 1967-68 to 1973-74; Jack Gordon, 1974-75 to 1976-77; Lou Nanne, 1977-78 to 1987-88; Jack Ferreira, 1988-89, 1989-90; Bob Clarke 1990-91, 1991-92; Bob Gainey, 1992-93 to 2000-01; Bob Gainey and Doug Armstrong, 2001-02; Doug Armstrong, 2002-03 to 2006-07; Doug Armstrong and Brett Hull/Les Jackson, 2007-08; Brett Hull/Les Jackson, 2008-09; Joe Nieuwendyk, 2009-10 to date.

Joe Nieuwendyk
General Manager
Born: Oshawa, Ont., September 10, 1966.

Joe Nieuwendyk was named general manager of the Dallas Stars on May 31, 2009. Nieuwendyk is considered by many to be one of the top up-and-coming hockey executives in the NHL. The former Stars player returned to Dallas from the Toronto Maple Leafs, where he served as special assistant to the general manager in 2008-09. Prior to joining the Leafs and after his 2006 retirement as a player, Nieuwendyk worked as a special consultant to the general manager with the Florida Panthers. He also helped lead Team Canada to a silver medal at the 2009 World Championship as assistant general manager.

A veteran of 20 seasons as a player in the National Hockey League, Nieuwendyk played seven with the Dallas Stars (1995 to 2002). He won the Stanley Cup for three different teams, in three different decades (Calgary in 1989, Dallas in 1999, New Jersey in 2003). Nieuwendyk was awarded the Conn Smythe Trophy as the Stanley Cup playoffs most valuable player in 1999 when he led Dallas in postseason scoring on their way to winning the Stanley Cup. Nieuwendyk played in 1,257 NHL games, scoring 564 goals and 562 assists for 1,126 points. He also appeared in 158 career playoff games, recording 116 points on 66 goals and 50 assists. Nieuwendyk played in 442 games for Dallas, scoring 178 goals and 162 assists for 340 points.

Captains' History

Bob Woytowich, 1967-68; Moose Vasko, 1968-69; Claude Larose, 1969-70; Ted Harris, 1970-71 to 1973-74; Bill Goldsworthy, 1974-75, 1975-76; Bill Hogaboam, 1976-77; Nick Beverley, 1977-78; J.P. Parise, 1978-79; Paul Shmyr, 1979-80, 1980-81; Tim Young, 1981-82; Craig Hartsburg, 1982-83; Craig Hartsburg and Brian Bellows, 1983-84; Craig Hartsburg, 1984-85 to 1987-88; Curt Fraser, Bob Rouse and Curt Giles, 1988-89; Curt Giles, 1989-90, 1990-91; Mark Tinordi, 1991-92 to 1993-94; Neal Broten and Derian Hatcher, 1994-95; Derian Hatcher, 1995-96 to 2002-03; Mike Modano, 2003-04 to 2005-06; Brenden Morrow, 2006-07 to date.

Detroit Red Wings

Key Off-Season Signings/Acquisitions

2010

June 1 • Re-signed D **Nicklas Lidstrom**.
4 • Re-signed LW **Tomas Holmstrom**.
16 • Re-signed RW **Todd Bertuzzi**.
July 6 • Re-signed LW **Drew Miller**.
6 • Signed G **Joey MacDonald**.
7 • Re-signed RW **Patrick Eaves**.
15 • Re-signed D **Derek Meech**.
Aug. 4 • Re-signed C **Darren Helm**.
5 • Signed C **Mike Modano**.
9 • Signed D **Ruslan Salei**.

2009-10 Results: 44W-24L-5OTL-9SOL 102PTS.
Second, Central Division

2010-11 Schedule

Oct.	Fri.	8	Anaheim
	Sat.	9	at Chicago
	Tue.	12	Colorado
	Thu.	14	at Dallas
	Sat.	16	at Phoenix
	Thu.	21	Calgary
	Sat.	23	Anaheim
	Thu.	28	Phoenix
	Sat.	30	Nashville
Nov.	Wed.	3	at Calgary
	Fri.	5	at Edmonton
	Sat.	6	at Vancouver
	Mon.	8	Phoenix
	Thu.	11	Edmonton
	Sat.	13	Colorado
	Wed.	17	St. Louis
	Fri.	19	Minnesota
	Sun.	21	Calgary*
	Wed.	24	at Atlanta
	Fri.	26	at Columbus
	Sun.	28	Columbus*
	Tue.	30	at San Jose
Dec.	Fri.	3	at Anaheim
	Sat.	4	at Los Angeles
	Mon.	6	San Jose
	Wed.	8	Nashville
	Fri.	10	Montreal
	Sat.	11	at New Jersey
	Mon.	13	Los Angeles
	Wed.	15	St. Louis
	Fri.	17	at Chicago
	Sun.	19	Dallas*
	Wed.	22	Vancouver
	Thu.	23	at St. Louis
	Sun.	26	at Minnesota
	Mon.	27	at Colorado
	Wed.	29	at Dallas
	Fri.	31	NY Islanders
Jan.	Sun.	2	Philadelphia*
	Tue.	4	at Edmonton
	Fri.	7	at Calgary
	Sat.	8	at Vancouver
	Mon.	10	at Colorado
	Fri.	14	at Columbus
	Sat.	15	Columbus
	Tue.	18	at Pittsburgh
	Thu.	20	at St. Louis
	Sat.	22	Chicago*
	Wed.	26	New Jersey
Feb.	Wed.	2	at Ottawa
	Fri.	4	Columbus
	Sat.	5	at Nashville
	Mon.	7	NY Rangers
	Wed.	9	Nashville
	Fri.	11	at Boston
	Sun.	13	Boston*
	Thu.	17	at Tampa Bay
	Fri.	18	at Florida
	Sun.	20	at Minnesota*
	Tue.	22	San Jose
	Thu.	24	Dallas
	Sat.	26	at Buffalo
	Mon.	28	at Los Angeles
Mar.	Wed.	2	at Anaheim
	Thu.	3	at San Jose
	Sat.	5	at Phoenix
	Wed.	9	Los Angeles
	Fri.	11	Edmonton
	Sat.	12	at St. Louis
	Wed.	16	Washington
	Thu.	17	at Columbus
	Sat.	19	at Nashville
	Mon.	21	Pittsburgh
	Wed.	23	Vancouver
	Sat.	26	Toronto
	Mon.	28	Chicago
	Wed.	30	St. Louis
Apr.	Sat.	2	at Nashville*
	Sun.	3	Minnesota*
	Wed.	6	at Carolina
	Fri.	8	Chicago
	Sun.	10	at Chicago*

* Denotes afternoon game.

Year-by-Year Record

		Home				Road				Overall								
Season	**GP**	**W**	**L**	**T**	**OL**	**W**	**L**	**T**	**OL**	**W**	**L**	**T**	**OL**	**GF**	**GA**	**Pts.**	**Finished**	**Playoff Result**
2009-10	82	25	10	....	6	19	14	....	8	44	24	....	14	229	216	102	2nd, Central Div.	Lost Conf. Semi-Final
2008-09	82	27	9	....	5	24	12	....	5	51	21	....	10	295	244	112	1st, Central Div.	Lost Final
2007-08	**82**	**29**	**9**	**....**	**3**	**25**	**12**	**....**	**4**	**54**	**21**	**....**	**7**	**257**	**184**	**115**	**1st, Central Div.**	**Won Stanley Cup**
2006-07	82	29	4	....	8	21	15	....	5	50	19	....	13	254	199	113	1st, Central Div.	Lost Conf. Championship
2005-06	82	27	9	....	5	31	7	....	3	58	16	....	8	305	209	124	1st, Central Div.	Lost Conf. Quarter-Final
2004-05	....	....	....	....	....	....	....	....	....	....	....	....	....	....	....	....		
2003-04	82	30	7	4	0	18	14	7	2	48	21	11	2	255	189	109	1st, Central Div.	Lost Conf. Semi-Final
2002-03	82	28	6	5	2	20	14	5	2	48	20	10	4	269	203	110	1st, Central Div.	Lost Conf. Quarter-Final
2001-02	**82**	**28**	**7**	**5**	**1**	**23**	**10**	**5**	**3**	**51**	**17**	**10**	**4**	**251**	**187**	**116**	**1st, Central Div.**	**Won Stanley Cup**
2000-01	82	27	9	3	2	22	11	6	2	49	20	9	4	253	202	111	1st, Central Div.	Lost Conf. Quarter-Final
1999-2000	82	28	9	3	1	20	13	7	1	48	22	10	2	278	210	108	2nd, Central Div.	Lost Conf. Semi-Final
1998-99	82	27	12	2	....	16	20	5	....	43	32	7	....	245	202	93	1st, Central Div.	Lost Conf. Semi-Final
1997-98	**82**	**25**	**8**	**8**	**....**	**19**	**15**	**7**	**....**	**44**	**23**	**15**	**....**	**250**	**196**	**103**	**2nd, Central Div.**	**Won Stanley Cup**
1996-97	**82**	**20**	**12**	**9**	**....**	**18**	**14**	**9**	**....**	**38**	**26**	**18**	**....**	**253**	**197**	**94**	**2nd, Central Div.**	**Won Stanley Cup**
1995-96	82	36	3	2	....	26	10	5	....	62	13	7	....	325	181	131	1st, Central Div.	Lost Conf. Championship
1994-95	48	17	4	3	....	16	7	1	....	33	11	4	....	180	117	70	1st, Central Div.	Lost Final
1993-94	84	23	13	6	....	23	17	2	....	46	30	8	....	356	275	100	1st, Central Div.	Lost Conf. Quarter-Final
1992-93	84	25	14	3	....	22	14	6	....	47	28	9	....	369	280	103	2nd, Norris Div.	Lost Div. Semi-Final
1991-92	80	24	12	4	....	19	13	8	....	43	25	12	....	320	256	98	1st, Norris Div.	Lost Div. Final
1990-91	80	26	14	0	....	8	24	8	....	34	38	8	....	273	298	76	3rd, Norris Div.	Lost Div. Semi-Final
1989-90	80	20	14	6	....	8	24	8	....	28	38	14	....	288	323	70	5th, Norris Div.	Out of Playoffs
1988-89	80	20	14	6	....	14	20	6	....	34	34	12	....	313	316	80	1st, Norris Div.	Lost Div. Semi-Final
1987-88	80	24	10	6	....	17	18	5	....	41	28	11	....	322	269	93	1st, Norris Div.	Lost Conf. Championship
1986-87	80	20	14	6	....	14	22	4	....	34	36	10	....	260	274	78	2nd, Norris Div.	Lost Conf. Championship
1985-86	80	10	26	4	....	7	31	2	....	17	57	6	....	266	415	40	5th, Norris Div.	Out of Playoffs
1984-85	80	19	14	7	....	8	27	5	....	27	41	12	....	313	357	66	3rd, Norris Div.	Lost Div. Semi-Final
1983-84	80	18	20	2	....	13	22	5	....	31	42	7	....	298	323	69	3rd, Norris Div.	Lost Div. Semi-Final
1982-83	80	14	19	7	....	7	25	8	....	21	44	15	....	263	344	57	5th, Norris Div.	Out of Playoffs
1981-82	80	15	19	6	....	6	28	6	....	21	47	12	....	270	351	54	6th, Norris Div.	Out of Playoffs
1980-81	80	16	15	9	....	3	28	9	....	19	43	18	....	252	339	56	5th, Norris Div.	Out of Playoffs
1979-80	80	14	21	5	....	12	22	6	....	26	43	11	....	268	306	63	5th, Norris Div.	Out of Playoffs
1978-79	80	15	17	8	....	8	24	8	....	23	41	16	....	252	295	62	5th, Norris Div.	Out of Playoffs
1977-78	80	22	11	7	....	10	23	7	....	32	34	14	....	252	266	78	2nd, Norris Div.	Lost Quarter-Final
1976-77	80	12	22	6	....	4	33	3	....	16	55	9	....	183	309	41	5th, Norris Div.	Out of Playoffs
1975-76	80	17	15	8	....	9	29	2	....	26	44	10	....	226	300	62	4th, Norris Div.	Out of Playoffs
1974-75	80	17	17	6	....	6	28	6	....	23	45	12	....	259	335	58	4th, Norris Div.	Out of Playoffs
1973-74	78	21	12	6	....	8	27	4	....	29	39	10	....	255	319	68	6th, East Div.	Out of Playoffs
1972-73	78	22	12	5	....	15	17	7	....	37	29	12	....	265	243	86	5th, East Div.	Out of Playoffs
1971-72	78	25	11	3	....	8	24	7	....	33	35	10	....	261	262	76	5th, East Div.	Out of Playoffs
1970-71	78	17	15	7	....	5	30	4	....	22	45	11	....	209	308	55	7th, East Div.	Out of Playoffs
1969-70	76	20	11	7	....	20	10	8	....	40	21	15	....	246	199	95	3rd, East Div.	Lost Quarter-Final
1968-69	76	23	8	7	....	10	23	5	....	33	31	12	....	239	221	78	5th, East Div.	Out of Playoffs
1967-68	74	18	15	4	....	9	20	8	....	27	35	12	....	245	257	66	6th, East Div.	Out of Playoffs
1966-67	70	21	11	3	....	6	28	1	....	27	39	4	....	212	241	58	5th,	Out of Playoffs
1965-66	70	20	8	7	....	11	19	5	....	31	27	12	....	221	194	74	4th,	Lost Final
1964-65	70	25	7	3	....	15	16	4	....	40	23	7	....	224	175	87	1st,	Lost Semi-Final
1963-64	70	23	9	3	....	7	20	8	....	30	29	11	....	191	204	71	4th,	Lost Final
1962-63	70	19	10	6	....	13	15	7	....	32	25	13	....	200	194	77	4th,	Lost Final
1961-62	70	17	11	7	....	6	22	7	....	23	33	14	....	184	219	60	5th,	Out of Playoffs
1960-61	70	15	13	7	....	10	16	9	....	25	29	16	....	195	215	66	4th,	Lost Final
1959-60	70	18	14	3	....	8	15	12	....	26	29	15	....	186	197	67	4th,	Lost Semi-Final
1958-59	70	13	17	5	....	12	20	3	....	25	37	8	....	167	218	58	6th,	Out of Playoffs
1957-58	70	16	11	8	....	13	18	4	....	29	29	12	....	176	207	70	3rd,	Lost Semi-Final
1956-57	70	23	7	5	....	15	13	7	....	38	20	12	....	198	157	88	1st,	Lost Semi-Final
1955-56	70	21	6	8	....	9	18	8	....	30	24	16	....	183	148	76	2nd,	Lost Final
1954-55	**70**	**25**	**5**	**5**	**....**	**17**	**12**	**6**	**....**	**42**	**17**	**11**	**....**	**204**	**134**	**95**	**1st,**	**Won Stanley Cup**
1953-54	**70**	**24**	**4**	**7**	**....**	**13**	**15**	**7**	**....**	**37**	**19**	**14**	**....**	**191**	**132**	**88**	**1st,**	**Won Stanley Cup**
1952-53	70	20	5	10	....	16	11	8	....	36	16	18	....	222	133	90	1st,	Lost Semi-Final
1951-52	**70**	**24**	**7**	**4**	**....**	**20**	**7**	**8**	**....**	**44**	**14**	**12**	**....**	**215**	**133**	**100**	**1st,**	**Won Stanley Cup**
1950-51	70	25	3	7	....	19	10	6	....	44	13	13	....	236	139	101	1st,	Lost Semi-Final
1949-50	**70**	**19**	**9**	**7**	**....**	**18**	**10**	**7**	**....**	**37**	**19**	**14**	**....**	**229**	**164**	**88**	**1st,**	**Won Stanley Cup**
1948-49	60	21	6	3	....	13	13	4	....	34	19	7	....	195	145	75	1st,	Lost Final
1947-48	60	16	9	5	....	14	9	7	....	30	18	12	....	187	148	72	2nd,	Lost Final
1946-47	60	14	10	6	....	8	17	5	....	22	27	11	....	190	193	55	4th,	Lost Semi-Final
1945-46	50	16	5	4	....	4	15	6	....	20	20	10	....	146	159	50	4th,	Lost Semi-Final
1944-45	50	19	5	1	....	12	9	4	....	31	14	5	....	218	161	67	2nd,	Lost Final
1943-44	50	18	5	2	....	8	13	4	....	26	18	6	....	214	177	58	2nd,	Lost Semi-Final
1942-43	**50**	**16**	**4**	**5**	**....**	**9**	**10**	**6**	**....**	**25**	**14**	**11**	**....**	**169**	**124**	**61**	**1st,**	**Won Stanley Cup**
1941-42	48	14	7	3	....	5	18	1	....	19	25	4	....	140	147	42	5th,	Lost Final
1940-41	48	14	5	5	....	7	11	6	....	21	16	11	....	112	102	53	3rd,	Lost Final
1939-40	48	11	10	3	....	5	16	3	....	16	26	6	....	91	126	38	5th,	Lost Semi-Final
1938-39	48	14	8	2	....	4	16	4	....	18	24	6	....	107	128	42	5th,	Lost Semi-Final
1937-38	48	8	10	6	....	4	15	5	....	12	25	11	....	99	133	35	4th, Amn. Div.	Out of Playoffs
1936-37	**48**	**14**	**5**	**5**	**....**	**11**	**9**	**4**	**....**	**25**	**14**	**9**	**....**	**128**	**102**	**59**	**1st, Amn. Div.**	**Won Stanley Cup**
1935-36	**48**	**14**	**5**	**5**	**....**	**10**	**11**	**3**	**....**	**24**	**16**	**8**	**....**	**124**	**103**	**56**	**1st, Amn. Div.**	**Won Stanley Cup**
1934-35	48	11	8	5	....	8	14	2	....	19	22	7	....	127	114	45	4th, Amn. Div.	Out of Playoffs
1933-34	48	15	5	4	....	9	9	6	....	24	14	10	....	113	98	58	1st, Amn. Div.	Lost Final
1932-33*	48	17	3	4	....	8	12	4	....	25	15	8	....	111	93	58	2nd, Amn. Div.	Lost Semi-Final
1931-32	48	15	3	6	....	3	17	4	....	18	20	10	....	95	108	46	3rd, Amn. Div.	Lost Quarter-Final
1930-31**	44	10	7	5	....	6	14	2	....	16	21	7	....	102	105	39	4th, Amn. Div.	Out of Playoffs
1929-30	44	9	10	3	....	5	14	3	....	14	24	6	....	117	133	34	4th, Amn. Div.	Out of Playoffs
1928-29	44	11	6	5	....	8	10	4	....	19	16	9	....	72	63	47	3rd, Amn. Div.	Lost Quarter-Final
1927-28	44	9	10	3	....	10	9	3	....	19	19	6	....	88	79	44	4th, Amn. Div.	Out of Playoffs
1926-27***	44	5	16	0	....	7	12	4	....	12	28	4	....	76	105	28	5th, Amn. Div.	Out of Playoffs

* Team name changed to Red Wings. ** Team name changed to Falcons. *** Team named Cougars.

CENTRAL DIVISION
85th NHL Season
Franchise date: September 25, 1926

2010-11 Player Personnel

FORWARDS	HT	WT	S	Place of Birth	*Age	2009-10 Club
ABDELKADER, Justin	6-2	215	L	Muskegon, MI	23	Detroit-Grand Rapids
BERTUZZI, Todd	6-3	225	L	Sudbury, Ont.	35	Detroit
CLEARY, Daniel	6-0	205	L	Carbonear, Nfld.	31	Detroit
DATSYUK, Pavel	5-11	194	L	Sverdlovsk, USSR	32	Detroit
DRAPER, Kris	5-10	188	L	Toronto, Ont.	39	Detroit
EAVES, Patrick	6-0	191	R	Calgary, Alta.	26	Detroit
FILPPULA, Valtteri	6-0	193	L	Vantaa, Finland	26	Detroit
FRANZEN, Johan	6-3	222	L	Landsbro, Sweden	30	Detroit
HELM, Darren	5-11	195	L	Winnipeg, Man.	23	Detroit
HOLMSTROM, Tomas	6-0	198	L	Pitea, Sweden	37	Detroit
HUDLER, Jiri	5-10	182	L	Olomouc, Czech.	26	Dynamo Moscow
MILLER, Drew	6-2	178	L	Dover, NJ	26	Tampa Bay-Detroit
MODANO, Mike	6-3	212	L	Livonia, MI	40	Dallas
RITOLA, Mattias	5-11	205	L	Borlange, Sweden	23	Detroit-Grand Rapids
ZETTERBERG, Henrik	5-11	195	L	Njurunda, Sweden	29	Detroit
DEFENSEMEN						
ERICSSON, Jonathan	6-4	220	L	Karlskrona, Sweden	26	Detroit
JANIK, Doug	6-1	215	L	Agawam, MA	30	Detroit-Grand Rapids
KINDL, Jakub	6-3	210	L	Sumperk, Czech.	23	Detroit-Grand Rapids
KRONWALL, Niklas	6-0	192	L	Stockholm, Sweden	29	Detroit
LIDSTROM, Nicklas	6-1	190	L	Vasteras, Sweden	40	Detroit
MEECH, Derek	5-11	200	L	Winnipeg, Man.	26	Detroit
RAFALSKI, Brian	5-10	194	R	Dearborn, MI	37	Detroit
SALEI, Ruslan	6-1	212	L	Minsk, USSR	35	Colorado
STUART, Brad	6-2	210	L	Rocky Mountain House, Alta.	30	Detroit

GOALTENDERS	HT	WT	C	Place of Birth	*Age	2009-10 Club
HOWARD, Jimmy	6-0	210	L	Syracuse, NY	26	Detroit
MacDONALD, Joey	6-0	197	L	Pictou, N.S.	30	Toronto-Toronto (AHL)
OSGOOD, Chris	5-10	180	L	Peace River, Alta.	37	Detroit

* – Age at start of 2010-11 season

Mike Babcock

Head Coach

Born: Manitouwadge, Ont., April 29, 1963.

Mike Babcock became the 26th coach in Detroit Red Wings history on July 14, 2005. In 2008, he led the Red Wings to the Stanley Cup. The Red Wings reached the Finals again in 2009 and topped 50 wins during the regular season in each of Babcock's first four years with the team. He coached Canada to an Olympic gold medal in 2010.

Babcock brought a winning track record to Detroit from all levels of play, including college and junior hockey, the American Hockey League, the NHL and international hockey. He is the only man to coach Team Canada to victories at both the World Junior Championship (1997) and the senior World Championship (2004.) Prior to joining the Red Wings, he had spent two seasons with Anaheim, leading the team to the Stanley Cup Finals in his first season behind the bench in 2002-03. He became the first rookie coach to reach the Finals since Florida's Doug MacLean in 1996. With a four-game sweep over Detroit in the first round of the playoffs, the Ducks became the first team since the 1952 Red Wings (over Toronto) to sweep a defending Stanley Cup champion.

Before joining Anaheim, Babcock spent two seasons as head coach of the Cincinnati Mighty Ducks (2000 to 2002), the primary development affiliate for both Detroit and Anaheim in the American Hockey League. He led the club to a franchise-best 41 wins and 95 points in 2000-01. Babcock moved to Cincinnati after a successful six-year run as the head coach of the Spokane Chiefs of the Western Hockey League (1994 through 2000). He was twice named WHL coach of the year (1996 and 2000) after taking the Chiefs to the league finals in both seasons. He began his WHL coaching career with the Moose Jaw Warriors in 1991-92. In Canadian university play, Babcock won a national championship and was named the coach of the year with the Lethbridge Pronghorns in 1993-94. In 1988, he was named head coach at Red Deer College in Red Deer, Alberta. He spent three seasons at the school, winning the Alberta college championship and coach of the year award in 1989.

Babcock played in the WHL for Saskatoon (1980-81) and Kelowna (1982-83), where he was team captain. In between, he spent a year at the University of Saskatoon. Babcock also played four years at McGill University (1983 to 1987), twice being named an All-Star defenseman. He earned his bachelor's degree in physical education and attended graduate school in sports psychology at McGill.

2009-10 Scoring

* – rookie

Regular Season

Pos	#	Player	Team	GP	G	A	Pts	TOI	+/–	PIM	PP	SH	GW	S	%
C	13	Pavel Datsyuk	DET	80	27	43	70	20:20	17	18	9	0	3	203	13.3
C	40	Henrik Zetterberg	DET	74	23	47	70	20:04	12	26	3	0	6	309	7.4
D	5	Nicklas Lidstrom	DET	82	9	40	49	25:25	22	24	5	0	1	194	4.6
L	96	Tomas Holmstrom	DET	68	25	20	45	15:48	5	60	13	0	5	131	19.1
R	44	Todd Bertuzzi	DET	82	18	26	44	16:46	–7	80	4	0	4	216	8.3
D	28	Brian Rafalski	DET	78	8	34	42	24:13	23	26	5	0	1	134	6.0
C	51	Valtteri Filppula	DET	55	11	24	35	18:14	–4	24	1	1	1	114	9.6
R	11	Daniel Cleary	DET	64	15	19	34	17:13	–3	29	2	0	2	140	10.7
C	43	Darren Helm	DET	75	11	13	24	14:29	–2	18	0	3	3	165	6.7
R	17	Patrick Eaves	DET	65	12	10	22	13:26	0	26	0	1	1	120	10.0
D	55	Niklas Kronwall	DET	48	7	15	22	21:54	5	32	3	0	0	68	10.3
C	33	Kris Draper	DET	81	7	15	22	11:32	–2	28	1	0	0	98	7.1
R	93	Johan Franzen	DET	27	10	11	21	18:42	1	22	6	0	1	91	11.0
D	23	Brad Stuart	DET	82	4	16	20	23:10	–12	22	1	0	2	153	2.6
L	20	Drew Miller	T.B.	14	0	0	0	12:13	–3	2	0	0	0	10	0.0
			DET	66	10	9	19	12:42	5	10	1	1	3	93	10.8
			Total	80	10	9	19	12:37	2	12	1	1	3	103	9.7
C	29	Jason Williams	DET	44	6	9	15	13:31	–7	8	3	0	1	96	6.3
D	52	Jonathan Ericsson	DET	62	4	9	13	16:42	–15	44	0	1	1	55	7.3
D	22	Brett Lebda	DET	63	1	7	8	14:59	–2	24	0	0	0	61	1.6
R	18	Kirk Maltby	DET	52	4	2	6	10:06	1	32	0	1	0	43	9.3
L	8	* Justin Abdelkader	DET	50	3	3	6	10:35	–11	35	0	0	0	79	3.8
D	14	Derek Meech	DET	49	2	4	6	11:54	–12	19	1	0	2	57	3.5
D	3	Andreas Lilja	DET	20	1	1	2	14:08	–2	4	0	0	0	19	5.3
D	37	Doug Janik	DET	13	0	2	2	13:28	–3	18	0	0	0	5	0.0
C	32	Kris Newbury	DET	4	1	0	1	8:41	1	4	0	0	0	3	33.3
L	24	Brad May	DET	40	0	1	1	6:58	–5	66	0	0	0	26	0.0
D	46	* Jakub Kindl	DET	3	0	0	0	10:49	–2	0	0	0	0	1	0.0
C	42	* Mattias Ritola	DET	5	0	0	0	11:41	0	0	0	0	0	9	0.0

Goaltending

No.	Goaltender	GPI	Mins	Avg	W	L	OT	EN	SO	GA	SA	S%	G	A	PIM
35	* Jimmy Howard	63	3740	2.26	37	15	10	3	3	141	1849	.924	0	2	2
30	Chris Osgood	23	1252	3.02	7	9	4	0	1	63	561	.888	0	1	0
	Totals	**82**	**5015**	**2.48**	**44**	**24**	**14**	**3**	**4**	**207**	**2413**	**.914**			

Playoffs

Pos	#	Player	Team	GP	G	A	Pts	TOI	+/–	PIM	PP	SH	GW	OT	S	%
R	93	Johan Franzen	DET	12	6	12	18	17:34	8	16	1	0	1	0	48	12.5
C	40	Henrik Zetterberg	DET	12	7	8	15	20:25	11	6	2	0	2	0	45	15.6
C	13	Pavel Datsyuk	DET	12	6	7	13	18:48	3	8	1	0	1	0	39	15.4
D	28	Brian Rafalski	DET	12	3	8	11	23:58	4	2	1	0	0	0	23	13.0
R	44	Todd Bertuzzi	DET	12	2	9	11	17:07	4	12	1	0	0	0	19	10.5
D	5	Nicklas Lidstrom	DET	12	4	6	10	26:22	7	2	3	0	0	0	39	10.3
C	51	Valtteri Filppula	DET	12	4	5	9	18:34	1	6	2	0	0	0	33	12.1
L	96	Tomas Holmstrom	DET	12	4	3	7	13:27	3	12	1	0	1	0	26	15.4
D	23	Brad Stuart	DET	12	2	4	6	22:04	6	8	0	0	0	0	23	8.7
D	55	Niklas Kronwall	DET	12	0	5	5	23:15	2	12	0	0	0	0	15	0.0
R	11	Daniel Cleary	DET	12	2	0	2	14:47	3	4	0	0	0	0	27	7.4
L	8	* Justin Abdelkader	DET	11	1	1	2	7:30	1	36	0	0	0	0	12	8.3
L	20	Drew Miller	DET	12	1	1	2	12:34	2	4	0	0	0	0	13	7.7
D	52	Jonathan Ericsson	DET	12	0	2	2	14:17	1	8	0	0	0	0	11	0.0
C	43	Darren Helm	DET	12	1	0	1	13:56	–4	4	0	0	0	0	16	6.3
C	42	* Mattias Ritola	DET	1	0	0	0	7:45	0	0	0	0	0	0	0	0.0
D	22	Brett Lebda	DET	2	0	0	0	5:55	0	0	0	0	0	0	1	0.0
C	29	Jason Williams	DET	3	0	0	0	8:12	–1	0	0	0	0	0	3	0.0
R	17	Patrick Eaves	DET	8	0	0	0	11:57	–3	2	0	0	0	0	14	0.0
D	3	Andreas Lilja	DET	11	0	0	0	11:00	1	14	0	0	0	0	6	0.0
C	33	Kris Draper	DET	12	0	0	0	7:23	0	16	0	0	0	0	4	0.0

Goaltending

No.	Goaltender	GPI	Mins	Avg	W	L	EN	SO	GA	SA	S%	G	A	PIM
35	* Jimmy Howard	12	720	2.75	5	7	0	1	33	387	.915	0	0	2
	Totals	**12**	**727**	**2.72**	**5**	**7**	**0**	**1**	**33**	**387**	**.915**			

Coaching Record

			Regular Season				Playoffs			
Season	Team	League	GC	W	L	O/T	GC	W	L	T
1991-92	Moose Jaw	WHL	72	33	36	3	4	0	4	....
1992-93	Moose Jaw	WHL	72	27	42	3	....	....	....	....
1993-94	U of Lethbridge	CIAU	28	19	7	2	....	....	....	....
1994-95	Spokane	WHL	72	32	36	4	11	6	5	....
1995-96	Spokane	WHL	72	50	18	4	9	3	6	....
1996-97	Spokane	WHL	72	35	33	4	9	4	5	....
1997-98	Spokane	WHL	72	45	23	4	18	10	8	....
1998-99	Spokane	WHL	72	19	44	9	....	....	....	....
99-2000	Spokane	WHL	72	47	19	6	20	15	5	....
2000-01	Cincinnati	AHL	80	41	26	13	4	1	3	....
2001-02	Cincinnati	AHL	80	33	33	14	3	1	2	....
2002-03	**Anaheim**	**NHL**	**82**	**40**	**27**	**15**	**21**	**15**	**6**	....
2003-04	**Anaheim**	**NHL**	**82**	**29**	**35**	**18**	....	....	....	....
2004-05	**Anaheim**				SEASON CANCELLED					
2005-06	**Detroit**	**NHL**	**82**	**58**	**16**	**8**	**6**	**2**	**4**	....
2006-07	**Detroit**	**NHL**	**82**	**50**	**19**	**13**	**18**	**10**	**8**	....
2007-08♦	**Detroit**	**NHL**	**82**	**54**	**21**	**7**	**22**	**16**	**6**	....
2008-09	**Detroit**	**NHL**	**82**	**51**	**21**	**10**	**23**	**15**	**8**	....
2009-10	**Detroit**	**NHL**	**82**	**44**	**24**	**14**	**12**	**5**	**7**	....
	NHL Totals		**574**	**326**	**163**	**85**	**102**	**63**	**39**	....

♦ Stanley Cup win.

Club Records

Team

(Figures in brackets for season records are games played; records for fewest points, wins, ties, losses, goals, goals against are for 70 or more games)

Most Points **131** 1995-96 (82)
Most Wins ***62** 1995-96 (82)
Most Ties **18** 1952-53 (70), 1980-81 (80), 1996-97 (82)
Most Losses **57** 1985-86 (80)
Most Goals **369** 1992-93 (84)
Most Goals Against **415** 1985-86 (80)
Fewest Points **40** 1985-86 (80)
Fewest Wins **16** 1976-77 (80)
Fewest Ties **4** 1966-67 (70)
Fewest Losses **13** 1950-51 (70), 1995-96 (82)
Fewest Goals **167** 1958-59 (70)
Fewest Goals Against **132** 1953-54 (70)
Longest Winning Streak
Overall .... **9** Seven times
Home .... **14** Jan. 21-Mar. 25/65
Away .... ***12** Mar. 1-Apr. 15/06
Longest Undefeated Streak
Overall .... **15** Nov. 27-Dec. 28/52 (8 wins, 7 ties)
Home .... **19** Dec. 31/00-Apr.7/01 (17 wins, 2 ties)
Away .... **15** Oct. 18-Dec. 20/51 (10 wins, 5 ties)
Longest Losing Streak
Overall .... **14** Feb. 24-Mar. 25/82
Home .... **7** Feb. 20-Mar. 25/82
Away .... **14** Oct. 19-Dec. 21/66
Longest Winless Streak
Overall .... **19** Feb. 26-Apr. 3/77 (18 losses, 1 tie)
Home .... **10** Dec. 11/85-Jan. 18/86 (9 losses, 1 tie)
Away .... **26** Dec. 15/76-Apr. 3/77 (23 losses, 3 ties)
Most Shutouts, Season **13** 1953-54 (70)
Most. PIM, Season **2,393** 1985-86 (80)
Most Goals, Game .... **15** Jan. 23/44 (NYR 0 at Det. 15)

Individual

Most Seasons .... **25** Gordie Howe
Most Games .... **1,687** Gordie Howe
Most Goals, Career .... **786** Gordie Howe
Most Assists, Career .... **1,063** Steve Yzerman
Most Points, Career .... **1,809** Gordie Howe (786G, 1,023A)
Most PIM, Career .... **2,090** Bob Probert
Most Shutouts, Career .... **85** Terry Sawchuk
Longest Consecutive Games Streak .... **548** Alex Delvecchio (Dec. 13/56-Nov. 11/64)
Most Goals, Season .... **65** Steve Yzerman (1988-89)
Most Assists, Season .... **90** Steve Yzerman (1988-89)
Most Points, Season .... **155** Steve Yzerman (1988-89; 65G, 90A)
Most PIM, Season .... **398** Bob Probert (1987-88)
Most Points, Defenseman, Season .... **80** Nicklas Lidstrom (2005-06; 16G, 64A)
Most Points, Center, Season .... **155** Steve Yzerman (1988-89; 65G, 90A)
Most Points, Right Wing, Season .... **103** Gordie Howe (1968-69; 44G, 59A)
Most Points, Left Wing, Season .... **105** John Ogrodnick (1984-85; 55G, 50A)
Most Points, Rookie, Season .... **87** Steve Yzerman (1983-84; 39G, 48A)
Most Shutouts, Season .... **12** Terry Sawchuk (1951-52), (1953-54), (1954-55) Glenn Hall (1955-56)
Most Goals, Game .... **6** Syd Howe (Feb. 3/44)
Most Assists, Game .... ***7** Billy Taylor (Mar. 16/47)
Most Points, Game .... **7** Carl Liscombe (Nov. 5/42; 3G, 4A), Don Grosso (Feb. 3/44; 1G, 6A), Billy Taylor (Mar. 16/47; 7A)

* NHL Record.

Retired Numbers

1	Terry Sawchuk	1949-55, 57-64, 68-69
7	Ted Lindsay	1944-57, 64-65
9	Gordie Howe	1946-1971
10	Alex Delvecchio	1951-1973
12	Sid Abel	1938-43, 45-52
19	Steve Yzerman	1983-2006

All-time Record vs. Other Clubs

Regular Season

	At Home								On Road								Total							
	GP	W	L	T	OL	GF	GA	PTS	GP	W	L	T	OL	GF	GA	PTS	GP	W	L	T	OL	GF	GA	PTS
Anaheim	32	26	3	3	0	114	67	55	32	14	13	4	1	86	85	33	64	40	16	7	1	200	152	88
Atlanta	7	5	2	0	0	23	18	10	5	4	1	0	0	31	17	8	12	9	3	0	0	54	35	18
Boston	287	155	80	52	0	957	726	362	289	91	154	43	1	765	1012	226	576	246	234	95	1	1722	1738	588
Buffalo	58	34	18	5	1	211	165	74	55	13	34	8	0	163	235	34	113	47	52	13	1	374	400	108
Calgary	69	37	21	10	1	253	207	85	70	25	39	6	0	201	249	56	139	62	60	16	1	454	456	141
Carolina	33	19	7	7	0	127	89	45	32	13	18	1	0	91	108	27	65	32	25	8	0	218	197	72
Chicago	353	215	102	33	3	1213	879	466	356	144	156	51	5	1011	1067	344	709	359	258	84	8	2224	1946	810
Colorado	50	30	16	1	3	178	146	64	52	25	22	4	1	172	170	55	102	55	38	5	4	350	316	119
Columbus	28	22	4	0	2	101	66	46	29	19	6	1	3	93	57	42	57	41	10	1	5	194	123	88
Dallas	116	59	40	16	1	439	362	135	116	41	54	18	3	344	393	103	232	100	94	34	4	783	755	238
Edmonton	54	31	16	3	4	208	171	69	54	18	20	10	6	187	203	52	108	49	36	13	10	395	374	121
Florida	10	5	1	3	1	36	25	14	11	7	1	2	1	32	22	17	21	12	2	5	2	68	47	31
Los Angeles	89	44	32	13	0	345	299	101	90	32	43	14	1	281	339	79	179	76	75	27	1	626	638	180
Minnesota	18	13	3	1	1	71	40	28	18	11	3	2	2	52	45	26	36	24	6	3	3	123	85	54
Montreal	282	131	98	53	0	808	720	315	284	69	172	43	0	643	997	181	566	200	270	96	0	1451	1717	496
Nashville	35	24	4	2	5	129	80	55	34	17	13	2	2	94	94	38	69	41	17	4	7	223	174	93
New Jersey	42	27	13	2	0	172	132	56	42	11	21	9	1	108	143	32	84	38	34	11	1	280	275	88
NY Islanders	47	26	19	2	0	166	139	54	48	20	24	4	0	141	173	44	95	46	43	6	0	307	312	98
NY Rangers	287	166	76	45	0	1013	706	377	286	94	134	58	0	745	872	246	573	260	210	103	0	1758	1578	623
Ottawa	11	7	4	0	0	39	23	14	12	7	4	1	0	34	33	15	23	14	8	1	0	73	56	29
Philadelphia	61	33	18	10	0	219	187	76	60	13	36	11	0	172	240	37	121	46	54	21	0	391	427	113
Phoenix	61	32	20	8	1	237	200	73	59	26	18	14	1	194	172	67	120	58	38	22	2	431	372	140
Pittsburgh	68	42	13	12	1	265	187	97	68	19	44	4	1	201	283	43	136	61	57	16	2	466	470	140
St. Louis	128	62	46	17	3	459	377	144	128	46	58	20	4	368	413	116	256	108	104	37	7	827	790	260
San Jose	35	29	4	1	1	136	60	60	36	19	14	3	0	138	126	41	71	48	18	4	1	274	186	101
Tampa Bay	14	12	1	1	0	54	23	25	16	11	4	1	0	71	49	23	30	23	5	2	0	125	72	48
Toronto	324	169	107	46	2	975	796	386	318	105	165	47	1	849	1053	258	642	274	272	93	3	1824	1849	644
Vancouver	76	46	19	8	3	304	220	103	75	32	32	10	1	240	266	75	151	78	51	18	4	544	486	178
Washington	49	23	15	11	0	168	140	57	49	21	23	5	0	155	178	47	98	44	38	16	0	323	318	104
Defunct Clubs	141	76	40	25	0	430	307	177	141	49	63	29	0	364	375	127	282	125	103	54	0	794	682	304
Totals	**2865**	**1600**	**842**	**390**	**33**	**9850**	**7557**	**3623**	**2865**	**1016**	**1389**	**425**	**35**	**8026**	**9469**	**2492**	**5730**	**2616**	**2231**	**815**	**68**	**17876**	**17026**	**6115**

Playoffs

	Series	W	L	GP	W	L	T	GF	GA	Last Mtg.	Rnd.	Result
Anaheim	5	3	2	25	14	11	0	75	57	2009	CSF	W 4-3
Boston	7	3	4	33	14	19	0	98	96	1957	SF	L 1-4
Calgary	3	2	1	14	8	6	0	38	26	2007	CQF	W 4-2
Carolina	1	1	0	5	4	1	0	14	7	2002	F	W 4-1
Chicago	15	7	8	74	35	39	0	209	220	2009	CF	W 4-1
Colorado	6	3	3	34	17	17	0	97	88	2008	CSF	W 4-0
Columbus	1	1	0	4	4	0	0	18	7	2009	CQF	W 4-0
Dallas	4	4	0	24	16	8	0	72	50	2008	CF	W 4-2
Edmonton	3	0	3	16	4	12	0	43	58	2006	CQF	L 2-4
Los Angeles	2	1	1	10	6	4	0	32	21	2001	CQF	L 2-4
Montreal	12	7	5	62	29	33	0	149	161	1978	QF	L 1-4
Nashville	2	2	0	12	8	4	0	29	21	2008	CQF	W 4-2
New Jersey	1	0	1	4	0	4	0	7	16	1995	F	L 0-4
NY Rangers	5	4	1	23	13	10	0	57	49	1950	F	W 4-3
Philadelphia	1	1	0	4	4	0	0	16	6	1997	F	W 4-0
Phoenix	3	3	0	19	12	7	0	70	46	2010	CQF	W 4-3
Pittsburgh	2	1	1	13	7	6	0	34	24	2009	F	L 3-4
St. Louis	7	5	2	40	24	16	0	125	103	2002	CSF	W 4-1
San Jose	4	2	2	22	12	10	0	81	51	2010	CSF	L 1-4
Toronto	23	11	12	117	59	58	0	321	311	1993	DSF	L 3-4
Vancouver	1	1	0	6	4	2	0	22	16	2002	CQF	W 4-2
Washington	1	1	0	4	4	0	0	13	7	1998	F	W 4-0
Defunct Clubs	4	3	1	10	7	2	1	21	13			
Totals	**113**	**66**	**47**	**575**	**305**	**269**	**1**	**1641**	**1454**			

Calgary totals include Atlanta Flames, 1972-73 to 1979-80.
Colorado totals include Quebec, 1979-80 to 1994-95.
New Jersey totals include Kansas City, 1974-75, 1975-76, and Colorado Rockies, 1976-77 to 1981-82.
Phoenix totals include Winnipeg, 1979-80 to 1995-96.
Carolina totals include Hartford, 1979-80 to 1996-97.
Dallas totals include Minnesota North Stars, 1967-68 to 1992-93.

Playoff Results 2010-2006

Year	Round	Opponent	Result	GF	GA
2010	CSF	San Jose	L 1-4	17	15
	CQF	Phoenix	W 4-3	26	18
2009	F	Pittsburgh	L 3-4	17	14
	CF	Chicago	W 4-1	19	10
	CSF	Anaheim	W 4-3	22	17
	CQF	Columbus	W 4-0	18	7
2008	**F**	**Pittsburgh**	**W 4-2**	**17**	**10**
	CF	Dallas	W 4-2	17	10
	CSF	Colorado	W 4-0	21	9
	CQF	Nashville	W 4-2	17	12
2007	CF	Anaheim	L 2-4	17	16
	CSF	San Jose	W 4-2	13	9
	CQF	Calgary	W 4-2	18	10
2006	CQF	Edmonton	L 2-4	17	19

Abbreviations: Round: F - Final; **CF** - conference final; **CSF** - conference semi-final; **CQF** - conference quarter-final; **DSF** - division semi-final; **SF** - semi-final; **QF** - quarter-final.

2009-10 Results

Month	Day	Opponent	Score	Month	Day	Opponent	Score
Oct.	2	St. Louis	3-4		5	at Anaheim	1-4
	3	at St. Louis	3-5		7	at Los Angeles	2-1
	8	Chicago	3-2		9	at San Jose	4-1
	10	Washington	3-2		12	at NY Islanders	0-6
	13	at Buffalo	2-6		14	Carolina	3-1
	15	Los Angeles	5-2		16	at Dallas	2-3†
	17	Colorado	3-4†		17	Chicago	3-4†
	22	at Phoenix	2-3*		19	at Washington	2-3
	24	at Colorado	1-3		21	at Minnesota	4-3†
	27	at Vancouver	5-4		23	Los Angeles	2-3
	29	at Edmonton	5-6†		26	Phoenix	4-5*
	31	at Calgary	3-1		27	at Minnesota	2-5
Nov.	3	Boston	2-0		29	Nashville	4-2
	5	San Jose	2-1†		31	at Pittsburgh	1-2†
	7	at Toronto	1-5	**Feb.**	2	at San Jose	4-2
	11	at Columbus	9-1		3	at Anaheim	1-3
	12	Vancouver	3-1		6	at Los Angeles	3-4
	14	Anaheim	7-4		9	at St. Louis	3-4†
	18	Dallas	1-3		11	San Jose	2-3†
	20	Florida	1-2*		13	Ottawa	4-1
	21	at Montreal	3-2†	**Mar.**	1	at Colorado	3-2
	23	at Nashville	1-3		3	Vancouver	3-6
	25	Atlanta	0-2		5	Nashville	5-2
	27	Calgary	0-3		7	at Chicago	5-4
	28	at St. Louis	4-3†		9	Calgary	2-4
	30	Dallas	4-1		11	Minnesota	5-1
Dec.	3	Edmonton	1-4		13	Buffalo	3-2*
	5	at New Jersey	3-4†		15	at Calgary	2-1
	6	at NY Rangers	3-1		19	at Edmonton	2-3†
	9	St. Louis	0-1		20	at Vancouver	4-3*
	11	Anaheim	3-2*		22	Pittsburgh	3-1
	12	at Nashville	3-2*		24	St. Louis	4-2
	14	Phoenix	3-2		26	Minnesota	6-2
	17	Tampa Bay	3-0		27	at Nashville	1-0†
	19	at Dallas	3-4		30	Edmonton	5-4
	20	at Chicago	0-3	**Apr.**	1	Columbus	3-2
	23	Chicago	0-3		3	Nashville	3-4*
	26	Columbus	2-1		4	at Philadelphia	3-4
	28	at Columbus	0-1*		7	Columbus	4-3
	31	Colorado	4-2		9	at Columbus	1-0†
Jan.	2	at Phoenix	4-1		11	at Chicago	3-2*

* – Overtime † – Shootout

Entry Draft Selections 2010-1996

Name in bold denotes played in NHL.

2010
Pick
- 21 Riley Sheahan
- 51 Calle Jarnkrok
- 81 Louis-Marc Aubry
- 111 Teemu Pulkkinen
- 141 Petr Mrazek
- 171 Brooks Macek
- 201 Benjamin Marshall

2009
Pick
- 32 Landon Ferraro
- 60 Tomas Tatar
- 75 Andrej Nestrasil
- 90 Gleason Fournier
- 150 Nick Jensen
- 180 Mitchell Callahan
- 210 Adam Almquist

2008
Pick
- 30 Thomas McCollum
- 91 Max Nicastro
- 121 Gustav Nyquist
- 151 Julien Cayer
- 181 Stephen Johnston
- 211 Jesper Samuelsson

2007
Pick
- 27 Brendan Smith
- 88 Joakim Andersson
- 148 Randy Cameron
- 178 Zack Torquato
- 208 Bryan Rufenach

2006
Pick
- 41 Cory Emmerton
- 47 **Shawn Matthias**
- 62 Dick Axelsson
- 92 Daniel Larsson
- 182 Jan Mursak
- 191 Nick Oslund
- 212 Logan Pyett

2005
Pick
- 19 **Jakub Kindl**
- 42 **Justin Abdelkader**
- 80 Christofer Lofberg
- 103 **Mattias Ritola**
- 132 **Darren Helm**
- 137 Johan Ryno
- 151 Jeff May
- 175 Juho Mielonen
- 214 Bretton Stamler

2004
Pick
- 97 **Johan Franzen**
- 128 Evan McGrath
- 151 Sergei Kolosov
- 162 Tyler Haskins
- 192 Anton Axelsson
- 226 Steven Covington
- 257 Gennady Stolyarov
- 290 Nils Backstrom

2003
Pick
- 64 **Jimmy Howard**
- 132 **Kyle Quincey**
- 164 Ryan Oulahen
- 170 Andreas Sundin
- 194 Stefan Blom
- 226 Tomas Kollar
- 258 Vladimir Kutny
- 289 Mikael Johansson

2002
Pick
- 58 **Jiri Hudler**
- 63 **Tomas Fleischmann**
- 95 **Valtteri Filppula**
- 131 Johan Berggren
- 166 Logan Koopmans
- 197 Jimmy Cuddihy
- 229 **Derek Meech**
- 260 Pierre-Olivier Beaulieu
- 262 Christian Soderstrom
- 291 **Jonathan Ericsson**

2001
Pick
- 62 Igor Grigorenko
- 121 **Drew MacIntyre**
- 129 Miroslav Blatak
- 157 Andreas Jamtin
- 195 Nick Pannoni
- 258 **Dmitri Bykov**
- 288 Francois Senez

2000
Pick
- 29 **Niklas Kronwall**
- 38 **Tomas Kopecky**
- 102 Stefan Liv
- 127 Dmitri Semenov
- 128 Alexander Seluyanov
- 130 Aaron Van Leusen
- 187 Per Backer
- 196 Paul Ballantyne
- 228 Jimmie Svensson
- 251 Todd Jackson
- 260 Yevgeny Bumagin

1999
Pick
- 120 Jari Tolsa
- 149 Andrei Maximenko
- 181 **Kent McDonell**
- 210 **Henrik Zetterberg**
- 238 Anton Borodkin
- 266 Ken Davis

1998
Pick
- 25 **Jiri Fischer**
- 55 **Ryan Barnes**
- 56 Tomek Valtonen
- 84 Jake McCracken
- 111 Brent Hobday
- 142 Calle Steen
- 151 Adam DeLeeuw
- 171 **Pavel Datsyuk**
- 198 Jeremy Goetzinger
- 226 David Petrasek
- 256 Petja Pietilainen

1997
Pick
- 49 **Yuri Butsayev**
- 76 **Petr Sykora**
- 102 **Quintin Laing**
- 129 John Wikstrom
- 157 **B.J. Young**
- 186 Mike Laceby
- 213 Steve Willejto
- 239 Greg Willers

1996
Pick
- 26 **Jesse Wallin**
- 52 Aren Miller
- 108 Johan Forsander
- 135 Michal Podolka
- 144 Magnus Nilsson
- 162 Alexandre Jacques
- 189 Colin Beardsmore
- 215 Craig Stahl
- 241 Eugeny Afanasiev

Club Directory

Joe Louis Arena

Detroit Red Wings
Joe Louis Arena
19 Steve Yzerman Drive
Detroit, MI 48226
Phone **313/394-7000**
FAX PR: 313/567-0296
Media Hotline: 313/396-7599
www.detroitredwings.com
Capacity: 20,066

Owner/Governor	Mike Ilitch
Owner/Secretary-Treasurer	Marian Ilitch
President and CEO, IlitchHoldings/ Alternate Governor Red Wings	Christopher Ilitch
Senior Vice President/Alternate Governor	Jim Devellano
Executive Vice President/General Manager	Ken Holland
Vice President/Assistant General Manager	Jim Nill
Assistant General Manager/HockeyAdmin.	Ryan Martin
Alternate Governor Red Wings	Tom Wilson
Vice President Olympia Entertainment/ General Counsel Red Wings	Robert E. Carr
Senior Vice President of Business Affairs	Steven Violetta
Head Coach	Mike Babcock
Assistant Coaches	Paul MacLean, Brad McCrimmon
Video Coach	Keith McKittrick
Goaltending Coach	Jim Bedard
Director of Pro Scouting	Mark Howe
Pro Scouts	Glenn Merkosky, Bruce Haralson
Director of Amateur Scouting	Joe McDonnell
Amateur Scouts	Mark Leach, Jeff Finley, Dave Kolb
Director of EuropeanScouting	Hakan Andersson
European Scouts	Vladimir Havluj, Ari Vouri, Nikolai Vakourov
Part-Time Scout	Marty Stein
Director of Player Development	Jiri Fischer
Vice President of Finance	Paul MacDonald
Executive Assistant	Kathi Wyatt
General Accountant	Bridget Merritt
Administrative Assistant	Julie Dailey
Head Athletic Therapist	Piet Van Zant
Head Equipment Manager	Paul Boyer
Assistant Athletic Therapist	Russ Baumann
Assistant Equipment Managers	John Remejes, Adam Sheehan
Team Masseur	Sergei Tchekmarev
Senior Director of Communications	John Hahn
Director, Detroit Red Wings Foundation	Anne Hayes
Media Relations Manager	Todd Beam
Community Relations Coordinator	Christy Hammond
Medical Director	Dr. Donald Weaver
Team Physicians	Dr. Anthony Colucci, Dr. Doug Plagens
Team Dentists	Dr. Jeffrey Boogren, Dr. Randy Freij
Team Photographer	Dave Reginek
Radio Announcers, 97.1 The Ticket	Ken Kal, Paul Woods
Television Announcers, Fox Sports Detroit	Ken Daniels, Mickey Redmond

Coaching History

Art Duncan and Duke Keats, 1926-27; Jack Adams, 1927-28 to 1946-47; Tommy Ivan, 1947-48 to 1953-54; Jimmy Skinner, 1954-55 to 1956-57; Jimmy Skinner and Sid Abel, 1957-58; Sid Abel, 1958-59 to 1967-68; Bill Gadsby, 1968-69; Bill Gadsby and Sid Abel, 1969-70; Ned Harkness and Doug Barkley, 1970-71; Doug Barkley and Johnny Wilson, 1971-72; Johnny Wilson, 1972-73; Ted Garvin and Alex Delvecchio, 1973-74; Alex Delvecchio, 1974-75; Doug Barkley and Alex Delvecchio, 1975-76; Alex Delvecchio and Larry Wilson, 1976-77; Bobby Kromm, 1977-78, 1978-79; Bobby Kromm and Ted Lindsay, 1979-80; Ted Lindsay and Wayne Maxner, 1980-81; Wayne Maxner and Billy Dea, 1981-82; Nick Polano, 1982-83 to 1984-85; Harry Neale and Brad Park, 1985-86; Jacques Demers, 1986-87 to 1989-90; Bryan Murray, 1990-91 to 1992-93; Scotty Bowman, 1993-94 to 1997-98; Dave Lewis, Barry Smith (co-coaches) and Scotty Bowman, 1998-99; Scotty Bowman, 1999-2000 to 2001-02; Dave Lewis, 2002-03 to 2004-05; Mike Babcock, 2005-06 to date.

General Managers' History

Art Duncan and Duke Keats, 1926-27; Jack Adams, 1927-28 to 1961-62; Sid Abel, 1962-63 to 1969-70; Sid Abel and Ned Harkness, 1970-71; Ned Harkness, 1971-72 to 1973-74; Alex Delvecchio, 1974-75, 1975-76; Alex Delvecchio and Ted Lindsay, 1976-77; Ted Lindsay, 1977-78 to 1979-80; Jimmy Skinner, 1980-81, 1981-82; Jim Devellano, 1982-83 to 1989-90; Bryan Murray, 1990-91 to 1993-94; Jim Devellano (Senior Vice President), 1994-95 to 1996-97; Ken Holland, 1997-98 to date.

Captains' History

Art Duncan, 1926-27; Reg Noble, 1927-28 to 1929-30; George Hay, 1930-31; Carson Cooper, 1931-32; Larry Aurie, 1932-33; Herbie Lewis, 1933-34; Ebbie Goodfellow, 1934-35; Doug Young, 1935-36 to 1937-38; Ebbie Goodfellow, 1938-39 to 1940-41; Ebbie Goodfellow and Syd Howe, 1941-42; Sid Abel, 1942-43; Mud Bruneteau, Flash Hollett, 1943-44; Flash Hollett, 1944-45; Flash Hollett and Sid Abel, 1945-46; Sid Abel, 1946-47 to 1951-52; Ted Lindsay, 1952-53 to 1955-56; Red Kelly, 1956-57, 1957-58; Gordie Howe, 1958-59 to 1961-62; Alex Delvecchio, 1962-63 to 1972-73; Alex Delvecchio, Nick Libett, Red Berenson, Gary Bergman, Ted Harris, Mickey Redmond and Larry Johnston, 1973-74; Marcel Dionne, 1974-75; Danny Grant and Terry Harper, 1975-76; Danny Grant and Dennis Polonich, 1976-77; Dan Maloney and Dennis Hextall, 1977-78; Dennis Hextall, Nick Libett and Paul Woods, 1978-79; Dale McCourt, 1979-80; Errol Thompson and Reed Larson, 1980-81; Reed Larson, 1981-82; Danny Gare, 1982-83 to 1985-86; Steve Yzerman, 1986-87 to 2005-06; Nicklas Lidstrom, 2006-07 to date.

Ken Holland

Executive Vice President and General Manager

Born: Vernon, B.C., November 10, 1955.

Ken Holland has served in the Red Wings front office since 1985, and has been the club's general manager since July 18, 1997. He has established himself as one of the most innovative and aggressive GMs in the National Hockey League. Detroit's Stanley Cup victory in 2008 marked the team's third championship under his leadership. Holland began his tenure as the club's general manager after serving as assistant general manager for the previous three seasons.

Holland oversees all aspects of hockey operations including all matters relating to player personnel, development, contract negotiations and player movements, though he now takes a less prominent role in the NHL draft than he did during his seven years as the club's director of amateur scouting.

At the conclusion of his playing days as a goaltender, spending most of his pro career at the American Hockey League level, Holland began his off-ice career in 1985 as a western Canada scout followed by five years as an amateur scouting director before promotions led to his current position as general manager.

A native of Vernon, British Columbia, Holland played in the junior ranks for Medicine Hat (WHL) in 1974-75. He was Toronto's 13th pick (188th overall) in the 1975 draft but never saw action with the Maple Leafs. Holland twice signed with NHL teams as a free agent — in 1980 with Hartford and 1983 with Detroit. He spent most of his pro career with AHL clubs in Binghamton and Springfield, along with Adirondack, but did appear in four NHL games, making his debut with Hartford in 1980-81 and playing three contests for Detroit in 1983-84.

Edmonton Oilers

Key Off-Season Signings/Acquisitions

2010

June 25 • Selected C **Taylor Hall** (Windsor Spitfires, OHL) with the 1st overall pick of the 2010 Entry Draft.

1 • Signed 2009 1st round pick (10th overall), LW **Magnus Paajarvi-Svensson** (Timra IK).

22 • Named **Tom Renney** head coach and **Pat Quinn** senior hockey advisor.

24 • Acquired C **Colin Fraser** from Chicago for Edmonton's 6th round pick in the 2010 Entry Draft.

30 • Acquired D **Jim Vandermeer** from Phoenix for C **Patrick O'Sullivan**.

July 1 • Signed D **Kurtis Foster**.

2 • Signed LW **Steve MacIntyre**.

3 • Signed LW **Alexandre Giroux**.

15 • Named **Steve Smith** assistant coach.

16 • Signed LW **Gregory Stewart**.

30 • Named **Ralph Krueger** associate coach.

Aug. 6 • Signed G **Martin Gerber**.

2009-10 Results: 27w-47L-2OTL-6SOL 62PTS.
Fifth, Northwest Division

Year-by-Year Record

Season	GP	Home W	L	T	OL	Road W	L	T	OL	Overall W	L	T	OL	GF	GA	Pts.	Finished	Playoff Result
2009-10	82	18	19	....	4	9	28	....	4	27	47	....	8	214	284	62	5th, Northwest Div.	Out of Playoffs
2008-09	82	18	17	....	6	20	18	....	3	38	35	....	9	234	248	85	4th, Northwest Div.	Out of Playoffs
2007-08	82	23	17	....	1	18	18	....	5	41	35	....	6	235	251	88	4th, Northwest Div.	Out of Playoffs
2006-07	82	19	19	....	3	13	24	....	4	32	43	....	7	195	248	71	5th, Northwest Div.	Out of Playoffs
2005-06	82	20	15	....	6	21	13	....	7	41	28	....	13	256	251	95	3rd, Northwest Div.	Lost Final
2004-05	....	....				....				....								
2003-04	82	22	12	4	3	14	17	8	2	36	29	12	5	221	208	89	4th, Northwest Div.	Out of Playoffs
2002-03	82	20	12	5	4	16	14	6	5	36	26	11	9	231	230	92	4th, Northwest Div.	Lost Conf. Quarter-Final
2001-02	82	23	14	4	0	15	14	8	4	38	28	12	4	205	182	92	3rd, Northwest Div.	Out of Playoffs
2000-01	82	23	9	7	2	16	19	5	1	39	28	12	3	243	222	93	2nd, Northwest Div.	Lost Conf. Quarter-Final
1999-2000	82	18	11	9	3	14	15	7	5	32	26	16	8	226	212	88	2nd, Northwest Div.	Lost Conf. Quarter-Final
1998-99	82	17	19	5	....	16	18	7	....	33	37	12	....	230	226	78	2nd, Northwest Div.	Lost Conf. Quarter-Final
1997-98	82	20	16	5	....	15	21	5	....	35	37	10	....	215	224	80	3rd, Pacific Div.	Lost Conf. Semi-Final
1996-97	82	21	16	4	....	15	21	5	....	36	37	9	....	252	247	81	3rd, Pacific Div.	Lost Conf. Semi-Final
1995-96	82	15	21	5	....	15	23	3	....	30	44	8	....	240	304	68	5th, Pacific Div.	Out of Playoffs
1994-95	48	11	12	1	....	6	15	3	....	17	27	4	....	136	183	38	5th, Pacific Div.	Out of Playoffs
1993-94	84	17	22	3	....	8	23	11	....	25	45	14	....	261	305	64	6th, Pacific Div.	Out of Playoffs
1992-93	84	16	21	5	....	10	29	3	....	26	50	8	....	242	337	60	5th, Smythe Div.	Out of Playoffs
1991-92	80	22	13	5	....	14	21	5	....	36	34	10	....	295	297	82	3rd, Smythe Div.	Lost Conf. Championship
1990-91	80	22	15	3	....	15	22	3	....	37	37	6	....	272	272	80	3rd, Smythe Div.	Lost Conf. Championship
1989-90	**80**	**23**	**11**	**6**	....	**15**	**17**	**8**	....	**38**	**28**	**14**	....	**315**	**283**	**90**	**2nd, Smythe Div.**	**Won Stanley Cup**
1988-89	80	21	16	3	....	17	18	5	....	38	34	8	....	325	306	84	3rd, Smythe Div.	Lost Div. Semi-Final
1987-88	**80**	**28**	**8**	**4**	....	**16**	**17**	**7**	....	**44**	**25**	**11**	....	**363**	**288**	**99**	**2nd, Smythe Div.**	**Won Stanley Cup**
1986-87	**80**	**29**	**6**	**5**	....	**21**	**18**	**1**	....	**50**	**24**	**6**	....	**372**	**284**	**106**	**1st, Smythe Div.**	**Won Stanley Cup**
1985-86	80	32	6	2	....	24	11	5	....	56	17	7	....	426	310	119	1st, Smythe Div.	Lost Div. Final
1984-85	**80**	**26**	**7**	**7**	....	**23**	**13**	**4**	....	**49**	**20**	**11**	....	**401**	**298**	**109**	**1st, Smythe Div.**	**Won Stanley Cup**
1983-84	**80**	**31**	**5**	**4**	....	**26**	**13**	**1**	....	**57**	**18**	**5**	....	**446**	**314**	**119**	**1st, Smythe Div.**	**Won Stanley Cup**
1982-83	80	25	9	6	....	22	12	6	....	47	21	12	....	424	315	106	1st, Smythe Div.	Lost Final
1981-82	80	31	5	4	....	17	12	11	....	48	17	15	....	417	295	111	1st, Smythe Div.	Lost Div. Semi-Final
1980-81	80	17	13	10	....	12	22	6	....	29	35	16	....	328	327	74	4th, Smythe Div.	Lost Quarter-Final
1979-80	80	17	14	9	....	11	25	4	....	28	39	13	....	301	322	69	4th, Smythe Div.	Lost Prelim. Round

2010-11 Schedule

Oct.	Thu.	7	Calgary		Thu.	13	at San Jose	
	Sun.	10	Florida		Sat.	15	at Los Angeles	
	Thu.	14	at Minnesota		Sun.	16	at Anaheim*	
	Sat.	16	at Calgary		Tue.	18	Minnesota	
	Thu.	21	Minnesota		Thu.	20	Dallas	
	Sat.	23	San Jose		Sun.	23	Nashville	
	Tue.	26	at Calgary		Tue.	25	at Phoenix	
	Thu.	28	at Columbus		Wed.	26	at Dallas	
	Fri.	29	at Chicago	**Feb.**	Wed.	2	Los Angeles	
Nov.	Tue.	2	Vancouver		Fri.	4	at St. Louis	
	Fri.	5	Detroit		Sat.	5	at Columbus	
	Sun.	7	at Chicago		Mon.	7	at Nashville	
	Tue.	9	at Carolina		Wed.	9	Chicago	
	Thu.	11	at Detroit		Sat.	12	Ottawa*	
	Fri.	12	at New Jersey		Sun.	13	Anaheim	
	Sun.	14	at NY Rangers*		Tue.	15	Dallas	
	Wed.	17	Chicago		Thu.	17	Montreal	
	Fri.	19	Phoenix		Sat.	19	Atlanta*	
	Sun.	21	at Anaheim*		Tue.	22	at Minnesota	
	Tue.	23	at Phoenix		Wed.	23	at Colorado	
	Thu.	25	Colorado		Fri.	25	St. Louis	
	Sat.	27	San Jose		Sun.	27	Boston	
	Mon.	29	at Ottawa	**Mar.**	Tue.	1	Nashville	
Dec.	Wed.	1	at Montreal		Thu.	3	Columbus	
	Thu.	2	at Toronto		Sat.	5	at Colorado	
	Sat.	4	St. Louis		Tue.	8	at Philadelphia	
	Tue.	7	Anaheim		Wed.	9	at Washington	
	Fri.	10	Tampa Bay		Fri.	11	at Detroit	
	Sun.	12	Vancouver		Sun.	13	at Pittsburgh*	
	Tue.	14	Toronto		Thu.	17	Phoenix	
	Thu.	16	Columbus		Sat.	19	Colorado	
	Tue.	21	at San Jose		Tue.	22	at Nashville	
	Thu.	23	at Los Angeles		Thu.	24	at St. Louis	
	Sun.	26	at Vancouver		Sat.	26	Calgary	
	Tue.	28	Buffalo		Tue.	29	Los Angeles	
	Thu.	30	Colorado		Thu.	31	at Minnesota	
Jan.	Sat.	1	Calgary	**Apr.**	Sat.	2	at Vancouver	
	Tue.	4	Detroit		Tue.	5	Vancouver	
	Thu.	6	NY Islanders		Wed.	6	at Calgary	
	Fri.	7	at Vancouver		Fri.	8	Minnesota	
	Tue.	11	at Dallas		Sun.	10	at Colorado*	

* Denotes afternoon game.

Dustin Penner established career highs in goals (32) and assists (31) to lead Edmonton with a career-best 63 points in 2009-10. His 32 goals were the most by an Oiler in four years.

**NORTHWEST DIVISION
32nd NHL Season**

Franchise date: June 22, 1979

2010-11 Player Personnel

FORWARDS

	HT	WT	S	Place of Birth	*Age	2009-10 Club
BRULE, Gilbert	5-10	180	R	Edmonton, Alta.	23	Edmonton
COGLIANO, Andrew	5-10	184	L	Toronto, Ont.	23	Edmonton
EBERLE, Jordan	5-10	174	R	Regina, Sask.	20	Regina-Springfield
FRASER, Colin	6-1	190	L	Surrey, B.C.	25	Chicago
GAGNER, Sam	5-11	191	R	London, Ont.	21	Edmonton
GIROUX, Alexandre	6-2	200	L	Quebec City, Que.	29	Washington-Hershey
HALL, Taylor	6-1	185	L	Calgary, Alta.	18	Windsor
HEMSKY, Ales	6-0	192	R	Pardubice, Czech.	27	Edmonton
HORCOFF, Shawn	6-1	208	L	Trail, B.C.	32	Edmonton
JACQUES, Jean-Francois	6-4	217	L	Montreal, Que.	25	Edmonton
JONES, Ryan	6-1	202	L	Chatham, Ont.	26	Nsh-Milwaukee-Edm
MacINTYRE, Steve	6-5	250	L	Brock, Sask.	30	Edm-Fla-Roch
MORAN, Brad	5-11	187	L	Abbotsford, B.C.	31	Skelleftea
OMARK, Linus	5-9	170	L	Overtornea, Sweden	23	Dynamo Moscow
O'MARRA, Ryan	6-2	193	R	Tokyo, Japan	23	Edmonton-Springfield
ONDRUS, Ben	6-0	194	L	Sherwood Park, Alta.	28	Toronto (AHL)
PAAJARVI-SVENSSON, Magnus	6-2	201	L	Norrkoping, Sweden	19	Timra
PENNER, Dustin	6-4	245	L	Winkler, Man.	28	Edmonton
REDDOX, Liam	5-10	180	L	East York, Ont.	24	Edmonton-Springfield
STEWART, Greg	6-2	197	L	Kitchener, Ont.	24	Mtl-Hamilton-Chi (AHL)
STORTINI, Zack	6-3	228	R	Elliot Lake, Ont.	25	Edmonton

DEFENSEMEN

	HT	WT	S	Place of Birth	*Age	2009-10 Club
BELLE, Shawn	6-1	240	L	Edmonton, Alta.	25	Montreal-Hamilton
CHORNEY, Taylor	5-11	182	L	Thunder Bay, Ont.	23	Edmonton-Springfield
FOSTER, Kurtis	6-5	223	R	Carp, Ont.	28	Tampa Bay
GILBERT, Tom	6-3	206	R	Bloomington, MN	27	Edmonton
PECKHAM, Theo	6-2	223	L	Richmond Hill, Ont.	22	Edmonton-Springfield
PETIOT, Richard	6-4	215	L	Daysland, Alta.	28	Rockford
PLANTE, Alex	6-4	225	L	Brandon, Man.	21	Edmonton-Springfield
SMID, Ladislav	6-3	226	L	Frydlant V Cechach, Czech.	24	Edmonton
SOURAY, Sheldon	6-4	233	L	Elk Point, Alta.	34	Edmonton
STRUDWICK, Jason	6-4	225	L	Edmonton, Alta.	35	Edmonton
VANDERMEER, Jim	6-1	210	L	Caroline, Alta.	30	Phoenix
WHITNEY, Ryan	6-4	219	L	Boston, MA	27	Anaheim-Edmonton

GOALTENDERS

	HT	WT	C	Place of Birth	*Age	2009-10 Club
DESLAURIERS, Jeff	6-4	200	R	St-Jean-Richelieu, Que.	26	Edmonton
DUBNYK, Devan	6-6	194	L	Regina, Sask.	24	Edmonton-Springfield
GERBER, Martin	5-11	199	L	Burgdorf, Switz.	36	Mytischi
KHABIBULIN, Nikolai	6-1	209	L	Sverdlovsk, USSR	37	Edmonton
PITTON, Bryan	6-2	168	L	Mississauga, Ont.	22	Springfield-Stockton

* – Age at start of 2010-11 season

2009-10 Scoring
* – rookie

Regular Season

Pos	#	Player	Team	GP	G	A	Pts	TOI	+/-	PIM	PP	SH	GW	S	%
R	27	Dustin Penner	EDM	82	32	31	63	18:22	-6	38	9	0	1	203	15.8
C	89	Sam Gagner	EDM	68	15	26	41	16:17	-8	33	6	0	1	170	8.8
D	6	Ryan Whitney	ANA	62	4	24	28	24:33	-6	48	3	0	0	107	3.7
			EDM	19	3	8	11	25:22	7	22	0	0	1	44	6.8
			Total	81	7	32	39	24:45	1	70	3	0	1	151	4.6
C	67	Gilbert Brule	EDM	65	17	20	37	14:13	-6	38	2	0	3	121	14.0
C	10	Shawn Horcoff	EDM	77	13	23	36	19:25	-29	51	4	0	1	123	10.6
C	19	Patrick O'Sullivan	EDM	73	11	23	34	17:31	-35	32	1	0	3	191	5.8
C	16	Ryan Potulny	EDM	64	15	17	32	16:16	-21	28	7	1	2	152	9.9
D	77	Tom Gilbert	EDM	82	5	26	31	22:25	-10	24	0	0	1	98	5.1
C	13	Andrew Cogliano	EDM	82	10	18	28	14:10	-5	31	1	0	1	139	7.2
C	12	Robert Nilsson	EDM	60	11	16	27	14:44	-17	12	3	0	1	104	10.6
R	83	Ales Hemsky	EDM	22	7	15	22	17:56	7	8	3	0	0	57	12.3
C	91	Mike Comrie	EDM	43	13	8	21	14:14	-9	30	5	0	0	97	13.4
L	18	Ethan Moreau	EDM	76	9	9	18	14:24	-18	62	0	3	2	143	6.3
C	78	Marc Pouliot	EDM	35	7	7	14	12:47	-4	21	1	0	1	60	11.7
D	44	Sheldon Souray	EDM	37	4	9	13	22:36	-19	65	0	0	0	113	3.5
R	46	Zack Stortini	EDM	77	4	9	13	9:17	3	155	1	0	1	46	8.7
R	28	Ryan Jones	NSH	41	7	4	11	10:42	3	18	2	0	0	53	13.2
			EDM	8	1	0	1	10:20	-3	8	0	0	0	9	11.1
			Total	49	8	4	12	10:38	0	26	2	0	0	62	12.9
L	22	J.F. Jacques	EDM	49	4	7	11	11:11	-15	13	0	0	0	49	8.2
D	2	Aaron Johnson	CGY	22	1	2	3	12:10	0	19	0	0	0	13	7.7
			EDM	19	3	4	7	19:40	-6	16	1	0	0	23	13.0
			Total	41	4	6	10	15:38	-6	35	1	0	0	36	11.1
D	5	Ladislav Smid	EDM	51	1	8	9	19:10	5	39	0	0	0	36	2.8
R	34	Fernando Pisani	EDM	40	4	4	8	14:35	-16	10	0	0	0	54	7.4
C	32	* Ryan Stone	EDM	27	0	6	6	10:51	2	48	0	0	0	25	0.0
D	43	Jason Strudwick	EDM	72	0	6	6	16:56	-18	50	0	0	0	19	0.0
D	41	* Taylor Chorney	EDM	42	0	3	3	17:23	-21	12	0	0	0	35	0.0
L	85	Liam Reddox	EDM	9	0	2	2	12:31	-2	4	0	0	0	11	0.0
R	57	* Colin McDonald	EDM	2	1	0	1	6:41	1	0	0	0	0	3	33.3
C	42	* Ryan O'Marra	EDM	3	0	1	1	6:37	0	2	0	0	0	2	0.0
D	48	* Alex Plante	EDM	4	0	1	1	13:36	1	2	0	0	0	4	0.0
L	39	Christopher Minard	EDM	5	0	1	1	9:44	-3	0	0	0	0	4	0.0
D	49	* Theo Peckham	EDM	15	0	1	1	16:04	-8	43	0	0	0	9	0.0
D	58	* Johan Motin	EDM	1	0	0	0	14:08	-1	0	0	0	0	0	0.0
L	36	Charles Linglet	EDM	5	0	0	0	10:15	-5	2	0	0	0	7	0.0
D	8	Dean Arsene	EDM	13	0	0	0	12:56	-3	41	0	0	0	4	0.0

Goaltending

No.	Goaltender	GPI	Mins	Avg	W	L	OT	EN	SO	GA	SA	S%	G	A	PIM
35	Nikolai Khabibulin	18	1089	3.03	7	9	2	2	0	55	602	.909	0	0	4
38	* Jeff Deslauriers	48	2798	3.26	16	28	4	4	3	152	1529	.901	0	3	8
40	* Devan Dubnyk	19	1075	3.57	4	10	2	1	0	64	579	.889	0	0	0
	Totals	82	4997	3.34	27	47	8	7	3	278	2716	.898			

Coaching History

Glen Sather, 1979-80; Bryan Watson and Glen Sather, 1980-81; Glen Sather, 1981-82 to 1988-89; John Muckler, 1989-90, 1990-91; Ted Green, 1991-92, 1992-93; Ted Green and Glen Sather, 1993-94; George Burnett and Ron Low, 1994-95; Ron Low, 1995-96 to 1998-99; Kevin Lowe, 1999-2000; Craig MacTavish, 2000-01 to 2008-09; Pat Quinn, 2009-10; Tom Renney, 2010-11.

Tom Renney
Head Coach
Born: Cranbrook, B.C., March 1, 1955.

General manager Steve Tambellini announced that Tom Renney had become the tenth head coach in franchise history on June 22, 2010. Renney had joined the Oilers on May 26, 2009 as an associate coach for the 2009-10 season.

Prior to joining the Oilers, Renney had spent five seasons as head coach of the New York Rangers. His tenure with the Rangers organization began as director of player personnel before being promoted to vice-president of player development in 2002. Renney was appointed head coach with 20 games left in the 2003-04 season. He led the Rangers into the postseason in each of his first three campaigns following the 2004-05 NHL lockout. The team's three consecutive 40-win seasons were a feat last accomplished in 1974.

Renney began his coaching career in 1990-91 with the Western Hockey League's Kamloops Blazers. He guided the Blazers to consecutive President's Cup championships as WHL champions and was named WHL coach of the year in 1990-91. He captured a Memorial Cup title in 1992.

Following his junior coaching career, Renney joined Hockey Canada in 1992, where he began coaching the Canadian national team. He guided Canada to a silver medal at the 1994 Winter Olympics in Lillehammer, Norway. Renney continued to represent his country, working on Team Canada's coaching staff at the 2004 (gold) and 2005 (silver) World Championships. In total, Tom Renney has coached in a range of capacities in 10 World Championships, capturing two gold, four silver and one bronze medal.

Coaching Record

Season	Team	League	Regular Season GC	W	L	O/T	Playoffs GC	W	L	T
1990-91	Kamloops	WHL	72	50	20	2	12	5	7	...
1991-92	Kamloops	WHL	72	51	17	4	17	12	5	...
1991-92	Kamloops	M-Cup	...	...	...	...	5	4	1	...
1993-94*	Canada	Exhib	63	33	26	4	8	5	2	...
1994-95**	Canada	Exhib	57	37	17	3	8	3	2	2
1995-96***	Canada	Exhib	53	33	12	8	8	4	2	2
1996-97	Vancouver	NHL	82	35	40	7	...	...	...	...
1997-98	Vancouver	NHL	19	4	13	2	...	...	...	...
99-2000	Canada	Exhib	56	27	23	6	...	...	...	...
2003-04	NY Rangers	NHL	20	5	11	4	...	...	...	...
2004-05	NY Rangers		SEASON CANCELLED							
2005-06	NY Rangers	NHL	82	44	26	12	4	0	4	...
2006-07	NY Rangers	NHL	82	42	30	10	10	6	4	...
2007-08	NY Rangers	NHL	82	42	27	13	10	5	5	...
2008-09	NY Rangers	NHL	61	31	23	7	...	...	...	...
	NHL Totals		428	203	170	55	24	11	13	

* Olympics (silver medal)
** World Championship (bronze)
*** World Championship (silver)

Club Records

Team

(Figures in brackets for season records are games played; records for fewest points, wins, ties, losses, goals, goals against are for 70 or more games)

Most Points .... 119 — 1983-84 (80), 1985-86 (80)
Most Wins .... 57 — 1983-84 (80)
Most Ties .... 16 — 1980-81 (80), 1999-2000 (82)
Most Losses .... 50 — 1992-93 (84)
Most Goals .... *446 — 1983-84 (80)
Most Goals Against .... 337 — 1992-93 (84)
Fewest Points .... 60 — 1992-93 (84)
Fewest Wins .... 25 — 1993-94 (84)
Fewest Ties .... 5 — 1983-84 (80)
Fewest Losses .... 17 — 1981-82 (80), 1985-86 (80)
Fewest Goals .... 195 — 2006-07 (82)
Fewest Goals Against .... 182 — 2001-02 (82)

Longest Winning Streak
- **Overall** .... 9 — Feb. 20-Mar. 13/01
- **Home** .... 8 — Jan. 19-Feb. 22/85, Feb. 24-Apr. 2/86
- **Away** .... 8 — Dec. 9/86-Jan. 17/87

Longest Undefeated Streak
- **Overall** .... 15 — Oct. 11-Nov. 9/84 (12 wins, 3 ties)
- **Home** .... 14 — Nov. 15/89-Jan. 6/90 (11 wins, 3 ties)
- **Away** .... 9 — Jan. 17-Mar. 2/82 (6 wins, 3 ties), Nov. 23/82-Jan. 18/83 (7 wins, 2 ties)

Longest Losing Streak
- **Overall** .... 13 — Dec. 31/09-Jan. 30/10
- **Home** .... 9 — Oct. 16-Nov. 24/93
- **Away** .... 11 — Dec. 23/09-Feb. 10/10

Longest Winless Streak
- **Overall** .... 14 — Oct. 11-Nov. 7/93 (13 losses, 1 tie)
- **Home** .... 9 — Oct. 16-Nov. 24/93 (9 losses)
- **Away** .... 11 — Dec. 18/01-Feb. 8/02 (7 losses, 4 ties), Dec. 23/09-Feb. 10/10 (11 loses)

Most Shutouts, Season .... 8 — 1997-98 (82); 2000-01 (82); 2001-02 (82)
Most PIM, Season .... 2,173 — 1987-88 (80)
Most Goals, Game .... 13 — Nov. 19/83 (N.J. 4 at Edm. 13), Nov. 8/85 (Van. 0 at Edm. 13)

Individual

Most Seasons .... 15 — Kevin Lowe
Most Games .... 1,037 — Kevin Lowe
Most Goals, Career .... 583 — Wayne Gretzky
Most Assists, Career .... 1,086 — Wayne Gretzky
Most Points, Career .... 1,669 — Wayne Gretzky (583G, 1,086A)
Most PIM, Career .... 1,747 — Kelly Buchberger
Most Shutouts, Career .... 23 — Tommy Salo
Longest Consecutive Games Streak .... 518 — Craig MacTavish (Oct. 12/86-Jan. 2/93)
Most Goals, Season .... *92 — Wayne Gretzky (1981-82)
Most Assists, Season .... *163 — Wayne Gretzky (1985-86)
Most Points, Season .... *215 — Wayne Gretzky (1985-86; 52G, 163A)
Most PIM, Season .... 286 — Steve Smith (1987-88)
Most Points, Defenseman, Season .... 138 — Paul Coffey (1985-86; 48G, 90A)
Most Points, Center, Season .... *215 — Wayne Gretzky (1985-86; 52G, 163A)
Most Points, Right Wing, Season .... 135 — Jari Kurri (1984-85; 71G, 64A)
Most Points, Left Wing, Season .... 106 — Mark Messier (1982-83; 48G, 58A)
Most Points, Rookie, Season .... 75 — Jari Kurri (1980-81; 32G, 43A)
Most Shutouts, Season .... 8 — Curtis Joseph (1997-98), Tommy Salo (2000-01)
Most Goals, Game .... 5 — Wayne Gretzky (Feb. 18/81), (Dec. 30/81), (Dec. 15/84), (Dec. 6/87); Jari Kurri (Nov. 19/83); Pat Hughes (Feb. 3/84)
Most Assists, Game .... *7 — Wayne Gretzky (Feb. 15/80), (Dec. 11/85), (Feb. 14/86)
Most Points, Game .... 8 — Wayne Gretzky (Nov. 19/83; 3G, 5A), (Jan. 4/84; 4G, 4A); Paul Coffey (Mar. 14/86; 2G, 6A)

* NHL Record.

Retired Numbers

3	Al Hamilton	1972-1980
7	Paul Coffey	1980-1987
9	Glenn Anderson	1980-91, 1996
11	Mark Messier	1980-1991
17	Jari Kurri	1980-1990
31	Grant Fuhr	1981-1991
99	Wayne Gretzky	1979-1988

Captains' History

Ron Chipperfield, 1979-80; Blair MacDonald and Lee Fogolin, Jr., 1980-81; Lee Fogolin, Jr., 1981-82, 1982-83; Wayne Gretzky, 1983-84 to 1987-88; Mark Messier, 1988-89 to 1990-91; Kevin Lowe, 1991-92; Craig MacTavish, 1992-93, 1993-94; Shayne Corson, 1994-95; Kelly Buchberger, 1995-96 to 1998-99; Doug Weight, 1999-2000, 2000-01; Jason Smith, 2001-02 to 2006-07; Ethan Moreau, 2007-08 to 2009-10.

All-time Record vs. Other Clubs

Regular Season

	At Home								On Road								Total							
	GP	W	L	T	OL	GF	GA	PTS	GP	W	L	T	OL	GF	GA	PTS	GP	W	L	T	OL	GF	GA	PTS
Anaheim	35	21	12	0	2	87	81	44	36	15	19	2	0	96	104	32	71	36	31	2	2	183	185	76
Atlanta	6	3	1	1	1	22	16	8	5	3	2	0	0	14	8	6	11	6	3	1	1	36	24	14
Boston	31	11	15	3	2	102	103	27	32	6	22	3	1	80	131	16	63	17	37	6	3	182	234	43
Buffalo	31	21	7	3	0	123	87	45	32	13	11	7	1	114	114	34	63	34	18	10	1	237	201	79
Calgary	99	50	36	10	3	350	313	113	99	34	56	9	0	311	385	77	198	84	92	19	3	661	698	190
Carolina	33	21	7	5	0	128	95	47	31	12	12	7	0	103	120	31	64	33	19	12	0	231	215	78
Chicago	55	27	23	5	0	194	177	59	54	19	28	7	0	177	203	45	109	46	51	12	0	371	380	104
Colorado	64	33	24	4	3	243	207	73	65	27	32	4	2	220	241	60	129	60	56	8	5	463	448	133
Columbus	18	13	4	0	1	61	42	27	18	9	4	3	2	61	46	23	36	22	8	3	3	122	88	50
Dallas	54	24	17	8	5	207	178	61	55	17	29	7	2	152	199	43	109	41	46	15	7	359	377	104
Detroit	54	26	17	10	1	203	187	63	54	20	29	3	2	171	208	45	108	46	46	13	3	374	395	108
Florida	9	5	3	1	0	28	19	11	11	4	5	2	0	31	29	10	20	9	8	3	0	59	48	21
Los Angeles	87	43	29	15	0	375	305	101	87	41	30	15	1	347	328	98	174	84	59	30	1	722	633	199
Minnesota	29	15	10	3	1	73	66	34	28	10	13	1	4	57	80	25	57	25	23	4	5	130	146	59
Montreal	38	21	17	0	0	132	120	42	33	10	16	4	3	104	117	27	71	31	33	4	3	236	237	69
Nashville	22	9	11	0	2	60	71	20	23	8	11	3	1	70	67	20	45	17	22	3	3	130	138	40
New Jersey	33	15	11	6	1	139	117	37	35	17	13	3	2	115	114	39	68	32	24	9	3	254	231	76
NY Islanders	31	18	8	5	0	114	89	41	33	7	16	9	1	113	134	24	64	25	24	14	1	227	223	65
NY Rangers	30	13	14	3	0	106	100	29	32	15	9	6	2	120	119	38	62	28	23	9	2	226	219	67
Ottawa	14	7	5	2	0	45	37	16	13	5	4	2	2	34	31	14	27	12	9	4	2	79	68	30
Philadelphia	30	16	8	6	0	104	86	38	33	11	20	2	0	93	134	24	63	27	28	8	0	197	220	62
Phoenix	82	53	21	6	2	359	260	114	81	42	29	5	5	343	316	94	163	95	50	11	7	702	576	208
Pittsburgh	32	22	9	1	0	152	105	45	32	13	15	3	1	134	123	30	64	35	24	4	1	286	228	75
St. Louis	54	27	21	4	2	189	176	60	54	22	24	7	1	186	185	52	108	49	45	11	3	375	361	112
San Jose	43	24	11	7	1	138	100	56	42	16	19	5	2	121	141	39	85	40	30	12	3	259	241	95
Tampa Bay	12	8	4	0	0	32	27	16	13	7	4	2	0	41	37	16	25	15	8	2	0	73	64	32
Toronto	46	24	15	6	1	185	147	55	40	16	22	2	0	165	165	34	86	40	37	8	1	350	312	89
Vancouver	99	59	29	7	4	403	308	129	100	45	39	12	4	366	355	106	199	104	68	19	8	769	663	235
Washington	31	16	11	4	0	126	95	36	31	10	18	2	1	102	125	23	62	26	29	6	1	228	220	59
Totals	**1202**	**645**	**400**	**125**	**32**	**4480**	**3714**	**1447**	**1202**	**474**	**551**	**137**	**40**	**4041**	**4359**	**1125**	**2404**	**1119**	**951**	**262**	**72**	**8521**	**8073**	**2572**

Playoffs

	Series	W	L	GP	W	L	T	GF	GA	Last Mtg.	Rnd.	Result
Anaheim	1	1	0	5	4	1	0	16	13	2006	CF	W 4-1
Boston	2	2	0	9	8	1	0	41	20	1990	F	W 4-1
Calgary	5	4	1	30	19	11	0	132	96	1991	DSF	W 4-3
Carolina	1	0	1	7	3	4	0	16	19	2006	F	L 3-4
Chicago	4	3	1	20	12	8	0	102	77	1992	CF	L 0-4
Colorado	2	1	1	12	5	7	0	30	35	1998	CQF	W 4-3
Dallas	8	2	6	42	15	27	0	104	118	2003	CQF	L 2-4
Detroit	3	3	0	16	12	4	0	58	43	2006	CQF	W 4-2
Los Angeles	7	5	2	36	24	12	0	154	127	1992	DSF	W 4-2
Montreal	1	1	0	3	3	0	0	15	6	1981	PRE	W 3-0
NY Islanders	3	1	2	15	6	9	0	47	58	1984	F	W 4-1
Philadelphia	3	2	1	15	8	7	0	49	44	1987	F	W 4-3
Phoenix	6	6	0	26	22	4	0	120	75	1990	DSF	W 4-3
San Jose	1	1	0	6	4	2	0	19	12	2006	CSF	W 4-2
Vancouver	2	2	0	9	7	2	0	35	20	1992	DF	W 4-2
Totals	**49**	**34**	**15**	**251**	**152**	**99**	**0**	**938**	**763**			

Playoff Results 2010-2006

Year	Round	Opponent	Result	GF	GA
2006	F	Carolina	L 3-4	16	19
	CF	Anaheim	W 4-1	16	13
	CSF	San Jose	W 4-2	19	12
	CQF	Detroit	W 4-2	19	17

Abbreviations: Round: F - Final; **CF** - conference final; **CSF** - conference semi-final; **CQF** - conference quarter-final; **DF** - division final; **DSF** - division semi-final; **PRE** - preliminary round.

Calgary totals include Atlanta Flames, 1979-80.
Colorado totals include Quebec, 1979-80 to 1994-95.
New Jersey totals include Colorado Rockies, 1979-80 to 1981-82.
Carolina totals include Hartford, 1979-80 to 1996-97.
Dallas totals include Minnesota North Stars, 1979-80 to 1992-93.
Phoenix totals include Winnipeg, 1979-80 to 1995-96.

2009-10 Results

Oct.	3	Calgary	3-4	Jan.	2	at San Jose	1-4
	6	Dallas	5-4†		5	Phoenix	4-5*
	8	Calgary	3-4†		7	Columbus	2-4
	10	Montreal	3-2		12	Nashville	3-5
	12	at Nashville	6-1		14	Pittsburgh	2-3
	14	at Chicago	3-4		16	at San Jose	2-4
	16	Minnesota	5-2		18	at Colorado	0-6
	19	Vancouver	2-1		20	Vancouver	2-3*
	22	Columbus	6-4		22	Dallas	3-4
	24	at Calgary	2-5		26	Chicago	2-4
	25	at Vancouver	0-2		28	St. Louis	1-2
	27	Colorado	0-3		30	at Calgary	1-6
	29	Detroit	6-5†	Feb.	1	Carolina	4-2
	31	at Boston	0-2		3	Philadelphia	1-0
Nov.	2	at NY Islanders	1-3		4	at Minnesota	2-4
	5	NY Rangers	2-4		6	at Colorado	0-3
	8	at Colorado	5-3		8	at Phoenix	1-6
	10	at Ottawa	3-4†		10	at Anaheim	2-3
	11	at Buffalo	1-3		11	at Los Angeles	3-2†
	15	at Atlanta	2-3		14	Anaheim	3-7
	16	at Columbus	2-3†	Mar.	2	at Nashville	3-4
	18	Colorado	6-4		3	at Chicago	2-5
	21	Chicago	2-5		5	Minnesota	2-1†
	23	Phoenix	4-0		7	New Jersey	2-0
	25	Los Angeles	1-3		9	Ottawa	1-4
	27	San Jose	4-5†		11	at Montreal	4-5†
	28	at Vancouver	3-7		13	at Toronto	4-6
Dec.	3	at Detroit	4-1		15	at Columbus	3-5
	5	at Dallas	3-2†		16	at Minnesota	2-4
	7	at Florida	3-2†		19	Detroit	3-2†
	9	at Tampa Bay	3-2		21	San Jose	5-1
	11	at St. Louis	5-3		23	Vancouver	3-2
	15	Los Angeles	2-3		26	Anaheim	2-3
	17	Nashville	3-6		28	at St. Louis	1-2
	19	Washington	2-4		30	at Detroit	4-5
	21	St. Louis	2-7	Apr.	2	at Dallas	3-6
	23	at Minnesota	1-3		3	at Phoenix	2-3†
	26	at Vancouver	1-4		5	Minnesota	4-1
	28	Calgary	1-4		7	Colorado	5-4*
	30	Toronto	3-1		10	at Los Angeles	4-3†
	31	at Calgary	1-2		11	at Anaheim	2-7

* – Overtime † – Shootout

Entry Draft Selections 2010-1996

Name in bold denotes played in NHL.

2010 Pick		2005 Pick		2002 Pick		1999 Pick	
1	Taylor Hall	25	**Andrew Cogliano**	15	Jesse Niinimaki	13	**Jani Rita**
31	Tyler Pitlick	36	**Taylor Chorney**	31	**Jeff Deslauriers**	36	**Alexei Semenov**
46	Martin Marincin	81	**Danny Syvret**	36	**Jarret Stoll**	41	**Tony Salmelainen**
48	Curtis Hamilton	86	Robby Dee	44	**Matt Greene**	81	**Adam Hauser**
61	Ryan Martindale	97	Chris Vande Velde	79	Brock Radunske	91	**Mike Comrie**
91	Jeremie Blain	120	Vyacheslav Trukhno	106	Ivan Koltsov	139	Jonathan Fauteux
121	Tyler Bunz	157	Fredrik Pettersson	111	Jonas Almtorp	171	Chris Legg
162	Brandon Davidson	220	Matthew Glasser	123	invalid pick	199	Christian Chartier
166	Drew Czerwonka			148	Glenn Fisher	256	Tamas Groschl
181	Kristians Pelss	**2004**		181	**Mikko Luoma**		
202	Kellen Jones	**Pick**		205	**J.F. Dufort**	**1998**	
		14	**Devan Dubnyk**	211	Patrick Murphy	**Pick**	
2009		25	**Rob Schremp**	244	**Dwight Helminen**	13	Michael Henrich
Pick		44	Roman Tesliuk	245	Tomas Micka	67	**Alex Henry**
10	Magnus	57	Geoff Paukovich	274	Fredrik Johansson	99	**Shawn Horcoff**
	Paajarvi-Svensson	112	**Liam Reddox**			113	Kristian Antila
40	Anton Lander	146	**Bryan Young**	**2001**		128	Paul Elliott
71	Troy Hesketh	177	Max Gordichuk	**Pick**		144	Oleg Smirnov
82	Cameron Abney	208	Stephane Goulet	13	**Ales Hemsky**	159	Trevor Ettinger
99	Kyle Bigos	242	Tyler Spurgeon	43	**Doug Lynch**	186	**Mike Morrison**
101	Toni Rajala	274	Bjorn Bjurling	52	Ed Caron	213	Christian Lefebvre
133	Olivier Roy			84	Kenny Smith	241	Maxim Spiridonov
		2003		133	**Jussi Markkanen**		
2008		**Pick**		154	Jake Brenk	**1997**	
Pick		22	**Marc Pouliot**	185	Mikael Svensk	**Pick**	
22	Jordan Eberle	51	**Colin McDonald**	215	Dan Baum	14	**Michel Riesen**
103	**Johan Motin**	68	**Jean-Francois Jacques**	248	**Kari Haakana**	41	Patrick Dovigi
133	Philippe Cornet	72	Mikhail Zhukov	272	**Ales Pisa**	68	Sergei Yerkovich
163	Teemu Hartikainen	94	**Zack Stortini**	278	**Shay Stephenson**	94	Jonas Elofsson
193	Jordan Bendfeld	147	Kalle Olsson			121	**Jason Chimera**
		154	David Rohlfs	**2000**		141	**Peter Sarno**
2007		184	Dragan Umicevic	**Pick**		176	Kevin Bolibruck
Pick		214	**Kyle Brodziak**	17	**Alexei Mikhnov**	187	Chad Hinz
6	**Sam Gagner**	215	**Mathieu Roy**	35	**Brad Winchester**	205	Chris Kerr
15	**Alex Plante**	248	Josef Hrabal	83	Alexander Liubimov	231	Alexander Fomichev
21	Riley Nash	278	**Troy Bodie**	113	Lou Dickenson		
97	Linus Omark			152	Paul Flache	**1996**	
127	Milan Kytnar			184	Shaun Norrie	**Pick**	
157	William Quist			211	Joe Cullen	6	**Boyd Devereaux**
				215	**Matthew Lombardi**	19	**Matthieu Descoteaux**
2006				247	Jason Platt	32	**Chris Hajt**
Pick				274	Yevgeny Muratov	59	**Tom Poti**
45	Jeff Petry					114	Brian Urick
75	**Theo Peckham**					141	Bryan Randall
133	Bryan Pitton					168	David Bernier
140	Cody Wild					170	Brandon Lafrance
170	Alexander Bumagin					195	**Fernando Pisani**
						221	John Hultberg

General Managers' History

Larry Gordon, 1979-80; Glen Sather, 1980-81 to 1999-2000; Kevin Lowe, 2000-01 to 2007-08; Steve Tambellini, 2008-09 to date.

Steve Tambellini

General Manager

Born: Trail, B.C., May 14, 1958.

Steve Tambellini joined the Edmonton Oilers as general manager on July 31, 2008 after 17 seasons as a member of the Vancouver Canucks management team. During his tenure with Vancouver, which began in 1990-91, Tambellini served in several positions. During his last three years with the club, he was vice president and assistant general manager. In that role, he was involved in all aspects of the team's hockey operations, including contract negotiations, scouting and minor league affiliates.

Tambellini took over in Edmonton from Kevin Lowe, who was promoted to the position of president of hockey operations. Tambellini and Lowe have previously worked together as members of Team Canada's management team, helping lead Canada to success on the international stage. As director of player personnel, Tambellini helped put together the roster that won the gold medal at the 2002 Winter Olympics in Salt Lake City and he was also a member of the management team for Team Canada's gold medal triumph at the 2004 World Cup of Hockey. He also served as the general manager of Team Canada at the 2003 and 2005 World Championships, winning gold in 2003 and silver in 2005.

Inducted into the B.C. Hockey Hall of Fame in 2004, Tambellini played 10 seasons in the NHL after being selected 15th overall in the 1978 NHL Amateur Draft by the New York Islanders. A member of the Islanders' 1980 Stanley Cup championship team, he played 553 career NHL games with five NHL teams between 1978-79 and 1987-88. He had 160 goals and 150 assists for 310 career points with 105 penalty minutes with the Islanders, Colorado Rockies, New Jersey Devils, Calgary Flames and Vancouver Canucks.

Besides his outstanding hockey resume, Tambellini has also been a contributor to the Canucks' off-ice activities. He served as the president of the Canucks for Kids Fund for 12 seasons and was awarded the B.C. Humanitarian of the Year Award by the B.C. Hockey Hall of Fame in 2006. He was also awarded the Jake Milford Plaque in 2004 for his significant and lasting contributions to hockey in his home province of British Columbia.

Club Directory

Rexall Place

Edmonton Oilers
11230 – 110 Street
Edmonton, Alberta T5G 3H7
Phone **780/414-GOAL(4625)**
Press Box 780/409-3780
Media Lounge 780/409-3778
FAX 780/409-5890
www.edmontonoilers.com
Capacity: 16,839

Owner	Daryl A. Katz (Rexall Sports Corp)
Governor	Daryl A. Katz
Alternate Governors	Patrick LaForge, Kevin Lowe
President & Chief Executive Officer	Patrick LaForge
President of Hockey Operations	Kevin Lowe
Executive Assistant to the Hockey President	Connie Hadden
Executive Vice President, Commercial Operations	Stew MacDonald
Senior Vice President, Marketing – Rexall Sports	Steve Katzman
Vice-President of Finance and CFO	Darryl Boessenkool
Executive Assistant to the President	Lisa Nicolson
Executive Assistant to the CFO	Bobbie-Jo Dawe
Security	Michael Fluker

Hockey Operations

General Manager	Steve Tambellini
Asst. G.M & Dir. of Hockey Ops/Legal Affairs	Ricky Olczyk
Senior Advisor, Hockey	Pat Quinn
Head Coach	Tom Renney
Assistant Coaches	Kelly Buchberger, Steve Smith
Goaltending Coach	Frederic Chabot
Video Coordinator	Myles Fee
Director of Player Development	Mike Sillinger
Coordinator of Player Development	Billy Moores
Skating & Skills Coach	Steve Serdachny
Fitness Consultant	Simon Bennett
Dir. of Research, Analysis & Software Development	Sean Draper
Coordinator of Hockey Operations	James McGregor
Head Amateur Scout	Stu MacGregor
Head Pro Scout	Morey Gare
Amateur Scouts	Bob Brown, Bill Dandy, Brad Davis, Kent Hawley, Mike Peluso
Pro Scouts	Michael Abbamont, Dave Semenko
European Scouts	Frank Musil, Kent Nilsson
Family Liaison	Jill Metz

Medical and Training Staff

Head Athletic Therapist	T.D. Forss
Head Equipment Manager	Jeff Lang
Assistant Medical Trainer	Chris Davie
Assistant Equipment Manager	Brad Harrison
Massage Therapist	Steve Lines
Team Medical Chief of Staff	Dr. David C. Reid
Medical Staff	Drs. John Clarke, Dhiren Naidu, Don Groot, Ben Eastwood, Tony Sneazwell, Gordon Bell, Dave Magee, Brent Saik

Communications and Broadcast

Vice President, Communications & Broadcast	Allan Watt
Director, Communications & Media Relations	J.J. Hebert
Director of Broadcast	Don Metz
Manager, Communications & Team Services	Patrick Garland
Coordinator, Communications & Media Relations	Rob Thomas

Finance and Administration

Senior Director, Business Development	Jason Quilley
Human Resource Manager	Tandy Kustiak
Director, Facilities Operations & GM Telus Field	TBD
Director of Administration & Legal Counsel	Keely Brown
Manager of Administrative Services	Sherry Smith
Controller / Assistant Controller	Zeina Charara / Zeshan Qureshi
Accounting	Christine Marceau, Jamie Schenknecht, Shawna Quigley, Corinne Amyotte
Director / Manager, IT	Alfred Ng / Rod Pruden
Infrastructure Administrator	Kevin Flemming
Senior Business Analyst / Business Analyst	Sharon Lyseng / Jason Lee
Manager / Supervisor, Ticket Operations	Gavin Morton / Travis Nielsen
Facilities Coordinator	Gilbert da Silva
Receptionists	Sandy Langley, Macy Beley

Corporate Partnerships

Vice President, Sales	Brad MacGregor
Sr. Directors, Corp. Partnerships	Lisa Munro, Martha Henderson, Daryl Zelinski, Scott Murray
Director, Executive Suites	Bob Haromy
Manager, Corporate Partnerships	Abe Hajar
Manager, Events / Digital Media Sales	Jody Young / Jessica Butts
Partner Activation Specialists	Angie Zander, Matt McPhee, David Reynar, Kendra Morton, Stephen Rausch, Sara Ripko, Brent Frew
Event Coordinators	Kevin Radomski, Corinne Ethier

Ticket Sales and Customer Relations

Director, Ticket Sales and Customer Relationships	Scott Murray
Manager, Customer Relationships	Carmen Day
Ticket Event Administrator	TBD
Ticket Account Executives	John Sutherland, Ryan Fengstad, Brent Frew, Julian Solberg, Don Robinson, David Benson, Field Pieterse, Conrad Langier, Erik Hapke, Derek Wold, Kevin Radomski
Customer Experience Representative	Brynn Tralnberg
Supervisor, Ticket Services	Curtis Griffith
Sr. Customer Services Representative	Paul Reid

Marketing

Vice President, Oilers Brand	Pat McLaughlin
Manager, Marketing	Christine Dmytryshyn
Manager, Digital Media	Marc Ciampa
Digital Media Specialist / Producer	Jen Sharpe / Nyki Scheuerman
Marketing Specialist / Coordinator	Debbie George / Avery Grbavac
Manager, Fan Community & Development	Trevor Murphy
Fan & Community Development Coordinator	Tyson Lazaruk
Manager, Corporate Communications	Jessica McPhee
Graphic Designer	Joey Angeles
Game Night Supervisor / Director	Trish Millard / Derek Dawley
Team Photographer	Andy Devlin

Community

Exec. Dir., Oilers Community Foundation	Natalie Minckler
Coordinators	Lindsay Gilbert, Dwain Tomkow, Sandy VanRiper, Amanda Weir
Fan Development Assistant	Cheryl Thomas

Radio/TV Broadcasters

Television Outlets	Sportsnet, CBXT TV and TSN
Radio Flagship Station	630 CHED (AM); TBD (play-by- play) & Bob Stauffer (color)

Florida Panthers

Key Off-Season Signings/Acquisitions

2010

May 17 • Named **Dale Tallon** general manager.

June 1 • Signed 2008 2nd round pick (31st overall), G **Jacob Markstrom** (Brynas IF).

22 • Acquired D **Dennis Wideman**, Boston's 1st round pick in the 2010 Entry Draft and and 3rd round pick in 2011 for RW **Nathan Horton** and C **Gregory Campbell**.

25 • Acquired RW **Steve Bernier**, RW **Michael Grabner** and Vancouver's 1st round pick in the 2010 Entry Draft from Vancouver for D **Keith Ballard** and RW **Victor Oreskovich**.

July 2 • Signed LW **Chris Higgins**.

6 • Named **Brian Skrudland** director of player development and **Gord Murphy** assistant coach.

7 • Signed D **Nathan Paetsch**.

22 • Acquired C **Marty Reasoner** from Chicago for C **Jeff Taffe**.

Aug. 3 • Signed D **Mike Weaver**.

5 • Acquired C **Mike Santorelli** from Nashville for a conditional pick in the 2011 Entry Draft.

2009-10 Results: 32w-37L-3OTL-10SOL 77PTS.
Fifth, Southeast Division

Year-by-Year Record

Season	GP	Home				Road				Overall						Pts	Finished	Playoff Result
		W	L	T	OL	W	L	T	OL	W	L	T	OL	GF	GA			
2009-10	82	16	16	....	9	16	21	....	4	32	37	....	13	208	244	77	5th, Southeast Div.	Out of Playoffs
2008-09	82	22	12	....	7	19	18	....	4	41	30	....	11	234	231	93	3rd, Southeast Div.	Out of Playoffs
2007-08	82	18	15	....	8	20	20	....	1	38	35	....	9	216	226	85	3rd, Southeast Div.	Out of Playoffs
2006-07	82	23	12	....	6	12	19	....	10	35	31	....	16	247	257	86	4th, Southeast Div.	Out of Playoffs
2005-06	82	25	11	....	5	12	23	....	6	37	34	....	11	240	257	85	4th, Southeast Div.	Out of Playoffs
2004-05														....		....		
2003-04	82	16	15	7	3	12	20	8	1	28	35	15	4	188	221	75	4th, Southeast Div.	Out of Playoffs
2002-03	82	8	21	7	5	16	15	6	4	24	36	13	9	176	237	70	4th, Southeast Div.	Out of Playoffs
2001-02	82	11	23	3	4	11	21	7	2	22	44	10	6	180	250	60	4th, Southeast Div.	Out of Playoffs
2000-01	82	12	18	7	4	10	20	6	5	22	38	13	9	200	246	66	3rd, Southeast Div.	Out of Playoffs
1999-2000	82	26	9	4	2	17	18	2	4	43	27	6	6	244	209	98	2nd, Southeast Div.	Lost Conf. Quarter-Final
1998-99	82	17	17	7	....	13	17	11	....	30	34	18	....	210	228	78	2nd, Southeast Div.	Out of Playoffs
1997-98	82	11	24	6	....	13	19	9	....	24	43	15	....	203	256	63	6th, Atlantic Div.	Out of Playoffs
1996-97	82	21	12	8	....	14	16	11	....	35	28	19	....	221	201	89	3rd, Atlantic Div.	Lost Conf. Quarter-Final
1995-96	82	25	12	4	....	16	19	6	....	41	31	10	....	254	234	92	3rd, Atlantic Div.	Lost Final
1994-95	48	9	12	3	....	11	10	3	....	20	22	6	....	115	127	46	5th, Atlantic Div.	Out of Playoffs
1993-94	84	15	18	9	....	18	16	8	....	33	34	17	....	233	233	83	5th, Atlantic Div.	Out of Playoffs

2010-11 Schedule

Oct.	Sun.	10	at Edmonton
	Mon.	11	at Vancouver
	Thu.	14	at Calgary
	Sat.	16	Tampa Bay
	Thu.	21	Dallas
	Sat.	23	NY Islanders
	Tue.	26	at Toronto
	Thu.	28	at Ottawa
	Sat.	30	at Montreal
Nov.	Wed.	3	Atlanta
	Fri.	5	Carolina
	Sat.	6	at Carolina
	Wed.	10	Toronto
	Fri.	12	Minnesota
	Sat.	13	at Philadelphia
	Wed.	17	at Atlanta
	Thu.	18	at Boston
	Sat.	20	at NY Islanders
	Mon.	22	Pittsburgh
	Wed.	24	Boston
	Fri.	26	NY Rangers
	Sat.	27	at Tampa Bay
Dec.	Wed.	1	at Anaheim
	Thu.	2	at Los Angeles
	Sat.	4	at Phoenix
	Tue.	7	Colorado
	Thu.	9	at Washington
	Sat.	11	at Nashville
	Wed.	15	Carolina
	Fri.	17	Buffalo
	Mon.	20	at Philadelphia
	Wed.	22	at Pittsburgh
	Thu.	23	at Buffalo
	Mon.	27	Boston
	Fri.	31	Montreal*
Jan.	Sun.	2	NY Rangers*
	Mon.	3	at Carolina
	Wed.	5	Atlanta
	Fri.	7	Carolina
	Sat.	8	at Washington
	Tue.	11	Washington
	Thu.	13	Nashville
	Sat.	15	New Jersey
	Mon.	17	Atlanta
	Wed.	19	Columbus
	Fri.	21	Tampa Bay
	Sun.	23	at New Jersey*
	Tue.	25	at NY Rangers
	Wed.	26	at Boston
Feb.	Tue.	1	at Toronto
	Wed.	2	at Montreal
	Fri.	4	at New Jersey
	Tue.	8	St. Louis
	Thu.	10	Buffalo
	Sun.	13	San Jose*
	Wed.	16	Philadelphia
	Fri.	18	Detroit
	Sat.	19	at Tampa Bay
	Mon.	21	at NY Islanders*
	Wed.	23	at Ottawa
	Fri.	25	at Atlanta
	Sun.	27	New Jersey*
Mar.	Tue.	1	at Carolina
	Thu.	3	Montreal
	Sat.	5	at Atlanta
	Sun.	6	Washington*
	Tue.	8	Chicago
	Thu.	10	Ottawa
	Sat.	12	Tampa Bay
	Tue.	15	Philadelphia
	Thu.	17	Toronto
	Sat.	19	NY Islanders
	Tue.	22	at NY Rangers
	Wed.	23	at Chicago
	Fri.	25	at Buffalo
	Sun.	27	at Pittsburgh*
	Tue.	29	at Columbus
	Thu.	31	Ottawa
Apr.	Sat.	2	Pittsburgh
	Wed.	6	at Washington
	Fri.	8	at Tampa Bay
	Sat.	9	Washington

* Denotes afternoon game.

Only 16 players in the NHL had more total ice time than Bryan McCabe, who averaged 23:19 per game in 82 games for the Panthers in 2009-10. He also led the team's defensemen with 35 assists and 43 points.

SOUTHEAST DIVISION
18th NHL Season
Franchise date: June 14, 1993

2010-11 Player Personnel

FORWARDS	HT	WT	S	Place of Birth	*Age	2009-10 Club
BERNIER, Steve	6-2	216	R	Quebec City, Que.	25	Vancouver
BITZ, Byron	6-5	215	R	Saskatoon, Sask.	26	Boston-Florida
BOOTH, David	6-0	212	L	Detroit, MI	25	Florida
CULLEN, Mark	5-11	182	L	Moorhead, MN	31	Rockford
DADONOV, Evgeny	5-10	178	L	Chelyabinsk, USSR	21	Florida-Rochester
DUCO, Mike	5-10	200	L	Toronto, Ont.	23	Florida-Rochester
DVORAK, Radek	6-2	200	R	Tabor, Czech.	33	Florida
FROLIK, Michael	6-1	185	L	Kladno, Czech.	22	Florida
GRABNER, Michael	6-0	170	L	Villach, Austria	23	Vancouver-Manitoba
GRANT, Triston	6-1	211	L	Neepawa, Man.	26	Nashville-Milwaukee
HIGGINS, Christopher	6-0	205	L	Smithtown, NY	27	NY Rangers-Calgary
MATTHIAS, Shawn	6-2	213	L	Mississauga, Ont.	22	Florida-Rochester
McARDLE, Kenndal	5-11	190	L	Toronto, Ont.	23	Florida-Rochester
OLESZ, Rostislav	6-1	214	L	Bilovec, Czech.	24	Florida
REASONER, Marty	6-1	205	L	Honeoye Falls, NY	33	Atlanta
REINPRECHT, Steve	6-0	195	L	Edmonton, Alta.	34	Florida
REPIK, Michal	5-10	180	R	Vlasim, Czech.	21	Florida-Rochester
SANTORELLI, Mike	6-0	189	R	Vancouver, B.C.	24	Nashville-Milwaukee
STILLMAN, Cory	6-0	200	L	Peterborough, Ont.	36	Florida
THOMAS, Bill	6-1	191	R	Pittsburgh, PA	27	Springfield-Lugano
WEISS, Stephen	5-11	185	L	Toronto, Ont.	27	Florida

DEFENSEMEN	HT	WT	S	Place of Birth	*Age	2009-10 Club
ALLEN, Bryan	6-4	220	L	Kingston, Ont.	30	Florida
CALLAHAN, Joe	6-3	220	R	Brockton, MA	27	San Jose-Worcester
ELLERBY, Keaton	6-4	186	L	Strathmore, Alta.	21	Florida-Rochester
GARRISON, Jason	6-2	220	L	White Rock, B.C.	25	Florida-Rochester
GUDBRANSON, Erik	6-4	195	R	Ottawa, Ont.	18	Kingston
HUDSON, Carl	6-1	210	R	Smooth Rock Falls, Ont.	24	Canisius-Rochester
KULIKOV, Dmitry	6-1	183	L	Lipetsk, USSR	19	Florida
McCABE, Bryan	6-2	220	L	St. Catharines, Ont.	35	Florida
PAETSCH, Nathan	6-1	195	L	Humboldt, Sask.	27	Buffalo-Columbus
WEAVER, Mike	5-9	186	R	Bramalea, Ont.	32	St. Louis
WIDEMAN, Dennis	6-0	196	R	Kitchener, Ont.	27	Boston
WILSON, Clay	6-0	195	L	Sturgeon Lake, MN	27	Florida-Rochester

GOALTENDERS	HT	WT	C	Place of Birth	*Age	2009-10 Club
CLEMMENSEN, Scott	6-3	205	L	Des Moines, IA	33	Florida
MARKSTROM, Jacob	6-3	178	L	Gavle, Sweden	20	Brynas Jr.-Brynas
PLANTE, Tyler	6-3	191	L	Milwaukee, WI	23	Rochester
SALAK, Alexander	6-1	189	L	Strakonice, Czech.	23	Florida-Rochester
VOKOUN, Tomas	6-0	195	R	Karlovy Vary, Czech.	34	Florida

* – Age at start of 2010-11 season

2009-10 Scoring

* – rookie

Regular Season

Pos		Player	Team	GP	G	A	Pts	TOI	+/-	PIM	PP	SH	GW	S	%
C	9	Stephen Weiss	FLA	80	28	32	60	19:59	-7	40	12	0	2	180	15.6
C	16	Nathan Horton	FLA	65	20	37	57	20:53	-1	42	7	2	4	159	12.6
C	67	Michael Frolik	FLA	82	21	22	43	17:28	-4	43	5	0	1	219	9.6
D	24	Bryan McCabe	FLA	82	8	35	43	23:19	-4	83	3	0	1	169	4.7
C	27	Steve Reinprecht	FLA	82	16	22	38	16:05	-1	18	3	0	1	124	12.9
C	61	Cory Stillman	FLA	58	15	22	37	17:34	-3	22	3	0	4	126	11.9
R	14	Radek Dvorak	FLA	76	14	18	32	17:26	-7	20	1	3	1	140	10.0
L	85	Rostislav Olesz	FLA	78	14	15	29	15:23	-4	28	3	0	3	178	7.9
D	2	Keith Ballard	FLA	82	8	20	28	22:24	-7	88	1	0	1	90	8.9
C	11	Gregory Campbell	FLA	60	2	15	17	15:23	-5	53	0	0	1	84	2.4
L	10	David Booth	FLA	28	8	8	16	18:07	-3	23	0	0	1	95	8.4
C	41 *	Shawn Matthias	FLA	55	7	9	16	10:47	-3	10	0	2	2	67	10.4
D	43 *	Dmitry Kulikov	FLA	68	3	13	16	17:56	-5	32	1	0	0	87	3.4
C	28	Kamil Kreps	FLA	76	5	9	14	12:42	-7	18	1	0	1	83	6.0
D	5	Bryan Allen	FLA	74	4	9	13	19:09	-8	99	0	1	2	78	5.1
R	12	Byron Bitz	BOS	45	4	5	9	10:56	-9	31	0	0	2	51	7.8
			FLA	7	1	1	2	11:37	1	2	0	0	0	7	14.3
			Total	52	5	6	11	11:02	-8	33	0	0	2	58	8.6
D	52 *	Jason Garrison	FLA	39	2	6	8	15:08	-5	23	0	0	0	48	8.3
R	65 *	Victor Oreskovich	FLA	50	2	4	6	8:53	-8	26	0	0	0	55	3.6
R	32 *	Michal Repik	FLA	19	3	2	5	8:34	1	6	0	0	0	23	13.0
D	6	Ville Koistinen	FLA	17	1	3	4	7:50	-1	8	0	0	0	12	8.3
L	71 *	Kenndal McArdle	FLA	19	1	2	3	8:53	-4	29	0	0	0	10	10.0
L	74	Nick Tarnasky	FLA	31	1	2	3	6:48	-5	85	0	0	0	19	5.3
L	22	Jeff Taffe	FLA	21	1	1	2	8:25	-1	4	0	0	0	18	5.6
L	33	Steve MacIntyre	EDM	4	0	0	0	1:34	0	7	0	0	0	0	0.0
			FLA	18	0	1	1	3:10	-3	17	0	0	0	3	0.0
			Total	22	0	1	1	2:52	-3	24	0	0	0	3	0.0
D	3	Clay Wilson	FLA	2	0	0	0	11:07	-5	0	0	0	0	3	0.0
R	63 *	Evgeny Dadonov	FLA	4	0	0	0	13:13	-1	0	0	0	0	6	0.0
R	68 *	Mike Duco	FLA	10	0	0	0	7:43	-3	50	0	0	0	6	0.0
D	39 *	Keaton Ellerby	FLA	22	0	0	0	5:25	-1	2	0	0	0	5	0.0

Goaltending

No.		Goaltender	GPI	Mins	Avg	W	L	OT	EN	SO	GA	SA	S%	G	A	PIM
29		Tomas Vokoun	63	3695	2.55	23	28	11	9	7	157	2081	.925	0	2	0
30		Scott Clemmensen	23	1215	2.91	9	8	2	3	1	59	668	.912	0	0	0
34	*	Alexander Salak	2	67	5.37	0	1	0	0	0	6	40	.850	0	0	0
		Totals	82	5008	2.80	32	37	13	12	8	234	2800	.916			

Michael Frolik and Stephen Weiss celebrate a goal. Frolik scored 21 for the second straight season in 2009-10. Weiss led the team with a career-high 28.

Peter DeBoer

Head Coach

Born: Dunnville, Ont., June 13, 1968.

The Florida Panthers named Peter DeBoer the 10th head coach in the club's history on June 13, 2008. DeBoer joined the Panthers from the Kitchener Rangers of the Ontario Hockey League, after guiding the team to the 2008 OHL championship before falling to the Spokane Chiefs in the Memorial Cup finals.

During his seven-year tenure as both coach and general manager in Kitchener, DeBoer earned 297 wins for a .676 winning percentage, while guiding his club to the 2003 Memorial Cup title. DeBoer earned his 500th OHL coaching victory in 2007-08, joining only five other coaches to have reached this milestone. He amassed a total of 539 OHL wins while coaching the Detroit Whalers (1995 to 1997), Plymouth Whalers (1997 to 2001) and the Kitchener Rangers (2001 to 2008), earning OHL coach of the year honors in 1999 and 2000. DeBoer was also named the 2000 Canadian Hockey League coach of the year, and was also a member of the coaching staff on Team Canada's 2005 gold medal-winning World Junior team.

As a player, DeBoer won the 1988 Memorial Cup as a member of the Windsor Spitfires. He was a 12th-round selection of the Toronto Maple Leafs in the 1988 NHL Entry Draft and played two full seasons professionally with the Milwaukee Admirals of the International Hockey League. He holds a law degree from the University of Windsor/University of Detroit.

Coaching Record

			Regular Season				Playoffs			
Season	Team	League	GC	W	L	O/T	GC	W	L	T
1995-96	Detroit	OHL	66	40	22	4	17	9	8	....
1996-97	Detroit	OHL	66	26	34	6	5	1	4	....
1997-98	Plymouth	OHL	66	37	22	7	15	8	7	....
1998-99	Plymouth	OHL	66	51	13	4	11	7	4	....
99-2000	Plymouth	OHL	68	45	18	5	23	15	8	....
2000-01	Plymouth	OHL	68	43	15	10	19	14	5	....
2001-02	Kitchener	OHL	68	35	22	11	4	0	4	....
2002-03	Kitchener	OHL	68	46	14	8	21	16	5	....
2002-03	Kitchener	M-Cup	....	....	....	....	4	4	0	....
2003-04	Kitchener	OHL	68	34	26	8	5	1	4	....
2004-05	Kitchener	OHL	68	35	20	13	15	9	6	....
2005-06	Kitchener	OHL	68	47	19	2	5	1	4	....
2006-07	Kitchener	OHL	68	47	17	4	9	5	4	....
2007-08	Kitchener	OHL	68	53	11	4	20	16	4	....
2007-08	Kitchener	M-Cup	....	....	....	....	5	2	3	....
2008-09	Florida	NHL	82	41	30	11	....	....	....	....
2009-10	Florida	NHL	82	32	37	13	....	....	....	....
	NHL Totals		164	73	67	24	....	....	....	....

Coaching History

Roger Neilson, 1993-94, 1994-95; Doug MacLean, 1995-96, 1996-97; Doug MacLean and Bryan Murray, 1997-98; Terry Murray, 1998-99, 1999-2000; Terry Murray and Duane Sutter, 2000-01; Duane Sutter and Mike Keenan, 2001-02; Mike Keenan, 2002-03; Mike Keenan, Rick Dudley and John Torchetti, 2003-04; Jacques Martin, 2004-05 to 2007-08; Peter DeBoer, 2008-09 to date.

General Managers' History

Bob Clarke, 1993-94; Bryan Murray, 1994-95 to 1999-2000; Bryan Murray and Bill Torrey, 2000-01; Bill Torrey and Chuck Fletcher, 2001-02; Rick Dudley, 2002-03, 2003-04; Mike Keenan, 2004-05, 2005-06; Jacques Martin, 2006-07 to 2008-09; Randy Sexton, 2009-10; Dale Tallon, 2010-11.

Club Records

Team

(Figures in brackets for season records are games played; records for fewest points, wins, ties, losses, goals, goals against are for 70 or more games)

Most Points	98	1999-2000 (82)
Most Wins	43	1999-2000 (82)
Most Ties	19	1996-97 (82)
Most Losses	44	2001-02 (82)
Most Goals	254	1995-96 (82)
Most Goals Against	257	2005-06 (82), 2006-07 (82)
Fewest Points	60	2001-02 (82)
Fewest Wins	22	2000-01 (82), 2001-02 (82)
Fewest Ties	6	1999-2000 (82)
Fewest Losses	27	1999-2000 (82)
Fewest Goals	176	2002-03 (82)
Fewest Goals Against	201	1996-97 (82)

Longest Winning Streak

Overall	7	Nov. 2-14/95, Mar. 17-29/06, Mar. 2-16/08
Home	5	Nov. 5-14/95, Mar. 17-Apr. 1/06, Mar. 6-16/08, Jan. 27-Feb. 13/09, Jan. 16-31/10
Away	5	Nov. 30-Dec. 12/08

Longest Undefeated Streak

Overall	12	Oct. 5-30/96 (8 wins, 4 ties)
Home	8	Nov. 5-26/95 (7 wins, 1 tie)
Away	7	Dec. 7-29/93 (5 wins, 2 ties), Oct. 5-29/96 (4 wins, 3 ties)

Longest Losing Streak

Overall	13	Feb. 7-Mar. 23/98
Home	6	Feb. 25-Mar. 23/98
Away	13	Oct. 27-Dec. 17/05

Longest Winless Streak

Overall	15	Feb. 1-Mar. 23/98 (14 losses, 1 tie)
Home	13	Feb. 5-Mar. 24/03 (11 losses, 2 ties)
Away	16	Jan. 2-Mar. 21/98 (12 losses, 4 ties)

Most Shutouts, Season	9	2008-09 (82)
Most PIM, Season	1,994	2001-02 (82)
Most Goals, Game	10	Nov. 26/97 (Bos. 5 at Fla. 10)

Individual

Most Seasons	9	Paul Laus
Most Games	573	Robert Svehla
Most Goals, Career	188	Olli Jokinen
Most Assists, Career	231	Olli Jokinen
Most Points, Career	419	Olli Jokinen (188G, 231A)
Most PIM, Career	1,702	Paul Laus
Most Shutouts, Career	26	Roberto Luongo

Longest Consecutive

Games Streak	342	Jay Bouwmeester (Feb. 27/04-Apr. 11/09)
Most Goals, Season	59	Pavel Bure (2000-01)
Most Assists, Season	53	Viktor Kozlov (1999-2000)
Most Points, Season	94	Pavel Bure (1999-2000; 58G, 36A)
Most PIM, Season	354	Peter Worrell (2001-02)

Most Points, Defenseman,

Season	57	Robert Svehla (1995-96; 8G, 49A)

Most Points, Center,

Season	91	Olli Jokinen (2006-07; 39G, 52A)

Most Points, Right Wing,

Season	94	Pavel Bure (1999-2000; 58G, 36A)

Most Points, Left Wing,

Season	71	Ray Whitney (1999-2000; 29G, 42A)

Most Points, Rookie,

Season	50	Jesse Belanger (1993-94; 17G, 33A)

Most Shutouts, Season

Most Shutouts, Season	7	Roberto Luongo (2003-04) Tomas Vokoun (2009-10)
Most Goals, Game	4	Mark Parrish (Oct. 30/98) Pavel Bure (Jan. 1/00), (Feb. 10/01)
Most Assists, Game	4	Six times
Most Points, Game	6	Olli Jokinen (Mar. 17/07; 2G, 4A)

Captains' History

Brian Skrudland, 1993-94 to 1996-97; Scott Mellanby, 1997-98 to 2000-01; Pavel Bure, 2001-02; no captain, 2002-03; Olli Jokinen, 2003-04 to 2007-08; no captain, 2008-09; Bryan McCabe, 2009-10 to date.

All-time Record vs. Other Clubs

Regular Season

	At Home								On Road								Total							
	GP	W	L	T	OL	GF	GA	PTS	GP	W	L	T	OL	GF	GA	PTS	GP	W	L	T	OL	GF	GA	PTS
Anaheim	10	4	4	2	0	27	25	10	11	6	3	1	1	33	29	14	21	10	7	3	1	60	54	24
Atlanta	31	15	13	4		79	89	33	31	9	14	4	4	86	106	26	62	24	27	5	6	165	195	59
Boston	31	13	13	2	3	92	90	31	32	17	11	4	0	83	81	38	63	30	24	6	3	175	171	69
Buffalo	31	14	15	1	1	81	89	30	33	8	20	3	2	66	100	21	64	22	35	4	3	147	189	51
Calgary	11	3	4	2	2	23	26	10	10	4	4	1	1	27	28	10	21	7	8	3	3	50	54	20
Carolina	44	21	7	8	8	134	102	58	43	11	26	3	3	107	141	28	87	32	33	11	11	241	243	86
Chicago	11	3	7	1	0	22	41	7	12	5	5	2	0	37	38	12	23	8	12	3	0	59	79	19
Colorado	14	3	10	0	1	42	57	7	13	4	5	3	1	31	38	12	27	7	15	3	2	73	95	19
Columbus	5	2	1	0	2	14	15	6	4	2	2	0	0	9	9	4	9	4	3	0	2	23	24	10
Dallas	12	5	6	1	0	25	33	11	11	5	4	2	0	37	37	12	23	10	10	3	0	62	70	23
Detroit	11	2	5	2	2	22	32	8	10	2	5	3	0	25	36	7	21	4	10	5	2	47	68	15
Edmonton	11	5	2	2	2	29	31	14	9	3	5	1	0	19	28	7	20	8	7	3	2	48	59	21
Los Angeles	10	4	3	2	1	26	25	12	11	4	7	0	0	32	33	8	21	8	9	3	1	58	58	20
Minnesota	5	1	4	0	0	10	17	2	5	1	3	1	0	6	16	3	10	2	7	1	0	16	33	5
Montreal	32	16	12	3	1	93	84	36	31	13	10	3	5	69	82	34	63	29	22	6	6	162	166	70
Nashville	7	4	0	1	2	23	14	11	8	2	3	2	1	16	19	7	15	6	3	3	3	39	33	18
New Jersey	35	12	16	4	3	80	89	31	34	9	20	3	2	65	103	23	69	21	36	7	5	145	192	54
NY Islanders	35	19	10	6	0	111	98	44	35	15	13	2	5	94	91	37	70	34	23	8	5	205	189	81
NY Rangers	35	15	13	2	5	89	96	37	34	12	18	4	0	76	103	28	69	27	31	6	5	165	199	65
Ottawa	32	12	18	1	1	99	106	26	32	14	14	2	2	83	95	32	64	26	32	3	3	182	201	58
Philadelphia	34	11	19	1	3	85	113	26	35	14	14	6	1	89	93	35	69	25	33	7	4	174	206	61
Phoenix	10	4	5	0	1	31	27	9	12	4	4	3	1	35	35	12	22	8	9	3	2	66	62	21
Pittsburgh	32	18	11	1	2	96	78	39	33	12	13	3	5	95	100	32	65	30	24	4	7	191	178	71
St. Louis	11	4	4	2	1	25	24	11	12	3	8	1	0	17	29	7	23	7	12	3	1	42	53	18
San Jose	11	3	3	5	0	30	32	11	11	3	6	2	0	22	34	8	22	6	9	7	0	52	66	19
Tampa Bay	46	29	9	4	4	155	115	66	46	20	18	6	2	131	112	48	92	49	27	10	6	286	227	114
Toronto	27	9	11	5	2	75	79	25	25	9	12	2	2	72	78	22	52	18	23	7	4	147	157	47
Vancouver	10	4	4	1	1	25	33	10	11	1	4	5	1	25	34	8	21	5	8	6	2	50	67	18
Washington	46	20	19	4	3	121	126	47	46	18	21	5	2	118	143	43	92	38	40	9	5	239	269	90
Totals	**640**	**275**	**247**	**65**	**53**	**1764**	**1786**	**668**	**640**	**230**	**292**	**77**	**41**	**1605**	**1871**	**578**	**1280**	**505**	**539**	**142**	**94**	**3369**	**3657**	**1246**

Playoffs

	Series	W	L	GP	W	L	T	GF	GA	Last Mtg.	Rnd.	Result
Boston	1	1	0	5	4	1	0	22	16	1996	CQF	W 4-1
Colorado	1	0	1	4	0	4	0	4	15	1996	F	L 0-4
New Jersey	1	0	1	4	0	4	0	6	12	2000	CQF	L 0-4
NY Rangers	1	0	1	5	1	4	0	10	13	1997	CQF	L 1-4
Philadelphia	1	1	0	6	4	2	0	15	11	1996	CSF	W 4-2
Pittsburgh	1	1	0	7	4	3	0	20	15	1996	CF	W 4-3
Totals	**6**	**3**	**3**	**31**	**13**	**18**	**0**	**77**	**82**			

Colorado totals include Quebec, 1993-94 to 1994-95.
Phoenix totals include Winnipeg, 1993-94 to 1995-96.
Carolina totals include Hartford, 1993-94 to 1996-97.

Playoff Results 2010-2006

(Last playoff appearance: 2000)

Abbreviations: Round: F - Final;
CF - conference final; **CSF** - conference semi-final;
CQF - conference quarter-final.

Entry Draft Selections 2010-1996

Name in bold denotes played in NHL.

2010
Pick
- 3 Erik Gudbranson
- 19 Nick Bjugstad
- 25 Quinton Howden
- 33 John McFarland
- 36 Alex Petrovic
- 50 Connor Brickley
- 69 Joe Basaraba
- 92 Sam Brittain
- 93 Benjamin Gallacher
- 99 Joonas Donskoi
- 123 Zach Hyman
- 153 Corey Durocher
- 183 Ronald Boyd

2009
Pick
- 14 **Dmitry Kulikov**
- 44 Drew Shore
- 67 Josh Birkholz
- 107 Garrett Wilson
- 135 Corban Knight
- 138 Wade Megan
- 165 Scott Timmins

2008
Pick
- 31 Jacob Markstrom
- 46 Colby Robak
- 80 Adam Comrie
- 100 A.J. Jenks
- 190 Matt Bartkowski

2007
Pick
- 10 **Keaton Ellerby**
- 40 **Michal Repik**
- 71 **Evgeni Dadonov**
- 101 Matt Rust
- 131 John Lee
- 181 Corey Syvret
- 191 Ryan Watson
- 202 Sergei Gayduchenko

2006
Pick
- 10 **Michael Frolik**
- 73 Brady Calla
- 103 Michael Caruso
- 116 Derrick Lapoint
- 155 Peter Aston
- 193 Marc Cheverie

2005
Pick
- 20 **Kenndal McArdle**
- 32 Tyler Plante
- 90 Dan Collins
- 93 Olivier Legault
- 104 Matt Duffy
- 161 Brian Foster
- 164 Roman Derlyuk
- 224 Zach Bearson

2004
Pick
- 7 **Rostislav Olesz**
- 37 David Shantz
- 53 **David Booth**
- 105 Evan Schafer
- 152 Bret Nasby
- 267 Spencer Dillon
- 283 Luke Beaverson

2003
Pick
- 3 **Nathan Horton**
- 25 **Anthony Stewart**
- 38 **Kamil Kreps**
- 55 **Stefan Meyer**
- 105 **Martin Lojek**
- 124 James Pemberton
- 141 Dan Travis
- 162 Martin Tuma
- 171 Denis Stasyuk
- 223 Dany Roussin
- 234 Petr Kadlec
- 264 John Hecimovic
- 265 **Tanner Glass**

2002
Pick
- 3 **Jay Bouwmeester**
- 9 **Petr Taticek**
- 40 **Rob Globke**
- 67 **Gregory Campbell**
- 134 Topi Jaakola
- 158 Vince Bellissimo
- 169 Jeremy Swanson
- 196 Mikael Vuorio
- 200 Denis Yachmenev
- 232 Peter Hafner

2001
Pick
- 4 **Stephen Weiss**
- 24 **Lukas Krajicek**
- 34 Greg Watson
- 64 **Tomas Malec**
- 68 **Grant McNeill**
- 117 Mike Woodford
- 136 Billy Thompson
- 169 Dustin Johner
- 200 Toni Koivisto
- 231 Kyle Bruce
- 263 Jan Blanar
- 267 **Ivan Majesky**

2000
Pick
- 58 Vladimir Sapozhnikov
- 77 Robert Fried
- 82 Sean O'Connor
- 115 Chris Eade
- 120 Davis Parley
- 190 Josh Olson
- 234 Janis Sprukts
- 253 Mathew Sommerfeld

1999
Pick
- 12 **Denis Shvidki**
- 40 **Alex Auld**
- 70 **Niklas Hagman**
- 80 Jean-Francois Laniel
- 103 Morgan McCormick
- 109 Rod Sarich
- 169 Brad Woods
- 198 Travis Eagles
- 227 Jonathon Charron

1998
Pick
- 30 **Kyle Rossiter**
- 61 **Joe DiPenta**
- 63 **Lance Ward**
- 89 **Ryan Jardine**
- 117 **Jaroslav Spacek**
- 148 Chris Ovington
- 176 B.J. Ketcheson
- 203 Ian Jacobs
- 231 Adrian Wichser

1997
Pick
- 20 **Mike Brown**
- 47 **Kristian Huselius**
- 56 Vratislav Cech
- 74 **Nick Smith**
- 95 **Ivan Novoseltsev**
- 127 Pat Parthenais
- 155 Keith Delaney
- 183 Tyler Palmer
- 211 Doug Schueller
- 237 Benoit Cote

1996
Pick
- 20 **Marcus Nilson**
- 60 **Chris Allen**
- 65 **Oleg Kvasha**
- 82 **Joey Tetarenko**
- 129 Andrew Long
- 156 Gaetan Poirier
- 183 Alexandre Couture
- 209 Denis Khloptonov
- 235 Russell Smith

Club Directory

BankAtlantic Center

Florida Panthers
BankAtlantic Center
One Panther Parkway
Sunrise, FL 33323
Phone **954/835-7000**
FAX 954/835-7700
www.floridapanthers.com
Capacity: 17,040

Ownership
General Partner/Chairman of the Board/
Chief Executive Officer/Governor . . . . Cliff Viner
Partners . . . . Alan Cohen, Steve Cohen, David Epstein, Dr. Elliott Hahn, H. Wayne Huizenga, Bernie Kosar, Richard C. Lehman, M.D., Al. E. Maroone, Michael E. Maroone, James L Nederlander, Stu Siegel, Jordan Zimmerman

Executive
President/Chief Operating Officer . . . . Michael Yormark
Exe. Vice President & G.M., Hockey Ops . . . . Dale Tallon
Exec.Vice President, Chief Marketing Officer . . . . . Pedro Goncalves
Exec. Vice President, Finance/CFO . . . . Eveyln Lopez
Senior Vice President, Human Resources . . . . Carol Duncanson
Vice President, Event Marketing . . . . Matt Bell
Vice President/G.M., Saveology.com Iceplex . . . . . Jeff Campol
Vice President, Corporate Marketing. . . . . Tim Kuhl
Vice President, Corporate Development . . . . R.J. Martino
Vice President, Ticket Sales . . . . Ryan McCoy
Vice President, Broadcasting & Panthers Alumni . . . Randy Moller
Vice President / G.M., BankAtlantic Center . . . . . . Erik Waldman
Vice President, Business Affairs . . . . Ed Wildermuth
Vice President, Marketing & Brand Activation . . . . Steve Ziff
Executive Assistant to the President / COO . . . . . . Heidi Leigh
Executive Assistant to the Chief Financial Officer . . . Cathy Stevenson

Hockey Operations
General Manager . . . . Dale Tallon
Assistant General Manager . . . . Mike Santos
Alternate Governor . . . . William Torrey
Executive Assistant to the General Manager . . . . . Giselle Seoane
Team Services Manager . . . . Mike Dixon
Director of Amateur Scouting . . . . Scott Luce
Director of Player Development . . . . Brian Skrudland
Pro Scout . . . . Peter Mahovlich, Al Tuer
Amateur Scouts . . . . Fred Bandel, Craig Demetrick, Paul Gallagher, Erin Ginnell, Jari Kekalainen, Kent Nilsson, Vadim Podrezov, Luke Williams, Mike Yandle

Coaching Staff
Head Coach . . . . Peter DeBoer
Assistant Coaches . . . . Jim Hulton, Gord Murphy
Goaltending Coach . . . . Robb Tallas
Strength & Conditioning Coach . . . . Craig Slaunwhite
Video Coach . . . . Jamie Pringle

Training Staff
Head Athletic Trainer . . . . David Zenobi
Assistant Athletic Trainer . . . . Steve Dischiavi
Equipment Manager . . . . Chris Scoppetto
Assistant Equipment Manager . . . . Chris Moody, Jason MacDonald

Communications and Media Content
Director, Communications . . . . Justin Copertino
Director, P.R./Editor, Panthers Insider . . . . Matthew F. Sacco
Manager, Websites & Social Media . . . . Glenn Odebralski

Broadcasting
Television . . . . FS Florida
Play-By-Play . . . . Steve Goldstein
Television Analyst . . . . Bill Lindsay
Panthers Preview/Review Host . . . . Craig Minervini
Radio . . . . 560 WQAM
Radio Play-By-Play . . . . Randy Moller

Dale Tallon
Executive Vice President and General Manager
Born: Noranda, Que., October 19, 1950.

Dale Tallon was named general manager of the Florida Panthers on May 17, 2010. Since joining Florida, Tallon conducted a successful 2010 NHL Entry Draft that saw the club stockpile 13 picks, including three first-round selections (No. 3 - D Erik Gudbranson, No. 19 - C Nick Bjugstad and No. 25 - C Quinton Howden). Tallon acquired forwards Steve Bernier and Michael Grabner, along with Vancouver's 2010 first-round pick in a draft-day trade. In addition, he acquired top-four defenseman Dennis Wideman and Boston's 2010 first-round pick, just days before the draft.

Prior to joining the Panthers, Tallon spent 33 years with the Blackhawks organization as a front office executive, player and broadcast personality. He served as Chicago's general manager from June of 2005 to July of 2009 after having served as assistant general manager from November of 2003 to June of 2005. Tallon was responsible for drafting or acquiring many of the players who led the Blackhawks to the Stanley Cup in 2010, including Jonathan Toews, Patrick Kane, Marian Hossa, Patrick Sharp, Kris Versteeg, John Madden and Brian Campbell.

As a player, Tallon was the Vancouver Canucks' first-round selection (second overall) in the 1970 NHL Draft. The Rouyn-Noranda, Quebec native played in 642 NHL contests with Vancouver (1970 to 1973), Chicago (1973 to 1978) and Pittsburgh (1978 to 1980) registering 336 points (98 goals, 238 assists) and 568 penalty minutes.Tallon recorded a career-high 17 goals in 69 games with Vancouver during the 1971-72 season and appeared in the 1971 and 1972 NHL All-Star Games. In 1972, Tallon was picked as an alternate for Team Canada for the Summit Series against the Soviet Union. After retiring following the 1979-80 season, Tallon served as a color analyst for Chicago radio and television broadcasts for 16 seasons.

Prior to joining the Panthers, Tallon spent the 2009-10 season serving as a senior advisor of hockey operations for the Blackhawks. He also served four years (1998 to 2002) as director of player personnel before returning to the radio and television booth prior to the 2002-03 season.

Los Angeles Kings

Key Off-Season Signings/Acquisitions

2010
June 24 • Named **John Stevens** assistant coach.
July 17 • Re-signed C **Brad Richardson**.
18 • Re-signed RW **Marc-Andre Cliche**, LW **Richard Clune**, C **Corey Elkins**, C **Trevor Lewis**.
27 • Signed LW **Alexei Ponikarovsky**.

2009-10 Results: 46w-27l-1otl-8sol 101pts.
Third, Pacific Division

2010-11 Schedule

Oct.	Sat.	9	at Vancouver		Mon.	10	Toronto
	Sun.	10	at Calgary		Thu.	13	St. Louis
	Tue.	12	Atlanta		Sat.	15	Edmonton
	Fri.	15	Vancouver		Mon.	17	at Dallas
	Wed.	20	Carolina		Tue.	18	at St. Louis
	Thu.	21	at Phoenix		Thu.	20	Phoenix
	Sat.	23	at Colorado		Sat.	22	at Phoenix
	Mon.	25	at Minnesota		Mon.	24	Boston
	Wed.	27	at Chicago		Wed.	26	San Jose
	Thu.	28	at Dallas	Feb.	Tue.	1	at Minnesota
	Sat.	30	New Jersey		Wed.	2	at Edmonton
Nov.	Thu.	4	Tampa Bay		Sat.	5	at Calgary
	Sat.	6	Nashville*		Thu.	10	at Pittsburgh
	Thu.	11	Dallas		Sat.	12	at Washington*
	Sat.	13	NY Islanders		Sun.	13	at Philadelphia
	Mon.	15	at San Jose		Wed.	16	at Columbus
	Wed.	17	Columbus		Thu.	17	at NY Rangers
	Fri.	19	at Buffalo		Sat.	19	at NY Islanders
	Sat.	20	at Boston		Wed.	23	at Anaheim
	Mon.	22	at Ottawa		Thu.	24	Minnesota
	Wed.	24	at Montreal		Sat.	26	Colorado*
	Sat.	27	Chicago		Mon.	28	Detroit
	Mon.	29	at Anaheim	Mar.	Thu.	3	Phoenix
Dec.	Thu.	2	Florida		Sat.	5	Vancouver*
	Sat.	4	Detroit		Mon.	7	Dallas
	Thu.	9	Calgary		Wed.	9	at Detroit
	Sat.	11	Minnesota		Fri.	11	at Columbus
	Mon.	13	at Detroit		Sun.	13	at Dallas*
	Thu.	16	at St. Louis		Tue.	15	at Nashville
	Sat.	18	at Nashville		Thu.	17	St. Louis
	Sun.	19	at Chicago		Sat.	19	Anaheim
	Tue.	21	at Colorado		Mon.	21	Calgary
	Thu.	23	Edmonton		Thu.	24	San Jose
	Sun.	26	Anaheim		Sat.	26	Colorado*
	Mon.	27	at San Jose		Tue.	29	at Edmonton
	Wed.	29	at Phoenix		Thu.	31	at Vancouver
	Thu.	30	Philadelphia	Apr.	Sat.	2	Dallas*
Jan.	Sat.	1	San Jose		Mon.	4	at San Jose
	Mon.	3	Chicago		Wed.	6	Phoenix
	Thu.	6	Nashville		Fri.	8	at Anaheim
	Sat.	8	Columbus		Sat.	9	Anaheim

* Denotes afternoon game.

Jonathan Quick took over the top goaltending job in Los Angeles in 2009-10 and set a club record with 39 wins in his first full NHL season.

Year-by-Year Record

Season	GP	Home W	L	T	OL	Road W	L	T	OL	Overall W	L	T	OL	GF	GA	Pts.	Finished	Playoff Result
2009-10	82	22	13	....	6	24	14	....	3	46	27	....	9	241	219	101	3rd, Pacific Div.	Lost Conf. Quarter-Final
2008-09	82	18	15	....	8	16	22	....	3	34	37	....	11	207	234	79	5th, Pacific Div.	Out of Playoffs
2007-08	82	17	21	....	3	15	22	....	4	32	43	....	7	231	266	71	5th, Pacific Div.	Out of Playoffs
2006-07	82	16	16	....	9	11	25	....	5	27	41	....	14	227	283	68	4th, Pacific Div.	Out of Playoffs
2005-06	82	26	14	....	1	16	21	....	4	42	35	....	5	249	270	89	4th, Pacific Div.	Out of Playoffs
2004-05	....																	
2003-04	82	15	16	9	1	13	13	7	8	28	29	16	9	205	217	81	3rd, Pacific Div.	Out of Playoffs
2002-03	82	19	19	2	1	14	18	4	5	33	37	6	6	203	221	78	3rd, Pacific Div.	Out of Playoffs
2001-02	82	22 -12	6	1	18	15	5	3	40	27	11	4	214	190	95	3rd, Pacific Div.	Lost Conf. Quarter-Final
2000-01	82	20	12	8	1	18	16	5	2	38	28	13	3	252	228	92	3rd, Pacific Div.	Lost Conf. Semi-Final
1999-2000	82	21	13	5	2	18 .14	7	2	39	27	12	4	245	228	94	3rd, Pacific Div.	Lost Conf. Quater-Final
1998-99	82	18	20	3	....	14	25	2	....	32	45	5	....	189	222	69	5th, Pacific Div.	Out of Playoffs
1997-98	82	22	16	3	....	16	17	8	....	38	33	11	....	227	225	87	2nd, Pacific Div.	Lost Conf. Quater-Final
1996-97	82	18	16	7	....	10	27	4	....	28	43	11	....	214	268	67	6th, Pacific Div.	Out of Playoffs
1995-96	82	16	16	9	....	8	24	9	....	24	40	18	....	256	302	66	6th, Pacific Div.	Out of Playoffs
1994-95	48	7	11	6	....	9	12	3	....	16	23	9	....	142	174	41	4th, Pacific Div.	Out of Playoffs
1993-94	84	18	19	5	....	9	26	7	....	27	45	12	....	294	322	66	5th, Pacific Div.	Out of Playoffs
1992-93	84	22	15	5	....	17	20	5	....	39	35	10	....	338	340	88	3rd, Smythe Div.	Lost Final
1991-92	80	20	11	9	....	15	20	5	....	35	31	14	....	287	296	84	2nd, Smythe Div.	Lost Div. Semi-Final
1990-91	80	26	9	5	....	20	15	5	....	46	24	10	....	340	254	102	1st, Smythe Div.	Lost Div. Final
1989-90	80	21	16	3	....	13	23	4	....	34	39	7	....	338	337	75	4th, Smythe Div.	Lost Div. Final
1988-89	80	25	12	3	....	17	19	4	....	42	31	7	....	376	335	91	2nd, Smythe Div.	Lost Div. Final
1987-88	80	19	18	3	....	11	24	5	....	30	42	8	....	318	359	68	4th, Smythe Div.	Lost Div. Semi-Final
1986-87	80	20	17	3	....	11	24	5	....	31	41	8	....	318	341	70	4th, Smythe Div.	Lost Div. Semi-Final
1985-86	80	9	27	4	....	14	22	4	....	23	49	8	....	284	389	54	5th, Smythe Div.	Out of Playoffs
1984-85	80	20	14	6	....	14	18	8	....	34	32	14	....	339	326	82	4th, Smythe Div.	Lost Div. Semi-Final
1983-84	80	13	19	8	....	10	25	5	....	23	44	13	....	309	376	59	5th, Smythe Div.	Out of Playoffs
1982-83	80	20	13	7	....	7	28	5	....	27	41	12	....	308	365	66	5th, Smythe Div.	Out of Playoffs
1981-82	80	19	15	6	....	5	26	9	....	24	41	15	....	314	369	63	4th, Smythe Div.	Lost Div. Final
1980-81	80	22	11	7	....	21	13	6	....	43	24	13	....	337	290	99	2nd, Norris Div.	Lost Prelim. Round
1979-80	80	18	13	9	....	12	23	5	....	30	36	14	....	290	313	74	2nd, Norris Div.	Lost Prelim. Round
1978-79	80	20	11	9	....	14	21	5	....	34	34	12	....	292	286	80	3rd, Norris Div.	Lost Prelim. Round
1977-78	80	18	16	6	....	13	18	9	....	31	34	15	....	243	245	77	3rd, Norris Div.	Lost Prelim. Round
1976-77	80	20	13	7	....	14	18	8	....	34	31	15	....	271	241	83	2nd, Norris Div.	Lost Quarter-Final
1975-76	80	22	13	5	....	16	20	4	....	38	33	9	....	263	265	85	2nd, Norris Div.	Lost Quarter-Final
1974-75	80	22	7	11	....	20	10	10	....	42	17	21	....	269	185	105	2nd, Norris Div.	Lost Prelim. Round
1973-74	78	22	13	4	....	11	20	8	....	33	33	12	....	233	231	78	3rd, West Div.	Lost Quarter-Final
1972-73	78	21	11	7	....	10	25	4	....	31	36	11	....	232	245	73	6th, West Div.	Out of Playoffs
1971-72	78	14	23	2	....	6	26	7	....	20	49	9	....	206	305	49	7th, West Div.	Out of Playoffs
1970-71	78	17	14	8	....	8	26	5	....	25	40	13	....	239	303	63	5th, West Div.	Out of Playoffs
1969-70	76	12	22	4	....	2	30	6	....	14	52	10	....	168	290	38	6th, West Div.	Out of Playoffs
1968-69	76	19	14	5	....	5	28	5	....	24	42	10	....	185	260	58	4th, West Div.	Lost Semi-Final
1967-68	74	20	13	4	....	11	20	6	....	31	33	10	....	200	224	72	2nd, West Div.	Lost Quarter-Final

PACIFIC DIVISION
44th NHL Season

Franchise date: June 5, 1967

2010-11 Player Personnel

FORWARDS	HT	WT	S	Place of Birth	*Age	2009-10 Club
BROWN, Dustin	6-0	208	R	Ithaca, NY	25	Los Angeles
CLUNE, Rich	5-10	198	L	Toronto, Ont.	23	Los Angeles
HANDZUS, Michal	6-4	216	L	Banska Bystrica, Czech.	33	Los Angeles
KAUNISTO, Ray	6-4	197	L	Sault Ste. Marie, MI	23	Northern Mich.
KOPITAR, Anze	6-3	222	L	Jesenice, Yugoslavia	23	Los Angeles
LEWIS, Trevor	6-0	199	R	Salt Lake City, UT	23	Los Angeles-Manchester
MOLLER, Oscar	5-10	186	R	Stockholm, Sweden	21	Los Angeles-Manchester
PARSE, Scott	5-11	197	R	Portage, MI	26	Los Angeles-Manchester
PONIKAROVSKY, Alexei	6-4	229	L	Kiev, USSR	30	Toronto-Pittsburgh
RICHARDSON, Brad	5-11	195	L	Belleville, Ont.	25	Los Angeles
SIMMONDS, Wayne	6-2	183	R	Scarborough, Ont.	22	Los Angeles
SMYTH, Ryan	6-2	189	L	Banff, Alta.	34	Los Angeles
STOLL, Jarret	6-1	215	R	Melville, Sask.	28	Los Angeles
WESTGARTH, Kevin	6-4	243	R	Amherstburg, Ont.	26	Manchester
WILLIAMS, Justin	6-1	193	R	Cobourg, Ont.	29	Los Angeles
ZEILER, John	6-0	203	R	Jefferson Hills, PA	27	Manchester
DEFENSEMEN						
DOUGHTY, Drew	6-0	211	R	London, Ont.	20	Los Angeles
DREWISKE, Davis	6-2	222	L	Hudson, WI	25	Los Angeles
FRANSSON, Johan	6-1	183	L	Kalix, Sweden	25	Lulea
GREENE, Matt	6-3	237	R	Grand Ledge, MI	27	Los Angeles
HARROLD, Peter	6-0	185	R	Kirtland Hills, OH	27	Los Angeles
JOHNSON, Jack	6-0	218	L	Indianapolis, IN	23	Los Angeles
SCUDERI, Rob	6-1	211	L	Syosset, NY	31	Los Angeles

GOALTENDERS	HT	WT	C	Place of Birth	*Age	2009-10 Club
BERNIER, Jonathan	5-11	184	L	Laval, Que.	22	Los Angeles-Manchester
ERSBERG, Erik	6-0	165	L	Sala, Sweden	28	Los Angeles
QUICK, Jonathan	6-1	223	L	Milford, CT	24	Los Angeles

* – Age at start of 2010-11 season

Terry Murray
Head Coach

Born: Shawville, Que., July 20, 1950.

The Los Angeles Kings named Terry Murray their head coach on July 17, 2008. Murray – formerly the head coach of the Washington Capitals, Florida Panthers and the Philadelphia Flyers, where he led that club to the 1997 Stanley Cup Finals – is the 22nd head coach in Kings history. In his second season behind the bench in 2009-10, Murray guided the team to the playoffs for the first time since 2001-02. The Kings tied a club record with 46 wins and their 101 points was the second-best total in franchise history.

Murray spent the four seasons prior to being hired by the Kings as an assistant coach with the Flyers, an organization he had worked for as a head coach, assistant coach, pro scout and player. In 2007-08, he helped the Flyers record 95 points and advance to Eastern Conference Finals after earning just 56 points in 2006-07. Murray compiled a 118-64-30 record as head coach of the Flyers for three seasons from 1994-95 through 1996-97. In addition to the 1997 Stanley Cup Finals / Eastern Conference Championship, Murray coached the team to two Atlantic Division Championships (1995 and 1996).

Murray's NHL head coaching career began with Washington for five seasons (1989-90 through 1993-94), where he compiled a 163-134-28 record. In his first season he helped lead the Capitals to the Eastern Conference Finals. Murray also coached Florida for three seasons (1998-99 through 2000-01), which included a franchise-record 98-point season and a team-record 43 wins in 1999-2000. He has also worked as an assistant coach with the Capitals (1983-84 through 1987-88); as head coach with the Baltimore Skipjacks of the American Hockey League; and as head coach with the Cincinnati Cyclones of the International Hockey League (1993-94).

As an NHL defenseman, Murray played in 302 career NHL regular-season games over eight seasons with Washington, Philadelphia (two stints), the Detroit Red Wings and the California Golden Seals / California Seals, who originally drafted Murray in the seventh-round (88th overall) of the 1970 NHL Amateur Draft. He recorded 80 points (four goals, 76 assists) and 199 penalty minutes during his NHL career and he also played in 18 career NHL playoff games, recording two goals, two assists and 10 penalty minutes.

Coaching Record

			Regular Season				Playoffs			
Season	Team	League	GC	W	L	O/T	GC	W	L	T
1988-89	Baltimore	AHL	80	30	46	4	....	....	....	....
1989-90	Baltimore	AHL	45	26	17	2	....	....	....	....
1989-90	**Washington**	**NHL**	**34**	**18**	**14**	**2**	**15**	**8**	**7**	....
1990-91	**Washington**	**NHL**	**80**	**37**	**36**	**7**	**11**	**5**	**6**	....
1991-92	**Washington**	**NHL**	**80**	**45**	**27**	**8**	**7**	**3**	**4**	....
1992-93	**Washington**	**NHL**	**84**	**43**	**34**	**7**	**6**	**2**	**4**	....
1993-94	Cincinnati	IHL	28	17	7	4	11	6	5	....
1993-94	**Washington**	**NHL**	**47**	**20**	**23**	**4**	....	....	....	....
1994-95	**Philadelphia**	**NHL**	**48**	**28**	**16**	**4**	**15**	**10**	**5**	....
1995-96	**Philadelphia**	**NHL**	**82**	**45**	**24**	**13**	**12**	**6**	**6**	....
1996-97	**Philadelphia**	**NHL**	**82**	**45**	**24**	**13**	**19**	**12**	**7**	....
1998-99	**Florida**	**NHL**	**82**	**30**	**34**	**18**	....	....	....	....
99-2000	**Florida**	**NHL**	**82**	**43**	**27**	**12**	**4**	**0**	**4**	....
2000-01	**Florida**	**NHL**	**36**	**6**	**18**	**12**	....	....	....	....
2008-09	**Los Angeles**	**NHL**	**82**	**34**	**37**	**11**	....	....	....	....
2009-10	**Los Angeles**	**NHL**	**82**	**46**	**27**	**9**	**6**	**2**	**4**	....
	NHL Totals		**901**	**440**	**341**	**120**	**95**	**48**	**47**	....

2009-10 Scoring

* – rookie

Regular Season

Pos	#	Player	Team	GP	G	A	Pts	TOI	+/-	PIM	PP	SH	GW	S	%
C	11	Anze Kopitar	L.A.	82	34	47	81	21:47	6	16	14	1	2	259	13.1
D	8	Drew Doughty	L.A.	82	16	43	59	24:58	20	54	9	0	5	142	11.3
R	23	Dustin Brown	L.A.	82	24	32	56	19:15	–6	41	7	0	3	248	9.7
L	94	Ryan Smyth	L.A.	67	22	31	53	19:40	8	42	11	0	3	206	10.7
L	24	Alexander Frolov	L.A.	81	19	32	51	18:26	–1	26	5	0	1	182	10.4
C	28	Jarret Stoll	L.A.	73	16	31	47	17:25	13	40	4	0	4	164	9.8
C	26	Michal Handzus	L.A.	81	20	22	42	18:18	4	38	5	1	6	117	17.1
R	17	Wayne Simmonds	L.A.	78	16	24	40	14:28	22	116	0	0	2	127	12.6
D	3	Jack Johnson	L.A.	80	8	28	36	22:36	–15	48	3	0	0	130	6.2
R	14	Justin Williams	L.A.	49	10	19	29	16:22	3	39	1	0	1	140	7.1
C	15	Brad Richardson	L.A.	81	11	16	27	12:50	1	37	0	1	4	148	7.4
R	63	* Scott Parse	L.A.	59	11	13	24	10:31	13	22	0	0	1	78	14.1
D	12	Randy Jones	L.A.	48	5	16	21	18:10	–3	28	1	1	1	54	9.3
C	22	Jeff Halpern	T.B.	55	9	8	17	15:38	–13	27	2	0	1	65	13.8
			L.A.	16	0	2	2	10:40	–1	12	0	0	0	6	0.0
			Total	71	9	10	19	14:31	–14	39	2	0	1	71	12.7
D	6	Sean O'Donnell	L.A.	78	3	12	15	18:44	14	70	0	0	1	44	6.8
L	33	Fredrik Modin	CBJ	24	2	4	6	14:40	–6	12	0	0	2	35	5.7
			L.A.	20	3	2	5	14:54	–2	14	2	0	0	32	9.4
			Total	44	5	6	11	14:46	–8	26	2	0	2	67	7.5
D	7	Rob Scuderi	L.A.	73	0	11	11	19:16	16	21	0	0	0	38	0.0
D	2	Matt Greene	L.A.	75	2	7	9	17:28	4	83	0	0	1	57	3.5
D	44	* Davis Drewiske	L.A.	42	1	7	8	15:14	–4	14	0	0	0	32	3.1
C	9	Oscar Moller	L.A.	34	4	3	7	8:35	–6	4	1	0	0	42	9.5
D	5	Peter Harrold	L.A.	39	1	2	3	9:14	–2	8	0	0	0	23	4.3
L	56	* Rich Clune	L.A.	14	0	2	2	7:17	1	26	0	0	0	7	0.0
C	47	* Corey Elkins	L.A.	3	1	0	1	11:54	–2	0	0	0	0	5	20.0
R	67	Marc-Andre Cliche	L.A.	1	0	0	0	7:23	1	0	0	0	0	0	0.0
C	48	* Andrei Loktionov	L.A.	1	0	0	0	11:52	0	0	0	0	0	1	0.0
C	55	* Brayden Schenn	L.A.	1	0	0	0	12:31	–1	0	0	0	0	0	0.0
D	53	* Alec Martinez	L.A.	4	0	0	0	15:24	–2	2	0	0	0	6	0.0
C	61	* Trevor Lewis	L.A.	5	0	0	0	9:07	–3	0	0	0	0	4	0.0
L	41	Raitis Ivanans	L.A.	61	0	0	0	4:53	–8	136	0	0	0	18	0.0

Goaltending

No.	Goaltender	GPI	Mins	Avg	W	L	OT	EN	SO	GA	SA	S%	G	A	PIM
45	* Jonathan Bernier	3	185	1.30	3	0	0	0	1	4	94	.957	0	1	0
31	Erik Ersberg	11	551	2.40	4	3	2	0	0	22	234	.906	0	0	0
32	Jonathan Quick	72	4258	2.54	39	24	7	5	4	180	1927	.907	0	1	2
	Totals	**82**	**5020**	**2.52**	**46**	**27**	**9**	**5**	**5**	**211**	**2260**	**.907**			

Playoffs

Pos	#	Player	Team	GP	G	A	Pts	TOI	+/-	PIM	PP	SH	GW	OT	S	%
D	8	Drew Doughty	L.A.	6	3	4	7	27:25	–5	4	2	0	0	0	13	23.1
D	3	Jack Johnson	L.A.	6	0	7	7	23:41	–5	6	0	0	0	0	15	0.0
C	26	Michal Handzus	L.A.	6	3	2	5	19:31	–5	4	3	0	0	0	17	17.6
C	11	Anze Kopitar	L.A.	6	2	3	5	21:13	–1	2	1	0	1	1	18	11.1
R	23	Dustin Brown	L.A.	6	1	4	5	18:53	–7	6	1	0	0	0	15	6.7
L	33	Fredrik Modin	L.A.	6	3	1	4	17:21	–3	2	2	0	0	0	13	23.1
L	24	Alexander Frolov	L.A.	6	1	3	4	16:48	–5	0	0	0	0	0	9	11.1
R	17	Wayne Simmonds	L.A.	6	2	1	3	14:21	1	9	0	0	0	0	14	14.3
L	94	Ryan Smyth	L.A.	6	1	1	2	18:38	0	6	0	0	0	0	11	9.1
C	15	Brad Richardson	L.A.	6	1	1	2	14:40	–7	2	0	0	1	0	12	8.3
C	28	Jarret Stoll	L.A.	6	1	0	1	15:50	–4	4	1	0	0	0	7	14.3
R	14	Justin Williams	L.A.	3	0	1	1	11:24	0	2	0	0	0	0	4	0.0
D	6	Sean O'Donnell	L.A.	6	0	1	1	18:27	–2	4	0	0	0	0	2	0.0
D	2	Matt Greene	L.A.	6	0	1	1	18:45	–4	0	0	0	0	0	4	0.0
L	41	Raitis Ivanans	L.A.	1	0	0	0	5:48	0	0	0	0	0	0	0	0.0
D	5	Peter Harrold	L.A.	2	0	0	0	11:57	0	0	0	0	0	0	1	0.0
D	12	Randy Jones	L.A.	4	0	0	0	17:41	–2	2	0	0	0	0	3	0.0
R	63	* Scott Parse	L.A.	4	0	0	0	6:37	–1	0	0	0	0	0	2	0.0
L	56	* Rich Clune	L.A.	4	0	0	0	5:11	–2	5	0	0	0	0	1	0.0
D	7	Rob Scuderi	L.A.	6	0	0	0	20:39	–4	6	0	0	0	0	4	0.0
C	22	Jeff Halpern	L.A.	6	0	0	0	10:12	–1	4	0	0	0	0	1	0.0

Goaltending

No.	Goaltender	GPI	Mins	Avg	W	L	EN	SO	GA	SA	S%	G	A	PIM
32	Jonathan Quick	6	360	3.50	2	4	2	0	21	181	.884	0	0	0
31	Erik Ersberg	1	13	9.23	0	0	0	0	2	4	.500	0	0	0
	Totals	**6**	**376**	**3.99**	**2**	**4**	**2**	**0**	**25**	**187**	**.866**			

Captains' History

Bob Wall, 1967-68, 1968-69; Larry Cahan, 1969-70, 1970-71; Bob Pulford, 1971-72, 1972-73; Terry Harper, 1973-74, 1974-75; Mike Murphy, 1975-76 to 1980-81; Dave Lewis, 1981-82, 1982-83; Terry Ruskowski, 1983-84, 1984-85; Dave Taylor, 1985-86 to 1988-89; Wayne Gretzky, 1989-90 to 1991-92; Wayne Gretzky and Luc Robitaille, 1992-93; Wayne Gretzky, 1993-94, 1994-95; Wayne Gretzky and Rob Blake, 1995-96; Rob Blake, 1996-97 to 2000-01; Mattias Norstrom, 2001-02 to 2006-07; Rob Blake, 2007-08; Dustin Brown, 2008-09 to date.

Club Records

Team

(Figures in brackets for season records are games played; records for fewest points, wins, ties, losses, goals, goals against are for 70 or more games)

Most Points	105	1974-75 (80)
Most Wins	46	1990-91 (80), 2009-10 (82)
Most Ties	21	1974-75 (80)
Most Losses	52	1969-70 (76)
Most Goals	376	1988-89 (80)
Most Goals Against	389	1985-86 (80)
Fewest Points	38	1969-70 (76)
Fewest Wins	14	1969-70 (76)
Fewest Ties	5	1998-99 (82)
Fewest Losses	17	1974-75 (80)
Fewest Goals	168	1969-70 (76)
Fewest Goals Against	185	1974-75 (80)
Longest Winning Streak		
Overall	9	Jan. 21-Feb. 6/10
Home	12	Oct. 10-Dec. 5/92
Away	8	Dec. 18/74-Jan. 16/75
Longest Undefeated Streak		
Overall	11	Feb. 28-Mar. 24/74 (9 wins, 2 ties)
Home	13	Oct. 10-Dec. 8/92 (12 wins, 1 tie)
Away	11	Oct. 10-Dec. 11/74 (6 wins, 5 ties)
Longest Losing Streak		
Overall	11	Mar. 16-Apr. 4/04
Home	9	Feb. 8-Mar. 12/86
Away	11	Jan. 11-Feb. 15/70
Longest Winless Streak		
Overall	17	Jan. 29-Mar. 5/70 (13 losses, 4 ties)
Home	9	Jan. 29-Mar. 5/70 (8 losses, 1 tie), Feb. 8-Mar. 12/86 (9 losses)
Away	20	Jan. 11-Apr. 3/70 (16 losses, 4 ties)
Most Shutouts, Season	10	2000-01 (82)
Most PIM, Season	2,247	1992-93 (84)
Most Goals, Game	12	Nov. 29/84 (Van. 1 at L.A. 12)

Individual

Most Seasons	17	Dave Taylor
Most Games	1,111	Dave Taylor
Most Goals, Career	557	Luc Robitaille
Most Assists, Career	757	Marcel Dionne
Most Points Career	1,307	Marcel Dionne (550G, 757A)
Most PIM, Career	1,846	Marty McSorley
Most Shutouts, Career	32	Rogie Vachon
Longest Consecutive Games Streak	324	Marcel Dionne (Jan. 7/78-Jan. 9/82)
Most Goals, Season	70	Bernie Nicholls (1988-89)
Most Assists, Season	122	Wayne Gretzky (1990-91)
Most Points, Season	168	Wayne Gretzky (1988-89; 54G, 114A)
Most PIM, Season	399	Marty McSorley (1992-93)
Most Points, Defenseman, Season	76	Larry Murphy (1980-81; 16G, 60A)
Most Points, Center, Season	168	Wayne Gretzky (1988-89; 54G, 114A)
Most Points, Right Wing, Season	112	Dave Taylor (1980-81; 47G, 65A)
Most Points, Left Wing, Season	*125	Luc Robitaille (1992-93; 63G, 62A)
Most Points, Rookie, Season	84	Luc Robitaille (1986-87; 45G, 39A)
Most Shutouts, Season	8	Rogie Vachon (1976-77)
Most Goals, Game	4	Seventeen times
Most Assists, Game	6	Bernie Nicholls (Dec. 1/88), Tomas Sandstrom (Oct. 9/93)
Most Points, Game	8	Bernie Nicholls (Dec. 1/88; 2G, 6A)

* NHL Record.

Coaching History

Red Kelly, 1967-68, 1968-69; Hal Laycoe and Johnny Wilson, 1969-70; Larry Regan, 1970-71; Larry Regan and Fred Glover, 1971-72; Bob Pulford, 1972-73 to 1976-77; Ron Stewart, 1977-78; Bob Berry, 1978-79 to 1980-81; Parker MacDonald and Don Perry, 1981-82; Don Perry, 1982-83; Don Perry, Rogie Vachon and Roger Neilson, 1983-84; Pat Quinn, 1984-85, 1985-86; Pat Quinn and Mike Murphy 1986-87; Mike Murphy, Rogie Vachon and Robbie Ftorek, 1987-88; Robbie Ftorek, 1988-89; Tom Webster, 1989-90 to 1991-92; Barry Melrose, 1992-93, 1993-94; Barry Melrose and Rogie Vachon, 1994-95; Larry Robinson, 1995-96 to 1998-99; Andy Murray, 1999-2000 to 2004-05; Andy Murray and John Torchetti, 2005-06; Marc Crawford, 2006-07, 2007-08; Terry Murray, 2008-09 to date.

Retired Numbers

16	Marcel Dionne	1975-1987
18	Dave Taylor	1977-1994
20	Luc Robitaille	1986-94, 97-01, 03-06
30	Rogie Vachon	1971-1978
99	Wayne Gretzky	1988-1996

All-time Record vs. Other Clubs

Regular Season

	At Home								On Road								Total							
	GP	W	L	T	OL	GF	GA	PTS	GP	W	L	T	OL	GF	GA	PTS	GP	W	L	T	OL	GF	GA	PTS
Anaheim	48	26	14	4	4	144	123	60	48	17	21	7	3	129	163	44	96	43	35	11	7	273	286	104
Atlanta	6	4	0	0	2	32	22	10	6	3	2	0	1	18	20	7	12	7	2	0	3	50	42	17
Boston	63	22	33	7	1	220	235	52	64	14	44	6	0	181	291	34	127	36	77	13	1	401	526	86
Buffalo	56	24	23	9	0	197	192	57	55	16	30	9	0	158	232	41	111	40	53	18	0	355	424	98
Calgary	101	50	42	9	0	364	346	109	104	28	61	12	3	330	451	71	205	78	103	21	3	694	797	180
Carolina	32	18	11	3	0	135	119	39	33	12	14	5	2	121	118	31	65	30	25	8	2	256	237	70
Chicago	84	39	34	8	3	284	275	89	85	34	40	9	2	241	293	79	169	73	74	17	5	525	568	168
Colorado	53	30	17	5	1	208	174	66	52	22	26	3	1	174	209	48	105	52	43	8	2	382	383	114
Columbus	18	11	6	1	0	51	34	23	18	7	8	0	3	56	49	17	36	18	14	1	3	107	83	40
Dallas	100	45	35	19	1	328	296	110	102	28	57	13	4	270	372	73	202	73	92	32	5	598	668	183
Detroit	90	44	31	14	1	339	281	103	89	32	41	13	3	299	345	80	179	76	72	27	4	638	626	183
Edmonton	87	31	35	15	6	328	347	83	87	29	43	15	0	305	375	73	174	60	78	30	6	633	722	156
Florida	11	7	4	0	0	33	32	14	10	3	4	3	0	25	26	9	21	10	8	3	0	58	58	23
Minnesota	18	8	6	2	2	46	45	20	18	8	6	3	1	42	39	20	36	16	12	5	3	88	84	40
Montreal	67	19	39	9	0	203	265	47	66	8	47	11	0	165	296	27	133	27	86	20	0	368	561	74
Nashville	22	10	11	0	1	62	64	21	22	11	7	3	1	58	49	26	44	21	18	3	2	120	113	47
New Jersey	44	29	9	6	0	205	137	64	46	21	19	5	1	157	151	48	90	50	28	11	1	362	288	112
NY Islanders	47	23	17	7	0	168	145	53	47	18	24	5	0	132	161	41	94	41	41	12	0	300	306	94
NY Rangers	63	25	26	10	2	207	221	62	60	18	36	6	0	178	239	42	123	43	62	16	2	385	460	104
Ottawa	12	10	1	1	0	54	24	21	11	5	5	1	0	30	35	11	23	15	6	2	0	84	59	32
Philadelphia	69	22	39	8	0	200	231	52	65	16	41	7	1	158	249	40	134	38	80	15	1	358	480	92
Phoenix	92	37	39	14	2	345	337	90	94	32	48	11	3	300	364	78	186	69	87	25	5	645	701	168
Pittsburgh	71	45	17	8	1	273	189	99	75	25	40	10	0	236	273	60	146	70	57	18	1	509	462	159
St. Louis	88	41	34	12	1	300	253	95	88	22	55	10	1	221	321	55	176	63	89	22	2	521	574	150
San Jose	55	28	21	4	2	159	150	62	55	19	28	3	5	150	183	46	110	47	49	7	7	309	333	108
Tampa Bay	13	1	10	2	0	26	43	4	12	6	5	0	1	26	27	13	25	7	15	2	1	52	70	17
Toronto	67	35	22	10	0	240	196	80	70	24	34	11	1	230	270	60	137	59	56	21	1	470	466	140
Vancouver	109	56	35	16	2	420	336	130	107	35	55	16	1	325	398	87	216	91	90	32	3	745	734	217
Washington	50	29	14	6	1	196	150	65	48	22	18	7	1	179	193	52	98	51	32	13	2	375	343	117
Defunct Clubs	35	27	6	2	0	141	76	56	34	11	14	9	0	91	109	31	69	38	20	11	0	232	185	87
Totals	**1671**	**796**	**631**	**211**	**33**	**5908**	**5338**	**1836**	**1671**	**546**	**873**	**213**	**39**	**4985**	**6301**	**1344**	**3342**	**1342**	**1504**	**424**	**72**	**10893**	**11639**	**3180**

Playoffs

	Series	W	L	GP	W	L	T	GF	GA	Last Mtg.	Rnd.	Result
Boston	2	0	2	13	5	8	0	38	56	1977	QF	L 2-4
Calgary	6	4	2	26	13	13	0	105	112	1993	DSF	W 4-2
Chicago	1	0	1	5	1	4	0	7	10	1974	QF	L 1-4
Colorado	2	0	2	14	6	8	0	23	33	2002	CQF	L 3-4
Dallas	1	0	1	7	3	4	0	21	26	1968	QF	L 3-4
Detroit	2	1	1	10	4	6	0	21	32	2001	CQF	W 4-2
Edmonton	7	2	5	36	12	24	0	127	154	1992	DSF	L 2-4
Montreal	1	0	1	5	1	4	0	12	15	1993	F	L 1-4
NY Islanders	1	0	1	4	1	3	0	10	21	1980	PRE	L 1-3
NY Rangers	2	0	2	6	1	5	0	14	32	1981	PRE	L 1-3
St. Louis	2	0	2	8	0	8	0	13	32	1998	CQF	L 0-4
Toronto	3	1	2	12	5	7	0	31	41	1993	CF	W 4-3
Vancouver	4	2	2	23	11	12	0	84	85	2010	CQF	L 2-4
Defunct Clubs	1	1	0	7	4	3	0	23	25			
Totals	**35**	**11**	**24**	**176**	**67**	**109**	**0**	**529**	**674**			

Calgary totals include Atlanta Flames, 1972-73 to 1979-80.
Colorado totals include Quebec, 1979-80 to 1994-95.
New Jersey totals include Kansas City, 1974-75, 1975-76, and Colorado Rockies, 1976-77 to 1981-82.
Phoenix totals include Winnipeg, 1979-80 to 1995-96.
Carolina totals include Hartford, 1979-80 to 1996-97.
Dallas totals include Minnesota North Stars, 1967-68 to 1992-93.

Playoff Results 2010-2006

Year	Round	Opponent	Result	GF	GA
2010	CQF	Vancouver	L 2-4	18	25

Abbreviations: Round: F - Final; **CF** - conference final; **CQF** - conference quarter-final; **DF** - division final; **DSF** - division semi-final; **QF** - quarter-final; **PRE** - preliminary round.

2009-10 Results

Oct.	3	Phoenix	3-6	Jan.	2	Washington	2-1
	6	San Jose	6-4		4	at San Jose	6-2
	8	Minnesota	6-3		7	Detroit	1-2
	10	at St. Louis	2-1		9	St. Louis	3-4
	12	at NY Islanders	2-1		11	San Jose	1-2
	14	at NY Rangers	2-4		14	Anaheim	4-0
	15	at Detroit	2-5		16	Boston	4-3†
	17	at Columbus	1-4		19	San Jose	1-5
	19	at Dallas	4-1		21	Buffalo	4-3†
	22	Dallas	5-4*		23	at Detroit	3-2
	24	at Phoenix	5-3		26	at Toronto	5-3
	25	Columbus	6-2		28	at Columbus	4-1
	28	at San Jose	1-2†		30	at Boston	3-2†
	29	Vancouver	1-2†		31	at New Jersey	3-2
Nov.	2	at Phoenix	5-3	Feb.	2	NY Rangers	2-1
	5	Pittsburgh	5-2		4	Anaheim	6-4
	7	Nashville	1-3		6	Detroit	4-3
	9	at Chicago	1-4		8	at Anaheim	2-4
	11	at Carolina	5-2		11	Edmonton	2-3†
	13	at Atlanta	0-7		13	Colorado	3-0
	14	at Tampa Bay	2-1†	Mar.	2	at Dallas	5-1
	16	at Florida	4-3†		4	at Nashville	2-4
	18	Philadelphia	2-3		6	Montreal	2-4
	21	Calgary	2-5		8	Columbus	6-0
	25	at Edmonton	3-1		10	at Chicago	2-3*
	26	at Vancouver	1-4		12	at Dallas	2-1†
	28	Chicago	2-1†		14	Nashville	2-3
Dec.	1	at Anaheim	4-3		18	Chicago	0-3
	3	Ottawa	6-3		20	NY Islanders	1-0
	5	St. Louis	4-5†		22	Colorado	4-3*
	7	Calgary	2-1		24	at Colorado	3-4†
	9	at San Jose	5-4*		25	at St. Louis	1-3
	10	Phoenix	3-2†		27	Dallas	1-4
	12	Dallas	3-2†		29	at Minnesota	2-3
	14	at Vancouver	1-3		30	at Nashville	2-0
	15	at Edmonton	3-2	Apr.	1	Vancouver	8-3
	17	at Calgary	1-2		3	Anaheim	1-2†
	26	at Phoenix	2-3		6	at Anaheim	5-4†
	28	Minnesota	3-4		8	Phoenix	2-3†
	30	at Calgary	1-2		10	Edmonton	3-4†
	31	at Minnesota	5-2		11	at Colorado	2-1*

* – Overtime † – Shootout

Entry Draft Selections 2010-1996

Name in bold denotes played in NHL.

2010
Pick
15	Derek Forbort
47	Tyler Toffoli
70	Jordan Weal
148	Kevin Gravel
158	Maxim Kitsyn

2009
Pick
5	**Brayden Schenn**
35	Kyle Clifford
84	Nicolas Deslauriers
95	Jean-Francois Berube
96	Linden Vey
126	David Kolomatis
156	Michael Pelech
179	Brandon Kozun
186	Jordan Nolan
198	Nic Dowd

2008
Pick
2	**Drew Doughty**
13	Colten Teubert
32	Viatcheslav Voynov
63	Robert Czarnik
74	Andrew Campbell
88	Geordie Wudrick
123	**Andrei Loktionov**
153	Justin Azevedo
183	Garrett Roe

2007
Pick
4	Thomas Hickey
52	**Oscar Moller**
61	**Wayne Simmonds**
82	Bryan Cameron
95	**Alec Martinez**
109	Dwight King
124	Linden Rowat
137	Joshua Turnbull
184	Josh Kidd
188	Matt Fillier

2006
Pick
11	**Jonathan Bernier**
17	**Trevor Lewis**
48	Joe Ryan
74	Jeff Zatkoff
86	Bud Holloway
114	Niclas Andersen
134	David Meckler
144	Martin Nolet
164	Constantin Braun

2005
Pick
11	**Anze Kopitar**
50	Dany Roussin
60	T.J. Fast
72	**Jonathan Quick**
139	Patrik Hersley
184	Ryan McGinnis
206	Josh Meyers
226	John Seymour

2004
Pick
11	**Lauri Tukonen**
95	Paul Baier
110	Ned Lukacevic
143	Eric Neilson
174	**Scott Parse**
205	Mike Curry
221	**Daniel Taylor**
238	Yutaka Fukufuji
264	Valtteri Tenkanen

2003
Pick
13	**Dustin Brown**
26	**Brian Boyle**
27	**Jeff Tambellini**
44	Konstantin Pushkarev
82	Ryan Munce
152	**Brady Murray**
174	**Esa Pirnes**
231	Matt Zaba
244	Mike Sullivan
274	Marty Guerin

2002
Pick
18	**Denis Grebeshkov**
50	Sergei Anshakov
66	**Petr Kanko**
104	**Aaron Rome**
115	Mark Rooneem
152	Greg Hogeboom
157	Joel Andresen
185	Ryan Murphy
215	Mikhail Lyubushin
248	Tuukka Pulliainen
279	**Connor James**

2001
Pick
18	Jens Karlsson
30	**David Steckel**
49	**Michael Cammalleri**
51	**Jaroslav Bednar**
83	Henrik Juntunen
116	**Richard Petiot**
152	Terry Denike
153	Tuukka Mantyla
214	**Cristobal Huet**
237	Mike Gabinet
277	Sebastien Laplante

2000
Pick
20	**Alexander Frolov**
54	**Andreas Lilja**
86	**Yanick Lehoux**
118	**Lubomir Visnovsky**
165	Nathan Marsters
201	Yevgeny Fedorov
206	Tim Eriksson
218	Craig Olynick
245	Dan Welch
250	Flavien Conne
282	Carl Grahn

1999
Pick
43	Andrei Shefer
74	Jason Crain
76	**Frantisek Kaberle**
92	Cory Campbell
104	**Brian McGrattan**
125	Daniel Johansson
133	Jean-Francois Nogues
193	Kevin Baker
222	**George Parros**
250	**Noah Clarke**

1998
Pick
21	**Mathieu Biron**
46	**Justin Papineau**
76	Alexei Volkov
103	**Kip Brennan**
133	Joe Rullier
163	**Tomas Zizka**
190	Tommi Hannus
217	Jim Henkel
248	**Matthew Yeats**

1997
Pick
3	**Olli Jokinen**
15	Matt Zultek
29	**Scott Barney**
83	**Joe Corvo**
99	Sean Blanchard
137	Richard Seeley
150	Jeff Katcher
193	Jay Kopischke
220	Konrad Brand

1996
Pick
30	**Josh Green**
37	**Marian Cisar**
57	Greg Phillips
84	Mikael Simons
96	**Eric Belanger**
120	Jesse Black
123	Peter Hogan
190	**Steve Valiquette**
193	**Kai Nurminen**
219	Sebastien Simard

General Managers' History

Larry Regan, 1967-68 to 1972-73; Larry Regan and Jake Milford, 1973-74; Jake Milford, 1974-75 to 1976-77; George Maguire, 1977-78 to 1982-83; George Maguire and Rogie Vachon, 1983-84; Rogie Vachon, 1984-85 to 1991-92; Nick Beverley, 1992-93, 1993-94; Sam McMaster, 1994-95 to 1996-97; Dave Taylor, 1997-98 to 2005-06; Dean Lombardi, 2006-07 to date.

Dean Lombardi
President and General Manager
Born: Holyoke, MA, March 5, 1958.

The Kings entered into a new executive era when the club hired Dean Lombardi as Kings President/General Manager on April 21, 2006. A veteran of 20 NHL seasons in the front office as an executive and a pro scout, Lombardi has a well-earned reputation for being one of hockey's true visionaries while possessing a solid track record of success, building from within, and of development on the ice and infrastructure off the ice. This past season he helped guide the Kings to their first playoff berth since 2001-02.

Lombardi was formerly a member of the San Jose Sharks front office for 13 years, including seven seasons as general manager, followed by three years as a pro scout for the Philadelphia Flyers from 2003 to 2006. As an executive in the San Jose front office beginning in 1990, Lombardi first served as assistant general manager (a post he held the previous two seasons with the Minnesota North Stars) for the expansion Sharks before being elevated to vice president, director of hockey operations in 1992. Four years later, he was promoted to executive vice president and general manager. During his tenure as general manager in San Jose from 1996 to 2003, Lombardi helped build the Sharks into one of the premier teams in the NHL.

Prior to joining the North Stars, Lombardi spent three seasons as a player representative, including the representation of five members of the 1988 United States Olympic team, and at the time he joined Minnesota's front office Lombardi was only the second former player agent to be employed in an NHL front office (Brian Burke/Vancouver Canucks was the other).

Born in Holyoke, Massachusetts, and raised in nearby Ludlow, Lombardi received his undergraduate degree from the University of New Haven where he finished third in his class. On the ice he was the hockey team's captain his final two seasons, and he received a full athletic scholarship and the school's student-athlete of the year award. In 1985, Lombardi earned his Law degree (with honors) from Tulane Law School where he specialized in Labor Law.

Club Directory

Los Angeles Kings
STAPLES Center
1111 South Figueroa Street
Los Angeles, CA 90015
Phone **213/742-7100**
GM FAX 310/535-4525
www.lakings.com
Capacity: 18,118

STAPLES Center

Ownership
Owner	Philip F. Anschutz
Owner	Edward P. Roski, Jr.
Governor	Timothy J. Leiweke
Chief Operating Officer/Chief Financial Officer	Dan Beckerman
Executive Administrative Assistant to the Governor	Carla Garcia
Executive Assistant to COO/CFO	Karen Zamora

Kings Executive
President/General Manager, Alternate Governor	Dean Lombardi
President, Business Operations, Alt. Governor	Luc Robitaille
Sr. V.P., Business Ops/Chief Marketing Officer	Chris McGowan
Executive Assistant to President/General Manager	Tiffany Grommon
Executive Assistant to President, Business Ops	Kehly Sloane
Executive Assistant to Senior Vice President, Business Operations/Chief Marketing Officer	Alicia Briones
Office Assistant	Jeff Monahan

Hockey Operations
Vice President/Assistant General Manager	Ron Hextall
Special Assistant to the General Manager	Jack Ferreira
Vice President/Hockey Ops and Legal Affairs	Jeff Solomon
Director of Team Operations	Marshall Dickerson

Coaches
Head Coach	Terry Murray
Assistant Coaches	John Stevens, Jamie Kompon
Goaltending Coach	Bill Ranford
Video Coordinator	Ryan Colville

Player Development
Player Development	Nelson Emerson
Pro Development and Special Assignments	Mike O'Connell
Goaltender Development	Kim Dillabaugh

Training Staff – Medical
Head Athletic Trainer	Chris Kingsley
Strength and Conditioning Coach	Tim Adams
Assistant Athletic Trainer	Myles Hirayama
Massage Therapist	TBD

Training Staff – Equipment
Head Equipment Manager	Darren Granger
Assistant Equipment Managers	Jason McMaster / Dana Bryson

Medical
Team Physician / Internist	Dr. Ronald Kvitne / Dr. Michael Mellman
Team Dentist / Opthalmologist	Dr. Jeffrey Hoy / Dr. Howard Lazerson

Scouts/Hockey Operations
Scouting Operations Coordinator	Lee Callans
Senior Pro Scout / Pro Scouts	Rob Laird / Steve Greeley, Alyn McCauley
Co-Directors of Amateur Scouting	Mark Yannetti, Michael Futa
Amateur Scouts	Brent McEwen, Tony Gasparini, Denis Fugere, Todd Woodcroft, Bob Crocker
Collegiate Scouts	Mike Donnelly, Mark Mullen
Video Technicians	Bob Friedlander, Bill Gurney

Broadcasters
TV Station / Play-by-Play / Analyst	FS West / Bob Miller / Jim Fox
Radio Falgship / Play-by-Play / Analyst	KTLK AM 1150 / Nick Nickson / Daryl Evans

Communications and Content
Vice President, Communications and Content	Michael Altieri
Senior Director, Communications	Jeff Moeller
Manager, Communications	Mike Kalinowski
Supervisor, Communications and Broadcasting	Jeremy Zager
Manager, Content/Host	Heidi Androl
Manager, Production	Aaron Brenner
Editor – Kings Vision	Paul Campbell
Beat Writer/Columnist – LAKings.com	Rich Hammond

Game Presentation
Director, Game Presentation and Events	Jon Adams

Group Sales
Vice President, Group Sales	Matt Rosenfeld
Fan Development and Community Relations	
Director, Fan Development/Community Relations	James Cefaly

Finance
Vice President, Finance	Peter Mazur

Humans Resources
Manager, Human Resources	LaShawnda Mikhael

Marketing
Vice President, Marketing	Jonathan Lowe

Sponsorship Sales and Service
Senior Vice President, Corporate Partnerships	Bill Pedigo
Senior Vice President, Partnership Activation	Tracy Hartman
Vice President, Partnership Activation	Kelly Staley
Director, Corporate Partnerships	Josh Veilleux

Ticket Sales and Service
Vice President, Ticket Sales and Service	Kelly Cheeseman
Director, Ticket Sales and Service	Josh Bender
Director, Ticket Operations	Elizabeth Tockstein

Minnesota Wild

2009-10 Results: 38w-36L-1OTL-7SOL 84PTS.
Fourth, Northwest Division

Year-by-Year Record

Season	GP	Home W	L	T	OL	Road W	L	T	OL	Overall W	L	T	OL	GF	GA	Pts.	Finished	Playoff Result
2009-10	82	25	12	....	4	13	24	....	4	38	36	....	8	219	246	84	4th, Northwest Div.	Out of Playoffs
2008-09	82	23	11	....	7	17	22	....	2	40	33	....	9	219	200	89	3rd, Northwest Div.	Out of Playoffs
2007-08	82	25	11	....	5	19	17	....	5	44	28	....	10	223	218	98	1st, Northwest Div.	Lost Conf. Quarter-Final
2006-07	82	29	7	....	5	19	19	....	3	48	26	....	8	235	191	104	2nd, Northwest Div.	Lost Conf. Quarter-Final
2005-06	82	23	16	....	2	15	20	....	6	38	36	....	8	231	215	84	5th, Northwest Div.	Out of Playoffs
2004-05	...	...	...	...	...	...	...	...	...	...	...	...	...	...	...	...	...	...
2003-04	82	19	13	7	2	11	16	13	1	30	29	20	3	188	183	83	5th, Northwest Div.	Out of Playoffs
2002-03	82	25	13	3	0	17	16	7	1	42	29	10	1	198	178	95	3rd, Northwest Div.	Lost Conf. Championship
2001-02	82	14	14	8	5	12	21	4	4	26	35	12	9	195	238	73	5th, Northwest Div.	Out of Playoffs
2000-01	82	14	13	10	4	11	26	3	1	25	39	13	5	168	210	68	5th, Northwest Div.	Out of Playoffs

2010-11 Schedule

Oct.						
Thu.	7	Carolina†	Sun.	9	Dallas*
Fri.	8	at Carolina†	Tue.	11	at Nashville
Thu.	14	Edmonton	Fri.	14	Colorado
Sat.	16	Columbus	Sun.	16	Vancouver*
Tue.	19	Vancouver	Tue.	18	at Edmonton
Thu.	21	at Edmonton	Wed.	19	at Calgary
Fri.	22	at Vancouver	Sat.	22	at San Jose
Mon.	25	Los Angeles	Tue.	25	at Chicago
Thu.	28	Washington	**Feb.** Tue.	1	Los Angeles
Sat.	30	Chicago	Thu.	3	at Colorado
Nov. Tue.	2	San Jose	Sat.	5	at Phoenix
Fri.	5	Calgary	Wed.	9	Colorado
Sat.	6	at Columbus	Fri.	11	at St. Louis
Thu.	11	at Atlanta	Sat.	12	St. Louis
Fri.	12	at Florida	Tue.	15	Vancouver
Sun.	14	at Tampa Bay	Wed.	16	at Chicago
Wed.	17	Anaheim	Fri.	18	Anaheim
Fri.	19	at Detroit	Sun.	20	Detroit*
Sat.	20	NY Rangers	Tue.	22	Edmonton
Wed.	24	Philadelphia	Thu.	24	at Los Angeles
Fri.	26	Nashville*	Fri.	25	at Anaheim
Sat.	27	at Colorado	Mon.	28	Chicago
Mon.	29	at Calgary	**Mar.** Wed.	2	at NY Islanders
Dec. Wed.	1	Phoenix	Thu.	3	at NY Rangers
Fri.	3	Calgary	Sun.	6	Buffalo*
Sat.	4	at Dallas	Tue.	8	Colorado
Thu.	9	at Phoenix	Thu.	10	at Nashville
Sat.	11	at Los Angeles	Fri.	11	at Dallas
Sun.	12	at Anaheim*	Mon.	14	at Vancouver
Thu.	16	Ottawa	Thu.	17	at San Jose
Sat.	18	at Calgary	Sat.	19	Columbus*
Mon.	20	Calgary	Sun.	20	Montreal*
Thu.	23	at Colorado	Tue.	22	Toronto
Sun.	26	Detroit	Sat.	26	St. Louis
Mon.	27	at Columbus	Tue.	29	at St. Louis
Wed.	29	San Jose	Thu.	31	Edmonton
Fri.	31	Nashville*	**Apr.** Sat.	2	Tampa Bay*
Jan. Sun.	2	Phoenix*	Sun.	3	at Detroit*
Tue.	4	at New Jersey	Thu.	7	at Vancouver
Thu.	6	at Boston	Fri.	8	at Edmonton
Sat.	8	at Pittsburgh	Sun.	10	Dallas*

* Denotes afternoon game.   † Games played in Helsinki, Fl.

Marek Zidlicky led the Wild in time on ice with an average of 24:10 per game in 2009-10, the highest total of his career. His 37 assists led all blueliners and marked the fifth time in six years he's had 30 or more.

NORTHWEST DIVISION
11th NHL Season

Franchise date: June 25, 1997

2010-11 Player Personnel

FORWARDS	HT	WT	S	Place of Birth	*Age	2009-10 Club
ALMOND, Cody	6-2	215	L	Calgary, Alta.	21	Minnesota-Houston
BOUCHARD, Pierre-Marc	5-10	173	L	Sherbrooke, Que.	26	Minnesota
BRODZIAK, Kyle	6-2	209	R	St. Paul, Alta.	26	Minnesota
BRUNETTE, Andrew	6-1	210	L	Sudbury, Ont.	37	Minnesota
CLUTTERBUCK, Cal	5-11	213	R	Welland, Ont.	22	Minnesota
CULLEN, Matt	6-1	200	L	Virginia, MN	33	Carolina-Ottawa
DiSALVATORE, Jon	6-1	200	R	Bangor, ME	29	Houston
EARL, Robbie	5-11	197	L	Chicago, IL	25	Minnesota-Houston
HAVLAT, Martin	6-2	217	L	Mlada Boleslav, Czech.	29	Minnesota
KALUS, Petr	6-1	197	L	Ostrava, Czech.	23	Minnesota-Houston
KASSIAN, Matt	6-5	245	L	Edmonton, Alta.	23	Houston
KOBASEW, Chuck	6-0	192	R	Vancouver, B.C.	28	Boston-Minnesota
KOIVU, Mikko	6-2	214	L	Turku, Finland	27	Minnesota
LATENDRESSE, Guillaume	6-2	230	L	Ste-Catherine, Que.	23	Montreal-Minnesota
MADDEN, John	5-11	190	L	Barrie, Ont.	37	Chicago
MIETTINEN, Antti	6-0	190	R	Hameenlinna, Finland	30	Minnesota
NYSTROM, Eric	6-1	193	L	Syosset, NY	27	Calgary
PALMER, Jarod	6-0	200	R	Fridley, MN	24	Miami U.
PETERS, Warren	6-0	195	L	Saskatoon, Sask.	28	Dallas-Texas
RAU, Chad	5-11	188	L	Eden Prairie, MN	23	Houston
SHEPPARD, James	6-2	210	L	Halifax, N.S.	22	Minnesota
STAUBITZ, Brad	6-1	210	R	Bright's Grove, Ont.	26	San Jose
WELLMAN, Casey	6-0	184	R	Brentwood, CA	22	Minnesota-Massachusetts

DEFENSEMEN						
BARKER, Cam	6-3	215	L	Winnipeg, Man.	24	Chicago-Minnesota
BURNS, Brent	6-5	219	R	Ajax, Ont.	25	Minnesota
FALK, Justin	6-5	217	L	Snowflake, Man.	21	Minnesota-Houston
FRASER, Jamie	6-0	198	L	Sarnia, Ont.	24	Houston
NOREAU, Maxim	5-11	192	R	Montreal, Que.	23	Minnesota-Houston
PROSSER, Nate	6-2	215	R	Elk River, MN	24	Minnesota-Colorado College
SCHULTZ, Nick	6-1	200	L	Strasbourg, Sask.	28	Minnesota
STONER, Clayton	6-3	225	L	Port McNeill, B.C.	25	Minnesota-Houston
ZANON, Greg	5-11	201	L	Burnaby, B.C.	30	Minnesota
ZIDLICKY, Marek	5-11	190	R	Most, Czech.	33	Minnesota

GOALTENDERS	HT	WT	C	Place of Birth	*Age	2009-10 Club
BACKSTROM, Niklas	6-1	189	L	Helsinki, Finland	32	Minnesota
HARDING, Josh	6-1	197	R	Regina, Sask.	26	Minnesota
KHUDOBIN, Anton	5-11	203	L	Ust-Kamenogorsk, USSR	24	Minnesota-Houston

* – Age at start of 2010-11 season

Todd Richards
Head Coach
Born: Robbinsdale, MN, October 20, 1966.

Minnesota Wild general manager Chuck Fletcher named Todd Richards as the second head coach in club history on June 16, 2009. Richards, who spent the 2008-09 season as an assistant coach with the San Jose Sharks, played collegiately at the University of Minnesota. Prior to the 2009-10 season, he had made the playoffs in all 13 of his professional seasons as a player, and in all seven as a head coach or assistant coach. Richards helped the Sharks to an NHL-best 53-18-11 record and the Presidents' Trophy in 2008-09. He was responsible for the power-play, which ranked third in the NHL at 24.2 percent.

Richards spent two seasons (2006 to 2008) as head coach of the Wilkes-Barre/Scranton Penguins in the American Hockey League, where he led the team to a berth in the Calder Cup Finals in 2008. (Chuck Fletcher was the Baby Pens general manager during that time.) Before joining Wilkes-Barre/Scranton, Richards served as an assistant coach (2002 to 2006) with the Milwaukee Admirals. During his time in Milwaukee, the Admirals won two West Division titles (2003-04 and 2005-06) and made two trips to the Calder Cup Finals, winning the AHL title in 2003-04. A former defenseman, Richards captured several championships throughout his career, including a pair of Western Collegiate Hockey Association titles with the University of Minnesota (1988 and 1989), the 1991 Calder Cup with Springfield, the 2001 Turner Cup (International Hockey League) in Orlando and a Swiss-B League title with Servette Geneve in 2002.

Richards was drafted by the Montreal Canadiens in the second round (33rd overall) of the 1985 NHL Entry Draft and made his NHL debut with the Hartford Whalers in 1990-91. He played eight games over the next two seasons and posted four assists. He also appeared in 11 Stanley Cup playoff games with Hartford, totaling three assists. During his four seasons at the University of Minnesota, Richards was named a member of the WCHA Second All-Star Team for three consecutive seasons (1987 to 1989) and was team captain during his senior season. The Gophers lost to Harvard 4-3 in overtime in the NCAA championship game in 1989.

Following his stints in the Montreal and Hartford organizations, Richards joined the IHL's Las Vegas Thunder and was named the league's top defenseman in 1994-95. He spent the next six seasons with the Orlando Solar Bears, captaining the squad for four seasons and winning the IHL Championship in 2000-01, the league's final year of existence. Richards concluded his playing career with Servette Geneve of Switzerland in 2001-02, where he was he was also named the league's top defenseman.

Coaching Record

			Regular Season				Playoffs			
Season	Team	League	GC	W	L	O/T	GC	W	L	T
2006-07	Wilkes-Barre	AHL	80	51	23	6	11	5	6	....
2007-08	Wilkes-Barre	AHL	80	47	26	6	23	14	9	....
2009-10	Minnesota	NHL	82	38	36	8	....	....	....	....
	NHL Totals		82	38	36	8	....	....	....	....

2009-10 Scoring
*– rookie

Regular Season

Pos	#	Player	Team	GP	G	A	Pts	TOI	+/–	PIM	PP	SH	GW	S	%
C	9	Mikko Koivu	MIN	80	22	49	71	20:44	-2	50	8	1	2	246	8.9
L	15	Andrew Brunette	MIN	82	25	36	61	17:01	-5	12	12	0	3	129	19.4
R	14	Martin Havlat	MIN	73	18	36	54	17:55	-19	34	4	0	3	169	10.7
D	3	Marek Zidlicky	MIN	78	6	37	43	24:10	-16	67	4	0	3	116	5.2
R	20	Antti Miettinen	MIN	79	20	22	42	18:02	-2	44	5	0	4	175	11.4
L	48	Guillaume Latendresse	MTL	23	2	1	3	11:21	-4	4	0	0	0	27	7.4
			MIN	55	25	12	37	16:27	1	12	7	0	4	133	18.8
			Total	78	27	13	40	14:57	-3	16	7	0	4	160	16.9
R	11	Owen Nolan	MIN	73	16	17	33	16:35	-12	40	4	1	3	151	10.6
C	21	Kyle Brodziak	MIN	82	9	23	32	15:19	-3	22	0	0	3	140	6.4
R	22	Cal Clutterbuck	MIN	74	13	8	21	14:16	-8	52	1	2	1	136	9.6
D	45	Cam Barker	CHI	51	4	10	14	13:05	7	58	3	0	1	74	5.4
			MIN	19	1	6	7	22:01	-2	10	1	0	0	31	3.2
			Total	70	5	16	21	15:31	5	68	4	0	1	105	4.8
D	8	Brent Burns	MIN	47	3	17	20	22:22	-15	32	2	0	0	104	2.9
D	55	Nick Schultz	MIN	80	1	19	20	20:58	-8	43	1	0	0	83	1.2
R	12	Chuck Kobasew	BOS	7	0	1	1	14:22	-2	0	0	0	0	13	0.0
			MIN	42	9	5	14	13:50	-9	16	2	0	2	58	15.5
			Total	49	9	6	15	13:54	-11	18	2	0	2	71	12.7
C	16	Andrew Ebbett	ANA	2	0	0	0	12:54	-1	0	0	0	0	1	0.0
			CHI	10	1	0	1	10:43	1	2	0	0	0	14	7.1
			MIN	49	8	6	14	13:05	-8	6	2	0	2	57	14.0
			Total	61	9	6	15	12:41	-8	8	2	0	2	72	12.5
D	6	Greg Zanon	MIN	81	2	13	15	22:22	-10	36	0	0	0	59	3.4
D	34	Shane Hnidy	MIN	70	2	12	14	13:32	-6	66	0	0	0	49	4.1
L	38 *	Robbie Earl	MIN	32	6	0	6	8:56	1	6	0	0	2	29	20.7
C	51	James Sheppard	MIN	64	2	4	6	11:59	-14	38	0	0	0	64	3.1
C	17 *	Casey Wellman	MIN	12	1	3	4	12:03	-2	0	0	0	0	18	5.6
L	24	Derek Boogaard	MIN	57	0	4	4	6:09	-12	105	0	0	0	26	0.0
R	17	Petr Sykora	MIN	14	2	1	3	11:59	-7	8	0	0	0	13	15.4
D	36	John Scott	MIN	51	1	1	2	8:36	-3	90	0	0	0	22	4.5
D	7 *	Clayton Stoner	MIN	10	0	2	2	13:18	1	12	0	0	0	5	0.0
C	23 *	Cody Almond	MIN	7	1	0	1	7:45	-3	9	0	0	0	6	16.7
D	39 *	Nate Prosser	MIN	3	0	1	1	19:36	2	0	0	0	0	4	0.0
C	96	Pierre-Marc Bouchard	MIN	1	0	0	0	10:44	0	2	0	0	0	0	0.0
D	4 *	Maxim Noreau	MIN	1	0	0	0	7:01	0	0	0	0	0	0	0.0
C	40 *	Danny Irmen	MIN	2	0	0	0	4:38	-1	0	0	0	0	0	0.0
R	29 *	Petr Kalus	MIN	2	0	0	0	7:44	0	0	0	0	0	0	0.0
D	41 *	Justin Falk	MIN	3	0	0	0	7:32	-2	0	0	0	0	1	0.0
C	19	Andy Hilbert	MIN	4	0	0	0	9:43	-2	0	0	0	0	6	0.0
C	27	Nathan Smith	MIN	9	0	0	0	7:50	-4	12	0	0	0	4	0.0
D	26	Jaime Sifers	MIN	14	0	0	0	12:59	1	6	0	0	0	0	0.0

Goaltending

No.	Goaltender	GPI	Mins	Avg	W	L	OT	EN	SO	GA	SA	S%	G	A	PIM
35	* Anton Khudobin	2	69	0.87	2	0	0	0	1		48	.979	0	0	0
32	Niklas Backstrom	60	3489	2.72	26	23	8	6	2	158	1632	.903	0	1	4
31	Wade Dubielewicz	3	101	2.97	1	1	0	0	0	5	34	.853	0	0	0
37	Josh Harding	25	1300	3.05	9	12	0	3	1	66	692	.905	0	1	4
	Totals	82	4995	2.87	38	36	8	9	3	239	2415	.901			

Mikko Koivu became the club's first permanent captain in 2009-10. He responded with a career year.

Club Records

Team

(Figures in brackets for season records are games played.)

Most Points	104	2006-07 (82)
Most Wins	48	2006-07 (82)
Most Ties	20	2003-04 (82)
Most Losses	39	2000-01 (82)
Most Goals	235	2006-07 (82)
Most Goals Against	246	2009-10 (82)
Fewest Points	68	2000-01 (82)
Fewest Wins	25	2000-01 (82)
Fewest Ties	10	2002-03 (82)
Fewest Losses	26	2006-07 (82)
Fewest Goals	168	2000-01 (82)
Fewest Goals Against	178	2002-03 (82)

Longest Winning Streak

Overall	9	Mar. 8-24/07
Home	8	Oct. 5-Nov. 2/06, Dec. 5/06-Jan. 2/07
Away	5	Mar. 8-17/07

Longest Undefeated Streak

Overall	9	Dec. 13-30/03 (4 wins, 5 ties) Mar. 8-24/07 (9 wins)
Home	9	Dec. 13/00-Jan. 10/01 (5 wins, 4 ties)
Away	7	Dec. 6-30/03 (2 wins, 5 ties)

Longest Losing Streak

Overall	6	Dec. 5-17/08
Home	4	Oct. 29-Nov. 15/00
Away	11	Nov. 20/06-Jan. 9/07

Longest Winless Streak

Overall	12	Mar. 11-Apr. 4/01 (9 losses, 3 ties)
Home	8	Feb. 26-Mar. 28/01 (5 losses, 3 ties)
Away	12	Dec. 18/03-Jan. 31/04 (5 losses, 7 ties)

Most Shutouts, Season	8	2006-07 (82), 2008-09 (82)
Most PIM, Season	1,209	2001-02 (82), 2005-06 (82)
Most Goals, Game	8	Mar. 25/04 (Min. 8 at Chi. 2) Apr. 10/09 (Nsh. 2 at Min. 8)

Individual

Most Seasons	8	Marian Gaborik, Nick Schultz
Most Games	607	Nick Schultz
Most Goals, Career	219	Marian Gaborik
Most Assists, Career	218	Marian Gaborik
Most Points, Career	437	Marian Gaborik (219G, 218A)
Most PIM, Career	698	Matt Johnson
Most Shutouts, Career	19	Niklas Backstrom
Longest Consecutive Games Streak	288	Antti Laaksonen (Oct. 6/00-Dec. 29/03)
Most Goals, Season	42	Marian Gaborik (2007-08)
Most Assists, Season	50	Pierre-Marc Bouchard (2007-08)
Most Points, Season	83	Marian Gaborik (2007-08; 42G, 41A)
Most PIM, Season	201	Matt Johnson (2002-03)

Most Points, Defenseman, Season	43	Brent Burns (2007-08; 15G, 28A) Marek Zidlicky (2009-10; 6G, 37A)
Most Points, Center, Season	71	Mikko Koivu (2009-10; 22G, 49A)
Most Points, Right Wing, Season	83	Marian Gaborik (2007-08; 42G, 41A)
Most Points, Left Wing, Season	79	Brian Rolston (2005-06; 34G, 45A)
Most Points, Rookie, Season	36	Marian Gaborik (2000-01; 18G, 18A)
Most Shutouts, Season	8	Nicklas Backstrom (2008-09)
Most Goals, Game	5	Marian Gaborik (Dec. 20/07)
Most Assists, Game	4	Andrew Brunette (Mar. 10/02) Marian Gaborik (Oct. 26/02) Pascal Dupuis (Mar. 25/04) Eric Belanger (Nov. 15/07) Mikko Koivu (Oct. 16/08)
Most Points, Game	6	Marian Gaborik (Oct. 26/02; 2G, 4A), (Dec. 20/07; 5G, 1A)

Captains' History

Sean O'Donnell, Scott Pellerin, Wes Walz, Brad Bombardir, Darby Hendrickson, 2000-01; Jim Dowd, Filip Kuba, Brad Brown, Andrew Brunette, 2001-02; Brad Bombardir, Matt Johnson, Sergei Zholtok, 2002-03; Brad Brown, Andrew Brunette, Richard Park, Brad Bombardir, Jim Dowd, 2003-04; Alex Henry, Filip Kuba, Willie Mitchell, Brian Rolston, Wes Walz, 2005-06; Brian Rolston, Keith Carney, Mark Parrish, 2006-07; Pavol Demitra, Brian Rolston, Mark Parrish, Nick Schultz, Marian Gaborik, 2007-08; Mikko Koivu, Kim Johnsson, Andrew Brunette, 2008-09; Mikko Koivu, 2009-10 to date.

General Managers' History

Doug Risebrough, 2000-01 to 2008-09; Chuck Fletcher, 2009-10 to date.

Coaching History

Jacques Lemaire, 2000-01 to 2008-09; Todd Richards, 2009-10 to date.

All-time Record vs. Other Clubs

Regular Season

	At Home								On Road								Total							
	GP	W	L	T	OL	GF	GA	PTS	GP	W	L	T	OL	GF	GA	PTS	GP	W	L	T	OL	GF	GA	PTS
Anaheim	18	11	4	2	1	47	36	25	18	7	10	0	1	42	46	15	36	18	14	2	2	89	82	40
Atlanta	5	3	1	1	0	15	9	7	4	3	0	0	1	16	11	7	9	6	1	1	1	31	20	14
Boston	5	3	1	0	1	14	10	7	5	5	0	0	0	16	5	10	10	8	1	0	1	30	15	17
Buffalo	5	1	3	0	1	9	14	3	5	4	0	0	0	16	10	8	10	5	4	0	1	25	24	11
Calgary	29	14	9	1	5	71	61	34	28	6	18	3	1	55	73	16	57	20	27	4	6	126	134	50
Carolina	7	4	1	2	0	20	20	10	4	0	3	0	1	6	11	1	11	4	4	2	1	26	31	11
Chicago	18	13	5	0	0	55	46	26	18	10	7	1	0	50	40	21	36	23	12	1	0	105	86	47
Colorado	28	15	9	1	3	77	81	34	29	10	15	2	2	65	79	24	57	25	24	3	5	142	160	58
Columbus	18	14	3	0	1	53	35	29	17	4	10	1	2	33	48	11	35	18	13	1	3	86	83	40
Dallas	18	9	7	0	2	47	40	20	18	3	11	1	3	41	69	10	36	12	18	1	5	88	109	30
Detroit	18	5	7	2	4	45	52	16	18	4	13	1	0	40	71	9	36	9	20	3	4	85	123	25
Edmonton	28	17	9	1	1	80	57	36	29	11	11	3	4	66	73	29	57	28	20	4	5	146	130	65
Florida	5	3	0	1	1	16	6	8	5	4	1	0	0	17	10	8	10	7	1	1	1	33	16	16
Los Angeles	18	7	6	3	2	39	42	19	18	8	6	2	2	45	46	20	36	15	12	5	4	84	88	39
Montreal	4	2	1	0	1	11	10	5	5	2	2	1	0	13	14	5	9	4	3	1	1	24	24	10
Nashville	18	10	5	3	0	62	50	23	18	6	10	2	0	41	52	14	36	16	15	5	0	103	102	37
New Jersey	5	1	2	1	1	13	17	4	5	0	3	1	1	10	20	2	10	1	5	2	2	23	37	6
NY Islanders	6	5	1	0	0	20	15	10	5	3	2	0	0	16	11	6	11	8	3	0	0	36	26	16
NY Rangers	6	3	2	0	1	20	18	7	5	1	4	0	0	9	15	2	11	4	6	0	1	29	33	9
Ottawa	5	1	2	1	1	14	19	4	4	1	3	0	0	8	13	2	9	2	5	1	1	22	32	6
Philadelphia	4	2	1	1	0	8	7	5	7	2	5	0	0	10	20	4	11	4	6	1	0	18	27	9
Phoenix	18	9	6	2	1	48	36	21	18	7	9	1	1	41	50	16	36	16	15	3	2	89	86	37
Pittsburgh	5	3	1	1	0	15	12	7	6	5	1	0	0	21	8	10	11	8	2	1	0	36	20	17
St. Louis	18	11	3	2	2	57	34	26	18	6	8	3	1	34	41	16	36	17	11	5	3	91	75	42
San Jose	18	6	9	1	2	41	48	15	18	7	9	1	1	38	51	16	36	13	18	2	3	79	99	31
Tampa Bay	5	4	1	0	0	19	13	8	6	3	1	1	1	16	14	8	11	7	2	1	1	35	27	16
Toronto	3	2	1	0	0	11	5	4	5	1	4	0	0	11	17	2	8	3	5	0	0	22	22	6
Vancouver	29	14	10	2	3	82	70	33	28	10	10	3	5	70	78	28	57	24	20	5	8	152	148	61
Washington	5	5	0	0	0	13	6	10	5	1	4	0	0	8	14	2	10	6	4	0	0	21	20	12
Totals	**369**	**197**	**110**	**28**	**34**	**1022**	**869**	**456**	**369**	**134**	**181**	**27**	**27**	**854**	**1010**	**322**	**738**	**331**	**291**	**55**	**61**	**1876**	**1879**	**778**

Playoffs

	Series	W	L	GP	W	L	T	GF	GA	Last Mtg.	Rnd.	Result
Anaheim	2	0	2	9	1	8	0	10	21	2007	CQF	L 1-4
Colorado	2	1	1	13	6	7	0	28	34	2008	CQF	L 2-4
Vancouver	1	1	0	7	4	3	0	26	17	2003	CSF	W 4-3
Totals	**5**	**2**	**3**	**29**	**11**	**18**	**0**	**64**	**72**			

Playoff Results 2010-2006

Year	Round	Opponent	Result	GF	GA
2008	CQF	Colorado	L 2-4	12	17
2007	CQF	Anaheim	L 1-4	9	12

Abbreviations: Round: CF – conference final; **CSF** – conference semi-final; **CQF** – conference quarter-final.

2009-10 Results

Oct.	3	at Columbus	1-2	Jan.	2	New Jersey	3-5
	6	Anaheim	4-3*		5	at Chicago	1-4
	8	at Los Angeles	3-6		6	Calgary	4-1
	10	at San Jose	2-4		9	Chicago	6-5†
	14	at Anaheim	2-3		11	Pittsburgh	4-3
	16	at Edmonton	2-5		13	Vancouver	5-2
	17	at Vancouver	1-2		14	at St. Louis	0-1
	21	Colorado	3-2†		16	at Phoenix	4-6
	23	at St. Louis	1-3		18	at Dallas	3-4
	24	Carolina	3-2*		21	Detroit	3-4†
	26	at Chicago	1-3		23	Columbus	4-2
	28	Nashville	3-4		27	Detroit	5-2
	30	NY Rangers	3-2		28	at Colorado	1-0
	31	at Pittsburgh	2-1		30	at San Jose	2-3
Nov.	5	Vancouver	2-5	Feb.	2	at Dallas	2-4
	7	Dallas	3-2		4	Edmonton	4-2
	10	at Toronto	5-2		6	Philadelphia	2-1
	12	at Tampa Bay	3-4†		10	Phoenix	2-3
	13	at Washington	1-3		12	Atlanta	2-3
	15	at Carolina	4-5†		14	Vancouver	6-2
	18	Phoenix	2-3	Mar.	3	at Calgary	4-0
	20	NY Islanders	3-2		5	at Edmonton	1-2†
	25	Boston	1-2†		7	Calgary	2-5
	27	Colorado	5-3		9	Florida	2-3†
	28	at Colorado	3-2†		11	at Detroit	1-5
Dec.	2	Nashville	5-4*		12	at Buffalo	3-2
	4	Anaheim	5-4†		14	St. Louis	4-2
	5	at Nashville	5-3		16	Edmonton	4-2
	7	at Phoenix	0-2		18	at Nashville	0-5
	9	at Colorado	1-0		19	at Columbus	2-4
	11	at Calgary	2-1*		21	Calgary	4-3
	12	at Vancouver	3-4		23	San Jose	1-4
	15	Columbus	2-1		25	at Philadelphia	4-3*
	17	at Montreal	3-1		26	at Detroit	2-6
	19	at Ottawa	1-4		29	Los Angeles	2-3
	21	Colorado	3-4		31	Chicago	0-4
	23	Edmonton	3-1	Apr.	2	San Jose	2-3
	26	St. Louis	4-3		4	at Vancouver	3-4*
	28	at Los Angeles	4-3		5	at Edmonton	1-4
	29	at Anaheim	2-4		8	at Calgary	2-1†
	31	Los Angeles	2-5		10	Dallas	3-4†

* – Overtime   † – Shootout

Entry Draft Selections 2010-2000

Name in bold denotes played in NHL.

2010 Pick		2006 Pick		2003 Pick		2000 Pick	
9	Mikael Granlund	9	**James Sheppard**	20	**Brent Burns**	3	**Marian Gaborik**
39	Brett Bulmer	40	Ondrej Fiala	56	**Patrick O'Sullivan**	33	**Nick Schultz**
56	Johan Larsson	72	**Cal Clutterbuck**	78	**Danny Irmen**	99	Marc Cavosie
59	Jason Zucker	102	Kyle Medvec	157	Marcin Kolusz	132	**Maxim Sushinsky**
159	Johan Gustafsson	132	Niko Hovinen	187	Miroslav Kopriva	170	**Erik Reitz**
189	Dylen McKinlay	162	Julian Walker	207	Georgy Misharin	199	Brian Passmore
		192	Chris Hickey	219	Adam Courchaine	214	**Peter Bartos**
2009				251	Mathieu Melanson	232	**Lubomir Sekeras**
Pick		**2005**		281	Jean-Michel Bolduc	255	Eric Johansson
16	Nick Leddy	Pick					
77	Matt Hackett	4	**Benoit Pouliot**	**2002**			
103	Kris Foucault	57	Matt Kassian	Pick			
116	Alexander Fallstrom	65	Kristofer Westblom	8	**Pierre-Marc Bouchard**		
161	Darcy Kuemper	110	Kyle Bailey	38	**Josh Harding**		
163	Jere Sallinen	122	Morten Madsen	72	Mike Erickson		
182	Erik Haula	129	Anthony Aiello	73	**Barry Brust**		
193	Anthony Hamburg	199	Riley Emmerson	155	Armands Berzins		
				175	**Matt Foy**		
2008		**2004**		204	Niklas Eckerblom		
Pick		Pick		237	**Christoph Brandner**		
23	Tyler Cuma	12	A.J. Thelen	268	Mikhail Tyulyapkin		
55	Marco Scandella	42	Roman Voloshenko	269	Mika Hannula		
115	Sean Lorenz	78	**Peter Olvecky**				
145	Eero Elo	79	**Clayton Stoner**	**2001**			
		111	**Ryan Jones**	Pick			
2007		114	Patrick Bordeleau	6	**Mikko Koivu**		
Pick		117	Julien Sprunger	36	**Kyle Wanvig**		
16	**Colton Gillies**	161	Jean-Claude Sawyer	74	Chris Heid		
110	**Justin Falk**	175	Aaron Boogaard	93	**Stephane Veilleux**		
140	**Cody Almond**	195	Jean-Michel Rizk	103	**Tony Virta**		
170	Harri Ilvonen	206	**Anton Khudobin**	202	**Derek Boogaard**		
200	Carson McMillan	272	Kyle Wilson	239	Jake Riddle		

Chuck Fletcher
General Manager
Born: Montreal, Que., April 29, 1967.

The Minnesota Wild announced the hiring of Chuck Fletcher as the second general manager in club history on May 22, 2009. Fletcher has been to the Stanley Cup Finals in management with three different teams (Florida, Anaheim and Pittsburgh). With the Penguins from 2006 to 2009, he worked closely with general manager Ray Shero on all hockey-related matters, including scouting, overseeing the development of young prospects and contract negotiations. Fletcher also managed hockey operations for the club's American Hockey League affiliate, the Wilkes-Barre/Scranton Penguins. Under his leadership, Wilkes-Barre/Scranton reached the AHL's Calder Cup finals in 2007-08, and the division finals in 2008-09.

Fletcher, the son of Hockey Hall of Famer Cliff Fletcher, had extensive NHL management experience before he joined the Penguins in July 2006 – including a four-year stint with the Anaheim Ducks from 2003 to 2006 as director of hockey operations, assistant general manager, and vice president of amateur scouting and player development.

The Montreal native also spent nine years in the front office of the Florida Panthers from 1993 to 2002, working seven seasons as assistant general manager and part of one season (2001-02) as interim general manager. In 1996, the Panthers advanced to the Stanley Cup Finals.

Fletcher graduated from Harvard in 1990 and spent one year as the sales and merchandising coordinator for Hockey Canada and two years as a player representative for Newport Sports Management before making the transition to the front office.

Club Directory

Xcel Energy Center

Minnesota Wild
317 Washington Street
St. Paul, MN 55102
Phone **651/602-6000**
FAX 651/222-1055
Tickets 651/222-9453
www.wild.com
Capacity: 18,064

Board Members . . . . Craig Leipold (Owner/Governor), Philip Falcone (Minority Owner), Mark Falcone, Quinn Martin, Robert O. Naegele, Jr., Mark Pacchini and Jac Sperling

Investors in MSE . . . Craig Leipold (Owner/Governor), Philip Falcone (Minority Owner), Robert Hubbard (Limited Partner), Stanley E. Hubbard (LP), Stanley S. Hubbard (LP), Horace H. Irvine III (LP), Robert Marvin (LP), Robert O. Naegele, Jr. (LP), Ford Nicholson (LP), Todd Nicholson (LP), Vance Opperman (LP), Michael Reilly (LP)

Executive Management
Owner/Governor. Craig Leipold
Minority Owner . . . . Philip Falcone
General Manager . . . . Chuck Fletcher
Executive Vice President, Chief Financial Officer. . . . Jeff Pellegrom
Chief Operating Officer . . . . Matt Majka
Vice President and General Counsel . . . . Steve Weinreich
Vice President, Customer Sales and Service;
  Exec. V.P., Houston Aeros and AHL Governor . . . Jamie Spencer
Vice President, Facility Admin. / G.M., RiverCentre . Jim Ibister
V.P./General Manager, Xcel Energy Center . . . . . . Jack Larson
Vice President, Communications and Broadcasting . . Bill Robertson
Vice President Corp. Partnerships and Retail Mgmt. . Carin Anderson
Vice President, Marketing and Brand Management . John Maher
Executive Assistants . . . . Stephanie Huseby, Laura Stevenson
Administrative Assistant, Sales and Service,
  Creative Services and Marketing . . . . Tawnya Vidnovic
Administrative Assistant, Communications/Broadcasting,
  Corp. Partnerships, Legal and Human Resources . Deb Hanson

Hockey Operations
Assistant General Manager . . . . Brent Flahr
Assistant to the G.M. and G.M. Houston Aeros . . . Jim Mill
Head Coach . . . . Todd Richards
Assistant Coach / Goaltending Coach . . . . Dave Barr / Bob Mason
Strength and Conditioning Coach . . . . Christopher Pietrzak-Wegner
Video Coordinator . . . . P.J. DeLuca
Coordinator of Amateur Scouting . . . . Guy Lapointe
Director of Player Development/Personnel . . . . . . Brad Bombardir/Blair Mackasey
Scouts . . . . Marc Chamard, Craig Channell, Paul Charles, Brian Fortin, Christopher Hamel, Jamie Hislop, Brian Hunter, Chris Kelleher, Martin Nanne, Ricard Perrson, Pavel Routa, Ernie Vargas
Head Athletic Trainer / Assistant . . . . Don Fuller / John Worley
Head Equipment Manager / Assistants . . . . Tony DaCosta / Matt Benz, Rick Bronwell
Message Therapist . . . . Travis Green
Director of Hockey Administration . . . . Shep Harder
Hockey Operations Administrator . . . . Cindy Sweiger
Travel Coordinator . . . . Mary Kenna
Medical Staff . . . . Drs. Sheldon Burns, Joel Boyd, Brad Nelson, Dan Peterson
Oral Surgeon / Team Dentists . . . . . . David Hamlar / Kyle Edlund, Mike Nanne, Mike Pelke

Sales and Service
Director, Customer Sales. . . . . Matt Cords
Manager, Ticket Operations . . . . Chris Turns
Account Manager, Group and Event Suites . . . . . . Cory Effertz
New Business Development . . . . Dexter Albrecht, Emily Iversen, Mike McDonough, Matt Sayer, Dusty Smieja, Jason Stern
Director, Fan Relations . . . . Maria Troje
Fan Relations Account Service Executives. . . . . Natalie Kaess, Erica McKenzie, Jennifer Watters
Account Executive Premium Seating . . . . Sarah Saubert

Retail Operation
Director, Retail Operations . . . . Matt Freiberg
Managers, Retail Operations. . . . . . . Scott Sarkis, Joe Ferens, Jennifer Meyers, Brian Talcott

Corporate Partnerships
Account Executives . . . . Bryan Bellows, Carl Levi
Interactive Account Executive . . . . Brandon Latack
Senior Manager, Corporate Service . . . . Kathleen Borschke
Corporate Service Coordinators . . . . Anna Johnson, Jessica Krebs, Ed Souter

Communications and Broadcasting
Manager, Media Relations and Team Services . . Aaron Sickman
Coordinator, Media Relations and Team Services. . . Ryan Stanzel
Manager of Broadcasting . . . . Maggie Kukar
Radio Operations Coordinator. . . . . Kevin Falness
Media Relations Intern . . . . Michael Placko
Radio Play-By-Play / Analyst . . . . Bob Kurtz / Tom Reid
Television Play-By-Play / Analyst. . . . . Dan Terhaar / Mike Greenlay

Brand Marketing
Director, Events and Promotions . . . . Wayne Petersen
Senior Manager, Digital & Interactive Group . . . . . Michael Brinkman
Manager, Game Presentation . . . . Paul Loomis
Manager, Production Services . . . . Hank Dolan
Manager, E-mail and Database . . . . Holly Doyle
Manager, Web and Creative Services . . . . Dewayne Hankins
Managing Editor, Web Sites . . . . Glen Andresen
Team Curator . . . . Roger Godin

Community Giving
Sr. Director, Community Partnerships . . . . Brad Bombardir
Manager, Community Giving . . . . Rachel Schuldt

Minnesota Wild Foundation
Executive Director . . . . Amy Woog-Patnode

Finance and Accounting
Controller and Senior Director Finance . . . . Molly Jungbauer
Director, Finance. Mitch Helgerson
Senior Manager, Accounting Services . . . . Molly McArdle

Human Resources
Senior Director, Human Resources . . . . Delores Murphy

Information Technology
Director, Information Technology . . . . David Weisbrod

Miscellaneous
Radio Network Flagship . . . . WCCO (830 AM)
Television Networks . . . . . . KSTC.TV Channel 45 (Over-the-Air), Fox Sports Net North (Cable)
Team Photographer / Public Address Announcer . . . Bruce Kluckhohn / Adam Abrams

Montreal Canadiens

Key Off-Season Signings/Acquisitions

2010

- **June 17** • Acquired C **Lars Eller** and RW **Ian Schultz** from St. Louis for G **Jaroslav Halak**.
- **22** • Re-signed C **Tomas Plekanec** and LW **Mathieu Darche**.
- **28** • Re-signed C **Tom Pyatt** and LW **Benoit Pouliot**.
- **29** • Acquired C **Dustin Boyd** from Nashville.
- **July 1** • Signed G **Alex Auld**.
- **13** • Re-signed C **Maxim Lapierre**.
- **15** • Re-signed C **David Desharnais**.
- **31** • Signed D **Alexandre Picard**.

2010-11 Schedule

Month	Day	Date	Opponent
Oct.	Thu.	7	at Toronto
	Sat.	9	at Pittsburgh
	Wed.	13	Tampa Bay
	Fri.	15	at Buffalo
	Sat.	16	Ottawa
	Thu.	21	New Jersey
	Sat.	23	at Ottawa
	Mon.	25	Phoenix
	Wed.	27	NY Islanders
	Fri.	29	at NY Islanders
	Sat.	30	Florida
Nov.	Tue.	2	at Columbus
	Fri.	5	at Buffalo
	Sat.	6	Ottawa
	Tue.	9	Vancouver
	Thu.	11	at Boston
	Sat.	13	Carolina
	Tue.	16	Philadelphia
	Thu.	18	Nashville
	Sat.	20	Toronto
	Mon.	22	at Philadelphia
	Wed.	24	Los Angeles
	Fri.	26	at Atlanta
	Sat.	27	Buffalo
Dec.	Wed.	1	Edmonton
	Thu.	2	at New Jersey
	Sat.	4	San Jose*
	Tue.	7	Ottawa
	Fri.	10	at Detroit
	Sat.	11	at Toronto
	Wed.	15	Philadelphia
	Thu.	16	Boston
	Sun.	19	at Colorado
	Tue.	21	at Dallas
	Thu.	23	at Carolina
	Sun.	26	at NY Islanders
	Tue.	28	at Washington
	Thu.	30	at Tampa Bay
	Fri.	31	at Florida*
Jan.	Sun.	2	Atlanta*
	Thu.	6	Pittsburgh
	Sat.	8	Boston
	Tue.	11	at NY Rangers
	Wed.	12	Pittsburgh
	Sat.	15	NY Rangers
	Mon.	17	Calgary
	Tue.	18	at Buffalo
	Fri.	21	at Ottawa
	Sat.	22	Anaheim
	Tue.	25	at Philadelphia
Feb.	Tue.	1	at Washington
	Wed.	2	Florida
	Sat.	5	NY Rangers*
	Sun.	6	New Jersey*
	Wed.	9	at Boston
	Thu.	10	NY Islanders
	Sat.	12	Toronto
	Tue.	15	Buffalo
	Thu.	17	at Edmonton
	Sun.	20	at Calgary*
	Tue.	22	at Vancouver
	Thu.	24	Toronto
	Sat.	26	Carolina
Mar.	Tue.	1	at Atlanta
	Thu.	3	at Florida
	Sat.	5	at Tampa Bay
	Tue.	8	Boston
	Thu.	10	at St. Louis
	Sat.	12	at Pittsburgh*
	Tue.	15	Washington
	Thu.	17	Tampa Bay
	Fri.	18	at NY Rangers
	Sun.	20	at Minnesota*
	Tue.	22	Buffalo
	Thu.	24	at Boston
	Sat.	26	Washington
	Tue.	29	Atlanta
	Wed.	30	at Carolina
Apr.	Sat.	2	at New Jersey
	Tue.	5	Chicago
	Thu.	7	at Ottawa
	Sat.	9	at Toronto

* Denotes afternoon game.

NORTHEAST DIVISION
94th NHL Season

Franchise date: November 22, 1917

2009-10 Results: 39W-33L-5OTL-5SOL 88PTS.
Fourth, Northeast Division

Year-by-Year Record

		Home				Road				Overall								
Season	GP	W	L	T	OL	W	L	T	OL	W	L	T	OL	GF	GA	Pts.	Finished	Playoff Result
2009-10	82	20	16	....	5	19	17	....	5	39	33	....	10	217	223	88	4th, Northeast Div.	Lost Conf. Championship
2008-09	82	24	10	....	7	17	20	....	4	41	30	....	11	249	247	93	2nd, Northeast Div.	Lost Conf. Quarter-Final
2007-08	82	22	13	....	6	25	12	....	4	47	25	....	10	262	222	104	1st, Northeast Div.	Lost Conf. Semi-Final
2006-07	82	26	12	....	3	16	22	....	3	42	34	....	6	245	256	90	4th, Northeast Div.	Out of Playoffs
2005-06	82	24	13	....	4	18	18	....	5	42	31	....	9	243	247	93	3rd, Northeast Div.	Lost Conf. Quarter-Final
2004-05	....	....	....	....	....	....	....	....	....	....	....	....	....	....	....	....		
2003-04	82	23	13	4	1	18	17	3	3	41	30	7	4	208	192	93	4th, Northeast Div.	Lost Conf. Semi-Final
2002-03	82	16	16	5	4	14	19	3	5	30	35	8	9	206	234	77	4th, Northeast Div.	Out of Playoffs
2001-02	82	21	13	6	1	15	18	6	2	36	31	12	3	207	209	87	4th, Northeast Div.	Lost Conf. Semi-Final
2000-01	82	15	20	4	2	13	20	4	4	28	40	8	6	206	232	70	5th, Northeast Div.	Out of Playoffs
1999-2000	82	18	17	5	1	17	17	4	3	35	34	9	4	196	194	83	4th, Northeast Div.	Out of Playoffs
1998-99	82	21	15	5	....	11	24	6	....	32	39	11	....	184	209	75	5th, Northeast Div.	Out of Playoffs
1997-98	82	15	17	9	....	22	15	4	....	37	32	13	....	235	208	87	4th, Northeast Div.	Lost Conf. Semi-Final
1996-97	82	17	17	7	....	14	19	8	....	31	36	15	....	249	276	77	4th, Northeast Div.	Lost Conf. Quarter-Final
1995-96	82	23	12	6	....	17	20	4	....	40	32	10	....	265	248	90	3rd, Northeast Div.	Lost Conf. Quarter-Final
1994-95	48	15	5	4	....	3	18	3	....	18	23	7	....	125	148	43	6th, Northeast Div.	Out of Playoffs
1993-94	84	26	12	4	....	15	17	10	....	41	29	14	....	283	248	96	3rd, Northeast Div.	Lost Conf. Quarter-Final
1992-93	**84**	**27**	**13**	**2**	....	**21**	**17**	**4**	....	**48**	**30**	**6**	....	**326**	**280**	**102**	**3rd, Adams Div.**	**Won Stanley Cup**
1991-92	80	27	8	5	....	14	20	6	....	41	28	11	....	267	207	93	1st, Adams Div.	Lost Div. Final
1990-91	80	23	12	5	....	16	18	6	....	39	30	11	....	273	249	89	2nd, Adams Div.	Lost Div. Final
1989-90	80	26	8	6	....	15	20	5	....	41	28	11	....	288	234	93	3rd, Adams Div.	Lost Div. Final
1988-89	80	30	6	4	....	23	12	5	....	53	18	9	....	315	218	115	1st, Adams Div.	Lost Final
1987-88	80	26	8	6	....	19	14	7	....	45	22	13	....	298	238	103	1st, Adams Div.	Lost Div. Final
1986-87	80	27	9	4	....	14	20	6	....	41	29	10	....	277	241	92	2nd, Adams Div.	Lost Conf. Championship
1985-86	**80**	**25**	**11**	**4**	....	**15**	**22**	**3**	....	**40**	**33**	**7**	....	**330**	**280**	**87**	**2nd, Adams Div.**	**Won Stanley Cup**
1984-85	80	24	10	6	....	17	17	6	....	41	27	12	....	309	262	94	1st, Adams Div.	Lost Div. Final
1983-84	80	19	19	2	....	16	21	3	....	35	40	5	....	286	295	75	4th, Adams Div.	Lost Conf. Championship
1982-83	80	25	6	9	....	17	18	5	....	42	24	14	....	350	286	98	2nd, Adams Div.	Lost Div. Semi-Final
1981-82	80	25	6	9	....	21	11	8	....	46	17	17	....	360	223	109	1st, Adams Div.	Lost Div. Semi-Final
1980-81	80	31	7	2	....	14	15	11	....	45	22	13	....	332	232	103	1st, Norris Div.	Lost Prelim. Round
1979-80	80	30	7	3	....	17	13	10	....	47	20	13	....	328	240	107	1st, Norris Div.	Lost Quarter-Final
1978-79	**80**	**29**	**6**	**5**	....	**23**	**11**	**6**	....	**52**	**17**	**11**	....	**337**	**204**	**115**	**1st, Norris Div.**	**Won Stanley Cup**
1977-78	**80**	**32**	**4**	**4**	....	**27**	**6**	**7**	....	**59**	**10**	**11**	....	**359**	**183**	**129**	**1st, Norris Div.**	**Won Stanley Cup**
1976-77	**80**	**33**	**1**	**6**	....	**27**	**7**	**6**	....	**60**	**8**	**12**	....	**387**	**171**	**132**	**1st, Norris Div.**	**Won Stanley Cup**
1975-76	**80**	**32**	**3**	**5**	....	**26**	**8**	**6**	....	**58**	**11**	**11**	....	**337**	**174**	**127**	**1st, Norris Div.**	**Won Stanley Cup**
1974-75	80	27	8	5	....	20	6	14	....	47	14	19	....	374	225	113	1st, Norris Div.	Lost Semi-Final
1973-74	78	24	12	3	....	21	12	6	....	45	24	9	....	293	240	99	2nd, East Div.	Lost Quarter-Final
1972-73	**78**	**29**	**4**	**6**	....	**23**	**6**	**10**	....	**52**	**10**	**16**	....	**329**	**184**	**120**	**1st, East Div.**	**Won Stanley Cup**
1971-72	78	29	3	7	....	17	13	9	....	46	16	16	....	307	205	108	3rd, East Div.	Lost Quarter-Final
1970-71	**78**	**29**	**7**	**3**	....	**13**	**16**	**10**	....	**42**	**23**	**13**	....	**291**	**216**	**97**	**3rd, East Div.**	**Won Stanley Cup**
1969-70	76	21	9	8	....	17	13	8	....	38	22	16	....	244	201	92	5th, East Div.	Out of Playoffs
1968-69	**76**	**26**	**7**	**5**	....	**20**	**12**	**6**	....	**46**	**19**	**11**	....	**271**	**202**	**103**	**1st, East Div.**	**Won Stanley Cup**
1967-68	**74**	**26**	**5**	**6**	....	**16**	**17**	**4**	....	**42**	**22**	**10**	....	**236**	**167**	**94**	**1st, East Div.**	**Won Stanley Cup**
1966-67	70	19	9	7	....	13	16	6	....	32	25	13	....	202	188	77	2nd,	Lost Final
1965-66	**70**	**23**	**11**	**1**	....	**18**	**10**	**7**	....	**41**	**21**	**8**	....	**239**	**173**	**90**	**1st,**	**Won Stanley Cup**
1964-65	**70**	**20**	**8**	**7**	....	**16**	**15**	**4**	....	**36**	**23**	**11**	....	**211**	**185**	**83**	**2nd,**	**Won Stanley Cup**
1963-64	70	22	7	6	....	14	14	7	....	36	21	13	....	209	167	85	1st,	Lost Semi-Final
1962-63	70	15	10	10	....	13	9	13	....	28	19	23	....	225	183	79	3rd,	Lost Semi-Final
1961-62	70	26	2	7	....	16	12	7	....	42	14	14	....	259	166	98	1st,	Lost Semi-Final
1960-61	70	24	6	5	....	17	13	5	....	41	19	10	....	254	188	92	1st,	Lost Semi-Final
1959-60	**70**	**23**	**4**	**8**	....	**17**	**14**	**4**	....	**40**	**18**	**12**	....	**255**	**178**	**92**	**1st,**	**Won Stanley Cup**
1958-59	**70**	**21**	**8**	**6**	....	**18**	**10**	**7**	....	**39**	**18**	**13**	....	**258**	**158**	**91**	**1st,**	**Won Stanley Cup**
1957-58	**70**	**23**	**8**	**4**	....	**20**	**9**	**6**	....	**43**	**17**	**10**	....	**250**	**158**	**96**	**1st,**	**Won Stanley Cup**
1956-57	**70**	**23**	**6**	**6**	....	**12**	**17**	**6**	....	**35**	**23**	**12**	....	**210**	**155**	**82**	**2nd,**	**Won Stanley Cup**
1955-56	**70**	**29**	**5**	**1**	....	**16**	**10**	**9**	....	**45**	**15**	**10**	....	**222**	**131**	**100**	**1st,**	**Won Stanley Cup**
1954-55	70	26	5	4	....	15	13	7	....	41	18	11	....	228	157	93	2nd,	Lost Final
1953-54	70	27	5	3	....	8	19	8	....	35	24	11	....	195	141	81	2nd,	Lost Final
1952-53	**70**	**18**	**12**	**5**	....	**10**	**11**	**14**	....	**28**	**23**	**19**	....	**155**	**148**	**75**	**2nd,**	**Won Stanley Cup**
1951-52	70	22	8	5	....	12	18	5	....	34	26	10	....	195	164	78	2nd,	Lost Final
1950-51	70	17	10	8	....	8	20	7	....	25	30	15	....	173	184	65	3rd,	Lost Final
1949-50	70	17	8	10	....	12	14	9	....	29	22	19	....	172	150	77	2nd,	Lost Semi-Final
1948-49	60	19	8	3	....	9	15	6	....	28	23	9	....	152	126	65	3rd,	Lost Semi-Final
1947-48	60	13	13	4	....	7	16	7	....	20	29	11	....	147	169	51	5th,	Out of Playoffs
1946-47	60	19	6	5	....	15	10	5	....	34	16	10	....	189	138	78	1st,	Lost Final
1945-46	**50**	**16**	**6**	**3**	....	**12**	**11**	**2**	....	**28**	**17**	**5**	....	**172**	**134**	**61**	**1st,**	**Won Stanley Cup**
1944-45	50	21	2	2	....	17	6	2	....	38	8	4	....	228	121	80	1st,	Lost Semi-Final
1943-44	**50**	**22**	**0**	**3**	....	**16**	**5**	**4**	....	**38**	**5**	**7**	....	**234**	**109**	**83**	**1st,**	**Won Stanley Cup**
1942-43	50	14	4	7	....	5	15	5	....	19	19	12	....	181	191	50	4th,	Lost Semi-Final
1941-42	48	12	10	2	....	6	17	1	....	18	27	3	....	134	173	39	6th,	Lost Quarter-Final
1940-41	48	11	9	4	....	5	17	2	....	16	26	6	....	121	147	38	6th,	Lost Quarter-Final
1939-40	48	5	14	5	....	5	19	0	....	10	33	5	....	90	168	25	7th,	Out of Playoffs
1938-39	48	8	11	5	....	7	13	4	....	15	24	9	....	115	146	39	6th,	Lost Quarter-Final
1937-38	48	13	4	7	....	5	13	6	....	18	17	13	....	123	128	49	3rd, Cdn. Div.	Lost Quarter-Final
1936-37	48	16	8	0	....	8	10	6	....	24	18	6	....	115	111	54	1st, Cdn. Div.	Lost Semi-Final
1935-36	48	5	11	8	....	6	15	3	....	11	26	11	....	82	123	33	4th, Cdn. Div.	Out of Playoffs
1934-35	48	11	11	2	....	8	12	4	....	19	23	6	....	110	145	44	3rd, Cdn. Div.	Lost Quarter-Final
1933-34	48	16	6	2	....	6	14	4	....	22	20	6	....	99	101	50	2nd, Cdn. Div.	Lost Quarter-Final
1932-33	48	15	5	4	....	3	20	1	....	18	25	5	....	92	115	41	3rd, Cdn. Div.	Lost Quarter-Final
1931-32	48	18	3	3	....	7	13	4	....	25	16	7	....	128	111	57	1st, Cdn. Div.	Lost Semi-Final
1930-31	**44**	**15**	**3**	**4**	....	**11**	**7**	**4**	....	**26**	**10**	**8**	....	**129**	**89**	**60**	**1st, Cdn. Div.**	**Won Stanley Cup**
1929-30	**44**	**13**	**5**	**4**	....	**8**	**9**	**5**	....	**21**	**14**	**9**	....	**142**	**114**	**51**	**2nd, Cdn. Div.**	**Won Stanley Cup**
1928-29	44	12	4	6	....	10	3	9	....	22	7	15	....	71	43	59	1st, Cdn. Div.	Lost Semi-Final
1927-28	44	12	7	3	....	14	4	4	....	26	11	7	....	116	48	59	1st, Cdn. Div.	Lost Semi-Final
1926-27	44	15	5	2	....	13	9	0	....	28	14	2	....	99	67	58	2nd, Cdn. Div.	Lost Semi-Final
1925-26	36	5	12	1	....	6	12	0	....	11	24	1	....	79	108	23	7th,	Out of Playoffs
1924-25	30	10	5	0	....	7	6	2	....	17	11	2	....	93	56	36	3rd,	Lost Final
1923-24	**24**	**10**	**2**	**0**	....	**3**	**9**	**0**	....	**13**	**11**	**0**	....	**59**	**48**	**26**	**2nd,**	**Won Stanley Cup**
1922-23	24	10	2	0	....	3	7	2	....	13	9	2	....	73	61	28	2nd,	Lost NHL Final
1921-22	24	8	3	1	....	4	8	0	....	12	11	1	....	88	94	25	3rd,	Out of Playoffs
1920-21	24	9	3	0	....	4	8	0	....	13	11	0	....	112	99	26	3rd and 2nd*	Out of Playoffs
1919-20	24	8	4	0	....	5	7	0	....	13	11	0	....	129	113	26	2nd and 3rd*	Out of Playoffs
1918-19	18	7	2	0	....	3	6	0	....	10	8	0	....	88	78	20	1st and 2nd*	Cup Final but no Decision
1917-18	22	8	3	0	....	5	6	0	....	13	9	0	....	115	84	26	1st and 3rd*	Lost NHL Final

* Season played in two halves with no combined standing at end.
From 1917-18 through 1925-26, NHL champions played against PCHA/WCHL champions for Stanley Cup.

2010-11 Player Personnel

FORWARDS	HT	WT	S	Place of Birth	*Age	2009-10 Club
BOYD, Dustin	6-0	187	L	Winnipeg, Man.	24	Calgary-Nashville
CAMMALLERI, Michael	5-9	182	L	Richmond Hill, Ont.	28	Montreal
DARCHE, Mathieu	6-1	215	L	St. Laurent, Que.	33	Montreal-Hamilton
GIONTA, Brian	5-7	173	R	Rochester, NY	31	Montreal
GOMEZ, Scott	5-11	202	L	Anchorage, AK	30	Montreal
KOSTITSYN, Andrei	6-0	214	L	Novopolotsk, USSR	25	Montreal
LAPIERRE, Maxim	6-2	207	R	St. Leonard, Que.	25	Montreal
MOEN, Travis	6-2	215	L	Stewart Valley, Sask.	28	Montreal
PLEKANEC, Tomas	5-11	198	L	Kladno, Czech.	27	Montreal
POULIOT, Benoit	6-3	199	L	Alfred, Ont.	24	Min-Mtl-Hamilton
PYATT, Tom	5-11	183	L	Thunder Bay, Ont.	23	Montreal-Hamilton
DEFENSEMEN						
GILL, Hal	6-7	241	L	Concord, MA	35	Montreal
GORGES, Josh	6-1	200	L	Kelowna, B.C.	26	Montreal
HAMRLIK, Roman	6-2	207	L	Zlin, Czech.	36	Montreal
MARKOV, Andrei	6-0	207	L	Voskresensk, USSR	31	Montreal
O'BYRNE, Ryan	6-5	234	R	Victoria, B.C.	26	Montreal
PICARD, Alexandre	6-3	215	L	Gatineau, Que.	25	Ottawa-Carolina
SPACEK, Jaroslav	6-0	210	L	Rokycany, Czech.	36	Montreal

GOALTENDERS	HT	WT	C	Place of Birth	*Age	2009-10 Club
AULD, Alex	6-4	223	L	Cold Lake, Alta.	29	Dallas-NY Rangers
PRICE, Carey	6-3	219	L	Vancouver, B.C.	23	Montreal

* – Age at start of 2010-11 season

Jacques Martin

Head Coach

Born: St. Pascal, Ont., October 1, 1952.

The Montreal Canadiens announced the appointment of Jacques Martin as the club's new head coach on June 1, 2009. Martin was the Florida Panthers' general manager the previous three seasons (2006 to 2009).He had originally been hired as Panthers coach in 2004 and served in both capacities through the 2007-08 season. In his first season with the Canadiens in 2009-10 he led the club to the Eastern Conference Final.

Midway through the 1995-96 season, Martin was hired as head coach of the Ottawa Senators. In his nine-year tenure with the Senators, he led his team to three division titles and had four seasons of at least 100 points. Martin was nominated for the Jack Adams Trophy as NHL coach of the year four times (1997, 1999, 2001, 2003), winning the award in 1999.

In 1986-87, Martin entered the NHL as head coach of the St. Louis Blues. From 1988 to 1993, Martin worked as an assistant coach with the Chicago Blackhawks and associate coach with the Quebec Nordiques and, following a one-year stint as head coach of the American Hockey League's Cornwall Aces, with the Colorado Avalanche. Martin also has extensive experience on the international level serving as an associate coach with Team Canada for two Winter Olympics (Salt Lake City and Turin), earning a gold medal in 2002. He was also a member of the Canadian Team coaching staff at the 2004 World Cup.

Martin began his coaching career in major junior hockey with the Ontario Hockey League's Peterborough Petes as an assistant to Dick Todd from 1982 to 1984. He then moved on to become Guelph's head coach in 1985-86 season leading the Platers to a Memorial Cup championship and winning the Matt Leyden Trophy as OHL coach of the year. As a player, Martin was a goaltender with the NCAA's St. Lawrence University from 1972 to 1974.

Coaching Record

			Regular Season				Playoffs			
Season	Team	League	GC	W	L	O/T	GC	W	L	T
1985-86	Guelph	OHL	66	41	23	2	20	15	3	2
1985-86	Guelph	M-Cup	....	....	....	....	4	3	1	....
1986-87	**St. Louis**	**NHL**	**80**	**32**	**33**	**15**	**6**	**2**	**4**	....
1987-88	**St. Louis**	**NHL**	**80**	**34**	**38**	**8**	**10**	**5**	**5**	....
1993-94	Cornwall	AHL	80	33	36	22	13	8	5	....
1995-96	**Ottawa**	**NHL**	**38**	**10**	**24**	**4**	....	....	....	....
1996-97	**Ottawa**	**NHL**	**82**	**31**	**36**	**15**	**7**	**3**	**4**	....
1997-98	**Ottawa**	**NHL**	**82**	**34**	**33**	**15**	**11**	**5**	**6**	....
1998-99	**Ottawa**	**NHL**	**82**	**44**	**23**	**15**	**4**	**0**	**4**	....
99-2000	**Ottawa**	**NHL**	**82**	**41**	**28**	**13**	**6**	**2**	**4**	....
2000-01	**Ottawa**	**NHL**	**82**	**48**	**21**	**13**	**4**	**0**	**4**	....
2001-02	**Ottawa**	**NHL**	**80**	**38**	**26**	**16**	**12**	**7**	**5**	....
2002-03	**Ottawa**	**NHL**	**82**	**52**	**21**	**9**	**18**	**11**	**7**	....
2003-04	**Ottawa**	**NHL**	**82**	**43**	**23**	**16**	**7**	**3**	**4**	....
2004-05	**Florida**				SEASON CANCELLED					
2005-06	**Florida**	**NHL**	**82**	**37**	**34**	**11**	....	....	....	....
2006-07	**Florida**	**NHL**	**82**	**35**	**31**	**16**	....	....	....	....
2007-08	**Florida**	**NHL**	**82**	**38**	**35**	**9**	....	....	....	....
2009-10	**Montreal**	**NHL**	**82**	**39**	**33**	**10**	**19**	**9**	**10**	....
	NHL Totals		**1180**	**556**	**439**	**185**	**104**	**47**	**57**	....

Won Jack Adams Award (1999)

Martin stepped aside (with NHL permission) during the final two games of the 2001-02 season in order to allow assistant coach Roger Neilson to reach the 1,000-game plateau, April 11 and 13, 2002.

2009-10 Scoring

* – rookie

Regular Season

Pos	#	Player	Team	GP	G	A	Pts	TOI	+/-	PIM	PP	SH	GW	S	%
C	14	Tomas Plekanec	MTL	82	25	45	70	19:57	5	50	3	1	4	216	11.6
C	91	Scott Gomez	MTL	78	12	47	59	19:56	1	60	5	0	1	180	6.7
L	13	Michael Cammalleri	MTL	65	26	24	50	19:31	7	16	4	0	4	218	11.9
R	21	Brian Gionta	MTL	61	28	18	46	20:45	3	26	10	0	3	237	11.8
D	47	Marc-Andre Bergeron	MTL	60	13	21	34	15:03	–7	16	7	0	4	123	10.6
D	79	Andrei Markov	MTL	45	6	28	34	23:48	11	32	4	0	1	85	7.1
L	46	Andrei Kostitsyn	MTL	59	15	18	33	15:59	1	32	6	0	2	136	11.0
C	15	Glen Metropolit	MTL	69	16	13	29	13:33	–1	24	10	0	1	115	13.9
L	57	Benoit Pouliot	MIN	14	2	2	4	11:56	0	12	0	0	0	19	10.5
			MTL	39	15	9	24	16:43	8	31	4	0	3	92	16.3
			Total	53	17	11	28	15:27	8	43	4	0	3	111	15.3
C	42	Dominic Moore	FLA	48	8	9	17	14:54	–7	35	2	1	0	81	9.9
			MTL	21	2	9	11	14:40	4	8	0	1	0	38	5.3
			Total	69	10	18	28	14:50	–3	43	2	2	0	119	8.4
D	44	Roman Hamrlik	MTL	75	6	20	26	23:26	–2	56	2	0	1	100	6.0
D	6	Jaroslav Spacek	MTL	74	3	18	21	21:47	9	50	1	0	0	99	3.0
L	32	Travis Moen	MTL	81	8	11	19	14:59	–2	57	1	2	0	107	7.5
L	74	Sergei Kostitsyn	MTL	47	7	11	18	14:09	4	8	0	0	2	59	11.9
C	40	Maxim Lapierre	MTL	76	7	7	14	12:16	–14	61	0	0	1	101	6.9
L	67	Max Pacioretty	MTL	52	3	11	14	12:42	–5	20	0	0	0	74	4.1
D	75	Hal Gill	MTL	68	2	9	11	18:20	–10	68	0	0	0	41	4.9
L	52	Mathieu Darche	MTL	29	5	5	10	10:50	2	4	0	0	3	43	11.6
D	26	Josh Gorges	MTL	82	3	7	10	21:00	2	39	0	0	1	52	5.8
D	22	Paul Mara	MTL	42	0	8	8	18:43	–16	48	0	0	0	30	0.0
C	94 *	Tom Pyatt	MTL	40	2	3	5	11:04	–5	10	0	0	0	48	4.2
D	20	Ryan O'Byrne	MTL	55	1	3	4	15:15	–3	74	0	0	1	27	3.7
R	17	Georges Laraque	MTL	28	1	2	3	5:45	–6	28	0	0	0	2	50.0
D	76 *	P.K. Subban	MTL	2	0	2	2	20:06	1	2	0	0	0	4	0.0
C	53 *	Ryan White	MTL	16	0	2	2	11:09	–6	16	0	0	0	5	0.0
C	58 *	David Desharnais	MTL	6	0	1	1	8:26	–1	0	0	0	0	2	0.0
D	34 *	Shawn Belle	MTL	2	0	0	0	10:38	–2	0	0	0	0	1	0.0
L	59 *	Brock Trotter	MTL	2	0	0	0	9:02	–1	0	0	0	0	6	0.0
R	48 *	James Wyman	MTL	3	0	0	0	4:23	–2	0	0	0	0	0	0.0
D	72 *	Mathieu Carle	MTL	3	0	0	0	14:28	1	4	0	0	0	2	0.0
L	70 *	Gregory Stewart	MTL	5	0	0	0	4:11	–3	11	0	0	0	4	0.0
D	68 *	Yannick Weber	MTL	5	0	0	0	13:52	–5	4	0	0	0	2	0.0
C	61 *	Ben Maxwell	MTL	13	0	0	0	8:46	–2	6	0	0	0	6	0.0

Goaltending

No.	Goaltender	GPI	Mins	Avg	W	L	OT	EN	SO	GA	SA	S%	G	A	PIM
41	Jaroslav Halak	45	2630	2.40	26	13	5	3	5	105	1386	.924	0	0	0
31	Carey Price	41	2358	2.77	13	20	5	1	0	109	1244	.912	0	1	8
	Totals	**82**	**5016**	**2.61**	**39**	**33**	**10**	**4**	**5**	**218**	**2634**	**.917**			

Playoffs

Pos	#	Player	Team	GP	G	A	Pts	TOI	+/-	PIM	PP	SH	GW	OT	S	%
L	13	Michael Cammalleri	MTL	19	13	6	19	20:40	–6	6	4	0	3	0	60	21.7
R	21	Brian Gionta	MTL	19	9	6	15	22:11	–6	14	4	0	1	0	70	12.9
C	91	Scott Gomez	MTL	19	2	12	14	21:10	–6	25	0	0	0	0	46	4.3
C	14	Tomas Plekanec	MTL	19	4	7	11	19:57	–4	20	1	0	1	1	39	10.3
D	44	Roman Hamrlik	MTL	19	0	9	9	20:08	–1	15	0	0	0	0	21	0.0
L	46	Andrei Kostitsyn	MTL	19	3	5	8	14:14	–1	12	1	0	0	0	29	10.3
D	76 *	P.K. Subban	MTL	14	1	7	8	20:44	2	6	0	0	0	0	23	4.3
D	47	Marc-Andre Bergeron	MTL	19	2	4	6	16:26	–12	10	2	0	0	0	36	5.6
C	42	Dominic Moore	MTL	19	4	1	5	14:33	1	6	0	0	1	0	20	20.0
C	40	Maxim Lapierre	MTL	19	3	1	4	12:20	–2	20	0	0	1	0	36	8.3
C	94 *	Tom Pyatt	MTL	18	2	2	4	13:02	–1	2	0	0	1	0	26	7.7
D	6	Jaroslav Spacek	MTL	10	1	3	4	18:28	–2	6	0	0	0	0	7	14.3
D	79	Andrei Markov	MTL	8	0	4	4	23:46	–3	0	0	0	0	0	9	0.0
L	32	Travis Moen	MTL	19	2	1	3	13:14	0	4	0	1	1	0	18	11.1
C	15	Glen Metropolit	MTL	16	0	2	2	6:43	–3	4	0	0	0	0	13	0.0
L	57	Benoit Pouliot	MTL	18	0	2	2	11:45	–5	6	0	0	0	0	22	0.0
D	26	Josh Gorges	MTL	19	0	2	2	22:41	–4	14	0	0	0	0	5	0.0
L	52	Mathieu Darche	MTL	11	0	1	1	6:14	–1	2	0	0	0	0	7	0.0
D	75	Hal Gill	MTL	18	0	1	1	19:54	–3	20	0	0	0	0	8	0.0
C	61 *	Ben Maxwell	MTL	1	0	0	0	1:03	–1	0	0	0	0	0	0	0.0
L	74	Sergei Kostitsyn	MTL	5	0	0	0	7:59	0	0	0	0	0	0	5	0.0
D	20	Ryan O'Byrne	MTL	13	0	0	0	12:42	1	10	0	0	0	0	7	0.0

Goaltending

No.	Goaltender	GPI	Mins	Avg	W	L	EN	SO	GA	SA	S%	G	A	PIM
41	Jaroslav Halak	18	1013	2.55	9	9	3	0	43	562	.923	0	0	0
31	Carey Price	4	135	3.56	0	1	3	0	8	73	.890	0	0	4
	Totals	**19**	**1154**	**2.96**	**9**	**10**	**6**	**0**	**57**	**641**	**.911**			

Coaching History

Jack Laviolette, 1909-10; Adolphe Lecours, 1910-11; Napoleon Dorval, 1911-12, 1912-13; Jimmy Gardner, 1913-14, 1914-15; Newsy Lalonde, 1915-16 to 1920-21; Newsy Lalonde and Léo Dandurand, 1921-22; Léo Dandurand, 1922-23 to 1925-26; Cecil Hart, 1926-27 to 1931-32; Newsy Lalonde, 1932-33, 1933-34; Newsy Lalonde and Léo Dandurand, 1934-35; Sylvio Mantha, 1935-36; Cecil Hart, 1936-37, 1937-38; Cecil Hart and Jules Dugal, 1938-39; Babe Siebert, 1939*; Pit Lepine, 1939-40; Dick Irvin 1940-41 to 1954-55; Toe Blake, 1955-56 to 1967-68; Claude Ruel, 1968-69, 1969-70; Claude Ruel and Al MacNeil, 1970-71; Scotty Bowman, 1971-72 to 1978-79; Bernie Geoffrion and Claude Ruel, 1979-80; Claude Ruel, 1980-81; Bob Berry, 1981-82, 1982-83; Bob Berry and Jacques Lemaire, 1983-84; Jacques Lemaire, 1984-85; Jean Perron, 1985-86 to 1987-88; Pat Burns, 1988-89 to 1991-92; Jacques Demers, 1992-93 to 1994-95; Jacques Demers, Jacques Laperriere, Mario Tremblay, 1995-96; Mario Tremblay, 1996-97; Alain Vigneault, 1997-98 to 1999-2000; Alain Vigneault and Michel Therrien, 2000-01; Michel Therrien, 2001-02; Michel Therrien and Claude Julien, 2002-03; Claude Julien, 2003-04, 2004-05; Claude Julien and Bob Gainey, 2005-06; Guy Carbonneau, 2006-07, 2007-08; Guy Carbonneau and Bob Gainey, 2008-09; Jacques Martin, 2009-10 to date.

Club Records

Team

(Figures in brackets for season records are games played; records for fewest points, wins, ties, losses, goals, goals against are for 70 or more games)

Most Points	*132	1976-77 (80)
Most Wins	60	1976-77 (80)
Most Ties	23	1962-63 (70)
Most Losses	40	1983-84 (80), 2000-01 (82)
Most Goals	387	1976-77 (80)
Most Goals Against	295	1983-84 (80)
Fewest Points	65	1950-51 (70)
Fewest Wins	25	1950-51 (70)
Fewest Ties	5	1983-84 (80)
Fewest Losses	*8	1976-77 (80)
Fewest Goals	155	1952-53 (70)
Fewest Goals Against	*131	1955-56 (70)
Longest Winning Streak		
Overall	12	Jan. 6-Feb. 3/68
Home	13	Nov. 2/43-Jan. 8/44, Jan. 30-Mar. 26/77
Away	8	Dec. 18/77-Jan. 18/78, Jan. 21-Feb. 21/82
Longest Undefeated Streak		
Overall	28	Dec. 18/77-Feb. 23/78 (23 wins, 5 ties)
Home	*34	Nov. 1/76-Apr. 2/77 (28 wins, 6 ties)
Away	*23	Nov. 27/74-Mar. 12/75 (14 wins, 9 ties)
Longest Losing Streak		
Overall	12	Feb. 13-Mar. 13/26
Home	7	Dec. 16/39-Jan. 18/40, Oct. 28-Nov. 25/00
Away	10	Jan. 16-Mar. 13/26
Longest Winless Streak		
Overall	12	Feb. 13-Mar. 13/26 (12 losses), Nov. 28-Dec. 29/35 (8 losses, 4 ties)
Home	15	Dec. 16/39-Mar. 7/40 (12 losses, 3 ties)
Away	12	Nov. 26/33-Jan. 28/34 (8 losses, 4 ties), Oct. 20-Dec. 13/51 (8 losses, 4 ties)
Most Shutouts, Season	*22	1928-29 (44)
Most PIM, Season	1,847	1995-96 (82)
Most Goals, Game	*16	Mar. 3/20 (Mtl. 16 at Que. 3)

Individual

Most Seasons	20	Henri Richard, Jean Béliveau
Most Games	1,256	Henri Richard
Most Goals, Career	544	Maurice Richard
Most Assists, Career	728	Guy Lafleur
Most Points, Career	1,246	Guy Lafleur (518G, 728A)
Most PIM, Career	2,248	Chris Nilan
Most Shutouts, Career	75	George Hainsworth
Longest Consecutive Games Streak	560	Doug Jarvis (Oct. 8/75-Apr. 4/82)
Most Goals, Season	60	Steve Shutt (1976-77), Guy Lafleur (1977-78)
Most Assists, Season	82	Pete Mahovlich (1974-75)
Most Points, Season	136	Guy Lafleur (1976-77; 56G, 80A)
Most PIM, Season	358	Chris Nilan (1984-85)
Most Points, Defenseman, Season	85	Larry Robinson (1976-77; 19G, 66A)
Most Points, Center, Season	117	Pete Mahovlich (1974-75; 35G, 82A)
Most Points, Right Wing, Season	136	Guy Lafleur (1976-77; 56G, 80A)
Most Points, Left Wing, Season	110	Mats Naslund (1985-86; 43G, 67A)
Most Points, Rookie, Season	71	Mats Naslund (1982-83; 26G, 45A), Kjell Dahlin (1985-86; 32G, 39A)
Most Shutouts, Season	*22	George Hainsworth (1928-29)
Most Goals, Game	6	Newsy Lalonde (Jan. 10/20)
Most Assists, Game	6	Elmer Lach (Feb. 6/43)
Most Points, Game	8	Maurice Richard (Dec. 28/44; 5G, 3A), Bert Olmstead (Jan. 9/54; 4G, 4A)

* NHL Record.

Retired Numbers

1	Jacques Plante	1952-1963
2	Doug Harvey	1947-1961
3	Butch Bouchard	1941-1956
4	Jean Béliveau	1950-1971
5	Bernard Geoffrion	1950-1964
7	Howie Morenz	1923-1937
9	Maurice Richard	1942-1960
10	Guy Lafleur	1971-1984
12	Dickie Moore	1951-1963
	Yvan Cournoyer	1963-1979
16	Henri Richard	1955-1975
	Elmer Lach	1940-1954
18	Serge Savard	1966-1981
19	Larry Robinson	1972-1989
23	Bob Gainey	1973-1989
29	Ken Dryden	1970-1979
33	Patrick Roy	1984-1996

All-time Record vs. Other Clubs

Regular Season

	At Home								On Road								Total							
	GP	W	L	T	OL	GF	GA	PTS	GP	W	L	T	OL	GF	GA	PTS	GP	W	L	T	OL	GF	GA	PTS
Anaheim	10	4	4	2	0	31	30	10	10	6	4	0	0	32	31	12	20	10	8	2	0	63	61	22
Atlanta	20	14	4	0	2	69	48	30	20	11	5	2	2	53	41	26	40	25	9	2	4	122	89	56
Boston	352	203	100	47	2	1184	829	455	353	136	157	56	4	956	1034	332	705	339	257	103	6	2140	1863	787
Buffalo	121	66	39	12	4	437	351	148	120	36	61	19	4	315	376	95	241	102	100	31	8	752	727	243
Calgary	49	28	13	8	0	172	118	64	52	26	18	7	1	171	159	60	101	54	31	15	1	343	277	124
Carolina	85	52	24	7	2	327	250	113	88	40	33	13	2	300	257	95	173	92	57	20	4	627	507	208
Chicago	278	176	54	48	0	1075	657	400	275	125	95	55	0	764	736	305	553	301	149	103	0	1839	1393	705
Colorado	66	39	16	10	1	271	206	89	65	27	32	5	1	227	220	60	131	66	48	15	2	498	426	149
Columbus	6	2	2	1	1	11	12	6	3	2	0	0	1	9	7	5	9	4	2	1	2	20	19	11
Dallas	60	39	12	9	0	259	149	87	61	31	18	12	0	207	158	74	121	70	30	21	0	466	307	161
Detroit	284	172	68	43	1	997	643	388	282	98	130	53	1	720	808	250	566	270	198	96	2	1717	1451	638
Edmonton	33	19	9	4	1	117	104	43	38	17	19	0	2	120	132	36	71	36	28	4	3	237	236	79
Florida	31	15	11	3	2	82	69	35	32	13	16	3	0	84	93	29	63	28	27	6	2	166	162	64
Los Angeles	66	47	8	11	0	296	165	105	67	39	19	9	0	265	203	87	133	86	27	20	0	561	368	192
Minnesota	5	2	2	1	0	14	13	5	4	2	1	0	1	10	11	5	9	4	3	1	1	24	24	10
Nashville	6	5	0	0	1	22	16	11	6	2	3	1	0	13	21	5	12	7	3	1	1	35	37	16
New Jersey	64	35	21	6	2	199	158	78	64	27	32	4	1	211	196	59	128	62	53	10	3	410	354	137
NY Islanders	70	43	16	9	2	250	189	97	70	31	30	6	3	202	209	71	140	74	46	15	5	452	398	168
NY Rangers	300	196	63	40	1	1166	702	433	300	122	122	54	2	869	867	300	600	318	185	94	3	2035	1569	733
Ottawa	51	26	20	4	1	149	146	57	49	21	24	1	3	135	156	46	100	47	44	5	4	284	302	103
Philadelphia	84	41	28	14	1	285	250	97	83	36	30	16	1	252	247	89	167	77	58	30	2	537	497	186
Phoenix	31	26	3	2	0	151	69	54	31	15	9	7	0	120	98	37	62	41	12	9	0	271	167	91
Pittsburgh	92	66	16	10	0	417	238	142	92	45	32	13	2	321	278	105	184	111	48	23	2	738	516	247
St. Louis	61	41	11	7	2	261	169	91	59	30	14	15	0	202	152	75	120	71	25	22	2	463	321	166
San Jose	13	9	2	2	0	45	24	20	13	4	6	2	1	34	42	11	26	13	8	4	1	79	66	31
Tampa Bay	32	17	13	1	1	90	78	36	33	15	13	5	0	89	79	35	65	32	26	6	1	179	157	71
Toronto	351	207	97	43	4	1224	884	461	351	125	178	45	3	927	1071	298	702	332	275	88	7	2151	1955	759
Vancouver	56	40	11	5	0	250	141	85	58	33	16	8	1	207	163	75	114	73	27	13	1	457	304	160
Washington	70	41	18	8	3	265	158	93	69	28	30	9	2	205	195	67	139	69	48	17	5	470	353	160
Defunct Clubs	231	148	58	25	0	779	469	321	230	98	97	35	0	586	606	231	461	246	155	60	0	1365	1075	552
Totals	**2978**	**1819**	**743**	**382**	**34**	**10895**	**7335**	**4054**	**2978**	**1241**	**1244**	**455**	**38**	**8606**	**8646**	**2975**	**5956**	**3060**	**1987**	**837**	**72**	**19501**	**15981**	**7029**

Playoffs

	Series	W	L	GP	W	L	T	GF	GA	Last Mtg.	Rnd.	Result
Boston	32	24	8	163	99	64	0	494	403	2009	CQF	L 0-4
Buffalo	7	4	3	35	18	17	0	124	111	1998	CSF	L 0-4
Calgary	2	1	1	11	6	5	0	31	32	1989	F	L 2-4
Carolina	7	5	2	39	23	16	0	125	106	2006	CQF	L 2-4
Chicago	17	12	5	81	50	29	2	261	185	1976	QF	W 4-0
Colorado	5	3	2	31	17	14	0	105	85	1993	DSF	W 4-2
Dallas	2	1	1	13	7	6	0	48	37	1980	QF	L 3-4
Detroit	12	5	7	62	33	29	0	161	149	1978	QF	W 4-1
Edmonton	1	0	1	3	0	3	0	6	15	1981	PRE	L 0-3
Los Angeles	1	1	0	5	4	1	0	15	12	1993	F	W 4-1
New Jersey	1	0	1	5	1	4	0	11	22	1997	CQF	L 1-4
NY Islanders	4	3	1	22	14	8	0	64	55	1993	CF	W 4-1
NY Rangers	14	7	7	61	34	25	2	188	158	1996	CQF	L 2-4
Philadelphia	6	3	3	31	16	15	0	93	89	2010	CF	L 1-4
Pittsburgh	2	2	0	13	8	5	0	37	33	2010	CSF	W 4-3
St. Louis	3	3	0	12	12	0	0	42	14	1977	QF	W 4-0
Tampa Bay	1	0	1	4	0	4	0	5	14	2004	CSF	L 0-4
Toronto	15	8	7	71	42	29	0	215	160	1979	QF	W 4-0
Vancouver	1	1	0	5	4	1	0	20	9	1975	QF	W 4-1
Washington	1	1	0	7	4	3	0	20	22	2010	CQF	W 4-3
Defunct Clubs	10*	5	4	28	15	9	4	70	71			
Totals	**144***	**89**	**54**	**702**	**407**	**287**	**8**	**2135**	**1782**			

Playoff Results 2010-2006

Year	Round	Opponent	Result	GF	GA
2010	CF	Philadelphia	L 1-4	7	17
	CSF	Pittsburgh	W 4-3	19	18
	CQF	Washington	W 4-3	20	22
2009	CQF	Boston	L 0-4	6	17
2008	CSF	Philadelphia	L 1-4	14	20
	CQF	Boston	W 4-3	19	15
2006	CQF	Carolina	L 2-4	17	15

Abbreviations: Round: F - Final; **CF** - conference final; **CSF** - conference semi-final; **CQF** - conference quarter-final; **DSF** - division semi-final; **QF** - quarter-final; **PRE** - preliminary round.

Calgary totals include Atlanta Flames, 1972-73 to 1979-80.
Carolina totals include Hartford, 1979-80 to 1996-97.
Colorado totals include Quebec, 1979-80 to 1994-95.
Dallas totals include Minnesota North Stars, 1967-68 to 1992-93.
New Jersey totals include Kansas City, 1974-75, 1975-76, and Colorado Rockies, 1976-77 to 1981-82.
Phoenix totals include Winnipeg, 1979-80 to 1995-96.

2009-10 Results

Oct.	1	at Toronto	4-3*
	3	at Buffalo	2-1*
	6	at Calgary	3-4
	7	at Vancouver	1-7
	10	at Edmonton	2-3
	15	Colorado	2-3
	17	Ottawa	1-3
	20	Atlanta	2-1†
	22	NY Islanders	5-1
	24	NY Rangers	5-4*
	26	NY Islanders	3-2*
	28	at Pittsburgh	1-6
	30	at Chicago	2-3
	31	Toronto	5-4†
Nov.	3	Atlanta	4-5
	5	at Boston	2-1†
	7	Tampa Bay	1-3
	10	Calgary	0-1
	12	at Phoenix	4-2
	14	at Nashville	0-2
	17	Carolina	3-2†
	20	at Washington	3-2
	21	Detroit	2-3†
	24	Columbus	5-3
	25	at Pittsburgh	1-3
	28	Washington	3-4†
Dec.	1	Toronto	0-3
	3	at Buffalo	2-6
	4	Boston	5-1
	7	Philadelphia	3-1
	8	at Ottawa	4-1
	10	Pittsburgh	2-3
	12	at Atlanta	3-4*
	14	Buffalo	3-4
	16	at New Jersey	1-2
	17	Minnesota	1-3
	19	at NY Islanders	3-0
	21	at Atlanta	4-3*
	23	at Carolina	5-1
	26	at Toronto	3-2*
	28	at Ottawa	2-4
	30	at Tampa Bay	2-1*
	31	at Florida	5-4
Jan.	3	Buffalo	0-1
	5	at Washington	2-4
	7	Florida	2-0
	9	New Jersey	1-2*
	14	Dallas	5-3
	16	Ottawa	2-4
	17	at NY Rangers	2-6
	20	St. Louis	3-4*
	22	at New Jersey	3-1
	23	NY Rangers	6-0
	26	at Florida	1-2
	27	at Tampa Bay	0-3
	30	at Ottawa	2-3*
Feb.	2	Vancouver	3-2
	4	at Boston	3-2†
	6	Pittsburgh	5-3
	7	Boston	0-3
	10	Washington	6-5*
	12	at Philadelphia	2-3
	13	Philadelphia	2-6
Mar.	2	at Boston	4-1
	4	at San Jose	2-3
	6	at Los Angeles	4-2
	7	at Anaheim	4-3†
	9	Tampa Bay	5-3
	11	Edmonton	5-4†
	13	Boston	3-2
	16	at NY Rangers	3-1
	20	at Toronto	2-3†
	22	Ottawa	0-2
	24	at Buffalo	2-3†
	25	Florida	4-1
	27	New Jersey	2-4
	31	Carolina	1-2
Apr.	2	at Philadelphia	1-0
	3	Buffalo	3-0
	6	at NY Islanders	3-4†
	8	at Carolina	2-5
	10	Toronto	3-4*

* – Overtime † – Shootout

Entry Draft Selections 2010-1996

Name in bold denotes played in NHL.

2010
Pick
22	Jarred Tinordi
113	Mark MacMillan
117	Morgan Ellis
147	Brendan Gallagher
207	John Westin

2009
Pick
18	Louis Leblanc
65	Joonas Nattinen
79	Mac Bennett
109	Alexander Avtsin
139	Gabriel Dumont
169	Dustin Walsh
199	Michael Cichy
211	Petteri Simila

2008
Pick
56	Danny Kristo
86	Steve Quailer
116	Jason Missiaen
138	Maxim Trunev
206	Patrick Johnson

2007
Pick
12	**Ryan McDonagh**
22	**Max Pacioretty**
43	**P.K. Subban**
65	Olivier Fortier
73	**Yannick Weber**
133	Joe Stejskal
142	Andrew Conboy
163	Nichlas Torp
192	Scott Kishel

2006
Pick
20	David Fischer
49	**Ben Maxwell**
53	**Mathieu Carle**
66	**Ryan White**
139	Pavel Valentenko
199	Cameron Cepek

2005
Pick
5	**Carey Price**
45	**Guillaume Latendresse**
121	Juraj Mikus
130	Mathieu Aubin
190	**Matt D'Agostini**
200	**Sergei Kostitsyn**
229	Philippe Paquet

2004
Pick
18	**Kyle Chipchura**
84	Alexei Yemelin
100	**James Wyman**
150	**Mikhail Grabovski**
181	Loic Lacasse
212	Jon Gleed
246	Greg Stewart
262	**Mark Streit**
278	Alex Dulac-Lemelin

2003
Pick
10	**Andrei Kostitsyn**
40	Cory Urquhart
61	**Maxim Lapierre**
79	**Ryan O'Byrne**
113	**Corey Locke**
123	Danny Stewart
177	Chris Heino-Lindberg
188	**Mark Flood**
217	Oskari Korpikari
241	Jimmy Bonneau
271	**Jaroslav Halak**

2002
Pick
14	**Christopher Higgins**
45	Tomas Linhart
99	Michael Lambert
182	Andre Deveaux
212	Jonathan Ferland
275	Konstantin Korneev

2001
Pick
7	**Mike Komisarek**
25	**Alexander Perezhogin**
37	**Duncan Milroy**
71	**Tomas Plekanec**
109	**Martti Jarventie**
171	Eric Himelfarb
203	Andrew Archer
266	Viktor Ujcik

2000
Pick
13	**Ron Hainsey**
16	**Marcel Hossa**
78	Jozef Balej
79	Tyler Hanchuck
109	Johan Eneqvist
114	Christian Larrivee
145	Ryan Glenn
172	Scott Selig
182	Petr Chvojka
243	Joni Puurula
275	Jonathan Gauthier

1999
Pick
39	Alexander Buturlin
58	**Matt Carkner**
97	Chris Dyment
107	Evan Lindsay
136	Dusty Jamieson
145	Marc-Andre Thinel
150	Matt Shasby
167	Sean Dixon
196	Vadim Tarasov
225	Mikko Hyytia
253	Jerome Marois

1998
Pick
16	**Eric Chouinard**
45	**Mike Ribeiro**
75	**Francois Beauchemin**
132	**Andrei Bashkirov**
152	**Gordie Dwyer**
162	**Andrei Markov**
189	Andrei Kruchinin
201	Craig Murray
216	**Michael Ryder**
247	Darcy Harris

1997
Pick
11	**Jason Ward**
37	Gregor Baumgartner
65	Ilkka Mikkola
91	Daniel Tetrault
118	Konstantin Sidulov
122	Gennady Razin
145	Jonathan Desroches
172	**Ben Guite**
197	Petr Kubos
202	Andrei Sidyakin
228	Jarl Espen Ygranes

1996
Pick
18	**Matt Higgins**
44	**Mathieu Garon**
71	**Arron Asham**
92	Kim Staal
99	Etienne Drapeau
127	Daniel Archambault
154	**Brett Clark**
181	Timo Vertala
207	Mattia Baldi
233	Michel Tremblay

Captains' History

Jack Laviolette, 1909-10; Newsy Lalonde, 1910-11; Jack Laviolette, 1911-12; Newsy Lalonde, 1912-13; Jimmy Gardner, 1913-14, 1914-15; Howard McNamara, 1915-16; Newsy Lalonde, 1916-17 to 1921-22; Sprague Cleghorn, 1922-23 to 1924-25; Bill Coutu, 1925-26; Sylvio Mantha, 1926-27 to 1931-32; George Hainsworth, 1932-33; Sylvio Mantha, 1933-34 to 1935-36; Babe Siebert, 1936-37 to 1938-39; Walt Buswell, 1939-40; Toe Blake, 1940-41 to 1946-47; Toe Blake and Bill Durnan, 1947-48; Butch Bouchard, 1948-49 to 1955-56; Maurice Richard, 1956-57 to 1959-60; Doug Harvey, 1960-61; Jean Béliveau, 1961-62 to 1970-71; Henri Richard, 1971-72 to 1974-75; Yvan Cournoyer, 1975-76 to 1978-79; Serge Savard, 1979-80, 1980-81; Bob Gainey, 1981-82 to 1988-89; Guy Carbonneau and Chris Chelios, 1989-90; Guy Carbonneau, 1990-91 to 1993-94; Kirk Muller and Mike Keane, 1994-95; Mike Keane and Pierre Turgeon, 1995-96; Pierre Turgeon and Vincent Damphousse, 1996-97; Vincent Damphousse, 1997-98, 1998-99; Saku Koivu, 1999-2000 to 2008-09; no captain, 2009-10.

General Managers' History

Jack Laviolette and Joseph Cattarinich, 1909-1910; George Kennedy, 1910-11 to 1920-21; Leo Dandurand, 1921-22 to 1934-35; Ernest Savard, 1935-36; Cecil Hart, 1936-37 to 1938-39; Jules Dugal, 1939-40; Tom P. Gorman, 1940-41 to 1945-46; Frank J. Selke, 1946-47 to 1963-64; Sam Pollock, 1964-65 to 1977-78; Irving Grundman, 1978-79 to 1982-83; Serge Savard, 1983-84 to 1994-95; Serge Savard and Réjean Houle, 1995-96; Réjean Houle, 1996-97 to 1999-2000; Réjean Houle and Andre Savard, 2000-01; Andre Savard, 2001-02, 2002-03; Bob Gainey, 2003-04 to 2008-09; Bob Gainey and Pierre Gauthier, 2009-10; Pierre Gauthier, 2010-11.

Pierre Gauthier
Executive Vice President and General Manager

Born: Montreal, Que., May 28, 1953.

Pierre Gauthier joined the Montreal Canadiens organization as director of professional scouting on July 21, 2003. On February 8, 2010, he was named general manager to replace Bob Gainey while keeping the responsibilities attached to professional scouting. Prior to his promotion, he held the assistant general manager position since June 2006.

Gauthier worked with the Mighty Ducks of Anaheim during six seasons, serving as the team's assistant general manager from 1993 to 1995. Following three seasons as general manager of the Ottawa Senators from 1995 to 1998, he returned to the Mighty Ducks' organization as president and general manager from 1998 to 2002. Gauthier originally came to the Anaheim organization from the Quebec Nordiques where he spent 12 seasons from 1981 to 1993, serving in all areas of scouting.

Gauthier also made his mark on the international hockey scene. Along with Bob Gainey and Bobby Clarke, he was one of three NHL general managers for the Canadian national team at the 1998 Olympic Games in Nagano. He was also Team Canada's general manager for the gold-medal winning team at the 1997 World Championships in Finland, as well as the silver medal-winning team at the 1996 World Championship in Austria.

Club Directory

Bell Centre

Club de hockey Canadien
1909, avenue des
Canadiens-de-Montréal
Montréal, QC H4B 5G0
Phone: **514/932-2582**
Media Hotline: 514/989-2835
Fax Lines (all area code 514):
Communications 932-8285
Hockey 989-2717
Press Lounge 932-5258
Marketing 925-2145
Community Relations 925-2144
www.canadiens.com
Capacity: 21,273

Executive Management
Chairman of the Board and Owner	Geoff Molson
President and CEO, Club de hockey Canadien, Bell Centre & evenko	Pierre Boivin
Executive Vice President Hockey and G.M.	Pierre Gauthier
Chief Financial Officer	Fred Steer
Vice President and Chief Sales and Marketing Officer	Ray Lalonde
Vice President, Communications and Community Relations	Donald Beauchamp
Vice President, Building Operations	Alain Gauthier
Vice President & General Manager, evenko	Jacques Aubé
President, Effix – Advertising and Sponsorship Sales	François Seigneur
President, Canadiens Alumni	Réjean Houle
Administrative Assistant to the President	Rolande Bernier

Hockey Operations
Assistant General Manager/Player Personnel	Larry Carrière
Special Advisor to the General Manager	Bob Gainey
Director of Hockey Operations	Patrick Boivin
Head Coach	Jacques Martin
Assistant Coaches	Perry Pearn, Kirk Muller
Assistant Coach and Goaltending Coach	Pierre Groulx
Video Coach	Mario Leblanc
Director of Player Recruitment and Development	Trevor Timmins
Professional Scouts	Doug Gibson, Vaughn Karpan
Amateur Scouting Staff	Elmer Benning, Bill Berglund, Serge Boisvert, Ryan Jankowski, Frank Jay, Hannu Laine, Mike McCann, Christer Rockstrom, Pat Westrum
Team Services and Hockey Admin. Manager	Claudine Crépin
Coordinator of Hockey Information	Ken Morin
Team Services Coordinator	Alain Gagnon

Medical and Training Staff
Club Physician and Chief Surgeon	Dr. David Mulder
Assistants to the Chief Surgeon	Dr. Tarek Razek, Dr. Kosar Khwaja
Dentist	Dr. Jean-François Desjardins
Consultant, Ophthalmologist	Dr. John Little
Head Athletic Therapist	Graham Rynbend
Athletic Therapist	Nick Addey-Jibb
Consultant, Ostheopathy	Dave Campbell
Consultant, Physiotherapy	Donald Balmforth
Strength & Conditioning Coordinator	Pierre Allard
Equipment Manager	Pierre Gervais
Assistants to the Equipment Manager	Richard Généreux, Patrick Langlois, Pierre Ouellette

Communications
Director of Media Relations	Dominick Saillant
Administrative Asst. to the V.P. Communications	Sylvie Lambert
Manager, Research and Translation	Carl Lavigne
Communications Coordinator	François Marchand

Community Relations
Director of Community Relations / Exec. Dir., Children's Foundation	Geneviève Paquette
Manager, Event and Communications, Children's Foundation	Marie-Christine Boucher
Community Relations Coordinator	Ryan Frank
Coordinator, Donations and Administration, Children's Foundation	Sylvie Nadeau
Project Manager, Children's Foundation	Patrick Mahoney

Marketing and Sales
Director, Group Sales and Administration	Pierre Constant
Executive Director, Luxury Suites and Services	Richard Primeau
Director, Ticket Sales	Vincent Lucier
Director, Marketing and Broadcast	Jon Trzcienski
Director, Consumer Products	Matt Zalkowitz
Director, Publications and Creative Services	Jean Simard
Group Manager, Game Production	Paul Gallant
Group Manager, Digital Media	Alexandre Harvey
Manager, Publications and Editorial	Manny Almela
Manager, Luxury Suites Services	Sabina D'Ascoli
Coordinator, Ticket Sales and Services	Sandra Fernandes TBC
Manager, Event Planning and Logistics	David McGinnis
Manager, Youth Hockey	Stéphane Verret

Building Operations
Director of Ticket Office	Cathy D'Ascoli
Assistant Director of Ticket Office	Lucie Masse
Director of Building Operations	Xavier Luydlin
Director of Concessions	Alec Beaudry
Director of Customer Satisfaction	Caroline Hamel
Administrative Assistant to the VP Operations	Maryse Cartwright

Finance
Exec. Dir, Info. and Communication Technology	Pierre-Éric Belzile
Controller	Dennis McKinley
Assistant Controller	Raymond Lamarche
Administrator, Human Resources	Susan Cryans
Administrative Assistant, Chief Financial Officer	Christine Ouellette

Broadcasting
Play-by-play - Radio/TV	Pierre Houde (RDS), Martin McGuire (CKAC), Rick Moffat (CJAD)
Colormen - Radio/TV	Benoit Brunet (RDS), Dany Dubé (CKAC), TBC (CJAD)
Radio/Television Flagships	RDS (Cable 33), CKAC (730 AM), CJAD (800 AM)

Nashville Predators

2009-10 Results: 47W-29L-2OTL-4SOL 100PTS.
Third, Central Division

Key Off-Season Signings/Acquisitions

2010

Apr. 29 • Re-signed RW **Wade Belak**.

June 15 • Signed 2006 2nd round pick and 2010 Hobey Baker Trophy winner, LW **Blake Geoffrion** (Univ. of Wisconsin).

18 • Re-signed D **Francis Bouillon**.

19 • Acquired D **Ryan Parent** from Philadelphia for the rights to D **Dan Hamhuis** and a conditional pick in the 2011 Entry Draft.

19 • Acquired RW **Matt Halischuk** and New Jersey's 2nd round pick in the 2011 Entry Draft from New Jersey for C **Jason Arnott**.

29 • Acquired LW **Sergei Kostitsyn** from Montreal for C **Dustin Boyd** and G **Dan Ellis**.

July 1 • Re-signed D **Teemu Laakso**.

2 • Signed C **Matthew Lombardi**.

16 • Signed C **Jamie Lundmark**.

Year-by-Year Record

		Home				Road				Overall						
Season	GP	W	L	T	OL	W	L	T	OL	W	L	T	OL	GF	GA	Pts.	Finished	Playoff Result
2009-10	82	24	14	....	3	23	15	....	3	47	29	....	6	225	225	100	3rd, Central Div.	Lost Conf. Quarter-Final
2008-09	82	24	13	....	4	16	21	....	4	40	34	....	8	213	233	88	5th, Central Div.	Out of Playoffs
2007-08	82	23	14	....	4	18	18	....	5	41	32	....	9	230	229	91	2nd, Central Div.	Lost Conf. Quarter-Final
2006-07	82	28	8	....	5	23	15	....	3	51	23	....	8	272	212	110	2nd, Central Div.	Lost Conf. Quarter-Final
2005-06	82	32	8	....	1	17	17	....	7	49	25	....	8	259	227	106	2nd, Central Div.	Lost Conf. Quarter-Final
2004-05	....	....								....				....				
2003-04	82	22	10	7	2	16	19	4	2	38	29	11	4	216	217	91	3rd, Central Div.	Lost Conf. Quarter-Final
2002-03	82	18	17	5	1	9	18	8	6	27	35	13	7	183	206	74	4th, Central Div.	Out of Playoffs
2001-02	82	17	16	8	0	11	25	5	0	28	41	13	0	196	230	69	4th, Central Div.	Out of Playoffs
2000-01	82	16	18	7	0	18	18	2	3	34	36	9	3	186	200	80	3rd, Central Div.	Out of Playoffs
1999-2000	82	15	21	3	2	13	19	4	5	28	40	7	7	199	240	70	4th, Central Div.	Out of Playoffs
1998-99	82	15	22	4	....	13	25	3	....	28	47	7	....	190	261	63	4th, Central Div.	Out of Playoffs

2010-11 Schedule

Oct.	Sat.	9	Anaheim	Tue.	11	Minnesota
	Wed.	13	at Chicago	Thu.	13	at Florida
	Thu.	14	St. Louis	Sat.	15	Chicago
	Sat.	16	Washington	Sun.	16	at Chicago
	Tue.	19	Calgary	Tue.	18	at Phoenix
	Thu.	21	Pittsburgh	Thu.	20	at Colorado
	Sat.	23	at Dallas	Sun.	23	at Edmonton
	Sun.	24	at Tampa Bay	Mon.	24	at Calgary
	Thu.	28	St. Louis	Wed.	26	at Vancouver
	Sat.	30	at Detroit	**Feb.** Tue.	1	Calgary
Nov.	Wed.	3	at Phoenix	Thu.	3	at Philadelphia
	Sat.	6	at Los Angeles*	Sat.	5	Detroit
	Sun.	7	at Anaheim*	Mon.	7	Edmonton
	Thu.	11	at St. Louis	Wed.	9	at Detroit
	Sat.	13	Chicago	Sat.	12	Colorado
	Tue.	16	at Toronto	Tue.	15	San Jose
	Thu.	18	at Montreal	Thu.	17	Vancouver
	Sat.	20	at Carolina	Sat.	19	Phoenix
	Mon.	22	at Columbus	Tue.	22	at Columbus
	Wed.	24	St. Louis	Thu.	24	Chicago
	Fri.	26	at Minnesota*	Sat.	26	at Dallas*
	Sat.	27	NY Rangers	Sun.	27	Columbus*
	Tue.	30	Phoenix	**Mar.** Tue.	1	at Edmonton
Dec.	Wed.	1	at Columbus	Thu.	3	at Vancouver
	Sat.	4	Carolina	Sun.	6	at Calgary
	Mon.	6	at Atlanta	Tue.	8	at San Jose
	Wed.	8	at Detroit	Thu.	10	Minnesota
	Sat.	11	Florida	Sat.	12	Colorado
	Mon.	13	NY Islanders	Tue.	15	Los Angeles
	Wed.	15	San Jose	Thu.	17	Boston
	Fri.	17	at New Jersey	Sat.	19	Detroit
	Sat.	18	Los Angeles	Sun.	20	at Buffalo*
	Wed.	22	at Chicago	Tue.	22	Edmonton
	Thu.	23	Ottawa	Thu.	24	Anaheim
	Sun.	26	at St. Louis	Sat.	26	Dallas
	Tue.	28	Dallas	Tue.	29	Vancouver
	Fri.	31	at Minnesota*	Thu.	31	at Colorado
Jan.	Sun.	2	Columbus*	**Apr.** Sat.	2	Detroit*
	Wed.	5	at Anaheim	Tue.	5	Atlanta
	Thu.	6	at Los Angeles	Fri.	8	Columbus
	Sat.	8	at San Jose*	Sat.	9	at St. Louis

* Denotes afternoon game.

After collecting just two goals in 28 games as a rookie in 2008-09, Patric Hornqvist scored a team-leading 30 goals in 80 games for the Predators in 2009-10

**CENTRAL DIVISION
13th NHL Season**

Franchise date: June 25, 1997

2010-11 Player Personnel

FORWARDS	HT	WT	S	Place of Birth	*Age	2009-10 Club
ANDERSSON, Jonas	6-3	204	L	Stockholm, Sweden	29	Dynamo Minsk
BELAK, Wade	6-5	222	R	Saskatoon, Sask.	34	Nashville
DUMONT, J.P.	6-1	205	L	Montreal, Que.	32	Nashville
ERAT, Martin	6-0	200	L	Trebic, Czech.	29	Nashville
GOC, Marcel	6-1	202	L	Calw, West Germany	27	Nashville
HALISCHUK, Matt	6-0	186	R	Toronto, Ont.	22	New Jersey-Lowell
HORNQVIST, Patric	5-11	188	L	Sollentuna, Sweden	23	Nashville
KLASEN, Linus	5-8	184	L	Stockholm, Sweden	24	Sodertalje
KOSTITSYN, Sergei	6-0	210	L	Novopolotsk, USSR	23	Montreal-Hamilton
LEGWAND, David	6-2	204	L	Detroit, MI	30	Nashville
LOMBARDI, Matthew	6-0	198	L	Montreal, Que.	28	Phoenix
LUNDMARK, Jamie	6-0	197	R	Edmonton, Alta.	29	Cgy-Abbotsford-Tor
O'REILLY, Cal	6-0	187	L	Toronto, Ont.	24	Nashville-Milwaukee
SMITHSON, Jerred	6-3	206	R	Vernon, B.C.	31	Nashville
SPALING, Nick	6-1	195	L	Palmerston, Ont.	22	Nashville-Milwaukee
SULLIVAN, Steve	5-8	161	R	Timmins, Ont.	36	Nashville
THURESSON, Andreas	6-1	212	R	Kristianstad, Sweden	22	Nashville-Milwaukee
TOOTOO, Jordin	5-9	197	R	Churchill, Man.	27	Nashville
WARD, Joel	6-1	218	R	Toronto, Ont.	29	Nashville
WILSON, Colin	6-1	219	L	Greenwich, CT	20	Nashville-Milwaukee
DEFENSEMEN						
BLUM, Jonathon	6-1	192	R	Long Beach, CA	21	Milwaukee
BOUILLON, Francis	5-8	198	L	New York, NY	34	Nashville
FRANSON, Cody	6-5	213	R	Salmon Arm, B.C.	23	Nashville-Milwaukee
JOSI, Roman	6-2	198	L	Bern, Switzerland	20	Bern
KLEIN, Kevin	6-1	201	R	Kitchener, Ont.	25	Nashville
LAAKSO, Teemu	6-1	209	R	Tuusula, Finland	23	Nashville-Milwaukee
PARENT, Ryan	6-3	198	L	Prince Albert, Sask.	23	Philadelphia
SULZER, Alexander	6-1	204	L	Kaufbeuren, W. Germany	26	Nashville-Milwaukee
SUTER, Ryan	6-1	198	L	Madison, WI	25	Nashville
WEBER, Shea	6-4	234	R	Sicamous, B.C.	25	Nashville

GOALTENDERS	HT	WT	C	Place of Birth	*Age	2009-10 Club
DEKANICH, Mark	6-2	190	L	N. Vancouver, B.C.	24	Milwaukee-Cincinnati (ECHL)
LINDBACK, Anders	6-6	212	L	Gavle, Sweden	22	Timra
PICKARD, Chet	6-2	210	L	Moncton, N.B.	20	Milwaukee
RINNE, Pekka	6-5	207	L	Kempele, Finland	27	Nashville

* – Age at start of 2010-11 season

Barry Trotz

Head Coach

Born: Winnipeg, Man., July 15, 1962.

The only head coach in the history of the Nashville Predators, Barry Trotz was hired on August 6, 1997. He is the second-longest tenured coach in the NHL behind Buffalo's Lindy Ruff. Trotz was hired after serving four seasons as head coach and director of hockey operations for the American Hockey League's Portland Pirates. He and assistant Paul Gardner spent the 1997-98 season scouting in preparation for the inaugural season of the Predators. In his sixth season behind the bench in 2003-04, Trotz led Nashville into the playoffs for the first time. During the 2006-07 season, Nashville was in contention for first overall in the NHL, setting club records with 51 wins and 110 points. In 2007-08, Trotz led a rebuilt Nashville roster back to the playoffs for the fourth consecutive season. After missing the playoffs in 2008-09, the Predators rebounded with a 100-point season in 2009-10 and a return to the postseason. Trotz was rewarded with a nomination for the Jack Adams Award as coach of the year.

Trotz began his coaching career in 1984 as assistant coach with the University of Manitoba for one season, before serving two seasons as the head coach and general manager of the Dauphin Kings Junior Hockey Club from 1985 to 1987. He became head coach of the University of Manitoba during the 1987 season and also served as a scout for the Spokane Chiefs of the Western Hockey League that season. Trotz joined the Washington Capitals organization as their chief western scout during the 1988 season. The Winnipeg, Manitoba native was appointed an assistant coach of the Capitals' American Hockey League affiliate in Baltimore prior to the 1991 season before being named head coach prior to the 1992 season. When the franchise relocated to Portland, he guided the Pirates to two AHL Calder Cup Final appearances in the club's first four seasons. He led the Pirates to a league-best 43-27-10 record, captured the Calder Cup championship and was named the American Hockey League coach of the year following the 1994-95 season.

In 1995, Trotz guided Portland to a new North American professional hockey league record 17-game unbeaten streak (14-0-3) to start the season. He was named head coach for the U.S. team at the American Hockey League All-Star Game in 1996.

Prior to his coaching career, Trotz played junior hockey for the Western Hockey League's Regina Pats from 1979-83. During that time, he recorded 39 goals, 121 assists for 160 points, along with 490 penalty minutes in 204 games.

Coaching Record

			Regular Season				Playoffs			
Season	Team	League	GC	W	L	O/T	GC	W	L	T
1992-93	Baltimore	AHL	80	28	40	12	7	3	4	....
1993-94	Portland	AHL	80	43	27	10	8	6	2	....
1994-95	Portland	AHL	80	46	22	12	7	3	4	....
1995-96	Portland	AHL	80	32	34	14	24	14	10	....
1996-97	Portland	AHL	80	37	26	17	5	2	3	....
1998-99	**Nashville**	**NHL**	**82**	**28**	**47**	**7**	....	....	....	....
99-2000	**Nashville**	**NHL**	**82**	**28**	**40**	**14**	....	....	....	....
2000-01	**Nashville**	**NHL**	**82**	**34**	**36**	**12**	....	....	....	....
2001-02	**Nashville**	**NHL**	**82**	**28**	**41**	**13**	....	....	....	....
2002-03	**Nashville**	**NHL**	**82**	**27**	**35**	**20**	....	....	....	....
2003-04	**Nashville**	**NHL**	**82**	**38**	**29**	**15**	**6**	**2**	**4**	....
2004-05	**Nashville**				SEASON CANCELLED					
2005-06	**Nashville**	**NHL**	**82**	**49**	**25**	**8**	**5**	**1**	**4**	....
2006-07	**Nashville**	**NHL**	**82**	**51**	**23**	**8**	**5**	**1**	**4**	....
2007-08	**Nashville**	**NHL**	**82**	**41**	**32**	**9**	**6**	**2**	**4**	....
2008-09	**Nashville**	**NHL**	**82**	**40**	**34**	**8**	....	....	....	....
2009-10	**Nashville**	**NHL**	**82**	**47**	**29**	**6**	**6**	**2**	**4**	....
	NHL Totals		**902**	**411**	**371**	**120**	**28**	**8**	**20**	....

2009-10 Scoring

* – rookie

Regular Season

Pos	#	Player	Team	GP	G	A	Pts	TOI	+/–	PIM	PP	SH	GW	S	%
R	27	Patric Hornqvist	NSH	80	30	21	51	15:41	18	40	10	0	8	275	10.9
L	26	Steve Sullivan	NSH	82	17	34	51	17:55	2	35	5	0	4	152	11.2
R	10	Martin Erat	NSH	74	21	28	49	17:59	–7	50	5	0	2	168	12.5
C	19	Jason Arnott	NSH	63	19	27	46	18:41	0	26	6	0	3	216	8.8
R	71	J.P. Dumont	NSH	74	17	28	45	14:46	8	20	3	1	3	112	15.2
D	6	Shea Weber	NSH	78	16	27	43	23:10	0	36	7	0	3	222	7.2
C	11	David Legwand	NSH	82	11	27	38	18:42	–5	24	0	1	3	151	7.3
D	20	Ryan Suter	NSH	82	4	33	37	23:58	4	48	2	0	1	125	3.2
R	29	Joel Ward	NSH	71	13	21	34	17:32	–5	18	3	1	1	134	9.7
C	9	Marcel Goc	NSH	73	12	18	30	14:41	10	14	0	0	1	118	10.2
C	14	Dustin Boyd	CGY	60	8	11	19	12:14	5	15	0	0	2	80	10.0
			NSH	18	3	2	5	12:11	1	4	0	0	1	32	9.4
			Total	78	11	13	24	12:13	6	19	0	0	3	112	9.8
D	2	Dan Hamhuis	NSH	78	5	19	24	21:15	4	49	0	0	0	115	4.3
D	37	Denis Grebeshkov	EDM	47	6	13	19	21:49	–16	26	1	0	0	43	14.0
			NSH	4	1	1	2	16:28	0	6	0	0	0	4	25.0
			Total	51	7	14	21	21:24	–16	32	1	0	0	47	14.9
D	32 *	Cody Franson	NSH	61	6	15	21	14:11	15	16	1	0	3	90	6.7
R	22	Jordin Tootoo	NSH	51	6	10	16	10:50	2	40	0	0	1	101	5.9
C	33 *	Colin Wilson	NSH	35	8	7	15	15:09	–2	7	1	0	3	58	13.8
C	25	Jerred Smithson	NSH	69	9	4	13	13:58	–4	54	0	2	1	54	16.7
D	51	Francis Bouillon	NSH	81	3	8	11	19:18	5	50	1	0	1	86	3.5
C	16 *	Cal O'Reilly	NSH	31	2	9	11	13:37	1	4	1	0	0	23	8.7
D	8	Kevin Klein	NSH	81	1	10	11	19:55	–13	27	0	0	0	67	1.5
C	38	Dave Scatchard	NSH	16	3	2	5	10:42	3	17	0	0	0	25	12.0
C	18 *	Mike Santorelli	NSH	25	2	1	3	10:57	–8	8	0	0	0	36	5.6
R	12 *	Andreas Thuresson	NSH	22	1	2	3	9:59	–5	4	0	0	0	30	3.3
C	13 *	Nick Spaling	NSH	28	0	3	3	11:03	3	0	0	0	0	26	0.0
D	52 *	Alexander Sulzer	NSH	20	0	2	2	13:22	4	4	0	0	0	15	0.0
R	3	Wade Belak	NSH	39	0	2	2	4:21	0	58	0	0	0	8	0.0
L	36	Peter Olvecky	NSH	1	0	0	0	7:53	0	0	0	0	0	0	0.0
L	21 *	Triston Grant	NSH	3	0	0	0	7:14	–1	9	0	0	0	2	0.0
C	24	Ben Guite	NSH	6	0	0	0	8:29	–3	4	0	0	0	5	0.0
D	4 *	Teemu Laakso	NSH	7	0	0	0	10:48	–2	2	0	0	0	5	0.0

Goaltending

No.	Goaltender	GPI	Mins	Avg	W	L	OT	EN	SO	GA	SA	S%	G	A	PIM
35	Pekka Rinne	58	3246	2.53	32	16	5	5	7	137	1541	.911	0	0	2
39	Dan Ellis	31	1715	2.69	15	13	1	2	1	77	848	.909	0	1	4
	Totals	**82**	**4991**	**2.66**	**47**	**29**	**6**	**7**	**8**	**221**	**2396**	**.908**			

Playoffs

Pos	#	Player	Team	GP	G	A	Pts	TOI	+/–	PIM	PP	SH	GW	OT	S	%
C	11	David Legwand	NSH	6	2	5	7	19:16	5	8	0	0	1	0	16	12.5
R	10	Martin Erat	NSH	6	4	1	5	18:55	–2	4	0	0	0	0	15	26.7
R	71	J.P. Dumont	NSH	6	2	2	4	14:18	3	0	0	0	1	0	7	28.6
R	29	Joel Ward	NSH	6	2	2	4	19:54	1	2	0	1	0	0	12	16.7
D	6	Shea Weber	NSH	6	2	1	3	24:26	–1	4	0	0	0	0	14	14.3
L	26	Steve Sullivan	NSH	6	0	3	3	17:58	2	2	0	0	0	0	7	0.0
C	19	Jason Arnott	NSH	6	2	0	2	17:50	–3	0	1	0	0	0	26	7.7
D	37	Denis Grebeshkov	NSH	2	0	2	2	11:22	2	0	0	0	0	0	0	0.0
D	2	Dan Hamhuis	NSH	6	0	2	2	22:24	–1	2	0	0	0	0	4	0.0
D	8	Kevin Klein	NSH	6	0	2	2	17:42	1	4	0	0	0	0	2	0.0
C	25	Jerred Smithson	NSH	6	1	0	1	15:35	–1	6	0	0	0	0	5	20.0
R	27	Patric Hornqvist	NSH	2	0	1	1	13:10	–2	4	0	0	0	0	1	0.0
D	32 *	Cody Franson	NSH	4	0	1	1	9:02	1	2	0	0	0	0	5	0.0
C	9	Marcel Goc	NSH	6	0	1	1	16:06	–2	2	0	0	0	0	13	0.0
R	22	Jordin Tootoo	NSH	6	0	1	1	7:57	0	2	0	0	0	0	5	0.0
C	33 *	Colin Wilson	NSH	6	0	1	1	13:42	–1	0	0	0	0	0	8	0.0
C	14	Dustin Boyd	NSH	4	0	0	0	7:03	–1	0	0	0	0	0	4	0.0
D	51	Francis Bouillon	NSH	6	0	0	0	19:37	–1	6	0	0	0	0	3	0.0
D	20	Ryan Suter	NSH	6	0	0	0	24:08	–1	0	0	0	0	0	16	0.0
C	13 *	Nick Spaling	NSH	6	0	0	0	8:23	0	0	0	0	0	0	3	0.0

Goaltending

No.	Goaltender	GPI	Mins	Avg	W	L	EN	SO	GA	SA	S%	G	A	PIM
35	Pekka Rinne	6	358	2.68	2	4	1	0	16	179	.911	0	0	0
	Totals	**6**	**364**	**2.80**	**2**	**4**	**1**	**0**	**17**	**180**	**.906**			

Captains' History

Tom Fitzgerald, 1998-99 to 2001-02; Greg Johnson, 2002-03 to 2005-06; Kimmo Timonen, 2006-07; Jason Arnott, 2007-08 to 2009-10; Shea Weber, 2010-11.

Coaching History

Barry Trotz, 1998-99 to date.

Club Records

Team

(Figures in brackets for season records are games played; records for fewest points, wins, ties, losses, goals, goals against are for 70 or more games)

Most Points	110	2006-07 (82)
Most Wins	51	2006-07 (82)
Most Ties	13	2001-02 (82), 2002-03 (82)
Most Losses	47	1998-99 (82)
Most Goals	272	2006-07 (82)
Most Goals Against	261	1998-99 (82)
Fewest Points	63	1998-99 (82)
Fewest Wins	27	2002-03 (82)
Fewest Ties	7	1998-99 (82)
		1999-2000 (82)
Fewest Losses	23	2006-07 (82)
Fewest Goals	183	2002-03 (82)
Fewest Goals Against	200	2000-01 (82)

Longest Winning Streak
- Overall......8 Oct. 5-25/05
- Home......8 Jan. 6-Feb. 8/07
- Away......7 Oct. 16-Nov. 4/06

Longest Undefeated Streak
- Overall......8 Dec. 18/99-Jan. 1/00
  (5 wins, 3 ties),
  Oct. 5-25/05
  (8 wins)
- Home......11 Dec. 20/03-Jan. 31/04
  (9 wins, 2 ties),
  Nov. 3-Dec. 23/01
  (8 wins, 3 ties)
- Away......7 Oct. 16-Nov. 4/06
  (7 wins)

Longest Losing Streak
- Overall......7 Nov. 20-Dec. 2/99
- Home......6 Jan. 21-Feb. 15/99,
  Feb. 26-Mar. 21/02,
  Feb. 21-Mar. 20/08

- Away......7 Jan. 26-Mar. 5/06,
  Dec. 8/08-Jan. 11/09

Longest Winless Streak
- Overall......15 Mar. 10-Apr. 6/03
  (10 losses, 2 OT losses, 3 ties)
- Home......9 Jan. 21-Mar. 2/99
  (8 losses, 1 tie)
- Away......9 Nov. 2-Dec. 2/01
  (3 losses, 4 OT losses, 2 ties),
  Oct. 11-Nov. 7/02
  (3 losses, 4 OT losses, 2 ties),
  Mar. 12-Apr. 6/03
  (6 losses, 1 OT loss, 2 ties)

Most Shutouts, Season	11	2006-07 (82)
Most PIM, Season	1,533	2005-06 (82)
Most Goals, Game	9	Mar. 4/04

(Nsh. 9 at Pit. 4),
Mar. 18/06
(Cgy. 4 at Nsh. 9)

Individual

Most Seasons	11	David Legwand
Most Games	704	David Legwand
Most Goals, Career	152	David Legwand
Most Assists, Career	255	David Legwand
Most Points, Career	407	David Legwand
		(152G, 255A)
Most PIM, Career	572	Jordin Tootoo
Most Shutouts, Career	21	Tomas Vokoun

Longest Consecutive
- Games Streak......269 Karlis Skrastins
  (Feb. 21/00-Apr. 6/03)
- Most Goals, Season......33 Jason Arnott
  (2008-09)
- Most Assists, Season......54 Paul Kariya
  (2005-06)
- Most Points, Season......85 Paul Kariya
  (2005-06; 31G, 54A)

Most PIM, Season	242	Patrick Cote
		(1998-99)

Most Points, Defenseman,
- Season......55 Kimmo Timonen
  (2006-07; 13G, 42A)

Most Points, Center,
- Season......72 Jason Arnott
  (2007-08; 28G, 44A)

Most Points, Right Wing,
- Season......72 J.P. Dumont
  (2007-08; 29G, 43A)

Most Points, Left Wing,
- Season......85 Paul Kariya
  (2005-06; 31G, 54A)

Most Points, Rookie,
- Season......37 Alexander Radulov
  (2006-07; 18G, 19A)

Most Shutouts, Season......7 Pekka Rinne
  (2008-09) (2009-10)

Most Goals, Game	3	Eighteen times
Most Assists, Game	5	Marek Zidlicky
		(Feb. 18/04)
Most Points, Game	5	Marek Zidlicky

(Feb. 18/04; 5A)
Dan Hamhuis
(Mar. 4/04; 1G, 4A)
J.P. Dumont
(Oct. 22/09; 1G, 4A)

All-time Record vs. Other Clubs

Regular Season

	At Home								On Road								Total							
	GP	W	L	T	OL	GF	GA	PTS	GP	W	L	T	OL	GF	GA	PTS	GP	W	L	T	OL	GF	GA	PTS
Anaheim	22	11	7	2	2	52	50	26	22	5	14	0	3	37	69	13	44	16	21	2	5	89	119	39
Atlanta	6	4	2	0	0	21	16	8	7	3	2	1	1	19	20	8	13	7	4	1	1	40	36	16
Boston	8	4	4	0	0	21	18	8	7	2	4	1	0	12	20	5	15	6	8	1	0	33	38	13
Buffalo	7	2	4	0	1	12	17	5	6	4	1	1	0	22	17	9	13	6	5	1	1	34	34	14
Calgary	23	13	9	1	0	74	58	27	22	9	7	3	3	54	64	24	45	22	16	4	3	128	122	51
Carolina	6	5	1	0	0	14	9	10	7	3	2	1	1	22	21	8	13	8	3	1	1	36	30	18
Chicago	34	17	11	3	3	108	97	40	35	14	20	1	0	90	97	29	69	31	31	4	3	198	194	69
Colorado	22	10	9	3	0	64	66	23	22	8	11	2	1	47	59	19	44	18	20	5	1	111	125	42
Columbus	29	24	3	1	1	100	60	50	28	16	9	0	3	81	65	35	57	40	12	1	4	181	125	85
Dallas	22	12	9	1	0	58	48	25	22	5	16	0	1	30	66	11	44	17	25	1	1	88	114	36
Detroit	34	15	15	2	2	94	94	34	35	9	19	2	5	80	129	25	69	24	34	4	7	174	223	59
Edmonton	23	12	8	3	0	67	70	27	22	13	7	0	2	71	60	28	45	25	15	3	2	138	130	55
Florida	8	4	2	2	0	19	16	10	7	2	4	1	0	14	23	5	15	6	6	3	0	33	39	15
Los Angeles	22	8	11	3	0	49	58	19	22	12	7	0	3	64	62	27	44	20	18	3	3	113	120	46
Minnesota	18	10	5	2	1	52	41	23	18	5	8	3	2	50	62	15	36	15	13	5	3	102	103	38
Montreal	6	3	1	1	1	21	13	8	6	1	4	0	1	16	22	3	12	4	5	1	2	37	35	11
New Jersey	8	2	5	0	1	16	23	5	7	4	2	0	1	20	23	9	15	6	7	0	2	36	46	14
NY Islanders	7	5	2	0	0	17	17	10	6	3	1	0	2	17	16	8	13	8	3	0	2	34	33	18
NY Rangers	6	2	4	0	0	16	23	4	7	5	1	0	1	20	19	11	13	7	5	0	1	36	42	15
Ottawa	6	3	3	0	0	14	13	6	7	3	4	0	0	19	25	6	13	6	7	0	0	33	38	12
Philadelphia	6	2	2	2	0	12	13	6	7	1	5	1	0	13	23	3	13	3	7	3	0	25	36	13
Phoenix	22	13	6	2	1	63	51	29	22	8	12	0	2	63	66	18	44	21	18	2	3	126	117	47
Pittsburgh	8	6	2	0	0	31	17	12	7	3	2	2	0	22	21	8	15	9	4	2	0	53	38	20
St. Louis	35	19	10	3	3	84	80	44	34	16	15	1	2	76	94	35	69	35	25	4	5	160	174	79
San Jose	22	11	10	1	0	57	60	23	22	7	11	1	3	57	67	18	44	18	21	2	3	114	127	41
Tampa Bay	8	3	4	1	0	20	22	7	6	1	3	2	0	14	19	4	14	4	7	3	0	34	41	11
Toronto	3	2	1	0	0	10	8	4	8	4	3	1	0	21	16	9	11	6	4	1	0	31	24	13
Vancouver	23	9	9	1	4	64	64	23	22	7	14	1	0	51	77	15	45	16	23	2	4	115	141	38
Washington	7	3	2	1	1	19	17	8	7	2	3	0	2	18	19	6	14	5	5	1	3	37	36	14
Totals	**451**	**234**	**161**	**34**	**22**	**1249**	**1139**	**524**	**451**	**177**	**210**	**26**	**38**	**1120**	**1341**	**418**	**902**	**411**	**371**	**60**	**60**	**2369**	**2480**	**942**

Playoffs

	Series	W	L	GP	W	L	T	GF	GA	Last Mtg.	Rnd.	Result
Chicago	1	0	1	6	2	4	0	15	17	2010	CQF	L 2-4
Detroit	2	0	2	12	4	8	0	21	29	2008	CQF	L 2-4
San Jose	2	0	2	10	2	8	0	24	33	2007	CQF	L 1-4
Totals	**5**	**0**	**5**	**28**	**8**	**20**	**0**	**60**	**79**			

Playoff Results 2010-2006

Year	Round	Opponent	Result	GF	GA
2010	CQF	Chicago	L 2-4	15	17
2008	CQF	Detroit	L 2-4	12	17
2007	CQF	San Jose	L 1-4	14	16
2006	CQF	San Jose	L 1-4	10	17

Abbreviations: Round: CQF - conference quarter-final.

2009-10 Results

Oct.				Jan.			
3	at Dallas	3-2†		2	Anaheim	3-1	
8	Colorado	3-2		5	Calgary	1-3	
10	Buffalo	0-1		7	Carolina	4-2	
12	Edmonton	1-6		9	Anaheim	2-3	
14	at Dallas	0-6		11	at Vancouver	3-2	
15	Chicago	1-3		12	at Edmonton	5-3	
17	at Washington	2-3†		15	at Calgary	1-0	
21	at Boston	2-3		18	Toronto	3-4	
22	at Ottawa	6-5*		21	at Phoenix	2-4	
24	at Chicago	0-2		22	at Colorado	1-2	
28	at Minnesota	4-3		26	at Columbus	2-3	
29	Chicago	2-0		29	at Detroit	2-4	
31	Dallas	4-2		30	Atlanta	4-3	

Nov.				Feb.			
5	at Anaheim	0-4		2	Phoenix	0-1†	
7	at Los Angeles	3-1		4	Colorado	5-3	
10	at San Jose	3-4		6	San Jose	3-4	
12	at St. Louis	3-1		9	at NY Islanders	3-4†	
14	Montreal	2-0		10	at NY Rangers	2-1	
17	San Jose	4-3		12	at New Jersey	4-3	
19	New Jersey	3-2†		14	at Pittsburgh	4-3†	
21	Columbus	4-3†	Mar.	2	Edmonton	4-3	
23	Detroit	3-1		4	Los Angeles	4-2	
25	at Colorado	4-3*		5	at Detroit	2-5	
27	St. Louis	1-3		7	Vancouver	2-4	
28	Florida	4-1		9	at Atlanta	2-1	
30	Calgary	0-5		11	at San Jose	5-8	

Dec.							
2	at Minnesota	4-5*		12	at Anaheim	1-0	
4	at Chicago	4-1		14	at Los Angeles	3-2	
5	Minnesota	3-5		16	Philadelphia	4-3†	
8	Vancouver	4-2		18	Minnesota	5-0	
10	Columbus	4-3†		20	Columbus	1-0*	
12	Detroit	2-3*		21	at St. Louis	3-2	
14	at Columbus	5-3		23	Dallas	1-3	
15	Tampa Bay	7-4		25	Phoenix	4-3†	
17	at Edmonton	6-3		27	Detroit	0-1†	
19	at Calgary	5-3		29	at Florida	3-2*	
22	at Vancouver	1-4		30	Los Angeles	0-2	
26	Chicago	1-4	Apr.	1	St. Louis	3-2	
27	at Chicago	4-5		3	at Detroit	4-3*	
29	at St. Louis	4-3		7	at Phoenix	2-5	
31	at Columbus	2-1*		10	St. Louis	2-1†	

* – Overtime   † – Shootout

Entry Draft Selections 2010-1998

Name in bold denotes played in NHL.

2010
Pick
18	Austin Watson
78	Taylor Aronson
126	Patrick Cehlin
168	Anthony Bitetto
194	David Elsner
198	Joonas Rask

2009
Pick
11	Ryan Ellis
41	Zach Budish
42	Charles-Olivier Roussel
70	Taylor Beck
72	Michael Latta
98	Craig Smith
102	Mattias Ekholm
110	Nick Oliver
132	Gabriel Bourque
192	Cameron Reid

2008
Pick
7	**Colin Wilson**
18	Chet Pickard
38	Roman Josi
136	Taylor Stefishen
166	Jeffrey Foss
201	Jani Lajunen
207	Anders Lindback

2007
Pick
23	Jonathon Blum
54	Jeremy Smith
58	**Nick Spaling**
81	Ryan Thang
114	Ben Ryan
119	Mark Santorelli
144	**Andreas Thuresson**
174	Robert Dietrich
204	Atte Engren

2006
Pick
56	Blake Geoffrion
105	Niko Snellman
146	Mark Dekanich
176	Ryan Flynn
206	Viktor Sjodin

2005
Pick
18	**Ryan Parent**
78	**Teemu Laakso**
79	**Cody Franson**
150	**Cal O'Reilly**
176	Ryan Maki
213	Scott Todd
230	**Patric Hornqvist**

2004
Pick
15	**Alexander Radulov**
81	Vaclav Meidl
107	Nick Fugere
139	Kyle Moir
147	**Janne Niskala**
178	**Mike Santorelli**
193	Kevin Schaeffer
209	Stanislav Balan
243	Denis Kulyash
258	**Pekka Rinne**
275	Craig Switzer

2003
Pick
7	**Ryan Suter**
35	Konstantin Glazachev
37	**Kevin Klein**
49	**Shea Weber**
76	Richard Stehlik
89	Paul Brown
92	**Alexander Sulzer**
98	Grigory Shafigulin
117	Teemu Lassila
133	Rustam Sidikov
210	Andrei Mukhachev
213	Miroslav Hanuljak
268	Lauris Darzins

2002
Pick
6	**Scottie Upshall**
102	**Brandon Segal**
138	Patrick Jarrett
172	**Mike McKenna**
203	Josh Morrow
235	Kaleb Betts
264	Matt Davis
266	Steven Spencer

2001
Pick
12	**Dan Hamhuis**
33	**Timofei Shishkanov**
42	Tomas Slovak
75	Denis Platonov
76	Oliver Setzinger
98	**Jordin Tootoo**
178	Anton Lavrentiev
240	Gustav Grasberg
271	**Mikko Lehtonen**

2000
Pick
6	**Scott Hartnell**
36	Daniel Widing
72	Mattias Nilsson
89	**Libor Pivko**
131	**Matt Hendricks**
137	**Mike Stuart**
154	**Matt Koalska**
173	Tomas Harant
197	Zbynek Irgl
203	Jure Penko
236	Mats Christeen
284	Martin Hohener

1999
Pick
6	**Brian Finley**
33	**Jonas Andersson**
52	**Adam Hall**
54	**Andrew Hutchinson**
61	Ed Hill
65	**Jan Lasak**
72	Brett Angel
121	Yevgeny Pavlov
124	Alexandre Krevsun
131	Konstantin Panov
162	**Timo Helbling**
191	**Martin Erat**
205	Kyle Kettles
220	Miroslav Durak
248	**Darren Haydar**

1998
Pick
2	**David Legwand**
60	**Denis Arkhipov**
85	Geoff Koch
88	Kent Sauer
138	Martin Beauchesne
147	Craig Brunel
202	Martin Bartek
230	**Karlis Skrastins**

General Managers' History

David Poile, 1998-99 to date.

David Poile
President of Hockey Operations and General Manager
Born: Toronto, Ont., February 14, 1949.

Hired as the first general manager in franchise history on July 9, 1997, David Poile has been committed to building the team through the NHL Draft. In 2003-04, Nashville reached the playoffs for the first time in franchise history. During the 2006-07 season, the team was in contention for first overall in the NHL, setting club records with 51 wins and 110 points. Though forced to rebuild the roster for 2007-08, the Predators reached the playoffs for the fourth year in a row. Poile has an impressive reputation as an NHL leader and in 2001 he received the Lester Patrick Trophy for his contributions to hockey in the United States. His father, Norman "Bud" Poile, had won the honor in 1989. He served as Associate G.M. for the 2010 U.S. Olympic Team and U.S. squads for the 2009 and 2010 IIHF World Championships. He was a finalist for the NHL's inaugural G.M. of the Year Award in 1910.

Prior to joining Nashville, Poile spent 15 seasons as vice president/general manager of the Washington Capitals. During his tenure in Washington, the Capitals made 14 postseason appearances, winning their only Patrick Division title in 1989 and advancing to the Conference Finals in 1990. During Poile's 15 years in Washington, the Capitals compiled a record of 594-454-132, finished second in the Patrick Division seven times and recorded 90-or-more points seven different seasons.

Poile started his professional hockey career as an administrative assistant for the Atlanta Flames in 1972, shortly after graduating from Northeastern University in Boston. At Northeastern, he was hockey team captain, leading scorer and most valuable player for two years.

In 1977, he was named assistant general manager of the Atlanta Flames (who moved to Calgary in 1980), serving as the manager and coordinator of the Flames farm club.

Poile was instrumental in the NHL's adoption of the instant replay rule in 1991. He was awarded *Inside Hockey*'s man of the year for his leadership on the issue. He has also been honored three times as *The Sporting News* NHL executive of the year in 1982-83, 1983-84 and 2006-07. Poile served as general manager of the 1998 and 1999 U.S. national teams for the World Championships.

Club Directory

Bridgestone Arena

Nashville Predators
Bridgestone Arena
501 Broadway
Nashville, TN 37203
Phone **615/770-2300**
FAX 615/770-2309
Ticket Information 615/770-PUCK
www.nashvillepredators.com
Capacity: 17,113

Owner	Predators Holdings LLC
Investor Group	Christopher Cigarran, Thomas Cigarran, Joel and Holly Dobberpuhl, David Freeman, Herbert Fritch, DeWitt Thompson V, John Thompson, Warren Woo.
Chairman and Alternate Governor	Thomas Cigarran
Governor	Joel Dobberpuhl
Chief Executive Officer	Jeff Cogen
President/COO	Sean Henry
Pres. of Hockey Ops/G.M./Alt. Gov.	David Poile
Executive Vice President/Chief Sales Officer	Chris Parker
Sr. V.P./Special Assistant to the President	Gerry Helper
Sr. V.P., Chief Admin. Officer, Corporate Counsel	Michelle Kennedy
Senior Vice President of Corporate Development	Chris Junghans

Hockey Operations
Assistant General Manager	Paul Fenton
Director of Hockey Operations	Brian Poile
Manager of Hockey Operations	Brandon Walker
Director of Player Development	Martin Gelinas
Executive Assistant	Connell Crow
Head Coach	Barry Trotz
Associate Coach	Brent Peterson
Assistant Coach	Peter Horachek
Goaltending Coach	Mitch Korn
Strength and Conditioning Coach	David Good
Video Coordinator	Lawrence Feloney
Chief Amateur Scout	Jeff Kealty
Professional Scout	Nick Beverley, Shawn Dineen
North American Amateur Scouts	Jason Bukala, Gary Knickle, Rick Knickle, Tom Nolan, Glen Sanders, David Westby
European Scouts	Martin Bakula, Lucas Bergman, Janne Kekalainen
Head Athletic Trainer	Dan Redmond
Assistant Athletic Trainer	Andy Hosler
Equipment Manger	Pete Rogers
Assistant Equipment Manager	Jeff Camelio
Equipment Assistant	Brad Peterson
Locker Room Attendant	Craig "Partner" Baugh

Medical Staff
Team Doctors	Drs. John E. Kuhn, Paul J. Rummo, James L. Carey, Charles L. Cox, Alex Diamond, Daniel S. Weikert, Mark Melson, Joseph L. Fredi Kevin Hagan, Blair Summitt, Wesley Thayer, Jason Wendel, Cristin M. Wallace

Communications/Development
Director of Communications	Tim Darling
Hockey Communications Coordinator	Kevin Wilson
Corporate Communications Coordinator	Jessica Jones
Director of Community Relations	Rebecca Ward
Community Relations Coordinator	Gina Maduri
Team Photographer	John Russell

Corporate Partnerships
Director of New Business Development	Bob Flynn
Director, Corporate Development	Delmar Smith
Director, Corporate Partnerships	Rock Upchurch
Account Executives, Corporate Partnerships	Jack Burk, Bradford Hollingsworth
Account Service Manager, Corporate Partnerships	Kathryn Cloud
Sr. Account Service Mgr., Corporate Partnerships	Jennifer Maxwell

Marketing
Director of Marketing	Jeff Schwartzenberg
Internet Development Manager	Jay Levin
Marketing Entertainment Manager	Adam DeVault
Youth and Amateur Hockey Manager	Andee Boiman

Premium Seats
Vice President of Premium Seat Service	Susie Masotti
Director of Premium Seat Service	Britt Kincheloe
Senior Manager of Premium Seat Sales	Tim Wilson
Manager, Premium Seating	Chris Burton

Finance/Administration/Human Resources
Vice President of Finance	Beth Snider
Senior Director, Human Resources	Allison Simms
Senior Manager, Administrative, Legal Affairs	Raquel Toombs

Event Technology
Senior Director of Event Presentation	Blake Grant
Event Presentation Manager	Patrick Abell
Game Operations Producer	Ron Zolkower
Game Entertainment Coordinator	Chris Smith

Broadcast
Broadcasting Director	Bob Kohl
Associate Producer	David White
Play-by-Play Announcer	Pete Weber
Color Analyst	Terry Crisp
Radio Play-by-Play Announcer	Tom Callahan
Manager, Video Production	Mitch Jordan
Videographer/Editor	Brett Newkirk
Broadcast Services Manager	Kelly Sparks

Ticket Operations
Vice President of Ticket Sales	Nat Harden
Director of Ticket Sales	Marty Mulford
Director of Ticket Operations	David Chadwell
Inside Sales Manager	Brad Gillispie
Senior Account Executives	Will Myers, Dan Schaefer
Account Executives	Chris Harrington, Brian Jamison, Travis Laufle, Charles Rand, Curry McKeel

New Jersey Devils

Key Off-Season Signings/Acquisitions

2010

May 14 • Signed 2008 1st round pick, LW **Mattias Tedenby** (HV 71) and 2009 1st round pick, C **Jacob Josefson** (Djurgarden).

June 17 • Named **John MacLean** head coach.

19 • Acquired C **Jason Arnott** from Nashville for RW **Matt Halischuk** and New Jersey's 2nd round pick in the 2011 Entry Draft.

29 • Named **Adam Oates** assistant coach.

30 • Re-signed RW **David Clarkson**.

July 1 • Signed D **Henrik Tallinder**, D **Anton Volchenkov** and G **Johan Hedberg**.

28 • Re-signed D **Mark Fraser**.

2009-10 Results: 48w-27l-2otl-5sol 103pts.
First, Atlantic Division

Martin Brodeur made 35 saves in a 4-0 win over Pittsburgh on December 21, 2009 to break Terry Sawchuk's NHL record with his 104th career shutout. Brodeur also surpassed 600 career wins in 2009-10.

2010-11 Schedule

Oct.	Fri.	8	Dallas
	Sat.	9	at Washington
	Mon.	11	Pittsburgh*
	Wed.	13	at Buffalo
	Fri.	15	Colorado
	Sat.	16	Boston
	Thu.	21	at Montreal
	Sat.	23	Buffalo
	Sun.	24	at NY Rangers
	Wed.	27	at San Jose
	Fri.	29	at Anaheim
	Sat.	30	at Los Angeles
Nov.	Mon.	1	at Vancouver
	Wed.	3	at Chicago
	Fri.	5	NY Rangers
	Wed.	10	Buffalo
	Fri.	12	Edmonton
	Mon.	15	at Boston
	Thu.	18	at Toronto
	Sat.	20	at St. Louis
	Mon.	22	Washington
	Wed.	24	Calgary
	Fri.	26	at NY Islanders*
	Sat.	27	Philadelphia*
Dec.	Thu.	2	Montreal
	Sat.	4	at Philadelphia*
	Mon.	6	at Pittsburgh
	Fri.	10	at Ottawa
	Sat.	11	Detroit
	Wed.	15	Phoenix
	Fri.	17	Nashville
	Sat.	18	at Atlanta
	Tue.	21	at Washington
	Thu.	23	NY Islanders
	Sun.	26	Toronto
	Wed.	29	NY Rangers
	Fri.	31	Atlanta*
Jan.	Sat.	1	at Carolina
	Tue.	4	Minnesota
	Thu.	6	Philadelphia
	Sat.	8	at Philadelphia*

	Sun.	9	Tampa Bay*
	Fri.	14	at Tampa Bay
	Sat.	15	at Florida
	Mon.	17	at NY Islanders*
	Thu.	20	Pittsburgh
	Sat.	22	at Philadelphia*
	Sun.	23	Florida*
	Wed.	26	at Detroit
Feb.	Tue.	1	Ottawa
	Thu.	3	at NY Rangers
	Fri.	4	Florida
	Sun.	6	at Montreal*
	Tue.	8	Carolina
	Thu.	10	at Toronto
	Fri.	11	San Jose
	Wed.	16	Carolina
	Fri.	18	NY Rangers
	Sat.	19	at Carolina
	Tue.	22	at Dallas
	Fri.	25	at Tampa Bay
	Sun.	27	at Florida*
Mar.	Wed.	2	Tampa Bay
	Fri.	4	Pittsburgh
	Sun.	6	at NY Islanders*
	Tue.	8	Ottawa
	Fri.	11	at Atlanta
	Sat.	12	NY Islanders
	Tue.	15	Atlanta
	Thu.	17	at Ottawa
	Fri.	18	Washington
	Sun.	20	at Columbus*
	Tue.	22	at Boston
	Fri.	25	at Pittsburgh
	Sat.	26	at Buffalo
	Wed.	30	NY Islanders
Apr.	Fri.	1	Philadelphia
	Sat.	2	Montreal
	Tue.	5	at Pittsburgh
	Wed.	6	Toronto
	Sat.	9	at NY Rangers*
	Sun.	10	Boston*

* Denotes afternoon game.

ATLANTIC DIVISION
37th NHL Season

Franchise date: June 11, 1974

Transferred from Denver to New Jersey, June 30, 1982.
Transferred from Kansas City to Denver, August 25, 1976.

Year-by-Year Record

Season	GP	Home W	L	T	OL	Road W	L	T	OL	Overall W	L	T	OL	GF	GA	Pts.	Finished	Playoff Result
2009-10	82	27	10	....	4	21	17	....	3	48	27	....	7	222	191	103	1st, Atlantic Div.	Lost Conf. Quarter-Final
2008-09	82	28	12	....	1	23	15	....	3	51	27	....	4	244	209	106	1st, Atlantic Div.	Lost Conf. Quarter-Final
2007-08	82	25	14	....	2	21	15	....	5	46	29	....	7	206	197	99	2nd, Atlantic Div.	Lost Conf. Quarter-Final
2006-07	82	25	10	....	6	24	14	....	3	49	24	....	9	216	201	107	1st, Atlantic Div.	Lost Conf. Semi-Final
2005-06	82	27	11	....	3	19	16	....	6	46	27	....	9	242	229	101	1st, Atlantic Div.	Lost Conf. Semi-Final
2004-05	....	....	....	....	....	....	....	....	....	....	....	....	....	....	....	....		
2003-04	82	22	13	5	1	21	12	7	1	43	25	12	2	213	164	100	2nd, Atlantic Div.	Lost Conf. Quarter-Final
2002-03	**82**	**25**	**11**	**3**	**2**	**21**	**9**	**7**	**4**	**46**	**20**	**10**	**6**	**216**	**166**	**108**	**1st, Atlantic Div.**	**Won Stanley Cup**
2001-02	82	22	13	4	2	19	15	5	2	41	28	9	4	205	187	95	3rd, Atlantic Div.	Lost Conf. Quarter-Final
2000-01	82	24	11	6	0	24	8	6	3	48	19	12	3	295	195	111	1st, Atlantic Div.	Lost Final
1999-2000	**82**	**28**	**9**	**3**	**1**	**17**	**15**	**5**	**4**	**45**	**24**	**8**	**5**	**251**	**203**	**103**	**2nd, Atlantic Div.**	**Won Stanley Cup**
1998-99	82	19	14	8		28	10	3		47	24	11	....	248	196	105	1st, Atlantic Div.	Lost Conf. Quarter-Final
1997-98	82	29	10	2		19	13	9		48	23	11	....	225	166	107	1st, Atlantic Div.	Lost Conf. Quarter-Final
1996-97	82	23	9	9		22	14	5		45	23	14	....	231	182	104	1st, Atlantic Div.	Lost Conf. Semi-Final
1995-96	82	22	17	2		15	16	10		37	33	12	....	215	202	86	6th, Atlantic Div.	Out of Playoffs
1994-95	**48**	**14**	**4**	**6**		**8**	**14**	**2**		**22**	**18**	**8**	....	**136**	**121**	**52**	**2nd, Atlantic Div.**	**Won Stanley Cup**
1993-94	84	29	11	2		18	14	10		47	25	12	....	306	220	106	2nd, Atlantic Div.	Lost Conf. Championship
1992-93	84	24	14	4		16	23	3		40	37	7	....	308	299	87	4th, Patrick Div.	Lost Div. Semi-Final
1991-92	80	24	12	4		14	19	7		38	31	11	....	289	259	87	4th, Patrick Div.	Lost Div. Semi-Final
1990-91	80	23	10	7		9	23	8		32	33	15	....	272	264	79	4th, Patrick Div.	Lost Div. Semi-Final
1989-90	80	22	15	3		15	19	6		37	34	9	....	295	288	83	2nd, Patrick Div.	Lost Div. Semi-Final
1988-89	80	17	18	5		10	23	7		27	41	12	....	281	325	66	5th, Patrick Div.	Out of Playoffs
1987-88	80	23	16	1		15	20	5		38	36	6	....	295	296	82	4th, Patrick Div.	Lost Conf. Championship
1986-87	80	20	17	3		9	28	3		29	45	6	....	293	368	64	6th, Patrick Div.	Out of Playoffs
1985-86	80	17	21	2		11	28	1		28	49	3	....	300	374	59	6th, Patrick Div.	Out of Playoffs
1984-85	80	13	21	6		9	27	4		22	48	10	....	264	346	54	5th, Patrick Div.	Out of Playoffs
1983-84	80	10	28	2		7	28	5		17	56	7	....	231	350	41	5th, Patrick Div.	Out of Playoffs
1982-83**	80	14	21	5		4	28	8		18	49	13	....	241	362	49	5th, Patrick Div.	Out of Playoffs
1981-82**	80	15	16	9		7	29	4		22	45	13	....	258	344	57	5th, Smythe Div.	Out of Playoffs
1980-81**	80	12	20	8		7	28	5		19	48	13	....	234	308	51	6th, Smythe Div.	Out of Playoffs
1979-80**	80	12	20	8		7	29	4		19	49	12	....	234	308	51	4th, Smythe Div.	Out of Playoffs
1978-79**	80	8	24	8		7	29	4		15	53	12	....	210	331	42	4th, Smythe Div.	Out of Playoffs
1977-78**	80	17	14	9		2	26	12		19	40	21	....	257	305	59	2nd, Smythe Div.	Lost Prelim. Round
1976-77**	80	8	24	8		8	26	6		20	46	14	....	226	307	54	5th, Smythe Div.	Out of Playoffs
1975-76*	80	8	24	8		4	32	4		12	56	12	....	190	351	36	5th, Smythe Div.	Out of Playoffs
1974-75*	80	12	20	8		3	34	3		15	54	11	....	184	328	41	5th, Smythe Div.	Out of Playoffs

* Kansas City Scouts. ** Colorado Rockies.

2010-11 Player Personnel

FORWARDS	HT	WT	S	Place of Birth	*Age	2009-10 Club
ARNOTT, Jason	6-5	220	R	Collingwood, Ont.	35	Nashville
BERUBE, Jean-Sebastien	6-4	210	L	Matane, Que.	20	Rouyn-Noranda-Lowell
CLARKSON, David	6-1	200	R	Toronto, Ont.	26	New Jersey
CORMIER, Kevin	6-2	230	L	Moncton, N.B.	24	Lowell-Trenton
DAVIS, Patrick	6-2	195	R	Sterling, MI	23	New Jersey-Lowell
ELIAS, Patrik	6-1	195	L	Trebic, Czech.	34	New Jersey
HENRIQUE, Adam	6-0	205	L	Brantford, Ont.	20	Windsor
JOSEFSON, Jacob	6-0	190	L	Stockholm, Sweden	19	Djurgarden
LANGENBRUNNER, Jamie	6-1	205	R	Cloquet, MN	35	New Jersey
LETOURNEAU-LEBLOND, Pierre-Luc	6-2	215	L	Levis, Que.	25	New Jersey-Lowell
McINTYRE, David	6-0	185	L	Oakville, Ont.	23	Lowell-Colgate
MILLS, Brad	6-0	195	R	Terrace, B.C.	27	Lowell
NAGY, Kory	5-11	195	L	London, Ont.	20	Lowell-Trenton
PALMIERI, Nick	6-3	220	R	Utica, NY	21	New Jersey-Lowell
PARISE, Zach	5-11	190	L	Minneapolis, MN	26	New Jersey
PELLEY, Rod	5-11	195	L	Kitimat, B.C.	26	New Jersey
PERKOVICH, Nathan	6-5	215	R	Canton, MI	24	Lowell
ROLSTON, Brian	6-2	210	L	Flint, MI	37	New Jersey
SESTITO, Tim	6-0	200	L	Rome, NY	26	New Jersey-Lowell
SWIFT, Michael	5-8	170	L	Peterborough, Ont.	23	Lowell
TEDENBY, Mattias	5-10	175	L	Vetlanda, Sweden	20	HV 71
VASYUNOV, Alexander	6-1	210	R	Yaroslavl, USSR	22	Lowell
WISEMAN, Chad	6-1	210	L	Burlington, Ont.	29	Springfield
ZAJAC, Travis	6-3	200	R	Winnipeg, Man.	25	New Jersey
ZHARKOV, Vladimir	6-1	200	L	Elektrostal, USSR	22	New Jersey-Lowell
ZUBRUS, Dainius	6-5	225	L	Elektrenai, USSR	32	New Jersey
DEFENSEMEN						
CORRENTE, Matthew	6-0	205	R	Mississauga, Ont.	22	New Jersey-Lowell
DAVISON, Rob	6-3	215	L	St. Catharines, Ont.	30	New Jersey-Lowell
ECKFORD, Tyler	6-1	205	L	Vancouver, B.C.	25	New Jersey-Lowell
FAYNE, Mark	6-3	220	R	Nashua, NH	23	Providence College
FRASER, Mark	6-3	220	L	Ottawa, Ont.	24	New Jersey
GELINAS, Eric	6-4	195	L	Vanier, Ont.	19	Lewiston-Chicoutimi
GREENE, Andy	5-11	190	L	Trenton, MI	27	New Jersey
KELLY, Dan	6-1	195	L	Morrisonville, NY	21	Kitchener
MAGNAN-GRENIER, Olivier	6-2	210	L	Sherbrooke, Que.	24	Lowell
SALMELA, Anssi	6-1	200	L	Nokia, Finland	26	Atlanta-New Jersey
SALVADOR, Bryce	6-3	215	L	Brandon, Man.	34	New Jersey
TALLINDER, Henrik	6-3	215	L	Stockholm, Sweden	31	Buffalo
TAORMINA, Matt	5-10	185	L	Washington Township, MI	23	Lowell
URBOM, Alexander	6-5	210	L	Stockholm, Sweden	19	Brandon
VOLCHENKOV, Anton	6-1	225	L	Moscow, USSR	28	Ottawa
WHITE, Colin	6-4	215	L	New Glasgow, N.S.	32	New Jersey
YOUNG, Harry	6-4	210	L	Windsor, Ont.	20	Windsor

GOALTENDERS	HT	WT	C	Place of Birth	*Age	2009-10 Club
BRODEUR, Martin	6-2	215	L	Montreal, Que.	38	New Jersey
CLERMONT, Maxime	6-1	195	L	Montreal, Que.	18	Gatineau
FRAZEE, Jeff	6-0	200	L	Edina, MN	23	Lowell
HEDBERG, Johan	6-0	190	L	Leksand, Sweden	37	Atlanta
McKENNA, Mike	6-3	195	R	St. Louis, MO	27	Lowell
WEDGEWOOD, Scott	6-1	190	L	Etobicoke, Ont.	18	Plymouth

* – Age at start of 2010-11 season

Captains' History

Simon Nolet, 1974-75 to 1976-77; Wilf Paiement, 1977-78; Gary Croteau, 1978-79; Mike Christie, Rene Robert and Lanny McDonald, 1979-80; Lanny McDonald, 1980-81; Lanny McDonald and Rob Ramage, 1981-82; Don Lever, 1982-83; Don Lever and Mel Bridgman, 1983-84; Mel Bridgman, 1984-85 to 1986-87; Kirk Muller, 1987-88 to 1990-91; Bruce Driver, 1991-92; Scott Stevens, 1992-93 to 2002-03; Scott Stevens and Scott Neidermayer, 2003-04; no captain, 2005-06; Patrik Elias, 2006-07; Patrik Elias and Jamie Langenbrunner, 2007-08; Jamie Langenbrunner, 2008-09 to date.

John MacLean

Head Coach

Born: Oshawa, Ont., November 20, 1964.

John MacLean became the 19th head coach in team history on June 17, 2010, replacing Jacques Lemaire, who retired at the end of the 2009-10 season. MacLean served as the head coach in Lowell (AHL) in 2009-10, guiding New Jersey's top minor league affiliate to the best record in franchise history (39-31-10) and a berth in the Calder Cup playoffs. This is the first NHL head coaching job for MacLean, who was a Devils assistant for seven seasons beginning with the 2003 run to the Stanley Cup.

Originally drafted sixth overall by New Jersey in 1983, MacLean still tops the franchise's all-time goals list with 347. He scored the overtime goal in the 1988 regular-season finale that clinched the Devils' first playoff berth, and was a key part of their first Stanley Cup championship in 1995. During his career, MacLean played in the NHL All-Star Game in 1989 and 1991 and represented Canada at the World Junior Championship in 1984 and World Championship in 1989.

MacLean's 19-year playing career included 14 as a Devil. He was traded with Ken Sutton to San Jose for Doug Bodger and Dody Wood on December 7, 1997, and finished with stops with the Rangers and Dallas Stars. He retired as an active player on June 7, 2002, and ended up with 413 goals, 429 assists and 842 points in 1,194 games.

Coaching Record

			Regular Season				Playoffs			
Season	Team	League	GC	W	L	O/T	GC	W	L	T
2009-10	Lowell	AHL	80	39	31	10	5	1	4	....

2009-10 Scoring

* – rookie

Regular Season

Pos	#	Player	Team	GP	G	A	Pts	TOI	+/–	PIM	PP	SH	GW	S	%
L	17	Ilya Kovalchuk	ATL	49	31	27	58	22:14	1	45	10	0	3	179	17.3
			N.J.	27	10	17	27	21:40	9	8	2	0	1	111	9.0
			Total	76	41	44	85	22:02	10	53	12	0	4	290	14.1
L	9	Zach Parise	N.J.	81	38	44	82	19:46	24	32	9	1	5	347	11.0
C	19	Travis Zajac	N.J.	82	25	42	67	20:12	22	24	6	0	4	210	11.9
R	15	Jamie Langenbrunner	N.J.	81	19	42	61	19:33	6	44	6	2	4	228	8.3
L	26	Patrik Elias	N.J.	58	19	29	48	17:37	18	40	3	1	4	145	13.1
C	12	Brian Rolston	N.J.	80	20	17	37	16:55	2	22	7	0	3	232	8.6
D	6	Andy Greene	N.J.	78	6	31	37	23:31	9	14	4	0	4	86	7.0
R	8	Dainius Zubrus	N.J.	51	10	17	27	16:28	4	28	1	0	4	86	11.6
R	23	David Clarkson	N.J.	46	11	13	24	14:26	3	85	3	0	2	106	10.4
L	21	Rob Niedermayer	N.J.	71	10	12	22	16:48	3	45	0	1	0	93	10.8
D	27	Mike Mottau	N.J.	79	2	16	18	22:15	4	41	0	0	0	74	2.7
L	11	Dean McAmmond	N.J.	62	8	9	17	12:51	–1	40	1	1	2	87	9.2
D	24	Bryce Salvador	N.J.	79	4	10	14	18:51	8	57	0	0	2	47	8.5
D	5	Colin White	N.J.	81	2	10	12	20:04	8	46	0	0	0	47	4.3
D	28	Martin Skoula	PIT	33	3	5	8	16:43	–4	6	1	0	0	23	13.0
			N.J.	19	0	3	3	18:36	7	4	0	0	0	11	0.0
			Total	52	3	8	11	17:24	3	10	1	0	0	34	8.8
D	7	Paul Martin	N.J.	22	2	9	11	22:30	10	2	1	0	0	21	9.5
C	10	Rod Pelley	N.J.	63	2	8	10	7:51	–4	40	0	0	0	74	2.7
R	18 *	Vladimir Zharkov	N.J.	40	0	10	10	11:26	2	8	0	0	0	54	0.0
L	20	Jay Pandolfo	N.J.	52	4	5	9	13:55	–10	6	0	0	3	71	5.6
D	29	Anssi Salmela	ATL	29	1	4	5	13:10	4	22	0	0	0	27	3.7
			N.J.	9	1	2	3	14:26	–5	0	0	1	0	14	7.1
			Total	38	2	6	8	13:28	–1	22	0	1	0	41	4.9
D	2 *	Mark Fraser	N.J.	61	3	3	6	12:22	3	36	0	0	0	24	12.5
R	17	Ilkka Pikkarainen	N.J.	31	1	3	4	8:08	–3	10	0	0	0	26	3.8
D	18	Cory Murphy	N.J.	12	2	1	3	12:26	–2	2	0	0	0	9	22.2
R	16 *	Matt Halischuk	N.J.	20	1	1	2	11:18	–4	2	0	0	0	22	4.5
R	22 *	P-L Letourneau-Leblond	N.J.	27	0	2	2	5:31	–4	48	0	0	0	9	0.0
C	14 *	Patrick Davis	N.J.	8	1	0	1	12:36	–2	0	0	0	0	8	12.5
D	28 *	Tyler Eckford	N.J.	3	0	1	1	7:22	0	4	0	0	0	1	0.0
R	16 *	Nick Palmieri	N.J.	6	0	1	1	11:45	0	0	0	0	0	10	0.0
C	14 *	Tim Sestito	N.J.	9	0	1	1	12:16	–2	2	0	0	0	7	0.0
D	18	Rob Davison	N.J.	1	0	0	0	3:59	0	0	0	0	0	0	0.0
C	17	Ben Walter	N.J.	2	0	0	0	5:47	0	2	0	0	0	0	0.0
D	32 *	Matthew Corrente	N.J.	12	0	0	0	8:51	0	24	0	0	0	6	0.0
L	25	Andrew Peters	N.J.	29	0	0	0	5:11	–5	93	0	0	0	15	0.0

Goaltending

No.	Goaltender	GPI	Mins	Avg	W	L	OT	EN	SO	GA	SA	S%	G	A	PIM
35	Yann Danis	12	467	2.06	3	2	1	1	0	16	207	.923	0	0	0
30	Martin Brodeur	77	4499	2.24	45	25	6	1	9	168	2004	.916	0	3	6
	Totals	**82**	**4990**	**2.24**	**48**	**27**	**7**	**2**	**9**	**186**	**2213**	**.916**			

Playoffs

Pos	#	Player	Team	GP	G	A	Pts	TOI	+/–	PIM	PP	SH	GW	OT	S	%
L	17	Ilya Kovalchuk	N.J.	5	2	4	6	23:37	0	6	1	0	0	0	19	10.5
L	9	Zach Parise	N.J.	5	1	3	4	20:44	0	0	0	1	0	0	20	5.0
L	26	Patrik Elias	N.J.	5	0	4	4	18:41	–2	2	0	0	0	0	12	0.0
C	12	Brian Rolston	N.J.	5	2	1	3	14:48	–1	0	2	0	0	0	12	16.7
C	19	Travis Zajac	N.J.	5	1	1	2	21:45	1	2	0	0	0	0	12	8.3
D	6	Andy Greene	N.J.	5	1	1	2	19:42	–1	6	1	0	0	0	8	12.5
R	8	Dainius Zubrus	N.J.	5	1	0	1	16:25	0	8	0	0	1	0	14	7.1
D	5	Colin White	N.J.	5	1	0	1	18:56	–1	8	0	0	0	0	1	100.0
R	15	Jamie Langenbrunner	N.J.	5	0	1	1	18:38	–1	4	0	0	0	0	10	0.0
D	27	Mike Mottau	N.J.	5	0	1	1	17:57	0	0	0	0	0	0	1	0.0
D	2 *	Mark Fraser	N.J.	1	0	0	0	5:52	–1	0	0	0	0	0	0	0.0
D	32 *	Matthew Corrente	N.J.	2	0	0	0	5:51	0	2	0	0	0	0	3	0.0
C	10	Rod Pelley	N.J.	3	0	0	0	9:11	0	2	0	0	0	0	3	0.0
D	28	Martin Skoula	N.J.	4	0	0	0	16:39	0	0	0	0	0	0	2	0.0
L	11	Dean McAmmond	N.J.	5	0	0	0	11:19	–1	4	0	0	0	0	5	0.0
L	21	Rob Niedermayer	N.J.	5	0	0	0	12:38	–1	6	0	0	0	0	3	0.0
D	24	Bryce Salvador	N.J.	5	0	0	0	16:03	0	6	0	0	0	0	1	0.0
D	7	Paul Martin	N.J.	5	0	0	0	22:23	–1	0	0	0	0	0	5	0.0
R	23	David Clarkson	N.J.	5	0	0	0	12:28	–1	22	0	0	0	0	4	0.0
R	22 *	P-L Letourneau-Leblond	N.J.	5	0	0	0	4:34	0	10	0	0	0	0	0	0.0

Goaltending

No.	Goaltender	GPI	Mins	Avg	W	L	EN	SO	GA	SA	S%	G	A	PIM
30	Martin Brodeur	5	299	3.01	1	4	0	0	15	126	.881	0	0	0
	Totals	**5**	**304**	**2.96**	**1**	**4**	**0**	**0**	**15**	**126**	**.881**			

Club Records

Team

(Figures in brackets for season records are games played; records for fewest points, wins, ties, losses, goals, goals against are for 70 or more games)

Most Points **111** 2000-01 (82)
Most Wins **51** 2008-09 (82)
Most Ties ***21** 1977-78 (80)
.... **15** 1990-91 (80)
Most Losses **56** 1975-76 (80), 1983-84 (80)
Most Goals **308** 1992-93 (84)
Most Goals Against **374** 1985-86 (80)
Fewest Points ***36** 1975-76 (80)
41 1983-84 (80)
Fewest Wins ***12** 1975-76 (80)
17 1982-83 (80), 1983-84 (80)
Fewest Ties **3** 1985-86 (80)
Fewest Losses **19** 2000-01 (82)
Fewest Goals ***184** 1974-75 (80)
205 2001-02 (82)
Fewest Goals Against **164** 2003-04 (82)

Longest Winning Streak
- **Overall** .... **13** Feb. 26-Mar. 23/01
- **Home** .... **11** Feb. 9-Mar. 20/09
- **Away** .... **10** Feb. 27-Apr. 7/01

Longest Undefeated Streak
- **Overall** .... **13** Four times
- **Home** .... **15** Jan. 8-Mar. 15/97 (9 wins, 6 ties)
- **Away** .... **10** Feb. 27-Apr. 7/01 (10 wins)

Longest Losing Streak
- **Overall** .... ***14** Dec. 30/75-Jan. 29/76
  10 Oct. 14-Nov. 4/83
- **Home** .... **9** Dec. 22/85-Feb. 6/86
- **Away** .... **12** Oct. 19-Dec. 1/83

Longest Winless Streak
- **Overall** .... ***27** Feb. 12-Apr. 4/76 (21 losses, 6 ties)
  18 Oct. 20-Nov. 26/82 (14 losses 4 ties)
- **Home** .... ***14** Feb. 12-Mar. 30/76 (10 losses, 4 ties), Feb. 4-Mar. 31/79 (12 losses, 2 ties)
  9 Dec. 22/85-Feb. 6/86 (9 losses)
- **Away** .... ***32** Nov. 12/77-Mar. 15/78 (22 losses, 10 ties)
  14 Dec. 26/82-Mar. 5/83 (13 losses, 1 tie)

Most Shutouts, Season **14** 2003-04 (82)
Most PIM, Season **2,494** 1988-89 (80)
Most Goals, Game .... **9** Nine times

Individual

Most Seasons .... **20** Ken Daneyko
Most Games .... **1,283** Ken Daneyko
Most Goals, Career .... **347** John MacLean
Most Assists, Career .... **440** Patrik Elias
Most Points, Career .... **754** Patrik Elias (314G, 440A)
Most PIM, Career .... **2,519** Ken Daneyko
Most Shutouts, Career ..... ****110** Martin Brodeur
Longest Consecutive Games Streak .... **388** Ken Daneyko (Nov. 4/89-Mar. 29/94)
Most Goals, Season .... **48** Brian Gionta (2005-06)
Most Assists, Season .... **60** Scott Stevens (1993-94)
Most Points, Season .... **96** Patrik Elias (2000-01; 40G, 56A)
Most PIM, Season .... **295** Krzysztof Oliwa (1997-98)
Most Points, Defenseman, Season .... **78** Scott Stevens (1993-94; 18G, 60A)
Most Points, Center, Season .... **94** Kirk Muller (1987-88; 37G, 57A)
Most Points, Right Wing, Season .... **89** Brian Gionta (2005-06; 48G, 41A)
Most Points, Left Wing, Season .... **96** Patrik Elias (2000-01; 40G, 56A)
Most Points, Rookie, Season .... **70** Scott Gomez (1999-2000; 19G, 51A)
Most Shutouts, Season .... **12** Martin Brodeur (2006-07)
Most Goals, Game .... **4** Six times
Most Assists, Game .... **5** Greg Adams (Oct. 10/85), Kirk Muller (Mar. 25/87), Tom Kurvers (Feb. 13/89), Scott Gomez (Mar. 30/03)
Most Points, Game .... **6** Kirk Muller (Oct. 29/86; 3G, 3A)

* Records include Kansas City Scouts and Colorado Rockies, 1974-75 through 1981-82.
** NHL Record.

General Managers' History

Sid Abel, 1974-75, 1975-76; Ray Miron, 1976-77 to 1980-81; Bill MacMillan, 1981-82, 1982-83; Bill MacMillan and Max McNab, 1983-84; Max McNab 1984-85 to 1986-87; Lou Lamoriello, 1987-88 to date.

Retired Numbers

3	Ken Daneyko	1982-2003
4	Scott Stevens	1991-2005

All-time Record vs. Other Clubs

Regular Season

	At Home								On Road								Total							
	GP	W	L	T	OL	GF	GA	PTS	GP	W	L	T	OL	GF	GA	PTS	GP	W	L	T	OL	GF	GA	PTS
Anaheim	10	8	2	0	0	35	17	16	12	5	6	1	0	31	34	11	22	13	8	1	0	66	51	27
Atlanta	20	10	6	1	3	57	46	24	20	13	3	2	2	73	43	30	40	23	9	3	5	130	89	54
Boston	63	22	29	11	1	161	191	56	66	24	32	8	2	202	244	58	129	46	61	19	3	363	435	114
Buffalo	64	25	30	9	0	182	198	59	64	21	33	8	2	192	237	52	128	46	63	17	2	374	435	111
Calgary	47	16	28	3	0	132	168	35	44	7	28	8	1	115	189	23	91	23	56	11	1	247	357	58
Carolina	55	32	19	4	0	188	163	68	54	23	21	8	2	159	161	56	109	55	40	12	2	347	324	124
Chicago	50	22	16	11	1	153	147	56	49	13	25	10	1	133	186	37	99	35	41	21	2	286	333	93
Colorado	38	20	13	4	1	154	125	45	37	14	19	4	0	103	129	32	75	34	32	8	1	257	254	77
Columbus	4	3	0	1	0	12	7	7	6	3	2	0	1	17	17	7	10	6	2	1	1	29	24	14
Dallas	46	24	19	3	0	159	134	51	48	13	28	6	1	123	176	33	94	37	47	9	1	282	310	84
Detroit	42	22	11	9	0	143	108	53	42	13	26	2	1	132	172	29	84	35	37	11	1	275	280	82
Edmonton	35	15	17	3	0	114	115	33	33	12	15	6	0	117	139	30	68	27	32	9	0	231	254	63
Florida	34	22	9	3	0	103	65	47	35	19	12	4	0	89	80	42	69	41	21	7	0	192	145	89
Los Angeles	46	20	21	5	0	151	157	45	44	9	27	6	2	137	205	26	90	29	48	11	2	288	362	71
Minnesota	5	4	0	1	0	20	10	9	5	3	1	1	0	17	13	7	10	7	1	2	0	37	23	16
Montreal	64	33	27	4	0	196	211	70	64	23	34	6	1	158	199	53	128	56	61	10	1	354	410	123
Nashville	7	3	3	0	1	23	20	7	8	6	1	0	1	23	16	13	15	9	4	0	2	46	36	20
NY Islanders	102	46	43	11	2	329	331	105	103	27	62	11	3	285	401	68	205	73	105	22	5	614	732	173
NY Rangers	104	55	39	7	3	350	326	120	102	30	48	20	4	289	366	84	206	85	87	27	7	639	692	204
Ottawa	33	21	10	2	0	96	77	44	34	21	9	3	1	86	78	46	67	42	19	5	1	182	155	90
Philadelphia	101	57	35	8	1	342	318	123	103	31	60	10	2	264	379	74	204	88	95	18	3	606	697	197
Phoenix	31	13	12	6	0	101	93	32	33	7	23	3	0	85	121	17	64	20	35	9	0	186	214	49
Pittsburgh	99	50	35	13	1	347	311	114	97	47	45	4	1	319	341	99	196	97	80	17	2	666	652	213
St. Louis	48	22	19	7	0	148	132	51	48	14	26	7	1	152	198	36	96	36	45	14	1	300	330	87
San Jose	14	9	4	1	0	53	31	19	12	7	3	1	1	36	29	16	26	16	7	2	1	89	60	35
Tampa Bay	36	24	8	2	2	128	76	52	35	19	9	5	2	106	79	45	71	43	17	7	4	234	155	97
Toronto	56	22	16	15	3	192	177	62	58	16	35	5	2	156	203	39	114	38	51	20	5	348	380	101
Vancouver	51	21	22	6	2	156	164	50	49	10	28	11	0	135	183	31	100	31	50	17	2	291	347	81
Washington	89	46	35	7	1	275	257	100	89	31	52	6	0	251	333	68	178	77	87	13	1	526	590	168
Defunct Clubs	8	4	2	2	0	25	19	10	8	2	3	3	0	19	27	7	16	6	5	5	0	44	46	17
Totals	**1402**	**691**	**530**	**159**	**22**	**4525**	**4194**	**1563**	**1402**	**483**	**716**	**169**	**34**	**4004**	**4978**	**1169**	**2804**	**1174**	**1246**	**328**	**56**	**8529**	**9172**	**2732**

Playoffs

	Series	W	L	GP	W	L	T	GF	GA	Last Mtg.	Rnd.	Result
Anaheim	1	1	0	7	4	3	0	19	12	2003	F	W 4-3
Boston	4	3	1	23	15	8	0	68	60	2003	CQF	W 4-1
Buffalo	1	1	0	7	4	3	0	14	14	1994	CQF	W 4-3
Carolina	4	1	3	24	10	14	0	56	51	2009	CQF	L 3-4
Colorado	1	0	1	7	3	4	0	11	19	2001	F	L 3-4
Dallas	1	1	0	6	4	2	0	15	9	2000	F	W 4-2
Detroit	1	1	0	4	4	0	0	16	7	1995	F	W 4-0
Florida	1	1	0	4	4	0	0	12	6	2000	CQF	W 4-0
Montreal	1	1	0	5	4	1	0	22	11	1997	CQF	W 4-1
NY Islanders	1	1	0	6	4	2	0	23	18	1988	DSF	W 4-2
NY Rangers	5	1	4	28	12	16	0	75	79	2008	CQF	L 1-4
Ottawa	3	1	2	18	7	11	0	40	41	2007	CSF	L 1-4
Philadelphia	5	2	3	25	10	15	0	59	64	2010	CQF	L 1-4
Pittsburgh	5	2	3	29	15	14	0	86	80	2001	CF	W 4-1
Tampa Bay	2	2	0	11	8	3	0	33	22	2007	CQF	W 4-2
Toronto	2	2	0	13	8	5	0	37	27	2001	CSF	W 4-3
Washington	2	1	1	13	6	7	0	43	44	1990	DSF	L 2-4
Totals	**40**	**22**	**18**	**230**	**122**	**108**	**0**	**629**	**564**			

Calgary totals include Atlanta Flames, 1974-75 to 1979-80.
Colorado totals include Quebec, 1979-80 to 1994-95.
Phoenix totals include Winnipeg, 1979-80 to 1995-96.
Carolina totals include Hartford, 1979-80 to 1996-97.
Dallas totals include Minnesota North Stars, 1974-75 to 1992-93.

Playoff Results 2010-2006

Year	Round	Opponent	Result	GF	GA
2010	CQF	Philadelphia	L 1-4	9	15
2009	CQF	Carolina	L 3-4	15	17
2008	CQF	NY Rangers	L 1-4	12	19
2007	CSF	Ottawa	L 1-4	11	15
	CQF	Tampa Bay	W 4-2	19	14
2006	CSF	Carolina	L 1-4	10	17
	CQF	NY Rangers	W 4-0	17	4

Abbreviations: Round: F – Final; **CF** – conference final; **CSF** – conference semi-final; **CQF** – conference quarter-final; **DSF** – division semi-final.

2009-10 Results

Oct.	3	Philadelphia	2-5		8	Tampa Bay	2-4
	5	NY Rangers	2-3		9	at Montreal	2-1*
	8	at Tampa Bay	4-3†		12	at NY Rangers	1-0†
	10	at Florida	3-2		14	at Phoenix	3-4
	12	at Washington	3-2†		16	at Colorado	1-3
	16	Atlanta	2-4		18	at NY Islanders	0-4
	17	Carolina	2-0		20	Florida	2-0
	22	at NY Rangers	4-2		22	Montreal	1-3
	24	at Pittsburgh	4-1		23	at NY Islanders	4-2
	28	Buffalo	1-4		26	at Ottawa	0-3
	29	at Boston	2-1		27	at Buffalo	1-2†
	31	at Tampa Bay	2-1†		29	Toronto	5-4*
Nov.	4	Washington	3-2		31	Los Angeles	2-3
	6	NY Islanders	2-1	**Feb.**	2	at Toronto	0-3
	7	at Ottawa	3-2		5	Toronto	4-3
	11	Anaheim	3-1		6	at NY Rangers	1-3
	12	at Pittsburgh	4-1		8	at Philadelphia	2-3
	14	Washington	5-2		10	Philadelphia	2-3*
	16	at Philadelphia	2-3		12	Nashville	5-2
	19	at Nashville	2-3†		13	at Carolina	2-5
	21	at Dallas	3-5	**Mar.**	2	at San Jose	4-3
	25	Ottawa	3-1		5	at Calgary	3-5
	27	at Boston	2-1†		7	at Edmonton	0-2
	28	NY Islanders	6-1		10	NY Rangers	6-3
Dec.	2	Vancouver	2-5		12	Pittsburgh	3-1
	4	Tampa Bay	3-2		13	at NY Islanders	2-4
	5	Detroit	4-3†		15	Boston	3-2
	7	at Buffalo	3-0		17	Pittsburgh	5-2
	9	Carolina	4-2		18	at Toronto	1-2†
	11	Florida	2-4		20	St. Louis	0-1
	12	Philadelphia	4-1		23	Columbus	6-3
	16	Montreal	2-1		25	NY Rangers	3-4†
	18	Ottawa	4-2		27	at Montreal	4-2
	19	at Atlanta	5-4		28	at Philadelphia	1-5
	21	at Pittsburgh	4-0		30	Boston	0-1*
	26	at Washington	1-4	**Apr.**	2	Chicago	1-2†
	28	Atlanta	3-2		3	at Carolina	4-0
	30	Pittsburgh	2-0		6	at Atlanta	3-0
	31	at Chicago	1-5		8	at Florida	2-3
Jan.	2	at Minnesota	5-3		10	NY Islanders	7-1
	5	Dallas	4-0		11	Buffalo	2-1

* – Overtime † – Shootout

Entry Draft Selections 2010-1996

Name in bold denotes played in NHL.

2010
Pick
38	Jonathon Merrill
84	Scott Wedgewood
114	Joe Faust
174	Maxime Clermont
204	Mauro Jorg

2009
Pick
20	Jacob Josefson
54	Eric Gelinas
73	Alexander Urbom
114	Seth Helgeson
144	Derek Rodwell
174	Ashton Bernard
204	Curtis Gedig

2008
Pick
24	Mattias Tedenby
52	Brandon Burlon
54	Patrice Cormier
82	Adam Henrique
112	Matt Delahey
142	Kory Nagy
172	David Wohlberg
202	Harry Young
205	Jean-Sebastien Berube

2007
Pick
57	Mike Hoeffel
79	**Nick Palmieri**
87	Corbin McPherson
117	**Matt Halischuk**
177	Vili Sopanen
207	Ryan Molle

2006
Pick
30	**Matthew Corrente**
58	Alexander Vasyunov
67	Kirill Tulupov
77	**Vladimir Zharkov**
107	Tyler Miller
148	Olivier Magnan-Grenier
178	Tony Romano
208	Kyell Henegan

2005
Pick
23	**Niclas Bergfors**
38	Jeff Frazee
84	**Mark Fraser**
99	**Patrick Davis**
155	Mark Fayne
170	Sean Zimmerman
218	Alexander Sundstrom

2004
Pick
20	**Travis Zajac**
155	Alexander Mikhailishin
185	Josh Disher
216	**Pierre-Luc Letourneau-Leblond**
217	Tyler Eckford
250	Nathan Perkovich
282	Valeri Klimov

2003
Pick
17	**Zach Parise**
42	Petr Vrana
93	Ivan Khomutov
167	Zach Tarkir
197	Jason Smith
261	**Joey Tenute**
292	Arseny Bondarev

2002
Pick
51	Anton Kadeykin
53	**Barry Tallackson**
64	**Jason Ryznar**
84	Marek Chvatal
85	Ahren Nittel
117	**Cam Janssen**
154	Krisjanis Redlihs
187	Eric Johansson
218	**Ilkka Pikkarainen**
250	Dan Glover
281	Bill Kinkel

2001
Pick
28	Adrian Foster
44	Igor Pohanka
48	**Tuomas Pihlman**
60	Victor Uchevatov
67	Robin Leblanc
72	**Brandon Nolan**
128	Andrei Posnov
163	**Andreas Salomonsson**
194	James Massen
229	**Aaron Voros**
257	Yevgeny Gamalei

2000
Pick
22	**David Hale**
39	Teemu Laine
56	**Alexander Suglobov**
57	Matt DeMarchi
62	**Paul Martin**
67	Max Birbraer
76	**Mike Rupp**
125	Phil Cole
135	**Mike Danton**
164	Matus Kostur
194	**Deryk Engelland**
198	Ken Magowan
257	Warren McCutcheon

1999
Pick
27	Ari Ahonen
42	**Mike Commodore**
50	Brett Clouthier
95	Andre Lakos
100	Teemu Kesa
185	Scott Cameron
214	Chris Hartsburg
242	Justin Dziama

1998
Pick
26	**Mike Van Ryn**
27	**Scott Gomez**
37	**Christian Berglund**
82	**Brian Gionta**
96	**Mikko Jokela**
105	**Pierre Dagenais**
119	Anton But
143	**Ryan Flinn**
172	Jacques Lariviere
199	Erik Jensen
227	Marko Ahosilta
257	Ryan Held

1997
Pick
24	**Jean-Francois Damphousse**
38	**Stanislav Gron**
104	Lucas Nehrling
131	**Jiri Bicek**
159	**Sascha Goc**
188	Mathieu Benoit
215	**Scott Clemmensen**
241	Jan Srdinko

1996
Pick
10	**Lance Ward**
38	Wes Mason
41	Josh DeWolf
47	**Pierre Dagenais**
49	**Colin White**
63	**Scott Parker**
91	**Josef Boumedienne**
101	Josh MacNevin
118	Glenn Crawford
145	Sean Ritchlin
173	Daryl Andrews
199	**Willie Mitchell**
205	Jay Bertsch
225	Pasi Petrilainen

Coaching History

Bep Guidolin, 1974-75; Bep Guidolin, Sid Abel and Eddie Bush, 1975-76; Johnny Wilson, 1976-77; Pat Kelly, 1977-78; Pat Kelly and Aldo Guidolin, 1978-79; Don Cherry, 1979-80; Bill MacMillan, 1980-81; Bert Marshall and Marshall Johnston, 1981-82; Bill MacMillan, 1982-83; Bill MacMillan and Tom McVie, 1983-84; Doug Carpenter, 1984-85 to 1986-87; Doug Carpenter and Jim Schoenfeld, 1987-88; Jim Schoenfeld, 1988-89; Jim Schoenfeld and John Cunniff, 1989-90; John Cunniff and Tom McVie, 1990-91; Tom McVie, 1991-92; Herb Brooks, 1992-93; Jacques Lemaire, 1993-94 to 1997-98; Robbie Ftorek, 1998-99; Robbie Ftorek and Larry Robinson, 1999-2000; Larry Robinson, 2000-01; Larry Robinson and Kevin Constantine, 2001-02; Pat Burns, 2002-03 to 2004-05; Larry Robinson and Lou Lamoriello, 2005-06; Claude Julien and Lou Lamoriello, 2006-07; Brent Sutter, 2007-08, 2008-09; Jacques Lemaire, 2009-10; John MacLean, 2010-11.

Lou Lamoriello
CEO, President and General Manager

Born: Providence, RI, October 21, 1942.

Lou Lamoriello has been president and general manager of the Devils since 1987-88 following more than 20 years with Providence College as a player, coach and administrator. He was inducted into the Hockey Hall of Fame's Builder category in November, 2009. His trades, signings and draft choices helped lead the Devils to their first Stanley Cup Championship in 1995 and were followed by victories again in 2000 and 2003. During his tenure, the Devils have had 12 100-point seasons, four Eastern Conference titles and nine Atlantic Division regular-season championships. In 2005-06, Lamoriello took over behind the bench and coached the Devils to first place in the Atlantic Division.

While at Providence, Lamoriello served as hockey coach for 15 seasons, compiling an impressive .578 winning percentage (248-179-13), while guiding the Friars to 12 post-season tournaments in a row. During his last five seasons (1978-83) of coaching, the school compiled a record of 107-58-4 and had more players drafted by the National Hockey League after entering college than any other college team during those years. Lamoriello helped propel numerous players and administrators toward NHL careers during his tenure at Providence. He was hired as president of the Devils on April 30, 1987, and assumed the responsibility of general manager on September 10, 1987. Lamoriello was G.M. of Team USA for the first World Cup of Hockey in 1996 as the U.S. captured the championship. He was also the G.M. for the 1998 U.S. Olympic Team.

Coaching Record

| Season | Team | League | Regular Season | | | | Playoffs | | | |
			GC	W	L	O/T	GC	W	L	T
2005-06	New Jersey	NHL	50	32	14	4	9	5	4	....
2006-07	New Jersey	NHL	3	2	0	1	11	5	6	....
NHL Totals			**53**	**34**	**14**	**5**	**20**	**10**	**10**	....

Posted an 0-1 playoff record as replacement coach when Jim Schoenfeld was suspended, May 10, 1988. Loss is credited to Schoenfeld's coaching record.

Club Directory

New Jersey Devils
Prudential Center
165 Mulberry Street
Newark, NJ 07102
Phone **973/757-6100**
FAX 973/757-6399
www.newjerseydevils.com
Capacity: 17,625

Prudential Center

Owners	Jeff Vanderbeek, Mike Gilfillan, Peter Simon
Chairman	Jeff Vanderbeek
Vice Chairman	Mike Gilfillan
President/CEO/General Manager	Lou Lamoriello
Sr. Exec. Vice President/Chief Operating Officer	Chris Modrzynski
Exec. Vice President, Hockey Ops/Director, Scouting	David Conte
Exec. Vice President, Operations	Peter McMullen
Sr. Vice President, Hockey Ops/ General Manager, Albany/Trenton and Scout	Chris Lamoriello
Senior Vice President, Communications	Mike Levine
Vice President, Hockey Operations	Stephen Pellegrini

Hockey Club Personnel
Head Coach	John MacLean
Assistant Coaches	Larry Robinson, Adam Oates
Goaltending Coach	Chris Terreri
Special Assignment Coaches	Jacques Lemaire, Jacques Laperriere, Scott Stevens, Pat Burns, Jacques Caron
Assistant Director, Scouting	Claude Carrier
Scouting Staff	Timo Blomqvist, Glen Dirk, Milt Fisher, Ferny Flaman, Dan Labraaten, Scott Lachance, Pierre Mondou, Gates Orlando, Larry Perris, Marcel Pronovost, Lou Reycroft, Vaclav Slansky, Jr., Steve Smith, Geoff Stevens, Ed Thomlinson, Les Widdifield
Pro Scouting Staff	Bob Hoffmeyer, Jan Ludvig, Andre Boudrias
Hockey Operations Video Coordinator	Taran Singleton
Hockey Operations Video Assistant	Mike Ford
Scouting Staff Assistant	Callie A. Smith
Head Trainer	Richard Stinziano
Equipment Manager	Rich Matthews
Assistant Equipment Managers	Alex Abasto, Jason McGrath, Mike Thibault
Strength/Conditioning Coordinator	Michael Vasalani
Massage Therapist	Tommy Plasko
Team Orthopedists	Dr. Barry Fisher, Dr. Len Jaffe
Team Cardiologist	Dr. Joseph Niznik
Team Dentist	Dr. H. Hugh Gardy
Team Optometrist	Dr. Paul Berman
Exercise Physiologist	Dr. Garret Caffrey
Physical Therapist	David Feniger
Video Consultant	Mitch Kaufman
Head Coach, Albany	Rick Kowalsky
Assistant Coach, Albany	Tommy Albelin
Video Coordinator, Albany	TBA
Athletic Trainer, Albany	Kevin Morley
Equipment Manager, Albany	TBA
Assistant Equipment Manager, Albany	Zach Dinga

President's Office
Hockey Operations Executive Assistant to the President/CEO/General Manager	Marie Carnevale
Corporate Exec. Asst. to Pres./CEO/G.M. and Director, Human Resources	Mary K. Morrison
Administrative Assistant	Christine Garcia

Communications
Senior Director, Communications	Jeff Altstadter
Assistant Director, Communications	Pete Albietz
Staff Writer	Eric Marin
Coordinator, Communications	Daniel Beam

Operations
Receptionist	Jelsa Belotta
Staff Assistant	Kyle Radzinski

Computer Operations
Director, Programming/Computer Operations	Jack Skelley

Alumni
Alumni Representatives	Ken Daneyko, Bruce Driver, Grant Marshall, Jim Dowd

Television/Radio
Television Outlet	MSG Plus
Television Play-by-Play / Color	Mike Emrick / Glenn Resch
Radio Outlet	SportsRadio 66 WFAN
Radio Play-by-Play / Color	Matt Loughlin / Sherry Ross

New York Islanders

Key Off-Season Signings/Acquisitions

2010

July 2 • Signed D **Mark Eaton**, D **Milan Jurcina**, LW **P.A. Parenteau** and C **Zenon Konopka**.
15 • Re-signed D **Dustin Kohn** and C **Rob Schremp**.
27 • Re-signed LW **Matt Moulson**.
30 • Acquired D **James Wisniewski** from Anaheim for a conditional pick in the 2011 Entry Draft.

Aug. 3 • Re-signed LW **Jon Sim**.

**2009-10 Results: 34w-37L-5OTL-6SOL 79PTS.
Fifth, Atlantic Division**

2010-11 Schedule

Oct.	Sat.	9	Dallas		Thu.	13	Ottawa
	Mon.	11	NY Rangers*		Sat.	15	Buffalo
	Wed.	13	at Washington		Mon.	17	New Jersey*
	Fri.	15	at Pittsburgh		Thu.	20	Washington
	Sat.	16	Colorado		Fri.	21	at Buffalo
	Mon.	18	at Toronto		Sun.	23	Buffalo*
	Thu.	21	at Tampa Bay		Tue.	25	at Pittsburgh
	Sat.	23	at Florida		Wed.	26	Carolina
	Wed.	27	at Montreal	**Feb.**	Tue.	1	at Atlanta
	Fri.	29	Montreal		Wed.	2	at Pittsburgh
	Sat.	30	at Philadelphia		Sat.	5	Ottawa
Nov.	Wed.	3	at Carolina		Tue.	8	Toronto
	Thu.	4	at Ottawa		Thu.	10	at Montreal
	Sat.	6	Philadelphia		Fri.	11	Pittsburgh
	Wed.	10	at Anaheim		Sun.	13	at Buffalo*
	Thu.	11	at San Jose		Tue.	15	at Ottawa
	Sat.	13	at Los Angeles		Thu.	17	Boston
	Wed.	17	Tampa Bay		Sat.	19	Los Angeles
	Sat.	20	Florida		Mon.	21	Florida*
	Sun.	21	at Atlanta*		Tue.	22	at Toronto
	Wed.	24	Columbus		Thu.	24	at Philadelphia
	Fri.	26	New Jersey*		Sat.	26	Washington
Dec.	Thu.	2	NY Rangers	**Mar.**	Tue.	1	at Washington
	Fri.	3	at New Jersey		Wed.	2	Minnesota
	Sun.	5	Philadelphia*		Sat.	5	St. Louis*
	Thu.	9	at Boston		Sun.	6	New Jersey*
	Sat.	11	Atlanta		Tue.	8	Toronto
	Mon.	13	at Nashville		Fri.	11	Boston
	Thu.	16	Anaheim		Sat.	12	at New Jersey
	Sat.	18	Phoenix		Tue.	15	at NY Rangers
	Wed.	22	Tampa Bay		Fri.	18	at Carolina
	Thu.	23	at New Jersey		Sat.	19	at Florida
	Sun.	26	Montreal		Tue.	22	at Tampa Bay
	Mon.	27	at NY Rangers		Thu.	24	Atlanta
	Wed.	29	Pittsburgh		Sat.	26	Philadelphia
	Fri.	31	at Detroit		Wed.	30	at New Jersey
Jan.	Mon.	3	at Calgary		Thu.	31	NY Rangers
	Thu.	6	at Edmonton	**Apr.**	Sat.	2	Carolina
	Sat.	8	at Colorado*		Wed.	6	at Boston
	Sun.	9	at Chicago		Fri.	8	Pittsburgh
	Tue.	11	Vancouver		Sat.	9	at Philadelphia

* Denotes afternoon game.

Josh Bailey, Kyle Okposo and John Tavares get together during a time out. Tavares and Okposo were the Islanders' top two point producers in 2009-10. Bailey more than doubled his rookie total of seven goals to 16 last season.

Year-by-Year Record

Season	GP	Home W	L	T	OL	Road W	L	T	OL	Overall W	L	T	OL	GF	GA	Pts.	Finished	Playoff Result
2009-10	82	23	14	....	4	11	23	....	7	34	37	....	11	222	264	79	5th, Atlantic Div.	Out of Playoffs
2008-09	82	17	18	....	6	9	29	....	3	26	47	....	9	201	279	61	5th, Atlantic Div.	Out of Playoffs
2007-08	82	18	18	....	5	17	20	....	4	35	38	....	9	194	243	79	5th, Atlantic Div.	Out of Playoffs
2006-07	82	22	13	....	6	18	17	....	6	40	30	....	12	248	240	92	4th, Atlantic Div.	Lost Conf. Quarter-Final
2005-06	82	20	18	....	3	16	22	....	3	36	40	....	6	230	278	78	4th, Atlantic Div.	Out of Playoffs
2004-05	....	....	....	....	....	....	....	....	....	....	....	....	....	....	....	....		
2003-04	82	25	11	4	1	13	18	7	3	38	29	11	4	237	210	91	3rd, Atlantic Div.	Lost Conf. Quarter-Final
2002-03	82	18	18	5	0	17	16	6	2	35	34	11	2	224	231	83	3rd, Atlantic Div.	Lost Conf. Quarter-Final
2001-02	82	21	13	5	2	21	15	3	2	42	28	8	4	239	220	96	2nd, Atlantic Div.	Lost Conf. Quarter-Final
2000-01	82	12	27	1	1	9	24	6	2	21	51	7	3	185	268	52	5th, Atlantic Div.	Out of Playoffs
1999-2000	82	10	25	5	1	14	23	4	0	24	48	9	1	194	275	58	5th, Atlantic Div.	Out of Playoffs
1998-99	82	11	23	7	....	13	25	3	....	24	48	10	....	194	244	58	5th, Atlantic Div.	Out of Playoffs
1997-98	82	17	20	4	....	13	21	7	....	30	41	11	....	212	225	71	4th, Atlantic Div.	Out of Playoffs
1996-97	82	19	18	4	....	10	23	8	....	29	41	12	....	240	250	70	7th, Atlantic Div.	Out of Playoffs
1995-96	82	14	21	6	....	8	29	4	....	22	50	10	....	229	315	54	7th, Atlantic Div.	Out of Playoffs
1994-95	48	10	11	3	....	5	17	2	....	15	28	5	....	126	158	35	7th, Atlantic Div.	Out of Playoffs
1993-94	84	23	15	4	....	13	21	8	....	36	36	12	....	282	264	84	4th, Atlantic Div.	Lost Conf. Quarter-Final
1992-93	84	20	19	3	....	20	18	4	....	40	37	7	....	335	297	87	3rd, Patrick Div.	Lost Conf. Championship
1991-92	80	20	15	5	....	14	20	6	....	34	35	11	....	291	299	79	5th, Patrick Div.	Out of Playoffs
1990-91	80	15	19	6	....	10	26	4	....	25	45	10	....	223	290	60	6th, Patrick Div.	Out of Playoffs
1989-90	80	15	17	8	....	16	21	3	....	31	38	11	....	281	288	73	4th, Patrick Div.	Lost Div. Semi-Final
1988-89	80	19	18	3	....	9	29	2	....	28	47	5	....	265	325	61	6th, Patrick Div.	Out of Playoffs
1987-88	80	24	10	6	....	15	21	4	....	39	31	10	....	308	267	88	1st, Patrick Div.	Lost Div. Semi-Final
1986-87	80	20	15	5	....	15	18	7	....	35	33	12	....	279	281	82	3rd, Patrick Div.	Lost Div. Final
1985-86	80	22	11	7	....	17	18	5	....	39	29	12	....	327	284	90	3rd, Patrick Div.	Lost Div. Semi-Final
1984-85	80	26	11	3	....	14	23	3	....	40	34	6	....	345	312	86	3rd, Patrick Div.	Lost Div. Final
1983-84	80	28	11	1	....	22	15	3	....	50	26	4	....	357	269	104	1st, Patrick Div.	Lost Final
1982-83	**80**	**26**	**11**	**3**	....	**16**	**15**	**9**	....	**42**	**26**	**12**	....	**302**	**226**	**96**	**2nd, Patrick Div.**	**Won Stanley Cup**
1981-82	**80**	**33**	**3**	**4**	....	**21**	**13**	**6**	....	**54**	**16**	**10**	....	**385**	**250**	**118**	**1st, Patrick Div.**	**Won Stanley Cup**
1980-81	**80**	**23**	**6**	**11**	....	**25**	**12**	**3**	....	**48**	**18**	**14**	....	**355**	**260**	**110**	**1st, Patrick Div.**	**Won Stanley Cup**
1979-80	**80**	**26**	**9**	**5**	....	**13**	**19**	**8**	....	**39**	**28**	**13**	....	**281**	**247**	**91**	**2nd, Patrick Div.**	**Won Stanley Cup**
1978-79	80	31	3	6	....	20	12	8	....	51	15	14	....	358	214	116	1st, Patrick Div.	Lost Semi-Final
1977-78	80	29	3	8	....	19	14	7	....	48	17	15	....	334	210	111	1st, Patrick Div.	Lost Quarter-Final
1976-77	80	24	11	5	....	23	10	7	....	47	21	12	....	288	193	106	2nd, Patrick Div.	Lost Semi-Final
1975-76	80	24	8	8	....	18	13	9	....	42	21	17	....	297	190	101	2nd, Patrick Div.	Lost Semi-Final
1974-75	80	22	6	12	....	11	19	10	....	33	25	22	....	264	221	88	3rd, Patrick Div.	Lost Semi-Final
1973-74	78	13	17	9	....	6	24	9	....	19	41	18	....	182	247	56	8th, East Div.	Out of Playoffs
1972-73	78	10	25	4	....	2	35	2	....	12	60	6	....	170	347	30	8th, East Div.	Out of Playoffs

ATLANTIC DIVISION
39th NHL Season

Franchise date: June 6, 1972

2010-11 Player Personnel

FORWARDS

	HT	WT	S	Place of Birth	*Age	2009-10 Club
BAILEY, Josh	6-1	188	L	Bowmanville, Ont.	21	NY Islanders
COMEAU, Blake	6-1	207	R	Meadow Lake, Sask.	24	NY Islanders
GILLIES, Trevor	6-3	215	L	Cambridge, Ont.	31	Bridgeport-NY Islanders
HUNTER, Trent	6-3	210	R	Red Deer, Alta.	30	NY Islanders
KONOPKA, Zenon	6-0	211	L	Niagara on the Lake, Ont.	29	Tampa Bay
MARTIN, Matthew	6-2	192	L	Windsor, Ont.	21	NY Islanders-Bridgeport
MOULSON, Matt	6-1	206	L	North York, Ont.	26	NY Islanders
NIELSEN, Frans	5-11	172	L	Herning, Denmark	26	NY Islanders
OKPOSO, Kyle	6-1	200	R	St. Paul, MN	22	NY Islanders
PARENTEAU, P.A.	6-0	198	R	Hull, Que.	27	NY Rangers-Hartford
SCHREMP, Rob	5-11	200	L	Syracuse, NY	24	NY Islanders
SIM, Jon	5-10	195	L	New Glasgow, N.S.	33	NY Islanders
TAVARES, John	6-0	195	L	Mississauga, Ont.	20	NY Islanders

DEFENSEMEN

EATON, Mark	6-2	204	L	Wilmington, DE	33	Pittsburgh
GERVAIS, Bruno	6-1	205	R	Longueuil, Que.	26	NY Islanders
HILLEN, Jack	5-11	200	L	Minnetonka, MN	24	NY Islanders
JURCINA, Milan	6-4	236	R	Liptovsky Mikulas, Czech.	27	Washington-Columbus
MacDONALD, Andrew	6-1	188	L	Judique, N.S.	24	NY Islanders-Bridgeport
MARTINEK, Radek	6-1	203	R	Havlicko Brod, Czech.	34	NY Islanders
STREIT, Mark	6-0	197	L	Bern, Switz.	32	NY Islanders
WISNIEWSKI, James	5-11	205	R	Canton, MI	26	Anaheim

GOALTENDERS

	HT	WT	C	Place of Birth	*Age	2009-10 Club
DiPIETRO, Rick	6-1	210	R	Winthrop, MA	29	Bridgeport-NY Islanders
ROLOSON, Dwayne	6-1	180	L	Simcoe, Ont.	40	NY Islanders

* – Age at start of 2010-11 season

2009-10 Scoring

* – rookie

Regular Season

Pos	#	Player	Team	GP	G	A	Pts	TOI	+/–	PIM	PP	SH	GW	S	%
C	91	* John Tavares	NYI	82	24	30	54	18:00	-15	22	11	0	2	186	12.9
R	21	Kyle Okposo	NYI	80	19	33	52	20:32	-22	34	4	0	4	249	7.6
D	2	Mark Streit	NYI	82	11	38	49	25:41	0	48	9	0	2	187	5.9
C	26	Matt Moulson	NYI	82	30	18	48	16:38	-1	16	8	0	5	208	14.4
C	51	Frans Nielsen	NYI	76	12	26	38	17:12	4	6	0	1	1	136	8.8
L	57	Blake Comeau	NYI	61	17	18	35	15:24	-2	40	0	1	2	133	12.8
C	12	Josh Bailey	NYI	73	16	19	35	15:08	5	18	3	1	2	112	14.3
R	10	Richard Park	NYI	81	9	22	31	15:45	-9	28	0	1	4	146	6.2
R	7	Trent Hunter	NYI	61	11	18	28	15:10	3	18	3	0	1	159	6.9
C	13	* Rob Schremp	NYI	44	7	18	25	13:54	-4	8	5	0	0	74	9.5
L	20	Sean Bergenheim	NYI	63	10	13	23	14:03	1	45	0	2	0	133	7.5
L	16	Jon Sim	NYI	77	13	9	22	11:39	-4	44	1	0	0	128	10.2
D	38	Jack Hillen	NYI	69	3	18	21	20:41	-5	44	1	0	0	78	3.8
D	8	Bruno Gervais	NYI	71	3	14	17	20:00	-15	31	1	0	1	83	3.6
C	93	Doug Weight	NYI	36	1	16	17	15:50	-1	8	0	0	0	61	1.6
D	44	Freddy Meyer	NYI	64	4	11	15	16:46	-2	40	0	0	0	56	7.1
L	15	Jeff Tambellini	NYI	36	7	7	14	11:28	-8	14	3	0	0	55	12.7
L	28	Tim Jackman	NYI	54	4	5	9	9:38	-4	98	0	0	1	51	7.8
D	47	* Andrew MacDonald	NYI	46	1	6	7	20:05	4	20	0	0	0	43	2.3
D	32	Brendan Witt	NYI	42	2	3	5	15:14	-18	45	0	0	1	25	8.0
D	42	* Dylan Reese	NYI	19	2	2	4	15:02	4	14	0	0	1	16	12.5
D	56	* Dustin Kohn	NYI	22	0	4	4	11:35	-2	4	0	0	0	7	0.0
D	24	Radek Martinek	NYI	16	2	1	3	22:47	-1	12	0	1	0	24	8.3
D	46	* Matt Martin	NYI	5	0	2	2	13:14	-1	26	0	0	0	10	0.0
L	58	* Jesse Joensuu	NYI	11	1	0	1	11:09	4	4	0	0	0	13	7.7
D	4	* Mark Flood	NYI	6	0	1	1	12:42	-4	0	0	0	0	5	0.0
L	14	Trevor Gillies	NYI	14	0	1	1	3:49	-2	75	0	0	0	6	0.0
C	62	Greg Mauldin	NYI	1	0	0	0	10:02	-1	0	0	0	0	2	0.0
D	48	* Anton Klementyev	NYI	1	0	0	0	6:20	0	0	0	0	0	0	0.0
C	59	* Micheal Haley	NYI	2	0	0	0	7:36	-3	9	0	0	0	0	0.0
R	40	* Joel Rechlicz	NYI	6	0	0	0	2:41	-2	27	0	0	0	1	0.0

Goaltending

No.	Goaltender	GPI	Mins	Avg	W	L	OT	EN	SO	GA	SA	S%	G	A	PIM
39	Rick DiPietro	8	462	2.60	2	5	0	2	1	20	201	.900	0	1	2
30	Dwayne Roloson	50	2897	3.00	23	18	7	2	1	145	1555	.907	0	0	14
43	Martin Biron	29	1634	3.27	9	14	4	0	1	89	859	.896	0	1	2
	Totals	82	5015	3.09	34	37	11	4	3	258	2619	.901			

Matt Moulson smiles after scoring his 30th goal of the 2009-10 season. Previously, Moulson had scored just six goals in 29 games over two seasons.

Scott Gordon
Head Coach
Born: Brockton, MA, February 6, 1963.

The New York Islanders announced the hiring of Scott Gordon as their head coach on August 12, 2008. Gordon spent the previous eight seasons with the Providence Bruins, Boston's affiliate in the American Hockey League. He began as an assistant coach in Providence in 2000-01 and was hired as the head coach on July 25, 2003 after serving as interim head coach for part of the 2002-03 season. In 2007-08, he guided the Bruins to top spot in the AHL standings with a record of 55-18-7 and was named coach of the year.

Gordon began his coaching career with the International Hockey League's Atlanta Knights as an assistant coach in 1994-95. When he was named head coach on January 5, 1996, he became at age 32 the youngest head coach in the league's 53-year history. The team spent the next two seasons as the Quebec Rafales, with Gordon serving as an assistant. His next move came in 1998-99, when he was named head coach of the Roanoke Express of the East Coast Hockey League. He led the club to consecutive first-place finishes in the Northeast Division, setting franchise records for wins (44), points (94) and fewest goals against (181) in 1999-2000.

As a player, Gordon spent four years as a goaltender at Boston College from 1982 to 1986, posting a 64-35-3 record over that span. He backstopped the Eagles to a NCAA Final Four appearance in 1985 and was named a Hockey East First-Team All-Star in 1986. Following the completion of his collegiate career, Gordon began his professional playing career with the AHL's Frederiction Express in 1986-87. He made his NHL debut in 1989-90 playing 10 games with the Quebec Nordiques. He played 13 more games for Quebec in 1990-91. Gordon played on the 1992 United States Olympic team and was a member of the IHL's 1994 Turner Cup champions Atlanta Knights squad. Gordon played 150 AHL games with Fredericton, the Baltimore Skipjacks, the Halifax Citadels and the New Haven Nighthawks through 1993-94.

Coaching Record

			Regular Season				Playoffs			
Season	Team	League	GC	W	L	O/T	GC	W	L	T
1995-96	Atlanta	IHL	40	15	19	6	3	0	3	....
1998-99	Roanoke	ECHL	70	38	22	10	12	6	6	....
99-2000	Roanoke	ECHL	70	44	20	6	4	1	3	....
2002-03	Providence	AHL	9	3	3	3	1	0	1	....
2003-04	Providence	AHL	80	36	29	15	2	0	2	....
2004-05	Providence	AHL	80	40	30	10	17	10	7	....
2005-06	Providence	AHL	80	43	31	6	6	2	4	....
2006-07	Providence	AHL	80	44	30	6	13	6	7	....
2007-08	Providence	AHL	80	55	18	7	10	6	4	....
2008-09	NY Islanders	NHL	82	26	47	9	....	....	....	....
2009-10	NY Islanders	NHL	82	34	37	11	....	....	....	....
	NHL Totals		164	60	84	20	....	....	....	....

Coaching History
Phil Goyette and Earl Ingarfield, 1972-73; Al Arbour, 1973-74 to 1985-86; Terry Simpson, 1986-87, 1987-88; Terry Simpson and Al Arbour, 1988-89; Al Arbour, 1989-90 to 1993-94; Lorne Henning, 1994-95; Mike Milbury, 1995-96; Mike Milbury and Rick Bowness, 1996-97; Rick Bowness and Mike Milbury, 1997-98; Mike Milbury and Bill Stewart, 1998-99; Butch Goring, 1999-2000; Butch Goring and Lorne Henning, 2000-01; Peter Laviolette, 2001-02, 2002-03; Steve Stirling, 2003-04, 2004-05; Steve Stirling and Brad Shaw, 2005-06; Ted Nolan, 2006-07, 2007-08; Scott Gordon, 2008-09 to date.

Club Records

Team

(Figures in brackets for season records are games played; records for fewest points, wins, ties, losses, goals, goals against are for 70 or more games)

Most Points	**118**	1981-82 (80)
Most Wins	**54**	1981-82 (80)
Most Ties	**22**	1974-75 (80)
Most Losses	**60**	1972-73 (78)
Most Goals	**385**	1981-82 (80)
Most Goals Against	**347**	1972-73 (78)
Fewest Points	**30**	1972-73 (78)
Fewest Wins	**12**	1972-73 (78)
Fewest Ties	**4**	1983-84 (80)
Fewest Losses	**15**	1978-79 (80)
Fewest Goals	**170**	1972-73 (78)
Fewest Goals Against	**190**	1975-76 (80)
Longest Winning Streak		
Overall	**15**	Jan. 21-Feb. 20/82
Home	**14**	Jan. 2-Feb. 25/82
Away	**8**	Feb. 27-Mar. 29/81
Longest Undefeated Streak		
Overall	**15**	Three times
Home	**23**	Oct. 17/78-Jan. 20/79 (19 wins, 4 ties), Jan. 2-Apr. 3/82 (21 wins, 2 ties)
Away	**8**	Three times
Longest Losing Streak		
Overall	**12**	Dec. 27/72-Jan. 16/73, Nov. 22-Dec. 15/88
Home	**7**	Nov. 13-Dec. 14/99
Away	**15**	Jan. 20-Mar. 31/73
Longest Winless Streak		
Overall	**15**	Nov. 22-Dec. 21/72 (12 losses, 3 ties)
Home	**9**	Mar. 2-Apr. 6/99 (7 losses, 2 ties)
Away	**20**	Nov. 3/72-Jan. 13/73 (19 losses, 1 tie)
Most Shutouts, Season	**10**	1975-76 (80)
Most PIM, Season	**1,857**	1986-87 (80)
Most Goals, Game	**11**	Dec. 20/83 (Pit. 3 at NYI 11), Mar. 3/84 (NYI 11 at Tor. 6)

Individual

Most Seasons	**17**	Billy Smith
Most Games	**1,123**	Bryan Trottier
Most Goals, Career	**573**	Mike Bossy
Most Assists, Career	**853**	Bryan Trottier
Most Points, Career	**1,353**	Bryan Trottier (500G, 853A)
Most PIM, Career	**1,879**	Mick Vukota
Most Shutouts, Career	**25**	Glenn Resch
Longest Consecutive Games Streak	**576**	Billy Harris (Oct. 7/72-Nov. 30/79)
Most Goals, Season	**69**	Mike Bossy (1978-79)
Most Assists, Season	**87**	Bryan Trottier (1978-79)
Most Points, Season	**147**	Mike Bossy (1981-82; 64G, 83A)
Most PIM, Season	**356**	Brian Curran (1986-87)
Most Points, Defenseman, Season	**101**	Denis Potvin (1978-79; 31G, 70A)
Most Points, Center, Season	**134**	Bryan Trottier (1978-79; 47G, 87A)
Most Points, Right Wing, Season	**147**	Mike Bossy (1981-82; 64G, 83A)
Most Points, Left Wing, Season	**100**	John Tonelli (1984-85; 42G, 58A)
Most Points, Rookie, Season	**95**	Bryan Trottier (1975-76; 32G, 63A)
Most Shutouts, Season	**7**	Glenn Resch (1975-76)
Most Goals, Game	**5**	Bryan Trottier (Dec. 23/78), (Feb. 13/82) John Tonelli (Jan. 6/81)
Most Assists, Game	**6**	Mike Bossy (Jan. 6/81)
Most Points, Game	**8**	Bryan Trottier (Dec. 23/78; 5G, 3A)

Captains' History

Ed Westfall, 1972-73 to 1975-76; Ed Westfall and Clark Gillies, 1976-77; Clark Gillies, 1977-78, 1978-79; Denis Potvin, 1979-80 to 1986-87; Brent Sutter, 1987-88 to 1990-91; Brent Sutter and Pat Flatley, 1991-92; Pat Flatley, 1992-93 to 1995-96; no captain, 1996-97; Bryan McCabe and Trevor Linden, 1997-98; Trevor Linden, 1998-99; Kenny Jonsson, 1999-2000, 2000-01; Michael Peca, 2001-02 to 2003-04; Alexei Yashin, 2005-06, 2006-07; Bill Guerin, 2007-08; Bill Guerin and no captain, 2008-09; Doug Weight, 2009-10.

Retired Numbers

5	Denis Potvin	1973-1988
9	Clark Gillies	1974-1986
19	Bryan Trottier	1975-1990
22	Mike Bossy	1977-1987
23	Bob Nystrom	1972-1986
31	Billy Smith	1972-1989

All-time Record vs. Other Clubs

Regular Season

	At Home								On Road								Total							
	GP	W	L	T	OL	GF	GA	PTS	GP	W	L	T	OL	GF	GA	PTS	GP	W	L	T	OL	GF	GA	PTS
Anaheim	10	5	4	1	0	26	27	11	11	5	2	3	1	33	27	14	21	10	6	4	1	59	54	25
Atlanta	20	11	9	0	0	71	55	22	20	11	5	2	2	78	64	26	40	22	14	2	2	149	119	48
Boston	71	30	31	10	0	230	223	70	69	20	35	11	3	191	252	54	140	50	66	21	3	421	475	124
Buffalo	71	32	29	9	1	199	195	74	71	22	38	9	2	195	242	55	142	54	67	18	3	394	437	129
Calgary	53	27	17	9	0	197	147	63	51	15	25	11	0	152	181	41	104	42	42	20	0	349	328	104
Carolina	54	24	25	4	1	158	158	53	55	22	28	5	0	174	194	49	109	46	53	9	1	332	352	102
Chicago	49	20	14	15	0	173	146	55	50	19	26	5	0	168	165	43	99	39	40	20	0	341	311	98
Colorado	34	20	13	1	0	138	115	41	36	12	20	3	1	101	127	28	70	32	33	4	1	239	242	69
Columbus	5	3	2	0	0	17	15	6	7	1	4	1	1	15	23	4	12	4	6	1	1	32	38	10
Dallas	50	26	15	8	1	181	142	61	49	22	19	8	0	176	143	52	99	48	34	16	1	357	285	113
Detroit	48	24	18	4	2	173	141	54	47	19	26	2	0	139	166	40	95	43	44	6	2	312	307	94
Edmonton	33	17	7	9	0	134	113	43	31	8	18	5	0	89	114	21	64	25	25	14	0	223	227	64
Florida	35	18	14	2	1	91	94	39	35	10	18	6	1	98	111	27	70	28	32	8	2	189	205	66
Los Angeles	47	24	17	5	1	161	132	54	47	17	23	7	0	145	168	41	94	41	40	12	1	306	300	95
Minnesota	5	2	3	0	0	11	16	4	6	1	4	0	1	15	20	3	11	3	7	0	1	26	36	7
Montreal	70	33	31	6	0	209	202	72	70	18	42	9	1	189	250	46	140	51	73	15	1	398	452	118
Nashville	6	3	2	0	1	16	17	7	7	2	5	0	0	17	17	4	13	5	7	0	1	33	34	11
New Jersey	103	65	25	11	2	401	285	143	102	45	43	11	3	331	329	104	205	110	68	22	5	732	614	247
NY Rangers	114	60	44	8	2	407	362	130	114	41	61	11	1	333	408	94	228	101	105	19	3	740	770	224
Ottawa	34	9	18	6	1	105	124	25	33	7	19	5	2	81	113	21	67	16	37	11	3	186	237	46
Philadelphia	116	55	44	15	2	402	348	127	113	34	67	11	1	308	400	80	229	89	111	26	3	710	748	207
Phoenix	32	15	9	8	0	119	95	38	33	16	13	4	0	117	111	36	65	31	22	12	0	236	206	74
Pittsburgh	104	55	35	8	6	404	345	124	106	38	52	14	2	356	407	92	210	93	87	22	8	760	752	216
St. Louis	52	26	13	11	2	191	138	65	49	21	18	9	1	160	173	52	101	47	31	20	3	351	311	117
San Jose	13	6	5	2	0	44	41	14	14	6	7	1	0	43	37	13	27	12	12	3	0	87	78	27
Tampa Bay	35	18	15	1	1	103	93	38	36	14	17	2	3	102	105	33	71	32	32	3	4	205	198	71
Toronto	63	37	21	3	2	241	178	79	65	26	33	4	2	213	232	58	128	63	54	7	4	454	410	137
Vancouver	49	27	12	10	0	177	138	64	49	22	23	3	1	160	160	48	98	49	35	13	1	337	298	112
Washington	91	47	39	2	3	330	282	99	91	35	42	11	3	286	301	84	182	82	81	13	6	616	583	183
Defunct Clubs	13	11	0	2	0	75	33	24	13	4	5	4	0	35	41	12	26	15	5	6	0	110	74	36
Totals	**1480**	**750**	**531**	**170**	**29**	**5184**	**4400**	**1699**	**1480**	**533**	**738**	**177**	**32**	**4500**	**5081**	**1275**	**2960**	**1283**	**1269**	**347**	**61**	**9684**	**9481**	**2974**

Playoffs

	Series	W	L	GP	W	L	T	GF	GA	Last Mtg.	Rnd.	Result
Boston	2	2	0	11	8	3	0	49	35	1983	CF	W 4-2
Buffalo	4	3	1	21	13	8	0	70	62	2007	CQF	L 1-4
Chicago	2	2	0	6	6	0	0	21	6	1979	QF	W 4-0
Colorado	1	1	0	4	4	0	0	18	9	1982	CF	W 4-0
Dallas	1	1	0	5	4	1	0	26	16	1981	F	W 4-1
Edmonton	3	2	1	15	9	6	0	58	47	1984	F	L 1-4
Los Angeles	1	1	0	4	3	1	0	21	10	1980	PRE	W 3-1
Montreal	4	1	3	22	8	14	0	55	64	1993	CF	L 1-4
New Jersey	1	0	1	6	2	4	0	18	23	1988	DSF	L 2-4
NY Rangers	8	5	3	39	20	19	0	129	132	1994	CQF	L 0-4
Ottawa	1	0	1	5	1	4	0	7	13	2003	CQF	L 1-4
Philadelphia	4	1	3	25	11	14	0	69	83	1987	DF	L 3-4
Pittsburgh	3	3	0	19	11	8	0	67	58	1993	DF	W 4-3
Tampa Bay	1	0	1	5	1	4	0	5	12	2004	CQF	L 1-4
Toronto	3	1	2	17	9	8	0	54	42	2002	CQF	L 3-4
Vancouver	2	2	0	6	6	0	0	26	14	1982	F	W 4-0
Washington	6	5	1	30	18	12	0	99	88	1993	DSF	W 4-2
Totals	**47**	**30**	**17**	**240**	**134**	**106**	**0**	**792**	**714**			

Playoff Results 2010-2006

Year	Round	Opponent	Result	GF	GA
2007	CQF	Buffalo	L 1-4	11	17

Abbreviations: Round: F – Final; **CF** – conference final; **CQF** – conference quarter-final; **DF** – division final; **DSF** – division semi-final; **QF** – quarter-final; **PRE** – preliminary round.

Calgary totals include Atlanta Flames, 1972-73 to 1979-80.
Carolina totals include Hartford, 1979-80 to 1996-97.
Colorado totals include Quebec, 1979-80 to 1994-95.
Dallas totals include Minnesota North Stars, 1972-73 to 1992-93.
New Jersey totals include Kansas City, 1974-75, 1975-76, and Colorado Rockies, 1976-77 to 1981-82.
Phoenix totals include Winnipeg, 1979-80 to 1995-96.

2009-10 Results

Oct.	3	Pittsburgh	3-4†
	8	at Ottawa	2-3*
	10	at Boston	3-4†
	12	Los Angeles	1-2
	16	at Buffalo	3-6
	17	San Jose	1-4
	21	Carolina	4-3†
	22	at Montreal	1-5
	24	Washington	2-3*
	26	at Montreal	2-3*
	28	NY Rangers	3-1
	30	at Washington	4-3*
	31	Buffalo	5-0
Nov.	2	Edmonton	3-1
	4	at Buffalo	0-3
	6	at New Jersey	1-2
	7	Atlanta	6-3
	11	at Washington	4-5†
	13	at Carolina	4-3*
	14	at Florida	4-5†
	16	at Boston	4-1
	20	at Minnesota	2-3
	21	at St. Louis	1-4
	23	at Toronto	4-3*
	25	Philadelphia	1-2
	27	Pittsburgh	3-2
	28	at New Jersey	1-6
Dec.	3	at Atlanta	4-1
	5	at Tampa Bay	0-4
	8	at Philadelphia	2-6
	9	at Toronto	2-3
	12	Boston	3-2*
	14	Florida	1-7
	16	at NY Rangers	2-1
	17	NY Rangers	2-5
	19	Montreal	0-3
	21	Tampa Bay	2-4
	23	Toronto	3-1
	26	at NY Rangers	3-2*
	27	Philadelphia	1-2
	29	Columbus	2-1†
	31	at Ottawa	2-3†
Jan.	2	Atlanta	6-5†
	6	at Colorado	3-2
	8	at Dallas	3-4
	9	at Phoenix	5-4†
	12	Detroit	6-0
	16	Buffalo	3-2†
	18	New Jersey	4-0
	19	at Pittsburgh	4-6
	21	Florida	2-1†
	23	New Jersey	2-4
	26	Washington	2-7
	28	at Carolina	1-4
	30	at Philadelphia	1-2
	31	at Florida	0-2
Feb.	4	at Tampa Bay	2-5
	6	Carolina	1-3
	9	Nashville	4-3†
	10	at Pittsburgh	1-3
	13	Tampa Bay	5-4
	14	Ottawa	3-4
Mar.	2	Chicago	5-3
	4	at Atlanta	3-6
	6	Boston	2-3
	9	at Philadelphia	2-3
	11	St. Louis	1-2†
	13	New Jersey	4-2
	14	Toronto	4-1
	16	at Vancouver	5-2
	19	at Anaheim	4-5*
	20	at Los Angeles	0-1
	24	at NY Rangers	0-5
	25	Calgary	3-2
	27	at Columbus	4-3*
	30	NY Rangers	3-4
Apr.	1	Philadelphia	6-4
	3	Ottawa	4-1
	6	Montreal	4-3†
	8	at Pittsburgh	3-7
	10	at New Jersey	1-7
	11	Pittsburgh	5-6*

* – Overtime † – Shootout

Entry Draft Selections 2010-1996

Name in bold denotes played in NHL.

2010		2006		2002		1998	
Pick		Pick		Pick		Pick	
5	Nino Niederreiter	7	**Kyle Okposo**	22	**Sean Bergenheim**	9	**Mike Rupp**
30	Brock Nelson	60	**Jesse Joensuu**	87	**Frans Nielsen**	36	**Chris Nielsen**
65	Kirill Kabanov	70	Robin Figren	149	Marcus Paulsson	95	Andy Burnham
82	Jason Clark	100	Rhett Rakhshani	189	Alexei Stonkus	123	**Jiri Dopita**
125	Tony Dehart	108	Jase Weslosky	220	Brad Topping	155	Kevin Clauson
185	Cody Rosen	115	Tomas Marcinko	252	Martin Chabada	182	**Evgeny Korolev**
		119	Doug Rogers	283	Per Braxenholm	209	Frederik Brindamour
2009		126	Shane Sims			237	Ben Blais
Pick		141	Kim Johansson	2001		242	Jason Doyle
1	**John Tavares**	160	**Andrew Macdonald**	Pick		250	Radek Matejovsky
12	**Calvin de Haan**	171	Brian Day	101	Cory Stillman		
31	**Mikko Koskinen**	173	Stefan Ridderwall	132	Dusan Salficky	1997	
62	**Anders Nilsson**	190	Troy Mattila	166	**Andy Chiodo**	Pick	
92	Casey Cizikas			197	Jan Holub	4	**Roberto Luongo**
122	**Anton Klementyev**	2005		228	Mike Bray	5	**Eric Brewer**
152	Anders Lee	Pick		260	Bryan Perez	31	**Jeff Zehr**
		15	**Ryan O'Marra**	280	Roman Kuhtinov	59	Jarrett Smith
2008		46	**Dustin Kohn**	287	Juha-Pekka Ketola	79	**Robert Schnabel**
Pick		76	Shea Guthrie			85	**Petr Mika**
9	**Josh Bailey**	144	**Masi Marjamaki**	2000		115	Adam Edinger
36	Corey Trivino	180	Tyrell Mason	Pick		139	Bobby Leavins
40	Aaron Ness	196	Nicholas Tuzzolino	1	**Rick DiPietro**	166	Kris Knoblauch
53	Travis Hamonic	210	Luciano Aquino	5	**Raffi Torres**	196	Jeremy Symington
66	David Toews			101	Arto Tukio	222	Ryan Clark
72	Jyri Niemi	2004		105	Vladimir Gorbunov		
93	Kirill Petrov	Pick		136	Dmitri Upper	1996	
96	Matt Donovan	16	**Petteri Nokelainen**	148	Kristofer Ottosson	Pick	
102	David Ullstrom	47	**Blake Comeau**	202	**Ryan Caldwell**	3	**J.P. Dumont**
126	Kevin Poulin	82	Sergei Ogorodnikov	264	Dmitri Altarev	29	**Dan LaCouture**
148	**Matthew Martin**	115	**Wes O'Neill**	267	**Tomi Pettinen**	56	**Zdeno Chara**
156	Jared Spurgeon	148	**Steve Regier**			83	**Tyrone Garner**
175	Justin Dibenedetto	179	Jaroslav Mrazek	1999		109	**Bubba Berenzweig**
		210	Emil Axelsson	Pick		128	Petr Sachl
2007		227	**Chris Campoli**	5	**Tim Connolly**	138	Todd Miller
Pick		244	Jason Pitton	8	**Taylor Pyatt**	165	J.R. Prestifilippo
62	**Mark Katic**	276	Sylvain Michaud	10	**Branislav Mezei**	192	**Evgeny Korolev**
76	Jason Gregoire			28	**Kristian Kudroc**	218	Mike Muzechka
106	Maxim Gratchev	2003		78	**Mattias Weinhandl**		
166	Blake Kessel	Pick		87	Brian Collins		
196	Simon Lacroix	15	**Robert Nilsson**	101	**Juraj Kolnik**		
		48	Dmitri Chernykh	102	Johan Halvardsson		
		53	Evgeny Tunik	130	**Justin Mapletoft**		
		58	**Jeremy Colliton**	140	Adam Johnson		
		120	Stefan Blaho	163	**Bjorn Melin**		
		182	**Bruno Gervais**	228	**Radek Martinek**		
		212	Denis Rehak	255	Brett Henning		
		238	Cody Blanshan	268	Tyler Scott		
		246	Igor Volkov				

Club Directory

New York Islanders
Executive Office
1535 Old Country Rd.
Plainview, NY 11803
Phone **516/501-6700**
FAX 516/501-6850
www.newyorkislanders.com
Arena
Nassau Veterans'
Memorial Coliseum
Uniondale, NY 11553
Capacity: 16,234

Nassau Veterans' Memorial Coliseum

Owner and Governor	Charles B. Wang
General Manager and Alternate Governor	Garth Snow
Alternate Governors	Art McCarthy, Michael Picker, Roy Reichbach
Sr. Vice President, Marketing and Sales	Paul Lancey
Sr. Vice President, Operations	Howard Saffan

Hockey Operations

Manager, Hockey Administration	Joanne Holewa
Director of Pro Scouting	Ken Morrow
Assistant to the General Manager	Kerry Gwydir
Head Coach	Scott Gordon
Assistant Coaches	Dean Chynoweth, Scott Allen
Goaltending Coach	Mike Dunham
Goaltending Consultant	Sudarshan Maharaj
Assistants, Player Development	Eric Cairns, Trent Klatt
Equipment Manager	Scott Boggs
Assistant Equipment Manager	Richard Krouse
Equipment Assistant	Tom Kitz
Head Athletic Trainer	Garrett Timms
Assistant Athletic Trainer	Nates Goto
Strength and Conditioning Coach	Jesse Demers
Video Coordinator	Ryan Ward
Chief European Scout	Vellu-Pekka Kautonen
Scouts	Anders Kallur, Mario Saraceno, Chris O'Sullivan, Toby O'Brien, Tim Maclean, David Hymovitz, Denny Scanlon, Tim Schurman

Administration

Assistant to Charles B. Wang	Susie Schaefer
Director of Legal Affairs	Jaimie Wolf
Human Resources Manager	Michele Finkelstein
IT Manager	Pawel Tauter
Receptionist	Bonnie Dreher
Office Attendant	Todd Aronovich

Corporate Partnerships and Islanders Business Club

Sr. Vice President, Corporate Partnerships	Justin Johnson
Coordinator, Partnership Marketing	Joshua Haynes
Exec. Director, Islanders Business Club	Mike Bossy
Vice President, Corporate Partnerships	Dave Decina
Senior Director, Corporate Partnerships	Sean Argaman
Director, Corporate Partnerships	Chris Lombardo
Manager, Executive Suites	Lori Ogden
Coordinator, Partnership Marketing	Steven Olwell
Manager, Partnership Marketing	Robert Hofmann
Manager, Executive Suite Sales	Stacy Gross

Ticket Sales and Operations

Vice President of Ticket Operations	Ralph Sellitti
Ticket Manager	Adam Ortiz
Ticket Operations Coordinators	Brianne Tompkins, Jon Welsh
Ticket Services & Box Office Manager	Kerry Cornils
Director of Group Sales	Rose Barre
Group Sales Coordinator	Dave DiLello
Senior Sales Executive, Group Tickets	Cliff Gault
Sales Executives, Group Tickets	Brian Aiello, Tom Giulietti, Nick Lombardo
Sales Executive, Tickets	Ariel Greenberg
Sales Executives, Group Tickets	Eric Mruczek, Eric Nadeau, Matthew Perry, Jeffrey Picker, Josh Rose, Stephen Smyth
Senior Sales Executive, Tickets	Steven Beisel, Chris Bukowski, Bryan Davis, Marc Gerstein, Jeffrey Guida
Sales Executive, Tickets	Edward Adelman, Michael Meinardus, Daniel Scatorchio, Devin Wilson, Jacob Russell, Joseph Rosato

Marketing and Client Services

Director of Marketing	Thomas Rakoczy
Marketing & Service Executive	Paul Dippolito
Marketing Assistant	Lauren Margiotta

Media Relations / Communications

Director, Communications	Kimber Auerbach
Manager, Digital Media	Katrina Doell
Corporate Communications Coordinator	David Hochman
Communications Coordinator	Jesse Eisenberg
Website Coordinator	Dyan LeBourdais
Social Media Coordinator	Dani Muccio
Radio Producer and Broadcaster	Chris King

Game Operations

Vice President, Operations	Tim Beach
Assistant to VP of Operations	Alexa Conforti
Director of Operations	Ken Zore
Community Relations Manager	Ann Rina
Operations Coordinator	John Dominici
Game Operations	Kimberly Bienia, Erin Willey
Manager, Video / Coordinator, Game Ops	Brian Jones
Manager, Amateur Hockey Development	Michelle Winter

Retail and Merchandise Operations

Director, Retail Operations	Terry Goldstein
Retail Sales Executive	Colleen Carolan
Islanders Pro Shop Manager	Tim Murray

Finance

Controller	Frank Romano
Accounting Manager	Chris Vardaro
Payroll Manager	Christine Bowler
Accounts Payable Coordinator	Janet Nelson
Staff Accountants	Laura Ferretti, Erica Palladino, Jennifer Penning

General Managers' History

Bill Torrey, 1972-73 to 1991-92; Don Maloney, 1992-93 to 1994-95; Don Maloney and Mike Milbury, 1995-96; Mike Milbury, 1996-97 to 2005-06; Neil Smith and Garth Snow, 2006-07; Garth Snow, 2007-08 to date.

Garth Snow
General Manager

Born: Wrentham, MA, June 28, 1969.

Former Islanders' goaltender Garth Snow retired as a player on July 18, 2006 to become the fifth general manager of the New York Islanders. In his first season as general manager, Snow successfully bolstered the lineup with several key additions that helped to propel the Islanders into the postseason for the first time since the 2003–04 season and earned Snow the title of NHL Executive of the Year from *Sports Illustrated.*

Snow spent four seasons with the Islanders and 12 in the NHL. The goaltender was 135-147-44 with a 2.80 goals-against average and .901 save percentage over 368 games with Quebec, Philadelphia, Vancouver, Pittsburgh and the Islanders. Originally selected in the sixth round by Quebec in the 1987 NHL Entry Draft, the native of Wrentham, Massachusetts signed with the Islanders as a free agent on July 1, 2001.

New York Rangers

Key Off-Season Signings/Acquisitions

2010

May 26 • Signed 2009-10 Swedish League MVP **Mats Zuccarello Aasen** (MoDo)

July 1 • Re-signed C **Vaclav Prospal** and C **Erik Christensen**.

1 • Signed G **Martin Biron** and LW **Derek Boogaard**.

2 • Re-signed LW **Brandon Prust**.

9 • Re-signed D **Dan Girardi**.

9 • Acquired D **Steve Eminger** from Anaheim for LW **Aaron Voros** and LW **Ryan Hillier**.

27 • Signed LW **Alexander Frolov**.

Aug. 2 • Acquired C **Todd White** from Atlanta for LW **Donald Brashear** and LW **Patrick Rissmiller**.

2010-11 Schedule

Oct.	Sat.	9	at Buffalo		Fri.	7	at Dallas
	Mon.	11	at NY Islanders*		Sat.	8	at St. Louis
	Fri.	15	Toronto		Tue.	11	Montreal
	Mon.	18	Colorado		Thu.	13	Vancouver
	Thu.	21	at Toronto		Sat.	15	at Montreal
	Sat.	23	at Boston		Sun.	16	Philadelphia
	Sun.	24	New Jersey		Wed.	19	Toronto
	Wed.	27	Atlanta		Thu.	20	at Carolina
	Fri.	29	Carolina		Sat.	22	at Atlanta
	Sat.	30	at Toronto		Mon.	24	at Washington
Nov.	Mon.	1	Chicago		Tue.	25	Florida
	Thu.	4	at Philadelphia	**Feb.**	Tue.	1	Pittsburgh
	Fri.	5	at New Jersey		Thu.	3	New Jersey
	Sun.	7	St. Louis		Sat.	5	at Montreal*
	Tue.	9	Washington		Mon.	7	at Detroit
	Thu.	11	Buffalo		Fri.	11	at Atlanta
	Sun.	14	Edmonton*		Sun.	13	Pittsburgh*
	Mon.	15	at Pittsburgh		Thu.	17	Los Angeles
	Wed.	17	Boston		Fri.	18	at New Jersey
	Fri.	19	at Colorado		Sun.	20	Philadelphia*
	Sat.	20	at Minnesota		Tue.	22	at Carolina
	Mon.	22	Calgary		Fri.	25	at Washington
	Wed.	24	at Tampa Bay		Sun.	27	Tampa Bay*
	Fri.	26	at Florida	**Mar.**	Tue.	1	Buffalo
	Sat.	27	at Nashville		Thu.	3	Minnesota
	Mon.	29	Pittsburgh		Fri.	4	at Ottawa
Dec.	Thu.	2	at NY Islanders		Sun.	6	Philadelphia*
	Fri.	3	NY Islanders		Wed.	9	at Anaheim
	Sun.	5	Ottawa*		Sat.	12	at San Jose
	Thu.	9	at Ottawa		Tue.	15	NY Islanders
	Sat.	11	at Columbus		Fri.	18	Montreal
	Sun.	12	Washington		Sun.	20	at Pittsburgh*
	Wed.	15	at Pittsburgh		Tue.	22	Florida
	Thu.	16	Phoenix		Thu.	24	Ottawa
	Sat.	18	at Philadelphia*		Sat.	26	at Boston*
	Thu.	23	Tampa Bay		Wed.	30	at Buffalo
	Mon.	27	NY Islanders		Thu.	31	at NY Islanders
	Wed.	29	at New Jersey	**Apr.**	Sun.	3	at Philadelphia*
Jan.	Sat.	1	at Tampa Bay		Mon.	4	Boston
	Sun.	2	at Florida*		Thu.	7	Atlanta
	Wed.	5	Carolina		Sat.	9	New Jersey*

* Denotes afternoon game.

ATLANTIC DIVISION
85th NHL Season

Franchise date: May 15, 1926

2009-10 Results: 38W-33L-7OTL-4SOL 87PTS.
Fourth, Atlantic Division

Year-by-Year Record

		Home				Road				Overall								
Season	**GP**	**W**	**L**	**T**	**OL**	**W**	**L**	**T**	**OL**	**W**	**L**	**T**	**OL**	**GF**	**GA**	**Pts.**	**Finished**	**Playoff Result**
2009-10	82	18	17	....	6	20	16	....	5	38	33	....	11	222	218	87	4th, Atlantic Div.	Out of Playoffs
2008-09	82	26	11	....	4	17	19	....	5	43	30	....	9	210	218	95	4th, Atlantic Div.	Lost Conf. Quarter-Final
2007-08	82	25	13	....	3	17	14	....	10	42	27	....	13	213	199	97	3rd, Atlantic Div.	Lost Conf. Semi-Final
2006-07	82	21	15	....	5	21	15	....	5	42	30	....	10	242	216	94	3rd, Atlantic Div.	Lost Conf. Semi-Final
2005-06	82	25	10	....	6	19	16	....	6	44	26	....	12	257	215	100	3rd, Atlantic Div.	Lost Conf. Quarter-Final
2004-05	....	....	....	....	....	....	....	....	....	....	....	....	....	....	....	....		
2003-04	82	13	21	3	4	14	19	4	4	27	40	7	8	206	250	69	4th, Atlantic Div.	Out of Playoffs
2002-03	82	17	18	4	2	15	18	6	2	32	36	10	4	210	231	78	4th, Atlantic Div.	Out of Playoffs
2001-02	82	19	19	2	1	17	19	2	3	36	38	4	4	227	258	80	4th, Atlantic Div.	Out of Playoffs
2000-01	82	17	20	3	1	16	23	2	0	33	43	5	1	250	290	72	4th, Atlantic Div.	Out of Playoffs
1999-2000	82	15	20	5	1	14	18	7	2	29	38	12	3	218	246	73	4th, Atlantic Div.	Out of Playoffs
1998-99	82	17	19	5	....	16	19	6	....	33	38	11	....	217	227	77	4th, Atlantic Div.	Out of Playoffs
1997-98	82	14	18	9	....	11	21	9	....	25	39	18	....	197	231	68	5th, Atlantic Div.	Out of Playoffs
1996-97	82	21	14	6	....	17	20	4	....	38	34	10	....	258	231	86	4th, Atlantic Div.	Lost Conf. Championship
1995-96	82	22	10	9	....	19	17	5	....	41	27	14	....	272	237	96	2nd, Atlantic Div.	Lost Conf. Semi-Final
1994-95	48	11	10	3	....	11	13	0	....	22	23	3	....	139	134	47	4th, Atlantic Div.	Lost Conf. Semi-Final
1993-94	**84**	**28**	**8**	**6**	....	**24**	**16**	**2**	....	**52**	**24**	**8**	....	**299**	**231**	**112**	**1st, Atlantic Div.**	**Won Stanley Cup**
1992-93	84	20	17	5	....	14	22	6	....	34	39	11	....	304	308	79	6th, Patrick Div.	Out of Playoffs
1991-92	80	28	8	4	....	22	17	1	....	50	25	5	....	321	246	105	1st, Patrick Div.	Lost Div. Final
1990-91	80	22	11	7	....	14	20	6	....	36	31	13	....	297	265	85	2nd, Patrick Div.	Lost Div. Semi-Final
1989-90	80	20	11	9	....	16	20	4	....	36	31	13	....	279	267	85	1st, Patrick Div.	Lost Div. Final
1988-89	80	21	17	2	....	16	18	6	....	37	35	8	....	310	307	82	3rd, Patrick Div.	Lost Div. Semi-Final
1987-88	80	22	13	5	....	14	21	5	....	36	34	10	....	300	283	82	5th, Patrick Div.	Out of Playoffs
1986-87	80	18	18	4	....	16	20	4	....	34	38	8	....	307	323	76	4th, Patrick Div.	Lost Div. Semi-Final
1985-86	80	20	18	2	....	16	20	4	....	36	38	6	....	280	276	78	4th, Patick Div.	Lost Conf. Championship
1984-85	80	16	18	6	....	10	26	4	....	26	44	10	....	295	345	62	4th, Patrick Div.	Lost Div. Semi-Final
1983-84	80	27	12	1	....	15	17	8	....	42	29	9	....	314	304	93	4th, Patrick Div.	Lost Div. Semi-Final
1982-83	80	24	13	3	....	11	22	7	....	35	35	10	....	306	287	80	4th, Patrick Div.	Lost Div. Final
1981-82	80	19	15	6	....	20	12	8	....	39	27	14	....	316	306	92	2nd, Patrick Div.	Lost Div. Final
1980-81	80	17	13	10	....	13	23	4	....	30	36	14	....	312	317	74	4th, Patrick Div.	Lost Semi-Final
1979-80	80	22	10	8	....	16	22	2	....	38	32	10	....	308	284	86	3rd, Patrick Div.	Lost Quarter-Final
1978-79	80	19	13	8	....	21	16	3	....	40	29	11	....	316	292	91	3rd, Patrick Div.	Lost Final
1977-78	80	18	15	7	....	12	22	6	....	30	37	13	....	279	280	73	4th, Patrick Div.	Lost Prelim. Round
1976-77	80	17	18	5	....	12	19	9	....	29	37	14	....	272	310	72	4th, Patrick Div.	Out of Playoffs
1975-76	80	16	16	8	....	13	26	1	....	29	42	9	....	262	333	67	4th, Patrick Div.	Out of Playoffs
1974-75	80	21	11	8	....	16	18	6	....	37	29	14	....	319	276	88	2nd, Patrick Div.	Lost Prelim. Round
1973-74	78	26	7	6	....	14	17	8	....	40	24	14	....	300	251	94	3rd, East Div.	Lost Semi-Final
1972-73	78	26	8	5	....	21	15	3	....	47	23	8	....	297	208	102	3rd, East Div.	Lost Semi-Final
1971-72	78	26	6	7	....	22	11	6	....	48	17	13	....	317	192	109	2nd, East Div.	Lost Final
1970-71	78	30	2	7	....	19	16	4	....	49	18	11	....	259	177	109	2nd, East Div.	Lost Semi-Final
1969-70	76	22	8	8	....	16	14	8	....	38	22	16	....	246	189	92	4th, East Div.	Lost Quarter-Final
1968-69	76	27	7	4	....	14	19	5	....	41	26	9	....	231	196	91	3rd, East Div.	Lost Quarter-Final
1967-68	74	22	8	7	....	17	15	5	....	39	23	12	....	226	183	90	2nd, East Div.	Lost Quarter-Final
1966-67	70	18	12	5	....	12	16	7	....	30	28	12	....	188	189	72	4th,	Lost Semi-Final
1965-66	70	12	16	7	....	6	25	4	....	18	41	11	....	195	261	47	6th,	Out of Playoffs
1964-65	70	8	19	8	....	12	19	4	....	20	38	12	....	179	246	52	5th,	Out of Playoffs
1963-64	70	14	13	8	....	8	25	2	....	22	38	10	....	186	242	54	5th,	Out of Playoffs
1962-63	70	12	17	6	....	10	19	6	....	22	36	12	....	211	233	56	5th,	Out of Playoffs
1961-62	70	16	11	8	....	10	21	4	....	26	32	12	....	195	207	64	4th,	Lost Semi-Final
1960-61	70	15	15	5	....	7	23	5	....	22	38	10	....	204	248	54	5th,	Out of Playoffs
1959-60	70	10	15	10	....	7	23	5	....	17	38	15	....	187	247	49	6th,	Out of Playoffs
1958-59	70	14	16	5	....	12	16	7	....	26	32	12	....	201	217	64	5th,	Out of Playoffs
1957-58	70	14	15	6	....	18	10	7	....	32	25	13	....	195	188	77	2nd,	Lost Semi-Final
1956-57	70	15	12	8	....	11	18	6	....	26	30	14	....	184	227	66	4th,	Lost Semi-Final
1955-56	70	20	7	8	....	12	21	2	....	32	28	10	....	204	203	74	3rd,	Lost Semi-Final
1954-55	70	10	12	13	....	7	23	5	....	17	35	18	....	150	210	52	5th,	Out of Playoffs
1953-54	70	18	12	5	....	11	19	5	....	29	31	10	....	161	182	68	5th,	Out of Playoffs
1952-53	70	11	14	10	....	6	23	6	....	17	37	16	....	152	211	50	6th,	Out of Playoffs
1951-52	70	16	13	6	....	7	21	7	....	23	34	13	....	192	219	59	5th,	Out of Playoffs
1950-51	70	14	11	10	....	6	18	11	....	20	29	21	....	169	201	61	5th,	Out of Playoffs
1949-50	70	19	12	4	....	9	19	7	....	28	31	11	....	170	189	67	4th,	Lost Final
1948-49	60	13	12	5	....	5	19	6	....	18	31	11	....	133	172	47	6th,	Out of Playoffs
1947-48	60	11	12	7	....	10	14	6	....	21	26	13	....	176	201	55	4th,	Lost Semi-Final
1946-47	60	11	14	5	....	11	18	1	....	22	32	6	....	167	186	50	5th,	Out of Playoffs
1945-46	50	8	12	5	....	5	16	4	....	13	28	9	....	144	191	35	6th,	Out of Playoffs
1944-45	50	7	11	7	....	4	18	3	....	11	29	10	....	154	247	32	6th,	Out of Playoffs
1943-44	50	4	17	4	....	2	22	1	....	6	39	5	....	162	310	17	6th,	Out of Playoffs
1942-43	50	7	13	5	....	4	18	3	....	11	31	8	....	161	253	30	6th,	Out of Playoffs
1941-42	48	15	8	1	....	14	9	1	....	29	17	2	....	177	143	60	1st,	Lost Semi-Final
1940-41	48	13	7	4	....	8	12	4	....	21	19	8	....	143	125	50	4th,	Lost Quarter-Final
1939-40	**48**	**17**	**4**	**3**	....	**10**	**7**	**7**	....	**27**	**11**	**10**	....	**136**	**77**	**64**	**2nd,**	**Won Stanley Cup**
1938-39	48	13	8	3	....	13	8	3	....	26	16	6	....	149	105	58	2nd,	Lost Semi-Final
1937-38	48	15	5	4	....	12	10	2	....	27	15	6	....	149	96	60	2nd, Amn. Div.	Lost Quarter-Final
1936-37	48	9	7	8	....	10	13	1	....	19	20	9	....	117	106	47	3rd, Amn. Div.	Lost Final
1935-36	48	11	6	7	....	8	11	5	....	19	17	12	....	91	96	50	4th, Amn. Div.	Out of Playoffs
1934-35	48	11	8	5	....	11	12	1	....	22	20	6	....	137	139	50	3rd, Amn. Div.	Lost Semi-Final
1933-34	48	11	7	6	....	10	12	2	....	21	19	8	....	120	113	50	3rd, Amn. Div.	Lost Quarter-Final
1932-33	**48**	**12**	**7**	**5**	....	**11**	**10**	**3**	....	**23**	**17**	**8**	....	**135**	**107**	**54**	**3rd, Amn. Div.**	**Won Stanley Cup**
1931-32	48	13	7	4	....	10	10	4	....	23	17	8	....	134	112	54	1st, Amn. Div.	Lost Final
1930-31	44	10	9	3	....	9	7	6	....	19	16	9	....	106	87	47	3rd, Amn. Div.	Lost Semi-Final
1929-30	44	11	5	6	....	6	12	4	....	17	17	10	....	136	143	44	3rd, Amn. Div.	Lost Semi-Final
1928-29	44	12	6	4	....	9	7	6	....	21	13	10	....	72	65	52	2nd, Amn. Div.	Lost Final
1927-28	**44**	**10**	**8**	**4**	....	**9**	**8**	**5**	....	**19**	**16**	**9**	....	**94**	**79**	**47**	**2nd, Amn. Div.**	**Won Stanley Cup**
1926-27	44	13	5	4	....	12	8	2	....	25	13	6	....	95	72	56	1st, Amn. Div.	Lost Quarter-Final

2010-11 Player Personnel

FORWARDS	HT	WT	S	Place of Birth	*Age	2009-10 Club
ANISIMOV, Artem	6-4	197	L	Yaroslavl, USSR	22	NY Rangers
AVERY, Sean	5-11	195	L	Pickering, Ont.	30	NY Rangers
BOOGAARD, Derek	6-7	260	R	Saskatoon, Sask.	28	Minnesota
BOYLE, Brian	6-7	252	L	Hingham, MA	25	NY Rangers
BYERS, Dane	6-3	204	L	Nipawin, Sask.	24	NY Rangers-Hartford
CALLAHAN, Ryan	5-11	188	R	Rochester, NY	25	NY Rangers
CHRISTENSEN, Erik	6-1	203	L	Edmonton, Alta.	26	Ana-Manitoba-NYR
DRURY, Chris	5-10	190	R	Trumbull, CT	34	NY Rangers
DUBINSKY, Brandon	6-1	205	L	Anchorage, AK	24	NY Rangers
DUPONT, Brodie	6-2	210	L	Russell, Man.	23	Hartford
FROLOV, Alexander	6-2	210	R	Moscow, USSR	28	Los Angeles
GABORIK, Marian	6-1	200	L	Trencin, Czech.	28	NY Rangers
GRACHEV, Yevgeny	6-4	222	L	Khabarovsk, USSR	20	Hartford
PROSPAL, Vinny	6-2	198	L	Ceske Budejovice, Czech.	35	NY Rangers
PRUST, Brandon	5-11	195	L	London, Ont.	26	Calgary-NY Rangers
WEISE, Dale	6-2	202	R	Winnipeg, Man.	22	Hartford
WHITE, Todd	5-10	195	L	Kanata, Ont.	35	Atlanta
ZUCCARELLO-AASEN, Mats	5-9	170	L	Oslo, Norway	23	MODO
DEFENSEMEN						
DEL ZOTTO, Michael	6-1	195	L	Stouffville, Ont.	20	NY Rangers
EMINGER, Steve	6-2	210	R	Woodbridge, Ont.	26	Anaheim
GILROY, Matt	6-1	201	R	North Bellmore, NY	26	NY Rangers-Hartford
GIRARDI, Dan	6-2	215	R	Welland, Ont.	26	NY Rangers
McDONAGH, Ryan	6-1	222	L	St.Paul, MN	21	U. of Wisconsin
REDDEN, Wade	6-2	210	L	Lloydminster, Sask.	33	NY Rangers
ROZSIVAL, Michal	6-2	205	R	Vlasim, Czech.	32	NY Rangers
STAAL, Marc	6-4	209	L	Thunder Bay, Ont.	23	NY Rangers

GOALTENDERS	HT	WT	C	Place of Birth	*Age	2009-10 Club
BIRON, Martin	6-3	180	L	Lac-St-Charles, Que.	33	NY Islanders-Bridgeport
LUNDQVIST, Henrik	6-1	198	L	Are, Sweden	28	NY Rangers

* – Age at start of 2010-11 season

2009-10 Scoring

* – rookie

Regular Season

Pos	#	Player	Team	GP	G	A	Pts	TOI	+/–	PIM	PP	SH	GW	S	%
R	10	Marian Gaborik	NYR	76	42	44	86	21:14	15	37	14	1	4	272	15.4
L	20	Vaclav Prospal	NYR	75	20	38	58	20:06	8	32	6	1	4	180	11.1
C	12	Olli Jokinen	CGY	56	11	24	35	18:30	2	53	2	0	2	162	6.8
			NYR	26	4	11	15	16:28	1	22	1	0	1	74	5.4
			Total	82	15	35	50	17:51	3	75	3	0	3	236	6.4
C	17	Brandon Dubinsky	NYR	69	20	24	44	19:33	9	54	6	2	5	165	12.1
R	24	Ryan Callahan	NYR	77	19	18	37	19:24	–12	48	9	0	3	204	9.3
D	4 *	Michael Del Zotto	NYR	80	9	28	37	18:58	–20	32	4	0	1	81	11.1
C	23	Chris Drury	NYR	77	14	18	32	17:46	–10	31	2	0	1	148	9.5
L	16	Sean Avery	NYR	69	11	20	31	13:22	0	160	3	0	1	139	7.9
C	42 *	Artem Anisimov	NYR	82	12	16	28	12:54	–2	32	1	0	2	124	9.7
D	18	Marc Staal	NYR	82	8	19	27	23:07	11	44	0	0	2	78	10.3
C	26	Erik Christensen	ANA	9	0	0	0	11:26	–3	2	0	0	0	9	0.0
			NYR	49	8	18	26	15:28	14	24	1	0	1	77	10.4
			Total	58	8	18	26	14:50	11	26	1	0	1	86	9.3
D	5	Dan Girardi	NYR	82	6	18	24	21:28	–2	53	1	1	1	108	5.6
D	33	Michal Rozsival	NYR	82	3	20	23	21:26	3	78	1	0	1	80	3.8
D	97 *	Matt Gilroy	NYR	69	4	11	15	16:18	0	23	0	0	1	82	4.9
R	81	Enver Lisin	NYR	57	6	8	14	11:10	–1	18	0	0	0	91	6.6
R	8	Brandon Prust	CGY	43	1	4	5	6:32	6	98	0	0	1	23	4.3
			NYR	26	4	5	9	9:19	3	65	0	0	2	21	19.0
			Total	69	5	9	14	7:35	9	163	0	0	3	44	11.4
D	6	Wade Redden	NYR	75	2	12	14	17:31	8	27	0	0	0	66	3.0
L	45	Jody Shelley	S.J.	36	0	3	3	6:33	1	78	0	0	0	20	0.0
			NYR	21	2	4	6	7:06	4	37	0	0	0	29	6.9
			Total	57	2	7	9	6:45	5	115	0	0	0	49	4.1
R	38	Pierre Parenteau	NYR	22	3	5	8	13:41	–2	4	1	0	0	38	7.9
L	34	Aaron Voros	NYR	41	3	4	7	6:08	–2	89	1	0	0	22	13.6
C	22	Brian Boyle	NYR	71	4	2	6	8:25	–6	47	0	0	1	73	5.5
D	25	Anders Eriksson	PHX	12	0	3	3	15:44	0	2	0	0	0	4	0.0
			NYR	8	0	2	2	14:29	2	0	0	0	0	2	0.0
			Total	20	0	5	5	15:14	2	2	0	0	0	6	0.0
L	36 *	Dane Byers	NYR	5	1	0	1	6:21	1	31	0	0	0	3	33.3
L	87	Donald Brashear	NYR	36	0	1	1	6:15	–9	73	0	0	0	18	0.0
C	84 *	Corey Locke	NYR	3	0	0	0	6:18	1	0	0	0	0	2	0.0
D	44 *	Corey Potter	NYR	3	0	0	0	12:07	0	2	0	0	0	2	0.0
D	54 *	Bobby Sanguinetti	NYR	5	0	0	0	11:32	0	4	0	0	0	5	0.0
D	49 *	Ilkka Heikkinen	NYR	7	0	0	0	8:51	2	0	0	0	0	4	0.0

Goaltending

No.	Goaltender	GPI	Mins	Avg	W	L	OT	EN	SO	GA	SA	S%	G	A	PIM
29	* Chad Johnson	5	281	2.35	1	2	1	1	0	11	135	.919	0	1	0
30	Henrik Lundqvist	73	4204	2.38	35	27	10	9	4	167	2109	.921	0	1	0
31	Alex Auld	3	119	2.52	0	1	0	0	0	5	52	.904	0	0	0
31	Matt Zaba	1	34	3.53	0	0	0	0	0	2	16	.875	0	0	0
40	Stephen Valiquette	6	305	3.74	2	3	0	0	1	19	128	.852	0	0	0
	Totals	**82**	**4977**	**2.58**	**38**	**33**	**11**	**10**	**5**	**214**	**2450**	**.913**			

John Tortorella

Head Coach

Born: Boston, MA, June 24, 1958.

John Tortorella was named head coach of the New York Rangers on February 23, 2009. He returned to the organization after serving as head coach of the Tampa Bay Lightning for seven seasons. In 2003-04, Tortorella guided Tampa Bay to the club's first Stanley Cup championship and was awarded the Jack Adams Award as the NHL's coach of the year.

Tortorella joined Tampa Bay following a one-year stint with the Rangers in 1999-2000 where he was an assistant coach and served as head coach for the final four games of the season. Prior to joining the Rangers, he spent two seasons as an assistant coach with the Phoenix Coyotes. He joined Phoenix during the 1997-98 season, after spending the previous eight seasons with the Buffalo Sabres organization. Tortorella served as an assistant coach with the Sabres from 1989-90 to 1994-95 and as head coach with their American Hockey League affiliate, the Rochester Americans, during the 1995-96 and 1996-97 campaigns. He guided the club to the Calder Cup championship in 1995-96.

The Boston native spent two seasons as general manager and head coach of the Virginia Lancers of the Atlantic Coast Hockey League from 1986-87 to 1987-88, winning coach of the year honors both seasons and the league championship in 1986-87. Following the 1987-88 season, Tortorella joined the Fort Wayne Komets of the International Hockey League during their 1988 playoff run before serving as an assistant coach with the New Haven Nighthawks (AHL) in 1988-89.

Prior to joining the coaching ranks, Tortorella played at Salem State College before transferring to the University of Maine Black Bears of the East Coast Athletic Conference, where he skated for three seasons as a right winger and was twice named an ECAC All-Star. After playing in Sweden, he returned to North America to skate in the ACHL with the Hampton Roads Gulls, Erie Golden Blades and Virginia Lancers, recording 98 goals and 160 assists for 258 points, along with 302 penalty minutes in 200 games over four seasons.

Coaching Record

			Regular Season				Playoffs			
Season	Team	League	GC	W	L	O/T	GC	W	L	T
1995-96	Rochester	AHL	80	37	34	9	19	15	4	....
1996-97	Rochester	AHL	80	40	30	10	10	6	4	....
99-2000	**NY Rangers**	**NHL**	**4**	**0**	**3**	**1**	....	....	....	....
2000-01	**Tampa Bay**	**NHL**	**43**	**12**	**27**	**4**	....	....	....	....
2001-02	**Tampa Bay**	**NHL**	**82**	**27**	**40**	**15**	....	....	....	....
2002-03	**Tampa Bay**	**NHL**	**82**	**36**	**25**	**21**	**11**	**5**	**6**	....
2003-04♦	**Tampa Bay**	**NHL**	**82**	**46**	**22**	**14**	**23**	**16**	**7**	....
2004-05	**Tampa Bay**		SEASON CANCELLED							
2005-06	**Tampa Bay**	**NHL**	**82**	**43**	**33**	**6**	**5**	**1**	**4**	....
2006-07	**Tampa Bay**	**NHL**	**82**	**44**	**33**	**5**	**6**	**2**	**4**	....
2007-08	**Tampa Bay**	**NHL**	**82**	**31**	**42**	**9**	....	....	....	....
2008-09	**NY Rangers**	**NHL**	**21**	**12**	**7**	**2**	**7**	**3**	**4**	....
2009-10	**NY Rangers**	**NHL**	**82**	**38**	**33**	**11**	....	....	....	....
	NHL Totals		**642**	**289**	**265**	**88**	**52**	**27**	**25**	....

♦ Stanley Cup win.
Won Jack Adams Award (2004)
Jim Schoenfeld posted an 0-1 playoff record as replacement coach when John Tortorella was suspended, April 26, 2009. Loss is credited to Tortorella's coaching record.

General Managers' History

Lester Patrick, 1926-27 to 1945-46; Frank Boucher, 1946-47 to 1954-55; Muzz Patrick, 1955-56 to 1963-64; Emile Francis, 1964-65 to 1974-75; Emile Francis and John Ferguson, 1975-76; John Ferguson, 1976-77, 1977-78; Fred Shero, 1978-79, 1979-80; Fred Shero and Craig Patrick, 1980-81; Craig Patrick, 1981-82 to 1985-86; Phil Esposito, 1986-87 to 1988-89; Neil Smith, 1989-90 to 1999-2000; Glen Sather, 2000-01 to date.

Captains' History

Bill Cook, 1926-27 to 1936-37; Art Coulter, 1937-38 to 1941-42; Ott Heller, 1942-43 to 1944-45; Neil Colville 1945-46 to 1948-49; Buddy O'Connor, 1949-50; Frank Eddolls, 1950-51; Frank Eddolls and Allan Stanley, 1951-52; Allan Stanley, 1952-53; Allan Stanley and Don Raleigh, 1953-54; Don Raleigh, 1954-55; Harry Howell, 1955-56, 1956-57; Red Sullivan, 1957-58 to 1960-61; Andy Bathgate, 1961-62, 1962-63; Andy Bathgate and Camille Henry, 1963-64; Camille Henry and Bob Nevin, 1964-65; Bob Nevin 1965-66 to 1970-71; Vic Hadfield, 1971-72 to 1973-74; Brad Park, 1974-75; Brad Park and Phil Esposito, 1975-76; Phil Esposito, 1976-77, 1977-78; Dave Maloney, 1978-79, 1979-80; Dave Maloney, Walt Tkaczuk and Barry Beck, 1980-81; Barry Beck, 1981-82 to 1985-86; Ron Greschner, 1986-87; Ron Greschner and Kelly Kisio, 1987-88; Kelly Kisio, 1988-89 to 1990-91; Mark Messier, 1991-92 to 1996-97; Brian Leetch, 1997-98 to 1999-2000; Mark Messier, 2000-01 to 2003-04; no captain, 2005-06; Jaromir Jagr, 2006-07, 2007-08; Chris Drury, 2008-09 to date.

Coaching History

Lester Patrick, 1926-27 to 1938-39; Frank Boucher, 1939-40 to 1947-48; Frank Boucher and Lynn Patrick, 1948-49; Lynn Patrick, 1949-50; Neil Colville, 1950-51; Neil Colville and Bill Cook, 1951-52; Bill Cook, 1952-53; Frank Boucher and Muzz Patrick, 1953-54; Muzz Patrick, 1954-55; Phil Watson, 1955-56 to 1958-59; Phil Watson, Muzz Patrick and Alf Pike, 1959-60; Alf Pike, 1960-61; Doug Harvey, 1961-62; Muzz Patrick and Red Sullivan, 1962-63; Red Sullivan, 1963-64, 1964-65; Red Sullivan and Emile Francis, 1965-66; Emile Francis, 1966-67, 1967-68; Bernie Geoffrion and Emile Francis, 1968-69; Emile Francis, 1969-70 to 1972-73; Larry Popein and Emile Francis, 1973-74; Emile Francis, 1974-75; Ron Stewart and John Ferguson, 1975-76; John Ferguson, 1976-77; Jean-Guy Talbot, 1977-78; Fred Shero, 1978-79, 1979-80; Fred Shero and Craig Patrick, 1980-81; Herb Brooks, 1981-82 to 1983-84; Herb Brooks and Craig Patrick, 1984-85; Ted Sator, 1985-86; Ted Sator, Tom Webster and Phil Esposito, 1986-87; Michel Bergeron, 1987-88; Michel Bergeron and Phil Esposito, 1988-89; Roger Neilson, 1989-90 to 1991-92; Roger Neilson and Ron Smith, 1992-93; Mike Keenan, 1993-94; Colin Campbell, 1994-95 to 1996-97; Colin Campbell and John Muckler, 1997-98; John Muckler, 1998-99; John Muckler and John Tortorella, 1999-2000; Ron Low, 2000-01, 2001-02; Bryan Trottier and Glen Sather, 2002-03; Glen Sather and Tom Renney, 2003-04; Tom Renney, 2004-05 to 2007-08; Tom Renney and John Tortorella, 2008-09; John Tortorella, 2009-10 to date.

Club Records

Team

(Figures in brackets for season records are games played; records for fewest points, wins, ties, losses, goals, goals against are for 70 or more games)

Most Points **112** 1993-94 (84)
Most Wins **52** 1993-94 (84)
Most Ties **21** 1950-51 (70)
Most Losses **44** 1984-85 (80)
Most Goals **321** 1991-92 (80)
Most Goals Against **345** 1984-85 (80)
Fewest Points **47** 1965-66 (70)
Fewest Wins **17** 1952-53 (70), 1954-55 (70), 1959-60 (70)
Fewest Ties **4** 2001-02 (82)
Fewest Losses **17** 1971-72 (78)
Fewest Goals **150** 1954-55 (70)
Fewest Goals Against **177** 1970-71 (78)
Longest Winning Streak
Overall .... **10** Dec. 19/39-Jan. 13/40, Jan. 19-Feb. 10/73
Home .... **14** Dec. 19/39-Feb. 25/40
Away .... **7** Jan. 12-Feb. 12/35, Oct. 28-Nov. 29/78
Longest Undefeated Streak
Overall .... **19** Nov. 23/39-Jan. 13/40 (14 wins, 5 ties)
Home .... **24** Oct. 14/70-Jan. 31/71 (18 wins, 6 ties), Oct. 24/95-Feb.15/96 (18 wins, 6 ties)
Away .... **11** Nov. 5/39-Jan. 13/40 (6 wins, 5 ties)
Longest Losing Streak
Overall .... **11** Oct. 30-Nov. 27/43
Home .... **7** Oct. 20-Nov. 14/76, Mar. 24-Apr. 14/93
Away .... **10** Oct. 30-Dec. 23/43, Feb. 8-Mar. 15/61
Longest Winless Streak
Overall .... **21** Jan. 23-Mar. 19/44 (17 losses, 4 ties)
Home .... **10** Jan. 30-Mar. 19/44 (7 losses, 3 ties)
Away .... **16** Oct. 9-Dec. 20/52 (12 losses, 4 ties)
Most Shutouts, Season **13** 1928-29 (44)
Most PIM, Season **2,018** 1989-90 (80)
Most Goals, Game .... **12** Nov. 21/71 (Cal. 1 at NYR 12)

Individual

Most Seasons .... **18** Rod Gilbert
Most Games .... **1,160** Harry Howell
Most Goals, Career .... **406** Rod Gilbert
Most Assists, Career .... **741** Brian Leetch
Most Points, Career .... **1,021** Rod Gilbert (406G, 615A)
Most PIM, Career .... **1,226** Ron Greschner
Most Shutouts, Career .... **49** Ed Giacomin
Longest Consecutive Games Streak .... **560** Andy Hebenton (Oct. 7/55-Mar. 24/63)
Most Goals, Season .... **54** Jaromir Jagr (2005-06)
Most Assists, Season .... **80** Brian Leetch (1991-92)
Most Points, Season .... **123** Jaromir Jagr (2005-06; 54G, 69A)
Most PIM, Season .... **305** Troy Mallette (1989-90)
Most Points, Defenseman, Season .... **102** Brian Leetch (1991-92; 22G, 80A)
Most Points, Center, Season .... **109** Jean Ratelle (1971-72; 46G, 63A)
Most Points, Right Wing, Season .... **123** Jaromir Jagr (2005-06; 54G, 69A)
Most Points, Left Wing, Season .... **106** Vic Hadfield (1971-72; 50G, 56A)
Most Points, Rookie, Season .... **76** Mark Pavelich (1981-82; 33G, 43A)
Most Shutouts, Season .... **13** John Ross Roach (1928-29)
Most Goals, Game .... **5** Don Murdoch (Oct. 12/76), Mark Pavelich (Feb. 23/83)
Most Assists, Game .... **5** Walt Tkaczuk (Feb. 12/72), Rod Gilbert (Mar. 2/75), (Mar. 30/75), (Oct. 8/76), Don Maloney (Jan. 3/87), Brian Leetch (Apr. 18/95), Wayne Gretzky (Feb. 15/99)
Most Points, Game .... **7** Steve Vickers (Feb. 18/76; 3G, 4A)

Retired Numbers

1	Ed Giacomin	1965-1975
2	Brian Leetch	1987-2004
3	Harry Howell	1952-1969
7	Rod Gilbert	1960-1977
9	Andy Bathgate	1952-1964
	Adam Graves	1991-2001
11	Mark Messier	1991-97; 2000-04
35	Mike Richter	1989-2003

All-time Record vs. Other Clubs

Regular Season

	At Home								On Road								Total							
	GP	W	L	T	OL	GF	GA	PTS	GP	W	L	T	OL	GF	GA	PTS	GP	W	L	T	OL	GF	GA	PTS
Anaheim	12	5	6	1	0	31	32	11	10	4	6	0	0	32	36	8	22	9	12	1	0	63	68	19
Atlanta	20	7	7	1	5	55	59	20	20	11	5	0	4	66	58	26	40	18	12	1	9	121	117	46
Boston	312	140	117	55	0	952	868	335	308	101	163	42	2	856	1093	246	620	241	280	97	2	1808	1961	581
Buffalo	76	32	26	15	3	241	206	82	78	23	43	10	2	237	312	58	154	55	69	25	5	478	518	140
Calgary	54	25	24	5	0	182	189	55	51	12	29	10	0	152	223	34	105	37	53	15	0	334	412	89
Carolina	55	33	16	4	2	195	138	72	53	20	30	3	0	158	172	43	108	53	46	7	2	353	310	115
Chicago	287	119	113	55	0	847	810	293	289	116	128	43	2	797	876	277	576	235	241	98	2	1644	1686	570
Colorado	36	20	10	4	2	141	102	46	37	14	18	3	2	136	148	33	73	34	28	7	4	277	250	79
Columbus	4	2	1	1	0	16	12	5	6	2	4	0	0	13	21	4	10	4	5	1	0	29	33	9
Dallas	65	37	17	11	0	221	172	85	63	31	20	11	1	228	199	74	128	68	37	22	1	449	371	159
Detroit	286	134	94	58	0	872	745	326	287	76	165	45	1	706	1013	198	573	210	259	103	1	1578	1758	524
Edmonton	32	11	14	6	1	119	120	29	30	14	12	3	1	100	106	32	62	25	26	9	2	219	226	61
Florida	34	18	12	4	0	103	76	40	35	18	11	2	4	96	89	42	69	36	23	6	4	199	165	82
Los Angeles	60	36	18	6	0	239	178	78	63	28	25	10	0	221	207	66	123	64	43	16	0	460	385	144
Minnesota	5	4	1	0	0	15	9	8	6	3	3	0	0	18	20	6	11	7	4	0	0	33	29	14
Montreal	300	124	121	54	1	867	869	303	300	64	194	40	2	702	1166	170	600	188	315	94	3	1569	2035	473
Nashville	8	2	4	1	1	19	20	6	6	4	1	0	1	23	16	9	14	6	5	1	2	42	36	15
New Jersey	102	52	28	20	2	366	289	126	104	42	52	7	3	326	350	94	206	94	80	27	5	692	639	220
NY Islanders	114	62	37	11	4	408	333	139	114	46	59	8	1	362	407	101	228	108	96	19	5	770	740	240
Ottawa	33	14	19	0	0	96	98	28	33	16	13	3	1	85	91	36	66	30	32	3	1	181	189	64
Philadelphia	128	56	45	23	4	402	376	139	127	52	58	14	3	355	398	121	255	108	103	37	7	757	774	260
Phoenix	32	20	10	2	0	138	110	42	33	15	14	4	0	110	113	34	65	35	24	6	0	248	223	76
Pittsburgh	119	63	45	9	2	453	388	137	118	48	51	14	5	406	417	115	237	111	96	23	7	859	805	252
St. Louis	62	45	11	6	0	251	149	96	66	29	27	10	0	209	198	68	128	74	38	16	0	460	347	164
San Jose	12	8	3	1	0	46	37	17	15	10	3	2	0	54	35	22	27	18	6	3	0	100	72	39
Tampa Bay	37	21	12	2	2	126	102	46	35	16	15	3	1	109	111	36	72	37	27	5	3	235	213	82
Toronto	293	126	109	56	2	908	860	310	292	89	161	39	3	771	1005	220	585	215	270	95	5	1679	1865	530
Vancouver	56	38	13	5	0	242	148	81	53	33	17	3	0	205	170	69	109	71	30	8	0	447	318	150
Washington	92	45	36	9	2	342	310	101	94	35	47	9	3	294	346	82	186	80	83	18	5	636	656	183
Defunct Clubs	139	87	30	22	0	460	290	196	139	82	34	23	0	441	291	187	278	169	64	45	0	901	581	383
Totals	**2865**	**1386**	**999**	**447**	**33**	**9353**	**8095**	**3252**	**2865**	**1054**	**1408**	**361**	**42**	**8268**	**9687**	**2511**	**5730**	**2440**	**2407**	**808**	**75**	**17621**	**17782**	**5763**

Playoffs

	Series	W	L	GP	W	L	T	GF	GA	Last Mtg.	Rnd.	Result
Atlanta	1	1	0	4	4	0	0	17	6	2007	CQF	W 4-0
Boston	9	3	6	42	18	22	2	104	114	1973	QF	W 4-1
Buffalo	2	0	2	9	3	6	0	19	28	2007	CSF	L 2-4
Calgary	1	1	0	4	3	1	0	14	8	1980	PRE	W 3-1
Chicago	5	1	4	24	10	14	0	54	66	1973	SF	L 1-4
Colorado	1	1	0	6	4	2	0	25	19	1995	CQF	W 4-2
Detroit	5	1	4	23	10	13	0	49	57	1950	F	L 3-4
Florida	1	1	0	5	4	1	0	13	10	1997	CQF	W 4-1
Los Angeles	2	2	0	6	5	1	0	32	14	1981	PRE	W 3-1
Montreal	14	7	7	61	25	34	2	158	188	1996	CQF	W 4-2
New Jersey	5	4	1	28	16	12	0	79	75	2008	CQF	W 4-1
NY Islanders	8	3	5	39	19	20	0	132	129	1994	CQF	W 4-0
Philadelphia	10	4	6	47	20	27	0	153	157	1997	CF	L 1-4
Pittsburgh	4	0	4	20	4	16	0	57	79	2008	CSF	L 1-4
St. Louis	1	1	0	6	4	2	0	29	22	1981	QF	W 4-2
Toronto	8	5	3	35	19	16	0	86	86	1971	QF	W 4-2
Vancouver	1	1	0	7	4	3	0	21	19	1994	F	W 4-3
Washington	5	2	3	29	14	15	0	82	94	2009	CQF	L 3-4
Defunct Clubs	9	6	3	22	11	7	4	43	29			
Totals	**92**	**44**	**48**	**417**	**197**	**212**	**8**	**1167**	**1200**			

Playoff Results 2010-2006

Year	Round	Opponent	Result	GF	GA
2009	CQF	Washington	L 3-4	11	19
2008	CSF	Pittsburgh	L 1-4	12	15
	CQF	New Jersey	W 4-1	19	12
2007	CSF	Buffalo	L 2-4	13	17
	CQF	Atlanta	W 4-0	17	6
2006	CQF	New Jersey	L 0-4	4	17

Abbreviations: Round: F – Final; **CF** – conference final; **CSF** – conference semi-final; **CQF** – conference quarter-final; **SF** – semi-final; **QF** – quarter-final; **PRE** – preliminary round.

Calgary totals include Atlanta Flames, 1972-73 to 1979-80. Carolina totals include Hartford, 1979-80 to 1996-97.
Colorado totals include Quebec, 1979-80 to 1994-95. Dallas totals include Minnesota North Stars, 1967-68 to 1992-93.
New Jersey totals include Kansas City, 1974-75, 1975-76, and Colorado Rockies, 1976-77 to 1981-82.
Phoenix totals include Winnipeg, 1979-80 to 1995-96.

2009-10 Results

Oct.	2	at Pittsburgh	2-3
	3	Ottawa	5-2
	5	at New Jersey	3-2
	8	at Washington	4-3
	11	Anaheim	3-0
	12	Toronto	7-2
	14	Los Angeles	4-2
	17	at Toronto	4-1
	19	San Jose	3-7
	22	New Jersey	2-4
	24	at Montreal	4-5*
	26	Phoenix	5-2
	28	at NY Islanders	1-3
	30	at Minnesota	2-3
Nov.	1	Boston	1-0
	3	at Vancouver	1-4
	5	at Edmonton	4-2
	7	at Calgary	1-3
	12	Atlanta	3-5
	14	at Ottawa	2-1†
	17	Washington	2-4
	21	Florida	2-3
	23	Columbus	7-4
	25	at Florida	2-1†
	27	at Tampa Bay	1-5
	28	at Pittsburgh	3-8
	30	Pittsburgh	2-5
Dec.	5	at Buffalo	2-1
	6	Detroit	1-3
	9	at Chicago	1-2*
	12	Buffalo	2-3
	14	Atlanta	2-3†
	16	NY Islanders	1-2
	17	at NY Islanders	5-2
	19	at Philadelphia	2-1
	21	at Carolina	3-1
	23	Florida	4-1
	26	NY Islanders	2-3*
	30	Philadelphia	0-6
	31	at Carolina	2-1
Jan.	2	Carolina	1-2*
	4	Boston	3-2
	6	Dallas	5-2
	7	at Atlanta	1-2†
	9	at Boston	3-1
	12	New Jersey	0-1†
	14	Ottawa	0-2
	16	at St. Louis	1-4
	17	Montreal	6-2
	19	Tampa Bay	8-2
	21	at Philadelphia	0-2
	23	at Montreal	0-6
	25	Pittsburgh	2-4
	27	Carolina	1-5
	30	at Phoenix	2-3
	31	at Colorado	3-1
Feb.	2	at Los Angeles	1-2
	4	Washington	5-6
	6	New Jersey	3-1
	10	Nashville	1-2
	12	at Pittsburgh	3-2*
	14	Tampa Bay	5-2
Mar.	2	at Ottawa	4-1
	4	Pittsburgh	4-5*
	6	at Washington	0-2
	7	Buffalo	1-2*
	10	at New Jersey	3-6
	12	at Atlanta	5-2
	14	Philadelphia	3-1
	16	Montreal	1-3
	18	St. Louis	3-4
	21	at Boston	1-2
	24	NY Islanders	5-0
	25	at New Jersey	4-3†
	27	at Toronto	2-3*
	30	at NY Islanders	4-3
Apr.	2	at Tampa Bay	5-0
	3	at Florida	4-1
	6	at Buffalo	2-5
	7	Toronto	5-1
	9	Philadelphia	4-3
	11	at Philadelphia	1-2†

* – Overtime † – Shootout

Entry Draft Selections 2010-1996

Name in bold denotes played in NHL.

2010

Pick	
10	Dylan McIlrath
40	Christian Thomas
100	Andrew Yogan
130	Jason Wilson
157	Jesper Fasth
190	Randy McNaught

2009

Pick	
19	Chris Kreider
47	Ethan Werek
80	Ryan Bourque
127	Roman Horak
140	Scott Stajcer
170	Daniel Maggio
200	Mikhail Pashnin

2008

Pick	
20	**Michael Del Zotto**
51	Derek Stepan
75	Yevgeny Grachev
90	Tomas Kundratek
111	Dale Weise
141	Chris Doyle
171	Mitch Gaulton

2007

Pick	
17	Alexei Cherepanov
48	Antoine Lafleur
138	Max Campbell
168	Carl Hagelin
193	David Skokan
198	Danny Hobbs

2006

Pick	
21	**Bobby Sanguinetti**
54	**Artem Anisimov**
84	Ryan Hillier
104	David Kveton
137	Tomas Zaborsky
174	Eric Hunter
204	Lukas Zeliska

2005

Pick	
12	**Marc Staal**
40	**Michael Sauer**
56	**Marc-Andre Cliche**
66	Brodie Dupont
77	Dalyn Flatt
107	**Tom Pyatt**
147	Trevor Koverko
178	Greg Beller
211	Ryan Russell

2004

Pick	
6	**Al Montoya**
19	**Lauri Korpikoski**
36	Darin Olver
48	**Dane Byers**
51	Bruce Graham
60	**Brandon Dubinsky**
73	Zdenek Bahensky
80	Billy Ryan
127	**Ryan Callahan**
135	Roman Psurny
169	Jordan Foote
247	Jonathan Paiement
266	**Jakub Petruzalek**

2003

Pick	
12	Hugh Jessiman
50	**Ivan Baranka**
75	Ken Roche
122	**Corey Potter**
149	**Nigel Dawes**
176	Ivan Dornic
179	Philippe Furrer
180	**Chris Holt**
209	**Dylan Reese**
243	Jan Marek

2002

Pick	
33	Lee Falardeau
81	Marcus Jonasen
127	**Nate Guenin**
143	Mike Walsh
177	Jake Taylor
194	Kim Hirschovits
226	**Joey Crabb**
240	**Petr Prucha**
270	Rob Flynn

2001

Pick	
10	**Dan Blackburn**
40	**Fedor Tyutin**
79	**Garth Murray**
113	**Bryce Lampman**
139	Shawn Collymore
176	**Marek Zidlicky**
206	Petr Preucil
226	Pontus Petterstrom
230	Leonid Zhvachkin
238	**Ryan Hollweg**
269	Juris Stals

2000

Pick	
64	**Filip Novak**
95	**Dominic Moore**
112	Premysl Duben
140	Nathan Martz
143	Brandon Snee
175	Sven Helfenstein
205	**Henrik Lundqvist**
238	Danny Eberly
269	Martin Richter

1999

Pick	
4	**Pavel Brendl**
9	**Jamie Lundmark**
59	David Inman
79	Johan Asplund
90	Patrick Aufiero
137	Garrett Bembridge
177	Jay Dardis
197	Arto Laatikainen
226	Yevgeny Gusakov
251	Petter Henning
254	Alexei Bulatov

1998

Pick	
7	**Manny Malhotra**
40	Randy Copley
66	**Jason LaBarbera**
114	**Boyd Kane**
122	**Patrick Leahy**
131	**Tomas Kloucek**
180	Stefan Lundqvist
207	**Johan Witehall**
235	**Jan Mertzig**

1997

Pick	
19	Stefan Cherneski
46	Wes Jarvis
73	**Burke Henry**
93	Tomi Kallarsson
126	Jason McLean
134	**Johan Lindbom**
136	**Mike York**
154	Shawn Degagne
175	**Johan Holmqvist**
182	**Mike Mottau**
210	Andrew Proskurnicki
236	Richard Miller

1996

Pick	
22	Jeff Brown
48	**Daniel Goneau**
76	Dmitri Subbotin
131	Colin Pepperall
158	Ola Sandberg
185	Jeff Dessner
211	Ryan McKie
237	**Ronnie Sundin**

Glen Sather

President and General Manager

Born: High River, Alta., September 2, 1943.

Glen Sather, who spent parts of four seasons with the New York Rangers as a player from 1970 to 1974, became the franchise's 12th president and tenth general manager on June 2, 2000. He also served as coach of the team from January 30, 2003, to February 25, 2004.

Sather joined the Rangers following a 24-year career with the Edmonton Oilers, where he was the architect of five Stanley Cup championships between 1984 and 1990. One of the most respected executives in the National Hockey League, Sather was honored for his tremendous achievements in 1997 by becoming the first member of the Oilers organization to be selected to the Hockey Hall of Fame.

Named coach and vice president of hockey operations for the Oilers when the franchise joined the NHL in June of 1979, Sather became general manager and club president in May of 1980. He coached through the 1988-89 season and also returned for 60 games behind the bench in 1993-94. Sather-coached teams won the Stanley Cup four times in the 1980s. As general manager, Sather was instrumental in the Oilers' fifth Cup triumph in 1990.

He played for six different teams during a 10-year NHL career. He scored 80 goals in 658 games.

Coaching Record

			Regular Season				Playoffs			
Season	Team	League	GC	W	L	O/T	GC	W	L	T
1979-80	Edmonton	NHL	80	28	39	13	3	0	3	....
1980-81	Edmonton	NHL	62	25	26	11	9	5	4	....
1981-82	Edmonton	NHL	80	48	17	15	5	2	3	....
1982-83	Edmonton	NHL	80	47	21	12	16	11	5	....
1983-84♦	Edmonton	NHL	80	57	18	5	19	15	4	....
1984-85♦	Edmonton	NHL	80	49	20	11	18	15	3	....
1985-86	Edmonton	NHL	80	56	17	7	10	6	4	....
1986-87♦	Edmonton	NHL	80	50	24	6	21	16	5	....
1987-88♦*	Edmonton	NHL	80	44	25	11	19	16	2	1
1988-89	Edmonton	NHL	80	38	34	8	7	3	4	....
1993-94	Edmonton	NHL	60	22	27	11	....	....	....	....
2002-03	NY Rangers	NHL	28	11	10	7	....	....	....	....
2003-04	NY Rangers	NHL	62	22	29	11	....	....	....	....
	NHL Totals		932	497	307	128	127	89	37	1

♦ Stanley Cup win.
Won Jack Adams Award (1986)
* Playoff game May 24, 1988 suspended due to power failure. Score tied.

Club Directory

Madison Square Garden

New York Rangers
14th Floor
2 Pennsylvania Plaza
New York, New York 10121
Phone **212/465-6486**
PR FAX 212/465-6494
www.newyorkrangers.com
Capacity: 18,200

Team Executive Management

Executive Chairman, MSG and Governor	James L. Dolan
President and CEO, MSG and Alternate Governor	Hank J. Ratner
President, MSG Sports and Alternate Governor	Scott O'Neil
President, G.M. and Alternate Governor	Glen Sather
Executive V.P., Business Development & Operations	Casey Coffman
Sr. V.P., Finance & Controller	John Cudmore
Sr. V.P., Marketing Partnerships	Greg Elliott
Sr. V.P., Marketing & Tickets Sales	Howard Jacobs
Sr. V.P., Sports Team Operations	Mark Piazza
Deputy General Counsel & Sr. V.P., Legal & Business Affairs – Team Ops.	Marc Schoenfeld
Sr. V.P., Legal & Business Affairs – Sports Ops	John Master
V.P., Public Relations and Player Recruitment	John Rosasco
V.P., Marketing	Jeanie Baumgartner

Hockey Club Personnel

Asst. G.M., Player Personnel, Assistant Coach and G.M., Hartford Wolf Pack	Jim Schoenfeld
Asst. G.M., Hockey Administration	Cameron Hope
Special Assistant to the President	Mark Messier
Head Coach	John Tortorella
Assistant Coaches	Mike Sullivan, Benoit Allaire
Director, Player Personnel	Gordie Clark
Assistant Director, Player Personnel	Jeff Gorton
Senior Advisor to the President and G.M. and Director of U.S. Amateur Scouting	Mike Barnett
Hockey and Business Operations	Adam Graves
Head Professional Scout, Europe	Anders Hedberg
European Scout	Jan Gajdosik
Amateur Scouting Staff	Larry Bernard, Rich Brown, Daniel Dore, Ernie Gare, Vladimir Lutchenko
Professional Scouting Staff	Rick Kehoe, Gilles Leger, Kevin Maxwell, Peter Stephan
Consultant	Doug Risebrough
Head Athletic Trainer	Jim Ramsay
Equipment Manager	Acacio Marques
Assistant Equipment Manager	Jason Levy
Massage Therapist/Assistant Trainer	Bruce Lifrieri
Strength and Conditioning Coach	Reg Grant
Strength and Conditioning Consultant – Europe	Daniel Hedin
Video Coach	Jerry Dineen
Video Analyst	Jim Sullivan
Manager, MSG Training Center Operations	Alex Case

Operations

V.P., Sports Team Operations	Jason Vogel
Manager of Scouting	Victor Saljanin
Manager of Hockey Administration	Sara Adamson
Executive Administrative Assistant	Barbara Steppe
Administrator, Sports Team Operations	Tim Criscitelli
Coordinator, Team Ops and Integrated Marketing	Caroline Giglio
Executive Assistant to the President, MSG Sports	Denise Schuler

Public Relations

V.P., Business Public Relations – MSG Sports	Stacey Escudero
V.P., Publicity, Sports Teams	Kaley Hoffman
Director, Public Relations	Brendan McIntyre
Manager, Public Relations	Lauren Buchman
Coordinator, Public Relations	Dino Ticinelli

Marketing Services

V.P., Marketing Services	Janet Duch
V.P., Event Presentation	Ryan Halkett
Manager, Marketing	Leigh Anne Berte
Coordinator, Marketing	Teanna DiMicco
Manager, Marketing Programs	Jayne Wise
Coordinator, Marketing Programs	Nicholas Brener
Administrative Assistant, Marketing	Meredith Malaga
Design Director	Joanecy Kagalingan
Art Directors	Brei Stevenson, Alex Mount
Manager, Event Presentation	Greg Kwizak
Music Director, MSG Sports	Ray Castoldi
Coordinating Producer, MSG Sports	Faith Astrada
Game Night Floor Director	Danielle Nardi

Community Relations and Fan Development

V.P., Comm. Relations and Field Mktg., Teams	Karin Buchholz
V.P., Community Relations, Teams	Kerryann Tomlinson
V.P., Fan Development & Field Marketing, Teams	Dan Gladstone
Director, Special Projects and Comm. Relations Rep.	Rod Gilbert
Director, Fan Development	Rick Nadeau
Coordinator, Fan Development and Field Marketing	Devin Pacheco
Manager, Community Relations	David Martella
Manager, Alumni and Community Relations	Anthony Zucconi

MSG Interactive

V.P., MSG Interactive	Heather Pariseau
Director, Interactive Sports Programming	Chris Creed
Manager, MSG Interactive Websites – Teams	Dan David

Finance

V.P., Finance	Jeanine McGrory
Director, Accounting	Paul Kohler
Senior Staff Accountant	Amy McGrath
Staff Accountant	Rob Lunetta
Coordinator, Accounts Payable	Dularie Harris
Senior Administrative Assistant	Maria Kovach

Legal and Business Affairs

V.P., Legal & Business Affairs – Team & Sports Ops	Jamaal Lesane

Human Resources

V.P., Human Resources – Teams	Alan Gershowitz

Medical Staff

Team Physician and Orthopedic Surgeon	Dr. Andrew Feldman
Assistant Team Physician	Dr. Anthony Maddalo
Medical Consultants	Drs. Ronald Weissman, Ron Preston, Martin Posner
Team Dentists	Drs. Don Salomon, Joe Esposito

Additional Information

Television / Radio Network	MSG Network / MSG Radio

Ottawa Senators

Key Off-Season Signings/Acquisitions

2010

May 26 • Re-signed G **Mike Brodeur**.

June 25 • Acquired D **David Rundblad** from St. Louis for Ottawa's 1st round pick in the 2010 Entry Draft.

July 1 • Signed D **Sergei Gonchar**.
1 • Re-signed C **Jesse Winchester**.
21 • Re-signed LW **Nick Foligno**.
29 • Re-signed C **Peter Regin**.
30 • Re-signed D **Chris Campoli**.

Aug. 4 • Signed D **David Hale**.

2009-10 Results: 44w-32L-1OTL-5SOL 94PTS.
Second, Northeast Division

Year-by-Year Record

Season	GP	Home W	Home L	Home T	Home OL	Road W	Road L	Road T	Road OL	Overall W	Overall L	Overall T	Overall OL	GF	GA	Pts.	Finished	Playoff Result
2009-10	82	26	11	....	4	18	21	....	2	44	32	....	6	225	238	94	2nd, Northeast Div.	Lost Conf. Quarter-Final
2008-09	82	22	12	....	7	14	23	....	4	36	35	....	11	217	237	83	4th, Northeast Div.	Out of Playoffs
2007-08	82	22	15	....	4	21	16	....	4	43	31	....	8	261	247	94	2nd, Northeast Div.	Lost Conf. Quarter-Final
2006-07	82	25	13	....	3	23	12	....	6	48	25	....	9	288	222	105	2nd, Northeast Div.	Lost Final
2005-06	82	29	9	....	3	23	12	....	6	52	21	....	9	314	211	113	1st, Northeast Div.	Lost Conf. Semi-Final
2004-05																		
2003-04	82	23	8	5	5	20	15	5	1	43	23	10	6	262	189	102	3rd, Northeast Div.	Lost Conf. Quarter-Final
2002-03	82	28	9	3	1	24	12	5	0	52	21	8	1	263	182	113	1st, Northeast Div.	Lost Conf. Championship
2001-02	82	21	13	3	4	18	14	6	3	39	27	9	7	243	208	94	3rd, Northeast Div.	Lost Conf. Semi-Final
2000-01	82	26	7	5	3	22	14	4	1	48	21	9	4	274	205	109	1st, Northeast Div.	Lost Conf. Quarter-Final
1999-2000	82	24	10	5	2	17	18	6	0	41	28	11	2	244	210	95	2nd, Northeast Div.	Lost Conf. Quarter-Final
1998-99	82	22	11	8	....	22	12	7	....	44	23	15	....	239	179	103	1st, Northeast Div.	Lost Conf. Quarter-Final
1997-98	82	18	16	7	....	16	17	8	....	34	33	15	....	193	200	83	5th, Northeast Div.	Lost Conf. Semi-Final
1996-97	82	16	17	8	....	15	19	7	....	31	36	15	....	226	234	77	3rd, Northeast Div.	Lost Conf. Quarter-Final
1995-96	82	8	28	5	....	10	31	0	....	18	59	5	....	191	291	41	6th, Northeast Div.	Out of Playoffs
1994-95	48	5	16	3	....	4	18	2	....	9	34	5	....	117	174	23	7th, Northeast Div.	Out of Playoffs
1993-94	84	8	30	4	....	6	31	5	....	14	61	9	....	201	397	37	7th, Northeast Div.	Out of Playoffs
1992-93	84	9	29	4	....	1	41	0	....	10	70	4	....	202	395	24	6th, Adams Div.	Out of Playoffs

2010-11 Schedule

Oct.						
Fri.	8	Buffalo	Sat.	8	Tampa Bay
Sat.	9	at Toronto	Tue.	11	at Boston
Mon.	11	at Washington	Thu.	13	at NY Islanders
Thu.	14	Carolina	Fri.	14	Calgary
Sat.	16	at Montreal	Sun.	16	at Washington*
Mon.	18	at Pittsburgh	Tue.	18	Anaheim
Fri.	22	at Buffalo	Thu.	20	at Philadelphia
Sat.	23	Montreal	Fri.	21	Montreal
Tue.	26	Phoenix	Tue.	25	Buffalo
Thu.	28	Florida	**Feb.** Tue.	1	at New Jersey
Sat.	30	Boston	Wed.	2	Detroit
Nov. Tue.	2	at Toronto	Sat.	5	at NY Islanders
Thu.	4	NY Islanders	Mon.	7	at Vancouver
Sat.	6	at Montreal	Wed.	9	at Calgary
Tue.	9	Atlanta	Sat.	12	at Edmonton*
Thu.	11	Vancouver	Tue.	15	NY Islanders
Sat.	13	at Boston	Fri.	18	Boston
Mon.	15	at Philadelphia	Sat.	19	at Toronto
Wed.	17	at Carolina	Wed.	23	Florida
Fri.	19	at St. Louis	Fri.	25	at Buffalo
Mon.	22	Los Angeles	Sat.	26	Philadelphia
Wed.	24	Dallas	**Mar.** Tue.	1	Boston
Fri.	26	at Pittsburgh*	Thu.	3	at Atlanta
Sat.	27	Toronto	Fri.	4	NY Rangers
Mon.	29	Edmonton	Tue.	8	at New Jersey
Dec. Thu.	2	San Jose	Thu.	10	at Florida
Sat.	4	Buffalo	Fri.	11	at Tampa Bay
Sun.	5	at NY Rangers*	Sun.	13	at Buffalo*
Tue.	7	at Montreal	Tue.	15	Pittsburgh
Thu.	9	NY Rangers	Thu.	17	New Jersey
Fri.	10	New Jersey	Sat.	19	Tampa Bay
Mon.	13	Atlanta	Tue.	22	at Carolina
Thu.	16	at Minnesota	Thu.	24	at NY Rangers
Fri.	17	at Colorado	Fri.	25	Washington
Sun.	19	Washington*	Sun.	27	at Atlanta*
Thu.	23	at Nashville	Tue.	29	at Tampa Bay
Sun.	26	Pittsburgh	Thu.	31	at Florida
Wed.	29	Carolina	**Apr.** Sat.	2	Toronto
Fri.	31	at Columbus	Tue.	5	Philadelphia
Jan. Sat.	1	Toronto	Thu.	7	Montreal
Fri.	7	at Chicago	Sat.	9	at Boston*

* Denotes afternoon game.

Mike Fisher's career-high 25 goals was tops on the Senators in 2009-10. Fisher also established new career marks with 28 assists and 53 points.

NORTHEAST DIVISION
19th NHL Season

Franchise date: December 16, 1991

2010-11 Player Personnel

FORWARDS	HT	WT	S	Place of Birth	*Age	2009-10 Club
ALFREDSSON, Daniel	5-11	200	R	Gothenburg, Sweden	37	Ottawa
BASS, Cody	6-1	211	R	Owen Sound, Ont.	23	Binghamton
BUTLER, Bobby	6-0	185	R	Marlborough, MA	23	New Hampshire-Ottawa
DAUGAVINS, Kaspars	5-11	209	L	Riga, USSR	22	Ottawa-Binghamton
FISHER, Mike	6-1	209	R	Peterborough, Ont.	30	Ottawa
FOLIGNO, Nick	6-0	209	L	Buffalo, NY	22	Ottawa
KELLER, Ryan	5-10	196	R	Saskatoon, Sask.	26	Ottawa-Binghamton
KELLY, Chris	6-0	198	L	Toronto, Ont.	29	Ottawa
KOVALEV, Alex	6-2	222	L	Togliatti, USSR	37	Ottawa
LESSARD, Francis	6-3	235	R	Montreal, Que.	31	San Antonio
LOCKE, Corey	5-9	189	L	Toronto, Ont.	26	NY Rangers-Hartford
MICHALEK, Milan	6-2	225	L	Jindrichuv Hradec, Czech.	25	Ottawa
NEIL, Chris	6-1	212	R	Markdale, Ont.	31	Ottawa
REGIN, Peter	6-2	197	L	Herning, Denmark	24	Ottawa
RUUTU, Jarkko	6-1	204	L	Vantaa, Finland	35	Ottawa
SHANNON, Ryan	5-9	171	R	Darien, CT	27	Ottawa
SMITH, Zack	6-2	210	L	Medicine Hat, Alta.	22	Ottawa-Binghamton
SPEZZA, Jason	6-3	215	R	Mississauga, Ont.	27	Ottawa
WICK, Roman	6-2	192	L	Kloten, Switz.	24	Kloten
WINCHESTER, Jesse	6-1	203	R	Long Sault, Ont.	27	Ottawa-Binghamton
DEFENSEMEN						
CAMPOLI, Chris	6-0	190	L	North York, Ont.	26	Ottawa
CARKNER, Matt	6-4	231	R	Winchester, Ont.	29	Ottawa
COWEN, Jared	6-5	228	L	Saskatoon, Sask.	19	Ottawa-Spokane
GONCHAR, Sergei	6-2	211	L	Chelyabinsk, USSR	36	Pittsburgh
HALE, David	6-1	218	L	Colorado Springs, CO	29	Tampa Bay-Norfolk
KARLSSON, Erik	5-11	175	R	Landsbro, Sweden	20	Ottawa-Binghamton
KINRADE, Geoff	6-0	195	L	Nelson, B.C.	25	Binghamton
KUBA, Filip	6-4	229	L	Ostrava, Czech.	33	Ottawa
LEE, Brian	6-3	206	R	Moorhead, MN	23	Ottawa-Binghamton
PHILLIPS, Chris	6-3	216	L	Calgary, Alta.	32	Ottawa
SCHIRA, Craig	6-0	196	R	Spiritwood, Sask.	22	Binghamton
SMITH, Derek	6-2	200	L	Belleville, Ont.	25	Ottawa-Binghamton

GOALTENDERS	HT	WT	C	Place of Birth	*Age	2009-10 Club
BRODEUR, Mike	6-2	186	L	Calgary, Alta.	27	Ottawa-Binghamton
ELLIOTT, Brian	6-2	201	L	Newmarket, Ont.	25	Ottawa
LECLAIRE, Pascal	6-2	202	L	Repentigny, Que.	27	Ottawa

* – Age at start of 2010-11 season

Cory Clouston

Head Coach

Born: Viking, Alta., September 19, 1969.

Cory Clouston was in his second season with the Binghamton Senators of the American Hockey League when it was announced on February 2, 2009 that he would take over behind the bench in Ottawa. His first game as an NHL head coach came on February 3. On April 8, 2009, the Senators announced that Clouston had signed a two-year contract as the team's head coach. In his first full season behind the bench in 2009-10, he guided the Senators back into the playoffs.

Clouston was named head coach of the B-Sens on July 19, 2007 and completed his first professional season with Binghamton in 2007-08. Prior to joining the Senators' organization, Clouston spent five seasons as head of the Western Hockey League's Kootenay Ice, where he also served as assistant coach from 1999-2000 to 2001-02. Kootenay won the Memorial Cup in 2002.

A native of Viking, Alberta, Clouston had a career regular-season record of 209 wins, 110 losses, 24 overtime losses and 15 shootout defeats with Kootenay. Kootenay made the playoffs in each of his seasons behind the bench, advancing as far as the conference final in 2004-05. Clouston was named both the WHL and Canadian Hockey League coach of the year for the 2004-05 season, notching 47 wins, 15 losses, seven in overtime and another three by shootout, for a 104-point season. Clouston was also named WHL coach of the year in 2006-07.

Clouston served as general manager and head coach of the Grande Prairie Storm prior to coaching with Kootenay. In his first year with Grande Prairie in 1995-96, he led the team to a first-place finish and was named coach of the year in the Rocky Mountain Junior League. The team moved into the Alberta Junior Hockey League the following year, and Clouston remained behind the bench through the 1998-99 season. In all, his Grande Prairie teams compiled a .627 winning percentage (143-82-15). Clouston was also an assistant coach with the Powell River Paper Kings of the British Columbia Junior Hockey League in 1994-95.

In addition to his junior hockey experience, Clouston has participated in Hockey Canada's national team program, serving as assistant coach for the national under-18 2005 Junior World Cup gold medalists and head coach for the 2006 team that also took home gold. As a player, he spent four seasons with the Sherwood Park Rangers in the AJHL and four years at the University of Alberta.

Coaching Record

			Regular Season				Playoffs			
Season	Team	League	GC	W	L	O/T	GC	W	L	T
2002-03	Kootenay	WHL	72	36	25	11	11	5	6	....
2003-04	Kootenay	WHL	72	32	30	10	4	0	4	....
2004-05	Kootenay	WHL	72	47	15	10	10	10	6	....
2005-06	Kootenay	WHL	72	45	23	4	6	2	4	....
2006-07	Kootenay	WHL	72	49	17	6	7	3	4	....
2007-08	Binghamton	AHL	80	34	32	14	....	....	....	....
2008-09	Binghamton	AHL	47	26	16	6	....	....	....	....
2008-09	**Ottawa**	**NHL**	**34**	**19**	**11**	**4**	....	....	....	....
2009-10	**Ottawa**	**NHL**	**82**	**44**	**32**	**6**	**6**	**2**	**4**	....
	NHL Totals		**116**	**63**	**43**	**10**	**6**	**2**	**4**	....

2009-10 Scoring

* – rookie

Regular Season

Pos	#	Player	Team	GP	G	A	Pts	TOI	+/–	PIM	PP	SH	GW	S	%
R	11	Daniel Alfredsson	OTT	70	20	51	71	19:39	8	22	4	1	5	168	11.9
C	19	Jason Spezza	OTT	60	23	34	57	19:03	0	20	11	0	5	165	13.9
C	12	Mike Fisher	OTT	79	25	28	53	18:58	1	59	10	0	6	212	11.8
R	27	Alex Kovalev	OTT	77	18	31	49	18:09	–8	54	4	0	5	165	10.9
C	7	Matt Cullen	CAR	60	12	28	40	19:01	0	26	1	2	1	137	8.8
			OTT	21	4	4	8	17:58	–7	8	1	0	1	58	6.9
			Total	81	16	32	48	18:45	–7	34	2	2	2	195	8.2
L	9	Milan Michalek	OTT	66	22	12	34	18:15	–12	18	8	2	3	163	13.5
L	22	Chris Kelly	OTT	81	15	17	32	14:57	–7	38	0	0	3	112	13.4
C	43 *	Peter Regin	OTT	75	13	16	29	12:53	10	20	1	0	1	135	9.6
D	17	Filip Kuba	OTT	53	3	25	28	22:51	–5	28	2	0	0	90	3.3
L	73	Jarkko Ruutu	OTT	82	12	14	26	13:21	–2	121	0	0	1	106	11.3
L	71	Nick Foligno	OTT	61	9	17	26	14:18	6	53	2	0	2	83	10.8
D	65 *	Erik Karlsson	OTT	60	5	21	26	20:06	–5	24	1	0	0	112	4.5
D	4	Chris Phillips	OTT	82	8	16	24	22:20	8	45	1	1	2	82	9.8
R	25	Chris Neil	OTT	68	10	12	22	11:58	–1	175	1	0	2	100	10.0
D	14	Chris Campoli	OTT	67	4	14	18	17:50	–3	16	1	0	1	71	5.6
R	26	Ryan Shannon	OTT	66	5	11	16	12:40	–12	20	1	0	1	109	4.6
R	41	Jonathan Cheechoo	OTT	61	5	9	14	11:56	–13	20	0	0	0	117	4.3
D	24	Anton Volchenkov	OTT	64	4	10	14	20:41	2	38	0	0	0	69	5.8
D	5	Andy Sutton	NYI	54	4	8	12	20:48	–3	73	0	0	0	58	6.9
			OTT	18	1	0	1	19:13	–7	34	0	0	0	19	5.3
			Total	72	5	8	13	20:24	–10	107	0	0	0	77	6.5
C	18	Jesse Winchester	OTT	52	2	11	13	10:01	–1	22	0	1	0	77	2.6
D	39	Matt Carkner	OTT	81	2	9	11	16:54	0	190	0	0	0	87	2.3
R	10	Shean Donovan	OTT	30	2	3	5	7:25	–4	40	0	0	0	24	8.3
C	47 *	Zack Smith	OTT	15	2	1	3	9:02	1	14	0	1	0	11	18.2
D	55	Brian Lee	OTT	23	2	1	3	15:33	–5	12	0	0	0	22	9.1
L	23 *	Kaspars Daugavins	OTT	1	0	0	0	8:26	0	0	0	0	0	2	0.0
D	48 *	Jared Cowen	OTT	1	0	0	0	6:46	0	2	0	0	0	0	0.0
D	51 *	Derek Smith	OTT	2	0	0	0	12:20	–4	0	0	0	0	4	0.0
R	16 *	Bobby Butler	OTT	2	0	0	0	8:20	–1	0	0	0	0	2	0.0
C	37	Martin St Pierre	OTT	3	0	0	0	9:37	–2	0	0	0	0	0	0.0
C	36 *	Joshua Hennessy	OTT	4	0	0	0	5:58	–1	0	0	0	0	2	0.0
R	44 *	Ryan Keller	OTT	6	0	0	0	6:12	–1	0	0	0	0	5	0.0

Goaltending

No.	Goaltender	GPI	Mins	Avg	W	L	OT	EN	SO	GA	SA	S%	G	A	PIM
31	Mike Brodeur	3	180	1.00	3	0	0	0	1	3	87	.966	0	0	0
30	Brian Elliott	55	3038	2.57	29	18	4	6	5	130	1424	.909	0	1	0
33	Pascal Leclaire	34	1745	3.20	12	14	2	1	0	93	822	.887	0	0	2
	Totals	**82**	**4986**	**2.80**	**44**	**32**	**6**	**7**	**6**	**233**	**2340**	**.900**			

Playoffs

Pos	#	Player	Team	GP	G	A	Pts	TOI	+/–	PIM	PP	SH	GW	OT	S	%
C	7	Matt Cullen	OTT	6	3	5	8	23:14	–3	0	2	0	0	0	14	21.4
R	11	Daniel Alfredsson	OTT	6	2	6	8	22:54	–2	2	0	0	0	0	9	22.2
C	19	Jason Spezza	OTT	6	1	6	7	22:45	–3	4	1	0	0	0	24	4.2
L	22	Chris Kelly	OTT	6	1	5	6	18:45	1	2	1	0	0	0	11	9.1
D	65 *	Erik Karlsson	OTT	6	1	5	6	25:51	–4	4	1	0	0	0	12	8.3
C	12	Mike Fisher	OTT	6	2	3	5	23:03	–2	6	2	0	0	0	13	15.4
R	25	Chris Neil	OTT	6	3	1	4	14:11	1	20	0	0	0	0	11	27.3
C	43 *	Peter Regin	OTT	6	3	1	4	18:05	–1	6	0	0	0	0	11	27.3
L	73	Jarkko Ruutu	OTT	6	2	1	3	18:19	2	34	0	0	1	0	14	14.3
D	24	Anton Volchenkov	OTT	6	0	2	2	22:30	–2	4	0	0	0	0	2	0.0
D	14	Chris Campoli	OTT	6	0	2	2	19:47	1	4	0	0	0	0	4	0.0
D	39	Matt Carkner	OTT	6	1	0	1	18:37	0	12	0	0	1	1	4	25.0
L	71	Nick Foligno	OTT	6	0	1	1	17:06	–1	2	0	0	0	0	11	0.0
R	41	Jonathan Cheechoo	OTT	1	0	0	0	7:13	0	0	0	0	0	0	0	0.0
L	9	Milan Michalek	OTT	1	0	0	0	12:08	0	0	0	0	0	0	3	0.0
R	10	Shean Donovan	OTT	2	0	0	0	6:54	–1	0	0	0	0	0	2	0.0
R	26	Ryan Shannon	OTT	2	0	0	0	6:12	0	0	0	0	0	0	1	0.0
D	4	Chris Phillips	OTT	6	0	0	0	24:56	–2	4	0	0	0	0	5	0.0
D	5	Andy Sutton	OTT	6	0	0	0	23:01	–2	8	0	0	0	0	3	0.0
C	47 *	Zack Smith	OTT	6	0	0	0	7:24	–4	5	0	0	0	0	7	0.0
C	18	Jesse Winchester	OTT	6	0	0	0	9:38	–3	0	0	0	0	0	12	0.0

Goaltending

No.	Goaltender	GPI	Mins	Avg	W	L	EN	SO	GA	SA	S%	G	A	PIM
33	Pascal Leclaire	3	211	2.84	1	2	0	0	10	125	.920	0	0	0
30	Brian Elliott	4	203	4.14	1	2	0	0	14	95	.853	0	0	0
	Totals	**6**	**417**	**3.45**	**2**	**4**	**0**	**0**	**24**	**220**	**.891**			

Coaching History

Rick Bowness, 1992-93 to 1994-95; Rick Bowness, Dave Allison and Jacques Martin, 1995-96; Jacques Martin, 1996-97 to 2000-01; Jacques Martin and Roger Neilson, 2001-02; Jacques Martin, 2002-03, 2003-04; Bryan Murray, 2004-05 to 2006-07; John Paddock and Bryan Murray, 2007-08; Craig Hartsburg and Cory Clouston, 2008-09; Cory Clouston, 2009-10 to date.

Club Records

Team

(Figures in brackets for season records are games played; records for fewest points, wins, ties, losses, goals, goals against are for 70 or more games)

Most Points	**113**	2002-03 (82), 2005-06 (82)
Most Wins	**52**	2002-03 (82), 2005-06 (82)
Most Ties	**15**	1996-97 (82), 1997-98 (82), 1998-99 (82)
Most Losses	**70**	1992-93 (84)
Most Goals	**312**	2005-06 (82)
Most Goals Against	**397**	1993-94 (84)
Fewest Points	**24**	1992-93 (84)
Fewest Wins	**10**	1992-93 (84)
Fewest Ties	**4**	1992-93 (84)
Fewest Losses	**21**	2000-01 (82), 2002-03 (82), 2005-06 (82)
Fewest Goals	**191**	1995-96 (82)
Fewest Goals Against	**179**	1998-99 (82)
Longest Winning Streak		
Overall	**11**	Jan. 14-Feb. 4/10
Home	**9**	Mar. 5-Apr. 7/09
Away	**6**	Mar. 18-Apr. 5/03, Jan. 14-Feb. 3/10
Longest Undefeated Streak		
Overall	**11**	Three times
Home	**12**	Dec. 18/03-Jan. 24/04 (10 wins, 2 ties)
Away	**7**	Three times
Longest Losing Streak		
Overall	**14**	Mar. 2-Apr. 7/93
Home	**11**	Oct. 27-Dec. 8/93
Away	***38**	Oct. 10/92-Apr. 3/93**
Longest Winless Streak		
Overall	**21**	Oct. 10-Nov. 23/92 (20 losses, 1 tie)
Home	***17**	Oct. 28/95-Jan. 27/96 (15 losses, 2 ties)
Away	***38**	Oct. 10/92-Apr. 3/93 (38 losses)
Most Shutouts, Season	**10**	2001-02 (82)
Most PIM, Season	**1,716**	1992-93 (84)
Most Goals, Game	**11**	Nov. 13/01 (Ott. 11 at Wsh. 5)

** NHL records do not include neutral site games

Individual

Most Seasons	**14**	Daniel Alfredsson
Most Games, Career	**1,002**	Daniel Alfredsson
Most Goals, Career	**375**	Daniel Alfredsson
Most Assists, Career	**617**	Daniel Alfredsson
Most Points, Career	**992**	Daniel Alfredsson (375G, 617A)
Most PIM, Career	**1,473**	Chris Neil
Most Shutouts, Career	**30**	Patrick Lalime
Longest Consecutive Games Streak	**292**	Alexei Yashin (Dec. 31/95-Apr. 17/99)
Most Goals, Season	**50**	Dany Heatley (2005-06), (2006-07)
Most Assists, Season	**71**	Jason Spezza (2005-06)
Most Points, Season	**105**	Dany Heatley (2006-07; 50G, 55A)
Most PIM, Season	**318**	Mike Peluso (1992-93)
Most Points, Defenseman, Season	**63**	Norm Maciver (1992-93; 17G, 46A)
Most Points, Center, Season	**94**	Alexei Yashin (1998-99; 44G, 50A)
Most Points, Right Wing, Season	**103**	Daniel Alfredsson (2005-06; 43G, 60A)
Most Points, Left Wing, Season	**105**	Dany Heatley (2006-07; 50G, 55A)
Most Points, Rookie, Season	**79**	Alexei Yashin (1993-94; 30G, 49A)
Most Shutouts, Season	**8**	Patrick Lalime (2002-03)
Most Goals, Game	**4**	Marian Hossa (Jan. 2/03); Dany Heatley (Oct. 29/05); Daniel Alfredsson (Nov. 2/05); Martin Havlat (Nov. 2/05); Alex Kovalev (Jan. 3/10)
Most Assists, Game	**5**	Marian Hossa (Jan. 4/01)
Most Points, Game	**7**	Daniel Alfredsson (Jan. 24/08; 3G, 4A)

* NHL Record.

General Managers' History

Mel Bridgman, 1992-93; Randy Sexton, 1993-94, 1994-95; Randy Sexton and Pierre Gauthier, 1995-96; Pierre Gauthier, 1996-97, 1997-98; Rick Dudley, 1998-99; Marshall Johnston, 1999-2000 to 2001-02; John Muckler, 2002-03 to 2006-07; Bryan Murray, 2007-08 to date.

Captains' History

Laurie Boschman, 1992-93; Brad Shaw, Mark Lamb and Gord Dineen, 1993-94; Randy Cunneyworth, 1994-95 to 1997-98; Alexei Yashin, 1998-99; Daniel Alfredsson, 1999-2000 to date.

Retired Numbers

8	Frank Finnigan	1924-1934

All-time Record vs. Other Clubs

Regular Season

	At Home								On Road								Total							
	GP	W	L	T	OL	GF	GA	PTS	GP	W	L	T	OL	GF	GA	PTS	GP	W	L	T	OL	GF	GA	PTS
Anaheim	10	4	4	1	1	30	27	10	11	4	5	2	0	23	27	10	21	8	9	3	1	53	54	20
Atlanta	20	12	4	1	3	85	55	28	20	10	8	1	1	72	73	22	40	22	12	2	4	157	128	50
Boston	49	21	23	3	2	124	146	47	51	16	28	5	2	137	174	39	100	37	51	8	4	261	320	86
Buffalo	51	23	17	7	4	144	136	57	49	19	23	3	4	119	149	45	100	42	40	10	8	263	285	102
Calgary	13	6	3	3	1	33	33	16	14	4	8	1	1	29	48	10	27	10	11	4	2	62	81	26
Carolina	39	19	14	4	2	117	99	44	37	11	22	4	0	91	107	26	76	30	36	8	2	208	206	70
Chicago	12	5	5	0	2	38	35	12	10	2	5	2	1	21	24	7	22	7	10	2	3	59	59	19
Colorado	20	8	9	3	0	57	70	19	17	3	12	1	1	49	75	8	37	11	21	4	1	106	145	27
Columbus	5	3	0	1	1	16	10	8	4	1	2	1	0	11	14	3	9	4	2	2	1	27	24	11
Dallas	11	5	6	0	0	27	30	10	13	5	8	0	0	36	51	10	24	10	14	0	0	63	81	20
Detroit	12	4	6	1	1	33	34	10	11	4	6	0	1	23	39	9	23	8	12	1	2	56	73	19
Edmonton	13	6	5	2	0	31	34	14	14	5	7	2	0	37	45	12	27	11	12	4	0	68	79	26
Florida	32	16	12	2	2	95	83	36	32	19	12	1	0	106	99	39	64	35	24	3	2	201	182	75
Los Angeles	11	5	4	1	1	35	30	12	12	1	10	1	0	24	54	3	23	6	14	2	1	59	84	15
Minnesota	4	3	1	0	0	13	8	6	5	3	1	1	0	19	14	7	9	6	2	1	0	32	22	13
Montreal	49	27	19	1	2	156	135	57	51	21	25	4	1	146	149	47	100	48	44	5	3	302	284	104
Nashville	7	4	2	0	1	25	19	9	6	3	3	0	0	13	14	6	13	7	5	0	1	38	33	15
New Jersey	34	10	18	3	3	78	86	26	33	10	17	2	4	77	96	26	67	20	35	5	7	155	182	52
NY Islanders	33	21	7	5	0	113	81	47	34	19	8	6	1	124	105	45	67	40	15	11	1	237	186	92
NY Rangers	33	14	15	3	1	91	85	32	33	19	13	0	1	98	96	39	66	33	28	3	2	189	181	71
Philadelphia	34	16	12	6	0	103	96	38	33	12	19	2	0	92	110	26	67	28	31	8	0	195	206	64
Phoenix	13	6	6	1	0	42	39	13	12	6	5	1	0	44	39	13	25	12	11	2	0	86	78	26
Pittsburgh	37	13	16	5	3	109	121	34	37	14	17	4	2	105	126	34	74	27	33	9	5	214	247	68
St. Louis	12	6	6	0	0	29	40	12	11	5	4	2	0	32	30	12	23	11	10	2	0	61	70	24
San Jose	11	4	3	4	0	37	30	12	11	4	6	0	1	20	26	9	22	8	9	4	1	57	56	21
Tampa Bay	33	23	10	0	0	122	71	46	33	18	10	2	3	117	96	41	66	41	20	2	3	239	167	87
Toronto	38	23	10	1	4	119	102	51	40	19	18	2	1	115	109	41	78	42	28	3	5	234	211	92
Vancouver	13	6	5	1	1	30	32	14	14	5	7	1	1	29	44	12	27	11	12	2	2	59	76	26
Washington	33	19	12	1	1	121	99	40	34	12	17	4	1	98	120	29	67	31	29	5	2	219	219	69
Totals	**682**	**332**	**254**	**60**	**36**	**2053**	**1866**	**760**	**682**	**274**	**326**	**55**	**27**	**1907**	**2153**	**630**	**1364**	**606**	**580**	**115**	**63**	**3960**	**4019**	**1390**

Playoffs

	Series	W	L	GP	W	L	T	GF	GA	Last Mtg.	Rnd.	Result
Anaheim	1	0	1	5	1	4	0	11	16	2007	F	L 1-4
Buffalo	4	1	3	21	8	13	0	47	52	2007	CF	W 4-1
New Jersey	3	2	1	18	11	7	0	41	40	2007	CSF	W 4-1
NY Islanders	1	1	0	5	4	1	0	13	7	2003	CQF	W 4-1
Philadelphia	2	2	0	11	8	3	0	28	12	2003	CSF	W 4-2
Pittsburgh	3	1	2	15	6	9	0	42	50	2010	CQF	L 2-4
Tampa Bay	1	1	0	5	4	1	0	23	13	2006	CQF	W 4-1
Toronto	4	0	4	24	8	16	0	42	57	2004	CQF	L 3-4
Washington	1	0	1	5	1	4	0	7	18	1998	CSF	L 1-4
Totals	**20**	**8**	**12**	**109**	**51**	**58**	**0**	**254**	**265**			

Playoff Results 2010-2006

Year	Round	Opponent	Result	GF	GA
2010	CQF	Pittsburgh	L 2-4	19	24
2008	CQF	Pittsburgh	L 0-4	5	16
2007	F	Anaheim	L 1-4	11	16
	CF	Buffalo	W 4-1	15	10
	CSF	New Jersey	W 4-1	15	11
	CQF	Pittsburgh	W 4-1	18	10
2006	CSF	Buffalo	L 1-4	13	16
	CQF	Tampa Bay	W 4-1	23	13

Abbreviations: Round: F - Final; **CF** – conference final; **CSF** – conference semi-final; **CQF** – conference quarter-final.

Colorado totals include Quebec, 1992-93 to 1994-95.
Dallas totals include Minnesota North Stars, 1992-93.

Carolina totals include Hartford, 1992-93 to 1996-97.
Phoenix totals include Winnipeg, 1992-93 to 1995-96.

2009-10 Results

Oct.	3	at NY Rangers	2-5	**Jan.**	3	Philadelphia	7-4
	6	at Toronto	2-1		5	Boston	1-4
	8	NY Islanders	3-2*		7	at Washington	2-5
	10	Atlanta	4-2		9	Florida	0-3
	12	Pittsburgh	1-4		10	at Carolina	1-4
	15	Tampa Bay	7-1		12	at Atlanta	1-6
	17	at Montreal	3-1		14	at NY Rangers	2-0
	22	Nashville	5-6*		16	at Montreal	4-2
	24	Boston	3-4†		18	at Boston	5-1
	28	at Florida	4-3		19	Chicago	4-1
	29	at Tampa Bay	2-5		21	St. Louis	3-2
	31	Atlanta	1-3		23	at Boston	2-1
Nov.	5	Tampa Bay	3-2*		26	New Jersey	3-0
	7	New Jersey	2-3		28	at Pittsburgh	4-1
	10	Edmonton	4-3†		30	Montreal	3-2*
	12	at Philadelphia	1-5	**Feb.**	3	at Buffalo	4-2
	14	NY Rangers	1-2†		4	Vancouver	3-1
	17	Toronto	3-2		6	at Toronto	0-5
	19	Pittsburgh	6-2		9	Calgary	3-2
	21	Buffalo	5-3		11	Washington	6-5
	23	Washington	4-3*		13	at Detroit	1-4
	25	at New Jersey	1-3		14	at NY Islanders	4-3
	26	Columbus	2-1	**Mar.**	2	NY Rangers	1-4
	28	at Boston	3-4†		4	at Carolina	1-4
Dec.	1	at San Jose	2-5		6	Toronto	1-2†
	3	at Los Angeles	3-6		9	at Edmonton	4-1
	5	at Phoenix	2-3		11	at Calgary	0-2
	6	at Anaheim	4-3†		13	at Vancouver	1-5
	8	Montreal	1-4		16	Toronto	1-4
	10	at Philadelphia	2-0		18	at Atlanta	3-6
	12	Carolina	4-2		20	at Dallas	4-5
	14	at Toronto	2-3		22	at Montreal	2-0
	16	Buffalo	2-0		23	Philadelphia	2-0
	18	at New Jersey	2-4		26	at Buffalo	4-2
	19	Minnesota	4-1		27	Florida	3-2
	21	Boston	0-2		30	at Washington	5-4*
	23	at Pittsburgh	2-8	**Apr.**	1	Carolina	4-3†
	26	at Buffalo	3-2†		3	at NY Islanders	1-4
	28	Montreal	4-2		6	at Florida	5-2
	30	Colorado	3-4		8	at Tampa Bay	3-4†
	31	NY Islanders	3-2†		10	Buffalo	2-5

* – Overtime † – Shootout

Entry Draft Selections 2010-1996

Name in bold denotes played in NHL.

2010

Pick	
76	Jakub Culek
106	Marcus Sorensen
178	Mark Stone
196	Bryce Aneloski

2009

Pick	
9	**Jared Cowen**
39	Jakob Silfverberg
46	Robin Lehner
100	Chris Wideman
130	Mike Hoffman
146	Jeff Costello
160	Corey Cowick
190	Brad Peltz
191	Michael Sdao

2008

Pick	
15	**Erik Karlsson**
42	Patrick Wiercioch
79	**Zack Smith**
109	Andre Petersson
119	Derek Grant
139	Mark Borowiecki
199	Emil Sandin

2007

Pick	
29	Jim O'Brien
60	Ruslan Bashkirov
90	Louie Caporusso
120	Ben Blood

2006

Pick	
28	**Nick Foligno**
68	Eric Gryba
91	**Kaspars Daugavins**
121	Pierre-Luc Lessard
151	Ryan Daniels
181	Kevin Koopman
211	Erik Condra

2005

Pick	
9	**Brian Lee**
70	Vitali Anikeyenko
95	**Cody Bass**
98	**Ilya Zubov**
115	Janne Kolehmainen
136	Tomas Kudelka
186	Dmitri Megalinsky
204	Colin Greening

2004

Pick	
23	**Andrej Meszaros**
58	Kirill Lyamin
77	Shawn Weller
87	**Peter Regin**
89	Jeff Glass
122	**Alexander Nikulin**
141	Jim McKenzie
156	Roman Wick
219	Joe Cooper
251	Matthew McIlvane
284	John Wikner

2003

Pick	
29	**Patrick Eaves**
67	Igor Mirnov
100	Philippe Seydoux
135	Mattias Karlsson
142	Tim Cook
166	Sergei Gimayev
228	Will Colbert
260	Ossi Louhivaara
291	**Brian Elliott**

2002

Pick	
16	**Jakub Klepis**
47	**Alexei Kaigorodov**
75	Arttu Luttinen
113	Scott Dobben
125	Johan Bjork
150	Brock Hooton
246	Josef Vavra
276	Vitali Atyushov

2001

Pick	
2	**Jason Spezza**
23	**Tim Gleason**
81	Neil Komadoski
99	**Ray Emery**
127	**Christoph Schubert**
162	Stefan Schauer
193	**Brooks Laich**
218	Jan Platil
223	**Brandon Bochenski**
235	Neil Petruic
256	Gregg Johnson
286	**Toni Dahlman**

2000

Pick	
21	**Anton Volchenkov**
45	**Mathieu Chouinard**
55	**Antoine Vermette**
87	Jan Bohac
122	Derrick Byfuglien
156	**Greg Zanon**
157	Grant Potulny
158	Sean Connolly
188	Jason Maleyko
283	James Demone

1999

Pick	
26	**Martin Havlat**
48	**Simon Lajeunesse**
62	Teemu Sainomaa
94	**Chris Kelly**
154	Andrew Ianiero
164	**Martin Prusek**
201	Mikko Ruutu
209	**Layne Ulmer**
213	**Alexandre Giroux**
269	Konstantin Gorovikov

1998

Pick	
15	**Mathieu Chouinard**
44	**Mike Fisher**
58	**Chris Bala**
74	**Julien Vauclair**
101	**Petr Schastlivy**
130	Gavin McLeod
161	**Chris Neil**
188	Michel Periard
223	Sergei Verenikin
246	Rastislav Pavlikovsky

1997

Pick	
12	**Marian Hossa**
58	**Jani Hurme**
66	**Josh Langfeld**
119	**Magnus Arvedson**
146	Jeff Sullivan
173	Robin Bacul
203	Nick Gillis
229	**Karel Rachunek**

1996

Pick	
1	**Chris Phillips**
81	**Antti-Jussi Niemi**
136	**Andreas Dackell**
163	Francois Hardy
212	**Erich Goldmann**
216	**Ivan Ciernik**
239	**Sami Salo**

Bryan Murray

Executive Vice President and General Manager

Born: Shawville, Que., December 5, 1942.

On June 18, 2007, Bryan Murray was appointed as the seventh general manager of the Ottawa Senators. Murray had joined the organization on June 8, 2004, when he was named the club's head coach. Murray resigned as senior vice president and general manager of Anaheim to take the coaching position in Ottawa. As coach in Ottawa in 2006–07, Murray led the Senators to the Stanley Cup Finals for the first time in franchise history, only to lose to his former Anaheim team. He also has previous front office experience as vice president and general manager of the Florida Panthers from 1994 to 2001, assembling a team that reached the Stanley Cup Finals in just its third year of existence in 1996.

Murray, who was back behind the bench in Ottawa briefly in 2007-08, began his NHL career as head coach of the Washington Capials in 1981. He has served 16+ years behind the bench, coaching more than 1,300 regular-season and playoff games, including 672 wins. He earned the Jack Adams Award as coach of the year in 1983-84. Murray's regular-season coaching record in Ottawa is 107-55-20 and includes winning the 2007 Prince of Wales Trophy as the NHL's Eastern Conference champions.

Coaching Record

			Regular Season				Playoffs			
Season	Team	League	GC	W	L	O/T	GC	W	L	T
1981-82	Washington	NHL	66	25	28	13	....	....	....	....
1982-83	Washington	NHL	80	39	25	16	4	1	3	....
1983-84	Washington	NHL	80	48	27	5	8	4	4	....
1984-85	Washington	NHL	80	46	25	9	5	2	3	....
1985-86	Washington	NHL	80	50	23	7	9	5	4	....
1986-87	Washington	NHL	80	38	32	10	7	3	4	....
1987-88	Washington	NHL	80	38	33	9	14	7	7	....
1988-89	Washington	NHL	80	41	29	10	6	2	4	....
1989-90	Washington	NHL	46	18	24	4	....	....	....	....
1990-91	Detroit	NHL	80	34	38	8	7	3	4	....
1991-92	Detroit	NHL	80	43	25	12	11	4	7	....
1992-93	Detroit	NHL	84	47	28	9	7	3	4	....
1997-98	Florida	NHL	59	17	31	11	....	....	....	....
2001-02	Anaheim	NHL	82	29	42	11	....	....	....	....
2004-05	Ottawa				SEASON CANCELLED					
2005-06	Ottawa	NHL	82	52	21	9	10	5	5	....
2006-07	Ottawa	NHL	82	48	25	9	20	13	7	....
2007-08	Ottawa	NHL	18	7	9	2	4	0	4	....
	NHL Totals		**1239**	**620**	**465**	**154**	**112**	**52**	**60**	....

Won Jack Adams Award (1984)

Club Directory

Scotiabank Place

Ottawa Senators
Scotiabank Place
1000 Palladium Drive
Ottawa, Ontario
K2V 1A5
Phone **613/599-0250**
FAX 613/599-0358
www.ottawasenators.com
Capacity: 19,153

Executive
Owner, Governor and Chairman .... Eugene Melnyk
President and Alternate Governor .... Cyril Leeder
Exec. V.P., CFO and Alternate Governor .... Erin Crowe
Exec. V.P., G.M. and Alternate Governor .... Bryan Murray
V.P. and Executive Director, Scotiabank Place .... Tom Conroy
Exec. Assistant to the President .... Kathy Downs
Exec. Assistant to the Exec. V.P. and CFO .... Colette Hiscotte

Hockey Operations
Assistant General Manager .... Tim Murray
Director of Player Personnel .... Pierre Dorion
Director of Player Development and Hockey Administration .... Randy Lee
Assistant to the General Manager .... Allison Vaughan
Head Coach .... Cory Clouston
Assistant Coaches .... Greg Carvel, Brad Lauer, Luke Richardson, Rick Wamsley
Video Coach .... Tim Pattyson
Conditioning Coach .... Chris Schwarz
Director of Player Services .... Chad Schella
Manager of Team Travel .... Jordan Silmser
Head Athletic Therapist .... Gerry Townend
Assistant Athletic Therapist .... Domenic Nicoletta
Equipment Manager .... Scott Allegrino
Assistant Equipment Manager .... Chris Cook
Massage Therapist .... Shawn Markwick

Scouts
Scouts .... Vaclav Burda, George Fargher, Bob Janecyk, Bob Lowes, Bill McCarthy, Trent Mann, Lew Mongelluzzo, Greg Royce, Mikko Ruutu
Pro Scouts .... Jim Clark, Rob Murphy, Nick Polano

Communications and Publications
Vice-President, Communications .... Phil Legault
Director, Publications .... Karen Ruttan
Director, Communications .... Brian Morris
Communications Co-ordinator .... Chris Moore
Writer/Edorial Manager .... Rob Brodie
Translator .... Eric Tremblay
Communications & Publications Assistant .... Amanda Nigh

Broadcasting
Vice-President, Broadcast .... Jim Steel

Legal
Senior Legal Council .... Richard Stacey

Corporate & Ticket Sales and Service
Sr, V.P., Corporate & Ticketing Sales .... Mark Bonneau
Exec. Ass't. to Sr. V.P., Corp. & Ticketing .... Cheryl Blake
Director, Corporate Sales .... Bill Courchaine
Sr. Corporate Account Managers .... Steve Chestnut, Francois Robert
Director, Business Development .... Gina Hillcoat
Director, Ticket Sales .... Jim Orban
Manager, Ticket Sales .... Chris Atack
Manager, Group Sales .... Devon Hogan
Manager, Premium Seating Sales .... Joe Lowes
Director, Premium Services .... Christine Clancy
Manager, Premium Client Services .... Tracey Bonner

Finance
Controller .... Derek Winch
Accounting Manager, Ottawa Senators .... Morgan Cranley

Information Technology
Director, Information Technology .... Sean Shrubsole
Systems Administrator, IT .... Robin Zanichkowsky
Help Desk Supervisor, IT .... Don Morin
Help Desk Support Technician, IT .... Tom Spooner

Marketing
Vice-President, Marketing .... Jeff Kyle
Exec. Assistant to the VP, Marketing .... Deborah Wilson
Director, Marketing .... Isabelle Perrault-Lachapelle
Director, Merchandise Operations .... Kevin Lawton
Director, Game Entertainment .... Glen Gower
Director, Fan and Community Development .... Aaron Robinson
Art Director .... Edtmun Jasvins
Director, Promotions & Marketing Services .... Lisa Trevisanutto

Operations and Events
Assistant to the V.P. & Executive Director .... Linda Julian
Director, Engineering & Operations .... Ed Healy
Director, Scotiabank Place Marketing .... Krista Galbraith

People Department
Director, People Department .... Sandi Horner

Sens Foundation
President .... Danielle Robinson

Miscellaneous
Radio .... Team 1200 (English), 104,7 FM (French)
Television .... Rogers Sportsnet and RDS
Team Photographer .... Freestyle Photography (André Ringuette)
Anthem singer .... Lyndon Slewidge
Mascot .... Spartacat

Philadelphia Flyers

Key Off-Season Signings/Acquisitions

2010

June 15 • Re-signed G **Johan Backlund**.

30 • Re-signed G **Michael Leighton**.

July 1 • Acquired D **Andrej Meszaros** from Tampa Bay for a 2nd round pick in the 2012 Entry Draft.

1 • Re-signed D **Braydon Coburn**.

1 • Signed D **Sean O'Donnell** and LW **Jody Shelley**.

9 • Signed RW **Nikolai Zherdev**.

13 • Re-signed LW **Dan Carcillo**.

19 • Acquired D **Matt Walker** and a 4th round pick in the 2011 Entry Draft from Tampa Bay for LW **Simon Gagne**.

22 • Re-signed C **Darroll Powe**.

2009-10 Results: 41W-35L-3OTL-3SOL 88PTS.
Third, Atlantic Division

Year-by-Year Record

Season	GP	Home W	L	T	OL	Road W	L	T	OL	Overall W	L	T	OL	GF	GA	Pts	Finished	Playoff Result
2009-10	82	24	14	....	3	17	21	....	3	41	35	....	6	236	225	88	3rd, Atlantic Div.	Lost Final
2008-09	82	24	13	....	4	20	14	....	7	44	27	....	11	264	238	99	3rd, Atlantic Div.	Lost Conf. Quarter-Final
2007-08	82	21	14	....	6	21	15	....	5	42	29	....	11	248	233	95	4th, Atlantic Div.	Lost Conf. Championship
2006-07	82	10	24	....	7	12	24	....	5	22	48	....	12	214	303	56	5th, Atlantic Div.	Out of Playoffs
2005-06	82	22	13	....	6	23	13	....	5	45	26	....	11	267	259	101	2nd, Atlantic Div.	Lost Conf. Quarter-Final
2004-05	....	....	....	....	....	....	....	....	....	....	....	....	....	....	....	....		
2003-04	82	24	11	3	3	16	10	12	3	40	21	15	6	229	186	101	1st, Atlantic Div.	Lost Conf. Championship
2002-03	82	21	10	8	2	24	10	5	2	45	20	13	4	211	166	107	2nd, Atlantic Div.	Lost Conf. Semi-Final
2001-02	82	20	13	5	3	22	14	5	0	42	27	10	3	234	192	97	1st, Atlantic Div.	Lost Conf. Quarter-Final
2000-01	82	26	11	4	0	17	14	7	3	43	25	11	3	240	207	100	2nd, Atlantic Div.	Lost Conf. Quarter-Final
1999-2000	82	25	6	7	3	20	16	5	0	45	22	12	3	237	179	105	1st, Atlantic Div.	Lost Conf. Championship
1998-99	82	21	9	11	....	16	17	8	....	37	26	19	....	231	196	93	2nd, Atlantic Div.	Lost Conf. Quarter-Final
1997-98	82	24	11	6	....	18	18	5	....	42	29	11	....	242	193	95	2nd, Atlantic Div.	Lost Conf. Quarter-Final
1996-97	82	23	12	6	....	22	12	7	....	45	24	13	....	274	217	103	2nd, Atlantic Div.	Lost Final
1995-96	82	27	9	5	....	18	15	8	....	45	24	13	....	282	208	103	1st, Atlantic Div.	Lost Conf. Semi-Final
1994-95	48	16	7	1	....	12	9	3	....	28	16	4	....	150	132	60	1st, Atlantic Div.	Lost Conf. Championship
1993-94	84	19	20	3	....	16	19	7	....	35	39	10	....	294	314	80	6th, Atlantic Div.	Out of Playoffs
1992-93	84	23	14	5	....	13	23	6	....	36	37	11	....	319	319	83	5th, Patrick Div.	Out of Playoffs
1991-92	80	22	11	7	....	10	26	4	....	32	37	11	....	252	273	75	6th, Patrick Div.	Out of Playoffs
1990-91	80	18	16	6	....	15	21	4	....	33	37	10	....	252	267	76	5th, Patrick Div.	Out of Playoffs
1989-90	80	17	19	4	....	13	20	7	....	30	39	11	....	290	297	71	6th, Patrick Div.	Out of Playoffs
1988-89	80	22	15	3	....	14	21	5	....	36	36	8	....	307	285	80	4th, Patrick Div.	Lost Conf. Championship
1987-88	80	20	14	6	....	18	24	3	....	38	33	9	....	292	292	85	3rd, Patrick Div.	Lost Div. Semi-Final
1986-87	80	29	9	2	....	17	17	6	....	46	26	8	....	310	245	100	1st, Patrick Div.	Lost Final
1985-86	80	33	6	1	....	20	17	3	....	53	23	4	....	335	241	110	1st, Patrick Div.	Lost Div. Semi-Final
1984-85	80	32	4	4	....	21	16	3	....	53	20	7	....	348	241	113	1st, Patrick Div.	Lost Final
1983-84	80	25	10	5	....	19	16	5	....	44	26	10	....	350	290	98	3rd, Patrick Div.	Lost Div. Semi-Final
1982-83	80	29	8	3	....	20	15	5	....	49	23	8	....	326	240	106	1st, Patrick Div.	Lost Div. Semi-Final
1981-82	80	25	10	5	....	13	21	6	....	38	31	11	....	325	313	87	3rd, Patrick Div.	Lost Div. Semi-Final
1980-81	80	23	9	8	....	18	15	7	....	41	24	15	....	313	249	97	2nd, Patrick Div.	Lost Quarter-Final
1979-80	80	27	5	8	....	21	7	12	....	48	12	20	....	327	254	116	1st, Patrick Div.	Lost Final
1978-79	80	26	10	4	....	14	15	11	....	40	25	15	....	281	248	95	2nd, Patrick Div.	Lost Quarter-Final
1977-78	80	29	6	5	....	16	14	10	....	45	20	15	....	296	200	105	2nd, Patrick Div.	Lost Semi-Final
1976-77	80	33	6	1	....	15	10	15	....	48	16	16	....	323	213	112	1st, Patrick Div.	Lost Semi-Final
1975-76	80	36	2	2	....	15	11	14	....	51	13	16	....	348	209	118	1st, Patrick Div.	Lost Final
1974-75	**80**	**32**	**6**	**2**	**....**	**19**	**12**	**9**	**....**	**51**	**18**	**11**	**....**	**293**	**181**	**113**	**1st, Patrick Div.**	**Won Stanley Cup**
1973-74	**78**	**28**	**6**	**5**	**....**	**22**	**10**	**7**	**....**	**50**	**16**	**12**	**....**	**273**	**164**	**112**	**1st, West Div.**	**Won Stanley Cup**
1972-73	78	27	8	4	....	10	22	7	....	37	30	11	....	296	256	85	2nd, West Div.	Lost Semi-Final
1971-72	78	19	13	7	....	7	25	7	....	26	38	14	....	200	236	66	5th, West Div.	Out of Playoffs
1970-71	78	20	10	9	....	8	23	8	....	28	33	17	....	207	225	73	3rd, West Div.	Lost Quarter-Final
1969-70	76	11	14	13	....	6	21	11	....	17	35	24	....	197	225	58	5th, West Div.	Out of Playoffs
1968-69	76	14	16	8	....	6	19	13	....	20	35	21	....	174	225	61	3rd, West Div.	Lost Quarter-Final
1967-68	74	17	13	7	....	14	19	4	....	31	32	11	....	173	179	73	1st, West Div.	Lost Quarter-Final

2010-11 Schedule

Oct.
Thu. 7 at Pittsburgh
Sat. 9 at St. Louis
Mon. 11 Colorado
Thu. 14 Tampa Bay
Sat. 16 Pittsburgh
Thu. 21 Anaheim
Sat. 23 Toronto
Mon. 25 at Columbus
Tue. 26 Buffalo
Fri. 29 at Pittsburgh
Sat. 30 NY Islanders

Nov.
Mon. 1 Carolina
Thu. 4 NY Rangers
Sat. 6 at NY Islanders
Sun. 7 at Washington*
Thu. 11 at Carolina
Sat. 13 Florida
Mon. 15 Ottawa
Tue. 16 at Montreal
Thu. 18 Tampa Bay
Sat. 20 at Washington
Mon. 22 Montreal
Wed. 24 at Minnesota
Fri. 26 Calgary*
Sat. 27 at New Jersey*

Dec.
Wed. 1 Boston
Sat. 4 New Jersey*
Sun. 5 at NY Islanders*
Wed. 8 San Jose
Thu. 9 at Toronto
Sat. 11 at Boston
Tue. 14 Pittsburgh
Wed. 15 at Montreal
Sat. 18 NY Rangers*
Mon. 20 Florida
Tue. 28 at Vancouver
Thu. 30 at Los Angeles
Fri. 31 at Anaheim*

Jan.
Sun. 2 at Detroit*
Thu. 6 at New Jersey
Sat. 8 New Jersey*

Tue. 11 at Buffalo
Thu. 13 at Boston
Fri. 14 at Atlanta
Sun. 16 at NY Rangers
Tue. 18 Washington
Thu. 20 Ottawa
Sat. 22 New Jersey*
Sun. 23 at Chicago*
Tue. 25 Montreal

Feb.
Tue. 1 at Tampa Bay
Thu. 3 Nashville
Sat. 5 Dallas
Thu. 10 Carolina
Sun. 13 Los Angeles
Tue. 15 at Tampa Bay
Wed. 16 at Florida
Fri. 18 at Carolina
Sun. 20 at NY Rangers*
Tue. 22 Phoenix
Thu. 24 NY Islanders
Sat. 26 at Ottawa

Mar.
Thu. 3 Toronto
Sat. 5 Buffalo*
Sun. 6 at NY Rangers*
Tue. 8 Edmonton
Thu. 10 at Toronto
Sat. 12 Atlanta
Tue. 15 at Florida
Thu. 17 at Atlanta
Sat. 19 at Dallas
Tue. 22 Washington
Thu. 24 Pittsburgh
Sat. 26 at NY Islanders
Sun. 27 Boston
Tue. 29 at Pittsburgh
Thu. 31 Atlanta

Apr.
Fri. 1 at New Jersey
Sun. 3 NY Rangers*
Tue. 5 at Ottawa
Fri. 8 at Buffalo
Sat. 9 NY Islanders

* Denotes afternoon game.

Philadelphia's first draft pick in 2006, Claude Giroux spent his first full season in the NHL in 2009-10. He scored 16 goals in 82 games, then added 10 more in 23 playoff games to rank among the postseason's leading scorers.

ATLANTIC DIVISION
44th NHL Season

Franchise date: June 5, 1967

2010-11 Player Personnel

FORWARDS	HT	WT	S	Place of Birth	*Age	2009-10 Club
BETTS, Blair	6-3	210	L	Edmonton, Alta.	30	Philadelphia
BRIERE, Danny	5-10	179	R	Gatineau, Que.	33	Philadelphia
CARCILLO, Daniel	6-0	205	L	King City, Ont.	25	Philadelphia
CARTER, Jeff	6-3	200	R	London, Ont.	25	Philadelphia
GIROUX, Claude	5-11	172	R	Hearst, Ont.	22	Philadelphia
HARTNELL, Scott	6-2	210	L	Regina, Sask.	28	Philadelphia
HOLMSTROM, Ben	6-1	202	R	Colorado Springs, CO	23	U. Mass-Lowell-Adirondack
KALINSKI, Jon	6-1	175	L	Bonnyville , Alta.	23	Philadelphia
LALIBERTE, David	6-1	194	R	St-Jean-Sur-Richelieu, Que.	24	Philadelphia-Adirondack
LAPERRIERE, Ian	6-1	200	R	Montreal, Que.	36	Philadelphia
LEINO, Ville	6-1	190	L	Savonlinna, Finland	27	Detroit-Philadelphia
MOORE, Greg	6-1	214	R	Lisbon, ME	26	Bridgeport-CBJ-Syr
NODL, Andreas	6-1	196	L	Vienna, Austria	23	Philadelphia-Adirondack
POWE, Darroll	5-11	212	L	Saskatoon, Sask.	25	Philadelphia
RICHARDS, Mike	5-11	195	L	Kenora, Ont.	25	Philadelphia
ROWE, Andrew	6-0	175	L	Muskegon, MI	22	Michigan State
SHELLEY, Jody	6-3	230	L	Thompson, Man.	34	San Jose-NY Rangers
TESTWUIDE, Mike	6-3	220	R	Vail, CO	23	Colorado College
van RIEMSDYK, James	6-3	200	L	Middletown, NJ	21	Philadelphia
ZHERDEV, Nikolai	6-2	203	R	Kiev, USSR	25	Mytischi
DEFENSEMEN						
BARTULIS, Oskars	6-2	184	L	Ogre, Latvia	23	Philadelphia-Adirondack
CARLE, Matt	6-0	205	L	Anchorage, AK	26	Philadelphia
COBURN, Braydon	6-5	220	L	Calgary, Alta.	25	Philadelphia
GUSTAFSSON, Erik	5-11	195	L	Kvissleby, Sweden	21	Northern Mich.-Adirondack
JANCEVSKI, Dan	6-3	222	L	Windsor, Ont.	29	Texas
MARSHALL, Kevin	6-1	191	L	Boucherville, Que.	21	Adirondack
MESZAROS, Andrej	6-2	223	L	Povazska Bystrica, Czech.	24	Tampa Bay
O'DONNELL, Sean	6-2	237	L	Ottawa, Ont.	38	Los Angeles
PRONGER, Chris	6-6	220	L	Dryden, Ont.	35	Philadelphia
TIMONEN, Kimmo	5-10	194	L	Kuopio, Finland	35	Philadelphia
WALKER, Matt	6-4	214	R	Beaverlodge, Alta.	30	Tampa Bay

GOALTENDERS	HT	WT	C	Place of Birth	*Age	2009-10 Club
BACKLUND, Johan	6-2	198	L	Skelleftea, Sweden	29	Philadelphia-Adirondack
BOBROVSKY, Sergei	6-1	174	L	Novokuznetsk, USSR	22	Novokuznetsk
BOUCHER, Brian	6-2	200	L	Woonsocket, RI	33	Philadelphia-Adirondack
LEIGHTON, Michael	6-3	186	L	Petrolia, Ont.	29	Carolina-Philadelphia

* – Age at start of 2010-11 season

Peter Laviolette

Head Coach

Born: Norwood, MA, December 7, 1964.

Peter Laviolette was named the 17th coach in Flyers history on December 4, 2009. Taking over the team two months into the season, Laviolette's Flyers would clinch a playoff berth in the final game on the schedule and go on to reach the Stanley Cup Finals before losing to the Chicago Blackhawks. Along the way, they became just the third team in NHL history to rally from a three-games-to-nothing deficit when they beat the Boston Bruins in the second round of the playoffs.

Previously, Laviolette had coached the Carolina Hurricanes from 2003-04 until partway through the 2008-09 season. He 2005-06 he led the Hurricanes to a club-record 52 wins and 112 points in the regular-season and a Stanley Cup championship. Laviolette's career as an NHL head coach began with the New York Islanders in 2001-02. He led the team to the playoffs two years in a row after the club had failed to reach the postseason for seven straight seasons. Prior to joining the Islanders, Laviolette served as an assistant coach with the Boston Bruins after two years of guiding Boston's AHL affiliate, Providence. In 1998-99, Laviolette led the Providence Bruins to a 56-16-8 regular-season record, and a 15-4 playoff record that culminated with Providence hoisting the Calder Cup and Laviolette being named AHL coach of the year.

Laviolette played 11 seasons of professional hockey, mostly in the AHL and IHL, but did play 12 games with the New York Rangers during the 1988-89 season. He was a member of the 1988 and 1994 U.S. Olympic hockey teams, and captained the 1994 Olympic squad.

In the spring of 2004, Laviolette helped assure the United States a spot in the 2006 Olympic Games in Torino, Italy, when he guided Team USA to a bronze medal at the 2004 World Championship in the Czech Republic. He also served as an assistant to San Jose Sharks head coach Ron Wilson behind the bench for Team USA in the 2004 World Cup of Hockey and was head coach again at the 2005 World Championship and 2006 Olympics.

Coaching Record

			Regular Season				Playoffs			
Season	Team	League	GC	W	L	O/T	GC	W	L	T
1997-98	Wheeling	ECHL	70	37	24	9	15	8	7	....
1998-99	Providence	AHL	80	56	16	8	19	15	4	....
99-2000	Providence	AHL	80	33	38	9	14	10	4	....
2001-02	**NY Islanders**	**NHL**	**82**	**42**	**28**	**12**	**7**	**3**	**4**	....
2002-03	**NY Islanders**	**NHL**	**82**	**35**	**34**	**13**	**5**	**1**	**4**	....
2003-04	**Carolina**	**NHL**	**52**	**20**	**22**	**10**	....	....	....	....
2004-05	**Carolina**		SEASON CANCELLED							
2005-06♦	**Carolina**	**NHL**	**82**	**52**	**22**	**8**	**25**	**16**	**9**	....
2006-07	**Carolina**	**NHL**	**82**	**40**	**34**	**8**	....	....	....	....
2007-08	**Carolina**	**NHL**	**82**	**43**	**33**	**6**	....	....	....	....
2008-09	**Carolina**	**NHL**	**25**	**12**	**11**	**2**	....	....	....	....
2009-10	**Philadelphia**	**NHL**	**57**	**28**	**24**	**5**	**23**	**14**	**9**	....
	NHL Totals		**544**	**272**	**208**	**64**	**60**	**34**	**26**	....

♦ Stanley Cup win.

2009-10 Scoring

* – rookie

Regular Season

Pos	#	Player	Team	GP	G	A	Pts	TOI	+/–	PIM	PP	SH	GW	S	%
C	18	Mike Richards	PHI	82	31	31	62	20:24	–2	79	13	1	3	237	13.1
C	17	Jeff Carter	PHI	74	33	28	61	19:18	2	38	11	2	6	319	10.3
D	20	Chris Pronger	PHI	82	10	45	55	25:55	22	79	5	0	2	175	5.7
C	48	Danny Briere	PHI	75	26	27	53	16:35	–2	71	8	0	1	193	13.5
R	28	Claude Giroux	PHI	82	16	31	47	16:36	–9	23	8	0	2	145	11.0
L	19	Scott Hartnell	PHI	81	14	30	44	15:43	–6	155	8	0	4	171	8.2
L	12	Simon Gagne	PHI	58	17	23	40	18:37	–1	47	5	0	4	183	9.3
D	44	Kimmo Timonen	PHI	82	6	33	39	22:52	–2	50	1	2	1	121	5.0
L	21 *	James van Riemsdyk	PHI	78	15	20	35	12:57	–1	30	4	0	6	173	8.7
D	25	Matt Carle	PHI	80	6	29	35	23:23	19	16	2	0	1	137	4.4
R	45	Arron Asham	PHI	72	10	14	24	10:04	–2	126	0	0	2	91	11.0
L	13	Daniel Carcillo	PHI	76	12	10	22	11:14	5	207	1	0	1	105	11.4
R	14	Ian Laperriere	PHI	82	3	17	20	12:30	–1	162	0	0	0	53	5.7
D	5	Braydon Coburn	PHI	81	5	14	19	21:08	–6	54	1	0	0	122	4.1
C	11	Blair Betts	PHI	63	8	10	18	12:36	7	14	1	1	2	63	12.7
C	36	Darroll Powe	PHI	63	9	6	15	12:05	0	54	0	0	0	103	8.7
L	22 *	Ville Leino	DET	42	4	3	7	13:12	–10	6	1	0	1	54	7.4
			PHI	13	2	2	4	12:39	2	4	0	0	1	23	8.7
			Total	55	6	5	11	13:05	–8	10	1	0	2	77	7.8
D	3 *	Oskars Bartulis	PHI	53	1	8	9	13:58	–12	28	0	0	0	26	3.8
D	26	Danny Syvret	PHI	21	2	2	4	12:28	1	12	0	0	0	14	14.3
C	27	Mika Pyorala	PHI	36	2	2	4	13:35	–3	10	0	0	0	41	4.9
R	9 *	David Laliberte	PHI	11	2	1	3	7:47	1	6	0	0	1	8	25.0
D	77	Ryan Parent	PHI	48	1	2	3	14:46	–14	20	0	0	0	27	3.7
D	2	Lukas Krajicek	T.B.	23	0	1	1	17:31	–4	21	0	0	0	17	0.0
			PHI	27	1	1	2	16:58	–10	14	0	0	0	25	4.0
			Total	50	1	2	3	17:13	–14	35	0	0	0	42	2.4
L	37 *	Jon Kalinski	PHI	10	0	2	2	6:57	–2	0	0	0	0	9	0.0
D	55	Ole-Kristian Tollefsen	PHI	18	0	2	2	9:51	1	23	0	0	0	12	0.0
R	15	Andreas Nodl	PHI	10	0	1	1	8:55	–2	0	0	0	0	2	0.0
C	42	Jared Ross	PHI	3	0	0	0	7:38	–1	0	0	0	0	4	0.0
L	32	Riley Cote	PHI	15	0	0	0	3:01	0	24	0	0	0	7	0.0

Goaltending

No.	Goaltender	GPI	Mins	Avg	W	L	OT	EN	SO	GA	SA	S%	G	A	PIM
49	Michael Leighton	27	1449	2.48	16	5	2	0	1	60	735	.918	0	1	0
29	Ray Emery	29	1684	2.64	16	11	1	3	3	74	783	.905	0	1	2
33	Brian Boucher	33	1742	2.76	9	18	3	2	1	80	796	.899	0	1	2
30	Johan Backlund	1	40	3.00	0	1	0	0	0	2	24	.917	0	0	0
35	* Jeremy Duchesne	1	17	3.53	0	0	0	0	0	1	4	.750	0	0	0
	Totals	**82**	**4969**	**2.68**	**41**	**35**	**6**	**5**	**5**	**222**	**2346**	**.905**			

Playoffs

Pos	#	Player	Team	GP	G	A	Pts	TOI	+/–	PIM	PP	SH	GW	OT	S	%
C	48	Danny Briere	PHI	23	12	18	30	19:37	9	18	4	0	4	0	63	19.0
C	18	Mike Richards	PHI	23	7	16	23	21:45	–1	18	2	1	1	0	59	11.9
R	28	Claude Giroux	PHI	23	10	11	21	18:44	7	4	3	0	2	1	47	21.3
L	22 *	Ville Leino	PHI	19	7	14	21	16:15	10	6	0	0	2	0	36	19.4
D	20	Chris Pronger	PHI	23	4	14	18	29:03	5	36	3	0	0	0	41	9.8
L	19	Scott Hartnell	PHI	23	8	9	17	16:13	4	25	3	0	0	0	30	26.7
D	25	Matt Carle	PHI	23	1	12	13	25:53	6	8	0	0	0	0	33	3.0
L	12	Simon Gagne	PHI	19	9	3	12	17:34	–2	0	5	0	2	1	52	17.3
D	44	Kimmo Timonen	PHI	23	1	10	11	26:37	6	20	0	0	0	0	45	2.2
C	17	Jeff Carter	PHI	12	5	2	7	17:56	–5	2	2	0	1	0	51	9.8
R	45	Arron Asham	PHI	23	4	3	7	11:14	4	10	0	0	0	0	32	12.5
L	21 *	James van Riemsdyk	PHI	21	3	3	6	11:54	–4	4	0	0	0	0	41	7.3
L	13	Daniel Carcillo	PHI	17	2	4	6	10:32	1	34	0	0	1	1	21	9.5
D	5	Braydon Coburn	PHI	23	1	3	4	25:09	–2	22	1	0	1	0	29	3.4
D	2	Lukas Krajicek	PHI	22	0	3	3	10:00	0	8	0	0	0	0	11	0.0
C	11	Blair Betts	PHI	23	1	1	2	11:19	–4	4	0	0	0	0	16	6.3
D	77	Ryan Parent	PHI	17	1	0	1	7:28	–2	2	0	0	0	0	3	33.3
R	14	Ian Laperriere	PHI	13	0	1	1	9:31	–3	6	0	0	0	0	3	0.0
C	36	Darroll Powe	PHI	23	0	1	1	12:33	–2	6	0	0	0	0	28	0.0
R	9 *	David Laliberte	PHI	1	0	0	0	5:32	0	2	0	0	0	0	0	0.0
C	42	Jared Ross	PHI	3	0	0	0	5:37	0	0	0	0	0	0	2	0.0
D	3 *	Oskars Bartulis	PHI	7	0	0	0	6:43	–1	4	0	0	0	0	1	0.0
R	15	Andreas Nodl	PHI	10	0	0	0	8:27	–1	0	0	0	0	0	2	0.0

Goaltending

No.	Goaltender	GPI	Mins	Avg	W	L	EN	SO	GA	SA	S%	G	A	PIM
30	Johan Backlund	1	1	0.00	0	0	0	0	0	0	.000	0	0	0
49	Michael Leighton	14	757	2.46	8	3	0	3	31	371	.916	0	0	2
33	Brian Boucher	12	656	2.47	6	6	3	1	27	298	.909	0	0	2
	Totals	**23**	**1422**	**2.57**	**14**	**9**	**3**	**5**	**61**	**672**	**.909**			

Coaching History

Keith Allen, 1967-68, 1968-69; Vic Stasiuk, 1969-70, 1970-71; Fred Shero, 1971-72 to 1977-78; Bob McCammon and Pat Quinn, 1978-79; Pat Quinn, 1979-80, 1980-81; Pat Quinn and Bob McCammon, 1981-82; Bob McCammon, 1982-83, 1983-84; Mike Keenan, 1984-85 to 1987-88; Paul Holmgren, 1988-89 to 1990-91; Paul Holmgren and Bill Dineen, 1991-92; Bill Dineen, 1992-93; Terry Simpson, 1993-94; Terry Murray, 1994-95 to 1996-97; Wayne Cashman and Roger Neilson, 1997-98; Roger Neilson, 1998-99, 1999-2000; Craig Ramsay and Bill Barber, 2000-01; Bill Barber, 2001-02; Ken Hitchcock, 2002-03 to 2005-06; Ken Hitchcock and John Stevens, 2006-07; John Stevens, 2007-08 to 2008-09; John Stevens and Peter Laviolette, 2009-10; Peter Laviolette, 2010-11.

Captains' History

Lou Angotti, 1967-68; Ed Van Impe, 1968-69 to 1971-72; Ed Van Impe and Bobby Clarke, 1972-73; Bobby Clarke, 1973-74 to 1978-79; Mel Bridgman, 1979-80, 1980-81; Bill Barber, 1981-82; Bill Barber and Bobby Clarke, 1982-83; Bobby Clarke, 1983-84; Dave Poulin, 1984-85 to 1988-89; Dave Poulin and Ron Sutter, 1989-90; Ron Sutter, 1990-91; Rick Tocchet, 1991-92; no captain, 1992-93; Kevin Dineen, 1993-94; Eric Lindros, 1994-95 to 1998-99; Eric Lindros and Eric Desjardins, 1999-2000; Eric Desjardins, 2000-01; Eric Desjardins and Keith Primeau, 2001-02; Keith Primeau, 2002-03, 2003-04; Keith Primeau and Derian Hatcher, 2005-06; Peter Forsberg, 2006-07; Jason Smith, 2007-08; Mike Richards, 2008-09 to date.

Club Records

Team

(Figures in brackets for season records are games played; records for fewest points, wins, ties, losses, goals, goals against are for 70 or more games)

Most Points	**118**	1975-76 (80)
Most Wins	**53**	1984-85 (80), 1985-86 (80)
Most Ties	***24**	1969-70 (76)
Most Losses	**48**	2006-07 (82)
Most Goals	**350**	1983-84 (80)
Most Goals Against	**319**	1992-93 (84)
Fewest Points	**56**	2006-07 (82)
Fewest Wins	**17**	1969-70 (76)
Fewest Ties	**4**	1985-86 (80)
Fewest Losses	**12**	1979-80 (80)
Fewest Goals	**173**	1967-68 (74)
Fewest Goals Against	**164**	1973-74 (78)
Longest Winning Streak		
Overall	**13**	Oct. 19-Nov. 17/85
Home	***20**	Jan. 4-Apr. 3/76
Away	**8**	Dec. 22/82-Jan. 16/83
Longest Undefeated Streak		
Overall	***35**	Oct. 14/79-Jan. 6/80 (25 wins, 10 ties)
Home	**26**	Oct. 11/79-Feb. 3/80 (19 wins, 7 ties)
Away	**16**	Oct. 20/79-Jan. 6/80 (11 wins, 5 ties)
Longest Losing Streak		
Overall	**9**	Dec. 8-27/06
Home	**13**	Nov. 29/06-Feb. 8/07
Away	**8**	Oct. 25-Nov. 26/72, Mar. 3-29/88
Longest Winless Streak		
Overall	**12**	Feb. 24-Mar. 16/99 (8 losses, 4 ties)
Home	**13**	Nov. 29/06-Feb. 8/07 (13 losses)
Away	**19**	Oct. 23/71-Jan. 27/72 (15 losses, 4 ties)
Most Shutouts, Season	**13**	1974-75 (80)
Most PIM, Season	**2,621**	1980-81 (80)
Most Goals, Game	**13**	Mar. 22/84 (Pit. 4 at Phi. 13), Oct. 18/84 (Van. 2 at Phi. 13)

Individual

Most Seasons	**15**	Bobby Clarke
Most Games	**1,144**	Bobby Clarke
Most Goals, Career	**420**	Bill Barber
Most Assists, Career	**852**	Bobby Clarke
Most Points, Career	**1,210**	Bobby Clarke (358G, 852A)
Most PIM, Career	**1,817**	Rick Tocchet
Most Shutouts, Career	**50**	Bernie Parent
Longest Consecutive Game Streak	**484**	Rod Brind'Amour (Feb. 24/93-Apr. 18/99)
Most Goals, Season	**61**	Reggie Leach (1975-76)
Most Assists, Season	**89**	Bobby Clarke (1974-75), (1975-76)
Most Points, Season	**123**	Mark Recchi (1992-93; 53G, 70A)
Most PIM, Season	***472**	Dave Schultz (1974-75)
Most Points, Defenseman, Season	**82**	Mark Howe (1985-86; 24G, 58A)
Most Points, Center, Season	**119**	Bobby Clarke (1975-76; 30G, 89A)
Most Points, Right Wing, Season	**123**	Mark Recchi (1992-93; 53G, 70A)
Most Points, Left Wing, Season	**112**	Bill Barber (1975-76; 50G, 62A)
Most Points, Rookie, Season	**82**	Mikael Renberg (1993-94; 38G, 44A)
Most Shutouts, Season	**12**	Bernie Parent (1973-74), (1974-75)
Most Goals, Game	**4**	Sixteen times
Most Assists, Game	**6**	Eric Lindros (Feb. 26/97)
Most Points, Game	**8**	Tom Bladon (Dec. 11/77; 4G, 4A)

* NHL Record.

Retired Numbers

1	Bernie Parent	1967-1971, 1973-1979
4	Barry Ashbee	1970-1974
7	Bill Barber	1972-1985
16	Bobby Clarke	1969-1984

All-time Record vs. Other Clubs

Regular Season

	At Home								On Road								Total							
	GP	W	L	T	OL	GF	GA	PTS	GP	W	L	T	OL	GF	GA	PTS	GP	W	L	T	OL	GF	GA	PTS
Anaheim	10	4	2	3	1	27	20	12	11	5	3	2	1	40	38	13	21	9	5	5	2	67	58	25
Atlanta	20	14	3	2	1	81	56	31	20	15	4	1	0	68	43	31	40	29	7	3	1	149	99	62
Boston	83	35	36	10	2	269	251	82	86	26	45	11	4	240	305	67	169	61	81	21	6	509	556	149
Buffalo	77	43	19	12	3	264	201	101	73	28	36	8	1	208	245	65	150	71	55	20	4	472	446	166
Calgary	53	34	15	3	1	201	142	72	54	20	25	9	0	178	210	49	107	54	40	12	1	379	352	121
Carolina	53	35	10	5	3	200	135	78	54	30	14	9	1	195	165	70	107	65	24	14	4	395	300	148
Chicago	64	37	16	11	0	210	164	85	62	16	27	19	0	176	212	51	126	53	43	30	0	386	376	136
Colorado	36	23	9	2	2	130	97	50	38	11	14	12	1	129	136	35	74	34	23	14	3	259	233	85
Columbus	4	3	0	1	0	15	8	7	5	2	1	2	0	10	10	6	9	5	1	3	0	25	18	13
Dallas	70	44	10	16	0	266	160	104	68	24	28	16	0	217	221	64	138	68	38	32	0	483	381	168
Detroit	60	36	13	11	0	240	172	83	61	18	33	10	0	187	219	46	121	54	46	21	0	427	391	129
Edmonton	33	20	11	2	0	134	93	42	30	8	16	6	0	86	104	22	63	28	27	8	0	220	197	64
Florida	35	15	12	6	2	93	89	38	34	22	11	1	0	113	85	45	69	37	23	7	2	206	174	83
Los Angeles	65	42	15	7	1	249	158	92	69	39	21	8	1	231	200	87	134	81	36	15	2	480	358	179
Minnesota	7	5	1	0	1	20	10	11	4	1	2	1	0	7	8	3	11	6	3	1	1	27	18	14
Montreal	83	31	34	16	2	247	252	80	84	29	39	14	2	250	285	74	167	60	73	30	4	497	537	154
Nashville	7	3	2	1	1	23	13	8	6	2	0	2	2	13	12	8	13	5	2	3	3	36	25	16
New Jersey	103	62	27	10	4	379	264	138	101	36	53	8	4	318	342	84	204	98	80	18	8	697	606	222
NY Islanders	113	68	32	11	2	400	308	149	116	46	53	15	2	348	402	109	229	114	85	26	4	748	710	258
NY Rangers	127	61	49	14	3	398	355	139	128	49	53	23	3	376	402	124	255	110	102	37	6	774	757	263
Ottawa	33	19	11	2	1	110	92	41	34	12	14	6	2	96	103	32	67	31	25	8	3	206	195	73
Phoenix	33	24	9	0	0	140	89	48	33	16	15	2	0	107	106	34	66	40	24	2	0	247	195	82
Pittsburgh	124	89	24	8	3	512	322	189	124	44	55	22	3	395	441	113	248	133	79	30	6	907	763	302
St. Louis	69	47	12	10	0	270	157	104	70	36	27	7	0	224	200	79	139	83	39	17	0	494	357	183
San Jose	14	6	5	2	1	44	41	15	15	7	5	2	1	39	39	17	29	13	10	4	2	83	80	32
Tampa Bay	35	18	8	7	2	107	80	45	36	21	14	1	0	113	105	43	71	39	22	8	2	220	185	88
Toronto	77	48	21	8	0	289	184	104	77	33	28	14	2	247	240	82	154	81	49	22	2	536	424	186
Vancouver	56	37	18	1	0	238	167	75	53	31	10	12	0	214	148	74	109	68	28	13	0	452	315	149
Washington	93	57	29	6	1	353	258	121	90	38	36	13	3	287	295	92	183	95	65	19	4	640	553	213
Defunct Clubs	34	24	4	6	0	137	67	54	35	13	14	8	0	102	89	34	69	37	18	14	0	239	156	88
Totals	**1671**	**984**	**457**	**193**	**37**	**6046**	**4405**	**2198**	**1671**	**678**	**696**	**264**	**33**	**5214**	**5410**	**1653**	**3342**	**1662**	**1153**	**457**	**70**	**11260**	**9815**	**3851**

Playoffs

	Series	W	L	GP	W	L	T	GF	GA	Last Mtg.	Rnd.	Result
Boston	5	3	2	27	13	14	0	79	80	2010	CSF	W 4-3
Buffalo	8	5	3	43	25	18	0	124	123	2006	CQF	L 2-4
Calgary	2	1	1	11	7	4	0	43	28	1981	QF	L 3-4
Chicago	2	0	2	10	2	8	0	30	45	2010	F	L 2-4
Colorado	2	2	0	11	7	4	0	39	29	1985	CF	W 4-2
Dallas	2	2	0	11	8	3	0	41	26	1980	SF	W 4-1
Detroit	1	0	1	4	0	4	0	6	16	1997	F	L 0-4
Edmonton	3	1	2	15	7	8	0	44	49	1987	F	L 3-4
Florida	1	0	1	6	2	4	0	11	15	1996	CSF	L 2-4
Montreal	6	3	3	31	15	16	0	89	93	2010	CF	W 4-1
New Jersey	5	3	2	25	15	10	0	64	59	2010	CQF	W 4-1
NY Islanders	4	3	1	25	14	11	0	83	69	1987	DF	W 4-3
NY Rangers	10	6	4	47	27	20	0	157	153	1997	CF	W 4-1
Ottawa	2	0	2	11	3	8	0	12	28	2003	CSF	L 2-4
Pittsburgh	5	3	2	29	15	14	0	91	89	2009	CQF	L 2-4
St. Louis	2	0	2	11	3	8	0	20	34	1969	QF	L 0-4
Tampa Bay	2	1	1	13	7	6	0	45	34	2004	CF	L 3-4
Toronto	6	5	1	36	22	14	0	119	85	2004	CSF	W 4-2
Vancouver	1	1	0	3	2	1	0	15	9	1979	PRE	W 2-1
Washington	4	2	2	23	11	12	0	78	85	2008	CQF	W 4-3
Totals	**73**	**41**	**32**	**392**	**205**	**187**	**0**	**1190**	**1149**			

Calgary totals include Atlanta Flames, 1972-73 to 1979-80.
Colorado totals include Quebec, 1979-80 to 1994-95.
New Jersey totals include Kansas City, 1974-75, 1975-76, and Colorado Rockies, 1976-77 to 1981-82.
Phoenix totals include Winnipeg, 1979-80 to 1995-96.
Carolina totals include Hartford, 1979-80 to 1996-97.
Dallas totals include Minnesota North Stars, 1967-68 to 1992-93.

Playoff Results 2010-2006

Year	Round	Opponent	Result	GF	GA
2010	F	Chicago	L 2-4	22	25
	CF	Montreal	W 4-1	17	7
	CSF	Boston	W 4-3	22	20
	CQF	New Jersey	W 4-1	15	9
2009	CQF	Pittsburgh	L 2-4	16	18
2008	CF	Pittsburgh	L 1-4	9	20
	CSF	Montreal	W 4-1	20	14
	CQF	Washington	W 4-3	23	20
2006	CQF	Buffalo	L 2-4	14	27

Abbreviations: Round: F – Final; **CF** – conference final; **CSF** – conference semi-final; **CQF** – conference quarter-final; **DF** – division final; **SF** – semi-final; **QF** – quarter-final; **PRE** – preliminary round.

2009-10 Results

Oct.	2	at Carolina	2-0
	3	at New Jersey	5-2
	6	Washington	6-5*
	8	Pittsburgh	4-5
	10	Anaheim	2-3†
	16	at Florida	2-4
	22	Boston	4-3†
	24	Florida	5-1
	25	San Jose	1-4
	27	at Washington	2-4
	31	Carolina	6-1
Nov.	2	Tampa Bay	6-2
	6	at Buffalo	5-2
	7	St. Louis	2-1†
	12	Ottawa	5-1
	14	Buffalo	2-3
	16	New Jersey	3-2
	18	at Los Angeles	3-2
	20	at San Jose	3-6
	21	at Phoenix	1-3
	23	at Colorado	4-5
	25	at NY Islanders	2-1
	27	Buffalo	2-4
	28	at Atlanta	0-1
Dec.	3	Vancouver	0-3
	5	Washington	2-8
	7	at Montreal	1-3
	8	NY Islanders	6-2
	10	Ottawa	0-2
	12	at New Jersey	1-4
	14	at Boston	3-1
	15	at Pittsburgh	1-6
	17	Pittsburgh	2-3†
	19	NY Rangers	1-2
	21	Florida	1-4
	23	at Tampa Bay	5-2
	26	at Carolina	4-3†
	27	at NY Islanders	2-1
	30	at NY Rangers	6-0
Jan.	1	at Boston	1-2*
	3	at Ottawa	4-7
	6	Toronto	6-2
	7	at Pittsburgh	7-4
	9	Tampa Bay	4-1
	12	Dallas	6-3
	14	at Toronto	0-4
	17	at Washington	3-5
	19	Columbus	5-3
	21	NY Rangers	2-0
	23	Carolina	4-2
	24	Pittsburgh	1-2
	28	Atlanta	3-4
	30	NY Islanders	2-1
Feb.	1	at Calgary	3-0
	3	at Edmonton	0-1
	6	at Minnesota	1-2
	8	New Jersey	3-2
	10	at New Jersey	3-2*
	12	Montreal	3-2
	13	at Montreal	6-2
Mar.	2	at Tampa Bay	7-2
	3	at Florida	4-7
	5	at Buffalo	2-3*
	7	Toronto	3-1
	9	NY Islanders	3-2
	11	Boston	1-5
	13	Chicago	3-2
	14	at NY Rangers	1-3
	16	at Nashville	3-4†
	18	at Dallas	3-2
	20	at Atlanta	2-5
	21	Atlanta	1-3
	23	at Ottawa	0-2
	25	Minnesota	3-4*
	27	at Pittsburgh	1-4
	28	New Jersey	5-1
Apr.	1	at NY Islanders	4-6
	2	Montreal	0-1
	4	Detroit	4-3
	6	at Toronto	2-0
	9	at NY Rangers	3-4
	11	NY Rangers	2-1†

* – Overtime † – Shootout

Entry Draft Selections 2010-1996

Name in bold denotes played in NHL.

2010
Pick
89 Michael Chaput
119 Tye McGinn
149 Michael Parks
179 Nicholas Luukko
206 Ricard Blidstrand
209 Brendan Ranford

2009
Pick
81 Adam Morrison
87 Simon Bertilsson
142 Nic Riopel
153 Dave Labrecque
172 Eric Wellwood
196 Oliver Lauridsen

2008
Pick
19 **Luca Sbisa**
67 Marc-Andre Bourdon
84 Jacob Deserres
178 Zac Rinaldo
196 Joacim Eriksson

2007
Pick
2 **James van Riemsdyk**
41 Kevin Marshall
66 Garrett Klotz
122 Mario Kempe
152 **Jon Kalinski**
161 Patrick Maroon
182 Brad Phillips

2006
Pick
22 **Claude Giroux**
39 **Andreas Nodl**
42 Michael Ratchuk
55 Denis Bodrov
79 Jonathan Matsumoto
101 Joonas Lehtivuori
109 Jakub Kovar
145 Jonathan Rheault
175 Michael Dupont
205 Andrei Popov

2005
Pick
29 **Steve Downie**
91 **Oskars Bartulis**
119 **Jeremy Duchesne**
152 Josh Beaulieu
174 John Flatters
215 Matt Clackson

2004
Pick
92 Rob Bellamy
101 R.J. Anderson
124 **David Laliberte**
144 Chris Zarb
149 Gino Pisellini
170 Ladislav Scurko
171 Frederik Cabana
232 **Martin Houle**
253 Travis Gawryletz
286 **Triston Grant**
291 John Carter

2003
Pick
11 **Jeff Carter**
24 **Mike Richards**
69 **Colin Fraser**
81 **Stefan Ruzicka**
85 **Alexandre Picard**
87 **Ryan Potulny**
95 Rick Kozak
108 Kevin Romy
140 David Tremblay
191 Rejean Beauchemin
193 Ville Hostikka

2002
Pick
4 **Joni Pitkanen**
105 Rosario Ruggeri
126 Konstantin Baranov
161 Dov Grumet-Morris
192 Nikita Korovkin
193 **Joey Mormina**
201 Mathieu Brunelle

2001
Pick
27 **Jeff Woywitka**
95 **Patrick Sharp**
146 **Jussi Timonen**
150 Bernd Bruckler
158 Roman Malek
172 **Dennis Seidenberg**
177 Andrei Razin
208 Thierry Douville
225 **David Printz**

2000
Pick
28 **Justin Williams**
94 Alexander Drozdetsky
171 **Roman Cechmanek**
195 Colin Shields
210 John Eichelberger
227 **Guillaume Lefebvre**
259 Regan Kelly
287 Milan Kopecky

1999
Pick
22 **Maxime Ouellet**
119 Jeff Feniak
160 Konstantin Rudenko
200 Pavel Kasparik
208 **Vaclav Pletka**
224 David Nystrom

1998
Pick
22 **Simon Gagne**
42 Jason Beckett
51 Ian Forbes
109 Jean-Philippe Morin
124 **Francis Belanger**
139 Garrett Prosofsky
168 **Antero Niittymaki**
175 Cam Ondrik
195 **Tomas Divisek**
222 Lubomir Pistek
243 **Petr Hubacek**
253 **Bruno St. Jacques**
258 Sergei Skrobot

1997
Pick
30 **Jean-Marc Pelletier**
50 **Pat Kavanagh**
62 Kris Mallette
103 Mikhail Chernov
158 Jordon Flodell
164 **Todd Fedoruk**
214 Marko Kauppinen
240 Par Styf

1996
Pick
15 **Dainius Zubrus**
64 Chester Gallant
124 Per-Ragna Bergqvist
133 **Jesse Boulerice**
187 Roman Malov
213 Jeff Milleker

General Managers' History

Bud Poile, 1967-68, 1968-69; Bud Poile and Keith Allen, 1969-70; Keith Allen, 1970-71 to 1982-83; Bob McCammon, 1983-84; Bob Clarke, 1984-85 to 1989-90; Russ Farwell, 1990-91 to 1993-94; Bob Clarke, 1994-95 to 2005-06; Bob Clarke and Paul Holmgren, 2006-07; Paul Holmgren, 2007-08 to date.

Paul Holmgren
General Manager
Born: St. Paul, MN, December 2, 1955.

Paul Holmgren was named interim general manager of the Philadelphia Flyers on November 11, 2006, replacing Bob Clarke who resigned on October 22. On March 14, 2007, Holmgren was officially announced as the club's new g.m. In his first full season on the job in 2007-08, the Flyers returned to the playoffs after finishing last overall in the NHL the year before. They reached the Stanley Cup Final in 2010. Prior to his promotion, Holmgren had served the previous seven seasons as the team's assistant general manager. He rejoined the Flyers organization as a scout after being replaced as the Hartford Whalers' head coach on November 6, 1995. He had served as a head coach with both the Whalers and the Flyers and also served as general manager in Hartford during the 1993–94 season.

Holmgren retired from playing after the 1984-85 season, having recorded 144 goals and 179 assists for 323 points and 1,684 penalty minutes in 527 career regular season NHL games with the Flyers and the Minnesota North Stars. He recorded 138 goals and 171 assists for 309 points and 1,600 penalty minutes in 500 games over parts of nine seasons with the Flyers (1975-76 to 1983-84). His 1,600 penalty minutes with the Flyers are second all-time in club history. Holmgren was drafted from the University of Minnesota by the Flyers in the sixth round (108th overall) of the 1975 NHL Entry Draft.

Coaching Record

			Regular Season				Playoffs			
Season	**Team**	**League**	**GC**	**W**	**L**	**O/T**	**GC**	**W**	**L**	**T**
1988-89	Philadelphia	NHL	80	36	36	8	19	10	9	....
1989-90	Philadelphia	NHL	80	30	39	11	....	....	....	....
1990-91	Philadelphia	NHL	80	33	37	10	....	....	....	....
1991-92	Philadelphia	NHL	24	8	14	2	....	....	....	....
1992-93	Hartford	NHL	84	26	52	6	....	....	....	....
1993-94	Hartford	NHL	17	4	11	2	....	....	....	....
1994-95	Hartford	NHL	48	19	24	5	....	....	....	....
1995-96	Hartford	NHL	12	5	6	1	....	....	....	....
	NHL Totals		**425**	**161**	**219**	**45**	**19**	**10**	**9**	....

Club Directory

Wells Fargo Center

Philadelphia Flyers
Wells Fargo Center
3601 South Broad Street
Philadelphia, PA 19148-5290
Phone **215/465-4500**
PR FAX 215/389-9403
www.philadelphiaflyers.com
Capacity: 19,537

Executive Management
Chairman . . . . Ed Snider
President and COO of Comcast-Spectacor. . . . . Peter A. Luukko
General Manager . . . . Paul Holmgren
Senior Vice President. . . . . Bob Clarke
Executive Vice President . . . . Keith Allen
Governor . . . . Ed Snider
Alternate Governors . . . . Paul Holmgren, Peter A. Luukko, Phil Weinberg
Senior Vice President, Business Operations . . . . Shawn Tilger

Hockey Club Personnel
Assistant General Managers . . . . Barry Hanrahan, John Paddock
Director of Hockey Operations . . . . Chris Pryor
Director of Player Development. . . . . Don Luce
Director of Player Personnel . . . . Dave Brown
Head Coach . . . . Peter Laviolette
Assistant Coaches. . . . . Craig Berube, Kevin McCarthy, Joe Mullen
Goaltending Coach. . . . . Jeff Reese
Player Development Coach . . . . Derian Hatcher
Video Coach. . . . . Adam Patterson
Pro Scouts . . . . Dave Brown, Patrick Burke, John Chapman, Al Hill
Scouting Staff. . . . . . . Andre Beaulieu, Wade Clarke, Ross Fitzpatrick, Mark Greig, Todd Hearty, Ken Hoodikoff, Matti Kautto, Neil Little, Jack McIlhargey, Simon Nolet, Dennis Patterson, John Riley, Ilkka Sinisalo, Vaclav Slansky
Scouting Consultant . . . . Bill Barber
Director, Team Services. . . . . Bryan Hardenbergh
Executive Assistant . . . . Dianna Taylor
Administrative Assistant . . . . Jody Clarke

Medical / Training Staff
Team Physicians . . . . Peter DeLuca, M.D.; Gary Dorshimer, M.D.; Guy Lanzi, D.M.D.; Frank Brady, D.C.
Athletic Trainer/Strength & Conditioning Coach . . . Jim McCrossin
Assistant Athletic Trainer. . . . . Sal Raffa
Massage Therapist . . . . Brad Smith
Head Equipment Manager . . . . Derek Settlemyre
Equipment Managers . . . . Harry Bricker, Anthony Oratorio, Luke Clarke
Training Center Maintenance . . . . Mike Craytor

Communications
Senior Director, Communications . . . . Zack Hill
Coordinator, Media Services & Publications. . . . . . . Joe Siville
Public Relations Assistant . . . . Brian Smith

Community Relations
Director, Community Relations & Special Events . . . Linda Mantai
Coordinator, Community Relations . . . . Jason Tempesta
Ambassador of Hockey . . . . Bob Kelly
Fan Relations Assistant . . . . Jerry Callahan
Ambassadors . . . . Gary Dornhoefer, Joe Kadlec, Bernie Parent

Customer Service
Vice President, Customer Solutions . . . . Cindy Stutman
Director, Customer Service . . . . Lauren Pawlowski
Manager, Client Communications. . . . . Nadine Enders
Customer Service Account Managers . . . . Vincent Galasso, Tom Griendling, Courtney Sams
Customer Service Coordinator . . . . Megan Bell

Game Presentation
Director, Game Presentation . . . . Anthony Gioia
Game Operations Coordinator . . . . Michaela Sweet
Producer/Director . . . . Artie Halstead
Graphics Designer / Video Editor. . . . . Mike Cahill / Chris Shay
Public Address Announcer / Anthem Singer . . . . . . Lou Nolan / Lauren Hart

Marketing
Director, Marketing. . . . . Lindsey Masciangelo
Marketing Manager . . . . Rob Johnson
Marketing Coordinator . . . . Alicia DeFillipo
New Media Manager . . . . Lauren Cochran
Publicist . . . . Shauna Adams

Ticket Sales
Vice President, Sales . . . . Jim Willits
Director, Ticket Sales. . . . . Bryan Anton
Director, Client Development . . . . Missy Keeler
Ticket Sales Coordinators . . . . Shannon Bowes, Angela Prendergast
Senior Account Executive . . . . Tim Gobs
Account Executives . . . . Mike Andrews, James Darlington, Erin Dunn, Austin Foley, Steve Greenblatt, Steve Hanson, Ilkka Kortesluoma, Dan Ryan, Melissa Sylvester, Josh Wentz
Client Development Executives. . . . . Warren Avart, Lindsay Heck, Travis Kraus, Tony Sukanick, Fran Walmsley
Sales Associates . . . . Marty Asalone, Bryan D'Ottavi, Paul Haines-LaPenta, Brad Rinehart, Ben Schegel, Andrew Sherman

Ticketing
Vice President, Ticket Operations . . . . Cecilia Baker
Ticket Office Manager / Asst. Manager . . . . Linda Fleischer / Lisa Albertson
Ticket Operations and Processing Manager . . . . Dan McGinnis
Ticket Office Administration . . . . Joan Kadlec

Finance
Chief Financial Officer. . . . . Angelo Cardone
Controller. . . . . Judy Zdunkiewicz
Staff Accountants. . . . . Kim Chuba, Tyler Deane
Payroll Accountant / Accounting Clerk . . . . Renee Eiler / Michele Dominic
Team Consultant . . . . Ron Ryan
Executive Assistants . . . . Sharon Allison, Cheri Arnao, Ann Marie Nasutt

Phoenix Coyotes

Key Off-Season Signings/Acquisitions

2010

May 24 • Signed 2009 1st round pick (6th overall), D **Oliver Ekman-Larsson** (Leksand).

June 9 • Re-signed LW **Scottie Upshall**.
- **17** • Re-signed D **Adrian Aucoin**.
- **21** • Re-signed LW **Taylor Pyatt**.
- **28** • Re-signed LW **Wojtek Wolski**.

July 1 • Signed LW **Ray Whitney**.
- **1** • Re-signed D **Derek Morris**.
- **2** • Signed C **Andrew Ebbett**.
- **2** • Re-signed D **Sami Lepisto** and G **Al Montoya**.
- **26** • Re-signed LW **Alexandre Picard**.

2009-10 Results: 50w-25l-1otl-6sol 107pts.
Second, Pacific Division

Year-by-Year Record

Season	GP	Home W	L	T	OL	Road W	L	T	OL	Overall W	L	T	OL	GF	GA	Pts.	Finished	Playoff Result
2009-10	82	29	10		2	21	15		5	50	25		7	225	202	107	2nd, Pacific Div.	Lost Conf. Quarter-Final
2008-09	82	23	15		3	13	24		4	36	39		7	208	252	79	4th, Pacific Div.	Out of Playoffs
2007-08	82	17	20		4	21	17		3	38	37		7	214	231	83	4th, Pacific Div.	Out of Playoffs
2006-07	82	18	20		3	13	26		2	31	46		5	216	284	67	5th, Pacific Div.	Out of Playoffs
2005-06	82	19	18		4	19	21		1	38	39		5	246	271	81	5th, Pacific Div.	Out of Playoffs
2004-05																		
2003-04	82	11	19	7	4	11	17	11	2	22	36	18	6	188	245	68	5th, Pacific Div.	Out of Playoffs
2002-03	82	17	16	6	2	14	19	5	3	31	35	11	5	204	230	78	4th, Pacific Div.	Out of Playoffs
2001-02	82	27	8	3	3	13	19	6	3	40	27	9	6	228	210	95	3rd, Pacific Div.	Lost Conf. Quarter-Final
2000-01	82	21	11	7	2	14	16	10	1	35	27	17	3	214	212	90	4th, Pacific Div.	Out of Playoffs
1999-2000	82	22	16	2	1	17	15	6	3	39	31	8	4	232	228	90	3rd, Pacific Div.	Lost Conf. Quarter-Final
1998-99	82	23	13	5	....	16	18	7	....	39	31	12	....	205	197	90	2nd, Pacific Div.	Lost Conf. Quarter-Final
1997-98	82	19	16	6	....	16	19	6	....	35	35	12	....	224	227	82	4th, Central Div.	Lost Conf. Quarter-Final
1996-97	82	15	19	7	....	23	18	0	....	38	37	7	....	240	243	83	3rd, Central Div.	Lost Conf. Quarter-Final
1995-96*	82	22	16	3	....	14	24	3	....	36	40	6	....	275	291	78	5th, Central Div.	Lost Conf. Quarter-Final
1994-95*	48	10	10	4	....	6	15	3	....	16	25	7	....	157	177	39	6th, Central Div.	Out of Playoffs
1993-94*	84	15	23	4	....	9	28	5	....	24	51	9	....	245	344	57	6th, Central Div.	Out of Playoffs
1992-93*	84	23	16	3	....	17	21	4	....	40	37	7	....	322	320	87	4th, Smythe Div.	Lost Div. Semi-Final
1991-92*	80	20	14	6	....	13	18	9	....	33	32	15	....	251	244	81	4th, Smythe Div.	Lost Div. Semi-Final
1990-91*	80	17	18	5	....	9	25	6	....	26	43	11	....	260	288	63	5th, Smythe Div.	Out of Playoffs
1989-90*	80	22	13	5	....	15	19	6	....	37	32	11	....	298	290	85	3rd, Smythe Div.	Lost Div. Semi-Final
1988-89*	80	17	18	5	....	9	24	7	....	26	42	12	....	300	355	64	5th, Smythe Div.	Out of Playoffs
1987-88*	80	20	14	6	....	13	22	5	....	33	36	11	....	292	310	77	3rd, Smythe Div.	Lost Div. Semi-Final
1986-87*	80	25	12	3	....	15	20	5	....	40	32	8	....	279	271	88	3rd, Smythe Div.	Lost Div. Final
1985-86*	80	18	19	3	....	8	28	4	....	26	47	7	....	295	372	59	3rd, Smythe Div.	Lost Div. Semi-Final
1984-85*	80	21	13	6	....	22	14	4	....	43	27	10	....	358	332	96	2nd, Smythe Div.	Lost Div. Final
1983-84*	80	17	15	8	....	14	23	3	....	31	38	11	....	340	374	73	4th, Smythe Div.	Lost Div. Semi-Final
1982-83*	80	22	16	2	....	11	23	6	....	33	39	8	....	311	333	74	4th, Smythe Div.	Lost Div. Semi-Final
1981-82*	80	18	13	9	....	15	20	5	....	33	33	14	....	319	332	80	2nd, Norris Div.	Lost Div. Semi-Final
1980-81*	80	7	25	8	....	2	32	6	....	9	57	14	....	246	400	32	6th, Smythe Div.	Out of Playoffs
1979-80*	80	13	19	8	....	7	30	3	....	20	49	11	....	214	314	51	5th, Smythe Div.	Out of Playoffs

* Winnipeg Jets

2010-11 Schedule

Oct.
- Sat. 9 at Boston†
- Sun. 10 Boston*†
- Sat. 16 Detroit
- Sun. 17 at Anaheim*
- Thu. 21 Los Angeles
- Sat. 23 Carolina
- Mon. 25 at Montreal
- Tue. 26 at Ottawa
- Thu. 28 at Detroit
- Sat. 30 Tampa Bay

Nov.
- Wed. 3 Nashville
- Fri. 5 at Dallas
- Sat. 6 Pittsburgh
- Mon. 8 at Detroit
- Wed. 10 at Chicago
- Fri. 12 Calgary
- Sat. 13 St. Louis
- Wed. 17 at Calgary
- Fri. 19 at Edmonton
- Sun. 21 at Vancouver
- Tue. 23 Edmonton
- Sat. 27 Anaheim
- Tue. 30 at Nashville

Dec.
- Wed. 1 at Minnesota
- Sat. 4 Florida
- Sun. 5 at Anaheim*
- Thu. 9 Minnesota
- Sat. 11 Dallas
- Wed. 15 at New Jersey
- Thu. 16 at NY Rangers
- Sat. 18 at NY Islanders
- Mon. 20 at Pittsburgh
- Thu. 23 at San Jose
- Sun. 26 at Dallas
- Tue. 28 Anaheim
- Wed. 29 Los Angeles
- Fri. 31 at St. Louis

Jan.
- Sun. 2 at Minnesota*
- Tue. 4 Columbus
- Thu. 6 at Colorado
- Sat. 8 Buffalo
- Mon. 10 at St. Louis
- Tue. 11 at Columbus
- Thu. 13 Toronto
- Sat. 15 Anaheim
- Mon. 17 San Jose*
- Tue. 18 Nashville
- Thu. 20 at Los Angeles
- Sat. 22 Los Angeles
- Tue. 25 Edmonton
- Wed. 26 at Colorado

Feb.
- Tue. 1 at San Jose
- Wed. 2 Vancouver
- Sat. 5 Minnesota
- Mon. 7 Colorado
- Wed. 9 at Dallas
- Sat. 12 Chicago
- Mon. 14 Washington
- Thu. 17 Atlanta
- Sat. 19 at Nashville
- Tue. 22 at Philadelphia
- Wed. 23 at Tampa Bay
- Fri. 25 at Columbus
- Sun. 27 at Chicago

Mar.
- Tue. 1 Dallas
- Thu. 3 at Los Angeles
- Sat. 5 Detroit
- Tue. 8 Vancouver
- Thu. 10 Calgary
- Sun. 13 at Anaheim*
- Tue. 15 at Calgary
- Thu. 17 at Edmonton
- Fri. 18 at Vancouver
- Sun. 20 Chicago*
- Tue. 22 St. Louis
- Thu. 24 Columbus
- Sat. 26 San Jose
- Tue. 29 Dallas

Apr.
- Fri. 1 Colorado
- Wed. 6 at Los Angeles
- Fri. 8 San Jose
- Sat. 9 at San Jose

* Denotes afternoon game. † Games played in Prague, CZ.

Ilya Bryzgalov was a big reason why the Coyotes set franchise records for wins and points in 2009-10, ranking among the NHL leaders in wins (42), goals-against average (2.29), save percentage (.920) and shutouts (8).

PACIFIC DIVISION
32nd NHL Season

Franchise date: June 22, 1979

Transferred from Winnipeg to Phoenix, July 1, 1996.

2010-11 Player Personnel

FORWARDS	HT	WT	S	Place of Birth	*Age	2009-10 Club
BEAUDOIN, Matt	5-11	190	R	Rock Forest, Que.	26	Texas
BISSONNETTE, Paul	6-3	220	L	Welland, Ont.	25	Phoenix
BOEDKER, Mikkel	5-11	202	L	Brondby, Denmark	20	Phoenix-San Antonio
DOAN, Shane	6-2	224	R	Halkirk, Alta.	33	Phoenix
EBBETT, Andrew	5-9	174	L	Calgary, Alta.	27	Ana-Chi-Min
FIDDLER, Vernon	5-11	201	L	Edmonton, Alta.	30	Phoenix
HANZAL, Martin	6-5	218	L	Pisek, Czech.	23	Phoenix
HOLLWEG, Ryan	5-10	212	L	Downey, CA	27	San Antonio
KEARNS, Bracken	6-0	195	R	Vancouver, B.C.	29	Rockford
KORPIKOSKI, Lauri	6-1	195	L	Turku, Finland	24	Phoenix
LONG, Colin	5-11	187	R	Santa Ana, CA	21	San Antonio
LUNDEN, Josh	6-2	202	L	Burnaby, B.C.	24	Alaska-Anchorage-San Antonio
MACLEAN, Brett	6-1	200	R	Port Elgin, Ont.	21	San Antonio
PICARD, Alexandre	6-2	206	L	Les Saules, Que.	24	CBJ-Syr-San Antonio
PRUCHA, Petr	6-0	175	R	Chrudim, Czech.	28	Phoenix
PYATT, Taylor	6-4	230	L	Thunder Bay, Ont.	29	Phoenix
TIKHONOV, Viktor	6-2	187	R	Riga, Latvia	22	San Antonio-Cherepovets
TURRIS, Kyle	6-1	188	R	New Westminster, B.C.	21	San Antonio
UPSHALL, Scottie	6-0	197	L	Fort McMurray, Alta.	27	Phoenix
VRBATA, Radim	6-1	190	R	Mlada Boleslav, Czech.	29	Phoenix
WATKINS, Matt	5-10	180	L	Aylesbury, Sask.	23	Las Vegas-San Antonio
WHITNEY, Ray	5-10	180	R	Fort Saskatchewan, Alta.	38	Carolina
WOLSKI, Wojtek	6-3	210	L	Zabrze, Poland	24	Colorado-Phoenix
DEFENSEMEN						
AHNELOV, Jonas	6-2	220	L	Huddinge, Sweden	22	San Antonio
AUCOIN, Adrian	6-2	213	R	Ottawa, Ont.	37	Phoenix
BRODEUR, Mathieu	6-5	190	L	Laval, Que.	20	Cape Breton-San Antonio
EKMAN-LARSSON, Oliver	6-2	176	L	Karlskrona, Sweden	19	Leksand
GONCHAROV, Maxim	6-0	176	R	Moscow, USSR	21	CSKA
HESHKA, Shaun	6-1	208	R	Melville, Sask.	25	Phoenix-San Antonio
JOVANOVSKI, Ed	6-3	218	L	Windsor, Ont.	34	Phoenix
LEPISTO, Sami	6-0	190	L	Espoo, Finland	25	Phoenix
MORRIS, Derek	6-0	221	R	Edmonton, Alta.	32	Boston-Phoenix
ROSS, Nick	6-1	196	L	Edmonton, Alta.	21	San Antonio-Las Vegas
SAUER, Kurt	6-4	222	L	St. Cloud, MN	29	Phoenix
SCHLEMKO, David	6-2	196	L	Edmonton, Alta.	23	Phoenix-San Antonio
STAFFORD, Garrett	6-1	207	R	Los Angeles, CA	30	Texas
STONE, Michael	6-3	200	R	Winnipeg, Man.	20	Calgary (WHL)
SUMMERS, Chris	6-2	180	L	Ann Arbor, MI	22	U. of Michigan-San Antonio
YANDLE, Keith	6-1	195	L	Boston, MA	24	Phoenix
YONKMAN, Nolan	6-6	253	R	Punnichy, Sask.	29	Milwaukee

GOALTENDERS	HT	WT	C	Place of Birth	*Age	2009-10 Club
BRYZGALOV, Ilya	6-3	210	L	Togliatti, USSR	30	Phoenix
CLIMIE, Matt	6-3	194	L	Leduc, Alta.	27	Dallas-Texas
LaBARBERA, Jason	6-3	234	L	Burnaby, B.C.	30	Phoenix
MONTOYA, Al	6-2	195	L	Chicago, IL	25	San Antonio

* – Age at start of 2010-11 season

Dave Tippett

Head Coach

Born: Moosomin, Sask., August 25, 1961.

Dave Tippett was named the 17th head coach in Coyotes/Jets history on September 24, 2009. In his first season with the team in 2009-10, he led the Coyotes to a club-record 50 wins and 107 points and the team's first playoff appearance since 2001-02. Tippett was rewarded with the Jack Adams Award as coach of the year.

Prior to Phoenix, Tippett spent seven seasons as the head coach of the Dallas Stars from 2002-03 to 2008-09. Under Tippett's leadership, the Stars won two Pacific Division titles (2002-03 and 2005-06), made the playoffs in five out of six years and reached the Western Conference Final in 2008. His 271 career regular-season coaching victories rank him second all-time in Stars history.

Tippett joined the Stars organization on May 16, 2002 after serving as an assistant coach with the Los Angeles Kings for three seasons. Prior to becoming a coach, Tippett played 11 years as a forward in the National Hockey League with the Hartford Whalers, Washington Capitals, Pittsburgh Penguins and Philadelphia Flyers. He ended his playing career in 1995 as a player-assistant coach with the Houston Aeros (IHL). Internationally, he captained the 1984 Canadian Olympic team in Sarajevo, Yugoslavia, and he earned a silver medal as a member of the Canadian Olympic team in Albertville, France, in 1992. He was a member of the 1982 NCAA Division I championship squad at the University of North Dakota with former Stars defenseman Craig Ludwig. Tippett became head coach of the Houston Aeros in 1995-96. In 1999, he led the team to the Turner Cup championship and was named the IHL coach of the year.

Coaching Record

			Regular Season				Playoffs			
Season	Team	League	GC	W	L	O/T	GC	W	L	T
1995-96	Houston	IHL	42	17	18	7	....	....	....	....
1996-97	Houston	IHL	82	44	30	8	13	8	5	....
1997-98	Houston	IHL	82	50	22	10	4	1	3	....
1998-99	Houston	IHL	82	54	15	13	19	11	8	....
2002-03	**Dallas**	**NHL**	**82**	**46**	**17**	**19**	**12**	**6**	**6**	....
2003-04	**Dallas**	**NHL**	**82**	**41**	**26**	**15**	**5**	**1**	**4**	....
2004-05	**Dallas**				SEASON CANCELLED					
2005-06	**Dallas**	**NHL**	**82**	**53**	**23**	**6**	**5**	**1**	**4**	....
2006-07	**Dallas**	**NHL**	**82**	**50**	**25**	**7**	**7**	**3**	**4**	....
2007-08	**Dallas**	**NHL**	**82**	**45**	**30**	**7**	**18**	**10**	**8**	....
2008-09	**Dallas**	**NHL**	**82**	**36**	**35**	**11**	....	....	....	....
2009-10	**Phoenix**	**NHL**	**82**	**50**	**25**	**7**	**7**	**3**	**4**	....
	NHL Totals		**574**	**321**	**181**	**72**	**54**	**24**	**30**	....

Won Jack Adams Award (2010)

Posted a 2-1-2 record as replacement coach when Andy Murray was sidelined following a car accident, February 26 to March 6, 2002, All games are credited to Murray's coaching record.

2009-10 Scoring

* – rookie

Regular Season

Pos	#	Player	Team	GP	G	A	Pts	TOI	+/–	PIM	PP	SH	GW	S	%
L	86	Wojtek Wolski	COL	62	17	30	47	18:56	15	21	2	0	4	156	10.9
			PHX	18	6	12	18	18:01	6	6	0	0	1	39	15.4
			Total	80	23	42	65	18:44	21	27	2	0	5	195	11.8
L	19	Shane Doan	PHX	82	18	37	55	19:09	3	41	5	0	4	234	7.7
C	15	Matthew Lombardi	PHX	78	19	34	53	17:56	8	36	4	0	2	174	10.9
R	22	Lee Stempniak	TOR	62	14	16	30	17:53	–10	18	5	1	1	164	8.5
			PHX	18	14	4	18	15:21	10	8	4	0	1	48	29.2
			Total	80	28	20	48	17:19	0	26	9	1	2	212	13.2
R	17	Radim Vrbata	PHX	82	24	19	43	16:13	6	24	7	0	4	266	9.0
D	3	Keith Yandle	PHX	82	12	29	41	20:13	16	45	5	0	2	145	8.3
D	55	Ed Jovanovski	PHX	66	10	24	34	21:37	–12	55	5	0	2	117	8.5
C	11	Martin Hanzal	PHX	81	11	22	33	18:28	0	104	2	0	0	147	7.5
L	8	Scottie Upshall	PHX	49	18	14	32	15:02	5	50	2	0	4	119	15.1
C	38	Vernon Fiddler	PHX	76	8	22	30	14:20	13	46	0	3	1	119	6.7
C	20	Robert Lang	PHX	64	9	20	29	15:04	–4	28	3	0	1	84	10.7
D	53	Derek Morris	BOS	58	3	22	25	22:00	–2	26	2	0	0	95	3.2
			PHX	18	1	3	4	19:39	4	11	0	0	0	25	4.0
			Total	76	4	25	29	21:26	2	37	2	0	0	120	3.3
D	33	Adrian Aucoin	PHX	82	8	20	28	22:33	2	56	1	0	2	144	5.6
L	14	Taylor Pyatt	PHX	74	12	11	23	13:27	13	39	1	0	3	121	9.9
R	16	Petr Prucha	PHX	79	13	9	22	14:02	–2	23	4	0	2	128	10.2
L	34	Daniel Winnik	PHX	74	4	15	19	13:08	1	12	0	0	1	83	4.8
D	4	Zbynek Michalek	PHX	72	3	14	17	22:38	5	30	2	0	1	104	2.9
C	71	Petteri Nokelainen	ANA	50	4	7	11	12:55	–7	21	0	0	0	70	5.7
			PHX	17	1	1	2	10:24	–2	6	0	0	0	18	5.6
			Total	67	5	8	13	12:17	–9	27	0	0	0	88	5.7
D	2	Jim Vandermeer	PHX	62	4	8	12	17:41	3	60	0	0	1	64	6.3
L	29	Lauri Korpikoski	PHX	71	5	6	11	12:18	–10	16	0	0	1	68	7.4
D	18	Sami Lepisto	PHX	66	1	10	11	18:13	14	60	0	0	1	68	1.5
D	23	Mathieu Schneider	VAN	17	2	3	5	15:14	0	12	1	0	0	14	14.3
			PHX	8	0	4	4	20:49	5	4	0	0	0	23	0.0
			Total	25	2	7	9	17:01	5	16	1	0	0	37	5.4
L	12	* Paul Bissonnette	PHX	41	3	2	5	5:51	–2	117	0	0	1	25	12.0
D	6	* David Schlemko	PHX	17	1	4	5	17:49	1	8	0	0	0	19	5.3
R	89	Mikkel Boedker	PHX	14	1	2	3	8:42	2	0	0	0	0	7	14.3
D	21	* Shaun Heshka	PHX	8	0	2	2	13:18	0	4	0	0	0	3	0.0
C	26	Joel Perrault	PHX	2	1	0	1	9:54	–1	0	0	0	0	7	14.3
D	44	Kurt Sauer	PHX	1	0	0	0	16:32	1	0	0	0	0	2	0.0
R	28	Jeff Hoggan	PHX	4	0	0	0	7:06	–1	2	0	0	0	5	0.0

Goaltending

No.	Goaltender	GPI	Mins	Avg	W	L	OT	EN	SO	GA	SA	S%	G	A	PIM
1	Jason Labarbera	17	928	2.13	8	5	1	1	0	33	459	.928	0	0	0
30	Ilya Bryzgalov	69	4084	2.29	42	20	6	6	8	156	1961	.920	0	1	4
	Totals	**82**	**5033**	**2.34**	**50**	**25**	**7**	**7**	**8**	**196**	**2427**	**.919**			

Playoffs

Pos	#	Player	Team	GP	G	A	Pts	TOI	+/–	PIM	PP	SH	GW	OT	S	%
C	15	Matthew Lombardi	PHX	7	1	5	6	17:36	2	2	0	0	0	0	19	5.3
L	86	Wojtek Wolski	PHX	7	4	1	5	17:24	1	0	1	0	0	0	14	28.6
D	3	Keith Yandle	PHX	7	2	3	5	17:11	–1	4	1	0	0	0	17	11.8
R	17	Radim Vrbata	PHX	7	2	2	4	15:41	–2	4	1	0	1	0	22	9.1
D	53	Derek Morris	PHX	7	1	3	4	19:34	–1	11	1	0	1	0	21	4.8
R	16	Petr Prucha	PHX	7	1	2	3	13:30	1	4	0	0	1	0	13	7.7
C	11	Martin Hanzal	PHX	7	0	3	3	18:57	–3	10	0	0	0	0	29	0.0
L	19	Shane Doan	PHX	3	1	1	2	13:21	0	4	0	0	0	0	7	14.3
C	38	Vernon Fiddler	PHX	6	1	1	2	14:03	–4	14	0	0	0	0	8	12.5
L	14	Taylor Pyatt	PHX	7	1	1	2	14:22	–4	2	1	0	0	0	11	9.1
D	33	Adrian Aucoin	PHX	7	0	2	2	21:16	3	10	0	0	0	0	7	0.0
D	4	Zbynek Michalek	PHX	7	0	2	2	20:27	–4	2	0	0	0	0	10	0.0
R	22	Lee Stempniak	PHX	7	0	2	2	14:28	–4	0	0	0	0	0	14	0.0
D	23	Mathieu Schneider	PHX	3	1	0	1	13:38	–1	0	1	0	0	0	3	33.3
D	55	Ed Jovanovski	PHX	7	1	0	1	21:13	–7	4	0	0	0	0	8	12.5
L	29	Lauri Korpikoski	PHX	7	1	0	1	16:15	–4	2	0	1	0	0	4	25.0
D	18	Sami Lepisto	PHX	7	1	0	1	15:49	–1	6	0	0	0	0	7	14.3
C	20	Robert Lang	PHX	4	0	1	1	9:03	0	0	0	0	0	0	1	0.0
C	71	Petteri Nokelainen	PHX	5	0	0	0	8:21	–1	2	0	0	0	0	0	0.0
L	34	Daniel Winnik	PHX	7	0	0	0	12:44	–2	0	0	0	0	0	6	0.0

Goaltending

No.	Goaltender	GPI	Mins	Avg	W	L	EN	SO	GA	SA	S%	G	A	PIM
30	Ilya Bryzgalov	7	419	3.44	3	4	2	0	24	255	.906	0	0	0
	Totals	**7**	**420**	**3.71**	**3**	**4**	**2**	**0**	**26**	**257**	**.899**			

Coaching History

Tom McVie and Bill Sutherland, 1979-80; Tom McVie, Bill Sutherland and Mike Smith, 1980-81; Tom Watt, 1981-82, 1982-83; Tom Watt and Barry Long, 1983-84; Barry Long, 1984-85; Barry Long and John Ferguson, 1985-86; Dan Maloney, 1986-87, 1987-88; Dan Maloney and Rick Bowness, 1988-89; Bob Murdoch, 1989-90, 1990-91; John Paddock, 1991-92 to 1993-94; John Paddock and Terry Simpson, 1994-95; Terry Simpson, 1995-96; Don Hay, 1996-97; Jim Schoenfeld, 1997-98, 1998-99; Bob Francis, 1999-2000 to 2002-03; Bob Francis and Rick Bowness, 2003-04; Rick Bowness, 2004-05; Wayne Gretzky, 2005-06 to 2008-09; Dave Tippett, 2009-10 to date.

Club Records

Team

(Figures in brackets for season records are games played; records for fewest points, wins, ties, losses, goals, goals against are for 70 or more games)

Most Points	**107**	2009-10 (82)
Most Wins	**50**	2009-10 (82)
Most Ties	**18**	2003-04 (82)
Most Losses	**57**	1980-81 (80)
Most Goals	**358**	1984-85 (80)
Most Goals Against	**400**	1980-81 (80)
Fewest Points	**32**	1980-81 (80)
Fewest Wins	**9**	1980-81 (80)
Fewest Ties	**6**	1995-96 (82)
Fewest Losses	**25**	2009-10 (82)
Fewest Goals	**188**	2003-04 (82)
Fewest Goals Against	**197**	1998-99 (82)
Longest Winning Streak		
Overall	**9**	Mar. 8-27/85, Mar. 4-21/10
Home	**10**	Nov. 21-Dec. 29/09
Away	**8**	Feb. 25-Apr. 6/85
Longest Undefeated Streak		
Overall	**14**	Oct. 25-Nov. 28/98 (12 wins, 2 ties)
Home	**11**	Dec. 23/83-Feb. 5/84 (6 wins, 5 ties), Oct. 15-Dec. 20/98 (10 wins, 1 tie)
Away	**9**	Feb. 25-Apr. 7/85 (8 wins, 1 tie), Dec. 7/03-Jan. 9/04 (5 wins, 4 ties)
Longest Losing Streak		
Overall	**10**	Nov. 30-Dec. 20/80, Feb. 6-25/94
Home	**6**	Oct. 6-Nov. 3/07, Jan. 27-Feb. 16/09
Away	**13**	Jan. 26-Apr. 14/94
Longest Winless Streak		
Overall	***30**	Oct. 19-Dec. 20/80 (23 losses, 7 ties)
Home	**14**	Oct. 19-Dec. 14/80 (9 losses, 5 ties)
Away	**18**	Oct. 10-Dec. 20/80 (16 losses, 2 ties)
Most Shutouts, Season	**9**	1998-99 (82)
Most PIM, Season	**2,278**	1987-88 (80)
Most Goals, Game	**12**	Feb. 25/85 (Wpg. 12 at NYR 5)

Individual

Most Seasons	**15**	Teppo Numminen
Most Games	**1,098**	Teppo Numminen
Most Goals, Career	**379**	Dale Hawerchuk
Most Assists, Career	**553**	Thomas Steen
Most Points, Career	**929**	Dale Hawerchuk (379G, 550A)
Most PIM, Career	**1,508**	Keith Tkachuk
Most Shutouts, Career	**21**	Nikolai Khabibulin
Longest Consecutive Games Streak	**475**	Dale Hawerchuk (Dec. 19/82-Dec. 10/88)
Most Goals, Season	**76**	Teemu Selanne (1992-93)
Most Assists, Season	**79**	Phil Housley (1992-93)
Most Points, Season	**132**	Teemu Selanne (1992-93; 76G, 56A)
Most PIM, Season	**347**	Tie Domi (1993-94)
Most Points, Defenseman, Season	**97**	Phil Housley (1992-93; 18G, 79A)
Most Points, Center, Season	**130**	Dale Hawerchuk (1984-85; 53G, 77A)
Most Points, Right Wing, Season	**132**	Teemu Selanne (1992-93; 76G, 56A)
Most Points, Left Wing, Season	**98**	Keith Tkachuk (1995-96; 50G, 48A)
Most Points, Rookie, Season	***132**	Teemu Selanne (1992-93; 76G, 56A)
Most Shutouts, Season	**8**	Nikolai Khabibulin (1998-99) Ilya Bryzgalov (2009-10)
Most Goals, Game	**5**	Willy Lindstrom (Mar. 2/82), Alexei Zhamnov (Apr. 1/95)
Most Assists, Game	**5**	Dale Hawerchuk (Mar. 6/84), (Mar. 18/89), (Mar. 4/90) Phil Housley (Jan. 18/93) Keith Tkachuk (Feb. 23/01)
Most Points, Game	**6**	Willy Lindstrom (Mar. 2/82; 5G, 1A) Dale Hawerchuk (Dec. 14/83; 3G, 3A), (Mar. 5/88; 2G, 4A), (Mar. 18/89; 1G, 5A) Thomas Steen (Oct. 24/84; 2G, 4A) Ed Olczyk (Dec. 21/91; 2G, 4A)

* NHL Record.

Records include Winnipeg Jets, 1979-80 through 1995-96.

Captains' History

Lars-Erik Sjoberg, 1979-80; Morris Lukowich and Scott Campbell, 1980-81; Dave Christian and Barry Long, 1981-82; Dave Christian and Lucien DeBlois, 1982-83; Lucien DeBlois, 1983-84; Dale Hawerchuk, 1984-85 to 1988-89; Randy Carlyle, Dale Hawerchuk and Thomas Steen (tri-captains), 1989-90; Randy Carlyle and Thomas Steen (co-captains), 1990-91; Troy Murray, 1991-92; Troy Murray and Dean Kennedy, 1992-93; Dean Kennedy and Keith Tkachuk, 1993-94; Keith Tkachuk, 1994-95; Kris King, 1995-96; Keith Tkachuk, 1996-97 to 2000-01; Teppo Numminen, 2001-02, 2002-03; Shane Doan, 2003-04 to date.

Winnipeg Jets Retired Numbers

9	Bobby Hull	1972-1980
10	Dale Hawerchuk	1981-1990
25	Thomas Steen	1981-1995
27	Teppo Numminen	1988-2003

All-time Record vs. Other Clubs

Regular Season

	At Home								On Road								Total							
	GP	W	L	T	OL	GF	GA	PTS	GP	W	L	T	OL	GF	GA	PTS	GP	W	L	T	OL	GF	GA	PTS
Anaheim	44	20	17	2	5	122	125	47	45	14	25	3	3	110	140	34	89	34	42	5	8	232	265	81
Atlanta	7	6	0	1	0	25	12	13	6	5	1	0	0	20	12	10	13	11	1	1	0	45	24	23
Boston	32	14	15	3	0	106	106	31	32	6	22	4	0	96	138	16	64	20	37	7	0	202	244	47
Buffalo	32	14	16	2	0	95	103	30	34	7	22	5	0	84	135	19	66	21	38	7	0	179	238	49
Calgary	80	38	31	11	0	289	273	87	81	27	44	9	1	250	325	64	161	65	75	20	1	539	598	151
Carolina	33	15	15	2	1	120	123	33	33	12	14	6	1	97	108	31	66	27	29	8	2	217	231	64
Chicago	60	32	21	5	2	192	187	71	58	16	31	10	1	143	212	43	118	48	52	15	3	335	399	114
Colorado	50	21	21	7	1	173	171	50	51	19	24	5	3	167	179	46	101	40	45	12	4	340	350	96
Columbus	18	10	5	3	0	53	40	23	18	10	7	1	0	45	42	21	36	20	12	4	0	98	82	44
Dallas	72	30	35	4	3	220	238	67	73	29	33	9	2	211	243	69	145	59	68	13	5	431	481	136
Detroit	59	19	25	14	1	172	194	53	61	21	31	8	1	200	237	51	120	40	56	22	2	372	431	104
Edmonton	81	34	40	5	2	316	343	75	82	23	51	6	2	260	359	54	163	57	91	11	4	576	702	129
Florida	12	5	3	3	1	35	35	14	10	6	4	0	0	27	31	12	22	11	7	3	1	62	66	26
Los Angeles	94	51	30	11	2	364	300	115	92	41	34	14	3	337	345	99	186	92	64	25	5	701	645	214
Minnesota	18	10	7	1	0	50	41	21	18	7	9	2	0	36	48	16	36	17	16	3	0	86	89	37
Montreal	31	9	15	7	0	98	120	25	31	3	26	2	0	69	151	8	62	12	41	9	0	167	271	33
Nashville	22	14	6	0	2	66	63	30	22	7	9	2	4	51	63	20	44	21	15	2	6	117	126	50
New Jersey	33	23	7	3	0	121	85	49	31	12	13	6	0	93	101	30	64	35	20	9	0	214	186	79
NY Islanders	33	13	15	4	1	111	117	31	32	9	15	8	0	95	119	26	65	22	30	12	1	206	236	57
NY Rangers	33	14	14	4	1	113	110	33	32	10	19	2	1	110	138	23	65	24	33	6	2	223	248	56
Ottawa	12	5	6	1	0	39	44	11	13	6	6	1	0	39	42	13	25	11	12	2	0	78	86	24
Philadelphia	33	15	16	2	0	106	107	32	33	9	23	0	1	89	140	19	66	24	39	2	1	195	247	51
Pittsburgh	33	15	14	3	1	122	115	34	32	11	21	0	0	90	123	22	65	26	35	3	1	212	238	56
St. Louis	61	31	23	7	0	194	191	69	60	20	28	11	1	163	199	52	121	51	51	18	1	357	390	121
San Jose	53	26	20	3	4	158	150	59	50	21	23	4	2	140	163	48	103	47	43	7	6	298	313	107
Tampa Bay	14	7	7	0	0	33	35	14	12	6	6	0	0	38	39	12	26	13	13	0	0	71	74	26
Toronto	41	22	13	6	0	172	146	50	45	23	20	2	0	171	163	48	86	45	33	8	0	343	309	98
Vancouver	79	39	29	10	1	285	270	89	82	21	51	10	0	220	303	52	161	60	80	20	1	505	573	141
Washington	32	16	9	7	0	115	112	39	33	9	18	5	1	90	125	24	65	25	27	12	1	205	237	63
Totals	**1202**	**568**	**475**	**131**	**28**	**4065**	**3956**	**1295**	**1202**	**410**	**630**	**135**	**27**	**3541**	**4423**	**982**	**2404**	**978**	**1105**	**266**	**55**	**7606**	**8379**	**2277**

Playoffs

	Series	W	L	GP	W	L	T	GF	GA	Last Mtg.	Rnd.	Result
Anaheim	1	0	1	7	3	4	0	17	17	1997	CQF	L 3-4
Calgary	3	2	1	13	7	6	0	45	43	1987	DSF	W 4-2
Colorado	1	0	1	5	1	4	0	10	17	2000	CQF	L 1-4
Detroit	3	0	3	19	7	12	0	46	70	2010	CQF	L 3-4
Edmonton	6	0	6	26	4	22	0	75	120	1990	DSF	L 3-4
St. Louis	2	0	2	11	4	7	0	29	39	1999	CQF	L 3-4
San Jose	1	0	1	5	1	4	0	7	13	2002	CQF	L 1-4
Vancouver	2	0	2	13	5	8	0	34	50	1993	DSF	L 2-4
Totals	**19**	**2**	**17**	**99**	**32**	**67**	**0**	**263**	**369**			

Calgary totals include Atlanta Flames, 1979-80.
Colorado totals include Quebec, 1979-80 to 1994-95.
New Jersey totals include Colorado Rockies, 1979-80 to 1981-82.
Carolina totals include Hartford, 1979-80 to 1996-97.
Dallas totals include Minnesota North Stars, 1979-80 to 1992-93.

Playoff Results 2010-2006

Year	Round	Opponent	Result	GF	GA
2010	CQF	Detroit	L 3-4	18	26

Abbreviations: Round: CQF – conference quarter-final; **DSF** – division semi-final.

2009-10 Results

Oct.	3	at Los Angeles	6-3		31	San Jose	2-3†
	7	at Pittsburgh	3-0	**Jan.**	2	Detroit	1-4
	8	at Buffalo	1-2		5	at Edmonton	5-4*
	10	Columbus	0-2		7	at Vancouver	0-4
	12	at San Jose	1-0†		9	NY Islanders	4-5†
	15	St. Louis	3-2*		12	San Jose	1-3
	17	Boston	4-1		14	New Jersey	4-3
	22	Detroit	3-2*		16	Minnesota	6-4
	24	Los Angeles	3-5		18	Buffalo	2-7
	26	at NY Rangers	2-5		21	Nashville	4-2
	28	at Columbus	4-1		23	at Washington	2-4
	29	at St. Louis	2-0		26	at Detroit	5-4*
	31	Anaheim	3-2†		28	Calgary	3-2†
Nov.	2	Los Angeles	3-5		30	NY Rangers	3-2
	4	at Colorado	1-4		31	at Dallas	4-2
	5	Chicago	3-1	**Feb.**	2	at Nashville	1-0†
	7	at Anaheim	3-4		5	at Chicago	2-1†
	12	Montreal	2-4		6	at Dallas	0-4
	14	Dallas	3-2		8	Edmonton	6-1
	16	Tampa Bay	1-4		10	at Minnesota	3-2
	18	at Minnesota	3-2		12	at Colorado	1-2
	19	at St. Louis	2-3*		13	Dallas	0-3
	21	Philadelphia	3-1	**Mar.**	2	St. Louis	2-5
	23	at Edmonton	0-4		4	Colorado	3-1
	25	at Calgary	1-2		6	Anaheim	4-0
	27	Dallas	5-2		10	Vancouver	4-3†
	29	at Anaheim	3-2*		13	at Carolina	4-0
Dec.	3	Calgary	2-1		14	at Atlanta	3-2†
	5	Ottawa	3-2		16	at Tampa Bay	2-1
	7	Minnesota	2-0		18	at Florida	4-3†
	10	at Los Angeles	2-3†		20	Chicago	5-4†
	12	San Jose	2-1		21	at Dallas	3-2†
	14	at Detroit	2-3		23	at Chicago	0-2
	16	at Toronto	6-3		25	at Nashville	3-4†
	17	at Columbus	2-1†		27	Colorado	6-2
	19	at Anaheim	2-4		30	at Vancouver	1-4
	21	Columbus	5-2		31	at Calgary	1-2
	23	Anaheim	4-0	**Apr.**	3	Edmonton	3-2†
	26	Los Angeles	3-2		7	Nashville	5-2
	28	at San Jose	2-3†		8	at Los Angeles	3-2†
	29	Vancouver	3-2†		10	at San Jose	2-3†

* – Overtime † – Shootout

Entry Draft Selections 2010-1996

Name in bold denotes played in NHL.

2010
Pick
13 Brandon Gormley
27 Mark Visentin
52 Philip Lane
57 Oscar Lindberg
138 Louis Domingue

2009
Pick
6 Oliver Ekman-Larsson
36 Chris Brown
91 Michael Lee
97 Jordan Szwarz
105 Justin Weller
157 Evan Bloodoff

2008
Pick
8 **Mikkel Boedker**
28 **Viktor Tikhonov**
49 Jared Staal
69 Michael Stone
76 Mathieu Brodeur
99 Colin Long
159 Brett Hextall
189 Tim Billingsley

2007
Pick
3 **Kyle Turris**
30 Nick Ross
32 Brett Maclean
36 Joel Gistedt
103 Vladimir Ruzicka
123 Maxim Goncharov
153 Scott Darling

2006
Pick
8 **Peter Mueller**
29 Chris Summers
88 Jonas Ahnelov
130 Brett Bennett
131 Martin Latal
152 Jordan Bendfeld
188 Chris Frank
196 **Benn Ferriero**

2005
Pick
17 **Martin Hanzal**
59 Pier-Olivier Pelletier
105 **Keith Yandle**
148 Anton Krysanov
212 Pat Brosnihan

2004
Pick
5 **Blake Wheeler**
35 Logan Stephenson
50 **Enver Lisin**
103 Roman Tomanek
119 **Kevin Porter**
168 Kevin Cormier
199 **Chad Kolarik**
240 **Aaron Gagnon**
261 Will Engasser
265 **Daniel Winnik**

2003
Pick
77 Tyler Redenbach
80 Dmitri Pestunov
115 Liam Lindstrom
178 Ryan Gibbons
208 Randall Gelech
242 Eduard Lewandowski
272 Sean Sullivan
290 Loic Burkhalter

2002
Pick
19 Jakub Koreis
23 **Ben Eager**
46 **David LeNeveu**
70 **Joe Callahan**
80 **Matt Jones**
97 Lance Monych
132 **John Zeiler**
186 Jeff Pietrasiak
216 Ladislav Kouba
249 Marcus Smith
280 Russell Spence

2001
Pick
11 **Fredrik Sjostrom**
31 **Matthew Spiller**
45 Martin Podlesak
78 Beat Forster
148 David Klema
180 Scott Polaski
210 Steve Belanger
243 Frantisek Lukes
273 Severin Blindenbacher

2000
Pick
19 **Krys Kolanos**
53 Alexander Tatarinov
85 **Ramzi Abid**
160 Nate Kiser
186 Brent Gauvreau
217 Igor Samoilov
249 Sami Venalainen
281 Peter Fabus

1999
Pick
15 Scott Kelman
19 **Kirill Safronov**
53 **Brad Ralph**
71 **Jason Jaspers**
116 Ryan Lauzon
123 Preston Mizzi
168 Erik Lewerstrom
234 **Goran Bezina**
262 Alexei Litvinenko

1998
Pick
14 **Patrick DesRochers**
43 **Ossi Vaananen**
73 Pat O'Leary
100 Ryan Vanbuskirk
115 **Jay Leach**
116 Josh Blackburn
129 **Robert Schnabel**
160 **Rickard Wallin**
187 **Erik Westrum**
214 Justin Hansen

1997
Pick
43 Juha Gustafsson
96 Scott McCallum
123 Curtis Suter
151 Robert Francz
207 Alexander Andreyev
233 **Wyatt Smith**

1996
Pick
11 **Dan Focht**
24 **Danny Briere**
62 Per-Anton Lundstrom
119 **Richard Lintner**
139 **Robert Esche**
174 **Trevor Letowski**
200 Nicholas Lent
226 Marc-Etienne Hubert

General Managers' History

John Ferguson, 1979-80 to 1987-88; John Ferguson and Mike Smith, 1988-89; Mike Smith, 1989-90 to 1992-93; Mike Smith and John Paddock, 1993-94; John Paddock, 1994-95, 1995-96; John Paddock and Bobby Smith, 1996-97; Bobby Smith, 1997-98 to 1999-2000; Bobby Smith and Cliff Fletcher, 2000-01; Cliff Fletcher and Michael Barnett, 2001-02; Michael Barnett, 2002-03 to 2006-07; Don Maloney, 2007-08 to date.

Don Maloney

General Manager

Born: Lindsay, Ont., September 5, 1958.

Don Maloney was signed as general manager of the Phoenix Coyotes on May 30, 2007. Maloney has steered the team through turbulent times and guided the Coyotes to the most successful season in franchise history in 2009-10, setting club records with 50 wins and 107 points. He was rewarded for his efforts by being named the inaugural winner of the NHL General Manager of the Year Award in 2010.

Maloney joined the Coyotes from the New York Rangers for whom he served as vice president of player personnel and assistant general manager. He assisted Rangers' president and g.m. Glen Sather in all player transactions and contract negotiations and was involved with the team's professional and amateur scouting operations. Maloney spent 10 seasons in the Rangers' front office. He played a key role in the Rangers' development of several prospects into productive NHL players, including Henrik Lundqvist. Maloney also served as assistant general manager for Team Canada squads that won gold medals at the 2003 and 2004 World Championships.

Maloney's first front office position in the NHL was as assistant general manager of the New York Islanders following his retirement as a player with the club on January 17, 1991. Maloney later served as Islanders' general manager from August 17, 1992 to December 2, 1995. Among the players drafted by the Islanders during Maloney's tenure with the club were Todd Bertuzzi, Bryan McCabe, Ziggy Palffy, Tommy Salo and Darius Kasparaitis. Maloney then served as Eastern professional scout for the San Jose Sharks during the 1996-97 season prior to joining the Rangers' front office.

As a player, Maloney registered 214 goals, 350 assists, and 564 points as well as 815 penalty minutes in 765 regular-season games over 13 NHL campaigns with the Rangers, Hartford Whalers and Islanders. He also collected 22 goals, 35 assists, and 57 points in 94 career playoff games. Maloney spent 11 seasons with the Rangers after being selected by the club in the second round (26th overall) of the 1978 NHL Entry Draft. He helped lead the Rangers to the 1980 Stanley Cup Final by posting 20 points (7 goals, 13 assists) that postseason, a playoff record for rookies at the time. Maloney played in the NHL All-Star Game in 1983 and 1984. He was named MVP of the 1984 game.

Club Directory

Jobing.com Arena

Phoenix Coyotes
6751 N. Sunset Blvd. #200
Glendale, AZ 85305
Phone **623/772-3200**
FAX 623/872-2000
Tickets 480/563-PUCK

Jobing.com Arena
9400 W. Maryland Avenue
Glendale, AZ 85305
Phone 623/772-3200
FAX 623/772-3201
www.PhoenixCoyotes.com
Capacity: 17,125

Club Officers and Executives	
Chief Operating Officer & Alt. Governor	Mike Nealy
Executive Vice President, G.M and Alt. Governor	Don Maloney
Vice President of Hockey Ops and Asst. G.M.	Brad Treliving
Executive Assistant to the C.O.O.	Cheryl Taylor
Exec. Support/Legal and Risk Mgmt.Coordintor	Gail Avisar
Hockey Operations	
Head Coach	Dave Tippett
Associate Coach	Ulf Samuelsson
Assistant Coaches	Dave King, Doug Sulliman
Goaltending Coach	Sean Burke
Video Coach	Steve Peters
Power Skating Coach	Mark Ciaccio
Director of Hockey Administration	Chris O'Hearn
Manager of Hockey Administration	Kimberly Trichel
Head Athletic Trainer	Jason Serbus
Assistant Athletic Trainer	John Bernal
Strength & Conditioning Coordinator	Mike Bahn
Manual Therapist	Mike Griebel
Head Equipment Manager	Stan Wilson
Equipment Manager	Tony Silva
Assistant Equipment Manager	Jason Rudee
Manager of Team Services	Rick Braunstein
Director of Amateur Scouting	Keith Gretzky
Director of Professional Scouting	Frank Effinger
Assistant Director of Amateur Scouting	Steve Lyons
Head European Scout	Christian Ruuttu
Professional Scout	Derek MacKinnon
European & Amateur Scouts	Norm Gosselin,David MacLean, Keith Sullivan, Jeff Twohey
Video Scout	Bob Teofilo
Team Services Coordinator/Security	Jim O'Neal
Team Internist	Robert Luberto, D.O.
Team Orthopedic Surgeons	Dr. Doug Freedberg, Dr. Gary Waslewski
Team Dentists	Byron J. Larsen, DDS, Dr. Lawrence Emmott, Dr. Rick Landgrin
Team Opthamologists	Dr. George Reiss, Dr. Jeffrey Edelstein
San Antonio (AHL) Head Coach	Ray Edwards
San Antonio (AHL) Assistant Coach	Jeff Truitt
San Antonio (AHL) Head Athletic Trainer	Mike Ermatinger
San Antonio (AHL) Equipment Manager	John Krouse
Broadcasting	
TV Play-by-Play / Analyst	Dave Strader, Tyson Nash
TV/Radio Host	Todd Walsh
Radio Play-by-Play / Host	Bob Heethuis / Luke Lapinski
Director of Broadcasting	Doug Cannon
Communications	
Director of Media Relations	Sergey Kocharov
Community Relations	
Director of Community Relations & Fan Development	Sarah Finecey
Manager of Hockey Development	TBD
Coyotes Charities Coordinator	Maggie Goble
News Content	
Senior Director of News Content	Dave Vest
Marketing	
Vice President of Marketing & Communications	Jim Brewer
Senior Director of Marketing	Stacey Cohen
Director of Advertising & Media	Ted Santiago
Manager of New Media	Michael Sharer
Manager of Creative Services	Scott Jenner
Production Artist	Kelly Gladden
Database Marketing Manager	Monica Leyba
Database Marketing Coordinator	Kyle Stephenson
Video Production Manager	Gannon Hubler
Producer/Editor	TBD
Video Graphic Coordinator	TBD
Event Presentation Manager	John Hess
Field Producer	Melanie Paramore
Video Production Coordinator	Colin Kelly
Corporate Sales and Service	
Corporate Partnerships Account Executives	Brittany Grant, Jenni Hansen
Partner & Suite Service Coordinators	Sara Morales, Stacy Gewecke
Suite Sales	
Suite Sales Director	Mike Briody
Ticket Operations	
Director of Ticket Operations	Douglas Vanderheyden
Ticket Sales and Service	
Vice President of Ticket Sales	David Burke
Senior Director of Ticket Sales	Grant Buckborough
Ticket Sales Coordinator	Stacie Morem
Finance and Accounting	
Vice President of Finance and Controller	Joe Leibfried
Assistant Controller	Burlenti Shaban
Legal	
Legal Counsel	Courtney Lewis
Human Resources	
Vice President of Human Resources	Julie Atherton
Technology	
Senior Director of IT	Jay Gaskin
Team Information	
Regional Sports Network / Radio Station	FOX Sports Arizona / XTRA Sports 910
Team Photographer	Norm Hall

Pittsburgh Penguins

Key Off-Season Signings/Acquisitions

2010

June **21** • Re-signed D **Ben Lovejoy**.
    22 • Re-signed LW **Matt Cooke**.
July **1** • Signed D **Paul Martin** and D **Zbynek Michalek**.
    13 • Re-signed RW **Chris Conner**.
    31 • Named **Todd Reirden** assistant coach.

2009-10 Results: 47w-28l-5otl-2sol 101pts.
Second, Atlantic Division

Sidney Crosby celebrates his 51st goal in the final game of the 2009-10 season. Crosby reached the 50-goal plateau for the first time in his career and shared the NHL goal-scoring lead with Tampa Bay's Steven Stamkos.

2010-11 Schedule

Oct. Thu.	7	Philadelphia
Sat.	9	Montreal
Mon.	11	at New Jersey*
Wed.	13	Toronto
Fri.	15	NY Islanders
Sat.	16	at Philadelphia
Mon.	18	Ottawa
Thu.	21	at Nashville
Sat.	23	at St. Louis
Wed.	27	at Tampa Bay
Fri.	29	Philadelphia
Sat.	30	at Carolina
Nov. Wed.	3	at Dallas
Fri.	5	at Anaheim
Sat.	6	at Phoenix
Wed.	10	Boston
Fri.	12	Tampa Bay
Sat.	13	at Atlanta
Mon.	15	NY Rangers
Wed.	17	Vancouver
Fri.	19	Carolina
Mon.	22	at Florida
Wed.	24	at Buffalo
Fri.	26	Ottawa*
Sat.	27	Calgary*
Mon.	29	at NY Rangers
Dec. Thu.	2	Atlanta
Sat.	4	at Columbus
Mon.	6	New Jersey
Wed.	8	Toronto
Sat.	11	at Buffalo
Tue.	14	at Philadelphia
Wed.	15	NY Rangers
Mon.	20	Phoenix
Wed.	22	Florida
Thu.	23	at Washington
Sun.	26	at Ottawa
Tue.	28	Atlanta
Wed.	29	at NY Islanders
Jan. Sat.	1	Washington*
Wed.	5	Tampa Bay

Thu.	6	at Montreal
Sat.	8	Minnesota
Mon.	10	Boston
Wed.	12	at Montreal
Sat.	15	at Boston*
Tue.	18	Detroit
Thu.	20	at New Jersey
Sat.	22	Carolina
Tue.	25	NY Islanders
Feb. Tue.	1	at NY Rangers
Wed.	2	NY Islanders
Fri.	4	Buffalo
Sun.	6	at Washington*
Tue.	8	Columbus
Thu.	10	Los Angeles
Fri.	11	at NY Islanders
Sun.	13	at NY Rangers*
Wed.	16	at Colorado
Sun.	20	at Chicago*
Mon.	21	Washington
Wed.	23	San Jose
Fri.	25	at Carolina
Sat.	26	at Toronto
Mar. Wed.	2	at Toronto
Fri.	4	at New Jersey
Sat.	5	at Boston
Tue.	8	Buffalo
Sat.	12	Montreal*
Sun.	13	Edmonton*
Tue.	15	at Ottawa
Sun.	20	NY Rangers*
Mon.	21	at Detroit
Thu.	24	at Philadelphia
Fri.	25	New Jersey
Sun.	27	Florida*
Tue.	29	Philadelphia
Thu.	31	at Tampa Bay
Apr. Sat.	2	at Florida
Tue.	5	New Jersey
Fri.	8	at NY Islanders
Sun.	10	at Atlanta*

* Denotes afternoon game.

Year-by-Year Record

		Home				Road				Overall							
Season	GP	W	L	T	OL	W	L	T	OL	W	L	T	OL	GF	GA	Pts.	Finished	Playoff Result
2009-10	82	25	12	....	4	22	16	....	3	47	28	....	7	257	237	101	2nd, Atlantic Div.	Lost Conf. Semi-Final
2008-09	**82**	**25**	**13**	**....**	**3**	**20**	**15**	**....**	**6**	**45**	**28**	**....**	**9**	**264**	**239**	**99**	**2nd, Atlantic Div.**	**Won Stanley Cup**
2007-08	82	26	10	....	5	21	17	....	3	47	27	....	8	247	216	102	1st, Atlantic Div.	Lost Final
2006-07	82	26	10	....	5	21	14	....	6	47	24	....	11	277	246	105	2nd, Atlantic Div.	Lost Conf. Quarter-Final
2005-06	82	12	21	....	8	10	25	....	6	22	46	....	14	244	316	58	5th, Atlantic Div.	Out of Playoffs
2004-05	....	....				....				....								
2003-04	82	13	22	6	0	10	25	2	4	23	47	8	4	190	303	58	5th, Atlantic Div.	Out of Playoffs
2002-03	82	15	22	2	2	12	22	4	3	27	44	6	5	189	255	65	5th, Atlantic Div.	Out of Playoffs
2001-02	82	16	20	4	1	12	21	4	4	28	41	8	5	198	249	69	5th, Atlantic Div.	Out of Playoffs
2000-01	82	24	15	2	0	18	13	7	3	42	28	9	3	281	256	96	3rd, Atlantic Div.	Lost Conf. Championship
1999-2000	82	23	11	7	0	14	20	1	6	37	31	8	6	241	236	88	3rd, Atlantic Div.	Lost Conf. Semi-Final
1998-99	82	21	10	10	....	17	20	4	....	38	30	14	....	242	225	90	3rd, Atlantic Div.	Lost Conf. Semi-Final
1997-98	82	21	10	10	....	19	14	8	....	40	24	18	....	228	188	98	1st, Northeast Div.	Lost Conf. Quarter-Final
1996-97	82	25	11	5	....	13	25	3	....	38	36	8	....	285	280	84	2nd, Northeast Div.	Lost Conf. Quarter-Final
1995-96	82	32	9	0	....	17	20	4	....	49	29	4	....	362	284	102	1st, Northeast Div.	Lost Conf. Championship
1994-95	48	18	5	1	....	11	11	2	....	29	16	3	....	181	158	61	2nd, Northeast Div.	Lost Conf. Semi-Final
1993-94	84	25	9	8	....	19	18	5	....	44	27	13	....	299	285	101	1st, Northeast Div.	Lost Conf. Quarter-Final
1992-93	84	32	6	4	....	24	15	3	....	56	21	7	....	367	268	119	1st, Patrick Div.	Lost Div. Final
1991-92	**80**	**21**	**13**	**6**	**....**	**18**	**19**	**3**	**....**	**39**	**32**	**9**	**....**	**343**	**308**	**87**	**3rd, Patrick Div.**	**Won Stanley Cup**
1990-91	**80**	**25**	**12**	**3**	**....**	**16**	**21**	**3**	**....**	**41**	**33**	**6**	**....**	**342**	**305**	**88**	**1st, Patrick Div.**	**Won Stanley Cup**
1989-90	80	22	13	5	....	10	25	5	....	32	40	8	....	318	359	72	5th, Patrick Div.	Out of Playoffs
1988-89	80	24	13	3	....	16	20	4	....	40	33	7	....	347	349	87	2nd, Patrick Div.	Lost Div. Final
1987-88	80	22	12	6	....	14	23	3	....	36	35	9	....	319	316	81	6th, Patrick Div.	Out of Playoffs
1986-87	80	19	15	6	....	11	23	6	....	30	38	12	....	297	290	72	5th, Patrick Div.	Out of Playoffs
1985-86	80	20	15	5	....	14	23	3	....	34	38	8	....	313	305	76	5th, Patrick Div.	Out of Playoffs
1984-85	80	17	20	3	....	7	31	2	....	24	51	5	....	276	385	53	6th, Patrick Div.	Out of Playoffs
1983-84	80	7	29	4	....	9	29	2	....	16	58	6	....	254	390	38	6th, Patrick Div.	Out of Playoffs
1982-83	80	14	22	4	....	4	31	5	....	18	53	9	....	257	394	45	6th, Patrick Div.	Out of Playoffs
1981-82	80	21	11	8	....	10	25	5	....	31	36	13	....	310	337	75	4th, Patrick Div.	Lost Div. Semi-Final
1980-81	80	21	16	3	....	9	21	10	....	30	37	13	....	302	345	73	3rd, Norris Div.	Lost Prelim. Round
1979-80	80	20	13	7	....	10	24	6	....	30	37	13	....	251	303	73	3rd, Norris Div.	Lost Prelim. Round
1978-79	80	23	12	5	....	13	19	8	....	36	31	13	....	281	279	85	2nd, Norris Div.	Lost Quarter-Final
1977-78	80	16	15	9	....	9	22	9	....	25	37	18	....	254	321	68	4th, Norris Div.	Out of Playoffs
1976-77	80	22	12	6	....	12	21	7	....	34	33	13	....	240	252	81	3rd, Norris Div.	Lost Prelim. Round
1975-76	80	23	11	6	....	12	22	6	....	35	33	12	....	339	303	82	3rd, Norris Div.	Lost Prelim. Round
1974-75	80	25	5	10	....	12	23	5	....	37	28	15	....	326	289	89	3rd, Norris Div.	Lost Quarter-Final
1973-74	78	15	18	6	....	13	23	3	....	28	41	9	....	242	273	65	5th, West Div.	Out of Playoffs
1972-73	78	24	11	4	....	8	26	5	....	32	37	9	....	257	265	73	5th, West Div.	Out of Playoffs
1971-72	78	18	15	6	....	8	23	8	....	26	38	14	....	220	258	66	4th, West Div.	Lost Quarter-Final
1970-71	78	18	12	9	....	3	25	11	....	21	37	20	....	221	240	62	6th, West Div.	Out of Playoffs
1969-70	76	17	13	8	....	9	25	4	....	26	38	12	....	182	238	64	2nd, West Div.	Lost Semi-Final
1968-69	76	12	20	6	....	8	25	5	....	20	45	11	....	189	252	51	5th, West Div.	Out of Playoffs
1967-68	74	15	12	10	....	12	22	3	....	27	34	13	....	195	216	67	5th, West Div.	Out of Playoffs

ATLANTIC DIVISION
44th NHL Season

Franchise date: June 5, 1967

2010-11 Player Personnel

FORWARDS	HT	WT	S	Place of Birth	*Age	2009-10 Club
ADAMS, Craig	6-0	197	R	Seria, Brunei	33	Pittsburgh
CONNER, Chris	5-8	180	L	Westland, MI	26	Pittsburgh-Wilkes-Barre
COOKE, Matt	5-11	205	L	Belleville, Ont.	32	Pittsburgh
CRAIG, Ryan	6-2	212	L	Abbotsford, B.C.	28	Tampa Bay-Norfolk
CROSBY, Sidney	5-11	200	L	Cole Harbour, N.S.	23	Pittsburgh
DUPUIS, Pascal	6-1	205	L	Laval, Que.	31	Pittsburgh
GODARD, Eric	6-4	214	R	Vernon, B.C.	30	Pittsburgh
HADDAD, Joey	6-2	200	L	Sydney, N.S.	21	Wilkes-Barre-Wheeling
JEFFREY, Dustin	6-1	205	L	Sarnia, Ont.	22	Pittsburgh-Wilkes-Barre
JOHNSON, Nick	6-1	202	R	Calgary, Alta.	24	Pittsburgh-Wilkes-Barre
KENNEDY, Tyler	5-11	183	R	Sault Ste. Marie, Ont.	24	Pittsburgh
KUNITZ, Chris	6-0	193	L	Regina, Sask.	31	Pittsburgh
LETESTU, Mark	5-11	195	R	Elk Point, Alta.	25	Pittsburgh-Wilkes-Barre
MALKIN, Evgeni	6-3	195	L	Magnitogorsk, USSR	24	Pittsburgh
PETERSEN, Nick	6-3	188	R	Wakefield, Que.	21	Saint John
PIERRO-ZABOTEL, Casey	6-1	205	L	Ashcroft, B.C.	21	Wilkes-Barre-Wheeling
RUPP, Mike	6-5	230	L	Cleveland, OH	30	Pittsburgh
STAAL, Jordan	6-4	220	L	Thunder Bay, Ont.	22	Pittsburgh
STERLING, Brett	5-7	175	L	Los Angeles, CA	26	Chicago (AHL)
TALBOT, Maxime	5-11	190	L	Lemoyne, Que.	26	Pittsburgh
TANGRADI, Eric	6-4	221	L	Philadelphia, PA	21	Pittsburgh-Wilkes-Barre
VEILLEUX, Keven	6-5	202	R	Saint-Renee, Que.	21	Wilkes-Barre
VITALE, Joe	6-0	205	R	St. Louis, MO	25	Wilkes-Barre
WALLACE, Tim	6-1	207	R	Anchorage, AK	26	Pittsburgh-Wilkes-Barre
DEFENSEMEN						
BORTUZZO, Robert	6-3	196	R	Thunder Bay, Ont.	21	Wilkes-Barre
ENGELLAND, Deryk	6-2	202	R	Edmonton, Alta.	28	Pittsburgh-Wilkes-Barre
GOLIGOSKI, Alex	5-11	180	L	Grand Rapids, MN	25	Pittsburgh
GRANT, Alex	6-2	185	R	Antigonish, N.S.	21	Wilkes-Barre-Wheeling
HUTCHINSON, Andrew	6-2	206	R	Evanston, IL	30	Texas
LETANG, Kris	6-0	201	R	Montreal, Que.	23	Pittsburgh
LOVEJOY, Ben	6-2	215	R	Concord, NH	26	Pittsburgh-Wilkes-Barre
MARTIN, Paul	6-1	200	L	Minneapolis, MN	29	New Jersey
MICHALEK, Zbynek	6-2	210	R	Jindrichuv Hradec, Czech.	27	Phoenix
ORPIK, Brooks	6-2	219	L	San Francisco, CA	30	Pittsburgh
POTTER, Corey	6-3	205	R	Lansing, MI	26	NY Rangers-Hartford
SNEEP, Carl	6-4	210	R	St. Louis Park, MN	22	Boston College
STRAIT, Brian	6-1	200	L	Boston, MA	22	Wilkes-Barre
WAGNER, Steve	6-2	200	L	Grand Rapids, MN	26	Peoria-Wilkes-Barre

GOALTENDERS	HT	WT	C	Place of Birth	*Age	2009-10 Club
CURRY, John	5-11	185	L	Shorewood, MN	26	Pittsburgh-Wilkes-Barre
FLEURY, Marc-Andre	6-2	180	L	Sorel, Que.	25	Pittsburgh
JOHNSON, Brent	6-3	199	L	Farmington, MI	33	Pittsburgh
KILLEEN, Patrick	6-4	194	L	Almonte, Ont.	20	Brampton
MODIG, Mattias	6-0	163	L	Lulea, Sweden	23	Lulea
THIESSEN, Brad	6-0	180	L	Aldergrove, B.C.	24	Wilkes-Barre-Wheeling

* – Age at start of 2010-11 season

Coaching History

Red Sullivan, 1967-68, 1968-69; Red Kelly, 1969-70 to 1971-72; Red Kelly and Ken Schinkel, 1972-73; Ken Schinkel and Marc Boileau, 1973-74; Marc Boileau, 1974-75; Marc Boileau and Ken Schinkel, 1975-76; Ken Schinkel, 1976-77; Johnny Wilson, 1977-78 to 1979-80; Eddie Johnston, 1980-81 to 1982-83; Lou Angotti, 1983-84; Bob Berry, 1984-85 to 1986-87; Pierre Creamer, 1987-88; Gene Ubriaco, 1988-89; Gene Ubriaco and Craig Patrick, 1989-90; Bob Johnson, 1990-91; Scotty Bowman, 1991-92, 1992-93; Eddie Johnston, 1993-94 to 1995-96; Eddie Johnston and Craig Patrick, 1996-97; Kevin Constantine, 1997-98, 1998-99; Kevin Constantine and Herb Brooks, 1999-2000; Ivan Hlinka, 2000-01; Ivan Hlinka and Rick Kehoe, 2001-02; Rick Kehoe, 2002-03; Ed Olczyk, 2003-04, 2004-05; Ed Olczyk and Michel Therrien, 2005-06; Michel Therrien, 2006-07, 2007-08; Michel Therrien and Dan Bylsma, 2008-09; Dan Bylsma, 2009-10 to date.

Dan Bylsma

Head Coach

Born: Grand Haven, MI, September 19, 1970.

Dan Bylsma was named interim head coach of the Pittsburgh Penguins on February 15, 2009 and had the interim tag removed on April 28. Bylsma had been serving as head coach of the team's American Hockey League affiliate in Wilkes-Barre/Scranton when he was promoted to Pittsburgh. He took over a slumping Penguins team that was six points out of a playoff spot with 25 games to go and guided them to the Stanley Cup. Bylsma was the 14th rookie head coach, and just the fourth in 50 years, to win the Stanley Cup. Of these, only Montreal's Al MacNeil (1970-71) took over in midseason.

Bylsma played nine NHL seasons as a right winger with Los Angeles and Anaheim from 1995 to 2004. A role player who excelled at killing penalties and blocking shots, he played 429 NHL regular-season games and also played in the 2003 Stanley Cup Final with Anaheim. He retired as a player following the 2003-04 season. The native of Grand Haven, Michigan began his coaching career as an assistant with the Cincinnati Mighty Ducks of the AHL in 2004-05. He made his NHL coaching debut as an assistant with the New York Islanders in 2005-06.

Bylsma joined the Penguins organization as an assistant to Todd Richards in Wilkes-Barre/Scranton in 2006-07. The Baby Penguins won the AHL East Division and Eastern Conference championships in 2007-08 and advanced to the Calder Cup Final. When Richards accepted the job as an assistant coach with the NHL's San Jose Sharks in the offseason, Bylsma was elevated to head coach at Wilkes-Barre/Scranton.

Bylsma was an outstanding athlete at West Michigan Christian High School, winning a state individual golf championship and starting in left field on a state championship baseball team. He played Junior B hockey for St. Mary's of the Ontario Hockey Association before playing four years of college hockey at Bowling Green. He was twice selected to the Central Collegiate Hockey Association (CCHA) All-Academic Team. Dan and his father, Jay, also have written four books about sports for kids and families, including "So Your Son Wants to Play in the NHL" and "So You Want to Play in the NHL." He operates Dan Bylsma's Western Michigan Hockey Camp and has established the Dan Bylsma Charitable Trust Fund, which provides a means to assist children with the high cost of participating in youth sports, especially hockey.

2009-10 Scoring

* – rookie

Regular Season

Pos	#	Player	Team	GP	G	A	Pts	TOI	+/–	PIM	PP	SH	GW	S	%
C	87	Sidney Crosby	PIT	81	51	58	109	21:57	15	71	13	2	6	298	17.1
C	71	Evgeni Malkin	PIT	67	28	49	77	20:50	–6	100	13	2	7	268	10.4
L	23	Alexei Ponikarovsky	TOR	61	19	22	41	16:49	5	44	4	0	1	147	12.9
			PIT	16	2	7	9	15:05	–6	17	1	0	0	37	5.4
			Total	77	21	29	50	16:27	–1	61	5	0	1	184	11.4
D	55	Sergei Gonchar	PIT	62	11	39	50	24:23	–4	49	6	0	3	138	8.0
C	11	Jordan Staal	PIT	82	21	28	49	19:23	19	57	1	2	1	195	10.8
R	13	Bill Guerin	PIT	78	21	24	45	17:31	–9	75	11	0	4	227	9.3
R	9	Pascal Dupuis	PIT	81	18	20	38	14:11	5	16	0	0	5	157	11.5
D	3	Alex Goligoski	PIT	69	8	29	37	21:25	7	22	2	0	0	98	8.2
L	14	Chris Kunitz	PIT	50	13	19	32	16:26	3	39	2	1	0	131	9.9
L	24	Matt Cooke	PIT	79	15	15	30	14:47	17	106	2	0	1	105	14.3
L	26	Ruslan Fedotenko	PIT	80	11	19	30	14:39	–17	50	3	0	3	158	7.0
D	58	Kris Letang	PIT	73	3	24	27	21:33	1	51	0	0	0	174	1.7
D	4	Jordan Leopold	FLA	61	7	11	18	22:25	–7	22	1	0	1	69	10.1
			PIT	20	4	4	8	20:26	5	6	0	0	2	26	15.4
			Total	81	11	15	26	21:55	–2	28	1	0	3	95	11.6
C	48	Tyler Kennedy	PIT	64	13	12	25	12:34	10	31	1	0	4	175	7.4
D	44	Brooks Orpik	PIT	73	2	23	25	20:05	6	64	0	0	0	61	3.3
L	17	Mike Rupp	PIT	81	13	6	19	9:02	5	120	0	0	1	87	14.9
D	7	Mark Eaton	PIT	79	3	13	16	19:45	5	26	0	0	1	65	4.6
D	74	Jay McKee	PIT	62	1	9	10	15:26	6	54	0	0	0	42	2.4
R	27	Craig Adams	PIT	82	0	10	10	11:05	–5	72	0	0	0	84	0.0
C	25	Maxime Talbot	PIT	45	2	5	7	12:13	–9	30	0	0	0	49	4.1
R	23	Chris Conner	PIT	8	2	1	3	9:35	–1	0	0	0	1	11	18.2
R	28	Eric Godard	PIT	45	1	2	3	4:11	2	76	0	0	0	17	5.9
D	6 *	Ben Lovejoy	PIT	12	0	3	3	16:37	8	2	0	0	0	14	0.0
R	42 *	Nick Johnson	PIT	6	1	1	2	10:06	–2	2	0	0	0	7	14.3
D	5	Deryk Engelland	PIT	9	0	2	2	16:08	–2	17	0	0	0	4	0.0
C	38 *	Mark Letestu	PIT	10	1	0	1	9:37	–2	2	0	0	0	9	11.1
R	22 *	Tim Wallace	PIT	1	0	0	0	5:50	0	0	0	0	0	0	0.0
C	56 *	Eric Tangradi	PIT	1	0	0	0	13:49	0	0	0	0	0	3	0.0
C	15 *	Dustin Jeffrey	PIT	1	0	0	0	8:35	0	0	0	0	0	0	0.0
D	2	Nathan Guenin	PIT	2	0	0	0	13:32	–2	0	0	0	0	1	0.0

Goaltending

No.	Goaltender	GPI	Mins	Avg	W	L	OT	EN	SO	GA	SA	S%	G	A	PIM
40	* Alexander Pechurski	1	36	1.67	0	0	0	0	0	1	13	.923	0	0	0
29	Marc-Andre Fleury	67	3798	2.65	37	21	6	4	1	168	1772	.905	0	1	10
1	Brent Johnson	23	1108	2.76	10	6	1	6	0	51	541	.906	0	1	0
36	* John Curry	1	24	12.50	0	1	0	0	0	5	14	.643	0	0	0
	Totals	**82**	**4998**	**2.82**	**47**	**28**	**7**	**10**	**1**	**235**	**2350**	**.900**			

Playoffs

Pos	#	Player	Team	GP	G	A	Pts	TOI	+/–	PIM	PP	SH	GW	OT	S	%
C	87	Sidney Crosby	PIT	13	6	13	19	23:31	6	6	1	0	1	0	41	14.6
D	55	Sergei Gonchar	PIT	13	2	10	12	26:26	4	4	1	0	1	0	24	8.3
C	71	Evgeni Malkin	PIT	13	5	6	11	21:53	0	6	4	0	1	0	58	8.6
L	14	Chris Kunitz	PIT	13	4	7	11	17:25	3	8	1	0	0	0	38	10.5
R	13	Bill Guerin	PIT	11	4	5	9	18:17	3	2	1	0	0	0	30	13.3
D	3	Alex Goligoski	PIT	13	2	7	9	20:34	4	2	1	0	0	0	28	7.1
R	9	Pascal Dupuis	PIT	13	2	6	8	16:51	5	4	0	0	1	1	33	6.1
D	58	Kris Letang	PIT	13	5	2	7	23:15	–5	6	4	0	1	0	23	21.7
L	24	Matt Cooke	PIT	13	4	2	6	15:10	–4	22	0	0	0	0	18	22.2
C	25	Maxime Talbot	PIT	13	2	4	6	14:15	1	11	0	1	1	0	23	8.7
C	11	Jordan Staal	PIT	11	3	2	5	18:14	–4	6	2	0	0	0	29	10.3
L	23	Alexei Ponikarovsky	PIT	11	1	4	5	13:12	0	4	0	0	0	0	20	5.0
R	27	Craig Adams	PIT	13	2	1	3	10:37	2	15	0	0	1	0	11	18.2
D	7	Mark Eaton	PIT	13	0	3	3	20:43	–4	4	0	0	0	0	13	0.0
D	44	Brooks Orpik	PIT	13	0	2	2	21:40	3	12	0	0	0	0	13	0.0
C	38 *	Mark Letestu	PIT	4	0	1	1	9:39	0	0	0	0	0	0	4	0.0
R	18	Chris Conner	PIT	1	0	0	0	11:03	0	0	0	0	0	0	0	0.0
D	74	Jay McKee	PIT	5	0	0	0	14:56	2	2	0	0	0	0	2	0.0
L	26	Ruslan Fedotenko	PIT	6	0	0	0	12:31	–3	4	0	0	0	0	3	0.0
D	4	Jordan Leopold	PIT	8	0	0	0	16:31	–2	2	0	0	0	0	6	0.0
C	48	Tyler Kennedy	PIT	10	0	0	0	11:57	–6	2	0	0	0	0	22	0.0
L	17	Mike Rupp	PIT	11	0	0	0	7:27	0	8	0	0	0	0	5	0.0

Goaltending

No.	Goaltender	GPI	Mins	Avg	W	L	EN	SO	GA	SA	S%	G	A	PIM
1	Brent Johnson	1	31	1.94	0	0	0	0	1	7	.857	0	0	0
29	Marc-Andre Fleury	13	798	2.78	7	6	0	1	37	339	.891	0	0	2
	Totals	**13**	**837**	**2.72**	**7**	**6**	**0**	**1**	**38**	**346**	**.890**			

Captains' History

Ab McDonald, 1967-68; Earl Ingarfield, 1968-69; no captain, 1968-69 to 1972-73; Ron Schock, 1973-74 to 1976-77; Jean Pronovost, 1977-78; Orest Kindrachuk, 1978-79 to 1980-81; Randy Carlyle, 1981-82 to 1983-84; Mike Bullard, 1984-85, 1985-86; Mike Bullard and Terry Ruskowski, 1986-87; Dan Frawley and Mario Lemieux, 1987-88; Mario Lemieux, 1988-89 to 1993-94; Ron Francis, 1994-95; Mario Lemieux, 1995-96, 1996-97; Ron Francis, 1997-98; Jaromir Jagr, 1998-99 to 2000-01; Mario Lemieux, 2001-02 to 2004-05; Mario Lemieux and no captain, 2005-06; no captain, 2006-07; Sidney Crosby, 2007-08 to date.

Coaching Record

			Regular Season				Playoffs			
Season	Team	League	GC	W	L	O/T	GC	W	L	T
2008-09	Wilkes-Barre	AHL	55	36	16	3	....	....	....	....
2008-09♦	**Pittsburgh**	**NHL**	**25**	**18**	**3**	**4**	**24**	**16**	**8**	....
2009-10	**Pittsburgh**	**NHL**	**82**	**47**	**28**	**7**	**13**	**7**	**6**	....
	NHL Totals		**107**	**65**	**31**	**11**	**37**	**23**	**14**	....

♦ Stanley Cup win.

Club Records

Team

(Figures in brackets for season records are games played; records for fewest points, wins, ties, losses, goals, goals against are for 70 or more games)

Record		Season / Date
Most Points	119	1992-93 (84)
Most Wins	56	1992-93 (84)
Most Ties	20	1970-71 (78)
Most Losses	58	1983-84 (80)
Most Goals	367	1992-93 (84)
Most Goals Against	394	1982-83 (80)
Fewest Points	38	1983-84 (80)
Fewest Wins	16	1983-84 (80)
Fewest Ties	4	1995-96 (82)
Fewest Losses	21	1992-93 (84)
Fewest Goals	182	1969-70 (76)
Fewest Goals Against	188	1997-98 (82)
Longest Winning Streak		
Overall	*17	Mar. 9-Apr. 10/93
Home	11	Jan. 5-Mar. 7/91
Away	7	Mar. 14-Apr. 9/93, Oct. 3-Nov. 3/09
Longest Undefeated Streak		
Overall	18	Mar. 9-Apr. 14/93 (17 wins, 1 tie)
Home	20	Nov. 30/74-Feb. 22/75 (12 wins, 8 ties)
Away	8	Mar. 14-Apr. 14/93 (7 wins, 1 tie)
Longest Losing Streak		
Overall	18	Jan. 13-Feb. 22/04
Home	*14	Dec. 31/03-Feb. 22/04
Away	18	Dec. 23/82-Mar. 4/83
Longest Winless Streak		
Overall	18	Jan. 2-Feb. 10/83 (17 losses, 1 tie), Jan. 13-Feb. 22/04 (18 losses)
Home	16	Dec. 31/03-Mar. 4/04 (15 losses, 1 tie)
Away	18	Oct. 25/70-Jan. 14/71 (11 losses, 7 ties), Dec. 23/82-Mar. 4/83 (18 losses)
Most Shutouts, Season	9	1998-99 (82)
Most PIM, Season	2,670	1988-89 (80)
Most Goals, Game	12	Mar. 15/75 (Wsh. 1 at Pit. 12), Dec. 26/91 (Tor. 1 at Pit. 12)

Individual

Record		Player
Most Seasons	17	Mario Lemieux
Most Games	915	Mario Lemieux
Most Goals, Career	690	Mario Lemieux
Most Assists, Career	1,033	Mario Lemieux
Most Points, Career	1,723	Mario Lemieux (690G, 1,033A)
Most PIM, Career	1,048	Kevin Stevens
Most Shutouts, Career	22	Tom Barrasso
Longest Consecutive Games Streak	313	Ron Schock (Oct. 24/73-Apr. 3/77)
Most Goals, Season	85	Mario Lemieux (1988-89)
Most Assists, Season	114	Mario Lemieux (1988-89)
Most Points, Season	199	Mario Lemieux (1988-89; 85G, 114A)
Most PIM, Season	409	Paul Baxter (1981-82)
Most Points, Defenseman, Season	113	Paul Coffey (1988-89; 30G, 83A)
Most Points, Center, Season	199	Mario Lemieux (1988-89; 85G, 114A)
Most Points, Right Wing, Season	*149	Jaromir Jagr (1995-96; 62G, 87A)
Most Points, Left Wing, Season	123	Kevin Stevens (1991-92; 54G, 69A)
Most Points, Rookie, Season	102	Sidney Crosby (2005-06; 39G, 63A)
Most Shutouts, Season	7	Tom Barrasso (1997-98)
Most Goals, Game	5	Mario Lemieux (Dec. 31/88), (Apr. 9/93), (Mar. 26/96)
Most Assists, Game	6	Ron Stackhouse (Mar. 8/75) Greg Malone (Nov. 28/79) Mario Lemieux (Oct. 15/88), (Dec. 5/92), (Nov. 1/95)
Most Points, Game	8	Mario Lemieux (Oct. 15/88; 2G, 6A), (Dec. 31/88; 5G, 3A)

* NHL Record.

General Managers' History

Jack Riley, 1967-68 to 1969-70; Red Kelly, 1970-71; Red Kelly and Jack Riley, 1971-72; Jack Riley, 1972-73; Jack Riley and Jack Button, 1973-74; Jack Button, 1974-75; Wren Blair, 1975-76; Wren Blair and Baz Bastien, 1976-77; Baz Bastien, 1977-78 to 1982-83; Eddie Johnston, 1983-84 to 1987-88; Tony Esposito, 1988-89; Tony Esposito and Craig Patrick, 1989-90; Craig Patrick, 1990-91 to 2005-06; Ray Shero, 2006-07 to date.

Retired Numbers

21	Michel Brière	1969-1970
66	Mario Lemieux	1984-2006

All-time Record vs. Other Clubs

Regular Season

	At Home								On Road								Total							
	GP	W	L	T	OL	GF	GA	PTS	GP	W	L	T	OL	GF	GA	PTS	GP	W	L	T	OL	GF	GA	PTS
Anaheim	12	8	2	2	0	42	34	18	10	4	4	0	2	30	35	10	22	12	6	2	2	72	69	28
Atlanta	20	16	3	0	1	79	49	33	20	13	5	0	2	65	57	28	40	29	8	0	3	144	106	61
Boston	90	37	36	15	2	309	319	91	88	20	61	6	1	245	379	47	178	57	97	21	3	554	698	138
Buffalo	81	42	20	18	1	302	247	103	81	25	38	17	1	219	301	68	162	67	58	35	2	521	548	171
Calgary	46	25	11	10	0	171	136	60	48	13	27	8	0	146	207	34	94	38	38	18	0	317	343	94
Carolina	56	27	22	6	1	214	200	61	58	24	25	5	4	203	212	57	114	51	47	11	5	417	412	118
Chicago	61	30	23	7	1	216	196	68	62	12	40	10	0	163	244	34	123	42	63	17	1	379	440	102
Colorado	39	17	17	5	0	153	156	39	34	13	18	2	1	127	150	29	73	30	35	7	1	280	306	68
Columbus	5	4	1	0	0	21	13	8	6	3	2	0	1	17	23	7	11	7	3	0	1	38	36	15
Dallas	65	40	19	6	0	246	182	86	66	23	36	6	1	221	250	53	131	63	55	12	1	467	432	139
Detroit	68	45	19	4	0	283	201	94	68	14	41	12	1	187	265	41	136	59	60	16	1	470	466	135
Edmonton	32	16	13	3	0	123	134	35	32	9	22	1	0	105	152	19	64	25	35	4	0	228	286	54
Florida	33	18	11	3	1	100	95	40	32	13	16	1	2	78	96	29	65	31	27	4	3	178	191	69
Los Angeles	75	40	25	10	0	273	236	90	71	18	44	8	1	189	273	45	146	58	69	18	1	462	509	135
Minnesota	6	1	4	0	1	8	21	3	5	1	3	1	0	12	15	3	11	2	7	1	1	20	36	6
Montreal	92	34	43	13	2	278	321	83	92	16	63	10	3	238	417	45	184	50	106	23	5	516	738	128
Nashville	7	2	2	2	1	21	22	7	8	2	6	0	0	17	31	4	15	4	8	2	1	38	53	11
New Jersey	97	46	43	4	4	341	319	100	99	36	47	13	3	311	347	88	196	82	90	17	7	652	666	188
NY Islanders	106	54	36	14	2	407	356	124	104	41	52	8	3	345	404	93	210	95	88	22	5	752	760	217
NY Rangers	118	56	45	14	3	417	406	129	119	47	59	9	4	388	453	107	237	103	104	23	7	805	859	236
Ottawa	37	19	12	4	2	126	105	44	37	19	13	5	0	121	109	43	74	38	25	9	2	247	214	87
Philadelphia	124	58	44	22	0	441	395	138	124	27	85	8	4	322	512	66	248	85	129	30	4	763	907	204
Phoenix	32	21	11	0	0	123	90	42	33	15	15	3	0	115	122	33	65	36	26	3	0	238	212	75
St. Louis	66	33	21	12	0	244	195	78	66	16	42	6	2	177	253	40	132	49	63	18	2	421	448	118
San Jose	11	5	4	1	1	44	35	12	16	6	8	2	0	57	44	14	27	11	12	3	1	101	79	26
Tampa Bay	33	18	9	3	3	112	87	42	33	14	16	2	1	82	98	31	66	32	25	5	4	194	185	73
Toronto	79	41	31	6	1	315	258	89	77	28	35	11	3	251	304	70	156	69	66	17	4	566	562	159
Vancouver	52	33	12	7	0	230	178	73	52	24	23	4	1	191	187	53	104	57	35	11	1	421	365	126
Washington	93	52	33	7	1	361	299	112	96	38	46	9	3	349	394	88	189	90	79	16	4	710	693	200
Defunct Clubs	35	22	6	7	0	148	93	51	34	13	10	11	0	108	101	37	69	35	16	18	0	256	194	88
Totals	**1671**	**860**	**578**	**205**	**28**	**6148**	**5378**	**1953**	**1671**	**547**	**902**	**178**	**44**	**5079**	**6435**	**1316**	**3342**	**1407**	**1480**	**383**	**72**	**11227**	**11813**	**3269**

Playoffs

	Series	W	L	GP	W	L	T	GF	GA	Last Mtg.	Rnd.	Result
Boston	4	2	2	19	10	9	0	67	62	1992	CF	W 4-0
Buffalo	2	2	0	10	6	4	0	26	26	2001	CSF	W 4-3
Carolina	1	1	0	4	4	0	0	20	9	2009	CF	W 4-0
Chicago	2	1	1	8	4	4	0	23	24	1992	F	W 4-0
Dallas	1	1	0	6	4	2	0	28	16	1991	F	W 4-2
Detroit	2	1	1	13	6	7	0	24	34	2009	F	W 4-3
Florida	1	0	1	7	3	4	0	15	20	1996	CF	L 3-4
Montreal	2	0	2	13	5	8	0	33	37	2010	CSF	L 3-4
New Jersey	5	3	2	29	14	15	0	80	86	2001	CF	L 1-4
NY Islanders	3	0	3	19	8	11	0	58	67	1993	DF	L 3-4
NY Rangers	4	4	0	20	16	4	0	79	57	2008	CSF	W 4-1
Ottawa	3	2	1	15	9	6	0	50	42	2010	CQF	W 4-2
Philadelphia	5	2	3	29	14	15	0	89	91	2009	CQF	W 4-2
St. Louis	3	1	2	13	6	7	0	40	45	1981	PRE	L 2-3
Toronto	3	0	3	12	4	8	0	27	39	1999	CSF	L 2-4
Washington	8	7	1	49	30	19	0	164	143	2009	CSF	W 4-3
Defunct Clubs	1	1	0	4	4	0	0	13	6			
Totals	**50**	**28**	**22**	**270**	**147**	**123**	**0**	**836**	**804**			

Playoff Results 2010-2006

Year	Round	Opponent	Result	GF	GA
2010	CSF	Montreal	L 3-4	18	19
	CQF	Ottawa	W 4-2	24	19
2009	**F**	**Detroit**	**W 4-3**	**14**	**17**
	CF	Carolina	W 4-0	20	9
	CSF	Washington	W 4-3	27	22
	CQF	Philadelphia	W 4-2	18	16
2008	F	Detroit	L 2-4	10	17
	CF	Philadelphia	W 4-1	20	9
	CSF	NY Rangers	W 4-1	15	12
	CQF	Ottawa	W 4-0	16	5
2007	CQF	Ottawa	L 1-4	10	18

Abbreviations: Round: F – Final; **CF** – conference final; **CSF** – conference semi-final; **CQF** – conference quarter-final; **DF** – division final; **PRE** – preliminary round.

Calgary totals include Atlanta Flames, 1972-73 to 1979-80.
Carolina totals include Hartford, 1979-80 to 1996-97.
Colorado totals include Quebec, 1979-80 to 1994-95.
Dallas totals include Minnesota North Stars, 1967-68 to 1992-93.
New Jersey totals include Kansas City, 1974-75, 1975-76, and Colorado Rockies, 1976-77 to 1981-82.
Phoenix totals include Winnipeg, 1979-80 to 1995-96.

2009-10 Results

Oct.	2	NY Rangers	3-2	**Jan.**	2	at Tampa Bay	1-3
	3	at NY Islanders	4-3†		3	at Florida	2-6
	7	Phoenix	0-3		5	Atlanta	5-2
	8	at Philadelphia	5-4		7	Philadelphia	4-7
	10	at Toronto	5-2		9	at Toronto	4-1
	12	at Ottawa	4-1		11	at Minnesota	3-4
	14	at Carolina	3-2†		13	at Calgary	3-1
	17	Tampa Bay	4-1		14	at Edmonton	3-2
	20	St. Louis	5-1		16	at Vancouver	2-6
	23	Florida	3-2†		19	NY Islanders	6-4
	24	New Jersey	1-4		21	Washington	3-6
	28	Montreal	6-1		24	at Philadelphia	2-1
	30	at Columbus	4-3†		25	at NY Rangers	4-2
	31	Minnesota	1-2		28	Ottawa	1-4
Nov.	3	at Anaheim	4-3		31	Detroit	2-1†
	5	at Los Angeles	2-5	**Feb.**	1	Buffalo	5-4
	7	at San Jose	0-5		6	at Montreal	3-5
	10	at Boston	0-3		7	at Washington	4-5*
	12	New Jersey	1-4		10	NY Islanders	3-1
	14	Boston	6-5*		12	NY Rangers	2-3*
	16	Anaheim	5-2		14	Nashville	3-4†
	19	at Ottawa	2-6	**Mar.**	2	Buffalo	3-2
	21	at Atlanta	3-2		4	at NY Rangers	5-4*
	23	at Florida	3-2*		6	Dallas	6-3
	25	Montreal	3-1		7	Boston	2-1
	27	at NY Islanders	2-3		11	at Carolina	3-4*
	28	NY Rangers	8-3		12	at New Jersey	1-3
	30	at NY Rangers	5-2		14	at Tampa Bay	2-1
Dec.	3	Colorado	4-1		17	at New Jersey	2-5
	5	Chicago	1-2*		18	at Boston	3-0
	7	Carolina	2-3		20	Carolina	2-3*
	10	at Montreal	3-2		22	at Detroit	1-3
	12	Florida	3-2*		24	at Washington	3-4†
	15	Philadelphia	6-1		27	Philadelphia	4-1
	17	at Philadelphia	3-2†		28	Toronto	5-4†
	19	at Buffalo	2-1†		31	Tampa Bay	0-2
	21	New Jersey	0-4	**Apr.**	3	Atlanta	4-3*
	23	Ottawa	8-2		6	Washington	3-6
	27	Toronto	3-4		8	NY Islanders	7-3
	29	at Buffalo	3-4		10	at Atlanta	0-1
	30	at New Jersey	0-2		11	at NY Islanders	6-5*

* – Overtime † – Shootout

Entry Draft Selections 2010-1996

Name in bold denotes played in NHL.

2010
Pick
20	Beau Bennett
80	**Bryan Rust**
110	Tom Kuhnhackl
140	Kenneth Agostino
152	Joe Rogalski
170	Reid McNeill

2009
Pick
30	Simon Despres
61	Philip Samuelsson
63	Ben Hanowski
121	Nick Petersen
123	Alex Velischek
151	Andy Bathgate
181	Viktor Ekbom

2008
Pick
120	Nathan Moon
150	**Alexander Pechurski**
180	Patrick Killeen
210	Nicholas D'Agostino

2007
Pick
20	Angelo Esposito
51	Keven Veilleux
78	Robert Bortuzzo
80	Casey Pierro-Zabotel
111	**Luca Caputi**
118	Alex Grant
141	Jake Muzzin
171	**Dustin Jeffrey**

2006
Pick
2	**Jordan Staal**
32	Carl Sneep
65	Brian Strait
125	**Chad Johnson**
185	Timo Seppanen

2005
Pick
1	**Sidney Crosby**
61	Michael Gergen
62	**Kris Letang**
125	Tommi Leinonen
126	Tim Crowder
194	Jean-Philippe Paquet
195	Joe Vitale

2004
Pick
2	**Evgeni Malkin**
31	Johannes Salmonsson
61	**Alex Goligoski**
67	**Nick Johnson**
85	Brian Gifford
99	**Tyler Kennedy**
130	Michal Sersen
164	Moises Gutierrez
194	Chris Peluso
222	Jordan Morrison
228	David Brown
259	Brian Ihnacak

2003
Pick
1	**Marc-Andre Fleury**
32	**Ryan Stone**
70	**Jonathan Filewich**
73	**Daniel Carcillo**
121	**Paul Bissonnette**
161	Evgeni Isakov
169	Lukas Bolf
199	**Andy Chiodo**
229	Stephen Dixon
232	**Joe Jensen**
263	**Matt Moulson**

2002
Pick
5	**Ryan Whitney**
35	Ondrej Nemec
69	**Erik Christensen**
101	Daniel Fernholm
136	Andrew Sertich
137	**Cam Paddock**
171	Robert Goepfert
202	Patrik Bartschi
234	**Maxime Talbot**
239	Ryan Lannon
265	Dwight Labrosse

2001
Pick
21	**Colby Armstrong**
54	**Noah Welch**
86	**Drew Fata**
96	Alexandre Rouleau
120	**Tomas Surovy**
131	Ben Eaves
156	Andy Schneider
217	Tomas Duba
250	Brandon Crawford-West

2000
Pick
18	**Brooks Orpik**
52	**Shane Endicott**
84	Peter Hamerlik
124	**Michel Ouellet**
146	**David Koci**
185	Patrick Foley
216	Jim Abbott
248	Steve Crampton
273	**Roman Simicek**
280	Nick Boucher

1999
Pick
18	**Konstantin Koltsov**
51	**Matt Murley**
57	Jeremy Van Hoof
86	**Sebastien Caron**
115	**Ryan Malone**
144	Tomas Skvaridlo
157	Vladimir Malenkykh
176	Doug Meyer
204	**Tom Kostopoulos**
233	Darcy Robinson
261	Andrew McPherson

1998
Pick
23	**Milan Kraft**
54	Alexander Zevakhin
80	David Cameron
110	Scott Myers
134	**Rob Scuderi**
169	Jan Fadrny
196	Joel Scherban
224	Mika Lehto
244	**Toby Petersen**
254	**Matt Hussey**

1997
Pick
17	**Robert Dome**
44	Brian Gaffaney
71	**Josef Melichar**
97	Alexandre Mathieu
124	Harlan Pratt
152	Petr Havelka
179	Mark Moore
208	**Andrew Ference**
234	Eric Lind

1996
Pick
23	Craig Hillier
28	**Pavel Skrbek**
72	**Boyd Kane**
77	Boris Protsenko
105	**Michal Rozsival**
150	Peter Bergman
186	**Eric Meloche**
238	Timo Seikkula

Ray Shero
Executive Vice President and General Manager
Born: St. Paul, MN, July 28, 1962.

The Pittsburgh Penguins signed Ray Shero to a five-year contract as their new general manager on May 25, 2006. His fresh ideas and calm but firm management style helped transform the Penguins organization in his first year on the job as the team made the playoffs in 2006-07 for the first time since 2000-01. In 2007-08 the team posted the second-best record in the Eastern Conference and advanced to the Stanley Cup Finals. They won the Stanley Cup in 2009. Shero is the son of the late Fred Shero, who coached the Philadelphia Flyers for seven years and led them to back-to-back Stanley Cup championships in 1973-74 and 1974-75. Fred Shero also was g.m. and coach of the New York Rangers from 1978 to 1980. Ray Shero played college hockey at St. Lawrence University, serving twice as team captain, and was drafted by the Los Angeles Kings in 1982. He worked as a player agent for seven years before entering NHL management.

Before joining the Penguins, Shero had been assistant general manager of the Nashville Predators for eight seasons, working closely with Predators g.m. David Poile on all aspects of the club's hockey operations. His specific responsibilities included scouting at the amateur and professional levels, contract negotiations, and personnel matters such as arbitration, in addition to overseeing operations of the Predators top minor-league affiliate, the Milwaukee Admirals of the American Hockey League. Before joining the Predators organization, Shero spent six seasons as assistant general manager of the Ottawa Senators – joining the club in its second year of existence as an expansion team.

Both Ottawa and Nashville made significant improvement during Shero's tenure as assistant g.m., building with youth while adhering to a budget and business plan. The Predators went 49-25-8 and established a club record with 106 points in 2005-06, qualifying for the Stanley Cup playoffs for the second straight season. They had the third-best record in the Western Conference and fifth-best in the NHL.

Shero also played an important role in the success of the Milwaukee Admirals, Nashville's top affiliate in the American Hockey League. In 2003-04, the Admirals led the AHL in wins (43) and points (102) and won the Calder Cup by defeating the Wilkes-Barre/Scranton Penguins in the league final. Milwaukee reached the Calder Cup Final again in 2005-06.

Club Directory

CONSOL Energy Center

Pittsburgh Penguins
CONSOL Energy Center
1001 Fifth Avenue
Pittsburgh, PA 15219
Phone **412/642-1300**
PR FAX 412/255-1988
www.pittsburghpenguins.com
Capacity: 18,087

Executive
CEO/President	David Morehouse
Sr. Vice President, Business & Legal Affairs	Travis Williams
Vice President & Controller	Kevin Hart
Vice President, Communications	Tom McMillan
Director of Government Affairs	Abass Kamara
Executive Assistants	Fay McNamara, Kimberly Wood
Mailroom Supervisor	Brett Hart
Receptionist	Kelly Hart

Hockey Operations
Executive V.P./General Manager	Ray Shero
Assistant General Manager	Jason Botterill
Assistant to the General Manager	Tom Fitzgerald
Head Coach	Dan Bylsma
Assistant Coaches	Tony Granato, Todd Reirden
Goaltending Coach	Gilles Meloche
Wilkes-Barre/Scranton Head Coach	John Hynes
Strength & Conditioning Coach	Michael Kadar
Sr. Director of Team Operations	Frank Buonomo
Executive Assistant	Kristen Yunn
Video Coordinator	Jim Britt
Head Athletic Trainer	Chris Stewart
Assistant Athletic Trainer	Scott Adams
Head Equipment Manager	Dana Heinze
Assistant Equipment Managers	Paul Defazio, Daniel Kroll
Physical Therapist	Mark Mortland

Scouting
Director of Pro Scouting	Derek Clancy
Professional Scouts	Andre Savard, Kevin Stevens
Director of Amateur Scouting	Daniel MacKinnon
Assistant Director of Amateur Scouting	Randy Sexton
Amateur Scouts	David Allison, Brian Fitzgerald, Luc Gauthier, Charles Grillo, Jay Heinbuck, James Madigan, David McNamara, Wayne Meier, Ron Pyette
European Scouts	Patrik Allvin, Rob Neuhauser

Communications
Director of Communications	Jennifer Bullano
Director of Content	Sam Kasan
Content Manager	Jason Seidling
Communications Coordinator	Erik Heasley

Marketing
Vice President, Marketing	James Santilli
Executive Director of Strategic Planning	Rich Hixon
Director of Marketing	Ross Miller
Director of Fan Development & Special Events	Jill Shipley
New Media Director / Coordinator	Jeremy Zimmer / Jonathan Meck
Director of Community/Alumni Relations	Cindy Himes
Director of Amateur Hockey	Mark Shuttleworth
Creative Director / Graphic Designers	Barbara Pilarski / Erin Halley, Lori Haramia
Manager of Amateur Hockey Development	Max Malone
Marketing Coordinator	Sarah Swartz
Community Relations Coordinator	Kathleen Unger
Fan Development Coordinator	Laura Spencer

Game Entertainment
Sr. Director, Event Entertainment & Production	Rod Murray
Director of Game Ops/Video Production	Billy Wareham
Director, Video Production & Technical Ops.	Andrew Warren
Manager of Arts and Graphics	Dori Minnis
Pens TV Host	Katie O'Malley
Game Entertainment Editors	James Archer, Michael Davenport, Stephen Finerty, Aaron Spiegel, Dave Weldon

Partnership Sales
Vice President of Business Partnerships	David Peart
Sr. Director of Corporate Sales	Kimberly Bogesdorfer
Corporate Sales Media Director	Mark Turley
Account Service, Sr. Manager / Manager	Lori Wineland / Ron Hay
Managers of Corporate Sales	Robbie Hofmann, Danny Smith
Coordinator, Client Services	Jeff Harshman
Corporate Sales Liaison	Pierre Larouche

Finance
Assistant Controller / Senior Accountant	Mark Kucziniski / Troy Ussack
Payroll Manager / Accounts Payable	Andrea Winschel / Tawni Love

CONSOL Energy Center Operations
Director, CONSOL Energy Center Project Devel.	Brian Magness
Director, Media Technology / IT	Chris Devivo / Erik Watts

Ticketing
Vice President of Ticket Sales	Chad Slencak
Director of Customer Service	Kathy Davis
Database Marketing Director / Coordinator	Erin Exley / Dana Cammer
Director of Premium Seating/Group Sales	Michael Guiffre
Manager of Box Office Ops / Ticket Sales	Jason Onufer / George Murphy
Box Office Manager / Assistant	Caroline Coulson / Kelly Gabany
Ticket Sales Account Execs	George Birman, Jeff Blizman, Bonnie Golinski, Nicole Kyslinger, Chuck Pukansky
Group Sales Account Executive	Michael Zatchey
Premium Sales / Seating Representatives	Amanda Gurney / Kyle Lux
Customer Service Representatives	Amber Auchey, Holly Homistek, Wayne Jones

Penguins Foundation
President, Penguins Foundation	David Soltesz
Manager / Event Coordinator, Foundation	Jaime Greenwald / Valerie Chouinard

Broadcasting
Executive Producer, Penguins Radio Network	Ray Walker
Radio Broadcasters / HD Radio Host	Phil Bourque, Mike Lange / Steve Mears

Key Off-Season Signings/Acquisitions

2010
June 1 • Named **Scott Mellanby** assistant coach.
17 • Acquired G **Jaroslav Halak** from Montreal for C **Lars Eller** and RW **Ian Schultz**.
17 • Acquired C **T.J. Hensick** from Colorado for LW **Julian Talbot**.
18 • Re-signed RW **Matt D'Agostini**.
26 • Acquired C **Vladimir Sobotka** from Boston for D **David Warsofsky**.
July 1 • Re-signed C **Alex Steen**.
2 • Re-signed LW **Brad Winchester**.
6 • Re-signed D **Carlo Colaiacovo** and RW **Cam Janssen**.
21 • Re-signed LW **David Perron**.
28 • Acquired LW **Stefan Della Rovere** from Washington for LW **D.J. King**.
Aug. 2 • Re-signed D **Erik Johnson**.

St. Louis Blues

2009-10 Results: 40w-32L-5OTL-5SOL 90PTS.
Fourth, Central Division

Andy McDonald was back on his game in 2009-10, tying Alex Steen for the Blues lead with 24 goals and leading the club outright with 33 assists and 57 points.

2010-11 Schedule

Oct.	Sat.	9	Philadelphia		Wed.	12	at Anaheim
	Mon.	11	Anaheim*		Thu.	13	at Los Angeles
	Thu.	14	at Nashville		Sat.	15	at San Jose
	Sat.	16	at Dallas		Tue.	18	Los Angeles
	Mon.	18	at Chicago		Thu.	20	Detroit
	Fri.	22	Chicago		Sat.	22	Columbus
	Sat.	23	Pittsburgh		Mon.	24	at Colorado
	Thu.	28	at Nashville		Wed.	26	at Calgary
	Sat.	30	Atlanta	Feb.	Tue.	1	Colorado
Nov.	Thu.	4	San Jose		Fri.	4	Edmonton
	Sat.	6	at Boston		Sun.	6	at Tampa Bay
	Sun.	7	at NY Rangers		Tue.	8	at Florida
	Wed.	10	at Columbus		Fri.	11	Minnesota
	Thu.	11	Nashville		Sat.	12	at Minnesota
	Sat.	13	at Phoenix		Mon.	14	Vancouver
	Mon.	15	at Colorado		Fri.	18	at Buffalo
	Wed.	17	at Detroit		Sat.	19	Anaheim
	Fri.	19	Ottawa		Mon.	21	Chicago*
	Sat.	20	New Jersey		Thu.	24	at Vancouver
	Wed.	24	at Nashville		Fri.	25	at Edmonton
	Fri.	26	at Dallas		Sun.	27	at Calgary
	Sat.	27	Dallas	Mar.	Tue.	1	Calgary
	Tue.	30	at Chicago		Thu.	3	at Washington
Dec.	Wed.	1	Washington		Sat.	5	at NY Islanders*
	Sat.	4	at Edmonton		Mon.	7	Columbus
	Sun.	5	at Vancouver		Wed.	9	at Columbus
	Thu.	9	Columbus		Thu.	10	Montreal
	Sat.	11	Carolina		Sat.	12	Detroit
	Wed.	15	at Detroit		Wed.	16	at Anaheim
	Thu.	16	Los Angeles		Thu.	17	at Los Angeles
	Sat.	18	San Jose		Sat.	19	at San Jose
	Mon.	20	Vancouver		Tue.	22	at Phoenix
	Tue.	21	at Atlanta		Thu.	24	Edmonton
	Thu.	23	Detroit		Sat.	26	at Minnesota
	Sun.	26	Nashville		Tue.	29	Minnesota
	Tue.	28	Chicago		Wed.	30	at Detroit
	Fri.	31	Phoenix	Apr.	Fri.	1	Calgary
Jan.	Sun.	2	Dallas*		Sun.	3	at Columbus*
	Thu.	6	at Toronto		Tue.	5	Colorado
	Sat.	8	NY Rangers		Wed.	6	at Chicago
	Mon.	10	Phoenix		Sat.	9	Nashville

* Denotes afternoon game.

**CENTRAL DIVISION
44th NHL Season**

Franchise date: June 5, 1967

Year-by-Year Record

		Home				Road				Overall							
Season	GP	W	L	T	OL	W	L	T	OL	W	L	T	OL	GF	GA	Pts.	Finished	Playoff Result
2009-10	82	18	18	....	5	22	14	....	5	40	32	....	10	225	223	90	4th, Central Div.	Out of Playoffs
2008-09	82	23	13	....	5	18	18	....	5	41	31	....	10	233	233	92	3rd, Central Div.	Lost Conf. Quarter-Final
2007-08	82	20	15	....	6	13	21	....	7	33	36	....	13	205	237	79	5th, Central Div.	Out of Playoffs
2006-07	82	18	19	....	4	16	16	....	9	34	35	....	13	214	254	81	3rd, Central Div.	Out of Playoffs
2005-06	82	12	23	....	6	9	23	....	9	21	46	....	15	197	292	57	5th, Central Div.	Out of Playoffs
2004-05	....	....	....	....	....	....	....	....	....	....	....	....	....	....	....	....		
2003-04	82	23	11	7	0	16	19	4	2	39	30	11	2	191	198	91	2nd, Central Div.	Lost Conf. Quarter-Final
2002-03	82	23	11	4	3	18	13	7	3	41	24	11	6	253	222	99	2nd, Central Div.	Lost Conf. Quarter-Final
2001-02	82	27	12	1	1	16	15	7	3	43	27	8	4	227	188	98	2nd, Central Div.	Lost Conf. Semi-Final
2000-01	82	28	5	5	3	15	17	7	2	43	22	12	5	249	195	103	2nd, Central Div.	Lost Conf. Championship
1999-2000	82	24	9	7	1	27	10	4	0	51	19	11	1	248	165	114	1st, Central Div.	Lost Conf. Quarter-Final
1998-99	82	18	17	6	....	19	15	7	....	37	32	13	....	237	209	87	2nd, Central Div.	Lost Conf. Semi-Final
1997-98	82	26	10	5	....	19	19	3	....	45	29	8	....	256	204	98	3rd, Central Div.	Lost Conf. Semi-Final
1996-97	82	17	20	4	....	19	15	7	....	36	35	11	....	236	239	83	4th, Central Div.	Lost Conf. Quarter-Final
1995-96	82	15	17	9	....	17	17	7	....	32	34	16	....	219	248	80	4th, Central Div.	Lost Conf. Semi-Final
1994-95	48	16	6	2	....	12	9	3	....	28	15	5	....	178	135	61	2nd, Central Div.	Lost Conf. Quarter-Final
1993-94	84	23	11	8	....	17	22	3	....	40	33	11	....	270	283	91	4th, Central Div.	Lost Conf. Quarter-Final
1992-93	84	22	13	7	....	15	23	4	....	37	36	11	....	282	278	85	4th, Norris Div.	Lost Div. Final
1991-92	80	25	12	3	....	11	21	8	....	36	33	11	....	279	266	83	3rd, Norris Div.	Lost Div. Semi-Final
1990-91	80	24	9	7	....	23	13	4	....	47	22	11	....	310	250	105	2nd, Norris Div.	Lost Div. Final
1989-90	80	20	15	5	....	17	19	4	....	37	34	9	....	295	279	83	2nd, Norris Div.	Lost Div. Final
1988-89	80	22	11	7	....	11	24	5	....	33	35	12	....	275	285	78	2nd, Norris Div.	Lost Div. Final
1987-88	80	18	17	5	....	16	21	3	....	34	38	8	....	278	294	76	2nd, Norris Div.	Lost Div. Final
1986-87	80	21	12	7	....	11	21	8	....	32	33	15	....	281	293	79	1st, Norris Div.	Lost Div. Semi-Final
1985-86	80	23	11	6	....	14	23	3	....	37	34	9	....	302	291	83	3rd, Norris Div.	Lost Conf. Championship
1984-85	80	21	12	7	....	16	19	5	....	37	31	12	....	299	288	86	1st, Norris Div.	Lost Div. Semi-Final
1983-84	80	23	14	3	....	9	27	4	....	32	41	7	....	293	316	71	2nd, Norris Div.	Lost Div. Final
1982-83	80	16	16	8	....	9	24	7	....	25	40	15	....	285	316	65	4th, Norris Div.	Lost Div. Semi-Final
1981-82	80	22	14	4	....	10	26	4	....	32	40	8	....	315	349	72	3rd, Norris Div.	Lost Div. Final
1980-81	80	29	7	4	....	16	11	13	....	45	18	17	....	352	281	107	1st, Smythe Div.	Lost Quarter-Final
1979-80	80	20	13	7	....	14	21	5	....	34	34	12	....	266	278	80	2nd, Smythe Div.	Lost Prelim. Round
1978-79	80	14	20	6	....	4	30	6	....	18	50	12	....	249	348	48	3rd, Smythe Div.	Out of Playoffs
1977-78	80	12	20	8	....	8	27	5	....	20	47	13	....	195	304	53	4th, Smythe Div.	Out of Playoffs
1976-77	80	22	13	5	....	10	26	4	....	32	39	9	....	239	276	73	1st, Smythe Div.	Lost Quarter-Final
1975-76	80	20	12	8	....	9	25	6	....	29	37	14	....	249	290	72	3rd, Smythe Div.	Lost Prelim. Round
1974-75	80	23	13	4	....	12	18	10	....	35	31	14	....	269	267	84	2nd, Smythe Div.	Lost Prelim. Round
1973-74	78	16	16	7	....	10	24	5	....	26	40	12	....	206	248	64	6th, West Div.	Out of Playoffs
1972-73	78	21	11	7	....	11	23	5	....	32	34	12	....	233	251	76	4th, West Div.	Lost Quarter-Final
1971-72	78	17	17	5	....	11	22	6	....	28	39	11	....	208	247	67	3rd, West Div.	Lost Semi-Final
1970-71	78	23	7	9	....	11	18	10	....	34	25	19	....	223	208	87	2nd, West Div.	Lost Quarter-Final
1969-70	76	24	9	5	....	13	18	7	....	37	27	12	....	224	179	86	1st, West Div.	Lost Final
1968-69	76	21	8	9	....	16	17	5	....	37	25	14	....	204	157	88	1st, West Div.	Lost Final
1967-68	74	18	12	7	....	9	19	9	....	27	31	16	....	177	191	70	3rd, West Div.	Lost Final

2010-11 Player Personnel

FORWARDS	HT	WT	S	Place of Birth	*Age	2009-10 Club
BACKES, David	6-3	225	R	Blaine, MN	26	St. Louis
BERGLUND, Patrik	6-4	215	L	Vasteras, Sweden	22	St. Louis
BOYES, Brad	6-0	200	R	Mississauga, Ont.	28	St. Louis
CRACKNELL, Adam	6-2	210	R	Prince Albert, Sask.	25	Peoria
CROMBEEN, B.J.	6-2	210	R	Denver, CO	25	St. Louis
D'AGOSTINI, Matt	6-0	200	R	Sault Ste. Marie, Ont.	23	Mtl-Hamilton-StL
DELLA ROVERE, Stefan	5-11	196	L	Richmond Hill, Ont.	20	Barrie-Hershey
DRAZENOVIC, Nicholas	6-0	205	L	Prince George, B.C.	23	Peoria
HENSICK, T.J.	5-10	185	R	Lansing, MI	24	Colorado-Lake Erie
JANSSEN, Cam	6-0	215	R	St. Louis, MO	26	St. Louis
McCLEMENT, Jay	6-1	200	L	Kingston, Ont.	27	St. Louis
McDONALD, Andy	5-11	190	L	Strathroy, Ont.	33	St. Louis
McRAE, Philip	6-2	195	L	Minneapolis, MN	20	London-Plymouth
MINK, Graham	6-3	220	R	Stowe, VT	31	Rochester
NIGRO, Anthony	6-0	187	L	Vaughan, Ont.	20	Ottawa (OHL)
OSHIE, T.J.	5-11	194	R	Mt. Vernon, WA	23	St. Louis
PERRON, David	6-0	200	R	Sherbrooke, Que.	22	St. Louis
PORTER, Chris	6-1	210	L	Toronto, Ont.	26	Peoria
REAVES, Ryan	6-1	225	R	Winnipeg, Man.	23	Peoria
SCATCHARD, Dave	6-3	210	R	Hinton, Alta.	34	Nashville-Milwaukee
SHATTOCK, Tyler	6-3	200	R	Vernon, B.C.	20	Kamloops-Calgary (WHL)
SOBOTKA, Vladimir	5-10	183	L	Trebic, Czech.	23	Boston-Providence (AHL)
SONNE, Brett	6-0	190	L	Chilliwack, B.C.	21	Peoria
STEEN, Alex	6-1	206	L	Winnipeg, Man.	26	St. Louis
WINCHESTER, Brad	6-5	231	L	Madison, WI	29	St. Louis

DEFENSEMEN	HT	WT	S	Place of Birth	*Age	2009-10 Club
ARSENE, Dean	6-2	195	L	Murrayville, B.C.	30	Edmonton-Springfield
BREWER, Eric	6-3	222	L	Vernon, B.C.	31	St. Louis
COLAIACOVO, Carlo	6-1	200	L	Toronto, Ont.	27	St. Louis
COLE, Ian	6-1	217	L	Ann Arbour, MI	21	U. of Notre Dame-Peoria
CUNDARI, Mark	5-9	200	L	Woodbridge, Ont.	20	Windsor
EVANS, Brennan	6-3	220	L	North Battleford, Sask.	28	Toronto (AHL)
JACKMAN, Barret	6-0	210	L	Trail, B.C.	29	St. Louis
JOHNSON, Erik	6-4	236	R	Bloomington, MN	22	St. Louis
NIKITIN, Nikita	6-3	215	L	Omsk, USSR	24	Omsk
OYSTRICK, Nathan	6-0	210	L	Regina, Sask.	27	Chicago (AHL)-Anaheim
PELUSO, Anthony	6-3	230	R	North York, Ont.	21	Peoria-Alaska
PIETRANGELO, Alex	6-3	206	R	King City, Ont.	20	St. Louis-Barrie
POLAK, Roman	6-1	225	R	Ostrava, Czech.	24	St. Louis
STRACHAN, Tyson	6-2	215	R	Melfort, Sask.	25	St. Louis-Peoria

GOALTENDERS	HT	WT	C	Place of Birth	*Age	2009-10 Club
ALLEN, Jake	6-1	190	L	Fredericton, N.B.	20	Montreal (QMJHL)-Drummondville
BISHOP, Ben	6-7	215	L	Denver, CO	23	Peoria
CONKLIN, Ty	6-1	190	L	Anchorage, AK	34	St. Louis
HALAK, Jaroslav	5-11	179	L	Bratislava, Czech.	25	Montreal

* – Age at start of 2010-11 season

2009-10 Scoring

* – rookie

Regular Season

Pos	#	Player	Team	GP	G	A	Pts	TOI	+/−	PIM	PP	SH	GW	S	%
C	10	Andy McDonald	STL	79	24	33	57	18:07	−9	18	6	0	3	191	12.6
C	74	T.J. Oshie	STL	76	18	30	48	18:19	−1	36	1	1	3	158	11.4
C	42	David Backes	STL	79	17	31	48	18:18	−4	106	5	0	3	163	10.4
C	20	Alex Steen	STL	68	24	23	47	16:16	6	30	7	2	4	189	12.7
L	57	David Perron	STL	82	20	27	47	16:09	−10	60	5	1	2	166	12.0
L	9	Paul Kariya	STL	75	18	25	43	17:09	−7	36	3	0	2	221	8.1
C	22	Brad Boyes	STL	82	14	28	42	16:47	1	26	2	0	3	197	7.1
D	6	Erik Johnson	STL	79	10	29	39	21:26	1	79	6	0	2	186	5.4
C	7	Keith Tkachuk	STL	67	13	19	32	13:30	−2	56	5	0	1	120	10.8
D	28	Carlo Colaiacovo	STL	67	7	25	32	17:18	8	60	4	1	1	74	9.5
C	18	Jay McClement	STL	82	11	18	29	16:43	0	22	0	3	3	109	10.1
C	21	Patrik Berglund	STL	71	13	16	29	13:13	−5	16	6	0	4	129	10.1
D	46	Roman Polak	STL	78	4	17	21	19:58	7	59	0	0	1	73	5.5
D	5	Barret Jackman	STL	66	2	15	17	22:40	3	81	0	1	0	73	2.7
D	4	Eric Brewer	STL	59	8	7	15	21:26	−17	46	0	0	8	84	9.5
R	26	Brandon Crombeen	STL	79	7	8	15	13:04	−5	168	0	1	1	120	5.8
D	43	Mike Weaver	STL	77	1	9	10	16:57	10	29	0	0	0	33	3.0
L	15	Brad Winchester	STL	64	3	5	8	9:03	3	108	1	0	0	69	4.3
D	44	Darryl Sydor	STL	47	0	8	8	16:42	−6	15	0	0	0	26	0.0
R	36	Matt D'Agostini	MTL	40	2	2	4	9:53	−12	26	0	0	0	48	4.2
			STL	7	0	0	0	9:13	−3	2	0	0	0	6	0.0
			Total	47	2	2	4	9:47	−15	28	0	0	0	54	3.7
C	61	* Lars Eller	STL	7	2	0	2	10:49	2	4	1	0	0	8	25.0
D	27	* Alex Pietrangelo	STL	9	1	1	2	16:34	−9	6	0	0	0	7	14.3
D	53	* Jonas Junland	STL	3	0	2	2	17:10	−3	0	0	0	0	7	0.0
D	33	Tyson Strachan	STL	8	0	2	2	14:02	3	4	0	0	0	7	0.0
C	25	Yan Stastny	STL	4	1	0	1	9:29	1	0	0	0	0	7	14.3
C	17	Derek Armstrong	STL	6	0	0	0	6:59	−2	2	0	0	0	6	0.0
L	19	Dwayne King	STL	12	0	0	0	4:30	−4	33	0	0	0	5	0.0
R	55	Cam Janssen	STL	43	0	0	0	4:42	−3	190	0	0	0	11	0.0

Goaltending

No.	Goaltender	GPI	Mins	Avg	W	L	OT	EN	SO	GA	SA	S%	G	A	PIM
29	Ty Conklin	26	1451	2.48	10	10	2	2	4	60	764	.921	0	1	4
50	Chris Mason	61	3512	2.53	30	22	8	8	2	148	1699	.913	0	0	0
	Totals	82	5002	2.61	40	32	10	10	6	218	2473	.912			

Davis Payne
Head Coach
Born: Port Alberni, B.C., September 24, 1970.

Davis Payne was named the 23rd head coach of the St. Louis Blues on January 2, 2010 after serving as head coach of the team's AHL club, the Peoria Rivermen. Originally named to the position on an interim basis, he was officially confirmed as the head coach on April 14, 2010. Payne guided the Rivermen to a 43-31-6 record in 2008-09 and returned Peoria to the postseason following a two-year drought.

Prior to joining the Rivermen before the 2007-08 campaign, Payne had spent a total of seven seasons as a head coach in the ECHL. He established a .691 winning percentage over four years as head coach for the Alaska Aces, the Blues' ECHL affiliate. The 2006-07 ECHL coach of the year, Payne led the Aces to the 2006 ECHL Kelly Cup championship and also guided the club to three consecutive trips to the Conference Finals; it was the first time in 15 years and only the second time in ECHL history that a team advanced to the ECHL's Final Four in three straight seasons. Payne owns a 289-142-45 record (.654) in seven seasons as an ECHL head coach between Alaska and the Pee Dee Pride. He had a record of 50-35 in the postseason.

A graduate of NCAA Division I Michigan Tech, Payne appeared in 22 NHL games with the Boston Bruins and played a total of eight professional seasons. He was originally drafted by the Edmonton Oilers in the seventh round of the 1989 NHL Entry Draft.

Coaching Record

			Regular Season				Playoffs			
Season	Team	League	GC	W	L	O/T	GC	W	L	T
2000-01	Pee Dee	ECHL	44	23	16	5	10	5	5	....
2001-02	Pee Dee	ECHL	72	41	25	6	9	4	5	....
2002-03	Pee Dee	ECHL	72	40	26	6	7	3	4	....
2003-04	Alaska	ECHL	72	38	28	6	7	4	3	....
2004-05	Alaska	ECHL	72	45	19	8	15	9	6	....
2005-06	Alaska	ECHL	72	53	12	7	22	16	6	....
2006-07	Alaska	ECHL	72	49	16	7	15	9	6	....
2008-09	Peoria	AHL	80	43	31	6	7	3	4	....
2009-10	Peoria	AHL	35	19	13	3	....	....	....	....
2009-10	St. Louis	NHL	42	23	15	4	....	....	....	....
	NHL Totals		42	23	15	4	....	....	....	....

General Managers' History
Lynn Patrick, 1967-68; Scotty Bowman, 1968-69 to 1970-71; Lynn Patrick, 1971-72; Sid Abel, 1972-73; Charles Catto, 1973-74; Gerry Ehman, 1974-75; Dennis Ball, 1975-76; Emile Francis, 1976-77 to 1982-83; Ron Caron, 1983-84 to 1993-94; Mike Keenan, 1994-95, 1995-96; Mike Keenan and Ron Caron, 1996-97; Larry Pleau, 1997-98 to 2009-10; Doug Armstrong, 2010-11.

Coaching History
Lynn Patrick and Scotty Bowman, 1967-68; Scotty Bowman, 1968-69, 1969-70; Al Arbour and Scotty Bowman, 1970-71; Sid Abel, Bill McCreary and Al Arbour, 1971-72; Al Arbour and Jean-Guy Talbot, 1972-73; Jean-Guy Talbot and Lou Angotti, 1973-74; Lou Angotti, Lynn Patrick and Garry Young, 1974-75; Garry Young, Lynn Patrick and Leo Boivin, 1975-76; Emile Francis, 1976-77; Leo Boivin and Barclay Plager, 1977-78; Barclay Plager, 1978-79; Barclay Plager and Red Berenson, 1979-80; Red Berenson, 1980-81; Red Berenson and Emile Francis, 1981-82; Emile Francis and Barclay Plager, 1982-83; Jacques Demers, 1983-84 to 1985-86; Jacques Martin, 1986-87, 1987-88; Brian Sutter, 1988-89 to 1991-92; Bob Plager and Bob Berry, 1992-93; Bob Berry, 1993-94; Mike Keenan, 1994-95, 1995-96; Mike Keenan, Jim Roberts and Joel Quenneville, 1996-97; Joel Quenneville, 1997-98 to 2002-03; Joel Quenneville and Mike Kitchen, 2003-04; Mike Kitchen, 2004-05, 2005-06; Mike Kitchen and Andy Murray, 2006-07; Andy Murray, 2007-08, 2008-09; Andy Murray and Davis Payne, 2009-10; Davis Payne, 2010-11.

Club Records

Team

(Figures in brackets for season records are games played; records for fewest points, wins, ties, losses, goals, goals against are for 70 or more games)

Most Points	**114**	1999-2000 (82)
Most Wins	**51**	1999-2000 (82)
Most Ties	**19**	1970-71 (78)
Most Losses	**50**	1978-79 (80)
Most Goals	**352**	1980-81 (80)
Most Goals Against	**349**	1981-82 (80)
Fewest Points	**48**	1978-79 (80)
Fewest Wins	**18**	1978-79 (80)
Fewest Ties	**7**	1983-84 (80)
Fewest Losses	**18**	1980-81 (80)
Fewest Goals	**177**	1967-68 (74)
Fewest Goals Against	**157**	1968-69 (76)
Longest Winning Streak		
Overall	**10**	Jan. 3-23/02
Home	**9**	Jan. 26-Feb. 26/91
Away	***10**	Jan. 21-Mar. 2/00
Longest Undefeated Streak		
Overall	**12**	Nov. 10-Dec. 8/68 (5 wins, 7 ties), Nov. 24-Dec. 26/00 (11 wins, 1 tie)
Home	**11**	Four times
Away	**11**	Jan. 21-Mar. 4/00 (10 wins, 1 tie)
Longest Losing Streak		
Overall	**13**	Mar. 16-Apr. 8/06
Home	**7**	Oct. 22-Nov. 26/05, Nov. 25-Dec. 17/06
Away	**10**	Jan. 20-Mar. 8/82, Dec. 29/05-Feb. 1/06, Feb. 16-Mar. 15/08
Longest Winless Streak		
Overall	**13**	Mar. 16-Apr. 8/06 (13 losses)
Home	**7**	Dec. 28/82-Jan. 25/83 (5 losses, 2 ties), Oct. 22-Nov. 26/05 (7 losses)
Away	**17**	Jan. 23-Apr. 7/74 (14 losses, 3 ties)
Most Shutouts, Season	**13**	1968-69 (76)
Most PIM, Season	**2,041**	1990-91 (80)
Most Goals, Game	**11**	Feb. 26/94 (St.L. 11 at Ott. 1)

Individual

Most Seasons	**13**	Bernie Federko
Most Games	**927**	Bernie Federko
Most Goals, Career	**527**	Brett Hull
Most Assists, Career	**721**	Bernie Federko
Most Points, Career	**1,073**	Bernie Federko (352G, 721A)
Most PIM, Career	**1,786**	Brian Sutter
Most Shutouts, Career	**16**	Glenn Hall
Longest Consecutive Games Streak	**662**	Garry Unger (Feb. 7/71-Apr. 8/79)
Most Goals, Season	**86**	Brett Hull (1990-91)
Most Assists, Season	**90**	Adam Oates (1990-91)
Most Points, Season	**131**	Brett Hull (1990-91; 86G, 45A)
Most PIM, Season	**306**	Bob Gassoff (1975-76)
Most Points, Defenseman, Season	**78**	Jeff Brown (1992-93; 25G, 53A)
Most Points, Center, Season	**115**	Adam Oates (1990-91; 25G, 90A)
Most Points, Right Wing, Season	**131**	Brett Hull (1990-91; 86G, 45A)
Most Points, Left Wing, Season	**102**	Brendan Shanahan (1993-94; 52G, 50A)
Most Points, Rookie, Season	**73**	Jorgen Pettersson (1980-81; 37G, 36A)
Most Shutouts, Season	**8**	Glenn Hall (1968-69)
Most Goals, Game	**6**	Red Berenson (Nov. 7/68)
Most Assists, Game	**5**	Brian Sutter (Nov. 22/83), Bernie Federko (Feb. 27/88), Adam Oates (Jan. 26/91), Dallas Drake (Oct. 29/03)
Most Points, Game	**7**	Red Berenson (Nov. 7/68; 6G, 1A), Garry Unger (Mar. 13/71; 3G, 4A)

* NHL Record.

Retired Numbers

2	Al MacInnis	1994-2004
3	Bob Gassoff	1973-1977
8	Barclay Plager	1967-1977
11	Brian Sutter	1976-1988
16	Brett Hull	1987-1998
24	Bernie Federko	1976-1989

All-time Record vs. Other Clubs

Regular Season

	At Home								On Road								Total							
	GP	W	L	T	OL	GF	GA	PTS	GP	W	L	T	OL	GF	GA	PTS	GP	W	L	T	OL	GF	GA	PTS
Anaheim	32	17	8	3	4	101	87	41	32	15	14	2	1	92	90	33	64	32	22	5	5	193	177	74
Atlanta	5	3	1	0	1	15	8	7	7	3	2	1	1	22	21	8	12	6	3	1	2	37	29	15
Boston	62	28	25	9	0	196	210	65	61	17	35	9	0	170	252	43	123	45	60	18	0	366	462	108
Buffalo	52	30	15	7	0	186	132	67	54	18	30	6	0	171	207	42	106	48	45	13	0	357	339	109
Calgary	74	34	29	9	2	255	231	79	72	31	33	5	3	199	231	70	146	65	62	14	5	454	462	149
Carolina	33	20	10	3	0	120	95	43	34	18	14	2	0	105	100	38	67	38	24	5	0	225	195	81
Chicago	133	66	47	17	3	441	406	152	136	41	72	18	5	387	493	105	269	107	119	35	8	828	899	257
Colorado	50	27	17	4	2	177	149	60	51	17	27	7	0	135	179	41	101	44	44	11	2	312	328	101
Columbus	29	21	6	1	1	103	66	44	28	12	12	2	2	75	76	28	57	33	18	3	3	178	142	72
Dallas	127	71	35	21	0	455	355	163	125	44	56	22	3	365	417	113	252	115	91	43	3	820	772	276
Detroit	128	62	45	20	1	413	368	145	128	49	59	17	3	377	459	118	256	111	104	37	4	790	827	263
Edmonton	54	25	19	7	3	185	186	60	54	23	25	4	2	176	189	52	108	48	44	11	5	361	375	112
Florida	12	8	3	1	0	29	17	17	11	5	4	2	0	24	25	12	23	13	7	3	0	53	42	29
Los Angeles	88	56	21	10	1	321	221	123	88	35	41	12	0	253	300	82	176	91	62	22	1	574	521	205
Minnesota	18	9	5	3	1	41	34	22	18	5	9	2	2	34	57	14	36	14	14	5	3	75	91	36
Montreal	59	14	29	15	1	152	202	44	61	13	41	7	0	169	261	33	120	27	70	22	1	321	463	77
Nashville	34	17	13	1	3	94	76	38	35	13	12	3	7	80	84	36	69	30	25	4	10	174	160	74
New Jersey	48	27	13	7	1	198	152	62	48	19	22	7	0	132	148	45	96	46	35	14	1	330	300	107
NY Islanders	49	19	19	9	2	173	160	49	52	15	26	11	0	138	191	41	101	34	45	20	2	311	351	90
NY Rangers	66	27	28	10	1	198	209	65	62	11	44	6	1	149	251	29	128	38	72	16	2	347	460	94
Ottawa	11	4	5	2	0	30	32	10	12	6	6	0	0	40	29	12	23	10	11	2	0	70	61	22
Philadelphia	70	27	34	7	2	200	224	63	69	12	45	10	2	157	270	36	139	39	79	17	4	357	494	99
Phoenix	60	29	20	11	0	199	163	69	61	23	27	7	4	191	194	57	121	52	47	18	4	390	357	126
Pittsburgh	66	44	16	6	0	253	177	94	66	21	32	12	1	195	244	55	132	65	48	18	1	448	421	149
San Jose	38	20	16	1	1	113	99	42	34	22	8	1	3	108	84	48	72	42	24	2	4	221	183	90
Tampa Bay	13	10	3	0	0	51	35	20	15	6	5	3	1	50	46	16	28	16	8	3	1	101	81	36
Toronto	104	59	30	14	1	353	285	133	101	32	58	11	0	300	375	75	205	91	88	25	1	653	660	208
Vancouver	81	47	22	9	3	301	228	106	82	37	33	9	3	257	242	86	163	84	55	18	6	558	470	192
Washington	43	22	13	8	0	173	133	52	41	15	21	4	1	123	145	35	84	37	34	12	1	296	278	87
Defunct Clubs	32	25	4	3	0	131	55	53	33	11	10	12	0	95	100	34	65	36	14	15	0	226	155	87
Totals	**1671**	**868**	**551**	**218**	**34**	**5657**	**4795**	**1988**	**1671**	**589**	**823**	**214**	**45**	**4769**	**5760**	**1437**	**3342**	**1457**	**1374**	**432**	**79**	**10426**	**10555**	**3425**

Playoffs

	Series	W	L	GP	W	L	T	GF	GA	Last Mtg.	Rnd.	Result
Boston	2	0	2	8	0	8	0	15	48	1972	SF	L 0-4
Buffalo	1	0	1	3	1	2	0	8	7	1976	PRE	L 1-2
Calgary	1	0	1	7	3	4	0	22	28	1986	CF	L 3-4
Chicago	10	3	7	50	22	28	0	142	171	2002	CQF	W 4-1
Colorado	1	0	1	5	1	4	0	11	17	2001	CF	L 1-4
Dallas	12	6	6	66	32	34	0	187	197	2001	CSF	W 4-0
Detroit	7	2	5	40	16	24	0	103	125	2002	CSF	L 1-4
Los Angeles	2	2	0	8	8	0	0	32	13	1998	CQF	W 4-0
Montreal	3	0	3	12	0	12	0	14	42	1977	QF	L 0-4
NY Rangers	1	0	1	6	2	4	0	22	29	1981	QF	L 2-4
Philadelphia	2	2	0	11	8	3	0	34	20	1969	QF	W 4-0
Phoenix	2	2	0	11	7	4	0	39	29	1999	CQF	W 4-3
Pittsburgh	3	2	1	13	7	6	0	45	40	1981	PRE	W 3-2
San Jose	3	1	2	18	8	10	0	47	43	2004	CQF	L 1-4
Toronto	5	3	2	31	17	14	0	88	90	1996	CQF	W 4-2
Vancouver	3	0	3	18	6	12	0	53	55	2009	CQF	L 0-4
Totals	**58**	**23**	**35**	**307**	**138**	**169**	**0**	**862**	**954**			

Calgary totals include Atlanta Flames, 1972-73 to 1979-80. Carolina totals include Hartford, 1979-80 to 1996-97.
Colorado totals include Quebec, 1979-80 to 1994-95. Dallas totals include Minnesota North Stars, 1967-68 to 1992-93.
New Jersey totals include Kansas City, 1974-75, 1975-76, and Colorado Rockies, 1976-77 to 1981-82.
Phoenix totals include Winnipeg, 1979-80 to 1995-96.

Playoff Results 2010-2006

Year	Round	Opponent	Result	GF	GA
2009	CQF	Vancouver	L 0-4	5	11

Abbreviations: Round: CF – conference final; **CSF** – conference semi-final; **CQF** – conference quarter-final; **SF** – semi-final; **QF** – quarter-final; **PRE** – preliminary round.

2009-10 Results

Oct.	2	at Detroit	4-3
	3	Detroit	5-3
	8	Atlanta	2-4
	10	Los Angeles	1-2
	15	at Phoenix	2-3*
	17	at Anaheim	5-0
	20	at Pittsburgh	1-5
	23	Minnesota	3-1
	24	Dallas	1-4
	28	at Carolina	5-2
	29	Phoenix	0-2
	31	Florida	0-4
Nov.	5	Calgary	1-2*
	7	at Philadelphia	1-2†
	8	at Atlanta	2-3†
	10	Vancouver	6-1
	12	Nashville	1-3
	14	San Jose	1-3
	19	Phoenix	3-2*
	21	NY Islanders	4-1
	23	Boston	2-4
	25	at Dallas	4-3†
	27	at Nashville	3-1
	28	Detroit	3-4†
	30	at Columbus	2-5
Dec.	3	at San Jose	3-2†
	5	at Los Angeles	5-4†
	7	Colorado	0-4
	9	at Detroit	1-0
	11	Edmonton	3-5
	15	Calgary	4-3
	16	at Chicago	0-3
	18	Tampa Bay	3-6
	20	at Vancouver	3-1
	21	at Edmonton	7-2
	23	at Calgary	2-1†
	26	at Minnesota	3-4
	27	Buffalo	3-5
	29	Nashville	3-4
	31	Vancouver	3-4*
Jan.	2	Chicago	3-6
	6	at San Jose	1-2*
	7	at Anaheim	2-4
	9	at Los Angeles	4-3
	12	Columbus	4-1
	14	Minnesota	1-0
	16	NY Rangers	4-1
	18	at Columbus	2-4
	20	at Montreal	4-3*
	21	at Ottawa	2-3
	23	Anaheim	3-4†
	25	at Calgary	2-0
	27	at Vancouver	2-3
	28	at Edmonton	2-1
	30	Columbus	2-3*
Feb.	3	at Chicago	3-2
	4	San Jose	2-4
	6	Chicago	1-2
	8	at Colorado	2-5
	9	Detroit	4-3†
	12	Toronto	4-0
	13	Washington	4-3†
Mar.	2	at Phoenix	5-2
	4	at Dallas	6-1
	6	at Colorado	3-7
	11	at NY Islanders	2-1†
	13	at Columbus	5-1
	14	at Minnesota	2-4
	16	Colorado	3-5
	18	at NY Rangers	4-3
	20	at New Jersey	1-0
	21	Nashville	2-3
	24	at Detroit	2-4
	25	Los Angeles	3-1
	28	Edmonton	2-1
	30	Chicago	4-2
Apr.	1	at Nashville	2-3
	3	Dallas	2-1
	5	Columbus	2-1*
	7	at Chicago	5-6
	9	Anaheim	6-3
	10	at Nashville	1-2†

* – Overtime † – Shootout

Entry Draft Selections 2010-1996

Name in bold denotes played in NHL.

2010
Pick
14 Jaden Schwartz
16 Vladimir Tarasenko
44 Sebastian Wannstrom
74 Max Gardiner
104 Jani Hakanpaa
134 Cody Beach
164 Stephen Macaulay

2009
Pick
17 David Rundblad
48 Brett Ponich
78 Sergei Andronov
108 Tyler Shattock
168 David Shields
202 Maxwell Tardy

2008
Pick
4 **Alex Pietrangelo**
33 Philip McRae
34 Jake Allen
65 Jori Lehtera
70 James Livingston
87 Ian Schultz
95 David Warsofsky
125 Kristofer Berglund
155 Anthony Nigro
185 Paul Karpowich

2007
Pick
13 **Lars Eller**
18 Ian Cole
26 **David Perron**
39 Simon Hjalmarsson
44 Aaron Palushaj
85 Brett Sonne
96 Cade Fairchild
100 Travis Erstad
160 Anthony Peluso
190 Trevor Nill

2006
Pick
1 **Erik Johnson**
25 **Patrik Berglund**
31 **Tomas Kana**
64 **Jonas Junland**
94 Ryan Turek
106 Reto Berra
124 Andy Sackrison
154 Matthew McCollem
184 Alexander Hellstrom

2005
Pick
24 **T.J. Oshie**
37 **Scott Jackson**
85 **Ben Bishop**
156 Ryan Reaves
169 Mike Gauthier
171 Nicholas Drazenovic
219 Nikolai Lemtyugov

2004
Pick
17 **Marek Schwarz**
49 Carl Soderberg
83 Viktor Alexandrov
116 Michal Birner
136 Nikita Nikitin
180 **Roman Polak**
211 David Fredriksson
277 Jonathan Michel Boutin

2003
Pick
30 **Shawn Belle**
62 **David Backes**
84 Konstantin Barulin
88 **Zach Fitzgerald**
101 Konstantin Zakharov
127 **Alexandre Bolduc**
148 **Lee Stempniak**
159 **Chris Beckford-Tseu**
189 Jonathan Lehun
221 Evgeny Skachkov
253 Andrei Pervyshin
284 Juhamatti Aaltonen

2002
Pick
48 Alexei Shkotov
62 Andrei Mikhnov
89 Tomas Troliga
120 Robin Jonsson
165 Justin Maiser
190 **D.J. King**
221 Jonas Johnson
253 **Tom Koivisto**
284 Ryan MacMurchy

2001
Pick
57 **Jay McClement**
89 Tuomas Nissinen
122 Igor Valeev
159 Dmitri Semin
190 Brett Scheffelmaier
253 **Petr Cajanek**
270 Grant Jacobsen
283 Simon Skoog

2000
Pick
30 **Jeff Taffe**
65 **Dave Morisset**
75 **Justin Papineau**
96 Antoine Bergeron
129 Troy Riddle
167 **Craig Weller**
229 Brett Lutes
261 **Reinhard Divis**
293 Lauri Kinos

1999
Pick
17 **Barret Jackman**
85 **Peter Smrek**
114 Chad Starling
143 Trevor Byrne
180 Tore Vikingstad
203 Phil Osaer
221 **Colin Hemingway**
232 **Alexander Khavanov**
260 Brian McMeekin
270 James Desmarais

1998
Pick
24 **Christian Backman**
41 Maxim Linnik
83 **Matt Walker**
157 Brad Voth
170 Andrei Troschinsky
197 Brad Twordik
225 Yevgeny Pastukh
255 **John Pohl**

1997
Pick
40 Tyler Rennette
86 Didier Tremblay
98 Jan Horacek
106 **Jame Pollock**
149 Nicholas Bilotto
177 **Ladislav Nagy**
206 Bobby Haglund
232 Dmitri Plekhanov
244 Marek Ivan

1996
Pick
14 **Marty Reasoner**
67 **Gordie Dwyer**
95 Jonathan Zukiwsky
97 Andrei Petrakov
159 Stephen Wagner
169 **Daniel Corso**
177 **Reed Low**
196 **Andrej Podkonicky**
203 Tony Hutchins
229 **Konstantin Shafranov**

Captains' History

Al Arbour, 1967-68 to 1969-70; Red Berenson and Barclay Plager, 1970-71; Barclay Plager, 1971-72 to 1975-76; no captain, 1976-77; Red Berenson, 1977-78; Barry Gibbs, 1978-79; Brian Sutter, 1979-80 to 1987-88; Bernie Federko, 1988-89; Rick Meagher, 1989-90; Scott Stevens, 1990-91; Garth Butcher, 1991-92; Brett Hull, 1992-93 to 1994-95; Brett Hull, Shayne Corson and Wayne Gretzky, 1995-96; no captain, 1996-97; Chris Pronger, 1997-98 to 2001-02; Al MacInnis, 2002-03, 2003-04; Dallas Drake, 2005-06, 2006-07; Eric Brewer, 2007-08 to date.

Doug Armstrong

Executive Vice President and General Manager

Born: Sarnia, Ont., September 24, 1964.

Doug Armstrong was named the Blues' executive vice president and general manager on July 1, 2010 after serving two seasons with the club as vice president of player personnel. Previously, Armstrong spent 17 years with the Dallas Stars organization and the last six seasons (from January 25, 2002, to 2008) as the club's general manager.

Armstrong was a part of the Stars' organization since the club moved to Dallas in 1993 and helped lead the franchise to two Presidents' Trophies, two Western Conference titles and the 1999 Stanley Cup championship. Prior to being named the team's seventh general manager, Armstrong served nine years as the assistant general manager under Bob Gainey. As Gainey's assistant, Armstrong worked on contract negotiations and season scheduling, and handled the day-to-day operations of the hockey department.

On the international level, Armstrong was the associate director of player personnel for Team Canada at the 2010 Winter Olympics in Vancouver. He also served as general manager for Team Canada and won the silver medal at the 2009 World Championship in Switzerland. He was the assistant general manager for Team Canada at the 2002 World Championship and 2008 World Championship (silver medal) and served as a special advisor to Steve Yzerman for the Canadian team that won gold at the 2007 World Championship. Armstrong is the son of former NHL linesman Neil Armstrong who was inducted into the Hockey Hall of Fame in 1991.

Club Directory

Scottrade Center

St. Louis Blues
Scottrade Center
1401 Clark Avenue
St. Louis, MO 63103
Phone **314/622-2500**
FAX 314/622-2582
www.stlouisblues.com
Capacity: 19,150

SCP Worldwide

Principal Owner and Chairman/Governor/ Chairman, SCP Worldwide	David W. Checketts
Vice Chairman/Alternate Governor/ Partner, SCP Worldwide	Michael McCarthy
Alternate Governor/Partner, SCP Worldwide	Kenneth Munoz
Partner, SCP Worldwide	Carl Vogel
Partner, SCP Worldwide	Steven Potter
Minority Owner	Tom Stillman

Executive

President of Hockey Operations/Alt. Governor	John Davidson
CEO of St. Louis Blues Enterprises/Alt. Governor	Peter McLoughlin
Exec. V.P., General Manager, St. Louis Blues	Doug Armstrong
Vice President, Hockey Operations	Al MacInnis
Exec. V.P., General Manager, Scottrade Center	Marty Brooks
Exec. V.P., Chief Marketing Officer	David Bullock
Exec. V.P., Corporate and Sponsorship Sales	Mark Toffolo
Sr. V.P., Sales	Todd Lambert
Sr. V.P., Finance and Administration	Phil Siddle
Sr. V.P., Business Development	Eric Stisser
Sr. V.P., Marketing	Karrie Yager
Vice President, Broadcasting and Blues Alumni	Bruce Affleck
Vice President, Public Relations	Mike Caruso
Vice President, Suite Sales	Chris Diiorio
Vice President, Corporate and Sponsorship Sales	Bryan Lucas
Vice President, Entertainment and Event Mktg.	Mark Tamar
Exec. Asst. to the President and G.M.	Donna Lembke
Exec. Asst. to the CEO, St. Louis Blues Enterprises	Amber Daniels
Exec. Asst. to the Chief Marketing Officer	Liz Holcomb

Hockey Operations

Director, Player Personnel	Dave Taylor
Senior Consultant	Larry Pleau
Assistant G.M./Director, Pro Scouting/Peoria G.M.	Kevin McDonald
Director, Amateur Scouting	Bill Armstrong
Head Coach	Davis Payne
Assistant Coaches	Ray Bennett, Scott Mellanby, Brad Shaw
Goaltending Coach	Corey Hirsch
Strength and Conditioning Coach	Nelson Ayotte
Video Coach	Scott Masters
Director, Hockey Administration	Ryan Miller
Director, Media Relations	Rich Jankowski
Coordinator, Media Relations	Dan O'Neill

Scouting

Professional Scouts	Rob DiMaio, Tony Feltrin, Jan Vopat
Part-Time Professional Scout	Wayne Mundey
Amateur Scouts	Mike Antonovich, Marshall Davidson, Dan Ginnell, J Niemiec, Ville Siren
Part-Time Amateur Scouts	Thomas Carlsson, Vladimir Havluj, Jr., Basil McRae, Rick Meagher, Blair Nicholson, Michel Picard

Training

Athletic Trainer	Ray Barile
Assistant Athletic Trainer	Mike Hannegan
Equipment Manager / Asst. Manager	Bert Godin / Joel Farnsworth
Assistant, Equipment / Strength & Conditioning	Ray Halle / Jon Benne
Massage Therapist	Jeff Wright

Medical

Orthopedic Surgeons	Drs. Jerome Gilden, Matt Matava, Rick Wright
Internists	Drs. Aaron Birenbaum, Dr. William Birenbaum
Neurosurgeon	Dr. Ralph Dacey
General / Plastic Surgeons	Dr. Michael Brunt / Dr. Tom Francel
Dentist / Oral Surgeon	Dr. Glenn Edwards / Dr. Ken Kram
Ophthalmologist / Optometrist	Dr. Gill Grand / Dr. David Seibel

Broadcasting

Radio / Television Stations	KMOX, 1120 AM / FS Midwest
Radio Play-by-play / Color & Comm. Relations	Chris Kerber / Kelly Chase
Community Relations and KMOX Radio	Bob Plager
Television Play-by-Play / Color	John Kelly / Darren Pang, Bernie Federko
FS Midwest Analyst / Host	Jim Hayes / Pat Parris

Marketing

Senior Director, Advertising/Promotions	Lisa Kampeter
Senior Director, Digital Media	Beth Schwartz
Director, Event Presentation	Chris Frome
Director, Community Relations/14 Fund	Renah Jones
Manager, Event Marketing / Website	Lamont Buford / Chris Pinkert

Sponsorship

Director, Sponsorship Sales	Deni Allen
Corporate Sales Executive	Matt Poling
Sr. Director, Corporate Sponsorship Services	Julie Drochelman
Marketing/Sponsorship Assistant	Donna Ferguson

Ticket Sales

Director, Client Services	Abby Jones
Managers, Ticket Sales / Suite Sales	Yancey Jones / Nick Wierciak
Coordinator, Suite Sales	Melissa Weissman

Group Ticket Sales

Senior Director, Group Sales	Jennifer Nevins
Manager, Group Sales	Kari Takmajian

Finance

Finance Controller	Keith Hegger
Managers, Accounting	Craig Bryant, Mike Tonjes
Manager, IT	Tony Kostansek

Retail

Director, Retail	George Pavlik
Manager, Retail	Barry Smith

Box Office

Manager, Ticket Operations	Kerry Emerson

San Jose Sharks

Key Off-Season Signings/Acquisitions

2010

June 24 • Re-signed C **Patrick Marleau** and C **Joe Pavelski**.

26 • Re-signed C **Scott Nichol** and D **Niclas Wallin**.

July 1 • Signed G **Antero Niittymaki**.

7 • Re-signed D **Jay Leach**.

29 • Re-signed D **Jason Demers**.

31 • Re-signed RW **Devin Setoguchi**

Aug. 4 • Signed RW **Jamal Mayers**.

5 • Re-signed D **Derek Joslin**.

2009-10 Results: 51w-20L-5oTL-6soL 113pts.
First, Pacific Division

Year-by-Year Record

Season	GP	Home				Road				Overall							Finished	Playoff Result
		W	L	T	OL	W	L	T	OL	W	L	T	OL	GF	GA	Pts.		
2009-10	82	27	6	....	8	24	14	....	3	51	20	....	11	264	215	113	1st, Pacific Div.	Lost Conf. Championship
2008-09	82	32	5	....	4	21	13	....	7	53	18	....	11	257	204	117	1st, Pacific Div.	Lost Conf. Quarter-Final
2007-08	82	22	13	....	6	27	10	....	4	49	23	....	10	222	193	108	1st, Pacific Div.	Lost Conf. Semi-Final
2006-07	82	25	12	....	4	26	14	....	1	51	26	....	5	258	199	107	2nd, Pacific Div.	Lost Conf. Semi-Final
2005-06	82	25	9	....	7	19	18	....	4	44	27	....	11	266	242	99	2nd, Pacific Div.	Lost Conf. Semi-Final
2004-05																		
2003-04	82	24	8	7	2	19	13	5	4	43	21	12	6	219	183	104	1st, Pacific Div.	Lost Conf. Championship
2002-03	82	17	16	5	3	11	21	4	5	28	37	9	8	214	239	73	5th, Pacific Div.	Out of Playoffs
2001-02	82	25	11	3	2	19	16	5	1	44	27	8	3	248	199	99	1st, Pacific Div.	Lost Conf. Semi-Final
2000-01	82	22	14	4	1	18	13	8	2	40	27	12	3	217	192	95	2nd, Pacific Div.	Lost Conf. Quarter-Final
1999-2000	82	21	14	3	3	14	16	7	4	35	30	10	7	225	214	87	4th, Pacific Div.	Lost Conf. Semi-Final
1998-99	82	17	15	9	....	14	18	9	....	31	33	18	....	196	191	80	4th, Pacific Div.	Lost Conf. Quarter-Final
1997-98	82	17	19	5	....	17	19	5	....	34	38	10	....	210	216	78	4th, Pacific Div.	Lost Conf. Quarter-Final
1996-97	82	14	23	4	....	13	24	4	....	27	47	8	....	211	278	62	7th, Pacific Div.	Out of Playoffs
1995-96	82	12	26	3	....	8	29	4	....	20	55	7	....	252	357	47	7th, Pacific Div.	Out of Playoffs
1994-95	48	10	13	1	....	9	12	3	....	19	25	4	....	129	161	42	3rd, Pacific Div.	Lost Conf. Semi-Final
1993-94	84	19	13	10	....	14	22	6	....	33	35	16	....	252	265	82	3rd, Pacific Div.	Lost Conf. Semi-Final
1992-93	84	8	33	1	....	3	38	1	....	11	71	2	....	218	414	24	6th, Smythe Div.	Out of Playoffs
1991-92	80	14	23	3	....	3	35	2	....	17	58	5	....	219	359	39	6th, Smythe Div.	Out of Playoffs

2010-11 Schedule

Oct.	Fri.	8	Columbus†		Sat.	8	Nashville*
	Sat.	9	at Columbus†		Sun.	9	at Anaheim*
	Sat.	16	Atlanta		Tue.	11	Toronto
	Tue.	19	Carolina		Thu.	13	Edmonton
	Thu.	21	at Colorado		Sat.	15	St. Louis
	Sat.	23	at Edmonton		Mon.	17	at Phoenix*
	Sun.	24	at Calgary		Thu.	20	at Vancouver
	Wed.	27	New Jersey		Sat.	22	Minnesota
	Sat.	30	Anaheim		Wed.	26	at Los Angeles
Nov.	Tue.	2	at Minnesota	Feb.	Tue.	1	Phoenix
	Thu.	4	at St. Louis		Wed.	2	at Anaheim
	Sat.	6	Tampa Bay		Sat.	5	at Boston*
	Tue.	9	Anaheim		Tue.	8	at Washington
	Thu.	11	NY Islanders		Wed.	9	at Columbus
	Sat.	13	Calgary		Fri.	11	at New Jersey
	Mon.	15	Los Angeles		Sun.	13	at Florida*
	Wed.	17	at Colorado		Tue.	15	at Nashville
	Thu.	18	at Dallas		Thu.	17	Washington
	Sat.	20	Columbus		Sat.	19	Colorado
	Wed.	24	Chicago		Tue.	22	at Detroit
	Fri.	26	at Vancouver		Wed.	23	at Pittsburgh
	Sat.	27	at Edmonton		Fri.	25	at Calgary
	Tue.	30	Detroit	Mar.	Tue.	1	Colorado
Dec.	Thu.	2	at Ottawa		Thu.	3	Detroit
	Sat.	4	at Montreal*		Sat.	5	Dallas
	Mon.	6	at Detroit		Tue.	8	Nashville
	Wed.	8	at Philadelphia		Thu.	10	Vancouver
	Thu.	9	at Buffalo		Sat.	12	NY Rangers
	Sat.	11	Chicago		Mon.	14	at Chicago
	Mon.	13	Dallas		Tue.	15	at Dallas
	Wed.	15	at Nashville		Thu.	17	Minnesota
	Thu.	16	at Dallas		Sat.	19	St. Louis
	Sat.	18	at St. Louis		Wed.	23	Calgary
	Tue.	21	Edmonton		Thu.	24	at Los Angeles
	Thu.	23	Phoenix		Sat.	26	at Phoenix
	Mon.	27	Los Angeles		Thu.	31	Dallas
	Wed.	29	at Minnesota	Apr.	Sat.	2	Anaheim
	Thu.	30	at Chicago		Mon.	4	Los Angeles
Jan.	Sat.	1	at Los Angeles		Wed.	6	at Anaheim
	Mon.	3	Vancouver		Fri.	8	at Phoenix
	Thu.	6	Buffalo		Sat.	9	Phoenix

* Denotes afternoon game.   † Games played in Stockholm, SE.

Joe Thornton scored 20 goals in 2009-10 to reach that plateau for the tenth straight season. His 69 assists were second in the NHL behind league scoring leader Henrik Sedin.

PACIFIC DIVISION
20th NHL Season

Franchise date: May 9, 1990

2010-11 Player Personnel

FORWARDS	HT	WT	S	Place of Birth	*Age	2009-10 Club
CLOWE, Ryane	6-2	225	L	St. John's, Nfld.	28	San Jose
COUTURE, Logan	6-1	195	L	Guelph, Ont.	21	San Jose-Worcester
DESJARDINS, Andrew	6-1	200	R	Lively, Ont.	24	Worcester
FERRIERO, Benn	5-11	195	R	Boston, MA	23	San Jose-Worcester
HEATLEY, Dany	6-4	220	L	Freiburg, West Germany	29	San Jose
HENDERSON, Kevin	6-3	210	L	Toronto, Ont.	23	Worcester
LUCIA, Tony	6-0	180	L	Wayzata, MN	23	U. of Minnesota-Worcester
MacINTYRE, Cam	6-1	225	R	Sooke, B.C.	25	Princeton
MARCOU, James	5-8	165	R	Huntington, NY	22	Massachusetts-Worcester
MARLEAU, Patrick	6-2	220	L	Aneroid, Sask.	31	San Jose
MASHINTER, Brandon	6-4	235	L	Bradford, Ont.	22	Worcester
MAYERS, Jamal	6-1	215	R	Toronto, Ont.	35	Toronto-Calgary
McCARTHY, John	6-1	200	L	Boston, MA	24	San Jose-Worcester
McGINN, Jamie	6-1	200	L	Fergus, Ont.	22	San Jose-Worcester
McLAREN, Frazer	6-5	250	L	Winnipeg, Man.	22	San Jose-Worcester
MITCHELL, Torrey	5-11	190	R	Montreal, Que.	25	San Jose-Worcester
NICHOL, Scott	5-9	180	R	Edmonton, Alta.	35	San Jose
PAVELSKI, Joe	5-11	195	R	Plover, WI	26	San Jose
SETOGUCHI, Devin	6-0	200	R	Taber, Alta.	23	San Jose
THORNTON, Joe	6-4	235	L	London, Ont.	31	San Jose
TREVELYAN, T.J.	5-9	180	L	Mississauga, Ont.	26	Worcester
VIEDENSKY, Marek	6-4	195	R	Handlova, Czechoslovakia	20	Prince George-Saskatoon
WINGELS, Tommy	6-0	195	R	Evanston, IL	22	Miami U.
ZALEWSKI, Steven	6-0	195	L	Utica, NY	24	San Jose-Worcester
DEFENSEMEN						
BOYLE, Dan	5-11	190	R	Ottawa, Ont.	34	San Jose
BRAUN, Justin	6-2	205	R	St. Paul, MN	23	Massachusetts-Worcester
DEMERS, Jason	6-1	195	R	Dorval, Que.	22	San Jose-Worcester
DOHERTY, Taylor	6-7	235	R	Cambridge, Ont.	19	Kingston
HUSKINS, Kent	6-4	205	L	Ottawa, Ont.	31	San Jose
IRWIN, Matt	6-2	205	L	Brentwood Bay, B.C.	22	Massachusetts-Worcester
JOSLIN, Derek	6-1	200	L	Richmond Hill, Ont.	23	San Jose-Worcester
LEACH, Jay	6-4	220	L	Syracuse, NY	31	Lowell-Montreal-San Jose
LOPRIENO, Joe	6-3	225	R	Bloomingdale, IL	23	Worcester
MOORE, Mike	6-1	200	L	Calgary, Alta.	25	Worcester
MURRAY, Douglas	6-3	240	L	Bromma, Sweden	30	San Jose
PETRECKI, Nicholas	6-3	230	L	Schenectady, NY	21	Worcester
SCHAUS, Nick	5-11	200	R	Orchard Park, NY	24	U. Mass-Lowell-Worcester
SULLIVAN, Sean	6-0	190	L	Boston, MA	26	San Antonio
VLASIC, Marc-Edouard	6-1	200	L	Montreal, Que.	23	San Jose
WALLIN, Niclas	6-3	220	L	Boden, Sweden	35	Carolina-San Jose
GOALTENDERS	**HT**	**WT**	**C**	**Place of Birth**	***Age**	**2009-10 Club**
GREISS, Thomas	6-1	210	L	Straubing, West Germany	24	San Jose
HEEMSKERK, Thomas	6-0	185	L	Chilliwack, B.C.	20	Everett
HUTTON, Carter	6-1	195	L	Thunder Bay, Ont.	24	U. Mass-Lowell-Adirondack
NIITTYMAKI, Antero	6-1	190	L	Turku, Finland	30	Tampa Bay
SATERI, Harri	6-1	210	L	Toijala, Finland	20	Tappara
SEXSMITH, Tyson	5-11	210	L	Calgary, Alta.	21	Worcester-Kalamazoo
STALOCK, Alex	6-0	180	L	St. Paul, MN	23	Worcester

* – Age at start of 2010-11 season

Todd McLellan

Head Coach

Born: Melville, Sask., October 3, 1967.

The San Jose Sharks introduced Todd McLellan as their new head coach on June 12, 2008. In his first season behind the bench in 2008-09, San Jose set new club records with 53 wins and 117 points and won the Presidents' Trophy for the first time. The Sharks won a second-straight Pacific Division title in 2009-10 and reached the Western Conference Final for just the second time in team history.

Prior to joining the Sharks, McLellan had captured the 2008 Stanley Cup in his third season as an assistant coach under Mike Babcock with the Detroit Red Wings. Over the course of those three seasons, the Red Wings won the Presidents' Trophy as the NHL's top regular season team twice. One of McLellan's key responsibilities was working with the Detroit power play, which finished third in the NHL in 2007-08 (20.7%) and first in 2005-06 (22.1%).

Prior to being hired in Detroit, McLellan spent four seasons as head coach of the Houston Aeros in the American Hockey League, including capturing the 2003 AHL Calder Cup championship. He also was selected to coach in two AHL All-Star Games during his tenure with Houston. In 2000-01, he served as the head coach of the Cleveland Lumberjacks of the International Hockey League.

From 1994-95 through 1999-2000, McLellan coached the Swift Current Broncos of the Western Hockey League, where he also served as general manager in his final four WHL seasons. He was named WHL coach of the year in 2000 and WHL executive of the year in 1997. In his 14 years of serving as a head and assistant coach prior to arriving in San Jose, McLellan's teams never missed the postseason.

McLellan played his junior hockey with Saskatoon (WHL) and was drafted by the New York Islanders in the fifth round (104th overall) in the 1986 NHL Entry Draft. He played parts of two seasons with Springfield in the American Hockey League and played in five games with the Islanders in 1987-88, posting two points (one goal, one assist) before a shoulder injury ended his NHL career.

Coaching Record

			Regular Season				Playoffs			
Season	Team	League	GC	W	L	O/T	GC	W	L	T
1994-95	Swift Current	WHL	72	31	34	7	6	2	4	....
1995-96	Swift Current	WHL	72	36	31	5	6	2	4	....
1996-97	Swift Current	WHL	72	44	23	5	10	4	4	....
1997-98	Swift Current	WHL	72	44	19	9	12	7	5	....
1998-99	Swift Current	WHL	72	34	32	6	6	2	4	....
99-2000	Swift Current	WHL	72	47	18	7	12	6	6	....
2000-01	Cleveland	IHL	82	43	32	7	4	0	4	....
2001-02	Houston	AHL	80	39	26	15	14	8	6	....
2002-03	Houston	AHL	80	47	23	10	23	15	8	....
2003-04	Houston	AHL	80	28	34	18	2	0	2	....
2004-05	Houston	AHL	80	40	28	12	5	1	4	....
2008-09	**San Jose**	**NHL**	**82**	**53**	**18**	**11**	**6**	**2**	**4**	....
2009-10	**San Jose**	**NHL**	**82**	**51**	**20**	**11**	**15**	**8**	**7**	....
	NHL Totals		**164**	**104**	**38**	**22**	**21**	**10**	**11**	....

2009-10 Scoring

* – rookie

Regular Season

Pos	#	Player	Team	GP	G	A	Pts	TOI	+/–	PIM	PP	SH	GW	S	%
C	19	Joe Thornton	S.J.	79	20	69	89	19:51	17	54	4	1	2	141	14.2
C	12	Patrick Marleau	S.J.	82	44	39	83	21:12	21	22	12	4	6	274	16.1
L	15	Dany Heatley	S.J.	82	39	43	82	20:13	14	54	18	1	9	280	13.9
D	22	Dan Boyle	S.J.	76	15	43	58	26:12	6	70	6	0	3	180	8.3
L	29	Ryane Clowe	S.J.	82	19	38	57	17:10	0	131	2	0	2	189	10.1
C	8	Joe Pavelski	S.J.	67	25	26	51	19:28	1	26	3	1	5	228	11.0
R	16	Devin Setoguchi	S.J.	70	20	16	36	15:17	0	19	8	0	4	165	12.1
C	27	Manny Malhotra	S.J.	71	14	19	33	15:37	17	41	2	0	4	111	12.6
D	4	Rob Blake	S.J.	70	7	23	30	21:21	14	60	4	0	1	182	3.8
D	40	Kent Huskins	S.J.	82	3	19	22	17:29	6	47	0	0	0	47	6.4
D	60 *	Jason Demers	S.J.	51	4	17	21	15:25	5	21	3	0	1	52	7.7
R	41	Jed Ortmeyer	S.J.	76	8	11	19	11:30	4	37	0	0	1	131	6.1
C	21	Scott Nichol	S.J.	79	4	15	19	13:03	0	72	0	1	0	93	4.3
D	3	Douglas Murray	S.J.	79	4	13	17	20:20	3	66	1	0	1	85	4.7
D	44	Marc-Edouard Vlasic	S.J.	64	3	13	16	22:05	21	33	1	0	0	74	4.1
L	64	Jamie McGinn	S.J.	59	10	3	13	9:59	–3	38	0	0	2	76	13.2
C	17	Torrey Mitchell	S.J.	56	2	9	11	11:25	6	27	0	0	0	59	3.4
C	39 *	Logan Couture	S.J.	25	5	4	9	10:15	4	6	1	0	1	42	11.9
D	7	Niclas Wallin	CAR	47	0	5	5	17:47	–5	26	0	0	0	50	0.0
			S.J.	23	0	2	2	16:22	0	23	0	0	0	22	0.0
			Total	70	0	7	7	17:19	–5	49	0	0	0	72	0.0
R	59	Brad Staubitz	S.J.	47	3	3	6	6:12	0	110	0	0	1	24	12.5
L	68 *	Frazer McLaren	S.J.	23	1	5	6	6:02	6	54	0	0	0	13	7.7
R	53	Ryan Vesce	S.J.	9	3	2	5	10:57	–1	0	0	0	1	20	15.0
C	78 *	Benn Ferriero	S.J.	24	2	3	5	11:08	4	8	0	0	0	42	4.8
D	65 *	Derek Joslin	S.J.	24	0	3	3	13:52	1	12	0	0	0	19	0.0
D	28	Jay Leach	MTL	7	0	0	0	13:02	0	5	0	0	0	4	0.0
			S.J.	28	1	1	2	15:11	3	20	0	0	0	26	3.8
			Total	35	1	1	2	14:45	3	25	0	0	0	30	3.3
C	36	Dwight Helminen	S.J.	4	1	0	1	10:59	–1	0	0	0	0	1	100.0
D	47	Joe Callahan	S.J.	1	0	1	1	9:34	1	0	0	0	0	0	0.0
C	48 *	Steven Zalewski	S.J.	3	0	0	0	8:19	–2	0	0	0	0	3	0.0
L	43 *	John McCarthy	S.J.	4	0	0	0	9:07	–3	0	0	0	0	3	0.0

Goaltending

No.	Goaltender	GPI	Mins	Avg	W	L	OT	EN	SO	GA	SA	S%	G	A	PIM
20	Evgeni Nabokov	71	4194	2.43	44	16	10	2	3	170	2168	.922	0	0	6
1	* Thomas Greiss	16	782	2.69	7	4	1	2	0	35	399	.912	0	0	2
	Totals	**82**	**4998**	**2.51**	**51**	**20**	**11**	**4**	**3**	**209**	**2571**	**.919**			

Playoffs

Pos	#	Player	Team	GP	G	A	Pts	TOI	+/–	PIM	PP	SH	GW	OT	S	%
C	8	Joe Pavelski	S.J.	15	9	8	17	21:31	6	6	5	0	3	1	65	13.8
D	22	Dan Boyle	S.J.	15	2	12	14	27:10	–1	8	1	0	0	0	47	4.3
C	12	Patrick Marleau	S.J.	14	8	5	13	22:06	–3	8	3	1	2	1	56	14.3
L	15	Dany Heatley	S.J.	14	2	11	13	20:41	–7	16	1	0	0	0	45	4.4
C	19	Joe Thornton	S.J.	15	3	9	12	21:19	–11	18	1	0	1	0	35	8.6
L	29	Ryane Clowe	S.J.	15	2	8	10	20:10	4	28	0	0	0	0	42	4.8
R	16	Devin Setoguchi	S.J.	15	5	4	9	18:25	3	6	1	0	1	1	58	8.6
D	3	Douglas Murray	S.J.	15	1	6	7	20:20	–1	8	0	0	0	0	14	7.1
D	60 *	Jason Demers	S.J.	15	1	4	5	11:10	0	8	1	0	0	0	12	8.3
C	39 *	Logan Couture	S.J.	15	4	0	4	11:23	1	4	0	0	1	0	18	22.2
D	44	Marc-Edouard Vlasic	S.J.	15	0	3	3	21:53	0	4	0	0	0	0	15	0.0
D	4	Rob Blake	S.J.	15	1	1	2	23:20	0	10	0	0	0	0	38	2.6
C	21	Scott Nichol	S.J.	15	1	1	2	8:54	–1	17	0	0	0	0	21	4.8
C	17	Torrey Mitchell	S.J.	15	0	2	2	13:05	–5	2	0	0	0	0	21	0.0
C	36	Dwight Helminen	S.J.	7	1	0	1	6:01	0	4	0	0	0	0	5	20.0
C	27	Manny Malhotra	S.J.	15	1	0	1	16:55	–1	0	1	0	0	0	37	2.7
R	41	Jed Ortmeyer	S.J.	4	0	1	1	6:58	–1	0	0	0	0	0	2	0.0
D	7	Niclas Wallin	S.J.	6	0	0	0	11:17	–3	2	0	0	0	0	2	0.0
D	40	Kent Huskins	S.J.	15	0	0	0	12:47	–5	6	0	0	0	0	3	0.0
L	64	Jamie McGinn	S.J.	15	0	0	0	7:45	1	8	0	0	0	0	11	0.0

Goaltending

No.	Goaltender	GPI	Mins	Avg	W	L	EN	SO	GA	SA	S%	G	A	PIM
20	Evgeni Nabokov	15	890	2.56	8	7	1	1	38	407	.907	0	0	0
1	* Thomas Greiss	1	40	3.00	0	0	0	0	2	28	.929	0	0	0
	Totals	**15**	**936**	**2.63**	**8**	**7**	**1**	**1**	**41**	**436**	**.906**			

General Managers' History

Jack Ferreira, 1991-92; Chuck Grillo (V.P. Director of Player Personnel), 1992-93 to 1995-96; Dean Lombardi, 1996-97 to 2002-03; Doug Wilson, 2003-04 to date.

Coaching History

George Kingston, 1991-92, 1992-93; Kevin Constantine, 1993-94, 1994-95; Kevin Constantine and Jim Wiley, 1995-96; Al Sims, 1996-97; Darryl Sutter, 1997-98 to 2001-02; Darryl Sutter, Cap Raeder and Ron Wilson, 2002-03; Ron Wilson, 2003-04 to 2007-08; Todd McLellan, 2008-09 to date.

Club Records

Team

(Figures in brackets for season records are games played; records for fewest points, wins, ties, losses, goals, goals against are for 70 or more games)

Most Points	117	2008-09 (82)
Most Wins	53	2008-09 (82)
Most Ties	18	1998-99 (82)
Most Losses	*71	1992-93 (84)
Most Goals	266	2005-06 (82)
Most Goals Against	414	1992-93 (84)
Fewest Points	24	1992-93 (84)
Fewest Wins	11	1992-93 (84)
Fewest Ties	*2	1992-93 (84)
Fewest Losses	18	2008-09 (82)
Fewest Goals	196	1998-99 (82)
Fewest Goals Against	183	2003-04 (82)

Longest Winning Streak

Overall	11	Feb. 21-Mar. 14/08
Home	9	Oct. 9-Nov. 8/08
Away	10	Nov. 14-Dec. 31/07

Longest Undefeated Streak

Overall	10	Nov. 27-Dec. 19/01 (9 wins, 1 tie)
Home	11	Nov. 15-Dec. 29/03 (8 wins, 3 ties)
Away	10	Dec. 26/00-Feb. 16/01 (6 wins, 4 ties)

Longest Losing Streak

Overall	*17	Jan. 4-Feb. 12/93
Home	9	Nov. 19-Dec. 19/92
Away	19	Nov. 27/92-Feb. 12/93

Longest Winless Streak

Overall	20	Dec. 29/92-Feb. 12/93 (19 losses, 1 tie)
Home	9	Nov. 19-Dec. 19/92 (9 losses), Oct. 16-Nov. 18/03 (4 losses, 5 ties)
Away	19	Nov. 27/92-Feb. 12/93 (19 losses)

Most Shutouts, Season	11	2003-04 (82), 2006-07 (82)
Most PIM, Season	2,134	1992-93 (84)
Most Goals, Game	10	Jan. 13/96 (S.J. 10 at Pit. 8), Mar. 30/02 (CBJ 2 at S.J. 10)

Individual

Most Seasons	12	Patrick Marleau
Most Games, Career	953	Patrick Marleau
Most Goals, Career	320	Patrick Marleau
Most Assists, Career	373	Patrick Marleau
Most Points, Career	693	Patrick Marleau (320G, 373A)
Most PIM, Career	1,001	Jeff Odgers
Most Shutouts, Career	50	Evgeni Nabokov
Longest Consecutive Games Streak	379	Joe Thornton (Dec. 1/05-Mar. 27/10)
Most Goals, Season	56	Jonathan Cheechoo (2005-06)
Most Assists, Season	92	Joe Thornton (2006-07)

Most Points, Season	114	Joe Thornton (2006-07; 22G, 92A)
Most PIM, Season	326	Link Gaetz (1991-92)
Most Points, Defenseman, Season	64	Sandis Ozolinsh (1993-94; 26G, 38A)
Most Points, Center, Season	114	Joe Thornton (2006-07; 22G, 92A)
Most Points, Right Wing, Season	93	Jonathan Cheechoo (2005-06; 56G, 37A)
Most Points, Left Wing, Season	83	Patrick Marleau (2009-10; 44G, 39A)
Most Points, Rookie, Season	59	Pat Falloon (1991-92; 25G, 34A)
Most Shutouts, Season	9	Evgeni Nabokov (2003-04)
Most Goals, Game	4	Owen Nolan (Dec. 19/95)
Most Assists, Game	4	Eighteen times
Most Points, Game	6	Owen Nolan (Oct. 4/99; 3G, 3A)

* NHL Record.

Captains' History

Doug Wilson, 1991-92, 1992-93; Bob Errey, 1993-94; Bob Errey and Jeff Odgers, 1994-95; Jeff Odgers, 1995-96; Todd Gill, 1996-97, 1997-98; Owen Nolan, 1998-99 to 2002-03; Mike Ricci, Vincent Damphousse, Alyn McCauley, Patrick Marleau, 2003-04; Patrick Marleau, 2005-06 to 2008-09; Rob Blake, 2009-10.

All-time Record vs. Other Clubs

Regular Season

	At Home								On Road								Total							
	GP	W	L	T	OL	GF	GA	PTS	GP	W	L	T	OL	GF	GA	PTS	GP	W	L	T	OL	GF	GA	PTS
Anaheim	48	23	21	2	2	132	126	50	48	27	15	2	4	144	126	60	96	50	36	4	6	276	252	110
Atlanta	6	5	0	1	0	24	11	11	6	4	1	1	0	20	11	10	12	9	0	2	1	44	22	21
Boston	13	4	6	2	1	32	42	11	12	2	7	3	0	37	43	7	25	6	13	5	1	69	85	18
Buffalo	12	6	2	4	0	42	42	16	14	1	12	0	1	38	61	3	26	7	14	4	1	80	103	19
Calgary	44	18	20	4	2	137	126	42	42	14	23	4	1	114	146	33	86	32	43	8	3	251	272	75
Carolina	13	8	4	0	1	57	38	17	13	6	7	0	0	32	41	12	26	14	11	0	1	89	79	29
Chicago	36	20	11	3	2	105	98	45	35	17	12	2	4	113	107	40	71	37	23	5	6	218	205	85
Colorado	34	15	18	1	0	96	112	31	33	10	17	4	2	72	116	26	67	25	35	5	2	168	228	57
Columbus	18	17	0	0	1	71	29	35	18	8	8	0	2	36	46	18	36	25	8	0	3	107	75	53
Dallas	48	18	22	1	7	112	132	44	47	21	21	4	1	115	131	47	95	39	43	5	8	227	263	91
Detroit	36	14	18	3	1	126	138	32	35	5	26	1	3	60	136	14	71	19	44	4	4	186	274	46
Edmonton	42	21	13	5	3	141	121	50	43	12	22	7	2	100	138	33	85	33	35	12	5	241	259	83
Florida	11	6	2	2	1	34	22	15	11	3	3	5	0	32	30	11	22	9	5	7	1	66	52	26
Los Angeles	55	33	17	3	2	183	150	71	55	23	26	4	2	150	159	52	110	56	43	7	4	333	309	123
Minnesota	18	10	5	1	2	51	38	23	18	11	4	1	2	48	41	25	36	21	9	2	4	99	79	48
Montreal	13	7	3	2	1	42	34	17	13	2	9	2	0	24	45	6	26	9	12	4	1	66	79	23
Nashville	22	14	5	1	2	67	57	31	22	10	10	1	1	60	57	22	44	24	15	2	3	127	114	53
New Jersey	12	4	6	1	1	29	36	10	14	4	8	1	1	31	53	10	26	8	14	2	2	60	89	20
NY Islanders	14	7	5	1	1	37	43	16	13	5	6	2	0	41	44	12	27	12	11	3	1	78	87	28
NY Rangers	15	3	10	2	0	35	54	8	12	3	7	1	1	37	46	8	27	6	17	3	1	72	100	16
Ottawa	11	7	4	0	0	26	20	14	11	3	4	4	0	30	37	10	22	10	8	4	0	56	57	24
Philadelphia	15	6	7	2	0	39	39	14	14	6	6	2	0	41	44	14	29	12	13	4	0	80	83	28
Phoenix	50	25	16	4	5	163	140	59	53	24	24	3	2	150	158	53	103	49	40	7	7	313	298	112
Pittsburgh	16	8	6	2	0	44	57	18	11	5	4	1	1	35	44	12	27	13	10	3	1	79	101	30
St. Louis	34	11	19	1	3	84	108	26	38	17	18	1	2	99	113	37	72	28	37	2	5	183	221	63
Tampa Bay	12	5	6	1	0	42	38	11	15	6	7	1	1	40	39	14	27	11	13	2	1	82	77	25
Toronto	17	7	7	3	0	40	44	17	20	6	12	2	0	55	75	14	37	13	19	5	0	95	119	31
Vancouver	44	20	17	5	2	131	126	47	42	16	21	4	1	116	142	37	86	36	38	9	3	247	268	84
Washington	13	9	3	1	0	45	31	19	14	8	6	0	0	40	40	16	27	17	9	1	0	85	71	35
Totals	**722**	**351**	**273**	**58**	**40**	**2167**	**2052**	**800**	**722**	**279**	**345**	**63**	**35**	**1910**	**2269**	**656**	**1444**	**630**	**618**	**121**	**75**	**4077**	**4321**	**1456**

Playoffs

	Series	W	L	GP	W	L	T	GF	GA	Last Mtg.
Anaheim	1	0	1	6	2	4	0	10	18	2009
Calgary	3	2	1	20	10	10	0	57	68	2008
Chicago	1	0	1	4	0	4	0	7	13	2010
Colorado	4	2	2	25	13	12	0	71	62	2010
Dallas	3	0	3	17	5	12	0	30	46	2008
Detroit	4	2	2	22	10	12	0	54	81	2010
Edmonton	1	0	1	6	2	4	0	12	19	2006
Nashville	2	2	0	10	8	2	0	33	24	2007
Phoenix	1	1	0	5	4	1	0	13	7	2002
St. Louis	3	2	1	18	10	8	0	43	47	2004
Toronto	1	0	1	7	3	4	0	21	26	1994
Totals	**24**	**11**	**13**	**140**	**67**	**73**	**0**	**348**	**411**	

Playoff Results 2010-2006

Year	Round	Opponent	Result	GF	GA
2010	CF	Chicago	L 0-4	7	13
	CSF	Detroit	W 4-1	15	17
	CQF	Colorado	W 4-2	19	11
2009	CQF	Anaheim	L 2-4	10	18
2008	CSF	Dallas	L 2-4	11	15
	CQF	Calgary	W 4-3	19	17
2007	CSF	Detroit	L 2-4	9	13
	CQF	Nashville	W 4-1	16	14
2006	CSF	Edmonton	L 2-4	12	19
	CQF	Nashville	W 4-1	17	10

Abbreviations: Round: CF – conference final; **CSF** – conference semi-final; **CQF** – conference quarter-final.

Carolina totals include Hartford, 1991-92 to 1996-97.
Dallas totals include Minnesota North Stars, 1991-92 to 1992-93.
Colorado totals include Quebec, 1991-92 to 1994-95.
Phoenix totals include Winnipeg, 1991-92 to 1995-96.

2009-10 Results

Oct.	1	at Colorado	2-5	Jan.	2	Edmonton	4-1
	3	at Anaheim	4-1		4	Los Angeles	2-6
	6	at Los Angeles	4-6		6	St. Louis	2-1*
	8	Columbus	6-3		9	Detroit	1-4
	10	Minnesota	4-2		11	at Los Angeles	2-1
	12	Phoenix	0-1†		12	at Phoenix	3-1
	15	at Washington	4-1		14	Boston	1-2†
	17	at NY Islanders	4-1		16	Edmonton	4-2
	19	at NY Rangers	7-3		18	Calgary	9-1
	22	at Tampa Bay	2-5		19	at Los Angeles	5-1
	24	at Atlanta	4-3		21	Anaheim	3-1
	25	at Philadelphia	4-1		23	Buffalo	5-2
	28	Los Angeles	2-1†		28	Chicago	3-4*
	30	Colorado	3-1		30	Minnesota	5-2
Nov.	1	at Carolina	5-1	Feb.	2	Detroit	2-4
	4	at Columbus	3-2†		3	at St. Louis	4-2
	5	at Detroit	1-2†		6	at Nashville	4-3
	7	Pittsburgh	5-0		8	at Toronto	3-2
	10	Nashville	4-3		10	at Columbus	0-3
	12	Dallas	2-3†		11	at Detroit	3-2†
	14	at St. Louis	3-1		13	at Buffalo	1-3
	15	at Chicago	3-4*	Mar.	2	New Jersey	3-4
	17	at Nashville	3-4		4	Montreal	3-2
	20	Philadelphia	6-3		6	Columbus	2-1
	21	at Anaheim	3-2		11	Nashville	8-5
	25	Chicago	2-7		13	Florida	2-3*
	27	at Edmonton	5-4†		14	at Anaheim	2-4
	29	at Vancouver	3-2		16	at Dallas	2-8
Dec.	1	Ottawa	5-2		18	at Vancouver	2-3
	3	St. Louis	2-3†		19	at Calgary	3-4
	5	Calgary	1-2		21	at Edmonton	1-5
	9	Los Angeles	4-5*		23	at Minnesota	4-1
	11	Dallas	2-3†		25	Dallas	3-0
	12	at Phoenix	1-2		27	Vancouver	4-2
	17	Anaheim	4-1		28	Colorado	4-3
	21	at Dallas	4-2		31	at Dallas	1-5
	22	at Chicago	3-2	Apr.	2	at Minnesota	3-2
	26	Anaheim	5-2		4	at Colorado	4-5*
	28	Phoenix	3-2†		6	at Calgary	2-1
	30	Washington	3-2†		8	Vancouver	4-2
	31	at Phoenix	3-2†		10	Phoenix	3-2†

* – Overtime   † – Shootout

Entry Draft Selections 2010-1996

Name in bold denotes played in NHL.

2010
Pick
28 Charlie Coyle
88 Max Gaede
127 Cody Ferriero
129 Freddie Hamilton
136 Isaac MacLeod
163 Konrad Abeltshauser
188 Lee Moffie
200 Chris Crane

2009
Pick
43 William Wrenn
57 Taylor Doherty
147 Philip Varone
189 Marek Viedensky
207 Dominik Bielke

2008
Pick
62 Justin Daniels
92 Samuel Groulx
106 Harri Sateri
146 Julien Demers
177 Tommy Wingels
186 **Jason Demers**
194 Drew Daniels

2007
Pick
9 **Logan Couture**
28 Nicholas Petrecki
83 Timo Pielmeier
91 Tyson Sexsmith
165 Patrik Zackrisson
173 **Nick Bonino**
201 Justin Braun
203 **Frazer McLaren**

2006
Pick
16 **Ty Wishart**
36 **Jamie McGinn**
98 James Delory
143 Ashton Rome
202 **John McCarthy**
203 Jay Barriball

2005
Pick
8 **Devin Setoguchi**
35 **Marc-Edouard Vlasic**
112 Alex Stalock
140 Taylor Dakers
149 **Derek Joslin**
162 P.J. Fenton
183 Will Colbert
193 Tony Lucia

2004
Pick
22 **Lukas Kaspar**
94 **Thomas Greiss**
126 **Torrey Mitchell**
129 Jason Churchill
153 **Steven Zalewski**
201 **Michael Vernace**
225 David MacDonald
234 Derek MacIntyre
288 Brian Mahoney-Wilson
289 Christian Jensen

2003
Pick
6 **Milan Michalek**
16 **Steve Bernier**
43 **Josh Hennessy**
47 **Matt Carle**
139 Patrick Ehelechner
201 Jonathan Tremblay
205 **Joe Pavelski**
216 Kai Hospelt
236 Alexander Hult
267 Brian O'Hanley
276 Carter Lee

2002
Pick
27 Mike Morris
52 Dan Spang
86 Jonas Fiedler
139 **Kris Newbury**
163 Tom Walsh
217 **Tim Conboy**
288 Michael Hutchins

2001
Pick
20 **Marcel Goc**
106 **Christian Ehrhoff**
107 **Dimitri Patzold**
140 **Tomas Plihal**
175 **Ryane Clowe**
182 **Tom Cavanagh**

2000
Pick
41 Tero Maatta
104 **Jon DiSalvatore**
142 Michal Pinc
166 **Nolan Schaefer**
183 Michal Macho
246 **Chad Wiseman**
256 Pasi Saarinen

1999
Pick
14 **Jeff Jillson**
82 Mark Concannon
111 Willie Levesque
155 **Niko Dimitrakos**
229 Eric Betournay
241 **Douglas Murray**
257 **Hannes Hyvonen**

1998
Pick
3 **Brad Stuart**
29 **Jonathan Cheechoo**
65 Eric Laplante
98 **Rob Davison**
104 **Miroslav Zalesak**
127 Brandon Coalter
145 **Mikael Samuelsson**
185 Robert Mulick
212 **Jim Fahey**

1997
Pick
2 **Patrick Marleau**
23 **Scott Hannan**
82 Adam Colagiacomo
107 Adam Nittel
163 Joe Dusbabek
192 **Cam Severson**
219 **Mark Smith**

1996
Pick
2 **Andrei Zyuzin**
21 **Marco Sturm**
55 Terry Friesen
102 **Matt Bradley**
137 **Michel Larocque**
164 Jake Deadmarsh
191 Cory Cyrenne
217 David Thibeault

Doug Wilson

Executive Vice President and General Manager

Born: Ottawa, Ont., July 5, 1957.

Through strong drafting, shrewd trades and timely free agent signings, Executive Vice President and General Manager Doug Wilson has crafted one of the National Hockey League's most successful on-ice franchises since being named to his post prior to the 2003-04 season.

In his six seasons in charge of the Sharks hockey department, Wilson, who also serves as the team's alternate governor to the NHL, has guided the team to its most successful era since the franchise's inception, capturing the Presidents' Trophy (2009), four Pacific Division titles (2004, 2008, 2009, 2010) and advancing to the Western Conference Final in 2004 and 2010.

In his tenure as general manager, only the Detroit Red Wings have appeared in more Stanley Cup Playoff rounds (16) than San Jose (13).

During that same span, the Sharks rank second in regular season points (648, 291-135-66 record), second in wins among all National Hockey League teams and has nearly posted six consecutive 100-point seasons (2003-04 – 104; 2005-06 – 99; 2006-07 – 107; 2007-08 – 108, 2008-09 – 117, 2009-10 – 113), an average of 108 points per season.

In his current role, Wilson has overall authority regarding all hockey-related operations. He oversees all player personnel decisions, negotiates player contracts, coordinates the efforts of the team's scouting department, leads the team in its draft day preparation and administers the club's player evaluation process at all professional, minor and junior levels.

In his previous role as the team's director of pro development (1997-03), the 16-year NHL veteran's responsibilities included evaluating talent at all professional and minor league levels and continuous assessment of the Sharks roster and reserve list.

Working closely with the entire hockey department, Wilson played a major role in creating a positive atmosphere in the dressing room and on-the-ice attractiveness to obtaining and retaining veteran free agents such as Vincent Damphousse, Mike Ricci, Gary Suter, Scott Thornton and Mike Vernon.

Wilson was an integral member of the NHL Players' Association for four years (1993-97) and is a past president of the NHLPA.

Wilson has extensive experience in talent evaluation. He served as management consultant for four consecutive Canadian World Junior gold medal-winning teams in the 1990s.

Wilson draws on a vast amount of hockey knowledge and expertise throughout his on- and off-the-ice experiences. His older brother, Murray, played seven NHL seasons, capturing four Stanley Cup Championships with the Montreal Canadiens (1973, 1976-78). As a member of the Ontario Hockey League's Ottawa 67s, Wilson played for Hall of Famer Brian Kilrea, junior hockey's all-time winningest coach. During his tenure with the Chicago Blackhawks, he was a teammate of NHL legend Bobby Orr and a roommate with Hall of Famer Stan Mikita.

Selected sixth overall in 1977 by Chicago after a stellar junior career with the Ottawa 67s, Wilson played 14 seasons in Chicago and still ranks as the club's highest scoring defenseman in points (779 — fifth overall), goals (225 — 12th overall) and assists (554 — third overall). Wilson ranks fifth all-time in games played (938) for Chicago. In addition, he led all Blackhawks defensemen in scoring for 10 consecutive seasons (1980-81 through 1990-91) and captured the 1982 James Norris Memorial Trophy, symbolic of the League's top defenseman, when he tallied 39 goals and 85 points — still Blackhawks single-season records for goals and points for a defenseman.

Club Directory

HP Pavilion at San Jose

San Jose Sharks
HP Pavilion at San Jose
525 West Santa Clara Street
San Jose, CA 95113
Phone **408/287-7070**
FAX 408/999-5797
www.sjsharks.com
Capacity: 17,562

San Jose Sports and Entertainment Enterprises Ownership Group
Kevin Compton, Hasso Plattner, Stratton Sclavos, Gary Valenzuela, Gordon Russell, Rudy Staedler, Floyd Kvamme, Greg Jamison, Harvey Armstrong, Tom McEnery, George Gund III

Executive Staff

President, CEO, NHL Exec. Committee	Greg Jamison
Executive Vice President of Business Operations	Malcolm Bordelon
Executive V.P. and Chief Financial Officer	Charlie Faas
Executive V.P. and G.M. (HP Pavilion at San Jose)	Jim Goddard
Executive V.P. and General Counsel	Don Gralnek
Executive V.P. of Business Development	Michael T. Lehr
Executive V.P. and General Manager (Sharks)	Doug Wilson
Vice President of Finance	Ken Caveney
Vice President of Corporate Partnerships	Eric Mastalir
Vice President of Sales and Marketing	Kent Russell
Vice President of Building Operations	Rich Sotelo
Vice President and Assistant G.M. (Sharks)	Wayne Thomas
Executive Assistants	Tricia Sullivan-Minsky, Michelle Simmons, Misty Macias

Hockey Operations

Director, Hockey Operations	Joe Will
Head Coach	Todd McLellan
Assistant Coaches	Trent Yawney, Matt Shaw, Jay Woodcroft
Goaltending Development Coach	Corey Schwab
Development Coach	Mike Ricci
Coaching Staff Assistant	Brett Heimlich
Director, Scouting	Tim Burke
Director, Pro Scouting	John Ferguson
Scouts	Gilles Cote, Pat Funk, Jack Gardiner, Dirk Graham, Rob Grillo, Brian Gross, Shin Larsson, Bryan Marchment, Karel Masopust, Jason Rowe
Director, Hockey Administration	Rosemary Tebaldi
Manager of Hockey Technology	Paul Fink
Head Athletic Trainer	Ray Tufts, ATC
Assistant Athletic Trainer	Wes Howard, ATC
Strength and Conditioning Coordinator	Mike Potenza
Massage Therapist	Arnulfo Aguirre, CMT
Equipment Manager	Mike Aldrich
Assistant Equipment Manager	Vinny Ferraiuolo
Equip. Assistant and Equip. Transport	Roy Sneesby
Cleaning Specialist	Norma Hernandez
Team Physician	Arthur J. Ting, M.D.
Team Internists	Greg Whitley M.D., John Chiu, M.D.
Team Dentists	Don Goudy, D.D.S., Robert Bonahoom, D.D.S.
Team Vision Specialist	Vincent S. Zuccaro, O.D., F.A.A.O.
Medical Staff	Steve Franzino, M.D., Robert Millard, M.D., Mark Sontag, M.D.
Chiropractic Consultant	Mike McMurray, D. C.
Manual Therapy Consultant	Tobe Hanson

SVS&E Business Operations

Senior Director, Communications	Ken Arnold
Director, Broadcasting	Frank Albin
Director, Marketing	Doug Bentz
Director, Ticket Sales	John Castro
Director, Media Relations	Scott Emmert
Director, Event Presentation	Steve Maroni
Director, Suite Sales and Service	Bruce Ross
Director, Communications and Internet	Roger Ross
Director, Public Relations	Jim Sparaco
Senior Sales Managers, Corporate Partnerships	Jennifer Birmingham, Bryan Deierling
Senior Ticket Operations Manager	Scott Fitzsimmons
Senior Service Manager, Corporate Partnerships	Heather Hunter
Sales Managers, Corporate Partnerships	Darren O'Donnell, Kevin Hilton, Christina Carrdellio
Account Sales Managers	Ted Chuba, Mike Hollywood, Patrick Frost, Adam King
Account Service Managers	Sharon Holman, Sarah Bauerle, Julie Kennedy
Marketing Manager	Deanna Miller
Internet Services Manager	Alex Aragon
Fan Development Managers	Erin Buchanan, Jeff Cafuir
Creative Services Manager	Derik Green
Media Relations Manager	Tom Holy
Suite Sales and Service Managers	Chris Hutchins, Kathy Payne-Tovar
Sharks Foundation Manager	TBD
Mascot Operations Manager	Tim Patnode
Media Relations and Team Services Manager	Ryan Stenn
Service Managers, Corporate Partnerships	Jennifer De Carlo, Kristin Toth
Executive Assistant	Mary Grace Miller

Finance

Director, Human Resources	Cathy Chandler
Director, Information Technology	Uy Ut
Controller	Stephanie Reitz

Building Operations

Director, Ticket Operations	Daniel DeBoer
Director, Booking and Events	Steve Kirsner, James Hamnett
Director, Guest Services	David Cahill
Director, Building Services	Monte Chavez
Facilities Technical Director	Greg Carrolan

Miscellaneous

Television Station	Comcast SportsNet California
Radio Network Flagship	98.5 K-FOX (KUFX FM)
Television Play-By-Play / Color Analyst	Randy Hahn / Drew Remenda
Radio Play-By-Play / Color Analyst	Dan Rusanowsky / Jamie Baker
Radio Reporter	David Maley
P.A. Announcer	Danny Miller
Mascot	S.J. Sharkie

Key Off-Season Signings/Acquisitions

2010

May 25 • Named **Steve Yzerman** vice president and general manager.

June 10 • Named **Guy Boucher** head coach.

July 1 • Re-signed RW **Martin St. Louis**.

1 • Signed G **Dan Ellis**.

2 • Signed D **Pavel Kubina**.

5 • Signed D **Brett Clark**.

19 • Acquired LW **Simon Gagne** from Philadelphia for D **Matt Walker** and a 4th round pick in the 2011 Entry Draft.

20 • Named **Daniel Lacroix** and **Martin Raymond** assistant coaches.

23 • Named **Wayne Fleming** assistant coach.

23 • Signed C **Marc-Antoine Pouliot**.

25 • Signed LW **Chris Durno**.

30 • Signed C **Dominic Moore**.

Tampa Bay Lightning

2009-10 Results: 34w-36L-5otl-7sol 80pts.
Fourth, Southeast Division

Year-by-Year Record

Season	GP	Home				Road				Overall				GF	GA	Pts	Finished	Playoff Result
		W	L	T	OL	W	L	T	OL	W	L	T	OL					
2009-10	82	21	14	...	6	13	22	...	6	34	36	...	12	217	260	80	4th, Southeast Div.	Out of Playoffs
2008-09	82	12	18	...	11	12	22	...	7	24	40	...	18	210	279	66	5th, Southeast Div.	Out of Playoffs
2007-08	82	20	18	...	3	11	24	...	6	31	42	...	9	223	267	71	5th, Southeast Div.	Out of Playoffs
2006-07	82	22	18	...	1	22	15	...	4	44	33	...	5	253	261	93	2nd, Southeast Div.	Lost Conf. Quarter-Final
2005-06	82	25	14	...	2	18	19	...	4	43	33	...	6	252	260	92	2nd, Southeast Div.	Lost Conf. Quarter-Final
2004-05																		
2003-04	**82**	**24**	**10**	**4**	**3**	**22**	**12**	**4**	**3**	**46**	**22**	**8**	**6**	**245**	**192**	**106**	**1st, Southeast Div.**	**Won Stanley Cup**
2002-03	82	22	9	7	3	14	16	9	2	36	25	16	5	219	210	93	1st, Southeast Div.	Lost Conf. Semi-Final
2001-02	82	16	17	5	3	11	23	6	1	27	40	11	4	178	219	69	3rd, Southeast Div.	Out of Playoffs
2000-01	82	17	19	3	2	7	28	3	...	24	47	6	5	201	280	59	5th, Southeast Div.	Out of Playoffs
1999-2000	82	13	20	4	4	6	27	5	3	19	47	9	7	204	310	54	4th, Southeast Div.	Out of Playoffs
1998-99	82	12	25	4	...	7	29	5	...	19	54	9	...	179	292	47	4th, Southeast Div.	Out of Playoffs
1997-98	82	11	23	7	...	6	32	3	...	17	55	10	...	151	269	44	7th, Atlantic Div.	Out of Playoffs
1996-97	82	15	18	8	...	17	22	2	...	32	40	10	...	217	247	74	6th, Atlantic Div.	Out of Playoffs
1995-96	82	22	14	5	...	16	18	7	...	38	32	12	...	238	248	88	5th, Atlantic Div.	Lost Conf. Quarter-Final
1994-95	48	10	14	0	...	7	14	3	...	17	28	3	...	120	144	37	6th, Atlantic Div.	Out of Playoffs
1993-94	84	14	22	6	...	16	21	5	...	30	43	11	...	224	251	71	7th, Atlantic Div.	Out of Playoffs
1992-93	84	12	27	3	...	11	27	4	...	23	54	7	...	245	332	53	6th, Norris Div.	Out of Playoffs

2010-11 Schedule

Oct.							
Sat.	9	Atlanta		Sat.	8	at Ottawa	
Wed.	13	at Montreal		Sun.	9	at New Jersey*	
Thu.	14	at Philadelphia		Wed.	12	Washington	
Sat.	16	at Florida		Fri.	14	New Jersey	
Mon.	18	Dallas		Sat.	15	at Carolina	
Thu.	21	NY Islanders		Tue.	18	Columbus	
Fri.	22	at Atlanta		Thu.	20	at Atlanta	
Sun.	24	Nashville		Fri.	21	at Florida	
Wed.	27	Pittsburgh		Sun.	23	Atlanta	
Sat.	30	at Phoenix		Tue.	25	Toronto	

Nov.				Feb.			
Wed.	3	at Anaheim		Tue.	1	Philadelphia	
Thu.	4	at Los Angeles		Fri.	4	Washington	
Sat.	6	at San Jose		Sun.	6	St. Louis	
Tue.	9	Toronto		Tue.	8	Buffalo	
Thu.	11	at Washington		Sat.	12	Carolina	
Fri.	12	at Pittsburgh		Tue.	15	Philadelphia	
Sun.	14	Minnesota		Thu.	17	Detroit	
Wed.	17	at NY Islanders		Sat.	19	Florida	
Thu.	18	at Philadelphia		Wed.	23	Phoenix	
Sat.	20	at Buffalo		Fri.	25	New Jersey	
Mon.	22	Boston		Sun.	27	at NY Rangers*	
Wed.	24	NY Rangers	Mar.	Wed.	2	at New Jersey	
Fri.	26	at Washington*		Thu.	3	at Boston	
Sat.	27	Florida		Sat.	5	Montreal	
Tue.	30	at Toronto		Mon.	7	Washington	

Dec.							
Thu.	2	at Boston		Wed.	9	Chicago	
Sat.	4	Colorado		Fri.	11	Ottawa	
Tue.	7	at Calgary		Sat.	12	at Florida	
Fri.	10	at Edmonton		Mon.	14	at Toronto	
Sat.	11	at Vancouver		Thu.	17	at Montreal	
Wed.	15	Atlanta		Sat.	19	at Ottawa	
Sat.	18	Buffalo		Tue.	22	NY Islanders	
Mon.	20	Carolina		Fri.	25	Carolina	
Wed.	22	at NY Islanders		Sat.	26	at Carolina	
Thu.	23	at NY Rangers		Tue.	29	Ottawa	
Sun.	26	at Atlanta		Thu.	31	Pittsburgh	
Tue.	28	Boston	Apr.	Sat.	2	at Minnesota*	
Thu.	30	Montreal		Sun.	3	at Chicago	

Jan.							
Sat.	1	NY Rangers		Tue.	5	at Buffalo	
Tue.	4	at Washington		Fri.	8	Florida	
Wed.	5	at Pittsburgh		Sat.	9	at Carolina	

* Denotes afternoon game.

Victor Hedman, Steven Stamkos, Ryan Malone and Martin St. Louis celebrate a Tampa Bay goal. Stamkos scored 51 times in 2009-10 to tie for the league lead while St. Louis ranked third with 65 assists.

SOUTHEAST DIVISION
19th NHL Season

Franchise date: December 16, 1991

2010-11 Player Personnel

FORWARDS	HT	WT	S	Place of Birth	*Age	2009-10 Club
ANGELIDIS, Mike	6-1	210	L	Woodbridge, Ont.	25	Albany
ASHTON, Carter	6-3	205	L	Winnipeg, Man.	19	Leth-Regn-Norfolk
DOWNIE, Steve	6-0	200	R	Newmarket, Ont.	23	Tampa Bay
DURNO, Chris	6-4	205	L	Scarborough, Ont.	29	Colorado-Lake Erie
FRITZ, Mitch	6-7	242	L	Osoyoos, B.C.	29	Norfolk
GAGNE, Simon	6-0	195	L	Ste-Foy, Que.	30	Philadelphia
HALL, Adam	6-3	206	R	Kalamazoo, MI	30	Norfolk
HARJU, Johan	6-3	205	L	Overtornea, Sweden	24	Dynamo Moscow
JONES, Blair	6-3	215	R	Central Butte, Sask.	24	Tampa Bay-Norfolk
LECAVALIER, Vincent	6-4	223	L	Ile Bizard, Que.	30	Tampa Bay
MALONE, Ryan	6-4	220	L	Pittsburgh, PA	30	Tampa Bay
MOORE, Dominic	6-0	196	L	Sarnia, Ont.	30	Florida-Montreal
PERSSON, Niklas	6-2	205	L	Osmo, Sweden	31	Nizhnekamsk
POULIOT, Marc	6-1	195	R	Quebec City, Que.	25	Edmonton-Springfield
PURCELL, Teddy	6-2	198	R	St. Johns, Nfld.	25	Los Angeles-Tampa Bay
ST. LOUIS, Martin	5-9	177	L	Laval, Que.	35	Tampa Bay
STAMKOS, Steven	6-1	196	R	Markham, Ont.	20	Tampa Bay
SZCZECHURA, Paul	5-11	190	R	Brantford, Ont.	24	Tampa Bay-Norfolk
THOMPSON, Nate	6-0	207	L	Anchorage, AK	26	NY Islanders-Tampa Bay
TYRELL, Dana	5-11	185	L	Airdrie, Alta.	21	Norfolk
WRIGHT, James	6-3	175	L	Saskatoon, Sask.	20	Tampa Bay-Vancouver (WHL)

DEFENSEMEN						
CLARK, Brett	6-0	195	L	Wapella, Sask.	33	Colorado
HEDMAN, Victor	6-6	230	L	Ornskoldsvik, Sweden	19	Tampa Bay
JACKSON, Scott	6-4	215	L	Salmon Arm, B.C.	23	Tampa Bay-Norfolk
KUBINA, Pavel	6-4	250	R	Celadna, Czech.	33	Atlanta
LASHOFF, Matt	6-2	205	L	Albany, NY	24	Tampa Bay-Norfolk
LUNDIN, Mike	6-2	197	L	Burnsville, MN	26	Tampa Bay-Norfolk
MIHALIK, Vladimir	6-7	240	L	Presov, Czech.	23	Tampa Bay-Norfolk
OHLUND, Mattias	6-4	225	L	Pitea, Sweden	34	Tampa Bay
RANGER, Paul	6-3	208	L	Whitby, Ont.	26	Tampa Bay
ROY, Mathieu	6-2	210	R	St-Georges, Que.	27	CBJ-Syr-Roch
SMABY, Matt	6-4	240	L	Minneapolis, MN	25	Tampa Bay-Norfolk
VERNACE, Michael	6-2	200	L	Toronto, Ont.	24	Chicago (AHL)-Hamilton
WISHART, Ty	6-4	215	L	Belleville, Ont.	22	Norfolk

GOALTENDERS	HT	WT	C	Place of Birth	*Age	2009-10 Club
ELLIS, Dan	6-0	193	L	Orangeville, Ont.	30	Nashville
SMITH, Mike	6-4	219	L	Kingston, Ont.	28	Tampa Bay

* – Age at start of 2010-11 season

2009-10 Scoring

* – rookie

Regular Season

Pos	#	Player	Team	GP	G	A	Pts	TOI	+/-	PIM	PP	SH	GW	S	%
C	91	Steven Stamkos	T.B.	82	51	44	95	20:33	-2	38	24	1	5	297	17.2
R	26	Martin St. Louis	T.B.	82	29	65	94	21:48	-8	12	7	1	7	242	12.0
C	4	Vincent Lecavalier	T.B.	82	24	46	70	19:47	-16	63	5	0	3	295	8.1
L	12	Ryan Malone	T.B.	69	21	26	47	18:45	-8	68	7	0	7	172	12.2
R	9	Steve Downie	T.B.	79	22	24	46	14:42	14	208	7	0	1	116	19.0
D	6	Kurtis Foster	T.B.	71	8	34	42	17:11	-5	48	3	0	1	165	4.8
L	13	Alex Tanguay	T.B.	80	10	27	37	15:47	-2	32	3	0	2	91	11.0
D	77*	Victor Hedman	T.B.	74	4	16	20	20:50	-3	79	0	0	0	90	4.4
D	14	Andrej Meszaros	T.B.	81	6	11	17	20:10	-14	50	2	0	1	145	4.1
R	16	Teddy Purcell	L.A.	41	3	3	6	11:21	-1	4	1	0	1	55	5.5
			T.B.	19	3	6	9	16:05	-8	6	1	0	0	46	6.5
			Total	60	6	9	15	12:51	-9	10	2	0	1	101	5.9
R	27	Brandon Bochenski	T.B.	28	4	9	13	12:16	-1	2	1	0	0	43	9.3
D	39	Mike Lundin	T.B.	49	3	10	13	21:56	-4	18	0	0	0	42	7.1
D	5	Mattias Ohlund	T.B.	67	0	13	13	22:49	-8	59	0	0	0	71	0.0
C	44	Nate Thompson	NYI	39	1	5	6	12:56	-14	39	0	0	0	48	2.1
			T.B.	32	1	3	4	13:57	-3	17	0	0	0	44	2.3
			Total	71	2	8	10	13:23	-17	56	0	0	0	92	2.2
L	19	Stephane Veilleux	T.B.	77	3	6	9	12:17	-14	48	0	0	0	94	3.2
C	38	Paul Szczechura	T.B.	52	5	2	7	13:05	-15	18	1	0	1	83	6.0
L	17	Todd Fedoruk	T.B.	50	3	3	6	7:31	-12	54	0	0	0	22	13.6
C	43*	James Wright	T.B.	48	2	3	5	11:38	-9	18	0	0	0	25	8.0
D	8	Matt Walker	T.B.	66	2	3	5	16:09	-11	90	0	0	0	54	3.7
C	28	Zenon Konopka	T.B.	74	2	3	5	8:08	-11	265	0	0	1	41	4.9
D	21	David Hale	T.B.	39	0	4	4	14:03	-2	25	0	0	0	25	0.0
D	54	Paul Ranger	T.B.	8	1	1	2	20:19	-2	6	0	0	0	11	9.1
R	37	Mark Parrish	T.B.	16	0	2	2	15:10	-5	4	0	0	0	10	0.0
D	32	Matt Smaby	T.B.	33	0	2	2	13:28	-4	27	0	0	0	17	0.0
D	58*	Scott Jackson	T.B.	1	0	0	0	13:44	0	0	0	0	0	0	0.0
C	34	Ryan Craig	T.B.	3	0	0	0	9:47	0	5	0	0	0	5	0.0
D	56*	Vladimir Mihalik	T.B.	4	0	0	0	11:32	-4	2	0	0	0	1	0.0
D	55	Matt Lashoff	T.B.	5	0	0	0	8:53	-2	21	0	0	0	0	0.0
C	49*	Blair Jones	T.B.	14	0	0	0	12:50	-5	0	0	0	0	26	0.0

Goaltending

No.	Goaltender	GPI	Mins	Avg	W	L	OT	EN	SO	GA	SA	S%	G	A	PIM
30	Antero Niittymaki	49	2657	2.87	21	18	5	3	1	127	1388	.909	0	1	0
41	Mike Smith	42	2273	3.09	13	18	7	3	2	117	1165	.900	0	0	14
40	* Dustin Tokarski	2	44	4.09	0	0	0	0	0	3	16	.813	0	0	0
	Totals	82	5002	3.03	34	36	12	6	3	253	2575	.902			

Coaching History

Terry Crisp, 1992-93 to 1996-97; Terry Crisp, Rick Paterson and Jacques Demers, 1997-98; Jacques Demers, 1998-99; Steve Ludzik, 1999-2000; Steve Ludzik and John Tortorella, 2000-01; John Tortorella, 2001-02 to 2007-08; Barry Melrose and Rick Tocchet, 2008-09; Rick Tocchet, 2009-10; Guy Boucher, 2010-11.

Guy Boucher
Head Coach

Born: Notre-Dame-du-Lac, Que., August 3, 1971.

The Tampa Bay Lightning agreed to terms with Guy Boucher on June 10, 2010 to become the seventh head coach in the organization's history. Boucher joined the Lightning after coaching the Hamilton Bulldogs of the American Hockey League to 52 wins and 115 points in the 2009-10 regular season.

Boucher becomes the youngest coach in the NHL after quickly building a track record of success in the Quebec Major Junior Hockey League and the AHL. In addition to winning the AHL's North Division Championship for 2009-10, Boucher's Bulldogs team allowed just 182 goals during the 80-game regular season, the lowest total in the league. Its 271 goals scored marked the league's third highest total. He was honored with the AHL's Louis A. R. Pieri Award as its coach of the year.

Boucher was named head coach of the Bulldogs for the 2009-10 season after leading the Drummondville Voltigeurs for three seasons. Boucher led Drummondville to QMJHL regular season and playoff championships and a berth in the Memorial Cup in 2008-09. That Voltigeurs team set franchise records with 54 wins and 112 points. He was also awarded the Paul Dumont Trophy as the QMJHL's personality of the year for 2008-09.

Boucher also has extensive experience working for Hockey Canada, most recently serving as an assistant coach under Pat Quinn on the gold medal-winning team for the 2009 World Junior Championship. He was an assistant coach with Canada's national men's under-18 team program three times, also helping that team to the gold medal in 2008.

Boucher is a graduate of Montreal's McGill University where he starred with the Redmen from 1991 to 1995. Boucher also has a unique resume for an NHL coach, with educational studies in four different fields – sports psychology, biosystems engineering, environmental biology and history.

The Lightning named Detroit Red Wings legend Steve Yzerman their new general manager on May 25, 2010. A month later, Yzerman selected Brett Connolly sixth overall at the NHL Entry Draft.

Coaching Record

Season	Team	League	Regular Season				Playoffs			
			GC	W	L	O/T	GC	W	L	T
2006-07	Drummondville	QMJHL	70	37	26	7	12	7	5	....
2007-08	Drummondville	QMJHL	70	14	51	5	....	....	....	....
2008-09	Drummondville	QMJHL	68	54	10	4	19	16	3	....
2008-09	Drummondville	M-Cup	....	....	....	....	4	2	2	....
2009-10	Hamilton	AHL	80	52	11	11	19	11	8	....

Club Records

Team

(Figures in brackets for season records are games played; records for fewest points, wins, ties, losses, goals, goals against are for 70 or more games)

Most Points	106	2003-04 (82)
Most Wins	46	2003-04 (82)
Most Ties	16	2002-03 (82)
Most Losses	55	1997-98 (82)
Most Goals	246	2005-06 (82)
Most Goals Against	332	1992-93 (84)
Fewest Points	44	1997-98 (82)
Fewest Wins	17	1997-98 (82)
Fewest Ties	6	2000-01 (82)
Fewest Losses	22	2003-04 (82)
Fewest Goals	151	1997-98 (82)
Fewest Goals Against	192	2003-04 (82)

Longest Winning Streak
Overall	8	Feb. 23-Mar. 6/04
Home	8	Mar. 17-Apr. 8/06
Away	7	Jan. 7-Feb. 1/07

Longest Undefeated Streak
Overall	13	Mar. 7-Apr. 2/03 (7 wins, 6 ties)
Home	10	Jan. 29-Mar. 12/04 (9 wins, 1 tie)
Away	7	Feb. 23-Mar. 10/04 (6 wins, 1 tie), Jan. 7-Feb. 1/07 (7 wins)

Longest Losing Streak
Overall	13	Jan. 3-Feb. 2/98
Home	10	Jan. 3-Feb. 26/98
Away	11	Oct. 24-Dec. 10/97

Longest Winless Streak
Overall	16	Oct. 10-Nov. 17/97 (15 losses, 1 tie), Jan. 2-Feb. 5/98 (14 losses, 2 ties)
Home	11	Jan. 2-Feb. 26/98 (10 losses, 1 tie)
Away	17	Dec. 2/99-Feb. 19/00 (14 losses, 3 ties)

Most Shutouts, Season	9	2001-02 (82)
Most PIM, Season	1,823	1997-98 (82)
Most Goals, Game	9	Nov. 8/03 (Pit. 0 at T.B. 9)

Individual

Most Seasons	11	Vincent Lecavalier
Most Games, Career	869	Vincent Lecavalier
Most Goals, Career	326	Vincent Lecavalier
Most Assists, Career	413	Vincent Lecavalier
Most Points, Career	739	Vincent Lecavalier (326G, 413A)
Most PIM, Career	828	Chris Gratton
Most Shutouts, Career	14	Nikolai Khabibulin

Longest Consecutive
Games Streak	390	Martin St. Louis (Nov. 17/05-to date)
Most Goals, Season	52	Vincent Lecavalier (2006-07)

Most Assists, Season	68	Brad Richards (2005-06)
Most Points, Season	108	Vincent Lecavalier (2006-07; 52G, 56A)
Most PIM, Season	265	Zenon Konopka (2009-10)
Most Points, Defenseman, Season	65	Roman Hamrlik (1995-96; 16G, 49A)
Most Points, Center, Season	108	Vincent Lecavalier (2006-07; 52G, 56A)
Most Points, Right Wing, Season	102	Martin St. Louis (2006-07; 43G, 59A)
Most Points, Left Wing, Season	80	Cory Stillman (2003-04; 25G, 55A) Vaclav Prospal (2005-06; 25G, 55A)
Most Points, Rookie, Season	62	Brad Richards (2000-01; 21G, 41A)
Most Shutouts, Season	7	Nikolai Khabibulin (2001-02)
Most Goals, Game	4	Chris Kontos (Oct. 7/92)
Most Assists, Game	5	Mark Recchi (Mar. 1/09)
Most Points, Game	6	Doug Crossman (Nov. 7/92; 3G, 3A)

Captains' History

No captain, 1992-93 to 1994-95; Paul Ysebaert, 1995-96, 1996-97; Paul Ysebaert and Mikael Renberg, 1997-98; Rob Zamuner, 1998-99; Bill Houlder, Chris Gratton and Vincent Lecavalier, 1999-2000; Vincent Lecavalier, 2000-01; no captain, 2001-02; Dave Andreychuk, 2002-03 to 2004-05; Dave Andreychuk and no captain, 2005-06; Tim Taylor, 2006-07, 2007-08; Vincent Lecavalier, 2008-09 to date.

All-time Record vs. Other Clubs

Regular Season

	At Home								On Road								Total							
	GP	W	L	T	OL	GF	GA	PTS	GP	W	L	T	OL	GF	GA	PTS	GP	W	L	T	OL	GF	GA	PTS
Anaheim	11	4	6	0	1	21	29	9	11	4	5	1	1	29	35	10	22	8	11	1	2	50	64	19
Atlanta	31	20	8	1	2	112	79	43	31	10	15	3	3	83	103	26	62	30	23	4	5	195	182	69
Boston	33	13	15	3	2	95	99	31	33	4	20	6	3	80	125	17	66	17	35	9	5	175	224	48
Buffalo	33	7	19	3	4	73	109	21	33	10	19	2	2	92	112	24	66	17	38	5	6	165	221	45
Calgary	12	6	5	1	0	39	42	13	12	6	5	0	1	35	40	13	24	12	10	1	1	74	82	26
Carolina	44	25	15	3	1	134	124	54	45	11	23	7	4	118	142	33	89	36	38	10	5	252	266	87
Chicago	13	5	4	3	1	32	35	14	16	4	10	2	0	36	54	10	29	9	14	5	1	68	89	24
Colorado	15	8	4	1	2	40	40	19	16	3	10	2	1	34	60	9	31	11	14	3	3	74	100	28
Columbus	5	4	1	0	0	11	6	8	5	1	3	1	0	9	13	3	10	5	4	1	0	20	19	11
Dallas	15	2	10	2	1	25	41	7	13	4	7	1	1	36	46	10	28	6	17	3	2	61	87	17
Detroit	16	4	10	1	1	49	71	10	14	1	12	1	0	23	54	3	30	5	22	2	1	72	125	13
Edmonton	13	4	6	2	1	37	41	11	12	4	8	0	0	27	32	8	25	8	14	2	1	64	73	19
Florida	46	20	18	6	2	112	131	48	46	13	25	4	4	115	155	34	92	33	43	10	6	227	286	82
Los Angeles	12	6	4	0	2	27	26	14	13	10	1	2	0	43	26	22	25	16	5	2	2	70	52	36
Minnesota	6	2	2	1	1	14	16	6	5	1	4	0	0	13	19	2	11	3	6	1	1	27	35	8
Montreal	33	13	12	5	3	79	89	34	32	14	16	1	1	78	90	30	65	27	28	6	4	157	179	64
Nashville	6	3	1	2	0	19	14	8	8	5	3	0	0	22	20	10	14	8	4	2	0	41	34	18
New Jersey	35	11	16	5	3	79	106	30	36	10	21	2	3	76	128	25	71	21	37	7	6	155	234	55
NY Islanders	36	20	12	2	2	105	102	44	35	16	17	1	1	93	103	34	71	36	29	3	3	198	205	78
NY Rangers	35	16	14	3	2	111	109	37	37	14	20	2	1	102	126	31	72	30	34	5	3	213	235	68
Ottawa	33	13	17	2	1	96	117	29	33	10	20	0	3	71	122	23	66	23	37	2	4	167	239	52
Philadelphia	36	14	20	1	1	105	113	30	35	10	17	7	1	80	107	28	71	24	37	8	2	185	220	58
Phoenix	12	6	6	0	0	39	38	12	14	7	7	0	0	35	33	14	26	13	13	0	0	74	71	26
Pittsburgh	33	17	14	2	0	98	82	36	33	12	16	3	2	87	112	29	66	29	30	5	2	185	194	65
St. Louis	15	6	5	3	1	46	50	16	13	3	9	0	1	35	51	7	28	9	14	3	2	81	101	23
San Jose	15	8	6	1	0	39	40	17	12	6	5	1	0	38	42	13	27	14	11	2	0	77	82	30
Toronto	30	9	18	1	2	71	99	21	31	10	17	1	3	81	112	24	61	19	35	2	5	152	211	45
Vancouver	11	5	5	0	1	38	41	11	11	0	8	2	1	19	47	3	22	5	13	2	2	57	88	14
Washington	47	17	27	2	1	119	151	37	47	13	28	4	2	121	172	32	94	30	55	6	3	240	323	69
Totals	**682**	**288**	**300**	**56**	**38**	**1865**	**2040**	**670**	**682**	**216**	**371**	**56**	**39**	**1711**	**2281**	**527**	**1364**	**504**	**671**	**112**	**77**	**3576**	**4321**	**1197**

Playoffs

	Series	W	L	GP	W	L	T	GF	GA	Last Mtg.	Rnd.	Result
Calgary	1	1	0	7	4	3	0	13	14	2004	F	W 4-3
Montreal	1	1	0	4	4	0	0	14	5	2004	CSF	W 4-0
New Jersey	2	0	2	11	3	8	0	22	33	2007	CQF	L 2-4
NY Islanders	1	1	0	5	4	1	0	12	5	2004	CQF	W 4-1
Ottawa	1	0	1	5	1	4	0	13	23	2006	CQF	L 1-4
Philadelphia	2	1	1	13	6	7	0	34	45	2004	CF	W 4-3
Washington	1	1	0	6	4	2	0	14	15	2003	CQF	W 4-2
Totals	**9**	**5**	**4**	**51**	**26**	**25**	**0**	**122**	**140**			

Carolina totals include Hartford, 1992-93 to 1996-97.
Dallas totals include Minnesota North Stars, 1992-93.
Colorado totals include Quebec, 1992-93 to 1994-95.
Phoenix totals include Winnipeg, 1992-93 to 1995-96.

Playoff Results 2010-2006

Year	Round	Opponent	Result	GF	GA
2007	CQF	New Jersey	L 2-4	14	19
2006	CQF	Ottawa	L 1-4	13	23

Abbreviations: Round: F – Final; CF – conference final; CSF – conference semi-final; CQF – conference quarter-final.

2009-10 Results

Oct.	3	at Atlanta	3-6		6	at Buffalo	3-5
	6	at Carolina	1-2†		8	at New Jersey	4-2
	8	New Jersey	3-4†		9	at Philadelphia	1-4
	10	Carolina	5-2		12	Washington	7-4
	12	Florida	3-2		14	Florida	2-3
	15	at Ottawa	1-7		16	at Florida	2-5
	17	at Pittsburgh	1-4		18	at Carolina	3-2
	22	San Jose	5-2		19	at NY Rangers	2-8
	24	Buffalo	2-3†		21	Toronto	3-2*
	29	Ottawa	5-2		23	Atlanta	2-1†
	31	New Jersey	1-2†		27	Montreal	3-0
Nov.	2	at Philadelphia	2-6		29	Anaheim	1-2†
	3	at Toronto	2-1*		31	at Washington	2-3
	5	at Ottawa	2-3*	Feb.	2	at Atlanta	2-1
	7	at Montreal	3-1		4	NY Islanders	5-2
	12	Minnesota	4-3†		6	Calgary	2-1*
	14	Los Angeles	1-2†		9	Vancouver	3-1
	16	at Phoenix	4-1		11	Boston	4-5
	19	at Anaheim	3-4*		13	at NY Islanders	4-5
	21	at Carolina	1-3		14	at NY Rangers	2-5
	22	at Atlanta	4-3*	Mar.	2	Philadelphia	2-7
	25	Toronto	3-4		4	at Washington	4-5
	27	NY Rangers	5-1		6	Atlanta	6-2
	28	at Dallas	3-4*		9	at Montreal	3-5
	30	Colorado	0-3		11	at Toronto	3-4*
Dec.	2	at Boston	1-4		12	at Washington	3-2
	4	at New Jersey	2-3		14	Pittsburgh	1-2
	5	NY Islanders	4-0		16	Phoenix	1-2
	7	Washington	0-3		18	Buffalo	2-6
	9	Edmonton	2-3		20	Washington	1-3
	11	at Colorado	1-2†		21	at Florida	2-5
	13	at Chicago	0-4		23	Carolina	3-2*
	15	at Nashville	4-7		25	at Boston	5-3
	17	at Detroit	0-3		27	at Buffalo	1-7
	18	at St. Louis	6-3		30	at Columbus	2-3
	21	at NY Islanders	4-2		31	at Pittsburgh	2-0
	23	Philadelphia	2-5	Apr.	2	NY Rangers	0-5
	26	Atlanta	4-3		6	Carolina	5-8
	28	Boston	4-3		8	Ottawa	4-3†
	30	Montreal	1-2*		10	Florida	4-3†
Jan.	2	Pittsburgh	3-1		11	at Florida	3-1

* – Overtime † – Shootout

Entry Draft Selections 2010-1996

Name in bold denotes played in NHL.

2010
Pick
6	Brett Connolly
63	Brock Beukeboom
66	Radko Gudas
72	Adam Janosik
96	Geoffrey Schemitsch
118	James Mullin
156	Brendan O'Donnell
186	Teigan Zahn

2009
Pick
2	**Victor Hedman**
29	Carter Ashton
52	Richard Panik
93	Alex Hutchings
148	Michael Zador
162	Jaroslav Janus
183	Kirill Gotovets

2008
Pick
1	**Steven Stamkos**
117	**James Wright**
122	**Dustin Tokarski**
147	Kyle De Coste
152	Mark Barberio
160	Luke Witkowski
182	Matias Sointu
203	David Carle

2007
Pick
47	Dana Tyrell
75	Luca Cunti
77	Alexander Killorn
107	Mitch Fadden
150	Matt Marshall
167	Johan Harju
183	Torrie Jung
197	Michael Ward
210	Justin Courtnall

2006
Pick
15	**Riku Helenius**
78	**Kevin Quick**
168	Dane Crowley
198	Denis Kazionov

2005
Pick
30	**Vladimir Mihalik**
73	**Radek Smolenak**
89	Chris Lawrence
92	Marek Bartanus
102	**Blair Jones**
133	Stanislav Lascek
163	Marek Kvapil
165	Kevin Beech
225	John Wessbecker

2004
Pick
30	Andy Rogers
65	Mark Tobin
102	**Mike Lundin**
158	Brandon Elliott
163	Dusty Collins
188	Jan Zapletal
191	**Karri Ramo**
245	Justin Keller

2003
Pick
34	Mike Egener
41	**Matt Smaby**
96	Jonathan Boutin
192	**Doug O'Brien**
224	**Gerald Coleman**
227	**Jay Rosehill**
255	Raimonds Danilics
256	Brady Greco
273	Albert Vishnyakov
286	Zbynek Hrdel
287	**Nick Tarnasky**

2002
Pick
60	Adam Henrich
100	Dmitri Kazionov
135	Joe Pearce
162	Gerard Dicaire
170	P.J. Atherton
174	Karri Akkanen
183	**Paul Ranger**
213	**Fredrik Norrena**
233	Vasily Koshechkin
255	**Ryan Craig**
256	**Darren Reid**
286	Alexei Glukhov
287	John Toffey

2001
Pick
3	**Alexander Svitov**
47	Alexander Polushin
61	Andreas Holmqvist
94	**Evgeny Artyukhin**
123	Aaron Lobb
138	Paul Lynch
188	Art Femenella
219	Dennis Packard
222	Jeremy Van Hoof
252	J.F. Soucy
259	Dmitri Bezrukov
261	Vitali Smolyaninov
281	Ilja Solarev
289	Henrik Bergfors

2000
Pick
8	**Nikita Alexeev**
34	Ruslan Zainullin
81	**Alexander Kharitonov**
126	Johan Hagglund
161	Pavel Sedov
191	Aaron Gionet
222	Marek Priechodsky
226	**Brian Eklund**
233	Alexander Polukeyev
263	**Thomas Ziegler**

1999
Pick
47	**Sheldon Keefe**
67	**Evgeny Konstantinov**
75	Brett Scheffelmaier
88	**Jimmie Olvestad**
127	**Kaspars Astashenko**
148	Michal Lanicek
182	**Fedor Fedorov**
187	Ivan Rachunek
216	Erkki Rajamaki
244	Mikko Kuparinen

1998
Pick
1	**Vincent Lecavalier**
64	**Brad Richards**
72	**Dmitry Afanasenkov**
92	**Eric Beaudoin**
121	Curtis Rich
146	Sergei Kuznetsov
174	Brett Allan
194	Oak Hewer
221	Daniel Hulak
229	Chris Lyness
252	**Martin Cibak**

1997
Pick
7	**Paul Mara**
33	Kyle Kos
61	**Matt Elich**
108	Mark Thompson
109	Jan Sulc
112	**Karel Betik**
153	**Andrei Skopintsev**
168	Justin Jack
170	Eero Somervuori
185	Samuel St-Pierre
198	Shawn Skolney
224	**Paul Comrie**

1996
Pick
16	Mario Larocque
69	Curtis Tipler
125	Jason Robinson
152	Nikolai Ignatov
157	**Xavier Delisle**
179	**Pavel Kubina**

General Managers' History

Phil Esposito, 1992-93 to 1997-98; Jacques Demers, 1998-99; Rick Dudley, 1999-2000, 2000-01; Rick Dudley and Jay Feaster, 2001-02; Jay Feaster, 2002-03 to 2007-08; Brian Lawton, 2008-09, 2009-10; Steve Yzerman, 2010-11.

Steve Yzerman
Vice President and General Manager
Born: Cranbrook, B.C., May 9, 1965.

Steve Yzerman – the iconic Detroit Red Wing player and executive – was named the sixth general manager in Lightning history on May 25, 2010. Yzerman spent five seasons as vice president with the Red Wings, working closely with general manager Ken Holland, senior vice president Jim Devellano and assistant general manager Jim Nill on evaluating talent at both the professional and amateur levels. He also contributed valuable input on trades, free agent signings and at the Entry Draft each summer. Yzerman served as general manager for Canada at the 2007 and 2008 World Championships, bringing home gold and silver respectively. He then led Canada to an Olympic gold medal victory on home ice in Vancouver at the 2010 Winter Olympics as executive director. Yzerman also won an Olympic gold medal as a player with Canada in 2002.

Yzerman is a four-time Stanley Cup champion, winning three as a player (1997, 1998 and 2002) and another as a member of Detroit's management team (2008). Overall he spent 27 seasons with the franchise. He was inducted into the Hockey Hall of Fame in 2009, his first year of eligibility. Recognized as one of the best centers in NHL history, Yzerman retired on July 3, 2006 after a remarkable 22-year NHL career with the Red Wings. He ranks among the NHL's all-time leaders with 1,514 career games, 692 goals, 1,063 assists and 1,755 career points. Even more impressive than his career statistics may be his 20-year run as captain in Detroit, the longest tenure in NHL and major sports history. Yzerman was named captain of the Red Wings prior to the 1986-87 season, making him the youngest captain in franchise history at 21-years-old.

During his illustrious career Yzerman was selected to the NHL All-Star Game on 10 occasions. He also won the Bill Masterton Trophy (perseverance, sportsmanship and dedication to hockey) in 2002, the Frank J. Selke Trophy (best defensive forward) in 2000, the Conn Smythe Trophy (playoff MVP) in 1998, the Lester B. Pearson Trophy (the NHLPA's top player) in 1989 and was also selected to the NHL All-Rookie Team in 1984.

Club Directory

St. Pete Times Forum

Tampa Bay Lightning
St. Pete Times Forum
401 Channelside Drive
Tampa, FL 33602
Phone **813/301-6500**
FAX 813/301-1480
Ticket Info. 813/301-6600
www.tampabaylightning.com
Capacity: 19,758

Executive Staff
Owner, Governor & Chairman	Jeff Vinik
Chief Executive Officer and Alternate Governor	Tod Leiweke
Vice President and General Manager	Steve Yzerman
Executive Vice President, Sales & Marketing	Brad Lott
Executive Vice President of Communications	Bill Wickett
Sr. Vice President, Corporate Sales	Patrick Duffy
Sr. Vice President, Human Resources	Keith Harris
Sr. Vice President / General Counsel	Paul Davis
Vice President, Partnership Services	Courtney Simons
Vice President, Operations	Mary Milne
Vice President, Event Booking	Elmer Straub
Vice President, Ticket Operations	Jim Mannino
Vice President, Event Prod/ and Entertainment	John Franzone
Executive Assistant	Michele Rooney

Hockey Operations
Asst. G.M. / G.M., Norfolk Admirals	Julien BriseBois
Assistant General Manager	Tom Kurvers
Director of Pro Scouting	Pat Verbeek
Director of Amateur Scouting	Al Murray
Head Pro Scout	Greg Malone
Head Amateur Scout	Darryl Plandowski
Director of Team Services	Ryan Belec
Manager of Hockey Administration	Elizabeth Sylvia
Head Athletic Trainer	Tom Mulligan
Assistant Athletic Trainer	Mike Poirier
Massage Therapist	TBD
Equipment Manager	Ray Thill
Assistant Equipment Managers	Rob Kennedy, Clay Roffer
Statistical Analyst	Michael Peterson
Head Coach, Norfolk Admirals	Jon Cooper
Head Athletic Trainer, Norfolk Admirals	Brad Chavis
Head Equipment Manager, Norfolk Admirals	JW Aiken

Coaching Staff
Head Coach	Guy Boucher
Assistant Coaches	Wayne Fleming, Dan Lacroix, Martin Raymond
Goaltending Coach	TBD
Video Coach	Nigel Kirwan

Public/Media Relations
Media Relations Manager	Brian Breseman
Digital Media Manager	Justen Fox

Community Relations and Lightning Foundation
Executive Director of Lightning Foundation	Kasey Smith
Community Representative	Dave Andreychuk
Community Relations Manager	Kelvin Woodson
Director of Youth Hockey	Brian Bradley
Manager of Community Hockey Initiatives	Mark Voyia
Lightning Foundation Coordinator	Heidi Hamlin

Finance
Controller	Doug Riefler
Accounts Payable / Receivable	Donna Clark / Angela Edwards
Staff Accountants	Kathleen Cook / Jill Harper

Internal Support Staff
Associate General Counsel	Danna Haydar
Front Desk Administrator	Charlene Beverly
Human Resources / Legal Coordinator	Sabrina Odria
Office Services Coordinator	Ryan Messier

Information Technology
Director of IT	Ian Steele

Box Office
Box Office Supervisor	Helen Junker
Box Office Coordinators	Tom Bradley, Missy Davis, Bobby Loman, Liz Mulhearn

Ticket Sales
Sr. Director of Sales	Ryan West
Director of Group Sales	Behn Custard
Sr. Director of New Business Development	Ryan Bringger
Director of Inside Sales	Ryan Cook
Suite Sales Managers	Adam Laws, Katie Valone
Sr. Corporate Account Manager	Michael Lopez

Sponsorship Sales and Partnerships
Vice Presidents, Corporate Partnerships	Kyle Draper, Rob Keith

Partnership Services
Director of Client Services	Amanda Graul
Sr. Director of Client Sales and Retention	Paul Wallace
Sr. Manager of Client Services	Erik Langner

Corporate Communications
Sr. Marketing Manager	Nashira Babooram
Marketing Coordinator	Jessica Eckley
Art Director	Justin Langley

Arena Management
General Manager, SportService	Bruce Ground
Managers, Arena Departments	Tony Castillo, Ricardo Collado, Amy Ford, Jenna Lemons, Tripp Turbiville, Stevan Simms
Event Booking Assistant	Jennifer Renspie
Operations Analyst	Sam Carr

Broadcast
Audio / Visual Manager	JC Kent
Production Systems Manager	Jorge Rosell
Video / Motion Graphics Coordinator	Brett Nehls
Video Production Coordinator	Jeff Cederbaum
Promotions and Entertainment Manager	Heather Chamberlain
Marketing Coordinator	Kelli Yeloushan
Television / Flagship Radio Station	SunSports Network / WHNZ 1250
Television Play-by-Play / Analyst	Rick Peckham / Bobby "The Chief" Taylor
Television Rinkside Reporter	Paul Kennedy
Radio Play-by-Play / Analyst	David Mishkin, Phil Esposito
Manager of Radio Programming	Matt Sammon

Toronto Maple Leafs

Key Off-Season Signings/Acquisitions

2010

Apr. 15 • Re-signed G **Jonas Gustavsson**.
June 26 • Acquired RW **Mike Brown** from Anaheim for Toronto's 5th round pick in the 2010 Entry Draft.
30 • Acquired RW **Kris Versteeg** from Chicago.
July 1 • Signed RW **Colby Armstrong**.
2 • Re-signed LW **Nikolai Kulemin**.
5 • Re-signed C **John Mitchell**.
7 • Signed D **Brett Lebda**.

2009-10 Results: 30W-38L-10OTL-4SOL 74PTS.
Fifth, Northeast Division

Year-by-Year Record

Season	GP	Home W	Home L	Home T	Home OL	Road W	Road L	Road T	Road OL	Overall W	Overall L	Overall T	Overall OL	GF	GA	Pts.	Finished	Playoff Result
2009-10	82	18	17	....	6	12	21	....	8	30	38	....	14	214	267	74	5th, Northeast Div.	Out of Playoffs
2008-09	82	16	16	....	9	18	19	....	4	34	35	....	13	250	293	81	5th, Northeast Div.	Out of Playoffs
2007-08	82	18	17	....	6	18	18	....	5	36	35	....	11	231	260	83	5th, Northeast Div.	Out of Playoffs
2006-07	82	21	15	....	5	19	16	....	6	40	31	....	11	258	269	91	3rd, Northeast Div.	Out of Playoffs
2005-06	82	26	12	....	3	15	21	....	5	41	33	....	8	257	270	90	4th, Northeast Div.	Out of Playoffs
2004-05	....	....	....	....	....	....	....	....	....	....	....	....	....	....	....	....		
2003-04	82	22	14	3	2	23	10	7	1	45	24	10	3	242	204	103	2nd, Northeast Div.	Lost Conf. Semi-Final
2002-03	82	24	13	4	0	20	15	3	3	44	28	7	3	236	208	98	2nd, Northeast Div.	Lost Conf. Quarter-Final
2001-02	82	24	11	6	0	19	14	4	4	43	25	10	4	249	207	100	2nd, Northeast Div.	Lost Conf. Championship
2000-01	82	19	11	7	4	18	18	4	1	37	29	11	5	232	207	90	3rd, Northeast Div.	Lost Conf. Semi-Final
1999-2000	82	24	12	5	0	21	15	2	3	45	27	7	3	246	222	100	1st, Northeast Div.	Lost Conf. Semi-Final
1998-99	82	23	13	5	....	22	17	2	....	45	30	7	....	268	231	97	2nd, Northeast Div.	Lost Conf. Championship
1997-98	82	16	20	5	....	14	23	4	....	30	43	9	....	194	237	69	6th, Central Div.	Out of Playoffs
1996-97	82	18	20	3	....	12	24	5	....	30	44	8	....	230	273	68	6th, Central Div.	Out of Playoffs
1995-96	82	19	15	7	....	15	21	5	....	34	36	12	....	247	252	80	3rd, Central Div.	Lost Conf. Quarter-Final
1994-95	48	15	7	2	....	6	12	6	....	21	19	8	....	135	146	50	4th, Central Div.	Lost Conf. Quarter-Final
1993-94	84	23	15	4	....	20	14	8	....	43	29	12	....	280	243	98	2nd, Central Div.	Lost Conf. Championship
1992-93	84	25	11	6	....	19	18	5	....	44	29	11	....	288	241	99	3rd, Norris Div.	Lost Conf. Championship
1991-92	80	21	16	3	....	9	27	4	....	30	43	7	....	234	294	67	5th, Norris Div.	Out of Playoffs
1990-91	80	15	21	4	....	8	25	7	....	23	46	11	....	241	318	57	5th, Norris Div.	Out of Playoffs
1989-90	80	24	14	2	....	14	24	2	....	38	38	4	....	337	358	80	3rd, Norris Div.	Lost Div. Semi-Final
1988-89	80	15	20	5	....	13	26	1	....	28	46	6	....	259	342	62	5th, Norris Div.	Out of Playoffs
1987-88	80	14	20	6	....	7	29	4	....	21	49	10	....	273	345	52	4th, Norris Div.	Lost Div. Semi-Final
1986-87	80	22	14	4	....	10	28	2	....	32	42	6	....	286	319	70	4th, Norris Div.	Lost Div. Final
1985-86	80	16	21	3	....	9	27	4	....	25	48	7	....	311	386	57	4th, Norris Div.	Lost Div. Final
1984-85	80	10	28	2	....	10	24	6	....	20	52	8	....	253	358	48	5th, Norris Div.	Out of Playoffs
1983-84	80	17	16	7	....	9	29	2	....	26	45	9	....	303	387	61	5th, Norris Div.	Out of Playoffs
1982-83	80	20	15	5	....	8	25	7	....	28	40	12	....	293	330	68	3rd, Norris Div.	Lost Div. Semi-Final
1981-82	80	12	20	8	....	8	24	8	....	20	44	16	....	298	380	56	5th, Norris Div.	Out of Playoffs
1980-81	80	14	21	5	....	14	16	10	....	28	37	15	....	322	367	71	5th, Adams Div.	Lost Prelim. Round
1979-80	80	17	19	4	....	18	21	1	....	35	40	5	....	304	327	75	4th, Adams Div.	Lost Prelim. Round
1978-79	80	20	12	8	....	14	21	5	....	34	33	13	....	267	252	81	3rd, Adams Div.	Lost Quarter-Final
1977-78	80	21	13	6	....	20	16	4	....	41	29	10	....	271	237	92	3rd, Adams Div.	Lost Semi-Final
1976-77	80	18	13	9	....	15	19	6	....	33	32	15	....	301	285	81	3rd, Adams Div.	Lost Quarter-Final
1975-76	80	23	12	5	....	11	19	10	....	34	31	15	....	294	276	83	3rd, Adams Div.	Lost Quarter-Final
1974-75	80	19	12	9	....	12	21	7	....	31	33	16	....	280	309	78	3rd, Adams Div.	Lost Quarter-Final
1973-74	78	21	11	7	....	14	16	9	....	35	27	16	....	274	230	86	4th, East Div.	Lost Quarter-Final
1972-73	78	20	12	7	....	7	29	3	....	27	41	10	....	247	279	64	6th, East Div.	Out of Playoffs
1971-72	78	21	11	7	....	12	20	7	....	33	31	14	....	209	208	80	4th, East Div.	Lost Quarter-Final
1970-71	78	24	9	6	....	13	24	2	....	37	33	8	....	248	211	82	4th, East Div.	Lost Quarter-Final
1969-70	76	18	13	7	....	11	21	6	....	29	34	13	....	222	242	71	6th, East Div.	Out of Playoffs
1968-69	76	20	8	10	....	15	18	5	....	35	26	15	....	234	217	85	4th, East Div.	Lost Quarter-Final
1967-68	74	24	9	4	....	9	22	6	....	33	31	10	....	209	176	76	5th, East Div.	Out of Playoffs
1966-67	**70**	**21**	**8**	**6**	....	**11**	**19**	**5**	....	**32**	**27**	**11**	....	**204**	**211**	**75**	**3rd,**	**Won Stanley Cup**
1965-66	70	22	9	4	....	12	16	7	....	34	25	11	....	208	187	79	3rd,	Lost Semi-Final
1964-65	70	17	15	3	....	13	11	11	....	30	26	14	....	204	173	74	4th,	Lost Semi-Final
1963-64	**70**	**22**	**7**	**6**	....	**11**	**18**	**6**	....	**33**	**25**	**12**	....	**192**	**172**	**78**	**3rd,**	**Won Stanley Cup**
1962-63	**70**	**21**	**8**	**6**	....	**14**	**15**	**6**	....	**35**	**23**	**12**	....	**221**	**180**	**82**	**1st,**	**Won Stanley Cup**
1961-62	**70**	**25**	**5**	**5**	....	**12**	**17**	**6**	....	**37**	**22**	**11**	....	**232**	**180**	**85**	**2nd,**	**Won Stanley Cup**
1960-61	70	21	6	8	....	18	13	4	....	39	19	12	....	234	176	90	2nd,	Lost Semi-Final
1959-60	70	20	9	6	....	15	17	3	....	35	26	9	....	199	195	79	2nd,	Lost Final
1958-59	70	17	13	5	....	10	19	6	....	27	32	11	....	189	201	65	4th,	Lost Final
1957-58	70	12	16	7	....	9	22	4	....	21	38	11	....	192	226	53	6th,	Out of Playoffs
1956-57	70	12	16	7	....	9	18	8	....	21	34	15	....	174	192	57	5th,	Out of Playoffs
1955-56	70	19	10	6	....	5	23	7	....	24	33	13	....	153	181	61	4th,	Lost Semi-Final
1954-55	70	14	10	11	....	10	14	11	....	24	24	22	....	147	135	70	3rd,	Lost Semi-Final
1953-54	70	22	6	7	....	10	18	7	....	32	24	14	....	152	131	78	3rd,	Lost Semi-Final
1952-53	70	17	12	6	....	10	18	7	....	27	30	13	....	156	167	67	5th,	Out of Playoffs
1951-52	70	17	10	8	....	12	15	8	....	29	25	16	....	168	157	74	3rd,	Lost Semi-Final
1950-51	**70**	**22**	**8**	**5**	....	**19**	**8**	**8**	....	**41**	**16**	**13**	....	**212**	**138**	**95**	**2nd,**	**Won Stanley Cup**
1949-50	70	18	9	8	....	13	18	4	....	31	27	12	....	176	173	74	3rd,	Lost Semi-Final
1948-49	**60**	**12**	**8**	**10**	....	**10**	**17**	**3**	....	**22**	**25**	**13**	....	**147**	**161**	**57**	**4th,**	**Won Stanley Cup**
1947-48	**60**	**22**	**3**	**5**	....	**10**	**12**	**8**	....	**32**	**15**	**13**	....	**182**	**143**	**77**	**1st,**	**Won Stanley Cup**
1946-47	**60**	**20**	**8**	**2**	....	**11**	**11**	**8**	....	**31**	**19**	**10**	....	**209**	**172**	**72**	**2nd,**	**Won Stanley Cup**
1945-46	50	10	13	2	....	9	11	5	....	19	24	7	....	174	185	45	5th,	Out of Playoffs
1944-45	**50**	**13**	**9**	**3**	....	**11**	**13**	**1**	....	**24**	**22**	**4**	....	**183**	**161**	**52**	**3rd,**	**Won Stanley Cup**
1943-44	50	13	11	1	....	10	12	3	....	23	23	4	....	214	174	50	3rd,	Lost Semi-Final
1942-43	50	17	6	2	....	5	13	7	....	22	19	9	....	198	159	53	3rd,	Lost Semi-Final
1941-42	**48**	**18**	**6**	**0**	....	**9**	**12**	**3**	....	**27**	**18**	**3**	....	**158**	**136**	**57**	**2nd,**	**Won Stanley Cup**
1940-41	48	16	5	3	....	12	9	3	....	28	14	6	....	145	99	62	2nd,	Lost Semi-Final
1939-40	48	15	3	6	....	10	14	0	....	25	17	6	....	134	110	56	3rd,	Lost Final
1938-39	48	13	8	3	....	6	12	6	....	19	20	9	....	114	107	47	3rd,	Lost Final
1937-38	48	13	6	5	....	11	9	4	....	24	15	9	....	151	127	57	1st, Cdn. Div.	Lost Final
1936-37	48	14	9	1	....	8	12	4	....	22	21	5	....	119	115	49	3rd, Cdn. Div.	Lost Quarter-Final
1935-36	48	15	4	5	....	8	15	1	....	23	19	6	....	126	106	52	2nd, Cdn. Div.	Lost Final
1934-35	48	16	6	2	....	14	8	2	....	30	14	4	....	157	111	64	1st, Cdn. Div.	Lost Final
1933-34	48	19	2	3	....	7	11	6	....	26	13	9	....	174	119	61	1st, Cdn. Div.	Lost Semi-Final
1932-33	48	16	4	4	....	8	14	2	....	24	18	6	....	119	111	54	1st, Cdn. Div.	Lost Final
1931-32	**48**	**17**	**4**	**3**	....	**6**	**14**	**4**	....	**23**	**18**	**7**	....	**155**	**127**	**53**	**2nd, Cdn. Div.**	**Won Stanley Cup**
1930-31	44	15	4	3	....	7	9	6	....	22	13	9	....	118	99	53	2nd, Cdn. Div.	Lost Quarter-Final
1929-30	44	10	8	4	....	7	13	2	....	17	21	6	....	116	124	40	4th, Cdn. Div.	Out of Playoffs
1928-29	44	15	5	2	....	6	13	3	....	21	18	5	....	85	69	47	3rd, Cdn. Div.	Lost Semi-Final
1927-28	44	9	8	5	....	9	10	3	....	18	18	8	....	89	88	44	4th, Cdn. Div.	Out of Playoffs
1926-27*	44	10	10	2	....	5	14	3	....	15	24	5	....	79	94	35	5th, Cdn. Div.	Out of Playoffs
1925-26	36	11	5	2	....	1	16	1	....	12	21	3	....	92	114	27	6th,	Out of Playoffs
1924-25	30	10	5	0	....	9	6	0	....	19	11	0	....	90	84	38	2nd,	Lost NHL S-Final
1923-24	24	7	5	0	....	3	9	0	....	10	14	0	....	59	85	20	3rd,	Out of Playoffs
1922-23	24	10	1	1	....	3	9	0	....	13	10	1	....	82	88	27	3rd,	Out of Playoffs
1921-22	**24**	**8**	**4**	**0**	....	**5**	**6**	**1**	....	**13**	**10**	**1**	....	**98**	**97**	**27**	**2nd,**	**Won Stanley Cup**
1920-21	24	9	3	0	....	6	6	0	....	15	9	0	....	105	100	30	2nd and 1st***	Lost NHL Final
1919-20**	24	8	4	0	....	4	8	0	....	12	12	0	....	119	106	24	3rd and 2nd***	Out of Playoffs
1918-19	18	5	4	0	....	0	9	0	....	5	13	0	....	64	92	10	3rd and 3rd***	Out of Playoffs
1917-18	**22**	**10**	**1**	**0**	....	**3**	**8**	**0**	....	**13**	**9**	**0**	....	**108**	**109**	**26**	**2nd and 1st*** **	**Won Stanley Cup**

* Name changed from St. Patricks to Maple Leafs (February, 1927). ** Name changed from Arenas to St. Patricks.
*** Season played in two halves with no combined standing at end.
From 1917-18 through 1925-26, NHL champions played against PCHA/WCHL champions for Stanley Cup.

2010-11 Schedule

Month	Day	Date	Opponent
Oct.	Thu.	7	Montreal
	Sat.	9	Ottawa
	Wed.	13	at Pittsburgh
	Fri.	15	at NY Rangers
	Mon.	18	NY Islanders
	Thu.	21	NY Rangers
	Sat.	23	at Philadelphia
	Tue.	26	Florida
	Thu.	28	at Boston
	Sat.	30	NY Rangers
Nov.	Tue.	2	Ottawa
	Wed.	3	at Washington
	Sat.	6	Buffalo
	Tue.	9	at Tampa Bay
	Wed.	10	at Florida
	Sat.	13	Vancouver
	Tue.	16	Nashville
	Thu.	18	New Jersey
	Sat.	20	at Montreal
	Mon.	22	Dallas
	Fri.	26	at Buffalo
	Sat.	27	at Ottawa
	Tue.	30	Tampa Bay
Dec.	Thu.	2	Edmonton
	Sat.	4	Boston
	Mon.	6	at Washington
	Wed.	8	at Pittsburgh
	Thu.	9	Philadelphia
	Sat.	11	Montreal
	Tue.	14	at Edmonton
	Thu.	16	at Calgary
	Sat.	18	at Vancouver
	Mon.	20	Atlanta
	Sun.	26	at New Jersey
	Tue.	28	Carolina
	Thu.	30	Columbus
Jan.	Sat.	1	at Ottawa
	Mon.	3	Boston
	Thu.	6	St. Louis
	Fri.	7	at Atlanta
	Mon.	10	at Los Angeles
	Tue.	11	at San Jose
	Thu.	13	at Phoenix
	Sat.	15	Calgary
	Wed.	19	at NY Rangers
	Thu.	20	Anaheim
	Sat.	22	Washington
	Mon.	24	at Carolina
	Tue.	25	at Tampa Bay
Feb.	Tue.	1	Florida
	Thu.	3	Carolina
	Sat.	5	at Buffalo
	Mon.	7	Atlanta
	Tue.	8	at NY Islanders
	Thu.	10	New Jersey
	Sat.	12	at Montreal
	Tue.	15	at Boston
	Wed.	16	at Buffalo
	Sat.	19	Ottawa
	Tue.	22	NY Islanders
	Thu.	24	at Montreal
	Sat.	26	Pittsburgh
	Sun.	27	at Atlanta*
Mar.	Wed.	2	Pittsburgh
	Thu.	3	at Philadelphia
	Sat.	5	Chicago
	Tue.	8	at NY Islanders
	Thu.	10	Philadelphia
	Sat.	12	Buffalo
	Mon.	14	Tampa Bay
	Wed.	16	at Carolina
	Thu.	17	at Florida
	Sat.	19	Boston
	Tue.	22	at Minnesota
	Thu.	24	at Colorado
	Sat.	26	at Detroit
	Tue.	29	Buffalo
	Thu.	31	at Boston
Apr.	Sat.	2	at Ottawa
	Tue.	5	Washington
	Wed.	6	at New Jersey
	Sat.	9	Montreal

* Denotes afternoon game.

NORTHEAST DIVISION
94th NHL Season

Franchise date: November 22, 1917

2010-11 Player Personnel

FORWARDS	HT	WT	S	Place of Birth	*Age	2009-10 Club
ARMSTRONG, Colby	6-2	195	R	Lloydminster, Sask.	27	Atlanta
BOZAK, Tyler	6-1	183	R	Regina, Sask.	24	Toronto-Toronto (AHL)
BRENT, Tim	6-0	197	R	Cambridge, Ont.	26	Toronto-Toronto (AHL)
BROWN, Mike	5-11	201	R	Northbrook, IL	25	Anaheim
CAPUTI, Luca	6-3	200	L	Toronto, Ont.	22	Pit-Wilkes-Barre-Tor
CRABB, Joey	6-1	190	R	Anchorage, AK	27	Chicago (AHL)
D'AMIGO, Jerry	5-11	208	L	Binghamton, NY	19	R.P.I.
GRABOVSKI, Mikhail	5-11	183	L	Potsdam, East Germany	26	Toronto
HANSON, Christian	6-3	228	R	Venetia, PA	24	Toronto-Toronto (AHL)
KADRI, Nazem	6-0	177	L	London, Ont.	20	London-Toronto
KESSEL, Phil	5-11	180	R	Madison, WI	23	Toronto
KULEMIN, Nikolai	6-1	225	L	Magnitogorsk, USSR	24	Toronto
MITCHELL, John	6-1	204	L	Oakville, Ont.	25	Toronto
MUELLER, Marcel	6-3	220	L	Berlin, East Germany	22	Kolner Haie
ORR, Colton	6-3	222	R	Winnipeg, Man.	28	Toronto
ROSEHILL, Jay	6-3	215	L	Olds, Alta.	25	Toronto-Toronto (AHL)
SJOSTROM, Fredrik	6-1	218	L	Fargelanda, Sweden	27	Calgary-Toronto
VERSTEEG, Kris	5-10	182	R	Lethbridge, Alta.	24	Chicago
DEFENSEMEN						
AULIE, Keith	6-5	217	L	Regina, Sask.	21	Abbotsford-Toronto (AHL)
BEAUCHEMIN, Francois	6-0	213	L	Sorel, Que.	30	Toronto
FINGER, Jeff	6-1	209	R	Houghton, MI	30	Toronto
GUNNARSSON, Carl	6-2	196	L	Orebro, Sweden	23	Toronto-Toronto (AHL)
HOLZER, Korbinian	6-3	205	R	Munich, West Germany	22	Dusseldorf
KABERLE, Tomas	6-1	214	L	Rakovnik, Czech.	32	Toronto
KOMISAREK, Mike	6-4	243	R	West Islip, NY	28	Toronto
LEBDA, Brett	5-9	195	L	Buffalo Grove, IL	28	Detroit
PHANEUF, Dion	6-3	214	L	Edmonton, Alta.	25	Calgary-Toronto
RICHMOND, Danny	6-0	192	L	Chicago, IL	26	Peoria-Rockford
SCHENN, Luke	6-2	215	R	Saskatoon, Sask.	20	Toronto

GOALTENDERS	HT	WT	C	Place of Birth	*Age	2009-10 Club
GIGUERE, Jean-Sebastien	6-1	202	L	Montreal, Que.	33	Anaheim-Toronto
GUSTAVSSON, Jonas	6-3	192	L	Danderyd, Sweden	25	Toronto

* – Age at start of 2010-11 season

2009-10 Scoring

* – rookie

Regular Season

Pos	#	Player	Team	GP	G	A	Pts	TOI	+/–	PIM	PP	SH	GW	S	%
C	81	Phil Kessel	TOR	70	30	25	55	19:32	–8	21	8	0	5	297	10.1
D	15	Tomas Kaberle	TOR	82	7	42	49	22:21	–16	24	3	0	1	158	4.4
L	41	Nikolai Kulemin	TOR	78	16	20	36	16:22	0	16	0	1	3	145	11.0
C	84	Mikhail Grabovski	TOR	59	10	25	35	16:47	3	10	2	1	3	126	7.9
D	3	Dion Phaneuf	CGY	55	10	12	22	23:14	3	49	5	0	2	138	7.2
			TOR	26	2	8	10	26:21	–2	34	0	0	1	87	2.3
			Total	81	12	20	32	24:14	1	83	5	0	3	225	5.3
C	42	* Tyler Bozak	TOR	37	8	19	27	19:13	–5	6	2	0	1	51	15.7
D	22	Francois Beauchemin	TOR	82	5	21	26	25:27	–13	33	4	0	1	170	2.9
C	39	John Mitchell	TOR	60	6	17	23	15:49	–7	31	1	0	1	90	6.7
D	2	Luke Schenn	TOR	79	5	12	17	16:52	2	50	0	0	1	101	5.0
D	36	* Carl Gunnarsson	TOR	43	3	12	15	21:26	8	10	0	0	0	45	6.7
L	45	* Viktor Stalberg	TOR	40	9	5	14	14:36	–13	30	0	0	0	117	7.7
C	16	Jamie Lundmark	CGY	21	4	5	9	15:22	–6	4	1	0	1	36	11.1
			TOR	15	1	2	3	11:34	–1	16	0	0	0	16	6.3
			Total	36	5	7	12	13:47	–7	20	1	0	1	52	9.6
L	11	Fredrik Sjostrom	CGY	46	1	5	6	9:31	2	8	0	0	0	33	3.0
			TOR	19	2	3	5	13:51	–4	4	0	0	0	31	6.5
			Total	65	3	8	11	10:47	–2	12	0	0	0	64	4.7
D	4	Jeff Finger	TOR	39	2	8	10	13:47	–11	20	0	0	0	29	6.9
C	51	Rickard Wallin	TOR	60	2	7	9	12:38	–7	20	0	0	0	72	2.8
C	18	Wayne Primeau	TOR	59	3	5	8	11:02	–1	35	0	0	0	47	6.4
L	33	* Luca Caputi	PIT	4	1	1	2	11:46	–1	2	0	0	0	4	25.0
			TOR	19	1	5	6	14:37	0	10	0	0	0	32	3.1
			Total	23	2	6	8	14:07	–1	12	0	0	0	36	5.6
C	20	* Christian Hanson	TOR	31	2	5	7	13:22	–2	16	0	1	0	45	4.4
R	28	Colton Orr	TOR	82	4	2	6	6:51	–4	239	0	0	1	43	9.3
D	7	Garnet Exelby	TOR	51	1	3	4	10:05	–8	73	0	0	0	14	7.1
D	8	Mike Komisarek	TOR	34	0	4	4	19:56	–9	40	0	0	0	35	0.0
D	38	* Jay Rosehill	TOR	15	1	1	2	6:14	–2	67	0	0	0	6	16.7
C	37	* Tim Brent	TOR	1	0	0	0	13:21	0	0	0	0	0	3	0.0
C	56	* Andre Deveaux	TOR	1	0	0	0	6:09	–1	0	0	0	0	1	0.0
C	43	* Nazem Kadri	TOR	1	0	0	0	17:26	–1	0	0	0	0	0	0.0
C	44	* Brayden Irwin	TOR	2	0	0	0	10:05	0	2	0	0	0	3	0.0

Goaltending

No.	Goaltender	GPI	Mins	Avg	W	L	OT	EN	SO	GA	SA	S%	G	A	PIM
35	Jean-Sebastien Giguere	15	915	2.49	6	7	2	2	2	38	451	.916	0	0	0
50	* Jonas Gustavsson	42	2340	2.87	16	15	9	5	1	112	1146	.902	0	2	2
30	Joey MacDonald	6	319	3.20	1	4	0	1	0	17	157	.892	0	0	0
35	Vesa Toskala	26	1393	3.66	7	12	3	3	1	85	676	.874	0	0	4
	Totals	**82**	**5003**	**3.15**	**30**	**38**	**14**	**11**	**5**	**263**	**2440**	**.892**			

Joey MacDonald and Jonas Gustavsson shared a shutout vs. Montreal on Dec 1, 2009.

Ron Wilson

Head Coach

Born: Windsor, Ont., May 28, 1955.

The Toronto Maple Leafs announced on June 10, 2008 that Ron Wilson had been named the 27th head coach in the club's history. Wilson previously held NHL head coaching duties with Anaheim, Washington, and the San Jose Sharks.

Under Wilson's guidance the Sharks were the only NHL team to have won at least one playoff round in each season from 2003-04 through 2007-08. In his four full seasons behind the Sharks bench, the team advanced to the Western Conference Final for the first time ever in 2004, and reached the Conference semifinals in 2006, 2007 and 2008. His Sharks teams garnered two Pacific Division championships (2004 and 2008); twice finished second in their division, and twice posted the second-best point total in the conference. With 206 victories in San Jose, Wilson surpassed Darryl Sutter as the Sharks' all-time wins leader on March 1, 2008.

Wilson coached the Washington Capitals from 1997 until 2002, with his tenure in the United State's capital highlighted by the team's only trip to the Stanley Cup Final in 1998. Prior to spending five seasons with the Capitals, Wilson had served as the first head coach of the expansion Mighty Ducks of Anaheim in 1993, and he led the team to the postseason for the very first time in 1996-97.

Throughout his professional and amateur career, Wilson has enjoyed a long-standing relationship with USA Hockey. He led Team USA to the gold medal in 1996 at the inaugural World Cup of Hockey and he coached the team again at the 2004 tournament. Wilson coached the U.S. team at the World Championship in 1994, 1996 and again in 2009. He also served as head coach for Team USA at the 1998 Nagano Olympics and will do again at the 2010 Vancouver Games.

Wilson was a seventh-round selection of the Toronto Maple Leafs (132nd overall) in the 1975 NHL Amateur Draft. He made his NHL debut by playing in 13 games for Toronto in 1977-78, followed by 46 games in 1978-79 and five games in 1979-80. In 177 career NHL games as a player with Toronto and Minnesota, Wilson recorded 26 goals and 67 assists for 93 points. He is one of 15 individuals that have both played for the Maple Leafs and then went on to coach at least one game for the Original Six franchise. He is the son of Larry Wilson and the nephew of Johnny Wilson, both former players on Stanley Cup winning teams from Detroit.

Coaching Record

			Regular Season				Playoffs			
Season	**Team**	**League**	**GC**	**W**	**L**	**O/T**	**GC**	**W**	**L**	**T**
1993-94	**Anaheim**	**NHL**	**84**	**33**	**46**	**5**	....	....	....	....
1994-95	**Anaheim**	**NHL**	**48**	**16**	**27**	**5**	....	....	....	....
1995-96	**Anaheim**	**NHL**	**82**	**35**	**39**	**8**	....	....	....	....
1996-97	**Anaheim**	**NHL**	**82**	**36**	**33**	**13**	**11**	**4**	**7**	....
1997-98	**Washington**	**NHL**	**82**	**40**	**30**	**12**	**21**	**12**	**9**	....
1998-99	**Washington**	**NHL**	**82**	**31**	**45**	**6**	....	....	....	....
99-2000	**Washington**	**NHL**	**82**	**44**	**24**	**14**	**5**	**1**	**4**	....
2000-01	**Washington**	**NHL**	**82**	**41**	**27**	**14**	**6**	**2**	**4**	....
2001-02	**Washington**	**NHL**	**82**	**36**	**33**	**13**	....	....	....	....
2002-03	**San Jose**	**NHL**	**57**	**19**	**25**	**13**	....	....	....	....
2003-04	**San Jose**	**NHL**	**82**	**43**	**21**	**18**	**17**	**10**	**7**	....
2004-05	**San Jose**				SEASON CANCELLED					
2005-06	**San Jose**	**NHL**	**82**	**44**	**27**	**11**	**11**	**6**	**5**	....
2006-07	**San Jose**	**NHL**	**82**	**51**	**26**	**5**	**11**	**6**	**5**	....
2007-08	**San Jose**	**NHL**	**82**	**49**	**23**	**10**	**13**	**6**	**7**	....
2008-09	**Toronto**	**NHL**	**82**	**34**	**35**	**13**	....	....	....	....
2009-10	**Toronto**	**NHL**	**82**	**30**	**38**	**14**	....	....	....	....
	NHL Totals		**1255**	**582**	**499**	**174**	**95**	**47**	**48**	....

Coaching History

Dick Carroll, 1917-18, 1918-19; Frank Heffernan and Harry Sproule, 1919-20; Frank Carroll, 1920-21; George O'Donohue, 1921-22; George O'Donohue and Charles Querrie, 1922-23; Charles Querrie, 1923-24; Eddie Powers, 1924-25, 1925-26; Charles Querrie, Mike Rodden and Alex Romeril, 1926-27; Conn Smythe, 1927-28 to 1929-30; Conn Smythe and Art Duncan, 1930-31; Art Duncan and Dick Irvin, 1931-32; Dick Irvin, 1932-33 to 1939-40; Hap Day, 1940-41 to 1949-50; Joe Primeau, 1950-51 to 1952-53; King Clancy, 1953-54 to 1955-56; Howie Meeker, 1956-57; Billy Reay, 1957-58; Billy Reay and Punch Imlach, 1958-59; Punch Imlach, 1959-60 to 1968-69; John McLellan, 1969-70 to 1972-73; Red Kelly, 1973-74 to 1976-77; Roger Neilson, 1977-78, 1978-79; Floyd Smith, Dick Duff and Punch Imlach, 1979-80; Joe Crozier and Mike Nykoluk, 1980-81; Mike Nykoluk, 1981-82 to 1983-84; Dan Maloney, 1984-85, 1985-86; John Brophy, 1986-87, 1987-88; John Brophy and George Armstrong, 1988-89; Doug Carpenter, 1989-90; Doug Carpenter and Tom Watt, 1990-91; Tom Watt, 1991-92; Pat Burns, 1992-93 to 1994-95; Pat Burns and Nick Beverley, 1995-96; Mike Murphy, 1996-97, 1997-98; Pat Quinn, 1998-99 to 2005-06; Paul Maurice, 2006-07, 2007-08; Ron Wilson, 2008-09 to date.

Captains' History

Bert Corbeau, 1926-27; Hap Day, 1927-28 to 1936-37; Charlie Conacher, 1937-38; Red Horner, 1938-39, 1939-40; Syl Apps, 1940-41 to 1942-43; Bob Davidson, 1943-44, 1944-45; Syl Apps, 1945-46 to 1947-48; Ted Kennedy, 1948-49 to 1954-55; Sid Smith, 1955-56; Jimmy Thomson, Ted Kennedy, 1956-57; George Armstrong, 1957-58 to 1968-69; Dave Keon, 1969-70 to 1974-75; Darryl Sittler, 1975-76 to 1980-81; Rick Vaive, 1981-82 to 1985-86; no captain, 1986-87 to 1988-89; Rob Ramage, 1989-90, 1990-91; Wendel Clark, 1991-92 to 1993-94; Doug Gilmour, 1994-95 to 1996-97; Mats Sundin, 1997-98 to 2007-08; no captain, 2008-09, 2009-10; Dion Phaneuf, 2010-11.

Club Records

Team

(Figures in brackets for season records are games played; records for fewest points, wins, ties, losses, goals, goals against are for 70 or more games)

Most Points **103** 2003-04 (82)
Most Wins **45** 1998-99 (82), 1999-2000 (82), 2003-04 (82)
Most Ties **22** 1954-55 (70)
Most Losses **52** 1984-85 (80)
Most Goals **337** 1989-90 (80)
Most Goals Against **387** 1983-84 (80)
Fewest Points **48** 1984-85 (80)
Fewest Wins **20** 1981-82 (80), 1984-85 (80)
Fewest Ties **4** 1989-90 (80)
Fewest Losses **16** 1950-51 (70)
Fewest Goals **147** 1954-55 (70)
Fewest Goals Against ***131** 1953-54 (70)
Longest Winning Streak
Overall .... **10** Oct. 7-28/93
Home .... **9** Nov. 11-Dec. 26/53, Mar. 6-Apr. 7/07
Away .... **7** Three times
Longest Undefeated Streak
Overall .... **11** Oct. 15-Nov. 8/50 (8 wins, 3 ties), Jan. 6-Feb. 1/94 (7 wins, 4 ties)
Home .... **18** Nov. 28/33-Mar. 10/34 (15 wins, 3 ties), Oct. 31/53-Jan. 23/54 (16 wins, 2 ties)
Away .... **9** Nov. 30/47-Jan. 11/48 (4 wins, 5 ties)
Longest Losing Streak
Overall .... **10** Jan. 15-Feb. 8/67
Home .... **7** Nov. 11-Dec. 5/84
Away .... **11** Feb. 20-Apr. 1/88
Longest Winless Streak
Overall .... **15** Dec. 26/87-Jan. 25/88 (11 losses, 4 ties)
Home .... **11** Dec. 19/87-Jan. 25/88 (7 losses, 4 ties)
Away .... **18** Oct. 6/82-Jan. 5/83 (13 losses, 5 ties)
Most Shutouts, Season **13** 1953-54 (70)
Most PIM, Season **2,419** 1989-90 (80)
Most Goals, Game .... **14** Mar. 16/57 (NYR 1 at Tor. 14)

Individual

Most Seasons .... **21** George Armstrong
Most Games .... **1,187** George Armstrong
Most Goals, Career .... **420** Mats Sundin
Most Assists, Career .... **620** Borje Salming
Most Points, Career .... **987** Mats Sundin (420G, 567A)
Most PIM, Career .... **2,265** Tie Domi
Most Shutouts, Career .... **62** Turk Broda
Longest Consecutive Games Streak .... **486** Tim Horton (Feb. 11/61-Feb. 4/68)
Most Goals, Season .... **54** Rick Vaive (1981-82)
Most Assists, Season .... **95** Doug Gilmour (1992-93)
Most Points, Season .... **127** Doug Gilmour (1992-93; 32G, 95A)
Most PIM, Season .... **365** Tie Domi (1997-98)
Most Points, Defenseman, Season .... **79** Ian Turnbull (1976-77; 22G, 57A)
Most Points, Center, Season .... **127** Doug Gilmour (1992-93; 32G, 95A)
Most Points, Right Wing, Season .... **97** Wilf Paiement (1980-81; 40G, 57A)
Most Points, Left Wing, Season .... **99** Dave Andreychuk (1993-94; 53G, 46A)
Most Points, Rookie, Season .... **66** Peter Ihnacak (1982-83; 28G, 38A)
Most Shutouts, Season .... **13** Harry Lumley (1953-54)
Most Goals, Game .... **6** Corb Denneny (Jan. 26/21), Darryl Sittler (Feb. 7/76)
Most Assists, Game .... **6** Babe Pratt (Jan. 8/44), Doug Gilmour (Feb. 13/93)
Most Points, Game .... ***10** Darryl Sittler (Feb. 7/76; 6G, 4A)

* NHL Record.

Retired Numbers

5	Bill Barilko	1946-1951
6	Ace Bailey	1926-1934

Honored Numbers

1	Turk Broda	1936-43, 45-52
	Johnny Bower	1958-1970
4	Hap Day	1926-1937
	Red Kelly	1959-1967
7	King Clancy	1930-1937
	Tim Horton	1949-50, 51-70
9	Charlie Conacher	1929-1938
	Ted Kennedy	1942-55, 56-57
10	Syl Apps	1936-43, 45-48
	George Armstrong	1949-50, 51-71
17	Wendel Clark	1985-94, 96-98, 2000
21	Borje Salming	1973-1989
27	Frank Mahovlich	1956-1968
	Darryl Sittler	1970-1982
93	Doug Gilmour	1992-97, 2003

All-time Record vs. Other Clubs

Regular Season

	At Home								On Road								Total							
	GP	W	L	T	OL	GF	GA	PTS	GP	W	L	T	OL	GF	GA	PTS	GP	W	L	T	OL	GF	GA	PTS
Anaheim	17	10	2	4	1	55	35	25	13	6	6	1	0	34	42	13	30	16	8	5	1	89	77	38
Atlanta	19	11	5	1	2	69	50	25	19	12	5	0	2	68	38	26	38	23	10	1	4	137	88	51
Boston	317	163	101	51	2	1051	828	379	316	96	168	47	5	844	1031	244	633	259	269	98	7	1895	1859	623
Buffalo	85	33	37	12	3	248	292	81	87	25	54	6	2	227	343	58	172	58	91	18	5	475	635	139
Calgary	56	30	18	7	1	217	204	68	64	22	35	5	2	199	247	51	120	52	53	12	3	416	451	119
Carolina	46	17	23	5	1	148	164	40	47	17	20	6	4	155	180	44	93	34	43	11	5	303	344	84
Chicago	317	164	98	54	1	1079	832	383	320	120	158	42	0	834	974	282	637	284	256	96	1	1913	1806	665
Colorado	37	16	17	4	0	120	141	36	31	8	18	5	0	97	120	21	68	24	35	9	0	217	261	57
Columbus	5	3	0	1	1	16	9	8	3	2	0	0	1	13	9	5	8	5	0	1	2	29	18	13
Dallas	103	49	37	17	0	359	329	115	99	36	51	11	1	310	372	84	202	85	88	28	1	669	701	199
Detroit	318	166	105	47	0	1053	849	379	324	109	169	46	0	796	975	264	642	275	274	93	0	1849	1824	643
Edmonton	40	22	16	2	0	165	165	46	46	16	23	6	1	147	185	39	86	38	39	8	1	312	350	85
Florida	25	14	8	2	1	78	72	31	27	13	8	5	1	79	75	32	52	27	16	7	2	157	147	63
Los Angeles	70	35	24	11	0	270	230	81	67	22	35	10	0	196	240	54	137	57	59	21	0	466	470	135
Minnesota	5	4	1	0	0	17	11	8	3	1	2	0	0	5	11	2	8	5	3	0	0	22	22	10
Montreal	351	181	119	45	6	1071	927	413	351	101	204	43	3	884	1224	248	702	282	323	88	9	1955	2151	661
Nashville	8	3	4	1	0	16	21	7	3	1	1	0	1	8	10	3	11	4	5	1	1	24	31	10
New Jersey	58	37	15	5	1	203	156	80	56	19	19	15	3	177	192	56	114	56	34	20	4	380	348	136
NY Islanders	65	35	24	4	2	232	213	76	63	23	34	3	3	178	241	52	128	58	58	7	5	410	454	128
NY Rangers	292	164	87	39	2	1005	771	369	293	111	123	56	3	860	908	281	585	275	210	95	5	1865	1679	650
Ottawa	40	19	15	2	4	109	115	44	38	14	20	1	3	102	119	32	78	33	35	3	7	211	234	76
Philadelphia	77	30	32	14	1	240	247	75	77	21	47	8	1	184	289	51	154	51	79	22	2	424	536	126
Phoenix	45	20	23	2	0	163	171	42	41	13	22	6	0	146	172	32	86	33	45	8	0	309	343	74
Pittsburgh	77	38	27	11	1	304	251	88	79	32	40	6	1	258	315	71	156	70	67	17	2	562	566	159
St. Louis	101	58	29	11	3	375	300	130	104	31	59	14	0	285	353	76	205	89	88	25	3	660	653	206
San Jose	20	12	6	2	0	75	55	26	17	7	7	3	0	44	40	17	37	19	13	5	0	119	95	43
Tampa Bay	31	20	9	1	1	112	81	42	30	20	6	1	3	99	71	44	61	40	15	2	4	211	152	86
Vancouver	63	28	23	11	1	225	209	68	67	24	32	11	0	222	236	59	130	52	55	22	1	447	445	127
Washington	58	32	20	6	0	241	192	70	60	21	35	4	0	169	218	46	118	53	55	10	0	410	410	116
Defunct Clubs	232	158	53	21	0	860	515	337	233	84	120	29	0	607	745	197	465	242	173	50	0	1467	1260	534
Totals	**2978**	**1572**	**978**	**393**	**35**	**10176**	**8435**	**3572**	**2978**	**1027**	**1521**	**390**	**40**	**8227**	**9975**	**2484**	**5956**	**2599**	**2499**	**783**	**75**	**18403**	**18410**	**6056**

Playoffs

	Series	W	L	GP	W	L	T	GF	GA	Last Mtg.	Rnd.	Result
Boston	13	8	5	62	31	30	1	150	153	1974	QF	L 0-4
Buffalo	1	0	1	5	1	4	0	16	21	1999	CF	L 1-4
Calgary	1	1	0	2	2	0	0	9	5	1979	PRE	W 2-0
Carolina	1	0	1	6	2	4	0	6	10	2002	CF	L 2-4
Chicago	9	6	3	38	22	15	1	111	89	1995	CQF	L 3-4
Dallas	2	0	2	7	1	6	0	26	35	1983	DSF	L 1-3
Detroit	23	12	11	117	58	59	0	311	321	1993	DSF	W 4-3
Los Angeles	3	2	1	12	7	5	0	41	31	1993	CF	L 3-4
Montreal	15	7	8	71	29	42	0	160	215	1979	QF	L 0-4
New Jersey	2	0	2	13	5	8	0	27	37	2001	CSF	L 3-4
NY Islanders	3	2	1	17	8	9	0	42	54	2002	CQF	W 4-3
NY Rangers	8	3	5	35	16	19	0	86	86	1971	QF	L 2-4
Ottawa	4	4	0	24	16	8	0	57	42	2004	CQF	W 4-3
Philadelphia	6	1	5	36	14	22	0	85	119	2004	CSF	L 2-4
Pittsburgh	3	3	0	12	8	4	0	39	27	1999	CSF	W 4-2
St. Louis	5	2	3	31	14	17	0	90	88	1996	CQF	L 2-4
San Jose	1	1	0	7	4	3	0	26	21	1994	CSF	W 4-3
Vancouver	1	0	1	5	1	4	0	9	16	1994	CF	L 1-4
Defunct Clubs	8	6	2	24	12	10	2	59	57			
Totals	**109**	**58**	**51**	**524**	**251**	**269**	**4**	**1350**	**1427**			

Playoff Results 2010-2006

(Last playoff appearance: 2004)

Abbreviations: Round: CF – conference final; **CSF** – conference semi-final; **CQF** – conference quarter-final; **DSF** – division semi-final; **QF** – quarter-final; **PRE** – preliminary round.

Calgary totals include Atlanta Flames, 1972-73 to 1979-80.
Carolina totals include Hartford, 1979-80 to 1996-97.
Colorado totals include Quebec, 1979-80 to 1994-95.
Dallas totals include Minnesota North Stars, 1967-68 to 1992-93.
New Jersey totals include Kansas City, 1974-75, 1975-76, and Colorado Rockies, 1976-77 to 1981-82.
Phoenix totals include Winnipeg, 1979-80 to 1995-96.

2009-10 Results

Oct.	1	Montreal	3-4*	**Jan.**	2	at Calgary	1-3
	3	at Washington	4-6		5	Florida	3-2
	6	Ottawa	1-2		6	at Philadelphia	2-6
	10	Pittsburgh	2-5		8	at Buffalo	2-3
	12	at NY Rangers	2-7		9	Pittsburgh	1-4
	13	Colorado	1-4		12	Carolina	2-4
	17	NY Rangers	1-4		14	Philadelphia	4-0
	24	at Vancouver	1-3		15	at Washington	1-6
	26	at Anaheim	6-3		18	at Nashville	4-3
	28	at Dallas	3-4*		19	at Atlanta	3-4
	30	at Buffalo	2-3*		21	at Tampa Bay	2-3*
	31	at Montreal	4-5†		23	at Florida	0-2
Nov.	3	Tampa Bay	1-2*		26	Los Angeles	3-5
	6	at Carolina	3-2		29	at New Jersey	4-5*
	7	Detroit	5-1		30	Vancouver	3-5
	10	Minnesota	2-5	**Feb.**	2	New Jersey	3-0
	13	at Chicago	2-3		5	at New Jersey	3-4
	14	Calgary	2-5		6	Ottawa	5-0
	17	at Ottawa	2-3		8	San Jose	2-3
	19	at Carolina	5-6†		12	at St. Louis	0-4
	21	Washington	2-1†	**Mar.**	2	Carolina	1-5
	23	NY Islanders	3-4*		4	at Boston	2-3†
	25	at Tampa Bay	4-3		6	at Ottawa	2-1†
	27	at Florida	6-4		7	at Philadelphia	1-3
	30	Buffalo	0-3		9	Boston	4-3*
Dec.	1	at Montreal	3-0		11	Tampa Bay	4-3*
	3	at Columbus	6-3		13	Edmonton	6-4
	5	at Boston	2-7		14	at NY Islanders	1-4
	7	Atlanta	5-2		16	at Ottawa	4-1
	9	NY Islanders	3-2		18	New Jersey	2-1†
	10	at Boston	2-5		20	Montreal	3-2†
	12	Washington	6-3		23	Florida	1-4
	14	Ottawa	3-2		25	at Atlanta	2-1*
	16	Phoenix	3-6		27	NY Rangers	3-2*
	18	at Buffalo	2-5		28	at Pittsburgh	4-5†
	19	Boston	2-0		30	Atlanta	2-3
	21	Buffalo	2-3*	**Apr.**	1	Buffalo	4-2
	23	at NY Islanders	1-3		3	Boston	1-2*
	26	Montreal	2-3*		6	Philadelphia	0-2
	27	at Pittsburgh	4-3		7	at NY Rangers	1-5
	30	at Edmonton	1-3		10	at Montreal	4-3*

* – Overtime † – Shootout

Entry Draft Selections 2010-1996

Name in bold denotes played in NHL.

2010 Pick		2005 Pick		2001 Pick		1998 Pick	
43	Brad Ross	21	**Tuukka Rask**	17	**Carlo Colaiacovo**	10	**Nik Antropov**
62	Greg McKegg	82	**Phil Oreskovic**	39	**Karel Pilar**	35	**Petr Svoboda**
79	Sondre Olden	153	Alex Berry	65	**Brendan Bell**	69	Jamie Hodson
116	Petter Granberg	173	Johan Dahlberg	82	**Jay Harrison**	87	**Alexei Ponikarovsky**
144	Sam Carrick	216	**Anton Stralman**	88	Nicolas Corbeil	126	Morgan Warren
146	Daniel Brodin	228	Chad Rau	134	**Kyle Wellwood**	154	**Allan Rourke**
182	Josh Nicholls			168	**Maxim Kondratiev**	181	Jonathan Gagnon

2009 Pick		2004 Pick				215	Dwight Wolfe
7	**Nazem Kadri**	90	**Justin Pogge**	183	Jaroslav Sklenar	228	Michal Travnicek
50	Kenny Ryan	113	Roman Kukumberg	198	Ivan Kolozvary	236	Sergei Rostov
58	Jesse Blacker	157	Dmitri Vorobiev	213	Jan Chovan		
68	Jamie Devane	187	**Robbie Earl**	246	**Tomas Mojzis**	**1997** Pick	
128	Eric Knodel	220	Maxim Semenov	276	Mike Knoepfli	57	Jeff Farkas
158	Jerry D'Amigo	252	Jan Steber			84	**Adam Mair**
188	Barron Smith	285	Pierce Norton	**2000** Pick		111	Frantisek Mrazek

2008 Pick		2003 Pick		24	**Brad Boyes**	138	Eric Gooldy
5	**Luke Schenn**	57	John Doherty	51	**Kris Vernarsky**	165	Hugo Marchand
60	Jimmy Hayes	91	Martin Sagat	70	**Mikael Tellqvist**	190	**Shawn Thornton**
98	Mikhail Stefanovich	125	Konstantin Volkov	90	Jean-Francois Racine	194	Russ Bartlett
128	Greg Pateryn	158	**John Mitchell**	100	Miguel Delisle	221	**Jonathan Hedstrom**
129	Joel Champagne	220	**Jeremy Williams**	179	Vadim Sozinov		
130	Jerome Flaake	237	Shaun Landolt	209	Markus Seikola	**1996** Pick	
158	Grant Rollheiser			223	Lubos Velebny	36	**Marek Posmyk**
188	Andrew MacWilliam	**2002** Pick		254	Alexander Shinkar	50	Francis Larivee

2007 Pick		24	**Alex Steen**	265	**Jean-Philippe Cote**	66	Mike Lankshear
74	Dale Mitchell	57	**Matt Stajan**			68	Konstantin Kalmikov
99	Matt Frattin	74	Todd Ford	**1999** Pick		86	Jason Sessa
104	Ben Winnett	88	Dominic D'Amour	24	Luca Cereda	103	Vladimir Antipov
134	Juraj Mikus	122	David Turon	60	Peter Reynolds	110	Peter Cava
164	Christopher Didomenico	191	**Ian White**	108	Mirko Murovic	111	Brandon Sugden
194	**Carl Gunnarsson**	222	Scott May	110	Jon Zion	140	**Dmitri Yakushin**
		254	**Jarkko Immonen**	151	Vaclav Zavoral	148	Chris Bogas
2006 Pick		285	**Staffan Kronwall**	161	Jan Sochor	151	Lucio DeMartinis
13	**Jiri Tlusty**			211	Vladimir Kulikov	178	Reggie Berg
44	**Nikolai Kulemin**			239	**Pierre Hedin**	204	**Tomas Kaberle**
99	**James Reimer**			267	Peter Metcalf	230	Jared Hope
111	Korbinian Holzer						
161	**Viktor Stalberg**						
166	Tyler Ruegsegger						
180	Leo Komarov						

General Managers' History

Charles Querrie, 1917-18 to 1926-27; Conn Smythe, 1927-28 to 1956-57; Hap Day, 1957-58; Punch Imlach, 1958-59 to 1968-69; Jim Gregory, 1969-70 to 1978-79; Punch Imlach, 1979-80, 1980-81; Punch Imlach and Gerry McNamara, 1981-82; Gerry McNamara, 1982-83 to 1987-88; Gord Stellick, 1988-89; Floyd Smith, 1989-90, 1990-91; Cliff Fletcher, 1991-92 to 1996-97; Ken Dryden, 1997-98, 1998-99; Pat Quinn, 1999-2000 to 2002-03; John Ferguson, 2003-04 to 2006-07; John Ferguson and Cliff Fletcher, 2007-08; Cliff Fletcher and Brian Burke, 2008-09; Brian Burke, 2009-10 to date.

Brian Burke
President and General Manager

Born: Providence, RI, June 30, 1955.

Brian Burke was named president and general manager of the Toronto Maple Leafs on November 29, 2008, bringing over 20 years of National Hockey League experience in various roles to the franchise. Most recently, Burke had served as executive vice president and general manager of the Anaheim Ducks from 2005 to 2008. In just over three seasons in Anaheim, Burke guided the Ducks to their first Stanley Cup (2007), first Pacific Division title (2007), and first-two 100+ point seasons (2006-07 and 2007-08).

Burke received two outstanding honours in the summer of 2008. On June 6, he was chosen by USA Hockey as general manager of the 2010 U.S. Olympic hockey team, and on August 7, he was named a recipient of the 2008 Lester Patrick Award for outstanding service to hockey in the United States. Burke was also ranked number one by The Hockey News in the magazine's Annual GM rankings in March of 2008, and was a finalist for The Hockey News Executive of the Year in 2006. He was named The Sporting News Executive of the Year in 2001, and was a runner-up for the same award following the 2005-06 season.

Burke joined the Ducks after a six-year stint (1998 to 2004) as president and general manager of the Vancouver Canucks where he revitalized the team en route to consecutive 100+ point seasons and the 2004 Northwest Division title. Under Burke's leadership, the Canucks improved their point total in four consecutive years from 1999-2003.

Born in Providence, Rhode Island and raised in Edina, Minnesota, Burke was named the vice president and director of hockey operations by the Vancouver Canucks in June of 1987. Burke left Vancouver to serve as general manager of the Hartford Whalers for one season in 1992, before joining the NHL front office as senior vice president and director of hockey operations in September of 1993.

After earning his Bachelor of Arts in history from Providence College in 1977, Burke signed with the Philadelphia Flyers prior to the 1977-78 season and won a Calder Cup championship with the Flyers' American Hockey League affiliate the Maine Mariners. He then returned to school and graduated from Harvard Law in 1981. Burke practiced law in Boston for the next six years, representing professional hockey players until joining the Canucks in 1987.

Club Directory

Air Canada Centre

Toronto Maple Leafs
Air Canada Centre
40 Bay St., Suite 400
Toronto, Ontario M5J 2X2
Phone **416/815-5700**
FAX 416/359-9331
www.mapleleafs.com
Capacity: 18,819

Board of Directors
Lawrence M. Tanenbaum (Chairman of the Board), Glen Silvestri, Robert G. Bertram, Ashvin Malkani, Robert MacLellan, Dale H. Lastman, Richard Peddie

Maple Leaf Sports & Entertainment
Chairman, NHL Governor . . . . Lawrence M. Tanenbaum
President, CEO and Alt. Governor . . . . Richard Peddie
Alternate NHL Governor . . . . Brian Burke
Alternate NHL Governor . . . . Dale H. Lastman
Exec. V.P. and Chief Operating Officer . . . . Tom Anselmi
Exec. V.P. and CFO, Business Development . . . . . . Ian Clarke
Exec. V.P., Venues and Entertainment . . . . Bob Hunter
Exec. V.P., General Counsel and Corp. Secretary . . . Robin Brudner
Senior Vice-President, People . . . . Mardi Walker
Senior Vice-President, Broadcast and Content . . . . Chris Hebb
Senior Vice-President, Business Partnerships . . . . . Dave Hopkinson
Senior Vice-President, Finance . . . . Kevin Nonomura
Senior Vice-President, Ticket Sales and Service . . . . Beth Robertson
Vice-President, Live Entertainment . . . . Patti-Anne Tarlton
Vice-President, Food & Beverage . . . . Michael Doyle

Hockey Operations
President, G.M. and Alternate NHL Governor . . . . . Brian Burke
Senior Vice-President of Hockey Operations . . . . . . David Nonis
Vice-President of Hockey Operations . . . . Dave Poulin
Senior Advisor . . . . Cliff Fletcher
Assistant General Manager . . . . Claude Loiselle
Head Coach . . . . Ron Wilson
Assistant Coaches . . . . Keith Acton, Tim Hunter, Rob Zettler
Goaltending Consultant . . . . Francois Allaire
Skating Coach . . . . Graeme Townshend
Director of Player Development . . . . Jim Hughes
Director, Hockey and Scouting Administration . . . . . Reid Mitchell
Strength and Conditioning Coordinator . . . . Anthony Belza
Manager, Team Services . . . . Dave Griffiths
Video Coach . . . . Chris Dennis
Director of Amateur Scouting . . . . Dave Morrison
Pro Scouts . . . . Rob Cowie, Steve Kasper, Mike Penny, Tom Watt
Amateur Scouts . . . . Scott Carter, Gary Harker, John Lilley, Garth Malarchuk, Mike Palmateer, Allan Power, George Armstrong, Pierre Rioux, Roy Stasiuk, John McMorrow, Dave Starman
European Scouts . . . . Thommie Bergman, Joe Gibbs, Peter Ihnacak, Nikolai Ladygin, Jari Gronstrand
Community Representatives . . . . Wendel Clark, Darryl Sittler
Executive Assistant, Hockey Operations . . . . Sandi Dunn
Exec. Assistant to the President and G.M. . . . . Catherine Grey

Medical and Training Staff
Head Athletic Therapist . . . . Andy Playter
Athletic Therapist . . . . Marty Dudgeon
Equipment Manager . . . . Brian Papineau
Assistant Equipment Managers . . . . Tom Blatchford, Bobby Hastings
Medical Director, Maple Leafs and Marlies . . . . Dr. Noah Forman
Orthopedic Consultant . . . . Dr. John Theodoropoulos
Team Dentists . . . . Dr. Marvin Lean, Dr. Charles Goldberg

Communications
Director, Media Relations . . . . Pat Park
Coordinators, Media Relations . . . . Craig Downey, Aaron Gogishvili

Broadcasting
Senior Vice-President, Broadcast and Content . . . . . Chris Hebb
Senior Director, Broadcast and Networks . . . . Liana Bristol
Director, Content and Networks G.M. . . . . Frank Hayward
Sr. Producer, Networks, Broadcast and Content . . . Mark Askin
Talent, Leafs TV . . . . Joe Bowen, Paul Hendrick, Bob McGill, Greg Millen, Andi Petrillo
AM 640 Toronto Radio, Play-By-Play . . . . Joe Bowen, Dennis Beyak (mid-week)
AM 640 Toronto Radio, Analyst . . . . Jim Ralph
Television Play-By-Play . . . . Joe Bowen (mid-week)
Television Analysts . . . . Bob McGill, Greg Millen

Key Off-Season Signings/Acquisitions

2010

June 2 • Re-signed G **Cory Schneider**.
15 • Re-signed D **Aaron Rome**.
25 • Acquired D **Keith Ballard** and RW **Victor Oreskovich** from Florida for RW **Steve Bernier**, RW **Michael Grabner** and Vancouver's 1st round pick in the 2010 Entry Draft.
July 1 • Signed D **Dan Hamhuis**, C **Manny Malhotra**, C **Joel Perrault** and LW **Jeff Tambellini**.
12 • Re-signed LW **Tanner Glass**, D **Shane O'Brien** and C **Alexandre Bolduc**.
22 • Re-signed RW **Jannik Hansen**.
26 • Re-signed LW **Mason Raymond**.
Aug. 3 • Named **Newell Brown** assistant coach.

Vancouver Canucks

2009-10 Results: 49w-28L-1OTL-4SOL 103PTS.
First, Northwest Division

Alexandre Burrows smiles after Henrik Sedin set him up for his third goal of the game on January 7, 2010. Burrows led the Canucks with a career-best 35 goals in 2009-10. Sedin led the NHL with 83 assists and 112 points.

2010-11 Schedule

Oct.	Sat.	9	Los Angeles	Tue.	11	at NY Islanders
	Mon.	11	Florida	Thu.	13	at NY Rangers
	Wed.	13	at Anaheim	Fri.	14	at Washington
	Fri.	15	at Los Angeles	Sun.	16	at Minnesota*
	Sun.	17	Carolina	Tue.	18	at Colorado
	Tue.	19	at Minnesota	Thu.	20	San Jose
	Wed.	20	at Chicago	Sat.	22	Calgary
	Fri.	22	Minnesota	Mon.	24	Dallas
	Tue.	26	Colorado	Wed.	26	Nashville
Nov.	Mon.	1	New Jersey	Feb. Tue.	1	at Dallas
	Tue.	2	at Edmonton	Wed.	2	at Phoenix
	Thu.	4	at Colorado	Fri.	4	Chicago
	Sat.	6	Detroit	Mon.	7	Ottawa
	Tue.	9	at Montreal	Wed.	9	Anaheim
	Thu.	11	at Ottawa	Sat.	12	Calgary
	Sat.	13	at Toronto	Mon.	14	at St. Louis
	Mon.	15	at Buffalo	Tue.	15	at Minnesota
	Wed.	17	at Pittsburgh	Thu.	17	at Nashville
	Sat.	20	Chicago	Sat.	19	Dallas
	Sun.	21	Phoenix	Tue.	22	Montreal
	Wed.	24	Colorado	Thu.	24	St. Louis
	Fri.	26	San Jose	Sat.	26	Boston
Dec.	Wed.	1	at Calgary	Mar. Tue.	1	Columbus
	Fri.	3	at Chicago	Thu.	3	Nashville
	Sun.	5	St. Louis	Sat.	5	at Los Angeles*
	Wed.	8	Anaheim	Sun.	6	at Anaheim*
	Sat.	11	Tampa Bay	Tue.	8	at Phoenix
	Sun.	12	at Edmonton	Thu.	10	at San Jose
	Wed.	15	Columbus	Sat.	12	at Calgary
	Sat.	18	Toronto	Mon.	14	Minnesota
	Mon.	20	at St. Louis	Wed.	16	Colorado
	Wed.	22	at Detroit	Fri.	18	Phoenix
	Thu.	23	at Columbus	Wed.	23	at Detroit
	Sun.	26	Edmonton	Fri.	25	at Atlanta
	Tue.	28	Philadelphia	Sun.	27	at Columbus*
	Fri.	31	at Dallas	Tue.	29	at Nashville
Jan.	Sun.	2	at Colorado	Thu.	31	Los Angeles
	Mon.	3	at San Jose	Apr. Sat.	2	Edmonton
	Wed.	5	Calgary	Tue.	5	at Edmonton
	Fri.	7	Edmonton	Thu.	7	Minnesota
	Sat.	8	Detroit	Sat.	9	at Calgary

* Denotes afternoon game.

NORTHWEST DIVISION
41st NHL Season
Franchise date: May 22, 1970

Year-by-Year Record

Season	GP	Home W	L	T	OL	Road W	L	T	OL	Overall W	L	T	OL	GF	GA	Pts.	Finished	Playoff Result
2009-10	82	30	8	....	3	19	20	....	2	49	28	....	5	272	222	103	1st, Northwest Div.	Lost Conf. Semi-Final
2008-09	82	24	12	....	5	21	15	....	5	45	27	....	10	246	220	100	1st, Northwest Div.	Lost Conf. Semi-Final
2007-08	82	21	15	....	5	18	18	....	5	39	33	....	10	213	215	88	5th, Northwest Div.	Out of Playoffs
2006-07	82	26	11	....	4	23	15	....	3	49	26	....	7	222	201	105	1st, Northwest Div.	Lost Conf. Semi-Final
2005-06	82	25	10	....	6	17	22	....	2	42	32	....	8	256	255	92	4th, Northwest Div.	Out of Playoffs
2004-05																		
2003-04	82	21	13	7	0	22	11	3	5	43	24	10	5	235	194	101	1st, Northwest Div.	Lost Conf. Quarter-Final
2002-03	82	22	13	6	0	23	10	7	1	45	23	13	1	264	208	104	2nd, Northwest Div.	Lost Conf. Semi-Final
2001-02	82	23	11	5	2	19	19	2	1	42	30	7	3	254	211	94	2nd, Northwest Div.	Lost Conf. Quarter-Final
2000-01	82	21	12	5	3	15	16	6	4	36	28	11	7	239	238	90	3rd, Northwest Div.	Lost Conf. Quarter-Final
1999-2000	82	16	14	5	6	14	15	10	2	30	29	15	8	227	237	83	3rd, Northwest Div.	Out of Playoffs
1998-99	82	14	21	6	....	9	26	6	....	23	47	12	....	192	258	58	4th, Northwest Div.	Out of Playoffs
1997-98	82	15	22	4	....	10	21	10	....	25	43	14	....	224	273	64	7th, Pacific Div.	Out of Playoffs
1996-97	82	20	17	4	....	15	23	3	....	35	40	7	....	257	273	77	4th, Pacific Div.	Out of Playoffs
1995-96	82	15	19	7	....	17	16	8	....	32	35	15	....	278	278	79	3rd, Pacific Div.	Lost Conf. Quarter-Final
1994-95	48	10	8	6	....	8	10	6	....	18	18	12	....	153	148	48	2nd, Pacific Div.	Lost Conf. Semi-Final
1993-94	84	24	19	3	....	17	24	1	....	41	40	3	....	279	276	85	2nd, Pacific Div.	Lost Final
1992-93	84	27	11	4	....	19	18	5	....	46	29	9	....	346	278	101	1st, Smythe Div.	Lost Div. Final
1991-92	80	23	10	7	....	19	16	5	....	42	26	12	....	285	250	96	1st, Smythe Div.	Lost Div. Final
1990-91	80	18	17	5	....	10	26	4	....	28	43	9	....	243	315	65	4th, Smythe Div.	Lost Div. Semi-Final
1989-90	80	13	16	11	....	12	25	3	....	25	41	14	....	245	306	64	5th, Smythe Div.	Out of Playoffs
1988-89	80	19	15	6	....	14	24	2	....	33	39	8	....	251	253	74	4th, Smythe Div.	Lost Div. Semi-Final
1987-88	80	15	20	5	....	10	26	4	....	25	46	9	....	272	320	59	5th, Smythe Div.	Out of Playoffs
1986-87	80	17	19	4	....	12	24	4	....	29	43	8	....	282	314	66	5th, Smythe Div.	Out of Playoffs
1985-86	80	17	18	5	....	6	26	8	....	23	44	13	....	282	333	59	4th, Smythe Div.	Lost Div. Semi-Final
1984-85	80	15	21	4	....	10	25	5	....	25	46	9	....	284	401	59	5th, Smythe Div.	Out of Playoffs
1983-84	80	20	16	4	....	12	23	5	....	32	39	9	....	306	328	73	3rd, Smythe Div.	Lost Div. Semi-Final
1982-83	80	20	12	8	....	10	23	7	....	30	35	15	....	303	309	75	3rd, Smythe Div.	Lost Div. Semi-Final
1981-82	80	20	8	12	....	10	25	5	....	30	33	17	....	290	286	77	2nd, Smythe Div.	Lost Final
1980-81	80	17	12	11	....	11	20	9	....	28	32	20	....	289	301	76	3rd, Smythe Div.	Lost Prelim. Round
1979-80	80	14	17	9	....	13	20	7	....	27	37	16	....	256	281	70	3rd, Smythe Div.	Lost Prelim. Round
1978-79	80	15	18	7	....	10	24	6	....	25	42	13	....	217	291	63	2nd, Smythe Div.	Lost Prelim. Round
1977-78	80	13	15	12	....	7	28	5	....	20	43	17	....	239	320	57	3rd, Smythe Div.	Out of Playoffs
1976-77	80	13	21	6	....	12	21	7	....	25	42	13	....	235	294	63	4th, Smythe Div.	Out of Playoffs
1975-76	80	22	11	7	....	11	21	8	....	33	32	15	....	271	272	81	2nd, Smythe Div.	Lost Prelim. Round
1974-75	80	23	12	5	....	15	20	5	....	38	32	10	....	271	254	86	1st, Smythe Div.	Lost Quarter-Final
1973-74	78	14	18	7	....	10	25	4	....	24	43	11	....	224	296	59	7th, East Div.	Out of Playoffs
1972-73	78	17	18	4	....	5	29	5	....	22	47	9	....	233	339	53	7th, East Div.	Out of Playoffs
1971-72	78	14	20	5	....	6	30	3	....	20	50	8	....	203	297	48	7th, East Div.	Out of Playoffs
1970-71	78	17	18	4	....	7	28	4	....	24	46	8	....	229	296	56	6th, East Div.	Out of Playoffs

2010-11 Player Personnel

FORWARDS	HT	WT	S	Place of Birth	*Age	2009-10 Club
BLIZNAK, Mario	6-0	185	L	Trencin, Czech.	23	Vancouver-Manitoba
BOLDUC, Alexandre	6-1	197	L	Montreal, Que.	25	Vancouver-Manitoba
BURROWS, Alexandre	6-1	188	L	Pincourt, Que.	29	Vancouver
DESBIENS, Guillaume	6-2	210	R	Alma, Que.	25	Vancouver-Manitoba
GLASS, Tanner	6-1	210	L	Regina, Sask.	26	Vancouver
HANSEN, Jannik	6-1	195	R	Herlev, Denmark	24	Vancouver-Manitoba
HODGSON, Cody	6-0	185	R	Toronto, Ont.	20	Brampton
HORDICHUK, Darcy	6-1	211	L	Kamsack, Sask.	30	Vancouver
KESLER, Ryan	6-2	202	R	Livonia, MI	26	Vancouver
MALHOTRA, Manny	6-2	220	L	Mississauga, Ont.	30	San Jose
ORESKOVICH, Victor	6-3	215	R	Whitby, Ont.	24	Florida-Rochester
PERRAULT, Joel	6-2	205	R	Montreal, Que.	27	Phoenix-San Antonio
RAYMOND, Mason	6-0	185	L	Cochrane, Alta.	25	Vancouver
RYPIEN, Rick	5-11	190	R	Coleman, Alta.	26	Vancouver
SAMUELSSON, Mikael	6-2	218	R	Mariefred, Sweden	33	Vancouver
SEDIN, Daniel	6-1	187	L	Ornskoldsvik, Sweden	30	Vancouver
SEDIN, Henrik	6-2	188	L	Ornskoldsvik, Sweden	30	Vancouver
SHIROKOV, Sergei	5-10	195	R	Ozery, USSR	24	Vancouver-Manitoba
TAMBELLINI, Jeff	5-11	186	L	Calgary, Alta.	26	NY Islanders
VOLPATTI, Aaron	6-1	201	L	Revelstoke, B.C.	25	Brown U.-Manitoba

DEFENSEMEN	HT	WT	S	Place of Birth	*Age	2009-10 Club
ALBERTS, Andrew	6-5	218	L	Minneapolis, MN	29	Carolina-Vancouver
BALLARD, Keith	5-11	208	L	Baudette, MN	27	Florida
BAUMGARTNER, Nolan	6-2	195	R	Calgary, Alta.	34	Vancouver-Manitoba
BIEKSA, Kevin	6-1	198	R	Grimsby, Ont.	29	Vancouver
EDLER, Alexander	6-3	215	L	Ostersund, Sweden	24	Vancouver
EHRHOFF, Christian	6-2	203	L	Moers, West Germany	28	Vancouver
HAMHUIS, Dan	6-1	209	L	Smithers, B.C.	27	Nashville
OBERG, Evan	6-0	178	L	Forestburg, Alta.	22	Vancouver-Manitoba
O'BRIEN, Shane	6-3	230	L	Port Hope, Ont.	27	Vancouver
ROME, Aaron	6-1	218	L	Nesbitt, Man.	27	Vancouver-Manitoba
SALO, Sami	6-3	212	R	Turku, Finland	36	Vancouver
SWEATT, Lee	5-9	195	R	Elburn, IL	25	Dynamo Riga-TPS
ZIMMERMAN, Sean	6-3	205	R	Denver, CO	23	San Antonio

GOALTENDERS	HT	WT	C	Place of Birth	*Age	2009-10 Club
LACK, Eddie	6-5	194	L	Norrtalje, Sweden	22	Brynas Jr.-Brynas
LUONGO, Roberto	6-3	217	L	Montreal, Que.	31	Vancouver
SCHNEIDER, Cory	6-2	195	L	Marblehead, MA	24	Vancouver-Manitoba
WEIMAN, Tyler	5-11	180	L	Saskatoon, Sask.	26	Lake Erie

* – Age at start of 2010-11 season

Alain Vigneault

Head Coach

Born: Quebec City, Que., May 14, 1961.

On June 20, 2006, Alain Vigneault became the 16th head coach in Vancouver Canucks history. He previously served in the NHL as head coach of the Montreal Canadiens from 1997 to 2001, becoming the second youngest coach in club history at the age of 36. Vigneault was nominated for the Jack Adams Award as NHL coach of the year following the 1999-2000 season. In 2006-07, he led the Canucks to first place in the Northwest Division by setting new club records with 49 wins and 105 points after the club had missed the playoffs the previous season. Vigneault was rewarded with the Jack Adams Award as NHL coach of the year. The Canucks won the Northwest Division title again in 2008-09 and for a third straight season in 2009-10 when they tied the club record for wins.

Vigneault joined the Canucks from the club's AHL affiliate, the Manitoba Moose, where he led the team to within one game of the conference finals in 2005-06. Prior to joining the Moose, Vigneault spent many years as a head coach in the QMJHL with Trois-Rivieres, Hull, Beauport and PEI. In 1988, Vigneault led the Hull Olympiques into the Memorial Cup and was subsequently named CHL coach of the year. He has also been honoured as coach of the QMJHL's Second All-Star team on three separate occasions. Vigneault has also achieved success on the international stage. He served as an assistant coach with Canada's national junior team in 1989 and 1991, winning a gold medal at the 1991 World Junior Championships in Saskatoon.

As a player, Vigneault was a member of the St. Louis Blues from 1981 to 1983. Drafted by the Blues in the eighth round, 167th overall, in the 1981 Entry Draft, the defenceman recorded two goals, five assists and 82 penalty minutes in his NHL career. Vigneault went on to serve as a scout for the Blues for two seasons and as an assistant coach for the Ottawa Senators from 1992 to 1996.

Coaching Record

			Regular Season				Playoffs			
Season	Team	League	GC	W	L	O/T	GC	W	L	T
1986-87	Trois-Rivieres	QMJHL	70	28	40	2	....	....	....	....
1987-88	Hull	QMJHL	70	43	23	4	19	12	7	....
1987-88	Hull	M-Cup	....	....	....	....	4	1	3	....
1988-89	Hull	QMJHL	70	40	25	5	9	5	4	....
1989-90	Hull	QMJHL	70	36	29	5	11	4	7	....
1990-91	Hull	QMJHL	70	36	27	7	6	2	4	....
1991-92	Hull	QMJHL	70	41	24	5	6	2	4	....
1995-96	Beauport	QMJHL	31	19	7	5	20	13	7	....
1996-97	Beauport	QMJHL	70	24	44	2	4	1	3	....
1997-98	**Montreal**	**NHL**	**82**	**37**	**32**	**13**	**10**	**4**	**6**	....
1998-99	**Montreal**	**NHL**	**82**	**32**	**39**	**11**	....	....	....	....
99-2000	**Montreal**	**NHL**	**82**	**35**	**34**	**13**	....	....	....	....
2000-01	**Montreal**	**NHL**	**20**	**5**	**13**	**2**	....	....	....	....
2003-04	PEI	QMJHL	70	40	19	11	11	6	5	....
2004-05	PEI	QMJHL	70	24	39	7	....	....	....	....
2005-06	Manitoba	AHL	80	44	24	12	13	7	6	....
2006-07	**Vancouver**	**NHL**	**82**	**49**	**26**	**7**	**12**	**5**	**7**	....
2007-08	**Vancouver**	**NHL**	**82**	**39**	**33**	**10**	....	....	....	....
2008-09	**Vancouver**	**NHL**	**82**	**45**	**27**	**10**	**10**	**6**	**4**	....
2009-10	**Vancouver**	**NHL**	**82**	**49**	**28**	**5**	**12**	**6**	**6**	....
	NHL Totals		**594**	**291**	**232**	**71**	**44**	**21**	**23**	....

Won Jack Adams Award (2007)

2009-10 Scoring

* – rookie

Regular Season

Pos	#	Player	Team	GP	G	A	Pts	TOI	+/–	PIM	PP	SH	GW	S	%
C	33	Henrik Sedin	VAN	82	29	83	112	19:41	35	48	4	2	5	166	17.5
L	22	Daniel Sedin	VAN	63	29	56	85	19:08	36	28	8	0	8	225	12.9
C	17	Ryan Kesler	VAN	82	25	50	75	19:37	1	104	12	1	5	214	11.7
L	14	Alexandre Burrows	VAN	82	35	32	67	17:51	34	121	4	5	3	209	16.7
R	26	Mikael Samuelsson	VAN	74	30	23	53	17:10	10	64	7	0	4	219	13.7
L	21	Mason Raymond	VAN	82	25	28	53	17:19	0	48	8	0	4	217	11.5
D	5	Christian Ehrhoff	VAN	80	14	30	44	22:47	36	42	6	0	3	181	7.7
D	23	Alexander Edler	VAN	76	5	37	42	22:38	0	40	2	0	0	161	3.1
D	6	Sami Salo	VAN	68	9	19	28	20:40	14	18	6	0	3	119	7.6
C	42	Kyle Wellwood	VAN	75	14	11	25	13:51	6	12	3	0	2	98	14.3
R	18	Steve Bernier	VAN	59	11	11	22	14:10	0	21	3	0	0	95	11.6
D	3	Kevin Bieksa	VAN	55	3	19	22	21:49	–5	85	1	0	0	95	3.2
R	38	Pavol Demitra	VAN	28	3	13	16	16:12	3	0	1	0	0	53	5.7
R	36	Jannik Hansen	VAN	47	9	6	15	12:20	–5	18	0	1	3	67	13.4
D	8	Willie Mitchell	VAN	48	4	8	12	22:36	13	48	0	0	1	47	8.5
D	41	Andrew Alberts	CAR	62	2	8	10	15:04	7	74	0	0	0	38	5.3
			VAN	14	1	1	2	16:45	–1	13	0	0	0	12	8.3
			Total	76	3	9	12	15:22	6	87	0	0	0	50	6.0
R	40 *	Michael Grabner	VAN	20	5	6	11	13:54	2	8	2	0	1	63	7.9
L	15	Tanner Glass	VAN	67	4	7	11	10:28	5	115	0	0	0	52	7.7
C	37	Rick Rypien	VAN	69	4	4	8	7:14	–3	126	0	0	1	61	6.6
D	55	Shane O'Brien	VAN	65	2	6	8	17:00	15	79	0	0	0	37	5.4
C	10	Ryan Johnson	VAN	58	1	4	5	10:37	–4	12	0	0	1	19	5.3
D	29	Aaron Rome	VAN	49	0	4	4	15:10	–2	24	0	0	0	49	0.0
L	13	Matt Pettinger	VAN	9	1	2	3	10:45	3	6	0	0	0	8	12.5
D	44	Nolan Baumgartner	VAN	12	1	1	2	14:12	7	2	0	0	0	12	8.3
D	34	Brad Lukowich	VAN	13	1	1	2	11:13	5	4	0	0	1	1	100.0
L	24	Darcy Hordichuk	VAN	56	1	1	2	6:01	–7	142	0	0	0	21	4.8
R	20 *	Guillaume Desbiens	VAN	1	0	0	0	9:25	0	2	0	0	0	0	0.0
C	62 *	Mario Bliznak	VAN	2	0	0	0	8:31	–2	0	0	0	0	1	0.0
D	64 *	Evan Oberg	VAN	2	0	0	0	6:17	0	0	0	0	0	0	0.0
R	25 *	Sergei Shirokov	VAN	6	0	0	0	12:49	–4	2	0	0	0	4	0.0
C	49 *	Alexandre Bolduc	VAN	15	0	0	0	9:58	–3	13	0	0	0	14	0.0

Goaltending

No.	Goaltender	GPI	Mins	Avg	W	L	OT	EN	SO	GA	SA	S%	G	A	PIM
30	Andrew Raycroft	21	967	2.42	9	5	1	3	1	39	438	.911	0	0	4
1	Roberto Luongo	68	3899	2.57	40	22	4	4	4	167	1915	.913	0	0	0
35	* Cory Schneider	2	79	3.80	0	1	0	0	0	5	59	.915	0	0	0
	Totals	**82**	**4973**	**2.63**	**49**	**28**	**5**	**7**	**5**	**218**	**2419**	**.910**			

Playoffs

Pos	#	Player	Team	GP	G	A	Pts	TOI	+/–	PIM	PP	SH	GW	OT	S	%
R	26	Mikael Samuelsson	VAN	12	8	7	15	17:58	7	16	3	0	1	1	42	19.0
L	22	Daniel Sedin	VAN	12	5	9	14	19:46	4	12	1	0	2	0	38	13.2
C	33	Henrik Sedin	VAN	12	3	11	14	20:38	3	6	0	0	1	0	23	13.0
C	17	Ryan Kesler	VAN	12	1	9	10	21:18	3	4	0	0	0	0	21	4.8
D	3	Kevin Bieksa	VAN	12	3	5	8	22:36	2	14	1	0	1	0	20	15.0
D	5	Christian Ehrhoff	VAN	12	3	4	7	24:08	–1	8	1	0	0	0	25	12.0
C	42	Kyle Wellwood	VAN	12	2	5	7	15:44	–1	0	1	0	0	0	18	11.1
L	14	Alexandre Burrows	VAN	12	3	3	6	18:50	4	22	0	0	0	0	27	11.1
R	38	Pavol Demitra	VAN	11	2	4	6	14:19	2	4	0	0	0	0	17	11.8
D	23	Alexander Edler	VAN	12	2	4	6	23:06	9	10	1	0	0	0	25	8.0
D	6	Sami Salo	VAN	12	1	5	6	20:39	2	2	1	0	0	0	18	5.6
R	18	Steve Bernier	VAN	12	4	1	5	9:58	–1	0	2	0	0	0	17	23.5
L	21	Mason Raymond	VAN	12	3	1	4	17:36	0	6	0	0	1	0	23	13.0
D	55	Shane O'Brien	VAN	12	1	2	3	17:43	3	25	0	0	0	0	10	10.0
R	36	Jannik Hansen	VAN	12	1	2	3	10:04	1	4	0	0	0	0	12	8.3
R	40 *	Michael Grabner	VAN	9	1	0	1	9:06	2	0	0	0	0	0	14	7.1
C	37	Rick Rypien	VAN	7	0	1	1	4:39	1	7	0	0	0	0	1	0.0
D	41	Andrew Alberts	VAN	10	0	1	1	12:26	1	27	0	0	0	0	6	0.0
D	44	Nolan Baumgartner	VAN	1	0	0	0	9:27	0	0	0	0	0	0	0	0.0
L	13	Matt Pettinger	VAN	1	0	0	0	4:12	0	0	0	0	0	0	0	0.0
D	29	Aaron Rome	VAN	1	0	0	0	9:32	0	0	0	0	0	0	0	0.0
C	10	Ryan Johnson	VAN	4	0	0	0	8:23	–2	2	0	0	0	0	1	0.0
L	15	Tanner Glass	VAN	4	0	0	0	3:08	0	0	0	0	0	0	0	0.0

Goaltending

No.	Goaltender	GPI	Mins	Avg	W	L	EN	SO	GA	SA	S%	G	A	PIM
30	Andrew Raycroft	1	25	2.40	0	0	0	0	1	7	.857	0	0	0
1	Roberto Luongo	12	707	3.22	6	6	2	0	38	362	.895	0	0	0
	Totals	**12**	**736**	**3.34**	**6**	**6**	**2**	**0**	**41**	**371**	**.889**			

Captains' History

Orland Kurtenbach, 1970-71 to 1973-74; no captain, 1974-75; Andre Boudrias, 1975-76; Chris Oddleifson, 1976-77; Don Lever, 1977-78; Don Lever and Kevin McCarthy, 1978-79; Kevin McCarthy, 1979-80 to 1981-82; Stan Smyl, 1982-83 to 1989-90; Dan Quinn, Doug Lidster and Trevor Linden, 1990-91; Trevor Linden, 1991-92 to 1996-97; Mark Messier, 1997-98 to 1999-2000; Markus Naslund, 2000-01 to 2007-08; Roberto Luongo, 2008-09 to date.

Coaching History

Hal Laycoe, 1970-71, 1971-72; Vic Stasiuk, 1972-73; Bill McCreary and Phil Maloney, 1973-74; Phil Maloney, 1974-75, 1975-76; Phil Maloney and Orland Kurtenbach, 1976-77; Orland Kurtenbach, 1977-78; Harry Neale, 1978-79 to 1980-81; Harry Neale and Roger Neilson, 1981-82; Roger Neilson, 1982-83; Roger Neilson and Harry Neale, 1983-84; Bill Laforge and Harry Neale, 1984-85; Tom Watt, 1985-86, 1986-87; Bob McCammon, 1987-88 to 1989-90; Bob McCammon and Pat Quinn, 1990-91; Pat Quinn, 1991-92 to 1993-94; Rick Ley, 1994-95; Rick Ley and Pat Quinn, 1995-96; Tom Renney, 1996-97; Tom Renney and Mike Keenan, 1997-98; Mike Keenan and Marc Crawford, 1998-99; Marc Crawford, 1999-2000 to 2005-06; Alain Vigneault, 2006-07 to date.

Club Records

Team

(Figures in brackets for season records are games played; records for fewest points, wins, ties, losses, goals, goals against are for 70 or more games)

Most Points	**105**	2006-07 (82)
Most Wins	**49**	2006-07 (82), 2009-10 (82)
Most Ties	**20**	1980-81 (80)
Most Losses	**50**	1971-72 (78)
Most Goals	**346**	1992-93 (84)
Most Goals Against	**401**	1984-85 (80)
Fewest Points	**48**	1971-72 (78)
Fewest Wins	**20**	1971-72 (78), 1977-78 (80)
Fewest Ties	**3**	1993-94 (84)
Fewest Losses	**24**	2002-03 (82)
Fewest Goals	**192**	1998-99 (82)
Fewest Goals Against	**194**	2003-04 (82)
Longest Winning Streak		
Overall	**10**	Nov. 9-30/02
Home	**11**	Feb. 3-Mar. 19/09
Away	**8**	Dec. 20/03-Jan. 13/04
Longest Undefeated Streak		
Overall	**14**	Jan.26-Feb. 25/03 (10 wins, 4 ties)
Home	**18**	Nov. 4/92-Jan. 16/93 (16 wins, 2 ties)
Away	**9**	Feb. 4-Mar. 3/03 (6 wins, 3 ties)
Longest Losing Streak		
Overall	**10**	Oct. 23-Nov. 11/97
Home	**6**	Dec. 18/70-Jan. 20/71
Away	**12**	Nov. 28/81-Feb. 6/82
Longest Winless Streak		
Overall	**13**	Nov. 9-Dec. 7/73 (10 losses, 3 ties)
Home	**11**	Dec. 18/70-Feb. 6/71 (10 losses, 1 tie)
Away	**20**	Jan. 2-Apr. 2/86 (14 losses, 6 ties)
Most Shutouts, Season	**10**	2008-09 (82)
Most PIM, Season	**2,326**	1992-93 (84)
Most Goals, Game	**11**	Mar. 28/71 (Cal. 5 at Van. 11), Nov. 25/86 (L.A. 5 at Van. 11), Mar. 1/92 (Cgy. 0 at Van. 11)

Individual

Most Seasons	**16**	Trevor Linden
Most Games	**1,140**	Trevor Linden
Most Goals, Career	**346**	Markus Naslund
Most Assists, Career	**434**	Henrik Sedin
Most Points, Career	**756**	Markus Naslund (346G, 410A)
Most PIM, Career	**2,127**	Gino Odjick
Most Shutouts, Career	**24**	Roberto Luongo
Longest Consecutive Games Streak	**534**	Brendan Morrison (Mar. 16/00-Dec. 10/07)
Most Goals, Season	**60**	Pavel Bure (1992-93), (1993-94)
Most Assists, Season	**83**	Henrik Sedin (2009-10)
Most Points, Season	**112**	Henrik Sedin (2009-10; 29G, 83A)
Most PIM, Season	**372**	Donald Brashear (1997-98)
Most Points, Defenseman, Season	**63**	Doug Lidster (1986-87; 12G, 51A)
Most Points, Center, Season	**112**	Henrik Sedin (2009-10; 29G, 83A)
Most Points, Right Wing, Season	**110**	Pavel Bure (1992-93; 60G, 50A)
Most Points, Left Wing, Season	**104**	Markus Naslund (2002-03; 48G, 56A)
Most Points, Rookie, Season	**60**	Ivan Hlinka (1981-82; 23G, 37A) Pavel Bure (1991-92; 34G, 26A)
Most Shutouts, Season	**9**	Roberto Luongo (2008-09)
Most Goals, Game	**4**	Twelve times
Most Assists, Game	**6**	Patrik Sundstrom (Feb. 29/84)
Most Points, Game	**7**	Patrik Sundstrom (Feb. 29/84; 1G, 6A)

General Managers' History

Bud Poile, 1970-71 to 1972-73; Hal Laycoe, 1973-74; Phil Maloney, 1974-75 to 1976-77; Jake Milford, 1977-78 to 1981-82; Harry Neale, 1982-83 to 1984-85; Jack Gordon, 1985-86, 1986-87; Pat Quinn, 1987-88 to 1997-98; Brian Burke, 1998-99 to 2003-04; David Nonis, 2004-05 to 2007-08; Mike Gillis, 2008-09 to date.

Retired Numbers

12	Stan Smyl	1978-1991
16	Trevor Linden	1988-98; 2001-08
19*	Markus Naslund	1996-2008

* - To be honored on December 11, 2010.

All-time Record vs. Other Clubs

Regular Season

	At Home								On Road								Total							
	GP	W	L	T	OL	GF	GA	PTS	GP	W	L	T	OL	GF	GA	PTS	GP	W	L	T	OL	GF	GA	PTS
Anaheim	36	20	13	2	1	116	88	43	35	16	11	7	1	105	100	40	71	36	24	9	2	221	188	83
Atlanta	5	3	1	1	0	17	9	7	5	3	1	0	1	17	16	7	10	6	2	1	1	34	25	14
Boston	53	17	27	8	1	171	212	43	54	8	38	7	1	127	221	24	107	25	65	15	2	298	433	67
Buffalo	54	27	16	11	0	200	165	65	54	18	27	8	1	157	195	45	108	45	43	19	1	357	360	110
Calgary	117	47	49	18	3	402	377	115	116	35	66	15	0	334	442	85	233	82	115	33	3	736	819	200
Carolina	32	16	10	6	0	113	87	38	31	12	14	5	0	104	102	29	63	28	24	11	0	217	189	67
Chicago	82	42	25	15	0	247	227	99	81	24	48	7	2	195	292	57	163	66	73	22	2	442	519	156
Colorado	65	26	27	7	5	208	236	64	65	24	30	8	3	184	215	59	130	50	57	15	8	392	451	123
Columbus	18	12	3	0	3	71	51	27	18	9	6	2	1	60	47	21	36	21	9	2	4	131	98	48
Dallas	81	38	31	10	2	282	241	88	81	25	42	12	2	232	283	64	162	63	73	22	4	514	524	152
Detroit	75	33	31	10	1	266	240	77	76	22	44	8	2	220	304	54	151	55	75	18	3	486	544	131
Edmonton	100	43	42	12	3	355	366	101	99	33	54	7	5	308	403	78	199	76	96	19	8	663	769	179
Florida	11	5	1	5	0	34	25	15	10	5	3	1	1	33	25	12	21	10	4	6	1	67	50	27
Los Angeles	107	56	33	16	2	398	325	130	109	37	55	16	1	336	420	91	216	93	88	32	3	734	745	221
Minnesota	28	15	5	3	5	78	70	38	29	13	13	2	1	70	82	29	57	28	18	5	6	148	152	67
Montreal	58	17	33	8	0	163	207	42	56	11	40	5	0	141	250	27	114	28	73	13	0	304	457	69
Nashville	22	14	6	1	1	77	51	30	23	13	9	1	0	64	64	27	45	27	15	2	1	141	115	57
New Jersey	49	28	10	11	0	183	135	67	51	24	21	6	0	164	156	54	100	52	31	17	0	347	291	121
NY Islanders	49	24	22	3	0	160	160	51	49	12	25	10	2	138	177	36	98	36	47	13	2	298	337	87
NY Rangers	53	17	33	3	0	170	205	37	56	13	38	5	0	148	242	31	109	30	71	8	0	318	447	68
Ottawa	14	8	5	1	0	44	29	17	13	6	6	1	0	32	30	13	27	14	11	2	0	76	59	30
Philadelphia	53	10	30	12	1	148	214	33	56	18	36	1	1	167	238	38	109	28	66	13	2	315	452	71
Phoenix	82	51	20	10	1	303	220	113	79	30	36	10	3	270	285	73	161	81	56	20	4	573	505	186
Pittsburgh	52	24	23	4	1	187	191	53	52	12	33	7	0	178	230	31	104	36	56	11	1	365	421	84
St. Louis	82	36	37	9	0	242	257	81	81	25	47	9	0	228	301	59	163	61	84	18	0	470	558	140
San Jose	42	22	15	4	1	142	116	49	44	19	19	5	1	126	131	44	86	41	34	9	2	268	247	93
Tampa Bay	11	9	0	2	0	47	19	20	11	6	5	0	0	41	38	12	22	15	5	2	0	88	57	32
Toronto	67	32	22	11	2	236	222	77	63	24	28	11	0	209	225	59	130	56	50	22	2	445	447	136
Washington	41	20	15	5	1	142	127	46	42	15	22	4	1	124	139	35	83	35	37	9	2	266	266	81
Defunct Clubs	19	14	3	2	0	82	48	30	19	10	8	1	0	71	68	21	38	24	11	3	0	153	116	51
Totals	**1558**	**726**	**588**	**210**	**34**	**5284**	**4920**	**1696**	**1558**	**522**	**825**	**181**	**30**	**4583**	**5721**	**1255**	**3116**	**1248**	**1413**	**391**	**64**	**9867**	**10641**	**2951**

Playoffs

	Series	W	L	GP	W	L	T	GF	GA	Last Mtg.	Rnd.	Result
Anaheim	1	0	1	5	1	4	0	8	14	2007	CSF	L 1-4
Buffalo	2	0	2	7	1	6	0	14	28	1981	PRE	L 0-3
Calgary	6	2	4	32	15	17	0	96	101	2004	CQF	L 3-4
Chicago	4	1	3	21	8	13	0	61	70	2010	CSF	L 2-4
Colorado	2	0	2	10	2	8	0	26	40	2001	CQF	L 0-4
Dallas	2	2	0	12	8	4	0	31	23	2007	CQF	W 4-3
Detroit	1	0	1	6	2	4	0	16	22	2002	CQF	L 2-4
Edmonton	2	0	2	9	2	7	0	20	35	1992	DF	L 2-4
Los Angeles	4	2	2	23	12	11	0	85	84	2010	CQF	W 4-2
Minnesota	1	0	1	7	3	4	0	17	26	2003	CSF	L 3-4
Montreal	1	0	1	5	1	4	0	9	20	1975	QF	L 1-4
NY Islanders	2	0	2	6	0	6	0	14	26	1982	F	L 0-4
NY Rangers	1	0	1	7	3	4	0	19	21	1994	F	L 3-4
Philadelphia	1	0	1	3	1	2	0	9	15	1979	PRE	L 1-2
Phoenix	2	2	0	13	8	5	0	50	34	1993	DSF	W 4-2
St. Louis	3	3	0	18	12	6	0	55	53	2009	CQF	W 4-0
Toronto	1	1	0	5	4	1	0	16	9	1994	CF	W 4-1
Totals	**36**	**13**	**23**	**189**	**83**	**106**	**0**	**546**	**621**			

Calgary totals include Atlanta Flames, 1972-73 to 1979-80.
Carolina totals include Hartford, 1979-80 to 1996-97.
Colorado totals include Quebec, 1979-80 to 1994-95.
Dallas totals include Minnesota North Stars, 1970-71 to 1992-93.
New Jersey totals include Kansas City, 1974-75, 1975-76, and Colorado Rockies, 1976-77 to 1981-82.
Phoenix totals include Winnipeg, 1979-80 to 1995-96.

Playoff Results 2010-2006

Year	Round	Opponent	Result	GF	GA
2010	CSF	Chicago	L 2-4	18	23
	CQF	Los Angeles	W 4-2	25	18
2009	CSF	Chicago	L 2-4	19	23
	CQF	St. Louis	W 4-0	11	5
2007	CSF	Anaheim	L 1-4	8	14
	CQF	Dallas	W 4-3	13	12

Abbreviations: Round: F – Final;
CF – conference final; **CSF** – conference semi-final;
CQF – conference quarter-final; **DF** – division final;
DSF – division semi-final; **QF** – quarter-final;
PRE – preliminary round.

2009-10 Results

Oct.	1	at Calgary	3-5	**Jan.**	2	at Dallas	3-1
	3	at Colorado	0-3		5	Columbus	7-3
	5	Columbus	3-5		7	Phoenix	4-0
	7	Montreal	7-1		9	Calgary	2-3†
	11	Dallas	4-3†		11	Nashville	2-3
	16	at Calgary	3-5		13	at Minnesota	2-5
	17	Minnesota	2-1		16	Pittsburgh	6-2
	19	at Edmonton	1-2		20	at Edmonton	3-2*
	21	at Chicago	3-2		21	Dallas	4-3
	24	Toronto	3-1		23	Chicago	5-1
	25	Edmonton	2-0		25	Buffalo	3-2
	27	Detroit	4-5		27	St. Louis	3-2
	29	at Los Angeles	2-1†		30	at Toronto	5-3
	30	at Anaheim	2-7	**Feb.**	2	at Montreal	2-3
Nov.	1	Colorado	3-0		4	at Ottawa	1-3
	3	NY Rangers	4-1		6	at Boston	3-2†
	5	at Minnesota	5-2		9	at Tampa Bay	1-3
	6	at Dallas	1-2		11	at Florida	3-0
	10	at St. Louis	1-6		12	at Columbus	4-3
	12	at Detroit	1-3		14	at Minnesota	2-6
	14	at Colorado	8-2	**Mar.**	2	at Columbus	4-3*
	20	Colorado	5-2		3	at Detroit	6-3
	22	Chicago	0-1		5	at Chicago	3-6
	26	Los Angeles	4-1		7	at Nashville	4-2
	28	Edmonton	7-3		9	at Colorado	6-4
	29	San Jose	2-4		10	at Phoenix	3-4†
Dec.	2	at New Jersey	5-2		13	Ottawa	5-1
	3	at Philadelphia	3-0		14	Calgary	3-1
	5	at Carolina	3-5		16	NY Islanders	2-5
	8	at Nashville	2-4		18	San Jose	3-2
	10	Atlanta	4-2		20	Detroit	3-4*
	12	Minnesota	4-3		23	at Edmonton	2-3
	14	Los Angeles	3-1		24	Anaheim	4-1
	16	Anaheim	2-3		27	at San Jose	2-4
	18	Washington	3-2		30	Phoenix	4-1
	20	St. Louis	1-3	**Apr.**	1	at Los Angeles	3-8
	22	Nashville	4-1		2	at Anaheim	5-4†
	26	Edmonton	4-1		4	Minnesota	4-3*
	27	at Calgary	5-1		6	Colorado	3-4†
	29	at Phoenix	2-3†		8	at San Jose	2-4
	31	at St. Louis	4-3*		10	Calgary	7-3

* – Overtime † – Shootout

Entry Draft Selections 2010-1996

Name in bold denotes played in NHL.

2010
Pick
- 115 Patrick McNally
- 145 Adam Polasek
- 172 Alex Friesen
- 175 Jonathan Iilahti
- 205 Sawyer Hannay

2009
Pick
- 22 Jordan Schroeder
- 53 Anton Rodin
- 83 Kevin Connauton
- 113 Jeremy Price
- 143 Peter Andersson
- 173 Joe Cannata
- 187 Steven Anthony

2008
Pick
- 10 Cody Hodgson
- 41 Yann Sauve
- 131 Prab Rai
- 161 Mats Froshaug
- 191 Morgan Clark

2007
Pick
- 25 Patrick White
- 33 Taylor Ellington
- 145 Charles-Antoine Messier
- 146 Ilja Kablukov
- 176 Taylor Matson
- 206 Dan Gendur

2006
Pick
- 14 **Michael Grabner**
- 82 Daniel Rahimi
- 163 **Sergei Shirokov**
- 167 Juraj Simek
- 197 Evan Fuller

2005
Pick
- 10 **Luc Bourdon**
- 51 **Mason Raymond**
- 114 Alexandre Vincent
- 138 Matt Butcher
- 185 Kris Fredheim
- 205 **Mario Bliznak**

2004
Pick
- 26 **Cory Schneider**
- 91 **Alexander Edler**
- 125 Andrew Sarauer
- 159 **Mike Brown**
- 189 Julien Ellis
- 254 David Schulz
- 287 **Jannik Hansen**

2003
Pick
- 23 **Ryan Kesler**
- 60 Marc-Andre Bernier
- 111 **Brandon Nolan**
- 128 Ty Morris
- 160 Nicklas Danielsson
- 190 Chad Brownlee
- 222 Francois-Pierre Guenette
- 252 Sergei Topol
- 254 **Nathan McIver**
- 285 Matthew Hansen

2002
Pick
- 49 Kirill Koltsov
- 55 Denis Grot
- 68 **Brett Skinner**
- 83 Lukas Mensator
- 114 John Laliberte
- 151 **Rob McVicar**
- 214 Marc-Andre Roy
- 223 Ilja Krikunov
- 247 Matt Violin
- 277 Thomas Nussli
- 278 Matt Gens

2001
Pick
- 16 **R.J. Umberger**
- 66 **Fedor Fedorov**
- 114 Evgeny Gladskikh
- 151 **Kevin Bieksa**
- 212 **Jason King**
- 245 Konstantin Mikhailov

2000
Pick
- 23 **Nathan Smith**
- 71 Thatcher Bell
- 93 Tim Branham
- 144 Pavel Duma
- 208 **Brandon Reid**
- 241 Nathan Barrett
- 272 Tim Smith

1999
Pick
- 2 **Daniel Sedin**
- 3 **Henrik Sedin**
- 69 Rene Vydareny
- 129 Ryan Thorpe
- 172 Josh Reed
- 189 Kevin Swanson
- 218 Markus Kankaanpera
- 271 Darrell Hay

1998
Pick
- 4 **Bryan Allen**
- 31 **Artem Chubarov**
- 68 **Jarkko Ruutu**
- 81 Justin Morrison
- 90 Regan Darby
- 136 David Ytfeldt
- 140 Rick Bertran
- 149 Paul Cabana
- 177 Vincent Malts
- 204 Greg Mischler
- 219 Curtis Valentine
- 232 Jason Metcalfe

1997
Pick
- 10 **Brad Ference**
- 34 **Ryan Bonni**
- 36 **Harold Druken**
- 64 Kyle Freadrich
- 90 Chris Stanley
- 114 David Darguzas
- 117 Matt Cockell
- 144 **Matt Cooke**
- 148 Larry Shapley
- 171 Rod Leroux
- 201 Denis Martynyuk
- 227 Peter Brady

1996
Pick
- 12 **Josh Holden**
- 75 **Zenith Komarniski**
- 93 Jonas Soling
- 121 Tyler Prosofsky
- 147 Nolan McDonald
- 175 Clint Cabana
- 201 Jeff Scissons
- 227 **Lubomir Vaic**

Mike Gillis
President and General Manager
Born: Sudbury, Ont., December 1, 1958.

The Vancouver Canucks announced on April 23, 2008, that Mike Gillis had been named the tenth general manager in club history. Gillis joined the Canucks organization after spending the previous 16 years as a player representative. In his two seasons with the club, the Canucks won the Northwest Division title.

Gillis began his NHL career in 1978 as a member of the Colorado Rockies. In 246 NHL regular season games, Gillis recorded 76 points (33 goals, 43 assists) and 186 penalty minutes with Colorado and Boston before a leg injury forced him to retire in 1985. He then returned to Kingston, Ontario, where he had grown up, to obtain his law degree from Queen's University in 1990. Gillis began his career as a NHL player representative in 1992 and became one of the most successful in his industry. His ability to evaluate players, negotiate contracts and his extensive knowledge of the Collective Bargaining Agreement, provided him the opportunity to work with a number of the NHL's most elite players.

Club Directory

Rogers Arena

Vancouver Canucks
Rogers Arena
800 Griffiths Way
Vancouver, B.C. V6B 6G1
Phone **604/899-4600**
FAX 604/899-4640
www.canucks.com
Capacity: 18,810

Executive Directory – Vancouver Canucks Limited Partnership
Chairman, Canucks L.P. and Governor, NHL	Francesco Aquilini
Alternate Governors, NHL	Paolo Aquilini, Roberto Aquilini
Executive Office Manager	Cheryl Loveseth
President, G.M. and Alt. Governor, NHL	Mike Gillis
Chief Operating Officer and Alt. Governor, NHL	Victor de Bonis
Executive Vice President, Sales and Service	Trent Carroll
Vice President, Hockey Ops and Assistant G.M.	Laurence Gilman
Vice President, Player Personnel and Assistant G.M.	Lorne Henning
Vice President and G.M., Arena Operations	Harvey Jones
Vice President, Business nd General Counsel	Chris Gear
Vice President, Finance and CFO	Todd Kobus
Vice President, Communications and Community Partnerships	TC Carling
Vice President, Marketing and Game Presentation	Ali Gardiner

Hockey Operations
President, G.M. and Alt. Governor, NHL	Mike Gillis
Executive Assistant	Joan Stobbs
Vice President, Player Personnel and Asst. G.M.	Lorne Henning
Vice President, Hockey Operations and Asst. G.M.	Laurence Gilman
Senior Advisor to the General Manager	Stan Smyl
Head Coach	Alain Vigneault
Associate Coach	Rick Bowness
Assistant Coach	Newell Brown
Assistant Coach, Video	Darryl Williams
Goaltending Consultant	Roland Melanson
Strength & Conditioning Coach	Roger Takahashi
Director, Player Development	Dave Gagner
Head Coach, Manitoba Moose	Claude Noel
Assistant Coaches, Manitoba Moose	Keith McCambridge, Rick St. Croix
Vice President, Communications and Community Partnerships	TC Carling
Manager, Media Relations and Team Operations	Ben Brown
Coordinator, Media Relations and Publications	Stephanie Maniago
Assistant, Media Relations	Jen Rollins
Director, Community Partnerships	Alex Mitchell
Director of Charitable, Corporate and On-Ice Events	Karen Christiansen
Coordinator, Community Partnerships and Education	Jessica Hoffman
Coordinator, Community Partnerships	Tara Clarke
Manager, Hockey Development and Alumni Liaison	Rod Brathwaite
Coordinator, Comm. Partnerships and Mascot Liaison	Paul Buckley

Scouting Staff
Chief Amateur Scout	Ron Delorme
Associate Head Scout	Thomas Gradin
Amateur Scouts	Brian Chapman, Sergei Chibisov, Frank Kollar, Tim Lenardon, Harold Snepsts, Darrell Young, Judd Brackett, Inge Hammarstrom, Richard Rose, Ken Cook
Director of Professional Scouting	Eric Crawford
Professional Scouts	Lucien DeBlois, Lars Lindgren, Brett Henning, Neil Komadoski, Don Granato, Jonathan Bates
Director of Hockey Administration	Jonathan Wall
Hockey Operations Assistant	Mike Brown

Medical and Training Staff
Head Athletic Trainer	Mike Burnstein
Assistant Athletic Trainers	Jon Sanderson, Dave Zarn
Equipment Manager	Pat O'Neill
Assistant Equipment Manager	Jamie Hendricks
Equipment Assistant	Brian Hamilton
Game Dressing Room Attendants	John Jukich, Ron Shute, Brian Brumwell
Team Physicians	Dr. Bill Regan, Dr. Mike Wilkinson
Team Dentist	Dr. Jeffrey Norden
Team Chiropractor	Dr. Sid Sheard
Team Optometrist	Dr. Alan R. Boyco

Broadcast
Director, Facilities & In-House Productions	Paul Brettell
Director, Production Services	Mike Hall
Senior Broadcast Technician	Greg Story
Multimedia Senior Producer/Producer	Jason Steensma/Gayla Anderson
Broadcast Business Manager	Shannon Baker
Production Assistant & Editor	Rory McGarry

Washington Capitals

2009-10 Results: 54w-15L-7otl-6sol 121pts.
First, Southeast Division

Key Off-Season Signings/Acquisitions

2010

May 17 • Re-signed C **Nicklas Backstrom**.

July 2 • Signed G **Dany Sabourin**.

6 • Re-signed C/RW **Boyd Gordon**.

7 • Re-signed D **Jeff Schultz**.

8 • Re-signed RW **Eric Fehr**.

14 • Signed RW **Brian Willsie**.

15 • Re-signed C **Jay Beagle** and RW **Andrew Gordon**.

27 • Re-signed LW/C **Tomas Fleischmann**.

28 • Acquired LW **D.J. King** from St. Louis for LW **Stefan Della Rovere**.

2010-11 Schedule

Oct.	Fri.	8	at Atlanta	Sat.	8	Florida
	Sat.	9	New Jersey	Tue.	11	at Florida
	Mon.	11	Ottawa	Wed.	12	at Tampa Bay
	Wed.	13	NY Islanders	Fri.	14	Vancouver
	Sat.	16	at Nashville	Sun.	16	Ottawa*
	Tue.	19	Boston	Tue.	18	at Philadelphia
	Thu.	21	at Boston	Thu.	20	at NY Islanders
	Sat.	23	Atlanta	Sat.	22	at Toronto
	Wed.	27	at Carolina	Mon.	24	NY Rangers
	Thu.	28	at Minnesota	Wed.	26	at Atlanta
	Sat.	30	at Calgary	**Feb.** Tue.	1	Montreal
Nov.	Wed.	3	Toronto	Fri.	4	at Tampa Bay
	Fri.	5	Boston	Sun.	6	Pittsburgh*
	Sun.	7	Philadelphia*	Tue.	8	San Jose
	Tue.	9	at NY Rangers	Sat.	12	Los Angeles*
	Thu.	11	Tampa Bay	Mon.	14	at Phoenix
	Sat.	13	at Buffalo	Wed.	16	at Anaheim
	Sun.	14	Atlanta*	Thu.	17	at San Jose
	Wed.	17	Buffalo	Sun.	20	at Buffalo*
	Fri.	19	at Atlanta	Mon.	21	at Pittsburgh
	Sat.	20	Philadelphia	Fri.	25	NY Rangers
	Mon.	22	at New Jersey	Sat.	26	at NY Islanders
	Wed.	24	at Carolina	**Mar.** Tue.	1	NY Islanders
	Fri.	26	Tampa Bay*	Thu.	3	St. Louis
	Sun.	28	Carolina*	Sun.	6	at Florida*
Dec.	Wed.	1	at St. Louis	Mon.	7	at Tampa Bay
	Thu.	2	at Dallas	Wed.	9	Edmonton
	Sat.	4	Atlanta	Fri.	11	Carolina
	Mon.	6	Toronto	Sun.	13	Chicago*
	Thu.	9	Florida	Tue.	15	at Montreal
	Sat.	11	Colorado	Wed.	16	at Detroit
	Sun.	12	at NY Rangers	Fri.	18	at New Jersey
	Wed.	15	Anaheim	Tue.	22	at Philadelphia
	Sat.	18	at Boston	Fri.	25	at Ottawa
	Sun.	19	at Ottawa*	Sat.	26	at Montreal
	Tue.	21	New Jersey	Tue.	29	Carolina
	Thu.	23	Pittsburgh	Thu.	31	Columbus
	Sun.	26	at Carolina	**Apr.** Sat.	2	Buffalo
	Tue.	28	Montreal	Tue.	5	at Toronto
Jan.	Sat.	1	at Pittsburgh*	Wed.	6	Florida
	Tue.	4	Tampa Bay	Sat.	9	at Florida

* Denotes afternoon game.

Two milestones with one puck. When Nicklas Backstrom (right) set up Alex Ovechkin for his 50th goal in the second last game of the 2009-10 season, the assist gave Backstrom his 100th point.

SOUTHEAST DIVISION
37th NHL Season

Franchise date: June 11, 1974

Year-by-Year Record

Season	GP	Home W	L	T	OL	Road W	L	T	OL	Overall W	L	T	OL	GF	GA	Pts.	Finished	Playoff Result
2009-10	82	30	5	....	6	24	10	....	7	54	15	....	13	318	233	121	1st, Southeast Div.	Lost Conf. Quarter-Final
2008-09	82	29	9	....	3	21	15	....	5	50	24	....	8	272	245	108	1st, Southeast Div.	Lost Conf. Semi-Final
2007-08	82	23	15	....	3	20	16	....	5	43	31	....	8	242	231	94	1st, Southeast Div.	Lost Conf. Quarter-Final
2006-07	82	17	17	....	7	11	23	....	7	28	40	....	14	235	286	70	5th, Southeast Div.	Out of Playoffs
2005-06	82	16	18	....	7	13	23	....	5	29	41	....	12	237	306	70	5th, Southeast Div.	Out of Playoffs
2004-05		....	....	....	....	....	....	....	....	....	....	....	....	....	....	....		
2003-04	82	13	20	6	2	10	26	4	1	23	46	10	3	186	253	59	5th, Southeast Div.	Out of Playoffs
2002-03	82	24	13	2	2	15	16	6	4	39	29	8	6	224	220	92	2nd, Southeast Div.	Lost Conf. Quarter-Final
2001-02	82	21	12	6	2	15	21	5	0	36	33	11	2	228	240	85	2nd, Southeast Div.	Out of Playoffs
2000-01	82	24	9	6	2	17	18	4	2	41	27	10	4	233	211	96	1st, Southeast Div.	Lost Conf. Quarter-Final
1999-2000	82	26	5	8	2	18	19	4	0	44	24	12	2	227	194	102	1st, Southeast Div.	Lost Conf. Quarter-Final
1998-99	82	16	23	2	....	15	22	4	....	31	45	6	....	200	218	68	3rd, Southeast Div.	Out of Playoffs
1997-98	82	23	12	6	....	17	18	6	....	40	30	12	....	219	202	92	3rd, Atlantic Div.	Lost Final
1996-97	82	19	17	5	....	14	23	4	....	33	40	9	....	214	231	75	5th, Atlantic Div.	Out of Playoffs
1995-96	82	21	15	5	....	18	17	6	....	39	32	11	....	234	204	89	4th, Atlantic Div.	Lost Conf. Quarter-Final
1994-95	48	15	6	3	....	7	12	5	....	22	18	8	....	136	120	52	3rd, Atlantic Div.	Lost Conf. Quarter-Final
1993-94	84	17	16	9	....	22	19	1	....	39	35	10	....	277	263	88	3rd, Atlantic Div.	Lost Conf. Semi-Final
1992-93	84	21	15	6	....	22	19	1	....	43	34	7	....	325	286	93	2nd, Patrick Div.	Lost Div. Semi-Final
1991-92	80	25	12	3	....	20	15	5	....	45	27	8	....	330	275	98	2nd, Patrick Div.	Lost Div. Semi-Final
1990-91	80	21	14	5	....	16	22	2	....	37	36	7	....	258	258	81	3rd, Patrick Div.	Lost Div. Final
1989-90	80	19	18	3	....	17	20	3	....	36	38	6	....	284	275	78	3rd, Patrick Div.	Lost Conf. Championship
1988-89	80	25	12	3	....	16	17	7	....	41	29	10	....	305	259	92	1st, Patrick Div.	Lost Div. Semi-Final
1987-88	80	22	14	4	....	16	19	5	....	38	33	9	....	281	249	85	2nd, Patrick Div.	Lost Div. Final
1986-87	80	22	15	3	....	16	17	7	....	38	32	10	....	285	278	86	2nd, Patrick Div.	Lost Div. Semi-Final
1985-86	80	30	8	2	....	20	15	5	....	50	23	7	....	315	272	107	2nd, Patrick Div.	Lost Div. Final
1984-85	80	27	11	2	....	19	14	7	....	46	25	9	....	322	240	101	2nd, Patrick Div.	Lost Div. Semi-Final
1983-84	80	26	11	3	....	22	16	2	....	48	27	5	....	308	226	101	2nd, Patrick Div.	Lost Div. Final
1982-83	80	22	12	6	....	17	13	10	....	39	25	16	....	306	283	94	3rd, Patrick Div.	Lost Div. Semi-Final
1981-82	80	16	16	8	....	10	25	5	....	26	41	13	....	319	338	65	5th, Patrick Div.	Out of Playoffs
1980-81	80	16	17	7	....	10	19	11	....	26	36	18	....	286	317	70	5th, Patrick Div.	Out of Playoffs
1979-80	80	20	14	6	....	7	26	7	....	27	40	13	....	261	293	67	5th, Patrick Div.	Out of Playoffs
1978-79	80	15	19	6	....	9	22	9	....	24	41	15	....	273	338	63	4th, Norris Div.	Out of Playoffs
1977-78	80	10	23	7	....	7	26	7	....	17	49	14	....	195	321	48	5th, Norris Div.	Out of Playoffs
1976-77	80	17	15	8	....	7	27	6	....	24	42	14	....	221	307	62	4th, Norris Div.	Out of Playoffs
1975-76	80	6	26	8	....	5	33	2	....	11	59	10	....	224	394	32	5th, Norris Div.	Out of Playoffs
1974-75	80	7	28	5	....	1	39	0	....	8	67	5	....	181	446	21	5th, Norris Div.	Out of Playoffs

2010-11 Player Personnel

FORWARDS	HT	WT	S	Place of Birth	*Age	2009-10 Club
AUCOIN, Keith	5-9	187	R	Waltham, MA	31	Washington-Hershey
BACKSTROM, Nicklas	6-1	210	L	Gavle, Sweden	22	Washington
BEAGLE, Jay	6-3	200	R	Calgary, Alta.	24	Washington-Hershey
BOUCHARD, Francois	6-0	180	L	Sherbrooke, Que.	22	Hershey
BRADLEY, Matt	6-3	201	R	Stittsville, Ont.	32	Washington
BRUESS, Trevor	6-0	209	R	Minneapolis, MN	24	Hershey-South Carolina
CHIMERA, Jason	6-2	216	L	Edmonton, Alta.	31	Columbus-Washington
FEHR, Eric	6-4	212	R	Winkler, Man.	25	Washington
FLEISCHMANN, Tomas	6-1	192	L	Koprivnice, Czech.	26	Washington-Hershey
GORDON, Andrew	5-11	180	R	Halifax, N.S.	24	Washington-Hershey
GORDON, Boyd	6-1	200	R	Unity, Sask.	26	Washington-Hershey
GREENTREE, Kyle	6-3	215	L	Victoria, B.C.	26	Rockford
GUSTAFSSON, Anton	6-2	194	L	Karlskoga, Sweden	20	Boras-Hershey
HAUSWIRTH, Jake	6-5	200	L	Merrill, WI	22	South Carolina
JOHANSSON, Marcus	6-0	196	L	Landskrona, Sweden	20	Farjestad
JOUDREY, Andrew	5-11	185	L	Halifax, N.S.	26	Hershey
KING, D.J.	6-3	230	L	Meadow Lake, Sask.	26	St. Louis-Peoria
KNUBLE, Mike	6-3	223	R	Toronto, Ont.	38	Washington
LAICH, Brooks	6-2	200	L	Wawota, Sask.	27	Washington
OVECHKIN, Alex	6-2	223	R	Moscow, USSR	25	Washington
PERREAULT, Mathieu	5-8	166	L	Drummondville, Que.	22	Washington-Hershey
PINIZZOTTO, Steve	6-1	195	R	Mississauga, Ont.	26	Hershey
SEMIN, Alexander	6-2	208	L	Krasnoyarsk, USSR	26	Washington
STECKEL, David	6-5	217	L	Westbend, WI	28	Washington
WILLSIE, Brian	6-1	202	R	Belmont, Ont.	32	Colorado-Lake Erie
DEFENSEMEN						
ALZNER, Karl	6-2	210	L	Burnaby, B.C.	22	Washington-Hershey
CARLSON, John	6-3	208	R	Natick, MA	20	Washington-Hershey
COLLINS, Sean	6-1	215	R	Troy, MI	26	Hershey
ERSKINE, John	6-4	220	L	Kingston, Ont.	30	Washington
FAHEY, Brian	6-1	216	R	Des Plaines, IL	29	Lake Erie
FINLEY, Joe	6-7	245	L	Edina, MN	23	South Carolina
GODFREY, Josh	6-1	202	R	Collingwood, Ont.	22	Hershey-South Carolina
GREEN, Mike	6-1	204	R	Calgary, Alta.	24	Washington
McNEILL, Patrick	6-1	200	L	Strathroy, Ont.	23	Hershey
MISKOVIC, Zach	6-1	158	R	River Forest, IL	25	Hershey
POTI, Tom	6-3	197	L	Worcester, MA	33	Washington
SCHULTZ, Jeff	6-6	230	L	Calgary, Alta.	24	Washington
SLOAN, Tyler	6-4	204	L	Calgary, Alta.	29	Washington-Hershey
STEVENSON, Dustin	6-5	220	L	Gull Lake, Sask.	21	La Ronge
GOALTENDERS	**HT**	**WT**	**C**	**Place of Birth**	***Age**	**2009-10 Club**
HOLTBY, Braden	6-1	202	L	Lloydminster, Sask.	21	Hershey-South Carolina
NEUVIRTH, Michal	6-1	200	L	Usti nad Labem, Czech.	22	Washington-Hershey
SABOURIN, Dany	6-4	200	L	Val-d'Or, Que.	30	Providence (AHL)
VARLAMOV, Semyon	6-2	209	L	Kuybyshev, USSR	22	Washington-Hershey

* – Age at start of 2010-11 season

Bruce Boudreau
Head Coach

Born: Toronto, Ont., January 9, 1955.

Bruce Boudreau became the 14th head coach in Washington Capitals history when he was named to the position on an interim basis on November 22, 2007. He had the interim tag removed on December 26. His tremendously successful first season behind the bench in Washington landed the Capitals a playoff berth and earned Boudreau the Jack Adams Award as the NHL's coach of the year. Boudreau led the Capitals on a remarkable comeback from 30th in the NHL when he took over the team to the Southeast Division championship. The Capitals won a second consecutive Southeast Division title in 2008-09, tying a franchise record with 50 wins and setting a new record with 108 points. They shattered those records with 54 wins and 121 points in 2009-10 and won the Presidents' Trophy for the first time in franchise history.

Boudreau spent nine seasons as a head coach in the American Hockey League, compiling a record of 340-216-99. He won the Calder Cup with the Hershey Bears in 2006 and won the Kelly Cup as head coach and director of hockey operations for the Mississippi Sea Wolves (ECHL) in 1999. He was named coach of the year in the International Hockey League in 1994 after leading the Fort Wayne Komets to the Turner Cup finals.

Boudreau played parts of eight seasons in the NHL with the Toronto Maple Leafs and Chicago Blackhawks, recording 70 points in 141 games. He enjoyed one of the best seasons ever by a Canadian junior player during 1974-75, collecting 165 points for the Toronto Marlboros, a Canadian Hockey League record until Wayne Gretzky surpassed the mark during the 1977-78 season. An outstanding minor league scorer, no AHL player in the 1980s notched more points than Boudreau.

Coaching Record

			Regular Season				Playoffs			
Season	Team	League	GC	W	L	O/T	GC	W	L	T
1992-93	Muskegon	CoHL	60	28	27	5	7	3	4	....
1993-94	Fort Wayne	IHL	81	41	29	11	18	10	8	....
1994-95	Fort Wayne	IHL	39	15	21	3	....	....	....	....
1996-97	Mississippi	ECHL	70	34	26	10	3	0	3	....
1997-98	Mississippi	ECHL	70	34	27	9	....	....	....	....
1998-99	Mississippi	ECHL	70	41	22	7	18	14	4	....
99-2000	Lowell	AHL	80	33	36	11	7	3	4	....
2000-01	Lowell	AHL	80	35	35	10	4	1	3	....
2001-02	Manchester	AHL	80	38	28	14	5	2	3	....
2002-03	Manchester	AHL	80	40	23	17	3	0	3	....
2003-04	Manchester	AHL	80	40	28	12	6	2	4	....
2004-05	Manchester	AHL	80	51	21	8	6	2	4	....
2005-06	Hershey	AHL	80	44	21	15	21	16	5	....
2006-07	Hershey	AHL	80	51	17	12	19	13	6	....
2007-08	Hershey	AHL	15	8	7	0	....	....	....	....
2007-08	**Washington**	**NHL**	**61**	**37**	**17**	**7**	**7**	**3**	**4**	....
2008-09	**Washington**	**NHL**	**82**	**50**	**24**	**8**	**14**	**7**	**7**	....
2009-10	**Washington**	**NHL**	**82**	**54**	**15**	**13**	**7**	**3**	**4**	....
	NHL Totals		**225**	**141**	**56**	**28**	**28**	**13**	**15**	....

Won Jack Adams Award (2008)

2009-10 Scoring

* – rookie

Regular Season

Pos	#	Player	Team	GP	G	A	Pts	TOI	+/–	PIM	PP	SH	GW	S	%
L	8	Alex Ovechkin	WSH	72	50	59	109	21:47	45	89	13	0	7	368	13.6
C	19	Nicklas Backstrom	WSH	82	33	68	101	20:26	37	50	11	0	4	222	14.9
L	28	Alexander Semin	WSH	73	40	44	84	19:07	36	66	8	2	5	278	14.4
D	52	Mike Green	WSH	75	19	57	76	25:28	39	54	10	0	4	205	9.3
C	21	Brooks Laich	WSH	78	25	34	59	18:17	16	34	12	1	4	222	11.3
R	22	Mike Knuble	WSH	69	29	24	53	16:52	23	59	6	0	5	151	19.2
R	14	Tomas Fleischmann	WSH	69	23	28	51	16:02	9	28	7	0	4	121	19.0
C	9	Brendan Morrison	WSH	74	12	30	42	15:44	23	40	3	0	3	105	11.4
C	18	Eric Belanger	MIN	60	13	22	35	15:45	–1	28	3	0	3	120	10.8
			WSH	17	2	4	6	14:39	3	4	0	0	0	31	6.5
			Total	77	15	26	41	15:30	2	32	3	0	3	151	9.9
R	16	Eric Fehr	WSH	69	21	18	39	12:07	18	24	3	0	3	145	14.5
L	25	Jason Chimera	CBJ	39	8	9	17	14:46	–7	47	1	0	1	92	8.7
			WSH	39	7	10	17	12:36	6	51	0	0	0	68	10.3
			Total	78	15	19	34	13:41	–1	98	1	0	1	160	9.4
R	10	Matt Bradley	WSH	77	10	14	24	11:01	6	47	0	1	5	98	10.2
D	3	Tom Poti	WSH	70	4	20	24	21:24	26	42	2	0	0	69	5.8
D	55	Jeff Schultz	WSH	73	3	20	23	19:51	50	32	0	0	0	43	7.0
D	77	Joe Corvo	CAR	34	4	8	12	25:13	–6	10	4	0	0	76	5.3
			WSH	18	2	4	6	19:40	–4	2	1	0	0	23	8.7
			Total	52	6	12	18	23:18	–10	12	5	0	0	99	6.1
C	39	David Steckel	WSH	79	5	11	16	12:24	4	19	1	0	1	90	5.6
D	26	Shaone Morrisonn	WSH	68	1	11	12	17:34	8	68	0	0	1	32	3.1
C	15	Boyd Gordon	WSH	36	4	6	10	10:17	4	12	0	0	0	40	10.0
C	85 *	Mathieu Perreault	WSH	21	4	5	9	11:21	4	6	1	0	0	27	14.8
R	24	Scott Walker	CAR	33	3	2	5	9:50	–4	23	1	0	0	50	6.0
			WSH	9	2	1	3	9:11	1	9	0	0	1	13	15.4
			Total	42	5	3	8	9:41	–3	32	1	0	1	63	7.9
D	89	Tyler Sloan	WSH	40	2	4	6	14:14	–1	22	0	0	0	34	5.9
D	74 *	John Carlson	WSH	22	1	5	6	15:14	11	8	0	0	0	21	4.8
D	4	John Erskine	WSH	50	1	5	6	15:58	16	66	0	0	0	50	2.0
C	20	Keith Aucoin	WSH	9	1	4	5	8:47	–2	0	0	0	0	4	25.0
D	27	Karl Alzner	WSH	21	0	5	5	16:24	–2	8	0	0	0	16	0.0
L	53	Quintin Laing	WSH	36	2	2	4	9:38	2	21	0	0	0	38	5.3
L	33	Alexandre Giroux	WSH	9	1	2	3	10:22	3	4	0	0	0	17	5.9
L	56 *	Chris Bourque	PIT	20	0	3	3	9:34	–4	10	0	0	0	20	0.0
			WSH	1	0	0	0	9:37	–2	0	0	0	0	1	0.0
			Total	21	0	3	3	9:34	–6	10	0	0	0	21	0.0
C	83 *	Jay Beagle	WSH	7	1	1	2	9:15	–1	2	0	0	0	10	10.0
C	57 *	Kyle Wilson	WSH	2	0	2	2	9:41	1	0	0	0	0	1	0.0
R	63 *	Andrew Gordon	WSH	2	0	0	0	6:41	–2	0	0	0	0	0	0.0
L	34	Boyd Kane	WSH	3	0	0	0	8:12	–1	2	0	0	0	2	0.0

Goaltending

No.	Goaltender	GPI	Mins	Avg	W	L	OT	EN	SO	GA	SA	S%	G	A	PIM
40	* Semyon Varlamov	26	1527	2.55	15	4	6	0	2	65	718	.909	0	1	0
30	* Michal Neuvirth	17	872	2.75	9	4	0	0	0	40	464	.914	0	0	0
60	Jose Theodore	47	2586	2.81	30	7	7	1	1	121	1352	.911	0	2	0
	Totals	**82**	**5009**	**2.72**	**54**	**15**	**13**	**1**	**3**	**227**	**2535**	**.910**			

Playoffs

Pos	#	Player	Team	GP	G	A	Pts	TOI	+/–	PIM	PP	SH	GW	OT	S	%
L	8	Alex Ovechkin	WSH	7	5	5	10	23:06	5	0	1	0	0	0	34	14.7
C	19	Nicklas Backstrom	WSH	7	5	4	9	21:03	7	4	0	0	1	1	27	18.5
R	22	Mike Knuble	WSH	7	2	4	6	17:49	2	6	0	1	0	0	23	8.7
R	16	Eric Fehr	WSH	7	3	1	4	11:24	2	4	0	0	0	0	20	15.0
D	74 *	John Carlson	WSH	7	1	3	4	20:14	6	0	0	0	0	0	14	7.1
D	3	Tom Poti	WSH	6	0	4	4	21:22	9	5	0	0	0	0	6	0.0
C	21	Brooks Laich	WSH	7	2	1	3	19:56	–2	4	0	0	1	0	21	9.5
R	10	Matt Bradley	WSH	7	1	2	3	10:35	2	2	0	0	0	0	8	12.5
L	25	Jason Chimera	WSH	7	1	2	3	11:45	2	2	0	0	1	0	15	6.7
D	52	Mike Green	WSH	7	0	3	3	26:01	1	12	0	0	0	0	23	0.0
C	15	Boyd Gordon	WSH	6	1	1	2	11:01	2	0	0	1	0	0	11	9.1
D	77	Joe Corvo	WSH	7	1	1	2	16:53	–2	4	0	0	0	0	21	4.8
L	28	Alexander Semin	WSH	7	0	2	2	19:20	0	4	0	0	0	0	44	0.0
C	9	Brendan Morrison	WSH	5	0	1	1	11:59	–1	2	0	0	0	0	6	0.0
R	14	Tomas Fleischmann	WSH	6	0	1	1	13:21	–1	6	0	0	0	0	8	0.0
C	18	Eric Belanger	WSH	7	0	1	1	14:05	0	4	0	0	0	0	6	0.0
D	55	Jeff Schultz	WSH	7	0	1	1	19:43	–1	4	0	0	0	0	4	0.0
R	24	Scott Walker	WSH	1	0	0	0	6:47	0	0	0	0	0	0	0	0.0
D	27	Karl Alzner	WSH	1	0	0	0	15:09	0	0	0	0	0	0	0	0.0
D	89	Tyler Sloan	WSH	2	0	0	0	13:05	–1	0	0	0	0	0	0	0.0
C	39	David Steckel	WSH	3	0	0	0	10:28	1	0	0	0	0	0	0	0.0
D	26	Shaone Morrisonn	WSH	5	0	0	0	15:54	1	2	0	0	0	0	1	0.0

Goaltending

No.	Goaltender	GPI	Mins	Avg	W	L	EN	SO	GA	SA	S%	G	A	PIM
40	* Semyon Varlamov	6	349	2.41	3	3	1	0	14	153	.908	0	0	0
60	Jose Theodore	2	81	3.70	0	1	0	0	5	40	.875	0	0	0
	Totals	**7**	**434**	**2.76**	**3**	**4**	**1**	**0**	**20**	**194**	**.897**			

Coaching History

Jim Anderson, Red Sullivan and Milt Schmidt, 1974-75; Milt Schmidt and Tom McVie, 1975-76; Tom McVie, 1976-77, 1977-78; Danny Belisle, 1978-79; Danny Belisle and Gary Green, 1979-80; Gary Green, 1980-81; Gary Green, Roger Crozier and Bryan Murray, 1981-82; Bryan Murray, 1982-83 to 1988-89; Bryan Murray and Terry Murray, 1989-90; Terry Murray, 1990-91 to 1992-93; Terry Murray and Jim Schoenfeld, 1993-94; Jim Schoenfeld, 1994-95 to 1996-97; Ron Wilson, 1997-98 to 2001-02; Bruce Cassidy, 2002-03; Bruce Cassidy and Glen Hanlon, 2003-04; Glen Hanlon, 2004-05 to 2006-07; Glen Hanlon and Bruce Boudreau, 2007-08; Bruce Boudreau, 2008-09 to date.

Club Records

Team

(Figures in brackets for season records are games played; records for fewest points, wins, ties, losses, goals, goals against are for 70 or more games)

Most Points **121** 2009-10 (82)
Most Wins **54** 2009-10 (82)
Most Ties **18** 1980-81 (80)
Most Losses **67** 1974-75 (80)
Most Goals **330** 1991-92 (80)
Most Goals Against ***446** 1974-75 (80)
Fewest Points ***21** 1974-75 (80)
Fewest Wins ***8** 1974-75 (80)
Fewest Ties **5** 1974-75 (80), 1983-84 (80)
Fewest Losses **15** 2009-10 (82)
Fewest Goals **181** 1974-75 (80)
Fewest Goals Against **194** 1999-00 (82)
Longest Winning Streak
  Overall .... **14** Jan. 13-Feb. 7/10
  Home .... **13** Jan. 5-Mar. 6/10
  Away .... **6** Feb. 26-Apr. 1/84
Longest Undefeated Streak
  Overall .... **14** Nov. 24-Dec. 23/82 (9 wins, 5 ties), Jan. 17-Feb. 18/84 (13 wins, 1 tie), Jan. 13-Feb. 7/10 (14 wins)
  Home .... **13** Nov. 25/92-Jan. 31/93 (9 wins, 4 ties), Dec. 27/99-Feb. 23/00 (11 wins, 2 ties), Jan. 5-Mar. 6/10 (13 wins)
  Away .... **10** Nov. 24/82-Jan. 8/83 (6 wins, 4 ties)
Longest Losing Streak
  Overall .... ***17** Feb. 18-Mar. 26/75
  Home .... **11** Feb. 18-Mar. 30/75
  Away .... **37** Oct. 9/74-Mar. 26/75
Longest Winless Streak
  Overall .... **25** Nov. 29/75-Jan. 21/76 (22 losses, 3 ties)
  Home .... **14** Dec. 3/75-Jan. 21/76 (11 losses, 3 ties)
  Away .... **37** Oct. 9/74-Mar. 26/75 (37 losses)
Most Shutouts, Season **9** 1995-96 (82)
Most PIM, Season **2,204** 1989-90 (80)
Most Goals, Game .... **12** Feb. 6/90 (Que. 2 at Wsh. 12), Jan. 11/03 (Fla. 2 at Wsh. 12)

Individual

Most Seasons .... **16** Olaf Kolzig
Most Games .... **983** Calle Johansson
Most Goals, Career .... **472** Peter Bondra
Most Assists, Career .... **418** Michal Pivonka
Most Points, Career .... **825** Peter Bondra (472G, 353A)
Most PIM, Career .... **2,003** Dale Hunter
Most Shutouts, Career .... **35** Olaf Kolzig
Longest Consecutive Games Streak .... **422** Bob Carpenter (Oct. 7/81-Nov. 22/86)
Most Goals, Season .... **65** Alex Ovechkin (2007-08)
Most Assists, Season .... **76** Dennis Maruk (1981-82)
Most Points, Season .... **136** Dennis Maruk (1981-82; 60G, 76A)
Most PIM, Season .... **339** Alan May (1989-90)
Most Points, Defenseman, Season .... **81** Larry Murphy (1986-87; 23G, 58A)
Most Points, Center, Season .... **136** Dennis Maruk (1981-82; 60G, 76A)
Most Points, Right Wing, Season .... **102** Mike Gartner (1984-85; 50G, 52A)
Most Points, Left Wing, Season .... **112** Alex Ovechkin (2007-08; 65G, 47A)
Most Points, Rookie, Season .... **106** Alex Ovechkin (2005-06; 52G, 54A)
Most Shutouts, Season .... **9** Jim Carey (1995-96)
Most Goals, Game .... **5** Bengt Gustafsson (Jan. 8/84), Peter Bondra (Feb. 5/94)
Most Assists, Game .... **6** Mike Ridley (Jan. 7/89)
Most Points, Game .... **7** Dino Ciccarelli (Mar. 18/89; 4G, 3A), Jaromir Jagr (Jan. 11/03; 3G, 4A)

* NHL Record.

Retired Numbers

5	Rod Langway	1982-1993
7	Yvon Labre	1974-1981
11	Mike Gartner	1979-1989
32	Dale Hunter	1987-1999

Captains' History

Doug Mohns, 1974-75; Bill Clement and Yvon Labre, 1975-76; Yvon Labre, 1976-77, 1977-78; Guy Charron, 1978-79; Ryan Walter, 1979-80 to 1981-82; Rod Langway, 1982-83 to 1991-92; Rod Langway and Kevin Hatcher, 1992-93; Kevin Hatcher, 1993-94; Dale Hunter, 1994-95 to 1998-99; Adam Oates, 1999-2000, 2000-01; Brendan Witt and Steve Konowalchuk, 2001-02; Steve Konowalchuk, 2002-03; Steve Konowalchuk and no captain, 2003-04; Jeff Halpern, 2005-06; Chris Clark, 2006-07 to 2008-09; Chris Clark and Alex Ovechkin, 2009-10; Alex Ovechkin, 2010-11.

All-time Record vs. Other Clubs

Regular Season

	At Home								On Road								Total							
	GP	W	L	T	OL	GF	GA	PTS	GP	W	L	T	OL	GF	GA	PTS	GP	W	L	T	OL	GF	GA	PTS
Anaheim	11	5	6	0	0	22	29	10	11	4	6	1	0	31	35	9	22	9	12	1	0	53	64	19
Atlanta	31	20	7	3	1	113	87	44	31	14	11	2	4	98	92	34	62	34	18	5	5	211	179	78
Boston	65	22	27	12	4	187	215	60	66	19	34	9	4	175	232	51	131	41	61	21	8	362	447	111
Buffalo	66	19	36	9	2	171	228	49	66	19	41	6	0	172	256	44	132	38	77	15	2	343	484	93
Calgary	43	22	15	6	0	159	146	50	40	8	25	7	0	98	161	23	83	30	40	13	0	257	307	73
Carolina	65	39	21	4	1	220	172	83	67	30	23	10	4	201	194	74	132	69	44	14	5	421	366	157
Chicago	43	22	15	5	1	152	133	50	42	13	23	6	0	124	159	32	85	35	38	11	1	276	292	82
Colorado	35	19	11	4	1	134	110	43	36	16	15	5	0	127	109	37	71	35	26	9	1	261	219	80
Columbus	5	2	1	1	1	15	15	6	7	5	2	0	0	22	19	10	12	7	3	1	1	37	34	16
Dallas	42	16	17	8	1	127	136	41	43	13	22	8	0	117	161	34	85	29	39	16	1	244	297	75
Detroit	49	23	21	5	0	178	155	51	49	15	21	11	2	140	168	43	98	38	42	16	2	318	323	94
Edmonton	31	19	10	2	0	125	102	40	31	11	16	4	0	95	126	26	62	30	26	6	0	220	228	66
Florida	46	23	13	5	5	143	118	56	46	22	19	4	1	126	121	49	92	45	32	9	6	269	239	105
Los Angeles	48	19	22	7	0	193	179	45	50	15	29	6	0	150	196	36	98	34	51	13	0	343	375	81
Minnesota	5	4	1	0	0	14	8	8	5	0	4	0	1	6	13	1	10	4	5	0	1	20	21	9
Montreal	69	32	28	9	0	195	205	73	70	21	39	8	2	158	265	52	139	53	67	17	2	353	470	125
Nashville	7	5	2	0	0	19	18	10	7	3	3	1	0	17	19	7	14	8	5	1	0	36	37	17
New Jersey	89	52	26	6	5	333	251	115	89	36	42	7	4	257	275	83	178	88	68	13	9	590	526	198
NY Islanders	91	45	33	11	2	301	286	103	91	42	46	2	1	282	330	87	182	87	79	13	3	583	616	190
NY Rangers	94	50	32	9	3	346	294	112	92	38	43	9	2	310	342	87	186	88	75	18	5	656	636	199
Ottawa	34	18	11	4	1	120	98	41	33	13	17	1	2	99	121	29	67	31	28	5	3	219	219	70
Philadelphia	90	39	38	13	0	295	287	91	93	30	56	6	1	258	353	67	183	69	94	19	1	553	640	158
Phoenix	33	19	8	5	1	125	90	44	32	9	16	7	0	112	115	25	65	28	24	12	1	237	205	69
Pittsburgh	96	49	35	9	3	394	349	110	93	34	51	7	1	299	361	76	189	83	86	16	4	693	710	186
St. Louis	41	22	15	4	0	145	123	48	43	13	21	8	1	133	173	35	84	35	36	12	1	278	296	83
San Jose	14	6	7	0	1	40	40	13	13	3	9	1	0	31	45	7	27	9	16	1	1	71	85	20
Tampa Bay	47	30	11	4	2	172	121	66	47	28	15	2	2	151	119	60	94	58	26	6	4	323	240	126
Toronto	60	35	20	4	1	218	169	75	58	20	29	6	3	192	241	49	118	55	49	10	4	410	410	124
Vancouver	42	23	15	4	0	139	124	50	41	16	19	5	1	127	142	38	83	39	34	9	1	266	266	88
Defunct Clubs	10	2	8	0	0	28	42	4	10	4	5	1	0	30	39	9	20	6	13	1	0	58	81	13
Totals	**1402**	**701**	**512**	**153**	**36**	**4823**	**4330**	**1591**	**1402**	**514**	**702**	**150**	**36**	**4138**	**4982**	**1214**	**2804**	**1215**	**1214**	**303**	**72**	**8961**	**9312**	**2805**

Playoffs

	Series	W	L	GP	W	L	T	GF	GA	Last Mtg.	Rnd.	Result
Boston	2	1	1	10	4	6	0	21	28	1998	CQF	W 4-2
Buffalo	1	1	0	6	4	2	0	13	11	1998	CF	W 4-2
Detroit	1	0	1	4	0	4	0	7	13	1998	F	L 0-4
Montreal	1	0	1	7	3	4	0	22	20	2010	CQF	L 3-4
New Jersey	2	1	1	13	7	6	0	44	43	1990	DSF	W 4-2
NY Islanders	6	1	5	30	12	18	0	88	99	1993	DSF	L 2-4
NY Rangers	5	3	2	29	15	14	0	94	82	2009	CQF	W 4-3
Ottawa	1	1	0	5	4	1	0	18	7	1998	CSF	W 4-1
Philadelphia	4	2	2	23	12	11	0	85	78	2008	CQF	L 3-4
Pittsburgh	8	1	7	49	19	30	0	143	164	2009	CSF	L 3-4
Tampa Bay	1	0	1	6	2	4	0	15	14	2003	CQF	L 2-4
Totals	**32**	**11**	**21**	**182**	**82**	**100**	**0**	**550**	**559**			

Calgary totals include Atlanta Flames, 1974-75 to 1979-80.
Carolina totals include Hartford, 1979-80 to 1996-97.
Colorado totals include Quebec, 1979-80 to 1994-95.
Dallas totals include Minnesota North Stars, 1974-75 to 1992-93.
New Jersey totals include Kansas City, 1974-75, 1975-76, and Colorado Rockies, 1976-77 to 1981-82.
Phoenix totals include Winnipeg, 1979-80 to 1995-96.

Playoff Results 2010-2006

Year	Round	Opponent	Result	GF	GA
2010	CQF	Montreal	L 3-4	22	20
2009	CSF	Pittsburgh	L 3-4	22	27
	CQF	NY Rangers	W 4-3	19	11
2008	CQF	Philadelphia	L 3-4	20	23

Abbreviations: Round: F – Final; **CF** – conference final; **CSF** – conference semi-final; **CQF** – conference quarter-final; **DSF** – division semi-final.

2009-10 Results

Oct.	1	at Boston	4-1		5	Montreal	4-2
	3	Toronto	6-4		7	Ottawa	5-2
	6	at Philadelphia	5-6*		9	at Atlanta	8-1
	8	NY Rangers	3-4		12	at Tampa Bay	4-7
	10	at Detroit	2-3		13	at Florida	5-4†
	12	New Jersey	2-3†		15	Toronto	6-1
	15	San Jose	4-1		17	Philadelphia	5-3
	17	Nashville	3-2†		19	Detroit	3-2
	22	at Atlanta	5-4		21	at Pittsburgh	6-3
	24	at NY Islanders	3-2*		23	Phoenix	4-2
	27	Philadelphia	4-2		26	at NY Islanders	7-2
	29	at Atlanta	4-3		27	Anaheim	5-1
	30	NY Islanders	3-4*		29	Florida	4-1
Nov.	1	Columbus	4-5*		31	Tampa Bay	3-2
	4	at New Jersey	2-3	**Feb.**	2	at Boston	4-1
	6	at Florida	4-1		4	at NY Rangers	6-5
	7	Florida	7-4		5	Atlanta	5-2
	11	NY Islanders	5-4†		7	Pittsburgh	5-4*
	13	Minnesota	3-1		10	at Montreal	5-6*
	14	at New Jersey	2-5		11	at Ottawa	5-6
	17	at NY Rangers	4-2		13	at St. Louis	3-4†
	20	Montreal	2-3	**Mar.**	3	at Buffalo	3-1
	21	at Toronto	1-2†		4	Tampa Bay	5-4
	23	at Ottawa	3-4*		6	NY Rangers	2-0
	25	Buffalo	2-0		8	Dallas	3-4†
	28	at Montreal	4-3†		10	Carolina	4-3*
	30	at Carolina	3-2		12	Tampa Bay	2-3
Dec.	3	Florida	6-2		14	at Chicago	4-3*
	5	at Philadelphia	8-2		16	at Florida	7-3
	7	at Tampa Bay	3-0		18	at Carolina	3-4*
	9	at Buffalo	0-3		20	at Tampa Bay	3-1
	11	Carolina	4-3*		24	Pittsburgh	4-3†
	12	at Toronto	3-6		25	at Carolina	2-3†
	15	at Colorado	6-1		28	Calgary	3-5
	18	at Vancouver	2-3		30	Ottawa	4-5*
	19	at Edmonton	4-2	**Apr.**	1	Atlanta	2-1
	23	Buffalo	5-2		3	at Columbus	3-2
	26	New Jersey	4-1		5	Boston	3-2*
	28	Carolina	3-6		6	at Pittsburgh	6-3
	30	at San Jose	2-5		9	Atlanta	5-2
Jan.	2	at Los Angeles	1-2		11	Boston	3-4†

* – Overtime † – Shootout

Entry Draft Selections 2010-1996

Name in bold denotes played in NHL.

2010
Pick
26 Yevgeny Kuznetsov
86 Stanislav Galiev
112 Philipp Grubauer
142 Caleb Herbert
176 Samuel Carrier

2009
Pick
24 Marcus Johansson
55 Dmitri Orlov
85 Cody Eakin
115 Patrick Wey
145 Brett Flemming
175 Garrett Mitchell
205 Benjamin Casavant

2008
Pick
21 Anton Gustafsson
27 **John Carlson**
57 Eric Mestery
58 Dmitry Kugryshev
93 Braden Holtby
144 Joel Broda
174 Greg Burke
204 Stefan Della Rovere

2007
Pick
5 **Karl Alzner**
34 Josh Godfrey
46 Theo Ruth
84 Phil Desimone
108 Brett Bruneteau
125 Brett Leffler
154 Dan Dunn
180 Justin Taylor
185 Nick Larson
199 Andrew Glass

2006
Pick
4 **Nicklas Backstrom**
23 **Semyon Varlamov**
34 **Michal Neuvirth**
35 Francois Bouchard
52 Keith Seabrook
97 **Oskar Osala**
122 Luke Lynes
127 Maxime Lacroix
157 Brent Gwidt
177 **Mathieu Perreault**

2005
Pick
14 Sasha Pokulok
27 Joe Finley
109 Andrew Thomas
118 Patrick McNeill
143 Daren Machesney
181 **Tim Kennedy**
209 Viktor Dovgan

2004
Pick
1 **Alex Ovechkin**
27 **Jeff Schultz**
29 **Mike Green**
33 **Chris Bourque**
62 Mikhail Yunkov
66 **Sami Lepisto**
88 Clayton Barthel
132 Oscar Hedman
138 Pasi Salonen
166 Peter Guggisberg
197 **Andrew Gordon**
230 Justin Mrazek
263 Travis Morin

2003
Pick
18 **Eric Fehr**
83 Steve Werner
109 Andreas Valdix
155 Josh Robertson
249 Andrew Joudrey
279 Mark Olafson

2002
Pick
12 **Steve Eminger**
13 **Alexander Semin**
17 **Boyd Gordon**
59 Maxime Daigneault
77 Patrick Wellar
92 Derek Krestanovich
109 Jevon Desautels
118 Petr Dvorak
145 Rob Gherson
179 Marian Havel
209 Joni Lindlof
242 Igor Ignatushkin
272 Patric Blomdahl

2001
Pick
58 **Nathan Paetsch**
90 **Owen Fussey**
125 Jeff Lucky
160 Artem Ternavsky
191 Zbynek Novak
221 **Johnny Oduya**
249 Matt Maglione
254 Peter Polcik
275 Robert Muller
284 Viktor Hubl

2000
Pick
26 **Brian Sutherby**
43 **Matt Pettinger**
61 **Jakub Cutta**
121 Ryan Vanbuskirk
163 Ivan Nepryayev
289 Bjorn Nord

1999
Pick
7 **Kris Beech**
29 **Michal Sivek**
31 **Charlie Stephens**
34 **Ross Lupaschuk**
37 **Nolan Yonkman**
132 **Roman Tvrdon**
175 Kyle Clark
192 David Bornhammar
219 Maxim Orlov
249 Igor Shadilov

1998
Pick
49 Jomar Cruz
59 Todd Hornung
106 **Krys Barch**
107 **Chris Corrinet**
118 **Mike Siklenka**
125 Erik Wendell
179 Nate Forster
193 **Rastislav Stana**
220 **Mike Farrell**
251 Blake Evans

1997
Pick
9 **Nick Boynton**
35 **Jean-Francois Fortin**
89 Curtis Cruickshank
116 Kevin Caulfield
143 Henrik Petre
200 Pierre-Luc Therrien
226 Matt Oikawa

1996
Pick
4 **Alexandre Volchkov**
17 **Jaroslav Svejkovsky**
43 **Jan Bulis**
58 Sergei Zimakov
74 Dave Weninger
78 Shawn McNeil
85 Justin Davis
126 Matthew Lahey
153 Andrew Van Bruggen
180 Michael Anderson
206 Oleg Orekhovsky
232 Chad Cavanagh

General Managers' History

Milt Schmidt, 1974-75; Milt Schmidt and Max McNab, 1975-76; Max McNab, 1976-77 to 1980-81; Max McNab and Roger Crozier, 1981-82; David Poile, 1982-83 to 1996-97; George McPhee, 1997-98 to date.

George McPhee

Vice President and General Manager

Born: Wallaceburg, Ont., July 2, 1958.

On June 9, 1997, George McPhee became the fifth general manager of the Washington Capitals. In his first year on the job, McPhee led the Caps to the Stanley Cup Finals for the first time in franchise history. He has since rebuilt the Capitals with younger players and used the first overall choice at the 2004 NHL Entry Draft to select Alex Ovechkin. In 2007-08 and 2008-09, the Capitals won the Southeast Division. They shattered club records with 54 wins and 121 points in 2009-10 and won the Presidents' Trophy for the first time in franchise history.

Prior to joining the Capitals, McPhee spent five years in the front office of the Vancouver Canucks where he served as vice president of hockey operations and alternate governor. He has earned degrees in both law and business and, while attending law school at Rutgers University, interned at the United States Court of International Trade in 1991.

A back injury forced McPhee to retire as an active player at the conclusion of the 1988-89 season, after a seven year playing career with the New York Rangers and New Jersey Devils. McPhee originally signed as a free agent with the Rangers in July, 1982, after graduating from Bowling Green State University with a business degree. McPhee did not waste any time in college, tallying 40 goals and 48 assists in his freshman season and easily winning CCHA rookie of the year honors. His outstanding collegiate hockey career was capped off when he was named the recipient of the Hobey Baker Award as the top U.S. collegiate player in his senior season. McPhee also earned All-America honors as a senior and finished his career at Bowling Green as the CCHA's all-time leading scorer with 114-153-267. He was the first player in CCHA history to make the Conference's all-academic team three straight seasons.

Club Directory

Verizon Center

Washington Capitals
627 N. Glebe Road, Suite 850
Arlington, VA 22203
Phone **202/266-2200**
PR FAX 202/266-2360
www.washingtoncaps.com
Capacity: 18,277

Ownership (Monumental Sports)	
Chairman and Majority Owner	Ted Leonsis
Vice Chairman and President, C.O.O.	Dick Patrick
Owner	Scott Brickman, Albert Cohen, Neil Cohen, Jack Davies, Richard Fairbank. Raul Fernandez, Michelle D. Freeman, Sheila Johnson, Richard Kay, Jeong Kim, Mark D. Lerner, Fred Schaufeld, George Stamas
Hockey Operations	
Vice President and General Manager	George McPhee
Assistant General Manager, Dir. of Legal Affairs	Don Fishman
Head Coach	Bruce Boudreau
Assistant Coaches	Dean Evason, Bob Woods
Assistant Coach/Video	Blaine Forsythe
Goaltending Coach	Arturs Irbe
Strength and Conditioning Coach	Mark Nemish
Physiologist	Jack Blatherwick
Director, Team Operations	Katy Headman
Hockey Operations Assistants	Eric Garvey, Evan Gold
Manager, Team Services	Ian Anderson
Head Coach, Hershey Bears	Mark French
Assistant Coach, Hershey Bears	Troy Mann
Scouting Staff	
Assistant General Manager, Player Personnel	Brian MacLellan
Pro Scouts	Jason Fitzsimmons, Chris Patrick
Director, Player Development	Steve Richmond
Director, Amateur Scouting	Ross Mahoney
Amateur Scouts	Darrell Baumgartner, Steve Bowman, Alan Haworth, Ed McColgan, Martin Pouliot, Terry Richardson, A.J. Toews
European Scouts	Vojtech Kucera, Petri Skriko, Mats Weiderstal
Director, Scouting Operations	Kris Wagner
Medical Staff	
Head Athletic Trainer	Greg Smith
Assistant Athletic Trainer	Ben Reisz
Massage Therapist	Curt Millar
Team Physician	Ben Shaffer, MD
Team Internist	Chris Walsh, MD
Team Ophthalmologist	Thomas Clinch, MD
Team Dentist	Thomas Lenz, DDS, PC
Equipment Staff	
Head Equipment Manager	Brock Myles
Assistant Equipment Manager	Craig Leydig
Equipment Assistant	Jeff Lewis
Business Operations	
Vice President, Administration	Michelle Trostle
Senior Director, Information Technology	Brian McPartland
Office Assistant	Valerie Garrett
Receptionist	Chuquita Pettus
Chief Building Engineer	Larry Hollen
Building Engineers	Pedro Pena / Justin Wilfong
Marketing	
Vice President, Chief Marketing Officer	Joe Dupriest
Director, Strategic Marketing	Mike Chan
Director, Fan Development & Promotions	Kim Frank
Director, Game Entertainment and TV Production	Michael Wurman
Game Entertainment Coordinator	Tyler Hines
Promotions Coordinator	Lauren Gilmore
Mascot Coordinator	Kevin Giambi
Amateur Hockey & Fan Development Coordinator	Peter Robinson
Communications	
Vice President, Communications	Nate Ewell
Director, New Media	Sean Parker
Director, Community Relations	Elizabeth Wodatch
Senior Writer	Mike Vogel
Graphic Designer	Andrew Mattice
Website Producer	Brett Leonhardt
Communications Coordinator	Kelly Murray
Community Relations Coordinator	Jennifer Vassil
Finance	
Vice President, Finance	Keith Burrows
Accounting Manager	Jill Ruehle
Accounts Payable Manager	Adam Porcelli
Accounting Coordinator	Liz Grant
Sales	
Senior Vice President, Ticket Sales	Jim Van Stone
Senior Director, Ticket Sales	Anthony Aspaas
Senior Director, Group and Arena Event Sales	Darren Montgomery
Director, Amateur Hockey Sales	Tim Bronaugh
Director, Group and Arena Event Sales	Jeff Keeney
Senior Regional Sales Managers	Nova Ackerman, David Boettinger, Travis Gendron
Senior Regional Sales Manager,s Groups	Jimm Bonk, Sara Plietz, Pete Sekulow
Regional Sales Manager	Joshua Gains, Greg Roberts
Corporate Sponsorships	
Vice President, Corporate Sponsorships	John Greeley
Directors, Corporate Sponsorships	Marco Gentile, Bruce Zalbe
Sr. Account Manager, Corporate Sponsorships	Joe LaBue
Sr. Sponsorship Activation Manager	Letitia Petrillo
Sponsorship Activation Manager	Graham Dunn
Ticket Operations	
Senior Director, Ticket Operations	Chris Sheap
Director, Ticket Operations	Jordan Cookler
Manager, Ticket Operations	Stephen Kaufman
Assistant Manager, Ticket Operations	Jill Salisbury
Guest Services	
Senior Director, Guest Services	Greg Monares
Director, Guest Services	Rick Olivieri
Specialists, Guest Services	Clayton Adams, Julie Bohling, Christi Carson, Justin Fenlon, Sean Goodman, Greg Gosselin, Scott Haberle, Kelly Jones, Ryan Kronebusch
Broadcasting	
Radio Rightsholder	WFED 1500 AM
Radio Play-by-Play / Analyst / Host	Steve Kolbe / Ken Sabourin, Jonathan Warner
Television Rightsholder	Comcast SportsNet
Television Play-by-Play / Analyst	Joe Beninati / Craig Laughlin
Television Reporters	Al Koken, Lisa Hillary

2009-10 Final Standings

Standings

Abbreviations: GP - games played; **W** - wins; **L** - losses; **OTL** - overtime losses; **SOL** - shootout losses; **GF** - goals for; **GA** - goals against; **PTS** - points; **%** - winning percentage.

EASTERN CONFERENCE

Northeast Division

		GP	W	L	OTL	SOL	GF	GA	PTS	%
Buffalo	(3)	82	45	27	4	6	235	207	100	.610
Ottawa	(5)	82	44	32	1	5	225	238	94	.573
Boston	(6)	82	39	30	4	9	206	200	91	.555
Montreal	(8)	82	39	33	5	5	217	223	88	.537
Toronto		82	30	38	10	4	214	267	74	.451

Atlantic Division

New Jersey	(2)	82	48	27	2	5	222	191	103	.628
Pittsburgh	(4)	82	47	28	5	2	257	237	101	.616
Philadelphia	(7)	82	41	35	3	3	236	225	88	.537
NY Rangers		82	38	33	7	4	222	218	87	.530
NY Islanders		82	34	37	5	6	222	264	79	.482

Southeast Division

Washington	(1)	82	54	15	7	6	318	233	121	.738
Atlanta		82	35	34	7	6	234	256	83	.506
Carolina		82	35	37	5	5	230	256	80	.488
Tampa Bay		82	34	36	5	7	217	260	80	.488
Florida		82	32	37	3	10	208	244	77	.470

WESTERN CONFERENCE

Central Division

Chicago	(2)	82	52	22	2	6	271	209	112	.683
Detroit	(5)	82	44	24	5	9	229	216	102	.622
Nashville	(7)	82	47	29	2	4	225	225	100	.610
St. Louis		82	40	32	5	5	225	223	90	.549
Columbus		82	32	35	5	10	216	259	79	.482

Pacific Division

San Jose	(1)	82	51	20	5	6	264	215	113	.689
Phoenix	(4)	82	50	25	1	6	225	202	107	.652
Los Angeles	(6)	82	46	27	1	8	241	219	101	.616
Anaheim		82	39	32	3	8	238	251	89	.543
Dallas		82	37	31	4	10	237	254	88	.537

Northwest Division

Vancouver	(3)	82	49	28	1	4	272	222	103	.628
Colorado	(8)	82	43	30	4	5	244	233	95	.579
Calgary		82	40	32	3	7	204	210	90	.549
Minnesota		82	38	36	1	7	219	246	84	.512
Edmonton		82	27	47	2	6	214	284	62	.378

INDIVIDUAL LEADERS

Goal Scoring

Player	Team	GP	G
Sidney Crosby	Pittsburgh	81	51
Steven Stamkos	Tampa Bay	82	51
Alex Ovechkin	Washington	72	50
Patrick Marleau	San Jose	82	44
Marian Gaborik	Ny Rangers	76	42
Ilya Kovalchuk	Atl-N.J	76	41
Alexander Semin	Washington	73	40
Dany Heatley	San Jose	82	39
Zach Parise	New Jersey	81	38
Bobby Ryan	Anaheim	81	35
Alex Burrows	Vancouver	82	35

Assists

Player	Team	GP	A
Henrik Sedin	Vancouver	82	83
Joe Thornton	San Jose	79	69
Nicklas Backstrom	Washington	82	68
Brad Richards	Dallas	80	67
Martin St. Louis	Tampa Bay	82	65
Alex Ovechkin	Washington	72	59
Paul Stastny	Colorado	81	59
Sidney Crosby	Pittsburgh	81	58
Patrick Kane	Chicago	82	58
Mike Green	Washington	75	57

Power-play Goals

Player	Team	GP	PP
Steven Stamkos	Tampa Bay	82	24
Dany Heatley	San Jose	82	18
Teemu Selanne	Anaheim	54	14
Marian Gaborik	Ny Rangers	76	14
Anze Kopitar	Los Angeles	82	14

Shorthand Goals

Player	Team	GP	SH
Marian Hossa	Chicago	57	5
Alex Burrows	Vancouver	82	5
Rene Bourque	Calgary	73	4
Patrick Marleau	San Jose	82	4
8 Players tied with			3

Game-winning Goals

Player	Team	GP	GW
Martin St. Louis	Tampa Bay	82	30
Daniel Alfredsson	Ottawa	70	27
Brad Richards	Dallas	80	27
Nicklas Backstrom	Washington	82	26
Mike Green	Washington	75	25
Joe Thornton	San Jose	79	25

Shots

Player	Team	GP	S
Alex Ovechkin	Washington	72	368
Zach Parise	New Jersey	81	347
Jeff Carter	Philadelphia	74	319
Henrik Zetterberg	Detroit	74	309
Sidney Crosby	Pittsburgh	81	298

Shooting Percentage

(minimum 82 shots)

Player	Team	GP	G	S	%
Andrew Brunette	Minnesota	82	25	129	19.4
Mike Knuble	Washington	69	29	151	19.2
Tomas Holmstrom	Detroit	68	25	131	19.1
Nik Antropov	Atlanta	76	24	126	19.0
Tomas Fleischmann	Washington	69	23	121	19.0
Troy Brouwer	Chicago	78	22	116	19.0
Steve Downie	Tampa Bay	79	22	116	19.0

Penalty Minutes

Player	Team	GP	PIM
Zenon Konopka	Tampa Bay	74	265
Colton Orr	Toronto	82	239
Steve Downie	Tampa Bay	79	208
Daniel Carcillo	Philadelphia	76	207
Cam Janssen	St. Louis	43	190
Matt Carkner	Ottawa	81	190

Plus/Minus

Player	Team	GP	+/–
Jeff Schultz	Washington	73	50
Alex Ovechkin	Washington	72	45
Mike Green	Washington	75	39
Nicklas Backstrom	Washington	82	37
Daniel Sedin	Vancouver	63	36
Alexander Semin	Washington	73	36
Christian Ehrhoff	Vancouver	80	36

Steven Stamkos celebrates his 50th goal of the 2009-10 season with his Tampa Bay teammates. Stamkos reached the milestone in the second last game of his second NHL season, then got his 51st into an open net late in the finale to tie Pittsburgh's Sidney Crosby for the league lead.

Individual Leaders

Abbreviations: GP – games played; **G** – goals; **A** – assists; **Pts** – points; **+/–** – difference between Goals For (**GF**) scored when a player is on the ice with his team at even strength or shorthanded and Goals Against (**GA**) scored when the same player is on the ice with his team at even strength or on a power play; **PIM** – penalties in minutes; **PP** – power play goals; **SH** – shorthanded goals; **GW** – game-winning goals; **S** – shots on goal; **%** – percentage of shots on goal resulting in goals.

Individual Scoring Leaders for Art Ross Trophy

Player	Team	GP	G	A	Pts	+/–	PIM	PP	SH	GW	S	%
Henrik Sedin	Vancouver	82	29	83	112	35	48	4	2	5	166	17.5
Sidney Crosby	Pittsburgh	81	51	58	109	15	71	13	2	6	298	17.1
Alex Ovechkin	Washington	72	50	59	109	45	89	13	0	7	368	13.6
Nicklas Backstrom	Washington	82	33	68	101	37	50	11	0	4	222	14.9
Steven Stamkos	Tampa Bay	82	51	44	95	–2	38	24	1	5	297	17.2
Martin St. Louis	Tampa Bay	82	29	65	94	–8	12	7	1	7	242	12.0
Brad Richards	Dallas	80	24	67	91	–12	14	13	0	2	284	8.5
Joe Thornton	San Jose	79	20	69	89	17	54	4	1	2	141	14.2
Patrick Kane	Chicago	82	30	58	88	16	20	9	0	6	261	11.5
Marian Gaborik	NY Rangers	76	42	44	86	15	37	14	1	4	272	15.4
Ilya Kovalchuk	Atl.-N.J.	76	41	44	85	10	53	12	0	4	290	14.1
Daniel Sedin	Vancouver	63	29	56	85	36	28	8	0	8	225	12.9
Alexander Semin	Washington	73	40	44	84	36	66	8	2	5	278	14.4
Patrick Marleau	San Jose	82	44	39	83	21	22	12	4	6	274	16.1
Dany Heatley	San Jose	82	39	43	82	14	54	18	1	9	280	13.9
Zach Parise	New Jersey	81	38	44	82	24	32	9	1	5	347	11.0
Anze Kopitar	Los Angeles	82	34	47	81	6	16	14	1	2	259	13.1
Paul Stastny	Colorado	81	20	59	79	2	50	9	0	2	199	10.1
Evgeni Malkin	Pittsburgh	67	28	49	77	–6	100	13	2	7	268	10.4
Corey Perry	Anaheim	82	27	49	76	0	111	6	1	2	270	10.0
Mike Green	Washington	75	19	57	76	39	54	10	0	4	205	9.3
Ryan Kesler	Vancouver	82	25	50	75	1	104	12	1	5	214	11.7
Loui Eriksson	Dallas	82	29	42	71	–4	26	6	2	4	214	13.6
Mikko Koivu	Minnesota	80	22	49	71	–2	50	8	1	2	246	8.9
Daniel Alfredsson	Ottawa	70	20	51	71	8	22	4	1	5	168	11.9
Eric Staal	Carolina	70	29	41	70	4	68	13	0	5	277	10.5

Defencemen Scoring Leaders

Player	Team	GP	G	A	Pts	+/–	PIM	PP	SH	GW	S	%
Mike Green	Washington	75	19	57	76	39	54	10	0	4	205	9.3
Duncan Keith	Chicago	82	14	55	69	21	51	3	1	1	213	6.6
Drew Doughty	Los Angeles	82	16	43	59	20	54	9	0	5	142	11.3
Dan Boyle	San Jose	76	15	43	58	6	70	6	0	3	180	8.3
Chris Pronger	Philadelphia	82	10	45	55	22	79	5	0	2	175	5.7
Sergei Gonchar	Pittsburgh	62	11	39	50	–4	49	6	0	3	138	8.0
Tobias Enstrom	Atlanta	82	6	44	50	–5	30	2	0	0	109	5.5
Mark Streit	NY Islanders	82	11	38	49	0	48	9	0	2	187	5.9
Nicklas Lidstrom	Detroit	82	9	40	49	22	24	5	0	1	194	4.6
Tomas Kaberle	Toronto	82	7	42	49	–16	24	3	0	1	158	4.4
Tyler Myers	Buffalo	82	11	37	48	13	32	3	0	1	104	10.6
Scott Niedermayer	Anaheim	80	10	38	48	–9	38	5	0	2	168	6.0
Joni Pitkanen	Carolina	71	6	40	46	–11	72	1	0	1	161	3.7
Lubomir Visnovsky	Edm.-Ana.	73	15	30	45	–10	20	5	0	2	131	11.5
Christian Ehrhoff	Vancouver	80	14	30	44	36	42	6	0	3	181	7.7
Zdeno Chara	Boston	80	7	37	44	19	87	4	0	1	242	2.9
Shea Weber	Nashville	78	16	27	43	0	36	7	0	3	222	7.2
Bryan McCabe	Florida	82	8	35	43	–4	83	3	0	1	169	4.7
Marek Zidlicky	Minnesota	78	6	37	43	–16	67	4	0	3	116	5.2
Kurtis Foster	Tampa Bay	71	8	34	42	–5	48	3	0	1	165	4.8
Brian Rafalski	Detroit	78	8	34	42	23	26	5	0	1	134	6.0
Alexander Edler	Vancouver	76	5	37	42	0	40	2	0	0	161	3.1
Keith Yandle	Phoenix	82	12	29	41	16	45	5	0	2	145	8.3
Stephane Robidas	Dallas	82	10	31	41	–10	70	7	0	1	199	5.0
Erik Johnson	St. Louis	79	10	29	39	1	79	6	0	2	186	5.4
Ryan Whitney	Ana.-Edm.	81	7	32	39	1	70	3	0	1	151	4.6

CONSECUTIVE SCORING STREAKS

Goals

Games	Player	Team	G
7	Steven Stamkos	Tampa Bay	9
6	Mikael Samuelsson	Vancouver	9
6	Steven Stamkos	Tampa Bay	8
6	Jason Spezza	Ottawa	7
6	Jeff Carter	Philadelphia	7
6	Zach Parise	New Jersey	7

Assists

Games	Player	Team	A
11	Daniel Sedin	Vancouver	14
10	Ryan Getzlaf	Anaheim	17
10	Martin St. Louis	Tampa Bay	12
10	Corey Perry	Anaheim	11
9	Joe Thornton	San Jose	15
9	Nicklas Backstrom	Washington	14
8	Tim Connolly	Buffalo	13
8	Evgeni Malkin	Pittsburgh	10
8	Mike Green	Washington	9
7	Henrik Sedin	Vancouver	14
7	Henrik Sedin	Vancouver	12
7	Joe Thornton	San Jose	11
7	Duncan Keith	Chicago	9

Points

Games	Player	Team	G	A	PTS
19	Corey Perry	Anaheim	10	16	26
18	Steven Stamkos	Tampa Bay	17	16	33
16	Tim Connolly	Buffalo	7	18	25
15	Evgeni Malkin	Pittsburgh	9	15	24
13	Ryan Kesler	Vancouver	6	9	15
12	Alex Burrows	Vancouver	13	6	19
11	Ryan Getzlaf	Anaheim	2	17	19
11	Patrick Kane	Chicago	9	9	18
11	Martin St. Louis	Tampa Bay	6	11	17
11	Daniel Sedin	Vancouver	3	14	17
11	Eric Staal	Carolina	10	7	17
11	Martin St. Louis	Tampa Bay	3	12	15

Henrik Sedin broke his own club record with 83 assists in 2009-10 and broke Pavel Bure's scoring record with 112 points. He became the ninth different player in the last nine seasons to lead the NHL in scoring, and the first Vancouver player ever to do so.

Individual Rookie Scoring Leaders

Player	Team	GP	G	A	Pts	+/−	PIM	PP	SH	GW	S	%
Matt Duchene	Colorado	81	24	31	55	1	16	10	1	2	180	13.3
John Tavares	NY Islanders	82	24	30	54	−15	22	11	0	2	186	12.9
Tyler Myers	Buffalo	82	11	37	48	13	32	3	0	1	104	10.6
Niclas Bergfors	N.J-Atl	81	21	23	44	−10	9	9	0	6	217	9.7
Jamie Benn	Dallas	82	22	19	41	−1	45	2	0	3	182	12.1
T.J. Galiardi	Colorado	70	15	24	39	6	28	2	1	3	120	12.5
Michael Del Zotto	NY Rangers	80	9	28	37	−20	32	4	0	1	81	11.1
James van Riemsdyk	Philadelphia	78	15	20	35	−1	30	4	0	6	173	8.7
Peter Regin	Ottawa	75	13	16	29	10	20	1	0	1	135	9.6
Artem Anisimov	NY Rangers	82	12	16	28	−2	32	1	0	2	124	9.7
Tyler Bozak	Toronto	37	8	19	27	−5	6	2	0	1	51	15.7
Evander Kane	Atlanta	66	14	12	26	2	62	0	1	3	127	11.0
Tim Kennedy	Buffalo	78	10	16	26	−3	50	1	0	3	98	10.2
Ryan O'Reilly	Colorado	81	8	18	26	4	18	0	2	2	135	5.9
Erik Karlsson	Ottawa	60	5	21	26	−5	24	1	0	0	112	4.5
Rob Schremp	NY Islanders	44	7	18	25	−4	8	5	0	0	74	9.5
Scott Parse	Los Angeles	59	11	13	24	13	22	0	0	1	78	14.1
Cody Franson	Nashville	61	6	15	21	15	16	1	0	3	90	6.7
Jason Demers	San Jose	51	4	17	21	5	21	3	0	1	52	7.7
Ryan Wilson	Colorado	61	3	18	21	13	36	0	0	0	46	6.5
Victor Hedman	Tampa Bay	74	4	16	20	−3	79	0	0	0	90	4.4
Brandon Yip	Colorado	32	11	8	19	5	22	4	0	2	65	16.9
Dan Sexton	Anaheim	41	9	10	19	−3	16	2	0	0	93	9.7
Matt Beleskey	Anaheim	60	11	7	18	−10	35	0	0	3	123	8.9
Shawn Matthias	Florida	55	7	9	16	−3	10	0	0	2	67	10.4
Dmitry Kulikov	Florida	68	3	13	16	−5	32	1	0	0	87	3.4

Goal Scoring

Player	Team	GP	G
Matt Duchene	Colorado	81	24
John Tavares	NY Islanders	82	24
Jamie Benn	Dallas	82	22
Niclas Bergfors	N.J-Atl	81	21
T.J. Galiardi	Colorado	70	15
James van Riemsdyk	Philadelphia	78	15
Evander Kane	Atlanta	66	14
Peter Regin	Ottawa	75	13
Artem Anisimov	NY Rangers	82	12

Assists

Player	Team	GP	A
Tyler Myers	Buffalo	82	37
Matt Duchene	Colorado	81	31
John Tavares	NY Islanders	82	30
Michael Del Zotto	NY Rangers	80	28
T.J. Galiardi	Colorado	70	24
Niclas Bergfors	N.J-Atl	81	23
Erik Karlsson	Ottawa	60	21
James van Riemsdyk	Philadelphia	78	20
Tyler Bozak	Toronto	37	19
Jamie Benn	Dallas	82	19

Power-play Goals

Player	Team	GP	PP
John Tavares	NY Islanders	82	11
Matt Duchene	Colorado	81	10
Niclas Bergfors	N.J-Atl	81	9
Rob Schremp	NY Islanders	44	5
Brandon Yip	Colorado	32	4
James van Riemsdyk	Philadelphia	78	4
Michael Del Zotto	NY Rangers	80	4

Shorthand Goals

Player	Team	GP	SH
Ryan O'Reilly	Colorado	81	2
Zack Smith	Ottawa	15	1
Christian Hanson	Toronto	31	1
Troy Bodie	Anaheim	44	1
Evander Kane	Atlanta	66	1
T.J. Galiardi	Colorado	70	1
Matt Duchene	Colorado	81	1

Game-winning Goals

Player	Team	GP	GW
James van Riemsdyk	Philadelphia	78	6
Niclas Bergfors	N.J-Atl	81	6
Colin Wilson	Nashville	35	3
Tom Wandell	Dallas	50	3
Matt Beleskey	Anaheim	60	3
Cody Franson	Nashville	61	3
Evander Kane	Atlanta	66	3
T.J. Galiardi	Colorado	70	3
Tim Kennedy	Buffalo	78	3
Jamie Benn	Dallas	82	3

Shots

Player	Team	GP	S
Niclas Bergfors	N.J-Atl	81	217
John Tavares	NY Islanders	82	186
Jamie Benn	Dallas	82	182
Matt Duchene	Colorado	81	180
James van Riemsdyk	Philadelphia	78	173
Peter Regin	Ottawa	75	135
Ryan O'Reilly	Colorado	81	135
Evander Kane	Atlanta	66	127
Artem Anisimov	NY Rangers	82	124
Matt Beleskey	Anaheim	60	123

Shooting Percentage
(minimum 82 shots)

Player	Team	GP	G	S	%
Matt Duchene	Colorado	81	24	180	13.3
John Tavares	NY Islanders	82	24	186	12.9
T.J. Galiardi	Colorado	70	15	120	12.5
Jamie Benn	Dallas	82	22	182	12.1
Evander Kane	Atlanta	66	14	127	11.0
Tyler Myers	Buffalo	82	11	104	10.6
Tim Kennedy	Buffalo	78	10	98	10.2
Niclas Bergfors	N.J-Atl	81	21	217	9.7
Artem Anisimov	NY Rangers	82	12	124	9.7
Dan Sexton	Anaheim	41	9	93	9.7

Penalty Minutes

Player	Team	GP	PIM
Paul Bissonnette	Phoenix	41	117
Troy Bodie	Anaheim	44	80
Victor Hedman	Tampa Bay	74	79
Jay Rosehill	Toronto	15	67
Evander Kane	Atlanta	66	62

Plus/Minus

Player	Team	GP	+/−
Cody Franson	Nashville	61	15
Scott Parse	Los Angeles	59	13
Ryan Wilson	Colorado	61	13
Tyler Myers	Buffalo	82	13
John Carlson	Washington	22	11

Three-or-More-Goal Games

Player	Team	Date	Final Score	G	Player	Team	Date	Final Score	G	Player	Team	Date	Final Score	G
Daniel Alfredsson	Ottawa	Jan. 18	Ott. 5 Bos. 1	3	Nathan Horton	Florida	Dec. 14	Fla. 7 NYI 1	3	Mike Richards	Philadelphia	Oct. 6	Wsh. 5 Phi. 6	3
Rene Bourque	Calgary	Dec. 28	Cgy. 4 Edm. 1	3	Jarome Iginla	Calgary	Nov. 21	Cgy. 5 L.A. 2	3	Derek Roy	Buffalo	Mar. 27	T.B. 1 Buf. 7	3
Danny Briere	Philadelphia	Feb. 13	Phi. 6 Mtl. 2	3	Jarome Iginla	Calgary	Mar. 7	Cgy. 5 Min. 2	3	Mike Rupp	Pittsburgh	Nov. 30	Pit. 5 NYR 2	3
Dustin Brown	Los Angeles	Apr. 1	Van. 3 L.A. 8	3	Chuck Kobasew	Minnesota	Nov. 27	Col. 3 Min. 5	3	Tuomo Ruutu	Carolina	Dec. 16	Dal. 3 Car. 5	3
Alex Burrows	Vancouver	Jan. 5	CBJ 3 Van. 7	3	Anze Kopitar	Los Angeles	Oct. 22	Dal. 4 L.A. 5	3	Mikael Samuelsson	Vancouver	Mar. 9	Van. 6 Col. 4	3
Alex Burrows	Vancouver	Jan. 7	Phx. 0 Van. 4	3	Alex Kovalev	Ottawa	Dec. 12	Car. 2 Ott. 4	3	Marc Savard	Boston	Dec. 5	Tor. 2 Bos. 7	3
Michael Cammalleri	Montreal	Oct. 24	NYR 4 Mtl. 5	3	Alex Kovalev	Ottawa	Jan. 3	Phi. 4 Ott. 7	4	Daniel Sedin	Vancouver	Dec. 10	Atl. 2 Van. 4	3
Michael Cammalleri	Montreal	Dec. 4	Bos. 1 Mtl. 5	3	Andrew Ladd	Chicago	Mar. 7	Det. 5 Chi. 4	3	Daniel Sedin	Vancouver	Apr. 10	Cgy. 3 Van. 7	3
Erik Cole	Carolina	Dec. 5	Van. 3 Car. 5	3	Brooks Laich	Washington	Feb. 10	Wsh. 5 Mtl. 6	3	Henrik Sedin	Vancouver	Nov. 14	Van. 8 Col. 2	3
Blake Comeau	NY Islanders	Mar. 2	Chi. 3 NYI 5	3	Jamie Langenbrunne	New Jersey	Jan. 2	N.J. 5 Min. 3	3	Alexander Semin	Washington	Feb. 11	Wsh. 5 Ott. 6	3
Sidney Crosby	Pittsburgh	Oct. 28	Mtl. 1 Pit. 6	3	Guillaume Latendresse	Minnesota	Jan. 16	Min. 4 Phx. 6	3	Jason Spezza	Ottawa	Mar. 20	Ott. 4 Dal. 5	3
Sidney Crosby	Pittsburgh	Nov. 28	NYR 3 Pit. 8	3	Evgeni Malkin	Pittsburgh	Dec. 23	Ott. 2 Pit. 8	3	Eric Staal	Carolina	Jan. 21	Car. 5 Atl. 2	3
Sidney Crosby	Pittsburgh	Feb. 1	Buf. 4 Pit. 5	3	Evgeni Malkin	Pittsburgh	Jan. 19	NYI 4 Pit. 6	3	Eric Staal	Carolina	Apr. 8	Mtl. 2 Car. 5	3
Radek Dvorak	Florida	Jan. 3	Pit. 2 Fla. 6	3	Ryan Malone	Tampa Bay	Oct. 10	Car. 2 T.B. 5	3	Chris Stewart	Colorado	Mar. 6	St.L. 3 Col. 7	3
Martin Erat	Nashville	Dec. 8	Van. 2 Nsh. 4	3	Patrick Marleau	San Jose	Nov. 27	S.J. 5 Edm. 4	3	Steve Sullivan	Nashville	Mar. 6	Nsh. 5 CBJ 3	3
Loui Eriksson	Dallas	Dec. 31	Ana. 3 Dal. 5	3	Milan Michalek	Ottawa	Oct. 15	T.B. 1 Ott. 7	3	Jeff Tambellini	NY Islanders	Oct. 31	Buf. 0 NYI 5	3
Marian Gaborik	NY Rangers	Jan. 31	NYR 3 Col. 1	3	Matt Moulson	NY Islanders	Dec. 3	NYI 4 Atl. 1	3	R.J. Umberger	Columbus	Nov. 30	St.L. 2 CBJ 5	3
Simon Gagne	Philadelphia	Dec. 30	Phi. 6 NYR 0	3	Steve Ott	Dallas	Mar. 31	S.J. 1 Dal. 5	3	Scottie Upshall	Phoenix	Jan. 21	Nsh. 2 Phx. 4	3
Curtis Glencross	Calgary	Feb. 3	Car. 1 Cgy. 4	3	Alex Ovechkin	Washington	Feb. 7	Pit. 4 Wsh. 5	3	Thomas Vanek	Buffalo	Apr. 10	Buf. 5 Ott. 2	3
*Michael Grabner	Vancouver	Apr. 2	Van. 5 Ana. 4	3	David Perron	St. Louis	Nov. 10	Van. 1 St.L. 6	3	Stephen Weiss	Florida	Dec. 2	Col. 5 Fla. 6	3
Niklas Hagman	Toronto	Oct. 26	Tor. 4 Ana. 3	3	Jason Pominville	Buffalo	Mar. 18	Buf. 4 T.B. 2	3	Henrik Zetterberg	Detroit	Nov. 14	Ana. 4 Det. 7	3
Dany Heatley	San Jose	Oct. 8	CBJ 3 S.J. 6	3	Mason Raymond	Vancouver	Dec. 27	Van. 5 Cgy. 1	3					
Dany Heatley	San Jose	Nov. 20	Phi. 3 S.J. 6	3	Steve Reinprecht	Florida	Oct. 30	Fla. 6 Dal. 5	3					

2009-10 Penalty Shots

(For shootout statistics, see page 149.)

Scored

Daniel Alfredsson (Ott.) scored against Jonas Gustavsson (Tor.) Oct. 6. Final Score: Ott. 2 at Tor. 1

Dany Heatley (S.J.) scored against Mathieu Garon (CBJ) Oct. 8. Final Score: CBJ 3 at S.J. 6

Clarke MacArthur (Buf.) scored against Dwayne Roloson (NYI) Oct. 16. Final Score: NYI 3 at Buf. 6

Wayne Simmonds (L.A.) scored against Brian Elliott (Ott.) Dec. 3. Final Score: Ott. 3 at L.A. 6

Drew Stafford (Buf.) scored against Marc-Andre Fleury (Pit.) Dec. 29. Final Score: Pit. 3 at Buf. 4

Ryane Clowe (S.J.) scored against Michal Neuvirth (Wsh.) Dec. 30. Final Score: Wsh. 2 at S.J. 5

Joe Thornton (S.J.) scored against Michal Neuvirth (Wsh.) Dec. 30. Final Score: Wsh. 2 at S.J. 5

Alex Ovechkin (Wsh.) scored against Ray Emery (Phi.) Jan. 17. Final Score: Phi. 3 at Wsh. 5

Shawn Matthias (Fla.) scored against Jaroslav Halak (Mtl.) Jan. 26. Final Score: Mtl. 1 at Fla. 2

Danny Briere (Phi.) scored against Carey Price (Mtl.) Feb. 13. Final Score: Phi. 6 at Mtl. 2

Sean Avery (NYR) scored against Mike Smith (T.B.) Feb. 14. Final Score: T.B. 2 at NYR 5

Teddy Purcell (T.B.) scored against Johan Hedberg (Atl.) Mar. 6. Final Score: Atl. 2 at T.B. 6

Chris Stewart (Col.) scored against Ty Conklin (St.L.) Mar. 6. Final Score: St.L. 3 at Col. 7

Jakub Voracek (CBJ) scored against Cristobal Huet (Chi.) Mar. 25. Final Score: Chi. 3 at CBJ 8

Brad Boyes (St.L.) scored against Antti Niemi (Chi.) Apr. 7. Final Score: St.L. 5 at Chi. 6

Thomas Vanek (Buf.) scored against Pascal Leclaire (Ott.) Apr. 10. Final Score: Buf. 5 at Ott. 2

Stopped

Valtteri Filppula (Det.) unsuccessful against Ryan Miller (Buf.) Oct. 13. Final Score: Det. 2 at Buf. 6

Patrick Sharp (Chi.) unsuccessful against Nikolai Khabibulin (Edm.) Oct. 14. Final Score: Edm. 3 at Chi. 4

Ray Whitney (Car.) unsuccessful against Craig Anderson (Col.) Oct. 23. Final Score: Car. 4 at Col. 5

Rick Nash (CBJ) unsuccessful against Jonathan Quick (L.A.) Oct. 25. Final Score: CBJ 2 at L.A. 6

Darroll Powe (Phi.) unsuccessful against Jose Theodore (Wsh.) Oct. 27. Final Score: Phi. 2 at Wsh. 4

Jim Slater (Atl.) unsuccessful against Semyon Varlamov (Wsh.) Oct. 29. Final Score: Wsh. 4 at Atl. 3

Martin St. Louis (T.B.) unsuccessful against Brian Elliott (Ott.) Oct. 29. Final Score: Ott. 2 at T.B. 5

Jamie Langenbrunner (N.J.) unsuccessful against Antero Niittymaki (T.B.) Oct. 31. Final Score: N.J. 2 at T.B. 1

Doug Weight (NYI) unsuccessful against Patrick Lalime (Buf.) Oct. 31. Final Score: Buf. 0 at NYI 5

Brenden Morrow (Dal.) unsuccessful against Curtis McElhinney (Cgy.) Nov. 4. Final Score: Cgy. 3 at Dal. 2

Shane Doan (Phx.) unsuccessful against Marty Turco (Dal.) Nov. 14. Final Score: Dal. 2 at Phx. 3

Maxime Talbot (Pit.) unsuccessful against Johan Hedberg (Atl.) Nov. 21. Final Score: Pit. 3 at Atl. 2

Ryan Callahan (NYR) unsuccessful against Jimmy Howard (Det.) Dec. 6. Final Score: Det. 3 at NYR 1

Troy Brouwer (Chi.) unsuccessful against Antero Niittymaki (T.B.) Dec. 13. Final Score: T.B. 0 at Chi. 4

Torrey Mitchell (S.J.) unsuccessful against Jean-Sebastien Giguere (Ana.) Dec. 17. Final Score: Ana. 1 at S.J. 4

Alexander Semin (Wsh.) unsuccessful against Roberto Luongo (Van.) Dec. 18. Final Score: Wsh. 2 at Van. 3

Todd Marchant (Ana.) unsuccessful against Ilya Bryzgalov (Phx.) Dec. 19. Final Score: Phx. 2 at Ana. 4

Dustin Brown (L.A.) unsuccessful against Miikka Kiprusoff (Cgy.) Dec. 30. Final Score: L.A. 1 at Cgy. 2

Vincent Lecavalier (T.B.) unsuccessful against Marc-Andre Fleury (Pit.) Jan. 2. Final Score: Pit. 1 at T.B. 3

Mason Raymond (Van.) unsuccessful against Ilya Bryzgalov (Phx.) Jan. 7. Final Score: Phx. 0 at Van. 4

Marco Sturm (Bos.) unsuccessful against Henrik Lundqvist (NYR) Jan. 9. Final Score: NYR 3 at Bos. 1

Martin St. Louis (T.B.) unsuccessful against Tomas Vokoun (Fla.) Jan. 14. Final Score: Fla. 3 at T.B. 2

Eric Staal (Car.) unsuccessful against Ondrej Pavelec (Atl.) Jan. 16. Final Score: Atl. 5 at Car. 3

Kyle Okposo (NYI) unsuccessful against Brent Johnson (Pit.) Jan. 19. Final Score: NYI 4 at Pit. 6

Patrick Kane (Chi.) unsuccessful against Miikka Kiprusoff (Cgy.) Jan. 21. Final Score: Chi. 3 at Cgy. 1

Mike Richards (Phi.) unsuccessful against Cam Ward (Car.) Jan. 23. Final Score: Car. 2 at Phi. 4

David Krejci (Bos.) unsuccessful against Jose Theodore (Wsh.) Feb. 2. Final Score: Wsh. 4 at Bos. 1

Dan Boyle (S.J.) unsuccessful against Carey Price (Mtl.) Mar. 4. Final Score: Mtl. 2 at S.J. 3

Mike Comrie (Edm.) unsuccessful against Brian Elliott (Ott.) Mar. 9. Final Score: Ott. 4 at Edm. 1

Brandon Sutter (Car.) unsuccessful against Jose Theodore (Wsh.) Mar. 10. Final Score: Car. 3 at Wsh. 4

Ilya Kovalchuk (N.J.) unsuccessful against Marc-Andre Fleury (Pit.) Mar. 12. Final Score: Pit. 1 at N.J. 3

Curtis Glencross (Cgy.) unsuccessful against Jimmy Howard (Det.) Mar. 15. Final Score: Det. 2 at Cgy. 1

Matthew Lombardi (Phx.) unsuccessful against Antti Niemi (Chi.) Mar. 20. Final Score: Chi. 4 at Phx. 5

Daniel Paille (Bos.) unsuccessful against Henrik Lundqvist (NYR) Mar. 21. Final Score: NYR 1 at Bos. 2

Colby Armstrong (Atl.) unsuccessful against Tuukka Rask (Bos,) Mar. 23. Final Score: Bos. 4 at Atl. 0

Marco Sturm (Bos.) unsuccessful against Ryan Miller (Buf.) Mar. 29. Final Score: Buf. 3 at Bos. 2

James Sheppard (Min.) unsuccessful against Evgeni Nabokov (S.J.) Apr. 2. Final Score: S.J. 3 at Min. 2

Darren Helm (Det.) unsuccessful against Steve Mason (CBJ) Apr. 9. Final Score: Det. 1 at CBJ 0

Fredrik Modin (L.A.) unsuccessful against Devan Dubnyk (Edm.) Apr. 10. Final Score: Edm. 4 at L.A. 3

Total Shots: 55

Total Goals: 16

Total Saves: 39

Jakub Voracek of the Columbus Blue Jackets puts the puck past Chicago's Cristobal Huet for a penalty shot goal during the second period of their game on March 25, 2010.

Goaltending Leaders

Minimum 25 games

Goals Against Average

Goaltender	Team	GPI	MINS	GA	Avg
*Tuukka Rask	Boston	45	2562	84	1.97
Ryan Miller	Buffalo	69	4047	150	2.22
Martin Brodeur	New Jersey	77	4499	168	2.24
Antti Niemi	Chicago	39	2190	82	2.25
*Jimmy Howard	Detroit	63	3740	141	2.26
Ilya Bryzgalov	Phoenix	69	4084	156	2.29
Miikka Kiprusoff	Calgary	73	4235	163	2.31
Henrik Lundqvist	NY Rangers	73	4204	167	2.38

Save Percentage

Goaltender	Team	GPI	MINS	GA	SA	S%	W	L	OT
*Tuukka Rask	Boston	45	2562	84	1221	.931	22	12	5
Ryan Miller	Buffalo	69	4047	150	2098	.929	41	18	8
Tomas Vokoun	Florida	63	3695	157	2081	.925	23	28	11
*Jimmy Howard	Detroit	63	3740	141	1849	.924	37	15	10
Jaroslav Halak	Montreal	45	2630	105	1386	.924	26	13	5
Evgeni Nabokov	San Jose	71	4194	170	2168	.922	44	16	10
Henrik Lundqvist	NY Rangers	73	4204	167	2109	.921	35	27	10
Ty Conklin	St. Louis	26	1451	60	764	.921	10	10	2

Wins

Goaltender	Team	GPI	MINS	W	L	OT
Martin Brodeur	New Jersey	77	4499	45	25	6
Evgeni Nabokov	San Jose	71	4194	44	16	10
Ilya Bryzgalov	Phoenix	69	4084	42	20	6
Ryan Miller	Buffalo	69	4047	41	18	8
Roberto Luongo	Vancouver	68	3899	40	22	4
Jonathan Quick	Los Angeles	72	4258	39	24	7
Craig Anderson	Colorado	71	4235	38	25	7

Shutouts

Goaltender	Team	GPI	MINS	SO	W	L	OT
Martin Brodeur	New Jersey	77	4499	9	45	25	6
Ilya Bryzgalov	Phoenix	69	4084	8	42	20	6
Antti Niemi	Chicago	39	2190	7	26	7	4
Pekka Rinne	Nashville	58	3246	7	32	16	5
Tomas Vokoun	Florida	63	3695	7	23	28	11

Team-by-Team Point Totals

2005-06 to 2009-10

(Ranked by five-year point %)

Team	09-10	08-09	07-08	06-07	05-06	Pts%
Detroit	102	112	115	113	124	.690
San Jose	113	117	108	107	99	.663
New Jersey	103	106	99	107	101	.629
Buffalo	100	91	90	113	110	.615
Nashville	100	88	91	110	106	.604
Anaheim	89	91	102	110	98	.598
Ottawa	94	83	94	105	113	.596
Vancouver	103	100	88	105	92	.595
Dallas	88	83	97	107	112	.593
Calgary	90	98	94	96	103	.587
NY Rangers	87	95	97	94	100	.577
Carolina	80	97	92	88	112	.572
Montreal	88	93	104	90	93	.571
Pittsburgh	101	99	102	105	58	.567
Washington	121	108	94	70	70	.565
Minnesota	84	89	98	104	84	.560
Boston	91	116	94	76	74	.550
Colorado	95	69	95	95	95	.548
Chicago	112	104	88	71	65	.537
Philadelphia	88	99	95	56	101	.535
Florida	77	93	85	86	85	.520
Atlanta	83	76	76	97	90	.515
Toronto	74	81	83	91	90	.511
Phoenix	107	79	83	67	81	.509
Los Angeles	101	79	71	68	89	.498
Tampa Bay	80	66	71	93	92	.490
Edmonton	62	85	88	71	95	.489
St. Louis	90	92	79	81	57	.487
Columbus	79	92	80	73	74	.485
NY Islanders	79	61	79	92	78	.474

Team Record When Scoring First Goal of a Game

Team	FG	W	L	OT
Anaheim	44	25	10	9
Atlanta	39	25	7	7
Boston	40	28	8	4
Buffalo	41	31	6	4
Calgary	50	33	11	6
Carolina	41	25	14	2
Chicago	56	40	9	7
Colorado	40	26	9	5
Columbus	38	20	12	6
Dallas	35	23	5	7
Detroit	38	25	6	7
Edmonton	34	20	11	3
Florida	39	18	12	9
Los Angeles	46	34	7	5
Minnesota	34	24	7	3
Montreal	39	28	8	3
Nashville	35	28	6	1
New Jersey	45	33	9	3
NY Islanders	39	25	8	6
NY Rangers	34	21	8	5
Ottawa	41	31	6	4
Philadelphia	49	33	10	6
Phoenix	42	36	3	3
Pittsburgh	41	28	9	4
San Jose	39	31	3	5
St. Louis	48	25	17	6
Tampa Bay	36	22	8	6
Toronto	30	18	6	6
Vancouver	39	31	7	1
Washington	52	38	7	7

Team Plus/Minus Differential

Team	GF	PPGF	Net GF	GA	PPGA	Net GA	Goal Differential
Washington	318	79	239	233	67	166	+73
Chicago	271	52	219	209	39	170	+49
Vancouver	272	68	204	222	59	163	+41
San Jose	264	65	199	215	49	166	+33
Phoenix	225	46	179	202	49	153	+26
New Jersey	222	51	171	191	41	150	+21
Los Angeles	241	64	177	219	60	159	+18
Pittsburgh	257	56	201	237	52	185	+16
Colorado	244	56	188	233	60	173	+15
Nashville	225	47	178	225	59	166	+12
Buffalo	235	55	180	207	38	169	+11
Calgary	204	43	161	210	54	156	+5
Philadelphia	236	68	168	225	57	168	0
NY Rangers	222	55	167	218	50	168	-1
Boston	206	44	162	200	37	163	-1
Detroit	229	59	170	216	43	173	-3
St. Louis	225	52	173	223	45	178	-5
Anaheim	238	63	175	251	67	184	-9
Montreal	217	57	160	223	53	170	-10
Ottawa	225	49	176	238	50	188	-12
Dallas	237	61	176	254	65	189	-13
Atlanta	234	51	183	256	57	199	-16
Carolina	230	56	174	256	62	194	-20
NY Islanders	222	49	173	264	71	193	-20
Florida	208	44	164	244	59	185	-21
Toronto	214	44	170	267	73	194	-24
Minnesota	219	59	160	246	53	193	-33
Columbus	216	56	160	259	61	198	-38
Tampa Bay	217	63	154	260	67	193	-39
Edmonton	214	52	162	284	67	217	-55

Team Record When Leading, Trailing, Tied

Team	Leading after 1 period W	L	OT	Leading after 2 periods W	L	OT	Trailing after 1 period W	L	OT	Trailing after 2 periods W	L	OT	Tied after 1 period W	L	OT	Tied after 2 periods W	L	OT
Anaheim	23	5	3	26	2	7	9	17	1	8	23	0	7	10	7	5	7	4
Atlanta	15	3	2	19	0	4	5	23	4	4	30	6	15	8	7	12	4	3
Boston	19	3	4	22	4	2	7	21	3	3	23	3	13	6	6	14	3	8
Buffalo	21	4	2	30	0	0	7	15	5	6	22	3	17	8	3	9	5	7
Calgary	20	4	4	33	2	3	4	17	2	3	22	3	16	11	4	6	4	3
Carolina	21	5	1	27	3	3	4	19	7	2	26	4	10	13	2	6	8	3
Chicago	30	6	6	35	1	3	5	8	0	7	18	1	17	8	2	10	3	4
Colorado	25	5	3	33	4	4	8	15	4	4	18	2	10	10	2	6	6	6
Columbus	13	8	6	24	7	4	5	18	5	4	25	5	14	9	4	4	3	6
Dallas	14	3	4	22	1	2	11	16	5	6	26	6	12	12	5	9	4	6
Detroit	18	5	5	28	2	4	12	13	5	5	18	8	14	6	4	11	4	2
Edmonton	14	2	2	17	2	2	6	29	2	4	34	3	7	16	4	6	11	3
Florida	15	5	5	21	3	6	7	18	0	5	28	4	10	14	8	6	6	5
Los Angeles	22	5	4	29	0	2	10	13	3	8	23	3	14	11	4	9	4	4
Minnesota	20	4	3	21	1	2	4	21	5	7	29	2	14	11	0	10	6	4
Montreal	19	8	3	26	2	3	11	19	6	4	25	4	9	6	1	9	6	3
Nashville	23	1	0	27	4	0	10	9	2	2	18	1	14	19	4	18	7	5
New Jersey	26	3	3	33	1	1	9	17	2	4	22	0	13	7	2	11	4	6
NY Islanders	18	8	4	27	3	4	3	24	3	3	31	5	13	5	4	5	7	4
NY Rangers	18	4	4	32	1	5	8	17	2	1	25	2	12	12	5	5	7	4
Ottawa	21	2	2	28	1	0	4	20	2	3	29	2	19	10	2	13	2	4
Philadelphia	22	4	2	30	1	3	7	17	1	3	26	1	12	14	3	8	4	2
Phoenix	23	1	0	33	1	2	6	16	4	7	20	4	21	8	3	10	4	1
Pittsburgh	20	3	3	28	3	2	6	15	2	8	23	2	21	10	2	11	2	3
San Jose	23	1	4	36	0	5	9	13	1	5	18	3	19	6	6	10	2	4
St. Louis	15	7	2	25	2	6	10	17	1	3	23	3	15	8	7	12	7	1
Tampa Bay	18	5	4	24	4	1	3	22	3	4	30	5	13	9	5	6	2	6
Toronto	12	5	2	18	2	2	10	23	3	2	33	7	8	10	9	10	3	5
Vancouver	26	4	1	32	1	0	10	17	1	11	21	3	13	7	3	6	6	4

Tuukka Rask led the NHL in goals-against average (1.97) and save percentage (.931) in 2009-10, just as his Bruins teammate Tim Thomas had done the year before.

Team Statistics

TEAMS' HOME AND ROAD RECORD

Eastern Conference

Team	GP	Home W	L	OT	GF	GA	PTS	GP	Road W	L	OT	GF	GA	PTS
WSH	41	30	5	6	159	109	66	41	24	10	7	159	124	55
N.J.	41	27	10	4	124	89	58	41	21	17	3	98	102	45
PIT	41	25	12	4	143	114	54	41	22	16	3	114	123	47
BUF	41	25	10	6	125	96	56	41	20	17	4	110	111	44
OTT	41	26	11	4	122	104	56	41	18	21	2	103	134	38
BOS	41	18	17	6	102	103	42	41	21	13	7	104	97	49
PHI	41	24	14	3	124	104	51	41	17	21	3	112	121	37
MTL	41	20	16	5	116	109	45	41	19	17	5	101	114	43
NYR	41	18	17	6	124	113	42	41	20	16	5	98	105	45
ATL	41	19	16	6	119	124	44	41	16	18	7	115	132	39
CAR	41	21	17	3	122	124	45	41	14	20	7	108	132	35
T.B.	41	21	14	6	116	112	48	41	13	22	6	101	148	32
NYI	41	23	14	4	125	114	50	41	11	23	7	97	150	29
FLA	41	16	16	9	111	123	41	41	16	21	4	97	121	36
TOR	41	18	17	6	106	117	42	41	12	21	8	108	150	32
TOTAL	615	331	206	78	1838	1655	740	615	264	273	78	1625	1864	606

Western Conference

Team	GP	Home W	L	OT	GF	GA	PTS	GP	Road W	L	OT	GF	GA	PTS
S.J.	41	27	6	8	142	100	62	41	24	14	3	122	115	51
CHI	41	29	8	4	140	100	62	41	23	14	4	131	109	50
PHX	41	29	10	2	128	101	60	41	21	15	5	97	101	47
VAN	41	30	8	3	149	88	63	41	19	20	2	123	134	40
DET	41	25	10	6	121	98	56	41	19	14	8	108	118	46
L.A.	41	22	13	6	127	112	50	41	24	14	3	114	107	51
NSH	41	24	14	3	108	101	51	41	23	15	3	117	124	49
COL	41	24	14	3	126	104	51	41	19	16	6	118	129	44
ST.L.	41	18	18	5	108	115	41	41	22	14	5	117	108	49
CGY	41	20	17	4	95	98	44	41	20	15	6	109	112	46
ANA	41	25	11	5	142	120	55	41	14	21	6	96	131	34
DAL	41	23	11	7	129	119	53	41	14	20	7	108	135	35
MIN	41	25	12	4	131	119	54	41	13	24	4	88	127	30
CBJ	41	20	12	9	111	111	49	41	12	23	6	105	148	30
EDM	41	18	19	4	119	132	40	41	9	28	4	95	152	22
TOTAL	615	359	183	73	1876	1618	791	615	276	267	72	1648	1850	624
	1230	690	389	151	3714	3273	1531	1230	540	540	150	3273	3714	1230

TEAMS' DIVISIONAL RECORD

Northeast Division

Team	GP	Against Own Division W	L	OT	GF	GA	PTS	GP	Against Other Divisions W	L	OT	GF	GA	PTS
BUF	24	12	8	4	59	59	28	58	33	19	6	176	148	72
OTT	24	14	7	3	60	58	31	58	30	25	3	165	180	63
BOS	24	13	8	3	61	55	29	58	26	22	10	145	145	62
MTL	24	11	9	4	57	61	26	58	28	24	6	160	162	62
TOR	24	10	7	7	61	65	27	58	20	31	7	153	202	47
TOTAL	120	60	39	21	298	298	141	290	137	121	32	799	837	306

Atlantic Division

Team	GP	Against Own Division W	L	OT	GF	GA	PTS	GP	Against Other Divisions W	L	OT	GF	GA	PTS
N.J.	24	14	8	2	73	53	30	58	34	19	5	149	138	73
PIT	24	15	8	1	84	73	31	58	32	20	6	173	164	70
PHI	24	14	9	1	70	60	29	58	27	26	5	166	165	59
NYR	24	10	10	4	59	72	24	58	28	23	7	163	146	63
NYI	24	7	15	2	58	86	16	58	27	22	9	164	178	63
TOTAL	120	60	50	10	344	344	130	290	148	110	32	815	791	328

Southeast Division

Team	GP	Against Own Division W	L	OT	GF	GA	PTS	GP	Against Other Divisions W	L	OT	GF	GA	PTS
WSH	24	19	3	2	101	66	40	58	35	12	11	217	167	81
ATL	24	8	14	2	64	83	18	58	27	20	11	170	173	65
CAR	24	12	9	3	78	73	27	58	23	28	7	152	183	53
T.B.	24	13	10	1	72	74	27	58	21	26	11	145	186	53
FLA	24	8	13	3	65	84	19	58	24	24	10	143	160	58
TOTAL	120	60	49	11	380	380	131	290	130	110	50	827	869	310

Central Division

Team	GP	Against Own Division W	L	OT	GF	GA	PTS	GP	Against Other Divisions W	L	OT	GF	GA	PTS
CHI	24	15	8	1	77	66	31	58	37	14	7	194	143	81
DET	24	14	6	4	67	58	32	58	30	18	10	162	158	70
NSH	24	14	8	2	59	57	30	58	33	21	4	166	168	70
ST.L.	24	10	11	3	64	69	23	58	30	21	7	161	154	67
CBJ	24	7	9	8	60	77	22	58	25	26	7	156	182	57
TOTAL	120	60	42	18	327	327	138	290	155	100	35	839	805	345

Pacific Division

Team	GP	Against Own Division W	L	OT	GF	GA	PTS	GP	Against Other Divisions W	L	OT	GF	GA	PTS
S.J.	24	14	6	4	67	62	32	58	37	14	7	197	153	81
PHX	24	13	7	4	64	60	30	58	37	18	3	161	142	77
L.A.	24	15	6	3	82	69	33	58	31	21	6	159	150	68
ANA	24	7	13	4	55	81	18	58	32	19	7	183	170	71
DAL	24	11	8	5	68	64	27	58	26	23	9	169	190	61
TOTAL	120	60	40	20	336	336	140	290	163	95	32	869	805	358

Northwest Division

Team	GP	Against Own Division W	L	OT	GF	GA	PTS	GP	Against Other Divisions W	L	OT	GF	GA	PTS
VAN	24	15	7	2	86	64	32	58	34	21	3	186	158	71
COL	24	10	11	3	64	70	23	58	33	19	6	180	163	72
CGY	24	12	9	3	67	67	27	58	28	23	7	137	143	63
MIN	24	15	7	2	69	57	32	58	23	29	6	150	189	52
EDM	24	8	14	2	54	82	18	58	19	33	6	160	202	44
TOTAL	120	60	48	12	340	340	132	290	137	125	28	813	855	302

TEAM STREAKS

Consecutive Wins

Games	Team	From	To
14	Washington	Jan. 13	Feb. 7
11	Ottawa	Jan. 14	Feb. 4
9	Los Angeles	Jan. 21	Feb. 6
9	Phoenix	Mar. 4	Mar. 21
8	New Jersey	Oct. 29	Nov. 14
8	Chicago	Nov. 9	Nov. 25
8	San Jose	Dec. 17	Jan. 2
7	NY Rangers	Oct. 3	Oct. 17
7	Pittsburgh	Oct. 8	Oct. 23
7	Nashville	Nov. 12	Nov. 25
7	Vancouver	Jan. 16	Jan. 30
7	Carolina	Feb. 5	Mar. 4
7	Detroit	Mar. 20	Apr. 1

Consecutive Home Wins

Games	Team	From	To
13	Washington	Jan. 5	Mar. 6
11	Anaheim	Dec. 8	Feb. 10
10	Phoenix	Nov. 21	Dec. 29
8	Chicago	Oct. 24	Dec. 1
8	Carolina	Jan. 24	Mar. 11
7	Nashville	Oct. 29	Nov. 23
7	Vancouver	Jan. 16	Mar. 14
7	Ottawa	Jan. 19	Feb. 11
7	Phoenix	Mar. 4	Apr. 7
7	Detroit	Mar. 11	Apr. 1

Consecutive Road Wins

Games	Team	From	To
9	New Jersey	Oct. 8	Nov. 12
9	San Jose	Dec. 21	Feb. 8
7	Pittsburgh	Oct. 3	Nov. 3
7	Los Angeles	Dec. 31	Jan. 31
6	Ottawa	Jan. 14	Feb. 3
5	Edmonton	Dec. 3	Dec. 11
5	Nashville	Dec. 29	Jan. 15
5	Washington	Jan. 13	Feb. 4
5	Boston	Feb. 7	Mar. 6
5	Nashville	Mar. 12	Apr. 3
5	Phoenix	Mar. 13	Mar. 21

As a team, the Chicago Blackhawks led the NHL with 13 shorthand goals in 2009-10. Marian Hossa tied for the league lead with five, while captain Jonathan Toews ranked among the leaders with three shorthand assists.

TEAM PENALTIES

Abbreviations: GP – games played; **PEN** – total penalty minutes including bench minutes; **BMI** – total bench minor minutes;
AVG – average penalty minutes/game calculated by dividing total penalty minutes by games played

Team	GP	PEN	BMI	AVG	Team	GP	PEN	BMI	AVG
NSH	82	710	12	8.7	COL	82	1027	26	12.5
DET	82	723	16	8.8	ATL	82	1053	8	12.8
N.J.	82	859	16	10.5	CBJ	82	1086	16	13.2
BUF	82	918	16	11.2	TOR	82	1091	20	13.3
CHI	82	924	16	11.3	EDM	82	1133	18	13.8
MIN	82	924	10	11.3	CGY	82	1143	14	13.9
PHX	82	925	20	11.3	OTT	82	1141	26	13.9
MTL	82	936	16	11.4	NYR	82	1159	22	14.1
WSH	82	940	20	11.5	S.J.	82	1155	18	14.1
BOS	82	953	24	11.6	PIT	82	1195	12	14.6
NYI	82	950	22	11.6	VAN	82	1269	8	15.5
DAL	82	963	8	11.7	ANA	82	1321	4	16.1
CAR	82	966	22	11.8	ST.L.	82	1318	22	16.1
FLA	82	977	16	11.9	PHI	82	1362	12	16.6
L.A.	82	979	16	11.9	T.B.	82	1377	20	16.8
					Total	**1230**	**31477**	**496**	**25.6**

TEAMS' POWER-PLAY RECORD

Abbreviations: ADV – total advantages; **PPGF** – power-play goals for;
% – calculated by dividing number of power-play goals by total advantages.

			Home					Road						Overall		
	Team	GP	ADV	PPGF	%	Team	GP	ADV	PPGF	%	Team	GP	ADV	PPGF	%
1	ANA	41	161	42	26.1	MTL	41	113	32	28.3	WSH	82	313	79	25.2
2	WSH	41	160	41	25.6	WSH	41	153	38	24.8	MTL	82	261	57	21.8
3	VAN	41	158	38	24.1	S.J.	41	151	34	22.5	PHI	82	317	68	21.5
4	NYR	41	166	38	22.9	CHI	41	136	30	22.1	S.J.	82	309	65	21.0
5	DET	41	173	38	22.0	L.A.	41	156	34	21.8	ANA	82	300	63	21.0
6	PHI	41	179	39	21.8	PHI	41	138	29	21.0	VAN	82	325	68	20.9
7	MIN	41	156	34	21.8	CBJ	41	144	29	20.1	L.A.	82	307	64	20.8
8	BUF	41	160	34	21.3	T.B.	41	164	32	19.5	T.B.	82	326	63	19.3
9	PIT	41	162	34	21.0	COL	41	145	28	19.3	DET	82	307	59	19.2
10	EDM	41	145	29	20.0	N.J.	41	131	24	18.3	MIN	82	309	59	19.1
11	CAR	41	166	33	19.9	VAN	41	167	30	18.0	N.J.	82	273	51	18.7
12	L.A.	41	151	30	19.9	DAL	41	168	30	17.9	DAL	82	328	61	18.6
13	S.J.	41	158	31	19.6	NYI	41	151	26	17.2	NYR	82	301	55	18.3
14	BOS	41	155	30	19.4	ST.L.	41	143	24	16.8	CBJ	82	308	56	18.2
15	DAL	41	160	31	19.4	MIN	41	153	25	16.3	COL	82	310	56	18.1
16	T.B.	41	162	31	19.1	OTT	41	142	23	16.2	CHI	82	294	52	17.7
17	N.J.	41	142	27	19.0	CGY	41	136	22	16.2	BUF	82	313	55	17.6
18	NSH	41	141	26	18.4	PHX	41	145	23	15.9	EDM	82	301	52	17.3
19	ATL	41	175	32	18.3	DET	41	134	21	15.7	PIT	82	326	56	17.2
20	OTT	41	148	26	17.6	ANA	41	139	21	15.1	CAR	82	332	56	16.9
21	FLA	41	160	28	17.5	EDM	41	156	23	14.7	ST.L.	82	307	52	16.9
22	ST.L.	41	164	28	17.1	NSH	41	145	21	14.5	OTT	82	290	49	16.9
23	COL	41	165	28	17.0	CAR	41	166	23	13.9	BOS	82	265	44	16.6
24	MTL	41	148	25	16.9	TOR	41	158	22	13.9	NSH	82	286	47	16.4
25	CBJ	41	164	27	16.5	BUF	41	153	21	13.7	ATL	82	316	51	16.1
26	CGY	41	132	21	15.9	ATL	41	141	19	13.5	CGY	82	268	43	16.0
27	NYI	41	155	23	14.8	PIT	41	164	22	13.4	NYI	82	306	49	16.0
28	TOR	41	157	22	14.0	BOS	41	110	14	12.7	PHX	82	314	46	14.6
29	CHI	41	158	22	13.9	NYR	41	135	17	12.6	FLA	82	309	44	14.2
30	PHX	41	169	23	13.6	FLA	41	149	16	10.7	TOR	82	315	44	14.0
		1230	4750	911	19.2		1230	4386	753	17.2		1230	9136	1664	18.2

SHORTHAND GOALS FOR

		Home			Road			Overall	
	Team	GP	SHGF	Team	GP	SHGF	Team	GP	SHGF
1	DET	41	7	CHI	41	7	CHI	82	13
2	CHI	41	6	S.J.	41	5	VAN	82	9
3	N.J.	41	6	ATL	41	5	ATL	82	9
4	ANA	41	6	MTL	41	4	DAL	82	9
5	VAN	41	6	CGY	41	4	COL	82	8
6	PIT	41	5	DAL	41	4	S.J.	82	8
7	DAL	41	5	COL	41	4	CGY	82	8
8	BOS	41	5	BUF	41	4	DET	82	8
9	COL	41	4	EDM	41	4	ANA	82	8
10	CGY	41	4	VAN	41	3	CAR	82	7
11	CAR	41	4	PHI	41	3	PIT	82	7
12	NYI	41	4	FLA	41	3	FLA	82	7
13	NYR	41	4	ST.L.	41	3	ST.L.	82	7
14	ATL	41	4	CAR	41	3	N.J.	82	7
15	FLA	41	4	TOR	41	3	NYI	82	7
16	ST.L.	41	4	CBJ	41	3	BOS	82	6
17	OTT	41	4	NYI	41	3	PHI	82	6
18	WSH	41	3	PIT	41	2	OTT	82	6
19	CBJ	41	3	OTT	41	2	CBJ	82	6
20	L.A.	41	3	NSH	41	2	EDM	82	6
21	PHI	41	3	ANA	41	2	NYR	82	5
22	MIN	41	3	BOS	41	2	NSH	82	5
23	NSH	41	3	WSH	41	1	WSH	82	4
24	S.J.	41	3	NYR	41	1	TOR	82	4
25	EDM	41	2	MIN	41	1	MTL	82	4
26	T.B.	41	2	DET	41	1	BUF	82	4
27	PHX	41	2	PHX	41	1	MIN	82	4
28	TOR	41	1	N.J.	41	1	L.A.	82	4
29	BUF	41	1	L.A.	41	1	PHX	82	3
30	MTL	41	0	T.B.	41	0	T.B.	82	2
		1230	109		1230	82		1230	191

TEAMS' PENALTY KILLING RECORD

Abbreviations: TSH – total times shorthanded; **PPGA** – power-play goals against;
% – calculated by dividing times short minus power-play goals against by times short.

			Home					Road						Overall		
	Team	GP	TSH	PPGA	%	Team	GP	TSH	PPGA	%	Team	GP	TSH	PPGA	%
1	BUF	41	128	13	89.8	ST.L.	41	174	21	87.9	ST.L.	82	342	45	86.8
2	CHI	41	132	14	89.4	PIT	41	170	25	85.3	BUF	82	284	38	86.6
3	BOS	41	144	16	88.9	NYR	41	165	25	84.8	BOS	82	272	37	86.4
4	VAN	41	150	21	86.0	S.J.	41	176	27	84.7	CHI	82	265	39	85.3
5	DET	41	141	20	85.8	ATL	41	156	24	84.6	S.J.	82	327	49	85.0
6	ST.L.	41	168	24	85.7	BUF	41	156	25	84.0	PHX	82	317	49	84.5
7	PHX	41	161	23	85.7	OTT	41	165	27	83.6	NYR	82	318	50	84.3
8	S.J.	41	151	22	85.4	BOS	41	128	21	83.6	OTT	82	318	50	84.3
9	OTT	41	153	23	85.0	MTL	41	163	27	83.4	PIT	82	327	52	84.1
10	MIN	41	139	22	84.2	PHX	41	156	26	83.3	DET	82	267	43	83.9
11	NYR	41	153	25	83.7	PHI	41	167	28	83.2	MTL	82	311	53	83.0
12	CBJ	41	153	25	83.7	CGY	41	160	28	82.5	PHI	82	335	57	83.0
13	DAL	41	116	19	83.6	N.J.	41	123	22	82.1	N.J.	82	239	41	82.8
14	WSH	41	149	25	83.2	L.A.	41	160	29	81.9	MIN	82	306	53	82.7
15	COL	41	148	25	83.1	FLA	41	143	26	81.8	CGY	82	305	54	82.3
16	PIT	41	157	27	82.8	DET	41	126	23	81.7	ATL	82	320	57	82.2
17	T.B.	41	169	29	82.8	CAR	41	178	33	81.5	CBJ	82	334	61	81.7
18	PHI	41	168	29	82.7	MIN	41	167	31	81.4	VAN	82	320	59	81.6
19	MTL	41	148	26	82.4	CHI	41	133	25	81.2	CAR	82	320	62	80.6
20	NYI	41	145	26	82.1	CBJ	41	181	36	80.1	L.A.	82	304	60	80.3
21	ANA	41	162	29	82.1	EDM	41	160	33	79.4	COL	82	303	60	80.2
22	NSH	41	113	22	80.5	DAL	41	154	33	78.6	T.B.	82	336	67	80.1
23	ATL	41	138	27	80.4	VAN	41	170	38	77.6	FLA	82	287	59	79.4
24	CAR	41	142	29	79.6	COL	41	155	35	77.4	ANA	82	324	69	79.3
25	L.A.	41	144	31	78.5	T.B.	41	167	38	77.2	WSH	82	316	67	78.8
26	TOR	41	127	29	77.2	ANA	41	162	38	76.5	EDM	82	305	67	78.0
27	FLA	41	144	33	77.1	WSH	41	167	42	74.9	DAL	82	288	65	77.4
28	EDM	41	145	34	76.6	NSH	41	145	37	74.5	NSH	82	258	59	77.1
29	DAL	41	134	32	76.1	NYI	41	162	44	72.8	NYI	82	300	71	76.3
30						TOR	41	161	44	72.7	TOR	82	288	73	74.7
		1230	4386	753	82.8		1230	4750	911	80.8		1230	9136	1664	81.8

SHORTHAND GOALS AGAINST

		Home			Road			Overall	
	Team	GP	SHGA	Team	GP	SHGA	Team	GP	SHGA
1	CAR	41	0	CGY	41	0	DET	82	1
2	DET	41	0	NYR	41	1	CGY	82	2
3	PIT	41	1	DET	41	1	BUF	82	3
4	CHI	41	1	BUF	41	1	NYI	82	3
5	NYI	41	1	BOS	41	1	BOS	82	4
6	COL	41	2	MTL	41	2	CHI	82	4
7	CGY	41	2	OTT	41	2	OTT	82	4
8	BUF	41	2	T.B.	41	2	ATL	82	4
9	N.J.	41	2	NSH	41	2	N.J.	82	5
10	ATL	41	2	NYI	41	2	EDM	82	5
11	FLA	41	2	ATL	41	2	VAN	82	6
12	EDM	41	2	EDM	41	3	ST.L.	82	6
13	ST.L.	41	2	S.J.	41	3	T.B.	82	6
14	PHI	41	2	VAN	41	3	NSH	82	6
15	OTT	41	2	TOR	41	3	L.A.	82	6
16	BOS	41	3	CHI	41	3	TOR	82	7
17	WSH	41	3	N.J.	41	3	NYR	82	7
18	CBJ	41	3	L.A.	41	3	PHX	82	7
19	EDM	41	3	ST.L.	41	4	WSH	82	8
20	L.A.	41	3	PHX	41	4	MTL	82	8
21	VAN	41	3	WSH	41	4	CAR	82	8
22	PHX	41	3	ANA	41	5	PHI	82	8
23	TOR	41	4	PHI	41	6	PIT	82	8
24	ANA	41	4	FLA	41	6	FLA	82	8
25	MIN	41	4	CBJ	41	6	DAL	82	9
26	T.B.	41	4	DAL	41	6	COL	82	9
27	NSH	41	4	PIT	41	7	S.J.	82	9
28	NYR	41	6	COL	41	7	CBJ	82	9
29	S.J.	41	6	CAR	41	8	ANA	82	9
30	MTL	41	6	MIN	41	9	MIN	82	13
		1230	82		1230	109		1230	191

Regular-Season Overtime Results

2009-10 to 1989-90

Team	2009-10 GP	W	L	SO	2008-09 GP	W	L	SO	2007-08 GP	W	L	SO	2006-07 GP	W	L	SO	2005-06 GP	W	L	SO	2003-04 GP	W	L	T	2002-03 GP	W	L	T	2001-02 GP	W	L	T	2000-01 GP	W	L	T	1999-2000 GP	W	L	T
ANA	19	3	3	13	19	5	4	10	20	4	1	15	23	5	4	14	18	3	5	10	22	4	8	10	21	6	6	9	14	3	3	8	20	4	5	11	18	3	3	12
ATL	19	2	7	10	17	4	5	8	23	6	2	15	25	7	7	11	18	5	3	10	18	6	4	8	19	7	5	7	19	3	5	11	16	2	2	12	11	0	4	7
BOS	27	4	4	19	17	3	4	10	21	3	5	13	19	4	2	13	22	4	8	10	30	8	7	15	21	6	4	11	24	9	9	6	20	4	8	8	26	1	6	19
BUF	20	6	4	10	19	2	4	13	21	5	3	13	22	5	3	14	16	6	1	10	13	2	4	7	19	2	6	11	16	4	1	11	10	4	1	5	20	5	4	11
CGY	15	2	3	10	12	3	4	5	16	3	7	6	15	2	5	8	15	2	4	9	15	2	4	9	15	4	3	8	17	2	3	12	22	3	4	15	26	11	5	10
CAR/HFD	19	5	5	9	17	7	2	8	13	5	3	5	18	3	2	13	20	4	6	10	25	5	6	14	15	4	3	8	17	3	1	13	18	6	3	9	14	4	0	10
CHI	23	6	2	15	22	6	5	11	17	4	4	9	22	7	7	8	15	3	3	9	23	4	8	11	23	6	4	13	17	3	1	13	15	2	5	8	17	5	2	10
COL/QUE	18	2	4	12	17	3	1	13	18	4	4	10	15	3	3	9	18	6	1	11	28	8	7	13	23	4	6	13	13	4	1	8	18	3	6	9	17	5	1	11
CBJ	20	3	5	12	21	5	3	13	17	2	4	11	16	4	2	10	18	3	2	13	18	3	2	13	24	5	4	15	15	2	5	8	16	6	2	8				
DAL/MIN	23	2	4	17	22	5	5	12	15	3	4	8	22	6	3	13	18	3	5	10	18	3	2	13	28	8	7	13	28	7	8	13	21	3	5	13	19	3	6	10
DET	25	5	5	15	19	3	6	10	14	2	2	10	18	3	5	10	15	3	5	7	23	6	5	12	21	7	2	11	21	7	4	10	23	10	4	9	27	3	8	16
EDM	17	1	2	14	16	1	5	10	25	4	2	19	11	1	4	6	26	6	4	16	24	5	4	15	27	2	9	16	19	6	7	6	24	10	4	10	27	3	8	16
FLA	21	2	3	16	18	4	3	11	18	4	3	11	21	3	8	10	23	8	6	9	24	5	4	15	26	4	9	13	16	0	6	10	20	5	3	12	15	3	6	6
L.A.	23	4	1	18	19	3	3	13	14	2	4	8	20	2	8	10	15	4	4	7	27	2	9	16	19	6	7	6	18	3	4	11	19	3	3	13	21	5	4	12
MIN	18	5	1	12	17	3	6	8	19	6	2	11	14	2	1	11	18	7	6	5	16	5	4	7	19	2	9	8	21	0	9	12	16	2	6	8				
MTL	25	8	5	12	22	4	4	14	20	5	4	11	17	3	3	11	17	3	5	9	19	2	9	8	22	7	4	11	18	5	0	13	17	5	3	9	17	4	4	9
NSH	20	6	2	12	20	6	3	11	17	5	4	8	19	5	6	8	22	3	1	18	21	7	2	12	25	5	7	13	19	6	5	8	20	5	3	12	16	3	5	8
N.J.	15	2	2	11	19	9	2	8	22	7	3	12	22	3	1	18	18	3	3	12	17	2	4	11	18	3	8	7	18	6	4	8	12	2	3	7	15	5	1	9
NYI	25	6	5	14	15	3	4	8	19	5	6	8	25	4	4	17	23	4	8	11	19	2	5	12	20	6	4	10	13	5	3	5	11	5	1	5	21	6	3	12
NYR	15	1	7	7	22	3	3	16	25	4	4	17	14	3	3	8	13	2	3	8	19	3	6	10	16	7	1	8	13	5	4	4	15	3	4	9	15	2	2	11
OTT	16	5	1	10	18	6	5	10	14	3	3	8	17	3	5	9	22	7	5	10	23	2	6	15	23	6	4	13	16	3	3	10	19	5	3	11	21	6	3	12
PHI	12	2	3	7	21	6	5	10	17	3	5	9	16	3	6	7	22	7	5	10	15	6	2	7	20	5	4	11	19	4	6	9	23	3	3	17	21	6	3	12
PHX/WPG	26	5	1	20	11	1	4	6	16	4	1	11	27	6	5	16	19	4	8	7	19	7	4	8	14	3	5	6	20	7	5	8	15	3	3	9	17	3	6	8
PIT	21	6	5	10	21	6	3	12	16	1	4	11	23	4	7	12	22	3	7	12	24	11	2	11	19	2	8	9	18	6	4	8	23	6	5	12	17	5	1	11
ST.L.	20	3	5	12	20	4	4	12	17	1	8	8	8	1	3	4	21	9	4	8	23	6	6	11	23	6	6	11	13	2	3	8	22	7	3	12	16	0	7	9
S.J.	19	1	5	13	21	4	6	11	19	3	4	12	20	5	3	12	18	6	2	10	18	4	6	12	23	6	11	5	23	2	5	16	19	4	4	11	16	0	7	9
T.B.	21	5	5	11	23	2	8	13	13	2	8	3	20	5	3	12	18	6	2	10	18	6	2	10	18	4	6	8	19	4	4	11	13	2	5	6	16	0	7	9
TOR	23	5	10	8	23	4	6	13	19	5	7	7	19	4	4	11	18	7	1	10	17	4	3	10	17	7	3	7	17	3	4	10	19	3	5	11	17	7	3	7
VAN	13	4	1	8	18	5	3	10	18	5	3	10	20	4	1	15	16	4	4	8	14	3	1	10	19	5	1	13	14	4	3	7	23	5	7	11	19	5	2	12
WSH	24	6	7	11	18	6	3	9	19	7	4	8	19	4	3	12	21	2	6	13	21	2	6	13	14	1	3	10	20	6	6	8	19	6	2	11	16	2	4	10
Totals	**301**	**117**		**184**	**282**	**123**		**159**	**272**	**116**		**156**	**281**	**117**		**164**	**281**	**136**		**145**	**315**	**145**		**170**	**313**	**156**		**157**	**270**	**121**		**149**	**274**	**122**		**152**	**260**	**114**		**146**

Team	1998-99 GP	W	L	T	1997-98 GP	W	L	T	1996-97 GP	W	L	T	1995-96 GP	W	L	T	1994-95 GP	W	L	T	1993-94 GP	W	L	T	1992-93 GP	W	L	T	1991-92 GP	W	L	T	1990-91 GP	W	L	T	1989-90 GP	W	L	T
ANA	17	1	3	13	20	3	4	13	16	3	0	13	16	6	2	8	7	2	0	5	12	2	5	5																
ATL																																								
BOS	17	2	2	13	17	3	1	13	15	3	3	9	19	2	6	11	8	2	3	3	17	2	2	13	15	5	3	7	18	4	4	10	20	6	2	12	14	3	2	9
BUF	23	3	3	17	21	3	1	17	21	5	4	12	15	2	6	7	9	1	1	7	13	0	4	9	18	4	4	10	16	2	2	12	24	3	2	19	15	4	3	8
CGY	16	3	1	12	22	4	3	15	16	3	4	9	16	2	3	11	9	1	1	7	18	3	2	13	18	3	9	6	18	2	3	13	19	2	5	12	21	3	3	15
CAR/HFD	24	1	5	18	12	2	2	8	18	3	4	11	19	1	4	14	7	2	0	5	16	2	5	9	16	1	3	12	19	2	2	15	12	3	1	8	10	2	2	6
CHI	15	1	2	12	18	1	4	13	19	1	5	13	15	2	3	10	8	0	0	8	15	3	3	9	15	4	1	10	17	0	5	12	18	1	3	14	8	0	1	7
COL/QUE	12	2	0	10	22	2	3	17	15	2	3	10	6	1	0	5	8	0	0	8																				
CBJ																																								
DAL/MIN	16	3	1	12	17	5	1	11	15	4	3	8	15	1	0	14	9	0	1	7	22	6	3	13	10	0	0	10	8	0	2	6	17	0	3	14	11	3	4	4
DET	10	2	1	7	15	0	0	15	27	7	2	18	11	3	1	7	11	4	2	5	15	5	2	8	11	2	0	9	14	3	1	12	14	2	4	8	12	2	1	14
EDM	20	3	5	12	15	3	2	10	16	1	6	9	16	3	3	10	9	0	3	6	21	1	6	14	17	5	4	8	17	5	4	8	15	4	5	6	20	5	1	14
FLA	21	1	2	18	20	3	2	15	26	3	4	19	13	0	3	10	9	0	3	6	24	2	5	17																
L.A.	12	5	2	5	16	3	2	11	14	0	3	11	23	3	2	18	10	1	2	7	18	3	3	12	18	3	3	12	16	1	1	14	16	4	2	10	12	3	2	7
MIN																																								
MTL	15	0	4	11	20	3	4	13	21	2	4	15	15	2	3	10	10	1	2	7	19	3	2	14	14	5	3	6	20	6	3	11	17	3	3	11	17	4	2	11
NSH	10	1	2	7																																				
N.J.	15	3	1	11	16	2	3	11	17	1	2	14	19	7	0	12	11	1	2	8	14	1	1	12	11	4	0	7	17	2	4	11	15	2	3	10	16	3	4	9
NYI	17	1	6	10	13	0	2	11	17	3	2	12	17	2	5	10	7	1	1	5	19	5	2	12	13	3	3	7	17	2	4	11	16	1	2	13	16	3	4	9
NYR	19	5	3	11	24	2	4	18	13	3	0	10	17	2	1	14	3	0	0	3	17	4	4	9	10	0	6	4	11	5	1	5	16	1	2	13	17	2	2	13
OTT	18	1	2	15	17	2	0	15	17	0	2	15	18	0	3	15	8	0	3	5	18	3	5	10	17	4	2	11												
PHI	24	2	3	19	15	3	1	11	18	2	3	13	20	4	3	13	8	3	1	4	18	3	5	10	11	2	2	7	17	2	4	11	11	1	0	10	18	2	5	11
PHX/WPG	15	2	1	12	14	0	2	12	16	5	4	7	8	2	0	6	9	0	2	7	15	1	5	9	11	2	2	7	20	1	4	15	14	1	2	11	19	4	4	11
PIT	22	7	1	14	13	2	3	8	13	1	4	8	13	1	4	8	9	1	1	7	19	4	2	13	14	4	2	11	15	2	1	12	12	4	2	6	14	3	3	8
ST.L.	15	1	1	13	12	2	2	8	13	1	1	11	18	1	1	16	9	1	1	7	17	4	2	11	16	3	2	11	12	5	2	5	18	3	4	11	15	2	4	9
S.J.	21	1	2	18	12	0	2	10	13	0	3	10	16	4	2	10	9	1	1	7	19	2	3	14	10	3	5	2	9	1	3	5								
T.B.	12	1	2	9	13	3	0	10	16	4	2	10	9	1	1	7	5	1	0	4	7	2	2	3	14	1	1	12												
TOR	14	6	1	7	10	1	0	9	10	1	1	8	18	4	2	12	8	0	0	8	17	4	1	12	13	1	1	11	11	4	0	7	17	4	2	11	11	3	4	4
VAN	13	0	1	12	17	0	3	14	14	5	2	7	16	4	1	11	9	0	1	8	14	2	2	10	11	2	2	7	12	2	2	8	15	3	3	9	9	2	1	6
WSH	11	2	3	6	17	4	1	12	13	2	2	9	16	1	1	11	9	0	1	8	14	2	2	10																
Totals	**222**	**60**		**162**	**219**	**54**		**165**	**214**	**70**		**144**	**201**	**64**		**137**	**101**	**26**		**75**	**214**	**74**		**140**	**165**	**65**		**100**	**169**	**52**		**117**	**166**	**54**		**112**	**155**	**55**		**100**

Abbreviations: GP – games played; **W** – overtime win; **L** – overtime loss;
SO – game tied after overtime. Game decided in shootout. (2005-06 to date); See page 143.
T – game tied after overtime. (Up to and including 2003-04.)

2009-10 Shootout Summary

Team Shootout Statistics

Team	GP	W	L	G	S	S%	GA	SA	Sv%	W	L	G	S	S%	GA	SA	Sv%	W	L	G	S	S%	GA	SA	Sv%
					OVERALL									HOME								ROAD			
Ana.	13	5	8	13	42	.310	18	43	.581	1	4	5	16	.313	8	14	.429	4	4	8	26	.308	13	42	.690
Atl.	10	4	6	10	33	.303	11	32	.656	2	2	5	14	.357	4	13	.692	2	4	5	19	.263	10	33	.697
Bos.	19	10	9	19	66	.288	19	66	.712	3	6	7	32	.219	10	30	.667	7	3	12	34	.353	19	66	.712
Buf.	10	4	6	15	47	.319	16	44	.636	3	4	10	30	.333	10	27	.630	1	2	5	17	.294	15	47	.681
Cgy.	10	3	7	10	28	.357	17	31	.452	0	3	1	7	.143	6	9	.333	3	4	9	21	.429	10	28	.643
Car.	9	4	5	9	31	.290	11	32	.656	4	2	8	21	.381	5	20	.750	0	3	1	10	.100	9	31	.710
Chi.	15	9	6	22	69	.319	19	70	.729	6	2	14	38	.368	9	38	.763	3	4	8	31	.258	22	69	.681
Col.	12	7	5	18	55	.327	17	56	.696	3	1	5	16	.313	4	16	.750	4	4	13	39	.333	18	55	.673
CBJ	12	2	10	13	50	.260	20	46	.565	2	6	9	28	.321	12	25	.520	0	4	4	22	.182	13	50	.740
Dal.	17	7	10	14	75	.187	17	72	.764	3	6	8	38	.211	10	35	.714	4	4	6	37	.162	14	75	.813
Det.	15	6	9	19	63	.302	21	62	.661	1	3	5	13	.385	6	11	.455	5	6	14	50	.280	19	63	.698
Edm.	14	8	6	20	61	.328	18	60	.700	4	2	8	21	.381	6	19	.684	4	4	12	40	.300	20	61	.672
Fla.	16	6	10	15	59	.254	20	60	.667	2	7	10	39	.256	15	37	.595	4	3	5	20	.250	15	59	.746
L.A.	18	10	8	27	74	.365	24	73	.671	5	6	17	45	.378	17	43	.605	5	2	10	29	.345	27	74	.635
Min.	12	5	7	14	51	.275	15	50	.700	3	4	8	35	.229	9	35	.743	2	3	6	16	.375	14	51	.725
Mtl.	12	7	5	11	37	.297	10	38	.737	4	2	6	21	.286	3	20	.850	3	3	5	16	.313	11	37	.703
Nsh.	12	8	4	18	52	.346	13	55	.764	6	2	13	38	.342	9	41	.780	2	2	5	14	.357	18	52	.654
N.J.	11	6	5	12	32	.375	12	34	.647	1	2	2	10	.200	3	9	.667	5	3	10	22	.455	12	32	.625
NYI	14	8	6	24	57	.421	21	55	.618	7	2	16	30	.533	10	28	.643	1	4	8	27	.296	24	57	.579
NYR	7	3	4	7	26	.269	9	27	.667	0	2	0	6	.000	3	6	.500	3	2	7	20	.350	7	26	.731
Ott.	10	5	5	13	32	.406	12	31	.613	3	3	9	21	.429	9	19	.526	2	2	4	11	.364	13	32	.594
Phi.	7	4	3	7	20	.350	6	18	.667	3	2	5	15	.333	5	14	.643	1	1	2	5	.400	7	20	.650
Phx.	20	14	6	34	90	.378	25	89	.719	6	2	12	37	.324	7	37	.811	8	4	22	53	.415	34	90	.622
Pit.	10	8	2	15	29	.517	6	29	.793	3	1	5	11	.455	2	9	.778	5	1	10	18	.556	15	29	.483
St.L.	12	7	5	17	39	.436	13	38	.658	2	2	6	18	.333	6	18	.667	5	3	11	21	.524	17	39	.564
S.J.	13	7	6	13	52	.250	13	56	.768	3	5	9	37	.243	11	38	.711	4	1	4	15	.267	13	52	.750
T.B.	11	4	7	6	36	.167	10	37	.730	4	5	6	31	.194	7	31	.774	0	2	0	5	.000	6	36	.833
Tor.	8	4	4	9	20	.450	9	19	.526	3	0	7	9	.778	2	7	.714	1	4	2	11	.182	9	20	.550
Van.	8	4	4	12	24	.500	11	26	.577	1	2	4	8	.500	4	8	.500	3	2	8	16	.500	12	24	.500
Wsh.	11	5	6	13	48	.271	16	49	.673	3	3	8	28	.286	9	28	.679	2	3	5	20	.250	13	48	.729

Team Shootout Leaders

Wins

	W	L	Win%
Phx.	14	6	.700
L.A.	10	8	.556
Bos.	10	9	.526
Chi.	9	6	.600
Pit.	8	2	.800
Nsh.	8	4	.667
Edm.	8	6	.571
NYI	8	6	.571
5 teams tied with	7		

Fewest Goals Against

	GA	SA	Sv%
Pit.	6	29	.793
Phi.	6	18	.667
Tor.	9	19	.526
NYR	9	27	.667
T.B.	10	37	.730
Mtl.	10	38	.737
Van.	11	26	.577
Car.	11	32	.656
Atl.	11	32	.656
Ott.	12	31	.613
N.J.	12	34	.647

Goals Scored

	G	S	S%
Phx.	34	90	.378
L.A.	27	74	.365
NYI	24	57	.421
Chi.	22	69	.319
Edm.	20	61	.328
Det.	19	63	.302
Bos.	19	66	.288
Col.	18	55	.327
Nsh.	18	52	.346
St.L.	17	39	.436

Winning Percentage

	Win%	W	L
Pit.	.800	8	2
Phx.	.700	14	6
Nsh.	.667	8	4
Chi.	.600	9	6
St.L.	.583	7	5
Col.	.583	7	5
Mtl.	.583	7	5
Edm.	.571	8	6
NYI	.571	8	6
Phi.	.571	4	3

Shootout Abbreviations

G ....Goals Scored
GA ......Goals Against
GDG ...Game Deciding Goal
S ....Shots Taken
SA ......Shots Against
S% ......Goal Scoring %
Sv% ....Save %

Individual Shootout Leaders – Goaltenders

Goaltender Shootout Wins

	Team	W	L
Ilya Bryzgalov	Phx.	8	5
Jonathan Quick	L.A.	8	6
Craig Anderson	Col.	7	4
Jason LaBarbera	Phx.	6	1
Antti Niemi	Chi.	6	2
Marc-Andre Fleury	Pit.	6	2
Pekka Rinne	Nsh.	6	3
Martin Brodeur	N.J.	6	4
Evgeni Nabokov	S.J.	6	6

Goaltender Shootout Shots Against

	Team	SA	GA	Sv%
Ilya Bryzgalov	Phx.	62	17	.726
Jimmy Howard	Det.	54	17	.685
Marty Turco	Dal.	53	15	.717
Jonathan Quick	L.A.	51	17	.667
Craig Anderson	Col.	51	16	.686
Evgeni Nabokov	S.J.	50	13	.740
Tomas Vokoun	Fla.	49	19	.612
Pekka Rinne	Nsh.	45	11	.756
Dwayne Roloson	NYI	39	15	.615
Cristobal Huet	Chi.	38	13	.658
Niklas Backstrom	Min.	38	14	.632

Goaltender Shootout Save Percentage

(min.10 shots faced)	Team	Sv%	SA	GA
Scott Clemmensen	Fla.	.909	11	1
Josh Harding	Min.	.900	10	1
Alex Auld	NYR	.867	15	2
Antti Niemi	Chi.	.812	32	6
Dan Ellis	Nsh.	.800	10	2
Antero Niittymaki	T.B.	.783	23	5
Jaroslav Halak	Mtl.	.762	21	5
Johan Hedberg	Atl.	.762	21	5
Pekka Rinne	Nsh.	.756	45	11
Manny Legace	Car.	.750	16	4

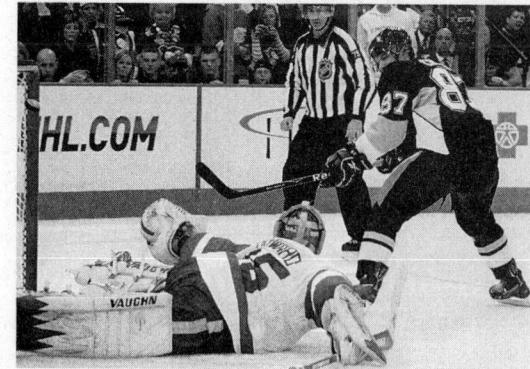

Pittsburgh's Sidney Crosby backhands the puck over Detroit's Jimmy Howard for one of his eight shootout goals on just 10 shots in 2009-10.

Individual Shootout Leaders – Skaters

Shootout Goals Scored

	Team	G	S	S%
Sidney Crosby	Pit.	8	10	80.0
Jonathan Toews	Chi.	8	14	57.1
Anze Kopitar	L.A.	8	16	50.0
Radim Vrbata	Phx.	8	18	44.4
Brad Boyes	St.L.	7	12	58.3
Frans Nielsen	NYI	7	12	58.3
Pavel Datsyuk	Det.	7	14	50.0
Lauri Korpikoski	Phx.	7	17	41.2
Adrian Aucoin	Phx.	6	9	66.7
Jack Johnson	L.A.	6	17	35.3

Shootout Shots Taken

	Team	S	G	S%
Radim Vrbata	Phx.	18	8	44.4
Lauri Korpikoski	Phx.	17	7	41.2
Jack Johnson	L.A.	17	6	35.3
Anze Kopitar	L.A.	16	8	50.0
Brad Richards	Dal.	16	4	25.0
Patrick Kane	Chi.	15	4	26.7
Wojtek Wolski	Phx.	15	1	6.7
Jonathan Toews	Chi.	14	8	57.1
Pavel Datsyuk	Det.	14	7	50.0
4 players tied with		13		

Shootout Scoring Percentage

(min. 5 shots taken)	Team	S%	S	G
Sidney Crosby	Pit.	80.0	10	8
Adrian Aucoin	Phx.	66.7	9	6
Vyacheslav Kozlov	Atl.	66.7	6	4
Robert Lang	Phx.	62.5	8	5
T.J. Oshie	St.L.	62.5	8	5
Michal Handzus	L.A.	62.5	8	5
Ryan Kesler	Van.	60.0	5	3
Claude Giroux	Phi.	60.0	5	3
Gilbert Brule	Edm.	60.0	5	3
Ryan Potulny	Edm.	60.0	5	3
Jeff Tambellini	NYI	60.0	5	3
Brian Gionta	Mtl.	60.0	5	3

Shootout Game-Deciding Goals

	Team	GDG	S	G
Adrian Aucoin	Phx.	6	9	6
Sidney Crosby	Pit.	4	10	8
Anze Kopitar	L.A.	4	16	8
8 players tied with		3		

Shootout Register, 2009-10

Skaters

Player	Team	S	G	S%	GDG
Afinogenov, Maxim	Atl.	3	0	0.0	0
Alfredsson, Daniel	Ott.	7	2	28.6	1
Anisimov, Artem	NYR	2	0	0.0	0
Antropov, Nik	Atl.	2	0	0.0	0
Arnott, Jason	Nsh.	2	1	50.0	0
Artyukhin, Evgeny	Atl.	1	0	0.0	0
Aucoin, Adrian	Phx.	9	6	66.7	6
Backes, David	St.L.	1	0	0.0	0
Backlund, Mikael	Cgy.	1	0	0.0	0
Backstrom, Nicklas	Wsh.	9	4	44.4	1
Bailey, Josh	NYI	3	1	33.3	0
Barker, Cam	Min.	1	0	0.0	0
Belanger, Eric	Wsh.	3	0	0.0	0
Beleskey, Matt	Ana.	1	0	0.0	0
Benn, Jamie	Dal.	5	1	20.0	1
Bergenheim, Sean	NYI	2	0	0.0	0
Bergeron, Patrice	Bos.	13	3	23.1	2
Bergfors, Nicklas	Atl.	1	0	0.0	0
Berglund, Patrik	St.L.	1	0	0.0	0
Bertuzzi, Todd	Det.	8	4	50.0	2
Bochenski, Brandon	T.B.	1	0	0.0	0
Bolland, Dave	Chi.	1	0	0.0	0
Booth, David	Fla.	2	1	50.0	0
Bouillon, Francis	Nsh.	1	0	0.0	0
Bourque, Rene	Cgy.	1	0	0.0	0
Boyd, Dustin	Nsh.	1	0	0.0	0
Boyes, Brad	St.L.	12	7	58.3	3
Boyle, Dan	S.J.	9	2	22.2	1
Bozak, Tyler	Tor.	1	0	0.0	0
Bradley, Matt	Wsh.	2	0	0.0	0
Brassard, Derick	CBJ	1	0	0.0	0
Briere, Danny	Phi.	6	2	33.3	1
Brind'Amour, Rod	Car.	1	0	0.0	0
Brodziak, Kyle	Min.	1	0	0.0	0
Brouwer, Troy	Chi.	5	1	20.0	1
Brown, Dustin	L.A.	11	2	18.2	1
Brule, Gilbert	Edm.	5	3	60.0	1
Burns, Brent	Min.	3	1	33.3	1
Burrows, Alexandre	Van.	1	1	100.0	0
Byfuglien, Dustin	Chi.	3	0	0.0	0
Callahan, Ryan	NYR	1	0	0.0	0
Cammalleri, Michael	Mtl.	8	2	25.0	2
Carter, Jeff	Phi.	1	0	0.0	0
Chara, Zdeno	Bos.	4	1	25.0	1
Chimera, Jason	Wsh.	1	0	0.0	0
Christensen, Erik	NYR	4	1	25.0	1
Clark, Chris	CBJ	1	1	100.0	1
Clarkson, David	N.J.	1	1	100.0	1
Cleary, Dan	Det.	4	0	0.0	0
Clowe, Ryane	S.J.	9	3	33.3	2
Clutterbuck, Cal	Min.	1	0	0.0	0
Comrie, Mike	Edm.	4	1	25.0	1
Connolly, Tim	Buf.	7	1	14.3	0
Couture, Logan	S.J.	1	1	100.0	1
Crosby, Sidney	Pit.	10	8	80.0	4
Cullen, Matt	Ott.	3	0	0.0	0
Datsyuk, Pavel	Det.	14	7	50.0	2
Dawes, Nigel	Cgy.	8	3	37.5	0
Del Zotto, Michael	NYR	1	0	0.0	0
Demitra, Pavol	Van.	4	2	50.0	2
Doan, Shane	Phx.	9	2	22.2	0
Doughty, Drew	L.A.	2	1	50.0	0
Downie, Steve	T.B.	1	0	0.0	0
Draper, Kris	Det.	1	0	0.0	0
Dubinsky, Brandon	NYR	2	0	0.0	0
Duchene, Matt	Col.	7	2	28.6	1
Dumont, J.P.	Nsh.	2	0	0.0	0
Dupuis, Pascal	Pit.	1	1	100.0	0
Eaves, Patrick	Det.	3	0	0.0	0
Ebbett, Andrew	Min.	2	1	50.0	0
Elias, Patrik	N.J.	5	2	40.0	2
Erat, Martin	Nsh.	11	5	45.4	3
Eriksson, Loui	Dal.	9	3	33.3	2
Fehr, Eric	Wsh.	2	0	0.0	0
Ferriero, Benn	S.J.	1	0	0.0	0
Fiddler, Vernon	Phx.	1	0	0.0	0
Filatov, Nikita	CBJ	2	0	0.0	0
Filppula, Valtteri	Det.	4	1	25.0	0
Fisher, Mike	Ott.	5	2	40.0	0
Fleischmann, Tomas	Wsh.	4	1	25.0	1
Foligno, Nick	Ott.	1	0	0.0	0
Foster, Kurtis	T.B.	1	0	0.0	0
Franson, Cody	Nsh.	1	0	0.0	0
Franzen, Johan	Det.	1	0	0.0	0
Frolik, Michael	Fla.	5	1	20.0	0
Frolov, Alexander	L.A.	1	0	0.0	0
Gaborik, Marian	NYR	5	1	20.0	0
Gagne, Simon	Phi.	1	0	0.0	0
Gagner, Sam	Edm.	7	0	0.0	0
Galiardi, T.J.	Col.	2	0	0.0	0
Getzlaf, Ryan	Ana.	8	4	50.0	0
Gilbert, Tom	Edm.	1	0	0.0	0
Gionta, Brian	Mtl.	5	3	60.0	1
Giroux, Claude	Phi.	5	3	60.0	2
Glencross, Curtis	Cgy.	1	0	0.0	0
Goc, Marcel	Nsh.	5	1	20.0	0
Goligoski, Alex	Pit.	1	0	0.0	0
Gomez, Scott	Mtl.	8	2	25.0	1
Gordon, Boyd	Wsh.	1	0	0.0	0
Green, Mike	Wsh.	2	0	0.0	0
Guerin, Bill	Pit.	3	0	0.0	0
Hagman, Niklas	Cgy.	1	1	100.0	0
Halpern, Jeff	L.A.	3	1	33.3	1
Handzus, Michal	L.A.	8	5	62.5	1
Havlat, Martin	Min.	4	0	0.0	0
Heatley, Dany	S.J.	6	1	16.7	0
Hecht, Jochen	Buf.	4	3	75.0	1
Hejduk, Milan	Col.	8	4	50.0	1
Hemsky, Ales	Edm.	4	2	50.0	1
Hendricks, Matt	Col.	2	1	50.0	1
Higgins, Christopher	Cgy.	1	0	0.0	0
Holmstrom, Tomas	Det.	1	0	0.0	0
Horcoff, Shawn	Edm.	7	4	57.1	3
Hornqvist, Patric	Nsh.	3	0	0.0	0
Horton, Nathan	Fla.	8	2	25.0	1
Hossa, Marian	Chi.	5	2	40.0	0
Hunter, Trent	NYI	2	1	50.0	1
Huselius, Kristian	CBJ	11	4	36.4	1
Iginla, Jarome	Cgy.	4	0	0.0	0
Johnson, Jack	L.A.	17	6	35.3	1
Jokinen, Jussi	Car.	9	4	44.4	1
Jokinen, Olli	NYR	10	5	50.0	1
Jones, David	Col.	1	0	0.0	0
Jones, Ryan	Edm.	1	0	0.0	0
Kaberle, Tomas	Tor.	1	0	0.0	0
Kaleta, Patrick	Buf.	1	0	0.0	0
Kane, Patrick	Chi.	15	4	26.7	0
Kariya, Paul	St.L.	1	0	0.0	0
Kennedy, Tim	Buf.	1	0	0.0	0
Kesler, Ryan	Van.	5	3	60.0	0
Kessel, Philip	Tor.	7	3	42.9	2
Knuble, Mike	Wsh.	2	1	50.0	1
Kobasew, Chuck	Min.	1	0	0.0	0
Koistinen, Ville	Fla.	2	1	50.0	1
Koivu, Mikko	Min.	12	5	41.7	2
Koivu, Saku	Ana.	3	1	33.3	1
Kopecky, Tomas	Chi.	3	1	33.3	0
Kopitar, Anze	L.A.	16	8	50.0	4
Korpikoski, Lauri	Phx.	17	7	41.2	2
Kostitsyn, Andrei	Mtl.	4	2	50.0	1
Kotalik, Ales	Cgy.	4	1	25.0	0
Kovalchuk, Ilya	N.J.	8	2	25.0	1
Kovalev, Alexei	Ott.	9	5	55.6	2
Kozlov, Vyacheslav	Atl.	6	4	66.7	0
Krejci, David	Bos.	10	4	40.0	3
Kreps, Kamil	Fla.	2	1	50.0	0
Kronwall, Niklas	Det.	2	1	50.0	1
Kulemin, Nikolai	Tor.	4	3	75.0	1
Kunitz, Chris	Pit.	2	1	50.0	1
Ladd, Andrew	Chi.	4	1	25.0	1
Laich, Brooks	Wsh.	3	1	33.3	0
Lang, Robert	Phx.	8	5	62.5	2
Langenbrunner, Jamie	N.J.	9	3	33.3	2
Lapierre, Maxim	Mtl.	3	1	33.3	1
Larose, Chad	Car.	1	1	100.0	1
Latendresse, Guillaume	Min.	6	1	16.7	1
Lecavalier, Vincent	T.B.	8	1	12.5	1
Legwand, David	Nsh.	9	4	44.4	2
Lehtinen, Jere	Dal.	4	1	25.0	0
Leino, Ville	Phi.	3	0	0.0	0
Letang, Kris	Pit.	10	4	40.0	3
Liles, John-Michael	Col.	1	0	0.0	0
Lisin, Enver	NYR	1	0	0.0	0
Little, Bryan	Atl.	4	1	25.0	1
Lombardi, Matthew	Phx.	3	1	33.3	1
Lundmark, Jamie	Tor.	5	2	40.0	2
Lupul, Joffrey	Ana.	2	1	50.0	0
MacArthur, Clarke	Atl.	3	0	0.0	0
Madden, John	Chi.	2	0	0.0	0
Mair, Adam	Buf.	1	0	0.0	0
Malhotra, Manny	S.J.	1	0	0.0	0
Malkin, Evgeni	Pit.	2	1	50.0	0
Malone, Ryan	T.B.	1	0	0.0	0
Markov, Andrei	Mtl.	1	0	0.0	0
Marleau, Patrick	S.J.	7	2	28.6	1
Matthias, Shawn	Fla.	1	0	0.0	0
McDonald, Andy	St.L.	9	4	44.4	1
McGinn, Jamie	S.J.	1	0	0.0	0
Meszaros, Andrej	T.B.	1	0	0.0	0
Michalek, Milan	Ott.	1	0	0.0	0
Miettinen, Antti	Min.	7	2	28.6	0
Miller, Drew	Det.	2	1	50.0	1
Mitchell, John	Tor.	3	2	66.7	1
Mitchell, Torrey	S.J.	1	0	0.0	0
Modano, Mike	Dal.	7	1	14.3	1
Moller, Oscar	L.A.	1	0	0.0	0
Morrison, Brendan	Wsh.	5	1	20.0	0
Morrow, Brenden	Dal.	2	0	0.0	0
Moulson, Matt	NYI	7	4	57.1	2
Mueller, Peter	Col.	8	3	37.5	0
Myers, Tyler	Buf.	3	1	33.3	1
Nash, Rick	CBJ	12	5	41.7	0
Neal, James	Dal.	10	0	0.0	0
Nielsen, Frans	NYI	12	7	58.3	2
Nilsson, Robert	Edm.	6	1	16.7	0
Niskanen, Matt	Dal.	3	1	33.3	1
Nolan, Owen	Min.	4	2	50.0	1
O'Reilly, Cal	Nsh.	4	2	50.0	1
O'Reilly, Ryan	Col.	3	1	33.3	0
O'Sullivan, Patrick	Edm.	11	4	36.4	1
Ohlund, Mattias	T.B.	1	0	0.0	0
Okposo, Kyle	NYI	4	0	0.0	0
Olesz, Rostislav	Fla.	9	2	22.2	1
Oshie, T.J.	St.L.	8	5	62.5	2
Ott, Steve	Dal.	2	1	50.0	1
Ovechkin, Alex	Wsh.	9	2	22.2	1
Pahlsson, Samuel	CBJ	1	0	0.0	0
Parenteau, Pierre	NYR	3	3	100.0	2
Parise, Zach	N.J.	11	5	45.4	1
Park, Richard	NYI	2	0	0.0	0
Parse, Scott	L.A.	1	0	0.0	0
Pavelski, Joe	S.J.	9	3	33.3	2
Penner, Dustin	Edm.	6	1	16.7	0
Perreault, Mathieu	Wsh.	1	0	0.0	0
Perron, David	St.L.	5	1	20.0	1
Perry, Corey	Ana.	13	3	23.1	0
Peverley, Rich	Atl.	8	3	37.5	2
Pisani, Fernando	Edm.	1	0	0.0	0
Plekanec, Tomas	Mtl.	6	1	16.7	1
Pominville, Jason	Buf.	9	5	55.6	2
Potulny, Ryan	Edm.	5	3	60.0	0
Pouliot, Benoit	Mtl.	1	0	0.0	0
Pouliot, Marc	Edm.	2	0	0.0	0
Prospal, Vinny	NYR	1	1	100.0	0
Prucha, Petr	Phx.	4	1	25.0	0
Purcell, Teddy	T.B.	2	1	50.0	1
Pyatt, Taylor	Phx.	1	0	0.0	0
Pyorala, Mika	Phi.	1	1	100.0	1
Raymond, Mason	Van.	4	1	25.0	0
Recchi, Mark	Bos.	4	1	25.0	1
Reinprecht, Steven	Fla.	13	3	23.1	0
Ribeiro, Mike	Dal.	12	1	8.3	0
Richards, Brad	Dal.	16	4	25.0	0
Richards, Mike	Phi.	6	1	16.7	0
Richardson, Brad	L.A.	1	0	0.0	0
Robidas, Stephane	Dal.	4	1	25.0	1
Rodney, Bryan	Car.	1	0	0.0	0
Roy, Derek	Buf.	5	1	20.0	0
Russell, Kris	CBJ	1	0	0.0	0
Ruutu, Jarkko	Ott.	1	0	0.0	0
Ruutu, Tuomo	Car.	6	2	33.3	1
Ryan, Bobby	Ana.	2	0	0.0	0
Ryder, Michael	Bos.	10	2	20.0	1
Samsonov, Sergei	Car.	5	1	20.0	1
Samuelsson, Mikael	Van.	3	1	33.3	1
Santorelli, Michael	Nsh.	3	3	100.0	1
Satan, Miroslav	Bos.	4	2	50.0	1
Savard, Marc	Bos.	6	3	50.0	1
Schremp, Rob	NYI	9	5	55.6	2
Seabrook, Brent	Chi.	1	1	100.0	1
Selanne, Teemu	Ana.	7	2	28.6	2
Semin, Alexander	Wsh.	7	2	28.6	0
Setoguchi, Devin	S.J.	3	1	33.3	0
Sexton, Dan	Ana.	2	0	0.0	0
Shannon, Ryan	Ott.	1	1	100.0	1
Sharp, Patrick	Chi.	10	2	20.0	2
Sim, Jon	NYI	1	0	0.0	0
Simmonds, Wayne	L.A.	3	1	33.3	0
Smyth, Ryan	L.A.	6	1	16.7	0
Spezza, Jason	Ott.	7	3	42.9	1
St Louis, Martin	T.B.	3	0	0.0	0
Staal, Eric	Car.	2	0	0.0	0
Stafford, Drew	Buf.	8	2	25.0	0
Stamkos, Steven	T.B.	9	3	33.3	1
Stastny, Paul	Col.	4	0	0.0	0
Steen, Alex	St.L.	1	0	0.0	0
Stempniak, Lee	Phx.	6	2	33.3	0
Stewart, Chris	Col.	7	3	42.9	3
Stillman, Cory	Fla.	6	2	33.3	2
Stoll, Jarret	L.A.	6	2	33.3	2
Stralman, Anton	CBJ	2	0	0.0	0
Streit, Mark	NYI	1	0	0.0	0
Sturm, Marco	Bos.	2	1	50.0	0
Sullivan, Steve	Nsh.	7	2	28.6	1
Svatos, Marek	Col.	7	4	57.1	0
Taffe, Jeff	Fla.	1	0	0.0	0
Tallinder, Henrik	Buf.	1	0	0.0	0
Tambellini, Jeff	NYI	5	3	60.0	0
Tanguay, Alex	T.B.	4	0	0.0	0
Tavares, John	NYI	8	3	37.5	1
Thornton, Joe	S.J.	2	0	0.0	0
Tkachuk, Keith	St.L.	1	0	0.0	0
Toews, Jonathan	Chi.	14	8	57.1	3
Torres, Raffi	Buf.	1	0	0.0	0
Tucker, Darcy	Col.	3	1	33.3	0
Tyutin, Fedor	CBJ	6	2	33.3	0
Umberger, R.J.	CBJ	2	0	0.0	0
Upshall, Scottie	Phx.	1	0	0.0	0
Vanek, Thomas	Buf.	5	2	40.0	0
Veilleux, Stephane	T.B.	1	0	0.0	0
Vermette, Antoine	CBJ	4	0	0.0	0
Versteeg, Kris	Chi.	5	2	40.0	1
Vesce, Ryan	S.J.	1	0	0.0	0
Visnovsky, Lubomir	Ana.	1	1	100.0	1
Vlasic, Marc-Edouard	S.J.	1	0	0.0	0
Voracek, Jakub	CBJ	6	2	33.3	1
Vrbata, Radim	Phx.	18	8	44.4	3
Wandell, Tom	Dal.	1	0	0.0	0
Ward, Joel	Nsh.	1	0	0.0	0
Weber, Shea	Nsh.	1	0	0.0	0
Weight, Doug	NYI	1	0	0.0	0
Weiss, Stephen	Fla.	10	2	20.0	1
Wellman, Casey	Min.	1	0	0.0	0
Wellwood, Kyle	Van.	7	4	57.1	1
Wheeler, Blake	Bos.	13	2	15.4	0
White, Todd	Atl.	1	0	0.0	0
Whitney, Ray	Car.	3	1	33.3	0
Williams, Jason	Det.	9	3	33.3	0
Williams, Justin	L.A.	1	1	100.0	1
Wilson, Colin	Nsh.	1	0	0.0	0
Wisniewski, James	Ana.	3	2	66.7	2
Wolski, Wojtek	Phx.	15	1	6.7	1
Yandle, Keith	Phx.	1	0	0.0	0
Yip, Brandon	Col.	1	0	0.0	0
Zajac, Travis	N.J.	5	1	20.0	0
Zetterberg, Henrik	Det.	11	2	18.2	0
Zidlicky, Marek	Min.	7	2	28.6	0

Goaltenders

Goaltender	Team	W	L	SA	GA	Sv %
Anderson, Craig	Col.	7	4	51	16	.686
Auld, Alex	NYR	2	2	15	2	.867
Backstrom, Niklas	Min.	2	7	38	14	.632
Bernier, Jonathan	L.A.	1	0	6	0	1.000
Biron, Martin	NYI	2	1	8	3	.625
Boucher, Brian	Phi.	1	2	7	4	.429
Brodeur, Martin	N.J.	6	4	31	9	.710
Bryzgalov, Ilya	Phx.	8	5	62	17	.726
Budaj, Peter	Col.	0	1	5	1	.800
Clemmensen, Scott	Fla.	2	1	11	1	.909
Conklin, Ty	St.L.	2	2	10	5	.500
Danis, Yann	N.J.	0	1	3	3	.000
DiPietro, Rick	NYI	1	0	8	3	.625
Drouin-Deslauriers, J.	Edm.	4	3	37	11	.703
Dubielewicz, Wade	Min.	1	0	2	0	1.000
Dubnyk, Devan	Edm.	2	1	11	3	.727
Elliott, Brian	Ott.	2	4	21	7	.667
Ellis, Dan	Nsh.	2	1	10	2	.800
Emery, Ray	Phi.	2	1	9	2	.778
Ersberg, Erik	L.A.	1	2	16	7	.562
Fleury, Marc-Andre	Pit.	6	2	23	6	.739
Garon, Mathieu	CBJ	2	3	18	8	.556
Giguere, J-S	Tor.	2	4	16	8	.500
Greiss, Thomas	S.J.	1	0	6	0	1.000
Gustavsson, Jonas	Tor.	2	1	7	3	.571
Halak, Jaroslav	Mtl.	5	2	21	5	.762
Harding, Josh	Min.	2	0	10	1	.900
Hedberg, Johan	Atl.	4	2	21	5	.762
Hiller, Jonas	Ana.	3	4	27	10	.630
Howard, Jimmy	Det.	5	7	54	17	.685
Huet, Cristobal	Chi.	3	4	38	13	.658
Johnson, Brent	Pit.	2	0	6	0	1.000
Johnson, Chad	NYR	0	1	5	2	.600
Khabibulin, Nikolai	Edm.	2	2	12	4	.667
Kiprusoff, Miikka	Cgy.	2	7	27	15	.444
LaBarbera, Jason	Phx.	6	1	27	8	.704
Lalime, Patrick	Buf.	0	2	13	5	.615
Leclaire, Pascal	Ott.	3	1	10	5	.500
Legace, Manny	Car.	2	2	16	4	.750
Lehtonen, Kari	Dal.	1	0	4	0	1.000
Leighton, Michael	Phi.	2	0	5	0	1.000
Lundqvist, Henrik	NYR	3	3	22	7	.682
Luongo, Roberto	Van.	2	3	14	5	.643
Mason, Chris	St.L.	5	3	28	8	.714
Mason, Steve	CBJ	0	7	28	12	.571
McElhinney, Curtis	Ana.	2	2	12	6	.500
Miller, Ryan	Buf.	4	4	31	11	.645
Nabokov, Evgeni	S.J.	6	6	50	13	.740
Niemi, Antti	Chi.	6	2	32	6	.812
Niittymaki, Antero	T.B.	3	4	23	5	.783
Osgood, Chris	Det.	1	2	8	4	.500
Pavelec, Ondrej	Atl.	0	4	11	6	.454
Price, Carey	Mtl.	2	3	17	5	.706
Quick, Jonathan	L.A.	8	6	51	17	.667
Rask, Tuukka	Bos.	5	4	33	10	.697
Raycroft, Andrew	Van.	2	1	12	6	.500
Rinne, Pekka	Nsh.	6	3	45	11	.756
Roloson, Dwayne	NYI	5	5	39	15	.615
Smith, Mike	T.B.	1	3	14	5	.643
Theodore, Jose	Wsh.	2	2	16	7	.562
Thomas, Tim	Bos.	5	5	33	9	.727
Toskala, Vesa	Cgy.	1	1	4	2	.500
Turco, Marty	Dal.	4	8	53	15	.717
Varlamov, Semyon	Wsh.	3	4	33	9	.727
Vokoun, Tomas	Fla.	4	9	49	19	.612
Ward, Cam	Car.	1	3	13	7	.462

NHL Record Book

Year-By-Year Final Standings & Leading Scorers

*Stanley Cup winner

1917-18

First Half

Team	GP	W	L	T	GF	GA	PTS
Montreal	14	10	4	0	81	47	20
Toronto	14	8	6	0	71	75	16
Ottawa	14	5	9	0	67	79	10
**Mtl. Wanderers	6	1	5	0	17	35	2

**Montreal Arena burned down and Wanderers forced to withdraw from League. Montreal Canadiens and Toronto each counted a win for defaulted games with Wanderers.

Second Half

Team	GP	W	L	T	GF	GA	PTS
*Toronto	8	5	3	0	37	34	10
Ottawa	8	4	4	0	35	35	8
Montreal	8	3	5	0	34	37	6

Leading Scorers

Player	Team	GP	G	A	PTS	PIM
Joe Malone	Montreal	20	44	4	48	30
Cy Denneny	Ottawa	20	36	10	46	80
Reg Noble	Toronto	20	30	10	40	35
Newsy Lalonde	Montreal	14	23	7	30	51
Corb Denneny	Toronto	21	20	9	29	14
Harry Cameron	Toronto	21	17	10	27	28
Didier Pitre	Montreal	20	17	6	23	29
Eddie Gerard	Ottawa	20	13	7	20	26
Jack Darragh	Ottawa	18	14	5	19	26
Frank Nighbor	Ottawa	10	11	8	19	6
Harry Meeking	Toronto	21	10	9	19	28

1918-19

First Half

Team	GP	W	L	T	GF	GA	PTS
• Montreal	10	7	3	0	57	50	14
Ottawa	10	5	5	0	39	39	10
Toronto	10	3	7	0	42	49	6

Second Half

Team	GP	W	L	T	GF	GA	PTS
Ottawa	8	7	1	0	32	14	14
Montreal	8	3	5	0	31	28	6
Toronto	8	2	6	0	22	43	4

• NHL Champion. Stanley Cup not awarded due to influenza epidemic.

Leading Scorers

Player	Team	GP	G	A	PTS	PIM
Newsy Lalonde	Montreal	17	22	10	32	40
Odie Cleghorn	Montreal	17	22	6	28	22
Frank Nighbor	Ottawa	18	19	9	28	27
Cy Denneny	Ottawa	18	18	4	22	58
Didier Pitre	Montreal	17	14	5	19	12
Alf Skinner	Toronto	17	12	4	16	26
Harry Cameron	Tor., Ott.	14	11	3	14	35
Jack Darragh	Ottawa	14	11	3	14	33
Ken Randall	Toronto	15	8	6	14	27
Sprague Cleghorn	Ottawa	18	7	6	13	27

1919-20

First Half

Team	GP	W	L	T	GF	GA	PTS
Ottawa	12	9	3	0	59	23	18
Montreal	12	8	4	0	62	51	16
Toronto	12	5	7	0	52	62	10
Quebec	12	2	10	0	44	81	4

Second Half

Team	GP	W	L	T	GF	GA	PTS
*Ottawa	12	10	2	0	62	41	20
Toronto	12	7	5	0	67	44	14
Montreal	12	5	7	0	67	62	10
Quebec	12	2	10	0	47	96	4

Leading Scorers

Player	Team	GP	G	A	PTS	PIM
Joe Malone	Quebec	24	39	10	49	12
Newsy Lalonde	Montreal	23	37	9	46	34
Frank Nighbor	Ottawa	23	26	15	41	18
Corb Denneny	Toronto	24	24	12	36	20
Jack Darragh	Ottawa	23	22	14	36	22
Reg Noble	Toronto	24	24	9	33	52
Amos Arbour	Montreal	22	21	5	26	13
Cully Wilson	Toronto	23	20	6	26	86
Didier Pitre	Montreal	22	14	12	26	6
Punch Broadbent	Ottawa	21	19	6	25	40

1920-21

First Half

Team	GP	W	L	T	GF	GA	PTS
*Ottawa	10	8	2	0	49	23	16
Toronto	10	5	5	0	39	47	10
Montreal	10	4	6	0	37	51	8
Hamilton	10	3	7	0	34	38	6

Second Half

Team	GP	W	L	T	GF	GA	PTS
Toronto	14	10	4	0	66	53	20
Montreal	14	9	5	0	75	48	18
Ottawa	14	6	8	0	48	52	12
Hamilton	14	3	11	0	58	94	6

Leading Scorers

Player	Team	GP	G	A	PTS	PIM
Newsy Lalonde	Montreal	24	33	10	43	36
Babe Dye	Ham., Tor.	24	35	5	40	32
Cy Denneny	Ottawa	24	34	5	39	10
Joe Malone	Hamilton	20	28	9	37	6
Frank Nighbor	Ottawa	24	19	10	29	10
Reg Noble	Toronto	24	19	8	27	54
Harry Cameron	Toronto	24	18	9	27	8
Goldie Prodgers	Hamilton	24	18	9	27	8
Corb Denneny	Toronto	20	19	7	26	29
Jack Darragh	Ottawa	24	11	15	26	20

All-Time Standings of NHL Teams

(ranked by percentage)

Active Clubs

Team	Games	Wins	Losses	Ties	OT Losses	SO Losses	Goals For	Goals Against	Points	Pts %	First Season
Montreal	5956	3060	1987	837	46	26	19501	15981	7029	.590	1917-18
Philadelphia	3342	1662	1153	457	43	27	11260	9815	3851	.576	1967-68
Buffalo	3116	1487	1158	409	33	29	10405	9416	3445	.553	1970-71
Boston	5796	2761	2153	791	57	34	18594	17062	6404	.552	1924-25
Edmonton	2404	1119	951	262	46	26	8521	8073	2572	.535	1979-80
Calgary	2960	1359	1156	379	42	24	9954	9422	3163	.534	1972-73
Detroit	5730	2616	2231	815	39	29	17876	17026	6115	.534	1926-27
Minnesota	738	331	291	55	33	28	1876	1879	778	.527	2000-01
Colorado	2404	1103	982	261	36	22	8129	7909	2525	.525	1979-80
Nashville	902	411	371	60	38	22	2369	2480	942	.522	1998-99
St. Louis	3342	1457	1374	432	49	30	10426	10555	3425	.512	1967-68
Ottawa	1364	606	580	115	35	28	3960	4019	1390	.510	1992-93
Toronto	5956	2599	2499	783	46	29	18403	18410	6056	.508	1917-18
Anaheim	1280	557	539	107	42	35	3420	3555	1298	.507	1993-94
Dallas	3342	1426	1393	459	40	24	10375	10647	3375	.505	1967-68
San Jose	1444	630	618	121	49	26	4077	4321	1456	.504	1991-92
NY Rangers	5730	2440	2407	808	47	28	17621	17782	5763	.503	1926-27
NY Islanders	2960	1283	1269	347	39	22	9684	9481	2974	.502	1972-73
Washington	2804	1215	1214	303	40	32	8961	9312	2805	.500	1974-75
Chicago	5730	2371	2473	814	42	30	17029	17339	5628	.491	1926-27
Pittsburgh	3342	1407	1480	383	48	24	11227	11813	3269	.489	1967-68
New Jersey	2804	1174	1246	328	33	23	8529	9172	2732	.487	1974-75
Florida	1280	505	539	142	57	37	3369	3657	1246	.487	1993-94
Los Angeles	3342	1342	1504	424	46	26	10893	11639	3180	.476	1967-68
Phoenix	2404	978	1105	266	35	20	7606	8379	2277	.474	1979-80
Vancouver	3116	1248	1413	391	36	28	9867	10641	2951	.474	1970-71
Carolina	2404	976	1106	263	39	20	7359	8117	2274	.473	1979-80
Columbus	738	279	360	33	33	33	1803	2224	657	.445	2000-01
Atlanta	820	308	401	45	44	22	2242	2745	727	.443	1999-2000
Tampa Bay	1364	504	671	112	53	24	3576	4321	1197	.439	1992-93

Defunct Clubs

Team	Games	Wins	Losses	Ties	Goals For	Goals Against	Points	Pts %	First Season	Last Season
Ottawa Senators	542	258	221	63	1458	1333	579	.534	1917-18	1933-34
Montreal Maroons	622	271	260	91	1474	1405	633	.509	1924-25	1937-38
NY/Brooklyn Americans	784	255	402	127	1643	2182	637	.406	1925-26	1941-42
Hamilton Tigers	126	47	78	1	414	475	95	.377	1920-21	1924-25
Cleveland Barons	160	47	87	26	470	617	120	.375	1976-77	1977-78
Pittsburgh Pirates	212	67	122	23	376	519	157	.370	1925-26	1929-30
Calif./Oakland Seals	698	182	401	115	1826	2580	479	.343	1967-68	1975-76
St. Louis Eagles	48	11	31	6	86	144	28	.292	1934-35	1934-35
Quebec Bulldogs	24	4	20	0	91	177	8	.167	1919-20	1919-20
Montreal Wanderers	6	1	5	0	17	35	2	.167	1917-18	1917-18
Philadelphia Quakers	44	4	36	4	76	184	12	.136	1930-31	1930-31

Calgary totals include Atlanta Flames, 1972-73 to 1979-80.
Carolina totals include Hartford, 1979-80 to 1996-97.
Colorado totals include Quebec, 1979-80 to 1994-95.
Dallas totals include Minnesota North Stars, 1967-68 to 1992-93.
Detroit totals include Cougars, 1926-27 to 1929-30, and Falcons, 1930-31 to 1931-32.
New Jersey totals include Kansas City, 1974-75 to 1975-76, and Colorado Rockies, 1976-77 to 1981-82.
Phoenix totals include Winnipeg, 1979-80 to 1995-96.
Toronto totals include Arenas, 1917-18 to 1918-19, and St. Patricks, 1919-20 to 1925-26.

1921-22

Team	GP	W	L	T	GF	GA	PTS
Ottawa	24	14	8	2	106	84	30
*Toronto	24	13	10	1	98	97	27
Montreal	24	12	11	1	88	94	25
Hamilton	24	7	17	0	88	105	14

Leading Scorers

Player	Team	GP	G	A	PTS	PIM
Punch Broadbent	Ottawa	24	32	14	46	28
Cy Denneny	Ottawa	22	27	12	39	20
Babe Dye	Toronto	24	31	7	38	39
Harry Cameron	Toronto	24	18	17	35	22
Joe Malone	Hamilton	24	24	7	31	4
Corb Denneny	Toronto	24	19	9	28	28
Reg Noble	Toronto	24	17	11	28	19
Sprague Cleghorn	Montreal	24	17	9	26	80
Georges Boucher	Ottawa	23	13	12	25	12
Odie Cleghorn	Montreal	23	21	3	24	26

1922-23

Team	GP	W	L	T	GF	GA	PTS
*Ottawa	24	14	9	1	77	54	29
Montreal	24	13	9	2	73	61	28
Toronto	24	13	10	1	82	88	27
Hamilton	24	6	18	0	81	110	12

Leading Scorers

Player	Team	GP	G	A	PTS	PIM
Babe Dye	Toronto	22	26	11	37	19
Cy Denneny	Ottawa	24	23	11	34	28
Billy Boucher	Montreal	24	24	7	31	55
Jack Adams	Toronto	23	19	9	28	42
Mickey Roach	Hamilton	24	17	10	27	8
Odie Cleghorn	Montreal	24	19	6	25	18
Georges Boucher	Ottawa	24	14	9	23	58
Reg Noble	Toronto	24	12	11	23	47
Cully Wilson	Hamilton	23	16	5	21	46
Aurel Joliat	Montreal	24	12	9	21	37

1923-24

Team	GP	W	L	T	GF	GA	PTS
Ottawa	24	16	8	0	74	54	32
*Montreal	24	13	11	0	59	48	26
Toronto	24	10	14	0	59	85	20
Hamilton	24	9	15	0	63	68	18

Leading Scorers

Player	Team	GP	G	A	PTS	PIM
Cy Denneny	Ottawa	22	22	2	24	10
Georges Boucher	Ottawa	21	13	10	23	38
Billy Boucher	Montreal	23	16	6	22	48
Billy Burch	Hamilton	24	16	6	22	6
Aurel Joliat	Montreal	24	15	5	20	27
Babe Dye	Toronto	19	16	3	19	23
Jack Adams	Toronto	22	14	4	18	51
Reg Noble	Toronto	24	12	5	17	79
Frank Nighbor	Ottawa	20	11	6	17	16
Howie Morenz	Montreal	24	13	3	16	20
King Clancy	Ottawa	24	8	8	16	26

1924-25

Team	GP	W	L	T	GF	GA	PTS
Hamilton	30	19	10	1	90	60	39
Toronto	30	19	11	0	90	84	38
• Montreal	30	17	11	2	93	56	36
Ottawa	30	17	12	1	83	66	35
Mtl. Maroons	30	9	19	2	45	65	20
Boston	30	6	24	0	49	119	12

• NHL Champion (Stanley Cup won by Victoria Cougars, WCHL)

Leading Scorers

Player	Team	GP	G	A	PTS	PIM
Babe Dye	Toronto	29	38	8	46	41
Cy Denneny	Ottawa	29	27	15	42	16
Aurel Joliat	Montreal	25	30	11	41	85
Howie Morenz	Montreal	30	28	11	39	46
Red Green	Hamilton	30	19	15	34	81
Jack Adams	Toronto	27	21	10	31	67
Billy Boucher	Montreal	30	17	13	30	92
Billy Burch	Hamilton	27	20	7	27	10
Jimmy Herberts	Boston	30	17	7	24	55
Hooley Smith	Ottawa	30	10	13	23	81

1925-26

Team	GP	W	L	T	GF	GA	PTS
Ottawa	36	24	8	4	77	42	52
*Mtl. Maroons	36	20	11	5	91	73	45
Pittsburgh	36	19	16	1	82	70	39
Boston	36	17	15	4	92	85	38
NY Americans	36	12	20	4	68	89	28
Toronto	36	12	21	3	92	114	27
Montreal	36	11	24	1	79	108	23

Leading Scorers

Player	Team	GP	G	A	PTS	PIM
Nels Stewart	Mtl. Maroons	36	34	8	42	119
Cy Denneny	Ottawa	36	24	12	36	18
Carson Cooper	Boston	36	28	3	31	10
Jimmy Herberts	Boston	36	26	5	31	47
Howie Morenz	Montreal	31	23	3	26	39
Jack Adams	Toronto	36	21	5	26	52
Aurel Joliat	Montreal	35	17	9	26	52
Billy Burch	NY Americans	36	22	3	25	33
Hooley Smith	Ottawa	28	16	9	25	53
Frank Nighbor	Ottawa	35	12	13	25	40

1926-27
Canadian Division

Team	GP	W	L	T	GF	GA	PTS
*Ottawa	44	30	10	4	86	69	64
Montreal	44	28	14	2	99	67	58
Mtl. Maroons	44	20	20	4	71	68	44
NY Americans	44	17	25	2	82	91	36
Toronto	44	15	24	5	79	94	35

American Division

Team	GP	W	L	T	GF	GA	PTS
NY Rangers	44	25	13	6	95	72	56
Boston	44	21	20	3	97	89	45
Chicago	44	19	22	3	115	116	41
Pittsburgh	44	15	26	3	79	108	33
Detroit	44	12	28	4	76	105	28

Leading Scorers

Player	Team	GP	G	A	PTS	PIM
Bill Cook	NY Rangers	44	33	4	37	58
Dick Irvin	Chicago	43	18	18	36	34
Howie Morenz	Montreal	44	25	7	32	49
Frank Fredrickson	Det., Bos.	41	18	13	31	46
Babe Dye	Chicago	41	25	5	30	14
Ace Bailey	Toronto	42	15	13	28	82
Frank Boucher	NY Rangers	44	13	15	28	17
Billy Burch	NY Americans	43	19	8	27	40
Harry Oliver	Boston	42	18	6	24	17
Duke Keats	Bos., Det.	42	16	8	24	52

1927-28
Canadian Division

Team	GP	W	L	T	GF	GA	PTS
Montreal	44	26	11	7	116	48	59
Mtl. Maroons	44	24	14	6	96	77	54
Ottawa	44	20	14	10	78	57	50
Toronto	44	18	18	8	89	88	44
NY Americans	44	11	27	6	63	128	28

American Division

Team	GP	W	L	T	GF	GA	PTS
Boston	44	20	13	11	77	70	51
*NY Rangers	44	19	16	9	94	79	47
Pittsburgh	44	19	17	8	67	76	46
Detroit	44	19	19	6	88	79	44
Chicago	44	7	34	3	68	134	17

Leading Scorers

Player	Team	GP	G	A	PTS	PIM
Howie Morenz	Montreal	43	33	18	51	66
Aurel Joliat	Montreal	44	28	11	39	105
Frank Boucher	NY Rangers	44	23	12	35	15
George Hay	Detroit	42	22	13	35	20
Nels Stewart	Mtl. Maroons	41	27	7	34	104
Art Gagne	Montreal	44	20	10	30	75
Bun Cook	NY Rangers	44	14	14	28	45
Bill Carson	Toronto	32	20	6	26	36
Frank Finnigan	Ottawa	38	20	5	25	34
Bill Cook	NY Rangers	43	18	6	24	42
Duke Keats	Det., Chi.	38	14	10	24	60

1928-29
Canadian Division

Team	GP	W	L	T	GF	GA	PTS
Montreal	44	22	7	15	71	43	59
NY Americans	44	19	13	12	53	53	50
Toronto	44	21	18	5	85	69	47
Ottawa	44	14	17	13	54	67	41
Mtl. Maroons	44	15	20	9	67	65	39

American Division

Team	GP	W	L	T	GF	GA	PTS
*Boston	44	26	13	5	89	52	57
NY Rangers	44	21	13	10	72	65	52
Detroit	44	19	16	9	72	63	47
Pittsburgh	44	9	27	8	46	80	26
Chicago	44	7	29	8	33	85	22

Leading Scorers

Player	Team	GP	G	A	PTS	PIM
Ace Bailey	Toronto	44	22	10	32	78
Nels Stewart	Mtl. Maroons	44	21	8	29	74
Carson Cooper	Detroit	43	18	9	27	14
Howie Morenz	Montreal	42	17	10	27	47
Andy Blair	Toronto	44	12	15	27	41
Frank Boucher	NY Rangers	44	10	16	26	8
Harry Oliver	Boston	43	17	6	23	24
Bill Cook	NY Rangers	43	15	8	23	41
Jimmy Ward	Mtl. Maroons	43	14	8	22	46

Seven players tied with 19 points

1929-30
Canadian Division

Team	GP	W	L	T	GF	GA	PTS
Mtl. Maroons	44	23	16	5	141	114	51
*Montreal	44	21	14	9	142	114	51
Ottawa	44	21	15	8	138	118	50
Toronto	44	17	21	6	116	124	40
NY Americans	44	14	25	5	113	161	33

American Division

Team	GP	W	L	T	GF	GA	PTS
Boston	44	38	5	1	179	98	77
Chicago	44	21	18	5	117	111	47
NY Rangers	44	17	17	10	136	143	44
Detroit	44	14	24	6	117	133	34
Pittsburgh	44	5	36	3	102	185	13

Leading Scorers

Player	Team	GP	G	A	PTS	PIM
Cooney Weiland	Boston	44	43	30	73	27
Frank Boucher	NY Rangers	42	26	36	62	16
Dit Clapper	Boston	44	41	20	61	48
Bill Cook	NY Rangers	44	29	30	59	56
Hec Kilrea	Ottawa	44	36	22	58	72
Nels Stewart	Mtl. Maroons	44	39	16	55	81
Howie Morenz	Montreal	44	40	10	50	72
Normie Himes	NY Americans	44	28	22	50	15
Joe Lamb	Ottawa	44	29	20	49	119
Dutch Gainor	Boston	42	18	31	49	39

1930-31
Canadian Division

Team	GP	W	L	T	GF	GA	PTS
*Montreal	44	26	10	8	129	89	60
Toronto	44	22	13	9	118	99	53
Mtl. Maroons	44	20	18	6	105	106	46
NY Americans	44	18	16	10	76	74	46
Ottawa	44	10	30	4	91	142	24

American Division

Team	GP	W	L	T	GF	GA	PTS
Boston	44	28	10	6	143	90	62
Chicago	44	24	17	3	108	78	51
NY Rangers	44	19	16	9	106	87	47
Detroit	44	16	21	7	102	105	39
Philadelphia	44	4	36	4	76	184	12

Leading Scorers

Player	Team	GP	G	A	PTS	PIM
Howie Morenz	Montreal	39	28	23	51	49
Ebbie Goodfellow	Detroit	44	25	23	48	32
Charlie Conacher	Toronto	37	31	12	43	78
Bill Cook	NY Rangers	43	30	12	42	39
Ace Bailey	Toronto	40	23	19	42	46
Joe Primeau	Toronto	38	9	32	41	18
Nels Stewart	Mtl. Maroons	42	25	14	39	75
Frank Boucher	NY Rangers	44	12	27	39	20
Cooney Weiland	Boston	44	25	13	38	14
Bun Cook	NY Rangers	44	18	17	35	72
Aurel Joliat	Montreal	43	13	22	35	73

1931-32

Canadian Division

Team	GP	W	L	T	GF	GA	PTS
Montreal	48	25	16	7	128	111	57
*Toronto	48	23	18	7	155	127	53
Mtl. Maroons	48	19	22	7	142	139	45
NY Americans	48	16	24	8	95	142	40

American Division

Team	GP	W	L	T	GF	GA	PTS
NY Rangers	48	23	17	8	134	112	54
Chicago	48	18	19	11	86	101	47
Detroit	48	18	20	10	95	108	46
Boston	48	15	21	12	122	117	42

Leading Scorers

Player	Team	GP	G	A	PTS	PIM
Busher Jackson	Toronto	48	28	25	53	63
Joe Primeau	Toronto	46	13	37	50	25
Howie Morenz	Montreal	48	24	25	49	46
Charlie Conacher	Toronto	44	34	14	48	66
Bill Cook	NY Rangers	48	34	14	48	33
Dave Trottier	Mtl. Maroons	48	26	18	44	94
Hooley Smith	Mtl. Maroons	43	11	33	44	49
Babe Siebert	Mtl. Maroons	48	21	18	39	64
Dit Clapper	Boston	48	17	22	39	21
Aurel Joliat	Montreal	48	15	24	39	46

1932-33

Canadian Division

Team	GP	W	L	T	GF	GA	PTS
Toronto	48	24	18	6	119	111	54
Mtl. Maroons	48	22	20	6	135	119	50
Montreal	48	18	25	5	92	115	41
NY Americans	48	15	22	11	91	118	41
Ottawa	48	11	27	10	88	131	32

American Division

Team	GP	W	L	T	GF	GA	PTS
Boston	48	25	15	8	124	88	58
Detroit	48	25	15	8	111	93	58
*NY Rangers	48	23	17	8	135	107	54
Chicago	48	16	20	12	88	101	44

Leading Scorers

Player	Team	GP	G	A	PTS	PIM
Bill Cook	NY Rangers	48	28	22	50	51
Busher Jackson	Toronto	48	27	17	44	43
Baldy Northcott	Mtl. Maroons	48	22	21	43	30
Hooley Smith	Mtl. Maroons	48	20	21	41	66
Paul Haynes	Mtl. Maroons	48	16	25	41	18
Aurel Joliat	Montreal	48	18	21	39	53
Marty Barry	Boston	48	24	13	37	40
Bun Cook	NY Rangers	48	22	15	37	35
Nels Stewart	Boston	47	18	18	36	62
Howie Morenz	Montreal	46	14	21	35	32
Johnny Gagnon	Montreal	48	12	23	35	64
Eddie Shore	Boston	48	8	27	35	102
Frank Boucher	NY Rangers	46	7	28	35	4

1933-34

Canadian Division

Team	GP	W	L	T	GF	GA	PTS
Toronto	48	26	13	9	174	119	61
Montreal	48	22	20	6	99	101	50
Mtl. Maroons	48	19	18	11	117	122	49
NY Americans	48	15	23	10	104	132	40
Ottawa	48	13	29	6	115	143	32

American Division

Team	GP	W	L	T	GF	GA	PTS
Detroit	48	24	14	10	113	98	58
*Chicago	48	20	17	11	88	83	51
NY Rangers	48	21	19	8	120	113	50
Boston	48	18	25	5	111	130	41

Leading Scorers

Player	Team	GP	G	A	PTS	PIM
Charlie Conacher	Toronto	42	32	20	52	38
Joe Primeau	Toronto	45	14	32	46	8
Frank Boucher	NY Rangers	48	14	30	44	4
Marty Barry	Boston	48	27	12	39	12
Cecil Dillon	NY Rangers	48	13	26	39	10
Nels Stewart	Boston	48	21	17	38	68
Busher Jackson	Toronto	38	20	18	38	38
Aurel Joliat	Montreal	48	22	15	37	27
Hooley Smith	Mtl. Maroons	47	18	19	37	58
Paul Thompson	Chicago	48	20	16	36	17

1934-35

Canadian Division

Team	GP	W	L	T	GF	GA	PTS
Toronto	48	30	14	4	157	111	64
*Mtl. Maroons	48	24	19	5	123	92	53
Montreal	48	19	23	6	110	145	44
NY Americans	48	12	27	9	100	142	33
St. Louis	48	11	31	6	86	144	28

American Division

Team	GP	W	L	T	GF	GA	PTS
Boston	48	26	16	6	129	112	58
Chicago	48	26	17	5	118	88	57
NY Rangers	48	22	20	6	137	139	50
Detroit	48	19	22	7	127	114	45

Leading Scorers

Player	Team	GP	G	A	PTS	PIM
Charlie Conacher	Toronto	47	36	21	57	24
Syd Howe	St.L., Det.	50	22	25	47	34
Larry Aurie	Detroit	48	17	29	46	24
Frank Boucher	NY Rangers	48	13	32	45	2
Busher Jackson	Toronto	42	22	22	44	27
Herbie Lewis	Detroit	47	16	27	43	26
Art Chapman	NY Americans	47	9	34	43	4
Marty Barry	Boston	48	20	20	40	33
Sweeney Schriner	NY Americans	48	18	22	40	6
Nels Stewart	Boston	47	21	18	39	45
Paul Thompson	Chicago	48	16	23	39	20

1935-36

Canadian Division

Team	GP	W	L	T	GF	GA	PTS
Mtl. Maroons	48	22	16	10	114	106	54
Toronto	48	23	19	6	126	106	52
NY Americans	48	16	25	7	109	122	39
Montreal	48	11	26	11	82	123	33

American Division

Team	GP	W	L	T	GF	GA	PTS
*Detroit	48	24	16	8	124	103	56
Boston	48	22	20	6	92	83	50
Chicago	48	21	19	8	93	92	50
NY Rangers	48	19	17	12	91	96	50

Leading Scorers

Player	Team	GP	G	A	PTS	PIM
Sweeney Schriner	NY Americans	48	19	26	45	8
Marty Barry	Detroit	48	21	19	40	16
Paul Thompson	Chicago	45	17	23	40	19
Bill Thoms	Toronto	48	23	15	38	29
Charlie Conacher	Toronto	44	23	15	38	74
Hooley Smith	Mtl. Maroons	47	19	19	38	75
Doc Romnes	Chicago	48	13	25	38	6
Art Chapman	NY Americans	47	10	28	38	14
Herbie Lewis	Detroit	45	14	23	37	25
Baldy Northcott	Mtl. Maroons	48	15	21	36	41

1936-37

Canadian Division

Team	GP	W	L	T	GF	GA	PTS
Montreal	48	24	18	6	115	111	54
Mtl. Maroons	48	22	17	9	126	110	53
Toronto	48	22	21	5	119	115	49
NY Americans	48	15	29	4	122	161	34

American Division

Team	GP	W	L	T	GF	GA	PTS
*Detroit	48	25	14	9	128	102	59
Boston	48	23	18	7	120	110	53
NY Rangers	48	19	20	9	117	106	47
Chicago	48	14	27	7	99	131	35

Leading Scorers

Player	Team	GP	G	A	PTS	PIM
Sweeney Schriner	NY Americans	48	21	25	46	17
Syl Apps	Toronto	48	16	29	45	10
Marty Barry	Detroit	48	17	27	44	6
Larry Aurie	Detroit	45	23	20	43	20
Busher Jackson	Toronto	46	21	19	40	12
Johnny Gagnon	Montreal	48	20	16	36	38
Bob Gracie	Mtl. Maroons	47	11	25	36	18
Nels Stewart	Bos., NYA	43	23	12	35	37
Paul Thompson	Chicago	47	17	18	35	28
Bill Cowley	Boston	46	13	22	35	4

1937-38

Canadian Division

Team	GP	W	L	T	GF	GA	PTS
Toronto	48	24	15	9	151	127	57
NY Americans	48	19	18	11	110	111	49
Montreal	48	18	17	13	123	128	49
Mtl. Maroons	48	12	30	6	101	149	30

American Division

Team	GP	W	L	T	GF	GA	PTS
Boston	48	30	11	7	142	89	67
NY Rangers	48	27	15	6	149	96	60
*Chicago	48	14	25	9	97	139	37
Detroit	48	12	25	11	99	133	35

Leading Scorers

Player	Team	GP	G	A	PTS	PIM
Gordie Drillon	Toronto	48	26	26	52	4
Syl Apps	Toronto	47	21	29	50	9
Paul Thompson	Chicago	48	22	22	44	14
Georges Mantha	Montreal	47	23	19	42	12
Cecil Dillon	NY Rangers	48	21	18	39	6
Bill Cowley	Boston	48	17	22	39	8
Sweeney Schriner	NY Americans	49	21	17	38	22
Bill Thoms	Toronto	48	14	24	38	14
Clint Smith	NY Rangers	48	14	23	37	0
Nels Stewart	NY Americans	48	19	17	36	29
Neil Colville	NY Rangers	45	17	19	36	11

1938-39

Team	GP	W	L	T	GF	GA	PTS
*Boston	48	36	10	2	156	76	74
NY Rangers	48	26	16	6	149	105	58
Toronto	48	19	20	9	114	107	47
NY Americans	48	17	21	10	119	157	44
Detroit	48	18	24	6	107	128	42
Montreal	48	15	24	9	115	146	39
Chicago	48	12	28	8	91	132	32

Leading Scorers

Player	Team	GP	G	A	PTS	PIM
Toe Blake	Montreal	48	24	23	47	10
Sweeney Schriner	NY Americans	48	13	31	44	20
Bill Cowley	Boston	34	8	34	42	2
Clint Smith	NY Rangers	48	21	20	41	2
Marty Barry	Detroit	48	13	28	41	4
Syl Apps	Toronto	44	15	25	40	4
Tom Anderson	NY Americans	48	13	27	40	14
Johnny Gottselig	Chicago	48	16	23	39	15
Paul Haynes	Montreal	47	5	33	38	27
Roy Conacher	Boston	47	26	11	37	12
Lorne Carr	NY Americans	46	19	18	37	16
Neil Colville	NY Rangers	48	18	19	37	12
Phil Watson	NY Rangers	48	15	22	37	42

1939-40

Team	GP	W	L	T	GF	GA	PTS
Boston	48	31	12	5	170	98	67
*NY Rangers	48	27	11	10	136	77	64
Toronto	48	25	17	6	134	110	56
Chicago	48	23	19	6	112	120	52
Detroit	48	16	26	6	91	126	38
NY Americans	48	15	29	4	106	140	34
Montreal	48	10	33	5	90	168	25

Leading Scorers

Player	Team	GP	G	A	PTS	PIM
Milt Schmidt	Boston	48	22	30	52	37
Woody Dumart	Boston	48	22	21	43	16
Bobby Bauer	Boston	48	17	26	43	2
Gordie Drillon	Toronto	43	21	19	40	13
Bill Cowley	Boston	48	13	27	40	24
Bryan Hextall	NY Rangers	48	24	15	39	52
Neil Colville	NY Rangers	48	19	19	38	22
Syd Howe	Detroit	46	14	23	37	17
Toe Blake	Montreal	48	17	19	36	48
Murray Armstrong	NY Americans	48	16	20	36	12

1940-41

Team	GP	W	L	T	GF	GA	PTS
*Boston	48	27	8	13	168	102	67
Toronto	48	28	14	6	145	99	62
Detroit	48	21	16	11	112	102	53
NY Rangers	48	21	19	8	143	125	50
Chicago	48	16	25	7	112	139	39
Montreal	48	16	26	6	121	147	38
NY Americans	48	8	29	11	99	186	27

Leading Scorers

Player	Team	GP	G	A	PTS	PIM
Bill Cowley	Boston	46	17	45	62	16
Bryan Hextall	NY Rangers	48	26	18	44	16
Gordie Drillon	Toronto	42	23	21	44	2
Syl Apps	Toronto	41	20	24	44	6
Lynn Patrick	NY Rangers	48	20	24	44	12
Syd Howe	Detroit	48	20	24	44	8
Neil Colville	NY Rangers	48	14	28	42	28
Eddie Wiseman	Boston	48	16	24	40	10
Bobby Bauer	Boston	48	17	22	39	2
Sweeney Schriner	Toronto	48	24	14	38	6
Roy Conacher	Boston	40	24	14	38	7
Milt Schmidt	Boston	44	13	25	38	23

1941-42

Team	GP	W	L	T	GF	GA	PTS
NY Rangers	48	29	17	2	177	143	60
*Toronto	48	27	18	3	158	136	57
Boston	48	25	17	6	160	118	56
Chicago	48	22	23	3	145	155	47
Detroit	48	19	25	4	140	147	42
Montreal	48	18	27	3	134	173	39
Brooklyn	48	16	29	3	133	175	35

Leading Scorers

Player	Team	GP	G	A	PTS	PIM
Bryan Hextall	NY Rangers	48	24	32	56	30
Lynn Patrick	NY Rangers	47	32	22	54	18
Don Grosso	Detroit	48	23	30	53	13
Phil Watson	NY Rangers	48	15	37	52	48
Sid Abel	Detroit	48	18	31	49	45
Toe Blake	Montreal	47	17	28	45	19
Bill Thoms	Chicago	47	15	30	45	8
Gordie Drillon	Toronto	48	23	18	41	6
Syl Apps	Toronto	38	18	23	41	0
Tom Anderson	Brooklyn	48	12	29	41	54

1942-43

Team	GP	W	L	T	GF	GA	PTS
*Detroit	50	25	14	11	169	124	61
Boston	50	24	17	9	195	176	57
Toronto	50	22	19	9	198	159	53
Montreal	50	19	19	12	181	191	50
Chicago	50	17	18	15	179	180	49
NY Rangers	50	11	31	8	161	253	30

Leading Scorers

Player	Team	GP	G	A	PTS	PIM
Doug Bentley	Chicago	50	33	40	73	18
Bill Cowley	Boston	48	27	45	72	10
Max Bentley	Chicago	47	26	44	70	2
Lynn Patrick	NY Rangers	50	22	39	61	28
Lorne Carr	Toronto	50	27	33	60	15
Billy Taylor	Toronto	50	18	42	60	2
Bryan Hextall	NY Rangers	50	27	32	59	28
Toe Blake	Montreal	48	23	36	59	28
Elmer Lach	Montreal	45	18	40	58	14
Buddy O'Connor	Montreal	50	15	43	58	2

1943-44

Team	GP	W	L	T	GF	GA	PTS
*Montreal	50	38	5	7	234	109	83
Detroit	50	26	18	6	214	177	58
Toronto	50	23	23	4	214	174	50
Chicago	50	22	23	5	178	187	49
Boston	50	19	26	5	223	268	43
NY Rangers	50	6	39	5	162	310	17

Leading Scorers

Player	Team	GP	G	A	PTS	PIM
Herb Cain	Boston	48	36	46	82	4
Doug Bentley	Chicago	50	38	39	77	22
Lorne Carr	Toronto	50	36	38	74	9
Carl Liscombe	Detroit	50	36	37	73	17
Elmer Lach	Montreal	48	24	48	72	23
Clint Smith	Chicago	50	23	49	72	4
Bill Cowley	Boston	36	30	41	71	12
Bill Mosienko	Chicago	50	32	38	70	10
Art Jackson	Boston	49	28	41	69	8
Gus Bodnar	Toronto	50	22	40	62	18

1944-45

Team	GP	W	L	T	GF	GA	PTS
Montreal	50	38	8	4	228	121	80
Detroit	50	31	14	5	218	161	67
*Toronto	50	24	22	4	183	161	52
Boston	50	16	30	4	179	219	36
Chicago	50	13	30	7	141	194	33
NY Rangers	50	11	29	10	154	247	32

Leading Scorers

Player	Team	GP	G	A	PTS	PIM
Elmer Lach	Montreal	50	26	54	80	37
Maurice Richard	Montreal	50	50	23	73	36
Toe Blake	Montreal	49	29	38	67	15
Bill Cowley	Boston	49	25	40	65	2
Ted Kennedy	Toronto	49	29	25	54	14
Bill Mosienko	Chicago	50	28	26	54	0
Joe Carveth	Detroit	50	26	28	54	6
Ab DeMarco	NY Rangers	50	24	30	54	10
Clint Smith	Chicago	50	23	31	54	0
Syd Howe	Detroit	46	17	36	53	6

1945-46

Team	GP	W	L	T	GF	GA	PTS
*Montreal	50	28	17	5	172	134	61
Boston	50	24	18	8	167	156	56
Chicago	50	23	20	7	200	178	53
Detroit	50	20	20	10	146	159	50
Toronto	50	19	24	7	174	185	45
NY Rangers	50	13	28	9	144	191	35

Leading Scorers

Player	Team	GP	G	A	PTS	PIM
Max Bentley	Chicago	47	31	30	61	6
Gaye Stewart	Toronto	50	37	15	52	8
Toe Blake	Montreal	50	29	21	50	2
Clint Smith	Chicago	50	26	24	50	2
Maurice Richard	Montreal	50	27	21	48	50
Bill Mosienko	Chicago	40	18	30	48	12
Ab DeMarco	NY Rangers	50	20	27	47	20
Elmer Lach	Montreal	50	13	34	47	34
Alex Kaleta	Chicago	49	19	27	46	17
Billy Taylor	Toronto	48	23	18	41	14
Pete Horeck	Chicago	50	20	21	41	34

1946-47

Team	GP	W	L	T	GF	GA	PTS
Montreal	60	34	16	10	189	138	78
*Toronto	60	31	19	10	209	172	72
Boston	60	26	23	11	190	175	63
Detroit	60	22	27	11	190	193	55
NY Rangers	60	22	32	6	167	186	50
Chicago	60	19	37	4	193	274	42

Leading Scorers

Player	Team	GP	G	A	PTS	PIM
Max Bentley	Chicago	60	29	43	72	12
Maurice Richard	Montreal	60	45	26	71	69
Billy Taylor	Detroit	60	17	46	63	35
Milt Schmidt	Boston	59	27	35	62	40
Ted Kennedy	Toronto	60	28	32	60	27
Doug Bentley	Chicago	52	21	34	55	18
Bobby Bauer	Boston	58	30	24	54	4
Roy Conacher	Detroit	60	30	24	54	6
Bill Mosienko	Chicago	59	25	27	52	2
Woody Dumart	Boston	60	24	28	52	12

1947-48

Team	GP	W	L	T	GF	GA	PTS
*Toronto	60	32	15	13	182	143	77
Detroit	60	30	18	12	187	148	72
Boston	60	23	24	13	167	168	59
NY Rangers	60	21	26	13	176	201	55
Montreal	60	20	29	11	147	169	51
Chicago	60	20	34	6	195	225	46

Leading Scorers

Player	Team	GP	G	A	PTS	PIM
Elmer Lach	Montreal	60	30	31	61	72
Buddy O'Connor	NY Rangers	60	24	36	60	8
Doug Bentley	Chicago	60	20	37	57	16
Gaye Stewart	Tor., Chi.	61	27	29	56	83
Max Bentley	Chi., Tor.	59	26	28	54	14
Bud Poile	Tor., Chi.	58	25	29	54	17
Maurice Richard	Montreal	53	28	25	53	89
Syl Apps	Toronto	55	26	27	53	12
Ted Lindsay	Detroit	60	33	19	52	95
Roy Conacher	Chicago	52	22	27	49	4

1948-49

Team	GP	W	L	T	GF	GA	PTS
Detroit	60	34	19	7	195	145	75
Boston	60	29	23	8	178	163	66
Montreal	60	28	23	9	152	126	65
*Toronto	60	22	25	13	147	161	57
Chicago	60	21	31	8	173	211	50
NY Rangers	60	18	31	11	133	172	47

Leading Scorers

Player	Team	GP	G	A	PTS	PIM
Roy Conacher	Chicago	60	26	42	68	8
Doug Bentley	Chicago	58	23	43	66	38
Sid Abel	Detroit	60	28	26	54	49
Ted Lindsay	Detroit	50	26	28	54	97
Jim Conacher	Det., Chi.	59	26	23	49	43
Paul Ronty	Boston	60	20	29	49	11
Harry Watson	Toronto	60	26	19	45	0
Billy Reay	Montreal	60	22	23	45	33
Gus Bodnar	Chicago	59	19	26	45	14
Johnny Peirson	Boston	59	22	21	43	45

1949-50

Team	GP	W	L	T	GF	GA	PTS
*Detroit	70	37	19	14	229	164	88
Montreal	70	29	22	19	172	150	77
Toronto	70	31	27	12	176	173	74
NY Rangers	70	28	31	11	170	189	67
Boston	70	22	32	16	198	228	60
Chicago	70	22	38	10	203	244	54

Leading Scorers

Player	Team	GP	G	A	PTS	PIM
Ted Lindsay	Detroit	69	23	55	78	141
Sid Abel	Detroit	69	34	35	69	46
Gordie Howe	Detroit	70	35	33	68	69
Maurice Richard	Montreal	70	43	22	65	114
Paul Ronty	Boston	70	23	36	59	8
Roy Conacher	Chicago	70	25	31	56	16
Doug Bentley	Chicago	64	20	33	53	28
Johnny Peirson	Boston	57	27	25	52	49
Metro Prystai	Chicago	65	29	22	51	31
Bep Guidolin	Chicago	70	17	34	51	42

1950-51

Team	GP	W	L	T	GF	GA	PTS
Detroit	70	44	13	13	236	139	101
*Toronto	70	41	16	13	212	138	95
Montreal	70	25	30	15	173	184	65
Boston	70	22	30	18	178	197	62
NY Rangers	70	20	29	21	169	201	61
Chicago	70	13	47	10	171	280	36

Leading Scorers

Player	Team	GP	G	A	PTS	PIM
Gordie Howe	Detroit	70	43	43	86	74
Maurice Richard	Montreal	65	42	24	66	97
Max Bentley	Toronto	67	21	41	62	34
Sid Abel	Detroit	69	23	38	61	30
Milt Schmidt	Boston	62	22	39	61	33
Ted Kennedy	Toronto	63	18	43	61	32
Ted Lindsay	Detroit	67	24	35	59	110
Tod Sloan	Toronto	70	31	25	56	105
Red Kelly	Detroit	70	17	37	54	24
Sid Smith	Toronto	70	30	21	51	10
Cal Gardner	Toronto	66	23	28	51	42

1951-52

Team	GP	W	L	T	GF	GA	PTS
*Detroit	70	44	14	12	215	133	100
Montreal	70	34	26	10	195	164	78
Toronto	70	29	25	16	168	157	74
Boston	70	25	29	16	162	176	66
NY Rangers	70	23	34	13	192	219	59
Chicago	70	17	44	9	158	241	43

Leading Scorers

Player	Team	GP	G	A	PTS	PIM
Gordie Howe	Detroit	70	47	39	86	78
Ted Lindsay	Detroit	70	30	39	69	123
Elmer Lach	Montreal	70	15	50	65	36
Don Raleigh	NY Rangers	70	19	42	61	14
Sid Smith	Toronto	70	27	30	57	6
Bernie Geoffrion	Montreal	67	30	24	54	66
Bill Mosienko	Chicago	70	31	22	53	10
Sid Abel	Detroit	62	17	36	53	32
Ted Kennedy	Toronto	70	19	33	52	33
Milt Schmidt	Boston	69	21	29	50	57
Johnny Peirson	Boston	68	20	30	50	30

1952-53

Team	GP	W	L	T	GF	GA	PTS
Detroit	70	36	16	18	222	133	90
*Montreal	70	28	23	19	155	148	75
Boston	70	28	29	13	152	172	69
Chicago	70	27	28	15	169	175	69
Toronto	70	27	30	13	156	167	67
NY Rangers	70	17	37	16	152	211	50

Leading Scorers

Player	Team	GP	G	A	PTS	PIM
Gordie Howe	Detroit	70	49	46	95	57
Ted Lindsay	Detroit	70	32	39	71	111
Maurice Richard	Montreal	70	28	33	61	112
Wally Hergesheimer	NY Rangers	70	30	29	59	10
Alex Delvecchio	Detroit	70	16	43	59	28
Paul Ronty	NY Rangers	70	16	38	54	20
Metro Prystai	Detroit	70	16	34	50	12
Red Kelly	Detroit	70	19	27	46	8
Bert Olmstead	Montreal	69	17	28	45	83
Fleming Mackell	Boston	65	27	17	44	63
Jim McFadden	Chicago	70	23	21	44	29

1953-54

Team	GP	W	L	T	GF	GA	PTS
*Detroit	70	37	19	14	191	132	88
Montreal	70	35	24	11	195	141	81
Toronto	70	32	24	14	152	131	78
Boston	70	32	28	10	177	181	74
NY Rangers	70	29	31	10	161	182	68
Chicago	70	12	51	7	133	242	31

Leading Scorers

Player	Team	GP	G	A	PTS	PIM
Gordie Howe	Detroit	70	33	48	81	109
Maurice Richard	Montreal	70	37	30	67	112
Ted Lindsay	Detroit	70	26	36	62	110
Bernie Geoffrion	Montreal	54	29	25	54	87
Bert Olmstead	Montreal	70	15	37	52	85
Red Kelly	Detroit	62	16	33	49	18
Dutch Reibel	Detroit	69	15	33	48	18
Ed Sandford	Boston	70	16	31	47	42
Fleming Mackell	Boston	67	15	32	47	60
Ken Mosdell	Montreal	67	22	24	46	64
Paul Ronty	NY Rangers	70	13	33	46	18

1954-55

Team	GP	W	L	T	GF	GA	PTS
*Detroit	70	42	17	11	204	134	95
Montreal	70	41	18	11	228	157	93
Toronto	70	24	24	22	147	135	70
Boston	70	23	26	21	169	188	67
NY Rangers	70	17	35	18	150	210	52
Chicago	70	13	40	17	161	235	43

Leading Scorers

Player	Team	GP	G	A	PTS	PIM
Bernie Geoffrion	Montreal	70	38	37	75	57
Maurice Richard	Montreal	67	38	36	74	125
Jean Béliveau	Montreal	70	37	36	73	58
Dutch Reibel	Detroit	70	25	41	66	15
Gordie Howe	Detroit	64	29	33	62	68
Red Sullivan	Chicago	69	19	42	61	51
Bert Olmstead	Montreal	70	10	48	58	103
Sid Smith	Toronto	70	33	21	54	14
Ken Mosdell	Montreal	70	22	32	54	82
Danny Lewicki	NY Rangers	70	29	24	53	8

1955-56

Team	GP	W	L	T	GF	GA	PTS
*Montreal	70	45	15	10	222	131	100
Detroit	70	30	24	16	183	148	76
NY Rangers	70	32	28	10	204	203	74
Toronto	70	24	33	13	153	181	61
Boston	70	23	34	13	147	185	59
Chicago	70	19	39	12	155	216	50

Leading Scorers

Player	Team	GP	G	A	PTS	PIM
Jean Béliveau	Montreal	70	47	41	88	143
Gordie Howe	Detroit	70	38	41	79	100
Maurice Richard	Montreal	70	38	33	71	89
Bert Olmstead	Montreal	70	14	56	70	94
Tod Sloan	Toronto	70	37	29	66	100
Andy Bathgate	NY Rangers	70	19	47	66	59
Bernie Geoffrion	Montreal	59	29	33	62	66
Dutch Reibel	Detroit	68	17	39	56	10
Alex Delvecchio	Detroit	70	25	26	51	24
Dave Creighton	NY Rangers	70	20	31	51	43
Bill Gadsby	NY Rangers	70	9	42	51	84

1956-57

Team	GP	W	L	T	GF	GA	PTS
Detroit	70	38	20	12	198	157	88
*Montreal	70	35	23	12	210	155	82
Boston	70	34	24	12	195	174	80
NY Rangers	70	26	30	14	184	227	66
Toronto	70	21	34	15	174	192	57
Chicago	70	16	39	15	169	225	47

Leading Scorers

Player	Team	GP	G	A	PTS	PIM
Gordie Howe	Detroit	70	44	45	89	72
Ted Lindsay	Detroit	70	30	55	85	103
Jean Béliveau	Montreal	69	33	51	84	105
Andy Bathgate	NY Rangers	70	27	50	77	60
Ed Litzenberger	Chicago	70	32	32	64	48
Maurice Richard	Montreal	63	33	29	62	74
Don McKenney	Boston	69	21	39	60	31
Dickie Moore	Montreal	70	29	29	58	56
Henri Richard	Montreal	63	18	36	54	71
Norm Ullman	Detroit	64	16	36	52	47

1957-58

Team	GP	W	L	T	GF	GA	PTS
*Montreal	70	43	17	10	250	158	96
NY Rangers	70	32	25	13	195	188	77
Detroit	70	29	29	12	176	207	70
Boston	70	27	28	15	199	194	69
Chicago	70	24	39	7	163	202	55
Toronto	70	21	38	11	192	226	53

Leading Scorers

Player	Team	GP	G	A	PTS	PIM
Dickie Moore	Montreal	70	36	48	84	65
Henri Richard	Montreal	67	28	52	80	56
Andy Bathgate	NY Rangers	65	30	48	78	42
Gordie Howe	Detroit	64	33	44	77	40
Bronco Horvath	Boston	67	30	36	66	71
Ed Litzenberger	Chicago	70	32	30	62	63
Fleming Mackell	Boston	70	20	40	60	72
Jean Béliveau	Montreal	55	27	32	59	93
Alex Delvecchio	Detroit	70	21	38	59	22
Don McKenney	Boston	70	28	30	58	22

1958-59

Team	GP	W	L	T	GF	GA	PTS
*Montreal	70	39	18	13	258	158	91
Boston	70	32	29	9	205	215	73
Chicago	70	28	29	13	197	208	69
Toronto	70	27	32	11	189	201	65
NY Rangers	70	26	32	12	201	217	64
Detroit	70	25	37	8	167	218	58

Leading Scorers

Player	Team	GP	G	A	PTS	PIM
Dickie Moore	Montreal	70	41	55	96	61
Jean Béliveau	Montreal	64	45	46	91	67
Andy Bathgate	NY Rangers	70	40	48	88	48
Gordie Howe	Detroit	70	32	46	78	57
Ed Litzenberger	Chicago	70	33	44	77	37
Bernie Geoffrion	Montreal	59	22	44	66	30
Red Sullivan	NY Rangers	70	21	42	63	56
Andy Hebenton	NY Rangers	70	33	29	62	8
Don McKenney	Boston	70	32	30	62	20
Tod Sloan	Chicago	59	27	35	62	79

1959-60

Team	GP	W	L	T	GF	GA	PTS
*Montreal	70	40	18	12	255	178	92
Toronto	70	35	26	9	199	195	79
Chicago	70	28	29	13	191	180	69
Detroit	70	26	29	15	186	197	67
Boston	70	28	34	8	220	241	64
NY Rangers	70	17	38	15	187	247	49

Leading Scorers

Player	Team	GP	G	A	PTS	PIM
Bobby Hull	Chicago	70	39	42	81	68
Bronco Horvath	Boston	68	39	41	80	60
Jean Béliveau	Montreal	60	34	40	74	57
Andy Bathgate	NY Rangers	70	26	48	74	28
Henri Richard	Montreal	70	30	43	73	66
Gordie Howe	Detroit	70	28	45	73	46
Bernie Geoffrion	Montreal	59	30	41	71	36
Don McKenney	Boston	70	20	49	69	28
Vic Stasiuk	Boston	69	29	39	68	121
Dean Prentice	NY Rangers	70	32	34	66	43

1960-61

Team	GP	W	L	T	GF	GA	PTS
Montreal	70	41	19	10	254	188	92
Toronto	70	39	19	12	234	176	90
*Chicago	70	29	24	17	198	180	75
Detroit	70	25	29	16	195	215	66
NY Rangers	70	22	38	10	204	248	54
Boston	70	15	42	13	176	254	43

Leading Scorers

Player	Team	GP	G	A	PTS	PIM
Bernie Geoffrion	Montreal	64	50	45	95	29
Jean Béliveau	Montreal	69	32	58	90	57
Frank Mahovlich	Toronto	70	48	36	84	131
Andy Bathgate	NY Rangers	70	29	48	77	22
Gordie Howe	Detroit	64	23	49	72	30
Norm Ullman	Detroit	70	28	42	70	34
Red Kelly	Toronto	64	20	50	70	12
Dickie Moore	Montreal	57	35	34	69	62
Henri Richard	Montreal	70	24	44	68	91
Alex Delvecchio	Detroit	70	27	35	62	26

1961-62

Team	GP	W	L	T	GF	GA	PTS
Montreal	70	42	14	14	259	166	98
*Toronto	70	37	22	11	232	180	85
Chicago	70	31	26	13	217	186	75
NY Rangers	70	26	32	12	195	207	64
Detroit	70	23	33	14	184	219	60
Boston	70	15	47	8	177	306	38

Leading Scorers

Player	Team	GP	G	A	PTS	PIM
Bobby Hull	Chicago	70	50	34	84	35
Andy Bathgate	NY Rangers	70	28	56	84	44
Gordie Howe	Detroit	70	33	44	77	54
Stan Mikita	Chicago	70	25	52	77	97
Frank Mahovlich	Toronto	70	33	38	71	87
Alex Delvecchio	Detroit	70	26	43	69	18
Ralph Backstrom	Montreal	66	27	38	65	29
Norm Ullman	Detroit	70	26	38	64	54
Bill Hay	Chicago	60	11	52	63	34
Claude Provost	Montreal	70	33	29	62	22

1962-63

Team	GP	W	L	T	GF	GA	PTS
*Toronto	70	35	23	12	221	180	82
Chicago	70	32	21	17	194	178	81
Montreal	70	28	19	23	225	183	79
Detroit	70	32	25	13	200	194	77
NY Rangers	70	22	36	12	211	233	56
Boston	70	14	39	17	198	281	45

Leading Scorers

Player	Team	GP	G	A	PTS	PIM
Gordie Howe	Detroit	70	38	48	86	100
Andy Bathgate	NY Rangers	70	35	46	81	54
Stan Mikita	Chicago	65	31	45	76	69
Frank Mahovlich	Toronto	67	36	37	73	56
Henri Richard	Montreal	67	23	50	73	57
Jean Béliveau	Montreal	69	18	49	67	68
John Bucyk	Boston	69	27	39	66	36
Alex Delvecchio	Detroit	70	20	44	64	8
Bobby Hull	Chicago	65	31	31	62	27
Murray Oliver	Boston	65	22	40	62	38

1963-64

Team	GP	W	L	T	GF	GA	PTS
Montreal	70	36	21	13	209	167	85
Chicago	70	36	22	12	218	169	84
*Toronto	70	33	25	12	192	172	78
Detroit	70	30	29	11	191	204	71
NY Rangers	70	22	38	10	186	242	54
Boston	70	18	40	12	170	212	48

Leading Scorers

Player	Team	GP	G	A	PTS	PIM
Stan Mikita	Chicago	70	39	50	89	146
Bobby Hull	Chicago	70	43	44	87	50
Jean Béliveau	Montreal	68	28	50	78	42
Andy Bathgate	NYR, Tor.	71	19	58	77	34
Gordie Howe	Detroit	69	26	47	73	70
Kenny Wharram	Chicago	70	39	32	71	18
Murray Oliver	Boston	70	24	44	68	41
Phil Goyette	NY Rangers	67	24	41	65	15
Rod Gilbert	NY Rangers	70	24	40	64	62
Dave Keon	Toronto	70	23	37	60	6

1964-65

Team	GP	W	L	T	GF	GA	PTS
Detroit	70	40	23	7	224	175	87
*Montreal	70	36	23	11	211	185	83
Chicago	70	34	28	8	224	176	76
Toronto	70	30	26	14	204	173	74
NY Rangers	70	20	38	12	179	246	52
Boston	70	21	43	6	166	253	48

Leading Scorers

Player	Team	GP	G	A	PTS	PIM
Stan Mikita	Chicago	70	28	59	87	154
Norm Ullman	Detroit	70	42	41	83	70
Gordie Howe	Detroit	70	29	47	76	104
Bobby Hull	Chicago	61	39	32	71	32
Alex Delvecchio	Detroit	68	25	42	67	16
Claude Provost	Montreal	70	27	37	64	28
Rod Gilbert	NY Rangers	70	25	36	61	52
Pierre Pilote	Chicago	68	14	45	59	162
John Bucyk	Boston	68	26	29	55	24
Ralph Backstrom	Montreal	70	25	30	55	41
Phil Esposito	Chicago	70	23	32	55	44

1965-66

Team	GP	W	L	T	GF	GA	PTS
*Montreal	70	41	21	8	239	173	90
Chicago	70	37	25	8	240	187	82
Toronto	70	34	25	11	208	187	79
Detroit	70	31	27	12	221	194	74
Boston	70	21	43	6	174	275	48
NY Rangers	70	18	41	11	195	261	47

Leading Scorers

Player	Team	GP	G	A	PTS	PIM
Bobby Hull	Chicago	65	54	43	97	70
Stan Mikita	Chicago	68	30	48	78	58
Bobby Rousseau	Montreal	70	30	48	78	20
Jean Béliveau	Montreal	67	29	48	77	50
Gordie Howe	Detroit	70	29	46	75	83
Norm Ullman	Detroit	70	31	41	72	35
Alex Delvecchio	Detroit	70	31	38	69	16
Bob Nevin	NY Rangers	69	29	33	62	10
Henri Richard	Montreal	62	22	39	61	47
Murray Oliver	Boston	70	18	42	60	30

1966-67

Team	GP	W	L	T	GF	GA	PTS
Chicago	70	41	17	12	264	170	94
Montreal	70	32	25	13	202	188	77
*Toronto	70	32	27	11	204	211	75
NY Rangers	70	30	28	12	188	189	72
Detroit	70	27	39	4	212	241	58
Boston	70	17	43	10	182	253	44

Leading Scorers

Player	Team	GP	G	A	PTS	PIM
Stan Mikita	Chicago	70	35	62	97	12
Bobby Hull	Chicago	66	52	28	80	52
Norm Ullman	Detroit	68	26	44	70	26
Kenny Wharram	Chicago	70	31	34	65	21
Gordie Howe	Detroit	69	25	40	65	53
Bobby Rousseau	Montreal	68	19	44	63	58
Phil Esposito	Chicago	69	21	40	61	40
Phil Goyette	NY Rangers	70	12	49	61	6
Doug Mohns	Chicago	61	25	35	60	58
Henri Richard	Montreal	65	21	34	55	28
Alex Delvecchio	Detroit	70	17	38	55	10

1967-68

East Division

Team	GP	W	L	T	GF	GA	PTS
*Montreal	74	42	22	10	236	167	94
NY Rangers	74	39	23	12	226	183	90
Boston	74	37	27	10	259	216	84
Chicago	74	32	26	16	212	222	80
Toronto	74	33	31	10	209	176	76
Detroit	74	27	35	12	245	257	66

West Division

Team	GP	W	L	T	GF	GA	PTS
Philadelphia	74	31	32	11	173	179	73
Los Angeles	74	31	33	10	200	224	72
St. Louis	74	27	31	16	177	191	70
Minnesota	74	27	32	15	191	226	69
Pittsburgh	74	27	34	13	195	216	67
Oakland	74	15	42	17	153	219	47

Leading Scorers

Player	Team	GP	G	A	PTS	PIM
Stan Mikita	Chicago	72	40	47	87	14
Phil Esposito	Boston	74	35	49	84	21
Gordie Howe	Detroit	74	39	43	82	53
Jean Ratelle	NY Rangers	74	32	46	78	18
Rod Gilbert	NY Rangers	73	29	48	77	12
Bobby Hull	Chicago	71	44	31	75	39
Norm Ullman	Det., Tor.	71	35	37	72	28
Alex Delvecchio	Detroit	74	22	48	70	14
John Bucyk	Boston	72	30	39	69	8
Kenny Wharram	Chicago	74	27	42	69	18

1968-69

East Division

Team	GP	W	L	T	GF	GA	PTS
*Montreal	76	46	19	11	271	202	103
Boston	76	42	18	16	303	221	100
NY Rangers	76	41	26	9	231	196	91
Toronto	76	35	26	15	234	217	85
Detroit	76	33	31	12	239	221	78
Chicago	76	34	33	9	280	246	77

West Division

Team	GP	W	L	T	GF	GA	PTS
St. Louis	76	37	25	14	204	157	88
Oakland	76	29	36	11	219	251	69
Philadelphia	76	20	35	21	174	225	61
Los Angeles	76	24	42	10	185	260	58
Pittsburgh	76	20	45	11	189	252	51
Minnesota	76	18	43	15	189	270	51

Leading Scorers

Player	Team	GP	G	A	PTS	PIM
Phil Esposito	Boston	74	49	77	126	79
Bobby Hull	Chicago	74	58	49	107	48
Gordie Howe	Detroit	76	44	59	103	58
Stan Mikita	Chicago	74	30	67	97	52
Ken Hodge	Boston	75	45	45	90	75
Yvan Cournoyer	Montreal	76	43	44	87	31
Alex Delvecchio	Detroit	72	25	58	83	8
Red Berenson	St. Louis	76	35	47	82	43
Jean Béliveau	Montreal	69	33	49	82	55
Frank Mahovlich	Detroit	76	49	29	78	38
Jean Ratelle	NY Rangers	75	32	46	78	26

1969-70

East Division

Team	GP	W	L	T	GF	GA	PTS
Chicago	76	45	22	9	250	170	99
*Boston	76	40	17	19	277	216	99
Detroit	76	40	21	15	246	199	95
NY Rangers	76	38	22	16	246	189	92
Montreal	76	38	22	16	244	201	92
Toronto	76	29	34	13	222	242	71

West Division

Team	GP	W	L	T	GF	GA	PTS
St. Louis	76	37	27	12	224	179	86
Pittsburgh	76	26	38	12	182	238	64
Minnesota	76	19	35	22	224	257	60
Oakland	76	22	40	14	169	243	58
Philadelphia	76	17	35	24	197	225	58
Los Angeles	76	14	52	10	168	290	38

Leading Scorers

Player	Team	GP	G	A	PTS	PIM
Bobby Orr	Boston	76	33	87	120	125
Phil Esposito	Boston	76	43	56	99	50
Stan Mikita	Chicago	76	39	47	86	50
Phil Goyette	St. Louis	72	29	49	78	16
Walt Tkaczuk	NY Rangers	76	27	50	77	38
Jean Ratelle	NY Rangers	75	32	42	74	28
Red Berenson	St. Louis	67	33	39	72	38
Jean-Paul Parise	Minnesota	74	24	48	72	72
Gordie Howe	Detroit	76	31	40	71	58
Frank Mahovlich	Detroit	74	38	32	70	59
Dave Balon	NY Rangers	76	33	37	70	100
John McKenzie	Boston	72	29	41	70	114

1970-71

East Division

Team	GP	W	L	T	GF	GA	PTS
Boston	78	57	14	7	399	207	121
NY Rangers	78	49	18	11	259	177	109
*Montreal	78	42	23	13	291	216	97
Toronto	78	37	33	8	248	211	82
Buffalo	78	24	39	15	217	291	63
Vancouver	78	24	46	8	229	296	56
Detroit	78	22	45	11	209	308	55

West Division

Team	GP	W	L	T	GF	GA	PTS
Chicago	78	49	20	9	277	184	107
St. Louis	78	34	25	19	223	208	87
Philadelphia	78	28	33	17	207	225	73
Minnesota	78	28	34	16	191	223	72
Los Angeles	78	25	40	13	239	303	63
Pittsburgh	78	21	37	20	221	240	62
California	78	20	53	5	199	320	45

Leading Scorers

Player	Team	GP	G	A	PTS	PIM
Phil Esposito	Boston	78	76	76	152	71
Bobby Orr	Boston	78	37	102	139	91
John Bucyk	Boston	78	51	65	116	8
Ken Hodge	Boston	78	43	62	105	113
Bobby Hull	Chicago	78	44	52	96	32
Norm Ullman	Toronto	73	34	51	85	24
Wayne Cashman	Boston	77	21	58	79	100
John McKenzie	Boston	65	31	46	77	120
Dave Keon	Toronto	76	38	38	76	4
Jean Béliveau	Montreal	70	25	51	76	40
Fred Stanfield	Boston	75	24	52	76	12

1971-72

East Division

Team	GP	W	L	T	GF	GA	PTS
*Boston	78	54	13	11	330	204	119
NY Rangers	78	48	17	13	317	192	109
Montreal	78	46	16	16	307	205	108
Toronto	78	33	31	14	209	208	80
Detroit	78	33	35	10	261	262	76
Buffalo	78	16	43	19	203	289	51
Vancouver	78	20	50	8	203	297	48

West Division

Team	GP	W	L	T	GF	GA	PTS
Chicago	78	46	17	15	256	166	107
Minnesota	78	37	29	12	212	191	86
St. Louis	78	28	39	11	208	247	67
Pittsburgh	78	26	38	14	220	258	66
Philadelphia	78	26	38	14	200	236	66
California	78	21	39	18	216	288	60
Los Angeles	78	20	49	9	206	305	49

Leading Scorers

Player	Team	GP	G	A	PTS	PIM
Phil Esposito	Boston	76	66	67	133	76
Bobby Orr	Boston	76	37	80	117	106
Jean Ratelle	NY Rangers	63	46	63	109	4
Vic Hadfield	NY Rangers	78	50	56	106	142
Rod Gilbert	NY Rangers	73	43	54	97	64
Frank Mahovlich	Montreal	76	43	53	96	36
Bobby Hull	Chicago	78	50	43	93	24
Yvan Cournoyer	Montreal	73	47	36	83	15
John Bucyk	Boston	78	32	51	83	4
Bobby Clarke	Philadelphia	78	35	46	81	87
Jacques Lemaire	Montreal	77	32	49	81	26

1972-73

East Division

Team	GP	W	L	T	GF	GA	PTS
*Montreal	78	52	10	16	329	184	120
Boston	78	51	22	5	330	235	107
NY Rangers	78	47	23	8	297	208	102
Buffalo	78	37	27	14	257	219	88
Detroit	78	37	29	12	265	243	86
Toronto	78	27	41	10	247	279	64
Vancouver	78	22	47	9	233	339	53
NY Islanders	78	12	60	6	170	347	30

West Division

Team	GP	W	L	T	GF	GA	PTS
Chicago	78	42	27	9	284	225	93
Philadelphia	78	37	30	11	296	256	85
Minnesota	78	37	30	11	254	230	85
St. Louis	78	32	34	12	233	251	76
Pittsburgh	78	32	37	9	257	265	73
Los Angeles	78	31	36	11	232	245	73
Atlanta	78	25	38	15	191	239	65
California	78	16	46	16	213	323	48

Leading Scorers

Player	Team	GP	G	A	PTS	PIM
Phil Esposito	Boston	78	55	75	130	87
Bobby Clarke	Philadelphia	78	37	67	104	80
Bobby Orr	Boston	63	29	72	101	99
Rick MacLeish	Philadelphia	78	50	50	100	69
Jacques Lemaire	Montreal	77	44	51	95	16
Jean Ratelle	NY Rangers	78	41	53	94	12
Mickey Redmond	Detroit	76	52	41	93	24
John Bucyk	Boston	78	40	53	93	12
Frank Mahovlich	Montreal	78	38	55	93	51
Jim Pappin	Chicago	76	41	51	92	82

Clark Gillies of the New York Islanders cracked the top 10 in scoring for the only time in his career with a career-high 91 points in 1978-79.

1973-74

East Division

Team	GP	W	L	T	GF	GA	PTS
Boston	78	52	17	9	349	221	113
Montreal	78	45	24	9	293	240	99
NY Rangers	78	40	24	14	300	251	94
Toronto	78	35	27	16	274	230	86
Buffalo	78	32	34	12	242	250	76
Detroit	78	29	39	10	255	319	68
Vancouver	78	24	43	11	224	296	59
NY Islanders	78	19	41	18	182	247	56

West Division

Team	GP	W	L	T	GF	GA	PTS
*Philadelphia	78	50	16	12	273	164	112
Chicago	78	41	14	23	272	164	105
Los Angeles	78	33	33	12	233	231	78
Atlanta	78	30	34	14	214	238	74
Pittsburgh	78	28	41	9	242	273	65
St. Louis	78	26	40	12	206	248	64
Minnesota	78	23	38	17	235	275	63
California	78	13	55	10	195	342	36

Leading Scorers

Player	Team	GP	G	A	PTS	PIM
Phil Esposito	Boston	78	68	77	145	58
Bobby Orr	Boston	74	32	90	122	82
Ken Hodge	Boston	76	50	55	105	43
Wayne Cashman	Boston	78	30	59	89	111
Bobby Clarke	Philadelphia	77	35	52	87	113
Rick Martin	Buffalo	78	52	34	86	38
Syl Apps Jr.	Pittsburgh	75	24	61	85	37
Darryl Sittler	Toronto	78	38	46	84	55
Lowell MacDonald	Pittsburgh	78	43	39	82	14
Brad Park	NY Rangers	78	25	57	82	148
Dennis Hextall	Minnesota	78	20	62	82	138

1974-75

PRINCE OF WALES CONFERENCE

Norris Division

Team	GP	W	L	T	GF	GA	PTS
Montreal	80	47	14	19	374	225	113
Los Angeles	80	42	17	21	269	185	105
Pittsburgh	80	37	28	15	326	289	89
Detroit	80	23	45	12	259	335	58
Washington	80	8	67	5	181	446	21

Adams Division

Team	GP	W	L	T	GF	GA	PTS
Buffalo	80	49	16	15	354	240	113
Boston	80	40	26	14	345	245	94
Toronto	80	31	33	16	280	309	78
California	80	19	48	13	212	316	51

CLARENCE CAMPBELL CONFERENCE

Patrick Division

Team	GP	W	L	T	GF	GA	PTS
*Philadelphia	80	51	18	11	293	181	113
NY Rangers	80	37	29	14	319	276	88
NY Islanders	80	33	25	22	264	221	88
Atlanta	80	34	31	15	243	233	83

Smythe Division

Team	GP	W	L	T	GF	GA	PTS
Vancouver	80	38	32	10	271	254	86
St. Louis	80	35	31	14	269	267	84
Chicago	80	37	35	8	268	241	82
Minnesota	80	23	50	7	221	341	53
Kansas City	80	15	54	11	184	328	41

Leading Scorers

Player	Team	GP	G	A	PTS	PIM
Bobby Orr	Boston	80	46	89	135	101
Phil Esposito	Boston	79	61	66	127	62
Marcel Dionne	Detroit	80	47	74	121	14
Guy Lafleur	Montreal	70	53	66	119	37
Pete Mahovlich	Montreal	80	35	82	117	64
Bobby Clarke	Philadelphia	80	27	89	116	125
Rene Robert	Buffalo	74	40	60	100	75
Rod Gilbert	NY Rangers	76	36	61	97	22
Gilbert Perreault	Buffalo	68	39	57	96	36
Rick Martin	Buffalo	68	52	43	95	72

1975-76

PRINCE OF WALES CONFERENCE

Norris Division

Team	GP	W	L	T	GF	GA	PTS
*Montreal	80	58	11	11	337	174	127
Los Angeles	80	38	33	9	263	265	85
Pittsburgh	80	35	33	12	339	303	82
Detroit	80	26	44	10	226	300	62
Washington	80	11	59	10	224	394	32

Adams Division

Team	GP	W	L	T	GF	GA	PTS
Boston	80	48	15	17	313	237	113
Buffalo	80	46	21	13	339	240	105
Toronto	80	34	31	15	294	276	83
California	80	27	42	11	250	278	65

CLARENCE CAMPBELL CONFERENCE

Patrick Division

Team	GP	W	L	T	GF	GA	PTS
Philadelphia	80	51	13	16	348	209	118
NY Islanders	80	42	21	17	297	190	101
Atlanta	80	35	33	12	262	237	82
NY Rangers	80	29	42	9	262	333	67

Smythe Division

Team	GP	W	L	T	GF	GA	PTS
Chicago	80	32	30	18	254	261	82
Vancouver	80	33	32	15	271	272	81
St. Louis	80	29	37	14	249	290	72
Minnesota	80	20	53	7	195	303	47
Kansas City	80	12	56	12	190	351	36

Leading Scorers

Player	Team	GP	G	A	PTS	PIM
Guy Lafleur	Montreal	80	56	69	125	36
Bobby Clarke	Philadelphia	76	30	89	119	136
Gilbert Perreault	Buffalo	80	44	69	113	36
Bill Barber	Philadelphia	80	50	62	112	104
Pierre Larouche	Pittsburgh	76	53	58	111	33
Jean Ratelle	Bos., NYR	80	36	69	105	18
Pete Mahovlich	Montreal	80	34	71	105	76
Jean Pronovost	Pittsburgh	80	52	52	104	24
Darryl Sittler	Toronto	79	41	59	100	90
Syl Apps Jr.	Pittsburgh	80	32	67	99	24

1976-77

PRINCE OF WALES CONFERENCE

Norris Division

Team	GP	W	L	T	GF	GA	PTS
*Montreal	80	60	8	12	387	171	132
Los Angeles	80	34	31	15	271	241	83
Pittsburgh	80	34	33	13	240	252	81
Washington	80	24	42	14	221	307	62
Detroit	80	16	55	9	183	309	41

Adams Division

Team	GP	W	L	T	GF	GA	PTS
Boston	80	49	23	8	312	240	106
Buffalo	80	48	24	8	301	220	104
Toronto	80	33	32	15	301	285	81
Cleveland	80	25	42	13	240	292	63

CLARENCE CAMPBELL CONFERENCE

Patrick Division

Team	GP	W	L	T	GF	GA	PTS
Philadelphia	80	48	16	16	323	213	112
NY Islanders	80	47	21	12	288	193	106
Atlanta	80	34	34	12	264	265	80
NY Rangers	80	29	37	14	272	310	72

Smythe Division

Team	GP	W	L	T	GF	GA	PTS
St. Louis	80	32	39	9	239	276	73
Minnesota	80	23	39	18	240	310	64
Chicago	80	26	43	11	240	298	63
Vancouver	80	25	42	13	235	294	63
Colorado	80	20	46	14	226	307	54

Leading Scorers

Player	Team	GP	G	A	PTS	PIM
Guy Lafleur	Montreal	80	56	80	136	20
Marcel Dionne	Los Angeles	80	53	69	122	12
Steve Shutt	Montreal	80	60	45	105	28
Rick MacLeish	Philadelphia	79	49	48	97	42
Gilbert Perreault	Buffalo	80	39	56	95	30
Tim Young	Minnesota	80	29	66	95	58
Jean Ratelle	Boston	78	33	61	94	22
Lanny McDonald	Toronto	80	46	44	90	77
Darryl Sittler	Toronto	73	38	52	90	89
Bobby Clarke	Philadelphia	80	27	63	90	71

1977-78

PRINCE OF WALES CONFERENCE

Norris Division

Team	GP	W	L	T	GF	GA	PTS
*Montreal	80	59	10	11	359	183	129
Detroit	80	32	34	14	252	266	78
Los Angeles	80	31	34	15	243	245	77
Pittsburgh	80	25	37	18	254	321	68
Washington	80	17	49	14	195	321	48

Adams Division

Team	GP	W	L	T	GF	GA	PTS
Boston	80	51	18	11	333	218	113
Buffalo	80	44	19	17	288	215	105
Toronto	80	41	29	10	271	237	92
Cleveland	80	22	45	13	230	325	57

CLARENCE CAMPBELL CONFERENCE

Patrick Division

Team	GP	W	L	T	GF	GA	PTS
NY Islanders	80	48	17	15	334	210	111
Philadelphia	80	45	20	15	296	200	105
Atlanta	80	34	27	19	274	252	87
NY Rangers	80	30	37	13	279	280	73

Smythe Division

Team	GP	W	L	T	GF	GA	PTS
Chicago	80	32	29	19	230	220	83
Colorado	80	19	40	21	257	305	59
Vancouver	80	20	43	17	239	320	57
St. Louis	80	20	47	13	195	304	53
Minnesota	80	18	53	9	218	325	45

Leading Scorers

Player	Team	GP	G	A	PTS	PIM
Guy Lafleur	Montreal	78	60	72	132	26
Bryan Trottier	NY Islanders	77	46	77	123	46
Darryl Sittler	Toronto	80	45	72	117	100
Jacques Lemaire	Montreal	76	36	61	97	14
Denis Potvin	NY Islanders	80	30	64	94	81
Mike Bossy	NY Islanders	73	53	38	91	6
Terry O'Reilly	Boston	77	29	61	90	211
Gilbert Perreault	Buffalo	79	41	48	89	20
Bobby Clarke	Philadelphia	71	21	68	89	83
Lanny McDonald	Toronto	74	47	40	87	54
Wilf Paiement	Colorado	80	31	56	87	114

1978-79

PRINCE OF WALES CONFERENCE

Norris Division

Team	GP	W	L	T	GF	GA	PTS
*Montreal	80	52	17	11	337	204	115
Pittsburgh	80	36	31	13	281	279	85
Los Angeles	80	34	34	12	292	286	80
Washington	80	24	41	15	273	338	63
Detroit	80	23	41	16	252	295	62

Adams Division

Team	GP	W	L	T	GF	GA	PTS
Boston	80	43	23	14	316	270	100
Buffalo	80	36	28	16	280	263	88
Toronto	80	34	33	13	267	252	81
Minnesota	80	28	40	12	257	289	68

CLARENCE CAMPBELL CONFERENCE

Patrick Division

Team	GP	W	L	T	GF	GA	PTS
NY Islanders	80	51	15	14	358	214	116
Philadelphia	80	40	25	15	281	248	95
NY Rangers	80	40	29	11	316	292	91
Atlanta	80	41	31	8	327	280	90

Smythe Division

Team	GP	W	L	T	GF	GA	PTS
Chicago	80	29	36	15	244	277	73
Vancouver	80	25	42	13	217	291	63
St. Louis	80	18	50	12	249	348	48
Colorado	80	15	53	12	210	331	42

Leading Scorers

Player	Team	GP	G	A	PTS	PIM
Bryan Trottier	NY Islanders	76	47	87	134	50
Marcel Dionne	Los Angeles	80	59	71	130	30
Guy Lafleur	Montreal	80	52	77	129	28
Mike Bossy	NY Islanders	80	69	57	126	25
Bob MacMillan	Atlanta	79	37	71	108	14
Guy Chouinard	Atlanta	80	50	57	107	14
Denis Potvin	NY Islanders	73	31	70	101	58
Bernie Federko	St. Louis	74	31	64	95	14
Dave Taylor	Los Angeles	78	43	48	91	124
Clark Gillies	NY Islanders	75	35	56	91	68

1979-80
PRINCE OF WALES CONFERENCE
Norris Division

Team	GP	W	L	T	GF	GA	PTS
Montreal	80	47	20	13	328	240	107
Los Angeles	80	30	36	14	290	313	74
Pittsburgh	80	30	37	13	251	303	73
Hartford	80	27	34	19	303	312	73
Detroit	80	26	43	11	268	306	63

Adams Division

Team	GP	W	L	T	GF	GA	PTS
Buffalo	80	47	17	16	318	201	110
Boston	80	46	21	13	310	234	105
Minnesota	80	36	28	16	311	253	88
Toronto	80	35	40	5	304	327	75
Quebec	80	25	44	11	248	313	61

CLARENCE CAMPBELL CONFERENCE
Patrick Division

Team	GP	W	L	T	GF	GA	PTS
Philadelphia	80	48	12	20	327	254	116
*NY Islanders	80	39	28	13	281	247	91
NY Rangers	80	38	32	10	308	284	86
Atlanta	80	35	32	13	282	269	83
Washington	80	27	40	13	261	293	67

Smythe Division

Team	GP	W	L	T	GF	GA	PTS
Chicago	80	34	27	19	241	250	87
St. Louis	80	34	34	12	266	278	80
Vancouver	80	27	37	16	256	281	70
Edmonton	80	28	39	13	301	322	69
Winnipeg	80	20	49	11	214	314	51
Colorado	80	19	48	13	234	308	51

Leading Scorers

Player	Team	GP	G	A	PTS	PIM
Marcel Dionne	Los Angeles	80	53	84	137	32
Wayne Gretzky	Edmonton	79	51	86	137	21
Guy Lafleur	Montreal	74	50	75	125	12
Gilbert Perreault	Buffalo	80	40	66	106	57
Mike Rogers	Hartford	80	44	61	105	10
Bryan Trottier	NY Islanders	78	42	62	104	68
Charlie Simmer	Los Angeles	64	56	45	101	65
Blaine Stoughton	Hartford	80	56	44	100	16
Darryl Sittler	Toronto	73	40	57	97	62
Blair MacDonald	Edmonton	80	46	48	94	6
Bernie Federko	St. Louis	79	38	56	94	24

1980-81
PRINCE OF WALES CONFERENCE
Norris Division

Team	GP	W	L	T	GF	GA	PTS
Montreal	80	45	22	13	332	232	103
Los Angeles	80	43	24	13	337	290	99
Pittsburgh	80	30	37	13	302	345	73
Hartford	80	21	41	18	292	372	60
Detroit	80	19	43	18	252	339	56

Adams Division

Team	GP	W	L	T	GF	GA	PTS
Buffalo	80	39	20	21	327	250	99
Boston	80	37	30	13	316	272	87
Minnesota	80	35	28	17	291	263	87
Quebec	80	30	32	18	314	318	78
Toronto	80	28	37	15	322	367	71

CLARENCE CAMPBELL CONFERENCE
Patrick Division

Team	GP	W	L	T	GF	GA	PTS
*NY Islanders	80	48	18	14	355	260	110
Philadelphia	80	41	24	15	313	249	97
Calgary	80	39	27	14	329	298	92
NY Rangers	80	30	36	14	312	317	74
Washington	80	26	36	18	286	317	70

Smythe Division

Team	GP	W	L	T	GF	GA	PTS
St. Louis	80	45	18	17	352	281	107
Chicago	80	31	33	16	304	315	78
Vancouver	80	28	32	20	289	301	76
Edmonton	80	29	35	16	328	327	74
Colorado	80	22	45	13	258	344	57
Winnipeg	80	9	57	14	246	400	32

Leading Scorers

Player	Team	GP	G	A	PTS	PIM
Wayne Gretzky	Edmonton	80	55	109	164	28
Marcel Dionne	Los Angeles	80	58	77	135	70
Kent Nilsson	Calgary	80	49	82	131	26
Mike Bossy	NY Islanders	79	68	51	119	32
Dave Taylor	Los Angeles	72	47	65	112	130
Peter Stastny	Quebec	77	39	70	109	37
Charlie Simmer	Los Angeles	65	56	49	105	62
Mike Rogers	Hartford	80	40	65	105	32
Bernie Federko	St. Louis	78	31	73	104	47
Jacques Richard	Quebec	78	52	51	103	39
Rick Middleton	Boston	80	44	59	103	16
Bryan Trottier	NY Islanders	73	31	72	103	74

1981-82
CLARENCE CAMPBELL CONFERENCE
Norris Division

Team	GP	W	L	T	GF	GA	PTS
Minnesota	80	37	23	20	346	288	94
Winnipeg	80	33	33	14	319	332	80
St. Louis	80	32	40	8	315	349	72
Chicago	80	30	38	12	332	363	72
Toronto	80	20	44	16	298	380	56
Detroit	80	21	47	12	270	351	54

Smythe Division

Team	GP	W	L	T	GF	GA	PTS
Edmonton	80	48	17	15	417	295	111
Vancouver	80	30	33	17	290	286	77
Calgary	80	29	34	17	334	345	75
Los Angeles	80	24	41	15	314	369	63
Colorado	80	18	49	13	241	362	49

PRINCE OF WALES CONFERENCE
Adams Division

Team	GP	W	L	T	GF	GA	PTS
Montreal	80	46	17	17	360	223	109
Boston	80	43	27	10	323	285	96
Buffalo	80	39	26	15	307	273	93
Quebec	80	33	31	16	356	345	82
Hartford	80	21	41	18	264	351	60

Patrick Division

Team	GP	W	L	T	GF	GA	PTS
*NY Islanders	80	54	16	10	385	250	118
NY Rangers	80	39	27	14	316	306	92
Philadelphia	80	38	31	11	325	313	87
Pittsburgh	80	31	36	13	310	337	75
Washington	80	26	41	13	319	338	65

Leading Scorers

Player	Team	GP	G	A	PTS	PIM
Wayne Gretzky	Edmonton	80	92	120	212	26
Mike Bossy	NY Islanders	80	64	83	147	22
Peter Stastny	Quebec	80	46	93	139	91
Dennis Maruk	Washington	80	60	76	136	128
Bryan Trottier	NY Islanders	80	50	79	129	88
Denis Savard	Chicago	80	32	87	119	82
Marcel Dionne	Los Angeles	78	50	67	117	50
Bobby Smith	Minnesota	80	43	71	114	82
Dino Ciccarelli	Minnesota	76	55	51	106	138
Dave Taylor	Los Angeles	78	39	67	106	130

1982-83
CLARENCE CAMPBELL CONFERENCE
Norris Division

Team	GP	W	L	T	GF	GA	PTS
Chicago	80	47	23	10	338	268	104
Minnesota	80	40	24	16	321	290	96
Toronto	80	28	40	12	293	330	68
St. Louis	80	25	40	15	285	316	65
Detroit	80	21	44	15	263	344	57

Smythe Division

Team	GP	W	L	T	GF	GA	PTS
Edmonton	80	47	21	12	424	315	106
Calgary	80	32	34	14	321	317	78
Vancouver	80	30	35	15	303	309	75
Winnipeg	80	33	39	8	311	333	74
Los Angeles	80	27	41	12	308	365	66

PRINCE OF WALES CONFERENCE
Adams Division

Team	GP	W	L	T	GF	GA	PTS
Boston	80	50	20	10	327	228	110
Montreal	80	42	24	14	350	286	98
Buffalo	80	38	29	13	318	285	89
Quebec	80	34	34	12	343	336	80
Hartford	80	19	54	7	261	403	45

Patrick Division

Team	GP	W	L	T	GF	GA	PTS
Philadelphia	80	49	23	8	326	240	106
*NY Islanders	80	42	26	12	302	226	96
Washington	80	39	25	16	306	283	94
NY Rangers	80	35	35	10	306	287	80
New Jersey	80	17	49	14	230	338	48
Pittsburgh	80	18	53	9	257	394	45

Leading Scorers

Player	Team	GP	G	A	PTS	PIM
Wayne Gretzky	Edmonton	80	71	125	196	59
Peter Stastny	Quebec	75	47	77	124	78
Denis Savard	Chicago	78	35	86	121	99
Mike Bossy	NY Islanders	79	60	58	118	20
Marcel Dionne	Los Angeles	80	56	51	107	22
Barry Pederson	Boston	77	46	61	107	47
Mark Messier	Edmonton	77	48	58	106	72
Michel Goulet	Quebec	80	57	48	105	51
Glenn Anderson	Edmonton	72	48	56	104	70
Kent Nilsson	Calgary	80	46	58	104	10
Jari Kurri	Edmonton	80	45	59	104	22

1983-84
CLARENCE CAMPBELL CONFERENCE
Norris Division

Team	GP	W	L	T	GF	GA	PTS
Minnesota	80	39	31	10	345	344	88
St. Louis	80	32	41	7	293	316	71
Detroit	80	31	42	7	298	323	69
Chicago	80	30	42	8	277	311	68
Toronto	80	26	45	9	303	387	61

Smythe Division

Team	GP	W	L	T	GF	GA	PTS
*Edmonton	80	57	18	5	446	314	119
Calgary	80	34	32	14	311	314	82
Vancouver	80	32	39	9	306	328	73
Winnipeg	80	31	38	11	340	374	73
Los Angeles	80	23	44	13	309	376	59

PRINCE OF WALES CONFERENCE
Adams Division

Team	GP	W	L	T	GF	GA	PTS
Boston	80	49	25	6	336	261	104
Buffalo	80	48	25	7	315	257	103
Quebec	80	42	28	10	360	278	94
Montreal	80	35	40	5	286	295	75
Hartford	80	28	42	10	288	320	66

Patrick Division

Team	GP	W	L	T	GF	GA	PTS
NY Islanders	80	50	26	4	357	269	104
Washington	80	48	27	5	308	226	101
Philadelphia	80	44	26	10	350	290	98
NY Rangers	80	42	29	9	314	304	93
New Jersey	80	17	56	7	231	350	41
Pittsburgh	80	16	58	6	254	390	38

Leading Scorers

Player	Team	GP	G	A	PTS	PIM
Wayne Gretzky	Edmonton	74	87	118	205	39
Paul Coffey	Edmonton	80	40	86	126	104
Michel Goulet	Quebec	75	56	65	121	76
Peter Stastny	Quebec	80	46	73	119	73
Mike Bossy	NY Islanders	67	51	67	118	8
Barry Pederson	Boston	80	39	77	116	64
Jari Kurri	Edmonton	64	52	61	113	14
Bryan Trottier	NY Islanders	68	40	71	111	59
Bernie Federko	St. Louis	79	41	66	107	43
Rick Middleton	Boston	80	47	58	105	14

1984-85
CLARENCE CAMPBELL CONFERENCE
Norris Division

Team	GP	W	L	T	GF	GA	PTS
St. Louis	80	37	31	12	299	288	86
Chicago	80	38	35	7	309	299	83
Detroit	80	27	41	12	313	357	66
Minnesota	80	25	43	12	268	321	62
Toronto	80	20	52	8	253	358	48

Smythe Division

Team	GP	W	L	T	GF	GA	PTS
*Edmonton	80	49	20	11	401	298	109
Winnipeg	80	43	27	10	358	332	96
Calgary	80	41	27	12	363	302	94
Los Angeles	80	34	32	14	339	326	82
Vancouver	80	25	46	9	284	401	59

PRINCE OF WALES CONFERENCE
Adams Division

Team	GP	W	L	T	GF	GA	PTS
Montreal	80	41	27	12	309	262	94
Quebec	80	41	30	9	323	275	91
Buffalo	80	38	28	14	290	237	90
Boston	80	36	34	10	303	287	82
Hartford	80	30	41	9	268	318	69

Patrick Division

Team	GP	W	L	T	GF	GA	PTS
Philadelphia	80	53	20	7	348	241	113
Washington	80	46	25	9	322	240	101
NY Islanders	80	40	34	6	345	312	86
NY Rangers	80	26	44	10	295	345	62
New Jersey	80	22	48	10	264	346	54
Pittsburgh	80	24	51	5	276	385	53

Leading Scorers

Player	Team	GP	G	A	PTS	PIM
Wayne Gretzky	Edmonton	80	73	135	208	52
Jari Kurri	Edmonton	73	71	64	135	30
Dale Hawerchuk	Winnipeg	80	53	77	130	74
Marcel Dionne	Los Angeles	80	46	80	126	46
Paul Coffey	Edmonton	80	37	84	121	97
Mike Bossy	NY Islanders	76	58	59	117	38
John Ogrodnick	Detroit	79	55	50	105	30
Denis Savard	Chicago	79	38	67	105	56
Bernie Federko	St. Louis	76	30	73	103	27
Mike Gartner	Washington	80	50	52	102	71

1985-86

CLARENCE CAMPBELL CONFERENCE

Norris Division

Team	GP	W	L	T	GF	GA	PTS
Chicago	80	39	33	8	351	349	86
Minnesota	80	38	33	9	327	305	85
St. Louis	80	37	34	9	302	291	83
Toronto	80	25	48	7	311	386	57
Detroit	80	17	57	6	266	415	40

Smythe Division

Team	GP	W	L	T	GF	GA	PTS
Edmonton	80	56	17	7	426	310	119
Calgary	80	40	31	9	354	315	89
Winnipeg	80	26	47	7	295	372	59
Vancouver	80	23	44	13	282	333	59
Los Angeles	80	23	49	8	284	389	54

PRINCE OF WALES CONFERENCE

Adams Division

Team	GP	W	L	T	GF	GA	PTS
Quebec	80	43	31	6	330	289	92
*Montreal	80	40	33	7	330	280	87
Boston	80	37	31	12	311	288	86
Hartford	80	40	36	4	332	302	84
Buffalo	80	37	37	6	296	291	80

Patrick Division

Team	GP	W	L	T	GF	GA	PTS
Philadelphia	80	53	23	4	335	241	110
Washington	80	50	23	7	315	272	107
NY Islanders	80	39	29	12	327	284	90
NY Rangers	80	36	38	6	280	276	78
Pittsburgh	80	34	38	8	313	305	76
New Jersey	80	28	49	3	300	374	59

Leading Scorers

Player	Team	GP	G	A	PTS	PIM
Wayne Gretzky	Edmonton	80	52	163	215	52
Mario Lemieux	Pittsburgh	79	48	93	141	43
Paul Coffey	Edmonton	79	48	90	138	120
Jari Kurri	Edmonton	78	68	63	131	22
Mike Bossy	NY Islanders	80	61	62	123	14
Peter Stastny	Quebec	76	41	81	122	60
Denis Savard	Chicago	80	47	69	116	111
Mats Naslund	Montreal	80	43	67	110	16
Dale Hawerchuk	Winnipeg	80	46	59	105	44
Neal Broten	Minnesota	80	29	76	105	47

1986-87

CLARENCE CAMPBELL CONFERENCE

Norris Division

Team	GP	W	L	T	GF	GA	PTS
St. Louis	80	32	33	15	281	293	79
Detroit	80	34	36	10	260	274	78
Chicago	80	29	37	14	290	310	72
Toronto	80	32	42	6	286	319	70
Minnesota	80	30	40	10	296	314	70

Smythe Division

Team	GP	W	L	T	GF	GA	PTS
*Edmonton	80	50	24	6	372	284	106
Calgary	80	46	31	3	318	289	95
Winnipeg	80	40	32	8	279	271	88
Los Angeles	80	31	41	8	318	341	70
Vancouver	80	29	43	8	282	314	66

PRINCE OF WALES CONFERENCE

Adams Division

Team	GP	W	L	T	GF	GA	PTS
Hartford	80	43	30	7	287	270	93
Montreal	80	41	29	10	277	241	92
Boston	80	39	34	7	301	276	85
Quebec	80	31	39	10	267	276	72
Buffalo	80	28	44	8	280	308	64

Patrick Division

Team	GP	W	L	T	GF	GA	PTS
Philadelphia	80	46	26	8	310	245	100
Washington	80	38	32	10	285	278	86
NY Islanders	80	35	33	12	279	281	82
NY Rangers	80	34	38	8	307	323	76
Pittsburgh	80	30	38	12	297	290	72
New Jersey	80	29	45	6	293	368	64

Leading Scorers

Player	Team	GP	G	A	PTS	PIM
Wayne Gretzky	Edmonton	79	62	121	183	28
Jari Kurri	Edmonton	79	54	54	108	41
Mario Lemieux	Pittsburgh	63	54	53	107	57
Mark Messier	Edmonton	77	37	70	107	73
Doug Gilmour	St. Louis	80	42	63	105	58
Dino Ciccarelli	Minnesota	80	52	51	103	92
Dale Hawerchuk	Winnipeg	80	47	53	100	54
Michel Goulet	Quebec	75	49	47	96	61
Tim Kerr	Philadelphia	75	58	37	95	57
Raymond Bourque	Boston	78	23	72	95	36

1987-88

CLARENCE CAMPBELL CONFERENCE

Norris Division

Team	GP	W	L	T	GF	GA	PTS
Detroit	80	41	28	11	322	269	93
St. Louis	80	34	38	8	278	294	76
Chicago	80	30	41	9	284	328	69
Toronto	80	21	49	10	273	345	52
Minnesota	80	19	48	13	242	349	51

Smythe Division

Team	GP	W	L	T	GF	GA	PTS
Calgary	80	48	23	9	397	305	105
*Edmonton	80	44	25	11	363	288	99
Winnipeg	80	33	36	11	292	310	77
Los Angeles	80	30	42	8	318	359	68
Vancouver	80	25	46	9	272	320	59

PRINCE OF WALES CONFERENCE

Adams Division

Team	GP	W	L	T	GF	GA	PTS
Montreal	80	45	22	13	298	238	103
Boston	80	44	30	6	300	251	94
Buffalo	80	37	32	11	283	305	85
Hartford	80	35	38	7	249	267	77
Quebec	80	32	43	5	271	306	69

Patrick Division

Team	GP	W	L	T	GF	GA	PTS
NY Islanders	80	39	31	10	308	267	88
Washington	80	38	33	9	281	249	85
Philadelphia	80	38	33	9	292	292	85
New Jersey	80	38	36	6	295	296	82
NY Rangers	80	36	34	10	300	283	82
Pittsburgh	80	36	35	9	319	316	81

Leading Scorers

Player	Team	GP	G	A	PTS	PIM
Mario Lemieux	Pittsburgh	77	70	98	168	92
Wayne Gretzky	Edmonton	64	40	109	149	24
Denis Savard	Chicago	80	44	87	131	95
Dale Hawerchuk	Winnipeg	80	44	77	121	59
Luc Robitaille	Los Angeles	80	53	58	111	82
Peter Stastny	Quebec	76	46	65	111	69
Mark Messier	Edmonton	77	37	74	111	103
Jimmy Carson	Los Angeles	80	55	52	107	45
Hakan Loob	Calgary	80	50	56	106	47
Michel Goulet	Quebec	80	48	58	106	56

1988-89

CLARENCE CAMPBELL CONFERENCE

Norris Division

Team	GP	W	L	T	GF	GA	PTS
Detroit	80	34	34	12	313	316	80
St. Louis	80	33	35	12	275	285	78
Minnesota	80	27	37	16	258	278	70
Chicago	80	27	41	12	297	335	66
Toronto	80	28	46	6	259	342	62

Smythe Division

Team	GP	W	L	T	GF	GA	PTS
*Calgary	80	54	17	9	354	226	117
Los Angeles	80	42	31	7	376	335	91
Edmonton	80	38	34	8	325	306	84
Vancouver	80	33	39	8	251	253	74
Winnipeg	80	26	42	12	300	355	64

PRINCE OF WALES CONFERENCE

Adams Division

Team	GP	W	L	T	GF	GA	PTS
Montreal	80	53	18	9	315	218	115
Boston	80	37	29	14	289	256	88
Buffalo	80	38	35	7	291	299	83
Hartford	80	37	38	5	299	290	79
Quebec	80	27	46	7	269	342	61

Patrick Division

Team	GP	W	L	T	GF	GA	PTS
Washington	80	41	29	10	305	259	92
Pittsburgh	80	40	33	7	347	349	87
NY Rangers	80	37	35	8	310	307	82
Philadelphia	80	36	36	8	307	285	80
New Jersey	80	27	41	12	281	325	66
NY Islanders	80	28	47	5	265	325	61

Leading Scorers

Player	Team	GP	G	A	PTS	PIM
Mario Lemieux	Pittsburgh	76	85	114	199	100
Wayne Gretzky	Los Angeles	78	54	114	168	26
Steve Yzerman	Detroit	80	65	90	155	61
Bernie Nicholls	Los Angeles	79	70	80	150	96
Rob Brown	Pittsburgh	68	49	66	115	118
Paul Coffey	Pittsburgh	75	30	83	113	193
Joe Mullen	Calgary	79	51	59	110	16
Jari Kurri	Edmonton	76	44	58	102	69
Jimmy Carson	Edmonton	80	49	51	100	36
Luc Robitaille	Los Angeles	78	46	52	98	65

1989-90

CLARENCE CAMPBELL CONFERENCE

Norris Division

Team	GP	W	L	T	GF	GA	PTS
Chicago	80	41	33	6	316	294	88
St. Louis	80	37	34	9	295	279	83
Toronto	80	38	38	4	337	358	80
Minnesota	80	36	40	4	284	291	76
Detroit	80	28	38	14	288	323	70

Smythe Division

Team	GP	W	L	T	GF	GA	PTS
Calgary	80	42	23	15	348	265	99
*Edmonton	80	38	28	14	315	283	90
Winnipeg	80	37	32	11	298	290	85
Los Angeles	80	34	39	7	338	337	75
Vancouver	80	25	41	14	245	306	64

PRINCE OF WALES CONFERENCE

Adams Division

Team	GP	W	L	T	GF	GA	PTS
Boston	80	46	25	9	289	232	101
Buffalo	80	45	27	8	286	248	98
Montreal	80	41	28	11	288	234	93
Hartford	80	38	33	9	275	268	85
Quebec	80	12	61	7	240	407	31

Patrick Division

Team	GP	W	L	T	GF	GA	PTS
NY Rangers	80	36	31	13	279	267	85
New Jersey	80	37	34	9	295	288	83
Washington	80	36	38	6	284	275	78
NY Islanders	80	31	38	11	281	288	73
Pittsburgh	80	32	40	8	318	359	72
Philadelphia	80	30	39	11	290	297	71

Leading Scorers

Player	Team	GP	G	A	PTS	PIM
Wayne Gretzky	Los Angeles	73	40	102	142	42
Mark Messier	Edmonton	79	45	84	129	79
Steve Yzerman	Detroit	79	62	65	127	79
Mario Lemieux	Pittsburgh	59	45	78	123	78
Brett Hull	St. Louis	80	72	41	113	24
Bernie Nicholls	L.A., NYR	79	39	73	112	86
Pierre Turgeon	Buffalo	80	40	66	106	29
Pat LaFontaine	NY Islanders	74	54	51	105	38
Paul Coffey	Pittsburgh	80	29	74	103	95
Joe Sakic	Quebec	80	39	63	102	27
Adam Oates	St. Louis	80	23	79	102	30

1990-91

CLARENCE CAMPBELL CONFERENCE

Norris Division

Team	GP	W	L	T	GF	GA	PTS
Chicago	80	49	23	8	284	211	106
St. Louis	80	47	22	11	310	250	105
Detroit	80	34	38	8	273	298	76
Minnesota	80	27	39	14	256	266	68
Toronto	80	23	46	11	241	318	57

Smythe Division

Team	GP	W	L	T	GF	GA	PTS
Los Angeles	80	46	24	10	340	254	102
Calgary	80	46	26	8	344	263	100
Edmonton	80	37	37	6	272	272	80
Vancouver	80	28	43	9	243	315	65
Winnipeg	80	26	43	11	260	288	63

PRINCE OF WALES CONFERENCE

Adams Division

Team	GP	W	L	T	GF	GA	PTS
Boston	80	44	24	12	299	264	100
Montreal	80	39	30	11	273	249	89
Buffalo	80	31	30	19	292	278	81
Hartford	80	31	38	11	238	276	73
Quebec	80	16	50	14	236	354	46

Patrick Division

Team	GP	W	L	T	GF	GA	PTS
*Pittsburgh	80	41	33	6	342	305	88
NY Rangers	80	36	31	13	297	265	85
Washington	80	37	36	7	258	258	81
New Jersey	80	32	33	15	272	264	79
Philadelphia	80	33	37	10	252	267	76
NY Islanders	80	25	45	10	223	290	60

Leading Scorers

Player	Team	GP	G	A	PTS	PIM
Wayne Gretzky	Los Angeles	78	41	122	163	16
Brett Hull	St. Louis	78	86	45	131	22
Adam Oates	St. Louis	61	25	90	115	29
Mark Recchi	Pittsburgh	78	40	73	113	48
John Cullen	Pit., Hfd.	78	39	71	110	101
Joe Sakic	Quebec	80	48	61	109	24
Steve Yzerman	Detroit	80	51	57	108	34
Theoren Fleury	Calgary	79	51	53	104	136
Al MacInnis	Calgary	78	28	75	103	90
Steve Larmer	Chicago	80	44	57	101	79

1991-92

CLARENCE CAMPBELL CONFERENCE

Norris Division

Team	GP	W	L	T	GF	GA	PTS
Detroit	80	43	25	12	320	256	98
Chicago	80	36	29	15	257	236	87
St. Louis	80	36	33	11	279	266	83
Minnesota	80	32	42	6	246	278	70
Toronto	80	30	43	7	234	294	67

Smythe Division

Team	GP	W	L	T	GF	GA	PTS
Vancouver	80	42	26	12	285	250	96
Los Angeles	80	35	31	14	287	296	84
Edmonton	80	36	34	10	295	297	82
Winnipeg	80	33	32	15	251	244	81
Calgary	80	31	37	12	296	305	74
San Jose	80	17	58	5	219	359	39

PRINCE OF WALES CONFERENCE

Adams Division

Team	GP	W	L	T	GF	GA	PTS
Montreal	80	41	28	11	267	207	93
Boston	80	36	32	12	270	275	84
Buffalo	80	31	37	12	289	299	74
Hartford	80	26	41	13	247	283	65
Quebec	80	20	48	12	255	318	52

Patrick Division

Team	GP	W	L	T	GF	GA	PTS
NY Rangers	80	50	25	5	321	246	105
Washington	80	45	27	8	330	275	98
*Pittsburgh	80	39	32	9	343	308	87
New Jersey	80	38	31	11	289	259	87
NY Islanders	80	34	35	11	291	299	79
Philadelphia	80	32	37	11	252	273	75

Leading Scorers

Player	Team	GP	G	A	PTS	PIM
Mario Lemieux	Pittsburgh	64	44	87	131	94
Kevin Stevens	Pittsburgh	80	54	69	123	254
Wayne Gretzky	Los Angeles	74	31	90	121	34
Brett Hull	St. Louis	73	70	39	109	48
Luc Robitaille	Los Angeles	80	44	63	107	95
Mark Messier	NY Rangers	79	35	72	107	76
Jeremy Roenick	Chicago	80	53	50	103	23
Steve Yzerman	Detroit	79	45	58	103	64
Brian Leetch	NY Rangers	80	22	80	102	26
Adam Oates	St.L., Bos.	80	20	79	99	22

1992-93

CLARENCE CAMPBELL CONFERENCE

Norris Division

Team	GP	W	L	T	GF	GA	PTS
Chicago	84	47	25	12	279	230	106
Detroit	84	47	28	9	369	280	103
Toronto	84	44	29	11	288	241	99
St. Louis	84	37	36	11	282	278	85
Minnesota	84	36	38	10	272	293	82
Tampa Bay	84	23	54	7	245	332	53

Smythe Division

Team	GP	W	L	T	GF	GA	PTS
Vancouver	84	46	29	9	346	278	101
Calgary	84	43	30	11	322	282	97
Los Angeles	84	39	35	10	338	340	88
Winnipeg	84	40	37	7	322	320	87
Edmonton	84	26	50	8	242	337	60
San Jose	84	11	71	2	218	414	24

PRINCE OF WALES CONFERENCE

Adams Division

Team	GP	W	L	T	GF	GA	PTS
Boston	84	51	26	7	332	268	109
Quebec	84	47	27	10	351	300	104
*Montreal	84	48	30	6	326	280	102
Buffalo	84	38	36	10	335	297	86
Hartford	84	26	52	6	284	369	58
Ottawa	84	10	70	4	202	395	24

Patrick Division

Team	GP	W	L	T	GF	GA	PTS
Pittsburgh	84	56	21	7	367	268	119
Washington	84	43	34	7	325	286	93
NY Islanders	84	40	37	7	335	297	87
New Jersey	84	40	37	7	308	299	87
Philadelphia	84	36	37	11	319	319	83
NY Rangers	84	34	39	11	304	308	79

Leading Scorers

Player	Team	GP	G	A	PTS	PIM
Mario Lemieux	Pittsburgh	60	69	91	160	38
Pat LaFontaine	Buffalo	84	53	95	148	63
Adam Oates	Boston	84	45	97	142	32
Steve Yzerman	Detroit	84	58	79	137	44
Teemu Selanne	Winnipeg	84	76	56	132	45
Pierre Turgeon	NY Islanders	83	58	74	132	26
Alexander Mogilny	Buffalo	77	76	51	127	40
Doug Gilmour	Toronto	83	32	95	127	100
Luc Robitaille	Los Angeles	84	63	62	125	100
Mark Recchi	Philadelphia	84	53	70	123	95

1993-94

EASTERN CONFERENCE

Northeast Division

Team		GP	W	L	T	GF	GA	PTS
Pittsburgh	(2)	84	44	27	13	299	285	101
Boston	(4)	84	42	29	13	289	252	97
Montreal	(5)	84	41	29	14	283	248	96
Buffalo	(6)	84	43	32	9	282	218	95
Quebec		84	34	42	8	277	292	76
Hartford		84	27	48	9	227	288	63
Ottawa		84	14	61	9	201	397	37

Atlantic Division

Team		GP	W	L	T	GF	GA	PTS
*NY Rangers	(1)	84	52	24	8	299	231	112
New Jersey	(3)	84	47	25	12	306	220	106
Washington	(7)	84	39	35	10	277	263	88
NY Islanders	(8)	84	36	36	12	282	264	84
Florida		84	33	34	17	233	233	83
Philadelphia		84	35	39	10	294	314	80
Tampa Bay		84	30	43	11	224	251	71

WESTERN CONFERENCE

Central Division

Team		GP	W	L	T	GF	GA	PTS
Detroit	(1)	84	46	30	8	356	275	100
Toronto	(3)	84	43	29	12	280	243	98
Dallas	(4)	84	42	29	13	286	265	97
St. Louis	(5)	84	40	33	11	270	283	91
Chicago	(6)	84	39	36	9	254	240	87
Winnipeg		84	24	51	9	245	344	57

Pacific Division

Team		GP	W	L	T	GF	GA	PTS
Calgary	(2)	84	42	29	13	302	256	97
Vancouver	(7)	84	41	40	3	279	276	85
San Jose	(8)	84	33	35	16	252	265	82
Anaheim		84	33	46	5	229	251	71
Los Angeles		84	27	45	12	294	322	66
Edmonton		84	25	45	14	261	305	64

Leading Scorers

Player	Team	GP	G	A	PTS	PIM
Wayne Gretzky	Los Angeles	81	38	92	130	20
Sergei Fedorov	Detroit	82	56	64	120	34
Adam Oates	Boston	77	32	80	112	45
Doug Gilmour	Toronto	83	27	84	111	105
Pavel Bure	Vancouver	76	60	47	107	86
Jeremy Roenick	Chicago	84	46	61	107	125
Mark Recchi	Philadelphia	84	40	67	107	46
Brendan Shanahan	St. Louis	81	52	50	102	211
Dave Andreychuk	Toronto	83	53	46	99	98
Jaromir Jagr	Pittsburgh	80	32	67	99	61

1994-95

EASTERN CONFERENCE

Northeast Division

Team		GP	W	L	T	GF	GA	PTS
Quebec	(1)	48	30	13	5	185	134	65
Pittsburgh	(3)	48	29	16	3	181	158	61
Boston	(4)	48	27	18	3	150	127	57
Buffalo	(7)	48	22	19	7	130	119	51
Hartford		48	19	24	5	127	141	43
Montreal		48	18	23	7	125	148	43
Ottawa		48	9	34	5	117	174	23

Atlantic Division

Team		GP	W	L	T	GF	GA	PTS
Philadelphia	(2)	48	28	16	4	150	132	60
*New Jersey	(5)	48	22	18	8	136	121	52
Washington	(6)	48	22	18	8	136	120	52
NY Rangers	(8)	48	22	23	3	139	134	47
Florida		48	20	22	6	115	127	46
Tampa Bay		48	17	28	3	120	144	37
NY Islanders		48	15	28	5	126	158	35

WESTERN CONFERENCE

Central Division

Team		GP	W	L	T	GF	GA	PTS
Detroit	(1)	48	33	11	4	180	117	70
St. Louis	(3)	48	28	15	5	178	135	61
Chicago	(4)	48	24	19	5	156	115	53
Toronto	(5)	48	21	19	8	135	146	50
Dallas	(8)	48	17	23	8	136	135	42
Winnipeg		48	16	25	7	157	177	39

Pacific Division

Team		GP	W	L	T	GF	GA	PTS
Calgary	(2)	48	24	17	7	163	135	55
Vancouver	(6)	48	18	18	12	153	148	48
San Jose	(7)	48	19	25	4	129	161	42
Los Angeles		48	16	23	9	142	174	41
Edmonton		48	17	27	4	136	183	38
Anaheim		48	16	27	5	125	164	37

Leading Scorers

Player	Team	GP	G	A	PTS	PIM
Jaromir Jagr	Pittsburgh	48	32	38	70	37
Eric Lindros	Philadelphia	46	29	41	70	60
Alex Zhamnov	Winnipeg	48	30	35	65	20
Joe Sakic	Quebec	47	19	43	62	30
Ron Francis	Pittsburgh	44	11	48	59	18
Theoren Fleury	Calgary	47	29	29	58	112
Paul Coffey	Detroit	45	14	44	58	72
Mikael Renberg	Philadelphia	47	26	31	57	20
John LeClair	Mtl., Phi.	46	26	28	54	30
Mark Messier	NY Rangers	46	14	39	53	40
Adam Oates	Boston	48	12	41	53	8

1995-96

EASTERN CONFERENCE

Northeast Division

Team		GP	W	L	T	GF	GA	PTS
Pittsburgh	(2)	82	49	29	4	362	284	102
Boston	(5)	82	40	31	11	282	269	91
Montreal	(6)	82	40	32	10	265	248	90
Hartford		82	34	39	9	237	259	77
Buffalo		82	33	42	7	247	262	73
Ottawa		82	18	59	5	191	291	41

Atlantic Division

Team		GP	W	L	T	GF	GA	PTS
Philadelphia	(1)	82	45	24	13	282	208	103
NY Rangers	(3)	82	41	27	14	272	237	96
Florida	(4)	82	41	31	10	254	234	92
Washington	(7)	82	39	32	11	234	204	89
Tampa Bay	(8)	82	38	32	12	238	248	88
New Jersey		82	37	33	12	215	202	86
NY Islanders		82	22	50	10	229	315	54

WESTERN CONFERENCE

Central Division

Team		GP	W	L	T	GF	GA	PTS
Detroit	(1)	82	62	13	7	325	181	131
Chicago	(3)	82	40	28	14	273	220	94
Toronto	(4)	82	34	36	12	247	252	80
St. Louis	(5)	82	32	34	16	219	248	80
Winnipeg	(8)	82	36	40	6	275	291	78
Dallas		82	26	42	14	227	280	66

Pacific Division

Team		GP	W	L	T	GF	GA	PTS
*Colorado	(2)	82	47	25	10	326	240	104
Calgary	(6)	82	34	37	11	241	240	79
Vancouver	(7)	82	32	35	15	278	278	79
Anaheim		82	35	39	8	234	247	78
Edmonton		82	30	44	8	240	304	68
Los Angeles		82	24	40	18	256	302	66
San Jose		82	20	55	7	252	357	47

Leading Scorers

Player	Team	GP	G	A	PTS	PIM
Mario Lemieux	Pittsburgh	70	69	92	161	54
Jaromir Jagr	Pittsburgh	82	62	87	149	96
Joe Sakic	Colorado	82	51	69	120	44
Ron Francis	Pittsburgh	77	27	92	119	56
Peter Forsberg	Colorado	82	30	86	116	47
Eric Lindros	Philadelphia	73	47	68	115	163
Paul Kariya	Anaheim	82	50	58	108	20
Teemu Selanne	Wpg., Ana.	79	40	68	108	22
Alexander Mogilny	Vancouver	79	55	52	107	16
Sergei Fedorov	Detroit	78	39	68	107	48

1996-97

EASTERN CONFERENCE

Northeast Division

Team		GP	W	L	T	GF	GA	PTS
Buffalo	(2)	82	40	30	12	237	208	92
Pittsburgh	(6)	82	38	36	8	285	280	84
Ottawa	(7)	82	31	36	15	226	234	77
Montreal	(8)	82	31	36	15	249	276	77
Hartford		82	32	39	11	226	256	75
Boston		82	26	47	9	234	300	61

Atlantic Division

Team		GP	W	L	T	GF	GA	PTS
New Jersey	(1)	82	45	23	14	231	182	104
Philadelphia	(3)	82	45	24	13	274	217	103
Florida	(4)	82	35	28	19	221	201	89
NY Rangers	(5)	82	38	34	10	258	231	86
Washington		82	33	40	9	214	231	75
Tampa Bay		82	32	40	10	217	247	74
NY Islanders		82	29	41	12	240	250	70

WESTERN CONFERENCE

Central Division

Team		GP	W	L	T	GF	GA	PTS
Dallas	(2)	82	48	26	8	252	198	104
*Detroit	(3)	82	38	26	18	253	197	94
Phoenix	(5)	82	38	37	7	240	243	83
St. Louis	(6)	82	36	35	11	236	239	83
Chicago	(8)	82	34	35	13	223	210	81
Toronto		82	30	44	8	230	273	68

Pacific Division

Team		GP	W	L	T	GF	GA	PTS
Colorado	(1)	82	49	24	9	277	205	107
Anaheim	(4)	82	36	33	13	245	233	85
Edmonton	(7)	82	36	37	9	252	247	81
Vancouver		82	35	40	7	257	273	77
Calgary		82	32	41	9	214	239	73
Los Angeles		82	28	43	11	214	268	67
San Jose		82	27	47	8	211	278	62

Leading Scorers

Player	Team	GP	G	A	PTS	PIM
Mario Lemieux	Pittsburgh	76	50	72	122	65
Teemu Selanne	Anaheim	78	51	58	109	34
Paul Kariya	Anaheim	69	44	55	99	6
John LeClair	Philadelphia	82	50	47	97	58
Wayne Gretzky	NY Rangers	82	25	72	97	28
Jaromir Jagr	Pittsburgh	63	47	48	95	40
Mats Sundin	Toronto	82	41	53	94	59
Ziggy Palffy	NY Islanders	80	48	42	90	43
Ron Francis	Pittsburgh	81	27	63	90	20
Brendan Shanahan	Hfd., Det.	81	47	41	88	131

1997-98

EASTERN CONFERENCE

Northeast Division

Team		GP	W	L	T	GF	GA	PTS
Pittsburgh	(2)	82	40	24	18	228	188	98
Boston	(5)	82	39	30	13	221	194	91
Buffalo	(6)	82	36	29	17	211	187	89
Montreal	(7)	82	37	32	13	235	208	87
Ottawa	(8)	82	34	33	15	193	200	83
Carolina		82	33	41	8	200	219	74

Atlantic Division

Team		GP	W	L	T	GF	GA	PTS
New Jersey	(1)	82	48	23	11	225	166	107
Philadelphia	(3)	82	42	29	11	242	193	95
Washington	(4)	82	40	30	12	219	202	92
NY Islanders		82	30	41	11	212	225	71
NY Rangers		82	25	39	18	197	231	68
Florida		82	24	43	15	203	256	63
Tampa Bay		82	17	55	10	151	269	44

WESTERN CONFERENCE

Central Division

Team		GP	W	L	T	GF	GA	PTS
Dallas	(1)	82	49	22	11	242	167	109
*Detroit	(3)	82	44	23	15	250	196	103
St. Louis	(4)	82	45	29	8	256	204	98
Phoenix	(6)	82	35	35	12	224	227	82
Chicago		82	30	39	13	192	199	73
Toronto		82	30	43	9	194	237	69

Pacific Division

Team		GP	W	L	T	GF	GA	PTS
Colorado	(2)	82	39	26	17	231	205	95
Los Angeles	(5)	82	38	33	11	227	225	87
Edmonton	(7)	82	35	37	10	215	224	80
San Jose	(8)	82	34	38	10	210	216	78
Calgary		82	26	41	15	217	252	67
Anaheim		82	26	43	13	205	261	65
Vancouver		82	25	43	14	224	273	64

Leading Scorers

Player	Team	GP	G	A	PTS	PIM
Jaromir Jagr	Pittsburgh	77	35	67	102	64
Peter Forsberg	Colorado	72	25	66	91	94
Pavel Bure	Vancouver	82	51	39	90	48
Wayne Gretzky	NY Rangers	82	23	67	90	28
John LeClair	Philadelphia	82	51	36	87	32
Ziggy Palffy	NY Islanders	82	45	42	87	34
Ron Francis	Pittsburgh	81	25	62	87	20
Teemu Selanne	Anaheim	73	52	34	86	30
Jason Allison	Boston	81	33	50	83	60
Jozef Stumpel	Los Angeles	77	21	58	79	53

1998-99

EASTERN CONFERENCE

Northeast Division

Team		GP	W	L	T	GF	GA	PTS
Ottawa	(2)	82	44	23	15	239	179	103
Toronto	(4)	82	45	30	7	268	231	97
Boston	(6)	82	39	30	13	214	181	91
Buffalo	(7)	82	37	28	17	207	175	91
Montreal		82	32	39	11	184	209	75

Atlantic Division

Team		GP	W	L	T	GF	GA	PTS
New Jersey	(1)	82	47	24	11	248	196	105
Philadelphia	(5)	82	37	26	19	231	196	93
Pittsburgh	(8)	82	38	30	14	242	225	90
NY Rangers		82	33	38	11	217	227	77
NY Islanders		82	24	48	10	194	244	58

Southeast Division

Team		GP	W	L	T	GF	GA	PTS
Carolina	(3)	82	34	30	18	210	202	86
Florida		82	30	34	18	210	228	78
Washington		82	31	45	6	200	218	68
Tampa Bay		82	19	54	9	179	292	47

WESTERN CONFERENCE

Central Division

Team		GP	W	L	T	GF	GA	PTS
Detroit	(3)	82	43	32	7	245	202	93
St Louis	(5)	82	37	32	13	237	209	87
Chicago		82	29	41	12	202	248	70
Nashville		82	28	47	7	190	261	63

Pacific Division

Team		GP	W	L	T	GF	GA	PTS
*Dallas	(1)	82	51	19	12	236	168	114
Phoenix	(4)	82	39	31	12	205	197	90
Anaheim	(6)	82	35	34	13	215	206	83
San Jose	(7)	82	31	33	18	196	191	80
Los Angeles		82	32	45	5	189	222	69

Northwest Division

Team		GP	W	L	T	GF	GA	PTS
Colorado	(2)	82	44	28	10	239	205	98
Edmonton	(8)	82	33	37	12	230	226	78
Calgary		82	30	40	12	211	234	72
Vancouver		82	23	47	12	192	258	58

Leading Scorers

Player	Team	GP	G	A	PTS	PIM
Jaromir Jagr	Pittsburgh	81	44	83	127	66
Teemu Selanne	Anaheim	75	47	60	107	30
Paul Kariya	Anaheim	82	39	62	101	40
Peter Forsberg	Colorado	78	30	67	97	108
Joe Sakic	Colorado	73	41	55	96	29
Alexei Yashin	Ottawa	82	44	50	94	54
Eric Lindros	Philadelphia	71	40	53	93	120
Theoren Fleury	Cgy., Col.	75	40	53	93	86
John LeClair	Philadelphia	76	43	47	90	30
Pavol Demitra	St Louis	82	37	52	89	16

1999-2000

EASTERN CONFERENCE

Northeast Division

Team		GP	W	L	T	OTL	GF	GA	PTS
Toronto	(3)	82	45	27	7	3	246	222	100
Ottawa	(6)	82	41	28	11	2	244	210	95
Buffalo	(8)	82	35	32	11	4	213	204	85
Montreal		82	35	34	9	4	196	194	83
Boston		82	24	33	19	6	210	248	73

Atlantic Division

Team		GP	W	L	T	OTL	GF	GA	PTS
Philadelphia	(1)	82	45	22	12	3	237	179	105
*New Jersey	(4)	82	45	24	8	5	251	203	103
Pittsburgh	(7)	82	37	31	8	6	241	236	88
NY Rangers		82	29	38	12	3	218	246	73
NY Islanders		82	24	48	9	1	194	275	58

Southeast Division

Team		GP	W	L	T	OTL	GF	GA	PTS
Washington	(2)	82	44	24	12	2	227	194	102
Florida	(5)	82	43	27	6	6	244	209	98
Carolina		82	37	35	10	0	217	216	84
Tampa Bay		82	19	47	9	7	204	310	54
Atlanta		82	14	57	7	4	170	313	39

WESTERN CONFERENCE

Central Division

Team		GP	W	L	T	OTL	GF	GA	PTS
St. Louis	(1)	82	51	19	11	1	248	165	114
Detroit	(4)	82	48	22	10	2	278	210	108
Chicago		82	33	37	10	2	242	245	78
Nashville		82	28	40	7	7	199	240	70

Pacific Division

Team		GP	W	L	T	OTL	GF	GA	PTS
Dallas	(2)	82	43	23	10	6	211	184	102
Los Angeles	(5)	82	39	27	12	4	245	228	94
Phoenix	(6)	82	39	31	8	4	232	228	90
San Jose	(8)	82	35	30	10	7	225	214	87
Anaheim		82	34	33	12	3	217	227	83

Northwest Division

Team		GP	W	L	T	OTL	GF	GA	PTS
Colorado	(3)	82	42	28	11	1	233	201	96
Edmonton	(7)	82	32	26	16	8	226	212	88
Vancouver		82	30	29	15	8	227	237	83
Calgary		82	31	36	10	5	211	256	77

Leading Scorers

Player	Team	GP	G	A	PTS	PIM
Jaromir Jagr	Pittsburgh	63	42	54	96	50
Pavel Bure	Florida	74	58	36	94	16
Mark Recchi	Philadelphia	82	28	63	91	50
Paul Kariya	Anaheim	74	42	44	86	24
Teemu Selanne	Anaheim	79	33	52	85	12
Owen Nolan	San Jose	78	44	40	84	110
Tony Amonte	Chicago	82	43	41	84	48
Mike Modano	Dallas	77	38	43	81	48
Joe Sakic	Colorado	60	28	53	81	28
Steve Yzerman	Detroit	78	35	44	79	34

2000-01

EASTERN CONFERENCE

Northeast Division

Team		GP	W	L	T	OTL	GF	GA	PTS
Ottawa	(2)	82	48	21	9	4	274	205	109
Buffalo	(5)	82	46	30	5	1	218	184	98
Toronto	(7)	82	37	29	11	5	232	207	90
Boston		82	36	30	8	8	227	249	88
Montreal		82	28	40	8	6	206	232	70

Atlantic Division

Team		GP	W	L	T	OTL	GF	GA	PTS
New Jersey	(1)	82	48	19	12	3	295	195	111
Philadelphia	(4)	82	43	25	11	3	240	207	100
Pittsburgh	(6)	82	42	28	9	3	281	256	96
NY Rangers		82	33	43	5	1	250	290	72
NY Islanders		82	21	51	7	3	185	268	52

Southeast Division

Team		GP	W	L	T	OTL	GF	GA	PTS
Washington	(3)	82	41	27	10	4	233	211	96
Carolina	(8)	82	38	32	9	3	212	225	88
Florida		82	22	38	13	9	200	246	66
Atlanta		82	23	45	12	2	211	289	60
Tampa Bay		82	24	47	6	5	201	280	59

WESTERN CONFERENCE

Central Division

Team		GP	W	L	T	OTL	GF	GA	PTS
Detroit	(2)	82	49	20	9	4	253	202	111
St. Louis	(4)	82	43	22	12	5	249	195	103
Nashville		82	34	36	9	3	186	200	80
Chicago		82	29	40	8	5	210	246	71
Columbus		82	28	39	9	6	190	233	71

Pacific Division

Team		GP	W	L	T	OTL	GF	GA	PTS
Dallas	(3)	82	48	24	8	2	241	187	106
San Jose	(5)	82	40	27	12	3	217	192	95
Los Angeles	(7)	82	38	28	13	3	252	228	92
Phoenix		82	35	27	17	3	214	212	90
Anaheim		82	25	41	11	5	188	245	66

Northwest Division

Team		GP	W	L	T	OTL	GF	GA	PTS
*Colorado	(1)	82	52	16	10	4	270	192	118
Edmonton	(6)	82	39	28	12	3	243	222	93
Vancouver	(8)	82	36	28	11	7	239	238	90
Calgary		82	27	36	15	4	197	236	73
Minnesota		82	25	39	13	5	168	210	68

Leading Scorers

Player	Team	GP	G	A	PTS	PIM
Jaromir Jagr	Pittsburgh	81	52	69	121	42
Joe Sakic	Colorado	82	54	64	118	30
Patrik Elias	New Jersey	82	40	56	96	51
Alex Kovalev	Pittsburgh	79	44	51	95	96
Jason Allison	Boston	82	36	59	95	85
Martin Straka	Pittsburgh	82	27	68	95	38
Pavel Bure	Florida	82	59	33	92	58
Doug Weight	Edmonton	82	25	65	90	91
Ziggy Palffy	Los Angeles	73	38	51	89	20
Peter Forsberg	Colorado	73	27	62	89	54

2001-02

EASTERN CONFERENCE

Northeast Division

Team		GP	W	L	T	OTL	GF	GA	PTS
Boston	(1)	82	43	24	6	9	236	201	101
Toronto	(4)	82	43	25	10	4	249	207	100
Ottawa	(7)	82	39	27	9	7	243	208	94
Montreal	(8)	82	36	31	12	3	207	209	87
Buffalo		82	35	35	11	1	213	200	82

Atlantic Division

Team		GP	W	L	T	OTL	GF	GA	PTS
Philadelphia	(2)	82	42	27	10	3	234	192	97
NY Islanders	(5)	82	42	28	8	4	239	220	96
New Jersey	(6)	82	41	28	9	4	205	187	95
NY Rangers		82	36	38	4	4	227	258	80
Pittsburgh		82	28	41	8	5	198	249	69

Southeast Division

Team		GP	W	L	T	OTL	GF	GA	PTS
Carolina	(3)	82	35	26	16	5	217	217	91
Washington		82	36	33	11	2	228	240	85
Tampa Bay		82	27	40	11	4	178	219	69
Florida		82	22	44	10	6	180	250	60
Atlanta		82	19	47	11	5	187	288	54

WESTERN CONFERENCE

Central Division

Team		GP	W	L	T	OTL	GF	GA	PTS
*Detroit	(1)	82	51	17	10	4	251	187	116
St. Louis	(4)	82	43	27	8	4	227	188	98
Chicago	(5)	82	41	27	13	1	216	207	96
Nashville		82	28	41	13	0	196	230	69
Columbus		82	22	47	8	5	164	255	57

Pacific Division

Team		GP	W	L	T	OTL	GF	GA	PTS
San Jose	(3)	82	44	27	8	3	248	199	99
Phoenix	(6)	82	40	27	9	6	228	210	95
Los Angeles	(7)	82	40	27	11	4	214	190	95
Dallas		82	36	28	13	5	215	213	90
Anaheim		82	29	42	8	3	175	198	69

Northwest Division

Team		GP	W	L	T	OTL	GF	GA	PTS
Colorado	(2)	82	45	28	8	1	212	169	99
Vancouver	(8)	82	42	30	7	3	254	211	94
Edmonton		82	38	28	12	4	205	182	92
Calgary		82	32	35	12	3	201	220	79
Minnesota		82	26	35	12	9	195	238	73

Leading Scorers

Player	Team	GP	G	A	PTS	PIM
Jarome Iginla	Calgary	82	52	44	96	77
Markus Naslund	Vancouver	81	40	50	90	50
Todd Bertuzzi	Vancouver	72	36	49	85	110
Mats Sundin	Toronto	82	41	39	80	94
Jaromir Jagr	Washington	69	31	48	79	30
Joe Sakic	Colorado	82	26	53	79	18
Pavol Demitra	St. Louis	82	35	43	78	46
Adam Oates	Wsh., Phi.	80	14	64	78	28
Mike Modano	Dallas	78	34	43	77	38
Ron Francis	Carolina	80	27	50	77	18

2002-03

EASTERN CONFERENCE
Northeast Division

Team		GP	W	L	T	OTL	GF	GA	PTS
Ottawa	(1)	82	52	21	8	1	263	182	113
Toronto	(5)	82	44	28	7	3	236	208	98
Boston	(7)	82	36	31	11	4	245	237	87
Montreal		82	30	35	8	9	206	234	77
Buffalo		82	27	37	10	8	190	219	72

Atlantic Division

Team		GP	W	L	T	OTL	GF	GA	PTS
*New Jersey	(2)	82	46	20	10	6	216	166	108
Philadelphia	(4)	82	45	20	13	4	211	166	107
NY Islanders	(8)	82	35	34	11	2	224	231	83
NY Rangers		82	32	36	10	4	210	231	78
Pittsburgh		82	27	44	6	5	189	255	65

Southeast Division

Team		GP	W	L	T	OTL	GF	GA	PTS
Tampa Bay	(3)	82	36	25	16	5	219	210	93
Washington	(6)	82	39	29	8	6	224	220	92
Atlanta		82	31	39	7	5	226	284	74
Florida		82	24	36	13	9	176	237	70
Carolina		82	22	43	11	6	171	240	61

WESTERN CONFERENCE
Central Division

Team		GP	W	L	T	OTL	GF	GA	PTS
Detroit	(2)	82	48	20	10	4	269	203	110
St. Louis	(5)	82	41	24	11	6	253	222	99
Chicago		82	30	33	13	6	207	226	79
Nashville		82	27	35	13	7	183	206	74
Columbus		82	29	42	8	3	213	263	69

Pacific Division

Team		GP	W	L	T	OTL	GF	GA	PTS
Dallas	(1)	82	46	17	15	4	245	169	111
Anaheim	(7)	82	40	27	9	6	203	193	95
Los Angeles		82	33	37	6	6	203	221	78
Phoenix		82	31	35	11	5	204	230	78
San Jose		82	28	37	9	8	214	239	73

Northwest Division

Team		GP	W	L	T	OTL	GF	GA	PTS
Colorado	(3)	82	42	19	13	8	251	194	105
Vancouver	(4)	82	45	23	13	1	264	208	104
Minnesota	(6)	82	42	29	10	1	198	178	95
Edmonton	(8)	82	36	26	11	9	231	230	92
Calgary		82	29	36	13	4	186	228	75

Leading Scorers

Player	Team	GP	G	A	PTS	PIM
Peter Forsberg	Colorado	75	29	77	106	70
Markus Naslund	Vancouver	82	48	56	104	52
Joe Thornton	Boston	77	36	65	101	109
Milan Hejduk	Colorado	82	50	48	98	52
Todd Bertuzzi	Vancouver	82	46	51	97	144
Pavol Demitra	St. Louis	78	36	57	93	32
Glen Murray	Boston	82	44	48	92	64
Mario Lemieux	Pittsburgh	67	28	63	91	43
Dany Heatley	Atlanta	77	41	48	89	58
Ziggy Palffy	Los Angeles	76	37	48	85	47
Mike Modano	Dallas	79	28	57	85	30

2003-04

EASTERN CONFERENCE
Northeast Division

Team		GP	W	L	T	OTL	GF	GA	PTS
Boston	(2)	82	41	19	15	7	209	188	104
Toronto	(4)	82	45	24	10	3	242	204	103
Ottawa	(5)	82	43	23	10	6	262	189	102
Montreal	(7)	82	41	30	7	4	208	192	93
Buffalo		82	37	34	7	4	220	221	85

Atlantic Division

Team		GP	W	L	T	OTL	GF	GA	PTS
Philadelphia	(3)	82	40	21	15	6	229	186	101
New Jersey	(6)	82	43	25	12	2	213	164	100
NY Islanders	(8)	82	38	29	11	4	237	210	91
NY Rangers		82	27	40	7	8	206	250	69
Pittsburgh		82	23	47	8	4	190	303	58

Southeast Division

Team		GP	W	L	T	OTL	GF	GA	PTS
*Tampa Bay	(1)	82	46	22	8	6	245	192	106
Atlanta		82	33	37	8	4	214	243	78
Carolina		82	28	34	14	6	172	209	76
Florida		82	28	35	15	4	188	221	75
Washington		82	23	46	10	3	186	253	59

WESTERN CONFERENCE
Central Division

Team		GP	W	L	T	OTL	GF	GA	PTS
Detroit	(1)	82	48	21	11	2	255	189	109
St. Louis	(7)	82	39	30	11	2	191	198	91
Nashville	(8)	82	38	29	11	4	216	217	91
Columbus		82	25	45	8	4	177	238	62
Chicago		82	20	43	11	8	188	259	59

Pacific Division

Team		GP	W	L	T	OTL	GF	GA	PTS
San Jose	(2)	82	43	21	12	6	219	183	104
Dallas	(5)	82	41	26	13	2	194	175	97
Los Angeles		82	28	29	16	9	205	217	81
Anaheim		82	29	35	10	8	184	213	76
Phoenix		82	22	36	18	6	188	245	68

Northwest Division

Team		GP	W	L	T	OTL	GF	GA	PTS
Vancouver	(3)	82	43	24	10	5	235	194	101
Colorado	(4)	82	40	22	13	7	236	198	100
Calgary	(6)	82	42	30	7	3	200	176	94
Edmonton		82	36	29	12	5	221	208	89
Minnesota		82	30	29	20	3	188	183	83

Leading Scorers

Player	Team	GP	G	A	PTS	PIM
Martin St. Louis	Tampa Bay	82	38	56	94	24
Ilya Kovalchuk	Atlanta	81	41	46	87	63
Joe Sakic	Colorado	81	33	54	87	42
Markus Naslund	Vancouver	78	35	49	84	58
Marian Hossa	Ottawa	81	36	46	82	46
Patrik Elias	New Jersey	82	38	43	81	44
Daniel Alfredsson	Ottawa	77	32	48	80	24
Cory Stillman	Tampa Bay	81	25	55	80	36
Robert Lang	Wsh., Det.	69	30	49	79	24
Brad Richards	Tampa Bay	82	26	53	79	12
Alex Tanguay	Colorado	69	25	54	79	42

2004-05
SEASON CANCELLED

2005-06

EASTERN CONFERENCE
Northeast Division

Team		GP	W	L	OL	GF	GA	PTS
Ottawa	(1)	82	52	21	9	314	211	113
Buffalo	(4)	82	52	24	6	281	239	110
Montreal	(7)	82	42	31	9	243	247	93
Toronto		82	41	33	8	257	270	90
Boston		82	29	37	16	230	266	74

Atlantic Division

Team		GP	W	L	OL	GF	GA	PTS
New Jersey	(3)	82	46	27	9	242	229	101
Philadelphia	(5)	82	45	26	11	267	259	101
NY Rangers	(6)	82	44	26	12	257	215	100
NY Islanders		82	36	40	6	230	278	78
Pittsburgh		82	22	46	14	244	316	58

Southeast Division

Team		GP	W	L	OL	GF	GA	PTS
*Carolina	(2)	82	52	22	8	294	260	112
Tampa Bay	(8)	82	43	33	6	252	260	92
Atlanta		82	41	33	8	281	275	90
Florida		82	37	34	11	240	257	85
Washington		82	29	41	12	237	306	70

WESTERN CONFERENCE
Central Division

Team		GP	W	L	OL	GF	GA	PTS
Detroit	(1)	82	58	16	8	305	209	124
Nashville	(4)	82	49	25	8	259	227	106
Columbus		82	35	43	4	223	279	74
Chicago		82	26	43	13	211	285	65
St. Louis		82	21	46	15	197	292	57

Pacific Division

Team		GP	W	L	OL	GF	GA	PTS
Dallas	(2)	82	53	23	6	265	218	112
San Jose	(5)	82	44	27	11	266	242	99
Anaheim	(6)	82	43	27	12	254	229	98
Los Angeles		82	42	35	5	249	270	89
Phoenix		82	38	39	5	246	271	81

Northwest Division

Team		GP	W	L	OL	GF	GA	PTS
Calgary	(3)	82	46	25	11	218	200	103
Colorado	(7)	82	43	30	9	283	257	95
Edmonton	(8)	82	41	28	13	256	251	95
Vancouver		82	42	32	8	256	255	92
Minnesota		82	38	36	8	231	215	84

Leading Scorers

Player	Team	GP	G	A	PTS	PIM
Joe Thornton	Bos., S.J.	81	29	96	125	61
Jaromir Jagr	NY Rangers	82	54	69	123	72
Alex Ovechkin	Washington	81	52	54	106	52
Dany Heatley	Ottawa	82	50	53	103	86
Daniel Alfredsson	Ottawa	77	43	60	103	50
Sidney Crosby	Pittsburgh	81	39	63	102	110
Eric Staal	Carolina	82	45	55	100	81
Ilya Kovalchuk	Atlanta	78	52	46	98	68
Marc Savard	Atlanta	82	28	69	97	100
Jonathan Cheechoo	San Jose	82	56	37	93	58

Peter Forsberg of the Colorado Avalanche passed countryman Markus Naslund of the Vancouver Canucks on the last day of the 2002-03 season to become the first Swedish player to lead the NHL in scoring.

2006-07

EASTERN CONFERENCE

Northeast Division

Team		GP	W	L	OL	GF	GA	PTS
Buffalo	(1)	82	53	22	7	308	242	113
Ottawa	(4)	82	48	25	9	288	222	105
Toronto		82	40	31	11	258	269	91
Montreal		82	42	34	6	245	256	90
Boston		82	35	41	6	219	289	76

Atlantic Division

Team		GP	W	L	OL	GF	GA	PTS
New Jersey	(2)	82	49	24	9	216	201	107
Pittsburgh	(5)	82	47	24	11	277	246	105
NY Rangers	(6)	82	42	30	10	242	216	94
NY Islanders	(8)	82	40	30	12	248	240	92
Philadelphia		82	22	48	12	214	303	56

Southeast Division

Team		GP	W	L	OL	GF	GA	PTS
Atlanta	(3)	82	43	28	11	246	245	97
Tampa Bay	(7)	82	44	33	5	253	261	93
Carolina		82	40	34	8	241	253	88
Florida		82	35	31	16	247	257	86
Washington		82	28	40	14	235	286	70

WESTERN CONFERENCE

Central Division

Team		GP	W	L	OL	GF	GA	PTS
Detroit	(1)	82	50	19	13	254	199	113
Nashville	(4)	82	51	23	8	272	212	110
St. Louis		82	34	35	13	214	254	81
Columbus		82	33	42	7	201	249	73
Chicago		82	31	42	9	201	258	71

Pacific Division

Team		GP	W	L	OL	GF	GA	PTS
*Anaheim	(2)	82	48	20	14	258	208	110
San Jose	(5)	82	51	26	5	258	199	107
Dallas	(6)	82	50	25	7	226	197	107
Los Angeles		82	27	41	14	227	283	68
Phoenix		82	31	46	5	216	284	67

Northwest Division

Team		GP	W	L	OL	GF	GA	PTS
Vancouver	(3)	82	49	26	7	222	201	105
Minnesota	(7)	82	48	26	8	235	191	104
Calgary	(8)	82	43	29	10	258	226	96
Colorado		82	44	31	7	272	251	95
Edmonton		82	32	43	7	195	248	71

Leading Scorers

Player	Team	GP	G	A	PTS	PIM
Sidney Crosby	Pittsburgh	79	36	84	120	60
Joe Thornton	San Jose	82	22	92	114	44
Vincent Lecavalier	Tampa Bay	82	52	56	108	44
Dany Heatley	Ottawa	82	50	55	105	74
Martin St. Louis	Tampa Bay	82	43	59	102	28
Marian Hossa	Atlanta	82	43	57	100	49
Joe Sakic	Colorado	82	36	64	100	46
Jaromir Jagr	NY Rangers	82	30	66	96	78
Marc Savard	Boston	82	22	74	96	96
Danny Briere	Buffalo	81	32	63	95	89

2007-08

EASTERN CONFERENCE

Northeast Division

Team		GP	W	L	OL	GF	GA	PTS
Montreal	(1)	82	47	25	10	262	222	104
Ottawa	(7)	82	43	31	8	261	247	94
Boston	(8)	82	41	29	12	212	222	94
Buffalo		82	39	31	12	255	242	90
Toronto		82	36	35	11	231	260	83

Atlantic Division

Team		GP	W	L	OL	GF	GA	PTS
Pittsburgh	(2)	82	47	27	8	247	216	102
New Jersey	(4)	82	46	29	7	206	197	99
NY Rangers	(5)	82	42	27	13	213	199	97
Philadelphia	(6)	82	42	29	11	248	233	95
NY Islanders		82	35	38	9	194	243	79

Southeast Division

Team		GP	W	L	OL	GF	GA	PTS
Washington	(3)	82	43	31	8	242	231	94
Carolina		82	43	33	6	252	249	92
Florida		82	38	35	9	216	226	85
Atlanta		82	34	40	8	216	272	76
Tampa Bay		82	31	42	9	223	267	71

WESTERN CONFERENCE

Central Division

Team		GP	W	L	OL	GF	GA	PTS
*Detroit	(1)	82	54	21	7	257	184	115
Nashville	(8)	82	41	32	9	230	229	91
Chicago		82	40	34	8	239	235	88
Columbus		82	34	36	12	193	218	80
St. Louis		82	33	36	13	205	237	79

Pacific Division

Team		GP	W	L	OL	GF	GA	PTS
San Jose	(2)	82	49	23	10	222	193	108
Anaheim	(4)	82	47	27	8	205	191	102
Dallas	(5)	82	45	30	7	242	207	97
Phoenix		82	38	37	7	214	231	83
Los Angeles		82	32	43	7	231	266	71

Northwest Division

Team		GP	W	L	OL	GF	GA	PTS
Minnesota	(3)	82	44	28	10	223	218	98
Colorado	(6)	82	44	31	7	231	219	95
Calgary	(7)	82	42	30	10	229	227	94
Edmonton		82	41	35	6	235	251	88
Vancouver		82	39	33	10	213	215	88

Leading Scorers

Player	Team	GP	G	A	PTS	PIM
Alex Ovechkin	Washington	82	65	47	112	40
Evgeni Malkin	Pittsburgh	82	47	59	106	78
Jarome Iginla	Calgary	82	50	48	98	83
Pavel Datsyuk	Detroit	82	31	66	97	20
Joe Thornton	San Jose	82	29	67	96	59
Henrik Zetterberg	Detroit	75	43	49	92	34
Vincent Lecavalier	Tampa Bay	81	40	52	92	89
Jason Spezza	Ottawa	76	34	58	92	66
Daniel Alfredsson	Ottawa	70	40	49	89	34
Ilya Kovalchuk	Atlanta	79	52	35	87	52

2008-09

EASTERN CONFERENCE

Northeast Division

Team		GP	W	L	OL	GF	GA	PTS
Boston	(1)	82	53	19	10	274	196	116
Montreal	(8)	82	41	30	11	249	247	93
Buffalo		82	41	32	9	250	234	91
Ottawa		82	36	35	11	217	237	83
Toronto		82	34	35	13	250	293	81

Atlantic Division

Team		GP	W	L	OL	GF	GA	PTS
New Jersey	(3)	82	51	27	4	244	209	106
*Pittsburgh	(4)	82	45	28	9	264	239	99
Philadelphia	(5)	82	44	27	11	264	238	99
NY Rangers	(7)	82	43	30	9	210	218	95
NY Islanders		82	26	47	9	201	279	61

Southeast Division

Team		GP	W	L	OL	GF	GA	PTS
Washington	(2)	82	50	24	8	272	245	108
Carolina	(6)	82	45	30	7	239	226	97
Florida		82	41	30	11	234	231	93
Atlanta		82	35	41	6	257	280	76
Tampa Bay		82	24	40	18	210	279	66

WESTERN CONFERENCE

Central Division

Team		GP	W	L	OL	GF	GA	PTS
Detroit	(2)	82	51	21	10	295	244	112
Chicago	(4)	82	46	24	12	264	216	104
St. Louis	(6)	82	41	31	10	233	233	92
Columbus	(7)	82	41	31	10	226	230	92
Nashville		82	40	34	8	213	233	88

Pacific Division

Team		GP	W	L	OL	GF	GA	PTS
San Jose	(1)	82	53	18	11	257	204	117
Anaheim	(8)	82	42	33	7	245	238	91
Dallas		82	36	35	11	230	257	83
Phoenix		82	36	39	7	208	252	79
Los Angeles		82	34	37	11	207	234	79

Northwest Division

Team		GP	W	L	OL	GF	GA	PTS
Vancouver	(3)	82	45	27	10	246	220	100
Calgary	(5)	82	46	30	6	254	248	98
Minnesota		82	40	33	9	219	200	89
Edmonton		82	38	35	9	234	248	85
Colorado		82	32	45	5	199	257	69

Leading Scorers

Player	Team	GP	G	A	PTS	PIM
Evgeni Malkin	Pittsburgh	82	35	78	113	80
Alex Ovechkin	Washington	79	56	54	110	72
Sidney Crosby	Pittsburgh	77	33	70	103	76
Pavel Datsyuk	Detroit	81	32	65	97	34
Zach Parise	New Jersey	82	45	49	94	24
Ilya Kovalchuk	Atlanta	79	43	48	91	50
Ryan Getzlaf	Anaheim	81	25	66	91	121
Jarome Iginla	Calgary	82	35	54	89	37
Marc Savard	Boston	82	25	63	88	70
Nicklas Backstrom	Washington	82	22	66	88	46

2009-10

EASTERN CONFERENCE

Northeast Division

Team		GP	W	L	OL	GF	GA	PTS
Buffalo	(3)	82	45	27	10	235	207	100
Ottawa	(5)	82	44	32	6	225	238	94
Boston	(6)	82	39	30	13	206	200	91
Montreal	(8)	82	39	33	10	217	223	88
Toronto		82	30	38	14	214	267	74

Atlantic Division

Team		GP	W	L	OL	GF	GA	PTS
New Jersey	(2)	82	48	27	7	222	191	103
Pittsburgh	(4)	82	47	28	7	257	237	101
Philadelphia	(7)	82	41	35	6	236	225	88
NY Rangers		82	38	33	11	222	218	87
NY Islanders		82	34	37	11	222	264	79

Southeast Division

Team		GP	W	L	OL	GF	GA	PTS
Washington	(1)	82	54	15	13	318	233	121
Atlanta		82	35	34	13	234	256	83
Carolina		82	35	37	10	230	256	80
Tampa Bay		82	34	36	12	217	260	80
Florida		82	32	37	13	208	244	77

WESTERN CONFERENCE

Central Division

Team		GP	W	L	OL	GF	GA	PTS
*Chicago	(2)	82	52	22	8	271	209	112
Detroit	(5)	82	44	24	14	229	216	102
Nashville	(7)	82	47	29	6	225	225	100
St. Louis		82	40	32	10	225	223	90
Columbus		82	32	35	15	216	259	79

Pacific Division

Team		GP	W	L	OL	GF	GA	PTS
San Jose	(1)	82	51	20	11	264	215	113
Phoenix	(4)	82	50	25	7	225	202	107
Los Angeles	(6)	82	46	27	9	241	219	101
Anaheim		82	39	32	11	238	251	89
Dallas		82	37	31	14	237	254	88

Northwest Division

Team		GP	W	L	OL	GF	GA	PTS
Vancouver	(3)	82	49	28	5	272	222	103
Colorado	(8)	82	43	30	9	244	233	95
Calgary		82	40	32	10	204	210	90
Minnesota		82	38	36	8	219	246	84
Edmonton		82	27	47	8	214	284	62

Leading Scorers

Player	Team	GP	G	A	PTS	PIM
Henrik Sedin	Vancouver	82	29	83	112	48
Sidney Crosby	Pittsburgh	81	51	58	109	71
Alex Ovechkin	Washington	72	50	59	109	89
Nicklas Backstrom	Washington	82	33	68	101	50
Steven Stamkos	Tampa Bay	82	51	44	95	38
Martin St. Louis	Tampa Bay	82	29	65	94	12
Brad Richards	Dallas	80	24	67	91	14
Joe Thornton	San Jose	79	20	69	89	54
Patrick Kane	Chicago	82	30	58	88	20
Marian Gaborik	NY Rangers	76	42	44	86	37

Note: Detailed statistics for 2009-10 are listed in the Final Statistics, 2009-10 section of the *NHL Guide & Record Book*. **See page 135.**

Team Records

Regular Season

FINAL STANDINGS

MOST POINTS, ONE SEASON:
- **132 – Montreal Canadiens**, 1976-77. 60w-8L-12T. 80GP
- 131 – Detroit Red Wings, 1995-96. 62w-13L-7T. 82GP
- 129 – Montreal Canadiens, 1977-78. 59w-10L-11T. 80GP

BEST POINTS PERCENTAGE, ONE SEASON:
- **.875 – Boston Bruins**, 1929-30. 38w-5L-1T. 77PTS in 44GP
- .830 – Montreal Canadiens, 1943-44. 38w-5L-7T. 83PTS in 50GP
- .825 – Montreal Canadiens, 1976-77. 60w-8L-12T. 132PTS in 80GP
- .806 – Montreal Canadiens, 1977-78. 59w-10L-11T. 129PTS in 80GP
- .800 – Montreal Canadiens, 1944-45. 38w-8L-4T. 80PTS in 50GP

FEWEST POINTS, ONE SEASON:
- **8 – Quebec Bulldogs**, 1919-20. 4w-20L-0T. 24GP
- 10 – Toronto Arenas, 1918-19. 5w-13L-0T. 18GP
- 12 – Hamilton Tigers, 1920-21. 6w-18L-0T. 24GP
  - Hamilton Tigers, 1922-23. 6w-18L-0T. 24GP
  - Boston Bruins, 1924-25. 6w-24L-0T. 30GP
  - Philadelphia Quakers, 1930-31. 4w-36L-4T. 44GP

FEWEST POINTS, ONE SEASON (MINIMUM 70-GAME SCHEDULE):
- **21 – Washington Capitals**, 1974-75. 8w-67L-5T. 80GP
- 24 – Ottawa Senators, 1992-93. 10w-70L-4T. 84GP
  - San Jose Sharks, 1992-93. 11w-71L-2T. 84GP
- 30 – New York Islanders, 1972-73. 12w-60L-6T. 78GP

WORST POINTS PERCENTAGE, ONE SEASON:
- **.131 – Washington Capitals**, 1974-75. 8w-67L-5T. 21PTS in 80GP
- .136 – Philadelphia Quakers, 1930-31. 4w-36L-4T. 12PTS in 44GP
- .143 – Ottawa Senators, 1992-93. 10w-70L-4T. 24PTS in 84GP
  - San Jose Sharks, 1992-93. 11w-71L-2T. 24PTS in 84GP
- .148 – Pittsburgh Pirates, 1929-30. 5w-36L-3T. 13PTS in 44GP

TEAM WINS

Most Wins

MOST WINS, ONE SEASON:
- **62 – Detroit Red Wings**, 1995-96. 82GP
- 60 – Montreal Canadiens, 1976-77. 80GP
- 59 – Montreal Canadiens, 1977-78. 80GP

MOST HOME WINS, ONE SEASON:
- **36 – Philadelphia Flyers**, 1975-76. 40GP
  - **Detroit Red Wings**, 1995-96. 41GP
- 33 – Boston Bruins, 1970-71. 39GP
  - Boston Bruins, 1973-74. 39GP
  - Montreal Canadiens, 1976-77. 40GP
  - Philadelphia Flyers, 1976-77. 40GP
  - New York Islanders, 1981-82. 40GP
  - Philadelphia Flyers, 1985-86. 40GP

MOST ROAD WINS, ONE SEASON:
- **31 – Detroit Red Wings**, 2005-06. 41GP
- 28 – New Jersey Devils, 1998-99. 41GP
- 27 – Montreal Canadiens, 1976-77. 40GP
  - Montreal Canadiens, 1977-78. 40GP
  - St. Louis Blues, 1999-2000. 41GP
  - San Jose Sharks, 2007-08. 41GP
- 26 – Boston Bruins, 1971-72. 39GP
  - Montreal Canadiens, 1975-76. 40GP
  - Edmonton Oilers, 1983-84. 40GP
  - Detroit Red Wings, 1995-96. 41GP
  - San Jose Sharks, 2006-07. 41GP

Fewest Wins

FEWEST WINS, ONE SEASON:
- **4 – Quebec Bulldogs**, 1919-20. 24GP
  - **Philadelphia Quakers**, 1930-31. 44GP
- 5 – Toronto Arenas, 1918-19. 18GP
  - Pittsburgh Pirates, 1929-30. 44GP

FEWEST WINS, ONE SEASON (MINIMUM 70-GAME SCHEDULE):
- **8 – Washington Capitals**, 1974-75. 80GP
- 9 – Winnipeg Jets, 1980-81. 80GP
- 10 – Ottawa Senators, 1992-93. 84GP

FEWEST HOME WINS, ONE SEASON:
- **2 – Chicago Blackhawks**, 1927-28. 22GP
- 3 – Boston Bruins, 1924-25. 15GP
  - Chicago Blackhawks, 1928-29. 22GP
  - Philadelphia Quakers, 1930-31. 22GP

FEWEST HOME WINS, ONE SEASON (MINIMUM 70-GAME SCHEDULE):
- **6 – Chicago Blackhawks**, 1954-55. 35GP
  - **Washington Capitals**, 1975-76. 40GP
- 7 – Boston Bruins, 1962-63. 35GP
  - Washington Capitals, 1974-75. 40GP
  - Winnipeg Jets, 1980-81. 40GP
  - Pittsburgh Penguins, 1983-84. 40GP

FEWEST ROAD WINS, ONE SEASON:
- **0 – Toronto Arenas**, 1918-19. 9GP
  - **Quebec Bulldogs**, 1919-20. 12GP
  - **Pittsburgh Pirates**, 1929-30. 22GP
- 1 – Hamilton Tigers, 1921-22. 12GP
  - Toronto St. Patricks, 1925-26. 18GP
  - Philadelphia Quakers, 1930-31. 22GP
  - New York Americans, 1940-41. 24GP
  - Washington Capitals, 1974-75. 40GP
- * – Ottawa Senators, 1992-93. 41GP

FEWEST ROAD WINS, ONE SEASON (MINIMUM 70-GAME SCHEDULE):
- **1 – Washington Capitals**, 1974-75. 40GP
- * – **Ottawa Senators**, 1992-93. 41GP
- 2 – Boston Bruins, 1960-61. 35GP
  - Los Angeles Kings, 1969-70. 38GP
  - New York Islanders, 1972-73. 39GP
  - California Golden Seals, 1973-74. 39GP
  - Colorado Rockies, 1977-78. 40GP
  - Winnipeg Jets, 1980-81. 40GP
  - Quebec Nordiques, 1991-92. 40GP

TEAM LOSSES

Fewest Losses

FEWEST LOSSES, ONE SEASON:
- **5 – Ottawa Senators**, 1919-20. 24GP
  - **Boston Bruins**, 1929-30. 44GP
  - **Montreal Canadiens**, 1943-44. 50GP

FEWEST HOME LOSSES, ONE SEASON:
- **0 – Ottawa Senators**, 1922-23. 12GP
  - **Montreal Canadiens**, 1943-44. 25GP
- 1 – Toronto Arenas, 1917-18. 11GP
  - Ottawa Senators, 1918-19. 9GP
  - Ottawa Senators, 1919-20. 12GP
  - Toronto St. Patricks, 1922-23. 12GP
  - Boston Bruins, 1929-30. 22GP
  - Boston Bruins, 1930-31. 22GP
  - Montreal Canadiens, 1976-77. 40GP
  - Quebec Nordiques, 1994-95. 24GP

FEWEST ROAD LOSSES, ONE SEASON:
- **3 – Montreal Canadiens**, 1928-29. 22GP
- 4 – Ottawa Senators, 1919-20. 12GP
  - Montreal Canadiens, 1927-28. 22GP
  - Boston Bruins, 1929-30. 20GP
  - Boston Bruins, 1940-41. 24GP

FEWEST LOSSES, ONE SEASON (MINIMUM 70-GAME SCHEDULE):
- **8 – Montreal Canadiens**, 1976-77. 80GP
- 10 – Montreal Canadiens, 1972-73. 78GP
  - Montreal Canadiens, 1977-78. 80GP
- 11 – Montreal Canadiens, 1975-76. 80GP

FEWEST HOME LOSSES, ONE SEASON (MINIMUM 70-GAME SCHEDULE):
- **1 – Montreal Canadiens**, 1976-77. 40GP
- 2 – Montreal Canadiens, 1961-62. 35GP
  - New York Rangers, 1970-71. 39GP
  - Philadelphia Flyers, 1975-76. 40GP

FEWEST ROAD LOSSES, ONE SEASON (MINIMUM 70-GAME SCHEDULE):
- **6 – Montreal Canadiens**, 1972-73. 39GP
  - **Montreal Canadiens**, 1974-75. 40GP
  - **Montreal Canadiens**, 1977-78. 40GP
- 7 – Detroit Red Wings, 1951-52. 35GP
  - Montreal Canadiens, 1976-77. 40GP
  - Philadelphia Flyers, 1979-80. 40GP
  - Boston Bruins, 2003-04. 41GP
  - Detroit Red Wings, 2005-06. 41GP

Most Losses

MOST LOSSES, ONE SEASON:
- **71 – San Jose Sharks**, 1992-93. 84GP
- 70 – Ottawa Senators, 1992-93. 84GP
- 67 – Washington Capitals, 1974-75. 80GP
- 61 – Quebec Nordiques, 1989-90. 80GP
  - Ottawa Senators, 1993-94. 84GP

MOST HOME LOSSES, ONE SEASON:
- ***32 – San Jose Sharks**, 1992-93. 41GP
- 29 – Pittsburgh Penguins, 1983-84. 40GP
- * – Ottawa Senators, 1993-94. 41GP

MOST ROAD LOSSES, ONE SEASON:
- ***40 – Ottawa Senators**, 1992-93. 41GP
- 39 – Washington Capitals, 1974-75. 40GP
- 37 – California Golden Seals, 1973-74. 39GP
- * – San Jose Sharks, 1992-93. 41GP

* – Does not include neutral site games

TEAM TIES
Most Ties
MOST TIES, ONE SEASON:
24 – **Philadelphia Flyers**, 1969-70. 76GP
23 – Montreal Canadiens, 1962-63. 70GP
 – Chicago Blackhawks, 1973-74. 78GP

MOST HOME TIES, ONE SEASON:
13 – **New York Rangers**, 1954-55. 35GP
 – **Philadelphia Flyers**, 1969-70. 38GP
 – **California Golden Seals**, 1971-72. 39GP
 – **California Golden Seals**, 1972-73. 39GP
 – **Chicago Blackhawks**, 1973-74. 39GP

MOST ROAD TIES, ONE SEASON:
15 – **Philadelphia Flyers**, 1976-77. 40GP
14 – Montreal Canadiens, 1952-53. 35GP
 – Montreal Canadiens, 1974-75. 40GP
 – Philadelphia Flyers, 1975-76. 40GP

Fewest Ties
FEWEST TIES, ONE SEASON (Since 1926-27):
1 – **Boston Bruins**, 1929-30. 44GP
2 – Montreal Canadiens, 1926-27. 44GP
 – New York Americans, 1926-27. 44GP
 – Boston Bruins, 1938-39. 48GP
 – New York Rangers, 1941-42. 48GP
 – San Jose Sharks, 1992-93. 84GP

FEWEST TIES, ONE SEASON (MINIMUM 70-GAME SCHEDULE):
2 – **San Jose Sharks**, 1992-93. 84GP
3 – New Jersey Devils, 1985-86. 80GP
 – Calgary Flames, 1986-87. 80GP
 – Vancouver Canucks, 1993-94. 84GP

WINNING STREAKS
LONGEST WINNING STREAK, ONE SEASON:
17 Games – **Pittsburgh Penguins**, Mar. 9 – Apr. 10, 1993.
15 Games – New York Islanders, Jan. 21 – Feb. 20, 1982.
14 Games – Boston Bruins, Dec. 3, 1929 – Jan. 9, 1930.
 – Washington Capitals, Jan.13 – Feb. 7, 2010.

LONGEST HOME WINNING STREAK, ONE SEASON:
20 Games – **Boston Bruins**, Dec. 3, 1929 – Mar. 18, 1930.
 – **Philadelphia Flyers**, Jan. 4 – Apr. 3, 1976.

LONGEST ROAD WINNING STREAK, ONE SEASON:
12 Games – **Detroit Red Wings**, Mar. 1 – Apr. 15, 2006.
10 Games – Buffalo Sabres, Dec. 10, 1983 – Jan. 23, 1984.
 – St. Louis Blues, Jan. 21 – Mar. 2, 2000.
 – New Jersey Devils, Feb. 27 – Apr. 7, 2001.
 – Buffalo Sabres, Oct. 4 – Nov. 13, 2006.
 – San Jose Sharks, Nov. 14 – Dec. 31, 2007.

LONGEST WINNING STREAK FROM START OF SEASON:
10 Games – **Toronto Maple Leafs**, 1993-94.
 – **Buffalo Sabres**, 2006-07.
8 Games – Toronto Maple Leafs, 1934-35.
 – Buffalo Sabres, 1975-76.
 – Nashville Predators, 2005-06.
7 Games – Edmonton Oilers, 1983-84.
 – Quebec Nordiques, 1985-86.
 – Pittsburgh Penguins, 1986-87.
 – Pittsburgh Penguins, 1994-95.

LONGEST HOME WINNING STREAK FROM START OF SEASON:
11 Games – **Chicago Blackhawks**, 1963-64.
10 Games – Ottawa Senators, 1925-26.
9 Games – Montreal Canadiens, 1953-54.
 – Chicago Blackhawks, 1971-72.
 – San Jose Sharks, 2008-09.

LONGEST ROAD WINNING STREAK FROM START OF SEASON:
10 Games – **Buffalo Sabres**, Oct.4 – Nov. 13, 2006.
9 Games – New Jersey Devils, Oct. 8 – Nov. 12, 2009.
7 Games – Toronto Maple Leafs, Nov. 14 – Dec. 15, 1940.
 – Philadelphia Flyers, Oct. 12 – Nov. 16, 1985.
 – Detroit Red Wings, Oct. 6 – Nov. 6, 2005.
 – Pittsburgh Penguins, Oct. 3 – Nov. 3, 2009

LONGEST WINNING STREAK, INCLUDING PLAYOFFS:
15 Games – **Detroit Red Wings**, Feb. 27 – Apr. 5, 1955.
(9 regular-season games, 6 playoff games)
 – **New Jersey Devils**, Mar. 28 – Apr. 29, 2006.
(11 regular-season games, 4 playoff games)

LONGEST HOME WINNING STREAK, INCLUDING PLAYOFFS:
24 Games – **Philadelphia Flyers**, Jan. 4 – Apr. 25, 1976.
(20 regular-season games, 4 playoff games)

LONGEST ROAD WINNING STREAK, INCLUDING PLAYOFFS:
11 Games – **New Jersey Devils**, Feb. 27 – Apr. 17, 2001.
(10 regular-season games, 1 playoff game)

UNDEFEATED STREAKS
LONGEST UNDEFEATED STREAK, ONE SEASON:
35 Games – **Philadelphia Flyers**, Oct. 14, 1979 – Jan. 6, 1980. 25w-10T
28 Games – Montreal Canadiens, Dec. 18, 1977 – Feb. 23, 1978. 23w-5T

LONGEST HOME UNDEFEATED STREAK, ONE SEASON:
34 Games – **Montreal Canadiens**, Nov. 1, 1976 – Apr. 2, 1977. 28w-6T
27 Games – Boston Bruins, Nov. 22, 1970 – Mar. 20, 1971. 26w-1T

LONGEST ROAD UNDEFEATED STREAK, ONE SEASON:
23 Games – **Montreal Canadiens**, Nov. 27, 1974 – Mar. 12, 1975. 14w-9T
17 Games – Montreal Canadiens, Dec. 18, 1977 – Mar. 1, 1978. 14w-3T

LONGEST UNDEFEATED STREAK FROM START OF SEASON:
15 Games – **Edmonton Oilers**, 1984-85. 12w-3T
14 Games – Montreal Canadiens, 1943-44. 11w-3T

LONGEST HOME UNDEFEATED STREAK FROM START OF SEASON:
26 Games – **Philadelphia Flyers**, Oct. 11, 1979 – Feb. 3, 1980. 19w-7T

LONGEST ROAD UNDEFEATED STREAK FROM START OF SEASON:
15 Games – **Detroit Red Wings**, Oct. 18 – Dec. 20, 1951. 10w-5T

LONGEST UNDEFEATED STREAK, INCLUDING PLAYOFFS:
24 Games – **Montreal Canadiens**, Feb. 21 – Apr. 11, 1980.
15w-6T in regular season and 3w in playoffs.
21 Games – Philadelphia Flyers, Mar. 9 – May 4, 1975.
13w-1T in regular season and 7w in playoffs.
 – Pittsburgh Penguins, Mar. 9 – Apr. 22, 1993.
17w-1T in regular season and 3w in playoffs.

LONGEST HOME UNDEFEATED STREAK, INCLUDING PLAYOFFS:
38 Games – **Montreal Canadiens**, Nov. 1, 1976 – Apr. 26, 1977.
28w-6T in regular season and 4w in playoffs.

LONGEST ROAD UNDEFEATED STREAK, INCLUDING PLAYOFFS:
13 Games – **Philadelphia Flyers**, Feb. 26 – Apr. 21, 1977. 6w-4T in
regular season and 3w in playoffs.
 – **Montreal Canadiens**, Feb. 26 – Apr. 20, 1980. 6w-4T in
regular season and 3w in playoffs.
 – **New York Islanders**, Mar. 16 – May 1, 1980. 3w-3T in regular
season and 7w in playoffs.

LOSING STREAKS
LONGEST LOSING STREAK, ONE SEASON:
17 Games – **Washington Capitals**, Feb. 18 – Mar. 26, 1975.
 – **San Jose Sharks**, Jan. 4 – Feb. 12, 1993.
15 Games – Philadelphia Quakers, Nov. 29, 1930 – Jan. 8, 1931.

LONGEST HOME LOSING STREAK, ONE SEASON:
14 Games – **Pittsburgh Penguins**, Dec. 31, 2003 – Feb. 22, 2004.
11 Games – Boston Bruins, Dec. 8, 1924 – Feb. 17, 1925.
 – Washington Capitals, Feb. 18 – Mar. 30, 1975.
 – Ottawa Senators, Oct. 27 – Dec. 8, 1993.

LONGEST ROAD LOSING STREAK, ONE SEASON:
***38 Games** – **Ottawa Senators**, Oct. 10, 1992 – Apr. 3, 1993.
37 Games – Washington Capitals, Oct. 9, 1974 – Mar. 26, 1975.

LONGEST LOSING STREAK FROM START OF SEASON:
11 Games – **New York Rangers**, 1943-44.
7 Games – Montreal Canadiens, 1938-39.
 – Chicago Blackhawks, 1947-48.
 – Washington Capitals, 1983-84.
 – Chicago Blackhawks, 1997-98.

LONGEST HOME LOSING STREAK FROM START OF SEASON:
8 Games – **Los Angeles Kings**, Oct. 13 – Nov. 6, 1971.

LONGEST ROAD LOSING STREAK FROM START OF SEASON:
***38 Games** – **Ottawa Senators**, Oct. 10, 1992 – Apr. 3, 1993.

WINLESS STREAKS
LONGEST WINLESS STREAK, ONE SEASON:
30 Games – **Winnipeg Jets**, Oct. 19 – Dec. 20, 1980. 23L-7T
27 Games – Kansas City Scouts, Feb. 12 – Apr. 4, 1976. 21L-6T
25 Games – Washington Capitals, Nov. 29, 1975 – Jan. 21, 1976. 22L-3T

LONGEST HOME WINLESS STREAK, ONE SEASON:
17 Games – **Ottawa Senators**, Oct. 28, 1995 – Jan. 27, 1996. 15L-2T
 – **Atlanta Thrashers**, Jan. 19 – Mar. 29, 2000. 15L-2T
16 Games – Pittsburgh Penguins, Dec. 31, 2003 – Mar. 4, 2004. 15L-1T

LONGEST ROAD WINLESS STREAK, ONE SEASON:
***38 Games** – **Ottawa Senators**, Oct. 10, 1992 – Apr. 3, 1993. 38L
37 Games – Washington Capitals, Oct. 9, 1974 – Mar. 26, 1975. 37L

LONGEST WINLESS STREAK FROM START OF SEASON:
15 Games – **New York Rangers**, 1943-44. 14L-1T
11 Games – Pittsburgh Pirates, 1927-28. 8L-3T
 – Minnesota North Stars, 1973-74. 5L-6T
 – San Jose Sharks, 1995-96. 7L-4T

LONGEST HOME WINLESS STREAK FROM START OF SEASON:
11 Games – **Pittsburgh Penguins**, Oct. 8 – Nov. 19, 1983. 9L-2T

LONGEST ROAD WINLESS STREAK FROM START OF SEASON:
***38 Games** – **Ottawa Senators**, Oct. 10, 1992 – Apr. 3, 1993. 38L

NON-SHUTOUT STREAKS
LONGEST NON-SHUTOUT STREAK:
264 Games – **Calgary Flames**, Nov. 12, 1981 – Jan. 9, 1985.
261 Games – Los Angeles Kings, Mar. 15, 1986 – Oct. 22, 1989.
244 Games – Washington Capitals, Oct. 31, 1989 – Nov. 11, 1993.
236 Games – New York Rangers, Dec. 20, 1989 – Dec. 13, 1992.
230 Games – Quebec Nordiques, Feb. 10, 1980 – Jan. 12, 1983.

LONGEST NON-SHUTOUT STREAK, INCLUDING PLAYOFFS:
264 Games – **Los Angeles Kings**, Mar. 15, 1986 – Apr. 6, 1989.
(5 playoff games in 1987; 5 in 1988; 2 in 1989).
262 Games – Chicago Blackhawks, Mar. 14, 1970 – Feb. 21, 1973.
(8 playoff games in 1970; 18 in 1971; 8 in 1972).
251 Games – Quebec Nordiques, Feb. 10, 1980 – Jan. 12, 1983.
(5 playoff games in 1981; 16 in 1982).
246 Games – Pittsburgh Penguins, Jan. 7, 1989 – Oct. 26, 1991.
(11 playoff games in 1989; 24 in 1991).

* – Does not include neutral site games

TEAM GOALS

Most Goals

MOST GOALS, ONE SEASON:
446 – Edmonton Oilers, 1983-84. 80GP
426 – Edmonton Oilers, 1985-86. 80GP
424 – Edmonton Oilers, 1982-83. 80GP
417 – Edmonton Oilers, 1981-82. 80GP
401 – Edmonton Oilers, 1984-85. 80GP

MOST GOALS, ONE TEAM, ONE GAME:
16 – Montreal Canadiens, Mar. 3, 1920, at Quebec. Montreal won 16-3.

MOST GOALS, BOTH TEAMS, ONE GAME:
21 – Montreal Canadiens (14), Toronto St. Patricks (7), Jan. 10, 1920, at Montreal.
– Edmonton Oilers (12), Chicago Blackhawks (9), Dec. 11, 1985, at Chicago.
20 – Edmonton Oilers (12), Minnesota North Stars (8), Jan. 4, 1984, at Edmonton.
– Toronto Maple Leafs (11), Edmonton Oilers (9), Jan. 8, 1986, at Toronto.
19 – Montreal Wanderers (10), Toronto Arenas (9), Dec. 19, 1917, at Montreal.
– Montreal Canadiens (16), Quebec Bulldogs (3), Mar. 3, 1920, at Quebec.
– Montreal Canadiens (13), Hamilton Tigers (6), Feb. 26, 1921, at Montreal.
– Boston Bruins (10), New York Rangers (9), Mar. 4, 1944, at Boston.
– Detroit Red Wings (10), Boston Bruins (9), Mar. 16, 1944, at Detroit.
– Vancouver Canucks (10), Minnesota North Stars (9), Oct. 7, 1983, at Vancouver.

MOST GOALS, ONE TEAM, ONE PERIOD:
9 – Buffalo Sabres, Mar. 19, 1981, at Buffalo, second period during 14-4 win over Toronto.
8 – Detroit Red Wings, Jan. 23, 1944, at Detroit, third period during 15-0 win over NY Rangers.
– Boston Bruins, Mar. 16, 1969, at Boston, second period during 11-3 win over Toronto.
– New York Rangers, Nov. 21, 1971, at NY Rangers, third period during 12-1 win over California.
– Philadelphia Flyers, Mar. 31, 1973, at Philadelphia, second period during 10-2 win over NY Islanders.
– Buffalo Sabres, Dec. 21, 1975, at Buffalo, third period during 14-2 win over Washington.
– Minnesota North Stars, Nov. 11, 1981, at Minnesota, second period during 15-2 win over Winnipeg.
– Pittsburgh Penguins, Dec. 17, 1991, at Pittsburgh, second period during 10-2 win over San Jose.
– Washington Capitals, Feb. 3, 1999, at Washington, second period during 10-1 win over Tampa Bay.

MOST GOALS, BOTH TEAMS, ONE PERIOD:
12 – Buffalo Sabres (9), Toronto Maple Leafs (3), Mar. 19, 1981, at Buffalo, second period. Buffalo won 14-4.
– Edmonton Oilers (6), Chicago Blackhawks (6), Dec. 11, 1985, at Chicago, second period. Edmonton won 12-9.
10 – New York Rangers (7), New York Americans (3), Mar. 16, 1939, at NY Americans, third period. NY Rangers won 11-5.
– Toronto Maple Leafs (6), Detroit Red Wings (4), Mar. 17, 1946, at Detroit, third period. Toronto won 11-7.
– Buffalo Sabres (6), Vancouver Canucks (4), Jan. 8, 1976, at Buffalo, third period. Buffalo won 8-5.
– Buffalo Sabres (5), Montreal Canadiens (5), Oct. 26, 1982, at Montreal, first period. Teams tied 7-7.
– Quebec Nordiques (6), Boston Bruins (4), Dec. 7, 1982, at Quebec, second period. Quebec won 10-5.
– Vancouver Canucks (6), Calgary Flames (4), Jan. 16, 1987, at Vancouver, first period. Vancouver won 9-5.
– Detroit Red Wings (7), Winnipeg Jets (3), Nov. 25, 1987, at Detroit, third period. Detroit won 10-8.
– Chicago Blackhawks (5), St. Louis Blues (5), Mar. 15, 1988, at St. Louis, third period. Teams tied 7-7.

MOST CONSECUTIVE GOALS, ONE TEAM, ONE GAME:
15 – Detroit Red Wings, Jan. 23, 1944, at Detroit during 15-0 win over NY Rangers.

Fewest Goals

FEWEST GOALS, ONE SEASON:
33 – Chicago Blackhawks, 1928-29. 44GP
45 – Montreal Maroons, 1924-25. 30GP
46 – Pittsburgh Pirates, 1928-29. 44GP

FEWEST GOALS, ONE SEASON (MINIMUM 70-GAME SCHEDULE):
133 – Chicago Blackhawks, 1953-54. 70GP
147 – Toronto Maple Leafs, 1954-55. 70GP
– Boston Bruins, 1955-56. 70GP
150 – New York Rangers, 1954-55. 70GP

TEAM POWER-PLAY GOALS

MOST POWER-PLAY GOALS, ONE SEASON:
119 – Pittsburgh Penguins, 1988-89. 80GP
113 – Detroit Red Wings, 1992-93. 84GP
111 – New York Rangers, 1987-88. 80GP
110 – Pittsburgh Penguins, 1987-88. 80GP
– Winnipeg Jets, 1987-88. 80GP

TEAM SHORTHAND GOALS

MOST SHORTHAND GOALS, ONE SEASON:
36 – Edmonton Oilers, 1983-84. 80GP
28 – Edmonton Oilers, 1986-87. 80GP
27 – Edmonton Oilers, 1985-86. 80GP
– Edmonton Oilers, 1988-89. 80GP

TEAM GOALS-PER-GAME

HIGHEST GOALS-PER-GAME AVERAGE, ONE SEASON:
5.58 – Edmonton Oilers, 1983-84. 446G in 80GP.
5.38 – Montreal Canadiens, 1919-20. 129G in 24GP.
5.33 – Edmonton Oilers, 1985-86. 426G in 80GP.
5.30 – Edmonton Oilers, 1982-83. 424G in 80GP.
5.23 – Montreal Canadiens, 1917-18. 115G in 22GP.

LOWEST GOALS-PER-GAME AVERAGE, ONE SEASON:
0.75 – Chicago Blackhawks, 1928-29. 33G in 44GP.
1.05 – Pittsburgh Pirates, 1928-29. 46G in 44GP.
1.20 – New York Americans, 1928-29. 53G in 44GP.

TEAM ASSISTS

MOST ASSISTS, ONE SEASON:
737 – Edmonton Oilers, 1985-86. 80GP
736 – Edmonton Oilers, 1983-84. 80GP
706 – Edmonton Oilers, 1981-82. 80GP

FEWEST ASSISTS, ONE SEASON (Since 1926-27):
45 – New York Rangers, 1926-27. 44GP

FEWEST ASSISTS, ONE SEASON (MINIMUM 70-GAME SCHEDULE):
206 – Chicago Blackhawks, 1953-54. 70GP

TEAM TOTAL POINTS

MOST SCORING POINTS, ONE SEASON:
1,182 – Edmonton Oilers, 1983-84. (446G-736A) 80GP
1,163 – Edmonton Oilers, 1985-86. (426G-737A) 80GP
1,123 – Edmonton Oilers, 1981-82. (417G-706A) 80GP

MOST SCORING POINTS, ONE TEAM, ONE GAME:
40 – Buffalo Sabres, Dec. 21, 1975, at Buffalo.
Buffalo defeated Washington 14-2, and had 26A.
39 – Minnesota North Stars, Nov. 11, 1981, at Minnesota.
Minnesota defeated Winnipeg 15-2, and had 24A.
37 – Detroit Red Wings, Jan. 23, 1944, at Detroit.
Detroit defeated NY Rangers 15-0, and had 22A.
– Toronto Maple Leafs, Mar. 16, 1957, at Toronto.
Toronto defeated NY Rangers 14-1, and had 23A.
– Buffalo Sabres, Feb. 25, 1978, at Cleveland.
Buffalo defeated Cleveland 13-3, and had 24A.
– Calgary Flames, Feb. 10, 1993, at Calgary.
Calgary defeated San Jose 13-1, and had 24A.

MOST SCORING POINTS, BOTH TEAMS, ONE GAME:
62 – Edmonton Oilers, Chicago Blackhawks, Dec. 11, 1985, at Chicago.
Edmonton won 12-9. Edmonton had 24A, Chicago, 17A.
53 – Quebec Nordiques, Washington Capitals, Feb. 22, 1981, at Washington.
Quebec won 11-7. Quebec had 22A, Washington, 13A.
– Edmonton Oilers, Minnesota North Stars, Jan. 4, 1984, at Edmonton.
Edmonton won 12-8. Edmonton had 20A, Minnesota, 13A.
– Minnesota North Stars, St. Louis Blues, Jan. 27, 1984, at St. Louis.
Minnesota won 10-8. Minnesota had 19A, St. Louis, 16A.
– Toronto Maple Leafs, Edmonton Oilers, Jan. 8, 1986, at Toronto.
Toronto won 11-9. Toronto had 17A, Edmonton, 16A.
52 – Montreal Maroons, New York Americans, Feb. 18, 1936, at NY Americans. Teams tied 8-8. NY Americans had 20A, Montreal, 16A. (3A allowed for each goal.)
– Vancouver Canucks, Minnesota North Stars, Oct. 7, 1983, at Vancouver.
Vancouver won 10-9. Vancouver had 16A, Minnesota, 17A.

MOST SCORING POINTS, ONE TEAM, ONE PERIOD:
23 – New York Rangers, Nov. 21, 1971, at NY Rangers, third period during 12-1 win over California. NY Rangers had 8G, 15A.
– Buffalo Sabres, Dec. 21, 1975, at Buffalo, third period during 14-2 win over Washington. Buffalo had 8G, 15A.
– Buffalo Sabres, Mar. 19, 1981, at Buffalo, second period during 14-4 win over Toronto. Buffalo had 9G, 14A.
22 – Detroit Red Wings, Jan. 23, 1944, at Detroit, third period during 15-0 win over NY Rangers. Detroit had 8G, 14A.
– Boston Bruins, Mar. 16, 1969, at Boston, second period during 11-3 win over Toronto. Boston had 8G, 14A.
– Minnesota North Stars, Nov. 11, 1981, at Minnesota, second period during 15-2 win over Winnipeg. Minnesota had 8G, 14A.
– Pittsburgh Penguins, Dec. 17, 1991, at Pittsburgh, second period during 10-2 win over San Jose. Pittsburgh had 8G, 14A.
– Washington Capitals, Feb. 3, 1999, at Washington, second period during 10-1 win over Tampa Bay. Washington had 8G, 14A.

MOST SCORING POINTS, BOTH TEAMS, ONE PERIOD:
35 – Edmonton, Oilers, Chicago Blackhawks, Dec. 11, 1985, at Chicago, second period. Edmonton won 12-9. Edmonton had 6G, 12A; Chicago, 6G, 11A.
31 – Buffalo Sabres, Toronto Maple Leafs, Mar. 19, 1981, at Buffalo, second period during 14-4. Buffalo won 14-4. Buffalo had 9G, 14A; Toronto, 3G, 5A.
29 – Winnipeg Jets, Detroit Red Wings, Nov. 25, 1987, at Detroit, third period. Detroit won 10-8. Detroit had 7G, 13A; Winnipeg, 3G, 6A.
– Chicago Blackhawks, St. Louis Blues, Mar. 15, 1988, at St. Louis, third period. Teams tied 7-7. St. Louis had 5G, 10A; Chicago, 5G, 9A.

FASTEST GOALS

FASTEST SIX GOALS, BOTH TEAMS:
3:00 – **Quebec Nordiques, Washington Capitals**, Feb. 22, 1981, at Washington. Scorers: Peter Stastny, Quebec, 18:51; Pierre Lacroix, Quebec, 19:57 (first period); Anton Stastny, Quebec, 0:34; Jacques Richard, Quebec, 1:07 and 1:37; Rick Green, Washington, 1:51 (second period). Quebec won 11-7.

3:15 – Montreal Canadiens, Toronto Maple Leafs, Jan. 4, 1944, at Montreal, first period. Scorers: Maurice Richard, Montreal, 14:10; Don Webster, Toronto, 15:13; Fern Majeau, Montreal, 15:41; Phil Watson, Montreal, 15:52; Lorne Carr, Toronto, 16:55; Butch Bouchard, Montreal, 17:25. Montreal won 6-3.

FASTEST FIVE GOALS, BOTH TEAMS:
1:24 – **Chicago Blackhawks, Toronto Maple Leafs**, Oct. 15, 1983, at Toronto, second period. Scorers: Gaston Gingras, Toronto, 16:49; Denis Savard, Chicago, 17:12; Steve Larmer, Chicago, 17:27; Denis Savard, Chicago, 17:42; John Anderson, Toronto, 18:13. Toronto won 10-8.

1:39 – Detroit Red Wings, Toronto Maple Leafs, Nov. 15, 1944, at Toronto, third period. Scorers: Ted Kennedy, Toronto, 10:36 and 10:55; Harold Jackson, Detroit, 11:48; Steve Wojciechowski, Detroit, 12:02; Don Grosso, Detroit, 12:15. Detroit won 8-4.

FASTEST FIVE GOALS, ONE TEAM:
2:07 – **Pittsburgh Penguins**, Nov. 22, 1972, at Pittsburgh, third period. Scorers: Bryan Hextall, Jr., 12:00; Jean Pronovost, 12:18; Al McDonough, 13:40; Ken Schinkel, 13:49; Ron Schock, 14:07. Pittsburgh defeated St. Louis 10-4.

2:37 – New York Islanders, Jan. 26, 1982, at NY Islanders, first period. Scorers: Duane Sutter, 1:31; John Tonelli, 2:30; Bryan Trottier, 2:46 and 3:31; Duane Sutter, 4:08. NY Islanders defeated Pittsburgh 9-2.

2:55 – Boston Bruins, Dec. 19, 1974, at Boston. Scorers: Bobby Schmautz, 19:13 (first period); Ken Hodge, 0:18; Phil Esposito, 0:43; Don Marcotte, 0:58; John Bucyk, 2:08 (second period). Boston defeated NY Rangers 11-3.

FASTEST FOUR GOALS, BOTH TEAMS:
0:53 – **Chicago Blackhawks, Toronto Maple Leafs**, Oct. 15, 1983, at Toronto, second period. Scorers: Gaston Gingras, Toronto, 16:49; Denis Savard, Chicago, 17:12; Steve Larmer, Chicago, 17:27; Denis Savard, Chicago, 17:42. Toronto won 10-8.

0:57 – Quebec Nordiques, Detroit Red Wings, Jan. 27, 1990, at Quebec, first period. Scorers: Paul Gillis, Quebec, 18:01; Claude Loiselle, Quebec, 18:12; Joe Sakic, Quebec, 18:27; Jimmy Carson, Detroit, 18:58. Detroit won 8-6.

1:01 – Colorado Rockies, New York Rangers, Jan. 15, 1980, at NY Rangers, first period. Scorers: Doug Sulliman, NY Rangers, 7:52; Eddie Johnstone, NY Rangers, 7:57; Warren Miller, NY Rangers, 8:20; Rob Ramage, Colorado, 8:53. Teams tied 6-6.

– Chicago Blackhawks, Toronto Maple Leafs, Oct. 15, 1983, at Toronto, second period. Scorers: Denis Savard, Chicago, 17:12; Steve Larmer, Chicago, 17:27; Denis Savard, Chicago, 17:42; John Anderson, Toronto, 18:13. Toronto won 10-8.

FASTEST FOUR GOALS, ONE TEAM:
1:20 – **Boston Bruins**, Jan. 21, 1945, at Boston, second period. Scorers: Bill Thoms, 6:34; Frank Mario, 7:08 and 7:27; Ken Smith, 7:54. Boston defeated NY Rangers 14-3.

FASTEST THREE GOALS, BOTH TEAMS:
0:15 – **Minnesota North Stars, New York Rangers**, Feb. 10, 1983, at Minnesota, second period. Scorers: Mark Pavelich, NY Rangers, 19:18; Ron Greschner, NY Rangers, 19:27; Willi Plett, Minnesota, 19:33. Minnesota won 7-5.

0:18 – Montreal Canadiens, New York Rangers, Dec. 12, 1963, at Montreal, first period. Scorers: Dave Balon, Montreal, 0:58; Gilles Tremblay, Montreal, 1:04; Camille Henry, NY Rangers, 1:16. Montreal won 6-4.

– California Golden Seals, Buffalo Sabres, Feb. 1, 1976, at California, third period. Scorers: Jim Moxey, California, 19:38; Wayne Merrick, California, 19:45; Danny Gare, Buffalo, 19:56. Buffalo won 9-5.

FASTEST THREE GOALS, ONE TEAM:
0:20 – **Boston Bruins**, Feb. 25, 1971, at Boston, third period. Scorers: John Bucyk, 4:50; Ed Westfall, 5:02; Ted Green, 5:10. Boston defeated Vancouver 8-3.

0:21 – Chicago Blackhawks, Mar. 23, 1952, at NY Rangers, third period. Bill Mosienko scored all three goals, at 6:09, 6:20 and 6:30. Chicago defeated NY Rangers 7-6.

– Washington Capitals, Nov. 23, 1990, at Washington, first period. Scorers: Michal Pivonka, 16:18; Stephen Leach, 16:29 and 16:39. Washington defeated Pittsburgh 7-3.

FASTEST THREE GOALS FROM START OF PERIOD, BOTH TEAMS:
1:05 – **Hartford Whalers, Montreal Canadiens**, Mar. 11, 1989, at Montreal, second period. Scorers: Kevin Dineen, Hartford, 0:11; Guy Carbonneau, Montreal, 0:36; Petr Svoboda, Montreal, 1:05. Montreal won 5-3.

FASTEST THREE GOALS FROM START OF PERIOD, ONE TEAM:
0:53 – **Calgary Flames**, Feb. 10, 1993, at Calgary, third period. Scorers: Gary Suter, 0:17; Chris Lindberg, 0:40; Ron Stern, 0:53. Calgary defeated San Jose 13-1.

FASTEST TWO GOALS, BOTH TEAMS:
0:02 – **St. Louis Blues, Boston Bruins**, Dec. 19, 1987, at Boston, third period. Scorers: Ken Linseman, Boston, 19:50; Doug Gilmour, St. Louis, 19:52. St. Louis won 7-5.

* **0:03** – Chicago Blackhawks, Minnesota North Stars, Nov. 5, 1988, at Minnesota, third period. Scorers: Steve Thomas, Chicago, 6:03; Dave Gagner, Minnesota, 6:06. Teams tied 5-5.

* – Newspaper accounts of this game note that the clock was slow to start after the first goal was scored.

FASTEST TWO GOALS, ONE TEAM:
0:03 – **Minnesota Wild**, Jan. 21, 2004, at Minnesota, third period. Scorers: Jim Dowd, 19:44; Richard Park, 19:47. Minnesota defeated Chicago 4-2.

0:04 – Montreal Maroons, Jan. 3, 1931, at Montreal, third period. Nels Stewart scored both goals, at 8:24 and 8:28. Mtl. Maroons defeated Boston 5-3.

– Buffalo Sabres, Oct. 17, 1974, at Buffalo, third period. Scorers: Lee Fogolin, Jr., 14:55; Don Luce, 14:59. Buffalo defeated California 6-1.

– Toronto Maple Leafs, Dec. 29, 1988, at Quebec, third period. Scorers: Ed Olczyk, 5:24; Gary Leeman, 5:28. Toronto defeated Quebec 6-5.

– Calgary Flames, Oct. 17, 1989, at Quebec, third period. Scorers: Doug Gilmour, 19:45; Paul Ranheim, 19:49. Teams tied 8-8.

– Winnipeg Jets, Dec. 15, 1995, at Winnipeg, second period. Deron Quint scored both goals, at 7:51 and 7:55. Winnipeg defeated Edmonton 9-4.

FASTEST TWO GOALS FROM START OF GAME, ONE TEAM:
0:24 – **Edmonton Oilers**, Mar. 28, 1982, at Los Angeles. Scorers: Mark Messier, 0:14; Dave Lumley, 0:24. Edmonton defeated Los Angeles 6-2.

0:27 – Boston Bruins, Feb. 14, 2003, at Florida. Mike Knuble scored both goals, at 0:10 and 0:27. Boston defeated Florida 6-5.

0:29 – Pittsburgh Penguins, Dec. 6, 1980, at Pittsburgh. Scorers: George Ferguson, 0:17; Greg Malone, 0:29. Pittsburgh defeated Chicago 6-4.

FASTEST TWO GOALS FROM START OF PERIOD, BOTH TEAMS:
0:14 – **New York Rangers, Quebec Nordiques**, Nov. 5, 1983, at Quebec, third period. Scorers: Andre Savard, Quebec, 0:08; Pierre Larouche, NY Rangers, 0:14. Teams tied 4-4.

0:25 – St. Louis Blues, Chicago Blackhawks, Feb. 2, 2006, at St. Louis, second period. Scorers: Peter Cajanek, St. Louis, 0:10; Tyler Arnason, Chicago, 0:25. St. Louis won 6-5.

0:28 – Boston Bruins, Montreal Canadiens, Oct. 11, 1989, at Montreal, third period. Scorers: Jim Wiemer, Boston 0:10; Tom Chorske, Montreal 0:28. Montreal won 4-2.

FASTEST TWO GOALS FROM START OF PERIOD, ONE TEAM:
0:21 – **Chicago Blackhawks**, Nov. 5, 1983, at Minnesota, second period. Scorers: Ken Yaremchuk, 0:12; Darryl Sutter, 0:21. Minnesota defeated Chicago 10-5.

0:24 – Edmonton Oilers, Mar. 28, 1982, at Los Angeles, first period. Scorers: Mark Messier, 0:14; Dave Lumley, 0:24. Edmonton defeated Los Angeles 6-2.

0:27 – Boston Bruins, Feb. 14, 2003, at Florida. Mike Knuble scored both goals, at 0:10 and 0:27. Boston defeated Florida 6-5.

50, 40, 30, 20-GOAL SCORERS

MOST 50-OR-MORE GOAL SCORERS, ONE SEASON:
3 – **Edmonton Oilers**, 1983-84. 80GP. Wayne Gretzky, 87; Glenn Anderson, 54; Jari Kurri, 52.

– **Edmonton Oilers**, 1985-86. 80GP. Jari Kurri, 68; Glenn Anderson, 54; Wayne Gretzky, 52.

2 – Boston Bruins, 1970-71. 78GP. Phil Esposito, 76; John Bucyk, 51.

– Boston Bruins, 1973-74. 78GP. Phil Esposito, 68; Ken Hodge, 50.

– Philadelphia Flyers, 1975-76. 80GP. Reggie Leach, 61; Bill Barber, 50.

– Pittsburgh Penguins, 1975-76. 80GP. Pierre Larouche, 53; Jean Pronovost, 52.

– Montreal Canadiens, 1976-77. 80GP. Steve Shutt, 60; Guy Lafleur, 56.

– Los Angeles Kings, 1979-80. 80GP. Charlie Simmer, 56; Marcel Dionne, 53.

– Montreal Canadiens, 1979-80. 80GP. Pierre Larouche, 50; Guy Lafleur, 50.

– Los Angeles Kings, 1980-81. 80GP. Marcel Dionne, 58; Charlie Simmer, 56.

– Edmonton Oilers, 1981-82. 80GP. Wayne Gretzky, 92; Mark Messier, 50.

– New York Islanders, 1981-82. 80GP. Mike Bossy, 64; Bryan Trottier, 50.

– Edmonton Oilers, 1984-85. 80GP. Wayne Gretzky, 73; Jari Kurri, 71.

– Washington Capitals, 1984-85. 80GP. Bob Carpenter, 53; Mike Gartner, 50.

– Edmonton Oilers, 1986-87. 80GP. Wayne Gretzky, 62; Jari Kurri, 54.

– Calgary Flames, 1987-88. 80GP. Joe Nieuwendyk, 51; Hakan Loob, 50.

– Los Angeles Kings, 1987-88. 80GP. Jimmy Carson, 55; Luc Robitaille, 53.

– Calgary Flames, 1988-89. 80GP. Joe Nieuwendyk, 51; Joe Mullen, 51.

– Los Angeles Kings, 1988-89. 80GP. Bernie Nicholls, 70; Wayne Gretzky, 54.

– Buffalo Sabres, 1992-93. 84GP. Alexander Mogilny, 76; Pat LaFontaine, 53.

– Pittsburgh Penguins, 1992-93. 84GP. Mario Lemieux, 69; Kevin Stevens, 55.

– St. Louis Blues, 1992-93. 84GP. Brett Hull, 54; Brendan Shanahan, 51.

– Detroit Red Wings, 1993-94. 84GP. Sergei Fedorov, 56; Ray Sheppard, 52.

– St. Louis Blues, 1993-94. 84GP. Brett Hull, 57; Brendan Shanahan, 52.

– Pittsburgh Penguins, 1995-96. 82GP. Mario Lemieux, 69; Jaromir Jagr, 62.

MOST 40-OR-MORE GOAL SCORERS, ONE SEASON:
4 – **Edmonton Oilers**, 1982-83. 80GP. Wayne Gretzky, 71; Glenn Anderson, 48; Mark Messier, 48; Jari Kurri, 45.

– **Edmonton Oilers**, 1983-84. 80GP. Wayne Gretzky, 87; Glenn Anderson, 54; Jari Kurri, 52; Paul Coffey, 40.

– **Edmonton Oilers**, 1984-85. 80GP. Wayne Gretzky, 73; Jari Kurri, 71; Mike Krushelnyski, 43; Glenn Anderson, 42.

– **Edmonton Oilers**, 1985-86. 80GP. Jari Kurri, 68; Glenn Anderson, 54; Wayne Gretzky, 52; Paul Coffey, 48.

– **Calgary Flames**, 1987-88. 80GP. Joe Nieuwendyk, 51; Hakan Loob, 50; Mike Bullard, 48; Joe Mullen, 40.

3 – Boston Bruins, 1970-71. 78GP. Phil Esposito, 76; John Bucyk, 51; Ken Hodge, 43.

– New York Rangers, 1971-72. 78GP. Vic Hadfield, 50; Jean Ratelle, 46; Rod Gilbert, 43.

– Buffalo Sabres, 1975-76. 80GP. Danny Gare, 50; Rick Martin, 49; Gilbert Perreault, 44.

– Montreal Canadiens, 1979-80. 80GP. Guy Lafleur, 50; Pierre Larouche, 50; Steve Shutt, 47.

– Buffalo Sabres, 1979-80. 80GP. Danny Gare, 56; Rick Martin, 45; Gilbert Perreault, 40.

– Los Angeles Kings, 1980-81. 80GP. Marcel Dionne, 58; Charlie Simmer, 56; Dave Taylor, 47.

– Los Angeles Kings, 1984-85. 80GP. Marcel Dionne, 46; Bernie Nicholls, 46; Dave Taylor, 41.

– New York Islanders, 1984-85. 80GP. Mike Bossy, 58; Brent Sutter, 42; John Tonelli, 42.

– Chicago Blackhawks, 1985-86. 80GP. Denis Savard, 47; Troy Murray, 45; Al Secord, 40.

– Chicago Blackhawks, 1987-88. 80GP. Denis Savard, 44; Rick Vaive, 43; Steve Larmer, 41.
– Edmonton Oilers, 1987-88. 80GP. Craig Simpson, 43; Jari Kurri, 43; Wayne Gretzky, 40.
– Los Angeles Kings, 1988-89. 80GP. Bernie Nicholls, 70; Wayne Gretzky, 54; Luc Robitaille, 46.
– Los Angeles Kings, 1990-91. 80GP. Luc Robitaille, 45; Tomas Sandstrom, 45; Wayne Gretzky, 41.
– Pittsburgh Penguins, 1991-92. 80GP. Kevin Stevens, 54; Mario Lemieux, 44; Joe Mullen, 42.
– Pittsburgh Penguins, 1992-93. 84GP. Mario Lemieux, 69; Kevin Stevens, 55; Rick Tocchet, 48.
– Calgary Flames, 1993-94. 84GP. Gary Roberts, 41; Robert Reichel, 40; Theoren Fleury, 40.
– Pittsburgh Penguins, 1995-96. 82GP. Mario Lemieux, 69; Jaromir Jagr, 62; Petr Nedved, 45.

MOST 30-OR-MORE GOAL SCORERS, ONE SEASON:
6 – Buffalo Sabres, 1974-75. 80GP. Rick Martin, 52; Rene Robert, 40; Gilbert Perreault, 39; Don Luce, 33; Rick Dudley, 31; Danny Gare, 31.
– New York Islanders, 1977-78. 80GP. Mike Bossy, 53; Bryan Trottier, 46; Clark Gillies, 35; Denis Potvin, 30; Bob Nystrom, 30; Bob Bourne, 30.
– Winnipeg Jets, 1984-85. 80GP. Dale Hawerchuk, 53; Paul MacLean, 41; Laurie Boschman, 32; Brian Mullen, 32; Doug Smail, 31; Thomas Steen, 30.
5 – Chicago Blackhawks, 1968-69. 76GP
– Boston Bruins, 1970-71. 78GP
– Montreal Canadiens, 1971-72. 78GP
– Philadelphia Flyers, 1972-73. 78GP
– Boston Bruins, 1973-74. 78GP
– Montreal Canadiens, 1974-75. 80GP
– Montreal Canadiens, 1975-76. 80GP
– Pittsburgh Penguins, 1975-76. 80GP
– New York Islanders, 1978-79. 80GP
– Detroit Red Wings, 1979-80. 80GP
– Philadelphia Flyers, 1979-80. 80GP
– New York Islanders, 1980-81. 80GP
– St. Louis Blues, 1980-81. 80GP
– Chicago Blackhawks, 1981-82. 80GP
– Edmonton Oilers, 1981-82. 80GP
– Montreal Canadiens, 1981-82. 80GP
– Quebec Nordiques, 1981-82. 80GP
– Washington Capitals, 1981-82. 80GP
– Edmonton Oilers, 1982-83. 80GP
– Edmonton Oilers, 1983-84. 80GP
– Edmonton Oilers, 1984-85. 80GP
– Los Angeles Kings, 1984-85. 80GP
– Edmonton Oilers, 1985-86. 80GP
– Edmonton Oilers, 1986-87. 80GP
– Edmonton Oilers, 1987-88. 80GP
– Edmonton Oilers, 1988-89. 80GP
– Detroit Red Wings, 1991-92. 80GP
– New York Rangers, 1991-92. 80GP
– Pittsburgh Penguins, 1991-92. 80GP
– Detroit Red Wings, 1992-93. 84GP
– Pittsburgh Penguins, 1992-93. 84GP

MOST 20-OR-MORE GOAL SCORERS, ONE SEASON:
11 – Boston Bruins, 1977-78. 80GP. Peter McNab, 41; Terry O'Reilly, 29; Bobby Schmautz, 27; Stan Jonathan, 27; Jean Ratelle, 25; Rick Middleton, 25; Wayne Cashman, 24; Gregg Sheppard, 23; Brad Park, 22; Don Marcotte, 20; Bob Miller, 20.
10 – Boston Bruins, 1970-71. 78GP
– Montreal Canadiens, 1974-75. 80GP
– St. Louis Blues, 1980-81. 80GP

100-POINT SCORERS

MOST 100 OR-MORE-POINT SCORERS, ONE SEASON:
4 – Boston Bruins, 1970-71. 78GP. Phil Esposito, 76G-76A-152PTS; Bobby Orr, 37G-102A-139PTS; John Bucyk, 51G-65A-116PTS; Ken Hodge, 43G-62A-105PTS.
– Edmonton Oilers, 1982-83. 80GP. Wayne Gretzky, 71G-125A-196PTS; Mark Messier, 48G-58A-106PTS; Glenn Anderson, 48G-56A-104PTS; Jari Kurri, 45G-59A-104PTS.
– Edmonton Oilers, 1983-84. 80GP. Wayne Gretzky, 87G-118A-205PTS; Paul Coffey, 40G-86A-126PTS; Jari Kurri, 52G-61A-113PTS; Mark Messier, 37G-64A-101PTS.
– Edmonton Oilers, 1985-86. 80GP. Wayne Gretzky, 52G-163A-215PTS; Paul Coffey, 48G-90A-138PTS; Jari Kurri, 68G-63A-131PTS; Glenn Anderson, 54G-48A-102PTS.
– Pittsburgh Penguins, 1992-93. 84GP. Mario Lemieux, 69G-91A-160PTS; Kevin Stevens, 55G-56A-111PTS; Rick Tocchet, 48G-61A-109PTS; Ron Francis, 24G-76A-100PTS.
3 – Boston Bruins, 1973-74. 78GP. Phil Esposito, 68G-77A-145PTS; Bobby Orr, 32G-90A-122PTS; Ken Hodge, 50G-55A-105PTS.
– New York Islanders, 1978-79. 80GP. Bryan Trottier, 47G-87A-134PTS; Mike Bossy, 69G-57A-126PTS; Denis Potvin, 31G-70A-101PTS.
– Los Angeles Kings, 1980-81. 80GP. Marcel Dionne, 58G-77A-135PTS; Dave Taylor, 47G-65A-112PTS; Charlie Simmer, 56G-49A-105PTS.
– Edmonton Oilers, 1984-85. 80GP. Wayne Gretzky, 73G-135A-208PTS; Jari Kurri, 71G-64A-135PTS; Paul Coffey, 37G-84A-121PTS.
– New York Islanders, 1984-85. 80GP. Mike Bossy, 58G-59A-117PTS; Brent Sutter, 42G-60A-102PTS; John Tonelli, 42G-58A-100PTS.
– Edmonton Oilers, 1986-87. 80GP. Wayne Gretzky, 62G-121A-183PTS; Jari Kurri, 54G-54A-108PTS; Mark Messier, 37G-70A-107PTS.
– Pittsburgh Penguins, 1988-89. 80GP. Mario Lemieux, 85G-114A-199PTS; Rob Brown, 49G-66A-115PTS; Paul Coffey, 30G-83A-113PTS.
– Pittsburgh Penguins, 1995-96. 82GP. Mario Lemieux, 69G-92A-161PTS; Jaromir Jagr, 62G-87A-149PTS; Ron Francis, 27G-92A-119PTS.

SHOTS ON GOAL

MOST SHOTS, BOTH TEAMS, ONE GAME:
141 – New York Americans, Pittsburgh Pirates, Dec. 26, 1925, at NY Americans. NY Americans won 3-1 with 73 shots; Pittsburgh had 68 shots.

MOST SHOTS, ONE TEAM, ONE GAME:
83 – Boston Bruins, Mar. 4, 1941, at Boston. Boston defeated Chicago 3-2.
73 – New York Americans, Dec. 26, 1925, at NY Americans. NY Americans defeated Pittsburgh 3-1.
– Boston Bruins, Mar. 21, 1991, at Boston. Boston tied Quebec 3-3.
72 – Boston Bruins, Dec. 10, 1970, at Boston. Boston defeated Buffalo 8-2.

MOST SHOTS, ONE TEAM, ONE PERIOD:
33 – Boston Bruins, Mar. 4, 1941, at Boston, second period. Boston defeated Chicago 3-2.

TEAM GOALS AGAINST

Fewest Goals Against

FEWEST GOALS AGAINST, ONE SEASON:
42 – Ottawa Senators, 1925-26. 36GP
43 – Montreal Canadiens, 1928-29. 44GP
48 – Montreal Canadiens, 1923-24. 24GP
– Montreal Canadiens, 1927-28. 44GP

FEWEST GOALS AGAINST, ONE SEASON (MINIMUM 70-GAME SCHEDULE):
131 – Toronto Maple Leafs, 1953-54. 70GP
– Montreal Canadiens, 1955-56. 70GP
132 – Detroit Red Wings, 1953-54. 70GP
133 – Detroit Red Wings, 1951-52. 70GP
– Detroit Red Wings, 1952-53. 70GP

LOWEST GOALS-AGAINST-PER-GAME AVERAGE, ONE SEASON:
0.98 – Montreal Canadiens, 1928-29. 43GA in 44GP.
1.09 – Montreal Canadiens, 1927-28. 48GA in 44GP.
1.17 – Ottawa Senators, 1925-26. 42GA in 36GP.

Most Goals Against

MOST GOALS AGAINST, ONE SEASON:
446 – Washington Capitals, 1974-75. 80GP
415 – Detroit Red Wings, 1985-86. 80GP
414 – San Jose Sharks, 1992-93. 84GP
407 – Quebec Nordiques, 1989-90. 80GP
403 – Hartford Whalers, 1982-83. 80GP

HIGHEST GOALS-AGAINST-PER-GAME AVERAGE, ONE SEASON:
7.38 – Quebec Bulldogs, 1919-20. 177GA in 24GP.
6.20 – New York Rangers, 1943-44. 310GA in 50GP.
5.58 – Washington Capitals, 1974-75. 446GA in 80GP.

MOST POWER-PLAY GOALS AGAINST, ONE SEASON:
122 – Chicago Blackhawks, 1988-89. 80GP
120 – Pittsburgh Penguins, 1987-88. 80GP
116 – Washington Capitals, 2005-06. 82GP
115 – New Jersey Devils, 1988-89. 80GP
– Ottawa Senators, 1992-93. 84GP
114 – Los Angeles Kings, 1992-93. 84GP

MOST SHORTHAND GOALS AGAINST, ONE SEASON:
22 – Pittsburgh Penguins, 1984-85. 80GP
– Minnesota North Stars, 1991-92. 80GP
– Colorado Avalanche, 1995-96. 82GP
21 – Calgary Flames, 1984-85. 80GP
– Pittsburgh Penguins, 1989-90. 80GP

SHUTOUTS

MOST SHUTOUTS, ONE SEASON:
22 – Montreal Canadiens, 1928-29. All by George Hainsworth. 44GP
16 – New York Americans, 1928-29. Roy Worters 13, Flat Walsh 3. 44GP
15 – Ottawa Senators, 1925-26. All by Alex Connell. 36GP
– Ottawa Senators, 1927-28. All by Alex Connell. 44GP
– Boston Bruins, 1927-28. All by Hal Winkler. 44GP
– Chicago Blackhawks, 1969-70. All by Tony Esposito. 76GP

MOST CONSECUTIVE SHUTOUTS, ONE SEASON:
6 – Ottawa Senators, Jan. 31 – Feb. 18, 1928. All by Alex Connell.

MOST CONSECUTIVE SHUTOUTS TO START SEASON:
5 – Toronto Maple Leafs, Nov. 13 – 22, 1930. Lorne Chabot 3, Benny Grant 2.

MOST GAMES SHUTOUT, ONE SEASON:
20 – Chicago Blackhawks, 1928-29. 44GP

MOST CONSECUTIVE GAMES SHUTOUT:
8 – Chicago Blackhawks, Feb. 7 – 28, 1929.

MOST CONSECUTIVE GAMES SHUTOUT TO START SEASON:
3 – Montreal Maroons, Nov. 11 – 18, 1930.

TEAM SHOOTOUT RECORDS

MOST SHOOTOUT GAMES, ONE SEASON:
20 – Phoenix, 2009-10 (14w, 6L)
19 – Edmonton, 2007-08 (15w, 4L)
– Boston, 2009-10 (10w, 9L)
18 – New Jersey, 2006-07 (10w, 8L)
– Los Angeles, 2009-10 (10w, 8L)

MOST SHOOTOUT GAMES, ALL-TIME:
65 – Edmonton (39w, 26L)
– NY Rangers (37w, 28L)
– Boston (31w, 34L)

MOST SHOOTOUT WINS, ONE SEASON:
15 – Edmonton, 2007-08, 19GP
14 – Phoenix, 2009-10, 20GP
12 – Dallas, 2005-06, 13GP

MOST SHOOTOUT WINS, ALL-TIME:
39 – New Jersey, 62GP
– Dallas, 63GP
– Edmonton, 65GP

MOST SHOOTOUT HOME WINS, ONE SEASON:
8 – Edmonton, 2007-08, 9GP
7 – NY Rangers, 2008-09, 9GP
– NY Islanders, 2009-10, 9GP
– Anaheim, 2007-08, 10GP
– Minnesota, 2006-07, 11GP

MOST SHOOTOUT HOME WINS, ALL-TIME:
20 – NY Islanders, 29GP
– New Jersey, 32GP19
19 – NY Rangers, 28GP

MOST SHOOTOUT ROAD WINS, ONE SEASON:
8 – Phoenix, 2009-10, 12GP
7 – Dallas, 2005-06, 8GP
– Dallas, 2006-07, 9GP
– Edmonton, 2007-08, 10GP
– Boston, 2009-10, 10GP

MOST SHOOTOUT ROAD WINS, ALL-TIME:
24 – Dallas, 36GP
21 – Edmonton, 36GP
19 – New Jersey, 30GP

MOST SHOOTOUT SHOTS TAKEN, ONE SEASON:
90 – Phoenix, 2009-10, 20GP
75 – Dallas, 2009-10, 17GP
74 – Los Angeles, 2009-10, 18GP

MOST SHOOTOUT SHOTS TAKEN, ALL-TIME:
241 – Dallas, 63GP
239 – NY Rangers, 65GP
230 – Edmonton, 65GP

MOST SHOOTOUT GOALS SCORED, ONE SEASON:
34 – Phoenix, 2009-10, 20GP
27 – Minnesota, 2006-07, 17GP
– Los Angeles, 2009-10, 18GP

MOST SHOOTOUT GOALS SCORED, ALL-TIME:
85 – Dallas, 63GP (241s)
82 – New Jersey, 62GP (206s)
80 – Los Angeles, 56GP (213s)
– Edmonton, 65GP (230s)

BEST SHOOTOUT SCORING PERCENTAGE, ONE SEASON:
.583 – San Jose, 2006-07, 4GP (7G, 12s)
.571 – Dallas, 2005-06, 13GP (24G, 42s)
.517 – Pittsburgh, 2009-10, 10GP (15G, 29s)
– Atlanta, 2006-07, 11GP (15G, 29s)

BEST SHOOTOUT SCORING PERCENTAGE, ALL-TIME:
.398 – New Jersey, 62GP (82G, 206s)
.376 – Nashville, 51GP (62G, 165s)
– Los Angeles, 56GP (80G, 213s)

FEWEST SHOOTOUT GOALS AGAINST, ONE SEASON:
3 – Los Angeles, 2005-06, 7GP (21SA)
– Tampa Bay, 2007-08, 3GP (9SA)
– Calgary, 2008-09, 5GP (14SA)

FEWEST SHOOTOUT GOALS AGAINST, ALL-TIME:
47 – Carolina, 37GP (123SA)
48 – Tampa Bay, 49GP (166SA)
49 – Calgary, 38GP (115SA)

BEST SHOOTOUT WINNING PERCENTAGE, ONE SEASON:
.923 – Dallas, 2005-06, 13GP (12w)
.875 – Atlanta, 2008-09, 8GP (7w)
.857 – Los Angeles, 2005-06, 7GP (6w)

BEST SHOOTOUT WINNING PERCENTAGE, ALL-TIME:
.629 – New Jersey, 62GP (39w)
.619 – Dallas, 63GP (39w)
.608 – Phoenix, 51GP (31w)

TEAM PENALTIES

MOST PENALTY MINUTES, ONE SEASON:
2,713 – Buffalo Sabres, 1991-92. 80GP
2,670 – Pittsburgh Penguins, 1988-89. 80GP
2,663 – Chicago Blackhawks, 1991-92. 80GP
2,643 – Calgary Flames, 1991-92. 80GP
2,621 – Philadelphia Flyers, 1980-81. 80GP

MOST PENALTIES, BOTH TEAMS, ONE GAME:
85 – **Edmonton Oilers (44), Los Angeles Kings (41)**, Feb. 28, 1990, at Los Angeles. Edmonton received 26 minors, 7 majors, 6 10-minute misconducts, 4 game misconducts and 1 match penalty; Los Angeles received 26 minors, 9 majors, 3 10-minute misconducts and 3 game misconducts.

MOST PENALTY MINUTES, BOTH TEAMS, ONE GAME:
419 – **Ottawa Senators (206), Philadelphia Flyers (213)**, Mar. 5, 2004, at Philadelphia. Ottawa received 8 minors, 10 majors, 4 10-minute misconducts and 10 game misconducts. Philadelphia received 9 minors, 11 majors, 4 10-minute misconducts and 10 game misconducts.

MOST PENALTIES, ONE TEAM, ONE GAME:
44 – **Edmonton Oilers**, Feb. 28, 1990, at Los Angeles. Edmonton received 26 minors, 7 majors, 6 10-minute misconducts, 4 game misconducts and 1 match penalty.
42 – Minnesota North Stars, Feb. 26, 1981, at Boston. Minnesota received 18 minors, 13 majors, 4 10-minute misconducts and 7 game misconducts.
– Boston Bruins, Feb. 26, 1981, at Boston vs. Minnesota. Boston received 20 minors, 13 majors, 3 10-minute misconducts and 6 game misconducts.

MOST PENALTY MINUTES, ONE TEAM, ONE GAME:
213 – **Philadelphia Flyers**, Mar. 5, 2004, at Philadelphia. Philadelphia received 9 minors, 11 majors, 4 10-minute misconducts and 10 game misconducts.

MOST PENALTIES, BOTH TEAMS, ONE PERIOD:
67 – **Minnesota North Stars (34), Boston Bruins (33)**, Feb. 26, 1981, at Boston, first period. Minnesota received 15 minors, 8 majors, 4 10-minute misconducts and 7 game misconducts. Boston had 16 minors, 8 majors, 3 10-minute misconducts and 6 game misconducts.

MOST PENALTY MINUTES, BOTH TEAMS, ONE PERIOD:
409 – **Ottawa Senators (200), Philadelphia Flyers (209)**, Mar. 5, 2004, at Philadelphia, third period. Ottawa received 5 minors, 10 majors, 4 10-minute misconducts and 10 game misconducts. Philadelphia received 7 minors, 11 majors, 4 10-minute misconducts and 10 game misconducts.

MOST PENALTIES, ONE TEAM, ONE PERIOD:
34 – **Minnesota North Stars**, Feb. 26, 1981, at Boston, first period. Minnesota received 15 minors, 8 majors, 4 10-minute misconducts and 7 game misconducts.

MOST PENALTY MINUTES, ONE TEAM, ONE PERIOD:
209 – **Philadelphia Flyers**, Mar. 5, 2004, at Philadelphia vs. Ottawa, third period. Philadelphia received 7 minors, 11 majors, 4 10-minute misconducts and 10 game misconducts.
200 – Ottawa Senators, Mar. 5, 2004, at Philadelphia, third period. Ottawa received 5 minors, 10 majors, 4 10-minute misconducts and 10 game misconducts.

NHL Individual Scoring Records – History

Six individual scoring records stand as benchmarks in the history of the game: most goals, single-season and career; most assists, single-season and career; and most points, single-season and career. The evolution of these six records is traced here, beginning with 1917-18, the NHL's first season. New research has resulted in changes to scoring records in the NHL's first nine seasons.

MOST GOALS, ONE SEASON

44 —Joe Malone, Montreal, 1917-18.
   Scored goal #44 against Toronto's Harry Holmes on March 2, 1918 and finished the season with 44 goals.
50 —Maurice Richard, Montreal, 1944-45.
   Scored goal #45 against Toronto's Frank McCool on February 25, 1945 and finished the season with 50 goals.
50 —Bernie Geoffrion, Montreal, 1960-61.
   Scored goal #50 against Toronto's Cesare Maniago on March 16, 1961 and finished the season with 50 goals.
50 —Bobby Hull, Chicago, 1961-62.
   Scored goal #50 against NY Rangers' Gump Worsley on March 25, 1962 and finished the season with 50 goals.
54 —Bobby Hull, Chicago, 1965-66.
   Scored goal #51 against NY Rangers' Cesare Maniago on March 12, 1966 and finished the season with 54 goals.
58 —Bobby Hull, Chicago, 1968-69.
   Scored goal #55 against Boston's Gerry Cheevers on March 20, 1969 and finished the season with 58 goals.
76 —Phil Esposito, Boston, 1970-71.
   Scored goal #59 against Los Angeles' Denis DeJordy on March 11, 1971 and finished the season with 76 goals.
92 —Wayne Gretzky, Edmonton, 1981-82.
   Scored goal #77 against Buffalo's Don Edwards on February 24, 1982 and finished the season with 92 goals.

MOST ASSISTS, ONE SEASON

10 —Cy Denneny, Ottawa, 1917-18.
   —Reg Noble, Toronto, 1917-18.
   —Harry Cameron, Toronto, 1917-18.
   —Newsy Lalonde, Montreal, 1918-19.
15 —Frank Nighbor, Ottawa, 1919-20.
   —Jack Darragh, Ottawa, 1920-21.
17 —Harry Cameron, Toronto, 1921-22.
18 —Dick Irvin, Chicago, 1926-27.
   —Howie Morenz, Montreal, 1927-28.
36 —Frank Boucher, NY Rangers, 1929-30.
37 —Joe Primeau, Toronto, 1931-32.
45 —Bill Cowley, Boston, 1940-41.
   —Bill Cowley, Boston, 1942-43.
49 —Clint Smith, Chicago, 1943-44.
54 —Elmer Lach, Montreal, 1944-45.
55 —Ted Lindsay, Detroit, 1949-50.
56 —Bert Olmstead, Montreal, 1955-56.
58 —Jean Beliveau, Montreal, 1960-61.
   —Andy Bathgate, NY Rangers/Toronto, 1963-64.
59 —Stan Mikita, Chicago, 1964-65.
62 —Stan Mikita, Chicago, 1966-67.
77 —Phil Esposito, Boston, 1968-69.
87 —Bobby Orr, Boston, 1969-70.
102 —Bobby Orr, Boston, 1970-71.
109 —Wayne Gretzky, Edmonton, 1980-81.
120 —Wayne Gretzky, Edmonton, 1981-82.
125 —Wayne Gretzky, Edmonton, 1982-83.
135 —Wayne Gretzky, Edmonton, 1984-85.
163 —Wayne Gretzky, Edmonton, 1985-86.

MOST POINTS, ONE SEASON

48 —Joe Malone, Montreal, 1917-18.
49 —Joe Malone, Montreal, 1919-20.
51 —Howie Morenz, Montreal, 1927-28.
73 —Cooney Weiland, Boston, 1929-30.
   —Doug Bentley, Chicago, 1942-43.
82 —Herb Cain, Boston, 1943-44.
86 —Gordie Howe, Detroit, 1950-51.
95 —Gordie Howe, Detroit, 1952-53.
96 —Dickie Moore, Montreal, 1958-59.
97 —Bobby Hull, Chicago, 1965-66.
   —Stan Mikita, Chicago, 1966-67.
126 —Phil Esposito, Boston, 1968-69.
152 —Phil Esposito, Boston, 1970-71.
164 —Wayne Gretzky, Edmonton, 1980-81.
212 —Wayne Gretzky, Edmonton, 1981-82.
215 —Wayne Gretzky, Edmonton, 1985-86.

MOST REGULAR-SEASON GOALS, CAREER

44 —Joe Malone, Montreal.
   Malone led the NHL in goals in the league's first season with 44 goals in 20 games in 1917-18.
54 —Cy Denneny, Ottawa.
   Denneny passed Malone during the 1918-19 season, and led the NHL in goals with 54 after two seasons.
143 —Joe Malone, Montreal, Quebec Bulldogs, Hamilton.
   Malone passed Denneny during the 1919-20 season and finished his career with 143 goals.
248 —Cy Denneny, Ottawa, Boston.
   Denneny passed Malone with goal #144 during the 1922-23 season and finished his career with 248 goals.
271 —Howie Morenz, Montreal, Chicago, NY Rangers.
   Morenz passed Denneny with goal #249 during the 1933-34 season and finished his career with 271 goals.
324 —Nels Stewart, Montreal Maroons, Boston, NY Americans.
   Stewart passed Morenz with goal #272 during the 1936-37 season and finished his career with 324 goals.
544 —Maurice Richard, Montreal.
   Richard passed Stewart with goal #325 on Nov. 8, 1952 and finished his career with 544 goals.
801 —Gordie Howe, Detroit, Hartford.
   Howe passed Richard with goal #545 on Nov. 10, 1963 and finished his career with 801 goals.
894 —Wayne Gretzky, Edmonton, Los Angeles, St. Louis, NY Rangers.
   Gretzky passed Howe with goal #802 on March 23, 1994 and finished his career with 894 goals.

Bobby Hull and Stan Mikita, above, revitalized the Chicago Blackhawks after joining the team in the late 1950s and re-wrote the NHL record book during the 1960s. Hull became the first player in league history to score more than 50 goals when he got 54 in 1965-66. He later pushed the single-season record to 58. Mikita was the first to top 60 assists in 1966-67 and his 97 points tied the NHL record set by Hull just one year before.

In addition to winning the Lady Byng Trophy seven times in eight years between 1928 and 1935, Frank Boucher piled up points too. Setting up goals for Rangers teammates Bill Cook and his brother Bun Cook saw Boucher become the NHL's early career leader in assists.

MOST REGULAR-SEASON ASSISTS, CAREER

(minimum 100 assists)

100 —Frank Boucher, Ottawa, NY Rangers.
In 1930-31, Boucher became the first NHL player to reach the 100-assist milestone.

263 —Frank Boucher, Ottawa, NY Rangers.
Boucher retired as the NHL's career assist leader in 1938 with 253. He returned to the NHL in 1943-44 and remained the NHL's career assist leader until he was overtaken by Bill Cowley in 1943-44. He finished his career with 263 assists.

353 —Bill Cowley, St. Louis Eagles, Boston.
Cowley passed Boucher with assist #264 in 1943-44. He retired as the NHL's career assist leader in 1947 with 353.

408 —Elmer Lach, Montreal.
Lach passed Cowley with assist #354 in 1951-52. He retired as the NHL's career assist leader in 1954 with 408.

1,049 —Gordie Howe, Detroit, Hartford.
Howe passed Lach with assist #409 in 1957-58. He retired as the NHL's career assist leader in 1980 with 1,049.

1,963 —Wayne Gretzky, Edmonton, Los Angeles, St. Louis, NY Rangers.
Gretzky passed Howe with assist #1,050 in 1987-88. He retired as the NHL's current career assist leader with 1,963.

MOST REGULAR-SEASON POINTS, CAREER

(minimum 100 points)

100 —Joe Malone, Montreal, Quebec Bulldogs, Hamilton.
In 1919-20, Malone became the first player in NHL history to record 100 points.

200 —Cy Denneny, Ottawa.
In 1923-24, Denneny became the first player in NHL history to record 200 points.

300 —Cy Denneny, Ottawa.
In 1926-27, Denneny became the first player in NHL history to record 300 points.

333 —Cy Denneny, Ottawa, Boston.
Denneny retired as the NHL's career point-scoring leader in 1929 with 333 points.

472 —Howie Morenz, Montreal, Chicago, NY Rangers.
Morenz passed Cy Denneny with point #334 in 1931-32. At the time his career ended in 1937, he was the NHL's career point- scoring leader with 472 points.

515 —Nels Stewart, Montreal Maroons, Boston, NY Americans.
Stewart passed Morenz with point #473 in 1938-39. He retired as the NHL's career point-scoring leader in 1940 with 515 points.

528 —Syd Howe, Ottawa, Philadelphia Quakers, Toronto, St. Louis Eagles, Detroit.
Howe passed Nels Stewart with point #516 on March 8, 1945. He retired as the NHL's career point-scoring leader in 1946 with 528 points.

548 —Bill Cowley, St. Louis Eagles, Boston.
Cowley passed Syd Howe with point #529 on Feb. 12, 1947. He retired as the NHL's career point-scoring leader in 1947 with 548 points.

610 —Elmer Lach, Montreal.
Lach passed Bill Cowley with point #549 on Feb. 23, 1952. He remained the NHL's career point-scoring leader until he was overtaken by Maurice Richard in 1953-54. He finished his career with 623 points.

946 —Maurice Richard, Montreal.
Richard passed teammate Elmer Lach with point #611 on Dec. 12, 1953. He remained the NHL's career point-scoring leader until he was overtaken by Gordie Howe in 1959-60. He finished his career with 965 points.

1,850 —Gordie Howe, Detroit, Hartford.
Howe passed Richard with point #947 on Jan. 16, 1960. He retired as the NHL's career point-scoring leader in 1980 with 1,850 points.

2,857 —Wayne Gretzky, Edmonton, Los Angeles, St. Louis, NY Rangers.
Gretzky passed Howe with point #1,851 on Oct. 15, 1989. He retired as the NHL's current career points leader with 2,857.

Individual Records

Regular Season

SEASONS

MOST SEASONS:
- **26 – Gordie Howe**, Detroit, 1946-47 – 1970-71; Hartford, 1979-80.
  - **Chris Chelios**, Montreal, Chicago, Detroit, Atlanta 1983-84 – 2003-04, 2005-06 – 2009-10.
- 25 – Mark Messier, Edmonton, NY Rangers, Vancouver, 1979-80 – 2003-04.
- 24 – Alex Delvecchio, Detroit, 1950-51 – 1973-74.
  - Tim Horton, Toronto, NY Rangers, Pittsburgh, Buffalo, 1949-50, 1951-52 – 1973-74.
- 23 – John Bucyk, Detroit, Boston, 1955-56 – 1977-78.
  - Ron Francis, Hartford, Pittsburgh, Carolina, Toronto, 1981-82 – 2003-04.
  - Al MacInnis, Calgary, St. Louis, 1981-82 – 2003-04.
  - Dave Andreychuk, Buffalo, Toronto, New Jersey, Boston, Colorado, Tampa Bay, 1982-83 – 2003-04, 2005-06.

GAMES

MOST GAMES:
- **1,767 – Gordie Howe**, Detroit, 1946-47 – 1970-71; Hartford, 1979-80.
- 1,756 – Mark Messier, Edmonton, NY Rangers, Vancouver, 1979-80 – 2003-04.
- 1,731 – Ron Francis, Hartford, Pittsburgh, Carolina, Toronto, 1981-82 – 2003-04.
- 1,651 – Chris Chelios, Montreal, Chicago, Detroit, Atlanta, 1983-84 – 2003-04, 2005-06 – 2009-10.
- 1,639 – Dave Andreychuk, Buffalo, Toronto, New Jersey, Boston, Colorado, Tampa Bay, 1982-83 – 2003-04, 2005-06.
- 1,635 – Scott Stevens, Washington, St. Louis, New Jersey, 1982-83 – 2003-04.

MOST GAMES, INCLUDING PLAYOFFS:
- **1,992 – Mark Messier**, Edmonton, NY Rangers, Vancouver, 1,756 regular-season games, 236 playoff games.
- 1,924 – Gordie Howe, Detroit, Hartford, 1,767 regular-season games, 157 playoff games.
- 1,917 – Chris Chelios, Montreal, Chicago, Detroit, Atlanta, 1,651 regular-season games, 266 playoff games.
- 1,902 – Ron Francis, Hartford, Pittsburgh, Carolina, Toronto, 1,731 regular-season games, 171 playoff games.
- 1,868 – Scott Stevens, Washington, St. Louis, New Jersey, 1,635 regular-season games, 233 playoff games.

MOST CONSECUTIVE GAMES:
- **964 – Doug Jarvis**, Montreal, Washington, Hartford, Oct. 8, 1975 – Oct. 10, 1987.
- 914 – Garry Unger, Toronto, Detroit, St. Louis, Atlanta, Feb. 24, 1968 – Dec. 21, 1979.
- 884 – Steve Larmer, Chicago, Oct. 6, 1982 – Apr. 15, 1993.
- 776 – Craig Ramsay, Buffalo, Mar. 27, 1973 – Feb. 10, 1983.
- 630 – Andy Hebenton, NY Rangers, Boston, Oct. 7, 1955 – Mar. 22, 1964.

GOALS

MOST GOALS:
- **894 – Wayne Gretzky**, Edmonton, Los Angeles, St. Louis, NY Rangers, in 20 seasons. 1,487GP
- 801 – Gordie Howe, Detroit, Hartford, in 26 seasons. 1,767GP
- 741 – Brett Hull, Calgary, St. Louis, Dallas, Detroit, Phoenix, in 19 seasons. 1,269GP
- 731 – Marcel Dionne, Detroit, Los Angeles, NY Rangers, in 18 seasons. 1,348GP
- 717 – Phil Esposito, Chicago, Boston, NY Rangers, in 18 seasons. 1,282GP

MOST GOALS, INCLUDING PLAYOFFS:
- **1,016 – Wayne Gretzky**, Edmonton, Los Angeles, St. Louis, NY Rangers, 894G in 1,487 regular-season games, 122G in 208 playoff games.
- 869 – Gordie Howe, Detroit, Hartford, 801G in 1,767 regular-season games, 68G in 157 playoff games.
- 844 – Brett Hull, Calgary, St. Louis, Dallas, Detroit, Phoenix, 741G in 1,269 regular-season games, 103G in 202 playoff games.
- 803 – Mark Messier, Edmonton, NY Rangers, Vancouver, 694G in 1,756 regular-season games, 109G in 236 playoff games.
- 778 – Phil Esposito, Chicago, Boston, NY Rangers, 717G in 1,282 regular-season games, 61G in 130 playoff games.

MOST GOALS, ONE SEASON:
- **92 – Wayne Gretzky**, Edmonton, 1981-82. 80GP – 80 game schedule.
- 87 – Wayne Gretzky, Edmonton, 1983-84. 74GP – 80 game schedule.
- 86 – Brett Hull, St. Louis, 1990-91. 78GP – 80 game schedule.
- 85 – Mario Lemieux, Pittsburgh, 1988-89. 76GP – 80 game schedule.
- 76 – Phil Esposito, Boston, 1970-71. 78GP – 78 game schedule.
  - Alexander Mogilny, Buffalo, 1992-93. 77GP – 84 game schedule.
  - Teemu Selanne, Winnipeg, 1992-93. 84GP – 84 game schedule.
- 73 – Wayne Gretzky, Edmonton, 1984-85. 80GP – 80 game schedule.
- 72 – Brett Hull, St. Louis, 1989-90. 80GP – 80 game schedule.
- 71 – Wayne Gretzky, Edmonton, 1982-83. 80GP – 80 game schedule.
  - Jari Kurri, Edmonton, 1984-85. 73GP – 80 game schedule.
- 70 – Mario Lemieux, Pittsburgh, 1987-88. 77GP – 80 game schedule.
  - Bernie Nicholls, Los Angeles, 1988-89. 79GP – 80 game schedule.
  - Brett Hull, St. Louis, 1991-92. 73GP – 80 game schedule.

MOST GOALS, ONE SEASON, INCLUDING PLAYOFFS:
- **100 – Wayne Gretzky**, Edmonton, 1983-84, 87G in 74 regular-season games, 13G in 19 playoff games.
- 97 – Wayne Gretzky, Edmonton, 1981-82, 92G in 80 regular-season games, 5G in 5 playoff games.
  - Mario Lemieux, Pittsburgh, 1988-89, 85G in 76 regular-season games, 12G in 11 playoff games.
  - Brett Hull, St. Louis, 1990-91, 86G in 78 regular-season games, 11G in 13 playoff games.
- 90 – Wayne Gretzky, Edmonton, 1984-85, 73G in 80 regular-season games, 17G in 18 playoff games.
  - Jari Kurri, Edmonton, 1984-85, 71G in 80 regular-season games, 19G in 18 playoff games.
- 85 – Mike Bossy, NY Islanders, 1980-81, 68G in 79 regular-season games, 17G in 18 playoff games.
  - Brett Hull, St. Louis, 1989-90, 72G in 80 regular-season games, 13G in 12 playoff games.
- 83 – Wayne Gretzky, Edmonton, 1982-83, 71G in 73 regular-season games, 12G in 16 playoff games.
  - Alexander Mogilny, Buffalo, 1992-93, 76G in 77 regular-season games, 7G in 7 playoff games.

MOST GOALS, 50 GAMES FROM START OF SEASON:
- **61 – Wayne Gretzky**, Edmonton, 1981-82. Oct. 7, 1981 – Jan. 22, 1982. (80-game schedule)
  - **Wayne Gretzky**, Edmonton, 1983-84. Oct. 5, 1983 – Jan. 25, 1984. (80-game schedule)
- 54 – Mario Lemieux, Pittsburgh, 1988-89. Oct. 7, 1988 – Jan. 31, 1989. (80-game schedule)
- 53 – Wayne Gretzky, Edmonton, 1984-85. Oct. 11, 1984 – Jan. 28, 1985. (80-game schedule)
- 52 – Brett Hull, St. Louis, 1990-91. Oct. 4, 1990 – Jan. 26, 1991. (80-game schedule)
- 50 – Maurice Richard, Montreal, 1944-45. Oct. 28, 1944 – Mar. 18, 1945. (50-game schedule)
  - Mike Bossy, NY Islanders, 1980-81. Oct. 11, 1980 – Jan. 24, 1981. (80-game schedule)
  - Brett Hull, St. Louis, 1991-92. Oct. 5, 1991 – Jan. 28, 1992. (80-game schedule)

MOST GOALS, ONE GAME:
- **7 – Joe Malone**, Quebec, Jan. 31, 1920, at Quebec. Quebec 10, Toronto 6.
- 6 – Newsy Lalonde, Montreal, Jan. 10, 1920, at Montreal. Montreal 14, Toronto 7.
  - Joe Malone, Quebec, Mar. 10, 1920, at Quebec. Quebec 10, Ottawa 4.
  - Corb Denneny, Toronto, Jan. 26, 1921, at Toronto. Toronto 10, Hamilton 3.
  - Cy Denneny, Ottawa, Mar. 7, 1921, at Ottawa. Ottawa 12, Hamilton 5.
  - Syd Howe, Detroit, Feb. 3, 1944, at Detroit. Detroit 12, NY Rangers 2.
  - Red Berenson, St. Louis, Nov. 7, 1968, at Philadelphia. St. Louis 8, Philadelphia 0.
  - Darryl Sittler, Toronto, Feb. 7, 1976, at Toronto. Toronto 11, Boston 4.

Although he got into only seven games with the Atlanta Thrashers, the 2009-10 season marked the 26th in the NHL for Chris Chelios which moved him into a tie with Gordie Howe for the most seasons played in NHL history. Chelios ranks fourth in games played with 1,651.

Darryl Sittler looks to pass the puck past Carol Vadnais of the Boston Bruins. No player in the NHL has managed to score six goals in a game since the Leafs captain did so against the Bruins on February 7, 1976. Sittler also had four assists that night for a record 10 points.

MOST GOALS, ONE ROAD GAME:

6 – **Red Berenson**, St. Louis, Nov. 7, 1968, at Philadelphia. St. Louis 8, Philadelphia 0.

5 – Joe Malone, Montreal, Dec. 19, 1917, at Ottawa. Montreal 7, Ottawa 4.
 – Red Green, Hamilton, Dec. 5, 1924, at Toronto. Hamilton 10, Toronto 3.
 – Babe Dye, Toronto, Dec. 22, 1924, at Boston. Toronto 10, Boston 1.
 – Punch Broadbent, Mtl. Maroons, Jan. 7, 1925, at Hamilton. Mtl. Maroons 6, Hamilton 2.
 – Don Murdoch, NY Rangers, Oct. 12, 1976, at Minnesota. NY Rangers 10, Minnesota 4.
 – Tim Young, Minnesota, Jan. 15, 1979, at NY Rangers. Minnesota 8, NY Rangers 1.
 – Willy Lindstrom, Winnipeg, Mar. 2, 1982, at Philadelphia. Winnipeg 7, Philadelphia 6.
 – Bengt Gustafsson, Washington, Jan. 8, 1984, at Philadelphia. Washington 7, Philadelphia 1.
 – Wayne Gretzky, Edmonton, Dec. 15, 1984, at St. Louis. Edmonton 8, St. Louis 2.
 – Dave Andreychuk, Buffalo, Feb. 6, 1986, at Boston. Buffalo 8, Boston 6.
 – Mats Sundin, Quebec, Mar. 5, 1992, at Hartford. Quebec 10, Hartford 4.
 – Mario Lemieux, Pittsburgh, Apr. 9, 1993, at NY Rangers. Pittsburgh 10, NY Rangers 4.
 – Mike Ricci, Quebec, Feb. 17, 1994, at San Jose. Quebec 8, San Jose 2.
 – Alex Zhamnov, Winnipeg, Apr. 1, 1995, at Los Angeles. Winnipeg 7, Los Angeles 7.

MOST GOALS, ONE PERIOD:

4 – **Busher Jackson**, Toronto, Nov. 20, 1934, at St. Louis, third period. Toronto 5, St. Louis 2.
 – **Max Bentley**, Chicago, Jan. 28, 1943, at Chicago, third period. Chicago 10, NY Rangers 1.
 – **Clint Smith**, Chicago, Mar. 4, 1945, at Chicago, third period. Chicago 6, Montreal 4.
 – **Red Berenson**, St. Louis, Nov. 7, 1968, at Philadelphia, second period. St. Louis 8, Philadelphia 0.
 – **Wayne Gretzky**, Edmonton, Feb. 18, 1981, at Edmonton, third period. Edmonton 9, St. Louis 2.
 – **Grant Mulvey**, Chicago, Feb. 3, 1982, at Chicago, first period. Chicago 9, St. Louis 5.
 – **Bryan Trottier**, NY Islanders, Feb. 13, 1982, at NY Islanders, second period. NY Islanders 8, Philadelphia 2.
 – **Al Secord**, Chicago, Jan. 7, 1987, at Chicago, second period. Chicago 6, Toronto 4.
 – **Joe Nieuwendyk**, Calgary, Jan. 11, 1989, at Calgary, second period. Calgary 8, Winnipeg 3.
 – **Peter Bondra**, Washington, Feb. 5, 1994, at Washington, first period. Washington 6, Tampa Bay 3.
 – **Mario Lemieux**, Pittsburgh, Jan. 26, 1997, at Montreal, third period. Pittsburgh 5, Montreal 2.

ASSISTS

MOST ASSISTS:

1,963 – **Wayne Gretzky,** Edmonton, Los Angeles, St. Louis, NY Rangers, in 20 seasons. 1,487GP

1,249 – Ron Francis, Hartford, Pittsburgh, Carolina, Toronto, in 23 seasons. 1,731GP

1,193 – Mark Messier, Edmonton, NY Rangers, Vancouver, in 25 seasons. 1,756GP

1,169 – Raymond Bourque, Boston, Colorado, in 22 seasons. 1,612GP

1,135 – Paul Coffey, Edmonton, Pittsburgh, Los Angeles, Detroit, Hartford, Philadelphia, Chicago, Carolina, Boston, in 21 seasons. 1,409GP

MOST ASSISTS, INCLUDING PLAYOFFS:

2,223 – **Wayne Gretzky**, Edmonton, Los Angeles, St. Louis, NY Rangers, 1,963A in 1,487 regular-season games, 260A in 208 playoff games.

1,379 – Mark Messier, Edmonton, NY Rangers, Vancouver, 1,193A in 1,756 regular-season games, 186A in 236 playoff games.

1,346 – Ron Francis, Hartford, Pittsburgh, Carolina, Toronto, 1,249A in 1,731 regular-season games, 97A in 171 playoff games.

1,308 – Raymond Bourque, Boston, Colorado, 1,169A in 1,612 regular-season games, 139A in 214 playoff games.

1,272 – Paul Coffey, Edmonton, Pittsburgh, Los Angeles, Detroit, Hartford, Philadelphia, Chicago, Carolina, Boston, 1,135A in 1,409 regular-season games, 137A in 194 playoff games.

MOST ASSISTS, ONE SEASON:

163 – **Wayne Gretzky**, Edmonton, 1985-86. 80GP – 80 game schedule.

135 – Wayne Gretzky, Edmonton, 1984-85. 80GP – 80 game schedule.

125 – Wayne Gretzky, Edmonton, 1982-83. 80GP – 80 game schedule.

122 – Wayne Gretzky, Los Angeles, 1990-91. 78GP – 80 game schedule.

121 – Wayne Gretzky, Edmonton, 1986-87. 79GP – 80 game schedule.

120 – Wayne Gretzky, Edmonton, 1981-82. 80GP – 80 game schedule.

118 – Wayne Gretzky, Edmonton, 1983-84. 74GP – 80 game schedule.

114 – Mario Lemieux, Pittsburgh, 1988-89. 76GP – 80 game schedule.
 – Wayne Gretzky, Los Angeles, 1988-89. 78GP – 80 game schedule.

109 – Wayne Gretzky, Edmonton, 1980-81. 80GP – 80 game schedule.
 – Wayne Gretzky, Edmonton, 1987-88. 64GP – 80 game schedule.

102 – Bobby Orr, Boston, 1970-71. 78GP – 78 game schedule.
 – Wayne Gretzky, Los Angeles, 1989-90. 73GP – 80 game schedule.

MOST ASSISTS, ONE SEASON, INCLUDING PLAYOFFS:
174 – **Wayne Gretzky**, Edmonton, 1985-86,
    163A in 80 regular-season games, 11A in 10 playoff games.
165 – Wayne Gretzky, Edmonton, 1984-85,
    135A in 80 regular-season games, 30A in 18 playoff games.
151 – Wayne Gretzky, Edmonton, 1982-83,
    125A in 80 regular-season games, 26A in 16 playoff games.
150 – Wayne Gretzky, Edmonton, 1986-87,
    121A in 79 regular-season games, 29A in 21 playoff games.
140 – Wayne Gretzky, Edmonton, 1983-84,
    118A in 74 regular-season games, 22A in 19 playoff games.
   – Wayne Gretzky, Edmonton, 1987-88,
    109A in 64 regular-season games, 31A in 19 playoff games.
133 – Wayne Gretzky, Los Angeles, 1990-91,
    122A in 78 regular-season games, 11A in 12 playoff games.
131 – Wayne Gretzky, Los Angeles, 1988-89,
    114A in 78 regular-season games, 17A in 11 playoff games.
127 – Wayne Gretzky, Edmonton, 1981-82,
    120A in 80 regular-season games, 7A in 5 playoff games.
123 – Wayne Gretzky, Edmonton, 1980-81,
    109A in 80 regular-season games, 14A in 9 playoff games.
121 – Mario Lemieux, Pittsburgh, 1988-89,
    114A in 76 regular-season games, 7A in 11 playoff games.

MOST ASSISTS, ONE GAME:
7 – **Billy Taylor**, Detroit, Mar. 16, 1947, at Chicago. Detroit 10, Chicago 6.
  – **Wayne Gretzky**, Edmonton, Feb. 15, 1980, at Edmonton.
    Edmonton 8, Washington 2.
  – **Wayne Gretzky**, Edmonton, Dec. 11, 1985, at Chicago.
    Edmonton 12, Chicago 9.
  – **Wayne Gretzky**, Edmonton, Feb. 14, 1986, at Edmonton.
    Edmonton 8, Quebec 2.
6 – Six assists have been recorded in one game on 24 occasions since
    Elmer Lach of Montreal first accomplished the feat vs. Boston on
    Feb. 6, 1943. The most recent player is Eric Lindros of Philadelphia
    on Feb. 26, 1997 at Ottawa.

MOST ASSISTS, ONE ROAD GAME:
7 – **Billy Taylor**, Detroit, Mar. 16, 1947, at Chicago. Detroit 10, Chicago 6.
  – **Wayne Gretzky**, Edmonton, Dec. 11, 1985, at Chicago.
    Edmonton 12, Chicago 9.
6 – Bobby Orr, Boston, Jan. 1, 1973, at Vancouver. Boston 8, Vancouver 2.
  – Patrik Sundstrom, Vancouver, Feb. 29, 1984, at Pittsburgh.
    Vancouver 9, Pittsburgh 5.
  – Mario Lemieux, Pittsburgh, Dec. 5, 1992, at San Jose.
    Pittsburgh 9, San Jose 4.
  – Eric Lindros, Philadelphia, Feb. 26, 1997, at Ottawa.
    Philadelphia 8, Ottawa 5.

MOST ASSISTS, ONE PERIOD:
5 – **Dale Hawerchuk**, Winnipeg, Mar. 6, 1984, at Los Angeles,
    second period. Winnipeg 7, Los Angeles 3.
4 – Four assists have been recorded in one period on 68 occasions since
    Mickey Roach of Hamilton first accomplished the feat vs. Toronto
    on Feb. 23, 1921. The most recent player is Matt Carle of Philadelphia
    on Oct. 6, 2009 vs. Washington.

POINTS

MOST POINTS:
2,857 – **Wayne Gretzky**, Edmonton, Los Angeles, St. Louis, NY Rangers,
    in 20 seasons. 1,487GP (894G–1,963A)
1,887 – Mark Messier, Edmonton, NY Rangers, Vancouver,
    in 25 seasons. 1,756GP (694G–1,193A)
1,850 – Gordie Howe, Detroit, Hartford, in 26 seasons. 1,767GP (801G–1,049A)
1,798 – Ron Francis, Hartford, Pittsburgh, Carolina, Toronto,
    in 23 seasons. 1,731GP (549G–1,249A)
1,771 – Marcel Dionne, Detroit, Los Angeles, NY Rangers,
    in 18 seasons. 1,348GP (731G–1,040A)

MOST POINTS, INCLUDING PLAYOFFS:
3,239 – **Wayne Gretzky**, Edmonton, Los Angeles, St. Louis, NY Rangers,
    2,857PTS in 1,487 regular-season games, 382PTS in 208 playoff games.
2,182 – Mark Messier, Edmonton, NY Rangers, Vancouver,
    1,887PTS in 1,756 regular-season games, 295PTS in 236 playoff games.
2,010 – Gordie Howe, Detroit, Hartford,
    1,850PTS in 1,767 regular-season games, 160PTS in 157 playoff games.
1,941 – Ron Francis, Hartford, Pittsburgh, Carolina, Toronto,
    1,798PTS in 1,731 regular-season games, 143PTS in 171 playoff games
1,940 – Steve Yzerman, Detroit,
    1,755PTS in 1,514 regular-season games, 185PTS in 196 playoff games.

MOST POINTS, ONE SEASON:
215 – **Wayne Gretzky**, Edmonton, 1985-86. 80GP – 80 game schedule.
212 – Wayne Gretzky, Edmonton, 1981-82. 80GP – 80 game schedule.
208 – Wayne Gretzky, Edmonton, 1984-85. 80GP – 80 game schedule.
205 – Wayne Gretzky, Edmonton, 1983-84. 74GP – 80 game schedule.
199 – Mario Lemieux, Pittsburgh, 1988-89. 76GP – 80 game schedule.
196 – Wayne Gretzky, Edmonton, 1982-83. 80GP – 80 game schedule.
183 – Wayne Gretzky, Edmonton, 1986-87. 79GP – 80 game schedule.
168 – Mario Lemieux, Pittsburgh, 1987-88. 77GP – 80 game schedule.
   – Wayne Gretzky, Los Angeles, 1988-89. 78GP – 80 game schedule.
164 – Wayne Gretzky, Edmonton, 1980-81. 80GP – 80 game schedule.
163 – Wayne Gretzky, Los Angeles, 1990-91. 78GP – 80 game schedule.
161 – Mario Lemieux, Pittsburgh, 1995-96. 70GP – 82 game schedule.
160 – Mario Lemieux, Pittsburgh, 1992-93. 60GP – 84 game schedule.

MOST POINTS, ONE SEASON, INCLUDING PLAYOFFS:
255 – **Wayne Gretzky**, Edmonton, 1984-85,
    208PTS in 80 regular-season games, 47PTS in 18 playoff games.
240 – Wayne Gretzky, Edmonton, 1983-84,
    205PTS in 74 regular-season games, 35PTS in 19 playoff games.
234 – Wayne Gretzky, Edmonton, 1982-83,
    196PTS in 80 regular-season games, 38PTS in 16 playoff games.
   – Wayne Gretzky, Edmonton, 1985-86,
    215PTS in 80 regular-season games, 19PTS in 10 playoff games.
224 – Wayne Gretzky, Edmonton, 1981-82,
    212PTS in 80 regular-season games, 12PTS in 5 playoff games.
218 – Mario Lemieux, Pittsburgh, 1988-89,
    199PTS in 76 regular-season games, 19PTS in 11 playoff games.
217 – Wayne Gretzky, Edmonton, 1986-87,
    183PTS in 79 regular-season games, 34PTS in 21 playoff games.
192 – Wayne Gretzky, Edmonton, 1987-88,
    149PTS in 64 regular-season games, 43PTS in 19 playoff games.
190 – Wayne Gretzky, Los Angeles, 1988-89,
    168PTS in 78 regular-season games, 22PTS in 11 playoff games.
188 – Mario Lemieux, Pittsburgh, 1995-96,
    161PTS in 70 regular-season games, 27PTS in 18 playoff games.
185 – Wayne Gretzky, Edmonton, 1980-81,
    164PTS in 80 regular-season games, 21PTS in 9 playoff games.

MOST POINTS, ONE GAME:
10 – **Darryl Sittler**, Toronto, Feb. 7, 1976, at Toronto, 6G-4A.
    Toronto 11, Boston 4.
8 – Maurice Richard, Montreal, Dec. 28, 1944, at Montreal, 5G-3A.
    Montreal 9, Detroit 1.
  – Bert Olmstead, Montreal, Jan. 9, 1954, at Montreal, 4G-4A.
    Montreal 12, Chicago 1.
  – Tom Bladon, Philadelphia, Dec. 11, 1977, at Philadelphia, 4G-4A.
    Philadelphia 11, Cleveland 1.
  – Bryan Trottier, NY Islanders, Dec. 23, 1978, at NY Islanders, 5G-3A.
    NY Islanders 9, NY Rangers 4.
  – Peter Stastny, Quebec, Feb. 22, 1981, at Washington, 4G-4A.
    Quebec 11, Washington 7.
  – Anton Stastny, Quebec, Feb. 22, 1981, at Washington, 3G-5A.
    Quebec 11, Washington 7.
  – Wayne Gretzky, Edmonton, Nov. 19, 1983, at Edmonton, 3G-5A.
    Edmonton 13, New Jersey 4.
  – Wayne Gretzky, Edmonton, Jan. 4, 1984, at Edmonton, 4G-4A.
    Edmonton 12, Minnesota 8.
  – Paul Coffey, Edmonton, Mar. 14, 1986, at Edmonton, 2G-6A.
    Edmonton 12, Detroit 3.
  – Mario Lemieux, Pittsburgh, Oct. 15, 1988, at Pittsburgh, 2G-6A.
    Pittsburgh 9, St. Louis 2.
  – Bernie Nicholls, Los Angeles, Dec. 1, 1988, at Los Angeles, 2G-6A.
    Los Angeles 9, Toronto 3.
  – Mario Lemieux, Pittsburgh, Dec. 31, 1988, at Pittsburgh, 5G-3A.
    Pittsburgh 8, New Jersey 6.

MOST POINTS, ONE ROAD GAME:
8 – **Peter Stastny**, Quebec, Feb. 22, 1981, at Washington. 4G-4A.
    Quebec 11, Washington 7.
  – **Anton Stastny**, Quebec, Feb. 22, 1981, at Washington. 3G-5A.
    Quebec 11, Washington 7.
7 – Red Green, Hamilton, Dec. 5, 1924, at Toronto. 5G-2A.
    Hamilton 10, Toronto 3.
  – Billy Taylor, Detroit, Mar. 16, 1947, at Chicago. 7A. Detroit 10, Chicago 6.
  – Red Berenson, St. Louis, Nov. 7, 1968, at Philadelphia. 6G-1A.
    St. Louis 8, Philadelphia 0.
  – Gilbert Perreault, Buffalo, Feb. 1, 1976, at California. 2G-5A.
    Buffalo 9, California 5.
  – Peter Stastny, Quebec, Apr. 1, 1982, at Boston. 3G-4A. Quebec 8, Boston 5.
  – Wayne Gretzky, Edmonton, Nov. 6, 1983, at Winnipeg. 4G-3A.
    Edmonton 8, Winnipeg 5.
  – Patrik Sundstrom, Vancouver, Feb. 29, 1984, at Pittsburgh. 1G-6A.
    Vancouver 9, Pittsburgh 5.
  – Wayne Gretzky, Edmonton, Dec. 11, 1985, at Chicago. 7A.
    Edmonton 12, Chicago 9.
  – Cam Neely, Boston, Oct. 16, 1988, at Chicago. 3G-4A.
    Boston 10, Chicago 3.
  – Mario Lemieux, Pittsburgh, Jan. 21, 1989, at Edmonton. 2G-5A.
    Pittsburgh 7, Edmonton 4.
  – Dino Ciccarelli, Washington, Mar. 18, 1989, at Hartford. 4G-3A.
    Washington 8, Hartford 2.
  – Mats Sundin, Quebec, Mar. 5, 1992, at Hartford. 5G-2A.
    Quebec 10, Hartford 4.
  – Mario Lemieux, Pittsburgh, Dec. 5, 1992, at San Jose. 1G-6A.
    Pittsburgh 9, San Jose 4.
  – Eric Lindros, Philadelphia, Feb. 26, 1997, at Ottawa. 1G-6A.
    Philadelphia 8, Ottawa 5.
  – Daniel Alfredsson, Ottawa, Jan. 24, 2008, at Tampa Bay. 3G-4A.
    Ottawa 8, Tampa Bay 4.

MOST POINTS, ONE PERIOD:
- **6 – Bryan Trottier**, NY Islanders, Dec. 23, 1978, at NY Islanders, second period. 3G-3A. NY Islanders 9, NY Rangers 4.
- 5 – Bill Cook, NY Rangers, Mar. 12, 1933, at NY Americans, third period. 3G-2A. NY Rangers 8, NY Americans 2.
  - Les Cunningham, Chicago, Jan. 28, 1940, at Chicago, third period. 2G-3A. Chicago 8, Montreal 1.
  - Max Bentley, Chicago, Jan. 28, 1943, at Chicago, third period. 4G-1A. Chicago 10, NY Rangers 1.
  - Leo Labine, Boston, Nov. 28, 1954, at Boston, second period. 3G-2A. Boston 6, Detroit 2.
  - Darryl Sittler, Toronto, Feb. 7, 1976, at Toronto, second period. 3G-2A. Toronto 11, Boston 4.
  - Grant Mulvey, Chicago, Feb. 3, 1982, at Chicago, first period. 4G-1A. Chicago 9, St. Louis 5.
  - Dale Hawerchuk, Winnipeg, Mar. 6, 1984, at Los Angeles, second period. 5A. Winnipeg 7, Los Angeles 3.
  - Jari Kurri, Edmonton, Oct. 26, 1984, at Edmonton, second period. 2G-3A. Edmonton 8, Los Angeles 2.
  - Pat Elynuik, Winnipeg, Jan. 20, 1989, at Winnipeg, second period. 2G-3A. Winnipeg 7, Pittsburgh 3.
  - Ray Ferraro, Hartford, Dec. 9, 1989, at Hartford, first period. 3G-2A. Hartford 7, New Jersey 3.
  - Stephane Richer, Montreal, Feb. 14, 1990, at Montreal, first period. 2G-3A. Montreal 10, Vancouver 1.
  - Cliff Ronning, Vancouver, Apr. 15, 1993, at Los Angeles, third period. 3G-2A. Vancouver 8, Los Angeles 6.
  - Peter Forsberg, Colorado, Mar. 3, 1999, at Florida, third period. 2G-3A. Colorado 7, Florida 5.

POWER-PLAY AND SHORTHAND GOALS

MOST POWER-PLAY GOALS, CAREER:
- **274 – Dave Andreychuk**, Buffalo, Toronto, New Jersey, Boston, Colorado, Tampa Bay, in 23 seasons. 1,639GP.
- 265 – Brett Hull, Calgary, St. Louis, Dallas, Detroit, Phoenix, in 19 seasons. 1,269GP.
- 249 – Phil Esposito, Chicago, Boston, NY Rangers, in 18 seasons. 1,282GP.

MOST POWER-PLAY GOALS, ONE SEASON:
- **34 – Tim Kerr**, Philadelphia, 1985-86. 76GP – 80 game schedule.
- 32 – Dave Andreychuk, Buffalo, Toronto, 1992-93. 83GP – 84 game schedule.
- 31 – Joe Nieuwendyk, Calgary, 1987-88. 75GP – 80 game schedule.
  - Mario Lemieux, Pittsburgh, 1988-89. 76GP – 80 game schedule.
  - Mario Lemieux, Pittsburgh, 1995-96. 70GP – 82 game schedule.
- 29 – Michel Goulet, Quebec, 1987-88. 80GP – 80 game schedule.
  - Brett Hull, St. Louis, 1990-91. 78GP – 80 game schedule.
  - Brett Hull, St. Louis, 1992-93. 80GP – 84 game schedule.

MOST POWER-PLAY GOALS, ONE GAME
- **4 – Camille Henry,** NY Rangers, Mar. 13, 1954, at Detroit. NY Rangers 5, Detroit 2.
- **Bernie Geoffrion**, Montreal, Feb. 19, 1955, at Montreal. Montreal 10, NY Rangers 2.
- **Bryan Trottier**, NY Islanders, Feb. 13, 1982, at NY Islanders. NY Islanders 8, Philadelphia 2.
- **Chris Valentine**, Washington, Feb. 27, 1982, at Washington. Washington 7, Hartford 1.
- **Dave Andreychuk**, Buffalo, Mar. 19, 1992, at Los Angeles. Buffalo 8, Los Angeles 2.
- **Mario Lemieux**, Pittsburgh, Mar. 20, 1993, at Pittsburgh. Pittsburgh 9, Philadelphia 3.
- **Luc Robitaille**, Los Angeles, Nov. 25, 1993, at Quebec. Quebec 8, Los Angeles 6.
- **Scott Mellanby**, St. Louis, Mar. 6, 2003, at St. Louis. St. Louis 6, Phoenix 3.

MOST SHORTHAND GOALS, ONE SEASON:
- **13 – Mario Lemieux**, Pittsburgh, 1988-89. 76GP – 80 game schedule.
- 12 – Wayne Gretzky, Edmonton, 1983-84. 74GP – 80 game schedule.
- 11 – Wayne Gretzky, Edmonton, 1984-85. 80GP – 80 game schedule.
- 10 – Marcel Dionne, Detroit, 1974-75. 80GP – 80 game schedule.
  - Mario Lemieux, Pittsburgh, 1987-88. 77GP – 80 game schedule.
  - Dirk Graham, Chicago, 1988-89. 80GP – 80 game schedule.

MOST SHORTHAND GOALS, ONE GAME:
- **3 – Theoren Fleury**, Calgary, Mar. 9, 1991, at St. Louis. Calgary 8, St. Louis 4.

OVERTIME SCORING

MOST OVERTIME GOALS, CAREER:
- **15 – Mats Sundin**, Quebec, Toronto.
- **Jaromir Jagr**, Pittsburgh, Washington, NY Rangers.
- **Sergei Fedorov**, Detroit, Anaheim, Columbus, Washington.
- **Patrik Elias**, New Jersey.
- 13 – Steve Thomas, Toronto, Chicago, NY Islanders, New Jersey, Anaheim.
  - Olli Jokinen, Los Angeles, NY Islanders, Florida, NY Rangers.
  - Scott Niedermayer, New Jersey, Anaheim.
- 12 – Nels Stewart, Mtl. Maroons, Boston, NY Americans.
  - Brett Hull, Calgary, St. Louis, Dallas, Detroit, Phoenix.
  - Brendan Shanahan, New Jersey, St. Louis, Hartford, Detroit, NY Rangers.

MOST OVERTIME ASSISTS, CAREER:
- **19 – Nicklas Lidstrom**, Detroit.
- 18 – Mark Messier, Edmonton, NY Rangers, Vancouver.
  - Pavol Demitra, Ottawa, St. Louis, Los Angeles, Minnesota, Vancouver.
- 17 – Adam Oates, Detroit, St. Louis, Boston, Washington, Philadelphia, Anaheim.
  - Tomas Kaberle, Toronto.
- 16 – Sergei Fedorov, Detroit, Anaheim, Columbus, Washington.

MOST OVERTIME POINTS, CAREER:
- **31 – Sergei Fedorov**, Detroit, Anaheim, Columbus, Washington. 15G-16A.
- 28 – Mats Sundin, Quebec, Toronto. 15G-13A.
- 27 – Jaromir Jagr, Pittsburgh, Washington, NY Rangers. 15G-12A.
  - Patrik Elias, New Jersey. 15G-12A.
  - Pavol Demitra, Ottawa, St. Louis, Los Angeles, Minnesota, Vancouver. 9G-18A.
- 26 – Mark Messier, Edmonton, NY Rangers, Vancouver. 8G-18A.
  - Jaromir Jagr, Pittsburgh, Washington, NY Rangers. 15G-11A.
- 24 – Tomas Kaberle, Toronto. 7G-17A.

MOST OVERTIME GOALS, ONE SEASON:
- **4 – Howie Morenz**, Montreal, 1929-30.
- **Frank Finnigan**, Ottawa, 1929-30.
- **Johnny Gagnon**, Montreal 1936-37.
- **Mats Sundin**, Toronto, 1999-2000.
- **Scott Niedermayer**, New Jersey, 2001-02.
- **Patrik Elias**, New Jersey, 2003-04.
- **Markus Naslund**, Vancouver, 2003-04.
- **Olli Jokinen**, Florida, 2005-06.
- **Daniel Sedin**, Vancouver 2006-07.

SHOOTOUT GOALS

MOST SHOOTOUT GOALS, ONE SEASON:
- 10 – Wojtek Wolski, Colorado, 2008-09, (12S)
  - Jussi Jokinen, Dallas, 2005-06, (13S)
- 8 – Sidney Crosby, Pittsburgh, 2009-10, (10S)
  - Viktor Kozlov, New Jersey, 2005-06, (12S)
  - Ales Kotalik, Buffalo, Edmonton, 2008-09, (13S)
  - Erik Christensen, Pittsburgh, 2006-07, (14S)
  - Jonathan Toews, Chicago, 2009-10, (14S)
  - Mikko Koivu, Minnesota, 2006-07, (15S)
  - Anze Kopitar, Los Angeles, 2009-10, (16S)
  - Radim Vrbata, Phoenix, 2009-10, (18S)

MOST SHOOTOUT GOALS, ALL-TIME:
- 27 – Vyacheslav Kozlov, Atlanta, (46S)
- 26 – Jussi Jokinen, Dallas, Tampa Bay, Carolina, (50S)
- 24 – Pavel Datsyuk, Detroit, (50S)
- 21 – Ales Kotalik, Buffalo, Edmonton, NY Rangers, Calgary, (42S)
  - Zach Parise, New Jersey, (47S)

MOST SHOOTOUT SHOTS TAKEN, ONE SEASON:
- 18 – Radim Vrbata, Phoenix, 2009-10, (8G)
- 17 – Lauri Korpikoski, Phoenix, 2009-10, (7G)
  - Jack Johnson, Los Angeles, 2009-10, (6G)
  - Sam Gagner, Edmonton, 2007-08, (5G)
- 16 – Anze Kopitar, Los Angeles, 2009-10, (8G)
  - Ales Hemsky, Edmonton, 2007-08, (6G)
  - Brad Richards, Dallas, 2009-10, (4G)

MOST SHOOTOUT SHOTS TAKEN, ALL-TIME:
- 50 – Jussi Jokinen, Dallas, Tampa Bay, Carolina, (26G)
  - Pavel Datsyuk, Detroit, (24G)
- 48 – Sidney Crosby, Pittsburgh, (20G)
  - Brad Richards, Tampa Bay, Dallas, (20G)
- 47 – Zach Parise, New Jersey, (21G)
  - Alex Ovechkin, Washington, (13G)

BEST SHOOTOUT SCORING PERCENTAGE, ONE SEASON: (minimum 5 shots)
- .857 – Petteri Nummelin, Minnesota, 2006-07, (6G, 7S)
- .833 – Wojtek Wolski, Colorado, 2008-09, (10G, 12S)
  - Patrik Elias, New Jersey, 2007-08, (5G, 6S)
- .800 – Sidney Crosby, Pittsburgh, 2009-10, (8G, 10S)
  - Patrick O'Sullivan, Los Angeles, 2007-08, (4G, 5S)
  - Kristian Huselius, Calgary, 2007-08, (4G, 5S)
  - Jeremy Roenick, San Jose, 2007-08, (4G, 5S)
  - Ray Whitney, Carolina, 2005-06, (4G, 5S)

BEST SHOOTOUT SCORING PERCENTAGE, CAREER: (minimum 10 shots)
- .800 – Petteri Nummelin, Minnesota, (8G, 10S)
- .587 – Vyacheslav Kozlov, Atlanta, (27G, 46S)
- .583 – Trevor Linden, Vancouver, (7G, 12S)
- .579 – Frans Nielsen, NY Islanders, (11G, 19S)
- .562 – Shawn Horcoff, Edmonton, (9G, 16S)

MOST GAME DECIDING SHOOTOUT GOALS, ONE SEASON:
- 6 – Adrian Aucoin, Phoenix, 2009-10, (9S)
- 5 – Miroslav Satan, NY Islanders, 2005-06, (10S)
  - Vyacheslav Kozlov, Atlanta, 2006-07, (11S)
  - Viktor Kozlov, New Jersey, 2005-06, (12S)
  - Phil Kessel, Boston, 2007-08, (13S)
  - Ales Kotalik, Buffalo, Edmonton, 2008-09, (13S)

MOST GAME DECIDING SHOOTOUT GOALS, CAREER:
- 13 – Sidney Crosby, Pittsburgh, (48S)
- 11 – Phil Kessel, Boston, Toronto, (35S)
  - Ales Kotalik, Buffalo, Edmonton, NY Rangers, Calgary, (42S)
  - Vyacheslav Kozlov, Atlanta, (46S)

SCORING BY A CENTER

MOST GOALS BY A CENTER, CAREER:
894 – Wayne Gretzky, Edmonton, Los Angeles, St. Louis, NY Rangers, in 20 seasons. 1,487GP
731 – Marcel Dionne, Detroit, Los Angeles, NY Rangers, in 18 seasons. 1,348GP
717 – Phil Esposito, Chicago, Boston, NY Rangers, in 18 seasons. 1,282GP
694 – Mark Messier, Edmonton, NY Rangers, Vancouver, in 25 seasons. 1,756GP
692 – Steve Yzerman, Detroit, in 22 seasons. 1,514GP

MOST GOALS BY A CENTER, ONE SEASON:
92 – Wayne Gretzky, Edmonton, 1981-82. 80GP – 80 game schedule.
87 – Wayne Gretzky, Edmonton, 1983-84. 74GP – 80 game schedule.
85 – Mario Lemieux, Pittsburgh, 1988-89. 76GP – 80 game schedule.
76 – Phil Esposito, Boston, 1970-71. 78GP – 78 game schedule.
73 – Wayne Gretzky, Edmonton, 1984-85. 80GP – 80 game schedule.

MOST ASSISTS BY A CENTER, CAREER:
1,963 – Wayne Gretzky, Edmonton, Los Angeles, St. Louis, NY Rangers, in 20 seasons. 1,487GP
1,249 – Ron Francis, Hartford, Pittsburgh, Carolina, Toronto, in 23 seasons. 1,731GP
1,193 – Mark Messier, Edmonton, NY Rangers, Vancouver, in 25 seasons. 1,756GP
1,079 – Adam Oates, Detroit, St. Louis, Boston, Washington, Philadelphia, Anaheim, Edmonton, in 19 seasons. 1,337GP
1,063 – Steve Yzerman, Detroit, in 22 seasons. 1,514GP

MOST ASSISTS BY A CENTER, ONE SEASON:
163 – Wayne Gretzky, Edmonton, 1985-86. 80GP – 80 game schedule.
135 – Wayne Gretzky, Edmonton, 1984-85. 80GP – 80 game schedule.
125 – Wayne Gretzky, Edmonton, 1982-83. 80GP – 80 game schedule.
122 – Wayne Gretzky, Los Angeles, 1990-91. 78GP – 80 game schedule.
121 – Wayne Gretzky, Edmonton, 1986-87. 79GP – 80 game schedule.

MOST POINTS BY A CENTER, CAREER:
2,857 – Wayne Gretzky, Edmonton, Los Angeles, St. Louis, NY Rangers, in 20 seasons. 1,487GP (894G-1,963A)
1,887 – Mark Messier, Edmonton, NY Rangers, Vancouver, in 25 seasons. 1,756GP (694G-1,193A)
1,798 – Ron Francis, Hartford, Pittsburgh, Carolina, Toronto, in 23 seasons. 1,731GP (549G-1,249A)
1,771 – Marcel Dionne, Detroit, Los Angeles, NY Rangers, in 18 seasons. 1,348GP (731G-1,040A)
1,755 – Steve Yzerman, Detroit, in 22 seasons. 1,514GP (692G-1,063A)

MOST POINTS BY A CENTER, ONE SEASON:
215 – Wayne Gretzky, Edmonton, 1985-86. 80GP – 80 game schedule.
212 – Wayne Gretzky, Edmonton, 1981-82. 80GP – 80 game schedule.
208 – Wayne Gretzky, Edmonton, 1984-85. 80GP – 80 game schedule.
205 – Wayne Gretzky, Edmonton, 1983-84. 74GP – 80 game schedule.
199 – Mario Lemieux, Pittsburgh, 1988-89. 76GP – 80 game schedule.

SCORING BY A LEFT WING

MOST GOALS BY A LEFT WING, CAREER:
668 – Luc Robitaille, Los Angeles, Pittsburgh, NY Rangers, Detroit, in 19 seasons. 1,431GP
656 – Brendan Shanahan, New Jersey, St. Louis, Hartford, Detroit, NY Rangers, in 21 seasons. 1,524GP
640 – Dave Andreychuk, Buffalo, Toronto, New Jersey, Boston, Colorado, Tampa Bay, in 23 seasons. 1,639GP
610 – Bobby Hull, Chicago, Winnipeg, Hartford, in 16 seasons. 1,063GP
556 – John Bucyk, Detroit, Boston, in 23 seasons. 1,540GP

MOST GOALS BY A LEFT WING, ONE SEASON:
65 – Alex Ovechkin, Washington, 2007-08. 82GP – 82 game schedule.
63 – Luc Robitaille, Los Angeles, 1992-93. 84GP – 84 game schedule.
60 – Steve Shutt, Montreal, 1976-77. 80GP – 80 game schedule.
58 – Bobby Hull, Chicago, 1968-69. 74GP – 76 game schedule.
57 – Michel Goulet, Quebec, 1982-83. 80GP – 80 game schedule.

MOST ASSISTS BY A LEFT WING, CAREER:
813 – John Bucyk, Detroit, Boston, in 23 seasons. 1,540GP
726 – Luc Robitaille, Los Angeles, Pittsburgh, NY Rangers, Detroit, in 19 seasons. 1,431GP
698 – Dave Andreychuk, Buffalo, Toronto, New Jersey, Boston, Colorado, Tampa Bay, in 23 seasons. 1,639GP
   – Brendan Shanahan, New Jersey, St. Louis, Hartford, Detroit, NY Rangers, in 21 seasons. 1,524GP
604 – Michel Goulet, Quebec, Chicago, in 15 seasons. 1,089GP

MOST ASSISTS BY A LEFT WING, ONE SEASON:
70 – Joe Juneau, Boston, 1992-93. 84GP – 84 game schedule.
69 – Kevin Stevens, Pittsburgh, 1991-92. 80GP – 80 game schedule.
67 – Mats Naslund, Montreal, 1985-86. 80GP – 80 game schedule.
65 – John Bucyk, Boston, 1970-71. 78GP – 78 game schedule.
   – Michel Goulet, Quebec, 1983-84. 75GP – 80 game schedule.
64 – Mark Messier, Edmonton, 1983-84. 73GP – 80 game schedule.

MOST POINTS BY A LEFT WING, CAREER:
1,394 – Luc Robitaille, Los Angeles, Pittsburgh, NY Rangers, Detroit, in 19 seasons. 1,431GP (668G-726A)
1,369 – John Bucyk, Detroit, Boston, in 23 seasons. 1,540GP (556G-813A)
1,354 – Brendan Shanahan, New Jersey, St. Louis, Hartford, Detroit, NY Rangers, in 21 seasons. 1,524GP (656G-698A)
1,338 – Dave Andreychuk, Buffalo, Toronto, New Jersey, Boston, Colorado, Tampa Bay, in 23 seasons. 1,639GP (640G-698A)
1,170 – Bobby Hull, Chicago, Winnipeg, Hartford, in 16 seasons. 1,063GP (610G-560A)

MOST POINTS BY A LEFT WING, ONE SEASON:
125 – Luc Robitaille, Los Angeles, 1992-93. 84GP – 84 game schedule.
123 – Kevin Stevens, Pittsburgh, 1991-92. 80GP – 80 game schedule.
121 – Michel Goulet, Quebec, 1983-84. 75GP – 80 game schedule.
116 – John Bucyk, Boston, 1970-71. 78GP – 78 game schedule.
112 – Bill Barber, Philadelphia, 1975-76. 80GP – 80 game schedule.
   – Alex Ovechkin, Washington, 2007-08. 82GP – 82 game schedule.

SCORING BY A RIGHT WING

MOST GOALS BY A RIGHT WING, CAREER:
801 – Gordie Howe, Detroit, Hartford, in 26 seasons. 1,767GP
741 – Brett Hull, Calgary, St. Louis, Dallas, Detroit, Phoenix, in 19 seasons. 1,269GP
708 – Mike Gartner, Washington, Minnesota, NY Rangers, Toronto, Phoenix, in 19 seasons. 1,432GP
646 – Jaromir Jagr, Pittsburgh, Washington, NY Rangers, in 17 seasons. 1,273GP
608 – Dino Ciccarelli, Minnesota, Washington, Detroit, Tampa Bay, Florida, in 19 seasons. 1,232GP

MOST GOALS BY A RIGHT WING, ONE SEASON:
86 – Brett Hull, St. Louis, 1990-91. 78GP – 80 game schedule.
76 – Alexander Mogilny, Buffalo, 1992-93. 77GP – 84 game schedule.
   – Teemu Selanne, Winnipeg, 1992-93. 84GP – 84 game schedule.
72 – Brett Hull, St. Louis, 1989-90. 80GP – 80 game schedule.
71 – Jari Kurri, Edmonton, 1984-85. 73GP – 80 game schedule.
70 – Brett Hull, St. Louis, 1991-92. 73GP – 80 game schedule.

MOST ASSISTS BY A RIGHT WING, CAREER:
1,049 – Gordie Howe, Detroit, Hartford, in 26 seasons. 1,767GP
953 – Jaromir Jagr, Pittsburgh, Washington, NY Rangers, in 17 seasons. 1,273GP
922 – Mark Recchi, Pittsburgh, Philadelphia, Montreal, Carolina, Atlanta, Boston, in 21 seasons. 1,571GP
797 – Jari Kurri, Edmonton, Los Angeles, NY Rangers, Anaheim, Colorado, in 17 seasons. 1,251GP
793 – Guy Lafleur, Montreal, NY Rangers, Quebec, in 17 seasons. 1,126GP

MOST ASSISTS BY A RIGHT WING, ONE SEASON:
87 – Jaromir Jagr, Pittsburgh, 1995-96. 82GP – 82 game schedule.
83 – Mike Bossy, NY Islanders, 1981-82. 80GP – 80 game schedule.
   – Jaromir Jagr, Pittsburgh, 1998-99. 81GP – 82 game schedule.
80 – Guy Lafleur, Montreal, 1976-77. 80GP – 80 game schedule.
77 – Guy Lafleur, Montreal, 1978-79. 80GP – 80 game schedule.

One of the most prolific left wingers in hockey history, Brendan Shanahan enjoyed the two most productive seasons of his 21-year career with the St. Louis Blues, topping 50 goals twice in his four years with the team during the early 1990s.

MOST POINTS BY A RIGHT WING, CAREER:
1,850 – Gordie Howe, Detroit, Hartford, in 26 seasons. 1,767GP (801G-1,049A)
1,599 – Jaromir Jagr, Pittsburgh, Washington, NY Rangers, in 17 seasons. 1,273GP (646G-953A)
1,485 – Mark Recchi, Pittsburgh, Philadelphia, Montreal, Carolina, Atlanta, Boston, in 21 seasons. 1,571GP (563G-922A)
1,398 – Jari Kurri, Edmonton, Los Angeles, NY Rangers, Anaheim, Colorado, in 17 seasons. 1,251GP (601G-797A)
1,391 – Brett Hull, Calgary, St. Louis, Dallas, Detroit, Phoenix, in 19 seasons. 1,269GP (741G-650A)

MOST POINTS BY A RIGHT WING, ONE SEASON:
149 – Jaromir Jagr, Pittsburgh, 1995-96. 82GP – 82 game schedule.
147 – Mike Bossy, NY Islanders, 1981-82. 80GP – 80 game schedule.
136 – Guy Lafleur, Montreal, 1976-77. 80GP – 80 game schedule.
135 – Jari Kurri, Edmonton, 1984-85. 73GP – 80 game schedule.
132 – Guy Lafleur, Montreal, 1977-78. 78GP – 80 game schedule.
    – Teemu Selanne, Winnipeg, 1992-93. 84GP – 84 game schedule.

SCORING BY A DEFENSEMAN

MOST GOALS BY A DEFENSEMAN, CAREER:
410 – Raymond Bourque, Boston, Colorado, in 22 seasons. 1,612GP
396 – Paul Coffey, Edmonton, Pittsburgh, Los Angeles, Detroit, Hartford, Philadelphia, Chicago, Carolina, Boston, in 21 seasons. 1,409GP
340 – Al MacInnis, Calgary, St. Louis, in 23 seasons. 1,416GP
338 – Phil Housley, Buffalo, Winnipeg, St. Louis, Calgary, New Jersey, Washington, Chicago, Toronto, in 21 seasons. 1,495GP
310 – Denis Potvin, NY Islanders, in 15 seasons. 1,060GP

MOST GOALS BY A DEFENSEMAN, ONE SEASON:
48 – Paul Coffey, Edmonton, 1985-86. 79GP – 80 game schedule.
46 – Bobby Orr, Boston, 1974-75. 80GP – 80 game schedule.
40 – Paul Coffey, Edmonton, 1983-84. 80GP – 80 game schedule.
39 – Doug Wilson, Chicago, 1981-82. 76GP – 80 game schedule.
37 – Bobby Orr, Boston, 1970-71. 78GP – 78 game schedule.
    – Bobby Orr, Boston, 1971-72. 76GP – 78 game schedule.
    – Paul Coffey, Edmonton, 1984-85. 80GP – 80 game schedule.

MOST GOALS BY A DEFENSEMAN, ONE GAME:
5 – Ian Turnbull, Toronto, Feb. 2, 1977, at Toronto. Toronto 9, Detroit 1.
4 – Harry Cameron, Toronto, Dec. 26, 1917, at Toronto. Toronto 7, Montreal 5.
  – Harry Cameron, Montreal, Mar. 3, 1920, at Quebec. Montreal 16, Quebec 3.
  – Sprague Cleghorn, Montreal, Jan. 14, 1922, at Montreal. Montreal 10, Hamilton 6.
  – John McKinnon, Pittsburgh, Nov. 19, 1929, at Pittsburgh. Pittsburgh 10, Toronto 5.
  – Hap Day, Toronto, Nov. 19, 1929, at Pittsburgh. Pittsburgh 10, Toronto 5.
  – Tom Bladon, Philadelphia, Dec. 11, 1977, at Philadelphia. Philadelphia 11, Cleveland 1.
  – Ian Turnbull, Los Angeles, Dec. 12, 1981, at Los Angeles. Los Angeles 7, Vancouver 5.
  – Paul Coffey, Edmonton, Oct. 26, 1984, at Calgary. Edmonton 6, Calgary 5.

MOST ASSISTS BY A DEFENSEMAN, CAREER:
1,169 – Raymond Bourque, Boston, Colorado, in 22 seasons. 1,612GP
1,135 – Paul Coffey, Edmonton, Pittsburgh, Los Angeles, Detroit, Hartford, Philadelphia, Chicago, Carolina, Boston, in 21 seasons. 1,409GP
934 – Al MacInnis, Calgary, St. Louis, in 23 seasons. 1,416GP
929 – Larry Murphy, Los Angeles, Washington, Minnesota, Pittsburgh, Toronto, Detroit, in 21 seasons. 1,615GP
894 – Phil Housley, Buffalo, Winnipeg, St. Louis, Calgary, New Jersey, Washington, Chicago, Toronto, in 21 seasons. 1,495GP

MOST ASSISTS BY A DEFENSEMAN, ONE SEASON:
102 – Bobby Orr, Boston, 1970-71. 78GP – 78 game schedule.
90 – Bobby Orr, Boston, 1973-74. 74GP – 78 game schedule.
  – Paul Coffey, Edmonton, 1985-86. 79GP – 80 game schedule.
89 – Bobby Orr, Boston, 1974-75. 80GP – 80 game schedule.
87 – Bobby Orr, Boston, 1969-70. 76GP – 78 game schedule.

MOST ASSISTS BY A DEFENSEMAN, ONE GAME:
6 – Babe Pratt, Toronto, Jan. 8, 1944, at Toronto. Toronto 12, Boston 3.
  – **Pat Stapleton**, Chicago, Mar. 30, 1969, at Chicago. Chicago 9, Detroit 5.
  – **Bobby Orr**, Boston, Jan. 1, 1973, at Vancouver. Boston 8, Vancouver 2.
  – **Ron Stackhouse**, Pittsburgh, Mar. 8, 1975, at Pittsburgh. Pittsburgh 8, Philadelphia 2.
  – **Paul Coffey**, Edmonton, Mar. 14, 1986, at Edmonton. Edmonton 12, Detroit 3.
  – **Gary Suter**, Calgary, Apr. 4, 1986, at Calgary. Calgary 9, Edmonton 3.

MOST POINTS BY A DEFENSEMAN, CAREER:
1,579 – Raymond Bourque, Boston, Colorado, in 22 seasons. 1,612GP (410G-1,169A)
1,531 – Paul Coffey, Edmonton, Pittsburgh, Los Angeles, Detroit, Hartford, Philadelphia, Chicago, Carolina, Boston, in 21 seasons. 1,409GP (396G-1,135A)
1,274 – Al MacInnis, Calgary, St. Louis, in 23 seasons. 1,416GP (340G-934A)
1,232 – Phil Housley, Buffalo, Winnipeg, St. Louis, Calgary, New Jersey, Washington, Chicago, Toronto, in 21 seasons. 1,495GP (338G-894A)
1,216 – Larry Murphy, Los Angeles, Washington, Minnesota, Pittsburgh, Toronto, Detroit, in 21 seasons. 1,615GP (287G-929A)

MOST POINTS BY A DEFENSEMAN, ONE SEASON:
139 – Bobby Orr, Boston, 1970-71. 78GP – 78 game schedule.
138 – Paul Coffey, Edmonton, 1985-86. 79GP – 80 game schedule.
135 – Bobby Orr, Boston, 1974-75. 80GP – 80 game schedule.
126 – Paul Coffey, Edmonton, 1983-84. 80GP – 80 game schedule.
122 – Bobby Orr, Boston, 1973-74. 74GP – 78 game schedule.

MOST POINTS BY A DEFENSEMAN, ONE GAME:
8 – Tom Bladon, Philadelphia, Dec. 11, 1977, at Philadelphia. 4G-4A. Philadelphia 11, Cleveland 1.
  – **Paul Coffey**, Edmonton, Mar. 14, 1986, at Edmonton. 2G-6A. Edmonton 12, Detroit 3.
7 – Bobby Orr, Boston, Nov. 15, 1973, at Boston. 3G-4A. Boston 10, NY Rangers 2.

SCORING BY A GOALTENDER

MOST POINTS BY A GOALTENDER, CAREER:
48 – Tom Barrasso, Buffalo, Pittsburgh, Ottawa, Carolina, Toronto, St. Louis, in 19 seasons. 777GP
46 – Grant Fuhr, Edmonton, Toronto, Buffalo, Los Angeles, St. Louis, Calgary, in 19 seasons. 868GP

MOST POINTS BY A GOALTENDER, ONE SEASON:
14 – Grant Fuhr, Edmonton, 1983-84. 45GP – 80 game schedule.
9 – Curtis Joseph, St. Louis, 1991-92. 60GP – 80 game schedule.
8 – Mike Palmateer, Washington, 1980-81. 49GP – 80 game schedule.
  – Grant Fuhr, Edmonton, 1987-88. 75GP – 80 game schedule.
  – Ron Hextall, Philadelphia, 1988-89. 64GP – 80 game schedule.
  – Tom Barrasso, Pittsburgh, 1992-93. 63GP – 84 game schedule.

MOST POINTS BY A GOALTENDER, ONE GAME:
3 – Jeff Reese, Calgary, Feb. 10, 1993, at Calgary. Calgary 13, San Jose 1.

Tom Bladon (top) of the Philadelphia Flyers broke Bobby Orr's record for points by a defenseman when he collected eight in a single game on December 11, 1977. Edmonton's Paul Coffey (above) tied the record during the 1985-86 season, the same year he scored 48 goals.

SCORING BY A ROOKIE

MOST GOALS BY A ROOKIE, ONE SEASON:
76 – Teemu Selanne, Winnipeg, 1992-93. 84GP – 84 game schedule.
53 – Mike Bossy, NY Islanders, 1977-78. 73GP – 80 game schedule.
52 – Alex Ovechkin, Washington, 2005-06. 81GP – 82 game schedule.
51 – Joe Nieuwendyk, Calgary, 1987-88. 75GP – 80 game schedule.
45 – Dale Hawerchuk, Winnipeg, 1981-82. 80GP – 80 game schedule.
– Luc Robitaille, Los Angeles, 1986-87. 79GP – 80 game schedule.

MOST GOALS BY A PLAYER IN HIS FIRST NHL SEASON, ONE GAME:
5 – Joe Malone, Montreal, three occasions, 1917-18.
– **Harry Hyland**, Mtl. Wanderers, Dec. 19, 1917, at Montreal.
Mtl Wanderers 10, Toronto 9.
– **Mickey Roach**, Toronto, Mar. 6, 1920, at Toronto. Toronto 11, Quebec 2.
– **Howie Meeker**, Toronto, Jan. 8, 1947, at Toronto. Toronto 10, Chicago 4.
– **Don Murdoch**, NY Rangers, Oct. 12, 1976, at Minnesota.
NY Rangers 10, Minnesota 4.

MOST GOALS BY A PLAYER IN HIS FIRST NHL GAME:
5 – Joe Malone, Montreal, Dec. 19, 1917, at Ottawa. Montreal 7, Ottawa 4.
– **Harry Hyland**, Mtl. Wanderers, Dec. 19, 1917, at Montreal.
Mtl Wanderers 10, Toronto 9.
3 – Alex Smart, Montreal, Jan. 14, 1943, at Montreal. Montreal 5, Chicago 1.
– Real Cloutier, Quebec, Oct. 10, 1979, at Quebec. Atlanta 5, Quebec 3.
– Fabian Brunnstrom, Dallas, Oct. 15, 2008, at Dallas.
Dallas 6, Nashville 4.

MOST ASSISTS BY A ROOKIE, ONE SEASON:
70 – Peter Stastny, Quebec, 1980-81. 77GP – 80 game schedule.
– **Joe Juneau**, Boston, 1992-93. 84GP – 84 game schedule.
63 – Bryan Trottier, NY Islanders, 1975-76. 80GP – 80 game schedule.
– Sidney Crosby, Pittsburgh, 2005–06. 81GP – 82 game schedule.
62 – Sergei Makarov, Calgary, 1989-90. 80GP – 80 game schedule.
60 – Larry Murphy, Los Angeles, 1980-81. 80GP – 80 game schedule.

MOST ASSISTS BY A PLAYER IN HIS FIRST NHL SEASON, ONE GAME:
7 – Wayne Gretzky, Edmonton, Feb. 15, 1980, at Edmonton.
Edmonton 8, Washington 2.
6 – Gary Suter, Calgary, Apr. 4, 1986, at Calgary. Calgary 9, Edmonton 3.

MOST ASSISTS BY A PLAYER IN HIS FIRST NHL GAME:
4 – Dutch Reibel, Detroit, Oct. 8, 1953, at Detroit. Detroit 4, NY Rangers 1.
– **Roland Eriksson**, Minnesota, Oct. 6, 1976, at NY Rangers.
NY Rangers 6, Minnesota 5.
3 – Al Hill, Philadelphia, Feb. 14, 1977, at Philadelphia. Philadelphia 6,
St. Louis 4.
– Jarno Kultanen, Boston, Oct. 5, 2000, at Boston. Boston 4, Ottawa 4.
– Stanislav Chistov, Anaheim, Oct. 10, 2002, at St. Louis. Anaheim 4,
St. Louis 3.
– Dominic Moore, NY Rangers, Nov. 1, 2003, at Montreal. NY Rangers 5,
Montreal 1.

MOST POINTS BY A ROOKIE, ONE SEASON:
132 – Teemu Selanne, Winnipeg, 1992-93. 84GP – 84 game schedule.
109 – Peter Stastny, Quebec, 1980-81. 77GP – 80 game schedule.
106 – Alex Ovechkin, Washington, 2005-06. 81GP – 82 game schedule.
103 – Dale Hawerchuk, Winnipeg, 1981-82. 80GP – 80 game schedule.
102 – Joe Juneau, Boston, 1992-93. 84GP – 84 game schedule.
– Sidney Crosby, Pittsburgh, 2005–06. 81GP – 82 game schedule.
100 – Mario Lemieux, Pittsburgh, 1984-85. 73GP – 80 game schedule.

MOST POINTS BY A PLAYER IN HIS FIRST NHL SEASON, ONE GAME:
8 – Peter Stastny, Quebec, Feb. 22, 1981, at Washington. 4G-4A.
Quebec 11, Washington 7.
– **Anton Stastny**, Quebec, Feb. 22, 1981, at Washington. 3G-5A.
Quebec 11, Washington 7.
7 – Wayne Gretzky, Edmonton, Feb. 15, 1980, at Edmonton. 7A.
Edmonton 8, Washington 2.
– Sergei Makarov, Calgary, Feb. 25, 1990, at Calgary. 2G-5A.
Calgary 10, Edmonton 4.
6 – Wayne Gretzky, Edmonton, Mar. 29, 1980, at Toronto. 2G-4A.
Edmonton 8, Toronto 5.
– Gary Suter, Calgary, Apr. 4, 1986, at Calgary. 6A.
Calgary 9, Edmonton 3.

MOST POINTS BY A PLAYER IN HIS FIRST NHL GAME:
5 – Joe Malone, Montreal, Dec. 19, 1917, at Ottawa. 5G*.
Montreal 7, Ottawa 4.
– **Harry Hyland**, Mtl. Wanderers, Dec. 19, 1917, at Montreal. 5G*.
Mtl Wanderers 10, Toronto 9.
– **Al Hill**, Philadelphia, Feb. 14, 1977, at Philadelphia. 2G-3A.
Philadelphia 6, St. Louis 4.
4 – Alex Smart, Montreal, Jan. 14, 1943, at Montreal. 3G-1A.
Montreal 5, Chicago 1.
– Dutch Reibel, Detroit, Oct. 8, 1953, at Detroit. 4A.
Detroit 4, NY Rangers 1.
– Roland Eriksson, Minnesota, Oct. 6, 1976, at NY Rangers. 4A.
NY Rangers 6, Minnesota 5.
– Stanislav Chistov, Anaheim, Oct. 10, 2002, at St. Louis. 1G-3A.
Anaheim 4, St. Louis 3.

– Official assists not awarded in 1917-18.

SCORING BY A ROOKIE DEFENSEMAN

MOST GOALS BY A ROOKIE DEFENSEMAN, ONE SEASON:
23 – Brian Leetch, NY Rangers, 1988-89. 68GP – 80 game schedule.
22 – Barry Beck, Colorado, 1977-78. 75GP – 80 game schedule.
20 – Dion Phaneuf, Calgary, 2005-06. 82GP – 82 game schedule.

MOST ASSISTS BY A ROOKIE DEFENSEMAN, ONE SEASON:
60 – Larry Murphy, Los Angeles, 1980-81. 80GP – 80 game schedule.
55 – Chris Chelios, Montreal, 1984-85. 74GP – 80 game schedule.
50 – Stefan Persson, NY Islanders, 1977-78. 66GP – 80 game schedule.
– Gary Suter, Calgary, 1985-86. 80GP – 80 game schedule.
49 – Nicklas Lidstrom, Detroit, 1991-92. 80GP – 80 game schedule.

MOST POINTS BY A ROOKIE DEFENSEMAN, ONE SEASON:
76 – Larry Murphy, Los Angeles, 1980-81. 80GP – 80 game schedule.
71 – Brian Leetch, NY Rangers, 1988-89. 68GP – 80 game schedule.
68 – Gary Suter, Calgary, 1985-86. 80GP – 80 game schedule.
66 – Phil Housley, Buffalo, 1982-83. 77GP – 80 game schedule.
65 – Raymond Bourque, Boston, 1979-80. 80GP – 80 game schedule.

*Excluding the NHL's first season, just three players have ever scored a hat trick in their very first NHL game. Fabian Brunnstrom (left)
of the Dallas Stars is the most recent to do so, scoring three times on October 15, 2008.
Real Cloutier (right) scored three in his first game back in 1979.*

PER-GAME SCORING AVERAGES

HIGHEST GOALS-PER-GAME AVERAGE, CAREER
(AMONG PLAYERS WITH 200-OR-MORE GOALS):
.762 – **Mike Bossy**, NY Islanders, 1977-78 – 1986-87, with 573G in 752GP.
.756 – Cy Denneny, Ottawa, Boston, 1917-18 – 1928-29, with 248G in 328GP.
.754 – Mario Lemieux, Pittsburgh, 1984-85 – 1996-97,
2000-01 – 2003-04, 2005-06, with 690G in 915GP.
.742 – Babe Dye, Toronto, Hamilton, Chicago, NY Americans,
1919-20 – 1930-31, with 201G in 271GP.
.679 – Alex Ovechkin, Washington, 2005-06 – 2009-10, with 269G in 396GP.

HIGHEST GOALS-PER-GAME AVERAGE, ONE SEASON
(AMONG PLAYERS WITH 20-OR-MORE GOALS):
2.20 – **Joe Malone**, Montreal, 1917-18, with 44G in 20GP.
1.80 – Cy Denneny, Ottawa, 1917-18, with 36G in 20GP.
1.64 – Newsy Lalonde, Montreal, 1917-18, with 23G in 14GP.
1.63 – Joe Malone, Quebec, 1919-20, with 39G in 24GP.
1.61 – Newsy Lalonde, Montreal, 1919-20, with 37G in 23GP.

HIGHEST GOALS-PER-GAME AVERAGE, ONE SEASON
(AMONG PLAYERS WITH 50-OR-MORE GOALS):
1.18 – **Wayne Gretzky**, Edmonton, 1983-84, with 87G in 74GP.
1.15 – Wayne Gretzky, Edmonton, 1981-82, with 92G in 80GP.
    – Mario Lemieux, Pittsburgh, 1992-93, with 69G in 60GP.
1.12 – Mario Lemieux, Pittsburgh, 1988-89, with 85G in 76GP.
1.10 – Brett Hull, St. Louis, 1990-91, with 86G in 78GP.
1.02 – Cam Neely, Boston, 1993-94, with 50G in 49GP.
1.00 – Maurice Richard, Montreal, 1944-45, with 50G in 50GP.

HIGHEST ASSISTS-PER-GAME AVERAGE, CAREER
(AMONG PLAYERS WITH 300-OR-MORE ASSISTS):
1.320 – **Wayne Gretzky**, Edmonton, Los Angeles, St. Louis, NY Rangers,
1979-80 – 1998-99, with 1,963A in 1,487GP.
1.129 – Mario Lemieux, Pittsburgh, 1984-85 – 1996-97,
2000-01 – 2003-04, 2005-06, with 1,033A in 915GP.
.982 – Bobby Orr, Boston, Chicago, 1966-67 – 1978-79, with 645A in 657GP.
.901 – Peter Forsberg, Quebec, Colorado, Philadelphia, Nashville, 1994-95 –
2000-01, 2002-03, 2003-04, 2005-06 – 2007-08 with 636A in 706GP.
.871 – Sidney Crosby, Pittsburgh, 2005-06 – 2009-10, with 323A in 371GP.

HIGHEST ASSISTS-PER-GAME AVERAGE, ONE SEASON
(AMONG PLAYERS WITH 35-OR-MORE ASSISTS):
2.04 – **Wayne Gretzky, Edmonton**, 1985-86, with 163A in 80GP.
1.70 – Wayne Gretzky, Edmonton, 1987-88, with 109A in 64GP.
1.69 – Wayne Gretzky, Edmonton, 1984-85, with 135A in 80GP.
1.59 – Wayne Gretzky, Edmonton, 1983-84, with 118A in 74GP.
1.56 – Wayne Gretzky, Edmonton, 1982-83, with 125A in 80GP.
    – Wayne Gretzky, Los Angeles, 1990-91, with 122A in 78GP.
1.53 – Wayne Gretzky, Edmonton, 1986-87, with 121A in 79GP.
1.52 – Mario Lemieux, Pittsburgh, 1992-93, with 91A in 60GP.
1.50 – Wayne Gretzky, Edmonton, 1981-82, with 120A in 80GP.
    – Mario Lemieux, Pittsburgh, 1988-89, with 114A in 76GP.

HIGHEST POINTS-PER-GAME AVERAGE, CAREER
(AMONG PLAYERS WITH 500-OR-MORE POINTS):
1.921 – **Wayne Gretzky**, Edmonton, Los Angeles, St. Louis, NY Rangers,
1979-80 – 1998-99, with 2,857PTS (894G-1,963A) in 1,487GP.
1.883 – Mario Lemieux, Pittsburgh, 1984-85 – 1996-97,
2000-01 – 2003-04, 2005-06, with 1,723PTS (690G-1,033A) in 915GP.
1.497 – Mike Bossy, NY Islanders, 1977-78 – 1986-87, with 1,126PTS
(573G-553A) in 752GP.
1.393 – Bobby Orr, Boston, Chicago, 1966-67 – 1978-79, with 915PTS
(270G-645A) in 657GP.
1.364 – Sidney Crosby, Pittsburgh, 2005-06 – 2009-10, with 506PTS
(183G-323A) in 371GP.
1.336 – Alex Ovechkin, Washington, 2005-06 – 2009-10, with 529PTS
(269G-260A) in 396GP.

HIGHEST POINTS-PER-GAME AVERAGE, ONE SEASON
(AMONG PLAYERS WITH 50-OR-MORE POINTS):
2.77 – **Wayne Gretzky**, Edmonton, 1983-84, with 205PTS in 74GP.
2.69 – Wayne Gretzky, Edmonton, 1985-86, with 215PTS in 80GP.
2.67 – Mario Lemieux, Pittsburgh, 1992-93, with 160PTS in 60GP.
2.65 – Wayne Gretzky, Edmonton, 1981-82, with 212PTS in 80GP.
2.62 – Mario Lemieux, Pittsburgh, 1988-89, with 199PTS in 76GP.
2.60 – Wayne Gretzky, Edmonton, 1984-85, with 208PTS in 80GP.
2.45 – Wayne Gretzky, Edmonton, 1982-83, with 196PTS in 80GP.
2.33 – Wayne Gretzky, Edmonton, 1987-88, with 149PTS in 64GP.
2.32 – Wayne Gretzky, Edmonton, 1986-87, with 183PTS in 79GP.
2.30 – Mario Lemieux, Pittsburgh, 1995-96, with 161PTS in 70GP.
2.18 – Mario Lemieux, Pittsburgh, 1987-88, with 168PTS in 77GP.
2.15 – Wayne Gretzky, Los Angeles, 1988-89, with 168PTS in 78GP.
2.09 – Wayne Gretzky, Los Angeles, 1990-91, with 163PTS in 78GP.
2.08 – Mario Lemieux, Pittsburgh, 1989-90, with 123PTS in 59GP.

SCORING PLATEAUS

MOST 20-OR-MORE GOAL SEASONS:
22 – **Gordie Howe**, Detroit, Hartford, in 26 seasons.
20 – Ron Francis, Hartford, Pittsburgh, Carolina, Toronto, in 23 seasons.
19 – Dave Andreychuk, Buffalo, Toronto, New Jersey, Boston, Colorado,
Tampa Bay, in 23 seasons.
    – Brendan Shanahan, New Jersey, St. Louis, Hartford, Detroit, NY Rangers,
in 21 seasons.
17 – Marcel Dionne, Detroit, Los Angeles, NY Rangers, in 18 seasons.
    – Mike Gartner, Washington, Minnesota, NY Rangers, Toronto,
Phoenix, in 19 seasons.
    – Wayne Gretzky, Edmonton, Los Angeles, St. Louis, NY Rangers,
in 20 seasons.
    – Mark Messier, Edmonton, NY Rangers, Vancouver, in 25 seasons.
    – Brett Hull, Calgary, St. Louis, Dallas, Detroit, Phoenix, in 19 seasons.
    – Joe Sakic, Quebec, Colorado, in 20 seasons.
    – Mats Sundin, Quebec, Toronto, Vancouver, in 18 seasons.
    – Jaromir Jagr, Pittsburgh, Washington, NY Rangers, in 17 seasons.

MOST CONSECUTIVE 20-OR-MORE GOAL SEASONS:
22 – **Gordie Howe**, Detroit, 1949-50 – 1970-71.
19 – Brendan Shanahan, New Jersey, St. Louis, Hartford, Detroit, NY Rangers,
1988-89 – 2007-08.
17 – Marcel Dionne, Detroit, Los Angeles, NY Rangers, 1971-72 – 1987-88.
    – Brett Hull, Calgary, St. Louis, Dallas, Detroit, 1987-88 – 2003-04.
    – Jaromir Jagr, Pittsburgh, Washington, NY Rangers, 1990-91 – 2007-08.
    – Mats Sundin, Quebec, Toronto, 1990-91 – 2007-08.

Among Mike Gartner's record 17 30-goal seasons (including 15 in a row) were nine years in which he topped 40 goals. Gartner collected a career-high 50 goals and 52 assists for the Washington Capitals in 1984-85.

MOST 30-OR-MORE GOAL SEASONS:
17 – Mike Gartner, Washington, Minnesota, NY Rangers, Toronto, Phoenix, in 19 seasons.
15 – Jaromir Jagr, Pittsburgh, Washington, NY Rangers, in 17 seasons.
14 – Gordie Howe, Detroit, Hartford, in 26 seasons.
 – Marcel Dionne, Detroit, Los Angeles, NY Rangers, in 18 seasons.
 – Wayne Gretzky, Edmonton, Los Angeles, St. Louis, NY Rangers, in 20 seasons.
13 – Bobby Hull, Chicago, Winnipeg, Hartford, in 16 seasons.
 – Phil Esposito, Chicago, Boston, NY Rangers, in 18 seasons.
 – Brett Hull, Calgary, St. Louis, Dallas, Detroit, Phoenix, in 19 seasons.
 – Mats Sundin, Quebec, Toronto, Vancouver, in 18 seasons.

MOST CONSECUTIVE 30-OR-MORE GOAL SEASONS:
15 – Mike Gartner, Washington, Minnesota, NY Rangers, Toronto, 1979-80 – 1993-94.
– Jaromir Jagr, Pittsburgh, Washington, NY Rangers, 1991-92 – 2006-07.
13 – Bobby Hull, Chicago, 1959-60 – 1971-72.
 – Phil Esposito, Boston, NY Rangers, 1967-68 – 1979-80.
 – Wayne Gretzky, Edmonton, Los Angeles, 1979-80 – 1991-92.

MOST 40-OR-MORE GOAL SEASONS:
12 – Wayne Gretzky, Edmonton, Los Angeles, St. Louis, NY Rangers, in 20 seasons.
10 – Marcel Dionne, Detroit, Los Angeles, NY Rangers, in 18 seasons.
 – Mario Lemieux, Pittsburgh, in 17 seasons.
 9 – Mike Bossy, NY Islanders, in 10 seasons.
 – Mike Gartner, Washington, Minnesota, NY Rangers, Toronto, Phoenix, in 19 seasons.

MOST CONSECUTIVE 40-OR-MORE GOAL SEASONS:
12 – Wayne Gretzky, Edmonton, Los Angeles, 1979-80 – 1990-91.
 9 – Mike Bossy, NY Islanders, 1977-78 – 1985-86.
 8 – Luc Robitaille, Los Angeles, 1986-87 – 1993-94.
 7 – Phil Esposito, Boston, 1968-69 – 1974-75.
 – Michel Goulet, Quebec, 1981-82 – 1987-88.
 – Jari Kurri, Edmonton, 1982-83 – 1988-89.

MOST 50-OR-MORE GOAL SEASONS:
9 – Mike Bossy, NY Islanders, in 10 seasons.
– Wayne Gretzky, Edmonton, Los Angeles, St. Louis, NY Rangers, in 20 seasons.
 6 – Guy Lafleur, Montreal, NY Rangers, Quebec, in 17 seasons.
 – Marcel Dionne, Detroit, Los Angeles, NY Rangers, in 18 seasons.
 – Mario Lemieux, Pittsburgh, in 17 seasons.
 5 – Bobby Hull, Chicago, Winnipeg, Hartford, in 16 seasons.
 – Phil Esposito, Chicago, Boston, NY Rangers, in 18 seasons.
 – Brett Hull, Calgary, St. Louis, Dallas, Detroit, Phoenix, in 19 seasons.
 – Steve Yzerman, Detroit, in 22 seasons.
 – Pavel Bure, Vancouver, Florida, NY Rangers, in 12 seasons.

MOST CONSECUTIVE 50-OR-MORE GOAL SEASONS:
9 – Mike Bossy, NY Islanders, 1977-78 – 1985-86.
 8 – Wayne Gretzky, Edmonton, 1979-80 – 1986-87.
 6 – Guy Lafleur, Montreal, 1974-75 – 1979-80.
 5 – Phil Esposito, Boston, 1970-71 – 1974-75.
 – Marcel Dionne, Los Angeles, 1978-79 – 1982-83.
 – Brett Hull, St. Louis, 1989-90 – 1993-94.

MOST 60-OR-MORE GOAL SEASONS:
5 – Mike Bossy, NY Islanders, in 10 seasons.
– Wayne Gretzky, Edmonton, Los Angeles, St. Louis, NY Rangers, in 20 seasons.
 4 – Phil Esposito, Chicago, Boston, NY Rangers, in 18 seasons.
 – Mario Lemieux, Pittsburgh, in 17 seasons.

MOST CONSECUTIVE 60-OR-MORE GOAL SEASONS:
4 – Wayne Gretzky, Edmonton, 1981-82 – 1984-85.
 3 – Mike Bossy, NY Islanders, 1980-81 – 1982-83.
 – Brett Hull, St. Louis, 1989-90 – 1991-92.
 2 – Phil Esposito, Boston, 1970-71 – 1971-72, 1973-74 – 1974-75.
 – Jari Kurri, Edmonton, 1984-85 – 1985-86.
 – Mario Lemieux, Pittsburgh, 1987-88 – 1988-89.
 – Steve Yzerman, Detroit, 1988-89 – 1989-90.
 – Pavel Bure, Vancouver, 1992-93 – 1993-94.

MOST 100-OR-MORE POINT SEASONS:
15 – Wayne Gretzky, Edmonton, Los Angeles, St. Louis, NY Rangers, in 20 seasons.
10 – Mario Lemieux, Pittsburgh, in 17 seasons.
 8 – Marcel Dionne, Detroit, Los Angeles, NY Rangers, in 18 seasons.
 7 – Mike Bossy, NY Islanders, in 10 seasons.
 – Peter Stastny, Quebec, New Jersey, St. Louis, in 15 seasons.

MOST CONSECUTIVE 100-OR-MORE POINT SEASONS:
13 – Wayne Gretzky, Edmonton, Los Angeles, 1979-80 – 1991-92.
 6 – Bobby Orr, Boston, 1969-70 – 1974-75.
 – Guy Lafleur, Montreal, 1974-75 – 1979-80.
 – Mike Bossy, NY Islanders, 1980-81 – 1985-86.
 – Peter Stastny, Quebec, 1980-81 – 1985-86.
 – Mario Lemieux, Pittsburgh, 1984-85 – 1989-90.
 – Steve Yzerman, Detroit, 1987-88 – 1992-93.

A great all-around athlete whose hockey career was hampered by an eye injury, Henry Boucha set an NHL record (since broken) when he scored for the Detroit Red Wings just six seconds into a game at the Montreal Forum on January 28, 1973.

THREE-OR-MORE-GOAL GAMES
MOST THREE-OR-MORE GOAL GAMES, CAREER:
50 – Wayne Gretzky, Edmonton, Los Angeles, St. Louis, NY Rangers, in 20 seasons, 37 three-goal games, 9 four-goal games, 4 five-goal games.
40 – Mario Lemieux, Pittsburgh, in 17 seasons, 27 three-goal games, 10 four-goal games, 3 five-goal games.
39 – Mike Bossy, NY Islanders, in 10 seasons, 30 three-goal games, 9 four-goal games.
33 – Brett Hull, Calgary, St. Louis, Dallas, Detroit, Phoenix, in 19 seasons, 30 three-goal games, 3 four-goal games.
32 – Phil Esposito, Chicago, Boston, NY Rangers, in 18 seasons, 27 three-goal games, 5 four-goal games.

MOST THREE-OR-MORE GOAL GAMES, ONE SEASON:
10 – Wayne Gretzky, Edmonton, 1981-82. 6 three-goal games, 3 four-goal games, 1 five-goal game.
– Wayne Gretzky, Edmonton, 1983-84. 6 three-goal games, 4 four-goal games.
 9 – Mike Bossy, NY Islanders, 1980-81. 6 three-goal games, 3 four-goal games.
 – Mario Lemieux, Pittsburgh, 1988-89. 7 three-goal games, 1 four-goal game, 1 five-goal game.
 8 – Brett Hull, St. Louis, 1991-92. 8 three-goal games.
 7 – Joe Malone, Montreal, 1917-18. 2 three-goal games, 2 four-goal games, 3 five-goal games.
 – Phil Esposito, Boston, 1970-71. 7 three-goal games.
 – Rick Martin, Buffalo, 1975-76. 6 three-goal games, 1 four-goal game.
 – Alexander Mogilny, Buffalo, 1992-93. 5 three-goal games, 2 four-goal games.

SCORING STREAKS
LONGEST CONSECUTIVE GOAL-SCORING STREAK:
16 Games – Punch Broadbent, Ottawa, 1921-22. 27G
14 Games – Joe Malone, Montreal, 1917-18. 35G
13 Games – Newsy Lalonde, Montreal, 1920-21. 24G
 – Charlie Simmer, Los Angeles, 1979-80. 17G
12 Games – Cy Denneny, Ottawa, 1917-18. 23G
 – Dave Lumley, Edmonton, 1981-82. 15G
 – Mario Lemieux, Pittsburgh, 1992-93. 18G

LONGEST CONSECUTIVE ASSIST-SCORING STREAK:
23 Games – Wayne Gretzky, Los Angeles, 1990-91. 48A
18 Games – Adam Oates, Boston, 1992-93. 28A
17 Games – Wayne Gretzky, Edmonton, 1983-84. 38A
 – Paul Coffey, Edmonton, 1985-86. 27A
 – Wayne Gretzky, Los Angeles, 1989-90. 35A
16 Games – Jaromir Jagr, Pittsburgh, 2000-01. 24A

LONGEST CONSECUTIVE POINT-SCORING STREAK:
51 Games – Wayne Gretzky, Edmonton, 1983-84. 61G-92A-153PTS
46 Games – Mario Lemieux, Pittsburgh, 1989-90. 39G-64A-103PTS
39 Games – Wayne Gretzky, Edmonton, 1985-86. 33G-75A-108PTS
30 Games – Wayne Gretzky, Edmonton, 1982-83. 24G-52A-76PTS
 – Mats Sundin, Quebec, 1992-93. 21G-25A-46PTS

LONGEST CONSECUTIVE POINT-SCORING STREAK
FROM START OF SEASON:
51 Games – **Wayne Gretzky**, Edmonton, 1983-84. 61G-92A-153PTS. Streak ended by Los Angeles and goaltender Markus Mattsson on Jan. 28, 1984.

LONGEST CONSECUTIVE POINT-SCORING STREAK BY A DEFENSEMAN:
28 Games – **Paul Coffey**, Edmonton, 1985-86. 16G-39A-55PTS
19 Games – Raymond Bourque, Boston, 1987-88. 6G-21A-27PTS
17 Games – Raymond Bourque, Boston, 1984-85. 4G-24A-28PTS
– Brian Leetch, NY Rangers, 1991-92. 5G-24A-29PTS
16 Games – Gary Suter, Calgary, 1987-88. 8G-17A-25PTS
15 Games – Bobby Orr, Boston, 1970-71. 10G-23A-33PTS
– Bobby Orr, Boston, 1973-74. 8G-15A-23PTS
– Steve Duchesne, Quebec, 1992-93. 4G-17A-21PTS
– Chris Chelios, Chicago, 1995-96. 4G-16A-20PTS

LONGEST CONSECUTIVE POINT-SCORING STREAK BY A ROOKIE:
20 Games – **Paul Stastny**, Colorado, 2006-07. 11G-18A-29PTS
17 Games – Teemu Selanne, Winnipeg, 1992-93. 20G-14A-34PTS
16 Games – Peter Stastny, Quebec, 1980-81
15 Games – Jude Drouin, Minnesota North Stars, 1970-71

FASTEST GOALS AND ASSISTS
FASTEST GOAL FROM START OF A GAME:
0:05 – **Doug Smail**, Winnipeg, Dec. 20, 1981, at Winnipeg. Winnipeg 5, St. Louis 4.
– **Bryan Trottier**, NY Islanders, Mar. 22, 1984, at Boston. NY Islanders 3, Boston 3.
– **Alexander Mogilny**, Buffalo, Dec. 21, 1991, at Toronto. Buffalo 4, Toronto 1.
0:06 – Henry Boucha, Detroit, Jan. 28, 1973, at Montreal. Detroit 4, Montreal 2.
– Jean Pronovost, Pittsburgh, Mar. 25, 1976, at St. Louis. St. Louis 5, Pittsburgh 2.
0:07 – Charlie Conacher, Toronto, Feb. 6, 1932, at Toronto. Toronto 6, Boston 0.
– Danny Gare, Buffalo, Dec. 17, 1978, at Buffalo. Buffalo 6, Vancouver 3.
– Tiger Williams, Los Angeles, Feb. 14, 1987, at Los Angeles. Los Angeles 5, Harford 2.
0:08 – A goal has been scored at 0:08 of the first period on 15 occasions since Ron Martin of NY Americans accomplished the feat at home vs. Montreal Canadiens on, Dec. 4, 1932. Final score: NY Americans 4, Montreal 2. The most recent players to score at 0:08 are Alexander Semin and Alexander Steen. Semin scored for Washington, Nov. 11, 2009 at Washington. (Final score: Washington 5, NY Islanders 4). Steen scored for St. Louis, Mar. 16, 2010 at St. Louis. Final score: Colorado 5, St. Louis 3.

FASTEST GOAL FROM START OF A PERIOD:
0:04 – **Claude Provost**, Montreal, Nov. 9, 1957, at Montreal, second period. Montreal 4, Boston 2.
– **Denis Savard**, Chicago, Jan. 12, 1986, at Chicago, third period. Chicago 4, Hartford 2.

FASTEST GOAL BY A PLAYER IN HIS FIRST NHL GAME:
0:15 – **Gus Bodnar**, Toronto, Oct. 30, 1943, at Toronto. Toronto 5, NY Rangers 2.
0:18 – Danny Gare, Buffalo, Oct. 10, 1974, at Buffalo. Buffalo 9, Boston 5.
0:20 – Alexander Mogilny, Buffalo, Oct. 5, 1989, at Buffalo. Buffalo 4, Quebec 3.

FASTEST TWO GOALS FROM START OF A GAME:
0:27 – **Mike Knuble**, Boston, Feb. 14, 2003, at Florida. 0:10 and 0:27. Boston 6, Florida 5.

FASTEST TWO GOALS:
0:04 – **Nels Stewart**, Mtl. Maroons, Jan. 3, 1931, at Mtl. Maroons. 8:24 and 8:28, third period. Mtl. Maroons 5, Boston 3.
– **Deron Quint**, Winnipeg, Dec. 15, 1995, at Winnipeg. 7:51 and 7:55, second period. Winnipeg 9, Edmonton 4.
0:05 – Pete Mahovlich, Montreal, Feb. 20, 1971, at Montreal. 12:16 and 12:21, third period. Montreal 7, Chicago 1.
0:06 – Jim Pappin, Chicago, Feb. 16, 1972, at Chicago. 2:57 and 3:03, third period. Chicago 3, Philadelphia 3.
– Ralph Backstrom, Los Angeles, Nov. 2, 1972, at Los Angeles. 8:30 and 8:36, third period. Los Angeles 6, Boston 2.
– Lanny McDonald, Calgary, Mar. 22, 1984, at Calgary. 16:23 and 16:29, first period. Detroit 6, Calgary 4.
– Sylvain Turgeon, Hartford, Mar. 28, 1987, at Hartford. 13:59 and 14:05, second period. Hartford 5, Pittsburgh 4.

FASTEST THREE GOALS:
0:21 – **Bill Mosienko**, Chicago, Mar. 23, 1952, at NY Rangers, against goaltender Lorne Anderson. Mosienko scored at 6:09, 6:20 and 6:30 of third period, all with both teams at full strength. Chicago 7, NY Rangers 6.
0:44 – Jean Béliveau, Montreal, Nov. 5, 1955, at Montreal, against goaltender Terry Sawchuk. Béliveau scored at 0:42, 1:08 and 1:26 of second period, all with Montreal holding a 6-4 man advantage. Montreal 4, Boston 2.

FASTEST THREE ASSISTS:
0:21 – **Gus Bodnar**, Chicago, Mar. 23, 1952, at NY Rangers, Bodnar assisted on Bill Mosienko's three goals at 6:09, 6:20 and 6:30 of third period. Chicago 7, NY Rangers 6.
0:44 – Bert Olmstead, Montreal, Nov. 5, 1955, at Montreal, Olmstead assisted on Jean Béliveau's three goals at 0:42, 1:08 and 1:26 of second period. Montreal 4, Boston 2.

SHOTS ON GOAL
MOST SHOTS ON GOAL, ONE SEASON:
550 – **Phil Esposito**, Boston, 1970-71. 78GP – 78 game schedule.
528 – Alex Ovechkin, Washington, 2008-09. 79GP – 82 game schedule.
446 – Alex Ovechkin, Washington, 2007-08. 82GP – 82 game schedule.
429 – Paul Kariya, Anaheim, 1998-99. 82GP – 82 game schedule.
426 – Phil Esposito, Boston, 1971-72. 76GP – 78 game schedule.

PENALTIES
MOST PENALTY MINUTES, CAREER:
3,966 – **Tiger Williams,** Toronto, Vancouver, Detroit, Los Angeles, Hartford, in 14 seasons. 962GP
3,565 – Dale Hunter, Quebec, Washington, Colorado, in 19 seasons. 1,407GP
3,515 – Tie Domi, Toronto, NY Rangers, Winnipeg, in 16 seasons. 1,020GP
3,381 – Marty McSorley, Pittsburgh, Edmonton, Los Angeles, NY Rangers, San Jose, Boston, in 17 seasons. 961GP
3,300 – Bob Probert, Detroit, Chicago, in 17 seasons. 935GP

MOST PENALTY MINUTES, CAREER, INCLUDING PLAYOFFS:
4,421 – **Tiger Williams**, Toronto, Vancouver, Detroit, Los Angeles, Hartford, 3,966 in 962 regular-season games; 455 in 83 playoff games.
4,294 – Dale Hunter, Quebec, Washington, Colorado, 3,565 in 1,407 regular-season games; 729 in 186 playoff games.
3,755 – Marty McSorley, Pittsburgh, Edmonton, Los Angeles, NY Rangers, San Jose, Boston, 3,381 in 961 regular-season games; 374 in 115 playoff games.
3,753 – Tie Domi, Toronto, NY Rangers, Winnipeg, 3,515 in 1,020 regular-season games; 238 in 98 playoff games.
3,584 – Chris Nilan, Montreal, NY Rangers, Boston, 3,043 in 688 regular-season games; 541 in 111 playoff games.

MOST PENALTY MINUTES, ONE SEASON:
472 – **Dave Schultz**, Philadelphia, 1974-75.
409 – Paul Baxter, Pittsburgh, 1981-82.
408 – Mike Peluso, Chicago, 1991-92.
405 – Dave Schultz, Los Angeles, Pittsburgh, 1977-78.

MOST PENALTIES, ONE GAME:
10 – **Chris Nilan**, Boston, Mar. 31, 1991, at Boston vs. Hartford. 6 minors, 2 majors, 1 10-minute misconduct, 1 game misconduct.
9 – Jim Dorey, Toronto, Oct. 16, 1968, at Toronto vs. Pittsburgh. 4 minors, 2 majors, 2 10-minute misconducts, 1 game misconduct.
– Dave Schultz, Pittsburgh, Apr. 6, 1978, at Detroit. 5 minors, 2 majors, 2 10-minute misconducts.
– Randy Holt, Los Angeles, Mar. 11, 1979, at Philadelphia. 1 minor, 3 majors, 2 10-minute misconducts, 3 game misconducts.
– Russ Anderson, Pittsburgh, Jan. 19, 1980, at Pittsburgh vs. Edmonton. 3 minors, 3 majors, 3 game misconducts.
– Kim Clackson, Quebec, Mar. 8, 1981, at Quebec vs. Chicago. 4 minors, 3 majors, 2 game misconducts.
– Terry O'Reilly, Boston, Dec. 19, 1984, at Hartford. 5 minors, 3 majors, 1 game misconduct.
– Larry Playfair, Los Angeles, Dec. 9, 1986, at NY Islanders. 6 minors, 2 majors, 1 10-minute misconduct.
– Marty McSorley, Los Angeles, Apr. 14, 1992, at Vancouver. 5 minors, 2 majors, 1 10-minute misconduct, 1 game misconduct.
– Reed Low, St. Louis, Dec. 31, 2002, at Detroit. 4 minors, 1 major, 1 10-minute misconduct, 3 game misconducts.

MOST PENALTY MINUTES, ONE GAME:
67 – **Randy Holt**, Los Angeles, Mar. 11, 1979, at Philadelphia. 1 minor, 3 majors, 2 10-minute misconducts, 3 game misconducts.
57 – Brad Smith, Toronto, Nov. 15, 1986, at Toronto vs. Detroit. 1 minor, 3 majors, 2 10-minute misconducts, 2 game misconducts.
– Reed Low, St. Louis, Feb. 28, 2002, at St. Louis vs. Calgary. 1 minor, 3 majors, 1 10-minute misconduct, 3 game misconducts.

MOST PENALTIES, ONE PERIOD:
9 – **Randy Holt**, Los Angeles, Mar. 11, 1979, at Philadelphia, first period. 1 minor, 3 majors, 2 10-minute misconducts, 3 game misconducts.

MOST PENALTY MINUTES, ONE PERIOD:
67 – **Randy Holt**, Los Angeles, Mar. 11, 1979, at Philadelphia, first period. 1 minor, 3 majors, 2 10-minute misconducts, 3 game misconducts.

GOALTENDING
MOST GAMES APPEARED IN BY A GOALTENDER, CAREER:
1,076 – **Martin Brodeur**, New Jersey, 1991-92 – 2003-04, 2005-06 – 2009-10.
1,029 – Patrick Roy, Montreal, Colorado, 1984-85 – 2002-03.
971 – Terry Sawchuk, Detroit, Boston, Toronto, Los Angeles, NY Rangers, 1949-50 – 1969-70.
963 – Ed Belfour, Chicago, San Jose, Dallas, Toronto, Florida, 1988-89 – 2003-04, 2005-06, 2006-07.
943 – Curtis Joseph, St. Louis, Edmonton, Toronto, Detroit, Phoenix, Calgary, 1989-90 – 2003-04, 2005-06 – 2008-09.

MOST CONSECUTIVE COMPLETE GAMES BY A GOALTENDER:
502 – **Glenn Hall**, Detroit, Chicago. Played 502 games from beginning of 1955-56 season through first 12 games of 1962-63 season. In his 503rd straight game, Nov. 7, 1962, at Chicago, Hall was removed from the game against Boston with a back injury in the first period.

MOST GAMES APPEARED IN BY A GOALTENDER, ONE SEASON:
79 – **Grant Fuhr**, St. Louis, 1995-96.
78 – Martin Brodeur, New Jersey, 2006-07.
77 – Martin Brodeur, New Jersey, 1995-96, 2007-08 and 2009-10.
– Bill Ranford, Edmonton, Boston, 1995-96.
– Arturs Irbe, Carolina, 2000-01.
– Marc Denis, Columbus, 2002-03.
– Evgeni Nabokov, San Jose, 2007-08.

MOST MINUTES PLAYED BY A GOALTENDER, CAREER:
63,521 – **Martin Brodeur**, New Jersey, 1991-92 – 2003-04, 2005-06 – 2009-10.
60,235 – Patrick Roy, Montreal, Colorado, 1984-85 – 2002-03.
57,194 – Terry Sawchuk, Detroit, Boston, Toronto, Los Angeles, NY Rangers, 1949-50 – 1969-70.

MOST MINUTES PLAYED BY A GOALTENDER, ONE SEASON:
4,697 – **Martin Brodeur**, New Jersey, 2006-07.
4,635 – Martin Brodeur, New Jersey, 2007-08.
4,561 – Evgeni Nabokov, San Jose, 2007-08.
4,555 – Martin Brodeur, New Jersey, 2003-04.
4,511 – Marc Denis, Columbus, 2002-03.

MOST SHUTOUTS, CAREER:
110 – **Martin Brodeur**, New Jersey, in 17 seasons.
    (1991-92, 1993-94 – 2003-04, 2005-06 – 2009-10)
103 – Terry Sawchuk, Detroit, Boston, Toronto, Los Angeles, NY Rangers,
    in 21 seasons. (1949-50 – 1969-70)
94 – George Hainsworth, Montreal, Toronto, in 11 seasons.
    (1926-27 – 1936-37)

MOST SHUTOUTS, ONE SEASON:
22 – **George Hainsworth**, Montreal, 1928-29. 44GP
15 – Alec Connell, Ottawa, 1925-26. 36GP
– Alec Connell, Ottawa, 1927-28. 44GP
– Hal Winkler, Boston, 1927-28. 44GP
– Tony Esposito, Chicago, 1969-70. 63GP
14 – George Hainsworth, Montreal, 1926-27. 44GP

LONGEST SHUTOUT SEQUENCE BY A GOALTENDER:
461:29 – **Alec Connell**, Ottawa, 1927-28, six consecutive shutouts.
    (Forward passing not permitted in attacking zones in 1927-28.)
343:05 – George Hainsworth, Montreal, 1928-29, four consecutive shutouts.
    (Forward passing not permitted in attacking zones in 1928-29.)
332:01 – Brian Boucher, Phoenix, 2003-04, five consecutive shutouts.
324:40 – Roy Worters, NY Americans, 1930-31, four consecutive shutouts.
309:21 – Bill Durnan, Montreal, 1948-49, four consecutive shutouts.

MOST WINS BY A GOALTENDER, CAREER:
602 – **Martin Brodeur**, New Jersey, in 17 seasons. 1,076 GP
551 – Patrick Roy, Montreal, Colorado, in 19 seasons. 1,029GP
484 – Ed Belfour, Chicago, San Jose, Dallas, Toronto, Florida,
    in 17 seasons. 963GP
454 – Curtis Joseph, St. Louis, Edmonton, Toronto, Detroit, Phoenix, Calgary,
    in 19 seasons. 943GP
447 – Terry Sawchuk, Detroit, Boston, Toronto, Los Angeles, NY Rangers,
    in 21 seasons. 971GP

MOST WINS BY A GOALTENDER, ONE SEASON:
48 – **Martin Brodeur**, New Jersey, 2006-07. 78GP
47 – Bernie Parent, Philadelphia, 1973-74. 73GP
– Roberto Luongo, Vancouver, 2006-07. 76GP
46 – Evgeni Nabokov, San Jose, 2007-08. 77GP
45 – Miikka Kiprusoff, Calgary, 2008-09. 76GP
– Martin Brodeur, New Jersey, 2009-10. 77GP

LONGEST WINNING STREAK BY A GOALTENDER, ONE SEASON:
17 – **Gilles Gilbert**, Boston, 1975-76.
14 – Tiny Thompson, Boston, 1929-30.
– Ross Brooks, Boston, 1973-74.
– Don Beaupre, Minnesota, 1985-86.
– Tom Barrasso, Pittsburgh, 1992-93.

LONGEST UNDEFEATED STREAK BY A GOALTENDER, ONE SEASON:
32 Games – **Gerry Cheevers**, Boston, 1971-72. 24w-8T
31 Games – Pete Peeters, Boston, 1982-83. 26w-5T
27 Games – Pete Peeters, Philadelphia, 1979-80. 22w-5T

LONGEST UNDEFEATED STREAK BY A GOALTENDER IN HIS FIRST NHL SEASON:
23 Games – **Grant Fuhr**, Edmonton, 1981-82. 15w-8T

LONGEST UNDEFEATED STREAK BY A GOALTENDER FROM START OF CAREER:
16 Games – **Patrick Lalime**, Pittsburgh, 1996-97. 14w-2T

MOST 30-OR-MORE WIN SEASONS BY A GOALTENDER:
13 – **Patrick Roy**, Montreal, Colorado, in 19 seasons.
– **Martin Brodeur**, New Jersey, in 17 seasons.
9 – Ed Belfour, Chicago, San Jose, Dallas, Toronto, Florida, in 17 seasons.
8 – Tony Esposito, Montreal, Chicago, in 16 seasons.
7 – Jacques Plante, Montreal, NY Rangers, St. Louis, Toronto, Boston,
    in 18 seasons.
– Ken Dryden, Montreal, in 8 seasons.
– Curtis Joseph, St. Louis, Edmonton, Toronto, Detroit, Phoenix, Calgary,
    in 19 seasons.
– Dominik Hasek, Chicago, Buffalo, Detroit, Ottawa, in 16 seasons.

MOST CONSECUTIVE 30-OR-MORE WIN SEASONS BY A GOALTENDER:
12 – **Martin Brodeur**, New Jersey, 1995-96 – 2003-04, 2005-06 – 2007-08.
8 – Patrick Roy, Montreal, Colorado, 1995-96 – 2002-03.
7 – Tony Esposito, Chicago, 1969-70 – 1975-76.
6 – Jacques Plante, Montreal, 1954-55 – 1959-60.
– Marty Turco, Dallas, 2002-03, 2003-04, 2005-06 – 2008-09.
5 – Terry Sawchuk, Detroit, 1950-51 – 1954-55.
– Ken Dryden, Montreal, 1974-75 – 1978-79.
– Ryan Miller, Buffalo, 2005-06 – 2009-10.
– Henrik Lundqvist, NY Rangers, 2005-06 – 2009-10.
– Miikka Kiprusoff, 2005-06 – 2009-10.

MOST 40-OR-MORE WIN SEASONS BY A GOALTENDER:
8 – **Martin Brodeur,** New Jersey, in 17 seasons.
3 – Terry Sawchuk, Detroit, Boston, Toronto, Los Angeles, NY Rangers,
    in 21 seasons.
– Jacques Plante, Montreal, NY Rangers, St. Louis, Toronto, Boston,
    in 18 seasons.
– Miikka Kiprusoff, San Jose, Calgary, in 9 seasons.
– Evgeni Nabokov, San Jose, in 10 seasons.
2 – Bernie Parent, Boston, Philadelphia, Toronto, in 13 seasons.
– Ken Dryden, Montreal, in 8 seasons.
– Ed Belfour, Chicago, San Jose, Dallas, Toronto, Florida, in 17 seasons.
– Ryan Miller, Buffalo, in 7 seasons.

MOST CONSECUTIVE 40-OR-MORE WIN SEASONS BY A GOALTENDER:
3 – **Martin Brodeur**, New Jersey, 2005-06 – 2007-08.
– **Evgeni Nabokov**, San Jose, 2007-08 – 2009-10.
2 – Terry Sawchuk, Detroit, 1950-51 – 1951-52.
– Bernie Parent, Philadelphia, 1973-74 – 1974-75.
– Ken Dryden, Montreal, 1975-76 – 1976-77.
– Martin Brodeur, New Jersey, 1999-2000 – 2000-01.
– Miikka Kiprusoff, Calgary, 2005-06 – 2006-07.

MOST LOSSES BY A GOALTENDER, CAREER:
352 – **Gump Worsley**, NY Rangers, Montreal, Minnesota, in 21 seasons. 861GP
– **Curtis Joseph**, St. Louis, Edmonton, Toronto, Detroit, Phoenix,
    in 19 seasons. 943GP
351 – Gilles Meloche, Chicago, California, Cleveland, Minnesota, Pittsburgh,
    in 18 seasons. 788GP
346 – John Vanbiesbrouck, NY Rangers, Florida, Philadelphia, NY Islanders,
    New Jersey, in 20 seasons. 882GP
341 – Sean Burke, New Jersey, Hartford, Carolina, Vancouver, Philadelphia,
    Florida, Phoenix, Tampa Bay, Los Angeles, in 18 seasons. 820GP

MOST LOSSES BY A GOALTENDER, ONE SEASON:
48 – **Gary Smith**, California, 1970-71. 71GP
47 – Al Rollins, Chicago, 1953-54. 66GP
46 – Peter Sidorkiewicz, Ottawa, 1992-93. 64GP

GOALTENDER SHOOTOUT RECORDS

MOST SHOOTOUT WINS, ONE SEASON:
10 – Mathieu Garon, Edmonton, 2007-08, (10GP)
– Ryan Miller, Buffalo, 2006-07, (14GP)
– Martin Brodeur, New Jersey, 2006-07, (16GP)
9 – Henrik Lundqvist, NY Rangers, 2008-09, (13GP)
– Marc-Andre Fleury, Pittsburgh, 2006-07, (14GP)

MOST SHOOTOUT WINS, CAREER:
34 – Martin Brodeur, New Jersey, (52GP)
30 – Henrik Lundqvist, NY Rangers, (51GP)
29 – Ryan Miller, Buffalo, (48GP)
28 – Marty Turco, Dallas, (50GP)

MOST SHOOTOUT SHOTS AGAINST, ONE SEASON:
62 – Ilya Bryzgalov, Phoenix, 2009-10, (17GA)
60 – Martin Brodeur, New Jersey, 2006-07, (20GA)
54 – Roberto Luongo, Vancouver, 2007-08, (15GA)
– Jimmy Howard, Detroit, 2009-10, (17GA)
53 – Marty Turco, Dallas, 2009-10, (15GA)

MOST SHOOTOUT SHOTS AGAINST, CAREER:
191 – Henrik Lundqvist, NY Rangers, (48GA)
189 – Marty Turco, Dallas, (57GA)
182 – Martin Brodeur, New Jersey, (52GA)
167 – Ryan Miller, Buffalo, (48GA)

BEST SHOOTOUT SAVE PERCENTAGE, ONE SEASON: (minimum 20 shots)
.938 – Mathieu Garon, Edmonton, 2007-08, (32s, 2GA)
.900 – Marc Denis, Tampa Bay, 2006-07, (20s, 2GA)
.879 – Johan Holmqvist, Tampa Bay, 2006-07, (33s, 4GA)
.850 – Kari Lehtonen, Atlanta, 2005-06, (20s, 3GA)

BEST SHOOTOUT SAVE PERCENTAGE, CAREER: (minimum 40 shots)
.854 – Marc Denis, Columbus, Tampa Bay, Montreal, (41s, 6GA)
.805 – Johan Hedberg, Dallas, Atlanta, (82s, 16GA)
.768 – Pekka Rinne, Nashville, (69s, 16GA)
.759 – Mathieu Garon, Los Angeles, Edmonton, Pittsburgh, Columbus
    (87s, 21GA)

Active NHL Players' Three-or-More-Goal Games

Regular Season

Teams named are the ones the players were with at the time of their multiple-scoring games. Players listed alphabetically.

Daniel Sedin scores his third goal of the game against Miikka Kiprusoff for his second hat trick of the season on April 10, 2010.

Player	Team(s)	3-Goals	4-Goals	5-Goals
Alfredsson, Daniel	Ottawa	6	1	—
Antropov, Nik	Toronto	2	—	—
Armstrong, Derek	Los Angeles	1	—	—
Arnason, Tyler	Chicago	1	—	—
Arnott, Jason	Edm., N.J., Dal., Nsh.	8	—	—
Backes, David	St. Louis	1	—	—
Battaglia, Bates	Carolina	1	—	—
Belanger, Eric	Los Angeles	1	—	—
Bergenheim, Sean	NY Islanders	1	—	—
Bergeron, Marc-Andre	Edmonton	1	—	—
Bertuzzi, Todd	Vancouver	5	—	—
Blake, Jason	NYI, Tor.	6	—	—
Bochenski, Brandon	Ottawa	1	—	—
Booth, David	Florida	2	—	—
Bourque, Rene	Calgary	2	—	—
Boyes, Brad	Boston	1	—	—
Boyle, Dan	Tampa Bay	1	—	—
Briere, Danny	Buf., Phi.	4	—	—
Brown, Dustin	Los Angeles	2	—	—
Brunette, Andrew	Colorado	1	—	—
Brunnstrom, Fabian	Dallas	1	—	—
Burrows, Alexandre	Vancouver	1	—	—
Byfuglien, Dustin	Chicago	1	—	—
Cammalleri, Michael	Cgy., Mtl.	4	—	—
Carcillo, Daniel	Phoenix	1	—	—
Carter, Jeff	Philadelphia	1	—	—
Cheechoo, Jonathan	San Jose	9	—	—
Clark, Chris	Washington	1	—	—
Cleary, Daniel	Detroit	1	—	—
Clowe, Ryane	San Jose	1	—	—
Cole, Erik	Car., Edm.	6	—	—
Comeau, Blake	NY Islanders	1	—	—
Conroy, Craig	St.L., L.A.	2	—	—
Corvo, Joe	Carolina	1	—	—
Crombeen, B.J.	St. Louis	1	—	—
Crosby, Sidney	Pittsburgh	5	—	—
Cullen, Matt	Carolina	1	—	—
Demitra, Pavol	St.L., L.A.	4	—	—
Donovan, Shean	Atlanta	1	—	—
Drury, Chris	Buf., NYR	2	—	—
Dumont, J.P.	Chi., Buf.	3	—	—
Dupuis, Pascal	Pittsburgh	1	—	—
Dvorak, Radek	NYR, Fla.	2	1	—
Elias, Patrik	New Jersey	6	1	—
Erat, Martin	Nashville	2	—	—
Eriksson, Loui	Dallas	2	—	—
Filatov, Nikita	Columbus	1	—	—
Fisher, Mike	Ottawa	1	—	—
Frolov, Alexander	Los Angeles	3	—	—
Gaborik, Marian	Min., NYR	7	—	1
Gagne, Simon	Philadelphia	3	—	—
Gagner, Sam	Edmonton	1	—	—
Gionta, Brian	New Jersey	1	—	—
Glencross, Curtis	Calgary	1	—	—
Gomez, Scott	New Jersey	2	—	—
Gonchar, Sergei	Washington	1	—	—
Grabner, Michael	Vancouver	1	—	—
Grier, Mike	Edmonton	1	—	—
Guerin, Bill	N.J., Bos., Dal., St.L., S.J., NYI	9	—	—
Hagman, Niklas	Dal., Tor.	2	—	—
Hamilton, Jeff	Chicago	2	—	—
Handzus, Michal	St.L., L.A.	2	—	—
Hanzal, Martin	Phoenix	1	—	—
Hartnell, Scott	Nsh., Phi.	5	—	—
Havlat, Martin	Ottawa	3	1	—
Heatley, Dany	Atl., Ott., S.J.	8	1	—
Hecht, Jochen	Buffalo	1	—	—
Hejduk, Milan	Colorado	4	—	—
Higgins, Chris	Montreal	1	—	—
Holmstrom, Tomas	Detroit	3	—	—
Horcoff, Shawn	Edmonton	1	—	—
Horton, Nathan	Florida	2	—	—
Hossa, Marian	Ott., Atl.	6	1	—
Huselius, Kristian	Calgary	1	—	—
Iginla, Jarome	Calgary	9	1	—
Jokinen, Jussi	Dallas	—	1	—
Jokinen, Olli	Fla., Phx., Cgy.	6	—	—
Kaberle, Tomas	Toronto	1	—	—
Kariya, Paul	Ana., Nsh., St.L.	10	—	—
Kessel, Phil	Boston	2	—	—
Knuble, Mike	Philadelphia	1	—	—
Kobasew, Chuck	Cgy., Min.	2	—	—
Koivu, Saku	Montreal	1	—	—
Kopitar, Anze	Los Angeles	1	—	—
Kostitsyn, Andrei	Montreal	1	—	—
Kovalchuk, Ilya	Atlanta	10	1	—
Kovalev, Alex	NYR, Pit., Ott.	11	1	—
Kozlov, Vyacheslav	Det., Atl.	4	1	—
Krejci, David	Boston	1	—	—
Kunitz, Chris	Anaheim	1	—	—
Ladd, Andrew	Chicago	1	—	—
Laich, Brooks	Washington	1	—	—
Lang, Robert	Wsh., Mtl.	2	—	—
Langenbrunner, Jamie	New Jersey	1	—	—
Langkow, Daymond	Phx., Cgy.	3	—	—
Laperriere, Ian	Los Angeles	1	—	—
Lapierre, Maxim	Montreal	1	—	—
Laraque, Georges	Edmonton	1	—	—
Larose, Chad	Carolina	1	—	—
Latendresse, Guillaume	Minnesota	1	—	—
Lecavalier, Vincent	Tampa Bay	6	—	—
Legwand, David	Nashville	2	—	—
Lehtinen, Jere	Dallas	2	—	—
Little, Bryan	Atlanta	1	—	—
Lombardi, Matthew	Calgary	1	—	—
Lucic, Milan	Boston	1	—	—
Lupul, Joffrey	Philadelphia	2	—	—
Madden, John	New Jersey	1	1	—
Malkin, Evgeni	Pittsburgh	5	—	—
Malone, Ryan	Pit., T.B.	3	—	—
Maltby, Kirk	Detroit	1	—	—
Marleau, Patrick	San Jose	3	—	—
Michalek, Milan	Ottawa	1	—	—
Modano, Mike	Min., Dal.	6	1	—
Modin, Fredrik	Tampa Bay	3	—	—
Moreau, Ethan	Edmonton	1	—	—
Morrison, Brendan	Vancouver	1	—	—
Morrow, Brenden	Dallas	1	—	—
Moss, Dave	Calgary	1	—	—
Moulson, Matt	NY Islanders	1	—	—
Mueller, Peter	Phoenix	2	—	—
Nash, Rick	Columbus	4	—	—
Neal, James	Dallas	1	—	—
Nolan, Owen	Que., S.J., Cgy.	10	1	—
Nylander, Michael	Hfd., Chi.	1	1	—
Ott, Steve	Dallas	1	—	—
Ovechkin, Alex	Washington	7	2	—
Pandolfo, Jay	New Jersey	1	—	—
Parise, Zach	New Jersey	1	—	—
Parrish, Mark	Fla., NYI, Min., Dal.	5	1	—
Perron, David	St. Louis	1	—	—
Petersen, Toby	Pittsburgh	1	—	—
Pisani, Fernando	Edmonton	1	—	—
Plekanec, Thomas	Montreal	1	—	—
Pominville, Jason	Buffalo	2	—	—
Prospal, Vaclav	Ana., T.B.	2	—	—
Pyatt, Taylor	Buffalo	2	—	—
Raymond, Mason	Vancouver	1	—	—
Recchi, Mark	Pit., Mtl., Phi.	7	—	—
Reinprecht, Steve	Col., Phx., Fla.	4	—	—
Ribeiro, Mike	Dallas	1	—	—
Richards, Mike	Philadelphia	2	—	—
Rolston, Brian	N.J., Min.	2	—	—
Roy, Derek	Buffalo	4	—	—
Rupp, Mike	Pittsburgh	1	—	—
Ruutu, Tuomo	Carolina	1	—	—
Ryan, Bobby	Anaheim	1	—	—
Ryder, Michael	Montreal	2	—	—
Salo, Sami	Ottawa	1	—	—
Samsonov, Sergei	Boston	1	—	—
Samuelsson, Mikael	Vancouver	1	—	—
Satan, Miroslav	Buf., NYI	6	1	—
Savard, Marc	Cgy., Bos.	2	1	—
Schneider, Mathieu	Detroit	1	—	—
Sedin, Daniel	Vancouver	3	1	—
Sedin, Henrik	Vancouver	1	—	—
Selanne, Teemu	Wpg., Ana., S.J.	19	2	—
Semin, Alexander	Washington	3	—	—
Sharp, Patrick	Chicago	1	—	—
Sim, Jon	Florida	1	—	—
Sjostrom, Fredrik	Phoenix	1	—	—
Smyth, Ryan	Edmonton	5	—	—
Souray, Sheldon	Montreal	1	—	—
Spezza, Jason	Ottawa	3	—	—
St. Louis, Martin	Tampa Bay	4	—	—
Staal, Eric	Carolina	9	1	—
Staal, Jordan	Pittsburgh	2	—	—
Stafford, Drew	Buffalo	2	—	—
Stamkos, Steven	Tampa Bay	1	—	—
Stastny, Paul	Colorado	1	—	—
Steen, Alex	Toronto	1	—	—
Stewart, Chris	Colorado	1	—	—
Stillman, Cory	Cgy., St.L., Car.	4	—	—
Sturm, Marco	S.J., Bos.	2	—	—
Sullivan, Steve	Tor., Chi., Nsh.	6	1	—
Svatos, Marek	Colorado	2	—	—
Sykora, Petr	Pittsburgh	1	—	—
Tambellini, Jeff	NY Islanders	1	—	—
Tanguay, Alex	Colorado	2	—	—
Thornton, Joe	Bos., S.J.	3	—	—
Tkachuk, Keith	Phoenix	7	2	—
Toews, Jonathan	Chicago	1	—	—
Umberger, R.J.	Phi., CBJ	2	—	—
Upshall, Scottie	Phoenix	1	—	—
Vanek, Thomas	Buffalo	5	1	—
Vermette, Antoine	Ottawa	1	—	—
Visnovsky, Lubomir	Los Angeles	1	—	—
Vrbata, Radim	Col., Car., Phx.	3	—	—
Walker, Scott	Nashville	2	—	—
Weight, Doug	Edm., St.L.	2	—	—
Weiss, Stephen	Florida	2	—	—
Wellwood, Kyle	Toronto	1	—	—
Wheeler, Blake	Boston	1	—	—
Whitney, Ray	CBJ, Car.	3	—	—
Williams, Jason	Detroit	1	—	—
Williams, Justin	Carolina	1	—	—
Zednik, Richard	Wsh., Fla.	2	—	—
Zetterberg, Henrik	Detroit	3	—	—
Zubrus, Dainus	Mtl., N.J.	1	1	—

Top 100 All-Time Goal-Scoring Leaders

* active player

Player	Seasons	Games	Goals	Goals per game
1. Wayne Gretzky, Edm., L.A., St.L., NYR .	20	1487	**894**	.601
2. Gordie Howe, Det., Hfd.	26	1767	**801**	.453
3. Brett Hull, Cgy., St.L., Dal., Det., Phx.	20	1269	**741**	.584
4. Marcel Dionne, Det., L.A., NYR	18	1348	**731**	.542
5. Phil Esposito, Chi., Bos., NYR	18	1282	**717**	.559
6. Mike Gartner, Wsh., Min., NYR, Tor., Phx.	19	1432	**708**	.494
7. Mark Messier, Edm., NYR, Van.	25	1756	**694**	.395
8. Steve Yzerman, Det.	22	1514	**692**	.457
9. Mario Lemieux, Pit.	18	915	**690**	.754
10. Luc Robitaille, L.A., Pit., NYR, Det. . . .	19	1431	**668**	.467
11. Brendan Shanahan, N.J., St.L., Hfd., Det., NYR	21	1524	**656**	.430
12. Jaromir Jagr, Pit., Wsh., NYR	17	1273	**646**	.507
13. Dave Andreychuk, Buf., Tor., N.J., Bos., Col., T.B.	23	1639	**640**	.390
14. Joe Sakic, Que., Col.	20	1378	**625**	.454
15. Bobby Hull, Chi., Wpg., Hfd.	16	1063	**610**	.574
16. Dino Ciccarelli, Min., Wsh., Det., T.B., Fla. . .	19	1232	**608**	.494
* 17. Teemu Selanne, Wpg., Ana., S.J., Col. . .	17	1186	**606**	.511
18. Jari Kurri, Edm., L.A., NYR, Ana., Col. . .	17	1251	**601**	.480
19. Mike Bossy, NYI	10	752	**573**	.762
20. Joe Nieuwendyk, Cgy., Dal., N.J., Tor., Fla. . .	20	1257	**564**	.449
21. Mats Sundin, Que., Tor., Van.	18	1346	**564**	.419
* 22. Mark Recchi, Pit., Phi., Mtl., Car., Atl., T.B., Bos.	21	1571	**563**	.358
23. Guy Lafleur, Mtl., NYR, Que.	17	1126	**560**	.497
* 24. Mike Modano, Min., Dal.	21	1459	**557**	.382
25. John Bucyk, Det., Bos.	23	1540	**556**	.361
26. Ron Francis, Hfd., Pit., Car., Tor. . . .	23	1731	**549**	.317
27. Michel Goulet, Que., Chi.	15	1089	**548**	.503
28. Maurice Richard, Mtl.	18	978	**544**	.556
29. Stan Mikita, Chi.	22	1394	**541**	.388
30. Keith Tkachuk, Wpg., Phx., St.L., Atl. . .	18	1201	**538**	.448
31. Frank Mahovlich, Tor., Det., Mtl.	18	1181	**533**	.451
32. Bryan Trottier, NYI, Pit.	18	1279	**524**	.410
33. Pat Verbeek, N.J., Hfd., NYR, Dal., Det.	20	1424	**522**	.367
34. Dale Hawerchuk, Wpg., Buf., St.L., Phi.	16	1188	**518**	.436
35. Pierre Turgeon, Buf., NYI, Mtl., St.L., Dal., Col.	19	1294	**515**	.398
36. Jeremy Roenick, Chi., Phx., Phi., L.A., S.J.	20	1363	**513**	.376
37. Gilbert Perreault, Buf.	17	1191	**512**	.430
38. Jean Beliveau, Mtl.	20	1125	**507**	.451
39. Peter Bondra, Wsh., Ott., Atl., Chi. . . .	16	1081	**503**	.465
40. Joe Mullen, St.L., Cgy., Pit., Bos. . . .	17	1062	**502**	.473
41. Lanny McDonald, Tor., Col., Cgy. . . .	16	1111	**500**	.450
42. Glenn Anderson, Edm., Tor., NYR, St.L.	16	1129	**498**	.441
43. Jean Ratelle, NYR, Bos.	21	1281	**491**	.383
44. Norm Ullman, Det., Tor.	20	1410	**490**	.348
45. Brian Bellows, Min., Mtl., T.B., Ana., Wsh. . .	17	1188	**485**	.408
46. Darryl Sittler, Tor., Phi., Det.	15	1096	**484**	.442
47. Sergei Fedorov, Det., Ana., CBJ, Wsh. . .	18	1248	**483**	.387
48. Bernie Nicholls, L.A., NYR, Edm., N.J., Chi., S.J.	18	1127	**475**	.421
49. Alexander Mogilny, Buf., Van., N.J., Tor.	16	990	**473**	.478
50. Denis Savard, Chi., Mtl., T.B.	17	1196	**473**	.395
51. Pat LaFontaine, NYI, Buf., NYR.	15	865	**468**	.541
52. Alex Delvecchio, Det.	24	1549	**456**	.294
53. Theoren Fleury, Cgy., Col., NYR, Chi. . .	15	1084	**455**	.420
54. Rod Brind'Amour, St.L., Phi., Car. . . .	21	1484	**452**	.305
55. Peter Stastny, Que., N.J., St.L.	15	977	**450**	.461
56. Doug Gilmour, St.L., Cgy., Tor., N.J., Chi., Buf., Mtl.	20	1474	**450**	.305
57. Rick Middleton, NYR, Bos.	14	1005	**448**	.446
58. Rick Vaive, Van., Tor., Chi., Buf. . . .	13	876	**441**	.503
59. Steve Larmer, Chi., NYR.	15	1006	**441**	.438
* 60. Jarome Iginla, Cgy.	14	1024	**441**	.431
61. Rick Tocchet, Phi., Pit., L.A., Bos., Wsh., Phx.	18	1144	**440**	.385
62. Gary Roberts, Cgy., Car., Tor., Fla., Pit., T.B.	22	1224	**438**	.358
63. Pavel Bure, Van., Fla., NYR	12	702	**437**	.623
64. Vincent Damphousse, Tor., Edm., Mtl., S.J.	18	1378	**432**	.313
65. Dave Taylor, L.A.	17	1111	**431**	.388
* 66. Bill Guerin, N.J., Edm., Bos., Dal., St.L., S.J., NYI, Pit.	18	1263	**429**	.340
67. Yvan Cournoyer, Mtl.	16	968	**428**	.442
68. Brian Propp, Phi., Bos., Min., Hfd. . .	15	1016	**425**	.418
69. Steve Shutt, Mtl., L.A.	13	930	**424**	.456
* 70. Owen Nolan, Que., Col., S.J., Tor., Phx., Cgy., Min.	18	1200	**422**	.352

In his first season with the Ottawa Senators, Alex Kovalev netted the 400th goal of his career versus the Carolina Hurricanes on December 12, 2009. He finished his 17th NHL season with 990 career points.

Player	Seasons	Games	Goals	Goals per game
71. Stephane Richer, Mtl., N.J., T.B., St.L., Pit.	17	1054	**421**	.399
72. Steve Thomas, Tor., Chi., NYI, N.J., Ana., Det.	20	1235	**421**	.341
73. Bill Barber, Phi.	14	903	**420**	.465
74. Tony Amonte, NYR, Chi., Phx., Phi., Cgy.	16	1174	**416**	.354
75. Garry Unger, Tor., Det., St.L., Atl., L.A., Edm.	16	1105	**413**	.374
76. John MacLean, N.J., S.J., NYR, Dal. . . .	18	1194	**413**	.346
* 77. Alex Kovalev, NYR, Pit., Mtl., Ott.	17	1228	**412**	.336
78. Raymond Bourque, Bos., Col. . . .	22	1612	**410**	.254
79. Ray Ferraro, Hfd., NYI, NYR, L.A., Atl., St.L.	18	1258	**408**	.324
80. John LeClair, Mtl., Phi., Pit.	16	967	**406**	.420
81. Rod Gilbert, NYR	18	1065	**406**	.381
82. John Ogrodnick, Det., Que., NYR . . .	14	928	**402**	.433
* 83. Paul Kariya, Ana., Col., Nsh., St.L. . .	15	989	**402**	.406
84. Dave Keon, Tor., Hfd.	18	1296	**396**	.306
85. Paul Coffey, Edm., Pit., L.A., Det., Hfd., Phi., Chi., Car., Bos.	21	1409	**396**	.281
86. Cam Neely, Van., Bos.	13	726	**395**	.544
87. Pierre Larouche, Pit., Mtl., Hfd., NYR .	14	812	**395**	.486
88. Markus Naslund, Pit., Van., NYR	15	1117	**395**	.354
89. Tomas Sandstrom, NYR, L.A., Pit., Det., Ana.	15	983	**394**	.401
90. Bernie Geoffrion, Mtl., NYR.	16	883	**393**	.445
91. Jean Pronovost, Pit., Atl., Wsh.	14	998	**391**	.392
92. Dean Prentice, NYR, Bos., Det., Pit., Min.	22	1378	**391**	.284
93. Rick Martin, Buf., L.A.	11	685	**384**	.561
* 94. Jason Arnott, Edm., N.J., Dal., Nsh. . .	16	1099	**383**	.348
95. Reggie Leach, Bos., Cal., Phi., Det. . .	13	934	**381**	.408
96. Ted Lindsay, Det., Chi.	17	1068	**379**	.355
97. Claude Lemieux, Mtl., N.J., Col., Phx., Dal., S.J.	21	1215	**379**	.312
* 98. Daniel Alfredsson, Ott.	14	1002	**375**	.374
99. Butch Goring, L.A., NYI, Bos.	16	1107	**375**	.339
100. Trevor Linden, Van., NYI, Mtl., Wsh. .	19	1382	**375**	.271

Top 100 Active Goal-Scoring Leaders

	Player	Seasons	Games	Goals	Goals per game
1.	**Teemu Selanne**, Wpg., Ana., S.J., Col.	17	1186	**606**	.511
2.	**Mark Recchi**, Pit., Phi., Mtl., Car., Atl., T.B., Bos.	21	1571	**563**	.358
3.	**Mike Modano**, Min., Dal.	21	1459	**557**	.382
4.	**Jarome Iginla**, Cgy.	14	1024	**441**	.431
5.	**Bill Guerin**, N.J., Edm., Bos., Dal., St.L., S.J., NYI, Pit.	18	1263	**429**	.340
6.	**Owen Nolan**, Que., Col., S.J., Tor., Phx., Cgy., Min.	18	1200	**422**	.352
7.	**Alex Kovalev**, NYR, Pit., Mtl., Ott.	17	1228	**412**	.336
8.	**Paul Kariya**, Ana., Col., Nsh., St.L.	15	989	**402**	.406
9.	**Jason Arnott**, Edm., N.J., Dal., Nsh.	16	1099	**383**	.348
10.	**Daniel Alfredsson**, Ott.	14	1002	**375**	.374
11.	**Marian Hossa**, Ott., Atl., Pit., Det., Chi.	12	832	**363**	.436
12.	**Miroslav Satan**, Edm., Buf., NYI, Pit., Bos.	14	1050	**363**	.346
13.	**Vyacheslav Kozlov**, Det., Buf., Atl.	18	1182	**356**	.301
14.	**Ilya Kovalchuk**, Atl., N.J.	8	621	**338**	.544
15.	**Milan Hejduk**, Col.	11	839	**335**	.399
16.	**Ryan Smyth**, Edm., NYI, Col., L.A.	15	987	**332**	.336
17.	**Vincent Lecavalier**, T.B.	11	869	**326**	.375
18.	**Ray Whitney**, S.J., Edm., Fla., CBJ, Det., Car.	18	1072	**324**	.302
19.	**Brian Rolston**, N.J., Col., Bos., Min.	15	1121	**321**	.286
20.	**Patrick Marleau**, S.J.	12	953	**320**	.336
21.	**Patrik Elias**, N.J.	14	880	**314**	.357
22.	**Pavol Demitra**, Ott., St.L., L.A., Min., Van.	16	847	**304**	.359
23.	**Petr Sykora**, N.J., Ana., NYR, Edm., Pit., Min.	14	935	**302**	.323
24.	**Dany Heatley**, Atl., Ott., S.J.	8	589	**299**	.508
25.	**Joe Thornton**, Bos., S.J.	12	915	**285**	.311
26.	**Shane Doan**, Wpg., Phx.	14	1047	**276**	.264
27.	**Doug Weight**, NYR, Edm., St.L., Car., Ana., NYI	19	1220	**276**	.226
28.	**Todd Bertuzzi**, NYI, Van., Fla., Det., Ana., Cgy.	14	941	**273**	.290
29.	**Alex Ovechkin**, Wsh.	5	396	**269**	.679
30.	**Martin St. Louis**, Cgy., T.B.	11	772	**267**	.346
31.	**Cory Stillman**, Cgy., St.L., T.B., Car., Ott., Fla.	15	960	**266**	.277
32.	**Marian Gaborik**, Min., NYR	9	578	**261**	.452
33.	**Robert Lang**, L.A., Bos., Pit., Wsh., Det., Chi., Mtl., Phx.	16	989	**261**	.264
34.	**Simon Gagne**, Phi.	10	664	**259**	.390
35.	**Daymond Langkow**, T.B., Phi., Phx., Cgy.	14	1013	**259**	.256
36.	**Steve Sullivan**, N.J., Tor., Chi., Nsh.	14	846	**256**	.303
37.	**Chris Drury**, Col., Cgy., Buf., NYR	11	868	**254**	.293
38.	**Olli Jokinen**, L.A., NYI, Fla., Phx., Cgy., NYR	12	881	**252**	.286
39.	**Mike Knuble**, Det., NYR, Bos., Phi., Wsh.	13	889	**244**	.274
40.	**Jere Lehtinen**, Dal.	14	875	**243**	.278
41.	**Andrew Brunette**, Wsh., Nsh., Atl., Min., Col.	14	950	**238**	.251
42.	**Nicklas Lidstrom**, Det.	18	1412	**237**	.168
43.	**Marco Sturm**, S.J., Bos.	12	855	**234**	.274
44.	**Danny Briere**, Phx., Buf., Phi.	12	666	**230**	.345
45.	**Jamie Langenbrunner**, Dal., N.J.	15	965	**228**	.236
46.	**Rick Nash**, CBJ	7	517	**227**	.439
47.	**Fredrik Modin**, Tor., T.B., CBJ, L.A.	13	858	**225**	.262
48.	**Mathieu Schneider**, Mtl., NYI, Tor., NYR, L.A., Det., Ana., Atl., Van., Phx.	21	1289	**223**	.173
49.	**Sergei Samsonov**, Bos., Edm., Mtl., Chi., Car.	12	810	**222**	.274
50.	**Vinny Prospal**, Phi., Ott., Fla., T.B., Ana., NYR.	13	949	**218**	.230
51.	**Mark Parrish**, Fla., NYI, L.A., Min., Dal., T.B.	11	720	**216**	.300
52.	**Darcy Tucker**, Mtl., T.B., Tor., Col.	14	947	**215**	.227
53.	**Tomas Holmstrom**, Det.	13	879	**214**	.243
54.	**Saku Koivu**, Mtl., Ana.	14	863	**210**	.243
55.	**Daniel Sedin**, Van.	9	705	**208**	.295
56.	**Radek Dvorak**, Fla., NYR, Edm., St.L.	14	1052	**208**	.198
57.	**Henrik Zetterberg**, Det.	7	506	**206**	.407
58.	**Marc Savard**, NYR, Cgy., Atl., Bos.	12	782	**205**	.262
59.	**J.P. Dumont**, Chi., Buf., Nsh.	11	752	**204**	.271
60.	**Alex Tanguay**, Col., Cgy., Mtl., T.B.	10	739	**203**	.275
61.	**Sergei Gonchar**, Wsh., Bos., Pit.	15	991	**202**	.204
62.	**Pavel Datsyuk**, Det.	8	606	**198**	.327
63.	**Eric Staal**, Car.	6	479	**193**	.403
64.	**Brenden Morrow**, Dal.	10	667	**193**	.289
65.	**Brad Richards**, T.B., Dal.	9	700	**192**	.274
66.	**Jason Blake**, L.A., NYI, Tor., Ana.	11	750	**190**	.253
67.	**Martin Havlat**, Ott., Chi., Min.	9	543	**187**	.344
68.	**Brendan Morrison**, N.J., Van., Ana., Dal., Wsh.	12	829	**187**	.226

Paul Kariya collected goal #400 of his career against the New York Rangers on March 18, 2010. Kariya completed the 15th season of his NHL career with 989 points in 989 games.

	Player	Seasons	Games	Goals	Goals per game
69.	**Dean McAmmond**, Chi., Edm., Phi., Cgy., Col., St.L., Ott., NYI, N.J.	17	996	**186**	.187
70.	**Todd Marchant**, NYR, Edm., CBJ, Ana.	16	1116	**185**	.166
71.	**Sidney Crosby**, Pit.	5	371	**183**	.493
72.	**Rob Niedermayer**, Fla., Cgy., Ana., N.J.	16	1082	**181**	.167
73.	**Brian Gionta**, N.J., Mtl.	8	534	**180**	.337
74.	**Craig Conroy**, Mtl., St.L., Cgy., L.A.	15	991	**180**	.182
75.	**Kristian Huselius**, Fla., Cgy., CBJ	8	621	**176**	.283
76.	**Dainius Zubrus**, Phi., Mtl., Wsh., Buf., N.J.	13	904	**176**	.195
77.	**Thomas Vanek**, Buf.	5	389	**172**	.442
78.	**Jason Spezza**, Ott.	7	464	**171**	.369
79.	**Jonathan Cheechoo**, S.J., Ott.	7	501	**170**	.339
80.	**Matt Cullen**, Ana., Fla., Car., NYR, Ott.	12	880	**169**	.192
81.	**Alexander Frolov**, L.A.	7	536	**168**	.313
82.	**Mike Comrie**, Edm., Phi., Phx., Ott., NYI	9	568	**167**	.294
83.	**Jochen Hecht**, St.L., Edm., Buf.	11	697	**165**	.237
84.	**Scott Hartnell**, Nsh., Phi.	9	679	**161**	.237
85.	**Zach Parise**, N.J.	5	407	**160**	.393
86.	**Michal Handzus**, St.L., Phx., Phi., Chi., L.A.	11	762	**160**	.210
87.	**Scott Gomez**, N.J., NYR, Mtl.	10	784	**160**	.204
88.	**Michael Cammalleri**, L.A., Cgy., Mtl.	7	429	**158**	.368
89.	**Erik Cole**, Car., Edm.	8	538	**158**	.294
90.	**Maxim Afinogenov**, Buf., Atl.	10	651	**158**	.243
91.	**Mike Grier**, Edm., Wsh., Buf., S.J.	13	987	**157**	.159
92.	**Nik Antropov**, Tor., NYR, Atl.	10	603	**156**	.259
93.	**Kris Draper**, Wpg., Det.	19	1110	**155**	.140
94.	**Mike Fisher**, Ott.	10	620	**153**	.247
95.	**David Legwand**, Nsh.	11	704	**152**	.216
96.	**Chris Pronger**, Hfd., St.L., Edm., Ana., Phi.	16	1104	**152**	.138
97.	**Scott Walker**, Van., Nsh., Car., Wsh.	15	829	**151**	.182
98.	**Ruslan Fedotenko**, Phi., T.B., NYI, Pit.	9	677	**150**	.222
99.	**John Madden**, N.J., Chi.	11	791	**150**	.190
100.	**Alexander Semin**, Wsh.	5	327	**148**	.453

Top 100 All-Time Assist Leaders

* active player

	Player	Seasons	Games	Assists	Assists per game
1.	**Wayne Gretzky**, Edm., L.A., St.L., NYR .	20	1487	**1963**	1.320
2.	**Ron Francis**, Hfd., Pit., Car., Tor.......	23	1731	**1249**	.722
3.	**Mark Messier**, Edm., NYR, Van.	25	1756	**1193**	.679
4.	**Raymond Bourque**, Bos., Col.	22	1612	**1169**	.725
5.	**Paul Coffey**, Edm., Pit., L.A., Det., Hfd., Phi., Chi., Car., Bos.	21	1409	**1135**	.806
6.	**Adam Oates**, Det., St.L., Bos., Wsh., Phi., Ana., Edm.	19	1337	**1079**	.807
7.	**Steve Yzerman**, Det.	22	1514	**1063**	.702
8.	**Gordie Howe**, Det., Hfd.	26	1767	**1049**	.594
9.	**Marcel Dionne**, Det., L.A., NYR	18	1348	**1040**	.772
10.	**Mario Lemieux**, Pit.	18	915	**1033**	1.129
11.	**Joe Sakic**, Que., Col.	20	1378	**1016**	.737
12.	**Doug Gilmour**, St.L., Cgy., Tor., N.J., Chi., Buf., Mtl.	20	1474	**964**	.654
13.	**Jaromir Jagr**, Pit., Wsh., NYR	17	1273	**953**	.749
14.	**Al MacInnis**, Cgy., St.L.	23	1416	**934**	.660
15.	**Larry Murphy**, L.A., Wsh., Min., Pit., Tor., Det.	21	1615	**929**	.575
16.	**Stan Mikita**, Chi.	22	1394	**926**	.664
* 17.	**Mark Recchi**, Pit., Phi., Mtl., Car., Atl., T.B., Bos.	21	1571	**922**	.587
18.	**Bryan Trottier**, NYI, Pit.	18	1279	**901**	.704
19.	**Phil Housley**, Buf., Wpg., St.L., Cgy., N.J., Wsh., Chi., Tor.	21	1495	**894**	.598
20.	**Dale Hawerchuk**, Wpg., Buf., St.L., Phi.	16	1188	**891**	.750
21.	**Phil Esposito**, Chi., Bos., NYR	18	1282	**873**	.681
22.	**Denis Savard**, Chi., Mtl., T.B.	17	1196	**865**	.723
23.	**Bobby Clarke**, Phi.	15	1144	**852**	.745
24.	**Alex Delvecchio**, Det.	24	1549	**825**	.533
25.	**Gilbert Perreault**, Buf.	17	1191	**814**	.683
26.	**John Bucyk**, Det., Bos.	23	1540	**813**	.528
27.	**Pierre Turgeon**, Buf., NYI, Mtl., St.L., Dal., Col.	19	1294	**812**	.628
* 28.	**Nicklas Lidstrom**, Det.	18	1412	**809**	.573
* 29.	**Mike Modano**, Min., Dal.	21	1459	**802**	.550
30.	**Jari Kurri**, Edm., L.A., NYR, Ana., Col...	17	1251	**797**	.637
31.	**Guy Lafleur**, Mtl., NYR, Que.	17	1126	**793**	.704
32.	**Peter Stastny**, Que., N.J., St.L.	15	977	**789**	.808
33.	**Mats Sundin**, Que., Tor., Van.	18	1346	**785**	.583
34.	**Brian Leetch**, NYR, Tor., Bos.	18	1205	**781**	.648
35.	**Jean Ratelle**, NYR, Bos..	21	1281	**776**	.606
36.	**Vincent Damphousse**, Tor., Edm., Mtl., S.J.	18	1378	**773**	.561
37.	**Chris Chelios**, Mtl., Chi., Det., Atl.	26	1651	**763**	.462
38.	**Bernie Federko**, St.L., Det.	14	1000	**761**	.761
39.	**Larry Robinson**, Mtl., L.A.	20	1384	**750**	.542
* 40.	**Doug Weight**, NYR, Edm., St.L., Car., Ana., NYI	19	1220	**748**	.613
41.	**Denis Potvin**, NYI	15	1060	**742**	.700
42.	**Norm Ullman**, Det., Tor.	20	1410	**739**	.524
43.	**Bernie Nicholls**, L.A., NYR, Edm., N.J., Chi., S.J.	18	1127	**734**	.651
44.	**Rod Brind'Amour**, St.L., Phi., Car.	21	1484	**732**	.493
45.	**Luc Robitaille**, L.A., Pit., NYR, Det.	19	1431	**726**	.507
46.	**Jean Beliveau**, Mtl..	20	1125	**712**	.633
47.	**Scott Stevens**, Wsh., St.L., N.J.	22	1635	**712**	.435
48.	**Jeremy Roenick**, Chi., Phx., Phi., L.A., S.J.	20	1363	**703**	.516
49.	**Brendan Shanahan**, N.J., St.L., Hfd., Det., NYR	21	1524	**698**	.458
50.	**Dave Andreychuk**, Buf., Tor., N.J., Bos., Col., T.B.	23	1639	**698**	.426
51.	**Dale Hunter**, Que., Wsh., Col.	19	1407	**697**	.495
52.	**Sergei Fedorov**, Det., Ana., CBJ, Wsh. ..	18	1248	**696**	.558
53.	**Henri Richard**, Mtl..	20	1256	**688**	.548
54.	**Brad Park**, NYR, Bos., Det.	17	1113	**683**	.614
55.	**Bobby Smith**, Min., Mtl.	15	1077	**679**	.630
* 56.	**Teemu Selanne**, Wpg., Ana., S.J., Col. ..	17	1186	**654**	.551
57.	**Brett Hull**, Cgy., St.L., Dal., Det., Phx. ...	20	1269	**650**	.512
* 58.	**Joe Thornton**, Bos., S.J.	12	915	**646**	.706
59.	**Bobby Orr**, Bos., Chi.	12	657	**645**	.982
60.	**Gary Suter**, Cgy., Chi., S.J.	17	1145	**641**	.560
61.	**Dave Taylor**, L.A.	17	1111	**638**	.574
62.	**Darryl Sittler**, Tor., Phi., Det.	15	1096	**637**	.581
63.	**Borje Salming**, Tor., Det.	17	1148	**637**	.555
64.	**Peter Forsberg**, Que., Col., Phi., Nsh. ...	13	706	**636**	.901
65.	**Neal Broten**, Min., Dal., N.J., L.A.	17	1099	**634**	.577
66.	**Theoren Fleury**, Cgy., Col., NYR, Chi...	15	1084	**633**	.584
67.	**Mike Gartner**, Wsh., Min., NYR, Tor., Phx.	19	1432	**627**	.438
68.	**Andy Bathgate**, NYR, Tor., Det., Pit...	17	1069	**624**	.584
69.	**Sergei Zubov**, NYR, Pit., Dal.	16	1068	**619**	.580
* 70.	**Daniel Alfredsson**, Ott.	14	1002	**617**	.616
71.	**Rod Gilbert**, NYR	18	1065	**615**	.577
72.	**Michel Goulet**, Que., Chi.	15	1089	**604**	.555
73.	**Kirk Muller**, N.J., Mtl., NYI, Tor., Fla., Dal.	19	1349	**602**	.446

Ottawa Senators captain Daniel Alfredsson collected the 600th assist of his career against Carolina on March 4, 2010. He reached 1,000 games played in his NHL career a few weeks later on April 6, 2010.

	Player	Seasons	Games	Assists	Assists per game
74.	**Glenn Anderson**, Edm., Tor., NYR, St.L.	16	1129	**601**	.532
75.	**Dino Ciccarelli**, Min., Wsh., Det., T.B., Fla..	19	1232	**592**	.481
76.	**Doug Wilson**, Chi., S.J.	16	1024	**590**	.576
77.	**Dave Keon**, Tor., Hfd..	18	1296	**590**	.455
* 78.	**Paul Kariya**, Ana., Col., Nsh., St.L.	15	989	**587**	.594
79.	**Dave Babych**, Wpg., Hfd., Van., Phi., L.A.	19	1195	**581**	.486
80.	**Brian Propp**, Phi., Bos., Min., Hfd......	15	1016	**579**	.570
* 81.	**Alex Kovalev**, NYR, Pit., Mtl., Ott.	17	1228	**578**	.471
82.	**Steve Larmer**, Chi., NYR..........	15	1006	**571**	.568
83.	**Frank Mahovlich**, Tor., Det., Mtl.	18	1181	**570**	.483
84.	**Scott Niedermayer**, N.J., Ana.	18	1263	**568**	.450
85.	**Craig Janney**, Bos., St.L., S.J., Wpg., Phx., T.B., NYI	12	760	**563**	.741
86.	**Cliff Ronning**, St.L., Van., Phx., Nsh., L.A., Min., NYI	18	1137	**563**	.495
87.	**Joe Nieuwendyk**, Cgy., Dal., N.J., Tor., Fla.	20	1257	**562**	.447
88.	**Joe Mullen**, St.L., Cgy., Pit., Bos........	17	1062	**561**	.528
89.	**Bobby Hull**, Chi., Wpg., Hfd.	16	1063	**560**	.527
90.	**Alexander Mogilny**, Buf., Van., N.J., Tor.	16	990	**559**	.565
91.	**Mike Bossy**, NYI	10	752	**553**	.735
92.	**Thomas Steen**, Wpg.	14	950	**553**	.582
93.	**Ken Linseman**, Phi., Edm., Bos., Tor....	14	860	**551**	.641
94.	**Tom Lysiak**, Atl., Chi.	13	919	**551**	.600
95.	**Pat LaFontaine**, NYI, Buf., NYR	15	865	**545**	.630
96.	**Mark Howe**, Hfd., Phi., Det.	16	929	**545**	.587
* 97.	**Ray Whitney**, S.J., Edm., Fla., CBJ, Det., Car.	18	1072	**545**	.508
98.	**Red Kelly**, Det., Tor.	20	1316	**542**	.412
99.	**Pat Verbeek**, N.J., Hfd., NYR, Dal., Det.	20	1424	**541**	.380
100.	**Rick Middleton**, NYR, Bos.	14	1005	**540**	.537

Top 100 Active Assist Leaders

	Player	Seasons	Games	Assists	Assists per game
1.	Mark Recchi, Pit., Phi., Mtl., Car., Atl., T.B., Bos.	21	1571	**922**	.587
2.	Nicklas Lidstrom, Det.	18	1412	**809**	.573
3.	Mike Modano, Min., Dal.	21	1459	**802**	.550
4.	Doug Weight, NYR, Edm., St.L., Car., Ana., NYI	19	1220	**748**	.613
5.	Teemu Selanne, Wpg., Ana., S.J., Col.	17	1186	**654**	.551
6.	Joe Thornton, Bos., S.J.	12	915	**646**	.706
7.	Daniel Alfredsson, Ott.	14	1002	**617**	.616
8.	Paul Kariya, Ana., Col., Nsh., St.L.	15	989	**587**	.594
9.	Alex Kovalev, NYR, Pit., Mtl., Ott.	17	1228	**578**	.471
10.	Ray Whitney, S.J., Edm., Fla., CBJ, Det., Car.	18	1072	**545**	.508
11.	Mathieu Schneider, Mtl., NYI, Tor., NYR, L.A., Det., Ana., Atl., Van., Phx.	21	1289	**520**	.403
12.	Chris Pronger, Hfd., St.L., Edm., Ana., Phi.	16	1104	**509**	.461
13.	Vyacheslav Kozlov, Det., Buf., Atl.	18	1182	**497**	.420
14.	Marc Savard, NYR, Cgy., Atl., Bos.	12	782	**491**	.628
15.	Jason Arnott, Edm., N.J., Dal., Nsh.	16	1099	**490**	.446
16.	Saku Koivu, Mtl., Ana.	14	863	**483**	.560
17.	Sergei Gonchar, Wsh., Bos., Pit.	15	991	**482**	.486
18.	Jarome Iginla, Cgy.	14	1024	**479**	.468
19.	Scott Gomez, N.J., NYR, Mtl.	10	784	**477**	.608
20.	Pavol Demitra, Ott., St.L., L.A., Min., Van.	16	847	**464**	.548
21.	Owen Nolan, Que., Col., S.J., Tor., Phx., Cgy., Min.	18	1200	**463**	.386
22.	Brad Richards, T.B., Dal.	9	700	**447**	.639
23.	Robert Lang, L.A., Bos., Pit., Wsh., Det., Chi., Mtl., Phx.	16	989	**442**	.447
24.	Roman Hamrlik, T.B., Edm., NYI, Cgy., Mtl.	17	1232	**442**	.359
25.	Patrik Elias, N.J.	14	880	**440**	.500
26.	Vinny Prospal, Phi., Ott., Fla., T.B., Ana., NYR.	13	949	**439**	.463
27.	Henrik Sedin, Van.	9	728	**434**	.596
28.	Bill Guerin, N.J., Edm., Bos., Dal., St.L., S.J., NYI, Pit.	18	1263	**427**	.338
29.	Andrew Brunette, Wsh., Nsh., Atl., Min., Col.	14	950	**422**	.444
30.	Cory Stillman, Cgy., St.L., T.B., Car., Ott., Fla.	15	960	**422**	.440
31.	Alex Tanguay, Col., Cgy., Mtl., T.B.	10	739	**414**	.560
32.	Vincent Lecavalier, T.B.	11	869	**413**	.475
33.	Martin St. Louis, Cgy., T.B.	11	772	**412**	.534
34.	Marian Hossa, Ott., Atl., Pit., Det., Chi.	12	832	**407**	.489
35.	Steve Sullivan, N.J., Tor., Chi., Nsh.	14	846	**404**	.478
36.	Tomas Kaberle, Tor.	11	820	**402**	.490
37.	Shane Doan, Wpg., Phx.	14	1047	**402**	.384
38.	Todd Bertuzzi, NYI, Van., Fla., Det., Ana., Cgy.	14	941	**395**	.420
39.	Pavel Datsyuk, Det.	8	606	**394**	.650
40.	Brian Rafalski, N.J., Det.	10	770	**392**	.509
41.	Daymond Langkow, T.B., Phi., Phx., Cgy.	14	1013	**382**	.377
42.	Brian Rolston, N.J., Col., Bos., Min.	15	1121	**382**	.341
43.	Ryan Smyth, Edm., NYI, Col., L.A.	15	987	**381**	.386
44.	Jamie Langenbrunner, Dal., N.J.	15	965	**378**	.392
45.	Petr Sykora, N.J., Ana., NYR, Edm., Pit., Min.	14	935	**375**	.401
46.	Patrick Marleau, S.J.	12	953	**373**	.391
47.	Miroslav Satan, Edm., Buf., NYI, Pit., Bos.	14	1050	**372**	.354
48.	Milan Hejduk, Col.	11	839	**366**	.436
49.	Bryan McCabe, NYI, Van., Chi., Tor., Fla.	14	1068	**362**	.339
50.	Brendan Morrison, N.J., Van., Ana., Dal., Wsh.	12	829	**360**	.434
51.	Craig Conroy, Mtl., St.L., Cgy., L.A.	15	991	**360**	.363
52.	Chris Drury, Col., Cgy., Buf., NYR	11	868	**356**	.410
53.	Wade Redden, Ott., NYR	13	994	**344**	.346
54.	Daniel Sedin, Van.	9	705	**339**	.481
55.	Ed Jovanovski, Fla., Van., Phx.	14	969	**339**	.350
56.	Kimmo Timonen, Nsh., Phi.	11	812	**331**	.408
57.	Dany Heatley, Atl., Ott., S.J.	8	589	**326**	.553
58.	Radek Dvorak, Fla., NYR, Edm., St.L.	14	1052	**326**	.310
59.	Sidney Crosby, Pit.	5	371	**323**	.871
60.	Olli Jokinen, L.A., NYI, Fla., Phx., Cgy., NYR	12	881	**316**	.359
61.	Sergei Samsonov, Bos., Edm., Mtl., Chi., Car.	12	810	**309**	.381
62.	Todd Marchant, NYR, Edm., CBJ, Ana.	16	1116	**305**	.273
63.	Jason Spezza, Ott.	7	464	**304**	.655
64.	Ilya Kovalchuk, Atl., N.J.	8	621	**304**	.490
65.	Dan Boyle, Fla., T.B., S.J.	11	676	**300**	.444
66.	J.P. Dumont, Chi., Buf., Nsh.	11	752	**300**	.399
67.	Danny Briere, Phx., Buf., Phi.	12	666	**296**	.444
68.	Matt Cullen, Ana., Fla., Car., NYR, Ott.	12	880	**292**	.332

Brad Richards matched a career high with 91 points for the Dallas Stars in 2009-10. His 67 assists pushed him over the 400 mark in that category with 447 in his career.

	Player	Seasons	Games	Assists	Assists per game
69.	Mike Ribeiro, Mtl., Dal.	10	581	**290**	.499
70.	Derek Morris, Cgy., Col., Phx., NYR, Bos.	12	869	**289**	.333
71.	Dainius Zubrus, Phi., Mtl., Wsh., Buf., N.J.	13	904	**289**	.320
72.	Andrei Markov, Mtl.	9	616	**283**	.459
73.	Jere Lehtinen, Dal.	14	875	**271**	.310
74.	Henrik Zetterberg, Det.	7	506	**269**	.532
75.	Rob Niedermayer, Fla., Cgy., Ana., N.J.	16	1082	**269**	.249
76.	Simon Gagne, Phi.	10	664	**265**	.399
77.	Martin Havlat, Ott., Chi., Min.	9	543	**263**	.484
78.	Marian Gaborik, Min., NYR	9	578	**262**	.453
79.	Lubomir Visnovsky, L.A., Edm., Ana.	9	622	**262**	.421
80.	Dean McAmmond, Chi., Edm., Phi., Cgy., Col., St.L., Ott., NYI, N.J.	17	996	**262**	.263
81.	Darcy Tucker, Mtl., T.B., Tor., Col.	14	947	**261**	.276
82.	Alex Ovechkin, Wsh.	5	396	**260**	.657
83.	David Legwand, Nsh.	11	704	**255**	.362
84.	Tomas Holmstrom, Det.	13	879	**255**	.290
85.	Ales Hemsky, Edm.	7	443	**253**	.571
86.	Kristian Huselius, Fla., Cgy., CBJ	8	621	**252**	.406
87.	Jason Blake, L.A., NYI, Tor., Ana.	11	750	**252**	.336
88.	Zdeno Chara, NYI, Ott., Bos.	12	847	**252**	.298
89.	Andy McDonald, Ana., St.L.	9	565	**251**	.444
90.	Tom Poti, Edm., NYR, NYI, Wsh.	11	787	**251**	.319
91.	Tim Connolly, NYI, Buf.	10	559	**248**	.444
92.	Jaroslav Spacek, Fla., Chi., CBJ, Edm., Buf., Mtl.	11	775	**248**	.320
93.	Adrian Aucoin, Van., T.B., NYI, Chi., Cgy., Phx.	15	933	**248**	.266
94.	Jochen Hecht, St.L., Edm., Buf.	11	697	**247**	.354
95.	Scott Walker, Van., Nsh., Car., Wsh.	15	829	**246**	.297
96.	Michal Handzus, St.L., Phx., Phi., Chi., L.A.	11	762	**245**	.322
97.	Pavel Kubina, T.B., Tor., Atl.	12	822	**245**	.298
98.	Mattias Ohlund, Van., T.B.	12	837	**245**	.293
99.	Brenden Morrow, Dal.	10	667	**242**	.363
100.	Shawn Horcoff, Edm.	9	637	**241**	.378

Top 100 All-Time Point Leaders

* active player

	Player	Seasons	Games	Goals	Assists	Points	Points per game
1.	**Wayne Gretzky**, Edm., L.A., St.L., NYR	20	1487	894	1963	**2857**	1.921
2.	**Mark Messier**, Edm., NYR, Van.	25	1756	694	1193	**1887**	1.075
3.	**Gordie Howe**, Det., Hfd.	26	1767	801	1049	**1850**	1.047
4.	**Ron Francis**, Hfd., Pit., Car., Tor.	23	1731	549	1249	**1798**	1.039
5.	**Marcel Dionne**, Det., L.A., NYR	18	1348	731	1040	**1771**	1.314
6.	**Steve Yzerman**, Det.	22	1514	692	1063	**1755**	1.159
7.	**Mario Lemieux**, Pit.	18	915	690	1033	**1723**	1.883
8.	**Joe Sakic**, Que., Col.	20	1378	625	1016	**1641**	1.191
9.	**Jaromir Jagr**, Pit., Wsh., NYR.	17	1273	646	953	**1599**	1.256
10.	**Phil Esposito**, Chi., Bos., NYR	18	1282	717	873	**1590**	1.240
11.	**Raymond Bourque**, Bos., Col.	22	1612	410	1169	**1579**	.980
12.	**Paul Coffey**, Edm., Pit., L.A., Det., Hfd., Phi., Chi., Car., Bos.	21	1409	396	1135	**1531**	1.087
* 13.	**Mark Recchi**, Pit., Phi., Mtl., Car., Atl., T.B., Bos.	21	1571	563	922	**1485**	.945
14.	**Stan Mikita**, Chi.	22	1394	541	926	**1467**	1.052
15.	**Bryan Trottier**, NYI, Pit.	18	1279	524	901	**1425**	1.114
16.	**Adam Oates**, Det., St.L., Bos., Wsh., Phi., Ana., Edm.	19	1337	341	1079	**1420**	1.062
17.	**Doug Gilmour**, St.L., Cgy., Tor., N.J., Chi., Buf., Mtl.	20	1474	450	964	**1414**	.959
18.	**Dale Hawerchuk**, Wpg., Buf., St.L., Phi.	16	1188	518	891	**1409**	1.186
19.	**Jari Kurri**, Edm., L.A., NYR, Ana., Col.	17	1251	601	797	**1398**	1.118
20.	**Luc Robitaille**, L.A., Pit., NYR, Det.	19	1431	668	726	**1394**	.974
21.	**Brett Hull**, Cgy., St.L., Dal., Det., Phx.	20	1269	741	650	**1391**	1.096
22.	**John Bucyk**, Det., Bos.	23	1540	556	813	**1369**	.889
* 23.	**Mike Modano**, Min., Dal.	21	1459	557	802	**1359**	.931
24.	**Brendan Shanahan**, N.J., St.L., Hfd., Det., NYR	21	1524	656	698	**1354**	.888
25.	**Guy Lafleur**, Mtl., NYR, Que.	17	1126	560	793	**1353**	1.202
26.	**Mats Sundin**, Que., Tor., Van.	18	1346	564	785	**1349**	1.002
27.	**Denis Savard**, Chi., Mtl., T.B.	17	1196	473	865	**1338**	1.119
28.	**Dave Andreychuk**, Buf., Tor., N.J., Bos., Col., T.B.	23	1639	640	698	**1338**	.816
29.	**Mike Gartner**, Wsh., Min., NYR, Tor., Phx.	19	1432	708	627	**1335**	.932
30.	**Pierre Turgeon**, Buf., NYI, Mtl., St.L., Dal., Col.	19	1294	515	812	**1327**	1.026
31.	**Gilbert Perreault**, Buf.	17	1191	512	814	**1326**	1.113
32.	**Alex Delvecchio**, Det.	24	1549	456	825	**1281**	.827
33.	**Al MacInnis**, Cgy., St.L.	23	1416	340	934	**1274**	.900
34.	**Jean Ratelle**, NYR, Bos.	21	1281	491	776	**1267**	.989
* 35.	**Teemu Selanne**, Wpg., Ana., S.J., Col.	17	1186	606	654	**1260**	1.062
36.	**Peter Stastny**, Que., N.J., St.L.	15	977	450	789	**1239**	1.268
37.	**Phil Housley**, Buf., Wpg., St.L., Cgy., N.J., Wsh., Chi., Tor.	21	1495	338	894	**1232**	.824
38.	**Norm Ullman**, Det., Tor.	20	1410	490	739	**1229**	.872
39.	**Jean Beliveau**, Mtl.	20	1125	507	712	**1219**	1.084
40.	**Jeremy Roenick**, Chi., Phx., Phi., L.A., S.J.	20	1363	513	703	**1216**	.892
41.	**Larry Murphy**, L.A., Wsh., Min., Pit., Tor., Det.	21	1615	287	929	**1216**	.753
42.	**Bobby Clarke**, Phi.	15	1144	358	852	**1210**	1.058
43.	**Bernie Nicholls**, L.A., NYR, Edm., N.J., Chi., S.J.	18	1127	475	734	**1209**	1.073
44.	**Vincent Damphousse**, Tor., Edm., Mtl., S.J.	18	1378	432	773	**1205**	.874
45.	**Dino Ciccarelli**, Min., Wsh., Det., T.B., Fla.	19	1232	608	592	**1200**	.974
46.	**Rod Brind'Amour**, St.L., Phi., Car.	21	1484	452	732	**1184**	.798
47.	**Sergei Fedorov**, Det., Ana., CBJ, Wsh.	18	1248	483	696	**1179**	.945
48.	**Bobby Hull**, Chi., Wpg., Hfd.	16	1063	610	560	**1170**	1.101
49.	**Michel Goulet**, Que., Chi.	15	1089	548	604	**1152**	1.058
50.	**Bernie Federko**, St.L., Det.	14	1000	369	761	**1130**	1.130
51.	**Mike Bossy**, NYI	10	752	573	553	**1126**	1.497
52.	**Joe Nieuwendyk**, Cgy., Dal., N.J., Tor., Fla.	20	1257	564	562	**1126**	.896
53.	**Darryl Sittler**, Tor., Phi., Det.	15	1096	484	637	**1121**	1.023
54.	**Frank Mahovlich**, Tor., Det., Mtl.	18	1181	533	570	**1103**	.934
55.	**Glenn Anderson**, Edm., Tor., NYR, St.L.	16	1129	498	601	**1099**	.973
56.	**Theoren Fleury**, Cgy., Col., NYR, Chi.	15	1084	455	633	**1088**	1.004
57.	**Dave Taylor**, L.A.	17	1111	431	638	**1069**	.962

Wayne Gretzky and Mark Messier, the two top scorers in NHL history, celebrate a goal during their glory days with the Edmonton Oilers.

	Player	Seasons	Games	Goals	Assists	Points	Points per game
58.	**Keith Tkachuk**, Wpg., Phx., St.L., Atl.	18	1201	538	527	**1065**	.887
59.	**Joe Mullen**, St.L., Cgy., Pit., Bos.	17	1062	502	561	**1063**	1.001
60.	**Pat Verbeek**, N.J., Hfd., NYR, Dal., Det.	20	1424	522	541	**1063**	.746
61.	**Denis Potvin**, NYI	15	1060	310	742	**1052**	.992
62.	**Henri Richard**, Mtl.	20	1256	358	688	**1046**	.833
* 63.	**Nicklas Lidstrom**, Det.	18	1412	237	809	**1046**	.741
64.	**Bobby Smith**, Min., Mtl.	15	1077	357	679	**1036**	.962
65.	**Alexander Mogilny**, Buf., Van., N.J., Tor.	16	990	473	559	**1032**	1.042
66.	**Brian Leetch**, NYR, Tor., Bos.	18	1205	247	781	**1028**	.853
* 67.	**Doug Weight**, NYR, Edm., St.L., Car., Ana., NYI	19	1220	276	748	**1024**	.839
68.	**Brian Bellows**, Min., Mtl., T.B., Ana., Wsh.	17	1188	485	537	**1022**	.860
69.	**Rod Gilbert**, NYR.	18	1065	406	615	**1021**	.959
70.	**Dale Hunter**, Que., Wsh., Col.	19	1407	323	697	**1020**	.725
71.	**Pat LaFontaine**, NYI, Buf., NYR	15	865	468	545	**1013**	1.171
72.	**Steve Larmer**, Chi., NYR	15	1006	441	571	**1012**	1.006
73.	**Lanny McDonald**, Tor., Col., Cgy.	16	1111	500	506	**1006**	.905
74.	**Brian Propp**, Phi., Bos., Min., Hfd.	15	1016	425	579	**1004**	.988
* 75.	**Daniel Alfredsson**, Ott.	14	1002	375	617	**992**	.990
* 76.	**Alex Kovalev**, NYR, Pit., Mtl., Ott.	17	1228	412	578	**990**	.806
* 77.	**Paul Kariya**, Ana., Col., Nsh., St.L.	15	989	402	587	**989**	1.000
78.	**Rick Middleton**, NYR, Bos.	14	1005	448	540	**988**	.983
79.	**Dave Keon**, Tor., Hfd.	18	1296	396	590	**986**	.761
80.	**Andy Bathgate**, NYR, Tor., Det., Pit.	17	1069	349	624	**973**	.910
81.	**Maurice Richard**, Mtl.	18	978	544	421	**965**	.987
82.	**Kirk Muller**, N.J., Mtl., NYI, Tor., Fla., Dal.	19	1349	357	602	**959**	.711
83.	**Larry Robinson**, Mtl., L.A.	20	1384	208	750	**958**	.692
84.	**Rick Tocchet**, Phi., Pit., L.A., Bos., Wsh., Phx.	18	1144	440	512	**952**	.832
85.	**Chris Chelios**, Mtl., Chi., Det., Atl.	26	1651	185	763	**948**	.574
86.	**Steve Thomas**, Tor., Chi., NYI, N.J., Ana., Det.	20	1235	421	512	**933**	.755
* 87.	**Joe Thornton**, Bos., S.J.	12	915	285	646	**931**	1.017
88.	**Neal Broten**, Min., Dal., N.J., L.A.	17	1099	289	634	**923**	.840
* 89.	**Jarome Iginla**, Cgy.	14	1024	441	479	**920**	.898
90.	**Bobby Orr**, Bos., Chi.	12	657	270	645	**915**	1.393
91.	**Gary Roberts**, Cgy., Car., Tor., Fla., Pit., T.B.	22	1224	438	472	**910**	.743
92.	**Scott Stevens**, Wsh., St.L., N.J.	22	1635	196	712	**908**	.555
93.	**Tony Amonte**, NYR, Chi., Phx., Phi., Cgy.	16	1174	416	484	**900**	.767
94.	**Ray Ferraro**, Hfd., NYI, NYR, L.A., Atl., St.L.	18	1258	408	490	**898**	.714
95.	**Brad Park**, NYR, Bos., Det.	17	1113	213	683	**896**	.805
96.	**Peter Bondra**, Wsh., Ott., Atl., Chi.	16	1081	503	389	**892**	.825
97.	**Butch Goring**, L.A., NYI, Bos.	16	1107	375	513	**888**	.802
98.	**Peter Forsberg**, Que., Col., Phi., Nsh.	13	706	249	636	**885**	1.254
* 99.	**Owen Nolan**, Que., Col., S.J., Tor., Phx., Cgy., Min.	18	1200	422	463	**885**	.738
100.	**Bill Barber**, Phi.	14	903	420	463	**883**	.978

Top 100 Active Points Leaders

Player	Seasons	Games	Goals	Assists	Points	Points per game
1. **Mark Recchi**, Pit., Phi., Mtl., Car., Atl., T.B., Bos.	21	1571	563	922	**1485**	.945
2. **Mike Modano**, Min., Dal. . . .	21	1459	557	802	**1359**	.931
3. **Teemu Selanne**, Wpg., Ana., S.J., Col.	17	1186	606	654	**1260**	1.062
4. **Nicklas Lidstrom**, Det.	18	1412	237	809	**1046**	.741
5. **Doug Weight**, NYR, Edm., St.L., Car., Ana., NYI	19	1220	276	748	**1024**	.839
6. **Daniel Alfredsson**, Ott.	14	1002	375	617	**992**	.990
7. **Alex Kovalev**, NYR, Pit., Mtl., Ott.	17	1228	412	578	**990**	.806
8. **Paul Kariya**, Ana., Col., Nsh., St.L.	15	989	402	587	**989**	1.000
9. **Joe Thornton**, Bos., S.J.	12	915	285	646	**931**	1.017
10. **Jarome Iginla**, Cgy.	14	1024	441	479	**920**	.898
11. **Owen Nolan**, Que., Col., S.J., Tor., Phx., Cgy., Min.	18	1200	422	463	**885**	.738
12. **Jason Arnott**, Edm., N.J., Dal., Nsh.	16	1099	383	490	**873**	.794
13. **Ray Whitney**, S.J., Edm., Fla., CBJ, Det., Car.	18	1072	324	545	**869**	.811
14. **Bill Guerin**, N.J., Edm., Bos., Dal., St.L., S.J., NYI, Pit.	18	1263	429	427	**856**	.678
15. **Vyacheslav Kozlov**, Det., Buf., Atl.	18	1182	356	497	**853**	.722
16. **Marian Hossa**, Ott., Atl., Pit., Det., Chi.	12	832	363	407	**770**	.925
17. **Pavol Demitra**, Ott., St.L., L.A., Min., Van.	16	847	304	464	**768**	.907
18. **Patrik Elias**, N.J.	14	880	314	440	**754**	.857
19. **Mathieu Schneider**, Mtl., NYI, Tor., NYR, L.A., Det., Ana., Atl., Van., Phx.	21	1289	223	520	**743**	.576
20. **Vincent Lecavalier**, T.B.	11	869	326	413	**739**	.850
21. **Miroslav Satan**, Edm., Buf., NYI, Pit., Bos.	14	1050	363	372	**735**	.700
22. **Ryan Smyth**, Edm., NYI, Col., L.A.	15	987	332	381	**713**	.722
23. **Robert Lang**, L.A., Bos., Pit., Wsh., Det., Chi., Mtl., Phx.	16	989	261	442	**703**	.711
24. **Brian Rolston**, N.J., Col., Bos., Min.	15	1121	321	382	**703**	.627
25. **Milan Hejduk**, Col.	11	839	335	366	**701**	.836
26. **Marc Savard**, NYR, Cgy., Atl., Bos.	12	782	205	491	**696**	.890
27. **Saku Koivu**, Mtl., Ana.	14	863	210	483	**693**	.803
28. **Patrick Marleau**, S.J.	12	953	320	373	**693**	.727
29. **Cory Stillman**, Cgy., St.L., T.B., Car., Ott., Fla.	15	960	266	422	**688**	.717
30. **Sergei Gonchar**, Wsh., Bos., Pit.	15	991	202	482	**684**	.690
31. **Martin St. Louis**, Cgy., T.B. . .	11	772	267	412	**679**	.880
32. **Shane Doan**, Wpg., Phx.	14	1047	276	402	**678**	.648
33. **Petr Sykora**, N.J., Ana., NYR, Edm., Pit., Min.	14	935	302	375	**677**	.724
34. **Todd Bertuzzi**, NYI, Van., Fla., Det., Ana., Cgy.	14	941	273	395	**668**	.710
35. **Chris Pronger**, Hfd., St.L., Edm., Ana., Phi.	16	1104	152	509	**661**	.599
36. **Steve Sullivan**, N.J., Tor., Chi., Nsh.	14	846	256	404	**660**	.780
37. **Andrew Brunette**, Wsh., Nsh., Atl., Min., Col.	14	950	238	422	**660**	.695
38. **Vinny Prospal**, Phi., Ott., Fla., T.B., Ana., NYR.	13	949	218	439	**657**	.692
39. **Ilya Kovalchuk**, Atl., N.J.	8	621	338	304	**642**	1.034
40. **Daymond Langkow**, T.B., Phi., Phx., Cgy.	14	1013	259	382	**641**	.633
41. **Brad Richards**, T.B., Dal.	9	700	192	447	**639**	.913
42. **Scott Gomez**, N.J., NYR, Mtl. . .	10	784	160	477	**637**	.813
43. **Dany Heatley**, Atl., Ott., S.J. . .	8	589	299	326	**625**	1.061
44. **Alex Tanguay**, Col., Cgy., Mtl., T.B.	10	739	203	414	**617**	.835
45. **Chris Drury**, Col., Cgy., Buf., NYR	11	868	254	356	**610**	.703
46. **Jamie Langenbrunner**, Dal., N.J.	15	965	228	378	**606**	.628
47. **Pavel Datsyuk**, Det.	8	606	198	394	**592**	.977
48. **Roman Hamrlik**, T.B., Edm., NYI, Cgy., Mtl.	17	1232	148	442	**590**	.479
49. **Henrik Sedin**, Van.	9	728	138	434	**572**	.786
50. **Olli Jokinen**, L.A., NYI, Fla., Phx., Cgy., NYR	12	881	252	316	**568**	.645
51. **Daniel Sedin**, Van.	9	705	208	339	**547**	.776
52. **Brendan Morrison**, N.J., Van., Ana., Dal., Wsh. . . .	12	829	187	360	**547**	.660
53. **Craig Conroy**, Mtl., St.L., Cgy., L.A.	15	991	180	360	**540**	.545
54. **Radek Dvorak**, Fla., NYR, Edm., St.L.	14	1052	208	326	**534**	.508

Marian Gaborik had 42 goals and 44 assists in his first year with the New York Rangers and cracked the top 10 in scoring in 2009-10. He also surpassed the 500-point plateau in his career.

Player	Seasons	Games	Goals	Assists	Points	Points per game
55. **Sergei Samsonov**, Bos., Edm., Mtl., Chi., Car.	12	810	222	309	**531**	.656
56. **Alex Ovechkin**, Wsh.	5	396	269	260	**529**	1.336
57. **Danny Briere**, Phx., Buf., Phi..	12	666	230	296	**526**	.790
58. **Simon Gagne**, Phi.	10	664	259	265	**524**	.789
59. **Marian Gaborik**, Min., NYR . .	9	578	261	262	**523**	.905
60. **Jere Lehtinen**, Dal.	14	875	243	271	**514**	.587
61. **Sidney Crosby**, Pit.	5	371	183	323	**506**	1.364
62. **J.P. Dumont**, Chi., Buf., Nsh. . .	11	752	204	300	**504**	.670
63. **Bryan McCabe**, NYI, Van., Chi., Tor., Fla.	14	1068	138	362	**500**	.468
64. **Todd Marchant**, NYR, Edm., CBJ, Ana.	16	1116	185	305	**490**	.439
65. **Tomas Kaberle**, Tor.	11	820	80	402	**482**	.588
66. **Mike Knuble**, Det., NYR, Bos., Phi., Wsh..	13	889	244	238	**482**	.542
67. **Darcy Tucker**, Mtl., T.B., Tor., Col.	14	947	215	261	**476**	.503
68. **Jason Spezza**, Ott.	7	464	171	304	**475**	1.024
69. **Henrik Zetterberg**, Det.	7	506	206	269	**475**	.939
70. **Tomas Holmstrom**, Det.	13	879	214	255	**469**	.534
71. **Brian Rafalski**, N.J., Det.	10	770	75	392	**467**	.606
72. **Ed Jovanovski**, Fla., Van., Phx.	14	969	128	339	**467**	.482
73. **Marco Sturm**, S.J., Bos.	12	855	234	232	**466**	.545
74. **Dainius Zubrus**, Phi., Mtl., Wsh., Buf., N.J.	13	904	176	289	**465**	.514
75. **Matt Cullen**, Ana., Fla., Car., NYR, Ott.	12	880	169	292	**461**	.524
76. **Fredrik Modin**, Tor., T.B., CBJ, L.A.	13	858	225	227	**452**	.527
77. **Martin Havlat**, Ott., Chi., Min.	9	543	187	263	**450**	.829
78. **Wade Redden**, Ott., NYR. . . .	13	994	106	344	**450**	.453
79. **Rob Niedermayer**, Fla., Cgy., Ana., N.J.	16	1082	181	269	**450**	.416
80. **Dean McAmmond**, Chi., Edm., Phi., Cgy., Col., St.L., Ott., NYI, N.J.	17	996	186	262	**448**	.450
81. **Jason Blake**, L.A., NYI, Tor., Ana.	11	750	190	252	**442**	.589
82. **Brenden Morrow**, Dal.	10	667	193	242	**435**	.652
83. **Eric Staal**, Car.	6	479	193	235	**428**	.894
84. **Kristian Huselius**, Fla., Cgy., CBJ.	8	621	176	252	**428**	.689
85. **Kimmo Timonen**, Nsh., Phi.. .	11	812	96	331	**427**	.526
86. **Mike Ribeiro**, Mtl., Dal..	10	581	136	290	**426**	.733
87. **Rick Nash**, CBJ.	7	517	227	195	**422**	.816
88. **Jochen Hecht**, St.L., Edm., Buf.	11	697	165	247	**412**	.591
89. **Dan Boyle**, Fla., T.B., S.J.	11	676	107	300	**407**	.602
90. **David Legwand**, Nsh.	11	704	152	255	**407**	.578
91. **Michal Handzus**, St.L., Phx., Phi., Chi., L.A.	11	762	160	245	**405**	.531
92. **Scott Walker**, Van., Nsh., Car., Wsh.	15	829	151	246	**397**	.479
93. **Andy McDonald**, Ana., St.L.. .	9	565	145	251	**396**	.701
94. **Maxim Afinogenov**, Buf., Atl.	10	651	158	237	**395**	.607
95. **Mark Parrish**, Fla., NYI, L.A., Min., Dal., T.B.	11	720	216	171	**387**	.538
96. **Evgeni Malkin**, Pit.	4	309	143	238	**381**	1.233
97. **Alexander Frolov**, L.A..	7	536	168	213	**381**	.711
98. **Todd White**, Chi., Phi., Ott., Min., Atl.	12	635	140	239	**379**	.597
99. **Shawn Horcoff**, Edm.	9	637	133	241	**374**	.587
100. **Steve Reinprecht**, L.A., Col., Cgy., Phx., Fla.	10	634	136	236	**372**	.587

Top 100 All-Time Games Played Leaders

* active player

Player	Seasons	Games Played
1. **Gordie Howe**, Det., Hfd.	26	1767
2. **Mark Messier**, Edm., NYR, Van.	25	1756
3. **Ron Francis**, Hfd., Pit., Car., Tor.	23	1731
4. **Chris Chelios**, Mtl., Chi., Det., Atl.	26	1651
5. **Dave Andreychuk**, Buf., Tor., N.J., Bos., Col., T.B.	23	1639
6. **Scott Stevens**, Wsh., St.L., N.J.	22	1635
7. **Larry Murphy**, L.A., Wsh., Min., Pit., Tor., Det.	21	1615
8. **Raymond Bourque**, Bos., Col.	22	1612
* 9. **Mark Recchi**, Pit., Phi., Mtl., Car., Atl., T.B., Bos.	21	1571
10. **Alex Delvecchio**, Det.	24	1549
11. **John Bucyk**, Det., Bos.	23	1540
12. **Brendan Shanahan**, N.J., St.L., Hfd., Det., NYR	21	1524
13. **Steve Yzerman**, Det.	22	1514
14. **Phil Housley**, Buf., Wpg., Cgy., N.J., Wsh., Chi., Tor.	21	1495
15. **Wayne Gretzky**, Edm., L.A., St.L., NYR	20	1487
16. **Rod Brind'Amour**, St.L., Phi., Car.	21	1484
17. **Doug Gilmour**, St.L., Cgy., Tor., N.J., Chi., Buf., Mtl.	20	1474
* 18. **Mike Modano**, Min., Dal.	21	1459
19. **Glen Wesley**, Bos., Hfd., Car., Tor.	20	1457
20. **Tim Horton**, Tor., NYR, Pit., Buf.	24	1446
21. **Mike Gartner**, Wsh., Min., NYR, Tor., Phx.	19	1432
22. **Luc Robitaille**, L.A., Pit., NYR, Det.	19	1431
23. **Scott Mellanby**, Phi., Edm., Fla., St.L., Atl.	21	1431
24. **Pat Verbeek**, N.J., Hfd., NYR, Dal., Det.	20	1424
25. **Luke Richardson**, Tor., Edm., Phi., CBJ, T.B., Ott.	21	1417
26. **Al MacInnis**, Cgy., St.L.	23	1416
* 27. **Nicklas Lidstrom**, Det.	18	1412
28. **Harry Howell**, NYR, Oak., Cal., L.A.	21	1411
29. **Norm Ullman**, Det., Tor.	20	1410
30. **Paul Coffey**, Edm., Pit., L.A., Det., Hfd., Phi., Chi., Car., Bos.	21	1409
31. **Dale Hunter**, Que., Wsh., Col.	19	1407
32. **Stan Mikita**, Chi.	22	1394
33. **Doug Mohns**, Bos., Chi., Min., Atl., Wsh.	22	1390
34. **Larry Robinson**, Mtl., L.A.	20	1384
35. **Trevor Linden**, Van., NYI, Mtl., Wsh.	19	1382
36. **Vincent Damphousse**, Tor., Edm., Mtl., S.J.	18	1378
37. **Joe Sakic**, Que., Col.	20	1378
38. **Dean Prentice**, NYR, Bos., Det., Pit., Min.	22	1378
39. **Teppo Numminen**, Wpg., Phx., Dal., Buf.	20	1372
40. **Jeremy Roenick**, Chi., Phx., Phi., L.A., S.J.	20	1363
41. **Ron Stewart**, Tor., Bos., St.L., NYR, Van., NYI	21	1353
42. **Kirk Muller**, N.J., Mtl., NYI, Tor., Fla., Dal.	19	1349
43. **Marcel Dionne**, Det., L.A., NYR	18	1348
44. **Mats Sundin**, Que., Tor., Van.	18	1346
45. **Adam Oates**, Det., St.L., Bos., Wsh., Phi., Ana., Edm.	19	1337
46. **Guy Carbonneau**, Mtl., St.L., Dal.	19	1318
47. **Red Kelly**, Det., Tor.	20	1316
48. **Bobby Holik**, Hfd., N.J., NYR, Atl.	18	1314
49. **Dave Keon**, Tor., Hfd.	18	1296
50. **Pierre Turgeon**, Buf., NYI, Mtl., St.L., Dal., Col.	19	1294
51. **Darryl Sydor**, L.A., Dal., CBJ, T.B., Pit., St.L.	18	1291
* 52. **Mathieu Schneider**, Mtl., NYI, Tor., NYR, L.A., Det., Ana., Atl., Van., Phx.	21	1289
53. **Ken Daneyko**, N.J.	20	1283
54. **Phil Esposito**, Chi., Bos., NYR	18	1282
55. **Jean Ratelle**, NYR, Bos.	21	1281
56. **James Patrick**, NYR, Hfd., Cgy., Buf.	21	1280
57. **Bryan Trottier**, NYI, Pit.	18	1279
58. **Jaromir Jagr**, Pit., Wsh., NYR	17	1273
59. **Martin Gelinas**, Edm., Que., Van., Car., Cgy., Fla., Nsh.	19	1273
60. **Rob Blake**, L.A., Col., S.J.	20	1270
61. **Brett Hull**, Cgy., St.L., Dal., Det., Phx.	20	1269
* 62. **Bill Guerin**, N.J., Edm., Bos., Dal., St.L., S.J., NYI, Pit.	18	1263
63. **Scott Niedermayer**, N.J., Ana.	18	1263
64. **Ray Ferraro**, Hfd., NYI, NYR, L.A., Atl., St.L.	18	1258
65. **Joe Nieuwendyk**, Cgy., Dal., N.J., Tor., Fla.	20	1257
66. **Craig Ludwig**, Mtl., NYI, Min., Dal.	17	1256
67. **Henri Richard**, Mtl.	20	1256
68. **Kevin Lowe**, Edm., NYR.	19	1254
69. **Jari Kurri**, Edm., L.A., NYR, Ana., Col.	17	1251
70. **Sergei Fedorov**, Det., Ana., CBJ, Wsh.	18	1248
71. **Bill Gadsby**, Chi., NYR, Det.	20	1248
72. **Allan Stanley**, NYR, Chi., Bos., Tor., Phi.	21	1244
73. **Steve Thomas**, Tor., Chi., NYI, N.J., Ana., Det.	20	1235
* 74. **Roman Hamrlik**, T.B., Edm., NYI, Cgy., Mtl.	17	1232
75. **Dino Ciccarelli**, Min., Wsh., Det., T.B., Fla.	19	1232
* 76. **Alex Kovalev**, NYR, Pit., Mtl., Ott.	17	1228
77. **Ed Westfall**, Bos., NYI.	18	1226
78. **Gary Roberts**, Cgy., Car., Tor., Fla., Pit., T.B.	22	1224
79. **Brad McCrimmon**, Bos., Phi., Cgy., Det., Hfd., Phx.	18	1222
* 80. **Doug Weight**, NYR, Edm., St.L., Car., Ana., NYI.	19	1220

Suiting up in 81 of 82 contests for the Boston Bruins in 2009-10, Mark Recchi climbed into the top 10 all time in games played. He reached the 1,500-games plateau early in the season on October 24, 2009.

Player	Seasons	Games Played
81. **Eric Nesterenko**, Tor., Chi.	21	1219
82. **Claude Lemieux**, Mtl., N.J., Col., Phx., Dal., S.J.	21	1215
83. **Marcel Pronovost**, Det., Tor.	21	1206
84. **Brian Leetch**, NYR, Tor., Bos.	18	1205
85. **Keith Tkachuk**, Wpg., Phx., St.L., Atl.	18	1201
* 86. **Owen Nolan**, Que., Col., S.J., Tor., Phx., Cgy., Min.	18	1200
87. **Denis Savard**, Chi., Mtl., T.B.	17	1196
88. **Dave Babych**, Wpg., Hfd., Van., Phi., L.A.	19	1195
89. **John MacLean**, N.J., S.J., NYR, Dal.	18	1194
90. **Gilbert Perreault**, Buf.	17	1191
91. **Marc Bergevin**, Chi., NYI, Hfd., T.B., St.L., Pit., Van.	20	1191
92. **Dale Hawerchuk**, Wpg., Buf., St.L., Phi.	16	1188
93. **Brian Bellows**, Min., Mtl., T.B., Ana., Wsh.	17	1188
94. **Kevin Dineen**, Hfd., Phi., Car., Ott., CBJ	19	1188
95. **George Armstrong**, Tor.	21	1187
* 96. **Teemu Selanne**, Wpg., Ana., S.J., Col.	17	1186
97. **Kelly Buchberger**, Edm., Atl., L.A., Phx., Pit.	18	1182
* 98. **Vyacheslav Kozlov**, Det., Buf., Atl.	18	1182
99. **Scott Young**, Hfd., Pit., Que., Col., Ana., St.L., Dal.	17	1181
100. **Frank Mahovlich**, Tor., Det., Mtl.	18	1181

Top 100 Active Games Played Leaders

	Player	Seasons	Games Played
1.	**Mark Recchi**, Pit., Phi., Mtl., Car., Atl., T.B., Bos.	21	1571
2.	**Mike Modano**, Min., Dal.	21	1459
3.	**Nicklas Lidstrom**, Det.	18	1412
4.	**Mathieu Schneider**, Mtl., NYI, Tor., NYR, L.A., Det., Ana., Atl., Van., Phx.	21	1289
5.	**Bill Guerin**, N.J., Edm., Bos., Dal., St.L., S.J., NYI, Pit.	18	1263
6.	**Roman Hamrlik**, T.B., Edm., NYI, Cgy., Mtl.	17	1232
7.	**Alex Kovalev**, NYR, Pit., Mtl., Ott.	17	1228
8.	**Doug Weight**, NYR, Edm., St.L., Car., Ana., NYI.	19	1220
9.	**Owen Nolan**, Que., Col., S.J., Tor., Phx., Cgy., Min.	18	1200
10.	**Teemu Selanne**, Wpg., Ana., S.J., Col.	17	1186
11.	**Vyacheslav Kozlov**, Det., Buf., Atl.	18	1182
12.	**Brian Rolston**, N.J., Col., Bos., Min.	15	1121
13.	**Todd Marchant**, NYR, Edm., CBJ, Ana.	16	1116
14.	**Kris Draper**, Wpg., Det.	19	1110
15.	**Adam Foote**, Que., Col., CBJ.	18	1107
16.	**Chris Pronger**, Hfd., St.L., Edm., Ana., Phi.	16	1104
17.	**Jason Arnott**, Edm., N.J., Dal., Nsh.	16	1099
18.	**Sean O'Donnell**, L.A., Min., N.J., Bos., Phx., Ana.	15	1092
19.	**Ian Laperriere**, St.L., NYR, L.A., Col., Phi.	16	1083
20.	**Rob Niedermayer**, Fla., Cgy., Ana., N.J.	16	1082
21.	**Martin Brodeur**, N.J.	17	1076
22.	**Kirk Maltby**, Edm., Det.	16	1072
23.	**Ray Whitney**, S.J., Edm., Fla., CBJ, Det., Car.	18	1072
24.	**Bryan McCabe**, NYI, Van., Chi., Tor., Fla.	14	1068
25.	**Radek Dvorak**, Fla., NYR, Edm., St.L.	14	1052
26.	**Miroslav Satan**, Edm., Buf., NYI, Pit., Bos.	14	1050
27.	**Shane Doan**, Wpg., Phx.	14	1047
28.	**Brad May**, Buf., Van., Phx., Col., Ana., Tor., Det.	18	1041
29.	**Donald Brashear**, Mtl., Van., Phi., Wsh., NYR	16	1025
30.	**Jarome Iginla**, Cgy.	14	1024
31.	**Daymond Langkow**, T.B., Phi., Phx., Cgy.	14	1013
32.	**Daniel Alfredsson**, Ott.	14	1002
33.	**Dean McAmmond**, Chi., Edm., Phi., Cgy., Col., St.L., Ott., NYI, N.J.	17	996
34.	**Wade Redden**, Ott., NYR.	13	994
35.	**Stephane Yelle**, Col., Cgy., Bos., Car.	14	991
36.	**Craig Conroy**, Mtl., St.L., Cgy., L.A.	15	991
37.	**Sergei Gonchar**, Wsh., Bos., Pit.	15	991
38.	**Paul Kariya**, Ana., Col., Nsh., St.L.	15	989
39.	**Robert Lang**, L.A., Bos., Pit., Wsh., Det., Chi., Mtl., Phx.	16	989
40.	**Mike Grier**, Edm., Wsh., Buf., S.J.	13	987
41.	**Ryan Smyth**, Edm., NYI, Col., L.A.	15	987
42.	**Ed Jovanovski**, Fla., Van., Phx.	14	969
43.	**Jamie Langenbrunner**, Dal., N.J.	15	965
44.	**Cory Stillman**, Cgy., St.L., T.B., Car., Ott., Fla.	15	960
45.	**Patrick Marleau**, S.J.	12	953
46.	**Shean Donovan**, S.J., Col., Atl., Pit., Cgy., Bos., Ott.	15	951
47.	**Andrew Brunette**, Wsh., Nsh., Atl., Min., Col.	14	950
48.	**Vinny Prospal**, Phi., Ott., Fla., T.B., Ana., NYR	13	949
49.	**Darcy Tucker**, Mtl., T.B., Tor., Col.	14	947
50.	**Todd Bertuzzi**, NYI, Van., Fla., Det., Ana., Cgy.	14	941
51.	**Petr Sykora**, N.J., Ana., NYR, Edm., Pit., Min.	14	935
52.	**Adrian Aucoin**, Van., T.B., NYI, Chi., Cgy., Phx.	15	933
53.	**Hal Gill**, Bos., Tor., Pit., Mtl.	12	919
54.	**Joe Thornton**, Bos., S.J.	12	915
55.	**Dainius Zubrus**, Phi., Mtl., Wsh., Buf., N.J.	13	904
56.	**Steve Staios**, Bos., Van., Atl., Edm., Cgy.	14	897
57.	**Brendan Witt**, Wsh., Nsh., NYI	14	890
58.	**Mike Knuble**, Det., NYR, Bos., Phi., Wsh.	13	889
59.	**Craig Rivet**, Mtl., S.J., Buf.	15	886
60.	**Olli Jokinen**, L.A., NYI, Fla., Phx., Cgy., NYR.	12	881
61.	**Matt Cullen**, Ana., Fla., Car., NYR, Ott.	12	880
62.	**Patrik Elias**, N.J.	14	880
63.	**Tomas Holmstrom**, Det.	13	879
64.	**Jere Lehtinen**, Dal.	14	875
65.	**Vincent Lecavalier**, T.B.	11	869
66.	**Derek Morris**, Cgy., Col., Phx., NYR, Bos.	12	869
67.	**Chris Drury**, Col., Cgy., Buf., NYR	11	868
68.	**Chris Phillips**, Ott.	12	863
69.	**Ethan Moreau**, Chi., Edm.	14	863
70.	**Saku Koivu**, Mtl., Ana.	14	863
71.	**Fredrik Modin**, Tor., T.B., CBJ, L.A.	13	858
72.	**Marco Sturm**, S.J., Bos.	12	855
73.	**Zdeno Chara**, NYI, Ott., Bos.	12	847
74.	**Pavol Demitra**, Ott., St.L., L.A., Min., Van.	16	847
75.	**Steve Sullivan**, N.J., Tor., Chi., Nsh.	14	846
76.	**Ruslan Salei**, Ana., Fla., Col.	13	842
77.	**Milan Hejduk**, Col.	11	839
78.	**Aaron Ward**, Det., Car., NYR, Bos., Ana.	15	839
79.	**Mattias Ohlund**, Van., T.B.	12	837
80.	**Marian Hossa**, Ott., Atl., Pit., Det., Chi.	12	832

Calgary's Jarome Iginla and Daymond Langkow reached 1,000 games played within a day of each other on a road trip in early February and were honored by the Flames back at home on February 11, 2010. The two teammates were among nine players who reached the milestone in 2009-10.

	Player	Seasons	Games Played
81.	**Brendan Morrison**, N.J., Van., Ana., Dal., Wsh.	12	829
82.	**Scott Walker**, Van., Nsh., Car., Wsh.	15	829
83.	**Pavel Kubina**, T.B., Tor., Atl.	12	822
84.	**Tomas Kaberle**, Tor.	11	820
85.	**Jay Pandolfo**, N.J.	13	819
86.	**Kimmo Timonen**, Nsh., Phi.	11	812
87.	**Sergei Samsonov**, Bos., Edm., Mtl., Chi., Car.	12	810
88.	**Jay McKee**, Buf., St.L., Pit.	14	802
89.	**John Madden**, N.J., Chi.	11	791
90.	**Tom Poti**, Edm., NYR, NYI, Wsh.	11	787
91.	**Scott Gomez**, N.J., NYR, Mtl.	10	784
92.	**Marc Savard**, NYR, Cgy., Atl., Bos.	12	782
93.	**Martin Skoula**, Col., Ana., Dal., Min., Pit., N.J.	10	776
94.	**Jassen Cullimore**, Van., Mtl., T.B., Chi., Fla.	14	776
95.	**Jaroslav Spacek**, Fla., Chi., CBJ, Edm., Buf., Mtl.	11	775
96.	**Wayne Primeau**, Buf., T.B., Pit., S.J., Bos., Cgy., Tor.	15	774
97.	**Martin St. Louis**, Cgy., T.B.	11	772
98.	**Brian Rafalski**, N.J., Det.	10	770
99.	**Michal Handzus**, St.L., Phx., Phi., Chi., L.A.	11	762
100.	**Karlis Skrastins**, Nsh., Col., Fla., Dal.	11	758

Goaltending Records

All-Time Shutout Leaders (Minimum 51 Shutouts)

	Goaltender	Team	Shutouts	Games	Seasons
1.	***Martin Brodeur** (1991-2010)	New Jersey	**110**	1,076	17
2.	**Terry Sawchuk** (1949-1970)	Detroit	85	734	14
		Boston	11	102	2
		Toronto	4	91	3
		Los Angeles	2	36	1
		NY Rangers	1	8	1
		Total	**103**	971	21
3.	**George Hainsworth** (1926-1937)	Montreal	75	318	7½
		Toronto	19	147	3½
		Total	**94**	465	11
4.	**Glenn Hall** (1952-1971)	Detroit	17	148	4
		Chicago	51	618	10
		St. Louis	16	140	4
		Total	**84**	906	18
5.	**Jacques Plante** (1952-1973)	Montreal	58	556	11
		NY Rangers	5	98	2
		St. Louis	10	69	2
		Toronto	7	106	2¾
		Boston	2	8	¼
		Total	**82**	837	18
6.	**Alec Connell** (1924-1937)	Ottawa	64	293	8
		Detroit	6	48	1
		NY Americans	0	1	1
		Mtl. Maroons	11	75	2
		Total	**81**	417	12
7.	**Tiny Thompson** (1928-1940)	Boston	74	468	10¼
		Detroit	7	85	1¾
		Total	**81**	553	12
8.	**Dominik Hasek** (1990-2008)	Chicago	1	25	2
		Buffalo	55	491	9
		Detroit	20	176	4
		Ottawa	5	43	1
		Total	**81**	735	16
9.	**Tony Esposito** (1968-1984)	Montreal	2	13	1
		Chicago	74	873	15
		Total	**76**	886	16
10.	**Ed Belfour** (1988-2007)	Chicago	30	415	7⅔
		San Jose	1	13	⅓
		Dallas	27	307	5
		Toronto	17	170	3
		Florida	1	58	1
		Total	**76**	963	17
11.	**Lorne Chabot** (1926-1937)	NY Rangers	21	80	2
		Toronto	31	214	5
		Montreal	8	47	1
		Chicago	8	48	1
		Mtl. Maroons	2	16	1
		NY Americans	1	6	1
		Total	**71**	411	11
12.	**Harry Lumley** (1943-1960)	Detroit	26	324	6½
		NY Rangers	0	1	½
		Chicago	5	134	2
		Toronto	34	267	4
		Boston	6	78	3
		Total	**71**	804	16
13.	**Roy Worters** (1925-1937)	Pittsburgh Pirates	22	123	3
		NY Americans	45	360	9
		**Montreal	0	1	
		Total	**67**	484	12
14.	**Patrick Roy** (1984-2003)	Montreal	29	551	11½
		Colorado	37	478	7½
		Total	**66**	1,029	19
15.	**Turk Broda** (1936-1952)	Toronto	**62**	629	14
16.	**John Ross Roach** (1921-1935)	Toronto	13	222	7
		NY Rangers	30	89	4
		Detroit	15	180	3
		Total	**58**	491	14
17.	**Clint Benedict** (1917-1930)	Ottawa	19	158	7
		Mtl. Maroons	38	204	6
		Total	**57**	362	13
18.	**Bernie Parent** (1965-1979)	Boston	1	57	2
		Philadelphia	50	486	9½
		Toronto	3	65	1½
		Total	**54**	608	13
19.	**Ed Giacomin** (1965-1978)	NY Rangers	49	539	10¼
		Detroit	5	71	2¾
		Total	**54**	610	13
20.	**Dave Kerr** (1930-1941)	Mtl. Maroons	11	101	3
		NY Americans	0	1	1
		NY Rangers	40	324	7
		Total	**51**	426	11
21.	***Roberto Luongo** (1999-2010)	NY Islanders	1	24	1
		Florida	26	317	5
		Vancouver	24	271	4
		Total	**51**	612	10
22.	**Rogie Vachon** (1966-1982)	Montreal	13	206	5¼
		Los Angeles	32	389	6¾
		Detroit	4	109	2
		Boston	2	91	2
		Total	**51**	795	16
23.	**Curtis Joseph** (1989-2009)	St. Louis	5	280	6
		Edmonton	14	177	3
		Toronto	17	270	5
		Detroit	7	92	2
		Phoenix	8	115	2
		Calgary	0	9	1
		Total	**51**	943	19

* Active goalie
** Played 1 game for Montreal in 1929-30.

Ten or More Shutouts, One Season

Number of Shutouts	Goaltender	Team	Season	Length of Schedule
22	George Hainsworth	Montreal	1928-29	44
15	Alec Connell	Ottawa	1925-26	36
	Alec Connell	Ottawa	1927-28	44
	Hal Winkler	Boston	1927-28	44
	Tony Esposito	Chicago	1969-70	76
14	George Hainsworth	Montreal	1926-27	44
13	Clint Benedict	Mtl. Maroons	1926-27	44
	Alec Connell	Ottawa	1926-27	44
	George Hainsworth	Montreal	1927-28	44
	John Ross Roach	NY Rangers	1928-29	44
	Roy Worters	NY Americans	1928-29	44
	Harry Lumley	Toronto	1953-54	70
	Dominik Hasek	Buffalo	1997-98	82
12	Tiny Thompson	Boston	1928-29	44
	Charlie Gardiner	Chicago	1930-31	44
	Terry Sawchuk	Detroit	1951-52	70
	Terry Sawchuk	Detroit	1953-54	70
	Terry Sawchuk	Detroit	1954-55	70
	Glenn Hall	Detroit	1955-56	70
	Bernie Parent	Philadelphia	1973-74	78
	Bernie Parent	Philadelphia	1974-75	80
	Martin Brodeur	New Jersey	2006-07	82
11	Lorne Chabot	NY Rangers	1927-28	44
	Hap Holmes	Detroit	1927-28	44
	Roy Worters	Pittsburgh Pirates	1927-28	44
	Clint Benedict	Mtl. Maroons	1928-29	44
	Joe Miller	Pittsburgh Pirates	1928-29	44
	Tiny Thompson	Boston	1932-33	48
	Terry Sawchuk	Detroit	1950-51	70
	Dominik Hasek	Buffalo	2000-01	82
	Martin Brodeur	New Jersey	2003-04	82
10	Lorne Chabot	NY Rangers	1926-27	44
	Lorne Chabot	Toronto	1928-29	44
	Dolly Dolson	Detroit	1928-29	44
	John Ross Roach	Detroit	1932-33	48
	Charlie Gardiner	Chicago	1933-34	48
	Tiny Thompson	Boston	1935-36	48
	Frank Brimsek	Boston	1938-39	48
	Bill Durnan	Montreal	1948-49	60
	Harry Lumley	Toronto	1952-53	70
	Gerry McNeil	Montreal	1952-53	70
	Tony Esposito	Chicago	1973-74	78
	Ken Dryden	Montreal	1976-77	80
	Martin Brodeur	New Jersey	1996-97	82
	Martin Brodeur	New Jersey	1997-98	82
	Byron Dafoe	Boston	1998-99	82
	Roman Cechmanek	Philadelphia	2000-01	82
	Ed Belfour	Toronto	2003-04	82
	Miikka Kiprusoff	Calgary	2005-06	82
	Henrik Lundqvist	NY Rangers	2007-08	82
	Steve Mason	Columbus	2008-09	82

All-Time Win Leaders

(Minimum 250 Wins)

	Goaltender	Wins	GP	Dec.	Losses	OT/Ties
1.	* Martin Brodeur	602	1076	1045	324	134
2.	Patrick Roy	551	1029	997	315	131
3.	Ed Belfour	484	963	929	320	125
4.	Curtis Joseph	454	943	902	352	96
5.	Terry Sawchuk	447	971	949	330	172
6.	Jacques Plante	437	837	829	247	145
7.	Tony Esposito	423	886	880	306	151
8.	Glenn Hall	407	906	896	326	163
9.	Grant Fuhr	403	868	812	295	114
10.	* Chris Osgood	396	733	702	213	93
11.	Dominik Hasek	389	735	707	223	95
12.	Mike Vernon	385	781	750	273	92
13.	John Vanbiesbrouck	374	882	839	346	119
14.	Andy Moog	372	713	669	209	88
15.	Tom Barrasso	369	777	732	277	86
16.	Rogie Vachon	355	795	773	291	127
17.	Gump Worsley	335	861	837	352	150
18.	Harry Lumley	330	803	801	329	142
19.	Sean Burke	324	820	775	341	110
20.	* Nikolai Khabibulin	306	696	666	276	84
21.	Billy Smith	305	680	643	233	105
22.	Olaf Kolzig	303	719	687	297	87
23.	Turk Broda	302	629	627	224	101
24.	Mike Richter	301	666	632	258	73
25.	Ron Hextall	296	608	579	214	69
26.	Mike Liut	294	664	639	271	74
27.	* Evgeni Nabokov	293	563	537	178	66
28.	Ed Giacomin	289	609	594	208	97
29.	Dan Bouchard	286	655	631	232	113
30.	Tiny Thompson	284	553	553	194	75
31.	Bernie Parent	271	608	590	198	121
32.	Kelly Hrudey	271	677	624	265	88
33.	* Roberto Luongo	270	602	592	254	68
34.	Gilles Meloche	270	788	752	351	131
35.	Don Beaupre	268	667	620	277	75
36.	Felix Potvin	266	635	611	260	85
37.	* Marty Turco	262	509	479	154	63
38.	Ken Dryden	258	397	389	57	74
39.	Frank Brimsek	252	514	514	182	80
40.	Johnny Bower	250	552	535	195	90

* active player

Active Shutout Leaders

(Minimum 25 Shutouts)

	Goaltender	Teams	Shutouts	Games	Seasons
1.	Martin Brodeur	New Jersey	110	1,076	17
2.	Roberto Luongo	NYI, Fla., Van.	51	612	10
3.	Evgeni Nabokov	San Jose	50	563	10
4.	Chris Osgood	Det., NYI, St.L.	50	733	16
5.	Nikolai Khabibulin	Wpg., Phx., T.B., Chi., Edm.	41	696	14
6.	Marty Turco	Dallas	40	509	9
7.	Tomas Vokoun	Mtl., Nas., Fla.	38	575	12
8.	Patrick Lalime	Pit., Ott., St.L., Chi., Buf.	35	437	11
9.	Miikka Kiprusoff	San Jose, Calgary	34	458	9
10.	Jean-Sebastien Giguere	Hfd., Cgy., Ana., Tor.	34	492	12
11.	Jose Theodore	Mtl., Col., Wsh.	29	548	13
12.	Martin Biron	Buf., Phi., NYI	26	462	12

All-Time Penalty-Minute Leaders

* active player

(Regular season. Minimum 2,900 minutes)

	Player	Seasons	Games	Penalty Minutes	Mins. per game
1.	Tiger Williams, Tor., Van., Det., L.A., Hfd.	14	962	3966	4.12
2.	Dale Hunter, Que., Wsh., Col.	19	1407	3565	2.53
3.	Tie Domi, Tor., NYR, Wpg.	16	1020	3515	3.45
4.	Marty McSorley, Pit., Edm., L.A., NYR, S.J., Bos.	17	961	3381	3.52
5.	Bob Probert, Det., Chi.	16	935	3300	3.53
6.	Rob Ray, Buf., Ott.	15	900	3207	3.56
7.	Craig Berube, Phi., Tor., Cgy., Wsh., NYI	17	1054	3149	2.99
8.	Tim Hunter, Cgy., Que., Van., S.J.	16	815	3146	3.86
9.	Chris Nilan, Mtl., NYR, Bos.	13	688	3043	4.42
10.	Rick Tocchet, Phi., Pit., L.A., Bos., Wsh., Phx.	18	1144	2972	2.60
11.	Pat Verbeek, N.J., Hfd., NYR, Dal., Det.	20	1424	2905	2.04

Goals-Against Average Leaders (Minimum 25 games played)

(Exceptions: Minimum 13 games played, 1994-95; minimum 26 games played, 1992-93 to 1993-94; minimum 15 games played, 1917-18 to 1925-26)

Season	Goaltender, Team	GP	Mins.	GA	SO	AVG.	Season	Goaltender, Team	GP	Mins.	GA	SO	AVG.
2009-10	Tuukka Rask, Boston	45	2,562	84	5	1.97	1962-63	Don Simmons, Toronto	28	1,680	69	1	2.46
2008-09	Tim Thomas, Boston	54	3,259	114	5	2.10	1961-62	Jacques Plante, Montreal	70	4,200	166	4	2.37
2007-08	Chris Osgood, Detroit	43	2,409	84	4	2.09	1960-61	Charlie Hodge, Montreal	30	1,800	74	4	2.47
2006-07	Niklas Backstrom, Minnesota	41	2,227	73	5	1.97	1959-60	Jacques Plante, Montreal	69	4,140	175	3	2.54
2005-06	Miikka Kiprusoff, Calgary	74	4,380	151	10	2.07	1958-59	Jacques Plante, Montreal	67	4,000	144	9	2.16
2003-04	Miikka Kiprusoff, Calgary	38	2,301	65	4	1.69	1957-58	Jacques Plante, Montreal	57	3,386	119	9	2.11
2002-03	Marty Turco, Dallas	55	3,203	92	7	1.72	1956-57	Jacques Plante, Montreal	61	3,660	122	9	2.00
2001-02	Patrick Roy, Colorado	63	3,773	122	9	1.94	1955-56	Jacques Plante, Montreal	64	3,840	119	7	1.86
2000-01	Marty Turco, Dallas	26	1,266	40	3	1.90	1954-55	Harry Lumley, Toronto	69	4,140	134	8	1.94
99-2000	Brian Boucher, Philadelphia	35	2,038	65	4	1.91	1953-54	Harry Lumley, Toronto	69	4,140	128	13	1.86
1998-99	Ron Tugnutt, Ottawa	43	2,508	75	3	1.79	1952-53	Terry Sawchuk, Detroit	63	3,780	120	9	1.90
1997-98	Ed Belfour, Dallas	61	3,581	112	9	1.88	1951-52	Terry Sawchuk, Detroit	70	4,200	133	12	1.90
1996-97	Martin Brodeur, New Jersey	67	3,838	120	10	1.88	1950-51	Al Rollins, Toronto	40	2,367	70	5	1.77
1995-96	Ron Hextall, Philadelphia	53	3,102	112	4	2.17	1949-50	Bill Durnan, Montreal	64	3,840	141	8	2.20
1994-95	Dominik Hasek, Buffalo	41	2,416	85	5	2.11	1948-49	Bill Durnan, Montreal	60	3,600	126	10	2.10
1993-94	Dominik Hasek, Buffalo	58	3,358	109	7	1.95	1947-48	Turk Broda, Toronto	60	3,600	143	5	2.38
1992-93	Felix Potvin, Toronto	48	2,781	116	2	2.50	1946-47	Bill Durnan, Montreal	60	3,600	138	4	2.30
1991-92	Patrick Roy, Montreal	67	3,935	155	5	2.36	1945-46	Bill Durnan, Montreal	40	2,400	104	4	2.60
1990-91	Ed Belfour, Chicago	74	4,127	170	4	2.47	1944-45	Bill Durnan, Montreal	50	3,000	121	1	2.42
1989-90	Mike Liut, Hartford, Washington	37	2,161	91	4	2.53	1943-44	Bill Durnan, Montreal	50	3,000	109	2	2.18
1988-89	Patrick Roy, Montreal	48	2,744	113	4	2.47	1942-43	Johnny Mowers, Detroit	50	3,010	124	6	2.47
1987-88	Pete Peeters, Washington	35	1,896	88	2	2.78	1941-42	Frank Brimsek, Boston	47	2,930	115	3	2.35
1986-87	Brian Hayward, Montreal	37	2,178	102	1	2.81	1940-41	Turk Broda, Toronto	48	2,970	99	5	2.00
1985-86	Bob Froese, Philadelphia	51	2,728	116	5	2.55	1939-40	Dave Kerr, NY Rangers	48	3,000	77	8	1.54
1984-85	Tom Barrasso, Buffalo	54	3,248	144	5	2.66	1938-39	Frank Brimsek, Boston	43	2,610	68	10	1.56
1983-84	Pat Riggin, Washington	41	2,299	102	4	2.66	1937-38	Tiny Thompson, Boston	48	2,970	89	7	1.80
1982-83	Pete Peeters, Philadelphia	62	3,611	142	8	2.36	1936-37	Normie Smith, Detroit	48	2,980	102	6	2.05
1981-82	Denis Herron, Montreal	27	1,547	68	3	2.64	1935-36	Tiny Thompson, Boston	48	2,930	82	10	1.68
1980-81	Richard Sevigny, Montreal	33	1,777	71	2	2.40	1934-35	Lorne Chabot, Chicago	48	2,940	88	8	1.80
1979-80	Bob Sauve, Buffalo	32	1,880	74	4	2.36	1933-34	Wilf Cude, Detroit, Montreal	30	1,920	47	5	1.47
1978-79	Ken Dryden, Montreal	47	2,814	108	5	2.30	1932-33	Tiny Thompson, Boston	48	3,000	88	11	1.76
1977-78	Ken Dryden, Montreal	52	3,071	105	5	2.05	1931-32	Charlie Gardiner, Chicago	48	2,989	92	4	1.85
1976-77	Michel Larocque, Montreal	26	1,525	53	4	2.09	1930-31	Roy Worters, NY Americans	44	2,760	74	8	1.61
1975-76	Ken Dryden, Montreal	62	3,580	121	8	2.03	1929-30	Tiny Thompson, Boston	44	2,680	98	3	2.19
1974-75	Bernie Parent, Philadelphia	68	4,041	137	12	2.03	1928-29	George Hainsworth, Montreal	44	2,800	43	22	0.92
1973-74	Bernie Parent, Philadelphia	73	4,314	136	12	1.89	1927-28	George Hainsworth, Montreal	44	2,730	48	13	1.05
1972-73	Ken Dryden, Montreal	54	3,165	119	6	2.26	1926-27	Clint Benedict, Mtl. Maroons	43	2,748	65	13	1.42
1971-72	Tony Esposito, Chicago	48	2,780	82	9	1.77	1925-26	Alec Connell, Ottawa	36	2,251	42	15	1.12
1970-71	Jacques Plante, Toronto	40	2,329	73	4	1.88	1924-25	Georges Vezina, Montreal	30	1,860	56	5	1.81
1969-70	Ernie Wakely, St. Louis	30	1,651	58	4	2.11	1923-24	Georges Vezina, Montreal	24	1,459	48	3	1.97
1968-69	Jacques Plante, St. Louis	37	2,139	70	5	1.96	1922-23	Clint Benedict, Ottawa	24	1,478	54	4	2.18
1967-68	Gump Worsley, Montreal	40	2,213	73	6	1.98	1921-22	Clint Benedict, Ottawa	24	1,508	84	2	3.34
1966-67	Glenn Hall, Chicago	32	1,664	66	2	2.38	1920-21	Clint Benedict, Ottawa	24	1,457	75	2	3.09
1965-66	Johnny Bower, Toronto	35	1,998	75	3	2.25	1919-20	Clint Benedict, Ottawa	24	1,444	64	5	2.66
1964-65	Johnny Bower, Toronto	34	2,040	81	3	2.38	1918-19	Clint Benedict, Ottawa	18	1,113	53	2	2.86
1963-64	Johnny Bower, Toronto	51	3,009	106	5	2.11	1917-18	Georges Vezina, Montreal	21	1,282	84	1	3.93

All-Time Regular-Season NHL Coaching Register

Regular Season, 1917-2010

Coach	Team	Games Coached	Wins	Losses	O/T	Years	Cup Wins	Career
Abel, Sid	Chicago	140	39	79	22	2		
	Detroit	811	340	339	132	12		
	St. Louis	10	3	6	1	1		
	Kansas City	3	0	3	0	1		
	Totals	964	382	427	155	16		1952-76
Adams, Jack	Detroit	964	413	390	161	20	3	1927-47
Agnew, Gary	Columbus	5	0	4	1	1		2006-07
Allen, Keith	Philadelphia	150	51	67	32	2		1967-69
Allison, Dave	Ottawa	25	2	22	1	1		1995-96
Anderson, Jim	Washington	54	4	45	5	1		1974-75
Anderson, John	Atlanta	164	70	75	19	2		2008-10
Angotti, Lou	St. Louis	32	6	20	6	2		
	Pittsburgh	80	16	58	6	1		
	Totals	112	22	78	12	3		1973-84
Arbour, Al	St. Louis	107	42	40	25	3		
	NY Islanders	1500	740	537	223	20	4	
	Totals	1607	782	577	248	23	4	1970-08
Armstrong, George	Toronto	47	17	26	4	1		1988-89
Babcock, Mike	Anaheim	164	69	62	33	3		
	Detroit	410	257	101	52	5	1	
	Totals	574	326	163	85	8	1	2002-10
Barber, Bill	Philadelphia	136	73	40	23	2		2000-02
Barkley, Doug	Detroit	77	20	46	11	3		1970-76
Beaulieu, Andre	Minnesota	32	6	23	3	1		1977-78
Belisle, Danny	Washington	96	28	51	17	2		1978-80
Berenson, Red	St. Louis	204	100	72	32	3		1979-82
Bergeron, Michel	Quebec	634	265	283	86	8		
	NY Rangers	158	73	67	18	2		
	Totals	792	338	350	104	10		1980-90
Berry, Bob	Los Angeles	240	107	94	39	3		
	Montreal	223	116	71	36	3		
	Pittsburgh	240	88	127	25	3		
	St. Louis	157	73	63	21	2		
	Totals	860	384	355	121	11		1978-94
Beverley, Nick	Toronto	17	9	6	2	1		1995-96
Blackburn, Don	Hartford	140	42	63	35	2		1979-81
Blair, Wren	Minnesota	147	48	65	34	3		1967-70
Blake, Toe	Montreal	914	500	255	159	13	8	1955-68
Boileau, Marc	Pittsburgh	151	66	61	24	3		1973-76
Boivin, Leo	St. Louis	97	28	53	16	2		1975-78
Boucher, Frank	NY Rangers	527	181	263	83	11	1	1939-54
Boucher, Georges	Mtl. Maroons	12	6	5	1	1		
	Ottawa	48	13	29	6	1		
	St. Louis	35	9	20	6	1		
	Boston	70	22	32	16	1		
	Totals	165	50	86	29	4		1930-50
Boudreau, Bruce	Washington	225	141	56	28	3		2007-10
Bowman, Scotty	St. Louis	238	110	83	45	4		
	Montreal	634	419	110	105	8	5	
	Buffalo	404	210	134	60	7		
	Pittsburgh	164	95	53	16	2	1	
	Detroit	701	410	193	98	9	3	
	Totals	2141	1244	573	324	30	9	1967-02
Bowness, Rick	Winnipeg	28	8	17	3	1		
	Boston	80	36	32	12	1		
	Ottawa	235	39	178	18	4		
	NY Islanders	100	38	50	12	2		
	Phoenix	20	2	12	6	2		
	Totals	463	123	289	51	10		1988-05
Brooks, Herb	NY Rangers	285	131	113	41	4		
	Minnesota	80	19	48	13	1		
	New Jersey	84	40	37	7	1		
	Pittsburgh	57	29	21	7	1		
	Totals	506	219	219	68	7		1981-00
Brophy, John	Toronto	193	64	111	18	3		1986-89
Burnett, George	Edmonton	35	12	20	3	1		1994-95
Burns, Charlie	Minnesota	86	22	50	14	2		1969-75
Burns, Pat	Montreal	320	174	104	42	4		
	Toronto	281	133	107	41	4		
	Boston	254	105	97	52	4		
	New Jersey	164	89	45	30	3	1	
	Totals	1019	501	353	165	15	1	1988-05
Bush, Eddie	Kansas City	32	1	23	8	1		1975-76
Bylsma, Dan	Pittsburgh	107	65	31	11	2	1	2008-10
Campbell, Colin	NY Rangers	269	118	108	43	4		1994-98
Carbonneau, Guy	Montreal	230	124	83	23	3		2006-09
Carlyle, Randy	Anaheim	410	219	139	52	5	1	2005-10
Carpenter, Doug	New Jersey	290	100	166	24	4		
	Toronto	91	39	47	5	2		
	Totals	381	139	213	29	6		1984-91
Carroll, Dick	Toronto	40	18	22	0	2	1	1917-19
Carroll, Frank	Toronto	24	15	9	0	1		1920-21
Cashman, Wayne	Philadelphia	61	32	20	9	1		1997-98
Cassidy, Bruce	Washington	110	47	47	16	2		2002-04
Chambers, Dave	Quebec	98	19	64	15	2		1990-92

Coach	Team	Games Coached	Wins	Losses	O/T	Years	Cup Wins	Career
Chapman, Art	NY Americans	48	8	29	11	1		
	Brooklyn	48	16	29	3	1		
	Totals	96	24	58	14	2		1940-42
Charron, Guy	Calgary	16	6	7	3	1		
	Anaheim	49	14	26	9	1		
	Totals	65	20	33	12	2		1991-01
Cheevers, Gerry	Boston	376	204	126	46	5		1980-85
Cherry, Don	Boston	400	231	105	64	5		
	Colorado	80	19	48	13	1		
	Totals	480	250	153	77	6		1974-80
Clancy, King	Mtl. Maroons	18	6	11	1	1		
	Toronto	210	80	81	49	3		
	Totals	228	86	92	50	4		1937-56
Clapper, Dit	Boston	230	102	88	40	4		1945-49
Cleghorn, Odie	Pittsburgh	168	62	86	20	4		1925-29
Cleghorn, Sprague	Mtl. Maroons	48	19	22	7	1		1931-32
Clouston, Cory	Ottawa	116	63	43	10	2		2008-10
Colville, Neil	NY Rangers	93	26	41	26	2		1950-52
Conacher, Charlie	Chicago	162	56	84	22	3		1947-50
Conacher, Lionel	NY Americans	44	14	25	5	1		1929-30
Constantine, Kevin	San Jose	157	55	78	24	3		
	Pittsburgh	189	86	64	39	3		
	New Jersey	31	20	8	3	1		
	Totals	377	161	150	66	7		1993-02
Cook, Bill	NY Rangers	117	34	59	24	2		1951-53
Crawford, Marc	Quebec	48	30	13	5	1		
	Colorado	246	135	75	36	3	1	
	Vancouver	529	246	189	94	8		
	Los Angeles	164	59	84	21	2		
	Dallas	82	37	31	14	1		
	Totals	1069	507	392	170	15	1	1994-10
Creamer, Pierre	Pittsburgh	80	36	35	9	1		1987-88
Creighton, Fred	Atlanta	348	156	136	56	5		
	Boston	73	40	20	13	1		
	Totals	421	196	156	69	6		1974-80
Crisp, Terry	Calgary	240	144	63	33	3	1	
	Tampa Bay	391	142	204	45	6		
	Totals	631	286	267	78	9	1	1987-98
Crozier, Joe	Buffalo	192	77	80	35	3		
	Toronto	40	13	22	5	1		
	Totals	232	90	102	40	4		1971-81
Crozier, Roger	Washington	1	0	1	0	1		1981-82
Cunniff, John	Hartford	13	3	9	1	1		
	New Jersey	133	59	56	18	2		
	Totals	146	62	65	19	3		1982-91
Curry, Alex	Ottawa	36	24	8	4	1		1925-26
Dandurand, Leo	Montreal	163	78	76	9	6	1	1921-35
Day, Hap	Toronto	546	259	206	81	10	5	1940-50
Dea, Billy	Detroit	11	3	8	0	1		1981-82
DeBoer, Peter	Florida	164	73	67	24	2		2008-10
Delvecchio, Alex	Detroit	245	82	131	32	4		1973-77
Demers, Jacques	Quebec	80	25	44	11	1		
	St. Louis	240	106	106	28	3		
	Detroit	320	137	136	47	4		
	Montreal	220	107	86	27	4	1	
	Tampa Bay	147	34	96	17	2		
	Totals	1007	409	468	130	14	1	1979-99
Denneny, Cy	Boston	44	26	13	5	1	1	
	Ottawa	48	11	27	10	1		
	Totals	92	37	40	15	2	1	1928-33
Dineen, Bill	Philadelphia	140	60	60	20	2		1991-93
Dudley, Rick	Buffalo	188	85	72	31	3		
	Florida	40	13	15	12	1		
	Totals	228	98	87	43	4		1989-04
Duff, Dick	Toronto	2	0	2	0	1		1979-80
Dugal, Jules	Montreal	18	9	6	3	1		1938-39
Duncan, Art	Detroit	33	10	21	2	1		
	Toronto	47	21	16	10	2		
	Totals	80	31	37	12	3		1926-32
Dutton, Red	NY Americans	192	66	97	29	4		1936-40
Eddolls, Frank	Chicago	70	13	40	17	1		1954-55
Esposito, Phil	NY Rangers	45	24	21	0	2		1986-89
Evans, Jack	California	80	27	42	11	1		
	Cleveland	160	47	87	26	2		
	Hartford	374	163	174	37	5		
	Totals	614	237	303	74	8		1975-88
Fashoway, Gordie	Oakland	10	4	5	1	1		1967-68
Ferguson, John	NY Rangers	121	43	59	19	2		
	Winnipeg	14	7	6	1	1		
	Totals	135	50	65	20	3		1975-86
Filion, Maurice	Quebec	6	1	3	2	1		1980-81
Francis, Bob	Phoenix	390	165	144	81	5		1999-04
Francis, Emile	NY Rangers	654	342	209	103	10		
	St. Louis	124	46	64	14	3		
	Totals	778	388	273	117	13		1965-83
Fraser, Curt	Atlanta	279	64	169	46	4		1999-03
Fredrickson, Frank	Pittsburgh	44	5	36	3	1		1929-30
Ftorek, Robbie	Los Angeles	132	65	56	11	2		
	New Jersey	156	88	44	24	2		
	Boston	155	76	52	27	2		
	Totals	443	229	152	62	6		1987-03
Gadsby, Bill	Detroit	78	35	31	12	2		1968-70

Coach	Team	Games Coached	Wins	Losses	O/T	Years	Cup Wins	Career
Gainey, Bob	Minnesota	244	95	119	30	3		
	Dallas	171	70	71	30	3		
	Montreal	57	29	21	7	2		
	Totals	472	194	211	67	8		1990-09
Gallant, Gerard	Columbus	142	56	76	10	4		2003-07
Gardiner, Herb	Chicago	32	5	23	4	1		1928-29
Gardner, Jimmy	Hamilton	30	19	10	1	1		1924-25
Garvin, Ted	Detroit	11	2	8	1	1		1973-74
Geoffrion, Bernie	NY Rangers	43	22	18	3	1		
	Atlanta	208	77	92	39	3		
	Montreal	30	15	9	6	1		
	Totals	281	114	119	48	5		1968-80
Gerard, Eddie	Ottawa	22	9	13	0	1		
	Mtl. Maroons	294	129	122	43	7	1	
	NY Americans	92	34	40	18	2		
	St. Louis	13	2	11	0	1		
	Totals	421	174	186	61	11	1	1917-35
Gilbert, Greg	Calgary	121	42	56	23	3		2000-03
Gill, David	Ottawa	132	64	41	27	3	1	1926-29
Glover, Fred	Oakland	152	51	76	25	2		
	California	204	45	131	28	4		
	Los Angeles	68	18	42	8	1		
	Totals	424	114	249	61	6		1968-74
Goodfellow, Ebbie	Chicago	140	30	91	19	2		1950-52
Gordon, Jackie	Minnesota	289	116	123	50	5		1970-75
Gordon, Scott	NY Islanders	164	60	84	20	2		2008-10
Goring, Butch	Boston	93	42	38	13	2		
	NY Islanders	147	41	88	18	2		
	Totals	240	83	126	31	4		1985-01
Gorman, Tommy	NY Americans	80	31	33	16	2		
	Chicago	73	28	28	17	2	1	
	Mtl. Maroons	174	74	71	29	4	1	
	Totals	327	133	132	62	8	2	1925-38
Gottselig, Johnny	Chicago	187	62	105	20	4		1944-48
Goyette, Phil	NY Islanders	48	6	38	4	1		1972-73
Graham, Dirk	Chicago	59	16	35	8	1		1998-99
Granato, Tony	Colorado	215	104	78	33	3		2002-09
Green, Gary	Washington	157	50	78	29	3		1979-82
Green, Pete	Ottawa	150	94	52	4	6	3	1919-25
Green, Shorty	NY Americans	44	11	27	6	1		1927-28
Green, Ted	Edmonton	188	65	102	21	3		1991-94
Gretzky, Wayne	Phoenix	328	143	161	24	4		2005-09
Guidolin, Aldo	Colorado	59	12	39	8	1		1978-79
Guidolin, Bep	Boston	104	72	23	9	2		
	Kansas City	125	26	84	15	2		
	Totals	229	98	107	24	4		1972-76
Hanlon, Glen	Washington	239	78	122	39	5		2003-08
Harkness, Ned	Detroit	38	12	22	4	1		1970-71
Harris, Ted	Minnesota	179	48	104	27	3		1975-78
Hart, Cecil	Montreal	394	196	125	73	9	2	1926-39
Hartley, Bob	Colorado	359	193	108	58	5	1	
	Atlanta	291	136	118	37	6		
	Totals	650	329	226	95	10	1	1998-08
Hartsburg, Craig	Chicago	246	104	102	40	3		
	Anaheim	197	80	82	35	3		
	Ottawa	48	17	24	7	1		
	Totals	491	201	208	82	7		1995-09
Harvey, Doug	NY Rangers	70	26	32	12	1		1961-62
Hay, Don	Phoenix	82	38	37	7	1		
	Calgary	68	23	28	17	1		
	Totals	150	61	65	24	2		1996-01
Heffernan, Frank	Toronto	12	5	7	0	1		1919-20
Helmer, Rosie	NY Americans	48	16	25	7	1		1935-36
Henning, Lorne	Minnesota	158	68	72	18	2		
	NY Islanders	65	19	39	7	2		
	Totals	223	87	111	25	4		1985-01
Hitchcock, Ken	Dallas	503	277	154	72	7	1	
	Philadelphia	254	131	73	50	5		
	Columbus	284	125	123	36	4		
	Totals	1041	533	350	158	15	1	1995-10
Hlinka, Ivan	Pittsburgh	86	42	32	12	2		2000-02
Holmgren, Paul	Philadelphia	264	107	126	31	4		
	Hartford	161	54	93	14	4		
	Totals	425	161	219	45	8		1988-96
Howell, Harry	Minnesota	11	3	6	2	1		1978-79
Imlach, Punch	Toronto	770	370	275	125	12	4	
	Buffalo	119	32	62	25	2		
	Totals	889	402	337	150	14	4	1958-80
Ingarfield, Earl	NY Islanders	30	6	22	2	1		1972-73
Inglis, Bill	Buffalo	56	28	18	10	1		1978-79
Irvin, Dick	Chicago	126	45	62	19	3		
	Toronto	427	216	152	59	9	1	
	Montreal	896	431	313	152	15	3	
	Totals	1449	692	527	230	27	4	1928-56
Ivan, Tommy	Detroit	470	262	118	90	7	3	
	Chicago	103	26	56	21	2		
	Totals	573	288	174	111	9	3	1947-58
Iverson, Emil	Chicago	21	8	7	6	1		1932-33
Johnson, Bob	Calgary	400	193	155	52	5		
	Pittsburgh	80	41	33	6	1	1	
	Totals	480	234	188	58	6	1	1982-91
Johnson, Tom	Boston	208	142	43	23	3	1	1970-73
Johnston, Eddie	Chicago	80	34	27	19	1		
	Pittsburgh	516	232	224	60	7		
	Totals	596	266	251	79	8		1979-97
Johnston, Marshall	California	69	13	45	11	2		
	Colorado	56	15	32	9	1		
	Totals	125	28	77	20	3		1973-82
Julien, Claude	Montreal	159	72	62	25	4		
	New Jersey	79	47	24	8	1		
	Boston	246	133	78	44	3		
	Totals	484	252	164	77	8		2002-10
Kasper, Steve	Boston	164	66	78	20	2		1995-97
Keats, Duke	Detroit	11	2	7	2	1		1926-27
Keenan, Mike	Philadelphia	320	190	102	28	4		
	Chicago	320	153	126	41	4		
	NY Rangers	84	52	24	8	1	1	
	St. Louis	163	75	66	22	3		
	Vancouver	108	36	54	18	2		
	Boston	74	33	26	15	1		
	Florida	153	45	73	35	3		
	Calgary	164	88	60	16	2		
	Totals	1386	672	531	183	20	1	1984-09
Kehoe, Rick	Pittsburgh	160	55	81	22	2		2001-03
Kelly, Pat	Colorado	101	22	54	25	2		1977-79
Kelly, Red	Los Angeles	150	55	75	20	2		
	Pittsburgh	274	90	132	52	4		
	Toronto	318	133	123	62	4		
	Totals	742	278	330	134	10		1967-77
King, Dave	Calgary	216	109	76	31	3		
	Columbus	204	64	106	34	3		
	Totals	420	173	182	65	6		1992-03
Kingston, George	San Jose	164	28	129	7	2		1991-93
Kish, Larry	Hartford	49	12	32	5	1		1982-83
Kitchen, Mike	St. Louis	131	38	70	23	4		2003-07
Kromm, Bobby	Detroit	231	79	111	41	3		1977-80
Kurtenbach, Orland	Vancouver	125	36	62	27	2		1976-78
LaForge, Bill	Vancouver	20	4	14	2	1		1984-85
Lalonde, Newsy	Montreal	207	96	97	14	8		
	NY Americans	44	17	25	2	1		
	Ottawa	88	31	45	12	2		
	Totals	339	144	167	28	11		1917-35
Lamoriello, Lou	New Jersey	53	34	14	5	2		2005-07
Laperriere, Jacques	Montreal	1	0	1	0	1		1995-96
Lapointe, Ron	Quebec	89	33	50	6	2		1987-89
Laviolette, Peter	NY Islanders	164	77	62	25	2		
	Carolina	323	167	122	34	6	1	
	Philadelphia	57	28	24	5	1		
	Totals	544	272	208	64	9	1	2001-10
Laycoe, Hal	Los Angeles	24	5	18	1	1		
	Vancouver	156	44	96	16	2		
	Totals	180	49	114	17	3		1969-72
Lehman, Hugh	Chicago	21	3	17	1	1		1927-28
Lemaire, Jacques	Montreal	97	48	37	12	2		
	New Jersey	460	247	149	64	6	1	
	Minnesota	656	293	255	108	9		
	Totals	1213	588	441	184	17	1	1983-10
Lepine, Pit	Montreal	48	10	33	5	1		1939-40
LeSueur, Percy	Hamilton	10	3	7	0	1		1923-24
Lewis, Dave	Detroit *	169	100	42	27	4		
	Boston	82	35	41	6	1		
	Totals	251	135	83	33	5		1998-07

* Shared a record of 4-1-0 with co-coach Barry Smith in 1998-99

Coach	Team	Games Coached	Wins	Losses	O/T	Years	Cup Wins	Career
Ley, Rick	Hartford	160	69	71	20	2		
	Vancouver	124	47	50	27	2		
	Totals	284	116	121	47	4		1989-96
Lindsay, Ted	Detroit	29	5	21	3	2		1979-81
Long, Barry	Winnipeg	205	87	93	25	3		1983-86
Loughlin, Clem	Chicago	144	61	63	20	3		1934-37
Low, Ron	Edmonton	341	139	162	40	5		
	NY Rangers	164	69	81	14	2		
	Totals	505	208	243	54	7		1994-02
Lowe, Kevin	Edmonton	82	32	26	24	1		1999-00
Ludzik, Steve	Tampa Bay	121	31	67	23	2		1999-01
MacDonald, Parker	Minnesota	61	20	30	11	1		
	Los Angeles	42	13	24	5	1		
	Totals	103	33	54	16	2		1973-82
MacLean, Doug	Florida	187	83	71	33	3		
	Columbus	79	24	43	12	2		
	Totals	266	107	114	45	5		1995-04
MacMillan, Bill	Colorado	80	22	45	13	1		
	New Jersey	100	19	67	14	2		
	Totals	180	41	112	27	3		1980-84
MacNeil, Al	Montreal	55	31	15	9	1	1	
	Atlanta	80	35	32	13	1		
	Calgary	171	72	66	33	3		
	Totals	306	138	113	55	5	1	1970-03
MacTavish, Craig	Edmonton	656	301	252	103	9		2000-09
Magnuson, Keith	Chicago	132	49	57	26	2		1980-82
Mahoney, Bill	Minnesota	93	42	39	12	2		1983-85
Maloney, Dan	Toronto	160	45	100	15	2		
	Winnipeg	212	91	93	28	3		
	Totals	372	136	193	43	5		1984-89
Maloney, Phil	Vancouver	232	95	105	32	4		1973-77
Mantha, Sylvio	Montreal	48	11	26	11	1		1935-36
Marshall, Bert	Colorado	24	3	17	4	1		1981-8

Coach	Team	Games Coached	Wins	Losses	O/T	Years	Cup Wins	Career
Martin, Jacques	St. Louis	160	66	71	23	2		
	Ottawa	692	341	235	116	9		
	Florida	246	110	100	36	4		
	Montreal	82	39	33	10	1		
	Totals	1180	556	439	185	16		1986-10
Matheson, Godfrey	Chicago	2	0	2	0	1		1932-33
Maurice, Paul	Hartford	152	61	72	19	2		
	Carolina	661	275	275	111	9		
	Toronto	164	76	66	22	2		
	Totals	977	412	413	152	13		1995-10
Maxner, Wayne	Detroit	129	34	68	27	2		1980-82
McCammon, Bob	Philadelphia	218	119	68	31	4		
	Vancouver	294	102	156	36	4		
	Totals	512	221	224	67	8		1978-91
McCreary, Bill	St. Louis	24	6	14	4	1		
	Vancouver	41	9	25	7	1		
	California	32	8	20	4	1		
	Totals	97	23	59	15	3		1971-75
McGuire, Pierre	Hartford	67	23	37	7	1		1993-94
McLellan, John	Toronto	310	126	139	45	4		1969-73
McLellan, Todd	San Jose	164	104	38	22	2		2008-10
McVie, Tom	Washington	204	49	122	33	3		
	Winnipeg	105	20	67	18	2		
	New Jersey	153	57	74	22	3		
	Totals	462	126	263	73	8		1975-92
Meeker, Howie	Toronto	70	21	34	15	1		1956-57
Melrose, Barry	Los Angeles	209	79	101	29	3		
	Tampa Bay	16	5	7	4	1		
	Totals	225	84	108	33	4		1992-09
Milbury, Mike	Boston	160	90	49	21	2		
	NY Islanders	191	56	111	24	4		
	Totals	351	146	160	45	6		1989-99
Molleken, Lorne	Chicago	47	18	19	10	2		1998-00
Muckler, John	Minnesota	35	6	23	6	1		
	Edmonton	160	75	65	20	2	1	
	Buffalo	268	125	109	34	4		
	NY Rangers	185	70	88	27	3		
	Totals	648	276	285	87	10	1	1968-00
Muldoon, Pete	Chicago	44	19	22	3	1		1926-27
Munro, Dunc	Mtl. Maroons	76	37	29	10	2		1929-31
Murdoch, Bob	Chicago	80	30	41	9	1		
	Winnipeg	160	63	75	22	2		
	Totals	240	93	116	31	3		1987-91
Murphy, Mike	Los Angeles	65	20	37	8	2		
	Toronto	164	60	87	17	2		
	Totals	229	80	124	25	4		1986-98
Murray, Andy	Los Angeles	480	215	176	89	7		
	St. Louis	258	118	102	38	4		
	Totals	738	333	278	127	11		1999-10
Murray, Bryan	Washington	672	343	246	83	9		
	Detroit	244	124	91	29	3		
	Florida	59	17	31	11	1		
	Anaheim	82	29	42	11	1		
	Ottawa	182	107	55	20	4		
	Totals	1239	620	465	154	18		1981-08
Murray, Terry	Washington	325	163	134	28	5		
	Philadelphia	212	118	64	30	3		
	Florida	200	79	79	42	3		
	Los Angeles	164	80	64	20	2		
	Totals	901	440	341	120	13		1989-10
Nanne, Lou	Minnesota	29	7	18	4	1		1977-78
Neale, Harry	Vancouver	407	142	189	76	6		
	Detroit	35	8	23	4	1		
	Totals	442	150	212	80	7		1978-86
Neilson, Roger	Toronto	160	75	62	23	2		
	Buffalo	80	39	20	21	1		
	Vancouver	133	51	61	21	3		
	Los Angeles	28	8	17	3	1		
	NY Rangers	280	141	104	35	4		
	Florida	132	53	56	23	2		
	Philadelphia	185	92	57	36	3		
	Ottawa	2	1	1	0	1		
	Totals	1000	460	378	162	16		1977-02
Noel, Claude	Columbus	24	10	8	6	1		2009-10
Nolan, Ted	Buffalo	164	73	72	19	2		
	NY Islanders	163	74	68	21	2		
	Totals	327	147	140	40	4		1995-08
Nykoluk, Mike	Toronto	280	89	144	47	4		1980-84
O'Connell, Mike	Boston	9	3	3	3	1		2002-03
O'Donoghue, George	Toronto	29	15	13	1	2	1	1921-23
Olczyk, Ed	Pittsburgh	113	31	64	18	3		2003-06
Oliver, Murray	Minnesota	37	18	12	7	1		1982-83
Olmstead, Bert	Oakland	64	11	37	16	1		1967-68
O'Reilly, Terry	Oakland	227	115	86	26	3		1986-89
Paddock, John	Winnipeg	281	106	138	37	4		
	Ottawa	64	36	22	6	1		
	Totals	345	142	160	43	5		1991-08
Page, Pierre	Minnesota	160	63	77	20	2		
	Quebec	230	98	103	29	3		
	Calgary	164	66	78	20	2		
	Anaheim	82	26	43	13	1		
	Totals	636	253	301	82	8		1988-98
Park, Brad	Detroit	45	9	34	2	1		1985-86
Paterson, Rick	Tampa Bay	6	0	6	0	1		1997-98
Patrick, Craig	NY Rangers	95	37	45	13	2		
	Pittsburgh	74	29	36	9	2		
	Totals	169	66	81	22	4		1980-97
Patrick, Frank	Boston	96	48	36	12	2		1934-36
Patrick, Lester	NY Rangers	604	281	216	107	13	2	1926-39
Patrick, Lynn	NY Rangers	107	40	51	16	2		
	NY Rangers	310	117	130	63	5		
	St. Louis	26	8	15	3	3		
	Totals	443	165	196	82	10		1948-76
Patrick, Muzz	NY Rangers	136	43	66	27	4		1953-63
Payne, Davis	St. Louis	42	23	15	4	1		2009-10
Perron, Jean	Montreal	240	126	84	30	3	1	
	Quebec	47	16	26	5	1		
	Totals	287	142	110	35	4	1	1985-89
Perry, Don	Los Angeles	168	52	85	31	3		1981-84
Pike, Alf	NY Rangers	123	36	66	21	2		1959-61
Pilous, Rudy	Chicago	387	162	151	74	6	1	1957-63
Plager, Barclay	St. Louis	178	49	96	33	4		1977-83
Plager, Bob	St. Louis	11	4	6	1	1		1992-93
Playfair, Jim	Calgary	82	43	29	10	1		2006-07
Pleau, Larry	Hartford	224	81	117	26	5		1980-89
Polano, Nick	Detroit	240	79	127	34	3		1982-85
Popein, Larry	NY Rangers	41	18	14	9	1		1973-74
Powers, Eddie	Toronto	66	31	32	3	2		1924-26
Primeau, Joe	Toronto	210	97	71	42	3	1	1950-53
Pronovost, Marcel	Buffalo	104	52	29	23	2		1977-79
Pulford, Bob	Los Angeles	396	178	150	68	5		
	Chicago	433	185	180	68	7		
	Totals	829	363	330	136	12		1972-00
Quenneville, Joel	St. Louis	593	307	191	95	8		
	Colorado	246	131	92	23	4		
	Chicago	160	97	44	19	2	1	
	Totals	999	535	327	137	14	1	1996-10
Querrie, Charles	Toronto	72	29	38	5	3		1922-27
Quinn, Mike	Quebec	24	4	20	0	1		1919-20
Quinn, Pat	Philadelphia	262	141	73	48	4		
	Los Angeles	202	75	101	26	3		
	Vancouver	280	141	111	28	5		
	Toronto	574	300	196	78	8		
	Edmonton	82	27	47	8	1		
	Totals	1400	684	528	188	21		1978-10
Raeder, Cap	San Jose	1	1	0	0	1		2002-03
Ramsay, Craig	Buffalo	21	4	15	2	1		
	Philadelphia	28	12	12	4	1		
	Totals	49	16	27	6	2		1986-01
Randall, Ken	Hamilton	14	6	8	0	1		1923-24
Reay, Billy	Toronto	90	26	50	14	2		
	Chicago	1012	516	335	161	14		
	Totals	1102	542	385	175	16		1957-77
Regan, Larry	Los Angeles	88	27	47	14	2		1970-72
Renney, Tom	Vancouver	101	39	53	9	2		
	NY Rangers	327	164	117	46	6		
	Totals	428	203	170	55	8		1996-09
Richards, Todd	Minnesota	82	38	36	8	1		2009-10
Risebrough, Doug	Calgary	144	71	56	17	2		1990-92
Roberts, Jim	Buffalo	45	21	16	8	1		
	Hartford	80	26	41	13	1		
	St. Louis	9	3	3	3	1		
	Totals	134	50	60	24	3		1981-97
Robinson, Larry	Los Angeles	328	122	161	45	4		
	New Jersey	173	87	56	30	4	1	
	Totals	501	209	217	75	8	1	1995-06
Rodden, Mike	Toronto	2	0	2	0	1		1926-27
Romeril, Alex	Toronto	13	7	5	1	1		1926-27
Ross, Art	Mtl. Wanderers	6	1	5	0	1		
	Hamilton	24	6	18	0	1		
	Boston	728	361	277	90	16	1	
	Totals	758	368	300	90	18	1	1917-45
Ruel, Claude	Montreal	305	172	82	51	5	1	1968-81
Ruff, Lindy	Buffalo	984	483	361	140	13		1997-10
Sacco, Joe	Colorado	82	43	30	9	1		2009-10
Sather, Glen	Colorado	842	464	268	110	11	4	
	NY Rangers	90	33	39	18	2		
	Totals	932	497	307	128	13	4	1979-04
Sator, Ted	NY Rangers	99	41	48	10	2		
	Buffalo	207	96	89	22	3		
	Totals	306	137	137	32	4		1985-89
Savard, Andre	Quebec	24	10	13	1	1		1987-88
Savard, Denis	Chicago	147	65	66	16	3		2006-09
Schinkel, Ken	Pittsburgh	203	83	92	28	4		1972-77
Schmidt, Milt	Boston	726	245	360	121	11		
	Washington	44	5	34	5	2		
	Totals	770	250	394	126	13		1954-76
Schoenfeld, Jim	Buffalo	43	19	19	5	1		
	New Jersey	124	50	59	15	3		
	Washington	249	113	102	34	4		
	Phoenix	164	74	66	24	2		
	Totals	580	256	246	78	10		1985-99
Shaughnessy, Tom	Chicago	21	10	8	3	1		1929-30
Shaw, Brad	NY Islanders	40	18	18	4	1		2005-06
Shero, Fred	Philadelphia	554	308	151	95	7	2	
	NY Rangers	180	82	74	24	3		
	Totals	734	390	225	119	10	2	1971-81
Simpson, Joe	NY Americans	144	42	72	30	3		1932-35

Coach	Team	Games Coached	Wins	Losses	O/T	Years	Cup Wins	Career
Simpson, Terry	NY Islanders	187	81	82	24	3		
	Philadelphia	84	35	39	10	1		
	Winnipeg	97	43	47	7	2		
	Totals	368	159	168	41	6		1986-96
Sims, Al	San Jose	82	27	47	8	1		1996-97
Sinden, Harry	Boston	327	153	116	58	6	1	1966-85
Skinner, Jimmy	Detroit	247	123	78	46	4	1	1954-58
Smeaton, Cooper	Philadelphia	44	4	36	4	1		1930-31
Smith, Alf	Ottawa	18	12	6	0	1		1918-19
Smith, Barry	Detroit *	5	4	1	0	1		1998-99
	Results Shared with co-coach Dave Lewis							
Smith, Floyd	Buffalo	241	143	62	36	4		
	Toronto	68	30	33	5	1		
	Totals	309	173	95	41	5		1971-80
Smith, Mike	Winnipeg	23	2	17	4	1		1980-81
Smith, Ron	NY Rangers	44	15	22	7	1		1992-93
Smythe, Conn	Toronto	134	57	57	20	4		1927-31
Sonmor, Glen	Minnesota	421	177	161	83	7		1978-87
Sproule, Harvey	Toronto	12	7	5	0	1		1919-20
Stanley, Barney	Chicago	23	4	17	2	1		1927-28
Stasiuk, Vic	Philadelphia	154	45	68	41	2		
	California	75	21	38	16	1		
	Vancouver	78	22	47	9	1		
	Totals	307	88	153	66	4		1969-73
Stevens, John	Philadelphia	263	120	109	34	4		2006-10
Stewart, Bill	NY Islanders	37	11	19	7	1		1998-99
Stewart, Bill	Chicago	69	22	35	12	2	1	1937-39
Stewart, Ron	NY Rangers	39	15	20	4	1		
	Los Angeles	80	31	34	15	1		
	Totals	119	46	54	19	2		1975-78
Stirling, Steve	NY Islanders	124	56	51	17	3		2003-06
Suhonen, Alpo	Chicago	82	29	41	12	1		2000-01
Sullivan, Mike	Boston	164	70	56	38	3		2003-06
Sullivan, Red	NY Rangers	196	58	103	35	4		
	Pittsburgh	150	47	79	24	2		
	Washington	18	2	16	0	1		
	Totals	364	107	198	59	7		1962-75
Sutherland, Bill	Winnipeg	32	7	22	3	2		1979-81
Sutter, Brent	New Jersey	164	97	56	11	2		
	Calgary	82	40	32	10	1		
	Totals	246	137	88	21	3		2007-10
Sutter, Brian	St. Louis	320	153	124	43	4		
	Boston	216	120	73	23	3		
	Calgary	246	87	117	42	3		
	Chicago	246	91	103	52	4		
	Totals	1028	451	417	160	14		1988-05
Sutter, Darryl	Chicago	216	110	80	26	3		
	San Jose	434	192	167	75	6		
	Calgary	210	107	73	30	4		
	Totals	860	409	320	131	12		1992-06
Sutter, Duane	Florida	72	22	35	15	2		2000-02
Talbot, Jean-Guy	St. Louis	120	52	53	15	2		
	NY Rangers	80	30	37	13	1		
	Totals	200	82	90	28	3		1972-78
Tessier, Orval	Chicago	213	99	93	21	3		1982-85
Therrien, Michel	Montreal	190	77	77	36	3		
	Pittsburgh	272	135	105	32	4		
	Totals	462	212	182	68	7		2000-09
Thompson, Paul	Chicago	272	104	127	41	7		1938-45
Thompson, Percy	Hamilton	48	13	35	0	2		1920-22
Tippett, Dave	Dallas	492	271	156	65	7		
	Phoenix	82	50	25	7	1		
	Totals	574	321	181	72	8		2002-10
Tobin, Bill	Chicago	71	29	29	13	2		1929-32
Tocchet, Rick	Tampa Bay	148	53	69	26	2		2008-10
Torchetti, John	Florida	27	10	12	5	1		
	Los Angeles	12	5	7	0	1		
	Totals	39	15	19	5	2		2003-06
Tortorella, John	NY Rangers	107	50	43	14	3		
	Tampa Bay	535	239	222	74	8	1	
	Totals	642	289	265	88	11	1	1999-10
Tremblay, Mario	Montreal	159	71	63	25	2		1995-97
Trottier, Bryan	NY Rangers	54	21	26	7	1		2002-03
Trotz, Barry	Nashville	902	411	371	120	12		1998-10
Ubriaco, Gene	Pittsburgh	106	50	47	9	2		1988-90
Vachon, Rogie	Los Angeles	10	4	3	3	3		1983-95
Vigneault, Alain	Montreal	266	109	118	39	4		
	Vancouver	328	182	114	32	4		
	Totals	594	291	232	71	8		1997-10
Waddell, Don	Atlanta	86	38	39	9	2		2002-08
Watson, Bryan	Edmonton	18	4	9	5	1		1980-81
Watson, Phil	NY Rangers	295	119	124	52	5		
	Boston	84	16	55	13	2		
	Totals	379	135	179	65	7		1955-63
Watt, Tom	Winnipeg	181	72	85	24	3		
	Vancouver	160	52	87	21	2		
	Toronto	149	52	80	17	2		
	Totals	490	176	252	62	7		1981-92
Webster, Tom	NY Rangers	18	5	9	4	1		
	Los Angeles	240	115	94	31	3		
	Totals	258	120	103	35	4		1986-92
Weiland, Cooney	Boston	96	58	20	18	2	1	1939-41
White, Bill	Chicago	46	16	24	6	1		1976-77
Wiley, Jim	San Jose	57	17	37	3	1		1995-96
Wilson, Johnny	Los Angeles	52	9	34	9	1		
	Detroit	145	67	56	22	2		
	Colorado	80	20	46	14	1		
	Pittsburgh	240	91	105	44	3		
	Totals	517	187	241	89	7		1969-80
Wilson, Larry	Detroit	36	3	29	4	1		1976-77
Wilson, Rick	Dallas	32	13	11	8	1		2001-02
Wilson, Ron	Anaheim	296	120	145	31	4		
	Washington	410	192	159	59	5		
	San Jose	385	206	122	57	6		
	Toronto	164	64	73	27	2		
	Totals	1255	582	499	174	17		1993-10
Yawney, Trent	Chicago	103	33	55	15	2		2005-07
Young, Garry	California	12	2	7	3	1		
	St. Louis	98	41	41	16	2		
	Totals	110	43	48	19	3		1972-76

Dave Tippett (left) joined the Phoenix Coyotes shortly before the start of the 2009-10 season. He led the team to a club-record 50 wins and 107 points and won the Jack Adams Award as coach of the year. Barry Trotz (center) was a first-time finalist for the Jack Adams Award after 12 years with the Nashville Predators. Joe Sacco (right) finished third in the voting after his first season as an NHL coach with the Colorado Avalanche in 2009-10.

Year-by-Year Individual Regular-Season Leaders

Season	Goals	G	Assists	A	Points	Pts.	Penalty Minutes	PIM
1917-18	Joe Malone	44	Cy Denneny, Reg Noble, Harry Cameron	10	Joe Malone	48	Joe Hall	100
1918-19	Newsy Lalonde	22	Newsy Lalonde	10	Newsy Lalonde	32	Joe Hall	135
1919-20	Joe Malone	39	Frank Nighbor	15	Joe Malone	49	Cully Wilson	86
1920-21	Babe Dye	35	Jack Darragh	15	Newsy Lalonde	43	Bert Corbeau	86
1921-22	Punch Broadbent	32	Harry Cameron	17	Punch Broadbent	46	Sprague Cleghorn	63
1922-23	Babe Dye	26	Eddie Gerard	13	Babe Dye	37	Georges Boucher	58
1923-24	Cy Denneny	22	Georges Boucher	10	Cy Denneny	24	Reg Noble	79
1924-25	Babe Dye	38	Cy Denneny, Red Green	15	Babe Dye	46	Georges Boucher	95
1925-26	Nels Stewart	34	Frank Nighbor	13	Nels Stewart	42	Bert Corbeau	121
1926-27	Bill Cook	33	Dick Irvin	18	Bill Cook	37	Nels Stewart	133
1927-28	Howie Morenz	33	Howie Morenz	18	Howie Morenz	51	Eddie Shore	165
1928-29	Ace Bailey	22	Frank Boucher	16	Ace Bailey	32	Red Dutton	139
1929-30	Cooney Weiland	43	Frank Boucher	36	Cooney Weiland	73	Joe Lamb	119
1930-31	Charlie Conacher	31	Joe Primeau	32	Howie Morenz	51	Harvey Rockburn	118
1931-32	Charlie Conacher, Bill Cook	34	Joe Primeau	37	Busher Jackson	53	Red Dutton	107
1932-33	Bill Cook	28	Frank Boucher	28	Bill Cook	50	Red Horner	144
1933-34	Charlie Conacher	32	Joe Primeau	32	Charlie Conacher	52	Red Horner	126 *
1934-35	Charlie Conacher	36	Art Chapman	34	Charlie Conacher	57	Red Horner	125
1935-36	Charlie Conacher, Bill Thoms	23	Art Chapman	28	Sweeney Schriner	45	Red Horner	167
1936-37	Larry Aurie, Nels Stewart	23	Syl Apps	29	Sweeney Schriner	46	Red Horner	124
1937-38	Gordie Drillon	26	Syl Apps	29	Gordie Drillon	52	Art Coulter	90
1938-39	Roy Conacher	26	Bill Cowley	34	Toe Blake	47	Red Horner	85
1939-40	Bryan Hextall	24	Milt Schmidt	30	Milt Schmidt	52	Red Horner	87
1940-41	Bryan Hextall	26	Bill Cowley	45	Bill Cowley	62	Jimmy Orlando	99
1941-42	Lynn Patrick	32	Phil Watson	37	Bryan Hextall	56	Pat Egan	124
1942-43	Doug Bentley	33	Bill Cowley	45	Doug Bentley	73	Jimmy Orlando	89 *
1943-44	Doug Bentley	38	Clint Smith	49	Herb Cain	82	Mike McMahon	98
1944-45	Maurice Richard	50	Elmer Lach	54	Elmer Lach	80	Pat Egan	86
1945-46	Gaye Stewart	37	Elmer Lach	34	Max Bentley	61	Jack Stewart	73
1946-47	Maurice Richard	45	Billy Taylor	46	Max Bentley	72	Gus Mortson	133
1947-48	Ted Lindsay	33	Doug Bentley	37	Elmer Lach	61	Bill Barilko	147
1948-49	Sid Abel	28	Doug Bentley	43	Roy Conacher	68	Bill Ezinicki	145
1949-50	Maurice Richard	43	Ted Lindsay	55	Ted Lindsay	78	Bill Ezinicki	144
1950-51	Gordie Howe	43	Gordie Howe, Ted Kennedy	43	Gordie Howe	86	Gus Mortson	142
1951-52	Gordie Howe	47	Elmer Lach	50	Gordie Howe	86	Gus Kyle	127
1952-53	Gordie Howe	49	Gordie Howe	46	Gordie Howe	95	Maurice Richard	112
1953-54	Maurice Richard	37	Gordie Howe	48	Gordie Howe	81	Gus Mortson	132
1954-55	Maurice Richard, Bernie Geoffrion	38	Bert Olmstead	48	Bernie Geoffrion	75	Fern Flaman	150
1955-56	Jean Beliveau	47	Bert Olmstead	56	Jean Beliveau	88	Lou Fontinato	202
1956-57	Gordie Howe	44	Ted Lindsay	55	Gordie Howe	89	Gus Mortson	147
1957-58	Dickie Moore	36	Henri Richard	52	Dickie Moore	84	Lou Fontinato	152
1958-59	Jean Beliveau	45	Dickie Moore	55	Dickie Moore	96	Ted Lindsay	184
1959-60	Bobby Hull, Bronco Horvath	39	Don McKenney	49	Bobby Hull	81	Carl Brewer	150
1960-61	Bernie Geoffrion	50	Jean Beliveau	58	Bernie Geoffrion	95	Pierre Pilote	165
1961-62	Bobby Hull	50	Andy Bathgate	56	Bobby Hull, Andy Bathgate	84	Lou Fontinato	167
1962-63	Gordie Howe	38	Henri Richard	50	Gordie Howe	86	Howie Young	273
1963-64	Bobby Hull	43	Andy Bathgate	58	Stan Mikita	89	Vic Hadfield	151
1964-65	Norm Ullman	42	Stan Mikita	59	Stan Mikita	87	Carl Brewer	177
1965-66	Bobby Hull	54	Stan Mikita, Bobby Rousseau, Jean Beliveau	48	Bobby Hull	97	Reggie Fleming	166
1966-67	Bobby Hull	52	Stan Mikita	62	Stan Mikita	97	John Ferguson	177
1967-68	Bobby Hull	44	Phil Esposito	49	Stan Mikita	87	Barclay Plager	153
1968-69	Bobby Hull	58	Phil Esposito	77	Phil Esposito	126	Forbes Kennedy	219
1969-70	Phil Esposito	43	Bobby Orr	87	Bobby Orr	120	Keith Magnuson	213
1970-71	Phil Esposito	76	Bobby Orr	102	Phil Esposito	152	Keith Magnuson	291
1971-72	Phil Esposito	66	Bobby Orr	80	Phil Esposito	133	Bryan Watson	212
1972-73	Phil Esposito	55	Phil Esposito	75	Phil Esposito	130	Dave Schultz	259
1973-74	Phil Esposito	68	Bobby Orr	90	Phil Esposito	145	Dave Schultz	348
1974-75	Phil Esposito	61	Bobby Orr, Bobby Clarke	89	Bobby Orr	135	Dave Schultz	472
1975-76	Reggie Leach	61	Bobby Clarke	89	Guy Lafleur	125	Steve Durbano	370
1976-77	Steve Shutt	60	Guy Lafleur	80	Guy Lafleur	136	Tiger Williams	338
1977-78	Guy Lafleur	60	Bryan Trottier	77	Guy Lafleur	132	Dave Schultz	405
1978-79	Mike Bossy	69	Bryan Trottier	87	Bryan Trottier	134	Tiger Williams	298
1979-80	Charlie Simmer, Danny Gare, Blaine Stoughton	56	Wayne Gretzky	86	Marcel Dionne, Wayne Gretzky	137	Jimmy Mann	287
1980-81	Mike Bossy	68	Wayne Gretzky	109	Wayne Gretzky	164	Tiger Williams	343
1981-82	Wayne Gretzky	92	Wayne Gretzky	120	Wayne Gretzky	212	Paul Baxter	409
1982-83	Wayne Gretzky	71	Wayne Gretzky	125	Wayne Gretzky	196	Randy Holt	275
1983-84	Wayne Gretzky	87	Wayne Gretzky	118	Wayne Gretzky	205	Chris Nilan	338
1984-85	Wayne Gretzky	73	Wayne Gretzky	135	Wayne Gretzky	208	Chris Nilan	358
1985-86	Jari Kurri	68	Wayne Gretzky	163	Wayne Gretzky	215	Joe Kocur	377
1986-87	Wayne Gretzky	62	Wayne Gretzky	121	Wayne Gretzky	183	Tim Hunter	361
1987-88	Mario Lemieux	70	Wayne Gretzky	109	Mario Lemieux	168	Bob Probert	398
1988-89	Mario Lemieux	85	Mario Lemieux, Wayne Gretzky	114	Mario Lemieux	199	Tim Hunter	375
1989-90	Brett Hull	72	Wayne Gretzky	102	Wayne Gretzky	142	Basil McRae	351
1990-91	Brett Hull	86	Wayne Gretzky	122	Wayne Gretzky	163	Rob Ray	350
1991-92	Brett Hull	70	Wayne Gretzky	90	Mario Lemieux	131	Mike Peluso	408
1992-93	Teemu Selanne, Alexander Mogilny	76	Adam Oates	97	Mario Lemieux	160	Marty McSorley	399
1993-94	Pavel Bure	60	Wayne Gretzky	92	Wayne Gretzky	130	Tie Domi	347
1994-95	Peter Bondra	34	Ron Francis	48	Jaromir Jagr, Eric Lindros	70	Enrico Ciccone	225
1995-96	Mario Lemieux	69	Mario Lemieux, Ron Francis	92	Mario Lemieux	161	Matthew Barnaby	335
1996-97	Keith Tkachuk	52	Mario Lemieux, Wayne Gretzky	72	Mario Lemieux	122	Gino Odjick	371
1997-98	Teemu Selanne, Peter Bondra	52	Jaromir Jagr, Wayne Gretzky	67	Jaromir Jagr	102	Donald Brashear	372
1998-99	Teemu Selanne	47	Jaromir Jagr	83	Jaromir Jagr	127	Rob Ray	261
99-2000	Pavel Bure	58	Mark Recchi	63	Jaromir Jagr	96	Denny Lambert	219
2000-01	Pavel Bure	59	Jaromir Jagr, Adam Oates	69	Jaromir Jagr	121	Matthew Barnaby	265
2001-02	Jarome Iginla	52	Adam Oates	64	Jarome Iginla	96	Peter Worrell	354
2002-03	Milan Hejduk	50	Peter Forsberg	77	Peter Forsberg	106	Jody Shelley	249
2003-04	Rick Nash, Jarome Iginla, Ilya Kovalchuk	41	Scott Gomez, Martin St. Louis	56	Martin St. Louis	94	Sean Avery	261
2004-05	....	....	....	....	....	....	....	....
2005-06	Jonathan Cheechoo	56	Joe Thornton	96	Joe Thornton	125	Sean Avery	257
2006-07	Vincent Lecavalier	52	Joe Thornton	92	Sidney Crosby	120	Ben Eager	233
2007-08	Alex Ovechkin	65	Joe Thornton	67	Alex Ovechkin	112	Daniel Carcillo	324
2008-09	Alex Ovechkin	56	Evgeni Malkin	78	Evgeni Malkin	113	Daniel Carcillo	254
2009-10	Sidney Crosby, Steven Stamkos	51	Henrik Sedin	83	Henrik Sedin	112	Zenon Konopka	265

* Match Misconduct penalty not included in total penalty minutes.
1946-47 was the first season that a Match penalty was automatically written into the player's total penalty minutes as 20 minutes.
Beginning in 1947-48 all penalties, Match, Game Misconduct, and Misconduct, are written as 10 minutes.

One Season Scoring Records

Goals-Per-Game Leaders, One Season

(Among players with 20 goals or more in one season)

Player	Team	Season	Games	Goals	Goals per game average
Joe Malone	Montreal	1917-18	20	44	2.20
Cy Denneny	Ottawa	1917-18	20	36	1.80
Newsy Lalonde	Montreal	1917-18	14	23	1.64
Joe Malone	Quebec	1919-20	24	39	1.63
Newsy Lalonde	Montreal	1919-20	23	37	1.61
Reg Noble	Toronto	1917-18	20	30	1.50
Babe Dye	Ham., Tor.	1920-21	24	35	1.46
Cy Denneny	Ottawa	1920-21	24	34	1.42
Joe Malone	Hamilton	1920-21	20	28	1.40
Newsy Lalonde	Montreal	1920-21	24	33	1.38
Punch Broadbent	Ottawa	1921-22	24	32	1.33
Babe Dye	Toronto	1924-25	29	38	1.31
Babe Dye	Toronto	1921-22	24	31	1.29
Newsy Lalonde	Montreal	1918-19	17	22	1.29
Odie Cleghorn	Montreal	1918-19	17	22	1.29
Cy Denneny	Ottawa	1921-22	22	27	1.23
Aurel Joliat	Montreal	1924-25	25	30	1.20
Wayne Gretzky	Edmonton	1983-84	74	87	1.18
Babe Dye	Toronto	1922-23	22	26	1.18
Wayne Gretzky	Edmonton	1981-82	80	92	1.15
Mario Lemieux	Pittsburgh	1992-93	60	69	1.15
Frank Nighbor	Ottawa	1919-20	23	26	1.13
Mario Lemieux	Pittsburgh	1988-89	76	85	1.12
Brett Hull	St. Louis	1990-91	78	86	1.10
Cam Neely	Boston	1993-94	49	50	1.02
Maurice Richard	Montreal	1944-45	50	50	1.00
Reg Noble	Toronto	1919-20	24	24	1.00
Corb Denneny	Toronto	1919-20	24	24	1.00
Joe Malone	Hamilton	1921-22	24	24	1.00
Billy Boucher	Montreal	1922-23	24	24	1.00
Cy Denneny	Ottawa	1923-24	22	22	1.00
Alexander Mogilny	Buffalo	1992-93	77	76	0.99
Mario Lemieux	Pittsburgh	1995-96	70	69	0.99
Cooney Weiland	Boston	1929-30	44	43	0.98
Phil Esposito	Boston	1970-71	78	76	0.97
Jari Kurri	Edmonton	1984-85	73	71	0.97

Bobby Clarke collected 89 assists in 80 games (1.11 per game) in 1974-75 and in 76 games (1.17) in 1975-76. At the time, only Bobby Orr had ever had more assists in a single season.

Assists-Per-Game Leaders, One Season

(Among players with 35 assists or more in one season)

Player	Team	Season	Games	Assists	Assists per game average
Wayne Gretzky	Edmonton	1985-86	80	163	2.04
Wayne Gretzky	Edmonton	1987-88	64	109	1.70
Wayne Gretzky	Edmonton	1984-85	80	135	1.69
Wayne Gretzky	Edmonton	1983-84	74	118	1.59
Wayne Gretzky	Edmonton	1982-83	80	125	1.56
Wayne Gretzky	Los Angeles	1990-91	78	122	1.56
Wayne Gretzky	Edmonton	1986-87	79	121	1.53
Mario Lemieux	Pittsburgh	1992-93	60	91	1.52
Wayne Gretzky	Edmonton	1981-82	80	120	1.50
Mario Lemieux	Pittsburgh	1988-89	76	114	1.50
Adam Oates	St. Louis	1990-91	61	90	1.48
Wayne Gretzky	Los Angeles	1988-89	78	114	1.46
Wayne Gretzky	Los Angeles	1989-90	73	102	1.40
Wayne Gretzky	Edmonton	1980-81	80	109	1.36
Mario Lemieux	Pittsburgh	1991-92	64	87	1.36
Mario Lemieux	Pittsburgh	1989-90	59	78	1.32
Bobby Orr	Boston	1970-71	78	102	1.31
Mario Lemieux	Pittsburgh	1995-96	70	92	1.31
Mario Lemieux	Pittsburgh	1987-88	77	98	1.27
Bobby Orr	Boston	1973-74	74	90	1.22
Wayne Gretzky	Los Angeles	1991-92	74	90	1.22
Joe Thornton	Bos., S.J.	2005-06	81	96	1.19
Ron Francis	Pittsburgh	1995-96	77	92	1.19
Mario Lemieux	Pittsburgh	1985-86	79	93	1.18
Bobby Clarke	Philadelphia	1975-76	76	89	1.17
Peter Stastny	Quebec	1981-82	80	93	1.16
Adam Oates	Boston	1992-93	84	97	1.15
Doug Gilmour	Toronto	1992-93	83	95	1.14
Wayne Gretzky	Los Angeles	1993-94	81	92	1.14
Paul Coffey	Edmonton	1985-86	79	90	1.14
Bobby Orr	Boston	1969-70	76	87	1.14
Bryan Trottier	NY Islanders	1978-79	76	87	1.14
Bobby Orr	Boston	1972-73	63	72	1.14
Bill Cowley	Boston	1943-44	36	41	1.14
Pat LaFontaine	Buffalo	1992-93	84	95	1.13
Steve Yzerman	Detroit	1988-89	80	90	1.13
Paul Coffey	Pittsburgh	1987-88	46	52	1.13
Joe Thornton	San Jose	2006-07	82	92	1.12
Bobby Orr	Boston	1974-75	80	89	1.11
Bobby Clarke	Philadelphia	1974-75	80	89	1.11
Paul Coffey	Pittsburgh	1988-89	75	83	1.11
Wayne Gretzky	Los Angeles	1992-93	45	49	1.11
Denis Savard	Chicago	1982-83	78	86	1.10
Denis Savard	Chicago	1981-82	80	87	1.09
Denis Savard	Chicago	1987-88	80	87	1.09
Wayne Gretzky	Edmonton	1979-80	79	86	1.09
Ron Francis	Pittsburgh	1994-95	44	48	1.09
Paul Coffey	Edmonton	1983-84	80	86	1.08
Elmer Lach	Montreal	1944-45	50	54	1.08
Peter Stastny	Quebec	1985-86	76	81	1.07
Jaromir Jagr	Pittsburgh	1995-96	82	87	1.06
Mark Messier	Edmonton	1989-90	79	84	1.06
Sidney Crosby	Pittsburgh	2006-07	79	84	1.06
Peter Forsberg	Colorado	1995-96	82	86	1.05
Paul Coffey	Edmonton	1984-85	80	84	1.05
Marcel Dionne	Los Angeles	1979-80	80	84	1.05
Bobby Orr	Boston	1971-72	76	80	1.05
Mike Bossy	NY Islanders	1981-82	80	83	1.04
Adam Oates	Boston	1993-94	77	80	1.04
Phil Esposito	Boston	1968-69	74	77	1.04
Bryan Trottier	NY Islanders	1983-84	68	71	1.04
Jason Spezza	Ottawa	2005-06	68	71	1.04
Pete Mahovlich	Montreal	1974-75	80	82	1.03
Kent Nilsson	Calgary	1980-81	80	82	1.03
Peter Stastny	Quebec	1982-83	75	77	1.03
Peter Forsberg	Colorado	2002-03	75	77	1.03
Denis Savard	Chicago	1988-89	58	59	1.02
Jaromir Jagr	Pittsburgh	1998-99	81	83	1.02
Doug Gilmour	Toronto	1993-94	83	84	1.01
Henrik Sedin	Vancouver	**2009-10**	82	83	1.01
Bernie Nicholls	Los Angeles	1988-89	79	80	1.01
Guy Lafleur	Montreal	1979-80	74	75	1.01
Guy Lafleur	Montreal	1976-77	80	80	1.00
Marcel Dionne	Los Angeles	1984-85	80	80	1.00
Brian Leetch	NY Rangers	1991-92	80	80	1.00
Bryan Trottier	NY Islanders	1977-78	77	77	1.00
Mike Bossy	NY Islanders	1983-84	67	67	1.00
Jean Ratelle	NY Rangers	1971-72	63	63	1.00
Steve Yzerman	Detroit	1993-94	58	58	1.00
Ron Francis	Hartford	1985-86	53	53	1.00
Guy Chouinard	Calgary	1980-81	52	52	1.00
Elmer Lach	Montreal	1943-44	48	48	1.00

Points-Per-Game Leaders, One Season

(Among players with 50 points or more in one season)

Player	Team	Season	Games	Points	Points per game average	Player	Team	Season	Games	Points	Points per game average
Wayne Gretzky	Edmonton	1983-84	74	205	2.77	Kent Nilsson	Calgary	1980-81	80	131	1.64
Wayne Gretzky	Edmonton	1985-86	80	215	2.69	Denis Savard	Chicago	1987-88	80	131	1.64
Mario Lemieux	Pittsburgh	1992-93	60	160	2.67	Wayne Gretzky	Los Angeles	1991-92	74	121	1.64
Wayne Gretzky	Edmonton	1981-82	80	212	2.65	Steve Yzerman	Detroit	1992-93	84	137	1.63
Mario Lemieux	Pittsburgh	1988-89	76	199	2.62	Marcel Dionne	Los Angeles	1978-79	80	130	1.63
Wayne Gretzky	Edmonton	1984-85	80	208	2.60	Dale Hawerchuk	Winnipeg	1984-85	80	130	1.63
Wayne Gretzky	Edmonton	1982-83	80	196	2.45	Mark Messier	Edmonton	1989-90	79	129	1.63
Wayne Gretzky	Edmonton	1987-88	64	149	2.33	Bryan Trottier	NY Islanders	1983-84	68	111	1.63
Wayne Gretzky	Edmonton	1986-87	79	183	2.32	Pat LaFontaine	Buffalo	1991-92	57	93	1.63
Mario Lemieux	Pittsburgh	1995-96	70	161	2.30	Charlie Simmer	Los Angeles	1980-81	65	105	1.62
Mario Lemieux	Pittsburgh	1987-88	77	168	2.18	Guy Lafleur	Montreal	1978-79	80	129	1.61
Wayne Gretzky	Los Angeles	1988-89	78	168	2.15	Bryan Trottier	NY Islanders	1981-82	80	129	1.61
Wayne Gretzky	Los Angeles	1990-91	78	163	2.09	Phil Esposito	Boston	1974-75	79	127	1.61
Mario Lemieux	Pittsburgh	1989-90	59	123	2.08	Steve Yzerman	Detroit	1989-90	79	127	1.61
Wayne Gretzky	Edmonton	1980-81	80	164	2.05	Peter Stastny	Quebec	1985-86	76	122	1.61
Mario Lemieux	Pittsburgh	1991-92	64	131	2.05	Mario Lemieux	Pittsburgh	1996-97	76	122	1.61
Bill Cowley	Boston	1943-44	36	71	1.97	Michel Goulet	Quebec	1983-84	75	121	1.61
Phil Esposito	Boston	1970-71	78	152	1.95	Wayne Gretzky	Los Angeles	1993-94	81	130	1.60
Wayne Gretzky	Los Angeles	1989-90	73	142	1.95	Bryan Trottier	NY Islanders	1977-78	77	123	1.60
Steve Yzerman	Detroit	1988-89	80	155	1.94	Bobby Orr	Boston	1972-73	63	101	1.60
Bernie Nicholls	Los Angeles	1988-89	79	150	1.90	Guy Chouinard	Calgary	1980-81	52	83	1.60
Adam Oates	St. Louis	1990-91	61	115	1.89	Elmer Lach	Montreal	1944-45	50	80	1.60
Phil Esposito	Boston	1973-74	78	145	1.86	Pierre Turgeon	NY Islanders	1992-93	83	132	1.59
Jari Kurri	Edmonton	1984-85	73	135	1.85	Steve Yzerman	Detroit	1987-88	64	102	1.59
Mike Bossy	NY Islanders	1981-82	80	147	1.84	Mike Bossy	NY Islanders	1978-79	80	126	1.58
Jaromir Jagr	Pittsburgh	1995-96	82	149	1.82	Paul Coffey	Edmonton	1983-84	80	126	1.58
Mario Lemieux	Pittsburgh	1985-86	79	141	1.78	Marcel Dionne	Los Angeles	1984-85	80	126	1.58
Bobby Orr	Boston	1970-71	78	139	1.78	Bobby Orr	Boston	1969-70	76	120	1.58
Jari Kurri	Edmonton	1983-84	64	113	1.77	Eric Lindros	Philadelphia	1995-96	73	115	1.58
Mario Lemieux	Pittsburgh	2000-01	43	76	1.77	Charlie Simmer	Los Angeles	1979-80	64	101	1.58
Pat LaFontaine	Buffalo	1992-93	84	148	1.76	Teemu Selanne	Winnipeg	1992-93	84	132	1.57
Bryan Trottier	NY Islanders	1978-79	76	134	1.76	Jaromir Jagr	Pittsburgh	1998-99	81	127	1.57
Mike Bossy	NY Islanders	1983-84	67	118	1.76	Bobby Clarke	Philadelphia	1975-76	76	119	1.57
Paul Coffey	Edmonton	1985-86	79	138	1.75	Guy Lafleur	Montreal	1975-76	80	125	1.56
Phil Esposito	Boston	1971-72	76	133	1.75	Dave Taylor	Los Angeles	1980-81	72	112	1.56
Peter Stastny	Quebec	1981-82	80	139	1.74	Denis Savard	Chicago	1982-83	78	121	1.55
Wayne Gretzky	Edmonton	1979-80	79	137	1.73	Ron Francis	Pittsburgh	1995-96	77	119	1.55
Jean Ratelle	NY Rangers	1971-72	63	109	1.73	Joe Thornton	Bos., S.J.	2005-06	81	125	1.54
Marcel Dionne	Los Angeles	1979-80	80	137	1.71	Mike Bossy	NY Islanders	1985-86	80	123	1.54
Herb Cain	Boston	1943-44	48	82	1.71	Kevin Stevens	Pittsburgh	1991-92	80	123	1.54
Guy Lafleur	Montreal	1976-77	80	136	1.70	Bobby Orr	Boston	1971-72	76	117	1.54
Dennis Maruk	Washington	1981-82	80	136	1.70	Mike Bossy	NY Islanders	1984-85	76	117	1.54
Phil Esposito	Boston	1968-69	74	126	1.70	Kevin Stevens	Pittsburgh	1992-93	72	111	1.54
Mario Lemieux	Pittsburgh	1986-87	63	107	1.70	Doug Bentley	Chicago	1943-44	50	77	1.54
Adam Oates	Boston	1992-93	84	142	1.69	Doug Gilmour	Toronto	1992-93	83	127	1.53
Bobby Orr	Boston	1974-75	80	135	1.69	Marcel Dionne	Los Angeles	1976-77	80	122	1.53
Marcel Dionne	Los Angeles	1980-81	80	135	1.69	Sidney Crosby	Pittsburgh	2006-07	79	120	1.52
Guy Lafleur	Montreal	1977-78	78	132	1.69	Jaromir Jagr	Pittsburgh	99-2000	63	96	1.52
Guy Lafleur	Montreal	1979-80	74	125	1.69	Eric Lindros	Philadelphia	1996-97	52	79	1.52
Rob Brown	Pittsburgh	1988-89	68	115	1.69	Eric Lindros	Philadelphia	1994-95	46	70	1.52
Jari Kurri	Edmonton	1985-86	78	131	1.68	Marcel Dionne	Detroit	1974-75	80	121	1.51
Brett Hull	St. Louis	1990-91	78	131	1.68	Mike Bossy	NY Islanders	1980-81	79	119	1.51
Phil Esposito	Boston	1972-73	78	130	1.67	Paul Coffey	Edmonton	1984-85	80	121	1.51
Cooney Weiland	Boston	1929-30	44	73	1.66	Dale Hawerchuk	Winnipeg	1987-88	80	121	1.51
Alexander Mogilny	Buffalo	1992-93	77	127	1.65	Paul Coffey	Pittsburgh	1988-89	75	113	1.51
Peter Stastny	Quebec	1982-83	75	124	1.65	Alex Ovechkin	Washington	**2009-10**	72	109	1.51
Bobby Orr	Boston	1973-74	74	122	1.65	Jaromir Jagr	Pittsburgh	1996-97	63	95	1.51
						Cam Neely	Boston	1993-94	49	74	1.51

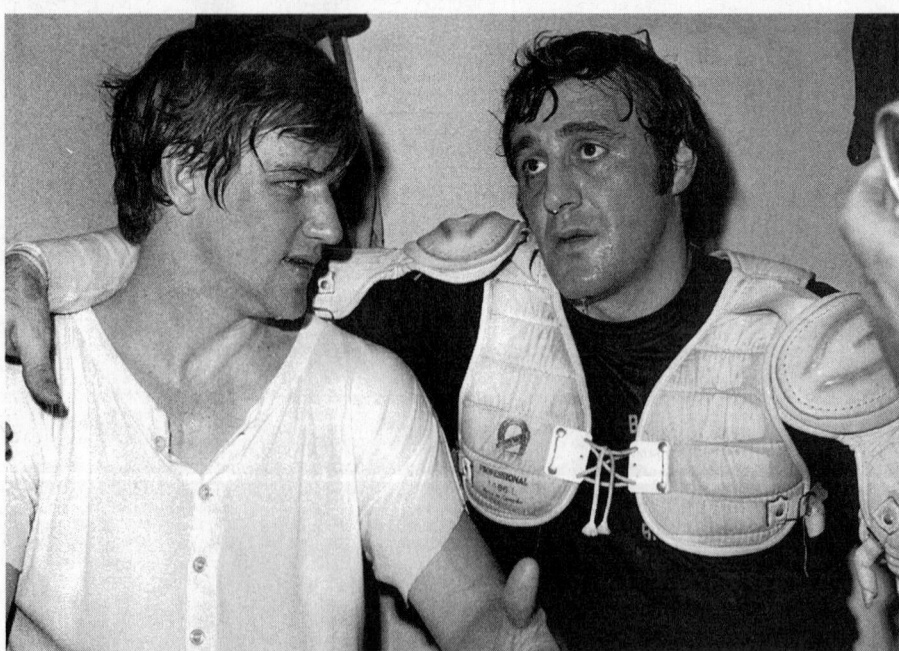

Bobby Orr and Phil Esposito combined to rewrite the NHL record book in 1970-71. In a 78-game season that year, Orr had 102 assists while Esposito had 76 goals and 152 points. Espo's points-per-game average of 1.95 was the highest since Bill Cowley collected 71 points in just 36 games back in 1943-44.

Number-one pick John Tavares of the Islanders and number-three pick Matt Duchene of Colorado both jumped directly to the NHL in 2009-10 and tied for the rookie lead with 24 goals. Duchene picked up one more assist (31) than Tavares to top all rookie scorers with 55 points.

Rookie Scoring Records

All-Time Top 50 Goal-Scoring Rookies

	Rookie	Team	Position	Season	GP	G	A	PTS
1.	* Teemu Selanne	Winnipeg	Right wing	1992-93	84	76	56	132
2.	* Mike Bossy	NY Islanders	Right wing	1977-78	73	53	38	91
3.	* Alex Ovechkin	Washington	Left wing	2005-06	81	52	54	106
4.	* Joe Nieuwendyk	Calgary	Center	1987-88	75	51	41	92
5.	* Dale Hawerchuk	Winnipeg	Center	1981-82	80	45	58	103
	* Luc Robitaille	Los Angeles	Left wing	1986-87	79	45	39	84
7.	Rick Martin	Buffalo	Left wing	1971-72	73	44	30	74
	Barry Pederson	Boston	Center	1981-82	80	44	48	92
9.	* Steve Larmer	Chicago	Right wing	1982-83	80	43	47	90
	* Mario Lemieux	Pittsburgh	Center	1984-85	73	43	57	100
11.	Eric Lindros	Philadelphia	Center	1992-93	61	41	34	75
12.	Darryl Sutter	Chicago	Left wing	1980-81	76	40	22	62
	Sylvain Turgeon	Hartford	Left wing	1983-84	76	40	32	72
	Warren Young	Pittsburgh	Left wing	1984-85	80	40	32	72
15.	* Eric Vail	Atlanta	Left wing	1974-75	72	39	21	60
	* Peter Stastny	Quebec	Center	1980-81	77	39	70	109
	Anton Stastny	Quebec	Left wing	1980-81	80	39	46	85
	Steve Yzerman	Detroit	Center	1983-84	80	39	48	87
	Sidney Crosby	Pittsburgh	Center	2005-06	81	39	63	102
20.	* Gilbert Perreault	Buffalo	Center	1970-71	78	38	34	72
	Neal Broten	Minnesota	Center	1981-82	73	38	60	98
	Ray Sheppard	Buffalo	Right wing	1987-88	74	38	27	65
	Mikael Renberg	Philadelphia	Left wing	1993-94	83	38	44	82
24.	Jorgen Pettersson	St. Louis	Left wing	1980-81	62	37	36	73
	Jimmy Carson	Los Angeles	Center	1986-87	80	37	42	79
26.	Mike Foligno	Detroit	Right wing	1979-80	80	36	35	71
	Paul MacLean	Winnipeg	Right wing	1981-82	74	36	25	61
	Mike Bullard	Pittsburgh	Center	1981-82	75	36	27	63
	Tony Granato	NY Rangers	Right wing	1988-89	78	36	27	63
30.	Marian Stastny	Quebec	Right wing	1981-82	74	35	54	89
	Brian Bellows	Minnesota	Right wing	1982-83	78	35	30	65
	Tony Amonte	NY Rangers	Right wing	1991-92	79	35	34	69
33.	Nels Stewart	Mtl. Maroons	Center	1925-26	36	34	8	42
	* Danny Grant	Minnesota	Left wing	1968-69	75	34	31	65
	Norm Ferguson	Oakland	Right wing	1968-69	76	34	20	54
	Brian Propp	Philadelphia	Left wing	1979-80	80	34	41	75
	Wendel Clark	Toronto	Left wing	1985-86	66	34	11	45
	* Pavel Bure	Vancouver	Right wing	1991-92	65	34	26	60
39.	* Willi Plett	Atlanta	Right wing	1976-77	64	33	23	56
	Dale McCourt	Detroit	Center	1977-78	76	33	39	72
	Steve Bozek	Los Angeles	Center	1981-82	71	33	23	56
	Ron Flockhart	Philadelphia	Center	1981-82	72	33	39	72
	Mark Pavelich	NY Rangers	Center	1981-82	79	33	43	76
	Jason Arnott	Edmonton	Center	1993-94	78	33	35	68
	* Evgeni Malkin	Pittsburgh	Center	2006-07	78	33	52	85
46.	Bill Mosienko	Chicago	Right wing	1943-44	50	32	38	70
	Michel Bergeron	Detroit	Right wing	1975-76	72	32	27	59
	* Bryan Trottier	NY Islanders	Center	1975-76	80	32	63	95
	Don Murdoch	NY Rangers	Right wing	1976-77	59	32	24	56
	Jari Kurri	Edmonton	Left wing	1980-81	75	32	43	75
	Bobby Carpenter	Washington	Center	1981-82	80	32	35	67
	Petr Klima	Detroit	Left wing	1985-86	74	32	24	56
	Kjell Dahlin	Montreal	Right wing	1985-86	77	32	39	71
	Darren Turcotte	NY Rangers	Right wing	1989-90	76	32	34	66
	Joe Juneau	Boston	Center	1992-93	84	32	70	102
	Marek Svatos	Colorado	Right wing	2005-06	61	32	18	50

* Calder Trophy Winner

All-Time Top 50 Point-Scoring Rookies

	Rookie	Team	Position	Season	GP	G	A	PTS
1.	* Teemu Selanne	Winnipeg	Right wing	1992-93	84	76	56	132
2.	* Peter Stastny	Quebec	Center	1980-81	77	39	70	109
3.	* Alex Ovechkin	Washington	Left wing	2005-06	81	52	54	106
4.	* Dale Hawerchuk	Winnipeg	Center	1981-82	80	45	58	103
	Joe Juneau	Boston	Center	1992-93	84	32	70	102
	Sidney Crosby	Pittsburgh	Center	2005-06	81	39	63	102
7.	* Mario Lemieux	Pittsburgh	Center	1984-85	73	43	57	100
8.	Neal Broten	Minnesota	Center	1981-82	73	38	60	98
9.	* Bryan Trottier	NY Islanders	Center	1975-76	80	32	63	95
10.	Barry Pederson	Boston	Center	1981-82	80	44	48	92
	* Joe Nieuwendyk	Calgary	Center	1987-88	75	51	41	92
12.	* Mike Bossy	NY Islanders	Right wing	1977-78	73	53	38	91
13.	* Steve Larmer	Chicago	Right wing	1982-83	80	43	47	90
14.	Marian Stastny	Quebec	Right wing	1981-82	74	35	54	89
15.	Steve Yzerman	Detroit	Center	1983-84	80	39	48	87
16.	* Sergei Makarov	Calgary	Right wing	1989-90	80	24	62	86
17.	Anton Stastny	Quebec	Left wing	1980-81	80	39	46	85
18.	* Evgeni Malkin	Pittsburgh	Center	2006-07	78	33	52	85
19.	* Luc Robitaille	Los Angeles	Left wing	1986-87	79	45	39	84
20.	Mikael Renberg	Philadelphia	Left wing	1993-94	83	38	44	82
21.	Jimmy Carson	Los Angeles	Center	1986-87	80	37	42	79
	Sergei Fedorov	Detroit	Center	1990-91	77	31	48	79
	Alexei Yashin	Ottawa	Center	1993-94	83	30	49	79
24.	Paul Stastny	Colorado	Center	2006-07	82	28	50	78
25.	Marcel Dionne	Detroit	Center	1971-72	78	28	49	77
26.	Larry Murphy	Los Angeles	Defense	1980-81	80	16	60	76
	Mark Pavelich	NY Rangers	Center	1981-82	79	33	43	76
	Dave Poulin	Philadelphia	Center	1983-84	73	31	45	76
29.	Brian Propp	Philadelphia	Left wing	1979-80	80	34	41	75
	Jari Kurri	Edmonton	Left wing	1980-81	75	32	43	75
	Denis Savard	Chicago	Center	1980-81	76	28	47	75
	Mike Modano	Minnesota	Center	1989-90	80	29	46	75
	Eric Lindros	Philadelphia	Center	1992-93	61	41	34	75
34.	Rick Martin	Buffalo	Left wing	1971-72	73	44	30	74
	* Bobby Smith	Minnesota	Center	1978-79	80	30	44	74
36.	Jorgen Pettersson	St. Louis	Left wing	1980-81	62	37	36	73
37.	* Gilbert Perreault	Buffalo	Center	1970-71	78	38	34	72
	Dale McCourt	Detroit	Center	1977-78	76	33	39	72
	Ron Flockhart	Philadelphia	Center	1981-82	72	33	39	72
	Sylvain Turgeon	Hartford	Left wing	1983-84	76	40	32	72
	Carey Wilson	Calgary	Center	1984-85	74	24	48	72
	Warren Young	Pittsburgh	Left wing	1984-85	80	40	32	72
	Alex Zhamnov	Winnipeg	Center	1992-93	68	25	47	72
	* Patrick Kane	Chicago	Right Wing	2007-08	82	21	51	72
45.	Mike Foligno	Detroit	Right wing	1979-80	80	36	35	71
	Dave Christian	Winnipeg	Center	1980-81	80	28	43	71
	Mats Naslund	Montreal	Left wing	1982-83	74	26	45	71
	Kjell Dahlin	Montreal	Right wing	1985-86	77	32	39	71
	* Brian Leetch	NY Rangers	Defense	1988-89	68	23	48	71
50.	Bill Mosienko	Chicago	Right wing	1943-44	50	32	38	70
	* Scott Gomez	New Jersey	Center	99-2000	82	19	51	70

* Calder Trophy Winner

50-Goal Seasons

Bobby Hull

Reggie Leach

Rick Vaive

Player	Team	Date of 50th Goal	Score		Goaltender	Player's Game No.	Team Game No.	Total Goals	Total Games	Age When First 50th Scored (Yrs. & Mos.)
Maurice Richard	Mtl.	Mar. 18/45	Mtl. 4	at Bos. 2	Harvey Bennett	50	50	50	50	23.7
Bernie Geoffrion	Mtl.	Mar. 16/61	Tor. 2	at Mtl. 5	Cesare Maniago	62	68	50	64	30.1
Bobby Hull	Chi.	Mar. 25/62	Chi. 1	at NYR 4	Gump Worsley	70	70	50	70	23.2
Bobby Hull	Chi.	Mar. 2/66	Det. 4	at Chi. 5	Hank Bassen	52	57	54	65	
Bobby Hull	Chi.	Mar. 18/67	Chi. 5	at Tor. 9	Bruce Gamble	63	66	52	66	
Bobby Hull	Chi.	Mar. 5/69	NYR 4	at Chi. 4	Ed Giacomin	64	66	58	74	
Phil Esposito	Bos.	Feb. 20/71	Bos. 4	at L.A. 5	Denis DeJordy	58	58	76	78	29.0
John Bucyk	Bos.	Mar. 16/71	Bos. 11	at Det. 4	Roy Edwards	69	69	51	78	35.10
Phil Esposito	Bos.	Feb. 20/72	Bos. 3	at Chi. 1	Tony Esposito	60	60	66	76	
Bobby Hull	Chi.	Apr. 2/72	Det. 1	at Chi. 6	Andy Brown	78	78	50	78	
Vic Hadfield	NYR	Apr. 2/72	Mtl. 6	at NYR 5	Denis DeJordy	78	78	50	78	31.6
Phil Esposito	Bos.	Mar. 25/73	Buf. 1	at Bos. 6	Roger Crozier	75	75	55	78	
Mickey Redmond	Det.	Mar. 27/73	Det. 8	at Tor. 1	Ron Low	73	75	52	76	25.3
Rick MacLeish	Phi.	Apr. 1/73	Phi. 4	at Pit. 5	Cam Newton	78	78	50	78	23.2
Phil Esposito	Bos.	Feb. 20/74	Bos. 5	at Min. 5	Cesare Maniago	56	56	68	78	
Mickey Redmond	Det.	Mar. 23/74	NYR 3	at Det. 5	Ed Giacomin	69	71	51	76	
Ken Hodge	Bos.	Apr. 6/74	Bos. 2	at Mtl. 6	Michel Larocque	75	77	50	76	29.10
Rick Martin	Buf.	Apr. 7/74	St.L. 2	at Buf. 5	Wayne Stephenson	78	78	52	78	22.9
Phil Esposito	Bos.	Feb. 8/75	Bos. 8	at Det. 5	Jim Rutherford	54	54	61	79	
Guy Lafleur	Mtl.	Mar. 29/75	K.C. 1	at Mtl. 4	Denis Herron	66	76	53	70	23.6
Danny Grant	Det.	Apr. 2/75	Wsh. 3	at Det. 8	John Adams	78	78	50	80	29.2
Rick Martin	Buf.	Apr. 3/75	Bos. 2	at Buf. 4	Ken Broderick	67	79	52	68	
Reggie Leach	Phi.	Mar. 14/76	Atl. 1	at Phi. 6	Dan Bouchard	69	69	61	80	25.11
Jean Pronovost	Pit.	Mar. 24/76	Bos. 5	at Pit. 5	Gilles Gilbert	74	74	52	80	30.3
Guy Lafleur	Mtl.	Mar. 27/76	K.C. 2	at Mtl. 8	Denis Herron	76	76	56	80	
Bill Barber	Phi.	Apr. 3/76	Buf. 2	at Phi. 5	Al Smith	79	79	50	80	23.9
Pierre Larouche	Pit.	Apr. 3/76	Wsh. 5	at Pit. 4	Ron Low	75	79	53	76	20.5
Danny Gare	Buf.	Apr. 4/76	Tor. 2	at Buf. 5	Gord McRae	79	80	50	79	21.11
Steve Shutt	Mtl.	Mar. 1/77	Mtl. 5	at NYI 4	Glenn Resch	65	65	60	80	24.8
Guy Lafleur	Mtl.	Mar. 6/77	Mtl. 1	at Buf. 4	Don Edwards	68	68	56	80	
Marcel Dionne	L.A.	Apr. 2/77	Min. 2	at L.A. 7	Pete LoPresti	79	79	53	80	25.8
Guy Lafleur	Mtl.	Mar. 8/78	Wsh. 3	at Mtl. 4	Jim Bedard	63	65	60	78	
Mike Bossy	NYI	Apr. 1/78	Wsh. 2	at NYI 3	Bernie Wolfe	69	76	53	73	21.2
Mike Bossy	NYI	Feb. 24/79	Det. 1	at NYI 3	Rogie Vachon	58	58	69	80	
Marcel Dionne	L.A.	Mar. 11/79	L.A. 3	at Phi. 6	Wayne Stephenson	68	68	59	80	
Guy Lafleur	Mtl.	Mar. 31/79	Pit. 3	at Mtl. 5	Denis Herron	76	76	52	80	
Guy Chouinard	Atl.	Apr. 6/79	NYR 2	at Atl. 9	John Davidson	79	79	50	80	22.5
Marcel Dionne	L.A.	Mar. 12/80	L.A. 2	at Pit. 4	Nick Ricci	70	70	53	80	
Mike Bossy	NYI	Mar. 16/80	NYI 6	at Chi. 1	Tony Esposito	68	71	51	75	
Charlie Simmer	L.A.	Mar. 19/80	Det. 3	at L.A. 4	Jim Rutherford	57	73	56	64	26.0
Pierre Larouche	Mtl.	Mar. 25/80	Chi. 4	at Mtl. 8	Tony Esposito	72	75	50	73	
Danny Gare	Buf.	Mar. 27/80	Det. 1	at Buf. 10	Jim Rutherford	71	75	56	76	
Blaine Stoughton	Hfd.	Mar. 28/80	Hfd. 4	at Van. 4	Glen Hanlon	75	75	56	80	27.0
Guy Lafleur	Mtl.	Apr. 2/80	Mtl. 7	at Det. 2	Rogie Vachon	72	78	50	74	
Wayne Gretzky	Edm.	Apr. 2/80	Min. 1	at Edm. 1	Gary Edwards	78	79	51	79	19.2
Reggie Leach	Phi.	Apr. 3/80	Wsh. 2	at Phi. 4	empty net	75	79	50	76	
Mike Bossy	NYI	Jan. 24/81	Que. 3	at NYI 7	Ron Grahame	50	50	68	79	
Charlie Simmer	L.A.	Jan. 26/81	L.A. 7	at Que. 5	Michel Dion	51	51	56	65	
Marcel Dionne	L.A.	Mar. 8/81	L.A. 4	at Wpg. 1	Markus Mattsson	68	68	58	80	
Wayne Babych	St.L.	Mar. 12/81	St.L. 3	at Mtl. 4	Richard Sevigny	70	68	54	78	22.9
Wayne Gretzky	Edm.	Mar. 15/81	Edm. 3	at Cgy. 3	Pat Riggin	69	69	55	80	
Rick Kehoe	Pit.	Mar. 16/81	Pit. 7	at Edm. 6	Eddie Mio	70	70	55	80	29.7
Jacques Richard	Que.	Mar. 29/81	Mtl. 0	at Que. 4	Richard Sevigny	76	75	52	78	28.6
Dennis Maruk	Wsh.	Apr. 5/81	Det. 2	at Wsh. 7	Larry Lozinski	80	80	50	80	25.3
Wayne Gretzky	Edm.	Dec. 30/81	Phi. 5	at Edm. 7	empty net	39	39	92	80	
Dennis Maruk	Wsh.	Feb. 21/82	Wpg. 3	at Wsh. 6	Doug Soetaert	61	61	60	80	
Mike Bossy	NYI	Mar. 4/82	Tor. 1	at NYI 10	Michel Larocque	66	66	64	80	
Dino Ciccarelli	Min.	Mar. 8/82	St.L. 1	at Min. 8	Mike Liut	67	68	55	76	22.1
Rick Vaive	Tor.	Mar. 24/82	St.L. 3	at Tor. 4	Mike Liut	72	75	54	77	22.10
Blaine Stoughton	Hfd.	Mar. 28/82	Min. 5	at Hfd. 2	Gilles Meloche	76	76	52	80	
Rick Middleton	Bos.	Mar. 28/82	Bos. 5	at Buf. 9	Paul Harrison	72	77	51	75	28.11
Marcel Dionne	L.A.	Mar. 30/82	Cgy. 7	at L.A. 5	Pat Riggin	75	77	50	78	
Mark Messier	Edm.	Mar. 31/82	L.A. 3	at Edm. 7	Mario Lessard	78	79	50	78	21.3
Bryan Trottier	NYI	Apr. 3/82	Phi. 3	at NYI 6	Pete Peeters	79	79	50	80	25.9
Lanny McDonald	Cgy.	Feb. 18/83	Cgy. 1	at Buf. 5	Bob Sauve	60	60	66	80	30.0
Wayne Gretzky	Edm.	Feb. 19/83	Edm. 10	at Pit. 7	Nick Ricci	60	60	71	80	
Michel Goulet	Que.	Mar. 5/83	Hfd. 3	at Que. 10	Mike Veisor	67	67	57	80	22.11
Mike Bossy	NYI	Mar. 12/83	Wsh. 2	at NYI 6	Al Jensen	70	71	60	79	
Marcel Dionne	L.A.	Mar. 17/83	Que. 3	at L.A. 4	Dan Bouchard	71	71	56	80	
Al Secord	Chi.	Mar. 20/83	Tor. 3	at Chi. 7	Mike Palmateer	73	73	54	80	25.0
Rick Vaive	Tor.	Mar. 30/83	Tor. 4	at Det. 2	Gilles Gilbert	76	78	51	78	
Wayne Gretzky	Edm.	Jan. 7/84	Hfd. 3	at Edm. 5	Greg Millen	42	42	87	74	
Michel Goulet	Que.	Mar. 8/84	Que. 8	at Pit. 6	Denis Herron	63	69	56	75	
Rick Vaive	Tor.	Mar. 14/84	Min. 3	at Tor. 3	Gilles Meloche	69	72	52	76	
Mike Bullard	Pit.	Mar. 14/84	Pit. 6	at L.A. 7	Markus Mattsson	71	72	51	76	23.0
Jari Kurri	Edm.	Mar. 15/84	Edm. 2	at Mtl. 3	Rick Wamsley	57	73	52	64	23.10
Glenn Anderson	Edm.	Mar. 21/84	Hfd. 3	at Edm. 5	Greg Millen	76	76	54	80	23.6
Tim Kerr	Phi.	Mar. 22/84	Pit. 4	at Phi. 13	Denis Herron	74	75	54	79	24.3

Player	Team	Date of 50th Goal	Score			Goaltender	Player's Game No.	Team Game No.	Total Goals	Total Games	Age When First 50th Scored (Yrs. & Mos.)
Mike Bossy	NYI	Mar. 31/84	NYI 3	at	Wsh. 1	Pat Riggin	67	79	51	67	
Wayne Gretzky	Edm.	Jan. 26/85	Pit. 3	at	Edm. 6	Denis Herron	49	49	73	80	
Jari Kurri	Edm.	Feb. 3/85	Hfd. 3	at	Edm. 6	Greg Millen	50	53	71	73	
Mike Bossy	NYI	Mar. 5/85	Phi. 5	at	NYI 4	Bob Froese	61	65	58	76	
Michel Goulet	Que.	Mar. 6/85	Buf. 3	at	Que. 4	Tom Barrasso	62	73	55	69	
Tim Kerr	Phi.	Mar. 7/85	Wsh. 6	at	Phi. 9	Pat Riggin	63	65	54	74	
John Ogrodnick	Det.	Mar. 13/85	Det. 6	at	Edm. 7	Grant Fuhr	69	69	55	79	25.9
Bob Carpenter	Wsh.	Mar. 21/85	Wsh. 2	at	Mtl. 3	Steve Penney	72	72	53	80	21.9
Dale Hawerchuk	Wpg.	Mar. 29/85	Chi. 5	at	Wpg. 5	W. Skorodenski	77	77	53	80	21.11
Mike Gartner	Wsh.	Apr. 7/85	Pit. 3	at	Wsh. 7	Brian Ford	80	80	50	80	25.5
Jari Kurri	Edm.	Mar. 4/86	Edm. 6	at	Van. 2	Richard Brodeur	63	65	68	78	
Mike Bossy	NYI	Mar. 11/86	Cgy. 4	at	NYI 8	Reggie Lemelin	67	67	61	80	
Glenn Anderson	Edm.	Mar. 14/86	Det. 3	at	Edm. 12	Greg Stefan	63	71	54	72	
Michel Goulet	Que.	Mar. 17/86	Que. 8	at	Mtl. 6	Patrick Roy	67	72	53	75	
Wayne Gretzky	Edm.	Mar. 18/86	Wpg. 2	at	Edm. 6	Brian Hayward	72	72	52	80	
Tim Kerr	Phi.	Mar. 20/86	Pit. 1	at	Phi. 5	Roberto Romano	68	72	58	76	
Wayne Gretzky	Edm.	Feb. 4/87	Edm. 6	at	Min. 5	Don Beaupre	55	55	62	79	
Dino Ciccarelli	Min.	Mar. 7/87	Pit. 7	at	Min. 3	Gilles Meloche	66	66	52	80	
Mario Lemieux	Pit.	Mar. 12/87	Que. 3	at	Pit. 6	Mario Gosselin	53	70	54	63	21.5
Tim Kerr	Phi.	Mar. 17/87	NYR 1	at	Phi. 4	J. Vanbiesbrouck	67	71	58	75	
Jari Kurri	Edm.	Mar. 17/87	N.J. 4	at	Edm. 7	Craig Billington	69	70	54	79	
Mario Lemieux	Pit.	Feb. 2/88	Wsh. 2	at	Pit. 3	Pete Peeters	51	54	70	77	
Steve Yzerman	Det.	Mar. 1/88	Buf. 0	at	Det. 4	Tom Barrasso	64	64	50	64	22.10
Joe Nieuwendyk	Cgy.	Mar. 12/88	Buf. 4	at	Cgy. 10	Tom Barrasso	66	70	51	75	21.5
Craig Simpson	Edm.	Mar. 15/88	Buf. 4	at	Edm. 6	Jacques Cloutier	71	71	56	80	21.1
Jimmy Carson	L.A.	Mar. 26/88	Chi. 5	at	L.A. 9	Darren Pang	77	77	55	88	19.8
Luc Robitaille	L.A.	Apr. 1/88	L.A. 6	at	Cgy. 3	Mike Vernon	79	79	53	80	21.10
Hakan Loob	Cgy.	Apr. 3/88	Min. 1	at	Cgy. 4	Don Beaupre	80	80	50	80	27.9
Stephane Richer	Mtl.	Apr. 3/88	Mtl. 4	at	Buf. 4	Tom Barrasso	72	80	50	72	21.10
Mario Lemieux	Pit.	Jan. 20/89	Pit. 3	at	Wpg. 7	Pokey Reddick	44	46	85	76	
Bernie Nicholls	L.A.	Jan. 28/89	Edm. 7	at	L.A. 6	Grant Fuhr	51	51	70	79	27.7
Steve Yzerman	Det.	Feb. 5/89	Det. 6	at	Wpg. 2	Pokey Reddick	55	55	65	80	
Wayne Gretzky	L.A.	Mar. 4/89	Phi. 2	at	L.A. 6	Ron Hextall	66	67	54	78	
Joe Nieuwendyk	Cgy.	Mar. 21/89	NYI 1	at	Cgy. 4	Mark Fitzpatrick	72	74	51	77	
Joe Mullen	Cgy.	Mar. 21/89	Wpg. 1	at	Cgy. 4	Bob Essensa	78	79	51	79	32.1
Brett Hull	St.L.	Feb. 6/90	Tor. 4	at	St.L. 6	Jeff Reese	54	54	72	80	25.6
Steve Yzerman	Det.	Feb. 24/90	Det. 3	at	NYI 3	Glenn Healy	63	63	62	79	
Cam Neely	Bos.	Mar. 10/90	Bos. 3	at	NYI 3	Mark Fitzpatrick	69	71	55	76	24.9
Brian Bellows	Min.	Mar. 22/90	Min. 5	at	Det. 1	Tim Cheveldae	75	75	55	80	25.6
Pat LaFontaine	NYI	Mar. 24/90	NYI 5	at	Edm. 5	Bill Ranford	71	77	54	74	25.1
Stephane Richer	Mtl.	Mar. 24/90	Mtl. 4	at	Hfd. 7	Peter Sidorkiewicz	75	77	51	75	
Gary Leeman	Tor.	Mar. 28/90	NYI 6	at	Tor. 3	Mark Fitzpatrick	78	78	51	80	26.1
Luc Robitaille	L.A.	Mar. 31/90	L.A. 3	at	Van. 6	Kirk McLean	79	79	52	80	
Brett Hull	St.L.	Jan. 25/91	St.L. 9	at	Det. 4	David Gagnon	49	49	86	78	
Cam Neely	Bos.	Mar. 26/91	Bos. 7	at	Que. 4	empty net	67	78	51	69	
Theoren Fleury	Cgy.	Mar. 26/91	Van. 2	at	Cgy. 7	Bob Mason	77	77	51	79	22.9
Steve Yzerman	Det.	Mar. 30/91	NYR 5	at	Det. 6	Mike Richter	79	79	51	80	
Brett Hull	St.L.	Jan. 28/92	St.L. 3	at	L.A. 3	Kelly Hrudey	50	50	70	73	
Jeremy Roenick	Chi.	Mar. 7/92	Chi. 2	at	Bos. 1	Daniel Berthiaume	67	67	53	80	22.2
Kevin Stevens	Pit.	Mar. 24/92	Pit. 3	at	Det. 4	Tim Cheveldae	74	74	54	80	26.11
Gary Roberts	Cgy.	Mar. 31/92	Edm. 2	at	Cgy. 5	Bill Ranford	73	77	53	76	25.10
Alexander Mogilny	Buf.	Feb. 3/93	Hfd. 2	at	Buf. 3	Sean Burke	46	53	76	77	23.11
Teemu Selanne	Wpg.	Feb. 28/93	Min. 6	at	Wpg. 7	Darcy Wakaluk	63	63	76	84	22.6
Pavel Bure	Van.	Mar. 1/93	Van. 5	at	Buf. 2*	Grant Fuhr	63	63	60	83	21.11
Steve Yzerman	Det.	Mar. 10/93	Det. 6	at	Edm. 3	Bill Ranford	70	70	58	84	
Luc Robitaille	L.A.	Mar. 15/93	L.A. 4	at	Buf. 2	Grant Fuhr	69	69	63	84	
Brett Hull	St.L.	Mar. 20/93	St.L. 2	at	L.A. 3	Robb Stauber	73	73	54	80	
Mario Lemieux	Pit.	Mar. 21/93	Pit. 6	at	Edm. 4**	Ron Tugnutt	48	72	69	60	
Kevin Stevens	Pit.	Mar. 21/93	Pit. 6	at	Edm. 4**	Ron Tugnutt	62	72	55	72	
Dave Andreychuk	Tor.	Mar. 23/93	Tor. 5	at	Wpg. 4	Bob Essensa	72	73	54	83	29.6
Pat LaFontaine	Buf.	Mar. 28/93	Ott. 1	at	Buf. 3	Peter Sidorkiewicz	75	75	53	84	
Pierre Turgeon	NYI	Apr. 2/93	NYI 3	at	NYR 2	Mike Richter	75	76	58	83	23.8
Mark Recchi	Phi.	Apr. 3/93	T.B. 2	at	Phi. 6	J-C Bergeron	77	77	53	84	25.2
Brendan Shanahan	St.L.	Apr. 15/93	T.B. 5	at	St.L. 6	Pat Jablonski	71	84	51	71	24.3
Jeremy Roenick	Chi.	Apr. 15/93	Tor. 2	at	Chi. 3	Felix Potvin	84	84	50	84	
Cam Neely	Bos.	Mar. 7/94	Wsh. 3	at	Bos. 6	Don Beaupre	44	66	50	49	
Sergei Fedorov	Det.	Mar. 15/94	Van. 2	at	Det. 5	Kirk McLean	67	69	56	82	24.3
Pavel Bure	Van.	Mar. 23/94	Van. 6	at	L.A. 3	empty net	65	73	60	76	
Adam Graves	NYR	Mar. 23/94	NYR 5	at	Edm. 3	Bill Ranford	74	74	51	84	25.11
Dave Andreychuk	Tor.	Mar. 24/94	S.J. 2	at	Tor. 1	Arturs Irbe	73	74	53	83	
Brett Hull	St.L.	Mar. 25/94	Dal. 3	at	St.L. 5	Andy Moog	71	74	52	81	
Ray Sheppard	Det.	Mar. 29/94	Hfd. 2	at	Det. 6	Sean Burke	74	76	52	82	27.10
Brendan Shanahan	St.L.	Apr. 12/94	St.L. 5	at	Dal. 3	Andy Moog	80	83	52	81	
Mike Modano	Dal.	Apr. 12/94	St.L. 5	at	Dal. 9	Curtis Joseph	75	83	50	76	23.11
Mario Lemieux	Pit.	Feb. 23/96	Hfd. 4	at	Pit. 5	Sean Burke	50	59	69	70	
Jaromir Jagr	Pit.	Feb. 23/96	Hfd. 4	at	Pit. 5	Sean Burke	59	59	62	82	24.0
Alexander Mogilny	Van.	Feb. 29/96	St.L. 2	at	Van. 2	Grant Fuhr	60	63	55	79	
Peter Bondra	Wsh.	Apr. 3/96	Wsh. 5	at	Buf. 1	Andrei Trefilov	62	77	52	67	28.1
Joe Sakic	Col.	Apr. 7/96	Col. 4	at	Dal. 1	empty net	79	79	51	82	26.7
John LeClair	Phi.	Apr. 10/96	Phi. 5	at	N.J. 1	Corey Schwab	80	80	51	82	26.7
Keith Tkachuk	Wpg.	Apr. 12/96	L.A. 3	at	Wpg. 5	empty net	75	81	50	76	24.0
Paul Kariya	Ana.	Apr. 14/96	Wpg. 2	at	Ana. 5	N. Khabibulin	82	82	50	82	21.5
Keith Tkachuk	Phx.	Apr. 6/97	Phx. 1	at	Col. 2	Patrick Roy	78	79	52	81	
Teemu Selanne	Ana.	Apr. 9/97	L.A. 1	at	Ana. 4	empty net	77	81	51	78	
Mario Lemieux	Pit.	Apr. 11/97	Pit. 2	at	Fla. 4	J. Vanbiesbrouck	75	81	50	76	

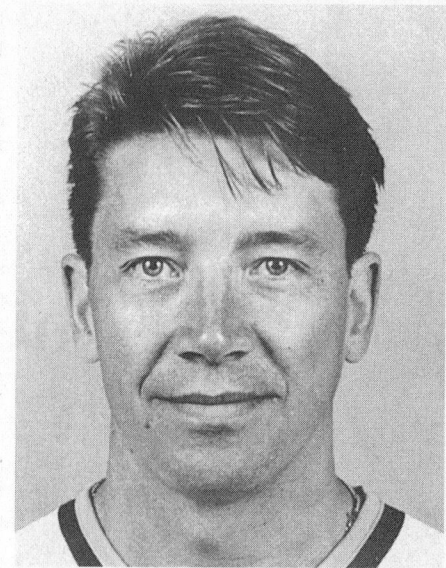

Jari Kurri

Stephane Richer

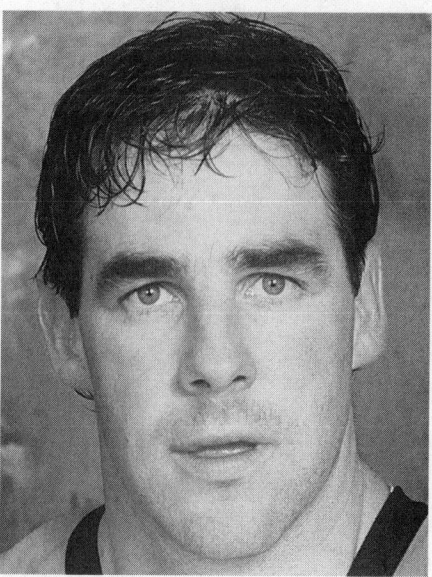

John LeClair

Steven Stamkos

Sidney Crosby

Ken Hodge

Player	Team	Date of 50th Goal	Score			Goaltender	Player's Game No.	Team Game No.	Total Goals	Total Games	Age When First 50th Scored (Yrs. & Mos.)
John LeClair	Phi.	Apr. 13/97	N.J. 4	at Phi. 5		Mike Dunham	82	82	50	82	
Teemu Selanne	Ana.	Mar. 25/98	Ana. 3	at Chi. 2		Jeff Hackett	66	71	52	73	
John LeClair	Phi.	Apr. 13/98	Phi. 1	at Buf. 2		Dominik Hasek	79	79	51	82	
Pavel Bure	Van.	Apr. 17/98	Cgy. 4	at Van. 2		Dwayne Roloson	81	81	51	82	
Peter Bondra	Wsh.	Apr. 18/98	Wsh. 4	at Car. 3		Mike Fountain	75	80	52	76	
Pavel Bure	Fla.	Mar. 18/00	Fla. 4	at NYI 2		empty net	63	71	58	74	
Pavel Bure	Fla.	Mar. 16/01	Pit. 6	at Fla. 3		Johan Hedberg	72	72	59	82	
Joe Sakic	Col.	Apr. 4/01	Ana. 1	at Col. 1		J-S Giguere	80	80	54	82	
Jaromir Jagr	Pit.	Apr. 4/01	T.B. 2	at Pit. 4		Kevin Weekes	80	80	52	81	
Jarome Iginla	Cgy.	Apr. 7/02	Cgy. 2	at Chi. 3		Jocelyn Thibault	79	79	52	82	24.9
Milan Hejduk	Col.	Apr. 6/03	St. L. 2	at Col. 5		Brent Johnson	82	82	50	82	27.1
Jaromir Jagr	NYR	Mar. 24/06	NYR 2	at Fla. 3		Roberto Luongo	70	70	54	82	
Ilya Kovalchuk	Atl.	Apr. 6/06	Atl. 2	at T.B. 3		Sean Burke	72	76	52	78	22.11
Jonathan Cheechoo	S.J.	Apr. 10/06	S.J. 3	at Phx. 2		David LeNeveu	78	78	56	82	25.8
Alex Ovechkin	Wsh.	Apr. 13/06	Wsh. 3	at Atl. 5		Mike Dunham	78	79	52	81	20.6
Dany Heatley	Ott.	Apr. 18/06	Ott. 5	at NYR 1		Henrik Lundqvist	82	82	50	82	25.2
Vincent Lecavalier	T.B.	Mar. 30/07	T.B. 4	at Car. 2		Cam Ward	78	78	52	82	26.11
Dany Heatley	Ott.	Apr. 7/07	Ott. 6	at Bos. 3		Tim Thomas	82	82	50	82	
Alex Ovechkin	Wsh.	Mar. 3/08	Bos. 2	at Wsh. 10		Tim Thomas	67	67	65	82	
Ilya Kovalchuk	Atl.	Mar. 18/08	Atl. 2	at Phi. 3		Antero Niittymaki	72	75	52	79	
Jarome Iginla	Cgy.	Apr. 5/08	Cgy. 7	at Van. 1		Curtis Sanford	82	82	50	82	
Alex Ovechkin	Wsh.	Mar. 19/09	Wsh. 5	at T.B. 2		Mike McKenna	70	73	56	79	
Alex Ovechkin	Wsh.	Apr. 9/10	Atl. 2	at Wsh. 5		Ondrej Pavelec	71	81	50	72	
Steven Stamkos	T.B.	Apr. 10/10	Fla. 3	at T.B. 4		S. Clemmensen	81	81	51	82	20.2
Sidney Crosby	Pit.	Apr. 11/10	Pit. 6	at NYI 5		Dwayne Roloson	81	82	51	81	22.8

* neutral site game played at Hamilton; ** neutral site game played at Cleveland

100-Point Seasons

Player	Team	Date of 100th Point	G or A	Score			Player's Game No.	Team Game No.	G - A	PTS	Total Games	Age when first 100th point scored (Yrs. & Mos.)
Phil Esposito	Bos.	Mar. 2/69	(G)	Pit. 0	at Bos. 4		60	62	49-77	126	74	27.1
Bobby Hull	Chi.	Mar. 20/69	(G)	Chi. 5	at Bos. 5		71	71	58-49	107	76	30.2
Gordie Howe	Det.	Mar. 30/69	(G)	Det. 5	at Chi. 9		76	76	44-59	103	76	41.0
Bobby Orr	Bos.	Mar. 15/70	(G)	Det. 5	at Bos. 5		67	67	33-87	120	76	22.11
Phil Esposito	Bos.	Feb. 6/71	(A)	Buf. 3	at Bos. 4		51	51	76-76	152	78	
Bobby Orr	Bos.	Feb. 20/71	(A)	Bos. 4	at L.A. 5		58	58	37-102	139	78	
John Bucyk	Bos.	Mar. 13/71	(G)	Bos. 6	at Van. 3		68	68	51-65	116	78	35.10
Ken Hodge	Bos.	Mar. 21/71	(A)	Buf. 7	at Bos. 5		72	72	43-62	105	78	26.9
Jean Ratelle	NYR	Feb. 18/72	(A)	NYR 2	at Cal. 2		58	58	46-63	109	63	31.4
Phil Esposito	Bos.	Feb. 19/72	(A)	Bos. 6	at Min. 4		59	59	66-67	133	76	
Bobby Orr	Bos.	Mar. 2/72	(A)	Van. 3	at Bos. 7		64	64	37-80	117	76	
Vic Hadfield	NYR	Mar. 25/72	(A)	NYR 3	at Mtl. 3		74	74	50-56	106	78	31.5
Phil Esposito	Bos.	Mar. 3/73	(A)	Bos. 1	at Mtl. 5		64	64	55-75	130	78	
Bobby Clarke	Phi.	Mar. 29/73	(G)	Atl. 2	at Phi. 4		76	76	37-67	104	78	23.7
Bobby Orr	Bos.	Mar. 31/73	(G)	Bos. 3	at Tor. 7		62	77	29-72	101	63	
Rick MacLeish	Phi.	Apr. 1/73	(G)	Phi. 4	at Pit. 5		78	78	50-50	100	78	23.3
Phil Esposito	Bos.	Feb. 13/74	(A)	Bos. 9	at Cal. 6		53	53	68-77	145	78	
Bobby Orr	Bos.	Mar. 12/74	(A)	Buf. 0	at Bos. 4		62	66	32-90	122	74	
Ken Hodge	Bos.	Mar. 24/74	(A)	Mtl. 3	at Bos. 6		72	72	50-55	105	76	
Phil Esposito	Bos.	Feb. 8/75	(A)	Bos. 8	at Det. 5		54	54	61-66	127	79	
Bobby Orr	Bos.	Feb. 13/75	(A)	Bos. 1	at Buf. 3		57	57	46-89	135	80	
Guy Lafleur	Mtl.	Mar. 7/75	(G)	Wsh. 4	at Mtl. 8		56	66	53-66	119	70	24.6
Marcel Dionne	Det.	Mar. 9/75	(A)	Det. 5	at Phi. 8		67	67	47-74	121	80	23.7
Pete Mahovlich	Mtl.	Mar. 9/75	(G)	Mtl. 5	at NYR 3		67	67	35-82	117	80	29.5
Bobby Clarke	Phi.	Mar. 22/75	(A)	Min. 0	at Phi. 4		72	72	27-89	116	80	
Rene Robert	Buf.	Apr. 5/75	(A)	Buf. 4	at Tor. 2		74	80	40-60	100	74	26.4
Guy Lafleur	Mtl.	Mar. 10/76	(G)	Mtl. 5	at Chi. 1		69	69	56-69	125	80	
Bobby Clarke	Phi.	Mar. 11/76	(A)	Buf. 1	at Phi. 6		64	68	30-89	119	76	
Bill Barber	Phi.	Mar. 18/76	(A)	Van. 2	at Phi. 3		71	71	50-62	112	80	23.8
Gilbert Perreault	Buf.	Mar. 21/76	(A)	K.C. 1	at Buf. 3		73	73	44-69	113	80	25.4
Pierre Larouche	Pit.	Mar. 24/76	(G)	Bos. 5	at Pit. 5		70	74	53-58	111	76	20.4
Pete Mahovlich	Mtl.	Mar. 28/76	(A)	Mtl. 2	at Bos. 2		77	77	34-71	105	80	
Jean Ratelle	Bos.	Mar. 30/76	(A)	Buf. 4	at Bos. 4		77	77	36-69	105	80	
Jean Pronovost	Pit.	Apr. 3/76	(A)	Wsh. 5	at Pit. 4		79	79	52-52	104	80	30.4
Darryl Sittler	Tor.	Apr. 3/76	(A)	Bos. 4	at Tor. 2		78	79	41-59	100	79	25.7
Guy Lafleur	Mtl.	Feb. 26/77	(A)	Cle. 3	at Mtl. 5		63	63	56-80	136	80	
Marcel Dionne	L.A.	Mar. 5/77	(G)	Pit. 3	at L.A. 3		67	67	53-69	122	80	
Steve Shutt	Mtl.	Mar. 27/77	(A)	Mtl. 6	at Det. 0		77	77	60-45	105	80	24.9
Bryan Trottier	NYI	Feb. 25/78	(A)	Chi. 1	at NYI 7		59	60	46-77	123	77	21.7
Guy Lafleur	Mtl.	Feb. 28/78	(G)	Det. 3	at Mtl. 9		69	61	60-72	132	78	
Darryl Sittler	Tor.	Mar. 12/78	(A)	Tor. 7	at Pit. 1		67	67	45-72	117	80	

Player	Team	Date of 100th Point	G or A	Score		Player's Game No.	Team Game No.	G - A PTS	Total Games	Age when first 100th point scored (Yrs. & Mos.)
Guy Lafleur	Mtl.	Feb. 27/79	(A)	Mtl. 3	at NYI 7	61	61	52-77 — 129	80	
Bryan Trottier	NYI	Mar. 6/79	(A)	Buf. 3	at NYI 2	59	63	47-87 — 134	76	
Marcel Dionne	L.A.	Mar. 8/79	(G)	L.A. 4	at Buf. 6	66	66	59-71 — 130	80	
Mike Bossy	NYI	Mar. 11/79	(G)	NYI 4	at Bos. 4	66	66	69-57 — 126	80	22.2
Bob MacMillan	Atl.	Mar. 15/79	(A)	Atl. 4	at Phi. 5	68	69	37-71 — 108	79	26.6
Guy Chouinard	Atl.	Mar. 30/79	(G)	L.A. 3	at Atl. 5	75	75	50-57 — 107	80	22.5
Denis Potvin	NYI	Apr. 8/79	(A)	NYI 5	at NYR 2	73	80	31-70 — 101	73	25.5
Marcel Dionne	L.A.	Feb. 6/80	(A)	L.A. 3	at Hfd. 7	53	53	53-84 — 137	80	
Guy Lafleur	Mtl.	Feb. 10/80	(A)	Mtl. 3	at Bos. 2	55	55	50-75 — 125	74	
Wayne Gretzky	Edm.	Feb. 24/80	(G)	Bos. 4	at Edm. 2	61	62	51-86 — 137	79	19.2
Bryan Trottier	NYI	Mar. 30/80	(G)	NYI 9	at Que. 6	75	77	42-62 — 104	78	
Gilbert Perreault	Buf.	Apr. 1/80	(A)	Buf. 5	at Atl. 2	77	77	40-66 — 106	80	
Mike Rogers	Hfd.	Apr. 4/80	(A)	Que. 2	at Hfd. 9	79	79	44-61 — 105	80	25.5
Charlie Simmer	L.A.	Apr. 5/80	(G)	Van. 5	at L.A. 3	64	80	56-45 — 101	64	26.0
Blaine Stoughton	Hfd.	Apr. 6/80	(A)	Det. 3	at Hfd. 5	80	80	56-44 — 100	80	27.0
Wayne Gretzky	Edm.	Feb. 6/81	(G)	Wpg. 4	at Edm. 10	53	53	55-109 — 164	80	
Marcel Dionne	L.A.	Feb. 12/81	(A)	L.A. 5	at Chi. 5	58	58	58-77 — 135	80	
Charlie Simmer	L.A.	Feb. 14/81	(A)	Bos. 5	at L.A. 4	59	59	56-49 — 105	65	
Kent Nilsson	Cgy.	Feb. 27/81	(G)	Hfd. 1	at Cgy. 5	64	64	49-82 — 131	80	24.6
Mike Bossy	NYI	Mar. 3/81	(G)	Edm. 8	at NYI 8	65	66	68-51 — 119	79	
Dave Taylor	L.A.	Mar. 14/81	(A)	Min. 4	at L.A. 10	63	70	47-65 — 112	72	25.3
Mike Rogers	Hfd.	Mar. 22/81	(A)	Tor. 3	at Hfd. 3	74	74	40-65 — 105	80	
Bernie Federko	St.L.	Mar. 28/81	(A)	Buf. 4	at St.L. 7	74	76	31-73 — 104	78	24.10
Rick Middleton	Bos.	Mar. 28/81	(A)	Chi. 2	at Bos. 5	76	76	44-59 — 103	80	27.4
Bryan Trottier	NYI	Mar. 29/81	(A)	NYI 5	at Wsh. 4	69	76	31-72 — 103	73	
Jacques Richard	Que.	Mar. 29/81	(G)	Mtl. 0	at Que. 4	75	76	52-51 — 103	78	28.6
Peter Stastny	Que.	Mar. 29/81	(A)	Mtl. 0	at Que. 4	73	76	39-70 — 109	77	24.6
Wayne Gretzky	Edm.	Dec. 27/81	(G)	L.A. 3	at Edm. 10	38	38	92-120 — 212	80	
Mike Bossy	NYI	Feb. 13/82	(A)	Phi. 2	at NYI 8	55	55	64-83 — 147	80	
Peter Stastny	Que.	Feb. 16/82	(A)	Wpg. 3	at Que. 7	60	60	46-93 — 139	80	
Dennis Maruk	Wsh.	Feb. 20/82	(A)	Wsh. 3	at Min. 7	60	60	60-76 — 136	80	26.3
Bryan Trottier	NYI	Feb. 23/82	(G)	Chi. 1	at NYI 5	61	61	50-79 — 129	80	
Denis Savard	Chi.	Feb. 27/82	(A)	Chi. 5	at L.A. 3	64	64	32-87 — 119	80	21.1
Bobby Smith	Min.	Mar. 3/82	(A)	Det. 4	at Min. 6	66	66	43-71 — 114	80	24.1
Marcel Dionne	L.A.	Mar. 6/82	(A)	L.A. 6	at Hfd. 7	64	66	50-67 — 117	78	
Dave Taylor	L.A.	Mar. 20/82	(A)	Pit. 5	at L.A. 7	71	72	39-67 — 106	78	
Dale Hawerchuk	Wpg.	Mar. 24/82	(G)	L.A. 3	at Wpg. 5	74	74	45-58 — 103	80	18.11
Dino Ciccarelli	Min.	Mar. 27/82	(A)	Min. 6	at Bos. 5	72	76	55-52 — 107	76	21.8
Glenn Anderson	Edm.	Mar. 28/82	(G)	Edm. 6	at L.A. 2	78	78	38-67 — 105	80	21.7
Mike Rogers	NYR	Apr. 2/82	(G)	Pit. 7	at NYR 5	79	79	38-65 — 103	80	
Wayne Gretzky	Edm.	Jan. 5/83	(A)	Edm. 8	at Wpg. 3	42	42	71-125 — 196	80	
Mike Bossy	NYI	Mar. 3/83	(A)	Tor. 1	at NYI 5	66	67	60-58 — 118	79	
Peter Stastny	Que.	Mar. 5/83	(A)	Hfd. 3	at Que. 10	62	67	47-77 — 124	75	
Denis Savard	Chi.	Mar. 6/83	(A)	Mtl. 4	at Chi. 5	65	67	35-86 — 121	78	
Mark Messier	Edm.	Mar. 23/83	(G)	Edm. 4	at Wpg. 7	73	76	48-58 — 106	77	22.2
Barry Pederson	Bos.	Mar. 26/83	(A)	Hfd. 4	at Bos. 7	73	76	46-61 — 107	77	22.0
Marcel Dionne	L.A.	Mar. 26/83	(A)	Edm. 9	at L.A. 3	75	75	56-51 — 107	80	
Michel Goulet	Que.	Mar. 27/83	(A)	Que. 6	at Buf. 6	77	77	57-48 — 105	80	22.11
Glenn Anderson	Edm.	Mar. 29/83	(A)	Edm. 7	at Van. 4	70	78	48-56 — 104	72	
Jari Kurri	Edm.	Mar. 29/83	(A)	Edm. 7	at Van. 4	78	78	45-59 — 104	80	22.10
Kent Nilsson	Cgy.	Mar. 29/83	(G)	L.A. 3	at Cgy. 5	78	78	46-58 — 104	80	
Wayne Gretzky	Edm.	Dec. 18/83	(G)	Edm. 7	at Wpg. 5	34	34	87-118 — 205	74	
Paul Coffey	Edm.	Mar. 4/84	(A)	Mtl. 1	at Edm. 6	68	68	40-86 — 126	80	22.9
Michel Goulet	Que.	Mar. 4/84	(A)	Que. 1	at Buf. 1	62	67	56-65 — 121	75	
Jari Kurri	Edm.	Mar. 7/84	(G)	Chi. 4	at Edm. 7	53	69	52-61 — 113	64	
Peter Stastny	Que.	Mar. 8/84	(A)	Que. 8	at Pit. 6	69	69	46-73 — 119	80	
Mike Bossy	NYI	Mar. 8/84	(G)	Tor. 5	at NYI 9	56	68	51-67 — 118	67	
Barry Pederson	Bos.	Mar. 14/84	(A)	Bos. 4	at Det. 2	71	71	39-77 — 116	80	
Bryan Trottier	NYI	Mar. 18/84	(G)	NYI 4	at Hfd. 5	62	73	40-71 — 111	68	
Bernie Federko	St.L.	Mar. 20/84	(A)	Wpg. 3	at St.L. 9	75	76	41-66 — 107	79	
Rick Middleton	Bos.	Mar. 27/84	(G)	Bos. 6	at Que. 4	77	77	47-58 — 105	80	
Dale Hawerchuk	Wpg.	Mar. 27/84	(G)	Wpg. 3	at L.A. 3	77	77	37-65 — 102	80	
Mark Messier	Edm.	Mar. 27/84	(G)	Edm. 9	at Cgy. 2	72	79	37-64 — 101	73	
Wayne Gretzky	Edm.	Dec. 29/84	(A)	Det. 3	at Edm. 6	35	35	73-135 — 208	80	
Jari Kurri	Edm.	Jan. 29/85	(G)	Edm. 4	at Cgy. 2	48	51	71-64 — 135	73	
Mike Bossy	NYI	Feb. 23/85	(A)	Bos. 1	at NYI 7	56	60	58-59 — 117	76	
Dale Hawerchuk	Wpg.	Feb. 25/85	(A)	Wpg. 12	at NYR 5	64	64	53-77 — 130	80	
Marcel Dionne	L.A.	Mar. 5/85	(A)	Pit. 0	at L.A. 6	66	66	46-80 — 126	80	
Brent Sutter	NYI	Mar. 12/85	(A)	NYI 6	at St.L. 5	68	68	42-60 — 102	72	22.10
John Ogrodnick	Det.	Mar. 22/85	(A)	NYR 3	at Det. 5	73	73	55-50 — 105	79	25.9
Paul Coffey	Edm.	Mar. 26/85	(G)	Edm. 7	at NYI 5	74	74	37-84 — 121	80	
Denis Savard	Chi.	Mar. 29/85	(A)	Chi. 5	at Wpg. 5	75	76	38-67 — 105	79	
Peter Stastny	Que.	Apr. 2/85	(A)	Bos. 4	at Que. 6	74	77	32-68 — 100	75	
Bernie Federko	St.L.	Apr. 4/85	(A)	NYR 5	at St.L. 4	74	78	30-73 — 103	76	
Paul MacLean	Wpg.	Apr. 6/85	(A)	Wpg. 6	at Edm. 5	78	79	41-60 — 101	79	27.1
Bernie Nicholls	L.A.	Apr. 6/85	(A)	Van. 4	at L.A. 4	80	80	46-54 — 100	80	22.9
John Tonelli	NYI	Apr. 6/85	(G)	N.J. 5	at NYI 5	80	80	42-58 — 100	80	28.1
Mike Gartner	Wsh.	Apr. 7/85	(G)	Pit. 3	at Wsh. 7	80	80	50-52 — 102	80	25.6
Mario Lemieux	Pit.	Apr. 7/85	(G)	Pit. 3	at Wsh. 7	73	80	43-57 — 100	73	19.6
Wayne Gretzky	Edm.	Jan. 4/86	(A)	Hfd. 3	at Edm. 4	39	39	52-163 — 215	80	
Mario Lemieux	Pit.	Feb. 15/86	(G)	Van. 4	at Pit. 9	55	56	48-93 — 141	79	
Paul Coffey	Edm.	Feb. 19/86	(A)	Tor. 5	at Edm. 3	59	60	48-90 — 138	79	
Peter Stastny	Que.	Mar. 1/86	(A)	Buf. 8	at Que. 4	66	68	41-81 — 122	76	
Jari Kurri	Edm.	Mar. 2/86	(G)	Phi. 1	at Edm. 2	62	64	68-63 — 131	78	

Bryan Trottier

Denis Savard

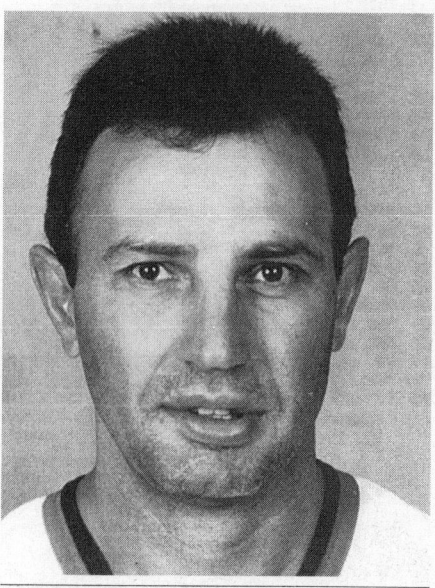

Brent Sutter

Hakan Loob

Rob Brown

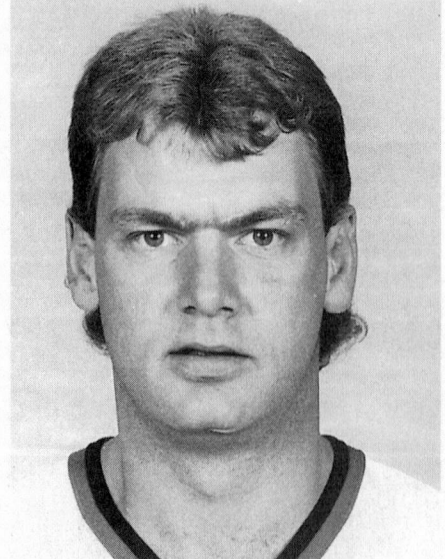

Steve Larmer

Player	Team	Date of 100th Point	G or A	Score		Player's Game No.	Team Game No.	G - A PTS	Total Games	Age when first 100th point scored (Yrs. & Mos.)
Mike Bossy	NYI	Mar. 8/86	(G)	Wsh. 6	at NYI 2	65	65	61-62 — 123	80	
Denis Savard	Chi.	Mar. 12/86	(A)	Buf. 7	at Chi. 6	69	69	47-69 — 116	80	
Mats Naslund	Mtl.	Mar. 13/86	(A)	Mtl. 2	at Bos. 3	70	70	43-67 — 110	80	26.4
Michel Goulet	Que.	Mar. 24/86	(A)	Que. 1	at Min. 0	70	75	53-50 — 103	75	
Glenn Anderson	Edm.	Mar. 25/86	(G)	Edm. 7	at Det. 2	66	74	54-48 — 102	72	
Neal Broten	Min.	Mar. 26/86	(A)	Min. 6	at Tor. 1	76	76	29-76 — 105	80	26.4
Dale Hawerchuk	Wpg.	Mar. 31/86	(A)	Wpg. 5	at L.A. 2	78	78	46-59 — 105	80	
Bernie Federko	St.L.	Apr. 5/86	(G)	Chi. 5	at St.L. 7	79	79	34-68 — 102	80	
Wayne Gretzky	Edm.	Jan. 11/87	(A)	Cgy. 3	at Edm. 5	42	42	62-121 — 183	79	
Jari Kurri	Edm.	Mar. 14/87	(A)	Buf. 3	at Edm. 5	67	68	54-54 — 108	79	
Mario Lemieux	Pit.	Mar. 18/87	(A)	St.L. 4	at Pit. 5	55	72	54-53 — 107	63	
Mark Messier	Edm.	Mar. 19/87	(A)	Edm. 4	at Cgy. 1	71	71	37-70 — 107	77	
Dino Ciccarelli	Min.	Mar. 30/87	(A)	NYR 6	at Min. 5	78	78	52-51 — 103	80	
Doug Gilmour	St.L.	Apr. 2/87	(A)	Buf. 3	at St.L. 5	78	78	42-63 — 105	80	23.10
Dale Hawerchuk	Wpg.	Apr. 5/87	(A)	Wpg. 3	at Cgy. 1	80	80	47-53 — 100	80	
Mario Lemieux	Pit.	Jan. 20/88	(G)	Pit. 8	at Chi. 3	45	48	70-98 — 168	77	
Wayne Gretzky	Edm.	Feb. 11/88	(A)	Edm. 7	at Van. 2	43	56	40-109 — 149	64	
Denis Savard	Chi.	Feb. 12/88	(A)	St.L. 3	at Chi. 4	57	57	44-87 — 131	80	
Dale Hawerchuk	Wpg.	Feb. 23/88	(G)	Wpg. 4	at Pit. 3	61	61	44-77 — 121	80	
Steve Yzerman	Det.	Feb. 27/88	(A)	Det. 4	at Que. 5	63	63	50-52 — 102	64	22.10
Peter Stastny	Que.	Mar. 8/88	(A)	Hfd. 4	at Que. 6	63	67	46-65 — 111	76	
Mark Messier	Edm.	Mar. 15/88	(A)	Buf. 4	at Edm. 6	68	71	37-74 — 111	77	
Jimmy Carson	L.A.	Mar. 26/88	(A)	Chi. 5	at L.A. 9	77	77	55-52 — 107	80	19.8
Hakan Loob	Cgy.	Mar. 26/88	(A)	Van. 1	at Cgy. 6	76	76	50-56 — 106	80	27.9
Mike Bullard	Cgy.	Mar. 26/88	(A)	Van. 1	at Cgy. 6	76	76	48-55 — 103	79	27.1
Michel Goulet	Que.	Mar. 27/88	(A)	Pit. 6	at Que. 3	76	76	48-58 — 106	80	
Luc Robitaille	L.A.	Mar. 30/88	(G)	Cgy. 7	at L.A. 9	78	78	53-58 — 111	80	22.1
Mario Lemieux	Pit.	Dec. 31/88	(A)	N.J. 6	at Pit. 8	36	38	85-114 — 199	76	
Wayne Gretzky	L.A.	Jan. 21/89	(A)	L.A. 4	at Hfd. 5	47	48	54-114 — 168	78	
Bernie Nicholls	L.A.	Jan. 21/89	(A)	L.A. 4	at Hfd. 5	48	48	70-80 — 150	79	
Steve Yzerman	Det.	Jan. 27/89	(G)	Tor. 1	at Det. 8	50	50	65-90 — 155	80	
Rob Brown	Pit.	Mar. 16/89	(A)	Pit. 2	at N.J. 1	60	72	49-66 — 115	68	20.11
Paul Coffey	Pit.	Mar. 20/89	(A)	Pit. 2	at Min. 7	69	74	30-83 — 113	75	
Joe Mullen	Cgy.	Mar. 23/89	(A)	L.A. 2	at Cgy. 4	74	75	51-59 — 110	79	32.1
Jari Kurri	Edm.	Mar. 29/89	(A)	Edm. 5	at Van. 2	75	79	44-58 — 102	76	
Jimmy Carson	Edm.	Apr. 2/89	(A)	Edm. 2	at Cgy. 4	80	80	49-51 — 100	80	
Mario Lemieux	Pit.	Jan. 28/90	(G)	Pit. 2	at Buf. 7	50	50	45-78 — 123	59	
Wayne Gretzky	L.A.	Jan. 30/90	(A)	N.J. 2	at L.A. 5	51	51	40-102 — 142	73	
Steve Yzerman	Det.	Feb. 19/90	(A)	Mtl. 5	at Det. 5	61	61	62-65 — 127	79	
Mark Messier	Edm.	Feb. 20/90	(A)	Edm. 4	at Van. 2	62	62	45-84 — 129	79	
Brett Hull	St.L.	Mar. 3/90	(A)	NYI 4	at St.L. 5	67	67	72-41 — 113	80	25.7
Bernie Nicholls	NYR	Mar. 12/90	(A)	L.A. 6	at NYR 2	70	71	39-73 — 112	79	
Pierre Turgeon	Buf.	Mar. 25/90	(G)	N.J. 4	at Buf. 3	76	76	40-66 — 106	80	20.7
Paul Coffey	Pit.	Mar. 25/90	(A)	Pit. 2	at Hfd. 4	77	77	29-74 — 103	80	
Pat LaFontaine	NYI	Mar. 27/90	(G)	Cgy. 4	at NYI 2	72	78	54-51 — 105	74	25.1
Adam Oates	St.L.	Mar. 29/90	(G)	Pit. 4	at St.L. 5	79	79	23-79 — 102	80	27.7
Joe Sakic	Que.	Mar. 31/90	(G)	Hfd. 3	at Que. 2	79	79	39-63 — 102	80	20.8
Ron Francis	Hfd.	Mar. 31/90	(G)	Hfd. 3	at Que. 2	79	79	32-69 — 101	80	27.0
Luc Robitaille	L.A.	Apr. 1/90	(A)	L.A. 4	at Cgy. 8	80	80	52-49 — 101	80	
Wayne Gretzky	L.A.	Jan. 30/91	(A)	N.J. 4	at L.A. 2	50	51	41-122 — 163	78	
Brett Hull	St.L.	Feb. 23/91	(G)	Bos. 2	at St.L. 9	60	62	86-45 — 131	78	
Mark Recchi	Pit.	Mar. 5/91	(G)	Van. 1	at Pit. 4	66	67	40-73 — 113	78	23.1
Steve Yzerman	Det.	Mar. 10/91	(G)	Det. 4	at St.L. 1	72	72	51-57 — 108	80	
John Cullen	Hfd.	Mar. 16/91	(G)	N.J. 2	at Hfd. 6	71	71	39-71 — 110	78	26.7
Adam Oates	St.L.	Mar. 17/91	(A)	St.L. 4	at Chi. 6	54	73	25-90 — 115	61	
Joe Sakic	Que.	Mar. 19/91	(G)	Edm. 7	at Que. 6	74	74	48-61 — 109	80	
Steve Larmer	Chi.	Mar. 24/91	(G)	Min. 4	at Chi. 5	76	76	44-57 — 101	80	29.9
Theoren Fleury	Cgy.	Mar. 26/91	(G)	Van. 2	at Cgy. 7	77	77	51-53 — 104	79	22.9
Al MacInnis	Cgy.	Mar. 28/91	(A)	Edm. 4	at Cgy. 4	78	78	28-75 — 103	78	27.8
Brett Hull	St.L.	Mar. 2/92	(G)	St.L. 5	at Van. 3	66	66	70-39 — 109	73	
Wayne Gretzky	L.A.	Mar. 3/92	(A)	Phi. 1	at L.A. 4	60	66	31-90 — 121	74	
Kevin Stevens	Pit.	Mar. 7/92	(A)	Pit. 3	at L.A. 5	66	66	54-69 — 123	80	26.11
Mario Lemieux	Pit.	Mar. 10/92	(A)	Cgy. 2	at Pit. 5	53	67	44-87 — 131	64	
Luc Robitaille	L.A.	Mar. 17/92	(A)	Wpg. 4	at L.A. 5	73	73	44-63 — 107	80	
Mark Messier	NYR	Mar. 22/92	(G)	N.J. 3	at NYR 6	74	75	35-72 — 107	79	
Jeremy Roenick	Chi.	Mar. 29/92	(A)	Tor. 1	at Chi. 5	77	77	53-50 — 103	80	22.2
Steve Yzerman	Det.	Apr. 14/92	(G)	Det. 7	at Min. 4	79	80	45-58 — 103	79	
Brian Leetch	NYR	Apr. 16/92	(G)	Pit. 1	at NYR 7	80	80	22-80 — 102	80	24.1
Mario Lemieux	Pit.	Dec. 31/92	(G)	Tor. 3	at Pit. 3	38	39	69-91 — 160	60	
Pat LaFontaine	Buf.	Feb. 10/93	(A)	Buf. 6	at Wpg. 2	55	55	53-95 — 148	84	
Adam Oates	Bos.	Feb. 14/93	(A)	Bos. 3	at T.B. 3	58	58	45-97 — 142	84	
Steve Yzerman	Det.	Feb. 24/93	(A)	Det. 7	at Buf. 10	64	64	58-79 — 137	84	
Pierre Turgeon	NYI	Feb. 28/93	(G)	NYI 7	at Hfd. 6	62	63	58-74 — 132	83	
Doug Gilmour	Tor.	Mar. 3/93	(A)	Min. 1	at Tor. 3	64	64	32-95 — 127	83	
Alexander Mogilny	Buf.	Mar. 5/93	(A)	Hfd. 4	at Buf. 2	58	65	76-51 — 127	77	24.1
Mark Recchi	Phi.	Mar. 7/93	(A)	Phi. 3	at N.J. 7	66	66	53-70 — 123	84	
Teemu Selanne	Wpg.	Mar. 9/93	(G)	Wpg. 4	at T.B. 2	68	68	76-56 — 132	84	22.7
Luc Robitaille	L.A.	Mar. 15/93	(A)	L.A. 4	at Buf. 2	69	69	63-62 — 125	84	
Kevin Stevens	Pit.	Mar. 23/93	(A)	S.J. 2	at Pit. 7	63	73	55-56 — 111	72	
Mats Sundin	Que.	Mar. 27/93	(G)	Phi. 3	at Que. 8	71	75	47-67 — 114	80	22.1
Pavel Bure	Van.	Apr. 1/93	(G)	Van. 5	at T.B. 3	77	77	60-50 — 110	83	22.0
Jeremy Roenick	Chi.	Apr. 4/93	(G)	St.L. 4	at Chi. 5	79	79	50-57 — 107	84	
Craig Janney	St.L.	Apr. 4/93	(G)	St.L. 4	at Chi. 5	79	79	24-82 — 106	84	25.7

Player	Team	Date of 100th Point	G or A	Score		Player's Game No.	Team Game No.	G - A PTS	Total Games	Age when first 100th point scored (Yrs. & Mos.)
Rick Tocchet	Pit.	Apr. 7/93	(G)	Mtl. 3	at Pit. 4	77	81	48-61 — 109	80	28.11
Joe Sakic	Que.	Apr. 8/93	(A)	Que. 2	at Bos. 6	75	81	48-57 — 105	78	
Ron Francis	Pit.	Apr. 9/93	(A)	Pit. 10	at NYR 4	82	82	24-76 — 100	84	
Brett Hull	St.L.	Apr. 11/93	(G)	Min. 1	at St.L. 5	78	82	54-47 — 101	80	
Theoren Fleury	Cgy.	Apr. 11/93	(G)	Cgy. 3	at Van. 6	82	82	34-66 — 100	83	
Joe Juneau	Bos.	Apr. 14/93	(A)	Bos. 4	at Ott. 2	84	84	32-70 — 102	84	25.3
Wayne Gretzky	L.A.	Feb. 14/94	(A)	Bos. 3	at L.A. 2	56	56	38-92 — 130	81	
Sergei Fedorov	Det.	Mar. 1/94	(A)	Cgy. 2	at Det. 5	63	63	56-64 — 120	82	24.2
Doug Gilmour	Tor.	Mar. 23/94	(G)	Tor. 1	at Fla. 1	74	74	27-84 — 111	83	
Adam Oates	Bos.	Mar. 26/94	(A)	Mtl. 3	at Bos. 6	68	75	32-80 — 112	77	
Mark Recchi	Phi.	Mar. 27/94	(A)	Ana. 3	at Phi. 2	76	76	40-67 — 107	84	
Pavel Bure	Van.	Mar. 28/94	(A)	Tor. 2	at Van. 3	68	68	60-47 — 107	76	
Jeremy Roenick	Chi.	Mar. 31/94	(A)	Chi. 3	at Wsh. 6	78	78	46-61 — 107	84	
Brendan Shanahan	St.L.	Apr. 12/94	(G)	St.L. 5	at Dal. 9	80	83	52-50 — 102	81	25.2
Mario Lemieux	Pit.	Jan. 16/96	(G)	Col. 5	at Pit. 2	38	44	69-92 — 161	70	
Jaromir Jagr	Pit.	Feb. 6/96	(G)	Bos. 5	at Pit. 6	52	52	62-87 — 149	82	23.11
Ron Francis	Pit.	Mar. 9/96	(A)	N.J. 4	at Pit. 3	61	66	27-92 — 119	77	
Peter Forsberg	Col.	Mar. 9/96	(A)	Col. 7	at Van. 5	68	68	30-86 — 116	82	22.7
Joe Sakic	Col.	Mar. 17/96	(A)	Edm. 1	at Col. 8	70	70	51-69 — 120	82	
Eric Lindros	Phi.	Mar. 25/96	(A)	Hfd. 0	at Phi. 3	65	73	47-68 — 115	73	23
Teemu Selanne	Ana.	Mar. 25/96	(A)	Ana. 1	at Det. 5	70	73	40-68 — 108	79	
Alexander Mogilny	Van.	Mar. 25/96	(A)	L.A. 1	at Van. 4	72	75	55-52 — 107	79	
Wayne Gretzky	St.L.	Mar. 28/96	(A)	N.J. 4	at St.L. 4	76	75	23-79 — 102	80	
Doug Weight	Edm.	Mar. 30/96	(G)	Tor. 4	at Edm. 3	76	76	25-79 — 104	82	25.3
Sergei Fedorov	Det.	Apr. 2/96	(A)	Det. 3	at S.J. 6	72	76	39-68 — 107	78	
Paul Kariya	Ana.	Apr. 7/96	(G)	Ana. 5	at S.J. 3	78	78	50-58 — 108	82	21.5
Mario Lemieux	Pit.	Mar. 8/97	(A)	Phi. 2	at Pit. 3	61	65	50-72 — 122	76	
Teemu Selanne	Ana.	Apr. 1/97	(A)	Chi. 3	at Ana. 3	74	78	51-58 — 109	78	
Jaromir Jagr	Pit.	Apr. 15/98	(G)	T.B. 1	at Pit. 5	76	80	35-67 — 102	77	
Jaromir Jagr	Pit.	Mar. 13/99	(G)	Phi. 0	at Pit. 4	65	65	44-83 — 127	81	
Teemu Selanne	Ana.	Apr. 5/99	(A)	Ana. 2	at Det. 3	69	76	47-60 — 107	75	
Paul Kariya	Ana.	Apr. 17/99	(G)	Ana. 3	at S.J. 3	82	82	39-62 — 101	82	
Jaromir Jagr	Pit.	Mar. 10/01	(G)	Cgy. 3	at Pit. 6	68	68	52-69 — 121	81	
Joe Sakic	Col.	Mar. 18/01	(G)	Min. 3	at Col. 4	72	72	54-64 — 118	82	
Markus Naslund	Van.	Mar. 27/03	(A)	Phx. 1	at Van. 5	78	78	48-56 — 104	82	29.8
Peter Forsberg	Col.	Mar. 31/03	(A)	S.J. 1	at Col. 3	72	79	29-77 — 106	79	
Joe Thornton	Bos.	Apr. 4/03	(A)	Buf. 5	at Bos. 8	77	82	36-65 — 101	77	23.9
Jaromir Jagr	NYR	Mar. 18/06	A	Tor. 2	at NYR 5	67	67	54-69 — 123	82	
Joe Thornton	S.J.	Mar. 21/06	A	S.J. 6	at St.L. 0	66	67	29-96 — 125	81	
Alex Ovechkin	Wsh.	Apr. 10/06	G	Wsh. 2	at Bos. 1	77	78	52-54 — 106	81	20.6
Dany Heatley	Ott.	Apr. 13/06	A	Fla. 5	at Ott. 4	80	80	50-53 — 103	82	25.2
Daniel Alfredsson	Ott.	Apr. 15/06	A	Fla. 5	at Ott. 4	76	81	43-60 — 103	77	33.4
Eric Staal	Car.	Apr. 15/06	A	Car. 2	at T.B. 3	81	81	45-55 — 100	82	21.5
Sidney Crosby	Pit.	Apr. 17/06	A	NYI 1	at Pit. 6	80	81	39-63 — 102	81	18.8
Sidney Crosby	Pit.	Mar. 10/07	G	NYR 2	at Pit. 3	65	68	36-84 — 120	79	
Joe Thornton	S.J.	Mar. 22/07	A	S.J. 5	at Atl. 1	75	75	22-92 — 114	82	
Vincent Lecavalier	T.B.	Mar. 24/07	A	Ott. 7	at T.B. 2	76	76	52-56 — 108	82	26.11
Dany Heatley	Ott.	Mar. 31/07	G	Ott. 5	at NYI 2	79	79	50-55 — 105	82	
Martin St. Louis	T.B.	Mar. 31/07	A	Wsh. 2	at T.B. 5	79	79	43-59 — 102	82	31.10
Marian Hossa	Atl.	Apr. 7/07	A	T.B. 2	at Atl. 3	82	82	43-57 — 100	82	28.3
Joe Sakic	Col.	Apr. 8/07	G	Cgy. 3	at Col. 6	82	82	36-64 — 100	82	
Alex Ovechkin	Wsh.	Mar. 18/08	A	Wsh. 4	at Nsh. 2	74	74	65-47 — 112	82	
Evgeni Malkin	Pit.	Mar. 22/08	G	N.J. 1	at Pit. 7	75	75	47-59 — 106	82	21.8
Evgeni Malkin	Pit.	Mar. 17/09	G	Atl. 2	at Pit. 6	72	72	35-78 — 113	82	
Alex Ovechkin	Wsh.	Mar. 27/09	G	T.B. 3	at Wsh. 5	73	76	56-54 — 110	79	
Sidney Crosby	Pit.	Apr. 7/09	G	Pit. 6	at T.B. 4	75	80	33-70 — 103	77	
Henrik Sedin	Van.	Mar. 27/10	A	Van. 2	at S.J. 4	75	75	29-83-112	82	29.7
Alex Ovechkin	Wsh.	Mar. 28/10	A	Cgy. 5	at Wsh. 3	65	75	50-59-109	72	
Sidney Crosby	Pit.	Apr. 6/10	A	Wsh. 6	at Pit. 3	78	79	51-58-109	81	
Nicklas Backstrom	Wsh.	Apr. 9/10	A	Atl. 2	at Wsh. 5	81	81	33-68-101	82	22.5

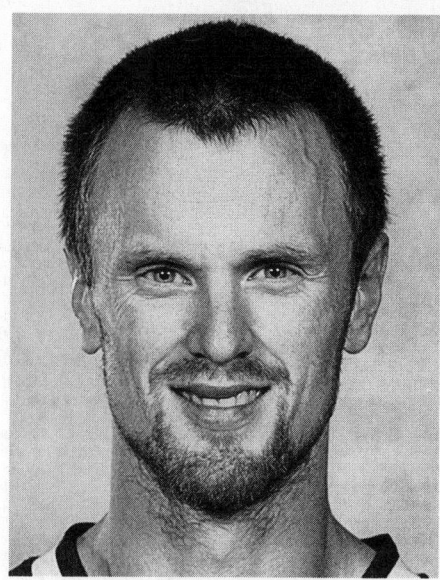

Henrik Sedin

Alex Ovechkin

Nicklas Backstrom

Five-or-more-Goal Games

Player	Team	Date	Score				Opposing Goaltender
SEVEN GOALS							
Joe Malone	Quebec Bulldogs	Jan. 31/20	Tor. 6	at	Que. 10		Ivan Mitchell (4)
							Howard Lockhart (3)
SIX GOALS							
Newsy Lalonde	Montreal	Jan. 10/20	Tor. 7	at	Mtl. 14		Ivan Mitchell (2)
							Howard Lockhart (4)
Joe Malone	Quebec Bulldogs	Mar. 10/20	Ott. 4	at	Que. 10		Clint Benedict
Corb Denneny	Toronto St. Pats	Jan. 26/21	Ham. 3	at	Tor. 10		Howard Lockhart
Cy Denneny	Ottawa Senators	Mar. 7/21	Ham. 5	at	Ott. 12		Howard Lockhart
Syd Howe	Detroit	Feb. 3/44	NYR 2	at	Det. 12		Ken McAuley
Red Berenson	St. Louis	Nov. 7/68	St.L. 8	at	Phi. 0		Doug Favell
Darryl Sittler	Toronto	Feb. 7/76	Bos. 4	at	Tor. 11		Dave Reece
FIVE GOALS							
Joe Malone	Montreal	Dec. 19/17	Mtl. 7	at	Ott. 4		Clint Benedict
Harry Hyland	Mtl. Wanderers	Dec. 19/17	Tor. 9	at	Mtl. W. 10		Art Brooks, Sammy Hebert
Joe Malone	Montreal	Jan. 12/18	Ott. 4	at	Mtl. 9		Clint Benedict
Joe Malone	Montreal	Feb. 2/18	Tor. 2	at	Mtl. 11		Hap Holmes
Mickey Roach	Toronto St. Pats	Mar. 6/20	Que. 2	at	Tor. 11		Howard Lockhart
Newsy Lalonde	Montreal	Feb. 16/21	Ham. 5	at	Mtl. 10		Howard Lockhart
Babe Dye	Toronto St. Pats	Dec. 16/22	Mtl. 2	at	Tor. 7		Georges Vezina
Red Green	Hamilton Tigers	Dec. 5/24	Ham. 10	at	Tor. 3		John Ross Roach
Babe Dye	Toronto St. Pats	Dec. 22/24	Tor. 10	at	Bos. 1		Hec Fowler
Punch Broadbent	Mtl. Maroons	Jan. 7/25	Mtl. 6	at	Ham. 2		Jake Forbes
Pit Lepine	Montreal	Dec. 14/29	Ott. 4	at	Mtl. 6		Alex Connell
Howie Morenz	Montreal	Mar. 18/30	NYA 3	at	Mtl. 8		Roy Worters
Charlie Conacher	Toronto	Jan. 19/32	NYA 3	at	Tor. 11		Roy Worters (3), Al Shields (2)
Ray Getliffe	Montreal	Feb. 6/43	Bos. 3	at	Mtl. 8		Frank Brimsek
Maurice Richard	Montreal	Dec. 28/44	Det. 1	at	Mtl. 9		Harry Lumley
Howie Meeker	Toronto	Jan. 8/47	Chi. 4	at	Tor. 10		Paul Bibeault
Bernie Geoffrion	Montreal	Feb. 19/55	NYR 2	at	Mtl. 10		Gump Worsley
Bobby Rousseau	Montreal	Feb. 1/64	Det. 3	at	Mtl. 9		Roger Crozier
Yvan Cournoyer	Montreal	Feb. 15/75	Chi. 3	at	Mtl. 12		Mike Veisor
Don Murdoch	NY Rangers	Oct. 12/76	NYR 10	at	Min. 4		Gary Smith
Ian Turnbull	Toronto	Feb. 2/77	Det. 1	at	Tor. 9		Ed Giacomin (2), Jim Rutherford (3)
Bryan Trottier	NY Islanders	Dec. 23/78	NYR 4	at	NYI 9		Wayne Thomas (4), John Davidson (1)
Tim Young	Minnesota	Jan. 15/79	Min. 8	at	NYR 1		Doug Soetaert (3), Wayne Thomas (2)
John Tonelli	NY Islanders	Jan. 6/81	Tor. 3	at	NYI 6		Jiri Crha (4), empty net (1)
Wayne Gretzky	Edmonton	Feb. 18/81	St.L. 2	at	Edm. 9		Mike Liut (3), Ed Staniowski (2)
Wayne Gretzky	Edmonton	Dec. 30/81	Phi. 5	at	Edm. 7		Pete Peeters (4), empty net (1)
Grant Mulvey	Chicago	Feb. 3/82	St.L. 5	at	Chi. 9		Mike Liut (4), Gary Edwards (1)
Bryan Trottier	NY Islanders	Feb. 13/82	Phi. 2	at	NYI 8		Pete Peeters
Willy Lindstrom	Winnipeg	Mar. 2/82	Wpg. 7	at	Phi. 6		Pete Peeters
Mark Pavelich	NY Rangers	Feb. 23/83	Hfd. 3	at	NYR 11		Greg Millen
Jari Kurri	Edmonton	Nov. 19/83	N.J. 4	at	Edm. 13		Glenn Resch (3), Ron Low (2)
Bengt Gustafsson	Washington	Jan. 8/84	Wsh. 7	at	Phi. 1		Pelle Lindbergh
Pat Hughes	Edmonton	Feb. 3/84	Cgy. 5	at	Edm. 10		Don Edwards (3), Reggie Lemelin (2)
Wayne Gretzky	Edmonton	Dec. 15/84	Edm. 8	at	St.L. 2		Rick Wamsley (3), Mike Liut (2)
Dave Andreychuk	Buffalo	Feb. 6/86	Buf. 8	at	Bos. 6		Pat Riggin (1), Doug Keans (4)
Wayne Gretzky	Edmonton	Dec. 6/87	Min. 4	at	Edm. 10		Don Beaupre (4), Kari Takko (1)
Mario Lemieux	Pittsburgh	Dec. 31/88	N.J. 6	at	Pit. 8		Bob Sauve (3), Chris Terreri (1), empty net (1)
Joe Nieuwendyk	Calgary	Jan. 11/89	Wpg. 3	at	Cgy. 8		Daniel Berthiaume
Mats Sundin	Quebec	Mar. 5/92	Que. 10	at	Hfd. 4		Peter Sidorkiewicz (3), Kay Whitmore (2)
Mario Lemieux	Pittsburgh	Apr. 9/93	Pit. 10	at	NYR 4		Corey Hirsch (3), Mike Richter (2)
Peter Bondra	Washington	Feb. 5/94	T.B. 3	at	Wsh. 6		Daren Puppa (4), Pat Jablonski (1)
Mike Ricci	Quebec	Feb. 17/94	Que. 8	at	S.J. 2		Arturs Irbe (3), Jimmy Waite (2)
Alex Zhamnov	Winnipeg	Apr. 1/95	Wpg. 7	at	L.A. 7		Kelly Hrudey (3), Grant Fuhr (2)
Mario Lemieux	Pittsburgh	Mar. 26/96	St.L. 4	at	Pit. 8		Grant Fuhr (1), Jon Casey (4)
Sergei Fedorov	Detroit	Dec. 26/96	Wsh. 4	at	Det. 5		Jim Carey
Marian Gaborik	Minnesota	Dec. 20/07	NYR 3	at	Min. 6		Henrik Lundqvist

Players' 500th Goals

Regular Season

Player	Team	Date	Game No.	Score				Opposing Goaltender	Total Goals	Total Games
Maurice Richard	Montreal	Oct. 19/57	863	Chi. 1	at	Mtl. 3		Glenn Hall	544	978
Gordie Howe	Detroit	Mar. 14/62	1,045	Det. 2	at	NYR 3		Gump Worsley	801	1,767
Bobby Hull	Chicago	Feb. 21/70	861	NYR. 2¹	at	Chi. 4		Ed Giacomin	610	1,063
Jean Béliveau	Montreal	Feb. 11/71	1,101	Min. 2	at	Mtl. 6		Gilles Gilbert	507	1,125
Frank Mahovlich	Montreal	Mar. 21/73	1,105	Van. 2	at	Mtl. 3		Dunc Wilson	533	1,181
Phil Esposito	Boston	Dec. 22/74	803	Det. 4	at	Bos. 5		Jim Rutherford	717	1,282
John Bucyk	Boston	Oct. 30/75	1,370	St.L. 2	at	Bos. 3		Yves Bélanger	556	1,540
Stan Mikita	Chicago	Feb. 27/77	1,221	Van. 4	at	Chi. 3		Cesare Maniago	541	1,394
Marcel Dionne	Los Angeles	Dec. 14/82	887	L.A. 2	at	Wsh. 7		Al Jensen	731	1,348
Guy Lafleur	Montreal	Dec. 20/83	918	Mtl. 6	at	N.J. 0		Glenn Resch	560	1,126
Mike Bossy	NY Islanders	Jan. 2/86	647	Bos. 5	at	NYI 7		empty net	573	752
Gilbert Perreault	Buffalo	Mar. 9/86	1,159	N.J. 3	at	Buf. 4		Alain Chevrier	512	1,191
Wayne Gretzky	Edmonton	Nov. 22/86	575	Van. 2	at	Edm. 5		empty net	894	1,487
Lanny McDonald	Calgary	Mar. 21/89	1,107	NYI 1	at	Cgy. 4		Mark Fitzpatrick	500	1,111
Bryan Trottier	NY Islanders	Feb. 13/90	1,104	Cgy. 4	at	NYI 2		Rick Wamsley	524	1,279
Mike Gartner	NY Rangers	Oct. 14/91	936	Wsh. 5	at	NYR 3		Mike Liut	708	1,432
Michel Goulet	Chicago	Feb. 16/92	951	Cgy. 5	at	Chi. 5		Jeff Reese	548	1,089
Jari Kurri	Los Angeles	Oct. 17/92	833	Bos. 6	at	L.A. 8		empty net	601	1,251
Dino Ciccarelli	Detroit	Jan. 8/94	946	Det. 6	at	L.A. 3		Kelly Hrudey	608	1,232
Mario Lemieux	Pittsburgh	Oct. 26/95	605	Pit. 7	at	NYI 5		Tommy Soderstrom	690	915
Mark Messier	NY Rangers	Nov. 6/95	1,141	Cgy. 2	at	NYR 4		Rick Tabaracci	694	1,756
Steve Yzerman	Detroit	Jan. 17/96	906	Col. 2	at	Det. 3		Patrick Roy	692	1,514
Dale Hawerchuk	St. Louis	Jan. 31/96	1,103	St.L. 4	at	Tor. 0		Felix Potvin	518	1,188
Brett Hull	St. Louis	Dec. 22/96	693	L.A. 4	at	St.L. 7		Stephane Fiset	741	1,269
Joe Mullen	Pittsburgh	Mar. 14/97	1,052	Pit. 3	at	Col. 6		Patrick Roy	502	1,062
Dave Andreychuk	New Jersey	Mar. 15/97	1,070	Wsh. 2	at	N.J. 3		Bill Ranford	640	1,639
Luc Robitaille	Los Angeles	Jan. 7/99	928	Buf. 2	at	L.A. 4		Dwayne Roloson	668	1,431
Pat Verbeek	Detroit	Mar. 22/00	1,285	Cgy. 2	at	Det. 2		Fred Brathwaite	522	1,424
Ron Francis	Carolina	Jan. 2/02	1,533	Bos. 6	at	Car. 3		Byron Dafoe	549	1,731
Brendan Shanahan	Detroit	Mar. 23/02	1,100	Det. 2	at	Col. 0		Patrick Roy	656	1,524
Joe Sakic	Colorado	Dec. 11/02	1,044	Col. 1	at	Van. 3		Dan Cloutier	625	1,378
Joe Nieuwendyk	New Jersey	Jan. 17/03	1,094	N.J. 2	at	Car. 1		Kevin Weekes	564	1,257
Jaromir Jagr	Washington	Feb. 4/03	928	Wsh. 5	at	T.B. 1		John Grahame	646	1,273
Pierre Turgeon	Colorado	Nov. 8/05	1,229	S.J. 2	at	Col. 5		Vesa Toskala	515	1,294
Mats Sundin	Toronto	Oct. 14/06	1,162	Cgy. 4	at	Tor. 5		Miikka Kiprusoff	564	1,346
*Teemu Selanne	Anaheim	Nov. 22/06	982	Ana. 2	at	Col. 3		Jose Theodore	606	1,186
Peter Bondra	Chicago	Dec. 22/06	1,050	Tor. 1	at	Chi. 3		J.S. Aubin	503	1,081
*Mark Recchi	Pittsburgh	Jan. 26/07	1,303	Pit. 4	at	Chi. 3		Marty Turco	563	1,571
*Mike Modano	Dallas	Mar. 13/07	1,225	Phi. 2	at	Dal. 3		Antero Niittymaki	557	1,459
Jeremy Roenick	San Jose	Nov. 10/07	1,267	Phx. 1	at	S.J. 4		Alex Auld	513	1,363
Keith Tkachuk	St. Louis	Apr. 6/08	1,055	St.L. 4	at	CBJ 1		empty net	538	1,201

*Active

Teemu Selanne is congratulated by fellow Finn Saku Koivu after scoring his 600th career goal on March 21, 2010. Selanne finished the season with 606 goals, five more than Finnish legend Jari Kurri and 40 behind Jaromir Jagr for the all-time lead among European-born NHLers.

Players' 1,000th Points

Regular Season

Player	Team	Date	Game No.	G or A	Score			Total Points G A PTS	Total Games
Gordie Howe	Detroit	Nov. 27/60	938	(A)	Tor. 0	at	Det. 2	801-1,049–1,850	1,767
Jean Béliveau	Montreal	Mar. 3/68	911	(A)	Mtl. 2	at	Det. 5	507-712–1,219	1,125
Alex Delvecchio	Detroit	Feb. 16/69	1,143	(A)	L.A. 3	at	Det. 6	456-825–1,281	1,549
Bobby Hull	Chicago	Dec. 13/70	909	(A)	Min. 2	at	Chi. 5	610-560–1,170	1,063
Norm Ullman	Toronto	Oct. 16/71	1,113	(A)	NYR 5	at	Tor. 3	490-739–1,229	1,410
Stan Mikita	Chicago	Oct. 15/72	924	(A)	St.L. 3	at	Chi. 1	541-926–1,467	1,394
John Bucyk	Boston	Nov. 9/72	1,144	(G)	Det. 3	at	Bos. 8	556-813–1,369	1,540
Frank Mahovlich	Montreal	Feb. 17/73	1,090	(A)	Phi. 7	at	Mtl. 6	533-570–1,103	1,181
Henri Richard	Montreal	Dec. 20/73	1,194	(A)	Mtl. 2	at	Buf. 2	358-688–1,046	1,256
Phil Esposito	Boston	Feb. 15/74	745	(A)	Bos. 4	at	Van. 2	717-873–1,590	1,282
Rod Gilbert	NY Rangers	Feb. 19/77	1,027	(G)	NYR 2	at	NYI 5	406-615–1,021	1,065
Jean Ratelle	Boston	Apr. 3/77	1,007	(A)	Tor. 4	at	Bos. 7	491-776–1,267	1,281
Marcel Dionne	Los Angeles	Jan. 7/81	740	(A)	L.A. 5	at	Hfd. 3	731-1,040–1,771	1,348
Guy Lafleur	Montreal	Mar. 4/81	720	(G)	Wpg. 3	at	Mtl. 9	560-793–1,353	1,126
Bobby Clarke	Philadelphia	Mar. 19/81	922	(G)	Bos. 3	at	Phi. 5	358-852–1,210	1,144
Gilbert Perreault	Buffalo	Apr. 3/82	871	(A)	Buf. 5	at	Mtl. 4	512-814–1,326	1,191
Darryl Sittler	Philadelphia	Jan. 20/83	927	(G)	Cgy. 2	at	Phi. 5	484-637–1,121	1,096
Wayne Gretzky	Edmonton	Dec. 19/84	424	(A)	L.A. 3	at	Edm. 7	894-1,963–2,875	1,487
Bryan Trottier	NY Islanders	Jan. 29/85	726	(A)	Min. 4	at	NYI 4	524-901–1,425	1,279
Mike Bossy	NY Islanders	Jan. 24/86	656	(A)	NYI 7	at	Wsh. 5	573-553–1,126	752
Denis Potvin	NY Islanders	Apr. 4/87	987	(G)	Buf. 6	at	NYI 6	310-742–1,052	1,060
Bernie Federko	St. Louis	Mar. 19/88	855	(A)	Hfd. 4	at	St.L. 3	369-761–1,130	1,000
Lanny McDonald	Calgary	Mar. 7/89	1,101	(G)	Wpg. 5	at	Cgy. 9	500-506–1,006	1,111
Peter Stastny	Quebec	Oct. 19/89	682	(G)	Que. 5	at	Chi. 3	450-789–1,239	977
Jari Kurri	Edmonton	Jan. 2/90	716	(A)	Edm. 6	at	St.L. 4	601-797–1,398	1,251
Denis Savard	Chicago	Mar. 11/90	727	(A)	St.L. 6	at	Chi. 4	473-865–1,338	1,196
Paul Coffey	Pittsburgh	Dec. 22/90	770	(A)	Pit. 4	at	NYI 3	396-1,135–1,531	1,409
Mark Messier	Edmonton	Jan. 13/91	822	(A)	Edm. 5	at	Phi. 3	694-1,193–1,887	1,756
Dave Taylor	Los Angeles	Feb. 5/91	930	(A)	L.A. 3	at	Phi. 2	431-638–1,069	1,111
Michel Goulet	Chicago	Feb. 23/91	878	(G)	Chi. 3	at	Min. 3	548-604–1,152	1,089
Dale Hawerchuk	Buffalo	Mar. 8/91	781	(G)	Chi. 5	at	Buf. 3	518-891–1,409	1,188
Bobby Smith	Minnesota	Nov. 30/91	986	(A)	Min. 4	at	Tor. 3	357-679–1,036	1,077
Mike Gartner	NY Rangers	Jan. 4/92	971	(G)	NYR 4	at	N.J. 6	708-627–1,335	1,432
Raymond Bourque	Boston	Feb. 29/92	933	(A)	Wsh. 5	at	Bos. 5	410-1,169–1,579	1,612
Mario Lemieux	Pittsburgh	Mar. 24/92	513	(A)	Pit. 3	at	Det. 4	690-1,033–1,723	915
Glenn Anderson	Toronto	Feb. 22/93	954	(G)	Tor. 8	at	Van. 1	498-601–1,099	1,129
Steve Yzerman	Detroit	Feb. 24/93	737	(A)	Det. 7	at	Buf. 10	692-1,063–1,755	1,514
Ron Francis	Pittsburgh	Oct. 28/93	893	(G)	Que. 7	at	Pit. 3	549-1,249–1,798	1,731
Bernie Nicholls	New Jersey	Feb. 13/94	858	(G)	N.J. 3	at	T.B. 3	475-734–1,209	1,127
Dino Ciccarelli	Detroit	Mar. 9/94	957	(G)	Det. 5	at	Cgy. 1	608-592–1,200	1,232
Brian Propp	Hartford	Mar. 19/94	1,008	(G)	Hfd. 5	at	Phi. 3	425-579–1,004	1,016
Joe Mullen	Pittsburgh	Feb. 7/95	935	(A)	Fla. 3	at	Pit. 7	502-561–1,063	1,062
Steve Larmer	NY Rangers	Mar. 8/95	983	(A)	N.J. 4	at	NYR 6	441-571–1,012	1,006
Doug Gilmour	Toronto	Dec. 23/95	935	(A)	Edm. 1	at	Tor. 6	450-964–1,414	1,474
Larry Murphy	Toronto	Mar. 27/96	1,228	(G)	Tor. 6	at	Van. 2	287-929–1,216	1,615
Dave Andreychuk	New Jersey	Apr. 7/96	998	(G)	NYR 2	at	N.J. 4	640-698–1,338	1,639
Adam Oates	Washington	Oct. 8/97	830	(G)	Wsh. 6	at	NYI 3	341-1,079–1,420	1,337
Phil Housley	Washington	Nov. 8/97	1,081	(A)	Edm. 1	at	Wsh. 2	338-894–1,232	1,495
Dale Hunter	Washington	Jan. 9/98	1,308	(A)	Phi. 1	at	Wsh. 4	323-697–1,020	1,407
Pat LaFontaine	NY Rangers	Jan. 22/98	847	(G)	Phi. 4	at	NYR 3	468-545–1,013	865
Luc Robitaille	Los Angeles	Jan. 29/98	882	(A)	Cgy. 3	at	L.A. 5	668-726–1,394	1,431
Al MacInnis	St. Louis	Apr. 7/98	1,056	(A)	St.L. 3	at	Det. 5	340-934–1,274	1,416
Brett Hull	Dallas	Nov. 14/98	815	(A)	Dal. 3	at	Bos. 1	741-650–1,391	1,269
Brian Bellows	Washington	Jan. 2/99	1,147	(A)	Tor. 2	at	Wsh. 5	485-537–1,022	1,188
Pierre Turgeon	St. Louis	Oct. 9/99	881	(G)	St.L. 4	at	Edm. 3	515-812–1,327	1,294
Joe Sakic	Colorado	Dec. 27/99	810	(A)	St.L. 1	at	Col. 5	625-1,016–1,641	1,378
Pat Verbeek	Detroit	Feb. 27/00	1,275	(A)	T.B. 1	at	Det. 3	522-541–1,063	1,424
V. Damphousse	San Jose	Oct. 14/00	1,090	(A)	Bos. 2	at	S.J. 5	432-773–1,205	1,378
Jaromir Jagr	Pittsburgh	Dec. 30/00	763	(G)	Ott. 3	at	Pit. 5	646-953–1,599	1,273
*Mark Recchi	Philadelphia	Mar. 13/01	920	(A)	St.L. 2	at	Phi. 5	563-922–1,485	1,571
Theoren Fleury	NY Rangers	Oct. 29/01	960	(A)	Dal. 2	at	NYR 4	455-633–1,088	1,084
B. Shanahan	Detroit	Jan. 12/02	1,073	(A)	Dal. 2	at	Det. 5	656-698–1,354	1,524
Jeremy Roenick	Philadelphia	Jan. 30/02	961	(G)	Phi. 1	at	Ott. 3	513-703–1,216	1,363
*Mike Modano	Dallas	Nov. 15/02	965	(A)	Col. 2	at	Dal. 4	557-802–1,359	1,459
Joe Nieuwendyk	New Jersey	Feb. 23/03	1,094	(A)	N.J. 4	at	Pit. 3	564-562–1,126	1,257
Mats Sundin	Toronto	Mar. 10/03	994	(G)	Tor. 3	at	Edm. 2	564-785–1,349	1,346
Sergei Fedorov	Anaheim	Feb. 14/04	965	(A)	Ana. 2	at	Van. 1	483-696–1,179	1,248
Alexander Mogilny	Toronto	Mar. 15/04	946	(A)	Tor. 6	at	Buf. 5	473-559–1,032	990
Brian Leetch	Boston	Oct. 18/05	1,151	(A)	Bos. 3	at	Mtl. 4	247-781–1,028	1,205
*Teemu Selanne	Anaheim	Jan. 30/06	928	(A)	L.A. 3	at	Ana. 4	606-654–1,260	1,186
Rod Brind'Amour	Carolina	Nov. 4/06	1,202	(G)	Car. 3	at	Ott. 2	452-732–1,184	1,484
Keith Tkachuk	St. Louis	Nov. 30/08	1,077	(G)	St.L. 4	at	Atl. 2	538-527–1,065	1,201
*Doug Weight	NY Islanders	Jan. 2/09	1,167	(A)	NYI 4	at	Phx. 5	276-748–1,024	1,220
*Nicklas Lidstrom	Detroit	Oct. 15/09	1,336	(A)	L.A. 2	at	Det. 5	237-809–1,046	1,412

*Active

Nicklas Lidstrom (above) and his wife receive a crystal globe from the Detroit Red Wings in honor of reaching the 1,000-point plateau on October 15, 2009. Denis Potvin (top) was the first defenseman in NHL history to collect 1,000 career points.

Individual Awards

Hart Memorial Trophy

Art Ross Trophy

Calder Memorial Trophy

James Norris Memorial Trophy

HART MEMORIAL TROPHY

An annual award "to the player adjudged to be the most valuable to his team." Winner selected in a poll by the Professional Hockey Writers' Association in the 30 NHL cities at the end of the regular schedule.

History: The Hart Memorial Trophy was presented by the National Hockey League in 1960 after the original Hart Trophy was retired to the Hockey Hall of Fame. The original Hart Trophy was donated to the NHL in 1924 by Dr. David A. Hart, father of Cecil Hart, former manager-coach of the Montreal Canadiens.

2009-10 Winner: Henrik Sedin, Vancouver Canucks
Runners-up: Alex Ovechkin, Washington Capitals
Sidney Crosby, Pittsburgh Penguins

Henrik Sedin of the Vancouver Canucks became the first player in the 40-year history of the franchise to win the Hart Memorial Trophy. Sedin received 46 first-place votes among the 133 ballots cast and accumulated 894 points to edge two-time defending Hart Trophy winner Alex Ovechkin of the Washington Capitals, who was the top selection on 40 ballots and earned 834 points. Pittsburgh's Sidney Crosby received 20 first-place votes and 729 points. Goalies Ryan Miller of Buffalo and Ilya Bryzgalov both received 13 first-place votes with Miller garnering 505 points overall and Bryzgalov 354. Colorado goalie Craig Anderson received the final first-place vote but finished ninth overall with 10 points behind Steven Stamkos of Tampa Bay (28 points), Patrick Kane of Chicago (17) and Martin Brodeur of New Jersey (16). San Jose's Patrick Marleau rounded out the top ten with 10 points as well.

Sedin flourished in 2009-10 despite having to play 19 games without his twin brother and career-long linemate Daniel, who missed a large chunk of the season with a broken foot. With 112 points - 30 more than his previous career high - Henrik became the first player in franchise history to win the Art Ross Trophy as NHL scoring champion. Sedin easily led the league with 83 assists, 14 more than runner-up Joe Thornton of San Jose. Five of Sedin's career-high 29 goals were game winners. With a plus-35 rating, Henrik Sedin has been a plus player in every one of his nine NHL seasons with the exception of his minus-2 rookie year.

ART ROSS TROPHY

An annual award "to the player who leads the league in scoring points at the end of the regular season."

History: Arthur Howey Ross, former manager-coach of the Boston Bruins, presented the trophy to the National Hockey League in 1947. If two players finish the schedule with the same number of points, the trophy is awarded in the following manner: 1. Player with most goals. 2. Player with fewer games played. 3. Player scoring first goal of the season.

2009-10 Winner: Henrik Sedin, Vancouver Canucks
Runners-up: Sidney Crosby, Pittsburgh Penguins
Alex Ovechkin, Washington Capitals

Center Henrik Sedin of the Vancouver Canucks received the Art Ross Trophy for the first time, finishing the 2009-10 regular season with a league-leading, career-high and franchise-record 112 points (29 goals, 83 assists). Sedin edged Pittsburgh Penguins center Sidney Crosby (51-58-109) and Washington Capitals left winger Alex Ovechkin (50-59-109) to become the first Canuck in franchise history and the ninth player in the past nine seasons to capture the Art Ross, joining Jaromir Jagr in 2001, Jarome Iginla in 2002, Peter Forsberg in 2003, Martin St. Louis in 2004, Joe Thornton in 2006, Crosby in 2007, Ovechkin in 2008 and Evgeni Malkin in 2009.

Sedin, Crosby and Ovechkin waged a neck-and-neck battle for the NHL points lead throughout the second half of the season, with Sedin regaining the lead by tallying four assists in a 7-3 win over the Calgary Flames in the Vancouver season finale. Ovechkin, needing three points to overhaul Sedin in his season-ending game, was held without a point in a 4-3 shootout loss to the Boston Bruins. Hours later, Crosby nosed past Ovechkin into second place by tallying five points (two goals, three assists) in a 6-5 overtime win over the New York Islanders.

CALDER MEMORIAL TROPHY

An annual award "to the player selected as the most proficient in his first year of competition in the National Hockey League." Winner selected in a poll by the Professional Hockey Writers' Association at the end of the regular schedule.

History: From 1936-37 until his death in 1943, Frank Calder, NHL President, bought a trophy each year to be given permanently to the outstanding rookie. After Calder's death, the NHL presented the Calder Memorial Trophy in his memory and the trophy is to be kept in perpetuity. To be eligible for the award, a player cannot have played more than 25 games in any single preceding season nor in six or more games in each of any two preceding seasons in any major professional league. Beginning in 1990-91, to be eligible for this award a player must not have attained his twenty-sixth birthday by September 15th of the season in which he is eligible.

2009-10 Winner: Tyler Myers, Buffalo Sabres
Runners-up: Jimmy Howard, Detroit Red Wings
Matt Duchene, Colorado Avalanche

Defenseman Tyler Myers of the Buffalo Sabres won the Calder Memorial Trophy. Myers received 94 of 133 first-place votes and 1,178 points, outdistancing Detroit Red Wings goalie Jimmy Howard, who polled 24 first-place votes and 778 points. Matt Duchene of Colorado received 12 first-place votes and 775 points. Tuukka Rask of Boston received the final two first-place votes, and finished fourth in the standings with 339 points. John Tavares of the New York Islanders (303 points) ranked fifth in the balloting.

Myers not only won an NHL roster spot as a 19-year-old, he posted statistics befitting an established veteran. The 6'8", 222-lb. defenseman led the Sabres in ice time per game (23:44), shared second place on the club in plus-minus (+13) and was fifth in scoring (11-37-48). Myers ranked at or near the top in several rookie categories, including average ice time (first), assists (first), blocked shots (first, 137), plus-minus (T-second) and points (third). He also was one of four rookies to play all 82 games. The Sabres' top pick, 12th overall, in the 2008 Entry Draft, Myers is the first defenseman to win the Calder since the Blues' Barret Jackman in 2003 and the third player in franchise history, following Gilbert Perreault (1971) and Tom Barrasso (1984).

JAMES NORRIS MEMORIAL TROPHY

An annual award "to the defense player who demonstrates throughout the season the greatest all-round ability in the position." Winner selected in a poll by the Professional Hockey Writers' Association at the end of the regular schedule.

History: The James Norris Memorial Trophy was presented in 1953 by the four children of the late James Norris in memory of the former owner-president of the Detroit Red Wings.

2009-10 Winner: Duncan Keith, Chicago Blackhawks
Runners-up: Mike Green, Washington Capitals
Drew Doughty, Los Angeles Kings

Duncan Keith of the Chicago Blackhawks won the James Norris Memorial Trophy for the first time. Keith received 76 of 133 first-place votes and 1,096 points to beat Mike Green of the Washington Capitals, who garnered 34 first-place votes and 831 points to finish as runner up for the second year in a row. Drew Doughty of the Los Angeles Kings received 15 first-place votes and 662 points while six-time winner Nicklas Lidstrom of Detroit finished fourth in the balloting with four first-place votes and 303 points. Chris Pronger of Philadelphia received two first-place votes and 168 points while Dan Boyle of San Jose (116 points) and Shea Weber of Nashville (96 points) each received one first-place vote.

Playing all 82 games for the third time in his five-year NHL career, Keith logged a total of 2,180:34 in ice time, the most among all NHL players. He took his offense to another level this season, registering career highs in goals (14), assists (55) and points (69). Keith ranked second to Washington's Mike Green among NHL defensemen in assists and points. He posted a plus-21 rating and is plus-84 over the past three seasons. Keith is the fourth Blackhawks defenseman to capture the Norris Trophy since it was first presented in 1954, joining Pierre Pilote (1963 through 1965), Doug Wilson (1982) and Chris Chelios (1993 and 1996). He is the fifth defenseman in the expansion era to win the Norris and the Stanley Cup in the same season, following Bobby Orr (Boston, 1970 and 1972), Larry Robinson (Montreal, 1977), Paul Coffey (Edmonton, 1985) and Nicklas Lidstrom (Detroit, 2002 and 2008). Keith also won an Olympic gold medal.

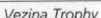

Vezina Trophy

Lady Byng Memorial Trophy

Frank J. Selke Trophy

Conn Smythe Trophy

VEZINA TROPHY

An annual award "to the goalkeeper adjudged to be the best at his position" as voted by the general managers of each of the 30 clubs.

History: Leo Dandurand, Louis Letourneau and Joe Cattarinich, former owners of the Montreal Canadiens, presented the trophy to the National Hockey League in 1926-27 in memory of Georges Vezina, outstanding goalkeeper of the Canadiens who collapsed during an NHL game on November 28, 1925, and died of tuberculosis a few months later. Until the 1981-82 season, the goalkeeper(s) of the team allowing the fewest number of goals during the regular season were awarded the Vezina Trophy.

2009-10 Winner: Ryan Miller, Buffalo
Runners-up: Ilya Bryzgalov, Phoenix Coyotes
Martin Brodeur, New Jersey Devils

Ryan Miller of the Buffalo Sabres captured the Vezina Trophy for the first time in his career. Miller was named on 28 of 30 ballots, including 23 first-place selections, and collected 126 points. Ilya Bryzgalov of the Phoenix Coyotes finished a strong second, receiving votes on 27 ballots including five first-place votes and 79 points. New Jersey's Martin Brodeur received one first-place vote and 32 points while San Jose's Evgeni Nabokov got the final first-place vote and nine points. Colorado's Craig Anderson also had nine points.

Miller led the Sabres to the Northeast Division title for the second time in the past four seasons. He set a franchise record and ranked fourth among NHL goaltenders with 41 wins; placed second in the league in goals-against average (2.22) and save percentage (.929); and tied a career high with five shutouts. Miller continued to excel following his MVP performance for Team USA at the 2010 Olympic Winter Games, going 9-2-1 in his first 12 decisions after collecting the silver medal in Vancouver.

LADY BYNG MEMORIAL TROPHY

An annual award "to the player adjudged to have exhibited the best type of sportsmanship and gentlemanly conduct combined with a high standard of playing ability." Winner selected in a poll by the Professional Hockey Writers' Association at the end of the regular schedule.

History: Lady Byng, wife of Canada's Governor-General at the time, presented the Lady Byng Trophy in the 1924-25 season. After Frank Boucher of the New York Rangers won the award seven times in eight seasons, he was given the trophy to keep and Lady Byng donated another trophy in 1936. After Lady Byng's death in 1949, the National Hockey League presented a new trophy, changing the name to Lady Byng Memorial Trophy.

2009-10 Winner: Martin St. Louis, Tampa Bay Lightning
Runners-up: Brad Richards, Dallas Stars
Pavel Datsyuk, Detroit Red Wings

Tampa Bay Lightning right winger Martin St. Louis won the Lady Byng Memorial Trophy after finishing as the runner-up in each of the last three seasons. It was the fifth time he was a finalist for the award. St. Louis earned 74 first-place votes among the 132 cast and earned 971 points to score a decisive victory over former teammate Brad Richards of the Dallas Stars (one first-place votes, 449 points). Detroit's Pavel Datsyuk, who was bidding for an unprecedented fifth straight win, received 14 first-place votes but only 438 points overall. Teammate Nicklas Lidstrom garnered 10 first-place votes, but finished fifth with 215 points. Anze Kopitar of Los Angeles had three first-place votes and 232 points.

St. Louis had a superb 2009-10 season, ranking sixth in the league in scoring with 94 points, the second-highest total of his 11-year NHL career. His 12 penalty minutes were the fewest among the league's top 50 scorers and the fewest among the 88 players who appeared in all 82 games. The winner of the Hart Trophy and Art Ross Trophy in Tampa Bay's Stanley Cup season of 2003-04, St. Louis has eclipsed 30 penalty minutes in a season only twice in a career that has seen him score 30 goals five times and appear in five NHL All-Star Games.

FRANK J. SELKE TROPHY

An annual award "to the forward who best excels in the defensive aspects of the game." Winner selected in a poll by the Professional Hockey Writers' Association at the end of the regular schedule.

History: Presented to the National Hockey League in 1977 by the Board of Governors of the NHL in honor of Frank J. Selke, one of the great architects of Montreal and Toronto championship teams.

2009-10 Winner: Pavel Datsyuk, Detroit Red Wings
Runners-up: Ryan Kesler, Vancouver Canucks
Jordan Staal, Pittsburgh Penguins

Detroit Red Wings center Pavel Datsyuk captured the Frank Selke Trophy for the third year in a row. Datsyuk edged Vancouver Canucks center Ryan Kesler 688-655 in the closest race of the 2009-10 NHL Awards voting. Datsyuk was named on 99 of 133 ballots and received 37 first-place votes while Kesler received 36 first-place votes. Pittsburgh's Jordan Staal earned 24 first-place votes and 528 points. Jonathan Toews of Chicago had 17 first-place votes and 408 points while Patrice Bergeron of Boston had eight and 158.

Datsyuk led the NHL in takeaways for the third time in the past four seasons with a career-high 132, nearly 60 percent more than second-place Kesler (83). Datsyuk had a plus-minus of +17 rating and posted a 55 percent face-off winning percentage (590 of 1,070). He is the first player to win the Selke Trophy three years in a row since Bob Gainey of the Montreal Canadiens won it the first four seasons it was presented, from 1978 through 1981.

WILLIAM M. JENNINGS TROPHY

An annual award "to the goalkeeper(s) having played a minimum of 25 games for the team with the fewest goals scored against it." Winners selected on regular-season play.

History: The Jennings Trophy was presented in 1981-82 by the National Hockey League's Board of Governors to honor the late William M. Jennings, longtime governor and president of the New York Rangers and one of the great builders of hockey in the United States.

2009-10 Winners: Martin Brodeur, New Jersey Devils
Runners-up: Tim Thomas/Tuukka Rask, Boston Bruins
Ilya Bryzgalov, Phoenix Coyotes

Martin Brodeur of the New Jersey Devils won the William M. Jennings Trophy for the fifth time in his career, tying Hall of Fame goaltender Patrick Roy for the most wins among all goaltenders since the award was introduced in 1981-82. Brodeur appeared in 77 of New Jersey's 82 games this season as the Devils finished with 191 goals against (186 goals, plus five shootout losses), nine fewer than the Boston Bruins and their goaltending tandem of 2009 Jennings winner Tim Thomas and rookie Tuukka Rask, who surrendered 191 goals and had nine shootout losses for a total of 200. Ilya Bryzgalov played in 69 of 82 games for Phoenix, who surrendered 196 goals plus six shootout losses for a total of 202.

CONN SMYTHE TROPHY

An annual award "to the most valuable player for his team in the playoffs." Winner selected by the Professional Hockey Writers' Association at the conclusion of the final game in the Stanley Cup Finals.

History: Presented by Maple Leaf Gardens Limited in 1964 to honor Conn Smythe, the former coach, manager, president and owner-governor of the Toronto Maple Leafs.

2009-10 Winner: Jonathan Toews, Chicago Blackhawks

Winning just a little more than a month after his 22nd birthday, Blackhawks center Jonathan Toews became the second-youngest player to capture the Conn Smythe Trophy behind goaltender Patrick Roy, who won the first of his three awards as a 20-year-old with the Montreal Canadiens in 1986. Toews ranked second among playoff scorers behind Philadelphia's Danny Briere, finishing the postseason with 7 goals and 22 assists for 29 points. His 277 face-off wins (in 460 changes) were by far the most of any player in the playoffs, and his 60.2 face-off winning percentage was surpassed only by those who saw significantly less playing time.

William M. Jennings Trophy

Jack Adams Award

Bill Masterton Memorial Trophy

Lester Patrick Trophy

JACK ADAMS AWARD

An annual award presented by the National Hockey League Broadcasters' Association to "the NHL coach adjudged to have contributed the most to his team's success." Winner selected by a poll among members of the NHL Broadcasters' Association at the end of the regular season.

History: The award was presented by the NHL Broadcasters' Association in 1974 to commemorate the late Jack Adams, coach and general manager of the Detroit Red Wings, whose lifetime dedication to hockey serves as an inspiration to all who aspire to further the game.

2009-10 Winner: Dave Tippett, Phoenix Coyotes
Runners-up: Barry Trotz, Nashville Predators
Joe Sacco, Colorado Avalanche

Phoenix Coyotes head coach Dave Tippett captured the Jack Adams Award for the first time. His highest previous finish in coach-of-the-year voting was fifth with the Dallas Stars in 2002-03, his rookie NHL season behind the bench. Tippett was a near-unanimous selection this year, receiving 57 of 59 first-place votes and collecting 291 points. Second-place Barry Trotz of the Nashville Predators garnered 60 points, while Joe Sacco of the Colorado Avalanche had 51. Mike Babcock received the two first-place votes that Tippett did not, but finished fourth in the balloting with 38 points.

Hired just days before the start of the regular season, Tippett led the Coyotes to the Stanley Cup playoffs for the first time since 2002 by posting a 50-27-5 record for 107 points. The club posted an NHL-best 28-point gain over its 2008-09 total, edging Colorado's 26-point improvement, and set franchise records for wins and points in a season, home wins (29) and longest home winning streak (10 games, Nov. 21 to Dec. 29). The Coyotes ranked third in the NHL in team defense (2.39 goals/game), up from 24th in 2008-09 (3.04), and were sixth in the league in penalty killing (84.5 percent).

BILL MASTERTON MEMORIAL TROPHY

An annual award under the trusteeship of the Professional Hockey Writers' Association to "the National Hockey League player who best exemplifies the qualities of perseverance, sportsmanship and dedication to hockey." Winner selected by a poll among the 30 chapters of the PHWA at the end of the regular season. A $2,500 grant from the PHWA is awarded annually to the Bill Masterton Scholarship Fund, based in Bloomington, MN, in the name of the Masterton Trophy winner.

History: The trophy was presented by the NHL Writers' Association in 1968 to commemorate the late Bill Masterton, a player with the Minnesota North Stars, who exhibited to a high degree the qualities of perseverance, sportsmanship and dedication to hockey, and who died January 15, 1968.

2009-10 Winner: Jose Theodore, Washington Capitals
Runners-up: Kurtis Foster, Tampa Bay Lightning
Jed Ortmeyer, San Jose Sharks

Washington Capitals goaltender Jose Theodore is the recipient of the Bill Masterton Memorial Trophy. Theodore had to deal with some adversity on the ice at the end of last season, but that was forgotten when his infant son Chace passed away last summer from complications stemming from his premature birth. Theodore not only regained the starting job, he had his best season since winning the Hart and Vezina Trophies in 2002, capped by a 20-0-3 run over the final three months. Of far greater importance was the way he handled himself in the dressing room, with fans and the media, and with his new charity "Saves for Kids" which benefits the NICU unit of the hospital Chace spent his entire brief life in.

LESTER PATRICK TROPHY

An annual award "for outstanding service to hockey in the United States." Eligible recipients are players, officials, coaches, executives and referees. Winners are selected by an award committee consisting of the commissioner of the NHL, an NHL governor, a representative of the New York Rangers, a member of the Hockey Hall of Fame builder's section, a member of the Hockey Hall of Fame player's section, a member of the U.S. Hockey Hall of Fame, a member of the NHL Broadcasters' Association and a member of the Professional Hockey Writers' Association. Each except the League Commissioner is rotated annually. The winner receives a miniature of the trophy.

History: Presented by the New York Rangers in 1966 to honor the late Lester Patrick, longtime general manager and coach of the New York Rangers, whose teams finished out of the playoffs only once in his first 16 years with the club.

2010 Winners: Cam Neely
Dave Andrews
Jack Parker
Jerry York

Cam Neely joined the Bruins in 1986 after three seasons with the Vancouver Canucks and his potent blend of offensive talent and a punishing physical presence quickly made him a fan favorite in Boston. Neely earned four Second-Team All-Star berths in his ten years with Boston, led the team in goals seven times and in points twice. He became just the fifth Bruin in team history to record a 50-goal season when he set a club record for goals by a right winger with 55 in 1989-90 and he was just the second player in team history to record consecutive 50-goal campaigns when he followed that with 51 tallies in 1990-91. His 50 goals in only 44 games in 1993-94 tied as the second fastest such feat in NHL history. After injuries forced him into retirement in 1996, Neely later joined the Bruins front office. On June 16, 2010, he was named president of the Boston Bruins.

Dave Andrews worked in his native Nova Scotia as the Edmonton Oilers' director of American Hockey League operations with the Cape Breton Oilers for seven years before becoming president of the AHL in 1994. During his time in office, the AHL has become the sole primary development league for all 30 National Hockey League organizations and will be at an all-time high of 30 active teams in 2010-11. Andrews has guided the AHL into unequaled times of prosperity, directing the league to record levels of attendance and exposure while expanding its geography across the United States and Canada. He has also worked to ensure the league's continuing success in smaller historical and traditional markets like Rochester, Springfield, Hershey, Portland and Providence.

Jack Parker, whose career with Boston University spans nearly four decades, was named the University's first Executive Director of Athletics in April 2002. Recognized primarily for his accomplishments as the Terriers' hockey coach since 1973, Parker continues to guide the B.U. hockey program. He has won 834 games, making him one of just three coaches to reach the 800-win plateau. No college hockey coach has won more games at the same institution than Coach Parker. His teams have won 20 or more games in 20 seasons, while 19 of his teams have advanced to the NCAA Tournament. Parker has posted 24 wins in the NCAA Tournament, the most of any Division 1 coach. His teams have won a combined total of 40 championships including two NCAA Division 1 titles, a record 17 Beanpots, five Hockey East titles, and four ECAC titles.

Jerry York enters the 2010-11 hockey season as the winningest active coach in NCAA history and second all time (behind Ron Mason's 924) with 850 victories. An All-American as a player at Boston College in the 1960s, York's head coaching career began at Clarkson in 1972 when he became the youngest head coach in the NCAA at age 26. After seven years (1972 to 1979) at Clarkson and 15 years (1979 to 1994) at Bowling Green, York returned to Boston College in 1994 to rebuild the program. In his career, he has led 18 teams to 25 or more wins and has guided four teams to 30 or more victories. He won his first NCAA title with Bowling Green in 1984 and has led Boston College to championships in 2001, 2008 and 2010.

King Clancy Memorial Trophy

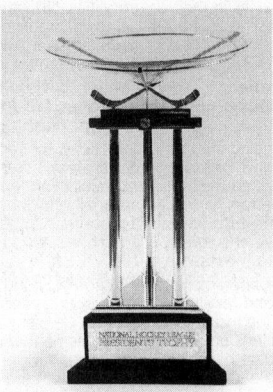

Presidents' Trophy

Maurice "Rocket" Richard Trophy

Ted Lindsay Award

KING CLANCY MEMORIAL TROPHY

An annual award "to the player who best exemplifies leadership qualities on and off the ice and has made a noteworthy humanitarian contribution in his community."

History: The King Clancy Memorial Trophy was presented to the National Hockey League by the Board of Governors in 1988 to honor the late Frank "King" Clancy.

2009-10 Winner: Shane Doan, Phoenix Coyotes

Phoenix Coyotes right winger Shane Doan is the recipient of the King Clancy Memorial Trophy. Doan's longtime dedication to the Arizona community was even more apparent in 2009-10. Throughout a turbulent offseason, Doan stood up for Phoenix, his home since 1996, as a great hockey market and a great place to live. The sixth-year captain helped Dave Tippett make a seamless transition into the head coaching position just nine days before the start of the regular season. The Coyotes got off to a dream start, tying the franchise record for most victories in October (9-4-0).

Doan's leadership kept the Coyotes together as they reached new heights on the ice, shattering the franchise records for most wins (50) and points (107) in a single season and breaking an eight-year playoff drought. Away from the rink, Doan served as a mentor to younger teammates and continued to make time for those less fortunate, making visits to sick children at Phoenix Children's Hospital. He also invited a group of students and teachers from Children First Academy in both Tempe and Phoenix to a game and spent time with them all afterward.

Aside from simply making appearances, Doan is well known in Phoenix for his ability to put a smile on fans' faces and engage them in conversations about nearly anything. During the Coyotes Carnival in March, during which Doan playfully interacted with each and every fan who stood in line awaiting the chance to participate in carnival games with him, he spontaneously decided to donate more time after the Carnival by auctioning off a personal tour of the Coyotes dressing room to benefit Coyotes Charities.

MAURICE "ROCKET" RICHARD TROPHY

An annual award "presented to the player finishing the regular season as the League's goal-scoring leader."

History: A gift to the NHL from the Montreal Canadiens in 1999, the Maurice "Rocket" Richard Trophy honors one of the game's greatest stars. During his 18-year career with the Canadiens from 1942-43 through 1959-60, Richard was the first player in NHL history to score 50 goals in a season and 500 in his career. He played on eight Stanley Cup champions and led the League in goal scoring five times.

2009-10 Winners: Sidney Crosby, Pittsburgh Penguins
**   Steven Stamkos, Tampa Bay Lightning**
**   Runner-up: Alex Ovechkin, Washington Capitals**

Pittsburgh Penguins center Sidney Crosby and Tampa Bay Lightning center Steven Stamkos each won his first Maurice Richard Trophy as the NHL goal-scoring leader. Crosby and Stamkos prevailed in a thrilling three-way race with Washington's Alex Ovechkin for the title, the outcome of which was still in doubt in the waning seconds of the regular season.

Entering the Penguins' final game of the season third in the goal-scoring race, Crosby's 50th and 51st tallies of the season in a 6-5 overtime win over the New York Islanders vaulted him past Ovechkin (50 goals) and, temporarily, Stamkos. Stamkos then grabbed a share of the NHL goal-scoring title in the dying seconds of his sensational sophomore season, nudging past Ovechkin and matching Crosby's 51-goal total by scoring an empty-net goal at 19:47 of the third period that sealed a 3-1 win over the Florida Panthers. He had reached the 50-goal mark the day before by scoring twice in a 4-3 shootout win over the Panthers. Stamkos, who turned 20 on February 7, became the youngest 50-goal man since Los Angeles' Jimmy Carson in 1987-88 (19 years, eight months) and the third youngest ever (Carson, Wayne Gretzky). He also became the youngest player to lead the NHL in goals since Columbus' Rick Nash (19 years, 10 months) joined Jarome Iginla and Ilya Kovalchuk in winning Maurice Richard Trophy honors in 2004. Crosby also reached the 50-goal milestone for the fist time in his career.

NHL GENERAL MANAGER OF THE YEAR AWARD

An annual award presented to recognize the work of the league's general managers, voting for this new award is conducted among the 30 club general managers and a panel of NHL executives, print and broadcast media at the conclusion of the regular season. The winner is announced during the Stanley Cup Final.

History: This award was first presented in 2010.

2009-10 Winner: Don Maloney, Phoenix Coyotes
**   Runners-up: George McPhee, Washington Capitals**
**   David Poile, Nashville Predators**

Don Maloney of the Phoenix Coyotes is the inaugural winner of the NHL General Manager of the Year Award. Maloney steered the Coyotes through an uncertain and turbulent offseason during the summer of 2009 and charted the course for the most successful regular season in franchise history in 2009-10. Maloney's biggest move was hiring head coach Dave Tippett, who guided the Coyotes to the Stanley Cup playoffs for the first time since 2002 by posting a 50-27-5 record for 107 points and setting franchise records for wins and points in a season.

Maloney added several players to the Coyotes roster over the summer, acquiring RW Radim Vrbata, D Sami Lepisto, LW Lauri Korpikoski and D Jim Vandermeer through trades and signing veteran free agent D Adrian Aucoin, C Vernon Fiddler, G Jason LaBarbera, LW Taylor Pyatt and C Robert Lang. Those players joined a veteran core that already included LW Shane Doan, D Ed Jovanovski, D Zbynek Michalek and G Ilya Bryzgalov. With the Coyotes already enjoying a breakout season, the acquisitions of forwards Lee Stempniak and Wojtek Wolski plus defensemen Derek Morris and Mathieu Schneider at the March 3 trade deadline propelled the club to even greater heights as Phoenix won nine consecutive games immediately following the deadline to tie a club record.

TED LINDSAY AWARD

The Ted Lindsay Award is presented annually to the "most outstanding player" in the NHL as voted by fellow members of the National Hockey League Players' Association. The winner receives $20,000, and the two finalists receive $10,000 each to donate to the grassroots hockey program of their choice, through the NHLPA's Goals & Dreams Fund.

History: On April 29, 2010, the Ted Lindsay Award was introduced to recognize Lindsay's pioneering efforts in the establishment of the NHL Players' Association. Carrying on the tradition established by the Lester B. Pearson Award, it remains the only award voted on by the players themselves. The award was originally created in 1971 in honor of the late Lester B. Pearson, former Prime Minister of Canada.

2009-10 Winner: Alex Ovechkin, Washington Capitals
**   Runners-up: Sidney Crosby, Pittsburgh Penguins**
**   Henrik Sedin, Vancouver Canucks**

As the inaugural winner of the Ted Lindsay Award, Alex Ovechkin of the Washington Capitals is the recipient of the NHLPA's "Most Outstanding Player" award for the third year in a row, having won it as the Lester B. Pearson award the previous two seasons. Ovechkin is the first player since Wayne Gretzky to capture the honor three years in a row and also just the third player out of the award's 22 recipients to accomplish this feat (along with Gretzky and Guy Lafleur, 1975-76 to 1977-78). He appeared in 72 games for the Washington Capitals in 2009-10, finishing amid the top-three players in the league in points (109) and goals (50), while leading the Capitals to their third consecutive Southeast Division title as well as to the first Presidents' Trophy in franchise history. This is the third straight season that Ovechkin reached the 100-point plateau and tallied more than 50 goals - reaching the 50-goal plateau for the fourth time in his five-year career.

MARK MESSIER NHL LEADERSHIP AWARD
presented by Bridgestone

An annual award presented "to the player who exemplifies great leadership qualitites to his team, on and off the ice during the regular season." Suggestions for nominees are solicited from fans, clubs and NHL personnel, but the selection of the three finalists and the ultimate winner is made by Mark Messier himself.

History: Presented by Bridgestone in honor of one of hockey's great leaders, this award was first handed out in 2007.

2009-10 Winner: Sidney Crosby, Pittsburgh Penguins
Runners-up: Shane Doan, Phoenix Coyotes
Ryan Miller, Buffalo Sabres

Pittsburgh Penguins captain Sidney Crosby is the recipient of the Mark Messier NHL Leadership Award. At the tender age of 22, Crosby already has led the Pittsburgh Penguins to back-to-back Stanley Cup Finals; became not only the youngest captain in NHL history but also the youngest captain to win the Stanley Cup; and scored the decisive goal in overtime to give Team Canada the gold medal in the 2010 Olympic hockey tournament. While many are familiar with his on-ice accomplishments, Crosby also leads by example off the ice with his extensive charitable work within the community. Sidney gives of his time generously during the season for Penguins' related charitable causes including: the Make-A-Wish Foundation, Project Bundle-up, Penguins' Charity practice and luncheon, several hospital visits and several postgame meet and greets for various charities. He also most recently established the Sidney Crosby Foundation, which focuses on youth charities. In each of the past two seasons, he has teamed up with the Penguins and Dick's Sporting Goods to introduce hockey to local youngsters by outfitting 600 area children from head to toe with hockey gear through the Little Penguins "Learn to Play Hockey" program. His home province recently honored the Cole Harbour native with the Order of Nova Scotia for his community service, another first for someone his age.

PRESIDENTS' TROPHY

An annual award to the club finishing the regular-season with the best overall record.

History: Presented to the National Hockey League in 1985-86 by the NHL Board of Governors to recognize the team compiling the top regular-season record.

2009-10 Winner: Washington Capitals
Runners-up: San Jose Sharks
Chicago Blackhawks

The Washington Capitals captured the Presidents' Trophy for the first time in franchise history, leading the NHL with 121 points by posting a record of 54-15-13. Both their 54 wins and 121 points set new club records. The Capitals won the Southeast Division title for the third year in a row and the fifth time in club history. (They also led the Patrick Division back in 1988-89.) The San Jose Sharks posted a record of 51-20-11 for 113 points and won the Pacific Division for the third year in a row. They finished atop the Western Conference standings for the second straight season. The Chicago Blackhawks won their first division title since 1992-93 with a record of 52-22-8 and 112 points.

NHL FOUNDATION PLAYER AWARD

An annual award presented to "an NHL player who applies the core values of hockey – commitment, perseverance and teamwork – to enrich the lives of people in his community." In recognition of this dedication, the NHL Foundation annually awards $25,000 to a current player's charity.

History: NHL players have a long-standing tradition of supporting charities and other important causes in their communities. NHL member clubs are constant in their quest to help local schools, hospitals and charitable organizations. Clubs submit nominations for the NHL Foundation Player Award and the finalists are selected by a judging panel. This award was first presented in 1998.

2009-10 Winner: Ryan Miller, Buffalo Sabres
Runners-up: Dustin Brown, Los Angeles Kings
Mike Green, Washington Capitals

Buffalo Sabres goaltender Ryan Miller is the recipient of the NHL Foundation Player Award. The NHL Foundation will present $25,000 to Miller's Steadfast Foundation. Miller established the Steadfast Foundation to benefit those afflicted and affected by the consequences of cancer, especially childhood forms of the disease. The organization, which has raised more than $500,000 since it was created in 2006, was inspired by Miller's cousin, Matt Schoals, who battled leukemia and eventually succumbed to the disease in 2007.

The primary benefactor of the Steadfast Foundation is Carly's Club, a support group for children and families who are fighting cancer. Miller-organized support programs for Carly's Club include the Saves for Cancer program in 2008, which raised $30,000 based on Miller's on-ice play; an agreement with Perry's Ice Cream that has provided $20,000 to date based on sales of a new Miller-inspired flavor, Breakaway Berrier; and a partnership with Buffalo Place to present the Downtown Christmas Tree Lighting Ceremony, at which members of the community can purchase Saves for Cancer holiday ornaments.

Miller also hosts an annual Catwalk for Charity, during which he and his teammates model clothing from Miller's The Refinery store in East Lansing, Michigan. Since its inception, the event has raised more than $400,000. In addition, he donates suite tickets for all Sabres home games and HSBC Arena special events to Carly's Club and is an active supporter of the Buffalo Sabres Foundation, the Buffalo Sabres Adopt-a-Family program and the Women and Children's Hospital of Buffalo.

As one of the Sabres' most popular players, Miller is often called upon to assist with the Buffalo Sabres Foundation in its numerous community events and activities.

NATIONAL HOCKEY LEAGUE INDIVIDUAL AWARD WINNERS

CONN SMYTHE TROPHY

2010	Jonathan Toews	Chicago
2009	Evgeni Malkin	Pittsburgh
2008	Henrik Zetterberg	Detroit
2007	Scott Niedermayer	Anaheim
2006	Cam Ward	Carolina
2005	....	
2004	Brad Richards	Tampa Bay
2003	Jean-Sebastien Giguere	Anaheim
2002	Nicklas Lidstrom	Detroit
2001	Patrick Roy	Colorado
2000	Scott Stevens	New Jersey
1999	Joe Nieuwendyk	Dallas
1998	Steve Yzerman	Detroit
1997	Mike Vernon	Detroit
1996	Joe Sakic	Colorado
1995	Claude Lemieux	New Jersey
1994	Brian Leetch	NY Rangers
1993	Patrick Roy	Montreal
1992	Mario Lemieux	Pittsburgh
1991	Mario Lemieux	Pittsburgh
1990	Bill Ranford	Edmonton
1989	Al MacInnis	Calgary
1988	Wayne Gretzky	Edmonton
1987	Ron Hextall	Philadelphia
1986	Patrick Roy	Montreal
1985	Wayne Gretzky	Edmonton
1984	Mark Messier	Edmonton
1983	Billy Smith	NY Islanders
1982	Mike Bossy	NY Islanders
1981	Butch Goring	NY Islanders
1980	Bryan Trottier	NY Islanders
1979	Bob Gainey	Montreal
1978	Larry Robinson	Montreal
1977	Guy Lafleur	Montreal
1976	Reggie Leach	Philadelphia
1975	Bernie Parent	Philadelphia
1974	Bernie Parent	Philadelphia
1973	Yvan Cournoyer	Montreal
1972	Bobby Orr	Boston
1971	Ken Dryden	Montreal
1970	Bobby Orr	Boston
1969	Serge Savard	Montreal
1968	Glenn Hall	St. Louis
1967	Dave Keon	Toronto
1966	Roger Crozier	Detroit
1965	Jean Beliveau	Montreal

FRANK J. SELKE TROPHY

	Winner	Runner-up
2010	Pavel Datsyuk, Det.	Ryan Kesler, Van.
2009	Pavel Datsyuk, Det.	Mike Richards, Phi.
2008	Pavel Datsyuk, Det.	John Madden, N.J.
2007	Rod Brind'Amour, Car.	Samuel Pahlsson, Ana.
2006	Rod Brind'Amour, Car.	Jere Lehtinen, Dal.
2005	....	
2004	Kris Draper, Det.	John Madden, N.J.
2003	Jere Lehtinen, Dal.	John Madden, N.J.
2002	Michael Peca, NYI	Craig Conroy, Cgy.
2001	John Madden, N.J.	Joe Sakic, Col.
2000	Steve Yzerman, Det.	Michal Handzus, St.L.
1999	Jere Lehtinen, Dal.	Magnus Arvedson, Ott.
1998	Jere Lehtinen, Dal.	Michael Peca, Buf.
1997	Michael Peca, Buf.	Peter Forsberg, Col.
1996	Sergei Fedorov, Det.	Ron Francis, Pit.
1995	Ron Francis, Pit.	Esa Tikkanen, St.L.
1994	Sergei Fedorov, Det.	Doug Gilmour, Tor.
1993	Doug Gilmour, Tor.	Dave Poulin, Bos.
1992	Guy Carbonneau, Mtl.	Sergei Fedorov, Det.
1991	Dirk Graham, Chi.	Esa Tikkanen, Edm.
1990	Rick Meagher, St.L.	Guy Carbonneau, Mtl.
1989	Guy Carbonneau, Mtl.	Esa Tikkanen, Edm.
1988	Guy Carbonneau, Mtl.	Steve Kasper, Bos.
1987	Dave Poulin, Phi.	Guy Carbonneau, Mtl.
1986	Troy Murray, Chi.	Ron Sutter, Phi.
1985	Craig Ramsay, Buf.	Doug Jarvis, Wsh.
1984	Doug Jarvis, Wsh.	Bryan Trottier, NYI
1983	Bobby Clarke, Phi.	Jari Kurri, Edm.
1982	Steve Kasper, Bos.	Bob Gainey, Mtl.
1981	Bob Gainey, Mtl.	Craig Ramsay, Buf.
1980	Bob Gainey, Mtl.	Craig Ramsay, Buf.
1979	Bob Gainey, Mtl.	Don Marcotte, Bos.
1978	Bob Gainey, Mtl.	Craig Ramsay, Buf.

BILL MASTERTON MEMORIAL TROPHY

2010	Jose Theodore	Washington
2009	Steve Sullivan	Nashville
2008	Jason Blake	Toronto
2007	Phil Kessel	Boston
2006	Teemu Selanne	Anaheim
2005	....	....
2004	Bryan Berard	Chicago
2003	Steve Yzerman	Detroit
2002	Saku Koivu	Montreal
2001	Adam Graves	NY Rangers
2000	Ken Daneyko	New Jersey
1999	John Cullen	Tampa Bay
1998	Jamie McLennan	St. Louis
1997	Tony Granato	San Jose
1996	Gary Roberts	Calgary
1995	Pat LaFontaine	Buffalo
1994	Cam Neely	Boston
1993	Mario Lemieux	Pittsburgh
1992	Mark Fitzpatrick	NY Islanders
1991	Dave Taylor	Los Angeles
1990	Gord Kluzak	Boston
1989	Tim Kerr	Philadelphia
1988	Bob Bourne	Los Angeles
1987	Doug Jarvis	Hartford
1986	Charlie Simmer	Boston
1985	Anders Hedberg	NY Rangers
1984	Brad Park	Detroit
1983	Lanny McDonald	Calgary
1982	Glenn Resch	Colorado
1981	Blake Dunlop	St. Louis
1980	Al MacAdam	Minnesota
1979	Serge Savard	Montreal
1978	Butch Goring	Los Angeles
1977	Ed Westfall	NY Islanders
1976	Rod Gilbert	NY Rangers
1975	Don Luce	Buffalo
1974	Henri Richard	Montreal
1973	Lowell MacDonald	Pittsburgh
1972	Bobby Clarke	Philadelphia
1971	Jean Ratelle	NY Rangers
1970	Pit Martin	Chicago
1969	Ted Hampson	Oakland
1968	Claude Provost	Montreal

ART ROSS TROPHY

	Winner	Runner-up
2010	Henrik Sedin, Van.	Sidney Crosby, Pit.
2009	Evgeni Malkin, Pit.	Alex Ovechkin, Wsh.
2008	Alex Ovechkin, Wsh.	Evgeni Malkin, Pit.
2007	Sidney Crosby, Pit.	Joe Thornton, S.J.
2006	Joe Thornton, Bos., S.J.	Jaromir Jagr, NYR
2005	....	....
2004	Martin St. Louis, T.B.	Ilya Kovalchuk, Atl.
2003	Peter Forsberg, Col.	Markus Naslund, Van.
2002	Jarome Iginla, Cgy.	Markus Naslund, Van.
2001	Jaromir Jagr, Pit.	Joe Sakic, Col.
2000	Jaromir Jagr, Pit.	Pavel Bure, Fla.
1999	Jaromir Jagr, Pit.	Teemu Selanne, Ana.
1998	Jaromir Jagr, Pit.	Peter Forsberg, Col.
1997	Mario Lemieux, Pit.	Teemu Selanne, Ana.
1996	Mario Lemieux, Pit.	Jaromir Jagr, Pit.
1995	Jaromir Jagr, Pit.	Eric Lindros, Phi.
1994	Wayne Gretzky, L.A.	Sergei Fedorov, Det.
1993	Mario Lemieux, Pit.	Pat LaFontaine, Buf.
1992	Mario Lemieux, Pit.	Kevin Stevens, Pit.
1991	Wayne Gretzky, L.A.	Brett Hull, St.L.
1990	Wayne Gretzky, L.A.	Mark Messier, Edm.
1989	Mario Lemieux, Pit.	Wayne Gretzky, L.A.
1988	Mario Lemieux, Pit.	Wayne Gretzky, Edm.
1987	Wayne Gretzky, Edm.	Jari Kurri, Edm.
1986	Wayne Gretzky, Edm.	Mario Lemieux, Pit.
1985	Wayne Gretzky, Edm.	Jari Kurri, Edm.
1984	Wayne Gretzky, Edm.	Paul Coffey, Edm.
1983	Wayne Gretzky, Edm.	Peter Stastny, Que.
1982	Wayne Gretzky, Edm.	Mike Bossy, NYI
1981	Wayne Gretzky, Edm.	Marcel Dionne, L.A.
1980	Marcel Dionne, L.A.	Wayne Gretzky, Edm.
1979	Bryan Trottier, NYI	Marcel Dionne, L.A.
1978	Guy Lafleur, Mtl.	Bryan Trottier, NYI
1977	Guy Lafleur, Mtl.	Marcel Dionne, L.A.
1976	Guy Lafleur, Mtl.	Bobby Clarke, Phi.
1975	Bobby Orr, Bos.	Phil Esposito, Bos.
1974	Phil Esposito, Bos.	Bobby Orr, Bos.
1973	Phil Esposito, Bos.	Bobby Clarke, Phi.
1972	Phil Esposito, Bos.	Bobby Orr, Bos.
1971	Phil Esposito, Bos.	Bobby Orr, Bos.
1970	Bobby Orr, Bos.	Phil Esposito, Bos.
1969	Phil Esposito, Bos.	Bobby Hull, Chi.
1968	Stan Mikita, Chi.	Phil Esposito, Bos.
1967	Stan Mikita, Chi.	Bobby Hull, Chi.
1966	Bobby Hull, Chi.	Stan Mikita, Chi.
1965	Stan Mikita, Chi.	Norm Ullman, Det.
1964	Stan Mikita, Chi.	Bobby Hull, Chi.
1963	Gordie Howe, Det.	Andy Bathgate, NYR
1962	Bobby Hull, Chi.	Andy Bathgate, NYR
1961	Bernie Geoffrion, Mtl.	Jean Beliveau, Mtl.
1960	Bobby Hull, Chi.	Bronco Horvath, Bos.
1959	Dickie Moore, Mtl.	Jean Beliveau, Mtl.
1958	Dickie Moore, Mtl.	Henri Richard, Mtl.
1957	Gordie Howe, Det.	Ted Lindsay, Det.
1956	Jean Beliveau, Mtl.	Gordie Howe, Det.
1955	Bernie Geoffrion, Mtl.	Maurice Richard, Mtl.
1954	Gordie Howe, Det.	Maurice Richard, Mtl.
1953	Gordie Howe, Det.	Ted Lindsay, Det.
1952	Gordie Howe, Det.	Ted Lindsay, Det.
1951	Gordie Howe, Det.	Maurice Richard, Mtl.
1950	Ted Lindsay, Det.	Sid Abel, Det.
1949	Roy Conacher, Chi.	Doug Bentley, Chi.
1948*	Elmer Lach, Mtl.	Buddy O'Connor, NYR
1947	Max Bentley, Chi.	Maurice Richard, Mtl.
1946	Max Bentley, Chi.	Gaye Stewart, Tor.
1945	Elmer Lach, Mtl.	Maurice Richard, Mtl.
1944	Herb Cain, Bos.	Doug Bentley, Chi.
1943	Doug Bentley, Chi.	Bill Cowley, Bos.
1942	Bryan Hextall, NYR	Lynn Patrick, NYR
1941	Bill Cowley, Bos.	Bryan Hextall, NYR
1940	Milt Schmidt, Bos.	Woody Dumart, Bos.
1939	Toe Blake, Mtl.	Sweeney Schriner, NYA
1938	Gordie Drillon, Tor.	Syl Apps, Tor.
1937	Sweeney Schriner, NYA	Syl Apps, Tor.
1936	Sweeney Schriner, NYA	Marty Barry, Det.
1935	Charlie Conacher, Tor.	Syd Howe, St.L., Det.
1934	Charlie Conacher, Tor.	Joe Primeau, Tor
1933	Bill Cook, NYR	Busher Jackson, Tor.
1932	Busher Jackson, Tor.	Joe Primeau, Tor.
1931	Howie Morenz, Mtl.	Ebbie Goodfellow, Det.
1930	Cooney Weiland, Bos.	Frank Boucher, NYR
1929	Ace Bailey, Tor.	Nels Stewart, Mtl.M
1928	Howie Morenz, Mtl.	Aurel Joliat, Mtl.
1927	Bill Cook, NYR	Dick Irvin, Chi.
1926	Nels Stewart, Mtl.M.	Cy Denneny, Ott.
1925	Babe Dye, Tor.	Cy Denneny, Ott.
1924	Cy Denneny, Ott.	Billy Boucher, Mtl.
1923	Babe Dye, Tor.	Cy Denneny, Ott.
1922	Punch Broadbent, Ott.	Cy Denneny, Ott.
1921	Newsy Lalonde, Mtl.	Babe Dye, Ham., Tor.
1920	Joe Malone, Que.	Newsy Lalonde, Mtl.
1919	Newsy Lalonde, Mtl.	Odie Cleghorn, Mtl.
1918	Joe Malone, Mtl.	Cy Denneny, Ott.

* Trophy first awarded in 1948.
   Scoring leaders listed from 1918 to 1947.

HART MEMORIAL TROPHY

	Winner	Runner-up
2010	Henrik Sedin, Van.	Alex Ovechkin, Wsh.
2009	Alex Ovechkin, Wsh.	Evgeni Malkin, Pit.
2008	Alex Ovechkin, Wsh.	Evgeni Malkin, Pit.
2007	Sidney Crosby, Pit.	Roberto Luongo, Van.
2006	Joe Thornton, Bos., S.J.	Jaromir Jagr, NYR
2005	....	....
2004	Martin St. Louis, T.B.	Jarome Iginla, Cgy.
2003	Peter Forsberg, Col.	Markus Naslund, Van.
2002	Jose Theodore, Mtl.	Jarome Iginla, Cgy.
2001	Joe Sakic, Col.	Mario Lemieux, Pit.
2000	Chris Pronger, St.L.	Jaromir Jagr, Pit.
1999	Jaromir Jagr, Pit.	Alexei Yashin, Ott.
1998	Dominik Hasek, Buf.	Jaromir Jagr, Pit.
1997	Dominik Hasek, Buf.	Paul Kariya, Ana.
1996	Mario Lemieux, Pit.	Mark Messier, NYR
1995	Eric Lindros, Phi.	Jaromir Jagr, Pit.
1994	Sergei Fedorov, Det.	Dominik Hasek, Buf.
1993	Mario Lemieux, Pit.	Doug Gilmour, Tor.
1992	Mark Messier, NYR	Patrick Roy, Mtl.
1991	Brett Hull, St.L.	Wayne Gretzky, L.A.
1990	Mark Messier, Edm.	Raymond Bourque, Bos.
1989	Wayne Gretzky, L.A.	Mario Lemieux, Pit.
1988	Mario Lemieux, Pit.	Grant Fuhr, Edm.
1987	Wayne Gretzky, Edm.	Raymond Bourque, Bos.
1986	Wayne Gretzky, Edm.	Mario Lemieux, Pit.
1985	Wayne Gretzky, Edm.	Dale Hawerchuk, Wpg.
1984	Wayne Gretzky, Edm.	Rod Langway, Wsh.
1983	Wayne Gretzky, Edm.	Pete Peeters, Bos.
1982	Wayne Gretzky, Edm.	Bryan Trottier, NYI
1981	Wayne Gretzky, Edm.	Mike Liut, St.L.
1980	Wayne Gretzky, Edm.	Marcel Dionne, L.A.
1979	Bryan Trottier, NYI	Guy Lafleur, Mtl
1978	Guy Lafleur, Mtl.	Bryan Trottier, NYI
1977	Guy Lafleur, Mtl.	Bobby Clarke, Phi.
1976	Bobby Clarke, Phi.	Denis Potvin, NYI
1975	Bobby Clarke, Phi.	Rogie Vachon, L.A.
1974	Phil Esposito, Bos.	Bernie Parent, Phi.
1973	Bobby Clarke, Phi.	Phil Esposito, Bos.
1972	Bobby Orr, Bos.	Ken Dryden, Mtl.
1971	Bobby Orr, Bos.	Phil Esposito, Bos.
1970	Bobby Orr, Bos.	Tony Esposito, Chi.
1969	Phil Esposito, Bos.	Jean Beliveau, Mtl.
1968	Stan Mikita, Chi.	Jean Beliveau, Mtl.
1967	Stan Mikita, Chi.	Ed Giacomin, NYR
1966	Bobby Hull, Chi.	Jean Beliveau, Mtl.
1965	Bobby Hull, Chi.	Norm Ullman, Det.
1964	Jean Beliveau, Mtl.	Bobby Hull, Chi.
1963	Gordie Howe, Det.	Stan Mikita, Chi.
1962	Jacques Plante, Mtl.	Doug Harvey, NYR
1961	Bernie Geoffrion, Mtl.	Johnny Bower, Tor.
1960	Gordie Howe, Det.	Bobby Hull, Chi.
1959	Andy Bathgate, NYR	Gordie Howe, Det.
1958	Gordie Howe, Det.	Andy Bathgate, NYR
1957	Gordie Howe, Det.	Jean Beliveau, Mtl.
1956	Jean Beliveau, Mtl.	Tod Sloan, Tor.
1955	Ted Kennedy, Tor.	Harry Lumley, Tor.
1954	Al Rollins, Chi.	Red Kelly, Det.
1953	Gordie Howe, Det.	Al Rollins, Chi.
1952	Gordie Howe, Det.	Elmer Lach, Mtl.
1951	Milt Schmidt, Bos.	Maurice Richard, Mtl.
1950	Chuck Rayner, NYR	Ted Kennedy, Tor.
1949	Sid Abel, Det.	Bill Durnan, Mtl.
1948	Buddy O'Connor, NYR	Frank Brimsek, Bos.
1947	Maurice Richard, Mtl.	Milt Schmidt, Bos.
1946	Max Bentley, Chi.	Gaye Stewart, Tor.
1945	Elmer Lach, Mtl.	Maurice Richard, Mtl.
1944	Babe Pratt, Tor.	Bill Cowley, Bos.
1943	Bill Cowley, Bos.	Doug Bentley, Chi.
1942	Tom Anderson, Bro.	Syl Apps, Tor.
1941	Bill Cowley, Bos.	Dit Clapper, Bos.
1940	Ebbie Goodfellow, Det.	Syl Apps, Tor.
1939	Toe Blake, Mtl.	Syl Apps, Tor.
1938	Eddie Shore, Bos.	Paul Thompson, Chi.
1937	Babe Siebert, Mtl.	Lionel Conacher, Mtl.M
1936	Eddie Shore, Bos.	Hooley Smith, Mtl.M
1935	Eddie Shore, Bos.	Charlie Conacher, Tor.
1934	Aurel Joliat, Mtl.	Lionel Conacher, Chi.
1933	Eddie Shore, Bos.	Bill Cook, NYR
1932	Howie Morenz, Mtl.	Ching Johnson, NYR
1931	Howie Morenz, Mtl.	Eddie Shore, Bos.
1930	Nels Stewart, Mtl.M.	Lionel Hitchman, Bos.
1929	Roy Worters, NYA	Ace Bailey, Tor.
1928	Howie Morenz, Mtl.	Roy Worters, Pit.
1927	Herb Gardiner, Mtl.	Bill Cook, NYR
1926	Nels Stewart, Mtl.M.	Sprague Cleghorn, Bos.
1925	Billy Burch, Ham.	Howie Morenz, Mtl.
1924	Frank Nighbor, Ott.	Sprague Cleghorn, Mtl.

WILLIAM M. JENNINGS TROPHY

	Winner	Runner-up
2010	Martin Brodeur, N.J.	Tim Thomas, Bos.
		Tuukka Rask, Bos.
2009	Tim Thomas, Bos.	Niklas Backstrom, Min.
	Manny Fernandez, Bos.	
2008	Chris Osgood, Det.	Jean-Sebastien Giguere, Ana.
	Dominik Hasek, Det.	
2007	Niklas Backstrom, Min.	Dominik Hasek, Det.
	Manny Fernandez, Min.	
2006	Miikka Kiprusoff, Cgy.	Manny Legace, Det.
		Chris Osgood, Det.
2005	....	....
2004	Martin Brodeur, N.J.	Marty Turco, Dal.
2003	Martin Brodeur, N.J.	Marty Turco, Dal.
	Roman Cechmanek, Phi.	Ron Tugnutt, Dal.
	Robert Esche, Phi.	
2002	Patrick Roy, Col.	Tommy Salo, Edm.
2001	Dominik Hasek, Buf.	Ed Belfour, Dal.
		Marty Turco, Dal.
2000	Roman Turek, St.L.	John Vanbiesbrouck, Phi.
		Brian Boucher, Phi.
1999	Ed Belfour, Dal.	Dominik Hasek, Buf.
	Roman Turek, Dal.	
1998	Martin Brodeur, N.J.	Ed Belfour, Dal.
1997	Martin Brodeur, N.J.	Chris Osgood, Det.
	Mike Dunham, N.J.	Mike Vernon, Det.
1996	Chris Osgood, Det.	Martin Brodeur, N.J.
	Mike Vernon, Det.	
1995	Ed Belfour, Chi.	Mike Vernon, Det.
		Chris Osgood, Det.
1994	Dominik Hasek, Buf.	Martin Brodeur, N.J.
	Grant Fuhr, Buf.	Chris Terreri, N.J.
1993	Ed Belfour, Chi.	Felix Potvin, Tor.
		Grant Fuhr, Tor.
1992	Patrick Roy, Mtl.	Ed Belfour, Chi.
1991	Ed Belfour, Chi.	Patrick Roy, Mtl.
1990	Andy Moog, Bos.	Patrick Roy, Mtl.
	Reggie Lemelin, Bos.	Brian Hayward, Mtl.
1989	Patrick Roy, Mtl.	Mike Vernon, Cgy.
	Brian Hayward, Mtl.	Rick Wamsley, Cgy.
1988	Patrick Roy, Mtl.	Clint Malarchuk, Wsh.
	Brian Hayward, Mtl.	Pete Peeters, Wsh.
1987	Patrick Roy, Mtl.	Ron Hextall, Phi.
	Brian Hayward, Mtl.	
1986	Bob Froese, Phi.	Al Jensen, Wsh.
	Darren Jensen, Phi.	Pete Peeters, Wsh.
1985	Tom Barrasso, Buf.	Pat Riggin, Wsh.
	Bob Sauve, Buf.	
1984	Al Jensen, Wsh.	Tom Barrasso, Buf.
	Pat Riggin, Wsh.	Bob Sauve, Buf.
1983	Roland Melanson, NYI	Pete Peeters, Bos.
	Billy Smith, NYI	
1982	Rick Wamsley, Mtl.	Billy Smith, NYI
	Denis Herron, Mtl.	Roland Melanson, NYI

MAURICE "ROCKET" RICHARD TROPHY

2010	Sidney Crosby	Pittsburgh
	Steven Stamkos	Tampa Bay
2009	Alex Ovechkin	Washington
2008	Alex Ovechkin	Washington
2007	Vincent Lecavalier	Tampa Bay
2006	Jonathan Cheechoo	San Jose
2005	....	
2004	Rick Nash	Columbus
	Jarome Iginla	Calgary
	Ilya Kovalchuk	Atlanta
2003	Milan Hejduk	Colorado
2002	Jarome Iginla	Calgary
2001	Pavel Bure	Florida
2000	Pavel Bure	Florida
1999	Teemu Selanne	Anaheim

MARK MESSIER NHL LEADERSHIP AWARD

	Winner	
2010	Sidney Crosby	Pittsburgh
2009	Jarome Iginla	Calgary
2008	Mats Sundin	Toronto
2007	Chris Chelios	Detroit

NHL GENERAL MANAGER OF THE YEAR AWARD

2010	Don Maloney	Phoenix

LADY BYNG MEMORIAL TROPHY

	Winner	Runner-up
2010	Martin St. Louis, T.B.	Brad Richards, Dal.
2009	Pavel Datsyuk, Det.	Martin St. Louis, T.B.
2008	Pavel Datsyuk, Det.	Martin St. Louis, T.B.
2007	Pavel Datsyuk, Det.	Martin St. Louis, T.B.
2006	Pavel Datsyuk, Det.	Brad Richards, T.B.
2005	....	....
2004	Brad Richards, T.B.	Daniel Alfredsson, Ott.
2003	Alexander Mogilny, Tor.	Nicklas Lidstrom, Det.
2002	Ron Francis, Car.	Joe Sakic, Col.
2001	Joe Sakic, Col.	Nicklas Lidstrom, Det.
2000	Pavol Demitra, St.L.	Nicklas Lidstrom, Det.
1999	Wayne Gretzky, NYR.	Nicklas Lidstrom, Det.
1998	Ron Francis, Pit.	Teemu Selanne, Ana.
1997	Paul Kariya, Ana.	Teemu Selanne, Ana.
1996	Paul Kariya, Ana.	Adam Oates, Bos.
1995	Ron Francis, Pit.	Adam Oates, Bos.
1994	Wayne Gretzky, L.A.	Adam Oates, Bos.
1993	Pierre Turgeon, NYI	Adam Oates, Bos.
1992	Wayne Gretzky, L.A.	Joe Sakic, Que.
1991	Wayne Gretzky, L.A.	Brett Hull, St.L.
1990	Brett Hull, St.L.	Wayne Gretzky, L.A.
1989	Joe Mullen, Cgy.	Wayne Gretzky, L.A.
1988	Mats Naslund, Mtl.	Wayne Gretzky, Edm.
1987	Joe Mullen, Cgy.	Wayne Gretzky, Edm.
1986	Mike Bossy, NYI	Jari Kurri, Edm.
1985	Jari Kurri, Edm.	Joe Mullen, St.L.
1984	Mike Bossy, NYI	Rick Middleton, Bos.
1983	Mike Bossy, NYI	Rick Middleton, Bos.
1982	Rick Middleton, Bos.	Mike Bossy, NYI
1981	Rick Kehoe, Pit.	Wayne Gretzky, Edm.
1980	Wayne Gretzky, Edm.	Marcel Dionne, L.A.
1979	Bob MacMillan, Atl.	Marcel Dionne, L.A.
1978	Butch Goring, L.A.	Peter McNab, Bos.
1977	Marcel Dionne, L.A.	Jean Ratelle, Bos.
1976	Jean Ratelle, NYR-Bos.	Jean Pronovost, Pit.
1975	Marcel Dionne, Det.	John Bucyk, Bos.
1974	John Bucyk, Bos.	Lowell MacDonald, Pit.
1973	Gilbert Perreault, Buf.	Jean Ratelle, NYR
1972	Jean Ratelle, NYR	John Bucyk, Bos.
1971	John Bucyk, Bos.	Dave Keon, Tor.
1970	Phil Goyette, St.L.	John Bucyk, Bos.
1969	Alex Delvecchio, Det.	Ted Hampson, Oak.
1968	Stan Mikita, Chi.	John Bucyk, Bos.
1967	Stan Mikita, Chi.	Dave Keon, Tor.
1966	Alex Delvecchio, Det.	Bobby Rousseau, Mtl.
1965	Bobby Hull, Chi.	Alex Delvecchio, Det.
1964	Kenny Wharram, Chi.	Dave Keon, Tor.
1963	Dave Keon, Tor.	Camille Henry, NYR
1962	Dave Keon, Tor.	Claude Provost, Mtl.
1961	Red Kelly, Tor.	Norm Ullman, Det.
1960	Don McKenney, Bos.	Andy Hebenton, NYR
1959	Alex Delvecchio, Det.	Andy Hebenton, NYR
1958	Camille Henry, NYR	Don Marshall, Mtl.
1957	Andy Hebenton, NYR	Dutch Reibel, Det.
1956	Dutch Reibel, Det.	Floyd Curry, Mtl.
1955	Sid Smith, Tor.	Danny Lewicki, NYR
1954	Red Kelly, Det.	Don Raleigh, NYR
1953	Red Kelly, Det.	Wally Hergesheimer, NYR
1952	Sid Smith, Tor.	Red Kelly, Det.
1951	Red Kelly, Det.	Woody Dumart, Bos.
1950	Edgar Laprade, NYR	Red Kelly, Det.
1949	Bill Quackenbush, Det.	Harry Watson, Tor.
1948	Buddy O'Connor, NYR	Syl Apps, Tor.
1947	Bobby Bauer, Bos.	Syl Apps, Tor.
1946	Toe Blake, Mtl.	Clint Smith, Chi.
1945	Bill Mosienko, Chi.	Syd Howe, Det.
1944	Clint Smith, Chi.	Herb Cain, Bos.
1943	Max Bentley, Chi.	Buddy O'Connor, Mtl.
1942	Syl Apps, Tor.	Gordie Drillon, Tor.
1941	Bobby Bauer, Bos.	Gordie Drillon, Tor.
1940	Bobby Bauer, Bos.	Clint Smith, NYR
1939	Clint Smith, NYR	Marty Barry, Det.
1938	Gordie Drillon, Tor.	Clint Smith, NYR
1937	Marty Barry, Det.	Gordie Drillon, Tor.
1936	Doc Romnes, Chi.	Sweeney Schriner, NYA
1935	Frank Boucher, NYR	Russ Blinco, Mtl.M
1934	Frank Boucher, NYR	Joe Primeau, Tor.
1933	Frank Boucher, NYR	Joe Primeau, Tor.
1932	Joe Primeau, Tor.	Frank Boucher, NYR
1931	Frank Boucher, NYR	Normie Himes, NYA
1930	Frank Boucher, NYR	Normie Himes, NYA
1929	Frank Boucher, NYR	Harold Darragh, Pit.
1928	Frank Boucher, NYR	George Hay, Det.
1927	Billy Burch, NYA	Dick Irvin, Chi.
1926	Frank Nighbor, Ott.	Billy Burch, NYA
1925	Frank Nighbor, Ott.	none

VEZINA TROPHY

	Winner	Runner-up
2010	Ryan Miller, Buf.	Ilya Bryzgalov, Phx.
2009	Tim Thomas, Bos.	Steve Mason, CBJ
2008	Martin Brodeur, N.J.	Evgeni Nabokov, S.J.
2007	Martin Brodeur, N.J.	Roberto Luongo, Van.
2006	Miikka Kiprusoff, Cgy.	Martin Brodeur, N.J.
2005	....	....
2004	Martin Brodeur, N.J.	Miikka Kiprusoff, Cgy.
2003	Martin Brodeur, N.J.	Marty Turco, Dal.
2002	Jose Theodore, Mtl.	Patrick Roy, Col.
2001	Dominik Hasek, Buf.	Roman Cechmanek, Phi.
2000	Olaf Kolzig, Wsh.	Roman Turek, St.L.
1999	Dominik Hasek, Buf.	Curtis Joseph, Tor.
1998	Dominik Hasek, Buf.	Martin Brodeur, N.J.
1997	Dominik Hasek, Buf.	Martin Brodeur, N.J.
1996	Jim Carey, Wsh.	Chris Osgood, Det.
1995	Dominik Hasek, Buf.	Ed Belfour, Chi.
1994	Dominik Hasek, Buf.	John Vanbiesbrouck, Fla.
1993	Ed Belfour, Chi.	Tom Barrasso, Pit.
1992	Patrick Roy, Mtl.	Kirk McLean, Van.
1991	Ed Belfour, Chi.	Patrick Roy, Mtl.
1990	Patrick Roy, Mtl.	Daren Puppa, Buf.
1989	Patrick Roy, Mtl.	Mike Vernon, Cgy.
1988	Grant Fuhr, Edm.	Tom Barrasso, Buf.
1987	Ron Hextall, Phi.	Mike Liut, Hfd.
1986	John Vanbiesbrouck, NYR	Bob Froese, Phi.
1985	Pelle Lindbergh, Phi.	Tom Barrasso, Buf.
1984	Tom Barrasso, Buf.	Reggie Lemelin, Cgy.
1983	Pete Peeters, Bos.	Roland Melanson, NYI
1982	Billy Smith, NYI	Grant Fuhr, Edm.
1981	Richard Sevigny, Mtl.	Pete Peeters, Phi.
	Denis Herron, Mtl.	Rick St. Croix, Phi.
	Michel Larocque, Mtl.	
1980	Bob Sauve, Buf.	Gerry Cheevers, Bos.
	Don Edwards, Buf.	Gilles Gilbert, Bos.
1979	Ken Dryden, Mtl.	Glenn Resch, NYI
	Michel Larocque, Mtl.	Billy Smith, NYI
1978	Ken Dryden, Mtl.	Bernie Parent, Phi.
	Michel Larocque, Mtl.	Wayne Stephenson, Phi.
1977	Ken Dryden, Mtl.	Glenn Resch, NYI
	Michel Larocque, Mtl.	Billy Smith, NYI
1976	Ken Dryden, Mtl.	Glenn Resch, NYI
		Billy Smith, NYI
1975	Bernie Parent, Phi.	Rogie Vachon, L.A.
		Gary Edwards, L.A.
1974	Bernie Parent, Phi. (tie)	Gilles Gilbert, Bos.
	Tony Esposito, Chi. (tie)	
1973	Ken Dryden, Mtl.	Ed Giacomin, NYR
		Gilles Villemure, NYR
1972	Tony Esposito, Chi.	Cesare Maniago, Min.
	Gary Smith, Chi.	Gump Worsley, Min.
1971	Ed Giacomin, NYR	Tony Esposito, Chi.
	Gilles Villemure, NYR	
1970	Tony Esposito, Chi.	Jacques Plante, St.L.
		Ernie Wakely, St.L.
1969	Jacques Plante, St.L.	Ed Giacomin, NYR
	Glenn Hall, St.L.	
1968	Gump Worsley, Mtl.	Johnny Bower, Tor.
	Rogie Vachon, Mtl.	Bruce Gamble, Tor.
1967	Glenn Hall, Chi.	Charlie Hodge, Mtl.
	Denis DeJordy, Chi.	
1966	Gump Worsley, Mtl.	Glenn Hall, Chi.
	Charlie Hodge, Mtl.	
1965	Terry Sawchuk, Tor.	Roger Crozier, Det.
	Johnny Bower, Tor.	
1964	Charlie Hodge, Mtl.	Glenn Hall, Chi.
1963	Glenn Hall, Chi.	Johnny Bower, Tor.
		Don Simmons, Tor.
1962	Jacques Plante, Mtl.	Johnny Bower, Tor.
1961	Johnny Bower, Tor.	Glenn Hall, Chi.
1960	Jacques Plante, Mtl.	Glenn Hall, Chi.
1959	Jacques Plante, Mtl.	Johnny Bower, Tor.
		Ed Chadwick, Tor.
1958	Jacques Plante, Mtl.	Gump Worsley, NYR
		Marcel Paille, NYR
1957	Jacques Plante, Mtl.	Glenn Hall, Det.
1956	Jacques Plante, Mtl.	Glenn Hall, Det.
1955	Terry Sawchuk, Det.	Harry Lumley, Tor.
1954	Harry Lumley, Tor.	Terry Sawchuk, Det.
1953	Terry Sawchuk, Det.	Gerry McNeil, Mtl.
1952	Terry Sawchuk, Det.	Al Rollins, Tor.
1951	Al Rollins, Tor.	Terry Sawchuk, Det.
1950	Bill Durnan, Mtl.	Harry Lumley, Det.
1949	Bill Durnan, Mtl.	Harry Lumley, Det.
1948	Turk Broda, Tor.	Harry Lumley, Det.
1947	Bill Durnan, Mtl.	Turk Broda, Tor.
1946	Bill Durnan, Mtl.	Frank Brimsek, Bos.
1945	Bill Durnan, Mtl.	Frank McCool, Tor. (tie)
		Harry Lumley, Det. (tie)
1944	Bill Durnan, Mtl.	Paul Bibeault, Tor.
1943	Johnny Mowers, Det.	Turk Broda, Tor.
1942	Frank Brimsek, Bos.	Turk Broda, Tor.
1941	Turk Broda, Tor.	Frank Brimsek, Bos. (tie)
		Johnny Mowers, Det. (tie)
1940	Dave Kerr, NYR	Frank Brimsek, Bos.
1939	Frank Brimsek, Bos.	Dave Kerr, NYR
1938	Tiny Thompson, Bos.	Dave Kerr, NYR
1937	Normie Smith, Det.	Dave Kerr, NYR
1936	Tiny Thompson, Bos.	Mike Karakas, Chi.
1935	Lorne Chabot, Chi.	Alex Connell, Mtl.M
1934	Charlie Gardiner, Chi.	Wilf Cude, Det.
1933	Tiny Thompson, Bos.	John Ross Roach, Det.
1932	Charlie Gardiner, Chi.	Alex Connell, Det.
1931	Roy Worters, NYA	Charlie Gardiner, Chi.
1930	Tiny Thompson, Bos.	Charlie Gardiner, Chi.
1929	George Hainsworth, Mtl.	Tiny Thompson, Bos.
1928	George Hainsworth, Mtl.	Alex Connell, Ott.
1927	George Hainsworth, Mtl.	Clint Benedict, Mtl.M

CALDER MEMORIAL TROPHY

	Winner	Runner-up
2010	Tyler Myers, Buf.	Jimmy Howard, Det.
2009	Steve Mason, CBJ	Bobby Ryan, Ana.
2008	Patrick Kane, Chi.	Nicklas Backstrom, Wsh.
2007	Evgeni Malkin, Pit.	Paul Stastny, Col.
2006	Alex Ovechkin, Wsh.	Sidney Crosby, Pit.
2005	....	....
2004	Andrew Raycroft, Bos.	Michael Ryder, Mtl.
2003	Barret Jackman, St.L.	Henrik Zetterberg, Det.
2002	Dany Heatley, Atl.	Ilya Kovalchuk, Atl.
2001	Evgeni Nabokov, S.J.	Brad Richards, T.B.
2000	Scott Gomez, N.J.	Brad Stuart, S.J.
1999	Chris Drury, Col.	Marian Hossa, Ott.
1998	Sergei Samsonov, Bos.	Mattias Ohlund, Van.
1997	Bryan Berard, NYI	Jarome Iginla, Cgy.
1996	Daniel Alfredsson, Ott.	Eric Daze, Chi.
1995	Peter Forsberg, Que.	Jim Carey, Wsh.
1994	Martin Brodeur, N.J.	Jason Arnott, Edm.
1993	Teemu Selanne, Wpg.	Joe Juneau, Bos.
1992	Pavel Bure, Van.	Nicklas Lidstrom, Det
1991	Ed Belfour, Chi.	Sergei Fedorov, Det.
1990	Sergei Makarov, Cgy.	Mike Modano, Min.
1989	Brian Leetch, NYR	Trevor Linden, Van.
1988	Joe Nieuwendyk, Cgy.	Ray Sheppard, Buf.
1987	Luc Robitaille, L.A.	Ron Hextall, Phi.
1986	Gary Suter, Cgy.	Wendel Clark, Tor.
1985	Mario Lemieux, Pit.	Chris Chelios, Mtl.
1984	Tom Barrasso, Buf.	Steve Yzerman, Det.
1983	Steve Larmer, Chi.	Phil Housley, Buf.
1982	Dale Hawerchuk, Wpg.	Barry Pederson, Bos.
1981	Peter Stastny, Que.	Larry Murphy, L.A.
1980	Raymond Bourque, Bos.	Mike Foligno, Det.
1979	Bobby Smith, Min	Ryan Walter, Wsh.
1978	Mike Bossy, NYI	Barry Beck, Col.
1977	Willi Plett, Atl.	Don Murdoch, NYR
1976	Bryan Trottier, NYI	Glenn Resch, NYI
1975	Eric Vail, Atl.	Pierre Larouche, Pit.
1974	Denis Potvin, NYI	Tom Lysiak, Atl.
1973	Steve Vickers, NYR	Bill Barber, Phi.
1972	Ken Dryden, Mtl.	Rick Martin, Buf.
1971	Gilbert Perreault, Buf.	Jude Drouin, Min.
1970	Tony Esposito, Chi.	Bill Fairbairn, NYR
1969	Danny Grant, Min.	Norm Ferguson, Oak.
1968	Derek Sanderson, Bos.	Jacques Lemaire, Mtl.
1967	Bobby Orr, Bos.	Ed Van Impe, Chi.
1966	Brit Selby, Tor.	Bert Marshall, Det.
1965	Roger Crozier, Det.	Ron Ellis, Tor.
1964	Jacques Laperriere, Mtl.	John Ferguson, Mtl.
1963	Kent Douglas, Tor.	Doug Barkley, Det.
1962	Bobby Rousseau, Mtl.	Cliff Pennington, Bos.
1961	Dave Keon, Tor.	Bob Nevin, Tor.
1960	Bill Hay, Chi.	Murray Oliver, Det.
1959	Ralph Backstrom, Mtl.	Carl Brewer, Tor.
1958	Frank Mahovlich, Tor.	Bobby Hull, Chi.
1957	Larry Regan, Bos.	Ed Chadwick, Tor.
1956	Glenn Hall, Det.	Andy Hebenton, NYR
1955	Ed Litzenberger, Chi.	Don McKenney, Bos.
1954	Camille Henry, NYR	Dutch Reibel, Det.
1953	Gump Worsley, NYR	Gord Hannigan, Tor.
1952	Bernie Geoffrion, Mtl.	Hy Buller, NYR
1951	Terry Sawchuk, Det.	Al Rollins, Tor.
1950	Jack Gelineau, Bos.	Phil Maloney, Bos.
1949	Pentti Lund, NYR	Allan Stanley, NYR
1948	Jim McFadden, Det.	Pete Babando, Bos.
1947	Howie Meeker, Tor.	Jim Conacher, Det.
1946	Edgar Laprade, NYR	George Gee, Chi.
1945	Frank McCool, Tor.	Ken Smith, Bos.
1944	Gus Bodnar, Tor.	Bill Durnan, Mtl.
1943	Gaye Stewart, Tor.	Glen Harmon, Mtl.
1942	Grant Warwick, NYR	Buddy O'Connor, Mtl.
1941	John Quilty, Mtl.	Johnny Mowers, Det.
1940	Kilby MacDonald, NYR	Wally Stanowski, Tor.
1939	Frank Brimsek, Bos.	Roy Conacher, Bos.
1938	Cully Dahlstrom, Chi.	Murph Chamberlain, Tor.
1937	Syl Apps, Tor.	Gordie Drillon, Tor.
1936	Mike Karakas, Chi.	Bucko McDonald, Det.
1935	Sweeney Schriner, NYA	Bert Connelly, NYR
1934	Russ Blinco, Mtl.M.	none
1933	Carl Voss, Det.	none

KING CLANCY MEMORIAL TROPHY

2010	Shane Doan	Phoenix
2009	Ethan Moreau	Edmonton
2008	Vincent Lecavalier	Tampa Bay
2007	Saku Koivu	Montreal
2006	Olaf Kolzig	Washington
2005	....	....
2004	Jarome Iginla	Calgary
2003	Brendan Shanahan	Detroit
2002	Ron Francis	Carolina
2001	Shjon Podein	Colorado
2000	Curtis Joseph	Toronto
1999	Rob Ray	Buffalo
1998	Kelly Chase	St. Louis
1997	Trevor Linden	Vancouver
1996	Kris King	Winnipeg
1995	Joe Nieuwendyk	Calgary
1994	Adam Graves	NY Rangers
1993	Dave Poulin	Boston
1992	Raymond Bourque	Boston
1991	Dave Taylor	Los Angeles
1990	Kevin Lowe	Edmonton
1989	Bryan Trottier	NY Islanders
1988	Lanny McDonald	Calgary

JAMES NORRIS MEMORIAL TROPHY

	Winner	Runner-up
2010	Duncan Keith, Chi.	Mike Green, Wsh.
2009	Zdeno Chara, Bos.	Mike Green, Wsh.
2008	Nicklas Lidstrom, Det.	Dion Phaneuf, Cgy.
2007	Nicklas Lidstrom, Det.	Scott Niedermayer, Ana.
2006	Nicklas Lidstrom, Det.	Scott Niedermayer, Ana.
2005	....	....
2004	Scott Niedermayer, N.J.	Zdeno Chara, Ott.
2003	Nicklas Lidstrom, Det.	Al MacInnis, St.L.
2002	Nicklas Lidstrom, Det.	Chris Chelios, Chi.
2001	Nicklas Lidstrom, Det.	Raymond Bourque, Col.
2000	Chris Pronger, St.L.	Nicklas Lidstrom, Det.
1999	Al MacInnis, St.L.	Nicklas Lidstrom, Det.
1998	Rob Blake, L.A.	Nicklas Lidstrom, Det.
1997	Brian Leetch, NYR	V. Konstantinov, Det.
1996	Chris Chelios, Chi.	Raymond Bourque, Bos.
1995	Paul Coffey, Det.	Chris Chelios, Chi.
1994	Raymond Bourque, Bos.	Scott Stevens, N.J.
1993	Chris Chelios, Chi.	Raymond Bourque, Bos.
1992	Brian Leetch, NYR	Raymond Bourque, Bos.
1991	Raymond Bourque, Bos.	Al MacInnis, Cgy.
1990	Raymond Bourque, Bos.	Al MacInnis, Cgy.
1989	Chris Chelios, Mtl	Paul Coffey, Pit.
1988	Raymond Bourque, Bos.	Scott Stevens, Wsh.
1987	Raymond Bourque, Bos.	Mark Howe, Phi.
1986	Paul Coffey, Edm.	Mark Howe, Phi.
1985	Paul Coffey, Edm.	Raymond Bourque, Bos.
1984	Rod Langway, Wsh.	Paul Coffey, Edm.
1983	Rod Langway, Wsh.	Mark Howe, Phi.
1982	Doug Wilson, Chi.	Raymond Bourque, Bos.
1981	Randy Carlyle, Pit.	Denis Potvin, NYI
1980	Larry Robinson, Mtl.	Borje Salming, Tor.
1979	Denis Potvin, NYI	Larry Robinson, Mtl.
1978	Denis Potvin, NYI	Brad Park, Bos.
1977	Larry Robinson, Mtl.	Borje Salming, Tor.
1976	Denis Potvin, NYI	Brad Park, NYR-Bos.
1975	Bobby Orr, Bos.	Denis Potvin, NYI
1974	Bobby Orr, Bos.	Brad Park, NYR
1973	Bobby Orr, Bos.	Guy Lapointe, Mtl.
1972	Bobby Orr, Bos.	Brad Park, NYR
1971	Bobby Orr, Bos.	Brad Park, NYR
1970	Bobby Orr, Bos.	Brad Park, NYR
1969	Bobby Orr, Bos.	Tim Horton, Tor.
1968	Bobby Orr, Bos.	J.C. Tremblay, Mtl
1967	Harry Howell, NYR	Pierre Pilote, Chi.
1966	Jacques Laperriere, Mtl.	Pierre Pilote, Chi.
1965	Pierre Pilote, Chi.	Jacques Laperriere, Mtl.
1964	Pierre Pilote, Chi.	Tim Horton, Tor.
1963	Pierre Pilote, Chi.	Carl Brewer, Tor.
1962	Doug Harvey, NYR	Pierre Pilote, Chi.
1961	Doug Harvey, Mtl.	Marcel Pronovost, Det.
1960	Doug Harvey, Mtl.	Allan Stanley, Tor.
1959	Tom Johnson, Mtl.	Bill Gadsby, NYR
1958	Doug Harvey, Mtl.	Bill Gadsby, NYR
1957	Doug Harvey, Mtl.	Red Kelly, Det.
1956	Doug Harvey, Mtl.	Bill Gadsby, NYR
1955	Doug Harvey, Mtl.	Red Kelly, Det.
1954	Red Kelly, Det.	Doug Harvey, Mtl.

JACK ADAMS AWARD

	Winner	Runner-up
2010	Dave Tippett, Phx.	Barry Trotz, Nsh.
2009	Claude Julien, Bos.	Andy Murray, St.L.
2008	Bruce Boudreau, Wsh.	Guy Carbonneau, Mtl.
2007	Alain Vigneault, Van.	Lindy Ruff, Buf.
2006	Lindy Ruff, Buf.	Peter Laviolette, Car.
2005	....	....
2004	John Tortorella, T.B.	Ron Wilson, S.J.
2003	Jacques Lemaire, Min.	John Tortorella, T.B.
2002	Bob Francis, Phx.	Brian Sutter, Chi.
2001	Bill Barber, Phi.	Scotty Bowman, Det.
2000	Joel Quenneville, St.L.	Alain Vigneault, Mtl.
1999	Jacques Martin, Ott.	Pat Quinn, Tor.
1998	Pat Burns, Bos.	Larry Robinson, L.A.
1997	Ted Nolan, Buf.	Ken Hitchcock, Dal.
1996	Scotty Bowman, Det.	Doug MacLean, Fla.
1995	Marc Crawford, Que.	Scotty Bowman, Det.
1994	Jacques Lemaire, N.J.	Kevin Constantine, S.J.
1993	Pat Burns, Tor.	Brian Sutter, Bos.
1992	Pat Quinn, Van.	Roger Neilson, NYR
1991	Brian Sutter, St.L.	Tom Webster, L.A.
1990	Bob Murdoch, Wpg.	Mike Milbury, Bos.
1989	Pat Burns, Mtl.	Bob McCammon, Van.
1988	Jacques Demers, Det.	Terry Crisp, Cgy.
1987	Jacques Demers, Det.	Jack Evans, Hfd.
1986	Glen Sather, Edm.	Jacques Demers, St.L.
1985	Mike Keenan, Phi.	Barry Long, Wpg.
1984	Bryan Murray, Wsh.	Scotty Bowman, Buf.
1983	Orval Tessier, Chi.	
1982	Tom Watt, Wpg.	
1981	Red Berenson, St.L.	Bob Berry, L.A.
1980	Pat Quinn, Phi.	
1979	Al Arbour, NYI	Fred Shero, NYR
1978	Bobby Kromm, Det.	Don Cherry, Bos.
1977	Scotty Bowman, Mtl.	Tom McVie, Wsh.
1976	Don Cherry, Bos.	
1975	Bob Pulford, L.A.	
1974	Fred Shero, Phi.	

LESTER PATRICK TROPHY

2010	Jerry York	Jack Parker
	Cam Neely	Dave Andrews
2009	Mark Messier	Jim Devellano
	Mike Richter	
2008	Brian Burke	Phil Housley
	Ted Lindsay	Bob Naegele, Jr.
2007	Brian Leetch	Cammi Granato
	Stan Fischler	John Halligan
2006	Red Berenson	Marcel Dionne
	Reed Larson	Glen Sonmor
	Steve Yzerman	
2005	....	
2004	John Davidson	Mike Emrick
	Ray Miron	
2003	Raymond Bourque	Ron DeGregorio
	Willie O'Ree	
2002	Herb Brooks	Larry Pleau
	1960 U.S. Olympic Team	
2001	Gary Bettman	Scotty Bowman
	David Poile	
2000	Mario Lemieux	Craig Patrick
	Lou Vairo	
1999	Harry Sinden	
	1998 U.S. Olympic Women's Team	
1998	Neal Broten	Peter Karmanos
	John Mayasich	Max McNab
1997	Bill Cleary	* Seymour H. Knox III
	Pat LaFontaine	
1996	George Gund	Ken Morrow
	Milt Schmidt	
1995	Bob Fleming	Brian Mullen
	Joe Mullen	
1994	Wayne Gretzky	Robert Ridder
1993	*Frank Boucher	* Mervyn "Red" Dutton
	Bruce McNall	Gil Stein
1992	Al Arbour	Art Berglund
	Lou Lamoriello	
1991	Rod Gilbert	Mike Ilitch
1990	Len Ceglarski	Lou Nanne
1989	Dan Kelly	Bud Poile
	*Lynn Patrick	Fred Cusick
1988	Keith Allen	
	Bob Johnson	
1987	*Hobey Baker	Frank Mathers
1986	John MacInnes	Jack Riley
1985	Jack Butterfield	Arthur M. Wirtz
1984	*Arthur Howey Ross	John A. Ziegler, Jr.
1983	Bill Torrey	
1982	Emile P. Francis	
1981	Charles M. Schulz	
1980	Bobby Clarke	Frederick A. Shero
	Edward M. Snider	1980 U.S. Olympic Team
1979	Bobby Orr	
1978	Phil Esposito	Tom Fitzgerald
	William T. Tutt	William W. Wirtz
1977	Murray A. Armstrong	John P. Bucyk
	John Mariucci	
1976	George A. Leader	Stanley Mikita
	Bruce A. Norris	
1975	William L. Chadwick	Donald M. Clark
	Thomas N. Ivan	
1974	*Weston W. Adams, Sr.	* Charles L. Crovat
	Alex Delvecchio	Murray Murdoch
1973	Walter L. Bush, Jr.	
1972	Clarence S. Campbell	John A. "Snooks" Kelly
	*James D. Norris	Ralph "Cooney" Weiland
1971	William M. Jennings	* Terrance G. Sawchuk
	*John B. Sollenberger	
1970	*James C. V. Hendy	Edward W. Shore
1969	Robert M. Hull	* Edward J. Jeremiah
1968	*Walter A. Brown	* Gen. John R. Kilpatrick
	Thomas F. Lockhart	
1967	*Charles F. Adams	Gordon Howe
	*James Norris, Sr.	
1966	J.J. "Jack" Adams	

* awarded posthumously

PRESIDENTS' TROPHY

	Winner	Runner-up
2010	Washington Capitals	San Jose Sharks
2009	San Jose Sharks	Boston Bruins
2008	Detroit Red Wings	San Jose Sharks
2007	Buffalo Sabres	Detroit Red Wings
2006	Detroit Red Wings	Ottawa Senators
2005	....	
2004	Detroit Red Wings	Tampa Bay Lightning
2003	Ottawa Senators	Dallas Stars
2002	Detroit Red Wings	Boston Bruins
2001	Colorado Avalanche	Detroit Red Wings
2000	St. Louis Blues	Detroit Red Wings
1999	Dallas Stars	New Jersey Devils
1998	Dallas Stars	New Jersey Devils
1997	Colorado Avalanche	Dallas Stars
1996	Detroit Red Wings	Colorado Avalanche
1995	Detroit Red Wings	Quebec Nordiques
1994	New York Rangers	New Jersey Devils
1993	Pittsburgh Penguins	Boston Bruins
1992	New York Rangers	Washington Capitals
1991	Chicago Blackhawks	St. Louis Blues
1990	Boston Bruins	Calgary Flames
1989	Calgary Flames	Montreal Canadiens
1988	Calgary Flames	Montreal Canadiens
1987	Edmonton Oilers	Philadelphia Flyers
1986	Edmonton Oilers	Philadelphia Flyers

TED LINDSAY AWARD

2010	Alex Ovechkin	Washington
2009	Alex Ovechkin	Washington
2008	Alex Ovechkin	Washington
2007	Sidney Crosby	Pittsburgh
2006	Jaromir Jagr	NY Rangers
2005	....	....
2004	Martin St. Louis	Tampa Bay
2003	Markus Naslund	Vancouver
2002	Jarome Iginla	Calgary
2001	Joe Sakic	Colorado
2000	Jaromir Jagr	Pittsburgh
1999	Jaromir Jagr	Pittsburgh
1998	Dominik Hasek	Buffalo
1997	Dominik Hasek	Buffalo
1996	Mario Lemieux	Pittsburgh
1995	Eric Lindros	Philadelphia
1994	Sergei Fedorov	Detroit
1993	Mario Lemieux	Pittsburgh
1992	Mark Messier	NY Rangers
1991	Brett Hull	St. Louis
1990	Mark Messier	Edmonton
1989	Steve Yzerman	Detroit
1988	Mario Lemieux	Pittsburgh
1987	Wayne Gretzky	Edmonton
1986	Mario Lemieux	Pittsburgh
1985	Wayne Gretzky	Edmonton
1984	Wayne Gretzky	Edmonton
1983	Wayne Gretzky	Edmonton
1982	Wayne Gretzky	Edmonton
1981	Mike Liut	St. Louis
1980	Marcel Dionne	Los Angeles
1979	Marcel Dionne	Los Angeles
1978	Guy Lafleur	Montreal
1977	Guy Lafleur	Montreal
1976	Guy Lafleur	Montreal
1975	Bobby Orr	Boston
1974	Phil Esposito	Boston
1973	Bobby Clarke	Philadelphia
1972	Jean Ratelle	NY Rangers
1971	Phil Esposito	Boston

NHL LIFETIME ACHIEVEMENT AWARD

	Winner
2010	not awarded
2009	Jean Beliveau
2008	Gordie Howe

NHL FOUNDATION AWARD

	Winner	
2010	Ryan Miller	Buffalo
2009	Rick Nash	Columbus
2008	Trevor Linden	Vancouver
	Vincent Lecavalier	Tampa Bay
2007	Joe Sakic	Colorado
2006	Marty Turco	Dallas
2004	Jarome Iginla	Calgary
2003	Darren McCarty	Detroit
2002	Ron Francis	Carolina
2001	Olaf Kolzig	Washington
2000	Adam Graves	NY Rangers
1999	Rob Ray	Buffalo
1998	Kelly Chase	St. Louis

NHL Entry Draft

Draft Summary

Following is a summary of the players drafted from the Ontario Hockey League (OHL), Quebec Major Junior Hockey League (QMJHL), Western Hockey League (WHL), United States colleges, United States high schools, European leagues and other North American leagues since 1969. "Other" may include Canadian and U.S. Jr. A and Jr. B, minor professional leagues (AHL, IHL), midget and other teams playing in leagues not listed above.

Year	Total Picks	OHL Picks	%	QMJHL Picks	%	WHL Picks	%	College Picks	%	Hi School Picks	%	Int'l Picks	%	Other Picks	%
1969	84	36	42.9	11	13.1	20	23.8	7	8.3	-	-	1	1.2	9	10.7
1970	115	51	44.3	13	11.3	22	19.1	16	13.9	-	-	-	-	13	11.3
1971	117	41	35.0	13	11.1	28	23.9	22	18.8	-	-	-	-	13	11.1
1972	152	46	30.3	30	19.7	44	28.9	21	13.8	-	-	-	-	11	7.2
1973	168	56	33.3	24	14.3	49	29.2	25	14.9	-	-	-	-	14	8.3
1974	247	69	27.9	40	16.2	66	26.7	41	16.6	-	-	6	2.4	25	10.1
1975	217	55	25.3	28	12.9	57	26.3	59	27.2	-	-	6	2.8	12	5.5
1976	135	47	34.8	18	13.3	33	24.4	26	19.3	-	-	8	5.9	3	2.2
1977	185	42	22.7	40	21.6	44	23.8	49	26.5	-	-	5	2.7	5	2.7
1978	234	59	25.2	22	9.4	48	20.5	73	31.2	-	-	16	6.8	16	6.8
1979	126	48	38.1	19	15.1	37	29.4	15	11.9	-	-	6	4.8	1	0.8
1980	210	73	34.8	24	11.4	41	19.5	42	20.0	7	3.3	13	6.2	10	4.8
1981	211	59	28.0	28	13.3	37	17.5	21	10.0	17	8.1	32	15.2	17	8.1
1982	252	60	23.8	17	6.7	55	21.8	20	7.9	47	18.7	35	13.9	18	7.1
1983	242	57	23.6	24	9.9	41	16.9	14	5.8	35	14.5	34	14.0	37	15.3
1984	250	55	22.0	16	6.4	37	14.8	22	8.8	44	17.6	40	16.0	36	14.4
1985	252	59	23.4	15	6.0	48	19.0	20	7.9	48	19.0	31	12.3	31	12.3
1986	252	66	26.2	22	8.7	32	12.7	22	8.7	40	15.9	28	11.1	42	16.7
1987	252	32	12.7	17	6.7	36	14.3	40	15.9	69	27.4	38	15.1	20	7.9
1988	252	32	12.7	22	8.7	30	11.9	48	19.0	56	22.2	39	15.5	25	9.9
1989	252	39	15.5	16	6.3	44	17.5	48	19.0	47	18.7	38	15.1	20	7.9
1990	250	39	15.6	14	5.6	33	13.2	38	15.2	57	22.8	53	21.2	16	6.4
1991	264	43	16.3	25	9.5	40	15.2	43	16.3	37	14.0	55	20.8	21	8.0
1992	264	57	21.6	22	8.3	45	17.0	9	3.4	25	9.5	84	31.8	22	8.3
1993	286	60	21.0	23	8.0	44	15.4	17	5.9	33	11.5	78	27.3	31	10.8
1994	286	45	15.7	28	9.8	66	23.1	6	2.1	28	9.8	80	28.0	33	11.5
1995	234	54	23.1	35	15.0	55	23.5	5	2.1	2	0.9	69	29.5	14	6.0
1996	241	51	21.2	31	12.9	54	22.4	25	10.4	6	2.5	58	24.1	16	6.6
1997	246	52	21.1	19	7.7	63	25.6	26	10.6	4	1.6	63	25.6	19	7.7
1998	258	50	19.4	41	15.9	44	17.1	27	10.5	7	2.7	75	29.1	14	5.4
1999	272	52	19.1	20	7.4	40	14.7	36	13.2	9	3.3	94	34.6	21	7.7
2000	293	39	13.3	21	7.2	41	14.0	35	11.9	7	2.4	123	42.0	27	9.2
2001	289	41	14.2	26	9.0	45	15.6	24	8.3	8	2.8	119	41.2	26	9.0
2002	290	35	12.1	23	7.9	43	14.8	41	14.1	6	2.1	110	37.9	32	11.0
2003	292	44	15.1	38	13.0	41	14.0	23	7.9	10	3.4	93	31.8	43	14.7
2004	291	42	14.4	27	9.3	44	15.1	28	9.6	18	6.2	88	30.2	44	15.1
2005	230	43	18.7	23	10.0	43	18.7	13	5.6	18	7.8	50	21.7	40	17.4
2006	213	29	13.6	25	11.7	24	11.2	18	8.4	19	8.9	63	29.5	35	16.4
2007	211	35	16.6	25	11.8	37	17.5	8	3.8	14	6.6	36	17.0	56	56.5
2008	211	46	21.8	27	12.8	37	17.5	9	4.2	15	7.1	39	18.5	38	18.0
2009	210	45	21.4	23	11.0	31	14.8	7	3.3	19	9.0	41	19.5	44	21.0
2010	210	42	20.0	22	10.4	43	20.5	9	4.2	22	10.5	39	18.6	33	15.7
Total		2026	21.2	997	10.4	1762	18.4	1098	11.5	774	8.1	1886	19.8	1003	10.5

Total Players Drafted (1969-2010): 9,546

Everyone agreed that Tyler Seguin (left) and Taylor Hall were the top two picks in the 2010 NHL Entry Draft, but nobody was certain who would selected first overall. When it came down to it, the Edmonton Oilers took the Hall first while Seguin went second to Boston.

History

Year	Location	Date	Players Drafted
1963–1968	Montreal	—	122
1969	Queen Elizabeth Hotel, Montreal	June 12	84
1970	Queen Elizabeth Hotel, Montreal	June 11	115
1971	Queen Elizabeth Hotel, Montreal	June 10	117
1972	Queen Elizabeth Hotel, Montreal	June 8	152
1973	Mount Royal Hotel, Montreal	May 15	168
1974	NHL Montreal Office	May 28	247
1975	NHL Montreal Office	June 3	217
1976	NHL Montreal Office	June 1	135
1977	NHL Montreal Office	June 14	185
1978	Queen Elizabeth Hotel, Montreal	June 15	234
1979	Queen Elizabeth Hotel, Montreal	August 9	126
1980	Montreal Forum	June 11	210
1981	Montreal Forum	June 10	211
1982	Montreal Forum	June 9	252
1983	Montreal Forum	June 8	242
1984	Montreal Forum	June 9	250
1985	Toronto Convention Centre	June 15	252
1986	Montreal Forum	June 21	252
1987	Joe Louis Arena, Detroit	June 13	252
1988	Montreal Forum	June 11	252
1989	Met Sports Center, Minnesota	June 17	252
1990	B.C. Place, Vancouver	June 16	250
1991	Memorial Auditorium, Buffalo	June 22	264
1992	Montreal Forum	June 20	264
1993	Le Colisée, Quebec	June 26	286
1994	Hartford Civic Center	June 28-29	286
1995	Edmonton Coliseum	July 8	234
1996	Kiel Center, St. Louis	June 22	241
1997	Civic Arena, Pittsburgh	June 21	246
1998	Marine Midland Arena, Buffalo	June 27	258
1999	FleetCenter, Boston	June 26	272
2000	Saddledome, Calgary	June 24-25	293
2001	National Car Rental Center, Florida	June 23-24	289
2002	Air Canada Centre, Toronto	June 22-23	290
2003	Gaylord Entertainment Center, Nashville	June 21-22	292
2004	RBC Center, Carolina	June 26-27	291
2005	Sheraton Hotel and Towers, Ottawa	July 30	230
2006	General Motors Place, Vancouver	June 24	213
2007	Nationwide Arena, Columbus	June 22-23	211
2008	Scotiabank Place, Ottawa	June 20-21	211
2009	Bell Centre, Montreal	June 26-27	210
2010	STAPLES Center, Los Angeles	June 25-26	210

First Selections

Year	Player	Pos	Team	Drafted From	Age
1963	Garry Monahan	LW	Montreal	St. Michael's Juveniles	16.7
1964	Claude Gauthier		Detroit	Comite des jeunes (Rosemont)	16.9
1965	Andre Veilleux	RW	NY Rangers	Montreal Ranger Jr. B	
1966	Barry Gibbs	D	Boston	Estevan Bruins	17.7
1967	Rick Pagnutti	D	Los Angeles	Garson Native Sons	20.6
1968	Michel Plasse	G	Montreal	Drummondville Rangers	20.0
1969	Rejean Houle	LW	Montreal	Montreal Jr. Canadiens	19.8
1970	Gilbert Perreault	C	Buffalo	Montreal Jr. Canadiens	19.7
1971	Guy Lafleur	RW	Montreal	Quebec Remparts	19.9
1972	Billy Harris	RW	NY Islanders	Toronto Marlboros	20.4
1973	Denis Potvin	D	NY Islanders	Ottawa 67's	19.7
1974	Greg Joly	D	Washington	Regina Pats	20.0
1975	Mel Bridgman	C	Philadelphia	Victoria Cougars	20.1
1976	Rick Green	D	Washington	London Knights	20.3
1977	Dale McCourt	C	Detroit	St. Catharines Fincups	20.4
1978	Bobby Smith	C	Minnesota	Ottawa 67's	20.4
1979	Rob Ramage	D	Colorado	London Knights	20.5
1980	Doug Wickenheiser	C	Montreal	Regina Pats	19.2
1981	Dale Hawerchuk	C	Winnipeg	Cornwall Royals	18.2
1982	Gord Kluzak	D	Boston	Nanaimo Islanders	18.3
1983	Brian Lawton	C	Minnesota	Mount St. Charles HS	18.11
1984	Mario Lemieux	C	Pittsburgh	Laval Voisins	18.8
1985	Wendel Clark	LW/D	Toronto	Saskatoon Blades	18.7
1986	Joe Murphy	C	Detroit	Michigan State Spartans	18.8
1987	Pierre Turgeon	C	Buffalo	Granby Bisons	17.10
1988	Mike Modano	C	Minnesota	Prince Albert Raiders	18.0
1989	Mats Sundin	RW	Quebec	Nacka (Sweden)	18.4
1990	Owen Nolan	RW	Quebec	Cornwall Royals	18.4
1991	Eric Lindros	C	Quebec	Oshawa Generals	18.3
1992	Roman Hamrlik	D	Tampa Bay	ZPS Zlin (Czech.)	18.2
1993	Alexandre Daigle	C	Ottawa	Victoriaville Tigres	18.5
1994	Ed Jovanovski	D	Florida	Windsor Spitfires	18.0
1995	Bryan Berard	D	Ottawa	Detroit Jr. Red Wings	18.4
1996	Chris Phillips	D	Ottawa	Prince Albert Raiders	18.3
1997	Joe Thornton	C	Boston	Sault Ste. Marie Greyhounds	17.11
1998	Vincent Lecavalier	C	Tampa Bay	Rimouski Oceanic	18.2
1999	Patrik Stefan	C	Atlanta	Long Beach Ice Dogs (IHL)	18.9
2000	Rick DiPietro	G	NY Islanders	Boston University Terriers	18.9
2001	Ilya Kovalchuk	LW	Atlanta	Spartak (Russia)	18.2
2002	Rick Nash	LW	Columbus	London Knights	18.0
2003	Marc-Andre Fleury	G	Pittsburgh	Cape Breton Screaming Eagles	18.0
2004	Alex Ovechkin	LW	Washington	Dynamo Moscow (Russia)	18.9
2005	Sidney Crosby	C	Pittsburgh	Rimouski Oceanic	17.11
2006	Erik Johnson	D	St. Louis	U.S. National U-18	18.3
2007	Patrick Kane	RW	Chicago	London Knights	18.7
2008	Steven Stamkos	C	Tampa Bay	Sarnia Sting	18.4
2009	John Tavares	C	NY Islanders	London Knights	18.9
2010	Taylor Hall	LW	Edmonton	Windsor Spitfires	18.7

Ontario Hockey League Draft Selections by Club

Total	Club	'10	'09	'08	'07	'06	'05	'04	'03	'02	'01	'00	'99	'98	'97	'96	'95	'94	'93	'92	'91	'90	'89	'88	'87	'86	'85	'84	'83	'82	'81	'80	'69 to '79
28	Barrie	2	2	2	—	—	1	—	—	1	1	3	6	3	4	2	—	—	—	—	—	—	—	—	—	—	—	—	—	—	—	—	—
66	Belleville	1	1	3	4	2	2	—	—	2	3	1	5	2	5	—	3	3	—	4	1	2	4	—	2	5	4	4	3	—	—	—	—
35	Brampton	2	2	3	—	4	4	2	4	3	3	6	2	—	—	—	—	—	—	—	—	—	—	—	—	—	—	—	—	—	—	—	—
28	Erie	2	3	1	5	—	2	—	2	2	3	2	1	3	—	—	—	—	—	—	—	—	—	—	—	—	—	—	—	—	—	—	—
76	Guelph	—	5	3	1	1	2	2	1	2	4	1	3	5	1	6	5	7	2	2	—	4	—	2	8	3	5	1	—	—	—	—	—
103	Kingston	2	2	2	—	4	2	—	1	1	2	—	4	1	4	4	3	2	5	3	2	2	—	1	1	4	3	3	1	2	5	8	29
144	Kitchener	1	1	2	4	—	4	2	1	4	1	1	—	5	3	2	4	2	4	1	3	5	7	1	2	3	6	4	8	5	5	4	49
147	London	2	3	1	3	1	3	6	4	2	2	1	4	8	1	4	1	1	4	3	1	3	3	6	2	3	1	7	3	5	5	2	52
16	Niagara/Mississauga	3	—	1	3	1	1	3	2	—	—	2	—	—	—	—	—	—	—	—	—	—	—	—	—	—	—	—	—	—	—	—	—
155	Oshawa	2	3	2	2	2	—	3	3	3	1	2	3	3	3	1	10	1	4	4	4	2	4	—	3	6	6	5	5	9	2	—	48
140	Ottawa	4	1	2	1	1	2	3	2	—	3	2	6	2	5	2	1	1	4	6	5	5	—	1	2	3	3	2	2	9	4	8	48
36	Owen Sound	4	3	1	1	2	2	1	1	1	—	1	—	1	2	3	2	3	4	2	1	1	—	—	—	—	—	—	—	—	—	—	0
168	Peterborough	2	2	2	1	1	2	5	5	1	2	1	4	1	5	4	5	2	4	4	3	4	2	2	5	2	9	3	7	5	3	10	60
63	Plymouth	3	2	2	2	3	3	3	3	3	6	2	2	4	3	6	2	7	2	2	—	—	—	—	—	—	—	—	—	—	—	—	—
71	Saginaw/North Bay	1	3	3	—	2	3	1	2	2	3	2	2	2	1	1	2	7	2	5	2	4	1	3	3	3	3	4	4	—	—	—	—
35	Sarnia	1	—	4	1	1	3	—	5	2	1	3	1	3	2	7	1	—	—	—	—	—	—	—	—	—	—	—	—	—	—	—	—
112	Sault Ste. Marie	2	1	2	3	—	1	3	1	2	1	1	4	1	4	3	4	3	7	2	1	3	2	1	7	5	4	6	1	8	3	—	25
27	St. Michael's	3	4	4	—	—	—	4	5	1	5	1	—	—	—	—	—	—	—	—	—	—	—	—	—	—	—	—	—	—	—	—	—
113	Sudbury	1	2	2	1	2	4	—	1	1	2	—	5	5	3	1	2	2	10	2	8	2	1	—	1	3	5	2	—	4	2	7	32
91	Windsor	4	5	4	2	2	3	2	2	2	2	1	5	1	4	3	—	3	—	1	2	5	—	7	3	2	2	3	5	3	9	—	—

Teams no longer operating

Total	Club	'10	'09	'08	'07	'06	'05	'04	'03	'02	'01	'00	'99	'98	'97	'96	'95	'94	'93	'92	'91	'90	'89	'88	'87	'86	'85	'84	'83	'82	'81	'80	'69 to '79
27	Brantford	—	—	—	—	—	—	—	—	—	—	—	—	—	—	—	—	—	—	—	—	—	—	—	—	—	2	7	2	5	8	0	
37	Cornwall	—	—	—	—	—	—	—	—	—	—	—	—	—	—	—	—	5	3	3	2	3	3	2	2	3	4	7	—	—	—	—	
62	Hamilton	—	—	—	—	—	—	—	—	—	—	—	—	—	—	—	—	—	—	2	—	4	4	6	3	—	—	—	—	—	—	43	
20	Montreal	—	—	—	—	—	—	—	—	—	—	—	—	—	—	—	—	—	—	—	—	—	—	—	—	—	—	—	—	—	—	20	
5	Newmarket	—	—	—	—	—	—	—	—	—	—	—	—	—	2	3	—	—	—	—	—	—	—	—	—	—	—	—	—	—	—	—	
72	Niagara Falls	—	—	—	—	—	—	—	—	—	—	—	6	2	3	4	4	4	4	—	—	—	—	—	6	6	8	21					
52	St. Catharines	—	—	—	—	—	—	—	—	—	—	—	—	—	—	—	—	—	—	—	—	—	—	—	—	—	—	—	—	—	—	—	52
97	Toronto	—	—	—	—	—	—	—	—	—	—	—	—	—	—	—	—	—	—	—	—	—	2	2	1	4	3	4	4	6	2	10	59

Quebec Major Junior Hockey League Draft Selections by Club

Total	Club	'10	'09	'08	'07	'06	'05	'04	'03	'02	'01	'00	'99	'98	'97	'96	'95	'94	'93	'92	'91	'90	'89	'88	'87	'86	'85	'84	'83	'82	'81	'80	'69 to '79
10	Acadie-Bathurst	1	—	—	—	2	—	3	2	—	2	—	—	—	—	—	—	—	—	—	—	—	—	—	—	—	—	—	—	—	—	—	—
21	Baie-Comeau	1	—	2	1	3	—	3	2	1	3	2	—	3	—	—	—	—	—	—	—	—	—	—	—	—	—	—	—	—	—	—	—
16	Cape Breton	1	1	—	1	—	3	2	2	1	—	3	—	—	—	—	—	—	—	—	—	—	—	—	—	—	—	—	—	—	—	—	—
54	Chicoutimi	—	—	3	—	—	4	—	1	3	1	1	—	1	2	—	2	3	1	1	—	1	1	2	2	1	3	—	3	1	6	3	8
57	Drummondville	—	3	—	—	2	2	1	1	—	1	1	—	2	2	3	4	1	2	2	4	—	1	4	2	2	2	1	—	—	—	—	14
77	Gatineau/Hull	3	—	1	1	2	—	4	4	5	2	—	4	3	—	3	3	1	3	3	3	2	2	3	4	—	1	3	—	1	3	10	
33	Halifax	3	—	—	2	3	1	3	6	—	3	2	—	3	3	1	3	—	—	—	—	—	—	—	—	—	—	—	—	—	—	—	—
80	Lewiston/Sher.	2	1	2	3	2	5	2	1	—	3	—	5	1	—	4	2	3	—	—	—	—	—	—	—	—	2	5	1	36			
23	Moncton	2	2	1	3	1	2	3	2	—	2	2	1	1	—	—	—	—	—	—	—	—	—	—	—	—	—	—	—	—	—	—	—
24	PEI/Mtl. Rocket	1	1	2	2	—	2	8	1	3	1	1	2	—	—	—	—	—	—	—	—	—	—	—	—	—	—	—	—	—	—	—	—
26	Quebec	1	1	3	2	2	2	1	1	3	1	3	—	3	4	—	—	—	—	—	—	—	—	—	—	—	—	—	—	—	—	—	—
32	Rimouski	2	2	2	4	—	2	3	4	—	4	2	2	5	—	—	—	—	—	—	—	—	—	—	—	—	—	—	—	—	—	—	—
19	Rouyn-Noranda	1	1	2	1	3	1	—	2	—	4	1	3	—	—	—	—	—	—	—	—	—	—	—	—	—	—	—	—	—	—	—	—
8	Saint John	2	2	1	2	1	—	—	—	—	—	—	—	—	—	—	—	—	—	—	—	—	—	—	—	—	—	—	—	—	—	—	—
8	Montreal/St. John's	1	1	2	4	—	—	—	—	—	—	—	—	—	—	—	—	—	—	—	—	—	—	—	—	—	—	—	—	—	—	—	—
82	Shawinigan	1	6	—	1	1	3	2	2	1	1	3	1	4	2	1	1	3	—	2	—	1	2	—	2	5	5	2	2	24			
24	Val-d'Or	1	—	2	—	2	1	1	1	2	—	2	4	2	1	—	—	—	—	—	—	—	—	—	—	—	—	—	—	—	—	—	—
35	Victoriaville	—	1	3	1	—	—	3	1	3	2	1	2	3	1	1	6	2	—	1	—	4	—	—	—	—	—	—	—	—	—	—	—

Teams no longer operating

Total	Club	'10	'09	'08	'07	'06	'05	'04	'03	'02	'01	'00	'99	'98	'97	'96	'95	'94	'93	'92	'91	'90	'89	'88	'87	'86	'85	'84	'83	'82	'81	'80	'69 to '79
21	Beauport	—	—	—	—	—	—	—	—	3	3	7	3	1	3	1	—	—	—	—	—	—	—	—	—	—	—	—	—	—	—	—	—
45	Cornwall	—	—	—	—	—	—	—	—	—	—	—	—	—	—	—	—	—	—	—	—	—	—	—	—	—	—	—	5	5	35		
30	Granby	—	—	—	—	—	—	—	1	3	2	5	1	—	2	—	2	—	4	2	2	3	1	2	—	—	—	—	—	—	—	—	—
54	Laval	—	—	—	—	—	—	3	1	2	4	5	2	1	4	3	3	1	3	5	—	2	1	2	—	12							
12	Longueuil	—	—	—	—	—	—	—	—	—	—	—	—	3	2	—	1	2	1	2	1	—	—	—	—	—	—	—	—	—	—	—	—
32	Montreal	—	—	—	—	—	—	—	—	—	—	—	—	—	—	—	—	—	—	—	—	—	—	—	—	—	3	—	3	26			
47	Quebec	—	—	—	—	—	—	—	—	—	—	—	—	—	—	—	—	—	—	—	—	3	2	2	1	2	2	35					
15	St. Hyacinthe	—	—	—	—	—	—	—	—	—	—	4	—	4	1	2	1	3	—	—	—	—	—	—	—	—	—	—	—	—	—	—	—
16	St. Jean	—	—	—	—	—	—	—	—	—	1	1	2	1	3	—	1	3	0	1	1	—	2	—	—	—	—	—	—	—	—	—	—
2	St. Jerome	—	—	—	—	—	—	—	—	—	—	—	—	—	—	—	—	—	—	—	—	—	—	—	—	—	—	—	—	—	—	—	2
28	Sorel	—	—	—	—	—	—	—	—	—	—	—	—	—	—	—	—	—	—	—	—	—	—	—	—	—	—	—	—	5	—	23	
47	Trois Rivieres	—	—	—	—	—	—	—	—	—	1	2	1	3	3	1	—	3	—	3	1	2	2	25									
27	Verdun	—	—	—	—	—	—	—	—	—	—	—	3	—	1	3	0	3	—	3	3	—	—	3	8								

2010 NHL Entry Draft Order of Selection

The first 14 picks of the 2010 Entry Draft were determined by the NHL's annual Draft Drawing, a weighted lottery system used to determine the order of selection.

The 14 teams that did not qualify for the 2010 Stanley Cup Playoffs, or clubs that acquired those clubs' 2010 first-round draft picks, participated in the drawing.

The club selected in the drawing may not move up more than four positions in the draft order, thus only the five clubs with the fewest regular-season points have the opportunity to select first overall. No club can move down more than one position as a result of the Draft Drawing. For 2010, the Edmonton Oilers won the right to the first overall pick.

In the first round of the 2010 Entry Draft, the order of selection was as follows:

a) The winner of the Draft Drawing followed by the remaining non-playoff teams, in inverse order of points. (Note that the original holder of each selection is listed followed by the club that acquired and used that selection in the first round of the 2010 Entry Draft.)

1. Edmonton
2. Tor. – Bos.
3. Florida
4. Columbus
5. NY Islanders
6. Tampa Bay
7. Carolina
8. Atlanta
9. Minnesota
10. NY Rangers
11. Dallas
12. Anaheim.
13. Cgy. – Phx.
14. St. Louis

b) Clubs eliminated in the first two rounds of the 2010 Stanley Cup Playoffs, regular-season division winners excluded, in inverse order of points;

15. Bos. – L.A.
16. Ott. – St.L.
17. Colorado
18. Nashville
19. L.A. – Fla.
20. Pittsburgh
21. Detroit
22. Phx. – Mtl

c) Regular-season division winning clubs eliminated in the first two rounds of the 2010 Stanley Cup Playoffs, in inverse order of points;

23. Buffalo
24. N.J. – Chi.
25. Van. – Fla.
26. Washington

d) Clubs eliminated in the 2010 Conference Finals, in inverse order of points;

27. Mtl. – Phx.
28. San Jose

e) Loser of Stanley Cup Final
29. Philadelphia – Anaheim

f) Stanley Cup champion
30. Chicago – NY Islanders

Because Edmonton Oilers were both the winner of the Draft Drawing and the Club with the fewest regular-season points, the order of selection in the second and subsequent rounds was identical to that used in the first round.

The Rangers' Michael Del Zotto (top) was selected 20th overall in 2008 from the Oshawa Generals of the OHL. He was the NHL's rookie of the month in October of 2009. Mathieu Perreault made his NHL debut in 2009-10 after being Washington's 10th pick (177th overall) from Acadia-Bathurst in the QMJHL back in 2006.

Western Hockey League Draft Selections by Club

Total	Club	'10	'09	'08	'07	'06	'05	'04	'03	'02	'01	'00	'99	'98	'97	'96	'95	'94	'93	'92	'91	'90	'89	'88	'87	'86	'85	'84	'83	'82	'81	'80	'69 to '79
104	Brandon	2	2	2	1	1	2	–	3	4	2	–	–	4	5	2	6	5	2	1	1	1	–	3	3	1	2	3	1	2	2	5	36
40	Calgary	2	2	2	4	1	2	5	3	2	1	4	6	3	–	3	–	–	–	–	–	–	–	–	–	–	–	–	–	–	–	–	–
6	Chilliwack	3	1	–	2	–	–	–	–	–	–	–	–	–	–	–	–	–	–	–	–	–	–	–	–	–	–	–	–	–	–	–	–
2	Edmonton	1	1	–	–	–	–	–	–	–	–	–	–	–	–	–	–	–	–	–	–	–	–	–	–	–	–	–	–	–	–	–	–
13	Everett	3	2	1	3	4	–	–	–	–	–	–	–	–	–	–	–	–	–	–	–	–	–	–	–	–	–	–	–	–	–	–	–
110	Kamloops	2	2	–	1	1	2	5	2	5	2	4	4	1	3	4	5	9	2	3	6	4	5	1	3	4	4	4	4	2	–	–	16
37	Kelowna	1	3	4	2	–	2	4	4	1	1	1	2	2	7	4	–	–	–	–	–	–	–	–	–	–	–	–	–	–	–	–	–
20	Kootenay	3	1	–	1	1	3	2	1	3	2	1	2	–	–	–	–	–	–	–	–	–	–	–	–	–	–	–	–	–	–	–	–
91	Lethbridge	–	1	2	2	1	–	2	2	2	1	3	–	1	5	1	3	3	4	3	7	4	3	3	–	1	5	1	2	7	4	1	17
110	Medicine Hat	2	1	2	–	2	4	2	3	3	2	–	1	4	2	7	2	6	1	3	3	1	4	1	5	2	6	1	2	1	2	4	31
65	Moose Jaw	3	–	3	1	1	3	3	3	3	3	5	1	2	4	4	4	3	2	3	2	1	3	–	3	1	4	–	–	–	–	–	–
115	Portland	8	1	–	2	1	3	2	1	2	–	6	1	3	3	1	2	3	4	4	1	1	4	1	3	4	2	5	7	7	6	8	19
81	Prince Albert	–	1	–	–	–	2	4	2	1	4	2	3	3	5	3	4	3	5	2	6	4	3	3	1	6	6	2	2	4	–	–	–
27	Prince George	1	1	–	1	4	1	2	2	–	4	–	2	4	2	2	2	–	–	–	–	–	–	–	–	–	–	–	–	–	–	–	–
48	Red Deer	1	4	1	1	1	1	1	4	4	6	1	1	5	3	4	2	5	3	–	–	–	–	–	–	–	–	–	–	–	–	–	–
114	Regina	2	1	3	3	1	1	–	2	1	2	2	4	2	3	4	2	3	–	4	–	1	5	–	2	3	4	4	8	6	5	3	33
115	Saskatoon	4	3	3	3	–	4	1	–	–	4	1	4	2	2	2	2	4	2	3	2	2	3	4	4	5	1	3	5	5	3	2	32
95	Seattle	1	–	2	1	1	3	2	5	1	5	4	6	2	8	1	5	5	4	2	3	6	2	4	2	1	3	1	–	6	–	3	6
65	Spokane	–	2	3	3	1	4	1	–	3	3	2	1	1	4	5	4	4	4	7	5	1	2	3	1	–	–	–	–	–	1	–	–
65	Swift Current	–	1	4	2	2	1	2	2	4	1	3	1	2	2	1	4	4	5	1	1	2	2	2	5	–	–	–	–	–	–	–	11
55	Tri-City	2	–	2	–	–	2	4	1	3	2	2	1	4	1	6	6	2	2	5	3	3	4	–	–	–	–	–	–	–	–	–	–
18	Vancouver	2	1	3	4	1	3	2	1	1	–	–	–	–	–	–	–	–	–	–	–	–	–	–	–	–	–	–	–	–	–	–	–
Teams no longer operating																																	
13	Billings	–	–	–	–	–	–	–	–	–	–	–	–	–	–	–	–	–	–	–	–	–	–	–	–	–	–	–	–	–	2	4	7
66	Calgary	–	–	–	–	–	–	–	–	–	–	–	–	–	–	–	–	–	–	–	–	–	–	–	–	2	3	3	3	4	5	2	44
38	Edmonton	–	–	–	–	–	–	–	–	–	–	–	–	–	4	–	–	–	–	–	–	–	–	–	–	–	–	–	–	–	–	–	34
12	Estevan	–	–	–	–	–	–	–	–	–	–	–	–	–	–	–	–	–	–	–	–	–	–	–	–	–	–	–	–	–	–	–	12
39	Flin Flon	–	–	–	–	–	–	–	–	–	–	–	–	–	–	–	–	–	–	–	–	–	–	–	–	–	–	–	–	–	–	–	39
11	Kelowna	–	–	–	–	–	–	–	–	–	–	–	–	–	–	–	–	–	–	–	–	–	–	–	–	–	5	4	2	–	–	–	–
6	Nanaimo	–	–	–	–	–	–	–	–	–	–	–	–	–	–	–	–	–	–	–	–	–	–	–	–	–	–	–	1	5	–	–	–
62	New Westm'r	–	–	–	–	–	–	–	–	–	–	–	–	–	–	–	–	–	–	–	–	–	–	1	2	1	1	2	–	–	–	1	54
12	Tacoma	–	–	–	–	–	–	–	–	–	–	–	–	–	–	–	2	5	2	3	–	–	–	–	–	–	–	–	–	–	–	–	–
2	Vancouver	–	–	–	–	–	–	–	–	–	–	–	–	–	–	–	–	–	–	–	–	–	–	–	–	–	–	–	–	–	–	–	2
70	Victoria	–	–	–	–	–	–	–	–	–	–	–	–	–	–	–	–	2	2	1	–	2	4	4	2	1	2	4	3	2	6	8	36
34	Winnipeg	–	–	–	–	–	–	–	–	–	–	–	–	–	–	–	–	–	–	–	–	–	–	–	–	–	–	–	1	4	1	–	28

U.S. College Hockey Draft Selections by School

Total	School	'10	'09	'08	'07	'06	'05	'04	'03	'02	'01	'00	'99	'98	'97	'96	'95	'94	'93	'92	'91	'90	'89	'88	'87	'86	'85	'84	'83	'82	'81	'80	'69 to '79
38	Boston College	–	–	1	–	1	1	1	1	3	2	3	–	3	3	2	–	–	–	–	–	–	2	–	2	1	–	–	–	1	1	2	8
53	Boston U.	–	1	1	–	1	–	1	–	3	2	1	3	2	1	1	1	–	1	1	2	2	1	3	2	2	1	1	–	–	1	–	18
28	Bowling Green	–	–	–	–	1	1	–	–	1	1	–	1	1	1	–	–	–	–	1	3	1	2	3	–	–	–	–	1	–	–	1	9
13	Brown	–	–	–	–	–	–	1	–	–	–	1	–	–	–	–	–	–	–	–	1	–	–	–	–	–	–	–	–	1	–	–	9
34	Clarkson	1	–	–	–	1	–	–	–	–	–	1	1	3	–	–	–	–	1	1	2	3	1	1	1	–	–	1	1	1	1	1	12
13	Colgate	–	–	–	–	1	–	1	–	1	–	–	–	–	–	–	–	–	–	–	2	2	1	1	–	–	–	–	–	–	–	–	4
33	Colorado	–	–	–	1	–	1	–	2	1	1	2	1	3	–	–	1	–	–	–	–	2	–	1	–	1	–	3	–	–	–	1	12
34	Cornell	–	–	–	–	–	1	2	2	1	–	2	2	–	1	–	–	–	–	–	–	2	5	2	1	–	2	1	–	1	1	1	7
10	Dartmouth	–	–	–	1	–	–	1	2	–	–	1	–	–	–	–	–	–	–	–	1	–	–	–	1	–	–	–	–	–	–	1	2
43	Denver	–	–	–	–	–	2	1	–	1	–	–	1	–	3	–	–	–	–	–	–	–	1	1	4	2	1	–	–	1	–	1	24
35	Harvard	1	–	–	–	–	1	–	–	3	2	2	1	2	1	3	–	1	2	–	–	–	2	1	1	–	2	–	1	1	–	–	8
25	Lake Superior	1	–	–	–	–	–	–	–	1	–	–	1	–	1	1	–	–	1	–	1	3	2	3	–	3	–	1	–	–	–	–	6
22	Maine	–	–	–	–	1	–	1	2	–	–	1	4	1	1	1	–	–	1	–	–	1	2	3	–	1	–	–	1	1	–	–	–
24	Miami U.	–	2	1	1	1	1	2	–	1	1	–	–	1	–	–	–	–	1	1	2	–	2	4	2	–	1	–	–	–	–	–	–
68	Michigan	1	–	–	1	2	1	3	2	3	2	1	2	3	1	3	–	1	1	2	4	5	3	2	1	–	1	1	–	–	–	4	18
49	Michigan State	1	–	–	–	1	–	2	1	4	–	2	2	1	1	1	–	1	1	1	4	5	4	4	1	1	–	2	–	2	–	2	5
46	Michigan Tech	–	–	–	–	–	–	–	–	–	1	–	–	–	–	1	–	2	1	–	2	1	2	1	1	2	2	2	–	1	–	4	23
69	Minnesota	–	1	–	1	1	1	–	2	3	–	3	3	1	2	3	2	–	–	–	–	–	1	1	1	2	–	–	1	1	1	3	35
13	Minn.-Duluth	–	–	–	–	–	–	–	–	–	–	–	–	1	–	–	–	–	–	–	1	2	1	2	–	–	–	–	–	–	1	–	5
31	New Hampshire	–	–	–	–	–	–	1	–	1	–	2	1	–	1	–	–	–	–	–	–	–	–	1	–	–	–	2	1	1	1	2	17
39	North Dakota	–	–	–	–	1	–	1	1	1	–	1	1	–	2	–	–	–	–	–	1	1	2	–	–	–	–	1	–	–	1	3	22
10	Northeastern	–	–	–	–	–	–	–	–	–	–	–	1	1	–	–	–	–	–	–	–	1	1	–	–	1	1	–	1	–	–	1	21
24	Northern Mich.	1	–	1	–	–	–	2	2	–	–	1	–	–	–	1	–	–	–	–	1	–	2	1	4	–	–	–	–	1	2	1	4
33	Notre Dame	1	–	–	1	1	–	2	–	2	1	1	2	–	2	1	–	–	–	–	–	–	–	–	–	–	–	–	–	–	–	1	18
21	Ohio State	–	–	–	–	–	1	–	1	2	2	–	1	–	1	1	–	–	1	1	1	1	–	2	2	–	–	1	–	–	–	–	3
10	Princeton	–	–	–	–	–	–	–	–	–	1	–	–	1	–	–	–	–	1	–	–	–	1	–	1	–	–	–	1	–	1	1	2
36	Providence	–	–	–	–	2	–	–	1	1	–	2	–	2	1	–	–	–	–	–	–	1	–	–	–	1	1	–	2	1	4	5	12
26	RPI	–	–	1	–	–	–	–	–	–	1	2	2	–	1	–	–	–	–	1	3	–	–	2	2	–	1	–	1	1	2	1	5
23	St. Lawrence	–	–	–	–	–	–	–	–	1	–	–	1	–	1	1	–	–	1	–	2	1	1	1	1	1	1	1	–	3	–	–	6
20	Vermont	–	–	–	–	–	1	–	–	–	2	–	–	–	–	1	–	1	–	–	1	–	–	1	–	–	2	1	1	–	1	1	7
25	W. Michigan	–	1	–	–	1	–	–	–	1	–	–	–	1	1	–	–	–	2	–	4	1	1	1	1	2	–	2	2	–	–	2	2
46	Wisconsin	1	–	2	–	–	–	2	–	–	–	3	2	–	–	–	–	–	–	–	1	–	1	–	1	–	1	1	–	2	3	–	26
16	Yale	–	–	–	–	1	–	2	–	3	–	–	–	–	–	–	–	–	1	–	–	–	1	–	2	1	–	–	–	–	–	1	4

Colleges with fewer than 10 players selected: 9 - Ferris State, Merrimack, St.Cloud State; 7 - Mass.-Lowell; 6 - Illinois-Chicago, St. Louis; 5 - Pennsylvania, Union College, Mass.-Amherst; 4 - Alaska-Anchorage, Nebraska-Omaha, Minnesota State (Mankato); 3 - Babson College, Alaska (Fairbanks); 1 - Air Force, American International College, Army, Bemidji State, Greenway, Hamilton, St. Anselm College, St. Thomas, Salem State, San Diego U., Wisconsin-River Falls.

U.S. High and Prep Schools Draft Selections by School (10 or more players drafted)

Total	School (State)	'10	'09	'08	'07	'06	'05	'04	'03	'02	'01	'00	'99	'98	'97	'96	'95	'94	'93	'92	'91	'90	'89	'88	'87	'86	'85	'84	'83	'82	'81	'80
12	Avon Old Farms (CT)	–	1	–	1	–	–	–	–	–	–	–	–	1	1	–	–	–	–	–	–	3	3	–	–	1	1	–	–	–	–	–
17	Belmont Hill (MA)	–	–	–	–	1	–	–	–	–	–	–	–	–	–	–	–	1	–	2	1	2	3	1	2	1	2	–	1	–	–	–
11	Canterbury (CT)	–	–	–	–	–	–	–	1	–	–	–	–	–	–	–	–	–	1	2	–	2	–	3	–	2	–	–	–	–	–	–
14	Catholic Memorial (MA)	–	–	–	–	–	–	2	–	–	–	–	–	1	–	–	–	2	1	2	–	–	2	1	1	–	2	–	–	–	–	–
10	Choate-Rosemary (CT)	–	–	–	–	–	–	–	–	–	–	1	–	–	–	–	–	–	–	1	1	1	–	3	2	–	1	–	–	–	–	–
12	Culver Mil. Acad. (IN)	–	–	–	–	–	–	–	–	–	–	–	–	–	–	–	–	–	2	2	1	2	2	1	2	–	–	–	–	–	–	–
22	Cushing Acad. (MA)	1	–	–	–	1	1	2	–	–	1	–	–	–	1	1	–	2	2	–	1	3	2	3	–	–	–	1	–	–	–	–
14	Deerfield (IL)	–	–	–	1	–	–	1	1	1	–	2	1	–	–	–	–	–	–	–	1	–	2	1	1	–	1	1	–	–	–	–
17	Edina (MN)	–	2	–	–	–	–	–	–	–	–	–	–	–	–	–	–	–	–	1	–	1	2	2	1	–	–	2	2	4	–	–
15	Hill-Murray (MN)	–	–	–	–	–	–	–	–	–	–	–	–	–	–	–	–	1	–	–	–	3	2	–	3	3	–	3	–	–	–	–
12	Hotchkiss (CT)	–	1	–	–	–	–	1	–	–	1	–	–	–	–	2	1	3	–	–	–	1	–	1	–	–	1	–	–	–	–	–
10	Lawrence Acad. (MA)	–	–	–	–	–	–	–	–	–	–	–	–	–	–	1	–	1	1	–	1	1	–	2	–	–	2	–	1	–	–	–
10	Matignon (MA)	–	–	–	–	–	–	–	–	–	–	–	–	–	–	–	–	–	–	–	1	–	–	–	3	–	–	3	–	1	1	1
12	Minnetonka (MN)	2	1	1	–	–	–	–	–	–	–	–	–	–	–	–	–	–	–	–	1	–	2	–	2	–	2	1	1	–	–	–
13	Mount St. Charles (RI)	–	–	–	–	–	–	–	–	–	–	–	–	–	–	–	–	–	–	–	–	1	1	3	1	2	–	1	3	–	1	–
20	Northwood Prep (NY)	–	–	1	–	–	–	1	–	–	–	1	–	–	–	–	–	1	1	–	–	3	1	1	3	2	2	–	1	2	–	–
12	Roseau (MN)	–	2	–	–	–	–	–	–	–	–	–	–	–	–	–	–	–	–	–	1	3	1	–	–	1	–	1	1	1	–	1
13	St. Sebastian's (MA)	–	–	–	–	1	–	–	4	1	1	–	–	1	–	–	–	1	2	2	–	–	–	–	–	–	–	–	–	–	–	–
15	Shattuck St. Mary's (MN)	3	3	3	1	1	2	–	1	–	–	–	–	–	–	1	–	–	–	–	–	–	–	–	–	–	–	–	–	–	–	–
10	Thayer Acad. (MA)	–	–	–	–	–	2	1	–	–	–	–	2	–	–	–	–	–	–	2	–	–	–	2	–	1	–	–	–	–	–	–

U.S. College and High School Firsts

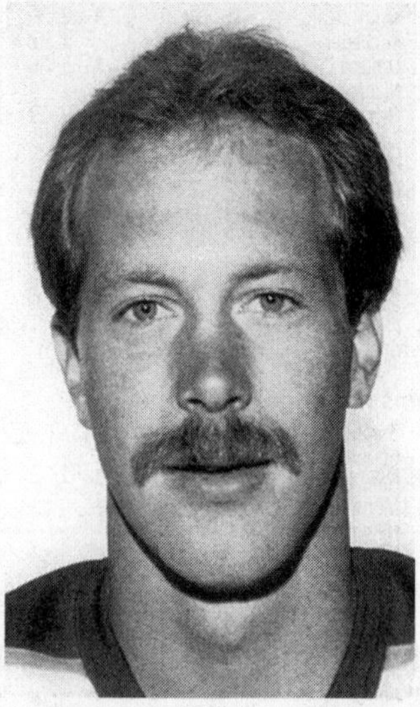

"Miracle on Ice" Olympian Mike Ramsey went on to play 1,070 games in the NHL.

1967 – First U.S. College Player Drafted • Michigan Tech center Al Karlander was selected 17th overall by the Detroit Red Wings.

1979 – First U.S. College First- Round Selection • Minnesota-born defenseman Mike Ramsey (currently an assistant coach with the Minnesota Wild) was selected 11th overall by the Buffalo Sabres.

1980 – First U.S. High School Player Drafted • Center Jay North of Bloomington-Jefferson H.S. was taken 62nd overall by the Buffalo Sabres in 1980.

1981 – First U.S. High School First- Round Selection • Center Bob Carpenter of St. John's prep school was selected third overall by Washington in 1981.

1983 – First U.S. High School Player Drafted First Overall • Minnesota North Stars selected left winger Brian Lawton from Mount St. Charles H.S. first overall in 1983.

1986 – First U.S. College Player Drafted First Overall • Detroit selected right winger Joe Murphy from Michigan State first overall in 1986.

2005 – Most U.S. College Players Selected in the First Round • The 2005 draft saw eight U.S. college players selected in the first round, the most in Entry Draft history. Seven were selected in the first round in 2003 and 1986, six in 2000, five in 2002, four in 2001 and three in each of the 1986 and 1999 Entry Drafts.

International

Ranked by total number of players drafted

Total	Country	'10	'09	'08	'07	'06	'05	'04	'03	'02	'01	'00	'99	'98	'97	'96	'95	'94	'93	'92	'91	'90	'89	'88	'87	'86	'85	'84	'83	'82	'81	'80	'69 to '79
529	Russia/CIS/USSR	4	6	9	7	16	11	24	32	33	36	44	29	22	16	17	27	35	31	45	25	14	18	11	2	1	2	1	5	3	–	–	3
507	Sweden	21	23	19	16	18	15	18	19	24	14	24	24	19	14	16	17	18	11	11	7	9	14	9	16	14	10	14	10	14	9	–	27
409	CzRep/Slovakia	1	3	2	4	11	15	24	20	21	28	28	20	20	17	14	21	18	15	17	9	21	8	5	11	6	8	13	9	13	4	–	3
327	Finland	7	8	6	4	13	8	14	12	26	29	19	17	12	11	7	12	8	9	8	6	9	3	7	6	10	4	10	9	5	12	4	12
49	Germany	3	1	1	4	2	1	1	4	1	7	1	–	–	1	3	1	1	3	2	1	–	–	2	1	–	1	2	1	–	2	–	2
45	Switzerland	1	–	1	3	–	4	5	4	5	7	3	2	3	1	–	1	2	–	1	–	–	–	–	–	–	–	–	–	–	–	–	1
8	Norway	–	–	1	–	–	–	–	–	1	–	–	–	–	1	–	–	–	–	1	2	–	1	–	–	2	–	–	–	–	–	–	–
5	Denmark	1	–	–	–	–	2	–	–	–	–	–	–	–	–	–	–	–	–	–	–	–	–	–	–	–	–	–	–	–	–	–	–
2	Japan	–	–	–	–	–	–	1	–	–	–	–	–	–	–	–	–	–	1	–	–	–	–	–	–	–	–	–	–	–	–	–	–
2	Poland	–	–	–	–	–	–	–	1	–	–	–	–	–	–	–	–	–	–	–	1	–	–	–	–	–	–	–	–	–	–	–	–
1	Hungary	–	–	–	–	–	–	–	–	–	–	–	1	–	–	–	–	–	–	–	–	–	–	–	–	–	–	–	–	–	–	–	–
1	Scotland	–	–	–	–	–	–	–	–	–	–	–	–	–	–	–	–	–	–	–	–	–	–	–	–	–	–	–	–	–	–	–	1
1	Belarus	1	–	–	–	–	–	–	–	–	–	–	–	–	–	–	–	–	–	–	–	–	–	–	–	–	–	–	–	–	–	–	–

Czech Republic and Slovakia

Total	Club	'10	'09	'08	'07	'06	'05	'04	'03	'02	'01	'00	'99	'98	'97	'96	'95	'94	'93	'92	'91	'90	'89	'88	'87	'86	'85	'84	'83	'82	'81	'80	'69 to '79
8	Brno	–	–	–	–	–	–	–	–	–	–	–	1	–	–	–	–	–	1	–	2	–	–	3	1	–	–	–	–	–	–	–	–
32	Ceske Budejovice	–	1	–	–	2	2	1	2	–	2	3	1	1	2	1	3	2	1	–	1	–	1	–	1	–	1	1	2	–	–	–	–
3	Havirov	–	–	–	–	–	–	–	2	–	1	–	–	–	–	–	–	–	–	–	–	–	–	–	–	–	–	–	–	–	–	–	–
28	Jihlava	–	–	–	–	–	–	–	–	–	–	–	–	2	2	1	–	1	2	3	1	1	3	–	1	3	4	2	–	–	–	–	–
4	Karlovy Vary	–	–	–	–	–	–	1	1	1	1	–	–	–	–	–	–	–	–	–	–	–	–	–	–	–	–	–	–	–	–	–	–
23	Kladno	–	–	–	3	1	1	1	–	1	1	2	–	–	2	1	–	2	1	–	–	1	–	1	–	–	1	1	2	–	–	–	–
15	Kosice	–	–	–	–	1	1	–	–	1	–	1	1	1	1	–	–	–	2	–	–	1	–	–	2	–	–	2	1	–	–	–	–
4	Liberec	–	–	–	–	1	1	–	2	–	1	–	–	–	–	–	–	–	–	–	–	–	–	–	–	–	–	–	–	–	–	–	–
34	Litvinov	–	–	–	–	–	3	2	–	1	–	1	1	2	2	6	1	4	2	3	1	2	2	–	–	–	2	1	3	–	–	–	–
6	Martin	–	–	–	–	–	–	1	–	1	–	1	1	–	–	–	2	–	–	–	1	–	–	–	–	–	–	–	–	–	–	–	–
7	Nitra	–	–	–	–	–	–	–	–	–	1	–	–	–	–	1	–	–	2	–	–	–	–	1	–	–	–	–	–	–	–	–	–
7	Olomouc	–	–	–	–	–	–	–	1	–	–	–	1	–	–	–	–	–	2	1	–	–	1	–	–	–	–	–	–	–	–	–	–
13	Pardubice	–	–	–	–	–	–	–	–	3	1	–	–	1	–	1	2	–	–	–	–	–	2	–	–	–	–	–	–	–	–	–	–
14	Plzen	–	–	1	–	–	–	–	–	2	1	1	–	1	1	–	1	3	–	1	1	–	1	–	–	–	–	–	–	–	–	–	–
3	Presov	–	–	–	–	1	–	–	–	–	–	–	–	–	–	–	–	–	–	–	–	–	–	–	–	1	–	–	–	–	–	–	–
28	Slavia Praha	–	–	–	1	–	1	1	2	2	5	3	2	5	4	–	–	–	1	–	–	–	–	–	–	–	–	–	–	–	–	–	–
22	Slovan Bratis.	–	–	–	–	–	–	3	1	–	2	2	1	1	1	–	3	–	–	–	1	1	–	–	1	–	–	2	–	–	2	–	–
28	Sparta Praha	–	–	–	–	1	2	4	1	2	1	–	1	1	–	1	–	1	–	2	1	2	1	1	1	2	–	1	–	–	–	–	–
30	Trencin	–	–	–	1	1	4	3	–	2	3	2	–	1	–	1	1	–	1	2	2	2	1	–	1	–	–	–	–	–	–	–	–
10	Trinec	–	1	1	–	1	–	1	1	1	1	1	2	–	–	–	–	–	–	–	–	–	–	–	–	–	–	–	–	–	–	–	–
19	Vitkovice	–	–	–	–	1	1	2	–	2	–	1	1	–	1	1	3	1	–	1	–	–	–	–	–	–	–	–	–	1	–	–	1
14	Vsetin	–	–	–	1	1	1	1	3	2	2	1	2	–	–	–	–	–	–	–	–	–	–	–	–	–	–	–	–	–	–	–	–
21	Zlin¹	–	–	–	1	2	–	2	–	2	2	1	–	1	2	2	1	–	1	–	–	1	–	–	–	1	–	–	–	–	–	–	–
8	Zvolen	–	1	–	–	–	–	–	–	–	2	2	–	–	1	1	–	1	–	–	–	–	–	–	–	–	–	–	–	–	–	–	–

Former club names: ¹—Gottwaldov. **Teams with two players selected:** Ingstav Brno, IS Banska Bystrica, Dubnica, Michalovce, Partizan Liptovsky Mikulas, VTJ Pisek, Skalica, Spisska Nova Ves, Topolcany. **Teams with one player selected:** Banik Sokolov, KLH Chomutov, Havlickuv Brod, Ostrava, KC SKP Poprad, Povazska Bystrica, HK Trnava, KHM Zvolen, Slovak U20.

Finland

Total	Club	'10	'09	'08	'07	'06	'05	'04	'03	'02	'01	'00	'99	'98	'97	'96	'95	'94	'93	'92	'91	'90	'89	'88	'87	'86	'85	'84	'83	'82	'81	'80	'69 to '79
16	Assat	–	–	–	2	–	–	1	–	–	1	–	–	–	1	1	–	1	–	–	–	–	2	2	–	1	–	2
21	Blues Espoo	1	3	1	–	–	1	–	1	–	2	–	1	2	–	2	1	1	–	1	–	–	–	–	–	–	–
40	HIFK Helsinki	1	–	–	4	1	2	–	5	2	2	4	2	1	–	1	2	–	–	1	2	2	1	1	–	–	3
12	HPK	–	–	–	–	1	–	1	1	3	1	1	1	–	–	–	–	–	–	–	–	–	–	–	–	–	–
37	Ilves	2	1	1	–	3	3	–	2	4	3	1	2	–	2	–	1	1	–	1	–	2	–	2	–	2	3
37	Jokerit	1	–	–	–	2	1	2	6	4	3	3	1	1	–	1	–	3	–	2	–	1	1	–	1	–	2
12	JyP Jyvaskyla	–	1	–	–	–	2	1	–	3	–	1	2	–	–	–	–	–	–	–	–	–	–	–	–	–	–
12	KalPa	–	1	–	1	–	–	1	–	2	1	–	1	–	–	–	–	1	–	–	–	–	–	–	–	–	–
26	Karpat	1	1	–	–	2	2	3	3	–	1	1	–	1	–	1	–	–	2	2	–	1	1	–	1	–	1
3	Kiekoo-67	–	–	–	–	–	–	–	–	–	–	3	–	–	–	–	–	–	–	–	–	–	–	–	–	–	–
20	Lukko	–	–	1	1	–	–	1	1	3	1	2	–	–	1	–	2	–	–	1	–	1	–	–	2	–	3
9	Pelicans	–	–	–	–	–	1	–	1	–	–	–	1	2	–	–	–	–	1	–	1	1	–	–	–	–	–
7	SaiPa	–	–	–	–	1	1	1	–	1	–	–	1	–	–	–	–	–	–	–	–	–	1	–	–	–	–
24	Tappara	–	2	2	2	–	1	2	2	2	1	–	–	–	–	–	–	1	–	4	–	–	2	–	1	–	–
35	TPS Turku	–	2	–	–	–	1	1	1	3	3	1	3	1	3	2	3	–	–	–	–	–	1	1	–	–	6	1

Teams with two players selected: KooKoo Kouvola, Sapko Savonlinna, Sport Vaasa, TuTo.
Teams with one player selected: Ahmat Hyvinkaa, Hermes Kokkola, Junkkarit Kalajoki, GrIFK Kauniainen, LeKi, S-Kiekko Seinajoki, K-Vantaa.

Selected 12th overall in 2008 from Kelowna in the WHL, 6'7" defenseman Tyler Myers (top) played all 82 games in 2009-10 and led all rookies with 37 assists. Swedish defenseman Victor Hedman was chosen second overall behind John Tavares in the 2009 Entry Draft and jumped directly into the NHL.

Note: International draft selections played outside North America in their draft year.

European-born players drafted from the OHL, QMJHL, WHL, U.S. colleges or other North American leagues are not counted as International players.

For analysis by birthplace, see the following page.

Russia/CIS/USSR

Total	Club	'10	'09	'08	'07	'06	'05	'04	'03	'02	'01	'00	'99	'98	'97	'96	'95	'94	'93	'92	'91	'90	'89	'88	'87	'86	'85	'84	'83	'82	'81	'80	'69 to '79
6	Ak Bars Kazan	–	–	1	–	–	–	–	1	–	1	1	–	1	–	–	–	1	–	–	–	–	–	–	–	–	–	–	–	–	–	–	–
3	Ak Bars Kazan 2	–	–	–	–	–	–	–	1	–	1	–	1	–	–	–	–	–	–	–	–	–	–	–	–	–	–	–	–	–	–	–	–
9	Avangard Omsk	–	–	–	–	–	–	–	–	1	3	1	–	–	–	1	–	3	–	–	–	–	–	–	–	–	–	–	–	–	–	–	–
5	Avangard Omsk 2	–	–	–	–	–	–	1	1	–	3	–	–	–	–	–	–	–	–	–	–	–	–	–	–	–	–	–	–	–	–	–	–
5	CSK VVS Samara	–	–	–	–	–	–	1	1	–	1	–	1	–	–	–	1	–	–	–	–	–	–	–	–	–	–	–	–	–	–	–	–
64	CSKA Moscow	–	–	–	2	1	1	3	3	–	–	–	3	1	–	3	2	5	3	7	4	3	8	5	1	1	1	–	4	1	–	–	2
13	CSKA Moscow 2	–	–	2	–	2	1	1	2	–	–	–	–	–	2	2	–	1	–	–	–	–	–	–	–	–	–	–	–	–	–	–	–
46	Dynamo Moscow	–	–	–	1	–	–	1	1	–	–	2	2	1	1	1	7	1	2	10	7	4	3	2	–	–	–	–	–	–	–	–	–
17	Dyn'o Moscow 2	–	1	–	–	–	–	–	1	–	–	4	–	3	3	–	–	2	1	2	–	–	–	–	–	–	–	–	–	–	–	–	–
4	Dyn-Energ. Yekat.[1]	–	–	–	–	–	–	–	1	–	–	–	1	1	–	1	–	–	–	–	–	–	–	–	–	–	–	–	–	–	–	–	–
16	Elektrostal	–	–	–	–	–	–	–	2	9	1	–	–	–	1	–	–	–	–	3	–	–	–	–	–	–	–	–	–	–	–	–	–
11	HC CSKA	–	–	–	–	–	–	–	–	4	–	5	2	–	–	–	–	–	–	–	–	–	–	–	–	–	–	–	–	–	–	–	–
3	Kristall Saratov	–	–	–	–	–	–	1	–	–	1	–	–	–	–	–	–	–	1	–	–	–	–	–	–	–	–	–	–	–	–	–	–
33	Krylja Sovetov	–	–	–	–	1	1	2	–	1	1	1	2	1	1	2	3	5	1	3	4	2	1	1	–	–	–	–	–	–	–	–	–
4	Krylja Sovetov 2	–	–	–	–	–	–	–	–	3	–	–	–	–	–	–	–	–	1	–	–	–	–	–	–	–	–	–	–	–	–	–	–
19	Lada Togliatti	–	1	–	–	2	–	2	–	2	–	2	2	1	3	1	–	–	2	1	–	–	–	–	–	–	–	–	–	–	–	–	–
6	Lada Togliatti 2	–	–	–	–	–	1	–	–	–	2	2	1	–	–	–	–	–	–	–	–	–	–	–	–	–	–	–	–	–	–	–	–
22	Lokomotiv Yaro.[2]	–	–	–	–	–	–	–	4	2	–	1	1	3	1	1	5	1	–	–	2	1	–	–	–	–	–	–	–	–	–	–	–
32	Lokomotiv Yaro.2	–	1	2	1	3	2	–	3	1	1	9	–	4	2	2	1	–	–	–	–	–	–	–	–	–	–	–	–	–	–	–	–
7	Magnitogorsk	–	–	–	–	1	–	1	1	1	3	–	–	–	–	–	–	–	–	–	–	–	–	–	–	–	–	–	–	–	–	–	–
3	Magnitogorsk 2	–	1	1	–	–	–	1	–	–	–	–	–	–	–	–	–	–	–	–	–	–	–	–	–	–	–	–	–	–	–	–	–
6	Nizhnekamsk	–	–	–	–	–	–	1	–	–	2	2	–	–	1	–	–	–	–	–	–	–	–	–	–	–	–	–	–	–	–	–	–
4	Nizhny Novgorod[3]	–	–	–	–	–	–	–	–	–	–	1	–	–	–	–	–	–	–	2	–	1	–	–	–	–	–	–	–	–	–	–	–
9	Novokuznetsk	1	1	–	–	–	–	1	1	–	1	2	2	–	–	–	–	–	–	–	–	–	–	–	–	–	–	–	–	–	–	–	–
9	Pardaugava Riga[4]	–	–	–	–	–	–	–	–	–	–	–	–	–	–	–	–	–	1	4	1	–	2	1	–	–	–	–	–	–	–	–	–
5	Perm	–	–	–	–	–	–	–	–	1	1	1	–	–	–	–	1	1	–	–	–	–	–	–	–	–	–	–	–	–	–	–	–
15	Severstal Cher.[5]	1	–	1	–	1	–	–	2	–	–	1	5	–	–	1	1	–	1	1	–	–	–	–	–	–	–	–	–	–	–	–	–
4	Severstal Cher. 2	–	–	1	–	–	–	–	–	1	–	1	1	–	–	–	–	–	–	–	–	–	–	–	–	–	–	–	–	–	–	–	–
12	SKA St. Pete.[6]	–	–	–	–	–	–	–	–	–	2	1	2	–	–	–	–	1	–	1	2	–	–	–	–	–	–	–	–	1	–	–	2
11	Sokol Kiev	–	–	–	–	–	–	–	–	–	–	–	–	–	–	–	2	–	1	3	2	1	–	1	–	–	–	1	–	–	–	–	–
22	Spartak Moscow	–	–	–	–	–	–	–	–	–	6	–	1	–	–	–	1	6	–	4	1	–	–	–	1	–	1	–	–	1	–	–	–
9	THC Tver	–	–	–	–	–	–	3	3	–	1	2	–	–	–	–	–	–	–	–	–	–	–	–	–	–	–	–	–	–	–	–	–
5	Tivali Minsk[7]	–	–	–	–	–	–	1	–	–	–	–	–	–	–	–	–	1	2	–	–	–	–	1	–	–	–	–	–	–	–	–	–
22	Traktor Chelyabinsk	1	–	1	1	1	2	–	–	1	–	–	–	1	1	–	1	1	7	2	–	–	2	–	–	–	–	–	–	–	–	–	–
9	Ufa	–	–	–	–	–	–	–	1	–	–	1	–	–	1	1	1	2	2	–	–	–	–	–	–	–	–	–	–	–	–	–	–
9	Ust-Kamenogorsk	–	–	–	–	–	–	–	1	–	–	–	1	2	–	–	1	2	1	1	–	–	–	–	–	–	–	–	–	–	–	–	–
14	Voskresensk	–	–	–	–	–	–	–	1	–	1	1	–	2	–	–	–	1	–	2	1	3	1	–	–	–	–	–	1	–	–	–	–

Former club names: 1–Avtomobilist Yekaterinburg, 2–Torpedo Yaroslavl, 3–Torpedo Gorky, 4–Dynamo Riga,HC Riga, 5–Metallurg Cherepovets, 6–SKA Leningrad, 7–Dynamo Minsk. **Teams with two players selected:** Dizelist Penza, Mechel Chelyabinsk, Metallurg Magnitogorsk 2, Metallurg Novokuznetsk 2, Salavat Yulayev Ufa 2, Spartak Moscow 2, Torpedo Nizhny Novgorod 2, Yunost Minsk.**Teams with one player selected:** Amur Khabarovsk, Argus Moscow, Avangard Omsk, HC CSKA Moscow 2, Dynamo Khazov, Dynamo-81 Riga, Gazovik Tyumen, HK Gomel, Izohets St. Petersburg, Kapitan Stupino, Khimik Novopolotsk, Khimik Voskresensk 2, Metalurgs Liepaja, Mostovik Kurgan, Neftekhimik Nizhnekamsk 2, Neftyanik Almetjevsk, SKA St. Petersburg 2, Spartak St. Petersburg, Sibir Novosibirsk, Sibir Novosibirsk 2, Stalkers-Juniors, Torpedo Nizhny Novgorod 2, THC Tver, Vityaz Podolsk, Vityaz Podolsk 2.

Sweden

Total	Club	'10	'09	'08	'07	'06	'05	'04	'03	'02	'01	'00	'99	'98	'97	'96	'95	'94	'93	'92	'91	'90	'89	'88	'87	'86	'85	'84	'83	'82	'81	'80	'69 to '79
28	AIK Solna	4	–	–	–	–	–	–	–	1	1	–	3	1	1	–	–	1	–	1	1	1	–	–	–	–	4	–	1	3	2	–	3
3	Almtuna	1	1	–	–	–	–	–	–	–	–	–	–	–	–	–	–	–	–	–	–	–	–	–	–	–	–	–	–	2	–	–	–
9	Bjorkloven	–	–	1	–	2	1	–	–	–	–	–	–	–	–	–	–	–	–	–	–	–	–	1	–	–	1	–	–	–	1	2	–
3	Boden	–	–	–	–	–	–	–	–	–	–	–	–	–	–	–	–	1	–	–	–	–	–	–	–	1	–	–	–	–	–	–	1
36	Brynas Gavle	4	3	4	1	1	–	–	2	–	2	1	1	2	1	1	–	–	1	–	–	–	–	–	4	–	–	2	1	–	1	1	3
44	Djurgarden	2	3	1	–	1	1	2	–	2	1	4	1	–	2	2	3	–	1	1	2	1	1	–	2	1	–	1	2	1	–	2	4
3	Falun	–	–	–	–	–	–	–	–	–	–	–	–	–	–	–	–	–	–	–	1	–	–	1	–	–	–	–	–	–	1	–	–
34	Farjestad	–	1	–	–	1	–	–	–	2	1	–	1	6	3	–	2	–	1	2	1	–	1	–	–	–	2	1	1	1	2	1	4
50	Frolunda	1	3	4	5	3	3	4	2	3	3	4	2	1	–	1	1	3	–	1	–	–	1	1	1	–	1	2	–	–	–	–	–
3	Grums	–	–	–	–	–	–	–	–	–	–	1	1	–	–	–	–	1	–	–	–	–	–	–	–	–	–	–	–	–	–	–	–
10	Hammarby	–	–	–	–	1	–	–	–	3	–	1	–	–	1	–	–	–	1	1	–	–	–	–	–	–	–	–	–	–	–	1	1
7	Huddinge	–	–	–	–	1	–	–	–	1	1	–	1	–	–	2	–	–	–	–	1	–	–	–	–	–	–	–	–	–	–	–	–
28	HV 71	1	1	3	1	–	1	2	1	1	–	1	3	4	1	2	–	2	–	–	–	1	–	1	1	–	–	–	–	–	1	–	–
31	Leksand	–	1	–	–	1	1	–	2	–	–	5	–	2	–	1	–	2	2	–	2	–	1	2	1	1	2	2	–	1	–	–	2
6	Linkoping	–	1	1	1	1	1	1	–	–	–	–	–	–	–	–	–	–	–	–	–	–	–	–	–	–	–	–	–	–	–	–	–
15	Lulea	–	1	–	3	–	–	1	–	–	–	2	–	1	1	–	–	–	–	1	–	–	–	1	1	1	–	–	–	–	1	1	–
19	Malmo	–	1	1	1	1	1	1	1	4	–	1	1	–	–	2	–	1	1	1	–	–	–	1	–	–	–	–	–	–	–	–	–
39	MODO	2	1	–	–	–	1	1	–	3	–	3	7	–	3	3	–	–	5	2	2	–	–	–	1	–	–	2	–	1	–	–	2
7	Mora	–	1	–	–	–	–	–	1	–	1	–	–	–	1	1	–	–	–	–	–	–	–	–	–	1	–	–	1	–	–	–	–
3	Morrum	–	–	–	–	–	–	–	–	2	1	–	–	–	–	–	–	–	–	–	–	–	–	–	–	–	–	–	–	–	–	–	–
4	Nacka	–	–	–	–	–	–	–	–	–	–	–	–	–	–	–	–	–	–	2	–	–	1	–	–	1	–	–	–	–	–	–	–
6	Orebro	–	–	–	–	–	–	1	–	–	–	–	–	–	–	–	–	–	–	–	–	–	–	–	1	–	1	–	1	–	–	–	2
3	Pitea	–	–	–	–	–	–	–	–	–	–	–	–	–	–	–	–	1	–	–	–	1	–	–	–	–	–	–	–	1	–	–	–
10	Rogle	–	–	–	1	–	–	–	–	–	–	–	1	–	–	–	1	2	2	–	–	–	–	2	1	–	–	–	–	–	–	–	–
15	Skelleftea	2	3	–	–	–	–	–	–	–	–	–	–	–	1	–	–	–	1	–	–	–	–	1	–	–	–	1	2	1	1	–	2
27	Sodertalje	2	–	–	1	2	3	1	2	–	1	1	–	1	–	–	–	–	1	–	–	–	2	–	–	2	2	2	1	1	1	–	1
3	Stocksund	–	–	–	–	–	–	2	–	–	–	–	–	–	–	–	–	–	–	–	–	–	–	–	–	–	–	–	–	1	–	–	–
3	Team Kiruna	–	–	–	–	–	–	–	–	–	–	–	–	–	–	–	–	–	1	–	–	–	–	–	–	–	–	–	–	1	–	–	1
11	Timra	1	2	–	–	–	–	–	–	1	–	–	1	–	–	–	–	1	–	–	–	–	–	–	–	1	1	–	–	–	2	1	–
4	Troja/Ljungby	–	–	–	–	–	–	–	1	–	–	–	1	–	–	–	–	–	–	–	–	–	–	1	–	–	1	–	–	–	–	–	–
16	Vasteras	–	–	1	1	3	–	1	–	1	–	1	–	–	–	–	–	1	1	–	1	1	2	2	–	–	–	–	–	–	–	–	–
3	Vita Hasten	–	–	1	–	–	–	–	–	–	1	–	–	–	–	1	–	–	–	–	–	–	–	–	–	–	–	–	–	–	–	–	–

Teams with two players selected: Almtuna, Bofors, Ostersund, Skare, Tingsryd. **Teams with one player selected:** Arboga, Arvika, Danderyd Hockey, Fagersta, Jamtland, Karskoga, Kumla, Stocksund, S/G Hockey 83 Gavle, Skovde, Sunne, Talje, Tunabro, Uppsala, Vallentuna, Vasby. Karskoga, Kumla, Stocksund, S/G Hockey 83 Gavle, Skovde, Sunne, Talje, Tunabro, Uppsala, Vallentuna, Vasby.

European Draft Firsts

1969 – First European (and Finn) • LW Tommi Salmelainen, 66th overall by St. Louis.

1974 – First Swede • C Per Alexandersson, 49th overall by Toronto. Four other Swedish-born players were selected that year, including defenseman Stefan Persson, 214th overall by the NY Islanders, who became the first European-trained player to be part of a Stanley Cup winner with the Islanders in 1980.

1975 – First Russian • C Viktor Khatulev, 160th overall by Philadelphia.

1976 – First European Taken in the First Round • Swedish D Bjorn Johansson, 5th overall by the California Seals.

1976 – First Swiss • C Jacques Soguel, 121st overall by St. Louis.

1978 – First Czechoslovak • LW Ladislav Svozil, 194th overall by Detroit.

1978 – First Germans • G Bernard Englbrecht, 196th overall by Atlanta and F Gerd Truntschka, 200th overall by St. Louis.

1989 – First European Taken First Overall • Swedish C Mats Sundin, 1st overall by Quebec in 1989.

2010 Entry Draft Analysis

BY BIRTHPLACE

Country of Origin

Country	Players Drafted
Canada	99
USA	59
Sweden	20
Russia	8
Finland	7
Czech Republic	5
Germany	5
Slovakia	2
Switzerland	2
Denmark	1
Latvia	1
Norway	1
Total	**210**

Canadian-Born Players

Province	Players Drafted
Ontario	37
British Columbia	17
Quebec	13
Alberta	13
Manitoba	7
Saskatchewan	7
Prince Edward Island	2
New Brunswick	2
Nova Scotia	1
Total	**99**

U.S.-Born Players

State	Players Drafted
Minnesota	14
Michigan	8
Massachusetts	6
New York	4
Pennsylvania	3
Missouri	3
Connecticut	3
California	3
Illinois	2
Florida	2
Oklahoma	1
Oregon	1
Washington	1
Virginia	1
Utah	1
Nevada	1
Maryland	1
Arizona	1
Ohio	1
North Dakota	1
New Jersey	1
Total	**59**

BY BIRTH YEAR

Year	Players Drafted
1992	139
1991	49
1990	21
1989	1

BY POSITION

Position	Players Drafted
Defense	68
Center	50
Right Wing	35
Left Wing	36
Goaltender	21

Notes on 2010 First-Round Selections

1. EDMONTON • **TAYLOR HALL** • LW • A dynamic skater who is fearless when he goes to the net, Taylor Hall led the OHL in playoff scoring and was named Memorial Cup MVP when the Windsor Spitfires won their second straight national junior title in 2010. He led the OHL with 66 assists and tied for the lead with 106 points in 2009-10 despite playing just 57 games. He was the only draft-eligible player on Canada's silver medal team at the 2010 World Junior Championship and was named to the tournament all-star team.

2. BOSTON • **TYLER SEGUIN** • C • A skilled forward who makes his teammates better, Tyler Seguin's 48 goals gave him the 2009-10 OHL scoring title although his 106 points were actually tied with Taylor Hall. He also won the Red Tilson Trophy as the league's most outstanding player. Seguin captained Team White at the Top Prospects game and was named the game's MVP. In 2009, he led Canada to gold at the Ivan Hlinka Under-18 tournament and was the leading scorer.

3. FLORIDA • **ERIK GUDBRANSON** • D • A tough defenseman who was hampered by injuries and illness in 2009-10, Erik Gudbranson is 6'4" with a strong shot. He is also a good passer. Gudbranson won the Bobby Smith Trophy as the OHL's Scholastic Player of the Year in 2009-10 and is compared by many to Chris Pronger in his style of play. He played for Canada's team at the 2010 Under-18 World Championship and won gold at the 2009 Ivan Hlinka Under-18 event.

4. COLUMBUS • **RYAN JOHANSEN** • C • An intelligent player with good on-ice vision, Ryan Johansen was second in scoring among rookies in the Western Hockey League with the Portland Winterhawks in 2009-10. He played most of the season on a line with fellow draft prospects Nino Niederreiter and Brad Ross. Just 5'9" during his bantam year, a growth spurt to 6'3" helped him put up big numbers as a WHL rookie after intending to go to Northeastern University.

5. NY ISLANDERS • **NINO NIEDERREITER** • RW • A physical player who his shifty and skilled, Nino Niederreiter led the Portland Winterhawks with 36 goals in 2009-10. He also starred for Switzerland at the 2010 World Junior Championship, collecting 10 points in six games, scoring in overtime to eliminate Russia in the quarterfinals, and being named to the tournament all-star team. Niederreiter is the highest-selected Swiss player in NHL Draft history.

6. TAMPA BAY • **BRETT CONNOLLY** • RW • A potential number-one pick if not for injuries in 2009-10, Brett Connolly is a gifted offensive player with great on-ice awareness. In 2008-09 he became the first 16-year-old WHL rookie to score 30 goals in a season since Patrick Marleau in 1995-96. He was the youngest Canadian player at the Under-18 World Championship in 2009 and was at the tourney again in 2010.

7. CAROLINA • **JEFF SKINNER** • C • A pure goal scorer with great moves and a hard shot, Jeff Skinner was one of only two 50-goal scorers in the Ontario Hockey League in 2009-10. His 90 points were seventh in the league. Skinner was the winner of the creative breakaway skills competition at the 2010 Top Prospects game. He won a bronze medal at the 2004 Skate Canada Junior Nationals figure skating championship.

8. ATLANTA • **ALEXANDER BURMISTROV** • C • Though he weighs only 165 pounds, Alexander Burmistrov is a hard worker with speed, agility and great on-ice vision. Burmistrov played his entire career for Ak Bars in Russia before joining the Barrie Colts of the OHL in 2009-10. He won a silver medal with Russia at the 2009 Under-18 World Championship and played at the 2010 World Junior tournament.

9. MINNESOTA • **MIKAEL GRANLUND** • C/W • A small player (5'10", 180 lbs.) who works hard and has a winning attitude, Mikael Granlund has been compared to fellow Finn Saku Koivu. He led all rookies with 40 points in 43 games in the Finnish elite league in 2009-10. He led Finland in scoring at the 2010 World Junior Championship and led the 2010 Under-18 World tourney in assists and won a bronze medal.

10. NY RANGERS • **DYLAN McILRATH** • D • At 6'4" and 218 pounds, Dylan McIlrath is a physical defenseman considered to be the toughest player available in the NHL Entry Draft. He had 19 fighting majors in 2009-10, but also has a good shot from the point. He had a productive second half of the WHL season, collecting 16 of his 24 points. McIlrath played for Team West at the 2009 Under-17 Hockey Challenge.

11. DALLAS • **JACK CAMPBELL** • G • A goalie with good size and quickness, Jack Campbell entered the gold medal game at the 2010 World Junior Championship against Canada in the second period with a 3-0 deficit and stopped 32 out of 34 shots to help the U.S. win in overtime. He also won gold at the Under-18 World Championship in 2009 and 2010. Campbell was named top goalie at the 2010 event after leading with a .965 save percentage and 0.83 average.

12. ANAHEIM • **CAM FOWLER** • D • An offensive defenseman with great skating and puck-control skills, Cam Fowler won the Memorial Cup with the Windsor Spitfires in 2010. He had 55 points in 55 games in 2009-10 and was a +38. Fowler previously spent two years with the U.S. National Team Development Program. He won a gold medal at the 2010 World Junior Championship and at the 2009 Under-18 World Championship, where he was also named top defenseman.

13. PHOENIX • **BRANDON GORMLEY** • D • A smart defenseman who can handle the puck and shoot well from the point, Brandon Gormley was the best player on Canada's gold medal-winning 2009 Under-18 Ivan Hlinka tournament team and helped the Moncton Wildcats win the QMJHL title in 2010. He was Moncton's rookie of the year in 2008-09 and the QMJHL's Mike Bossy Trophy winner as the top professional prospect in 2009-10.

14. ST. LOUIS • **JADEN SCHWARTZ** • C • A skilled player who is deceptive and tricky, Jaden Schwartz is hard to knock off the puck. He became the youngest player since 1982-83 to win the USHL scoring title in 2009-10 and his 83 points in 60 games were the highest since Thomas Vanek scored 91 in 2001-02. Schwartz previously broke the league scoring record held by Vincent Lecavalier and Brad Richards as a midget with the Notre Dame Hounds in 2007-08.

15. LOS ANGELES • **DEREK FORBORT** • D • At 6'5"and 198 pounds, Derek Forbort is strong on both sides of the puck. He's smart and skates well and has great offensive instincts. Forbort is a member of the U.S. National Team Development Program and was +9 in seven games when the United States won gold at the 2010 Under-18 World Championship. He has committed to the University of North Dakota for 2010-11.

16. ST. LOUIS • **VLADIMIR TARASENKO** • RW • A strong, mobile skater who is very effective around the net, Vladimir Tarasenko has a quick shot and excellent vision. He is also a good passer and playmaker. Tarasenko has spent the last two seasons in the Kontinental Hockey League and tied for the Russian team lead in goals at the 2010 World Junior Championship. He won a silver medal and was second in tournament scoring at the 2009 Under-18 World tourney.

17. COLORADO • **JOEY HISHON** • C • A high-energy player with a great work ethic and good skills, Joey Hishon was limited to 36 games with the Owen Sound Attack in 2009-10 but still collected 40 points. He was voted the best playmaker and best stickhandler in the OHL's Western Conference by the league's coaches in 2008-09. Hishon represented Canada at the 2009 Under-18 World Championship.

18. NASHVILLE • **AUSTIN WATSON** • LW • A power forward who plays an aggressive, two-way game, Austin Watson has good hands and a hard shot. He was a role-player on a talented Windsor team, but collected 20 points in just 10 games after being traded to Peterborough. Watson won the Memorial Cup with Windsor in 2009 and a gold medal with the U.S. team at the 2010 Under-18 World Championship.

19. FLORIDA • **NICK BJUGSTAD** • C • The nephew of former NHLer Scott Bjugstad who played nine NHL seasons between 1983-84 and 1991-92, Nick Bjudstad is a big player (6'4") with a good shot and good on-ice vision. He won the 2010 Mr. Hockey Award as the most outstanding high school senior in the state of Minnesota. Bjugstad accelerated his academic workload in order to be able to attend the University of Minnesota in 2010-11.

20. PITTSBURGH • **BEAU BENNETT** • RW • A player with great offensive instincts, Beau Bennett led the BCHL with 120 points in 2009-10 and was the first rookie to top 100 points in the last seven years. Bennett was born and raised in Southern California, playing for the L.A. Junior Kings before joining the Penticton Vees. He was a member of the California Selects that won the under-14 U.S. championship in 2006.

21. DETROIT • **RILEY SHEAHAN** • C • A complete player who is mature for his age, Riley Sheahan plays in a defensive system at the University of Notre Dame and is very aware in the defensive zone. Sheahan was named the Junior B Top Prospect in 2009 while playing in St. Catharines, Ontario. He comes from an athletic family and is the nephew of Canadian Football League star Rocky DiPietro.

22. MONTREAL • **JARRED TINORDI** • D • The son of former NHL defenseman Mark Tinordi, Jarred Tinordi is 6'6" and has an excellent shot from the point. He's a good skater and good passer who can play with an edge to his game. Tinordi did not play a lot of high-level hockey growing up in Maryland, but he was captain of the U.S. National Team Development Program's Under-18 team in 2009-10 and won a gold medal at the 2010 Under-18 World Championship.

23. BUFFALO • **MARK PYSYK** • D • A smooth-skating defenseman who moves the puck well, Mark Pysyk can lead the rush or make the crisp outlet pass. His 2009-10 season was cut short by injuries but he was still named the Edmonton Oil Kings' most valuable player, top defenseman and top scholastic player. Pysyk was Edmonton's first pick ever in the WHL Bantam Draft and averaged more than 20 minutes playing time per game as a 16-year-old in 2008-09.

24. CHICAGO • **KEVIN HAYES** • RW • A skilled power forward who plays with enthusiasm and drive, Kevin Hayes has very good hands and is an excellent playmaker. He is a strong skater with a long stride, and uses his long reach and puck protection to beat defenders. He has an excellent wrist shot with a sneaky quick release. After starring at Nobles H.S., he is expected to move on to Boston College in 2010-11 and play with his brother Jimmy who was drafted by Toronto in 2008.

25. FLORIDA • **QUINTON HOWDEN** • C • A two-way player who can use his speed to score goals or cause turnovers, Quinton Howden won the accuracy shooting contest at the 2010 Top Prospects game. Howden was the first pick in the 2007 WHL Bantam Draft and was Moose Jaw's rookie of the year in 2008-09. He won a gold medal at the 2009 Ivan Hlinka Under-18 tournament and tied for the Team Canada lead in goals at the 2010 Under-18 World Championship.

26. WASHINGTON • **EVGENY KUZNETSOV** • C • A highly skilled player with plenty of speed, Evgeny Kuznetsov captained the Russian team at the 2010 Under-18 World Championship and recorded a team-high 12 points (five goals, seven assists) in seven games. He also played for the Russian team at the 2010 World Junior Championship and won a silver medal at the 2009 Under-18 event.

27. PHOENIX • **MARK VISENTIN** • G • A butterfly goalie with great quickness and net coverage, Mark Visentin is technically very sound. He is very mobile and has great instincts. Visentin patterns his game after Carolina's Cam Ward and Pittsburgh's Marc-Andre Fleury and his childhood hero was Curtis Joseph. He played for the gold medal-winning Team Ontario at the 2009 Under-17 World Challenge along with Tyler Seguin, Jeff Skinner and several other 2010 draft picks.

28. SAN JOSE • **CHARLIE COYLE** • W/C • A skilled forward, who can play a power game as well as a finesse game, Charlie Coyle is the cousin of former NHL players Tony Amonte and Bobby Sheehan. He has very soft hands and is a confident puck handler. Coyle was named the Eastern Junior Hockey League rookie of the year after finishing fifth in scoring with 63 points (21-42-63) in 42 games in 2009-10 and will attend Boston University in 2010-11.

29. ANAHEIM • **EMERSON ETEM** • RW • A great skater who can handle the puck at high speeds, Emerson Etem is a native of Long Beach, California who went to Shattuck-St. Mary's in Minnesota at the age of 14 to further his hockey career. He played for the U.S. National Team Development Program in 2008-09 before joining the Medicine Hat Tigers of the WHL in 2009-10. His mother is a former Olympic rower.

30. NY ISLANDERS • **BROCK NELSON** • C • A hard-skating power forward who is very coachable, Brock Nelson was a finalist for the Mr. Hockey Award as the most outstanding high school senior in the state of Minnesota in 2010. He is the nephew of 1980 U.S. gold medalist Dave Christian and the grandson of 1960 Olympic champion Bill Christian. Nelson will attend the University of North Dakota in 2010-11.

1: Taylor Hall
LW – Edmonton

2: Tyler Seguin
C – Boston

3: Erik Gudbranson
D – Florida

4: Ryan Johansen
C – Columbus

5: Nino Niederreiter
RW – NY Islanders

6: Brett Connolly
RW – Tampa Bay

7: Jeff Skinner
C – Carolina

8: Alexander Burmistrov
C – Atlanta

9: Mikael Granlund
C/W – Minnesota

10: Dylan McIlrath
D – NY Rangers

Players selected first through tenth in the 2010 NHL Entry Draft.

Pick	Claimed by	Amateur Club	Position

2010 NHL ENTRY DRAFT

FIRST ROUND

Pick		Claimed by	Amateur Club	Position
1	EDM	Taylor Hall	Windsor	LW
2	BOS	Tyler Seguin	Plymouth	C
3	FLA	Erik Gudbranson	Kingston	D
4	CBJ	Ryan Johansen	Portland	C
5	NYI	Nino Niederreiter	Portland	RW
6	T.B.	Brett Connolly	Prince George	RW
7	CAR	Jeff Skinner	Kitchener	C
8	ATL	Alexander Burmistrov	Barrie	C
9	MIN	Mikael Granlund	HIFK	C/W
10	NYR	Dylan McIlrath	Moose Jaw	D
11	DAL	Jack Campbell	USA U-18	G
12	ANA	Cam Fowler	Windsor	D
13	PHX	Brandon Gormley	Moncton	D
14	STL	Jaden Schwartz	Tri-City	C
15	L.A.	Derek Forbort	USA U-18	D
16	STL	Vladimir Tarasenko	Novosibirsk	RW
17	COL	Joey Hishon	Owen Sound	C
18	NSH	Austin Watson	Peterborough	LW
19	FLA	Nick Bjugstad	Blaine	C
20	PIT	Beau Bennett	Penticton	RW
21	DET	Riley Sheahan	U of Notre Dame	C
22	MTL	Jarred Tinordi	USA U-18	D
23	BUF	Mark Pysyk	Edmonton	D
24	CHI	Kevin Hayes	Nobles	RW
25	FLA	Quinton Howden	Moose Jaw	C
26	WSH	Evgeny Kuznetsov	Chelyabinsk	C
27	PHX	Mark Visentin	Niagara	G
28	S.J.	Charlie Coyle	South Shore	C/RW
29	ANA	Emerson Etem	Medicine Hat	C
30	NYI	Brock Nelson	Warroad	C

SECOND ROUND

Pick		Claimed by	Amateur Club	Position
31	EDM	Tyler Pitlick	Minnesota State	C
32	BOS	Jared Knight	London	C
33	FLA	John McFarland	Sudbury	LW
34	CBJ	Dalton Smith	Ottawa	LW
35	CHI	Ludvig Rensfeldt	Brynas Jr.	LW
36	FLA	Alexander Petrovic	Red Deer	D
37	CAR	Justin Faulk	USA U-18	D
38	N.J.	Jonathon Merrill	USA U-18	D
39	MIN	Brett Bulmer	Kelowna	RW
40	NYR	Christian Thomas	Oshawa	RW
41	DAL	Patrik Nemeth	AIK-Jr.	D
42	ANA	Devante Smith-Pelly	Mississauga	RW
43	TOR	Brad Ross	Portland	LW
44	STL	Sebastian Wannstrom	Brynas Jr.	RW
45	BOS	Ryan Spooner	Peterborough	C
46	MTL	Martin Marincin	Slovakia U-20	D
47	L.A.	Tyler Toffoli	Ottawa	C
48	EDM	Curtis Hamilton	Saskatoon	LW
49	COL	Calvin Pickard	Seattle	G
50	FLA	Connor Brickley	Des Moines	C
51	DET	Calle Jarnkrok	Brynas	C
52	PHX	Philip Lane	Brampton	RW
53	CAR	Mark Alt	Cretin-Derham	D
54	CHI	Justin Holl	Minnetonka	D
55	CBJ	Petr Straka	Rimouski	RW
56	MIN	Johan Larsson	Brynas Jr.	LW
57	PHX	Oscar Lindberg	Skelleftea Jr.	C
58	CHI	Kent Simpson	Everett	G
59	MIN	Jason Zucker	USA U-18	LW
60	CHI	Stephen Johns	USA U-18	D

THIRD ROUND

Pick		Claimed by	Amateur Club	Position
61	EDM	Ryan Martindale	Ottawa	C
62	TOR	Greg McKegg	Erie	C
63	T.B.	Brock Beukeboom	Sault Ste. Marie	D
64	CGY	Max Reinhart	Kootenay	C
65	NYI	Kirill Kabanov	Moncton	LW
66	T.B.	Radko Gudas	Everett	D
67	CAR	Danny Biega	Harvard	D
68	BUF	Jerome Gauthier-Leduc	Rouyn-Noranda	D
69	FLA	Joe Basaraba	Shattuck St. Mary's	RW
70	L.A.	Jordan Weal	Regina	C
71	COL	Michael Bournival	Shawinigan	LW
72	T.B.	Adam Janosik	Gatineau	D
73	CGY	Joey Leach	Kootenay	D
74	STL	Max Gardiner	Minnetonka	C
75	BUF	Kevin Sundher	Chilliwack	C
76	OTT	Jakub Culek	Rimouski	LW
77	DAL	Alexander Guptill	Orangeville	LW
78	NSH	Taylor Aronson	Portland	D
79	TOR	Sondre Olden	Modo Jr.	W
80	PIT	Bryan Rust	USA U-18	RW
81	DET	Louis-Marc Aubry	Montreal	C
82	NYI	Jason Clark	Shattuck St. Mary's	C/LW
83	BUF	Matt MacKenzie	Calgary	D
84	N.J.	Scott Wedgewood	Plymouth	G
85	CAR	Austin Levi	Plymouth	D
86	WSH	Stanislav Galiev	Saint John	RW
87	ATL	Julian Melchiori	Newmarket	D
88	S.J.	Max Gaede	Woodbury HS	RW
89	PHI	Michael Chaput	Lewiston	C
90	CHI	Joakim Nordstrom	AIK Jr.	C

FOURTH ROUND

Pick		Claimed by	Amateur Club	Position
91	EDM	Jeremie Blain	Acadie-Bathurst	D
92	FLA	Sam Brittain	Canmore	G
93	FLA	Benjamin Gallacher	Camrose	D
94	CBJ	Brandon Archibald	Sault Ste. Marie	D
95	COL	Stephen Silas	Belleville	D
96	T.B.	Geoffrey Schemitsch	Owen Sound	D
97	BOS	Craig Cunningham	Vancouver	LW
98	BUF	Steven Shipley	Owen Sound	C
99	FLA	Joonas Donskoi	Karpat Jr.	RW
100	NYR	Andrew Yogan	Erie	C;LW
101	ATL	Ivan Telegin	Saginaw	LW
102	CBJ	Mathieu Corbeil-Theriault	Halifax	G
103	CGY	John Ramage	U. of Wisconsin	D
104	STL	Jani Hakanpaa	K-Vantaa Jr.	D
105	CAR	Justin Shugg	Windsor	LW
106	OTT	Markus Sorensen	Sodertalje Jr.	RW
107	COL	Sami Aittokallio	Ilves Jr.	G
108	CGY	Bill Arnold	USA U-18	C
109	DAL	Alex Theriau	Everett	D
110	PIT	Tom Kuehnhackl	Landshut Cann.	RW
111	DET	Teemu Pulkkinen	Jokerit	LW
112	WSH	Philipp Grubauer	Windsor	G
113	MTL	Mark MacMillan	Alberni Valley	F
114	N.J.	Joe Faust	Bloomington-Jeff.	D
115	VAN	Patrick Mcnally	Milton Academy	D
116	TOR	Petter Granberg	Skelleftea Jr.	D
117	MTL	Morgan Ellis	Cape Breton	D
118	T.B.	James Mullin	Shattuck St. Mary's	C/RW
119	PHI	Tye McGinn	Gatineau	LW
120	CHI	Rob Flick	Mississauga	C

FIFTH ROUND

Pick		Claimed by	Amateur Club	Position
121	EDM	Tyler Bunz	Medicine Hat	G
122	ANA	Chris Wagner	South Shore	RW
123	FLA	Zach Hyman	Hamilton	C
124	CBJ	Austin Madaisky	Kamloops	D
125	NYI	Tony Dehart	Oshawa	D
126	NSH	Patrick Cehlin	Djurgarden	RW
127	S.J.	Cody Ferriero	Governor's Acad.	C
128	ATL	Fredrik Pettersson-Wentzel	Almtuna	G
129	S.J.	Freddie Hamilton	Niagara	C
130	NYR	Jason Wilson	Owen Sound	D
131	DAL	John Klingberg	Frolunda Jr.	D
132	ANA	Tim Heed	Sodertalje	D
133	CGY	Michael Ferland	Brandon	LW
134	STL	Cody Beach	Calgary	RW
135	BOS	Justin Florek	Northern Mich.	LW
136	S.J.	Isaac MacLeod	Penticton	D
137	COL	Troy Rutkowski	Portland	D
138	PHX	Louis Domingue	Quebec	G
139	COL	Luke Walker	Portland	C
140	PIT	Kenneth Agostino	Delbarton	LW
141	DET	Petr Mrazek	Ottawa	G
142	WSH	Caleb Herbert	Bloomington-Jeff.	C
143	BUF	Gregg Sutch	Mississauga	RW
144	TOR	Sam Carrick	Brampton	C
145	VAN	Adam Polasek	PEI	D
146	TOR	Daniel Brodin	Djurgarden	LW
147	MTL	Brendan Gallagher	Vancouver	RW
148	L.A.	Kevin Gravel	Sioux City	D
149	PHI	Michael Parks	Cedar Rapids	RW
150	ATL	Yasin Cisse	Des Moines	RW

SIXTH ROUND

Pick		Claimed by	Amateur Club	Position
151	CHI	Mirko Hoefflin	Mannheim Jr.	C
152	PIT	Joe Rogalski	Sarnia	D
153	FLA	Corey Durocher	Kingston	LW
154	CBJ	Dalton Prout	Barrie	D
155	ATL	Kendall McFaull	Moose Jaw	D
156	T.B.	Brendan O'Donnell	Winnipeg South	C
157	NYR	Jesper Fasth	HV 71 Jr.	RW
158	L.A.	Maxim Kitsyn	Novokuznetsk	LW
159	MIN	Johan Gustafsson	Farjestad Jr.	G
160	ATL	Tanner Lane	Detroit Lakes	D
161	ANA	Andreas Dahlstrom	AIK	C;W
162	EDM	Brandon Davidson	Regina	D
163	S.J.	Konrad Abeltshauser	Halifax	D
164	STL	Stephen Macaulay	Saint John	LW
165	BOS	Zane Gothberg	Thief River Falls	G
166	EDM	Drew Czerwonka	Kootenay	LW
167	CAR	Tyler Stahl	Chilliwack	D
168	NSH	Anthony Bitetto	Indiana	D
169	ATL	Sebastian Owuya	Timra Jr.	D
170	PIT	Reid McNeill	London	D
171	DET	Brooks Macek	Tri-City	C
172	VAN	Alex Friesen	Niagara	C
173	BUF	Cedrick Henley	Val D'Or	LW
174	N.J.	Maxime Clermont	Gatineau	G
175	VAN	Jonathan Iilahti	Blues Jr.	G
176	WSH	Samuel Carrier	Lewiston	D
177	ANA	Kevin Lind	Chicago	D
178	OTT	Mark Stone	Brandon	RW
179	PHI	Nicholas Luukko	The Gunnery	D
180	CHI	Nick Mattson	Indiana	D

SEVENTH ROUND

Pick	Claimed by	Amateur Club	Position
181 EDM	Kristians Pelss	Dynamo Jr.	F
182 TOR	Josh Nicholls	Saskatoon	RW
183 FLA	Ronald (R.J.) Boyd	Cushing Academy	D
184 CBJ	Martin Ouellette	Kimball Union	G
185 NYI	Cody Rosen	Clarkson	G
186 T.B.	Teigan Zahn	Saskatoon	D
187 CAR	Frederik Andersen	Frederikshavn	G
188 S.J.	Lee Moffie	U of Michigan	D
189 MIN	Dylen McKinlay	Chilliwack	RW
190 NYR	Randy McNaught	Saskatoon	RW
191 CHI	Mac Carruth	Portland	G
192 ANA	Brett Perlini	Michigan State	RW
193 CGY	Patrick Holland	Tri-City	RW
194 NSH	David Elsner	Landshut Cann.	W
195 BOS	Maxim Chudinov	Cherepovets	D
196 OTT	Bryce Aneloski	Cedar Rapids	D
197 COL	Luke Moffatt	USA U-18	C
198 NSH	Joonas Rask	Ilves	C
199 ATL	Peter Stoykewych	Winnipeg South	D
200 S.J.	Chris Crane	Green Bay	RW
201 DET	Benjamin Marshall	Mahtomedi	D
202 EDM	Kellen Jones	Vernon	F
203 BUF	Christian Isackson	St. Thomas	RW
204 N.J.	Mauro Jorg	Lugano	RW
205 VAN	Sawyer Hannay	Halifax	D
206 PHI	Ricard Blidstrand	AIK Jr.	D
207 MTL	John Westin	Modo Jr.	LW
208 BUF	Riley Boychuk	Portland	LW
209 PHI	Brendan Ranford	Kamloops	LW
210 BOS	Zach Trotman	Lake Superior	D

First Two Rounds, 2009–2007

2009

FIRST ROUND

Pick	Claimed by	Amateur Club	Position
1 NYI	John Tavares	London	C
2 T.B.	Victor Hedman	MODO	D
3 COL	Matt Duchene	Brampton	C
4 ATL	Evander Kane	Vancouver	C
5 L.A.	Brayden Schenn	Brandon	C
6 PHX	Oliver Ekman-Larsson	Leksand	D
7 TOR	Nazem Kadri	London	C
8 DAL	Scott Glennie	Brandon	RW
9 OTT	Jared Cowen	Spokane	D
10 EDM	Magnus Paajarvi-Svensson.	Timra	LW
11 NSH	Ryan Ellis	Windsor	D
12 NYI	Calvin De Haan	Oshawa	D
13 BUF	Zack Kassian	Peterborough	RW
14 FLA	Dmitry Kulikov	Drummondville	D
15 ANA	Peter Holland	Guelph	C
16 MIN	Nick Leddy	Eden Prairie	D
17 STL	David Rundblad	Skelleftea	D
18 MTL	Louis Leblanc	Omaha	C
19 NYR	Chris Kreider	Andover	C
20 N.J.	Jacob Josefson	Djurgarden	C
21 CBJ	John Moore	Chicago	D
22 VAN	Jordan Schroeder	U of Minnesota	C
23 CGY	Tim Erixon	Skelleftea	D
24 WSH	Marcus Johansson	Farjestad	C
25 BOS	Jordan Caron	Rimouski	RW
26 ANA	Kyle Palmieri	USA U-18	C/RW
27 CAR	Philippe Paradis	Shawinigan	C
28 CHI	Dylan Olsen	Camrose	D
29 T.B.	Carter Ashton	Lethbridge	RW
30 PIT	Simon Despres	Saint John	D

SECOND ROUND

Pick	Claimed by	Amateur Club	Position
31 NYI	Mikko Koskinen	Blues	G
32 DET	Landon Ferraro	Red Deer	C
33 COL	Ryan O'Reilly	Erie	C
34 ATL	Carl Klingberg	Frolunda Jr.	LW
35 L.A.	Kyle Clifford	Barrie	LW
36 PHX	Chris Brown	USA U-18	C
37 ANA	Matt Clark	Brampton	D
38 DAL	Alex Chiasson	Des Moines	RW
39 OTT	Jakob Silfverberg	Brynas	LW
40 EDM	Anton Lander	Timra	C
41 NSH	Zach Budish	Edina High	RW
42 NSH	Charles-Olivier Roussel	Shawinigan	D
43 S.J.	William Wrenn	USA U-18	D
44 FLA	Drew Shore	USA U-18	C
45 ATL	Jeremy Morin	USA U-18	LW
46 OTT	Robin Lehner	Frolunda Jr.	G
47 NYR	Ethan Werek	Kingston	C
48 STL	Brett Ponich	Portland	D
49 COL	Stefan Elliott	Saskatoon	D
50 TOR	Kenny Ryan	USA U-18.	RW
51 CAR	Brian Dumoulin	Jr. Monarchs	D
52 T.B.	Richard Panik	Trinec	RW
53 VAN	Anton Rodin	Brynas Jr.	RW
54 N.J.	Eric Gelinas	Lewiston	D
55 WSH	Dmitri Orlov	Novokuznetsk	D
56 CBJ	Kevin Lynch	USA U-18	C
57 S.J.	Taylor Doherty	Kingston	D
58 TOR	Jesse Blacker	Windsor	D
59 CHI	Brandon Pirri	Georgetown	C
60 DET	Tomas Tatar	Zvolen	C
61 PIT	Philip Samuelsson	Chicago	D

2008

FIRST ROUND

Pick	Claimed by	Amateur Club	Position
1 T.B.	Steven Stamkos	Sarnia	C
2 L.A.	Drew Doughty	Guelph	D
3 ATL	Zach Bogosian	Peterborough	D
4 STL	Alex Pietrangelo	Niagara	D
5 TOR	Luke Schenn	Kelowna	D
6 CBJ	Nikita Filatov	CSKA 2.	LW
7 NSH	Colin Wilson	Boston University.	C
8 PHX	Mikkel Boedker	Kitchener	LW
9 NYI	Joshua Bailey	Windsor	C
10 VAN	Cody Hodgson	Brampton	C
11 CHI	Kyle Beach	Everett	C
12 BUF	Tyler Myers	Kelowna	D
13 L.A.	Colten Teubert	Regina	D
14 CAR	Zach Boychuk	Lethbridge	C
15 OTT	Erik Karlsson	Frolunda Jr.	D
16 BOS	Joe Colborne	Camrose	C
17 ANA	Jake Gardiner	Minnetonka.	D
18 NSH	Chet Pickard	Tri-City	G
19 PHI	Luca Sbisa	Lethbridge	D
20 NYR	Michael Del Zotto	Oshawa	D
21 WSH	Anton Gustafsson	Frolunda Jr.	C
22 EDM	Jordan Eberle	Regina	C
23 MIN	Tyler Cuma	Ottawa	D
24 N.J.	Mattias Tedenby	HV 71	LW
25 CGY	Greg Nemisz	Windsor	C
26 BUF	Tyler Ennis	Medicine Hat	C
27 WSH	John Carlson	Indiana	D
28 PHX	Viktor Tikhonov	Cherepovets	W
29 ATL	Daultan Leveille	St. Catharines	C
30 DET	Thomas McCollum	Guelph	G

SECOND ROUND

Pick	Claimed by	Amateur Club	Position
31 FLA	Jacob Markstrom	Brynas Jr.	G
32 L.A.	Vjateslav Voinov	Chelyabinsk	D
33 STL	Philip McRae	London	C
34 STL	Jake Allen	St. John's	G
35 ANA	Nicolas Deschamps	Chicoutimi	C
36 NYI	Corey Trivino	Stouffville	C
37 CBJ	Cody Goloubef	U. of Wisconsin	D
38 NSH	Roman Josi	Bern	D
39 ANA	Eric O'Dell	Sudbury	C
40 NYI	Aaron Ness	Roseau High	D
41 VAN	Yann Sauve	Saint John	D
42 OTT	Patrick Wiercioch	Omaha	D
43 ANA	Justin Schultz	Westside	D
44 BUF	Luke Adam	St. John's	C
45 CAR	Zac Dalpe	Penticton	C/RW
46 FLA	Colby Robak	Brandon	D
47 BOS	Maxime Sauve	Val d'Or.	C
48 CGY	Mitch Wahl	Spokane	C
49 PHX	Jared Staal	Sudbury	RW
50 COL	Cameron Gaunce	St. Michael's	D
51 NYR	Derek Stepan	Shattuck St.Mary's	C
52 N.J.	Brandon Burlon	St. Michael's	D
53 NYI	Travis Hamonic	Moose Jaw	D
54 N.J.	Patrice Cormier	Rimouski	C
55 MIN	Marco Scandella	Val d'Or.	D
56 MTL	Danny Kristo	U-18	RW
57 WSH	Eric Mestery	Tri-City	D
58 WSH	Dmitri Kugryshev	CSKA 2	RW
59 DAL	Tyler Beskorowany	Owen Sound	G
60 TOR	Jimmy Hayes	Lincoln	RW
61 COL	Peter Delmas	Lewiston	G

Selected second overall by Los Angeles in the 2008 NHL Entry Draft, Drew Doughty followed up a successful 2008-09 rookie season with a remarkable 2009-10 campaign that saw the 20-year-old win an Olympic gold medal with Team Canada and finish as a finalist in voting for the Norris Trophy as the NHL's best defenseman.

Pick	Claimed by		Amateur Club	Position	Pick	Claimed by		Amateur Club	Position	Pick	Claimed by		Amateur Club	Position

Selected second overall from the United States National Team Development Program in the 2007 Entry Draft, James van Riemsdyk then spent two years at the University of New Hampshire before joining the Philadelphia Flyers in 2009-10. He scored this goal (above) against Chicago in game five of the 2010 Stanley Cup Finals ... but Patrick Kane (who was chosen first overall in 2007) would score an even bigger goal three days later!

2007

FIRST ROUND

1	CHI	Patrick Kane	London	RW
2	PHI	James van Riemsdyk	USA U-18	LW
3	PHX	Kyle Turris	Burnaby	C
4	LA	Thomas Hickey	Seattle	D
5	WSH	Karl Alzner	Calgary	D
6	EDM	Sam Gagner	London	C/W
7	CBJ	Jakub Voracek	Halifax	RW
8	BOS	Zach Hamill	Everett	C
9	SJ	Logan Couture	Ottawa	C
10	FLA	Keaton Ellerby	Kamloops	D
11	CAR	Brandon Sutter	Red Deer	C/RW
12	MTL	Ryan McDonagh	Cretin-Derham	D
13	STL	Lars Eller	Frolunda Jr.	C
14	COL	Kevin Shattenkirk	USA U-18	D
15	EDM	Alex Plante	Calgary	D
16	MIN	Colton Gillies	Saskatoon	C
17	NYR	Alexei Cherepanov	Omsk	RW
18	STL	Ian Cole	USA U-18	D
19	ANA	Logan MacMillan	Halifax	C
20	PIT	Angelo Esposito	Quebec	C
21	EDM	Riley Nash	Salmon Arm	C
22	MTL	Max Pacioretty	Sioux City	LW
23	NSH	Jonathon Blum	Vancouver	D
24	CGY	Mikael Backlund	Vasteras	C
25	VAN	Patrick White	Tri-City	C
26	STL	David Perron	Lewiston	LW
27	DET	Brendan Smith	St. Michael's	D
28	SJ	Nicholas Petrecki	Omaha	D
29	OTT	James O'Brien	U of Minnesota	C
30	PHX	Nick Ross	Regina	D

SECOND ROUND

31	BUF	T.J. Brennan	St. John's	D
32	PHX	Brett MacLean	Oshawa	LW
33	VAN	Taylor Ellington	Everett	D
34	WSH	Josh Godfrey	Sault Ste. Marie	D
35	BOS	Tommy Cross	Westminster	D
36	PHX	Joel Gistedt	Frolunda	G
37	CBJ	Stefan Legein	Mississauga	RW
38	CHI	William Sweatt	Colorado College	LW
39	STL	Simon Hjalmarsson	Frolunda Jr.	RW
40	FLA	Michal Repik	Vancouver	RW
41	PHI	Kevin Marshall	Lewiston	D
42	ANA	Eric Tangradi	Belleville	C
43	MTL	P.K. Subban	Belleville	D
44	STL	Aaron Palushaj	Des Moines	RW
45	COL	Colby Cohen	Lincoln	D
46	WSH	Theo Ruth	USA U-18	D
47	TB	Dana Tyrell	Prince George	C/RW
48	NYR	Antoine Lafleur	PEI	G
49	COL	Trevor Cann	Peterborough	G
50	LA	Nico Sacchetti	Virginia High	C
51	PIT	Keven Veilleux	Victoriaville	C
52	L.A	Oscar Moller	Chilliwack	RW
53	CBJ	Will Weber	Gaylord High	D
54	NSH	Jeremy Smith	Plymouth	G
55	COL	T.J. Galiardi	Dartmouth	W
56	CHI	Akim Aliu	Sudbury	C/RW
57	NJ	Mike Hoeffel	USA U-18	W
58	NSH	Nick Spaling	Kitchener	C
59	BUF	Drew Schiestel	Mississauga	D
60	OTT	Ruslan Bashkirov	Quebec	LW
61	LA	Wayne Simmonds	Owen Sound	RW

First Round and Other Notable Selections, 2006–1969

2006

FIRST ROUND

1	STL	Erik Johnson	USA U-18	D
2	PIT	Jordan Staal	Peterborough	C
3	CHI	Jonathan Toews	U. of North Dakota	C
4	WSH	Nicklas Backstrom	Brynas	C
5	BOS	Phil Kessel	U. of Minnesota	C
6	CBJ	Derick Brassard	Drummondville	C
7	NYI	Kyle Okposo	Des Moines	RW
8	PHX	Peter Mueller	Everett	C
9	MIN	James Sheppard	Cape Breton	C
10	FLA	Michael Frolik	Kladno	C
11	L.A.	Jonathan Bernier	Lewiston	G
12	ATL	Bryan Little	Barrie	C
13	TOR	Jiri Tlusty	Kladno	C
14	VAN	Michael Grabner	Spokane	RW
15	T.B.	Riku Helenius	Ilves	G
16	S.J.	Ty Wishart	Prince George	D
17	L.A.	Trevor Lewis	Des Moines	C
18	COL	Chris Stewart	Kingston	RW
19	ANA	Mark Mitera	U. of Michigan	D
20	MTL	David Fischer	Apple Valley	D
21	NYR	Bobby Sanguinetti	Owen Sound	D
22	PHI	Claude Giroux	Gatineau	RW
23	WSH	Simeon Varlamov	Yaroslavl 2	G
24	BUF	Dennis Persson	Vasteras	D
25	STL	Patrik Berglund	Vasteras	C
26	CGY	Leland Irving	Everett	G
27	DAL	Ivan Vishnevskiy	Rouyn Noranda	D
28	OTT	Nick Foligno	Sudbury	LW
29	PHX	Chris Summers	USA U-18	D
30	N.J.	Matthew Corrente	Saginaw	D

OTHER NOTABLE SELECTIONS

Pick	Claimed by	Player	Amateur Club	Position
34	Wsh.	Michal Neuvirth	Sparta Jr.	G
39	Phi.	Andreas Nodl	Sioux Falls	RW
44	Tor.	Nikolai Kulemin	Magnitogorsk	W
50	Bos.	Milan Lucic	Vancouver	LW
54	NYR	Artem Anisimov	Yaroslavl	C
60	NYI	Jesse Joensuu	Assat	LW
69	CBJ	Steve Mason	London	G
128	Bos.	Andrew Bodnarchuk	Halifax	D
141	NYI	Kim Johansson	Malmo Jr.	W
161	Tor.	Viktor Stahlberg	Frolunda	LW

2005

FIRST ROUND

Pick	Claimed by	Player	Amateur Club	Position
1	PIT	Sidney Crosby	Rimouski	C
2	ANA	Bobby Ryan	Owen Sound	RW
3	CAR	Jack Johnson	USA U-18	D
4	MIN	Benoit Pouliot	Sudbury	LW
5	MTL	Carey Price	Tri-City	G
6	CBJ	Gilbert Brule	Vancouver	C
7	CHI	Jack Skille	USA U-18	RW
8	S.J.	Devin Setoguchi	Saskatoon	RW
9	OTT	Brian Lee	Moorhead	D
10	VAN	Luc Bourdon	Val D'or	D
11	L.A.	Anze Kopitar	Sodertalje Jr.	C
12	NYR	Marc Staal	Sudbury	D
13	BUF	Marek Zagrapan	Chicoutimi	C
14	WSH	Sasha Pokulok	Cornell	D
15	NYI	Ryan O'Marra	Erie	C
16	ATL	Alex Bourret	Lewiston	RW
17	PHX	Martin Hanzal	C. Budejovice	C
18	NSH	Ryan Parent	Guelph	D
19	DET	Jakub Kindl	Kitchener	D
20	FLA	Kenndal McArdle	Moose Jaw	LW
21	TOR	Tuukka Rask	Ilves Jr.	G
22	BOS	Matt Lashoff	Kitchener	D
23	N.J.	Nicklas Bergfors	Sodertalje	RW
24	STL	T.J. Oshie	Warroad	C
25	EDM	Andrew Cogliano	St. Mike's B's	C
26	CGY	Matt Pelech	Sarnia	D
27	WSH	Joe Finley	Sioux Falls	D
28	DAL	Matt Niskanen	Virginia	D
29	PHI	Steve Downie	Windsor	RW
30	T.B.	Vladimir Mihalik	Presov	D

OTHER NOTABLE SELECTIONS

Pick	Claimed by	Player	Amateur Club	Position
33	DAL	James Neal	Plymouth	LW
35	S.J.	Marc-Edouard Vlasic	Quebec	D
42	DET	Justin Abdelkader	Cedar Rapids	LW
44	COL	Paul Stastny	U. of Denver	C
45	MTL	Guillaume Latendresse	Drummondville	RW
51	VAN	Mason Raymond	Camrose	LW
62	PIT	Kris Letang	Val d'Or	D
72	L.A.	Jonathan Quick	Avon Old Farms	G
200	MTL	Sergei Kostitsyn	Gomel	LW

2004

FIRST ROUND

Pick	Claimed by	Player	Amateur Club	Position
1	WSH	Alex Ovechkin	Dynamo	LW
2	PIT	Evgeni Malkin	Magnitogorsk	C
3	CHI	Cam Barker	Medicine Hat	D
4	CAR	Andrew Ladd	Calgary	LW
5	PHX	Blake Wheeler	Breck	RW
6	NYR	Al Montoya	U. of Michigan	G
7	FLA	Rostislav Olesz	Vitkovice	C
8	CBJ	Alexandre Picard	Lewiston	LW
9	ANA	Ladislav Smid	Liberec	D
10	ATL	Boris Valabik	Kitchener	D
11	L.A.	Lauri Tukonen	Blues Espoo	RW
12	MIN	A.J. Thelen	Michigan State	D
13	BUF	Drew Stafford	U. of North Dakota	RW
14	EDM	Devan Dubnyk	Kamloops	G
15	NSH	Alexander Radulov	Tver	LW
16	NYI	Petteri Nokelainen	SaiPa	C
17	STL	Marek Schwarz	Sparta Praha	G
18	MTL	Kyle Chipchura	Prince Albert	C
19	NYR	Lauri Korpikoski	TPS Turku Jr.	LW
20	N.J.	Travis Zajac	Salmon Arm	C
21	COL	Wojtek Wolski	Brampton	LW
22	S.J.	Lukas Kaspar	Litvinov	RW
23	OTT	Andrej Meszaros	Trencin	D
24	CGY	Kris Chucko	Salmon Arm	LW
25	EDM	Rob Schremp	London	C
26	VAN	Cory Schneider	Phillips-Andover	G
27	WSH	Jeff Schultz	Calgary	D
28	DAL	Mark Fistric	Vancouver	D
29	WSH	Mike Green	Saskatoon	D
30	T.B.	Andy Rogers	Calgary	D

OTHER NOTABLE SELECTIONS

Pick	Claimed by	Player	Amateur Club	Position
32	CHI	Dave Bolland	London	C
53	FLA	David Booth	Michigan State	LW
60	NYR	Brandon Dubinsky	Portland	C
63	BOS	David Krejci	Kladno Jr.	C
91	VAN	Alexander Edler	Jamtland	D
97	DET	Johan Franzen	Linkoping	C
99	PIT	Tyler Kennedy	Sault Ste. Marie	C
127	NYR	Ryan Callahan	Guelph	RW

Pick	Claimed by	Player	Amateur Club	Position
134	BOS	Kris Versteeg	Lethbridge	RW
150	MTL	Mikhail Grabovski	Nizhnekamsk	C
214	CHI	Troy Brouwer	Moose Jaw	RW
227	NYI	Chris Campoli	Erie	D
258	NSH	Pekka Rinne	Karpat	G
262	MTL	Mark Streit	Zurich	D

2003

FIRST ROUND

Pick	Claimed by	Player	Amateur Club	Position
1	PIT	Marc-Andre Fleury	Cape Breton	G
2	CAR	Eric Staal	Peterborough	C
3	FLA	Nathan Horton	Oshawa	C
4	CBJ	Nikolai Zherdev	CSKA Moscow	W
5	BUF	Thomas Vanek	U. of Minnesota	LW
6	S.J.	Milan Michalek	Budejovice	RW
7	NSH	Ryan Suter	U.S. National U-18	D
8	ATL	Braydon Coburn	Portland	D
9	CGY	Dion Phaneuf	Red Deer	D
10	MTL	Andrei Kostitsyn	CSKA Moscow 2	RW
11	PHI	Jeff Carter	Sault Ste. Marie	C
12	NYR	Hugh Jessiman	Dartmouth	RW
13	L.A.	Dustin Brown	Guelph	RW
14	CHI	Brent Seabrook	Lethbridge	D
15	NYI	Robert Nilsson	Leksand	RW
16	S.J.	Steve Bernier	Moncton	RW
17	N.J.	Zach Parise	North Dakota	C
18	WSH	Eric Fehr	Brandon	RW
19	ANA	Ryan Getzlaf	Calgary	C
20	MIN	Brent Burns	Brampton	RW
21	BOS	Mark Stuart	Colorado College	D
22	EDM	Marc-Antoine Pouliot	Rimouski	C
23	VAN	Ryan Kesler	Ohio State	C
24	PHI	Mike Richards	Kitchener	C
25	FLA	Anthony Stewart	Kingston	C
26	L.A.	Brian Boyle	St. Sebastian's H.S.	C
27	L.A.	Jeff Tambellini	U. of Michigan	LW
28	ANA	Corey Perry	London	RW
29	OTT	Patrick Eaves	Boston College	RW
30	STL	Shawn Belle	Tri-City	D

OTHER NOTABLE SELECTIONS

Pick	Claimed by	Player	Amateur Club	Position
33	DAL	Loui Eriksson	Vastra Frolunda Jr	LW
45	BOS	Patrice Bergeron	Acadie-Bathurst	C
47	S.J.	Matt Carle	River City	D
49	NSH	Shea Weber	Kelowna	D
61	MTL	Maxim Lapierre	Montreal	C
62	ST.L.	David Backes	Lincoln	C
64	DET	Jimmy Howard	U. of Maine	G
73	PHX	Daniel Carcillo	Sarnia	LW
148	STL	Lee Stempniak	Dartmouth College	RW
205	S.J.	Joe Pavelski	Waterloo Jr. A	C
239	ATL	Tobias Enstrom	MoDo	D
245	CHI	Dustin Byfuglien	Prince George	RW
271	MTL	Jaroslav Halak	Bratislava Jr.	G
291	OTT	Brian Elliott	Ajax	G

2002

FIRST ROUND

Pick	Claimed by	Player	Amateur Club	Position
1	CBJ	Rick Nash	London	LW
2	ATL	Kari Lehtonen	Jokerit	G
3	FLA	Jay Bouwmeester	Medicine Hat	D
4	PHI	Joni Pitkanen	Karpat	D
5	PIT	Ryan Whitney	Boston U.	D
6	NSH	Scottie Upshall	Kamloops	RW
7	ANA	Joffrey Lupul	Medicine Hat	C
8	MIN	Pierre-Marc Bouchard	Chicoutimi	C
9	FLA	Petr Taticek	Sault Ste. Marie	C
10	CGY	Eric Nystrom	U. of Michigan	LW
11	BUF	Keith Ballard	U. of Minnesota	D
12	WSH	Steve Eminger	Kitchener	D
13	WSH	Alexander Semin	Chelyabinsk	LW
14	MTL	Christopher Higgins	Yale	C
15	EDM	Jesse Niinimaki	Ilves Tampere	C
16	OTT	Jakub Klepis	Portland	C
17	WSH	Boyd Gordon	Red Deer	RW
18	L.A.	Denis Grebeshkov	Yaroslavl	D
19	PHX	Jakub Koreis	Plzen	C
20	BUF	Dan Paille	Guelph	LW
21	CHI	Anton Babchuk	Elektrostal	D
22	NYI	Sean Bergenheim	Jokerit	C
23	PHX	Ben Eager	Oshawa	LW
24	TOR	Alexander Steen	Vastra Frolunda	C
25	CAR	Cam Ward	Red Deer	G
26	DAL	Martin Vagner	Hull	D
27	S.J.	Mike Morris	St. Sebastian's H.S.	RW
28	COL	Jonas Johansson	HV 71 Jonkoping Jr.	RW
29	BOS	Hannu Toivonen	HPK Jr.	G
30	ATL	Jim Slater	Michigan State	C

OTHER NOTABLE SELECTIONS

Pick	Claimed by	Player	Amateur Club	Position
36	EDM	Jarret Stoll	Kootenay	C
54	CHI	Duncan Keith	Michigan State	D
57	TOR	Matt Stajan	Belleville	C
58	DET	Jiri Hudler	Vsetin	C
90	CGY	Matthew Lomardi	Victoriaville	C
95	DET	Valtteri Filppula	Jokerit Jr.	C
183	TB	Paul Ranger	Oshawa	D
191	TOR	Ian White	Swift Current	D

Pick	Claimed by	Player	Amateur Club	Position
234	PIT	Maxime Talbot	Hull	C
240	NYR	Petr Prucha	Pardubice	RW
241	BUF	Dennis Wideman	London	D
282	CHI	Adam Burish	Green Bay	RW
291	DET	Jonathan Ericsson	Hasten Jr.	D

2001

FIRST ROUND

Pick	Claimed by	Player	Amateur Club	Position
1	ATL	Ilya Kovalchuk	Spartak	LW
2	OTT	Jason Spezza	Windsor	C
3	T.B.	Alexander Svitov	Avangard Omsk	C
4	FLA	Stephen Weiss	Plymouth	C
5	ANA	Stanislav Chistov	Avangard Omsk	LW
6	MIN	Mikko Koivu	TPS Turku	C
7	MTL	Mike Komisarek	U. of Michigan	D
8	CBJ	Pascal Leclaire	Halifax	G
9	CHI	Tuomo Ruutu	Jokerit	C/LW
10	NYR	Dan Blackburn	Kootenay	G
11	PHX	Fredrik Sjostrom	Vastra Frolunda	RW
12	NSH	Dan Hamhuis	Prince George	D
13	EDM	Ales Hemsky	Hull	RW
14	CGY	Chuck Kobasew	Boston College	C
15	CAR	Igor Knyazev	Spartak	D
16	VAN	R.J. Umberger	Ohio State	C
17	TOR	Carlo Colaiacovo	Erie	D
18	L.A.	Jens Karlsson	Vastra Frolunda	RW
19	BOS	Shaone Morrisonn	Kamloops	D
20	S.J.	Marcel Goc	Schwenningen	C
21	PIT	Colby Armstrong	Red Deer	RW
22	BUF	Jiri Novotny	Budejovice	C
23	OTT	Tim Gleason	Windsor	D
24	FLA	Lukas Krajicek	Peterborough	D
25	MTL	Alexander Perezhogin	Avangard Omsk	C
26	DAL	Jason Bacashihua	Chicago (NAHL)	G
27	PHI	Jeff Woywitka	Red Deer	D
28	N.J.	Adrian Foster	Saskatoon	C
29	CHI	Adam Munro	Erie	G
30	L.A.	Dave Steckel	Ohio State	C

OTHER NOTABLE SELECTIONS

Pick	Claimed by	Player	Amateur Club	Position
32	BUF	Derek Roy	Kitchener	C
49	L.A.	Mike Cammalleri	U. of Michigan	C
55	BUF	Jason Pominville	Shawinigan	RW
71	MTL	Tomas Plekanec	Kladno	LW
95	PHI	Patrick Sharp	U. of Vermont	C
98	NSH	Jordin Tootoo	Brandon	RW
106	S.J.	Christoph Ehrhoff	Krefeld	D
134	TOR	Kyle Wellwood	Belleville	C
151	VAN	Kevin Bieksa	Bowling Green	D
172	PHI	Dennis Seidenberg	Mannheim	D
175	SJ	Ryan Clowe	Rimouski	RW
176	NSH	Marek Zidlicky	HIFK	D
192	DAL	Jussi Jokinen	Karpat Jr.	F
193	OTT	Brooks Laich	Moose Jaw	C
214	L.A.	Cristobal Huet	HC Lugano	G
232	ANA	Martin Gerber	Langnau	G

2000

FIRST ROUND

Pick	Claimed by	Player	Amateur Club	Position
1	NYI	Rick DiPietro	Boston U.	G
2	ATL	Dany Heatley	U. of Wisconsin	RW
3	MIN	Marian Gaborik	Dukla Trencin	RW
4	CBJ	Rostislav Klesla	Brampton	D
5	NYI	Raffi Torres	Brampton	LW
6	NSH	Scott Hartnell	Prince Albert	LW
7	BOS	Lars Jonsson	Leksand	D
8	T.B.	Nikita Alexeev	Erie	RW
9	CGY	Brent Krahn	Calgary	G
10	CHI	Mikhail Yakubov	Lada Togliatti	C
11	CHI	Pavel Vorobiev	Yaroslavl	RW
12	ANA	Alexei Smirnov	Tver	LW
13	MTL	Ron Hainsey	U. of Mass-Lowell	D
14	COL	Vaclav Nedorost	Budejovice	C
15	BUF	Artem Kryukov	Yaroslavl	C
16	MTL	Marcel Hossa	Portland	LW
17	EDM	Alexei Mikhnov	Yaroslavl	LW
18	PIT	Brooks Orpik	Boston College	D
19	PHX	Krys Kolanos	Boston College	C
20	L.A.	Alexander Frolov	Yaroslavl 2	LW
21	OTT	Anton Volchenkov	HC Moscow	D
22	N.J.	David Hale	Sioux City	D
23	VAN	Nathan Smith	Swift Current	C
24	TOR	Brad Boyes	Erie	C
25	DAL	Steve Ott	Windsor	C
26	WSH	Brian Sutherby	Moose Jaw	C
27	BOS	Martin Samuelsson	MoDo Ornskoldsvik	RW
28	PHI	Justin Williams	Plymouth	RW
29	DET	Niklas Kronwall	Djurgarden	D
30	STL	Jeff Taffe	U. of Minnesota	C

OTHER NOTABLE SELECTIONS

Pick	Claimed by	Player	Amateur Club	Position
33	MIN	Nick Schultz	Prince Albert	D
44	ANA	Ilya Bryzgalov	Lada Togliatti	G
46	CGY	Jarret Stoll	Kootenay	C
55	OTT	Antoine Vermette	Victoriaville	D
62	COL	Paul Martin	Elk River H.S.	D
95	NYR	Dominic Moore	Harvard	C
155	CGY	Travis Moen	Kelowna	LW

Pick	Claimed by		Amateur Club	Position
159	COL	John-Michael Liles	Michigan State	D
205	NYR	Henrik Lundqvist	Vastre Frolunda Jr.	G
215	BUF	Matthew Lombardi	Victoriaville	C
220	BUF	Paul Gaustad	Portland	C
224	DAL	Antti Miettinen	HPK Jr.	RW

1999

FIRST ROUND

Pick	Claimed by		Amateur Club	Position
1	ATL	Patrik Stefan	Long Beach	C
2	VAN	Daniel Sedin	MoDo Ornskoldsvik	LW
3	VAN	Henrik Sedin	MoDo Ornskoldsvik	C
4	NYR	Pavel Brendl	Calgary	RW
5	NYI	Tim Connolly	Erie	C
6	NSH	Brian Finley	Barrie	G
7	WSH	Kris Beech	Calgary	C
8	NYI	Taylor Pyatt	Sudbury	LW
9	NYR	Jamie Lundmark	Moose Jaw	C
10	NYI	Branislav Mezei	Belleville	D
11	CGY	Oleg Saprykin	Seattle	LW
12	FLA	Denis Shvidki	Barrie	RW
13	EDM	Jani Rita	Jokerit	LW
14	S.J.	Jeff Jillson	U. of Michigan	D
15	PHX	Scott Kelman	Seattle	C
16	CAR	David Tanabe	U. of Wisconsin	D
17	STL	Barret Jackman	Regina	D
18	PIT	Konstantin Koltsov	Cherepovets	RW
19	PHX	Kirill Safronov	St. Petersburg	D
20	BUF	Barrett Heisten	U. of Maine	LW
21	BOS	Nick Boynton	Ottawa	D
22	PHI	Maxime Ouellet	Quebec	G
23	CHI	Steve McCarthy	Kootenay	D
24	TOR	Luca Cereda	Ambri	C
25	COL	Mikhail Kuleshov	Cherepovets	LW
26	OTT	Martin Havlat	Trinec	LW
27	N.J.	Ari Ahonen	JyP HT Jr.	G
28	NYI	Kristian Kudroc	Michalovce	D

OTHER NOTABLE SELECTIONS

Pick	Claimed by		Amateur Club	Position
44	ANA	Jordan Leopold	U. of Minnesota	D
70	FLA	Niklas Hagman	HIFK Helsinki	LW
83	ANA	Niclas Havelid	Malmo	D
91	EDM	Mike Comrie	U. of Michigan	C
115	PIT	Ryan Malone	Omaha	LW
138	BUF	Ryan Miller	Soo	G
165	CHI	Michael Leighton	Windsor	G
191	NSH	Martin Erat	ZPS Zlin Jr.	LW
204	PIT	Tom Kostopolous	London	RW
210	DET	Henrik Zetterberg	Timra	LW
212	COL	Radim Vrbata	Hull	RW
222	L.A.	George Parros	Chicago Freeze	RW

1998

FIRST ROUND

Pick	Claimed by		Amateur Club	Position
1	T.B.	Vincent Lecavalier	Rimouski	C
2	NSH	David Legwand	Plymouth	C
3	S.J.	Brad Stuart	Regina	D
4	VAN	Bryan Allen	Oshawa	D
5	ANA	Vitaly Vishnevski	Yaroslavl 2	D
6	CGY	Rico Fata	London	RW
7	NYR	Manny Malhotra	Guelph	C
8	CHI	Mark Bell	Ottawa	C
9	NYI	Mike Rupp	Erie	RW
10	TOR	Nik Antropov	Ust-Kamenogorsk	C
11	CAR	Jeff Heerema	Sarnia	RW
12	COL	Alex Tanguay	Halifax	C
13	EDM	Michael Henrich	Barrie	RW
14	PHX	Patrick DesRochers	Sarnia	G
15	OTT	Mathieu Chouinard	Shawinigan	G
16	MTL	Eric Chouinard	Quebec	LW
17	COL	Martin Skoula	Barrie	D
18	BUF	Dmitri Kalinin	Chelyabinsk	D
19	COL	Robyn Regehr	Kamloops	D
20	COL	Scott Parker	Kelowna	RW
21	L.A.	Mathieu Biron	Shawinigan	D
22	PHI	Simon Gagne	Quebec	LW
23	PIT	Milan Kraft	Keramika Plzen Jr.	C
24	STL	Christian Backman	Vastra Frolunda Jr.	D
25	DET	Jiri Fischer	Hull	D
26	N.J.	Mike Van Ryn	U. of Michigan	D
27	N.J.	Scott Gomez	Tri-City	C

OTHER NOTABLE SELECTIONS

Pick	Claimed by		Amateur Club	Position
29	S.J.	Jonathan Cheechoo	Belleville	RW
44	OTT	Mike Fisher	Sudbury	C
45	MTL	Mike Ribiero	Rouyan-Noranda	C
64	T.B.	Brad Richards	Rimouski	C
68	VAN	Jarkko Ruutu	HIFK Helsinki	RW
71	CAR	Erik Cole	Clarkson	LW
75	MTL	Francois Beauchemin	Laval	D
82	NJ	Brian Gionta	Boston College	RW
87	TOR	Alexei Ponikarovsky	Dyn-2 Moscow	LW
99	EDM	Shawn Horcoff	Michigan State	C
117	FLA	Jaroslav Spacek	Farjestad Karlstad	D
145	SJ	Mikael Samuelsson	Sodertalje	LW
161	OTT	Chris Neil	North Bay	RW
162	MTL	Andrei Markov	Khimik	D
164	BUF	Ales Kotalik	Ceske Budejovice Jr.	RW
168	PHI	Antero Niittymaki	TPS Turku Jr.	G
171	DET	Pavel Datsyuk	Yekateringburg	C
216	MTL	Michael Ryder	Hull	RW

1997

FIRST ROUND

Pick	Claimed by		Amateur Club	Position
1	BOS	Joe Thornton	Sault Ste. Marie	C
2	S.J.	Patrick Marleau	Seattle	C
3	L.A.	Olli Jokinen	HIFK Helsinki	C
4	NYI	Roberto Luongo	Val-d'Or	G
5	NYI	Eric Brewer	Prince George	D
6	CGY	Daniel Tkaczuk	Barrie	C
7	T.B.	Paul Mara	Sudbury	D
8	BOS	Sergei Samsonov	Detroit	LW
9	WSH	Nick Boynton	Ottawa	D
10	VAN	Brad Ference	Spokane	D
11	MTL	Jason Ward	Erie	RW
12	OTT	Marian Hossa	Dukla Trencin	RW
13	CHI	Daniel Cleary	Belleville	RW
14	EDM	Michel Riesen	Biel-Bienne	RW
15	L.A.	Matt Zultek	Ottawa	LW
16	CHI	Ty Jones	Spokane	RW
17	PIT	Robert Dome	Las Vegas (IHL)	RW
18	ANA	Mikael Holmqvist	Djurgarden	C
19	NYR	Stefan Cherneski	Brandon	RW
20	FLA	Mike Brown	Red Deer	LW
21	BUF	Mika Noronen	Tappara Tampere	G
22	CAR	Nikos Tselios	Belleville	D
23	S.J.	Scott Hannan	Kelowna	D
24	N.J.	J-F Damphousse	Moncton	G
25	DAL	Brenden Morrow	Portland	LW
26	COL	Kevin Grimes	Kingston	D

OTHER NOTABLE SELECTIONS

Pick	Claimed by		Amateur Club	Position
47	FLA	Kristian Huselius	Farjestad Karlstad	LW
48	BUF	Henrik Tallinder	AIK Solna	D
69	BUF	Maxim Afinogenov	Dynamo Moscow	RW
78	COL	Ville Nieminen	Tappara Tampere	RW
83	L.A.	Joe Corvo	U. of Western Michigan	D
144	VAN	Matt Cooke	Windsor	C
156	BUF	Brian Campbell	Ottawa	D
177	STL	Ladislav Nagy	Dragon Presov	LW

1996

FIRST ROUND

Pick	Claimed by		Amateur Club	Position
1	OTT	Chris Phillips	Prince Albert	D
2	S.J.	Andrei Zyuzin	Salavat Yulayev Ufa	D
3	NYI	J.P. Dumont	Val-d'Or	RW
4	WSH	Alexandre Volchkov	Barrie	C
5	DAL	Ric Jackman	Sault Ste. Marie	D
6	EDM	Boyd Devereaux	Kitchener	C
7	BUF	Erik Rasmussen	U. of Minnesota	LW/C
8	BOS	Johnathan Aitken	Medicine Hat	D
9	ANA	Ruslan Salei	Las Vegas (IHL)	D
10	N.J.	Lance Ward	Red Deer	D
11	PHX	Dan Focht	Tri-City	D
12	VAN	Josh Holden	Regina	C
13	CGY	Derek Morris	Regina	D
14	STL	Marty Reasoner	Boston College	C
15	PHI	Dainius Zubrus	Pembroke Jr. A	RW
16	T.B.	Mario Larocque	Hull	D
17	WSH	Jaroslav Svejkovsky	Tri-City	RW
18	MTL	Matt Higgins	Moose Jaw	C
19	EDM	Matthieu Descoteaux	Shawinigan	D
20	FLA	Marcus Nilson	Djurgarden	LW
21	S.J.	Marco Sturm	Landshut	LW
22	NYR	Jeff Brown	Sarnia	D
23	PIT	Craig Hillier	Ottawa	G
24	PHX	Daniel Briere	Drummondville	C
25	COL	Peter Ratchuk	Shattuck St. Mary's H.S.	D
26	DET	Jesse Wallin	Red Deer	D

OTHER NOTABLE SELECTIONS

Pick	Claimed by		Amateur Club	Position
35	ANA	Matt Cullen	St. Cloud State	C
49	N.J.	Colin White	Hull	D
56	NYI	Zdeno Chara	Dukla Trencin	D
59	EDM	Tom Poti	Cushing Academy	D
71	MTL	Arron Asham	Red Deer	RW
79	COL	Mark Parrish	St. Cloud State	RW
89	CGY	Toni Lydman	Reipas Lahti	D
96	L.A.	Eric Belanger	Beauport	C
102	S.J.	Matt Bradley	Kingston	RW
154	MTL	Brett Clark	U. of Maine	D
176	COL	Samuel Pahlsson	MoDo	C
179	T.B.	Pavel Kubina	Vitkovice	D
199	N.J.	Willie Mitchell	Melfort Jr. A	D
204	TOR	Tomas Kaberle	Kladno	D
223	HFD	Craig Adams	Harvard	RW
239	OTT	Sami Salo	TPS Turku	D

1995

FIRST ROUND

Pick	Claimed by		Amateur Club	Position
1	OTT	Bryan Berard	Detroit	D
2	NYI	Wade Redden	Brandon	D
3	L.A.	Aki Berg	Kiekko-67 Turku	D
4	ANA	Chad Kilger	Kingston	C
5	T.B.	Daymond Langkow	Tri-City	C
6	EDM	Steve Kelly	Prince Albert	C
7	WPG	Shane Doan	Kamloops	RW
8	MTL	Terry Ryan	Tri-City	LW
9	BOS	Kyle McLaren	Tacoma	D
10	FLA	Radek Dvorak	HC Ceske Budejovice	RW
11	DAL	Jarome Iginla	Kamloops	RW
12	S.J.	Teemu Riihijarvi	Kiekko-Espoo	LW
13	HFD	Jean-Sebastien Giguere	Halifax	G
14	BUF	Jay McKee	Niagara Falls	D
15	TOR	Jeff Ware	Oshawa	D
16	BUF	Martin Biron	Beauport	G
17	WSH	Brad Church	Prince Albert	LW
18	N.J.	Petr Sykora	Detroit	RW
19	CHI	Dmitri Nabokov	Krylja Sovetov	C/LW
20	CGY	Denis Gauthier	Drummondville	D
21	BOS	Sean Brown	Belleville	D
22	PHI	Brian Boucher	Tri-City	G
23	WSH	Miika Elomo	Kiekko-67 Turku	LW
24	PIT	Aleksey Morozov	Krylja Sovetov	RW
25	COL	Marc Denis	Chicoutimi	G
26	DET	Maxim Kuznetsov	Dynamo	D

OTHER NOTABLE SELECTIONS

Pick	Claimed by		Amateur Club	Position
31	EDM	Georges Laraque	St-Jean	RW
49	STL	Jochen Hecht	Mannheim	C
67	WPG	Brad Isbister	Portland	LW
79	N.J.	Alyn McCauley	Ottawa	C
87	HFD	Sami Kapanen	HIFK Helsinki	RW
90	S.J.	Vesa Toskala	Ilves Tampere	G
91	NYR	Marc Savard	Oshawa	C
101	STL	Michal Handzus	IS Banska Bystrica	C
116	S.J.	Miikka Kiprusoff	TPS Turku Jr.	G
122	N.J.	Chris Mason	Prince George	G
129	COL	Brent Johnson	Owen Sound	G
144	VAN	Brent Sopel	Swift Current	D
164	MTL	Stephane Robidas	Shawinigan	D
166	FLA	Peter Worrell	Hull	LW
177	BOS	P.J. Axelsson	Vastra Frolunda	LW
192	FLA	Filip Kuba	HC Vitkovice Jr.	D

1994

FIRST ROUND

Pick	Claimed by		Amateur Club	Position
1	FLA	Ed Jovanovski	Windsor	D
2	ANA	Oleg Tverdovsky	Krylja Sovetov	D
3	OTT	Radek Bonk	Las Vegas (IHL)	C
4	EDM	Jason Bonsignore	Niagara Falls	C
5	HFD	Jeff O'Neill	Guelph	RW
6	EDM	Ryan Smyth	Moose Jaw	LW
7	L.A.	Jamie Storr	Owen Sound	G
8	T.B.	Jason Wiemer	Portland	C
9	NYI	Brett Lindros	Kingston	RW
10	WSH	Nolan Baumgartner	Kamloops	D
11	S.J.	Jeff Friesen	Regina	LW
12	QUE	Wade Belak	Saskatoon	D/RW
13	VAN	Mattias Ohlund	Pitea	D
14	CHI	Ethan Moreau	Niagara Falls	LW
15	WSH	Alexander Kharlamov	CSKA Moscow	C
16	TOR	Eric Fichaud	Chictoutimi	G
17	BUF	Wayne Primeau	Owen Sound	C
18	MTL	Brad Brown	North Bay	D
19	CGY	Chris Dingman	Brandon	LW
20	DAL	Jason Botterill	U. of Michigan	LW
21	BOS	Evgeni Ryabchikov	Molot Perm	G
22	QUE	Jeffrey Kealty	Catholic Memorial H.S.	D
23	DET	Yan Golubovsky	Dynamo 2	D
24	PIT	Chris Wells	Seattle	C
25	N.J.	Vadim Sharifijanov	Salavat Yulayev Ufa	LW
26	NYR	Dan Cloutier	Sault Ste. Marie	G

OTHER NOTABLE SELECTIONS

Pick	Claimed by		Amateur Club	Position
44	MTL	Jose Theodore	St-Jean	G
49	DET	Mathieu Dandenault	Sherbrooke	RW/D
50	PIT	Richard Park	Belleville	D
51	N.J.	Patrik Elias	Kladno	C
64	TOR	Fredrik Modin	Timra	LW
71	N.J.	Sheldon Souray	Tri-City	D
72	QUE	Chris Drury	Fairfield Prep	C
87	QUE	Milan Hejduk	Pardubice	RW
90	NYI	Brad Lukowich	Kamloops	D
124	DAL	Marty Turco	Cambridge Jr. A	G
133	OTT	Daniel Alfredsson	Vastra Frolunda	RW
151	BOS	Andre Roy	Chicoutimi	RW
217	QUE	Tim Thomas	U. of Vermont	G
218	PHI	Johan Hedberg	Leksand	G
219	S.J.	Evgeni Nabokov	Ust-Kamengorsk	G
226	MTL	Tomas Vokoun	HC Kladno	G
233	N.J.	Steve Sullivan	Sault Ste. Marie	RW
249	WSH	Richard Zednik	IS Banka Bystricia	RW
257	DET	Tomas Holmstrom	Bodens IK	LW
286	NYR	Kim Johnsson	Malmo	D

Pick	Claimed by	Amateur Club	Position	Pick	Claimed by	Amateur Club	Position	Pick	Claimed by	Amateur Club	Position

1993

FIRST ROUND

1	OTT	Alexandre Daigle	Victoriaville	C
2	HFD	Chris Pronger	Peterborough	D
3	T.B.	Chris Gratton	Kingston	C
4	ANA	Paul Kariya	U. of Maine	LW
5	FLA	Rob Niedermayer	Medicine Hat	C
6	S.J.	Viktor Kozlov	Dynamo	C
7	EDM	Jason Arnott	Oshawa	C
8	NYR	Niklas Sundstrom	MoDo Ornskoldsvik	RW
9	DAL	Todd Harvey	Detroit	RW/C
10	QUE	Jocelyn Thibault	Sherbrooke	G
11	WSH	Brendan Witt	Seattle	D
12	TOR	Kenny Jonsson	Rogle Angelholm	D
13	N.J.	Denis Pederson	Prince Albert	C/RW
14	QUE	Adam Deadmarsh	Portland	RW
15	WPG	Mats Lindgren	Skelleftea	C/LW
16	EDM	Nick Stajduhar	London	D
17	WSH	Jason Allison	London	C
18	CGY	Jesper Mattsson	Malmo	C
19	TOR	Landon Wilson	Dubuque Jr. A	RW
20	VAN	Mike Wilson	Sudbury	D
21	MTL	Saku Koivu	TPS Turku	C
22	DET	Anders Eriksson	MoDo Ornskoldsvik	D
23	NYI	Todd Bertuzzi	Guelph	RW
24	CHI	Eric Lecompte	Hull	LW
25	BOS	Kevyn Adams	Miami of Ohio	C
26	PIT	Stefan Bergkvist	Leksand	D

OTHER NOTABLE SELECTIONS

28	S.J.	Shean Donovan	Ottawa	RW
32	N.J.	Jay Pandolfo	Boston University	LW
35	DAL	Jamie Langenbrunner	Cloquet	C
39	NJ	Brendan Morrison	Spokane	D
40	NYI	Bryan McCabe	Spokane	D
41	FLA	Kevin Weekes	Owen Sound	G
71	PHI	Vaclav Prospal	Motor Ceske Budejovice	C
72	HFD	Marek Malik	Vitkovice	D
90	CHI	Eric Daze	Beauport	RW
111	EDM	Miroslav Satan	Dukla Trencin	LW
118	NYI	Tommy Salo	Vasteras	G
124	VAN	Scott Walker	Owen Sound	RW
151	MTL	Darcy Tucker	Kamloops	RW
164	NYR	Todd Marchant	Clarkson	C
174	WSH	Andrew Brunette	Owen Sound	LW
188	HFD	Manny Legace	Niagara Falls	G
207	BOS	Hal Gill	Nashoba H.S.	D
219	STL	Mike Grier	St. Sebastien's	RW
227	OTT	Pavol Demitra	Dukla Trencin	LW
250	LA	Kimmo Timonen	KalPa Kuopio	D

1992

FIRST ROUND

1	T.B.	Roman Hamrlik	ZPS Zlin	D
2	OTT	Alexei Yashin	Dynamo	C
3	S.J.	Mike Rathje	Medicine Hat	D
4	QUE	Todd Warriner	Windsor	LW
5	NYI	Darius Kasparaitis	Dynamo	D
6	CGY	Cory Stillman	Windsor	LW
7	PHI	Ryan Sittler	Nichols H.S.	LW
8	TOR	Brandon Convery	Sudbury	C
9	HFD	Robert Petrovicky	Dukla Trencin	C
10	S.J.	Andrei Nazarov	Dynamo	LW
11	BUF	David Cooper	Medicine Hat	D
12	CHI	Sergei Krivokrasov	CSKA Moscow	RW
13	EDM	Joe Hulbig	St. Sebastian's H.S.	LW
14	WSH	Sergei Gonchar	Chelyabinsk	D
15	PHI	Jason Bowen	Tri-City	D
16	BOS	Dmitri Kvartalnov	San Diego (IHL)	LW
17	WPG	Sergei Bautin	Dynamo	D
18	N.J.	Jason Smith	Regina	D
19	PIT	Martin Straka	HC Skoda Plzen	C
20	MTL	David Wilkie	Kamloops	D
21	VAN	Libor Polasek	Vitkovice	C
22	DET	Curtis Bowen	Ottawa	LW
23	TOR	Grant Marshall	Ottawa	RW
24	NYR	Peter Ferraro	Waterloo Jr. A	LW

OTHER NOTABLE SELECTIONS

32	WSH	Jim Carey	Catholic Memorial	G
33	MTL	Valeri Bure	Spokane	RW
38	STL	Igor Korolev	Dynamo	C
40	VAN	Michael Peca	Ottawa	C
42	N.J.	Sergei Brylin	CSKA Moscow	C
46	DET	Darren McCarty	Belleville	RW
48	NYR	Mattias Norstrom	AIK Solna	D
52	QUE	Manny Fernandez	Laval	G
65	EDM	Kirk Maltby	Owen Sound	RW
68	MTL	Craig Rivet	Kingston	D
88	MIN	Jere Lehtinen	Kiekko-Espoo	RW
117	VAN	Adrian Aucoin	Boston University	D
158	STL	Ian Laperriere	Drummondville	C/RW
186	N.J.	Stephane Yelle	Oshawa	C
204	WPG	Nikolai Khabibulin	CSKA Moscow	G
220	QUE	Anson Carter	Wexford Jr. A	C

1991

FIRST ROUND

1	QUE	Eric Lindros	Oshawa	C
2	S.J.	Pat Falloon	Spokane	RW
3	N.J.	Scott Niedermayer	Kamloops	D
4	NYI	Scott Lachance	Boston U.	D
5	WPG	Aaron Ward	U. of Michigan	D
6	PHI	Peter Forsberg	MoDo Ornskoldsvik	C
7	VAN	Alek Stojanov	Hamilton	RW
8	MIN	Richard Matvichuk	Saskatoon	D
9	HFD	Patrick Poulin	St-Hyacinthe	C
10	DET	Martin Lapointe	Laval	RW
11	N.J.	Brian Rolston	Detroit Compuware Jr. A	C/RW
12	EDM	Tyler Wright	Swift Current	C
13	BUF	Philippe Boucher	Granby	D
14	WSH	Pat Peake	Detroit	C
15	NYR	Alex Kovalev	Dynamo	RW
16	PIT	Markus Naslund	MoDo Ornskoldsvik	LW
17	MTL	Brent Bilodeau	Seattle	D
18	BOS	Glen Murray	Sudbury	RW
19	CGY	Niklas Sundblad	AIK Solna	RW
20	EDM	Martin Rucinsky	CHZ Litvinov	LW
21	WSH	Trevor Halverson	North Bay	LW
22	CHI	Dean McAmmond	Prince Albert	LW

OTHER NOTABLE SELECTIONS

23	S.J.	Ray Whitney	Spokane	LW
26	NYI	Ziggy Palffy	AC Nitra	RW
27	STL	Steve Staios	Niagara Falls	D
30	S.J.	Sandis Ozolinsh	Dynamo Riga	D
40	BOS	Jozef Stumpel	AC Nitra	C
47	TOR	Yanic Perreault	Trois-Rivieres	C
54	DET	Chris Osgood	Medicine Hat	G
58	WSH	Steve Konowalchuk	Portland	LW
59	HFD	Michael Nylander	Huddinge	C
76	DET	Mike Knuble	Kalamazoo Jr. A	RW
81	L.A.	Alexei Zhitnik	Sokol Kiev	D
106	BOS	Mariusz Czerkawski	GKS Tychy	RW
122	PHI	Dmitry Yushkevich	Yaroslavl	D
123	BUF	Sean O'Donnell	Sudbury	D
171	MTL	Brian Savage	Miami of Ohio	LW
203	WPG	Igor Ulanov	Khimik Voskresensk	D

Chris Pronger was selected second overall by the Hartford Whalers in the 1993 NHL Entry Draft but spent only two seasons with the team before being traded to the St. Louis Blues for Brendan Shanahan.

Pick	Claimed by	Amateur Club	Position

1990

FIRST ROUND

Pick	Claimed by	Amateur Club	Position
1	QUE	Owen Nolan	Cornwall	RW
2	VAN	Petr Nedved	Seattle	C
3	DET	Keith Primeau	Niagara Falls	C
4	PHI	Mike Ricci	Peterborough	C
5	PIT	Jaromir Jagr	Kladno	RW
6	NYI	Scott Scissons	Saskatoon	C
7	L.A.	Darryl Sydor	Kamloops	D
8	MIN	Derian Hatcher	North Bay	D
9	WSH	John Slaney	Cornwall	D
10	TOR	Drake Berehowsky	Kingston	D
11	CGY	Trevor Kidd	Brandon	G
12	MTL	Turner Stevenson	Seattle	RW
13	NYR	Michael Stewart	Michigan State	D
14	BUF	Brad May	Niagara Falls	LW
15	HFD	Mark Greig	Lethbridge	RW
16	CHI	Karl Dykhuis	Hull	D
17	EDM	Scott Allison	Prince Albert	C
18	VAN	Shawn Antoski	North Bay	LW
19	WPG	Keith Tkachuk	Malden Catholic H.S.	LW
20	N.J.	Martin Brodeur	St-Hyacinthe	G
21	BOS	Bryan Smolinski	Michigan State	C

OTHER NOTABLE SELECTIONS

Pick	Claimed by	Amateur Club	Position
25	PHI	Chris Simon	Ottawa	LW
31	TOR	Felix Potvin	Chicoutimi	G
34	NYR	Doug Weight	Lake Superior State	C
36	HFD	Geoff Sanderson	Swift Current	LW
45	DET	Vyacheslav Kozlov	Khimik Voskresensk	RW
77	WPG	Alexei Zhamnov	Dynamo Moscow	C
85	NYR	Sergei Zubov	CSKA Moscow	D
113	MIN	Roman Turek	Plzen	G
123	MTL	Craig Conroy	Northwood Prep	C
133	L.A.	Robert Lang	CHZ Litvinov	C
156	WSH	Peter Bondra	Kosice	RW
158	QUE	Alexander Karpovtsev	VSZ Dynamo	D
177	WSH	Ken Klee	Bowling Green	D
244	NYR	Sergei Nemchinov	Krylja Sovetov	LW

1989

FIRST ROUND

Pick	Claimed by	Amateur Club	Position
1	QUE	Mats Sundin	Nacka	C
2	NYI	Dave Chyzowski	Kamloops	LW
3	TOR	Scott Thornton	Belleville	LW
4	WPG	Stu Barnes	Tri-City	C
5	N.J.	Bill Guerin	Springfield Jr. B.	RW
6	CHI	Adam Bennett	Sudbury	D
7	MIN	Doug Zmolek	John Marshall H.S.	D
8	VAN	Jason Herter	North Dakota	D
9	STL	Jason Marshall	Vernon Jr. A.	D
10	HFD	Bobby Holik	Dukla Jihlava	C
11	DET	Mike Sillinger	Regina	C
12	TOR	Rob Pearson	Belleville	RW
13	MTL	Lindsay Vallis	Seattle	D
14	BUF	Kevin Haller	Regina	D
15	EDM	Jason Soules	Niagara Falls	D
16	PIT	Jamie Heward	Regina	D
17	BOS	Shayne Stevenson	Kitchener	RW
18	N.J.	Jason Miller	Medicine Hat	LW
19	WSH	Olaf Kolzig	Tri-City	G
20	NYR	Steven Rice	Kitchener	RW
21	TOR	Steve Bancroft	Belleville	D

OTHER NOTABLE SELECTIONS

Pick	Claimed by	Amateur Club	Position
22	QUE	Adam Foote	Sault Ste. Marie	D
30	MTL	Patrice Brisebois	Laval	D
53	DET	Nicklas Lidstrom	Vasteras	D
62	WPG	Kris Draper	Canadian National	C
70	CGY	Robert Reichel	Litvinov	C
109	CHI	Dan Bylsma	Bowling Green	RW
74	DET	Sergei Fedorov	CSKA Moscow	C
113	VAN	Pavel Bure	CSKA Moscow	RW
116	DET	Dallas Drake	Northern Michigan	LW
183	BUF	Donald Audette	Laval	RW
191	NYI	Vladimir Malakhov	CSKA Moscow	D
196	MIN	Arturs Irbe	Dynamo Riga	G
221	DET	Vladimir Konstantinov	CSKA Moscow	D

1988

FIRST ROUND

Pick	Claimed by	Amateur Club	Position
1	MIN	Mike Modano	Prince Albert	C
2	VAN	Trevor Linden	Medicine Hat	RW
3	QUE	Curtis Leschyshyn	Saskatoon	D
4	PIT	Darrin Shannon	Windsor	LW
5	QUE	Daniel Dore	Drummondville	RW
6	TOR	Scott Pearson	Kingston	LW
7	L.A.	Martin Gelinas	Hull	LW
8	CHI	Jeremy Roenick	Thayer Academy	C
9	STL	Rod Brind'Amour	Notre Dame Jr. A.	C
10	WPG	Teemu Selanne	Jokerit	RW
11	HFD	Chris Govedaris	Toronto	LW
12	N.J.	Corey Foster	Peterborough	D
13	BUF	Joel Savage	Victoria	RW
14	PHI	Claude Boivin	Drummondville	LW
15	WSH	Reggie Savage	Victoriaville	C

The Maple Leafs picked Wendel Clark first overall in 1985 when the NHL Entry Draft was held in Toronto. Clark quickly became a fan favorite and later became captain of the team

Pick	Claimed by	Amateur Club	Position
16	NYI	Kevin Cheveldayoff	Brandon	D
17	DET	Kory Kocur	Saskatoon	RW
18	BOS	Rob Cimetta	Toronto	W
19	EDM	Francois Leroux	St-Jean	D
20	MTL	Eric Charron	Trois-Rivieres	D
21	CGY	Jason Muzzatti	Michigan State	G

OTHER NOTABLE SELECTIONS

Pick	Claimed by	Amateur Club	Position
27	TOR	Tie Domi	Peterborough	RW
67	PIT	Mark Recchi	Kamloops	RW
68	NYR	Tony Amonte	Thayer Academy	RW
70	L.A.	Rob Blake	Bowling Green	D
76	BUF	Keith Carney	Mount St. Charles	D
81	BOS	Joe Juneau	R.P.I.	C
89	BUF	Alexander Mogilny	CSKA Moscow	LW
97	BUF	Rob Ray	Cornwall	RW
129	QUE	Valeri Kamensky	CSKA Moscow	D
198	STL	Bret Hedican	North St. Paul H.S.	D
234	QUE	Claude Lapointe	Laval	LW/C

1987

FIRST ROUND

Pick	Claimed by	Amateur Club	Position
1	BUF	Pierre Turgeon	Granby	C
2	N.J.	Brendan Shanahan	London	LW
3	BOS	Glen Wesley	Portland	D
4	L.A.	Wayne McBean	Medicine Hat	D
5	PIT	Chris Joseph	Seattle	D
6	MIN	Dave Archibald	Portland	C/LW
7	TOR	Luke Richardson	Peterborough	D
8	CHI	Jimmy Waite	Chicoutimi	G
9	QUE	Bryan Fogarty	Kingston	D
10	NYR	Jay More	New Westminster	D
11	DET	Yves Racine	Longueuil	D
12	STL	Keith Osborne	North Bay	RW
13	NYI	Dean Chynoweth	Medicine Hat	D
14	BOS	Stephane Quintal	Granby	D
15	QUE	Joe Sakic	Swift Current	C
16	WPG	Bryan Marchment	Belleville	D
17	MTL	Andrew Cassels	Ottawa	C
18	HFD	Jody Hull	Peterborough	RW
19	CGY	Bryan Deasley	U. of Michigan	LW
20	PHI	Darren Rumble	Kitchener	D
21	EDM	Peter Soberlak	Swift Current	LW

OTHER NOTABLE SELECTIONS

Pick	Claimed by	Amateur Club	Position
33	MTL	John LeClair	Bellows Academy	LW
38	MTL	Eric Desjardins	Granby	D
44	MTL	Mathieu Schneider	Cornwall	D
71	TOR	Joe Sacco	Medford H.S.	RW
110	PIT	Shawn McEachern	Matignon H.S.	RW
114	QUE	Garth Snow	Mount St. Charles H.S.	G
118	NYI	Rob DiMaio	Medicine Hat	RW
149	N.J.	Jim Dowd	Brick H.S.	C
166	CGY	Theoren Fleury	Moose Jaw	RW

1986

FIRST ROUND

Pick	Claimed by	Amateur Club	Position
1	DET	Joe Murphy	Michigan State	RW
2	L.A.	Jimmy Carson	Verdun	C
3	N.J.	Neil Brady	Medicine Hat	C
4	PIT	Zarley Zalapski	Canadian National	D
5	BUF	Shawn Anderson	Canadian National	D
6	TOR	Vincent Damphousse	Laval	C
7	VAN	Dan Woodley	Portland	RW
8	WPG	Pat Elynuik	Prince Albert	RW
9	NYR	Brian Leetch	Avon Old Farms H.S.	D
10	STL	Jocelyn Lemieux	Laval	RW
11	HFD	Scott Young	Boston U.	RW
12	MIN	Warren Babe	Lethbridge	LW
13	BOS	Craig Janney	Boston College	C
14	CHI	Everett Sanipass	Verdun	LW
15	MTL	Mark Pederson	Medicine Hat	LW
16	CGY	George Pelawa	Bemidji H.S.	RW
17	NYI	Tom Fitzgerald	Austin Prep	RW
18	QUE	Ken McRae	Sudbury	C
19	WSH	Jeff Greenlaw	Canadian National	LW
20	PHI	Kerry Huffman	Guelph	D
21	EDM	Kim Issel	Prince Albert	RW

OTHER NOTABLE SELECTIONS

Pick	Claimed by	Amateur Club	Position
22	DET	Adam Graves	Windsor	LW
29	WPG	Teppo Numminen	Tappara Tampere	D
67	PIT	Rob Brown	Kamloops	RW
72	NYR	Mark Janssens	Regina	C
81	QUE	Ron Tugnutt	Peterborough	G
85	DET	Johan Garpenlov	Nacka	LW
114	NYR	Darren Turcotte	North Bay	C
141	MTL	Lyle Odelein	Moose Jaw	D
143	NYI	Rich Pilon	Prince Albert AAA	D
202	BOS	Greg Hawgood	Kamloops	D

1985

FIRST ROUND

Pick	Claimed by	Amateur Club	Position
1	TOR	Wendel Clark	Saskatoon	LW/D
2	PIT	Craig Simpson	Michigan State	LW
3	N.J.	Craig Wolanin	Kitchener	D
4	VAN	Jim Sandlak	London	RW
5	HFD	Dana Murzyn	Calgary	D
6	NYI	Brad Dalgarno	Hamilton	RW
7	NYR	Ulf Dahlen	Ostersund	LW
8	DET	Brent Fedyk	Regina	LW
9	L.A.	Craig Duncanson	Sudbury	LW
10	L.A.	Dan Gratton	Oshawa	C
11	CHI	Dave Manson	Prince Albert	D
12	MTL	Jose Charbonneau	Drummondville	RW
13	NYI	Derek King	Sault Ste. Marie	LW

14	BUF	Calle Johansson	Vastra Frolunda	D
15	QUE	David Latta	Kitchener	LW
16	MTL	Tom Chorske	Minneapolis SW H.S.	LW
17	CGY	Chris Biotti	Belmont Hill H.S.	D
18	WPG	Ryan Stewart	Kamloops	C
19	WSH	Yvon Corriveau	Toronto	LW
20	EDM	Scott Metcalfe	Kingston	LW
21	PHI	Glen Seabrooke	Peterborough	C

OTHER NOTABLE SELECTIONS

24	N.J.	Sean Burke	Toronto	G
27	CGY	Joe Nieuwendyk	Cornell	C
28	NYR	Mike Richter	Northwood Prep	G
32	N.J.	Eric Weinrich	North Yarmouth Academy	D
35	BUF	Benoit Hogue	St-Jean	C
50	DET	Steve Chiasson	Guelph	D
52	BOS	Bill Ranford	New Westminster	G
81	WPG	Fredrik Olausson	Farjestad Karlstad	D
113	DET	Randy McKay	Michigan Tech	RW
157	BOS	Randy Burridge	Peterborough	LW
188	EDM	Kelly Buchberger	Moose Jaw	RW
189	PHI	Gord Murphy	Oshawa	D
214	VAN	Igor Larionov	CSKA Moscow	C
245	BUF	Ken Baumgartner	Prince Albert	D

1984

FIRST ROUND

1	PIT	Mario Lemieux	Laval	C
2	N.J.	Kirk Muller	Guelph	LW
3	CHI	Eddie Olczyk	Team USA	C
4	TOR	Al Iafrate	Belleville	D
5	MTL	Petr Svoboda	CHZ Litvinov	D
6	L.A.	Craig Redmond	U. of Denver	D
7	DET	Shawn Burr	Kitchener	LW/C
8	MTL	Shayne Corson	Brantford	LW
9	PIT	Doug Bodger	Kamloops	D
10	VAN	J.J. Daigneault	Longueuil	D
11	HFD	Sylvain Cote	Quebec	D
12	CGY	Gary Roberts	Ottawa	LW
13	MIN	David Quinn	Kent H.S.	D
14	NYR	Terry Carkner	Peterborough	D
15	QUE	Trevor Stienburg	Guelph	RW
16	PIT	Roger Belanger	Kingston	C
17	WSH	Kevin Hatcher	North Bay	D
18	BUF	Mikael Andersson	Vastra Frolunda	LW
19	BOS	Dave Pasin	Prince Albert	RW
20	NYI	Duncan MacPherson	Saskatoon	D
21	EDM	Selmar Odelein	Regina	D

OTHER NOTABLE SELECTIONS

25	TOR	Todd Gill	Windsor	D
27	PHI	Scott Mellanby	Henry Carr Jr. B.	RW
29	MTL	Stephane Richer	Granby	RW
36	QUE	Jeff Brown	Sudbury	D
51	MTL	Patrick Roy	Granby	G
107	N.J.	Kirk McLean	Oshawa	G
117	CGY	Brett Hull	Penticton Jr. A	RW
119	NYR	Kjell Samuelsson	Leksand	D
166	BOS	Don Sweeney	St. Paul's H.S.	D
171	L.A.	Luc Robitaille	Hull	LW
180	CGY	Gary Suter	U. of Wisconsin	D

1983

FIRST ROUND

1	MIN	Brian Lawton	Mount St. Charles H.S.	LW
2	HFD	Sylvain Turgeon	Hull	LW
3	NYI	Pat LaFontaine	Verdun	C
4	DET	Steve Yzerman	Peterborough	C
5	BUF	Tom Barrasso	Acton-Boxborough	G
6	N.J.	John MacLean	Oshawa	RW
7	TOR	Russ Courtnall	Victoria	RW
8	WPG	Andrew McBain	North Bay	RW
9	VAN	Cam Neely	Portland	RW
10	BUF	Normand Lacombe	New Hampshire	RW
11	BUF	Adam Creighton	Ottawa	C
12	NYR	Dave Gagner	Brantford	C
13	CGY	Dan Quinn	Belleville	C
14	WPG	Bobby Dollas	Laval	D
15	PIT	Bob Errey	Peterborough	LW
16	NYI	Gerald Diduck	Lethbridge	D
17	MTL	Alfie Turcotte	Portland	C
18	CHI	Bruce Cassidy	Ottawa	D
19	EDM	Jeff Beukeboom	Sault Ste. Marie	D
20	HFD	David Jensen	Lawrence Academy	C
21	BOS	Nevin Markwart	Regina	LW

OTHER NOTABLE SELECTIONS

26	MTL	Claude Lemieux	Trois-Rivieres	RW
27	MTL	Sergio Momesso	Shawinigan	LW
41	PHI	Peter Zezel	Toronto	C
82	EDM	Esa Tikkanen	HIFK Helsinki	LW
88	DET	Petr Klima	Dukla Jihlava	W
91	DET	Joe Kocur	Saskatoon	RW
112	L.A.	Kevin Stevens	Silvere Lake H.S.	LW
125	PHI	Rick Tocchet	Sault Ste. Marie	RW
139	BUF	Christian Ruuttu	Assat Pori	C
150	N.J.	Viacheslav Fetisov	CSKA Moscow	D
207	CHI	Dominik Hasek	Pardubice	G
223	BUF	Uwe Krupp	Koln	D
241	CGY	Sergei Makarov	CSKA Moscow	RW

1982

FIRST ROUND

1	BOS	Gord Kluzak	Billings	D
2	MIN	Brian Bellows	Kitchener	LW
3	TOR	Gary Nylund	Portland	D
4	PHI	Ron Sutter	Lethbridge	C
5	WSH	Scott Stevens	Kitchener	D
6	BUF	Phil Housley	South St. Paul H.S.	D
7	CHI	Ken Yaremchuk	Portland	C
8	N.J.	Rocky Trottier	Nanaimo	RW
9	BUF	Paul Cyr	Victoria	LW
10	PIT	Rich Sutter	Lethbridge	RW
11	VAN	Michel Petit	Sherbrooke	D
12	WPG	Jim Kyte	Cornwall	D
13	QUE	David Shaw	Kitchener	D
14	HFD	Paul Lawless	Windsor	LW
15	NYR	Chris Kontos	Toronto	LW/C
16	BUF	Dave Andreychuk	Oshawa	LW
17	DET	Murray Craven	Medicine Hat	LW
18	N.J.	Ken Daneyko	Seattle	D
19	MTL	Alain Heroux	Chicoutimi	LW
20	EDM	Jim Playfair	Portland	D
21	NYI	Pat Flatley	U. of Wisconsin	RW

OTHER NOTABLE SELECTIONS

36	NYR	Tomas Sandstrom	Farjestad Karlstad	RW
43	N.J.	Pat Verbeek	Sudbury	RW
45	TOR	Ken Wregget	Lethbridge	G
56	HFD	Kevin Dineen	U. of Denver	RW
67	HFD	Ulf Samuelsson	Leksand	D
75	WPG	Dave Ellett	Ottawa Jr. A	D
80	MIN	Bob Rouse	Nanaimo	D
88	HFD	Ray Ferraro	Penticton Jr. A	C
119	PHI	Ron Hextall	Brandon	G
120	NYR	Tony Granato	Northwood Prep	RW
134	STL	Doug Gilmour	Cornwall	C
140	PHI	Dave Brown	Saskatoon	RW

1981

FIRST ROUND

1	WPG	Dale Hawerchuk	Cornwall	C
2	L.A.	Doug Smith	Ottawa	C
3	WSH	Bob Carpenter	St. John's Prep	C
4	HFD	Ron Francis	Sault Ste. Marie	C
5	COL	Joe Cirella	Oshawa	D
6	TOR	Jim Benning	Portland	D
7	MTL	Mark Hunter	Brantford	RW
8	EDM	Grant Fuhr	Victoria	G
9	NYR	James Patrick	Prince Albert	D
10	VAN	Garth Butcher	Regina	D
11	QUE	Randy Moller	Lethbridge	D
12	CHI	Tony Tanti	Oshawa	RW
13	MIN	Ron Meighan	Niagara Falls	D
14	BOS	Normand Leveille	Chicoutimi	LW
15	CGY	Al MacInnis	Kitchener	D
16	PHI	Steve Smith	Sault Ste. Marie	D
17	BUF	Jiri Dudacek	Kladno	RW
18	MTL	Gilbert Delorme	Chicoutimi	D
19	MTL	Jan Ingman	Farjestad Karlstad	LW
20	STL	Marty Ruff	Lethbridge	D
21	NYI	Paul Boutilier	Sherbrooke	D

OTHER NOTABLE SELECTIONS

22	WPG	Scott Arniel	Cornwall	LW
40	MTL	Chris Chelios	Moose Jaw	D
56	CGY	Mike Vernon	Calgary	G
72	NYR	John Vanbiesbrouck	Sault Ste. Marie	G
107	DET	Gerard Gallant	Sherbrooke	LW
108	COL	Bruce Driver	U. of Wisconsin	D
111	EDM	Steve Smith	London	D
145	MTL	Tom Kurvers	Minnesota-Duluth	D
152	WSH	Gaetan Duchesne	Quebec	LW

1980

FIRST ROUND

1	MTL	Doug Wickenheiser	Regina	C
2	WPG	Dave Babych	Portland	D
3	CHI	Denis Savard	Montreal	C
4	L.A.	Larry Murphy	Peterborough	D
5	WSH	Darren Veitch	Regina	D
6	EDM	Paul Coffey	Kitchener	D
7	VAN	Rick Lanz	Oshawa	D
8	HFD	Fred Arthur	Cornwall	D
9	PIT	Mike Bullard	Brantford	C
10	L.A.	Jim Fox	Ottawa	RW
11	DET	Mike Blaisdell	Regina	RW
12	STL	Rik Wilson	Kingston	D
13	CGY	Denis Cyr	Montreal	RW
14	NYR	Jim Malone	Toronto	C
15	CHI	Jerome Dupont	Toronto	D
16	MIN	Brad Palmer	Victoria	LW
17	NYI	Brent Sutter	Red Deer Jr. A	C
18	BOS	Barry Pederson	Victoria	C
19	COL	Paul Gagne	Windsor	LW
20	BUF	Steve Patrick	Brandon	RW
21	PHI	Mike Stothers	Kingston	D

OTHER NOTABLE SELECTIONS

37	MIN	Don Beaupre	Sudbury	G
38	NYI	Kelly Hrudey	Medicine Hat	G
57	CHI	Troy Murray	St. Albert Jr. A	C
61	MTL	Craig Ludwig	North Dakota	D
69	EDM	Jari Kurri	Jokerit	RW
73	L.A.	Bernie Nicholls	Kingston	C
80	NYI	Greg Gilbert	Toronto	LW
81	BOS	Steve Kasper	Verdun	C
106	COL	Aaron Broten	Minnesota-Duluth	LW/C
120	CHI	Steve Larmer	Niagara Falls	RW
124	MTL	Mike McPhee	RPI	LW
128	WPG	Brian Mullen	U.S. Jr. National	RW
132	EDM	Andy Moog	Billings	G
181	CGY	Hakan Loob	Farjestad Karlstad	RW

1979

FIRST ROUND

1	COL	Rob Ramage	London	D
2	STL	Perry Turnbull	Portland	C
3	DET	Mike Foligno	Sudbury	RW
4	WSH	Mike Gartner	Niagara Falls	RW
5	VAN	Rick Vaive	Sherbrooke	RW
6	MIN	Craig Hartsburg	Sault Ste. Marie	D
7	CHI	Keith Brown	Portland	D
8	BOS	Raymond Bourque	Verdun	D
9	TOR	Laurie Boschman	Brandon	C
10	MIN	Tom McCarthy	Oshawa	LW
11	BUF	Mike Ramsey	U. of Minnesota	D
12	ATL	Paul Reinhart	Kitchener	D
13	NYR	Doug Sulliman	Kitchener	RW
14	PHI	Brian Propp	Brandon	LW
15	BOS	Brad McCrimmon	Brandon	D
16	L.A.	Jay Wells	Kingston	D
17	NYI	Duane Sutter	Lethbridge	RW
18	HFD	Ray Allison	Brandon	RW
19	WPG	Jimmy Mann	Sherbrooke	RW
20	QUE	Michel Goulet	Quebec	LW
21	EDM	Kevin Lowe	Quebec	D

OTHER NOTABLE SELECTIONS

32	BUF	Lindy Ruff	Lethbridge	D/LW
37	MTL	Mats Naslund	Brynas Gavle	LW
40	WPG	Dave Christian	North Dakota	RW
41	QUE	Dale Hunter	Sudbury	C
42	MIN	Neal Broten	Minnesota-Duluth	C
44	MTL	Guy Carbonneau	Chicoutimi	C
48	EDM	Mark Messier	St. Albert Jr. A	C
54	ATL	Tim Hunter	Seattle	RW
57	BOS	Keith Crowder	Peterborough	RW
58	MTL	Rick Wamsley	Brantford	G
66	DET	John Ogrodnick	New Westminster	LW
69	EDM	Glenn Anderson	U. of Denver	RW
75	ATL	Jim Peplinski	Toronto	RW
83	QUE	Anton Stastny	Slovan Bratislava	LW
89	VAN	Dirk Graham	Regina	RW/LW
103	WPG	Thomas Steen	Leksand	C
120	BOS	Mike Krushelnyski	Montreal	LW/C

1978

FIRST ROUND

1	MIN	Bobby Smith	Ottawa	C
2	WSH	Ryan Walter	Seattle	C/LW
3	STL	Wayne Babych	Portland	RW
4	VAN	Bill Derlago	Brandon	C
5	COL	Mike Gillis	Kingston	LW
6	PHI	Behn Wilson	Kingston	D
7	PHI	Ken Linseman	Kingston	C
8	MTL	Danny Geoffrion	Cornwall	RW
9	DET	Willie Huber	Hamilton	D
10	CHI	Tim Higgins	Ottawa	RW
11	ATL	Brad Marsh	London	D
12	DET	Brent Peterson	Portland	C
13	BUF	Larry Playfair	Portland	D
14	PHI	Danny Lucas	Sault Ste. Marie	RW
15	NYI	Steve Tambellini	Lethbridge	C
16	BOS	Al Secord	Hamilton	LW
17	MTL	Dave Hunter	Sudbury	LW
18	WSH	Tim Coulis	Hamilton	LW

OTHER NOTABLE SELECTIONS

19	MIN	Steve Payne	Ottawa	LW
21	TOR	Joel Quenneville	Windsor	D
22	VAN	Curt Fraser	Victoria	LW
26	NYR	Don Maloney	Kitchener	LW
32	BUF	Tony McKegney	Kingston	LW
40	VAN	Stan Smyl	New Westminster	RW
54	MIN	Curt Giles	Minnesota-Duluth	D
55	WSH	Bengt Gustafsson	Farjestad Karlstad	RW
93	NYR	Tom Laidlaw	Northern Michigan	D
103	MTL	Keith Acton	Peterborough	C
109	STL	Paul MacLean	Hull	RW
153	BOS	Craig MacTavish	University of Lowell	C
173	STL	Risto Siltanen	Ilves Tampere	D
179	CHI	Darryl Sutter	Lethbridge	LW
231	MTL	Chris Nilan	Northeastern	RW

1977

FIRST ROUND

#	Team	Player	From	Pos
1	DET	Dale McCourt	St. Catharines	C
2	COL	Barry Beck	New Westminster	D
3	WSH	Robert Picard	Montreal	D
4	VAN	Jere Gillis	Sherbrooke	LW
5	Cle.	Mike Crombeen	Kingston	RW
6	CHI	Doug Wilson	Ottawa	D
7	MIN	Brad Maxwell	New Westminster	D
8	NYR	Lucien DeBlois	Sorel	C
9	STL	Scott Campbell	London	D
10	MTL	Mark Napier	Toronto	RW
11	TOR	John Anderson	Toronto	RW
12	TOR	Trevor Johansen	Toronto	D
13	NYR	Ron Duguay	Sudbury	C/RW
14	BUF	Ric Seiling	St. Catharines	RW/C
15	NYI	Mike Bossy	Laval	RW
16	BOS	Dwight Foster	Kitchener	RW
17	PHI	Kevin McCarthy	Winnipeg	D
18	MTL	Norm Dupont	Montreal	LW

OTHER NOTABLE SELECTIONS

#	Team	Player	From	Pos
25	MIN	Dave Semenko	Brandon	LW
33	NYI	John Tonelli	Toronto	LW
36	MTL	Rod Langway	New Hampshire	D
40	VAN	Glen Hanlon	Brandon	G
54	MTL	Gordie Roberts	Victoria	D
66	PIT	Mark Johnson	U. of Wisconsin	C
102	PIT	Greg Millen	Peterborough	G
135	PHI	Pete Peeters	Medicine Hat	G
162	MTL	Craig Laughlin	Clarkson	RW

1976

FIRST ROUND

#	Team	Player	From	Pos
1	WSH	Rick Green	London	D
2	PIT	Blair Chapman	Saskatoon	RW
3	MIN	Glen Sharpley	Hull	C
4	DET	Fred Williams	Saskatoon	C
5	CAL	Bjorn Johansson	Orebro	D
6	NYR	Don Murdoch	Medicine Hat	RW
7	STL	Bernie Federko	Saskatoon	C
8	ATL	Dave Shand	Peterborough	D
9	CHI	Real Cloutier	Quebec	RW
10	ATL	Harold Phillipoff	New Westminster	LW
11	K.C.	Paul Gardner	Oshawa	C
12	MTL	Peter Lee	Ottawa	RW
13	MTL	Rod Schutt	Sudbury	LW
14	NYI	Alex McKendry	Sudbury	W
15	WSH	Greg Carroll	Medicine Hat	C
16	BOS	Clayton Pachal	New Westminster	C/LW
17	PHI	Mark Suzor	Kingston	D
18	MTL	Bruce Baker	Ottawa	RW

OTHER NOTABLE SELECTIONS

#	Team	Player	From	Pos
19	PIT	Greg Malone	Oshawa	C
20	STL	Brian Sutter	Lethbridge	LW
22	DET	Reed Larson	Minnesota-Duluth	D
30	TOR	Randy Carlyle	Sudbury	D
45	CHI	Thomas Gradin	MoDo Ornskoldsvik	D
47	PIT	Morris Lukowich	Medicine Hat	LW
56	STL	Mike Liut	Bowling Green	G
64	ATL	Kent Nilsson	Djurgarden	C
68	NYI	Ken Morrow	Bowling Green	D
133	MTL	Ron Wilson	St. Catharines	C

1975

FIRST ROUND

#	Team	Player	From	Pos
1	PHI	Mel Bridgman	Victoria	C
2	K.C.	Barry Dean	Medicine Hat	LW
3	CAL	Ralph Klassen	Saskatoon	C
4	MIN	Bryan Maxwell	Medicine Hat	D
5	DET	Rick Lapointe	Victoria	D
6	TOR	Don Ashby	Calgary	C
7	CHI	Greg Vaydik	Medicine Hat	C
8	ATL	Richard Mulhern	Sherbrooke	D
9	MTL	Robin Sadler	Edmonton	D
10	VAN	Rick Blight	Brandon	RW
11	NYI	Pat Price	Saskatoon	D
12	NYR	Wayne Dillon	Toronto	C
13	PIT	Gord Laxton	New Westminster	G
14	BOS	Doug Halward	Peterborough	D
15	MTL	Pierre Mondou	Montreal	C
16	L.A.	Tim Young	Ottawa	C

OTHER NOTABLE SELECTIONS

#	Team	Player	From	Pos
17	BUF	Bob Sauve	Laval	G
21	CAL	Dennis Maruk	London	C
22	MTL	Brian Engblom	Wisconsin	D
24	TOR	Doug Jarvis	Peterborough	C
43	CHI	Mike O'Connell	Kingston	D
57	CAL	Greg Smith	Colorado College	D
80	ATL	Willi Plett	St. Catharines	RW
108	PHI	Paul Holmgren	U. of Minnesota	RW
210	L.A.	Dave Taylor	Clarkson	RW

1974

FIRST ROUND

#	Team	Player	From	Pos
1	WSH	Greg Joly	Regina	D
2	K.C.	Wilf Paiement	St. Catharines	RW
3	CAL	Rick Hampton	St. Catharines	LW/D
4	NYI	Clark Gillies	Regina	LW
5	MTL	Cam Connor	Flin Flon	RW
6	MIN	Doug Hicks	Flin Flon	D
7	MTL	Doug Risebrough	Kitchener	C
8	PIT	Pierre Larouche	Sorel	C
9	DET	Bill Lochead	Oshawa	LW
10	MTL	Rick Chartraw	Kitchener	D/RW
11	BUF	Lee Fogolin Jr.	Oshawa	D
12	MTL	Mario Tremblay	Montreal	RW
13	TOR	Jack Valiquette	Sault Ste. Marie	C
14	NYR	Dave Maloney	Kitchener	D
15	MTL	Gord McTavish	Sudbury	C
16	CHI	Grant Mulvey	Calgary	RW
17	CAL	Ron Chipperfield	Brandon	C
18	BOS	Don Larway	Swift Current	RW

OTHER NOTABLE SELECTIONS

#	Team	Player	From	Pos
22	NYI	Bryan Trottier	Swift Current	C
25	BOS	Mark Howe	Toronto	D
29	BUF	Danny Gare	Calgary	RW
31	TOR	Tiger Williams	Swift Current	LW
32	NYR	Ron Greschner	New Westminster	D
38	K.C.	Bob Bourne	Saskatoon	C
39	CAL	Charlie Simmer	Sault Ste. Marie	LW
52	CHI	Bob Murray	Cornwall	D
70	CHI	Terry Ruskowski	Swift Current	C
77	VAN	Mike Rogers	Calgary	C
85	TOR	Mike Palmateer	Toronto	G
125	PHI	Reggie Lemelin	Sherbrooke	G
199	MTL	Dave Lumley	New Hampshire	RW
214	NYI	Stefan Persson	Brynas Gavle	D

1973

FIRST ROUND

#	Team	Player	From	Pos
1	NYI	Denis Potvin	Ottawa	D
2	ATL	Tom Lysiak	Medicine Hat	C
3	VAN	Dennis Ververgaert	London	RW
4	TOR	Lanny McDonald	Medicine Hat	RW
5	STL	John Davidson	Calgary	G
6	BOS	Andre Savard	Quebec	C
7	PIT	Blaine Stoughton	Flin Flon	RW
8	MTL	Bob Gainey	Peterborough	LW
9	VAN	Bob Dailey	Toronto	D
10	TOR	Bob Neely	Peterborough	LW
11	DET	Terry Richardson	New Westminster	G
12	BUF	Morris Titanic	Sudbury	LW
13	CHI	Darcy Rota	Edmonton	LW
14	NYR	Rick Middleton	Oshawa	RW
15	TOR	Ian Turnbull	Ottawa	D
16	ATL	Vic Mercredi	New Westminster	C

OTHER NOTABLE SELECTIONS

#	Team	Player	From	Pos
21	ATL	Eric Vail	Sudbury	LW
27	PIT	Colin Campbell	Peterborough	D
30	NYR	Pat Hickey	Hamilton	LW
33	NYI	Dave Lewis	Saskatoon	D
49	NYI	Andre St. Laurent	Montreal	C
85	ATL	Ken Houston	Chatham Jr. B.	RW
130	CAL	Larry Patey	Braintree H.S.	C
134	PIT	Gord Lane	New Westminster	D
162	ATL	Greg Fox	U. of Michigan	D

1972

FIRST ROUND

#	Team	Player	From	Pos
1	NYI	Billy Harris	Toronto	RW
2	ATL	Jacques Richard	Quebec	LW
3	VAN	Don Lever	Niagara Falls	LW
4	MTL	Steve Shutt	Toronto	LW
5	BUF	Jim Schoenfeld	Niagara Falls	D
6	MTL	Michel Larocque	Ottawa	G
7	PHI	Bill Barber	Kitchener	LW
8	MTL	Dave Gardner	Toronto	C
9	STL	Wayne Merrick	Ottawa	C
10	NYR	Al Blanchard	Kitchener	LW
11	TOR	George Ferguson	Toronto	C
12	MIN	Jerry Byers	Kitchener	LW
13	CHI	Phil Russell	Edmonton	D
14	MTL	John Van Boxmeer	Guelph	D
15	NYR	Bob MacMillan	St. Catharines	RW
16	BOS	Mike Bloom	St. Catharines	LW

OTHER NOTABLE SELECTIONS

#	Team	Player	From	Pos
17	NYI	Lorne Henning	New Westminster	C
23	PHI	Tom Bladon	Edmonton	D
33	NYI	Bob Nystrom	Calgary	RW
39	PHI	Jimmy Watson	Calgary	D
55	PHI	Al MacAdam	University of PEI	RW
85	BUF	Peter McNab	U. of Denver	C
97	NYI	Richard Brodeur	Cornwall	G
139	TOR	Pat Boutette	Minnesota-Duluth	C/RW
144	NYI	Garry Howatt	Flin Flon	LW

1971

FIRST ROUND

#	Team	Player	From	Pos
1	MTL	Guy Lafleur	Quebec	RW
2	DET	Marcel Dionne	St. Catharines	C
3	VAN	Jocelyn Guevremont	Montreal	D
4	STL	Gene Carr	Flin Flon	C
5	BUF	Rick Martin	Montreal	LW
6	BOS	Ron Jones	Edmonton	D
7	MTL	Chuck Arnason	Flin Flon	RW
8	PHI	Larry Wright	Regina	C
9	PHI	Pierre Plante	Drummondville	RW
10	NYR	Steve Vickers	Toronto	LW
11	MTL	Murray Wilson	Ottawa	LW
12	CHI	Dan Spring	Edmonton	C
13	NYR	Steve Durbano	Toronto	D
14	BOS	Terry O'Reilly	Oshawa	RW

OTHER NOTABLE SELECTIONS

#	Team	Player	From	Pos
17	VAN	Bobby Lalonde	Montreal	C
19	BUF	Craig Ramsay	Peterborough	LW
20	MTL	Larry Robinson	Kitchener	D
22	TOR	Rick Kehoe	Hamilton	RW
33	BUF	Bill Hajt	Saskatoon	D
48	L.A.	Neil Komadoski	Winnipeg	D
55	NYR	Jerry Butler	Hamilton	RW

1970

FIRST ROUND

#	Team	Player	From	Pos
1	BUF	Gilbert Perreault	Montreal	C
2	VAN	Dale Tallon	Toronto	D
3	BOS	Reggie Leach	Flin Flon	RW
4	BOS	Rick MacLeish	Peterborough	C
5	MTL	Ray Martyniuk	Flin Flon	G
6	MTL	Chuck Lefley	Canadian National	LW
7	PIT	Greg Polis	Estevan	LW
8	TOR	Darryl Sittler	London	C
9	BOS	Ron Plumb	Peterborough	D
10	CAL	Chris Oddleifson	Winnipeg	C
11	NYR	Norm Gratton	Montreal	LW
12	DET	Serge Lajeunesse	Montreal	D/RW
13	BOS	Bob Stewart	Oshawa	D
14	CHI	Dan Maloney	London	LW

OTHER NOTABLE SELECTIONS

#	Team	Player	From	Pos
18	PHI	Bill Clement	Ottawa	C
20	MIN	Fred Barrett	Toronto	D
22	TOR	Errol Thompson	Charlottetown Sr.	LW
25	NYR	Mike Murphy	Toronto	RW
27	BOS	Dan Bouchard	London	G
32	PHI	Bob Kelly	Oshawa	LW
40	DET	Yvon Lambert	Drummondville	LW
59	L.A.	Billy Smith	Cornwall	G
70	CHI	Gilles Meloche	Verdun	G
88	OAK	Terry Murray	Ottawa	D
103	TOR	Ron Low	Dauphin Jr. A.	G

1969

FIRST ROUND

#	Team	Player	From	Pos
1	MTL	Rejean Houle	Montreal	W
2	MTL	Marc Tardif	Montreal	LW
3	BOS	Don Tannahill	Niagara Falls	LW
4	BOS	Frank Spring	Edmonton	RW
5	MIN	Dick Redmond	St. Catharines	D
6	PHI	Bob Currier	Cornwall	C
7	OAK	Tony Featherstone	Peterborough	RW
8	NYR	Andre Dupont	Montreal	D
9	TOR	Ernie Moser	Estevan	RW
10	DET	Jim Rutherford	Hamilton	G
11	BOS	Ivan Boldirev	Oshawa	C
12	NYR	Pierre Jarry	Ottawa	LW

OTHER NOTABLE SELECTIONS

#	Team	Player	From	Pos
13	CHI	J.P. Bordeleau	Montreal	RW
17	PHI	Bobby Clarke	Flin Flon	C
18	OAK	Ron Stackhouse	Peterborough	D
25	MIN	Gilles Gilbert	London	G
26	PIT	Michel Briere	Shawinigan	C
51	L.A.	Butch Goring	Dauphin Jr. A.	C
52	PHI	Dave Schultz	Sorel	LW
55	TOR	Brian Spencer	Swift Current	LW
64	PHI	Don Saleski	Regina	RW

NHL All-Stars

Active Players' All-Star Selection Records

	Total	First Team Selections		Second Team Selections	
GOALTENDER					
Martin Brodeur	7	(3)	2002-03; 2003-04; 2006-07.	(4)	1996-97; 1997-98; 2005-06; 2007-08.
Roberto Luongo	2	(0)		(2)	2003-04; 2006-07.
Miikka Kiprusoff	1	(1)	2005-06.	(0)	
Evgeni Nabokov	1	(1)	2007-08.	(0)	
Tim Thomas	1	(1)	2008-09.	(0)	
Ryan Miller	1	(1)	2009-10.	(0)	
Chris Osgood	1	(0)		(1)	1995-96.
Jose Theodore	1	(0)		(1)	2001-02.
Marty Turco	1	(0)		(1)	2002-03.
Steve Mason	1	(0)		(1)	2008-09.
Ilya Bryzgalov	1	(0)		(1)	2009-10.
DEFENSE					
Nicklas Lidstrom	11	(9)	1997-98; 1998-99; 99-2000; 2000-01; 2001-02; 2002-03; 2005-06; 2006-07; 2007-08.	(2)	2008-09; 2009-10.
Zdeno Chara	4	(2)	2003-04; 2008-09.	(2)	2005-06; 2007-08.
Chris Pronger	4	(1)	99-2000.	(3)	1997-98; 2003-04; 2006-07.
Mike Green	2	(2)	2008-09; 2009-10.	(0)	
Sergei Gonchar	2	(0)		(2)	2001-02; 2002-03.
Dan Boyle	2	(0)		(2)	2006-07; 2008-09.
Dion Phaneuf	1	(1)	2007-08.	(0)	
Duncan Keith	1	(1)	2009-10.	(0)	
Bryan McCabe	1	(0)		(1)	2003-04.
Sergei Zubov	1	(0)		(1)	2005-06.
Brian Campbell	1	(0)		(1)	2007-08.
Drew Doughty	1	(0)		(1)	2009-10.
CENTER					
Joe Thornton	3	(1)	2005-06.	(2)	2002-03; 2007-08.
Evgeni Malkin	2	(2)	2007-08; 2008-09	(0)	
Sidney Crosby	2	(1)	2006-07.	(1)	2009-10.
Henrik Sedin	1	(1)	2009-10.	(0)	
Mike Modano	1	(0)		(1)	99-2000.
Eric Staal	1	(0)		(1)	2005-06.
Vincent Lecavalier	1	(0)		(1)	2006-07.
Pavel Datsyuk	1	(0)		(1)	2008-09.
RIGHT WING					
Jarome Iginla	4	(3)	2001-02; 2007-08; 2008-09.	(1)	2003-04.
Teemu Selanne	4	(2)	1992-93; 1996-97.	(2)	1997-98; 1998-99.
Martin St. Louis	3	(1)	2003-04.	(2)	2006-07; 2009-10.
Todd Bertuzzi	1	(1)	2002-03.	(0)	
Dany Heatley	1	(1)	2006-07.	(0)	
Patrick Kane	1	(1)	2009-10	(0)	
Mark Recchi	1	(0)		(1)	1991-92.
Bill Guerin	1	(0)		(1)	2001-02.
Milan Hejduk	1	(0)		(1)	2002-03.
Daniel Alfredsson	1	(0)		(1)	2005-06.
Alex Kovalev	1	(0)		(1)	2007-08.
Marian Hossa	1	(0)		(1)	2008-09.
LEFT WING					
Alex Ovechkin	5	(5)	2005-06; 2006-07; 2007-08; 2008-09; 2009-10.	(0)	
Paul Kariya	5	(3)	1995-96; 1996-97; 1998-99.	(2)	99-2000; 2002-03.
Patrik Elias	1	(1)	2000-01.	(0)	
Ilya Kovalchuk	1	(0)		(1)	2003-04.
Dany Heatley	1	(0)		(1)	2005-06.
Thomas Vanek	1	(0)		(1)	2006-07.
Henrik Zetterberg	1	(0)		(1)	2007-08.
Zach Parise	1	(0)		(1)	2008-09.
Daniel Sedin	1	(0)		(1)	2009-10.

Leading NHL All-Stars 1930-31 to 2009-10

Player	Pos.	Team(s)	Total Selections	First Team Selections	Second Team Selections	NHL Seasons
Gordie Howe	RW	Detroit	21	12	9	26
Raymond Bourque	D	Bos., Col.	19	13	6	22
Wayne Gretzky	C	Edm., L.A., NYR	15	8	7	20
Maurice Richard	RW	Montreal	14	8	6	18
Bobby Hull	LW	Chicago	12	10	2	16
Doug Harvey	D	Mtl., NYR	11	10	1	19
* Nicklas Lidstrom	D	Detroit	11	9	2	18
Glenn Hall	G	Det., Chi., St.L.	11	7	4	18
Jean Beliveau	C	Montreal	10	6	4	20
Earl Seibert	D	NYR, Chi.	10	4	6	15
Bobby Orr	D	Boston	9	8	1	12
Ted Lindsay	LW	Detroit	9	8	1	17
Mario Lemieux	C	Pittsburgh	9	5	4	17
Frank Mahovlich	LW	Tor., Det., Mtl.	9	3	6	18
Eddie Shore	D	Boston	8	7	1	14
Jaromir Jagr	RW	Pit., NYR	8	7	1	17
Phil Esposito	C	Boston	8	6	2	18
Red Kelly	D	Detroit	8	6	2	20
Stan Mikita	C	Chicago	8	6	2	22
Mike Bossy	RW	NY Islanders	8	5	3	10
Pierre Pilote	D	Chicago	8	5	3	14
Luc Robitaille	LW	Los Angeles	8	5	3	19
Paul Coffey	D	Edm., Pit., Det.	8	4	4	21
Frank Brimsek	G	Boston	8	2	6	10
Denis Potvin	D	NY Islanders	7	5	2	15
Brad Park	D	NYR, Bos.	7	5	2	17
Chris Chelios	D	Mtl., Chi., Det.	7	5	2	25
Al MacInnis	D	Cgy., St.L.	7	4	3	23
Jacques Plante	G	Mtl., Tor.	7	3	4	18
Bill Gadsby	D	Chi., NYR, Det.	7	3	4	20
Terry Sawchuk	G	Detroit	7	3	4	21
* Martin Brodeur	G	New Jersey	7	3	4	17
Bill Durnan	G	Montreal	6	6	0	7
Dominik Hasek	G	Buffalo	6	6	0	15
Guy Lafleur	RW	Montreal	6	6	0	17
Ken Dryden	G	Montreal	6	5	1	8
Patrick Roy	G	Mtl., Col.	6	4	2	19
Dit Clapper	RW/D	Boston	6	3	3	20
Larry Robinson	D	Montreal	6	3	3	20
Tim Horton	D	Toronto	6	3	3	24
Borje Salming	D	Toronto	6	1	5	17
* Alex Ovechkin	LW	Washington	5	5	0	5
Bill Cowley	C	Boston	5	4	1	13
Busher Jackson	LW	Toronto	5	4	1	15
Mark Messier	LW/C	Edm., NYR	5	4	1	25
Charlie Conacher	RW	Toronto	5	3	2	12
Jack Stewart	D	Detroit	5	3	2	12
Toe Blake	LW	Montreal	5	3	2	14
Elmer Lach	C	Montreal	5	3	2	14
Bill Quackenbush	D	Det., Bos.	5	3	2	14
Michel Goulet	LW	Quebec	5	3	2	15
* Paul Kariya	LW	Anaheim	5	3	2	15
Tony Esposito	G	Chicago	5	3	2	16
Ken Reardon	D	Montreal	5	2	3	7
Syl Apps	C	Toronto	5	2	3	10
John LeClair	LW	Mtl., Phi.	5	2	3	16
Ed Giacomin	G	NY Rangers	5	2	3	13
Brian Leetch	D	NY Rangers	5	2	3	17
Jari Kurri	RW	Edmonton	5	2	3	17
Scott Stevens	D	Wsh., N.J.	5	2	3	21

* Active

Position Leaders in All-Star Selections

Position	Player	Total	First Team	Second Team	NHL Seasons	Career
GOALTENDER	Glenn Hall	11	7	4	18	1952-53 to 1970-71
	Frank Brimsek	8	2	6	10	1938-39 to 1949-50
	* Martin Brodeur	7	3	4	17	1991-92 to 2009-10
	Jacques Plante	7	3	4	18	1952-53 to 1972-73
	Terry Sawchuk	7	3	4	21	1949-50 to 1969-70
	Bill Durnan	6	6	0	7	1943-44 to 1949-50
	Dominik Hasek	6	6	0	15	1990-91 to 2007-08
	Ken Dryden	6	5	1	8	1970-71 to 1978-79
	Patrick Roy	6	4	2	19	1984-85 to 2002-03
DEFENSE	Raymond Bourque	19	13	6	22	1979-80 to 2000-01
	Doug Harvey	11	10	1	20	1947-48 to 1968-69
	* Nicklas Lidstrom	11	9	2	18	1991-92 to 2009-10
	Earl Seibert	10	4	6	15	1931-32 to 1945-46
	Bobby Orr	9	8	1	12	1966-67 to 1978-79
	Eddie Shore	8	7	1	14	1926-27 to 1939-40
	Red Kelly	8	6	2	20	1947-48 to 1966-67
	Pierre Pilote	8	5	3	14	1955-56 to 1968-69
	Paul Coffey	8	4	4	21	1980-81 to 2000-01
CENTER	Wayne Gretzky	15	8	7	20	1979-80 to 1998-99
	Jean Beliveau	10	6	4	20	1950-51 to 1970-71
	Mario Lemieux	9	5	4	18	1984-85 to 2005-06
	Phil Esposito	8	6	2	18	1963-64 to 1980-81
	Stan Mikita	8	6	2	22	1958-59 to 1979-80
RIGHT WING	Gordie Howe	21	12	9	26	1946-47 to 1979-80
	Maurice Richard	14	8	6	18	1942-43 to 1959-60
	Jaromir Jagr	8	7	1	17	1990-91 to 2007-08
	Mike Bossy	8	5	3	10	1977-78 to 1986-87
	Guy Lafleur	6	6	0	17	1971-72 to 1990-91
LEFT WING	Bobby Hull	12	10	2	16	1957-58 to 1979-80
	Ted Lindsay	9	8	1	17	1944-45 to 1964-65
	Frank Mahovlich	9	3	6	18	1956-57 to 1973-74
	Luc Robitaille	8	5	3	19	1986-87 to 2005-06

* active player

All-Star Teams

1930-2010

Voting for the NHL All-Star Team is conducted among the representatives of the Professional Hockey Writers' Association at the end of the season.

Following is a list of the First and Second All-Star Teams since their inception in 1930-31.

2009-10

First Team	Pos	Second Team
Ryan Miller, Buf.	G	Ilya Bryzgalov, Phx.
Duncan Keith, Chi.	D	Drew Doughty, L.A..
Mike Green, Wsh.	D	Nicklas Lidstrom, Det.
Henrik Sedin, Van.	C	Sidney Crosby, Pit.
Patrick Kane, Chi.	RW	Martin St. Louis, T.B.
Alex Ovechkin, Wsh.	LW	Daniel Sedin, Van.

2008-09

First Team	Pos	Second Team
Tim Thomas, Bos.	G	Steve Mason, CBJ
Zdeno Chara, Bos	D	Nicklas Lidstrom, Det.
Mike Green, Wsh.	D	Dan Boyle, S.J.
Evgeni Malkin, Pit.	C	Pavel Datsyuk, Det.
Jarome Iginla, Cgy.	RW	Marian Hossa, Det.
Alex Ovechkin, Wsh.	LW	Zach Parise, N.J.

2007-08

First Team	Pos	Second Team
Evgeni Nabokov, S.J.	G	Martin Brodeur, N.J.
Nicklas Lidstrom, Det.	D	Brian Campbell, Buf., S.J.
Dion Phaneuf, Cgy.	D	Zdeno Chara, Bos.
Evgeni Malkin, Pit.	C	Joe Thornton, S.J.
Jarome Iginla, Cgy.	RW	Alex Kovalev, Mtl.
Alex Ovechkin, Wsh.	LW	Henrik Zetterberg, Det.

2006-07

First Team	Pos	Second Team
Martin Brodeur, N.J.	G	Roberto Luongo, Van.
Nicklas Lidstrom, Det.	D	Chris Pronger, Ana.
Scott Niedermayer, Ana.	D	Dan Boyle, T.B.
Sidney Crosby, Pit.	C	Vincent Lecavalier, T.B.
Dany Heatley, Ott.	RW	Martin St. Louis, T.B.
Alex Ovechkin, Wsh.	LW	Thomas Vanek, Buf.

2005-06

First Team	Pos	Second Team
Miikka Kiprusoff, Cgy.	G	Martin Brodeur, N.J.
Nicklas Lidstrom, Det.	D	Zdeno Chara, Ott.
Scott Niedermayer, Ana.	D	Sergei Zubov, Dal.
Joe Thornton, Bos., S.J.	C	Eric Staal, Car.
Jaromir Jagr, NYR	RW	Daniel Alfredsson, Ott.
Alex Ovechkin, Wsh.	LW	Dany Heatley, Ott.

2004-05

Season Cancelled

2003-04

First Team	Pos	Second Team
Martin Brodeur, N.J.	G	Roberto Luongo, Fla.
Scott Niedermayer, N.J.	D	Chris Pronger, St.L.
Zdeno Chara, Ott.	D	Bryan McCabe, Tor.
Joe Sakic, Col.	C	Mats Sundin, Tor.
Martin St. Louis, T.B.	RW	Jarome Iginla, Cgy.
Markus Naslund, Van.	LW	Ilya Kovalchuk, Atl.

2002-03

First Team	Pos	Second Team
Martin Brodeur, N.J.	G	Marty Turco, Dal.
Al MacInnis, St.L.	D	Sergei Gonchar, Wsh.
Nicklas Lidstrom, Det.	D	Derian Hatcher, Dal.
Peter Forsberg, Col.	C	Joe Thornton, Bos.
Todd Bertuzzi, Van.	RW	Milan Hejduk, Col.
Markus Naslund, Van.	LW	Paul Kariya, Ana.

2001-02

First Team	Pos	Second Team
Patrick Roy, Col.	G	Jose Theodore, Mtl.
Nicklas Lidstrom, Det.	D	Rob Blake, Col.
Chris Chelios, Det.	D	Sergei Gonchar, Wsh.
Joe Sakic, Col.	C	Mats Sundin, Tor.
Jarome Iginla, Cgy.	RW	Bill Guerin, Bos.
Markus Naslund, Van.	LW	Brendan Shanahan, Det.

2000-01

First Team	Pos	Second Team
Dominik Hasek, Buf.	G	Roman Cechmanek, Phi.
Nicklas Lidstrom, Det.	D	Rob Blake, L.A., Col.
Raymond Bourque, Col.	D	Scott Stevens, N.J.
Joe Sakic, Col.	C	Mario Lemieux, Pit.
Jaromir Jagr, Pit.	RW	Pavel Bure, Fla.
Patrik Elias, N.J.	LW	Luc Robitaille, L.A.

1999-2000

First Team	Pos	Second Team
Olaf Kolzig, Wsh.	G	Roman Turek, St.L.
Chris Pronger, St.L.	D	Rob Blake, L.A.
Nicklas Lidstrom, Det.	D	Eric Desjardins, Phi.
Steve Yzerman, Det.	C	Mike Modano, Dal.
Jaromir Jagr, Pit.	RW	Pavel Bure, Fla.
Brendan Shanahan, Det.	LW	Paul Kariya, Ana.

1998-99

First Team	Pos	Second Team
Dominik Hasek, Buf.	G	Byron Dafoe, Bos.
Al MacInnis, St.L.	D	Raymond Bourque, Bos.
Nicklas Lidstrom, Det.	D	Eric Desjardins, Phi.
Peter Forsberg, Col.	C	Alexei Yashin, Ott.
Jaromir Jagr, Pit.	RW	Teemu Selanne, Ana.
Paul Kariya, Ana.	LW	John LeClair, Phi.

1997-98

First Team	Pos	Second Team
Dominik Hasek, Buf.	G	Martin Brodeur, N.J.
Nicklas Lidstrom, Det.	D	Chris Pronger, St.L.
Rob Blake, L.A.	D	Scott Niedermayer, N.J.
Peter Forsberg, Col.	C	Wayne Gretzky, NYR
Jaromir Jagr, Pit.	RW	Teemu Selanne, Ana.
John LeClair, Phi.	LW	Keith Tkachuk, Phx.

1996-97

First Team	Pos	Second Team
Dominik Hasek, Buf.	G	Martin Brodeur, N.J.
Brian Leetch, NYR	D	Chris Chelios, Chi.
Sandis Ozolinsh, Col.	D	Scott Stevens, N.J.
Mario Lemieux, Pit.	C	Wayne Gretzky, NYR
Teemu Selanne, Ana.	RW	Jaromir Jagr, Pit.
Paul Kariya, Ana.	LW	John LeClair, Phi.

1995-96

First Team	Pos	Second Team
Jim Carey, Wsh.	G	Chris Osgood, Det.
Chris Chelios, Chi.	D	V. Konstantinov, Det.
Raymond Bourque, Bos.	D	Brian Leetch, NYR
Mario Lemieux, Pit.	C	Eric Lindros, Phi.
Jaromir Jagr, Pit.	RW	Alexander Mogilny, Van.
Paul Kariya, Ana.	LW	John LeClair, Phi.

1994-95

First Team	Pos	Second Team
Dominik Hasek, Buf.	G	Ed Belfour, Chi.
Paul Coffey, Det.	D	Raymond Bourque, Bos.
Chris Chelios, Chi.	D	Larry Murphy, Pit.
Eric Lindros, Phi.	C	Alexei Zhamnov, Wpg.
Jaromir Jagr, Pit.	RW	Theoren Fleury, Cgy.
John LeClair, Mtl., Phi.	LW	Keith Tkachuk, Wpg.

1993-94

First Team	Pos	Second Team
Dominik Hasek, Buf.	G	John Vanbiesbrouck, Fla.
Raymond Bourque, Bos.	D	Al MacInnis, Cgy.
Scott Stevens, N.J.	D	Brian Leetch, NYR
Sergei Fedorov, Det.	C	Wayne Gretzky, L.A.
Pavel Bure, Van.	RW	Cam Neely, Bos.
Brendan Shanahan, St.L.	LW	Adam Graves, NYR

1992-93

First Team	Pos	Second Team
Ed Belfour, Chi.	G	Tom Barrasso, Pit.
Chris Chelios, Chi.	D	Larry Murphy, Pit.
Raymond Bourque, Bos.	D	Al Iafrate, Wsh.
Mario Lemieux, Pit.	C	Pat LaFontaine, Buf.
Teemu Selanne, Wpg.	RW	Alexander Mogilny, Buf.
Luc Robitaille, L.A.	LW	Kevin Stevens, Pit.

1991-92

First Team	Pos	Second Team
Patrick Roy, Mtl.	G	Kirk McLean, Van.
Brian Leetch, NYR	D	Phil Housley, Wpg.
Raymond Bourque, Bos.	D	Scott Stevens, N.J.
Mark Messier, NYR	C	Mario Lemieux, Pit.
Brett Hull, St.L.	RW	Mark Recchi, Pit., Phi.
Kevin Stevens, Pit.	LW	Luc Robitaille, L.A.

1990-91

First Team	Pos	Second Team
Ed Belfour, Chi.	G	Patrick Roy, Mtl.
Raymond Bourque, Bos.	D	Chris Chelios, Chi.
Al MacInnis, Cgy.	D	Brian Leetch, NYR
Wayne Gretzky, L.A.	C	Adam Oates, St.L.
Brett Hull, St.L.	RW	Cam Neely, Bos.
Luc Robitaille, L.A.	LW	Kevin Stevens, Pit.

1989-90

First Team	Pos	Second Team
Patrick Roy, Mtl.	G	Daren Puppa, Buf.
Raymond Bourque, Bos.	D	Paul Coffey, Pit.
Al MacInnis, Cgy.	D	Doug Wilson, Chi.
Mark Messier, Edm.	C	Wayne Gretzky, L.A.
Brett Hull, St.L.	RW	Cam Neely, Bos.
Luc Robitaille, L.A.	LW	Brian Bellows, Min.

1988-89

First Team	Pos	Second Team
Patrick Roy, Mtl.	G	Mike Vernon, Cgy.
Chris Chelios, Mtl.	D	Al MacInnis, Cgy.
Paul Coffey, Pit.	D	Raymond Bourque, Bos.
Mario Lemieux, Pit.	C	Wayne Gretzky, L.A.
Joe Mullen, Cgy.	RW	Jari Kurri, Edm.
Luc Robitaille, L.A.	LW	Gerard Gallant, Det.

1987-88

First Team	Pos	Second Team
Grant Fuhr, Edm.	G	Patrick Roy, Mtl.
Raymond Bourque, Bos.	D	Gary Suter, Cgy.
Scott Stevens, Wsh.	D	Brad McCrimmon, Cgy.
Mario Lemieux, Pit.	C	Wayne Gretzky, Edm.
Hakan Loob, Cgy.	RW	Cam Neely, Bos.
Luc Robitaille, L.A.	LW	Michel Goulet, Que.

1986-87

First Team	Pos	Second Team
Ron Hextall, Phi.	G	Mike Liut, Hfd.
Raymond Bourque, Bos.	D	Larry Murphy, Wsh.
Mark Howe, Phi.	D	Al MacInnis, Cgy.
Wayne Gretzky, Edm.	C	Mario Lemieux, Pit.
Jari Kurri, Edm.	RW	Tim Kerr, Phi.
Michel Goulet, Que.	LW	Luc Robitaille, L.A.

1985-86

First Team	Pos	Second Team
John Vanbiesbrouck, NYR	G	Bob Froese, Phi.
Paul Coffey, Edm.	D	Larry Robinson, Mtl.
Mark Howe, Phi.	D	Raymond Bourque, Bos.
Wayne Gretzky, Edm.	C	Mario Lemieux, Pit.
Mike Bossy, NYI	RW	Jari Kurri, Edm.
Michel Goulet, Que.	LW	Mats Naslund, Mtl.

1984-85

First Team	Pos	Second Team
Pelle Lindbergh, Phi.	G	Tom Barrasso, Buf.
Paul Coffey, Edm.	D	Rod Langway, Wsh.
Raymond Bourque, Bos.	D	Doug Wilson, Chi.
Wayne Gretzky, Edm.	C	Dale Hawerchuk, Wpg.
Jari Kurri, Edm.	RW	Mike Bossy, NYI
John Ogrodnick, Det.	LW	John Tonelli, NYI

1983-84

First Team	Pos	Second Team
Tom Barrasso, Buf.	G	Pat Riggin, Wsh.
Rod Langway, Wsh.	D	Paul Coffey, Edm.
Raymond Bourque, Bos.	D	Denis Potvin, NYI
Wayne Gretzky, Edm.	C	Bryan Trottier, NYI
Mike Bossy, NYI	RW	Jari Kurri, Edm.
Michel Goulet, Que.	LW	Mark Messier, Edm.

1982-83

First Team	Pos	Second Team
Pete Peeters, Bos.	G	Roland Melanson, NYI
Mark Howe, Phi.	D	Raymond Bourque, Bos.
Rod Langway, Wsh.	D	Paul Coffey, Edm.
Wayne Gretzky, Edm.	C	Denis Savard, Chi.
Mike Bossy, NYI	RW	Lanny McDonald, Cgy.
Mark Messier, Edm.	LW	Michel Goulet, Que.

1981-82

First Team	Pos	Second Team
Billy Smith, NYI	G	Grant Fuhr, Edm.
Doug Wilson, Chi.	D	Paul Coffey, Edm.
Raymond Bourque, Bos.	D	Brian Engblom, Mtl.
Wayne Gretzky, Edm.	C	Bryan Trottier, NYI
Mike Bossy, NYI	RW	Rick Middleton, Bos.
Mark Messier, Edm.	LW	John Tonelli, NYI

1980-81

First Team	Pos	Second Team
Mike Liut, St.L.	G	Mario Lessard, L.A.
Denis Potvin, NYI	D	Larry Robinson, Mtl.
Randy Carlyle, Pit.	D	Raymond Bourque, Bos.
Wayne Gretzky, Edm.	C	Marcel Dionne, L.A.
Mike Bossy, NYI	RW	Dave Taylor, L.A.
Charlie Simmer, L.A.	LW	Bill Barber, Phi.

1979-80

First Team	Pos	Second Team
Tony Esposito, Chi.	G	Don Edwards, Buf.
Larry Robinson, Mtl.	D	Borje Salming, Tor.
Raymond Bourque, Bos.	D	Jim Schoenfeld, Buf.
Marcel Dionne, L.A.	C	Wayne Gretzky, Edm.
Guy Lafleur, Mtl.	RW	Danny Gare, Buf.
Charlie Simmer, L.A.	LW	Steve Shutt, Mtl.

1978-79

First Team	Pos	Second Team
Ken Dryden, Mtl.	G	Glenn Resch, NYI
Denis Potvin, NYI	D	Borje Salming, Tor.
Larry Robinson, Mtl.	D	Serge Savard, Mtl.
Bryan Trottier, NYI	C	Marcel Dionne, L.A.
Guy Lafleur, Mtl.	RW	Mike Bossy, NYI
Clark Gillies, NYI	LW	Bill Barber, Phi.

1977-78

First Team	Pos	Second Team
Ken Dryden, Mtl.	G	Don Edwards, Buf.
Denis Potvin, NYI	D	Larry Robinson, Mtl.
Brad Park, Bos.	D	Borje Salming, Tor.
Bryan Trottier, NYI	C	Darryl Sittler, Tor.
Guy Lafleur, Mtl.	RW	Mike Bossy, NYI
Clark Gillies, NYI	LW	Steve Shutt, Mtl.

1976-77

First Team	Pos	Second Team
Ken Dryden, Mtl.	G	Rogie Vachon, L.A.
Larry Robinson, Mtl.	D	Denis Potvin, NYI
Borje Salming, Tor.	D	Guy Lapointe, Mtl.
Marcel Dionne, L.A.	C	Gilbert Perreault, Buf.
Guy Lafleur, Mtl.	RW	Lanny McDonald, Tor.
Steve Shutt, Mtl.	LW	Rick Martin, Buf.

1975-76

First Team	Pos	Second Team
Ken Dryden, Mtl.	G	Glenn Resch, NYI
Denis Potvin, NYI	D	Borje Salming, Tor.
Brad Park, Bos.	D	Guy Lapointe, Mtl.
Bobby Clarke, Phi.	C	Gilbert Perreault, Buf.
Guy Lafleur, Mtl.	RW	Reggie Leach, Phi.
Bill Barber, Phi.	LW	Rick Martin, Buf.

1974-75

First Team	Pos	Second Team
Bernie Parent, Phi.	G	Rogie Vachon, L.A.
Bobby Orr, Bos.	D	Guy Lapointe, Mtl.
Denis Potvin, NYI	D	Borje Salming, Tor.
Bobby Clarke, Phi.	C	Phil Esposito, Bos.
Guy Lafleur, Mtl.	RW	René Robert, Buf.
Rick Martin, Buf.	LW	Steve Vickers, NYR

1973-74

First Team	Pos	Second Team
Bernie Parent, Phi.	G	Tony Esposito, Chi.
Bobby Orr, Bos.	D	Bill White, Chi.
Brad Park, NYR	D	Barry Ashbee, Phi.
Phil Esposito, Bos.	C	Bobby Clarke, Phi.
Ken Hodge, Bos.	RW	Mickey Redmond, Det.
Rick Martin, Buf.	LW	Wayne Cashman, Bos.

1972-73

First Team	Pos	Second Team
Ken Dryden, Mtl.	G	Tony Esposito, Chi.
Bobby Orr, Bos.	D	Brad Park, NYR
Guy Lapointe, Mtl.	D	Bill White, Chi.
Phil Esposito, Bos.	C	Bobby Clarke, Phi.
Mickey Redmond, Det.	RW	Yvan Cournoyer, Mtl.
Frank Mahovlich, Mtl.	LW	Dennis Hull, Chi.

1971-72

First Team	Pos	Second Team
Tony Esposito, Chi.	G	Ken Dryden, Mtl.
Bobby Orr, Bos.	D	Bill White, Chi.
Brad Park, NYR	D	Pat Stapleton, Chi.
Phil Esposito, Bos.	C	Jean Ratelle, NYR
Rod Gilbert, NYR	RW	Yvan Cournoyer, Mtl.
Bobby Hull, Chi.	LW	Vic Hadfield, NYR

1970-71

First Team	Pos	Second Team
Ed Giacomin, NYR	G	Jacques Plante, Tor.
Bobby Orr, Bos.	D	Brad Park, NYR
J.C. Tremblay, Mtl.	D	Pat Stapleton, Chi.
Phil Esposito, Bos.	C	Dave Keon, Tor.
Ken Hodge, Bos.	RW	Yvan Cournoyer, Mtl.
John Bucyk, Bos.	LW	Bobby Hull, Chi.

1969-70

First Team	Pos	Second Team
Tony Esposito, Chi.	G	Ed Giacomin, NYR
Bobby Orr, Bos.	D	Carl Brewer, Det.
Brad Park, NYR	D	Jacques Laperriere, Mtl.
Phil Esposito, Bos.	C	Stan Mikita, Chi.
Gordie Howe, Det.	RW	John McKenzie, Bos.
Bobby Hull, Chi.	LW	Frank Mahovlich, Det.

1968-69

First Team	Pos	Second Team
Glenn Hall, St.L.	G	Ed Giacomin, NYR
Bobby Orr, Bos.	D	Ted Green, Bos.
Tim Horton, Tor.	D	Ted Harris, Mtl.
Phil Esposito, Bos.	C	Jean Béliveau, Mtl.
Gordie Howe, Det.	RW	Yvan Cournoyer, Mtl.
Bobby Hull, Chi.	LW	Frank Mahovlich, Det.

1967-68

First Team	Pos	Second Team
Gump Worsley, Mtl.	G	Ed Giacomin, NYR
Bobby Orr, Bos.	D	J.C. Tremblay, Mtl.
Tim Horton, Tor.	D	Jim Neilson, NYR
Stan Mikita, Chi.	C	Phil Esposito, Bos.
Gordie Howe, Det.	RW	Rod Gilbert, NYR
Bobby Hull, Chi.	LW	John Bucyk, Bos.

1966-67

First Team	Pos	Second Team
Ed Giacomin, NYR	G	Glenn Hall, Chi.
Pierre Pilote, Chi.	D	Tim Horton, Tor.
Harry Howell, NYR	D	Bobby Orr, Bos.
Stan Mikita, Chi.	C	Norm Ullman, Det.
Kenny Wharram, Chi.	RW	Gordie Howe, Det.
Bobby Hull, Chi.	LW	Don Marshall, NYR

1965-66

First Team	Pos	Second Team
Glenn Hall, Chi.	G	Gump Worsley, Mtl.
Jacques Laperriere, Mtl.	D	Allan Stanley, Tor.
Pierre Pilote, Chi.	D	Pat Stapleton, Chi.
Stan Mikita, Chi.	C	Jean Béliveau, Mtl.
Gordie Howe, Det.	RW	Bobby Rousseau, Mtl.
Bobby Hull, Chi.	LW	Frank Mahovlich, Tor.

1964-65

First Team	Pos	Second Team
Roger Crozier, Det.	G	Charlie Hodge, Mtl.
Pierre Pilote, Chi.	D	Bill Gadsby, Det.
Jacques Laperriere, Mtl.	D	Carl Brewer, Tor.
Norm Ullman, Det.	C	Stan Mikita, Chi.
Claude Provost, Mtl.	RW	Gordie Howe, Det.
Bobby Hull, Chi.	LW	Frank Mahovlich, Tor.

1963-64

First Team	Pos	Second Team
Glenn Hall, Chi.	G	Charlie Hodge, Mtl.
Pierre Pilote, Chi.	D	Moose Vasko, Chi.
Tim Horton, Tor.	D	Jacques Laperriere, Mtl.
Stan Mikita, Chi.	C	Jean Béliveau, Mtl.
Kenny Wharram, Chi.	RW	Gordie Howe, Det.
Bobby Hull, Chi.	LW	Frank Mahovlich, Tor.

1962-63

First Team	Pos	Second Team
Glenn Hall, Chi.	G	Terry Sawchuk, Det.
Pierre Pilote, Chi.	D	Tim Horton, Tor.
Carl Brewer, Tor.	D	Moose Vasko, Chi.
Stan Mikita, Chi.	C	Henri Richard, Mtl.
Gordie Howe, Det.	RW	Andy Bathgate, NYR
Frank Mahovlich, Tor.	LW	Bobby Hull, Chi.

1961-62

First Team	Pos	Second Team
Jacques Plante, Mtl.	G	Glenn Hall, Chi.
Doug Harvey, NYR	D	Carl Brewer, Tor.
Jean-Guy Talbot, Mtl.	D	Pierre Pilote, Chi.
Stan Mikita, Chi.	C	Dave Keon, Tor.
Andy Bathgate, NYR	RW	Gordie Howe, Det.
Bobby Hull, Chi.	LW	Frank Mahovlich, Tor.

1960-61

First Team	Pos	Second Team
Johnny Bower, Tor.	G	Glenn Hall, Chi.
Doug Harvey, Mtl.	D	Allan Stanley, Tor.
Marcel Pronovost, Det.	D	Pierre Pilote, Chi.
Jean Béliveau, Mtl.	C	Henri Richard, Mtl.
Bernie Geoffrion, Mtl.	RW	Gordie Howe, Det.
Frank Mahovlich, Tor.	LW	Dickie Moore, Mtl.

1959-60

First Team	Pos	Second Team
Glenn Hall, Chi.	G	Jacques Plante, Mtl.
Doug Harvey, Mtl.	D	Allan Stanley, Tor.
Marcel Pronovost, Det.	D	Pierre Pilote, Chi.
Jean Béliveau, Mtl.	C	Bronco Horvath, Bos.
Gordie Howe, Det.	RW	Bernie Geoffrion, Mtl.
Bobby Hull, Chi.	LW	Dean Prentice, NYR

1958-59

First Team	Pos	Second Team
Jacques Plante, Mtl.	G	Terry Sawchuk, Det.
Tom Johnson, Mtl.	D	Marcel Pronovost, Det.
Bill Gadsby, NYR	D	Doug Harvey, Mtl.
Jean Béliveau, Mtl.	C	Henri Richard, Mtl.
Andy Bathgate, NYR	RW	Gordie Howe, Det.
Dickie Moore, Mtl.	LW	Alex Delvecchio, Det.

1957-58

First Team	Pos	Second Team
Glenn Hall, Chi.	G	Jacques Plante, Mtl.
Doug Harvey, Mtl.	D	Fern Flaman, Bos.
Bill Gadsby, NYR	D	Marcel Pronovost, Det.
Henri Richard, Mtl.	C	Jean Béliveau, Mtl.
Gordie Howe, Det.	RW	Andy Bathgate, NYR
Dickie Moore, Mtl.	LW	Camille Henry, NYR

1956-57

First Team	Pos	Second Team
Glenn Hall, Det.	G	Jacques Plante, Mtl.
Doug Harvey, Mtl.	D	Fern Flaman, Bos.
Red Kelly, Det.	D	Bill Gadsby, NYR
Jean Béliveau, Mtl.	C	Ed Litzenberger, Chi.
Gordie Howe, Det.	RW	Maurice Richard, Mtl.
Ted Lindsay, Det.	LW	Real Chevrefils, Bos.

1955-56

First Team		Second Team
Jacques Plante, Mtl.	G	Glenn Hall, Det.
Doug Harvey, Mtl.	D	Red Kelly, Det.
Bill Gadsby, NYR	D	Tom Johnson, Mtl.
Jean Béliveau, Mtl.	C	Tod Sloan, Tor.
Maurice Richard, Mtl.	RW	Gordie Howe, Det.
Ted Lindsay, Det.	LW	Bert Olmstead, Mtl.

1954-55

First Team		Second Team
Harry Lumley, Tor.	G	Terry Sawchuk, Det.
Doug Harvey, Mtl.	D	Bob Goldham, Det.
Red Kelly, Det.	D	Fern Flaman, Bos.
Jean Béliveau, Mtl.	C	Ken Mosdell, Mtl.
Maurice Richard, Mtl.	RW	Bernie Geoffrion, Mtl.
Sid Smith, Tor.	LW	Danny Lewicki, NYR

1953-54

First Team		Second Team
Harry Lumley, Tor.	G	Terry Sawchuk, Det.
Red Kelly, Det.	D	Bill Gadsby, Chi.
Doug Harvey, Mtl.	D	Tim Horton, Tor.
Ken Mosdell, Mtl.	C	Ted Kennedy, Tor.
Gordie Howe, Det.	RW	Maurice Richard, Mtl.
Ted Lindsay, Det.	LW	Ed Sandford, Bos.

1952-53

First Team		Second Team
Terry Sawchuk, Det.	G	Gerry McNeil, Mtl.
Red Kelly, Det.	D	Bill Quackenbush, Bos.
Doug Harvey, Mtl.	D	Bill Gadsby, Chi.
Fleming MacKell, Bos.	C	Alex Delvecchio, Det.
Gordie Howe, Det.	RW	Maurice Richard, Mtl.
Ted Lindsay, Det.	LW	Bert Olmstead, Mtl.

1951-52

First Team		Second Team
Terry Sawchuk, Det.	G	Jim Henry, Bos.
Red Kelly, Det.	D	Hy Buller, NYR
Doug Harvey, Mtl.	D	Jimmy Thomson, Tor.
Elmer Lach, Mtl.	C	Milt Schmidt, Bos.
Gordie Howe, Det.	RW	Maurice Richard, Mtl.
Ted Lindsay, Det.	LW	Sid Smith, Tor.

1950-51

First Team		Second Team
Terry Sawchuk, Det.	G	Chuck Rayner, NYR
Red Kelly, Det.	D	Jimmy Thomson, Tor.
Bill Quackenbush, Bos.	D	Leo Reise Jr., Det.
Milt Schmidt, Bos.	C	Sid Abel, Det.
		Ted Kennedy, Tor. (tied)
Gordie Howe, Det.	RW	Maurice Richard, Mtl.
Ted Lindsay, Det.	LW	Sid Smith, Tor.

1949-50

First Team		Second Team
Bill Durnan, Mtl.	G	Chuck Rayner, NYR
Gus Mortson, Tor.	D	Leo Reise Jr., Det.
Ken Reardon, Mtl.	D	Red Kelly, Det.
Sid Abel, Det.	C	Ted Kennedy, Tor.
Maurice Richard, Mtl.	RW	Gordie Howe, Det.
Ted Lindsay, Det.	LW	Tony Leswick, NYR

1948-49

First Team		Second Team
Bill Durnan, Mtl.	G	Chuck Rayner, NYR
Bill Quackenbush, Det.	D	Glen Harmon, Mtl.
Jack Stewart, Det.	D	Ken Reardon, Mtl.
Sid Abel, Det.	C	Doug Bentley, Chi.
Maurice Richard, Mtl.	RW	Gordie Howe, Det.
Roy Conacher, Chi.	LW	Ted Lindsay, Det.

1947-48

First Team		Second Team
Turk Broda, Tor.	G	Frank Brimsek, Bos.
Bill Quackenbush, Det.	D	Ken Reardon, Mtl.
Jack Stewart, Det.	D	Neil Colville, NYR
Elmer Lach, Mtl.	C	Buddy O'Connor, NYR
Maurice Richard, Mtl.	RW	Bud Poile, Chi.
Ted Lindsay, Det.	LW	Gaye Stewart, Chi.

1946-47

First Team		Second Team
Bill Durnan, Mtl.	G	Frank Brimsek, Bos.
Ken Reardon, Mtl.	D	Jack Stewart, Det.
Butch Bouchard, Mtl.	D	Bill Quackenbush, Det.
Milt Schmidt, Bos.	C	Max Bentley, Chi.
Maurice Richard, Mtl.	RW	Bobby Bauer, Bos.
Doug Bentley, Chi.	LW	Woody Dumart, Bos.

1945-46

First Team		Second Team
Bill Durnan, Mtl.	G	Frank Brimsek, Bos.
Jack Crawford, Bos.	D	Ken Reardon, Mtl.
Butch Bouchard, Mtl.	D	Jack Stewart, Det.
Max Bentley, Chi.	C	Elmer Lach, Mtl.
Maurice Richard, Mtl.	RW	Bill Mosienko, Chi.
Gaye Stewart, Tor.	LW	Toe Blake, Mtl.
Dick Irvin, Mtl.	Coach	Johnny Gottselig, Chi.

1944-45

First Team		Second Team
Bill Durnan, Mtl.	G	Mike Karakas, Chi.
Butch Bouchard, Mtl.	D	Glen Harmon, Mtl.
Flash Hollett, Det.	D	Babe Pratt, Tor.
Elmer Lach, Mtl.	C	Bill Cowley, Bos.
Maurice Richard, Mtl.	RW	Bill Mosienko, Chi.
Toe Blake, Mtl.	LW	Syd Howe, Det.
Dick Irvin, Mtl.	Coach	Jack Adams, Det.

1943-44

First Team		Second Team
Bill Durnan, Mtl.	G	Paul Bibeault, Tor.
Earl Seibert, Chi.	D	Butch Bouchard, Mtl.
Babe Pratt, Tor.	D	Dit Clapper, Bos.
Bill Cowley, Bos.	C	Elmer Lach, Mtl.
Lorne Carr, Tor.	RW	Maurice Richard, Mtl.
Doug Bentley, Chi.	LW	Herb Cain, Bos.
Dick Irvin, Mtl.	Coach	Hap Day, Tor.

1942-43

First Team		Second Team
Johnny Mowers, Det.	G	Frank Brimsek, Bos.
Earl Seibert, Chi.	D	Jack Crawford, Bos.
Jack Stewart, Det.	D	Flash Hollett, Bos.
Bill Cowley, Bos.	C	Syl Apps, Tor.
Lorne Carr, Tor.	RW	Bryan Hextall, NYR
Doug Bentley, Chi.	LW	Lynn Patrick, NYR
Jack Adams, Det.	Coach	Art Ross, Bos.

1941-42

First Team		Second Team
Frank Brimsek, Bos.	G	Turk Broda, Tor.
Earl Seibert, Chi.	D	Pat Egan, Bro.
Tom Anderson, Bro.	D	Bucko McDonald, Tor.
Syl Apps, Tor.	C	Phil Watson, NYR
Bryan Hextall, NYR	RW	Gordie Drillon, Tor.
Lynn Patrick, NYR	LW	Sid Abel, Det.
Frank Boucher, NYR	Coach	Paul Thompson, Chi.

1940-41

First Team		Second Team
Turk Broda, Tor.	G	Frank Brimsek, Bos.
Dit Clapper, Bos.	D	Earl Seibert, Chi.
Wally Stanowski, Tor.	D	Ott Heller, NYR
Bill Cowley, Bos.	C	Syl Apps, Tor.
Bryan Hextall, NYR	RW	Bobby Bauer, Bos.
Sweeney Schriner, Tor.	LW	Woody Dumart, Bos.
Cooney Weiland, Bos.	Coach	Dick Irvin, Mtl.

1939-40

First Team		Second Team
Dave Kerr, NYR	G	Frank Brimsek, Bos.
Dit Clapper, Bos.	D	Art Coulter, NYR
Ebbie Goodfellow, Det.	D	Earl Seibert, Chi.
Milt Schmidt, Bos.	C	Neil Colville, NYR
Bryan Hextall, NYR	RW	Bobby Bauer, Bos.
Toe Blake, Mtl.	LW	Woody Dumart, Bos.
Paul Thompson, Chi.	Coach	Frank Boucher, NYR

1938-39

First Team		Second Team
Frank Brimsek, Bos.	G	Earl Robertson, NYA
Eddie Shore, Bos.	D	Earl Seibert, Chi.
Dit Clapper, Bos.	D	Art Coulter, NYR
Syl Apps, Tor.	C	Neil Colville, NYR
Gordie Drillon, Tor.	RW	Bobby Bauer, Bos.
Toe Blake, Mtl.	LW	Johnny Gottselig, Chi.
Art Ross, Bos.	Coach	Red Dutton, NYA

1937-38

First Team		Second Team
Tiny Thompson, Bos.	G	Dave Kerr, NYR
Eddie Shore, Bos.	D	Art Coulter, NYR
Babe Siebert, Mtl.	D	Earl Seibert, Chi.
Bill Cowley, Bos.	C	Syl Apps, Tor.
Cecil Dillon, NYR	RW	
Gordie Drillon, Tor. *(tied)*		
Paul Thompson, Chi.	LW	Toe Blake, Mtl.
Lester Patrick, NYR	Coach	Art Ross, Bos.

1936-37

First Team		Second Team
Normie Smith, Det.	G	Wilf Cude, Mtl.
Babe Siebert, Mtl.	D	Earl Seibert, Chi.
Ebbie Goodfellow, Det.	D	Lionel Conacher, Mtl. M.
Marty Barry, Det.	C	Art Chapman, NYA
Larry Aurie, Det.	RW	Cecil Dillon, NYR
Busher Jackson, Tor.	LW	Sweeney Schriner, NYA
Jack Adams, Det.	Coach	Cecil Hart, Mtl.

1935-36

First Team		Second Team
Tiny Thompson, Bos.	G	Wilf Cude, Mtl.
Eddie Shore, Bos.	D	Earl Seibert, Chi.
Babe Siebert, Bos.	D	Ebbie Goodfellow, Det.
Hooley Smith, Mtl. M.	C	Bill Thoms, Tor.
Charlie Conacher, Tor.	RW	Cecil Dillon, NYR
Sweeney Schriner, NYA	LW	Paul Thompson, Chi.
Lester Patrick, NYR	Coach	Tommy Gorman, Mtl. M.

1934-35

First Team		Second Team
Lorne Chabot, Chi.	G	Tiny Thompson, Bos.
Eddie Shore, Bos.	D	Cy Wentworth, Mtl. M.
Earl Seibert, NYR	D	Art Coulter, Chi.
Frank Boucher, NYR	C	Cooney Weiland, Det.
Charlie Conacher, Tor.	RW	Dit Clapper, Bos.
Busher Jackson, Tor.	LW	Aurel Joliat, Mtl.
Lester Patrick, NYR	Coach	Dick Irvin, Tor.

1933-34

First Team		Second Team
Charlie Gardiner, Chi.	G	Roy Worters, NYA
King Clancy, Tor.	D	Eddie Shore, Bos.
Lionel Conacher, Chi.	D	Ching Johnson, NYR
Frank Boucher, NYR	C	Joe Primeau, Tor.
Charlie Conacher, Tor.	RW	Bill Cook, NYR
Busher Jackson, Tor.	LW	Aurel Joliat, Mtl.
Lester Patrick, NYR	Coach	Dick Irvin, Tor.

1932-33

First Team		Second Team
John Ross Roach, Det.	G	Charlie Gardiner, Chi.
Eddie Shore, Bos.	D	King Clancy, Tor.
Ching Johnson, NYR	D	Lionel Conacher, Mtl. M.
Frank Boucher, NYR	C	Howie Morenz, Mtl.
Bill Cook, NYR	RW	Charlie Conacher, Tor.
Baldy Northcott, Mtl. M.	LW	Busher Jackson, Tor.
Lester Patrick, NYR	Coach	Dick Irvin, Tor.

1931-32

First Team		Second Team
Charlie Gardiner, Chi.	G	Roy Worters, NYA
Eddie Shore, Bos.	D	Sylvio Mantha, Mtl.
Ching Johnson, NYR	D	King Clancy, Tor.
Howie Morenz, Mtl.	C	Hooley Smith, Mtl. M.
Bill Cook, NYR	RW	Charlie Conacher, Tor.
Busher Jackson, Tor.	LW	Aurel Joliat, Mtl.
Lester Patrick, NYR	Coach	Dick Irvin, Tor.

1930-31

First Team		Second Team
Charlie Gardiner, Chi.	G	Tiny Thompson, Bos.
Eddie Shore, Bos.	D	Sylvio Mantha, Mtl.
King Clancy, Tor.	D	Ching Johnson, NYR
Howie Morenz, Mtl.	C	Frank Boucher, NYR
Bill Cook, NYR	RW	Dit Clapper, Bos.
Aurel Joliat, Mtl.	LW	Bun Cook, NYR
Lester Patrick, NYR	Coach	Dick Irvin, Chi.

NHL ALL-ROOKIE TEAM

Voting for the NHL All-Rookie Team is conducted among the representatives of the Professional Hockey Writers' Association at the end of the season. The rookie all-star team was first selected for the 1982-83 season.

2009-10
Goal	Jimmy Howard, Detroit
Defense	Tyler Myers, Buffalo
Defense	Michael Del Zotto, NY Rangers
Forward	John Tavares, NY Islanders
Forward	Matt Duchene, Colorado
Forward	Niclas Bergfors, N.J., Atl.

2008-09
Goal	Steve Mason, Columbus
Defense	Drew Doughty, Los Angeles
Defense	Luke Schenn, Toronto
Forward	Patrik Berglund, St. Louis
Forward	Bobby Ryan, Anaheim
Forward	Kris Versteeg, Chicago

2007-08
Goal	Carey Price, Montreal
Defense	Tobias Enstrom, Atlanta
Defense	Tom Gilbert, Edmonton
Forward	Nicklas Backstrom, Washington
Forward	Patrick Kane, Chicago
Forward	Jonathan Toews, Chicago

2006-07
Goal	Mike Smith, Dallas
Defense	Matt Carle, San Jose
Defense	Marc-Edouard Vlasic, San Jose
Forward	Evgeni Malkin, Pittsburgh
Forward	Jordan Staal, Pittsburgh
Forward	Paul Stastny, Colorado

2005-06
Goal	Henrik Lundqvist, NY Rangers
Defense	Andrej Meszaros, Ottawa
Defense	Dion Phaneuf, Calgary
Forward	Brad Boyes, Boston
Forward	Sidney Crosby, Pittsburgh
Forward	Alex Ovechkin, Washington

2004-05
Goal	
Defense	
Defense	*Season Cancelled*
Forward	
Forward	
Forward	

2003-04
Goal	Andrew Raycroft, Boston
Defense	John-Michael Liles, Colorado
Defense	Joni Pitkanen, Philadelphia
Forward	Trent Hunter, NY Islanders
Forward	Ryan Malone, Pittsburgh
Forward	Michael Ryder, Montreal

2002-03
Goal	Sebastien Caron, Pittsburgh
Defense	Jay Bouwmeester, Florida
Defense	Barret Jackman, St. Louis
Forward	Tyler Arnason, Chicago
Forward	Rick Nash, Columbus
Forward	Henrik Zetterberg, Detroit

2001-02
Goal	Dan Blackburn, NY Rangers
Defense	Nick Boynton, Boston
Defense	Rostislav Klesla, Columbus
Forward	Dany Heatley, Atlanta
Forward	Ilya Kovalchuk, Atlanta
Forward	Kristian Huselius, Florida

2000-01
Goal	Evgeni Nabokov, San Jose
Defense	Lubomir Visnovsky, Los Angeles
Defense	Colin White, New Jersey
Forward	Martin Havlat, Ottawa
Forward	Brad Richards, Tampa Bay
Forward	Shane Willis, Carolina

1999-2000
Goal	Brian Boucher, Philadelphia
Defense	Brian Rafalski, New Jersey
Defense	Brad Stuart, San Jose
Forward	Simon Gagne, Philadelphia
Forward	Scott Gomez, New Jersey
Forward	Michael York, NY Rangers

1998-99
Goal	Jamie Storr, Los Angeles
Defense	Tom Poti, Edmonton
Defense	Sami Salo, Ottawa
Forward	Chris Drury, Colorado
Forward	Milan Hejduk, Colorado
Forward	Marian Hossa, Ottawa

1997-98
Goal	Jamie Storr, Los Angeles
Defense	Mattias Ohlund, Vancouver
Defense	Derek Morris, Calgary
Forward	Sergei Samsonov, Boston
Forward	Patrick Elias, New Jersey
Forward	Mike Johnson, Toronto

1996-97
Goal	Patrick Lalime, Pittsburgh
Defense	Bryan Berard, NY Islanders
Defense	Janne Niinimaa, Philadelphia
Forward	Jarome Iginla, Calgary
Forward	Jim Campbell, St. Louis
Forward	Sergei Berezin, Toronto

1995-96
Goal	Corey Hirsch, Vancouver
Defense	Ed Jovanovski, Florida
Defense	Kyle McLaren, Boston
Forward	Daniel Alfredsson, Ottawa
Forward	Eric Daze, Chicago
Forward	Petr Sykora, New Jersey

1994-95
Goal	Jim Carey, Washington
Defense	Chris Therien, Philadelphia
Defense	Kenny Jonsson, Toronto
Forward	Peter Forsberg, Quebec
Forward	Jeff Friesen, San Jose
Forward	Paul Kariya, Anaheim

1993-94
Goal	Martin Brodeur, New Jersey
Defense	Chris Pronger, Hartford
Defense	Boris Mironov, Wpg./Edm.
Forward	Jason Arnott, Edmonton
Forward	Mikael Renberg, Philadelphia
Forward	Oleg Petrov, Montreal

1992-93
Goal	Felix Potvin, Toronto
Defense	Vladimir Malakhov, NY Islanders
Defense	Scott Niedermayer, New Jersey
Forward	Eric Lindros, Philadelphia
Forward	Teemu Selanne, Winnipeg
Forward	Joe Juneau, Boston

1991-92
Goal	Dominik Hasek, Chicago
Defense	Nicklas Lidstrom, Detroit
Defense	Vladimir Konstantinov, Detroit
Forward	Kevin Todd, New Jersey
Forward	Tony Amonte, NY Rangers
Forward	Gilbert Dionne, Montreal

1990-91
Goal	Ed Belfour, Chicago
Defense	Eric Weinrich, New Jersey
Defense	Rob Blake, Los Angeles
Forward	Sergei Fedorov, Detroit
Forward	Ken Hodge, Boston
Forward	Jaromir Jagr, Pittsburgh

1989-90
Goal	Bob Essensa, Winnipeg
Defense	Brad Shaw, Hartford
Defense	Geoff Smith, Edmonton
Forward	Mike Modano, Minnesota
Forward	Sergei Makarov, Calgary
Forward	Rod Brind'Amour, St. Louis

1988-89
Goal	Peter Sidorkiewicz, Hartford
Defense	Brian Leetch, NY Rangers
Defense	Zarley Zalapski, Pittsburgh
Forward	Trevor Linden, Vancouver
Forward	Tony Granato, NY Rangers
Forward	David Volek, NY Islanders

1987-88
Goal	Darren Pang, Chicago
Defense	Glen Wesley, Boston
Defense	Calle Johansson, Buffalo
Forward	Joe Nieuwendyk, Calgary
Forward	Ray Sheppard, Buffalo
Forward	Iain Duncan, Winnipeg

1986-87
Goal	Ron Hextall, Philadelphia
Defense	Steve Duchesne, Los Angeles
Defense	Brian Benning, St. Louis
Forward	Jimmy Carson, Los Angeles
Forward	Jim Sandlak, Vancouver
Forward	Luc Robitaille, Los Angeles

1985-86
Goal	Patrick Roy, Montreal
Defense	Gary Suter, Calgary
Defense	Dana Murzyn, Hartford
Forward	Mike Ridley, NY Rangers
Forward	Kjell Dahlin, Montreal
Forward	Wendel Clark, Toronto

1984-85
Goal	Steve Penney, Montreal
Defense	Chris Chelios, Montreal
Defense	Bruce Bell, Quebec
Forward	Mario Lemieux, Pittsburgh
Forward	Tomas Sandstrom, NY Rangers
Forward	Warren Young, Pittsburgh

1983-84
Goal	Tom Barrasso, Buffalo
Defense	Thomas Eriksson, Philadelphia
Defense	Jamie Macoun, Calgary
Forward	Steve Yzerman, Detroit
Forward	Hakan Loob, Calgary
Forward	Sylvain Turgeon, Hartford

1982-83
Goal	Pelle Lindbergh, Philadelphia
Defense	Scott Stevens, Washington
Defense	Phil Housley, Buffalo
Forward	Dan Daoust, Mtl./Tor.
Forward	Steve Larmer, Chicago
Forward	Mats Naslund, Montreal

Chicago's Duncan Keith (left) led all NHL players in total ice time in 2009-10 (2,180:34 minutes in 82 games for 26:36 per game) while registering career highs in goals (14), assists (55) and points (69). He was rewarded with the Norris Trophy and a First-Team All-Star selection. Eddie Shore (right) played before there was a trophy for the game's best defenseman, but he was a First-Team All-Star seven times in the first nine years such honors were bestowed.

All-Star Game Results

Year	Venue	Score	Coaches	Attendance
2009	Montreal	East 12, West 11	Claude Julien, Todd McLellan	21,273
2008	Atlanta	East 8, West 7	John Paddock, Mike Babcock	18,644
2007	Dallas	West 12, East 9	Lindy Ruff, Randy Carlyle	18,532
2004	Minnesota	East 6, West 4	Pat Quinn, Dave Lewis	19,434
2003	Florida	West 6, East 5	Marc Crawford, Jacques Martin	19,250
2002	Los Angeles	World 8, North America 5	Scotty Bowman, Pat Quinn	18,118
2001	Colorado	North America 14, World 12	Joel Quenneville, Jacques Martin	18,646
2000	Toronto	World 9, North America 4	Scotty Bowman, Pat Quinn	19,300
1999	Tampa Bay	North America 8, World 6	Lindy Ruff, Ken Hitchcock	19,758
1998	Vancouver	North America 8, World 7	Jacques Lemaire, Ken Hitchcock	18,422
1997	San Jose	East 11, West 7	Doug MacLean, Ken Hitchcock	17,422
1996	Boston	East 5, West 4	Doug MacLean, Scotty Bowman	17,565
1994	NY Rangers	East 9, West 8	Jacques Demers, Barry Melrose	18,200
1993	Montreal	Wales 16, Campbell 6	Scotty Bowman, Mike Keenan	17,137
1992	Philadelphia	Campbell 10, Wales 6	Bob Gainey, Scotty Bowman	17,380
1991	Chicago	Campbell 11, Wales 5	John Muckler, Mike Milbury	18,472
1990	Pittsburgh	Wales 12, Campbell 7	Pat Burns, Terry Crisp	16,236
1989	Edmonton	Campbell 9, Wales 5	Glen Sather, Terry O'Reilly	17,503
1988	St. Louis	Wales 6, Campbell 5 OT	Mike Keenan, Glen Sather	17,878
1986	Hartford	Wales 4, Campbell 3 OT	Mike Keenan, Glen Sather	15,100
1985	Calgary	Wales 6, Campbell 4	Al Arbour, Glen Sather	16,825
1984	New Jersey	Wales 7, Campbell 6	Al Arbour, Glen Sather	18,939
1983	NY Islanders	Campbell 9, Wales 3	Roger Neilson, Al Arbour	15,230
1982	Washington	Wales 4, Campbell 2	Al Arbour, Glen Sonmor	18,130
1981	Los Angeles	Campbell 4, Wales 1	Pat Quinn, Scotty Bowman	15,761
1980	Detroit	Wales 6, Campbell 3	Scotty Bowman, Al Arbour	21,002
1978	Buffalo	Wales 3, Campbell 2 OT	Scotty Bowman, Fred Shero	16,433
1977	Vancouver	Wales 4, Campbell 3	Scotty Bowman, Fred Shero	15,607
1976	Philadelphia	Wales 7, Campbell 5	Floyd Smith, Fred Shero	16,436
1975	Montreal	Wales 7, Campbell 1	Bep Guidolin, Fred Shero	16,080
1974	Chicago	West 6, East 4	Billy Reay, Scotty Bowman	16,426
1973	NY Rangers	East 5, West 4	Tom Johnson, Billy Reay	16,986
1972	Minnesota	East 3, West 2	Al MacNeil, Billy Reay	15,423
1971	Boston	West 2, East 1	Scotty Bowman, Harry Sinden	14,790
1970	St. Louis	East 4, West 1	Claude Ruel, Scotty Bowman	16,587
1969	Montreal	East 3, West 3	Toe Blake, Scotty Bowman	16,260
1968	Toronto	Toronto 4, All-Stars 3	Punch Imlach, Toe Blake	15,753
1967	Montreal	Montreal 3, All-Stars 0	Toe Blake, Sid Abel	14,284
1965	Montreal	All-Stars 5, Montreal 2	Billy Reay, Toe Blake	13,529
1964	Toronto	All-Stars 3, Toronto 2	Sid Abel, Punch Imlach	14,232
1963	Toronto	All-Stars 3, Toronto 3	Sid Abel, Punch Imlach	14,034
1962	Toronto	Toronto 4, All-Stars 1	Punch Imlach, Rudy Pilous	14,236
1961	Chicago	All-Stars 3, Chicago 1	Sid Abel, Rudy Pilous	14,534
1960	Montreal	All-Stars 2, Montreal 1	Punch Imlach, Toe Blake	13,949
1959	Montreal	Montreal 6, All-Stars 1	Toe Blake, Punch Imlach	13,818
1958	Montreal	Montreal 6, All-Stars 3	Toe Blake, Milt Schmidt	13,989
1957	Montreal	All-Stars 5, Montreal 3	Milt Schmidt, Toe Blake	13,003
1956	Montreal	All-Stars 1, Montreal 1	Jim Skinner, Toe Blake	13,095
1955	Detroit	Detroit 3, All-Stars 1	Jim Skinner, Dick Irvin	10,111
1954	Detroit	All-Stars 2, Detroit 2	King Clancy, Jim Skinner	10,689
1953	Montreal	All-Stars 3, Montreal 1	Lynn Patrick, Dick Irvin	14,153
1952	Detroit	1st Team 1, 2nd Team 1	Tommy Ivan, Dick Irvin	10,680
1951	Toronto	1st Team 2, 2nd Team 2	Joe Primeau, Dick Irvin	11,469
1950	Detroit	Detroit 7, All-Stars 1	Tommy Ivan, Lynn Patrick	9,166
1949	.Toronto	All-Stars 3, Toronto 1	Tommy Ivan, Hap Day	13,541
1948	Chicago	All-Stars 3, Toronto 1	Tommy Ivan, Hap Day	12,794
1947	Toronto	All-Stars 3, Toronto 3	Dick Irvin, Hap Day	14,169

There was no All-Star contest during the calendar year of 1966 because the game was moved from the start of season to mid-season. In 1979, the Challenge Cup series between the Soviet Union and Team NHL replaced the All-Star Game. In 1987, Rendez-Vous '87, two games between the Soviet Union and Team NHL replaced the All-Star Game. In 1995 and 2005 the All-Star Game was not played due to a labour disruption affecting the NHL. In both 2006 and 2010 the All-Star Game was not played because of NHL players' participation in the Olympics.

NHL ALL-STAR GAME MVP

2009	Alex Kovalev, Mtl.	1992	Brett Hull, St.L.	1976	Pete Mahovlich, Mtl.
2008	Eric Staal, Car.	1991	Vincent Damphousse, Tor.	1975	Syl Apps Jr., Pit.
2007	Danny Briere, Buf.	1990	Mario Lemieux, Pit.	1974	Garry Unger, St.L.
2004	Joe Sakic, Col..	1989	Wayne Gretzky, L.A.	1973	Greg Polis, Pit.
2003	Dany Heatley, Atl.	1988	Mario Lemieux, Pit.	1972	Bobby Orr, Bos.
2002	Eric Daze, Chi.	1986	Grant Fuhr, Edm.	1971	Bobby Hull, Chi.
2001	Bill Guerin, Bos.	1985	Mario Lemieux, Pit.	1970	Bobby Hull, Chi.
2000	Pavel Bure, Fla.	1984	Don Maloney, NYR	1969	Frank Mahovlich, Det.
1999	Wayne Gretzky, NYR	1983	Wayne Gretzky, Edm.	1968	Bruce Gamble, Tor.
1998	Teemu Selanne, Ana.	1982	Mike Bossy, NYI	1967	Henri Richard, Mtl.
1997	Mark Recchi, Mtl.	1981	Mike Liut, St.L.	1965	Gordie Howe, Det.
1996	Raymond Bourque, Bos.	1980	Reggie Leach, Phi.	1964	Jean Beliveau, Mtl.
1994	Mike Richter, NYR	1978	Billy Smith, NYI	1963	Frank Mahovlich, Tor.
1993	Mike Gartner, NYR	1977	Rick Martin, Buf.	1962	Eddie Shack, Tor.

All-Star Game Records 1947 through 2010

TEAM RECORDS

MOST GOALS, BOTH TEAMS, ONE GAME:
26 — North America 14, World 12, 2001 at Colorado
23 — East 12, West 11, 2009 at Montreal
22 — Wales 16, Campbell 6, 1993 at Montreal
21 — West 12, East 9, 2007 at Dallas
19 — Wales 12, Campbell 7, 1990 at Pittsburgh
18 — East 11, West 7, 1997 at San Jose
17 — East 9, West 8, 1994 at NY Rangers

FEWEST GOALS, BOTH TEAMS, ONE GAME:
2 — First Team All-Stars 1, Second Team All-Stars 1, 1952 at Detroit
  — NHL All-Stars 1, Montreal Canadiens 1, 1956 at Montreal
3 — NHL All-Stars 2, Montreal Canadiens 1, 1960 at Montreal
  — Montreal Canadiens 3, NHL All-Stars 0, 1967 at Montreal
  — West 2, East 1, 1971 at Boston

MOST GOALS, ONE TEAM, ONE GAME:
16 — Wales 16, Campbell 6, 1993 at Montreal
14 — North America 14, World 12, 2001 at Colorado
12 — Wales 12, Campbell 7, 1990 at Pittsburgh
  — World 12, North America 14, 2001 at Colorado
  — West 12, East 9, 2007 at Dallas
  — East 12, West 11, 2009 at Montreal

FEWEST GOALS, ONE TEAM, ONE GAME:
0 — NHL All-Stars 0, Montreal Canadiens 3, 1967 at Montreal
1 — 17 times (1981, 1975, 1971, 1970, 1962, 1961, 1960, 1959, both teams 1956, 1955, 1953, both teams 1952, 1950, 1949, 1948)

MOST SHOTS, BOTH TEAMS, ONE GAME (SINCE 1955):
102 — 1994 at NY Rangers —	East 9 (56 shots), West 8 (46 shots)
2009 at Montreal	— East 12 (48 shots) — West 11 (54 shots)
98 — 2001 at Denver	— North America 14 (53 shots), World 12 (45 shots)
90 — 1993 at Montreal	— Wales 16 (49 shots), Campbell 6 (41 shots)

FEWEST SHOTS, BOTH TEAMS, ONE GAME (SINCE 1955):
52 — 1978 at Buffalo	— Campbell 2 (12 shots) Wales 3 (40 shots)
53 — 1960 at Montreal	— NHL All-Stars 2 (27 shots) Montreal Canadiens 1 (26 shots)
55 — 1956 at Montreal	— NHL All-Stars 1 (28 shots) Montreal Canadiens 1 (27 shots)
— 1971 at Boston	— West 2 (28 shots) East 1 (27 shots)

MOST SHOTS, ONE TEAM, ONE GAME (SINCE 1955):
56 — 1994 at NY Rangers — East (9-8 vs. West)
54 — 2009 at Montreal — East (12-11 vs. West)
53 — 2001 at Colorado — North America (14-12 vs. World)
51 — 2008 at Atlanta — West (7-8 vs. East)

FEWEST SHOTS, ONE TEAM, ONE GAME (SINCE 1955):
12 — 1978 at Buffalo — Campbell (2-3 vs. Wales)
17 — 1970 at St. Louis — West (1-4 vs. East)
23 — 1961 at Chicago — Chicago Black Hawks (1-3 vs. NHL All-Stars)
24 — 1976 at Philadelphia — Campbell (5-7 vs. Wales)

MOST POWER-PLAY GOALS, BOTH TEAMS, ONE GAME (SINCE 1950):
3 — 1953 at Montreal	— NHL All-Stars 3 (2 power-play goals), Montreal Canadiens 1 (1 power-play goal)
— 1954 at Detroit	— NHL All-Stars 2 (1 power-play goal) Detroit Red Wings 2 (2 power-play goals)
— 1958 at Montreal	— NHL All-Stars 3 (1 power-play goal) Montreal Canadiens 6 (2 power-play goals)

FEWEST POWER-PLAY GOALS, BOTH TEAMS, ONE GAME (SINCE 1950):
0 — 25 times (1952, 1959, 1960, 1967, 1968, 1969, 1972, 1973, 1976, 1980, 1981, 1984, 1985, 1992, 1994, 1996, 1999, 2000, 2001, 2002, 2003, 2004, 2007, 2008, 2009)

FASTEST TWO GOALS, BOTH TEAMS, FROM START OF GAME:
0:37 — 1970 at St. Louis — Jacques Laperriere of East scored at 0:20 and Dean Prentice of West scored at 0:37. Final score: East 4, West 1.

1:20 — 2008 at Atlanta — Rick Nash of West scored at 0:12 and Eric Staal of East scored at 1:20. Final score: East 8, West 7.

2:15 — 1998 at Vancouver — Teemu Selanne scored at 0:53 and Jaromir Jagr scored at 2:15 for World. Final score: North America 8, World 7.

FASTEST TWO GOALS, BOTH TEAMS:
0:08 — 1997 at San Jose — Owen Nolan scored at 18:54 and 19:02 of second period for West. Final Score: East 11, West 7.

0:10 — 1976 at Philadelphia — Dennis Ververgaert scored at 4:33 and at 4:43 of third period for Campbell. Final score: Wales 7, Campbell 5.

0:13 — 1998 at Vancouver — Teemu Selanne scored at 4:00 of first period for World and John LeClair scored at 4:13 for North America. Final score: North America 8, World 7.

FASTEST THREE GOALS, BOTH TEAMS:
0:48 — 2007 at Dallas — Martin Havlat scored at 19:00 of third period for West; Sheldon Souray scored at 19:25 for East; Dion Phaneuf scored at 19:48 for West. Final score: West 12, East 9.
1:08 — 1993 at Montreal — all by Wales — Mike Gartner scored at 3:15 and at 3:37 of first period; Peter Bondra scored at 4:23. Final score: Wales 16, Campbell 6.
1:14 — 1994 at NY Rangers — Bob Kudelski scored at 9:46 of first period for East; Sergei Fedorov scored at 10:20 for West; Eric Lindros scored at 11:00 for East. Final score: East 9, West 8.

FASTEST FOUR GOALS, BOTH TEAMS:
2:24 — 1997 at San Jose — Brendan Shanahan scored at 16:38 of second period for West; Dale Hawerchuk scored at 17:28 for East; Owen Nolan scored at 18:54 and 19:02 for West. Final score: East 11, West 7.
2:49 — 2009 at Montreal — Evgeni Malkin scored at 7:45 of second period for East; Rick Nash scored at 8:27 for West; Milan Hejduk scored at 9:02 for West; Sheldon Souray scored at 10:34 for West.
2:52 — 2007 at Dallas — Rick Nash scored at 10:40 of second period for West; Martin Havlat scored at 11:34 for West; Yanic Perreault scored at 12:47 for West; Alex Ovechkin scored at 13:32 for East. Final score: West 12, East 9.

FASTEST TWO GOALS, ONE TEAM, FROM START OF GAME:
2:15 — 1998 at Vancouver — World — Teemu Selanne scored at 0:53 and Jaromir Jagr scored at 2:15. Final score: North America 8, World 7.
3:37 — 1993 at Montreal — Wales — Mike Gartner scored at 3:15 and at 3:37. Final score: Wales 16, Campbell 6.
4:19 — 1980 at Detroit — Wales — Larry Robinson scored at 3:58 and Steve Payne scored at 4:19. Final score: Wales 6, Campbell 3.

FASTEST TWO GOALS, ONE TEAM:
0:08 — 1997 at San Jose — West — Owen Nolan scored at 18:54 and at 19:02 of second period. Final score: East 11, West 7.
0:10 — 1976 at Philadelphia — Campbell — Dennis Ververgaert scored at 4:33 and at 4:43 of third period. Final score: Wales 7, Campbell 5.
0:14 — 1989 at Edmonton — Campbell — Steve Yzerman and Gary Leeman scored at 17:21 and 17:35 of second period. Final score: Campbell 9, Wales 5.

FASTEST THREE GOALS, ONE TEAM:
1:08 — 1993 at Montreal — Wales — Mike Gartner scored at 3:15 and 3:37 of first period; Peter Bondra scored at 4:23. Final score: Wales 16, Campbell 6.
1:32 — 1980 at Detroit — Wales — Ron Stackhouse scored at 11:40 of third period; Craig Hartsburg scored at 12:40; Reed Larson scored at 13:12. Final score: Wales 6, Campbell 3.
1:39 — 2002 at Los Angeles — Markus Naslund scored at 18:17 of third period; Alex Zhamnov scored at 19:12; Sami Kapanen scored at 19:56. Final score: World 8, North America 5.

FASTEST FOUR GOALS, ONE TEAM:
2:57 — 2002 at Los Angeles — World — Sergei Fedorov scored at 16:59 of third period; Markus Naslund scored at 18:17; Alex Zhamnov scored at 19:12; Sami Kapanen scored at 19:56. Final score: World 8, North America 5.
4:17 — 2007 at Dallas — Brian Rolston scored at 8:30 of second period; Rick Nash scored at 10:40; Martin Havlat scored at 11:34; Yanic Perreault scored at 12:47. Final score: West 12, East 9.
4:19 — 1992 at Philadelphia — Campbell — Brian Bellows scored at 7:40 of second period; Jeremy Roenick scored at 8:13; Theoren Fleury scored at 11:06, Brett Hull scored at 11:59. Final score: Campbell 10, Wales 6.

MOST GOALS, BOTH TEAMS, ONE PERIOD:
10 — 1997 at San Jose — Second period — East (6), West (4). Final score: East 11, West 7.
— 2001 at Colorado — Second period — North America (6), World (4). Final score: North America 14, World 12.
— 2001 at Colorado — Third period — North America (5), World (5). Final score: North America 14, World 12.
— 2009 at Montreal — Second period — West (6), East (4). Final Score: East 12, West 11.
9 — 1990 at Pittsburgh — First period — Wales (7), Campbell (2). Final score: Wales 12, Campbell 7.
— 2007 at Dallas — Second period — West (6), East (3). Final score: West 12, East 9.

MOST GOALS, ONE TEAM, ONE PERIOD:
7 — 1990 at Pittsburgh — First period — Wales. Final score: Wales 12, Campbell 7.
6 — 1983 at NY Islanders — Third period — Campbell. Final score: Campbell 9, Wales 3.
— 1992 at Philadelphia — Second period — Campbell. Final score: Campbell 10, Wales 6.
— 1993 at Montreal — First period — Wales. Final score: Wales 16, Campbell 6.
— 1993 at Montreal — Second period — Wales. Final score: Wales 16, Campbell 6.
— 1997 at San Jose — Second period — East. Final score: East 11, West 7.
— 2001 at Colorado — Second period — North America. Final score: North America 14, World 12.
— 2007 at Dallas — Second period — West. Final score: West 12, East 9.
— 2009 at Montreal — Second period — West. Final score: East 12, West 11.

MOST SHOTS, BOTH TEAMS, ONE PERIOD:
42 — 2009 at Montreal — Second period — West (21), East (21). Final score: East 12, West 11.
39 — 1994 at NY Rangers — Second period — West (21), East (18). Final score: East 9, West 8.
— 2001 at Colorado — Third period — World (23), North America (16). Final score: North America 14, World 12.
36 — 1990 at Pittsburgh — Third period — Campbell (22), Wales (14). Final score: Wales 12, Campbell 7.
— 1994 at NY Rangers — First period — East (19), West (17). Final score: East 9, West 8.
— 2002 at Los Angeles — Third period — North America (20), World (16). Final score: World 8, North America 5.

MOST SHOTS, ONE TEAM, ONE PERIOD:
23 — 2001 at Colorado — Third period — World. Final score: North America 14, World 12.
22 — 1990 at Pittsburgh — Third period — Campbell. Final score: Wales 12, Campbell 7.
— 1991 at Chicago — Third period — Wales. Final score: Campbell 11, Wales 5.
— 1993 at Montreal — First period — Wales. Final score: Wales 16, Campbell 6.

FEWEST SHOTS, BOTH TEAMS, ONE PERIOD:
9 — 1971 at Boston — Third period — East (2), West (7). Final score: West 2, East 1.
— 1980 at Detroit — Second period — Campbell (4), Wales (5). Final score: Wales 6, Campbell 3.
13 — 1982 at Washington — Third period — Campbell (6), Wales (7). Final score: Wales 4, Campbell 2.
14 — 1978 at Buffalo — First period — Campbell (7), Wales (7). Final score: Wales 3, Campbell 2.
— 1986 at Hartford — First period — Campbell (6), Wales (8). Final score: Wales 4, Campbell 3.

FEWEST SHOTS, ONE TEAM, ONE PERIOD:
2 — 1971 at Boston — Third period — East. Final score: West 2, East 1.
— 1978 at Buffalo — Second period — Campbell. Final score: Wales 3, Campbell 2.
3 — 1978 at Buffalo — Third period — Campbell. Final score: Wales 3, Campbell 2.
4 — 1955 at Detroit — First period — NHL All-Stars. Final score: Detroit Red Wings 3, NHL All-Stars 1.
— 1980 at Detroit — Second period — Campbell. Final score: Wales 6, Campbell 3.

INDIVIDUAL RECORDS

Games

MOST GAMES PLAYED:
23 — **Gordie Howe**, 1948 through 1980
19 — Raymond Bourque, 1981 through 2001
18 — Wayne Gretzky, 1980 through 1999
15 — Frank Mahovlich, 1959 through 1974
— Mark Messier, 1982 through 2004

Goals

MOST GOALS, CAREER:
13 — **Wayne Gretzky** in 18GP
— **Mario Lemieux** in 10GP
10 — Gordie Howe in 23GP
9 — Teemu Selanne in 10GP
8 — Frank Mahovlich in 15GP
— Luc Robitaille in 8GP

MOST GOALS, ONE GAME:
4 — **Wayne Gretzky,** Campbell, 1983
— **Mario Lemieux,** Wales, 1990
— **Vince Damphousse,** Campbell, 1991
— **Mike Gartner,** Wales, 1993
— **Dany Heatley,** East, 2003
3 — Ted Lindsay, Detroit, 1950
— Mario Lemieux, Wales, 1988
— Pierre Turgeon, Wales, 1993
— Mark Recchi, East, 1997
— Owen Nolan, West, 1997
— Teemu Selanne, World, 1998
— Pavel Bure, World, 2000
— Bill Guerin, North America, 2001
— Joe Sakic, West, 2004
— Rick Nash, West, 2008

MOST GOALS, ONE PERIOD:
4 — **Wayne Gretzky,** Campbell, Third period, 1983
3 — Mario Lemieux, Wales, First period, 1990
— Vincent Damphousse, Campbell, Third period, 1991
— Mike Gartner, Wales, First period, 1993

Assists

MOST ASSISTS, CAREER:
16 — **Joe Sakic** in 12GP
14 — Mark Messier in 15GP
13 — Raymond Bourque in 19GP
12 — Adam Oates in 5GP
— Mats Sundin in 8GP
— Wayne Gretzky in 18GP

MOST ASSISTS, ONE GAME:
5 — **Mats Naslund,** Wales, 1988
4 — Raymond Bourque, Wales, 1985
— Adam Oates, Campbell, 1991
— Adam Oates, Wales, 1993
— Mark Recchi, Wales, 1993
— Pierre Turgeon, East, 1994
— Fredrik Modin, World, 2001
— Joe Sakic, West, 2007
— Danny Briere, East, 2007
— Marian Hossa, East, 2007

MOST ASSISTS, ONE PERIOD:
4 — **Adam Oates,** Wales, First period, 1993
3 — Mark Messier, Campbell, Third period, 1983
3 — Marian Hossa, East, Third period, 2007

Points

MOST POINTS, CAREER:
25 — **Wayne Gretzky** (13G-12A in 18GP)
23 — Mario Lemieux (13G-10A in 10GP)
22 — Joe Sakic (6G-16A in 12GP)
20 — Mark Messier (6G-14A in 15GP)
19 — Gordie Howe (10G-9A in 23GP)

MOST POINTS, ONE GAME:
6 — **Mario Lemieux,** Wales, 1988 (3G-3A)
5 — Mats Naslund, Wales, 1988 (5A)
— Adam Oates, Campbell, 1991 (1G-4A)
— Mike Gartner, Wales, 1993 (4G-1A)
— Mark Recchi, Wales, 1993 (1G-4A)
— Pierre Turgeon, Wales, 1993 (3G-2A)
— Bill Guerin, North America, 2001 (3G-2A)
— Dany Heatley, East, 2003 (4G-1A)
— Danny Briere, East, 2007 (1G-4A)

MOST POINTS, ONE PERIOD:
4 — **Wayne Gretzky,** Campbell, Third period, 1983 (4G)
— **Mike Gartner,** Wales, First period, 1993 (3G-1A)
— **Adam Oates,** Wales, First period, 1993 (4A)
3 — Gordie Howe, NHL All-Stars, Second period, 1965 (1G-2A)
— Pete Mahovlich, Wales, First period, 1976 (1G-2A)
— Mark Messier, Campbell, Third period, 1983 (3A)
— Mario Lemieux, Wales, Second period, 1988 (1G-2A)
— Mario Lemieux, Wales, First period, 1990 (3G)
— Vince Damphousse, Campbell, Third period, 1991 (3G)
— Mark Recchi, Wales, Second period, 1993 (1G-2A)
— Tony Amonte, North America, Second period, 2001 (2G-1A)
— Daniel Alfredsson, East, Second period, 2004 (2G-1A)
— Marian Hossa, East, Third period, 2007 (3A)

Power-Play Goals

MOST POWER-PLAY GOALS, CAREER:
6 — **Gordie Howe** in 23GP
3 — Bobby Hull in 12GP
— Maurice Richard in 13GP

Fastest Goals

FASTEST GOAL FROM START OF GAME:
0:12 — **Rick Nash,** West, 2008
0:19 — Ted Lindsay, Detroit, 1950
0:20 — Jacques Laperriere, East, 1970
0:21 — Mario Lemieux, Wales, 1990
0:35 — Vincent Damphousse, North America, 2002

FASTEST GOAL FROM START OF A PERIOD:
0:12 — **Rick Nash,** West, 2008 (first period)
0:17 — Raymond Bourque, North America, 1999 (second period)
0:19 — Ted Lindsay, Detroit, 1950 (first period)
— Rick Tocchet, Wales, 1993 (second period)
0:20 — Jacques Laperriere, East, 1970 (first period)

FASTEST TWO GOALS, ONE PLAYER, FROM START OF GAME:
3:37 — **Mike Gartner,** Wales, 1993, at 3:15 and 3:37.
4:00 — Teemu Selanne, World, 1998, at 0:53 and 4:00.
5:25 — Wally Hergesheimer, NHL All-Stars, 1953, at 4:06 and 5:25.

FASTEST TWO GOALS, ONE PLAYER, FROM START OF A PERIOD:
3:37 — **Mike Gartner,** Wales, 1993, at 3:15 and 3:37 of first period.
4:00 — Teemu Selanne, World, 1998, at 0:53 and 4:00 of first period.
4:43 — Dennis Ververgaert, Campbell, 1976, at 4:33 and 4:43 of third period.

FASTEST TWO GOALS, ONE PLAYER:
0:08 — **Owen Nolan,** West, 1997. Scored at 18:54 and 19:02 of second period.
0:10 — Dennis Ververgaert, Campbell, 1976. Scored at 4:33 and 4:43 of third period.
0:22 — Mike Gartner, Wales, 1993. Scored at 3:15 and 3:37 of first period.

Penalties

MOST PENALTY MINUTES:
25 — **Gordie Howe** in 23GP
21 — Gus Mortson in 9GP
16 — Harry Howell in 7GP

Goaltenders

MOST GAMES PLAYED:
13 — **Glenn Hall** from 1955 through 1969
11 — Terry Sawchuk from 1950 through 1968
— Patrick Roy from 1988 through 2003
9 — Martin Brodeur from 1996 through 2007
8 — Jacques Plante from 1956 through 1970

MOST MINUTES PLAYED:
540 — **Glenn Hall** in 13GP
467 — Terry Sawchuk in 11GP
370 — Jacques Plante in 8GP
250 — Patrick Roy in 11GP
209 — Turk Broda in 4GP

MOST GOALS AGAINST:
31 — **Patrick Roy** in 11GP
22 — Martin Brodeur in 9GP
— Glenn Hall in 13GP
21 — Mike Vernon in 5GP
19 — Terry Sawchuk in 11GP

BEST GOALS-AGAINST-AVERAGE AMONG THOSE WITH AT LEAST TWO GAMES PLAYED:
0.68 — **Gilles Villemure** in 3GP
1.49 — Gerry McNeil in 3GP
1.50 — Johnny Bower in 4GP
1.51 — Frank Brimsek in 3GP
1.64 — Gump Worsley in 4GP

Rick Nash of Columbus beat Tomas Vokoun for his second of three goals during the 2008 All-Star Game in Atlanta. Nash's first goal of the game came just 12 seconds after the opening face-off to set an All-Star record.

Hockey Hall of Fame

(Year of induction is listed after each Honoured Members name)

Location: Brookfield Place, at the corner of Front and Yonge Streets in the heart of downtown Toronto. Easy access from all major highways running into Toronto. Close to TTC subway and Union Station.

Telephone: administration (416) 360-7735; information (416) 360-7765.

Public Hours of Operation: Open every day except Christmas Day, New Year's Day and Induction Day (November 8, 2010). Please call our information number (above) or visit our website (below) for times.

The Hockey Hall of Fame can be booked for private functions after hours.

Website address: www.hhof.com

History: The Hockey Hall of Fame was established in 1943. Members were first honoured in 1945. On August 26, 1961, the Hockey Hall of Fame opened its doors to the public in a building located on the grounds of the Canadian National Exhibition in Toronto. The Hockey Hall of Fame relocated to its current location and welcomed the hockey world on June 18, 1993.

Honour Roll: There are 362 Honoured Members in the Hockey Hall of Fame. 247 have been inducted as players including the first two women in 2010, 100 as builders and 15 as Referees/Linesmen. In addition, there are 84 media honourees.

Founding/Premiere Sponsors: Imperial Oil, International Ice Hockey Federation, Molson Canada, National Hockey League, National Hockey League Players' Association, Panasonic Canada, Pepsi-Cola Canada, RBC Financial Group, The Toronto Sun, The Sports Network (TSN/RDS), Verizon.

Dino Ciccarelli made his NHL debut with the Minnesota North Stars in 1980-81. He had 55 goals and 106 points in his first full season in 1981-82 and went on to collect 608 goals and 592 assists in his 19-year career.

PLAYERS

* Abel, Sidney Gerald 1969
* Adams, John James "Jack" 1959
  Anderson, Glenn 2008
* Apps, Charles Joseph Sylvanus "Syl" 1961
  Armstrong, George Edward 1975
* Bailey, Irvine Wallace "Ace" 1975
* Bain, Donald H. "Dan" 1949
* Baker, Hobart "Hobey" 1945
  Barber, William Charles "Bill" 1990
* Barry, Martin J. "Marty" 1965
  Bathgate, Andrew James "Andy" 1978
* Bauer, Robert Theodore "Bobby" 1996
  Béliveau, Jean Arthur 1972
* Benedict, Clinton S. 1965
* Bentley, Douglas Wagner 1964
* Bentley, Maxwell H. L. 1966
* Blake, Hector "Toe" 1966
  Boivin, Leo Joseph 1986
* Boon, Richard R. "Dickie" 1952
  Bossy, Michael 1991
* Bouchard, Emile Joseph "Butch" 1966
* Boucher, Frank 1958
* Boucher, Georges "Buck" 1960
  Bourque, Raymond 2004
  Bower, John William 1976
* Bowie, Russell 1947
* Brimsek, Francis Charles 1966
* Broadbent, Harry L. "Punch" 1962
* Broda, Walter Edward "Turk" 1967
  Bucyk, John Paul 1981
* Burch, Billy 1974
* Cameron, Harold Hugh "Harry" 1962
  Cheevers, Gerald Michael "Gerry" 1985

Ciccarelli, Dino 2010
* Clancy, Francis Michael "King" 1958
* Clapper, Aubrey "Dit" 1947
  Clarke, Robert "Bobby" 1987
* Cleghorn, Sprague 1958
  Coffey, Paul 2004
* Colville, Neil MacNeil 1967
* Conacher, Charles W. 1961
* Conacher, Lionel Pretoria 1994
* Conacher, Roy Gordon 1998
* Connell, Alex 1958
* Cook, Fred "Bun" 1995
* Cook, William Osser 1952
* Coulter, Arthur Edmund 1974
  Cournoyer, Yvan Serge 1982
* Cowley, William Mailes 1968
* Crawford, Samuel Russell "Rusty" 1962
* Darragh, John Proctor "Jack" 1962
* Davidson, Allan M. "Scotty" 1950

* Day, Clarence Henry "Hap" 1961
  Delvecchio, Alex 1977
* Denneny, Cyril "Cy" 1959
  Dionne, Marcel 1992
* Drillon, Gordon Arthur 1975
* Drinkwater, Charles Graham 1950
  Dryden, Kenneth Wayne 1983
  Duff, Dick 2006
* Dumart, Woodrow "Woody" 1992
* Dunderdale, Thomas 1974
* Durnan, William Ronald 1964
* Dutton, Mervyn A. "Red" 1958
* Dye, Cecil Henry "Babe" 1970
  Esposito, Anthony James "Tony" 1988
  Esposito, Philip Anthony 1984
* Farrell, Arthur F. 1965
  Federko, Bernie 2002
  Fetisov, Viacheslav 2001
  Flaman, Ferdinand Charles "Fern" 1990
* Foyston, Frank 1958
  Francis, Ron 2007
* Fredrickson, Frank 1958
  Fuhr, Grant 2003
  Gadsby, William Alexander 1970
  Gainey, Bob 1992
* Gardiner, Charles Robert "Chuck" 1945
* Gardiner, Herbert Martin "Herb" 1958
* Gardner, James Henry "Jimmy" 1962
  Gartner, Michael Alfred 2001
* Geoffrion, Jos. A. Bernard "Boom Boom" 1972
* Gerard, Eddie 1945
  Giacomin, Edward "Eddie" 1987
  Gilbert, Rodrigue Gabriel "Rod" 1982
  Gillies, Clark 2002
* Gilmour, Hamilton Livingstone "Billy" 1962
* Goheen, Frank Xavier "Moose" 1952
* Goodfellow, Ebenezer R. "Ebbie" 1963
  Goulet, Michel 1998
  Granato, Cammi 2010
* Grant, Michael "Mike" 1950
* Green, Wilfred "Shorty" 1962
  Gretzky, Wayne Douglas 1999
* Griffis, Silas Seth "Si" 1950
* Hainsworth, George 1961
  Hall, Glenn Henry 1975
* Hall, Joseph Henry 1961
* Harvey, Douglas Norman 1973
  Hawerchuk, Dale Martin 2001
* Hay, George 1958
* Hern, William Milton "Riley" 1962
* Hextall, Bryan Aldwyn 1969

* Holmes, Harry "Hap" 1972
* Hooper, Charles Thomas "Tom" 1962
* Horner, George Reginald "Red" 1965
* Horton, Miles Gilbert "Tim" 1977
  Howe, Gordon 1972
* Howe, Sydney Harris 1965
  Howell, Henry Vernon "Harry" 1979
  Hull, Brett 2009
  Hull, Robert Marvin 1983
* Hutton, John Bower "Bouse" 1962
* Hyland, Harry M. 1962
* Irvin, James Dickenson "Dick" 1958
* Jackson, Harvey "Busher" 1971
  James, Angela 2010
* Johnson, Ernest "Moose" 1952
* Johnson, Ivan "Ching" 1958
* Johnson, Thomas Christian 1970
* Joliat, Aurel 1947
* Keats, Gordon "Duke" 1958
  Kelly, Leonard Patrick "Red" 1969
* Kennedy, Theodore Samuel "Teeder" 1966
  Keon, David Michael 1986
* Kharlamov, Valeri 2005
  Kurri, Jari 2001
  Lach, Elmer James 1966
  Lafleur, Guy Damien 1988
  LaFontaine, Pat 2003
* Lalonde, Edouard Charles "Newsy" 1950
  Langway, Rod Corry 2002
  Laperriere, Jacques 1987
  Lapointe, Guy 1993
  Laprade, Edgar 1993
  Larionov, Igor 2008
* Laviolette, Jean Baptiste "Jack" 1962
* Lehman, Hugh 1958
  Lemaire, Jacques Gerard 1984
  Lemieux, Mario 1997
* LeSueur, Percy 1961
  Leetch, Brian 2009
* Lewis, Herbert A. 1989
  Lindsay, Robert Blake Theodore "Ted" 1966
* Lumley, Harry 1980
  MacInnis, Al 2007
* MacKay, Duncan "Mickey" 1952
  Mahovlich, Frank William 1981
* Malone, Joseph "Joe" 1950
  Mantha, Sylvio 1960
* Marshall, John "Jack" 1965
* Maxwell, Fred G. "Steamer" 1962
  McDonald, Lanny 1992
* McGee, Frank 1945

* McGimsie, William George "Billy" 1962
* McNamara, George 1958
  Messier, Mark 2007
  Mikita, Stanley 1983
  Moore, Richard Winston "Dickie" 1974
* Moran, Patrick Joseph "Paddy" 1958
  Morenz, Howie 1945
* Mosienko, William "Billy" 1965
  Mullen, Joseph P. 2000
  Murphy, Larry 2004
  Neely, Cam 2005
* Nighbor, Frank 1947
* Noble, Edward Reginald "Reg" 1962
* O'Connor, Herbert William "Buddy" 1988
* Oliver, Harry 1967
  Olmstead, Murray Bert "Bert" 1985
  Orr, Robert Gordon 1979
  Parent, Bernard Marcel 1984
  Park, Douglas Bradford "Brad" 1988
* Patrick, Joseph Lynn 1980
* Patrick, Lester 1947
  Perreault, Gilbert 1990
* Phillips, Tommy 1945
  Pilote, Joseph Albert Pierre Paul 1975
* Pitre, Didier "Pit" 1962
* Plante, Joseph Jacques Omer 1978
  Potvin, Denis 1991
* Pratt, Walter "Babe" 1966
* Primeau, A. Joseph 1963
  Pronovost, Joseph René Marcel 1978
  Pulford, Bob 1991
* Pulford, Harvey 1945
* Quackenbush, Hubert George "Bill" 1976
* Rankin, Frank 1961
  Ratelle, Joseph Gilbert Yvan Jean "Jean" 1985
* Rayner, Claude Earl "Chuck" 1973
* Reardon, Kenneth Joseph 1966
  Richard, Joseph Henri 1979
* Richard, Joseph Henri Maurice "Rocket" 1961
* Richardson, George Taylor 1950
* Roberts, Gordon 1971
  Robinson, Larry 1995
  Robitaille, Luc 2009
* Ross, Arthur Howey 1949
  Roy, Patrick 2006
* Russell, Blair 1965
* Russell, Ernest 1965
* Ruttan, J.D. "Jack" 1962
  Salming, Borje Anders 1996
  Savard, Denis Joseph 2000

Savard, Serge 1986
* Sawchuk, Terrance Gordon "Terry" 1971
* Scanlan, Fred 1965
Schmidt, Milton Conrad "Milt" 1961
* Schriner, David "Sweeney" 1962
* Seibert, Earl Walter 1963
* Seibert, Oliver Levi 1961
* Shore, Edward W. "Eddie" 1947
Shutt, Stephen 1993
* Siebert, Albert C. "Babe" 1964
* Simpson, Harold Edward "Bullet Joe" 1962
Sittler, Darryl Glen 1989
* Smith, Alfred E. 1962
* Smith, Clint 1991
* Smith, Reginald "Hooley" 1972
* Smith, Thomas James 1973
Smith, William John "Billy" 1993
Stanley, Allan Herbert 1981
* Stanley, Russell "Barney" 1962
Stastny, Peter 1998
Stevens, Scott 2007
* Stewart, John Sherratt "Black Jack" 1964
* Stewart, Nelson "Nels" 1952
* Stuart, Bruce 1961
* Stuart, Hod 1945
* Taylor, Frederick "Cyclone" (O.B.E.) 1947
* Thompson, Cecil R. "Tiny" 1959
Tretiak, Vladislav 1989
* Trihey, Col. Harry J. 1950
Trottier, Bryan 1997
Ullman, Norman V. Alexander "Norm" 1982
* Vezina, Georges 1945
* Walker, John Phillip "Jack" 1960
* Walsh, Martin "Marty" 1962
* Watson, Harry E. 1962
* Watson, Harry 1994
* Weiland, Ralph "Cooney" 1971
* Westwick, Harry 1962
* Whitcroft, Fred 1962
* Wilson, Gordon Allan "Phat" 1962

* Worsley, Lorne John "Gump" 1980
* Worters, Roy 1969
Yzerman, Steve 2009

BUILDERS

* Adams, Charles 1960
* Adams, Weston W. 1972
* Ahearn, Thomas Franklin "Frank" 1962
* Ahearne, John Francis "Bunny" 1977
* Allan, Sir Montagu (C.V.O.) 1945
Allen, Keith 1992
Arbour, Alger Joseph "Al" 1996
* Ballard, Harold Edwin 1977
* Bauer, Father David 1989
* Bickell, John Paris 1978
Bowman, Scotty 1991
* Brooks, Herb 2006
* Brown, George V. 1961
* Brown, Walter A. 1962
* Buckland, Frank 1975
Bush, Walter 2000
Butterfield, Jack Arlington 1980
* Calder, Frank 1947
* Campbell, Angus D. 1964
* Campbell, Clarence Sutherland 1966
* Cattarinich, Joseph 1977
* Chynoweth, Ed 2008
Costello, Murray 2005
* Dandurand, Joseph Viateur "Leo" 1963
Devellano, Jim 2010
* Dilio, Francis Paul 1964
* Dudley, George S. 1958
* Dunn, James A. 1968
Fletcher, Cliff 2004
Francis, Emile 1982
* Gibson, Dr. John L. "Jack" 1976
* Gorman, Thomas Patrick "Tommy" 1963
Gregory, Jim 2007
* Griffiths, Frank A. 1993
* Hanley, William 1986
* Hay, Charles 1974

* Hendy, James C. 1968
* Hewitt, Foster 1965
* Hewitt, William Abraham 1947
Hotchkiss, Harley 2006
* Hume, Fred J. 1962
Illitch, Mike 2003
* Imlach, George "Punch" 1984
* Ivan, Thomas N. 1974
* Jennings, William M. 1975
* Johnson, Bob 1992
* Juckes, Gordon W. 1979
* Kilpatrick, Gen. John Reed 1960
Kilrea, Brian Blair 2003
* Knox, Seymour H. III 1993
Lamoriello, Lou 2009
* Leader, George Alfred 1969
* LeBel, Robert 1970
* Lockhart, Thomas F. 1965
* Loicq, Paul 1961
* Mariucci, John 1985
* Mathers, Frank 1992
* McLaughlin, Major Frederic 1963
* Milford, John "Jake" 1984
* Molson, Hon. Hartland de Montarville 1973
Morrison, Ian "Scotty" 1999
* Murray, Monsignor Athol 1998
* Neilson, Roger 2002
* Nelson, Francis 1947
* Norris, Bruce A. 1969
* Norris, Sr., James 1958
* Norris, James Dougan 1962
* Northey, William M. 1947
* O'Brien, John Ambrose 1962
O'Neill, Brian 1994
* Page, Fred 1993
Patrick, Craig 2001
* Patrick, Frank 1950
* Pickard, Allan W. 1958
* Pilous, Rudy 1985
* Poile, Norman "Bud" 1990
* Pollock, Samuel Patterson Smyth 1978
* Raymond, Sen. Donat 1958
* Robertson, John Ross 1947
* Robinson, Claude C. 1947

* Ross, Philip D. 1976
* Sabetzki, Dr. Gunther 1995
Sather, Glen 1997
Seaman, Daryl "Doc" 2010
* Selke, Frank J. 1960
Sinden, Harry James 1983
* Smith, Frank D. 1962
* Smythe, Conn 1958
Snider, Edward M. 1988
* Stanley of Preston, Lord (G.C.B.) 1945
* Sutherland, Cap. James T. 1947
* Tarasov, Anatoli V. 1974
Torrey, Bill 1995
* Turner, Lloyd 1958
* Tutt, William Thayer 1978
* Voss, Carl Potter 1974
* Waghorne, Fred 1961
* Wirtz, Arthur Michael 1971
* Wirtz, William W. "Bill" 1976
Ziegler, John A. Jr. 1987

REFEREES/LINESMEN

Armstrong, Neil 1991
* Ashley, John George 1981
* Chadwick, William L. 1964
* D'Amico, John 1993
* Elliott, Chaucer 1961
* Hayes, George William 1988
* Hewitson, Robert W. 1963
* Ion, Fred J. "Mickey" 1961
Pavelich, Matt 1987
* Rodden, Michael J. "Mike" 1962
Scapinello, Ray 2008
* Smeaton, J. Cooper 1961
* Storey, Roy Alvin "Red" 1967
Udvari, Frank Joseph 1973
Van Hellemond, Andy 1999

International hockey stars Cammi Granato (left) of the United States and Angela James (right) of Canada made history in 2010 as the first women elected to the Hockey Hall of Fame.

Foster Hewitt Memorial Award Winners

In recognition of members of the radio and television industry who made outstanding contributions to their profession and the game during their career in hockey broadcasting. Selected by the NHL Broadcasters' Association.

Cole, Bob, Hockey Night in Canada 1996
* Cusick, Fred, Boston 1984
* Darling, Ted, Buffalo 1994
Emrick, Mike, New Jersey, U.S. networks, 2008
Davidson, John, MSG Network/HNIC 2009
* Gallivan, Danny, Montreal 1984
Garneau, Richard, Montreal 1999
* Hart, Gene, Philadelphia 1997
* Hewitt, Bill, Hockey Night in Canada 2007
* Hewitt, Foster, Toronto 1984
Irvin, Dick, Montreal 1988
Kaiton, Chuck, Hartford/Carolina 2004
* Kelly, Dan, St. Louis 1989
Lange, Mike, Pittsburgh 2001
* Lecavelier, René, Montreal 1984
Lynch, Budd, Detroit 1985
Maher, Peter, Calgary 2006
Martyn, Bruce, Detroit 1991
McDonald, Jiggs, Los Angeles, Atlanta, NY Islanders 1990
McFarlane, Brian, Hockey Night in Canada 1995
* McKnight, Wes, Toronto 1986
Meeker, Howie, Hockey Night in Canada 1998
Messina, Sal, New York 2005
Miller, Bob, Los Angeles 2000
* Pettit, Lloyd, Chicago 1986
Phillips, Rod, Edmonton 2003
Robson, Jim, Vancouver 1992
Shaver, Al, Minnesota 1993
* Smith, Doug, Montreal 1985
Tremblay, Gilles, La Soirée du Hockey 2002
Weber, Ron, Washington 2010
Wilson, Bob, Boston 1987

* Deceased

Elmer Ferguson Memorial Award Winners

In recognition of distinguished members of the newspaper profession whose words have brought honor to journalism and to hockey. Selected by the Professional Hockey Writers' Association.

* Barton, Charlie, Buffalo-Courier Express 1985
* Beauchamp, Jacques, Montreal Matin/Journal de Montréal 1984
* Brennan, Bill, Detroit News 1987
* Burchard, Jim, New York World Telegram 1984
* Burnett, Red, Toronto Star 1984
* Carroll, Dink, Montreal Gazette 1984
* Coleman, Jim, Southam Newspapers 1984
  Conway, Russ, Eagle-Tribune 1999
* Damata, Ted, Chicago Tribune 1984
  de Foy, Marc, Le Journal de Montreal/ ruefrontenac.com 2010
  Delano, Hugh, New York Post 1991
  Desjardins, Marcel, Montréal La Presse 1984
  Duhatschek, Eric, Calgary Herald/Globe and Mail 2001
* Dulmage, Jack, Windsor Star 1984
* Dunnell, Milt, Toronto Star 1984
  Dupont, Kevin Paul, Boston Globe 2002
  Elliott, Helene, Los Angeles Times 2005
  Farber, Michael, Montreal Gazette/Sports Illustrated 2003
  Fay, Dave, Washington Times 2007
* Ferguson, Elmer, Montreal Herald/Star 1984
* Fitzgerald, Tom, Boston Globe 1984
  Frayne, Trent, Toronto Telegram/Globe and Mail/Sun 1984
  Gatecliff, Jack, St. Catharines Standard 1995
* Gross, George, Toronto Telegram/Sun 1985
  Johnston, Dick, Buffalo News 1986
  Kelley, Jim, Buffalo News 2004
* Laney, Al, New York Herald-Tribune 1984
* Larochelle, Claude, Le Soleil 1989
  L'Esperance, Zotique, Journal de Montréal/ le Petit Journal 1985
* MacLeod, Rex, Toronto Globe and Mail/Star 1987
  Matheson, Jim, Edmonton Journal 2000
* Mayer, Charles, Journal de Montréal/la Patrie 1985
* McKenzie, Ken, The Hockey News 1997
  Molinari, Dave, Pittsburgh Post-Gazette 2009
  Monahan, Leo, Boston Daily Record/Record-American/ Herald American 1986
  Moriarty, Tim, UPI/Newsday 1986
  Morrison, Scott, Toronto Sun/Rogers Sportsnet 2006
* Nichols, Joe, New York Times 1984
* O'Brien, Andy, Weekend Magazine 1985
  Orr, Frank, Toronto Star 1989
  Olan, Ben, New York Associated Press 1987
* O'Meara, Basil, Montreal Star 1984
  Pedneault, Yvon, La Presse/Journal de Montréal 1998
* Proudfoot, Jim, Toronto Star 1988
  Raymond, Bertrand, Journal de Montréal 1990
  Rosa, Fran, Boston Globe 1987
  Stevens, Neil, Canadian Press 2008
  Strachan, Al, Globe and Mail/Toronto Sun 1993
* Vipond, Jim, Toronto Globe and Mail 1984
  Walter, Lewis, Detroit Times 1984

U.S. HOCKEY HALL of FAME

United States Hockey Hall of Fame

On May 11, 2007, the U.S. Hockey Hall of Fame and USA Hockey came to a historic agreement that transferred rights to the selection process and induction event associated with the Hall, including the Wayne Gretzky International Award, to USA Hockey. As part of the agreement, the U.S. Hockey Hall of Fame Museum, located in Eveleth, Minn., formed a separate Board of Directors to govern the national shrine for American Hockey.

There are 148 enshrined members in the U.S. Hockey Hall of Fame (www.ushockeyhalloffame.com). New members are inducted annually and must have made a significant contribution to hockey in the United States during the course of their career. A special Wayne Gretzky International Award pays tribute to international individuals who have made major contributions to hockey in the USA.

The United States Hockey Hall of Fame Museum was opened on June 21, 1973. It is dedicated to honoring the sport of ice hockey in the United States by preserving those previous memories and legends of the game. It is located in Eveleth, Minn., 60 miles north of Duluth on Highway 53. The facility is open Memorial Day through Labor Day, Monday to Saturday, 9 a.m. to 5 p.m. and Sundays from 10 a.m. to 3 p.m. After Labor Day, it is open Friday through Sunday. Admission is $8.00 for adults, $7.00 for seniors and youths (13-17) and $6.00 for children (6-12). Children under 6 are free. For further information, call 800-443-7825 or 218-744-5167, or visit www.ushockeyhall.com.

INDIVIDUALS

* Abel, Clarence "Taffy" 1973
* Almquist, Oscar 1983
  Amonte, Tony 2009
* Baker, Hobart "Hobey" 1973
  Barrasso, Tom 2009
* Bartholome, Earl 1977
  Berglund, Art 2010
  Bessone, Amo 1992
* Bessone, Peter 1978
* Blake, Robert 1985
  Boucha, Henry 1995
* Brimsek, Frank 1973
* Brink, Milton "Curly" 2006
* Brooks, Herb 1990
  Broten, Aaron 2007
  Broten, Neal 2000
  Brown, George V. 1973
  Brown, Walter A. 1973
  Bush, Walter 1980
  Carpenter, Bobby 2007
  Cavanagh, Joe 1994
  Ceglarski, Len 1992
* Chadwick, William 1974
* Chaisson, Ray 1974
* Chase, John P. 1973
  Christian, Dave 2001
  Christian, Roger 1989
* Christian, William "Bill" 1984
  Christiansen, Keith 2005
* Clark, Donald 1978
  Claypool, James 1995
  Cleary, Robert 1981
  Cleary, William 1976
* Conroy, Anthony 1975
  Coppo, Paul 2004
* Cunniff, John 2003
  Curran, Mike 1998
* Dahlstrom, Carl "Cully" 1973
* Desjardins, Victor 1974
* Desmond, Richard 1988
* Dill, Robert 1979
  Dougherty, Richard "Dick" 2003
* Everett, Doug 1974
  Ftorek, Robbie 1991
* Fullerton, James 1992
  Fusco, Mark 2002
  Fusco, Scott 2002
  Gambucci, Gary 2006
  Gambucci, Sergio 1996
* Garrison, John B. 1973
  Garrity, Jack 1986
* Gibson, J.C. "Doc" 1973
* Goheen, Frank "Moose" 1973
* Gordon, Malcolm K. 1973
  Granato, Cammi 2008

Grant, Wally 1994
* Harding, Francis "Austie" 1975
* Harkness, Nevin D. "Ned" 1994
  Hatcher, Derian 2010
  Hatcher, Kevin 2010
* Heyliger, Victor 1974
* Holt, Jr. Charles E. 1997
  Housley, Phil 2004
  Howe, Mark 2003
  Hull, Brett 2008
* Iglehart, Stewart 1975
  Ikola, Willard 1990
  Ilitch, Mike 2004
* Jennings, William M. 1981
* Jeremiah, Edward J. 1973
* Johnson, Bob 1991
  Johnson, Mark 2004
  Johnson, Paul 2001
* Johnson, Virgil 1974
* Kahler, Nick 1980
* Karakas, Mike 1973
* Kelley, John "Snooks" 1974
  Kelley, John H. "Jack" 1993
  Kirrane, Jack 1987
  LaFontaine, Pat 2003
* Lane, Myles J. 1973
  Langevin, David R. 1993
  Langway, Rod 1999
  Larson, Reed 1996
  LeClair, John 2009
  Leetch, Brian 2008
* Linder, Joseph 1975
* Lockhart, Thomas F. 1973
* LoPresti, Sam L. 1973
  MacDonald, Lane 2005
* MacInnes, John 2007
* Mariucci, John 1973
* Marvin, Cal 1982
  Matchefts, John 1991
* Mather, Bruce 1998
  Mayasich, John 1976
  McCartan, Jack 1983
  Milbury, Mike 2006
* Moe, William 1974
  Morrow, Ken 1995
* Moseley, Fred 1975
  Mullen, Joe 1998
* Murray, Sr. Hugh "Muzz" 1987
  Nagobads, Dr. V. George 2010
  Nanne, Lou 1998
* Nelson, Hubert "Hub" 1978
* Nyrop, William D. 1997
* Olson, Eddie 1977
* Owen, Jr. George 1973
  Palazzari, Doug 2000

* Palmer, Winthrop 1973
  Paradise, Robert 1989
  Patrick, Craig 1996
  Pleau, Larry 2000
* Pleban, Jon "Connie" 1990
* Purpur, Clifford "Fido" 1974
  Ramsey, Mike 2001
  Richter, Mike 2008
* Ridder, Robert 1976
  Riley, Jack 1979
* Riley, Joe 2002
* Riley, William 1977
  Roberts, Gordie 1999
* Roberts, Moe 2005
  Roenick, Jeremy 2010
* Romnes, Elwin "Doc" 1973
* Rondeau, Richard 1985
* Ross, Larry 1988
* Schulz, Charles M. 1993
  Sheehy, Timothy K. 1997
* Stewart, William 1982
* Thompson, Clifford R. 1973
  Trumble, Harold 1985
* Tutt, William Thayer 1973
  Vanbiesbrouck, John 2007
* Watson, Sid 1999
* Williams, Thomas 1981
  Williamson, Murray 2005
  Winsor, Alfred "Ralph" 1973
* Winters, Frank "Coddy" 1973
* Wirtz, William W. "Bill" 1984
  Woog, Doug 2002
* Wright, Lyle Z. 1973
* Yackel, Ken 1986
  Zamboni, Frank 2009

TEAMS

1960 Olympic Men's Team 2000
1980 Olympic Men's Team 2003
1998 Olympic Women's Team 2009

WAYNE GRETZKY AWARD

Wayne Gretzky 1999
The Howe family 2000
Scotty Morrison 2001
Scotty Bowman 2002
Bobby Hull 2003
* Herb Brooks 2004
* Anatoli Tarasov 2008

* Deceased

International Ice Hockey Federation Hall of Fame

The IIHF Hall of Fame was founded in 1997.

Candidates for election as Honoured Members in the player category shall be chosen on the basis of their playing ability, sportsmanship, character and their contribution to their team or teams and to the game of ice hockey in general.

Candidates for election as Honoured Members in the builder category shall be chosen on the basis of their coaching, managerial or executive ability, where applicable, their sportsmanship and character, and their contribution to their organization or organizations and to the game of ice hockey in general.

Candidates for election as Honoured Members in the referee or linesman category shall be chosen on the basis of their officiating ability, sportsmanship, character and their contribution to the game of ice hockey in general. The Paul Loicq Award, named for the longtime former IIHF president, is presented to honor a person for his service to the international hockey community.

Inductees' names are followed by their country and year of induction.

PLAYERS

Alexandrov, Veniamin, RUS, 2007
Balderis, Helmut, LAT, 1998
Ball, Rudi, GER, 2004
Bergqvist, Sven, SWE, 1999
Bjorn, Lars, SWE, 1998
Bobrov, Vsevolod, RUS, 1997
Bourbonnais, Roger, CAN, 1999
Bouzek, Vladimir, CzRep, 2007
Bozon, Phillippe, FRA 2008
Bubnik, Vlastimil, CzRep, 1997
Cattini, Ferdinand, SUI, 1998
Cattini, Hans, SUI, 1998
Cerny, Josef, CzRep, 2007
Christian, Bill, USA, 1998
Cleary, Bill, USA, 1997
Cosby, Gerry, USA, 1997
Craig, Jim, USA, 1999
Curran, Mike, USA, 1999
Davydov, Vitaly, RUS, 2004
Drobny, Jaroslav, CzRep, 1997
Dzurilla, Vladimir, SVK, 1998
Erhardt, Carl, G.B., 1998
Fetisov, Viacheslav, RUS, 2005
Firsov, Anatoli, RUS, 1998
Golonka, Josef, SVK, 1998
Granato, Cammi, USA 2008
Gretzky, Wayne, CAN, 2000
Gruth, Henryk, POL, 2006
Gustafsson, Bengt-Ake, SWE, 2003
Gut, Karel, CzRep, 1998
Heaney, Geraldine, CAN 2008
Hedberg, Anders, SWE, 1997
Hegen, Dieter, GER 2010
Hiti, Rudi, SLO, 2009
Hlinka, Ivan, CzRep, 2002
Holecek, Jiri, CzRep, 1998
Holik, Jiri, CzRep, 1999
Holmqvist, Leif, SWE, 1999
Huck, Fran, CAN, 1999
Irbe, Arturs, LAT 2010
Jaenecke, Gustav, GER, 1998
James, Angela, CAN 2008
Johnson, Mark, USA, 1999
Johnston, Marshall, CAN, 1998
Jonsson, Tomas, SWE, 2000
Jutila, Timo, FIN, 2003
Kasatonov, Alexei, RUS, 2009
Keinonen, Matti, FIN, 2002
Kharlamov, Valeri, RUS, 1998
Kiessling, Udo, GER, 2000
Kolliker, Jakob, SUI, 2007
Konovalenko, Viktor, RUS, 2007
Krutov, Vladimir, RUS 2010
Kuhnhackl, Erich, GER, 1997
Kurri, Jari, FIN, 2000
Kuzkin, Viktor, RUS, 2005
Lacarriere, Jacques, FRA, 1998
Larionov, Igor RUS 2008
Lemieux, Mario CAN 2008
Loktev, Konstantin, RUS, 2007
Loob, Hakan, SWE, 1998
Lundquist, Vic, CAN, 1997
Machac, Oldrich, CzRep, 1999
MacKenzie, Barry, CAN, 1999
Makarov, Sergei, RUS, 2001
Malecek, Josef, CzRep, 2003
Maltsev, Alexander, RUS, 1999
Marjamaki, Pekka, FIN, 1998
Martin, Seth, CAN, 1997
Martinec, Vladimir, CzRep, 2001
Mayasich, John, USA, 1997
Mayorov, Boris, RUS, 1999
McCartan, Jack, USA, 1998
McLeod, Jackie, CAN, 1999
Mikhailov, Boris, RUS, 2000
Nanne, Lou, USA, 2004
Naslund, Mats, SWE, 2005
Nedomansky, Vaclav, CzRep, 1997

Nieminen-Valila, Riika, FIN, 2010
Nilsson, Kent, SWE, 2006
Nilsson, Nisse, SWE, 2002
O'Malley, Terry, CAN, 1998
Oksanen, Lasse, FIN, 1999
Pana, Eduard, ROM, 1998
Patton, Peter, G.B., 2002
Peltonen, Esa, FIN, 2007
Petrov, Vladimir, RUS, 2006
Pettersson, Ronald, SWE, 2004
Pospisil, Frantisek, CzRep, 1999
Puschnig, Josef, AUT, 1999
Ragulin, Alexander, RUS, 1997
Rampf, Hans, GER, 2001
Rundqvist, Thomas, SWE, 2007
Salming, Borje, SWE, 1998
Schloder, Alois, GER, 2005
Sinden, Harry, CAN, 1997
Sologubov, Nikolai, RUS, 2004
Starshinov, Vyacheslav, RUS, 2007
Stastny, Peter, SVK, 2000
Sterner, Ulf, SWE, 2001
Stoltz, Roland, SWE, 1999
Suchy, Jan, CzRep, 2009
Tikal, Frantisek, CzRep, 2004
Torriani, Bibi, SUI, 1997
Tretiak, Vladislav, RUS, 1997
Tumba, Sven, SWE, 1997
Valtonen, Jorma, FIN, 1999
Vasiliev, Valeri, RUS, 1998
Wahlsten, Vladimir, FIN, 2006
Watson, Harry, CAN, 1998
Yakushev, Alexander, RUS, 2003
Ylonen, Urpo, FIN, 1997
Zabrodsky, Vladimir, CzRep, 1997
Ziesche, Joachim, GER, 1999

BUILDERS

Ahearne, Bunny, G.B., 1997
Aljancic Sr., Ernest, SLO, 2002
Bauer, Father David, CAN, 1997
Berglund, Art USA 2008
Berglund, Curt, SWE, 2003
Bokac, Ludek, CzRep, 2007
Brooks, Herb, USA, 1999
Brown, Walter, USA, 1997
Buckna, Mike, CAN, 2004
Bush, Walter Jr. USA, 2009
Calcaterra, Enrico, ITA, 1999
Chernyshev, Arkady, RUS, 1999
Dimitriev, Igor, RUS, 2007
Dobida, Hans, AUT, 2007
Eklow, Rudolf, SWE, 1999
Fagerlund, Rickard SWE 2010
Grunander, Arne, SWE, 1997
Henschel, Heinz, GER, 2003
Hewitt, William, CAN, 1998
Holmes, Derek, CAN, 1999
Horsky, Ladislav, SVK, 2004
Hviid, Jorgen, DEN, 2005
Johannessen, Tore, NOR, 1999
Juckes, Gordon, CAN, 1997
Kawabuchi, Tsutomu, JPN, 2004
Khorozov, Anatoli, UKR, 2006
King, Dave, CAN, 2001
Kostka, Vladimir, CzRep, 1997
LeBel, Bob, CAN, 1997
Lindblad, Harry, FIN, 1999
Loicq, Paul, BEL, 1997
Luhti, Cesar W., SUI, 1998
Magnus, Louis, FRA, 1997
Pasztor, Gyorgy, HUN, 2001
Renwick, Gordon, CAN, 2002
Ridder, Bob, USA, 1998
Riley, Jack, USA, 1998
Sabetzki, Dr. Gunther, GER, 1997
Starovoitov, Andrei, RUS, 1997

Starsi, Jan, SVK, 1999
Stromberg, Arne, SWE, 1998
Stubb, Goran, FIN, 2000
Subrt, Miroslav, CzRep, 2004
Tarasov, Anatoli, RUS, 1997
Tikhonov, Viktor, RUS, 1998
Tomita, Shoichi, JPN, 2006
Trumble, Hal, USA, 1999
Tsutsumi, Yoshiaki, JPN, 1999
Tutt, Thayer, USA, 2002
Unsinn, Xaver, GER, 1998
Wasservogel, Walter, AUT, 1997
Yurzinov, Vladimir, RUS, 2002

REFEREES

Adamec, Quido, CzRep, 2005
Dahlberg, Ove, SWE, 2004
Karandin, Yuri, RUS, 2004
Kompalla, Josef, GER, 2003
Schell, Laszlo, HUN, 2009
Wiitala, Unto, FIN, 2003

PAUL LOICQ AWARD

Montag, Wolf-Dieter, GER, 1998
Neumayer, Roman, GER, 1999
Kukushkin, Vsevolod, RUS, 2000
Kataoka, Isao, JPN, 2001
Marsh, Pat, G.B., 2002
Nagobads, George, USA, 2003
Kukulowicz, Aggie, CAN, 2004
Hrabcek, Rita, AUS, 2005
Tovland, Bo, SWE, 2006
Nadin, Bob, CAN, 2007
Okolicany, Juraj, SVK 2008
Griebel, Harald, GER, 2009
Vairo, Lou, USA 2010

CENTENNIAL ALL-STAR TEAM (1908-2008)

Goaltender: Vladislav Tretiak, RUS
Defenseman: Viacheslav Fetisov, RUS
Defenseman: Borje Salming, SWE
Winger: Valeri Kharlamov, RUS
Winger: Sergei Makarov, RUS
Center: Wayne Gretzky, CAN

TRIPLE GOLD CLUB

(Olympics, World Championship, Stanley Cup)
Tomas Jonsson, SWE
Mats Naslund, SWE
Hakan Loob, SWE
Valeri Kamensky, RUS
Alexei Gusarov, RUS
Peter Forsberg, SWE
Vyacheslav Fetisov, RUS
Igor Larionov, RUS
Alexander Mogilny, RUS
Vladimir Malakhov, RUS
Rob Blake, CAN
Joe Sakic, CAN
Brendan Shanahan, CAN
Scott Niedermayer, CAN
Jaromir Jagr, CzRep
Jiri Slegr, CzRep
Nicklas Lidstrom, SWE
Fredrik Modin, SWE
Chris Pronger, CAN
Niklas Kronwall, SWE
Henrik Zetterberg, SWE
Mikael Samuelsson, SWE
Eric Staal, CAN
Jonathan Toews, CAN
Mike Babcock (coach), CAN

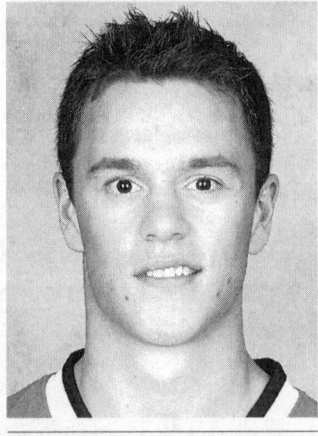

With Canada's victory on home ice in Vancouver at the 2010 Winter Olympics, Mike Babcock (top) became the first coach in history to guide teams to victory in the Stanley Cup, the World Championship and at the Olympics. The Olympic victory made Eric Staal (middle) the 23rd player in history to win all three prizes while Jonathan Toews (bottom) joined the club after the Chicago Blackhawks' Stanley Cup victory in June.

Results

2010

Stanley Cup Playoffs

CONFERENCE QUARTER-FINALS
(Best-of-seven series)

Eastern Conference

Series 'A'
Thu. Apr. 15	(8) Montreal 3	at	(1) Washington 2*
Sat. Apr. 17	Montreal 5	at	Washington 6**
Mon. Apr. 19	Washington 5	at	Montreal 1
Wed. Apr. 21	Washington 6	at	Montreal 3
Fri. Apr. 23	Montreal 2	at	Washington 1
Mon. Apr. 26	Washington 1	at	Montreal 4
Wed. Apr. 28	Montreal 2	at	Washington 1

    * Tomas Plekanec scored at 13:19 of overtime
    ** Nicklas Backstrom scored at 0:31 of overtime
(Montreal won series 4-3)

Series 'B'
Wed. Apr. 14	(7) Philadelphia 2	at	(2) New Jersey 1
Fri. Apr. 16	Philadelphia 3	at	New Jersey 5
Sun. Apr. 18	New Jersey 2	at	Philadelphia 3*
Tue. Apr. 20	New Jersey 1	at	Philadelphia 4
Thu. Apr. 22	Philadelphia 3	at	New Jersey 0

    *Daniel Carcillo scored at 3:35 of overtime
(Philadelphia won series 4-1)

Series 'C'
Thu. Apr. 15	(6) Boston 1	at	(3) Buffalo 2
Sat. Apr. 17	Boston 5	at	Buffalo 3
Mon. Apr. 19	Buffalo 1	at	Boston 2
Wed. Apr. 21	Buffalo 4	at	Boston 3*
Fri. Apr. 23	Boston 1	at	Buffalo 4
Mon. Apr. 26	Buffalo 3	at	Boston 4

    * Miroslav Satan scored at 27:41 of overtime
(Boston won series 4-2)

Series 'D'
Wed. Apr. 14	(5) Ottawa 5	at	(4) Pittsburgh 4
Fri. Apr. 16	Ottawa 1	at	Pittsburgh 2
Sun. Apr. 18	Pittsburgh 4	at	Ottawa 2
Tue. Apr. 20	Pittsburgh 7	at	Ottawa 4
Thu. Apr. 22	Ottawa 4	at	Pittsburgh 3*
Sat. Apr. 24	Pittsburgh 4	at	Ottawa 3**

    * Matt Carkner scored at 47:06 of overtime
    ** Pascal Dupuis scored at 9:56 of overtime
(Pittsburgh won series 4-2)

Western Conference

Series 'E'
Wed. Apr. 14	(8) Colorado 2	at	(1) San Jose 1
Fri. Apr. 16	Colorado 5	at	San Jose 6*
Sun. Apr. 18	San Jose 0	at	Colorado 1**
Tue. Apr. 20	San Jose 2	at	Colorado 1***
Thu. Apr. 22	Colorado 0	at	San Jose 5
Sat. Apr. 24	San Jose 5	at	Colorado 2

    * Devin Setoguchi scored at 5:22 of overtime
    ** Ryan O'Reilly scored at 0:51 of overtime
    *** Joe Pavelski scored at 10:24 of overtime
(San Jose won series 4-2)

Series 'F'
Fri. Apr. 16	(7) Nashville 4	at	(2) Chicago 1
Sun. Apr. 18	Nashville 0	at	Chicago 2
Tue. Apr. 20	Chicago 1	at	Nashville 4
Thu. Apr. 22	Chicago 3	at	Nashville 4
Sat. Apr. 24	Nashville 4	at	Chicago 5*
Mon. Apr. 26	Chicago 5	at	Nashville 3

    * Marian Hossa scored at 4:07 of overtime
(Chicago won series 4-2)

Series 'G'
Thu. Apr. 15	(6) Los Angeles 2	at	(3) Vancouver 3*
Sat. Apr. 17	Los Angeles 3	at	Vancouver 2**
Mon. Apr. 19	Vancouver 3	at	Los Angeles 5
Wed. Apr. 21	Vancouver 6	at	Los Angeles 4
Fri. Apr. 23	Los Angeles 2	at	Vancouver 7
Sun. Apr. 25	Vancouver 4	at	Los Angeles 2

    * Mikael Samuelsson scored at 8:52 of overtime
    ** Anze Kopitar scored at 7:28 of overtime
(Vancouver won series 4-2)

Series 'H'
Wed. Apr. 14	(5) Detroit 2	at	(4) Phoenix 3
Fri. Apr. 16	Detroit 7	at	Phoenix 4
Sun. Apr. 18	Phoenix 4	at	Detroit 2
Tue. Apr. 20	Phoenix 0	at	Detroit 3
Fri. Apr. 23	Detroit 4	at	Phoenix 1
Sun. Apr. 25	Phoenix 5	at	Detroit 2
Tue. Apr. 27	Detroit 6	at	Phoenix 1

(Detroit won series 4-3)

CONFERENCE SEMI-FINALS
(Best-of-seven series)

Eastern Conference

Series 'I'
Fri. Apr. 30	(8) Montreal 3	at	(4) Pittsburgh 6
Sun. May 2	Montreal 3	at	Pittsburgh 1
Tue. May 4	Pittsburgh 2	at	Montreal 0
Thu. May 6	Pittsburgh 2	at	Montreal 3
Sat. May 8	Montreal 1	at	Pittsburgh 2
Mon. May 10	Pittsburgh 3	at	Montreal 4
Wed. May 12	Montreal 5	at	Pittsburgh 2

(Montreal won series 4-3)

Series 'J'
Sat. May 1	(7) Philadelphia 4	at	(6) Boston 5*
Mon. May 3	Philadelphia 2	at	Boston 3
Wed. May 5	Boston 4	at	Philadelphia 1
Fri. May 7	Boston 4	at	Philadelphia 5**
Mon. May 10	Philadelphia 4	at	Boston 0
Wed. May 12	Boston 1	at	Philadelphia 2
Fri. May 14	Philadelphia 4	at	Boston 3

    * Marc Savard scored at 13:52 of overtime
    ** Simon Gagne scored at 14:40 of overtime
(Philadelphia won series 4-3)

Western Conference

Series 'K'
Thu. Apr. 29	(5) Detroit 3	at	(1) San Jose 4
Sun. May 2	Detroit 3	at	San Jose 4
Tue. May 4	San Jose 4	at	Detroit 3*
Thu. May 6	San Jose 1	at	Detroit 7
Sat. May 8	Detroit 1	at	San Jose 2

    * Patrick Marleau scored at 7:07 of overtime
(San Jose won series 4-1)

Series 'L'
Sat. May 1	(3) Vancouver 5	at	(2) Chicago 1
Mon. May 3	Vancouver 2	at	Chicago 4
Wed. May 5	Chicago 5	at	Vancouver 2
Fri. May 7	Chicago 7	at	Vancouver 4
Sun. May 9	Vancouver 4	at	Chicago 1
Tue. May 11	Chicago 5	at	Vancouver 1

(Chicago won series 4-2)

CONFERENCE FINALS
(Best-of-seven series)

Eastern Conference

Series 'M'
Sun. May 16	(8) Montreal 0	at	(7) Philadelphia 6
Tue. May 18	Montreal 0	at	Philadelphia 3
Thu. May 20	Philadelphia 1	at	Montreal 5
Sat. May 22	Philadelphia 3	at	Montreal 0
Mon. May 24	Montreal 2	at	Philadelphia 4

(Philadelphia won series 4-1)

Western Conference

Series 'N'
Sun. May 16	(2) Chicago 2	at	(1) San Jose 1
Tue. May 18	Chicago 4	at	San Jose 2
Fri. May 21	San Jose 2	at	Chicago 3*
Sun. May 23	San Jose 2	at	Chicago 4

    * Dustin Byfuglien scored at 12:24 of overtime
(Chicago won series 4-0)

STANLEY CUP FINAL
(Best-of-seven series)

Series 'O'
Sat. May 29	(7) Philadelphia 5	at	(2) Chicago 6
Mon. May 31	Philadelphia 1	at	Chicago 2
Wed. June 2	Chicago 3	at	Philadelphia 4*
Fri. June 4	Chicago 3	at	Philadelphia 5
Sun. June 6	Philadelphia 4	at	Chicago 7
Wed. June 9	Chicago 4	at	Philadelphia 3**

    * Claude Giroux scored at 5:59 of overtime
    ** Patrick Kane scored at 4:06 of overtime
(Chicago won series 4-2)

Team Playoff Records

	GP	W	L	GF	GA	%
Chicago	22	16	6	78	62	.727
Philadelphia	23	14	9	76	61	.609
Montreal	19	9	10	46	57	.474
San Jose	15	8	7	41	41	.533
Pittsburgh	13	7	6	42	38	.538
Boston	13	7	6	36	37	.538
Vancouver	12	6	6	43	41	.500
Detroit	12	5	7	43	33	.417
Washington	7	3	4	22	20	.429
Phoenix	7	3	4	18	26	.429
Buffalo	6	2	4	15	16	.333
Nashville	6	2	4	15	17	.333
Ottawa	6	2	4	19	24	.333
Los Angeles	6	2	4	18	25	.333
Colorado	6	2	4	11	19	.333
New Jersey	5	1	4	9	15	.200

Individual Leaders

Abbreviations: GP – games played; **G** – goals; **A** – assists; **PTS** – points; **+/–** – difference between Goals For **(GF)** scored when a player is on the ice with his team at even strength or shorthanded and Goals Against **(GA)** scored when the same player is on the ice with his team at even strength or on a power play; **PIM** – penalties in minutes; **PP** – power play goals; **SH** – shorthanded goals; **GW** – game-winning goals; **OT** – overtime goals; **S** – shots on goal; **%** – percentage of shots resulting in goals.

Playoff Scoring Leaders

Player	Team	GP	G	A	PTS	+/–	PIM	PP	SH	GW	OT	S	%
Danny Briere	Philadelphia	23	12	18	30	9	18	4	0	4	0	63	19.0
Jonathan Toews	Chicago	22	7	22	29	-1	4	5	0	3	0	58	12.1
Patrick Kane	Chicago	22	10	18	28	-2	6	1	1	1	1	64	15.6
Mike Richards	Philadelphia	23	7	16	23	-1	18	2	1	1	0	59	11.9
Patrick Sharp	Chicago	22	11	11	22	10	16	3	1	1	0	76	14.5
Claude Giroux	Philadelphia	23	10	11	21	7	4	3	0	2	1	47	21.3
Ville Leino*	Philadelphia	19	7	14	21	10	6	0	0	2	0	36	19.4
Michael Cammalleri	Montreal	19	13	6	19	-6	6	4	0	3	0	60	21.7
Sidney Crosby	Pittsburgh	13	6	13	19	6	6	1	0	1	0	41	14.6
Johan Franzen	Detroit	12	6	12	18	8	16	1	0	1	0	48	12.5
Chris Pronger	Philadelphia	23	4	14	18	5	36	3	0	0	0	41	9.8
Joe Pavelski	San Jose	15	9	8	17	6	6	5	0	3	1	65	13.8
Scott Hartnell	Philadelphia	23	8	9	17	4	25	3	0	0	0	30	26.7
Duncan Keith	Chicago	22	2	15	17	2	10	0	0	0	0	61	3.3
Dustin Byfuglien	Chicago	22	11	5	16	-4	20	5	0	5	1	45	24.4
Dave Bolland	Chicago	22	8	8	16	6	30	2	2	1	0	35	22.9
Brian Gionta	Montreal	19	9	6	15	-6	14	4	0	1	0	70	12.9
Mikael Samuelsson	Vancouver	12	8	7	15	7	16	3	0	1	1	42	19.0
Henrik Zetterberg	Detroit	12	7	8	15	11	6	2	0	2	0	45	15.6
Marian Hossa	Chicago	22	3	12	15	7	25	0	0	1	1	73	4.1

Playoff Defencemen Scoring Leaders

Player	Team	GP	G	A	PTS	+/–	PIM	PP	SH	GW	OT	S	%
Chris Pronger	Philadelphia	23	4	14	18	5	36	3	0	0	0	41	9.8
Duncan Keith	Chicago	22	2	15	17	2	10	0	0	0	0	61	3.3
Dan Boyle	San Jose	15	2	12	14	-1	8	1	0	0	0	47	4.3
Matt Carle	Philadelphia	23	1	12	13	6	8	0	0	0	0	33	3.0
Sergei Gonchar	Pittsburgh	13	2	10	12	4	4	1	0	1	0	24	8.3
Dennis Wideman	Boston	13	1	11	12	3	4	0	0	0	0	29	3.4
Brent Seabrook	Chicago	22	4	7	11	8	14	1	0	0	0	39	10.3
Brian Rafalski	Detroit	12	3	8	11	4	2	1	0	0	0	23	13.0
Kimmo Timonen	Philadelphia	23	1	10	11	6	20	0	0	0	0	45	2.2
Nicklas Lidstrom	Detroit	12	4	6	10	7	2	3	0	0	0	39	10.3
Alex Goligoski	Pittsburgh	13	2	7	9	4	2	1	0	0	0	28	7.1
Roman Hamrlik	Montreal	19	0	9	9	-1	15	0	0	0	0	21	0.0
Kevin Bieksa	Vancouver	12	3	5	8	2	14	1	0	1	0	20	15.0
P.K. Subban*	Montreal	14	1	7	8	2	6	0	0	0	0	23	4.3
Niklas Hjalmarsson	Chicago	22	1	7	8	9	6	0	0	0	0	17	5.9

GOALTENDING LEADERS

Goals Against Average

Goaltender	Team	GP	Mins	GA	Avg.
Michael Leighton	Philadelphia	14	757	31	2.46
Brian Boucher	Philadelphia	12	656	27	2.47
Jaroslav Halak	Montreal	18	1013	43	2.55
Evgeni Nabokov	San Jose	15	890	38	2.56
Tuukka Rask*	Boston	13	829	36	2.61
Antti Niemi	Chicago	22	1322	58	2.63
Jimmy Howard*	Detroit	12	720	33	2.75
Marc-Andre Fleury	Pittsburgh	13	798	37	2.78
Roberto Luongo	Vancouver	12	707	38	3.22

Wins

Goaltender	Team	GP	Mins	W	L
Antti Niemi	Chicago	22	1322	16	6
Jaroslav Halak	Montreal	18	1013	9	9
Michael Leighton	Philadelphia	14	757	8	3
Evgeni Nabokov	San Jose	15	890	8	7
Marc-Andre Fleury	Pittsburgh	13	798	7	6
Tuukka Rask*	Boston	13	829	7	6
Brian Boucher	Philadelphia	12	656	6	6
Roberto Luongo	Vancouver	12	707	6	6
Jimmy Howard*	Detroit	12	720	5	7

Save Percentage

Goaltender	Team	GP	Mins	GA	SA	S%	W	L
Jaroslav Halak	Montreal	18	1013	43	562	.923	9	9
Michael Leighton	Philadelphia	14	757	31	371	.916	8	3
Jimmy Howard*	Detroit	12	720	33	387	.915	5	7
Tuukka Rask*	Boston	13	829	36	409	.912	7	6
Antti Niemi	Chicago	22	1322	58	645	.910	16	6
Brian Boucher	Philadelphia	12	656	27	298	.909	6	6
Evgeni Nabokov	San Jose	15	890	38	407	.907	8	7
Roberto Luongo	Vancouver	12	707	38	362	.895	6	6
Marc-Andre Fleury	Pittsburgh	13	798	37	339	.891	7	6

Shutouts

Goaltender	Team	GP	Mins	SO
Michael Leighton	Philadelphia	14	757	3
Antti Niemi	Chicago	22	1322	2
Craig Anderson	Colorado	6	366	1
Brian Boucher	Philadelphia	12	656	1
Jimmy Howard*	Detroit	12	720	1
Marc-Andre Fleury	Pittsburgh	13	798	1
Evgeni Nabokov	San Jose	15	890	1

* Rookie

Goals

Player	Team	GP	G
Michael Cammalleri	Montreal	19	13
Danny Briere	Philadelphia	23	12
Patrick Sharp	Chicago	22	11
Dustin Byfuglien	Chicago	22	11
Patrick Kane	Chicago	22	10
Claude Giroux	Philadelphia	23	10
Joe Pavelski	San Jose	15	9
Simon Gagne	Philadelphia	19	9
Brian Gionta	Montreal	19	9

Assists

Player	Team	GP	A
Jonathan Toews	Chicago	22	22
Patrick Kane	Chicago	22	18
Danny Briere	Philadelphia	23	18
Mike Richards	Philadelphia	23	16
Duncan Keith	Chicago	22	15

Power-play Goals

Player	Team	GP	PP
Joe Pavelski	San Jose	15	5
Simon Gagne	Philadelphia	19	5
Dustin Byfuglien	Chicago	22	5
Jonathan Toews	Chicago	22	5
Evgeni Malkin	Pittsburgh	13	4
Kris Letang	Pittsburgh	13	4
Brian Gionta	Montreal	19	4
Michael Cammalleri	Montreal	19	4
Danny Briere	Philadelphia	23	4

Game-winning Goals

Player	Team	GP	GW
Dustin Byfuglien	Chicago	22	5
Danny Briere	Philadelphia	23	4
Miroslav Satan	Boston	13	3
Joe Pavelski	San Jose	15	3
Michael Cammalleri	Montreal	19	3

Shorthanded Goals

Player	Team	GP	SH
Dave Bolland	Chicago	22	2
Zach Parise	New Jersey	5	1
Joel Ward	Nashville	6	1
Boyd Gordon	Washington	6	1
Mike Knuble	Washington	7	1
Lauri Korpikoski	Phoenix	7	1
Maxime Talbot	Pittsburgh	13	1
Patrick Marleau	San Jose	14	1
Travis Moen	Montreal	19	1
Patrick Sharp	Chicago	22	1
Patrick Kane	Chicago	22	1
Mike Richards	Philadelphia	23	1

Overtime Goals

Player	Team	GP	OT
Matt Carkner	Ottawa	6	1
Anze Kopitar	Los Angeles	6	1
Ryan O'Reilly*	Colorado	6	1
Marc Savard	Boston	7	1
Nicklas Backstrom	Washington	7	1
Mikael Samuelsson	Vancouver	12	1
Miroslav Satan	Boston	13	1
Pascal Dupuis	Pittsburgh	13	1
Patrick Marleau	San Jose	14	1
Joe Pavelski	San Jose	15	1
Devin Setoguchi	San Jose	15	1
Daniel Carcillo	Philadelphia	17	1
Simon Gagne	Philadelphia	19	1
Tomas Plekanec	Montreal	19	1
Marian Hossa	Chicago	22	1
Dustin Byfuglien	Chicago	22	1
Patrick Kane	Chicago	22	1
Claude Giroux	Philadelphia	23	1

Shots

Player	Team	GP	S
Patrick Sharp	Chicago	22	76
Marian Hossa	Chicago	22	73
Brian Gionta	Montreal	19	70
Joe Pavelski	San Jose	15	65
Patrick Kane	Chicago	22	64

Plus/Minus

Player	Team	GP	+/–
Henrik Zetterberg	Detroit	12	11
Brian Campbell	Chicago	19	11
Ville Leino*	Philadelphia	19	10
Patrick Sharp	Chicago	22	10
Tom Poti	Washington	6	9

TEAMS' PLAYOFF HOME/ROAD RECORD

Team	HOME GP	W	L	GF	GA	Win %	ROAD GP	W	L	GF	GA	Win %
Chicago	11	8	3	36	33	.727	11	8	3	42	29	.727
Philadelphia	11	9	2	40	24	.818	12	5	7	36	37	.417
Montreal	8	4	4	20	23	.500	11	5	6	26	34	.455
San Jose	8	5	3	25	20	.625	7	3	4	16	21	.429
Pittsburgh	7	3	4	20	22	.429	6	4	2	22	16	.667
Boston	7	5	2	20	20	.714	6	2	4	16	17	.333
Vancouver	6	2	4	19	24	.333	6	4	2	24	17	.667
Detroit	5	2	3	17	14	.400	7	3	4	26	19	.429
Washington	4	1	3	10	12	.250	3	2	1	12	8	.667
Phoenix	4	1	3	9	19	.250	3	2	1	9	7	.667
Buffalo	3	2	1	9	7	.667	3	0	3	6	9	.000
Nashville	3	1	2	7	9	.333	3	1	2	8	8	.333
Ottawa	3	0	3	9	15	.000	3	2	1	10	9	.667
Los Angeles	3	1	2	11	13	.333	3	1	2	7	12	.333
Colorado	3	1	2	4	7	.333	3	1	2	7	12	.333
New Jersey	3	1	2	6	8	.333	2	0	2	3	7	.000
Totals	**89**	**46**	**43**	**262**	**270**	**.517**	**89**	**43**	**46**	**270**	**262**	**.483**

TEAMS' POWER-PLAY RECORD

Abbreviations: ADV-total advantages; **PPGF**-power play goals for; **%** arrived by dividing number of power-play goals by total advantages.

	Team	HOME GP	ADV	PPGF	%	Team	ROAD GP	ADV	PPGF	%	Team	OVERALL GP	ADV	PPGF	%
1	L.A.	3	12	5	41.7	L.A.	3	14	5	35.7	L.A.	6	26	10	38.5
2	Ott.	3	11	4	36.4	Chi.	11	43	12	27.9	Ott.	6	22	7	31.8
3	Bos.	7	26	7	26.9	Ott.	3	11	3	27.3	Pit.	13	57	15	26.3
4	Pit.	7	30	8	26.7	Pit.	6	27	7	25.9	Bos.	13	45	11	24.4
5	S.J.	8	42	11	26.2	Van.	6	27	6	22.2	Chi.	22	80	18	22.5
6	Phi.	11	52	12	23.1	Bos.	6	19	4	21.1	Van.	12	50	11	22.0
7	Det.	5	23	5	21.7	Phi.	12	53	11	20.8	Phi.	23	105	23	21.9
8	Van.	6	23	5	21.7	Det.	7	34	7	20.6	Det.	12	57	12	21.1
9	Col.	3	6	1	16.7	Phx.	3	15	3	20.0	S.J.	15	71	14	19.7
10	Phx.	4	18	3	16.7	N.J.	2	16	3	18.8	Phx.	7	33	6	18.2
11	Chi.	11	37	6	16.2	Mtl.	11	44	8	18.2	Mtl.	19	73	12	16.4
12	Mtl.	8	29	4	13.8	Col.	3	9	1	11.1	Col.	6	15	2	13.3
13	Nsh.	3	15	1	6.7	S.J.	7	29	3	10.3	N.J.	5	32	4	12.5
14	N.J.	3	16	1	6.3	Wsh.	3	18	1	5.6	Nsh.	6	27	1	3.7
15	Buf.	3	11	0	0.0	Buf.	3	8	0	0.0	Wsh.	7	33	1	3.0
16	Wsh.	4	15	0	0.0	Nsh.	3	12	0	0.0	Buf.	6	19	0	0.0
	Total	**89**	**366**	**73**	**19.9**		**89**	**379**	**74**	**19.5**		**89**	**745**	**147**	**19.7**

TEAMS' PENALTY KILLING RECORD

Abbreviations: TSH – Total times shorthanded; **PPGA** – power-play goals against; **%** arrived by dividing times shorthanded minus power-play goals against by times short.

	Team	HOME GP	TSH	PPGA	%	Team	ROAD GP	TSH	PPGA	%	Team	OVERALL GP	TSH	PPGA	%
1	Col.	3	10	1	90.0	Bos.	6	21	1	95.2	Bos.	13	50	5	90.0
2	Mtl.	8	37	4	89.2	Nsh.	3	11	1	90.9	Phi.	23	95	14	85.3
3	S.J.	8	26	3	88.5	Phx.	3	13	2	84.6	Mtl.	19	84	13	84.5
4	Chi.	11	46	6	87.0	Phi.	12	44	7	84.1	Chi.	22	90	15	83.3
5	Phi.	11	51	7	86.3	Mtl.	11	47	9	80.9	Nsh.	6	23	4	82.6
6	Bos.	7	29	4	86.2	Chi.	11	44	9	79.5	S.J.	15	49	9	81.6
7	Det.	5	26	4	84.6	Det.	7	38	8	78.9	Det.	12	64	12	81.3
8	Wsh.	4	16	3	81.3	Wsh.	3	14	3	78.6	Col.	6	26	5	80.8
9	Buf.	3	9	2	77.8	Ott.	3	14	3	78.6	Wsh.	7	30	6	80.0
10	Nsh.	3	12	3	75.0	Pit.	6	18	4	77.8	Phx.	7	34	8	76.5
11	L.A.	3	11	3	72.7	N.J.	2	13	3	76.9	Ott.	6	28	7	75.0
12	Ott.	3	14	4	71.4	L.A.	3	13	3	76.9	L.A.	6	24	6	75.0
13	Phx.	4	21	6	71.4	Col.	3	16	4	75.0	Buf.	6	22	6	72.7
14	N.J.	3	16	5	68.8	Van.	6	24	6	75.0	N.J.	5	29	8	72.4
15	Pit.	7	25	8	68.0	S.J.	7	23	6	73.9	Pit.	13	43	12	72.1
16	Van.	6	30	11	63.3	Buf.	3	13	4	69.2	Van.	12	54	17	68.5
	Total	**89**	**379**	**74**	**80.5**		**89**	**366**	**73**	**80.1**		**89**	**745**	**147**	**80.3**

SHORTHAND GOALS

Team	GOALS FOR GP	GF	Team	GOALS AGAINST GP	GA
Chi.	22	4	S.J.	15	0
Wsh.	7	2	Bos.	13	0
N.J.	5	1	Wsh.	7	0
Nsh.	6	1	Phx.	7	0
Phx.	7	1	Buf.	6	0
Pit.	13	1	Col.	6	0
S.J.	15	1	L.A.	6	0
Mtl.	19	1	N.J.	5	0
Phi.	23	1	Pit.	13	1
Buf.	6	0	Det.	12	1
Ott.	6	0	Ott.	6	1
Col.	6	0	Nsh.	6	1
L.A.	6	0	Phi.	23	2
Van.	12	0	Chi.	22	2
Det.	12	0	Van.	12	2
Bos.	13	0	Mtl.	19	3
Total	**89**	**13**		**89**	**13**

TEAM PENALTIES

Abbreviations: GP – games played; **PEN** – total penalty minutes, including bench penalties; **BMI** – total bench minor minutes; **AVG** – average penalty minutes/game arrived by dividing total penalty minutes by games played

Team	GP	PEN	BMI	AVG
Nashville	6	52	4	8.7
Washington	7	69	4	9.9
Chicago	22	223	8	10.1
Pittsburgh	13	136	4	10.5
San Jose	15	163	0	10.9
Philadelphia	23	253	10	11.0
Colorado	6	67	4	11.2
Montreal	19	216	10	11.4
Phoenix	7	81	0	11.6
Los Angeles	6	70	2	11.7
Boston	13	175	4	13.5
Vancouver	12	175	4	14.6
Detroit	12	178	4	14.8
New Jersey	5	92	4	18.4
Buffalo	6	114	2	19.0
Ottawa	6	123	6	20.5
Total	**89**	**2187**	**72**	**24.6**

Though he slipped to second in scoring after leading the playoffs for much of the spring, the all-around excellence of Blackhawks captain Jonathan Toews — especially his ability to win face-offs — saw him rewarded with the Conn Smythe Trophy as playoff MVP.

Stanley Cup Record Book

History: The Stanley Cup, the oldest trophy competed for by professional athletes in North America, was donated by Frederick Arthur, Lord Stanley of Preston and son of the Earl of Derby, in 1893. Lord Stanley purchased the trophy for 10 guineas ($50 at that time) for presentation to the amateur hockey champions of Canada. Since 1906, when Canadian teams began to pay their players openly, the Stanley Cup has been the symbol of professional hockey supremacy. It has been competed for only by NHL teams since 1926-27 and has been under the exclusive control of the NHL since 1947.

Stanley Cup Standings

1918-2010

(ranked by Cup wins)

Teams	Cup Wins	Yrs.	Series	Wins	Losses	Games	Wins	Losses	Ties	Goals For	Goals Against	Winning %
Montreal[1,2]	23	78	144	89	54	702	407	287	8	2135	1782	.585
Toronto[3]	13	64	109	58	51	524	251	269	4	1350	1427	.483
Detroit	11	58	113	66	47	575	305	269	1	1641	1454	.531
Boston	5	65	109	49	60	543	259	278	6	1573	1594	.483
Edmonton	5	20	49	34	15	251	152	99	0	938	763	.606
Chicago	4	55	97	46	51	450	213	232	5	1291	1411	.479
NY Rangers	4	52	92	44	48	417	197	212	8	1167	1200	.482
NY Islanders	4	21	47	30	17	240	134	106	0	792	714	.558
Pittsburgh	3	25	50	28	22	270	147	123	0	836	804	.544
New Jersey[4]	3	21	40	22	18	230	122	108	0	629	564	.530
Philadelphia	2	34	73	41	32	392	205	187	0	1190	1149	.523
Colorado[5]	2	21	44	25	19	249	132	117	0	726	703	.530
Dallas[6]	1	29	56	28	28	307	154	153	0	897	910	.502
Calgary[7]	1	26	40	15	25	208	94	114	0	648	701	.452
Carolina[8]	1	13	22	10	12	127	59	68	0	323	368	.465
Anaheim	1	7	17	11	6	92	53	39	0	228	220	.576
Tampa Bay	1	5	9	5	4	51	26	25	0	122	140	.510
St. Louis	0	35	58	23	35	307	138	169	0	862	954	.450
Buffalo	0	28	49	21	28	249	121	128	0	745	743	.486
Los Angeles	0	24	35	11	24	176	67	109	0	529	674	.381
Vancouver	0	23	36	13	23	189	83	106	0	546	621	.439
Washington	0	21	32	11	21	182	82	100	0	550	559	.451
Phoenix[9]	0	17	19	2	17	99	32	67	0	263	369	.323
San Jose	0	13	24	11	13	140	67	73	0	348	411	.479
Ottawa[10]	0	12	20	8	12	109	51	58	0	254	265	.468
Nashville	0	5	5	0	5	28	8	20	0	60	79	.286
Florida	0	3	6	3	3	31	13	18	0	77	82	.419
Minnesota	0	3	5	2	3	29	11	18	0	64	72	.379
Atlanta	0	1	1	0	1	4	0	4	0	6	17	.000
Columbus	0	1	1	0	1	4	0	4	0	7	18	.000

1 Montreal also won the Stanley Cup in 1916.
2 1919 final incomplete due to influenza epidemic.
3 Toronto Blueshirts also won the Stanley Cup in 1914.
4 Includes totals of Colorado Rockies 1976-82.
5 Includes totals of Quebec Nordiques 1979-95.
6 Includes totals of Minnesota North Stars 1967-93.
7 Includes totals of Atlanta Flames 1972-80.
8 Includes totals of Hartford Whalers 1979-97.
9 Includes totals of Winnipeg Jets 1979-96.
10 Modern Ottawa Senators franchise only, 1992 to date.

Stanley Cup Winners Prior to Formation of NHL in 1917

Season	Champions	Manager	Coach
1916-17	Seattle Metropolitans	Pete Muldoon	Pete Muldoon
1915-16	Montreal Canadiens	George Kennedy	George Kennedy
1914-15	Vancouver Millionaires	Frank Patrick	Frank Patrick
1913-14	Toronto Blueshirts	Jack Marshall	Scotty Davidson*
1912-13**	Quebec Bulldogs	M.J. Quinn	Joe Malone*
1911-12	Quebec Bulldogs	M.J. Quinn	Charley Nolan
1910-11	Ottawa Senators		Percy LeSueur
1909-10	Montreal Wanderers (Mar. 1910)	Dickie Boon	Pud Glass*
1909-10	Ottawa Senators (Jan. 1910)		Bruce Stuart*
1908-09	Ottawa Senators		Bruce Stuart*
1907-08	Montreal Wanderers	Dickie Boon	Cecil Blachford
1906-07	Montreal Wanderers (Mar. 25, 1907)	Dickie Boon	Cecil Blachford
1906-07	Kenora Thistles (Jan./Mar. 18, 1907)	F.A. Hudson	Tom Phillips*
1905-06	Montreal Wanderers (Mar. 1906)	Cecil Blachford*	
1905-06	Ottawa Silver Seven (Feb. 1906)		Alf Smith
1904-05	Ottawa Silver Seven		Alf Smith
1903-04	Ottawa Silver Seven		Alf Smith
1902-03	Ottawa Silver Seven (Mar. 1903)		Alf Smith
1902-03	Montreal A.A.A. (Feb. 1903)		C. McKerrow
1901-02	Montreal A.A.A. (Mar. 1902)		C. McKerrow
1901-02	Winnipeg Victorias (Jan. 1902)		
1900-01	Winnipeg Victorias		Dan Bain*
1899-1900	Montreal Shamrocks		Harry Trihey*
1898-99	Montreal Shamrocks (Mar. 1899)		Harry Trihey*
1898-99	Montreal Victorias (Feb. 1899)		Mike Grant*
1897-98	Montreal Victorias		Frank Richardson
1896-97	Montreal Victorias		Mike Grant*
1895-96	Montreal Victorias (Dec. 1896)		Mike Grant*
1895-96	Winnipeg Victorias (Feb. 1896)		Jack Armitage
1894-95	Montreal Victorias		Mike Grant*
1893-94	Montreal A.A.A.		
1892-93	Montreal A.A.A.		

* In the early years the teams were frequently run by the Captain. *Indicates Captain
** Victoria defeated Quebec in challenge series. No official recognition.

Stanley Cup Winners

Year	W-L-T in Finals	Winner	Coach	Finalist	Coach
2010	4-2	Chicago	Joel Quenneville	Philadelphia	Peter Laviolette
2009	4-3	Pittsburgh	Dan Bylsma	Detroit	Mike Babcock
2008	4-2	Detroit	Mike Babcock	Pittsburgh	Michel Therrien
2007	4-1	Anaheim	Randy Carlyle	Ottawa	Bryan Murray
2006	4-3	Carolina	Peter Laviolette	Edmonton	Craig MacTavish
2005	....	....	....	....	....
2004	4-3	Tampa Bay	John Tortorella	Calgary	Darryl Sutter
2003	4-3	New Jersey	Pat Burns	Anaheim	Mike Babcock
2002	4-1	Detroit	Scotty Bowman	Carolina	Paul Maurice
2001	4-3	Colorado	Bob Hartley	New Jersey	Larry Robinson
2000	4-2	New Jersey	Larry Robinson	Dallas	Ken Hitchcock
1999	4-2	Dallas	Ken Hitchcock	Buffalo	Lindy Ruff
1998	4-0	Detroit	Scotty Bowman	Washington	Ron Wilson
1997	4-0	Detroit	Scotty Bowman	Philadelphia	Terry Murray
1996	4-0	Colorado	Marc Crawford	Florida	Doug MacLean
1995	4-0	New Jersey	Jacques Lemaire	Detroit	Scotty Bowman
1994	4-3	NY Rangers	Mike Keenan	Vancouver	Pat Quinn
1993	4-1	Montreal	Jacques Demers	Los Angeles	Barry Melrose
1992	4-0	Pittsburgh	Scotty Bowman	Chicago	Mike Keenan
1991	4-2	Pittsburgh	Bob Johnson	Minnesota	Bob Gainey
1990	4-1	Edmonton	John Muckler	Boston	Mike Milbury
1989	4-2	Calgary	Terry Crisp	Montreal	Pat Burns
1988	4-0	Edmonton	Glen Sather	Boston	Terry O'Reilly
1987	4-3	Edmonton	Glen Sather	Philadelphia	Mike Keenan
1986	4-1	Montreal	Jean Perron	Calgary	Bob Johnson
1985	4-1	Edmonton	Glen Sather	Philadelphia	Mike Keenan
1984	4-1	Edmonton	Glen Sather	NY Islanders	Al Arbour
1983	4-0	NY Islanders	Al Arbour	Edmonton	Glen Sather
1982	4-0	NY Islanders	Al Arbour	Vancouver	Roger Neilson
1981	4-1	NY Islanders	Al Arbour	Minnesota	Glen Sonmor
1980	4-2	NY Islanders	Al Arbour	Philadelphia	Pat Quinn
1979	4-1	Montreal	Scotty Bowman	NY Rangers	Fred Shero
1978	4-2	Montreal	Scotty Bowman	Boston	Don Cherry
1977	4-0	Montreal	Scotty Bowman	Boston	Don Cherry
1976	4-0	Montreal	Scotty Bowman	Philadelphia	Fred Shero
1975	4-2	Philadelphia	Fred Shero	Buffalo	Floyd Smith
1974	4-2	Philadelphia	Fred Shero	Boston	Bep Guidolin
1973	4-2	Montreal	Scotty Bowman	Chicago	Billy Reay
1972	4-2	Boston	Tom Johnson	NY Rangers	Emile Francis
1971	4-3	Montreal	Al MacNeil	Chicago	Billy Reay
1970	4-0	Boston	Harry Sinden	St. Louis	Scotty Bowman
1969	4-0	Montreal	Claude Ruel	St. Louis	Scotty Bowman
1968	4-0	Montreal	Toe Blake	St. Louis	Scotty Bowman
1967	4-2	Toronto	Punch Imlach	Montreal	Toe Blake
1966	4-2	Montreal	Toe Blake	Detroit	Sid Abel
1965	4-3	Montreal	Toe Blake	Chicago	Billy Reay
1964	4-3	Toronto	Punch Imlach	Detroit	Sid Abel
1963	4-1	Toronto	Punch Imlach	Detroit	Sid Abel
1962	4-2	Toronto	Punch Imlach	Chicago	Rudy Pilous
1961	4-2	Chicago	Rudy Pilous	Detroit	Sid Abel
1960	4-0	Montreal	Toe Blake	Toronto	Punch Imlach
1959	4-1	Montreal	Toe Blake	Toronto	Punch Imlach
1958	4-2	Montreal	Toe Blake	Boston	Milt Schmidt
1957	4-1	Montreal	Toe Blake	Boston	Milt Schmidt
1956	4-1	Montreal	Toe Blake	Detroit	Jimmy Skinner
1955	4-3	Detroit	Jimmy Skinner	Montreal	Dick Irvin
1954	4-3	Detroit	Tommy Ivan	Montreal	Dick Irvin
1953	4-1	Montreal	Dick Irvin	Boston	Lynn Patrick
1952	4-0	Detroit	Tommy Ivan	Montreal	Dick Irvin
1951	4-1	Toronto	Joe Primeau	Montreal	Dick Irvin
1950	4-3	Detroit	Tommy Ivan	NY Rangers	Lynn Patrick
1949	4-0	Toronto	Hap Day	Detroit	Tommy Ivan
1948	4-0	Toronto	Hap Day	Detroit	Tommy Ivan
1947	4-2	Toronto	Hap Day	Montreal	Dick Irvin
1946	4-1	Montreal	Dick Irvin	Boston	Dit Clapper
1945	4-3	Toronto	Hap Day	Detroit	Jack Adams
1944	4-0	Montreal	Dick Irvin	Chicago	Paul Thompson
1943	4-0	Detroit	Jack Adams	Boston	Art Ross
1942	4-3	Toronto	Hap Day	Detroit	Jack Adams
1941	4-0	Boston	Cooney Weiland	Detroit	Ebbie Goodfellow
1940	4-2	NY Rangers	Frank Boucher	Toronto	Dick Irvin
1939	4-1	Boston	Art Ross	Toronto	Dick Irvin
1938	3-1	Chicago	Bill Stewart	Toronto	Dick Irvin
1937	3-2	Detroit	Jack Adams	NY Rangers	Lester Patrick
1936	3-1	Detroit	Jack Adams	Toronto	Dick Irvin
1935	3-0	Mtl. Maroons	Tommy Gorman	Toronto	Dick Irvin
1934	3-1	Chicago	Tommy Gorman	Detroit	Herbie Lewis
1933	3-1	NY Rangers	Lester Patrick	Toronto	Dick Irvin
1932	3-0	Toronto	Dick Irvin	NY Rangers	Lester Patrick
1931	3-2	Montreal	Cecil Hart	Chicago	Dick Irvin
1930	2-0	Montreal	Cecil Hart	Boston	Art Ross
1929	2-0	Boston	Cy Denneny	NY Rangers	Lester Patrick
1928	3-2	NY Rangers	Lester Patrick	Mtl. Maroons	Eddie Gerard
1927	2-0-2	Ottawa	Dave Gill	Boston	Art Ross
		The National Hockey League assumed control of Stanley Cup competition after 1926			
1926	3-1	Mtl. Maroons	Eddie Gerard	Victoria	Lester Patrick
1925	3-1	Victoria	Lester Patrick	Montreal	Leo Dandurand
1924	2-0	Montreal	Leo Dandurand	Cgy. Tigers	Eddie Oatman
1923	2-0	Ottawa	Pete Green	Edm. Eskimos	Ken McKenzie
1922	3-2	Tor. St. Pats	George O'Donoghue	Van. Millionaires	Lloyd Cook/Frank Patrick
1921	3-2	Ottawa	Pete Green	Van. Millionaires	Lloyd Cook/Frank Patrick
1920	3-2	Ottawa	Pete Green	Seattle	Pete Muldoon
1919	2-2-1	No decision - series between Montreal and Seattle cancelled due to influenza epidemic			
1918	3-2	Tor. Arenas	Dick Carroll	Van. Millionaires	Frank Patrick

Championship Trophies

PRINCE OF WALES TROPHY

Beginning with the 1993-94 season, the club which advances to the Stanley Cup Finals as the winner of the Eastern Conference Championship is presented with the Prince of Wales Trophy.

History: His Royal Highness, the Prince of Wales, donated the trophy to the National Hockey League in 1925. It was originally awarded to the winner of the first game played in Madison Square Garden, December 15, 1925 (Montreal Canadiens 3 at NY Americans 1). It was then awarded to the NHL playoff champion in 1925-26 and 1926-27. From 1927-28 through 1937-38, the award was presented to the regular-season champion of the American Division of the NHL. (The team finishing first in the Canadian Division received the O'Brien Trophy during these years.) From 1938-39, when the NHL reverted to one section, to 1966-67, it was presented to the team winning the NHL regular-season championship. With expansion in 1967-68, it again became a divisional trophy, awarded to the regular-season champions of the East Division through to the end of the 1973-74 season. Beginning in 1974-75, it was awarded to the regular-season winner of the conference bearing the name of the trophy. From 1981-82 to 1992-93 the trophy was presented to the playoff champion in the Wales Conference. Since 1993-94, the trophy has been presented to the playoff champion in the Eastern Conference.

2009-10 Winner: Philadelphia Flyers

The Philadelphia Flyers won the Prince of Wales Trophy on May 24, 2010 after defeating the Montreal Canadiens 4-2 in game 5 of the Eastern Conference Finals. Before defeating the Canadiens, Philadelphia had series wins over the New Jersey Devils and the Boston Bruins.

Prince of Wales Trophy

Clarence S. Campbell Bowl

Stanley Cup

PRINCE OF WALES TROPHY WINNERS

2009-10	Philadelphia	1979-80	Buffalo	1950-51	Detroit
2008-09	Pittsburgh	1978-79	Montreal	1949-50	Detroit
2007-08	Pittsburgh	1977-78	Montreal	1948-49	Detroit
2006-07	Ottawa	1976-77	Montreal	1947-48	Toronto
2005-06	Carolina	1975-76	Montreal	1946-47	Montreal
2003-04	Tampa Bay	1974-75	Buffalo	1945-46	Montreal
2002-03	New Jersey	1973-74	Boston	1944-45	Montreal
2001-02	Carolina	1972-73	Montreal	1943-44	Montreal
2000-01	New Jersey	1971-72	Boston	1942-43	Detroit
99-2000	New Jersey	1970-71	Boston	1941-42	NY Rangers
1998-99	Buffalo	1969-70	Chicago	1940-41	Boston
1997-98	Washington	1968-69	Montreal	1939-40	Boston
1996-97	Philadelphia	1967-68	Montreal	1938-39	Boston
1995-96	Florida	1966-67	Chicago	1937-38	Boston
1994-95	New Jersey	1965-66	Montreal	1936-37	Detroit
1993-94	NY Rangers	1964-65	Detroit	1935-36	Detroit
1992-93	Montreal	1963-64	Montreal	1934-35	Boston
1991-92	Pittsburgh	1962-63	Toronto	1933-34	Detroit
1990-91	Pittsburgh	1961-62	Montreal	1932-33	Boston
1989-90	Boston	1960-61	Montreal	1931-32	NY Rangers
1988-89	Montreal	1959-60	Montreal	1930-31	Boston
1987-88	Boston	1958-59	Montreal	1929-30	Boston
1986-87	Philadelphia	1957-58	Montreal	1928-29	Boston
1985-86	Montreal	1956-57	Detroit	1927-28	Boston
1984-85	Philadelphia	1955-56	Montreal	1926-27	Ottawa
1983-84	NY Islanders	1954-55	Detroit	1925-26	Mtl. Maroons
1982-83	NY Islanders	1953-54	Detroit	Dec. 15/25	Montreal
1981-82	NY Islanders	1952-53	Detroit	1923-24	Montreal*
1980-81	Montreal	1951-52	Detroit		

* Engraved by Montreal Canadiens in 1925-26.

CLARENCE S. CAMPBELL BOWL

Beginning with the 1993-94 season, the club which advances to the Stanley Cup Finals as the winner of the Western Conference Championship is presented with the Clarence S. Campbell Bowl.

History: Presented by the member clubs in 1968 for perpetual competition by the National Hockey League in recognition of the services of Clarence S. Campbell, President of the NHL from 1946 to 1977. From 1967-68 through 1973-74, the trophy was awarded to the regular-season champions of the West Division. Beginning in 1974-75, it was awarded to the regular-season winner of the conference bearing the name of the trophy. From 1981-82 to 1992-93 the trophy was presented to the playoff champion in the Campbell Conference. Since 1993-94, the trophy has been presented to the playoff champion in the Western Conference. The trophy itself is a hallmark piece made of sterling silver and was crafted by a British silversmith in 1878.

2009-10 Winner: Chicago Blackhawks

The Chicago Blackhawks won the Clarence Campbell Bowl on May 23, 2010 after defeating the San Jose Sharks 4-2 in game 4 of the Western Conference Finals. Before defeating the Sharks, Chicago had series wins over the Nashville Predators and the Vancouver Canucks.

CLARENCE S. CAMPBELL BOWL WINNERS

2009-10	Chicago	1994-95	Detroit	1980-81	NY Islanders
2008-09	Detroit	1993-94	Vancouver	1979-80	Philadelphia
2007-08	Detroit	1992-93	Los Angeles	1978-79	NY Islanders
2006-07	Anaheim	1991-92	Chicago	1977-78	NY Islanders
2005-06	Edmonton	1990-91	Minnesota	1976-77	Philadelphia
2003-04	Calgary	1989-90	Edmonton	1975-76	Philadelphia
2002-03	Anaheim	1988-89	Calgary	1974-75	Philadelphia
2001-02	Detroit	1987-88	Edmonton	1973-74	Philadelphia
2000-01	Colorado	1986-87	Edmonton	1972-73	Chicago
99-2000	Dallas	1985-86	Calgary	1971-72	Chicago
1998-99	Dallas	1984-85	Edmonton	1970-71	Chicago
1997-98	Detroit	1983-84	Edmonton	1969-70	St. Louis
1996-97	Detroit	1982-83	Edmonton	1968-69	St. Louis
1995-96	Colorado	1981-82	Vancouver	1967-68	Philadelphia

Stanley Cup Winners

Rosters and Final Series Scores

2009-10 — Chicago Blackhawks — Jonathan Toews (Captain), Dave Bolland, Nick Boynton, Troy Brouwer, Adam Burish, Dustin Byfuglien, Brian Campbell, Ben Eager, Colin Fraser, Jordan Hendry, Niklas Hjalmarsson, Marian Hossa, Cristobal Huet, Patrick Kane, Duncan Keith, Tomas Kopecky, Andrew Ladd, John Madden, Antti Niemi, Brent Seabrook, Patrick Sharp, Brent Sopel, Kris Versteeg, W. Rockwell Wirtz (Chairman), John McDonough (President), Jay Blunk (Senior VP, Business Operations), Stan Bowman (General Manager), Kevin Cheveldayoff (Assistant General Manager), Al MacIsaac (Senior Director, Hockey Administration/Assistant to the President), Scotty Bowman, Dale Tallon (Senior Advisors, Hockey Operations), Joel Quenneville (Head Coach), John Torchetti, Mike Haviland (Assistant Coaches), Stephane Waite (Goaltending Coach), Paul Goodman (Strength and Conditioning Coach), Brad Aldrich (Video Coach), Paul Vincent (Skating Coach), Marc Bergevin (Director, Player Personnel), Mark Bernard (G.M., Minor League Affiliations), Norm Maciver (Director, Player Development), Mark Kelley (Director, Amateur Scouting), Ron Anderson (Director, Player Recruitment), Michel Dumas (Chief Amateur Scout), Tony Ommen (Director Team Services), Dr. Michael Terry (Head Team Physician), Mike Gapski (Head Athletic Trainer), Troy Parchman (Equipment Manager), Pawel Prylinski (Massage Therapist), Jeff Thomas (Assistant Athletic Trainer), Clint Reif (Assistant Equipment Manager), Jim Heintzelman (Equipment Assistant).

Scores: May 29, at Chicago — Chicago 6, Philadelphia 5; May 31, at Chicago — Chicago 2, Philadelphia 1; June 2 at Philadelphia — Philadelphia 4, Chicago 3; June 4 at Philadelphia — Philadelphia 5, Chicago 3; June 6, at Chicago — Chicago 7, Philadelphia 4; June 9 at Philadelphia — Chicago 4, Philadelphia 3.

2008-09 — Pittsburgh Penguins — Sidney Crosby (Captain), Craig Adams, Philippe Boucher, Matt Cooke, Pascal Dupuis, Mark Eaton, Ruslan Fedotenko, Marc-Andre Fleury, Mathieu Garon, Hal Gill, Eric Godard, Alex Goligoski, Sergei Gonchar, Bill Guerin, Tyler Kennedy, Chris Kunitz, Kris Letang, Evgeni Malkin, Brooks Orpik, Miroslav Satan, Rob Scuderi, Jordan Staal, Petr Sykora, Maxime Talbot, Mike Zigomanis, Mario Lemieux (Co-owner/Chairman), Ron Burkle (Co-owner), Bill Kassling, Tom Grealish, Tony Liberati (Directors), Ken Sawyer (Chief Executive Officer), David Morehouse (President), Ray Shero (Executive Vice President amd General Manager), Chuck Fletcher (Assistant General Manager), Ed Johnston (Senior Advisor, Hockey Operations), Jason Botterill (Director of Hockey Administration), Dan Bylsma (Head Coach), Mike Yeo (Assistant Coach), Tom Fitzgerald (Director of Player Development), Gilles Meloche (Goaltending Coach), Mike Kadar (Strength and Conditioning Coach), Travis Ramsay (Video Coordinator), Chris Stewart (Head Athletic Trainer), Scott Adams (Assistant Athletic Trainer), Mark Mortland (Physical Therapist), Dana Heinze (Equipment Manager), Paul DeFazio, Danny Kroll (Assistant Equipment Managers), Frank Buonomo (Senior Director of Team Services and Communications), Tom McMillan (Vice President, Communications), Dan McKinnon (Director of Professional Scouting), Jay Heinbuck (Director of Amateur Scouting).

Scores: May 30, at Detroit — Detroit 3, Pittsburgh 1; May 31 at Detroit — Detroit 3, Pittsburgh 1; June 2, at Pittsburgh — Pittsburgh 4, Detroit 2; June 4, at Pittsburgh — Pittsburgh 4, Detroit 2; June 6 at Detroit — Detroit 5, Pittsburgh 0; June 9, at Pittsburgh — Pittsburgh 2, Detroit 1; June 12, at Detroit — Pittsburgh 2, Detroit 1.

2007-08 — Detroit Red Wings — Nicklas Lidstrom (Captain), Chris Chelios, Daniel Cleary, Pavel Datsyuk, Aaron Downey, Dallas Drake, Kris Draper, Valtteri Filppula, Johan Franzen, Dominik Hasek, Darren Helm, Tomas Holmstrom, Jiri Hudler, Tomas Kopecky, Niklas Kronwall, Brett Lebda, Andreas Lilja, Kirk Maltby, Darren McCarty, Derek Meech, Chris Osgood, Brian Rafalski, Mikael Samuelsson, Brad Stuart, Henrik Zetterberg, Michael Ilitch (Owner/Governor), Marian Ilitch (Owner/Secretary-Treasurer), Christopher Ilitch (Vice President/Alternate Governor), Denise Ilitch, Ronald Ilitch, Michael Ilitch Jr., Lisa Ilitch Murray, Atanas Ilitch, Carole Ilitch. Jim Devellano (Senior Vice President/Alternate Governor), Ken Holland (General Manager/Alternate Governor), Steve Yzerman (Vice President/Alternate Governor), Jim Nill (Assistant General Manager), Ryan Martin (Director, Hockey Operations), Scotty Bowman (Consultant), Mike Babcock (Head Coach), Todd McLellan (Associate Coach), Paul MacLean (Assistant Coach), Jim Bedard (Goaltending Consultant), Jay Woodcroft (Video Coordinator), Mark Howe (Director, Pro Scouting), Joe McDonnell (Director, Amateur Scouting), Hakan Andersson (Director, Amateur Scouting Europe), Piet Van Zant (Athletic Trainer), Paul Boyer (Equipment Manager), Russ Baumann, Christopher Scoppetto (Assistant Athletic Trainers).

Scores: May 24, at Detroit — Detroit 4, Pittsburgh 0; May 26, at Detroit — Detroit 3, Pittsburgh 0; May 28, at Pittsburgh — Pittsburgh 3, Detroit 2; May 31, at Pittsburgh — Detroit 2, Pittsburgh 1; June 2, at Detroit — Pittsburgh 4, Detroit 3; June 4, at Pittsburgh — Detroit 3, Pittsburgh 2.

2006-07 — Anaheim Ducks — Scott Niedermayer (Captain), Rob Niedermayer, Chris Pronger, Teemu Selanne, Sean O'Donnell, Brad May, Todd Marchant, Jean-Sebastien Giguere, Andy McDonald, Samuel Pahlsson, Shawn Thornton, Ric Jackman, Joe DiPenta, Kent Huskins, Chris Kunitz, George Parros, Joe Motzko, Ilya Bryzgalov, Francois Beauchemin, Travis Moen, Ryan Carter, Drew Miller, Ryan Shannon, Dustin Penner, Ryan Getzlaf, Corey Perry; Henry Samueli, Susan Samueli (Owners), Michael Schulman (CEO), Brian Burke (Executive Vice President/General Manager), Tim Ryan (Executive Vice President/COO), Bob Wagner (Senior Vice President/Chief Marketing Officer), Bob Murray (Senior Vice President-Hockey Operations), David McNab (Assistant General Manager), Al Coates (Senior Advisor to GM), Randy Carlyle (Head Coach), Dave Farrish, Newell Brown (Assistant Coaches), Francois Allaire (Goaltending Consultant), Sean Skahan (Strength and Conditioning Coach), Joe Trotta (Video Coordinator), Tim Clark (Head Trainer), Mark O'Neill (Equipment Manager), John Allaway (Assistant Equipment Manager), James Partida (Massage Therapist), Rick Paterson (Director of Professional Scouting), Alain Chainey (Director of Amateur Scouting).

Scores: May 28, at Anaheim - Anaheim 3, Ottawa 2; May 30, at Anaheim - Anaheim 1, Ottawa 0; June 2, at Ottawa - Ottawa 5, Anaheim 3; June 4, at Ottawa - Anaheim 3, Ottawa 2; June 6, at Anaheim - Anaheim 6, Ottawa 2.

2005-06 — Carolina Hurricanes — Rod Brind'Amour (Captain), Glen Wesley, Cory Stillman, Kevyn Adams, Craig Adams, Anton Babchuk, Erik Cole, Mike Commodore, Matt Cullen, Martin Gerber, Bret Hedican, Andrew Hutchinson, Frantisek Kaberle, Andrew Ladd, Chad LaRose, Mark Recchi, Eric Staal, Oleg Tverdovsky, Josef Vasicek, Niclas Wallin, Aaron Ward, Cam Ward, Doug Weight, Ray Whitney, Justin Williams; Peter Karmanos Jr., Thomas Thewes (Owners), Jim Rutherford (President/General Manager), Jason Karmanos (Vice President/Assistant General Manager), Mike Amendola (Chief Financial Officer), Peter Laviolette (Head Coach), Kevin McCarthy, Jeff Daniels (Assistant Coaches), Greg Stefan (Goaltending Coach), Chris Huffine (Video Coordinator), Skip Cunningham, Wally Tatomir, Bob Gorman (Equipment Managers), Peter Friesen (Head Athletic Therapist/Strength and Conditioning Coach), Chris Stewart (Associate Athletic Trainer), Brian Tatum (Team Services Manager), Kelly Kirwin (Event Coordinator-Hockey Operations), Mike Sundheim (Director of Media Relations), Kyle Hanlin (Manager of Media Relations), Sheldon Ferguson (Director of Amateur Scouting), Marshall Johnston (Director of Professional Scouting), Claude Larose, Ron Smith (Professional Scouts), Bert Marshall, Tony MacDonald, Martin Madden (Amateur Scouts), Tom Rowe (Lowell (AHL) - Coach).

Scores: June 5, at Carolina - Carolina 5, Edmonton 4; June 7, at Carolina - Carolina 5, Edmonton 0; June 10, at Edmonton - Edmonton 2, Carolina 1; June 12, at Edmonton - Carolina 2, Edmonton 1; June 14, at Carolina - Edmonton 4, Carolina 3; June 17, at Edmonton - Edmonton 4, Carolina 0; June 19, at Carolina - Carolina 3, Edmonton 1.

2003-04 — Tampa Bay Lightning — Dave Andreychuk (Captain), Fredrik Modin, Vincent Lecavalier, Martin St. Louis, Brad Richards, Nikolai Khabibulin, Pavel Kubina, Dan Boyle, Ruslan Fedotenko, Darryl Sydor, Cory Sarich, Tim Taylor, Cory Stillman, Jassen Cullimore, John Grahame, Chris Dingman, Nolan Pratt, Brad Lukowich, Andre Roy, Dmitry Afanasenkov, Martin Cibak, Ben Clymer, Darren Rumble, Stan Neckar, Eric Perrin; William Davidson (Owner), Tom Wilson (Governor), Ron Campbell (President), Jay Feaster (General Manager), John Tortorella (Head Coach), Craig Ramsay (Associate Coach), Jeff Reese (Assistant Coach), Nigel Kirwan (Video Coach), Eric Lawson (Strength and Conditioning Coach), Tom Mulligan (Trainer), Adam Rambo (Assistant Trainer), Ray Thill (Equipment Manager), Dana Heinze, Jim Pickard (Assistant Equipment Managers), Mike Griebel (Massage Therapist), Bill Barber (Director of Player Personnel), Jake Goertzen (Head Scout), Phil Thibodeau (Director of Team Services), Ryan Belec (Assistant to the GM), Rick Paterson (Chief Pro Scout), Kari Kettunen, Glen Zacharias, Steve Baker, Dave Heitz, Yuri Yanchenkov, (Scouts), Bill Wickett (Senior Vice President - Communications), Sean Henry (Executive Vice President/COO).

Scores: May 25, at Tampa Bay - Calgary 4, Tampa Bay 1; May 27, at Tampa Bay - Tampa Bay 4, Calgary 1; May 29, at Calgary - Calgary 3, Tampa Bay 0; May 31, at Calgary - Tampa Bay 1, Calgary 0; June 3, at Tampa Bay - Calgary 3, Tampa Bay 2; June 5, at Calgary - Tampa Bay 3, Calgary 2; June 7, at Tampa Bay - Tampa Bay 2, Calgary 1.

2002-03 — New Jersey Devils — Tommy Albelin, Jiri Bicek, Martin Brodeur, Sergei Brylin, Ken Daneyko, Patrik Elias, Jeff Friesen, Brian Gionta, Scott Gomez, Jamie Langenbrunner, John Madden, Grant Marshall, Jim McKenzie, Scott Niedermayer, Joe Nieuwendyk, Jay Pandolfo, Brian Rafalski, Pascal Rheaume, Mike Rupp, Corey Schwab, Richard Smehlik, Scott Stevens (Captain), Turner Stevenson, Oleg Tverdovsky, Colin White; Raymond Chambers, Lewis Catz (Owners), Peter Simon (Chairman), Lou Lamoriello (CEO/President/General Manager), Pat Burns (Head Coach), Bob Carpenter, John MacLean (Assistant Coaches), Jacques Caron (Goaltending Coach), Larry Robinson (Special Assignment Coach), David Conte (Director - Scouting), Claude Carrier (Assistant Director - Scouting), Chris Lamoriello (Scout/Albany (AHL) - General Manager), Milt Fisher, Dan Labraaten, Marcel Pronovost (Scouts), Bob Hoffmeyer, Jan Ludvig (Pro Scouts), Dr. Barry Fisher (Orthopedist), Chris Modrzynski (Executive Vice President), Terry Farmer (Vice President - Ticket Operations), Vladimir Bure (Fitness Consultant), Taran Singleton (Hockey Operations), Bill Murray (Medical Trainer), Michael Vasalani (Strength and Conditioning Coordinator), Rick Matthews (Equipment Manager), Juergen Merz (Massage Therapist), Alex Abasto (Assistant Equipment Manager).

Scores: May 27, at New Jersey - New Jersey 3, Anaheim 0; May 29, at New Jersey - New Jersey 3, Anaheim 0; May 31, at Anaheim - Anaheim 3, New Jersey 2; June 2, at Anaheim - Anaheim 1, New Jersey 0; June 5, at New Jersey - New Jersey 6, Anaheim 3; June 7, at Anaheim - Anaheim 5, New Jersey 2; June 9, at New Jersey - New Jersey 3, Anaheim 0.

2001-02 — Detroit Red Wings — Steve Yzerman (Captain), Dominik Hasek, Manny Legace, Chris Chelios, Mathieu Dandenault, Steve Duchesne, Jiri Fischer, Nicklas Lidstrom, Fredrik Olausson, Jiri Slegr, Pavel Datsyuk, Boyd Devereaux, Kris Draper, Sergei Fedorov, Tomas Holmstrom, Brett Hull, Igor Larionov, Kirk Maltby, Darren McCarty, Luc Robitaille, Brendan Shanahan, Jason Williams; Michael Ilitch (Owner/Governor), Marian Ilitch (Owner/Secretary Treasurer), Christoper Ilitch (Vice President), Denise Ilitch (Alternate Governor), Ronald Ilitch, Michael Ilitch Jr., Lisa Ilitch Murray, Atanas Ilitch, Carole Ilitch, Jim Devellano (Senior Vice President), Ken Holland (General Manager), Jim Nill (Assistant General Manager), Scotty Bowman (Head Coach), Dave Lewis, Barry Smith (Associate Coaches), Jim Berard (Goaltending Consultant), Joe Kocur (Video Coordinator), John Wharton (Athletic Trainer), Piet Van Zant (Assistant Athletic Trainer), Paul Boyer (Equipment Manager), Paul MacDonald (Senior Director of Finance), Nancy Beard (Executive Assistant), Dan Belisle, Mark Howe, Bob McCammon (Pro Scouts), Hakan Andersson (Director of European Scouting), Bruce Haralson, Mark Leach, Joe McDonnell, Glenn Merkosky (Scouts).

Scores: June 4, at Detroit - Carolina 3, Detroit 2; June 6, at Detroit - Detroit 3, Carolina 1; June 8, at Carolina - Detroit 3, Carolina 2; June 10, at Carolina - Detroit 3, Carolina 0; June 13, at Detroit - Detroit 3, Carolina 1.

2000-01 — Colorado Avalanche — David Aebischer, Rob Blake, Raymond Bourque, Greg de Vries, Chris Dingman, Chris Drury, Adam Foote, Peter Forsberg, Milan Hejduk, Dan Hinote, Jon Klemm, Eric Messier, Bryan Muir, Ville Nieminen, Scott Parker, Shjon Podein, Nolan Pratt, Dave Reid, Steve Reinprecht, Patrick Roy, Joe Sakic (Captain), Martin Skoula, Alex Tanguay, Stephane Yelle; E. Stanley Kroenke (Owner/Governor), Pierre Lacroix (President/ General Manager), Bob Hartley (Head Coach), Jacques Cloutier, Bryan Trottier (Assistant Coaches), Paul Fixter (Video Coach), Francois Giguere (Vice President - Hockey Operations), Brian MacDonald (Assistant General Manager), Michel Goulet (Vice President - Player Personnel), Jean Martineau (Vice President - Communications and Team Services), Pat Karns (Head Athletic Trainer), Matthew Sokolowski (Assistant Athletic Trainer), Wayne Flemming, Mark Miller (Equipment Managers), Dave Randolph (Assistant Equipment Manager), Paul Goldberg (Strength and Conditioning Coach), Gregorio Pradera (Massage Therapist), Brad Smith (Pro Scout), Jim Hammett (Chief Scout), Garth Joy, Steve Lyons, Joni Lehto, Orval Tessier (Scouts), Charlotte Grahame (Director of Hockey Administration).

Scores: May 26, at Colorado - Colorado 5, New Jersey 0; May 29, at Colorado - New Jersey 2, Colorado 1; May 31, at New Jersey - Colorado 3, New Jersey 1; June 2, at New Jersey - New Jersey 3, Colorado 2; June 4, at Colorado - New Jersey 4, Colorado 1; June 7, at New Jersey - Colorado 4, New Jersey 0; June 9, at Colorado - Colorado 3, New Jersey 1.

1999-2000 — New Jersey Devils — Jason Arnott, Brad Bombardir, Martin Brodeur, Steve Brule, Sergei Brylin, Ken Daneyko, Patrik Elias, Scott Gomez, Bobby Holik, Steve Kelly, Claude Lemieux, John Madden, Vladimir Malakhov, Randy McKay, Alexander Mogilny, Sergei Nemchinov, Scott Niedermayer, Krzysztof Oliwa, Jay Pandolfo, Brian Rafalski, Ken Sutton, Scott Stevens (Captain), Petr Sykora, Chris Terreri, Colin White; Dr. John J. McMullen (Owner/Chairman), Peter S. McMullen (Owner), Lou Lamoriello (President/General Manager), Larry Robinson (Head Coach), Viacheslav Fetisov (Assistant Coach), Jacques Caron (Goaltending Coach), Bob Carpenter (Assistant Coach), John Cuniff (Albany (AHL) - Coach), David Conte (Director of Scouting), Claude Carrier (Assistant Director of Scouting), Milt Fisher, Dan Labraaten, Marcel Pronovost (Scouts), Bob Hoffmeyer (Pro Scout), Dr. Barry Fisher (Orthopedist), Dennis Gendron (Albany (AHL) - Assistant Coach), Robbie Ftorek (Coach), Vladimir Bure (Consultant), Taran Singleton, Marie Carnevale, Callie Smith (Hockey Operations), Bill Murray (Medical Trainer), Michael Vasalani (Strength and Conditioning Coordinator), Dana McGuane (Equipment Manager), Juergen Merz (Massage Therapist), Harry Bricker, Lou Centanni Jr. (Assistant Equipment Managers).

Scores: May 30, at New Jersey - New Jersey 7, Dallas 3; June 1, at New Jersey - Dallas 2, New Jersey 1; June 3, at Dallas - New Jersey 2, Dallas 1; June 5, at Dallas - New Jersey 3, Dallas 1; June 8, at New Jersey - Dallas 1 - New Jersey 0; June 10, at Dallas, New Jersey 2 - Dallas 1.

1998-99 — Dallas Stars — Derian Hatcher (Captain), Mike Modano, Joe Nieuwendyk, Craig Ludwig, Sergei Zubov, Ed Belfour, Guy Carbonneau, Shawn Chambers, Benoit Hogue, Tony Hrkac, Brett Hull, Mike Keane, Jamie Langenbrunner, Jere Lehtinen, Grant Marshall, Richard Matvichuk, Derek Plante, Dave Reid, Brent Severyn, Jon Sim, Brian Skrudland, Blake Sloan, Darryl Sydor, Roman Turek, Pat Verbeek; Thomas Hicks (Chairman/Owner), Jim Lites (President), Bob Gainey (Vice President - Hockey Operations/General Manager), Doug Armstrong (Assistant General Manager), Craig Button (Director of Player Personnel), Ken Hitchcock (Head Coach), Doug Jarvis, Rick Wilson (Assistant Coaches), Rick McLaughlin (Vice President/Chief Financial Officer), Jeff Cogen (Vice President - Marketing and Promotion), Bill Strong (Vice President - Marketing and Broadcasting), Tim Bernhardt (Director of Amateur Scouting), Doug Overton (Director of Pro Scouting), Bob Gernander (Chief Scout), Stu MacGregor (Western Scout), Dave Suprenant (Medical Trainer), Dave Smith, Rich Matthews (Equipment Managers), J.J. McQueen (Strength and Conditioning Coach), Rick St. Croix (Goaltending Consultant), Dan Stuchal (Director of Team Services), Larry Kelly (Director of Public Relations).

Scores: June 8, at Dallas - Buffalo 3, Dallas 2; June 10, at Dallas - Dallas 4, Buffalo 2; June 12, at Buffalo - Dallas 2, Buffalo 1; June 15, at Buffalo - Buffalo 2, Dallas 1; June 17, at Dallas - Dallas 2, Buffalo 0; June 19, at Buffalo - Dallas 2, Buffalo 1.

1997-98 — Detroit Red Wings — Steve Yzerman (Captain), Doug Brown, Mathieu Dandenault, Kris Draper, Anders Eriksson, Sergei Fedorov, Viacheslav Fetisov, Brent Gilchrist, Kevin Hodson, Tomas Holmstrom, Mike Knuble, Joe Kocur, Vladimir Konstantinov, Vyacheslav Kozlov, Martin Lapointe, Igor Larionov, Nicklas Lidstrom, Jamie Macoun, Kirk Maltby, Darren McCarty, Dmitri Mironov, Larry Murphy, Chris Osgood, Bob Rouse, Brendan Shanahan, Aaron Ward; Mike Ilitch, (Owner/Chairman), Marian Ilitch (Owner), Atanas Ilitch, Christopher Ilitch (Vice Presidents), Denise Ilitch, Ronald Ilitch, Michael Ilitch Jr., Lisa Ilitch Murray, Carole Ilitch Trepeck, Jim Devellano (Senior Vice President), Ken Holland (General Manager), Don Waddell (Assistant General Manager), Scotty Bowman (Head Coach), Barry Smith, Dave Lewis (Associate Coaches), Jim Nill (Director of Player Development), Dan Belisle, Mark Howe (Pro Scouts), Jim Bedard (Goaltending Consultant), Hakan Andersson (Director of European Scouting), Mark Leach (USA Scout), Joe McDonnell (Eastern Scout), Bruce Haralson (Western Scout), John Wharton (Athletic Trainer), Paul Boyer (Equipment Manager), Tim Abbott (Assistant Equipment Manager), Bob Huddleston (Masseur), Sergei Mnatsakanov, Wally Crossman (Dressing Room Assistant).

Scores: June 9, at Detroit — Detroit 2, Washington 1; June 11, at Detroit — Detroit 5, Washington 4; June 13, at Washington — Detroit 2, Washington 1; June 16, at Washington — Detroit 4, Washington 1.

1996-97 — Detroit Red Wings — Steve Yzerman (Captain), Doug Brown, Mathieu Dandenault, Kris Draper, Sergei Fedorov, Viacheslav Fetisov, Kevin Hodson, Tomas Holmstrom, Joe Kocur, Vladimir Konstantinov, Vyacheslav Kozlov, Martin Lapointe, Igor Larionov, Nicklas Lidstrom, Kirk Maltby, Darren McCarty, Larry Murphy, Chris Osgood, Jamie Pushor, Bob Rouse, Tomas Sandstrom, Brendan Shanahan, Tim Taylor, Mike Vernon, Aaron Ward; Mike Ilitch (Owner/Chairman), Marian Ilitch (Owner), Atanas Ilitch, Christopher Ilitch (Vice Presidents), Denise Ilitch Lites, Ronald Ilitch, Michael Ilitch Jr., Lisa Ilitch Murray, Carole Ilitch Trepeck, Jim Devellano (Senior Vice President), Scotty Bowman (Head Coach/Director of Player Personnel), Ken Holland (Assistant General Manager), Barry Smith, Dave Lewis (Associate Coaches), Mike Krushelnyski (Assistant Coach), Jim Nill (Director of Player Development), Dan Belisle, Bruce Haralson, Mark Howe (Scouts), Hakan Andersson (Director of European Scouting), John Wharton (Athletic Trainer), Wally Crossman (Dressing Room Assistant), Mark Leach (Scout), Paul Boyer (Equipment Manager), Tim Abbott (Assistant Equipment Manager), Sergei Mnatsakanov (Masseur), Joe McDonnell (Scout).

Scores: May 31, at Philadelphia — Detroit 4, Philadelphia 2; June 3, at Philadelphia — Detroit 4, Philadelphia 2; June 5, at Detroit — Detroit 6, Philadelphia 1; June 7, at Detroit — Detroit 2, Philadelphia 1.

1995-96 — Colorado Avalanche — Rene Corbet, Adam Deadmarsh, Stephane Fiset, Adam Foote, Peter Forsberg, Alexei Gusarov, Dave Hannan, Valeri Kamensky, Mike Keane, Jon Klemm, Uwe Krupp, Sylvain Lefebvre, Claude Lemieux, Curtis Leschyshyn, Troy Murray, Sandis Ozolinsh, Mike Ricci, Patrick Roy, Warren Rychel, Joe Sakic (Captain), Chris Simon, Craig Wolanin, Stephane Yelle, Scott Young; Charlie Lyons (Chairman/CEO), Pierre Lacroix (Executive Vice President/General Manager), Marc Crawford (Head Coach), Joel Quenneville, Jacques Cloutier (Assistant Coaches), Francois Giguere (Assistant General Manager), Michel Goulet (Director of Player Personnel), Dave Draper (Chief Scout), Jean Martineau (Director of Public Relations), Pat Karns (Trainer), Matthew Sokolowski (Assistant Trainer), Rob McLean (Equipment Manager), Mike Kramer, Brock Gibbins (Assistant Equipment Managers), Skip Allen (Strength and Conditioning Coach), Paul Fixter (Video Coordinator), Leo Vyssokov (Massage Therapist).

Scores: June 4, at Colorado — Colorado 3, Florida 1; June 6, at Colorado — Colorado 8, Florida 1; June 8, at Florida — Colorado 3, Florida 2; June 10, at Florida — Colorado 1, Florida 0.

1994-95 — New Jersey Devils — Tommy Albelin, Martin Brodeur, Neal Broten, Sergei Brylin, Bob Carpenter, Shawn Chambers, Tom Chorske, Danton Cole, Ken Daneyko, Kevin Dean, Jim Dowd, Bruce Driver, Bill Guerin, Bobby Holik, Claude Lemieux, John MacLean, Chris McAlpine, Randy McKay, Scott Niedermayer, Mike Peluso, Stephane Richer, Brian Rolston, Scott Stevens (Captain), Chris Terreri, Valeri Zelepukin; Dr. John J. McMullen (Owner/Chairman), Peter S. McMullen (Owner), Lou Lamoriello (President/General Manager), Jacques Lemaire (Head Coach), Jacques Caron (Goaltender Coach), Dennis Gendron, Larry Robinson (Assistant Coaches), Robbie Ftorek (Albany (AHL) - Coach), Alex Abasto (Assistant Equipment Manager), Bob Huddleston (Massage Therapist), David Nichols (Equipment Manager), Ted Schuch (Medical Trainer), Michael Vasalani (Strength and Conditioning Coach), David Conte (Director of Scouting), Milt Fisher, Claude Carrier, Dan Labraaten, Marcel Pronovost (Scouts).

Scores: June 17, at Detroit — New Jersey 2, Detroit 1; June 20, at Detroit — New Jersey 4, Detroit 2; June 22, at New Jersey — New Jersey 5, Detroit 2; June 24, at New Jersey — New Jersey 5, Detroit 2.

1993-94 — New York Rangers — Mark Messier (Captain), Brian Leetch, Kevin Lowe, Adam Graves, Steve Larmer, Glenn Anderson, Jeff Beukeboom, Greg Gilbert, Glenn Healy, Mike Hudson, Alexander Karpovtsev, Joe Kocur, Alex Kovalev, Nick Kypreos, Doug Lidster, Stephane Matteau, Craig MacTavish, Sergei Nemchinov, Brian Noonan, Esa Tikkanen, Mike Richter, Jay Wells, Sergei Zubov, Ed Olczyk, Mike Hartman; Neil Smith (President/General Manager/Governor), Robert Gutkowski, Stanley Jaffe, Kenneth Munoz (Governors), Larry Pleau (Assistant General Manager), Mike Keenan (Head Coach), Colin Campbell (Associate Coach), Dick Todd (Assistant Coach), Matthew Loughren (Manager - Team Operations), Barry Watkins (Director - Communications), Christer Rockstrom, Tony Feltrin, Martin Madden, Herb Hammond, Darwin Bennett (Scouts), Dave Smith, Joe Murphy, Mike Folga, Bruce Lifrieri (Trainers).

Scores: May 31, at New York — Vancouver 3, NY Rangers 2; June 2, at New York — NY Rangers 3, Vancouver 1; June 4, at Vancouver — NY Rangers 5, Vancouver 1; June 7, at Vancouver — NY Rangers 4, Vancouver 2; June 9, at New York — Vancouver 6, at NY Rangers 3; June 11, at Vancouver — Vancouver 4, NY Rangers 1; June 14, at New York — NY Rangers 3, Vancouver 2.

1992-93 — Montreal Canadiens — Guy Carbonneau (Captain), Patrick Roy, Andre Racicot, Rob Ramage, Kirk Muller, Mike Keane, Kevin Haller, Paul DiPietro, John LeClair, Denis Savard, Benoit Brunet, Brian Bellows, Lyle Odelein, Vincent Damphousse, Gary Leeman, Mathieu Schneider, Eric Desjardins, Jesse Belanger, Ed Ronan, Mario Roberge, Donald Dufresne, Todd Ewen, Sean Hill, Patrice Brisebois, Gilbert Dionne, Stephan Lebeau, J.J. Daigneault; Ronald Corey (President), Serge Savard (Managing Director/Vice President - Hockey), Jacques Demers (Head Coach), Jacques Laperriere, Charles Thiffault (Assistant Coaches), Francois Allaire (Goaltending Instructor), Jean Béliveau (Senior Vice President - Corporate Affairs), Jacques Lemaire (Assistant to the Managing Director), André Boudrias (Assistant to the Managing Director/Director of Scouting), Gaeten Lefebvre (Athletic Trainer), John Shipman (Assistant to the Athletic Trainer), Eddy Palchak (Equipment Manager), Pierre Gervais, Robert Boulanger (Assistants to the Equipment Manager).

Scores: June 1, at Montreal — Los Angeles 4, Montreal 1; June 3, at Montreal — Montreal 3, Los Angeles 2; June 5, at Los Angeles — Montreal 4, Los Angeles 3; June 7, at Los Angeles — Montreal 3, Los Angeles 2; June 9, at Montreal — Montreal 4, Los Angeles 1.

1991-92 — Pittsburgh Penguins — Mario Lemieux (Captain), Ron Francis, Bryan Trottier, Kevin Stevens, Bob Errey, Phil Bourque, Troy Loney, Rick Tocchet, Joe Mullen, Jaromir Jagr, Jiri Hrdina, Shawn McEachern, Ulf Samuelsson, Kjell Samuelsson, Larry Murphy, Gordie Roberts, Jim Paek, Paul Stanton, Tom Barrasso, Ken Wregget, Jay Caufield, Jamie Leach, Wendell Young, Grant Jennings, Peter Taglianetti, Jock Callander, Dave Michayluk, Mike Needham, Jeff Chychrun, Ken Priestlay, Jeff Daniels; Morris Belzberg, Howard Baldwin, Thomas Ruta (Owners), Donn Patton (Executive Vice President/Chief Financial Officer), Paul Martha (Executive Vice President/General Counsel), Craig Patrick (Executive Vice President/General Manager), Bob Johnson (Head Coach), Scotty Bowman (Director of Player Development/Coach), Barry Smith, Rick Kehoe, Pierre McGuire, Gilles Meloche, Rick Paterson (Assistant Coaches), Steve Latin (Equipment Manager), Skip Thayer (Trainer), John Welday (Strength and Conditioning Coach), Greg Malone, Les Binkley, Charlie Hodge, John Gill, Ralph Cox (Scouts).

Scores: May 26, at Pittsburgh — Pittsburgh 5, Chicago 4; May 28, at Pittsburgh — Pittsburgh 3, Chicago 1; May 30, at Chicago — Pittsburgh 1, Chicago 0; June 1, at Chicago — Pittsburgh 6, Chicago 5.

1990-91 — Pittsburgh Penguins — Mario Lemieux (Captain), Paul Coffey, Randy Hillier, Bob Errey, Tom Barrasso, Phil Bourque, Jay Caufield, Ron Francis, Randy Gilhen, Jiri Hrdina, Jaromir Jagr, Grant Jennings, Troy Loney, Joe Mullen, Larry Murphy, Jim Paek, Frank Pietrangelo, Barry Pederson, Mark Recchi, Gordie Roberts, Ulf Samuelsson, Paul Stanton, Kevin Stevens, Peter Taglianetti, Bryan Trottier, Scott Young, Wendell Young; Edward J. DeBartolo Sr. (Owner), Marie D. DeBartolo York (President), Paul Martha (Vice President/General Counsel), Craig Patrick (General Manager), Scotty Bowman (Director of Player Development and Recruitment), Bob Johnson (Head Coach), Rick Kehoe, Rick Paterson, Barry Smith (Assistant Coaches), Gilles Meloche (Goaltending Coach/Scout), Steve Latin (Equipment Manager), Skip Thayer (Trainer), John Welday (Strength and Conditioning Coach), Greg Malone (Scout).

Scores: May 15, at Pittsburgh — Minnesota 5, Pittsburgh 4; May 17, at Pittsburgh — Pittsburgh 4, Minnesota 1; May 19, at Minnesota — Minnesota 3, Pittsburgh 1; May 21, at Minnesota — Pittsburgh 5, Minnesota 3; May 23, at Pittsburgh — Pittsburgh 6, Minnesota 4; May 25, at Minnesota — Pittsburgh 8, Minnesota 0.

1989-90 — Edmonton Oilers — Mark Messier (Captain), Jari Kurri, Kevin Lowe, Steve Smith, Jeff Beukeboom, Mark Lamb, Joe Murphy, Glenn Anderson, Adam Graves, Craig MacTavish, Kelly Buchberger, Craig Simpson, Martin Gelinas, Randy Gregg, Charlie Huddy, Geoff Smith, Reijo Ruotsalainen, Craig Muni, Bill Ranford, Dave Brown, Pokey Reddick, Petr Klima, Esa Tikkanen, Grant Fuhr; Peter Pocklington (Owner), Glen Sather (President/General Manager), John Muckler (Head Coach), Ted Green (Co-Coach), Ron Low (Assistant Coach), Bruce MacGregor (Assistant General Manager), Barry Fraser (Director of Player Personnel), Bill Tuele (Director of Public Relations), Werner Baum (Vice President), Dr. Gordon Cameron (Medical Chief of Staff), Dr. David Reid (Team Physician), Ken Lowe (Athletic Therapist), Barrie Stafford (Athletic Trainer), Stuart Poirier (Massage Therapist), Lyle Kulchisky (Assistant Trainer), John Blackwell (Cape Breton (AHL) - Director of Operations), Ace Bailey, Ed Chadwick, Lorne Davis, Harry Howell, Albert Reeves, Matti Vaisanen (Scouts).

Scores: May 15, at Boston — Edmonton 3, Boston 2; May 18, at Boston — Edmonton 7, Boston 2; May 20, at Edmonton — Boston 2, Edmonton 1; May 22, at Edmonton — Edmonton 5, Boston 1; May 24, at Boston — Edmonton 4, Boston 1.

1988-89 — Calgary Flames — Lanny McDonald (Co- Captain), Jim Peplinski (Co-Captain), Tim Hunter, Mike Vernon, Rick Wamsley, Al MacInnis, Brad McCrimmon, Dana Murzyn, Ric Nattress, Joe Mullen, Gary Roberts, Colin Patterson, Hakan Loob, Theoren Fleury, Jiri Hrdina, Gary Suter, Mark Hunter, Joe Nieuwendyk, Brian MacLellan, Joel Otto, Jamie Macoun, Doug Gilmour, Rob Ramage; Norman Green, Harley Hotchkiss, Norman Kwong, Sonia Scurfield, B.J. Seaman, D.K. Seaman (Owners), Cliff Fletcher (President/General Manager), Al MacNeil (Assistant General Manager), Al Coates (Assistant to the President), Terry Crisp (Head Coach), Doug Risebrough, Tom Watt (Assistant Coaches), Glenn Hall (Goaltending Consultant), Jim Murray (Trainer), Al Murray (Assistant Trainer), Bob Stewart (Equipment Manager).

Scores: May 14, at Calgary — Calgary 3, Montreal 2; May 17, at Calgary— Montreal 4, Calgary 2; May 19, at Montreal — Montreal 4, Calgary 3; May 21, at Montreal — Calgary 4, Montreal 2; May 23, at Calgary — Calgary 3, Montreal 2; May 25, at Montreal — Calgary 4, Montreal 2.

1987-88 — Edmonton Oilers — Wayne Gretzky (Captain), Keith Acton, Glenn Anderson, Jeff Beukeboom, Geoff Courtnall, Grant Fuhr, Randy Gregg, Dave Hannan, Charlie Huddy, Mike Krushelnyski, Jari Kurri, Normand Lacombe, Kevin Lowe, Craig MacTavish, Kevin McClelland, Marty McSorley, Mark Messier, Craig Muni, Bill Ranford, Craig Simpson, Steve Smith, Esa Tikkanen; Peter Pocklington (Owner), Glen Sather (General Manager/Coach), John Muckler (Co-Coach), Ted Green (Assistant Coach), Bruce MacGregor (Assistant General Manager), Barry Fraser (Director of Player Personnel), Bill Tuele (Director of Public Relations), Dr. Gordon Cameron (Team Doctor), Peter Millar (Athletic Therapist), Juergen Merz (Massage Therapist), Barrie Stafford (Trainer), Lyle Kulchisky (Assistant Trainer).

Scores: May 18, at Edmonton — Edmonton 2, Boston 1; May 20, at Edmonton — Edmonton 4, Boston 2; May 22, at Boston — Edmonton 6, Boston 3; May 24, at Boston — Boston 3, Edmonton 3 (suspended due to power failure); May 26, at Edmonton — Edmonton 6, Boston 3.

1986-87 — Edmonton Oilers — Wayne Gretzky (Captain), Glenn Anderson, Jeff Beukeboom, Kelly Buchberger, Paul Coffey, Grant Fuhr, Randy Gregg, Charlie Huddy, Dave Hunter, Mike Krushelnyski, Jari Kurri, Moe Lemay, Kevin Lowe, Craig MacTavish, Kevin McClelland, Marty McSorley, Mark Messier, Andy Moog, Craig Muni, Kent Nilsson, Jaroslav Pouzar, Reijo Ruotsalainen, Steve Smith, Esa Tikkanen; Peter Pocklington (Owner), Glen Sather (General Manager/Coach), Bruce MacGregor (Assistant General Manager), John Muckler (Co-Coach), Ted Green, Ron Low (Assistant Coaches), Barry Fraser (Director of Player Personnel), Garnet Bailey, Ed Chadwick, Lorne Davis, Matti Vaisanen (Scouts), Peter Millar (Athletic Therapist), Juergen Merz (Massage Therapist), Dr. Gordon Cameron (Team Doctor), Barrie Stafford (Trainer), Lyle Kulchisky (Assistant Trainer).

Scores: May 17, at Edmonton — Edmonton 4, Philadelphia 2; May 20, at Edmonton — Edmonton 3, Philadelphia 2; May 22, at Philadelphia — Philadelphia 5, Edmonton 3; May 24, at Philadelphia — Edmonton 4, Philadelphia 1; May 26, at Edmonton — Philadelphia 4, Edmonton 3; May 28, at Philadelphia — Philadelphia 3, Edmonton 2; May 31, at Edmonton — Edmonton 3, Philadelphia 1.

246 • STANLEY CUP SCORES, ROSTERS, 1986–1971

1985-86 — Montreal Canadiens — Bob Gainey (Captain), Doug Soetaert, Patrick Roy, Rick Green, David Maley, Ryan Walter, Serge Boisvert, Mario Tremblay, Bobby Smith, Craig Ludwig, Tom Kurvers, Kjell Dahlin, Larry Robinson, Guy Carbonneau, Chris Chelios, Petr Svoboda, Mats Naslund, Lucien DeBlois, Steve Rooney, Gaston Gingras, Mike Lalor, Chris Nilan, John Kordic, Claude Lemieux, Mike McPhee, Brian Skrudland, Stephane Richer; Ronald Corey (President), Serge Savard (General Manager), Jean Perron (Coach), Jacques Laperrière (Assistant Coach), Jean Béliveau, Francois-Xavier Seigneur, Fred Steer (Vice Presidents), Jacques Lemaire, André Boudrias (Assistant General Managers), Claude Ruel (Player Development), Yves Belanger (Athletic Therapist), Gaetan Lefebvre (Assistant Athletic Therapist), Eddy Palchak (Trainer), Sylvain Toupin (Assistant Trainer).
Scores: May 16, at Calgary — Calgary 5, Montreal 2; May 18, at Calgary — Montreal 3, Calgary 2; May 20, at Montreal — Montreal 5, Calgary 3; May 22, at Montreal — Montreal 1, Calgary 0; May 24, at Calgary — Montreal 4, Calgary 3.

1984-85 — Edmonton Oilers — Wayne Gretzky (Captain), Glenn Anderson, Billy Carroll, Paul Coffey, Lee Fogolin Jr., Grant Fuhr, Randy Gregg, Charlie Huddy, Pat Hughes, Dave Hunter, Don Jackson, Mike Krushelnyski, Jari Kurri, Willy Lindstrom, Kevin Lowe, Dave Lumley, Kevin McClelland, Larry Melnyk, Mark Messier, Andy Moog, Mark Napier, Jaroslav Pouzar, Dave Semenko, Esa Tikkanen; Peter Pocklington (Owner), Glen Sather (General Manager/Coach), Bruce MacGregor (Assistant General Manager), John Muckler, Ted Green (Assistant Coaches), Barry Fraser (Director of Player Personnel/Chief Scout), Garnet Bailey, Ed Chadwick, Lorne Davis, Matti Vaisanen (Scouts), Peter Millar (Athletic Therapist), Dr. Gordon Cameron (Team Doctor), Barrie Stafford (Trainer), Lyle Kulchisky (Assistant Trainer).
Scores: May 21, at Philadelphia — Philadelphia 4, Edmonton 1; May 23, at Philadelphia — Edmonton 3, Philadelphia 1; May 25, at Edmonton — Edmonton 4, Philadelphia 3; May 28, at Edmonton — Edmonton 5, Philadelphia 3; May 30, at Edmonton — Edmonton 8, Philadelphia 3.

1983-84 — Edmonton Oilers — Wayne Gretzky (Captain), Glenn Anderson, Paul Coffey, Pat Conacher, Lee Fogolin Jr., Grant Fuhr, Randy Gregg, Charlie Huddy, Pat Hughes, Dave Hunter, Don Jackson, Jari Kurri, Willy Lindstrom, Ken Linseman, Kevin Lowe, Dave Lumley, Kevin McClelland, Mark Messier, Andy Moog, Jaroslav Pouzar, Dave Semenko; Peter Pocklington (Owner), Glen Sather (General Manager/Coach), Bruce MacGregor (Assistant General Manager), John Muckler, Ted Green (Assistant Coaches), Barry Fraser (Director of Player Personnel/Chief Scout), Pete Millar (Athletic Therapist), Barrie Stafford (Trainer), Lyle Kulchisky (Assistant Trainer).
Scores: May 10, at New York — Edmonton 1, NY Islanders 0; May 12, at New York — NY Islanders 6, Edmonton 1; May 15, at Edmonton — Edmonton 7, NY Islanders 2; May 17, at Edmonton — Edmonton 7, NY Islanders 2; May 19, at Edmonton — Edmonton 5, NY Islanders 2.

1982-83 — New York Islanders — Denis Potvin (Captain), Mike Bossy, Bob Bourne, Paul Boutilier, Billy Carroll, Greg Gilbert, Clark Gillies, Butch Goring, Mats Hallin, Tomas Jonsson, Anders Kallur, Gord Lane, Dave Langevin, Mike McEwen, Roland Melanson, Wayne Merrick, Ken Morrow, Bob Nystrom, Stefan Persson, Billy Smith, Brent Sutter, Duane Sutter, John Tonelli, Bryan Trottier; Bill Torrey (President/General Manager), John Pickett Jr. (Chairman), Gerry Ehman (Assistant General Manager/Director of Scouting), Al Arbour (Coach), Lorne Henning (Assistant Coach), Ron Waske (Trainer), Jim Pickard (Assistant Trainer).
Scores: May 10, at Edmonton — NY Islanders 2, Edmonton 0; May 12, at Edmonton — NY Islanders 6, Edmonton 3; May 14, at New York — NY Islanders 5, Edmonton 1; May 17, at New York — NY Islanders 4, Edmonton 2

1981-82 — New York Islanders — Denis Potvin (Captain), Mike Bossy, Bob Bourne, Billy Carroll, Greg Gilbert, Clark Gillies, Butch Goring, Tomas Jonsson, Anders Kallur, Gord Lane, Dave Langevin, Hector Marini, Mike McEwen, Roland Melanson, Wayne Merrick, Ken Morrow, Bob Nystrom, Stefan Persson, Billy Smith, Brent Sutter, Duane Sutter, John Tonelli, Bryan Trottier; Bill Torrey (President/General Manager), John Pickett Jr. (Chairman), Jim Devellano (Assistant General Manager/Director of Scouting), Al Arbour (Coach), Lorne Henning (Assistant Coach), Gerry Ehman (Head Scout), Ron Waske (Trainer), Jim Pickard (Assistant Trainer).
Scores: May 8, at New York — NY Islanders 6, Vancouver 5; May 11, at New York — NY Islanders 6, Vancouver 4; May 13, at Vancouver — NY Islanders 3, Vancouver 0; May 16, at Vancouver — NY Islanders 3, Vancouver 1

1980-81 — New York Islanders — Denis Potvin (Captain), Mike Bossy, Bob Bourne, Billy Carroll, Clark Gillies, Butch Goring, Garry Howatt, Anders Kallur, Gord Lane, Dave Langevin, Bob Lorimer, Hector Marini, Mike McEwen, Roland Melanson, Wayne Merrick, Ken Morrow, Bob Nystrom, Stefan Persson, Jean Potvin, Billy Smith, Duane Sutter, John Tonelli, Bryan Trottier; Bill Torrey (President/General Manager), John Pickett Jr. (Chairman), Al Arbour (Coach), Lorne Henning (Player/Assistant Coach), Jim Devellano (Chief Scout), Gerry Ehman, Mario Saraceno, Harry Boyd (Scouts), Ron Waske (Trainer), Jim Pickard (Assistant Trainer).
Scores: May 12, at New York — NY Islanders 6, Minnesota 3; May 14, at New York — NY Islanders 6, Minnesota 3; May 17, at Minnesota — NY Islanders 7, Minnesota 5; May 19, at Minnesota— Minnesota 4, NY Islanders 2; May 21, at New York — NY Islanders 5, Minnesota 1.

1979-80 — New York Islanders — Denis Potvin (Captain), Mike Bossy, Bob Bourne, Clark Gillies, Butch Goring, Lorne Henning, Garry Howatt, Anders Kallur, Gord Lane, Dave Langevin, Bob Lorimer, Alex McKendry, Wayne Merrick, Ken Morrow, Bob Nystrom, Stefan Persson, Jean Potvin, Glenn Resch, Billy Smith, Duane Sutter, Steve Tambellini, John Tonelli, Bryan Trottier; Bill Torrey (President/General Manager), John Pickett Jr. (Chairman), Al Arbour (Coach), Billy MacMillan (Assistant Coach), Jim Devellano (Chief Scout), Gerry Ehman, Mario Saraceno, Harry Boyd (Scouts), Ron Waske (Trainer), Jim Pickard (Assistant Trainer).
Scores: May 13, at Philadelphia — NY Islanders 4, Philadelphia 3; May 15, at Philadelphia — Philadelphia 8, NY Islanders 3; May 17, at New York — NY Islanders 6, Philadelphia 2; May 19, at New York — NY Islanders 5, Philadelphia 2; May 22, at Philadelphia — Philadelphia 6, NY Islanders 3; May 24, at New York — NY Islanders 5, Philadelphia 4.

1978-79 — Montreal Canadiens — Yvan Cournoyer (Captain), Guy Lafleur, Ken Dryden, Rick Chartraw, Brian Engblom, Bob Gainey, Mario Tremblay, Guy Lapointe, Doug Risebrough, Réjean Houle, Pat Hughes, Michel Larocque, Doug Jarvis, Yvon Lambert, Pierre Larouche, Gilles Lupien, Rod Langway, Jacques Lemaire, Pierre Mondou, Larry Robinson, Mark Napier, Serge Savard, Steve Shutt, Cam Connor, Richard Sévigny; Jacques Courtois (President), Sam Pollock (Director), Irving Grundman (Vice President/Managing Director), Jean Beliveau (Vice President - Corporate Affairs), Scotty Bowman (Coach), Claude Ruel (Director of Player Development), Al MacNeil (Director of Player Personnel), Morgan McCammon (Director), Ron Caron (Director of Recruitment), Eddy Palchak (Trainer), Pierre Meilleur (Assistant Trainer).
Scores: May 13, at Montreal — NY Rangers 4, Montreal 1; May 15, at Montreal — Montreal 6, NY Rangers 2; May 17, at New York — Montreal 4, NY Rangers 1; May 19, at New York — Montreal 4, NY Rangers 3; May 21, at Montreal — Montreal 4, NY Rangers 1.

1977-78 — Montreal Canadiens — Yvan Cournoyer (Captain), Guy Lafleur, Ken Dryden, Michel Larocque, Rick Chartraw, Réjean Houle, Pierre Larouche, Brian Engblom, Yvon Lambert, Jacques Lemaire, Bob Gainey, Guy Lapointe, Doug Jarvis, Gilles Lupien, Pierre Mondou, Larry Robinson, Bill Nyrop, Murray Wilson, Serge Savard, Steve Shutt, Mario Tremblay, Pierre Bouchard, Doug Risebrough; Jacques Courtois (President), Sam Pollock (Vice President/General Manager), Jean Beliveau (Vice President/Director of Corporate Relations), Scotty Bowman (Coach), Peter Bronfman, Edward Bronfman (Directors), Al MacNeil (Director of Player Development), Eddy Palchak (Trainer), Pierre Meilleur (Assistant Trainer), Claude Ruel (Director of Player Development), Floyd Curry, Ron Caron (Assistant General Managers).
Scores: May 13, at Montreal — Montreal 4, Boston 1; May 16, at Montreal — Montreal 3, Boston 2; May 18, at Boston — Boston 4, Montreal 0; May 21, at Boston — Boston 4, Montreal 3; May 23, at Montreal — Montreal 4, Boston 1; May 25, at Boston — Montreal 4, Boston 1.

1976-77 — Montreal Canadiens — Yvan Cournoyer (Captain), Larry Robinson, Guy Lafleur, Pierre Bouchard, Rejean Houle, Yvon Lambert, Bob Gainey, Jacques Lemaire, Guy Lapointe, Ken Dryden, Rick Chartraw, Bill Nyrop, Michel Larocque, Pierre Mondou, Serge Savard, Steve Shutt, Mario Tremblay, Murray Wilson, Doug Jarvis, Mike Polich, Jimmy Roberts, Pete Mahovlich, Doug Risebrough, Jacques Courtois (President), Sam Pollock (Vice President/General Manager), Jean Beliveau (Vice President/Director of Corporate Relations), Scotty Bowman (Coach), Peter Bronfman, Edward Bronfman (Directors), Claude Ruel (Director of Player Development), Floyd Curry, Ron Caron (Assistant General Managers), Pierre Meilleur (Assistant Trainer), Eddy Palchak (Trainer).
Scores: May 7, at Montreal — Montreal 7, Boston 3; May 10, at Montreal — Montreal 3, Boston 0; May 12, at Boston — Montreal 4, Boston 2; May 14, at Boston — Montreal 2, Boston 1.

1975-76 — Montreal Canadiens — Yvan Cournoyer (Captain), Bob Gainey, Larry Robinson, Pierre Bouchard, Rick Chartraw, Ken Dryden, Pete Mahovlich, Guy Lafleur, Yvon Lambert, Michel Larocque, Serge Savard, Doug Jarvis, Jacques Lemaire, Guy Lapointe, Jimmy Roberts, Doug Risebrough, Steve Shutt, Murray Wilson, Mario Tremblay, Bill Nyrop; Jacques Courtois (President), Jean Beliveau (Vice President), Peter Bronfman (Chairman), Edward Bronfman (Director), Sam Pollock (Vice President/General Manager), Scotty Bowman (Coach), Eddy Palchak (Trainer), Pierre Meilleur (Assistant Trainer), Claude Ruel (Director of Player Development).
Scores: May 9, at Montreal — Montreal 4, Philadelphia 3; May 11, at Montreal — Montreal 2, Philadelphia 1; May 13, at Philadelphia — Montreal 3, Philadelphia 2; May 16, at Philadelphia — Montreal 5, Philadelphia 3.

1974-75 — Philadelphia Flyers — Bobby Clarke (Captain), Bernie Parent, Bobby Taylor, Wayne Stephenson, Ed Van Impe, Don Saleski, Tom Bladon, Larry Goodenough, Bill Barber, Gary Dornhoefer, Dave Schultz, Joe Watson, Ross Lonsberry, André Dupont, Terry Crisp, Orest Kindrachuk, Bill Clement, Bob Kelly, Rick MacLeish, Jimmy Watson, Reggie Leach, Ted Harris; Ed Snider (Chairman), Joe Scott (President), Eugene Dixon Jr. (Vice Chairman), Fred Shero (Coach), Keith Allen (Vice President/General Manager), Lou Scheinfeld (Vice President), Mike Nykoluk (Assistant Coach), Marcel Pelletier (Player Personnel Director), Barry Ashbee (Assistant Coach), Frank Lewis (Trainer), Jim McKenzie (Assistant Trainer).
Scores: May 15, at Philadelphia — Philadelphia 4, Buffalo 1; May 18, at Philadelphia — Philadelphia 2, Buffalo 1; May 20, at Buffalo — Buffalo 5, Philadelphia 4; May 22, at Buffalo — Buffalo 4, Philadelphia 2; May 25, at Philadelphia — Philadelphia 5, Buffalo 1; May 27, at Buffalo — Philadelphia 2, Buffalo 0.

1973-74 — Philadelphia Flyers — Bobby Clarke (Captain), Bernie Parent, Bobby Taylor, Bill Clement, Ross Lonsberry, Bill Barber, Orest Kindrachuk, Ed Van Impe, Don Saleski, Gary Dornhoefer, Barry Ashbee, Jimmy Watson, Dave Schultz, André Dupont, Bruce Cowick, Rick MacLeish, Terry Crisp, Bill Flett, Simon Nolet, Joe Watson, Bob Kelly, Tom Bladon; Ed Snider (Chairman), Joe Scott (President), Eugene Dixon Jr. (Vice Chairman), Fred Shero (Coach), Keith Allen (Vice President/General Manager), Mike Nykoluk (Assistant Coach), Marcel Pelletier (Player Personnel Director), Frank Lewis (Trainer), Jim McKenzie (Assistant Trainer).
Scores: May 7, at Boston — Boston 3, Philadelphia 2; May 9, at Boston — Philadelphia 3, Boston 2; May 12, at Philadelphia — Philadelphia 4, Boston 1; May 14, at Philadelphia — Philadelphia 4, Boston 2; May 16, at Boston — Boston 5, Philadelphia 1; May 19, at Philadelphia — Philadelphia 1, Boston 0.

1972-73 — Montreal Canadiens — Henri Richard (Captain), Jacques Laperrière, Ken Dryden, Yvan Cournoyer, Jacques Lemaire, Marc Tardif, Serge Savard, Pete Mahovlich, Guy Lapointe, Réjean Houle, Claude Larose, Pierre Bouchard, Frank Mahovlich, Jimmy Roberts, Chuck Lefley, Guy Lafleur, Bob Murdoch, Michel Plasse, Murray Wilson, Larry Robinson, Steve Shutt; Jacques Courtois (President), Jean Beliveau (Vice President), Peter Bronfman (Chairman), Sam Pollock (Vice President/General Manager), Edward Bronfman (Executive Director), Scotty Bowman (Coach), Bob Williams (Trainer).
Scores: April 29, at Montreal — Montreal 8, Chicago 3; May 1, at Montreal — Montreal 4, Chicago 1; May 3, at Chicago — Chicago 7, Montreal 4; May 6, at Chicago — Montreal 4, Chicago 0; May 8, at Montreal — Chicago 8, Montreal 7; May 10, at Chicago — Montreal 6, Chicago 4.

1971-72 — Boston Bruins — Bobby Orr, Gerry Cheevers, Eddie Johnston, Dallas Smith, Derek Sanderson, Carol Vadnais, Phil Esposito, Fred Stanfield, Don Awrey, Ted Green, Ken Hodge, John Bucyk, Wayne Cashman, John McKenzie, Ed Westfall, Mike Walton, Garnet Bailey, Don Marcotte; Weston Adams (Chairman), Weston Adams Jr. (President), Shelby Davis (Vice President), Charles Mulcahy (Junior Vice President/General Counsel), Eddie Powers (Vice President/Treasurer), Milt Schmidt (General Manager), Tom Johnson (Coach), Dan Canney (Trainer), John Forristall (Assistant Trainer).
Scores: April 30, at Boston — Boston 6, NY Rangers 5; May 2, at Boston — Boston 2, NY Rangers 1; May 4, at New York — NY Rangers 5, Boston 2; May 7, at New York — Boston 3, NY Rangers 2; May 9, at Boston — NY Rangers 3, Boston 2; May 11, at New York — Boston 3, NY Rangers 0.

1970-71 — Montreal Canadiens — Jean Béliveau (Captain), Pierre Bouchard, Yvan Cournoyer, John Ferguson, Jacques Laperrière, Terry Harper, Réjean Houle, Guy Lapointe, Claude Larose, Marc Tardif, Chuck Lefley, Jacques Lemaire, Frank Mahovlich, Henri Richard, Phil Roberto, Pete Mahovlich, Bob Murdoch, Serge Savard (37GP – injured), Bobby Sheehan, Leon Rochefort, J.C. Tremblay, Ken Dryden, Rogie Vachon; David Molson (President), William Molson, Peter Molson (Vice Presidents), Sam Pollock (Vice President/General Manager), Ron Caron (Assistant General Manager), Al MacNeil (Coach), Yves Belanger (Trainer), Phil Langlois, Eddie Palchak (Assistant Trainers).
Scores: May 4, at Chicago — Chicago 2, Montreal 1; May 6, at Chicago — Chicago 5, Montreal 3; May 9, at Montreal — Montreal 4, Chicago 2; May 11, at Montreal — Montreal 5, Chicago 2; May 13, at Chicago — Chicago 2, Montreal 0; May 16, at Montreal — Montreal 4, Chicago 3; May 18, at Chicago — Montreal 3, Chicago 2.

1969-70 — Boston Bruins — Don Awrey, John Bucyk, Garnet Bailey, Wayne Carleton, Wayne Cashman, Gary Doak, Phil Esposito, Ted Green, Ken Hodge, Bobby Orr, Don Marcotte, John McKenzie, Derek Sanderson, Dallas Smith, Rick Smith, Bill Speer, Fred Stanfield, Ed Westfall, Gerry Cheevers, Eddie Johnston, John Adams, Jim Lorentz, Ron Murphy, Bill Lesuk, Ivan Boldirev, Danny Schock; Weston Adams Sr. (Chairman), Weston Adams Jr. (President), Charles Mulcahy, Eddie Powers, Shelby Davis (Vice Presidents), Harry Sinden (Coach), Milt Schmidt (General Manager), Tom Johnson (Assistant General Manager), Dan Canney (Trainer), John Forristall (Assistant Trainer).
Scores: May 3, at St. Louis — Boston 6, St. Louis 1; May 5, at St. Louis — Boston 6, St. Louis 2; May 7, at Boston — Boston 4, St. Louis 1; May 10, at Boston — Boston 4, St. Louis 3.

1968-69 — Montreal Canadiens — Jean Béliveau (Captain), Ralph Backstrom, Jacques Lemaire, Dick Duff, Christian Bordeleau, Mickey Redmond, Yvan Cournoyer, Henri Richard, Bobby Rousseau, John Ferguson, Serge Savard, Terry Harper, Gilles Tremblay, Ted Harris, J.C. Tremblay, Larry Hillman, Jacques Laperrière, Claude Provost, Tony Esposito, Rogie Vachon, Gump Worsley; David Molson (President), William Molson, Peter Molson (Vice Presidents), Sam Pollock (Vice President/General Manager), Claude Ruel (Coach), Larry Aubut (Trainer), Eddie Palchak (Assistant Trainer).
Scores: April 27, at Montreal — Montreal 3, St. Louis 1; April 29, at Montreal — Montreal 3, St. Louis 1; May 1, at St. Louis — Montreal 4, St. Louis 0; May 4, at St. Louis — Montreal 2, St. Louis 1.

1967-68 — Montreal Canadiens — Jean Béliveau (Captain), Ralph Backstrom, Yvan Cournoyer, Dick Duff, John Ferguson, Danny Grant, Terry Harper, Ted Harris, Serge Savard, Jacques Laperrière, Claude Larose, Jacques Lemaire, Claude Provost, Mickey Redmond, Henri Richard, Bobby Rousseau, Gilles Tremblay, J.C. Tremblay, Carol Vadnais, Rogie Vachon, Ernie Wakely, Gump Worsley; Hartland Molson (Chairman), David Molson (President), Sam Pollock (Vice President/General Manager), Toe Blake (Coach), Larry Aubut (Trainer), Eddie Palchak (Assistant Trainer).
Scores: May 5, at St. Louis — Montreal 3, St. Louis 2; May 7, at St. Louis — Montreal 1, St. Louis 0; May 9, at Montreal — Montreal 4, St. Louis 3; May 11, at Montreal — Montreal 3, St. Louis 2.

1966-67 — Toronto Maple Leafs — George Armstrong (Captain), Bob Baun, Johnny Bower, Brian Conacher, Ron Ellis, Aut Erickson, Larry Hillman, Tim Horton, Red Kelly, Larry Jeffrey, Dave Keon, Frank Mahovlich, Milan Marcetta, Jim Pappin, Marcel Pronovost, Bob Pulford, Terry Sawchuk, Eddie Shack, Allan Stanley, Pete Stemkowski, Mike Walton; Stafford Smythe (President), Harold Ballard (Executive Vice President), John Bassett (Chairman), Punch Imlach (General Manager/Coach), King Clancy (Assistant Coach/Assistant General Manager), Bob Davidson (Chief Scout), John Anderson (Business Manager), Bob Haggert (Trainer), Tom Nayler (Assistant Trainer), Karl Elieff (Physiotherapist), Richard Smythe (Mascot).
Scores: April 20, at Montreal — Toronto 2, Montreal 6; April 22, at Montreal — Toronto 3, Montreal 0; April 25, at Toronto — Toronto 3, Montreal 2; April 27, at Toronto — Toronto 2, Montreal 6; April 29, at Montreal — Toronto 4, Montreal 1; May 2, at Toronto — Toronto 3, Montreal 1.

1965-66 — Montreal Canadiens — Jean Béliveau (Captain), Ralph Backstrom, Dave Balon, Yvan Cournoyer, Bobby Rousseau, Dick Duff, John Ferguson, Terry Harper, Ted Harris, Charlie Hodge, Jacques Laperrière, Claude Larose, Noel Price, Claude Provost, Henri Richard, Jimmy Roberts, Leon Rochefort, Jean-Guy Talbot, Gilles Tremblay, J.C. Tremblay, Gump Worsley; Hartland Molson (Chairman), David Molson (President), Sam Pollock (General Manager), Toe Blake (Coach), Andy Galley (Trainer), Larry Aubut (Assistant Trainer).
Scores: April 24, at Montreal — Detroit 3, Montreal 2; April 26, at Montreal — Detroit 5, Montreal 2; April 28, at Detroit — Montreal 4, Detroit 2; May 1, at Detroit — Montreal 2, Detroit 1; May 3, at Montreal — Montreal 5, Detroit 1; May 5, at Detroit — Montreal 3, Detroit 2.

1964-65 — Montreal Canadiens — Jean Béliveau (Captain), Ralph Backstrom, Dave Balon, Red Berenson, Yvan Cournoyer, Dick Duff, John Ferguson, Jean Gauthier, Charlie Hodge, Terry Harper, Ted Harris, Jacques Laperrière, Claude Larose, Garry Peters, Noel Picard, Claude Provost, Henri Richard, Jimmy Roberts, Bobby Rousseau, Jean-Guy Talbot, Gilles Tremblay, J.C. Tremblay, Ernie Wakely, Bryan Watson, Gump Worsley; Hartland Molson (Chairman), David Molson (President), Maurice Richard (Assistant to the President), Sam Pollock (General Manager), Toe Blake (Coach), Andy Galley (Trainer), Larry Aubut (Assistant Trainer).
Scores: April 17, at Montreal — Montreal 3, Chicago 2; April 20, at Montreal — Montreal 2, Chicago 0; April 22, at Chicago — Montreal 1, Chicago 3; April 25, at Chicago — Montreal 1, Chicago 5; April 7, at Montreal — Montreal 6, Chicago 0; April 29, at Chicago — Montreal 1, Chicago 2; May 1, at Montreal — Montreal 4, Chicago 0.

1963-64 — Toronto Maple Leafs — George Armstrong (Captain), Andy Bathgate, Bob Baun, Johnny Bower, Carl Brewer, Gerry Ehman, Billy Harris, Larry Hillman, Dave Keon, Tim Horton, Red Kelly, Frank Mahovlich, Don McKenney, Jim Pappin, Bob Pulford, Eddie Shack, Don Simmons, Allan Stanley, Ron Stewart, Al Arbour, Ed Litzenberger; Stafford Smythe (President), Harold Ballard (Executive Vice President), John Bassett (Chairman), Punch Imlach (Coach/General Manager), King Clancy (Assistant Coach/Assistant General Manager), Bob Haggert (Trainer), Tom Nayler (Assistant Trainer), Hugh Hoult (Stick Boy).
Scores April 11, at Toronto — Toronto 3, Detroit 2; April 14, at Toronto — Toronto 3, Detroit 4; April 16, at Detroit — Toronto 3, Detroit 4; April 18, at Detroit — Toronto 4, Detroit 2; April 21, at Toronto — Toronto 1, Detroit 2; April 23, at Detroit — Toronto 4, Detroit 3; April 25, at Toronto — Toronto 4, Detroit 0.

1962-63 — Toronto Maple Leafs — George Armstrong (Captain), Bob Baun, Johnny Bower, Carl Brewer, Kent Douglas, Dick Duff, Billy Harris, Larry Hillman, Tim Horton, Red Kelly, Dave Keon, Ed Litzenberger, John MacMillan, Frank Mahovlich, Bob Nevin, Bob Pulford, Eddie Shack, Don Simmons, Allan Stanley, Ron Stewart; Stafford Smythe (President), Harold Ballard (Executive Vice President), John Bassett (Chairman), Punch Imlach (Coach/General Manager), King Clancy (Assistant Coach/Assistant General Manager), Bob Haggert (Trainer), Tom Nayler (Assistant Trainer), Hugh Hoult (Stick Boy).
Scores: April 9, at Toronto — Toronto 4, Detroit 2; April 11, at Toronto — Toronto 4, Detroit 2; April 14, at Detroit — Toronto 2, Detroit 3; April 16, at Detroit — Toronto 4, Detroit 2; April 18, at Toronto — Toronto 3, Detroit 1.

1961-62 — Toronto Maple Leafs — George Armstrong (Captain), Al Arbour, Bob Baun, Johnny Bower, Carl Brewer, Dick Duff, Billy Harris, Larry Hillman, Dave Keon, Tim Horton, Red Kelly, Ed Litzenberger, John MacMillan, Frank Mahovlich, Bob Nevin, Bert Olmstead, Bob Pulford, Eddie Shack, Allan Stanley, Don Simmons, Ron Stewart; Stafford Smythe (President), Harold Ballard (Executive Vice President), John Bassett (Vice President), Conn Smythe (Chairman), Punch Imlach (Coach/General Manager), King Clancy (Assistant Coach), Bob Davidson (Chief Scout), Bob Haggert (Trainer), Tom Nayler (Assistant Trainer), Hugh Hoult (Stick Boy).
Scores: April 10, at Toronto — Toronto 4, Chicago 1; April 12, at Toronto — Toronto 3, Chicago 2; April 15, at Chicago — Toronto 0, Chicago 3; April 17, at Chicago — Toronto 1, Chicago 4; April 19, at Toronto —Toronto 8, Chicago 4; April 22, at Chicago — Toronto 2, Chicago 1.

1960-61 — Chicago Black Hawks — Ed Litzenberger (Captain), Al Arbour, Earl Balfour, Murray Balfour, Glenn Hall, Jack Evans, Roy Edwards, Denis DeJordy, Bill Hay, Wayne Hicks, Reggie Fleming, Wayne Hillman, Bobby Hull, Chico Maki, Ab McDonald, Moose Vasko, Stan Mikita, Ron Murphy, Eric Nesterenko, Pierre Pilote, Tod Sloan, Dollard St. Laurent, Kenny Wharram; Arthur Wirtz (President), Arthur Wirtz Jr. (Vice President), James Norris (Chairman), Tommy Ivan (General Manager), Rudy Pilous (Coach), Nick Garen, Walter Humeniuk (Trainers).
Scores: April 6, at Chicago — Chicago 3, Detroit 2; April 8, at Detroit — Detroit 3, Chicago 1; April 10, at Chicago — Chicago 3, Detroit 1; April 12, at Detroit — Detroit 2, Chicago 1; April 14, at Chicago — Chicago 6, Detroit 3; April 16, at Detroit — Chicago 5, Detroit 1.

1959-60 — Montreal Canadiens — Maurice Richard (Captain), Ralph Backstrom, Marcel Bonin, Jean Béliveau, Bernie Geoffrion, Phil Goyette, Doug Harvey, Bill Hicke, Charlie Hodge, Tom Johnson, Albert Langlois, Don Marshall, Dickie Moore, Ab McDonald, Jacques Plante, Henri Richard, André Pronovost, Claude Provost, Bob Turner, Jean-Guy Talbot; Senator Hartland Molson (President), Frank Selke (Managing Director), Ken Reardon (Vice President), Sam Pollock (Personnel Director), Toe Blake (Coach), Hector Dubois, Larry Aubut (Trainers).
Scores: April 7, at Montreal — Montreal 4, Toronto 2; April 9, at Montreal — Montreal 2, Toronto 1; April 12, at Toronto — Montreal 5, Toronto 2; April 14, at Toronto — Montreal 4, Toronto 0.

1958-59 — Montreal Canadiens — Maurice Richard (Captain), Ralph Backstrom, Marcel Bonin, Jean Béliveau, Ian Cushenan, Bernie Geoffrion, Charlie Hodge, Phil Goyette, Doug Harvey, Bill Hicke, Tom Johnson, Albert Langlois, Don Marshall, Ab McDonald, Dickie Moore, Jacques Plante, Ken Mosdell, André Pronovost, Claude Provost, Henri Richard, Jean-Guy Talbot, Bob Turner; Senator Hartland Molson (President), Frank Selke (Managing Director), Ken Reardon (Vice President), Sam Pollock (Personnel Director), Toe Blake (Coach), Hector Dubois, Larry Aubut (Trainers).
Scores: April 9, at Montreal — Montreal 5, Toronto 3; April 11, at Montreal — Montreal 3, Toronto 1; April 14, at Toronto — Toronto 3, Montreal 2; April 16, at Toronto — Montreal 3, Toronto 2; April 18, at Montreal — Montreal 5, Toronto 3.

1957-58 — Montreal Canadiens — Maurice Richard (Captain), Jean Béliveau, Marcel Bonin, Floyd Curry, Connie Broden, Bernie Geoffrion, Phil Goyette, Doug Harvey, Charlie Hodge, Tom Johnson, Albert Langlois, Don Marshall, Ab McDonald, Gerry McNeil, Dickie Moore, Bert Olmstead, Jacques Plante, André Pronovost, Henri Richard, Claude Provost, Dollard St. Laurent, Jean-Guy Talbot, Bob Turner; Senator Hartland Molson (President), Frank Selke (Managing Director), Ken Reardon (Vice President), Toe Blake (Coach), Hector Dubois, Larry Aubut (Trainers).
Scores: April 8, at Montreal —Montreal 2, Boston 1; April 10, at Montreal — Boston 5, Montreal 2; April 13, at Boston — Montreal 3, Boston 0; April 15, at Boston — Boston 3, Montreal 1; April 17, at Montreal — Montreal 3, Boston 2; April 20, at Boston — Montreal 5, Boston 3.

1956-57 — Montreal Canadiens — Maurice Richard (Captain), Jean Béliveau, Connie Broden, Floyd Curry, Bernie Geoffrion, Phil Goyette, Doug Harvey, Tom Johnson, Don Marshall, Gerry McNeil, Dickie Moore, Bert Olmstead, Jacques Plante, André Pronovost, Claude Provost, Henri Richard, Dollard St. Laurent, Jean-Guy Talbot, Bob Turner; William Northey (President), Donat Raymond (Chairman), Ken Reardon (Vice President), Frank Selke (Managing Director), Toe Blake (Coach), Hector Dubois, Larry Aubut (Trainers).
Scores: April 6, at Montreal — Montreal 5, Boston 1; April 9, at Montreal — Montreal 1, Boston 0; April 11, at Boston — Montreal 4, Boston 2; April 14, at Boston — Boston 2, Montreal 0; April 16, at Montreal — Montreal 5, Boston 1.

1955-56 — Montreal Canadiens — Butch Bouchard (Captain), Bob Turner, Jean Béliveau, Bert Olmstead, Floyd Curry, Bernie Geoffrion, Jacques Plante, Doug Harvey, Claude Provost, Charlie Hodge, Henri Richard, Tom Johnson, Maurice Richard, Jackie LeClair, Dollard St. Laurent, Don Marshall, Jean-Guy Talbot, Dickie Moore, Ken Mosdell; Donat Raymond (President), Frank Selke (Managing Director), D'Alton Coleman, William Northey (Vice Presidents), Ken Reardon (Assistant Manager), Toe Blake (Coach), Hector Dubois, Gaston Bettez (Trainers).
Scores: March 31, at Montreal — Montreal 6, Detroit 4; April 3, at Montreal — Montreal 5, Detroit 1; April 5, at Detroit — Detroit 3, Montreal 1; April 8, at Detroit — Montreal 3, Detroit 0; April 10, at Montreal — Montreal 3, Detroit 1.

1954-55 — Detroit Red Wings — Dutch Reibel, Terry Sawchuk, Jim Hay, Vic Stasiuk, Johnny Wilson, Gordie Howe, Red Kelly, Tony Leswick, Ted Lindsay (Captain), Marty Pavelich, Marcel Pronovost, Marcel Bonin, Alex Delvecchio, Bill Dineen, Bob Goldham, Benny Woit, Larry Hillman, Glen Skov; Bruce Norris (President), Marguerite Norris (President), Jack Adams (Manager), Jimmy Skinner (Coach), John Mitchell (Chief Scout), Fred Huber (Publicity Director), Carl Mattson, Lefty Wilson (Trainers).
Scores: April 3, at Detroit — Detroit 4, Montreal 2; April 5, at Detroit — Detroit 7, Montreal 1; April 7, at Montreal — Montreal 4, Detroit 2; April 9, at Montreal — Montreal 5, Detroit 3; April 10, at Detroit — Detroit 5, Montreal 1; April 12, at Montreal — Montreal 6, Detroit 3; April 14, at Detroit — Detroit 3, Montreal 1.

1953-54 — Detroit Red Wings — Marty Pavelich, Jimmy Peters, Marcel Pronovost, Metro Prystai, Dutch Reibel, Terry Sawchuk, Bob Goldham, Gordie Howe, Earl Johnson, Red Kelly, Tony Leswick, Ted Lindsay (Captain), Keith Allen, Al Arbour, Alex Delvecchio, Bill Dineen, Gilles Dube, Dave Gatherum, Glen Skov, Johnny Wilson, Benny Woit; Bruce Norris (Owner), Marguerite Norris (President), Jack Adams (Manager), Tommy Ivan (Coach), John Mitchell (Chief Scout), Fred Huber (Publicity Director), Carl Mattson, Lefty Wilson (Trainers), Wally Crossman (Assistant Trainer).
Scores: April 4, at Detroit — Detroit 3, Montreal 1; April 6, at Detroit — Montreal 3, Detroit 1; April 8, at Montreal — Detroit 5, Montreal 2; April 10, at Montreal — Detroit 2, Montreal 0; April 11, at Detroit — Montreal 1, Detroit 0; April 13, at Montreal — Montreal 4, Detroit 1; April 16, at Detroit — Detroit 2, Montreal 1.

1952-53 — Montreal Canadiens — Floyd Curry, Bernie Geoffrion, Bert Olmstead, Paul Meger, Dick Gamble, Dickie Moore, Tom Johnson, Bud MacPherson, Billy Reay, Ken Mosdell, Paul Masnick, John McCormack, Butch Bouchard (Captain), Maurice Richard, Elmer Lach, Gerry McNeil, Doug Harvey, Dollard St. Laurent, Jacques Plante, Lorne Davis, Calum MacKay, Eddie Mazur, Donat Raymond (President), Dalton Coleman (Director), William Northey (Special Advisor), Frank Selke (Manager), Dick Irvin (Coach), Hector Dubois, Gaston Bettez (Trainers).
Scores: April 9, at Montreal — Montreal 4, Boston 2; April 11, at Montreal — Boston 4, Montreal 1; April 12, at Boston — Montreal 3, Boston 0; April 14, at Boston — Montreal 7, Boston 3; April 16, at Montreal — Montreal 1, Boston 0.

1951-52 — Detroit Red Wings — Metro Prystai, Leo Reise Jr., Terry Sawchuk, Enio Sclisizzi, Glen Skov, Vic Stasiuk, Gordie Howe, Red Kelly, Tony Leswick, Ted Lindsay, Marty Pavelich, Marcel Pronovost, Sid Abel (Captain), Alex Delvecchio, Fred Glover, Bob Goldham, Glenn Hall, Benny Woit, Johnny Wilson, Larry Zeidel; James Norris (President), Bruce Norris (Owner), Jack Adams (Manager), Tommy Ivan (Coach), Fred Huber (Publicity Director), Carson Cooper (Scout), Carl Mattson, Lefty Wilson (Trainers), Wally Crossman (Assistant Trainer).
Scores: April 10, at Montreal — Detroit 3, Montreal 1; April 12, at Montreal — Detroit 2, Montreal 1; April 13, at Detroit — Detroit 3, Montreal 0; April 15, at Detroit — Detroit 3, Montreal 0.

1950-51 — Toronto Maple Leafs — Bill Barilko, Max Bentley, Hugh Bolton, Turk Broda, Fern Flaman, Cal Gardner, Bob Hassard, Bill Juzda, Ted Kennedy (Captain), Joe Klukay, Danny Lewicki, Fleming MacKell, Howie Meeker, Gus Mortson, John McCormack, Al Rollins, Tod Sloan, Sid Smith, Jimmy Thomson, Ray Timgren, Harry Watson; Joe Primeau (Coach), Bill MacBrien (Chairman), Conn Smythe (President/Manager), Hap Day (Assistant Manager), George McCullagh, J.Y. Murdoch (Vice Presidents), J.P. Bickell, Ed Bickle (Directors), Tim Daly (Trainer), Archie Campbell, Tommy Naylor (Assistant Trainers), Dr. Norman Delarue, Dr. James Murray, Dr. Horace MacIntyre (Club Doctors), Ed Fitkin (Publicity Director), Squib Walker (Chief Scout).
Scores: April 11, at Toronto — Toronto 3, Montreal 2; April 14, at Toronto — Montreal 3, Toronto 2; April 17, at Montreal — Toronto 2, Montreal 1; April 19, at Montreal — Toronto 3, Montreal 2; April 21, at Toronto — Toronto 3, Montreal 2.

1949-50 — Detroit Red Wings — Sid Abel (Captain), Pete Babando, Steve Black, Joe Carveth, Gerry Couture, Al Dewsbury, Lee Fogolin, George Gee, Gordie Howe, Red Kelly, Ted Lindsay, Harry Lumley, Clare Martin, Jim McFadden, Max McNab, Marty Pavelich, Jimmy Peters, Marcel Pronovost, Leo Reise Jr., Jack Stewart, Johnny Wilson, Larry Wilson, Doug McKay; James Norris (President), James Norris Jr. (Vice President), Arthur Wirtz (Secretary Treasurer), Jack Adams (Manager), Tommy Ivan (Coach), Fred Huber Jr. (Publicity Director), Carson Cooper (Head Scout), Carl Mattson (Trainer), Walter Humeniuk (Assistant Trainer).
Scores: April 11, at Detroit — Detroit 4, NY Rangers 1; April 13, at Toronto* — NY Rangers 3, Detroit 1; April 15, at Toronto* — Detroit 4, NY Rangers 0; April 18, at Detroit — NY Rangers 4, Detroit 3; April 20, at Detroit — NY Rangers 2, Detroit 1; April 22, at Detroit — Detroit 5, NY Rangers 4; April 23, at Detroit — Detroit 4, NY Rangers 3.
*Ice was unavailable in Madison Square Garden and NY Rangers elected to play second and third games on Toronto ice.

1948-49 — Toronto Maple Leafs — Bill Barilko, Max Bentley, Garth Boesch, Turk Broda, Bob Dawes, Bill Ezinicki, Cal Gardner, Bill Juzda, Ted Kennedy (Captain), Joe Klukay, Vic Lynn, Howie Meeker, Don Metz, Fleming MacKell, Gus Mortson, Sid Smith, Harry Taylor, Ray Timgren, Jimmy Thomson, Harry Watson; Hap Day (Coach), Bill MacBrien (Chairman), Conn Smythe (President/Manager), George McCullagh, J.Y. Murdoch (Vice Presidents), J.P. Bickell, Ed Bickle (Directors), Tim Daly (Trainer), Archie Campbell (Assistant Trainer), Dr. Norman Delarue, Dr. James Murray, Dr. Horace MacIntyre (Club Doctors), Ed Fitkin (Publicity Director), Squib Walker (Chief Scout), Kerry Day (Mascot).
Scores: April 8, at Detroit — Toronto 3, Detroit 2; April 10, at Detroit — Toronto 3, Detroit 1; April 13, at Toronto — Toronto 3, Detroit 1; April 16, at Toronto — Toronto 3, Detroit 1.

1947-48 — Toronto Maple Leafs — Syl Apps (Captain), Bill Barilko, Max Bentley, Garth Boesch, Turk Broda, Les Costello, Bill Ezinicki, Ted Kennedy, Joe Klukay, Vic Lynn, Howie Meeker, Nick Metz, Don Metz, Gus Mortson, Phil Samis, Sid Smith, Wally Stanowski, Jimmy Thomson, Harry Watson; Hap Day (Coach), Conn Smythe (Manager), Tim Daly (Trainer).
Scores: April 7, at Toronto — Toronto 5, Detroit 3; April 10, at Toronto — Toronto 4, Detroit 2; April 11, at Detroit — Toronto 2, Detroit 0; April 14, at Detroit — Toronto 7, Detroit 2.

1946-47 — Toronto Maple Leafs — Turk Broda, Garth Boesch, Gus Mortson, Jimmy Thomson, Wally Stanowski, Bill Barilko, Harry Watson, Bud Poile, Ted Kennedy, Syl Apps (Captain), Don Metz, Nick Metz, Bill Ezinicki, Vic Lynn, Howie Meeker, Gaye Stewart, Joe Klukay, Gus Bodnar, Bob Goldham; Conn Smythe (Manager), Hap Day (Coach), Tim Daly (Trainer).
Scores: April 8, at Montreal — Montreal 6, Toronto 0; April 10, at Montreal — Toronto 4, Montreal 0; April 12, at Toronto — Toronto 4, Montreal 2; April 15, at Toronto — Toronto 2, Montreal 1; April 17, at Montreal — Montreal 3, Toronto 1; April 19, at Toronto — Toronto 2, Montreal 1.

1945-46 — Montreal Canadiens — Elmer Lach, Toe Blake (Captain), Maurice Richard, Bob Fillion, Dutch Hiller, Murph Chamberlain, Ken Mosdell, Buddy O'Connor, Glen Harmon, Jimmy Peters, Butch Bouchard, Billy Reay, Ken Reardon, Leo Lamoureux, Frank Eddolls, Gerry Plamondon, Joe Benoit, Bill Durnan; Tommy Gorman (Manager), Dick Irvin (Coach), Ernie Cook (Trainer).
Scores: March 30, at Montreal — Montreal 4, Boston 3; April 2, at Montreal — Montreal 3, Boston 2; April 4, at Boston — Montreal 4, Boston 2; April 7, at Boston — Boston 3, Montreal 2; April 9, at Montreal — Montreal 6, Boston 3.

1944-45 — Toronto Maple Leafs — Don Metz, Frank McCool, Wally Stanowski, Reg Hamilton, Moe Morris, John McCreedy, Tom O'Neill, Ted Kennedy, Babe Pratt, Gus Bodnar, Art Jackson, Jack McLean, Mel Hill, Nick Metz, Bob Davidson (Captain), Sweeney Schriner, Lorne Carr, Pete Backor, Ross Johnstone; Conn Smythe (Manager), Frank Selke (Business Manager), Hap Day (Coach), Tim Daly (Trainer).
Scores: April 6, at Detroit — Toronto 1, Detroit 0; April 8, at Detroit — Toronto 2, Detroit 0; April 12, at Toronto — Toronto 1, Detroit 0; April 14, at Toronto — Detroit 5, Toronto 3; April 19, at Detroit — Detroit 2, Toronto 0; April 21, at Toronto — Detroit 1, Toronto 0; April 22, at Detroit — Toronto 2, Detroit 1.

1943-44 — Montreal Canadiens — Toe Blake (Captain), Maurice Richard, Elmer Lach, Ray Getliffe, Murph Chamberlain, Phil Watson, Butch Bouchard, Glen Harmon, Buddy O'Connor, Gerry Heffernan, Mike McMahon, Leo Lamoureux, Fern Majeau, Bob Fillion, Bill Durnan; Tommy Gorman (Manager), Dick Irvin (Coach), Ernie Cook (Trainer).
Scores: April 4, at Montreal — Montreal 5, Chicago 1; April 6, at Chicago — Montreal 3, Chicago 1; April 9, at Chicago — Montreal 3, Chicago 2; April 13, at Montreal — Montreal 5, Chicago 4.

1942-43 — Detroit Red Wings — Jack Stewart, Jimmy Orlando, Sid Abel (captain), Alex Motter, Harry Watson, Joe Carveth, Mud Bruneteau, Eddie Wares, Johnny Mowers, Cully Simon, Don Grosso, Carl Liscombe, Connie Brown, Syd Howe, Les Douglas, Harold Jackson, Joe Fisher, Adam Brown; Jack Adams (Manager), Ebbie Goodfellow (Playing Coach), Honey Walker (Trainer).
Scores: April 1, at Detroit — Detroit 6, Boston 2; April 4, at Detroit — Detroit 4, Boston 3; April 7, at Boston — Detroit 4, Boston 0; April 8, at Boston — Detroit 2, Boston 0.

1941-42 — Toronto Maple Leafs — Wally Stanowski, Syl Apps (Captain), Bob Goldham, Gordie Drillon, Hank Goldup, Ernie Dickens, Sweeney Schriner, Bucko McDonald, Bob Davidson, Nick Metz, Bingo Kampman, Don Metz, Gaye Stewart, Turk Broda, John McCreedy, Lorne Carr, Pete Langelle, Billy Taylor, Reg Hamilton; Conn Smythe (Manager), Hap Day (Coach), Frank Selke (Business Manager), Tim Daly (Trainer).
Scores: April 4, at Toronto — Detroit 3, Toronto 2; April 7, at Toronto — Detroit 4, Toronto 2; April 9, at Detroit — Detroit 5, Toronto 2; April 12, at Detroit — Toronto 4, Detroit 3; April 14, at Toronto — Toronto 9, Detroit 3; April 16, at Detroit — Toronto 3, Detroit 0; April 18, at Toronto — Toronto 3, Detroit 1.

1940-41 — Boston Bruins — Bill Cowley, Des Smith, Dit Clapper (Captain), Frank Brimsek, Flash Hollett, Jack Crawford, Bobby Bauer, Pat McReavy, Herb Cain, Mel Hill, Milt Schmidt, Woody Dumart, Roy Conacher, Terry Reardon, Art Jackson, Eddie Wiseman, Jack Shewchuck; Art Ross (Manager), Cooney Weiland (Coach), Win Green (Trainer).
Scores: April 6, at Boston — Detroit 2, Boston 3; April 8, at Boston — Detroit 1, Boston 2; April 10, at Detroit — Boston 4, Detroit 2; April 12, at Detroit — Boston 3, Detroit 1.

1939-40 — New York Rangers — Dave Kerr, Art Coulter (Captain), Ott Heller, Alex Shibicky, Mac Colville, Neil Colville, Phil Watson, Lynn Patrick, Clint Smith, Muzz Patrick, Babe Pratt, Bryan Hextall, Kilby MacDonald, Dutch Hiller, Alf Pike, Stan Smith; Lester Patrick (Manager), Frank Boucher (Coach), Harry Westerby (Trainer).
Scores: April 2, at New York — NY Rangers 2, Toronto 1; April 3, at New York — NY Rangers 6, Toronto 2; April 6, at Toronto — NY Rangers 1, Toronto 2; April 9, at Toronto — NY Rangers 0, Toronto 3; April 11, at Toronto — NY Rangers 2, Toronto 1; April 13, at Toronto — NY Rangers 3, Toronto 2.

1938-39 — Boston Bruins — Bobby Bauer, Mel Hill, Flash Hollett, Roy Conacher, Gord Pettinger, Charlie Sands, Milt Schmidt, Woody Dumart, Jack Crawford, Ray Getliffe, Frank Brimsek, Eddie Shore, Dit Clapper, Bill Cowley, Jack Portland, Red Hamill, Harry Frost, Cooney Weiland (Captain); Art Ross (Manager/Coach), Win Green (Trainer).
Scores: April 6, at Boston — Toronto 1, Boston 2; April 9, at Boston — Toronto 3, Boston 2; April 11, at Toronto — Toronto 1, Boston 3; April 13, at Toronto — Toronto 0, Boston 2; April 16, at Boston — Toronto 1, Boston 3.

1937-38 — Chicago Black Hawks — Art Wiebe, Carl Voss, Harold Jackson, Mike Karakas, Mush March, Jack Shill, Earl Seibert, Cully Dahlstrom, Alex Levinsky, Johnny Gottselig (Captain), Lou Trudel, Pete Palangio, Bill MacKenzie, Doc Romnes, Paul Thompson, Roger Jenkins, Alfie Moore, Bert Connelly, Virgil Johnson, Paul Goodman; Bill Stewart (Manager/Coach), Eddie Froelich (Trainer).
Scores: April 5, at Toronto — Chicago 3, Toronto 1; April 7, at Toronto — Chicago 1, Toronto 5; April 10, at Chicago — Chicago 2, Toronto 1; April 12, at Chicago — Chicago 4, Toronto 1.

1936-37 — Detroit Red Wings — Normie Smith, Pete Kelly, Larry Aurie, Herbie Lewis, Hec Kilrea, Mud Bruneteau, Syd Howe, Wally Kilrea, Jimmy Franks, Bucko McDonald, Gord Pettinger, Ebbie Goodfellow, John Gallagher, Ralph Bowman, John Sorrell, Marty Barry, Earl Robertson, John Sherf, Howie Mackie, Rolly Roulston, Doug Young (Captain); Jack Adams (Manager/Coach), Honey Walker (Trainer).
Scores: April 6, at New York — Detroit 1, NY Rangers 5; April 8, at Detroit — Detroit 4, NY Rangers 2; April 11, at Detroit — Detroit 0, NY Rangers 1; April 13, at Detroit — Detroit 1, NY Rangers 0; April 15, at Detroit — Detroit 3, NY Rangers 0.

1935-36 — Detroit Red Wings — John Sorrell, Syd Howe, Marty Barry, Herbie Lewis, Mud Bruneteau, Wally Kilrea, Hec Kilrea, Gord Pettinger, Bucko McDonald, Ralph Bowman, Pete Kelly, Doug Young (Captain), Ebbie Goodfellow, Normie Smith, Larry Aurie; Jack Adams (Manager/Coach), Honey Walker (Trainer).
Scores: April 5, at Detroit — Detroit 3, Toronto 1; April 7, at Detroit — Detroit 9, Toronto 4; April 9, at Toronto — Detroit 3, Toronto 4; April 11, at Toronto — Detroit 3, Toronto 2.

1934-35 — Montreal Maroons — Lionel Conacher, Cy Wentworth, Alec Connell, Toe Blake, Stewart Evans, Earl Robinson, Bill Miller, Dave Trottier, Jimmy Ward, Baldy Northcott, Hooley Smith (Captain), Russ Blinco, Al Shields, Sammy McManus, Gus Marker, Bob Gracie, Herb Cain, Dutch Gainor; Tommy Gorman (Manager/Coach), Bill O'Brien (Trainer).
Scores: April 4, at Toronto — Mtl. Maroons 3, Toronto 2; April 6, at Toronto — Mtl. Maroons 3, Toronto 1; April 9, at Montreal — Mtl. Maroons 4, Toronto 1.

1933-34 — Chicago Black Hawks — Clarence Abel, Rosie Couture, Lou Trudel, Lionel Conacher, Paul Thompson, Leroy Goldsworthy, Art Coulter, Roger Jenkins, Don McFadyen, Tom Cook, Doc Romnes, Johnny Gottselig, Mush March, Johnny Sheppard, Charlie Gardiner (Captain), Bill Kendall, Jack Leswick; Tommy Gorman (Manager/Coach), Eddie Froelich (Trainer).
Scores: April 3, at Detroit — Chicago 2, Detroit 1; April 5, at Detroit — Chicago 4, Detroit 1; April 8, at Chicago — Detroit 5, Chicago 2; April 10, at Chicago — Chicago 1, Detroit 0.

1932-33 — New York Rangers — Ching Johnson, Butch Keeling, Frank Boucher, Art Somers, Babe Siebert, Bun Cook, Andy Aitkenhead, Ott Heller, Oscar Asmundson, Gord Pettinger, Doug Brennan, Cecil Dillon, Bill Cook (Captain), Murray Murdoch, Earl Seibert; Lester Patrick (Manager/Coach), Harry Westerby (Trainer).
Scores: April 4, at New York — NY Rangers 5, Toronto 1; April 8, at Toronto — NY Rangers 3, Toronto 1; April 11, at Toronto — Toronto 3, NY Rangers 2; April 13, at Toronto — NY Rangers 1, Toronto 0.

1931-32 — Toronto Maple Leafs — Charlie Conacher, Busher Jackson, King Clancy, Andy Blair, Red Horner, Lorne Chabot, Alex Levinsky, Joe Primeau, Harold Darragh, Baldy Cotton, Frank Finnigan, Hap Day (Captain), Ace Bailey, Bob Gracie, Fred Robertson, Earl Miller; Conn Smythe (Manager), Dick Irvin (Coach), Tim Daly (Trainer).
Scores: April 5, at New York — Toronto 6, NY Rangers 4; April 7, at Boston* — Toronto 6, NY Rangers 2; April 9, at Toronto — Toronto 6, NY Rangers 4.

WIEBE • VOSS • GOODMAN • STANLEY CUP EMBLEMATIC WORLD'S HOCKEY CHAMPIONSHIP • KARAKAS • MARCH

SEIBERT • LEVINSKY

SHILL • DAHLSTROM

W.ᵐ J. TOBIN VICE-PRESIDENT • FREDERIC McLAUGHLIN PRESIDENT • W.ᵐ STEWART MANAGER

TRUDELL • MAC KENZIE

CHICAGO BLACKHAWKS
WORLD'S CHAMPIONS ★ WINNERS STANLEY CUP 1937-38
COPYRIGHT CHICAGO BLACKHAWKS AND NESTOR JOHNSON SKATE CO.

GOTTSELIG • ROMNES • THOMPSON • FROELICH Trainer • JOHNSON • JENKINS • PALANGIO

Chicago's unexpected Stanley Cup victory in 1938 was the team's second in just five seasons. It would take 23 years for them to win their third in 1961. The youthful makeup of the 2010 Blackhawks Stanley Cup team put many people in mind of the 1961 squad.

1930-31 — Montreal Canadiens — George Hainsworth, Wildor Larochelle, Marty Burke, Sylvio Mantha (Captain), Howie Morenz, Johnny Gagnon, Aurel Joliat, Armand Mondou, Pit Lepine, Albert Leduc, Georges Mantha, Art Lesieur, Nick Wasnie, Gus Rivers, Jean Pusie; Léo Dandurand (Manager), Cecil Hart (Coach), Ed Dufour (Trainer).
Scores: April 3, at Chicago — Montreal 2, Chicago 1; April 5, at Chicago — Chicago 2, Montreal 1; April 9, at Montreal — Chicago 3, Montreal 2; April 11, at Montreal — Montreal 4, Chicago 2; April 14, at Montreal — Montreal 2, Chicago 0.

1929-30 — Montreal Canadiens — George Hainsworth, Marty Burke, Sylvio Mantha (Captain), Howie Morenz, Bert McCaffrey, Aurel Joliat, Albert Leduc, Pit Lepine, Wildor Larochelle, Nick Wasnie, Gerry Carson, Armand Mondou, Georges Mantha, Gus Rivers; Léo Dandurand (Manager), Cecil Hart (Coach), Ed Dufour (Trainer).
Scores: April 1, at Boston — Montreal 3, Boston 0; April 3, at Montreal — Montreal 4, Boston 3.

1928-29 — Boston Bruins — Tiny Thompson, Eddie Shore, Lionel Hitchman (Captain), Percy Galbraith, Mickey MacKay, Red Green, Dutch Gainor, Harry Oliver, Eddie Rodden, Dit Clapper, Cooney Weiland, Lloyd Klein, Cy Denneny, Bill Carson, George Owen, Myles Lane; Art Ross (Manager/Coach), Win Green (Trainer).
Scores: March 28, at Boston — Boston 2, NY Rangers 0; March 29, at New York — Boston 2, NY Rangers 1.

1927-28 — New York Rangers — Lorne Chabot, Clarence Abel, Leo Bourgeault, Ching Johnson, Bill Cook (Captain), Bun Cook, Frank Boucher, Bill Boyd, Murray Murdoch, Paul Thompson, Alex Gray, Joe Miller, Patsy Callighen; Lester Patrick (Manager/Coach), Harry Westerby (Trainer).
Scores: April 5, at Montreal — Mtl. Maroons 2, NY Rangers 0; April 7, at Montreal — NY Rangers 2, Mtl. Maroons 1; April 10, at Montreal — Mtl. Maroons 2, NY Rangers 0; April 12, at Montreal — NY Rangers 1, Mtl. Maroons 0; April 14, at Montreal — NY Rangers 2, Mtl. Maroons 1.

1926-27 — Ottawa Senators — Alec Connell, King Clancy, Georges Boucher (Captain), Ed Gorman, Frank Finnigan, Alex Smith, Hec Kilrea, Hooley Smith, Cy Denneny, Frank Nighbor, Jack Adams, Milt Halliday; Dave Gill (Manager/Coach).
Scores: April 7, at Boston — Ottawa 0, Boston 0; April 9, at Boston — Ottawa 3, Boston 1; April 11, at Ottawa — Boston 1, Ottawa 1; April 13, at Ottawa — Ottawa 3, Boston 1.

1925-26 — Montreal Maroons — Clint Benedict, Reg Noble, Frank Carson, Dunc Munro (Captain), Nels Stewart, Punch Broadbent, Babe Siebert, Chuck Dinsmore, Merlyn Phillips, Hobie Kitchen, Sam Rothschild, Albert Holway, George Horne, Bernie Brophy; Eddie Gerard (Manager/Coach), Bill O'Brien (Trainer).
Scores: March 30, at Montreal — Mtl. Maroons 3, Victoria 0; April 1, at Montreal — Mtl. Maroons 3, Victoria 0; April 3, at Montreal — Victoria 3, Mtl. Maroons 2; April 6, at Montreal — Mtl. Maroons 2, Victoria 0.

The series in the spring of 1926 ended the annual playoffs between the champions of the East and the champions of the West. Since 1926-27 the annual playoffs in the National Hockey League have decided the Stanley Cup champions.

1924-25 — Victoria Cougars — Hap Holmes, Clem Loughlin (Captain), Gord Fraser, Frank Fredrickson, Jack Walker, Gizzy Hart, Harold Halderson, Frank Foyston, Wally Elmer, Harry Meeking, Jocko Anderson; Lester Patrick (Manager/Coach).
Scores: March 21, at Victoria — Victoria 5, Montreal 2; March 23, at Vancouver — Victoria 3, Montreal 1; March 27, at Victoria — Montreal 4, Victoria 2; March 30, at Victoria — Victoria 6, Montreal 1.

1923-24 — Montreal Canadiens — Georges Vezina, Sprague Cleghorn (Captain), Billy Coutu, Howie Morenz, Aurel Joliat, Billy Boucher, Odie Cleghorn, Sylvio Mantha, Bobby Boucher, Billy Bell, Billy Cameron, Joe Malone, Charles Fortier; Leo Dandurand (Manager/Coach).
Scores: March 22, at Montreal — Montreal 6, Cgy. Tigers 1; March 25, at Ottawa* — Montreal 3, Cgy. Tigers 0.

* Game transferred to Ottawa to benefit from artificial ice surface.

1922-23 — Ottawa Senators — Georges Boucher, Lionel Hitchman, Frank Nighbor, King Clancy, Harry Helman, Clint Benedict, Jack Darragh, Eddie Gerard (Captain), Cy Denneny, Punch Broadbent; Tommy Gorman (Manager), Pete Green (Coach), F. Dolan (Trainer).
Scores: March 29, at Vancouver — Ottawa 2, Edm. Eskimos 1; March 31, at Vancouver — Ottawa 1, Edm. Eskimos 0.

1921-22 — Toronto St. Patricks — Ted Stackhouse, Corb Denneny, Rod Smylie, Lloyd Andrews, John Ross Roach, Harry Cameron, Billy Stuart, Babe Dye, Ken Randall, Reg Noble (borrowed for one game from Ottawa), Stan Jackson, Ivan Mitchell; Charlie Querrie (Manager), George O'Donoghue (Coach).
Scores: March 17, at Toronto — Van. Millionaires 4, Toronto 3; March 20, at Toronto — Toronto 2, Van. Millionaires 1; March 23, at Toronto — Van. Millionaires 3, Toronto 0; March 25, at Toronto — Toronto 6, Van. Millionaires 0; March 28, at Toronto — Toronto 5, Van. Millionaires 1.

1920-21 — Ottawa Senators — Jack MacKell, Jack Darragh, Morley Bruce, Georges Boucher, Eddie Gerard (Captain), Clint Benedict, Sprague Cleghorn, Frank Nighbor, Punch Broadbent, Cy Denneny, Leth Graham; Tommy Gorman (Manager), Pete Green (Coach), F. Dolan (Trainer).
Scores: March 21, at Vancouver — Van. Millionaires 2, Ottawa 1; March 24, at Vancouver — Ottawa 4, Van. Millionaires 3; March 28, at Vancouver — Ottawa 3, Van. Millionaires 2; March 31, at Vancouver — Van. Millionaires 3, Ottawa 2; April 4, at Vancouver — Ottawa 2, Van. Millionaires 1

1919-20 — Ottawa Senators — Jack MacKell, Jack Darragh, Morley Bruce, Horace Merrill, Georges Boucher, Eddie Gerard (Captain), Clint Benedict, Sprague Cleghorn, Frank Nighbor, Punch Broadbent, Cy Denneny, Tommy Gorman (Manager), Pete Green (Coach).
Scores: March 22, at Ottawa — Ottawa 3, Seattle 2; March 24, at Ottawa — Ottawa 3, Seattle 0; March 27, at Ottawa — Seattle 3, Ottawa 1; March 30, at Toronto* — Seattle 5, Ottawa 2; April 1, at Toronto* — Ottawa 6, Seattle 1.

* Games transferred to Toronto to benefit from artificial ice surface.

1918-19 — No decision, Series halted by Spanish influenza epidemic, illness of several players and death of Joe Hall of Montreal Canadiens from the flu. Five games had been played when the series was halted, each team having won two and tied one. Final scores are listed below.
Scores: March 19, at Seattle — Seattle 7, Montreal 0; March 22, at Seattle — Montreal 4, Seattle 2; March 24, at Seattle — Seattle 7, Montreal 2; March 26, at Seattle — Montreal 0, Seattle 0; March 30, at Seattle — Montreal 4, Seattle 3.

1917-18 — Toronto Arenas — Rusty Crawford, Harry Meeking, Ken Randall (Captain), Corb Denneny, Harry Cameron, Jack Adams, Alf Skinner, Harry Mummery, Hap Holmes, Reg Noble, Sammy Hebert, Jack Marks, Jack Coughlin; Charlie Querrie (Manager), Dick Carroll (Coach), Frank Carroll (Trainer).
Scores: March 20, at Toronto — Toronto 5, Van. Millionaires 3; March 23, at Toronto — Van. Millionaires 6, Toronto 4; March 26, at Toronto — Toronto 6, Van. Millionaires 3; March 28, at Toronto — Van. Millionaires 8, Toronto 1; March 30, at Toronto — Toronto 2, Van. Millionaires 1.

1916-17 — Seattle Metropolitans — Hap Holmes, Ed Carpenter, Cully Wilson, Jack Walker, Bernie Morris, Frank Foyston, Roy Rickey, Jim Riley, Bobby Rowe (Captain); Peter Muldoon (Manager).
Scores: March 17, at Seattle — Montreal 8, Seattle 4; March 20, at Seattle — Seattle 6, Montreal 1; March 23, at Seattle — Seattle 4, Montreal 1; March 26, at Seattle — Seattle 9, Montreal 1.

1915-16 — Montreal Canadiens — Georges Vezina, Bert Corbeau, Jack Laviolette, Newsy Lalonde, Louis Berlinquette, Goldie Prodger, Howard McNamara (Captain), Didier Pitre, Skene Ronan, Amos Arbour, Skinner Poulin, Jack Fournier; George Kennedy (Manager).
Scores: March 20, at Montreal — Portland 2, Montreal 0; March 22, at Montreal — Montreal 2, Portland 1; March 25, at Montreal — Montreal 6, Portland 3; March 28, at Montreal — Portland 6, Montreal 5; March 30, at Montreal — Montreal 2, Portland 1.

1914-15 — Vancouver Millionaires — Ken Mallen, Frank Nighbor, Cyclone Taylor, Hugh Lehman, Lloyd Cook, Mickey MacKay, Barney Stanley, Jim Seaborn, Si Griffis (Captain), Johnny Matz; Frank Patrick (Playing Manager).
Scores: March 22, at Vancouver — Van. Millionaires 6, Ottawa 2; March 24, at Vancouver — Van. Millionaires 8, Ottawa 3; March 26, at Vancouver — Van. Millionaires 12, Ottawa 3.

1913-14 — Toronto Blueshirts — Con Corbeau, Roy McGiffen, Jack Walker, George McNamara, Cully Wilson, Frank Foyston, Harry Cameron, Hap Holmes, Scotty Davidson (Captain), Harriston; Jack Marshall (Playing Manager), Frank Carroll, Dick Carroll (Trainers).
Scores: March 14, at Toronto — Toronto 5, Victoria 2; March 17, at Toronto — Toronto 6, Victoria 5; March 19, at Toronto — Toronto 2, Victoria 1.

Prior to 1914, teams could challenge the Stanley Cup champions for the title, thus there was more than one Championship Series played in most of the seasons between 1894 and 1913.

1912-13 — Quebec Bulldogs — Joe Malone (Captain), Joe Hall, Paddy Moran, Harry Mummery, Tommy Smith, Jack Marks, Rusty Crawford, Billy Creighton, Jeff Malone, Rocket Power; M.J. Quinn (Manager), D. Beland (Trainer).
Scores: March 8, at Quebec — Que. Bulldogs 14, Sydney 3; March 10, at Quebec — Que. Bulldogs 6, Sydney 2.

Victoria challenged Quebec but the Bulldogs refused to put the Stanley Cup in competition so the two teams played an exhibition series with Victoria winning two games to one by scores of 7-5, 3-6, 6-1. It was the first meeting between the Eastern champions and the Western champions. The following year, and until the Western Hockey League disbanded after the 1926 playoffs, the Cup went to the winner of the series between East and West.

1911-12 — Quebec Bulldogs — Goldie Prodger, Joe Hall, Walter Rooney, Paddy Moran, Jack Marks, Jack McDonald, Eddie Oatman, George Leonard, Joe Malone (Captain); Charley Nolan (Coach), M.J. Quinn (Manager), D. Beland (Trainer).
Scores: March 11, at Quebec — Que. Bulldogs 9, Moncton 3; March 13, at Quebec — Que. Bulldogs 8, Moncton 0.

1910-11 — Ottawa Senators — Hamby Shore, Percy LeSueur (Captain), Jack Darragh, Bruce Stuart, Marty Walsh, Bruce Ridpath, Fred Lake, Dubbie Kerr, Alex Currie, Horace Gaul.
Scores: March 13, at Ottawa — Ottawa 7, Galt 4; March 16, at Ottawa — Ottawa 13, Port Arthur 4.

1909-10 — (March) — **Montreal Wanderers** — Cecil Blachford, Moose Johnson, Ernie Russell, Riley Hern, Harry Hyland, Jack Marshall, Pud Glass (Captain), Jimmy Gardner; Dickie Boon (Manager).
Scores: March 12, at Montreal — Mtl. Wanderers 7, Berlin (Kitchener) 3.

By winning the 1910 NHA title, the Montreal Wanderers took possession of the Stanley Cup from Ottawa and accepted a challenge from Berlin, 1910 champions of the OPHL

1909-10 — (January) — **Ottawa Senators** — Dubbie Kerr, Fred Lake, Percy LeSueur, Ken Mallen, Bruce Ridpath, Gord Roberts, Hamby Shore, Bruce Stuart (Captain), Marty Walsh.

The Senators accepted two challenges as defending Cup champions. The first was against Galt in a 2-game, total-goals series, and the second was against Edmonton, also a 2-game, total-goals series.
Scores: January 5, at Ottawa — Ottawa 12, Galt 3; January 7, at Ottawa — Ottawa 3, Galt 1; January 18, at Ottawa — Ottawa 8, Edm. Eskimos 4; January 20, at Ottawa — Ottawa 13, Edm. Eskimos 7.

1908-09 — Ottawa Senators — Fred Lake, Percy LeSueur, Cyclone Taylor, Billy Gilmour, Dubbie Kerr, Edgar Dey, Marty Walsh, Bruce Stuart (Captain).

Ottawa, as champions of the Eastern Canada Hockey Association took over the Stanley Cup in 1909 and, although a challenge was accepted by the Cup trustees from Winnipeg Shamrocks, games could not be arranged because of the lateness of the season. No other challenges were made in 1909.

1907-08 — Montreal Wanderers — Riley Hern, Art Ross, Walter Smaill, Pud Glass, Bruce Stuart, Ernie Russell, Moose Johnson, Cecil Blachford (Captain), Tom Hooper, Larry Gilmour, Ernie Liffiton; Dickie Boon (Manager).
Scores: Wanderers accepted four challenges for the Cup: January 9, at Montreal — Mtl. Wanderers 9, Ott. Victorias 3; January 13, at Montreal — Mtl. Wanderers 13, Ott. Victorias 1; March 10, at Montreal — Mtl. Wanderers 11, Wpg. Maple Leafs 5; March 12, at Montreal — Mtl. Wanderers 9, Wpg. Maple Leafs 3; March 14, at Montreal — Mtl. Wanderers 6, Toronto (OPHL) 4. At start of following season, 1908-09, Wanderers were challenged by Edmonton. Results: December 28, at Montreal — Mtl. Wanderers 7, Edm. Eskimos 3; December 30, at Montreal — Edm. Eskimos 7, Mtl. Wanderers 6. Total goals: Mtl. Wanderers 13, Edm. Eskimos 10.

1906-07 — (March 25) — **Montreal Wanderers** — Billy Strachan, Riley Hern, Lester Patrick, Hod Stuart, Pud Glass, Ernie Russell, Cecil Blachford (Captain), Moose Johnson, Rod Kennedy, Jack Marshall; Dickie Boon (Manager).

1906-07 — (March 18) — **Kenora Thistles** — Eddie Giroux, Si Griffis, Tom Hooper, Fred Whitcroft, Alf Smith, Harry Westwick, Roxy Beaudro, Tommy Phillips (Captain), Russell Phillips.
Scores: March 16, at Winnipeg — Kenora 8, Brandon 6; March 18, at Winnipeg — Kenora 4, Brandon 1; March 23, at Winnipeg — Mtl. Wanderers 7, Kenora 2; March 25, at Winnipeg — Kenora 6, Mtl. Wanderers 5. Total goals: Mtl. Wanderers 12, Kenora 8.

1906-07 — (January) — **Kenora Thistles** — Eddie Giroux, Art Ross, Si Griffis, Tom Hooper, Billy McGimsie, Roxy Beaudro, Tommy Phillips (Captain), Joe Hall, Russell Phillips.
Scores: January 17, at Montreal — Kenora 4, Mtl. Wanderers 2; Jan. 21, at Montreal — Kenora 8, Mtl. Wanderers 6.

1906-07 — (December) — **Montreal Wanderers** — Riley Hern, Billy Strachan, Rod Kennedy, Lester Patrick, Pud Glass, Ernie Russell, Moose Johnson, Cecil Blachford (Captain), Dickie Boon (Manager).

1905-06 — (March) — **Montreal Wanderers** — Henri Menard, Billy Strachan, Rod Kennedy, Lester Patrick, Pud Glass, Ernie Russell, Moose Johnson, Cecil Blachford (Captain), Josh Arnold; Dickie Boon (Manager).
Scores: March 14, at Montreal — Mtl. Wanderers 9, Ottawa 1; March 17, at Ottawa — Ottawa 9, Mtl. Wanderers 3. Total goals: Mtl. Wanderers 12, Ottawa 10.
Wanderers accepted a challenge from New Glasgow, N.S., prior to the start of the 1906-07 season. Results: December 27, at Montreal — Mtl. Wanderers 10, New Glasgow 3; December 29, at Montreal — Mtl. Wanderers 7, New Glasgow 2.

1905-06 — (February) — **Ottawa Silver Seven** — Harvey Pulford (Captain), Arthur Moore, Harry Westwick, Frank McGee, Alf Smith (Playing Coach), Billy Gilmour, Billy Hague, Percy LeSueur, Harry Smith, Tommy Smith, Dion, Ebbs.
Scores: February 27, at Ottawa — Ottawa 16, Queen's University 7; February 28, at Ottawa — Ottawa 12, Queen's University 7; March 6, at Ottawa — Ottawa 6, Smiths Falls 5; March 8, at Ottawa — Ottawa 8, Smiths Falls 2.

1904-05 — Ottawa Silver Seven — Dave Finnie, Harvey Pulford (Captain), Arthur Moore, Harry Westwick, Frank McGee, Alf Smith (Playing Coach), Billy Gilmour, Frank White, Horace Gaul, Hamby Shore, Bones Allen.
Scores: January 13, at Ottawa — Ottawa 9, Dawson City 2; January 16, at Ottawa — Ottawa 23, Dawson City 2; March 7, at Ottawa — Rat Portage 9, Ottawa 3; March 9, at Ottawa — Ottawa 4, Rat Portage 2; March 11, at Ottawa — Ottawa 5, Rat Portage 4.

1903-04 — Ottawa Silver Seven — Suddy Gilmour, Arthur Moore, Frank McGee, Bouse Hutton, Billy Gilmour, Jim McGee, Harry Westwick, Harvey Pulford (Captain), Scott, Alf Smith (Playing Coach).
Scores: December 30, at Ottawa — Ottawa 9, Wpg. Rowing Club 1; January 1, at Ottawa — Wpg. Rowing Club 6, Ottawa 2; January 4, at Ottawa — Ottawa 2, Wpg. Rowing Club 0. February 23, at Ottawa — Ottawa 6, Tor. Marlboros 3; February 25, at Ottawa — Ottawa 11, Tor. Marlboros 2; March 2, at Montreal — Ottawa 5, Mtl. Wanderers 5. Following the tie game, a new two-game series was ordered to be played in Ottawa but the Wanderers refused unless the tie game was replayed in Montreal. When no settlement could be reached, the series was abandoned and Ottawa retained the Cup and accepted a two-game challenge from Brandon. Results: (both games at Ottawa), March 9, Ottawa 6, Brandon 3; March 11, Ottawa 9, Brandon 3.

1902-03 — (March) — Ottawa Silver Seven — Suddy Gilmour, Percy Sims, Bouse Hutton, Dave Gilmour, Billy Gilmour, Harry Westwick, Frank McGee, F.H. Wood, A.A. Fraser, Charles Spittal, Harvey Pulford (Captain), Arthur Moore; Alf Smith (Coach).
Scores: March 7, at Montreal — Ottawa 1, Mtl. Victorias 1; March 10, at Ottawa — Ottawa 8, Mtl. Victorias 0. Total goals: Ottawa 9, Mtl. Victorias 1; March 12, at Ottawa — Ottawa 6, Rat Portage 2; March 14, at Ottawa — Ottawa 4, Rat Portage 2.

1902-03 — (February) — Montreal AAA — Tom Hodge, Dickie Boon, Billy Nicholson, Tommy Phillips, Art Hooper, Billy Bellingham, Charles Liffiton, Jack Marshall, Jimmy Gardner, Cecil Blachford, George Smith.
Scores: January 29, at Montreal — Mtl. AAA 8, Wpg. Victorias 1; January 31, at Montreal — Wpg. Victorias 2, Mtl. AAA 2; February 2, at Montreal — Wpg. Victorias 4, Mtl. AAA 2; February 4, at Montreal — Mtl. AAA 5, Wpg. Victorias 1.

1901-02 — (March) — Montreal AAA — Tom Hodge, Dickie Boon, Billy Nicholson, Art Hooper, Billy Bellingham, Charles Liffiton, Jack Marshall, Roland Elliot, Jimmy Gardner.
Scores: March 13, at Winnipeg — Wpg. Victorias 1, Mtl. AAA 0; March 15, at Winnipeg — Mtl. AAA 5, Wpg. Victorias 0; March 17, at Winnipeg — Mtl. AAA 2, Wpg. Victorias 1.

1901-02 — (January) — Winnipeg Victorias — Burke Wood, Tony Gingras, Charles Johnstone, Rod Flett, Magnus Flett, Dan Bain (Captain), Fred Scanlon, F. Cadham, Art Brown.
Scores: January 21, at Winnipeg — Wpg. Victorias 5, Tor Wellingtons 3; January 23, at Winnipeg — Wpg. Victorias 5, Tor. Wellingtons 3.

1900-01 — Winnipeg Victorias — Burke Wood, Jack Marshall, Tony Gingras, Charles Johnstone, Rod Flett, Magnus Flett, Dan Bain (Captain), Art Brown, George Carruthers.
Scores: January 29, at Montreal — Wpg. Victorias 4, Mtl. Shamrocks 3; January 31, at Montreal — Wpg. Victorias 2, Mtl. Shamrocks 1.

1899-1900 — Montreal Shamrocks — oe McKenna, Frank Tansey, Frank Wall, Art Farrell, Fred Scanlon, Harry Trihey (Captain), Jack Brannen.
Scores: February 12, at Montreal — Mtl. Shamrocks 4, Wpg. Victorias 3; February 14, at Montreal — Wpg. Victorias 3, Mtl. Shamrocks 2; February 16, at Montreal — Mtl. Shamrocks 5, Wpg. Victorias 4; March 5, at Montreal — Mtl. Shamrocks 10, Halifax 2; March 7, at Montreal — Mtl. Shamrocks 11, Halifax 0.

1898-99 — (March) — Montreal Shamrocks — Joe McKenna, Frank Tansey, Frank Wall, Harry Trihey (Captain), Art Farrell, Fred Scanlon, Jack Brannen, John Dobby, Charles Hoerner.
Scores: March 14, at Montreal — Mtl. Shamrocks 6, Queen's University 2.

1898-99 — (February) — Montreal Victorias — Gordon Lewis, Mike Grant (Captain), Graham Drinkwater, Cam Davidson, Bob McDougall, Ernie McLea, Frank Richardson, Jack Ewing, Russell Bowie, Douglas Acer, Fred McRobie.
Scores: February 15, at Montreal — Mtl. Victorias 2, Wpg. Victorias 1; February 18, at Montreal — Mtl. Victorias 3, Wpg. Victorias 2.

1897-98 — Montreal Victorias — Gordon Lewis, Hartland McDougall, Mike Grant, Graham Drinkwater, Cam Davidson, Bob McDougall, Ernie McLea, Frank Richardson (Captain), Jack Ewing.

1896-97 — Montreal Victorias — Gordon Lewis, Harold Henderson, Mike Grant (Captain), Cam Davidson, Graham Drinkwater, Bob McDougall, Ernie McLea, Shirley Davidson, Hartland McDougall, Jack Ewing, Percy Molson, David Gillilan, McLellan.
Scores: December 27, at Montreal — Mtl. Victorias 15, Ott. Capitals 2.

1895-96 — (December) — Montreal Victorias — Harold Henderson, Mike Grant (Captain), Bob McDougall, Graham Drinkwater, Shirley Davidson, Hartland McDougall, Ernie McLea, Cam Davidson, David Gillilan, Stanley Willett, Gordon Lewis, W. Wallace.
Scores: December 30, at Winnipeg — Mtl. Victorias 6, Wpg. Victorias 5.

1895-96 — (February) — Winnipeg Victorias — Whitey Merritt, Rod Flett, Fred Higginbotham, Jack Armitage (Captain), Tote Campbell, Dan Bain, Charles Johnstone, Attie Howard.
Scores: February 14, at Montreal — Wpg. Victorias 2, Mtl. Victorias 0.

1894-95 — Montreal Victorias — Robert Jones, Harold Henderson, Mike Grant (Captain), Shirley Davidson, Hartland McDougall, Bob McDougall, Norman Rankin, Graham Drinkwater, Roland Elliot, William Pullan, Arthur Fenwick, A. McDougall.

1893-94 — Montreal AAA — Herb Collins, Allan Cameron, George James, Billy Barlow, Clare Mussen, Archie Hodgson, Haviland Routh, Alex Irving, James Stewart, E. O'Brien, Toad Wand, Alex Kingan.
Scores: March 17, at Mtl. Victorias — Mtl. AAA 3, Mtl. Victorias 2; March 22, at Montreal — Mtl. AAA 3, Ott. Capitals 1.

1892-93 — Montreal AAA — Tom Paton, James Stewart, Allan Cameron, Haviland Routh, Archie Hodgson, Billy Barlow, Alex Irving, Alex Kingan, G.S. Low.

All-Time NHL Playoff Formats

1917-18 — The regular-season was split into two halves. The winners of both halves faced each other in a two-game, total-goals series for the NHL championship and the right to meet the PCHA champion in the best-of-five Stanley Cup Finals.

1918-19 — Same as 1917-18, except that the Stanley Cup Finals was extended to a best-of-seven series.

1919-20 — Same as 1917-1918, except that Ottawa won both halves of the split regular-season schedule to earn an automatic berth into the best-of-five Stanley Cup Finals against the PCHA champions.

1921-22 — The top two teams at the conclusion of the regular-season faced each other in a two-game, total-goals series for the NHL championship. The NHL champion then moved on to play the winner of the PCHA-WCHL playoff series in the best-of-five Stanley Cup Finals.

1922-23 — The top two teams at the conclusion of the regular-season faced each other in a two-game, total-goals series for the NHL championship. The NHL champion then moved on to play the PCHA champion in the best-of-three Stanley Cup Semi-Finals, and the winner of the Semi-Finals played the WCHL champion, which had been given a bye, in the best-of-three Stanley Cup Finals.

1923-24 — The top two teams at the conclusion of the regular-season faced each other in a two-game, total-goals series for the NHL championship. The NHL champion then moved on to play the loser of the PCHA-WCHL playoff (the winner of the PCHA-WCHL playoff earned a bye into the Stanley Cup Finals) in the best-of-three Stanley Cup Semi-Finals. The winner of this series met the PCHA-WCHL playoff winner in the best-of-three Stanley Cup Finals.

1924-25 — The first place team (Hamilton) at the conclusion of the regular-season was supposed to play the winner of a two-game, total-goals series between the second (Toronto) and third (Montreal) place clubs. However, Hamilton refused to abide by this new format, demanding greater compensation than offered by the League. Thus, Toronto and Montreal played their two-game, total-goals series, and the winner (Montreal) earned the NHL title and then played the WCHL champion (Victoria) in the best-of-five Stanley Cup Finals.

1925-26 — The format which was intended for 1924-25 went into effect. The winner of the two-game, total-goals series between the second and third place teams squared off against the first place team in the two-game, total-goals NHL championship series. The NHL champion then moved on to play the WHL champion in the best-of-five Stanley Cup Finals.

After the 1925-26 season, the NHL was the only major professional hockey league still in existence and consequently took over sole control of the Stanley Cup competition.

1926-27 — The 10-team league was divided into two divisions — Canadian and American — of five teams apiece. In each division, the winner of the two-game, total-goals series between the second and third place teams faced the first place team in a two-game, total-goals series for the division title. The two division title winners then met in the best-of-five Stanley Cup Finals.

1928-29 — Both first place teams in the two divisions played each other in a best-of-five series. Both second place teams in the two divisions played each other in a two-game, total-goals series as did the two third place teams. The winners of these latter two series then played each other in a best-of-three series for the right to meet the winner of the series between the two first place clubs. This Stanley Cup Final was a best-of-three.

Series A: First in Canadian Division vs. first in American (best-of-five)
Series B: Second in Canadian Division vs. second in American (two-game, total-goals)
Series C: Third in Canadian Division vs. third in American (two-game, total-goals)
Series D: Winner of Series B vs. winner of Series C (best-of-three)
Series E: Winner of Series A vs. winner of Series D (best-of-three) for Stanley Cup

1931-32 — Same as 1928-29, except that Series D was changed to a two-game, total-goals format and Series E was changed to best-of-five.

1936-37 — Same as 1931-32, except that Series B, C, and D were each best-of-three.

1938-39 — With the NHL reduced to seven teams, the two-division system was replaced by one seven-team league. Based on final regular-season standings, the following playoff format was adopted:

Series A: First vs. Second (best-of-seven)
Series B: Third vs. Fourth (best-of-three)
Series C: Fifth vs. Sixth (best-of-three)
Series D: Winner of Series B vs. winner of Series C (best-of-three)
Series E: Winner of Series A vs. winner of Series D (best-of-seven)

1942-43 — With the NHL reduced to six teams (the "original six"), only the top four finishers qualified for playoff action. The best-of-seven Semi-Finals pitted Team #1 vs. Team #3 and Team #2 vs. Team #4. The winners of each Semi-Final series met in the best-of-seven Stanley Cup Finals.

1967-68 — When it doubled in size from 6 to 12 teams, the NHL once again was divided into two divisions — East and West — of six teams apiece. The top four clubs in each division qualified for the playoffs (all series were best-of-seven):

Series A: Team #1 (East) vs. Team #3 (East)
Series B: Team #2 (East) vs. Team #4 (East)
Series C: Team #1 (West) vs. Team #3 (West)
Series D: Team #2 (West) vs. Team #4 (West)
Series E: Winner of Series A vs. winner of Series B
Series F: Winner of Series C vs. winner of Series D
Series G: Winner of Series E vs. Winner of Series F

1970-71 — Same as 1967-68 except that Series E matched the winners of Series A and D, and Series F matched the winners of Series B and C.

1971-72 — Same as 1970-71, except that Series A and C matched Team #1 vs. Team #4, and Series B and D matched Team #2 vs. Team #3.

1974-75 — With the League now expanded to 18 teams in four divisions, a completely new playoff format was introduced. First, the #2 and #3 teams in each of the four divisions were pooled together in the Preliminary round. These eight (#2 and #3) clubs were ranked #1 to #8 based on regular-season record:

Series A: Team #1 vs. Team #8 (best-of-three)
Series B: Team #2 vs. Team #7 (best-of-three)
Series C: Team #3 vs. Team #6 (best-of-three)
Series D: Team #4 vs. Team #5 (best-of-three)
The winners of this Preliminary round then pooled together with the four division winners, which had received byes into this Quarter-Final round. These eight teams were again ranked #1 to #8 based on regular-season record:
Series E: Team #1 vs. Team #8 (best-of-seven)
Series F: Team #2 vs. Team #7 (best-of-seven)
Series G: Team #3 vs. Team #6 (best-of-seven)
Series H: Team #4 vs. Team #5 (best-of-seven)
The four Quarter-Finals winners, which moved on to the Semi-Finals, were then ranked #1 to #4 based on regular season record:
Series I: Team #1 vs. Team #4 (best-of-seven)
Series J: Team #2 vs. Team #3 (best-of-seven)
Series K: Winner of Series I vs. winner of Series J (best-of-seven)

1977-78 — Same as 1974-75, except that the Preliminary round consisted of the #2 teams in the four divisions and the next four teams based on regular-season record (not their standings within their divisions).

1979-80 — With the addition of four WHA franchises, the League expanded its playoff structure to include 16 of its 21 teams. The four first place teams in the four divisions automatically earned playoff berths. Among the 17 other clubs, the top 12, according to regular-season record, also earned berths. All 16 teams were then pooled together and ranked #1 to #16 based on regular-season record:

Series A: Team #1 vs. Team #16 (best-of-five)
Series B: Team #2 vs. Team #15 (best-of-five)
Series C: Team #3 vs. Team #14 (best-of-five)
Series D: Team #4 vs. Team #13 (best-of-five)
Series E: Team #5 vs. Team #12 (best-of-five)
Series F: Team #6 vs. Team #11 (best-of-five)
Series G: Team #7 vs. Team #10 (best-of-five)
Series H: Team #8 vs. Team # 9 (best-of-five)
The eight Preliminary round winners, ranked #1 to #8 based on regular-season record, moved on to the Quarter-Finals:
Series I: Team #1 vs. Team #8 (best-of-seven)
Series J: Team #2 vs. Team #7 (best-of-seven)
Series K: Team #3 vs. Team #6 (best-of-seven)
Series L: Team #4 vs. Team #5 (best-of-seven)
The four Quarter-Finals winners, ranked #1 to #4 based on regular-season record, moved on to the semi-finals:
Series M: Team #1 vs. Team #4 (best-of-seven)
Series N: Team #2 vs. Team #3 (best-of-seven)
Series O: Winner of Series M vs. winner of Series N (best-of-seven)

1981-82 — The first four teams in each division earned playoff berths. In each division, the first-place team opposed the fourth-place team and the second-place team opposed the third-place team in a best-of-five Division Semi-Final series (DSF). In each division, the two winners of the DSF met in a best-of-seven Division Final series (DF). The two DF winners in each conference met in a best-of-seven Conference Final series (CF). In the Prince of Wales Conference, the Adams Division winner opposed the Patrick Division winner; in the Clarence Campbell Conference, the Smythe Division winner opposed the Norris Division winner. The two CF winners met in a best-of-seven Stanley Cup Final (F) series.

1986-87 — Division Semi-Final series changed from best-of-five to best-of-seven.

1993-94 — The NHL's playoff draw is conference-based rather than division-based. At the conclusion of the regular season, the top eight teams in each of the Eastern and Western Conferences qualify for the playoffs. The teams that finish in first place in each of the League's divisions are seeded first and second in each conference's playoff draw and are assured of home ice advantage in the first two playoff rounds. The remaining teams are seeded based on their regular-season point totals. In each conference, the team seeded #1 plays #8; #2 vs. #7; #3 vs. #6; and #4 vs. #5. All series are best-of-seven with home ice rotating on a 2-2-1-1-1 basis, with the exception of matchups between Central and Pacific Division teams. These matchups will be played on a 2-3-2 basis to reduce travel. In a 2-3-2 series, the team with the most points will have its choice to start the series at home or on the road. The Eastern Conference champion will face the Western Conference champion in the Stanley Cup Final.

1994-95 — Same as 1993-94, except that in first, second or third-round playoff series involving Central and Pacific Division teams, the team with the better record has the choice of using either a 2-3-2 or a 2-2-1-1-1 format. When a 2-3-2 format is selected, the higher-ranked team also has the choice of playing games 1, 2, 6 and 7 at home or playing games 3, 4 and 5 at home. The format for the Stanley Cup Final remains 2-2-1-1-1.

1998-99 — The NHL's clubs are re-aligned into two conferences each consisting of three divisions. The number of teams qualifying for the Stanley Cup Playoffs remains unchanged at 16.

First-round playoff berths will be awarded to the first-place team in each division as well as to the next five best teams based on regular-season point totals in each conference. The three division winners in each conference will be seeded first through third, in order of points, for the playoffs and the next five best teams, in order of points, will be seeded fourth through eighth. In each conference, the team seeded #1 will play #8; #2 vs. #7; #3 vs. #6; and #4 vs. #5 in the quarterfinal round. Home-ice in the Conference Quarter-Finals is granted to those teams seeded first through fourth in each conference.

In the Conference Semi-Finals and Conference Finals, teams will be re-seeded according to the same criteria as the Conference Quarter-Finals. Higher seeded teams will have home-ice advantage.

Home-ice advantage for the Stanley Cup Finals will be determined by points.

All series remain best-of-seven.

Guy Lafleur, Rejean Houle, Rick Chartraw and Pierre Mondou smile behind captain Serge Savard as the Montreal Canadiens celebrate their fourth straight Stanley Cup title in 1979 … one short of the all-time record held by the Canadiens of 1956 to 1960.

Team Records

1918-2010

GAMES PLAYED

MOST GAMES PLAYED BY ALL TEAMS, ONE PLAYOFF YEAR:
92 — 1991. There were 51 DSF, 24 DF, 11 CF and 6 F games.
90 — 1994. There were 48 CQF, 23 CSF, 12 CF and 7 F games.
— 2002. There were 47 CQF, 25 CSF, 13 CF and 5 F games.

MOST GAMES PLAYED, ONE TEAM, ONE PLAYOFF YEAR:
26 — Philadelphia Flyers, 1987. Won DSF 4-2 vs. NY Rangers, DF 4-3 vs. NY Islanders, CF 4-2 vs. Montreal, and lost F 4-3 vs. Edmonton.
— **Calgary Flames,** 2004. Won DSF 4-3 vs. Vancouver, DF 4-2 vs. Detroit, CF 4-2 vs. San Jose, and lost F 4-3 vs. Tampa Bay.
25 — New Jersey Devils, 2001. Won CQF 4-2 vs. Carolina, CSF 4-3 vs. Toronto, CF 4-1 vs. Pittsburgh, and lost F 4-3 vs. Colorado.
— Carolina Hurricanes, 2006. Won CQF 4-2 vs. Montreal, CSF 4-1 vs. New Jersey, CF 4-3 vs. Buffalo, and F 4-3 vs. Edmonton

PLAYOFF APPEARANCES

MOST STANLEY CUP CHAMPIONSHIPS:
23 — Montreal Canadiens (1924-30-31-44-46-53-56-57-58-59-60-65-66-68-69-71-73-76-77-78-79-86-93)
13 — Toronto Maple Leafs (1918-22-32-42-45-47-48-49-51-62-63-64-67)
11 — Detroit Red Wings (1936-37-43-50-52-54-55-97-98-2002-08)

MOST CONSECUTIVE STANLEY CUP CHAMPIONSHIPS:
5 — Montreal Canadiens (1956-57-58-59-60)
4 — Montreal Canadiens (1976-77-78-79)
— NY Islanders (1980-81-82-83)

MOST FINAL SERIES APPEARANCES:
32 — Montreal Canadiens in 93-year history.
24 — Detroit Red Wings in 84-year history.
21 — Toronto Maple Leafs in 93-year history.

MOST CONSECUTIVE FINAL SERIES APPEARANCES:
10 — Montreal Canadiens, (1951-60, inclusive)
5 — Montreal Canadiens, (1965-69, inclusive)
— NY Islanders, (1980-84, inclusive)

MOST YEARS IN PLAYOFFS:
78 — Montreal Canadiens in 93-year history.
65 — Boston Bruins in 86-year history.
64 — Toronto Maple Leafs in 93-year history.

MOST CONSECUTIVE PLAYOFF APPEARANCES:
29 — Boston Bruins (1968-96, inclusive)
28 — Chicago Blackhawks (1970-97, inclusive)
25 — St. Louis Blues (1980-2004, inclusive)
24 — Montreal Canadiens (1971-94, inclusive)
21 — Montreal Canadiens (1949-69, inclusive)

TEAM WINS

MOST HOME WINS, ONE TEAM, ONE PLAYOFF YEAR:
12 — New Jersey Devils, 2003 in 13 home games.
11 — Edmonton Oilers, 1988 in 11 home games.
— Detroit Red Wings, 2009 in 13 home games.
10 — Edmonton Oilers, 1985 in 10 home games.
— Montreal Canadiens, 1986 in 11 home games.
— Montreal Canadiens, 1993 in 11 home games.
— Carolina Hurricanes, 2006 in 14 home games.
— Anaheim Ducks, 2007 in 12 home games.

MOST HOME WINS, ALL TEAMS, ONE PLAYOFF YEAR:
57 — 1991. Of 92 games played, home teams won 57 (29 DSF, 17 DF, 8 CF and 3 in F).

MOST ROAD WINS, ONE TEAM, ONE PLAYOFF YEAR:
10 — New Jersey Devils, 1995. Won three at Boston in CQF; two at Pittsburgh in CSF; three at Philadelphia in CF; and two at Detroit in F.
— **New Jersey Devils,** 2000. Won two at Florida in CQF; two at Toronto in CSF; three at Philadelphia in CF; and three at Dallas in F.
— **Calgary Flames,** 2004. Won three at Vancouver in DSF; two at Detroit in DF; three at San Jose in CF; and two at Tampa Bay in F.
8 — NY Islanders, 1980. Won two at Los Angeles in PR; three at Boston in QF; two at Buffalo in SF; and one at Philadelphia in F.
— Philadelphia Flyers, 1987. Won two at NY Rangers in DSF; two at NY Islanders in DF; three at Montreal in CF; and one at Edmonton in F.
— Edmonton Oilers, 1990. Won one at Winnipeg in DSF; two at Los Angeles in DF; two at Chicago in CF and three at Boston in F.
— Pittsburgh Penguins, 1992. Won two at Washington in DSF; two at NY Rangers in DF; two at Boston in CF; and two at Chicago in F.
— Vancouver Canucks, 1994. Won three at Calgary in CQF; two at Dallas in CSF; one at Toronto in CF; and two at NY Rangers in F.
— Colorado Avalanche, 1996. Won two at Vancouver in CQF; two at Chicago in CSF; two at Detroit in CF; and two at Florida in F.
— Detroit Red Wings, 1998. Won two at Phoenix in CQF; three at St. Louis in CSF; one at Dallas in CF; and two at Washington in F.
— Colorado Avalanche, 1999. Won three at San Jose in CQF; three at Detroit in CSF; and two at Dallas in CF.
— New Jersey Devils, 2001. Won two at Carolina in CQF; two at Toronto in CSF; two at Pittsburgh in CF; and two at Colorado in F.
— Detroit Red Wings, 2002. Won three at Vancouver in CQF; one at St. Louis in CSF; two at Colorado in CF; and two at Carolina in F.
— Chicago Blackhawks, 2010. Won two at Nashville in CQF; three at Vancouver in CSF; two at San Jose in CF; and one at Philadelphia in F.

MOST ROAD WINS, ALL TEAMS, ONE PLAYOFF YEAR:
46 — 1987. Of 87 games played, road teams won 46 (22 DSF, 14 DF, 8 CF and 2 in F).

MOST OVERTIME WINS, ONE TEAM, ONE PLAYOFF YEAR:
10 — Montreal Canadiens, 1993. Won two vs. Quebec in DSF; three vs. Buffalo in DF; two vs. NY Islanders in CF; and three vs. Los Angeles in F.
7 — Carolina Hurricanes, 2002. Won two vs. New Jersey in CQF; one vs. Montreal in CSF; three vs. Toronto in CF; and one vs. Detroit in F.
— Anaheim Mighty Ducks, 2003. Won two vs. Detroit in CQF; two vs. Dallas in CSF; one vs. Minnesota in CF; and two vs. New Jersey in F.

MOST OVERTIME WINS AT HOME, ONE TEAM, ONE PLAYOFF YEAR:
- **4 — St. Louis Blues, 1968.** Won one vs. Philadelphia in QF; three vs. Minnesota in SF.
- **— Montreal Canadiens, 1993.** Won one vs. Quebec in DSF; one vs. Buffalo in DF, one vs. NY Islanders in CF; one vs. Los Angeles in F.

MOST OVERTIME WINS ON THE ROAD, ONE TEAM, ONE PLAYOFF YEAR:
- **6 — Montreal Canadiens, 1993.** Won one vs. Quebec in DSF; two vs. Buffalo in DF; one vs. NY Islanders in CF; two vs. Los Angeles in F.

TEAM LOSSES

MOST LOSSES, ONE TEAM, ONE PLAYOFF YEAR:
- **11 — Philadelphia Flyers, 1987.** Lost two vs. NY Rangers in DSF; three vs. NY Islanders in DF; two vs. Montreal in CF; four vs. Edmonton in F.
- **— Calgary Flames, 2004.** Lost three vs. Vancouver in CQF; two vs. Detroit in CSF; two vs. San Jose in CF; four vs. Tampa Bay in F

MOST HOME LOSSES, ONE TEAM, ONE PLAYOFF YEAR:
- **7 — Calgary Flames, 2004.** Lost two vs. Vancouver in CQF; one vs. Detroit in CSF; two vs. San Jose in CF; two vs. Tampa Bay in F.
- **6 — Philadelphia Flyers, 1987.** Lost one vs. NY Rangers in DSF; two vs. NY Islanders in DF; two vs. Montreal in CF; one vs. Edmonton in F.
- **— Washington Capitals, 1998.** Lost two vs. Boston in CQF; two vs. Buffalo in CF; two vs. Detroit in F.
- **— Colorado Avalanche, 1999.** Lost two vs. San Jose in CQF; two vs. Detroit in CSF; two vs. Dallas in CF.
- **— New Jersey Devils, 2001.** Lost one vs. Carolina in CQF; two vs. Toronto in CSF; one vs. Pittsburgh in CF; two vs Colorado in F.
- **— Minnesota Wild, 2003.** Lost two vs. Colorado in CQF; two vs. Vancouver in CSF; two vs. Anaheim in CF.

MOST ROAD LOSSES, ONE TEAM, ONE PLAYOFF YEAR:
- **7 — New Jersey Devils, 2003.** Lost one at Boston in CQF; one at Tampa Bay in CSF; two at Ottawa in CF; three at Anaheim in F.
- **— Philadelphia Flyers, 2010.** Lost one at New Jersey in CQF; two at Boston in CSF; one at Montreal in CF; three at Chicago in F.

MOST OVERTIME LOSSES, ONE TEAM, ONE PLAYOFF YEAR:
- **4 — Montreal Canadiens, 1951.** Lost four vs. Toronto in F.
- **— St. Louis Blues, 1968.** Lost one vs. Philadelphia in QF; one vs. Minnesota in SF; two vs. Montreal in F.
- **— New York Rangers, 1979.** Lost one vs. Philadelphia in QF; two vs. NY Islanders in SF; one vs. Montreal in F.
- **— Los Angeles Kings, 1991.** Lost one vs. Vancouver in DSF; three vs. Edmonton in DF.
- **— Los Angeles Kings, 1993.** Lost one vs. Toronto in CF; three vs. Montreal in F.
- **— New Jersey Devils, 1994.** Lost one vs. Buffalo in CQF; one vs. Boston in CSF; two vs. NY Rangers in CF.
- **— Chicago Blackhawks, 1995.** Lost one vs. Toronto in CQF; three vs. Detroit in CF.
- **— Philadelphia Flyers, 1996.** Lost two vs. Tampa Bay in CQF; two vs. Florida in CSF.
- **— Dallas Stars, 1999.** Lost two vs. St. Louis in CSF; one vs. Colorado in CF; one vs. Buffalo in F.
- **— Detroit Red Wings, 2002.** Lost one vs. Vancouver in CQF; two vs. Colorado in CF; one vs. Carolina in F.
- **— New Jersey Devils, 2003.** Lost two vs. Ottawa in CF; two vs. Anaheim in F.

MOST OVERTIME LOSSES AT HOME, ONE TEAM, ONE PLAYOFF YEAR:
- **4 — Detroit Red Wings, 2002.** Lost one vs. Vancouver in CQF; two vs. Colorado in CF; one vs. Carolina in F.

MOST OVERTIME LOSSES ON THE ROAD, ONE TEAM, ONE PLAYOFF YEAR:
- **3 — Los Angeles Kings, 1991.** Lost one at Vancouver in DSF; two at Edmonton in DF.
- **— Chicago Blackhawks, 1995.** Lost one at Toronto in CQF; two at Detroit in CF.
- **— St. Louis Blues, 1996.** Lost two at Toronto in CQF; one at Detroit in CSF.
- **— Dallas Stars, 1999.** Lost two at St. Louis in CSF; one at Colorado in CF.
- **— New Jersey Devils, 2003.** Lost one at Ottawa in CF; two at Anaheim in F.

PLAYOFF WINNING STREAKS

LONGEST PLAYOFF WINNING STREAK:
- **14 — Pittsburgh Penguins.** Streak started May 9, 1992 as Pittsburgh won the first of three straight games in DF vs. NY Rangers. Continued with four wins vs. Boston in 1992 CF and four wins vs. Chicago in 1992 F. Pittsburgh then won the first three games of 1993 DSF vs. New Jersey. New Jersey ended the streak April 25, 1993, at New Jersey with a 4-1 win vs. Pittsburgh in the fourth game of 1993 DSF.
- **12 —** Edmonton Oilers. Streak started May 15, 1984 as Edmonton won the first of three straight games in F vs. NY Islanders. Continued with three wins vs. Los Angeles in 1985 DSF and four wins vs. Winnipeg in 1985 DF. Edmonton then won the first two games of 1985 CF vs. Chicago. Chicago ended the streak May 9, 1985, at Chicago with a 5-2 win vs. Edmonton in the third game of 1985 CF.

MOST CONSECUTIVE WINS, ONE TEAM, ONE PLAYOFF YEAR:
- **11 — Chicago Blackhawks** in 1992. Chicago won last three games of DSF vs. St. Louis to win series 4-2, defeated Detroit 4-0 in DF and Edmonton 4-0 in CF.
- **— Pittsburgh Penguins** in 1992. Pittsburgh won last three games of DF vs. NY Rangers to win series 4-2, defeated Boston 4-0 in CF and Chicago 4-0 in F.
- **— Montreal Canadiens** in 1993. Montreal won last four games of DSF vs. Quebec to win series 4-2, defeated Buffalo 4-0 in DF and won first three games of CF vs. NY Islanders.

PLAYOFF LOSING STREAKS

LONGEST PLAYOFF LOSING STREAK:
- **16 — Chicago Black Hawks.** Streak started April 20, 1975 at Chicago with a 6-2 loss in fourth game of QF vs. Buffalo, won by Buffalo 4-1. Continued with four consecutive losses vs. Montreal, in 1976 QF and two straight losses vs. NY Islanders in 1977 best-of-three PRE. Chicago then lost four games vs. Boston in 1978 QF and four games vs. NY Islanders in 1979 QF. Chicago ended the streak April 8, 1980, at Chicago with a 3-2 win vs. St. Louis in the opening game of 1980 PRE.
- **14 —** Los Angeles Kings. Streak started June 3, 1993 at Montreal with a 3-2 loss in second game of F vs. Montreal, won by Montreal 4-1. Los Angeles failed to qualify for the playoffs for the next four years. Then Los Angeles lost four games vs. St. Louis in 1998 CQF; missed the 1999 playoffs and lost four games vs. Detroit in 2000 CQF. Los Angeles then lost the first two games of 2001 CQF vs. Detroit. Los Angeles ended the streak April 15, 2001, at Los Angeles with a 2-1 win vs. Detroit in the third game of 2001 CQF.

The Blackhawks celebrate their 2010 championship with a group picture on the ice in Philadelphia. Chicago was 8-3 at home and 8-3 on the road en route to the Stanley Cup.

MOST GOALS IN A SERIES, ONE TEAM

MOST GOALS, ONE TEAM, ONE PLAYOFF SERIES:
44 — Edmonton Oilers in 1985. Edmonton won best-of-seven CF 4-2, outscoring Chicago 44-25.
35 — Edmonton Oilers in 1983. Edmonton won best-of-seven DF 4-1, outscoring Calgary 35-13.
— Calgary Flames in 1995. Calgary lost best-of-seven CQF 4-3, outscoring San Jose 35-26.

MOST GOALS, ONE TEAM, TWO-GAME SERIES:
11 — Buffalo Sabres in 1977. Buffalo won best-of-three PRE 2-0, outscoring Minnesota 11-3.
— **Toronto Maple Leafs** in 1978. Toronto won best-of-three PRE 2-0, outscoring Los Angeles 11-3.

MOST GOALS, ONE TEAM, THREE-GAME SERIES:
23 — Chicago Blackhawks in 1985. Chicago won best-of-five DSF 3-0, outscoring Detroit 23-8.
20 — Minnesota North Stars in 1981. Minnesota won best-of-five PRE 3-0, outscoring Boston 20-13.
— NY Islanders in 1981. NY Islanders won best-of-five PRE 3-0, outscoring Toronto 20-4.

MOST GOALS, ONE TEAM, FOUR-GAME SERIES:
28 — Boston Bruins in 1972. Boston won best-of-seven SF 4-0, outscoring St. Louis 28-8.

MOST GOALS, ONE TEAM, FIVE-GAME SERIES:
35 — Edmonton Oilers in 1983. Edmonton won best-of-seven DF 4-1, outscoring Calgary 35-13.
32 — Edmonton Oilers in 1987. Edmonton won best-of-seven DSF 4-1, outscoring Los Angeles 32-20.
30 — Calgary Flames in 1988. Calgary won best-of-seven DSF 4-1, outscoring Los Angeles 30-18.

MOST GOALS, ONE TEAM, SIX-GAME SERIES:
44 — Edmonton Oilers in 1985. Edmonton won best-of-seven CF 4-2, outscoring Chicago 44-25.
33 — Montreal Canadiens in 1973. Montreal won best-of-seven F 4-2, outscoring Chicago 33-23.
— Chicago Blackhawks in 1985. Chicago won best-of-seven DF 4-2, outscoring Minnesota 33-29.
— Los Angeles Kings in 1993. Los Angeles won best-of-seven DSF 4-2, outscoring Calgary 33-28.

MOST GOALS, ONE TEAM, SEVEN-GAME SERIES:
35 — Calgary Flames in 1995. Calgary lost best-of-seven CQF 4-3, outscoring San Jose 35-26.
33 — Philadelphia Flyers in 1976. Philadelphia won best-of-seven QF 4-3, outscoring Toronto 33-23.
— Boston Bruins in 1983. Boston won best-of-seven DF 4-3, outscoring Buffalo 33-23.
— Edmonton Oilers in 1984. Edmonton won best-of-seven DF 4-3, outscoring Calgary 33-27.

FEWEST GOALS IN A SERIES, ONE TEAM

FEWEST GOALS, ONE TEAM, TWO-GAME SERIES:
0 — Toronto St. Patricks in 1921. Toronto lost two-game, total-goals NHL F 7-0 vs. Ottawa.
— **New York Americans** in 1929. NY Americans lost two-game, total-goals QF 1-0 vs. NY Rangers.
— **New York Rangers** in 1931. NY Rangers lost two-game, total-goals SF 3-0 vs. Chicago.
— **Chicago Black Hawks** in 1935. Chicago lost two-game, total-goals SF 1-0 vs. Mtl. Maroons.
— **Montreal Maroons** in 1937. Mtl. Maroons lost best-of-three SF 2-0, outscored by NY Rangers 5-0.
— **New York Americans** in 1939. NY Americans lost best-of-three QF 2-0, outscored by Toronto 5-0.

FEWEST GOALS, ONE TEAM, THREE-GAME SERIES:
1 — Montreal Maroons in 1936. Mtl. Maroons lost best-of-five SF 3-0, outscored by Detroit 6-1.

FEWEST GOALS, ONE TEAM, FOUR-GAME SERIES:
1 — Minnesota Wild in 2003. Minnesota lost best-of-seven CF 4-0, outscored by Anaheim 9-1.

FEWEST GOALS, ONE TEAM, FIVE-GAME SERIES:
2 — Philadelphia Flyers in 2002. Ottawa won best-of-seven CQF 4-1, while outscoring Philadelphia 11-2.

FEWEST GOALS, ONE TEAM, SIX-GAME SERIES:
5 — Boston Bruins in 1951. Toronto won best-of-seven SF 4-1 with 1 tie, outscoring Boston 17-5.

FEWEST GOALS, ONE TEAM, SEVEN-GAME SERIES:
9 — Toronto Maple Leafs, in 1945. Toronto won best-of-seven F 4-3; teams tied in scoring 9-9.
— **Detroit Red Wings,** in 1945. Toronto won best-of-seven F 4-3; teams tied in scoring 9-9.

The 1985 Chicago Blackhawks were involved in some of the highest-scoring series in playoff history. Denis Savard set a club record with 29 points that spring, a mark that was tied by Jonathan Toews in 2010.

MOST GOALS IN A SERIES, BOTH TEAMS

MOST GOALS, BOTH TEAMS, ONE PLAYOFF SERIES:
69 — Edmonton Oilers (44), Chicago Black Hawks (25) in 1985. Edmonton won best-of-seven CF 4-2.
62 — Chicago Black Hawks (33), Minnesota North Stars (29) in 1985. Chicago won best-of-seven DF 4-2.
61 — Los Angeles Kings (33), Calgary Flames (28) in 1993. Los Angeles won best-of-seven DSF 4-2.
— Calgary Flames (35), San Jose Sharks (26) in 1995. San Jose won best-of-seven CQF 4-3.

MOST GOALS, BOTH TEAMS, TWO-GAME SERIES:
17 — Toronto St. Patricks (10), Montreal Canadiens (7) in 1918. Toronto won two-game total-goals NHL F.
15 — Boston Bruins (10), Chicago Black Hawks (5) in 1927. Boston won two-game total-goals QF.
— Pittsburgh Penguins (9), St. Louis Blues (6) in 1975. Pittsburgh won best-of-three PRE 2-0.

MOST GOALS, BOTH TEAMS, THREE-GAME SERIES:
33 — Minnesota North Stars (20), Boston Bruins (13) in 1981. Minnesota won best-of-five PRE 3-0.
31 — Chicago Black Hawks (23), Detroit Red Wings (8) in 1985. Chicago won best-of-five DSF 3-0.
28 — Toronto Maple Leafs (18), New York Rangers (10) in 1932. Toronto won best-of-five F 3-0.

MOST GOALS, BOTH TEAMS, FOUR-GAME SERIES:
36 — Boston Bruins (28), St. Louis Blues (8) in 1972. Boston won best-of-seven SF 4-0.
— **Minnesota North Stars (18), Toronto Maple Leafs (18)** in 1983. Minnesota won best-of-five DSF 3-1.
— **Edmonton Oilers (25), Chicago Black Hawks (11)** in 1983. Edmonton won best-of-seven CF 4-0.
35 — New York Rangers (23), Los Angeles Kings (12) in 1981. NY Rangers won best-of-five PRE 3-1.

MOST GOALS, BOTH TEAMS, FIVE-GAME SERIES:
 52 — Edmonton Oilers (32), Los Angeles Kings (20) in 1987. Edmonton won
   best-of-seven DSF 4-1.
 50 — Los Angeles Kings (27), Edmonton Oilers (23) in 1982. Los Angeles won
   best-of-five DSF 3-2.
 48 — Edmonton Oilers (35), Calgary Flames (13) in 1983. Edmonton won
   best-of-seven DF 4-1.
  — Calgary Flames (30), Los Angeles Kings (18) in 1988. Calgary won
   best-of-seven DSF 4-1.

MOST GOALS, BOTH TEAMS, SIX-GAME SERIES:
 69 — Edmonton Oilers (44), Chicago Black Hawks (25) in 1985. Edmonton won
   best-of-seven CF 4-2.
 62 — Chicago Black Hawks (33), Minnesota North Stars (29) in 1985. Chicago won
   best-of-seven DF 4-2.
 61 — Los Angeles Kings (33), Calgary Flames (28) in 1993. Los Angeles won
   best-of-seven DSF 4-2.

MOST GOALS, BOTH TEAMS, SEVEN-GAME SERIES:
 61 — Calgary Flames (35), San Jose Sharks (26) in 1995. San Jose won
   best-of-seven CQF 4-3.
 60 — Edmonton Oilers (33), Calgary Flames (27) in 1984. Edmonton won
   best-of-seven DF 4-3.

FEWEST GOALS IN A SERIES, BOTH TEAMS

FEWEST GOALS, BOTH TEAMS, TWO-GAME SERIES:
 1 — New York Rangers (1), New York Americans (0) in 1929. NY Rangers won
   two-game total-goals QF.
  — Montreal Maroons (1), Chicago Black Hawks (0) in 1935. Mtl. Maroons
   won two-game total-goals SF.

FEWEST GOALS, BOTH TEAMS, THREE-GAME SERIES:
 7 — Boston Bruins (5), Montreal Canadiens (2) in 1929. Boston won
   best-of-five SF 3-0.
  — Detroit Red Wings (6), Montreal Maroons (1) in 1936. Detroit won
   best-of-five SF 3-0.

FEWEST GOALS, BOTH TEAMS, FOUR-GAME SERIES:
 9 — Toronto Maple Leafs (7), Boston Bruins (2) in 1935. Toronto won
   best-of-five SF 3-1.

FEWEST GOALS, BOTH TEAMS, FIVE-GAME SERIES:
 11 — Montreal Maroons (6), New York Rangers (5) in 1928. NY Rangers won
   best-of-five F 3-2.

FEWEST GOALS, BOTH TEAMS, SIX-GAME SERIES:
 16 — Carolina Hurricanes (10), Toronto Maple Leafs (6) in 2002. Carolina won
   best-of-seven CF 4-2.

FEWEST GOALS, BOTH TEAMS, SEVEN-GAME SERIES:
 18 — Toronto Maple Leafs (9), Detroit Red Wings (9) in 1945. Toronto won
   best-of-seven F 4-3.

MOST GOALS IN A GAME OR PERIOD

MOST GOALS, ONE TEAM, ONE GAME:
 13 — Edmonton Oilers April 9, 1987, vs. Los Angeles at Edmonton. Edmonton
   won 13-3.
 12 — Los Angeles Kings, April 10, 1990, vs. Calgary at Los Angeles. Los Angeles
   won 12-4.
 11 — Montreal Canadiens, March 30, 1944, vs. Toronto at Montreal. Montreal won
   11-0.
  — Edmonton Oilers, May 4, 1985, vs. Chicago at Edmonton. Edmonton won
   11-2.

MOST GOALS, ONE TEAM, ONE PERIOD:
 7 — Montreal Canadiens, March 30, 1944, vs. Toronto at Montreal, third period.
   Montreal won 11-0.

MOST GOALS, BOTH TEAMS, ONE GAME:
 18 — Los Angeles Kings (10), Edmonton Oilers (8), April 7, 1982, at Edmonton.
   Los Angeles won best-of-five DSF 3-2.
 17 — Pittsburgh Penguins (10), Philadelphia Flyers (7), April 25, 1989, at Pittsburgh.
   Pittsburgh won best-of-seven DF 4-3.
 16 — Edmonton Oilers (13), Los Angeles Kings (3), April 9, 1987, at Edmonton.
   Edmonton won best-of-seven DSF 4-1.
  — Los Angeles Kings (12), Calgary Flames (4), April 10, 1990, at Los Angeles.
   Los Angeles won best-of-seven DF 4-2.

MOST GOALS, BOTH TEAMS, ONE PERIOD:
 9 — New York Rangers (6), Philadelphia Flyers (3), April 24, 1979, third
   period, at Philadelphia. NY Rangers won 8-3.
  — Los Angeles Kings (5), Calgary Flames (4), April 10, 1990, second period,
   at Los Angeles. Los Angeles won 12-4.
 8 — Chicago Black Hawks (5), Montreal Canadiens (3), May 8, 1973, second
   period, at Montreal. Chicago won 8-7.
  — Chicago Black Hawks (5), Edmonton Oilers (3), May 12, 1985, first period, at
   Chicago. Chicago won 8-6.
  — Edmonton Oilers (6), Winnipeg Jets (2), April 6, 1988, third period, at
   Edmonton. Edmonton won 7-4.
  — Hartford Whalers (5), Montreal Canadiens (3), April 10, 1988, third period, at
   Montreal. Hartford won 7-5.
  — Vancouver Canucks (5), New York Rangers (3), June 9, 1994, third period, at
   NY Rangers. Vancouver won 6-3.
  — Pittsburgh Penguins (5), Ottawa Senators (3), April 20, 2010, second period,
   at Ottawa. Pittsburgh won 7-4.

TEAM POWER-PLAY GOALS

MOST POWER-PLAY GOALS BY ALL TEAMS, ONE PLAYOFF YEAR:
 199 — 1988 in 83 games.

MOST POWER-PLAY GOALS, ONE TEAM, ONE PLAYOFF YEAR:
 35 — Minnesota North Stars, 1991 in 23 games.
 32 — Edmonton Oilers, 1988 in 18 games.
 31 — New York Islanders, 1981 in 18 games.

MOST POWER-PLAY GOALS, ONE TEAM, ONE SERIES:
 15 — New York Islanders in 1980 F vs. Philadelphia. NY Islanders won series 4-2.
  — Minnesota North Stars in 1991 DSF vs. Chicago. Minnesota won series 4-2.
 13 — New York Islanders in 1981 QF vs. Edmonton. NY Islanders won series 4-2.
  — Calgary Flames in 1986 CF vs. St. Louis. Calgary won series 4-3.
 12 — Toronto Maple Leafs in 1976 QF vs. Philadelphia. Philadelphia won series 4-3.

MOST POWER-PLAY GOALS, BOTH TEAMS, ONE SERIES:
 21 — New York Islanders (15), Philadelphia Flyers (6) in 1980 best-of-seven F
   won by NY Islanders 4-2.
  — New York Islanders (13), Edmonton Oilers (8) in 1981 best-of-seven QF
   won by NY Islanders 4-2.
  — Philadelphia Flyers (11), Pittsburgh Penguins (10) in 1989 best-of-seven
   DF won by Philadelphia 4-3.
  — Minnesota North Stars (15), Chicago Black Hawks (6) in 1991
   best-of-seven DSF won by Minnesota 4-2.
 20 — Toronto Maple Leafs (12), Philadelphia Flyers (8) in 1976 best-of-seven QF
   won by Philadelphia 4-3.

MOST POWER-PLAY GOALS, ONE TEAM, ONE GAME:
 6 — Boston Bruins, April 2, 1969, at Boston vs. Toronto. Boston won 10-0.

MOST POWER-PLAY GOALS, BOTH TEAMS, ONE GAME:
 8 — Minnesota North Stars (4), St. Louis Blues (4), April 24, 1991, at
   Minnesota. Minnesota won 8-4.
 7 — Minnesota North Stars (4), Edmonton Oilers (3), April 28, 1984, at Minnesota.
   Edmonton won 8-5.
  — Philadelphia Flyers (4), New York Rangers (3), April 13, 1985, at NY Rangers.
   Philadelphia won 6-5.
  — Chicago Black Hawks (5), Edmonton Oilers (2), May 14, 1985, at Edmonton.
   Edmonton won 10-5.
  — Edmonton Oilers (5), Los Angeles Kings (2), April 9, 1987, at Edmonton.
   Edmonton won 13-3.
  — Vancouver Canucks (4), Calgary Flames (3), April 9, 1989, at Vancouver.
   Vancouver won 5-3.

MOST POWER-PLAY GOALS, ONE TEAM, ONE PERIOD:
 4 — Toronto Maple Leafs, March 26, 1936, second period vs. Boston at
   Toronto. Toronto won 8-3.
  — Minnesota North Stars, April 28, 1984, second period vs. Edmonton at
   Minnesota. Edmonton won 8-5.
  — Boston Bruins, April 11, 1991, third period vs. Hartford at Boston. Boston
   won 6-1.
  — Minnesota North Stars, April 24, 1991, second period vs. St. Louis at
   Minnesota. Minnesota won 8-4.
  — St. Louis Blues, April 27, 1998, third period at Los Angeles. St. Louis won
   4-3.

MOST POWER-PLAY GOALS, BOTH TEAMS, ONE PERIOD:
 5 — Minnesota North Stars (4), Edmonton Oilers (1), April 28, 1984, at
   Minnesota. Edmonton won 8-5.
  — Vancouver Canucks (3), Calgary Flames (2), April 9, 1989, at Vancouver.
   Vancouver won 5-3.
  — Minnesota North Stars (4), St. Louis Blues (1), April 24, 1991, at
   Minnesota. Minnesota won 8-4.

TEAM SHORTHAND GOALS

MOST SHORTHAND GOALS BY ALL TEAMS, ONE PLAYOFF YEAR:
 33 — 1988, in 83 games.

MOST SHORTHAND GOALS, ONE TEAM, ONE PLAYOFF YEAR:
 10 — Edmonton Oilers, 1983, in 16 games.
 9 — New York Islanders, 1981, in 19 games.
 8 — Philadelphia Flyers, 1989, in 19 games.

MOST SHORTHAND GOALS, ONE TEAM, ONE SERIES:
 6 — Calgary Flames in 1995 vs. San Jose best-of-seven CQF won by San Jose
   4-3.
  — Vancouver Canucks in 1995 vs. St. Louis in best-of-seven CQF won by
   Vancouver 4-3.
 5 — New York Rangers in 1979 vs. Philadelphia in best-of-seven QF won by
   NY Rangers 4-1.
  — Edmonton Oilers in 1983 vs. Calgary in best-of-seven DF won by Edmonton
   4-1.

MOST SHORTHAND GOALS, BOTH TEAMS, ONE SERIES:
 7 — Boston Bruins (4), New York Rangers (3), in 1958 SF won by Boston 4-2.
  — Edmonton Oilers (5), Calgary Flames (2), in 1983 DF won by Edmonton
   4-1.
  — Vancouver Canucks (6), St. Louis Blues (1), in 1995 CQF won by
   Vancouver 4-3.

MOST SHORTHAND GOALS, ONE TEAM, ONE GAME:
 3 — Boston Bruins, April 11, 1981, at Minnesota North Stars. Minnesota won
   6-3.
  — New York Islanders, April 17, 1983, at NY Rangers. NY Rangers won 7-6.
  — Toronto Maple Leafs, May 8, 1994, at San Jose Sharks. Toronto won 8-3.

MOST SHORTHAND GOALS, BOTH TEAMS, ONE GAME:

4 — **Boston Bruins (3), Minnesota North Stars (1)**, April 11, 1981, at Minnesota. Minnesota won 6-3.
- **New York Islanders (3), New York Rangers (1)**, April 17, 1983, at NY Rangers. NY Rangers won 7-6.
- **Toronto Maple Leafs (3), San Jose Sharks (1)**, May 8, 1994, at San Jose. Toronto won 8-3.

3 — Toronto Maple Leafs (2), Detroit Red Wings (1), April 5, 1947, at Toronto. Toronto won 6-1.
- New York Rangers (2), Boston Bruins (1), April 1, 1958, at Boston. NY Rangers won 5-2.
- Minnesota North Stars (2), Philadelphia Flyers (1), May 4, 1980, at Minnesota. Philadelphia won 5-3.
- Winnipeg Jets (2), Edmonton Oilers (1), April 9, 1988, at Winnipeg. Winnipeg won 6-4.
- New York Islanders (2), New Jersey Devils (1), April 14, 1988, at New Jersey. New Jersey won 6-5.
- Montreal Canadiens (2), New Jersey Devils (1), April 17, 1997, at New Jersey. New Jersey won 5-2.
- Dallas Stars (2), San Jose Sharks (1), May 5, 2000, at San Jose. Dallas won 5-4.
- Detroit Red Wings (2), Calgary Flames (1), April 21, 2007, at Detroit. Detroit won 5-1.

MOST SHORTHAND GOALS, ONE TEAM, ONE PERIOD:

2 — **Toronto Maple Leafs**, April 5, 1947, first period vs. Detroit at Toronto. Toronto won 6-1.
- **Toronto Maple Leafs**, April 13, 1965, first period vs. Montreal at Toronto. Montreal won 4-3.
- **Boston Bruins**, April 20, 1969, first period vs. Montreal at Boston. Boston won 3-2.
- **Boston Bruins**, April 8, 1970, second period vs. NY Rangers at Boston. Boston won 8-2.
- **Boston Bruins**, April 30, 1972, first period vs. NY Rangers at Boston. Boston won 6-5.
- **Chicago Black Hawks**, May 3, 1973, first period vs. Montreal at Chicago. Chicago won 7-4.
- **Montreal Canadiens**, April 23, 1978, first period at Detroit. Montreal won 8-0.
- **New York Islanders**, April 8, 1980, second period vs. Los Angeles at NY Islanders. NY Islanders won 8-1.
- **Los Angeles Kings**, April 9, 1980, first period at NY Islanders. Los Angeles won 6-3.
- **Boston Bruins**, April 13, 1980, second period at Pittsburgh. Boston won 8-3.
- **Minnesota North Stars**, May 4, 1980, second period vs. Philadelphia at Minnesota. Philadelphia won 5-3.
- **Boston Bruins**, April 11, 1981, third period at Minnesota North Stars. Minnesota won 6-3.
- **New York Islanders**, May 12, 1981, first period vs. Minnesota North Stars at NY Islanders. NY Islanders won 6-3.
- **Montreal Canadiens**, April 7, 1982, third period vs. Quebec at Montreal. Montreal won 5-1.
- **Edmonton Oilers**, April 24, 1983, third period vs. Chicago at Edmonton. Edmonton won 8-4.
- **Winnipeg Jets**, April 14, 1985, second period at Calgary. Winnipeg won 5-3.
- **Boston Bruins**, April 6, 1988, first period vs. Buffalo at Boston. Boston won 7-3.
- **New York Islanders**, April 14, 1988, third period at New Jersey. New Jersey won 6-5.
- **Detroit Red Wings**, April 29, 1993, second period at Toronto. Detroit won 7-3.
- **Toronto Maple Leafs**, May 8, 1994, third period at San Jose. Toronto won 8-3.
- **Calgary Flames**, May 11, 1995, first period at San Jose. Calgary won 9-2.
- **Vancouver Canucks**, May 15, 1995, second period at St. Louis. Vancouver won 6-5.
- **Montreal Canadiens**, April 17, 1997, second period at New Jersey. New Jersey won 5-2.
- **Philadelphia Flyers**, April 26, 1997, first period vs. Pittsburgh at Philadelphia. Philadelphia won 6-3.
- **Phoenix Coyotes**, April 24, 1998, second period at Detroit. Phoenix won 7-4.
- **Buffalo Sabres**, April 27, 1998, second period vs. Philadelphia at Buffalo. Buffalo won 6-1.
- **San Jose Sharks**, April 30, 1999, third period at Colorado. San Jose won 7-3.
- **Detroit Red Wings**, April 27, 2002, second period at Vancouver. Detroit won 6-4.
- **Detroit Red Wings**, April 21, 2007, second period at Detroit. Detroit won 5-1.

MOST SHORTHAND GOALS, BOTH TEAMS, ONE PERIOD:

3 — **Toronto Maple Leafs (2), Detroit Red Wings (1)**, April 5, 1947, first period at Toronto. Toronto won 6-1.
- **Toronto Maple Leafs (2), San Jose Sharks (1)**, May 8, 1994, third period at San Jose. Toronto won 8-3.

FASTEST GOALS

FASTEST FIVE GOALS, BOTH TEAMS:

3:06 — **Minnesota North Stars, Chicago Black Hawks**, April 21, 1985, at Chicago. Keith Brown scored for Chicago at 1:12 of the second period; Ken Yaremchuk, Chicago, 1:27; Dino Ciccarelli, Minnesota, 2:48; Tony McKegney, Minnesota, 4:07; and Curt Fraser, Chicago, 4:18. Chicago won 6-2 and won best-of-seven DF 4-2.

3:20 — Minnesota North Stars, Philadelphia Flyers, April 29, 1980, at Philadelphia. Paul Shmyr scored for Minnesota at 13:20 of the first period; Steve Christoff, Minnesota, 13:59; Ken Linseman, Philadelphia, 14:54; Tom Gorence, Philadelphia, 15:36; and Ken Linseman, Philadelphia, 16:40. Minnesota won 6-5. Philadelphia won best-of-seven SF 4-1.

3:58 — Detroit Red Wings, Phoenix Coyotes, April 16, 2010, at Phoenix. Henrik Zetterberg scored for Detroit at 6:27 of the second period; Wojtek Wolski,

Phoenix, 7:05; Pavel Datsyuk, Detroit, 8:20; Matthew Lombardi, Phoenix, 9:09; Valtteri Filppula, Detroit, 10:25. Detroit won 7-4 and won best-of-seven CQF 4-3.

FASTEST FIVE GOALS, ONE TEAM:

3:36 — **Montreal Canadiens**, March 30, 1944, at Montreal vs. Toronto. Toe Blake scored at 7:58 and 8:37 of the third period; Maurice Richard, 9:17; Ray Getliffe, 10:33; and Buddy O'Connor, 11:34. Canadiens won 11-0 and won best-of-seven SF 4-1.

FASTEST FOUR GOALS, BOTH TEAMS:

1:33 — **Toronto Maple Leafs, Philadelphia Flyers**, April 20, 1976, at Philadelphia. Don Saleski scored for Philadelphia at 10:04 of the second period; Bob Neely, Toronto, 10:42; Gary Dornhoefer, Philadelphia, 11:24; and Don Saleski, Philadelphia, 11:37. Philadelphia won 7-1 and won best-of-seven QF 4-3.

1:34 — Calgary Flames, Montreal Canadiens, May 20, 1986, at Montreal. Joel Otto scored for Calgary at 17:59 of the first period; Bobby Smith, Montreal, 18:25; Mats Naslund, Montreal, 19:17; and Bob Gainey, Montreal, 19:33. Montreal won 5-3 and won best-of-seven F 4-1.

1:38 — Boston Bruins, Philadelphia Flyers, April 26, 1977, at Philadelphia. Gregg Sheppard scored for Boston at 14:01 of the second period; Mike Milbury, Boston, 15:01; Gary Dornhoefer, Philadelphia, 15:16; and Jean Ratelle, Boston, 15:39. Boston won 5-4 and won best-of-seven SF 4-0.

FASTEST FOUR GOALS, ONE TEAM:

2:35 — **Montreal Canadiens**, March 30, 1944, at Montreal. Toe Blake scored at 7:58 and 8:37 of the third period; Maurice Richard, 9:17; and Ray Getliffe, 10:33. Montreal won 11-0 and won best-of-seven SF 4-1.

FASTEST THREE GOALS, BOTH TEAMS:

0:21 — **Chicago Black Hawks, Edmonton Oilers**, May 7, 1985, at Edmonton. Behn Wilson scored for Chicago at 19:22 of the third period; Jari Kurri, Edmonton, 19:36; and Glenn Anderson, Edmonton, 19:43. Edmonton won 7-3 and won best-of-seven CF 4-2.

0:27 — Phoenix Coyotes, Detroit Red Wings, April 24, 1998, at Detroit. Jeremy Roenick scored for Phoenix at 13:24 of the second period; Mathieu Dandenault, Detroit, 13:32; and Keith Tkachuk, Phoenix, 13:51. Phoenix won 7-4. Detroit won best-of-seven CQF 4-2.

0:30 — Pittsburgh Penguins, Chicago Blackhawks, June 1, 1992, at Chicago. Dirk Graham scored for Chicago at 6:21 of the first period; Kevin Stevens, Pittsburgh, 6:33; and Dirk Graham, Chicago, 6:51. Pittsburgh won 6-5 and won best-of-seven F 4-0.

FASTEST THREE GOALS, ONE TEAM:

0:23 — **Toronto Maple Leafs**, April 12, 1979, at Toronto vs. Atlanta Flames. Darryl Sittler scored at 4:04 and 4:16 of the first period; and Ron Ellis, 4:27. Toronto won 7-4 and won best-of-three PRE 2-0.

0:38 — New York Rangers, April 12, 1986, at NY Rangers vs. Philadelphia. Jim Weimer scored at 12:29 of the third period; Bob Brooke, 12:43; and Ron Greschner, 13:07. NY Rangers won 5-2 and won best-of-five DSF 3-2.
- Colorado Avalanche, April 18, 2001, at Vancouver. Peter Forsberg scored at 9:11 of the third period; Joe Sakic, 9:28; and Eric Messier, 9:49. Colorado won 5-1 and won best-of-seven CQF 4-0.

FASTEST TWO GOALS, BOTH TEAMS:

0:05 — **Pittsburgh Penguins, Buffalo Sabres**, April 14, 1979, at Buffalo. Gilbert Perreault scored for Buffalo at 12:59 of the first period; and Jim Hamilton, Pittsburgh, 13:04. Pittsburgh won 4-3 and won best-of-three PRE 2-1.

0:08 — St. Louis Blues, Minnesota North Stars, April 9, 1989, at Minnesota. Bernie Federko scored for St. Louis at 2:28 of the third period; and Perry Berezan, Minnesota, 2:36. Minnesota won 5-4. St. Louis won best-of-seven DSF 4-1.
- Phoenix Coyotes, Detroit Red Wings, April 24, 1998, at Detroit. Jeremy Roenick scored for Phoenix at 13:24 of the second period; and Mathieu Dandenault, Detroit, 13:32. Phoenix won 7-4. Detroit won best-of-seven CQF 4-2.

FASTEST TWO GOALS, ONE TEAM:

0:05 — **Detroit Red Wings**, April 11, 1965, at Detroit vs. Chicago. Norm Ullman scored at 17:35 and 17:40 of the second period. Detroit won 4-2. Chicago won best-of-seven SF 4-3.

Montreal's Michael Cammalleri led all postseason performers with 13 goals during the 2010 playoffs.

Known as "Ulcers" because of his nerves, Frank McCool lasted less than two seasons in the NHL, but made his mark as a rookie in the spring of 1945 when he recorded three straight shutouts to open the Stanley Cup Finals.

OVERTIME

SHORTEST OVERTIME:
0:09 — Montreal Canadiens, Calgary Flames, May 18, 1986, at Calgary. Montreal won 3-2 on Brian Skrudland's goal at 0:09 of the first overtime period. Montreal won best-of-seven F 4-1.
0:11 — New York Islanders, New York Rangers, April 11, 1975, at NY Rangers. NY Islanders won 4-3 on J.P. Parise's goal at 0:11 of the first overtime period. NY Islanders won best-of-three PRE 2-1.

LONGEST OVERTIME:
116:30 — Detroit Red Wings, Montreal Maroons, March 24, 1936, at Montreal. Mtl. Maroons won 1-0 on Mud Bruneteau's goal at 16:30 of the sixth overtime period. Detroit won best-of-five SF 3-0.

MOST OVERTIME GAMES, ONE PLAYOFF YEAR:
28 — 1993. Of 85 games played, 28 went into overtime.
26 — 2001. Of 86 games played, 26 went into overtime.
22 — 2003. Of 89 games played, 22 went into overtime.

FEWEST OVERTIME GAMES, ONE PLAYOFF YEAR:
0 — 1963. None of the 16 games went into overtime, the only year since 1926 that no overtime was required in any playoff series.

MOST OVERTIME GAMES, ONE SERIES:
5 — Toronto Maple Leafs, Montreal Canadiens in 1951. Toronto won best-of-seven F 4-1.
4 — Toronto Maple Leafs, Boston Bruins in 1933. Toronto won best-of-five SF 3-2.
— Boston Bruins, NY Rangers in 1939. Boston won best-of-seven SF 4-3.
— St. Louis Blues, Minnesota North Stars in 1968. St. Louis won best-of-seven SF 4-3.
— Dallas Stars, St. Louis Blues in 1999. Dallas won best-of-seven CSF 4-2.
— Dallas Stars, Edmonton Oilers in 2001. Dallas won best-of-seven CQF 4-2.
— Dallas Stars, San Jose Sharks in 2008. Dallas won best-of-seven CSF 4-2

TEAM HAT-TRICKS

MOST HAT-TRICKS, BY ALL TEAMS, ONE PLAYOFF YEAR:
12 — 1983 in 66 games.
— **1988** in 83 games.
11 — 1985 in 70 games.
— 1992 in 86 games.

MOST HAT-TRICKS, ONE TEAM, ONE PLAYOFF YEAR:
6 — Edmonton Oilers in 16 games, 1983.
— **Edmonton Oilers** in 18 games, 1985.

SHUTOUTS

MOST SHUTOUTS, ONE PLAYOFF YEAR, ALL TEAMS:
25 — 2002. Of 90 games played, Detroit had 6; Ottawa had 4; Carolina, Colorado, St. Louis and Toronto had 3 each; while Los Angeles, New Jersey and Philadelphia had 1 each.
23 — 2004. Of 89 games played, Tampa Bay and Calgary had 5 each; Toronto and San Jose had 3 each; while Boston, Colorado, Detroit, Montreal, Nashville, NY Islanders and Philadelphia had 1 each.
19 — 2001. Of 86 games played, Colorado and New Jersey had 4 each, Toronto had 3, Pittsburgh and Los Angeles had 2 each, while Buffalo, Washington, Detroit and San Jose had 1 each.

FEWEST SHUTOUTS, ONE PLAYOFF YEAR, ALL TEAMS:
0 — 1959. 18 games played.

MOST SHUTOUTS, BOTH TEAMS, ONE SERIES:
5 — Toronto Maple Leafs (3), Detroit Red Wings (2), in 1945. Toronto won best-of-seven F 4-3.
— **Toronto Maple Leafs (3), Detroit Red Wings (2),** in 1950. Detroit won best-of-seven SF 4-3.

TEAM PENALTIES

FEWEST PENALTIES, BOTH TEAMS, BEST-OF-SEVEN SERIES:
19 — Detroit Red Wings, Toronto Maple Leafs in 1945. Detroit received 10 minors, Toronto received 9 minors. Detroit won best-of-seven F 4-3.

FEWEST PENALTIES, ONE TEAM, BEST-OF-SEVEN SERIES:
9 — Toronto Maple Leafs in 1945 vs. Detroit. Toronto received 9 minors. Detroit won best-of-seven F 4-3.

MOST PENALTIES, BOTH TEAMS, ONE SERIES:
218 — New Jersey Devils, Washington Capitals in 1988. New Jersey received 97 minors, 11 majors, 9 misconducts and 1 match penalty. Washington received 80 minors, 11 majors, 8 misconducts and 1 match penalty. New Jersey won best-of-seven DF 4-3.

MOST PENALTY MINUTES, BOTH TEAMS, ONE SERIES:
654 — New Jersey Devils (349), Washington Capitals (305) in 1988. New Jersey won best-of-seven DF 4-3.

MOST PENALTIES, ONE TEAM, ONE SERIES:
118 — New Jersey Devils in 1988 vs. Washington. New Jersey received 97 minors, 11 majors, 9 misconducts and 1 match penalty. New Jersey won best-of-seven DF 4-3.

MOST PENALTY MINUTES, ONE TEAM, ONE SERIES:
349 — New Jersey Devils in 1988 vs. Washington. New Jersey won best-of-seven DF 4-3.

MOST PENALTIES, BOTH TEAMS, ONE GAME:
66 — Detroit Red Wings (33), St. Louis Blues (33), April 12, 1991, at St. Louis. St. Louis won 6-1.
63 — Minnesota North Stars (34), Chicago Blackhawks (29), April 6, 1990, at Chicago. Chicago won 5-3.
62 — New Jersey Devils (32), Washington Capitals (30), April 22, 1988, at New Jersey. New Jersey won 10-4.

MOST PENALTY MINUTES, BOTH TEAMS, ONE GAME:
298 — Detroit Red Wings (152), St. Louis Blues (146), April 12, 1991, at St. Louis. Detroit received 33 penalties; St. Louis received 33 penalties. St. Louis won 6-1.
267 — New York Rangers (142), Los Angeles Kings (125), April 9, 1981, at Los Angeles. NY Rangers received 31 penalties; LA received 28 penalties. Los Angeles won 5-4.

MOST PENALTIES, ONE TEAM, ONE GAME:
34 — Minnesota North Stars, April 6, 1990, at Chicago. Chicago won 5-3.
33 — Detroit Red Wings, April 12, 1991, at St. Louis. St. Louis won 6-1.
— St. Louis Blues, April 12, 1991, at St. Louis vs. Detroit. St. Louis won 6-1.

MOST PENALTY MINUTES, ONE TEAM, ONE GAME:
152 — Detroit Red Wings, April 12, 1991, at St. Louis. St. Louis won 6-1.
146 — St. Louis Blues, April 12, 1991, at St. Louis vs. Detroit. St. Louis won 6-1.
142 — New York Rangers, April 9, 1981, at Los Angeles. Los Angeles won 5-4.

MOST PENALTIES, BOTH TEAMS, ONE PERIOD:
43 — New York Rangers (24), Los Angeles Kings (19), April 9, 1981, first period at Los Angeles. Los Angeles won 5-4.

MOST PENALTY MINUTES, BOTH TEAMS, ONE PERIOD:
248 — New York Islanders (124), Boston Bruins (124), April 17, 1980, first period at Boston. NY Islanders won 5-4.

MOST PENALTIES, ONE TEAM, ONE PERIOD:
24 — New York Rangers, April 9, 1981, first period at Los Angeles. Los Angeles won 5-4.

MOST PENALTY MINUTES, ONE TEAM, ONE PERIOD:
125 — New York Rangers, April 9, 1981, first period at Los Angeles. Los Angeles won 5-4.

Individual Records

GAMES PLAYED

MOST YEARS IN PLAYOFFS:
24 — Chris Chelios, Montreal, Chicago, Detroit (1984-97 inclusive; 1999-2004 inclusive, 2006-2009 inclusive)
21 — Raymond Bourque, Boston, Colorado (1980-96 inclusive; 98-2001 inclusive)
20 — Gordie Howe, Detroit, Hartford
— Larry Robinson, Montreal, Los Angeles
— Larry Murphy, Los Angeles, Washington, Minnesota, Pittsburgh, Toronto, Detroit
— Scott Stevens, Washington, St. Louis, New Jersey
— Steve Yzerman, Detroit

MOST CONSECUTIVE YEARS IN PLAYOFFS:
20 — Larry Robinson, Montreal, Los Angeles (1973-92, inclusive)
19 — Brett Hull, Calgary, St. Louis, Dallas, Detroit (1986-2004, inclusive).
18 — Larry Murphy, Los Angeles, Washington, Minnesota, Pittsburgh, Toronto, Detroit (1984-2001, inclusive).
— Nicklas Lidstrom, Detroit (1992-2004 inclusive; 2006-2010 inclusive)
17 — Brad Park, NY Rangers, Boston, Detroit (1969-85, inclusive).
— Raymond Bourque, Boston (1980-96, inclusive).

MOST PLAYOFF GAMES:
266 — Chris Chelios, Montreal, Chicago, Detroit
247 — Patrick Roy, Montreal, Colorado
— Nicklas Lidstrom, Detroit
236 — Mark Messier, Edmonton, NY Rangers
234 — Claude Lemieux, Montreal, New Jersey, Colorado, Phoenix, Dallas, San Jose

GOALS

MOST GOALS IN PLAYOFFS, CAREER:
122 — Wayne Gretzky, Edmonton, Los Angeles, St. Louis, NY Rangers
109 — Mark Messier, Edmonton, NY Rangers
106 — Jari Kurri, Edmonton, Los Angeles, NY Rangers, Anaheim
103 — Brett Hull, Calgary, St. Louis, Dallas, Detroit
93 — Glenn Anderson, Edmonton, Toronto, NY Rangers, St. Louis

MOST GOALS, ONE PLAYOFF YEAR:
19 — Reggie Leach, Philadelphia, 1976. 16 games.
— Jari Kurri, Edmonton, 1985. 18 games.
18 — Joe Sakic, Colorado, 1996. 22 games.
17 — Newsy Lalonde, Montreal, 1919. 10 games.
— Mike Bossy, NY Islanders, 1981. 18 games.
— Steve Payne, Minnesota, 1981. 19 games.
— Mike Bossy, NY Islanders, 1982. 19 games.
— Mike Bossy, NY Islanders, 1983. 19 games.
— Wayne Gretzky, Edmonton, 1985. 18 games.
— Kevin Stevens, Pittsburgh, 1991. 24 games.

MOST GOALS IN ONE SERIES (OTHER THAN FINAL):
12 — Jari Kurri, Edmonton, in 1985 CF, 6 games vs. Chicago.
11 — Newsy Lalonde, Montreal, in 1919 NHL F, 5 games vs. Ottawa.
10 — Tim Kerr, Philadelphia, in 1989 DF, 7 games vs. Pittsburgh.
9 — Reggie Leach, Philadelphia, in 1976 SF, 5 games vs. Boston.
— Bill Barber, Philadelphia, in 1980 SF, 5 games vs. Minnesota.
— Mike Bossy, NY Islanders, in 1983 CF, 6 games vs. Boston.
— Mario Lemieux, Pittsburgh, in 1989 DF, 7 games vs. Philadelphia.
— John Druce, Washington, in 1990 DF, 5 games vs. NY Rangers.
— Johan Franzen, Detroit, in 2008 CSF, 4 games vs. Colorado.

MOST GOALS IN FINAL SERIES (NHL PLAYERS ONLY):
9 — Babe Dye, Toronto, in 1922, 5 games vs. Van. Millionaires.
8 — Alf Skinner, Toronto, in 1918, 5 games vs. Van. Millionaires.
7 — Jean Beliveau, Montreal, in 1956, 5 games vs. Detroit.
— Mike Bossy, NY Islanders, in 1982, 4 games vs. Vancouver.
— Wayne Gretzky, Edmonton, in 1985, 5 games vs. Philadelphia.

MOST GOALS, ONE GAME:
5 — Newsy Lalonde, Montreal, March 1, 1919, at Montreal. Final score: Montreal 6, Ottawa 3.
— Maurice Richard, Montreal, March 23, 1944, at Montreal. Final score: Montreal 5, Toronto 1.
— Darryl Sittler, Toronto, April 22, 1976, at Toronto. Final score: Toronto 8, Philadelphia 5.
— Reggie Leach, Philadelphia, May 6, 1976, at Philadelphia. Final score: Philadelphia 6, Boston 3.
— Mario Lemieux, Pittsburgh, April 25, 1989, at Pittsburgh. Final score: Pittsburgh 10, Philadelphia 7.

MOST GOALS, ONE PERIOD:
4 — Tim Kerr, Philadelphia, April 13, 1985, at NY Rangers, second period. Final score: Philadelphia 6, NY Rangers 5.
— Mario Lemieux, Pittsburgh, April 25, 1989, at Pittsburgh vs. Philadelphia, first period. Final score: Pittsburgh 10, Philadelphia 7.

ASSISTS

MOST ASSISTS IN PLAYOFFS, CAREER:
260 — Wayne Gretzky, Edmonton, Los Angeles, St. Louis, NY Rangers
186 — Mark Messier, Edmonton, NY Rangers
139 — Raymond Bourque, Boston, Colorado
137 — Paul Coffey, Edmonton, Pittsburgh, Los Angeles, Detroit, Philadelphia, Carolina
128 — Doug Gilmour, St. Louis, Calgary, Toronto, New Jersey, Buffalo, Montreal

MOST ASSISTS, ONE PLAYOFF YEAR:
31 — Wayne Gretzky, Edmonton, 1988. 19 games.
30 — Wayne Gretzky, Edmonton, 1985. 18 games.
29 — Wayne Gretzky, Edmonton, 1987. 21 games.
28 — Mario Lemieux, Pittsburgh, 1991. 23 games.
26 — Wayne Gretzky, Edmonton, 1983. 16 games.

MOST ASSISTS IN ONE SERIES (OTHER THAN FINAL):
14 — Rick Middleton, Boston, in 1983 DF, 7 games vs. Buffalo.
— Wayne Gretzky, Edmonton, in 1985 CF, 6 games vs. Chicago.
13 — Wayne Gretzky, Edmonton, in 1987 DSF, 5 games vs. Los Angeles.
— Doug Gilmour, Toronto, in 1994 CSF, 7 games vs. San Jose.
11 — Al MacInnis, Calgary, in 1984 DF, 7 games vs. Edmonton.
— Mark Messier, Edmonton, in 1989 DSF, 7 games vs. Los Angeles.
— Mike Ridley, Washington, in 1992 DSF, 7 games vs. Pittsburgh.
— Ron Francis, Pittsburgh, in 1995 CQF, 7 games vs. Washington.
10 — Fleming Mackell, Boston, in 1958 SF, 6 games vs. NY Rangers.
— Stan Mikita, Chicago, in 1962 SF, 6 games vs. Montreal.
— Bob Bourne, NY Islanders, in 1983 DF, 6 games vs. NY Rangers.
— Wayne Gretzky, Edmonton, in 1988 DSF, 5 games vs. Winnipeg.
— Mario Lemieux, Pittsburgh, in 1992 DSF, 6 games vs. Washington.

MOST ASSISTS IN FINAL SERIES:
10 — Wayne Gretzky, Edmonton, in 1988, 4 games plus suspended game vs. Boston.
9 — Jacques Lemaire, Montreal, in 1973, 6 games vs. Chicago.
— Wayne Gretzky, Edmonton, in 1987, 7 games vs. Philadelphia.
— Larry Murphy, Pittsburgh, in 1991, 6 games vs. Minnesota.
— Danny Briere, Philadelphia, in 2010, 6 games vs. Chicago.

MOST ASSISTS, ONE GAME:
6 — Mikko Leinonen, NY Rangers, April 8, 1982, at NY Rangers. Final score: NY Rangers 7, Philadelphia 3.
— Wayne Gretzky, Edmonton, April 9, 1987, at Edmonton. Final score: Edmonton 13, Los Angeles 3.
5 — Toe Blake, Montreal, March 23, 1944, at Montreal. Final score: Montreal 5, Toronto 1.
— Maurice Richard, Montreal, March 27, 1956, at Montreal. Final score: Montreal 7, NY Rangers 0.
— Bert Olmstead, Montreal, March 30, 1957, at Montreal. Final score: Montreal 8, NY Rangers 3.
— Don McKenney, Boston, April 5, 1958, at Boston. Final score: Boston 8, NY Rangers 2.
— Stan Mikita, Chicago, April 4, 1973, at Chicago. Final score: Chicago 7, St. Louis 1.
— Wayne Gretzky, Edmonton, April 8, 1981, at Montreal. Final score: Edmonton 6, Montreal 3.
— Paul Coffey, Edmonton, May 14, 1985, at Edmonton. Final score: Edmonton 10, Chicago 5.
— Doug Gilmour, St. Louis, April 15, 1986, at Minnesota. Final score: St. Louis 6, Minnesota 3.
— Risto Siltanen, Quebec, April 14, 1987, at Hartford. Final score: Quebec 7, Hartford 5.
— Patrik Sundstrom, New Jersey, April 22, 1988, at New Jersey. Final score: New Jersey 10, Washington 4.
— Geoff Courtnall, St. Louis, April 23, 1998, at St. Louis. Final score: St. Louis 8, Los Angeles 3.

MOST ASSISTS, ONE PERIOD:
3 — Three assists by one player in one period of a playoff game has been recorded on 82 occasions. Daniel Sedin of the Vancouver Canucks is the most recent to equal this mark with 3 assists in the third period at Los Angeles, April 21, 2010. Final score: Vancouver 6, Los Angeles 4.
— Wayne Gretzky has had 3 assists in one period 5 times; Raymond Bourque, 3 times; Toe Blake, Jean Beliveau, Doug Harvey and Bobby Orr, twice each. Joe Primeau of Toronto was the first player to be credited with 3 assists in one period of a playoff game; third period at Boston vs. NY Rangers, April 7, 1932. Final score: Toronto 6, NY Rangers 2.

POINTS

MOST POINTS IN PLAYOFFS, CAREER:
382 — Wayne Gretzky, Edmonton, Los Angeles, St. Louis, NY Rangers, 122G, 260A
295 — Mark Messier, Edmonton, NY Rangers, 109G, 186A
233 — Jari Kurri, Edmonton, Los Angeles, NY Rangers, Anaheim, 106G, 127A
214 — Glenn Anderson, Edmonton, Toronto, NY Rangers, St. Louis, 93G, 121A
196 — Paul Coffey, Edmonton, Pittsburgh, Los Angeles, Detroit, Philadelphia, Carolina, 59G, 137A

MOST POINTS, ONE PLAYOFF YEAR:
47 — Wayne Gretzky, Edmonton, in 1985. 17 goals, 30 assists in 18 games.
44 — Mario Lemieux, Pittsburgh, in 1991. 16 goals, 28 assists in 23 games.
43 — Wayne Gretzky, Edmonton, in 1988. 12 goals, 31 assists in 19 games.
40 — Wayne Gretzky, Los Angeles, in 1993. 15 goals, 25 assists in 24 games.
38 — Wayne Gretzky, Edmonton, in 1983. 12 goals, 26 assists in 16 games.

MOST POINTS IN ONE SERIES (OTHER THAN FINAL):
19 — Rick Middleton, Boston, in 1983 DF, 7 games vs. Buffalo. 5 goals, 14 assists.
18 — Wayne Gretzky, Edmonton, in 1985 CF, 6 games vs. Chicago. 4 goals, 14 assists.
17 — Mario Lemieux, Pittsburgh, in 1992 DSF, 6 games vs. Washington. 7 goals, 10 assists.
16 — Barry Pederson, Boston, in 1983 DF, 7 games vs. Buffalo. 7 goals, 9 assists.
— Doug Gilmour, Toronto, in 1994 CSF, 7 games vs. San Jose. 3 goals, 13 assists.
15 — Jari Kurri, Edmonton, in 1985 CF, 6 games vs. Chicago. 12 goals, 3 assists.
— Wayne Gretzky, Edmonton, in 1987 DSF, 5 games vs. Los Angeles. 2 goals, 13 assists.
— Tim Kerr, Philadelphia, in 1989 DF, 7 games vs. Pittsburgh. 10 goals, 5 assists.
— Mario Lemieux, Pittsburgh, in 1991 CF, 6 games vs. Boston. 6 goals, 9 assists.

MOST POINTS IN FINAL SERIES:
13 — Wayne Gretzky, Edmonton, in 1988, 4 games plus suspended game vs. Boston. 3 goals, 10 assists.
12 — Gordie Howe, Detroit, in 1955, 7 games vs. Montreal. 5 goals, 7 assists.
— Yvan Cournoyer, Montreal, in 1973, 6 games vs. Chicago. 6 goals, 6 assists.
— Jacques Lemaire, Montreal, in 1973, 6 games vs. Chicago. 3 goals, 9 assists.
— Mario Lemieux, Pittsburgh, in 1991, 5 games vs. Minnesota. 5 goals, 7 assists.
— Danny Briere, Philadelphia, in 2010, 6 games vs. Chicago. 3 goals, 9 assists.

MOST POINTS, ONE GAME:
8 — Patrik Sundstrom, New Jersey, April 22, 1988, at New Jersey in 10-4 win over Washington. Sundstrom had 3 goals, 5 assists.
— **Mario Lemieux, Pittsburgh,** April 25, 1989, at Pittsburgh in 10-7 win over Philadelphia. Lemieux had 5 goals, 3 assists.
7 — Wayne Gretzky, Edmonton, April 17, 1983, at Calgary in 10-2 win. Gretzky had 4 goals, 3 assists.
— Wayne Gretzky, Edmonton, April 25,1985, at Winnipeg in 8-3 win. Gretzky had 3 goals, 4 assists.
— Wayne Gretzky, Edmonton, April 9, 1987, at Edmonton in 13-3 win over Los Angeles. Gretzky had 1 goal, 6 assists.
6 — Dickie Moore, Montreal, March 25, 1954, at Montreal in 8-1 win over Boston. Moore had 2 goals, 4 assists.
— Phil Esposito, Boston, April 2, 1969, at Boston in 10-0 win over Toronto. Esposito had 4 goals, 2 assists.
— Darryl Sittler, Toronto, April 22, 1976, at Toronto in 8-5 win over Philadelphia. Sittler had 5 goals, 1 assist.
— Guy Lafleur, Montreal, April 11, 1977, at Montreal in 7-2 win over St. Louis. Lafleur had 3 goals, 3 assists.
— Mikko Leinonen, NY Rangers, April 8, 1982, at NY Rangers in 7-3 win over Philadelphia. Leinonen had 6 assists.
— Paul Coffey, Edmonton, May 14, 1985, at Edmonton in 10-5 win over Chicago. Coffey had 1 goal, 5 assists.
— John Anderson, Hartford, April 12, 1986, at Hartford in 9-4 win over Quebec. Anderson had 2 goals, 4 assists.
— Mario Lemieux, Pittsburgh, April 23, 1992, at Pittsburgh in 6-4 win over Washington. Lemieux had 3 goals, 3 assists.
— Geoff Courtnall, St. Louis, April 23, 1998, at St. Louis in 8-3 win over Los Angeles. Courtnall had 1 goal, 5 assists.
— Johan Franzen, Detroit, May 6, 2010, at Detroit in 7-1 win over San Jose. Franzen had 4 goals, 2 assists.

MOST POINTS, ONE PERIOD:
4 — Maurice Richard, Montreal, March 29, 1945, at Montreal, third period, in 10-3 win vs. Toronto. 3 goals, 1 assist.
— **Dickie Moore,** Montreal, March 25, 1954, at Montreal, first period, in 8-1 win vs. Boston. 2 goals, 2 assists.
— **Barry Pederson,** Boston, April 8, 1982, at Boston, second period, in 7-3 win vs. Buffalo. 3 goals, 1 assist.
— **Peter McNab,** Boston, April 11, 1982, at Buffalo, second period, in 5-2 win vs. Buffalo. 1 goal, 3 assists.
— **Tim Kerr,** Philadelphia, April 13, 1985, at NY Rangers, second period, in 6-5 win vs. NY Rangers. 4 goals.
— **Ken Linseman,** Boston, April 14, 1985, at Boston, second period, in 7-6 win vs. Montreal. 2 goals, 2 assists.
— **Wayne Gretzky,** Edmonton, April 12, 1987, at Los Angeles, third period, in 6-3 win vs. Los Angeles. 1 goal, 3 assists.
— **Glenn Anderson,** Edmonton, April 6, 1988, at Edmonton, third period, in 7-4 win vs. Winnipeg. 3 goals, 1 assist.
— **Mario Lemieux,** Pittsburgh, April 25, 1989, at Pittsburgh, first period, in 10-7 win vs. Philadelphia. 4 goals.
— **Dave Gagner,** Minnesota North Stars, April 8, 1991, at Minnesota, first period, in 6-5 loss vs. Chicago. 2 goals, 2 assists.
— **Mario Lemieux,** Pittsburgh, April 23, 1992, at Pittsburgh, second period, in 6-4 win vs. Washington. 2 goals, 2 assists.
— **Alexander Mogilny,** New Jersey, April 28, 2001, at New Jersey, second period, in 6-5 win vs. Toronto. 1 goal, 3 assists.
— **Brad Richards,** Dallas, April 27, 2008, at San Jose, third period, in 5-2 win vs. San Jose. 1 goal, 3 assists.
— **Johan Franzen,** Detroit, May 6, 2010, at Detroit, first period, in 7-1 win over San Jose. 3 goals, 1 assist.

POWER-PLAY GOALS

MOST POWER-PLAY GOALS IN PLAYOFFS, CAREER:
38 — Brett Hull, St. Louis, Dallas, Detroit
35 — Mike Bossy, NY Islanders
34 — Dino Ciccarelli, Minnesota, Washington, Detroit
— Wayne Gretzky, Edmonton, Los Angeles, St. Louis, NY Rangers
29 — Mario Lemieux, Pittsburgh

MOST POWER-PLAY GOALS, ONE PLAYOFF YEAR:
9 — Mike Bossy, NY Islanders, 1981. 18 games vs. Toronto, Edmonton, NY Rangers and Minnesota.
— **Cam Neely, Boston,** 1991. 19 games vs. Hartford, Montreal and Pittsburgh.
8 — Tim Kerr, Philadelphia, 1989. 19 games.
— John Druce, Washington, 1990. 15 games.
— Brian Propp, Minnesota, 1991. 23 games.
— Mario Lemieux, Pittsburgh, 1992. 15 games.

MOST POWER-PLAY GOALS, ONE PLAYOFF SERIES:
6 — Chris Kontos, Los Angeles, 1989 DSF vs. Edmonton, won by Los Angeles 4-3.
5 — Andy Bathgate, Detroit, 1966 SF vs. Chicago, won by Detroit 4-2.
— Denis Potvin, NY Islanders, 1981 QF vs. Edmonton, won by NY Islanders 4-2.
— Ken Houston, Calgary, 1981 QF vs. Philadelphia, won by Calgary 4-3.
— Rick Vaive, Chicago, 1988 DSF vs. St. Louis, won by St. Louis 4-1.
— Tim Kerr, Philadelphia, 1989 DF vs. Pittsburgh, won by Philadelphia 4-3.
— Mario Lemieux, Pittsburgh, 1989 DF vs. Philadelphia, won by Philadelphia 4-3.
— John Druce, Washington, 1990 DF vs. NY Rangers, won by Washington 4-1.
— Pat LaFontaine, Buffalo, 1992 DSF vs. Boston, won by Boston 4-3.
— Adam Graves, NY Rangers, 1996 CQF vs Montreal, won by NY Rangers 4-2.

MOST POWER-PLAY GOALS, ONE GAME:
3 — Syd Howe, Detroit, March 23, 1939, at Detroit vs. Montreal. Detroit won 7-3.
— **Sid Smith, Toronto,** April 10, 1949, at Detroit. Toronto won 3-1.
— **Phil Esposito, Boston,** April 2, 1969, at Boston vs. Toronto. Boston won 10-0.
— **John Bucyk, Boston,** April 21, 1974, at Boston vs. Chicago. Boston won 8-6.
— **Denis Potvin, NY Islanders,** April 17, 1981, at NY Islanders vs. Edmonton. NY Islanders won 6-3.
— **Tim Kerr, Philadelphia,** April 13, 1985, at NY Rangers. Philadelphia won 6-5.
— **Jari Kurri, Edmonton,** April 9, 1987, at Edmonton vs. Los Angeles. Edmonton won 13-3.
— **Mark Johnson, New Jersey,** April 22, 1988, at New Jersey vs. Washington. New Jersey won 10-4.
— **Dino Ciccarelli, Detroit,** April 29, 1993, at Toronto. Detroit won 7-3.
— **Dino Ciccarelli, Detroit,** May 11, 1995, at Dallas. Detroit won 5-1.
— **Valeri Kamensky, Colorado,** April 24, 1997, at Colorado vs. Chicago. Colorado won 7-0.
— **Jonathan Toews, Chicago** May 7, 2010, at Vancouver. Chicago won 7-4.

MOST POWER-PLAY GOALS, ONE PERIOD:
3 — Tim Kerr, Philadelphia, April 13, 1985, at NY Rangers, second period in 6-5 win.
2 — Two power-play goals have been scored by one player in one period on 57 occasions. Charlie Conacher of Toronto was the first to score two power-play goals in one period, setting the mark with two power-play goals in the second period at Toronto vs. Boston, March 26, 1936. Final score: Toronto 8, Boston 3. Jonathan Toews of the Chicago Blackhawks is the most recent to equal this mark with two power-play goals in the second period at Vancouver, May 7, 2010. Final score: Chicago 7, Vancouver 4.

SHORTHAND GOALS

MOST SHORTHAND GOALS IN PLAYOFFS, CAREER:
14 — Mark Messier, Edmonton, NY Rangers
11 — Wayne Gretzky, Edmonton, Los Angeles, St. Louis
10 — Jari Kurri, Edmonton, Los Angeles, NY Rangers
8 — Ed Westfall, Boston, NY Islanders
— Hakan Loob, Calgary

MOST SHORTHAND GOALS, ONE PLAYOFF YEAR:
3 — Derek Sanderson, Boston, 1969. 1 vs. Toronto in QF, won by Boston 4-0; 2 vs. Montreal in SF, won by Montreal, 4-2.
— **Bill Barber, Philadelphia,** 1980. All vs. Minnesota in SF, won by Philadelphia 4-1.
— **Lorne Henning, NY Islanders,** 1980. 1 vs. Boston in QF, won by NY Islanders 4-1; 1 vs. Buffalo in SF, won by NY Islanders 4-2, 1 vs. Philadelphia in F, won by NY Islanders 4-2.
— **Wayne Gretzky, Edmonton,** 1983. 2 vs. Winnipeg in DSF, won by Edmonton 3-0; 1 vs. Calgary in DF, won by Edmonton 4-1.
— **Wayne Presley, Chicago,** 1989. All vs. Detroit in DSF, won by Chicago 4-2.
— **Todd Marchant, Edmonton,** 1997. 1 vs. Dallas in CQF, won by Edmonton 4-3; 2 vs. Colorado in CSF, won by Colorado 4-1.

Dave Bolland had only six goals in 39 games in 2009-10, but then scored eight times in 22 postseason games. He was the only player in the NHL to score two shorthand goals during the playoffs, including one against Philadelphia in the first game of the Stanley Cup Finals.

MOST SHORTHAND GOALS, ONE PLAYOFF SERIES:
3 — Bill Barber, Philadelphia, 1980 SF vs. Minnesota, won by Philadelphia 4-1.
  — **Wayne Presley, Chicago,** 1989 DSF vs. Detroit, won by Chicago 4-2.
2 — Mac Colville, NY Rangers, 1940 SF vs. Boston, won by NY Rangers 4-2.
  — Jerry Toppazzini, Boston, 1958 SF vs. NY Rangers, won by Boston 4-2.
  — Dave Keon, Toronto, 1963 F vs. Detroit, won by Toronto 4-1.
  — Bob Pulford, Toronto, 1964 F vs. Detroit, won by Toronto 4-3.
  — Serge Savard, Montreal, 1968 F vs. St. Louis, won by Montreal 4-0.
  — Derek Sanderson, Boston, 1969 SF vs. Montreal, won by Montreal 4-2.
  — Bryan Trottier, NY Islanders, 1980 PR vs. Los Angeles, won by NY Islanders 3-1.
  — Bobby Lalonde, Boston, 1981 PR vs. Minnesota, won by Minnesota 3-0.
  — Butch Goring, NY Islanders, 1981 SF vs. NY Rangers, won by NY Islanders 4-0.
  — Wayne Gretzky, Edmonton, 1983 DSF vs. Winnipeg, won by Edmonton 3-0.
  — Mark Messier, Edmonton, 1983 DF vs. Calgary, won by Edmonton 4-1.
  — Jari Kurri, Edmonton, 1983 CF vs. Chicago, won by Edmonton 4-0.
  — Wayne Gretzky, Edmonton, 1985 DF vs. Winnipeg, won by Edmonton 4-0.
  — Kevin Lowe, Edmonton, 1987 F vs. Philadelphia, won by Edmonton 4-3.
  — Bob Gould, Washington, 1988 DSF vs. Philadelphia, won by Washington 4-3.
  — Dave Poulin, Philadelphia, 1989 DF vs. Pittsburgh, won by Philadelphia 4-3.
  — Russ Courtnall, Montreal, 1991 DF vs. Boston, won by Boston 4-3.
  — Sergei Fedorov, Detroit, 1992 DSF vs. Minnesota, won by Detroit 4-3.
  — Mark Messier, NY Rangers, 1992 DSF vs. New Jersey, won by NY Rangers 4-3.
  — Tom Fitzgerald, NY Islanders, 1993 DF vs. Pittsburgh, won by NY Islanders 4-3.
  — Mark Osborne, Toronto, 1994 CSF vs. San Jose, won by Toronto 4-3.
  — Tony Amonte, Chicago, 1997 CQF vs. Colorado, won by Colorado 4-2.
  — Brian Rolston, New Jersey, 1997 CQF vs. Montreal, won by New Jersey 4-1.
  — Rod Brind'Amour, Philadelphia, 1997 CQF vs. Pittsburgh, won by Philadelphia 4-1.
  — Todd Marchant, Edmonton, 1997 CSF vs. Colorado, won by Colorado 4-1.
  — Jeremy Roenick, Phoenix, 1998 CQF vs. Detroit, won by Detroit 4-2.
  — Vincent Damphousse, San Jose, 1999 CQF vs. Colorado, won by Colorado 4-2.
  — Dixon Ward, Buffalo, 1999 CF vs. Toronto, won by Buffalo 4-1.
  — Curtis Brown, Buffalo, 2001 CSF vs. Pittsburgh, won by Pittsburgh 4-3.
  — John Madden, New Jersey, 2006 CQF vs. NY Rangers, won by New Jersey 4-0.

MOST SHORTHAND GOALS, ONE GAME:
2 — Dave Keon, Toronto, April 18, 1963, at Toronto, in 3-1 win vs. Detroit.
  — **Bryan Trottier, NY Islanders,** April 8, 1980, at NY Islanders, in 8-1 win vs. Los Angeles.
  — **Bobby Lalonde, Boston,** April 11, 1981, at Minnesota, in 6-3 loss vs. Minnesota.
  — **Wayne Gretzky, Edmonton,** April 6, 1983, at Edmonton, in 6-3 win vs. Winnipeg.
  — **Jari Kurri, Edmonton,** April 24, 1983, at Edmonton, in 8-3 win vs. Chicago.
  — **Wayne Gretzky, Edmonton,** April 25, 1985, at Winnipeg, in 8-3 win by Edmonton.
  — **Mark Messier, NY Rangers,** April 21, 1992, at NY Rangers, in 7-3 loss vs. New Jersey.
  — **Tom Fitzgerald, NY Islanders,** May 8, 1993, at NY Islanders, in 6-5 win vs. Pittsburgh.
  — **Rod Brind'Amour, Philadelphia,** April 26, 1997, at Philadelphia, in 6-3 win vs. Pittsburgh.
  — **Jeremy Roenick, Phoenix,** April 24, 1998, at Detroit, in 7-4 win by Phoenix.
  — **Vincent Damphousse, San Jose,** April 30, 1999, at Colorado, in 7-3 win by San Jose.
  — **John Madden, New Jersey,** April 24, 2006, at New Jersey, in 4-1 win vs. NY Rangers.

MOST SHORTHAND GOALS, ONE PERIOD:
2 — Bryan Trottier, NY Islanders, April 8, 1980, second period, at NY Islanders, in 8-1 win vs. Los Angeles.
  — **Bobby Lalonde, Boston,** April 11, 1981, third period, at Minnesota, in 6-3 loss vs. Minnesota.
  — **Jari Kurri, Edmonton,** April 24, 1983, third period, at Edmonton, in 8-4 win vs. Chicago.
  — **Rod Brind'Amour, Philadelphia,** April 26, 1997, first period, at Philadelphia, in 6-3 win vs. Pittsburgh.
  — **Jeremy Roenick, Phoenix,** April 24, 1998, second period, at Detroit, in 7-4 win by Phoenix.
  — **Vincent Damphousse, San Jose,** April 30, 1999, third period, at Colorado, in 7-3 win vs. Colorado.

GAME-WINNING GOALS

MOST GAME-WINNING GOALS IN PLAYOFFS, CAREER:
24 — Wayne Gretzky, Edmonton, Los Angeles, St. Louis, NY Rangers
  — **Brett Hull, St. Louis, Dallas, Detroit**
19 — Claude Lemieux, Montreal, New Jersey, Colorado
  — Joe Sakic, Colorado
18 — Maurice Richard, Montreal

MOST GAME-WINNING GOALS, ONE PLAYOFF YEAR:
7 — Brad Richards, Tampa Bay, 2004. 23 games.
6 — Joe Sakic, Colorado, 1996. 22 games.
  — Joe Nieuwendyk, Dallas, 1999. 23 games.
5 — Mike Bossy, NY Islanders, 1983. 19 games.
  — Jari Kurri, Edmonton, 1987. 21 games.
  — Bobby Smith, Minnesota, 1991. 23 games.
  — Mario Lemieux, Pittsburgh, 1992. 15 games.
  — Fernando Pisani, Edmonton, 2006. 24 games.
  — Johan Franzen, Detroit, 2008. 16 games.
  — Dustin Byfuglien, Chicago, 2010. 22 games.

MOST GAME-WINNING GOALS, ONE PLAYOFF SERIES:
4 — Mike Bossy, NY Islanders, 1983 CF vs. Boston, won by NY Islanders 4-2.

OVERTIME GOALS

MOST OVERTIME GOALS IN PLAYOFFS, CAREER:
8 — Joe Sakic, Colorado (2 in 1996; 1 in 1998; 1 in 2001; 2 in 2004; 1 in 2006; 1 in 2008)
6 — Maurice Richard, Montreal
5 — Glenn Anderson, Edmonton, Toronto, St. Louis
4 — Bob Nystrom, NY Islanders
  — Dale Hunter, Quebec, Washington
  — Wayne Gretzky, Edmonton, Los Angeles
  — Stephane Richer, Montreal, New Jersey
  — Joe Murphy, Edmonton, Chicago
  — Esa Tikkanen, Edmonton, NY Rangers
  — Jaromir Jagr, Pittsburgh
  — Kirk Muller, Montreal, Dallas
  — Jeremy Roenick, Chicago, Philadelphia
  — Chris Drury, Colorado, Buffalo
  — Jamie Langenbrunner, Dallas, New Jersey

MOST OVERTIME GOALS, ONE PLAYOFF YEAR:
3 — Mel Hill, Boston, 1939. All vs. NY Rangers in best-of-seven SF, won by Boston 4-3.
  — **Maurice Richard, Montreal,** 1951. 2 vs. Detroit in best-of-seven SF, won by Montreal 4-2; 1 vs. Toronto best-of-seven F, won by Toronto 4-1.

MOST OVERTIME GOALS, ONE PLAYOFF SERIES:
3 — Mel Hill, Boston, 1939, SF vs. NY Rangers, won by Boston 4-3. Hill scored at 59:25 of overtime March 21 for a 2-1 win; at 8:24 of overtime, March 23 for a 3-2 win; and at 48:00 of overtime, April 2 for a 2-1 win.

SCORING BY A DEFENSEMAN

MOST GOALS BY A DEFENSEMAN, ONE PLAYOFF YEAR:
12 — Paul Coffey, Edmonton, 1985. 18 games.
11 — Brian Leetch, NY Rangers, 1994. 23 games.
9 — Bobby Orr, Boston, 1970. 14 games.
  — Brad Park, Boston, 1978. 15 games.
8 — Denis Potvin, NY Islanders, 1981. 18 games.
  — Raymond Bourque, Boston, 1983. 17 games.
  — Denis Potvin, NY Islanders, 1983. 20 games.
  — Paul Coffey, Edmonton, 1984. 19 games.

MOST GOALS BY A DEFENSEMAN, ONE GAME:
3 — Bobby Orr, Boston, April 11, 1971, at Montreal. Final score: Boston 5, Montreal 2.
  — **Dick Redmond, Chicago,** April 4, 1973, at Chicago. Final score: Chicago 7, St. Louis 1.
  — **Denis Potvin, NY Islanders,** April 17, 1981, at NY Islanders. Final score: NY Islanders 6, Edmonton 3.
  — **Paul Reinhart, Calgary,** April 14, 1983, at Edmonton. Final score: Edmonton 6, Calgary 3.
  — **Doug Halward, Vancouver,** April 7, 1984, at Vancouver. Final score: Vancouver 7, Calgary 0.
  — **Paul Reinhart, Calgary,** April 8, 1984, at Vancouver. Final score: Calgary 5, Vancouver 1.
  — **Al Iafrate, Washington,** April 26, 1993, at Washington. Final score: Washington 6, NY Islanders 4.
  — **Eric Desjardins, Montreal,** June 3, 1993, at Montreal. Final score: Montreal 3, Los Angeles 2.
  — **Gary Suter, Chicago,** April 24, 1994, at Chicago. Final score: Chicago 4, Toronto 3.
  — **Brian Leetch, NY Rangers,** May 22, 1995, at Philadelphia. Final score: Philadelphia 4, NY Rangers 3.
  — **Andy Delmore, Philadelphia,** May 7, 2000, at Philadelphia. Final score: Philadelphia 6, Pittsburgh 3.

MOST ASSISTS BY A DEFENSEMAN, ONE PLAYOFF YEAR:
25 — Paul Coffey, Edmonton, 1985. 18 games.
24 — Al MacInnis, Calgary, 1989. 22 games.
23 — Brian Leetch, NY Rangers, 1994. 23 games.
19 — Bobby Orr, Boston, 1972. 15 games.
18 — Raymond Bourque, Boston, 1988. 23 games.
  — Raymond Bourque, Boston, 1991. 19 games.
  — Larry Murphy, Pittsburgh, 1991. 23 games.
  — Chris Pronger, Philadelphia, 2010. 23 games.

MOST ASSISTS BY A DEFENSEMAN, ONE GAME:
5 — Paul Coffey, Edmonton, May 14, 1985, at Edmonton vs. Chicago. Edmonton won 10-5.
  — **Risto Siltanen, Quebec,** April 14, 1987, at Hartford. Quebec won 7-5.

MOST POINTS BY A DEFENSEMAN, ONE PLAYOFF YEAR:
37 — Paul Coffey, Edmonton, 1985. 12 goals, 25 assists in 18 games.
34 — Brian Leetch, NY Rangers, 1994. 11 goals, 23 assists in 23 games.
31 — Al MacInnis, Calgary, 1989. 7 goals, 24 assists in 22 games.
25 — Denis Potvin, NY Islanders, 1981. 8 goals, 17 assists in 18 games.
  — Raymond Bourque, Boston, 1991. 7 goals, 18 assists in 19 games.

MOST POINTS BY A DEFENSEMAN, ONE GAME:
6 — Paul Coffey, Edmonton, May 14, 1985, at Edmonton vs. Chicago. 1 goal, 5 assists. Edmonton won 10-5.
5 — Eddie Bush, Detroit, April 9, 1942, at Detroit vs. Toronto. 1 goal, 4 assists. Detroit won 5-2.
  — Bob Dailey, Philadelphia, May 1, 1980, at Philadelphia vs. Minnesota. 1 goal, 4 assists. Philadelphia won 7-0.
  — Denis Potvin, NY Islanders, April 17, 1981, at NY Islanders vs. Edmonton. 3 goals, 2 assists. NY Islanders won 6-3.
  — Risto Siltanen, Quebec, April 14, 1987, at Hartford. 5 assists. Quebec won 7-5.

SCORING BY A ROOKIE

MOST GOALS BY A ROOKIE, ONE PLAYOFF YEAR:
14 — Dino Ciccarelli, Minnesota, 1981. 19 games.
11 — Jeremy Roenick, Chicago, 1990. 20 games.
10 — Claude Lemieux, Montreal, 1986. 20 games.
9 — Pat Flatley, NY Islanders, 1984. 21 games.
8 — Steve Christoff, Minnesota, 1981. 19 games.
  — Brad Palmer, Minnesota, 1981. 19 games.
  — Mike Krushelnyski, Boston, 1983. 17 games.
  — Bob Joyce, Boston, 1988. 23 games.

MOST ASSISTS BY A ROOKIE, ONE PLAYOFF YEAR:
14 — Ville Leino, Philadelphia, 2010. 19 games.
13 — Don Maloney, NY Rangers, 1979. 18 games.

MOST POINTS BY A ROOKIE, ONE PLAYOFF YEAR:
21 — Dino Ciccarelli, Minnesota, 1981. 14 goals, 7 assists in 19 games.
  — Ville Leino, Philadelphia, 2010. 7 goals, 14 assists in 19 games.
20 — Don Maloney, NY Rangers, 1979. 7 goals, 13 assists in 18 games.

THREE-OR-MORE-GOAL GAMES

MOST THREE-OR-MORE-GOAL GAMES IN PLAYOFFS, CAREER:
10 — Wayne Gretzky, Edmonton, Los Angeles, NY Rangers. Eight three-goal games; two four-goal games.
7 — Maurice Richard, Montreal. Four three-goal games; two four-goal games; one five-goal game.
  — Jari Kurri, Edmonton. Six three-goal games; one four-goal game.
6 — Dino Ciccarelli, Minnesota, Washington, Detroit. Five three-goal games; one four-goal game.
5 — Mike Bossy, NY Islanders. Four three-goal games; one four-goal game.

MOST THREE-OR-MORE-GOAL GAMES, ONE PLAYOFF YEAR:
4 — Jari Kurri, Edmonton, 1985. 1 four-goal game, 3 three-goal games.
3 — Mark Messier, Edmonton, 1983. 3 three-goal games.
  — Mike Bossy, NY Islanders, 1983. 1 four-goal game, 2 three-goal games
2 — Newsy Lalonde, Montreal, 1919. 1 five-goal game, 1 four-goal game.
  — Maurice Richard, Montreal, 1944. 1 five-goal game; 1 three-goal game.
  — Doug Bentley, Chicago, 1944. 2 three-goal games.
  — Norm Ullman, Detroit, 1964. 2 three-goal games.
  — Phil Esposito, Boston, 1970. 2 three-goal games.
  — Pit Martin, Chicago, 1973. 2 three-goal games.
  — Rick MacLeish, Philadelphia, 1975. 2 three-goal games.
  — Lanny McDonald, Toronto, 1977. 1 four-goal game; 1 three-goal game.
  — Wayne Gretzky, Edmonton, 1981. 2 three-goal games.
  — Wayne Gretzky, Edmonton, 1983. 2 four-goal games.
  — Wayne Gretzky, Edmonton, 1985. 2 three-goal games.
  — Petr Klima, Detroit, 1988. 2 three-goal games.
  — Cam Neely, Boston, 1991. 2 three-goal games.
  — Wayne Gretzky, NY Rangers, 1997. 2 three-goal games.
  — Daniel Alfredsson, Ottawa, 1998. 2 three-goal games.
  — Patrick Marleau, San Jose, 2004. 2 three-goal games.
  — Johan Franzen, Detroit, 2008. 2 three-goal games.

MOST THREE-OR-MORE-GOAL GAMES, ONE PLAYOFF SERIES:
3 — Jari Kurri, Edmonton, 1985 CF vs. Chicago, won by Edmonton 4-2. Kurri scored 3 goals May 7 at Edmonton in 7-3 win, 3 goals May 14 at Edmonton in 10-5 win and 4 goals May 16 at Chicago in 8-2 win.
2 — Doug Bentley, Chicago, 1944 SF vs. Detroit, won by Chicago 4-1. Bentley scored 3 goals March 28 at Chicago in 7-1 win and 3 goals March 30 at Detroit in 5-2 win.
  — Norm Ullman, Detroit, 1964 SF vs. Chicago, won by Detroit 4-3. Ullman scored 3 goals March 29 at Chicago in 5-4 win and 3 goals April 7 at Detroit in 7-2 win.
  — Mark Messier, Edmonton, 1983 DF vs. Calgary, won by Edmonton 4-1. Messier scored 4 goals April 14 at Edmonton in 6-3 win and 3 goals April 17 at Calgary in 10-2 win.
  — Mike Bossy, NY Islanders, 1983 CF vs. Boston, won by NY Islanders 4-2. Bossy scored 3 goals May 3 at NY Islanders in 8-3 win and 4 goals May 7 at New York in 8-4 win.
  — Johan Franzen, Detroit, 2008 CSF vs. Colorado, won by Detroit 4-0. Franzen scored 3 goals Apr. 26 at Detroit in 5-1 win and 3 goals May 1 at Colorado in 8-2 win.

SCORING STREAKS

LONGEST CONSECUTIVE GOAL-SCORING STREAK, ONE PLAYOFF YEAR:
10 Games — Reggie Leach, Philadelphia, 1976. Streak started April 17 at Toronto and ended May 9 at Montreal. He scored one goal in each of eight games; two in one game; and five in another; a total of 15 goals.

LONGEST CONSECUTIVE POINT-SCORING STREAK, ONE PLAYOFF YEAR:
18 games — Bryan Trottier, NY Islanders, 1981. 11 goals, 18 assists, 29 points.
17 games — Wayne Gretzky, Edmonton, 1988. 12 goals, 29 assists, 41 points.
  — Al MacInnis, Calgary, 1989. 7 goals, 19 assists, 26 points.

LONGEST CONSECUTIVE POINT-SCORING STREAK, MORE THAN ONE PLAYOFF YEAR:
27 games — Bryan Trottier, NY Islanders, 1980, 1981 and 1982. 7 games in 1980 (3 goals, 5 assists, 8 points), 18 games in 1981 (11 goals, 18 assists, 29 points), and two games in 1982 (2 goals, 3 assists, 5 points). Total points, 42.
19 games — Wayne Gretzky, Edmonton, Los Angeles, 1988 and 1989. 17 games in 1988 (12 goals, 29 assists, 41 points with Edmonton), 2 games in 1989 (1 goal, 2 assists, 3 points with Los Angeles). Total points, 44.
  — Al MacInnis, Calgary, 1989 and 1990. 17 games in 1989 (7 goals, 19 assists, 26 points), and two games in 1990 (2 goals, 1 assist, 3 points). Total points, 29.

FASTEST GOALS

FASTEST GOAL FROM START OF GAME:
0:06 — Don Kozak, Los Angeles, April 17, 1977, at Los Angeles vs. Boston and goaltender Gerry Cheevers. Los Angeles won 7-4.
0:07 — Bob Gainey, Montreal, May 5, 1977, at NY Islanders vs. goaltender Chico Resch. Montreal won 2-1.
  — Terry Murray, Philadelphia, April 12, 1981, at Quebec vs. goaltender Dan Bouchard. Quebec won 4-3 in overtime.

FASTEST GOAL FROM START OF PERIOD (OTHER THAN FIRST):
0:06 — Pelle Eklund, Philadelphia, April 25, 1989, at Pittsburgh vs. goaltender Tom Barrasso, second period. Pittsburgh won 10-7.
0:09 — Bill Collins, Minnesota, April 9, 1968, at Minnesota vs. Los Angeles and goaltender Wayne Rutledge, third period. Minnesota won 7-5.
  — Dave Balon, Minnesota, April 25, 1968, at St. Louis vs. goaltender Glenn Hall, third period. Minnesota won 5-1.
  — Murray Oliver, Minnesota, April 8, 1971, at St. Louis vs. goaltender Ernie Wakely, third period. St. Louis won 4-2.
  — Clark Gillies, NY Islanders, April 15, 1977, at Buffalo vs. goaltender Don Edwards, third period. NY Islanders won 4-3.
  — Eric Vail, Atlanta, April 11, 1978, at Atlanta vs. Detroit and goaltender Ron Low, third period. Detroit won 5-3.
  — Stan Smyl, Vancouver, April 10, 1979, at Philadelphia vs. goaltender Wayne Stephenson, third period. Vancouver won 3-2.
  — Wayne Gretzky, Edmonton, April 6, 1983, at Edmonton vs. Winnipeg and goaltender Brian Hayward, second period. Edmonton won 6-3.
  — Mark Messier, Edmonton, April 16, 1984, at Calgary vs. goaltender Don Edwards, third period. Edmonton won 5-3.
  — Brian Skrudland, Montreal, May 18, 1986, at Calgary vs. goaltender Mike Vernon, first overtime period. Montreal won 3-2.

FASTEST TWO GOALS:
0:05 — Norm Ullman, Detroit, April 11, 1965, at Detroit vs. Chicago and goaltender Glenn Hall. Ullman scored at 17:35 and 17:40 of second period. Detroit won 4-2.

FASTEST TWO GOALS FROM START OF A GAME:
1:08 — Dick Duff, Toronto, April 9, 1963, at Toronto vs. Detroit and goaltender Terry Sawchuk. Duff scored at 0:49 and 1:08. Toronto won 4-2.

FASTEST TWO GOALS FROM START OF A PERIOD:
0:35 — Pat LaFontaine, NY Islanders, May 19, 1984, at Edmonton vs. goaltender Andy Moog. LaFontaine scored at 0:13 and 0:35 of third period. Edmonton won 5-2.

PENALTIES

MOST PENALTY MINUTES IN PLAYOFFS, CAREER:
729 — Dale Hunter, Quebec, Washington, Colorado
541 — Chris Nilan, Montreal, NY Rangers, Boston
529 — Claude Lemieux, Montreal, New Jersey, Colorado, Phoenix, Dallas
471 — Rick Tocchet, Philadelphia, Pittsburgh, Boston, Phoenix
466 — Willi Plett, Atlanta, Calgary, Minnesota, Boston

MOST PENALTIES, ONE GAME:
8 — Forbes Kennedy, Toronto, April 2, 1969, at Boston. Kennedy was assessed 4 minors, 2 majors, 1 10-minute misconduct, 1 game misconduct. Boston won 10-0.
  — Kim Clackson, Pittsburgh, April 14, 1980, at Boston. Clackson was assessed 5 minors, 2 majors, 1 10-minute misconduct. Boston won 6-2.

MOST PENALTY MINUTES, ONE GAME:
42 — Dave Schultz, Philadelphia, April 22, 1976, at Toronto. Schultz was assessed 1 minor, 2 majors, 1 10-minute misconduct and 2 game-misconducts. Toronto won 8-5.

MOST PENALTIES, ONE PERIOD AND MOST PENALTY MINUTES, ONE PERIOD:
6 Penalties; 39 Minutes — Ed Hospodar, NY Rangers, April 9, 1981, at Los Angeles, first period. Hospodar was assessed 2 minors, 1 major, 1 10-minute misconduct, 2 game misconducts. Los Angeles won 5-4.

GOALTENDING

MOST PLAYOFF GAMES APPEARED IN BY A GOALTENDER, CAREER:
247 — Patrick Roy, Montreal, Colorado
181 — Martin Brodeur, New Jersey
161 — Ed Belfour, Chicago, Dallas, Toronto
150 — Grant Fuhr, Edmonton, Buffalo, St. Louis
138 — Mike Vernon, Calgary, Detroit, San Jose, Florida

MOST MINUTES PLAYED BY A GOALTENDER, CAREER:
15,209 — Patrick Roy, Montreal, Colorado
11,248 — Martin Brodeur, New Jersey
9,945 — Ed Belfour, Chicago, Dallas, Toronto
8,834 — Grant Fuhr, Edmonton, Buffalo, St. Louis
8,214 — Mike Vernon, Calgary, Detroit, San Jose, Florida

MOST MINUTES PLAYED BY A GOALTENDER, ONE PLAYOFF YEAR:
1,655 — Miikka Kiprusoff, Calgary, 2004. 26 games.
1,544 — Kirk McLean, Vancouver, 1994. 24 games.
  — Ed Belfour, Dallas, 1999. 23 games.
1,540 — Ron Hextall, Philadelphia, 1987. 26 games.
1,505 — Martin Brodeur, New Jersey, 2001. 25 games.

MOST SHUTOUTS IN PLAYOFFS, CAREER:
23 — Patrick Roy, Montreal, Colorado
  — **Martin Brodeur, New Jersey**
16 — Curtis Joseph, St. Louis, Edmonton, Toronto, Detroit

MOST SHUTOUTS, ONE PLAYOFF YEAR:
7 — **Martin Brodeur, New Jersey,** 2003. 24 games.
6 — Dominik Hasek, Detroit, 2002. 23 games.
5 — Jean-Sebastien Giguere, Anaheim, 2003. 21 games.
— Nikolai Khabibulin, Tampa Bay, 2004. 23 games.
— Miikka Kiprusoff, Calgary, 2004. 26 games.

MOST SHUTOUTS, ONE PLAYOFF SERIES:
3 — **Clint Benedict, Mtl. Maroons,** 1926 F vs. Victoria. 4 games.
— **Dave Kerr, NY Rangers,** 1940 SF vs. Boston. 6 games.
— **Frank McCool, Toronto,** 1945 F vs. Detroit. 7 games.
— **Turk Broda, Toronto,** 1950 SF vs. Detroit. 7 games.
— **Felix Potvin, Toronto,** 1994 CQF vs. Chicago. 6 games.
— **Martin Brodeur, New Jersey,** 1995 CQF vs. Boston. 5 games.
— **Brent Johnson, St. Louis,** 2002 CQF vs. Chicago. 5 games.
— **Patrick Lalime, Ottawa,** 2002 CQF vs. Philadelphia. 5 games.
— **Jean-Sebastien Giguere, Anaheim,** 2003 CF vs. Minnesota. 4 games.
— **Martin Brodeur, New Jersey,** 2003 F vs. Anaheim. 7 games.
— **Ed Belfour, Toronto,** 2004 CQF vs. Ottawa. 7 games.
— **Nikolai Khabibulin, Tampa Bay,** 2004 CQF vs. NY Islanders. 5 games.
— **Marty Turco, Dallas,** 2007 CQF vs. Vancouver. 7 games.
— **Michael Leighton, Philadelphia,** 2010 CF vs. Montreal. 5 games.

MOST WINS BY A GOALTENDER, CAREER:
151 — **Patrick Roy, Montreal, Colorado**
99 — Martin Brodeur, New Jersey
92 — Grant Fuhr, Edmonton, Buffalo, St. Louis
88 — Billy Smith, NY Islanders
— Ed Belfour, Chicago, Dallas, Toronto

MOST WINS BY A GOALTENDER, ONE PLAYOFF YEAR:
16 — **Sixteen wins** by a goaltender in one playoff year has been recorded on 19 occasions. Antti Niemi of the Chicago Blackhawks is the most recent to equal this mark, posting a record of 16 wins and 6 losses in 22 games in 2010. It was first accomplished by Grant Fuhr in 1988.

MOST CONSECUTIVE WINS BY A GOALTENDER,
MORE THAN ONE PLAYOFF YEAR:
14 — **Tom Barrasso, Pittsburgh,** 1992, 1993; 3 wins vs. NY Rangers in 1992 DF, won by Pittsburgh 4-2; 4 wins vs. Boston in 1992 CF, won by Pittsburgh 4-0; 4 wins vs. Chicago in 1992 F, won by Pittsburgh 4-0; 3 wins vs. New Jersey in 1993 DSF, won by Pittsburgh 4-1.

MOST CONSECUTIVE WINS BY A GOALTENDER, ONE PLAYOFF YEAR:
11 — **Ed Belfour, Chicago,** 1992. 3 wins vs. St. Louis in DSF, won by Chicago 4-2; 4 wins vs. Detroit in DF, won by Chicago 4-0; and 4 wins vs. Edmonton in CF, won by Chicago 4-0.
— **Tom Barrasso, Pittsburgh,** 1992. 3 wins vs. NY Rangers in DF, won by Pittsburgh 4-2; 4 wins vs. Boston in CF, won by Pittsburgh 4-0; and 4 wins vs. Chicago in F, won by Pittsburgh 4-0.
— **Patrick Roy, Montreal,** 1993. 4 wins vs. Quebec in DSF, won by Montreal 4-2; 4 wins vs. Buffalo in DF, won by Montreal 4-0; and 3 wins vs. NY Islanders in CF, won by Montreal 4-1.

LONGEST SHUTOUT SEQUENCE:
270:08 — **George Hainsworth,** Montreal, 1930. Hainsworth's shutout streak began after Murray Murdoch scored a goal for the NY Rangers at 15:34 of the first period in the first game of a SF series on March 28, 1930. Hainsworth did not allow another goal in the final 113:18 of that game, won by Montreal 2-1 at 8:52 of the 4th overtime period. Hainsworth then shutout the NY Rangers in the next and final game of the series on March 30, 1930, won by Montreal 2-0. The streak continued with a 3-0 win over Boston in the opening game of the F series on April 1, 1930. His streak ended on April 3, 1930 when Boston's Eddie Shore scored at 16:50 of the second period in the second game of the F series.

MOST CONSECUTIVE SHUTOUTS:
3 — **Clint Benedict, Mtl. Maroons,** 1926. Benedict shut out Ottawa 1-0, March 27; he then shut out Victoria twice, 3-0, March 30; 3-0, April 1. Mtl. Maroons won NHL F vs. Ottawa 2 goals to 1 and won the best-of-five F vs. Victoria 3-1.
— **John Ross Roach, NY Rangers,** 1929. Roach shut out NY Americans twice, 0-0, March 19; 1-0, March 21; he then shut out Toronto 1-0, March 24. NY Rangers won QF vs. NY Americans 1 goal to 0 and won the best-of-three SF vs. Toronto 2-0.
— **Frank McCool, Toronto,** 1945. McCool shut out Detroit 1-0, April 6; 2-0, April 8; 1-0, April 12. Toronto won the best-of-seven F 4-3.
— **Brent Johnson, St. Louis,** 2002. Johnson shut out Chicago three times; 2-0, April 20; 4-0, April 21; 1-0, April 23. St. Louis won the best-of-seven CQF 4-1.
— **Patrick Lalime, Ottawa,** 2002. Lalime shut out Philadelphia three times; 3-0, April 20; 3-0, April 22; 3-0, April 24. Ottawa won the best-of-seven CQF 4-1.
— **Jean-Sebastien Giguere, Anaheim,** 2003. Giguere shut out Minnesota 1-0, May 10; 2-0, May 12; 4-0, May 14. Anaheim won the best-of-seven CF 4-0.

Early Playoff Records

1893-1918
Team Records

MOST GOALS, BOTH TEAMS, ONE GAME:
25 — **Ottawa Silver Seven, Dawson City** at Ottawa, Jan. 16, 1905. Ottawa 23, Dawson City 2. Ottawa won best-of-three series 2-0.

MOST GOALS, ONE TEAM, ONE GAME:
23 — **Ottawa Silver Seven** at Ottawa, Jan. 16, 1905. Ottawa defeated Dawson City 23-2.

MOST GOALS, BOTH TEAMS, BEST-OF-THREE SERIES:
42 — **Ottawa Silver Seven, Queen's University** at Ottawa, 1906. Ottawa defeated Queen's 16-7, Feb. 27, and 12-7, Feb. 28.

MOST GOALS, ONE TEAM, BEST-OF-THREE SERIES:
32 — **Ottawa Silver Seven** in 1905 at Ottawa. Defeated Dawson City 9-2, Jan. 13, and 23-2, Jan. 16.

MOST GOALS, BOTH TEAMS, BEST-OF-FIVE SERIES:
39 — **Toronto Arenas, Vancouver Millionaires** at Toronto, 1918. Toronto won 5-3, Mar. 20; 6-3, Mar. 26; 2-1, Mar. 30. Vancouver won 6-4, Mar. 23, and 8-1, Mar. 28. Toronto scored 18 goals; Vancouver 21.

MOST GOALS, ONE TEAM, BEST-OF-FIVE SERIES:
26 — **Vancouver Millionaires** in 1915 at Vancouver. Defeated Ottawa Senators 6-2, Mar. 22; 8-3, Mar. 24; and 12-3, Mar. 26.

Individual Records

MOST GOALS IN PLAYOFFS:
63 — **Frank McGee, Ottawa Silver Seven,** in 22 playoff games. Seven goals in four games, 1903; 21 goals in eight games, 1904; 18 goals in four games, 1905; 17 goals in six games, 1906.

MOST GOALS, ONE PLAYOFF SERIES:
15 — **Frank McGee, Ottawa Silver Seven,** in two games in 1905 at Ottawa. Scored one goal, Jan. 13, in 9-2 victory over Dawson City and 14 goals, Jan. 16, in 23-2 victory.

MOST GOALS, ONE PLAYOFF GAME:
14 — **Frank McGee, Ottawa Silver Seven,** at Ottawa, Jan. 16, 1905, in 23-2 victory over Dawson City.

FASTEST THREE GOALS:
40 Seconds — **Marty Walsh, Ottawa Senators,** at Ottawa, March 16, 1911, at 3:00, 3:10, and 3:40 of third period. Ottawa defeated Port Arthur 13-4.

Antti Niemi became the latest goalie in NHL history to post 16 wins in one playoff year when he led the Blackhawks to a Stanley Cup win in 2010.

All-Time Playoff Goal Leaders since 1918

(40 or more goals)

Player	Teams	Yrs.	GP	G
Wayne Gretzky	Edm., L.A., St.L., NYR	16	208	122
Mark Messier	Edm., NYR, Van.	17	236	109
Jari Kurri	Edm., L.A., NYR, Ana., Col.	15	200	106
Brett Hull	Cgy., St.L., Dal., Det., Phx.	19	202	103
Glenn Anderson	Edm., Tor., NYR, St.L.	15	225	93
Mike Bossy	NYI	10	129	85
Joe Sakic	Que., Col.	13	172	84
Maurice Richard	Mtl.	15	133	82
Claude Lemieux	Mtl., N.J., Col., Phx., Dal., S.J.	18	234	80
Jean Beliveau	Mtl.	17	162	79
Jaromir Jagr	Pit., Wsh., NYR	15	169	77
Mario Lemieux	Pit.	8	107	76
Dino Ciccarelli	Min., Wsh., Det., T.B., Fla.	14	141	73
Esa Tikkanen	Edm., NYR, St.L., N.J., Van., Fla., Wsh.	13	186	72
Bryan Trottier	NYI, Pit.	17	221	71
Steve Yzerman	Det.	20	196	70
Gordie Howe	Det., Hfd.	20	157	68
Joe Nieuwendyk	Cgy., Dal., N.J., Tor., Fla.	16	158	66
Denis Savard	Chi., Mtl., T.B.	16	169	66
Yvan Cournoyer	Mtl.	12	147	64
Peter Forsberg	Que., Col., Phi., Nsh.	13	151	64
Brian Propp	Phi., Bos., Min., Hfd.	13	160	64
Bobby Smith	Min., Mtl.	13	184	64
Bobby Hull	Chi., Wpg., Hfd.	14	119	62
Phil Esposito	Chi., Bos., NYR	15	130	61
Jacques Lemaire	Mtl.	11	145	61
Joe Mullen	St.L., Cgy., Pit., Bos.	15	143	60
Doug Gilmour	St.L., Cgy., Tor., N.J., Chi., Buf., Mtl.	17	182	60
Brendan Shanahan	N.J., St.L., Hfd., Det., NYR	19	184	60
Stan Mikita	Chi.	18	155	59
Paul Coffey	Edm., Pit., L.A., Det., Hfd., Phi., Chi., Car., Bos.	16	194	59
Guy Lafleur	Mtl., NYR, Que.	14	128	58
Bernie Geoffrion	Mtl., NYR	16	132	58
Luc Robitaille	L.A., Pit., NYR, Det.	15	159	58
* Mike Modano	Min., Dal.	15	174	58
Cam Neely	Van., Bos.	9	93	57
Steve Larmer	Chi., NYR	13	140	56
* Mark Recchi	Pit., Phi., Mtl., Car., Atl., T.B., Bos.	13	164	56
Denis Potvin	NYI	14	185	56
Rick MacLeish	Phi., Hfd., Pit., Det.	11	114	54
Steve Thomas	Tor., Chi., NYI, N.J., Ana., Det.	16	174	54
Bill Barber	Phi.	11	129	53
Stephane Richer	Mtl., N.J., T.B., St.L., Pit.	13	134	53
Jeremy Roenick	Chi., Phx., Phi., L.A., S.J.	17	154	53
Rick Tocchet	Phi., Pit., L.A., Bos., Wsh., Phx.	13	145	52
Sergei Fedorov	Det., Ana., CBJ, Wsh.	15	183	52
Frank Mahovlich	Tor., Det., Mtl.	14	137	51
Brian Bellows	Min., Mtl., T.B., Ana., Wsh.	13	143	51
Rod Brind'Amour	St.L., Phi., Car.	12	159	51
Steve Shutt	Mtl., L.A.	12	99	50
* Nicklas Lidstrom	Det.	17	247	50
Henri Richard	Mtl.	18	180	49
Reggie Leach	Bos., Cal., Phi., Det.	8	94	47
* Chris Drury	Col., Cgy., Buf., NYR	8	130	47
Ted Lindsay	Det., Chi.	16	133	47
Clark Gillies	NYI, Buf.	13	164	47
* Henrik Zetterberg	Det.	6	97	46
Kevin Stevens	Pit., Bos., L.A., NYR, Phi.	7	103	46
Dickie Moore	Mtl., Tor., St.L.	14	135	46
Ron Francis	Hfd., Pit., Car., Tor.	17	171	46
* Patrick Marleau	S.J.	10	106	45
* Daniel Alfredsson	Ott.	11	107	45
Rick Middleton	NYR, Bos.	12	114	45
* Alex Kovalev	NYR, Pit., Mtl., Ott.	10	116	44
Lanny McDonald	Tor., Col., Cgy.	13	117	44
Scott Young	Hfd., Pit., Que., Col., Ana., St.L., Dal.	14	141	44
Ken Linseman	Phi., Edm., Bos., Tor.	11	113	43
Mike Gartner	Wsh., Min., NYR, Tor., Phx.	15	122	43
Dave Andreychuk	Buf., Tor., N.J., Bos., Col., T.B.	18	162	43
* Vyacheslav Kozlov	Det., Buf., Atl.	10	118	42
Bernie Nicholls	L.A., NYR, Edm., N.J., Chi., S.J.	13	118	42
Bobby Clarke	Phi.	13	136	42
John LeClair	Mtl., Phi., Pit.	14	154	42
Adam Oates	Det., St.L., Bos., Wsh., Phi., Ana., Edm.	15	163	42
* Tomas Holmstrom	Det.	12	164	42
Dale Hunter	Que., Wsh., Col	18	186	42
John Bucyk	Det., Bos.	14	124	41
Vincent Damphousse	Tor., Edm., Mtl., S.J.	14	140	41
Raymond Bourque	Bos., Col.	21	214	41
Tim Kerr	Phi., NYR, Hfd.	10	81	40
Peter McNab	Buf., Bos., Van., N.J.	10	107	40
* Patrik Elias	N.J.	12	138	40
Bob Bourne	NYI, L.A.	13	139	40
John Tonelli	NYI, Cgy., L.A., Chi., Que.	13	172	40

* Active

All-Time Playoff Assist Leaders since 1918

(65 or more assists)

Player	Teams	Yrs.	GP	A
Wayne Gretzky	Edm., L.A., St.L., NYR	16	208	260
Mark Messier	Edm., NYR, Van.	17	236	186
Raymond Bourque	Bos., Col.	21	214	139
Paul Coffey	Edm., Pit., L.A., Det., Hfd., Phi., Chi., Car., Bos.	16	194	137
Doug Gilmour	St.L., Cgy., Tor., N.J., Chi., Buf., Mtl.	17	182	128
Jari Kurri	Edm., L.A., NYR, Ana., Col.	15	200	127
* Nicklas Lidstrom	Det.	17	247	125
Sergei Fedorov	Det., Ana., CBJ, Wsh.	15	183	124
Al MacInnis	Cgy., St.L.	19	177	121
Glenn Anderson	Edm., Tor., NYR, St.L.	15	225	121
Larry Robinson	Mtl., L.A.	20	227	116
Steve Yzerman	Det.	20	196	115
Larry Murphy	L.A., Wsh., Min., Pit., Tor., Det.	20	215	115
Adam Oates	Det., St.L., Bos., Wsh., Phi., Ana., Edm.	15	163	114
Bryan Trottier	NYI, Pit.	17	221	113
Chris Chelios	Mtl., Chi., Det., Atl.	24	266	113
Denis Savard	Chi., Mtl., T.B.	16	169	109
Denis Potvin	NYI	14	185	108
Peter Forsberg	Que., Col., Phi., Nsh.	13	151	107
Jaromir Jagr	Pit., Wsh., NYR	15	169	104
Joe Sakic	Que., Col.	13	172	104
Jean Beliveau	Mtl.	17	162	97
Ron Francis	Hfd., Pit., Car., Tor.	17	171	97
Mario Lemieux	Pit.	8	107	96
Bobby Smith	Min., Mtl.	13	184	96
* Chris Pronger	Hfd., St.L., Edm., Ana., Phi.	13	170	94
Sergei Zubov	NYR, Pit., Dal.	13	164	93
Gordie Howe	Det., Hfd.	20	157	92
Scott Stevens	Wsh., St.L., N.J.	20	233	92
Stan Mikita	Chi.	18	155	91
Brad Park	NYR, Bos., Det.	17	161	90
* Mike Modano	Min., Dal.	15	174	87
Brett Hull	Cgy., St.L., Dal., Det., Phx.	19	202	87
Craig Janney	Bos., St.L., S.J., Wpg., Phx., T.B., NYI	11	120	86
Brian Propp	Phi., Bos., Min., Hfd.	13	160	84
Henri Richard	Mtl.	18	180	80
Jacques Lemaire	Mtl.	11	145	78
Claude Lemieux	Mtl., N.J., Col., Phx., Dal., S.J.	18	234	78
Ken Linseman	Phi., Edm., Bos., Tor.	11	113	77
Bobby Clarke	Phi.	13	136	77
* Patrik Elias	N.J.	12	138	77
* Mark Recchi	Pit., Phi., Mtl., Car., Atl., T.B., Bos.	13	164	77
Guy Lafleur	Mtl., NYR, Que.	14	128	76
Phil Esposito	Chi., Bos., NYR	15	130	76
Dale Hunter	Que., Wsh., Col.	18	186	76
Mike Bossy	NYI	10	129	75
Steve Larmer	Chi., NYR	13	140	75
John Tonelli	NYI, Cgy., L.A., Chi., Que.	13	172	75
Brendan Shanahan	N.J., St.L., Hfd., Det., NYR	19	184	74
Scott Niedermayer	N.J., Ana.	15	202	73
Peter Stastny	Que., N.J., St.L.	12	93	72
Bernie Nicholls	L.A., NYR, Edm., N.J., Chi., S.J.	13	118	72
Brian Bellows	Min., Mtl., T.B., Ana., Wsh.	13	143	71
Gilbert Perreault	Buf.	11	90	70
* Brian Rafalski	N.J., Det.	9	154	70
Geoff Courtnall	Bos., Edm., Wsh., St.L., Van.	15	156	70
Brian Leetch	NYR, Tor., Bos.	8	95	69
Dale Hawerchuk	Wpg., Buf., St.L., Phi.	15	97	69
Alex Delvecchio	Det.	14	121	69
Jeremy Roenick	Chi., Phx., Phi., L.A., S.J.	17	154	69
Luc Robitaille	L.A., Pit., NYR, Det.	15	159	69
Bobby Hull	Chi., Wpg., Hfd.	14	119	67
Sandis Ozolinsh	S.J., Col., Car., Fla., Ana., NYR	10	137	67
Frank Mahovlich	Tor., Det., Mtl.	14	137	67
Igor Larionov	Van., S.J., Det., Fla., N.J.	13	150	67
Bobby Orr	Bos., Chi.	8	74	66
Bernie Federko	St.L., Det.	11	91	66
Jean Ratelle	NYR, Bos.	15	123	66
* Scott Gomez	N.J., NYR, Mtl.	8	133	66
Charlie Huddy	Edm., L.A., Buf., St.L.	14	183	66
Trevor Linden	Van., NYI, Mtl., Wsh.	12	124	65

All-Time Playoff Point Leaders since 1918

(110 or more points)

Player	Teams	Yrs.	GP	G	A	Pts.
Wayne Gretzky	Edm., L.A., St.L., NYR	16	208	122	260	382
Mark Messier	Edm., NYR, Van.	17	236	109	186	295
Jari Kurri	Edm., L.A., NYR, Ana., Col.	15	200	106	127	233
Glenn Anderson	Edm., Tor., NYR, St.L.	15	225	93	121	214
Paul Coffey	Edm., Pit., L.A., Det., Hfd., Phi., Chi., Car., Bos.	16	194	59	137	196
Brett Hull	Cgy., St.L., Dal., Det., Phx.	19	202	103	87	190
Joe Sakic	Que., Col.	13	172	84	104	188
Doug Gilmour	St.L., Cgy., Tor., N.J., Chi., Buf., Mtl.	17	182	60	128	188
Steve Yzerman	Det.	20	196	70	115	185
Bryan Trottier	NYI, Pit.	17	221	71	113	184
Jaromir Jagr	Pit., Wsh., NYR	15	169	77	104	181
Raymond Bourque	Bos., Col.	21	214	41	139	180
Jean Beliveau	Mtl.	17	162	79	97	176
Sergei Fedorov	Det., Ana., CBJ, Wsh.	15	183	52	124	176
Denis Savard	Chi., Mtl., T.B.	16	169	66	109	175
* Nicklas Lidstrom	Det.	17	247	50	125	175
Mario Lemieux	Pit.	8	107	76	96	172
Peter Forsberg	Que., Col., Phi., Nsh.	13	151	64	107	171
Denis Potvin	NYI	14	185	56	108	164
Mike Bossy	NYI	10	129	85	75	160
Gordie Howe	Det., Hfd.	20	157	68	92	160
Al MacInnis	Cgy., St.L.	19	177	39	121	160
Bobby Smith	Min., Mtl.	13	184	64	96	160
Claude Lemieux	Mtl., N.J., Col., Phx., Dal., S.J.	18	234	80	78	158
Adam Oates	Det., St.L., Bos., Wsh., Phi., Ana., Edm.	15	163	42	114	156
Larry Murphy	L.A., Wsh., Min., Pit., Tor., Det.	20	215	37	115	152
Stan Mikita	Chi.	18	155	59	91	150
Brian Propp	Phi., Bos., Min., Hfd.	13	160	64	84	148
* Mike Modano	Min., Dal.	15	174	58	87	145
Larry Robinson	Mtl., L.A.	20	227	28	116	144
Chris Chelios	Mtl., Chi., Det., Atl.	24	266	31	113	144
Ron Francis	Hfd., Pit., Car., Tor.	17	171	46	97	143
Jacques Lemaire	Mtl.	11	145	61	78	139
Phil Esposito	Chi., Bos., NYR	15	130	61	76	137
Guy Lafleur	Mtl., NYR, Que.	14	128	58	76	134
Brendan Shanahan	N.J., St.L., Hfd., Det., NYR	19	184	60	74	134
* Mark Recchi	Pit., Phi., Mtl., Car., Atl., T.B., Bos.	13	164	56	77	133
Esa Tikkanen	Edm., NYR, St.L., N.J., Van., Fla., Wsh.	13	186	72	60	132
Steve Larmer	Chi., NYR	13	140	56	75	131
Bobby Hull	Chi., Wpg., Hfd.	14	119	62	67	129
Henri Richard	Mtl.	18	180	49	80	129
Yvan Cournoyer	Mtl.	12	147	64	63	127
Luc Robitaille	L.A., Pit., NYR, Det.	15	159	58	69	127
Maurice Richard	Mtl.	15	133	82	44	126
Brad Park	NYR, Bos., Det.	17	161	35	90	125
Brian Bellows	Min., Mtl., T.B., Ana., Wsh.	13	143	51	71	122
Jeremy Roenick	Chi., Phx., Phi., L.A., S.J.	17	154	53	69	122
Ken Linseman	Phi., Edm., Bos., Tor.	11	113	43	77	120
* Chris Pronger	Hfd., St.L., Edm., Ana., Phi.	13	170	26	94	120
Bobby Clarke	Phi.	13	136	42	77	119
Bernie Geoffrion	Mtl., NYR	16	132	58	60	118
Frank Mahovlich	Tor., Det., Mtl.	14	137	51	67	118
Dino Ciccarelli	Min., Wsh., Det., T.B., Fla.	14	141	73	45	118
Dale Hunter	Que., Wsh., Col.	18	186	42	76	118
Scott Stevens	Wsh., St.L., N.J.	20	233	26	92	118
* Patrik Elias	N.J.	12	138	40	77	117
Sergei Zubov	NYR, Pit., Dal.	13	164	24	93	117
Joe Nieuwendyk	Cgy., Dal., N.J., Tor., Fla.	16	158	66	50	116
John Tonelli	NYI, Cgy., L.A., Chi., Que.	13	172	40	75	115
Bernie Nicholls	L.A., NYR, Edm., N.J., Chi., S.J.	13	118	42	72	114
Rick Tocchet	Phi., Pit., L.A., Bos., Wsh., Phx.	13	145	52	60	112
Rod Brind'Amour	St.L., Phi., Car.	12	159	51	60	111
Craig Janney	Bos., St.L., S.J., Wpg., Phx., T.B., NYI	11	120	24	86	110
Dickie Moore	Mtl., Tor., St.L.	14	135	46	64	110

With 12 points (three goals, nine assists) in the Finals, Danny Briere emerged as the top playoff scorer in 2009-10. Ville Leino behind him led all rookies with seven goals, 14 assists and 21 points.

Leading Playoff Scorers, 1918–2010

Season	Player, Team	Games Played	Goals	Assists	Points
2009-10	Danny Briere, Philadelphia	23	12	18	30
2008-09	Evgeni Malkin, Pittsburgh	24	14	22	36
2007-08	Henrik Zetterberg, Detroit	22	13	14	27
	Sidney Crosby, Pittsburgh	20	6	21	27
2006-07	Daniel Alfredsson, Ottawa	20	14	8	22
	Dany Heatley, Ottawa	20	7	15	22
	Jason Spezza, Ottawa	20	7	15	22
2005-06	Eric Staal, Carolina	25	9	19	28
2004-05	*Season Cancelled*				
2003-04	Brad Richards, Tampa Bay	23	12	14	26
2002-03	Jamie Langenbrunner, New Jersey	24	11	7	18
	Scott Niedermayer, New Jersey	24	2	16	18
2001-02	Peter Forsberg, Colorado	20	9	18	27
2000-01	Joe Sakic, Colorado	21	13	13	26
99-2000	Brett Hull, Dallas	23	11	13	24
1998-99	Peter Forsberg, Colorado	19	8	16	24
1997-98	Steve Yzerman, Detroit	22	6	18	24
1996-97	Eric Lindros, Philadelphia	19	12	14	26
1995-96	Joe Sakic, Colorado	22	18	16	34
1994-95	Sergei Fedorov, Detroit	17	7	17	24
1993-94	Brian Leetch, NY Rangers	23	11	23	34
1992-93	Wayne Gretzky, Los Angeles	24	15	25	40
1991-92	Mario Lemieux, Pittsburgh	15	16	18	34
1990-91	Mario Lemieux, Pittsburgh	23	16	28	44
1989-90	Craig Simpson, Edmonton	22	16	15	31
	Mark Messier, Edmonton	22	9	22	31
1988-89	Al MacInnis, Calgary	22	7	24	31
1987-88	Wayne Gretzky, Edmonton	19	12	31	43
1986-87	Wayne Gretzky, Edmonton	21	5	29	34
1985-86	Doug Gilmour, St. Louis	19	9	12	21
	Bernie Federko, St. Louis	19	7	14	21
1984-85	Wayne Gretzky, Edmonton	18	17	30	47
1983-84	Wayne Gretzky, Edmonton	19	13	22	35
1982-83	Wayne Gretzky, Edmonton	16	12	26	38
1981-82	Bryan Trottier, NY Islanders	19	6	23	29
1980-81	Mike Bossy, NY Islanders	18	17	18	35
1979-80	Bryan Trottier, NY Islanders	21	12	17	29
1978-79	Jacques Lemaire, Montreal	16	11	12	23
	Guy Lafleur, Montreal	16	10	13	23
1977-78	Guy Lafleur, Montreal	15	10	11	21
	Larry Robinson, Montreal	15	4	17	21
1976-77	Guy Lafleur, Montreal	14	9	17	26
1975-76	Reggie Leach, Philadelphia	16	19	5	24
1974-75	Rick MacLeish, Philadelphia	17	11	9	20
1973-74	Rick MacLeish, Philadelphia	17	13	9	22
1972-73	Yvan Cournoyer, Montreal	17	15	10	25
1971-72	Phil Esposito, Boston	15	9	15	24
	Bobby Orr, Boston	15	5	19	24
1970-71	Frank Mahovlich, Montreal	20	14	13	27
1969-70	Phil Esposito, Boston	14	13	14	27
1968-69	Phil Esposito, Boston	10	8	10	18
1967-68	Bill Goldsworthy, Minnesota	14	8	7	15
1966-67	Jim Pappin, Toronto	12	7	8	15
1965-66	Norm Ullman, Detroit	12	6	9	15
1964-65	Bobby Hull, Chicago	14	10	7	17
1963-64	Gordie Howe, Detroit	14	9	10	19
1962-63	Gordie Howe, Detroit	11	7	9	16
	Norm Ullman, Detroit	11	4	12	16
1961-62	Stan Mikita, Chicago	12	6	15	21
1960-61	Gordie Howe, Detroit	11	4	11	15
	Pierre Pilote, Chicago	12	3	12	15
1959-60	Henri Richard, Montreal	8	3	9	12
	Bernie Geoffrion, Montreal	8	2	10	12
1958-59	Dickie Moore, Montreal	11	5	12	17
1957-58	Fleming MacKell, Boston	12	5	14	19
1956-57	Bernie Geoffrion, Montreal	11	11	7	18
1955-56	Jean Béliveau, Montreal	10	12	7	19
1954-55	Gordie Howe, Detroit	11	9	11	20
1953-54	Dickie Moore, Montreal	11	5	8	13
1952-53	Ed Sandford, Boston	11	8	3	11
1951-52	Ted Lindsay, Detroit	8	5	2	7
	Floyd Curry, Montreal	11	4	3	7
	Metro Prystai, Detroit	8	2	5	7
	Gordie Howe, Detroit	8	2	5	7
1950-51	Maurice Richard, Montreal	11	9	4	13
	Max Bentley, Toronto	11	2	11	13
1949-50	Pentti Lund, NY Rangers	12	6	5	11
1948-49	Gordie Howe, Detroit	11	8	3	11
1947-48	Ted Kennedy, Toronto	9	8	6	14
1946-47	Maurice Richard, Montreal	10	6	5	11
1945-46	Elmer Lach, Montreal	9	5	12	17
1944-45	Joe Carveth, Detroit	14	5	6	11
1943-44	Toe Blake, Montreal	9	7	11	18
1942-43	Carl Liscombe, Detroit	10	6	8	14
1941-42	Don Grosso, Detroit	12	8	6	14
	Syl Apps, Toronto	13	5	9	14
1940-41	Milt Schmidt, Boston	11	5	6	11
1939-40	Phil Watson, NY Rangers	12	3	6	9
	Neil Colville, NY Rangers	12	2	7	9
1938-39	Bill Cowley, Boston	12	3	11	14
1937-38	Johnny Gottselig, Chicago	10	5	3	8
	Gordie Drillon, Toronto	7	7	1	8
1936-37	Marty Barry, Detroit	10	4	7	11
1935-36	Frank Boll, Toronto	9	7	3	10
1934-35	Baldy Northcott, Mtl. Maroons	7	4	1	5
	Busher Jackson, Toronto	7	3	2	5
	Cy Wentworth, Mtl. Maroons	7	3	2	5
	Charlie Conacher, Toronto	7	1	4	5
1933-34	Larry Aurie, Detroit	9	3	7	10
1932-33	Cecil Dillon, NY Rangers	8	8	2	10
1931-32	Frank Boucher, NY Rangers	7	3	6	9
1930-31	Cooney Weiland, Boston	5	6	3	9
1929-30	Marty Barry, Boston	6	3	3	6
	Cooney Weiland, Boston	6	1	5	6
1928-29	Andy Blair, Toronto	4	3	0	3
	Butch Keeling, NY Rangers	6	3	0	3
	Ace Bailey, Toronto	4	1	2	3
1927-28	Frank Boucher, NY Rangers	9	7	3	10
1926-27	Harry Oliver, Boston	8	4	2	6
	Percy Galbraith, Boston	8	3	3	6
1925-26	Nels Stewart, Mtl. Maroons	8	6	3	9
1924-25	Howie Morenz, Montreal	6	7	1	8
1923-24	Howie Morenz, Montreal	6	7	3	10
1922-23	Punch Broadbent, Ottawa	8	6	1	7
1921-22	Babe Dye, Toronto	7	11	1	12
1920-21	Cy Denneny, Ottawa	7	4	2	6
1919-20	Frank Nighbor, Ottawa	5	6	1	7
	Jack Darragh, Ottawa	5	5	2	7
1918-19	Newsy Lalonde, Montreal	10	17	2	19
1917-18	Alf Skinner, Toronto	7	8	3	11

Three-or-more-Goal Games, Playoffs 1918–2010

Player	Team	Date	City	Total Goals	Opposing Goaltender	Score
Wayne Gretzky (10)	Edm.	Apr. 11/81	Edm.	3	Richard Sevigny	Edm. 6 Mtl. 2
		Apr. 19/81	Edm.	3	Billy Smith	Edm. 5 NYI 2
		Apr. 6/83	Edm.	4	Brian Hayward	Edm. 6 Wpg. 3
		Apr. 17/83	Cgy.	3	Reggie Lemelin	Edm. 10 Cgy. 2
		Apr. 25/85	Wpg.	3	Brian Hayward (2) / Marc Behrend (1)	Edm. 8 Wpg. 3
		May 25/85	Edm.	3	Pelle Lindbergh	Edm. 4 Phi. 3
		Apr. 24/86	Cgy.	3	Mike Vernon	Edm. 7 Cgy. 4
	L.A.	May 29/93	Tor.	3	Felix Potvin	L.A. 5 Tor. 4
	NYR	Apr. 23/97	NYR	3	John Vanbiesbrouck	NYR 3 Fla. 2
		May 18/97	Phi.	3	Garth Snow	NYR 5 Phi. 4
Maurice Richard (7)	Mtl.	Mar. 23/44	Mtl.	5	Paul Bibeault	Mtl. 5 Tor. 1
		Apr. 6/44	Chi.	3	Mike Karakas	Mtl. 3 Chi. 1
		Mar. 29/45	Mtl.	4	Frank McCool	Mtl. 10 Tor. 3
		Apr. 14/53	Bos.	3	Gord Henry	Mtl. 7 Bos. 3
		Mar. 20/56	Mtl.	3	Gump Worsley	Mtl. 7 NYR 1
		Apr. 6/57	Mtl.	3	Don Simmons	Mtl. 5 Bos. 1
		Apr. 1/58	Det.	3	Terry Sawchuk	Mtl. 4 Det. 3
Jari Kurri (7)	Edm.	Apr. 4/84	Edm.	3	Doug Soetaert (1) / Mike Veisor (2)	Edm. 9 Wpg. 2
		Apr. 25/85	Wpg.	3	Brian Hayward (2) / Marc Behrend (1)	Edm. 8 Wpg. 3
		May 7/85	Edm.	3	Murray Bannerman	Edm. 7 Chi. 3
		May 14/85	Edm.	3	Murray Bannerman	Edm. 10 Chi. 5
		May 16/85	Chi.	4	Murray Bannerman	Edm. 8 Chi. 2
		Apr. 9/87	Edm.	4	Rollie Melanson (2) / Darren Eliot (2)	Edm. 13 L.A. 3
		May 18/90	Bos.	3	Andy Moog (2) / Reggie Lemelin (1)	Edm. 7 Bos. 2
Dino Ciccarelli (6)	Min.	May 5/81	Min.	3	Pat Riggin	Min. 7 Cgy. 4
		Apr. 10/82	Min.	3	Murray Bannerman	Min. 7 Chi. 1
	Wsh.	Apr. 5/90	N.J.	3	Sean Burke	Wsh. 5 N.J. 4
		Apr. 25/92	Pit.	4	Tom Barrasso (1) / Ken Wregget (3)	Wsh. 7 Pit. 2
	Det.	Apr. 29/93	Tor.	3	Felix Potvin (1) / Daren Puppa (1)	Det. 7 Tor. 3
		May 11/95	Dal.	3	Andy Moog (2) / Darcy Wakaluk (1)	Det. 5 Dal. 1
Mike Bossy (5)	NYI	Apr. 16/79	NYI	3	Tony Esposito	NYI 6 Chi. 2
		May 8/82	NYI	3	Richard Brodeur	NYI 6 Van. 5
		Apr. 10/83	Wsh.	3	Al Jensen	NYI 6 Wsh. 3
		May 3/83	NYI	3	Pete Peeters	NYI 8 Bos. 3
		May 7/83	NYI	4	Pete Peeters	NYI 8 Bos. 4
Phil Esposito (4)	Bos.	Apr. 2/69	Bos.	4	Bruce Gamble	Bos. 10 Tor. 0
		Apr. 8/70	Bos.	3	Ed Giacomin	Bos. 8 NYR 2
		Apr. 19/70	Chi.	3	Tony Esposito	Bos. 6 Chi. 3
		Apr. 8/75	Bos.	3	Tony Esposito (2) / Michel Dumas (1)	Bos. 8 Chi. 2
Mark Messier (4)	Edm.	Apr. 14/83	Edm.	3	Reggie Lemelin	Edm. 6 Cgy. 3
		Apr. 17/83	Cgy.	3	Reggie Lemelin (1) / Don Edwards (2)	Edm. 10 Cgy. 2
		Apr. 26/83	Edm.	3	Murray Bannerman	Edm. 8 Chi. 2
	NYR	May 25/94	N.J.	3	Martin Brodeur (2) / ENG (1)	NYR 4 N.J. 2
Steve Yzerman (4)	Det.	Apr. 6/89	Det.	3	Alain Chevrier	Chi. 5 Det. 4
		Apr. 4/91	St.L.	3	Vincent Riendeau (2) / Pat Jablonski (1)	Det. 6 St.L. 3
		May 8/96	St.L.	3	Jon Casey	St.L. 5 Det. 4
		Apr. 21/99	Det.	3	Guy Hebert (2) / Pat Jablonski (1)	Det. 5 Ana. 3
Bernie Geoffrion (3)	Mtl.	Mar. 27/52	Mtl.	3	Jim Henry	Mtl. 4 Bos. 0
		Apr. 7/55	Mtl.	3	Terry Sawchuk	Mtl. 4 Det. 2
		Mar. 30/57	Mtl.	3	Gump Worsley	Mtl. 8 NYR 3
Norm Ullman (3)	Det.	Mar. 29/64	Chi.	3	Glenn Hall	Det. 5 Chi. 4
		Apr. 7/64	Det.	3	Glenn Hall (1) / Denis DeJordy (1)	Det. 7 Chi. 2
		Apr. 11/65	Det.	3	Glenn Hall	Det. 4 Chi. 2
John Bucyk (3)	Bos.	May 3/70	St.L.	3	Jacques Plante (1) / Ernie Wakely (1)	Bos. 6 St.L. 1
		Apr. 20/72	Bos.	3	Jacques Caron (1) / Ernie Wakely (2)	Bos. 10 St.L. 2
		Apr. 21/74	Bos.	3	Tony Esposito	Bos. 8 Chi. 6
Rick MacLeish (3)	Phi.	Apr. 11/74	Phi.	3	Phil Myre	Phi. 5 Atl. 1
		Apr. 13/75	Phi.	3	Gord McRae	Phi. 6 Tor. 3
		May 13/75	Phi.	3	Glenn Resch	Phi. 4 NYI 1
Denis Savard (3)	Chi.	Apr. 19/82	Chi.	3	Mike Liut	Chi. 7 St.L. 4
		Apr. 10/86	Chi.	4	Ken Wregget	Tor. 6 Chi. 4
		Apr. 9/88	St.L.	3	Greg Millen	Chi. 6 St.L. 3
Tim Kerr (3)	Phi.	Apr. 13/85	NYR	4	Glen Hanlon	Phi. 6 NYR 5
		Apr. 20/87	Phi.	3	Kelly Hrudey	Phi. 4 NYI 2
		Apr. 19/89	Pit.	3	Tom Barrasso	Phi. 4 Pit. 2
Cam Neely (3)	Bos.	Apr. 9/87	Mtl.	3	Patrick Roy	Mtl. 4 Bos. 3
		Apr. 5/91	Bos.	3	Peter Sidorkiewicz	Bos. 4 Hfd. 3
		Apr. 25/91	Bos.	3	Patrick Roy	Bos. 4 Mtl. 1
Petr Klima (3)	Det.	Apr. 7/88	Tor.	3	Allan Bester (2) / Ken Wregett (1)	Det. 6 Tor. 2
		Apr. 21/88	St.L.	3	Greg Millen	Det. 6 St.L. 0
	Edm.	May 4/91	Edm.	3	Jon Casey	Edm. 7 Min. 2
Esa Tikkanen (3)	Edm.	May 22/88	Edm.	3	Reggie Lemelin	Edm. 6 Bos. 3
		Apr. 16/91	Cgy.	3	Mike Vernon	Edm. 5 Cgy. 4
	L.A.	Apr. 26/92	L.A.	3	Kelly Hrudey (2) / Tom Askey (1)	Edm. 5 L.A. 2
Mike Gartner (3)	NYR	Apr. 13/90	NYR	3	Mark Fitzpatrick (2) / Glenn Healy (1)	NYR 6 NYI 5
		Apr. 27/92	NYR	3	Chris Terreri	NYR 8 N.J. 5
	Tor.	Apr. 25/96	Tor.	3	Jon Casey	Tor. 5 St.L. 4
Mario Lemieux (3)	Pit.	Apr. 25/89	Pit.	5	Ron Hextall	Pit. 10 Phi. 7
		Apr. 23/92	Pit.	3	Don Beaupre	Pit. 6 Wsh. 4
		May 11/96	Pit.	3	Mike Richter	Pit. 7 NYR 3
Patrick Marleau (3)	S.J.	Apr. 10/04	S.J.	3	Chris Osgood	S.J. 3 St.L. 1
		Apr. 22/04	S.J.	3	David Aebischer	S.J. 5 Col. 2
		Apr. 27/06	S.J.	3	Chris Mason	Nsh. 4 S.J. 5
Johan Franzen (3)	Det.	Apr. 26/08	Det.	3	Jose Theodore (2) / Peter Budaj (1)	Det. 5 Col. 1
		May 1/08	Col.	3	Jose Theodore (1) / Peter Budaj (2)	Det. 8 Col. 2
		May 6/10	Det.	4	Evgeni Nabokov (3) / Thomas Greiss	Det. 7 S.J. 1
Newsy Lalonde (2)	Mtl.	Mar. 1/19	Mtl.	5	Clint Benedict	Mtl. 6 Ott. 3
		Mar. 22/19	Sea.	4	Hap Holmes	Mtl. 4 Sea. 2
Howie Morenz (2)	Mtl.	Mar. 22/24	Mtl.	3	Charles Reid	Mtl. 6 Cgy.T. 1
		Mar. 27/25	Mtl.	3	Hap Holmes	Mtl. 4 Vic. 2
Doug Bentley (2)	Chi.	Mar. 28/44	Chi.	3	Connie Dion	Chi. 7 Det. 1
		Mar. 30/44	Det.	3	Connie Dion	Chi. 5 Det. 2
Toe Blake (2)	Mtl.	Mar. 22/38	Mtl.	3	Mike Karakas	Mtl. 6 Chi. 4
		Mar. 26/46	Chi.	3	Mike Karakas	Mtl. 7 Chi. 2
Ted Kennedy (2)	Tor.	Apr. 14/45	Tor.	3	Harry Lumley	Det. 5 Tor. 3
		Mar. 27/48	Tor.	3	Frank Brimsek	Tor. 5 Bos. 3
F. St. Marseille (2)	St.L.	Apr. 28/70	St.L.	3	Al Smith	St.L. 5 Pit. 0
		Apr. 6/72	Min.	3	Cesare Maniago	Min. 6 St.L. 5
Bobby Hull (2)	Chi.	Apr. 7/63	Det.	3	Terry Sawchuk	Det. 7 Chi. 4
		Apr. 9/72	Chi.	3	Jim Rutherford	Chi. 6 Pit. 5
Pit Martin (2)	Chi.	Apr. 4/73	Chi.	3	Wayne Stephenson	Chi. 7 St.L. 1
		May 10/73	Chi.	3	Ken Dryden	Mtl. 6 Chi. 4
Yvan Cournoyer (2)	Mtl.	Apr. 5/73	Mtl.	3	Dave Dryden	Mtl. 7 Buf. 3
		Apr. 11/74	Mtl.	3	Ed Giacomin	Mtl. 4 NYR 1
Guy Lafleur (2)	Mtl.	May 1/75	Mtl.	3	Roger Crozier (1) / Gerry Desjardins (2)	Mtl. 7 Buf. 0
		Apr. 11/77	Mtl.	3	Ed Staniowski	Mtl. 7 St.L. 2
Lanny McDonald (2)	Tor.	Apr. 9/77	Pit.	3	Denis Herron	Tor. 5 Pit. 2
		Apr. 17/77	Tor.	4	Wayne Stephenson	Phi. 6 Tor. 5
Bill Barber (2)	Phi.	May 4/80	Min.	3	Gilles Meloche	Phi. 5 Min. 3
		Apr. 9/81	Phi.	3	Dan Bouchard	Phi. 8 Que. 5
Bryan Trottier (2)	NYI	Apr. 8/80	NYI	3	Doug Keans	NYI 8 L.A. 1
		Apr. 9/81	NYI	3	Michel Larocque	NYI 5 Tor. 1
Butch Goring (2)	L.A.	Apr. 9/77	L.A.	3	Phil Myre	L.A. 4 Atl. 2
	NYI	May 17/81	Min.	3	Gilles Meloche	NYI 7 Min. 5
Paul Reinhart (2)	Cgy.	Apr. 14/83	Edm.	3	Andy Moog	Edm. 6 Cgy. 3
		Apr. 8/84	Van	3	Richard Brodeur	Cgy. 5 Van. 1
Brian Propp (2)	Phi.	Apr. 22/81	Phi.	3	Pat Riggin	Phi. 9 Cgy. 4
		Apr. 21/85	Phi.	3	Billy Smith	Phi. 5 NYI 2
Peter Stastny (2)	Que.	Apr. 5/83	Bos.	3	Pete Peeters	Bos. 4 Que. 3
		Apr. 11/87	Que.	3	Mike Liut (2) / Steve Weeks (1)	Que. 5 Hfd. 1
Michel Goulet (2)	Que.	Apr. 23/85	Que.	3	Steve Penney	Que. 7 Mtl. 6
		Apr. 12/87	Que.	3	Mike Liut	Que. 4 Hfd. 1
Glenn Anderson (2)	Edm.	Apr. 26/83	Edm.	3	Murray Bannerman	Edm. 8 Chi. 2
		Apr. 6/88	Wpg.	3	Daniel Berthiaume	Edm. 7 Wpg. 4
Peter Zezel (2)	Phi.	Apr. 13/86	NYR	3	John Vanbiesbrouck	Phi. 7 NYR 1
	St.L.	Apr. 11/89	St.L.	3	Jon Casey (2) / Kari Takko (1)	St.L. 6 Min. 1
Geoff Courtnall (2)	Van.	Apr. 4/91	L.A.	3	Kelly Hrudey	Van. 6 L.A. 5
		Apr. 30/92	Van.	3	Rick Tabaracci	Van. 5 Win. 0
Joe Sakic (2)	Que.	May 6/95	Que.	3	Mike Richter	Que. 5 NYR 4
	Col.	Apr. 25/96	Col.	3	Corey Hirsch	Col. 5 Van. 4
Daniel Alfredsson (2)	Ott.	Apr. 28/98	Ott.	3	Martin Brodeur	Ott. 4 N.J. 3
		May 11/98	Ott.	3	Olaf Kolzig	Ott. 4 Wsh. 3
Harry Meeking	Tor.	Mar. 11/18	Tor.	3	Georges Vezina	Tor. 7 Mtl. 3
Alf Skinner	Tor.	Mar. 23/18	Tor.	3	Hugh Lehman	Van.M. 6 Tor. 4
Joe Malone	Mtl.	Feb. 23/19	Mtl.	3	Clint Benedict	Mtl. 8 Ott. 4
Odie Cleghorn	Mtl.	Feb. 27/19	Mtl.	3	Clint Benedict	Mtl. 5 Ott. 3
Jack Darragh	Ott.	Apr. 1/20	Ott.	3	Hap Holmes	Ott. 6 Sea. 1
George Boucher	Ott.	Mar. 10/21	Ott.	3	Jake Forbes	Ott. 5 Tor. 0
Babe Dye	Tor.	Mar. 28/22	Tor.	3	Hugh Lehman	Tor. 5 Van.M. 1
Percy Galbraith	Bos.	Mar. 31/27	Bos.	3	Hugh Lehman	Bos. 4 Chi. 4
Busher Jackson	Tor.	Apr. 5/32	NYR	3	John Ross Roach	Tor. 6 NYR 4
Frank Boucher	NYR	Apr. 9/32	Tor.	3	Lorne Chabot	Tor. 6 NYR 4
Charlie Conacher	Tor.	Mar. 26/36	Tor.	3	Tiny Thompson	Tor. 8 Bos. 3
Syd Howe	Det.	Mar. 23/39	Det.	3	Claude Bourque	Det. 7 Mtl. 3
Bryan Hextall	NYR	Apr. 3/40	NYR	3	Turk Broda	NYR 6 Tor. 2
Joe Benoit	Mtl.	Mar. 22/41	Mtl.	3	Sam LoPresti	Mtl. 4 Chi. 3
Syl Apps	Tor.	Mar. 25/41	Tor.	3	Frank Brimsek	Tor. 7 Bos. 2
Jack McGill	Bos.	Mar. 29/42	Bos.	3	Johnny Mowers	Det. 6 Bos. 4
Don Metz	Tor.	Apr. 14/42	Tor.	3	Johnny Mowers	Tor. 9 Det. 3
Mud Bruneteau	Det.	Apr. 1/43	Det.	3	Frank Brimsek	Det. 6 Bos. 2
Don Grosso	Det.	Apr. 7/43	Det.	3	Frank Brimsek	Det. 4 Bos. 0
Carl Liscombe	Det.	Apr. 3/45	Bos.	4	Paul Bibeault	Det. 5 Bos. 3
Billy Reay	Mtl.	Apr. 1/47	Bos.	4	Frank Brimsek	Mtl. 5 Bos. 1

Three-or-more-Goal Games, Playoffs — *continued*

Player	Team	Date	City	Total Goals	Opposing Goaltender	Score
Gerry Plamondon	Mtl.	Mar. 24/49	Det.	3	Harry Lumley	Mtl. 4 Det. 3
Sid Smith	Tor.	Apr. 10/49	Det.	3	Harry Lumley	Tor. 3 Det. 1
Pentti Lund	NYR	Apr. 2/50	NYR	3	Bill Durnan	NYR 4 Mtl. 1
Ted Lindsay	Det.	Apr. 5/55	Det.	4	Charlie Hodge (1) / Jacques Plante (3)	Det. 7 Mtl. 1
Gordie Howe	Det.	Apr. 10/55	Det.	3	Jacques Plante	Det. 5 Mtl. 1
Phil Goyette	Mtl.	Mar. 25/58	Mtl.	3	Terry Sawchuk	Mtl. 8 Det. 1
Jerry Toppazzini	Bos.	Apr. 5/58	Bos.	3	Gump Worsley	Bos. 8 NYR 2
Bob Pulford	Tor.	Apr. 19/62	Tor.	3	Glenn Hall	Tor. 8 Chi. 4
Dave Keon	Tor.	Apr. 9/64	Mtl.	3	Charlie Hodge (2) ENG (1)	Tor. 3 Mtl. 1
Henri Richard	Mtl.	Apr. 20/67	Mtl.	3	Terry Sawchuk (2) / Johnny Bower (1)	Mtl. 6 Tor. 2
Rosaire Paiement	Phi.	Apr. 13/68	Phi.	3	Glenn Hall (1) / Seth Martin (2)	Phi. 6 St.L. 1
Jean Beliveau	Mtl.	Apr. 20/68	Mtl.	3	Denis DeJordy	Mtl. 4 Chi. 1
Red Berenson	St.L.	Apr. 15/69	St.L.	3	Gerry Desjardins	St.L. 4 L.A. 0
Ken Schinkel	Pit.	Apr. 11/70	Oak.	3	Gary Smith	Pit. 5 Oak. 2
Jim Pappin	Chi.	Apr. 11/71	Phi.	3	Bruce Gamble	Chi. 6 Phi. 2
Bobby Orr	Bos.	Apr. 11/71	Bos.	3	Ken Dryden	Bos. 5 Mtl. 2
Jacques Lemaire	Mtl.	Apr. 20/71	Mtl.	3	Gump Worsley	Mtl. 7 Min. 2
Vic Hadfield	NYR	Apr. 22/71	NYR	3	Tony Esposito	NYR 4 Chi. 1
Fred Stanfield	Bos.	Apr. 18/72	Bos.	3	Jacques Caron	Bos. 6 St.L. 1
Ken Hodge	Bos.	Apr. 30/72	Bos.	3	Ed Giacomin	Bos. 6 NYR 5
Dick Redmond	Chi.	Apr. 4/73	Chi.	3	Wayne Stephenson	Chi. 7 St.L. 1
Steve Vickers	NYR	Apr. 10/73	NYR	3	Ross Brooks (2) / Eddie Johnston (1)	NYR 6 Bos. 3
Tom Williams	L.A.	Apr. 14/74	L.A.	3	Mike Veisor	L.A. 5 Chi. 1
Marcel Dionne	L.A.	Apr. 15/76	L.A.	3	Gilles Gilbert	L.A. 6 Bos. 4
Don Saleski	Phi.	Apr. 20/76	Phi.	3	Wayne Thomas	Phi. 7 Tor. 1
Darryl Sittler	Tor.	Apr. 22/76	Tor.	5	Bernie Parent	Tor. 8 Phi. 5
Reggie Leach	Phi.	May 6/76	Phi.	5	Gilles Gilbert	Phi. 6 Bos. 3
Jim Lorentz	Buf.	Apr. 7/77	Min.	3	Pete LoPresti (2) / Gary Smith (1)	Buf. 7 Min. 1
Bobby Schmautz	Bos.	Apr. 11/77	Bos.	3	Rogie Vachon	Bos. 8 L.A. 3
Billy Harris	NYI	Apr. 23/77	Mtl.	3	Ken Dryden	Mtl. 4 NYI 3
George Ferguson	Tor.	Apr. 11/78	Tor.	3	Rogie Vachon	Tor. 7 L.A. 3
Jean Ratelle	Bos.	May 3/79	Bos.	3	Ken Dryden	Bos. 4 Mtl. 3
Stan Jonathan	Bos.	May 8/79	Bos.	3	Ken Dryden	Bos. 5 Mtl. 2
Ron Duguay	NYR	Apr. 20/80	NYR	3	Pete Peeters	NYR 4 Phi. 2
Steve Shutt	Mtl.	Apr. 22/80	Mtl.	3	Gilles Meloche	Mtl. 6 Min. 2
Gilbert Perreault	Buf.	May 6/80	NYI	3	Billy Smith (2) ENG (1)	Buf. 7 NYI 4
Paul Holmgren	Phi.	May 15/80	Phi.	3	Billy Smith	Phi. 8 NYI 3
Steve Payne	Min.	Apr. 8/81	Bos.	3	Rogie Vachon	Min. 5 Bos. 4
Denis Potvin	NYI	Apr. 17/81	NYI	3	Andy Moog	NYI 6 Edm. 3
Barry Pederson	Bos.	Apr. 8/82	Bos.	3	Don Edwards	Bos. 7 Buf. 3
Duane Sutter	NYI	Apr. 15/83	NYI	3	Glen Hanlon	NYI 5 NYR 0
Doug Halward	Van.	Apr. 7/84	Van.	3	Reggie Lemelin (2) / Don Edwards (1)	Van. 7 Cgy. 0
Jorgen Pettersson	St.L.	Apr. 8/84	Det.	3	Eddie Mio	St.L. 3 Det. 2
Clark Gillies	NYI	May 12/84	NYI	3	Grant Fuhr	NYI 6 Edm. 1
Ken Linseman	Bos.	Apr. 14/85	Bos.	3	Steve Penney	Bos. 7 Mtl. 6
Dave Andreychuk	Buf.	Apr. 14/85	Buf.	3	Dan Bouchard	Buf. 7 Que. 4
Greg Paslawski	St.L.	Apr. 15/86	Min.	3	Don Beaupre	St.L. 6 Min. 3
Doug Risebrough	Cgy.	May 4/86	Cgy.	3	Rick Wamsley	Cgy. 8 St.L. 2
Mike McPhee	Mtl.	Apr. 11/87	Bos.	3	Doug Keans	Mtl. 5 Bos. 4
John Ogrodnick	Que.	Apr. 14/87	Hfd.	3	Mike Liut	Que. 7 Hfd. 5
Pelle Eklund	Phi.	May 10/87	Mtl.	3	Patrick Roy (1) / Brian Hayward (2)	Phi. 6 Mtl. 3
John Tucker	Buf.	Apr. 9/88	Bos.	4	Andy Moog	Buf. 6 Bos. 2
Tony Hrkac	St.L.	Apr. 10/88	St.L.	4	Darren Pang	St.L. 6 Chi. 5
Hakan Loob	Cgy.	Apr. 10/88	Cgy.	3	Glenn Healy	Cgy. 7 L.A. 3
Ed Olczyk	Tor.	Apr. 12/88	Tor.	3	Greg Stefan (2) / Glen Hanlon (1)	Tor. 6 Det. 5
Aaron Broten	N.J.	Apr. 20/88	N.J.	3	Pete Peeters	N.J. 5 Wsh. 2
Mark Johnson	N.J.	Apr. 22/88	Wsh.	4	Pete Peeters	N.J. 10 Wsh. 4
Patrik Sundstrom	N.J.	Apr. 22/88	Wsh.	3	Pete Peeters (2) / Clint Malarchuk (1)	N.J. 10 Wsh. 4
Bob Brooke	Min.	Apr. 5/89	St.L.	3	Greg Millen	St.L. 4 Min. 3
Chris Kontos	L.A.	Apr. 6/89	L.A.	3	Grant Fuhr	L.A. 5 Edm. 2
Wayne Presley	Chi.	Apr. 13/89	Chi.	3	Greg Stefan (1) / Glen Hanlon (2)	Chi. 7 Det. 1
Tony Granato	L.A.	Apr. 10/90	L.A.	3	Mike Vernon (2) / Rick Wamsley (2)	L.A. 12 Cgy. 4
Tomas Sandstrom	L.A.	Apr. 10/90	L.A.	3	Mike Vernon (1) / Rick Wamsley (2)	L.A. 12 Cgy. 4
Dave Taylor	L.A.	Apr. 10/90	L.A.	3	Mike Vernon (1) / Rick Wamsley (2)	L.A. 12 Cgy. 4
Bernie Nicholls	NYR	Apr. 19/90	NYR	3	Mike Liut	NYR 7 Wsh. 3
John Druce	Wsh.	Apr. 21/90	NYR	3	John Vanbiesbrouck	Wsh. 6 NYR 3
Adam Oates	St.L.	Apr. 12/91	St.L.	3	Tim Chevaldae	St.L. 6 Det. 1
Luc Robitaille	L.A.	Apr. 26/91	L.A.	3	Grant Fuhr	L.A. 5 Edm. 2
Ray Sheppard	Det.	Apr. 24/92	Min.	3	Jon Casey	Min. 5 Det. 2
Pavel Bure	Van.	Apr. 28/92	Wpg.	3	Rick Tabaracci	Van. 4 Wpg. 3
Joe Murphy	Edm.	May 6/92	Edm.	3	Kirk McLean	Edm. 5 Van. 2
Ron Francis	Pit.	May 9/92	Pit.	3	Mike Richter (2) / John V'brouck (1)	Pit. 5 NYR 4
Kevin Stevens	Pit.	May 21/92	Bos.	4	Andy Moog	Pit. 5 Bos. 2
Dirk Graham	Chi.	Jun. 1/92	Chi.	3	Tom Barrasso	Pit. 6 Chi. 5
Brian Noonan	Chi.	Apr. 18/93	Chi.	3	Curtis Joseph	St.L. 4 Chi. 3
Dale Hunter	Wsh.	Apr. 20/93	Wsh.	3	Glenn Healy	NYI 5 Wsh. 4
Teemu Selanne	Wpg.	Apr. 23/93	Wpg.	3	Kirk McLean	Wpg. 5 Van. 4
Ray Ferraro	NYI	Apr. 26/93	Wsh.	4	Don Beaupre	Wsh. 6 NYI 4
Al Iafrate	Wsh.	Apr. 26/93	Wsh.	3	Glenn Healy (2) / Mark Fitzpatrick (1)	Wsh. 6 NYI 4
Paul DiPietro	Mtl.	Apr. 28/93	Mtl.	3	Ron Hextall	Mtl. 6 Que. 2
Wendel Clark	Tor.	May 27/93	L.A.	3	Kelly Hrudey	L.A. 5 Tor. 4
Eric Desjardins	Mtl.	Jun. 3/93	Mtl.	3	Kelly Hrudey	Mtl. 3 L.A. 2
Tony Amonte	Chi.	Apr. 23/94	Chi.	4	Felix Potvin	Chi. 5 Tor. 4
Gary Suter	Chi.	Apr. 24/94	Chi.	3	Felix Potvin	Chi. 4 Tor. 3
Ulf Dahlen	S.J.	May 6/94	S.J.	3	Felix Potvin	S.J. 5 Tor. 2
Mike Sullivan	Cgy.	May 11/95	S.J.	3	Arturs Irbe (2) / Wade Flaherty (1)	Cgy. 9 S.J. 2
Theoren Fleury	Cgy.	May 13/95	S.J.	4	Arturs Irbe (3) ENG (1)	Cgy. 6 S.J. 4
Brendan Shanahan	St.L.	May 13/95	Van.	3	Kirk McLean	St.L. 5 Van. 2
John LeClair	Phi.	May 21/95	Phi.	3	Mike Richter	Phi. 5 NYR 4
Brian Leetch	NYR	May 22/95	Phi.	3	Ron Hextall	Phi. 4 NYR 3
Trevor Linden	Van.	Apr. 25/96	Col.	3	Patrick Roy	Col. 5 Van. 4
Jaromir Jagr	Pit.	May 11/96	Pit.	3	Mike Richter	Pit. 7 NYR 3
Peter Forsberg	Col.	Jun. 6/96	Col.	3	John Vanbiesbrouck	Col. 8 Fla. 1
Valeri Zelepukin	N.J.	Apr. 22/97	Mtl.	3	Jocelyn Thibault	N.J. 6 Mtl. 4
Valeri Kamensky	Col.	Apr. 24/97	Col.	3	Jeff Hackett (2) / Chris Terreri (1)	Col. 7 Chi. 0
Eric Lindros	Phi.	May 20/97	NYR	3	Mike Richter	Phi. 6 NYR 3
Matthew Barnaby	Buf.	May 10/98	Buf.	3	Andy Moog (2) ENG (1)	Buf. 6 Mtl. 3
Martin Straka	Pit.	Apr. 25/99	Pit.	3	Martin Brodeur	Pit. 4 N.J. 2
Martin Lapointe	Det.	Apr. 15/00	Det.	3	Stephane Fiset (2) / Jamie Storr (1)	Det. 8 L.A. 5
Doug Weight	Edm.	Apr. 16/00	Edm.	3	Ed Belfour	Edm. 5 Dal. 2
Bill Guerin	Edm.	Apr. 18/00	Edm.	3	Ed Belfour	Dal. 4 Edm. 3
Scott Young	St.L.	Apr. 23/00	S.J.	3	Steve Shields	St.L. 6 S.J. 2
Andy Delmore	Phi.	May 7/00	Phi.	3	Ron Tugnutt (2) / Peter Skudra (1)	Phi. 6 Pit. 3
Brett Hull	Det.	Apr. 27/02	Van.	3	Peter Skudra	Det. 6 Van. 4
Keith Tkachuk	St.L.	May 7/02	St.L.	3	Dominik Hasek	St.L. 6 Det. 1
Darren McCarty	Det.	May 18/02	Det.	3	Patrick Roy	Det. 5 Col. 3
Alexander Mogilny	Tor.	Apr. 9/03	Tor.	3	Roman Cechmanek (2) ENG (1)	Tor. 5 Phi. 2
Mike Sillinger	St.L.	Apr. 12/04	St.L.	3	Evgeni Nabokov (2) ENG (1)	St.L. 4 S.J. 1
Keith Primeau	Phi.	May 2/04	Phi.	3	Ed Belfour (2) / Trevor Kidd (1)	Phi. 7 Tor. 2
J.P. Dumont	Buf.	Apr. 24/06	Buf.	3	Antero Niittymaki (1) / Robert Esche (2)	Phi. 2 Buf. 8
John Madden	N.J.	Apr. 24/06	N.J.	3	Kevin Weekes	NYR 1 N.J. 4
Jason Pominville	Buf.	Apr. 24/06	Buf.	3	Antero Niittymaki (1) / Robert Esche (1)	Phi. 2 Buf. 8
Joffrey Lupul	Ana.	May 9/06	Col.	4	Jose Theodore	Ana. 4 Col. 3
Michael Nylander	NYR	Apr. 17/07	NYR	3	Kari Lehtonen	NYR 7 Atl. 0
Andy McDonald	Ana.	Apr. 25/07	Ana.	3	Dany Sabourin (1) / Roberto Luongo (2)	Ana. 5 Van. 1
Pavel Datsyuk	Det.	May 12/08	Dal.	3	Marty Turco	Det. 5 Dal. 2
Alex Ovechkin	Wsh.	May 4/09	Wsh.	3	Marc-Andre Fleury	Wsh. 4 Pit. 3
Sidney Crosby	Pit.	May 4/09	Wsh.	3	Semyon Varlamov	Wsh. 4 Pit. 3
Patrick Kane	Chi.	May 11/09	Chi.	3	Roberto Luongo	Chi. 7 Van. 5
Evgeni Malkin	Pit.	May 21/09	Pit.	3	Cam Ward	Pit. 7 Car. 4
Henrik Zetterberg	Det.	Apr. 16/10	Phx.	3	Ilya Bryzgalov	Det. 7 Phx. 4
Andrei Kostitsyn	Mtl.	Apr. 17/10	Wsh.	3	Jose Theodore (1) / Semyon Varlamov (2)	Wsh. 6 Mtl. 5
Nicklas Backstrom	Wsh.	Apr. 17/10	Wsh.	3	Jaroslav Halak	Wsh. 6 Mtl. 5
Dustin Byfuglien	Chi.	May 5/10	Van.	3	Roberto Luongo	Chi. 5 Van. 2
Jonathan Toews	Chi.	May 7/10	Van.	3	Roberto Luongo	Chi. 7 Van. 2

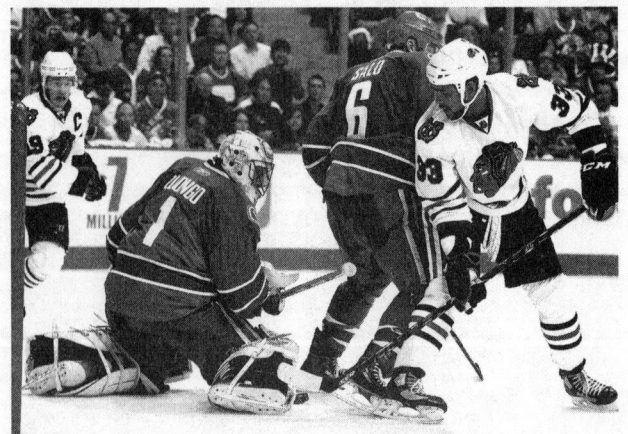

Chicago's Dustin Byfuglien (out front) and Jonathan Toews (far left) both scored their first career playoff hat trick during the Blackhawks' second-round series with Vancouver.

Overtime Games since 1918

Abbreviations: Teams/Cities: — **Ana.** - Anaheim; **Atl.** - Atlanta; **Bos.** - Boston; **Buf.** - Buffalo; **Cgy.** - Calgary; **Cgy. T.** - Calgary Tigers (Western Canada Hockey League); **Car.** - Carolina; **Chi.** - Chicago; **Col.** - Colorado; **Dal.** - Dallas; **Det.** - Detroit; **Edm.** - Edmonton; **Edm. E.** - Edmonton Eskimos (WCHL); **Fla.** - Florida; **Hfd.** - Hartford; **L.A.** - Los Angeles; **Min.** - Minnesota; **Mtl.** - Montreal; **Mtl. M.** - Montreal Maroons; **Nsh.** - Nashville, **N.J.** - New Jersey; **NYA** - NY Americans; **NYI** - New York Islanders; **NYR** - New York Rangers; **Oak.** - Oakland; **Ott.** - Ottawa; **Phi.** - Philadelphia; **Phx.** - Phoenix; **Pit.** - Pittsburgh; **Que.** - Quebec; **St.L.** - St. Louis; **Sea.** - Seattle Metropolitans (Pacific Coast Hockey Association); **S.J.** - San Jose; **T.B.** - Tampa Bay; **Tor.** - Toronto; **Van.** - Vancouver; **Van. M.** - Vancouver Millionaires (PCHA); **Vic.** - Victoria Cougars (WCHL); **Wpg.** - Winnipeg; **Wsh.** - Washington.

SERIES — **CF** - conference final; **CQF** - conference quarter-final; **CSF** - conference semi-final; **DF** - division final; **DSF** - division semi-final; **F** - final; **PRE** - preliminary round; **QF** - quarter-final; **SF** - semi-final.

Date	City	Series	Score		Scorer	Overtime	Series Winner
Mar. 26/19	Sea.	F	Mtl. 0	Sea. 0	no scorer	20:00	....
Mar. 29/19	Sea.	F	Mtl. 4	Sea. 3	Jack McDonald	15:57	....
Mar. 20/22	Tor.	F	Tor. 2	Van. M. 1	Babe Dye	4:50	Tor.
Mar. 29/23	Van.	F	Ott. 2	Edm. E. 1	Cy Denneny	2:08	Ott.
Mar. 31/27	Mtl.	QF	Mtl. 1	Mtl. M. 0	Howie Morenz	12:05	Mtl.
Apr. 7/27	Bos.	F	Ott. 0	Bos. 0	no scorer	20:00	Ott.
Apr. 11/27	Ott.	F	Bos. 1	Ott. 1	no scorer	20:00	Ott.
Apr. 3/28	Mtl.	QF	Mtl. M. 1	Mtl. 0	Russell Oatman	8:20	Mtl. M.
Apr. 7/28	Mtl.	F	NYR 2	Mtl. M. 1	Frank Boucher	7:05	NYR
Mar. 21/29	NYR	QF	NYR 1	NYA 0	Butch Keeling	29:50	NYR
Mar. 26/29	Tor.	SF	NYR 2	Tor. 1	Frank Boucher	2:03	NYR
Mar. 20/30	Mtl.	SF	Bos. 2	Mtl. M. 1	Harry Oliver	45:35	Bos.
Mar. 25/30	Bos.	SF	Mtl. M. 1	Bos. 0	Archie Wilcox	26:27	Bos.
Mar. 26/30	Mtl.	QF	Chi. 2	Mtl. 2	Howie Morenz (Mtl.)	51:43	Mtl.
Mar. 28/30	Mtl.	SF	Mtl. 2	NYR 1	Gus Rivers	68:52	Mtl.
Mar. 24/31	Bos.	SF	Bos. 5	Mtl. 4	Cooney Weiland	18:56	Mtl.
Mar. 26/31	Chi.	QF	Chi. 2	Tor. 1	Stew Adams	19:20	Chi.
Mar. 28/31	Mtl.	SF	Mtl. 4	Bos. 3	Georges Mantha	5:10	Mtl.
Apr. 1/31	Mtl.	SF	Mtl. 3	Bos. 2	Wildor Larochelle	19:00	Mtl.
Apr. 5/31	Chi.	F	Chi. 2	Mtl. 1	Johnny Gottselig	24:50	Mtl.
Apr. 9/31	Mtl.	F	Chi. 3	Mtl. 2	Cy Wentworth	53:50	Mtl.
Mar. 26/32	Mtl.	SF	NYR 4	Mtl. 3	Fred Cook	59:32	NYR
Apr. 2/32	Tor.	SF	Tor. 3	Mtl. M. 2	Bob Gracie	17:59	Tor.
Mar. 25/33	Bos.	SF	Bos. 2	Tor. 1	Marty Barry	14:14	Tor.
Mar. 28/33	Bos.	SF	Tor. 1	Bos. 0	Busher Jackson	15:03	Tor.
Mar. 30/33	Tor.	SF	Bos. 2	Tor. 1	Eddie Shore	4:23	Tor.
Apr. 3/33	Tor.	SF	Tor. 1	Bos. 0	Ken Doraty	104:46	Tor.
Apr. 13/33	Tor.	F	NYR 1	Tor. 0	Bill Cook	7:33	NYR
Mar. 22/34	Tor.	SF	Det. 2	Tor. 1	Herbie Lewis	1:33	Det.
Mar. 25/34	Chi.	QF	Chi. 1	Mtl. 1	Mush March (Chi)	11:05	Chi.
Apr. 3/34	Det.	F	Chi. 2	Det. 1	Paul Thompson	21:10	Chi.
Apr. 10/34	Chi.	F	Chi. 1	Det. 0	Mush March	30:05	Chi.
Mar. 23/35	Bos.	SF	Bos. 1	Tor. 0	Dit Clapper	33:26	Tor.
Mar. 26/35	Chi.	QF	Mtl. M. 1	Chi. 0	Baldy Northcott	4:02	Mtl. M.
Mar. 30/35	Tor.	SF	Tor. 2	Bos. 1	Pep Kelly	1:36	Tor.
Apr. 4/35	Tor.	F	Mtl. M. 3	Tor. 2	Dave Trottier	5:28	Mtl. M.
Mar. 24/36	Mtl.	SF	Det. 1	Mtl. M. 0	Mud Bruneteau	116:30	Det.
Apr. 9/36	Tor.	F	Tor. 4	Det. 3	Buzz Boll	0:31	Det.
Mar. 25/37	NYR	QF	NYR 2	Tor. 1	Babe Pratt	13:05	NYR
Apr. 1/37	Mtl.	SF	Det. 2	Mtl. 1	Hec Kilrea	51:49	Det.
Mar. 22/38	NYR	QF	NYA 2	NYR 1	John Sorrell	21:25	NYA
Mar. 24/38	Tor.	SF	Tor. 1	Bos. 0	George Parsons	21:31	Tor.
Mar. 26/38	Mtl.	QF	Chi. 3	Mtl. 2	Paul Thompson	11:49	Chi.
Mar. 27/38	NYR	QF	NYA 3	NYR 2	Lorne Carr	60:40	NYA
Mar. 29/38	Bos.	SF	Tor. 3	Bos. 2	Gordie Drillon	10:04	Tor.
Mar. 31/38	Chi.	SF	Chi. 1	NYA 0	Cully Dahlstrom	33:01	Chi.
Mar. 21/39	NYR	SF	Bos. 2	NYR 1	Mel Hill	59:25	Bos.
Mar. 23/39	Bos.	SF	Bos. 3	NYR 2	Mel Hill	8:24	Bos.
Mar. 26/39	Det.	QF	Det. 1	Mtl. 0	Marty Barry	7:47	Det.
Mar. 30/39	Bos.	SF	NYR 2	Bos. 1	Clint Smith	17:19	Bos.
Apr. 1/39	Tor.	SF	Tor. 5	Det. 4	Gordie Drillon	5:42	Tor.
Apr. 2/39	Bos.	SF	Bos. 2	NYR 1	Mel Hill	48:00	Bos.
Apr. 9/39	Bos.	F	Tor. 3	Bos. 2	Doc Romnes	10:38	Bos.
Mar. 19/40	Det.	QF	Det. 2	NYA 1	Syd Howe	0:25	Det.
Mar. 19/40	Tor.	QF	Tor. 3	Chi. 2	Syl Apps	6:35	Tor.
Apr. 2/40	NYR	F	NYR 2	Tor. 1	Alf Pike	15:30	NYR
Apr. 11/40	Tor.	F	NYR 2	Tor. 1	Muzz Patrick	31:43	NYR
Apr. 13/40	Tor.	F	NYR 3	Tor. 2	Bryan Hextall	2:07	NYR
Mar. 20/41	Det.	QF	Det. 2	NYR 1	Syd Howe	12:01	Det.
Mar. 22/41	Mtl.	QF	Mtl. 4	Chi. 3	Charlie Sands	34:04	Chi.
Mar. 29/41	Bos.	SF	Tor. 2	Bos. 1	Pete Langelle	17:31	Bos.
Mar. 30/41	Chi.	SF	Det. 2	Chi. 1	Gus Giesebrecht	9:15	Det.
Mar. 22/42	Chi.	QF	Bos. 2	Chi. 1	Des Smith	6:51	Bos.
Mar. 21/43	Bos.	SF	Bos. 5	Mtl. 4	Don Gallinger	12:30	Bos.
Mar. 23/43	Det.	SF	Tor. 3	Det. 2	Jack McLean	70:18	Det.
Mar. 25/43	Mtl.	SF	Bos. 3	Mtl. 2	Busher Jackson	3:20	Bos.
Mar. 30/43	Tor.	SF	Det. 3	Tor. 2	Adam Brown	9:21	Det.
Mar. 30/43	Bos.	SF	Bos. 5	Mtl. 4	Ab DeMarco	3:41	Bos.
Apr. 13/44	Mtl.	F	Mtl. 5	Chi. 4	Toe Blake	9:12	Mtl.
Mar. 27/45	Tor.	SF	Tor. 4	Mtl. 3	Gus Bodnar	12:36	Tor.
Mar. 29/45	Det.	SF	Det. 3	Bos. 2	Mud Bruneteau	17:12	Det.
Apr. 21/45	Tor.	F	Det. 1	Tor. 0	Eddie Bruneteau	14:16	Tor.
Mar. 28/46	Bos.	SF	Bos. 4	Det. 3	Don Gallinger	9:51	Bos.
Mar. 30/46	Mtl.	F	Mtl. 4	Bos. 3	Maurice Richard	9:08	Mtl.
Apr. 2/46	Mtl.	F	Mtl. 3	Bos. 2	Jimmy Peters	16:55	Mtl.
Apr. 7/46	Bos.	F	Bos. 3	Mtl. 2	Terry Reardon	15:13	Mtl.
Mar. 26/47	Tor.	SF	Tor. 3	Det. 2	Howie Meeker	3:05	Tor.
Mar. 27/47	Mtl.	SF	Mtl. 2	Bos. 1	Ken Mosdell	5:38	Mtl.
Apr. 3/47	Mtl.	SF	Mtl. 4	Bos. 3	John Quilty	36:40	Mtl.
Apr. 15/47	Tor.	F	Tor. 2	Mtl. 1	Syl Apps	16:36	Tor.
Mar. 24/48	Tor.	SF	Tor. 5	Bos. 4	Nick Metz	17:03	Tor.
Mar. 22/49	Det.	SF	Det. 2	Mtl. 1	Max McNab	44:52	Det.
Mar. 24/49	Det.	SF	Mtl. 4	Det. 3	Gerry Plamondon	2:59	Det.
Mar. 26/49	Tor.	SF	Bos. 5	Tor. 4	Woody Dumart	16:14	Tor.
Apr. 8/49	Det.	F	Tor. 3	Det. 2	Joe Klukay	17:31	Tor.
Apr. 4/50	Tor.	SF	Det. 2	Tor. 1	Leo Reise Jr.	20:38	Det.
Apr. 4/50	Mtl.	SF	Mtl. 3	NYR 2	Elmer Lach	15:19	NYR
Apr. 9/50	Det.	SF	Det. 1	Tor. 0	Leo Reise Jr.	8:39	Det.
Apr. 18/50	Det.	F	NYR 4	Det. 3	Don Raleigh	8:34	Det.
Apr. 20/50	Det.	F	NYR 2	Det. 1	Don Raleigh	1:38	Det.
Apr. 23/50	Det.	F	Det. 4	NYR 3	Pete Babando	28:31	Det.
Mar. 27/51	Det.	SF	Mtl. 3	Det. 2	Maurice Richard	61:09	Mtl.
Mar. 29/51	Det.	SF	Mtl. 1	Det. 0	Maurice Richard	42:20	Mtl.
Mar. 31/51	Tor.	SF	Bos. 1	Tor. 1	no scorer	20:00	Tor.
Apr. 11/51	Tor.	F	Tor. 3	Mtl. 2	Sid Smith	5:51	Tor.
Apr. 14/51	Tor.	F	Mtl. 3	Tor. 2	Maurice Richard	2:55	Tor.
Apr. 17/51	Mtl.	F	Tor. 2	Mtl. 1	Ted Kennedy	4:47	Tor.
Apr. 19/51	Mtl.	F	Tor. 3	Mtl. 2	Harry Watson	5:15	Tor.
Apr. 21/51	Tor.	F	Tor. 3	Mtl. 2	Bill Barilko	2:53	Tor.
Apr. 6/52	Bos.	SF	Mtl. 3	Bos. 2	Paul Masnick	27:49	Mtl.
Mar. 29/53	Bos.	SF	Bos. 2	Det. 1	Jack McIntyre	12:29	Bos.
Mar. 29/53	Chi.	SF	Chi. 2	Mtl. 1	Al Dewsbury	5:18	Mtl.
Apr. 16/53	Mtl.	F	Mtl. 1	Bos. 0	Elmer Lach	1:22	Mtl.
Apr. 1/54	Det.	SF	Det. 4	Tor. 3	Ted Lindsay	21:01	Det.
Apr. 11/54	Det.	F	Mtl. 1	Det. 0	Ken Mosdell	5:45	Det.
Apr. 16/54	Det.	F	Det. 2	Mtl. 1	Tony Leswick	4:29	Det.
Mar. 29/55	Bos.	SF	Mtl. 4	Bos. 3	Don Marshall	3:05	Mtl.
Mar. 24/56	Tor.	SF	Det. 5	Tor. 4	Ted Lindsay	4:22	Det.
Mar. 28/57	NYR	SF	NYR 4	Mtl. 3	Andy Hebenton	13:38	Mtl.
Apr. 4/57	Mtl.	SF	Mtl. 4	NYR 3	Maurice Richard	1:11	Mtl.
Mar. 27/58	NYR	SF	Bos. 4	NYR 3	Jerry Toppazzini	4:46	Bos.
Mar. 30/58	Det.	SF	Mtl. 2	Det. 1	André Pronovost	11:52	Mtl.
Apr. 17/58	Mtl.	F	Mtl. 3	Bos. 2	Maurice Richard	5:45	Mtl.
Mar. 28/59	Tor.	SF	Tor. 3	Bos. 2	Gerry Ehman	5:02	Tor.
Mar. 31/59	Tor.	SF	Tor. 3	Bos. 2	Frank Mahovlich	11:21	Tor.
Apr. 14/59	Tor.	F	Tor. 3	Mtl. 2	Dick Duff	10:06	Mtl.
Mar. 26/60	Mtl.	SF	Mtl. 4	Chi. 3	Doug Harvey	8:38	Mtl.
Mar. 27/60	Det.	SF	Tor. 5	Det. 4	Frank Mahovlich	43:00	Tor.
Mar. 29/60	Det.	SF	Det. 2	Tor. 1	Gerry Melnyk	1:54	Tor.
Mar. 22/61	Tor.	SF	Tor. 3	Det. 2	George Armstrong	24:51	Det.
Mar. 26/61	Chi.	SF	Chi. 2	Mtl. 1	Murray Balfour	52:12	Chi.
Apr. 5/62	Tor.	SF	Tor. 3	NYR 2	Red Kelly	24:23	Tor.
Apr. 2/64	Det.	SF	Chi. 3	Det. 2	Murray Balfour	8:21	Det.
Apr. 14/64	Tor.	F	Det. 4	Tor. 3	Larry Jeffrey	7:52	Tor.
Apr. 23/64	Det.	F	Tor. 4	Det. 3	Bob Baun	1:43	Tor.
Apr. 6/65	Tor.	SF	Tor. 3	Mtl. 2	Dave Keon	4:17	Mtl.
Apr. 13/65	Tor.	SF	Mtl. 4	Tor. 3	Claude Provost	16:33	Mtl.
May 5/66	Det.	F	Mtl. 3	Det. 2	Henri Richard	2:20	Mtl.
Apr. 13/67	NYR	SF	Mtl. 2	NYR 1	John Ferguson	6:28	Mtl.
Apr. 25/67	Tor.	F	Tor. 3	Mtl. 2	Bob Pulford	28:26	Tor.
Apr. 10/68	St.L.	QF	St.L. 3	Phi. 2	Larry Keenan	24:10	St.L.
Apr. 16/68	St.L.	QF	Phi. 2	St.L. 1	Don Blackburn	31:18	St.L.
Apr. 16/68	Min.	QF	Min. 4	L.A. 3	Milan Marcetta	9:11	Min.
Apr. 22/68	Min.	SF	Min. 3	St.L. 2	Parker MacDonald	3:41	St.L.
Apr. 27/68	St.L.	SF	St.L. 4	Min. 3	Gary Sabourin	1:32	St.L.
Apr. 28/68	Mtl.	SF	Mtl. 4	Chi. 3	Jacques Lemaire	2:14	Mtl.
Apr. 29/68	St.L.	SF	St.L. 3	Min. 2	Bill McCreary	17:27	St.L.
May 3/68	St.L.	SF	St.L. 2	Min. 1	Ron Schock	22:50	St.L.
May 5/68	St.L.	F	Mtl. 3	St.L. 2	Jacques Lemaire	1:41	Mtl.
May 9/68	Mtl.	F	Mtl. 4	St.L. 3	Bobby Rousseau	1:13	Mtl.
Apr. 2/69	Oak.	QF	L.A. 5	Oak. 4	Ted Irvine	0:19	L.A.
Apr. 10/69	Mtl.	SF	Mtl. 3	Bos. 2	Ralph Backstrom	0:42	Mtl.
Apr. 13/69	Mtl.	SF	Mtl. 4	Bos. 3	Mickey Redmond	4:55	Mtl.
Apr. 24/69	Bos.	SF	Mtl. 2	Bos. 1	Jean Béliveau	31:28	Mtl.
Apr. 12/70	Oak.	QF	Pit. 3	Oak. 2	Michel Briere	8:28	Pit.
May 10/70	Bos.	F	Bos. 4	St.L. 3	Bobby Orr	0:40	Bos.
Apr. 15/71	Tor.	QF	NYR 2	Tor. 1	Bob Nevin	9:07	NYR
Apr. 18/71	Chi.	SF	NYR 2	Chi. 1	Pete Stemkowski	1:37	Chi.
Apr. 27/71	Chi.	SF	Chi. 3	NYR 2	Bobby Hull	6:35	Chi.
Apr. 29/71	NYR	SF	NYR 3	Chi. 2	Pete Stemkowski	41:29	Chi.
May 4/71	Chi.	F	Chi. 2	Mtl. 1	Jim Pappin	21:11	Mtl.
Apr. 6/72	Bos.	QF	Tor. 4	Bos. 3	Jim Harrison	2:58	Bos.
Apr. 6/72	Min.	QF	Min. 6	St.L. 5	Bill Goldsworthy	1:36	St.L.
Apr. 9/72	Pit.	QF	Chi. 6	Pit. 5	Pit Martin	0:12	Chi.
Apr. 16/72	Min.	QF	St.L. 2	Min. 1	Kevin O'Shea	10:07	St.L.
Apr. 1/73	Mtl.	QF	Buf. 3	Mtl. 2	René Robert	9:18	Mtl.
Apr. 10/73	Phi.	QF	Phi. 3	Min. 2	Gary Dornhoefer	8:35	Phi.
Apr. 14/73	Mtl.	SF	Phi. 5	Mtl. 4	Rick MacLeish	2:56	Mtl.
Apr. 17/73	Mtl.	SF	Mtl. 4	Phi. 3	Larry Robinson	6:45	Mtl.
Apr. 14/74	Tor.	QF	Bos. 4	Tor. 3	Ken Hodge	1:27	Bos.
Apr. 14/74	Atl.	QF	Phi. 4	Atl. 3	Dave Schultz	5:40	Phi.
Apr. 16/74	Mtl.	QF	NYR 3	Mtl. 2	Ron Harris	4:07	NYR
Apr. 23/74	Chi.	SF	Chi. 4	Bos. 3	Jim Pappin	3:48	Bos.
Apr. 28/74	NYR	SF	NYR 2	Phi. 1	Rod Gilbert	4:20	Phi.
May 9/74	Bos.	F	Phi. 3	Bos. 2	Bobby Clarke	12:01	Phi.
Apr. 8/75	L.A.	PRE	L.A. 3	Tor. 2	Mike Murphy	8:53	Tor.
Apr. 10/75	Tor.	PRE	Tor. 3	L.A. 2	Blaine Stoughton	10:19	Tor.
Apr. 10/75	Chi.	PRE	Chi. 4	Bos. 3	Ivan Boldirev	7:33	Chi.
Apr. 11/75	NYR	PRE	NYI 4	NYR 3	J.P. Parise	0:11	NYI
Apr. 17/75	Chi.	QF	Chi. 5	Buf. 4	Stan Mikita	2:31	Buf.
Apr. 19/75	Tor.	QF	Phi. 4	Tor. 3	André Dupont	1:45	Phi.
Apr. 22/75	Mtl.	QF	Mtl. 5	Van. 4	Guy Lafleur	17:06	Mtl.
Apr. 27/75	Buf.	SF	Buf. 6	Mtl. 5	Danny Gare	4:42	Buf.
May 1/75	Phi.	SF	Phi. 5	NYI 4	Bobby Clarke	2:56	Phi.
May 6/75	Buf.	SF	Buf. 5	Mtl. 4	René Robert	5:56	Buf.
May 7/75	NYI	SF	NYI 4	Phi. 3	Jude Drouin	1:53	Phi.
May 20/75	Buf.	F	Buf. 5	Phi. 4	René Robert	18:29	Phi.
Apr. 8/76	Buf.	PRE	Buf. 3	St.L. 2	Danny Gare	11:43	Buf.

Overtime Games since 1918 — *continued*

Date	City	Series	Score		Scorer	Overtime	Series Winner
Apr. 9/76	Buf.	PRE	Buf. 2	St.L. 1	Don Luce	14:27	Buf.
Apr. 13/76	Bos.	QF	L.A. 3	Bos. 2	Butch Goring	0:27	Bos.
Apr. 13/76	Buf.	QF	Buf. 3	NYI 2	Danny Gare	14:04	NYI
Apr. 22/76	L.A.	QF	L.A. 4	Bos. 3	Butch Goring	18:28	Bos.
Apr. 29/76	Phi.	SF	Phi. 2	Bos. 1	Reggie Leach	13:38	Phi.
Apr. 15/77	Tor.	QF	Phi. 4	Tor. 3	Rick MacLeish	2:55	Phi.
Apr. 17/77	Tor.	QF	Phi. 6	Tor. 5	Reggie Leach	19:10	Phi.
Apr. 24/77	Phi.	SF	Bos. 4	Phi. 3	Rick Middleton	2:57	Bos.
Apr. 26/77	Phi.	SF	Bos. 5	Phi. 4	Terry O'Reilly	30:07	Bos.
May 3/77	Mtl.	SF	NYI 4	Mtl. 3	Billy Harris	3:58	Mtl.
May 14/77	Bos.	F	Mtl. 2	Bos. 1	Jacques Lemaire	4:32	Mtl.
Apr. 11/78	Phi.	PRE	Phi. 3	Col. 2	Mel Bridgman	0:23	Phi.
Apr. 13/78	NYR	PRE	NYR 4	Buf. 3	Don Murdoch	1:37	Buf.
Apr. 19/78	Bos.	QF	Bos. 4	Chi. 3	Terry O'Reilly	1:50	Bos.
Apr. 19/78	NYI	QF	NYI 3	Tor. 2	Mike Bossy	2:50	Tor.
Apr. 21/78	Chi.	QF	Bos. 4	Chi. 3	Peter McNab	10:17	Bos.
Apr. 25/78	NYI	QF	NYI 2	Tor. 1	Bob Nystrom	8:02	Tor.
Apr. 29/78	NYI	QF	Tor. 2	NYI 1	Lanny McDonald	4:13	Tor.
May 2/78	Bos.	SF	Bos. 3	Phi. 2	Rick Middleton	1:43	Bos.
May 16/78	Mtl.	F	Mtl. 3	Bos. 2	Guy Lafleur	13:09	Mtl.
May 21/78	Bos.	F	Bos. 4	Mtl. 3	Bobby Schmautz	6:22	Mtl.
Apr. 12/79	L.A.	PRE	NYR 2	L.A. 1	Phil Esposito	6:11	NYR
Apr. 14/79	Buf.	PRE	Pit. 4	Buf. 3	George Ferguson	0:47	Pit.
Apr. 16/79	Phi.	QF	Phi. 3	NYR 2	Ken Linseman	0:44	NYR
Apr. 18/79	NYI	QF	NYI 1	Chi. 0	Mike Bossy	2:31	NYI
Apr. 21/79	Tor.	QF	Mtl. 4	Tor. 3	Cam Connor	25:25	Mtl.
Apr. 22/79	Tor.	QF	Mtl. 5	Tor. 4	Larry Robinson	4:14	Mtl.
Apr. 28/79	NYI	SF	NYI 4	NYR 3	Denis Potvin	8:02	NYR
May 3/79	NYR	SF	NYI 3	NYR 2	Bob Nystrom	3:40	NYR
May 3/79	Bos.	SF	Bos. 4	Mtl. 3	Jean Ratelle	3:46	Mtl.
May 10/79	Mtl.	SF	Mtl. 5	Bos. 4	Yvon Lambert	9:33	Mtl.
May 19/79	NYR	F	Mtl. 4	NYR 3	Serge Savard	7:25	Mtl.
Apr. 8/80	NYR	PRE	NYR 2	Atl. 1	Steve Vickers	0:33	NYR
Apr. 8/80	Phi.	PRE	Phi. 4	Edm. 3	Bobby Clarke	8:06	Phi.
Apr. 8/80	Chi.	PRE	Chi. 3	St.L. 2	Doug Lecuyer	12:34	Chi.
Apr. 11/80	Hfd.	PRE	Mtl. 4	Hfd. 3	Yvon Lambert	0:29	Mtl.
Apr. 11/80	Tor.	PRE	Min. 4	Tor. 3	Al MacAdam	0:32	Min.
Apr. 11/80	L.A.	PRE	NYI 4	L.A. 3	Ken Morrow	6:55	NYI
Apr. 11/80	Edm.	PRE	Phi. 3	Edm. 2	Ken Linseman	23:56	Phi.
Apr. 16/80	Bos.	QF	NYI 2	Bos. 1	Clark Gillies	1:02	NYI
Apr. 17/80	Bos.	QF	NYI 5	Bos. 4	Bob Bourne	1:24	NYI
Apr. 21/80	NYI	QF	Bos. 4	NYI 3	Terry O'Reilly	17:13	NYI
May 1/80	Buf.	SF	NYI 2	Buf. 1	Bob Nystrom	21:20	NYI
May 13/80	Phi.	F	NYI 4	Phi. 3	Denis Potvin	4:07	NYI
May 24/80	NYI	F	NYI 5	Phi. 4	Bob Nystrom	7:11	NYI
Apr. 8/81	Buf.	PRE	Buf. 3	Van. 2	Alan Haworth	5:00	Buf.
Apr. 8/81	Bos.	PRE	Min. 5	Bos. 4	Steve Payne	3:34	Min.
Apr. 11/81	Chi.	PRE	Cgy. 5	Chi. 4	Willi Plett	35:17	Cgy.
Apr. 12/81	Que.	PRE	Que. 4	Phi. 3	Dale Hunter	0:37	Phi.
Apr. 14/81	St.L.	PRE	St.L. 4	Pit. 3	Mike Crombeen	25:16	St.L.
Apr. 16/81	Buf.	QF	Min. 4	Buf. 3	Steve Payne	0:22	Min.
Apr. 20/81	Min.	QF	Buf. 5	Min. 4	Craig Ramsay	16:32	Min.
Apr. 20/81	Edm.	QF	NYI 5	Edm. 4	Ken Morrow	5:41	NYI
Apr. 7/82	Min.	DSF	Chi. 3	Min. 2	Greg Fox	3:34	Chi.
Apr. 8/82	Edm.	DSF	Edm. 3	L.A. 2	Wayne Gretzky	6:20	L.A.
Apr. 8/82	Van.	DSF	Van. 2	Cgy. 1	Tiger Williams	14:20	Van.
Apr. 10/82	Pit.	DSF	Pit. 2	NYI 1	Rick Kehoe	4:14	NYI
Apr. 10/82	L.A.	DSF	L.A. 6	Edm. 5	Daryl Evans	2:35	L.A.
Apr. 13/82	Mtl.	DSF	Que. 3	Mtl. 2	Dale Hunter	0:22	Que.
Apr. 13/82	NYI	DSF	NYI 4	Pit. 3	John Tonelli	6:19	NYI
Apr. 16/82	Van.	DF	L.A. 3	Van. 2	Steve Bozek	4:33	Van.
Apr. 18/82	Que.	DF	Que. 3	Bos. 2	Wilf Paiement	11:44	Que.
Apr. 18/82	NYR	DF	NYI 4	NYR 3	Bryan Trottier	3:00	NYI
Apr. 18/82	L.A.	DF	Van. 4	L.A. 3	Colin Campbell	1:23	Van.
Apr. 21/82	St.L.	DF	St.L. 3	Chi. 2	Bernie Federko	3:28	Chi.
Apr. 23/82	Que.	DF	Bos. 6	Que. 5	Peter McNab	10:54	Que.
Apr. 27/82	Chi.	CF	Van. 2	Chi. 1	Jim Nill	28:58	Van.
May 1/82	Que.	CF	NYI 5	Que. 4	Wayne Merrick	16:52	NYI
May 8/82	NYI	F	NYI 6	Van. 5	Mike Bossy	19:58	NYI
Apr. 5/83	Bos.	DSF	Bos. 4	Que. 3	Barry Pederson	1:46	Bos.
Apr. 6/83	Cgy.	DSF	Cgy. 4	Van. 3	Eddy Beers	12:27	Cgy.
Apr. 7/83	Min.	DSF	Min. 5	Tor. 4	Bobby Smith	5:03	Min.
Apr. 10/83	Tor.	DSF	Min. 5	Tor. 4	Dino Ciccarelli	8:05	Min.
Apr. 10/83	Van.	DSF	Cgy. 4	Van. 3	Greg Meredith	1:06	Cgy.
Apr. 18/83	Min.	DF	Chi. 4	Min. 3	Rich Preston	10:34	Chi.
Apr. 24/83	Bos.	DF	Bos. 3	Buf. 2	Brad Park	1:52	Bos.
Apr. 5/84	Edm.	DSF	Edm. 5	Wpg. 4	Randy Gregg	0:21	Edm.
Apr. 7/84	Det.	DSF	St.L. 4	Det. 3	Mark Reeds	37:07	St.L.
Apr. 8/84	Det.	DSF	St.L. 3	Det. 2	Jorgen Pettersson	2:42	St.L.
Apr. 10/84	NYI	DSF	NYI 3	NYR 2	Ken Morrow	8:56	NYI
Apr. 13/84	Min.	DF	St.L. 4	Min. 3	Doug Gilmour	16:16	Min.
Apr. 13/84	Edm.	DF	Cgy. 6	Edm. 5	Carey Wilson	3:42	Edm.
Apr. 13/84	NYI	DF	NYI 5	Wsh. 4	Anders Kallur	7:35	NYI
Apr. 16/84	Mtl.	DF	Que. 4	Mtl. 3	Bo Berglund	3:00	Mtl.
Apr. 20/84	Cgy.	DF	Cgy. 5	Edm. 4	Lanny McDonald	1:04	Edm.
Apr. 22/84	Min.	DF	Min. 4	St.L. 3	Steve Payne	6:00	Min.
Apr. 10/85	Phi.	DSF	Phi. 5	NYR 4	Mark Howe	8:01	Phi.
Apr. 10/85	Wsh.	DSF	Wsh. 4	NYI 3	Alan Haworth	2:28	NYI
Apr. 10/85	Edm.	DSF	Edm. 3	L.A. 2	Lee Fogolin	3:01	Edm.
Apr. 10/85	Wpg.	DSF	Wpg. 5	Cgy. 4	Brian Mullen	7:56	Wpg.
Apr. 11/85	Wsh.	DSF	Wsh. 2	NYI 1	Mike Gartner	21:23	NYI
Apr. 13/85	L.A.	DSF	Edm. 4	L.A. 3	Glenn Anderson	0:46	Edm.
Apr. 18/85	Mtl.	DF	Que. 2	Mtl. 1	Mark Kumpel	12:23	Que.
Apr. 23/85	Que.	DF	Que. 7	Mtl. 6	Dale Hunter	18:36	Que.
Apr. 25/85	Min.	DF	Chi. 7	Min. 6	Darryl Sutter	21:57	Chi.
Apr. 28/85	Chi.	DF	Min. 5	Chi. 4	Dennis Maruk	1:14	Chi.
Apr. 30/85	Min.	DF	Chi. 6	Min. 5	Darryl Sutter	15:41	Chi.
May 2/85	Mtl.	DF	Que. 3	Mtl. 2	Peter Stastny	2:22	Que.
May 5/85	Que.	CF	Que. 2	Phi. 1	Peter Stastny	6:20	Phi.
Apr. 9/86	Que.	DSF	Hfd. 3	Que. 2	Sylvain Turgeon	2:36	Hfd.
Apr. 12/86	Wpg.	DSF	Cgy. 4	Wpg. 3	Lanny McDonald	8:25	Cgy.
Apr. 17/86	Wsh.	DF	NYR 4	Wsh. 3	Brian MacLellan	1:16	NYR
Apr. 20/86	Edm.	DF	Edm. 6	Cgy. 5	Glenn Anderson	1:04	Cgy.
Apr. 23/86	Hfd.	DF	Hfd. 2	Mtl. 1	Kevin Dineen	1:07	Mtl.
Apr. 23/86	NYR	DF	NYR 6	Wsh. 5	Bob Brooke	2:40	NYR
Apr. 26/86	St L.	DF	St L. 4	Tor. 3	Mark Reeds	7:11	St L.
Apr. 29/86	Mtl.	DF	Mtl. 2	Hfd. 1	Claude Lemieux	5:55	Mtl.
May 5/86	NYR	CF	Mtl. 4	NYR 3	Claude Lemieux	9:41	Mtl.
May 12/86	St L.	CF	St L. 6	Cgy. 5	Doug Wickenheiser	7:30	Cgy.
May 18/86	Cgy.	F	Mtl. 3	Cgy. 2	Brian Skrudland	0:09	Mtl.
Apr. 8/87	Hfd.	DSF	Hfd. 3	Que. 2	Paul MacDermid	2:20	Que.
Apr. 9/87	Mtl.	DSF	Mtl. 4	Bos. 3	Mats Naslund	2:38	Mtl.
Apr. 9/87	St.L.	DSF	Tor. 3	St.L. 2	Rick Lanz	10:17	Tor.
Apr. 11/87	Wpg.	DSF	Cgy. 3	Wpg. 2	Mike Bullard	3:53	Wpg.
Apr. 11/87	Chi.	DSF	Det. 4	Chi. 3	Shawn Burr	4:51	Det.
Apr. 16/87	Que.	DSF	Que. 5	Hfd. 4	Peter Stastny	6:05	Que.
Apr. 18/87	Wsh.	DSF	NYI 3	Wsh. 2	Pat LaFontaine	68:47	NYI
Apr. 21/87	Edm.	DF	Edm. 3	Wpg. 2	Glenn Anderson	0:36	Edm.
Apr. 26/87	Que.	DF	Mtl. 3	Que. 2	Mats Naslund	5:30	Mtl.
Apr. 27/87	Tor.	DF	Tor. 3	Det. 2	Mike Allison	9:31	Det.
May 4/87	Phi.	CF	Phi. 4	Mtl. 3	Ilkka Sinislao	9:11	Phi.
May 20/87	Edm.	F	Edm. 3	Phi. 2	Jari Kurri	6:50	Edm.
Apr. 6/88	NYI	DSF	NYI 4	N.J. 3	Pat LaFontaine	6:11	N.J.
Apr. 10/88	Phi.	DSF	Phi. 5	Wsh. 4	Murray Craven	1:18	Wsh.
Apr. 10/88	N.J.	DSF	NYI 5	N.J. 4	Brent Sutter	15:07	N.J.
Apr. 10/88	Buf.	DSF	Buf. 6	Bos. 5	John Tucker	5:32	Bos.
Apr. 12/88	Det.	DSF	Tor. 6	Det. 5	Ed Olczyk	0:34	Det.
Apr. 16/88	Wsh.	DSF	Wsh. 5	Phi. 4	Dale Hunter	5:57	Wsh.
Apr. 21/88	Cgy.	DF	Edm. 5	Cgy. 4	Wayne Gretzky	7:54	Edm.
May 4/88	Bos.	CF	N.J. 3	Bos. 2	Doug Brown	17:46	Bos.
May 9/88	Det.	CF	Edm. 4	Det. 3	Jari Kurri	11:02	Edm.
Apr. 5/89	St.L.	DSF	St.L. 4	Min. 3	Brett Hull	11:55	St.L.
Apr. 5/89	Cgy.	DSF	Van. 4	Cgy. 3	Paul Reinhart	2:47	Cgy.
Apr. 6/89	St.L.	DSF	St.L. 4	Min. 3	Rick Meagher	5:30	St.L.
Apr. 6/89	Det.	DSF	Chi. 5	Det. 4	Duane Sutter	14:36	Chi.
Apr. 8/89	Hfd.	DSF	Mtl. 5	Hfd. 4	Stephane Richer	5:01	Mtl.
Apr. 8/89	Phi.	DSF	Wsh. 4	Phi. 3	Kelly Miller	0:51	Phi.
Apr. 9/89	Hfd.	DSF	Mtl. 4	Hfd. 3	Russ Courtnall	15:12	Mtl.
Apr. 15/89	Cgy.	DSF	Cgy. 4	Van. 3	Joel Otto	19:21	Cgy.
Apr. 18/89	Cgy.	DF	Cgy. 4	L.A. 3	Doug Gilmour	7:47	Cgy.
Apr. 19/89	Mtl.	DF	Mtl. 3	Bos. 2	Bobby Smith	12:24	Mtl.
Apr. 20/89	St.L.	DF	St.L. 5	Chi. 4	Tony Hrkac	33:49	Chi.
Apr. 21/89	Phi.	DF	Pit. 4	Phi. 3	Phil Bourque	12:08	Phi.
May 8/89	Chi.	CF	Cgy. 2	Chi. 1	Al MacInnis	15:05	Cgy.
May 9/89	Mtl.	CF	Phi. 2	Mtl. 1	Dave Poulin	5:02	Mtl.
May 19/89	Mtl.	F	Mtl. 4	Cgy. 3	Ryan Walter	38:08	Cgy.
Apr. 5/90	N.J.	DSF	Wsh. 5	N.J. 4	Dino Ciccarelli	5:34	Wsh.
Apr. 6/90	Edm.	DSF	Edm. 3	Wpg. 2	Mark Lamb	4:21	Edm.
Apr. 8/90	Tor.	DSF	St.L. 6	Tor. 5	Sergio Momesso	6:04	St.L.
Apr. 8/90	L.A.	DSF	L.A. 2	Cgy. 1	Tony Granato	8:37	L.A.
Apr. 9/90	Mtl.	DSF	Mtl. 2	Buf. 1	Brian Skrudland	12:35	Mtl.
Apr. 9/90	NYI	DSF	NYI 4	NYR 3	Brent Sutter	20:59	NYR
Apr. 10/90	Wpg.	DSF	Wpg. 4	Edm. 3	Dave Ellett	21:08	Edm.
Apr. 14/90	L.A.	DSF	L.A. 4	Cgy. 3	Mike Krushelnyski	23:14	L.A.
Apr. 15/90	Hfd.	DSF	Hfd. 3	Bos. 2	Kevin Dineen	12:30	Bos.
Apr. 21/90	Bos.	DF	Bos. 5	Mtl. 4	Garry Galley	3:42	Bos.
Apr. 24/90	L.A.	DF	Edm. 6	L.A. 5	Joe Murphy	4:42	Edm.
Apr. 25/90	Wsh.	DF	Wsh. 4	NYR 3	Rod Langway	0:34	Wsh.
Apr. 27/90	NYR	DF	Wsh. 2	NYR 1	John Druce	6:48	Wsh.
May 15/90	Bos.	F	Edm. 3	Bos. 2	Petr Klima	55:13	Edm.
Apr. 4/91	Chi.	DSF	Min. 4	Chi. 3	Brian Propp	4:14	Min.
Apr. 5/91	Pit.	DSF	Pit. 5	N.J. 4	Jaromir Jagr	8:52	Pit.
Apr. 6/91	L.A.	DSF	L.A. 3	Van. 2	Wayne Gretzky	11:08	L.A.
Apr. 8/91	Van.	DSF	Van. 2	L.A. 1	Cliff Ronning	3:12	L.A.
Apr. 11/91	NYR	DSF	Wsh. 5	NYR 4	Dino Ciccarelli	6:44	Wsh.
Apr. 11/91	Mtl.	DSF	Mtl. 4	Buf. 3	Russ Courtnall	5:56	Mtl.
Apr. 14/91	Edm.	DSF	Cgy. 2	Edm. 1	Theoren Fleury	4:40	Edm.
Apr. 16/91	Cgy.	DSF	Edm. 5	Cgy. 4	Esa Tikkanen	6:58	Edm.
Apr. 18/91	L.A.	DF	L.A. 4	Edm. 3	Luc Robitaille	2:13	Edm.
Apr. 19/91	Bos.	DF	Mtl. 4	Bos. 3	Stephane Richer	0:27	Bos.
Apr. 19/91	Pit.	DF	Pit. 7	Wsh. 6	Kevin Stevens	8:10	Pit.
Apr. 20/91	L.A.	DF	Edm. 4	L.A. 3	Petr Klima	24:48	Edm.
Apr. 22/91	Edm.	DF	Edm. 4	L.A. 3	Esa Tikkanen	20:48	Edm.
Apr. 27/91	Mtl.	DF	Mtl. 3	Bos. 2	Shayne Corson	17:47	Bos.
Apr. 28/91	Edm.	DF	Edm. 4	L.A. 3	Craig MacTavish	16:57	Edm.
May 3/91	Bos.	CF	Bos. 5	Pit. 4	Vladimir Ruzicka	8:14	Pit.
Apr. 21/92	Bos.	DSF	Bos. 3	Buf. 2	Adam Oates	11:14	Bos.
Apr. 22/92	Min.	DSF	Det. 5	Min. 4	Yves Racine	1:15	Det.
Apr. 22/92	St.L.	DSF	St.L. 5	Chi. 4	Brett Hull	23:33	Chi.
Apr. 25/92	Buf.	DSF	Bos. 5	Buf. 4	Ted Donato	2:08	Bos.
Apr. 28/92	Min.	DSF	Det. 1	Min. 0	Sergei Fedorov	16:13	Det.
Apr. 29/92	Hfd.	DSF	Hfd. 2	Mtl. 1	Yvon Corriveau	0:24	Mtl.
May 1/92	Mtl.	DSF	Mtl. 3	Hfd. 2	Russ Courtnall	25:26	Mtl.
May 3/92	Van.	DF	Edm. 4	Van. 3	Joe Murphy	8:36	Edm.
May 5/92	Mtl.	DF	Bos. 3	Mtl. 2	Peter Douris	3:12	Bos.
May 7/92	Pit.	DF	NYR 6	Pit. 5	Kris King	1:29	Pit.
May 9/92	Pit.	DF	Pit. 5	NYR 4	Ron Francis	2:47	Pit.
May 17/92	Pit.	CF	Pit. 4	Bos. 3	Jaromir Jagr	9:44	Pit.

Overtime Games since 1918 — *continued*

Date	City	Series	Score		Scorer	Overtime	Series Winner
May 20/92	Edm.	CF	Chi. 4	Edm. 3	Jeremy Roenick	2:45	Chi.
Apr. 18/93	Bos.	DSF	Buf. 5	Bos. 4	Bob Sweeney	11:03	Buf.
Apr. 18/93	Que.	DSF	Que. 3	Mtl. 2	Scott Young	16:49	Mtl.
Apr. 20/93	Wsh.	DSF	NYI 5	Wsh. 4	Brian Mullen	34:50	NYI
Apr. 22/93	Mtl.	DSF	Mtl. 2	Que. 1	Vincent Damphousse	10:30	Mtl.
Apr. 22/93	Buf.	DSF	Buf. 4	Bos. 3	Yuri Khmylev	1:05	Buf.
Apr. 22/93	NYI	DSF	NYI 4	Wsh. 3	Ray Ferraro	4:46	NYI
Apr. 24/93	Buf.	DSF	Buf. 6	Bos. 5	Brad May	4:48	Buf.
Apr. 24/93	NYI	DSF	NYI 4	Wsh. 3	Ray Ferraro	25:40	NYI
Apr. 25/93	St.L.	DSF	St.L. 4	Chi. 3	Craig Janney	10:43	St.L.
Apr. 26/93	Que.	DSF	Mtl. 5	Que. 4	Kirk Muller	8:17	Mtl.
Apr. 27/93	Det.	DSF	Tor. 5	Det. 4	Mike Foligno	2:05	Tor.
Apr. 27/93	Van.	DSF	Wpg. 4	Van. 3	Teemu Selanne	6:18	Van.
Apr. 29/93	Wpg.	DSF	Van. 4	Wpg. 3	Greg Adams	4:30	Van.
May 1/93	Det.	DSF	Tor. 4	Det. 3	Nikolai Borschevsky	2:35	Tor.
May 3/93	Tor.	DF	Tor. 2	St.L. 1	Doug Gilmour	23:16	Tor.
May 4/93	Mtl.	DF	Mtl. 4	Buf. 3	Guy Carbonneau	2:50	Mtl.
May 5/93	Tor.	DF	St.L. 2	Tor. 1	Jeff Brown	23:03	Tor.
May 6/93	Buf.	DF	Mtl. 4	Buf. 3	Gilbert Dionne	8:28	Mtl.
May 8/93	Buf.	DF	Mtl. 4	Buf. 3	Kirk Muller	11:37	Mtl.
May 11/93	Van.	DF	L.A. 4	Van. 3	Gary Shuchuk	26:31	L.A.
May 14/93	Pit.	DF	NYI 4	Pit. 3	Dave Volek	5:16	NYI
May 18/93	Mtl.	CF	Mtl. 4	NYI 3	Stephan Lebeau	26:21	Mtl.
May 20/93	NYI	CF	Mtl. 2	NYI 1	Guy Carbonneau	12:34	Mtl.
May 25/93	Tor.	CF	Tor. 3	L.A. 2	Glenn Anderson	19:20	L.A.
May 27/93	L.A.	CF	L.A. 5	Tor. 4	Wayne Gretzky	1:41	L.A.
Jun. 3/93	Mtl.	F	Mtl. 3	L.A. 2	Eric Desjardins	0:51	Mtl.
Jun. 5/93	L.A.	F	Mtl. 4	L.A. 3	John LeClair	0:34	Mtl.
Jun. 7/93	L.A.	F	Mtl. 3	L.A. 2	John LeClair	14:37	Mtl.
Apr. 20/94	Tor.	CQF	Tor. 1	Chi. 0	Todd Gill	2:15	Tor.
Apr. 22/94	St.L.	CQF	Dal. 5	St.L. 4	Paul Cavallini	8:34	Dal.
Apr. 24/94	Chi.	CQF	Chi. 4	Tor. 3	Jeremy Roenick	1:23	Tor.
Apr. 25/94	Bos.	CQF	Mtl. 2	Bos. 1	Kirk Muller	17:18	Bos.
Apr. 26/94	Cgy.	CQF	Van. 2	Cgy. 1	Geoff Courtnall	7:15	Van.
Apr. 27/94	Buf.	CQF	Buf. 1	N.J. 0	Dave Hannan	65:43	N.J.
Apr. 28/94	Van.	CQF	Van. 3	Cgy. 2	Trevor Linden	16:43	Van.
Apr. 30/94	Cgy.	CQF	Van. 4	Cgy. 3	Pavel Bure	22:20	Van.
May 3/94	N.J.	CSF	Bos. 6	N.J. 5	Don Sweeney	9:08	N.J.
May 7/94	Bos.	CSF	N.J. 5	Bos. 4	Stephane Richer	14:19	N.J.
May 8/94	Van.	CSF	Van. 2	Dal. 1	Sergio Momesso	11:01	Van.
May 12/94	Tor.	CSF	Tor. 3	S.J. 2	Mike Gartner	8:53	Tor.
May 15/94	NYR	CF	N.J. 4	NYR 3	Stephane Richer	35:23	NYR
May 16/94	Tor.	CF	Tor. 3	Van. 2	Peter Zezel	16:55	Van.
May 19/94	N.J.	CF	NYR 3	N.J. 2	Stephane Matteau	26:13	NYR
May 24/94	Van.	CF	Van. 4	Tor. 3	Greg Adams	20:14	Van.
May 27/94	NYR	CF	NYR 2	N.J. 1	Stephane Matteau	24:24	NYR
May 31/94	NYR	F	Van. 3	NYR 2	Greg Adams	19:26	NYR
May 7/95	Phi.	CQF	Phi. 4	Buf. 3	Karl Dykhuis	10:06	Phi.
May 9/95	Cgy.	CQF	S.J. 5	Cgy. 4	Ulf Dahlen	12:21	S.J.
May 12/95	NYR	CQF	NYR 3	Que. 2	Steve Larmer	8:09	NYR
May 12/95	N.J.	CQF	N.J. 1	Bos. 0	Randy McKay	8:51	N.J.
May 14/95	Pit.	CQF	Pit. 6	Wsh. 5	Luc Robitaille	4:30	Pit.
May 15/95	St.L.	CQF	Van. 6	St.L. 5	Cliff Ronning	1:48	Van.
May 17/95	Tor.	CQF	Tor. 5	Chi. 4	Randy Wood	10:00	Chi.
May 19/95	Cgy.	CQF	S.J. 5	Cgy. 4	Ray Whitney	21:54	S.J.
May 21/95	Phi.	CSF	Phi. 5	NYR 4	Eric Desjardins	7:03	Phi.
May 21/95	Chi.	CSF	Chi. 2	Van. 1	Joe Murphy	9:04	Chi.
May 22/95	Phi.	CSF	Phi. 4	NYR 3	Kevin Haller	0:25	Phi.
May 25/95	Van.	CSF	Chi. 3	Van. 2	Chris Chelios	6:22	Chi.
May 26/95	N.J.	CSF	N.J. 2	Pit. 1	Neal Broten	18:36	N.J.
May 27/95	Van.	CSF	Chi. 4	Van. 3	Chris Chelios	5:35	Chi.
Jun. 1/95	Det.	CF	Det. 2	Chi. 1	Nicklas Lidstrom	1:01	Det.
Jun. 6/95	Chi.	CF	Det. 4	Chi. 3	Vladimir Konstantinov	29:25	Det.
Jun. 7/95	N.J.	CF	Phi. 3	N.J. 2	Eric Lindros	4:19	N.J.
Jun. 11/95	Det.	CF	Det. 2	Chi. 1	Vyacheslav Kozlov	22:25	Det.
Apr. 16/96	NYR	CQF	Mtl. 3	NYR 2	Vincent Damphousse	5:04	NYR
Apr. 18/96	Tor.	CQF	Tor. 5	St.L. 4	Mats Sundin	4:02	St.L.
Apr. 18/96	Phi.	CQF	T.B. 2	Phi. 1	Brian Bellows	9:05	Phi.
Apr. 21/96	St.L.	CQF	St.L. 3	Tor. 2	Glenn Anderson	1:24	St.L.
Apr. 21/96	T.B.	CQF	T.B. 5	Phi. 4	Alexander Selivanov	2:04	Phi.
Apr. 23/96	Cgy.	CQF	Chi. 2	Cgy. 1	Joe Murphy	50:02	Chi.
Apr. 24/96	Wsh.	CQF	Pit. 3	Wsh. 2	Petr Nedved	79:15	Pit.
Apr. 25/96	Col.	CQF	Col. 5	Van. 4	Joe Sakic	0:51	Col.
Apr. 25/96	Tor.	CQF	Tor. 5	St.L. 4	Mike Gartner	7:31	St.L.
May 2/96	Col.	CSF	Chi. 3	Col. 2	Jeremy Roenick	6:29	Col.
May 6/96	Chi.	CSF	Chi. 4	Col. 3	Sergei Krivokrasov	0:46	Col.
May 8/96	St.L.	CSF	St.L. 5	Det. 4	Igor Kravchuk	3:23	Det.
May 8/96	Chi.	CSF	Col. 3	Chi. 2	Joe Sakic	44:33	Col.
May 9/96	Fla.	CSF	Fla. 4	Phi. 3	Dave Lowry	4:06	Fla.
May 12/96	Phi.	CSF	Fla. 2	Phi. 1	Mike Hough	28:05	Fla.
May 13/96	Chi.	CSF	Col. 4	Chi. 3	Sandis Ozolinsh	25:18	Col.
May 16/96	Det.	CSF	Det. 1	St.L. 0	Steve Yzerman	21:15	Det.
May 19/96	Det.	CF	Col. 3	Det. 2	Mike Keane	17:31	Col.
Jun. 10/96	Fla.	F	Col. 1	Fla. 0	Uwe Krupp	44:31	Col.
Apr. 20/97	Chi.	CQF	Chi. 4	Col. 3	Sergei Krivokrasov	31:03	Col.
Apr. 20/97	Edm.	CQF	Edm. 4	Dal. 3	Kelly Buchberger	9:15	Edm.
Apr. 22/97	NYR	CQF	NYR 4	Fla. 3	Esa Tikkanen	16:29	NYR
Apr. 23/97	Ott.	CQF	Ott. 1	Buf. 0	Daniel Alfredsson	2:34	Buf.
Apr. 24/97	Mtl.	CQF	Mtl. 4	N.J. 3	Patrice Brisebois	47:37	N.J.
Apr. 25/97	Fla.	CQF	NYR 3	Fla. 2	Esa Tikkanen	12:02	NYR
Apr. 25/97	Dal.	CQF	Edm. 1	Dal. 0	Ryan Smyth	20:22	Edm.
Apr. 27/97	Phx.	CQF	Ana. 3	Phx. 2	Paul Kariya	7:29	Ana.
Apr. 29/97	Buf.	CQF	Buf. 3	Ott. 2	Derek Plante	5:24	Buf.
Apr. 29/97	Dal.	CQF	Edm. 4	Dal. 3	Todd Marchant	12:26	Edm.
May 2/97	Det.	CSF	Det. 2	Ana. 1	Martin Lapointe	0:59	Det.
May 4/97	Det.	CSF	Det. 3	Ana. 2	Vyacheslav Kozlov	41:31	Det.
May 8/97	Ana.	CSF	Det. 3	Ana. 2	Brendan Shanahan	37:03	Det.
May 9/97	Phi.	CSF	Buf. 5	Phi. 4	Ed Ronan	6:24	Phi.
May 9/97	Edm.	CSF	Col. 3	Edm. 2	Claude Lemieux	8:35	Col.
May 11/97	N.J.	CSF	NYR 2	N.J. 1	Adam Graves	14:08	NYR
Apr. 22/98	N.J.	CQF	Ott. 2	N.J. 1	Bruce Gardiner	5:58	Ott.
Apr. 23/98	Pit.	CQF	Mtl. 3	Pit. 2	Benoit Brunet	18:43	Mtl.
Apr. 24/98	Wsh.	CQF	Bos. 4	Wsh. 3	Darren Van Impe	20:54	Wsh.
Apr. 26/98	Ott.	CQF	Ott. 2	N.J. 1	Alexei Yashin	2:47	Ott.
Apr. 26/98	Bos.	CQF	Wsh. 3	Bos. 2	Joe Juneau	26:31	Wsh.
Apr. 26/98	Edm.	CQF	Col. 5	Edm. 4	Joe Sakic	15:25	Edm.
Apr. 28/98	S.J.	CQF	S.J. 1	Dal. 0	Andrei Zyuzin	6:31	Dal.
May 1/98	Phi.	CQF	Buf. 3	Phi. 2	Michal Grosek	5:40	Buf.
May 2/98	S.J.	CQF	Dal. 3	S.J. 2	Mike Keane	3:43	Dal.
May 3/98	Bos.	CQF	Wsh. 3	Bos. 2	Brian Bellows	15:24	Wsh.
May 3/98	Buf.	CQF	Buf. 3	Mtl. 2	Geoff Sanderson	2:37	Buf.
May 11/98	Edm.	CSF	Dal. 1	Edm. 0	Benoit Hogue	13:07	Dal.
May 12/98	Mtl.	CSF	Buf. 5	Mtl. 4	Michael Peca	21:24	Buf.
May 12/98	St.L.	CSF	Det. 3	St.L. 2	Brendan Shanahan	31:12	Det.
May 25/98	Wsh.	CF	Wsh. 3	Buf. 2	Todd Krygier	3:01	Wsh.
May 28/98	Buf.	CF	Wsh. 4	Buf. 3	Peter Bondra	9:37	Wsh.
Jun. 3/98	Dal.	CF	Dal. 3	Det. 2	Jamie Langenbrunner	0:46	Det.
Jun. 4/98	Buf.	CF	Wsh. 3	Buf. 2	Joe Juneau	6:24	Wsh.
Jun. 11/98	Det.	F	Det. 5	Wsh. 4	Kris Draper	15:24	Det.
Apr. 23/99	Ott.	CQF	Buf. 3	Ott. 2	Miroslav Satan	30:35	Buf.
Apr. 24/99	Car.	CQF	Car. 3	Bos. 2	Ray Sheppard	17:05	Bos.
Apr. 24/99	Phx.	CQF	Phx. 4	St.L. 3	Shane Doan	8:58	St.L.
Apr. 26/99	S.J.	CQF	Col. 2	S.J. 1	Milan Hejduk	7:53	Col.
Apr. 27/99	Edm.	CQF	Dal. 3	Edm. 2	Joe Nieuwendyk	57:34	Dal.
Apr. 30/99	Tor.	CQF	Tor. 2	Phi. 1	Yanic Perreault	11:51	Tor.
Apr. 30/99	Car.	CQF	Bos. 4	Car. 3	Anson Carter	34:45	Bos.
Apr. 30/99	Phx.	CQF	St.L. 2	Phx. 1	Scott Young	5:43	St.L.
May 2/99	Pit.	CQF	Pit. 3	N.J. 2	Jaromir Jagr	8:59	Pit.
May 3/99	S.J.	CQF	Col. 3	S.J. 2	Milan Hejduk	13:12	Col.
May 4/99	Phx.	CQF	St.L. 1	Phx. 0	Pierre Turgeon	17:59	St.L.
May 7/99	Col.	CSF	Det. 3	Col. 2	Kirk Maltby	4:18	Col.
May 8/99	Dal.	CSF	Dal. 5	St.L. 4	Joe Nieuwendyk	8:22	Dal.
May 10/99	St.L.	CSF	St.L. 3	Dal. 2	Pavol Demitra	2:43	Dal.
May 12/99	St.L.	CSF	St.L. 3	Dal. 2	Pierre Turgeon	5:52	Dal.
May 13/99	Pit.	CSF	Tor. 3	Pit. 2	Sergei Berezin	2:18	Tor.
May 17/99	Pit.	CSF	Tor. 4	Pit. 3	Garry Valk	1:57	Tor.
May 17/99	St.L.	CSF	Dal. 2	St.L. 1	Mike Modano	2:21	Dal.
May 28/99	Col.	CF	Col. 3	Dal. 2	Chris Drury	19:29	Dal.
Jun. 8/99	Dal.	F	Buf. 3	Dal. 2	Jason Woolley	15:30	Dal.
Jun. 19/99	Buf.	F	Dal. 2	Buf. 1	Brett Hull	54:51	Dal.
Apr. 15/00	Pit.	CQF	Pit. 2	Wsh. 1	Jaromir Jagr	5:49	Pit.
Apr. 18/00	Buf.	CQF	Buf. 3	Phi. 2	Stu Barnes	4:42	Phi.
Apr. 22/00	Tor.	CQF	Tor. 2	Ott. 1	Steve Thomas	14:47	Tor.
May 2/00	Pit.	CSF	Phi. 4	Pit. 3	Andy Delmore	11:01	Phi.
May 3/00	Det.	CSF	Col. 3	Det. 2	Chris Drury	10:21	Col.
May 4/00	Pit.	CSF	Phi. 2	Pit. 1	Keith Primeau	92:01	Phi.
May 23/00	Dal.	CF	Dal. 3	Col. 2	Joe Nieuwendyk	12:10	Dal.
Jun. 8/00	N.J.	F	Dal. 1	N.J. 0	Mike Modano	46:21	N.J.
Jun. 10/00	Dal.	F	N.J. 2	Dal. 1	Jason Arnott	28:20	N.J.
Apr. 11/01	Dal.	CQF	Dal. 2	Edm. 1	Jamie Langenbrunner	2:08	Dal.
Apr. 13/01	Ott.	CQF	Tor. 1	Ott. 0	Mats Sundin	10:49	Tor.
Apr. 14/01	Phi.	CQF	Buf. 4	Phi. 3	Jay McKee	18:02	Buf.
Apr. 15/01	Edm.	CQF	Dal. 3	Edm. 2	Benoit Hogue	19:48	Dal.
Apr. 16/01	Tor.	CQF	Tor. 3	Ott. 2	Cory Cross	2:16	Tor.
Apr. 16/01	Van.	CQF	Col. 4	Van. 3	Peter Forsberg	2:50	Col.
Apr. 17/01	Buf.	CQF	Buf. 4	Phi. 3	Curtis Brown	6:13	Buf.
Apr. 17/01	Edm.	CQF	Edm. 2	Dal. 1	Mike Comrie	17:19	Dal.
Apr. 18/01	Car.	CQF	Car. 3	N.J. 2	Rod Brind'Amour	:46	N.J.
Apr. 18/01	Pit.	CQF	Wsh. 4	Pit. 3	Jeff Halpern	4:01	Pit.
Apr. 18/01	L.A.	CQF	L.A. 4	Det. 3	Eric Belanger	2:36	L.A.
Apr. 19/01	Dal.	CQF	Dal. 4	Edm. 3	Kirk Muller	8:01	Dal.
Apr. 19/01	St.L.	CQF	St.L. 3	S.J. 2	Bryce Salvador	9:54	St.L.
Apr. 23/01	Pit.	CQF	Pit. 4	Wsh. 3	Martin Straka	13:04	Pit.
Apr. 23/01	L.A.	CQF	L.A. 3	Det. 2	Adam Deadmarsh	4:48	L.A.
Apr. 26/01	Col.	CSF	L.A. 4	Col. 3	Jaroslav Modry	14:23	Col.
Apr. 28/01	N.J.	CSF	N.J. 6	Tor. 5	Randy McKay	5:31	N.J.
May 1/01	Tor.	CSF	N.J. 3	Tor. 2	Brian Rafalski	7:00	N.J.
May 1/01	St.L.	CSF	St.L. 3	Dal. 2	Cory Stillman	29:26	St.L.
May 5/01	Buf.	CSF	Buf. 3	Pit. 2	Stu Barnes	8:34	Pit.
May 6/01	L.A.	CSF	L.A. 1	Col. 0	Glen Murray	22:41	Col.
May 8/01	Pit.	CSF	Pit. 3	Buf. 2	Martin Straka	11:29	Pit.
May 10/01	Buf.	CSF	Pit. 3	Buf. 2	Darius Kasparaitis	13:01	Pit.
May 16/01	St.L.	CF	St.L. 4	Col. 3	Scott Young	30:27	Col.
May 18/01	St.L.	CF	Col. 4	St.L. 3	Stephane Yelle	4:23	Col.
May 21/01	Col.	CF	Col. 2	St.L. 1	Joe Sakic	:24	Col.
Apr. 17/02	Phi.	CQF	Phi. 1	Ott. 0	Ruslan Fedotenko	7:47	Ott.
Apr. 17/02	Det.	CQF	Van. 4	Det. 3	Henrik Sedin	13:59	Det.
Apr. 19/02	Car.	CQF	Car. 2	N.J. 1	Bates Battaglia	15:26	Car.
Apr. 24/02	Car.	CQF	Car. 3	N.J. 2	Josef Vasicek	8:16	Car.
Apr. 25/02	Col.	CQF	L.A. 1	Col. 0	Craig Johnson	2:19	Col.
Apr. 26/02	Phi.	CQF	Ott. 2	Phi. 1	Martin Havlat	7:33	Ott.
May 4/02	Tor.	CSF	Tor. 3	Ott. 2	Gary Roberts	44:30	Tor.
May 7/02	Mtl.	CSF	Mtl. 2	Car. 1	Donald Audette	2:26	Car.
May 9/02	Mtl.	CSF	Car. 4	Mtl. 3	Niclas Wallin	3:14	Car.
May 13/02	S.J.	CSF	Col. 2	S.J. 1	Peter Forsberg	2:47	Col.
May 19/02	Car.	CF	Car. 2	Tor. 1	Niclas Wallin	13:42	Car.
May 20/02	Det.	CF	Col. 4	Det. 3	Chris Drury	2:17	Det.

Overtime Games since 1918 — *continued*

Date	City	Series	Score		Scorer	Overtime	Series Winner
May 21/02	Tor.	CF	Car. 2	Tor. 1	Jeff O'Neill	6:01	Car.
May 22/02	Col.	CF	Det. 2	Col. 1	Fredrik Olausson	12:44	Det.
May 27/02	Det.	CF	Col. 2	Det. 1	Peter Forsberg	6:24	Det.
May 28/02	Tor.	CF	Car. 2	Tor. 1	Martin Gelinas	8:05	Car.
Jun. 4/02	Det.	F	Car. 3	Det. 2	Ron Francis	:58	Det.
Jun. 8/02	Car.	F	Det. 3	Car. 2	Igor Larionov	54:47	Det.
Apr. 10/03	Det.	CQF	Ana. 2	Det. 1	Paul Kariya	43:18	Ana.
Apr. 14/03	NYI	CQF	Ott. 3	NYI 2	Todd White	22:25	Ott.
Apr. 14/03	Tor.	CQF	Tor. 4	Phi. 3	Tomas Kaberle	27:20	Phi.
Apr. 15/03	Wsh.	CQF	T.B. 4	Wsh. 3	Vincent Lecavalier	2:29	T.B.
Apr. 16/03	Tor.	CQF	Phi. 3	Tor. 2	Mark Recchi	53:54	Phi.
Apr. 16/03	Ana.	CQF	Ana. 3	Det. 2	Steve Rucchin	6:53	Ana.
Apr. 20/03	Wsh.	CQF	T.B. 2	Wsh. 1	Martin St. Louis	44:03	T.B.
Apr. 21/03	Tor.	CQF	Tor. 2	Phi. 1	Travis Green	30:51	Phi.
Apr. 21/03	Min.	CQF	Min. 3	Col. 2	Richard Park	4:22	Min.
Apr. 22/03	Col.	CQF	Min. 3	Col. 2	Andrew Brunette	3:25	Min.
Apr. 24/03	Dal.	CSF	Ana. 4	Dal. 3	Petr Sykora	80:48	Ana.
Apr. 25/03	Van.	CSF	Van. 4	Min. 3	Trent Klatt	3:42	Min.
Apr. 26/03	N.J.	CSF	N.J. 3	T.B. 2	Jamie Langenbrunner	2:09	N.J.
Apr. 26/03	Dal.	CSF	Ana. 3	Dal. 2	Mike Leclerc	1:44	Ana.
Apr. 29/03	Phi.	CSF	Ott. 3	Phi. 2	Wade Redden	6:43	Ott.
May 2/03	Min.	CSF	Van. 3	Min. 2	Brent Sopel	15:52	Min.
May 2/03	N.J.	CSF	N.J. 2	T.B. 1	Grant Marshall	51:12	N.J.
May 10/03	Min.	CF	Ana. 1	Min. 0	Petr Sykora	28:06	Ana.
May 10/03	Ott.	CF	Ott. 3	N.J. 2	Shaun Van Allen	3:08	N.J.
May 21/03	N.J.	CF	Ott. 2	N.J. 1	Chris Phillips	15:51	N.J.
May 31/03	Ana.	F	Ana. 3	N.J. 2	Ruslan Salei	6:59	N.J.
Jun. 2/03	Ana.	F	Ana. 1	N.J. 0	Steve Thomas	0:39	N.J.
Apr. 8/04	S.J.	CQF	S.J. 1	St.L. 0	Niko Dimitrakos	9:16	S.J.
Apr. 9/04	Bos.	CQF	Bos. 2	Mtl. 1	Patrice Bergeron	1:26	Mtl.
Apr. 12/04	Dal.	CQF	Dal. 4	Col. 3	Steve Ott	2:11	Col.
Apr. 13/04	Mtl.	CQF	Bos. 4	Mtl. 3	Glen Murray	29:27	Mtl.
Apr. 14/04	Dal.	CQF	Col. 3	Dal. 2	Marek Svatos	25:21	Col.
Apr. 16/04	T.B.	CQF	T.B. 3	NYI 2	Martin St. Louis	4:07	T.B.
Apr. 17/04	Cgy.	CQF	Van. 5	Cgy. 4	Brendan Morrison	42:28	Cgy.
Apr. 18/04	Ott.	CQF	Ott. 2	Tor. 1	Mike Fisher	21:47	Tor.
Apr. 19/04	Van.	CQF	Cgy. 3	Van. 2	Martin Gelinas	1:25	Cgy.
Apr. 22/04	Det.	CSF	Cgy. 2	Det. 1	Marcus Nilson	2:39	Cgy.
Apr. 27/04	Mtl.	CSF	T.B. 4	Mtl 3	Brad Richards	1:05	T.B.
Apr. 28/04	Col	CSF	Col. 1	S.J. 0	Joe Sakic	5:15	S.J.
May 1/04	S.J.	CSF	Col. 2	S.J. 1	Joe Sakic	1:54	S.J.
May 3/04	Cgy.	CSF	Cgy. 1	Det. 0	Martin Gelinas	19:13	Cgy.
May 4/04	Phi.	CSF	Phi. 3	Tor. 2	Jeremy Roenick	7:39	Phi.
May 9/04	S.J.	CF	Cgy. 4	S.J. 3	Steve Montador	18:43	Cgy.
May 20/04	Phi.	CF	Phi. 5	T.B. 4	Simon Gagne	18:18	T.B.
Jun. 3/04	T.B.	F	Cgy. 3	T.B. 2	Oleg Saprykin	14:40	T.B.
Jun. 5/04	Cgy.	F	T.B. 3	Cgy. 2	Martin St. Louis	20:33	T.B.
Apr. 21/06	Det.	CQF	Det. 3	Edm. 2	Kirk Maltby	22:39	Edm.
Apr. 21/06	Cgy.	CQF	Cgy. 2	Ana. 1	Darren McCarty	9:45	Ana.
Apr. 22/06	Buf.	CQF	Buf. 3	Phi. 2	Danny Briere	27:31	Buf.
Apr. 24/06	Car.	CQF	Mtl. 6	Car. 5	Michael Ryder	22:32	Car.
Apr. 24/06	Dal.	CQF	Col. 5	Dal. 4	Joe Sakic	4:36	Col.
Apr. 25/06	Edm.	CQF	Edm. 4	Det. 3	Jarret Stoll	28:44	Edm.
Apr. 26/06	Mtl.	CQF	Car. 2	Mtl. 1	Eric Staal	3:38	Car.
Apr. 26/06	Col.	CQF	Col. 4	Dal. 3	Alex Tanguay	1:09	Col.
Apr. 27/06	Ana.	CQF	Ana. 3	Cgy. 2	Sean O'Donnell	1:36	Ana.
Apr. 30/06	Col.	CQF	Col. 3	Dal. 2	Andrew Brunette	13:55	Col.
May 2/06	Mtl.	CQF	Car. 2	Mtl. 1	Cory Stillman	1:19	Car.
May 5/06	Ott.	CSF	Buf. 7	Ott. 6	Chris Drury	0:18	Buf.
May 8/06	Car.	CSF	Car. 3	N.J. 2	Niclas Wallin	3:09	Car.
May 9/06	Col.	CSF	Ana. 4	Col. 3	Joffrey Lupul	16:30	Ana.
May 10/06	Buf.	CSF	Buf. 3	Ott. 2	J.P. Dumont	5:05	Buf.
May 10/06	Edm.	CSF	Edm. 3	S.J. 2	Shawn Horcoff	42:24	Edm.
May 13/06	Ott.	CSF	Buf. 3	Ott. 2	Jason Pominville	2:26	Buf.
May 28/06	Car.	CF	Car. 4	Buf. 3	Cory Stillman	8:46	Car.
May 30/06	Buf.	CF	Buf. 2	Car. 1	Danny Briere	4:22	Car.
June 14/06	Car.	F	Edm. 4	Car. 3	Fernando Pisani	3:31	Car.
Apr. 11/07	Nsh.	CQF	S.J. 5	Nsh. 4	Patrick Rissmiller	28:14	S.J.
Apr. 11/07	Van.	CQF	Van. 5	Dal. 4	Henrik Sedin	78:06	Van.
Apr. 15/07	Dal.	CQF	Van. 2	Dal. 1	Taylor Pyatt	7:47	Van.
Apr. 18/07	T.B.	CQF	N.J. 4	T.B. 3	Scott Gomez	12:54	N.J.
Apr. 19/07	Van.	CQF	Dal. 1	Van. 0	Brenden Morrison	6:22	Van.
Apr. 22/07	Cgy.	CQF	Det. 2	Cgy. 1	Johan Franzen	24:23	Det.
Apr. 27/07	Ana.	CSF	Van. 2	Ana. 1	Jeff Cowan	27:49	Ana.
Apr. 28/07	N.J.	CSF	N.J. 3	Ott. 2	Jamie Langenbrunner	21:55	Ott.
Apr. 29/07	NYR	CSF	NYR 2	Buf. 1	Michal Rozsival	36:43	Buf.
May 1/07	Van.	CSF	Ana. 3	Van. 2	Travis Moen	2:07	Ana.
May 2/07	S.J.	CSF	Det. 3	S.J. 2	Mathieu Schneider	16:04	Det.
May 3/07	Ana.	CSF	Ana. 2	Van. 1	Scott Niedermayer	24:30	Ana.
May 4/07	Buf.	CSF	Buf. 2	NYR 1	Maxim Afinogenov	4:39	Buf.
May 12/07	Buf.	CF	Ott. 4	Buf. 3	Joe Corvo	24:58	Ott.
May 13/07	Det.	CF	Ana. 3	Det. 2	Scott Niedermayer	14:17	Ana.
May 19/07	Buf.	CF	Ott. 3	Buf. 2	Daniel Alfredsson	9:32	Ott.
May 20/07	Det.	CF	Ana. 2	Det. 1	Teemu Selanne	11:57	Ana.
Apr. 9/08	Min.	CQF	Col. 3	Min. 2	Joe Sakic	11:11	Col.
Apr. 11/08	Min.	CQF	Min. 3	Col. 2	Keith Carney	1:14	Col.
Apr. 12/08	Mtl.	CQF	Mtl. 3	Bos. 2	Alex Kovalev	2:30	Mtl.
Apr. 13/08	Mtl.	CQF	Bos. 2	Mtl.1	Marc Savard	9:25	Mtl.
Apr. 13/08	NYR	CQF	N.J. 4	NYR 3	John Madden	6:01	NYR
Apr. 14/08	Col.	CQF	Min. 3	Col. 2	Pierre-Marc Bouchard	11:58	Col.
Apr. 17/08	Phi.	CQF	Phi. 4	Wsh. 3	Mike Knuble	26:40	Phi.
Apr. 18/08	Det.	CQF	Det. 2	Nsh. 1	Johan Franzen	1:48	Det.
Apr. 22/08	Wsh.	CQF	Phi. 3	Wsh. 2	Joffrey Lupul	6:06	Phi.
Apr. 24/08	Mtl.	CSF	Mtl. 4	Phi. 3	Tom Kostopoulos	0:48	Phi.

Date	City	Series	Score		Scorer	Overtime	Series Winner
Apr. 25/08	S.J.	CSF	Dal. 3	S.J. 2	Brenden Morrow	4:39	Dal.
Apr. 29/08	Dal.	CSF	Dal. 2	S.J. 1	Mattias Norstrom	4:37	Dal.
May 2/08	S.J.	CSF	S.J. 3	Dal. 2	Joe Pavelski	1:05	Dal.
May 4/08	Pit.	CSF	Pit. 3	NYR 2	Marian Hossa	7:10	Pit.
May 4/08	Dal.	CSF	Dal. 2	S.J. 1	Brenden Morrow	69:03	Dal.
June 2/08	Det.	F	Pit. 3	Det. 2	Petr Sykora	49:57	Det.
Apr. 16/09	Chi.	CQF	Chi. 3	Cgy. 2	Martin Havlat	0:12	Chi.
Apr. 17/09	Pit.	CQF	Pit. 3	Phi. 2	Bill Guerin	18:29	Pit.
Apr. 17/09	N.J.	CQF	Car. 2	N.J. 1	Tim Gleason	2:40	Car.
Apr. 19/09	Car.	CQF	N.J. 3	Car. 2	Travis Zajac	4:58	Car.
Apr. 21/09	St.L.	CQF	Van. 3	St.L. 2	Alex Burrows	19:41	Van.
Apr. 25/09	S.J.	CQF	S.J. 3	Ana. 2	Patrick Marleau	6:02	Ana.
May 3/09	Det.	CSF	Ana. 4	Det. 3	Todd Marchant	41:15	Det.
May 6/09	Pit.	CSF	Pit. 3	Wsh. 2	Kris Letang	11:23	Pit.
May 6/09	Car.	CSF	Car. 3	Bos. 2	Jussi Jokinen	2:48	Car.
May 7/09	Chi.	CSF	Chi. 2	Van. 1	Andrew Ladd	2:52	Chi.
May 9/09	Wsh.	CSF	Pit. 4	Wsh. 3	Evgeni Malkin	3:28	Pit.
May 11/09	Pit.	CSF	Wsh. 5	Pit. 4	David Steckel	6:22	Pit.
May 14/09	Bos.	CSF	Car. 3	Bos. 2	Scott Walker	18:46	Car.
May 19/09	Det.	CF	Det. 3	Chi. 2	Mikael Samuelsson	5:14	Det.
May 22/09	Chi.	CF	Chi. 4	Det. 3	Patrick Sharp	1:52	Det.
May 27/09	Det.	CF	Det. 2	Chi. 1	Darren Helm	3:58	Det.
Apr. 15/10	Wsh.	CQF	Mtl. 3	Wsh. 2	Tomas Plekanec	13:19	Mtl.
Apr. 15/10	Van.	CQF	Van. 3	L.A. 2	Mikael Samuelsson	8:52	Van.
Apr. 16/10	S.J.	CQF	S.J. 6	Col. 5	Devin Setoguchi	5:22	S.J.
Apr. 17/10	Wsh.	CQF	Wsh. 6	Mtl. 5	Nicklas Backstrom	0:31	Mtl.
Apr. 17/10	Van.	CQF	L.A. 3	Van. 2	Anze Kopitar	7:28	Van.
Apr. 18/10	Phi.	CQF	Phi. 3	N.J. 2	Daniel Carcillo	3:35	Phi.
Apr. 18/10	S.J.	CQF	Col. 1	S.J. 0	Ryan O'Reilly	0:51	S.J.
Apr. 20/10	Col.	CQF	S.J. 2	Col. 1	Joe Pavelski	10:24	S.J.
Apr. 21/10	Bos.	CQF	Bos. 3	Buf. 2	Miroslav Satan	27:41	Bos.
Apr. 22/10	Pit.	CQF	Ott. 4	Pit. 3	Matt Carkner	47:06	Pit.
Apr. 24/10	Chi.	CQF	Chi. 5	Nsh. 4	Marian Hossa	4:07	Chi.
Apr. 24/10	Ott.	CQF	Pit. 4	Ott. 3	Pascal Dupuis	9:56	Pit.
May 1/10	Bos.	CSF	Bos. 5	Phi. 4	Marc Savard	13:52	Phi.
May 4/10	Det.	CSF	S.J. 4	Det. 3	Patrick Marleau	7:07	S.J.
May 7/10	Phi.	CSF	Phi. 5	Bos. 4	Simon Gagne	14:40	Phi.
May 21/10	Chi.	CSF	Chi. 3	S.J. 2	Dustin Byfuglien	12:24	Chi.
June 2/10	Phi.	F	Phi. 4	Chi. 3	Claude Giroux	5:59	Chi.
June 9/10	Phi.	F	Chi. 4	Phi. 3	Patrick Kane	4:06	Chi.

Patrick Kane (with Nick Boynton behind him) begins to celebrate after scoring in overtime to give Chicago the Stanley Cup. It took a while to sort out for sure that Kane's shot had actually gone in the net.

Ten Longest Overtime Games

Date	City	Series	Score		Scorer	Overtime	Series Winner
Mar. 24/36	Mtl.	SF	Det. 1	Mtl. M. 0	Mud Bruneteau	116:30	Det.
Apr. 3/33	Tor.	SF	Tor. 1	Bos. 0	Ken Doraty	104:46	Tor.
May 4/00	Pit.	CSF	Phi. 2	Pit. 1	Keith Primeau	92:01	Phi.
Apr. 24/03	Dal.	CSF	Ana. 4	Dal. 3	Petr Sykora	80:48	Ana.
Apr. 24/96	Wsh.	CQF	Pit. 3	Wsh. 2	Petr Nedved	79:15	Pit.
Apr. 11/07	Van.	CQF	Van. 5	Dal. 4	Henrik Sedin	78:06	Van.
Mar. 23/43	Det.	SF	Tor. 3	Det. 2	Jack McLean	70:18	Det.
May 4/08	Dal.	CSF	Dal. 2	S.J. 1	Brenden Morrow	69:03	Dal.
Mar. 28/30	Mtl.	SF	Mtl. 2	NYR 1	Gus Rivers	68:52	Mtl.
Apr. 18/87	Wsh.	DSF	NYI 3	Wsh. 2	Pat LaFontaine	68:47	NYI

Overtime Record of Current Teams

Listed by number of OT games played)

Team	Overall GP	W	L	T	Home GP	W	L	T	Last OT Game	Road GP	W	L	T	Last OT Game
Montreal	135	75	57	3	63	39	23	1	Apr. 24/08	72	36	34	2	Apr. 17/10
Boston	108	43	62	3	50	24	25	1	May 1/10	58	19	37	2	May 7/10
Toronto	106	54	51	1	68	36	31	1	May 4/04	38	18	20	0	Apr. 18/04
Detroit	89	39	50	0	54	20	34	0	May 4/10	35	19	16	0	May 22/09
Chicago	71	36	33	2	35	21	13	1	May 21/10	36	15	20	1	Jun. 9/10
Philadelphia	68	33	35	0	31	17	14	0	Jun. 9/10	37	16	21	0	May 7/10
NY Rangers	67	31	36	0	29	13	16	0	Apr. 13/08	38	18	20	0	May 4/08
Dallas[1]	64	28	36	0	32	13	19	0	May 4/08	32	15	17	0	May 2/08
Colorado[2]	59	33	26	0	23	10	13	0	Apr. 20/10	36	23	13	0	Apr. 16/10
Buffalo	57	31	26	0	32	20	12	0	May 19/07	25	11	14	0	Apr. 21/10
St. Louis	51	27	24	0	27	20	7	0	Apr. 21/09	24	7	17	0	Apr. 8/04
Vancouver	45	22	23	0	20	8	12	0	Apr. 17/10	25	14	11	0	May 7/09
Edmonton	42	24	18	0	23	13	10	0	May 10/06	19	11	8	0	Jun. 14/06
Calgary[3]	41	17	24	0	19	6	13	0	Apr. 22/07	22	11	11	0	Apr. 16/09
NY Islanders	40	29	11	0	18	14	4	0	Apr. 14/03	22	15	7	0	Apr. 16/04
New Jersey[4]	40	14	26	0	16	6	10	0	Apr. 17/09	24	8	16	0	Apr. 18/10
Washington	38	16	22	0	17	7	10	0	Apr. 17/10	21	9	12	0	May 11/09
Los Angeles	37	18	19	0	19	11	8	0	May 6/01	18	7	11	0	Apr. 17/10
Pittsburgh	37	21	16	0	24	13	11	0	Apr. 22/10	13	8	5	0	Apr. 24/10
Carolina[5]	34	21	13	0	20	12	8	0	May 6/09	14	9	5	0	May 14/09
San Jose	26	10	16	0	13	5	8	0	Apr. 16/10	13	5	8	0	May 21/10
Ottawa	24	12	12	0	9	4	5	0	Apr. 24/10	15	8	7	0	Apr. 22/10
Anaheim	21	15	6	0	7	5	2	0	May 3/07	14	10	4	0	May 3/09
Tampa Bay	12	7	5	0	4	2	2	0	Apr. 18/07	8	5	3	0	Jun. 5/04
Phoenix[6]	12	5	7	0	8	3	5	0	May 4/99	4	2	2	0	Apr. 27/93
Minnesota	8	4	4	0	5	2	3	0	Apr. 11/08	3	2	1	0	Apr. 14/08
Florida	5	2	3	0	3	1	2	0	Apr. 25/97	2	1	1	0	Apr. 22/97
Nashville	3	0	3	0	1	0	1	0	Apr. 11/07	2	0	2	0	Apr. 24/10

1 Totals include those of Minnesota North Stars 1967-93.
2 Totals include those of Quebec 1979-95.
3 Totals include those of Atlanta Flames 1972-80.
4 Totals include those of Kansas City and Colorado Rockies 1974-82.
5 Totals include those of Hartford 1979-97.
6 Totals include those of Winnipeg 1979-96.

Penalty Shots in Stanley Cup Playoff Games

Date	Player, Team	Goaltender, Team	Scored	Final Score	Series
Mar. 25/37	Lionel Conacher, Mtl. Maroons	Tiny Thompson, Boston	No	Mtl. M. 0 at Bos. 4	QF
Apr. 15/37	Alex Shibicky, NY Rangers	Earl Robertson, Detroit	No	NYR 0 at Det. 3	F
Mar. 24/38	Mush March, Chicago	Wilf Cude, Montreal	No	Mtl. 0 at Chi. 4	QF
Mar. 29/38	Lorne Carr, NY Americans	Mike Karakas, Chicago	No	Chi. 1 at NYA 3	SF
Apr. 10/38	Art Wiebe, Chicago	Turk Broda, Toronto	No	Tor. 1 at Chi. 2	F
Mar. 24/42	Charlie Sands, Montreal	Johnny Mowers, Detroit	No	Det. 0 at Mtl. 5	QF
Apr. 13/44	Virgil Johnson, Chicago	Bill Durnan, Montreal	No	Chi. 4 at Mtl. 5*	F
Apr. 9/68	Wayne Connelly, Minnesota	Terry Sawchuk, Los Angeles	Yes	L.A. 5 at Min. 7	QF
Apr. 27/68	Jim Roberts, St. Louis	Cesare Maniago, Minnesota	No	St.L. 4 at Min. 3	SF
May 16/71	Frank Mahovlich, Montreal	Tony Esposito, Chicago	No	Chi. 3 at Mtl. 4	F
May 7/75	Bill Barber, Philadelphia	Glenn Resch, NY Islanders	No	Phi. 3 at NYI 4*	SF
Apr. 20/79	Mike Walton, Chicago	Glenn Resch, NY Islanders	No	NYI 4 at Chi. 0	QF
Apr. 9/81	Peter McNab, Boston	Don Beaupre, Minnesota	No	Min. 5 at Bos. 4*	PR
Apr. 17/81	Anders Hedberg, NY Rangers	Mike Liut, St. Louis	Yes	NYR 6 at St.L. 4	QF
Apr. 9/83	Denis Potvin, NY Islanders	Pat Riggin, Washington	No	NYI 6 at Wsh. 2	DSF
Apr. 28/84	Wayne Gretzky, Edmonton	Don Beaupre, Minnesota	Yes	Edm. 8 at Min. 5	CF
May 1/84	Mats Naslund, Montreal	Billy Smith, NY Islanders	No	Mtl. 1 at NYI 3	CF
Apr. 14/85	Bob Carpenter, Washington	Billy Smith, NY Islanders	No	Wsh. 4 at NYI 6	DF
Apr. 28/85	Ron Sutter, Philadelphia	Grant Fuhr, Edmonton	No	Phi. 3 at Edm. 5	F
May 30/85	Dave Poulin, Philadelphia	Grant Fuhr, Edmonton	No	Phi. 3 at Edm. 8	F
Apr. 9/88	John Tucker, Buffalo	Andy Moog, Boston	Yes	Bos. 2 at Buf. 6	DSF
Apr. 9/88	Petr Klima, Detroit	Allan Bester, Toronto	Yes	Det. 6 at Tor. 3	DSF
Apr. 8/89	Neal Broten, Minnesota	Greg Millen, St. Louis	Yes	St.L. 5 at Min. 3	DSF
Apr. 4/90	Al MacInnis, Calgary	Kelly Hrudey, Los Angeles	Yes	L.A. 5 at Cgy. 3	DSF
Apr. 5/90	Randy Wood, NY Islanders	Mike Richter, NY Rangers	No	NYI 1 at NYR 2	DSF
May 3/90	Kelly Miller, Washington	Andy Moog, Boston	No	Wsh. 3 at Bos. 5	CF
May 18/90	Petr Klima, Edmonton	Reggie Lemelin, Boston	No	Edm. 7 at Bos. 2	F
Apr. 6/91	Basil McRae, Minnesota	Ed Belfour, Chicago	Yes	Min. 2 at Chi. 5	DSF
Apr. 10/91	Steve Duchesne, Los Angeles	Kirk McLean, Vancouver	Yes	L.A. 6 at Van. 1	DSF
May 11/92	Jaromir Jagr, Pittsburgh	John Vanbiesbrouck, NYR	Yes	Pit. 3 at NYR 2	DF
May 13/92	Shawn McEachern, Pittsburgh	John Vanbiesbrouck, NYR	No	NYR 1 at Pit. 5	DF
June 7/94	Pavel Bure, Vancouver	Mike Richter, NYR	No	NYR 4 at Van. 2	F
May 9/95	Patrick Poulin, Chicago	Felix Potvin, Toronto	No	Tor. 3 at Chi. 0	CQF
May 10/95	Michal Pivonka, Washington	Tom Barrasso, Pittsburgh	No	Pit. 2 at Wsh. 6	CQF
Apr. 24/96	Joe Juneau, Washington	Ken Wregget, Pittsburgh	No	Pit. 3 at Wsh. 2**	CSF
May 11/97	Eric Lindros, Philadelphia	Steve Shields, Buffalo	Yes	Phi. 6 at Buf. 3	CSF
Apr. 23/98	Aleksey Morozov, Pittsburgh	Andy Moog, Montreal	No	Mtl. 3 at Pit. 2**	CQF
Apr. 22/99	Mats Sundin, Toronto	John Vanbiesbrouck, Phi.	No	Phi. 3 at Tor. 0	CQF
May 29/99	Mats Sundin, Toronto	Dominik Hasek, Buffalo	Yes	Tor. 2 at Buf. 5	CF
Apr. 16/00	Eric Desjardins, Philadelphia	Dominik Hasek, Buffalo	No	Phi. 2 at Buf. 0	CQF
Apr. 11/01	Mark Recchi, Philadelphia	Dominik Hasek, Buffalo	No	Buf. 2 at Phi. 1	CQF
May 2/01	Martin Straka, Pittsburgh	Dominik Hasek, Buffalo	No	Buf. 5 at Pit. 2	CSF
May 12/01	Joe Sakic, Colorado	Roman Turek, St. Louis	Yes	St.L. 1 at Col. 4	CF
Apr. 21/02	Todd Bertuzzi, Vancouver	Dominik Hasek, Detroit	No	Det. 3 at Van. 1	CQF
Apr. 24/02	Shawn Bates, NY Islanders	Curtis Joseph, Toronto	Yes	Tor. 3 at NYI 4	CQF
Apr. 26/02	Mike Johnson, Phoenix	Evgeni Nabokov, San Jose	Yes	Phx. 1 at S.J. 4	CQF
Apr. 15/03	Dainius Zubrus, Washington	Nikolai Khabibulin, Tampa Bay	No	T.B. 4 at Wsh. 3	CQF
Apr. 21/03	Robert Reichel, Toronto	Roman Cechmanek, Philadelphia	No	Phi. 1 at Tor. 2	CQF
Apr. 7/04	Steve Sullivan, Nashville	Manny Legace, Detroit	No	Nsh. 1 at Det. 3	CQF
Apr. 28/06	Derek Roy, Buffalo	Robert Esche, Philadelphia	No	Buf. 4 at Phi. 5	CQF
June 5/06	Chris Pronger, Edmonton***	Cam Ward, Carolina	Yes	Edm. 4 at Car. 5	F
Apr. 21/07	Daniel Cleary, Detroit	Miikka Kiprusoff, Calgary	Yes	Cgy. 1 at Det. 5	CQF
June 5/07	Antoine Vermette, Ottawa	J.S. Giguere, Anaheim	No	Ott. 2 at Ana. 6	F
Apr. 9/08	Ryan Smyth, Colorado	Niklas Backstrom, Minnesota	No	Col. 3 at Min. 2	CQF
Apr. 15/08	Mike Richards, Philadelphia	Cristobal Huet, Washington	Yes	Wsh. 3 at Phi. 6	CQF
Apr. 18/08	John Madden, New Jersey	Henrik Lundqvist, NY Rangers	No	NYR 5 at N.J. 3	CQF
Apr. 24/08	Andrei Kostitsyn, Montreal	Martin Biron, Philadelphia	No	Phi. 3 at Mtl. 4	CSF
Apr. 29/08	Niklas Hagman, Dallas	Evgeni Nabokov, San Jose	No	S.J. 1 at Dal. 2	CSF
May 1/08	Evgeni Malkin, Pittsburgh	Henrik Lundqvist, NY Rangers	No	Pit. 0 at NYR 3	CSF
Apr. 20/10	Martin Erat, Nashville	Antti Niemi, Chicago	Yes	Chi. 1 at Nsh. 4	CQF
May 4/10	Henrik Zetterberg, Detroit	Evgeni Nabokov, San Jose	No	S.J. 4 at Det. 3	CSF
May 8/10	Joe Pavelski, San Jose	Jimmy Howard, Detroit	No	S.J. 2 at Det. 1	CSF
May 12/10	Ville Leino, Philadelphia	Tuukka Rask, Boston	No	Phi. 1 at Bos. 1	CSF

* Game was decided in overtime, but shot taken during regulation time.
** Shot taken in overtime.
*** First penalty shot scored in Stanley Cup Final history

Anze Kopitar's overtime goal against Vancouver on April 17, 2010 gave the Kings their first playoff victory since April 27, 2002. Their last overtime win had also come in 2002.

Jason Arnott had been the last player to score the Stanley Cup-winning goal in overtime, netting the winner for the New Jersey Devils at 8:20 of the second extra period back on June 10, 2000.

All-Time Playoff NHL Coaching Register

Playoffs, 1917-2010

Coach	Team	Games Coached	Wins	Losses	T	Years	Cup Wins	Career
Abel, Sid	Chicago	7	3	4		1		
	Detroit	69	29	40		8		
	Totals	76	32	44		9		1952-76
Adams, Jack	Detroit	105	52	52	1	15	3	1927-47
Allen, Keith	Philadelphia	11	3	8		2		1967-69
Arbour, Al	St. Louis	11	4	7		1		
	NY Islanders	198	119	79		15	4	
	Totals	209	123	86		16	4	1970-08
Babcock, Mike	Anaheim	21	15	6		1		
	Detroit	81	48	33		5	1	
	Totals	102	63	39		6	1	2002-10
Barber, Bill	Philadelphia	11	3	8		2		2000-02
Berenson, Red	St. Louis	14	5	9		2		1979-82
Bergeron, Michel	Quebec	68	31	37		7		1980-90
Berry, Bob	Los Angeles	10	2	8		3		
	Montreal	8	2	6		2		
	St. Louis	15	7	8		2		
	Totals	33	11	22		7		1978-94
Beverley, Nick	Toronto	6	2	4		1		1995-96
Blackburn, Don	Hartford	3	0	3		1		1979-81
Blair, Wren	Minnesota	14	7	7		1		1967-70
Blake, Toe	Montreal	119	82	37		13	8	1955-68
Boileau, Marc	Pittsburgh	9	5	4		1		1973-76
Boivin, Leo	St. Louis	3	1	2		1		1975-78
Boucher, Georges	Mtl. Maroons	2	0	2	0	1		1930-50
Boucher, Frank	NY Rangers	27	13	14		4	1	1939-54
Boudreau, Bruce	Washington	28	13	15		3		2007-10
Bowman, Scotty	St. Louis	52	26	26		4		
	Montreal	98	70	28		8	5	
	Buffalo	36	18	18		5		
	Pittsburgh	33	23	10		2	1	
	Detroit	134	86	48		9	3	
	Totals	353	223	130		28	9	1967-02
Bowness, Rick	Boston	15	8	7		1		1988-05
Brooks, Herb	NY Rangers	24	12	12		3		
	New Jersey	5	1	4		1		
	Pittsburgh	11	6	5		1		
	Totals	40	19	21		5		1981-00
Brophy, John	Toronto	19	9	10		2		1986-89
Burns, Charlie	Minnesota	6	2	4		1		1969-75
Burns, Pat	Montreal	56	30	26		4		
	Toronto	46	23	23		3		
	Boston	18	8	10		2		
	New Jersey	29	17	12		1	1	
	Totals	149	78	71		11	1	1988-05
Bylsma, Dan	Pittsburgh	37	23	14		2	1	2008-10
Campbell, Colin	NY Rangers	36	18	18		3		1994-98
Carbonneau, Guy	Montreal	12	5	7		2		2006-09
Carlyle, Randy	Anaheim	56	34	22		4	1	2005-10
Carpenter, Doug	Toronto	5	1	4		1		1984-91
Carroll, Dick	Toronto	2	1	1	0	1	1	1917-19
Carroll, Frank	Toronto	2	0	2	0	1		1920-21
Cassidy, Bruce	Washington	6	2	4		1		2002-04
Cheevers, Gerry	Boston	34	15	19		4		1980-85
Cherry, Don	Boston	55	31	24		5		1974-80
Clancy, King	Toronto	14	2	12		3		1937-56
Clapper, Dit	Boston	25	8	17		4		1945-49
Cleghorn, Sprague	Mtl. Maroons	4	1	1	2	1		1931-32
Cleghorn, Odie	Pittsburgh	4	1	2	1	2		1925-29
Clouston, Cory	Ottawa	6	2	4		1		2008-10
Constantine, Kevin	San Jose	25	11	14		2		
	Pittsburgh	19	8	11		2		
	New Jersey	6	2	4		1		
	Totals	50	21	29		5		1993-02
Crawford, Marc	Quebec	6	2	4		1		
	Colorado	46	29	17		3	1	
	Vancouver	27	12	15		3		
	Totals	79	43	36		7	1	1994-10
Creighton, Fred	Atlanta	9	2	7		4		1974-80
Crisp, Terry	Calgary	37	22	15		3	1	
	Tampa Bay	6	2	4		1		
	Totals	43	24	19		4	1	1987-98
Crozier, Joe	Buffalo	6	2	4		1		1971-81
Cunniff, John	New Jersey	6	2	4		1		1982-91
Curry, Alex	Ottawa	2	0	1	1	1		1925-26
Dandurand, Leo	Montreal	8	5	3	0	4	1	1921-35
Day, Hap	Toronto	80	49	31		9	5	1940-50
Demers, Jacques	St. Louis	33	16	17		3		
	Detroit	38	20	18		3		
	Montreal	27	19	8		1	1	
	Totals	98	55	43		8	1	1979-99
Denneny, Cy	Boston	5	5	0	0	1	1	1928-33
Dudley, Rick	Buffalo	12	4	8		2		1989-04
Dugal, Jules	Montreal	3	1	2		1		1938-39
Duncan, Art	Toronto	2	0	1	1	1		1926-32
Dutton, Red	NY Americans	11	4	7		3		1936-40
Esposito, Phil	NY Rangers	10	2	8		2		1986-89

Coach	Team	Games Coached	Wins	Losses	Ties	Years	Cup Wins	Career
Evans, Jack	Hartford	16	8	8		2		1975-88
Ferguson, John	Winnipeg	3	0	3		1		1975-86
Francis, Bob	Phoenix	10	2	8		2		1999-04
Francis, Emile	NY Rangers	75	34	41		9		
	St. Louis	14	5	9		2		
	Totals	89	39	50		11		1965-83
Ftorek, Robbie	Los Angeles	16	5	11		2		
	New Jersey	7	3	4		1		
	Boston	6	2	4		1		
	Totals	29	10	19		4		1987-03
Gainey, Bob	Minnesota	30	17	13		2		
	Dallas	14	6	8		2		
	Montreal	10	2	8		2		
	Totals	54	25	29		6		1990-09
Geoffrion, Bernie	Atlanta	4	0	4		1		1968-80
Gerard, Eddie	Mtl. Maroons	21	8	8	5	5	1	1917-35
Gill, David	Ottawa	8	3	2	3	2	1	1926-29
Glover, Fred	Oakland	11	3	8		2		1968-74
Gordon, Jackie	Minnesota	25	11	14		3		1970-75
Goring, Butch	Boston	3	0	3		1		1985-01
Gorman, Tommy	NY Americans	2	0	1	1	1		
	Chicago	8	6	1	1	1	1	
	Mtl. Maroons	15	7	6	2	3	1	
	Totals	25	13	8	4	5	2	1925-38
Gottselig, Johnny	Chicago	4	0	4		1		1944-48
Granato, Tony	Colorado	18	9	9		2		2002-09
Green, Pete	Ottawa	8	3	4	1	4	3	1919-25
Green, Ted	Edmonton	16	8	8		1		1991-94
Guidolin, Bep	Boston	21	11	10		2		1972-76
Harris, Ted	Minnesota	2	0	2		1		1975-78
Hart, Cecil	Montreal	37	16	17	4	8	2	1926-39
Hartley, Bob	Colorado	80	49	31		4	1	
	Atlanta	4	0	4		1		
	Totals	84	49	35		5	1	1998-08
Hartsburg, Craig	Chicago	16	8	8		2		
	Anaheim	4	0	4		1		
	Totals	20	8	12		3		1995-09
Harvey, Doug	NY Rangers	6	2	4		1		1961-62
Hay, Don	Phoenix	7	3	4		1		1996-01
Helmer, Rosie	NY Americans	5	2	3	0	1		1935-36
Henning, Lorne	Minnesota	5	2	3		1		1985-01
Hitchcock, Ken	Dallas	80	47	33		5	1	
	Philadelphia	37	19	18		3		
	Columbus	4	0	4		1		
	Totals	121	66	55		9	1	1995-10
Hlinka, Ivan	Pittsburgh	18	9	9		1		2000-02
Holmgren, Paul	Philadelphia	19	10	9		1		1988-96
Imlach, Punch	Toronto	92	44	48		11	4	1958-80
Inglis, Bill	Buffalo	3	1	2		1		1978-79
Irvin, Dick	Chicago	9	5	3	1	1		
	Toronto	66	33	32	1	9	1	
	Montreal	115	62	53		14	3	
	Totals	190	100	88	2	24	4	1928-56
Ivan, Tommy	Detroit	67	36	31		7	3	1947-58
Johnson, Tom	Boston	22	15	7		2	1	1970-73
Johnson, Bob	Calgary	52	25	27		5		
	Pittsburgh	24	16	8		1	1	
	Totals	76	41	35		6	1	1982-91
Johnston, Eddie	Chicago	7	3	4		1		
	Pittsburgh	46	22	24		5		
	Totals	53	25	28		6		1979-97
Julien, Claude	Montreal	11	4	7		2		
	Boston	31	17	14		3		
	Totals	42	21	21		4		2002-10
Kasper, Steve	Boston	5	1	4		1		1995-97
Keenan, Mike	Philadelphia	57	32	25		4		
	Chicago	60	33	27		4		
	NY Rangers	23	16	7		1	1	
	St. Louis	20	10	10		2		
	Calgary	13	5	8		2		
	Totals	173	96	77		13	1	1984-09
Kelly, Red	Los Angeles	18	7	11		2		
	Pittsburgh	14	6	8		2		
	Toronto	30	11	19		4		
	Totals	62	24	38		8		1967-77
Kelly, Pat	Colorado	2	0	2		1		1977-79
King, Dave	Calgary	20	8	12		2		1992-03
Kromm, Bobby	Detroit	7	3	4		1		1977-80
Lalonde, Newsy	Montreal	11	5	4	2	4		
	Ottawa	2	0	1	1	1		
	Totals	13	5	5	3	5		1917-35
Lamoriello, Lou	New Jersey	20	10	10		2		2005-07
Laviolette, Peter	NY Islanders	12	4	8		2		
	Carolina	25	16	9		1	1	
	Philadelphia	23	14	9		1		
	Totals	60	34	26		4	1	2001-10
Lemaire, Jacques	Montreal	27	15	12		2		
	New Jersey	61	35	26		5	1	
	Minnesota	29	11	18		3		
	Totals	117	61	56		10	1	1983-07
Lewis, Dave	Minnesota	16	6	10		2		1998-07
Ley, Rick	Hartford	13	5	8		2		
	Vancouver	11	4	7		1		
	Totals	24	9	15		3		1989-96
Long, Barry	Winnipeg	11	3	8		2		1983-86
Loughlin, Clem	Chicago	4	1	2	1	2		1934-37

Coach	Team	Games Coached	Wins	Losses	Ties	Years	Cup Wins	Career
Low, Ron	Edmonton	28	10	18		3		1994-02
Lowe, Kevin	Edmonton	5	1	4		1		1999-00
MacLean, Doug	Florida	27	13	14		2		1995-04
MacNeil, Al	Montreal	20	12	8		1	1	
	Atlanta	4	1	3		1		
	Calgary	19	9	10		2		
	Totals	43	22	21		4	1	1970-03
MacTavish, Craig	Edmonton	36	19	17		3		2000-09
Magnuson, Keith	Chicago	3	0	3		1		1980-82
Mahoney, Bill	Minnesota	16	7	9		1		1983-85
Maloney, Phil	Vancouver	7	1	6		2		1973-77
Maloney, Dan	Toronto	10	6	4		1		
	Winnipeg	15	5	10		2		
	Totals	25	11	14		3		1984-89
Martin, Jacques	St. Louis	16	7	9		2		
	Ottawa	69	31	38		8		
	Montreal	19	9	10		1		
	Totals	104	47	57		11		1986-10
Maurice, Paul	Carolina	53	25	37		4		1995-10
McCammon, Bob	Philadelphia	10	1	9		3		
	Vancouver	7	3	4		1		
	Totals	17	4	13		4		1978-91
McLellan, Todd	San Jose	21	10	11		2		2008-10
McLellan, John	Toronto	11	3	8		2		1969-73
McVie, Tom	New Jersey	14	6	8		2		1975-92
Melrose, Barry	Los Angeles	24	13	11		1		1992-09
Milbury, Mike	Boston	40	23	17		2		1989-99
Muckler, John	Edmonton	40	25	15		2	1	
	Buffalo	27	11	16		4		
	Totals	67	36	31		6	1	1968-00
Muldoon, Pete	Chicago	2	0	1	1	1		1926-27
Munro, Dunc	Mtl. Maroons	4	1	3	0	1		1929-31
Murdoch, Bob	Chicago	5	1	4		1		
	Winnipeg	7	3	4		1		
	Totals	12	4	8		2		1987-91
Murphy, Mike	Los Angeles	5	1	4		1		1986-98
Murray, Bryan	Washington	53	24	29		7		
	Detroit	25	10	15		3		
	Ottawa	34	18	16		3		
	Totals	112	52	60		13		1981-08
Murray, Terry	Washington	39	18	21		4		
	Philadelphia	46	28	18		3		
	Florida	4	0	4		1		
	Los Angeles	6	2	4		1		
	Totals	95	48	47		9		1989-10
Murray, Andy	Los Angeles	24	10	14		3		
	St. Louis	4	0	4		1		
	Totals	28	10	18		4		1999-10
Neale, Harry	Vancouver	14	3	11		4		1978-86
Neilson, Roger	Toronto	19	8	11		2		
	Buffalo	8	4	4		1		
	Vancouver	21	12	9		2		
	NY Rangers	29	13	16		3		
	Philadelphia	29	14	15		3		
	Totals	106	51	55		11		1977-02
Nolan, Ted	Buffalo	12	5	7		1		
	NY Islanders	5	1	4		1		
	Totals	17	6	11		2		1995-08
Nykoluk, Mike	Toronto	7	1	6		2		1980-84
O'Connell, Mike	Boston	5	1	4		1		2002-03
O'Donoghue, George	Toronto	2	1	0	1	1	1	1921-23
Oliver, Murray	Minnesota	9	4	5		1		1982-83
O'Reilly, Terry	Boston *	37	17	19	1	3		1986-89

* Playoff game May 24, 1988 suspended due to power failure. Score tied.

Coach	Team	Games Coached	Wins	Losses	Ties	Years	Cup Wins	Career
Paddock, John	Winnipeg	13	5	8		2		1991-08
Page, Pierre	Minnesota	12	4	8		2		
	Quebec	6	2	4		1		
	Calgary	4	0	4		1		
	Totals	22	6	16		4		1988-98
Patrick, Frank	Boston	6	2	4	0	2		1934-36
Patrick, Craig	NY Rangers	17	7	10		4		
	Pittsburgh	5	1	4		1		
	Totals	22	8	14		3		1980-97
Patrick, Lynn	NY Rangers	12	7	5		1		
	Boston *	28	9	18	1	4		
	Totals	40	16	23	1	5		1948-76

* Playoff game March 31, 1951 suspended due to Toronto city curfew. Score tied.

Coach	Team	Games Coached	Wins	Losses	Ties	Years	Cup Wins	Career
Patrick, Lester	NY Rangers	65	32	26	7	12	2	1926-39
Perron, Jean	Montreal	48	30	18		3	1	1985-89
Perry, Don	Los Angeles	10	4	6		1		1981-84
Pilous, Rudy	Chicago	41	19	22		5	1	1957-63
Plager, Barclay	St. Louis	4	1	3		1		1977-83
Playfair, Jim	Calgary	6	2	4		1		2006-07
Pleau, Larry	Hartford	10	2	8		2		1980-89
Polano, Nick	Detroit	7	1	6		2		1982-85
Powers, Eddie	Toronto	2	0	2	0	1		1924-26
Primeau, Joe	Toronto *	15	8	6	1	2	1	1950-53

* Playoff game March 31, 1951 suspended due to Toronto city curfew. Score tied.

Coach	Team	Games Coached	Wins	Losses	Ties	Years	Cup Wins	Career
Pronovost, Marcel	Buffalo	8	3	5		1		1977-79
Pulford, Bob	Los Angeles	26	10	16		4		
	Chicago	45	17	28		6		
	Totals	71	27	44		10		1972-00
Quenneville, Joel	St. Louis	68	34	34		7		
	Colorado	19	8	11		2		
	Chicago	39	25	14		1	1	
	Totals	126	67	59		11	1	1996-10
Quinn, Pat	Philadelphia	39	22	17		3		
	Los Angeles	3	0	3		1		
	Vancouver	61	31	30		5		
	Toronto	80	41	39		6		
	Totals	183	94	89		15		1978-10
Reay, Billy	Chicago	116	56	60		12		1957-77
Renney, Tom	NY Rangers	24	11	13		3		1996-09
Risebrough, Doug	Calgary	7	3	4		1		1990-92
Roberts, Jim	Hartford	7	3	4		1		1981-97
Robinson, Larry	Los Angeles	4	0	4		1		
	New Jersey	48	31	17		2	1	
	Totals	52	31	21		3	1	1995-06
Ross, Art	Boston	65	27	33	5	11	1	1917-45
Ruel, Claude	Montreal	27	18	9		3	1	1968-81
Ruff, Lindy	Buffalo	94	54	40		7		1997-10
Sacco, Joe	Colorado	6	2	4		1		2009-10
Sather, Glen	Edmonton *	127	89	37	1	10	4	1979-04

* Playoff game May 24, 1988 suspended due to power failure. Score tied.

Coach	Team	Games Coached	Wins	Losses	Ties	Years	Cup Wins	Career
Sator, Ted	NY Rangers	16	8	8		1		
	Buffalo	11	3	8		2		
	Totals	27	11	16		3		1985-89
Schinkel, Ken	Pittsburgh	6	2	4		2		1972-77
Schmidt, Milt	Boston	34	15	19		4		1954-76
Schoenfeld, Jim	New Jersey	20	11	9		1		
	Washington	24	10	14		3		
	Phoenix	13	5	8		2		
	Totals	57	26	31		6		1985-99
Shero, Fred	Philadelphia	83	48	35		6	2	
	NY Rangers	27	15	12		2		
	Totals	110	63	47		8	2	1971-81
Simpson, Terry	NY Islanders	20	9	11		2		
	Winnipeg	6	2	4		1		
	Totals	26	11	15		3		1986-96
Sinden, Harry	Boston	43	24	19		5	1	1966-85
Skinner, Jimmy	Detroit	26	14	12		3	1	1954-74
Smith, Alf	Ottawa	5	1	4	0	1		1918-19
Smith, Floyd	Buffalo	32	16	16		3		1971-80
Smythe, Conn	Toronto	4	2	2	0	1		1927-31
Sonmor, Glen	Minnesota	47	26	21		4		1978-87
Stasiuk, Vic	Philadelphia	4	0	4		1		1969-73
Stevens, John	Philadelphia	23	11	12		2		2006-09
Stewart, Bill	Chicago	10	7	3		2	1	1937-39
Stewart, Ron	Los Angeles	2	0	2		1		1975-78
Sutter, Darryl	Chicago	26	11	15		3		
	San Jose	42	18	24		5		
	Calgary	33	18	15		2		
	Totals	101	47	54		10		1992-06
Sutter, Brian	St. Louis	41	20	21		4		
	Boston	22	7	15		3		
	Chicago	5	1	4		1		
	Totals	68	28	40		8		1988-05
Sutter, Brent	New Jersey	12	4	8		2		2007-09
Talbot, Jean-Guy	St. Louis	5	1	4		1		
	NY Rangers	3	1	2		1		
	Totals	8	2	6		2		1972-78
Tessier, Orval	Chicago	18	9	9		2		1982-85
Therrien, Michel	Montreal	12	6	6		1		
	Pittsburgh	25	15	10		2		
	Totals	37	21	16		3		2000-09
Thompson, Paul	Chicago	19	7	12		4		1938-45
Tippett, Dave	Dallas	47	21	26		5		
	Phoenix	7	3	4		1		
	Totals	54	24	30		6		2002-10
Tobin, Bill	Chicago	4	1	2	1	2		1929-32
Tortorella, John	NY Rangers	7	3	4		1		
	Tampa Bay	45	24	21		4	1	
	Totals	52	27	25		5	1	1999-10
Tremblay, Mario	Montreal	11	3	8		2		1995-97
Trotz, Barry	Nashville	28	8	20		5		1998-10
Ubriaco, Gene	Pittsburgh	11	7	4		1		1988-90
Vigneault, Alain	Montreal	10	4	6		1		
	Vancouver	34	17	17		3		
	Totals	44	21	23		4		1997-10
Watson, Phil	NY Rangers	16	4	12		3		1955-63
Watt, Tom	Winnipeg	7	1	6		2		
	Vancouver	3	0	3		1		
	Totals	10	1	9		3		1981-92
Webster, Tom	Los Angeles	28	12	16		3		1986-92
Weiland, Cooney	Boston	17	10	7		2	1	1939-41
White, Bill	Chicago	2	0	2		1		1976-77
Wilson, Ron	Anaheim	11	4	7		1		
	Washington	32	15	17		3		
	San Jose	52	28	24		4		
	Totals	95	47	48		8		1993-10
Wilson, Johnny	Pittsburgh	12	4	8		2		1969-80
Young, Garry	St. Louis	2	0	2		1		1972-76

Key to Prospect, NHL Player and Goaltender Registers

Demographics: Position, shooting side (catching hand for goaltenders), height, weight, place and date of birth as well as draft information, if any, is located on this line.

Major and tier-II junior, NCAA, minor pro, European and NHL clubs form a permanent part of each player's data panel. If a player sees action with more than one club in any of the above categories, a separate line is included for each one.

Olympic Team statistics are also listed.

Player's NHL organization as of August 15, 2010. This includes players under contract, unsigned draft choices and other players on reserve lists. Free agents as of this date show a blank here.

The complete career data panels of players with NHL experience who announced their retirement before the start of the 2010-11 season are included in the Player Register and Golatender Register.

These newly-retired players also show a blank here.

Each NHL club's minor-pro affiliates are listed on page 14.

							Regular Season															Playoffs						
Season	Club	League	GP	G	A	Pts	PIM	PP	SH	GW	S	%	+/-	TF	F%	Min	GP	G	A	Pts	PIM	PP	SH	GW	Min

KEITH Duncan (KEETH, DUHN-kuhn) **CHI.**

Defense. Shoots left. 6'1", 196 lbs. Born, Winnipeg, Man., July 16, 1983. Chicago's 2nd choice, 54th overall, in 2002 Entry Draft.

Season	Club	League	GP	G	A	Pts	PIM	PP	SH	GW	S	%	+/-	TF	F%	Min	GP	G	A	Pts	PIM	PP	SH	GW	Min
1998-99	Penticton	Minor-BC	44	51	57	108	45	....	....	....	....	....	....	....	....	....	....	....	....	....	....				
99-2000	Penticton	BCHL	59	9	27	36	37	....	....	....	....	....	....	....	....	....	....	....	....	....	....				
2000-01	Penticton	BCHL	60	18	64	82	61	....	....	....	....	....	....	....	....	....	9	4	6	10	18				
2001-02	Michigan State	CCHA	41	3	12	15	18	....	....	....	....	....	....	....	....	....	....	....	....	....	....				
2002-03	Michigan State	CCHA	15	3	6	9	8	....	....	....	....	....	....	....	....	....	....	....	....	....	....				
	Kelowna Rockets	WHL	37	11	35	46	60	....	....	....	....	....	....	....	....	....	19	3	11	14	2				
2003-04	Norfolk Admirals	AHL	75	7	18	25	44	....	....	....	....	....	....	....	....	....	8	1	1	2	6				
2004-05	Norfolk Admirals	AHL	79	9	17	26	78	....	....	....	....	....	....	....	....	....	6	0	0	0	14				
2005-06	Chicago	NHL	81	9	12	21	79	1	1	0	134	6.7	-11	0	0.0	23:26	....	....	....	....	....				
2006-07	Chicago	NHL	82	2	29	31	76	0	0	0	122	1.6	0	0	0.0	23:36	....	....	....	....	....				
2007-08	Chicago	NHL	82	12	20	32	56	1	1	0	148	8.1	30	0	0.0	25:34	....	....	....	....	....				
2008-09	Chicago	NHL	77	8	36	44	60	2	1	1	173	4.6	33	0	0.0	25:34	17	0	6	6	10	0	0	0	24:39
2009-10 ♦	Chicago	NHL	82	14	55	69	51	3	1	1	213	6.6	21	0	0.0	26:36	22	2	15	17	10	0	0	0	28:11
	Canada	Olympics	7	0	6	6	2																		
	NHL Totals		404	45	152	197	322	7	4	2	790	5.7		0	0.0	24:57	39	2	21	23	20	0	0	0	26:38

NHL First All-Star Team (2010) • James Norris Memorial Trophy (2010)
Played in NHL All-Star Game (2008)
• Left **Michigan State** (CCHA) and signed as a free agent by **Kelowna** (WHL), December 27, 2002.

Diamond (♦) indicates member of Stanley Cup-winning team.

"Did not play" Indicates that a player did not participate in a professional, junior or college league for an entire season.

Asterisks (*) indicates league leader in individual statistical categories.

All trades, free agent signings and other transactions involving NHL clubs are listed here and are presented in chronological order. First draft selection for players who re-enter the NHL Entry Draft is noted here as well. Also listed are other special notes. These are highlighted with a bullet (•).

Dates for trades or free agent signings often differ depending upon source. Signings can be reported based on when contracts are filed with NHL Central Registry or on the date a club announces that it has made a trade or come to terms with a free agent.

All-Star Team selections and awards are listed below player's year-by-year data.
NHL All-Star Game appearances are listed above trade notes.

THIS 79TH EDITION OF THE *NHL Official Guide & Record Book* is the 12th to include additional statistical categories for forwards and defensemen in the National Hockey League. These categories are, from left to right in the sample panel above, power-play goals (PP), shorthand goals (SH), game-winning goals (GW), shots on goal (S), percentage of shots that score (%), plus-minus rating (+/−), total faceoffs taken (TF), faceoff winning percentage (F%), and average time-on-ice per game played (Min).

To integrate this data, the Player Register has been is split into two sections. The Prospect Register presents data on players who have yet to play in the NHL. The NHL Player Register, containing more information and a photo of each player, lists all active players who have appeared in an NHL regular-season or playoff game at any time.

Goaltenders, whether prospects or active NHLers, are included in one register. With the addition of the shootout to NHL regular-season play, the column formerly used to record tie games for goaltenders has been renamed "O/T." For NHL goaltenders beginning in 2005-06, it lists overtime losses and shootout losses; previous to 2005-06, it lists tie games.

Registers (with their starting page) are presented in the following order: Prospects (275), NHL Players (345), Goaltenders (583), Retired Players (610) and Retired Goaltenders (650).

League abbreviations, page 662. Late additions to the Registers, page 609.

Pronunciation of Player Names

United Press International phonetic style.

AY	long A as in mate
A	short A as in cat
AI	nasal A as on air
AH	short A as in father
AW	broad A as in talk
EE	long E as in meat
EH	short E as in get
UH	hollow E as in the
AY	French long E with acute accent as in Pathe
IH	middle E as in pretty
EW	EW dipthong as in few
IGH	long I as in time
EE	French long I as in machine
IH	short I as in pity
OH	long O as in note
AH	short O as in hot
AW	broad O as in fought
OI	OI dipthong as in noise
OO	long double OO as in fool
U	short double O as in foot
OW	OW dipthong as in how
EW	long U as in mule
OO	long U as in rule
U	middle U as in put
UH	short U as in shut or hurt
K	hard C as in cat
S	soft C as in cease
SH	soft CH as in machine
CH	hard CH or TCH as in catch
Z	hard S as in bells
S	soft S as in sun
G	hard G as in gang
J	soft G as in general
ZH	soft J as in French version of Joliet
KH	gutteral CH as in Scottish version of Loch

Some information is unavailable at press time. Readers are encouraged to contribute.
See page 5 for contact names and addresses.

2010-11 Prospect Register

Note: The 2010-11 Prospect Register lists forwards and defensemen only. Goaltenders are listed separately. The Prospect Register lists every player drafted in the 2010 Entry Draft, players on NHL Reserve Lists and other players who have not yet played in the NHL. Trades and roster changes are current as of August 15, 2010.

Abbreviations: GP – games played; **G** – goals; **A** – assists; **Pts** – points; **PIM** – penalties in minutes; ***** – league-leading total.

NHL Player Register begins on page 345.

Goaltender Register begins on page 583.

League Abbreviations are listed on page 662.

ABELTSHAUSER, Konrad   (ah-behlts-HAHW-zuhr, KAWN-rad)   **S.J.**

Defense. Shoots left. 6'5", 210 lbs.   Born, Bad Tolz, Germany, September 2, 1992.
(San Jose's 6th choice, 163rd overall, in 2010 Entry Draft).

			Regular Season					Playoffs				
Season	Club	League	GP	G	A	Pts	PIM	GP	G	A	Pts	PIM
2007-08	EC Bad Tolz Jr.	Ger-Jr.	36	1	10	11	32	8	0	6	6	2
2008-09	EC Bad Tolz Jr.	Ger-Jr.	36	16	28	44	26	4	1	0	1	0
2009-10	Halifax	QMJHL	48	5	20	25	28	....	....	....	....	....

ABNEY, Cameron   (AB-nee, KAM-ih-RUHN)   **EDM.**

Right wing. Shoots right. 6'4", 192 lbs.   Born, Aldergrove, B.C., May 23, 1991.
(Edmonton's 4th choice, 82nd overall, in 2009 Entry Draft).

			Regular Season					Playoffs				
Season	Club	League	GP	G	A	Pts	PIM	GP	G	A	Pts	PIM
2007-08	North Delta Devils	PIJHL	42	12	14	26	110	5	1	0	1	27
	Everett Silvertips	WHL	4	0	0	0	0	....	....	....	....	....
2008-09	Everett Silvertips	WHL	48	1	3	4	103	5	0	0	0	2
2009-10	Everett Silvertips	WHL	34	3	3	6	60	....	....	....	....	....
	Edmonton	WHL	34	3	4	7	63	....	....	....	....	....

ADAM, Luke   (A-duhm, LEWK)   **BUF.**

Center. Shoots left. 6'2", 215 lbs.   Born, St. John's, Nfld., June 18, 1990.
(Buffalo's 3rd choice, 44th overall, in 2008 Entry Draft).

			Regular Season					Playoffs				
Season	Club	League	GP	G	A	Pts	PIM	GP	G	A	Pts	PIM
2006-07	St. John's	QMJHL	63	6	9	15	51	4	0	2	2	4
2007-08	St. John's	QMJHL	70	36	30	66	72	6	3	5	8	8
2008-09	Montreal	QMJHL	47	22	27	49	59	....	....	....	....	....
2009-10	Cape Breton	QMJHL	56	49	41	90	75	5	3	1	4	2
	Portland Pirates	AHL	....	....	....	....	....	3	0	2	2	0

QMJHL First All-Star Team (2010)

ADAMS, Mark   (A-duhmz, MAHRK)   **BUF.**

Defense. Shoots right. 6'1", 187 lbs.   Born, Boston, MA, May 23, 1991.
(Buffalo's 4th choice, 134th overall, in 2009 Entry Draft).

			Regular Season					Playoffs				
Season	Club	League	GP	G	A	Pts	PIM	GP	G	A	Pts	PIM
2007-08	Malden Cath.	High-MA	23	4	13	17	....	....	....	....	....	....	....
2008-09	Malden Cath.	High-MA	23	6	23	29	....	....	....	....	....	....	....
	Bos. Jr. Bruins	EJHL	32	5	10	15	18	....	....	....	....	....	....
2009-10	Chicago Steel	USHL	53	4	10	14	85	....	....	....	....	....	....

• Signed Letter of Intent to attend **Providence College** (Hockey East) in fall of 2010.

AGOSTINO, Kenneth   (a-goh-STEE-noh, KEH-nehth)   **PIT.**

Left wing. Shoots left. 5'11", 190 lbs.   Born, Morristown, NJ, April 30, 1992.
(Pittsburgh's 4th choice, 140th overall, in 2010 Entry Draft).

			Regular Season					Playoffs				
Season	Club	League	GP	G	A	Pts	PIM	GP	G	A	Pts	PIM
2006-07	Delbarton	High-NJ	....	12	20	32	....	....	....	....	....	....
2007-08	Delbarton	High-NJ	....	24	48	72	....	....	....	....	....	....
2008-09	Delbarton	High-NJ	....	....	....	74	....	....	....	....	....	....
2009-10	Delbarton	High-NJ	27	50	33	83	40	....	....	....	....	....
	USNTDP	U-18	2	0	0	0	2	....	....	....	....	....

• Signed Letter of Intent to attend **Yale University** (ECAC) in fall of 2010.

AHNELOV, Jonas   (AH-neh-lawv, YOH-nuhs)   **PHX.**

Defense. Shoots left. 6'2", 220 lbs.   Born, Huddinge, Sweden, December 11, 1987.
(Phoenix's 3rd choice, 88th overall, in 2006 Entry Draft).

			Regular Season					Playoffs				
Season	Club	League	GP	G	A	Pts	PIM	GP	G	A	Pts	PIM
2003-04	Huddinge IK U18	Swe-U18	6	0	3	3	8	....	....	....	....	....
	Huddinge IK Jr.	Swe-Jr.	9	0	1	1	6	....	....	....	....	....
2004-05	Huddinge IK U18	Swe-U18	2	0	0	0	2	....	....	....	....	....
	Huddinge IK Jr.	Swe-Jr.	29	3	3	6	94	3	0	0	0	2
2005-06	Frolunda Jr.	Swe-Jr.	29	4	11	15	84	7	2	4	6	22
	Frolunda	Sweden	15	0	0	0	2	....	....	....	....	....
2006-07	Frolunda Jr.	Swe-Jr.	9	4	5	9	22	8	2	3	5	8
	Frolunda	Sweden	46	1	3	4	20	....	....	....	....	....
2007-08	Boras HC	Sweden-2	1	0	0	0	0	....	....	....	....	....
	Frolunda	Sweden	51	3	4	7	30	6	0	0	0	0
2008-09	San Antonio	AHL	43	1	6	7	35	....	....	....	....	....
2009-10	San Antonio	AHL	11	0	1	1	2	....	....	....	....	....

ALBERT, John   (AL-buhrt, JAWN)   **ATL.**

Center. Shoots left. 5'11", 190 lbs.   Born, Cleveland, OH, January 19, 1989.
(Atlanta's 3rd choice, 175th overall, in 2007 Entry Draft).

			Regular Season					Playoffs				
Season	Club	League	GP	G	A	Pts	PIM	GP	G	A	Pts	PIM
2004-05	Cleveland Barons	MWEHL	67	34	60	94	48	....	....	....	....	....
	Cleveland Barons	NAHL	3	0	0	0	0	....	....	....	....	....
2005-06	USNTDP	U-17	19	8	15	23	25	....	....	....	....	....
	NAHL		36	8	15	23	23	....	....	....	....	....
2006-07	USNTDP	U-18	41	8	16	24	10	....	....	....	....	....
	USNTDP	NAHL	15	4	9	13	4	....	....	....	....	....
2007-08	Ohio State	CCHA	41	4	17	21	10	....	....	....	....	....
2008-09	Ohio State	CCHA	42	11	28	39	20	....	....	....	....	....
2009-10	Ohio State	CCHA	39	6	24	30	20	....	....	....	....	....

ALEXANDROV, Viktor   (al-ehx-AN-drawv, VIHK-tohr)   **ST.L.**

Left wing. Shoots left. 5'11", 183 lbs.   Born, Ust-Kamenogorsk, USSR, December 28, 1985.
(St. Louis' 3rd choice, 83rd overall, in 2004 Entry Draft).

			Regular Season					Playoffs				
Season	Club	League	GP	G	A	Pts	PIM	GP	G	A	Pts	PIM
2001-02	Ust-Kamenogorsk	Russia-2	45	12	17	29	48	2	0	1	1	2
2002-03	Yaroslavl	Russia	2	0	0	0	2	....	....	....	....	....
	Energiya Kemerovo	Russia-2	15	2	4	6	12	....	....	....	....	....
	Novokuznetsk	Russia	11	0	0	0	4	....	....	....	....	....
2003-04	Novokuznetsk	Russia	57	5	4	9	26	4	1	1	2	4
2004-05	Novokuznetsk	Russia	50	8	10	18	16	4	1	1	2	0
2005-06	SKA St. Petersburg	Russia	41	4	6	10	55	....	....	....	....	....
	St. Petersburg 2	Russia-3	1	0	3	3	0	....	....	....	....	....
2006-07	SKA St. Petersburg	Russia	19	1	10	11	18	....	....	....	....	....
	St. Petersburg 2	Russia-3	5	2	7	9	12	....	....	....	....	....
	MVD	Russia	20	2	6	8	8	2	0	2	2	2
2007-08	Novokuznetsk	Russia	55	20	24	44	26	....	....	....	....	....
2008-09	Omsk	Rus-KHL	35	2	8	10	18	8	2	0	2	8
2009-10	Nizhny Novgorod	Rus-KHL	55	11	14	25	34	....	....	....	....	....

ALEXANDROV, Yury   (al-ehx-AN-drawv, YOO-ree)   **BOS.**

Defense. Shoots left. 6'1", 185 lbs.   Born, Cherepovets, USSR, June 24, 1988.
(Boston's 2nd choice, 37th overall, in 2006 Entry Draft).

			Regular Season					Playoffs				
Season	Club	League	GP	G	A	Pts	PIM	GP	G	A	Pts	PIM
2003-04	Cherepovets 2	Russia-3	32	0	2	2	10	4	0	0	0	0
2004-05	Cherepovets 2	Russia-3	STATISTICS NOT AVAILABLE									
2005-06	Cherepovets	Russia	37	1	0	1	18	2	0	0	0	2
2006-07	Cherepovets	Russia	45	1	1	2	38	5	0	0	0	8
2007-08	Cherepovets	Russia	45	5	4	9	32	8	0	0	0	8
2008-09	Cherepovets	Rus-KHL	26	3	5	8	40	....	....	....	....	....
2009-10	Cherepovets	Rus-KHL	56	6	15	21	56	....	....	....	....	....
	Cherepovets Jr.	Russia-Jr.	....	....	....	....	....	3	0	1	1	2

ALIU, Akim   (ah-lee-OO, a-KEEM)   **ATL.**

Center. Shoots right. 6'3", 225 lbs.   Born, Okene, Nigeria, April 24, 1989.
(Chicago's 3rd choice, 56th overall, in 2007 Entry Draft).

			Regular Season					Playoffs				
Season	Club	League	GP	G	A	Pts	PIM	GP	G	A	Pts	PIM
2004-05	Toronto Marlboros	GTHL	68	35	50	85	197	....	....	....	....	....
2005-06	Windsor Spitfires	OHL	18	3	4	7	25	....	....	....	....	....
	Sudbury Wolves	OHL	29	7	6	13	54	6	0	1	1	7
2006-07	Sudbury Wolves	OHL	53	20	22	42	104	21	1	5	6	50
2007-08	London Knights	OHL	60	28	33	61	133	5	2	1	3	15
	Rockford IceHogs	AHL	2	0	0	0	2	....	....	....	....	....
2008-09	London Knights	OHL	16	8	10	18	30	....	....	....	....	....
	Sudbury Wolves	OHL	29	10	16	26	61	6	2	1	3	14
	Rockford IceHogs	AHL	5	2	0	2	14	1	1	0	1	0
2009-10	Rockford IceHogs	AHL	48	11	6	17	69	....	....	....	....	....
	Toledo Walleye	ECHL	13	5	9	14	18	2	1	1	2	16

Traded to **Atlanta** by **Chicago** with Brent Sopel, Dustin Byfuglien and Ben Eager for Marty Reasoner, Joey Crabb, Jeremy Morin and New Jersey's 1st (previously acquired, Chicago selected Kevin Hayes) and 2nd (previously acquired, Chicago selected Justin Holl) round choices in 2010 Entry Draft, June 24, 2010.

ALMQVIST, Adam (AHLM-kwihst, A-duhm) DET.

Defense. Shoots left. 5'10", 169 lbs. Born, Jonkoping, Sweden, February 27, 1991.
(Detroit's 7th choice, 210th overall, in 2009 Entry Draft).

			Regular Season					Playoffs				
Season	Club	League	GP	G	A	Pts	PIM	GP	G	A	Pts	PIM
2006-07	HV 71 U18	Swe-U18	1	0	0	0	0	1	0	0	0	0
2007-08	HV 71 U18	Swe-U18	18	8	12	20	28	....	....	....	....	....
	HV 71 Jr.	Swe-Jr.	23	1	6	7	12	3	0	0	0	4
2008-09	HV 71 Jr.	Swe-Jr.	41	8	28	36	44	....	....	....	....	....
2009-10	HV 71 Jonkoping	Sweden	28	2	6	8	10	16	1	10	11	8
	HV 71 Jr.	Swe-Jr.	15	5	29	34	14	....	....	....	....	....

ALT, Mark (AHLT, MAHRK) CAR.

Defense. Shoots right. 6'3", 200 lbs. Born, Kansas City, MO, October 18, 1991.
(Carolina's 3rd choice, 53rd overall, in 2010 Entry Draft).

			Regular Season					Playoffs				
Season	Club	League	GP	G	A	Pts	PIM	GP	G	A	Pts	PIM
2007-08	Cretin-Derham	High-MN	17	1	5	6	4	....	....	....	....	....
2008-09	Cretin-Derham	High-MN	26	11	16	27	10	....	....	....	....	....
2009-10	Team Northeast	UMHSEL	24	13	9	22	....	....	....	....	....	....
	Cretin-Derham	High-MN	24	6	14	20	....	....	....	....	....	....

• Signed Letter of Intent to attend **University of Minnesota** (WCHA) in fall of 2010.

AMBUHL, Andres (AM-b'yool, AWN-drehs)

Right wing. Shoots right. 5'10", 190 lbs. Born, Davos, Switz., September 14, 1983.

			Regular Season					Playoffs				
Season	Club	League	GP	G	A	Pts	PIM	GP	G	A	Pts	PIM
2000-01	HC Davos Jr.	Swiss-Jr.	31	24	17	41	36	6	4	3	7	6
	HC Davos	Swiss	3	0	1	1	0	....	....	....	....	....
2001-02	HC Davos	Swiss	38	5	3	8	26	6	1	0	1	4
	HC Davos Jr.	Swiss-Jr.	3	2	2	4	12	1	0	1	1	2
2002-03	HC Davos	Swiss	40	6	11	17	18	17	0	2	2	10
2003-04	HC Davos	Swiss	487	6	16	22	40	6	0	1	1	2
2004-05	HC Davos	Swiss	43	7	11	18	67	15	3	2	5	12
2005-06	HC Davos	Swiss	44	7	14	21	50	15	4	1	5	12
	Switzerland	Olympics	1	0	0	0	0	....	....	....	....	....
2006-07	HC Davos	Swiss	44	5	13	18	88	19	2	2	4	20
2007-08	HC Davos	Swiss	49	11	15	26	46	13	5	3	8	8
2008-09	HC Davos	Swiss	50	17	24	41	90	21	4	3	7	44
2009-10	Hartford Wolf Pack	AHL	64	8	5	13	37	....	....	....	....	....
	Switzerland	Olympics	5	[illegible]	0	0	0	....	....	....	....	....

Signed as a free agent by **NY Rangers**, May 27, 20[illegible].

ANDERSON, Chad (AN-duhr-suhn, CHAD)

Defense. Shoots right. 6'4", 217 lbs. Born, Chisago City, MN, June 16, 1982.

			Regular Season					Playoffs				
Season	Club	League	GP	G	A	Pts	PIM	GP	G	A	Pts	PIM
2000-01	Tri-City Storm	USHL	50	0	1	1	34	7	0	1	1	2
2001-02	Tri-City Storm	USHL	60	3	10	13	53	....	....	....	....	....
2002-03	Tri-City Storm	USHL	60	8	20	28	119	3	0	0	0	10
2003-04	Alaska Anchorage	WCHA	38	2	6	8	24	....	....	....	....	....
2004-05	Alaska Anchorage	WCHA	36	4	11	15	46	....	....	....	....	....
2005-06	Alaska Anchorage	WCHA	30	3	3	6	49	....	....	....	....	....
2006-07	Alaska Anchorage	WCHA	34	7	13	20	96	....	....	....	....	....
	Las Vegas	ECHL	2	0	0	0	0	....	....	....	....	....
2007-08	Philadelphia	AHL	55	2	11	13	35	12	0	2	2	8
2008-09	Hamilton Bulldogs	AHL	56	5	2	7	55	5	0	2	2	6
2009-10	Hamilton Bulldogs	AHL	52	1	6	7	26	18	0	3	3	8

Signed as a free agent by **Montreal**, August 6, 2008.

ANDERSSON, Joakim (AN-duhr-suhn, YOH-ah-kihm) DET.

Center. Shoots left. 6'2", 198 lbs. Born, Munkedal, Sweden, February 5, 1989.
(Detroit's 2nd choice, 88th overall, in 2007 Entry Draft).

			Regular Season					Playoffs				
Season	Club	League	GP	G	A	Pts	PIM	GP	G	A	Pts	PIM
2004-05	Munkedals BK	Sweden-5		STATISTICS NOT AVAILABLE								
2005-06	Frolunda U18	Swe-U18	1	0	0	0	0	2	0	1	1	0
	Frolunda Jr.	Swe-Jr.	35	9	11	20	10	7	2	5	7	4
2006-07	Frolunda U18	Swe-U18	2	1	2	3	2	6	3	2	5	28
	Frolunda Jr.	Swe-Jr.	41	20	26	46	60	8	0	7	7	4
	Frolunda	Sweden	1	0	0	0	0	....	....	....	....	....
2007-08	Boras HC	Sweden-2	33	6	17	23	26	....	....	....	....	....
	Frolunda Jr.	Swe-Jr.	6	8	2	10	30	5	6	3	9	4
	Frolunda	Sweden	9	1	0	1	2	4	1	1	2	0
2008-09	Boras HC	Sweden-2	4	2	2	4	2	....	....	....	....	....
	Frolunda	Sweden	49	6	6	12	22	11	0	0	0	4
	Grand Rapids	AHL	1	0	1	1	2	10	1	2	3	4
2009-10	Frolunda	Sweden	55	6	12	18	42	7	1	2	3	0

ANDERSSON, Peter (AN-duhr-suhn, PEE-tuhr) VAN.

Defense. Shoots left. 6'4", 195 lbs. Born, Kvidinge, Sweden, April 13, 1991.
(Vancouver's 5th choice, 143rd overall, in 2009 Entry Draft).

			Regular Season					Playoffs				
Season	Club	League	GP	G	A	Pts	PIM	GP	G	A	Pts	PIM
2007-08	Frolunda U18	Swe-U18	12	2	3	5	18	5	0	1	1	14
	Frolunda Jr.	Swe-Jr.	8	0	2	2	4	1	0	0	0	0
	Frolunda	Sweden	1	0	0	0	0	....	....	....	....	....
2008-09	Frolunda U18	Swe-U18	5	0	1	1	4	5	1	1	2	2
	Frolunda Jr.	Swe-Jr.	36	3	5	8	42	4	0	1	1	0
2009-10	Frolunda	Sweden	21	1	4	5	4	....	....	....	....	....
	Frolunda Jr.	Swe-Jr.	1	1	0	1	0	....	....	....	....	....
	Boras HC	Sweden-2	10	2	4	6	12	....	....	....	....	....

ANDRONOV, Sergei (an-DROH-nahv, SAIR-gay) ST.L.

Right wing. Shoots left. 6'2", 183 lbs. Born, Penza, USSR, July 19, 1989.
(St. Louis' 3rd choice, 78th overall, in 2009 Entry Draft).

			Regular Season					Playoffs				
Season	Club	League	GP	G	A	Pts	PIM	GP	G	A	Pts	PIM
2006-07	Lada Togliatti	Russia	3	0	0	0	2	....	....	....	....	....
2007-08	Lada Togliatti 2	Russia-3	16	10	2	12	16	8	7	2	9	0
	Lada Togliatti	Russia	38	2	5	7	2	4	1	0	1	6
2008-09	Lada Togliatti 2	Russia-3	7	5	2	7	6	3	0	2	2	32
	Lada Togliatti	Rus-KHL	47	9	5	14	22	5	0	1	1	8
2009-10	Lada Togliatti	Rus-KHL	33	5	9	14	20	....	....	....	....	....
	CSKA Moscow	Rus-KHL	19	5	3	8	6	3	0	0	0	0

ANELOSKI, Bryce (a-nehl-AWZ-kee, BRIGHS) OTT.

Defense. Shoots right. 6'2", 204 lbs. Born, Pekin, IL, April 27, 1990.
(Ottawa's 4th choice, 196th overall, in 2010 Entry Draft).

			Regular Season					Playoffs				
Season	Club	League	GP	G	A	Pts	PIM	GP	G	A	Pts	PIM
2007-08	Cedar Rapids	USHL	59	8	12	20	39	3	0	0	0	0
2008-09	Providence College	H-East	16	0	1	1	8	....	....	....	....	....
	Cedar Rapids	USHL	38	4	8	12	38	5	0	0	0	20
2009-10	Cedar Rapids	USHL	60	15	39	54	34	5	0	4	4	0

USHL First All-Star Team (2010)

ANGELIDIS, Mike (AN-gehl-EE-dihs, MIGHK) T.B.

Left wing. Shoots left. 6'1", 210 lbs. Born, Woodbridge, Ont., June 27, 1985.

			Regular Season					Playoffs				
Season	Club	League	GP	G	A	Pts	PIM	GP	G	A	Pts	PIM
2002-03	Owen Sound	OHL	65	7	10	17	81	4	1	1	2	0
2003-04	Owen Sound	OHL	66	9	9	18	118	7	4	1	5	4
2004-05	Owen Sound	OHL	41	9	10	19	126	8	3	2	5	10
2005-06	Owen Sound	OHL	68	53	25	78	167	11	5	9	14	38
2006-07	Albany River Rats	AHL	27	4	5	9	44	4	0	0	0	10
	Florida Everblades	ECHL	24	10	8	18	54	....	....	....	....	....
2007-08	Albany River Rats	AHL	74	11	16	27	151	7	0	2	2	6
2008-09	Albany River Rats	AHL	67	15	10	25	142	....	....	....	....	....
2009-10	Albany River Rats	AHL	67	12	12	24	119	8	2	4	6	12

OHL First All-Star Team (2006) • Canadian Major Junior Humanitarian Player of the Year (2006)

Signed as a free agent by **Carolina**, July 27, 2006. Signed as a free agent by **Tampa Bay**, August 3, 2010.

ANIKEYENKO, Vitali (ah-nih-KEH-ehn-koh, vih-TAL-ee) OTT.

Defense. Shoots right. 6'3", 198 lbs. Born, Kiev, USSR, January 2, 1987.
(Ottawa's 2nd choice, 70th overall, in 2005 Entry Draft).

			Regular Season					Playoffs				
Season	Club	League	GP	G	A	Pts	PIM	GP	G	A	Pts	PIM
2003-04	Yaroslavl 2	Russia-3	40	2	9	11	68	....	....	....	....	....
2004-05	Yaroslavl 2	Russia-3	58	3	11	14	62	....	....	....	....	....
2005-06	Yaroslavl 2	Russia-3	19	3	5	8	20	....	....	....	....	....
	Yaroslavl	Russia	26	0	1	1	28	1	0	0	0	0
2006-07	Yaroslavl 2	Russia-3	15	1	6	7	59	....	....	....	....	....
	Yaroslavl	Russia	25	1	3	4	16	3	0	0	0	12
2007-08	Novokuznetsk	Russia	10	1	1	2	10	....	....	....	....	....
	Yaroslavl	Russia	40	4	9	13	48	16	0	0	0	20
2008-09	Yaroslavl	Rus-KHL	40	2	10	12	44	19	0	2	2	10
2009-10	Yaroslavl	Rus-KHL	52	7	11	18	50	9	1	0	1	8

ANSHAKOV, Sergei (an-sha-KAHV, SAIR-gay) PIT.

Left wing. Shoots left. 6'3", 179 lbs. Born, Moscow, USSR, January 13, 1984.
(Los Angeles' 2nd choice, 50th overall, in 2002 Entry Draft).

			Regular Season					Playoffs				
Season	Club	League	GP	G	A	Pts	PIM	GP	G	A	Pts	PIM
2000-01	Dyn'o Moscow 18	Exhib.	6	7	1	8	2	....	....	....	....	....
2001-02	HK CSKA 2	Russia-3	3	3	1	4	0	....	....	....	....	....
	HK CSKA Moscow	Russia-2	46	20	12	22	10	....	....	....	....	....
2002-03	CSKA Moscow	Russia	25	1	2	3	4	....	....	....	....	....
2003-04	CSKA Moscow	Russia	33	3	2	5	12	....	....	....	....	....
2004-05	CSKA Moscow	Russia	11	0	0	0	2	....	....	....	....	....
	Ufa	Russia	23	9	3	12	4	....	....	....	....	....
2005-06	Ufa	Russia	6	1	1	2	12	....	....	....	....	....
	Dynamo Moscow	Russia	1	0	0	0	0	....	....	....	....	....
	HK MVD-THK Tver	Russia-3	1	2	0	2	0	....	....	....	....	....
	MVD	Russia	12	1	3	4	2	2	0	1	1	0
2006-07	CSKA Moscow	Russia	29	2	3	5	12	....	....	....	....	....
	Sibir Novosibirsk 2	Russia-3	2	2	1	3	0	....	....	....	....	....
	Sibir Novosibirsk	Russia	17	2	4	6	4	3	1	0	1	2
2007-08	Khabarovsk 2	Russia-3	2	0	0	0	2	....	....	....	....	....
	Amur Khabarovsk	Russia	22	4	2	6	4	....	....	....	....	....
2008-09	Nizhnekamsk	Rus-KHL	41	7	3	10	10	2	0	0	0	0
2009-10	CSKA Moscow	Rus-KHL	34	2	3	5	4	....	....	....	....	....

Traded to **Pittsburgh** by **Los Angeles** with Martin Strbak for Martin Straka, November 30, 2003.

ANTHONY, Steven (AN-thuh-nee, STEE-vehn) VAN.

Left wing. Shoots left. 6'1", 195 lbs. Born, Halifax, N.S., March 21, 1991.
(Vancouver's 7th choice, 187th overall, in 2009 Entry Draft).

			Regular Season					Playoffs				
Season	Club	League	GP	G	A	Pts	PIM	GP	G	A	Pts	PIM
2006-07	Dartmouth	NSMHL	35	33	31	64	78	9	8	16	24	10
2007-08	Saint John	QMJHL	55	6	8	14	38	10	1	1	2	2
2008-09	Saint John	QMJHL	67	19	29	48	47	4	1	2	3	4
2009-10	Saint John	QMJHL	61	18	23	41	28	5	0	0	0	6

ARCHIBALD, Brandon (AHR-chih-bawld, BRAN-duhn) CBJ

Defense. Shoots right. 6'4", 195 lbs. Born, Port Huron, MI, March 31, 1992.
(Columbus' 4th choice, 94th overall, in 2010 Entry Draft).

			Regular Season					Playoffs				
Season	Club	League	GP	G	A	Pts	PIM	GP	G	A	Pts	PIM
2007-08	Det. Honeybaked	MWEHL	26	1	3	4	28	....	....	....	....	....
	Det. Honeybaked	Minor-MI	38	6	18	24	20	....	....	....	....	....
	Det. Honeybaked	Exhib.	7	1	1	2	8	....	....	....	....	....
2008-09	Sault Ste. Marie	OHL	61	0	8	8	45	....	....	....	....	....
2009-10	Sault Ste. Marie	OHL	68	5	28	33	81	5	1	1	2	6

ARMSTRONG, John (AHRM-strawng, JAWN) CGY.

Center. Shoots right. 6'2", 205 lbs. Born, Unionville, Ont., February 26, 1988.
(Calgary's 2nd choice, 87th overall, in 2006 Entry Draft).

			Regular Season					Playoffs				
Season	Club	League	GP	G	A	Pts	PIM	GP	G	A	Pts	PIM
2004-05	Plymouth Whalers	OHL	52	6	13	19	39	4	0	0	0	4
2005-06	Plymouth Whalers	OHL	65	14	23	37	75	13	4	7	11	18
2006-07	Plymouth Whalers	OHL	34	8	13	21	26	....	....	....	....	....
	Peterborough	OHL	27	11	13	24	34	....	....	....	....	....
2007-08	Peterborough	OHL	65	21	36	57	77	5	0	1	1	6
2008-09	Quad City Flames	AHL	68	5	15	20	72	....	....	....	....	....
2009-10	Abbotsford Heat	AHL	14	1	5	6	13	....	....	....	....	....

ARNIEL, Jamie (ahr-NEEL, JAY-mee) BOS.

Center. Shoots right. 5'11", 191 lbs. Born, Kingston, Ont., November 16, 1989.
(Boston's 4th choice, 97th overall, in 2008 Entry Draft).

			Regular Season					Playoffs				
Season	Club	League	GP	G	A	Pts	PIM	GP	G	A	Pts	PIM
2005-06	Guelph Storm	OHL	61	11	8	19	30	15	2	0	2	4
2006-07	Guelph Storm	OHL	68	31	31	62	51	4	2	2	4	0
2007-08	Guelph Storm	OHL	20	9	4	13	16	....	....	....	....	....
	Sarnia Sting	OHL	40	18	16	34	22	9	2	2	4	6
2008-09	Sarnia Sting	OHL	63	32	36	68	28	5	1	2	3	4
	Providence Bruins	AHL	....	....	....	....	....	8	1	0	1	0
2009-10	Providence Bruins	AHL	67	12	16	28	16	....	....	....	....	....

ARNOLD, Bill (AHR-nohld, BIHL) CGY.

Center. Shoots right. 6', 215 lbs. Born, Boston, MA, May 13, 1992.
(Calgary's 4th choice, 108th overall, in 2010 Entry Draft).

			Regular Season					Playoffs				
Season	Club	League	GP	G	A	Pts	PIM	GP	G	A	Pts	PIM
2008-09	Nobles	High-MA	29	28	27	55	....	....	....	....	....	....
	Little Bruins	Minor-MA	33	26	21	47	24	....	....	....	....	....
2009-10	USNTDP	USHL	26	8	15	23	20	....	....	....	....	....
	USNTDP	U-18	38	12	16	28	30	....	....	....	....	....

• Signed Letter of Intent to attend **Boston College** (Hockey East) in fall of 2010.

ARONSON, Taylor (AIR-uhn-suhn, TAY-luhr) NSH.

Defense. Shoots right. 6', 196 lbs. Born, Placentia, CA, December 30, 1991.
(Nashville's 2nd choice, 78th overall, in 2010 Entry Draft).

			Regular Season					Playoffs				
Season	Club	League	GP	G	A	Pts	PIM	GP	G	A	Pts	PIM
2008-09	L.A. Jr. Kings	T1EHL	45	9	16	25	68	....	....	....	....	....
2009-10	Portland	WHL	71	5	25	30	65	11	2	7	9	13

ASHTON, Carter (ASH-tuhn, KAHR-tuhr) T.B.

Right wing. Shoots left. 6'3", 205 lbs. Born, Winnipeg, Man., April 1, 1991.
(Tampa Bay's 2nd choice, 29th overall, in 2009 Entry Draft).

			Regular Season					Playoffs				
Season	Club	League	GP	G	A	Pts	PIM	GP	G	A	Pts	PIM
2006-07	Sask. Contacts	SMHL	41	28	38	66	99	....	....	....	....	....
	Lethbridge	WHL	2	0	0	0	0	....	....	....	....	....
2007-08	Lethbridge	WHL	40	5	4	9	21	19	0	1	1	12
2008-09	Lethbridge	WHL	70	30	20	50	93	11	1	2	3	15
2009-10	Lethbridge	WHL	28	13	13	26	52	....	....	....	....	....
	Regina Pats	WHL	37	11	14	25	57	....	....	....	....	....
	Norfolk Admirals	AHL	11	1	0	1	6	....	....	....	....	....

ATKINSON, Cam (AT-kihn-suhn, KAM-ih-RUHN) CBJ

Right wing. Shoots right. 5'9", 173 lbs. Born, Riverside, CT, June 5, 1989.
(Columbus' 8th choice, 157th overall, in 2008 Entry Draft).

			Regular Season					Playoffs				
Season	Club	League	GP	G	A	Pts	PIM	GP	G	A	Pts	PIM
2005-06	Avon Old Farms	High-CT	25	15	20	35	16	....	....	....	....	....
2006-07	Avon Old Farms	High-CT	27	28	24	52	12	....	....	....	....	....
2007-08	Avon Old Farms	High-CT	28	26	37	63	10	....	....	....	....	....
2008-09	Boston College	H-East	36	7	12	19	28	....	....	....	....	....
2009-10	Boston College	H-East	42	*30	23	53	30	....	....	....	....	....

Hockey East Second All-Star Team (2010) • NCAA Championship All-Tournament Team (2010)

ATYUSHOV, Vitali (a-tew-SHAWF, vih-TAL-ee) OTT.

Defense. Shoots left. 6'1", 205 lbs. Born, Penza, USSR, July 4, 1979.
(Ottawa's 8th choice, 276th overall, in 2002 Entry Draft).

			Regular Season					Playoffs				
Season	Club	League	GP	G	A	Pts	PIM	GP	G	A	Pts	PIM
1997-98	Krylja Sovetov	Russia	4	0	0	0	2	....	....	....	....	....
1998-99	Dizelist Penza 2	Russia-4	2	1	1	2	2	....	....	....	....	....
	Dizelist Penza	Russia-2	22	0	0	0	22	....	....	....	....	....
	Krylja Sovetov	Russia	17	1	0	1	20	....	....	....	....	....
	Krylja Sovetov	Russia-Q	21	0	5	5	50	....	....	....	....	....
99-2000	Perm	Russia	38	4	0	4	50	3	0	0	0	12
2000-01	Perm	Russia	44	3	9	12	32	....	....	....	....	....
2001-02	Perm	Russia	51	4	8	12	66	....	....	....	....	....
2002-03	Ak Bars Kazan	Russia	33	0	9	9	12	2	0	0	0	0
2003-04	Magnitogorsk	Russia	56	5	9	14	26	14	2	3	5	6
2004-05	Magnitogorsk	Russia	58	6	18	24	42	5	2	0	2	0
2005-06	Magnitogorsk	Russia	51	7	12	19	64	11	2	0	2	4
2006-07	Magnitogorsk	Russia	54	7	20	27	46	15	3	9	12	10
2007-08	Magnitogorsk	Russia	56	10	33	43	32	10	1	4	5	2
2008-09	Magnitogorsk	Rus-KHL	55	8	27	35	34	12	1	6	7	8
2009-10	Magnitogorsk	Rus-KHL	49	5	17	22	45	10	1	3	4	6

AUBRY, Louis-Marc (AW-bree, LOO-ee-MAHRK) DET.

Center. Shoots left. 6'3", 186 lbs. Born, Arthabaska, Que., November 11, 1991.
(Detroit's 3rd choice, 81st overall, in 2010 Entry Draft).

			Regular Season					Playoffs				
Season	Club	League	GP	G	A	Pts	PIM	GP	G	A	Pts	PIM
2007-08	Trois-Rivieres	QAAA	20	9	20	29	30	7	1	1	2	20
2008-09	Montreal	QMJHL	65	10	12	22	53	10	2	2	4	8
2009-10	Montreal	QMJHL	66	15	18	33	69	7	1	1	2	6

AULIE, Keith (AW-lee, KEETH) TOR.

Defense. Shoots left. 6'5", 217 lbs. Born, Regina, Sask., June 11, 1989.
(Calgary's 3rd choice, 116th overall, in 2007 Entry Draft).

			Regular Season					Playoffs				
Season	Club	League	GP	G	A	Pts	PIM	GP	G	A	Pts	PIM
2004-05	Notre Dame	SJHL	38	2	7	9	53	....	....	....	....	....
2005-06	Brandon	WHL	38	0	2	2	32	4	0	0	0	4
2006-07	Brandon	WHL	66	1	8	9	82	11	0	2	2	14
2007-08	Brandon	WHL	72	5	12	17	81	6	0	3	3	11
2008-09	Brandon	WHL	58	6	27	33	83	12	2	7	9	12
2009-10	Abbotsford Heat	AHL	43	2	4	6	32	....	....	....	....	....
	Toronto Marlies	AHL	5	0	0	0	6	....	....	....	....	....

WHL East First All-Star Team (2009)

Traded to **Toronto** by **Calgary** with Dion Phaneuf and Fredrik Sjostrom for Matt Stajan, Niklas Hagman, Jamal Mayers and Ian White, January 31, 2010.

AVTSIN, Alexander (AV-tsihn, al-ehx-AN-duhr) MTL.

Right wing. Shoots right. 6'2", 198 lbs. Born, Moscow, USSR, March 19, 1991.
(Montreal's 4th choice, 109th overall, in 2009 Entry Draft).

			Regular Season					Playoffs				
Season	Club	League	GP	G	A	Pts	PIM	GP	G	A	Pts	PIM
2008-09	Dyn'o Moscow 2	Russia-3	STATISTICS NOT AVAILABLE									
2009-10	Dynamo Moscow	Rus-KHL	30	3	6	9	10	....	....	....	....	....
	Dyn'o Moscow Jr.	Russia-Jr.	12	4	5	9	20	....	....	....	....	....

AXELSSON, Dick (AHX-ehl-suhn, DIHK) DET.

Wing. Shoots left. 6'2", 198 lbs. Born, Stockholm, Sweden, April 25, 1987.
(Detroit's 3rd choice, 62nd overall, in 2006 Entry Draft).

			Regular Season					Playoffs				
Season	Club	League	GP	G	A	Pts	PIM	GP	G	A	Pts	PIM
2003-04	Huddinge IK U18	Swe-U18	13	3	1	4	38	....	....	....	....	....
2004-05	Huddinge IK U18	Swe-U18	1	0	0	0	0	....	....	....	....	....
	Huddinge IK Jr.	Swe-Jr.	31	12	4	16	34	3	1	0	1	0
2005-06	Huddinge IK Jr.	Swe-Jr.	28	19	15	34	157	....	....	....	....	....
2006-07	Huddinge IK	Sweden-2	33	16	15	31	145	....	....	....	....	....
2007-08	Djurgarden	Sweden	47	12	13	25	44	5	1	0	1	2
2008-09	Djurgarden	Sweden	18	5	7	12	10	....	....	....	....	....
	Farjestad	Sweden	21	6	12	18	32	9	1	3	4	2
2009-10	Grand Rapids	AHL	17	2	3	5	6	....	....	....	....	....
	Farjestad	Sweden	15	6	4	10	24	7	1	2	3	6

AZEVEDO, Justin (a-zeh-VAY-doh, JUHS-tihn) L.A.

Center. Shoots right. 5'7", 180 lbs. Born, West Lorne, Ont., April 1, 1988.
(Los Angeles' 8th choice, 153rd overall, in 2008 Entry Draft).

			Regular Season					Playoffs				
Season	Club	League	GP	G	A	Pts	PIM	GP	G	A	Pts	PIM
2004-05	Kitchener Rangers	OHL	58	18	21	39	34	15	3	1	4	14
2005-06	Kitchener Rangers	OHL	60	29	40	69	80	5	0	3	3	12
2006-07	Kitchener Rangers	OHL	50	17	39	56	42	9	4	11	15	22
2007-08	Kitchener Rangers	OHL	67	43	*81	*124	69	20	10	*26	*36	33
2008-09	Manchester	AHL	49	12	24	36	31	....	....	....	....	....
2009-10	Manchester	AHL	46	14	13	27	31	16	3	6	9	12

OHL First All-Star Team (2008) • Memorial Cup All-Star Team (2008) • Ed Chynoweth Trophy (Memorial Cup Tournament - Leading Scorer) (2008) • Canadian Major Junior First All-Star Team (2008) • Canadian Major Junior Player of the Year (2008)

BACKMAN, Sean (BAK-man, SHAWN) DAL.

Right wing. Shoots right. 5'8", 165 lbs. Born, Cos Cob, CT, April 29, 1986.

			Regular Season					Playoffs				
Season	Club	League	GP	G	A	Pts	PIM	GP	G	A	Pts	PIM
2006-07	Yale	ECAC	29	18	13	31	38	....	....	....	....	....
2007-08	Yale	ECAC	32	18	9	27	16	....	....	....	....	....
2008-09	Yale	ECAC	32	20	13	33	44	....	....	....	....	....
2009-10	Yale	ECAC	29	21	14	35	12	....	....	....	....	....

ECAC Second All-Star Team (2009) • ECAC First All-Star Team (2010) • NCAA East Second All-American Team (2010)

Signed as a free agent by **Dallas**, March 30, 2010.

BAGNALL, Drew (BAG-nuhl, DROO) MIN.

Defense. Shoots left. 6'3", 220 lbs. Born, Oakbank, Man., October 26, 1983.
(Dallas' 9th choice, 195th overall, in 2003 Entry Draft).

			Regular Season					Playoffs				
Season	Club	League	GP	G	A	Pts	PIM	GP	G	A	Pts	PIM
2000-01	Battlefords	SJHL	58	7	20	27	205	....	....	....	....	....
2001-02	Battlefords	SJHL	60	16	23	39	247	....	....	....	....	....
2002-03	Battlefords	SJHL	55	17	46	63	248	4	0	1	1	4
2003-04	St. Lawrence	ECAC	40	5	13	18	61	....	....	....	....	....
2004-05	St. Lawrence	ECAC	37	7	12	19	68	....	....	....	....	....
2005-06	St. Lawrence	ECAC	24	1	9	10	32	....	....	....	....	....
2006-07	St. Lawrence	ECAC	39	6	19	25	74	....	....	....	....	....
2007-08	Manchester	AHL	54	1	11	12	115	4	0	0	0	4
	Reading Royals	ECHL	10	1	2	3	32	....	....	....	....	....
2008-09	Manchester	AHL	79	0	6	6	150	....	....	....	....	....
2009-10	Manchester	AHL	58	2	10	12	113	16	0	3	3	21

Traded to **Florida** by **Dallas** with Dallas' 2nd round compensatory choice (later traded to Phoenix - Phoenix selected Enver Lisin) in 2004 Entry Draft for Valeri Bure, March 8, 2004. Signed as a free agent by **Los Angeles**, August 23, 2007. Signed as a free agent by **Minnesota**, July 2, 2010.

BAIER, Paul (BAI-uhr, PAWL)

Defense. Shoots right. 6'3", 212 lbs. Born, Summit, NJ, February 2, 1985.
(Los Angeles' 2nd choice, 95th overall, in 2004 Entry Draft).

			Regular Season					Playoffs				
Season	Club	League	GP	G	A	Pts	PIM	GP	G	A	Pts	PIM
2002-03	Deerfield Academy	High-MA	25	2	15	17	24	....	....	....	....	....
2003-04	Deerfield Academy	High-MA	23	6	4	10	22	....	....	....	....	....
2004-05	Brown U.	ECAC	32	2	8	10	24	....	....	....	....	....
2005-06	Brown U.	ECAC	30	0	6	6	18	....	....	....	....	....
2006-07	Brown U.	ECAC	32	1	4	5	55	....	....	....	....	....
2007-08	Brown U.	ECAC	31	2	5	7	38	....	....	....	....	....
	Rochester	AHL	9	1	3	4	5	....	....	....	....	....
2008-09	Portland Pirates	AHL	62	3	8	11	67	3	0	0	0	6
2009-10	Binghamton	AHL	62	2	8	10	49	....	....	....	....	....

BAILEY, Jason (BAY-lee, JAY-sohn) OTT.

Right wing. Shoots right. 6', 205 lbs. Born, Ottawa, Ont., June 4, 1987.
(Anaheim's 3rd choice, 63rd overall, in 2005 Entry Draft).

			Regular Season					Playoffs				
Season	Club	League	GP	G	A	Pts	PIM	GP	G	A	Pts	PIM
2003-04	Nepean Raiders	CJHL	45	14	14	28	119	18	2	7	9	35
2004-05	USNTDP	U-18	26	3	2	5	91	....	....	....	....	....
	USNTDP	NAHL	13	2	4	6	50	....	....	....	....	....
2005-06	U. of Michigan	CCHA	27	5	2	7	57	....	....	....	....	....
2006-07	U. of Michigan	CCHA	19	0	0	0	28	....	....	....	....	....
	Ottawa 67's	OHL	35	7	9	16	88	4	0	0	0	6
2007-08	Ottawa 67's	OHL	34	8	9	17	78	4	0	2	2	11
2008-09	Bakersfield	ECHL	35	0	2	2	44	2	0	0	0	0
	Iowa Chops	AHL	2	0	0	0	0	....	....	....	....	....
2009-10	Binghamton	AHL	62	6	1	7	78	....	....	....	....	....

Traded to **Ottawa** by **Anaheim** for Shawn Weller, September 4, 2009.

BALAN, Stanislav (BAY-luhn, STAN-ihs-lahv) NSH.

Center. Shoots left. 6'2", 161 lbs. Born, Hodonin, Czech., January 30, 1986.
(Nashville's 8th choice, 209th overall, in 2004 Entry Draft).

			Regular Season					Playoffs				
Season	Club	League	GP	G	A	Pts	PIM	GP	G	A	Pts	PIM
2001-02	HC Zlin Jr.	CzRep-Jr.	48	21	23	44	60	4	1	1	2	0
2002-03	HC Zlin Jr.	CzRep-Jr.	35	24	21	45	59	3	2	0	2	16
2003-04	HC Zlin Jr.	CzRep-Jr.	53	23	33	56	122	5	2	0	2	31
	HC Hame Zlin	CzRep	4	1	0	1	2	....	....	....	....	....
2004-05	SHK Hodonin	CzRep-3	5	3	2	5	20	....	....	....	....	....
	HC Zlin Jr.	CzRep-Jr.	37	10	13	23	131	2	0	0	0	2
2005-06	Portland	WHL	67	14	23	37	102	12	1	4	5	18
2006-07	HC Hame Zlin	CzRep	44	4	3	7	48	5	0	0	0	2
	Trebic	CzRep-2	7	3	2	5	12	....	....	....	....	....
2007-08	RI Okna Zlin	CzRep	57	4	6	10	54	....	....	....	....	....
2008-09	HC Dukla Jihlava	CzRep-2	5	4	3	7	4	....	....	....	....	....
	RI Okna Zlin	CzRep	46	5	3	8	61	4	0	0	0	0
2009-10	PSG Zlin	CzRep	52	5	11	16	85	6	0	2	2	4

BALDWIN, Gord (BAHLD-wihn, GOHRD) CGY.

Defense. Shoots left. 6'5", 199 lbs. Born, Winnipeg, Man., March 1, 1987.
(Calgary's 2nd choice, 69th overall, in 2005 Entry Draft).

			Regular Season					Playoffs				
Season	Club	League	GP	G	A	Pts	PIM	GP	G	A	Pts	PIM
2003-04	Wpg. Thrashers	MMHL	39	5	16	21	66	....	....	....	....	....
2004-05	Medicine Hat	WHL	66	3	8	11	73	....	....	....	....	....
2005-06	Medicine Hat	WHL	71	4	20	24	119	13	0	9	9	22
2006-07	Medicine Hat	WHL	53	7	19	26	70	23	2	6	8	32
2007-08	Quad City Flames	AHL	37	0	5	5	26	....	....	....	....	....
	Las Vegas	ECHL	12	0	1	1	9	....	....	....	....	....
2008-09	Quad City Flames	AHL	55	2	4	6	39	....	....	....	....	....
	Las Vegas	ECHL	3	0	1	1	23	....	....	....	....	....
2009-10	Abbotsford Heat	AHL	67	4	20	24	84	12	1	1	2	18

BALDWIN, Lee (BAHLD-wihn, LEE) NYR

Defense. Shoots left. 6'4", 205 lbs. Born, Victoria, B.C., April 26, 1988.

			Regular Season					Playoffs				
Season	Club	League	GP	G	A	Pts	PIM	GP	G	A	Pts	PIM
2006-07	Burnaby Express	BCHL	59	0	16	16	55	14	2	3	5	6
2007-08	Burnaby Express	BCHL	35	7	17	24	40	5	1	5	6	4
2008-09	Victoria Grizzlies	BCHL	56	13	41	54	79	14	2	6	8	10
2009-10	Alaska-Anchorage	WCHA	32	1	9	10	51	....	....	....	....	....
	Hartford Wolf Pack	AHL	7	1	0	1	4	....	....	....	....	....

Signed as a free agent by **NY Rangers**, March 22, 2010.

BANCKS, Carter CGY.

Left wing. Shoots left. 5'11", 180 lbs. Born, Marysville, B.C., August 9, 1989.

			Regular Season					Playoffs				
Season	Club	League	GP	G	A	Pts	PIM	GP	G	A	Pts	PIM
2004-05	Kimberley	KIJHL	11	1	5	6	10	....	....	....	....	....
2005-06	Kimberley	KIJHL	50	24	49	73	57	13	5	7	12	6
	Lethbridge	WHL	2	0	0	0	0	6	0	0	0	4
2006-07	Lethbridge	WHL	67	11	20	31	64	....	....	....	....	....
2007-08	Lethbridge	WHL	70	15	30	45	56	19	6	4	10	19
2008-09	Lethbridge	WHL	53	13	34	47	68	3	0	0	0	4
2009-10	Lethbridge	WHL	70	19	36	55	96	....	....	....	....	....
	Abbotsford Heat	AHL	9	0	0	0	0	13	0	1	1	7

• Missed majority of 2004-05 season recovering from leg injury suffered during the 2003-04 season. Signed to a ATO (amateur tryout) contract by **Abbotsford** (AHL), March 18, 2010.

BARANOV, Konstantin (buh-RA-nawf, KAWN-stan-tihn) PHI.

Right wing. Shoots left. 6'2", 185 lbs. Born, Omsk, USSR, January 11, 1982.
(Philadelphia's 3rd choice, 126th overall, in 2002 Entry Draft).

			Regular Season					Playoffs				
Season	Club	League	GP	G	A	Pts	PIM	GP	G	A	Pts	PIM
1998-99	Omsk 2	Russia-4	23	18	8	26	40	....	....	....	....	....
	Avangard Omsk	Russia	1	0	0	0	0	2	0	0	0	0
99-2000	Omsk 2	Russia-3	33	15	8	23	46	....	....	....	....	....
	Avangard Omsk	Russia	1	0	0	0	2	....	....	....	....	....
2000-01	Kristall Saratov	Russia-2	26	6	9	15	26	....	....	....	....	....
	Ufa	Russia	8	1	0	1	4	....	....	....	....	....
2001-02	Avangard Omsk	Russia	5	0	0	0	6	....	....	....	....	....
	Mechel	Russia	6	1	2	3	2	....	....	....	....	....
	Lada Togliatti	Russia	20	2	4	6	18	3	0	2	2	0
2002-03	Avangard Omsk	Russia	6	0	1	1	2	....	....	....	....	....
	Ufa	Russia	11	2	2	4	0	....	....	....	....	....
	CSKA Moscow	Russia	14	4	1	5	10	....	....	....	....	....
	Omsk 2	Russia-3	3	4	6	10	2	....	....	....	....	....
2003-04	Avangard Omsk	Russia	51	6	10	16	50	11	2	2	4	6
2004-05	Omsk 2	Russia-3	7	5	7	12	20	....	....	....	....	....
	Avangard Omsk	Russia	21	3	2	5	16	....	....	....	....	....
2005-06	Dynamo Moscow	Russia	19	0	5	5	10	....	....	....	....	....
	SKA St. Petersburg	Russia	12	1	2	3	18	3	0	0	0	2
2006-07	Amur Khabarovsk	Russia	7	0	1	1	16	....	....	....	....	....
	Novokuznetsk	Russia	21	2	2	4	28	3	3	1	4	0
2007-08	Avtomobilist	Russia-2	4	0	0	0	26	....	....	....	....	....
	Avtomobilist 2	Russia-3	6	3	2	5	10	....	....	....	....	....
	HK Dmitrov	Russia-2	33	5	14	19	56	2	1	0	1	0
2008-09	Gazovik Tyumen	Russia-2	31	5	11	16	50	....	....	....	....	....
	Kapitan Stupino	Russia-2	21	8	13	21	36	9	1	3	4	16
2009-10	HK Sarov	Russia-2	54	23	17	40	68	....	....	....	....	....

BARBERIO, Mark (bahr-BAIR-ee-oh, MAHRK) T.B.

Defense. Shoots left. 6'1", 185 lbs. Born, Montreal, Que., March 23, 1990.
(Tampa Bay's 5th choice, 152nd overall, in 2008 Entry Draft).

			Regular Season					Playoffs				
Season	Club	League	GP	G	A	Pts	PIM	GP	G	A	Pts	PIM
2005-06	Lac St-Louis Lions	QAAA	43	2	12	14	80	10	1	7	8	26
2006-07	Cape Breton	QMJHL	41	2	8	10	42	....	....	....	....	....
	Moncton Wildcats	QMJHL	19	1	6	7	21	7	0	2	2	8
2007-08	Moncton Wildcats	QMJHL	70	11	35	46	75	....	....	....	....	....
2008-09	Moncton Wildcats	QMJHL	66	15	30	45	42	10	0	4	4	8
2009-10	Moncton Wildcats	QMJHL	65	17	43	60	72	21	5	17	22	12

QMJHL All-Rookie Team (2007) • QMJHL Second All-Star Team (2010)

BARRIBALL, Jay (BEHR-ih-bahl, JAY) ST.L.

Left wing. Shoots left. 5'9", 171 lbs. Born, Prior Lake, MN, May 27, 1987.
(San Jose's 6th choice, 203rd overall, in 2006 Entry Draft).

			Regular Season					Playoffs				
Season	Club	League	GP	G	A	Pts	PIM	GP	G	A	Pts	PIM
2004-05	Holy Angels	High-MN	30	32	49	81	....	....	....	....	....	....
2005-06	Holy Angels	High-MN	20	28	38	66	....	....	....	....	....	....
	Sioux Falls	USHL	13	5	7	12	2	5	2	1	3	0
2006-07	U. of Minnesota	WCHA	44	20	23	43	16	....	....	....	....	....
2007-08	U. of Minnesota	WCHA	41	6	15	21	34	....	....	....	....	....
2008-09	U. of Minnesota	WCHA	34	11	23	34	52	....	....	....	....	....
2009-10	U. of Minnesota	WCHA	5	2	2	4	10	....	....	....	....	....

Traded to **St. Louis** by **San Jose** with Ville Nieminen and New Jersey's 1st round choice (previously acquired, St. Louis selected David Perron) in 2007 Entry Draft for Bill Guerin, February 27, 2007.

BARRIE, Tyson (BAIR-ree, TIGH-suhn) COL.

Defense. Shoots right. 5'10", 190 lbs. Born, Victoria, B.C., July 26, 1991.
(Colorado's 4th choice, 64th overall, in 2009 Entry Draft).

			Regular Season					Playoffs				
Season	Club	League	GP	G	A	Pts	PIM	GP	G	A	Pts	PIM
2006-07	Juan de Fuca	Minor-BC	72	43	87	130	....	....	....	....	....	....
	Kelowna Rockets	WHL	7	0	3	3	2	....	....	....	....	....
2007-08	Kelowna Rockets	WHL	64	9	34	43	32	7	1	3	4	0
2008-09	Kelowna Rockets	WHL	68	12	40	52	31	22	4	14	18	12
2009-10	Kelowna Rockets	WHL	63	19	53	72	31	12	3	8	11	6

Canadian Major Junior All-Rookie Team (2008) • WHL West First All-Star Team (2010) • WHL Defenseman of the Year (2010) • Canadian Major Junior Second All-Star Team (2010)

BARTKOWSKI, Matt (bahrt-KOW-skee, MATT) BOS.

Defense. Shoots left. 6'1", 196 lbs. Born, Pittsburgh, PA, June 4, 1988.
(Florida's 5th choice, 190th overall, in 2008 Entry Draft).

			Regular Season					Playoffs				
Season	Club	League	GP	G	A	Pts	PIM	GP	G	A	Pts	PIM
2006-07	Lincoln Stars	USHL	57	3	6	9	95	3	0	0	0	2
2007-08	Lincoln Stars	USHL	60	4	37	41	135	8	1	4	5	10
2008-09	Ohio State	CCHA	41	5	15	20	46	....	....	....	....	....
2009-10	Ohio State	CCHA	39	6	12	18	*99	....	....	....	....	....

CCHA All-Rookie Team (2009) • USHL First All-Star Team (2008)

Traded to **Boston** by **Florida** with Dennis Seidenberg for Byron Bitz, Craig Weller and Tampa Bay's 2nd round choice (previously acquired, Florida selected Alexander Petrovic) in 2010 Entry Draft, March 3, 2010.

BASARABA, Joe (ba-sa-RA-bah, JOH) FLA.

Right wing. Shoots right. 6'2", 190 lbs. Born, Fort Frances, Ont., May 2, 1992.
(Florida's 7th choice, 69th overall, in 2010 Entry Draft).

			Regular Season					Playoffs				
Season	Club	League	GP	G	A	Pts	PIM	GP	G	A	Pts	PIM
2008-09	Shat.-St. Mary's	High-MN	54	20	24	44	54	....	....	....	....	....
2009-10	Shat.-St. Mary's	High-MN	52	24	22	46	39	....	....	....	....	....

• Signed Letter of Intent to attend **University of Minnesota-Duluth** (WCHA) in fall of 2010.

BASHKIROV, Ruslan (bash-KIHR-ahv, roos-LAHN) OTT.

Left wing. Shoots left. 5'11", 193 lbs. Born, Moscow, USSR, March 7, 1989.
(Ottawa's 2nd choice, 60th overall, in 2007 Entry Draft).

			Regular Season					Playoffs				
Season	Club	League	GP	G	A	Pts	PIM	GP	G	A	Pts	PIM
2005-06	Spartak Moscow 2	Russia-3	35	16	9	25	44	....	....	....	....	....
2006-07	Quebec Remparts	QMJHL	64	30	37	67	117	5	1	3	4	6
2007-08	Mytischi	Russia	4	0	0	0	0	....	....	....	....	....
	Kristall Elektrostal	Russia-2	12	4	0	4	22	....	....	....	....	....
2008-09	Lada Togliatti	Rus-KHL	2	0	0	0	2	....	....	....	....	....
	Rys Podolsk	Russia-2	48	9	8	17	20	3	1	3	4	2
2009-10	Perm	Russia-2	37	10	8	18	12	10	2	3	5	4

Signed as a free agent by **Mytischi** (Russia), August 23, 2007.

BATHGATE, Andy (BATH-gayt, AHN-dee) PIT.

Center. Shoots left. 6', 164 lbs. Born, Brampton, Ont., February 26, 1991.
(Pittsburgh's 6th choice, 151st overall, in 2009 Entry Draft).

			Regular Season					Playoffs				
Season	Club	League	GP	G	A	Pts	PIM	GP	G	A	Pts	PIM
2007-08	Georgetown	OPJHL	40	14	30	44	24	10	1	6	7	10
	Belleville Bulls	OHL	5	0	1	1	2	5	0	0	0	0
2008-09	Belleville Bulls	OHL	44	4	12	16	10	....	....	....	....	....
2009-10	Belleville Bulls	OHL	59	13	27	40	16	....	....	....	....	....

BEACH, Cody (BEECH, KOH-dee) ST.L.

Right wing. Shoots right. 6'5", 180 lbs. Born, Nanaimo, B.C., August 8, 1992.
(St. Louis' 6th choice, 134th overall, in 2010 Entry Draft).

			Regular Season					Playoffs				
Season	Club	League	GP	G	A	Pts	PIM	GP	G	A	Pts	PIM
2007-08	Okanagan Rockets	BCMML	37	8	17	25	68	6	1	3	4	16
2008-09	Calgary Hitmen	WHL	3	0	0	0	2	....	....	....	....	....
	Okanagan Rockets	BCMML	23	10	13	23	58	2	1	0	1	2
2009-10	Calgary Hitmen	WHL	51	3	11	14	157	19	1	7	8	34

BEACH, Kyle (BEECH, KIGH-uhl) CHI.

Center. Shoots right. 6'3", 210 lbs. Born, Vancouver, B.C., January 13, 1990.
(Chicago's 1st choice, 11th overall, in 2008 Entry Draft).

			Regular Season					Playoffs				
Season	Club	League	GP	G	A	Pts	PIM	GP	G	A	Pts	PIM
2005-06	Okanagan Rockets	BCMML	25	23	18	41	220	....	....	....	....	....
	Everett Silvertips	WHL	4	2	1	3	4	9	1	3	4	31
2006-07	Everett Silvertips	WHL	65	29	32	61	196	11	5	6	11	19
2007-08	Everett Silvertips	WHL	60	27	33	60	222	4	0	0	0	4
2008-09	Everett Silvertips	WHL	30	9	21	30	106	....	....	....	....	....
	Lethbridge	WHL	24	15	18	33	59	10	1	1	2	31
	Rockford IceHogs	AHL	2	0	0	0	15	1	0	0	0	0
2009-10	Spokane Chiefs	WHL	68	*52	34	86	186	7	7	2	9	19
	Rockford IceHogs	AHL	4	0	0	0	0	4	3	0	3	6

WHL Rookie of the Year (2007) • WHL West First All-Star Team (2010)

BEAUDOIN, Matt (boh-DWEH, MAT) **PHX.**

Right wing. Shoots right. 5'11", 190 lbs. Born, Rock Forest, Que., April 6, 1984.

			Regular Season					Playoffs				
Season	Club	League	GP	G	A	Pts	PIM	GP	G	A	Pts	PIM
2003-04	Ohio State	CCHA	40	7	7	14	26	....	....	....	....	....
2004-05	Ohio State	CCHA	40	23	11	34	50	....	....	....	....	....
2005-06	Ohio State	CCHA	32	8	8	16	18	....	....	....	....	....
2006-07	Ohio State	CCHA	37	14	11	25	24	....	....	....	....	....
	Arizona Sundogs	CHL	....	....	....	....	....	14	2	1	3	14
2007-08	Iowa Stars	AHL	3	0	0	0	0	....	....	....	....	....
	Rochester	AHL	1	0	0	0	0	....	....	....	....	....
	Hershey Bears	AHL	7	0	0	0	0	1	0	0	0	0
	Las Vegas	ECHL	1	0	1	1	0	....	....	....	....	....
	Dayton Bombers	ECHL	61	38	30	68	44	2	0	0	0	0
2008-09	San Antonio	AHL	1	0	1	1	2	....	....	....	....	....
	Milwaukee	AHL	2	0	0	0	0	....	....	....	....	....
	Houston Aeros	AHL	41	11	8	19	17	20	8	9	17	12
	Las Vegas	ECHL	15	10	6	16	10	....	....	....	....	....
2009-10	Texas Stars	AHL	72	19	25	44	22	22	4	3	7	4

Signed as a free agent by **Phoenix**, July 3, 2010.

BEAULIEU, Josh (BOI-l'yew, JAWSH)

Right wing. Shoots left. 6'1", 180 lbs. Born, Windsor, Ont., January 10, 1987.
(Philadelphia's 4th choice, 152nd overall, in 2005 Entry Draft).

			Regular Season					Playoffs				
Season	Club	League	GP	G	A	Pts	PIM	GP	G	A	Pts	PIM
2003-04	London Knights	OHL	41	3	6	9	32	9	0	0	0	5
2004-05	London Knights	OHL	65	9	13	22	159	13	2	3	5	13
2005-06	London Knights	OHL	60	15	13	28	140	18	4	5	9	12
2006-07	London Knights	OHL	44	10	6	16	93	10	3	6	9	31
2007-08	Philadelphia	AHL	50	3	3	6	50	....	....	....	....	....
2008-09	Philadelphia	AHL	40	1	1	2	36	....	....	....	....	....
2009-10	Adirondack	AHL	46	2	2	4	11	....	....	....	....	....

BECK, Taylor (BEHK, TAY-luhr) **NSH.**

Left wing. Shoots right. 6'2", 205 lbs. Born, St. Catharines, Ont., May 13, 1991.
(Nashville's 4th choice, 70th overall, in 2009 Entry Draft).

			Regular Season					Playoffs				
Season	Club	League	GP	G	A	Pts	PIM	GP	G	A	Pts	PIM
2006-07	Niagara Falls	Minor-ON	69	64	75	139	76	....	....	....	....	....
2007-08	Guelph Storm	OHL	56	7	14	21	43	7	0	0	0	4
2008-09	Guelph Storm	OHL	67	22	36	58	36	4	0	0	0	2
2009-10	Guelph Storm	OHL	61	39	54	93	54	5	3	3	6	2

OHL Second All-Star Team (2010)

BELLAMY, Rob (BEHL-ah-mee, RAWB)

Right wing. Shoots right. 6'1", 190 lbs. Born, Providence, RI, May 30, 1985.
(Philadelphia's 1st choice, 92nd overall, in 2004 Entry Draft).

			Regular Season					Playoffs				
Season	Club	League	GP	G	A	Pts	PIM	GP	G	A	Pts	PIM
2002-03	Berkshire Bears	High-MA	32	21	21	42	128	....	....	....	....	....
2003-04	N.E. Jr. Coyotes	EJHL	36	19	21	40	95	....	....	....	....	....
2004-05	U. of Maine	H-East	28	3	4	7	34	....	....	....	....	....
2005-06	U. of Maine	H-East	40	6	9	15	77	....	....	....	....	....
2006-07	U. of Maine	H-East	37	1	7	8	82	....	....	....	....	....
2007-08	U. of Maine	H-East	33	5	13	18	61	....	....	....	....	....
	Philadelphia	AHL	1	0	0	0	0	....	....	....	....	....
2008-09	Philadelphia	AHL	51	2	3	5	18	....	....	....	....	....
2009-10	Adirondack	AHL	62	2	5	7	20	....	....	....	....	....

BELLEMORE, Brett (BEHL-mohr, BREHT) **CAR.**

Defense. Shoots right. 6'4", 205 lbs. Born, Windsor, Ont., June 25, 1988.
(Carolina's 5th choice, 162nd overall, in 2007 Entry Draft).

			Regular Season					Playoffs				
Season	Club	League	GP	G	A	Pts	PIM	GP	G	A	Pts	PIM
2005-06	Plymouth Whalers	OHL	46	0	0	0	16	10	0	0	0	0
2006-07	Plymouth Whalers	OHL	50	0	12	12	50	20	0	5	5	28
2007-08	Plymouth Whalers	OHL	56	6	18	24	70	4	0	2	2	8
	Albany River Rats	AHL	4	0	0	0	6	5	0	0	0	6
2008-09	Plymouth Whalers	OHL	29	2	10	12	39	11	1	2	3	16
	Albany River Rats	AHL	6	0	0	0	4	....	....	....	....	....
2009-10	Albany River Rats	AHL	75	1	6	7	81	8	0	1	1	2

BENDFELD, Jordan (BENHD-felhd, JOHR-dahn) **EDM.**

Defense. Shoots right. 6'2", 216 lbs. Born, Leduc, Alta., February 9, 1988.
(Edmonton's 5th choice, 193rd overall, in 2008 Entry Draft).

			Regular Season					Playoffs				
Season	Club	League	GP	G	A	Pts	PIM	GP	G	A	Pts	PIM
2003-04	Leduc Oil Kings	AMHL	36	0	9	9	22	....	....	....	....	....
2004-05	Leduc Oil Kings	AMHL	21	1	5	6	96	....	....	....	....	....
	Medicine Hat	WHL	16	0	0	0	4	2	0	0	0	2
2005-06	Medicine Hat	WHL	65	2	10	12	92	13	0	4	4	27
2006-07	Medicine Hat	WHL	72	9	21	30	136	23	0	5	5	*62
2007-08	Medicine Hat	WHL	72	6	19	25	160	5	0	2	2	2
2008-09	Stockton Thunder	ECHL	17	1	2	3	25	....	....	....	....	....
2009-10	Springfield Falcons	AHL	10	0	1	1	7	....	....	....	....	....
	Stockton Thunder	ECHL	52	0	10	10	91	15	1	4	5	23

• Re-entered NHL Entry Draft. Originally Phoenix's 6th choice, 152nd overall, in 2006 Entry Draft.
• Missed majority of 2008-09 season recovering from knee injury suffered in game vs. Ontario (ECHL), November, 2008.

BENNETT, Beau (BEH-neht, BOH) **PIT.**

Right wing. Shoots right. 6'1", 173 lbs. Born, Gardena, CA, November 27, 1991.
(Pittsburgh's 1st choice, 20th overall, in 2010 Entry Draft).

			Regular Season					Playoffs				
Season	Club	League	GP	G	A	Pts	PIM	GP	G	A	Pts	PIM
2008-09	L.A. Jr. Kings	T1EHL	46	25	33	58	10	....	....	....	....	....
2009-10	Penticton Vees	BCHL	56	41	79	*120	20	15	5	9	14	6

• Signed Letter of Intent to attend **University of Denver** (WCHA) in fall of 2010.

BENNETT, Mac (BEHN-neht, MAK) **MTL.**

Defense. Shoots left. 6', 170 lbs. Born, Warwick, RI, March 25, 1991.
(Montreal's 3rd choice, 79th overall, in 2009 Entry Draft).

			Regular Season					Playoffs				
Season	Club	League	GP	G	A	Pts	PIM	GP	G	A	Pts	PIM
2006-07	Hotchkiss	High-CT	25	7	6	13	....	....	....	....	....	....
2007-08	Hotchkiss	High-CT	25	6	9	15	....	....	....	....	....	....
2008-09	Neponset Valley	Minor-MA	16	5	19	24	....	....	....	....	....	....
	Hotchkiss	High-CT	15	4	11	15	....	....	....	....	....	....
2009-10	Cedar Rapids	USHL	53	9	15	24	34	2	1	0	1	0

USHL All-Rookie Team (2010)

BENNETT, Spencer (BEHN-neht, SPEHN-suhr) **CGY.**

Left wing. Shoots left. 6'4", 185 lbs. Born, White Rock, B.C., October 31, 1990.
(Calgary's 4th choice, 141st overall, in 2009 Entry Draft).

			Regular Season					Playoffs				
Season	Club	League	GP	G	A	Pts	PIM	GP	G	A	Pts	PIM
2006-07	Delta Ice Hawks	PIJHL	40	6	12	18	14	3	0	0	0	2
	Burnaby Express	BCHL	7	1	0	1	2	13	1	1	2	2
2007-08	Burnaby Express	BCHL	58	6	11	17	41	5	1	2	3	4
2008-09	Surrey Eagles	BCHL	60	20	21	41	32	9	2	4	6	7
2009-10	Portland	WHL	71	19	21	40	53	13	1	2	3	2

BENOIT, Andre (behn-WAH, AWN-dray)

Defense. Shoots left. 5'11", 186 lbs. Born, St. Albert, Ont., January 6, 1984.

			Regular Season					Playoffs				
Season	Club	League	GP	G	A	Pts	PIM	GP	G	A	Pts	PIM
2000-01	Kitchener Rangers	OHL	65	16	19	35	37	....	....	....	....	....
2001-02	Kitchener Rangers	OHL	62	13	32	45	77	4	1	0	1	8
2002-03	Kitchener Rangers	OHL	65	22	45	67	77	21	1	16	17	16
2003-04	Kitchener Rangers	OHL	65	24	51	75	67	5	1	1	2	6
2004-05	Kitchener Rangers	OHL	67	24	53	77	72	15	5	13	18	6
2005-06	Hamilton Bulldogs	AHL	70	7	19	26	60	....	....	....	....	....
2006-07	Hamilton Bulldogs	AHL	64	10	21	31	41	22	2	11	13	22
2007-08	Tappara Tampere	Finland	54	12	26	38	96	11	2	3	5	10
2008-09	Sodertalje SK	Sweden	54	4	16	20	34	....	....	....	....	....
	Sodertalje SK	Sweden-Q	10	0	2	2	10	....	....	....	....	....
2009-10	Hamilton Bulldogs	AHL	78	6	30	36	63	19	3	11	14	8

Signed as a free agent by **Montreal**, January 9, 2006. Signed as a free agent by **Tappara Tampere** (Finland), June 21, 2007. Signed as a free agent by **Montreal**, May 13, 2009.

BERGIN, Mike (BUHR-gihn, MIGHK) **DAL.**

Defense. Shoots left. 6'3", 197 lbs. Born, Kanata, Ont., June 30, 1988.
(Dallas' 5th choice, 209th overall, in 2008 Entry Draft).

			Regular Season					Playoffs				
Season	Club	League	GP	G	A	Pts	PIM	GP	G	A	Pts	PIM
2006-07	Smiths Falls Bears	CJHL	53	10	35	45	116	11	2	7	9	18
2007-08	Smiths Falls Bears	CJHL	45	14	27	41	60	15	2	5	7	19
2008-09	RPI Engineers	ECAC	6	0	1	1	6	....	....	....	....	....
2009-10	RPI Engineers	ECAC	30	4	7	11	52	....	....	....	....	....

• Missed majority of 2008-09 season recovering from shoulder injury suffered in game vs. University of Massachusetts (Hockey East), October 21, 2008.

BERGLUND, Kristofer (BUHR-gluhnd, KRIHS-toh-fuhr) **ST.L.**

Defense. Shoots left. 5'10", 180 lbs. Born, Umea, Sweden, August 12, 1988.
(St. Louis' 8th choice, 125th overall, in 2008 Entry Draft).

			Regular Season					Playoffs				
Season	Club	League	GP	G	A	Pts	PIM	GP	G	A	Pts	PIM
2003-04	Bjorkloven U18	Swe-U18	10	4	4	8	2	....	....	....	....	....
2004-05	Bjorkloven U18	Swe-U18	STATISTICS NOT AVAILABLE									
2005-06	Bjorkloven Jr.	Swe-Jr.	38	3	11	14	36	6	0	3	3	8
	IF Bjorkloven Umea	Sweden-2	1	0	0	0	0	....	....	....	....	....
2006-07	Bjorkloven Jr.	Swe-Jr.	30	4	22	26	38	....	....	....	....	....
	Tegs SK Umea	Sweden-3	2	0	1	1	2	....	....	....	....	....
	IF Bjorkloven Umea	Sweden-2	42	0	4	4	18	....	....	....	....	....
2007-08	Bjorkloven Jr.	Swe-Jr.	1	0	0	0	0	....	....	....	....	....
	IF Bjorkloven Umea	Sweden-2	42	4	21	25	14	2	0	1	1	0
2008-09	Lulea HF	Sweden	52	3	22	25	36	5	0	3	3	4
2009-10	Lulea HF	Sweden	55	6	16	22	22	....	....	....	....	....

BERNIKOV, Ruslan (BAIR-nih-kahf, roos-LAHN) **DAL.**

Right wing. Shoots left. 6'3", 216 lbs. Born, Vidnoye, USSR, December 4, 1977.
(Dallas' 6th choice, 139th overall, in 2000 Entry Draft).

			Regular Season					Playoffs				
Season	Club	League	GP	G	A	Pts	PIM	GP	G	A	Pts	PIM
1996-97	Dyn'o Moscow 2	Russia-3	32	11	4	15	20	....	....	....	....	....
	Dynamo Moscow	Russia	2	0	0	0	0	....	....	....	....	....
1997-98	Yekaterinburg 2	Russia-3	2	1	1	2	0	....	....	....	....	....
	Yekaterinburg	Russia	43	7	7	14	55	....	....	....	....	....
1998-99	Dynamo Moscow	Russia	6	0	1	1	2	....	....	....	....	....
	Krylja Sovetov	Russia	20	3	1	4	24	....	....	....	....	....
	CSKA Moscow	Russia	1	0	0	0	0	....	....	....	....	....
	Cherepovets	Russia	5	0	0	0	0	1	0	0	0	0
99-2000	Dynamo Moscow	Russia	6	2	1	3	2	....	....	....	....	....
	Amur Khabarovsk	Russia	14	3	6	9	10	5	3	1	4	2
2000-01	Amur Khabarovsk	Russia	33	1	4	5	40	....	....	....	....	....
2001-02	Amur Khabarovsk	Russia	38	7	10	17	20	....	....	....	....	....
2002-03	Krylja Sovetov	Russia	50	15	10	25	40	....	....	....	....	....
2003-04	Lada Togliatti	Russia	49	8	10	18	51	6	0	0	0	4
2004-05	Lada Togliatti	Russia	16	3	1	4	14	....	....	....	....	....
	Cherepovets	Russia	33	9	6	15	8	....	....	....	....	....
2005-06	Mytischi	Russia	21	2	3	5	40	....	....	....	....	....
	Ak Bars Kazan	Russia	5	0	0	0	0	....	....	....	....	....
	Ufa	Russia	16	3	2	5	26	6	1	0	1	4
2006-07	Ufa	Russia	32	6	3	9	14	5	1	1	2	6
	Ufa 2	Russia-3	4	4	3	7	28	....	....	....	....	....
2007-08	Sibir Novosibirsk	Russia	20	3	4	7	16	....	....	....	....	....
	Nizhnekamsk	Russia	27	8	3	11	34	5	1	2	3	2
2008-09	Nizhnekamsk	Rus-KHL	16	1	2	3	39	....	....	....	....	....
	Vityaz Chekhov	Rus-KHL	10	0	2	2	4	....	....	....	....	....
2009-10	Amur Khabarovsk	Rus-KHL	9	0	1	1	4	....	....	....	....	....
	Krylja Sovetov	Russia-2	18	9	11	20	10	....	....	....	....	....
	Gazovik Tyumen	Russia-2	4	2	1	3	4	3	0	0	0	0

BERRY, Alex (BAIR-ee, AL-ehx) TOR.

Right wing. Shoots right. 6'3", 215 lbs. Born, Danvers, MA, March 6, 1986.
(Toronto's 3rd choice, 153rd overall, in 2005 Entry Draft).

			Regular Season					Playoffs				
Season	Club	League	GP	G	A	Pts	PIM	GP	G	A	Pts	PIM
2003-04	Cushing	High-MA	31	19	16	35	50	....	....	....	....	....
2004-05	Bos. Jr. Bruins	EJHL	53	17	25	42	170	....	....	....	....	....
2005-06	Massachusetts	H-East	24	1	1	2	33	....	....	....	....	....
2006-07	Massachusetts	H-East	29	7	6	13	34	....	....	....	....	....
2007-08	Massachusetts	H-East	34	10	7	17	63	....	....	....	....	....
2008-09	Massachusetts	H-East	37	11	19	30	83	....	....	....	....	....
	Toronto Marlies	AHL	8	0	0	0	15	....	....	....	....	....
2009-10	Toronto Marlies	AHL	55	3	4	7	97	....	....	....	....	....
	Reading Royals	ECHL	5	0	5	5	2	16	2	4	6	4

BERTILSSON, Simon (BUHR-tihl-suhn, SEE-muhn) PHI.

Defense. Shoots left. 6', 185 lbs. Born, Karlskoga, Sweden, April 19, 1991.
(Philadelphia's 2nd choice, 87th overall, in 2009 Entry Draft).

			Regular Season					Playoffs				
Season	Club	League	GP	G	A	Pts	PIM	GP	G	A	Pts	PIM
2006-07	Bofors U18	Swe-U18	19	8	10	18	6	....	....	....	....	....
2007-08	Brynas U18	Swe-U18	4	1	1	2	27	5	0	0	0	4
	Brynas IF Gavle Jr.	Swe-Jr.	27	2	3	5	52	7	0	0	0	8
2008-09	Brynas U18	Swe-U18	5	2	3	5	50	1	2	0	2	4
	Brynas IF Gavle Jr.	Swe-Jr.	30	9	22	31	54	6	0	1	1	0
	Brynas IF Gavle	Sweden	21	0	1	1	2	4	0	0	0	0
2009-10	Brynas IF Gavle	Sweden	32	1	3	4	43	5	0	0	0	2
	Brynas IF Gavle Jr.	Swe-Jr.	....	....	....	....	....	2	0	0	0	0

BERUBE, Jean-Sebastien (beh-ROO-bay, ZHAWN-seh-BAS-t'yehn) N.J.

Left wing. Shoots left. 6'4", 210 lbs. Born, Matane, Que., July 20, 1990.
(New Jersey's 9th choice, 205th overall, in 2008 Entry Draft).

			Regular Season					Playoffs				
Season	Club	League	GP	G	A	Pts	PIM	GP	G	A	Pts	PIM
2006-07	Rouyn-Noranda	QMJHL	40	3	7	10	22	16	0	0	0	4
2007-08	Rouyn-Noranda	QMJHL	64	12	12	24	118	17	1	3	4	16
2008-09	Rouyn-Noranda	QMJHL	64	15	11	26	143	6	0	1	1	10
2009-10	Rouyn-Noranda	QMJHL	64	24	21	45	130	11	1	1	2	10
	Lowell Devils	AHL	....	....	....	....	....	1	0	0	0	0

BEUKEBOOM, Brock (BOO-kuh-BOOM, BRAWK) T.B.

Defense. Shoots right. 6'1", 202 lbs. Born, Greenwich, CT, April 1, 1992.
(Tampa Bay's 2nd choice, 63rd overall, in 2010 Entry Draft).

			Regular Season					Playoffs				
Season	Club	League	GP	G	A	Pts	PIM	GP	G	A	Pts	PIM
2007-08	Cent. Ont. Wolves	Minor-ON	40	15	30	45	50	....	....	....	....	....
2008-09	Sault Ste. Marie	OHL	55	2	9	11	26	....	....	....	....	....
2009-10	Sault Ste. Marie	OHL	66	7	19	26	64	1	0	0	0	0

BICKEL, Stu (BIH-kuhl, STEW) ANA.

Defense. Shoots right. 6'4", 207 lbs. Born, Chanhassen, MN, October 2, 1986.

			Regular Season					Playoffs				
Season	Club	League	GP	G	A	Pts	PIM	GP	G	A	Pts	PIM
2004-05	Green Bay	USHL	13	0	0	0	20	....	....	....	....	....
2005-06	Green Bay	USHL	14	0	0	0	25	....	....	....	....	....
2006-07	Sioux Falls	USHL	57	2	11	13	*215	8	0	3	3	29
2007-08	U. of Minnesota	WCHA	45	1	6	7	*92	....	....	....	....	....
2008-09	Iowa Chops	AHL	21	0	1	1	51	....	....	....	....	....
2009-10	San Antonio	AHL	36	2	2	4	38	....	....	....	....	....
	Bakersfield	ECHL	24	1	12	13	50	9	0	2	2	14

Signed as a free agent by **Anaheim**, July 2, 2008.

BIEGA, Alex (bee-AY-guh, AL-ehx) BUF.

Defense. Shoots right. 5'11", 188 lbs. Born, Montreal, Que., April 4, 1988.
(Buffalo's 5th choice, 147th overall, in 2006 Entry Draft).

			Regular Season					Playoffs				
Season	Club	League	GP	G	A	Pts	PIM	GP	G	A	Pts	PIM
2004-05	Salisbury School	High-CT	27	9	22	31	45	....	....	....	....	....
2005-06	Salisbury School	High-CT	28	10	17	27	51	....	....	....	....	....
2006-07	Harvard Crimson	ECAC	33	6	12	18	36	....	....	....	....	....
2007-08	Harvard Crimson	ECAC	34	3	19	22	28	....	....	....	....	....
2008-09	Harvard Crimson	ECAC	31	4	16	20	46	....	....	....	....	....
2009-10	Harvard Crimson	ECAC	33	2	8	10	30	....	....	....	....	....

ECAC All-Rookie Team (2007)

BIEGA, Danny (bee-AY-ga, DAN-ee) CAR.

Defense. Shoots right. 6', 200 lbs. Born, Montreal, Que., September 29, 1991.
(Carolina's 4th choice, 67th overall, in 2010 Entry Draft).

			Regular Season					Playoffs				
Season	Club	League	GP	G	A	Pts	PIM	GP	G	A	Pts	PIM
2007-08	Salisbury School	High-CT	26	4	13	17	....	....	....	....	....	....
2008-09	Salisbury School	High-CT	29	8	14	22	....	....	....	....	....	....
2009-10	Harvard Crimson	ECAC	32	5	4	9	47	....	....	....	....	....

BIELKE, Dominik (BIGHL-keh, DOHM-ihn-ihk) S.J.

Defense. Shoots left. 6'3", 190 lbs. Born, Berlin, Germany, October 23, 1990.
(San Jose's 5th choice, 207th overall, in 2009 Entry Draft).

			Regular Season					Playoffs				
Season	Club	League	GP	G	A	Pts	PIM	GP	G	A	Pts	PIM
2005-06	Eisb. Jrs. Berl. Jr.	Ger-Jr.	28	1	0	1	16	2	0	0	0	2
2006-07	Eisb. Jrs. Berl. Jr.	Ger-Jr.	33	12	22	34	36	3	1	1	2	6
	Eisb. Jrs. Berlin	German-3	3	0	0	0	2	....	....	....	....	....
2007-08	Eisb. Jrs. Berl. Jr.	Ger-Jr.	10	7	6	13	22	3	0	0	0	16
	Eisb. Jrs. Berlin	German-3	46	5	7	12	74	7	2	4	6	12
2008-09	Eisb. Jrs. Berlin	German-3	47	14	25	39	104	....	....	....	....	....
	Eisbaren Berlin	Germany	7	0	1	1	2	....	....	....	....	....
2009-10	Eisbaren Berlin	Germany	10	0	1	1	8	....	....	....	....	....
	Dresdner Eislowen	German-2	36	1	5	6	71	3	1	0	1	14

BIGOS, Kyle (BEE-gohs, KIGHL) EDM.

Defense. Shoots right. 6'5", 230 lbs. Born, Upland, CA, May 12, 1989.
(Edmonton's 5th choice, 99th overall, in 2009 Entry Draft).

			Regular Season					Playoffs				
Season	Club	League	GP	G	A	Pts	PIM	GP	G	A	Pts	PIM
2006-07	Notre Dame	SMHL	39	12	24	36	165	....	....	....	....	....
	Notre Dame	SJHL	3	0	0	0	0	....	....	....	....	....
2007-08	Vernon Vipers	BCHL	58	2	15	17	152	10	0	2	2	28
2008-09	Vernon Vipers	BCHL	58	8	25	33	126	17	2	4	6	37
2009-10	Merrimack College	H-East	36	4	7	11	94	....	....	....	....	....

BIRCH, Braden (BUHRCH, BRAY-duhn) CHI.

Defense. Shoots left. 6'3", 192 lbs. Born, Hamilton, Ont., September 25, 1989.
(Chicago's 6th choice, 179th overall, in 2008 Entry Draft).

			Regular Season					Playoffs				
Season	Club	League	GP	G	A	Pts	PIM	GP	G	A	Pts	PIM
2006-07	Stoney Creek	OJHL-B	43	10	11	21	86	....	....	....	....	....
2007-08	Nanaimo Clippers	BCHL	19	0	2	2	15	....	....	....	....	....
	Oakville Blades	OPJHL	13	1	4	5	6	19	0	2	2	4
2008-09	Oakville Blades	OJHL	35	7	18	25	46	27	4	6	10	20
2009-10	Cornell Big Red	ECAC	32	0	2	2	10	....	....	....	....	....

BIRKHOLZ, Josh (BUHRK-hohlz, JAWSH) FLA.

Right wing. Shoots right. 6'1", 182 lbs. Born, St. Louis Park, MN, March 28, 1991.
(Florida's 3rd choice, 67th overall, in 2009 Entry Draft).

			Regular Season					Playoffs				
Season	Club	League	GP	G	A	Pts	PIM	GP	G	A	Pts	PIM
2005-06	Blake Bears	High-MN	29	3	2	5	12	....	....	....	....	....
2006-07	Blake Bears	High-MN	21	11	8	19	20	....	....	....	....	....
2007-08	Blake Bears	High-MN	30	34	24	58	42	....	....	....	....	....
2008-09	Fargo Force	USHL	55	21	15	36	52	9	3	2	5	4
2009-10	U. of Minnesota	WCHA	36	5	1	6	20	....	....	....	....	....

BISHOP, Hunter (BIH-shuhp, HUHN-tuhr) MTL.

Left wing. Shoots left. 6', 196 lbs. Born, Fairbanks, AK, September 5, 1987.

			Regular Season					Playoffs				
Season	Club	League	GP	G	A	Pts	PIM	GP	G	A	Pts	PIM
2003-04	Fairbanks Ice Dogs	NAHL	52	7	14	21	33	....	....	....	....	....
2004-05	Cedar Rapids	USHL	50	2	10	12	17	1	0	0	0	2
2005-06	Vernon Vipers	BCHL	56	25	29	54	39	....	....	....	....	....
2006-07	Vernon Vipers	BCHL	24	11	15	26	16	....	....	....	....	....
	North Dakota	WCHA	4	0	1	1	4	....	....	....	....	....
2007-08	Vernon Vipers	BCHL	60	57	40	97	45	....	....	....	....	....
2008-09	Ohio State	CCHA	42	14	17	31	18	....	....	....	....	....
2009-10	Ohio State	CCHA	33	15	12	27	22	....	....	....	....	....
	Hamilton Bulldogs	AHL	9	2	3	5	0	12	0	1	1	6

Signed as a free agent by **Montreal**, March 18, 2010.

BITETTO, Anthony (bih-TEH-toh, AN-thuh-nee) NSH.

Defense. Shoots left. 6'1", 210 lbs. Born, Island Park, NY, July 15, 1990.
(Nashville's 4th choice, 168th overall, in 2010 Entry Draft).

			Regular Season					Playoffs				
Season	Club	League	GP	G	A	Pts	PIM	GP	G	A	Pts	PIM
2007-08	NY Apple Core	EmJHL	12	4	10	14	32	....	....	....	....	....
	NY Apple Core	EJHL	17	2	6	8	28	....	....	....	....	....
2008-09	NY Apple Core	EJHL	30	2	9	11	50	....	....	....	....	....
	Indiana Ice	USHL	24	1	3	4	29	13	0	3	3	6
2009-10	Indiana Ice	USHL	58	11	29	40	99	9	2	2	4	19

USHL Second All-Star Team (2010)

• Signed Letter of Intent to attend **Northeastern University** (Hockey East) in fall of 2010.

BJORKLUND, Henrik (B'YOURK-luhnd, HEHN-rihk) CGY.

Right wing. Shoots right. 6'2", 202 lbs. Born, Karlstad, Sweden, September 22, 1990.
(Calgary's 3rd choice, 111th overall, in 2009 Entry Draft).

			Regular Season					Playoffs				
Season	Club	League	GP	G	A	Pts	PIM	GP	G	A	Pts	PIM
2005-06	Farjestad U18	Swe-U18	10	3	2	5	6	5	1	0	1	2
2006-07	Farjestad U18	Swe-U18	14	13	12	25	53	8	4	3	7	20
	Farjestad	Sweden	1	0	0	0	0	....	....	....	....	....
2007-08	Farjestad U18	Swe-U18	29	31	28	59	104	8	8	3	11	12
	Farjestad	Sweden	1	0	0	0	0	2	0	0	0	0
	Skare BK	Sweden-3	17	7	4	11	6	....	....	....	....	....
2008-09	Farjestad	Sweden	10	0	0	0	0	....	....	....	....	....
	Skare Jr.	Swe-Jr.	1	2	0	2	4	....	....	....	....	....
	Skare BK Karlstad	Sweden-3	38	21	14	35	83	3	3	2	5	2
2009-10	Boras HC	Sweden-2	31	8	6	14	51	....	....	....	....	....
	Farjestad	Sweden	19	1	3	4	4	....	....	....	....	....
	Skare BK	Sweden-3	4	1	1	2	4	....	....	....	....	....

BJUGSTAD, Nick (BYOOG-stad, NIHK) FLA.

Center. Shoots right. 6'4", 188 lbs. Born, Minneapolis, MN, July 17, 1992.
(Florida's 2nd choice, 19th overall, in 2010 Entry Draft).

			Regular Season					Playoffs				
Season	Club	League	GP	G	A	Pts	PIM	GP	G	A	Pts	PIM
2007-08	Blaine Bengals	High-MN	24	6	14	20	10	....	....	....	....	....
2008-09	Blaine Bengals	High-MN	25	26	25	51	20	....	....	....	....	....
2009-10	Team Northwest	UMHSEL	23	13	8	21	18	....	....	....	....	....
	Blaine Bengals	High-MN	30	35	34	69	26	....	....	....	....	....
	USNTDP	U-18	4	0	0	0	0	....	....	....	....	....

• Signed Letter of Intent to attend **University of Minnesota** (WCHA) in fall of 2010.

BLACKER, Jesse (BLA-kuhr, JEH-see) TOR.

Defense. Shoots right. 6'1", 190 lbs. Born, Toronto, Ont., April 19, 1991.
(Toronto's 3rd choice, 58th overall, in 2009 Entry Draft).

			Regular Season					Playoffs				
Season	Club	League	GP	G	A	Pts	PIM	GP	G	A	Pts	PIM
2007-08	Chatham Maroons	OJHL-B	8	1	2	3	25	....	....	....	....	....
	Windsor Spitfires	OHL	17	0	4	4	6	5	0	1	1	2
2008-09	Windsor Spitfires	OHL	67	4	17	21	54	20	0	4	4	18
2009-10	Windsor Spitfires	OHL	9	0	3	3	12	....	....	....	....	....
	Owen Sound	OHL	48	6	24	30	62	....	....	....	....	....
	Toronto Marlies	AHL	6	0	1	1	0	....	....	....	....	....

BLAIN, Jeremie (BLAYN, JAIR-uh-mee) EDM.

Defense. Shoots right. 6'2", 190 lbs. Born, Le Moyne, Que., March 19, 1992.
(Edmonton's 6th choice, 91st overall, in 2010 Entry Draft).

			Regular Season					Playoffs				
Season	Club	League	GP	G	A	Pts	PIM	GP	G	A	Pts	PIM
2007-08	C.C. Lemoyne	QAAA	45	2	21	23	16	8	4	3	7	2
2008-09	Victoriaville Tigres	QMJHL	27	1	3	4	0	....	....	....	....	....
	Acadie-Bathurst	QMJHL	22	0	3	3	6	5	0	2	2	4
2009-10	Acadie-Bathurst	QMJHL	64	4	34	38	72	5	2	2	4	10

BLANCHARD, Nicolas (BLAN-shard, NIHK-oh-las) CAR.

Center/Right wing. Shoots left. 6'3", 200 lbs. Born, Granby, Que., May 31, 1987.
(Carolina's 8th choice, 192nd overall, in 2005 Entry Draft).

			Regular Season					Playoffs				
Season	Club	League	GP	G	A	Pts	PIM	GP	G	A	Pts	PIM
2003-04	Antoine-Girouard	QAAA	42	24	28	52	28	13	9	6	15	4
2004-05	Chicoutimi	QMJHL	69	13	26	39	31	17	2	2	4	10
2005-06	Chicoutimi	QMJHL	60	15	29	44	51	9	1	2	3	4
2006-07	Chicoutimi	QMJHL	62	22	35	57	41	4	0	2	2	8
	Albany River Rats	AHL	7	1	2	3	2	5	0	0	0	2
2007-08	Albany River Rats	AHL	64	11	12	23	70	7	0	2	2	2
2008-09	Albany River Rats	AHL	55	7	12	19	132	....	....	....	....	....
2009-10	Albany River Rats	AHL	76	14	8	22	171	8	0	0	0	13

BLIDSTRAND, Ricard (BLIHD-strahnd, REE-kahrd) PHI.

Defense. Shoots left. 6'3", 202 lbs. Born, Stockholm, Sweden, April 20, 1992.
(Philadelphia's 5th choice, 206th overall, in 2010 Entry Draft).

			Regular Season					Playoffs				
Season	Club	League	GP	G	A	Pts	PIM	GP	G	A	Pts	PIM
2007-08	Djurgarden U18	Swe-U18	22	1	2	3	18	2	0	0	0	0
2008-09	Djurgarden U18	Swe-U18	17	1	8	9	26	....	....	....	....	....
	Djurgarden Jr.	Swe-Jr.	2	0	0	0	0	....	....	....	....	....
	Balsta HC	Sweden-3	2	0	1	1	0	....	....	....	....	....
	AIK IF Solna U18	Swe-U18	6	2	0	2	0	7	2	2	4	0
	AIK IF Solna Jr.	Swe-Jr.	5	0	0	0	2	....	....	....	....	....
2009-10	AIK IF Solna U18	Swe-U18	10	2	4	6	0	3	0	1	1	12
	AIK IF Solna Jr.	Swe-Jr.	33	2	6	8	4	....	....	....	....	....

BLOMQVIST, Anton (BLAWM-kvihst, AN-tawn) CBJ

Defense. Shoots left. 6'5", 192 lbs. Born, Kristianstad, Sweden, March 7, 1990.
(Columbus' 5th choice, 167th overall, in 2009 Entry Draft).

			Regular Season					Playoffs				
Season	Club	League	GP	G	A	Pts	PIM	GP	G	A	Pts	PIM
2005-06	Osby IK	Sweden-3	22	1	1	2	6	....	....	....	....	....
2006-07	Linkopings HC U18	Swe-U18	10	2	1	3	16	....	....	....	....	....
	Linkopings HC Jr.	Swe-Jr.	1	0	1	1	0	....	....	....	....	....
2007-08	Malmo U18	Swe-U18	20	2	2	4	57	2	0	0	0	2
	Malmo Jr.	Swe-Jr.	18	0	1	1	20	5	0	1	1	2
2008-09	Malmo Jr.	Swe-Jr.	31	2	14	16	73	....	....	....	....	....
	Malmo	Sweden-2	13	0	3	3	8	....	....	....	....	....
2009-10	Malmo	Sweden-2	49	3	2	5	55	5	0	0	0	10
	Malmo Jr.	Swe-Jr.	....	....	....	....	....	1	0	0	0	0

BLOOD, Ben (BLUHD, BEHN) OTT.

Defense. Shoots left. 6'3", 232 lbs. Born, Plymouth, MN, March 15, 1989.
(Ottawa's 4th choice, 120th overall, in 2007 Entry Draft).

			Regular Season					Playoffs				
Season	Club	League	GP	G	A	Pts	PIM	GP	G	A	Pts	PIM
2005-06	Shat.-St. Mary's	High-MN	73	3	22	25	32	....	....	....	....	....
2006-07	Shat.-St. Mary's	High-MN	63	11	25	36	144	....	....	....	....	....
2007-08	Des Moines	USHL	11	0	7	7	17	....	....	....	....	....
	Indiana Ice	USHL	46	10	6	16	83	4	1	2	3	14
2008-09	North Dakota	WCHA	31	0	1	1	12	....	....	....	....	....
2009-10	North Dakota	WCHA	43	5	9	14	96	....	....	....	....	....

BLOODOFF, Evan (BLUHD-awf, EH-vuhn) PHX.

Left wing. Shoots left. 5'11", 190 lbs. Born, Nelson, B.C., November 21, 1990.
(Phoenix's 6th choice, 157th overall, in 2009 Entry Draft).

			Regular Season					Playoffs				
Season	Club	League	GP	G	A	Pts	PIM	GP	G	A	Pts	PIM
2005-06	Castlegar Rebels	Minor-BC	50	32	21	53	....	....	....	....	....	....
2006-07	Kelowna Rockets	WHL	59	4	4	8	20	....	....	....	....	....
2007-08	Kelowna Rockets	WHL	69	15	12	27	69	7	1	0	1	4
2008-09	Kelowna Rockets	WHL	71	12	9	21	77	22	3	3	6	10
	Kelowna Rockets	M-Cup	....	....	....	....	....	4	0	0	0	0
2009-10	Kelowna Rockets	WHL	9	3	0	3	13	12	0	3	3	6

• Missed majority of 2009-10 season recovering from knee injury.

BLUM, Jonathon (BLUHM, JAWN-ah-thuhn) NSH.

Defense. Shoots right. 6'1", 192 lbs. Born, Long Beach, CA, January 30, 1989.
(Nashville's 1st choice, 23rd overall, in 2007 Entry Draft).

			Regular Season					Playoffs				
Season	Club	League	GP	G	A	Pts	PIM	GP	G	A	Pts	PIM
2004-05	California Wave	Minor-CA	55	15	50	65	65	....	....	....	....	....
2005-06	Vancouver Giants	WHL	61	7	17	24	25	18	1	7	8	16
2006-07	Vancouver Giants	WHL	72	8	43	51	48	22	3	6	9	8
2007-08	Vancouver Giants	WHL	64	18	45	63	44	10	3	4	7	10
2008-09	Vancouver Giants	WHL	51	16	50	66	30	17	7	11	18	6
	Milwaukee	AHL	....	....	....	....	....	5	0	0	0	0
2009-10	Milwaukee	AHL	80	11	30	41	32	7	1	7	8	0

WHL West Second All-Star Team (2008) • WHL West First All-Star Team (2009) • WHL Defenseman of the Year (2009) • Canadian Major Junior First All-Star Team (2009) • Canadian Major Junior Defenseman of the Year (2009)

BODROV, Denis (bawd-RAWV, DEH-nihs) PHI.

Defense. Shoots left. 6', 185 lbs. Born, Togliatti, USSR, August 22, 1986.
(Philadelphia's 4th choice, 55th overall, in 2006 Entry Draft).

			Regular Season					Playoffs				
Season	Club	League	GP	G	A	Pts	PIM	GP	G	A	Pts	PIM
2002-03	Lada Togliatti 2	Russia-3	9	0	0	0	2	....	....	....	....	....
2003-04	Lada Togliatti 2	Russia-3	45	3	4	7	58	....	....	....	....	....
2004-05	CSK VVS Samara	Russia-2	33	1	6	7	57	....	....	....	....	....
2005-06	Lada Togliatti	Russia	35	2	2	4	42	8	0	0	0	8
2006-07	Lada Togliatti	Russia	49	1	5	6	70	3	0	1	1	6
2007-08	Lada Togliatti 2	Russia-3	8	3	4	7	38	....	....	....	....	....
	Lada Togliatti	Russia	46	2	9	11	74	4	1	0	1	2
2008-09	Lada Togliatti	Rus-KHL	24	1	5	6	20	....	....	....	....	....
	Mytischi	Rus-KHL	21	1	4	5	24	4	0	1	1	0
2009-10	Mytischi	Rus-KHL	12	1	0	1	6	....	....	....	....	....
	Adirondack	AHL	17	1	3	4	6	....	....	....	....	....

BOLLIG, Brandon (BOH-lihg, BRAN-duhn) CHI.

Left wing. Shoots left. 6'3", 215 lbs. Born, St. Charles, MO, January 31, 1987.

			Regular Season					Playoffs				
Season	Club	League	GP	G	A	Pts	PIM	GP	G	A	Pts	PIM
2005-06	Lincoln Stars	USHL	58	8	8	16	175	9	1	2	3	12
2006-07	Lincoln Stars	USHL	57	14	12	26	207	4	0	2	2	2
2007-08	Lincoln Stars	USHL	58	15	16	31	211	8	2	4	6	40
2008-09	St. Lawrence	ECAC	36	6	7	13	51	....	....	....	....	....
2009-10	St. Lawrence	ECAC	42	7	18	25	83	....	....	....	....	....
	Rockford IceHogs	AHL	3	1	1	2	7	....	....	....	....	....

Signed as a free agent by **Chicago**, April 3, 2010.

BONNEAU, Jimmy (BAW-noh, JIHM-mee)

Left wing. Shoots left. 6'3", 214 lbs. Born, Baie-Comeau, Que., March 22, 1985.
(Montreal's 10th choice, 241st overall, in 2003 Entry Draft).

			Regular Season					Playoffs				
Season	Club	League	GP	G	A	Pts	PIM	GP	G	A	Pts	PIM
2000-01	Jonquiere Elites	QAAA	1	0	0	0	0	....	....	....	....	....
2001-02	Jonquiere Elites	QAAA	40	5	10	15	55	3	1	1	2	2
2002-03	Montreal Rocket	QMJHL	65	1	5	6	261	7	0	0	0	12
2003-04	P.E.I. Rocket	QMJHL	70	7	12	19	263	11	1	0	1	12
2004-05	P.E.I. Rocket	QMJHL	70	11	11	22	234	....	....	....	....	....
2005-06	Long Beach	ECHL	65	1	5	6	137	....	....	....	....	....
2006-07	Hamilton Bulldogs	AHL	9	0	0	0	59	....	....	....	....	....
	Cincinnati	ECHL	46	2	5	7	89	10	0	0	0	23
2007-08	Hamilton Bulldogs	AHL	6	1	0	1	5	....	....	....	....	....
	Cincinnati	ECHL	18	0	4	4	61	3	0	0	0	0
2008-09	Portland Pirates	AHL	46	0	6	6	122	....	....	....	....	....
2009-10	Rochester	AHL	57	4	2	6	187	....	....	....	....	....

Signed as a free agent by **Buffalo**, August 13, 2008.

BOOGAARD, Aaron (BOO-gard, AIR-ruhn)

Right wing. Shoots right. 6'3", 220 lbs. Born, Newmarket, Ont., August 11, 1986.
(Minnesota's 9th choice, 175th overall, in 2004 Entry Draft).

			Regular Season					Playoffs				
Season	Club	League	GP	G	A	Pts	PIM	GP	G	A	Pts	PIM
2002-03	Calgary Hitmen	WHL	39	3	0	3	52	5	0	0	0	0
2003-04	Calgary Hitmen	WHL	12	0	1	1	24	....	....	....	....	....
	Tri-City Americans	WHL	23	3	1	4	33	6	0	0	0	8
2004-05	Tri-City Americans	WHL	65	4	11	15	96	5	0	0	0	4
2005-06	Tri-City Americans	WHL	65	6	4	10	211	5	0	2	2	4
2006-07	Tri-City Americans	WHL	69	10	11	21	173	5	1	0	1	14
2007-08	Wilkes-Barre	AHL	2	0	0	0	5	....	....	....	....	....
	Wheeling Nailers	ECHL	58	6	9	15	105	....	....	....	....	....
2008-09	Wilkes-Barre	AHL	41	2	1	3	112	1	0	0	0	0
2009-10	Wilkes-Barre	AHL	21	1	0	1	65	....	....	....	....	....
	Wheeling Nailers	ECHL	11	0	2	2	12	....	....	....	....	....

Signed as a free agent by **Pittsburgh**, April 23, 2007.

BORDSON, Rob (BOHRD-suhn, RAWB) ANA.

Left wing. Shoots left. 6'2", 190 lbs. Born, Duluth, MN, June 9, 1988.

			Regular Season					Playoffs				
Season	Club	League	GP	G	A	Pts	PIM	GP	G	A	Pts	PIM
2006-07	Cedar Rapids	USHL	47	6	29	35	26	5	0	1	1	0
2007-08	U. Minn-Duluth	WCHA	27	1	6	7	6	....	....	....	....	....
2008-09	U. Minn-Duluth	WCHA	15	0	0	0	6	....	....	....	....	....
2009-10	U. Minn-Duluth	WCHA	40	12	28	40	18	....	....	....	....	....

Signed as a free agent by **Anaheim**, March 23, 2010.

BOROWIECKI, Mark (boh-roh-WIH-kee, MAHRK) OTT.

Defense. Shoots left. 6'1", 205 lbs. Born, Ottawa, Ont., July 12, 1989.
(Ottawa's 6th choice, 139th overall, in 2008 Entry Draft).

			Regular Season					Playoffs				
Season	Club	League	GP	G	A	Pts	PIM	GP	G	A	Pts	PIM
2006-07	Smiths Falls Bears	CJHL	53	3	25	28	85	6	0	0	0	10
2007-08	Smiths Falls Bears	CJHL	46	2	24	26	80	15	1	10	11	22
2008-09	Clarkson Knights	ECAC	33	1	1	2	24	....	....	....	....	....
2009-10	Clarkson Knights	ECAC	35	8	11	19	55	....	....	....	....	....

BORTUZZO, Robert (bohr-TOOZ-oh, RAW-buhrt) PIT.

Defense. Shoots right. 6'3", 196 lbs. Born, Thunder Bay, Ont., March 18, 1989.
(Pittsburgh's 3rd choice, 78th overall, in 2007 Entry Draft).

			Regular Season					Playoffs				
Season	Club	League	GP	G	A	Pts	PIM	GP	G	A	Pts	PIM
2005-06	F-Wm. North Stars	SIJHL	40	4	18	22	....	....	....	....	....	....
2006-07	Kitchener Rangers	OHL	63	2	12	14	67	9	1	2	3	8
2007-08	Kitchener Rangers	OHL	52	3	15	18	61	18	0	8	8	14
2008-09	Kitchener Rangers	OHL	23	1	16	17	24	....	....	....	....	....
2009-10	Wilkes-Barre	AHL	75	2	10	12	109	4	0	0	0	0

BOUCHARD, Francois (BOO-shahrd, frahn-SWUH) WSH.

Right wing. Shoots left. 6', 180 lbs. Born, Sherbrooke, Que., April 26, 1988.
(Washington's 4th choice, 35th overall, in 2006 Entry Draft).

			Regular Season					Playoffs				
Season	Club	League	GP	G	A	Pts	PIM	GP	G	A	Pts	PIM
2004-05	Baie-Comeau	QMJHL	54	11	13	24	13	6	1	1	2	2
2005-06	Baie-Comeau	QMJHL	69	33	69	102	66	4	1	0	1	6
2006-07	Baie-Comeau	QMJHL	68	45	*80	*125	72	11	7	11	18	4
2007-08	Baie-Comeau	QMJHL	68	36	56	92	70	5	1	1	2	6
	Hershey Bears	AHL	4	1	0	1	2	1	0	0	0	2
2008-09	Hershey Bears	AHL	64	15	20	35	34	11	1	2	3	8
2009-10	Hershey Bears	AHL	77	21	31	52	55	21	5	5	10	28

QMJHL Second All-Star Team (2007)

BOUMA, Lance (BOW-ma, LANTZ) CGY.

Center. Shoots left. 6'1", 210 lbs. Born, Provost, Alta., March 25, 1990.
(Calgary's 3rd choice, 78th overall, in 2008 Entry Draft).

			Regular Season					Playoffs				
Season	Club	League	GP	G	A	Pts	PIM	GP	G	A	Pts	PIM
2005-06	Wainwright	RAMHL	37	21	29	50	....	....	....	....	....	....
	Vancouver Giants	WHL	5	1	3	4	0	....	....	....	....	....
2006-07	Vancouver Giants	WHL	49	3	5	8	31	22	3	3	6	12
2007-08	Vancouver Giants	WHL	71	12	23	35	93	10	0	1	1	8
2008-09	Vancouver Giants	WHL	48	9	16	25	116	17	7	5	12	30
2009-10	Vancouver Giants	WHL	57	14	29	43	134	16	4	13	17	*47
	Abbotsford Heat	AHL	....	....	....	....	....	5	1	0	1	2

BOURDON, Marc-Andre (boor-DOHN, MAHRK-AHN-dray) PHI.

Defense. Shoots left. 6', 206 lbs. Born, St-Hyacinthe, Que., September 17, 1989.
(Philadelphia's 2nd choice, 67th overall, in 2008 Entry Draft).

			Regular Season					Playoffs				
Season	Club	League	GP	G	A	Pts	PIM	GP	G	A	Pts	PIM
2006-07	Rouyn-Noranda	QMJHL	63	2	26	28	80	16	0	4	4	21
2007-08	Rouyn-Noranda	QMJHL	69	12	47	59	114	17	2	16	18	25
2008-09	Rouyn-Noranda	QMJHL	37	11	27	38	89	....	....	....	....	....
	Rimouski Oceanic	QMJHL	17	7	15	22	23	13	1	12	13	25
2009-10	Adirondack	AHL	61	2	17	19	53	....	....	....	....	....

QMJHL First All-Star Team (2008, 2009) • Canadian Major Junior Second All-Star Team (2008)

BOURNIVAL, Michael (boor-nee-VAHL, MIGH-kuhl) COL.

Left wing. Shoots left. 5'11", 179 lbs. Born, Shawinigan, Que., May 31, 1992.
(Colorado's 3rd choice, 71st overall, in 2010 Entry Draft).

			Regular Season					Playoffs				
Season	Club	League	GP	G	A	Pts	PIM	GP	G	A	Pts	PIM
2007-08	Trois-Rivieres	QAAA	52	33	23	56	66	7	3	3	6	10
2008-09	Shawinigan	QMJHL	46	11	11	22	29	21	1	3	4	12
2009-10	Shawinigan	QMJHL	58	24	38	62	37	6	2	2	4	6

BOURQUE, Gabriel (BOHRK, gah-BREE-ehl) NSH.

Left wing. Shoots left. 5'10", 193 lbs. Born, Rimouski, Que., September 23, 1990.
(Nashville's 9th choice, 132nd overall, in 2009 Entry Draft).

			Regular Season					Playoffs				
Season	Club	League	GP	G	A	Pts	PIM	GP	G	A	Pts	PIM
2006-07	Ecole Notre Dame	QAAA	43	15	35	50	115	13	8	16	24	14
2007-08	Baie-Comeau	QMJHL	65	10	18	28	38	5	0	0	0	0
2008-09	Baie-Comeau	QMJHL	60	22	39	61	82	5	0	2	2	16
2009-10	Baie-Comeau	QMJHL	30	13	25	38	61	....	....	....	....	....
	Moncton Wildcats	QMJHL	25	3	11	14	37	21	19	10	29	18

BOURQUE, Ryan (BOHRK, RIGH-uhn) NYR

Center. Shoots left. 5'9", 171 lbs. Born, Boxford, MA, January 3, 1991.
(NY Rangers' 3rd choice, 80th overall, in 2009 Entry Draft).

			Regular Season					Playoffs				
Season	Club	League	GP	G	A	Pts	PIM	GP	G	A	Pts	PIM
2006-07	Cushing	High-MA	29	19	31	50	....	....	....	....	....	....
2007-08	USNTDP	NAHL	34	11	9	20	14	....	....	....	....	....
	USNTDP	U-17	7	4	3	7	10	....	....	....	....	....
	USNTDP	U-18	27	4	12	16	18	....	....	....	....	....
2008-09	USNTDP	NAHL	14	7	9	16	10	....	....	....	....	....
	USNTDP	U-18	43	14	24	38	48	....	....	....	....	....
2009-10	Quebec Remparts	QMJHL	44	19	24	43	20	9	3	7	10	6

BOYCHUK, Riley (BOY-chuhk, RIGH-lee) BUF.

Left wing. Shoots left. 6'5", 218 lbs. Born, Vancouver, B.C., February 20, 1991.
(Buffalo's 9th choice, 208th overall, in 2010 Entry Draft).

			Regular Season					Playoffs				
Season	Club	League	GP	G	A	Pts	PIM	GP	G	A	Pts	PIM
2006-07	Fraser Valley	BCMML	29	18	18	36	72	....	....	....	....	....
2007-08	Portland	WHL	5	0	1	1	0	....	....	....	....	....
2008-09	Portland	WHL	62	7	10	17	86	....	....	....	....	....
2009-10	Portland	WHL	66	14	16	30	157	13	2	1	3	24

• Missed majority of 2007-08 seasons recovering from surgeries to both hips.

BOYD, Ronald (BOID, RAW-nuhld (AHR-JAY)) FLA.

Defense. Shoots left. 6'2", 175 lbs. Born, Sarasota, FL, February 7, 1991.
(Florida's 13th choice, 183rd overall, in 2010 Entry Draft).

			Regular Season					Playoffs				
Season	Club	League	GP	G	A	Pts	PIM	GP	G	A	Pts	PIM
2007-08	Cushing	High-MA	35	0	3	3	....	....	....	....	....	....
2008-09	Cushing	High-MA	35	2	11	13	35	....	....	....	....	....
2009-10	Cushing	High-MA	31	4	18	22	0	....	....	....	....	....

• Signed Letter of Intent to attend **Sacred Heart University** (AH) in fall of 2010.

BRADFORD, Brock (BRAD-fohrd, BRAWK)

Center. Shoots right. 5'9", 168 lbs. Born, Burnaby, B.C., January 7, 1987.
(Boston's 8th choice, 217th overall, in 2005 Entry Draft).

			Regular Season					Playoffs				
Season	Club	League	GP	G	A	Pts	PIM	GP	G	A	Pts	PIM
2002-03	Richmond	PIJHL	18	12	12	24	....	....	....	....	....	....
	Coquitlam Express	BCHL	36	11	23	34	14	....	....	....	....	....
2003-04	Coquitlam Express	BCHL	57	36	49	85	....	....	....	....	....	....
2004-05	Omaha Lancers	USHL	60	24	33	57	16	5	0	1	1	0
2005-06	Boston College	H-East	42	6	12	18	8	....	....	....	....	....
2006-07	Boston College	H-East	42	19	26	45	28	....	....	....	....	....
2007-08	Boston College	H-East	5	3	2	5	2	....	....	....	....	....
2008-09	Boston College	H-East	37	*25	17	42	19	....	....	....	....	....
2009-10	Lake Erie Monsters	AHL	54	9	11	20	18	....	....	....	....	....
	Charlotte	ECHL	6	0	5	5	6	....	....	....	....	....

Hockey East Second All-Star Team (2009)

BRAUN, Constantin (BRAWN, kawn-stuhn-TIHN) L.A.

Defense. Shoots left. 6'3", 198 lbs. Born, Lampertheim, West Germany, March 11, 1988.
(Los Angeles' 9th choice, 164th overall, in 2006 Entry Draft).

			Regular Season					Playoffs				
Season	Club	League	GP	G	A	Pts	PIM	GP	G	A	Pts	PIM
2003-04	Mannheim Jr.	Ger-Jr.	30	12	5	17	42	....	....	....	....	....
2004-05	Eisb. Jrs. Berlin	German-3	1	0	0	0	0	....	....	....	....	....
	Eisb. Jrs. Berl. Jr.	Ger-Jr.	29	14	20	34	125	6	5	4	9	16
2005-06	Eisb. Jrs. Berl. Jr.	Ger-Jr.	7	8	4	12	14	1	1	0	1	6
	Eisbaren Berlin	Germany	6	0	0	0	0	....	....	....	....	....
	Eisb. Jrs. Berlin	German-3	24	13	10	23	34	....	....	....	....	....
2006-07	Eisb. Jrs. Berlin	German-3	10	4	3	7	37	2	2	1	3	0
	Eisbaren Berlin	Germany	34	1	3	4	14	....	....	....	....	....
2007-08	Eisb. Jrs. Berlin	German-3	2	0	0	0	0	....	....	....	....	....
	Eisbaren Berlin	Germany	50	4	7	11	32	14	3	7	10	2
2008-09	Eisbaren Berlin	Germany	43	6	9	15	20	12	0	2	2	2
2009-10	Eisbaren Berlin	Germany	40	6	12	18	26	5	0	2	2	2

BRAUN, Justin (BRAWN, JUHS-tihn) S.J.

Defense. Shoots right. 6'2", 205 lbs. Born, St. Paul, MN, February 10, 1987.
(San Jose's 7th choice, 201st overall, in 2007 Entry Draft).

			Regular Season					Playoffs				
Season	Club	League	GP	G	A	Pts	PIM	GP	G	A	Pts	PIM
2004-05	White Bear Lake	High-MN	STATISTICS NOT AVAILABLE									
	Green Bay	USHL	10	0	0	0	2	....	....	....	....	....
2005-06	Green Bay	USHL	59	2	11	13	69	3	0	0	0	2
2006-07	Massachusetts	H-East	39	4	10	14	20	....	....	....	....	....
2007-08	Massachusetts	H-East	36	4	16	20	20	....	....	....	....	....
2008-09	Massachusetts	H-East	39	7	16	23	50	....	....	....	....	....
2009-10	Massachusetts	H-East	36	8	23	31	30	....	....	....	....	....
	Worcester Sharks	AHL	3	0	3	3	0	11	0	3	3	4

Hockey East All-Rookie Team (2007) • Hockey East Second All-Star Team (2009) • Hockey East First All-Star Team (2010) • NCAA East Second All-American Team (2010)

BREEN, Christopher (BREEN, KRIHS-toh-fuhr) CGY.

Defense. Shoots left. 6'6", 225 lbs. Born, Uxbridge, Ont., June 29, 1989.

			Regular Season					Playoffs				
Season	Club	League	GP	G	A	Pts	PIM	GP	G	A	Pts	PIM
2005-06	Mississauga	OPJHL	33	1	6	7	10	....	....	....	....	....
	Saginaw Spirit	OHL	25	0	0	0	10	....	....	....	....	....
2006-07	Saginaw Spirit	OHL	39	1	2	3	32	2	0	0	0	2
2007-08	Saginaw Spirit	OHL	55	0	6	6	67	4	0	1	1	0
2008-09	Saginaw Spirit	OHL	6	0	1	1	9	....	....	....	....	....
	Erie Otters	OHL	59	0	12	12	31	5	0	1	1	7
2009-10	Erie Otters	OHL	12	0	2	2	11	....	....	....	....	....
	Peterborough	OHL	53	4	8	12	36	4	1	0	1	5
	Abbotsford Heat	AHL	1	0	1	1	4	....	....	....	....	....

Signed to an ATO (amateur tryout) contract by **Abbotsford** (AHL), March 30, 2010. Signed as a free agent by **Calgary**, May 28, 2010.

BRENNAN, Mike (BREH-nan, MIGHK)

Defense. Shoots right. 6', 205 lbs. Born, Smithtown, NY, January 24, 1986.

			Regular Season					Playoffs				
Season	Club	League	GP	G	A	Pts	PIM	GP	G	A	Pts	PIM
2002-03	USNTDP	U-17	18	2	4	6	8	....	....	....	....	....
	USNTDP	NAHL	44	1	2	3	89	....	....	....	....	....
2003-04	USNTDP	U-17	43	2	5	7	58	....	....	....	....	....
	USNTDP	NAHL	11	2	3	5	19	....	....	....	....	....
2004-05	Boston College	H-East	40	2	6	8	46	....	....	....	....	....
2005-06	Boston College	H-East	40	2	9	11	89	....	....	....	....	....
2006-07	Boston College	H-East	42	0	11	11	89	....	....	....	....	....
2007-08	Boston College	H-East	44	3	5	8	52	....	....	....	....	....
2008-09	Rockford IceHogs	AHL	64	0	6	6	77	2	0	0	0	2
2009-10	Rockford IceHogs	AHL	72	3	6	9	113	3	0	0	0	0

NCAA Championship All-Tournament Team (2008)

Signed as a free agent by **Chicago**, April 16, 2008.

BRENNAN, T.J. (BREH-nan, TEE-JAY) BUF.

Defense. Shoots left. 6'1", 202 lbs. Born, Willingboro, NJ, April 3, 1989.
(Buffalo's 1st choice, 31st overall, in 2007 Entry Draft).

			Regular Season					Playoffs				
Season	Club	League	GP	G	A	Pts	PIM	GP	G	A	Pts	PIM
2005-06	Phi. Little Flyers	AtJHL	42	9	23	32	....	....	....	....	....	....
2006-07	Saint John	QMJHL	68	16	25	41	79	4	1	1	2	4
2007-08	St. John's	QMJHL	65	16	25	41	92	6	2	4	6	12
2008-09	Montreal	QMJHL	59	5	29	34	63	10	4	8	12	34
2009-10	Portland Pirates	AHL	65	6	17	23	64	4	0	1	1	2

BRICKLEY, Connor (BRIH-klee, KAW-nuhr) FLA.

Center. Shoots left. 6', 190 lbs. Born, Malden, MA, February 25, 1992.
(Florida's 6th choice, 50th overall, in 2010 Entry Draft).

			Regular Season					Playoffs				
Season	Club	League	GP	G	A	Pts	PIM	GP	G	A	Pts	PIM
2008-09	Belmont Hill	High-MA	30	17	18	35	60	....	....	....	....	....
2009-10	Des Moines	USHL	52	22	21	43	68	....	....	....	....	....
	USNTDP	U-18	14	2	5	7	6	....	....	....	....	....

• Signed Letter of Intent to attend **University of Vermont** (Hockey East) in fall of 2010.

BRITTAIN, Josh (BRIH-tehn, JAWSH) **ANA.**

Left wing. Shoots left. 6'5", 217 lbs. Born, Milton, Ont., January 3, 1990.
(Anaheim's 5th choice, 71st overall, in 2008 Entry Draft).

			Regular Season					Playoffs				
Season	Club	League	GP	G	A	Pts	PIM	GP	G	A	Pts	PIM
2005-06	Tor. Jr. Canadiens	GTHL	33	19	21	40	47	....	....	....	....	....
2006-07	Kingston	OHL	54	5	12	17	38	2	0	0	0	0
2007-08	Kingston	OHL	68	28	23	51	106	....	....	....	....	....
2008-09	Kingston	OHL	27	17	7	24	31	....	....	....	....	....
	Barrie Colts	OHL	41	15	13	28	65	5	1	2	3	4
2009-10	Barrie Colts	OHL	12	3	5	8	29	....	....	....	....	....
	Plymouth Whalers	OHL	56	12	12	24	101	9	1	0	1	5

BRODA, Joel (BROH-da, JOHL) **MIN.**

Center. Shoots left. 6', 208 lbs. Born, Yorkton, Sask., November 24, 1989.
(Washington's 6th choice, 144th overall, in 2008 Entry Draft).

			Regular Season					Playoffs				
Season	Club	League	GP	G	A	Pts	PIM	GP	G	A	Pts	PIM
2004-05	Beardy's	SMHL	44	13	13	26	28	....	....	....	....	....
	Tri-City Americans	WHL	2	0	0	0	0	....	....	....	....	....
2005-06	Tri-City Americans	WHL	51	3	1	4	10	5	0	0	0	0
2006-07	Tri-City Americans	WHL	71	16	28	44	62	6	2	0	2	0
2007-08	Tri-City Americans	WHL	3	2	1	3	2	....	....	....	....	....
	Moose Jaw	WHL	70	28	22	50	72	6	1	1	2	0
2008-09	Moose Jaw	WHL	39	*36	12	48	45	....	....	....	....	....
	Calgary Hitmen	WHL	28	*17	22	39	19	18	11	13	24	8
2009-10	Calgary Hitmen	WHL	66	39	34	73	65	23	*13	4	17	16

WHL East Second All-Star Team (2009)

Signed as a free agent by **Minnesota**, July 14, 2010.

BRODEUR, Mathieu (broh-DUHR, MA-tyew) **PHX.**

Defense. Shoots left. 6'5", 190 lbs. Born, Laval, Que., June 21, 1990.
(Phoenix's 5th choice, 76th overall, in 2008 Entry Draft).

			Regular Season					Playoffs				
Season	Club	League	GP	G	A	Pts	PIM	GP	G	A	Pts	PIM
2006-07	Laurentides	QAAA	44	5	7	12	58	15	2	4	6	18
2007-08	Cape Breton	QMJHL	69	1	6	7	27	11	0	0	0	6
2008-09	Cape Breton	QMJHL	61	3	12	15	15	11	1	3	4	4
2009-10	Cape Breton	QMJHL	65	4	25	29	31	5	0	0	0	9
	San Antonio	AHL	2	0	1	1	0	....	....	....	....	....

BRODIE, T.J. (BROH-dee, TEE-JAY) **CGY.**

Defense. Shoots left. 6'1", 180 lbs. Born, Chatham, Ont., June 7, 1990.
(Calgary's 5th choice, 114th overall, in 2008 Entry Draft).

			Regular Season					Playoffs				
Season	Club	League	GP	G	A	Pts	PIM	GP	G	A	Pts	PIM
2006-07	Leamington Flyers	OJHL-B	43	8	38	46	104	5	1	2	3	12
	Saginaw Spirit	OHL	20	0	4	4	23	3	0	1	1	2
2007-08	Saginaw Spirit	OHL	68	4	26	30	73	4	0	3	3	2
2008-09	Saginaw Spirit	OHL	63	12	38	50	67	8	3	6	9	8
2009-10	Saginaw Spirit	OHL	19	4	19	23	20	....	....	....	....	....
	Barrie Colts	OHL	46	3	30	33	38	17	1	14	15	14

BRODIN, Daniel (broh-DEEN, DAN-yehl) **TOR.**

Left wing. Shoots right. 6'1", 172 lbs. Born, Tyreso, Sweden, February 9, 1990.
(Toronto's 6th choice, 146th overall, in 2010 Entry Draft).

			Regular Season					Playoffs				
Season	Club	League	GP	G	A	Pts	PIM	GP	G	A	Pts	PIM
2006-07	Almtuna U18	Swe-U18	....	14	7	21	36	....	....	....	....	....
	Almtuna Jr.	Swe-Jr.	24	3	3	6	16	2	0	0	0	0
2007-08	Djurgarden U18	Swe-U18	35	9	16	25	30	4	0	0	0	0
	Djurgarden Jr.	Swe-Jr.	2	0	0	0	0	....	....	....	....	....
2008-09	Djurgarden Jr.	Swe-Jr.	41	11	12	23	90	6	1	1	2	8
	Djurgarden	Sweden	1	0	0	0	0	....	....	....	....	....
2009-10	Djurgarden Jr.	Swe-Jr.	20	5	2	7	12	....	....	....	....	....
	Djurgarden	Sweden	30	2	3	5	26	16	0	0	0	2

BROPHEY, Evan (BROH-fee, EH-vuhn) **CHI.**

Center/Left wing. Shoots left. 6'2", 199 lbs. Born, Kitchener, Ont., December 3, 1986.
(Chicago's 4th choice, 68th overall, in 2005 Entry Draft).

			Regular Season					Playoffs				
Season	Club	League	GP	G	A	Pts	PIM	GP	G	A	Pts	PIM
2002-03	Barrie Colts	OHL	61	12	14	26	36	6	0	0	0	2
2003-04	Barrie Colts	OHL	67	14	11	25	63	12	4	3	7	4
2004-05	Barrie Colts	OHL	10	3	7	10	13	....	....	....	....	....
	Belleville Bulls	OHL	53	25	36	61	42	5	2	1	3	2
2005-06	Belleville Bulls	OHL	22	9	17	26	39	....	....	....	....	....
	Plymouth Whalers	OHL	40	10	25	35	42	13	4	7	11	18
2006-07	Plymouth Whalers	OHL	68	36	71	107	91	20	9	14	23	26
2007-08	Rockford IceHogs	AHL	74	4	15	19	64	1	0	0	0	0
2008-09	Rockford IceHogs	AHL	79	16	23	39	65	4	1	0	1	0
2009-10	Rockford IceHogs	AHL	79	14	17	31	39	4	0	0	0	2

BROWN, Chris (BROWN, KRIHS) **PHX.**

Center. Shoots right. 6'2", 191 lbs. Born, Flower Mound, TX, February 3, 1991.
(Phoenix's 2nd choice, 36th overall, in 2009 Entry Draft).

			Regular Season					Playoffs				
Season	Club	League	GP	G	A	Pts	PIM	GP	G	A	Pts	PIM
2007-08	USNTDP	NAHL	43	8	6	14	66	3	0	0	0	0
	USNTDP	U-17	17	5	1	6	8	....	....	....	....	....
2008-09	USNTDP	NAHL	15	6	2	8	37	....	....	....	....	....
	USNTDP	U-18	47	14	16	30	83	....	....	....	....	....
2009-10	U. of Michigan	CCHA	45	13	15	28	58	....	....	....	....	....

CCHA All-Rookie Team (2010)

BRUESS, Trevor (BRIHS, TREH-vuhr) **WSH.**

Right wing. Shoots right. 6', 209 lbs. Born, Minneapolis, MN, January 6, 1986.

			Regular Season					Playoffs				
Season	Club	League	GP	G	A	Pts	PIM	GP	G	A	Pts	PIM
2004-05	Fargo-Moorhead	NAHL	51	11	17	28	72	....	....	....	....	....
2005-06	Lincoln Stars	USHL	56	10	17	27	108	9	1	0	1	8
2006-07	Minnesota State	WCHA	37	3	11	14	102	....	....	....	....	....
2007-08	Minnesota State	WCHA	38	9	21	30	54	....	....	....	....	....
2008-09	Minnesota State	WCHA	35	12	5	17	117	....	....	....	....	....
2009-10	Hershey Bears	AHL	14	1	1	2	15	....	....	....	....	....
	South Carolina	ECHL	46	8	17	25	74	5	1	0	1	10

Signed as a free agent by **Washington**, March 20, 2009.

BUBNICK, Jimmy (BUHB-nihk, JIH-mee) **ATL.**

Center. Shoots right. 6'2", 200 lbs. Born, Esterhazy, Sask., January 19, 1991.
(Atlanta's 7th choice, 155th overall, in 2009 Entry Draft).

			Regular Season					Playoffs				
Season	Club	League	GP	G	A	Pts	PIM	GP	G	A	Pts	PIM
2006-07	Sask. Contacts	SMHL	41	33	37	70	32	....	....	....	....	....
	Kamloops Blazers	WHL	2	0	1	1	0	....	....	....	....	....
2007-08	Kamloops Blazers	WHL	64	9	18	27	24	4	0	0	0	4
2008-09	Kamloops Blazers	WHL	72	25	32	57	41	4	0	1	1	6
2009-10	Kamloops Blazers	WHL	44	17	23	40	44	....	....	....	....	....
	Calgary Hitmen	WHL	21	5	8	13	15	23	2	12	14	8

Memorial Cup All-Star Team (2010)

BUDISH, Zach (BOO-dihsh, ZAK) **NSH.**

Right wing. Shoots right. 6'3", 221 lbs. Born, Edina, MN, May 9, 1991.
(Nashville's 2nd choice, 41st overall, in 2009 Entry Draft).

			Regular Season					Playoffs				
Season	Club	League	GP	G	A	Pts	PIM	GP	G	A	Pts	PIM
2006-07	Edina Hornets	High-MN	31	22	25	47	....	....	....	....	....	....
2007-08	Edina Hornets	High-MN	30	26	37	63	....	....	....	....	....	....
2008-09	Edina Hornets	High-MN	DID NOT PLAY – INJURED									
	Team Southwest	UMHSEL	15	14	13	27	12	....	....	....	....	....
2009-10	U. of Minnesota	WCHA	39	7	10	17	45	....	....	....	....	....

• Missed entire 2008-09 High School season recovering from knee injury suffered during football season.

BULMER, Brett (BUHL-muhr, BREHT) **MIN.**

Right wing. Shoots right. 6'2", 182 lbs. Born, Prince George, B.C., April 26, 1992.
(Minnesota's 2nd choice, 39th overall, in 2010 Entry Draft).

			Regular Season					Playoffs				
Season	Club	League	GP	G	A	Pts	PIM	GP	G	A	Pts	PIM
2007-08	Cariboo Cougars	BCMML	40	20	19	39	40	6	2	7	9	4
2008-09	Cariboo Cougars	BCMML	36	28	35	63	56	5	4	2	6	8
	Kelowna Rockets	WHL	3	0	0	0	2	....	....	....	....	....
2009-10	Kelowna Rockets	WHL	65	13	27	40	95	12	3	2	5	6

BUMAGIN, Alexander (buh-MAH-gihn, al-EHX-AN-duhr) **EDM.**

Wing. Shoots left. 6', 180 lbs. Born, Togliatti, USSR, March 1, 1987.
(Edmonton's 5th choice, 170th overall, in 2006 Entry Draft).

			Regular Season					Playoffs				
Season	Club	League	GP	G	A	Pts	PIM	GP	G	A	Pts	PIM
2002-03	Lada Togliatti 2	Russia-3	9	4	1	5	2	....	....	....	....	....
2003-04	Lada Togliatti 2	Russia-3	22	4	9	13	12	4	0	1	1	4
2004-05	Lada Togliatti 2	Russia-3	STATISTICS NOT AVAILABLE									
	Lada Togliatti	Russia	7	2	0	2	2	....	....	....	....	....
	Lada Togliatti	Russia	7	2	0	2	2	....	....	....	....	....
2005-06	Lada Togliatti	Russia	40	9	12	21	28	8	0	3	3	4
2006-07	Lada Togliatti	Russia	41	2	3	5	18	3	0	0	0	0
2007-08	Mytischi	Russia	31	8	7	15	37	5	0	0	0	0
2008-09	Mytischi	Rus-KHL	40	4	7	11	20	6	2	1	3	0
2009-10	Nizhnekamsk	Rus-KHL	51	8	13	21	28	3	0	0	0	0

BURAVCHIKOV, Vyacheslav (burh-AV-chih-kawf, V'YATCH-ih-slav) **BUF.**

Defense. Shoots left. 6'1", 189 lbs. Born, Moscow, USSR, May 22, 1987.
(Buffalo's 7th choice, 191st overall, in 2005 Entry Draft).

			Regular Season					Playoffs				
Season	Club	League	GP	G	A	Pts	PIM	GP	G	A	Pts	PIM
2003-04	Krylja Sovetov 2	Russia-3	STATISTICS NOT AVAILABLE									
2004-05	Krylja Sovetov 2	Russia-3	15	5	6	11	22	....	....	....	....	....
	Krylja Sovetov	Russia-2	26	4	1	5	14	3	0	0	0	2
2005-06	Mytischi	Russia	43	1	2	3	24	9	1	0	1	4
2006-07	Ak Bars Kazan	Russia	35	0	3	3	20	....	....	....	....	....
2007-08	Ak Bars Kazan	Russia	46	1	0	1	12	10	1	0	1	4
2008-09	Ak Bars Kazan	Rus-KHL	44	4	6	10	14	18	0	1	1	16
2009-10	Ak Bars Kazan	Rus-KHL	35	3	3	6	26	6	0	1	1	0

BURKE, Greg (BUHRK, GREHG) **WSH.**

Left wing. Shoots left. 6'3", 205 lbs. Born, Portsmouth, NH, May 16, 1990.
(Washington's 7th choice, 174th overall, in 2008 Entry Draft).

			Regular Season					Playoffs				
Season	Club	League	GP	G	A	Pts	PIM	GP	G	A	Pts	PIM
2006-07	N.H. Jr. Monarchs	EJHL	34	6	12	18	22	....	....	....	....	....
2007-08	N.H. Jr. Monarchs	EJHL	40	21	25	46	46	6	5	4	9	6
2008-09	Cedar Rapids	USHL	8	2	0	2	8	....	....	....	....	....
2009-10	New Hampshire	H-East	32	2	8	10	18	....	....	....	....	....

• Missed majority of 2008-09 season recovering from shoulder injury.

BURLON, Brandon (BUHR-lohn, BRAN-duhn) **N.J.**

Defense. Shoots left. 6', 190 lbs. Born, Nobleton, Ont., March 5, 1990.
(New Jersey's 2nd choice, 52nd overall, in 2008 Entry Draft).

			Regular Season					Playoffs				
Season	Club	League	GP	G	A	Pts	PIM	GP	G	A	Pts	PIM
2005-06	Vaughan Kings	GTHL	55	19	29	48	38	....	....	....	....	....
2006-07	St. Michael's	OPJHL	45	4	19	23	46	4	0	1	1	4
2007-08	St. Michael's	OPJHL	32	7	17	24	41	10	2	4	6	8
2008-09	U. of Michigan	CCHA	33	5	10	15	14	....	....	....	....	....
2009-10	U. of Michigan	CCHA	45	3	11	14	24	....	....	....	....	....

CCHA All-Rookie Team (2009)

BURMISTROV, Alexander (buhr-MIHS-trawf, al-ehx-AN-duhr) **ATL.**

Center. Shoots left. 6', 175 lbs. Born, Kazan, USSR, October 21, 1991.
(Atlanta's 1st choice, 8th overall, in 2010 Entry Draft).

			Regular Season					Playoffs				
Season	Club	League	GP	G	A	Pts	PIM	GP	G	A	Pts	PIM
2008-09	Ak Bars Kazan 2	Russia-3	34	25	25	50	54	....	....	....	....	....
	Ak Bars Kazan	Rus-KHL	1	0	0	0	0	....	....	....	....	....
2009-10	Barrie Colts	OHL	62	22	43	65	49	17	8	8	16	22

BUT, Anton (BOOT, AN-tawn) **T.B.**

Left wing. Shoots left. 6'1", 189 lbs. Born, Kharkov, USSR, July 3, 1980.
(New Jersey's 7th choice, 119th overall, in 1998 Entry Draft).

			Regular Season					Playoffs				
Season	Club	League	GP	G	A	Pts	PIM	GP	G	A	Pts	PIM
1995-96	Yaroslavl 2	CIS-2	60	30	12	42	10	....	....	....	....	....
1996-97	Yaroslavl 2	Russia-3	70	30	20	50	20	....	....	....	....	....
1997-98	Yaroslavl 2	Russia-2	48	12	5	17	28	....	....	....	....	....
1998-99	Yaroslavl 2	Russia-3	22	12	8	20	59	....	....	....	....	....
	Torpedo Yaroslavl	Russia	5	0	0	0	0	....	....	....	....	....
99-2000	Yaroslavl 2	Russia-3	1	0	0	0	2	....	....	....	....	....
	Torpedo Yaroslavl	Russia	26	2	5	7	16	8	2	1	3	0
2000-01	Yaroslavl	Russia	42	14	6	20	14	11	1	3	4	8
2001-02	Yaroslavl	Russia	48	14	11	25	14	6	0	1	1	2
2002-03	Yaroslavl	Russia	44	16	13	29	16	9	1	2	3	6
2003-04	Yaroslavl	Russia	51	11	10	21	24	3	0	0	0	0
2004-05	Yaroslavl	Russia	60	12	22	34	58	8	3	3	6	0
2005-06	Yaroslavl	Russia	49	16	21	37	26	11	2	1	3	2
2006-07	SKA St. Petersburg	Russia	52	13	13	26	61	2	0	1	1	2
2007-08	SKA St. Petersburg	Russia	57	15	13	28	40	9	4	1	5	6
2008-09	CSKA Moscow	Rus-KHL	55	12	21	33	36	8	2	1	3	2
2009-10	SKA St. Petersburg	Rus-KHL	56	19	9	28	30	4	0	0	0	2

• Rights traded to **Tampa Bay** by **New Jersey** with Josef Boumedienne and Sascha Goc for Andrei Zyuzin, November 9, 2001.

BUTTON, Ryan (BUH-tuhn, RIGH-uhn) **BOS.**

Defense. Shoots left. 6'1", 193 lbs. Born, Edmonton, Alta., March 26, 1991.
(Boston's 2nd choice, 86th overall, in 2009 Entry Draft).

			Regular Season					Playoffs				
Season	Club	League	GP	G	A	Pts	PIM	GP	G	A	Pts	PIM
2006-07	Edmonton CAC	AMHL	28	2	6	8	74	....	....	....	....	....
2007-08	Prince Albert	WHL	58	0	8	8	30	....	....	....	....	....
2008-09	Prince Albert	WHL	70	5	32	37	43	....	....	....	....	....
2009-10	Prince Albert	WHL	67	6	27	33	46	....	....	....	....	....

BYRON, Paul (BIGH-ruhn, PAWL) **BUF.**

Center. Shoots left. 5'9", 144 lbs. Born, Ottawa, Ont., April 27, 1989.
(Buffalo's 6th choice, 179th overall, in 2007 Entry Draft).

			Regular Season					Playoffs				
Season	Club	League	GP	G	A	Pts	PIM	GP	G	A	Pts	PIM
2005-06	Ottawa West	OJHL-B	33	20	23	43	33	7	3	8	11	4
2006-07	Gatineau	QMJHL	68	21	23	44	46	5	5	1	6	2
2007-08	Gatineau	QMJHL	52	37	31	68	25	19	*21	11	32	12
2008-09	Gatineau	QMJHL	64	33	66	99	32	10	2	14	16	4
2009-10	Portland Pirates	AHL	57	14	19	33	59	4	0	0	0	0

QMJHL Second All-Star Team (2009)

CALLA, Brady (KAL-luh, BRAY-dee) **FLA.**

Right wing. Shoots right. 6', 190 lbs. Born, North Vancouver, B.C., March 14, 1988.
(Florida's 2nd choice, 73rd overall, in 2006 Entry Draft).

			Regular Season					Playoffs				
Season	Club	League	GP	G	A	Pts	PIM	GP	G	A	Pts	PIM
2004-05	Everett Silvertips	WHL	68	11	10	21	38	11	1	1	2	0
2005-06	Everett Silvertips	WHL	66	8	25	33	52	11	1	2	3	4
2006-07	Everett Silvertips	WHL	29	3	6	9	23	....	....	....	....	....
	Moose Jaw	WHL	39	12	20	32	19	....	....	....	....	....
2007-08	Moose Jaw	WHL	14	2	8	10	10	....	....	....	....	....
	Kamloops Blazers	WHL	52	10	20	30	52	4	0	2	2	4
	Rochester	AHL	6	2	2	4	2	....	....	....	....	....
2008-09	Kamloops Blazers	WHL	19	5	8	13	31	....	....	....	....	....
	Spokane Chiefs	WHL	31	11	14	25	27	12	1	3	4	6
	Rochester	AHL	8	0	1	1	9	....	....	....	....	....
2009-10	Rochester	AHL	33	1	5	6	14	....	....	....	....	....
	Florida Everblades	ECHL	16	2	2	4	23	....	....	....	....	....

CALLAHAN, Mitchell (kal-AH-han, MIH-chuhl) **DET.**

Right wing. Shoots right. 5'11", 175 lbs. Born, Whittier, CA, August 17, 1991.
(Detroit's 6th choice, 180th overall, in 2009 Entry Draft).

			Regular Season					Playoffs				
Season	Club	League	GP	G	A	Pts	PIM	GP	G	A	Pts	PIM
2007-08	L.A. Jr. Kings	Minor-CA	52	32	37	69	62	....	....	....	....	....
2008-09	Kelowna Rockets	WHL	70	14	13	27	188	22	1	3	4	43
2009-10	Kelowna Rockets	WHL	72	20	27	47	165	12	2	4	6	10

CALVERT, Matt (KAL-vuhrt, MAT) **CBJ**

Left wing. Shoots left. 5'11", 180 lbs. Born, Brandon, Man., December 24, 1989.
(Columbus' 5th choice, 127th overall, in 2008 Entry Draft).

			Regular Season					Playoffs				
Season	Club	League	GP	G	A	Pts	PIM	GP	G	A	Pts	PIM
2005-06	Brandon	MMHL	38	24	30	54	48	6	3	6	9	18
2006-07	Brandon	MMHL	30	28	55	83	46	16	5	13	18	16
	Winkler Flyers	MJHL	1	0	0	0	15	....	....	....	....	....
2007-08	Brandon	WHL	72	24	40	64	53	6	1	2	3	2
2008-09	Brandon	WHL	58	28	39	67	58	12	9	8	17	22
2009-10	Brandon	WHL	68	47	52	99	70	15	9	7	16	15

WHL East Second All-Star Team (2010) • Memorial Cup All-Star Team (2010)

CAMERON, Bryan (KAM-ruhn, BRIGH-uhn) **CGY.**

Right wing. Shoots right. 5'10", 180 lbs. Born, Brampton, Ont., February 25, 1989.
(Los Angeles' 4th choice, 82nd overall, in 2007 Entry Draft).

			Regular Season					Playoffs				
Season	Club	League	GP	G	A	Pts	PIM	GP	G	A	Pts	PIM
2004-05	Toronto Marlboros	GTHL	75	73	47	120	76	....	....	....	....	....
	Milton Icehawks	OPJHL	2	0	0	0	0	....	....	....	....	....
2005-06	Belleville Bulls	OHL	64	20	9	29	46	6	1	2	3	6
2006-07	Belleville Bulls	OHL	60	33	25	58	50	15	4	8	12	15
2007-08	Belleville Bulls	OHL	68	41	37	78	56	21	4	9	13	10
2008-09	Belleville Bulls	OHL	64	37	44	81	51	17	7	7	14	18
2009-10	Barrie Colts	OHL	62	*53	25	78	68	17	11	9	20	16

OHL All-Rookie Team (2006) • OHL First All-Star Team (2009, 2010)

Signed as a free agent by **Calgary**, April 30, 2010.

CAMPBELL, Andrew (KAM-buhl, AN-droo) **L.A.**

Defense. Shoots left. 6'4", 206 lbs. Born, Caledonia, Ont., February 4, 1988.
(Los Angeles' 5th choice, 74th overall, in 2008 Entry Draft).

			Regular Season					Playoffs				
Season	Club	League	GP	G	A	Pts	PIM	GP	G	A	Pts	PIM
2005-06	Sault Ste. Marie	OHL	31	1	3	4	23	3	0	0	0	4
2006-07	Sault Ste. Marie	OHL	63	4	14	18	75	13	0	1	1	6
2007-08	Sault Ste. Marie	OHL	68	13	22	35	64	14	2	3	5	13
2008-09	Manchester	AHL	72	3	5	8	72	....	....	....	....	....
2009-10	Manchester	AHL	74	2	9	11	68	16	1	4	5	6

CAMPBELL, Max (KAM-behl, MAX) **NYR**

Center. Shoots left. 6'1", 185 lbs. Born, Strathroy, Ont., December 21, 1988.
(NY Rangers' 3rd choice, 138th overall, in 2007 Entry Draft).

			Regular Season					Playoffs				
Season	Club	League	GP	G	A	Pts	PIM	GP	G	A	Pts	PIM
2005-06	Strathroy Rockets	OJHL-B	48	17	18	35	10	....	....	....	....	....
2006-07	Strathroy Rockets	OJHL-B	46	46	49	95	84	....	....	....	....	....
2007-08	Western Mich.	CCHA	38	6	16	22	10	....	....	....	....	....
2008-09	Western Mich.	CCHA	40	16	15	31	44	....	....	....	....	....
2009-10	Western Mich.	CCHA	34	6	13	19	43	....	....	....	....	....

CAPORUSSO, Louie (kap-oh-ROO-soh, LOO-ee) **OTT.**

Center/Left wing. Shoots left. 5'10", 190 lbs. Born, Toronto, Ont., June 21, 1989.
(Ottawa's 3rd choice, 90th overall, in 2007 Entry Draft).

			Regular Season					Playoffs				
Season	Club	League	GP	G	A	Pts	PIM	GP	G	A	Pts	PIM
2004-05	Tor. Red Wings	GTHL	53	38	28	66	28	....	....	....	....	....
2005-06	St. Michael's	OPJHL	48	29	44	73	44	25	8	10	18	16
2006-07	St. Michael's	OPJHL	37	23	27	50	45	20	14	19	33	14
2007-08	U. of Michigan	CCHA	33	12	9	21	18	....	....	....	....	....
2008-09	U. of Michigan	CCHA	41	*24	25	49	30	....	....	....	....	....
2009-10	U. of Michigan	CCHA	45	*21	22	43	26	....	....	....	....	....

CCHA First All-Star Team (2009) • NCAA West First All-American Team (2009)

CAREY, Paul (KAIR-ee, PAWL) **COL.**

Center. Shoots left. 6', 175 lbs. Born, Boston, MA, September 24, 1988.
(Colorado's 7th choice, 135th overall, in 2007 Entry Draft).

			Regular Season					Playoffs				
Season	Club	League	GP	G	A	Pts	PIM	GP	G	A	Pts	PIM
2005-06	Salisbury School	High-CT	27	14	11	25	18	....	....	....	....	....
2006-07	Salisbury School	High-CT	24	16	11	27	16	....	....	....	....	....
2007-08	Indiana Ice	USHL	60	34	32	66	32	4	1	2	3	2
2008-09	Boston College	H-East	24	5	4	9	8	....	....	....	....	....
2009-10	Boston College	H-East	41	9	12	21	29	....	....	....	....	....

USHL All-Rookie Team (2008) • USHL Second All-Star Team (2008)

CARLSSON, Jonathan (KAHRL-suhn, JAWN-ah-thuhn) **CHI.**

Defense. Shoots right. 6'2", 187 lbs. Born, Uppsala, Sweden, August 5, 1988.
(Chicago's 4th choice, 162nd overall, in 2008 Entry Draft).

			Regular Season					Playoffs				
Season	Club	League	GP	G	A	Pts	PIM	GP	G	A	Pts	PIM
2004-05	Brynas IF Gavle Jr.	Swe-Jr.	19	1	0	1	6	....	....	....	....	....
2005-06	Brynas U18	Swe-U18	1	0	0	0	0	....	....	....	....	....
	Brynas IF Gavle Jr.	Swe-Jr.	37	2	9	11	24	2	0	1	1	0
2006-07	Brynas IF Gavle Jr.	Swe-Jr.	39	12	5	17	16	4	2	1	3	6
	Brynas IF Gavle	Sweden	6	1	0	1	2	....	....	....	....	....
2007-08	Brynas IF Gavle Jr.	Swe-Jr.	8	3	2	5	6	4	2	0	2	0
	IF Bjorkloven Umea	Sweden-2	16	2	3	5	6	....	....	....	....	....
	Brynas IF Gavle	Sweden	26	0	0	0	27	....	....	....	....	....
	Brynas IF Gavle	Sweden-Q	9	0	0	0	2	....	....	....	....	....
2008-09	Brynas IF Gavle	Sweden	55	0	1	1	78	4	0	0	0	4
2009-10	Toledo Walleye	ECHL	27	4	6	10	13	3	0	0	0	0
	Rockford IceHogs	AHL	19	1	0	1	8	....	....	....	....	....

CARMAN, Michael (KAR-mahn, MIGH-kuhl) **COL.**

Center. Shoots left. 6', 180 lbs. Born, Augusta, GA, April 14, 1988.
(Colorado's 4th choice, 81st overall, in 2006 Entry Draft).

			Regular Season					Playoffs				
Season	Club	League	GP	G	A	Pts	PIM	GP	G	A	Pts	PIM
2003-04	Holy Angels	High-MN	29	19	40	59	....	....	....	....	....	....
2004-05	USNTDP	U-17	14	2	9	11	40	....	....	....	....	....
	USNTDP	NAHL	39	12	15	27	38	10	2	4	6	10
2005-06	USNTDP	U-18	43	15	23	38	78	....	....	....	....	....
	USNTDP	NAHL	17	6	10	16	24	....	....	....	....	....
2006-07	U. of Minnesota	WCHA	41	9	11	20	55	....	....	....	....	....
2007-08	U. of Minnesota	WCHA	23	4	7	11	28	....	....	....	....	....
2008-09	U. of Minnesota	WCHA	32	8	9	17	32	....	....	....	....	....
2009-10	U. of Minnesota	WCHA	39	8	10	18	39	....	....	....	....	....
	Lake Erie Monsters	AHL	10	2	0	2	10	....	....	....	....	....

CARON, Jordan (kuh-RAWN, JOHR-dihn) **BOS.**

Right wing. Shoots left. 6'3", 204 lbs. Born, Sayabec, Que., November 2, 1990.
(Boston's 1st choice, 25th overall, in 2009 Entry Draft).

			Regular Season					Playoffs				
Season	Club	League	GP	G	A	Pts	PIM	GP	G	A	Pts	PIM
2005-06	Notre Dame	SMHL	35	8	16	24	32	....	....	....	....	....
2006-07	Rimouski Oceanic	QMJHL	59	18	22	40	41	....	....	....	....	....
2007-08	Rimouski Oceanic	QMJHL	46	20	23	43	42	9	3	1	4	18
2008-09	Rimouski Oceanic	QMJHL	56	36	31	67	66	13	6	5	11	16
2009-10	Rimouski Oceanic	QMJHL	20	9	11	20	8	....	....	....	....	....
	Rouyn-Noranda	QMJHL	23	17	16	33	16	11	7	11	18	15

CARPENTIER, Hugo (kar-PUHNT-yay, HEW-goh) **CGY.**

Center. Shoots left. 6'2", 205 lbs. Born, Hull, Que., March 17, 1988.
(Calgary's 4th choice, 118th overall, in 2006 Entry Draft).

			Regular Season					Playoffs				
Season	Club	League	GP	G	A	Pts	PIM	GP	G	A	Pts	PIM
2004-05	Rouyn-Noranda	QMJHL	49	6	9	15	32	5	0	1	1	6
2005-06	Rouyn-Noranda	QMJHL	70	31	39	70	64	5	1	2	3	4
2006-07	Rouyn-Noranda	QMJHL	69	17	37	54	86	16	0	6	6	24
2007-08	Rouyn-Noranda	QMJHL	69	27	38	65	114	17	14	8	22	20
2008-09	Quad City Flames	AHL	17	2	2	4	8	....	....	....	....	....
	Las Vegas	ECHL	45	9	15	24	33	8	0	3	3	0
2009-10	Abbotsford Heat	AHL	35	0	6	6	27	....	....	....	....	....
	Utah Grizzlies	ECHL	24	3	6	9	38	....	....	....	....	....

CARRICK, Sam (KAIR-ihk, SAM) TOR.

Center. Shoots right. 6', 188 lbs. Born, Markham, Ont., February 4, 1992.
(Toronto's 5th choice, 144th overall, in 2010 Entry Draft).

			Regular Season					Playoffs				
Season	Club	League	GP	G	A	Pts	PIM	GP	G	A	Pts	PIM
2007-08	Tor. Red Wings	GTHL	55	40	30	70	130	....	....	....	....	....
2008-09	Brampton	OHL	61	10	11	21	47	21	1	0	1	16
2009-10	Brampton	OHL	66	21	21	42	96	8	2	2	4	8

CARRIER, Samuel (kair-ee-AIR, SAM-yoo-ehl) WSH.

Defense. Shoots right. 6'1", 186 lbs. Born, Laval, Que., April 28, 1992.
(Washington's 5th choice, 176th overall, in 2010 Entry Draft).

			Regular Season					Playoffs				
Season	Club	League	GP	G	A	Pts	PIM	GP	G	A	Pts	PIM
2007-08	Antoine-Girouard	QAAA	45	8	25	33	64	15	7	4	11	14
2008-09	Quebec Remparts	QMJHL	56	4	5	9	49	3	1	0	1	4
2009-10	Lewiston	QMJHL	66	10	32	42	65	4	1	0	1	14

CARUSO, Michael (kah-ROO-soh, MIGH-kuhl) FLA.

Defense. Shoots left. 6'2", 191 lbs. Born, Mississauga, Ont., July 5, 1988.
(Florida's 3rd choice, 103rd overall, in 2006 Entry Draft).

			Regular Season					Playoffs				
Season	Club	League	GP	G	A	Pts	PIM	GP	G	A	Pts	PIM
2004-05	Guelph Storm	OHL	56	0	3	3	31	4	0	0	0	2
2005-06	Guelph Storm	OHL	66	1	15	16	85	15	1	2	3	24
2006-07	Guelph Storm	OHL	64	4	16	20	119	4	0	0	0	8
2007-08	Guelph Storm	OHL	62	10	24	34	103	10	2	6	8	22
2008-09	Rochester	AHL	73	1	9	10	66	....	....	....	....	....
2009-10	Rochester	AHL	67	1	10	11	42	....	....	....	....	....

CAYER, Julien (KAY-uhr, JOO-lee-ehn) DET.

Center. Shoots left. 6'4", 186 lbs. Born, Longueuil, Que., July 6, 1989.
(Detroit's 4th choice, 151st overall, in 2008 Entry Draft).

			Regular Season					Playoffs				
Season	Club	League	GP	G	A	Pts	PIM	GP	G	A	Pts	PIM
2005-06	C.C. Lemoyne	QAAA	42	11	21	32	46	8	1	2	3	14
2006-07	St-Jerome	QJHL	45	6	23	29	84	10	1	3	4	2
2007-08	Northwood	High-NY	42	24	32	56	56	....	....	....	....	....
2008-09	Clarkson Knights	ECAC	29	4	6	10	30	....	....	....	....	....
2009-10	Clarkson Knights	ECAC	22	2	3	5	18	....	....	....	....	....

CEHLIN, Patrick (seh-LIHN, PAHT-rihk) NSH.

Right wing. Shoots right. 5'11", 170 lbs. Born, Huddinge, Sweden, July 27, 1991.
(Nashville's 3rd choice, 126th overall, in 2010 Entry Draft).

			Regular Season					Playoffs				
Season	Club	League	GP	G	A	Pts	PIM	GP	G	A	Pts	PIM
2006-07	Djurgarden U18	Swe-U18	27	10	18	28	49	3	1	2	3	0
2007-08	Djurgarden U18	Swe-U18	12	7	16	23	10	8	0	5	5	12
	Djurgarden Jr.	Swe-Jr.	22	5	3	8	8	4	0	1	1	4
2008-09	Djurgarden U18	Swe-U18	4	5	2	7	0	1	0	0	0	2
	Djurgarden Jr.	Swe-Jr.	36	10	25	35	110	6	1	2	3	6
	Djurgarden	Sweden	2	0	0	0	0	....	....	....	....	....
2009-10	Djurgarden Jr.	Swe-Jr.	9	3	3	6	4	....	....	....	....	....
	Djurgarden	Sweden	54	5	6	11	10	16	0	2	2	2

CHAMPAGNE, Joel (sham-PAYN, JOHL)

Center. Shoots left. 6'4", 210 lbs. Born, Chateauguay, Que., January 24, 1990.
(Toronto's 5th choice, 129th overall, in 2008 Entry Draft).

			Regular Season					Playoffs				
Season	Club	League	GP	G	A	Pts	PIM	GP	G	A	Pts	PIM
2005-06	Chateauguay	QAAA	42	9	29	38	22	19	7	10	17	20
2006-07	Chicoutimi	QMJHL	62	6	16	22	51	4	0	0	0	6
2007-08	Chicoutimi	QMJHL	70	18	22	40	45	6	1	1	2	6
2008-09	Chicoutimi	QMJHL	28	10	11	21	34	....	....	....	....	....
	P.E.I. Rocket	QMJHL	24	14	26	40	18	3	0	1	1	4
2009-10	P.E.I. Rocket	QMJHL	36	18	25	43	32	....	....	....	....	....
	Victoriaville Tigres	QMJHL	29	20	16	36	15	16	7	6	13	16

CHAPPELL, Chris (CHA-puhl, KRIHS) NYR

Left wing. Shoots left. 6'4", 209 lbs. Born, Pickering, Ont., March 21, 1988.

			Regular Season					Playoffs				
Season	Club	League	GP	G	A	Pts	PIM	GP	G	A	Pts	PIM
2003-04	Pickering Panthers	OPJHL	10	2	2	4	2	....	....	....	....	....
2004-05	Pickering Panthers	OPJHL	49	8	27	35	11	....	....	....	....	....
2005-06	Saginaw Spirit	OHL	60	8	12	20	53	4	0	0	0	2
2006-07	Saginaw Spirit	OHL	66	10	14	24	47	6	0	1	1	6
2007-08	Saginaw Spirit	OHL	54	14	20	34	55	4	2	1	3	4
2008-09	Saginaw Spirit	OHL	68	38	38	76	88	8	2	6	8	8
2009-10	Hartford Wolf Pack	AHL	6	0	0	0	5	....	....	....	....	....
	Charlotte	ECHL	11	1	3	4	2	....	....	....	....	....

Signed as a free agent by **NY Rangers**, July 2, 2009.

CHAPUT, Michael (sha-PUT, MIGH-kuhl) PHI.

Center. Shoots left. 6'2", 194 lbs. Born, Ile Bizard, Que., April 9, 1992.
(Philadelphia's 1st choice, 89th overall, in 2010 Entry Draft).

			Regular Season					Playoffs				
Season	Club	League	GP	G	A	Pts	PIM	GP	G	A	Pts	PIM
2007-08	Lac St-Louis Royals	Minor-QU	STATISTICS NOT AVAILABLE									
	Lac St-Louis Lions	QAAA	4	0	0	0	0	....	....	....	....	....
2008-09	Lewiston	QMJHL	29	3	7	10	34	....	....	....	....	....
2009-10	Lewiston	QMJHL	68	28	27	55	60	4	0	1	1	2

• Missed majority of 2008-09 season recovering from shoulder injury.

CHAPUT, Stefan (sha-PEW, STEH-fan) CAR.

Center. Shoots left. 6', 190 lbs. Born, Montreal, Que., March 11, 1988.
(Carolina's 4th choice, 153rd overall, in 2006 Entry Draft).

			Regular Season					Playoffs				
Season	Club	League	GP	G	A	Pts	PIM	GP	G	A	Pts	PIM
2003-04	West Island Lions	QAAA	29	7	12	19	32	7	1	3	4	4
2004-05	West Island Lions	QAAA	39	29	25	54	86	5	2	2	4	16
	Lewiston	QMJHL	8	2	3	5	2	8	1	0	1	2
2005-06	Lewiston	QMJHL	69	19	29	48	44	6	0	1	1	4
2006-07	Lewiston	QMJHL	57	17	29	46	43	17	6	5	11	20
2007-08	Lewiston	QMJHL	62	33	36	69	56	6	2	1	3	12
	Albany River Rats	AHL	1	0	0	0	0	....	....	....	....	....
2008-09	Albany River Rats	AHL	15	4	7	11	10	....	....	....	....	....
2009-10	Albany River Rats	AHL	75	10	28	38	18	2	0	1	1	2

CHIAROT, Ben (CHAIR-awt, BEHN) ATL.

Defense. Shoots left. 6'3", 220 lbs. Born, Hamilton, Ont., May 9, 1991.
(Atlanta's 5th choice, 120th overall, in 2009 Entry Draft).

			Regular Season					Playoffs				
Season	Club	League	GP	G	A	Pts	PIM	GP	G	A	Pts	PIM
2006-07	Mississauga Reps	GTHL	60	21	42	63	166	....	....	....	....	....
2007-08	Guelph Storm	OHL	31	0	0	0	14	....	....	....	....	....
2008-09	Guelph Storm	OHL	67	2	10	12	111	4	0	3	3	8
2009-10	Guelph Storm	OHL	41	4	9	13	106	....	....	....	....	....
	Sudbury Wolves	OHL	26	4	4	8	61	4	1	1	2	6
	Chicago Wolves	AHL	1	0	0	0	4	....	....	....	....	....

CHIASSON, Alex (CHAY-sahn, Al-ehx) DAL.

Right wing. Shoots right. 6'4", 187 lbs. Born, Montreal, Que., October 1, 1990.
(Dallas' 2nd choice, 38th overall, in 2009 Entry Draft).

			Regular Season					Playoffs				
Season	Club	League	GP	G	A	Pts	PIM	GP	G	A	Pts	PIM
2007-08	Northwood	High-NY	45	35	46	81		....	....	....	....	....
2008-09	Des Moines	USHL	56	17	33	50	101	....	....	....	....	....
2009-10	Boston University	H-East	35	7	12	19	44	....	....	....	....	....

CHOUINARD, Joel (SHWEE-nahrd, JOHL) COL.

Defense. Shoots left. 6'1", 186 lbs. Born, Longueuil, Que., April 8, 1990.
(Colorado's 5th choice, 167th overall, in 2008 Entry Draft).

			Regular Season					Playoffs				
Season	Club	League	GP	G	A	Pts	PIM	GP	G	A	Pts	PIM
2005-06	Magog	QAAA	44	4	14	18	70	13	1	5	6	6
2006-07	Magog	QAAA	33	8	30	38	88	....	....	....	....	....
	Victoriaville Tigres	QMJHL	23	3	3	6	20	6	0	1	1	0
2007-08	Victoriaville Tigres	QMJHL	69	7	28	35	95	6	2	0	2	4
2008-09	Victoriaville Tigres	QMJHL	64	12	23	35	65	4	0	1	1	6
2009-10	Victoriaville Tigres	QMJHL	65	23	45	68	56	16	3	10	13	6

QMJHL First All-Star Team (2010)

CHUDINOV, Maxim (choo-DEE-nawf, max-EEM) BOS.

Defense. Shoots right. 5'11", 187 lbs. Born, Cherepovets, USSR, March 25, 1990.
(Boston's 7th choice, 195th overall, in 2010 Entry Draft).

			Regular Season					Playoffs				
Season	Club	League	GP	G	A	Pts	PIM	GP	G	A	Pts	PIM
2006-07	Cherepovets	Russia	2	0	0	0	0	3	0	0	0	2
2007-08	Cherepovets 2	Russia-3	STATISTICS NOT AVAILABLE									
	Cherepovets	Russia	18	0	0	0	10	1	0	0	0	0
2008-09	Cherepovets	Rus-KHL	26	0	0	0	14	....	....	....	....	....
2009-10	Cherepovets Jr.	Russia-Jr.	4	1	0	1	12	2	0	1	1	4
	Cherepovets	Rus-KHL	47	6	8	14	30	....	....	....	....	....

CICHY, Michael (KEE-chee, MIGH-kuhl) MTL.

Center. Shoots left. 5'11", 187 lbs. Born, New Britain, CT, July 8, 1990.
(Montreal's 7th choice, 199th overall, in 2009 Entry Draft).

			Regular Season					Playoffs				
Season	Club	League	GP	G	A	Pts	PIM	GP	G	A	Pts	PIM
2006-07	USNTDP	NAHL	32	2	8	10	35	....	....	....	....	....
	USNTDP	U-17	7	4	1	5	4	....	....	....	....	....
2007-08	Tri-City Storm	USHL	59	16	29	45	45	....	....	....	....	....
2008-09	Tri-City Storm	USHL	26	*10	19	29	11	....	....	....	....	....
	Indiana Ice	USHL	30	*24	23	47	12	13	6	*19	*25	6
2009-10	North Dakota	WCHA	23	2	2	4	6	....	....	....	....	....

USHL First All-Star Team (2009)

CISSE, Yasin (SIH-say, YA-sihn) ATL.

Right wing. Shoots right. 6'3", 210 lbs. Born, Montreal, Que., March 11, 1992.
(Atlanta's 5th choice, 150th overall, in 2010 Entry Draft).

			Regular Season					Playoffs				
Season	Club	League	GP	G	A	Pts	PIM	GP	G	A	Pts	PIM
2007-08	Lac St-Louis Lions	QAAA	44	20	38	58	66	13	6	10	16	28
2008-09	Des Moines	USHL	31	2	6	8	46	....	....	....	....	....
2009-10	Des Moines	USHL	18	13	6	19	16	....	....	....	....	....

• Missed majority of 2009-10 season recovering from a severed tendon injury to his ankle. • Signed Letter of Intent to attend **Boston University** (Hockey East) in fall of 2011.

CIZIKAS, Casey (sih-ZEE-kuhs, KAY-see) NYI

Center. Shoots left. 5'11", 184 lbs. Born, Toronto, Ont., February 27, 1991.
(NY Islanders' 5th choice, 92nd overall, in 2009 Entry Draft).

			Regular Season					Playoffs				
Season	Club	League	GP	G	A	Pts	PIM	GP	G	A	Pts	PIM
2006-07	Mississauga Reps	GTHL	77	46	60	106	88	....	....	....	....	....
2007-08	St. Michael's	OHL	62	18	23	41	41	4	1	2	3	6
2008-09	St. Michael's	OHL	55	16	20	36	39	11	5	4	9	11
2009-10	St. Michael's	OHL	68	25	37	62	77	16	7	7	14	16

CLACKSON, Matt (KLAK-suhn, MA-thyew) PHI.

Left wing. Shoots right. 6', 196 lbs. Born, Saskatoon, Sask., April 26, 1985.
(Philadelphia's 6th choice, 215th overall, in 2005 Entry Draft).

			Regular Season					Playoffs				
Season	Club	League	GP	G	A	Pts	PIM	GP	G	A	Pts	PIM
2002-03	Pittsburgh Hornets	MWEHL	64	22	22	44	169	....	....	....	....	....
2003-04	Chicago Steel	USHL	42	5	4	9	108	5	0	1	1	8
2004-05	Chicago Steel	USHL	56	10	15	25	270	....	....	....	....	....
2005-06	Western Mich.	CCHA	34	1	1	2	52	....	....	....	....	....
2006-07	Western Mich.	CCHA	36	0	8	8	80	....	....	....	....	....
2007-08	Western Mich.	CCHA	35	3	3	6	87	....	....	....	....	....
	Philadelphia	AHL	2	0	0	0	19	....	....	....	....	....
2008-09	Philadelphia	AHL	80	3	6	9	263	4	0	0	0	4
2009-10	Adirondack	AHL	60	2	4	6	174	....	....	....	....	....

CLARK, Jason (KLARK, JAY-suhn) NYI

Center/Left wing. Shoots left. 6'2", 180 lbs. Born, Eden Prairie, MN, February 27, 1992.
(NY Islanders' 4th choice, 82nd overall, in 2010 Entry Draft).

			Regular Season					Playoffs				
Season	Club	League	GP	G	A	Pts	PIM	GP	G	A	Pts	PIM
2008-09	Shat.-St. Mary's	High-MN	52	18	26	44	68	....	....	....	....	....
2009-10	Shat.-St. Mary's	High-MN	54	23	23	46	80	....	....	....	....	....

• Signed Letter of Intent to attend **University of Wisconsin** (WCHA) in fall of 2010.

CLARK, Mat (KLAHRK, MAT) ANA.

Defense. Shoots right. 6'3", 211 lbs. Born, Lakewood, CO, October 17, 1990.
(Anaheim's 3rd choice, 37th overall, in 2009 Entry Draft).

			Regular Season					Playoffs				
Season	Club	League	GP	G	A	Pts	PIM	GP	G	A	Pts	PIM
2006-07	Brampton Capitals	OPJHL	47	2	7	9	50	8	1	1	2	19
2007-08	Brampton Capitals	OPJHL	46	6	11	17	64	8	1	4	5	45
2008-09	Brampton	OHL	63	3	20	23	91	21	0	5	5	37
2009-10	Brampton	OHL	66	7	16	23	88	7	2	4	6	9
	Manitoba Moose	AHL	1	0	0	0	0	6	0	0	0	2

CLIFFORD, Kyle (KLIHF-fuhrd, KIGHL) L.A.

Left wing. Shoots left. 6'1", 200 lbs. Born, Ayr, Ont., January 13, 1991.
(Los Angeles' 2nd choice, 35th overall, in 2009 Entry Draft).

			Regular Season					Playoffs				
Season	Club	League	GP	G	A	Pts	PIM	GP	G	A	Pts	PIM
2006-07	Cambridge Hawks	Minor-ON	70	31	49	80	119	....	....	....	....	....
2007-08	Barrie Colts	OHL	66	1	14	15	83	9	0	1	1	4
2008-09	Barrie Colts	OHL	60	16	12	28	133	5	0	0	0	13
2009-10	Barrie Colts	OHL	58	28	29	57	111	17	5	9	14	28
	Manchester	AHL	....	....	....	....	....	7	0	2	2	12

COETZEE, Willie (KOHT-zee, WIHL-ee) DET.

Right wing. Shoots right. 5'10", 186 lbs. Born, Maple Ridge, B.C., November 7, 1990.

			Regular Season					Playoffs				
Season	Club	League	GP	G	A	Pts	PIM	GP	G	A	Pts	PIM
2007-08	Cowichan Valley	BCHL	33	5	11	16	19	....	....	....	....	....
	Red Deer Rebels	WHL	23	2	0	2	14	....	....	....	....	....
2008-09	Red Deer Rebels	WHL	72	18	24	42	42	....	....	....	....	....
2009-10	Red Deer Rebels	WHL	72	29	52	81	32	4	1	0	1	0
	Grand Rapids	AHL	2	0	0	0	0	....	....	....	....	....

Signed as a free agent by **Detroit**, September 18, 2009.

COHEN, Colby (KOH-uhn, KOHL-bee) COL.

Defense. Shoots right. 6'2", 200 lbs. Born, Villanova, PA, April 25, 1989.
(Colorado's 2nd choice, 45th overall, in 2007 Entry Draft).

			Regular Season					Playoffs				
Season	Club	League	GP	G	A	Pts	PIM	GP	G	A	Pts	PIM
2004-05	Syracuse Stars	EmJHL	50	13	30	41	....	....	....	....	....	....
2005-06	USNTDP	U-17	18	2	3	5	22	....	....	....	....	....
	USNTDP	NAHL	37	5	9	14	33	10	1	1	2	0
2006-07	USNTDP	NAHL	4	1	3	4	0	....	....	....	....	....
	Lincoln Stars	USHL	53	13	47	60	110	4	0	0	0	2
2007-08	Boston University	H-East	39	3	13	16	34	....	....	....	....	....
2008-09	Boston University	H-East	43	8	24	32	65	....	....	....	....	....
2009-10	Boston University	H-East	36	14	16	30	82	....	....	....	....	....
	Lake Erie Monsters	AHL	3	0	1	1	9	....	....	....	....	....

USHL Second All-Star Team (2007) • NCAA Championship All-Tournament Team (2009) • NCAA Championship Tournament MVP (2009) • Hockey East First All-Star Team (2010) • NCAA East First All-American Team (2010)

COHEN, Zach (KOHN, ZAK) COL.

Left wing. Shoots left. 6'3", 208 lbs. Born, Schaumburg, IL, February 6, 1987.

			Regular Season					Playoffs				
Season	Club	League	GP	G	A	Pts	PIM	GP	G	A	Pts	PIM
2004-05	Tri-City Storm	USHL	48	8	10	18	32	....	....	....	....	....
2005-06	Tri-City Storm	USHL	60	18	15	33	46	....	....	....	....	....
2006-07	Boston University	H-East	33	1	2	3	8	....	....	....	....	....
2007-08	Boston University	H-East	18	2	4	6	8	....	....	....	....	....
2008-09	Boston University	H-East	41	13	5	18	22	....	....	....	....	....
2009-10	Boston University	H-East	38	15	10	25	30	....	....	....	....	....
	Lake Erie Monsters	AHL	10	1	3	4	4	....	....	....	....	....

Signed as a free agent by **Colorado**, March 23, 2010.

COLBORNE, Joe (KOHL-bohrn, JOH) BOS.

Center. Shoots left. 6'5", 216 lbs. Born, Calgary, Alta., January 30, 1990.
(Boston's 1st choice, 16th overall, in 2008 Entry Draft).

			Regular Season					Playoffs				
Season	Club	League	GP	G	A	Pts	PIM	GP	G	A	Pts	PIM
2005-06	Notre Dame	SMHL	48	13	14	27	26	....	....	....	....	....
2006-07	Camrose Kodiaks	AJHL	53	20	28	48	44	16	5	1	6	10
2007-08	Camrose Kodiaks	AJHL	55	33	*57	90	48	18	8	8	*16	26
2008-09	U. of Denver	WCHA	40	10	21	31	24	....	....	....	....	....
2009-10	U. of Denver	WCHA	39	22	19	41	30	....	....	....	....	....
	Providence Bruins	AHL	6	0	2	2	2	....	....	....	....	....

WCHA All-Rookie Team (2009)

COLE, Brad (KOHL, BRAD)

Defense. Shoots left. 6'4", 200 lbs. Born, Miniota, Man., October 21, 1986.

			Regular Season					Playoffs				
Season	Club	League	GP	G	A	Pts	PIM	GP	G	A	Pts	PIM
2003-04	Seattle	WHL	6	0	0	0	12	....	....	....	....	....
	Kootenay Ice	WHL	52	0	1	1	39	4	1	0	1	2
2004-05	Kootenay Ice	WHL	39	1	2	3	35	8	0	1	1	2
2005-06	Kootenay Ice	WHL	16	1	2	3	20	....	....	....	....	....
	Saskatoon Blades	WHL	56	3	12	15	64	9	1	0	1	23
2006-07	Saskatoon Blades	WHL	63	16	25	41	83	....	....	....	....	....
2007-08	Quad City Flames	AHL	25	1	4	5	13	....	....	....	....	....
	Las Vegas	ECHL	19	0	4	4	11	....	....	....	....	....
2008-09	Quad City Flames	AHL	73	3	8	11	53	....	....	....	....	....
2009-10	Abbotsford Heat	AHL	63	1	9	10	37	1	0	0	0	0

Signed as a free agent by **Calgary**, May 22, 2007.

COLE, Ian (KOHL, EE-an) ST.L.

Defense. Shoots left. 6'1", 217 lbs. Born, Ann Arbour, MI, February 21, 1989.
(St. Louis' 2nd choice, 18th overall, in 2007 Entry Draft).

			Regular Season					Playoffs				
Season	Club	League	GP	G	A	Pts	PIM	GP	G	A	Pts	PIM
2004-05	Det. Victory Honda	MWEHL	60	15	25	40	....	....	....	....	....	....
2005-06	USNTDP	U-17	18	2	1	3	14	....	....	....	....	....
	USNTDP	NAHL	40	2	8	10	75	12	0	3	3	14
2006-07	USNTDP	U-18	42	6	11	17	36	....	....	....	....	....
	USNTDP	NAHL	16	2	7	9	28	....	....	....	....	....
2007-08	U. of Notre Dame	CCHA	43	8	12	20	40	....	....	....	....	....
2008-09	U. of Notre Dame	CCHA	38	6	20	26	58	....	....	....	....	....
2009-10	U. of Notre Dame	CCHA	30	3	16	19	55	....	....	....	....	....
	Peoria Rivermen	AHL	9	1	4	5	4	....	....	....	....	....

CCHA First All-Star Team (2009) • NCAA West First All-American Team (2009)

COLLINS, Sean (KAW-lihnz, SHAWN) CBJ

Center. Shoots left. 6'1", 199 lbs. Born, Saskatoon, Sask., December 29, 1988.
(Columbus' 9th choice, 187th overall, in 2008 Entry Draft).

			Regular Season					Playoffs				
Season	Club	League	GP	G	A	Pts	PIM	GP	G	A	Pts	PIM
2006-07	Waywayseecappo	MJHL	70	20	69	89	34	....	....	....	....	....
2007-08	Waywayseecappo	MJHL	60	51	64	115	34	7	9	4	13	10
2008-09	Cornell Big Red	ECAC	33	3	3	6	16	....	....	....	....	....
2009-10	Cornell Big Red	ECAC	34	7	3	10	12	....	....	....	....	....

COMRIE, Adam (KAWM-ree, A-duhm) FLA.

Defense. Shoots left. 6'4", 205 lbs. Born, Kanata, Ont., July 31, 1990.
(Florida's 3rd choice, 80th overall, in 2008 Entry Draft).

			Regular Season					Playoffs				
Season	Club	League	GP	G	A	Pts	PIM	GP	G	A	Pts	PIM
2006-07	Ohio	USHL	19	6	4	10	28	....	....	....	....	....
	Omaha Lancers	USHL	38	1	6	7	27	5	0	0	0	4
2007-08	Saginaw Spirit	OHL	58	10	18	28	90	4	0	0	0	4
2008-09	Saginaw Spirit	OHL	52	9	21	30	70	8	0	2	2	8
2009-10	Guelph Storm	OHL	68	14	26	40	79	5	1	2	3	4

CONBOY, Andrew (KAWN-boi, AN-droo) MTL.

Left wing. Shoots left. 6'4", 199 lbs. Born, Burnsville, MN, May 16, 1988.
(Montreal's 7th choice, 142nd overall, in 2007 Entry Draft).

			Regular Season					Playoffs				
Season	Club	League	GP	G	A	Pts	PIM	GP	G	A	Pts	PIM
2005-06	Wichita Falls	NAHL	51	7	8	15	158	5	0	2	2	2
2006-07	Omaha Lancers	USHL	56	25	25	50	105	....	....	....	....	....
2007-08	Omaha Lancers	USHL	58	17	21	38	188	14	*9	1	10	24
2008-09	Michigan State	CCHA	21	3	2	5	76	....	....	....	....	....
	Hamilton Bulldogs	AHL	15	0	1	1	6	1	0	0	0	2
2009-10	Hamilton Bulldogs	AHL	68	8	5	13	73	19	1	2	3	28

CONDON, Nathan (KOHN-duhn, NAY-thun) COL.

Center. Shoots left. 6', 180 lbs. Born, Wausau, WI, May 29, 1990.
(Colorado's 7th choice, 200th overall, in 2008 Entry Draft).

			Regular Season					Playoffs				
Season	Club	League	GP	G	A	Pts	PIM	GP	G	A	Pts	PIM
2004-05	Wausau West	High-WI	22	1	4	5	4	....	....	....	....	....
2005-06	Wausau West	High-WI	22	21	22	43	6	....	....	....	....	....
	Team Wisconsin	UMHSEL	24	16	13	29	10	....	....	....	....	....
2006-07	Wausau West	High-WI	21	21	27	48	10	....	....	....	....	....
	Team Wisconsin	UMHSEL	23	14	9	23	6	....	....	....	....	....
2007-08	Wausau West	High-WI	23	33	26	59	10	....	....	....	....	....
	Team Wisconsin	UMHSEL	24	20	25	45	6	....	....	....	....	....
2008-09	Fargo Force	USHL	58	11	18	29	20	10	1	5	6	2
2009-10	Fargo Force	USHL	60	23	28	51	20	13	3	2	5	6

CONDRA, Erik (KAWN-druh, AIR-ihk) OTT.

Right wing. Shoots right. 6', 186 lbs. Born, Trenton, MI, August 6, 1986.
(Ottawa's 7th choice, 211th overall, in 2006 Entry Draft).

			Regular Season					Playoffs				
Season	Club	League	GP	G	A	Pts	PIM	GP	G	A	Pts	PIM
2004-05	Lincoln Stars	USHL	60	30	30	60	56	4	0	2	2	4
2005-06	U. of Notre Dame	CCHA	36	6	28	34	32	....	....	....	....	....
2006-07	U. of Notre Dame	CCHA	42	14	34	48	18	....	....	....	....	....
2007-08	U. of Notre Dame	CCHA	41	15	23	38	26	....	....	....	....	....
2008-09	U. of Notre Dame	CCHA	40	13	25	38	34	....	....	....	....	....
2009-10	Binghamton	AHL	80	11	27	38	61	....	....	....	....	....

CCHA All-Rookie Team (2006) • CCHA Second All-Star Team (2009) • NCAA West Second All-American Team (2009)

CONNAUTON, Kevin (kuh-NAW-tuhn, KEH-vihn) VAN.

Defense. Shoots left. 6'2", 200 lbs. Born, Edmonton, Alta., February 23, 1990.
(Vancouver's 3rd choice, 83rd overall, in 2009 Entry Draft).

			Regular Season					Playoffs				
Season	Club	League	GP	G	A	Pts	PIM	GP	G	A	Pts	PIM
2007-08	Spruce Grove	AJHL	56	13	32	45	59	15	5	0	5	18
2008-09	Western Mich.	CCHA	40	7	11	18	44	....	....	....	....	....
2009-10	Vancouver Giants	WHL	69	24	48	72	107	16	3	10	13	21

WHL West First All-Star Team (2010) • Canadian Major Junior All-Rookie Team (2010)

CONNELLY, Brian (KAW-nuh-lee, BRIGH-uhn) CHI.

Defense. Shoots left. 5'10", 167 lbs. Born, Bloomington, MN, June 10, 1986.

			Regular Season					Playoffs				
Season	Club	League	GP	G	A	Pts	PIM	GP	G	A	Pts	PIM
2004-05	Bloomington-Jeff.	High-MN	....	18	45	63	....	....	....	....	....	....
	Tri-City Storm	USHL	20	0	3	3	12	9	0	1	1	2
2005-06	Tri-City Storm	USHL	54	3	9	12	16	5	1	0	1	0
2006-07	Colorado College	WCHA	35	2	15	17	22	....	....	....	....	....
2007-08	Colorado College	WCHA	41	3	16	19	32	....	....	....	....	....
2008-09	Colorado College	WCHA	38	3	24	27	46	....	....	....	....	....
	Rockford IceHogs	AHL	9	1	2	3	6	3	0	0	0	2
2009-10	Rockford IceHogs	AHL	78	4	31	35	28	4	0	3	3	2

Signed to an ATO (amateur tryout) contract by **Chicago**, March 23, 2009.

CONNOLLY, Brett (KAW-noh-lee, BREHT) T.B.

Right wing. Shoots right. 6'2", 181 lbs. Born, Campbell River, B.C., May 2, 1992.
(Tampa Bay's 1st choice, 6th overall, in 2010 Entry Draft).

			Regular Season					Playoffs				
Season	Club	League	GP	G	A	Pts	PIM	GP	G	A	Pts	PIM
2007-08	Cariboo Cougars	BCMML	38	16	16	32	80	6	4	1	5	10
	Prince George	WHL	4	0	0	0	0	....	....	....	....	....
2008-09	Prince George	WHL	65	30	30	60	38	4	0	2	2	6
2009-10	Prince George	WHL	16	10	9	19	8	....	....	....	....	....

WHL Rookie of the Year (2009) • Canadian Major Junior All-Rookie Team (2009) • Canadian Major Junior Rookie of the Year (2009)

• Missed majority of 2009-10 season recovering from hip injury.

CORMIER, Kevin (KOHR-mee-ay, KEH-vihn) N.J.

Right wing. Shoots left. 6'2", 230 lbs. Born, Moncton, N.B., January 27, 1986.
(Phoenix's 6th choice, 168th overall, in 2004 Entry Draft).

			Regular Season					Playoffs				
Season	Club	League	GP	G	A	Pts	PIM	GP	G	A	Pts	PIM
2003-04	Moncton	MJrHL	42	3	2	5	235	4	0	0	0	52
	Halifax	QMJHL	1	0	0	0	5	....	....	....	....	....
2004-05	Halifax	QMJHL	60	2	5	7	235	9	0	0	0	8
2005-06	Halifax	QMJHL	69	16	11	27	202	11	0	1	1	18
2006-07	Rimouski Oceanic	QMJHL	28	5	4	9	97	....	....	....	....	....
	Shawinigan	QMJHL	25	7	5	12	70	3	0	0	0	4
2007-08	Arizona Sundogs	CHL	23	3	2	5	104	....	....	....	....	....
2008-09	Lowell Devils	AHL	1	0	0	0	5	....	....	....	....	....
	Trenton Devils	ECHL	29	2	2	4	94	3	0	0	0	0
2009-10	Lowell Devils	AHL	9	0	0	0	17	....	....	....	....	....
	Trenton Devils	ECHL	10	1	0	1	24	....	....	....	....	....

Traded to **New Jersey** by **Phoenix** for Sean Zimmerman, September 12, 2008.

CORMIER, Patrice (KOHR-mee-ay, pa-TREEZ) ATL.

Center. Shoots left. 6'2", 210 lbs. Born, Moncton, N.B., June 14, 1990.
(New Jersey's 3rd choice, 54th overall, in 2008 Entry Draft).

			Regular Season					Playoffs				
Season	Club	League	GP	G	A	Pts	PIM	GP	G	A	Pts	PIM
2006-07	Rimouski Oceanic	QMJHL	53	11	10	21	73	....	....	....	....	....
2007-08	Rimouski Oceanic	QMJHL	51	18	23	41	84	9	4	5	9	10
2008-09	Rimouski Oceanic	QMJHL	54	23	28	51	118	13	4	6	10	30
2009-10	Rimouski Oceanic	QMJHL	28	11	15	26	57	....	....	....	....	....
	Rouyn-Noranda	QMJHL	3	0	5	5	7	....	....	....	....	....
	Chicago Wolves	AHL	....	....	....	....	....	9	0	0	0	8

Traded to **Atlanta** by **New Jersey** with Johnny Oduya, Niclas Bergfors and New Jersey's 1st (later traded to Chicago - Chicago selected Kevin Hayes) and 2nd (later traded to Chicago - Chicago selected Justin Holl) round choices in 2010 Entry Draft for Ilya Kovalchuk, Anssi Salmela and Atlanta's 2nd round choice (Jonathon Merrill) in 2010 Entry Draft, February 4, 2010.

CORNET, Philippe (kohr-NAY, fih-LEEP) EDM.

Left wing. Shoots left. 6', 173 lbs. Born, Val-Senneville, Que., March 28, 1990.
(Edmonton's 3rd choice, 133rd overall, in 2008 Entry Draft).

			Regular Season					Playoffs				
Season	Club	League	GP	G	A	Pts	PIM	GP	G	A	Pts	PIM
2006-07	Rimouski Oceanic	QMJHL	46	7	14	21	8	....	....	....	....	....
2007-08	Rimouski Oceanic	QMJHL	61	23	26	49	24	9	3	3	6	6
2008-09	Rimouski Oceanic	QMJHL	63	29	48	77	34	13	4	11	15	14
2009-10	Rouyn-Noranda	QMJHL	65	28	49	77	32	11	5	6	11	6

COSTELLO, Jeff (kaw-STEHL-oh, JEHF) OTT.

Left wing. Shoots left. 5'11", 198 lbs. Born, Milwaukee, WI, November 20, 1990.
(Ottawa's 6th choice, 146th overall, in 2009 Entry Draft).

			Regular Season					Playoffs				
Season	Club	League	GP	G	A	Pts	PIM	GP	G	A	Pts	PIM
2005-06	Catholic Memorial	High-WI	....	13	16	29	....	....	....	....	....	....
2006-07	Catholic Memorial	High-WI	....	34	20	54	....	....	....	....	....	....
2007-08	Catholic Memorial	High-WI	22	31	17	48	60	....	....	....	....	....
	Team Wisconsin	UMHSEL	....	18	18	36	....	....	....	....	....	....
2008-09	Cedar Rapids	USHL	54	24	9	33	73	5	0	2	2	0
2009-10	Cedar Rapids	USHL	54	29	19	48	149	5	2	3	5	8

• Signed Letter of Intent to attend **University of Notre Dame** (CCHA) in fall of 2010.

COWICK, Corey (KOW-ihk, KOH-ree) OTT.

Left wing. Shoots left. 6'3", 208 lbs. Born, Gloucester, Ont., August 1, 1989.
(Ottawa's 7th choice, 160th overall, in 2009 Entry Draft).

			Regular Season					Playoffs				
Season	Club	League	GP	G	A	Pts	PIM	GP	G	A	Pts	PIM
2006-07	Oshawa Generals	OHL	67	4	4	8	54	9	0	0	0	2
2007-08	Oshawa Generals	OHL	63	11	14	25	79	15	1	1	2	22
2008-09	Ottawa 67's	OHL	68	34	26	60	48	7	7	2	9	14
2009-10	Ottawa 67's	OHL	27	15	6	21	33	12	9	3	12	27

• Missed majority of 2009-10 season recovering from shoulder injury suffered in pre-season game at Kingston, August 30, 2009.

COYLE, Charlie (KOYL, CHAR-lee) S.J.

Center/Right wing. Shoots right. 6'2", 205 lbs. Born, E. Weymouth, MA, March 2, 1992.
(San Jose's 1st choice, 28th overall, in 2010 Entry Draft).

			Regular Season					Playoffs				
Season	Club	League	GP	G	A	Pts	PIM	GP	G	A	Pts	PIM
2007-08	Thayer Academy	High-MA	....	14	23	37	....	....	....	....	....	....
2008-09	Thayer Academy	High-MA	26	20	28	48	4	....	....	....	....	....
2009-10	South Shore	EJHL	42	21	42	63	50	....	....	....	....	....
	USNTDP	U-18	4	1	0	1	2	....	....	....	....	....

• Signed Letter of Intent to attend **Boston University** (Hockey East) in fall of 2010.

COYLE, Jace (KOYL, JAYS) DAL.

Defense. Shoots right. 5'11", 180 lbs. Born, Cranbrook, B.C., May 24, 1990.

			Regular Season					Playoffs				
Season	Club	League	GP	G	A	Pts	PIM	GP	G	A	Pts	PIM
2007-08	Spokane Chiefs	WHL	52	1	8	9	23	....	....	....	....	....
2008-09	Medicine Hat	WHL	72	8	16	24	74	11	1	2	3	6
2009-10	Medicine Hat	WHL	68	10	36	46	64	12	3	1	4	14

Signed as a free agent by **Dallas**, July 9, 2010.

CRACKNELL, Adam (krak-NEHL, A-duhm) ST.L.

Right wing. Shoots right. 6'2", 210 lbs. Born, Prince Albert, Sask., July 15, 1985.
(Calgary's 10th choice, 279th overall, in 2004 Entry Draft).

			Regular Season					Playoffs				
Season	Club	League	GP	G	A	Pts	PIM	GP	G	A	Pts	PIM
2002-03	Kootenay Ice	WHL	67	7	4	11	37	11	0	0	0	2
2003-04	Kootenay Ice	WHL	72	26	35	61	63	4	1	1	2	2
2004-05	Kootenay Ice	WHL	72	19	29	48	65	16	8	8	16	6
2005-06	Kootenay Ice	WHL	72	42	51	93	85	6	1	4	5	6
	Omaha	AHL	6	1	2	3	2	....	....	....	....	....
2006-07	Las Vegas	ECHL	31	8	14	22	35	8	3	3	6	6
2007-08	Quad City Flames	AHL	4	1	0	1	0	....	....	....	....	....
	Las Vegas	ECHL	61	29	30	59	47	21	9	13	22	4
2008-09	Quad City Flames	AHL	79	10	16	26	36	....	....	....	....	....
2009-10	Peoria Rivermen	AHL	76	17	21	38	40	....	....	....	....	....

WHL West Second All-Star Team (2006)

Signed as a free agent by **St. Louis**, July 23, 2009.

CRANE, Chris (KRAYN, KRIHS-tuh-fuhr) S.J.

Right wing. Shoots right. 6'1", 185 lbs. Born, Virginia Beach, VA, December 2, 1991.
(San Jose's 8th choice, 200th overall, in 2010 Entry Draft).

			Regular Season					Playoffs				
Season	Club	League	GP	G	A	Pts	PIM	GP	G	A	Pts	PIM
2008-09	Green Bay	USHL	48	10	9	19	120	5	2	1	3	2
2009-10	Green Bay	USHL	52	15	14	29	107	12	2	3	5	27

• Signed Letter of Intent to attend **Ohio State University** (CCHA) in fall of 2010 or 2011.

CRAWFORD, Nick (KRAW-fuhrd, NIHK) BUF.

Defense. Shoots left. 6'1", 199 lbs. Born, Brampton, Ont., February 23, 1990.
(Buffalo's 8th choice, 164th overall, in 2008 Entry Draft).

			Regular Season					Playoffs				
Season	Club	League	GP	G	A	Pts	PIM	GP	G	A	Pts	PIM
2006-07	Saginaw Spirit	OHL	63	1	7	8	32	5	0	1	1	0
2007-08	Saginaw Spirit	OHL	68	4	16	20	58	4	1	1	2	2
2008-09	Saginaw Spirit	OHL	65	7	35	42	41	8	1	4	5	4
2009-10	Saginaw Spirit	OHL	19	4	17	21	4	....	....	....	....	....
	Barrie Colts	OHL	49	7	42	49	20	17	0	12	12	4

OHL First All-Star Team (2010) • Canadian Major Junior Second All-Star Team (2010)

CROSS, Tommy (KRAWS, TAW-mee) BOS.

Defense. Shoots left. 6'3", 215 lbs. Born, Hartford, CT, September 12, 1989.
(Boston's 2nd choice, 35th overall, in 2007 Entry Draft).

			Regular Season					Playoffs				
Season	Club	League	GP	G	A	Pts	PIM	GP	G	A	Pts	PIM
2004-05	Simsbury	High-CT	23	5	40	45	18	....	....	....	....	....
2005-06	Simsbury	High-CT	22	15	35	50	....	....	....	....	....	....
2006-07	Westminster	High-CT	25	8	12	20	20	....	....	....	....	....
	USNTDP	NAHL	2	0	2	2	0	....	....	....	....	....
	USNTDP	U-18	11	0	1	1	8	....	....	....	....	....
2007-08	Westminster	High-CT	25	9	12	21	....	....	....	....	....	....
	Ohio	USHL	9	0	4	4	8	....	....	....	....	....
2008-09	Boston College	H-East	24	0	8	8	24	....	....	....	....	....
2009-10	Boston College	H-East	38	5	5	10	36	....	....	....	....	....

CROWDER, Paul (KROW-duhr, PAWL)

Center. Shoots right. 6'3", 180 lbs. Born, Victoria, B.C., February 12, 1985.

			Regular Season					Playoffs				
Season	Club	League	GP	G	A	Pts	PIM	GP	G	A	Pts	PIM
2002-03	Powell River Kings	BCHL	STATISTICS NOT AVAILABLE									
2003-04	Powell River Kings	BCHL	58	19	39	58	57	7	1	3	4	2
2004-05	South Surrey	BCHL	20	2	9	11	20	....	....	....	....	....
	Coquitlam Express	BCHL	27	12	25	37	32	1	0	0	0	0
2005-06	Burnaby Express	BCHL	14	3	10	13	13	....	....	....	....	....
2006-07	Alaska Anchorage	WCHA	37	11	13	24	26	....	....	....	....	....
2007-08	Alaska-Anchorage	WCHA	35	7	16	23	10	....	....	....	....	....
2008-09	Alaska-Anchorage	WCHA	35	14	19	33	44	....	....	....	....	....
	Hartford Wolf Pack	AHL	11	0	3	3	6	5	0	0	0	4
2009-10	Hartford Wolf Pack	AHL	79	12	14	26	26	....	....	....	....	....

Signed as a free agent by **NY Rangers**, March 19, 2009.

CULEK, Jakub (TSOO-lehk, YA-koob) OTT.

Left wing. Shoots left. 6'2", 177 lbs. Born, Klatovy, Czechoslovakia, September 7, 1992.
(Ottawa's 1st choice, 76th overall, in 2010 Entry Draft).

			Regular Season					Playoffs				
Season	Club	League	GP	G	A	Pts	PIM	GP	G	A	Pts	PIM
2006-07	HC Kladno U17	CzR-U17	5	1	0	1	0	....	....	....	....	....
2007-08	HC Plzen U17	CzR-U17	44	12	22	34	76	8	1	4	5	10
2008-09	HC Plzen U17	CzR-U17	29	15	16	31	98	1	0	0	0	0
	HC Plzen Jr.	CzRep-Jr.	12	3	2	5	10	5	3	0	3	0
2009-10	Rimouski Oceanic	QMJHL	63	13	34	47	54	12	6	3	9	4

CUMA, Tyler (KOO-ma, TIGH-luhr) MIN.

Defense. Shoots left. 6'1", 198 lbs. Born, Toronto, Ont., January 19, 1990.
(Minnesota's 1st choice, 23rd overall, in 2008 Entry Draft).

			Regular Season					Playoffs				
Season	Club	League	GP	G	A	Pts	PIM	GP	G	A	Pts	PIM
2005-06	Mississauga Reps	GTHL	40	15	20	35	52	....	....	....	....	....
2006-07	Ottawa 67's	OHL	63	3	16	19	55	5	0	2	2	6
2007-08	Ottawa 67's	OHL	59	4	28	32	69	4	1	1	2	2
2008-09	Ottawa 67's	OHL	21	1	8	9	27	....	....	....	....	....
2009-10	Ottawa 67's	OHL	52	5	17	22	73	12	0	5	5	20

• Missed majority of 2008-09 season recovering from knee injury suffered at Team Canada Juniors training camp, December 12, 2008.

CUNDARI, Mark (kuhn-DAHR-ee, MAHRK) ST.L.

Defense. Shoots left. 5'9", 200 lbs. Born, Woodbridge, Ont., April 23, 1990.

			Regular Season					Playoffs				
Season	Club	League	GP	G	A	Pts	PIM	GP	G	A	Pts	PIM
2005-06	Vaughan Vipers	OPJHL	2	0	0	0	0	....	....	....	....	....
2006-07	Windsor Spitfires	OHL	62	6	16	22	130	....	....	....	....	....
2007-08	Windsor Spitfires	OHL	63	6	17	23	141	3	0	0	0	10
2008-09	Windsor Spitfires	OHL	60	10	22	32	143	20	1	8	9	38
2009-10	Windsor Spitfires	OHL	63	8	46	54	139	19	3	15	18	42

Signed as a free agent by **St. Louis**, September 24, 2008.

CUNNING, Cam (KUH-nihng, KAM) CGY.

Left wing. Shoots left. 6'1", 213 lbs. Born, Powell River, B.C., June 4, 1985.
(Calgary's 8th choice, 240th overall, in 2003 Entry Draft).

			Regular Season					Playoffs				
Season	Club	League	GP	G	A	Pts	PIM	GP	G	A	Pts	PIM
2002-03	Kamloops Blazers	WHL	71	7	12	19	54	6	1	0	1	2
2003-04	Kamloops Blazers	WHL	65	14	13	27	62	5	1	1	2	10
2004-05	Kamloops Blazers	WHL	39	14	8	22	63	....	....	....	....	....
	Vancouver Giants	WHL	30	3	7	10	19	6	1	3	4	14
2005-06	Red Deer Rebels	WHL	40	19	13	32	52	....	....	....	....	....
	Omaha	AHL	30	2	4	6	24	....	....	....	....	....
2006-07	Omaha	AHL	60	12	5	17	45	6	0	2	2	2
2007-08	Quad City Flames	AHL	68	11	4	15	80	....	....	....	....	....
2008-09	Quad City Flames	AHL	63	7	14	21	38	....	....	....	....	....
2009-10	Abbotsford Heat	AHL	69	19	19	38	64	13	1	2	3	6

CUNNINGHAM, Craig (KUN-ihng-ham, KRAYG) BOS.

Left wing. Shoots right. 5'10", 186 lbs. Born, Trail, B.C., September 13, 1990.
(Boston's 4th choice, 97th overall, in 2010 Entry Draft).

			Regular Season					Playoffs				
Season	Club	League	GP	G	A	Pts	PIM	GP	G	A	Pts	PIM
2005-06	Beaver Valley	KIJHL	47	19	25	44	22	16	4	5	9	29
2006-07	Vancouver Giants	WHL	48	0	5	5	38	15	0	1	1	15
2007-08	Vancouver Giants	WHL	67	11	14	25	72	10	1	2	3	6
2008-09	Vancouver Giants	WHL	72	28	22	50	62	17	5	9	14	12
2009-10	Vancouver Giants	WHL	72	37	60	97	44	16	12	12	24	12

WHL West First All-Star Team (2010)

CURRY, Sean (KUH-ree, SHAWN)

Defense. Shoots right. 6'4", 230 lbs. Born, Burnsville, MN, April 29, 1982.
(Carolina's 6th choice, 211th overall, in 2001 Entry Draft).

			Regular Season					Playoffs				
Season	Club	League	GP	G	A	Pts	PIM	GP	G	A	Pts	PIM
99-2000	Burnsville	High-MN	23	8	18	26	....	....	....	....	....	....
2000-01	Tri-City Americans	WHL	72	5	12	17	113	....	....	....	....	....
2001-02	Tri-City Americans	WHL	36	6	6	12	84	....	....	....	....	....
	Medicine Hat	WHL	24	4	13	17	43	....	....	....	....	....
2002-03	Lowell	AHL	35	0	2	2	62	....	....	....	....	....
	Florida Everblades	ECHL	32	1	6	7	77	1	0	0	0	0
2003-04	Lowell	AHL	74	1	8	9	66	....	....	....	....	....
2004-05	Lowell	AHL	61	2	7	9	103	7	0	1	1	4
2005-06	Providence Bruins	AHL	72	4	4	8	144	6	0	1	1	20
2006-07	Providence Bruins	AHL	64	5	8	13	122	13	2	9	11	28
2007-08	Providence Bruins	AHL	72	13	25	38	139	10	0	4	4	27
2008-09	Philadelphia	AHL	80	5	13	18	72	4	0	0	0	2
2009-10	Adirondack	AHL	67	4	7	11	73	....	....	....	....	....

Signed as a free agent by **Boston**, August 8, 2007. Signed as a free agent by **Philadelphia**, July 1, 2008.

CZARNIK, Robert (CHAHR-nihk, RAW-buhrt) L.A.

Right wing. Shoots right. 6', 178 lbs. Born, Detroit, MI, January 25, 1990.
(Los Angeles' 4th choice, 63rd overall, in 2008 Entry Draft).

			Regular Season					Playoffs				
Season	Club	League	GP	G	A	Pts	PIM	GP	G	A	Pts	PIM
2005-06	Det. Honeybaked	MWEHL	....	53	78	131	....	....	....	....	....	....
2006-07	USNTDP	U-17	19	10	2	12	22	....	....	....	....	....
	USNTDP	NAHL	46	7	10	17	46	....	....	....	....	....
2007-08	USNTDP	U-18	43	15	18	33	30	....	....	....	....	....
	USNTDP	NAHL	14	4	2	6	12	....	....	....	....	....
2008-09	U. of Michigan	CCHA	39	5	11	16	32	....	....	....	....	....
2009-10	U. of Michigan	CCHA	12	3	3	6	4	....	....	....	....	....

CZERWONKA, Drew (chuhr-WAWN-kuh, DROO) EDM.

Left wing. Shoots left. 6'2", 189 lbs. Born, Wolseley, Sask., July 1, 1992.
(Edmonton's 9th choice, 166th overall, in 2010 Entry Draft).

			Regular Season					Playoffs				
Season	Club	League	GP	G	A	Pts	PIM	GP	G	A	Pts	PIM
2007-08	Reg. Pat Cdns.	SMHL	42	18	10	28	113	5	2	0	2	44
	Kootenay Ice	WHL	2	0	0	0	0	....	....	....	....	....
2008-09	Kootenay Ice	WHL	55	16	2	18	83	4	0	0	0	5
2009-10	Kootenay Ice	WHL	54	4	9	13	106	6	1	2	3	9

D'AGOSTINO, Nicholas (DA-goh-STEE-noh, NIHK-oh-las) PIT.

Defense. Shoots left. 6'1", 177 lbs. Born, Mississauga, Ont., June 24, 1990.
(Pittsburgh's 4th choice, 210th overall, in 2008 Entry Draft).

			Regular Season					Playoffs				
Season	Club	League	GP	G	A	Pts	PIM	GP	G	A	Pts	PIM
2006-07	Tor. Young Nats	GTHL	30	5	21	26	....	5	0	4	4	....
	Young Nats	Exhib.	8	1	5	6	....	....	....	....	....	....
2007-08	St. Michael's	OPJHL	46	5	18	23	22	12	0	3	3	8
2008-09	St. Michael's	OJHL	43	9	24	33	34	6	2	3	5	8
2009-10	Cornell Big Red	ECAC	32	4	14	18	6	....	....	....	....	....

DAHLSTROM, Andreas (DAHL-stuhm, an–DRAY-uhs) ANA.

Center. Shoots left. 5'11", 176 lbs. Born, Huddinge, Sweden, June 22, 1991.
(Anaheim's 6th choice, 161st overall, in 2010 Entry Draft).

			Regular Season					Playoffs				
Season	Club	League	GP	G	A	Pts	PIM	GP	G	A	Pts	PIM
2007-08	AIK IF Solna U18	Swe-U18	25	6	10	16	16	....	....	....	....	....
	AIK IF Solna Jr.	Swe-Jr.	9	1	2	3	8	....	....	....	....	....
2008-09	AIK IF Solna U18	Swe-U18	11	6	9	15	33	7	2	11	13	31
	AIK IF Solna Jr.	Swe-Jr.	28	5	5	10	67	....	....	....	....	....
	AIK IF Solna	Sweden-2	4	0	0	0	0	....	....	....	....	....
2009-10	AIK IF Solna Jr.	Swe-Jr.	5	4	6	10	2	....	....	....	....	....
	AIK IF Solna	Sweden-2	6	1	2	3	4	....	....	....	....	....

DALPE, Zac (DAL-pee, ZAK) CAR.

Right wing. Shoots right. 6'1", 195 lbs. Born, Paris, Ont., November 1, 1989.
(Carolina's 2nd choice, 45th overall, in 2008 Entry Draft).

			Regular Season					Playoffs				
Season	Club	League	GP	G	A	Pts	PIM	GP	G	A	Pts	PIM
2006-07	Stratford Cullitons	OJHL-B	52	30	43	73	68	....	....	....	....	....
2007-08	Penticton Vees	BCHL	46	27	36	63	14	15	8	9	17	4
2008-09	Ohio State	CCHA	37	13	12	25	25	....	....	....	....	....
2009-10	Ohio State	CCHA	39	*21	24	45	19	....	....	....	....	....
	Albany River Rats	AHL	9	6	2	8	0	8	3	3	6	0

CCHA All-Rookie Team (2009) • CCHA First All-Star Team (2010) • NCAA West Second All-American Team (2010)

D'AMIGO, Jerry (dah-MEE-goh, JAIR-ree) TOR.

Right wing. Shoots left. 5'11", 208 lbs. Born, Binghamton, NY, February 19, 1991.
(Toronto's 6th choice, 158th overall, in 2009 Entry Draft).

			Regular Season					Playoffs				
Season	Club	League	GP	G	A	Pts	PIM	GP	G	A	Pts	PIM
2007-08	USNTDP	NAHL	44	5	12	17	59	3	1	1	2	6
	USNTDP	U-17	17	5	4	9	10	....	....	....	....	....
2008-09	USNTDP	NAHL	11	8	6	14	4	....	....	....	....	....
	USNTDP	U-18	42	15	27	42	57	....	....	....	....	....
2009-10	RPI Engineers	ECAC	35	10	24	34	37	....	....	....	....	....

ECAC All-Rookie Team (2010) • ECAC Rookie of the Year (2010)

DANIELS, Drew (DA-nyehlz, DROO) S.J.

Right wing. Shoots right. 6'2", 185 lbs. Born, Suffern, NY, June 7, 1989.
(San Jose's 7th choice, 194th overall, in 2008 Entry Draft).

			Regular Season					Playoffs				
Season	Club	League	GP	G	A	Pts	PIM	GP	G	A	Pts	PIM
2006-07	Kent Prep School	High-CT	....	12	22	34	....	....	....	....	....	....
2007-08	Kent Prep School	High-CT	25	12	35	47	14	....	....	....	....	....
2008-09	Sioux City	USHL	53	9	19	28	24	....	....	....	....	....
2009-10	Northeastern	H-East	32	4	4	8	4	....	....	....	....	....

DANIELS, Justin (DA-nyehlz, JUHS-tihn) S.J.

Center. Shoots right. 6'1", 175 lbs. Born, Suffern, NY, June 7, 1989.
(San Jose's 1st choice, 62nd overall, in 2008 Entry Draft).

			Regular Season					Playoffs				
Season	Club	League	GP	G	A	Pts	PIM	GP	G	A	Pts	PIM
2006-07	Kent Prep School	High-CT	....	14	32	46	....	....	....	....	....	....
2007-08	Kent Prep School	High-CT	25	17	37	54	10	....	....	....	....	....
2008-09	Sioux City	USHL	56	9	28	37	17	....	....	....	....	....
2009-10	Northeastern	H-East	32	8	7	15	10	....	....	....	....	....

DANIS-PEPIN, Simon (da-NEE-peh-PEHN, see-MOHN) CHI.

Defense. Shoots right. 6'6", 229 lbs. Born, Gatineau, Que., April 11, 1988.
(Chicago's 3rd choice, 61st overall, in 2006 Entry Draft).

			Regular Season					Playoffs				
Season	Club	League	GP	G	A	Pts	PIM	GP	G	A	Pts	PIM
2003-04	Gatineau Intrepide	QAAA	33	2	14	16	20	2	0	0	0	0
2004-05	Gatineau Intrepide	QAAA	39	6	31	37	64	14	6	7	13	25
2005-06	N.H. Jr. Monarchs	EJHL	2	0	0	0	0	....	....	....	....	....
	U. of Maine	H-East	23	0	5	5	14	....	....	....	....	....
2006-07	U. of Maine	H-East	40	2	4	6	18	....	....	....	....	....
2007-08	U. of Maine	H-East	34	4	8	12	20	....	....	....	....	....
2008-09	U. of Maine	H-East	36	0	13	13	29	....	....	....	....	....
2009-10	Rockford IceHogs	AHL	38	1	7	8	10	....	....	....	....	....
	Toledo Walleye	ECHL	13	1	9	10	13	4	1	3	4	0

DAOUST, Jean-Michel (DAH-oo, ZHAWN-MEE-shehl) MIN.

Right wing. Shoots right. 5'7", 175 lbs. Born, Valleyfield, Que., November 24, 1983.

			Regular Season					Playoffs				
Season	Club	League	GP	G	A	Pts	PIM	GP	G	A	Pts	PIM
2000-01	Hull Olympiques	QMJHL	68	23	27	50	84	5	0	0	0	8
2001-02	Hull Olympiques	QMJHL	72	16	20	36	91	10	2	1	3	11
2002-03	Hull Olympiques	QMJHL	72	34	60	94	104	20	12	25	37	28
2003-04	Gatineau	QMJHL	60	31	65	96	82	15	7	15	22	16
2005-06	Danbury Trashers	UHL	70	30	35	65	73	18	7	4	11	8
2006-07	Cincinnati	ECHL	71	32	30	62	63	10	3	5	8	8
2007-08	Cincinnati	ECHL	36	27	24	51	54	17	6	12	18	14
	Rockford IceHogs	AHL	1	0	0	0	0	....	....	....	....	....
	Wilkes-Barre	AHL	37	5	13	18	4	2	0	0	0	0
2008-09	Wilkes-Barre	AHL	58	10	18	28	24	12	5	4	9	12
2009-10	Houston Aeros	AHL	78	21	34	55	38	....	....	....	....	....

Signed as a free agent by **Houston** (AHL), October 13, 2009. Signed as a free agent by **Minnesota**, May 13, 2010.

DASILVA, Dan (duh-SIHL-vah, DAN)

Right wing. Shoots right. 6'1", 195 lbs. Born, Saskatoon, Sask., April 30, 1985.

			Regular Season					Playoffs				
Season	Club	League	GP	G	A	Pts	PIM	GP	G	A	Pts	PIM
2002-03	Portland	WHL	64	9	13	22	81	7	0	4	4	16
2003-04	Portland	WHL	65	36	20	56	120	5	0	1	1	6
2004-05	Portland	WHL	71	31	42	73	127	5	1	1	2	6
2005-06	Lowell	AHL	25	3	2	5	27	....	....	....	....	....
	San Diego Gulls	ECHL	4	5	3	8	2	....	....	....	....	....
2006-07	Albany River Rats	AHL	43	11	8	19	33	....	....	....	....	....
	Arizona Sundogs	CHL	14	9	13	22	10	....	....	....	....	....
2007-08	Lake Erie Monsters	AHL	54	9	14	23	50	....	....	....	....	....
2008-09	Worcester Sharks	AHL	26	6	7	13	27	12	3	7	10	6
	Phoenix	ECHL	36	9	12	21	40	....	....	....	....	....
2009-10	Worcester Sharks	AHL	72	21	32	53	65	11	2	6	8	8

Signed as a free agent by **Colorado**, October 11, 2005.

D'AVERSA, Jonathan (dah-VEHR-sah, JAWN-ah-thuhn)

Defense. Shoots right. 6'2", 200 lbs. Born, Richmond Hill, Ont., March 2, 1986.

			Regular Season					Playoffs				
Season	Club	League	GP	G	A	Pts	PIM	GP	G	A	Pts	PIM
2002-03	Stouffville Spirit	OPJHL	49	4	21	25	18	....	....	....	....	....
2003-04	Sudbury Wolves	OHL	63	1	14	15	22	7	0	1	1	2
2004-05	Sudbury Wolves	OHL	67	5	24	29	42	12	4	6	10	8
2005-06	Sudbury Wolves	OHL	62	7	39	46	83	10	2	0	2	17
2006-07	Sudbury Wolves	OHL	67	13	47	60	53	21	3	15	18	16
2007-08	Wilkes-Barre	AHL	27	4	2	6	6	....	....	....	....	....
	Wheeling Nailers	ECHL	25	1	13	14	10	....	....	....	....	....
2008-09	Wilkes-Barre	AHL	68	1	22	23	36	11	0	2	2	4
	Wheeling Nailers	ECHL	3	1	3	4	2	....	....	....	....	....
2009-10	Wilkes-Barre	AHL	21	0	1	1	23	....	....	....	....	....
	Wheeling Nailers	ECHL	22	6	11	17	26	....	....	....	....	....

Signed as a free agent by **Pittsburgh**, May 24, 2007.

DAVIDSON, Brandon (DAY-vihn-suhn, BRAN-duhn) EDM.

Defense. Shoots left. 6'1", 190 lbs. Born, Lethbridge, Alta., August 21, 1991.
(Edmonton's 8th choice, 162nd overall, in 2010 Entry Draft).

			Regular Season					Playoffs				
Season	Club	League	GP	G	A	Pts	PIM	GP	G	A	Pts	PIM
2008-09	Lethbridge	AMHL	31	7	14	21	52	7	2	5	7	14
2009-10	Regina Pats	WHL	59	1	33	34	37	....	....	....	....	....

DAVIS, Nathan (DAY-vihs, NAY-thuhn) **CHI.**

Center/Left wing. Shoots left. 6'1", 205 lbs. Born, Cleveland, OH, May 23, 1986.
(Chicago's 6th choice, 113th overall, in 2005 Entry Draft).

			Regular Season					Playoffs				
Season	Club	League	GP	G	A	Pts	PIM	GP	G	A	Pts	PIM
2002-03	USNTDP	NAHL	20	2	3	5	23	....	....	....	....	....
2003-04	USNTDP	U-18	46	7	8	15	16	....	....	....	....	....
	USNTDP	NAHL	11	3	6	9	17	....	....	....	....	....
2004-05	Miami U.	CCHA	38	14	11	25	30	....	....	....	....	....
2005-06	Miami U.	CCHA	37	20	20	40	34	....	....	....	....	....
2006-07	Miami U.	CCHA	42	21	29	50	24	....	....	....	....	....
2007-08	Miami U.	CCHA	21	8	9	17	14	....	....	....	....	....
2008-09	Rockford IceHogs	AHL	49	5	7	12	16	....	....	....	....	....
2009-10	Rockford IceHogs	AHL	23	8	3	11	10	....	....	....	....	....

CCHA First All-Star Team (2006) • CCHA Second All-Star Team (2007) • NCAA West Second All-American Team (2007)

DAY, Brian (DAY, BRIGH-uhn) **NYI**

Right wing. Shoots right. 6', 195 lbs. Born, Boston, MA, August 4, 1988.
(NY Islanders' 11th choice, 171st overall, in 2006 Entry Draft).

			Regular Season					Playoffs				
Season	Club	League	GP	G	A	Pts	PIM	GP	G	A	Pts	PIM
2003-04	Gov. Dummer	High-MA	25	8	15	23	....	....	....	....	....	....
2004-05	Gov. Dummer	High-MA	25	11	13	24	30	....	....	....	....	....
2005-06	Gov. Dummer	High-MA	28	9	13	22	34	....	....	....	....	....
2006-07	Gov. Academy	High-MA	27	20	18	38	....	....	....	....	....	....
2007-08	Colgate	ECAC	41	9	13	22	53	....	....	....	....	....
2008-09	Colgate	ECAC	34	14	13	27	26	....	....	....	....	....
2009-10	Colgate	ECAC	34	21	15	36	26	....	....	....	....	....

DE HAAN, Calvin (DUH HAWN, CAL-vihn) **NYI**

Defense. Shoots left. 6', 184 lbs. Born, Ottawa, Ont., May 9, 1991.
(NY Islanders' 2nd choice, 12th overall, in 2009 Entry Draft).

			Regular Season					Playoffs				
Season	Club	League	GP	G	A	Pts	PIM	GP	G	A	Pts	PIM
2006-07	Ottawa Valley	Minor-ON	32	4	22	26	20	....	....	....	....	....
2007-08	Kemptville 73's	CJHL	58	3	39	42	14	....	....	....	....	....
2008-09	Oshawa Generals	OHL	68	8	55	63	40	....	....	....	....	....
2009-10	Oshawa Generals	OHL	34	5	19	24	14	....	....	....	....	....

DEE, Robby (DEE, RAW-bee) **EDM.**

Center/Wing. Shoots left. 6'2", 185 lbs. Born, Minneapolis, MN, April 9, 1987.
(Edmonton's 4th choice, 86th overall, in 2005 Entry Draft).

			Regular Season					Playoffs				
Season	Club	League	GP	G	A	Pts	PIM	GP	G	A	Pts	PIM
2004-05	Breck Mustangs	High-MN	28	49	38	87	14	....	....	....	....	....
2005-06	Omaha Lancers	USHL	32	6	6	12	20	3	1	0	1	2
2006-07	Omaha Lancers	USHL	34	11	14	25	60	....	....	....	....	....
2007-08	U. of Maine	H-East	24	1	2	3	18	....	....	....	....	....
2008-09	U. of Maine	H-East	33	6	5	11	24	....	....	....	....	....
2009-10	U. of Maine	H-East	33	13	12	25	32	....	....	....	....	....

DEGON, Marvin (DEE-gawn, MAR-vihn) **MTL.**

Defense. Shoots right. 6', 175 lbs. Born, Worcester, MA, July 20, 1983.

			Regular Season					Playoffs				
Season	Club	League	GP	G	A	Pts	PIM	GP	G	A	Pts	PIM
2002-03	Massachusetts	H-East	36	2	14	16	14	....	....	....	....	....
2003-04	Massachusetts	H-East	36	5	15	20	18	....	....	....	....	....
2004-05	Massachusetts	H-East	38	10	8	18	44	....	....	....	....	....
2005-06	Massachusetts	H-East	36	10	19	29	33	....	....	....	....	....
	Hartford Wolf Pack	AHL	14	2	4	6	4	13	0	5	5	6
2006-07	Hartford Wolf Pack	AHL	71	8	26	34	40	7	0	1	1	0
2007-08	Hamilton Bulldogs	AHL	79	9	22	31	56	....	....	....	....	....
2008-09	Wolfsburg	Germany	52	11	29	40	42	10	3	2	5	8
2009-10	Eisbaren Berlin	Germany	55	4	19	23	32	5	0	1	1	2

Signed as a free agent by **Montreal**, July 5, 2007.

de GRAY, John (DIH-gray, JAWN) **ANA.**

Defense. Shoots left. 6'4", 215 lbs. Born, Richmond Hill, Ont., March 14, 1988.
(Anaheim's 3rd choice, 83rd overall, in 2006 Entry Draft).

			Regular Season					Playoffs				
Season	Club	League	GP	G	A	Pts	PIM	GP	G	A	Pts	PIM
2003-04	Richmond Hill	Minor-ON	76	5	35	40	107	....	....	....	....	....
2004-05	Brampton	OHL	52	2	8	10	51	6	0	0	0	2
2005-06	Brampton	OHL	68	0	10	10	103	11	0	0	0	8
2006-07	Brampton	OHL	65	4	13	17	75	4	1	0	1	10
2007-08	Brampton	OHL	67	4	13	17	140	5	0	0	0	12
	Portland Pirates	AHL	6	0	0	0	0	3	0	0	0	0
2008-09	Iowa Chops	AHL	62	2	5	7	67	....	....	....	....	....
2009-10	Bakersfield	ECHL	29	5	6	11	28	....	....	....	....	....
	Rochester	AHL	41	1	5	6	31	2	0	0	0	2

Loaned to **Rochester** (AHL) by **Anaheim** (Bakersfield-ECHL), December 30, 2009.

DEHART, Tony (deh-HAHRT, TOH-nee) **NYI**

Defense. Shoots right. 6'2", 187 lbs. Born, St. Louis, MO, March 20, 1990.
(NY Islanders' 5th choice, 125th overall, in 2010 Entry Draft).

			Regular Season					Playoffs				
Season	Club	League	GP	G	A	Pts	PIM	GP	G	A	Pts	PIM
2005-06	St. Louis Jr. Blues	Minor-MO	50	5	10	15	40	....	....	....	....	....
2006-07	London Knights	OHL	38	1	4	5	29	....	....	....	....	....
2007-08	London Knights	OHL	34	1	3	4	33	3	0	0	0	0
2008-09	Oshawa Generals	OHL	63	7	20	27	76	....	....	....	....	....
2009-10	Oshawa Generals	OHL	68	10	40	50	82	....	....	....	....	....
	Springfield Falcons	AHL	2	0	0	0	0	....	....	....	....	....

DEILERT, Alexander (DAY-luhrt, al-ehx-AN-duhr) **CGY.**

Defense. Shoots right. 6', 180 lbs. Born, Stockholm, Sweden, February 10, 1989.
(Calgary's 7th choice, 198th overall, in 2008 Entry Draft).

			Regular Season					Playoffs				
Season	Club	League	GP	G	A	Pts	PIM	GP	G	A	Pts	PIM
2004-05	Hammarby U18	Swe-U18	2	2	1	3		....	....	....	....	....
2005-06	Djurgarden U18	Swe-U18	24	6	8	14	41	4	0	0	0	4
2006-07	Djurgarden U18	Swe-U18	11	2	2	4	41	2	0	1	1	6
	Djurgarden Jr.	Swe-Jr.	28	1	4	5	10	7	0	0	0	0
2007-08	Djurgarden Jr.	Swe-Jr.	38	6	12	18	70	7	1	2	3	14
2008-09	Djurgarden Jr.	Swe-Jr.	19	4	7	11	45	....	....	....	....	....
	Almtuna	Sweden-2	6	0	1	1	2	....	....	....	....	....
	Djurgarden	Sweden	6	0	0	0	0	....	....	....	....	....
	Frisk	Norway	4	0	1	1	0	....	....	....	....	....
2009-10	Mora IK	Sweden-2	32	5	11	16	30	....	....	....	....	....
	Djurgarden	Sweden	26	0	1	1	0	5	0	0	0	0

DELISLE, Dan (deh-LIGH-uhl, DAN) **CHI.**

Center/Left wing. Shoots left. 6'4", 222 lbs. Born, Minneapolis, MN, September 24, 1990.
(Chicago's 3rd choice, 89th overall, in 2009 Entry Draft).

			Regular Season					Playoffs				
Season	Club	League	GP	G	A	Pts	PIM	GP	G	A	Pts	PIM
2006-07	Totino-Grace	High-MN	....	21	26	47	....	....	....	....	....	....
2007-08	Totino-Grace	High-MN	27	25	31	56	26	....	....	....	....	....
2008-09	Totino-Grace	High-MN	27	32	24	56	16	....	....	....	....	....
	Team Northeast	UMHSEL	24	12	11	23	....	....	....	....	....	....
2009-10	U. Minn-Duluth	WCHA	25	0	1	1	24	....	....	....	....	....

DELISLE, Steven (deh-LIH-uhl, STEE-vehn) **CBJ**

Defense. Shoots right. 6'6", 224 lbs. Born, Levise, Que., July 30, 1990.
(Columbus' 3rd choice, 107th overall, in 2008 Entry Draft).

			Regular Season					Playoffs				
Season	Club	League	GP	G	A	Pts	PIM	GP	G	A	Pts	PIM
2006-07	Gatineau	QMJHL	56	1	11	12	47	5	0	0	0	0
2007-08	Gatineau	QMJHL	70	6	23	29	82	19	0	10	10	16
2008-09	Gatineau	QMJHL	63	5	25	30	94	10	2	3	5	15
2009-10	Gatineau	QMJHL	39	4	19	23	61	....	....	....	....	....
	Rouyn-Noranda	QMJHL	25	1	5	6	16	11	1	3	4	12

DELLA ROVERE, Stefan (DEHL-ah ROH-vair, STEH-fan) **ST.L.**

Left wing. Shoots left. 5'11", 196 lbs. Born, Richmond Hill, Ont., February 25, 1990.
(Washington's 8th choice, 204th overall, in 2008 Entry Draft).

			Regular Season					Playoffs				
Season	Club	League	GP	G	A	Pts	PIM	GP	G	A	Pts	PIM
2005-06	Tor. Jr. Canadiens	GTHL	47	25	31	56	69	....	....	....	....	....
2006-07	Barrie Colts	OHL	48	7	7	14	37	6	0	0	0	0
2007-08	Barrie Colts	OHL	68	13	19	32	171	9	1	2	3	16
2008-09	Barrie Colts	OHL	57	27	24	51	146	5	2	2	4	19
	South Carolina	ECHL	2	0	1	1	6	....	....	....	....	....
2009-10	Barrie Colts	OHL	57	18	23	41	125	17	8	1	9	29
	Hershey Bears	AHL	....	....	....	....	....	2	0	0	0	0

Traded to **St. Louis** by **Washington** for D.J. King, July 28, 2010.

DELORY, James (deh-LOR-ee, JAYMZ) **FLA.**

Defense. Shoots right. 6'4", 220 lbs. Born, Scarborough, Ont., March 3, 1988.
(San Jose's 3rd choice, 98th overall, in 2006 Entry Draft).

			Regular Season					Playoffs				
Season	Club	League	GP	G	A	Pts	PIM	GP	G	A	Pts	PIM
2004-05	Oshawa Generals	OHL	61	1	4	5	82	....	....	....	....	....
2005-06	Oshawa Generals	OHL	67	6	26	32	136	....	....	....	....	....
2006-07	Oshawa Generals	OHL	61	4	21	25	167	9	0	4	4	16
2007-08	Oshawa Generals	OHL	54	2	20	22	154	15	1	8	9	26
2008-09	Oshawa Generals	OHL	33	4	6	10	53	....	....	....	....	....
	Florida Everblades	ECHL	1	0	0	0	0	....	....	....	....	....
2009-10	Bossier-Shreve.	CHL	36	2	1	3	78	11	0	0	0	19

Signed as a free agent by **Florida**, July 3, 2008.

DENISOV, Denis (den-NEES-ahf, deh-NEES) **BUF.**

Left wing. Shoots left. 6', 183 lbs. Born, Kalinin, USSR, December 31, 1981.
(Buffalo's 4th choice, 149th overall, in 2000 Entry Draft).

			Regular Season					Playoffs				
Season	Club	League	GP	G	A	Pts	PIM	GP	G	A	Pts	PIM
1997-98	HK CSKA Moscow	Russia	7	0	0	0	4	....	....	....	....	....
1998-99	HK CSKA Moscow	Russia-2	42	1	6	7	16	....	....	....	....	....
99-2000	HK Moscow	Russia-2	39	1	8	9	16	....	....	....	....	....
2000-01	HK Moscow	Russia-2	41	0	3	3	6	....	....	....	....	....
2001-02	Krylja Sovetov	Russia	47	3	4	7	37	....	....	....	....	....
	Krylja Sovetov 2	Russia-3	3	0	1	1	18	....	....	....	....	....
2002-03	Ufa	Russia	50	2	8	10	12	3	0	1	1	0
2003-04	Ak Bars Kazan	Russia	51	4	11	15	34	7	0	0	0	4
2004-05	Ak Bars Kazan	Russia	57	4	7	11	30	4	0	0	0	2
2005-06	Ak Bars Kazan	Russia	22	0	2	2	51	2	0	0	0	4
2006-07	Avangard Omsk	Russia	52	2	10	12	32	9	1	2	3	4
2007-08	Avangard Omsk	Russia	51	7	12	19	34	4	0	2	2	4
2008-09	Dynamo Moscow	Rus-KHL	56	7	15	22	95	10	2	2	4	10
2009-10	Dynamo Moscow	Rus-KHL	54	8	12	20	69	4	1	0	1	4

DERLYUK, Roman (duhr-LYUHK, ROH-muhn) **FLA.**

Defense. Shoots left. 6'3", 198 lbs. Born, Leningrad, USSR, October 27, 1986.
(Florida's 7th choice, 164th overall, in 2005 Entry Draft).

			Regular Season					Playoffs				
Season	Club	League	GP	G	A	Pts	PIM	GP	G	A	Pts	PIM
2003-04	Lokom. St. Pete.	Russia-3	STATISTICS NOT AVAILABLE									
2004-05	Spartak St. Pet.	Russia-2	51	0	3	3	74	....	....	....	....	....
2005-06	SKA St. Petersburg	Russia	32	0	3	3	63	2	1	0	1	0
	St. Petersburg 2	Russia-3	2	0	1	1	0	....	....	....	....	....
2006-07	SKA St. Petersburg	Russia	6	0	1	1	4	....	....	....	....	....
	St. Petersburg 2	Russia-3	6	1	4	5	6	....	....	....	....	....
	THK Tver	Russia-3	2	0	2	2	0	....	....	....	....	....
	MVD	Russia	19	0	3	3	14	1	0	0	0	0
2007-08	MVD 2	Russia-3	24	1	5	6	36	....	....	....	....	....
	MVD	Russia	26	3	3	6	26	3	0	0	0	2
2008-09	MVD	Rus-KHL	54	3	8	11	50	....	....	....	....	....
2009-10	MVD	Rus-KHL	25	2	7	9	34	15	1	3	4	16

DESCHAMPS, Nicolas (day-SHAWMP, NIHK-oh-las) ANA.

Center. Shoots left. 6'1", 189 lbs. Born, Lasalle, Que., January 6, 1990.
(Anaheim's 2nd choice, 35th overall, in 2008 Entry Draft).

			Regular Season					Playoffs				
Season	Club	League	GP	G	A	Pts	PIM	GP	G	A	Pts	PIM
2005-06	C.C. Lemoyne	QAAA	23	5	4	9	14	8	0	0	0	12
2006-07	C.C. Lemoyne	QAAA	35	20	28	48	60	10	4	7	11	22
2007-08	Chicoutimi	QMJHL	70	24	43	67	63	6	2	3	5	6
2008-09	Chicoutimi	QMJHL	65	24	41	65	40	4	3	1	4	12
	Iowa Chops	AHL	2	0	1	1	0	....	....	....	....	....
2009-10	Chicoutimi	QMJHL	31	18	26	*44	20	....	....	....	....	....
	Moncton Wildcats	QMJHL	33	21	31	*52	20	15	5	9	14	10

QMJHL All-Rookie Team (2008) • Canadian Major Junior All-Rookie Team (2008) • QMJHL Second All-Star Team (2010)

DESIMONE, Phil (DEE-sihr-mohn, FIHL) WSH.

Center. Shoots left. 6', 185 lbs. Born, East Amherst, NY, March 19, 1987.
(Washington's 4th choice, 84th overall, in 2007 Entry Draft).

			Regular Season					Playoffs				
Season	Club	League	GP	G	A	Pts	PIM	GP	G	A	Pts	PIM
2004-05	Sioux City	USHL	44	2	7	9	28	6	0	1	1	4
2005-06	Sioux City	USHL	60	15	38	53	71	....	....	....	....	....
2006-07	Sioux City	USHL	60	26	47	73	60	7	6	6	12	2
2007-08	New Hampshire	H-East	38	3	10	13	28	....	....	....	....	....
2008-09	New Hampshire	H-East	38	7	11	18	46	....	....	....	....	....
2009-10	New Hampshire	H-East	39	10	27	37	38	....	....	....	....	....

USHL First All-Star Team (2007) • USHL Player of the Year (2007)

DESJARDINS, Andrew (deh-ZHAHR-dai, AN-droo) S.J.

Center. Shoots right. 6'1", 200 lbs. Born, Lively, Ont., July 27, 1986.

			Regular Season					Playoffs				
Season	Club	League	GP	G	A	Pts	PIM	GP	G	A	Pts	PIM
2003-04	Sault Ste. Marie	OHL	55	3	6	9	41	....	....	....	....	....
2004-05	Sault Ste. Marie	OHL	68	17	17	34	49	7	0	0	0	2
2005-06	Sault Ste. Marie	OHL	6	12	16	28	78	4	2	3	5	10
2006-07	Sault Ste. Marie	OHL	65	16	26	42	96	13	2	5	7	18
2007-08	Laredo Bucks	CHL	64	22	37	59	112	11	2	4	6	21
2008-09	Phoenix	ECHL	5	2	0	2	6	....	....	....	....	....
	Worcester Sharks	AHL	74	8	14	22	99	12	4	2	6	12
2009-10	Worcester Sharks	AHL	80	19	27	46	126	11	2	2	4	32

Signed as a free agent by **San Jose**, June 26, 2010.

DESLAURIERS, Nicolas (duh-LOHR-ree-AY, NIH-koh-las) L.A.

Defense. Shoots left. 6', 198 lbs. Born, LaSalle, Que., February 22, 1991.
(Los Angeles' 3rd choice, 84th overall, in 2009 Entry Draft).

			Regular Season					Playoffs				
Season	Club	League	GP	G	A	Pts	PIM	GP	G	A	Pts	PIM
2006-07	Chateauguay	QAAA	43	2	10	12	28	3	1	0	1	4
2007-08	Rouyn-Noranda	QMJHL	42	2	7	9	38	4	0	0	0	0
2008-09	Rouyn-Noranda	QMJHL	68	11	19	30	80	6	2	2	4	8
2009-10	Rouyn-Noranda	QMJHL	65	9	36	45	72	11	2	6	8	2

DESPRES, Simon (duh-PRAY, see-MOHN) PIT.

Defense. Shoots left. 6'4", 205 lbs. Born, Laval, Que., July 27, 1991.
(Pittsburgh's 1st choice, 30th overall, in 2009 Entry Draft).

			Regular Season					Playoffs				
Season	Club	League	GP	G	A	Pts	PIM	GP	G	A	Pts	PIM
2006-07	Laval-Bourassa	QAAA	42	8	31	39	36	5	0	2	2	8
2007-08	Saint John	QMJHL	64	1	13	14	30	14	0	4	4	18
2008-09	Saint John	QMJHL	66	2	30	32	74	4	0	4	4	2
2009-10	Saint John	QMJHL	63	9	38	47	87	21	2	17	19	18

QMJHL All-Rookie Team (2008)

DEVANE, Jamie (deh-VAYN, JAY-mee) TOR.

Left wing. Shoots left. 6'5", 217 lbs. Born, Mississauga, Ont., February 20, 1991.
(Toronto's 4th choice, 68th overall, in 2009 Entry Draft).

			Regular Season					Playoffs				
Season	Club	League	GP	G	A	Pts	PIM	GP	G	A	Pts	PIM
2007-08	Vaughan Kings	GTHL	15	4	11	15	24	....	....	....	....	....
	Vaughan Vipers	OPJHL	19	2	0	2	17	1	0	0	0	0
2008-09	Plymouth Whalers	OHL	64	5	12	17	92	11	0	0	0	17
2009-10	Plymouth Whalers	OHL	51	6	8	14	84	9	0	1	1	12
	Toronto Marlies	AHL	2	0	0	0	4	....	....	....	....	....

DIBENEDETTO, Justin (dih-behn-ih-DEH-toh, JUHS-tihn) NYI

Center. Shoots left. 5'11", 194 lbs. Born, Etobicoke, Ont., August 25, 1988.
(NY Islanders' 13th choice, 175th overall, in 2008 Entry Draft).

			Regular Season					Playoffs				
Season	Club	League	GP	G	A	Pts	PIM	GP	G	A	Pts	PIM
2004-05	St. Michael's	OHL	64	3	6	9	37	9	0	0	0	0
2005-06	St. Michael's	OHL	61	17	13	30	58	4	1	0	1	11
2006-07	Sarnia Sting	OHL	58	28	35	63	46	4	2	1	3	4
2007-08	Sarnia Sting	OHL	58	39	54	93	61	9	3	7	10	12
2008-09	Sarnia Sting	OHL	62	45	48	93	85	5	0	3	3	12
	Bridgeport	AHL	....	....	....	....	....	3	1	0	1	4
2009-10	Bridgeport	AHL	67	6	8	14	62	....	....	....	....	....

OHL Second All-Star Team (2009)

DIDIOMETE, Devin (dih-dee-OH-meht, DEH-vihn) NYR

Left wing. Shoots left. 5'11", 200 lbs. Born, Stratford, Ont., May 9, 1988.
(Calgary's 7th choice, 187th overall, in 2006 Entry Draft).

			Regular Season					Playoffs				
Season	Club	League	GP	G	A	Pts	PIM	GP	G	A	Pts	PIM
2004-05	Sudbury Wolves	OHL	58	7	8	15	113	11	0	1	1	11
2005-06	Sudbury Wolves	OHL	60	15	21	36	202	10	0	4	4	26
2006-07	Sudbury Wolves	OHL	62	21	19	40	205	21	6	6	12	62
2007-08	Sarnia Sting	OHL	56	23	33	56	216	9	1	2	3	*40
2008-09	Hartford Wolf Pack	AHL	73	4	5	9	239	4	0	0	0	6
2009-10	Hartford Wolf Pack	AHL	34	0	2	2	119	....	....	....	....	....
	Charlotte	ECHL	15	2	2	4	128	....	....	....	....	....

Signed as a free agent by **NY Rangers**, October 20, 2008.

DIDOMENICO, Chris (dee-DOH-mehn-ih-koh, KRIHS) CHI.

Center. Shoots right. 5'11", 165 lbs. Born, Toronto, Ont., February 20, 1989.
(Toronto's 5th choice, 164th overall, in 2007 Entry Draft).

			Regular Season					Playoffs				
Season	Club	League	GP	G	A	Pts	PIM	GP	G	A	Pts	PIM
2005-06	North York	GTHL	36	28	35	63	....	....	....	....	....	....
	North York	OPJHL	2	2	0	2	0	....	....	....	....	....
2006-07	Saint John	QMJHL	70	25	50	75	60	....	....	....	....	....
2007-08	Saint John	QMJHL	70	39	56	95	103	14	8	11	19	20
2008-09	Saint John	QMJHL	26	11	23	34	34	....	....	....	....	....
	Drummondville	QMJHL	25	8	17	25	28	15	4	*31	35	24
2009-10	Drummondville	QMJHL	12	7	15	22	10	14	7	14	21	18

QMJHL All-Rookie Team (2007)

• Missed majority of 2009-10 season recovering from leg injury suffered during playoff game vs. Shawinigan (QMJHL), May 5, 2009. Traded to **Chicago** by **Toronto** with Viktor Stalberg and Phillipe Paradis for Kris Versteeg and Bill Sweatt, June 30, 2010.

DIETRICH, Robert (DEET-rihkh, RAW-buhrt) NSH.

Defense. Shoots right. 5'10", 178 lbs. Born, Ordzhonikidze, USSR, July 25, 1986.
(Nashville's 8th choice, 174th overall, in 2007 Entry Draft).

			Regular Season					Playoffs				
Season	Club	League	GP	G	A	Pts	PIM	GP	G	A	Pts	PIM
2001-02	Kaufbeuren Jr.	Ger-Jr.	9	1	2	3	2	....	....	....	....	....
2002-03	Mannheim Jr.	Ger-Jr.	33	4	13	17	39	3	0	1	1	4
2003-04	EC Peiting	German-3	42	5	9	24	83	....	....	....	....	....
2004-05	ETC Crimmitschau	German-2	45	3	14	17	34	10	0	0	0	6
2005-06	Straubing Tigers	German-2	46	5	3	8	55	15	0	1	1	8
	Dusseldorf	Germany	4	0	0	0	2	....	....	....	....	....
2006-07	Dusseldorf	Germany	52	3	19	22	28	9	2	4	6	22
2007-08	Dusseldorf	Germany	9	1	1	2	12	13	1	2	3	4
2008-09	Milwaukee	AHL	63	4	15	19	32	11	1	7	8	2
2009-10	Milwaukee	AHL	79	6	37	43	28	2	0	1	1	2

Signed as a free agent by **Mannheim** (Germany), June 8, 2010.

DINGLE, Ryan (DIHN-guhl, RIGH-uhn)

Left wing. Shoots left. 5'10", 190 lbs. Born, Steamboat Springs, CO, April 4, 1984.

			Regular Season					Playoffs				
Season	Club	League	GP	G	A	Pts	PIM	GP	G	A	Pts	PIM
2001-02	Des Moines	USHL	61	7	10	17	63	3	1	0	1	[illegible]
2002-03	Tri-City Storm	USHL	32	17	17	34	31	3	0	0	0	[illegible]
	Des Moines	USHL	26	8	6	14	16	....	....	....	....	....
2003-04	Tri-City Storm	USHL	38	13	23	36	14	9	3	7	10	[illegible]
2004-05	U. of Denver	WCHA	41	6	12	18	32	....	....	....	....	....
2005-06	U. of Denver	WCHA	38	27	16	43	37	....	....	....	....	....
2006-07	U. of Denver	WCHA	40	22	15	37	38	....	....	....	....	....
	Portland Pirates	AHL	4	0	1	1	4	....	....	....	....	....
2007-08	Portland Pirates	AHL	19	1	5	6	10	2	0	1	1	[illegible]
	Augusta Lynx	ECHL	50	10	17	27	51	5	0	1	1	[illegible]
2008-09	Iowa Chops	AHL	70	11	7	18	21	....	....	....	....	....
2009-10	Adirondack	AHL	54	5	5	10	18	....	....	....	....	....

Signed as a free agent by **Anaheim**, March 26, 2007. Traded to **Philadelphia** by **Anaheim** with Chris Pronger for Joffrey Lupul, Luca Sbisa, Philadelphia's 1st round choices in 2009 (later traded to Columbus - Columbus selected John Moore) and 2010 (Emerson Etem) Entry Drafts and future considerations, June 26, 2009.

DIXON, Stephen (DIHX-uhn, STEE-vehn) ANA

Center. Shoots left. 5'11", 188 lbs. Born, Halifax, N.S., September 7, 1985.
(Pittsburgh's 9th choice, 229th overall, in 2003 Entry Draft).

			Regular Season					Playoffs				
Season	Club	League	GP	G	A	Pts	PIM	GP	G	A	Pts	PIM
2001-02	Cape Breton	QMJHL	64	16	15	31	12	16	3	5	8	[illegible]
2002-03	Cape Breton	QMJHL	72	28	42	70	54	4	0	0	0	[illegible]
2003-04	Cape Breton	QMJHL	55	22	50	72	33	5	1	0	1	[illegible]
2004-05	Cape Breton	QMJHL	45	17	34	51	40	....	....	....	....	....
2005-06	Wilkes-Barre	AHL	80	12	17	29	45	11	0	1	1	[illegible]
2006-07	Wilkes-Barre	AHL	80	17	24	41	43	11	2	3	5	[illegible]
2007-08	Portland Pirates	AHL	80	17	28	45	43	18	6	4	10	[illegible]
2008-09	Brynas IF Gavle	Sweden	53	8	19	27	32	4	0	0	0	[illegible]
2009-10	Brynas IF Gavle	Sweden	53	20	15	35	55	5	0	0	0	[illegible]

Traded to **Anaheim** by **Pittsburgh** for Tim Brent, June 23, 2007.

DOBRYSHKIN, Yuri (doh-BRIHSH-kihn, YOO-ree) ATL

Right wing. Shoots right. 6', 190 lbs. Born, Penza, USSR, July 19, 1979.
(Atlanta's 7th choice, 159th overall, in 1999 Entry Draft).

			Regular Season					Playoffs				
Season	Club	League	GP	G	A	Pts	PIM	GP	G	A	Pts	PIM
1996-97	Krylja Sovetov 2	Russia-3	35	13	5	18	42	....	....	....	....	....
	Krylja Sovetov	Russia	2	0	0	0	0	2	0	0	0	[illegible]
1997-98	Krylja Sovetov 2	Russia-3	26	12	5	17	68	....	....	....	....	....
	Krylja Sovetov	Russia	22	4	0	4	12	....	....	....	....	....
1998-99	Krylja Sovetov	Russia	50	11	5	16	86	....	....	....	....	....
99-2000	Ak Bars Kazan	Russia	27	6	9	15	24	17	2	0	2	[illegible]
2000-01	Ak Bars Kazan	Russia	40	10	5	15	32	4	2	0	2	[illegible]
2001-02	Ak Bars Kazan	Russia	38	9	8	17	22	11	0	2	2	[illegible]
2002-03	Cherepovets	Russia	49	19	7	26	82	12	5	2	7	[illegible]
2003-04	Cherepovets	Russia	53	11	7	18	75	....	....	....	....	....
2004-05	Magnitogorsk	Russia	54	14	6	20	42	2	0	0	0	[illegible]
2005-06	Magnitogorsk	Russia	15	3	1	4	22	8	0	0	0	[illegible]
	Magnitogorsk 2	Russia-3	2	3	1	4	2	....	....	....	....	....
2006-07	CSKA Moscow	Russia	50	5	10	15	65	12	3	0	3	[illegible]
2007-08	Nizhny Novgorod	Russia	48	15	6	21	60	....	....	....	....	....
2008-09	Nizhny Novgorod	Rus-KHL	19	2	1	3	12	....	....	....	....	....
	Mytischi	Rus-KHL	8	1	0	1	2	2	0	0	0	[illegible]
2009-10	MVD	Rus-KHL	33	13	5	18	12	9	1	0	1	[illegible]

DODGE, Nick (DAWGE, NIHK) CAR

Right wing. Shoots right. 5'10", 185 lbs. Born, Oakville, Ont., May 1, 1986.
(Carolina's 5th choice, 183rd overall, in 2006 Entry Draft).

			Regular Season					Playoffs				
Season	Club	League	GP	G	A	Pts	PIM	GP	G	A	Pts	PIM
2004-05	Clarkson Knights	ECAC	37	6	12	18	42	....	....	....	....	....
2005-06	Clarkson Knights	ECAC	38	16	25	41	72	....	....	....	....	....
2006-07	Clarkson Knights	ECAC	36	18	21	39	32	....	....	....	....	....
2007-08	Clarkson Knights	ECAC	39	12	14	26	26	....	....	....	....	....
2008-09	Albany River Rats	AHL	80	13	26	39	34	....	....	....	....	....
2009-10	Albany River Rats	AHL	80	16	20	36	30	8	4	1	5	[illegible]

ECAC First All-Star Team (2007) • NCAA East Second All-American Team (2007)

DOHERTY, Taylor (DOHR-eh-tee, TAY-luhr) **S.J.**

Defense. Shoots right. 6'7", 235 lbs. Born, Cambridge, Ont., March 2, 1991.
(San Jose's 2nd choice, 57th overall, in 2009 Entry Draft).

			Regular Season					Playoffs				
Season	**Club**	**League**	**GP**	**G**	**A**	**Pts**	**PIM**	**GP**	**G**	**A**	**Pts**	**PIM**
2006-07	Cambridge Hawks	Minor-ON	70	10	37	47	169	....	....	....	....	....
2007-08	Kingston	OHL	64	6	14	20	118	....	....	....	....	....
2008-09	Kingston	OHL	68	2	18	20	140	....	....	....	....	....
2009-10	Kingston	OHL	63	16	28	44	114	5	1	4	5	0

DONIKA, Mikhail (DAW-nih-ka, mih-kigh-EHL) **DAL.**

Defense. Shoots left. 6', 185 lbs. Born, Yaroslavl, USSR, May 15, 1979.
(Dallas' 11th choice, 272nd overall, in 1999 Entry Draft).

			Regular Season					Playoffs				
Season	**Club**	**League**	**GP**	**G**	**A**	**Pts**	**PIM**	**GP**	**G**	**A**	**Pts**	**PIM**
1996-97	Yaroslavl 2	Russia-3	15	3	5	8	6	....	....	....	....	....
	Torpedo Yaroslavl	Russia	22	1	0	1	6	2	0	0	0	0
1997-98	Yaroslavl 2	Russia-2	19	1	2	3	32	....	....	....	....	....
	Torpedo Yaroslavl	Russia	30	0	2	2	14	....	....	....	....	....
1998-99	Yaroslavl 2	Russia-3	6	2	1	3	4	....	....	....	....	....
	Torpedo Yaroslavl	Russia	37	0	1	1	10	....	....	....	....	....
99-2000	Torpedo Yaroslavl	Russia	35	0	1	1	22	10	0	0	0	4
2000-01	Dynamo Moscow	Russia	43	1	3	4	12	....	....	....	....	....
2001-02	Amur Khabarovsk	Russia	51	1	3	4	66	....	....	....	....	....
2002-03	Spartak Moscow	Russia	51	4	7	11	16	....	....	....	....	....
2003-04	Spartak Moscow	Russia-2	55	4	14	18	14	12	2	1	3	2
2004-05	Spartak Moscow	Russia	49	0	2	2	34	....	....	....	....	....
2005-06	Perm	Russia	26	0	0	0	18	....	....	....	....	....
	Sibir Novosibirsk	Russia	14	1	3	4	8	3	0	1	1	0
2006-07	Nizhny Novgorod	Russia-2	47	8	16	24	38	14	3	0	3	14
2007-08	Nizhny Novgorod	Russia	31	0	5	5	28	....	....	....	....	....
	Lada Togliatti	Russia	2	0	0	0	0	....	....	....	....	....
	Yunost Minsk	Belarus	10	1	1	2	2	....	....	....	....	....
	Yunior Minsk	Belarus-2	....	....	....	....	....	1	0	0	0	0
2008-09	Khanty-Mansiisk	Russia-2	46	3	11	14	46	15	1	1	2	16
2009-10	Khanty-Mansiisk	Russia-2	16	0	5	5	20	....	....	....	....	....
	Gazovik Tyumen	Russia-2	4	0	0	0	0	5	0	0	0	2

DONOVAN, Matt (DAWN-uh-vuhn, MAT) **NYI**

Defense. Shoots left. 6', 195 lbs. Born, Edmond, OK, May 9, 1990.
(NY Islanders' 8th choice, 96th overall, in 2008 Entry Draft).

			Regular Season					Playoffs				
Season	**Club**	**League**	**GP**	**G**	**A**	**Pts**	**PIM**	**GP**	**G**	**A**	**Pts**	**PIM**
2006-07	Dallas Stars AAA	NTHL	....	22	46	68	54	....	....	....	....	....
2007-08	Cedar Rapids	USHL	59	12	18	30	41	3	0	1	1	4
2008-09	Cedar Rapids	USHL	57	19	32	51	43	5	0	4	4	2
2009-10	U. of Denver	WCHA	36	7	14	21	50	....	....	....	....	....

USHL All-Rookie Team (2008) • USHL First All-Star Team (2009) • WCHA All-Rookie Team (2010)

DONSKOI, Joonas (DAWN-skoy, YOH-nuhs) **FLA.**

Right wing. Shoots right. 6', 180 lbs. Born, Raahe, Finland, April 13, 1992.
(Florida's 10th choice, 99th overall, in 2010 Entry Draft).

			Regular Season					Playoffs				
Season	**Club**	**League**	**GP**	**G**	**A**	**Pts**	**PIM**	**GP**	**G**	**A**	**Pts**	**PIM**
2007-08	Karpat Oulu U18	Fin-U18	30	18	20	38	26	5	3	4	7	0
2008-09	Karpat Oulu U18	Fin-U18	4	2	5	7	0	6	6	7	13	0
	Karpat Oulu Jr.	Fin-Jr.	32	7	17	24	12	....	....	....	....	....
2009-10	Suomi U20	Finland-2	4	1	0	1	0	....	....	....	....	....
	Karpat Oulu Jr.	Fin-Jr.	18	14	15	29	2	12	5	10	15	4
	Karpat Oulu	Finland	18	2	2	4	4	....	....	....	....	....
	Karpat Oulu U18	Fin-U18	....	....	....	....	....	1	1	1	2	0

DOWD, Nic (DOWD, NIHK) **L.A.**

Center. Shoots right. 6'1", 175 lbs. Born, Huntsville, AL, May 27, 1990.
(Los Angeles' 10th choice, 198th overall, in 2009 Entry Draft).

			Regular Season					Playoffs				
Season	**Club**	**League**	**GP**	**G**	**A**	**Pts**	**PIM**	**GP**	**G**	**A**	**Pts**	**PIM**
2007-08	Culver Academy	High-IN	45	15	31	46	38	....	....	....	....	....
2008-09	Wenatchee Wild	NAHL	43	16	33	49	71	13	8	*14	*22	34
2009-10	Indiana Ice	USHL	46	16	23	39	48	9	2	4	6	2

• Signed Letter of Intent to attend **St. Cloud State University** (WCHA) in fall of 2010.

DOWZAK, Tysen (DOW-zak, TIGH-suhn) **NYR**

Defense. Shoots left. 6'5", 215 lbs. Born, Fergus Falls, MN, March 8, 1988.

			Regular Season					Playoffs				
Season	**Club**	**League**	**GP**	**G**	**A**	**Pts**	**PIM**	**GP**	**G**	**A**	**Pts**	**PIM**
2005-06	Kelowna Rockets	WHL	43	1	3	4	68	8	0	0	0	16
2006-07	Kelowna Rockets	WHL	55	3	4	7	68	....	....	....	....	....
2007-08	Kelowna Rockets	WHL	68	0	13	13	91	7	0	1	1	13
	Texas Wildcatters	ECHL	....	....	....	....	....	5	0	0	0	4
2008-09	Kelowna Rockets	WHL	54	0	14	14	77	22	0	4	4	14
	Hartford Wolf Pack	AHL	1	0	0	0	2	....	....	....	....	....
	Charlotte	ECHL	4	0	0	0	9	....	....	....	....	....
2009-10	Hartford Wolf Pack	AHL	2	0	0	0	0	....	....	....	....	....
	Charlotte	ECHL	35	1	3	4	29	....	....	....	....	....
	Bossier-Shreve.	CHL	16	0	2	2	22	....	....	....	....	....

Signed as a free agent by **NY Rangers**, October 14, 2008.

DRAZENOVIC, Nicholas (DRAY-zehn-oh-vihk, NIH-koh-las) **ST.L.**

Center. Shoots left. 6', 205 lbs. Born, Prince George, B.C., January 14, 1987.
(St. Louis' 6th choice, 171st overall, in 2005 Entry Draft).

			Regular Season					Playoffs				
Season	**Club**	**League**	**GP**	**G**	**A**	**Pts**	**PIM**	**GP**	**G**	**A**	**Pts**	**PIM**
2003-04	Prince George	WHL	65	7	30	37	38	....	....	....	....	....
2004-05	Prince George	WHL	72	18	38	56	24	....	....	....	....	....
2005-06	Prince George	WHL	71	30	33	63	51	5	0	0	0	4
2006-07	Prince George	WHL	58	18	32	50	63	15	9	10	19	6
2007-08	Peoria Rivermen	AHL	69	16	26	42	38	....	....	....	....	....
2008-09	Peoria Rivermen	AHL	76	12	21	33	43	5	1	0	1	2
2009-10	Peoria Rivermen	AHL	58	19	20	39	40	....	....	....	....	....

DROZDETSKY, Alexander (drawz-DEHT-skee, al-EHX-AN-duhr) **PHI.**

Right wing. Shoots left. 6', 180 lbs. Born, Moscow, USSR, November 10, 1981.
(Philadelphia's 2nd choice, 94th overall, in 2000 Entry Draft).

			Regular Season					Playoffs				
Season	**Club**	**League**	**GP**	**G**	**A**	**Pts**	**PIM**	**GP**	**G**	**A**	**Pts**	**PIM**
1997-98	St. Petersburg 2	Russia-3	19	0	1	1	0	....	....	....	....	....
1998-99	St. Petersburg 2	Russia-4	24	5	3	8	12	....	....	....	....	....
99-2000	St. Petersburg 2	Russia-3	4	4	1	5	2	....	....	....	....	....
	SKA St. Petersburg	Russia	32	2	0	2	10	4	0	0	0	0
2000-01	SKA St. Petersburg	Russia	42	6	7	13	74	....	....	....	....	....
2001-02	CSKA Moscow	Russia	49	11	6	17	26	....	....	....	....	....
2002-03	CSKA Moscow	Russia	46	14	13	27	30	....	....	....	....	....
2003-04	Ak Bars Kazan	Russia	57	16	15	31	62	1	0	0	0	2
2004-05	Ak Bars Kazan	Russia	32	3	4	7	28	....	....	....	....	....
	Ak Bars Kazan 2	Russia-3	....	10	8	18	....	....	....	....	....	....
	Nizhnekamsk	Russia	7	5	1	6	4	....	....	....	....	....
2005-06	Avangard Omsk	Russia	30	6	6	12	26	....	....	....	....	....
	SKA St. Petersburg	Russia	16	4	10	14	6	3	0	0	0	0
2006-07	SKA St. Petersburg	Russia	45	11	15	26	66	3	0	2	2	0
2007-08	St. Petersburg 2	Russia-3	12	9	9	18	6	....	....	....	....	....
	Spartak Moscow	Russia	32	11	6	17	40	5	4	3	7	2
2008-09	Spartak Moscow	Rus-KHL	47	14	13	27	38	6	1	3	4	2
2009-10	Cherepovets	Rus-KHL	11	1	0	1	4	....	....	....	....	....
	Nizhnekamsk	Rus-KHL	26	4	7	11	14	9	0	1	1	4

DUMONT, Gabriel (doo-MAWNT, gah-BREE-ehl) **MTL.**

Center. Shoots right. 5'9", 170 lbs. Born, Ville Degelis, Que., October 6, 1990.
(Montreal's 5th choice, 139th overall, in 2009 Entry Draft).

			Regular Season					Playoffs				
Season	**Club**	**League**	**GP**	**G**	**A**	**Pts**	**PIM**	**GP**	**G**	**A**	**Pts**	**PIM**
2006-07	Ecole Notre Dame	QAAA	39	30	42	72	127	13	11	12	23	20
	Drummondville	QMJHL	8	1	1	2	6	6	0	2	2	0
2007-08	Drummondville	QMJHL	59	11	14	25	103	....	....	....	....	....
2008-09	Drummondville	QMJHL	51	28	21	49	63	19	6	13	19	32
2009-10	Drummondville	QMJHL	62	*51	42	93	127	14	*11	10	21	19
	Hamilton Bulldogs	AHL	....	....	....	....	....	11	2	0	2	12

QMJHL First All-Star Team (2010) • Canadian Major Junior Second All-Star Team (2010)

DUMOULIN, Brian (DOO-moh-lihn, BRIGH-uhn) **CAR.**

Defense. Shoots left. 6'3", 205 lbs. Born, Biddeford, ME, September 6, 1991.
(Carolina's 2nd choice, 51st overall, in 2009 Entry Draft).

			Regular Season					Playoffs				
Season	**Club**	**League**	**GP**	**G**	**A**	**Pts**	**PIM**	**GP**	**G**	**A**	**Pts**	**PIM**
2007-08	Biddeford Tigers	High-ME	24	13	48	61	10	....	....	....	....	....
2008-09	N.H. Jr. Monarchs	EJHL	41	7	23	30	30	7	0	3	3	2
2009-10	Boston College	H-East	42	1	21	22	16	....	....	....	....	....

NCAA Championship All-Tournament Team (2010)

DUPONT, Brodie (DOO-pawnt, BROH-dee) **NYR**

Center. Shoots left. 6'2", 210 lbs. Born, Russell, Man., February 17, 1987.
(NY Rangers' 4th choice, 66th overall, in 2005 Entry Draft).

			Regular Season					Playoffs				
Season	**Club**	**League**	**GP**	**G**	**A**	**Pts**	**PIM**	**GP**	**G**	**A**	**Pts**	**PIM**
2003-04	Swan Valley	MJHL	51	25	16	41	88	12	5	1	6	36
	Calgary Hitmen	WHL	2	0	1	1	0	....	....	....	....	....
2004-05	Calgary Hitmen	WHL	70	14	11	25	111	12	2	8	10	21
2005-06	Calgary Hitmen	WHL	72	30	23	53	123	13	4	5	9	24
2006-07	Calgary Hitmen	WHL	70	37	33	70	90	18	9	7	16	33
2007-08	Hartford Wolf Pack	AHL	66	9	13	22	75	1	0	0	0	0
2008-09	Hartford Wolf Pack	AHL	79	18	24	42	112	6	0	2	2	15
2009-10	Hartford Wolf Pack	AHL	80	17	22	39	124	....	....	....	....	....

DUROCHER, Corey (doo-ROH-shay, KOH-ree) **FLA.**

Left wing. Shoots left. 6'2", 173 lbs. Born, Ottawa, Ont., May 30, 1992.
(Florida's 12th choice, 153rd overall, in 2010 Entry Draft).

			Regular Season					Playoffs				
Season	**Club**	**League**	**GP**	**G**	**A**	**Pts**	**PIM**	**GP**	**G**	**A**	**Pts**	**PIM**
2007-08	Ott. Senators	Minor-ON	53	18	22	40	12	....	....	....	....	....
2008-09	Gloucester	CJHL	60	7	20	27	16	4	0	2	2	0
2009-10	Kingston	OHL	66	15	11	26	31	7	2	0	2	4

DZIURZYNSKI, David (z'yuhr-IHN-skee, DAY-vihd) **OTT.**

Center. Shoots left. 6'3", 205 lbs. Born, Lloydminster, Alta., October 6, 1989.

			Regular Season					Playoffs				
Season	**Club**	**League**	**GP**	**G**	**A**	**Pts**	**PIM**	**GP**	**G**	**A**	**Pts**	**PIM**
2007-08	Lloydminster	AJHL	52	8	12	20	82	....	....	....	....	....
2008-09	Lloydminster	AJHL	54	12	25	37	185	....	....	....	....	....
2009-10	Alberni Valley	BCHL	57	21	53	74	79	13	9	10	19	8

Signed as a free agent by **Ottawa**, April 6, 2010.

EAKIN, Cody (EE-kihn, KOH-dee) **WSH.**

Center. Shoots left. 5'11", 187 lbs. Born, Winnipeg, Man., May 24, 1991.
(Washington's 3rd choice, 85th overall, in 2009 Entry Draft).

			Regular Season					Playoffs				
Season	**Club**	**League**	**GP**	**G**	**A**	**Pts**	**PIM**	**GP**	**G**	**A**	**Pts**	**PIM**
2006-07	Winnipeg Wild	MMHL	38	29	35	64	62	7	5	4	9	10
	Swift Current	WHL	3	0	0	0	0	....	....	....	....	....
2007-08	Swift Current	WHL	55	11	6	17	52	12	3	4	7	6
2008-09	Swift Current	WHL	54	24	24	48	42	7	3	0	3	10
2009-10	Swift Current	WHL	70	47	44	91	71	4	1	0	1	2
	Hershey Bears	AHL	4	2	0	2	2	5	0	0	0	2

WHL East Second All-Star Team (2010)

EBERLE, Jordan (EH-buhr-lee, JOHR-dahn) **EDM.**

Center. Shoots right. 5'10", 174 lbs. Born, Regina, Sask., May 15, 1990.
(Edmonton's 1st choice, 22nd overall, in 2008 Entry Draft).

			Regular Season					Playoffs				
Season	**Club**	**League**	**GP**	**G**	**A**	**Pts**	**PIM**	**GP**	**G**	**A**	**Pts**	**PIM**
2005-06	Calgary Buffaloes	AMHL	31	14	20	34	6	11	7	1	8	8
2006-07	Regina Pats	WHL	66	28	27	55	32	6	2	5	7	2
2007-08	Regina Pats	WHL	70	42	33	75	20	5	2	4	6	7
2008-09	Regina Pats	WHL	61	35	39	74	20	....	....	....	....	....
	Springfield Falcons	AHL	9	3	6	9	4	....	....	....	....	....
2009-10	Regina Pats	WHL	57	50	56	106	32	....	....	....	....	....
	Springfield Falcons	AHL	11	6	8	14	0	....	....	....	....	....

WHL East First All-Star Team (2008, 2010) • WHL Player of the Year (2010) • Canadian Major Junior First All-Star Team (2010) • Canadian Major Junior Player of the Year (2010)

EHRHARDT, Travis (AIR-hahrt, TRA-vihs) DET.

Defense. Shoots left. 5'11", 203 lbs. Born, Calgary, Alta., April 12, 1989.

			Regular Season					Playoffs				
Season	Club	League	GP	G	A	Pts	PIM	GP	G	A	Pts	PIM
2004-05	Cgy. North Stars	AMHL	11	0	0	0	0	....	....	....	....	....
	Moose Jaw	WHL	2	0	1	1	2	....	....	....	....	....
2005-06	Moose Jaw	WHL	45	1	10	11	37	18	0	2	2	18
2006-07	Moose Jaw	WHL	69	0	29	29	83	....	....	....	....	....
2007-08	Moose Jaw	WHL	18	3	9	12	27	....	....	....	....	....
	Portland	WHL	54	7	22	29	53	....	....	....	....	....
2008-09	Portland	WHL	68	9	28	37	109	....	....	....	....	....
	Manitoba Moose	AHL	3	0	0	0	0	....	....	....	....	....
2009-10	Grand Rapids	AHL	42	0	5	5	38	....	....	....	....	....
	Toledo Walleye	ECHL	3	1	1	2	0	....	....	....	....	....

Signed as a free agent by **Detroit**, July 7, 2009.

EKBOM, Viktor (EHK-bawm, VIHK-tohr) PIT.

Defense. Shoots left. 6'2", 194 lbs. Born, Falkoping, Sweden, June 1, 1989.
(Pittsburgh's 7th choice, 181st overall, in 2009 Entry Draft).

			Regular Season					Playoffs				
Season	Club	League	GP	G	A	Pts	PIM	GP	G	A	Pts	PIM
2004-05	Skovde IK Jr.	Swe-Jr.	37	3	3	6	24	....	....	....	....	....
2005-06	Skovde IK Jr.	Swe-Jr.	....	3	2	5	....	....	....	....	....	....
	Skovde IK	Sweden-3	17	1	1	2	0	....	....	....	....	....
2006-07	Skovde IK	Sweden-3	36	3	14	17	30	....	....	....	....	....
2007-08	Linkopings HC Jr.	Swe-Jr.	25	3	7	10	10	5	0	2	2	6
	IK Oskarshamn	Sweden-2	9	0	0	0	2	....	....	....	....	....
2008-09	IK Oskarshamn	Sweden-2	29	2	4	6	22	....	....	....	....	....
	Linkopings HC	Sweden	14	0	1	1	6	5	0	0	0	2
	Linkopings HC Jr.	Swe-Jr.	....	....	....	....	....	5	1	1	2	2
2009-10	Linkopings HC	Sweden	47	0	2	2	16	12	0	0	0	8
	IK Oskarshamn	Sweden-2	3	2	0	2	2	....	....	....	....	....

EKHOLM, Mattias (EHK-hohlm, ma-TEE-uhs) NSH.

Defense. Shoots left. 6'4", 204 lbs. Born, Borlange, Sweden, May 24, 1990.
(Nashville's 7th choice, 102nd overall, in 2009 Entry Draft).

			Regular Season					Playoffs				
Season	Club	League	GP	G	A	Pts	PIM	GP	G	A	Pts	PIM
2006-07	Mora IK U18	Swe-U18	5	2	2	4	6	....	....	....	....	....
	Mora IK Jr.	Swe-Jr.	36	0	4	4	28	2	0	0	0	0
2007-08	Mora IK U18	Swe-U18	9	4	5	9	12	....	....	....	....	....
	Mora IK Jr.	Swe-Jr.	37	5	7	12	54	....	....	....	....	....
	Mora IK	Sweden	1	0	0	0	0	....	....	....	....	....
	Mora IK	Sweden-Q	6	0	0	0	2	....	....	....	....	....
2008-09	Mora IK Jr.	Swe-Jr.	21	3	5	8	32	....	....	....	....	....
	Mora IK	Sweden-2	38	2	11	13	12	3	0	0	0	4
2009-10	Mora IK	Sweden-2	41	1	21	22	54	2	0	0	0	6

• Loaned to **Timra** (Sweden) by **Mora** (Sweden-2) for 2010-11 season.

EKMAN-LARSSON, Oliver (EHK-man-LAHR-suhn, AW-lih-vuhr) PHX.

Defense. Shoots left. 6'2", 176 lbs. Born, Karlskrona, Sweden, July 17, 1991.
(Phoenix's 1st choice, 6th overall, in 2009 Entry Draft).

			Regular Season					Playoffs				
Season	Club	League	GP	G	A	Pts	PIM	GP	G	A	Pts	PIM
2005-06	Tingsryds AIF Jr.	Swe-Jr.	1	0	0	0	2	....	....	....	....	....
2006-07	Tingsryds AIF U18	Swe-U18	23	0	3	3	28	....	....	....	....	....
2007-08	Tingsryds AIF U18	Swe-U18	12	2	3	5	57	....	....	....	....	....
	Tingsryds AIF Jr.	Swe-Jr.	7	2	4	6	16	....	....	....	....	....
	Tingsryds AIF	Sweden-3	27	3	5	8	10	....	....	....	....	....
2008-09	Leksands IF	Sweden-2	47	5	16	21	38	....	....	....	....	....
2009-10	Leksands IF	Sweden-2	52	11	22	33	106	....	....	....	....	....

ELLINGTON, Taylor (EHL-ihng-tuhn, TAY-luhr) VAN.

Defense. Shoots left. 6'1", 200 lbs. Born, Victoria, B.C., October 31, 1988.
(Vancouver's 2nd choice, 33rd overall, in 2007 Entry Draft).

			Regular Season					Playoffs				
Season	Club	League	GP	G	A	Pts	PIM	GP	G	A	Pts	PIM
2004-05	Everett Silvertips	WHL	47	0	0	0	48	8	0	1	1	4
2005-06	Everett Silvertips	WHL	63	0	7	7	62	15	1	2	3	16
2006-07	Everett Silvertips	WHL	60	5	8	13	65	6	1	0	1	2
2007-08	Everett Silvertips	WHL	48	3	11	14	66	4	0	0	0	0
2008-09	Everett Silvertips	WHL	69	6	26	32	130	5	0	5	5	6
	Manitoba Moose	AHL	1	1	0	1	0	....	....	....	....	....
2009-10	Manitoba Moose	AHL	19	1	3	4	9	....	....	....	....	....
	Victoria	ECHL	48	3	11	14	49	....	....	....	....	....

ELLIOTT, Stefan (ehl-LEE-awt, STEH-fan) COL.

Defense. Shoots right. 6'1", 180 lbs. Born, Vancouver, B.C., January 30, 1991.
(Colorado's 3rd choice, 49th overall, in 2009 Entry Draft).

			Regular Season					Playoffs				
Season	Club	League	GP	G	A	Pts	PIM	GP	G	A	Pts	PIM
2006-07	Van. NW Giants	BCMML	36	12	19	31	18	....	....	....	....	....
	Saskatoon Blades	WHL	1	0	0	0	0	....	....	....	....	....
2007-08	Saskatoon Blades	WHL	67	9	31	40	17	....	....	....	....	....
2008-09	Saskatoon Blades	WHL	71	16	39	55	26	7	1	3	4	4
2009-10	Saskatoon Blades	WHL	72	26	39	65	24	10	3	5	8	4

Canadian Major Junior Scholastic Player of the Year (2009)

ELLIS, Morgan (EHL-ihs, MOHR-guhn) MTL.

Defense. Shoots right. 6'1", 197 lbs. Born, Summerside, P.E.I., April 30, 1992.
(Montreal's 3rd choice, 117th overall, in 2010 Entry Draft).

			Regular Season					Playoffs				
Season	Club	League	GP	G	A	Pts	PIM	GP	G	A	Pts	PIM
2007-08	Charlottetown	NBPEI	33	3	4	7	28	7	0	2	2	10
	Charlottetown	Exhib.	16	2	6	8	16	....	....	....	....	....
2008-09	Cape Breton	QMJHL	52	0	6	6	45	10	0	1	1	4
2009-10	Cape Breton	QMJHL	60	4	25	29	56	5	1	0	1	10

ELLIS, Ryan (EHL-ihs, RIGH-uhn) NSH.

Defense. Shoots right. 5'10", 186 lbs. Born, Hamilton, Ont., January 3, 1991.
(Nashville's 1st choice, 11th overall, in 2009 Entry Draft).

			Regular Season					Playoffs				
Season	Club	League	GP	G	A	Pts	PIM	GP	G	A	Pts	PIM
2006-07	Cambridge Hawks	Minor-ON	75	37	56	93	151	....	....	....	....	....
2007-08	Windsor Spitfires	OHL	63	15	48	63	51	5	2	3	5	2
2008-09	Windsor Spitfires	OHL	57	22	*67	89	57	20	8	*23	31	20
2009-10	Windsor Spitfires	OHL	48	12	49	61	38	19	3	*30	33	14

Canadian Major Junior All-Rookie Team (2008) • OHL First All-Star Team (2009) • Canadian Major Junior First All-Star Team (2009) • OHL Second All-Star Team (2010)

ELSNER, David (EHLZ-nuhr, DAY-vihd) NSH.

Left wing. Shoots right. 6', 184 lbs. Born, Landshut, Germany, March 22, 1992.
(Nashville's 5th choice, 194th overall, in 2010 Entry Draft).

			Regular Season					Playoffs				
Season	Club	League	GP	G	A	Pts	PIM	GP	G	A	Pts	PIM
2007-08	EV Landshut Jr.	Ger-Jr.	36	11	8	19	16	3	1	0	1	4
2008-09	EV Landshut Jr.	Ger-Jr.	36	17	18	35	46	9	2	8	10	10
2009-10	EV Landshut Jr.	Ger-Jr.	17	10	7	17	63	5	2	4	6	12
	Landshut Cann.	German-2	29	6	3	9	6	6	0	0	0	16

• Loaned to **Ingolstadt** (Germany) by **Landshut** (German-2) for 2010-11 season.

EMMERTON, Cory (EHM-uhr-tuhn, KOH-ree) DET.

Center. Shoots left. 6', 188 lbs. Born, St. Thomas, Ont., June 1, 1988.
(Detroit's 1st choice, 41st overall, in 2006 Entry Draft).

			Regular Season					Playoffs				
Season	Club	League	GP	G	A	Pts	PIM	GP	G	A	Pts	PIM
2003-04	Elgin-Mid. Chiefs	Minor-ON	32	33	24	57	26	....	....	....	....	....
2004-05	Kingston	OHL	58	17	21	38	8	....	....	....	....	....
2005-06	Kingston	OHL	66	26	64	90	32	6	2	0	2	6
2006-07	Kingston	OHL	40	29	37	66	22	5	5	2	7	2
	Grand Rapids	AHL	....	....	....	....	....	2	0	0	0	0
2007-08	Kingston	OHL	24	13	18	31	6	....	....	....	....	....
	Brampton	OHL	30	12	18	30	10	5	0	2	2	2
	Grand Rapids	AHL	7	0	1	1	0	....	....	....	....	....
2008-09	Grand Rapids	AHL	69	10	25	35	18	9	1	0	1	2
2009-10	Grand Rapids	AHL	76	12	25	37	22	....	....	....	....	....

ENGQVIST, Andreas (ENG-kvihst, awn-DRAY-uhs) MTL.

Center. Shoots right. 6'4", 199 lbs. Born, Stockholm, Sweden, December 23, 1987.

			Regular Season					Playoffs				
Season	Club	League	GP	G	A	Pts	PIM	GP	G	A	Pts	PIM
2004-05	Spanga U18	Swe-U18	6	3	6	9	6	....	....	....	....	....
	Spanga Jr.	Swe-Jr.	13	15	9	24	12	....	....	....	....	....
2005-06	Djurgarden Jr.	Swe-Jr.	26	6	13	19	6	4	1	1	2	2
	Djurgarden	Sweden	1	0	0	0	0	....	....	....	....	....
2006-07	Djurgarden Jr.	Swe-Jr.	5	1	3	4	4	7	3	4	7	10
	Djurgarden	Sweden	43	1	3	4	16	....	....	....	....	....
2007-08	Djurgarden Jr.	Swe-Jr.	1	1	0	1	0	....	....	....	....	....
	Djurgarden	Sweden	51	5	7	12	16	5	0	0	0	0
2008-09	Djurgarden	Sweden	31	9	7	16	12	....	....	....	....	....
2009-10	Djurgarden	Sweden	55	14	12	26	30	16	5	8	13	10

Signed as a free agent by **Montreal**, July 13, 2009.

ERIXON, Tim (AIR-ihx-uhn, TIHM) CGY.

Defense. Shoots left. 6'2", 200 lbs. Born, Port Chester, NY, February 24, 1991.
(Calgary's 1st choice, 23rd overall, in 2009 Entry Draft).

			Regular Season					Playoffs				
Season	Club	League	GP	G	A	Pts	PIM	GP	G	A	Pts	PIM
2005-06	Skelleftea U18	Swe-U18	9	0	2	2	4	....	....	....	....	....
2006-07	Skelleftea U18	Swe-U18	8	2	2	4	20	....	....	....	....	....
	Skelleftea Jr.	Swe-Jr.	8	0	2	2	2	2	0	0	0	4
2007-08	Skelleftea U18	Swe-U18	4	0	1	1	10	....	....	....	....	....
	Skelleftea Jr.	Swe-Jr.	28	3	11	14	78	1	0	1	1	4
	Skelleftea AIK HK	Sweden	2	0	0	0	0	....	....	....	....	....
2008-09	Skelleftea AIK U18	Swe-U18	1	0	2	2	10	5	1	5	6	14
	Skelleftea AIK Jr.	Swe-Jr.	9	2	12	14	10	5	1	2	3	4
	Malmo	Sweden-2	3	0	2	2	0	....	....	....	....	....
	Skelleftea AIK	Sweden	45	2	5	7	12	9	0	0	0	4
2009-10	Skelleftea AIK	Sweden	45	7	6	13	44	12	1	0	1	8

ERSTAD, Travis (UHR-stad, TRA-vihs) ST.L.

Center/Right wing. Shoots right. 6'4", 199 lbs. Born, Madison, WI, November 9, 1988.
(St. Louis' 8th choice, 100th overall, in 2007 Entry Draft).

			Regular Season					Playoffs				
Season	Club	League	GP	G	A	Pts	PIM	GP	G	A	Pts	PIM
2005-06	Stevens Point High	High-WI	STATISTICS NOT AVAILABLE									
2006-07	Stevens Point High	High-WI	24	31	33	64	....	....	....	....	....	....
	Lincoln Stars	USHL	8	0	0	0	4	3	1	0	1	0
2007-08	Lincoln Stars	USHL	52	9	10	19	104	8	1	2	3	8
2008-09	Wisc.-Stevens Pt.	NCHA	26	10	7	17	56	....	....	....	....	....
2009-10	Wisc.-Stevens Pt.	NCHA	23	5	10	15	....	....	....	....	....	....

ESPOSITO, Angelo (EHS-poh-ZEE-toh, AN-jul-loh) ATL.

Center. Shoots left. 6'1", 195 lbs. Born, Montreal, Que., February 20, 1989.
(Pittsburgh's 1st choice, 20th overall, in 2007 Entry Draft).

			Regular Season					Playoffs				
Season	Club	League	GP	G	A	Pts	PIM	GP	G	A	Pts	PIM
2004-05	Shat.-St. Mary's	High-MN	68	31	35	66	47	....	....	....	....	....
2005-06	Quebec Remparts	QMJHL	57	39	59	98	45	23	6	5	11	4
2006-07	Quebec Remparts	QMJHL	60	27	52	79	63	5	4	3	7	2
2007-08	Quebec Remparts	QMJHL	56	30	39	69	69	11	4	6	10	6
	Chicago Wolves	AHL	1	0	0	0	0	....	....	....	....	....
2008-09	Montreal	QMJHL	35	24	18	42	25	....	....	....	....	....
2009-10	Chicago Wolves	AHL	12	0	4	4	2	....	....	....	....	....

QMJHL All-Rookie Team (2006) • QMJHL Offensive Rookie of the Year (2006)

Traded to **Atlanta** by **Pittsburgh** with Colby Armstrong, Erik Christensen and Pittsburgh's 1st round choice (Daultan Leveille) in 2008 Entry Draft for Marian Hossa and Pascal Dupuis, February 26, 2008. • Missed majority of 2009-10 season recovering from knee injury suffered in game vs. Texas (AHL), November 22, 2009.

ETEM, Emerson (EE-tehm, EHM-ur-suhn) ANA.

Right wing. Shoots left. 6', 190 lbs. Born, Long Beach, CA, June 16, 1992.
(Anaheim's 2nd choice, 29th overall, in 2010 Entry Draft).

			Regular Season					Playoffs				
Season	Club	League	GP	G	A	Pts	PIM	GP	G	A	Pts	PIM
2007-08	Shat.-St. Mary's	High-MN	58	13	15	28	20	....	....	....	....	....
2008-09	USNTDP	NAHL	19	14	33	23	1	9	4	4	8	4
	USNTDP	U-17	13	6	7	13	0	....	....	....	....	....
2009-10	Medicine Hat	WHL	72	37	28	65	26	12	7	3	10	0

EVSEEV, Vladislav (yehv-SAY-ehv, VLA-dih-slav) BOS.

Left wing. Shoots left. 6'2", 196 lbs. Born, Moscow, USSR, September 10, 1984.
(Boston's 2nd choice, 56th overall, in 2002 Entry Draft).

			Regular Season					Playoffs				
Season	Club	League	GP	G	A	Pts	PIM	GP	G	A	Pts	PIM
99-2000	Dyn'o Moscow 2	Russia-3	5	2	3	5	6	....	....	....	....	....
2000-01	Dyn'o Moscow 2	Russia-3	6	5	2	7	2	....	....	....	....	....
2001-02	CSKA Moscow 2	Russia-3	8	2	1	3	2	....	....	....	....	....
	HK CSKA Moscow	Russia-2	15	2	5	7	10	....	....	....	....	....
2002-03	Dynamo Moscow	Russia	22	1	1	2	2	1	0	0	0	0
2003-04	Vityaz Podolsk	Russia-2	8	1	2	3	2	7	0	0	0	2
2004-05	Dynamo Moscow	Russia	12	1	1	2	2	....	....	....	....	....
	Ufa	Russia	5	0	0	0	2	....	....	....	....	....
2005-06	Cherepovets	Russia	30	3	0	3	18	....	....	....	....	....
2006-07	Dynamo Moscow	Russia	30	1	3	4	32	2	0	0	0	0
2007-08	Dynamo Moscow	Russia	3	0	0	0	12	....	....	....	....	....
	Vityaz Chekhov	Russia	30	5	5	10	10	....	....	....	....	....
2008-09	Vityaz Chekhov	Rus-KHL	52	4	3	7	16	....	....	....	....	....
2009-10	Vityaz Chekhov	Rus-KHL	8	1	0	1	0	....	....	....	....	....

EZHOV, Denis (YEHZH-awf, DEH-nihs) BUF.

Defense. Shoots left. 5'11", 200 lbs. Born, Togliatti, USSR, February 28, 1985.
(Buffalo's 5th choice, 114th overall, in 2003 Entry Draft).

			Regular Season					Playoffs				
Season	Club	League	GP	G	A	Pts	PIM	GP	G	A	Pts	PIM
99-2000	Lada Togliatti 2	Russia-3	4	0	0	0	4	....	....	....	....	....
2000-01	Lada Togliatti 2	Russia-3	STATISTICS NOT AVAILABLE									
2001-02	Lada Togliatti 2	Russia-3	4	2	4	6	6	....	....	....	....	....
	Lada Togliatti	Russia	15	0	0	0	6	....	....	....	....	....
2002-03	Lada Togliatti 2	Russia-3	15	2	7	9	4	....	....	....	....	....
	CSK VVS Samara	Russia-2	9	0	1	1	8	....	....	....	....	....
2003-04	Novokuznetsk	Russia	19	0	1	1	2	3	0	0	0	0
	CSKA Moscow 2	Russia-3	4	1	2	3	2	....	....	....	....	....
2004-05	Novokuznetsk	Russia	28	0	0	0	16	4	0	0	0	2
2005-06	Mytischi	Russia	24	1	0	1	10	....	....	....	....	....
	Kristall Elektrostal	Russia-3	STATISTICS NOT AVAILABLE									
2006-07	Chelyabinsk	Russia	54	2	6	8	73	....	....	....	....	....
2007-08	Chelyabinsk	Russia	57	4	9	13	64	3	0	0	0	10
2008-09	Omsk	Rus-KHL	55	2	8	10	58	8	1	0	1	2
2009-10	Omsk	Rus-KHL	31	0	4	4	58	....	....	....	....	....

FADDEN, Mitch (FA-dehn, MIHTCH) T.B.

Center. Shoots left. 6', 200 lbs. Born, Victoria, B.C., April 3, 1988.
(Tampa Bay's 4th choice, 107th overall, in 2007 Entry Draft).

			Regular Season					Playoffs				
Season	Club	League	GP	G	A	Pts	PIM	GP	G	A	Pts	PIM
2003-04	Victoria Cougars	VIJHL	47	36	31	67	63	11	11	4	15	24
	Seattle	WHL	2	0	0	0	0	....	....	....	....	....
2004-05	Seattle	WHL	64	9	12	21	30	12	2	0	2	4
2005-06	Seattle	WHL	38	9	11	20	19	....	....	....	....	....
	Lethbridge	WHL	30	11	17	28	22	6	2	5	7	14
2006-07	Lethbridge	WHL	71	36	48	84	54	....	....	....	....	....
2007-08	Lethbridge	WHL	72	34	55	89	72	19	5	15	20	19
2008-09	Lethbridge	WHL	9	2	3	5	8	....	....	....	....	....
	Tri-City Americans	WHL	54	35	36	71	41	10	3	13	16	8
2009-10	Norfolk Admirals	AHL	53	7	12	19	8	....	....	....	....	....

WHL East Second All-Star Team (2008)

FAHEY, Brian (FAY-hee, BRIGH-uhn) WSH.

Defense. Shoots right. 6'1", 216 lbs. Born, Des Plaines, IL, March 2, 1981.
(Colorado's 7th choice, 119th overall, in 2000 Entry Draft).

			Regular Season					Playoffs				
Season	Club	League	GP	G	A	Pts	PIM	GP	G	A	Pts	PIM
1997-98	USNTDP	U-18	17	1	10	11	12	....	....	....	....	....
	USNTDP	USHL	5	1	1	2	8	....	....	....	....	....
	USNTDP	NAHL	39	5	10	15	35	7	0	0	0	2
1998-99	USNTDP	U-18	6	1	0	1	4	....	....	....	....	....
	USNTDP	USHL	52	9	9	18	34	....	....	....	....	....
99-2000	U. of Wisconsin	WCHA	41	6	11	17	42	....	....	....	....	....
2000-01	U. of Wisconsin	WCHA	38	1	5	6	16	....	....	....	....	....
2001-02	U. of Wisconsin	WCHA	38	2	8	10	55	....	....	....	....	....
2002-03	U. of Wisconsin	WCHA	39	5	4	9	34	....	....	....	....	....
2003-04	Worcester IceCats	AHL	2	0	0	0	2	....	....	....	....	....
	Atlantic City	ECHL	55	11	26	37	49	2	0	0	0	2
	Hershey Bears	AHL	12	0	1	1	6	....	....	....	....	....
2004-05	Atlantic City	ECHL	46	10	16	26	47	3	0	2	2	0
	Worcester IceCats	AHL	20	0	4	4	12	....	....	....	....	....
2005-06	Iowa Stars	AHL	64	6	11	17	74	7	0	1	1	8
	Idaho Steelheads	ECHL	3	1	1	2	4	....	....	....	....	....
2006-07	Chicago Wolves	AHL	75	11	18	29	81	15	3	2	5	20
2007-08	Chicago Wolves	AHL	76	14	23	37	123	24	2	8	10	24
2008-09	Hartford Wolf Pack	AHL	66	4	20	24	67	5	0	1	1	6
2009-10	Lake Erie Monsters	AHL	71	11	14	25	97	....	....	....	....	....

WCHA All-Rookie Team (2000) • ECHL All-Rookie Team (2004)

Signed as a free agent by **Chicago** (AHL), August 31, 2006. Signed as a free agent by **NY Rangers**, July 17, 2008. Traded to **Colorado** by **NY Rangers** for Nigel Wiliams, July 16, 2009. Signed as a free agent by **Washington**, July 7, 2010.

FAIRCHILD, Cade (FAIR-chighld, KAYD) ST.L.

Defense. Shoots left. 5'11", 190 lbs. Born, Duluth, MN, January 15, 1989.
(St. Louis' 7th choice, 96th overall, in 2007 Entry Draft).

			Regular Season					Playoffs				
Season	Club	League	GP	G	A	Pts	PIM	GP	G	A	Pts	PIM
2004-05	Duluth East	High-MN	29	10	32	42	....	....	....	....	....	....
2005-06	USNTDP	U-17	18	2	7	9	4	....	....	....	....	....
	USNTDP	NAHL	36	8	9	17	10	2	0	0	0	0
2006-07	USNTDP	U-18	36	3	16	19	34	....	....	....	....	....
	USNTDP	NAHL	13	1	6	7	16	....	....	....	....	....
2007-08	U. of Minnesota	WCHA	40	2	13	15	22	....	....	....	....	....
2008-09	U. of Minnesota	WCHA	35	9	24	33	52	....	....	....	....	....
2009-10	U. of Minnesota	WCHA	39	4	17	21	36	....	....	....	....	....

WCHA All-Rookie Team (2008)

FALLSTROM, Alexander (FAHL-struhm, al-ehx-AN-duhr) BOS.

Right wing. Shoots right. 6'2", 205 lbs. Born, Goteborg, Sweden, September 15, 1990.
(Minnesota's 4th choice, 116th overall, in 2009 Entry Draft).

			Regular Season					Playoffs				
Season	Club	League	GP	G	A	Pts	PIM	GP	G	A	Pts	PIM
2005-06	Djurgarden U18	Swe-U18	11	1	2	3	2	....	....	....	....	....
2006-07	Djurgarden U18	Swe-U18	33	22	15	37	52	3	2	1	3	2
	Djurgarden Jr.	Swe-Jr.	2	0	0	0	0	1	0	0	0	0
2007-08	Shat.-St. Mary's	High-MN	62	20	27	47	56	....	....	....	....	....
2008-09	Shat.-St. Mary's	High-MN	52	40	47	87	52	....	....	....	....	....
2009-10	Harvard Crimson	ECAC	32	4	8	12	23	....	....	....	....	....

Traded to **Boston** by **Minnesota** with Craig Weller and Minnesota's 2nd round choice in 2011 Entry Draft for Chuck Kobasew, October 18, 2009.

FAST, T.J. (FAST, TEE-JAY) FLA.

Defense. Shoots left. 6'1", 190 lbs. Born, Calgary, Alta., September 2, 1987.
(Los Angeles' 3rd choice, 60th overall, in 2005 Entry Draft).

			Regular Season					Playoffs				
Season	Club	League	GP	G	A	Pts	PIM	GP	G	A	Pts	PIM
2003-04	Cgy. North Stars	AMHL	31	7	7	14	42	....	....	....	....	....
2004-05	Camrose Kodiaks	AJHL	58	8	28	36	40	....	....	....	....	....
2005-06	U. of Denver	WCHA	39	1	6	7	26	....	....	....	....	....
2006-07	U. of Denver	WCHA	19	0	4	4	14	....	....	....	....	....
	Tri-City Americans	WHL	26	3	19	22	30	6	0	1	1	14
2007-08	Tri-City Americans	WHL	71	17	37	54	92	16	1	8	9	16
2008-09	Peoria Rivermen	AHL	46	1	4	5	12	....	....	....	....	....
	Alaska Aces	ECHL	9	0	1	1	6	18	0	5	5	11
2009-10	Peoria Rivermen	AHL	18	0	1	1	4	....	....	....	....	....
	Alaska Aces	ECHL	46	10	21	31	26	4	2	1	3	0

AJHL All-Rookie Team (2005) • WHL West First All-Star Team (2008)

Traded to **St. Louis** by **Los Angeles** for St. Louis' 5th round choice (later traded to Florida – Florida selected Wade Megan) in 2009 Entry Draft, June 4, 2008. Traded to **Florida** by **St. Louis** for Graham Mink, August 3, 2010.

FASTH, Jesper (FAHST, YEHS-puhr) NYR

Right wing. Shoots right. 5'11", 176 lbs. Born, Nassjo, Sweden, December 2, 1991.
(NY Rangers' 5th choice, 157th overall, in 2010 Entry Draft).

			Regular Season					Playoffs				
Season	Club	League	GP	G	A	Pts	PIM	GP	G	A	Pts	PIM
2007-08	HV 71 U18	Swe-U18	30	15	11	26	14	....	....	....	....	....
	HV 71 Jr.	Swe-Jr.	3	0	0	0	2	....	....	....	....	....
2008-09	HV 71 U18	Swe-U18	3	2	2	4	2	....	....	....	....	....
	HV 71 Jr.	Swe-Jr.	37	7	7	14	16	7	2	1	3	6
2009-10	HV 71 Jr.	Swe-Jr.	37	23	26	49	10	3	0	2	2	0
	HV 71 Jonkoping	Sweden	2	0	0	0	0	....	....	....	....	....

FAULK, Justin (FAWLK, JUHS-tihn) CAR.

Defense. Shoots right. 6', 205 lbs. Born, South St. Paul, MN, March 20, 1992.
(Carolina's 2nd choice, 37th overall, in 2010 Entry Draft).

			Regular Season					Playoffs				
Season	Club	League	GP	G	A	Pts	PIM	GP	G	A	Pts	PIM
2007-08	South St. Paul	High-MN	26	6	15	21	32	....	....	....	....	....
2008-09	USNTDP	NAHL	38	3	9	12	20	9	3	3	6	6
	USNTDP	U-17	17	7	9	16	35	....	....	....	....	....
	USNTDP	U-18	1	0	0	0	0	....	....	....	....	....
2009-10	USNTDP	USHL	21	9	3	12	46	....	....	....	....	....
	USNTDP	U-18	39	12	9	21	20	....	....	....	....	....

• Signed Letter of Intent to attend **University of Minnesota-Duluth** (WCHA) in fall of 2010.

FAUST, Joe (FOWST, JOH) N.J.

Defense. Shoots right. 5'11", 190 lbs. Born, Edina, MN, November 15, 1991.
(New Jersey's 3rd choice, 114th overall, in 2010 Entry Draft).

			Regular Season					Playoffs				
Season	Club	League	GP	G	A	Pts	PIM	GP	G	A	Pts	PIM
2007-08	Bloomington-Jeff.	High-MN	28	4	14	18	10	....	....	....	....	....
2008-09	Bloomington-Jeff.	High-MN	28	14	26	40	12	....	....	....	....	....
2009-10	Team Southeast	UMHSEL	24	3	6	9	....	....	....	....	....	....
	Bloomington-Jeff.	High-MN	25	12	28	40	18	3	2	4	6	2

• Signed Letter of Intent to attend **University of Wisconsin** (WCHA) in fall of 2011.

FAYNE, Mark (FAYN, MAHRK) N.J.

Defense. Shoots right. 6'3", 220 lbs. Born, Nashua, NH, May 15, 1987.
(New Jersey's 5th choice, 155th overall, in 2005 Entry Draft).

			Regular Season					Playoffs				
Season	Club	League	GP	G	A	Pts	PIM	GP	G	A	Pts	PIM
2003-04	Nobles	High-MA	20	3	5	8	14	....	....	....	....	....
2004-05	Nobles	High-MA	24	1	17	18	16	....	....	....	....	....
2005-06	Nobles	High-MA	29	10	24	34	....	....	....	....	....	....
2006-07	Providence College	H-East	36	5	7	12	43	....	....	....	....	....
2007-08	Providence College	H-East	36	2	4	6	18	....	....	....	....	....
2008-09	Providence College	H-East	33	4	5	9	30	....	....	....	....	....
2009-10	Providence College	H-East	34	5	17	22	14	....	....	....	....	....

FEDOROV, Yevgeny (FEH-duh-rahf, yehv-GEH-nee) **DAL.**

Center. Shoots left. 5'10", 187 lbs. Born, Sverdlovsk, USSR, November 11, 1980.
(Los Angeles' 6th choice, 201st overall, in 2000 Entry Draft).

			Regular Season					Playoffs				
Season	Club	League	GP	G	A	Pts	PIM	GP	G	A	Pts	PIM
1997-98	Krylja Sovetov 2	Russia-3	20	1	6	7	48	....	....	....	....	....
	Krylja Sovetov	Russia	32	1	0	1	12	....	....	....	....	....
1998-99	Krylja Sovetov	Russia	52	5	3	8	61	....	....	....	....	....
99-2000	Perm	Russia	37	5	5	10	20	3	0	1	1	4
2000-01	Perm	Russia	43	9	9	18	18	....	....	....	....	....
2001-02	Ak Bars Kazan	Russia	45	10	12	22	12	11	0	0	0	2
2002-03	Ak Bars Kazan	Russia	46	4	11	15	26	5	1	0	1	2
2003-04	Ak Bars Kazan	Russia	47	7	4	11	14	4	0	0	0	0
2004-05	Ak Bars Kazan	Russia	47	4	10	14	10	....	....	....	....	....
2005-06	Dynamo Moscow	Russia	35	7	9	16	16	....	....	....	....	....
2006-07	Dynamo Moscow	Russia	48	15	9	24	42	3	0	0	0	0
2007-08	Magnitogorsk	Russia	49	9	10	19	64	13	1	1	2	2
2008-09	Magnitogorsk	Rus-KHL	54	0	4	4	14	11	1	1	2	8
2009-10	MVD	Rus-KHL	53	5	12	17	24	22	4	2	6	2

Traded to **Dallas** by **Los Angeles** for Dallas' 6th round choice (later traded to Chicago - Chicago selected Braden Birch) in 2008 Entry Draft, December 10, 2007.

FERLAND, Michael (FAIR-land, MIGH-kuhl) **CGY.**

Left wing. Shoots left. 6', 195 lbs. Born, Swan River, Man., April 20, 1992.
(Calgary's 5th choice, 133rd overall, in 2010 Entry Draft).

			Regular Season					Playoffs				
Season	Club	League	GP	G	A	Pts	PIM	GP	G	A	Pts	PIM
2007-08	Brandon	MMHL	40	12	8	20	20	6	3	2	5	4
2008-09	Brandon	MMHL	44	45	40	85	52	6	4	5	9	8
2009-10	Brandon	WHL	61	9	19	28	85	15	3	1	4	8

FERNHOLM, Daniel (FUHRN-hohlm, DAN-yehl) **PIT.**

Defense. Shoots left. 6'4", 218 lbs. Born, Stockholm, Sweden, December 20, 1983.
(Pittsburgh's 4th choice, 101st overall, in 2002 Entry Draft).

			Regular Season					Playoffs				
Season	Club	League	GP	G	A	Pts	PIM	GP	G	A	Pts	PIM
99-2000	Mora IK Jr.	Swe-Jr.	33	3	3	6	8	1	0	0	0	0
2000-01	Mora IK Jr.	Swe-Jr.	3	0	1	1	2	....	....	....	....	....
	Mora IK	Sweden-2	2	0	0	0	0	....	....	....	....	....
2001-02	Djurgarden Jr.	Swe-Jr.	8	6	13	19	12	3	0	0	0	0
2002-03	Huddinge IK	Sweden-2	39	6	10	16	20	2	1	0	1	0
	Huddinge IK Jr.	Swe-Jr.	1	0	0	0	2	....	....	....	....	....
2003-04	Djurgarden	Sweden	37	4	7	11	28	4	0	0	0	4
	Hammarby	Sweden-2	15	1	3	4	6	....	....	....	....	....
2004-05	Djurgarden Jr.	Swe-Jr.	2	0	0	0	4	....	....	....	....	....
	HC Forst Bolzano	Italy	7	0	2	2	2	....	....	....	....	....
	Djurgarden	Sweden	31	3	2	5	22	11	0	0	0	14
2005-06	Wilkes-Barre	AHL	27	1	6	7	10	....	....	....	....	....
	Wheeling Nailers	ECHL	29	2	4	6	20	9	1	3	4	6
2006-07	Wheeling Nailers	ECHL	13	0	3	3	14	....	....	....	....	....
	Djurgarden	Sweden	32	4	12	16	16	....	....	....	....	....
2007-08	Linkopings HC	Sweden	54	8	21	29	28	16	3	7	10	20
2008-09	Linkopings HC	Sweden	40	5	8	13	22	7	2	2	4	6
2009-10	Linkopings HC	Sweden	52	3	16	19	42	12	0	2	2	12

FERRARO, Landon (fuh-RAHR-oh, LAN-duhn) **DET.**

Center. Shoots right. 5'11", 165 lbs. Born, Trail, B.C., August 8, 1991.
(Detroit's 1st choice, 32nd overall, in 2009 Entry Draft).

			Regular Season					Playoffs				
Season	Club	League	GP	G	A	Pts	PIM	GP	G	A	Pts	PIM
2006-07	Van. NW Giants	BCMML	25	21	13	34	77	....	....	....	....	....
	Red Deer Rebels	WHL	4	0	0	0	0	1	0	0	0	0
2007-08	Red Deer Rebels	WHL	54	13	11	24	65	....	....	....	....	....
2008-09	Red Deer Rebels	WHL	68	37	18	55	99	....	....	....	....	....
2009-10	Red Deer Rebels	WHL	53	16	30	46	55	3	0	0	0	2
	Grand Rapids	AHL	2	0	0	0	0	....	....	....	....	....

FERRIERO, Cody (fair-ee-AIR-oh, KOH-dee) **S.J.**

Center. Shoots right. 5'10", 195 lbs. Born, Boston, MA, December 19, 1991.
(San Jose's 3rd choice, 127th overall, in 2010 Entry Draft).

			Regular Season					Playoffs				
Season	Club	League	GP	G	A	Pts	PIM	GP	G	A	Pts	PIM
2006-07	Gov. Academy	High-MA	27	6	3	9	26	....	....	....	....	....
2007-08	Gov. Academy	High-MA	25	13	9	22	26	....	....	....	....	....
2008-09	Gov. Academy	High-MA	27	10	10	20	87	....	....	....	....	....
2009-10	Gov. Academy	High-MA	27	21	19	40	112	....	....	....	....	....

• Signed Letter of Intent to attend **Northeastern University** (Hockey East) in fall of 2010.

FIENHAGE, Corey (fihn-AW-gee, KOH-ree) **BUF.**

Defense. Shoots right. 6'2", 223 lbs. Born, Topeka, KS, May 4, 1990.
(Buffalo's 4th choice, 81st overall, in 2008 Entry Draft).

			Regular Season					Playoffs				
Season	Club	League	GP	G	A	Pts	PIM	GP	G	A	Pts	PIM
2005-06	Eastview High	High-MN	25	1	6	7	32	....	....	....	....	....
2006-07	Eastview High	High-MN	20	4	11	15	....	....	....	....	....	....
	Team Southeast	UMWEHL	11	4	4	8	....	....	....	....	....	....
2007-08	Eastview High	High-MN	26	6	10	16	87	....	....	....	....	....
	Team Southeast	UMWEHL	12	2	4	6	....	....	....	....	....	....
	Indiana Ice	USHL	12	1	2	3	12	2	0	0	0	0
2008-09	North Dakota	WCHA	9	0	1	1	28	....	....	....	....	....
2009-10	North Dakota	WCHA	30	0	2	2	28	....	....	....	....	....

FIGREN, Robin (FIH-grehn, RAW-bihn) **NYI**

Wing. Shoots right. 5'11", 176 lbs. Born, Stockholm, Sweden, March 7, 1988.
(NY Islanders' 3rd choice, 70th overall, in 2006 Entry Draft).

			Regular Season					Playoffs				
Season	Club	League	GP	G	A	Pts	PIM	GP	G	A	Pts	PIM
2003-04	Hammarby U18	Swe-U18	11	5	5	10	22	....	....	....	....	....
2004-05	Frolunda U18	Swe-U18	12	13	8	21	94	7	4	4	8	10
	Frolunda Jr.	Swe-Jr.	4	1	2	3	0	....	....	....	....	....
2005-06	Frolunda Jr.	Swe-Jr.	38	10	18	28	72	7	4	2	6	6
	Frolunda	Sweden	2	0	0	0	0	....	....	....	....	....
	Frolunda U18	Swe-U18	1	1	0	1	2	2	2	0	2	0
2006-07	Calgary Hitmen	WHL	62	10	17	27	54	18	4	4	8	18
2007-08	Edmonton	WHL	35	18	13	31	46	....	....	....	....	....
2008-09	Djurgarden	Sweden	49	3	6	9	28	....	....	....	....	....
	Bridgeport	AHL	3	0	1	1	2	....	....	....	....	....
2009-10	Bridgeport	AHL	62	3	4	7	24	4	1	1	2	6

FILPPULA, Ilari (FIHL-poo-luh) **DET.**

Left wing. Shoots left. 5'11", 191 lbs. Born, Vantaa, Finland, November 5, 1981.

			Regular Season					Playoffs				
Season	Club	League	GP	G	A	Pts	PIM	GP	G	A	Pts	PIM
1996-97	Kiekko-Vantaa Jr.	Fin-Jr.	1	0	2	2	0	....	....	....	....	....
1997-98	K-Vantaa U18	Fin-U18	21	10	17	27	12	....	....	....	....	....
	Kiekko-Vantaa Jr.	Fin-Jr.	1	1	1	2	0	....	....	....	....	....
1998-99	Kiekko-Vantaa Jr.	Fin-Jr.	19	7	5	12	4	....	....	....	....	....
99-2000	K-Vantaa U18	Fin-U18	4	2	1	3	0	....	....	....	....	....
	Kiekko-Vantaa Jr.	Fin-Jr.	28	12	44	56	39	....	....	....	....	....
	Kiekko-Vantaa	Finland-3	2	0	0	0	0	....	....	....	....	....
2000-01	Jokerit Helsinki Jr.	Fin-Jr.	38	18	40	58	16	2	1	0	1	0
2001-02	Kiekko-Vantaa	Finland-2	44	13	22	35	20	5	4	2	6	2
2002-03	Kiekko-Vantaa	Finland-2	41	19	28	47	14	12	0	7	7	4
	Jokerit Helsinki	Finland	1	0	0	0	0	....	....	....	....	....
2003-04	JYP Jyvaskyla	Finland	47	3	6	9	12	1	0	0	0	0
2004-05	JYP Jyvaskyla	Finland	55	8	10	18	10	3	1	0	1	0
2005-06	Jokerit Helsinki	Finland	56	9	16	25	14	....	....	....	....	....
2006-07	JYP Jyvaskyla	Finland	54	15	26	41	36	....	....	....	....	....
2007-08	JYP Jyvaskyla	Finland	56	7	15	22	20	6	0	1	1	0
2008-09	TPS Turku	Finland	48	6	17	23	47	8	0	3	3	6
2009-10	TPS Turku	Finland	58	12	37	49	24	15	2	*12	14	6

Signed as a free agent by **Detroit**, June 16, 2010.

FINLEY, Joe (FIHN-lee, JOH) **WSH.**

Defense. Shoots left. 6'7", 245 lbs. Born, Edina, MN, June 29, 1987.
(Washington's 2nd choice, 27th overall, in 2005 Entry Draft).

			Regular Season					Playoffs				
Season	Club	League	GP	G	A	Pts	PIM	GP	G	A	Pts	PIM
2004-05	Sioux Falls	USHL	55	3	10	13	181	....	....	....	....	....
2005-06	North Dakota	WCHA	43	0	3	3	96	....	....	....	....	....
2006-07	North Dakota	WCHA	41	1	6	7	72	....	....	....	....	....
2007-08	North Dakota	WCHA	43	4	11	15	79	....	....	....	....	....
2008-09	North Dakota	WCHA	27	2	8	10	56	....	....	....	....	....
	Hershey Bears	AHL	1	0	0	0	7	....	....	....	....	....
2009-10	South Carolina	ECHL	17	1	3	4	43	....	....	....	....	....

• Missed majority of 2009-10 season recovering from hand injury.

FISCHER, David (FIH-shuhr, DAY-vihd)

Defense. Shoots right. 6'3", 185 lbs. Born, Minneapolis, MN, February 19, 1988.
(Montreal's 1st choice, 20th overall, in 2006 Entry Draft).

			Regular Season					Playoffs				
Season	Club	League	GP	G	A	Pts	PIM	GP	G	A	Pts	PIM
2003-04	Apple Valley	High-MN	27	2	9	11	10	....	....	....	....	....
2004-05	Apple Valley	High-MN	28	8	20	28	36	....	....	....	....	....
2005-06	Apple Valley	High-MN	28	8	31	39	22	....	....	....	....	....
2006-07	U. of Minnesota	WCHA	42	0	5	5	14	....	....	....	....	....
2007-08	U. of Minnesota	WCHA	45	2	12	14	18	....	....	....	....	....
2008-09	U. of Minnesota	WCHA	31	2	11	13	16	....	....	....	....	....
2009-10	U. of Minnesota	WCHA	39	2	4	6	28	....	....	....	....	....

FLAAKE, Jerome (FLAH-keh, juh-ROHM) **TOR.**

Left wing. Shoots left. 6'2", 187 lbs. Born, Guben, East Germany, March 2, 1990.
(Toronto's 6th choice, 130th overall, in 2008 Entry Draft).

			Regular Season					Playoffs				
Season	Club	League	GP	G	A	Pts	PIM	GP	G	A	Pts	PIM
2005-06	Riessersee Jr.	Ger-Jr.	36	20	18	38	36	3	0	2	2	0
2006-07	Heil./Mann. Jr.	Ger-Jr.	36	32	31	63	36	6	4	3	7	8
2007-08	Kolner Haie	Germany	30	0	1	1	4	....	....	....	....	....
	Koln Jr.	Ger-Jr.	32	33	41	74	68	4	2	4	6	41
2008-09	Kolner Haie	Germany	43	5	11	16	22	....	....	....	....	....
2009-10	Kolner Haie	Germany	42	3	6	9	45	....	....	....	....	....
	Bremerhaven	German-2	2	0	3	3	0	....	....	....	....	....

FLEMMING, Brett (FLEH-mihng, BREHT) **WSH.**

Defense. Shoots right. 5'11", 178 lbs. Born, Regina, Sask., February 26, 1991.
(Washington's 5th choice, 145th overall, in 2009 Entry Draft).

			Regular Season					Playoffs				
Season	Club	League	GP	G	A	Pts	PIM	GP	G	A	Pts	PIM
2006-07	Burlington Eagles	Minor-ON	67	15	36	51	130	....	....	....	....	....
2007-08	St. Michael's	OHL	47	1	9	10	30	4	0	0	0	6
2008-09	St. Michael's	OHL	64	3	25	28	89	10	1	3	4	2
2009-10	St. Michael's	OHL	68	1	23	24	90	16	0	5	5	10

FLETCHER, Justin (FLEH-chuhr, JUHS-tihn)

Defense. Shoots left. 5'11", 185 lbs. Born, Maryville, IL, March 30, 1983.

			Regular Season					Playoffs				
Season	Club	League	GP	G	A	Pts	PIM	GP	G	A	Pts	PIM
2000-01	Sioux City	USHL	38	0	5	5	28	3	0	0	0	0
2001-02	Sioux City	USHL	56	3	10	13	48	12	2	1	3	6
2002-03	Sioux City	USHL	60	12	31	43	28	4	0	3	3	6
2003-04	St. Cloud State	WCHA	29	6	7	13	22	....	....	....	....	....
2004-05	St. Cloud State	WCHA	36	8	14	22	86	....	....	....	....	....
2005-06	St. Cloud State	WCHA	40	6	21	27	55	....	....	....	....	....
2006-07	St. Cloud State	WCHA	38	6	18	24	37	....	....	....	....	....
	Springfield Falcons	AHL	10	3	1	4	4	....	....	....	....	....
2007-08	Norfolk Admirals	AHL	39	1	4	5	37	....	....	....	....	....
	Rockford IceHogs	AHL	20	4	7	11	43	11	0	1	1	6
2008-09	Peoria Rivermen	AHL	68	8	24	32	50	7	0	2	2	6
2009-10	Peoria Rivermen	AHL	42	3	14	17	19	....	....	....	....	....

Signed as a free agent by **Tampa Bay**, April 30, 2007. Signed as a free agent by **St. Louis**, July 20, 2009.

FLICK, Rob (FLIHK, RAWB) **CHI.**

Center. Shoots left. 6'2", 205 lbs. Born, London, Ont., March 28, 1991.
(Chicago's 7th choice, 120th overall, in 2010 Entry Draft).

			Regular Season					Playoffs				
Season	Club	League	GP	G	A	Pts	PIM	GP	G	A	Pts	PIM
2007-08	London Nationals	OJHL-B	8	0	1	1	25	....	....	....	....	...
	Lon. Jr. Knights	Minor-ON	57	32	29	61	160	....	....	....	....	....
2008-09	St. Michael's	OHL	48	4	4	8	69	10	1	1	2	14
2009-10	St. Michael's	OHL	65	15	19	34	157	16	2	2	4	*44

FLOREK, Justin (FLOHR-ehk, JUHS-tihn) BOS.

Left wing. Shoots left. 6'4", 202 lbs. Born, Marquette, MI, May 18, 1990.
(Boston's 5th choice, 135th overall, in 2010 Entry Draft).

			Regular Season					Playoffs				
Season	Club	League	GP	G	A	Pts	PIM	GP	G	A	Pts	PIM
2006-07	USNTDP	NAHL	47	11	10	21	40	6	3	0	3	4
	USNTDP	U-17	13	6	1	7	8	....	....	....	....	....
2007-08	USNTDP	NAHL	13	3	3	6	8	....	....	....	....	....
	USNTDP	U-17	1	0	0	0	2	....	....	....	....	....
	USNTDP	U-18	41	5	5	10	20	....	....	....	....	....
2008-09	Northern Mich.	CCHA	40	9	8	17	6	....	....	....	....	....
2009-10	Northern Mich.	CCHA	41	12	23	35	22	....	....	....	....	....

FLYNN, Ryan (FLIHN, RIGH-uhn) NSH.

Right wing. Shoots right. 6'3", 211 lbs. Born, St. Paul, MN, March 22, 1988.
(Nashville's 4th choice, 176th overall, in 2006 Entry Draft).

			Regular Season					Playoffs				
Season	Club	League	GP	G	A	Pts	PIM	GP	G	A	Pts	PIM
2003-04	Centennial	High-MN	30	29	39	68	....	....	....	....	....	....
2004-05	USNTDP	U-17	14	4	5	9	12	....	....	....	....	....
	USNTDP	NAHL	41	11	8	19	31	9	2	4	6	7
2005-06	USNTDP	U-18	42	10	12	22	57	....	....	....	....	....
	USNTDP	NAHL	17	6	5	11	20	....	....	....	....	....
2006-07	U. of Minnesota	WCHA	43	5	8	13	58	....	....	....	....	....
2007-08	U. of Minnesota	WCHA	38	4	11	15	51	....	....	....	....	....
2008-09	U. of Minnesota	WCHA	37	6	13	19	62	....	....	....	....	....
2009-10	U. of Minnesota	WCHA	38	2	8	10	36	....	....	....	....	....
	Milwaukee	AHL	2	0	0	0	0	1	0	0	0	0

FOLIGNO, Marcus (foh-LEE-noh, MAHR-kuhs) BUF.

Left wing. Shoots left. 6'3", 222 lbs. Born, Buffalo, NY, August 10, 1991.
(Buffalo's 3rd choice, 104th overall, in 2009 Entry Draft).

			Regular Season					Playoffs				
Season	Club	League	GP	G	A	Pts	PIM	GP	G	A	Pts	PIM
2006-07	Sudbury	Minor-ON	30	21	15	36	70	....	....	....	....	....
2007-08	Sudbury Wolves	OHL	66	5	6	11	38	....	....	....	....	....
2008-09	Sudbury Wolves	OHL	65	12	18	30	96	6	1	2	3	9
2009-10	Sudbury Wolves	OHL	67	14	25	39	156	4	1	1	2	6

FORBORT, Derek (FOHR-bohrt, DAIR-ihk) L.A.

Defense. Shoots left. 6'5", 198 lbs. Born, Duluth, MN, March 4, 1992.
(Los Angeles' 1st choice, 15th overall, in 2010 Entry Draft).

			Regular Season					Playoffs				
Season	Club	League	GP	G	A	Pts	PIM	GP	G	A	Pts	PIM
2008-09	Duluth East	High-MN	25	7	21	28	....	....	....	....	....	....
	USNTDP	NAHL	2	0	1	1	6	....	....	....	....	....
	USNTDP	U-17	7	1	4	5	4	....	....	....	....	....
2009-10	USNTDP	USHL	26	4	10	14	26	....	....	....	....	....
	USNTDP	U-18	39	1	13	14	20	....	....	....	....	....

• Signed Letter of Intent to attend **University of North Dakota** (WCHA) in fall of 2010.

FORD, Matthew (FOHRD, MA-thew)

Right wing. Shoots right. 6'1", 207 lbs. Born, West Hills, CA, October 9, 1984.
(Chicago's 16th choice, 256th overall, in 2004 Entry Draft).

			Regular Season					Playoffs				
Season	Club	League	GP	G	A	Pts	PIM	GP	G	A	Pts	PIM
2003-04	Sioux Falls	USHL	60	*37	31	68	60	....	....	....	....	....
2004-05	U. of Wisconsin	WCHA	21	5	5	10	18	....	....	....	....	....
2005-06	U. of Wisconsin	WCHA	31	5	2	7	14	....	....	....	....	....
2006-07	U. of Wisconsin	WCHA	39	7	6	13	38	....	....	....	....	....
2007-08	U. of Wisconsin	WCHA	33	4	5	9	30	....	....	....	....	....
2008-09	Hartford Wolf Pack	AHL	25	1	2	3	10	....	....	....	....	....
	Lake Erie Monsters	AHL	5	0	0	0	2	....	....	....	....	....
	Charlotte	ECHL	28	21	17	38	25	6	2	3	5	21
2009-10	Lake Erie Monsters	AHL	45	13	14	27	28	....	....	....	....	....
	Charlotte	ECHL	3	0	2	2	6	....	....	....	....	....

USHL Rookie of the Year (2004)

FORNEY, Michael (FOHR-NEE, MIGH-kuhl) ATL.

Right wing. Shoots right. 6'2", 200 lbs. Born, Thief River Falls, MN, May 14, 1988.
(Atlanta's 3rd choice, 80th overall, in 2006 Entry Draft).

			Regular Season					Playoffs				
Season	Club	League	GP	G	A	Pts	PIM	GP	G	A	Pts	PIM
2002-03	Thief River Falls	High-MN	28	4	10	14	....	....	....	....	....	....
2003-04	Thief River Falls	High-MN	24	14	22	36	....	....	....	....	....	....
2004-05	Thief River Falls	High-MN	28	34	33	67	....	....	....	....	....	....
2005-06	Thief River Falls	High-MN	21	23	37	60	28	....	....	....	....	....
	Des Moines	USHL	3	0	0	0	0	....	....	....	....	....
2006-07	North Dakota	WCHA	16	0	2	2	10	....	....	....	....	....
2007-08	North Dakota	WCHA	3	0	0	0	2	....	....	....	....	....
2008-09	Green Bay	USHL	59	26	34	60	53	7	3	7	10	2
2009-10	Chicago Wolves	AHL	3	0	0	0	0	....	....	....	....	....
	Gwinnett	ECHL	63	11	15	26	66	....	....	....	....	....

FORTIER, Olivier (FOHR-t'yay, OH-lihv-ee-ay) MTL.

Center. Shoots left. 5'11", 181 lbs. Born, Quebec City, Que., May 2, 1989.
(Montreal's 4th choice, 65th overall, in 2007 Entry Draft).

			Regular Season					Playoffs				
Season	Club	League	GP	G	A	Pts	PIM	GP	G	A	Pts	PIM
2004-05	Sem. St-Francois	QAAA	31	7	17	24	8	4	2	1	3	4
2005-06	Drummondville	QMJHL	13	2	2	4	14	....	....	....	....	....
	Rimouski Oceanic	QMJHL	27	4	8	12	16	....	....	....	....	....
2006-07	Rimouski Oceanic	QMJHL	69	28	36	64	28	....	....	....	....	....
2007-08	Rimouski Oceanic	QMJHL	67	23	23	46	37	3	1	0	1	4
2008-09	Rimouski Oceanic	QMJHL	29	8	27	35	12	13	4	5	9	12
2009-10	Hamilton Bulldogs	AHL	1	0	0	0	0	10	1	0	1	0

• Missed majority of 2008-09 season revovering from knee injury suffered in game at Baie-Comeau (QMJHL), October 31, 2008. • Missed majority of 2009-10 season recovering from shoulder injury and resulting surgery.

FOSS, Jeffrey (FAWS, JEHF-ree) NSH.

Defense. Shoots right. 6'2", 206 lbs. Born, Fargo, ND, December 12, 1988.
(Nashville's 5th choice, 166th overall, in 2008 Entry Draft).

			Regular Season					Playoffs				
Season	Club	League	GP	G	A	Pts	PIM	GP	G	A	Pts	PIM
2004-05	Moorhead Spuds	High-MN	22	1	4	5	6	....	....	....	....	....
2005-06	Moorhead Spuds	High-MN	26	4	17	21	16	....	....	....	....	....
	Team Great Plains	UMWEHL	11	4	9	13	....	....	....	....	....	....
2006-07	Moorhead Spuds	High-MN	26	15	31	46	28	....	....	....	....	....
	Team Great Plains	UMWEHL	12	3	13	16	....	....	....	....	....	....
	Sioux Falls	USHL	11	0	1	1	10	4	0	1	1	2
2007-08	RPI Engineers	ECAC	38	1	3	4	28	....	....	....	....	....
2008-09	RPI Engineers	ECAC	39	2	9	11	58	....	....	....	....	....
2009-10	RPI Engineers	ECAC	39	2	7	9	32	....	....	....	....	....

FOUCAULT, Kris (foo-KOH, KRIHS) MIN.

Left wing. Shoots left. 6'1", 207 lbs. Born, Calgary, Alta., December 12, 1990.
(Minnesota's 3rd choice, 103rd overall, in 2009 Entry Draft).

			Regular Season					Playoffs				
Season	Club	League	GP	G	A	Pts	PIM	GP	G	A	Pts	PIM
2006-07	Calgary Buffaloes	AMHL	35	7	6	13	46	....	....	....	....	....
	Swift Current	WHL	3	0	0	0	0	....	....	....	....	....
2007-08	Kootenay Ice	WHL	33	0	3	3	12	8	2	1	3	2
2008-09	Kootenay Ice	WHL	4	0	1	1	4	....	....	....	....	....
	Canmore Eagles	AJHL	32	18	23	41	84	....	....	....	....	....
	Calgary Hitmen	WHL	22	9	7	16	12	18	11	5	16	10
2009-10	Calgary Hitmen	WHL	68	22	21	43	31	23	9	7	16	21

FOURNIER, Gleason (FOHR-nyay, GLEE-suhn) DET.

Defense. Shoots left. 6', 176 lbs. Born, Rimouski, Que., September 8, 1991.
(Detroit's 4th choice, 90th overall, in 2009 Entry Draft).

			Regular Season					Playoffs				
Season	Club	League	GP	G	A	Pts	PIM	GP	G	A	Pts	PIM
2006-07	Ecole Notre Dame	QAAA	44	3	17	20	32	13	0	2	2	30
2007-08	Rimouski Oceanic	QMJHL	56	3	8	11	26	3	0	0	0	0
2008-09	Rimouski Oceanic	QMJHL	66	3	25	28	64	4	0	0	0	0
2009-10	Rimouski Oceanic	QMJHL	58	13	37	50	76	12	2	10	12	10

FOWLER, Cam (FOW-luhr, KAM) ANA.

Defense. Shoots left. 6'1", 190 lbs. Born, Windsor, Ont., December 5, 1991.
(Anaheim's 1st choice, 12th overall, in 2010 Entry Draft).

			Regular Season					Playoffs				
Season	Club	League	GP	G	A	Pts	PIM	GP	G	A	Pts	PIM
2006-07	Det. Honeybaked	MWEHL	21	5	13	18	18	....	....	....	....	....
	Det. Honeybaked	Minor-MI	31	3	7	10	....	....	....	....	....	....
2007-08	USNTDP	NAHL	38	3	10	13	2	3	0	0	0	2
	USNTDP	U-17	18	0	2	2	8	....	....	....	....	....
	USNTDP	U-18	1	0	0	0	0	....	....	....	....	....
2008-09	USNTDP	NAHL	14	2	7	9	12	....	....	....	....	....
	USNTDP	U-18	33	6	25	31	32	....	....	....	....	....
2009-10	Windsor Spitfires	OHL	55	8	47	55	14	19	3	11	14	10

Memorial Cup All-Star Team (2010)

FRANSSON, Johan (FRAN-suhn, YOH-han) L.A.

Defense. Shoots left. 6'1", 183 lbs. Born, Kalix, Sweden, February 18, 1985.
(Dallas' 2nd choice, 34th overall, in 2004 Entry Draft).

			Regular Season					Playoffs				
Season	Club	League	GP	G	A	Pts	PIM	GP	G	A	Pts	PIM
2000-01	Kalix HF	Sweden-3	19	0	6	6	8	....	....	....	....	....
2001-02	Lulea HF U18	Swe-U18	5	2	0	2	0	....	....	....	....	....
	Lulea HF Jr.	Swe-Jr.	29	4	4	8	28	5	0	1	1	8
2002-03	Lulea HF Jr.	Swe-Jr.	24	2	4	6	67	....	....	....	....	....
	Lulea HF U18	Swe-U18	2	0	0	0	2	....	....	....	....	....
	Lulea HF	Sweden	3	0	0	0	0	....	....	....	....	....
2003-04	Lulea HF Jr.	Swe-Jr.	5	0	2	2	10	....	....	....	....	....
	Lulea HF	Sweden	44	3	3	6	28	2	0	0	0	4
2004-05	Lulea HF Jr.	Swe-Jr.	1	1	1	2	0	7	1	2	3	4
	Lulea HF	Sweden	43	1	6	7	30	3	0	0	0	0
2005-06	Lulea HF	Sweden	50	3	5	8	74	6	1	1	2	6
2006-07	Frolunda	Sweden	35	0	6	6	18	....	....	....	....	....
	Assat Pori	Finland	6	0	1	1	2	....	....	....	....	....
	Linkopings HC	Sweden	8	0	0	0	4	15	0	0	0	2
2007-08	Linkopings HC	Sweden	48	5	9	14	24	16	0	5	5	16
2008-09	Linkopings HC	Sweden	40	3	7	10	24	....	....	....	....	....
	HC Lugano	Swiss	7	2	3	5	2	4	2	0	2	0
2009-10	Lulea HF	Sweden	54	11	19	30	26	....	....	....	....	....

• Rights traded to **Los Angeles** by **Dallas** with Jaroslav Modry, Dallas' 2nd (Oscar Moller) and 3rd (Bryan Cameron) round choices in 2007 Entry Draft and Dallas' 1st round choice (later traded to Phoenix - Phoenix selected Viktor Tikhonov) in 2008 Entry Draft for Mattias Norstrom, Konstantin Pushkarev and Los Angeles' 3rd (Sergei Korostin) and 4th (later traded to Columbus - Columbus selected Maxim Mayorov) round choices in 2007 Entry Draft, February 27, 2007.

FRATTIN, Matt (FRA-tihn, MAT) TOR.

Right wing. Shoots right. 5'11", 187 lbs. Born, Edmonton, Alta., January 3, 1988.
(Toronto's 2nd choice, 99th overall, in 2007 Entry Draft).

			Regular Season					Playoffs				
Season	Club	League	GP	G	A	Pts	PIM	GP	G	A	Pts	PIM
2004-05	Gregg Distributors	AMHL	34	12	13	25	14	....	....	....	....	....
2005-06	Gregg Distributors	AMHL	34	20	17	37	48	6	5	1	6	4
	Ft. Saskatchewan	AJHL	3	2	0	2	0	....	....	....	....	....
2006-07	Ft. Saskatchewan	AJHL	58	49	34	83	75	15	5	6	11	10
2007-08	North Dakota	WCHA	43	4	11	15	18	....	....	....	....	....
2008-09	North Dakota	WCHA	42	13	12	25	48	....	....	....	....	....
2009-10	North Dakota	WCHA	24	11	8	19	21	....	....	....	....	....

FRETTER, Colton (FREH-tuhr, KOHL-tuhn)

Right wing. Shoots right. 5'10", 187 lbs. Born, Harrow, Ont., March 12, 1982.
(Atlanta's 8th choice, 230th overall, in 2002 Entry Draft).

			Regular Season					Playoffs				
Season	Club	League	GP	G	A	Pts	PIM	GP	G	A	Pts	PIM
99-2000	Chatham Maroons	OHA-B	40	12	22	34	34	....	....	....	....	....
2000-01	Chatham Maroons	OHA-B	54	33	39	72	....	15	7	6	13	....
2001-02	Chatham Maroons	OHA-B	52	51	53	104	62	15	5	3	8	2
2002-03	Michigan State	CCHA	35	7	15	22	36	....	....	....	....	....
2003-04	Michigan State	CCHA	39	6	11	17	22	....	....	....	....	....
2004-05	Michigan State	CCHA	40	20	24	44	28	....	....	....	....	....
2005-06	Michigan State	CCHA	45	10	19	29	28	....	....	....	....	....
2006-07	Gwinnett	ECHL	51	36	32	68	46	4	3	0	3	4
2007-08	Chicago Wolves	AHL	8	1	3	4	2	....	....	....	....	....
	Gwinnett	ECHL	2	2	0	2	4	....	....	....	....	....
	Bridgeport	AHL	18	9	2	11	14	....	....	....	....	....
2008-09	Portland Pirates	AHL	80	24	16	40	43	5	0	1	1	0
2009-10	Springfield Falcons	AHL	79	26	29	55	51	....	....	....	....	....

ECHL All-Rookie Team (2007) • ECHL – Rookie of the Year (2007)

Signed as a free agent by **Buffalo**, August 4, 2008. Signed as a free agent by **Springfield** (AHL), August 3, 2009.

FRIESEN, Alex (FREE-zuhn, Al-ehx) VAN.

Center. Shoots left. 5'9", 191 lbs. Born, St. Catharines, Ont., January 30, 1991.
(Vancouver's 3rd choice, 172nd overall, in 2010 Entry Draft).

			Regular Season					Playoffs				
Season	Club	League	GP	G	A	Pts	PIM	GP	G	A	Pts	PIM
2006-07	Niagara Falls	Minor-ON	69	45	67	112	66	....	....	....	....	....
2007-08	Niagara Ice Dogs	OHL	46	5	9	14	26	10	0	2	2	6
2008-09	Niagara Ice Dogs	OHL	64	11	22	33	94	12	3	7	10	25
2009-10	Niagara Ice Dogs	OHL	60	23	37	60	94	5	1	6	7	8

FRITSCHE, Tom (FRIHCH, TAWM) COL.

Left wing. Shoots left. 5'11", 183 lbs. Born, Parma, OH, September 30, 1986.
(Colorado's 3rd choice, 47th overall, in 2005 Entry Draft).

			Regular Season					Playoffs				
Season	Club	League	GP	G	A	Pts	PIM	GP	G	A	Pts	PIM
2002-03	USNTDP	U-17	19	7	11	18	16	....	....	....	....	....
	USNTDP	NAHL	44	14	9	23	43	....	....	....	....	....
2003-04	USNTDP	U-18	46	19	23	42	46	....	....	....	....	....
	USNTDP	NAHL	11	5	4	9	0	....	....	....	....	....
2004-05	Ohio State	CCHA	42	11	*34	45	38	....	....	....	....	....
2005-06	Ohio State	CCHA	37	11	19	30	16	....	....	....	....	....
2006-07	Ohio State	CCHA	19	5	8	13	8	....	....	....	....	....
2007-08	Ohio State	CCHA	39	5	14	19	28	....	....	....	....	....
	Lake Erie Monsters	AHL	15	2	3	5	2	....	....	....	....	....
2008-09	Lake Erie Monsters	AHL	48	10	10	20	40	....	....	....	....	....
2009-10	Lake Erie Monsters	AHL	47	0	10	10	8	....	....	....	....	....

CCHA All-Rookie Team (2005) • CCHA Second All-Star Team (2005)

FROESE, Byron (FROHZ, BIGH-ruhn) CHI.

Center. Shoots right. 6', 176 lbs. Born, Winkler, Man., March 12, 1991.
(Chicago's 4th choice, 119th overall, in 2009 Entry Draft).

			Regular Season					Playoffs				
Season	Club	League	GP	G	A	Pts	PIM	GP	G	A	Pts	PIM
2007-08	Pembina Valley	MMHL	23	14	20	34	8	11	7	7	14	8
2008-09	Everett Silvertips	WHL	72	19	38	57	30	5	0	3	3	4
2009-10	Everett Silvertips	WHL	70	29	32	61	37	7	3	2	5	0

FROSHAUG , Mats (FRAWZ-howg, MATS) VAN.

Center. Shoots left. 6'1", 207 lbs. Born, Oslo, Norway, July 31, 1988.
(Vancouver's 4th choice, 161st overall, in 2008 Entry Draft).

			Regular Season					Playoffs				
Season	Club	League	GP	G	A	Pts	PIM	GP	G	A	Pts	PIM
2004-05	Sunne IK U18	Swe-U18	18	8	8	16	35	....	....	....	....	....
	Sunne IK Jr.	Swe-Jr.	16	0	3	3	4	....	....	....	....	....
2005-06	Sunne IK U18	Swe-U18	16	8	11	19	10	....	....	....	....	....
	Sunne IK Jr.	Swe-Jr.	17	14	10	24	6	....	....	....	....	....
	Sunne IK	Sweden-3	14	1	1	2	0	....	....	....	....	....
2006-07	Linkopings HC Jr.	Swe-Jr.	37	10	11	21	20	5	0	1	1	6
2007-08	Linkopings HC Jr.	Swe-Jr.	35	18	18	36	41	5	3	4	7	2
	Nykoping	Sweden-2	2	0	1	1	2	....	....	....	....	....
	Linkopings HC	Sweden	2	0	0	0	0	....	....	....	....	....
2008-09	Linkopings HC Jr.	Swe-Jr.	7	2	6	8	2	....	....	....	....	....
	Linkopings HC	Sweden	20	0	1	1	0	....	....	....	....	....
	Lulea HF	Sweden	14	0	1	1	0	....	....	....	....	....
	Sparta Sarpsborg	Norway	7	2	6	8	6	14	1	3	4	2
2009-10	Linkopings HC Jr.	Swe-Jr.	2	1	3	4	2	....	....	....	....	....
	Linkopings HC	Sweden	1	0	0	0	0	....	....	....	....	....
	Manglerud	Norway	11	2	9	11	6	5	2	1	3	18

GAEDE, Max (GAYD, MAX) S.J.

Right wing. Shoots right. 6'2", 190 lbs. Born, Maryland, MN, March 27, 1992.
(San Jose's 2nd choice, 88th overall, in 2010 Entry Draft).

			Regular Season					Playoffs				
Season	Club	League	GP	G	A	Pts	PIM	GP	G	A	Pts	PIM
2007-08	Woodbury	High-MN	26	5	11	16	2	....	....	....	....	....
2008-09	Woodbury	High-MN	27	16	28	44	66	....	....	....	....	....
2009-10	Team Southeast	UMHSEL	23	5	6	11	....	....	....	....	....	....
	Woodbury	High-MN	25	19	17	36	36	3	3	0	3	0

• Signed Letter of Intent to attend **Minnesota State University** (WCHA) in fall of 2011.

GALIEV, Stanislav (gah-LEE-ehv, stan-ihs-LAHV) WSH.

Right wing. Shoots right. 6'1", 178 lbs. Born, Moscow, Russia, January 17, 1992.
(Washington's 2nd choice, 86th overall, in 2010 Entry Draft).

			Regular Season					Playoffs				
Season	Club	League	GP	G	A	Pts	PIM	GP	G	A	Pts	PIM
2008-09	Indiana Ice	USHL	60	29	35	64	46	13	5	4	9	8
2009-10	Saint John	QMJHL	67	15	45	60	38	21	8	11	19	14

QMJHL All-Rookie Team (2010)

GALLACHER, Benjamin (gal-lah-CHUR, BEHN-jah-mihn) FLA.

Defense. Shoots left. 5'11", 183 lbs. Born, Calgary, Alta., September 11, 1992.
(Florida's 9th choice, 93rd overall, in 2010 Entry Draft).

			Regular Season					Playoffs				
Season	Club	League	GP	G	A	Pts	PIM	GP	G	A	Pts	PIM
2008-09	Camrose Kodiaks	AJHL	43	4	6	10	58	9	0	1	1	4
2009-10	Camrose Kodiaks	AJHL	34	3	19	22	61	11	1	1	2	43

• Signed Letter of Intent to attend **Ohio State University** (CCHA) in fall of 2011.

GALLAGHER, Brendan (gal-lah-GUR, BREHN-duhn) MTL.

Right wing. Shoots right. 5'9", 163 lbs. Born, Edmonton, Alta., May 6, 1992.
(Montreal's 4th choice, 147th overall, in 2010 Entry Draft).

			Regular Season					Playoffs				
Season	Club	League	GP	G	A	Pts	PIM	GP	G	A	Pts	PIM
2007-08	Greater Van.	BCMML	39	23	33	56	66	2	0	1	1	0
2008-09	Vancouver Giants	WHL	52	10	21	31	61	16	1	2	3	10
2009-10	Vancouver Giants	WHL	72	41	40	81	111	16	11	10	21	14

GARDINER, Jake (GAHR-dih-nuhr, JAYK) ANA.

Defense. Shoots left. 6'2", 188 lbs. Born, Deephaven, MN, July 4, 1990.
(Anaheim's 1st choice, 17th overall, in 2008 Entry Draft).

			Regular Season					Playoffs				
Season	Club	League	GP	G	A	Pts	PIM	GP	G	A	Pts	PIM
2005-06	Minnetonka High	High-MN	21	2	14	16	6	....	....	....	....	....
2006-07	Minnetonka High	High-MN	19	10	22	32	20	....	....	....	....	....
	Team Southwest	UMWEHL	11	4	3	7	....	....	....	....	....	....
2007-08	Minnetonka High	High-MN	24	20	28	48	14	....	....	....	....	....
	Team Southwest	UMWEHL	11	8	7	15	....	....	....	....	....	....
2008-09	U. of Wisconsin	WCHA	39	3	18	21	16	....	....	....	....	....
2009-10	U. of Wisconsin	WCHA	41	6	7	13	20	....	....	....	....	....

WCHA All-Rookie Team (2009)

GARDINER, Max (GAR-dih-nuhr, MAX) ST.L.

Center. Shoots left. 6'3", 176 lbs. Born, Edina, MN, May 7, 1992.
(St. Louis' 4th choice, 74th overall, in 2010 Entry Draft).

			Regular Season					Playoffs				
Season	Club	League	GP	G	A	Pts	PIM	GP	G	A	Pts	PIM
2007-08	Minnetonka High	High-MN	27	9	12	21	16	....	....	....	....	....
2008-09	Minnetonka High	High-MN	28	15	28	43	8	....	....	....	....	....
2009-10	Team Southwest	UMHSEL	22	6	6	12	....	....	....	....	....	....
	Minnetonka High	High-MN	17	17	26	43	14	6	5	6	11	0

• Signed Letter of Intent to attend **University of Minnesota** (WCHA) in fall of 2010.

GAUNCE, Cameron (GAWNS, KAM-ih-RUHN) COL.

Defense. Shoots left. 6'1", 203 lbs. Born, Sudbury, Ont., March 19, 1990.
(Colorado's 1st choice, 50th overall, in 2008 Entry Draft).

			Regular Season					Playoffs				
Season	Club	League	GP	G	A	Pts	PIM	GP	G	A	Pts	PIM
2005-06	Markham Waxers	Minor-ON	72	11	60	71	122	....	....	....	....	....
2006-07	Markham Waxers	OPJHL	45	2	12	14	68	11	0	3	3	26
2007-08	St. Michael's	OHL	63	10	30	40	99	4	0	1	1	6
2008-09	St. Michael's	OHL	67	17	47	64	110	11	4	6	10	20
2009-10	St. Michael's	OHL	55	6	31	37	112	16	0	13	13	34

OHL Second All-Star Team (2009, 2010)

GAUTHIER-LEDUC, Jerome (GOH-t'yay-leh-DOOK, Jah-ROHM) BUF.

Defense. Shoots right. 6'1", 196 lbs. Born, Quebec City, Que., July 30, 1992.
(Buffalo's 2nd choice, 68th overall, in 2010 Entry Draft).

			Regular Season					Playoffs				
Season	Club	League	GP	G	A	Pts	PIM	GP	G	A	Pts	PIM
2007-08	Sem. St-Francois	QAAA	43	10	12	22	10	17	2	6	8	26
2008-09	Rouyn-Noranda	QMJHL	52	1	16	17	8	6	0	2	2	5
2009-10	Rouyn-Noranda	QMJHL	68	20	26	46	16	11	2	4	6	2

GAZDIC, Luke (GAZ-dihk, LEWK) DAL.

Left wing. Shoots left. 6'3", 226 lbs. Born, Toronto, Ont., July 25, 1989.
(Dallas' 8th choice, 172nd overall, in 2007 Entry Draft).

			Regular Season					Playoffs				
Season	Club	League	GP	G	A	Pts	PIM	GP	G	A	Pts	PIM
2005-06	Wexford Raiders	OPJHL	47	17	16	33	105	....	....	....	....	....
	North York	GTHL	38	13	16	29	24	....	....	....	....	....
2006-07	Erie Otters	OHL	58	5	8	13	136	....	....	....	....	....
2007-08	Erie Otters	OHL	67	17	12	29	144	....	....	....	....	....
2008-09	Erie Otters	OHL	63	20	10	30	127	5	0	0	0	9
	Idaho Steelheads	ECHL	2	1	0	1	14	2	0	0	0	0
2009-10	Texas Stars	AHL	49	3	1	4	155	....	....	....	....	....
	Idaho Steelheads	ECHL	4	1	1	2	10	....	....	....	....	....

GEDIG, Curtis (GEH-dihg, KUHR-tihs) N.J.

Defense. Shoots left. 6'3", 190 lbs. Born, Penticton, B.C., September 14, 1991.
(New Jersey's 7th choice, 204th overall, in 2009 Entry Draft).

			Regular Season					Playoffs				
Season	Club	League	GP	G	A	Pts	PIM	GP	G	A	Pts	PIM
2007-08	Okanagan Rockets	BCMML	40	4	14	18	36	....	....	....	....	....
	Princeton Posse	KIJHL	9	0	2	2	4	1	0	0	0	0
2008-09	Merritt	BCHL	16	2	4	6	2	....	....	....	....	....
	Cowichan Valley	BCHL	30	2	10	12	16	10	0	3	3	2
2009-10	Cowichan Valley	BCHL	23	6	3	9	14	....	....	....	....	....
	Vernon Vipers	BCHL	30	5	7	12	6	19	1	5	6	10

GELINAS, Eric (ZHEHL-ih-nuh, AIR-ihk) N.J.

Defense. Shoots left. 6'4", 195 lbs. Born, Vanier, Ont., May 8, 1991.
(New Jersey's 2nd choice, 54th overall, in 2009 Entry Draft).

			Regular Season					Playoffs				
Season	Club	League	GP	G	A	Pts	PIM	GP	G	A	Pts	PIM
2006-07	C.C. Lemoyne	QAAA	44	5	14	19	50	10	1	4	5	14
2007-08	Lewiston	QMJHL	54	3	16	19	34	5	0	0	0	2
2008-09	Lewiston	QMJHL	67	10	29	39	80	4	0	1	1	12
2009-10	Lewiston	QMJHL	33	3	16	19	33	....	....	....	....	....
	Chicoutimi	QMJHL	28	3	9	12	26	6	1	4	5	6

GENDUR, Dan (JEHN-duhr, DAN) **VAN.**

Right wing. Shoots right. 5'11", 195 lbs. Born, Vancouver, B.C., May 21, 1987.
(Vancouver's 6th choice, 206th overall, in 2007 Entry Draft).

			Regular Season					Playoffs				
Season	**Club**	**League**	**GP**	**G**	**A**	**Pts**	**PIM**	**GP**	**G**	**A**	**Pts**	**PIM**
2003-04	Victoria Cougars	VIJHL	31	26	30	56	70	....	....	....	....	....
	Cowichan Valley	BCHL	17	3	8	11	22	1	0	0	0	0
2004-05	Prince George	WHL	60	2	6	8	75	....	....	....	....	....
2005-06	Prince George	WHL	19	2	1	3	24	....	....	....	....	....
2006-07	Prince George	WHL	13	2	5	7	18	....	....	....	....	....
	Everett Silvertips	WHL	48	20	22	42	44	12	4	4	8	8
2007-08	Everett Silvertips	WHL	60	29	55	84	68	4	1	2	3	8
2008-09	Manitoba Moose	AHL	10	1	0	1	2	....	....	....	....	....
	Victoria	ECHL	52	9	29	38	97	2	1	2	3	0
2009-10	Victoria	ECHL	8	0	4	4	6	....	....	....	....	....
	Johnstown Chiefs	ECHL	21	2	6	8	8	....	....	....	....	....

WHL West Second All-Star Team (2008)

GENEROUS, Matt (GEHN-uhr-uhs, MAT)

Defense. Shoots right. 6'3", 208 lbs. Born, Methuen, MA, May 4, 1985.
(Buffalo's 8th choice, 208th overall, in 2005 Entry Draft).

			Regular Season					Playoffs				
Season	**Club**	**League**	**GP**	**G**	**A**	**Pts**	**PIM**	**GP**	**G**	**A**	**Pts**	**PIM**
2003-04	N.E. Jr. Falcons	EJHL	43	6	9	15	134	....	....	....	....	....
2004-05	N.E. Jr. Falcons	EJHL	49	8	16	24	105	....	....	....	....	....
2005-06	St. Lawrence	ECAC	34	4	11	15	34	....	....	....	....	....
2006-07	St. Lawrence	ECAC	37	3	6	9	34	....	....	....	....	....
2007-08	St. Lawrence	ECAC	33	3	12	15	31	....	....	....	....	....
2008-09	St. Lawrence	ECAC	35	8	9	17	34	....	....	....	....	....
	Portland Pirates	AHL	4	1	0	1	13	4	0	0	0	0
2009-10	Portland Pirates	AHL	61	2	11	13	74	....	....	....	....	....

ECAC All-Rookie Team (2006)

GEOFFRION, Blake (JEHF-REE-ohn, BLAYK) **NSH.**

Left wing. Shoots left. 6'1", 194 lbs. Born, Plantation, FL, February 3, 1988.
(Nashville's 1st choice, 56th overall, in 2006 Entry Draft).

			Regular Season					Playoffs				
Season	**Club**	**League**	**GP**	**G**	**A**	**Pts**	**PIM**	**GP**	**G**	**A**	**Pts**	**PIM**
2003-04	Culver Academy	High-IN	45	....	....	65	....	....	....	....	....	....
2004-05	USNTDP	U-17	11	2	3	5	24	....	....	....	....	....
	USNTDP	NAHL	37	7	15	22	62	10	2	5	7	23
2005-06	USNTDP	U-18	41	12	14	26	38	....	....	....	....	....
	USNTDP	NAHL	13	6	9	15	30	....	....	....	....	....
2006-07	U. of Wisconsin	WCHA	36	2	4	6	62	....	....	....	....	....
2007-08	U. of Wisconsin	WCHA	36	10	20	30	52	....	....	....	....	....
2008-09	U. of Wisconsin	WCHA	35	15	13	28	73	....	....	....	....	....
2009-10	U. of Wisconsin	WCHA	40	*28	22	50	56	....	....	....	....	....
	Milwaukee	AHL	....	....	....	....	....	3	2	0	2	0

WCHA First All-Star Team (2010) • NCAA West First All-American Team (2010) • Hobey Baker Memorial Award (Top U.S. Collegiate Player) (2010)

GILBERT, David (zhihl-BAIR, DAY-vihd) **CHI.**

Center. Shoots left. 6'2", 186 lbs. Born, Chateauguay, Que., February 9, 1991.
(Chicago's 8th choice, 209th overall, in 2009 Entry Draft).

			Regular Season					Playoffs				
Season	**Club**	**League**	**GP**	**G**	**A**	**Pts**	**PIM**	**GP**	**G**	**A**	**Pts**	**PIM**
2006-07	Antoine-Girouard	QAAA	44	19	26	45	10	4	2	1	3	2
2007-08	Antoine-Girouard	QAAA	29	29	24	53	54	....	....	....	....	....
	Quebec Remparts	QMJHL	28	7	7	14	12	11	1	0	1	2
2008-09	Quebec Remparts	QMJHL	67	11	32	43	24	17	6	2	8	11
2009-10	Quebec Remparts	QMJHL	31	6	12	18	15	....	....	....	....	....
	Acadie-Bathurst	QMJHL	31	18	12	30	22	5	5	2	7	6
	Rockford IceHogs	AHL	1	0	1	1	0	....	....	....	....	....

GILIATI, Stefano (jihl-ee-A-tee, steh-FA-noh) **TOR.**

Left wing. Shoots left. 5'11", 200 lbs. Born, Montreal, Que., October 7, 1987.

			Regular Season					Playoffs				
Season	**Club**	**League**	**GP**	**G**	**A**	**Pts**	**PIM**	**GP**	**G**	**A**	**Pts**	**PIM**
2004-05	Shawinigan	QMJHL	54	9	5	14	23	3	0	0	0	2
2005-06	Lewiston	QMJHL	70	21	28	49	72	6	2	0	2	6
2006-07	Lewiston	QMJHL	68	24	33	57	73	17	4	11	15	22
2007-08	Lewiston	QMJHL	65	40	47	87	103	....	....	....	....	....
	Toronto Marlies	AHL	1	0	0	0	0	....	....	....	....	....
2008-09	Toronto Marlies	AHL	53	6	9	15	16	....	....	....	....	....
2009-10	Toronto Marlies	AHL	25	3	6	9	8	....	....	....	....	....
	Reading Royals	ECHL	46	23	32	55	76	13	4	4	8	18

QMJHL First All-Star Team (2008)

Signed as a free agent by **Toronto**, April 3, 2008.

GIMAYEV, Sergei (gih-MIGH-ehv, SAIR-gay) **OTT.**

Defense. Shoots left. 6'1", 183 lbs. Born, Moscow, USSR, February 16, 1984.
(Ottawa's 6th choice, 166th overall, in 2003 Entry Draft).

			Regular Season					Playoffs				
Season	**Club**	**League**	**GP**	**G**	**A**	**Pts**	**PIM**	**GP**	**G**	**A**	**Pts**	**PIM**
2001-02	CSKA Moscow 2	Russia-3	36	0	10	10	50	....	....	....	....	....
2002-03	Cherepovets	Russia	11	0	0	0	4	....	....	....	....	....
2003-04	Cherepovets	Russia	50	1	3	4	32	....	....	....	....	....
2004-05	Cherepovets	Russia	5	0	1	1	2	....	....	....	....	....
	Sibir Novosibirsk	Russia	31	1	6	7	34	....	....	....	....	....
2005-06	Dynamo Moscow	Russia	46	1	3	4	36	2	0	0	0	0
2006-07	Dynamo Moscow	Russia	23	0	2	2	28	2	0	0	0	6
2007-08	Cherepovets	Russia	39	1	0	1	30	8	1	1	2	4
2008-09	Barys Astana	Rus-KHL	45	0	2	2	79	....	....	....	....	....
2009-10	Barys Astana	Rus-KHL	54	6	6	12	73	3	0	0	0	8

GIONTA, Stephen (jee-OHN-tuh, STEE-vehn)

Right wing. Shoots right. 5'7", 180 lbs. Born, Rochester, NY, October 9, 1983.

			Regular Season					Playoffs				
Season	**Club**	**League**	**GP**	**G**	**A**	**Pts**	**PIM**	**GP**	**G**	**A**	**Pts**	**PIM**
2002-03	Boston College	H-East	33	5	10	15	36	....	....	....	....	....
2003-04	Boston College	H-East	41	9	15	24	36	....	....	....	....	....
2004-05	Boston College	H-East	38	8	11	19	44	....	....	....	....	....
2005-06	Boston College	H-East	37	11	21	32	66	....	....	....	....	....
	Albany River Rats	AHL	3	5	1	6	2	....	....	....	....	....
2006-07	Lowell Devils	AHL	67	7	8	15	15	....	....	....	....	....
2007-08	Lowell Devils	AHL	63	16	13	29	33	....	....	....	....	....
2008-09	Lowell Devils	AHL	52	2	9	11	30	....	....	....	....	....
2009-10	Lowell Devils	AHL	68	15	19	34	26	5	0	1	1	0

Signed to an ATO (amateur tryout) contract by **Albany** (AHL), April 12, 2006. Signed as a free agent by **New Jersey**, September 26, 2006.

GLADSKIKH, Evgeny (glad-SKEEKH, ehv-GEH-nee) **VAN.**

Right wing. Shoots left. 6', 176 lbs. Born, Magnitogorsk, USSR, April 24, 1982.
(Vancouver's 3rd choice, 114th overall, in 2001 Entry Draft).

			Regular Season					Playoffs				
Season	**Club**	**League**	**GP**	**G**	**A**	**Pts**	**PIM**	**GP**	**G**	**A**	**Pts**	**PIM**
1998-99	Magnitogorsk 2	Russia-4	16	3	3	6	6	....	....	....	....	....
99-2000	Magnitogorsk 2	Russia-3	39	17	2	19	24	....	....	....	....	....
	Magnitogorsk	Russia	1	0	0	0	0	....	....	....	....	....
2000-01	Magnitogorsk 2	Russia-3	11	10	7	17	6	....	....	....	....	....
	Magnitogorsk	Russia	31	3	5	8	10	12	0	2	2	2
2001-02	Magnitogorsk	Russia	32	5	6	11	6	4	0	0	0	4
2002-03	Magnitogorsk	Russia	42	4	7	11	18	3	0	0	0	2
2003-04	Magnitogorsk	Russia	47	13	13	26	22	14	3	1	4	10
2004-05	Magnitogorsk 2	Russia-3	2	0	2	2	0	....	....	....	....	....
	Magnitogorsk	Russia	42	11	12	23	24	4	1	0	1	4
2005-06	Magnitogorsk	Russia	43	12	8	20	20	7	1	1	2	2
2006-07	Magnitogorsk	Russia	47	5	9	14	16	15	2	4	6	6
2007-08	Magnitogorsk	Russia	52	12	12	24	12	12	2	2	4	2
2008-09	Omsk	Rus-KHL	17	1	4	5	4	....	....	....	....	....
	Mytischi	Rus-KHL	26	2	8	10	22	7	1	0	1	2
2009-10	Magnitogorsk	Rus-KHL	37	4	6	10	14	6	0	0	0	2

GLASS, Andrew (GLAS, AN-droo) **WSH.**

Left wing. Shoots left. 6', 175 lbs. Born, Wrentham, MA, July 14, 1989.
(Washington's 10th choice, 199th overall, in 2007 Entry Draft).

			Regular Season					Playoffs				
Season	**Club**	**League**	**GP**	**G**	**A**	**Pts**	**PIM**	**GP**	**G**	**A**	**Pts**	**PIM**
2003-04	Junior Bruins	Minor-MA	61	15	23	38	2	....	....	....	....	....
2004-05	Little Bruins	Minor-MA	33	5	13	18	15	....	....	....	....	....
	Nobles	High-MA	29	7	15	22	6	....	....	....	....	....
2005-06	Little Bruins	Minor-MA	19	9	11	20	17	....	....	....	....	....
	Nobles	High-MA	29	15	24	39	8	....	....	....	....	....
2006-07	Little Bruins	Minor-MA	12	7	8	15	4	....	....	....	....	....
	Nobles	High-MA	18	7	10	17	6	....	....	....	....	....
2007-08	Nobles	High-MA	29	27	23	50	....	....	....	....	....	....
2008-09	Boston University	H-East	15	2	1	3	2	....	....	....	....	....
2009-10	Boston University	H-East	24	1	1	2	14	....	....	....	....	....

GLASSER, Matthew (GLAS-uhr, MA-thew) **EDM.**

Left wing. Shoots left. 5'10", 175 lbs. Born, Saskatoon, Sask., January 11, 1987.
(Edmonton's 8th choice, 220th overall, in 2005 Entry Draft).

			Regular Season					Playoffs				
Season	**Club**	**League**	**GP**	**G**	**A**	**Pts**	**PIM**	**GP**	**G**	**A**	**Pts**	**PIM**
2003-04	Fort McMurray	AJHL	55	13	12	25	24	....	....	....	....	....
2004-05	Fort McMurray	AJHL	62	25	24	49	14	....	....	....	....	....
2005-06	Fort McMurray	AJHL	58	15	20	35	36	17	5	2	7	38
2006-07	U. of Denver	WCHA	12	0	0	0	2	....	....	....	....	....
2007-08	U. of Denver	WCHA	40	6	2	8	20	....	....	....	....	....
2008-09	U. of Denver	WCHA	40	4	3	7	18	....	....	....	....	....
2009-10	U. of Denver	WCHA	41	3	3	6	20	....	....	....	....	....

GLAZACHEV, Konstantin (GLAH-zuh-chehv, KAWN-stan-tihn) **NSH.**

Left wing. Shoots right. 6', 186 lbs. Born, Arkhangelsk, USSR, February 18, 1985.
(Nashville's 2nd choice, 35th overall, in 2003 Entry Draft).

			Regular Season					Playoffs				
Season	**Club**	**League**	**GP**	**G**	**A**	**Pts**	**PIM**	**GP**	**G**	**A**	**Pts**	**PIM**
2001-02	Yaroslavl 2	Russia-3	7	5	6	11	6	....	....	....	....	....
2002-03	Yaroslavl 2	Russia-3	STATISTICS NOT AVAILABLE									
	Yaroslavl	Russia	13	3	4	7	4	4	0	0	0	0
2003-04	Yaroslavl 2	Russia-3	9	6	5	11	8	....	....	....	....	....
	Yaroslavl	Russia	35	4	3	7	4	2	0	0	0	0
2004-05	Sibir Novosibirsk	Russia	24	4	9	13	6	....	....	....	....	....
	Yaroslavl	Russia	9	0	3	3	2	....	....	....	....	....
	Yaroslavl 2	Russia-3	20	17	9	26	14	....	....	....	....	....
2005-06	Yaroslavl	Russia	29	7	4	11	8	9	0	2	2	0
2006-07	Yaroslavl	Russia	14	4	1	5	10	....	....	....	....	....
	Yaroslavl 2	Russia-3	4	2	5	7	0	....	....	....	....	....
	Amur Khabarovsk	Russia	22	4	7	11	14	....	....	....	....	....
2007-08	Novokuznetsk	Russia	50	7	9	16	10	....	....	....	....	....
2008-09	Barys Astana	Rus-KHL	56	28	24	52	30	3	3	0	3	2
2009-10	Barys Astana	Rus-KHL	42	16	17	33	18	2	0	0	0	0

GLEASON, Joe (GLEE-suhn, JOH) **CHI.**

Defense. Shoots right. 5'9", 171 lbs. Born, Edina, MN, March 30, 1990.
(Chicago's 7th choice, 192nd overall, in 2008 Entry Draft).

			Regular Season					Playoffs				
Season	**Club**	**League**	**GP**	**G**	**A**	**Pts**	**PIM**	**GP**	**G**	**A**	**Pts**	**PIM**
2006-07	Edina Hornets	High-MN	21	10	23	33	....	....	....	....	....	....
	Team Southwest	UMWEHL	11	4	6	10	....	....	....	....	....	....
2007-08	Edina Hornets	High-MN	23	9	33	42	....	....	....	....	....	....
	Team Southwest	UMWEHL	12	6	14	20	....	....	....	....	....	....
2008-09	Des Moines	USHL	59	5	16	21	40	....	....	....	....	....
2009-10	North Dakota	WCHA	39	0	9	9	31	....	....	....	....	....

GLENNIE, Scott (GLEH-nee, SKAWT) **DAL.**

Right wing. Shoots right. 6'1", 185 lbs. Born, Oakville, Ont., February 22, 1991.
(Dallas' 1st choice, 8th overall, in 2009 Entry Draft).

			Regular Season					Playoffs				
Season	**Club**	**League**	**GP**	**G**	**A**	**Pts**	**PIM**	**GP**	**G**	**A**	**Pts**	**PIM**
2006-07	Winnipeg Wild	MMHL	38	31	37	68	64	7	3	3	6	16
2007-08	Brandon	WHL	61	26	32	58	50	6	1	0	1	7
2008-09	Brandon	WHL	55	28	42	70	25	12	3	15	18	11
2009-10	Brandon	WHL	66	32	57	89	50	15	3	7	10	14

GLUKHOV, Alexei (GLUH-khawv, al-EHX-ay) T.B.

Right wing. Shoots left. 6'3", 176 lbs. Born, Voskresensk, USSR, April 5, 1984.
(Tampa Bay's 12th choice, 286th overall, in 2002 Entry Draft).

			Regular Season					Playoffs				
Season	Club	League	GP	G	A	Pts	PIM	GP	G	A	Pts	PIM
99-2000	Voskresensk 2	Russia-3	10	2	2	4	2	....	....	....	....	....
2000-01	Voskresensk	Russia-2	9	0	1	1	6	....	....	....	....	....
2001-02	Voskresensk 2	Russia-3	34	8	22	30	54	....	....	....	....	....
	Voskresensk	Russia-2	4	0	0	0	0	....	....	....	....	....
2002-03	Voskresensk	Russia-2	38	4	4	8	30	....	....	....	....	....
2003-04	Voskresensk	Russia	28	0	0	0	12	....	....	....	....	....
2004-05	Kristall Elektrostal	Russia-2	16	2	2	4	20	....	....	....	....	....
	Voskresensk	Russia	9	0	0	0	6	....	....	....	....	....
	Victoria	ECHL	32	5	12	17	12	....	....	....	....	....
	Springfield Falcons	AHL	3	0	1	1	6	....	....	....	....	....
2005-06	Mytischi	Russia	45	2	14	16	70	9	2	1	3	10
2006-07	Cherepovets	Russia	52	2	14	16	97	5	0	0	0	4
2007-08	Cherepovets	Russia	57	7	13	20	86	8	2	0	2	12
2008-09	Mytischi	Rus-KHL	43	10	10	20	28	7	1	1	2	4
2009-10	Mytischi	Rus-KHL	51	5	12	17	34	4	0	0	0	0

Signed to PTO (professional tryout) contract by **Springfield** (AHL), April 14, 2005.

GODFREY, Josh (GAWD-free, JAWSH) WSH.

Defense. Shoots right. 6'1", 202 lbs. Born, Collingwood, Ont., January 15, 1988.
(Washington's 2nd choice, 34th overall, in 2007 Entry Draft).

			Regular Season					Playoffs				
Season	Club	League	GP	G	A	Pts	PIM	GP	G	A	Pts	PIM
2004-05	Guelph Storm	OHL	18	0	4	4	9	1	0	0	0	0
2005-06	Guelph Storm	OHL	33	2	8	10	38	....	....	....	....	....
	Sault Ste. Marie	OHL	30	6	5	11	26	1	0	1	1	0
2006-07	Sault Ste. Marie	OHL	68	24	33	57	80	13	9	5	14	18
2007-08	Sault Ste. Marie	OHL	60	17	34	51	61	14	5	1	6	20
	Hershey Bears	AHL	....	....	....	....	....	1	0	0	0	0
2008-09	Hershey Bears	AHL	13	0	6	6	21	....	....	....	....	....
	South Carolina	ECHL	37	5	20	25	30	6	1	3	4	10
2009-10	Hershey Bears	AHL	2	0	0	0	0	....	....	....	....	....
	South Carolina	ECHL	29	5	11	16	20	1	0	0	0	2

GOGGIN, Mark (GAW-gihn, MAHRK) BOS.

Center. Shoots left. 5'11", 198 lbs. Born, Chicago, IL, July 29, 1990.
(Boston's 6th choice, 197th overall, in 2008 Entry Draft).

			Regular Season					Playoffs				
Season	Club	League	GP	G	A	Pts	PIM	GP	G	A	Pts	PIM
2006-07	Choate-Rosemary	High-CT	....	15	20	35	....	....	....	....	....	....
2007-08	Choate-Rosemary	High-CT	21	15	21	36	10	....	....	....	....	....
	USNTDP	U-17	3	1	1	2	0	....	....	....	....	....
	USNTDP	NAHL	5	1	1	2	2	....	....	....	....	....
2008-09	Choate-Rosemary	High-CT	25	14	20	34	....	....	....	....	....	....
	Chicago Steel	USHL	17	5	4	9	10	....	....	....	....	....
2009-10	Dartmouth	ECAC	21	4	2	6	10	....	....	....	....	....

GOGULLA, Philip (GOH-goo-lah, FIHL-ihp) BUF.

Right wing. Shoots left. 6'2", 182 lbs. Born, Dusseldorf, West Germany, July 31, 1987.
(Buffalo's 2nd choice, 48th overall, in 2005 Entry Draft).

			Regular Season					Playoffs				
Season	Club	League	GP	G	A	Pts	PIM	GP	G	A	Pts	PIM
2002-03	Krefelder EV Jr.	Ger-Jr.	32	11	23	34	42	2	0	0	0	2
2003-04	Krefelder EV Jr.	Ger-Jr.	35	35	44	79	22	2	0	2	2	27
2004-05	Essen	German-2	3	0	0	0	0	....	....	....	....	....
	Koln Jr.	Ger-Jr.	7	4	5	9	18	....	....	....	....	....
	Kolner Haie	Germany	47	1	1	2	14	7	0	0	0	2
2005-06	Kolner Haie	Germany	48	7	15	22	49	9	3	2	5	40
2006-07	Kolner Haie	Germany	44	8	13	21	26	7	0	0	0	8
2007-08	Kolner Haie	Germany	51	11	33	44	30	14	3	9	12	6
2008-09	Kolner Haie	Germany	48	17	21	38	58	....	....	....	....	....
2009-10	Portland Pirates	AHL	76	15	20	35	27	3	0	0	0	0

GOLOUBEF, Cody (GOH-luh-behf, KOH-dee) CBJ

Defense. Shoots right. 6'1", 186 lbs. Born, Mississauga, Ont., November 30, 1989.
(Columbus' 2nd choice, 37th overall, in 2008 Entry Draft).

			Regular Season					Playoffs				
Season	Club	League	GP	G	A	Pts	PIM	GP	G	A	Pts	PIM
2003-04	Toronto Marlboros	GTHL	89	10	27	37	44	....	....	....	....	....
2004-05	Toronto Marlboros	GTHL	69	14	47	61	56	....	....	....	....	....
2005-06	Milton Icehawks	OPJHL	42	9	29	38	38	7	1	3	4	10
2006-07	Oakville Blades	OPJHL	9	5	5	10	46	10	2	10	12	18
2007-08	U. of Wisconsin	WCHA	40	4	6	10	36	....	....	....	....	....
2008-09	U. of Wisconsin	WCHA	36	5	8	13	38	....	....	....	....	....
2009-10	U. of Wisconsin	WCHA	42	3	11	14	64	....	....	....	....	....

• Missed majority of 2006-07 season recovering from various injuries.

GONCHAROV, Maxim (gohn-CHAR-ahv, mahx-EEM) PHX.

Defense. Shoots right. 6', 176 lbs. Born, Moscow, USSR, June 15, 1989.
(Phoenix's 6th choice, 123rd overall, in 2007 Entry Draft).

			Regular Season					Playoffs				
Season	Club	League	GP	G	A	Pts	PIM	GP	G	A	Pts	PIM
2005-06	CSKA Moscow 2	Russia-3	STATISTICS NOT AVAILABLE									
2006-07	CSKA Moscow 2	Russia-3	STATISTICS NOT AVAILABLE									
	CSKA Moscow	Russia	18	0	0	0	10	5	0	0	0	2
2007-08	CSKA Moscow	Russia	47	3	2	5	38	6	0	2	2	0
	CSKA Moscow 2	Russia-3	4	0	2	2	35	3	0	0	0	8
2008-09	CSKA Moscow	Rus-KHL	47	7	8	15	50	7	0	0	0	4
2009-10	CSKA Moscow	Rus-KHL	51	4	13	17	52	3	1	0	1	2

GORMLEY, Brandon (GOHRM-lee, BRAN-duhn) PHX.

Defense. Shoots left. 6'2", 185 lbs. Born, Charlottetown, P.E.I., February 18, 1992.
(Phoenix's 1st choice, 13th overall, in 2010 Entry Draft).

			Regular Season					Playoffs				
Season	Club	League	GP	G	A	Pts	PIM	GP	G	A	Pts	PIM
2007-08	Notre Dame	SMHL	42	23	33	56	63	9	1	6	7	18
2008-09	Moncton Wildcats	QMJHL	62	7	20	27	34	10	1	3	4	6
2009-10	Moncton Wildcats	QMJHL	58	9	34	43	54	21	2	15	17	10

QMJHL All-Rookie Team (2009) • QMJHL Second All-Star Team (2010)

GOTOVETS, Kirill (goh-TOH-vets, kih-RIHL) T.B.

Defense. Shoots left. 5'11", 175 lbs. Born, Minsk, USSR, June 25, 1991.
(Tampa Bay's 7th choice, 183rd overall, in 2009 Entry Draft).

			Regular Season					Playoffs				
Season	Club	League	GP	G	A	Pts	PIM	GP	G	A	Pts	PIM
2007-08	Yunior Minsk	Belarus-2	45	2	8	10	54	....	....	....	....	....
2008-09	Shat.-St. Mary's	High-MN	54	7	25	32	70	....	....	....	....	....
2009-10	Shat.-St. Mary's	High-MN	44	8	19	27	73	....	....	....	....	....

• Signed Letter of Intent to attend **Cornell University** (ECAC) in fall of 2010.

GOULET, Alain (goo-LAY, AL-eh) BOS.

Defense. Shoots right. 6'2", 186 lbs. Born, Kapuskasing, Ont., September 22, 1988.
(Boston's 4th choice, 159th overall, in 2007 Entry Draft).

			Regular Season					Playoffs				
Season	Club	League	GP	G	A	Pts	PIM	GP	G	A	Pts	PIM
2005-06	Ottawa Jr. Sens	CJHL	41	6	14	20	22	....	....	....	....	....
2006-07	Aurora Tigers	OPJHL	43	10	32	42	34	25	5	16	21	32
2007-08	Nebraska-Omaha	CCHA	37	6	8	14	14	....	....	....	....	....
2008-09	Nebraska-Omaha	CCHA	17	2	3	5	21	....	....	....	....	....
	Gatineau	QMJHL	32	16	19	35	10	10	0	10	10	18
2009-10	Providence Bruins	AHL	71	3	15	18	28	....	....	....	....	....

GRACHEV, Yevgeny (gra-CHAWF, yehv-GEH-nee) NYR

Center. Shoots left. 6'4", 222 lbs. Born, Khabarovsk, USSR, February 21, 1990.
(NY Rangers' 3rd choice, 75th overall, in 2008 Entry Draft).

			Regular Season					Playoffs				
Season	Club	League	GP	G	A	Pts	PIM	GP	G	A	Pts	PIM
2005-06	Yaroslavl 2	Russia-3	1	0	0	0	2	....	....	....	....	....
2006-07	Yaroslavl 2	Russia-3	28	7	6	13	6	....	....	....	....	....
2007-08	Yaroslavl 2	Russia-3	STATISTICS NOT AVAILABLE									
	Yaroslavl	Russia	1	0	0	0	0	....	....	....	....	....
2008-09	Brampton	OHL	60	40	40	80	22	19	11	14	25	4
2009-10	Hartford Wolf Pack	AHL	80	12	16	28	14	....	....	....	....	....

OHL Rookie of the Year (2009) • Canadian Major Junior All-Rookie Team (2009)

GRACIK, Juraj (GRAH-chihk, YUHR-ay) ATL.

Right wing. Shoots right. 6'3", 190 lbs. Born, Topolcany, Czech., August 14, 1986.
(Atlanta's 5th choice, 142nd overall, in 2004 Entry Draft).

			Regular Season					Playoffs				
Season	Club	League	GP	G	A	Pts	PIM	GP	G	A	Pts	PIM
2002-03	Topolcany Jr.	Slovak-Jr.	24	10	7	17	28	....	....	....	....	....
2003-04	Topolcany Jr.	Slovak-Jr.	28	22	12	34	78	....	....	....	....	....
	Topolcany	Slovak-2	28	16	8	24	8	4	1	0	1	0
2004-05	Tri-City Americans	WHL	33	4	2	6	18	....	....	....	....	....
2005-06	Tri-City Americans	WHL	53	22	23	45	36	....	....	....	....	....
2006-07	Bratislava	Slovakia	37	5	1	6	6	3	0	0	0	0
	HC Topolcany	Slovak-2	7	8	1	9	18	....	....	....	....	....
	Ruzinov	Slovak-2	13	7	5	12	16	3	1	1	2	0
2007-08	Bratislava	Slovakia	40	3	4	7	10	11	0	0	0	0
	Ruzinov	Slovak-2	10	5	3	8	10	4	1	2	3	4
2008-09	Ruzinov	Slovak-2	6	5	2	7	26	2	1	1	2	2
	Bratislava	Slovakia	50	1	3	4	8	12	2	2	4	4
2009-10	HK Nitra	Slovakia	44	6	7	13	36	10	2	0	2	2

Signed as a free agent by **Bratislava** (Slovakia), October 14, 2006.

GRANBERG, Petter (GRAN-buhrg, PEH-tuhr) TOR.

Defense. Shoots right. 6'3", 200 lbs. Born, Gallivare, Sweden, August 27, 1992.
(Toronto's 4th choice, 116th overall, in 2010 Entry Draft).

			Regular Season					Playoffs				
Season	Club	League	GP	G	A	Pts	PIM	GP	G	A	Pts	PIM
2007-08	Skelleftea U18	Swe-U18	28	1	3	4	4	....	....	....	....	....
2008-09	Skelleftea AIK U18	Swe-U18	32	0	8	8	20	8	0	0	0	4
	Skelleftea AIK Jr.	Swe-Jr.	4	0	0	0	0	2	0	0	0	6
2009-10	Skelleftea AIK U18	Swe-U18	6	0	1	1	2	3	0	3	3	4
	Skelleftea AIK Jr.	Swe-Jr.	40	2	7	9	39	4	1	0	1	4
	Skelleftea AIK	Sweden	1	0	0	0	0	....	....	....	....	....

GRANLUND, Mikael (GRAHN-lund, mih-kigh-EHL) MIN.

Center. Shoots left. 5'10", 180 lbs. Born, Oulu, Finland, February 26, 1992.
(Minnesota's 1st choice, 9th overall, in 2010 Entry Draft).

			Regular Season					Playoffs				
Season	Club	League	GP	G	A	Pts	PIM	GP	G	A	Pts	PIM
2007-08	Karpat Oulu U18	Fin-U18	31	22	27	49	20	5	3	5	8	0
2008-09	Suomi U20	Finland-2	6	4	3	7	0	....	....	....	....	....
	Karpat Oulu Jr.	Fin-Jr.	38	22	44	66	45	....	....	....	....	....
	Karpat Oulu	Finland	2	0	0	0	0	....	....	....	....	....
	Karpat Oulu U18	Fin-U18	....	....	....	....	....	3	2	4	6	2
2009-10	Suomi U20	Finland-2	1	0	0	0	0	....	....	....	....	....
	HIFK Helsinki	Finland	43	13	27	40	2	6	1	5	6	0

GRANT, Alex (GRANT, AL-ehx) PIT.

Defense. Shoots right. 6'2", 185 lbs. Born, Antigonish, N.S., January 20, 1989.
(Pittsburgh's 6th choice, 118th overall, in 2007 Entry Draft).

			Regular Season					Playoffs				
Season	Club	League	GP	G	A	Pts	PIM	GP	G	A	Pts	PIM
2004-05	Antigonish	MJrHL	50	7	9	16	36	3	1	1	2	2
2005-06	Saint John	QMJHL	47	4	9	13	58	....	....	....	....	....
2006-07	Saint John	QMJHL	68	12	20	32	108	....	....	....	....	....
2007-08	Saint John	QMJHL	70	15	33	48	96	14	3	11	14	12
2008-09	Saint John	QMJHL	37	9	22	31	51	....	....	....	....	....
	Shawinigan	QMJHL	23	4	15	19	11	21	4	5	9	18
2009-10	Wilkes-Barre	AHL	14	3	2	5	28	2	0	0	0	0
	Wheeling Nailers	ECHL	40	7	20	27	36	....	....	....	....	....

GRANT, Derek (GRANT, DAIR-ihk) OTT.

Center. Shoots left. 6'3", 196 lbs. Born, Abbotsford, B.C., April 20, 1990.
(Ottawa's 5th choice, 119th overall, in 2008 Entry Draft).

			Regular Season					Playoffs				
Season	Club	League	GP	G	A	Pts	PIM	GP	G	A	Pts	PIM
2006-07	Abbotsford Pilots	PIJHL	47	31	20	51	42	11	6	5	11	20
2007-08	Langley Chiefs	BCHL	57	24	39	63	44	12	5	5	10	15
2008-09	Langley Chiefs	BCHL	35	25	35	60	22	4	2	1	3	2
2009-10	Michigan State	CCHA	38	12	18	30	10	....	....	....	....	....

GRANTHAM, Ryley (GRAN-thum, RIGH-lee) **CGY.**

Center. Shoots left. 6'4", 200 lbs. Born, Hanna, Alta., January 7, 1988.
(Calgary's 6th choice, 168th overall, in 2008 Entry Draft).

			Regular Season					Playoffs				
Season	Club	League	GP	G	A	Pts	PIM	GP	G	A	Pts	PIM
2005-06	Brooks Bandits	AJHL	43	6	3	9	98	13	2	0	2	16
2006-07	Brooks Bandits	AJHL	....	3	11	14	....	....	....	....	....	....
	Moose Jaw	WHL	33	1	1	2	50	....	....	....	....	....
2007-08	Moose Jaw	WHL	66	10	9	19	163	6	0	0	0	8
2008-09	Moose Jaw	WHL	38	8	5	13	132	....	....	....	....	....
	Kelowna Rockets	WHL	29	4	12	16	61	22	4	1	5	16
2009-10	Abbotsford Heat	AHL	67	1	3	4	163	....	....	....	....	....

GRATCHEV, Maxim (GRAT-chehv, max-EEM)

Left wing. Shoots left. 5'11", 196 lbs. Born, Novosibirsk, USSR, September 26, 1988.
(NY Islanders' 3rd choice, 106th overall, in 2007 Entry Draft).

			Regular Season					Playoffs				
Season	Club	League	GP	G	A	Pts	PIM	GP	G	A	Pts	PIM
2003-04	Thayer Academy	High-MA	....	7	9	16	....	....	....	....	....	....
2004-05	Quebec Remparts	QMJHL	54	7	11	18	36	....	....	....	....	....
2005-06	Quebec Remparts	QMJHL	22	5	5	10	40	....	....	....	....	....
	Rimouski Oceanic	QMJHL	33	6	11	17	57	....	....	....	....	....
2006-07	Rimouski Oceanic	QMJHL	70	35	42	77	88	....	....	....	....	....
2007-08	Rimouski Oceanic	QMJHL	39	9	20	29	48	9	2	0	2	12
2008-09	Lewiston	QMJHL	64	30	31	61	108	....	....	....	....	....
	Bridgeport	AHL	1	0	0	0	2	1	0	0	0	0
2009-10	Binghamton	AHL	17	2	3	5	10	....	....	....	....	....
	Elmira Jackals	ECHL	40	17	24	41	51	5	2	2	4	8
	Rochester	AHL	13	2	2	4	6	2	0	0	0	0

GRAVEL, Kevin (gra-VEHL, KEH-vihn) **L.A.**

Defense. Shoots left. 6'4", 185 lbs. Born, Kingsford, MI, March 6, 1992.
(Los Angeles' 4th choice, 148th overall, in 2010 Entry Draft).

			Regular Season					Playoffs				
Season	Club	League	GP	G	A	Pts	PIM	GP	G	A	Pts	PIM
2008-09	Marquette	NAHL	58	3	11	14	29	....	....	....	....	....
	USNTDP	U-17	3	0	1	1	4	....	....	....	....	....
2009-10	Sioux City	USHL	53	3	3	6	36	....	....	....	....	....

• Signed Letter of Intent to attend **St. Cloud State University** (WCHA) in fall of 2010.

GREENING, Colin (GREEN-ihng, KAW-lihn) **OTT.**

Center/Left wing. Shoots left. 6'3", 212 lbs. Born, St. John's, Nfld., March 9, 1986.
(Ottawa's 8th choice, 204th overall, in 2005 Entry Draft).

			Regular Season					Playoffs				
Season	Club	League	GP	G	A	Pts	PIM	GP	G	A	Pts	PIM
2002-03	St. John's	NFAHA	60	24	34	58	48	....	....	....	....	....
2003-04	Upper Canada	High-ON	53	30	43	73	40	....	....	....	....	....
2004-05	Upper Canada	High-ON	35	24	22	46	24	....	....	....	....	....
2005-06	Nanaimo Clippers	BCHL	56	27	35	62	46	5	3	0	3	2
2006-07	Cornell Big Red	ECAC	31	11	8	19	26	....	....	....	....	....
2007-08	Cornell Big Red	ECAC	36	14	19	33	41	....	....	....	....	....
2008-09	Cornell Big Red	ECAC	36	15	16	31	28	....	....	....	....	....
2009-10	Cornell Big Red	ECAC	34	15	20	35	31	....	....	....	....	....

ECAC Second All-Star Team (2008, 2009, 2010)

GREENOP, Richard (GREEN-awp, RIH-chuhrd) **TOR.**

Center. Shoots right. 6'4", 225 lbs. Born, Oshawa, Ont., February 24, 1989.
(Chicago's 7th choice, 156th overall, in 2007 Entry Draft).

			Regular Season					Playoffs				
Season	Club	League	GP	G	A	Pts	PIM	GP	G	A	Pts	PIM
2005-06	Oshawa	OPJHL	47	10	4	14	97	....	....	....	....	....
2006-07	Windsor Spitfires	OHL	48	3	9	12	149	....	....	....	....	....
2007-08	Windsor Spitfires	OHL	60	2	3	5	194	5	0	0	0	2
2008-09	Windsor Spitfires	OHL	60	4	4	8	156	15	0	0	0	28
2009-10	Toronto Marlies	AHL	42	2	3	5	136	....	....	....	....	....

Signed as a free agent by **Toronto**, July 6, 2009.

GREGOIRE, Jason (GREHG-wahr, JAY-suhn) **NYI**

Left wing. Shoots left. 6'1", 196 lbs. Born, Winnipeg, Man., February 24, 1989.
(NY Islanders' 2nd choice, 76th overall, in 2007 Entry Draft).

			Regular Season					Playoffs				
Season	Club	League	GP	G	A	Pts	PIM	GP	G	A	Pts	PIM
2005-06	Wpg. South Blues	MJHL	57	22	28	50	46	14	12	11	23	....
2006-07	Lincoln Stars	USHL	32	16	20	36	10	4	4	0	4	2
2007-08	Lincoln Stars	USHL	54	*37	32	69	41	8	3	9	*12	6
2008-09	North Dakota	WCHA	42	12	17	29	28	....	....	....	....	....
2009-10	North Dakota	WCHA	43	20	17	37	10	....	....	....	....	....

USHL First All-Star Team (2008) • USHL Player of the Year (2008)

GROT, Denis (GROHT, DEH-nihs) **VAN.**

Defense. Shoots left. 6', 185 lbs. Born, Minsk, USSR, January 6, 1984.
(Vancouver's 2nd choice, 55th overall, in 2002 Entry Draft).

			Regular Season					Playoffs				
Season	Club	League	GP	G	A	Pts	PIM	GP	G	A	Pts	PIM
2000-01	Yaroslavl 2	Russia-3	34	5	1	6	10	....	....	....	....	....
	Russia	Nat-Tm	5	0	2	2	8	....	....	....	....	....
2001-02	Yaroslavl 2	Russia-3	14	1	0	1	10	....	....	....	....	....
	Elektrostal 2	Russia-3	3	0	1	1	2	....	....	....	....	....
	Elektrostal	Russia-2	33	1	1	2	42	....	....	....	....	....
2002-03	HK Lipetsk	Russia-2	27	4	4	8	28	....	....	....	....	....
2003-04	Yaroslavl	Russia	31	0	2	2	4	3	0	0	0	2
2004-05	Yaroslavl 2	Russia-3	20	2	3	5	22	....	....	....	....	....
	Yaroslavl	Russia	1	0	0	0	2	....	....	....	....	....
	Sibir Novosibirsk	Russia	23	0	4	4	32	....	....	....	....	....
	Amur Khabarovsk	Russia-2	9	1	5	6	2	12	0	0	0	31
2005-06	Spartak Moscow	Russia	48	1	4	5	28	3	0	0	0	0
2006-07	Nizhnekamsk	Russia	38	2	7	9	59	1	0	0	0	2
2007-08	Nizhnekamsk	Russia	48	0	3	3	32	5	0	0	0	4
2008-09	Sibir Novosibirsk	Rus-KHL	54	0	5	5	36	....	....	....	....	....
2009-10	Avtomobilist	Rus-KHL	38	1	3	4	34	4	0	0	0	2

GROULX, Danny (GROO, DA-nee)

Defense. Shoots left. 6', 205 lbs. Born, LaSalle, Que., June 23, 1981.

			Regular Season					Playoffs				
Season	Club	League	GP	G	A	Pts	PIM	GP	G	A	Pts	PIM
1996-97	Charles-Lemoyne	QAAA	40	2	26	28	....	15	3	15	18	....
1997-98	Val-d'Or Foreurs	QMJHL	63	4	16	20	61	19	1	4	5	18
1998-99	Val-d'Or Foreurs	QMJHL	36	3	26	29	55	....	....	....	....	....
	Acadie-Bathurst	QMJHL	36	2	15	17	51	18	0	2	2	6
99-2000	Victoriaville Tigres	QMJHL	66	12	55	67	131	6	0	4	4	14
2000-01	Victoriaville Tigres	QMJHL	72	16	71	87	164	13	2	19	21	46
2001-02	Victoriaville Tigres	QMJHL	68	29	83	112	165	22	9	*30	39	68
2002-03	Grand Rapids	AHL	71	3	7	10	52	7	0	1	1	7
2003-04	Grand Rapids	AHL	79	8	13	21	93	3	0	0	0	0
2004-05	Grand Rapids	AHL	53	1	11	12	90	....	....	....	....	....
	Manitoba Moose	AHL	16	2	6	8	16	13	1	3	4	14
2005-06	Kassel Huskies	Germany	51	2	11	13	93	5	0	1	1	6
2006-07	Hamilton Bulldogs	AHL	58	0	16	16	62	22	6	6	12	14
2007-08	Manitoba Moose	AHL	58	4	20	24	32	6	2	1	3	12
2008-09	Rockford IceHogs	AHL	80	6	34	40	58	4	0	2	2	2
2009-10	Worcester Sharks	AHL	80	14	52	66	80	10	1	6	7	6

QMJHL First All-Star Team (2001, 2002) • Canadian Major Junior First All-Star Team (2002) • Memorial Cup Tournament All-Star Team (2002) • Stafford Smythe Memorial Trophy (Memorial Cup Tournament MVP) (2002) • Eddie Shore Award (AHL – Outstanding Defenseman) (2010)

Signed as a free agent by **Detroit**, August 12, 2002. • Loaned to **Manitoba** (AHL) by **Detroit** (Grand Rapids-AHL) for cash, March 15, 2005. Signed as a free agent by **Kassel** (Germany), August 25, 2005. Signed as a free agent by **San Jose**, July 16, 2009.

GRYBA, Eric (GREE-buh, AIR-ihk) **OTT.**

Defense. Shoots right. 6'4", 222 lbs. Born, Saskatoon, Sask., April 14, 1988.
(Ottawa's 2nd choice, 68th overall, in 2006 Entry Draft).

			Regular Season					Playoffs				
Season	Club	League	GP	G	A	Pts	PIM	GP	G	A	Pts	PIM
2003-04	Sask. Contacts	SMHL	39	1	10	11	89	10	4	8	12	20
2004-05	Sask. Contacts	SMHL	32	11	29	40	83	11	5	7	12	22
2005-06	Green Bay	USHL	56	3	12	15	*205	3	1	1	2	27
2006-07	Boston University	H-East	38	1	3	4	76	....	....	....	....	....
2007-08	Boston University	H-East	32	1	1	2	54	....	....	....	....	....
2008-09	Boston University	H-East	45	0	6	6	106	....	....	....	....	....
2009-10	Boston University	H-East	38	4	6	10	*118	....	....	....	....	....
	Binghamton	AHL	6	1	0	1	2	....	....	....	....	....

GUDAS, Radko (GOO-duhs, RAHD-koh) **T.B.**

Defense. Shoots right. 5'11", 192 lbs. Born, Prague, Czechoslovakia, June 5, 1990.
(Tampa Bay's 3rd choice, 66th overall, in 2010 Entry Draft).

			Regular Season					Playoffs				
Season	Club	League	GP	G	A	Pts	PIM	GP	G	A	Pts	PIM
2004-05	HC Kladno U17	CzR-U17	46	1	5	6	70	7	0	0	0	10
2005-06	HC Kladno U17	CzR-U17	46	12	14	26	178	5	1	2	3	8
2006-07	HC Kladno U17	CzR-U17	16	6	7	13	34	7	4	1	5	14
	HC KEB Kladno Jr.	CzRep-Jr.	15	0	1	1	18	1	0	0	0	0
	Beroun	CzRep-2	9	0	1	1	6	....	....	....	....	....
2007-08	Beroun	CzRep-2	43	1	5	6	90	....	....	....	....	....
	Kladno	CzRep	....	....	....	....	....	1	0	0	0	0
2008-09	HC KEB Kladno Jr.	CzRep-Jr.	2	0	1	1	0	....	....	....	....	....
	Beroun	CzRep-2	32	1	6	7	110	....	....	....	....	....
	Kladno	CzRep	14	0	1	1	10	....	....	....	....	....
2009-10	Everett Silvertips	WHL	65	7	30	37	151	3	0	2	2	4

WHL West Second All-Star Team (2010)

GUDBRANSON, Erik (guhd-BRAN-suhn, AIR-ihk) **FLA.**

Defense. Shoots right. 6'4", 195 lbs. Born, Ottawa, Ont., January 7, 1992.
(Florida's 1st choice, 3rd overall, in 2010 Entry Draft).

			Regular Season					Playoffs				
Season	Club	League	GP	G	A	Pts	PIM	GP	G	A	Pts	PIM
2007-08	Ottawa Jr. 67's	Minor-ON	70	15	40	55	118	....	....	....	....	....
2008-09	Kingston	OHL	63	3	19	22	69	....	....	....	....	....
2009-10	Kingston	OHL	41	2	21	23	68	7	1	2	3	6

GUPTILL, Alexander (GUP-tihl, al-ehx-AN-duhr) **DAL.**

Left wing. Shoots left. 6'3", 175 lbs. Born, Burlington, Ont., March 5, 1992.
(Dallas' 3rd choice, 77th overall, in 2010 Entry Draft).

			Regular Season					Playoffs				
Season	Club	League	GP	G	A	Pts	PIM	GP	G	A	Pts	PIM
2008-09	Brampton Capitals	OJHL	49	30	34	64	28	3	0	1	1	0
2009-10	Brampton Capitals	OJAHL	10	6	5	11	24	....	....	....	....	....
	Orangeville	CCHL	19	13	13	26	26	2	1	0	1	2

• Signed Letter of Intent to attend **University of Michigan** (CCHA) in fall of 2011.

GUSTAFSSON, Anton (goos-TAHF-suhn, AN-tawn) **WSH.**

Center. Shoots left. 6'2", 194 lbs. Born, Karlskoga, Sweden, February 25, 1990.
(Washington's 1st choice, 21st overall, in 2008 Entry Draft).

			Regular Season					Playoffs				
Season	Club	League	GP	G	A	Pts	PIM	GP	G	A	Pts	PIM
2005-06	Karlskoga HC	Sweden-4	....	3	0	3	0	....	....	....	....	....
2006-07	Frolunda U18	Swe-U18	8	3	4	7	8	6	3	1	4	2
	Frolunda Jr.	Swe-Jr.	26	5	3	8	24	8	0	0	0	8
2007-08	Frolunda U18	Swe-U18	1	0	1	1	2	....	....	....	....	....
	Frolunda Jr.	Swe-Jr.	33	15	17	32	55	2	1	0	1	2
	Frolunda	Sweden	1	0	0	0	0	....	....	....	....	....
2008-09	Bofors	Sweden-2	25	6	4	10	22	....	....	....	....	....
	Frolunda Jr.	Swe-Jr.	2	0	0	0	4	5	3	4	7	4
2009-10	Boras HC	Sweden-2	34	6	12	18	20	....	....	....	....	....
	Hershey Bears	AHL	1	0	2	2	0	....	....	....	....	....

GUSTAFSSON, Erik (GOOS-tahf-suhn, AIR-ihk) PHI.

Defense. Shoots left. 5'11", 195 lbs. Born, Kvissleby, Sweden, December 15, 1988.

			Regular Season					Playoffs				
Season	Club	League	GP	G	A	Pts	PIM	GP	G	A	Pts	PIM
2004-05	Timra IK U18	Swe-U18	14	4	2	6	12	3	0	0	0	0
2005-06	Timra IK U18	Swe-U18	8	2	1	3	8	....	....	....	....	....
	Timra IK Jr.	Swe-Jr.	38	3	4	7	26	1	0	0	0	0
2006-07	Timra IK Jr.	Swe-Jr.	41	7	13	20	93	3	0	0	0	14
2007-08	Northern Mich.	CCHA	44	0	27	27	12	....	....	....	....	....
2008-09	Northern Mich.	CCHA	40	4	30	34	10	....	....	....	....	....
2009-10	Northern Mich.	CCHA	39	3	29	32	26	....	....	....	....	....
	Adirondack	AHL	5	2	5	7	0	....	....	....	....	....

CCHA All-Rookie Team (2008) • CCHA First All-Star Team (2009, 2010) • NCAA West Second All-American Team (2009, 2010)

Signed as a free agent by **Philadelphia**, March 31, 2010.

GYSBERS, Simon (GIGHZ-buhrz, SIGH-muhn) TOR.

Defense. Shoots right. 6'4", 200 lbs. Born, Richmond Hill, Ont., May 7, 1987.

			Regular Season					Playoffs				
Season	Club	League	GP	G	A	Pts	PIM	GP	G	A	Pts	PIM
2004-05	Stouffville Spirit	OPJHL	46	11	23	34	32	....	....	....	....	....
2005-06	Stouffville Spirit	OPJHL	46	8	24	32	94	....	....	....	....	....
2006-07	Lake Superior	CCHA	41	4	8	12	45	....	....	....	....	....
2007-08	Lake Superior	CCHA	37	6	13	19	46	....	....	....	....	....
2008-09	Lake Superior	CCHA	39	3	18	21	28	....	....	....	....	....
2009-10	Lake Superior	CCHA	38	6	9	15	46	....	....	....	....	....
	Toronto Marlies	AHL	14	0	1	1	2	....	....	....	....	....

Signed to an ATO (amateur tryout) contact by **Toronto** (AHL), March 11, 2010.

HADDAD, Joey (HA-DAD, JOH-ee) PIT.

Left wing. Shoots left. 6'2", 200 lbs. Born, Sydney, N.S., December 10, 1988.

			Regular Season					Playoffs				
Season	Club	League	GP	G	A	Pts	PIM	GP	G	A	Pts	PIM
2005-06	P.E.I. Rocket	QMJHL	48	3	12	15	73	1	0	0	0	0
2006-07	P.E.I. Rocket	QMJHL	68	9	12	21	78	5	0	0	0	6
2007-08	Cape Breton	QMJHL	70	31	31	62	103	11	7	5	12	12
2008-09	Cape Breton	QMJHL	50	30	25	55	91	11	8	4	12	32
2009-10	Wilkes-Barre	AHL	29	1	5	6	24	....	....	....	....	....
	Wheeling Nailers	ECHL	34	7	13	20	52	....	....	....	....	....

Signed as a free agent by **Pittsburgh**, October 10, 2008.

HAGELIN, Carl (HAG-eh-lihn, KARL) NYR

Left wing. Shoots left. 5'11", 176 lbs. Born, Sodertalje, Sweden, August 23, 1988.
(NY Rangers' 4th choice, 168th overall, in 2007 Entry Draft).

			Regular Season					Playoffs				
Season	Club	League	GP	G	A	Pts	PIM	GP	G	A	Pts	PIM
2004-05	Sodertalje SK U18	Swe-U18	14	10	7	17	16	2	0	2	2	0
2005-06	Sodertalje SK U18	Swe-U18	7	4	8	12	2	....	....	....	....	....
	Sodertalje SK Jr.	Swe-Jr.	41	20	20	40	42	4	1	2	3	22
2006-07	Sodertalje SK Jr.	Swe-Jr.	40	24	31	55	42	3	1	5	6	20
2007-08	U. of Michigan	CCHA	41	11	11	22	28	....	....	....	....	....
2008-09	U. of Michigan	CCHA	41	13	18	31	32	....	....	....	....	....
2009-10	U. of Michigan	CCHA	45	19	*31	*50	34	....	....	....	....	....

HAKANPAA, Jani (HAHK-an-pah, YAH-nee) ST.L.

Defense. Shoots right. 6'5", 218 lbs. Born, Kirkkonummi, Finland, March 31, 1992.
(St. Louis' 5th choice, 104th overall, in 2010 Entry Draft).

			Regular Season					Playoffs				
Season	Club	League	GP	G	A	Pts	PIM	GP	G	A	Pts	PIM
2007-08	K-Vantaa U18	Fin-U18	2	0	1	1	2	2	0	0	0	0
2008-09	K-Vantaa U18	Fin-U18	10	3	4	7	14	....	....	....	....	....
2009-10	K-Vantaa U18	Fin-U18	32	3	16	19	69	6	0	2	2	6

HALL, Taylor (HAWL, TAY-luhr) EDM.

Left wing. Shoots left. 6'1", 185 lbs. Born, Calgary, Alta., November 14, 1991.
(Edmonton's 1st choice, 1st overall, in 2010 Entry Draft).

			Regular Season					Playoffs				
Season	Club	League	GP	G	A	Pts	PIM	GP	G	A	Pts	PIM
2006-07	King. Jr. Frontenacs	Minor-ON	29	44	41	85	10	....	....	....	....	....
2007-08	Windsor Spitfires	OHL	63	45	39	84	22	5	2	3	5	2
2008-09	Windsor Spitfires	OHL	63	38	52	90	60	20	*16	20	*36	12
2009-10	Windsor Spitfires	OHL	57	40	*66	*106	56	19	17	18	*35	32

Canadian Major Junior All-Rookie Team (2008) • Canadian Major Junior Rookie of the Year (2008) • OHL First All-Star Team (2009, 2010) • Canadian Major Junior Second All-Star Team (2010) • Memorial Cup All-Star Team (2010) • Ed Chynoweth Trophy (Memorial Cup Tournament - Leading Scorer) (2010) • Stafford Smythe Memorial Trophy (Memorial Cup Tournament - MVP) (2010)

HAMBURG, Anthony (HAM-buhrg, AN-thuh-nee) MIN.

Center. Shoots right. 6'1", 199 lbs. Born, Houston, TX, August 30, 1991.
(Minnesota's 8th choice, 193rd overall, in 2009 Entry Draft).

			Regular Season					Playoffs				
Season	Club	League	GP	G	A	Pts	PIM	GP	G	A	Pts	PIM
2007-08	Dallas Stars AAA	Exhib.	65	20	57	77	68	....	....	....	....	....
2008-09	Dallas Stars AAA	T1EHL	46	16	38	54	38	....	....	....	....	....
	Dallas Stars AAA	Exhib.	24	13	32	45	38	....	....	....	....	....
2009-10	Omaha Lancers	USHL	54	5	17	22	35	3	0	0	0	2

HAMILTON, Curtis (HAM-ihl-tuhn, KUHR-tihs) EDM.

Left wing. Shoots left. 6'2", 209 lbs. Born, Tacoma, WA, December 4, 1991.
(Edmonton's 4th choice, 48th overall, in 2010 Entry Draft).

			Regular Season					Playoffs				
Season	Club	League	GP	G	A	Pts	PIM	GP	G	A	Pts	PIM
2006-07	Okanagan Rockets	BCMML	37	26	27	53	68	....	....	....	....	....
	Saskatoon Blades	WHL	2	0	0	0	0	....	....	....	....	....
2007-08	Saskatoon Blades	WHL	68	14	13	27	43	....	....	....	....	....
2008-09	Saskatoon Blades	WHL	58	20	28	48	24	7	1	1	2	2
2009-10	Saskatoon Blades	WHL	26	7	9	16	6	5	2	1	3	6

HAMILTON, Freddie (HAM-ihl-tuhn, FREH-dee) S.J.

Center. Shoots right. 6'1", 190 lbs. Born, Toronto, Ont., January 1, 1992.
(San Jose's 4th choice, 129th overall, in 2010 Entry Draft).

			Regular Season					Playoffs				
Season	Club	League	GP	G	A	Pts	PIM	GP	G	A	Pts	PIM
2007-08	Toronto Marlboros	GTHL	51	39	42	81	4	....	....	....	....	....
2008-09	Niagara Ice Dogs	OHL	65	10	18	28	8	12	2	2	4	4
2009-10	Niagara Ice Dogs	OHL	64	25	30	55	12	5	1	1	2	6

HAMILTON, Ryan (HAM-ihl-tuhn, RIGH-uhn) TOR.

Left wing. Shoots left. 6'2", 219 lbs. Born, Oshawa, Ont., April 15, 1985.

			Regular Season					Playoffs				
Season	Club	League	GP	G	A	Pts	PIM	GP	G	A	Pts	PIM
2002-03	Couchiching	OPJHL	11	5	8	13	2	....	....	....	....	....
	Peterborough Bees	OPJHL	27	3	10	13	43	....	....	....	....	....
	Trenton Sting	OPJHL	17	3	8	11	24	....	....	....	....	....
	Barrie Colts	OHL	24	3	2	5	10	6	1	0	1	0
2003-04	Kingston	OPJHL	14	1	5	6	23	....	....	....	....	....
	Barrie Colts	OHL	46	17	10	27	21	7	0	1	1	8
2004-05	Barrie Colts	OHL	37	13	11	24	6	6	2	0	2	2
2005-06	Barrie Colts	OHL	63	46	26	72	58	14	8	9	17	11
	Houston Aeros	AHL	....	....	....	....	....	1	0	0	0	0
2006-07	Houston Aeros	AHL	62	7	9	16	36	....	....	....	....	....
2007-08	Houston Aeros	AHL	72	20	19	39	38	2	1	0	1	0
2008-09	Houston Aeros	AHL	29	8	4	12	24	....	....	....	....	....
	Toronto Marlies	AHL	36	7	6	13	33	6	1	2	3	4
2009-10	Toronto Marlies	AHL	47	16	9	25	37	....	....	....	....	....

Signed as a free agent by **Minnesota**, July 5, 2006. Traded to **Toronto** by **Minnesota** for Robbie Earl, January 21, 2009.

HAMONIC, Travis (HA-mohn-ihk, TRA-vihs) NYI

Defense. Shoots right. 6'2", 215 lbs. Born, Winnipeg, Man., August 16, 1990.
(NY Islanders' 4th choice, 53rd overall, in 2008 Entry Draft).

			Regular Season					Playoffs				
Season	Club	League	GP	G	A	Pts	PIM	GP	G	A	Pts	PIM
2006-07	Winnipeg Saints	MJHL	....	2	13	15	....	....	....	....	....	....
	Moose Jaw	WHL	22	0	3	3	30	....	....	....	....	....
2007-08	Moose Jaw	WHL	61	5	17	22	101	6	0	1	1	6
2008-09	Moose Jaw	WHL	57	13	27	40	126	....	....	....	....	....
2009-10	Moose Jaw	WHL	31	10	29	39	48	....	....	....	....	....
	Brandon	WHL	10	1	4	5	17	15	4	7	11	23

WHL East Second All-Star Team (2010) • Memorial Cup All-Star Team (2010)

HANNAY, Sawyer (HA-NAY, SOY-yuhr) VAN.

Defense. Shoots right. 6'4", 194 lbs. Born, Moncton, N.B., September 6, 1992.
(Vancouver's 5th choice, 205th overall, in 2010 Entry Draft).

			Regular Season					Playoffs				
Season	Club	League	GP	G	A	Pts	PIM	GP	G	A	Pts	PIM
2007-08	Moncton Flyers	NBPEI	35	2	1	3	50	8	0	0	0	12
2008-09	Moncton Flyers	NBPEI	34	5	17	22	74	8	2	4	6	36
2009-10	Halifax	QMJHL	54	1	5	6	158	....	....	....	....	....

HANOWSKI, Ben (ha-NOW-skee, BEHN) PIT.

Wing. Shoots left. 6'2", 198 lbs. Born, Little Falls, MN, October 18, 1990.
(Pittsburgh's 3rd choice, 63rd overall, in 2009 Entry Draft).

			Regular Season					Playoffs				
Season	Club	League	GP	G	A	Pts	PIM	GP	G	A	Pts	PIM
2005-06	Little Falls Flyers	High-MN	31	35	29	64	....	....	....	....	....	....
2006-07	Little Falls Flyers	High-MN	29	40	71	111	....	....	....	....	....	....
2007-08	Little Falls Flyers	High-MN	26	48	47	95	....	....	....	....	....	....
	Team North	UMHSEL	....	17	16	33	....	....	....	....	....	....
2008-09	Little Falls Flyers	High-MN	31	73	62	135	16	....	....	....	....	....
	Team North	UMHSEL	19	14	8	22	....	....	....	....	....	....
2009-10	St. Cloud State	WCHA	43	9	10	19	19	....	....	....	....	....

HANSEN, Jake (HAHN-suhn, JAYK) CBJ

Wing. Shoots right. 6'1", 190 lbs. Born, St.Paul, MN, August 21, 1989.
(Columbus' 4th choice, 68th overall, in 2007 Entry Draft).

			Regular Season					Playoffs				
Season	Club	League	GP	G	A	Pts	PIM	GP	G	A	Pts	PIM
2005-06	White Bear Lake	High-MN	STATISTICS NOT AVAILABLE									
2006-07	White Bear Lake	High-MN	25	28	43	71		....	....	....	....	....
	Sioux Falls	USHL	15	4	4	8	14	7	0	2	2	6
2007-08	Sioux Falls	USHL	60	31	27	58	57	3	1	0	1	0
2008-09	U. of Minnesota	WCHA	33	2	5	7	38	....	....	....	....	....
2009-10	U. of Minnesota	WCHA	38	7	5	12	20	....	....	....	....	....

USHL Second All-Star Team (2008)

HARJU, Johan (HAHR-yoo, YOH-hahn) T.B.

Left wing. Shoots left. 6'3", 205 lbs. Born, Overtornea, Sweden, May 15, 1986.
(Tampa Bay's 6th choice, 167th overall, in 2007 Entry Draft).

			Regular Season					Playoffs				
Season	Club	League	GP	G	A	Pts	PIM	GP	G	A	Pts	PIM
2002-03	Lulea HF U18	Swe-U18	11	7	2	9	14	....	....	....	....	....
	Lulea HF Jr.	Swe-Jr.	7	2	0	2	0	....	....	....	....	....
2003-04	Lulea HF U18	Swe-U18	3	1	3	4	0	7	4	3	7	8
	Lulea HF Jr.	Swe-Jr.	35	14	12	26	8	....	....	....	....	....
2004-05	Lulea HF Jr.	Swe-Jr.	33	18	13	31	14	7	2	2	4	2
	Pitea HC	Sweden-2	1	0	0	0	0	....	....	....	....	....
	Lulea HF	Sweden	4	0	0	0	0	....	....	....	....	....
2005-06	Lulea HF Jr.	Swe-Jr.	17	14	9	23	4	4	3	1	4	8
	Lulea HF	Sweden	39	3	1	4	8	4	0	0	0	20
2006-07	Lulea HF	Sweden	55	12	10	22	30	4	2	0	2	4
2007-08	Lulea HF	Sweden	51	20	8	28	55	....	....	....	....	....
2008-09	Lulea HF	Sweden	55	27	22	49	30	5	4	1	5	0
2009-10	Dynamo Moscow	Rus-KHL	55	4	14	18	38	2	1	0	1	8

Signed as a free agent by **Dynamo Moscow** (Russia-KHL), April 8, 2009.

HARPER, Shane (HAHR-puhr, SHAYN) PHI.

Right wing. Shoots right. 5'11", 193 lbs. Born, Valencia, CA, February 1, 1989.

			Regular Season					Playoffs				
Season	**Club**	**League**	**GP**	**G**	**A**	**Pts**	**PIM**	**GP**	**G**	**A**	**Pts**	**PIM**
2005-06	Everett Silvertips	WHL	62	6	4	10	8	5	1	0	1	0
2006-07	Everett Silvertips	WHL	58	3	12	15	23	8	1	2	3	0
2007-08	Everett Silvertips	WHL	71	17	26	43	18	4	0	2	2	0
2008-09	Everett Silvertips	WHL	72	32	34	66	10	5	0	4	4	0
2009-10	Everett Silvertips	WHL	72	42	38	80	38	7	6	4	10	6
	Adirondack	AHL	5	1	0	1	2	....	....	....	....	....

WHL West Second All-Star Team (2010)

Signed as a free agent by **Philadelphia**, March 4, 2010.

HARTIKAINEN, Teemu (har-tih-KIGH-nehn, TEE-moo) EDM.

Center. Shoots left. 6'1", 198 lbs. Born, Kuopio, Finland, May 3, 1990.
(Edmonton's 4th choice, 163rd overall, in 2008 Entry Draft).

			Regular Season					Playoffs				
Season	**Club**	**League**	**GP**	**G**	**A**	**Pts**	**PIM**	**GP**	**G**	**A**	**Pts**	**PIM**
2006-07	KalPa Kuopio U18	Fin-U18	19	24	13	37	51	....	....	....	....	....
	KalPa Kuopio Jr.	Fin-Jr.	11	2	1	3	0	3	0	0	0	4
2007-08	KalPa Kuopio U18	Fin-U18	7	9	6	15	6	....	....	....	....	....
	KalPa Kuopio Jr.	Fin-Jr.	37	10	7	17	24	11	1	4	5	6
	KalPa Kuopio	Finland	1	0	0	0	0	....	....	....	....	....
2008-09	Suomi U20	Finland-2	3	0	2	2	8	....	....	....	....	....
	KalPa Kuopio	Finland	51	17	6	23	12	12	3	0	3	0
2009-10	KalPa Kuopio	Finland	53	15	18	33	22	13	6	1	7	28
	Suomi U20	Finland-2	1	0	0	0	0	....	....	....	....	....

HAULA, Erik (HOW-la, AIR-ihk) MIN.

Left wing. Shoots left. 5'11", 177 lbs. Born, Pori, Finland, March 23, 1991.
(Minnesota's 7th choice, 182nd overall, in 2009 Entry Draft).

			Regular Season					Playoffs				
Season	**Club**	**League**	**GP**	**G**	**A**	**Pts**	**PIM**	**GP**	**G**	**A**	**Pts**	**PIM**
2006-07	Assat Pori U18	Fin-U18	29	19	24	43	24	6	1	3	4	4
2007-08	Assat Pori U18	Fin-U18	3	1	1	2	0	2	4	2	6	14
	Assat Pori Jr.	Fin-Jr.	40	7	15	22	26	12	2	0	2	4
2008-09	Shat.-St. Mary's	High-MN	53	26	58	84	46	....	....	....	....	....
2009-10	Omaha Lancers	USHL	56	28	44	72	59	8	2	9	11	2

USHL All-Rookie Team (2010) • USHL Second All-Star Team (2010)

• Signed Letter of Intent to attend **University of Minnesota** (WCHA) in fall of 2010.

HAUSWIRTH, Jake (HAWZ-wuhrth, JAYK) WSH.

Left wing. Shoots left. 6'5", 200 lbs. Born, Merrill, WI, February 16, 1988.

			Regular Season					Playoffs				
Season	**Club**	**League**	**GP**	**G**	**A**	**Pts**	**PIM**	**GP**	**G**	**A**	**Pts**	**PIM**
2006-07	Marquette	NAHL	55	21	19	40	74	....	....	....	....	....
2007-08	Omaha Lancers	USHL	57	13	10	23	36	13	2	4	6	10
2008-09	Omaha Lancers	USHL	58	28	24	52	22	3	1	0	1	0
2009-10	South Carolina	ECHL	62	17	27	44	24	2	0	1	1	0

Signed as a free agent by **Washington**, May 26, 2009.

HAYES, Jimmy (HAYZ, JIH-mee) CHI.

Right wing. Shoots right. 6'5", 210 lbs. Born, Boston, MA, November 21, 1989.
(Toronto's 2nd choice, 60th overall, in 2008 Entry Draft).

			Regular Season					Playoffs				
Season	**Club**	**League**	**GP**	**G**	**A**	**Pts**	**PIM**	**GP**	**G**	**A**	**Pts**	**PIM**
2006-07	USNTDP	U-17	42	17	14	31	37	....	....	....	....	....
	USNTDP	NAHL	14	6	8	14	4	....	....	....	....	....
2007-08	USNTDP	U-18	18	2	5	7	6	....	....	....	....	....
	USNTDP	NAHL	19	2	8	10	6	....	....	....	....	....
	Lincoln Stars	USHL	21	4	11	15	18	8	4	5	9	8
2008-09	Boston College	H-East	36	8	5	13	22	....	....	....	....	....
2009-10	Boston College	H-East	42	13	22	35	14	....	....	....	....	....

Traded to **Chicago** by **Toronto** for Calgary's 2nd round choice (previously acquired, Toronto selected Brad Ross) in 2010 Entry Draft, June 25, 2010.

HAYES, Kevin (HAYZ, KEH-vihn) CHI.

Right wing. Shoots left. 6'2", 201 lbs. Born, Boston, MA, May 8, 1992.
(Chicago's 1st choice, 24th overall, in 2010 Entry Draft).

			Regular Season					Playoffs				
Season	**Club**	**League**	**GP**	**G**	**A**	**Pts**	**PIM**	**GP**	**G**	**A**	**Pts**	**PIM**
2007-08	Nobles	High-MA	29	8	5	13	2	....	....	....	....	....
2008-09	Nobles	High-MA	23	28	27	55	15	....	....	....	....	....
2009-10	Cape Cod Whalers	Minor-MA	25	21	30	51	....	....	....	....	....	....
	Nobles	High-MA	29	25	44	69	8	....	....	....	....	....
	USNTDP	U-18	2	2	0	2	0	....	....	....	....	....

• Signed Letter of Intent to attend **Boston College** (Hockey East) in fall of 2010.

HEED, Tim (HEH-ehd, TIHM) ANA.

Defense. Shoots right. 5'11", 165 lbs. Born, Gothenburg, Sweden, January 27, 1991.
(Anaheim's 5th choice, 132nd overall, in 2010 Entry Draft).

			Regular Season					Playoffs				
Season	**Club**	**League**	**GP**	**G**	**A**	**Pts**	**PIM**	**GP**	**G**	**A**	**Pts**	**PIM**
2007-08	Sodertalje SK U18	Swe-U18	36	4	23	27	34	2	0	0	0	4
	Sodertalje SK Jr.	Swe-Jr.	2	0	0	0	0	....	....	....	....	....
2008-09	Sodertalje SK U18	Swe-U18	14	7	10	17	10	3	3	2	5	2
	Sodertalje SK Jr.	Swe-Jr.	32	1	7	8	10	2	0	1	1	0
2009-10	Sodertalje SK Jr.	Swe-Jr.	32	8	29	37	20	....	....	....	....	....
	Sodertalje SK	Sweden	27	1	9	10	2	....	....	....	....	....
	Sodertalje SK	Sweden-Q	10	0	4	4	0	....	....	....	....	....

HEGARTY, Ryan (HEH-gahr-tee, RIGH-uhn) ANA.

Defense. Shoots left. 6', 196 lbs. Born, Stoneham, MA, May 16, 1990.
(Anaheim's 8th choice, 113th overall, in 2008 Entry Draft).

			Regular Season					Playoffs				
Season	**Club**	**League**	**GP**	**G**	**A**	**Pts**	**PIM**	**GP**	**G**	**A**	**Pts**	**PIM**
2006-07	USNTDP	U-17	15	1	2	3	10	....	....	....	....	....
	USNTDP	NAHL	43	2	2	4	54	6	0	0	0	4
2007-08	USNTDP	U-18	41	5	8	13	38	....	....	....	....	....
	USNTDP	NAHL	14	2	8	10	18	....	....	....	....	....
2008-09	U. of Maine	H-East	24	0	3	3	22	....	....	....	....	....
2009-10	U. of Maine	H-East	33	1	7	8	36	....	....	....	....	....

HELGESON, Seth (HEHL-guh-suhn, SEHTH) N.J.

Defense. Shoots left. 6'5", 220 lbs. Born, Faribault, MN, October 8, 1990.
(New Jersey's 4th choice, 114th overall, in 2009 Entry Draft).

			Regular Season					Playoffs				
Season	**Club**	**League**	**GP**	**G**	**A**	**Pts**	**PIM**	**GP**	**G**	**A**	**Pts**	**PIM**
2006-07	Faribault Falcons	High-MN	27	19	17	36	....	....	....	....	....	....
2007-08	Sioux City	USHL	58	3	8	11	41	4	0	1	1	2
2008-09	Sioux City	USHL	58	4	12	16	64	....	....	....	....	....
2009-10	U. of Minnesota	WCHA	31	1	0	1	24	....	....	....	....	....

HENDERSON, Kevin (HEHN-duhr-SOHN, KEH-vihn) S.J.

Left wing. Shoots left. 6'3", 210 lbs. Born, Toronto, Ont., December 3, 1986.

			Regular Season					Playoffs				
Season	**Club**	**League**	**GP**	**G**	**A**	**Pts**	**PIM**	**GP**	**G**	**A**	**Pts**	**PIM**
2003-04	Pickering Panthers	OPJHL	47	11	23	34	44	....	....	....	....	....
2004-05	Kitchener Rangers	OHL	47	5	8	13	46	15	0	3	3	8
	Tor. T-Birds	OPJHL	11	5	9	14	33	....	....	....	....	....
2005-06	Kitchener Rangers	OHL	63	6	11	17	66	2	1	0	1	0
2006-07	Kitchener Rangers	OHL	56	33	15	48	69	9	4	6	10	13
2007-08	New Brunswick	AUAA	27	5	10	15	22	....	....	....	....	....
2008-09	New Brunswick	AUAA	28	19	31	50	28	....	....	....	....	....
2009-10	Worcester Sharks	AHL	64	2	13	15	45	11	0	1	1	4

Signed as a free agent by **San Jose**, April 22, 2009.

HENLEY, Cedrick (HEHN-lee, SEH-drihk) BUF.

Left wing. Shoots left. 6'5", 195 lbs. Born, Val D'Or, Que., January 10, 1992.
(Buffalo's 7th choice, 173rd overall, in 2010 Entry Draft).

			Regular Season					Playoffs				
Season	**Club**	**League**	**GP**	**G**	**A**	**Pts**	**PIM**	**GP**	**G**	**A**	**Pts**	**PIM**
2007-08	Filon De Malartic	Minor-QC	STATISTICS NOT AVAILABLE									
	Amos Foresters	QAAA	14	6	12	18	12	....	....	....	....	....
2008-09	Val-d'Or Foreurs	QMJHL	61	7	12	19	26	....	....	....	....	....
2009-10	Val-d'Or Foreurs	QMJHL	44	5	7	12	43	6	0	0	0	6

HENRIQUE, Adam (HEHN-reek, A-duhm) N.J.

Center. Shoots left. 6', 205 lbs. Born, Brantford, Ont., February 6, 1990.
(New Jersey's 4th choice, 82nd overall, in 2008 Entry Draft).

			Regular Season					Playoffs				
Season	**Club**	**League**	**GP**	**G**	**A**	**Pts**	**PIM**	**GP**	**G**	**A**	**Pts**	**PIM**
2006-07	Windsor Spitfires	OHL	62	23	21	44	20	....	....	....	....	....
2007-08	Windsor Spitfires	OHL	66	20	24	44	28	5	2	3	5	4
2008-09	Windsor Spitfires	OHL	56	30	33	63	47	20	8	9	17	19
2009-10	Windsor Spitfires	OHL	54	38	39	77	57	19	*20	5	25	12

HERBERT, Caleb (HUHR-buhrt, KAY-lehb) WSH.

Center. Shoots right. 5'10", 180 lbs. Born, St. Paul, MN, October 12, 1991.
(Washington's 4th choice, 142nd overall, in 2010 Entry Draft).

			Regular Season					Playoffs				
Season	**Club**	**League**	**GP**	**G**	**A**	**Pts**	**PIM**	**GP**	**G**	**A**	**Pts**	**PIM**
2007-08	Bloomington-Jeff.	High-MN	6	4	3	7	6	....	....	....	....	....
2008-09	Bloomington-Jeff.	High-MN	27	29	24	53	36	....	....	....	....	....
2009-10	Team Southeast	UMHSEL	24	14	8	22	....	....	....	....	....	....
	Bloomington-Jeff.	High-MN	25	26	28	54	42	3	4	4	8	2

• Signed Letter of Intent to attend **University of Minnesota-Duluth** (WCHA) in fall of 2010.

HESKETH, Troy (HEHS-kehth, TROY) EDM.

Defense. Shoots left. 6'2", 178 lbs. Born, Minnetonka, MN, July 5, 1991.
(Edmonton's 3rd choice, 71st overall, in 2009 Entry Draft).

			Regular Season					Playoffs				
Season	**Club**	**League**	**GP**	**G**	**A**	**Pts**	**PIM**	**GP**	**G**	**A**	**Pts**	**PIM**
2007-08	Minnetonka High	High-MN	9	0	0	0	2	....	....	....	....	....
2008-09	Team Southwest	UMHSEL	22	2	7	9	....	....	....	....	....	....
	Minnetonka High	High-MN	28	7	15	22	46	....	....	....	....	....
2009-10	Team Southwest	UMHSEL	22	2	7	9	....	....	....	....	....	....
	Minnetonka High	High-MN	30	3	17	20	55	....	....	....	....	....

• Signed Letter of Intent to attend **University of Wisconsin** (WCHA) in fall of 2011.

HEXTALL, Brett (HEHX-tahl, BREHT) PHX.

Center. Shoots right. 5'10", 176 lbs. Born, Philadelphia, PA, April 2, 1988.
(Phoenix's 7th choice, 159th overall, in 2008 Entry Draft).

			Regular Season					Playoffs				
Season	**Club**	**League**	**GP**	**G**	**A**	**Pts**	**PIM**	**GP**	**G**	**A**	**Pts**	**PIM**
2006-07	Penticton Vees	BCHL	59	18	27	45	156	11	2	2	4	8
2007-08	Penticton Vees	BCHL	54	24	48	72	52	15	*12	3	15	12
2008-09	North Dakota	WCHA	42	12	24	36	91	....	....	....	....	....
2009-10	North Dakota	WCHA	34	14	12	26	88	....	....	....	....	....

HICKEY, Thomas (HIH-kee, TAW-muhs) L.A.

Defense. Shoots left. 6', 190 lbs. Born, Calgary, Alta., February 8, 1989.
(Los Angeles' 1st choice, 4th overall, in 2007 Entry Draft).

			Regular Season					Playoffs				
Season	**Club**	**League**	**GP**	**G**	**A**	**Pts**	**PIM**	**GP**	**G**	**A**	**Pts**	**PIM**
2003-04	Cgy. Royals	CBHL	32	13	25	38	51	....	....	....	....	....
2004-05	Calgary Royals	AMHL	33	9	13	22	36	....	....	....	....	....
	Seattle	WHL	5	2	1	3	6	....	....	....	....	....
2005-06	Seattle	WHL	69	1	27	28	53	7	1	3	4	10
2006-07	Seattle	WHL	68	9	41	50	70	11	3	4	7	4
2007-08	Seattle	WHL	63	11	34	45	49	9	1	9	10	4
2008-09	Seattle	WHL	57	16	35	51	30	5	2	1	3	4
	Manchester	AHL	7	1	6	7	2	....	....	....	....	....
2009-10	Manchester	AHL	19	1	5	6	12	4	0	3	3	0

WHL West Second All-Star Team (2007) • WHL West First All-Star Team (2008, 2009)

HILLIER, Ryan (HIHL-lee-uhr, RIGH-uhn) **ANA.**

Left wing. Shoots left. 6'1", 195 lbs. Born, Halifax, N.S., January 25, 1988.
(NY Rangers' 3rd choice, 84th overall, in 2006 Entry Draft).

			Regular Season					Playoffs				
Season	Club	League	GP	G	A	Pts	PIM	GP	G	A	Pts	PIM
2003-04	Dartmouth	NSMHL	55	31	36	67	97	....	....	....	....	....
2004-05	Halifax	QMJHL	21	1	1	2	13	7	0	2	2	2
2005-06	Halifax	QMJHL	68	19	38	57	76	11	2	2	4	12
2006-07	Halifax	QMJHL	70	32	27	59	79	12	3	6	9	20
2007-08	Halifax	QMJHL	70	34	38	72	55	14	8	7	15	22
2008-09	Charlotte	ECHL	66	10	16	26	33	....	....	....	....	....
2009-10	Hartford Wolf Pack	AHL	4	0	0	0	2	....	....	....	....	....
	Charlotte	ECHL	7	0	2	2	2	....	....	....	....	....
	Wheeling Nailers	ECHL	15	2	3	5	4	....	....	....	....	....

Traded to **Anaheim** by **NY Rangers** with Aaron Voros for Steve Eminger, July 9, 2010.

HISHON, Joey (HIHS-hawn, JOH-ee) **COL.**

Center. Shoots left. 5'10", 170 lbs. Born, Stratford, Ont., October 20, 1991.
(Colorado's 1st choice, 17th overall, in 2010 Entry Draft).

			Regular Season					Playoffs				
Season	Club	League	GP	G	A	Pts	PIM	GP	G	A	Pts	PIM
2006-07	Stratford Warriors	Minor-ON	50	44	42	86	114	....	....	....	....	....
2007-08	Owen Sound	OHL	63	20	27	47	38	....	....	....	....	....
2008-09	Owen Sound	OHL	65	37	44	81	34	4	4	3	7	6
2009-10	Owen Sound	OHL	36	16	24	40	26	....	....	....	....	....

HOBBS, Danny (HAWBZ, DA-nee) **NYR**

Center/Right wing. Shoots left. 5'11", 194 lbs. Born, Shawville, Ont., June 21, 1989.
(NY Rangers' 6th choice, 198th overall, in 2007 Entry Draft).

			Regular Season					Playoffs				
Season	Club	League	GP	G	A	Pts	PIM	GP	G	A	Pts	PIM
2005-06	Stanstead	QJHL	46	58	32	90	15	....	....	....	....	....
2006-07	Ohio	USHL	60	10	11	21	36	4	0	2	2	2
2007-08	Ohio	USHL	54	15	16	31	22	....	....	....	....	....
2008-09	Massachusetts	H-East	24	1	1	2	20	....	....	....	....	....
2009-10	Massachusetts	H-East	33	3	6	9	12	....	....	....	....	....

HODGSON, Cody (HAWJ-suhn, KOH-dee) **VAN.**

Center. Shoots right. 6', 185 lbs. Born, Toronto, Ont., February 18, 1990.
(Vancouver's 1st choice, 10th overall, in 2008 Entry Draft).

			Regular Season					Playoffs				
Season	Club	League	GP	G	A	Pts	PIM	GP	G	A	Pts	PIM
2005-06	Markham Waxers	Minor-ON	30	27	24	51	22	15	13	14	27	8
2006-07	Brampton	OHL	63	23	23	46	24	4	1	3	4	0
2007-08	Brampton	OHL	68	40	45	85	36	5	5	0	5	2
2008-09	Brampton	OHL	53	43	49	92	33	21	11	20	31	18
	Manitoba Moose	AHL	....	....	....	....	....	11	2	4	6	4
2009-10	Brampton	OHL	13	8	12	20	9	11	3	7	10	4

OHL First All-Star Team (2009) • OHL Player of the Year (2009) • Canadian Major Junior First All-Star Team (2009) • Canadian Major Junior Player of the Year (2009)

HOEFFEL, Mike (HOH-fuhl, MIGHK) **N.J.**

Left wing. Shoots left. 6'3", 205 lbs. Born, North Oaks, MN, April 9, 1989.
(New Jersey's 1st choice, 57th overall, in 2007 Entry Draft).

			Regular Season					Playoffs				
Season	Club	League	GP	G	A	Pts	PIM	GP	G	A	Pts	PIM
2004-05	Hill-Murray	High-MN	26	24	19	43	10	....	....	....	....	....
2005-06	Hill-Murray	High-MN	30	27	46	73	20	....	....	....	....	....
2006-07	USNTDP	U-18	33	10	2	12	18	....	....	....	....	....
	USNTDP	NAHL	11	6	5	11	10	....	....	....	....	....
2007-08	U. of Minnesota	WCHA	45	9	10	19	22	....	....	....	....	....
2008-09	U. of Minnesota	WCHA	35	12	8	20	38	....	....	....	....	....
2009-10	U. of Minnesota	WCHA	34	14	10	24	22	....	....	....	....	....

HOFFLIN, Mirko (HOHF-lihn, MIHR-koh) **CHI.**

Center. Shoots left. 6', 174 lbs. Born, Freiburg, Germany, June 18, 1992.
(Chicago's 8th choice, 151st overall, in 2010 Entry Draft).

			Regular Season					Playoffs				
Season	Club	League	GP	G	A	Pts	PIM	GP	G	A	Pts	PIM
2007-08	Heil./Mann. Jr.	Ger-Jr.	34	8	7	15	28	8	0	2	2	4
2008-09	Heil./Mann. Jr.	Ger-Jr.	36	14	30	44	26	8	6	8	14	0
2009-10	Heil./Mann. Jr.	Ger-Jr.	24	32	35	67	20	8	5	9	14	2
	Heilbronner Falken	German-2	18	0	3	3	0	5	0	0	0	2

HOFFMAN, Mike (HAWF-muhn, MIGHK) **OTT.**

Center/Left wing. Shoots left. 6'1", 172 lbs. Born, Kitchener, Ont., November 24, 1989.
(Ottawa's 5th choice, 130th overall, in 2009 Entry Draft).

			Regular Season					Playoffs				
Season	Club	League	GP	G	A	Pts	PIM	GP	G	A	Pts	PIM
2006-07	Kitchener	OJHL-B	47	28	29	57	70	6	3	5	8	6
	Kitchener Rangers	OHL	2	0	0	0	2	4	0	0	0	0
2007-08	Gatineau	QMJHL	19	5	7	12	16	....	....	....	....	....
	Drummondville	QMJHL	43	19	17	36	77	....	....	....	....	....
2008-09	Drummondville	QMJHL	62	52	42	94	86	19	21	13	34	26
2009-10	Saint John	QMJHL	56	46	39	85	38	21	11	13	24	23

QMJHL First All-Star Team (2009, 2010) • QMJHL Player of the Year (2010) • Canadian Major Junior Second All-Star Team (2010)

HOLDEN, Nick (HOHL-dehn, NIHK) **CBJ**

Defense. Shoots left. 6'4", 200 lbs. Born, St. Albert, Alta., May 15, 1987.

			Regular Season					Playoffs				
Season	Club	League	GP	G	A	Pts	PIM	GP	G	A	Pts	PIM
2004-05	Camrose Kodiaks	AJHL	4	0	0	0	0	....	....	....	....	....
2005-06	Sherwood Park	AJHL	57	7	23	30	46	....	....	....	....	....
2006-07	Chilliwack Bruins	WHL	67	8	23	31	62	5	1	1	2	6
2007-08	Chilliwack Bruins	WHL	70	22	38	60	54	4	1	3	4	0
	Syracuse Crunch	AHL	1	0	0	0	2	....	....	....	....	....
2008-09	Syracuse Crunch	AHL	61	4	18	22	46	....	....	....	....	....
2009-10	Syracuse Crunch	AHL	68	6	17	23	52	....	....	....	....	....

Signed as a free agent by **Columbus**, March 28, 2008.

HOLL, Justin (HOHL, JUHS-tihn) **CHI.**

Defense. Shoots right. 6'2", 170 lbs. Born, Edina, MN, January 30, 1992.
(Chicago's 3rd choice, 54th overall, in 2010 Entry Draft).

			Regular Season					Playoffs				
Season	Club	League	GP	G	A	Pts	PIM	GP	G	A	Pts	PIM
2007-08	Minnetonka High	High-MN	24	0	1	1	0	....	....	....	....	....
2008-09	Minnetonka High	High-MN	28	1	6	7	4	....	....	....	....	....
2009-10	Team Southwest	UMHSEL	STATISTICS NOT AVAILABLE									
	Minnetonka High	High-MN	25	17	14	31	8	6	3	3	6	0

• Signed Letter of Intent to attend **University of Minnesota** (WCHA) in fall of 2010.

HOLLAND, Patrick (HAW-luhnd, PAT-rihk) **CGY.**

Right wing. Shoots right. 6', 170 lbs. Born, Lethbridge, Alta., January 7, 1992.
(Calgary's 6th choice, 193rd overall, in 2010 Entry Draft).

			Regular Season					Playoffs				
Season	Club	League	GP	G	A	Pts	PIM	GP	G	A	Pts	PIM
2007-08	Leth. Hurricanes	Minor-AB	32	33	21	54	34	....	....	....	....	....
2008-09	Lethbridge	AMHL	34	17	28	45	20	7	5	11	16	2
	Lethbridge	Exhib.	6	5	3	8	0	....	....	....	....	....
	Tri-City Americans	WHL	1	0	0	0	0	....	....	....	....	....
2009-10	Tri-City Americans	WHL	59	16	20	36	14	22	3	7	10	10

HOLLAND, Peter (HAW-luhnd, PEE-tuhr) **ANA.**

Center. Shoots left. 6'2", 187 lbs. Born, Toronto, Ont., January 14, 1991.
(Anaheim's 1st choice, 15th overall, in 2009 Entry Draft).

			Regular Season					Playoffs				
Season	Club	League	GP	G	A	Pts	PIM	GP	G	A	Pts	PIM
2006-07	Brampton	Minor-ON	60	59	60	119	107	....	....	....	....	....
2007-08	Guelph Storm	OHL	62	8	15	23	31	10	0	1	1	4
2008-09	Guelph Storm	OHL	68	28	39	67	42	4	4	0	4	2
2009-10	Guelph Storm	OHL	59	30	50	80	40	5	3	5	8	12

HOLLOWAY, Bud (HAHL-OH-way, BUHD) **L.A.**

Center. Shoots right. 6'1", 200 lbs. Born, Wapella, Sask., March 1, 1988.
(Los Angeles' 5th choice, 86th overall, in 2006 Entry Draft).

			Regular Season					Playoffs				
Season	Club	League	GP	G	A	Pts	PIM	GP	G	A	Pts	PIM
2003-04	Yorkton Harvest	SMHL	43	15	21	36	22	....	....	....	....	....
	Seattle	WHL	2	0	0	0	0	....	....	....	....	....
2004-05	Seattle	WHL	67	4	11	15	27	12	0	1	1	0
2005-06	Seattle	WHL	72	21	13	34	18	7	3	2	5	4
2006-07	Seattle	WHL	71	27	38	65	50	11	3	3	6	8
2007-08	Seattle	WHL	70	43	40	83	55	12	5	5	10	4
2008-09	Manchester	AHL	38	7	5	12	6	....	....	....	....	....
	Ontario Reign	ECHL	23	14	8	22	8	7	5	9	14	8
2009-10	Manchester	AHL	75	19	28	47	26	16	7	7	14	9

HOLMSTROM, Ben (HOHLM-struhm, BEHN) **PHI.**

Right wing. Shoots right. 6'1", 202 lbs. Born, Colorado Springs, CO, April 9, 1987.

			Regular Season					Playoffs				
Season	Club	League	GP	G	A	Pts	PIM	GP	G	A	Pts	PIM
2006-07	U. Mass-Lowell	H-East	30	4	9	13	18	....	....	....	....	....
2007-08	U. Mass-Lowell	H-East	37	7	20	27	62	....	....	....	....	....
2008-09	U. Mass-Lowell	H-East	38	6	15	21	52	....	....	....	....	....
2009-10	U. Mass-Lowell	H-East	39	9	14	23	69	....	....	....	....	....
	Adirondack	AHL	13	3	0	3	9	....	....	....	....	....

Signed as a free agent by **Philadelphia**, March 17, 2010.

HOLOS, Jonas (hoh-LAWS, YOH-nuhs) **COL.**

Defense. Shoots right. 5'11", 196 lbs. Born, Sarpsborg, Norway, August 27, 1987.
(Colorado's 6th choice, 170th overall, in 2008 Entry Draft).

			Regular Season					Playoffs				
Season	Club	League	GP	G	A	Pts	PIM	GP	G	A	Pts	PIM
2002-03	Sarpsborg Jr.	Norway-Jr.	20	1	1	2	0	....	....	....	....	....
2003-04	Sarpsborg Jr.	Norway-Jr.	35	10	7	17	24	1	0	1	1	2
	Sarpsborg	Norway	1	0	0	0	0	....	....	....	....	....
2004-05	Sarpsborg Jr.	Norway-Jr.	1	1	1	2	0	1	0	0	0	0
	Sarpsborg	Norway	41	3	2	5	18	4	0	0	0	2
2005-06	Sarpsborg	Norway	26	3	4	7	14	6	0	0	0	0
2006-07	Sarpsborg 2	Norway-2	1	2	0	2	0	....	....	....	....	....
	Sarpsborg	Norway	40	11	19	30	32	13	2	2	4	18
2007-08	Sarpsborg	Norway	40	2	20	22	67	6	1	0	1	2
2008-09	Farjestad	Sweden	55	8	8	16	12	13	3	3	6	8
2009-10	Farjestad	Sweden	51	1	13	14	24	7	0	0	0	2
	Norway	Olympics	4	0	1	1	2	....	....	....	....	....

HOLZAPFEL, Riley (HOHL-za-fehl, RIGH-lee) **ATL.**

Center. Shoots left. 5'11", 195 lbs. Born, Regina, Sask., August 18, 1988.
(Atlanta's 2nd choice, 43rd overall, in 2006 Entry Draft).

			Regular Season					Playoffs				
Season	Club	League	GP	G	A	Pts	PIM	GP	G	A	Pts	PIM
2004-05	Moose Jaw	WHL	63	15	13	28	32	5	1	2	3	8
2005-06	Moose Jaw	WHL	64	19	38	57	46	22	7	9	16	20
2006-07	Moose Jaw	WHL	72	39	43	82	94	....	....	....	....	....
2007-08	Moose Jaw	WHL	49	18	23	41	43	6	3	5	8	12
	Chicago Wolves	AHL	1	0	0	0	0	....	....	....	....	....
2008-09	Chicago Wolves	AHL	73	13	19	32	38	....	....	....	....	....
2009-10	Chicago Wolves	AHL	60	7	16	23	30	14	0	3	3	6

WHL East First All-Star Team (2007)

HOLZER, Korbinian (HOHL-zuhr, kohr-BEEHN-yuhn) **TOR.**

Defense. Shoots right. 6'3", 205 lbs. Born, Munich, West Germany, February 16, 1988.
(Toronto's 4th choice, 111th overall, in 2006 Entry Draft).

			Regular Season					Playoffs				
Season	Club	League	GP	G	A	Pts	PIM	GP	G	A	Pts	PIM
2004-05	EC Bad Tolz Jr.	Ger-Jr.	34	7	11	18	66	5	0	2	2	2
2005-06	EC Bad Tolz Jr.	Ger-Jr.	2	1	1	2	6	....	....	....	....	....
	Tolzer Lowen	German-2	46	3	3	6	94	....	....	....	....	....
2006-07	Regensburg	German-2	42	2	6	8	68	4	0	0	0	2
2007-08	Dusseldorf	Germany	35	2	5	7	66	13	0	2	2	20
2008-09	Dusseldorf	Germany	38	4	5	9	89	16	0	1	1	18
2009-10	Dusseldorf	Germany	52	6	16	22	96	3	0	0	0	4
	Germany	Olympics	4	0	0	0	2	....	....	....	....	....

HORAK, Roman (HOH-rak, ROH-muhn) NYR

Center. Shoots left. 6', 171 lbs. Born, Ceske Budejovice, Czechoslovakia, May 21, 1991.
(NY Rangers' 4th choice, 127th overall, in 2009 Entry Draft).

			Regular Season					Playoffs				
Season	Club	League	GP	G	A	Pts	PIM	GP	G	A	Pts	PIM
2004-05	C. Budejovice U17	CzR-U17	2	0	0	0	0	....	....	....	....	....
2005-06	C. Budejovice U17	CzR-U17	34	5	3	8	10	3	0	0	0	4
2006-07	C. Budejovice U17	CzR-U17	24	22	16	38	38	2	1	0	1	4
	C. Budejovice Jr.	CzRep-Jr.	16	1	4	5	6	1	0	0	0	0
2007-08	C. Budejovice U17	CzR-U17	2	3	2	5	0	....	....	....	....	....
	C. Budejovice Jr.	CzRep-Jr.	34	17	11	28	14	3	0	1	1	0
	C. Budejovice	CzRep	1	0	0	0	0	....	....	....	....	....
2008-09	C. Budejovice Jr.	CzRep-Jr.	31	16	17	33	14	2	0	0	0	0
	C. Budejovice	CzRep	17	1	0	1	0	....	....	....	....	....
2009-10	Chilliwack Bruins	WHL	66	21	26	47	39	6	2	4	6	4

HOSTETTER, Tyler (HAWS-the-tuhr, TIGH-luhr) PHI.

Defense. Shoots right. 5'11", 182 lbs. Born, Lititz, PA, January 30, 1991.

			Regular Season					Playoffs				
Season	Club	League	GP	G	A	Pts	PIM	GP	G	A	Pts	PIM
2007-08	Erie Otters	OHL	57	1	10	11	31	....	....	....	....	....
2008-09	Erie Otters	OHL	61	6	17	23	49	5	1	1	2	2
2009-10	Erie Otters	OHL	59	2	24	26	37	4	0	1	1	2

Signed as a free agent by **Philadelphia**, September 22, 2009.

HOWDEN, Quinton (HOW-duhn, KWIHN-tuhn) FLA.

Center. Shoots left. 6'2", 182 lbs. Born, Winnipeg, Man., January 21, 1992.
(Florida's 3rd choice, 25th overall, in 2010 Entry Draft).

			Regular Season					Playoffs				
Season	Club	League	GP	G	A	Pts	PIM	GP	G	A	Pts	PIM
2007-08	Eastman Selects	MMHL	37	23	27	50	36	....	....	....	....	....
	Moose Jaw	WHL	5	0	0	0	0	....	....	....	....	....
2008-09	Moose Jaw	WHL	62	13	17	30	22	....	....	....	....	....
2009-10	Moose Jaw	WHL	65	28	37	65	44	2	0	2	2	2

HOWSE, Ryan (HOWS, RIGH-uhn) CGY.

Left wing. Shoots left. 5'11", 205 lbs. Born, Prince George, B.C., July 6, 1991.
(Calgary's 2nd choice, 74th overall, in 2009 Entry Draft).

			Regular Season					Playoffs				
Season	Club	League	GP	G	A	Pts	PIM	GP	G	A	Pts	PIM
2006-07	Cariboo Cougars	BCMML	30	21	16	37	40	....	....	....	....	....
	Chilliwack Bruins	WHL	5	1	0	1	2	1	0	0	0	0
2007-08	Chilliwack Bruins	WHL	54	10	7	17	12	4	1	1	2	2
2008-09	Chilliwack Bruins	WHL	61	31	13	44	12	....	....	....	....	....
2009-10	Chilliwack Bruins	WHL	72	47	25	72	27	6	5	1	6	2

HROMAS, Karel (huh-ROM-mahs, KAH-rehl) CHI.

Left wing. Shoots left. 6'2", 189 lbs. Born, Beroun, Czech., January 27, 1986.
(Chicago's 8th choice, 123rd overall, in 2004 Entry Draft).

			Regular Season					Playoffs				
Season	Club	League	GP	G	A	Pts	PIM	GP	G	A	Pts	PIM
2000-01	Sparta U17	CzR-U17	34	4	18	22	6	....	....	....	....	....
2001-02	Sparta U17	CzR-U17	39	19	15	34	55	6	3	2	5	6
2002-03	Sparta U17	CzR-U17	1	3	1	4	4	....	....	....	....	....
	Sparta Jr.	CzRep-Jr.	32	6	7	13	14	3	0	1	1	4
2003-04	Sparta Jr.	CzRep-Jr.	21	10	10	20	16	....	....	....	....	....
	HC Sparta Praha	CzRep	13	0	0	0	0	2	0	0	0	0
2004-05	Everett Silvertips	WHL	65	18	11	29	22	11	2	2	4	4
2005-06	Everett Silvertips	WHL	52	11	11	22	14	14	2	0	2	10
2006-07	HC Sparta Praha	CzRep	48	1	0	1	20	11	1	0	1	0
2007-08	HC Sparta Praha	CzRep	52	0	1	1	42	4	0	0	0	0
2008-09	HC Sparta Praha	CzRep	52	2	4	6	64	11	0	3	3	20
2009-10	HC Sparta Praha	CzRep	48	2	12	14	75	7	0	1	1	10

HUDSON, Carl (HUHD-suhn, KARL) FLA.

Defense. Shoots right. 6'1", 210 lbs. Born, Smooth Rock Falls, Ont., January 2, 1986.

			Regular Season					Playoffs				
Season	Club	League	GP	G	A	Pts	PIM	GP	G	A	Pts	PIM
2006-07	Canisius College	AH	34	10	11	21	93	....	....	....	....	....
2007-08	Canisius College	AH	28	6	6	12	*96	....	....	....	....	....
2008-09	Canisius College	AH	35	14	9	23	44	....	....	....	....	....
2009-10	Canisius College	AH	35	14	20	34	120	....	....	....	....	....
	Rochester	AHL	7	0	0	0	16	5	0	1	1	12

Signed as a free agent by **Florida**, July 9, 2010.

HUTCHINGS, Alex (HUH-chihngz, Al-ehx) T.B.

Left wing. Shoots right. 5'10", 173 lbs. Born, Burlington, Ont., November 7, 1990.
(Tampa Bay's 4th choice, 93rd overall, in 2009 Entry Draft).

			Regular Season					Playoffs				
Season	Club	League	GP	G	A	Pts	PIM	GP	G	A	Pts	PIM
2006-07	Barrie Colts	OHL	30	1	4	5	24	....	....	....	....	....
2007-08	Barrie Colts	OHL	68	29	25	54	48	9	0	5	5	18
2008-09	Barrie Colts	OHL	63	34	34	68	60	5	3	4	7	6
2009-10	Barrie Colts	OHL	68	47	34	81	58	13	2	8	10	12

HYMAN, Zach (HIGH-muhn, ZAK) FLA.

Center. Shoots right. 6', 182 lbs. Born, Toronto, Ont., June 9, 1992.
(Florida's 11th choice, 123rd overall, in 2010 Entry Draft).

			Regular Season					Playoffs				
Season	Club	League	GP	G	A	Pts	PIM	GP	G	A	Pts	PIM
2008-09	Hamilton	OJHL	49	13	24	37	24	5	2	2	4	4
2009-10	Hamilton	CCHL	49	35	40	75	30	11	7	9	16	4

• Signed Letter of Intent to attend **Princeton University** (ECAC) in fall of 2011.

IGNATUSHKIN, Igor (ihg-nah-TOOSH-kihn, EE-gohr) WSH.

Center. Shoots left. 5'11", 161 lbs. Born, Elektrostal, USSR, April 7, 1984.
(Washington's 12th choice, 242nd overall, in 2002 Entry Draft).

			Regular Season					Playoffs				
Season	Club	League	GP	G	A	Pts	PIM	GP	G	A	Pts	PIM
99-2000	Elektrostal 2	Russia-3	5	0	0	0	0	....	....	....	....	....
2000-01	Team Center 84	Exhib.	5	1	1	2	0	....	....	....	....	....
	Elektrostal 2	Russia-3	STATISTICS NOT AVAILABLE									
2001-02	Elektrostal 2	Russia-3	6	2	3	5	6	....	....	....	....	....
	Elektrostal	Russia-2	46	1	4	5	20	....	....	....	....	....
2002-03	Elektrostal	Russia-2	36	9	10	19	8	....	....	....	....	....
2003-04	Kristall Elektrostal	Russia-2	49	6	2	8	22	....	....	....	....	....
2004-05	Kristall Elektrostal	Russia-2	45	9	3	12	28	....	....	....	....	....
	Leninogorsk	Russia-2	6	1	1	2	6	4	1	0	1	4
2005-06	Mytischi	Russia	7	0	0	0	2	....	....	....	....	....
	Kristall Elektrostal	Russia-3	STATISTICS NOT AVAILABLE									
2006-07	Kristall Elektrostal	Russia-2	49	14	23	37	48	....	....	....	....	....
2007-08	Khabarovsk 2	Russia-3	2	0	0	0	0	....	....	....	....	....
	Amur Khabarovsk	Russia	49	4	4	8	12	4	0	0	0	2
2008-09	Amur Khabarovsk	Rus-KHL	49	6	8	14	16	....	....	....	....	....
2009-10	Amur Khabarovsk	Rus-KHL	47	10	10	20	20	....	....	....	....	....

ILLO, Radoslav (IHL-oh, RAD-oh-slav) ANA.

Center. Shoots left. 6', 178 lbs. Born, Povazska Bystrica, Czech., January 21, 1990.
(Anaheim's 6th choice, 136th overall, in 2009 Entry Draft).

			Regular Season					Playoffs				
Season	Club	League	GP	G	A	Pts	PIM	GP	G	A	Pts	PIM
2005-06	P. Bystrica U18	Svk-U18	4	1	1	2	2	....	....	....	....	....
2006-07	Bratislava U18	Svk-U18	26	9	14	23	12	....	....	....	....	....
2007-08	Hampton Roads	MJHL	....	48	38	86	....	....	....	....	....	....
2008-09	Tri-City Storm	USHL	47	21	12	33	37	....	....	....	....	....
2009-10	Tri-City Storm	USHL	50	24	19	43	56	1	1	0	1	0

IRWIN, Matt (UHR-wihn, MAT) S.J.

Defense. Shoots left. 6'2", 205 lbs. Born, Brentwood Bay, B.C., November 29, 1987.

			Regular Season					Playoffs				
Season	Club	League	GP	G	A	Pts	PIM	GP	G	A	Pts	PIM
2004-05	Nanaimo Clippers	BCHL	3	0	0	0	2	....	....	....	....	....
2005-06	Nanaimo Clippers	BCHL	56	3	6	9	41	....	....	....	....	....
2006-07	Nanaimo Clippers	BCHL	60	22	27	49	67	....	....	....	....	....
2007-08	Nanaimo Clippers	BCHL	59	16	37	53	40	....	....	....	....	....
2008-09	Massachusetts	H-East	31	7	11	18	8	....	....	....	....	....
2009-10	Massachusetts	H-East	36	7	17	24	16	....	....	....	....	....
	Worcester Sharks	AHL	3	0	0	0	2	1	0	0	0	0

Signed as a free agent by **San Jose**, March 23, 2010.

ISACKSON, Christian (IGH-zak-suhn, KRIHS-ch'yehn) BUF.

Right wing. Shoots right. 6', 174 lbs. Born, Pine City, MN, January 20, 1992.
(Buffalo's 8th choice, 203rd overall, in 2010 Entry Draft).

			Regular Season					Playoffs				
Season	Club	League	GP	G	A	Pts	PIM	GP	G	A	Pts	PIM
2006-07	Saint Thomas	High-MN	31	6	12	18	....	....	....	....	....	....
2007-08	Saint Thomas	High-MN	31	22	34	56	....	....	....	....	....	....
2008-09	Saint Thomas	High-MN	27	18	39	57	....	....	....	....	....	....
2009-10	Team Southeast	UMHSEL	24	11	11	22	....	....	....	....	....	....
	Saint Thomas	High-MN	25	24	33	57	26	3	1	2	3	0

• Signed Letter of Intent to attend **University of Minnesota** (WCHA) in fall of 2010.

ISAKOV, Evgeni (ih-SA-kawf, ehv-GEH-nee) PIT.

Right wing. Shoots left. 6'1", 196 lbs. Born, Krasnoyarsk, USSR, October 13, 1984.
(Pittsburgh's 6th choice, 161st overall, in 2003 Entry Draft).

			Regular Season					Playoffs				
Season	Club	League	GP	G	A	Pts	PIM	GP	G	A	Pts	PIM
99-2000	Rubin Tyumen 2	Russia-3	7	0	2	2	16	....	....	....	....	....
2000-01	Rubin Tyumen 2	Russia-3	....	....	....	....	....	....	....	....	....	....
	Gazovik Tyumen	Russia-3	11	1	1	2	12	....	....	....	....	....
2001-02	Gazovik Tyumen	Russia-2	19	2	2	4	2	....	....	....	....	....
	Elektrostal	Russia-2	29	3	2	5	24	....	....	....	....	....
	Elektrostal 2	Russia-3	11	3	3	6	43	....	....	....	....	....
2002-03	Cherepovets	Russia	36	0	3	3	12	1	0	0	0	0
2003-04	Cherepovets	Russia	38	3	2	5	18	....	....	....	....	....
	Cherepovets 2	Russia-3	14	4	8	12	48	....	....	....	....	....
2004-05	Kristall Saratov	Russia-2	1	0	0	0	0	....	....	....	....	....
	Tyumen 2	Russia-3	2	1	3	4	14	....	....	....	....	....
	Gazovik Tyumen	Russia-2	4	0	2	2	2	3	0	0	0	2
2005-06	Gazovik Tyumen	Russia-2	46	9	12	21	90	3	0	0	0	6
2006-07	Gazovik Tyumen	Russia-2	51	6	11	17	48	....	....	....	....	....
	Tyumen 2	Russia-3	2	1	2	3	0	....	....	....	....	....
2007-08	Gazovik Tyumen	Russia-2	43	10	11	21	119	....	....	....	....	....
2008-09	Khanty-Mansiisk	Russia-2	18	1	4	5	12	....	....	....	....	....
	Metallurg Serov	Russia-2	33	11	18	29	40	3	1	0	1	22
2009-10	Dizel Penza	Russia-2	53	11	21	32	104	12	4	2	6	12

JANOSIK, Adam (YA-noh-shihk, A-duhm) T.B.

Defense. Shoots left. 5'11", 170 lbs. Born, Spisska Nova Ves, SVK, September 7, 1992.
(Tampa Bay's 4th choice, 72nd overall, in 2010 Entry Draft).

			Regular Season					Playoffs				
Season	Club	League	GP	G	A	Pts	PIM	GP	G	A	Pts	PIM
2006-07	HC Liberec U17	CzR-U17	12	0	0	0	12	....	....	....	....	....
2007-08	HC Liberec U17	CzR-U17	42	4	15	19	38	4	1	0	1	2
2008-09	HC Liberec U17	CzR-U17	20	7	19	26	39	7	2	6	8	2
	HC Liberec Jr.	CzRep-Jr.	22	1	8	9	12	....	....	....	....	....
2009-10	Gatineau	QMJHL	63	9	26	35	45	10	5	2	7	4

JARNKROK, Calle (YAHRN-krohk, KAHL-leh) DET.

Center. Shoots right. 5'11", 165 lbs. Born, Gavle, Sweden, September 25, 1991.
(Detroit's 2nd choice, 51st overall, in 2010 Entry Draft).

			Regular Season					Playoffs				
Season	Club	League	GP	G	A	Pts	PIM	GP	G	A	Pts	PIM
2007-08	Brynas U18	Swe-U18	13	4	4	8	4	5	0	1	1	0
	Brynas IF Gavle Jr.	Swe-Jr.	2	0	0	0	2	....	....	....	....	....
2008-09	Brynas U18	Swe-U18	7	5	7	12	12	2	0	1	1	2
	Brynas IF Gavle Jr.	Swe-Jr.	41	8	18	26	37	7	4	3	7	2
2009-10	Brynas IF Gavle Jr.	Swe-Jr.	19	11	20	31	30	2	0	1	1	0
	Brynas IF Gavle	Sweden	33	4	6	10	2	5	1	1	2	0

JENKS, A.J. (JEHKS, AY-JAY) FLA.

Left wing. Shoots left. 6'2", 206 lbs. Born, Detroit, MI, June 27, 1990.
(Florida's 4th choice, 100th overall, in 2008 Entry Draft).

			Regular Season					Playoffs				
Season	Club	League	GP	G	A	Pts	PIM	GP	G	A	Pts	PIM
2004-05	Det. Compuware	MWEHL	28	7	12	19	54	....	....	....	....	....
2005-06	Det. Honeybaked	MWEHL	21	7	10	17	23	....	....	....	....	....
2006-07	Plymouth Whalers	OHL	68	9	14	23	50	20	0	1	1	8
2007-08	Plymouth Whalers	OHL	68	26	29	55	94	4	1	0	1	4
2008-09	Plymouth Whalers	OHL	61	21	31	52	78	11	1	2	3	18
2009-10	Plymouth Whalers	OHL	52	23	40	63	58	9	4	8	12	14

JENSEN, Nick (JEHN-suhn, NIHK) DET.

Defense. Shoots right. 6'1", 187 lbs. Born, St. Paul, MN, September 21, 1990.
(Detroit's 5th choice, 150th overall, in 2009 Entry Draft).

			Regular Season					Playoffs				
Season	Club	League	GP	G	A	Pts	PIM	GP	G	A	Pts	PIM
2006-07	Rogers Royals	High-MN	21	20	17	37	....	....	....	....	....	....
2007-08	Rogers Royals	High-MN	14	14	13	27	....	....	....	....	....	....
2008-09	Green Bay	USHL	52	5	17	22	27	7	0	1	1	2
2009-10	Green Bay	USHL	53	6	21	27	35	12	2	6	8	6

• Signed Letter of Intent to attend **St. Cloud State University** (WCHA) in fall of 2010.

JESSIMAN, Hugh (JEHS-ih-muhn, HEW) CHI.

Right wing. Shoots right. 6'6", 221 lbs. Born, New York, NY, March 28, 1984.
(NY Rangers' 1st choice, 12th overall, in 2003 Entry Draft).

			Regular Season					Playoffs				
Season	Club	League	GP	G	A	Pts	PIM	GP	G	A	Pts	PIM
2001-02	Brunswick Bruins	High-CT	18	25	27	52	40	....	....	....	....	....
2002-03	Dartmouth	ECAC	34	23	24	47	48	....	....	....	....	....
2003-04	Dartmouth	ECAC	34	16	17	33	71	....	....	....	....	....
2004-05	Dartmouth	ECAC	12	1	1	2	18	....	....	....	....	....
2005-06	Hartford Wolf Pack	AHL	46	7	12	19	66	2	0	0	0	0
	Charlotte	ECHL	25	13	10	23	56	....	....	....	....	....
2006-07	Hartford Wolf Pack	AHL	49	7	6	13	79	7	1	0	1	9
	Charlotte	ECHL	20	12	10	22	52	....	....	....	....	....
2007-08	Hartford Wolf Pack	AHL	71	18	24	42	154	5	0	1	1	21
2008-09	Hartford Wolf Pack	AHL	6	0	0	0	2	....	....	....	....	....
	Milwaukee	AHL	63	20	7	27	100	10	2	0	2	10
2009-10	Milwaukee	AHL	78	20	22	42	111	....	....	....	....	....

ECAC All-Rookie Team (2003) • ECAC Rookie of the Year (2003) • ECAC Second All-Star Team (2004)

Traded to **Nashville** by **NY Rangers** for future considerations, October 30, 2008. Signed as a free agent by **Chicago**, July 24, 2010.

JOHANSEN, Ryan (joh-HAN-suhn, RIGH-uhn) CBJ

Center. Shoots right. 6'3", 192 lbs. Born, Port Moody, B.C., July 31, 1992.
(Columbus' 1st choice, 4th overall, in 2010 Entry Draft).

			Regular Season					Playoffs				
Season	Club	League	GP	G	A	Pts	PIM	GP	G	A	Pts	PIM
2007-08	Van. NE Chiefs	BCMML	41	18	30	48	26	....	....	....	....	....
2008-09	Penticton Vees	BCHL	47	5	12	17	21	10	4	3	7	2
2009-10	Portland	WHL	71	25	44	69	53	13	6	12	18	18

JOHANSSON, Marcus (yoh-HAHN-suhn, MAHR-kuhs) WSH.

Center. Shoots left. 6', 196 lbs. Born, Landskrona, Sweden, October 6, 1990.
(Washington's 1st choice, 24th overall, in 2009 Entry Draft).

			Regular Season					Playoffs				
Season	Club	League	GP	G	A	Pts	PIM	GP	G	A	Pts	PIM
2005-06	Malmo U18	Swe-U18	12	0	7	7	0	6	0	4	4	0
2006-07	Farjestad U18	Swe-U18	12	5	9	14	8	8	7	3	10	2
2007-08	Farjestad U18	Swe-U18	24	12	26	38	16	8	4	8	12	0
	Skare BK	Sweden-3	19	2	10	12	10	....	....	....	....	....
	Farjestad	Sweden	....	....	....	....	....	3	0	0	0	0
2008-09	Farjestad U18	Swe-U18	2	2	0	2	0	....	....	....	....	....
	Skare BK Karlstad	Sweden-3	5	5	5	10	0	....	....	....	....	....
	Farjestad	Sweden	45	5	5	10	10	6	0	0	0	0
2009-10	Farjestad	Sweden	42	10	10	20	10	7	0	5	5	2

JOHANSSON, Mikael (yoh-HAHN-suhn, MIGH-kuhl)

Center. Shoots left. 5'10", 188 lbs. Born, Arvika, Sweden, June 27, 1985.
(Detroit's 8th choice, 289th overall, in 2003 Entry Draft).

			Regular Season					Playoffs				
Season	Club	League	GP	G	A	Pts	PIM	GP	G	A	Pts	PIM
2001-02	Truro Bearcats	MJrHL	31	1	13	14	34	6	0	0	0	6
2002-03	Arvika HC	Sweden-3	30	13	28	41	89	....	....	....	....	....
2003-04	Skare BK Karlstad	Sweden-3	10	1	5	6	6	....	....	....	....	....
2004-05	Bofors	Sweden-2	45	5	7	12	22	5	0	0	0	0
2005-06	Farjestad	Sweden	46	1	5	6	16	18	0	2	2	4
2006-07	Farjestad	Sweden	55	7	9	16	42	8	2	3	5	4
2007-08	Farjestad	Sweden	53	15	24	39	80	11	4	5	9	37
2008-09	Farjestad	Sweden	49	6	28	34	20	11	1	3	4	2
2009-10	Hamilton Bulldogs	AHL	20	3	3	6	2	....	....	....	....	....
	Farjestad	Sweden	12	0	6	6	6	7	2	0	2	0

Signed as a free agent by **Montreal**, May 27, 2009. • Assigned to **Farjestad** (Sweden) by **Montreal**, January 23, 2010.

JOHNS, Stephen (JAWNZ, STEE-vehn) CHI.

Defense. Shoots right. 6'3", 215 lbs. Born, Ellwood City, PA, April 18, 1992.
(Chicago's 5th choice, 60th overall, in 2010 Entry Draft).

			Regular Season					Playoffs				
Season	Club	League	GP	G	A	Pts	PIM	GP	G	A	Pts	PIM
2007-08	Pittsburgh Hornets	MWEHL	26	4	7	11	24	....	....	....	....	....
	Pittsburgh Hornets	Minor-PA	50	12	22	34	46	....	....	....	....	....
2008-09	USNTDP	NAHL	31	3	5	8	30	....	....	....	....	....
	USNTDP	U-17	16	2	6	8	20	....	....	....	....	....
2009-10	USNTDP	USHL	23	1	7	8	29	....	....	....	....	....
	USNTDP	U-18	39	2	9	11	38	....	....	....	....	....

• Signed Letter of Intent to attend **University of Notre Dame** (CCHA) in fall of 2010.

JOHNSON, Jamie (JAHN-suhn, JAY-mee) DET.

Center. Shoots right. 5'11", 185 lbs. Born, Port Franks, Ont., January 23, 1982.

			Regular Season					Playoffs				
Season	Club	League	GP	G	A	Pts	PIM	GP	G	A	Pts	PIM
99-2000	Sarnia Sting	OHL	61	6	14	20	24	7	0	2	2	2
2000-01	Sarnia Sting	OHL	9	0	5	5	7	....	....	....	....	....
	Oshawa Generals	OHL	56	8	38	46	14	....	....	....	....	....
2001-02	Oshawa Generals	OHL	68	17	61	78	46	5	2	4	6	2
2002-03	Oshawa Generals	OHL	68	24	76	100	34	13	1	13	14	16
2003-04	Louisiana	ECHL	71	12	45	57	46	9	3	6	9	4
2004-05	Augusta Lynx	ECHL	72	22	58	80	26	....	....	....	....	....
2005-06	Augusta Lynx	ECHL	7	2	4	6	6	....	....	....	....	....
	Iowa Stars	AHL	68	9	28	37	24	7	0	4	4	21
2006-07	Augusta Lynx	ECHL	31	14	30	44	26	....	....	....	....	....
	Iowa Stars	AHL	8	1	3	4	2	....	....	....	....	....
	Bridgeport	AHL	34	5	11	16	18	....	....	....	....	....
2007-08	Albany River Rats	AHL	79	21	37	58	28	7	0	2	2	0
2008-09	TPS Turku	Finland	42	8	20	28	24	6	0	3	3	2
2009-10	Rochester	AHL	80	27	44	71	24	7	2	4	6	5

Signed as a free agent by **Florida**, July 15, 2009. Signed as a free agent by **Detroit**, July 6, 2010.

JOHNSON, Patrick (JAWN-suhn, PAT-rihk) MTL.

Left wing. Shoots left. 5'9", 155 lbs. Born, Madison, WI, April 21, 1989.
(Montreal's 5th choice, 206th overall, in 2008 Entry Draft).

			Regular Season					Playoffs				
Season	Club	League	GP	G	A	Pts	PIM	GP	G	A	Pts	PIM
2006-07	Lincoln Stars	USHL	49	11	16	27	50	4	1	0	1	14
2007-08	U. of Wisconsin	WCHA	40	8	13	21	36	....	....	....	....	....
2008-09	U. of Wisconsin	WCHA	35	3	4	7	44	....	....	....	....	....
2009-10	U. of Wisconsin	WCHA	37	3	4	7	14	....	....	....	....	....

JOKINEN, Justin (YOH-kihn-ihn, JUHS-tihn) BUF.

Right wing. Shoots right. 6'3", 188 lbs. Born, Cloquet, MN, November 25, 1989.
(Buffalo's 5th choice, 101st overall, in 2008 Entry Draft).

			Regular Season					Playoffs				
Season	Club	League	GP	G	A	Pts	PIM	GP	G	A	Pts	PIM
2005-06	Cloquet	High-MN	....	7	11	18	....	....	....	....	....	....
2006-07	Cloquet	High-MN	....	26	25	51	18	....	....	....	....	....
	Team North	UMWEHL	11	6	5	11	....	....	....	....	....	....
2007-08	Cloquet	High-MN	30	22	21	43	....	....	....	....	....	....
	Team North	UMWEHL	12	5	13	18	....	....	....	....	....	....
2008-09	Minnesota State	WCHA	24	3	2	5	6	....	....	....	....	....
2009-10	Minnesota State	WCHA	24	3	1	4	14	....	....	....	....	....

JONES, Kellen (JOHNZ, KEHL-ehn) EDM.

Forward. Shoots left. 5'9", 164 lbs. Born, Montrose, B.C., August 16, 1990.
(Edmonton's 11th choice, 202nd overall, in 2010 Entry Draft).

			Regular Season					Playoffs				
Season	Club	League	GP	G	A	Pts	PIM	GP	G	A	Pts	PIM
2006-07	Beaver Valley	KIJHL	50	32	35	67	48	13	8	4	12	6
	Vernon Vipers	BCHL	2	0	1	1	0	16	3	5	8	8
2007-08	Vernon Vipers	BCHL	60	12	55	67	30	10	7	4	11	8
2008-09	Vernon Vipers	BCHL	51	15	37	52	16	17	6	12	18	8
2009-10	Vernon Vipers	BCHL	41	12	41	53	18	19	5	14	19	14

• Signed Letter of Intent to attend **Quinnipiac University** (ECAC) in fall of 2010.

JORDAN, Michal (JOHR-duhn, MEE-khuhl) CAR.

Defense. Shoots left. 6'1", 186 lbs. Born, Zlin, Czech., July 17, 1990.
(Carolina's 3rd choice, 105th overall, in 2008 Entry Draft).

			Regular Season					Playoffs				
Season	Club	League	GP	G	A	Pts	PIM	GP	G	A	Pts	PIM
2005-06	HC Zlin U17	CzR-U17	43	7	15	22	12	5	0	1	1	2
2006-07	HC Zlin U17	CzR-U17	1	0	0	0	4	....	....	....	....	....
	HC Zlin Jr.	CzRep-Jr.	40	7	11	18	20	12	1	5	6	12
2007-08	Windsor Spitfires	OHL	22	1	5	6	12	....	....	....	....	....
	Plymouth Whalers	OHL	39	5	17	22	32	4	0	3	3	6
2008-09	Plymouth Whalers	OHL	58	12	30	42	39	11	0	3	3	12
2009-10	Plymouth Whalers	OHL	41	13	19	32	18	9	0	5	5	8

JORG, Mauro (YOHRG, MAHW-roh) N.J.

Left wing. Shoots left. 6', 190 lbs. Born, Chur, Switzerland, April 29, 1990.
(New Jersey's 5th choice, 204th overall, in 2010 Entry Draft).

			Regular Season					Playoffs				
Season	Club	League	GP	G	A	Pts	PIM	GP	G	A	Pts	PIM
2006-07	HC Lugano Jr.	Swiss-Jr.	4	2	3	5	6	....	....	....	....	....
	EHC Arosa	Swiss-3	7	4	1	5	8	1	0	0	0	2
	EHC Chur	Swiss-2	20	1	1	2	0	....	....	....	....	....
2007-08	Switzerland U20	Swiss-2	1	0	0	0	0	....	....	....	....	....
	EHC Chur Jr.	Swiss-Jr.	4	4	1	5	18	....	....	....	....	....
	EHC Chur	Swiss-2	40	11	9	20	33	....	....	....	....	....
	HC Lugano Jr.	Swiss-Jr.	8	5	2	7	12	....	....	....	....	....
	HC Lugano	Swiss	....	....	....	....	....	1	0	0	0	0
2008-09	Switzerland U20	Swiss-2	5	1	0	1	0	....	....	....	....	....
	HC Lugano	Swiss	47	3	3	6	6	7	0	0	0	0
	HC Ceresio Lugano	Swiss-3	1	0	0	0	0	....	....	....	....	....
	HC Lugano Jr.	Swiss-Jr.	3	0	3	3	0	2	0	3	3	4
2009-10	HC Lugano	Swiss	44	1	7	8	14	4	0	0	0	0
	HC Lugano Jr.	Swiss-Jr.	1	0	0	0	0	....	....	....	....	....
	EHC Visp	Swiss-2	....	....	....	....	....	7	0	1	1	0

JOSEFSON, Jacob (JOH-sehf-suhn, YA-kuhb) N.J.

Center. Shoots left. 6', 190 lbs. Born, Stockholm, Sweden, March 2, 1991.
(New Jersey's 1st choice, 20th overall, in 2009 Entry Draft).

			Regular Season					Playoffs				
Season	Club	League	GP	G	A	Pts	PIM	GP	G	A	Pts	PIM
2005-06	Djurgarden U18	Swe-U18	5	1	1	2	0	....	....	....	....	....
2006-07	Djurgarden U18	Swe-U18	25	14	17	31	22	3	0	0	0	0
2007-08	Djurgarden U18	Swe-U18	4	1	2	3	12	6	0	6	6	4
	Djurgarden Jr.	Swe-Jr.	34	14	17	31	22	7	2	3	5	8
	Djurgarden	Sweden	1	0	0	0	0	....	....	....	....	....
2008-09	Djurgarden Jr.	Swe-Jr.	5	1	2	3	8	6	1	3	4	4
	Djurgarden	Sweden	50	5	11	16	14	....	....	....	....	....
	Djurgarden U18	Swe-U18	....	....	....	....	....	1	0	0	0	0
2009-10	Djurgarden	Sweden	43	8	12	20	20	14	3	2	5	4

JOSI, Roman
(YAW-see, ROH-man) **NSH.**

Defense. Shoots left. 6'2", 198 lbs. Born, Bern, Switzerland, June 1, 1990.
(Nashville's 3rd choice, 38th overall, in 2008 Entry Draft).

			Regular Season					Playoffs				
Season	Club	League	GP	G	A	Pts	PIM	GP	G	A	Pts	PIM
2005-06	SC Bern Future Jr.	Swiss-Jr.	5	0	0	0	0	....	....	....	....	....
2006-07	SC Bern Future Jr.	Swiss-Jr.	33	14	16	30	28	14	1	3	4	2
	Switzerland U20	Swiss-2	5	1	1	2	2	....	....	....	....	....
	SC Bern	Swiss	3	0	1	1	0	....	....	....	....	....
2007-08	Switzerland U20	Swiss-2	2	0	1	1	0	....	....	....	....	....
	HC Neuchatel	Swiss-2	3	2	0	2	4	....	....	....	....	....
	SC Bern	Swiss	35	2	6	8	10	6	0	0	0	0
2008-09	SC Bern	Swiss	42	7	17	24	16	6	0	0	0	2
2009-10	SC Bern	Swiss	26	9	12	21	12	15	6	7	13	8

JOUDREY, Andrew
(JOO-dree, AN-droo) **WSH.**

Center. Shoots left. 5'11", 185 lbs. Born, Halifax, N.S., July 15, 1984.
(Washington's 5th choice, 249th overall, in 2003 Entry Draft).

			Regular Season					Playoffs				
Season	Club	League	GP	G	A	Pts	PIM	GP	G	A	Pts	PIM
2000-01	Dartmouth	NSMHL	82	51	70	121	....	....	....	....	....	....
2001-02	Notre Dame	SJHL	57	24	38	62	14	....	....	....	....	....
2002-03	Notre Dame	SJHL	53	27	51	78	16	....	....	....	....	....
2003-04	U. of Wisconsin	WCHA	42	7	15	22	2	....	....	....	....	....
2004-05	U. of Wisconsin	WCHA	41	7	17	24	18	....	....	....	....	....
2005-06	U. of Wisconsin	WCHA	37	8	10	18	14	....	....	....	....	....
2006-07	U. of Wisconsin	WCHA	40	9	20	29	18	....	....	....	....	....
	Hershey Bears	AHL	5	2	1	3	0	10	0	2	2	0
2007-08	Hershey Bears	AHL	61	11	14	25	22	5	0	1	1	0
2008-09	Hershey Bears	AHL	69	7	20	27	22	22	1	3	4	6
2009-10	Hershey Bears	AHL	78	15	19	34	11	21	1	2	3	4

KABANOV, Kirill
(kuh-BAH-nawf, kih-RIHL) **NYI**

Left wing. Shoots right. 6'2", 176 lbs. Born, Moscow, Russia, July 16, 1992.
(NY Islanders' 3rd choice, 65th overall, in 2010 Entry Draft).

			Regular Season					Playoffs				
Season	Club	League	GP	G	A	Pts	PIM	GP	G	A	Pts	PIM
2008-09	Spartak Moscow 2	Russia-3	STATISTICS NOT AVAILABLE									
	Spartak Moscow	Rus-KHL	6	0	0	0	2	5	0	0	0	0
2009-10	Moncton Wildcats	QMJHL	22	10	13	23	34	1	0	0	0	2

KABLUKOV, Ilja
(ka-BLOO-hahv, IHL-yah) **VAN.**

Center. Shoots left. 6'2", 183 lbs. Born, Moscow, USSR, January 18, 1988.
(Vancouver's 4th choice, 146th overall, in 2007 Entry Draft).

			Regular Season					Playoffs				
Season	Club	League	GP	G	A	Pts	PIM	GP	G	A	Pts	PIM
2005-06	CSKA Moscow 2	Russia-3	STATISTICS NOT AVAILABLE									
2006-07	CSKA Moscow 2	Russia-3	STATISTICS NOT AVAILABLE									
	CSKA Moscow	Russia	24	0	0	0	2	2	0	0	0	2
2007-08	CSKA Moscow	Russia	50	4	9	13	18	6	1	3	4	2
	CSKA Moscow 2	Russia-3	....	....	....	....	....	2	1	3	4	2
2008-09	Nizhny Novgorod	Rus-KHL	42	1	3	4	8	3	0	0	0	4
2009-10	Spartak Moscow	Rus-KHL	54	5	7	12	24	4	0	0	0	0

KAIP, Rylan
(KAYP, RIH-luhn)

Center. Shoots left. 6', 175 lbs. Born, Wilcox, Sask., March 19, 1984.
(Atlanta's 9th choice, 269th overall, in 2003 Entry Draft).

			Regular Season					Playoffs				
Season	Club	League	GP	G	A	Pts	PIM	GP	G	A	Pts	PIM
2000-01	Notre Dame	SJHL	5	0	0	0	0	1	0	0	0	0
2001-02	Notre Dame	SJHL	61	14	18	32	77	....	....	....	....	....
2002-03	Notre Dame	SJHL	57	20	36	56	164	6	1	6	7	21
2003-04	Notre Dame	SJHL	54	30	36	66	133	4	1	1	2	6
2004-05	North Dakota	WCHA	22	0	4	4	20	....	....	....	....	....
2005-06	North Dakota	WCHA	42	3	5	8	76	....	....	....	....	....
2006-07	North Dakota	WCHA	38	5	7	12	55	....	....	....	....	....
2007-08	North Dakota	WCHA	42	8	7	15	81	....	....	....	....	....
2008-09	Chicago Wolves	AHL	42	1	2	3	17	....	....	....	....	....
2009-10	Chicago Wolves	AHL	68	4	7	11	59	9	0	0	0	8

KAMPFER, Steven
(KAMP-fuhr, STEE-vehn) **BOS.**

Defense. Shoots right. 5'10", 188 lbs. Born, Ann Arbor, MI, September 24, 1988.
(Anaheim's 5th choice, 93rd overall, in 2007 Entry Draft).

			Regular Season					Playoffs				
Season	Club	League	GP	G	A	Pts	PIM	GP	G	A	Pts	PIM
2004-05	Sioux City	USHL	47	6	13	19	91	13	2	5	7	12
2005-06	Sioux City	USHL	56	6	10	16	99	....	....	....	....	....
2006-07	U. of Michigan	CCHA	35	1	3	4	24	....	....	....	....	....
2007-08	U. of Michigan	CCHA	42	2	15	17	36	....	....	....	....	....
2008-09	U. of Michigan	CCHA	25	1	12	13	24	....	....	....	....	....
2009-10	U. of Michigan	CCHA	45	3	23	26	50	....	....	....	....	....
	Providence Bruins	AHL	6	1	2	3	4	....	....	....	....	....

Traded to **Boston** by **Anaheim** for Boston's 4th round choice (later traded to Carolina - Carolina selected Justin Shugg) in 2010 Entry Draft, March 2, 2010.

KARLSSON, Mattias
(KARL-suhn, mat-TEE-uhs) **OTT.**

Defense. Shoots left. 6'2", 192 lbs. Born, Stora, Sweden, April 15, 1985.
(Ottawa's 4th choice, 135th overall, in 2003 Entry Draft).

			Regular Season					Playoffs				
Season	Club	League	GP	G	A	Pts	PIM	GP	G	A	Pts	PIM
2001-02	Brynas U18	Swe-U18	5	2	1	3	6	....	....	....	....	....
	Brynas IF Gavle Jr.	Swe-Jr.	13	0	1	1	12	....	....	....	....	....
2002-03	Brynas IF Gavle Jr.	Swe-Jr.	27	11	6	17	93	2	0	0	0	4
	Brynas IF Gavle	Sweden	3	0	0	0	0	....	....	....	....	....
	Brynas IF Gavle	Sweden-Q	3	0	0	0	0	....	....	....	....	....
2003-04	Brynas IF Gavle Jr.	Swe-Jr.	20	5	8	13	67	5	0	4	4	10
	Brynas IF Gavle	Sweden	39	0	0	0	6	....	....	....	....	....
2004-05	Brynas IF Gavle Jr.	Swe-Jr.	13	3	5	8	40	....	....	....	....	....
	Almtuna	Sweden-2	22	0	2	2	18	....	....	....	....	....
	Brynas IF Gavle	Sweden	9	0	0	0	2	....	....	....	....	....
	Brynas IF Gavle	Sweden-Q	1	0	0	0	0	....	....	....	....	....
2005-06	Almtuna Jr.	Swe-Jr.	2	0	1	1	4	....	....	....	....	....
	Almtuna	Sweden-2	32	3	4	7	40	....	....	....	....	....
2006-07	Bofors	Sweden-2	44	11	21	32	34	....	....	....	....	....
2007-08	Binghamton	AHL	2	0	0	0	0	....	....	....	....	....
	Farjestad	Sweden	13	2	2	4	4	12	1	3	4	20
2008-09	Binghamton	AHL	73	9	42	51	40	....	....	....	....	....
2009-10	Timra IK	Sweden	37	5	10	15	38	5	1	0	1	29

AHL All-Rookie Team (2009)

KASSIAN, Matt
(KAS-ee-uhn, MAT) **MIN.**

Left wing. Shoots left. 6'5", 245 lbs. Born, Edmonton, Alta., October 28, 1986.
(Minnesota's 2nd choice, 57th overall, in 2005 Entry Draft).

			Regular Season					Playoffs				
Season	Club	League	GP	G	A	Pts	PIM	GP	G	A	Pts	PIM
2002-03	Sherwood Park	AJHL	33	5	7	12	38	....	....	....	....	....
2003-04	Vancouver Giants	WHL	37	1	0	1	42	3	0	0	0	4
2004-05	Vancouver Giants	WHL	41	0	3	3	89	....	....	....	....	....
	Kamloops Blazers	WHL	28	3	0	3	83	6	1	2	3	14
2005-06	Kamloops Blazers	WHL	67	5	6	11	147	....	....	....	....	....
2006-07	Kamloops Blazers	WHL	72	8	10	18	162	4	0	1	1	0
2007-08	Houston Aeros	AHL	19	0	0	0	48	....	....	....	....	....
	Texas Wildcatters	ECHL	47	6	4	10	90	....	....	....	....	....
2008-09	Houston Aeros	AHL	56	1	2	3	130	4	0	0	0	10
2009-10	Houston Aeros	AHL	59	2	4	6	149	....	....	....	....	....

KASSIAN, Zack
(KA-see-uhn, ZAK) **BUF.**

Right wing. Shoots right. 6'3", 226 lbs. Born, Windsor, Ont., January 24, 1991.
(Buffalo's 1st choice, 13th overall, in 2009 Entry Draft).

			Regular Season					Playoffs				
Season	Club	League	GP	G	A	Pts	PIM	GP	G	A	Pts	PIM
2006-07	Wind. Jr. Spitfires	Minor-ON	57	32	48	80	136	....	....	....	....	....
2007-08	Peterborough	OHL	58	9	12	21	74	5	1	0	1	2
2008-09	Peterborough	OHL	61	24	39	63	136	4	0	2	2	8
2009-10	Peterborough	OHL	33	8	19	27	58	....	....	....	....	....
	Windsor Spitfires	OHL	5	4	0	4	23	19	7	9	16	38

KATIC, Mark
(KA-tihk, MAHRK) **NYI**

Defense. Shoots left. 5'11", 185 lbs. Born, Timmins, Ont., May 9, 1989.
(NY Islanders' 1st choice, 62nd overall, in 2007 Entry Draft).

			Regular Season					Playoffs				
Season	Club	League	GP	G	A	Pts	PIM	GP	G	A	Pts	PIM
2003-04	Timmins Majors	GNMHL	40	12	20	32	35	....	....	....	....	....
2004-05	Timmins Majors	GNMHL	35	11	21	32	74	....	....	....	....	....
2005-06	Sarnia Sting	OHL	51	5	29	34	33	....	....	....	....	....
2006-07	Sarnia Sting	OHL	68	5	35	40	31	4	1	3	4	8
2007-08	Sarnia Sting	OHL	45	5	26	31	28	6	0	3	3	8
2008-09	Sarnia Sting	OHL	63	13	41	54	45	4	1	0	1	6
2009-10	Bridgeport	AHL	48	3	11	14	16	....	....	....	....	....

OHL All-Rookie Team (2006)

KAUNISTO, Ray
(kow-NEES-tow, RAY) **L.A.**

Left wing. Shoots left. 6'4", 197 lbs. Born, Sault Ste. Marie, MI, February 7, 1987.

			Regular Season					Playoffs				
Season	Club	League	GP	G	A	Pts	PIM	GP	G	A	Pts	PIM
2003-04	Soo Indians	NAHL	4	1	1	2	6	....	....	....	....	....
2004-05	Soo	NAHL	55	20	20	40	72	....	....	....	....	....
2005-06	Cedar Rapids	USHL	53	5	14	19	78	....	....	....	....	....
2006-07	Northern Mich.	CCHA	41	3	0	3	30	....	....	....	....	....
2007-08	Northern Mich.	CCHA	40	8	5	13	44	....	....	....	....	....
2008-09	Northern Mich.	CCHA	40	7	7	14	56	....	....	....	....	....
2009-10	Northern Mich.	CCHA	40	18	14	32	78	....	....	....	....	....

Signed as a free agent by **Los Angeles**, March 31, 2010.

KAZIONOV, Denis
(ka-zee-OH-nahv, DEH-nihs) **T.B.**

Left wing. Shoots left. 6'3", 187 lbs. Born, Perm, USSR, December 8, 1987.
(Tampa Bay's 4th choice, 198th overall, in 2006 Entry Draft).

			Regular Season					Playoffs				
Season	Club	League	GP	G	A	Pts	PIM	GP	G	A	Pts	PIM
2003-04	CSKA Moscow 2	Russia-3	2	0	1	1	2	....	....	....	....	....
2004-05	Dyn'o Moscow 2	Russia-3	STATISTICS NOT AVAILABLE									
2005-06	MVD	Russia	26	0	0	0	12	3	0	0	0	0
	HK MVD-THK Tver	Russia-3	31	6	13	19	34	....	....	....	....	....
2006-07	THK Tver	Russia-3	13	23	15	38	42	....	....	....	....	....
	MVD	Russia	24	2	0	2	8	2	0	0	0	2
2007-08	Novokuznetsk	Russia	8	0	0	0	8	....	....	....	....	....
	Avangard Omsk 2	Russia-3	13	10	6	16	16	....	....	....	....	....
	Avangard Omsk	Russia	18	0	0	0	4	3	0	0	0	6
2008-09	Amur Khabarovsk	Rus-KHL	6	0	0	0	6	....	....	....	....	....
	Trebic	CzRep-2	2	0	1	1	2	....	....	....	....	....
	BK Mlada Boleslav	CzRep	33	4	6	10	99	....	....	....	....	....
	BK Mlada Boleslav	CzRep-Q	....	....	....	....	....	2	0	0	0	0
2009-10	Avtomobilist	Rus-KHL	51	5	4	9	20	4	0	0	0	6

KAZIONOV, Dmitri
(ka-zee-OH-nahv, dih-MEE-tree) **T.B.**

Center. Shoots left. 6'3", 185 lbs. Born, Moscow, USSR, May 13, 1984.
(Tampa Bay's 2nd choice, 100th overall, in 2002 Entry Draft).

			Regular Season					Playoffs				
Season	Club	League	GP	G	A	Pts	PIM	GP	G	A	Pts	PIM
99-2000	Dyn'o Moscow 2	Russia-3	2	1	0	1	0	....	....	....	....	....
2000-01	THK Tver	Russia-2	33	1	1	2	6	....	....	....	....	....
2001-02	HK CSKA Moscow	Russia-2	2	0	1	1	0	....	....	....	....	....
	HK CSKA 2	Russia-3	10	1	0	1	4	....	....	....	....	....
	Lada Togliatti	Russia	3	0	0	0	0	....	....	....	....	....
	Lada Togliatti 2	Russia-3	16	10	9	19	0	....	....	....	....	....
2002-03	Lada Togliatti	Russia	5	0	1	1	4	....	....	....	....	....
	Lada Togliatti 2	Russia-3	34	14	13	27	26	....	....	....	....	....
2003-04	Lada Togliatti 2	Russia-3	5	3	2	5	0	4	0	0	0	0
	Lada Togliatti	Russia	47	5	5	10	34	5	0	0	0	4
2004-05	Lada Togliatti	Russia	46	3	7	10	32	2	0	0	0	0
	Lada Togliatti 2	Russia-3	2	1	0	1	4	....	....	....	....	....
2005-06	Lada Togliatti	Russia	13	0	3	3	18	....	....	....	....	....
	Dynamo Moscow	Russia	27	2	2	4	24	4	1	0	1	6
2006-07	Ak Bars Kazan	Russia	48	10	11	21	34	13	2	3	5	4
2007-08	Ak Bars Kazan	Russia	56	7	13	20	46	10	0	3	3	16
2008-09	Ak Bars Kazan	Rus-KHL	55	10	11	21	30	21	2	6	8	12
2009-10	Ak Bars Kazan	Rus-KHL	52	18	9	27	18	22	3	5	8	12

KEARNS, Bracken
(KUHNRZ, DEH-nihs) **PHX.**

Center. Shoots right. 6', 195 lbs. Born, Vancouver, B.C., May 12, 1981.

			Regular Season					Playoffs				
Season	**Club**	**League**	**GP**	**G**	**A**	**Pts**	**PIM**	**GP**	**G**	**A**	**Pts**	**PIM**
2001-02	U. of Calgary	CWUAA	26	0	8	8	2	....	....	....	....	....
2002-03	U. of Calgary	CWUAA	29	8	9	17	14	....	....	....	....	....
2003-04	U. of Calgary	CWUAA	38	11	12	23	22	....	....	....	....	....
2004-05	U. of Calgary	CWUAA	43	12	23	35	18	....	....	....	....	....
2005-06	Cleveland Barons	AHL	1	0	1	1	0	....	....	....	....	....
	Toledo Storm	ECHL	71	33	36	69	66	13	7	6	13	6
2006-07	Milwaukee	AHL	79	11	15	26	59	4	0	0	0	8
2007-08	Norfolk Admirals	AHL	53	9	16	25	40	....	....	....	....	....
	Reading Royals	ECHL	17	5	13	18	17	....	....	....	....	....
2008-09	Norfolk Admirals	AHL	53	12	10	22	63	....	....	....	....	....
2009-10	Rockford IceHogs	AHL	80	15	36	51	99	4	0	2	2	2

Signed as a free agent by **Phoenix**, July 27, 2010.

KELLER, Justin
(KEHL-uhr, JUHS-tihn)

Left wing. Shoots left. 5'11", 185 lbs. Born, Nelson, B.C., March 4, 1986.
(Tampa Bay's 8th choice, 245th overall, in 2004 Entry Draft).

			Regular Season					Playoffs				
Season	**Club**	**League**	**GP**	**G**	**A**	**Pts**	**PIM**	**GP**	**G**	**A**	**Pts**	**PIM**
2001-02	Spokane Chiefs	WHL	25	7	6	13	10	....	....	....	....	....
	Saskatoon Blades	WHL	36	7	6	13	6	2	0	0	0	2
2002-03	Saskatoon Blades	WHL	2	0	0	0	0	....	....	....	....	....
	Regina Pats	WHL	16	3	3	6	6	....	....	....	....	....
2003-04	Kelowna Rockets	WHL	72	25	21	46	44	17	4	5	9	18
2004-05	Kelowna Rockets	WHL	72	31	22	53	103	23	12	10	22	44
2005-06	Kelowna Rockets	WHL	72	*51	37	88	82	12	3	6	9	14
2006-07	Springfield Falcons	AHL	60	13	11	24	26	....	....	....	....	....
2007-08	Norfolk Admirals	AHL	70	15	22	37	45	....	....	....	....	....
2008-09	Norfolk Admirals	AHL	58	18	19	37	52	....	....	....	....	....
2009-10	Norfolk Admirals	AHL	68	17	7	24	45	....	....	....	....	....

WHL West First All-Star Team (2006)

KELLY, Dan
(KEHL-lee, DAN) **N.J.**

Defense. Shoots left. 6'1", 195 lbs. Born, Morrisonville, NY, May 17, 1989.

			Regular Season					Playoffs				
Season	**Club**	**League**	**GP**	**G**	**A**	**Pts**	**PIM**	**GP**	**G**	**A**	**Pts**	**PIM**
2005-06	Kitchener Rangers	OHL	9	0	3	3	8	....	....	....	....	....
2006-07	Kitchener Rangers	OHL	59	0	19	19	79	9	1	1	2	10
2007-08	Kitchener Rangers	OHL	65	1	17	18	61	8	0	2	2	4
	Kitchener Rangers	M-Cup	....	....	....	....	....	5	0	1	1	6
2008-09	Kitchener Rangers	OHL	44	4	11	15	30	....	....	....	....	....
2009-10	Kitchener Rangers	OHL	58	6	21	27	99	20	4	9	13	23

Signed as a free agent by **New Jersey**, May 19, 2010.

KENNEDY, Matt
(KEH-nuh-dee, MAT) **CAR.**

Right wing. Shoots right. 6'2", 202 lbs. Born, Richmond Hill, Ont., March 4, 1989.
(Carolina's 4th choice, 131st overall, in 2009 Entry Draft).

			Regular Season					Playoffs				
Season	**Club**	**League**	**GP**	**G**	**A**	**Pts**	**PIM**	**GP**	**G**	**A**	**Pts**	**PIM**
2005-06	Seguin Bruins	OPJHL	47	11	16	27	71	6	0	0	0	8
	Guelph Storm	OHL	13	1	0	1	31	13	0	2	2	8
2006-07	Guelph Storm	OHL	63	10	12	22	78	4	1	1	2	10
2007-08	Guelph Storm	OHL	45	17	4	21	99	10	3	1	4	25
2008-09	Guelph Storm	OHL	67	33	40	73	95	4	3	2	5	0
	Syracuse Crunch	AHL	4	1	0	1	2	....	....	....	....	....
2009-10	Guelph Storm	OHL	14	10	6	16	15	....	....	....	....	....
	Barrie Colts	OHL	29	8	10	18	18	17	9	6	15	11

KESSEL, Blake
(KEH-suhl, BLAYK) **NYI**

Defense. Shoots right. 6'2", 205 lbs. Born, Madison, WI, April 13, 1989.
(NY Islanders' 4th choice, 166th overall, in 2007 Entry Draft).

			Regular Season					Playoffs				
Season	**Club**	**League**	**GP**	**G**	**A**	**Pts**	**PIM**	**GP**	**G**	**A**	**Pts**	**PIM**
2005-06	Madison Capitols	MAHL	62	33	47	80	....	....	....	....	....	....
2006-07	Waterloo	USHL	59	11	27	38	38	9	1	5	6	8
2007-08	Waterloo	USHL	59	19	38	57	26	11	1	*10	11	12
2008-09	New Hampshire	H-East	37	6	7	13	24	....	....	....	....	....
2009-10	New Hampshire	H-East	38	10	28	38	28	....	....	....	....	....

USHL All-Rookie Team (2007) • USHL Defenseman of the Year (2008) • USHL First All-Star Team (2008) • Hockey East First All-Star Team (2010) • NCAA East Second All-American Team (2010)

KHOMITSKI, Vadim
(khoh-MIHT-skee, va-DEEM) **DAL.**

Defense. Shoots left. 6'1", 185 lbs. Born, Voskresensk, USSR, July 21, 1982.
(Dallas' 5th choice, 123rd overall, in 2000 Entry Draft).

			Regular Season					Playoffs				
Season	**Club**	**League**	**GP**	**G**	**A**	**Pts**	**PIM**	**GP**	**G**	**A**	**Pts**	**PIM**
1998-99	Voskresensk	Russia	9	0	0	0	10	....	....	....	....	....
99-2000	Voskresensk	Russia-2	17	0	0	0	31	....	....	....	....	....
	HK Moscow	Russia-2	11	0	1	1	10	....	....	....	....	....
2000-01	HK Moscow	Russia-2	44	2	7	9	89	....	....	....	....	....
2001-02	HK CSKA Moscow	Russia-2	68	2	18	20	63	....	....	....	....	....
2002-03	CSKA Moscow	Russia	51	3	2	5	58	....	....	....	....	....
2003-04	CSKA Moscow	Russia	54	3	3	6	46	....	....	....	....	....
2004-05	CSKA Moscow	Russia	60	1	5	6	105	....	....	....	....	....
2005-06	CSKA Moscow	Russia	51	5	6	11	110	7	0	0	0	6
2006-07	Iowa Stars	AHL	9	1	6	7	24	....	....	....	....	....
	Mytischi	Russia	29	6	5	11	50	9	1	1	2	22
2007-08	Iowa Stars	AHL	7	1	0	1	10	....	....	....	....	....
	Mytischi	Russia	27	1	3	4	34	5	1	2	3	8
2008-09	Mytischi	Rus-KHL	45	2	4	6	68	7	2	0	2	25
2009-10	Mytischi	Rus-KHL	51	1	4	5	57	4	1	0	1	4

KHOMUTOV, Ivan
(khoh-moo-TAWF, ee-VAHN) **N.J.**

Center. Shoots left. 6'3", 200 lbs. Born, Saratov, USSR, March 11, 1985.
(New Jersey's 3rd choice, 93rd overall, in 2003 Entry Draft).

			Regular Season					Playoffs				
Season	**Club**	**League**	**GP**	**G**	**A**	**Pts**	**PIM**	**GP**	**G**	**A**	**Pts**	**PIM**
2001-02	HK CSKA 2	Russia-3	30	11	8	19	14	....	....	....	....	....
2002-03	Elektrostal	Russia-2	20	1	1	2	8	....	....	....	....	....
2003-04	London Knights	OHL	40	9	12	21	25	15	3	1	4	7
2004-05	Albany River Rats	AHL	66	6	11	17	30	....	....	....	....	....
2005-06	Albany River Rats	AHL	60	9	20	29	44	....	....	....	....	....
2006-07	Lowell Devils	AHL	3	1	1	2	2	....	....	....	....	....
	Trenton Titans	ECHL	5	0	1	1	2	....	....	....	....	....
2007-08	Lowell Devils	AHL	72	13	19	32	53	....	....	....	....	....
2008-09	CSKA Moscow	Rus-KHL	47	9	7	16	32	7	1	0	1	4
2009-10	Avtomobilist	Rus-KHL	17	0	5	5	14	....	....	....	....	....

KILLORN, Alexander
(KIHL-ohrn, al-ehx-AN-duhr) **T.B.**

Center. Shoots left. 6', 161 lbs. Born, Halifax, N.S., September 14, 1989.
(Tampa Bay's 3rd choice, 77th overall, in 2007 Entry Draft).

			Regular Season					Playoffs				
Season	**Club**	**League**	**GP**	**G**	**A**	**Pts**	**PIM**	**GP**	**G**	**A**	**Pts**	**PIM**
2005-06	Lac St-Louis Lions	QAAA	43	18	34	52	94	10	9	6	15	8
2006-07	Deerfield Academy	High-MA	25	18	14	32	....	....	....	....	....	....
2007-08	Deerfield Academy	High-MA	24	28	27	55	....	....	....	....	....	....
2008-09	Harvard Crimson	ECAC	30	6	8	14	46	....	....	....	....	....
2009-10	Harvard Crimson	ECAC	32	9	11	20	26	....	....	....	....	....

KING, Dwight
(KIHNG, DWIGHT) **L.A.**

Center/Left wing. Shoots left. 6'3", 227 lbs. Born, Meadowlake, Sask., July 5, 1989.
(Los Angeles' 6th choice, 109th overall, in 2007 Entry Draft).

			Regular Season					Playoffs				
Season	**Club**	**League**	**GP**	**G**	**A**	**Pts**	**PIM**	**GP**	**G**	**A**	**Pts**	**PIM**
2004-05	Beardy's	SMHL	44	26	30	56	16	3	0	1	1	4
	Lethbridge	WHL	7	0	0	0	2	4	0	0	0	2
2005-06	Lethbridge	WHL	68	8	8	16	22	6	0	0	0	6
2006-07	Lethbridge	WHL	62	12	32	44	39	....	....	....	....	....
2007-08	Lethbridge	WHL	72	34	35	69	56	19	8	6	14	12
2008-09	Lethbridge	WHL	64	25	35	60	51	11	1	7	8	2
2009-10	Manchester	AHL	52	10	16	26	42	16	2	7	9	4
	Ontario Reign	ECHL	20	4	5	9	9	....	....	....	....	....

KING, Tristan
(KIHNG, TRIHS-tuhn) **DAL.**

Center. Shoots right. 6'2", 190 lbs. Born, Elk River, MN, November 7, 1990.

			Regular Season					Playoffs				
Season	**Club**	**League**	**GP**	**G**	**A**	**Pts**	**PIM**	**GP**	**G**	**A**	**Pts**	**PIM**
2006-07	Portland	WHL	64	6	9	15	26	....	....	....	....	....
2007-08	Portland	WHL	69	9	16	25	39	....	....	....	....	....
2008-09	Medicine Hat	WHL	47	14	22	36	33	2	0	0	0	0
2009-10	Medicine Hat	WHL	70	21	44	65	65	12	3	3	6	12

Signed as a free agent by **Dallas**, September 18, 2009.

KISHEL, Scott
(KIH-shuhl, SKAWT) **MTL.**

Defense. Shoots left. 5'11", 170 lbs. Born, Virginia, MN, April 21, 1989.
(Montreal's 9th choice, 192nd overall, in 2007 Entry Draft).

			Regular Season					Playoffs				
Season	**Club**	**League**	**GP**	**G**	**A**	**Pts**	**PIM**	**GP**	**G**	**A**	**Pts**	**PIM**
2004-05	Virginia Blue Devils	High-MN	....	4	9	13	....	....	....	....	....	....
2005-06	Virginia Blue Devils	High-MN	....	5	25	30	....	....	....	....	....	....
2006-07	Virginia Blue Devils	High-MN	24	14	34	48	....	....	....	....	....	....
2007-08	Sioux Falls	USHL	57	3	11	14	34	3	0	0	0	0
2008-09	U. Minn-Duluth	WCHA	12	0	2	2	2	....	....	....	....	....
2009-10	U. Minn-Duluth	WCHA	28	0	8	8	14	....	....	....	....	....

KITSYN, Maxim
(KIHT-sihn, max-EEM) **L.A.**

Left wing. Shoots right. 6'2", 194 lbs. Born, Novokuznetsk, USSR, December 24, 1991.
(Los Angeles' 5th choice, 158th overall, in 2010 Entry Draft).

			Regular Season					Playoffs				
Season	**Club**	**League**	**GP**	**G**	**A**	**Pts**	**PIM**	**GP**	**G**	**A**	**Pts**	**PIM**
2007-08	Novokuznetsk 2	Russia-3	4	1	0	1	0	....	....	....	....	....
2008-09	Novokuznetsk 2	Russia-3	STATISTICS NOT AVAILABLE									
	Novokuznetsk	Rus-KHL	31	5	2	7	26	....	....	....	....	....
2009-10	Novokuznetsk Jr.	Russia-Jr.	11	6	12	18	26	17	9	12	21	42
	Novokuznetsk	Rus-KHL	21	1	1	2	12	....	....	....	....	....

KIVISTO, Tommi
(K'VIHS-toh, TAW-mee) **CAR.**

Defense. Shoots left. 6'1", 195 lbs. Born, Vantaa, Finland, June 7, 1991.
(Carolina's 6th choice, 208th overall, in 2009 Entry Draft).

			Regular Season					Playoffs				
Season	**Club**	**League**	**GP**	**G**	**A**	**Pts**	**PIM**	**GP**	**G**	**A**	**Pts**	**PIM**
2006-07	Jokerit U18	Fin-U18	24	0	2	2	10	....	....	....	....	....
2007-08	Jokerit U18	Fin-U18	26	6	10	16	50	4	0	3	3	4
	Jokerit Helsinki Jr.	Fin-Jr.	9	2	0	2	4	4	0	3	3	2
2008-09	Red Deer Rebels	WHL	65	1	21	22	49	....	....	....	....	....
2009-10	Suomi U20	Finland-2	2	0	0	0	2	....	....	....	....	....
	Jokerit Helsinki	Finland	22	0	2	2	12	3	0	0	0	0
	Kiekko-Vantaa	Finland-2	2	0	0	0	2	....	....	....	....	....
	Jokerit Helsinki Jr.	Fin-Jr.	18	2	5	7	58	2	0	0	0	0

KLASEN, Linus (KLAW-suhn, LEE-nuhs) NSH.

Left wing. Shoots left. 5'8", 184 lbs. Born, Stockholm, Sweden, February 19, 1986.

			Regular Season					Playoffs				
Season	Club	League	GP	G	A	Pts	PIM	GP	G	A	Pts	PIM
2001-02	Huddinge IK U18	Swe-U18	14	7	5	12	4	7	0	0	0	0
2002-03	Huddinge IK U18	Swe-U18	13	3	4	7	4	2	0	0	0	0
	Huddinge IK Jr.	Swe-Jr.	2	0	0	0	0	....	....	....	....	....
2003-04	Huddinge IK U18	Swe-U18	11	8	12	20	14	....	....	....	....	....
	Huddinge IK Jr.	Swe-Jr.	21	3	2	5	6	2	0	0	0	0
2004-05	Lincoln Stars	USHL	26	7	9	16	13	....	....	....	....	....
	Huddinge IK	Sweden-2	2	0	0	0	0	....	....	....	....	....
	Huddinge IK Jr.	Swe-Jr.	9	4	5	9	27	3	0	2	2	0
2005-06	Huddinge IK Jr.	Swe-Jr.	8	3	6	9	29	....	....	....	....	....
	Huddinge IK	Sweden-3	43	24	51	75	38	5	3	3	6	2
2006-07	Huddinge IK	Sweden-2	52	19	44	63	30	....	....	....	....	....
2007-08	Sodertalje SK Jr.	Swe-Jr.	1	0	2	2	0	....	....	....	....	....
	Sodertalje SK	Sweden	52	14	20	34	24	....	....	....	....	....
2008-09	Sodertalje SK	Sweden	53	14	15	29	8	....	....	....	....	....
	Sodertalje SK	Sweden-Q	9	2	3	5	0	....	....	....	....	....
2009-10	Sodertalje SK	Sweden	51	19	32	51	20	....	....	....	....	....
	Sodertalje SK	Sweden-Q	10	4	4	8	4	....	....	....	....	....

Signed as a free agent by **Nashville**, April 20, 2010.

KLASSEN, Sam (klah-SIHN, SAM) NYR

Defense. Shoots left. 6'2", 199 lbs. Born, Watrous, Sask., January 1, 1989.

			Regular Season					Playoffs				
Season	Club	League	GP	G	A	Pts	PIM	GP	G	A	Pts	PIM
2006-07	Humboldt Broncos	SJHL	32	2	9	11	74	....	....	....	....	....
	Saskatoon Blades	WHL	39	1	5	6	52	....	....	....	....	....
2007-08	Saskatoon Blades	WHL	71	1	24	25	103	....	....	....	....	....
2008-09	Saskatoon Blades	WHL	72	2	18	20	92	7	0	1	1	10
2009-10	Saskatoon Blades	WHL	67	3	27	30	98	10	0	2	2	8

Signed as a free agent by **NY Rangers**, July 27, 2009.

KLINGBERG, Carl (KLIHNG-buhrg, KAHRL) ATL.

Left wing. Shoots right. 6'3", 205 lbs. Born, Goteborg, Sweden, January 28, 1991.
(Atlanta's 2nd choice, 34th overall, in 2009 Entry Draft).

			Regular Season					Playoffs				
Season	Club	League	GP	G	A	Pts	PIM	GP	G	A	Pts	PIM
2006-07	Frolunda U18	Swe-U18	7	3	1	4	0	....	....	....	....	....
	Frolunda Jr.	Swe-Jr.	2	0	0	0	0	....	....	....	....	....
2007-08	Frolunda U18	Swe-U18	31	19	24	43	22	5	2	1	3	8
2008-09	Frolunda U18	Swe-U18	3	4	1	5	0	5	2	2	4	2
	Frolunda Jr.	Swe-Jr.	35	13	13	26	34	2	0	0	0	4
	Boras HC	Sweden-2	8	4	2	6	2	....	....	....	....	....
	Frolunda	Sweden	10	2	1	3	0	....	....	....	....	....
2009-10	Frolunda	Sweden	42	6	7	13	16	7	0	0	0	2
	Boras HC	Sweden-2	4	0	5	5	2	....	....	....	....	....

KLINGBERG, John (KLIHNG-buhrg, JAWN) DAL.

Defense. Shoots right. 6', 158 lbs. Born, Lerum, Sweden, August 14, 1992.
(Dallas' 5th choice, 131st overall, in 2010 Entry Draft).

			Regular Season					Playoffs				
Season	Club	League	GP	G	A	Pts	PIM	GP	G	A	Pts	PIM
2008-09	Frolunda U18	Swe-U18	30	3	12	15	12	3	0	0	0	0
2009-10	Frolunda U18	Swe-U18	20	3	13	16	22	7	2	9	11	10
	Frolunda Jr.	Swe-Jr.	27	0	5	5	32	5	1	0	1	6

KLINKHAMMER, Robert (KLIHNK-ham-uhr, RAW-buhrt) CHI.

Left wing. Shoots left. 6'3", 206 lbs. Born, Lethbridge, Alta., August 12, 1986.

			Regular Season					Playoffs				
Season	Club	League	GP	G	A	Pts	PIM	GP	G	A	Pts	PIM
2003-04	Lethbridge	AMHL	29	20	22	42	8	....	....	....	....	....
	Lethbridge	WHL	25	2	3	5	12	....	....	....	....	....
2004-05	Lethbridge	WHL	72	14	12	26	81	5	0	1	1	4
2005-06	Lethbridge	WHL	35	5	7	12	15	....	....	....	....	....
	Seattle	WHL	32	3	5	8	37	7	0	1	1	6
2006-07	Seattle	WHL	1	0	0	0	9	....	....	....	....	....
	Portland	WHL	37	23	19	42	70	....	....	....	....	....
	Brandon	WHL	28	10	21	31	29	11	4	4	8	22
2007-08	Norfolk Admirals	AHL	66	12	12	24	41	....	....	....	....	....
2008-09	Rockford IceHogs	AHL	76	15	18	33	32	4	0	1	1	0
2009-10	Rockford IceHogs	AHL	72	10	13	23	38	4	1	1	2	7

Signed as a free agent by **Tampa Bay**, July, 2007. Signed as a free agent by **Chicago**, June 8, 2009.

KLOTZ, Garrett (KLAWTZ, GAIR-reht) PHI.

Left wing. Shoots left. 6'6", 235 lbs. Born, Regina, Sask., November 27, 1988.
(Philadelphia's 3rd choice, 66th overall, in 2007 Entry Draft).

			Regular Season					Playoffs				
Season	Club	League	GP	G	A	Pts	PIM	GP	G	A	Pts	PIM
2004-05	Reg. Midget Hawks	SMMHL	STATISTICS NOT AVAILABLE									
	Reg. Pat Cdns.	SMHL	5	0	1	1	0	....	....	....	....	....
2005-06	Red Deer Rebels	WHL	35	2	0	2	26	....	....	....	....	....
2006-07	Saskatoon Blades	WHL	63	2	2	4	107	....	....	....	....	....
2007-08	Saskatoon Blades	WHL	52	1	3	4	96	....	....	....	....	....
2008-09	Philadelphia	AHL	36	0	1	1	59	....	....	....	....	....
2009-10	Adirondack	AHL	73	2	4	6	94	....	....	....	....	....

KLUBERTANZ, Kyle (KLOO-buhr-tanz, KIGHL) MTL.

Defense. Shoots right. 6', 186 lbs. Born, Madison, WI, September 23, 1985.
(Anaheim's 3rd choice, 74th overall, in 2004 Entry Draft).

			Regular Season					Playoffs				
Season	Club	League	GP	G	A	Pts	PIM	GP	G	A	Pts	PIM
2002-03	Green Bay	USHL	60	8	26	34	74	....	....	....	....	....
2003-04	Green Bay	USHL	57	6	21	27	124	....	....	....	....	....
2004-05	U. of Wisconsin	WCHA	41	3	15	18	64	....	....	....	....	....
2005-06	U. of Wisconsin	WCHA	43	4	17	21	44	....	....	....	....	....
2006-07	U. of Wisconsin	WCHA	34	1	12	13	46	....	....	....	....	....
2007-08	U. of Wisconsin	WCHA	40	4	16	20	52	....	....	....	....	....
	Portland Pirates	AHL	5	0	0	0	2	1	0	0	0	0
2008-09	TPS Turku	Finland	51	5	7	12	62	8	3	0	3	20
2009-10	Djurgarden	Sweden	55	12	19	31	32	16	3	2	5	18

WCHA All-Rookie Team (2005)

Signed as a free agent by **Montreal**, May 27, 2010.

KNACKSTEDT, Jordan (NAK-stehd, JOHR-dahn) BOS.

Right wing. Shoots right. 6'3", 195 lbs. Born, Saskatoon, Sask., September 28, 1988.
(Boston's 6th choice, 189th overall, in 2007 Entry Draft).

			Regular Season					Playoffs				
Season	Club	League	GP	G	A	Pts	PIM	GP	G	A	Pts	PIM
2003-04	Beardy's	SMHL	44	22	19	41	20	4	2	1	3	0
2004-05	Red Deer Rebels	WHL	52	1	2	3	34	7	0	0	0	2
2005-06	Red Deer Rebels	WHL	72	12	28	40	36	....	....	....	....	....
2006-07	Red Deer Rebels	WHL	33	10	7	17	54	....	....	....	....	....
	Moose Jaw	WHL	39	13	26	39	44	....	....	....	....	....
2007-08	Moose Jaw	WHL	72	31	54	85	116	6	1	1	2	8
	Providence Bruins	AHL	5	2	0	2	2	4	1	0	1	0
2008-09	Providence Bruins	AHL	71	10	16	26	55	16	3	1	4	11
2009-10	Providence Bruins	AHL	67	14	24	38	30	....	....	....	....	....

KNIGHT, Corban (NIGHT, KOHR-buhn) FLA.

Center. Shoots right. 6'1", 180 lbs. Born, Oliver, B.C., September 10, 1990.
(Florida's 5th choice, 135th overall, in 2009 Entry Draft).

			Regular Season					Playoffs				
Season	Club	League	GP	G	A	Pts	PIM	GP	G	A	Pts	PIM
2006-07	UFA Bisons	AMHL	36	6	18	24	44	8	2	4	6	16
2007-08	UFA Bisons	AMHL	36	29	36	65	64	6	5	4	9	10
	Okotoks Oilers	AJHL	4	1	0	1	0	7	0	0	0	0
2008-09	Okotoks Oilers	AJHL	61	34	38	72	55	9	10	2	12	12
2009-10	North Dakota	WCHA	37	6	7	13	35	....	....	....	....	....

KNIGHT, Jared (NIGHT, JAIR-uhd) BOS.

Center. Shoots right. 5'10", 198 lbs. Born, Battle Creek, MI, January 16, 1992.
(Boston's 2nd choice, 32nd overall, in 2010 Entry Draft).

			Regular Season					Playoffs				
Season	Club	League	GP	G	A	Pts	PIM	GP	G	A	Pts	PIM
2007-08	Det. Compuware	MWEHL	22	8	21	29	21	....	....	....	....	....
	Det. Compuware	Exhib.	5	1	2	3	8	....	....	....	....	....
2008-09	London Knights	OHL	67	15	15	30	60	14	3	0	3	2
2009-10	London Knights	OHL	63	36	21	57	39	12	10	7	17	12

KNODEL, Eric (NOH-dehl, AIR-ihk) TOR.

Defense. Shoots left. 6'6", 216 lbs. Born, West Chesteer, PA, June 8, 1990.
(Toronto's 5th choice, 128th overall, in 2009 Entry Draft).

			Regular Season					Playoffs				
Season	Club	League	GP	G	A	Pts	PIM	GP	G	A	Pts	PIM
2007-08	Phi. Jr. Flyers	AYHL	16	5	6	11	6	....	....	....	....	....
	Phi. Jr. Flyers	Exhib.	35	11	17	28	30	....	....	....	....	....
2008-09	Phi. Jr. Flyers	AYHL	16	2	13	15	12	....	....	....	....	....
	Phi. Jr. Flyers	Exhib.	35	11	19	30	18	....	....	....	....	....
2009-10	Des Moines	USHL	50	3	17	20	37	....	....	....	....	....

KOLOMATIS, David (koh-loh-MA-tihs, DAY-vihd) L.A.

Defense. Shoots right. 5'11", 189 lbs. Born, Livingston, NJ, February 25, 1989.
(Los Angeles' 6th choice, 126th overall, in 2009 Entry Draft).

			Regular Season					Playoffs				
Season	Club	League	GP	G	A	Pts	PIM	GP	G	A	Pts	PIM
2005-06	USNTDP	NAHL	16	1	0	1	4	....	....	....	....	....
	USNTDP	U-17	3	0	0	0	2	....	....	....	....	....
2006-07	Owen Sound	OHL	67	4	16	20	54	4	0	0	0	0
2007-08	Owen Sound	OHL	68	9	36	45	68	....	....	....	....	....
2008-09	Owen Sound	OHL	63	18	28	46	52	4	2	2	4	0
	Providence Bruins	AHL	4	0	0	0	0	16	0	1	1	2
2009-10	Manchester	AHL	76	8	21	29	30	15	0	1	1	2

KOLOSOV, Sergei (KOH-leh-sawf, SAIR-gay) DET.

Defense. Shoots left. 6'4", 210 lbs. Born, Novopolotsk, USSR, May 22, 1986.
(Detroit's 3rd choice, 151st overall, in 2004 Entry Draft).

			Regular Season					Playoffs				
Season	Club	League	GP	G	A	Pts	PIM	GP	G	A	Pts	PIM
2003-04	Dynamo Minsk	Belarus	STATISTICS NOT AVAILABLE									
2004-05	Dynamo Minsk	BelOpen	37	2	6	8	24	....	....	....	....	....
	Yunost-Minsk	BelOpen	1	0	0	0	2	9	0	0	0	4
2005-06	Cedar Rapids	USHL	50	2	8	10	66	8	0	0	0	10
2006-07	Cedar Rapids	USHL	51	1	10	11	79	5	0	0	0	4
2007-08	Dynamo Minsk	Belarus	55	5	9	14	83	....	....	....	....	....
2008-09	Grand Rapids	AHL	70	4	7	11	36	10	0	0	0	9
2009-10	Grand Rapids	AHL	66	2	6	8	29	....	....	....	....	....
	Belarus	Olympics	4	0	0	0	0	....	....	....	....	....

KOMAROV, Leo (koh-mah-RAWV, L'YAY-oh) TOR.

Center. Shoots left. 5'10", 187 lbs. Born, Narva, USSR, January 23, 1987.
(Toronto's 7th choice, 180th overall, in 2006 Entry Draft).

			Regular Season					Playoffs				
Season	Club	League	GP	G	A	Pts	PIM	GP	G	A	Pts	PIM
2003-04	Sport Vaasa U18	Fin-U18	30	9	15	24	8	....	....	....	....	....
2004-05	Assat Pori U18	Fin-U18	9	4	5	9	62	....	....	....	....	....
	Assat Pori Jr.	Fin-Jr.	38	8	6	13	59	2	0	0	0	2
2005-06	Suomi U20	Finland-2	5	0	3	3	4	....	....	....	....	....
	Assat Pori Jr.	Fin-Jr.	10	5	6	11	59	2	2	1	3	10
	Assat Pori	Finland	44	3	3	6	106	14	1	3	4	22
2006-07	Suomi U20	Finland-2	1	1	0	1	0	....	....	....	....	....
	Pelicans Lahti	Finland	49	3	9	12	108	6	1	0	1	6
2007-08	Pelicans Lahti Jr.	Fin-Jr.	2	0	3	3	0	....	....	....	....	....
	Pelicans Lahti	Finland	53	4	10	14	76	6	1	1	2	8
2008-09	Pelicans Lahti	Finland	56	8	16	24	144	10	0	1	1	16
2009-10	Dynamo Moscow	Rus-KHL	47	5	11	16	44	4	0	1	1	16

KOPER, Levko (KOE-puhr, LEHV-koh) ATL.

Left wing. Shoots left. 6'1", 190 lbs. Born, Edmonton, Alta., October 5, 1990.
(Atlanta's 8th choice, 185th overall, in 2009 Entry Draft).

			Regular Season					Playoffs				
Season	Club	League	GP	G	A	Pts	PIM	GP	G	A	Pts	PIM
2005-06	SSAC Bulldogs	Minor-AB	36	39	50	89	34	....	....	....	....	....
	SSAC Athletics	AMHL	1	0	1	1	0	....	....	....	....	....
2006-07	Spokane Chiefs	WHL	50	3	2	5	14	5	0	0	0	0
2007-08	Spokane Chiefs	WHL	69	12	14	26	45	21	4	5	9	14
2008-09	Spokane Chiefs	WHL	71	23	36	59	57	12	3	7	10	6
2009-10	Spokane Chiefs	WHL	68	27	27	54	51	7	2	3	5	13

KORNEEV, Konstantin (kor-NEE-ehv, KAWN-stan-tihn) MTL.

Defense. Shoots left. 5'11", 176 lbs. Born, Moscow, USSR, June 5, 1984.
(Montreal's 6th choice, 275th overall, in 2002 Entry Draft).

			Regular Season					Playoffs				
Season	Club	League	GP	G	A	Pts	PIM	GP	G	A	Pts	PIM
99-2000	Krylja Sovetov 2	Russia-3	1	0	0	0	0	....	....	....	....	....
2000-01	Russia Jr.	Exhib.	12	0	4	4	10	....	....	....	....	....
2001-02	Krylja Sovetov 2	Russia-3	26	9	19	28	44	....	....	....	....	....
	Krylja Sovetov	Russia	4	0	2	2	0	2	0	0	0	2
2002-03	Krylja Sovetov	Russia	49	2	8	10	28	....	....	....	....	....
2003-04	Ak Bars Kazan	Russia	55	1	4	5	8	8	0	1	1	2
2004-05	Ak Bars Kazan 2	Russia-3	....	6	16	22	....	....	....	....	....	....
	Ak Bars Kazan	Russia	35	0	4	4	10	1	0	0	0	0
2005-06	Ak Bars Kazan	Russia	30	1	3	4	14	4	0	0	0	0
2006-07	CSKA Moscow	Russia	54	8	14	22	40	12	2	4	6	6
2007-08	CSKA Moscow	Russia	57	6	18	24	52	6	0	1	1	0
2008-09	CSKA Moscow	Rus-KHL	54	6	18	24	46	8	1	0	1	6
2009-10	CSKA Moscow	Rus-KHL	55	7	22	29	28	3	0	2	2	0
	Russia	Olympics	4	0	0	0	4	....	....	....	....	....

KOROSTIN, Sergei (koh-ROH-stihn, SAIR-gay) DAL.

Right wing. Shoots left. 5'11", 180 lbs. Born, Prokopjevsk, USSR, July 5, 1989.
(Dallas' 2nd choice, 64th overall, in 2007 Entry Draft).

			Regular Season					Playoffs				
Season	Club	League	GP	G	A	Pts	PIM	GP	G	A	Pts	PIM
2005-06	Dyn'o Moscow 2	Russia-3		STATISTICS NOT AVAILABLE								
	Dynamo Moscow	Russia	1	0	0	0	0	....	....	....	....	....
2006-07	Dyn'o Moscow 2	Russia-3		STATISTICS NOT AVAILABLE								
	Dynamo Moscow	Russia	7	0	0	0	8	....	....	....	....	....
2007-08	Dynamo Moscow	Russia	2	0	0	0	2	....	....	....	....	....
	Prokopjevsk	Russia-3	2	2	2	4	0	....	....	....	....	....
	Texas Tornado	NAHL	19	8	10	18	12	3	2	0	2	2
2008-09	London Knights	OHL	13	2	5	7	17	....	....	....	....	....
	Peterborough	OHL	36	11	18	29	16	4	1	2	3	0
2009-10	Texas Stars	AHL	63	13	12	25	41	2	0	0	0	0
	Idaho Steelheads	ECHL	4	4	2	6	2	....	....	....	....	....

KOSMACHEV, Dmitry (kaws-ma-CHEHV, dih-MEE-tree) CBJ

Defense. Shoots right. 6'4", 227 lbs. Born, Nizhny Novgorod, USSR, June 7, 1985.
(Columbus' 3rd choice, 71st overall, in 2003 Entry Draft).

			Regular Season					Playoffs				
Season	Club	League	GP	G	A	Pts	PIM	GP	G	A	Pts	PIM
2001-02	HK CSKA 2	Russia-3	6	1	0	1	2	....	....	....	....	....
	HK CSKA Moscow	Russia-2	49	0	1	1	12	....	....	....	....	....
2002-03	CSKA Moscow	Russia	27	0	0	0	2	....	....	....	....	....
2003-04	CSKA Moscow	Russia	34	0	2	2	12	....	....	....	....	....
2004-05	Nizhny Novgorod	Russia-2	34	3	4	7	22	15	0	1	1	0
2005-06	Mytischi	Russia	38	2	2	4	14	9	0	0	0	4
	Kristall Elektrostal	Russia-3		STATISTICS NOT AVAILABLE								
2006-07	Mytischi	Russia	32	0	0	0	18	9	0	0	0	2
2007-08	Mytischi	Russia	56	0	6	6	34	4	0	0	0	2
2008-09	Ak Bars Kazan	Rus-KHL	28	0	3	3	24	....	....	....	....	....
2009-10	Nizhny Novgorod	Rus-KHL	43	0	1	1	26	....	....	....	....	....

KOSTKA, Mike (KOHST-kuh, MIGHK)

Defense. Shoots right. 6'2", 210 lbs. Born, Ajax, Ont., November 28, 1985.

			Regular Season					Playoffs				
Season	Club	League	GP	G	A	Pts	PIM	GP	G	A	Pts	PIM
2001-02	Ajax Axemen	OPJHL	19	1	4	5	8	....	....	....	....	....
2002-03	Ajax Axemen	OPJHL	39	4	11	15	32	....	....	....	....	....
2003-04	Aurora Tigers	OPJHL	42	9	27	36	4	....	....	....	....	....
2004-05	Massachusetts	H-East	32	1	5	6	14	....	....	....	....	....
2005-06	Massachusetts	H-East	36	2	6	8	20	....	....	....	....	....
2006-07	Massachusetts	H-East	39	3	15	18	20	....	....	....	....	....
2007-08	Massachusetts	H-East	36	9	12	21	20	....	....	....	....	....
	Rochester	AHL	1	0	0	0	2	....	....	....	....	....
2008-09	Portland Pirates	AHL	80	4	26	30	33	4	1	0	1	6
2009-10	Portland Pirates	AHL	76	2	25	27	37	4	0	0	0	0

Hockey East Second All-Star Team (2008)

Signed as a free agent by **Buffalo**, March 25, 2008.

KOZEK, Andrew (KOH-zehk, AN-droo) ATL.

Left wing. Shoots left. 5'10", 200 lbs. Born, Revelstoke, B.C., May 26, 1986.
(Atlanta's 4th choice, 53rd overall, in 2005 Entry Draft).

			Regular Season					Playoffs				
Season	Club	League	GP	G	A	Pts	PIM	GP	G	A	Pts	PIM
2003-04	South Surrey	BCHL	58	19	22	41	67	....	....	....	....	....
2004-05	South Surrey	BCHL	60	48	49	97	81	....	....	....	....	....
2005-06	North Dakota	WCHA	46	7	6	13	22	....	....	....	....	....
2006-07	North Dakota	WCHA	41	5	6	11	12	....	....	....	....	....
2007-08	North Dakota	WCHA	42	18	3	21	18	....	....	....	....	....
2008-09	North Dakota	WCHA	38	8	12	20	40	....	....	....	....	....
	Chicago Wolves	AHL	5	2	0	2	2	....	....	....	....	....
2009-10	Chicago Wolves	AHL	69	12	10	22	36	7	0	1	1	0

KOZUN, Brandon (KOH-zuhn, BRAN-duhn) L.A.

Right wing. Shoots right. 5'9", 164 lbs. Born, Los Angeles, CA, March 8, 1990.
(Los Angeles' 8th choice, 179th overall, in 2009 Entry Draft).

			Regular Season					Playoffs				
Season	Club	League	GP	G	A	Pts	PIM	GP	G	A	Pts	PIM
2006-07	Calgary Royals	AJHL	39	20	22	42	38	4	2	1	3	2
	Calgary Hitmen	WHL	11	1	1	2	4	....	....	....	....	....
2007-08	Calgary Hitmen	WHL	69	19	34	53	46	16	4	14	18	6
2008-09	Calgary Hitmen	WHL	72	40	68	108	58	18	7	12	19	8
2009-10	Calgary Hitmen	WHL	65	32	*75	*107	50	23	8	*22	*30	12

WHL East First All-Star Team (2009, 2010) • Canadian Major Junior First All-Star Team (2010)

KREIDER, Chris (KRIGH-duhr, KRIHS) NYR

Center. Shoots left. 6'3", 217 lbs. Born, Boxford, MA, April 30, 1991.
(NY Rangers' 1st choice, 19th overall, in 2009 Entry Draft).

			Regular Season					Playoffs				
Season	Club	League	GP	G	A	Pts	PIM	GP	G	A	Pts	PIM
2005-06	Masconomet	High-MA	19	5	10	15	....	....	....	....	....	....
2006-07	Masconomet	High-MA	20	28	13	41	....	....	....	....	....	....
2007-08	Andover	High-MA	24	26	15	41	....	....	....	....	....	....
2008-09	Andover	High-MA	26	33	23	56	10	....	....	....	....	....
	Valley Jr. Warriors	Minor-MA	5	4	2	6	....	....	....	....	....	....
2009-10	Boston College	H-East	38	15	8	23	26	....	....	....	....	....

Hockey East All-Rookie Team (2010)

KRIKUNOV, Ilja (krih-koo-NAWF, IHL-yah) VAN.

Left wing. Shoots left. 5'11", 169 lbs. Born, Elektrostal, USSR, February 27, 1984.
(Vancouver's 8th choice, 223rd overall, in 2002 Entry Draft).

			Regular Season					Playoffs				
Season	Club	League	GP	G	A	Pts	PIM	GP	G	A	Pts	PIM
2000-01	Elektrostal 2	Russia-3	4	0	0	0	2	....	....	....	....	....
2001-02	Elektrostal 2	Russia-3	5	3	6	9	4	....	....	....	....	....
	Elektrostal	Russia-2	48	12	10	22	28	....	....	....	....	....
2002-03	Elektrostal	Russia-2	48	19	9	28	34	....	....	....	....	....
2003-04	Voskresensk	Russia	50	10	9	19	14	....	....	....	....	....
2004-05	Voskresensk	Russia	58	9	14	23	20	....	....	....	....	....
2005-06	Mytischi	Russia	46	10	5	15	57	8	1	1	2	2
	Kristall Elektrostal	Russia-3		STATISTICS NOT AVAILABLE								
2006-07	Mytischi	Russia	48	9	6	15	56	9	2	1	3	12
2007-08	Mytischi	Russia	34	7	12	19	18	5	1	1	2	4
2008-09	Mytischi	Rus-KHL	5	0	1	1	0	....	....	....	....	....
	Nizhny Novgorod	Rus-KHL	27	6	6	12	10	3	0	2	2	0
2009-10	Nizhny Novgorod	Rus-KHL	55	9	17	26	30	....	....	....	....	....

KRISTO, Danny (KRIHS-toh, DAN-ee) MTL.

Right wing. Shoots right. 5'11", 172 lbs. Born, Edina, MN, June 18, 1990.
(Montreal's 1st choice, 56th overall, in 2008 Entry Draft).

			Regular Season					Playoffs				
Season	Club	League	GP	G	A	Pts	PIM	GP	G	A	Pts	PIM
2006-07	USNTDP	U-17	14	4	5	9	0	....	....	....	....	....
	USNTDP	NAHL	39	8	10	18	34	6	0	1	1	2
2007-08	USNTDP	U-18	43	18	14	32	18	....	....	....	....	....
	USNTDP	NAHL	14	4	4	8	6	....	....	....	....	....
2008-09	Omaha Lancers	USHL	50	22	35	57	18	3	3	0	3	2
2009-10	North Dakota	WCHA	41	15	21	36	8	....	....	....	....	....

WCHA All-Rookie Team (2010) • WCHA Rookie of the Year (2010)

KRUEGER, Justin (KROO-guhr, JUHS-tihn) CAR.

Defense. Shoots right. 6'2", 205 lbs. Born, Dusseldorf, West Germany, October 6, 1986.
(Carolina's 6th choice, 213th overall, in 2006 Entry Draft).

			Regular Season					Playoffs				
Season	Club	League	GP	G	A	Pts	PIM	GP	G	A	Pts	PIM
2002-03	HC Davos Jr.	Swiss-Jr.	12	0	0	0	4	2	0	0	0	0
2003-04	HC Davos Jr.	Swiss-Jr.	33	2	0	2	14	....	....	....	....	....
2004-05	HC Davos Jr.	Swiss-Jr.	38	5	12	17	76	4	1	2	3	2
2005-06	Penticton Vees	BCHL	55	7	15	22	25	....	....	....	....	....
2006-07	Cornell Big Red	ECAC	31	1	5	6	24	....	....	....	....	....
2007-08	Cornell Big Red	ECAC	35	4	5	9	33	....	....	....	....	....
2008-09	Cornell Big Red	ECAC	35	1	4	5	24	....	....	....	....	....
2009-10	Cornell Big Red	ECAC	34	1	11	12	22	....	....	....	....	....

KRUGER, Marcus (KROO-guhr, MAHR-kuhs) CHI.

Center. Shoots left. 5'11", 172 lbs. Born, Stockholm, Sweden, May 27, 1990.
(Chicago's 5th choice, 149th overall, in 2009 Entry Draft).

			Regular Season					Playoffs				
Season	Club	League	GP	G	A	Pts	PIM	GP	G	A	Pts	PIM
2006-07	Djurgarden U18	Swe-U18	23	5	14	19	10	3	2	1	3	2
2007-08	Djurgarden U18	Swe-U18	22	11	20	31	22	7	3	8	11	6
	Djurgarden Jr.	Swe-Jr.	22	3	13	16	16	7	5	3	8	0
2008-09	Djurgarden Jr.	Swe-Jr.	34	9	30	39	24	6	1	5	6	2
	Djurgarden	Sweden	15	2	2	4	2	....	....	....	....	....
2009-10	Djurgarden	Sweden	38	11	20	31	14	16	3	7	10	6

KRUPP, Bjorn (KROOP, B'YOHRN) MIN.

Defense. Shoots right. 6'2", 201 lbs. Born, Manhattan Beach, CA, March 6, 1991.

			Regular Season					Playoffs				
Season	Club	League	GP	G	A	Pts	PIM	GP	G	A	Pts	PIM
2007-08	USNTDP	NAHL	43	0	3	3	40	....	....	....	....	....
2008-09	Belleville Bulls	OHL	57	1	3	4	22	17	0	0	0	9
2009-10	Belleville Bulls	OHL	67	0	11	11	53	....	....	....	....	....

Signed as a free agent by **Minnesota**, September 18, 2009.

KRYSANOV, Anton (KREE-sa-nahf, AN-tawn) PHX.

Center. Shoots left. 6'3", 198 lbs. Born, Togliatti, USSR, March 25, 1987.
(Phoenix's 4th choice, 148th overall, in 2005 Entry Draft).

			Regular Season					Playoffs				
Season	Club	League	GP	G	A	Pts	PIM	GP	G	A	Pts	PIM
2002-03	Lada Togliatti 2	Russia-3	9	1	3	4	2	....	....	....	....	....
2003-04	Lada Togliatti 2	Russia-3	18	2	3	5	2	....	....	....	....	....
2004-05	Lada Togliatti 2	Russia-3	34	13	13	26	32	....	....	....	....	....
	Lada Togliatti	Russia	15	1	0	1	2	....	....	....	....	....
2005-06	Lada Togliatti	Russia	46	3	3	6	24	8	0	0	0	2
2006-07	Lada Togliatti	Russia	48	1	15	16	14	3	0	0	0	4
2007-08	Lada Togliatti 2	Russia-3	2	2	1	3	2	....	....	....	....	....
	Lada Togliatti	Russia	54	9	11	20	22	4	0	1	1	0
2008-09	Lada Togliatti	Rus-KHL	46	8	10	18	14	5	0	3	3	4
2009-10	Dynamo Moscow	Rus-KHL	41	8	6	14	14	2	0	0	0	2

KRYUKOV, Artem (KREE-oo-kahf, AHR-tehm) BUF.

Center. Shoots left. 6'3", 180 lbs. Born, Novosibirsk, USSR, March 5, 1982.
(Buffalo's 1st choice, 15th overall, in 2000 Entry Draft).

			Regular Season					Playoffs				
Season	Club	League	GP	G	A	Pts	PIM	GP	G	A	Pts	PIM
1997-98	Torpedo Yaroslavl	Russia	7	0	0	0	2	....	....	....	....	....
1998-99	Yaroslavl 2	Russia-3	20	2	2	4	6	....	....	....	....	....
99-2000	Yaroslavl 2	Russia-3	14	1	1	2	12	....	....	....	....	....
	Torpedo Yaroslavl	Russia	3	0	0	0	4	....	....	....	....	....
2000-01	Yaroslavl 2	Russia-3	6	0	0	0	2	11	0	0	0	8
	SKA St. Petersburg	Russia	14	0	2	2	14	....	....	....	....	....
2001-02	Yaroslavl	Russia	15	1	3	4	10	6	1	0	1	8
2002-03	Sibir Novosibirsk	Russia	9	0	0	0	27	....	....	....	....	....
2003-04	Yaroslavl 2	Russia-3	30	5	4	9	26	....	....	....	....	....
	Yaroslavl	Russia	4	0	2	2	0	....	....	....	....	....
2004-05	Yaroslavl	Russia	60	8	9	17	44	7	1	0	1	4
2005-06	Yaroslavl	Russia	33	1	2	3	42	1	0	0	0	0
	Yaroslavl 2	Russia-3	6	3	3	6	18	....	....	....	....	....
2006-07	Vityaz Chekhov	Russia	12	0	0	0	20	....	....	....	....	....
	Yaroslavl 2	Russia-3	13	4	10	14	10	....	....	....	....	....
	Yaroslavl	Russia	19	1	3	4	20	....	....	....	....	....
2007-08	SKA St. Petersburg	Russia	51	7	8	15	54	9	0	2	2	8
2008-09	SKA St. Petersburg	Rus-KHL	50	8	3	11	48	....	....	....	....	....
2009-10				DID NOT PLAY – INJURED								

• Missed entire 2009-10 season recovering from knee injury suffered in pre-season.

KUBALIK, Tomas (koo-BAHL-ihk, TAW-mahsh) CBJ

Right wing. Shoots right. 6'3", 209 lbs. Born, Plzen, Czech., May 1, 1990.
(Columbus' 6th choice, 135th overall, in 2008 Entry Draft).

			Regular Season					Playoffs				
Season	Club	League	GP	G	A	Pts	PIM	GP	G	A	Pts	PIM
2003-04	HC Plzen U17	CzR-U17	4	0	0	0	0	....	....	....	....	....
2004-05	HC Plzen U17	CzR-U17	37	4	1	5	18	....	....	....	....	....
2005-06	HC Plzen U17	CzR-U17	35	26	21	47	91	6	1	5	6	16
	HC Plzen Jr.	CzRep-Jr.	5	1	2	3	6	....	....	....	....	....
2006-07	HC Plzen U17	CzR-U17	2	4	1	5	6	8	5	5	10	30
	HC Plzen Jr.	CzRep-Jr.	34	23	15	38	76	3	1	2	3	24
	Plzen	CzRep	23	1	0	1	18	....	....	....	....	....
2007-08	HC Plzen Jr.	CzRep-Jr.	22	8	13	21	50	5	1	3	4	22
	Beroun	CzRep-2	7	0	0	0	2	....	....	....	....	....
	Plzen	CzRep	20	2	1	3	8	1	0	0	0	0
2008-09	HC Plzen Jr.	CzRep-Jr.	4	1	2	3	10	....	....	....	....	....
	Plzen	CzRep	32	1	1	2	64	17	1	0	1	8
2009-10	Victoriaville Tigres	QMJHL	58	33	42	75	95	16	4	10	14	8

KUDELKA, Tomas (koo-DEHL-kah, TAW-mahsh)

Defense. Shoots left. 6'3", 195 lbs. Born, Gottwaldov, Czech., March 10, 1987.
(Ottawa's 6th choice, 136th overall, in 2005 Entry Draft).

			Regular Season					Playoffs				
Season	Club	League	GP	G	A	Pts	PIM	GP	G	A	Pts	PIM
2002-03	HC Zlin U17	CzR-U17	45	1	16	17	28	3	1	0	1	12
2003-04	HC Zlin U17	CzR-U17	1	0	0	0	2	3	0	0	0	0
	HC Zlin Jr.	CzRep-Jr.	51	1	12	13	95	7	0	0	0	0
	HC Hame Zlin	CzRep	3	0	0	0	0	....	....	....	....	....
2004-05	HC Zlin Jr.	CzRep-Jr.	38	9	8	17	38	....	....	....	....	....
	HC Hame Zlin	CzRep	4	0	0	0	6	....	....	....	....	....
2005-06	Lethbridge	WHL	64	6	25	31	77	6	1	1	2	12
	Binghamton	AHL	5	0	0	0	4	....	....	....	....	....
2006-07	Lethbridge	WHL	59	14	27	41	74	....	....	....	....	....
	Binghamton	AHL	11	1	2	3	8	....	....	....	....	....
2007-08	Binghamton	AHL	35	1	1	2	17	....	....	....	....	....
	Elmira Jackals	ECHL	23	5	14	19	26	1	0	0	0	0
2008-09	Binghamton	AHL	76	7	16	23	67	....	....	....	....	....
2009-10	Binghamton	AHL	55	3	17	20	81	....	....	....	....	....

Signed as a free agent by **Kiev** (Russia-KHL), May 20, 2010.

KUEHNHACKL, Tom (koon-HAH-kuhl, TAWM) PIT.

Center. Shoots left. 6'2", 172 lbs. Born, Landshut, Germany, January 21, 1992.
(Pittsburgh's 3rd choice, 110th overall, in 2010 Entry Draft).

			Regular Season					Playoffs				
Season	Club	League	GP	G	A	Pts	PIM	GP	G	A	Pts	PIM
2007-08	EV Landshut Jr.	Ger-Jr.	30	21	20	41	102	3	1	0	1	2
2008-09	EV Landshut Jr.	Ger-Jr.	6	4	3	7	31	7	5	5	10	27
	Landshut Cann.	German-2	42	11	10	21	34	6	1	0	1	6
2009-10	EV Landshut Jr.	Ger-Jr.	2	1	3	4	0	3	4	4	8	12
	Landshut Cann.	German-2	38	12	9	21	38	6	0	0	0	2
	Augsburg	Germany	4	0	0	0	0	....	....	....	....	....

KUGRYSHEV, Dmitry (koo-GRIH-shev, dih-MEE-tree) WSH.

Right wing. Shoots right. 5'11", 192 lbs. Born, Balakovo, USSR, January 18, 1990.
(Washington's 4th choice, 58th overall, in 2008 Entry Draft).

			Regular Season					Playoffs				
Season	Club	League	GP	G	A	Pts	PIM	GP	G	A	Pts	PIM
2005-06	CSKA Moscow 2	Russia-3	STATISTICS NOT AVAILABLE									
2006-07	CSKA Moscow 2	Russia-3	STATISTICS NOT AVAILABLE									
2007-08	CSKA Moscow 2	Russia-3	29	25	25	50	60	7	5	6	11	6
2008-09	Quebec Remparts	QMJHL	57	34	40	74	38	17	6	14	20	24
2009-10	Quebec Remparts	QMJHL	66	29	58	87	52	9	4	6	10	8

QMJHL All-Rookie Team (2009) • Canadian Major Junior All-Rookie Team (2009)

KULYASH, Denis (kuh-L'YASH, DEH-nihs) NSH.

Defense. Shoots left. 6'3", 199 lbs. Born, Omsk, USSR, May 31, 1983.
(Nashville's 9th choice, 243rd overall, in 2004 Entry Draft).

			Regular Season					Playoffs				
Season	Club	League	GP	G	A	Pts	PIM	GP	G	A	Pts	PIM
2003-04	CSK VVS Samara 2	Russia-3	STATISTICS NOT AVAILABLE									
	CSKA Moscow	Russia	10	1	0	1	8	....	....	....	....	....
2004-05	CSKA Moscow	Russia	59	8	10	18	58	....	....	....	....	....
2005-06	Dynamo Moscow	Russia	44	12	5	17	117	4	0	2	2	6
2006-07	Dynamo Moscow	Russia	48	3	9	12	58	2	0	0	0	2
2007-08	CSKA Moscow	Russia	53	9	13	22	79	6	1	1	2	34
2008-09	CSKA Moscow	Rus-KHL	56	16	10	26	62	8	2	1	3	20
2009-10	CSKA Moscow	Rus-KHL	35	11	10	21	34	....	....	....	....	....
	Omsk	Rus-KHL	6	1	1	2	6	3	0	0	0	4

KUNDRATEK, Tomas (kuhn-DRAT-ehk, TAW-mahsh) NYR

Defense. Shoots right. 6'2", 200 lbs. Born, Prerov, Czech., December 26, 1989.
(NY Rangers' 4th choice, 90th overall, in 2008 Entry Draft).

			Regular Season					Playoffs				
Season	Club	League	GP	G	A	Pts	PIM	GP	G	A	Pts	PIM
2003-04	HC Prerov U17	CzR-U17	6	0	0	0	0	....	....	....	....	....
2004-05	HC Prerov U17	CzR-U17	38	2	7	9	26	4	0	1	1	4
2005-06	HC Trinec U17	CzR-U17	39	5	13	18	96	2	0	1	1	10
	HC Trinec Jr.	CzRep-Jr.	12	1	1	2	16	7	1	1	2	4
2006-07	HC Trinec Jr.	CzRep-Jr.	33	4	13	17	93	3	1	1	2	10
	HC Ocelari Trinec	CzRep	22	0	1	1	4	4	0	0	0	6
2007-08	HC Trinec Jr.	CzRep-Jr.	14	3	6	9	28	....	....	....	....	....
	Prostejov	CzRep-2	15	1	0	1	10	....	....	....	....	....
	HC Havirov	CzRep-2	2	0	0	0	2	....	....	....	....	....
	HC Ocelari Trinec	CzRep	14	0	1	1	10	7	0	2	2	8
2008-09	Hartford Wolf Pack	AHL	....	....	....	....	....	1	0	0	0	0
	Medicine Hat	WHL	51	4	19	23	63	11	0	6	6	12
2009-10	Medicine Hat	WHL	65	2	33	35	62	12	1	5	6	23

KUZNETSOV, Evgeny (kooz-neht-SAWF, ehv-GEH-nee) WSH.

Center. Shoots left. 6', 172 lbs. Born, Chelyabinsk, Russia, May 19, 1992.
(Washington's 1st choice, 26th overall, in 2010 Entry Draft).

			Regular Season					Playoffs				
Season	Club	League	GP	G	A	Pts	PIM	GP	G	A	Pts	PIM
2007-08	Chelyabinsk 2	Russia-3	2	0	0	0	0	....	....	....	....	....
2008-09	Chelyabinsk 2	Russia-3	22	5	11	16	40	....	....	....	....	....
2009-10	Chelyabinsk Jr.	Russia-Jr.	9	4	12	16	8	2	1	2	3	4
	Chelyabinsk	Rus-KHL	35	2	6	8	10	4	1	0	1	0

KVETON, David (KVEH-tuhn, DAY-vihd) NYR

Right wing. Shoots left. 6', 190 lbs. Born, Novy Jicin, Czech., January 3, 1988.
(NY Rangers' 4th choice, 104th overall, in 2006 Entry Draft).

			Regular Season					Playoffs				
Season	Club	League	GP	G	A	Pts	PIM	GP	G	A	Pts	PIM
2003-04	HC Vsetin U17	CzR-U17	14	9	11	20	35	....	....	....	....	....
	HC Vsetin Jr.	CzRep-Jr.	41	12	11	23	14	5	2	3	5	2
	TJ Novy Jicin	CzRep-3	1	0	1	1	0	....	....	....	....	....
	HC Vsetin	CzRep	1	0	0	0	0	....	....	....	....	....
2004-05	HC Vsetin U17	CzR-U17	1	1	0	1	0	....	....	....	....	....
	HC Vsetin Jr.	CzRep-Jr.	36	21	27	48	66	8	6	5	11	4
	TJ Novy Jicin	CzRep-3	7	0	1	1	6	....	....	....	....	....
	HC Vsetin	CzRep	6	1	0	1	0	....	....	....	....	....
2005-06	HC Vsetin Jr.	CzRep-Jr.	1	1	1	2	0	1	0	1	1	0
	HC Sareza Ostrava	CzRep-2	7	2	1	3	2	....	....	....	....	....
	HC Vsetin	CzRep	45	6	4	10	18	....	....	....	....	....
	TJ Novy Jicin	CzRep-3	....	....	....	....	....	5	5	0	5	18
	HC Vsetin	CzRep-Q	....	....	....	....	....	3	1	1	2	2
2006-07	Gatineau	QMJHL	31	5	27	32	17	5	0	0	0	4
	HC Vsetin	CzRep	19	2	0	2	8	....	....	....	....	....
2007-08	HC Ocelari Trinec	CzRep	28	10	5	15	10	....	....	....	....	....
2008-09	HC Ocelari Trinec	CzRep	46	22	22	44	20	5	3	2	5	16
2009-10	HC Ocelari Trinec	CzRep	52	18	17	35	59	5	1	1	2	24

KYTNAR, Milan (KIHT-nahr, MEE-lan) EDM.

Center. Shoots left. 6', 180 lbs. Born, Topolcany, Czech., May 19, 1989.
(Edmonton's 5th choice, 127th overall, in 2007 Entry Draft).

			Regular Season					Playoffs				
Season	Club	League	GP	G	A	Pts	PIM	GP	G	A	Pts	PIM
2003-04	Topolcany U18	Svk-U18	42	17	22	39	90	....	....	....	....	....
2004-05	Topolcany U18	Svk-U18	53	36	65	101	105	....	....	....	....	....
	Topolcany Jr.	Slovak-Jr.	10	2	2	4	8	....	....	....	....	....
2005-06	HK Trnava U18	Svk-U18	30	18	23	41	106	....	....	....	....	....
	HK Trnava Jr.	Slovak-Jr.	12	1	2	3	20	....	....	....	....	....
	Topolcany U18	Svk-U18	8	4	4	8	4	....	....	....	....	....
	Topolcany Jr.	Slovak-Jr.	6	6	4	10	8	....	....	....	....	....
2006-07	HC Topolcany U18	Svk-U18	53	37	54	91	84	....	....	....	....	....
	HC Topolcany	Slovak-2	22	4	7	11	53	5	1	1	2	4
2007-08	Kelowna Rockets	WHL	62	9	13	22	66	7	0	0	0	4
2008-09	Saskatoon Blades	WHL	65	27	37	64	89	7	3	1	4	14
2009-10	Saskatoon Blades	WHL	3	0	1	1	2	....	....	....	....	....
	Vancouver Giants	WHL	42	14	25	39	40	16	3	12	15	23

LABRECQUE, Dave (lah-BREHK, DAYV) PHI.

Center. Shoots left. 6', 170 lbs. Born, Vanier, Que., January 27, 1990.
(Philadelphia's 4th choice, 153rd overall, in 2009 Entry Draft).

			Regular Season					Playoffs				
Season	Club	League	GP	G	A	Pts	PIM	GP	G	A	Pts	PIM
2005-06	Sem. St-Francois	QAAA	43	18	30	48	82	3	2	1	3	2
2006-07	Sem. St-Francois	QAAA	38	21	39	60	92	18	13	17	30	28
	Shawinigan	QMJHL	4	1	0	1	0	....	....	....	....	....
2007-08	Que. AssurExperts	QJHL	36	17	30	47	22	....	....	....	....	....
	Shawinigan	QMJHL	22	4	7	11	26	5	1	2	3	6
2008-09	Shawinigan	QMJHL	59	13	48	61	76	20	3	16	19	34
2009-10	Shawinigan	QMJHL	63	23	40	63	88	4	1	1	2	4

LABRIE, Hubert (la-BREE, hew-BAIR) DAL.

Defense. Shoots left. 5'11", 170 lbs. Born, Victoriaville, Que., July 12, 1991.

			Regular Season					Playoffs				
Season	Club	League	GP	G	A	Pts	PIM	GP	G	A	Pts	PIM
2007-08	Gatineau	QMJHL	61	2	15	17	79	19	1	3	4	26
2008-09	Gatineau	QMJHL	55	1	3	4	82	5	0	0	0	14
2009-10	Gatineau	QMJHL	67	4	16	20	99	11	3	4	7	20

Signed as a free agent by **Dallas**, September 18, 2009.

LABRIE, Pierre-Cedric (la-BREE, pee-AIR-SEH-DRIHK)

Left wing. Shoots right. 6'2", 218 lbs. Born, Baie Comeau, Que., December 6, 1986.

			Regular Season					Playoffs				
Season	Club	League	GP	G	A	Pts	PIM	GP	G	A	Pts	PIM
2003-04	Coaticook	QJHL	46	13	12	25	96	....	....	....	....	....
	Quebec Remparts	QMJHL	1	0	0	0	0	....	....	....	....	....
2004-05	Coaticook	QJHL	15	3	4	7	59	....	....	....	....	....
2005-06	Restigouche Tigers	MJrHL	54	43	43	86	153	....	....	....	....	....
	Baie-Comeau	QMJHL	....	....	....	....	....	4	2	2	4	6
2006-07	Baie-Comeau	QMJHL	68	35	28	63	113	11	8	6	14	35
2007-08	Manitoba Moose	AHL	67	7	11	18	108	3	0	0	0	2
2008-09	Manitoba Moose	AHL	63	6	9	15	79	14	0	1	1	37
2009-10	Manitoba Moose	AHL	45	5	1	6	69	....	....	....	....	....
	Peoria Rivermen	AHL	16	0	1	1	16	....	....	....	....	....

Signed as a free agent by **Vancouver**, July 3, 2007. Traded to **St. Louis** by **Vancouver** for Yan Stastny, March 3, 2010.

LAGACE, Jacob (LEH-gah-see, JAY-kawb) BUF.

Left wing. Shoots left. 5'11", 204 lbs. Born, Beloeil, Que., January 9, 1990.
(Buffalo's 7th choice, 134th overall, in 2008 Entry Draft).

			Regular Season					Playoffs				
Season	Club	League	GP	G	A	Pts	PIM	GP	G	A	Pts	PIM
2005-06	C.A.-Girouord	QAAA	38	10	11	21	....	8	0	2	2	4
2006-07	C.A.-Girouord	QAAA	44	24	29	53	46	4	1	4	5	2
2007-08	Chicoutimi	QMJHL	67	23	39	62	40	6	3	2	5	7
2008-09	Chicoutimi	QMJHL	64	32	37	69	52	4	1	2	3	4
2009-10	Chicoutimi	QMJHL	35	30	23	53	20	....	....	....	....	....
	Cape Breton	QMJHL	25	5	15	20	32	5	0	3	3	4
	Portland Pirates	AHL	....	....	....	....	....	1	0	0	0	0

QMJHL All-Rookie Team (2008)

LAJUNEN, Jani (LA-joo-nehn, YAH-nee) **NSH.**

Center. Shoots left. 6'1", 190 lbs. Born, Helsinki, Finland, June 16, 1990.
(Nashville's 6th choice, 201st overall, in 2008 Entry Draft).

			Regular Season					Playoffs				
Season	Club	League	GP	G	A	Pts	PIM	GP	G	A	Pts	PIM
2005-06	K-Vantaa U18	Fin-U18	2	0	0	0	0	....	....	....	....	....
2006-07	Blues Espoo U18	Fin-U18	28	5	12	17	20	6	1	1	2	4
2007-08	Blues Espoo U18	Fin-U18	1	1	0	1	2	4	2	2	4	0
	Blues Espoo Jr.	Fin-Jr.	25	4	10	14	14	3	0	0	0	0
	Blues Espoo	Finland	1	0	0	0	0	....	....	....	....	....
2008-09	Suomi U20	Finland-2	2	2	2	4	0	....	....	....	....	....
	Blues Espoo Jr.	Fin-Jr.	25	16	10	26	24	8	2	1	3	12
2009-10	Suomi U20	Finland-2	2	0	0	0	0	....	....	....	....	....
	Blues Espoo	Finland	46	6	9	15	34	3	0	0	0	2
	Blues Espoo Jr.	Fin-Jr.	4	1	1	2	0	....	....	....	....	....

LALONDE, Shawn (la-LAWND, SHAWN) **CHI.**

Defense. Shoots right. 6'1", 192 lbs. Born, Ottawa, Ont., March 10, 1990.
(Chicago's 2nd choice, 68th overall, in 2008 Entry Draft).

			Regular Season					Playoffs				
Season	Club	League	GP	G	A	Pts	PIM	GP	G	A	Pts	PIM
2005-06	Cumberland	Minor-ON	60	18	36	54	98	....	....	....	....	....
2006-07	Belleville Bulls	OHL	58	6	20	26	71	13	1	1	2	6
2007-08	Belleville Bulls	OHL	66	9	22	31	67	21	2	7	9	25
2008-09	Belleville Bulls	OHL	66	19	34	53	73	17	3	9	12	36
2009-10	Belleville Bulls	OHL	58	13	43	56	87	....	....	....	....	....
	Rockford IceHogs	AHL	8	1	1	2	11	3	0	0	0	2

LAMMERS, John (LA-muhrs, JAWN)

Left wing. Shoots left. 5'11", 184 lbs. Born, Bowmanville, Ont., January 29, 1986.
(Dallas' 5th choice, 86th overall, in 2004 Entry Draft).

			Regular Season					Playoffs				
Season	Club	League	GP	G	A	Pts	PIM	GP	G	A	Pts	PIM
2001-02	Langley Bantams	Minor-BC	64	51	69	120	30	....	....	....	....	....
	Lethbridge	WHL	5	0	0	0	0	....	....	....	....	....
2002-03	Lethbridge	WHL	53	17	15	32	11	....	....	....	....	....
2003-04	Lethbridge	WHL	62	21	24	45	31	....	....	....	....	....
2004-05	Lethbridge	WHL	66	17	30	47	43	5	0	0	0	2
2005-06	Everett Silvertips	WHL	70	38	37	75	25	15	5	6	11	12
2006-07	Iowa Stars	AHL	52	6	8	14	14	....	....	....	....	....
	Idaho Steelheads	ECHL	9	2	2	4	4	22	7	12	19	2
2007-08	Iowa Stars	AHL	1	0	0	0	0	....	....	....	....	....
	Idaho Steelheads	ECHL	36	27	16	43	22	4	0	3	3	2
	Assat Pori	Finland	23	0	4	4	24	....	....	....	....	....
2008-09	Houston Aeros	AHL	57	12	14	26	40	18	0	8	8	4
2009-10	Manitoba Moose	AHL	11	0	0	0	2	....	....	....	....	....
	Providence Bruins	AHL	31	8	9	17	8	....	....	....	....	....
	Alaska Aces	ECHL	25	20	15	35	12	....	....	....	....	....
	Abbotsford Heat	AHL	4	1	4	5	2	12	2	5	7	2

Signed as a free agent by **Manitoba** (AHL), October 27 2009.

LANDER, Anton (LAN-duhr, AN-tawn) **EDM.**

Center. Shoots left. 6', 194 lbs. Born, Sundsvall, Sweden, April 24, 1991.
(Edmonton's 2nd choice, 40th overall, in 2009 Entry Draft).

			Regular Season					Playoffs				
Season	Club	League	GP	G	A	Pts	PIM	GP	G	A	Pts	PIM
2005-06	Timra IK U18	Swe-U18	14	1	6	7	14	....	....	....	....	....
2006-07	Timra IK U18	Swe-U18	12	6	10	16	14	2	1	2	3	0
	Timra IK Jr.	Swe-Jr.	10	2	1	3	10	....	....	....	....	....
2007-08	Timra IK U18	Swe-U18	4	6	4	10	8	....	....	....	....	....
	Timra IK Jr.	Swe-Jr.	18	5	14	19	39	....	....	....	....	....
	Timra IK	Sweden	32	1	2	3	4	10	0	0	0	0
2008-09	Timra IK Jr.	Swe-Jr.	8	5	1	6	8	....	....	....	....	....
	Timra IK	Sweden	47	4	6	10	12	7	0	0	0	4
2009-10	Timra IK	Sweden	49	7	9	16	14	5	0	2	2	2

LANE, Philip (LAYN, FIHL-ihp) **PHX.**

Right wing. Shoots right. 6'2", 194 lbs. Born, Rochester, NY, May 29, 1992.
(Phoenix's 3rd choice, 52nd overall, in 2010 Entry Draft).

			Regular Season					Playoffs				
Season	Club	League	GP	G	A	Pts	PIM	GP	G	A	Pts	PIM
2008-09	Buffalo Jr. Sabres	OJHL	45	18	24	42	72	5	0	0	0	6
2009-10	Brampton	OHL	64	18	14	32	52	11	3	0	3	14

LANE, Tanner (LAYN, TA-nuhr) **ATL.**

Center. Shoots left. 6'2", 172 lbs. Born, Detroit Lakes, MN, August 13, 1992.
(Atlanta's 7th choice, 160th overall, in 2010 Entry Draft).

			Regular Season					Playoffs				
Season	Club	League	GP	G	A	Pts	PIM	GP	G	A	Pts	PIM
2007-08	Detroit Lakes	High-MN	26	24	20	44	28	....	....	....	....	....
2008-09	Detroit Lakes	High-MN	26	26	26	52	50	....	....	....	....	....
2009-10	Team Great Plains	UMHSEL	21	8	7	15	....	....	....	....	....	....
	Detroit Lakes	High-MN	25	49	41	*90	62	1	0	0	0	2

• Signed Letter of Intent to attend **University of Nebraska-Omaha** (WCHA) in fall of 2011 or 2012.

LANNON, Ryan (LA-nuhn, RIGH-uhn)

Defense. Shoots left. 6'2", 220 lbs. Born, Worcester, MA, December 14, 1982.
(Pittsburgh's 10th choice, 239th overall, in 2002 Entry Draft).

			Regular Season					Playoffs				
Season	Club	League	GP	G	A	Pts	PIM	GP	G	A	Pts	PIM
1998-99	USNTDP	NAHL	56	3	4	7	36	....	....	....	....	....
99-2000	Cushing	High-MA	STATISTICS NOT AVAILABLE									
2000-01	Cushing	High-MA	STATISTICS NOT AVAILABLE									
2001-02	Harvard Crimson	ECAC	34	0	2	2	38	....	....	....	....	....
2002-03	Harvard Crimson	ECAC	34	3	11	14	39	....	....	....	....	....
2003-04	Harvard Crimson	ECAC	35	0	9	9	36	....	....	....	....	....
2004-05	Harvard Crimson	ECAC	33	1	12	13	34	....	....	....	....	....
2005-06	Wilkes-Barre	AHL	74	2	8	10	65	11	0	0	0	8
2006-07	Wilkes-Barre	AHL	68	0	19	19	71	11	0	2	2	14
2007-08	Wilkes-Barre	AHL	75	3	10	13	29	23	1	6	7	2
2008-09	San Antonio	AHL	63	0	5	5	33	....	....	....	....	....
2009-10	Houston Aeros	AHL	27	1	1	2	8	....	....	....	....	....

Signed as a free agent by **Phoenix**, July 15, 2008. Signed as a free agent by **Minnesota** July 23, 2009.

LAPOINT, Derrick (luh-POYNT, DAIR-ihk) **FLA**

Defense. Shoots left. 6'3", 175 lbs. Born, Eau Claire, MA, May 13, 1988.
(Florida's 4th choice, 116th overall, in 2006 Entry Draft).

			Regular Season					Playoffs				
Season	Club	League	GP	G	A	Pts	PIM	GP	G	A	Pts	PIM
2004-05	Eau Claire North	High-WI	23	9	28	37	14	....	....	....	....	....
2005-06	Eau Claire North	High-WI	23	6	26	32	34	....	....	....	....	....
2006-07	Green Bay	USHL	59	13	36	49	48	4	0	2	2	2
2007-08	North Dakota	WCHA	31	2	5	7	34	....	....	....	....	....
2008-09	North Dakota	WCHA	32	1	4	5	12	....	....	....	....	....
2009-10	North Dakota	WCHA	43	2	20	22	16	....	....	....	....	....

USHL All-Rookie Team (2007) • USHL First All-Star Team (2007)

LARKIN, Thomas (LAHR-kihn, TAW-muhs) **CBJ**

Defense. Shoots right. 6'5", 223 lbs. Born, London, England, December 31, 1990.
(Columbus' 4th choice, 137th overall, in 2009 Entry Draft).

			Regular Season					Playoffs				
Season	Club	League	GP	G	A	Pts	PIM	GP	G	A	Pts	PIM
2006-07	Exeter	High-NH	28	1	7	8	5	....	....	....	....	....
2007-08	Exeter	High-NH	29	6	15	21	18	....	....	....	....	....
2008-09	Exeter	High-NH	35	14	38	52	30	....	....	....	....	....
	Little Bruins	Minor-MA	18	1	1	2	10	....	....	....	....	....
2009-10	Colgate	ECAC	33	3	16	19	32	....	....	....	....	....

LARSON, Nick (LAHR-suhn, NIHK-oh-las) **CGY.**

Left wing. Shoots left. 6'1", 195 lbs. Born, St.Paul, MN, November 14, 1989.
(Calgary's 4th choice, 108th overall, in 2008 Entry Draft).

			Regular Season					Playoffs				
Season	Club	League	GP	G	A	Pts	PIM	GP	G	A	Pts	PIM
2006-07	Saint Thomas	High-MN	25	20	30	50	....	....	....	....	....	....
	Team Southeast	UMWEHL	11	5	6	11	....	....	....	....	....	....
2007-08	Waterloo	USHL	57	19	19	38	66	9	3	2	5	31
2008-09	Waterloo	USHL	51	19	17	36	144	3	0	0	0	4
2009-10	U. of Notre Dame	CCHA	35	6	5	11	47	....	....	....	....	....

LARSON, Nick (LAR-suhn, NIHK) **WSH.**

Center. Shoots right. 6'1", 186 lbs. Born, Stillwater, MN, January 16, 1989.
(Washington's 9th choice, 185th overall, in 2007 Entry Draft).

			Regular Season					Playoffs				
Season	Club	League	GP	G	A	Pts	PIM	GP	G	A	Pts	PIM
2004-05	Hill-Murray	High-MN	26	9	15	24	6	....	....	....	....	....
2005-06	Hill-Murray	High-MN	....	41	38	79	....	....	....	....	....	....
2006-07	Hill-Murray	High-MN	29	31	30	61	16	....	....	....	....	....
	Omaha Lancers	USHL	10	3	2	5	6	....	....	....	....	....
2007-08			DID NOT PLAY – INJURED									
2008-09	U. of Minnesota	WCHA	13	1	1	2	2	....	....	....	....	....
2009-10	U. of Minnesota	WCHA	33	4	4	8	10	....	....	....	....	....

• Missed entire 2007-08 season and start of 2008-09 season recovering from back injury.

LARSSON, Johan (LAHR-suhn, YOH-han) **MIN.**

Left wing. Shoots left. 5'11", 200 lbs. Born, Lau, Sweden, July 25, 1992.
(Minnesota's 3rd choice, 56th overall, in 2010 Entry Draft).

			Regular Season					Playoffs				
Season	Club	League	GP	G	A	Pts	PIM	GP	G	A	Pts	PIM
2005-06	Sudrets HC Hemse	Sweden-4	2	0	2	2	2	....	....	....	....	....
2006-07	Sudrets HC Hemse	Sweden-4	29	13	7	20	40	....	....	....	....	....
2007-08	Sudrets HC Hemse	Sweden-4	25	11	11	22	71	....	....	....	....	....
2008-09	Brynas U18	Swe-U18	11	6	4	10	76	3	0	3	3	2
	Brynas IF Gavle Jr.	Swe-Jr.	33	4	5	9	55	5	0	0	0	2
2009-10	Brynas U18	Swe-U18	4	1	1	2	2	4	4	4	8	6
	Brynas IF Gavle Jr.	Swe-Jr.	40	15	19	34	80	5	1	1	2	2

LASHOFF, Brian (LASH-awf, BRIGH-uhn) **DET.**

Defense. Shoots left. 6'3", 204 lbs. Born, Albany, NY, July 16, 1990.

			Regular Season					Playoffs				
Season	Club	League	GP	G	A	Pts	PIM	GP	G	A	Pts	PIM
2006-07	Barrie Colts	OHL	47	2	10	12	20	5	0	1	1	2
2007-08	Barrie Colts	OHL	50	5	15	20	44	8	0	1	1	4
2008-09	Barrie Colts	OHL	25	1	12	13	19	....	....	....	....	....
	Kingston	OHL	35	6	13	19	32	....	....	....	....	....
	Grand Rapids	AHL	6	1	4	5	0	8	1	4	5	2
2009-10	Kingston	OHL	58	6	21	27	71	7	0	0	0	12
	Grand Rapids	AHL	6	0	2	2	2	....	....	....	....	....

Signed as a free agent by **Detroit**, October 1, 2008.

LASU, Nicklas (LA-soo, NIHK-luhs) **ATL.**

Left wing. Shoots left. 6', 180 lbs. Born, Molndal, Sweden, September 16, 1989.
(Atlanta's 5th choice, 124th overall, in 2008 Entry Draft).

			Regular Season					Playoffs				
Season	Club	League	GP	G	A	Pts	PIM	GP	G	A	Pts	PIM
2005-06	Frolunda U18	Swe-U18	14	3	3	6	2	2	1	0	1	2
2006-07	Frolunda U18	Swe-U18	5	5	5	10	12	7	2	6	8	6
	Frolunda Jr.	Swe-Jr.	39	11	14	25	30	7	0	0	0	4
2007-08	Frolunda Jr.	Swe-Jr.	41	19	34	53	42	8	5	5	10	4
	Frolunda	Sweden	2	0	0	0	0	....	....	....	....	....
2008-09	Frolunda Jr.	Swe-Jr.	4	3	1	4	33	....	....	....	....	....
	Boras HC	Sweden-2	21	4	6	10	35	....	....	....	....	....
	Frolunda	Sweden	14	3	1	4	4	11	0	1	1	8
2009-10	Boras HC	Sweden-2	8	5	2	7	2	....	....	....	....	....
	Frolunda	Sweden	51	2	7	9	10	7	0	1	1	2

LATTA, Michael (LA-tuh, MIGH-kuhl) **NSH.**

Center. Shoots right. 6', 214 lbs. Born, Kitchener, Ont., May 25, 1991.
(Nashville's 5th choice, 72nd overall, in 2009 Entry Draft).

			Regular Season					Playoffs				
Season	Club	League	GP	G	A	Pts	PIM	GP	G	A	Pts	PIM
2006-07	Waterloo Wolves	Minor-ON	73	52	66	118	213	....	....	....	....	....
2007-08	Ottawa 67's	OHL	50	14	14	28	78	4	0	1	1	2
2008-09	Ottawa 67's	OHL	23	8	13	21	32	....	....	....	....	....
	Guelph Storm	OHL	42	14	22	36	60	4	0	2	2	12
2009-10	Guelph Storm	OHL	58	33	40	73	157	5	2	7	9	14
	Milwaukee	AHL	....	....	....	....	....	1	0	0	0	0

AURIDSEN, Oliver (LAWR-ihd-suhn, AW-lih-vuhr) PHI.

efense. Shoots left. 6'6", 220 lbs. Born, Gentofte, Denmark, March 24, 1989.
'hiladelphia's 6th choice, 196th overall, in 2009 Entry Draft).

			Regular Season					Playoffs				
eason	Club	League	GP	G	A	Pts	PIM	GP	G	A	Pts	PIM
004-05	IC Gentofte Jr.	Den-Jr.	24	4	12	16	22	....	....	....	....	....
	IC Gentofte	Den-2	8	0	1	1	0	....	....	....	....	....
005-06	Rogle Jr.	Swe-Jr.	28	1	1	2	32	....	....	....	....	....
006-07	Linkopings HC Jr.	Swe-Jr.	34	0	2	2	95	5	0	0	0	8
007-08	Linkopings HC U18	Swe-U18	2	1	3	4	0	....	....	....	....	....
	Tranas AIF	Sweden-3	1	0	0	0	0	....	....	....	....	....
	Linkopings HC Jr.	Swe-Jr.	35	5	6	11	159	1	0	1	1	0
008-09	St. Cloud State	WCHA	28	0	1	1	38	....	....	....	....	....
009-10	St. Cloud State	WCHA	43	6	6	12	54	....	....	....	....	....

AVIN, Joe (LA-vihn, JOH) CHI.

efense. Shoots left. 6'1", 199 lbs. Born, Worcester, MA, July 17, 1989.
Chicago's 6th choice, 126th overall, in 2007 Entry Draft).

			Regular Season					Playoffs				
eason	Club	League	GP	G	A	Pts	PIM	GP	G	A	Pts	PIM
004-05	Boston Jr. Bruins	EmJHL	64	11	44	55	....	....	....	....	....	....
005-06	USNTDP	U-17	19	2	1	3	30	....	....	....	....	....
	USNTDP	NAHL	37	8	10	18	16	12	3	2	5	4
006-07	USNTDP	U-18	23	1	0	1	18	....	....	....	....	....
	USNTDP	NAHL	18	1	8	9	22	6	0	2	2	4
007-08	Providence College	H-East	36	0	8	8	26	....	....	....	....	....
008-09	Providence College	H-East	12	0	1	1	10	....	....	....	....	....
	Omaha Lancers	USHL	33	7	16	23	28	3	0	4	4	8
009-10	Omaha Lancers	USHL	24	5	12	17	16	....	....	....	....	....
	U. of Notre Dame	CCHA	18	3	7	10	4	....	....	....	....	....

AWRENCE, Chris (LOH-rehnts, KRIHS)

enter. Shoots right. 6'4", 210 lbs. Born, Toronto, Ont., February 5, 1987.
Tampa Bay's 3rd choice, 89th overall, in 2005 Entry Draft).

			Regular Season					Playoffs				
eason	Club	League	GP	G	A	Pts	PIM	GP	G	A	Pts	PIM
003-04	Sault Ste. Marie	OHL	62	7	6	13	34	....	....	....	....	....
004-05	Sault Ste. Marie	OHL	68	11	40	51	57	7	3	3	6	4
005-06	Sault Ste. Marie	OHL	29	3	14	17	31	....	....	....	....	....
	Mississauga	OHL	38	20	16	36	60	....	....	....	....	....
006-07	Mississauga	OHL	64	47	41	88	113	5	3	1	4	14
007-08	Norfolk Admirals	AHL	53	5	11	16	32	....	....	....	....	....
008-09	Norfolk Admirals	AHL	48	5	3	8	37	....	....	....	....	....
	Augusta Lynx	ECHL	7	1	2	3	25	....	....	....	....	....
	Mississippi	ECHL	3	0	1	1	5	....	....	....	....	....
009-10	Norfolk Admirals	AHL	72	0	7	7	49	....	....	....	....	....

AWSON, Kyle (LAW-suhn, KIGHL) CAR.

efense. Shoots right. 5'11", 205 lbs. Born, Southfield, MI, January 11, 1987.
Carolina's 9th choice, 198th overall, in 2005 Entry Draft).

			Regular Season					Playoffs				
eason	Club	League	GP	G	A	Pts	PIM	GP	G	A	Pts	PIM
003-04	Det. Honeybaked	MWEHL	61	17	41	58	68	....	....	....	....	....
	Texarkana Bandits	NAHL	....	....	....	....	....	3	0	1	1	0
004-05	USNTDP	U-18	23	2	12	14	6	....	....	....	....	....
	USNTDP	NAHL	8	1	3	4	0	....	....	....	....	....
005-06	Tri-City Storm	USHL	49	9	13	22	40	1	0	0	0	0
006-07	U. of Notre Dame	CCHA	38	4	15	19	14	....	....	....	....	....
007-08	U. of Notre Dame	CCHA	45	5	21	26	36	....	....	....	....	....
008-09	U. of Notre Dame	CCHA	40	4	19	23	44	....	....	....	....	....
009-10	U. of Notre Dame	CCHA	38	4	18	22	44	....	....	....	....	....
	Albany River Rats	AHL	10	0	1	1	0	....	....	....	....	....

CHA All-Rookie Team (2007) • NCAA Championship All-Tournament Team (2008) • CCHA
econd All-Star Team (2009)

EACH, Joey (LEECH, JOH-ee) CGY.

efense. Shoots left. 6'3", 185 lbs. Born, Wadena, Sask., January 29, 1992.
Calgary's 2nd choice, 73rd overall, in 2010 Entry Draft).

			Regular Season					Playoffs				
Season	Club	League	GP	G	A	Pts	PIM	GP	G	A	Pts	PIM
2007-08	Tisdale Trojans	SMHL	42	1	13	14	30	9	1	1	2	2
	Tisdale Trojans	Exhib.	3	1	2	3	0	....	....	....	....	....
2008-09	Tisdale Trojans	SMHL	42	3	26	29	99	6	1	0	1	8
	Kootenay Ice	WHL	12	1	0	1	4	3	0	0	0	0
2009-10	Kootenay Ice	WHL	70	3	23	26	77	6	1	0	1	16

LEBLANC, Louis (luh-BLAWNK, LOU-ee) MTL.

Center. Shoots right. 6', 178 lbs. Born, Pointe-Claire, Que., January 26, 1991.
(Montreal's 1st choice, 18th overall, in 2009 Entry Draft).

			Regular Season					Playoffs				
Season	Club	League	GP	G	A	Pts	PIM	GP	G	A	Pts	PIM
2006-07	Lac St-Louis Lions	QAAA	40	31	18	49	72	22	14	7	21	10
2007-08	Lac St-Louis Lions	QAAA	43	54	37	91	152	14	8	14	22	76
2008-09	Omaha Lancers	USHL	60	28	31	59	78	3	2	1	3	2
2009-10	Harvard Crimson	ECAC	31	11	12	23	50	....	....	....	....	....

USHL All-Rookie Team (2009) • USHL Rookie of the Year (2009) • ECAC All-Rookie Team (2010)

LEBLANC, Peter (luh-BLAHNK, PEE-tuhr) CHI.

Center. Shoots left. 5'9", 186 lbs. Born, Hamilton, Ont., February 3, 1988.
(Chicago's 9th choice, 186th overall, in 2006 Entry Draft).

			Regular Season					Playoffs				
Season	Club	League	GP	G	A	Pts	PIM	GP	G	A	Pts	PIM
2004-05	Hamilton	OPJHL	49	14	22	36	....	....	....	....	....	....
2005-06	Hamilton	OPJHL	22	10	12	22	25	....	....	....	....	....
2006-07	New Hampshire	H-East	39	1	4	5	4	....	....	....	....	....
2007-08	New Hampshire	H-East	37	5	10	15	37	....	....	....	....	....
2008-09	New Hampshire	H-East	38	14	16	30	8	....	....	....	....	....
2009-10	New Hampshire	H-East	39	14	21	35	24	....	....	....	....	....

OPJHL Rookie of the Year (2005)

• Missed majority of 2005-06 season recovering from mononucleosis.

LEDDY, Nick (LEH-dee, NIHK) CHI.

Defense. Shoots left. 5'11", 179 lbs. Born, Eden Prairie, MN, March 20, 1991.
(Minnesota's 1st choice, 16th overall, in 2009 Entry Draft).

			Regular Season					Playoffs				
Season	Club	League	GP	G	A	Pts	PIM	GP	G	A	Pts	PIM
2006-07	Eden Prairie Eagles	High-MN	28	2	16	18	10	....	....	....	....	....
2007-08	Eden Prairie Eagles	High-MN	27	6	22	28	14	....	....	....	....	....
	USNTDP	U-18	4	0	2	2	....	....	....	....	....	....
2008-09	Eden Prairie Eagles	High-MN	31	12	33	45	26	....	....	....	....	....
	Team Southwest	UMHSEL	24	9	11	20	....	....	....	....	....	....
2009-10	U. of Minnesota	WCHA	30	3	8	11	4	....	....	....	....	....

Traded to **Chicago** by **Minnesota** with Kim Johnsson for Cam Barker, February 12, 2010.

LEE, Anders (LEE, AN-duhrz) NYI

Center. Shoots left. 6'2", 209 lbs. Born, St.Paul, MN, July 3, 1990.
(NY Islanders' 7th choice, 152nd overall, in 2009 Entry Draft).

			Regular Season					Playoffs				
Season	Club	League	GP	G	A	Pts	PIM	GP	G	A	Pts	PIM
2006-07	Saint Thomas	High-MN	31	24	17	41	....	....	....	....	....	....
2007-08	Edina Hornets	High-MN	31	32	22	54	....	....	....	....	....	....
2008-09	Edina Hornets	High-MN	31	25	59	84	30	....	....	....	....	....
	Team Southwest	UMHSEL	18	12	17	29	....	....	....	....	....	....
2009-10	Green Bay	USHL	59	35	31	66	54	12	*10	*12	*22	13

USHL All-Rookie Team (2010) • USHL First All-Star Team (2010) • USHL Rookie of the Year (2010)

• Signed Letter of Intent to attend **University of Notre Dame** (CCHA) in fall of 2010.

LEE, Chris (LEE, KRIHS)

Defense. Shoots left. 6', 185 lbs. Born, MacTier, Ont., October 3, 1980.

			Regular Season					Playoffs				
Season	Club	League	GP	G	A	Pts	PIM	GP	G	A	Pts	PIM
2004-05	Florida Everblades	ECHL	68	5	22	27	16	15	2	9	11	6
2005-06	Florida Everblades	ECHL	52	10	27	37	56	8	2	1	3	4
2006-07	Albany River Rats	AHL	3	0	1	1	4	....	....	....	....	....
	Bridgeport	AHL	1	0	0	0	0	....	....	....	....	....
	Omaha	AHL	32	4	13	17	16	6	3	0	3	6
	Florida Everblades	ECHL	37	6	19	25	22	9	3	1	4	0
2007-08	Iowa Stars	AHL	68	7	21	28	42	....	....	....	....	....
2008-09	Bridgeport	AHL	66	6	24	30	36	5	0	3	3	2
2009-10	Wilkes-Barre	AHL	79	9	30	39	30	4	0	1	1	0

Signed as a free agent by **NY Islanders**, July 3, 2008. Signed as a free agent by **Pittsburgh**, July 5. 2009. Signed as a free agent by **Koln** (Germany), August 3, 2010.

LEE, John (LEE, JAWN) FLA.

Defense. Shoots right. 6'2", 173 lbs. Born, Fargo, ND, January 16, 1989.
(Florida's 5th choice, 131st overall, in 2007 Entry Draft).

			Regular Season					Playoffs				
Season	Club	League	GP	G	A	Pts	PIM	GP	G	A	Pts	PIM
2004-05	Moorhead Spuds	High-MN	3	0	1	1	0	....	....	....	....	....
2005-06	Moorhead Spuds	High-MN	26	6	21	27	50	....	....	....	....	....
2006-07	Moorhead Spuds	High-MN	26	6	33	39	62	....	....	....	....	....
	Waterloo	USHL	27	2	7	9	56	9	0	3	3	4
2007-08	Waterloo	USHL	59	1	11	12	106	11	0	4	4	24
2008-09	U. of Denver	WCHA	39	0	5	5	38	....	....	....	....	....
2009-10	U. of Denver	WCHA	41	2	10	12	55	....	....	....	....	....

LEFEBVRE, Philippe (luh-FAYV, fihl-EEP) MTL.

Left wing. Shoots left. 6'1", 193 lbs. Born, Trois-Rivieres, Que., February 28, 1991.

			Regular Season					Playoffs				
Season	Club	League	GP	G	A	Pts	PIM	GP	G	A	Pts	PIM
2006-07	Trois-Rivieres	QAAA	43	25	23	48	56	8	3	6	9	6
2007-08	Drummondville	QMJHL	62	10	15	25	16	....	....	....	....	....
2008-09	Drummondville	QMJHL	68	21	27	48	38	19	3	5	8	2
2009-10	Drummondville	QMJHL	66	26	29	55	38	14	2	4	6	9

Signed as a free agent by **Montreal**, September 15, 2009.

LEGAULT, Maxime (luh-GOH, max-EEM) BUF.

Right wing. Shoots right. 6'2", 195 lbs. Born, Ste. Agathe, Que., March 28, 1989.
(Buffalo's 6th choice, 194th overall, in 2009 Entry Draft).

			Regular Season					Playoffs				
Season	Club	League	GP	G	A	Pts	PIM	GP	G	A	Pts	PIM
2005-06	Laval-Laurentides	QAAA	36	13	15	28	138	4	2	1	3	21
2006-07	Shawinigan	QMJHL	55	7	12	19	98	4	0	0	0	4
2007-08	Shawinigan	QMJHL	31	6	4	10	61	....	....	....	....	....
2008-09	Shawinigan	QMJHL	63	28	16	44	66	21	10	3	13	23
2009-10	Shawinigan	QMJHL	22	10	10	20	29	....	....	....	....	....
	Cape Breton	QMJHL	21	7	12	19	25	5	1	0	1	4
	Portland Pirates	AHL	5	0	0	0	4	....	....	....	....	....

LEGEIN, Stefan (LEE-gihn, STEH-fan) PHI.

Right wing. Shoots right. 5'9", 170 lbs. Born, Oakville, Ont., November 24, 1988.
(Columbus' 2nd choice, 37th overall, in 2007 Entry Draft).

			Regular Season					Playoffs				
Season	Club	League	GP	G	A	Pts	PIM	GP	G	A	Pts	PIM
2003-04	Tor. Red Wings	GTHL	33	19	14	33	63	....	....	....	....	....
2004-05	Milton Icehawks	OPJHL	26	7	12	19	18	....	....	....	....	....
	Mississauga	OHL	49	3	5	8	37	5	0	1	1	0
2005-06	Mississauga	OHL	59	7	9	16	101	....	....	....	....	....
2006-07	Mississauga	OHL	64	43	32	75	115	5	3	2	5	0
2007-08	Niagara Ice Dogs	OHL	30	24	13	37	80	10	7	11	18	28
	Syracuse Crunch	AHL	....	....	....	....	....	2	0	0	0	0
2008-09	Syracuse Crunch	AHL	26	1	0	1	4	....	....	....	....	....
2009-10	Syracuse Crunch	AHL	6	2	1	3	0	....	....	....	....	....
	Adirondack	AHL	71	24	10	34	48	....	....	....	....	....

OHL Second All-Star Team (2008)

Traded to **Philadelphia** by **Columbus** for Michael Ratchuk, October 20, 2009.

LEHTERA, Jori (LEH-tuhr-a, YOHR-ee) **ST.L.**

Center. Shoots left. 6'2", 191 lbs. Born, Helsinki, Finland, December 23, 1987.
(St. Louis' 4th choice, 65th overall, in 2008 Entry Draft).

			Regular Season					Playoffs				
Season	Club	League	GP	G	A	Pts	PIM	GP	G	A	Pts	PIM
2003-04	Jokerit U18	Fin-U18	19	0	6	6	2	5	3	1	4	0
2004-05	Jokerit U18	Fin-U18	30	13	37	50	24	7	6	5	11	2
2005-06	Suomi U20	Finland-2	2	0	0	0	0	....	....	....	....	....
	Jokerit Helsinki Jr.	Fin-Jr.	39	14	33	47	16	4	1	4	5	0
2006-07	Suomi U20	Finland-2	10	4	7	11	10	....	....	....	....	....
	Jokerit Helsinki Jr.	Fin-Jr.	24	18	48	66	20	5	1	7	8	2
	Jokerit Helsinki	Finland	28	6	6	12	14	....	....	....	....	....
2007-08	Tappara Tampere	Finland	54	13	29	42	32	11	4	2	6	8
2008-09	Tappara Tampere	Finland	58	9	38	47	34	3	4	5	9	4
	Peoria Rivermen	AHL	7	0	1	1	2	7	1	1	2	10
2009-10	Tappara Tampere	Finland	57	19	*50	*69	58	9	1	9	10	8

LEHTIVUORI, Joonas (leh-tee-VWOO-aw-ree, YOH-nuhs) **PHI.**

Defense. Shoots left. 5'11", 167 lbs. Born, Tampere, Finland, July 19, 1988.
(Philadelphia's 6th choice, 101st overall, in 2006 Entry Draft).

			Regular Season					Playoffs				
Season	Club	League	GP	G	A	Pts	PIM	GP	G	A	Pts	PIM
2004-05	Ilves Tampere U18	Fin-U18	25	5	11	16	12	5	1	1	2	8
2005-06	Ilves Tampere U18	Fin-U18	2	0	1	1	0	6	1	4	5	4
	Ilves Tampere Jr.	Fin-Jr.	39	9	16	25	22	3	0	0	0	4
	Ilves Tampere	Finland	1	0	0	0	0	....	....	....	....	....
2006-07	Ilves Tampere Jr.	Fin-Jr.	15	3	8	11	51	5	0	1	1	2
	Suomi U20	Finland-2	2	0	0	0	0	....	....	....	....	....
	Ilves Tampere	Finland	40	0	0	0	18	4	0	0	0	0
2007-08	Suomi U20	Finland-2	2	0	1	1	2	....	....	....	....	....
	Ilves Tampere	Finland	48	8	13	21	10	9	1	1	2	2
2008-09	Ilves Tampere	Finland	44	4	8	12	16	3	0	0	0	0
2009-10	Adirondack	AHL	66	5	18	23	18	....	....	....	....	....

LERG, Bryan (LEHRG, BRIGH-uhn)

Center. Shoots left. 5'10", 175 lbs. Born, Livonia, MI, January 20, 1986.

			Regular Season					Playoffs				
Season	Club	League	GP	G	A	Pts	PIM	GP	G	A	Pts	PIM
2002-03	USNTDP	U-17	19	11	6	17	5	....	....	....	....	....
	USNTDP	NAHL	46	10	12	22	32	....	....	....	....	....
2003-04	USNTDP	U-18	46	22	25	47	....	....	....	....	....	....
	USNTDP	NAHL	11	5	7	12	10	....	....	....	....	....
2004-05	Michigan State	CCHA	41	10	5	15	14	....	....	....	....	....
2005-06	Michigan State	CCHA	45	15	23	38	26	....	....	....	....	....
2006-07	Michigan State	CCHA	41	23	13	36	21	....	....	....	....	....
2007-08	Michigan State	CCHA	42	20	19	39	18	....	....	....	....	....
	Springfield Falcons	AHL	4	0	2	2	2	....	....	....	....	....
2008-09	Springfield Falcons	AHL	42	9	8	17	24	....	....	....	....	....
	Stockton Thunder	ECHL	7	2	8	10	4	....	....	....	....	....
2009-10	Springfield Falcons	AHL	36	4	3	7	11	....	....	....	....	....

Signed as a free agent by **Edmonton**, April 2, 2008.

LEVEILLE, Daultan (leh-VAY-yay, DAWL-tuhn) **ATL.**

Center. Shoots left. 6', 175 lbs. Born, St. Catharines, Ont., August 10, 1990.
(Atlanta's 2nd choice, 29th overall, in 2008 Entry Draft).

			Regular Season					Playoffs				
Season	Club	League	GP	G	A	Pts	PIM	GP	G	A	Pts	PIM
2005-06	St. Catharines	Minor-ON	46	25	31	56	32	....	....	....	....	....
2006-07	St. Catharines	OJHL-B	48	19	26	45	30	....	....	....	....	....
2007-08	St. Catharines	OJHL-B	45	29	27	56	38	16	*14	16	30	14
2008-09	Michigan State	CCHA	38	9	8	17	12	....	....	....	....	....
2009-10	Michigan State	CCHA	38	6	19	25	16	....	....	....	....	....

LEVI, Austin (LEH-vee, AW-stuhn) **CAR.**

Defense. Shoots left. 6'3", 192 lbs. Born, Columbus, OH, February 16, 1992.
(Carolina's 5th choice, 85th overall, in 2010 Entry Draft).

			Regular Season					Playoffs				
Season	Club	League	GP	G	A	Pts	PIM	GP	G	A	Pts	PIM
2007-08	Det. Compuware	MWEHL	22	0	5	5	33	....	....	....	....	....
2008-09	Plymouth Whalers	OHL	12	0	2	2	4	5	0	0	0	5
2009-10	Plymouth Whalers	OHL	68	3	9	12	116	9	0	0	0	8

LIND, Kevin (LIHND, KEH-vihn) **ANA.**

Defense. Shoots left. 6'3", 202 lbs. Born, Homer Glen, IL, March 31, 1992.
(Anaheim's 7th choice, 177th overall, in 2010 Entry Draft).

			Regular Season					Playoffs				
Season	Club	League	GP	G	A	Pts	PIM	GP	G	A	Pts	PIM
2008-09	Chicago Mission	T1EHL	25	3	0	3	16	....	....	....	....	....
	Chicago Steel	USHL	50	2	3	5	45	....	....	....	....	....
2009-10	Chicago Steel	USHL	55	6	10	16	76	....	....	....	....	....

• Signed Letter of Intent to attend **University of Notre Dame** (CCHA) in fall of 2010.

LINDBERG, Oscar (LIHND-buhrg, AWS-kuhr) **PHX.**

Center. Shoots left. 6', 187 lbs. Born, Skelleftea, Sweden, October 29, 1991.
(Phoenix's 4th choice, 57th overall, in 2010 Entry Draft).

			Regular Season					Playoffs				
Season	Club	League	GP	G	A	Pts	PIM	GP	G	A	Pts	PIM
2007-08	Skelleftea U18	Swe-U18	31	19	29	48	36	....	....	....	....	....
	Skelleftea Jr.	Swe-Jr.	1	0	0	0	2	2	0	1	1	0
2008-09	Skelleftea AIK U18	Swe-U18	6	8	10	18	14	7	4	5	9	8
	Skelleftea AIK Jr.	Swe-Jr.	38	14	19	33	54	5	0	1	1	4
2009-10	Skelleftea AIK Jr.	Swe-Jr.	30	14	23	37	44	1	1	1	2	12
	Skelleftea AIK	Sweden	36	1	1	2	35	10	2	0	2	2

LINDSTROM, Mattias (LIHND-struhm, ma-TEE-uhs) **CAR.**

Left wing. Shoots left. 6'4", 203 lbs. Born, Lulea, Sweden, March 21, 1991.
(Carolina's 3rd choice, 88th overall, in 2009 Entry Draft).

			Regular Season					Playoffs				
Season	Club	League	GP	G	A	Pts	PIM	GP	G	A	Pts	PIM
2007-08	Skelleftea U18	Swe-U18	3	1	0	1	0	....	....	....	....	....
	Skelleftea Jr.	Swe-Jr.	21	5	1	6	40	....	....	....	....	....
2008-09	Skelleftea AIK U18	Swe-U18	2	0	0	0	6	5	0	1	1	10
	Skelleftea AIK Jr.	Swe-Jr.	31	8	5	13	46	5	2	0	2	0
	Skelleftea AIK	Sweden	7	1	0	1	0	7	1	0	1	0
2009-10	Skelleftea AIK Jr.	Swe-Jr.	1	0	0	0	0	....	....	....	....	....

• Missed majority of 2009-10 season recovering from knee injury.

LOGINOV, Denis (LOG-gih-nawv, DEH-nihs) **AT**

Center. Shoots left. 6'1", 210 lbs. Born, Kazan, USSR, May 5, 1985.
(Atlanta's 7th choice, 203rd overall, in 2003 Entry Draft).

			Regular Season					Playoffs				
Season	Club	League	GP	G	A	Pts	PIM	GP	G	A	Pts	PIM
99-2000	Ak Bars Kazan 2	Russia-3	4	0	0	0	0	....	....	....	....	
2000-01	Ak Bars Kazan 2	Russia-3	STATISTICS NOT AVAILABLE									
2001-02	Ak Bars Kazan 2	Russia-3	38	6	10	16	40	....	....	....	....	
	Team Volga	Exhib.	3	0	3	3	27	....	....	....	....	
2002-03	Ak Bars Kazan 2	Russia-3	52	17	24	41	98	....	....	....	....	
	Perm	Russia	1	0	0	0	0	....	....	....	....	
2003-04	Ak Bars Kazan	Russia	16	2	1	3	0	7	1	0	1	
2004-05	Ak Bars Kazan	Russia	2	0	0	0	0	....	....	....	....	
2005-06	Almetjevsk	Russia-2	7	1	0	1	8	....	....	....	....	
	Ak Bars Kazan	Russia	16	1	1	2	10	....	....	....	....	
2006-07	Ak Bars Kazan 2	Russia-3	STATISTICS NOT AVAILABLE									
2007-08	Nizhnekamsk	Russia	6	0	0	0	6	....	....	....	....	
	Volzhsk	Russia-2	10	2	3	5	14	....	....	....	....	
	Orenburg	Russia-2	12	3	3	6	30	....	....	....	....	
2008-09	Rys Podolsk	Russia-2	51	10	5	15	97	3	0	1	1	
2009-10	Almetjevsk	Russia-2	20	7	9	16	24	13	3	6	9	4

LONG, Colin (LAWNG, KAW-lihn) **PHX**

Center. Shoots right. 5'11", 187 lbs. Born, Santa Ana, CA, June 19, 1989.
(Phoenix's 6th choice, 99th overall, in 2008 Entry Draft).

			Regular Season					Playoffs				
Season	Club	League	GP	G	A	Pts	PIM	GP	G	A	Pts	PIM
2005-06	Kelowna Rockets	WHL	20	1	3	4	6	3	0	0	0	
2006-07	Kelowna Rockets	WHL	69	11	17	28	38	....	....	....	....	
2007-08	Kelowna Rockets	WHL	72	31	69	100	41	7	2	10	12	
2008-09	Kelowna Rockets	WHL	68	33	58	91	28	22	4	12	16	
2009-10	San Antonio	AHL	29	2	2	4	10	....	....	....	....	

WHL West First All-Star Team (2008) • WHL West Second All-Star Team (2009)

LOPRIENO, Joe (loh-PRE-eh-noh, JOH) **S.**

Defense. Shoots right. 6'3", 225 lbs. Born, Bloomingdale, IL, October 8, 1986.

			Regular Season					Playoffs				
Season	Club	League	GP	G	A	Pts	PIM	GP	G	A	Pts	PIM
2004-05	Chicago Steel	USHL	50	0	3	3	78	1	0	0	0	
2005-06	Chicago Steel	USHL	45	3	10	13	73	....	....	....	....	
2006-07	Merrimack College	H-East	32	1	3	4	66	....	....	....	....	
2007-08	Merrimack College	H-East	34	2	3	5	74	....	....	....	....	
2008-09	Merrimack College	H-East	22	2	2	4	50	....	....	....	....	
2009-10	Worcester Sharks	AHL	46	0	4	4	52	....	....	....	....	

Signed as a free agent by **San Jose**, March 30, 2009.

LORENZ, Sean (lohr-EHNZ, SHAWN) **MIN**

Defense. Shoots right. 6'1", 191 lbs. Born, Littleton, CO, March 10, 1990.
(Minnesota's 3rd choice, 115th overall, in 2008 Entry Draft).

			Regular Season					Playoffs				
Season	Club	League	GP	G	A	Pts	PIM	GP	G	A	Pts	PIM
2006-07	USNTDP	U-17	6	6	9	15	28	....	....	....	....	
	USNTDP	NAHL	45	1	7	8	26	6	0	0	0	
2007-08	USNTDP	U-18	50	0	8	8	28	....	....	....	....	
	USNTDP	NAHL	14	2	1	3	4	....	....	....	....	
2008-09	U. of Notre Dame	CCHA	40	0	3	3	18	....	....	....	....	
2009-10	U. of Notre Dame	CCHA	34	2	1	3	14	....	....	....	....	

LOVE, Mitch (LUHV, MIHTCH)

Defense. Shoots left. 6', 200 lbs. Born, Quesnel, B.C., June 15, 1984.

			Regular Season					Playoffs				
Season	Club	League	GP	G	A	Pts	PIM	GP	G	A	Pts	PIM
2000-01	Moose Jaw	WHL	51	5	4	9	97	4	0	0	0	
2001-02	Moose Jaw	WHL	16	0	1	1	40	....	....	....	....	
	Swift Current	WHL	52	5	11	16	132	12	0	0	0	3
2002-03	Swift Current	WHL	70	2	15	17	*327	4	1	0	1	1
2003-04	Everett Silvertips	WHL	70	12	15	27	163	21	2	6	8	4
2004-05	Everett Silvertips	WHL	59	9	20	29	142	4	0	2	2	
2005-06	Lowell	AHL	27	0	4	4	68	....	....	....	....	
2006-07	Albany River Rats	AHL	69	1	5	6	184	....	....	....	....	
2007-08	Lake Erie Monsters	AHL	59	2	5	7	213	....	....	....	....	
	Johnstown Chiefs	ECHL	4	0	0	0	16	....	....	....	....	
2008-09	Houston Aeros	AHL	63	2	4	6	214	16	1	0	1	3
2009-10	Peoria Rivermen	AHL	60	1	3	4	129	....	....	....	....	

Signed as a free agent by **Colorado**, October 25, 2005.

LoVECCHIO, Jeff (LOH-veh-kee-oh, JEHF) **BOS**

Left wing. Shoots left. 6'2", 198 lbs. Born, Arlington Heights, IL, August 26, 1985.

			Regular Season					Playoffs				
Season	Club	League	GP	G	A	Pts	PIM	GP	G	A	Pts	PIM
2003-04	River City Lancers	USHL	58	16	13	29	29	3	0	1	1	
2004-05	Omaha Lancers	USHL	57	17	27	44	82	5	1	0	1	
2005-06	Western Mich.	CCHA	40	7	11	18	46	....	....	....	....	
2006-07	Western Mich.	CCHA	37	19	16	35	24	....	....	....	....	
2007-08	Western Mich.	CCHA	36	9	12	21	28	....	....	....	....	
	Providence Bruins	AHL	14	3	2	5	6	6	0	1	1	
2008-09			DID NOT PLAY – INJURED									
2009-10	Providence Bruins	AHL	65	15	9	24	32					

Signed as a free agent by **Boston**, March 18, 2008. • Missed entire 2008-09 season recovering from head injury.

LUCIA, Tony (loo-CHEE-ah, TOH-nee) **S.J**

Left wing. Shoots left. 6', 180 lbs. Born, Wayzata, MN, August 23, 1987.
(San Jose's 8th choice, 193rd overall, in 2005 Entry Draft).

			Regular Season					Playoffs				
Season	Club	League	GP	G	A	Pts	PIM	GP	G	A	Pts	PIM
2003-04	Wayzata	High-MN	31	13	22	35		....	....	....	....	
2004-05	Wayzata	High-MN	24	27	36	63	32	....	....	....	....	
	Omaha Lancers	USHL	11	1	0	1	0	....	....	....	....	
2005-06	Omaha Lancers	USHL	56	12	23	35	25	5	0	0	0	
2006-07	U. of Minnesota	WCHA	43	7	12	19	28	....	....	....	....	
2007-08	U. of Minnesota	WCHA	44	7	11	18	41	....	....	....	....	
2008-09	U. of Minnesota	WCHA	34	9	8	17	43	....	....	....	....	
2009-10	U. of Minnesota	WCHA	39	11	17	28	22	....	....	....	....	
	Worcester Sharks	AHL	4	1	0	1	0	1	0	0	0	

LUDWIG, Trevor (LUHD-wihg, TREH-vuhr) **DAL.**

Defense. Shoots left. 6', 205 lbs. Born, Rhinelander, WI, May 24, 1985.
(Dallas' 7th choice, 183rd overall, in 2004 Entry Draft).

			Regular Season					Playoffs				
Season	Club	League	GP	G	A	Pts	PIM	GP	G	A	Pts	PIM
2002-03	Texas Tornado	NAHL	55	4	5	9	39	....	....	....	....	....
2003-04	Texas Tornado	NAHL	54	5	25	30	50	....	....	....	....	....
2004-05	Providence College	H-East	33	1	6	7	36	....	....	....	....	....
2005-06	Providence College	H-East	27	0	2	2	6	....	....	....	....	....
2006-07	Providence College	H-East	26	0	2	2	37	....	....	....	....	....
2007-08	Providence College	H-East	29	1	3	4	28	....	....	....	....	....
	Iowa Stars	AHL	7	0	3	3	12	....	....	....	....	....
2008-09	Manitoba Moose	AHL	16	0	0	0	18	....	....	....	....	....
	Idaho Steelheads	ECHL	35	2	8	10	41	4	0	0	0	13
2009-10	Texas Stars	AHL	47	3	5	8	62	19	0	1	1	18
	Idaho Steelheads	ECHL	14	1	5	6	24	....	....	....	....	....

NAHL All-Rookie Team (2003) • NAHL First All-Star Team (2004)

LUNDEN, Josh (LUHN-dehn, JAWSH) **PHX.**

Left wing. Shoots left. 6'2", 202 lbs. Born, Burnaby, B.C., February 24, 1986.

			Regular Season					Playoffs				
Season	Club	League	GP	G	A	Pts	PIM	GP	G	A	Pts	PIM
2006-07	Alaska Anchorage	WCHA	31	11	9	20	36	....	....	....	....	....
2007-08	Alaska-Anchorage	WCHA	36	14	13	27	26	....	....	....	....	....
2008-09	Alaska-Anchorage	WCHA	34	14	6	20	26	....	....	....	....	....
2009-10	Alaska-Anchorage	WCHA	25	8	9	17	22	....	....	....	....	....
	San Antonio	AHL	8	0	2	2	7	....	....	....	....	....

Signed as a free agent by **Phoenix**, March 19, 2010.

LUUKKO, Nicholas (LOO-koh, NIH-koh-las) **PHI.**

Defense. Shoots right. 6'2", 180 lbs. Born, West Chester, PA, November 29, 1991.
(Philadelphia's 4th choice, 179th overall, in 2010 Entry Draft).

			Regular Season					Playoffs				
Season	Club	League	GP	G	A	Pts	PIM	GP	G	A	Pts	PIM
2008-09	Team Comcast	AYHL	3	0	1	1	2	....	....	....	....	....
	The Gunnery	High-CT	34	4	11	15	....	....	....	....	....	....
2009-10	The Gunnery	High-CT	....	3	22	25	....	....	....	....	....	....

• Signed Letter of Intent to attend **University of Vermont** (Hockey-East) in fall of 2011.

LYAMIN, Kirill (L'YAH-mihn, kih-RIHL) **OTT.**

Defense. Shoots left. 6'3", 198 lbs. Born, Moscow, USSR, January 13, 1986.
(Ottawa's 2nd choice, 58th overall, in 2004 Entry Draft).

			Regular Season					Playoffs				
Season	Club	League	GP	G	A	Pts	PIM	GP	G	A	Pts	PIM
2001-02	Moscow 18	Exhib.	5	0	3	3	4	....	....	....	....	....
2002-03	CSKA Moscow 2	Russia-3	5	0	0	0	10	....	....	....	....	....
	Moscow 18	Exhib.	5	0	0	0	6	....	....	....	....	....
2003-04	CSKA Moscow 2	Russia-3	STATISTICS NOT AVAILABLE									
	CSKA Moscow	Russia	28	0	3	3	12	....	....	....	....	....
2004-05	CSKA Moscow 2	Russia-3	STATISTICS NOT AVAILABLE									
2005-06	CSKA Moscow	Russia	25	0	1	1	28	2	0	0	0	0
2006-07	CSKA Moscow	Russia	47	1	7	8	48	12	1	0	1	8
2007-08	Mytischi	Russia	40	1	6	7	77	3	0	0	0	0
2008-09	Spartak Moscow	Rus-KHL	54	1	7	8	82	6	0	0	0	4
2009-10	Spartak Moscow	Rus-KHL	48	3	9	12	52	9	0	1	1	8

LYNCH, Kevin (LIHNCH, KEH-vihn) **CBJ**

Center. Shoots right. 6'2", 194 lbs. Born, Grosse Pointe, MI, April 23, 1991.
(Columbus' 2nd choice, 56th overall, in 2009 Entry Draft).

			Regular Season					Playoffs				
Season	Club	League	GP	G	A	Pts	PIM	GP	G	A	Pts	PIM
2006-07	Det. Honeybaked	MWEHL	28	14	14	28	16	....	....	....	....	....
	Det. Honeybaked	Exhib.	24	22	10	32	....	....	....	....	....	....
2007-08	USNTDP	NAHL	43	11	4	15	24	3	2	0	2	2
	USNTDP	U-17	17	6	2	8	18	....	....	....	....	....
2008-09	USNTDP	NAHL	16	8	7	15	14	....	....	....	....	....
	USNTDP	U-18	47	16	17	33	40	....	....	....	....	....
2009-10	U. of Michigan	CCHA	45	6	10	16	44	....	....	....	....	....

LYUBUSHIN, Mikhail (l'yoo-BOOSH-ihn, mih-kigh-EHL) **L.A.**

Defense. Shoots left. 6'2", 216 lbs. Born, Moscow, USSR, July 24, 1983.
(Los Angeles' 9th choice, 215th overall, in 2002 Entry Draft).

			Regular Season					Playoffs				
Season	Club	League	GP	G	A	Pts	PIM	GP	G	A	Pts	PIM
99-2000	Vityaz Podolsk 2	Russia-3	24	2	2	4	69	....	....	....	....	....
2000-01	Krylja Sovetov	Russia-2	2	0	1	1	0	1	0	0	0	0
2001-02	Krylja Sovetov 2	Russia-3	20	3	6	9	24	....	....	....	....	....
	THK Tver	Russia-2	22	1	0	1	18	....	....	....	....	....
	Krylja Sovetov	Russia	13	0	1	1	14	3	0	0	0	0
2002-03	Krylja Sovetov	Russia	49	0	6	6	26	....	....	....	....	....
2003-04	Dynamo Moscow	Russia	38	1	2	3	18	2	0	0	0	2
2004-05	Voskresensk	Russia	21	1	2	3	16	....	....	....	....	....
	Vityaz Chekhov	Russia-2	8	0	2	2	6	14	1	0	1	8
2005-06	Cherepovets	Russia	23	1	4	5	10	....	....	....	....	....
	Avangard Omsk	Russia	26	0	1	1	20	8	0	0	0	4
2006-07	Avangard Omsk	Russia	21	0	1	1	16	3	0	0	0	2
	Avangard Omsk 2	Russia-3	2	0	1	1	4	....	....	....	....	....
2007-08	Avangard Omsk	Russia	42	1	3	4	28	4	0	0	0	2
2008-09	Omsk	Rus-KHL	4	0	1	1	4	....	....	....	....	....
	Nizhny Novgorod	Rus-KHL	25	0	2	2	32	2	0	0	0	2
2009-10	Nizhny Novgorod	Rus-KHL	14	1	0	1	8	....	....	....	....	....

MacARTHUR, Pete (muh-KAR-thuhr, PEET)

Left wing. Shoots left. 5'10", 181 lbs. Born, Clifton Park, NY, June 20, 1985.

			Regular Season					Playoffs				
Season	Club	League	GP	G	A	Pts	PIM	GP	G	A	Pts	PIM
2003-04	Waterloo	USHL	52	18	24	42	33	10	2	8	10	11
2004-05	Boston University	H-East	40	13	14	27	32	....	....	....	....	....
2005-06	Boston University	H-East	40	14	25	39	38	....	....	....	....	....
2006-07	Boston University	H-East	39	16	20	36	26	....	....	....	....	....
2007-08	Boston University	H-East	40	21	24	45	24	....	....	....	....	....
	Bridgeport	AHL	9	0	1	1	6	....	....	....	....	....
2008-09	Rockford IceHogs	AHL	64	14	11	25	27	4	0	0	0	0
	Fresno Falcons	ECHL	3	2	2	4	2	....	....	....	....	....
2009-10	Rockford IceHogs	AHL	71	8	34	42	33	3	0	1	1	0

Signed as a free agent by **Chicago**, July 9, 2009.

MacAULAY, Stephen (muh-KAWL-ee, STEE-vehn) **ST.L.**

Left wing. Shoots left. 6'1", 175 lbs. Born, Halifax, N.S., April 20, 1992.
(St. Louis' 7th choice, 164th overall, in 2010 Entry Draft).

			Regular Season					Playoffs				
Season	Club	League	GP	G	A	Pts	PIM	GP	G	A	Pts	PIM
2007-08	Cole Harbour	NSMHL	34	7	15	22	34	14	8	6	14	....
2008-09	Saint John	QMJHL	47	2	4	6	8	2	0	0	0	0
2009-10	Saint John	QMJHL	56	8	13	21	39	21	2	8	10	10

MacDERMID, Lane (MAK-duhr-mihd, LAYN) **BOS.**

Left wing. Shoots left. 6'3", 205 lbs. Born, Hartford, CT, August 25, 1989.
(Boston's 3rd choice, 112th overall, in 2009 Entry Draft).

			Regular Season					Playoffs				
Season	Club	League	GP	G	A	Pts	PIM	GP	G	A	Pts	PIM
2005-06	Owen Sound	OJHL-B	48	1	7	8	....	....	....	....	....	....
2006-07	Owen Sound	OHL	57	2	5	7	115	4	1	0	1	2
2007-08	Owen Sound	OHL	66	13	11	24	190	....	....	....	....	....
2008-09	Owen Sound	OHL	26	8	6	14	85	....	....	....	....	....
	Windsor Spitfires	OHL	38	7	14	21	112	20	4	5	9	38
2009-10	Providence Bruins	AHL	65	2	3	5	155	....	....	....	....	....

MACEK, Brooks (MA-chehk, BRUKS) **DET.**

Center. Shoots right. 5'11", 180 lbs. Born, Winnipeg, Man., May 15, 1992.
(Detroit's 6th choice, 171st overall, in 2010 Entry Draft).

			Regular Season					Playoffs				
Season	Club	League	GP	G	A	Pts	PIM	GP	G	A	Pts	PIM
2007-08	Notre Dame	SMHL	44	32	30	62	37	10	10	6	16	10
	Notre Dame	Exhib.	1	0	1	1	0	....	....	....	....	....
2008-09	Tri-City Americans	WHL	60	8	16	24	24	11	3	0	3	0
2009-10	Tri-City Americans	WHL	72	21	52	73	26	21	6	11	17	17

MACENAUER, Maxime (MAY-sehn-owr, mahx-EEM) **ANA.**

Center. Shoots left. 6', 205 lbs. Born, Laval, Que., January 4, 1989.
(Anaheim's 3rd choice, 63rd overall, in 2007 Entry Draft).

			Regular Season					Playoffs				
Season	Club	League	GP	G	A	Pts	PIM	GP	G	A	Pts	PIM
2004-05	Ecole Montpetit	QAAA	37	17	22	39	56	3	0	0	0	0
2005-06	Rimouski Oceanic	QMJHL	41	8	14	22	30	....	....	....	....	....
2006-07	Rouyn-Noranda	QMJHL	14	1	3	4	10	....	....	....	....	....
2007-08	Rouyn-Noranda	QMJHL	67	23	37	60	53	17	6	10	16	8
2008-09	Rouyn-Noranda	QMJHL	35	15	9	24	34	....	....	....	....	....
	Shawinigan	QMJHL	19	7	9	16	18	21	5	9	14	20
2009-10	Bakersfield	ECHL	45	5	16	21	49	6	1	0	1	0

MacINTYRE, Cam (MAK-ihn-tighr, KAM) **S.J.**

Right wing. Shoots right. 6'1", 225 lbs. Born, Sooke, B.C., October 3, 1985.

			Regular Season					Playoffs				
Season	Club	League	GP	G	A	Pts	PIM	GP	G	A	Pts	PIM
2006-07	Princeton	ECAC	32	9	4	13	34	....	....	....	....	....
2007-08	Princeton	ECAC	31	13	18	31	35	....	....	....	....	....
2008-09	Princeton	ECAC	15	1	5	6	4	....	....	....	....	....
2009-10	Princeton	ECAC	10	6	4	10	8	....	....	....	....	....

Signed as a free agent by **San Jose**, April 5, 2010.

MACKENZIE, Drew (muh-KEHN-zee , DROO) **BUF.**

Defense. Shoots left. 6'2", 200 lbs. Born, Stamford, CT, December 17, 1988.
(Buffalo's 8th choice, 209th overall, in 2007 Entry Draft).

			Regular Season					Playoffs				
Season	Club	League	GP	G	A	Pts	PIM	GP	G	A	Pts	PIM
2004-05	Taft Rhinos	High-CT	....	0	1	1	....	....	....	....	....	....
2005-06	Taft Rhinos	High-CT	....	0	11	11	....	....	....	....	....	....
2006-07	Taft Rhinos	High-CT	24	3	10	13	10	....	....	....	....	....
2007-08	Waterloo	USHL	57	4	14	18	103	11	0	6	6	4
2008-09	U. of Vermont	H-East	31	1	9	10	14	....	....	....	....	....
2009-10	U. of Vermont	H-East	36	4	10	14	16	....	....	....	....	....

MacKENZIE, Matt (muh-KEHN-zee, MAT) **BUF.**

Defense. Shoots right. 6'1", 191 lbs. Born, New Westminster, B.C., October 15, 1991.
(Buffalo's 4th choice, 83rd overall, in 2010 Entry Draft).

			Regular Season					Playoffs				
Season	Club	League	GP	G	A	Pts	PIM	GP	G	A	Pts	PIM
2006-07	Van. NW Giants	BCMML	40	5	11	16	64	....	....	....	....	....
2007-08	Calgary Hitmen	WHL	39	2	6	8	8	6	1	2	3	2
2008-09	Calgary Hitmen	WHL	49	3	9	12	24	16	0	2	2	4
2009-10	Calgary Hitmen	WHL	64	6	34	40	62	23	6	10	16	31

MACLEAN, Brett (muh-KLAIN, BREHT) **PHX.**

Left wing. Shoots right. 6'1", 200 lbs. Born, Port Elgin, Ont., December 24, 1988.
(Phoenix's 3rd choice, 32nd overall, in 2007 Entry Draft).

			Regular Season					Playoffs				
Season	Club	League	GP	G	A	Pts	PIM	GP	G	A	Pts	PIM
2003-04	Listowel Cyclones	OJHL-B	9	4	6	10	10	2	3	2	5	12
	Grey-Bruce	Minor-ON	66	71	47	118	117	....	....	....	....	....
2004-05	Erie Otters	OHL	68	7	16	23	31	6	1	1	2	6
2005-06	Erie Otters	OHL	13	3	5	8	6	....	....	....	....	....
	Oshawa Generals	OHL	35	13	25	38	29	....	....	....	....	....
2006-07	Oshawa Generals	OHL	68	47	53	100	43	7	6	9	15	9
2007-08	Oshawa Generals	OHL	61	*61	58	119	42	15	5	11	16	12
2008-09	San Antonio	AHL	74	21	19	40	33	....	....	....	....	....
2009-10	San Antonio	AHL	76	30	35	65	43	....	....	....	....	....

OHL Second All-Star Team (2007) • OHL First All-Star Team (2008) • Canadian Major Junior Second All-Star Team (2008)

MacLEOD, Isaac (muh-KLOWD, IGH-zihk) **S.J.**

Defense. Shoots left. 6'4", 205 lbs. Born, Nelson, B.C., February 22, 1992.
(San Jose's 5th choice, 136th overall, in 2010 Entry Draft).

			Regular Season					Playoffs				
Season	Club	League	GP	G	A	Pts	PIM	GP	G	A	Pts	PIM
2008-09	Nelson Leafs	KIJHL	45	3	16	19	68	13	3	2	5	48
	Penticton Vees	BCHL	3	0	1	1	0	....	....	....	....	....
2009-10	Penticton Vees	BCHL	56	0	23	23	51	14	0	1	1	6

• Signed Letter of Intent to attend **Boston College** (Hockey East) in fall of 2010.

MacMILLAN, Logan (muhk-MIHL-uhn , LOH-guhn) CGY.

Center. Shoots left. 6'1", 205 lbs. Born, Charlottetown, P.E.I., July 5, 1989.
(Anaheim's 1st choice, 19th overall, in 2007 Entry Draft).

			Regular Season					Playoffs				
Season	**Club**	**League**	**GP**	**G**	**A**	**Pts**	**PIM**	**GP**	**G**	**A**	**Pts**	**PIM**
2004-05	Notre Dame	SJHL	41	9	19	28	27	....	....	....	....	....
2005-06	Halifax	QMJHL	62	9	9	18	31	11	1	0	1	0
2006-07	Halifax	QMJHL	68	20	35	55	82	12	9	11	20	6
2007-08	Halifax	QMJHL	46	15	26	41	77	15	3	10	13	20
2008-09	Halifax	QMJHL	15	4	6	10	27	....	....	....	....	....
	Rimouski Oceanic	QMJHL	28	5	16	21	37	13	3	3	6	20
2009-10	Abbotsford Heat	AHL	7	0	0	0	7	....	....	....	....	....
	Bakersfield	ECHL	30	2	4	6	20	....	....	....	....	....

Traded to **Calgary** by **Anaheim** with future considerations for Jason Jaffray and future considerations, June 30, 2010.

MacMILLAN, Mark (muhk-MIHL-uhn, MAHRK) MTL.

Forward. Shoots left. 6', 150 lbs. Born, Penticton, B.C., January 23, 1992.
(Montreal's 2nd choice, 113th overall, in 2010 Entry Draft).

			Regular Season					Playoffs				
Season	**Club**	**League**	**GP**	**G**	**A**	**Pts**	**PIM**	**GP**	**G**	**A**	**Pts**	**PIM**
2008-09	Okanagan Prep	Minor-BC	50	16	21	37	34	....	....	....	....	....
2009-10	Alberni Valley	BCHL	59	26	54	80	44	13	5	9	14	16

• Signed Letter of Intent to attend **University of North Dakota** (WCHA) in fall of 2011.

MacWILLIAM, Andrew (MAK-WIHL-yuhm, AN-droo) TOR.

Defense. Shoots left. 6'2", 214 lbs. Born, Calgary, Alta., March 25, 1990.
(Toronto's 8th choice, 188th overall, in 2008 Entry Draft).

			Regular Season					Playoffs				
Season	**Club**	**League**	**GP**	**G**	**A**	**Pts**	**PIM**	**GP**	**G**	**A**	**Pts**	**PIM**
2006-07	Calgary Royals	AMHL	35	5	13	18	125	....	....	....	....	....
	Camrose Kodiaks	AJHL	2	0	0	0	0	1	0	0	0	0
2007-08	Camrose Kodiaks	AJHL	54	0	13	13	130	18	0	5	5	49
2008-09	Camrose Kodiaks	AJHL	57	8	21	29	220	11	0	4	4	39
2009-10	North Dakota	WCHA	43	0	3	3	87	....	....	....	....	....

MADAISKY, Austin (muh-DAY-skee, AW-stuhn) CBJ

Defense. Shoots right. 6'2", 191 lbs. Born, Surrey, B.C., January 30, 1992.
(Columbus' 6th choice, 124th overall, in 2010 Entry Draft).

			Regular Season					Playoffs				
Season	**Club**	**League**	**GP**	**G**	**A**	**Pts**	**PIM**	**GP**	**G**	**A**	**Pts**	**PIM**
2007-08	Valley West Hawks	BCMML	35	6	23	29	38	....	....	....	....	....
2008-09	Calgary Hitmen	WHL	48	2	7	9	16	2	0	0	0	2
2009-10	Calgary Hitmen	WHL	39	5	13	18	46	....	....	....	....	....
	Kamloops Blazers	WHL	26	2	7	9	28	4	3	3	6	6

MAGGIO, Daniel (MA-jee-oh, DAN-yehl) NYR

Defense. Shoots right. 6'3", 202 lbs. Born, Windsor, Ont., March 4, 1991.
(NY Rangers' 6th choice, 170th overall, in 2009 Entry Draft).

			Regular Season					Playoffs				
Season	**Club**	**League**	**GP**	**G**	**A**	**Pts**	**PIM**	**GP**	**G**	**A**	**Pts**	**PIM**
2006-07	Wind. Jr. Spitfires	Minor-ON	59	16	38	54	94	....	....	....	....	....
2007-08	Sudbury Wolves	OHL	64	5	15	20	96	....	....	....	....	....
2008-09	Sudbury Wolves	OHL	44	2	14	16	60	6	1	0	1	12
2009-10	Sudbury Wolves	OHL	66	9	22	31	121	3	0	2	2	2

MAGNAN-GRENIER, Olivier (MAHG-nah-GREH-n'yay) N.J.

Defense. Shoots left. 6'2", 210 lbs. Born, Sherbrooke, Que., May 1, 1986.
(New Jersey's 6th choice, 148th overall, in 2006 Entry Draft).

			Regular Season					Playoffs				
Season	**Club**	**League**	**GP**	**G**	**A**	**Pts**	**PIM**	**GP**	**G**	**A**	**Pts**	**PIM**
2004-05	Rouyn-Noranda	QMJHL	70	5	15	20	82	10	0	2	2	14
2005-06	Rouyn-Noranda	QMJHL	69	14	27	41	97	5	0	1	1	6
2006-07	Lowell Devils	AHL	24	1	1	2	13	....	....	....	....	....
	Trenton Titans	ECHL	45	1	9	10	63	1	0	0	0	0
2007-08	Lowell Devils	AHL	75	1	15	16	69	....	....	....	....	....
2008-09	Lowell Devils	AHL	76	2	8	10	66	....	....	....	....	....
2009-10	Lowell Devils	AHL	71	3	16	19	68	5	0	0	0	4

MAKAROV, Igor (MAK-ah-rahv, EE-gohr) CHI.

Right wing. Shoots right. 6'1", 195 lbs. Born, Moscow, USSR, September 19, 1987.
(Chicago's 2nd choice, 33rd overall, in 2006 Entry Draft).

			Regular Season					Playoffs				
Season	**Club**	**League**	**GP**	**G**	**A**	**Pts**	**PIM**	**GP**	**G**	**A**	**Pts**	**PIM**
2003-04	Krylja Sovetov 2	Russia-3	1	0	0	0	0	....	....	....	....	....
2004-05	Krylja Sovetov 2	Russia-3	38	13	15	28	44	....	....	....	....	....
	Krylja Sovetov	Russia-2	6	2	2	4	4	1	0	0	0	0
2005-06	Krylja Sovetov	Russia-2	35	9	7	16	20	17	3	4	7	20
2006-07	SKA St. Petersburg	Russia	49	7	2	9	47	3	1	0	1	2
2007-08	St. Petersburg 2	Russia-3	3	1	3	4	2	2	1	2	3	2
	SKA St. Petersburg	Russia	50	4	11	15	26	9	2	1	3	35
2008-09	SKA St. Petersburg	Rus-KHL	42	9	8	17	61	3	1	0	1	2
2009-10	SKA St. Petersburg	Rus-KHL	26	4	2	6	28	....	....	....	....	....
	Dynamo Moscow	Rus-KHL	25	1	2	3	33	4	0	0	0	0

MAKI, Ryan (MA-kee, RIGH-uhn)

Right wing. Shoots right. 6'2", 206 lbs. Born, Medford, NJ, April 23, 1985.
(Nashville's 5th choice, 176th overall, in 2005 Entry Draft).

			Regular Season					Playoffs				
Season	**Club**	**League**	**GP**	**G**	**A**	**Pts**	**PIM**	**GP**	**G**	**A**	**Pts**	**PIM**
2001-02	USNTDP	U-17	17	3	11	14	6	....	....	....	....	....
	USNTDP	NAHL	31	4	11	15	24	....	....	....	....	....
2002-03	USNTDP	U-18	42	5	6	11	18	....	....	....	....	....
	USNTDP	NAHL	10	1	0	1	8	....	....	....	....	....
2003-04	Harvard Crimson	ECAC	34	4	4	8	18	....	....	....	....	....
2004-05	Harvard Crimson	ECAC	30	10	9	19	20	....	....	....	....	....
2005-06	Harvard Crimson	ECAC	33	10	12	22	32	....	....	....	....	....
2006-07	Harvard Crimson	ECAC	32	12	11	23	36	....	....	....	....	....
	Milwaukee	AHL	2	0	1	1	0	2	0	0	0	0
2007-08	Milwaukee	AHL	54	2	3	5	23	3	0	0	0	2
	Cincinnati	ECHL	5	1	0	1	4	6	1	0	1	4
2008-09	Milwaukee	AHL	65	12	13	25	37	11	1	1	2	4
2009-10	Milwaukee	AHL	61	6	9	15	17	7	2	2	4	0

MALENKYKH, Vladimir (MAH-lihn-keh, vla-DIH-meer) PIT.

Defense. Shoots left. 6'1", 187 lbs. Born, Togliatti, USSR, October 1, 1980.
(Pittsburgh's 7th choice, 157th overall, in 1999 Entry Draft).

			Regular Season					Playoffs				
Season	**Club**	**League**	**GP**	**G**	**A**	**Pts**	**PIM**	**GP**	**G**	**A**	**Pts**	**PIM**
1997-98	Lada Togliatti 2	Russia-3	39	6	4	10	112	....	....	....	....	....
1998-99	Lada Togliatti 2	Russia-4	38	6	3	9	68	....	....	....	....	....
	Lada Togliatti	Russia	9	0	0	0	2	....	....	....	....	....
99-2000	Lada Togliatti 2	Russia-3	34	7	9	16	98	....	....	....	....	....
	CSK VVS Samara	Russia	7	0	1	1	14	....	....	....	....	....
	Lada Togliatti	Russia	1	0	0	0	0	....	....	....	....	....
	CSK VVS Samara 2	Russia-3	1	0	1	1	2	....	....	....	....	....
2000-01	Lada Togliatti	Russia	25	1	1	2	14	5	0	0	0	26
2001-02	Lada Togliatti	Russia	47	5	4	9	88	4	0	0	0	2
2002-03	Lada Togliatti	Russia	30	3	1	4	36	10	0	0	0	6
2003-04	Lada Togliatti	Russia	44	2	4	6	42	3	0	0	0	0
2004-05	Lada Togliatti	Russia	37	1	4	5	20	....	....	....	....	....
2005-06	Magnitogorsk	Russia	36	0	2	2	8	11	0	1	1	16
	Magnitogorsk 2	Russia-3	5	1	1	2	2	....	....	....	....	....
2006-07	Magnitogorsk	Russia	54	2	9	11	92	15	1	2	3	28
2007-08	Magnitogorsk 2	Russia-3	1	1	0	1	0	....	....	....	....	....
	Magnitogorsk	Russia	19	0	2	2	18	12	0	0	0	8
2008-09	Magnitogorsk	Rus-KHL	53	3	4	7	22	12	3	0	3	35
2009-10	Magnitogorsk	Rus-KHL	52	3	6	9	38	9	0	1	1	0

MALONE, Brad (MA-lohn, BRAD) COL.

Center/Left wing. Shoots left. 6'2", 207 lbs. Born, Miramichi, N.B., May 20, 1989.
(Colorado's 5th choice, 105th overall, in 2007 Entry Draft).

			Regular Season					Playoffs				
Season	**Club**	**League**	**GP**	**G**	**A**	**Pts**	**PIM**	**GP**	**G**	**A**	**Pts**	**PIM**
2005-06	Cushing	High-MA		STATISTICS NOT AVAILABLE								
2006-07	Sioux Falls	USHL	57	14	19	33	134	8	3	1	4	24
2007-08	North Dakota	WCHA	34	1	2	3	44	....	....	....	....	....
2008-09	North Dakota	WCHA	41	5	12	17	75	....	....	....	....	....
2009-10	North Dakota	WCHA	43	11	14	25	*102	....	....	....	....	....

MARCINKO, Tomas (mahr-TSIHN-koh, TAW-mahsh) NYI

Center. Shoots right. 6'4", 207 lbs. Born, Poprad, Czech., April 11, 1988.
(NY Islanders' 6th choice, 115th overall, in 2006 Entry Draft).

			Regular Season					Playoffs				
Season	**Club**	**League**	**GP**	**G**	**A**	**Pts**	**PIM**	**GP**	**G**	**A**	**Pts**	**PIM**
2003-04	HC Kosice U18	Svk-U18	42	19	23	42	60	2	0	0	0	4
	HC Kosice Jr.	Slovak-Jr.	7	0	2	2	4	3	0	1	1	0
2004-05	HC Kosice Jr.	Slovak-Jr.	38	11	18	29	28	8	1	2	3	6
	HC Kosice	Slovakia	6	0	0	0	0	....	....	....	....	....
	HC Kosice	Slovakia	6	0	0	0	0	....	....	....	....	....
2005-06	HC Kosice Jr.	Slovak-Jr.	35	26	21	47	50	3	1	0	1	4
	HKm Humenne	Slovak-2	9	3	5	8	10	....	....	....	....	....
	HC Kosice	Slovakia	18	2	0	2	2	5	0	0	0	0
2006-07	Barrie Colts	OHL	56	19	21	40	56	8	0	1	1	8
2007-08	Barrie Colts	OHL	48	19	26	45	54	9	4	3	7	14
2008-09	Bridgeport	AHL	58	4	7	11	30	4	0	0	0	0
2009-10	Bridgeport	AHL	54	4	2	6	27	5	0	1	1	2

MARCOU, James (mar-KOO, JAYMZ) S.J.

Right wing. Shoots right. 5'8", 165 lbs. Born, Huntington, NY, February 19, 1988.

			Regular Season					Playoffs				
Season	**Club**	**League**	**GP**	**G**	**A**	**Pts**	**PIM**	**GP**	**G**	**A**	**Pts**	**PIM**
2004-05	USNTDP	NAHL	6	0	2	2	0	....	....	....	....	....
2005-06	Waterloo	USHL	51	18	14	32	26	....	....	....	....	....
2006-07	Waterloo	USHL	58	24	47	71	60	9	6	6	12	4
2007-08	Massachusetts	H-East	36	8	24	32	20	....	....	....	....	....
2008-09	Massachusetts	H-East	39	15	32	47	34	....	....	....	....	....
2009-10	Massachusetts	H-East	36	11	40	51	36	....	....	....	....	....
	Worcester Sharks	AHL	4	1	2	3	0	1	0	0	0	0

USHL Second All-Star Team (2007) • Hockey East All-Rookie Team (2008) • Hockey East First All-Star Team (2009) • NCAA East Second All-American Team (2009) • Hockey East Second All-Star Team (2010)

Signed as a free agent by **San Jose**, March 23, 2010.

MAREK, Jan (MAIR-ehk, YAHN) L.A.

Center. Shoots right. 5'10", 185 lbs. Born, Jindrichuv Hradec, Czech., December 31, 1979.
(NY Rangers' 10th choice, 243rd overall, in 2003 Entry Draft).

			Regular Season					Playoffs				
Season	**Club**	**League**	**GP**	**G**	**A**	**Pts**	**PIM**	**GP**	**G**	**A**	**Pts**	**PIM**
1998-99	Trinec	CzRep	32	2	2	4	2	6	0	0	0	0
99-2000	HC Trinec Jr.	CzRep-Jr.	6	5	5	10	10	1	0	0	0	0
	HC Slezan Opava	CzRep-2	3	0	1	1	4	....	....	....	....	....
	Jind. Hradec	CzRep-2	4	0	3	3	10	....	....	....	....	....
	HC Ocelari Trinec	CzRep	32	1	5	6	4	2	0	0	0	0
2000-01	HC Ocelari Trinec	CzRep	38	7	4	11	2	....	....	....	....	....
2001-02	HC Ocelari Trinec	CzRep	52	13	27	40	44	6	1	3	4	6
2002-03	HC Ocelari Trinec	CzRep	51	*32	30	62	42	12	6	4	10	22
2003-04	HC Sparta Praha	CzRep	50	21	30	51	62	11	4	9	13	26
2004-05	HC Sparta Praha	CzRep	38	7	21	28	26	5	2	2	4	2
2005-06	HC Sparta Praha	CzRep	48	22	32	*54	66	17	4	4	8	24
2006-07	Magnitogorsk	Russia	47	17	30	47	70	15	7	10	17	10
2007-08	Magnitogorsk	Russia	49	16	32	48	40	11	4	3	7	2
2008-09	Magnitogorsk	Rus-KHL	53	*38	37	75	62	12	6	4	10	26
2009-10	Magnitogorsk	Rus-KHL	35	7	13	20	14	10	3	1	4	4

Traded to **Los Angeles** by **NY Rangers** with Jason Ward, Marc-Andre Cliche and NY Rangers' 3rd round choice (later traded to Buffalo - Buffalo selected Corey Fienhage) in 2008 Entry Draft for Sean Avery and John Seymour, February 5, 2007.

MARINCIN, Martin (mah-RIHN-chihn, MAHR-tihn) EDM.

Defense. Shoots left. 6'4", 187 lbs. Born, Kosice, Czechoslovakia, February 18, 1992.
(Edmonton's 3rd choice, 46th overall, in 2010 Entry Draft).

			Regular Season					Playoffs				
Season	**Club**	**League**	**GP**	**G**	**A**	**Pts**	**PIM**	**GP**	**G**	**A**	**Pts**	**PIM**
2006-07	HC Kosice U18	Svk-U18	16	0	3	3	6	....	....	....	....	....
2007-08	HC Kosice U18	Svk-U18	59	3	29	32	36	....	....	....	....	....
2008-09	HC Kosice U18	Svk-U18	5	4	4	8	35	....	....	....	....	....
	HC Kosice Jr.	Slovak-Jr.	46	11	15	26	50	3	0	0	0	0
2009-10	Slovakia U20	Slovakia	35	2	4	6	71	....	....	....	....	....
	HC Kosice Jr.	Slovak-Jr.	....	....	....	....	....	2	0	0	0	0

AROON, Patrick (ma-ROON, PAT-rihk) **PHI.**

eft wing. Shoots left. 6'4", 225 lbs. Born, St Louis, MO, April 23, 1988.
Philadelphia's 6th choice, 161st overall, in 2007 Entry Draft).

			Regular Season					Playoffs				
eason	Club	League	GP	G	A	Pts	PIM	GP	G	A	Pts	PIM
'005-06	Texarkana Bandits	NAHL	57	23	37	60	61	8	3	1	4	22
'006-07	St. Louis Bandits	NAHL	57	40	55	*95	152	12	*10	*13	*23	12
'007-08	London Knights	OHL	64	35	55	90	57	5	0	1	1	10
	Philadelphia	AHL	1	0	0	0	0	....	....	....	....	....
'008-09	Philadelphia	AHL	80	23	31	54	62	4	1	2	3	13
009-10	Adirondack	AHL	67	11	33	44	125	....	....	....	....	....

ARQUARDT, Matt (MAR-kwart, MAT) **EDM.**

eft wing. Shoots left. 6'3", 222 lbs. Born, North Bay, Ont., July 19, 1987.
Columbus' 10th choice, 194th overall, in 2006 Entry Draft).

			Regular Season					Playoffs				
eason	Club	League	GP	G	A	Pts	PIM	GP	G	A	Pts	PIM
'003-04	Huntsville Wildcats	OPJHL	STATISTICS NOT AVAILABLE									
	Brockville Braves	CJHL	11	1	2	3	17	....	....	....	....	....
004-05	Brockville Braves	CJHL	55	19	22	41	78	7	2	1	3	8
005-06	Moncton Wildcats	QMJHL	68	16	9	25	69	20	5	3	8	12
006-07	Moncton Wildcats	QMJHL	67	41	29	70	68	7	1	3	4	14
007-08	Moncton Wildcats	QMJHL	35	20	13	33	38	....	....	....	....	....
	Baie-Comeau	QMJHL	33	23	13	36	33	5	1	1	2	6
008-09	Providence Bruins	AHL	71	9	13	22	45	9	1	1	2	2
009-10	Providence Bruins	AHL	42	1	9	10	21	....	....	....	....	....
	Reading Royals	ECHL	9	1	2	3	14	....	....	....	....	....
	Springfield Falcons	AHL	4	0	0	0	4	....	....	....	....	....
	Stockton Thunder	ECHL	7	1	1	2	4	15	6	4	10	15

.JHL Rookie of the Year (2005)

raded to **Boston** by **Columbus** for Jonathon Sigalet, May 27, 2008. Traded to **Edmonton** by **oston** for Cody Wild, March 2, 2010.

ARSHALL, Benjamin (MAR-shuhl, BEHN-jah-mihn) **DET.**

efense. Shoots left. 5'9", 160 lbs. Born, St. Paul, MN, August 30, 1992.
Detroit's 7th choice, 201st overall, in 2010 Entry Draft).

			Regular Season					Playoffs				
eason	Club	League	GP	G	A	Pts	PIM	GP	G	A	Pts	PIM
007-08	Mahtomedi	High-MN	6	3	0	3	....	....	....	....	....	....
008-09	Mahtomedi	High-MN	29	21	29	50	30	....	....	....	....	....
009-10	Team Northeast	UMHSEL	16	1	3	4	....	....	....	....	....	....
	Minnetonka High	High-MN	23	18	30	48	40	6	2	10	12	10

Signed Letter of Intent to attend **University of Minnesota** (WCHA) in fall of 2011.

ARSHALL, Kevin (MAR-shuhl, KEH-vihn) **PHI.**

efense. Shoots left. 6'1", 191 lbs. Born, Boucherville, Que., March 10, 1989.
Philadelphia's 2nd choice, 41st overall, in 2007 Entry Draft).

			Regular Season					Playoffs				
eason	Club	League	GP	G	A	Pts	PIM	GP	G	A	Pts	PIM
004-05	C.C. Lemoyne	QAAA	39	2	9	11	88	5	0	1	1	16
005-06	Lewiston	QMJHL	60	1	10	11	112	6	0	1	1	14
006-07	Lewiston	QMJHL	70	5	27	32	141	17	0	7	7	38
007-08	Lewiston	QMJHL	66	11	24	35	143	6	1	1	2	12
008-09	Quebec Remparts	QMJHL	61	9	29	38	125	17	1	10	11	32
009-10	Adirondack	AHL	75	2	7	9	80	....	....	....	....	....

MJHL Second All-Star Team (2008)

ARSHALL, Matt (MAR-shuhl, MAT) **T.B.**

enter/Right wing. Shoots right. 6'1", 175 lbs. Born, Boston, MA, August 30, 1988.
Tampa Bay's 5th choice, 150th overall, in 2007 Entry Draft).

			Regular Season					Playoffs				
eason	Club	League	GP	G	A	Pts	PIM	GP	G	A	Pts	PIM
005-06	Hingham	High-MA	STATISTICS NOT AVAILABLE									
006-07	Nobles	High-MA	27	14	10	24	6	....	....	....	....	....
007-08	Nobles	High-MA	29	25	26	51	....	....	....	....	....	....
008-09	U. of Vermont	H-East	24	1	3	4	12	....	....	....	....	....
009-10	U. of Vermont	H-East	33	1	4	5	16	....	....	....	....	....

ARTIN, Jesse (MAHR-tihn, JEH-see) **ATL.**

enter. Shoots right. 5'11", 180 lbs. Born, Edmonton, Alta., September 7, 1988.
Atlanta's 6th choice, 195th overall, in 2006 Entry Draft).

			Regular Season					Playoffs				
eason	Club	League	GP	G	A	Pts	PIM	GP	G	A	Pts	PIM
003-04	K of C Pats	AMHL	34	10	11	21	6	....	....	....	....	....
004-05	K of C Pats	AMHL	30	17	28	45	70	8	4	8	12	....
005-06	Spruce Grove	AJHL	40	15	29	44	122	....	....	....	....	....
006-07	Tri-City Storm	USHL	59	19	37	56	31	9	2	4	6	4
007-08	U. of Denver	WCHA	41	7	8	15	26	....	....	....	....	....
008-09	U. of Denver	WCHA	37	10	13	23	34	....	....	....	....	....
009-10	U. of Denver	WCHA	34	14	8	22	26	....	....	....	....	....

ARTINDALE, Ryan (MAHR-tihn-dayl, RIGH-uhn) **EDM.**

enter. Shoots left. 6'3", 183 lbs. Born, Oshawa, Ont., October 27, 1991.
dmonton's 5th choice, 61st overall, in 2010 Entry Draft).

			Regular Season					Playoffs				
eason	Club	League	GP	G	A	Pts	PIM	GP	G	A	Pts	PIM
006-07	Whitby Wildcats	Minor-ON	79	65	67	132	....	....	....	....	....	....
007-08	Ottawa 67's	OHL	64	9	8	17	18	4	0	0	0	2
008-09	Ottawa 67's	OHL	53	23	24	47	14	7	2	1	3	7
009-10	Ottawa 67's	OHL	61	19	41	60	37	12	4	5	9	6

ARVIN, Aaron (MAHR-vihn, AIR-ruhn) **CGY.**

orward. Shoots left. 6'3", 210 lbs. Born, Warrod, MN, May 27, 1988.
Calgary's 3rd choice, 89th overall, in 2006 Entry Draft).

			Regular Season					Playoffs				
eason	Club	League	GP	G	A	Pts	PIM	GP	G	A	Pts	PIM
004-05	Warroad Warriors	High-MN	31	23	25	48	18	....	....	....	....	....
005-06	Warroad Warriors	High-MN	23	9	21	30	40	....	....	....	....	....
006-07	Tri-City Storm	USHL	13	1	3	4	8	9	1	0	1	8
007-08	St. Cloud State	WCHA	40	3	10	13	33	....	....	....	....	....
008-09	St. Cloud State	WCHA	38	10	17	27	46	....	....	....	....	....
009-10	St. Cloud State	WCHA	39	5	11	16	73	....	....	....	....	....

MASHINTER, Brandon (ma-SHIHN-tuhr, BRAN-duhn) **S.J.**

Center. Shoots left. 6'4", 235 lbs. Born, Bradford, Ont., September 20, 1988.

			Regular Season					Playoffs				
Season	Club	League	GP	G	A	Pts	PIM	GP	G	A	Pts	PIM
2004-05	Tor. T-Birds	OPJHL	49	3	6	9	19	....	....	....	....	....
	Sarnia Sting	OHL	8	0	0	0	9	....	....	....	....	....
2005-06	Sarnia Sting	OHL	65	6	1	7	65	....	....	....	....	....
2006-07	Sarnia Sting	OHL	55	7	8	15	49	4	0	2	2	0
2007-08	Kitchener Rangers	OHL	62	10	10	20	84	20	2	2	4	16
2008-09	Kitchener Rangers	OHL	21	14	12	26	24	....	....	....	....	....
	Belleville Bulls	OHL	31	20	12	32	32	17	8	3	11	13
2009-10	Worcester Sharks	AHL	79	22	15	37	117	11	1	5	6	6

Signed as a free agent by **San Jose**, July, 2009.

MASSE, Dany (ma-SAY, DA-nee) **MTL.**

Left wing. Shoots left. 5'10", 177 lbs. Born, La Pocatière, Que., May 12, 1988.

			Regular Season					Playoffs				
Season	Club	League	GP	G	A	Pts	PIM	GP	G	A	Pts	PIM
2004-05	Val-d'Or Foreurs	QMJHL	58	2	8	10	43	....	....	....	....	....
2005-06	Val-d'Or Foreurs	QMJHL	67	9	20	29	64	5	0	0	0	0
2006-07	Acadie-Bathurst	QMJHL	69	26	30	56	84	12	1	6	7	12
2007-08	Acadie-Bathurst	QMJHL	70	29	50	79	38	12	1	6	7	14
2008-09	Drummondville	QMJHL	68	44	66	110	52	19	15	21	36	18
2009-10	Hamilton Bulldogs	AHL	25	3	2	5	6	9	0	1	1	0

QMJHL First All-Star Team (2009)

Signed as a free agent by **Montreal**, April 15, 2009.

MATSON, Taylor (MAT-suhn, TAY-luhr) **VAN.**

Center. Shoots right. 5'10", 183 lbs. Born, Mound, MN, September 16, 1988.
(Vancouver's 5th choice, 176th overall, in 2007 Entry Draft).

			Regular Season					Playoffs				
Season	Club	League	GP	G	A	Pts	PIM	GP	G	A	Pts	PIM
2005-06	Holy Angels	High-MN	27	30	40	70	28	....	....	....	....	....
2006-07	Holy Angels	High-MN	11	16	15	31	16	....	....	....	....	....
	Des Moines	USHL	10	1	2	3	6	6	0	1	1	10
2007-08	Des Moines	USHL	55	13	24	37	38	....	....	....	....	....
2008-09	U. of Minnesota	WCHA	13	1	0	1	2	....	....	....	....	....
2009-10	U. of Minnesota	WCHA	19	2	3	5	6	....	....	....	....	....

MATSUMOTO, Jonathan (mat-suh-MOH-toh, JAWN-ah-thuhn) **CAR.**

Center. Shoots left. 6', 184 lbs. Born, Ottawa, Ont., October 13, 1986.
(Philadelphia's 5th choice, 79th overall, in 2006 Entry Draft).

			Regular Season					Playoffs				
Season	Club	League	GP	G	A	Pts	PIM	GP	G	A	Pts	PIM
2002-03	Cumberland	CJHL	8	2	3	5	2	10	4	7	11	2
2003-04	Cumberland	CJHL	51	31	32	63	26	7	5	5	10	6
2004-05	Bowling Green	CCHA	36	18	14	32	22	....	....	....	....	....
2005-06	Bowling Green	CCHA	36	20	28	48	43	....	....	....	....	....
2006-07	Bowling Green	CCHA	38	11	22	33	70	....	....	....	....	....
	Philadelphia	AHL	16	2	2	4	10	....	....	....	....	....
2007-08	Philadelphia	AHL	77	20	24	44	52	12	2	2	4	10
2008-09	Philadelphia	AHL	78	29	34	63	77	4	1	2	3	4
2009-10	Adirondack	AHL	80	30	32	62	50	....	....	....	....	....

Traded to **Carolina** by **Philadelphia** for Washington's 7th round choice (previously acquired, Philadelphia selected Ricard Blidstrand) in 2010 Entry Draft, June 25, 2010.

MATTSON, Nick (MAT-suhn, NIHK) **CHI.**

Defense. Shoots left. 6'1", 189 lbs. Born, Salem, OR, October 25, 1991.
(Chicago's 9th choice, 180th overall, in 2010 Entry Draft).

			Regular Season					Playoffs				
Season	Club	League	GP	G	A	Pts	PIM	GP	G	A	Pts	PIM
2006-07	Chaska Hawks	High-MN	41	5	15	20	....	....	....	....	....	....
2007-08	USNTDP	NAHL	43	1	10	11	16	3	0	0	0	0
	USNTDP	U-17	17	0	9	9	....	....	....	....	....	....
2008-09	USNTDP	NAHL	16	1	5	6	4	....	....	....	....	....
	USNTDP	U-18	47	3	14	17	4	....	....	....	....	....
2009-10	Indiana Ice	USHL	51	5	14	19	14	9	0	6	6	2

• Signed Letter of Intent to attend **University of North Dakota** (WCHA) in fall of 2010.

McCAULEY, Dennis (muh-KAW-lee, DEH-nihs) **BUF.**

Left wing. Shoots left. 6'3", 225 lbs. Born, Billerica, MA, August 15, 1985.

			Regular Season					Playoffs				
Season	Club	League	GP	G	A	Pts	PIM	GP	G	A	Pts	PIM
2003-04	Sioux City	USHL	58	12	9	21	176	7	1	0	1	26
2004-05	Sioux City	USHL	54	18	21	39	236	12	2	3	5	46
2005-06	Northeastern	H-East	32	7	7	14	57	....	....	....	....	....
2006-07	Northeastern	H-East	33	5	9	14	90	....	....	....	....	....
2007-08	Northeastern	H-East	28	4	2	6	70	....	....	....	....	....
2008-09	Northeastern	H-East	36	6	5	11	49	....	....	....	....	....
2009-10	Worcester Sharks	AHL	45	10	4	14	84	8	0	2	2	2

Signed as a free agent by **Buffalo**, July 30, 2010.

McCOLLEM, Matthew (muh-KAHL-uhm, MA-thew) **ST.L.**

Left wing. Shoots left. 6', 185 lbs. Born, Somerville, MA, May 6, 1988.
(St. Louis' 8th choice, 154th overall, in 2006 Entry Draft).

			Regular Season					Playoffs				
Season	Club	League	GP	G	A	Pts	PIM	GP	G	A	Pts	PIM
2004-05	Belmont Hill	High-MA	....	2	7	9	....	....	....	....	....	....
2005-06	Belmont Hill	High-MA	....	15	11	26	....	....	....	....	....	....
2006-07	Belmont Hill	High-MA	28	16	19	35	64	....	....	....	....	....
2007-08	Harvard Crimson	ECAC	31	5	9	14	28	....	....	....	....	....
2008-09	Harvard Crimson	ECAC	29	6	8	14	28	....	....	....	....	....
2009-10	Harvard Crimson	ECAC	8	1	1	2	0	....	....	....	....	....

McCUE, Matt (muh-KEW, MAHT) NYR

Defense. Shoots left. 6'5", 220 lbs. Born, Cochrane, Alta., July 5, 1988.

			Regular Season					Playoffs				
Season	Club	League	GP	G	A	Pts	PIM	GP	G	A	Pts	PIM
2003-04	Medicine Hat	AMHL	28	2	7	9	101	....	....	....	....	....
	Spokane Chiefs	WHL	3	0	0	0	0	....	....	....	....	....
2004-05	Spokane Chiefs	WHL	21	1	2	3	35	....	....	....	....	....
2005-06	Spokane Chiefs	WHL	56	5	10	15	125	....	....	....	....	....
2006-07	Spokane Chiefs	WHL	4	1	1	2	4	....	....	....	....	....
	Chilliwack Bruins	WHL	32	2	5	7	71	5	0	0	0	14
2007-08	Chilliwack Bruins	WHL	42	0	4	4	111	....	....	....	....	....
	Brandon	WHL	28	0	7	7	84	6	1	0	1	12
2008-09	Brandon	WHL	9	1	1	2	*35	....	....	....	....	....
	Medicine Hat	WHL	52	5	18	23	*160	9	1	2	3	12
2009-10	Manitoba Moose	AHL	10	1	0	1	24	....	....	....	....	....
	Bakersfield	ECHL	19	0	2	2	68	....	....	....	....	....

• Missed majority of 2004-05 season recovering from leg injury. Signed as a free agent by **Anaheim**, December 30, 2008. Traded to **NY Rangers** by **Anaheim** for Tomas Zaborsky, July 19, 2010.

McCUTCHEON, Mark (muh-KUH-chuhn, MAHRK)

Center. Shoots right. 6', 190 lbs. Born, Ithaca, NY, May 21, 1984.
(Colorado's 3rd choice, 146th overall, in 2003 Entry Draft).

			Regular Season					Playoffs				
Season	Club	League	GP	G	A	Pts	PIM	GP	G	A	Pts	PIM
2001-02	N.E. Jr. Coyotes	EJHL	36	24	26	50	84	....	....	....	....	....
2002-03	N.E. Jr. Coyotes	EJHL	35	27	22	49	76	10	8	5	13	24
2003-04	Cornell Big Red	ECAC	32	0	4	4	12	....	....	....	....	....
2004-05	Cornell Big Red	ECAC	22	0	5	5	12	....	....	....	....	....
2005-06	Cornell Big Red	ECAC	34	9	6	15	34	....	....	....	....	....
2006-07	Cornell Big Red	ECAC	29	10	10	20	32	....	....	....	....	....
2007-08	Lake Erie Monsters	AHL	63	2	7	9	73	....	....	....	....	....
2008-09	Lake Erie Monsters	AHL	65	6	11	17	70	....	....	....	....	....
	Johnstown Chiefs	ECHL	9	3	1	4	14	....	....	....	....	....
2009-10	Idaho Steelheads	ECHL	34	14	32	46	52	15	8	10	18	14
	Portland Pirates	AHL	5	2	0	2	2	....	....	....	....	....
	Manitoba Moose	AHL	12	0	0	0	13	....	....	....	....	....

Signed as a free agent by **Idaho** (ECHL), October 10, 2009. Signed as a free agent by **Portland** (AHL), October 23, 2009. Signed as a free agent by **Manitoba** (AHL), November 3, 2009.

McDONAGH, Ryan (muhk-DUHN-uh, RIGH-uhn) NYR

Defense. Shoots left. 6'1", 222 lbs. Born, St.Paul, MN, June 13, 1989.
(Montreal's 1st choice, 12th overall, in 2007 Entry Draft).

			Regular Season					Playoffs				
Season	Club	League	GP	G	A	Pts	PIM	GP	G	A	Pts	PIM
2004-05	Cretin-Derham	High-MN	28	12	18	30	....	....	....	....	....	....
2005-06	Cretin-Derham	High-MN	25	12	33	45	....	....	....	....	....	....
2006-07	Cretin-Derham	High-MN	26	14	26	40	....	....	....	....	....	....
2007-08	U. of Wisconsin	WCHA	40	5	7	12	42	....	....	....	....	....
2008-09	U. of Wisconsin	WCHA	36	5	11	16	59	....	....	....	....	....
2009-10	U. of Wisconsin	WCHA	43	4	14	18	73	....	....	....	....	....

WCHA All-Rookie Team (2008) • WCHA Second All-Star Team (2010)

Traded to **NY Rangers** by **Montreal** with Christopher Higgins and Pavel Valentenko for Scott Gomez, Tom Pyatt and Michael Busto, June 30, 2009.

McFARLAND, John (muhk-FAHR-luhnd, JAWN) FLA.

Left wing. Shoots right. 6', 192 lbs. Born, Richmond Hill, Ont., April 2, 1992.
(Florida's 4th choice, 33rd overall, in 2010 Entry Draft).

			Regular Season					Playoffs				
Season	Club	League	GP	G	A	Pts	PIM	GP	G	A	Pts	PIM
2007-08	Tor. Jr. Canadiens	GTHL	76	96	69	165	176	....	....	....	....	....
2008-09	Sudbury Wolves	OHL	58	21	31	52	36	6	1	3	4	2
2009-10	Sudbury Wolves	OHL	64	20	30	50	70	4	3	0	3	2

McFAULL, Kendall (muhk-FAWL, KEN-duhl) ATL.

Defense. Shoots left. 6'3", 190 lbs. Born, Rosetown, Sask., April 10, 1992.
(Atlanta's 6th choice, 155th overall, in 2010 Entry Draft).

			Regular Season					Playoffs				
Season	Club	League	GP	G	A	Pts	PIM	GP	G	A	Pts	PIM
2008-09	Sask. Contacts	SMHL	42	4	14	18	73	10	1	5	6	21
	Sask. Contacts	Exhib.	8	2	4	6	21	....	....	....	....	....
2009-10	Moose Jaw	WHL	62	4	6	10	70	7	0	1	1	10

McGINN, Tye (muhk-GIHN, TIGH) PHI.

Left wing. Shoots left. 6'2", 205 lbs. Born, Fergus, Ont., July 29, 1990.
(Philadelphia's 2nd choice, 119th overall, in 2010 Entry Draft).

			Regular Season					Playoffs				
Season	Club	League	GP	G	A	Pts	PIM	GP	G	A	Pts	PIM
2006-07	Waterloo Wolves	Minor-ON	62	41	55	96	42	....	....	....	....	....
2007-08	Ottawa 67's	OHL	59	3	8	11	25	4	0	0	0	2
2008-09	Listowel Cyclones	OJHL-B	14	10	18	28	10	....	....	....	....	....
	Gatineau	QMJHL	48	8	22	30	25	10	7	6	13	19
2009-10	Gatineau	QMJHL	50	27	35	62	50	10	2	5	7	12

McGRATH, Evan (muh-GRATH, EH-vuhn)

Center. Shoots left. 6', 200 lbs. Born, Oakville, Ont., January 14, 1986.
(Detroit's 2nd choice, 128th overall, in 2004 Entry Draft).

			Regular Season					Playoffs				
Season	Club	League	GP	G	A	Pts	PIM	GP	G	A	Pts	PIM
2001-02	Oakville Blades	OPJHL	49	43	44	87	24	....	....	....	....	....
2002-03	Kitchener Rangers	OHL	64	16	31	47	40	21	6	2	8	6
2003-04	Kitchener Rangers	OHL	68	15	36	51	28	5	2	1	3	2
2004-05	Kitchener Rangers	OHL	67	28	59	87	51	15	7	6	13	6
2005-06	Kitchener Rangers	OHL	67	37	77	114	63	5	1	3	4	4
2006-07	Grand Rapids	AHL	59	6	8	14	41	7	0	0	0	0
	Toledo Storm	ECHL	9	6	9	15	12	....	....	....	....	....
2007-08	Grand Rapids	AHL	78	18	17	35	26	....	....	....	....	....
2008-09	Grand Rapids	AHL	68	17	30	47	24	....	....	....	....	....
2009-10	Grand Rapids	AHL	57	8	11	19	25	....	....	....	....	....
	Syracuse Crunch	AHL	15	4	2	6	2	....	....	....	....	....

OHL All-Rookie Team (2003)

McILRATH, Dylan (MAK-ihl-rayth, DIH-luhn) NYR

Defense. Shoots right. 6'4", 218 lbs. Born, Winnipeg, Man., April 20, 1992.
(NY Rangers' 1st choice, 10th overall, in 2010 Entry Draft).

			Regular Season					Playoffs				
Season	Club	League	GP	G	A	Pts	PIM	GP	G	A	Pts	PIM
2007-08	Winnipeg Warriors	Minor-MB	34	5	17	22	68	....	....	....	....	....
2008-09	Moose Jaw	WHL	53	1	3	4	102	....	....	....	....	....
2009-10	Moose Jaw	WHL	65	7	17	24	169	7	0	1	1	21

McINTYRE, David (MAK-ihn-tigh-uhr, DAY-vihd) N.J.

Center. Shoots left. 6', 185 lbs. Born, Oakville, Ont., February 4, 1987.
(Dallas' 4th choice, 138th overall, in 2006 Entry Draft).

			Regular Season					Playoffs				
Season	Club	League	GP	G	A	Pts	PIM	GP	G	A	Pts	PIM
2004-05	Newmarket	OPJHL	46	17	14	31	33	16	8	7	15	20
2005-06	Newmarket	OPJHL	46	42	50	92	143	11	4	8	12	42
2006-07	Colgate	ECAC	40	9	8	17	75	....	....	....	....	....
2007-08	Colgate	ECAC	39	15	17	32	38	....	....	....	....	....
2008-09	Colgate	ECAC	37	21	22	43	54	....	....	....	....	....
2009-10	Lowell Devils	AHL	12	3	2	5	8	5	1	1	2	0
	Colgate	ECAC	35	11	28	39	60	....	....	....	....	....

ECAC First All-Star Team (2009) • NCAA East First All-American Team (2009) • ECAC Second All-Star Team (2010)

Traded to **Anaheim** by **Dallas** with Dallas' 6th round choice (Andreas Dahlstrom) in 2010 Entry Draft for Brian Sutherby, December 14, 2008. Traded to **New Jersey** by **Anaheim** for Sheldon Brookbank, February 3, 2009.

McKEGG, Greg (Muhk-ehg, GREHG) TOR.

Center. Shoots left. 6', 191 lbs. Born, St.Thomas, Ont., June 17, 1992.
(Toronto's 2nd choice, 62nd overall, in 2010 Entry Draft).

			Regular Season					Playoffs				
Season	Club	League	GP	G	A	Pts	PIM	GP	G	A	Pts	PIM
2007-08	Elgin-Mid. Chiefs	Minor-ON	64	73	53	126	....	....	....	....	....	....
2008-09	Erie Otters	OHL	64	8	10	18	22	5	2	1	3	4
2009-10	Erie Otters	OHL	67	37	48	85	32	4	2	1	3	0

McKELVIE, Zach (muh-KEHL-vee, ZAK) BOS.

Defense. Shoots . 6'2", 196 lbs. Born, St. Paul, MN, February 22, 1985.

			Regular Season					Playoffs				
Season	Club	League	GP	G	A	Pts	PIM	GP	G	A	Pts	PIM
2004-05	Bozeman IceDogs	NAHL	53	0	6	6	108	....	....	....	....	....
2005-06	Army	AH	32	2	8	10	64	....	....	....	....	....
2006-07	Army	AH	34	3	9	12	48	....	....	....	....	....
2007-08	Army	AH	35	4	13	17	48	....	....	....	....	....
2008-09	Army	AH	33	5	12	17	48	....	....	....	....	....
2009-10	Army	AH	MILITARY SERVICE									

Signed as a free agent by **Boston**, July 13, 2009. • Missed entire 2009-10 season fulfilling his U.S. military service requirements per his enrollment at West Point.

McKENZIE, Curtis (muh-KEHN-zee, KUHR-tihs) DAL.

Left wing. Shoots left. 6'2", 192 lbs. Born, Golden, B.C., February 22, 1991.
(Dallas' 5th choice, 159th overall, in 2009 Entry Draft).

			Regular Season					Playoffs				
Season	Club	League	GP	G	A	Pts	PIM	GP	G	A	Pts	PIM
2007-08	Penticton Vees	BCHL	49	3	7	10	81	7	0	1	1	9
2008-09	Penticton Vees	BCHL	53	30	34	64	90	10	3	7	10	81
2009-10	Miami U.	CCHA	42	6	21	27	88	....	....	....	....	....

McKENZIE, Ian (muh-KEHN-zee, EE-an) NSH.

Right wing. Shoots right. 6'5", 239 lbs. Born, Weyburn, Sask., May 23, 1987.

			Regular Season					Playoffs				
Season	Club	League	GP	G	A	Pts	PIM	GP	G	A	Pts	PIM
2003-04	Saskatoon Blazers	SMHL	STATISTICS NOT AVAILABLE									
	Moose Jaw	WHL	8	0	0	0	0	....	....	....	....	....
2004-05	Moose Jaw	WHL	44	3	4	7	18	5	0	0	0	11
2005-06	Moose Jaw	WHL	42	4	3	7	68	22	5	3	8	8
2006-07	Moose Jaw	WHL	6	1	0	1	10	....	....	....	....	....
	Seattle	WHL	60	12	9	21	77	11	2	1	3	17
2007-08	Seattle	WHL	68	19	21	40	103	12	8	6	14	12
2008-09	Milwaukee	AHL	26	3	1	4	31	....	....	....	....	....
	Cincinnati	ECHL	40	12	3	15	56	8	4	4	8	8
2009-10	Milwaukee	AHL	24	1	0	1	14	....	....	....	....	....
	Cincinnati	ECHL	24	3	2	5	48	15	3	3	6	33

Signed as a free agent by **Nashville**, May 6, 2008.

McKINLAY, Dylen (muh-KIHN-lee, DIH-luhn) MIN

Right wing. Shoots left. 5'11", 162 lbs. Born, Langley, B.C., April 20, 1992.
(Minnesota's 6th choice, 189th overall, in 2010 Entry Draft).

			Regular Season					Playoffs				
Season	Club	League	GP	G	A	Pts	PIM	GP	G	A	Pts	PIM
2007-08	Valley West Hawks	BCMML	35	13	13	26	70	....	....	....	....	....
2008-09	Princeton Posse	KIJHL	13	5	3	8	31	....	....	....	....	....
	Chilliwack Bruins	WHL	55	3	7	10	47	....	....	....	....	....
2009-10	Chilliwack Bruins	WHL	72	20	23	43	57	6	2	3	5	2

McMILLAN, Brandon (muhk-MIHL-uhn, BRAN-duhn) ANA

Center. Shoots left. 5'11", 185 lbs. Born, Richmond, B.C., March 22, 1990.
(Anaheim's 7th choice, 85th overall, in 2008 Entry Draft).

			Regular Season					Playoffs				
Season	Club	League	GP	G	A	Pts	PIM	GP	G	A	Pts	PIM
2006-07	Kelowna Rockets	WHL	55	2	10	12	27	....	....	....	....	....
2007-08	Kelowna Rockets	WHL	71	15	26	41	56	7	0	0	0	[illegible]
2008-09	Kelowna Rockets	WHL	70	14	35	49	75	22	0	5	5	2[illegible]
2009-10	Kelowna Rockets	WHL	55	25	42	67	63	12	5	10	15	1[illegible]

McMILLAN, Carson (muhk-MIHL-lihn, KAHR-suhn) MIN.

Right wing. Shoots right. 6'1", 190 lbs. Born, Brandon, Man., September 10, 1988.
(Minnesota's 5th choice, 200th overall, in 2007 Entry Draft).

			Regular Season					Playoffs				
Season	Club	League	GP	G	A	Pts	PIM	GP	G	A	Pts	PIM
2003-04	Crocus Plains	High-MB	STATISTICS NOT AVAILABLE									
	Brandon	MMHL	4	0	0	0	0	....	....	....	....	....
2004-05	Brandon	MMHL	40	17	19	36	34	5	3	4	7	8
	Winkler Flyers	MJHL	4	1	1	2	2	....	....	....	....	....
2005-06	Calgary Hitmen	WHL	59	3	2	5	42	13	0	0	0	2
2006-07	Calgary Hitmen	WHL	72	7	15	22	76	18	2	0	2	17
2007-08	Calgary Hitmen	WHL	72	16	26	42	87	16	1	0	1	22
2008-09	Calgary Hitmen	WHL	68	31	41	72	93	18	3	8	11	18
2009-10	Houston Aeros	AHL	56	4	4	8	70	....	....	....	....	....

McNABB, Brayden (muhk-NAB, BRAY-duhn) BUF.

Defense. Shoots left. 6'5", 216 lbs. Born, Saskatoon, Sask., January 21, 1991.
(Buffalo's 2nd choice, 66th overall, in 2009 Entry Draft).

			Regular Season					Playoffs				
Season	Club	League	GP	G	A	Pts	PIM	GP	G	A	Pts	PIM
2006-07	Notre Dame	SMHL	41	5	13	18	72	....	....	....	....	....
	Kootenay Ice	WHL	3	0	0	0	0	....	....	....	....	....
2007-08	Kootenay Ice	WHL	65	2	9	11	63	10	0	1	1	10
2008-09	Kootenay Ice	WHL	67	10	26	36	140	4	0	5	5	2
2009-10	Kootenay Ice	WHL	64	17	40	57	121	6	0	4	4	18

WHL East First All-Star Team (2010)

McNALLY, Patrick (muhk-NAL-ee, PAT-rihk) VAN.

Defense. Shoots left. 6'2", 182 lbs. Born, Glen Head, NY, December 4, 1991.
(Vancouver's 1st choice, 115th overall, in 2010 Entry Draft).

			Regular Season					Playoffs				
Season	Club	League	GP	G	A	Pts	PIM	GP	G	A	Pts	PIM
2008-09	Suffolk PAL S.S.	MtJHL	52	25	41	66	72	....	....	....	....	....
2009-10	Milton Academy	High-MA	28	14	21	35	....	....	....	....	....	....

• Signed Letter of Intent to attend **Harvard University** (ECAC) in fall of 2011.

McNAUGHT, Randy (muhk-NAWT, RAN-dee) NYR

Right wing. Shoots right. 6'4", 220 lbs. Born, Nanaimo, B.C., August 5, 1990.
(NY Rangers' 6th choice, 190th overall, in 2010 Entry Draft).

			Regular Season					Playoffs				
Season	Club	League	GP	G	A	Pts	PIM	GP	G	A	Pts	PIM
2006-07	Nanaimo Clippers	BCHL	39	3	4	7	59	2	0	0	0	4
2007-08	Nanaimo Clippers	BCHL	25	2	3	5	54	....	....	....	....	....
	Chilliwack Bruins	WHL	30	3	1	4	53	4	0	0	0	2
2008-09	Chilliwack Bruins	WHL	51	5	4	9	78	....	....	....	....	....
2009-10	Chilliwack Bruins	WHL	6	0	0	0	32	....	....	....	....	....
	Saskatoon Blades	WHL	59	6	6	12	131	5	0	0	0	11

McNEILL, Patrick (muhk-NEEL, PAT-rihk) WSH.

Defense. Shoots left. 6'1", 200 lbs. Born, Strathroy, Ont., March 17, 1987.
(Washington's 4th choice, 118th overall, in 2005 Entry Draft).

			Regular Season					Playoffs				
Season	Club	League	GP	G	A	Pts	PIM	GP	G	A	Pts	PIM
2002-03	Strathroy Rockets	OHA-B	45	6	13	19	53	....	....	....	....	....
2003-04	Saginaw Spirit	OHL	57	3	11	14	28	....	....	....	....	....
2004-05	Saginaw Spirit	OHL	66	7	26	33	31	....	....	....	....	....
2005-06	Saginaw Spirit	OHL	68	21	56	77	64	4	1	3	4	6
2006-07	Saginaw Spirit	OHL	58	22	36	58	49	6	3	2	5	6
2007-08	Hershey Bears	AHL	48	1	13	14	16	2	0	0	0	0
	South Carolina	ECHL	19	5	11	16	16	5	0	2	2	4
2008-09	Hershey Bears	AHL	46	3	15	18	20	10	0	3	3	4
2009-10	Hershey Bears	AHL	62	8	27	35	36	11	3	3	6	2

OHL Second All-Star Team (2006)

McNEILL, Reid (muhk-NEEL, REED) PIT.

Defense. Shoots left. 6'3", 191 lbs. Born, London, Ont., April 29, 1992.
(Pittsburgh's 6th choice, 170th overall, in 2010 Entry Draft).

			Regular Season					Playoffs				
Season	Club	League	GP	G	A	Pts	PIM	GP	G	A	Pts	PIM
2008-09	Lambeth Lancers	OJHL-D	16	0	4	4	12	....	....	....	....	....
	Lucas High School	High-ON	STATISTICS NOT AVAILABLE									
2009-10	London Nationals	OJHL-B	20	0	7	7	6	....	....	....	....	....
	London Knights	OHL	53	2	3	5	32	12	0	1	1	0

McNICOLL, Cedric (mihk-NIH-kohl, SEH-DRIHK) CAR.

Center. Shoots left. 5'10", 180 lbs. Born, Longueuil, Que., August 28, 1988.

			Regular Season					Playoffs				
Season	Club	League	GP	G	A	Pts	PIM	GP	G	A	Pts	PIM
2004-05	C.C. Lemoyne	QAAA	41	20	24	44	30	4	2	2	4	21
	Shawinigan	QMJHL	1	0	1	1	0	1	0	0	0	0
2005-06	Shawinigan	QMJHL	67	13	17	30	34	10	1	7	8	2
2006-07	Shawinigan	QMJHL	47	16	30	46	14	4	4	1	5	0
2007-08	Shawinigan	QMJHL	69	43	40	83	20	5	0	8	8	6
2008-09	Shawinigan	QMJHL	65	38	66	104	22	....	....	....	....	....
2009-10	Lake Erie Monsters	AHL	45	5	8	13	0	....	....	....	....	....
	Charlotte	ECHL	3	1	3	4	0	....	....	....	....	....
	Albany River Rats	AHL	7	2	0	2	0	....	....	....	....	....
	Florida Everblades	ECHL	5	1	3	4	0	6	0	2	2	0

QMJHL First All-Star Team (2009) • Canadian Major Junior Second All-Star Team (2009) • Canadian Major Junior Sportsman of the Year (2008, 2009)

Signed as a free agent by **Colorado**, March 6, 2009. Traded to **Carolina** by **Colorado** with Colorado's 6th round choice (Tyler Stahl) in 2010 Entry Draft for Stephane Yelle and Harrison Reed, March 3, 2010.

McPHERSON, Corbin (muhk-FUHR-suhn, KOHR-bihn) N.J.

Defense. Shoots right. 6'4", 210 lbs. Born, Folsom, CA, September 7, 1988.
(New Jersey's 3rd choice, 87th overall, in 2007 Entry Draft).

			Regular Season					Playoffs				
Season	Club	League	GP	G	A	Pts	PIM	GP	G	A	Pts	PIM
2005-06	San Jose Jr. Sharks	Minor-CA	59	5	16	21	45	....	....	....	....	....
2006-07	Cowichan Valley	BCHL	44	4	10	14	63	18	1	3	4	14
2007-08	Cowichan Valley	BCHL	55	3	14	17	84	....	....	....	....	....
2008-09	Colgate	ECAC	37	0	5	5	50	....	....	....	....	....
2009-10	Colgate	ECAC	35	2	6	8	20	....	....	....	....	....

McRAE, Philip (muh-KRAY, FIHL-ihp) ST.L.

Center. Shoots left. 6'2", 195 lbs. Born, Minneapolis, MN, March 15, 1990.
(St. Louis' 2nd choice, 33rd overall, in 2008 Entry Draft).

			Regular Season					Playoffs				
Season	Club	League	GP	G	A	Pts	PIM	GP	G	A	Pts	PIM
2005-06	USNTDP	U-17	15	1	1	2	0	....	....	....	....	....
	USNTDP	NAHL	33	8	8	16	9	10	1	2	3	2
2006-07	London Knights	OHL	63	2	8	10	27	16	0	0	0	6
2007-08	London Knights	OHL	66	18	28	46	61	4	0	0	0	7
2008-09	London Knights	OHL	59	29	31	60	54	14	5	5	10	12
2009-10	London Knights	OHL	33	11	26	37	43	....	....	....	....	....
	Plymouth Whalers	OHL	19	5	9	14	21	9	6	9	15	11

MECKLER, David (MEHK-luhr, DAY-vihd) L.A.

Center. Shoots right. 6', 214 lbs. Born, Highland Park, IL, July 9, 1987.
(Los Angeles' 7th choice, 134th overall, in 2006 Entry Draft).

			Regular Season					Playoffs				
Season	Club	League	GP	G	A	Pts	PIM	GP	G	A	Pts	PIM
2004-05	Waterloo	USHL	60	30	15	45	32	5	3	2	5	2
2005-06	Yale	ECAC	31	7	3	10	28	....	....	....	....	....
2006-07	London Knights	OHL	67	38	35	73	53	16	*15	7	22	20
2007-08	Manchester	AHL	76	23	13	36	24	4	1	1	2	2
2008-09	Manchester	AHL	74	14	15	29	28	....	....	....	....	....
2009-10	Manchester	AHL	73	11	9	20	22	14	1	0	1	2

MEDVEC, Kyle (MEHD-vek, KIGHL) MIN.

Defense. Shoots left. 6'6", 227 lbs. Born, Westminster, CO, June 16, 1988.
(Minnesota's 4th choice, 102nd overall, in 2006 Entry Draft).

			Regular Season					Playoffs				
Season	Club	League	GP	G	A	Pts	PIM	GP	G	A	Pts	PIM
2003-04	Apple Valley	High-MN	27	1	12	13	30	....	....	....	....	....
2004-05	Apple Valley	High-MN	23	4	16	20	18	....	....	....	....	....
2005-06	Apple Valley	High-MN	28	13	22	35	44	....	....	....	....	....
	Sioux City	USHL	3	0	0	0	0	....	....	....	....	....
2006-07	Sioux City	USHL	57	4	14	18	83	7	0	0	0	4
2007-08	U. of Vermont	H-East	30	1	4	5	18	....	....	....	....	....
2008-09	U. of Vermont	H-East	39	2	10	12	40	....	....	....	....	....
2009-10	U. of Vermont	H-East	39	5	10	15	50	....	....	....	....	....

MEGALINSKY, Dmitri (meh-gahl-IHN-skee, dih-MEE-tree) OTT.

Defense. Shoots left. 6'2", 212 lbs. Born, Perm, USSR, April 15, 1985.
(Ottawa's 7th choice, 186th overall, in 2005 Entry Draft).

			Regular Season					Playoffs				
Season	Club	League	GP	G	A	Pts	PIM	GP	G	A	Pts	PIM
2003-04	HK Voronezh	Russia-2	42	4	8	12	159	....	....	....	....	....
	Yaroslavl	Russia	1	0	0	0	0	....	....	....	....	....
	Yaroslavl 2	Russia-3	11	0	4	4	16	....	....	....	....	....
2004-05	Yaroslavl	Russia	1	0	0	0	2	....	....	....	....	....
	Yaroslavl 2	Russia-3	30	6	12	18	82	....	....	....	....	....
2005-06	Yaroslavl 2	Russia-3	12	4	10	14	6	....	....	....	....	....
	Yaroslavl	Russia	20	0	1	1	8	8	0	0	0	6
2006-07	Khimik	Russia-2	33	4	7	11	34	7	0	1	1	16
2007-08	Vityaz Chekhov	Russia	25	2	7	9	20	....	....	....	....	....
2008-09	Vityaz Chekhov	Rus-KHL	52	2	5	7	72	....	....	....	....	....
2009-10	Vityaz Chekhov	Rus-KHL	52	4	16	20	98	....	....	....	....	....

MEGAN, Wade (MEE-guhn, WAYD) FLA.

Center. Shoots left. 6'1", 185 lbs. Born, Canton, NY, July 22, 1990.
(Florida's 6th choice, 138th overall, in 2009 Entry Draft).

			Regular Season					Playoffs				
Season	Club	League	GP	G	A	Pts	PIM	GP	G	A	Pts	PIM
2007-08	Kent Prep School	High-CT	34	24	29	53	....	....	....	....	....	....
2008-09	Kent Prep School	High-CT	32	27	36	63	18	....	....	....	....	....
	Neponset Valley	Minor-MA	16	8	8	16	....	....	....	....	....	....
2009-10	Boston University	H-East	35	5	7	12	22	....	....	....	....	....

MELCHIORI, Julian (mehl-KEE-awr-ee, JOO-lee-ehn) ATL.

Defense. Shoots left. 6'3", 200 lbs. Born, Richmond Hill, Ont., December 6, 1991.
(Atlanta's 2nd choice, 87th overall, in 2010 Entry Draft).

			Regular Season					Playoffs				
Season	Club	League	GP	G	A	Pts	PIM	GP	G	A	Pts	PIM
2007-08	Toronto Marlboros	GTHL	43	2	13	15	36	....	....	....	....	....
2008-09	Newmarket	OJHL	48	2	20	22	34	9	1	2	3	14
2009-10	Newmarket	CCHL	39	7	16	23	16	20	2	9	11	10

• Signed Letter of Intent to attend **University of Massachusetts-Lowell** (Hockey East) in fall of 2010.

MELYAKOV, Igor (mehl-yuh-KAHF, EE-gohr) L.A.

Left wing. Shoots left. 5'10", 200 lbs. Born, Lipetsk, USSR, December 23, 1976.
(Los Angeles' 6th choice, 137th overall, in 1995 Entry Draft).

			Regular Season					Playoffs				
Season	Club	League	GP	G	A	Pts	PIM	GP	G	A	Pts	PIM
1993-94	Torpedo Yaroslavl	CIS	39	4	3	7	10	4	0	0	0	0
1994-95	Torpedo Yaroslavl	CIS	50	6	8	14	34	4	0	1	1	0
1995-96	Torpedo Yaroslavl	CIS	39	5	1	6	6	3	0	0	0	2
1996-97	Torpedo Yaroslavl	Russia	8	0	0	0	0	....	....	....	....	....
	Nizhny Novgorod	Russia	12	2	3	5	10	....	....	....	....	....
1997-98	Nizhny Novgorod	Russia	13	3	3	6	6	....	....	....	....	....
1998-99	Nizhny Novgorod	Russia-2	36	13	17	30	14	....	....	....	....	....
99-2000	Nizhny Novgorod	Russia	34	1	8	9	10	5	1	0	1	4
2000-01	Nizhny Novgorod	Russia	24	2	3	5	10	....	....	....	....	....
2001-02	HK Lipetsk	Russia-2	68	16	37	53	94	....	....	....	....	....
2002-03	Voskresensk	Russia-2	48	9	22	31	16	....	....	....	....	....
2003-04	Nizhny Novgorod	Russia	45	5	10	15	18	....	....	....	....	....
	Nizh. Novgorod 2	Russia-3	4	1	6	7	4	....	....	....	....	....
2004-05	Nizhny Novgorod	Russia-2	52	14	30	44	32	11	2	4	6	18
2005-06	Magnitogorsk	Russia	25	7	8	15	10	3	0	0	0	2
2006-07	Novokuznetsk	Russia	22	0	1	1	8	....	....	....	....	....
	Nizhny Novgorod	Russia-2	16	2	6	8	10	12	2	5	7	6
2007-08	Nizhny Novgorod	Russia	8	1	0	1	6	....	....	....	....	....
	Zauralje Kurgan	Russia-2	24	2	11	13	38	....	....	....	....	....
2008-09	Zauralje Kurgan	Russia-2	46	3	22	25	32	....	....	....	....	....
2009-10	Titan Klin	Russia-2	54	10	25	35	30	13	2	2	4	6

MERRILL, Jonathon
(MAIR-ihl, JAWN-ah-thuhn) **N.J.**

Defense. Shoots left. 6'3", 200 lbs. Born, Oklahoma City, OK, February 3, 1992.
(New Jersey's 1st choice, 38th overall, in 2010 Entry Draft).

			Regular Season					Playoffs				
Season	**Club**	**League**	**GP**	**G**	**A**	**Pts**	**PIM**	**GP**	**G**	**A**	**Pts**	**PIM**
2007-08	Det. Caesars	MWEHL	25	2	9	11	26	....	....	....	....	....
	Det. Caesars	Minor-MI	....	7	21	28	....	....	....	....	....	....
2008-09	USNTDP	NAHL	26	2	2	4	14	....	....	....	....	....
	USNTDP	U-17	8	0	1	1	6	....	....	....	....	....
	USNTDP	U-18	9	1	2	3	4	....	....	....	....	....
2009-10	USNTDP	USHL	22	1	8	9	12	....	....	....	....	....
	USNTDP	U-18	34	4	19	23	6	....	....	....	....	....

• Signed Letter of Intent to attend **University of Michigan** (CCHA) in fall of 2010.

MEYERS, Josh
(MIGH-uhrs, JAWSH) **CGY.**

Defense. Shoots right. 6'2", 190 lbs. Born, Alexandria, MN, December 7, 1985.
(Los Angeles' 7th choice, 206th overall, in 2005 Entry Draft).

			Regular Season					Playoffs				
Season	**Club**	**League**	**GP**	**G**	**A**	**Pts**	**PIM**	**GP**	**G**	**A**	**Pts**	**PIM**
2003-04	Minnesota Blizzard	NAHL	27	2	12	14	....	....	....	....	....	....
2004-05	Sioux City	USHL	57	8	24	32	92	13	1	9	10	18
2005-06	U. Minn-Duluth	WCHA	27	3	7	10	20	....	....	....	....	....
2006-07	U. Minn-Duluth	WCHA	37	11	13	24	30	....	....	....	....	....
2007-08	U. Minn-Duluth	WCHA	36	6	8	14	72	....	....	....	....	....
2008-09	U. Minn-Duluth	WCHA	43	10	18	28	42	....	....	....	....	....
2009-10	Utah Grizzlies	ECHL	12	0	3	3	2	....	....	....	....	....
	Abbotsford Heat	AHL	54	3	15	18	28	11	1	0	1	13

Signed as a free agent by **Calgary**, December 28, 2009.

MIKUS, Juraj
(MEE-kuhsh, YUHR-ay) **TOR.**

Defense. Shoots left. 6'4", 185 lbs. Born, Trencin, Czech., November 30, 1988.
(Toronto's 4th choice, 134th overall, in 2007 Entry Draft).

			Regular Season					Playoffs				
Season	**Club**	**League**	**GP**	**G**	**A**	**Pts**	**PIM**	**GP**	**G**	**A**	**Pts**	**PIM**
2004-05	Piestany U18	Svk-U18	2	1	2	3	2	....	....	....	....	....
	Dukla Trencin U18	Svk-U18	39	2	7	9	20	5	0	0	0	0
2005-06	Piestany Jr.	Slovak-Jr.	6	0	4	4	2	....	....	....	....	....
	Dukla Trencin Jr.	Slovak-Jr.	17	1	4	5	2	....	....	....	....	....
	Dukla Trencin U18	Svk-U18	40	3	18	21	36	7	1	5	6	12
2006-07	Dukla Trencin Jr.	Slovak-Jr.	42	9	15	24	72	7	2	1	3	10
	P. Bystrica	Slovak-2	7	0	3	3	2	1	0	0	0	0
	Dukla Trencin	Slovakia	22	0	0	0	2	7	0	0	0	0
2007-08	HK VSR SR 20	Slovakia	21	1	4	5	30	....	....	....	....	....
	Dukla Trencin	Slovakia	14	0	3	3	4	14	0	1	1	2
2008-09	HC Dukla Senica	Slovak-2	9	1	1	2	4	1	0	0	0	0
	Dukla Trencin	Slovakia	51	2	1	3	18	4	2	0	2	0
	Dukla Trencin Jr.	Slovak-Jr.	....	....	....	....	....	2	0	0	0	2
2009-10	Toronto Marlies	AHL	68	5	18	23	38	....	....	....	....	....

MILLER, Tyler
(MIHL-luhr, TIGH-luhr) **N.J.**

Defense. Shoots left. 6'4", 230 lbs. Born, Placentia, CA, September 15, 1986.
(New Jersey's 5th choice, 107th overall, in 2006 Entry Draft).

			Regular Season					Playoffs				
Season	**Club**	**League**	**GP**	**G**	**A**	**Pts**	**PIM**	**GP**	**G**	**A**	**Pts**	**PIM**
2004-05	South Surrey	BCHL	53	3	9	12	85	....	....	....	....	....
2005-06	Penticton Vees	BCHL	60	16	32	48	73	....	....	....	....	....
2006-07	Northern Mich.	CCHA	37	2	12	14	12	....	....	....	....	....
2007-08	Northern Mich.	CCHA	42	2	7	9	53	....	....	....	....	....
2008-09	Northern Mich.	CCHA	16	0	2	2	14	....	....	....	....	....
2009-10	Northern Mich.	CCHA	39	4	11	15	38	....	....	....	....	....

MILLS, Brad
(MIHLS, BRAD) **N.J.**

Right wing. Shoots right. 6', 195 lbs. Born, Terrace, B.C., May 3, 1983.

			Regular Season					Playoffs				
Season	**Club**	**League**	**GP**	**G**	**A**	**Pts**	**PIM**	**GP**	**G**	**A**	**Pts**	**PIM**
2002-03	Fort McMurray	AJHL	62	20	47	67	73	....	....	....	....	....
2003-04	Yale	ECAC	27	4	7	11	18	....	....	....	....	....
2004-05	Yale	ECAC	27	12	14	26	30	....	....	....	....	....
2005-06	Yale	ECAC	22	8	8	16	65	....	....	....	....	....
2006-07	Yale	ECAC	20	2	6	8	39	....	....	....	....	....
	Lowell Devils	AHL	8	0	1	1	4	....	....	....	....	....
2007-08	Lowell Devils	AHL	16	1	2	3	44	....	....	....	....	....
	Trenton Devils	ECHL	26	9	7	16	67	....	....	....	....	....
2008-09	Lowell Devils	AHL	75	5	16	21	108	....	....	....	....	....
2009-10	Lowell Devils	AHL	51	12	7	19	67	2	1	2	3	4

Signed as a free agent by **Lowell** (AHL), March 16, 2007. Signed as a free agent by **New Jersey**, June 1, 2009.

MIRNOV, Igor
(mihr-NAWF, EE-gohr) **OTT.**

Left wing. Shoots left. 6', 187 lbs. Born, Chita, USSR, September 19, 1984.
(Ottawa's 2nd choice, 67th overall, in 2003 Entry Draft).

			Regular Season					Playoffs				
Season	**Club**	**League**	**GP**	**G**	**A**	**Pts**	**PIM**	**GP**	**G**	**A**	**Pts**	**PIM**
2001-02	Dyn'o Moscow 2	Russia-3	30	33	17	50	34	....	....	....	....	....
	Dynamo Moscow	Russia	6	0	0	0	0	....	....	....	....	....
2002-03	Dynamo Moscow	Russia	50	3	7	10	49	5	0	0	0	2
2003-04	Dynamo Moscow	Russia	53	11	10	21	26	3	0	0	0	2
2004-05	Dynamo Moscow	Russia	55	13	13	26	50	9	2	4	6	0
2005-06	Dynamo Moscow	Russia	32	8	10	18	36	4	0	2	2	4
2006-07	Dynamo Moscow	Russia	49	21	25	46	54	3	2	1	3	4
2007-08	Dynamo Moscow	Russia	24	3	3	6	16	....	....	....	....	....
	Magnitogorsk	Russia	23	9	6	15	20	13	3	1	4	4
2008-09	Magnitogorsk	Rus-KHL	39	11	8	19	24	11	2	7	9	8
2009-10	Mytischi	Rus-KHL	20	2	4	6	0	....	....	....	....	....
	MVD	Rus-KHL	10	1	3	4	4	....	....	....	....	....
	Sibir Novosibirsk	Rus-KHL	12	7	5	12	8	....	....	....	....	....

MISKOVIC, Zach
(MIHS-koh-vihch, ZAK) **WSH.**

Defense. Shoots right. 6'1", 158 lbs. Born, River Forest, IL, May 8, 1985.

			Regular Season					Playoffs				
Season	**Club**	**League**	**GP**	**G**	**A**	**Pts**	**PIM**	**GP**	**G**	**A**	**Pts**	**PIM**
2002-03	Cedar Rapids	USHL	60	2	6	8	91	7	0	0	0	12
2003-04	Cedar Rapids	USHL	60	6	15	21	139	4	1	1	2	2
2004-05	Cedar Rapids	USHL	60	4	16	20	149	8	1	0	1	14
2005-06	St. Lawrence	ECAC	40	1	15	16	30	....	....	....	....	....
2006-07	St. Lawrence	ECAC	39	2	10	12	48	....	....	....	....	....
2007-08	St. Lawrence	ECAC	37	8	12	20	36	....	....	....	....	....
2008-09	St. Lawrence	ECAC	38	16	9	25	32	....	....	....	....	....
2009-10	Hershey Bears	AHL	59	6	20	26	25	6	1	1	2	0

ECAC First All-Star Team (2009) • NCAA East First All-American Team (2009)

Signed as a free agent by **Washington**, March 25, 2009.

MITCHELL, Dale
(MIH-chuhl, DAYL) **TOR.**

Right wing. Shoots right. 5'9", 200 lbs. Born, Etobicoke, Ont., April 9, 1989.
(Toronto's 1st choice, 74th overall, in 2007 Entry Draft).

			Regular Season					Playoffs				
Season	**Club**	**League**	**GP**	**G**	**A**	**Pts**	**PIM**	**GP**	**G**	**A**	**Pts**	**PIM**
2005-06	Oshawa Generals	OHL	65	20	23	43	63	....	....	....	....	....
2006-07	Oshawa Generals	OHL	67	43	37	80	81	9	1	4	5	12
2007-08	Oshawa Generals	OHL	63	24	36	60	79	15	10	6	16	23
	Toronto Marlies	AHL	....	....	....	....	....	2	0	1	1	2
2008-09	Windsor Spitfires	OHL	66	33	35	68	87	20	14	15	29	24
2009-10	Windsor Spitfires	OHL	32	16	27	43	44	19	7	10	17	16
	Toronto Marlies	AHL	9	2	1	3	2	....	....	....	....	....

MITCHELL, Garrett
(MIH-chuhl, GAIR-reht) **WSH.**

Right wing. Shoots right. 5'11", 185 lbs. Born, Regina, Sask., September 2, 1991.
(Washington's 6th choice, 175th overall, in 2009 Entry Draft).

			Regular Season					Playoffs				
Season	**Club**	**League**	**GP**	**G**	**A**	**Pts**	**PIM**	**GP**	**G**	**A**	**Pts**	**PIM**
2006-07	Reg. Pat Cdns.	SMHL	42	14	11	25	140	....	....	....	....	....
	Regina Pats	WHL	4	0	1	1	2	....	....	....	....	....
2007-08	Regina Pats	WHL	62	8	5	13	73	6	1	0	1	6
2008-09	Regina Pats	WHL	71	10	5	15	140	....	....	....	....	....
2009-10	Regina Pats	WHL	57	15	16	31	110	....	....	....	....	....
	Hershey Bears	AHL	1	0	0	0	0	....	....	....	....	....

MITERA, Mark
(MIH-tair-a, MAHRK) **ANA.**

Defense. Shoots left. 6'4", 214 lbs. Born, Royal Oak, MI, October 22, 1987.
(Anaheim's 1st choice, 19th overall, in 2006 Entry Draft).

			Regular Season					Playoffs				
Season	**Club**	**League**	**GP**	**G**	**A**	**Pts**	**PIM**	**GP**	**G**	**A**	**Pts**	**PIM**
2003-04	USNTDP	U-17	16	2	6	8	22	....	....	....	....	....
	USNTDP	NAHL	43	2	13	15	69	7	0	2	2	10
2004-05	USNTDP	U-18	45	5	10	15	91	....	....	....	....	....
	USNTDP	NAHL	16	2	6	8	32	....	....	....	....	....
2005-06	U. of Michigan	CCHA	39	0	10	10	59	....	....	....	....	....
2006-07	U. of Michigan	CCHA	41	1	17	18	52	....	....	....	....	....
2007-08	U. of Michigan	CCHA	43	2	21	23	60	....	....	....	....	....
2008-09	U. of Michigan	CCHA	8	1	2	3	4	....	....	....	....	....
	Iowa Chops	AHL	5	0	2	2	2	....	....	....	....	....
2009-10	San Antonio	AHL	5	0	0	0	6	....	....	....	....	....
	Abbotsford Heat	AHL	27	0	3	3	12	13	0	2	2	9
	Bakersfield	ECHL	36	3	11	14	62	....	....	....	....	....

CCHA Second All-Star Team (2008)

MOFFATT, Luke
(MAW-fuht, LEWK) **COL.**

Center. Shoots right. 6'1", 187 lbs. Born, Scottsdale, AZ, June 11, 1992.
(Colorado's 8th choice, 197th overall, in 2010 Entry Draft).

			Regular Season					Playoffs				
Season	**Club**	**League**	**GP**	**G**	**A**	**Pts**	**PIM**	**GP**	**G**	**A**	**Pts**	**PIM**
2007-08	Det. Compuware	MWEHL	30	37	19	56	....	....	....	....	....	....
	Det. Compuware	Minor-MI	5	4	1	5	4	....	....	....	....	....
2008-09	USNTDP	NAHL	42	17	10	27	30	9	0	3	3	4
	USNTDP	U-17	16	4	7	11	2	....	....	....	....	....
2009-10	USNTDP	USHL	28	5	10	15	22	....	....	....	....	....
	USNTDP	U-18	37	13	9	22	14	....	....	....	....	....

• Signed Letter of Intent to attend **University of Michigan** (CCHA) in fall of 2010.

MOFFIE, Lee
(MAW-fee, LEE) **S.J.**

Defense. Shoots left. 6'1", 205 lbs. Born, Wallingford, CT, August 29, 1990.
(San Jose's 7th choice, 188th overall, in 2010 Entry Draft).

			Regular Season					Playoffs				
Season	**Club**	**League**	**GP**	**G**	**A**	**Pts**	**PIM**	**GP**	**G**	**A**	**Pts**	**PIM**
2008-09	Waterloo	USHL	55	9	35	44	97	3	0	0	0	6
2009-10	U. of Michigan	CCHA	29	4	8	12	27	....	....	....	....	....

MONAST, Guillaume
(moh-NAST, GEE-OHM) **DAL.**

Defense. Shoots right. 6'2", 199 lbs. Born, Longueuil, Que., May 12, 1988.

			Regular Season					Playoffs				
Season	**Club**	**League**	**GP**	**G**	**A**	**Pts**	**PIM**	**GP**	**G**	**A**	**Pts**	**PIM**
2005-06	Val-d'Or Foreurs	QMJHL	65	2	7	9	54	5	0	0	0	0
2006-07	Val-d'Or Foreurs	QMJHL	35	0	4	4	31	....	....	....	....	....
	Halifax	QMJHL	32	3	11	14	28	12	2	7	9	6
2007-08	Halifax	QMJHL	65	8	22	30	68	15	2	4	6	22
2008-09	Quebec Remparts	QMJHL	63	5	38	43	59	17	3	7	10	22
2009-10	Idaho Steelheads	ECHL	68	0	6	6	69	13	1	4	5	4

Signed as a free agent by **Dallas**, September 25, 2008.

IONTGOMERY, Kevin (mawnt-GUHM-uhr-ee, KEH-vihn) **COL.**

efense. Shoots left. 6'1", 185 lbs. Born, Rochester, NY, April 4, 1988.
Colorado's 5th choice, 110th overall, in 2006 Entry Draft).

			Regular Season					Playoffs				
eason	Club	League	GP	G	A	Pts	PIM	GP	G	A	Pts	PIM
003-04	Syracuse Jr. Stars	EmJHL	62	7	28	35	....	....	....	....	....	....
004-05	USNTDP	U-17	8	1	4	5	4	....	....	....	....	....
	USNTDP	NAHL	38	4	12	16	46	9	1	3	4	6
005-06	USNTDP	U-18	42	2	10	12	61	....	....	....	....	....
	USNTDP	NAHL	17	4	6	10	15	....	....	....	....	....
006-07	Ohio State	CCHA	17	1	4	5	18	....	....	....	....	....
	London Knights	OHL	31	1	16	17	50	9	0	0	0	6
007-08	London Knights	OHL	63	9	34	43	95	5	0	1	1	4
	Lake Erie Monsters	AHL	5	0	0	0	2	....	....	....	....	....
008-09	London Knights	OHL	46	2	34	36	41	14	0	4	4	6
	Lake Erie Monsters	AHL	5	0	1	1	2	....	....	....	....	....
009-10	Lake Erie Monsters	AHL	65	1	6	7	37	....	....	....	....	....

IOORE, John (MOOR, JAWN) **CBJ**

efense. Shoots left. 6'3", 198 lbs. Born, Winnetka, IL, November 19, 1990.
Columbus' 1st choice, 21st overall, in 2009 Entry Draft).

			Regular Season					Playoffs				
eason	Club	League	GP	G	A	Pts	PIM	GP	G	A	Pts	PIM
006-07	Chicago Mission	MWEHL	31	1	12	13	26	....	....	....	....	....
	Chicago Mission	Exhib.	30	13	37	50	14	....	....	....	....	....
007-08	Chicago Steel	USHL	56	4	11	15	26	7	0	2	2	2
008-09	Chicago Steel	USHL	57	14	25	39	50	....	....	....	....	....
009-10	Kitchener Rangers	OHL	61	10	37	47	53	20	4	12	16	2

SHL First All-Star Team (2009) • USHL Defenseman of the Year (2009)

IOORE, Mike (MOOR, MIGHK) **S.J.**

efense. Shoots left. 6'1", 200 lbs. Born, Calgary, Alta., December 12, 1984.

			Regular Season					Playoffs				
eason	Club	League	GP	G	A	Pts	PIM	GP	G	A	Pts	PIM
003-04	South Surrey	BCHL	52	6	21	27	148	10	0	2	2	6
004-05	Princeton	ECAC	25	3	7	10	22	....	....	....	....	....
005-06	Princeton	ECAC	30	0	4	4	42	....	....	....	....	....
006-07	Princeton	ECAC	32	4	10	14	50	....	....	....	....	....
007-08	Princeton	ECAC	34	7	17	24	40	....	....	....	....	....
	Worcester Sharks	AHL	3	0	0	0	16	....	....	....	....	....
008-09	Worcester Sharks	AHL	76	5	13	18	132	12	0	1	1	17
009-10	Worcester Sharks	AHL	64	3	19	22	82	11	0	0	0	14

CAC First All-Star Team (2008) • NCAA East First All-American Team (2008)

igned as a free agent by **San Jose**, April 8, 2008.

IORIN, Jeremy (moh-REHN, JAIR-eh-mee) **CHI.**

ft wing. Shoots right. 6'1", 190 lbs. Born, Auburn, NY, April 16, 1991.
Atlanta's 3rd choice, 45th overall, in 2009 Entry Draft).

			Regular Season					Playoffs				
eason	Club	League	GP	G	A	Pts	PIM	GP	G	A	Pts	PIM
006-07	Syracuse Stars	EJHL	45	26	28	54	80	....	....	....	....	....
007-08	USNTDP	NAHL	30	17	17	34	26	....	....	....	....	....
	USNTDP	U-17	7	11	1	12	4	....	....	....	....	....
	USNTDP	U-18	28	20	14	34	36	....	....	....	....	....
008-09	USNTDP	NAHL	14	12	15	27	28	....	....	....	....	....
	USNTDP	U-18	41	21	11	32	79	....	....	....	....	....
009-10	Kitchener Rangers	OHL	58	47	36	83	76	20	12	9	21	32

HL Second All-Star Team (2010)

aded to **Chicago** by **Atlanta** with Marty Reasoner, Joey Crabb and New Jersey's 1st (previously :quired, Chicago selected Kevin Hayes) and 2nd (previously acquired, Chicago selected Justin oll) round choices in 2010 Entry Draft for Brent Sopel, Dustin Byfuglien, Ben Eager and Akim iu, June 24, 2010.

IOZYAKIN, Sergei (mohz-YA-kihn, SAIR-gay) **CBJ**

ft wing. Shoots right. 5'10", 171 lbs. Born, Yaroslavl, USSR, March 30, 1981.
Columbus' 13th choice, 263rd overall, in 2002 Entry Draft).

			Regular Season					Playoffs				
eason	Club	League	GP	G	A	Pts	PIM	GP	G	A	Pts	PIM
998-99	Val-d'Or Foreurs	QMJHL	4	0	1	1	2	....	....	....	....	....
9-2000	HK Moscow 2	Russia-3	6	9	3	12	6	....	....	....	....	....
	HK Moscow	Russia-2	44	23	25	48	10	....	....	....	....	....
000-01	HK Moscow	Russia-2	37	22	28	50	18	....	....	....	....	....
	CSKA Moscow	Russia	9	0	2	2	0	....	....	....	....	....
001-02	HK CSKA Moscow	Russia-2	54	34	30	64	10	12	9	12	21	4
002-03	CSKA Moscow	Russia	33	12	15	27	18	....	....	....	....	....
003-04	CSKA Moscow	Russia	45	21	19	40	6	....	....	....	....	....
004-05	CSKA Moscow	Russia	49	11	12	23	22	....	....	....	....	....
005-06	CSKA Moscow	Russia	51	20	*31	*51	28	7	1	2	3	4
006-07	Mytischi	Russia	54	27	33	60	10	9	5	3	8	4
007-08	Mytischi	Russia	57	*37	29	*66	22	5	3	1	4	0
008-09	Mytischi	Rus-KHL	56	36	*42	*78	14	7	2	5	7	0
009-10	Mytischi	Rus-KHL	56	27	39	*66	44	4	1	3	4	0

IUELLER, Marcel (MUHL-uhr, MAHR-sehl) **TOR.**

ft wing. Shoots left. 6'3", 220 lbs. Born, Berlin, East Germany, July 10, 1988.

			Regular Season					Playoffs				
eason	Club	League	GP	G	A	Pts	PIM	GP	G	A	Pts	PIM
003-04	Mannheim Jr.	Ger-Jr.	27	3	5	8	51	4	1	2	3	4
004-05	Mannheim Jr.	Ger-Jr.	26	21	13	34	100	....	....	....	....	....
	Mannheimer ERC	German-5	3	1	1	2	4	....	....	....	....	....
005-06	Eisb. Jrs. Berl. Jr.	Ger-Jr.	8	9	4	13	50	1	0	0	0	0
	Eisb. Jrs. Berlin	German-3	27	7	8	15	91	....	....	....	....	....
	Eisbaren Berlin	Germany	24	1	1	2	20	....	....	....	....	....
006-07	Eisb. Jrs. Berlin	German-3	9	1	3	4	18	....	....	....	....	....
	Eisbaren Berlin	Germany	36	1	7	8	53	3	0	0	0	14
007-08	Kolner Haie	Germany	44	6	7	13	61	14	1	1	2	6
008-09	Kolner Haie	Germany	41	11	14	25	60	....	....	....	....	....
009-10	Kolner Haie	Germany	53	24	32	56	122	3	0	4	4	2

igned as a free agent by **Toronto**, July 14, 2010.

MULLEN, Patrick (MUHL-uhn, PA-trihk) **L.A.**

Defense. Shoots right. 6', 181 lbs. Born, Pittsburgh, PA, May 6, 1986.

			Regular Season					Playoffs				
Season	Club	League	GP	G	A	Pts	PIM	GP	G	A	Pts	PIM
2004-05	Sioux City	USHL	60	14	23	37	8	....	....	....	....	....
2005-06	U. of Denver	WCHA	37	7	10	17	24	....	....	....	....	....
	U. of Denver	WCHA	37	7	10	17	24	....	....	....	....	....
2006-07	U. of Denver	WCHA	37	5	12	17	20	....	....	....	....	....
2007-08	U. of Denver	WCHA	40	4	18	22	65	....	....	....	....	....
2008-09	U. of Denver	WCHA	38	4	21	25	39	....	....	....	....	....
2009-10	Manchester	AHL	44	4	6	10	16	2	0	0	0	2
	Ontario Reign	ECHL	1	0	0	0	0	....	....	....	....	....

Signed as a free agent by **Los Angeles**, April 3, 2009.

MULLIN, Jimmy (MUH-lihn, JIHM-ee) **T.B.**

Right wing. Shoots right. 5'10", 152 lbs. Born, Philadelphia, PA, February 24, 1992.
(Tampa Bay's 6th choice, 118th overall, in 2010 Entry Draft).

			Regular Season					Playoffs				
Season	Club	League	GP	G	A	Pts	PIM	GP	G	A	Pts	PIM
2006-07	Shattuck Bantam	High-MN	67	24	34	58	24	....	....	....	....	....
2007-08	Shattuck U-16	High-MN	52	20	29	49	32	....	....	....	....	....
2008-09	Shattuck U-16	High-MN	56	62	44	106	38	....	....	....	....	....
2009-10	Shat.-St. Mary's	High-MN	55	32	40	72	26	....	....	....	....	....

• Signed Letter of Intent to attend **Miami University** (CCHA) in fall of 2011.

MURSAK, Jan (MUHR-sak, YAHN) **DET.**

Left wing. Shoots right. 5'11", 184 lbs. Born, Maribor, Yugoslavia, January 20, 1988.
(Detroit's 5th choice, 182nd overall, in 2006 Entry Draft).

			Regular Season					Playoffs				
Season	Club	League	GP	G	A	Pts	PIM	GP	G	A	Pts	PIM
2002-03	HK Maribor U18	Sloven-U18	13	27	18	45	14	....	....	....	....	....
2003-04	HK Maribor U18	Sloven-U18	22	27	17	44	14	....	....	....	....	....
	HK Maribor Jr.	Sloven-Jr.	19	8	8	16	37	....	....	....	....	....
	HK Maribor	Slovenia	14	3	3	6	16	....	....	....	....	....
2004-05	HK Maribor Jr.	Sloven-Jr.	19	17	16	33	39	....	....	....	....	....
	HK Maribor	Slovenia	24	16	29	45	10	....	....	....	....	....
2005-06	C. Budejovice Jr.	CzRep-Jr.	43	15	15	30	32	5	0	2	2	2
2006-07	Saginaw Spirit	OHL	62	27	53	80	50	6	1	2	3	10
	Grand Rapids	AHL	....	....	....	....	....	7	0	2	2	2
2007-08	Saginaw Spirit	OHL	26	6	20	26	15	....	....	....	....	....
	Belleville Bulls	OHL	31	11	27	38	8	21	9	15	24	10
2008-09	Grand Rapids	AHL	51	2	7	9	25	6	0	1	1	0
2009-10	Grand Rapids	AHL	79	24	18	42	46	....	....	....	....	....

MUZZIN, Jake (MUH-zihn, JAYK) **L.A.**

Defense. Shoots left. 6'2", 216 lbs. Born, Woodstock, Ont., February 21, 1989.
(Pittsburgh's 7th choice, 141st overall, in 2007 Entry Draft).

			Regular Season					Playoffs				
Season	Club	League	GP	G	A	Pts	PIM	GP	G	A	Pts	PIM
2004-05	Brantford 99ers	Minor-ON	57	20	23	43	78	....	....	....	....	....
2005-06	Sault Ste. Marie	OHL		DID NOT PLAY – INJURED								
2006-07	Soo Thunderbirds	NOJHL	4	0	3	3	2	....	....	....	....	....
	Sault Ste. Marie	OHL	37	1	3	4	10	13	0	4	4	6
2007-08	Sault Ste. Marie	OHL	67	6	12	18	53	10	1	3	4	4
2008-09	Sault Ste. Marie	OHL	62	6	23	29	57	....	....	....	....	....
2009-10	Sault Ste. Marie	OHL	64	15	52	67	76	5	0	1	1	2
	Manchester	AHL	1	0	1	1	0	13	1	3	4	6

OHL First All-Star Team (2010) • Canadian Major Junior First All-Star Team (2010)

• Missed entire 2005-06 season recovering from off-season back surgery. Signed as a free agent by **Los Angeles**, January 4, 2010.

NAGY, Kory (NAH-gee, KOHR-ee) **N.J.**

Left wing. Shoots left. 5'11", 195 lbs. Born, London, Ont., October 12, 1989.
(New Jersey's 6th choice, 142nd overall, in 2008 Entry Draft).

			Regular Season					Playoffs				
Season	Club	League	GP	G	A	Pts	PIM	GP	G	A	Pts	PIM
2005-06	Lindsay Muskies	OPJHL	47	11	12	23	14	4	0	0	0	0
	Oshawa Generals	OHL	16	0	1	1	8	....	....	....	....	....
2006-07	Oshawa Generals	OHL	64	0	5	5	18	9	0	0	0	4
2007-08	Oshawa Generals	OHL	57	5	12	17	47	15	6	3	9	4
2008-09	Oshawa Generals	OHL	63	17	38	55	83	....	....	....	....	....
2009-10	Lowell Devils	AHL	31	2	4	6	10	2	0	0	0	2
	Trenton Devils	ECHL	33	4	9	13	27	....	....	....	....	....

NASH, Brendon (NASH, BREHN-duhn) **MTL.**

Defense. Shoots left. 6'3", 205 lbs. Born, Calgary, Alta., March 31, 1987.

			Regular Season					Playoffs				
Season	Club	League	GP	G	A	Pts	PIM	GP	G	A	Pts	PIM
2005-06	Salmon Arm	BCHL	53	9	33	42	80	....	....	....	....	....
2006-07	Cornell Big Red	ECAC	29	2	12	14	38	....	....	....	....	....
2007-08	Cornell Big Red	ECAC	24	2	14	16	49	....	....	....	....	....
2008-09	Cornell Big Red	ECAC	34	2	16	18	38	....	....	....	....	....
2009-10	Cornell Big Red	ECAC	33	2	17	19	48	....	....	....	....	....

ECAC Second All-Star Team (2009) • ECAC First All-Star Team (2010) • NCAA East First All-American Team (2010)

Signed as a free agent by **Montreal**, March 30, 2010.

NASH, Riley (NASH, RIGH-lee) **CAR.**

Center. Shoots right. 6'1", 191 lbs. Born, Consort, Alta., May 9, 1989.
(Edmonton's 3rd choice, 21st overall, in 2007 Entry Draft).

			Regular Season					Playoffs				
Season	Club	League	GP	G	A	Pts	PIM	GP	G	A	Pts	PIM
2005-06	Thompson Blazers	BCMML	31	29	31	60	100	....	....	....	....	....
	Salmon Arm	BCHL	1	0	0	0	0	5	1	2	3	0
2006-07	Salmon Arm	BCHL	55	38	46	84	87	11	4	7	11	31
2007-08	Cornell Big Red	ECAC	36	12	20	32	28	....	....	....	....	....
2008-09	Cornell Big Red	ECAC	36	13	22	35	34	....	....	....	....	....
2009-10	Cornell Big Red	ECAC	30	12	23	35	39	....	....	....	....	....

ECAC All-Rookie Team (2008) • ECAC Rookie of the Year (2008) • ECAC First All-Star Team (2009)

Traded to **Carolina** by **Edmonton** for Ottawa's 2nd round choice (previously acquired, Edmonton selected Martin Marincin) in 2010 Entry Draft, June 25, 2010.

NATTINEN, Joonas

(NA-tih-nuhn, YOH-nuhs)   **MTL.**

Center. Shoots right. 6'2", 183 lbs.   Born, Jamsa, Finland, January 3, 1991.
(Montreal's 2nd choice, 65th overall, in 2009 Entry Draft).

			Regular Season					Playoffs			
Season	Club	League	GP	G	A	Pts	PIM	GP	G	A	Pts	PIM
2006-07	JyP Jyvaskyla U18	Fin-U18	30	10	25	35	22	8	5	7	12	0
2007-08	JyP Jyvaskyla U18	Fin-U18	34	14	34	48	22	2	0	0	0	0
	JyP Jyvaskyla Jr.	Fin-Jr.	8	0	2	2	2	3	0	2	2	2
2008-09	Suomi U20	Finland-2	5	2	2	4	0	....	....	....	....	....
	Blues Espoo Jr.	Fin-Jr.	30	9	29	38	6	10	3	10	13	4
	Blues Espoo	Finland	14	0	0	0	4	....	....	....	....	....
2009-10	Blues Espoo	Finland	23	0	3	3	4	1	0	0	0	0
	Suomi U20	Finland-2	7	0	8	8	6	....	....	....	....	....
	Hokki Kajaani	Finland-2	10	2	2	4	4	....	....	....	....	....
	Blues Espoo Jr.	Fin-Jr.	11	7	6	13	2	....	....	....	....	....

NEAL, Michael

(NEEL, MIGH-kuhl)   **DAL.**

Left wing. Shoots left. 6'3", 205 lbs.   Born, Whitby, Ont., April 3, 1989.
(Dallas' 7th choice, 149th overall, in 2007 Entry Draft).

			Regular Season					Playoffs			
Season	Club	League	GP	G	A	Pts	PIM	GP	G	A	Pts	PIM
2004-05	Whitby Wildcats	Minor-ON	52	20	29	49	67	....	....	....	....	....
2005-06	Belleville Bulls	OHL	46	1	3	4	6	....	....	....	....	....
2006-07	Belleville Bulls	OHL	52	4	4	8	25	15	0	1	1	6
2007-08	Belleville Bulls	OHL	....	....	....	....	....	7	0	0	0	2
2008-09	Belleville Bulls	OHL	3	0	0	0	0	....	....	....	....	....
	Sarnia Sting	OHL	63	9	12	21	48	5	0	1	1	4
2009-10	Texas Stars	AHL	6	0	0	0	2	....	....	....	....	....
	Idaho Steelheads	ECHL	57	5	10	15	33	5	0	1	1	0

• Missed entire 2007-08 regular season recovering from knee injury.

NELSON, Brock

(NEHL-suhn, BRAWK)   **NYI**

Center. Shoots left. 6'3", 205 lbs.   Born, Minneapolis, MN, October 15, 1991.
(NY Islanders' 2nd choice, 30th overall, in 2010 Entry Draft).

			Regular Season					Playoffs			
Season	Club	League	GP	G	A	Pts	PIM	GP	G	A	Pts	PIM
2007-08	Warroad Warriors	High-MN	31	14	9	23	....	....	....	....	....	....
2008-09	Warroad Warriors	High-MN	31	45	36	81	....	....	....	....	....	....
2009-10	Team Great Plains	UMHSEL	24	5	10	15	....	....	....	....	....	....
	Warroad Warriors	High-MN	25	39	34	73	38	6	14	8	22	8

• Signed Letter of Intent to attend **University of North Dakota** (WCHA) in fall of 2010 or 2011.

NELSON, Levi

(NELH-suhn, LEE-vigh)   **BOS.**

Center. Shoots left. 6', 187 lbs.   Born, Calgary, Alta., April 28, 1988.
(Boston's 6th choice, 158th overall, in 2006 Entry Draft).

			Regular Season					Playoffs			
Season	Club	League	GP	G	A	Pts	PIM	GP	G	A	Pts	PIM
2004-05	Cgy. North Stars	AMHL	35	15	13	28	70	....	....	....	....	....
	Swift Current	WHL	2	1	0	1	0	....	....	....	....	....
2005-06	Swift Current	WHL	63	21	17	38	63	4	0	0	0	4
2006-07	Swift Current	WHL	66	18	34	52	125	6	4	3	7	4
	Providence Bruins	AHL	1	0	0	0	2	4	1	0	1	2
2007-08	Swift Current	WHL	67	25	36	61	152	12	7	8	15	16
2008-09	Providence Bruins	AHL	59	2	5	7	37	5	1	1	2	2
	Reading Royals	ECHL	8	2	1	3	28	....	....	....	....	....
2009-10	Providence Bruins	AHL	44	8	5	13	29	....	....	....	....	....

NEMETH, Patrik

(NEH-meht, PAHT-rihk)   **DAL.**

Defense. Shoots left. 6'3", 210 lbs.   Born, Stockholm, Sweden, February 8, 1992.
(Dallas' 2nd choice, 41st overall, in 2010 Entry Draft).

			Regular Season					Playoffs			
Season	Club	League	GP	G	A	Pts	PIM	GP	G	A	Pts	PIM
2007-08	Hammarby U18	Swe-U18	13	1	3	4	12	....	....	....	....	....
2008-09	AIK IF Solna	Swe-U18	27	3	10	13	123	4	1	0	1	29
	AIK IF Solna Jr.	Swe-Jr.	19	0	0	0	43	....	....	....	....	....
	AIK IF Solna	Sweden-2	1	0	1	1	0	....	....	....	....	....
2009-10	AIK IF Solna U18	Swe-U18	3	0	1	1	4	1	0	1	1	0
	AIK IF Solna Jr.	Swe-Jr.	38	1	19	20	120	5	1	2	3	10
	AIK IF Solna	Sweden-2	19	0	3	3	8	....	....	....	....	....

NEMISZ, Greg

(NEH-mihtz, GREHG)   **CGY.**

Center. Shoots right. 6'3", 195 lbs.   Born, Courtice, Ont., June 5, 1990.
(Calgary's 1st choice, 25th overall, in 2008 Entry Draft).

			Regular Season					Playoffs			
Season	Club	League	GP	G	A	Pts	PIM	GP	G	A	Pts	PIM
2005-06	Clarington	Minor-ON	32	29	24	53	24	....	....	....	....	....
2006-07	Windsor Spitfires	OHL	62	11	23	34	23	....	....	....	....	....
2007-08	Windsor Spitfires	OHL	68	34	33	67	52	5	2	1	3	8
2008-09	Windsor Spitfires	OHL	65	36	41	77	48	20	8	12	20	22
2009-10	Windsor Spitfires	OHL	51	34	36	70	50	15	2	10	12	12

OHL Second All-Star Team (2009)

NEPRYAYEV, Ivan

(neh-pree-YIGH-ehv, IGH-vuhn)   **WSH.**

Center. Shoots left. 6'1", 180 lbs.   Born, Yaroslavl, USSR, February 4, 1982.
(Washington's 5th choice, 163rd overall, in 2000 Entry Draft).

			Regular Season					Playoffs			
Season	Club	League	GP	G	A	Pts	PIM	GP	G	A	Pts	PIM
1997-98	Torpedo Yaroslavl	Russia	6	0	0	0	0	....	....	....	....	....
1998-99	Yaroslavl 2	Russia-3	15	1	0	1	0	....	....	....	....	....
99-2000	Yaroslavl 2	Russia-3	40	8	14	22	....	....	....	....	....	....
2000-01	Yaroslavl	Russia	10	0	0	0	2	....	....	....	....	....
2001-02	Yaroslavl 2	Russia-3	2	1	0	1	18	....	....	....	....	....
	Yaroslavl	Russia	36	3	8	11	28	....	....	....	....	....
2002-03	Yaroslavl	Russia	26	3	6	9	12	6	1	0	1	0
2003-04	Yaroslavl 2	Russia-3	13	5	10	15	12	....	....	....	....	....
2004-05	Yaroslavl	Russia	56	10	10	20	73	9	1	0	1	16
2005-06	Yaroslavl	Russia	43	7	16	23	70	11	0	0	0	8
	Russia	Olympics	2	0	0	0	2	....	....	....	....	....
2006-07	Yaroslavl	Russia	52	17	9	26	66	7	0	4	4	2
2007-08	Yaroslavl	Russia	56	9	17	26	84	15	3	6	9	41
2008-09	Dynamo Moscow	Rus-KHL	52	14	13	27	48	12	0	4	4	10
2009-10	Dynamo Moscow	Rus-KHL	44	4	9	13	46	4	0	0	0	4

NESS, Aaron

(NEHS, AIR-uhn)   **NY**

Defense. Shoots left. 5'10", 170 lbs.   Born, Bemidji, MN, May 18, 1990.
(NY Islanders' 3rd choice, 40th overall, in 2008 Entry Draft).

			Regular Season					Playoffs			
Season	Club	League	GP	G	A	Pts	PIM	GP	G	A	Pts	PIM
2005-06	Roseau Rams	High-MN	30	3	18	21	8	....	....	....	....	....
2006-07	Roseau Rams	High-MN	31	13	38	51	12	....	....	....	....	....
	Team Great Plains	UMWEHL	11	0	8	8	....	....	....	....	....	....
2007-08	Roseau Rams	High-MN	31	28	44	72	16	....	....	....	....	....
	Team Great Plains	UMWEHL	11	2	11	13	....	....	....	....	....	....
2008-09	U. of Minnesota	WCHA	37	2	15	17	16	....	....	....	....	....
2009-10	U. of Minnesota	WCHA	39	2	10	12	24	....	....	....	....	....

NESTRASIL, Andrej

(NEHS-tra-shihl, ahn-DRAY)   **DET**

Right wing. Shoots left. 6'2", 200 lbs.   Born, Prague, Czechoslovakia, February 22, 1991.
(Detroit's 3rd choice, 75th overall, in 2009 Entry Draft).

			Regular Season					Playoffs			
Season	Club	League	GP	G	A	Pts	PIM	GP	G	A	Pts	PIM
2004-05	Slavia U17	CzR-U17	3	0	1	1	2	....	....	....	....	....
2005-06	Slavia U17	CzR-U17	41	6	12	18	18	....	....	....	....	....
2006-07	Slavia U17	CzR-U17	43	24	37	61	75	5	2	2	4	
2007-08	Slavia U17	CzR-U17	....	....	....	....	....	2	1	0	1	
	HC Slavia Praha Jr.	CzRep-Jr.	40	12	16	28	58	5	1	2	3	
2008-09	Victoriaville Tigres	QMJHL	66	22	35	57	67	4	2	1	3	
2009-10	Victoriaville Tigres	QMJHL	50	16	35	51	40	16	2	4	6	1

NEUBER, Kyle

(NEW-buhr, KIGHL)   **CB**

Right wing. Shoots right. 6'2", 240 lbs.   Born, Sarnia, Ont., March 22, 1989.
(Columbus' 6th choice, 197th overall, in 2009 Entry Draft).

			Regular Season					Playoffs			
Season	Club	League	GP	G	A	Pts	PIM	GP	G	A	Pts	PIM
2006-07	St. Michael's	OHL	26	0	1	1	70	....	....	....	....	....
	St. Michael's	OPJHL	4	2	0	2	12	15	0	3	3	
2007-08	St. Michael's	OHL	54	4	4	8	133	4	0	0	0	
2008-09	St. Michael's	OHL	59	9	3	12	135	10	0	0	0	
2009-10	Sarnia Sting	OHL	60	5	5	10	188	....	....	....	....	....
	Syracuse Crunch	AHL	1	0	0	0	2	....	....	....	....	....

NEWTON, Jake

(NOO-tuhn, JAYK)   **ANA**

Defense. Shoots left. 6'3", 205 lbs.   Born, San Jacinto, CA, September 22, 1988.

			Regular Season					Playoffs			
Season	Club	League	GP	G	A	Pts	PIM	GP	G	A	Pts	PIM
2006-07	Texas Tornado	NAHL	61	12	15	27	35	....	....	....	....	....
2007-08	Lincoln Stars	USHL	56	11	14	25	22	8	3	3	6	
2008-09	Lincoln Stars	USHL	59	10	28	38	22	7	2	2	4	
2009-10	Northeastern	H-East	34	9	13	22	10	....	....	....	....	....

Hockey East All-Rookie Team (2010)
Signed as a free agent by **Anaheim**, March 17, 2010.

NICASTRO, Max

(nih-KAS-troh, MAX)   **DET**

Defense. Shoots right. 6'2", 189 lbs.   Born, Thousand Oaks, CA, March 2, 1990.
(Detroit's 2nd choice, 91st overall, in 2008 Entry Draft).

			Regular Season					Playoffs			
Season	Club	League	GP	G	A	Pts	PIM	GP	G	A	Pts	PI
2006-07	L.A. Jr. Kings	Minor-CA	48	17	19	36	44	....	....	....	....	....
2007-08	Chicago Steel	USHL	58	6	14	20	78	7	1	2	3	
2008-09	Chicago Steel	USHL	57	9	22	31	84	....	....	....	....	....
2009-10	Boston University	H-East	37	3	12	15	26	....	....	....	....	....

Hockey East All-Rookie Team (2010)

NICHOLLS, Josh

(NIH-kuhls, JAWSH)   **TO**

Right wing. Shoots right. 6'2", 174 lbs.   Born, Tsawwassen, B.C., April 27, 1992.
(Toronto's 7th choice, 182nd overall, in 2010 Entry Draft).

			Regular Season					Playoffs			
Season	Club	League	GP	G	A	Pts	PIM	GP	G	A	Pts	PIM
2007-08	Greater Van.	BCMML	39	18	30	48	68	2	0	0	0	2
2008-09	Saskatoon Blades	WHL	63	9	16	25	37	7	2	0	2	
2009-10	Saskatoon Blades	WHL	71	18	30	48	55	10	0	5	5	

NIEDERREITER, Nino

(nee-duhr-RIGH-tuhr, NEE-noh)   **N**

Right wing. Shoots left. 6'2", 201 lbs.   Born, Chur, Switzerland, September 8, 1992.
(NY Islanders' 1st choice, 5th overall, in 2010 Entry Draft).

			Regular Season					Playoffs			
Season	Club	League	GP	G	A	Pts	PIM	GP	G	A	Pts	P
2006-07	HC Davos U18	Swiss-U18	32	43	19	62	38	....	....	....	....	....
	HC Davos Jr.	Swiss-Jr.	....	....	....	....	....	1	0	0	0	
2007-08	HC Davos U18	Swiss-U18	32	39	26	65	62	5	6	3	9	
	HC Davos Jr.	Swiss-Jr.	8	7	3	10	4	3	0	1	1	
2008-09	HC Davos U18	Swiss-U18	6	6	6	12	6	....	....	....	....	....
	HC Davos Jr.	Swiss-Jr.	30	20	14	34	44	8	5	6	11	
	HC Davos	Swiss						3	0	1	1	
2009-10	Portland	WHL	65	36	24	60	68	13	8	8	16	

WHL West Second All-Star Team (2010)

NIEMI, Jyri

(nee-YEH-mee, YEW-ree)   **NY**

Defense. Shoots left. 6'2", 208 lbs.   Born, Hameenkyro, Finland, June 15, 1990.
(NY Islanders' 6th choice, 72nd overall, in 2008 Entry Draft).

			Regular Season					Playoffs			
Season	Club	League	GP	G	A	Pts	PIM	GP	G	A	Pts	P
2006-07	HPK U18	Fin-U18	1	0	1	1	4	....	....	....	....	....
	HPK Jr.	Fin-Jr.	40	7	5	12	82	....	....	....	....	....
2007-08	Saskatoon Blades	WHL	49	14	20	34	57	....	....	....	....	....
2008-09	Saskatoon Blades	WHL	60	7	25	32	74	6	1	6	7	
2009-10	Saskatoon Blades	WHL	50	8	21	29	67	10	2	0	2	

Traded to **NY Rangers** by **NY Islanders** for NY Rangers' 6th round choice (later traded to Atlan
– Atlanta selected Tanner Lane) in 2010 Entry Draft, May 25, 2010.

NIGRO, Anthony (NIGH-groh, AN-thuh-nee) ST.L.

Center. Shoots left. 6', 187 lbs. Born, Vaughan, Ont., January 11, 1990.
(St. Louis' 9th choice, 155th overall, in 2008 Entry Draft).

			Regular Season					Playoffs				
Season	Club	League	GP	G	A	Pts	PIM	GP	G	A	Pts	PIM
2006-07	Guelph Storm	OHL	56	4	13	17	26	4	0	0	0	2
2007-08	Guelph Storm	OHL	67	24	24	48	65	10	2	3	5	7
2008-09	Guelph Storm	OHL	25	7	11	18	31	....	....	....	....	....
	Ottawa 67's	OHL	42	23	28	51	28	7	4	4	8	4
2009-10	Ottawa 67's	OHL	61	16	46	62	49	12	6	7	13	12

NIKITIN, Nikita (nih-KEE-tihn, nih-KEE-tuh) ST.L.

Defense. Shoots left. 6'3", 215 lbs. Born, Omsk, USSR, June 16, 1986.
(St. Louis' 5th choice, 136th overall, in 2004 Entry Draft).

			Regular Season					Playoffs				
Season	Club	League	GP	G	A	Pts	PIM	GP	G	A	Pts	PIM
2002-03	Omsk 2	Russia-3	34	3	7	10	4	....	....	....	....	....
2003-04	Omsk 2	Russia-3	34	3	8	11	22	....	....	....	....	....
2004-05	Avangard Omsk	Russia	12	0	0	0	2	3	0	0	0	0
	Omsk 2	Russia-3	31	3	8	11	20	....	....	....	....	....
2005-06	Avangard Omsk	Russia	43	1	2	3	22	13	1	2	3	6
	Omsk 2	Russia-3	1	0	0	0	0	....	....	....	....	....
2006-07	Avangard Omsk	Russia	54	1	15	16	99	9	0	4	4	35
2007-08	Avangard Omsk	Russia	57	3	11	14	48	4	0	1	1	2
2008-09	Omsk	Rus-KHL	53	4	11	15	28	9	1	2	3	8
2009-10	Omsk	Rus-KHL	43	4	9	13	14	3	0	0	0	0

NIKULIN, Ilja (nih-KOO-lihn, IHL-yah) ATL.

Defense. Shoots left. 6'3", 215 lbs. Born, Moscow, USSR, March 12, 1982.
(Atlanta's 2nd choice, 31st overall, in 2000 Entry Draft).

			Regular Season					Playoffs				
Season	Club	League	GP	G	A	Pts	PIM	GP	G	A	Pts	PIM
1998-99	Dyn'o Moscow 2	Russia-3	23	0	2	2	18	....	....	....	....	....
99-2000	Dyn'o Moscow 2	Russia-3	4	2	1	3	10	....	....	....	....	....
	THK Tver	Russia-2	39	3	6	9	84	....	....	....	....	....
2000-01	Dynamo Moscow	Russia	44	0	4	4	61	....	....	....	....	....
2001-02	Dyn'o Moscow 2	Russia-3	2	0	1	1	2	....	....	....	....	....
	Dynamo Moscow	Russia	47	2	1	3	44	3	0	0	0	0
2002-03	Dynamo Moscow	Russia	40	1	4	5	46	5	0	1	1	4
2003-04	Dynamo Moscow	Russia	54	1	5	6	56	3	0	0	0	2
2004-05	Dynamo Moscow	Russia	50	1	9	10	65	10	0	3	3	8
2005-06	Ak Bars Kazan	Russia	49	9	9	18	48	13	4	0	4	36
2006-07	Ak Bars Kazan	Russia	51	11	14	25	99	16	4	5	9	18
2007-08	Ak Bars Kazan	Russia	57	3	15	18	95	10	1	3	4	14
2008-09	Ak Bars Kazan	Rus-KHL	53	7	26	33	72	17	2	8	10	22
2009-10	Ak Bars Kazan	Rus-KHL	49	6	27	33	86	22	5	6	11	14
	Russia	Olympics	4	0	1	1	2	....	....	....	....	....

NILL, Trevor (NIHL, TREH-vuhr) ST.L.

Center. Shoots right. 6'1", 194 lbs. Born, Detroit, MI, April 11, 1989.
(St. Louis' 10th choice, 190th overall, in 2007 Entry Draft).

			Regular Season					Playoffs				
Season	Club	League	GP	G	A	Pts	PIM	GP	G	A	Pts	PIM
2004-05	Det. Compuware	MWEHL	25	10	8	18	8	4	2	1	3	0
2005-06	Det. Compuware	MWEHL	21	4	9	13	20	4	1	0	1	2
2006-07	Det. Compuware	MWEHL	24	6	10	16	23	6	2	4	6	2
2007-08	Penticton Vees	BCHL	53	5	6	11	16	11	0	2	2	0
2008-09	Michigan State	CCHA	34	1	2	3	6	....	....	....	....	....
2009-10	Michigan State	CCHA	26	2	7	9	12	....	....	....	....	....

NOLAN, Jordan (NOH-luhn, JOHR-dahn) L.A.

Center. Shoots left. 6'3", 216 lbs. Born, St. Catharines, Ont., June 23, 1989.
(Los Angeles' 9th choice, 186th overall, in 2009 Entry Draft).

			Regular Season					Playoffs				
Season	Club	League	GP	G	A	Pts	PIM	GP	G	A	Pts	PIM
2005-06	Erie Otters	OHL	33	3	4	7	20	....	....	....	....	....
2006-07	Windsor Spitfires	OHL	60	11	16	27	100	....	....	....	....	....
2007-08	Windsor Spitfires	OHL	62	13	14	27	69	5	3	0	3	2
2008-09	Sault Ste. Marie	OHL	64	16	27	43	158	....	....	....	....	....
2009-10	Sault Ste. Marie	OHL	49	23	25	48	88	5	1	1	2	4
	Ontario Reign	ECHL	3	1	1	2	4	....	....	....	....	....

NOLET, Martin (noh-LAY, MAHR-tihn) L.A.

Defense. Shoots left. 6'3", 209 lbs. Born, Quebec City, Que., October 2, 1986.
(Los Angeles' 8th choice, 144th overall, in 2006 Entry Draft).

			Regular Season					Playoffs				
Season	Club	League	GP	G	A	Pts	PIM	GP	G	A	Pts	PIM
2002-03	St-Francois	QAAA	31	3	3	6	62	....	....	....	....	....
2003-04	St-Francois	QAAA	31	5	11	16	91	8	2	2	4	24
2004-05	Champlain College	QJHL	43	4	23	27	97	14	2	3	5	14
2005-06	Champlain College	QJHL	19	5	7	12	26	10	1	1	2	24
2006-07	Massachusetts	H-East	32	1	3	4	35	....	....	....	....	....
2007-08	Massachusetts	H-East	31	2	4	6	53	....	....	....	....	....
2008-09	Massachusetts	H-East	38	2	7	9	84	....	....	....	....	....
2009-10	Massachusetts	H-East	36	5	4	9	59	....	....	....	....	....

• Missed majority of 2005-06 season recovering from off-season shoulder surgery.

NORDSTROM, Joakim (NOHRD-stuhm, YOH-a-kihm) CHI.

Center. Shoots left. 6'2", 174 lbs. Born, Tyreso, Sweden, February 25, 1992.
(Chicago's 6th choice, 90th overall, in 2010 Entry Draft).

			Regular Season					Playoffs				
Season	Club	League	GP	G	A	Pts	PIM	GP	G	A	Pts	PIM
2008-09	AIK IF Solna U18	Swe-U18	35	8	16	24	32	7	2	2	4	2
	AIK IF Solna Jr.	Swe-Jr.	4	2	0	2	2	....	....	....	....	....
2009-10	AIK IF Solna U18	Swe-U18	2	1	1	2	0	3	1	2	3	4
	AIK IF Solna Jr.	Swe-Jr.	28	6	9	15	53	....	....	....	....	....
	AIK IF Solna	Sweden-2	2	0	0	0	0	....	....	....	....	....

NYQUIST, Gustav (NEW-kwihst, GUHS-tav) DET.

Right wing. Shoots left. 5'10", 169 lbs. Born, Halmstad, Sweden, September 1, 1989.
(Detroit's 3rd choice, 121st overall, in 2008 Entry Draft).

			Regular Season					Playoffs				
Season	Club	League	GP	G	A	Pts	PIM	GP	G	A	Pts	PIM
2005-06	Malmo U18	Swe-U18	14	9	3	12	10	6	1	3	4	0
2006-07	Malmo Jr.	Swe-Jr.	42	21	23	44	57	4	2	2	4	6
2007-08	Malmo Jr.	Swe-Jr.	24	11	20	31	20	7	5	5	10	6
2008-09	U. of Maine	H-East	38	13	19	32	28	....	....	....	....	....
2009-10	U. of Maine	H-East	39	19	*42	*61	20	....	....	....	....	....

Hockey East All-Rookie Team (2009) • Hockey East First All-Star Team (2010) • NCAA East First All-American Team (2010)

O'BRIEN, Jim (oh-BRIGH-uhn, JIHM) OTT.

Center. Shoots right. 6'3", 204 lbs. Born, Maplewood, MN, January 29, 1989.
(Ottawa's 1st choice, 29th overall, in 2007 Entry Draft).

			Regular Season					Playoffs				
Season	Club	League	GP	G	A	Pts	PIM	GP	G	A	Pts	PIM
2003-04	Det. Caesars	MWEHL	68	19	24	43	72	....	....	....	....	....
2004-05	USNTDP	U-17	13	6	6	12	10	....	....	....	....	....
	USNTDP	NAHL	40	10	12	22	41	1	0	0	0	0
2005-06	USNTDP	U-18	38	11	14	25	62	....	....	....	....	....
	USNTDP	NAHL	13	6	10	16	14	....	....	....	....	....
2006-07	U. of Minnesota	WCHA	43	7	8	15	51	....	....	....	....	....
2007-08	Seattle	WHL	70	21	34	55	66	12	2	6	8	14
2008-09	Seattle	WHL	63	27	35	62	55	5	1	0	1	10
	Binghamton	AHL	6	0	1	1	0	....	....	....	....	....
2009-10	Binghamton	AHL	76	8	9	17	49	....	....	....	....	....

O'DELL, Eric (OH-DEHL, AIR-ihk) ATL.

Center. Shoots right. 6', 185 lbs. Born, Ottawa, Ont., June 21, 1990.
(Anaheim's 3rd choice, 39th overall, in 2008 Entry Draft).

			Regular Season					Playoffs				
Season	Club	League	GP	G	A	Pts	PIM	GP	G	A	Pts	PIM
2006-07	Ottawa West	OJHL-B	40	28	20	48	45	....	....	....	....	....
	Ottawa Jr. Sens	CJHL	2	1	0	1	0	....	....	....	....	....
2007-08	Cumberland	CJHL	34	23	33	56	12	....	....	....	....	....
	Sudbury Wolves	OHL	26	14	18	32	19	....	....	....	....	....
2008-09	Sudbury Wolves	OHL	65	33	30	63	55	6	0	4	4	4
2009-10	Sudbury Wolves	OHL	68	33	35	68	63	4	0	2	2	7
	Chicago Wolves	AHL	3	0	0	0	0	....	....	....	....	....

Traded to **Atlanta** by **Anaheim** for Erik Christensen, March 4, 2009.

O'DONNELL, Brendan (OH'DAW-nuhl, BREHN-duhn) T.B.

Center. Shoots left. 6', 185 lbs. Born, Flin Flon, Man., June 25, 1992.
(Tampa Bay's 7th choice, 156th overall, in 2010 Entry Draft).

			Regular Season					Playoffs				
Season	Club	League	GP	G	A	Pts	PIM	GP	G	A	Pts	PIM
2008-09	Winnipeg Wild	MMHL	38	....	....	83	....	10	....	....	20	....
2009-10	Wpg. South Blues	MJHL	53	29	32	61	55	4	2	1	3	4

• Signed Letter of Intent to attend **University of North Dakota** (WCHA) in fall of 2010.

OLDEN, Sondre (OHL-duhn, SAWN-dreh) TOR.

Center. Shoots left. 6'4", 176 lbs. Born, Oslo, Norway, August 29, 1992.
(Toronto's 3rd choice, 79th overall, in 2010 Entry Draft).

			Regular Season					Playoffs				
Season	Club	League	GP	G	A	Pts	PIM	GP	G	A	Pts	PIM
2007-08	Manglerud Jr.	Norway-Jr.	19	20	18	38	12	3	0	2	2	4
2008-09	Manglerud U17	Norway-U17	1	2	3	5	0	4	8	6	14	33
	Manglerud Jr.	Norway-Jr.	19	32	35	67	18	7	5	9	14	16
	Manglerud	Norway-2	29	11	19	30	6	....	....	....	....	....
2009-10	MODO U18	Swe-U18	24	21	18	39	22	5	1	0	1	6
	MODO Jr.	Swe-Jr.	32	7	20	27	22	....	....	....	....	....

OLIMB, Mathis (OH-lihmb, MA-this) CHI.

Center. Shoots left. 5'10", 175 lbs. Born, Oslo, Norway, February 1, 1986.

			Regular Season					Playoffs				
Season	Club	League	GP	G	A	Pts	PIM	GP	G	A	Pts	PIM
2001-02	Valerenga Jr.	Norway-Jr.	1	0	0	0	0	....	....	....	....	....
2002-03	Valerenga U18	Nor-U18	....	....	....	....	....	3	2	4	6	0
	Valerenga Jr.	Norway-Jr.	29	15	22	37	16	5	1	4	5	0
	Valerengen IF Oslo	Norway	10	4	3	7	4	....	....	....	....	....
2003-04	Valerenga Jr.	Norway-Jr.	2	4	8	12	2	....	....	....	....	....
	Valerengen IF Oslo	Norway	3	0	0	0	0	....	....	....	....	....
	Manglerud	Norway	29	5	7	12	16	....	....	....	....	....
2004-05	London Knights	OHL	10	0	2	2	4	....	....	....	....	....
	Sarnia Sting	OHL	47	8	23	31	12	....	....	....	....	....
2005-06	Valerengen IF Oslo	Norway	39	11	14	25	46	13	4	3	7	8
2006-07	Valerengen IF Oslo	Norway	42	19	44	63	59	15	3	7	10	4
2007-08	Augsburg	Germany	54	14	25	39	71	....	....	....	....	....
2008-09	Augsburg	Germany	43	13	28	41	14	....	....	....	....	....
2009-10	Frolunda	Sweden	55	9	25	34	20	7	1	3	4	4

Signed as a free agent by **Chicago**, June 17, 2010.

OLIVER, Nick (aw-LIH-vuhr, NIHK) NSH.

Center/Left wing. Shoots left. 6'1", 194 lbs. Born, Grand Forks, ND, May 4, 1991.
(Nashville's 8th choice, 110th overall, in 2009 Entry Draft).

			Regular Season					Playoffs				
Season	Club	League	GP	G	A	Pts	PIM	GP	G	A	Pts	PIM
2006-07	Roseau Rams	High-MN	31	12	14	26	51	....	....	....	....	....
2007-08	Roseau Rams	High-MN	30	17	25	42	45	....	....	....	....	....
2008-09	Roseau Rams	High-MN	11	5	11	16	8	....	....	....	....	....
	Fargo Force	USHL	12	1	1	2	11	1	0	0	0	0
2009-10	Fargo Force	USHL	53	5	13	18	95	13	1	1	2	4

• Signed Letter of Intent to attend **St. Cloud State University** (WCHA) in fall of 2011.

OLSEN, Dylan (OHL-suhn, DIH-luhn) CHI.

Defense. Shoots left. 6'2", 206 lbs. Born, Salt Lake City, UT, January 3, 1991.
(Chicago's 1st choice, 28th overall, in 2009 Entry Draft).

			Regular Season					Playoffs				
Season	Club	League	GP	G	A	Pts	PIM	GP	G	A	Pts	PIM
2006-07	Calgary Blazers	SAMHL	53	19	41	60	119	....	....	....	....	....
	Camrose Kodiaks	AJHL	2	1	0	1	0	....	....	....	....	....
2007-08	Camrose Kodiaks	AJHL	49	8	16	24	45	16	1	5	6	6
2008-09	Camrose Kodiaks	AJHL	53	10	19	29	123	10	1	6	7	12
2009-10	U. Minn-Duluth	WCHA	36	1	10	11	49	....	....	....	....	....

OLSON, Drew (OHL-suhn, DROO) CBJ

Defense. Shoots left. 6', 206 lbs. Born, Brainerd, MN, April 4, 1990.
(Columbus' 4th choice, 118th overall, in 2008 Entry Draft).

			Regular Season					Playoffs				
Season	Club	League	GP	G	A	Pts	PIM	GP	G	A	Pts	PIM
2006-07	Brainerd	High-MN	STATISTICS NOT AVAILABLE									
	Team North	UMWEHL	11	2	4	6	....	....	....	....	....	....
2007-08	Brainerd	High-MN	27	20	16	36	....	....	....	....	....	....
	Team North	UMWEHL	11	3	4	7	....	....	....	....	....	....
2008-09	Omaha Lancers	USHL	39	2	6	8	43	....	....	....	....	....
2009-10	U. Minn-Duluth	WCHA	34	0	2	2	12	....	....	....	....	....

OLVER, Mark (AWL-vuhr, MAHRK) COL.

Center. Shoots left. 5'10", 155 lbs. Born, Burnaby, B.C., January 1, 1988.
(Colorado's 4th choice, 140th overall, in 2008 Entry Draft).

			Regular Season					Playoffs				
Season	Club	League	GP	G	A	Pts	PIM	GP	G	A	Pts	PIM
2005-06	Omaha Lancers	USHL	59	5	20	25	72	2	0	0	0	0
2006-07	Omaha Lancers	USHL	57	29	35	64	84	5	3	3	6	18
2007-08	Northern Mich.	CCHA	39	21	17	38	59	....	....	....	....	....
2008-09	Northern Mich.	CCHA	40	16	19	35	84	....	....	....	....	....
2009-10	Northern Mich.	CCHA	40	19	30	49	48	....	....	....	....	....
	Lake Erie Monsters	AHL	6	2	0	2	4	....	....	....	....	....

CCHA All-Rookie Team (2008) • CCHA First All-Star Team (2010) • NCAA West First All-American Team (2010)

OMARK, Linus (OH-mahrk, LIH-nuhs) EDM.

Left wing. Shoots left. 5'9", 170 lbs. Born, Overtornea, Sweden, February 5, 1987.
(Edmonton's 4th choice, 97th overall, in 2007 Entry Draft).

			Regular Season					Playoffs				
Season	Club	League	GP	G	A	Pts	PIM	GP	G	A	Pts	PIM
2003-04	Lulea HF U18	Swe-U18	14	14	8	22	18	7	3	4	7	0
	Lulea HF Jr.	Swe-Jr.	1	0	0	0	0	....	....	....	....	....
2004-05	Lulea HF U18	Swe-U18	1	2	0	2	0	....	....	....	....	....
	Lulea HF Jr.	Swe-Jr.	32	8	9	17	44	7	4	2	6	2
2005-06	Lulea HF Jr.	Swe-Jr.	32	22	21	43	56	5	1	2	3	28
	Lulea HF	Sweden	19	0	1	1	10	3	0	0	0	0
2006-07	Lulea HF	Sweden	50	8	9	17	32	4	1	0	1	2
2007-08	Lulea HF	Sweden	55	11	21	32	46	....	....	....	....	....
2008-09	Lulea HF	Sweden	53	23	32	55	66	5	0	5	5	4
2009-10	Dynamo Moscow	Rus-KHL	56	20	16	36	34	4	0	0	0	4

O'NEILL, Will (oh-NEEL, WIHL) ATL.

Defense. Shoots left. 6'1", 190 lbs. Born, Boston, MA, April 28, 1988.
(Atlanta's 8th choice, 210th overall, in 2006 Entry Draft).

			Regular Season					Playoffs				
Season	Club	League	GP	G	A	Pts	PIM	GP	G	A	Pts	PIM
2004-05	Tabor	High-MA	....	1	16	17	....	....	....	....	....	....
2005-06	Tabor	High-MA	28	5	25	30	38	....	....	....	....	....
2006-07	Omaha Lancers	USHL	57	4	9	13	73	5	0	0	0	8
2007-08	Omaha Lancers	USHL	58	5	19	24	95	14	1	6	7	38
2008-09	U. of Maine	H-East	34	4	12	16	82	....	....	....	....	....
2009-10	U. of Maine	H-East	39	8	23	31	69	....	....	....	....	....

ORLOV, Dmitri (ohr-LAWF, dih-MEE-tree) WSH.

Defense. Shoots left. 6', 197 lbs. Born, Novokuznetsk, USSR, July 23, 1991.
(Washington's 2nd choice, 55th overall, in 2009 Entry Draft).

			Regular Season					Playoffs				
Season	Club	League	GP	G	A	Pts	PIM	GP	G	A	Pts	PIM
2007-08	Novokuznetsk	Russia	6	0	0	0	0	....	....	....	....	....
2008-09	Novokuznetsk 2	Russia-3	STATISTICS NOT AVAILABLE									
	Novokuznetsk	Rus-KHL	16	1	0	1	4	....	....	....	....	....
2009-10	Novokuznetsk	Rus-KHL	41	4	3	7	49	....	....	....	....	....
	Novokuznetsk Jr.	Russia-Jr.	7	7	6	13	6	17	9	10	19	26

ORLOV, Maxim (ohr-LAHF, max-EEM) WSH.

Center. Shoots left. 6', 176 lbs. Born, Moscow, USSR, March 31, 1981.
(Washington's 9th choice, 219th overall, in 1999 Entry Draft).

			Regular Season					Playoffs				
Season	Club	League	GP	G	A	Pts	PIM	GP	G	A	Pts	PIM
1998-99	CSKA Moscow	Russia	2	0	0	0	2	1	0	0	0	0
99-2000	CSKA Moscow	Russia	25	0	0	0	2	2	0	0	0	2
2000-01	CSKA Moscow	Russia	41	5	4	9	14	....	....	....	....	....
2001-02	CSKA Moscow 2	Russia-3	7	7	4	11	4	....	....	....	....	....
	CSKA Moscow	Russia	35	3	5	8	14	....	....	....	....	....
2002-03	MGU Moscow	Russia-3	2	0	0	0	0	....	....	....	....	....
	Leninogorsk	Russia-2	25	3	8	11	24	....	....	....	....	....
2003-04	Leninogorsk	Russia-2	35	5	9	14	39	2	0	0	0	0
2004-05	Kristall Saratov	Russia-2	47	13	23	36	46	4	0	0	0	2
2005-06	Ufa 2	Russia-3	20	8	8	16	10	....	....	....	....	....
	Ufa	Russia	5	0	0	0	0	....	....	....	....	....
2006-07	Toros Neftekamsk	Russia-2	55	5	22	27	46	....	....	....	....	....
2007-08	Toros Neftekamsk	Russia-2	50	7	12	19	20	3	1	2	3	0
2008-09	Toros Neftekamsk	Russia-2	41	10	9	19	14	7	3	0	3	6
2009-10	Kristall Saratov	Russia-2	35	9	6	15	20	5	1	0	1	0

OSLUND, Nick (OZ-luhnd, NIHK) DET.

Right wing. Shoots right. 6'3", 195 lbs. Born, Burnsville, MN, November 15, 1987.
(Detroit's 6th choice, 191st overall, in 2006 Entry Draft).

			Regular Season					Playoffs				
Season	Club	League	GP	G	A	Pts	PIM	GP	G	A	Pts	PIM
2004-05	Burnsville	High-MN	27	29	18	47	28	....	....	....	....	....
2005-06	Burnsville	High-MN	26	22	30	52	30	....	....	....	....	....
2006-07	Tri-City Storm	USHL	56	7	14	21	24	9	0	1	1	0
2007-08	St. Cloud State	WCHA	38	4	1	5	27	....	....	....	....	....
2008-09	St. Cloud State	WCHA	35	4	3	7	26	....	....	....	....	....
2009-10	St. Cloud State	WCHA	43	4	5	9	24	....	....	....	....	....

OSTRCIL, Radim (AWS-tuhr-chihl, RA-dihm) BOS.

Defense. Shoots left. 5'11", 194 lbs. Born, Vsetin, Czech., January 15, 1989.
(Boston's 5th choice, 169th overall, in 2007 Entry Draft).

			Regular Season					Playoffs				
Season	Club	League	GP	G	A	Pts	PIM	GP	G	A	Pts	PIM
2002-03	HC Vsetin U17	CzR-U17	33	1	2	3	8	11	1	1	2	2
2003-04	HC Vsetin U17	CzR-U17	43	0	12	12	44	2	0	0	0	0
2004-05	HC Vsetin U17	CzR-U17	31	8	15	23	85	3	1	3	4	4
	HC Vsetin Jr.	CzRep-Jr.	19	0	3	3	14	3	0	0	0	2
2005-06	HC Vsetin U17	CzR-U17	1	1	1	2	0	3	2	2	4	0
	HC Vsetin Jr.	CzRep-Jr.	41	6	8	14	50	5	1	1	2	6
	Hr. Kralove	CzRep-2	1	0	0	0	0	1	0	0	0	0
	HC Vsetin	CzRep	3	0	0	0	6	....	....	....	....	....
2006-07	HC Vsetin Jr.	CzRep-Jr.	25	8	13	21	69	8	4	4	8	6
	HC Vsetin	CzRep	37	1	1	2	20	....	....	....	....	....
2007-08	Ottawa 67's	OHL	59	0	13	13	69	4	0	0	0	2
2008-09	HC Olomouc Jr.	CzRep-Jr.	5	3	2	5	10	....	....	....	....	....
	HC Olomouc	CzRep-2	38	1	3	4	18	5	0	0	0	4
2009-10	HC Kometa Brno	CzRep	2	0	0	0	2	3	0	0	0	0
	Trebic	CzRep-2	41	1	12	13	38	11	2	5	7	12

OWENS, Jordan (OH-wehns , JOHR-dahn) DET.

Left wing. Shoots left. 6', 189 lbs. Born, Toronto, Ont., May 1, 1986.

			Regular Season					Playoffs				
Season	Club	League	GP	G	A	Pts	PIM	GP	G	A	Pts	PIM
2004-05	Mississauga	OHL	66	11	14	25	45	5	0	0	0	2
2005-06	Mississauga	OHL	66	26	28	54	47	....	....	....	....	....
2006-07	Mississauga	OHL	60	32	42	74	51	5	1	2	3	6
	Hartford Wolf Pack	AHL	2	0	0	0	0	6	0	0	0	9
2007-08	Hartford Wolf Pack	AHL	41	7	7	14	44	5	0	0	0	0
	Charlotte	ECHL	20	3	10	13	28	2	0	0	0	0
2008-09	Hartford Wolf Pack	AHL	67	12	25	37	66	6	1	2	3	0
2009-10	Hartford Wolf Pack	AHL	50	6	13	19	53	....	....	....	....	....
	Grand Rapids	AHL	17	1	4	5	22	....	....	....	....	....

Signed as a free agent by **Hartford** (AHL), June 12, 2007. Signed as a free agent by **NY Rangers**, May 5, 2009. Traded to **Detroit** by **NY Rangers** for Kris Newbury, March 3, 2010.

OWUYA, Sebastian (oh-WUH-yuh, seh-BAS-t'yehn) ATL.

Defense. Shoots left. 6'4", 205 lbs. Born, Stockholm, Sweden, October 8, 1991.
(Atlanta's 8th choice, 169th overall, in 2010 Entry Draft).

			Regular Season					Playoffs				
Season	Club	League	GP	G	A	Pts	PIM	GP	G	A	Pts	PIM
2006-07	Djurgarden U18	Swe-U18	1	0	0	0	0	....	....	....	....	....
2007-08	Timra IK U18	Swe-U18	36	3	6	9	50	....	....	....	....	....
2008-09	Timra IK U18	Swe-U18	31	0	9	9	54	1	0	1	1	14
	Timra IK Jr.	Swe-Jr.	4	0	1	1	4	....	....	....	....	....
2009-10	Timra IK Jr.	Swe-Jr.	42	4	15	19	120	....	....	....	....	....
	Timra IK	Sweden	11	0	0	0	0	....	....	....	....	....

PAAJARVI-SVENSSON, Magnus pe-ya-YAR-vee-SVEHN-suhn, MAG-nuhs EDM.

Left wing. Shoots left. 6'2", 201 lbs. Born, Norrkoping, Sweden, April 12, 1991.
(Edmonton's 1st choice, 10th overall, in 2009 Entry Draft).

			Regular Season					Playoffs				
Season	Club	League	GP	G	A	Pts	PIM	GP	G	A	Pts	PIM
2005-06	Malmo U18	Swe-U18	13	2	3	5	4	1	0	0	0	0
	Malmo Jr.	Swe-Jr.	2	0	0	0	0	....	....	....	....	....
2006-07	Malmo U18	Swe-U18	3	3	3	6	0	....	....	....	....	....
	Malmo Jr.	Swe-Jr.	20	4	2	6	6	4	0	1	1	0
2007-08	Timra IK U18	Swe-U18	5	1	6	7	4	....	....	....	....	....
	Timra IK Jr.	Swe-Jr.	18	7	15	22	6	....	....	....	....	....
	Timra IK	Sweden	35	1	2	3	2	11	0	0	0	2
2008-09	Timra IK Jr.	Swe-Jr.	1	0	0	0	0	....	....	....	....	....
	Timra IK	Sweden	50	7	10	17	4	7	1	0	1	0
2009-10	Timra IK	Sweden	49	12	17	29	6	5	0	1	1	2

PACAN, David (PAY-cuhn, DAY-vihd) CHI

Center. Shoots right. 6'3", 187 lbs. Born, Ottawa, Ont., March 31, 1991.
(Chicago's 6th choice, 177th overall, in 2009 Entry Draft).

			Regular Season					Playoffs				
Season	Club	League	GP	G	A	Pts	PIM	GP	G	A	Pts	PIM
2007-08	Cumberland	CJHL	60	12	22	34	30	6	3	7	10	[illegible]
2008-09	Cumberland	CJHL	58	22	38	60	78	6	2	6	8	[illegible]
2009-10	U. of Vermont	H-East	39	7	7	14	22	....	....	....	....	[illegible]

PALIN, Brett (PAY-lihn, BREHT) NSH

Defense. Shoots right. 6'2", 203 lbs. Born, Nanaimo, B.C., June 23, 1984.

			Regular Season					Playoffs				
Season	Club	League	GP	G	A	Pts	PIM	GP	G	A	Pts	PIM
2000-01	Kelowna Rockets	WHL	39	0	0	0	25	....	....	....	....	....
2001-02	Kelowna Rockets	WHL	70	0	1	1	88	15	0	0	0	[illegible]
2002-03	Kelowna Rockets	WHL	71	1	17	18	118	19	0	4	4	[illegible]
2003-04	Kelowna Rockets	WHL	72	1	16	17	106	17	0	5	5	[illegible]
2004-05	Kelowna Rockets	WHL	72	4	21	25	71	24	4	6	10	[illegible]
2005-06	Omaha	AHL	64	0	5	5	46	....	....	....	....	....
2006-07	Omaha	AHL	78	1	9	10	71	6	1	0	1	[illegible]
2007-08	Quad City Flames	AHL	67	0	10	10	68	....	....	....	....	....
2008-09	Quad City Flames	AHL	57	5	10	15	40	....	....	....	....	....
2009-10	Abbotsford Heat	AHL	21	0	3	3	17	2	0	0	0	[illegible]

Signed as a free agent by **Calgary**, August 5, 2005. Signed as a free agent by **Nashville**, July 9, 2010.

PALMER, Jarod (PAHL-muhr, JAIR-uhd) MIN

Right wing. Shoots right. 6', 200 lbs. Born, Fridley, MN, February 10, 1986.

			Regular Season					Playoffs				
Season	Club	League	GP	G	A	Pts	PIM	GP	G	A	Pts	PIM
2004-05	Tri-City Storm	USHL	52	15	26	41	67	9	1	0	1	[illegible]
2005-06	Tri-City Storm	USHL	58	15	37	52	91	5	1	1	2	[illegible]
2006-07	Miami U.	CCHA	42	11	19	30	26	....	....	....	....	....
2007-08	Miami U.	CCHA	42	10	25	35	32	....	....	....	....	....
2008-09	Miami U.	CCHA	41	8	19	27	34	....	....	....	....	....
2009-10	Miami U.	CCHA	44	18	27	45	40	....	....	....	....	....

CCHA First All-Star Team (2010)

Signed as a free agent by **Minnesota**, April 26, 2010.

PALMIERI, Kyle (pawl-mee-AIR-ee, KIGHL) ANA.

Right wing. Shoots right. 5'10", 194 lbs. Born, Smithtown, NY, February 1, 1991.
(Anaheim's 2nd choice, 26th overall, in 2009 Entry Draft).

			Regular Season					Playoffs				
Season	Club	League	GP	G	A	Pts	PIM	GP	G	A	Pts	PIM
2007-08	USNTDP	NAHL	32	15	10	25	43	....	....	....	....	....
	USNTDP	U-17	7	5	0	5	8	....	....	....	....	....
	USNTDP	U-18	27	9	9	18	20	....	....	....	....	....
2008-09	USNTDP	NAHL	5	1	1	2	2	....	....	....	....	....
	USNTDP	U-18	28	14	14	28	49	....	....	....	....	....
2009-10	U. of Notre Dame	CCHA	33	9	8	17	36	....	....	....	....	....

PALUSHAJ, Aaron (puh-LOO-shigh, AIR-ruhn) MTL.

Right wing. Shoots right. 5'11", 187 lbs. Born, Livonia, MI, September 7, 1989.
(St. Louis' 5th choice, 44th overall, in 2007 Entry Draft).

			Regular Season					Playoffs				
Season	Club	League	GP	G	A	Pts	PIM	GP	G	A	Pts	PIM
2005-06	Des Moines	USHL	58	10	23	33	53	11	2	4	6	15
2006-07	Des Moines	USHL	56	22	45	67	62	8	6	5	11	6
2007-08	U. of Michigan	CCHA	43	10	*34	44	22	....	....	....	....	....
2008-09	U. of Michigan	CCHA	39	13	*37	*50	26	....	....	....	....	....
	Peoria Rivermen	AHL	4	2	0	2	4	4	0	1	1	2
2009-10	Peoria Rivermen	AHL	44	5	17	22	22	....	....	....	....	....
	Hamilton Bulldogs	AHL	18	3	7	10	8	19	2	10	12	28

CCHA First All-Star Team (2009) • NCAA West First All-American Team (2009)

Traded to **Montreal** by **St. Louis** for Matt D'Agostini, March 2, 2010.

PANIK, Richard (PAH-nihk, RIH-chuhrd) T.B.

Right wing. Shoots left. 6'2", 203 lbs. Born, Martin, Czechoslovakia, February 7, 1991.
(Tampa Bay's 3rd choice, 52nd overall, in 2009 Entry Draft).

			Regular Season					Playoffs				
Season	Club	League	GP	G	A	Pts	PIM	GP	G	A	Pts	PIM
2005-06	MHC Martin U18	Svk-U18	40	11	13	24	20	4	4	2	6	4
2006-07	HC Trinec U17	CzR-U17	12	10	6	16	48	3	1	4	5	8
	HC Trinec Jr.	CzRep-Jr.	27	16	9	25	30	4	1	4	5	6
2007-08	HC Trinec Jr.	CzRep-Jr.	39	35	27	62	70	8	8	4	12	52
	HC Ocelari Trinec	CzRep	6	0	0	0	0	....	....	....	....	....
2008-09	HC Trinec Jr.	CzRep-Jr.	16	10	9	19	36	8	6	1	7	41
	HC Havirov	CzRep-2	3	2	1	3	0	....	....	....	....	....
	HC Ocelari Trinec	CzRep	15	1	1	2	4	4	0	0	0	0
2009-10	Windsor Spitfires	OHL	33	9	9	18	19	....	....	....	....	....
	Belleville Bulls	OHL	27	12	11	23	36	....	....	....	....	....
	Norfolk Admirals	AHL	5	0	1	1	0	....	....	....	....	....

PAQUETTE, Danick (pa-KETT, DA-nihk) ATL.

Right wing. Shoots right. 6', 210 lbs. Born, Montreal, Que., July 17, 1990.
(Atlanta's 3rd choice, 64th overall, in 2008 Entry Draft).

			Regular Season					Playoffs				
Season	Club	League	GP	G	A	Pts	PIM	GP	G	A	Pts	PIM
2005-06	Ecole Montpetit	QAAA	36	17	16	33	191	3	0	1	1	6
2006-07	Lewiston	QMJHL	63	4	14	18	112	14	0	0	0	18
2007-08	Lewiston	QMJHL	63	29	13	42	213	5	1	2	3	30
2008-09	Lewiston	QMJHL	61	25	25	50	230	2	1	2	3	25
	Chicago Wolves	AHL	4	0	0	0	12	....	....	....	....	....
2009-10	Quebec Remparts	QMJHL	64	36	29	65	136	5	1	3	4	21

PARADIS, Philippe (PAIR-a-dee, fihl-EEP) CHI.

Center. Shoots left. 6'2", 205 lbs. Born, Dolbeau, Que., January 2, 1991.
(Carolina's 1st choice, 27th overall, in 2009 Entry Draft).

			Regular Season					Playoffs				
Season	Club	League	GP	G	A	Pts	PIM	GP	G	A	Pts	PIM
2006-07	Jonquiere Elites	QAAA	38	5	12	17	76	3	1	1	2	6
2007-08	Shawinigan	QMJHL	45	11	12	23	44	3	0	0	0	0
2008-09	Shawinigan	QMJHL	66	19	31	50	74	21	6	6	12	20
2009-10	Shawinigan	QMJHL	63	24	20	44	104	6	2	1	3	4
	Toronto Marlies	AHL	4	0	2	2	0	....	....	....	....	....

Traded to **Toronto** by **Carolina** for Jiri Tlusty, December 3, 2009. Traded to **Chicago** by **Toronto** with Viktor Stalberg and Christopher Didomenico for Kris Versteeg and Bill Sweatt, June 30, 2010.

PARE, Francis (pa-RAY, FRAN-sihs) DET.

Center. Shoots right. 5'10", 188 lbs. Born, Lemoyne, Que., June 30, 1987.

			Regular Season					Playoffs				
Season	Club	League	GP	G	A	Pts	PIM	GP	G	A	Pts	PIM
2003-04	Shawinigan	QMJHL	5	2	0	2	2	....	....	....	....	....
2004-05	Shawinigan	QMJHL	70	24	23	47	52	4	0	3	3	4
2005-06	Shawinigan	QMJHL	50	26	48	74	66	5	1	3	4	4
2006-07	Shawinigan	QMJHL	68	29	44	73	37	4	1	1	2	8
2007-08	Chicoutimi	QMJHL	69	54	48	102	54	6	5	3	8	4
2008-09	Grand Rapids	AHL	63	24	24	48	14	10	2	2	4	2
2009-10	Grand Rapids	AHL	77	16	23	39	20	....	....	....	....	....

QMJHL First All-Star Team (2008) • Canadian Major Junior Second All-Star Team (2008)

Signed as a free agent by **Grand Rapids** (AHL), June 13, 2008. Signed as a free agent by **Detroit**, April 7, 2009.

PARKS, Michael (PARKS, MIGH-kuhl) PHI.

Right wing. Shoots right. 5'11", 188 lbs. Born, St. Louis, MO, February 15, 1992.
(Philadelphia's 3rd choice, 149th overall, in 2010 Entry Draft).

			Regular Season					Playoffs				
Season	Club	League	GP	G	A	Pts	PIM	GP	G	A	Pts	PIM
2008-09	St. Louis Selects	Exhib.	46	38	47	85	26	....	....	....	....	....
2009-10	Cedar Rapids	USHL	51	11	11	22	57	5	0	1	1	0

• Signed Letter of Intent to attend **University of Notre Dame** (CCHA) in fall of 2010.

PARSHIN, Denis (PAHR-shihn, DEH-nihs) COL.

Right wing. Shoots left. 5'10", 165 lbs. Born, Rybinsk, USSR, February 1, 1986.
(Colorado's 3rd choice, 72nd overall, in 2004 Entry Draft).

			Regular Season					Playoffs				
Season	Club	League	GP	G	A	Pts	PIM	GP	G	A	Pts	PIM
2002-03	CSKA Moscow 2	Russia-3	4	1	0	1	2	....	....	....	....	....
2003-04	CSKA Moscow	Russia	27	2	4	6	4	....	....	....	....	....
	CSKA Moscow 2	Russia-3	STATISTICS NOT AVAILABLE									
2004-05	CSKA Moscow	Russia	42	3	4	7	18	....	....	....	....	....
2005-06	CSKA Moscow 2	Russia-3	STATISTICS NOT AVAILABLE									
	CSKA Moscow	Russia	37	2	8	10	22	6	0	2	2	2
2006-07	CSKA Moscow	Russia	54	18	14	32	24	12	2	2	4	8
2007-08	CSKA Moscow	Russia	56	12	23	35	46	6	1	0	1	0
2008-09	CSKA Moscow	Rus-KHL	48	13	14	27	34	8	1	0	1	6
2009-10	CSKA Moscow	Rus-KHL	56	21	22	43	28	3	0	1	1	6

PASHNIN, Mikhail (pahsh-NIHN, mih-KHIGH-eel) NYR

Defense. Shoots left. 6'1", 191 lbs. Born, Chelyabinsk, USSR, May 11, 1989.
(NY Rangers' 7th choice, 200th overall, in 2009 Entry Draft).

			Regular Season					Playoffs				
Season	Club	League	GP	G	A	Pts	PIM	GP	G	A	Pts	PIM
2005-06	Mechel 2	Russia-3	25	0	5	5	30	....	....	....	....	....
2006-07	Mechel 2	Russia-3	12	1	3	4	26	....	....	....	....	....
	Mechel	Russia-2	41	0	2	2	40	4	0	0	0	8
2007-08	Mechel 2	Russia-3	8	4	1	5	12	....	....	....	....	....
	Mechel	Russia-2	49	2	5	7	58	....	....	....	....	....
2008-09	Mechel 2	Russia-3	3	0	1	1	4	....	....	....	....	....
	Mechel	Russia-2	35	2	4	6	40	7	0	2	2	8
2009-10	CSKA Moscow	Rus-KHL	44	1	4	5	52	1	0	0	0	0
	CSKA Jr.	Russia-Jr.	4	0	3	3	2	4	1	1	2	20

PATERYN, Greg (PA-tuhr-ihn, GREHG) MTL.

Defense. Shoots right. 6'2", 212 lbs. Born, Sterling Heights, MI, June 20, 1990.
(Toronto's 4th choice, 128th overall, in 2008 Entry Draft).

			Regular Season					Playoffs				
Season	Club	League	GP	G	A	Pts	PIM	GP	G	A	Pts	PIM
2004-05	Brother Rice	High-MI	29	2	8	10	42	....	....	....	....	....
2005-06	Brother Rice	High-MI	24	0	8	8	34	....	....	....	....	....
2006-07	Brother Rice	High-MI	27	9	19	28	44	....	....	....	....	....
2007-08	Ohio	USHL	60	3	24	27	145	....	....	....	....	....
2008-09	U. of Michigan	CCHA	28	0	5	5	32	....	....	....	....	....
2009-10	U. of Michigan	CCHA	33	1	5	6	18	....	....	....	....	....

Traded to **Montreal** by **Toronto** with Toronto's 2nd round choice (later traded to Chicago, later traded back to Toronto, later traded to Boston - Boston selected Jared Knight) in 2010 Entry Draft for Mikhail Grabovski, July 3, 2008.

PATTERSON, Gaelan (PA-tuhr-suhn, GAY-luhn) CGY.

Center. Shoots left. 6', 210 lbs. Born, La Ronge, Sask., August 22, 1990.
(Calgary's 6th choice, 201st overall, in 2009 Entry Draft).

			Regular Season					Playoffs				
Season	Club	League	GP	G	A	Pts	PIM	GP	G	A	Pts	PIM
2005-06	Beardy's	SMHL	38	7	10	17	16	....	....	....	....	....
2006-07	Saskatoon Blades	WHL	53	3	1	4	24	....	....	....	....	....
2007-08	Saskatoon Blades	WHL	51	4	6	10	38	....	....	....	....	....
2008-09	Saskatoon Blades	WHL	71	22	35	57	41	7	1	1	2	2
2009-10	Saskatoon Blades	WHL	71	26	33	59	31	10	4	6	10	6
	Abbotsford Heat	AHL	....	....	....	....	....	3	1	0	1	0

PAUKOVICH, Geoff (paw-KOH-vihch, JEHF)

Left wing. Shoots left. 6'4", 208 lbs. Born, Englewood, CO, April 24, 1986.
(Edmonton's 4th choice, 57th overall, in 2004 Entry Draft).

			Regular Season					Playoffs				
Season	Club	League	GP	G	A	Pts	PIM	GP	G	A	Pts	PIM
2002-03	Tri-City Storm	USHL	31	1	3	4	29	....	....	....	....	....
2003-04	USNTDP	U-18	44	6	9	15	46	....	....	....	....	....
	USNTDP	NAHL	11	4	2	6	31	....	....	....	....	....
2004-05	U. of Denver	WCHA	41	12	10	22	120	....	....	....	....	....
2005-06	U. of Denver	WCHA	37	4	6	10	72	....	....	....	....	....
2006-07	U. of Denver	WCHA	39	8	9	17	65	....	....	....	....	....
2007-08	Stockton Thunder	ECHL	70	13	13	26	94	6	1	0	1	4
2008-09	Springfield Falcons	AHL	46	5	4	9	51	....	....	....	....	....
	Stockton Thunder	ECHL	6	1	0	1	4	....	....	....	....	....
2009-10	Springfield Falcons	AHL	63	5	3	8	75	....	....	....	....	....

PELECH, Michael (PEH-lehch, MIGH-kuhl) L.A.

Center/Left wing. Shoots left. 6'3", 206 lbs. Born, Toronto, Ont., October 6, 1989.
(Los Angeles' 7th choice, 156th overall, in 2009 Entry Draft).

			Regular Season					Playoffs				
Season	Club	League	GP	G	A	Pts	PIM	GP	G	A	Pts	PIM
2004-05	St. Mike's B's	OPJHL	47	12	25	37	22	23	1	7	8	20
2005-06	Kitchener Rangers	OHL	48	3	6	9	32	2	0	0	0	0
2006-07	St. Michael's	OHL	65	12	35	47	54	....	....	....	....	....
2007-08	St. Michael's	OHL	68	17	32	49	72	4	1	1	2	6
2008-09	St. Michael's	OHL	68	19	46	65	121	11	4	9	13	23
2009-10	Ontario Reign	ECHL	72	10	25	35	133	....	....	....	....	....

PELSS, Kristians (PEHLSH, KRIHS-tyehns) EDM.

Left wing. Shoots left. 5'11", 198 lbs. Born, Preili, Latvia, September 9, 1992.
(Edmonton's 10th choice, 181st overall, in 2010 Entry Draft).

			Regular Season					Playoffs				
Season	Club	League	GP	G	A	Pts	PIM	GP	G	A	Pts	PIM
2007-08	Daugavpils U18	LatviaU18	27	33	21	54	26	....	....	....	....	....
2008-09	Daugavpils Jr.	Latvia-Jr.	8	3	9	12	16	....	....	....	....	....
	Latgale 2	Latvia	22	9	11	20	24	....	....	....	....	....
	Latgale	Belarus	31	3	4	7	14	....	....	....	....	....
2009-10	Dyn. Jr. Riga	Belarus	46	6	3	9	28	....	....	....	....	....

PELTZ, Brad (PEHLTZ, BRAD) OTT.

Left wing. Shoots right. 6'1", 175 lbs. Born, New York, NY, October 2, 1989.
(Ottawa's 8th choice, 190th overall, in 2009 Entry Draft).

			Regular Season					Playoffs				
Season	Club	League	GP	G	A	Pts	PIM	GP	G	A	Pts	PIM
2005-06	Avon Old Farms	High-CT	19	2	0	2	6	....	....	....	....	....
2006-07	Avon Old Farms	High-CT	26	8	7	15	8	....	....	....	....	....
2007-08	Avon Old Farms	High-CT	27	12	19	31	12	....	....	....	....	....
2008-09	Avon Old Farms	High-CT	DID NOT PLAY – INJURED									
2009-10	Bos. Jr. Bruins	EJHL	45	19	15	34	28	3	2	0	2	0

• Signed Letter of Intent to attend **Yale University** (ECAC) in fall of 2010.

PELUSO, Anthony (puh-LOO-soh, AN-toh-nee) **ST.L.**

Defense. Shoots right. 6'3", 230 lbs. Born, North York, Ont., April 18, 1989.
(St. Louis' 9th choice, 160th overall, in 2007 Entry Draft).

			Regular Season					Playoffs				
Season	Club	League	GP	G	A	Pts	PIM	GP	G	A	Pts	PIM
2004-05	Richmond Hill	Minor-ON	30	22	20	42	80	....	....	....	....	....
2005-06	Erie Otters	OHL	68	5	3	8	66	....	....	....	....	....
2006-07	Erie Otters	OHL	52	7	3	10	176	....	....	....	....	....
2007-08	Erie Otters	OHL	21	3	3	6	41	....	....	....	....	....
	Sault Ste. Marie	OHL	42	4	11	15	83	14	2	1	3	12
2008-09	Sault Ste. Marie	OHL	36	9	6	15	68	....	....	....	....	....
	Brampton	OHL	27	11	11	22	57	21	8	7	15	29
2009-10	Peoria Rivermen	AHL	22	1	1	2	57	....	....	....	....	....
	Alaska Aces	ECHL	27	4	7	11	48	4	1	0	1	6

PELUSO, Chris (puh-LOO-soh, KRIHS) **TOR.**

Defense. Shoots left. 5'11", 180 lbs. Born, Wadena, MN, August 21, 1986.
(Pittsburgh's 9th choice, 194th overall, in 2004 Entry Draft).

			Regular Season					Playoffs				
Season	Club	League	GP	G	A	Pts	PIM	GP	G	A	Pts	PIM
2003-04	Brainerd	High-MN	25	10	33	43	....	....	....	....	....	....
2004-05	Sioux Falls	USHL	53	1	7	8	54	....	....	....	....	....
2005-06	Sioux Falls	USHL	57	5	19	24	49	14	0	4	4	8
2006-07	Bemidji State	CHA	26	0	6	6	24	....	....	....	....	....
2007-08	Bemidji State	CHA	36	1	9	10	26	....	....	....	....	....
2008-09	Bemidji State	CHA	35	0	13	13	34	....	....	....	....	....
2009-10	Bemidji State	CHA	29	1	8	9	20	....	....	....	....	....

Traded to **Toronto**by **Pittsburgh** for Toronto's 6th round choice (Joe Rogalski) in 2010 Entry Draft, March 3, 2010.

PERKOVICH, Nathan (puhr-KOH-vihch, NAY-thuhn) **N.J.**

Right wing. Shoots right. 6'5", 215 lbs. Born, Canton, MI, October 15, 1985.
(New Jersey's 6th choice, 250th overall, in 2004 Entry Draft).

			Regular Season					Playoffs				
Season	Club	League	GP	G	A	Pts	PIM	GP	G	A	Pts	PIM
2003-04	Cedar Rapids	USHL	35	1	7	8	23	4	1	0	1	0
2004-05	Chicago Steel	USHL	37	6	2	8	55	7	2	2	4	4
2005-06	Chicago Steel	USHL	56	28	24	52	121	....	....	....	....	....
2006-07	Lake Superior	CCHA	42	15	7	22	59	....	....	....	....	....
2007-08	Lake Superior	CCHA	36	17	8	25	52	....	....	....	....	....
2008-09	Lake Superior	CCHA	35	12	12	24	68	....	....	....	....	....
	Trenton Devils	ECHL	....	....	....	....	....	6	1	3	4	4
2009-10	Lowell Devils	AHL	68	19	14	33	81	5	0	1	1	0

PERLINI, Brett (PUHR-lee-nee, BREHT) **ANA.**

Right wing. Shoots right. 6'2", 200 lbs. Born, Sault Ste. Marie, Ont., June 14, 1990.
(Anaheim's 8th choice, 192nd overall, in 2010 Entry Draft).

			Regular Season					Playoffs				
Season	Club	League	GP	G	A	Pts	PIM	GP	G	A	Pts	PIM
2006-07	Soo Thunderbirds	NOJHL	48	38	19	57	20	12	6	6	12	6
2007-08	Ohio	USHL	19	1	4	5	0	....	....	....	....	....
	Soo Thunderbirds	NOJHL	16	16	16	32	12	6	4	3	7	6
2008-09	Michigan State	CCHA	26	2	1	3	4	....	....	....	....	....
2009-10	Michigan State	CCHA	20	7	5	12	10	....	....	....	....	....

PERSSON, Dennis (PAIR-suhn, DEH-nihs) **BUF.**

Defense. Shoots left. 6'1", 192 lbs. Born, Nykoping, Sweden, June 2, 1988.
(Buffalo's 1st choice, 24th overall, in 2006 Entry Draft).

			Regular Season					Playoffs				
Season	Club	League	GP	G	A	Pts	PIM	GP	G	A	Pts	PIM
2004-05	Vasteras U18	Swe-U18	3	0	1	1	2	4	0	1	1	0
	Vasteras Jr.	Swe-Jr.	27	3	3	6	24	....	....	....	....	....
2005-06	Vasteras Jr.	Swe-Jr.	28	11	15	26	22	....	....	....	....	....
	VIK Vasteras HK	Sweden-2	19	0	2	2	6	....	....	....	....	....
2006-07	Djurgarden	Sweden	9	0	0	0	2	....	....	....	....	....
	Almtuna	Sweden-2	3	0	0	0	2	....	....	....	....	....
	Nykoping	Sweden-2	29	4	4	8	38	....	....	....	....	....
	Djurgarden Jr.	Swe-Jr.	11	1	3	4	8	5	2	3	5	2
2007-08	Djurgarden Jr.	Swe-Jr.	4	0	0	0	10	....	....	....	....	....
	Djurgarden	Sweden	21	0	1	1	6	....	....	....	....	....
	Nykoping	Sweden-2	21	1	3	4	14	....	....	....	....	....
2008-09	Timra IK	Sweden	46	1	5	6	24	7	0	0	0	0
	Timra IK Jr.	Swe-Jr.	1	0	0	0	0	....	....	....	....	....
	Portland Pirates	AHL	8	0	2	2	6	3	0	0	0	0
2009-10	Portland Pirates	AHL	60	1	6	7	16	....	....	....	....	....

PERSSON, Niklas (PAIR-suhn, NIHK-luhs) **T.B.**

Right wing. Shoots left. 6'2", 205 lbs. Born, Osmo, Sweden, March 26, 1979.

			Regular Season					Playoffs				
Season	Club	League	GP	G	A	Pts	PIM	GP	G	A	Pts	PIM
1994-95	Huddinge IK Jr.	Swe-Jr.	3	0	0	0	0	....	....	....	....	....
1995-96	Leksands IF Jr.	Swe-Jr.	8	1	2	3	0	....	....	....	....	....
1996-97	Leksands IF Jr.	Swe-Jr.	29	18	15	33	....	....	....	....	....	....
1997-98	Leksands IF Jr.	Swe-Jr.	20	10	12	22	30	....	....	....	....	....
	Leksands IF	Sweden	17	2	3	5	4	2	0	0	0	0
1998-99	Leksands IF	Sweden	47	1	2	3	6	1	0	0	0	0
99-2000	Leksands IF	Sweden	49	2	5	7	34	....	....	....	....	....
2000-01	Leksands IF Jr.	Swe-Jr.	2	4	1	5	12	....	....	....	....	....
	Leksands IF	Sweden	48	3	4	7	43	....	....	....	....	....
	Leksands IF	Sweden-Q	7	2	1	3	6	....	....	....	....	....
2001-02	Leksands IF	Sweden-2	51	18	15	33	66	....	....	....	....	....
2002-03	Leksands IF	Sweden	49	4	21	25	51	5	0	0	0	10
2003-04	Leksands IF	Sweden	50	14	19	33	42	....	....	....	....	....
	Leksands IF	Sweden-Q	10	3	1	4	33	....	....	....	....	....
2004-05	Leksands IF	Sweden-2	53	17	28	45	44	....	....	....	....	....
2005-06	Leksands IF	Sweden	34	7	10	17	30	....	....	....	....	....
	Leksands IF	Sweden-Q	10	2	3	5	4	....	....	....	....	....
2006-07	Linkopings HC	Sweden	55	15	17	32	32	15	5	9	14	6
2007-08	Linkopings HC	Sweden	54	10	22	32	44	15	3	6	9	10
2008-09	Linkopings HC	Sweden	55	21	21	42	38	7	4	4	8	4
2009-10	Nizhnekamsk	Rus-KHL	55	13	25	38	30	7	0	2	2	2

Signed as a free agent by **Tampa Bay**, July 2, 2010.

PERVYSHIN, Andrei (pair-VIHSH-ihn, AWN-dray) **ST.L**

Defense. Shoots left. 5'9", 165 lbs. Born, Arkhangelsk, USSR, February 2, 1985.
(St. Louis' 11th choice, 253rd overall, in 2003 Entry Draft).

			Regular Season					Playoffs				
Season	Club	League	GP	G	A	Pts	PIM	GP	G	A	Pts	PIM
2003-04	Spartak Moscow	Russia-2	59	3	6	9	14	13	0	1	1	[illegible]
2004-05	Ak Bars Kazan	Russia	52	0	3	3	10	2	0	0	0	[illegible]
	Ak Bars Kazan 2	Russia-3	....	0	1	1	....	....	....	....	....	[illegible]
2005-06	Ak Bars Kazan	Russia	48	3	7	10	22	13	0	3	3	1[illegible]
2006-07	Ak Bars Kazan	Russia	45	5	8	13	71	12	2	3	5	[illegible]
2007-08	Ak Bars Kazan	Russia	55	7	8	15	40	10	1	1	2	[illegible]
2008-09	Ak Bars Kazan	Rus-KHL	54	6	21	27	28	21	1	9	10	1[illegible]
2009-10	Ak Bars Kazan	Rus-KHL	53	5	15	20	26	17	0	2	2	[illegible]

PESTUNOV, Dmitri (pehs-too-NAWF, dih-MEE-tree) **PHX**

Center. Shoots left. 5'9", 196 lbs. Born, Ust-Kamenogorsk, USSR, January 22, 1985.
(Phoenix's 2nd choice, 80th overall, in 2003 Entry Draft).

			Regular Season					Playoffs				
Season	Club	League	GP	G	A	Pts	PIM	GP	G	A	Pts	PIM
2002-03	Magnitogorsk	Russia	32	4	0	4	0	....	....	....	....	....
2003-04	Magnitogorsk	Russia	51	6	7	13	40	14	0	3	3	2[illegible]
	Magnitogorsk 2	Russia-3	6	3	15	18	2	3	0	2	2	[illegible]
2004-05	Magnitogorsk	Russia	37	4	4	8	46	....	....	....	....	....
	Spartak Moscow	Russia	12	1	1	2	14	....	....	....	....	....
2005-06	Magnitogorsk	Russia	48	6	13	19	58	4	0	1	1	[illegible]
2006-07	Magnitogorsk	Russia	53	5	18	23	26	11	0	0	0	[illegible]
2007-08	Spartak Moscow	Russia	51	8	17	25	56	5	0	0	0	1[illegible]
2008-09	Omsk	Rus-KHL	56	7	34	41	58	9	0	3	3	1[illegible]
2009-10	Omsk	Rus-KHL	48	5	18	23	30	2	0	0	0	[illegible]

Signed as a free agent by **Spartak Moscow** (Russia), February 16, 2005. Signed as a free agent by **Omsk** (Russia-KHL), May 16, 2008. Signed as a free agent by **Chelyabinsk** (Russia-KHL), July 15, 2010.

PETERSEN, Nick (PEE-tuhr-suhn, NIHK) **PIT.**

Right wing. Shoots right. 6'3", 188 lbs. Born, Wakefield, Que., May 27, 1989.
(Pittsburgh's 4th choice, 121st overall, in 2009 Entry Draft).

			Regular Season					Playoffs				
Season	Club	League	GP	G	A	Pts	PIM	GP	G	A	Pts	PIM
2006-07	Georgetown Prep.	High-MD	....	28	14	42	....	....	....	....	....	....
	Wsh. Jr. Nationals	AtJHL	40	24	34	58	40	....	....	....	....	....
2007-08	Shawinigan	QMJHL	51	11	18	29	38	5	5	1	6	[illegible]
2008-09	Shawinigan	QMJHL	68	37	53	90	42	21	10	12	22	22
2009-10	Saint John	QMJHL	59	39	40	79	55	21	7	*21	28	14

PETERSSON, Andre (PEH-tuhr-suhn, AHN-dray) **OTT.**

Right wing. Shoots right. 5'9", 179 lbs. Born, Olofstrom, Sweden, September 11, 1990.
(Ottawa's 4th choice, 109th overall, in 2008 Entry Draft).

			Regular Season					Playoffs				
Season	Club	League	GP	G	A	Pts	PIM	GP	G	A	Pts	PIM
2005-06	Tingsryds AIF U18	Swe-U18	9	5	3	8	0	....	....	....	....	....
2006-07	HV 71 U18	Swe-U18	10	14	10	24	6	2	1	2	3	0
	HV 71 Jr.	Swe-Jr.	6	1	1	2	8	....	....	....	....	....
2007-08	HV 71 U18	Swe-U18	4	4	5	9	4	....	....	....	....	....
	HV 71 Jr.	Swe-Jr.	36	16	22	38	34	3	0	0	0	2
2008-09	HV 71 Jonkoping	Sweden	10	0	1	1	0	....	....	....	....	....
	HV 71 Jr.	Swe-Jr.	36	24	31	55	28	7	7	4	11	8
2009-10	HV 71 Jonkoping	Sweden	37	10	5	15	14	6	0	1	1	2
	Boras HC	Sweden-2	1	1	0	1	0	....	....	....	....	....

PETRECKI, Nicholas (peh-TREH-kee, NIH-koh-las) **S.J.**

Defense. Shoots left. 6'3", 230 lbs. Born, Schenectady, NY, July 11, 1989.
(San Jose's 2nd choice, 28th overall, in 2007 Entry Draft).

			Regular Season					Playoffs				
Season	Club	League	GP	G	A	Pts	PIM	GP	G	A	Pts	PIM
2004-05	Capital District	EmJHL	53	5	18	23	159	....	....	....	....	....
2005-06	Omaha Lancers	USHL	53	0	3	3	110	5	0	0	0	0
2006-07	Omaha Lancers	USHL	54	11	14	25	177	5	0	0	0	10
2007-08	Boston College	H-East	42	5	7	12	*102	....	....	....	....	....
2008-09	Boston College	H-East	35	0	7	7	*161	....	....	....	....	....
2009-10	Worcester Sharks	AHL	65	2	12	14	106	....	....	....	....	....

USHL Second All-Star Team (2007)

PETROV, Kirill (peh-TRAWF, kih-RIHL) **NYI**

Right wing. Shoots left. 6'3", 198 lbs. Born, Kazan, USSR, April 13, 1990.
(NY Islanders' 7th choice, 73rd overall, in 2008 Entry Draft).

			Regular Season					Playoffs				
Season	Club	League	GP	G	A	Pts	PIM	GP	G	A	Pts	PIM
2005-06	Ak Bars Kazan 2	Russia-3	STATISTICS NOT AVAILABLE									
2006-07	Ak Bars Kazan 2	Russia-3	STATISTICS NOT AVAILABLE									
	Ak Bars Kazan	Russia	9	1	1	2	8	3	0	0	0	2
2007-08	Ak Bars Kazan	Russia	47	4	6	10	54	8	1	1	2	0
2008-09	Ak Bars Kazan 2	Russia-3	9	4	10	14	26	....	....	....	....	....
	Ak Bars Kazan	Rus-KHL	6	1	0	1	2	....	....	....	....	....
2009-10	Ak Bars Kazan	Rus-KHL	8	0	0	0	4	3	0	1	1	0
	Bars Kazan Jr.	Russia-Jr.	4	2	1	3	4	....	....	....	....	....
	Almetjevsk	Russia-2	22	7	13	20	48	13	12	7	19	24

PETROVIC, Alex (peh-TROH-vihch, AL-ehx) **FLA.**

Defense. Shoots right. 6'4", 193 lbs. Born, Edmonton, Alta., March 3, 1992.
(Florida's 5th choice, 36th overall, in 2010 Entry Draft).

			Regular Season					Playoffs				
Season	Club	League	GP	G	A	Pts	PIM	GP	G	A	Pts	PIM
2007-08	Edm. MLAC	AMHL	31	3	8	11	80	....	....	....	....	....
	Red Deer Rebels	WHL	10	1	0	1	2	....	....	....	....	....
2008-09	Red Deer Rebels	WHL	66	1	12	13	70	....	....	....	....	....
2009-10	Red Deer Rebels	WHL	57	8	19	27	87	4	0	0	0	4

ETRY, Jeff (PEH-tree, JEHF) **EDM.**

efense. Shoots right. 6'3", 176 lbs. Born, Ann Arbor, MI, December 9, 1987.
dmonton's 1st choice, 45th overall, in 2006 Entry Draft).

			Regular Season					Playoffs				
eason	Club	League	GP	G	A	Pts	PIM	GP	G	A	Pts	PIM
004-05	St. Mary's Prep	High-MI	23	2	8	10	....	6	2	5	7	....
005-06	Det. Caesers	MWEHL	33	7	21	28	24	....	....	....	....	....
	Des Moines	USHL	48	1	14	15	68	11	2	5	7	8
006-07	Des Moines	USHL	55	18	27	45	71	8	0	6	6	10
007-08	Michigan State	CCHA	42	3	21	24	28	....	....	....	....	....
008-09	Michigan State	CCHA	38	2	12	14	32	....	....	....	....	....
009-10	Springfield Falcons	AHL	8	0	3	3	2	....	....	....	....	....
	Michigan State	CCHA	38	4	25	29	26	....	....	....	....	....

SHL First All-Star Team (2007) • USHL Defenseman of the Year (2007) • CCHA All-Rookie Team
008) • CCHA Second All-Star Team (2010) • NCAA West Second All-American Team (2010)

HILLIPS, Paul (FIHL-ihps, PAWL) **CHI.**

efense. Shoots left. 6'1", 195 lbs. Born, Darien, IL, July 16, 1991.
hicago's 7th choice, 195th overall, in 2009 Entry Draft).

			Regular Season					Playoffs				
eason	Club	League	GP	G	A	Pts	PIM	GP	G	A	Pts	PIM
006-07	Chicago Fury	MWEHL	26	7	5	12	40	....	....	....	....	....
007-08	Cedar Rapids	USHL	43	1	2	3	25	3	0	0	0	4
008-09	Cedar Rapids	USHL	60	8	25	33	56	5	0	0	0	6
009-10	U. of Denver	WCHA	31	0	4	4	16	....	....	....	....	....

ICHE, Sebastien (PEE-shay, suh-BAS-tee-yehn) **DET.**

efense. Shoots left. 6', 202 lbs. Born, Lasarre, Que., February 4, 1988.

			Regular Season					Playoffs				
eason	Club	League	GP	G	A	Pts	PIM	GP	G	A	Pts	PIM
004-05	Rouyn-Noranda	QMJHL	2	0	0	0	2	....	....	....	....	....
	Lewiston	QMJHL	24	0	3	3	33	8	0	1	1	18
005-06	Lewiston	QMJHL	65	1	14	15	83	6	0	1	1	12
006-07	Lewiston	QMJHL	62	4	23	27	122	10	3	3	6	8
007-08	Shawinigan	QMJHL	18	1	11	12	21	....	....	....	....	....
	Rouyn-Noranda	QMJHL	32	1	27	28	44	17	4	19	23	39
008-09	Rimouski Oceanic	QMJHL	62	23	49	72	69	12	2	4	6	14
009-10	Grand Rapids	AHL	9	0	0	0	4	....	....	....	....	....
	Toledo Walleye	ECHL	46	5	23	28	67	4	0	2	2	4

MJHL Second All-Star Team (2009)

gned as a free agent by **Detroit**, April 12, 2009.

IERRO-ZABOTEL, Casey (PEE-air-oh-ZA-boh-tuhl, KAY-see) **PIT.**

enter. Shoots left. 6'1", 205 lbs. Born, Ashcroft, B.C., November 8, 1988.
ittsburgh's 4th choice, 80th overall, in 2007 Entry Draft).

			Regular Season					Playoffs				
eason	Club	League	GP	G	A	Pts	PIM	GP	G	A	Pts	PIM
004-05	Merritt	BCHL	58	6	6	12	19	5	0	0	0	0
005-06	Merritt	BCHL	60	20	35	55	29	9	9	4	13	10
006-07	Merritt	BCHL	55	51	65	116	42	7	8	3	11	13
007-08	Vancouver Giants	WHL	49	19	29	48	8	10	2	4	6	4
008-09	Vancouver Giants	WHL	72	36	*79	*115	52	17	4	13	17	16
009-10	Wilkes-Barre	AHL	9	0	1	1	0	....	....	....	....	....
	Wheeling Nailers	ECHL	49	12	29	41	26	....	....	....	....	....

HL West First All-Star Team (2009) • Canadian Major Junior Second All-Star Team (2009)

INIZZOTTO, Steve (pih-nih-ZAW-toh, STEEV) **WSH.**

enter. Shoots right. 6'1", 195 lbs. Born, Mississauga, Ont., April 26, 1984.

			Regular Season					Playoffs				
eason	Club	League	GP	G	A	Pts	PIM	GP	G	A	Pts	PIM
001-02	Oakville Blades	OPJHL	34	10	16	26	40	....	....	....	....	....
002-03	Oakville Blades	OPJHL	44	16	24	40	152	2	0	0	0	2
003-04	Oakville Blades	OPJHL	39	17	34	51	177	....	....	....	....	....
004-05	Oakville Blades	OPJHL	48	33	62	95	86	....	....	....	....	....
005-06	RIT Tigers	NCAA	20	7	6	13	32	....	....	....	....	....
006-07	RIT Tigers	AH	34	13	31	44	76	....	....	....	....	....
	Hershey Bears	AHL	5	0	0	0	4	....	....	....	....	....
007-08	Hershey Bears	AHL	23	0	4	4	12	5	0	0	0	13
	South Carolina	ECHL	40	15	17	32	58	10	1	2	3	34
008-09	Hershey Bears	AHL	45	4	7	11	61	21	3	2	5	28
	South Carolina	ECHL	11	4	6	10	19	....	....	....	....	....
009-10	Hershey Bears	AHL	69	13	28	41	124	21	5	3	8	33

gned as a free agent by **Washington**, March 16, 2007.

IRRI, Brandon (PIHR-ee, BRAN-duhn) **CHI.**

enter. Shoots left. 6', 160 lbs. Born, Toronto, Ont., April 10, 1991.
hicago's 2nd choice, 59th overall, in 2009 Entry Draft).

			Regular Season					Playoffs				
ason	Club	League	GP	G	A	Pts	PIM	GP	G	A	Pts	PIM
006-07	Tor. Young Nats	GTHL	44	54	72	128	18	....	....	....	....	....
007-08	Streetsville Derbys	OPJHL	40	18	32	50	42	....	....	....	....	....
008-09	Streetsville Derbys	OJHL	18	21	28	49	24	....	....	....	....	....
	Georgetown	OJHL	26	25	20	45	22	....	....	....	....	....
009-10	RPI Engineers	ECAC	39	11	32	43	67	....	....	....	....	....

AC All-Rookie Team (2010)

STILLI, Matthew (pihs-TIHL-lee, MATH-yew) **CAR.**

ght wing. Shoots right. 6'2", 219 lbs. Born, Montreal, Que., October 17, 1988.

			Regular Season					Playoffs				
ason	Club	League	GP	G	A	Pts	PIM	GP	G	A	Pts	PIM
04-05	Trois-Rivieres	QAAA	41	20	28	48	34	....	....	....	....	....
	Shawinigan	QMJHL	2	1	1	2	6	....	....	....	....	....
05-06	Shawinigan	QMJHL	34	5	5	10	20	....	....	....	....	....
	Gatineau	QMJHL	32	10	13	23	16	17	2	2	4	8
06-07	Gatineau	QMJHL	65	22	29	51	44	5	1	1	2	2
07-08	Gatineau	QMJHL	63	37	56	93	51	19	11	17	28	14
08-09	Shawinigan	QMJHL	63	45	41	86	37	21	13	7	20	4
09-10	Florida Everblades	ECHL	11	2	2	4	4	8	3	6	9	2
	Albany River Rats	AHL	41	5	3	8	10	....	....	....	....	....

anadian Major Junior Humanitarian Player of the Year (2009)

gned as a free agent by **Carolina**, May 20, 2009.

PITHER, Lukas (PIH-tuhr, LOO-kuhs) **PHI.**

Center. Shoots left. 6', 195 lbs. Born, Burketon, Ont., April 26, 1989.

			Regular Season					Playoffs				
Season	Club	League	GP	G	A	Pts	PIM	GP	G	A	Pts	PIM
2004-05	Bowmanville	OPJHL	2	1	0	1	0	....	....	....	....	....
2005-06	Kingston	OHL	68	4	9	13	26	6	0	1	1	2
2006-07	Kingston	OHL	5	1	0	1	2	....	....	....	....	....
	Guelph Storm	OHL	52	15	13	28	22	4	1	0	1	2
2007-08	Guelph Storm	OHL	51	13	29	42	31	10	0	2	2	0
2008-09	Guelph Storm	OHL	41	16	14	30	22	....	....	....	....	....
	Belleville Bulls	OHL	23	19	23	42	10	17	6	13	19	6
2009-10	Barrie Colts	OHL	67	36	58	94	44	17	9	11	20	4

Signed as a free agent by **Philadelphia**, March 4, 2010.

PITLICK, Tyler (PIHT-lihk, TIGH-luhr) **EDM.**

Center. Shoots right. 6'2", 194 lbs. Born, Minneapolis, MN, November 1, 1991.
(Edmonton's 2nd choice, 31st overall, in 2010 Entry Draft).

			Regular Season					Playoffs				
Season	Club	League	GP	G	A	Pts	PIM	GP	G	A	Pts	PIM
2007-08	Centennial	High-MN	....	25	34	59	....	....	....	....	....	....
2008-09	Centennial	High-MN	25	31	33	64	....	....	....	....	....	....
2009-10	Minnesota State	WCHA	38	11	8	19	27	....	....	....	....	....

POLASEK, Adam (poh-LAH-shehk, A-duhm) **VAN.**

Defense. Shoots left. 6'3", 190 lbs. Born, Ostrava, Czechoslovakia, July 12, 1991.
(Vancouver's 2nd choice, 145th overall, in 2010 Entry Draft).

			Regular Season					Playoffs				
Season	Club	League	GP	G	A	Pts	PIM	GP	G	A	Pts	PIM
2005-06	HC Vitkovice U17	CzR-U17	17	1	0	1	2	....	....	....	....	....
2006-07	HC Vitkovice U17	CzR-U17	43	6	13	19	83	9	0	1	1	12
	HC Vitkovice Jr.	CzRep-Jr.	1	0	0	0	2	....	....	....	....	....
2007-08	HC Vitkovice U17	CzR-U17	18	3	2	5	50	2	0	0	0	0
	HC Vitkovice Jr.	CzRep-Jr.	23	0	3	3	16	2	0	1	1	0
2008-09	HC Vitkovice Jr.	CzRep-Jr.	38	7	13	20	68	9	0	9	9	18
2009-10	P.E.I. Rocket	QMJHL	66	13	28	41	91	5	0	0	0	2

QMJHL All-Rookie Team (2010) • Canadian Major Junior All-Rookie Team (2010)

PONICH, Brett (PAW-nihch, BREHT) **ST.L.**

Defense. Shoots left. 6'7", 204 lbs. Born, Edmonton, Alta., February 22, 1991.
(St. Louis' 2nd choice, 48th overall, in 2009 Entry Draft).

			Regular Season					Playoffs				
Season	Club	League	GP	G	A	Pts	PIM	GP	G	A	Pts	PIM
2006-07	Leduc Oil Kings	AMHL	35	1	10	11	64	13	1	6	7	24
	Portland	WHL	2	0	0	0	0	....	....	....	....	....
2007-08	Portland	WHL	64	0	3	3	63	....	....	....	....	....
2008-09	Portland	WHL	72	1	17	18	117	....	....	....	....	....
2009-10	Portland	WHL	66	1	13	14	87	13	1	2	3	13

POPE, Matt (POHP, MAT)

Right wing. Shoots right. 6'1", 185 lbs. Born, Langley, B.C., August 5, 1984.

			Regular Season					Playoffs				
Season	Club	League	GP	G	A	Pts	PIM	GP	G	A	Pts	PIM
2003-04	Langley Hornets	BCHL	60	27	44	71	92	....	....	....	....	....
2004-05	Bemidji State	CHA	37	7	7	14	28	....	....	....	....	....
2005-06	Bemidji State	CHA	37	7	14	21	44	....	....	....	....	....
2006-07	Bemidji State	CHA	33	5	8	13	14	....	....	....	....	....
2007-08	Bemidji State	CHA	36	14	9	23	40	....	....	....	....	....
2008-09	Binghamton	AHL	4	2	1	3	4	....	....	....	....	....
	Manitoba Moose	AHL	8	2	3	5	6	12	3	3	6	2
	Bakersfield	ECHL	54	30	33	63	72	....	....	....	....	....
2009-10	Manitoba Moose	AHL	40	3	5	8	23	2	0	1	1	10
	Bakersfield	ECHL	6	4	4	8	2	....	....	....	....	....

Signed as a free agent by **Vancouver**, July 2, 2009. Signed as a free agent by **Victoria** (ECHL), August 3, 2010.

POPOV, Andrei (PAH-pawv, AWN-dray) **PHI.**

Right wing. Shoots left. 6', 187 lbs. Born, Chelyabinsk, USSR, July 15, 1988.
(Philadelphia's 10th choice, 205th overall, in 2006 Entry Draft).

			Regular Season					Playoffs				
Season	Club	League	GP	G	A	Pts	PIM	GP	G	A	Pts	PIM
2003-04	Chelyabinsk 2	Russia-3	6	3	0	3	4	....	....	....	....	....
2004-05	Chelyabinsk 2	Russia-3	17	7	1	8	4	....	....	....	....	....
2005-06	Chelyabinsk 2	Russia-3	2	1	4	5	0	....	....	....	....	....
	Chelyabinsk	Russia-2	37	8	8	16	26	5	2	0	2	2
2006-07	Chelyabinsk 2	Russia-3	2	1	1	2	0	....	....	....	....	....
	Chelyabinsk	Russia	44	2	10	12	36	....	....	....	....	....
2007-08	Chelyabinsk 2	Russia-3	6	4	3	7	4	....	....	....	....	....
	Chelyabinsk	Russia	33	5	2	7	12	2	0	0	0	4
2008-09	Chelyabinsk	Rus-KHL	54	4	5	9	38	3	0	0	0	0
2009-10	Chelyabinsk	Rus-KHL	50	15	11	26	24	4	0	1	1	2
	Chelyabinsk Jr.	Russia-Jr.	5	6	6	12	4	9	5	9	14	8

POSTMA, Paul (POHST-muh, PAWL) **ATL.**

Defense. Shoots right. 6'3", 195 lbs. Born, Red Deer, Alta., February 22, 1989.
(Atlanta's 4th choice, 205th overall, in 2007 Entry Draft).

			Regular Season					Playoffs				
Season	Club	League	GP	G	A	Pts	PIM	GP	G	A	Pts	PIM
2004-05	Red Deer	AMHL	36	6	5	11	24	....	....	....	....	....
	Swift Current	WHL	4	0	0	0	0	....	....	....	....	....
2005-06	Swift Current	WHL	58	2	9	11	6	4	0	0	0	0
2006-07	Swift Current	WHL	70	5	19	24	42	6	0	1	1	0
2007-08	Swift Current	WHL	2	0	0	0	2	....	....	....	....	....
	Calgary Hitmen	WHL	66	14	28	42	30	16	6	4	10	4
2008-09	Calgary Hitmen	WHL	70	23	61	84	28	18	5	8	13	10
2009-10	Chicago Wolves	AHL	63	15	14	29	24	7	0	2	2	0

WHL East First All-Star Team (2009) • Canadian Major Junior Second All-Star Team (2009)

PRICE, Jeremy (PRIGHS, JAIR-eh-mee) **VAN.**

Defense. Shoots right. 6'1", 194 lbs. Born, Milton, Ont., September 26, 1990.
(Vancouver's 4th choice, 113th overall, in 2009 Entry Draft).

			Regular Season					Playoffs				
Season	Club	League	GP	G	A	Pts	PIM	GP	G	A	Pts	PIM
2006-07	Milton Icehawks	OPJHL	37	1	6	7	51	5	2	1	3	9
2007-08	Milton Icehawks	OPJHL	44	10	22	32	28	10	0	6	6	4
2008-09	Nepean Raiders	CJHL	55	12	29	41	50	14	2	4	6	14
2009-10	Colgate	ECAC	35	6	8	14	32	....	....	....	....	....

PROUT, Dalton (PROWT, DAHL-tuhn) **CBJ**

Defense. Shoots right. 6'3", 221 lbs. Born, LaSalle, Ont., March 13, 1990.
(Columbus' 7th choice, 154th overall, in 2010 Entry Draft).

			Regular Season					Playoffs				
Season	**Club**	**League**	**GP**	**G**	**A**	**Pts**	**PIM**	**GP**	**G**	**A**	**Pts**	**PIM**
2005-06	Wind. Jr. Spitfires	Minor-ON	58	11	19	30	78	....	....	....	....	....
2006-07	Sarnia Sting	OHL	49	1	2	3	36	4	0	0	0	0
2007-08	Sarnia Sting	OHL	32	0	2	2	43	....	....	....	....	....
	Barrie Colts	OHL	25	0	3	3	39	8	0	2	2	16
2008-09	Barrie Colts	OHL	65	0	6	6	98	5	0	1	1	10
2009-10	Barrie Colts	OHL	63	7	14	21	121	17	1	6	7	20

PRYOR, Nick (PRIGH-uhr, NIHK) **ANA.**

Defense. Shoots left. 5'11", 184 lbs. Born, St. Paul, MN, September 9, 1990.
(Anaheim's 10th choice, 208th overall, in 2008 Entry Draft).

			Regular Season					Playoffs				
Season	**Club**	**League**	**GP**	**G**	**A**	**Pts**	**PIM**	**GP**	**G**	**A**	**Pts**	**PIM**
2006-07	USNTDP	U-17	7	2	3	5	2	....	....	....	....	....
	USNTDP	NAHL	37	1	3	4	10	4	1	0	1	0
2007-08	USNTDP	U-18	41	3	9	12	6	....	....	....	....	....
	USNTDP	NAHL	12	0	2	2	6	....	....	....	....	....
2008-09	Des Moines	USHL	31	6	12	18	26	....	....	....	....	....
	Waterloo	USHL	12	1	5	6	10	....	....	....	....	....
2009-10	U. of Maine	H-East	6	0	0	0	2	....	....	....	....	....

PULKKINEN, Teemu (PUHL-kih-nuhn, TEE-moo) **DET.**

Left wing. Shoots right. 5'11", 183 lbs. Born, Vantaa, Finland, January 2, 1992.
(Detroit's 4th choice, 111th overall, in 2010 Entry Draft).

			Regular Season					Playoffs				
Season	**Club**	**League**	**GP**	**G**	**A**	**Pts**	**PIM**	**GP**	**G**	**A**	**Pts**	**PIM**
2007-08	Jokerit U18	Fin-U18	32	36	24	60	8	6	11	6	17	6
2008-09	Suomi U20	Finland-2	1	0	0	0	0	....	....	....	....	....
	Jokerit U18	Fin-U18	9	16	19	35	4	....	....	....	....	....
	Jokerit Helsinki Jr.	Fin-Jr.	24	15	13	28	12	....	....	....	....	....
	Jokerit Helsinki	Finland	3	0	0	0	6	....	....	....	....	....
2009-10	Jokerit Helsinki Jr.	Fin-Jr.	17	20	21	41	41	4	3	3	6	0
	Jokerit Helsinki	Finland	12	1	2	3	6	....	....	....	....	....

PYETT, Logan (PIGH-eht, LOH-guhn) **DET.**

Defense. Shoots right. 5'10", 200 lbs. Born, Regina, Sask., May 26, 1988.
(Detroit's 7th choice, 212th overall, in 2006 Entry Draft).

			Regular Season					Playoffs				
Season	**Club**	**League**	**GP**	**G**	**A**	**Pts**	**PIM**	**GP**	**G**	**A**	**Pts**	**PIM**
2002-03	Balgonie	SSMHL	35	27	46	73	40	....	....	....	....	....
2003-04	Reg. Pat Cdns.	SMHL	44	18	27	45	34	....	....	....	....	....
	Regina Pats	WHL	2	0	1	1	0	3	0	0	0	0
2004-05	Regina Pats	WHL	67	5	19	24	67	....	....	....	....	....
2005-06	Regina Pats	WHL	71	10	35	45	89	6	1	6	7	12
2006-07	Regina Pats	WHL	71	14	48	62	84	10	3	6	9	4
2007-08	Regina Pats	WHL	62	20	34	54	54	6	1	3	4	0
2008-09	Grand Rapids	AHL	61	3	11	14	12	1	0	0	0	0
2009-10	Grand Rapids	AHL	80	9	21	30	41	....	....	....	....	....

WHL East First All-Star Team (2008) • Canadian Major Junior Second All-Star Team (2008)

PYSYK, Mark (PIH-zihk, MAHRK) **BUF.**

Defense. Shoots right. 6'1", 174 lbs. Born, Edmonton, Alta., January 11, 1992.
(Buffalo's 1st choice, 23rd overall, in 2010 Entry Draft).

			Regular Season					Playoffs				
Season	**Club**	**League**	**GP**	**G**	**A**	**Pts**	**PIM**	**GP**	**G**	**A**	**Pts**	**PIM**
2007-08	Sherwood Park	AMHL	34	10	10	20	60	2	1	0	1	16
	Edmonton	WHL	14	1	2	3	8	....	....	....	....	....
2008-09	Edmonton	WHL	61	5	15	20	27	4	0	0	0	2
2009-10	Edmonton	WHL	48	7	17	24	47	....	....	....	....	....

QUAILER, Steve (KWAY-luhr, STEEV) **MTL.**

Left wing. Shoots left. 6'4", 184 lbs. Born, Arvada, CO, August 5, 1989.
(Montreal's 2nd choice, 86th overall, in 2008 Entry Draft).

			Regular Season					Playoffs				
Season	**Club**	**League**	**GP**	**G**	**A**	**Pts**	**PIM**	**GP**	**G**	**A**	**Pts**	**PIM**
2006-07	Rocky Mountain	Minor-CO	53	14	23	37	25	....	....	....	....	....
2007-08	Sioux City	USHL	60	19	30	49	55	4	1	2	3	4
2008-09	Northeastern	H-East	41	10	15	25	12	....	....	....	....	....
2009-10	Northeastern	H-East	DID NOT PLAY – INJURED									

USHL All-Rookie Team (2008) • Hockey East All-Rookie Team (2009)

• Missed entire 2009-10 season recovering from knee injury suffered in exhibition game vs. St. Thomas University (MIAC), October 3, 2009.

RABBIT, Wacey (RA-biht, WAY-see)

Center. Shoots left. 5'10", 169 lbs. Born, Lethbridge, Alta., November 16, 1986.
(Boston's 6th choice, 154th overall, in 2005 Entry Draft).

			Regular Season					Playoffs				
Season	**Club**	**League**	**GP**	**G**	**A**	**Pts**	**PIM**	**GP**	**G**	**A**	**Pts**	**PIM**
2001-02	Cgy. North Stars	AMHL	35	24	28	52	....	....	....	....	....	....
	Saskatoon Blades	WHL	3	0	1	1	0	....	....	....	....	....
2002-03	Saskatoon Blades	WHL	62	21	24	45	33	5	1	3	4	6
2003-04	Saskatoon Blades	WHL	60	9	8	17	51	....	....	....	....	....
2004-05	Saskatoon Blades	WHL	70	22	45	67	70	4	1	2	3	0
2005-06	Saskatoon Blades	WHL	64	28	28	56	45	10	5	3	8	4
2006-07	Vancouver Giants	WHL	30	11	25	36	34	22	*11	9	20	16
	Providence Bruins	AHL	22	1	2	3	25	....	....	....	....	....
2007-08	Providence Bruins	AHL	66	9	17	26	51	4	2	0	2	2
2008-09	Providence Bruins	AHL	74	16	18	34	74	14	1	5	6	8
2009-10	Milwaukee	AHL	76	8	10	18	53	5	0	0	0	0

Signed as a free agent by **Milwaukee** (AHL), October 2, 2009.

RAEDEKE, Brent (RAD-kee, BREHNT) **DET.**

Left wing. Shoots left. 6', 190 lbs. Born, Regina, Sask., May 29, 1990.

			Regular Season					Playoffs				
Season	**Club**	**League**	**GP**	**G**	**A**	**Pts**	**PIM**	**GP**	**G**	**A**	**Pts**	**PIM**
2005-06	Regina Pat Cdns.	SAHA	41	7	7	14	36	2	0	0	0	0
2006-07	Regina Pat Cdns.	SAHA	40	16	20	36	74	1	1	0	1	0
2007-08	Edmonton	WHL	72	15	16	31	62	....	....	....	....	....
2008-09	Edmonton	WHL	70	19	36	55	80	4	1	1	2	6
	Grand Rapids	AHL	2	0	0	0	0	....	....	....	....	....
2009-10	Edmonton	WHL	39	16	15	31	60	....	....	....	....	....
	Brandon	WHL	33	7	18	25	35	15	5	7	12	16

Signed as a free agent by **Detroit**, October 1, 2008.

RAI, Prab (RIGH, PRAB) **VAN**

Center. Shoots left. 5'11", 185 lbs. Born, Surrey, B.C., November 22, 1989.
(Vancouver's 3rd choice, 131st overall, in 2008 Entry Draft).

			Regular Season					Playoffs				
Season	**Club**	**League**	**GP**	**G**	**A**	**Pts**	**PIM**	**GP**	**G**	**A**	**Pts**	**PIM**
2006-07	Prince George	WHL	24	2	3	5	12	....	....	....	....	....
	Seattle	WHL	38	5	14	19	18	8	1	4	5	[illegible]
2007-08	Seattle	WHL	72	20	45	65	21	11	2	4	6	[illegible]
2008-09	Seattle	WHL	61	25	40	65	29	5	1	1	2	[illegible]
2009-10	Seattle	WHL	67	41	28	69	20	....	....	....	....	....

WHL West Second All-Star Team (2010)

RAJALA, Toni (ray-YAH-lah, TOH-nee) **EDM**

Left wing. Shoots left. 5'10", 163 lbs. Born, Parkano, Finland, March 29, 1991.
(Edmonton's 6th choice, 101st overall, in 2009 Entry Draft).

			Regular Season					Playoffs				
Season	**Club**	**League**	**GP**	**G**	**A**	**Pts**	**PIM**	**GP**	**G**	**A**	**Pts**	**PIM**
2006-07	Ilves Tampere U18	Fin-U18	30	18	26	44	32	3	2	1	3	[illegible]
	Ilves Tampere Jr.	Fin-Jr.	1	0	0	0	0	....	....	....	....	....
2007-08	Ilves Tampere U18	Fin-U18	13	10	15	25	18	....	....	....	....	....
	Ilves Tampere Jr.	Fin-Jr.	33	13	22	35	10	5	1	3	4	[illegible]
2008-09	Suomi U20	Finland-2	4	1	2	3	2	....	....	....	....	....
	Ilves Tampere Jr.	Fin-Jr.	31	14	17	31	18	....	....	....	....	....
	Ilves Tampere	Finland	21	2	3	5	0	3	0	0	0	[illegible]
2009-10	Brandon	WHL	60	26	37	63	24	15	4	3	7	[illegible]

George Parsons Trophy (Memorial Cup Tournament - Most Sportsmanlike Player) (2010)

RAKHSHANI, Rhett (rahk-SHAH-nee, REHT) **NY**

Right wing. Shoots right. 5'10", 170 lbs. Born, Orange, CA, March 6, 1988.
(NY Islanders' 4th choice, 100th overall, in 2006 Entry Draft).

			Regular Season					Playoffs				
Season	**Club**	**League**	**GP**	**G**	**A**	**Pts**	**PIM**	**GP**	**G**	**A**	**Pts**	**PIM**
2003-04	California Wave	Minor-CA	56	54	67	121	....	....	....	....	....	....
2004-05	USNTDP	U-17	14	6	5	11	32	....	....	....	....	....
	USNTDP	NAHL	40	12	15	27	21	9	1	4	5	[illegible]
2005-06	USNTDP	U-18	43	11	12	23	30	....	....	....	....	....
	USNTDP	NAHL	16	13	13	26	35	....	....	....	....	....
2006-07	U. of Denver	WCHA	40	10	26	36	38	....	....	....	....	....
2007-08	U. of Denver	WCHA	37	14	14	28	52	....	....	....	....	....
2008-09	U. of Denver	WCHA	38	15	22	37	50	....	....	....	....	....
2009-10	U. of Denver	WCHA	41	21	29	50	40	....	....	....	....	....
	Bridgeport	AHL	5	0	2	2	2	5	0	0	0	[illegible]

WCHA First All-Star Team (2010) • NCAA West First All-American Team (2010)

RAMAGE, John (RAM-ihj, JAWN) **CGY**

Defense. Shoots right. 6'1", 184 lbs. Born, Mississauga, Ont., February 7, 1991.
(Calgary's 3rd choice, 103rd overall, in 2010 Entry Draft).

			Regular Season					Playoffs				
Season	**Club**	**League**	**GP**	**G**	**A**	**Pts**	**PIM**	**GP**	**G**	**A**	**Pts**	**PIM**
2007-08	St. Louis Bandits	NAHL	45	4	5	9	75	11	0	2	2	[illegible]
	USNTDP	U-17	3	0	0	0	0	....	....	....	....	....
2008-09	USNTDP	NAHL	14	1	4	5	12	....	....	....	....	....
	USNTDP	U-18	40	1	4	5	32	....	....	....	....	....
2009-10	U. of Wisconsin	WCHA	41	2	10	12	51	....	....	....	....	....

RANDELL, Tyler (RAN-duhl, TIGH-luhr) **BOS**

Right wing. Shoots right. 6'1", 194 lbs. Born, Scarborough, Ont., June 15, 1991.
(Boston's 4th choice, 176th overall, in 2009 Entry Draft).

			Regular Season					Playoffs				
Season	**Club**	**League**	**GP**	**G**	**A**	**Pts**	**PIM**	**GP**	**G**	**A**	**Pts**	**PIM**
2006-07	Brampton	Minor-ON	63	53	38	91	81	....	....	....	....	....
2007-08	Belleville Bulls	OHL	62	5	6	11	24	19	0	0	0	[illegible]
2008-09	Belleville Bulls	OHL	36	10	5	15	60	....	....	....	....	....
	Kitchener Rangers	OHL	37	14	8	22	39	....	....	....	....	....
2009-10	Kitchener Rangers	OHL	47	9	12	21	88	20	1	4	5	[illegible]

RANFORD, Brendan (RAN-fohrd, BREHN-duhn) **PH**

Left wing. Shoots left. 5'10", 182 lbs. Born, Edmonton, Alta., May 3, 1992.
(Philadelphia's 6th choice, 209th overall, in 2010 Entry Draft).

			Regular Season					Playoffs				
Season	**Club**	**League**	**GP**	**G**	**A**	**Pts**	**PIM**	**GP**	**G**	**A**	**Pts**	**PIM**
2007-08	G.D. Canadians	AMHL	35	*33	46	*79	58	12	10	5	15	[illegible]
	Kamloops Blazers	WHL	3	0	0	0	0	....	....	....	....	....
2008-09	Kamloops Blazers	WHL	66	13	14	27	46	4	0	3	3	[illegible]
2009-10	Kamloops Blazers	WHL	72	29	36	65	83	4	2	3	5	[illegible]

RASK, Joonas (RASK, YOH-nuhs) **NS**

Center. Shoots right. 5'10", 176 lbs. Born, Savonlinna, Finland, March 24, 1990.
(Nashville's 6th choice, 198th overall, in 2010 Entry Draft).

			Regular Season					Playoffs				
Season	**Club**	**League**	**GP**	**G**	**A**	**Pts**	**PIM**	**GP**	**G**	**A**	**Pts**	**PIM**
2005-06	SaPKo Jr.	Fin-Jr.	2	3	1	4	0	....	....	....	....	....
2006-07	Ilves Tampere U18	Fin-U18	32	17	23	40	46	....	....	....	....	....
	Ilves Tampere Jr.	Fin-Jr.	1	0	0	0	0	....	....	....	....	....
2007-08	Ilves Tampere U18	Fin-U18	6	3	9	12	22	....	....	....	....	....
	Ilves Tampere Jr.	Fin-Jr.	32	11	18	29	34	5	1	3	4	[illegible]
2008-09	Suomi U20	Finland-2	8	0	6	6	0	....	....	....	....	....
	Ilves Tampere Jr.	Fin-Jr.	25	8	11	19	8	....	....	....	....	....
	LeKi Lempaala	Finland-2	1	1	2	3	2	....	....	....	....	....
	Ilves Tampere	Finland	24	1	0	1	8	3	0	1	1	[illegible]
2009-10	Ilves Tampere	Finland	43	10	9	19	32	....	....	....	....	....
	Suomi U20	Finland-2	1	0	0	0	0	....	....	....	....	....
	Ilves Tampere Jr.	Fin-Jr.	2	0	0	0	2	4	2	2	4	[illegible]
	Ilves Tampere	Finland-Q	....	....	....	....	....	5	3	0	3	[illegible]

RATCHUK, Michael (RAT-chuhk, MIGH-kuhl) **CBJ**

Defense. Shoots left. 5'11", 186 lbs. Born, Buffalo, NY, February 20, 1988.
(Philadelphia's 3rd choice, 42nd overall, in 2006 Entry Draft).

			Regular Season					Playoffs				
Season	Club	League	GP	G	A	Pts	PIM	GP	G	A	Pts	PIM
2004-05	USNTDP	U-17	15	1	4	5	16	....	....	....	....	....
	USNTDP	NAHL	33	3	6	9	14	10	1	1	2	2
2005-06	USNTDP	U-18	39	8	14	22	52	....	....	....	....	....
	USNTDP	NAHL	16	4	4	8	4	....	....	....	....	....
2006-07	Michigan State	CCHA	40	4	8	12	28	....	....	....	....	....
2007-08	Michigan State	CCHA	42	6	19	25	48	....	....	....	....	....
	Philadelphia	AHL	3	1	2	3	2	5	0	1	1	0
2008-09	Philadelphia	AHL	77	5	12	17	44	4	0	1	1	2
2009-10	Adirondack	AHL	5	0	1	1	2	....	....	....	....	....
	Syracuse Crunch	AHL	35	3	7	10	10	....	....	....	....	....

Traded to **Columbus** by **Philadelphia** for Stefan Legein, October 20, 2009.

RAU, Chad (ROW, CHAD) **MIN.**

Center. Shoots right. 5'11", 188 lbs. Born, Eden Prairie, MN, January 18, 1987.
(Toronto's 6th choice, 228th overall, in 2005 Entry Draft).

			Regular Season					Playoffs				
Season	Club	League	GP	G	A	Pts	PIM	GP	G	A	Pts	PIM
2004-05	Des Moines	USHL	57	31	40	71	32	....	....	....	....	....
2005-06	Colorado College	WCHA	42	13	17	30	8	....	....	....	....	....
2006-07	Colorado College	WCHA	39	14	17	31	4	....	....	....	....	....
2007-08	Colorado College	WCHA	40	*28	14	42	8	....	....	....	....	....
2008-09	Colorado College	WCHA	38	18	19	37	6	....	....	....	....	....
2009-10	Houston Aeros	AHL	79	19	19	38	7	....	....	....	....	....

USHL All-Rookie Team (2005) • USHL First All-Star Team (2005) • USHL Rookie of the Year (2005) • WCHA First All-Star Team (2008, 2009) • NCAA West Second All-American Team (2008, 2009)

Signed as a free agent by **Houston** (AHL), October 6, 2009. Signed as a free agent by **Minnesota**, May 17, 2010.

REAVES, Ryan (REEVZ, RIGH-uhn) **ST.L.**

Right wing. Shoots right. 6'1", 225 lbs. Born, Winnipeg, Man., January 20, 1987.
(St. Louis' 4th choice, 156th overall, in 2005 Entry Draft).

			Regular Season					Playoffs				
Season	Club	League	GP	G	A	Pts	PIM	GP	G	A	Pts	PIM
2004-05	Brandon	WHL	64	7	9	16	79	23	2	4	6	43
2005-06	Brandon	WHL	68	14	14	28	91	6	0	1	1	8
2006-07	Brandon	WHL	69	15	20	35	76	11	1	4	5	19
2007-08	Peoria Rivermen	AHL	31	4	3	7	46	....	....	....	....	....
	Alaska Aces	ECHL	9	2	0	2	42	2	0	0	0	22
2008-09	Peoria Rivermen	AHL	57	8	9	17	130	4	0	0	0	2
2009-10	Peoria Rivermen	AHL	76	4	7	11	167	....	....	....	....	....

REDMOND, Zach (REHD-muhnd, ZAK) **ATL.**

Defense. Shoots right. 6'2", 205 lbs. Born, Houston, TX, July 26, 1988.
(Atlanta's 7th choice, 184th overall, in 2008 Entry Draft).

			Regular Season					Playoffs				
Season	Club	League	GP	G	A	Pts	PIM	GP	G	A	Pts	PIM
2005-06	Sioux Falls	USHL	48	4	7	11	57	11	1	2	3	4
2006-07	Sioux Falls	USHL	60	8	31	39	37	8	3	7	10	8
2007-08	Ferris State	CCHA	37	6	13	19	33	....	....	....	....	....
2008-09	Ferris State	CCHA	38	3	21	24	48	....	....	....	....	....
2009-10	Ferris State	CCHA	40	6	21	27	46	....	....	....	....	....

CCHA Second All-Star Team (2010)

REED, Harrison (REED, HAIR-rih-suhn) **COL.**

Center/Right wing. Shoots right. 6'1", 185 lbs. Born, Newmarket, Ont., January 18, 1988.
(Carolina's 2nd choice, 93rd overall, in 2006 Entry Draft).

			Regular Season					Playoffs				
Season	Club	League	GP	G	A	Pts	PIM	GP	G	A	Pts	PIM
2004-05	Petrolia Jets	OJHL-B	43	11	18	29	43	....	....	....	....	....
	London Knights	OHL	6	0	0	0	0	4	0	1	1	0
2005-06	Sarnia Sting	OHL	68	26	24	50	50	....	....	....	....	....
2006-07	Sarnia Sting	OHL	67	29	52	81	30	4	0	4	4	8
2007-08	Sarnia Sting	OHL	28	6	12	18	20	....	....	....	....	....
	Guelph Storm	OHL	41	8	21	29	20	10	3	2	5	12
2008-09	Albany River Rats	AHL	70	5	4	9	22	....	....	....	....	....
	Florida Everblades	ECHL	1	1	1	2	0	....	....	....	....	....
2009-10	Albany River Rats	AHL	49	1	5	6	10	....	....	....	....	....
	Lake Erie Monsters	AHL	17	0	1	1	19	....	....	....	....	....
	Florida Everblades	ECHL	9	8	5	13	9	....	....	....	....	....

Traded to **Colorado** by **Carolina** with Stephane Yelle for Cedric Lalonde-McNicoll and Colorado's 6th round choice (Tyler Stahl) in 2010 Entry Draft, March 3, 2010.

REGAN, Eric (REE-guhn, AIR-ihk) **ANA.**

Defenseman. Shoots right. 6'2", 206 lbs. Born, Ajax, Ont., May 20, 1988.

			Regular Season					Playoffs				
Season	Club	League	GP	G	A	Pts	PIM	GP	G	A	Pts	PIM
2004-05	Erie Otters	OHL	61	2	2	4	6	6	0	0	0	0
2005-06	Erie Otters	OHL	25	0	3	3	14	....	....	....	....	....
	Oshawa Generals	OHL	35	3	10	13	16	....	....	....	....	....
2006-07	Oshawa Generals	OHL	64	3	42	45	64	9	1	1	2	7
2007-08	Oshawa Generals	OHL	67	8	40	48	56	15	1	7	8	26
2008-09	Iowa Chops	AHL	59	1	7	8	36	....	....	....	....	....
2009-10	San Antonio	AHL	5	0	0	0	6	....	....	....	....	....
	Bakersfield	ECHL	59	16	34	50	46	10	2	4	6	4

Signed as a free agent by **Anaheim**, September 22, 2008.

REGNER, Brent (REHG-nuhr, BREHNT) **CBJ**

Defense. Shoots right. 6', 185 lbs. Born, Westlock, Alta., May 17, 1989.
(Columbus' 7th choice, 137th overall, in 2008 Entry Draft).

			Regular Season					Playoffs				
Season	Club	League	GP	G	A	Pts	PIM	GP	G	A	Pts	PIM
2004-05	Ft. Saskatchewan	AMHL	36	2	13	15	24	....	....	....	....	....
2005-06	Ft. Saskatchewan	AMHL	36	9	25	34	30	14	1	7	8	2
	Vancouver Giants	WHL	1	0	0	0	0	....	....	....	....	....
2006-07	Vancouver Giants	WHL	64	1	5	6	19	22	0	6	6	10
2007-08	Vancouver Giants	WHL	72	8	39	47	45	10	0	10	10	10
2008-09	Vancouver Giants	WHL	70	15	52	67	42	17	2	11	13	6
2009-10	Syracuse Crunch	AHL	50	4	16	20	22	....	....	....	....	....

WHL West Second All-Star Team (2009)

REID, Cameron (REED, KAM-uhr-UHN) **NSH.**

Center. Shoots left. 6'2", 198 lbs. Born, Delta, B.C., August 25, 1991.
(Nashville's 10th choice, 192nd overall, in 2009 Entry Draft).

			Regular Season					Playoffs				
Season	Club	League	GP	G	A	Pts	PIM	GP	G	A	Pts	PIM
2007-08	Victoria Grizzlies	BCHL	55	10	16	26	25	11	2	3	5	4
2008-09	Victoria Grizzlies	BCHL	41	6	17	23	32	....	....	....	....	....
	Westside Warriors	BCHL	17	6	11	17	10	8	4	3	7	0
2009-10	Westside Warriors	BCHL	54	27	45	72	70	11	2	6	8	16

• Signed Letter of Intent to attend **St. Cloud State University** (WCHA) in fall of 2010.

REINHART, Max (RIGHN-hart, MAX) **CGY.**

Center. Shoots left. 6'1", 180 lbs. Born, West Vancouver, B.C., February 4, 1992.
(Calgary's 1st choice, 64th overall, in 2010 Entry Draft).

			Regular Season					Playoffs				
Season	Club	League	GP	G	A	Pts	PIM	GP	G	A	Pts	PIM
2008-09	Kootenay Ice	WHL	62	11	16	27	21	4	1	0	1	2
2009-10	Kootenay Ice	WHL	72	21	30	51	38	6	1	1	2	6

RENSFELDT, Ludvig (REHNS-fehldt, LOOD-vihg) **CHI.**

Left wing. Shoots left. 6'3", 192 lbs. Born, Gavle, Sweden, January 29, 1992.
(Chicago's 2nd choice, 35th overall, in 2010 Entry Draft).

			Regular Season					Playoffs				
Season	Club	League	GP	G	A	Pts	PIM	GP	G	A	Pts	PIM
2007-08	Brynas U18	Swe-U18	5	1	2	3	0	....	....	....	....	....
2008-09	Brynas U18	Swe-U18	31	13	23	36	14	3	0	1	1	0
	Brynas IF Gavle Jr.	Swe-Jr.	2	0	0	0	2	1	0	0	0	0
2009-10	Brynas U18	Swe-U18	6	5	7	12	16	4	3	5	8	0
	Brynas IF Gavle Jr.	Swe-Jr.	39	21	29	50	37	5	3	0	3	0

REUL, Denis (ROIL, DEH-nihs) **BOS.**

Defense. Shoots right. 6'4", 214 lbs. Born, Marktredwitz, West Germany, June 29, 1989.
(Boston's 3rd choice, 130th overall, in 2007 Entry Draft).

			Regular Season					Playoffs				
Season	Club	League	GP	G	A	Pts	PIM	GP	G	A	Pts	PIM
2004-05	Mannheimer ERC	German-5	1	0	0	0	0	....	....	....	....	....
	Mannheim Jr.	Ger-Jr.	34	0	3	3	18	7	1	0	1	12
2005-06	Mannheim Jr.	Ger-Jr.	36	6	13	19	40	5	0	1	1	4
2006-07	Heilbronner Falken	German-3	16	0	1	1	16	....	....	....	....	....
	Heil./Mann. Jr.	Ger-Jr.	34	9	17	26	82	6	0	1	1	16
2007-08	Lewiston	QMJHL	67	3	11	14	99	6	0	0	0	4
2008-09	Lewiston	QMJHL	60	4	14	18	91	4	0	0	0	10
	Providence Bruins	AHL	5	0	1	1	6	....	....	....	....	....
2009-10	Adler Mannheim	Germany	54	0	8	8	62	2	0	0	0	0
	Heilbronner Falken	German-2	9	0	0	0	28	....	....	....	....	....

Signed as a free agent by **Lewiston** (QMJHL), August 14, 2007.

RHEAULT, Jon (RAY-oh, JAWN) **CGY.**

Right wing. Shoots right. 5'11", 200 lbs. Born, Arlington, TX, August 1, 1986.
(Philadelphia's 8th choice, 145th overall, in 2006 Entry Draft).

			Regular Season					Playoffs				
Season	Club	League	GP	G	A	Pts	PIM	GP	G	A	Pts	PIM
2003-04	N.H. Jr. Monarchs	EJHL	....	49	46	*95		....	....	....	....	....
2004-05	Providence College	H-East	36	11	8	19	36	....	....	....	....	....
2005-06	Providence College	H-East	35	16	14	30	29	....	....	....	....	....
2006-07	Providence College	H-East	35	12	13	25	38	....	....	....	....	....
2007-08	Providence College	H-East	36	17	14	31	23	....	....	....	....	....
2008-09	Ontario Reign	ECHL	51	19	22	41	56	7	4	4	8	4
	Manchester	AHL	24	2	3	5	12	....	....	....	....	....
2009-10	Ontario Reign	ECHL	30	19	16	35	24	....	....	....	....	....
	Providence Bruins	AHL	4	0	0	0	4	....	....	....	....	....
	Manchester	AHL	35	3	3	6	14	....	....	....	....	....
	Abbotsford Heat	AHL	5	3	2	5	0	13	6	2	8	2

Signed as a free agent by **Ontario** (ECHL), August 29, 2008. Signed to a PTO (professional tryout) contract by **Manchester** (AHL), December 13, 2008. Signed as a free agent by **Ontario** (ECHL), July 21, 2009. Signed to a PTO (professional tryout) contract by **Providence** (AHL), November 13, 2009. Signed to a PTO (professional tryout) contract by **Manchester** (AHL), December 1, 2009. Signed to a PTO (professional tryout) contract by **Abbotsford** (AHL), March 29, 2010. Signed as a free agent by **Abbotsford** (AHL), June 16, 2010.

RIENDEAU, Yannick (ree-EHN-doh, YAH-nihk) **BOS.**

Right wing. Shoots left. 5'11", 187 lbs. Born, Boucherville, Que., June 18, 1988.

			Regular Season					Playoffs				
Season	Club	League	GP	G	A	Pts	PIM	GP	G	A	Pts	PIM
2004-05	Rouyn-Noranda	QMJHL	58	10	15	25	22	6	0	1	1	0
2005-06	Rouyn-Noranda	QMJHL	67	27	38	65	40	5	0	2	2	6
2006-07	Rouyn-Noranda	QMJHL	67	32	40	72	38	10	9	5	14	6
2007-08	HC Chamonix	France	24	11	11	22	87	5	7	7	14	20
	Rouyn-Noranda	QMJHL	42	23	26	49	18	17	8	13	21	14
2008-09	Drummondville	QMJHL	64	*58	*68	*126	31	19	*29	23	*52	16
2009-10	Providence Bruins	AHL	22	1	4	5	6	....	....	....	....	....
	Reading Royals	ECHL	6	3	2	5	0	5	3	2	5	0

QMJHL First All-Star Team (2009) • Canadian Major Junior First All-Star Team (2009)

Signed as a free agent by **Boston**, April 2, 2009.

RINALDO, Zac (rih-NAL-doh, ZAK) **PHI.**

Center. Shoots left. 5'11", 169 lbs. Born, Mississauga, Ont., June 15, 1990.
(Philadelphia's 4th choice, 178th overall, in 2008 Entry Draft).

			Regular Season					Playoffs				
Season	Club	League	GP	G	A	Pts	PIM	GP	G	A	Pts	PIM
2006-07	Hamilton	OPJHL	44	16	16	32	193	16	4	4	8	48
	St. Michael's	OHL	6	0	0	0	2	....	....	....	....	....
2007-08	St. Michael's	OHL	63	7	7	14	191	4	0	0	0	9
2008-09	St. Michael's	OHL	34	6	7	13	*112	....	....	....	....	....
	London Knights	OHL	22	4	13	17	*89	8	1	1	2	26
2009-10	London Knights	OHL	34	8	7	15	*148	....	....	....	....	....
	Barrie Colts	OHL	26	2	8	10	*107	4	2	0	2	11

RISSANEN, Rasmus (RIH-sa-nehn, RAS-mus) **CAR.**

Defense. Shoots left. 6'2", 202 lbs. Born, Kuopio, Finland, July 13, 1991.
(Carolina's 5th choice, 178th overall, in 2009 Entry Draft).

			Regular Season					Playoffs				
Season	Club	League	GP	G	A	Pts	PIM	GP	G	A	Pts	PIM
2006-07	KalPa Kuopio U18	Fin-U18	9	1	1	2	28	3	0	1	1	8
2007-08	KalPa Kuopio U18	Fin-U18	29	7	9	16	99	2	0	0	0	8
	KalPa Kuopio Jr.	Fin-Jr.	5	0	0	0	10	....	....	....	....	....
2008-09	KalPa Kuopio Jr.	Fin-Jr.	29	1	8	9	56	4	0	1	1	6
2009-10	Everett Silvertips	WHL	71	4	11	15	103	7	0	1	1	8

ROBAK, Colby (ROH-bak, KOHL-bee) **FLA.**

Defense. Shoots left. 6'3", 194 lbs. Born, Dauphin, Man., April 24, 1990.
(Florida's 2nd choice, 46th overall, in 2008 Entry Draft).

			Regular Season					Playoffs				
Season	Club	League	GP	G	A	Pts	PIM	GP	G	A	Pts	PIM
2005-06	Parkland Rangers	MMHL	40	14	20	34	14	....	....	....	....	....
2006-07	Brandon	WHL	39	2	3	5	12	1	0	0	0	0
2007-08	Brandon	WHL	71	6	24	30	25	6	0	2	2	8
2008-09	Brandon	WHL	65	13	29	42	41	12	6	8	14	4
2009-10	Brandon	WHL	71	16	50	66	9	15	3	9	12	2

WHL East Second All-Star Team (2010)

RODIN, Anton (ROH-dihn, AN-tawn) **VAN.**

Right wing. Shoots left. 5'11", 178 lbs. Born, Stockholm, Sweden, November 21, 1990.
(Vancouver's 2nd choice, 53rd overall, in 2009 Entry Draft).

			Regular Season					Playoffs				
Season	Club	League	GP	G	A	Pts	PIM	GP	G	A	Pts	PIM
2006-07	Brynas U18	Swe-U18	14	7	4	11	4	3	0	0	0	2
	Brynas IF Gavle Jr.	Swe-Jr.	1	0	0	0	0	....	....	....	....	....
2007-08	Brynas U18	Swe-U18	6	2	7	9	8	5	2	5	7	0
	Brynas IF Gavle Jr.	Swe-Jr.	35	8	11	19	36	7	1	0	1	0
2008-09	Brynas IF Gavle Jr.	Swe-Jr.	37	29	26	55	34	7	2	10	12	4
	IK Oskarshamn	Sweden-2	6	0	0	0	2	....	....	....	....	....
2009-10	Brynas IF Gavle	Sweden	36	1	4	5	8	5	1	0	1	4
	Brynas IF Gavle Jr.	Swe-Jr.	4	0	3	3	4	3	0	0	3	0
	Mora IK	Sweden-2	8	2	2	4	0	....	....	....	....	....

RODWELL, Derek (RAWD-wehl, DAIR-ihk) **N.J.**

Left wing. Shoots right. 6'2", 190 lbs. Born, Taber, Alta., July 8, 1990.
(New Jersey's 5th choice, 144th overall, in 2009 Entry Draft).

			Regular Season					Playoffs				
Season	Club	League	GP	G	A	Pts	PIM	GP	G	A	Pts	PIM
2007-08	Okotoks Oilers	AJHL	62	9	10	19	69	9	0	3	3	6
2008-09	Okotoks Oilers	AJHL	41	17	12	29	69	9	1	2	3	6
2009-10	Okotoks Oilers	AJHL	55	18	35	53	38	11	6	3	9	20

• Signed Letter of Intent to attend **University of North Dakota** (WCHA) in fall of 2010.

ROE, Garrett (ROH, GAIR-eht) **L.A.**

Left wing. Shoots left. 5'8", 162 lbs. Born, Vienna, VA, February 22, 1988.
(Los Angeles' 9th choice, 183rd overall, in 2008 Entry Draft).

			Regular Season					Playoffs				
Season	Club	League	GP	G	A	Pts	PIM	GP	G	A	Pts	PIM
2004-05	Indiana Ice	USHL	49	6	15	21	62	3	0	3	3	4
2005-06	Indiana Ice	USHL	49	21	32	53	93	2	3	0	3	0
2006-07	Indiana Ice	USHL	57	24	39	63	143	6	3	10	13	8
2007-08	St. Cloud State	WCHA	39	18	27	45	55	....	....	....	....	....
2008-09	St. Cloud State	WCHA	38	17	31	48	72	....	....	....	....	....
2009-10	St. Cloud State	WCHA	41	20	29	49	65	....	....	....	....	....

WCHA All-Rookie Team (2008)

ROGALSKI, Joe (roh-GAL-skee, JOH) **PIT.**

Defense. Shoots right. 6'1", 195 lbs. Born, Buffalo, NY, November 29, 1991.
(Pittsburgh's 5th choice, 152nd overall, in 2010 Entry Draft).

			Regular Season					Playoffs				
Season	Club	League	GP	G	A	Pts	PIM	GP	G	A	Pts	PIM
2006-07	Buffalo Saints	Minor-NY	54	11	30	41	62	....	....	....	....	....
2007-08	Sarnia Sting	OHL	53	0	5	5	33	9	0	0	0	2
2008-09	Sarnia Sting	OHL	68	2	11	13	40	5	0	0	0	4
2009-10	Sarnia Sting	OHL	66	6	23	29	75	....	....	....	....	....

ROGERS, Brandon (RAW-juhrs, BRAN-duhn)

Defense. Shoots right. 6'1", 198 lbs. Born, Rochester, NH, February 27, 1982.
(Anaheim's 6th choice, 118th overall, in 2001 Entry Draft).

			Regular Season					Playoffs				
Season	Club	League	GP	G	A	Pts	PIM	GP	G	A	Pts	PIM
1998-99	Hotchkiss	High-CT	22	8	13	21	....	....	....	....	....	....
99-2000	Hotchkiss	High-CT	25	9	12	21	35	....	....	....	....	....
2000-01	Hotchkiss	High-CT	22	10	13	23	45	....	....	....	....	....
2001-02	U. of Michigan	CCHA	32	2	1	3	30	....	....	....	....	....
2002-03	U. of Michigan	CCHA	43	4	21	25	65	....	....	....	....	....
2003-04	U. of Michigan	CCHA	43	7	16	23	46	....	....	....	....	....
2004-05	U. of Michigan	CCHA	42	5	22	27	70	....	....	....	....	....
2005-06	Omaha	AHL	42	0	8	8	24	....	....	....	....	....
	Norfolk Admirals	AHL	27	3	7	10	28	2	0	0	0	4
2006-07	Norfolk Admirals	AHL	64	0	9	9	92	6	0	0	0	14
2007-08	Houston Aeros	AHL	63	4	24	28	77	5	0	1	1	2
2008-09	Houston Aeros	AHL	74	3	29	32	80	20	0	3	3	12
2009-10	Houston Aeros	AHL	60	3	5	8	44	....	....	....	....	....

CCHA Second All-Star Team (2004) • Yanick Dupre Memorial Award (AHL - Outstanding Humanitarian Contribution) (2009)

Signed as a free agent by **Minnesota**, July 15, 2008.

ROGERS, Doug (RAW-juhrs, DUHG) **NYI**

Center. Shoots right. 6'1", 195 lbs. Born, Watertown, MA, January 20, 1988.
(NY Islanders' 7th choice, 119th overall, in 2006 Entry Draft).

			Regular Season					Playoffs				
Season	Club	League	GP	G	A	Pts	PIM	GP	G	A	Pts	PIM
2003-04	St. Sebastian's	High-MA	28	24	24	48	....	....	....	....	....	....
2004-05	St. Sebastian's	High-MA	28	17	26	43	....	....	....	....	....	....
2005-06	St. Sebastian's	High-MA	28	24	38	62	20	....	....	....	....	....
2006-07	Harvard Crimson	ECAC	33	7	17	24	18	....	....	....	....	....
2007-08	Harvard Crimson	ECAC	34	13	19	32	30	....	....	....	....	....
2008-09	Harvard Crimson	ECAC	31	8	13	21	40	....	....	....	....	....
2009-10	Harvard Crimson	ECAC	28	6	6	12	24	....	....	....	....	....

ROGERS, Kyle (RAW-juhrs, KIGHL)

Right wing. Shoots right. 6'3", 210 lbs. Born, Philadelphia, PA, December 20, 1984.

			Regular Season					Playoffs				
Season	Club	League	GP	G	A	Pts	PIM	GP	G	A	Pts	PIM
2005-06	Niagara University	CHA	28	2	2	4	12	....	....	....	....	....
2006-07	Niagara University	CHA	35	6	7	13	37	....	....	....	....	....
2007-08	Niagara University	CHA	34	10	13	23	40	....	....	....	....	....
	Toronto Marlies	AHL	2	0	0	0	0	10	0	0	0	7
2008-09	Toronto Marlies	AHL	71	4	7	11	63	4	1	0	1	0
2009-10	Toronto Marlies	AHL	67	5	5	10	32	....	....	....	....	....

Signed as a free agent by **Toronto**, March 29, 2008.

ROMAN, Ondrej (ROH-mahn, AWN-dray) **DAL.**

Center. Shoots left. 6', 168 lbs. Born, Ostrava, Czech., April 8, 1989.
(Dallas' 6th choice, 136th overall, in 2007 Entry Draft).

			Regular Season					Playoffs				
Season	Club	League	GP	G	A	Pts	PIM	GP	G	A	Pts	PIM
2002-03	HC Ostrava U17	CzR-U17	6	1	1	2	0	....	....	....	....	....
2003-04	HC Ostrava U17	CzR-U17	55	38	27	65	61	....	....	....	....	....
2004-05	HC Ostrava U17	CzR-U17	8	8	16	24	22	....	....	....	....	....
	HC Ostrava Jr.	CzRep-Jr.	7	2	2	4	6	....	....	....	....	....
	HC Vitkovice U17	CzR-U17	2	0	3	3	2	....	....	....	....	....
	HC Vitkovice Jr.	CzRep-Jr.	30	8	3	11	12	....	....	....	....	....
2005-06	HC Vitkovice U17	CzR-U17	....	....	....	....	....	4	1	8	9	0
	HC Vitkovice Jr.	CzRep-Jr.	46	17	27	44	42	5	0	3	3	4
	HC Vitkovice Steel	CzRep	1	0	0	0	0	....	....	....	....	....
2006-07	Spokane Chiefs	WHL	70	4	44	48	42	6	1	4	5	0
2007-08	Spokane Chiefs	WHL	72	15	46	61	28	21	9	11	20	6
2008-09	HC Vitkovice Jr.	CzRep-Jr.	4	1	3	4	0	....	....	....	....	....
	HC Vitkovice Steel	CzRep	26	3	6	9	2	....	....	....	....	....
	Spokane Chiefs	WHL	32	10	22	32	19	12	1	4	5	10
2009-10	HC Vitkovice Jr.	CzRep-Jr.	10	9	17	26	8	....	....	....	....	....
	HC Vitkovice Steel	CzRep	26	1	2	3	6	....	....	....	....	....
	Havirov	CzRep-2	11	1	6	7	16	....	....	....	....	....

ROMANO, Tony (roh-MAHN-oh, TOH-nee) **NYI**

Center. Shoots right. 5'10", 170 lbs. Born, Smithtown, NY, January 5, 1988.
(New Jersey's 7th choice, 178th overall, in 2006 Entry Draft).

			Regular Season					Playoffs				
Season	Club	League	GP	G	A	Pts	PIM	GP	G	A	Pts	PIM
2004-05	New York Bobcats	AtJHL	....	47	54	101	....	....	....	....	....	....
2005-06	New York Bobcats	AtJHL	40	*50	52	*102	38	....	....	....	....	....
2006-07	Cornell Big Red	ECAC	29	9	10	19	18	....	....	....	....	....
2007-08	London Knights	OHL	66	12	10	22	40	4	1	0	1	0
2008-09	Peterborough	OHL	65	36	33	69	86	2	2	1	3	4
2009-10	Bridgeport	AHL	21	1	1	2	12	....	....	....	....	....
	Utah Grizzlies	ECHL	34	9	15	24	35	....	....	....	....	....
	Toledo Walleye	ECHL	12	6	6	12	19	4	1	0	1	4

Traded to **NY Islanders** by **New Jersey** for Ben Walter and future considerations, June 30, 2009.

ROSS, Brad (RAWS, BRAD) **TOR.**

Left wing. Shoots left. 6', 175 lbs. Born, Lethbridge, Alta., May 28, 1992.
(Toronto's 1st choice, 43rd overall, in 2010 Entry Draft).

			Regular Season					Playoffs				
Season	Club	League	GP	G	A	Pts	PIM	GP	G	A	Pts	PIM
2007-08	Lethbridge	AMHL	35	10	14	24	82	6	6	5	11	22
	Portland	WHL	3	0	0	0	0	....	....	....	....	....
2008-09	Portland	WHL	61	9	17	26	119	....	....	....	....	....
2009-10	Portland	WHL	71	27	41	68	*203	13	2	7	9	36

ROSS, Nick (RAWS, NIHK) **PHX.**

Defense. Shoots left. 6'1", 196 lbs. Born, Edmonton, Alta., February 10, 1989.
(Phoenix's 2nd choice, 30th overall, in 2007 Entry Draft).

			Regular Season					Playoffs				
Season	Club	League	GP	G	A	Pts	PIM	GP	G	A	Pts	PIM
2004-05	Lethbridge	AMHL	33	8	20	28	123	....	....	....	....	....
	Regina Pats	WHL	10	0	1	1	2	....	....	....	....	....
2005-06	Regina Pats	WHL	62	7	16	23	38	6	0	1	1	2
2006-07	Regina Pats	WHL	70	7	24	31	87	10	1	5	6	14
2007-08	Regina Pats	WHL	41	3	25	28	60	....	....	....	....	....
	Kamloops Blazers	WHL	31	5	14	19	55	4	0	2	2	10
	San Antonio	AHL	4	1	0	1	0	....	....	....	....	....
2008-09	Kamloops Blazers	WHL	40	4	18	22	51	....	....	....	....	....
	Vancouver Giants	WHL	34	7	14	21	32	17	1	8	9	14
2009-10	San Antonio	AHL	47	0	2	2	19	....	....	....	....	....
	Las Vegas	ECHL	7	0	1	1	2	....	....	....	....	....

ROUSSEL, Charles-Olivier (roo-SEHL, CHAR-uhlz-OH-lihv-ee-ay) **NSH**

Defense. Shoots right. 6'1", 205 lbs. Born, St. Eustache, Que., September 13, 1991.
(Nashville's 3rd choice, 42nd overall, in 2009 Entry Draft).

			Regular Season					Playoffs				
Season	Club	League	GP	G	A	Pts	PIM	GP	G	A	Pts	PIM
2006-07	Laurentides	QAAA	44	8	24	32	90	15	2	9	11	24
2007-08	Shawinigan	QMJHL	50	3	13	16	28	5	1	2	3	2
2008-09	Shawinigan	QMJHL	68	11	33	44	77	21	5	13	18	14
2009-10	Shawinigan	QMJHL	64	15	36	51	70	6	0	1	1	4

QMJHL Second All-Star Team (2009)

ROWE, Andrew (ROH, AN-droo) **PHI**

Left wing. Shoots left. 6', 175 lbs. Born, Muskegon, MI, January 22, 1988.

			Regular Season					Playoffs				
Season	Club	League	GP	G	A	Pts	PIM	GP	G	A	Pts	PIM
2005-06	Sioux City	USHL	50	8	8	16	30	....	....	....	....	....
2006-07	Sioux City	USHL	60	19	15	34	28	7	2	1	3	0
2007-08	Michigan State	CCHA	21	3	4	7	8	....	....	....	....	....
2008-09	Michigan State	CCHA	35	6	8	14	14	....	....	....	....	....
2009-10	Michigan State	CCHA	38	17	11	28	38	....	....	....	....	....

Signed as a free agent by **Philadelphia**, May 6, 2010.

UDENKO, Konstantin (roo-DEHN-koh, KAWN-stan-tihn) PHI.

eft wing. Shoots right. 5'11", 180 lbs. Born, Ust-Kamenogorsk, USSR, July 23, 1981.
'hiladelphia's 3rd choice, 160th overall, in 1999 Entry Draft).

			Regular Season					Playoffs				
eason	Club	League	GP	G	A	Pts	PIM	GP	G	A	Pts	PIM
997-98	Omsk 2	Russia-3	22	7	8	15	4	....	....	....	....	....
998-99	Cherepovets	Russia	28	15	9	24	67	....	....	....	....	....
	Cherepovets 2	Russia-3	3	0	1	1	4	....	....	....	....	....
9-2000	St. Petersburg 2	Russia-3	7	2	4	6	2	....	....	....	....	....
	SKA St. Petersburg	Russia	19	1	1	2	10	1	0	0	0	0
000-01	Yaroslavl	Russia	18	2	3	5	28	9	2	1	3	8
001-02	Yaroslavl 2	Russia-3	2	1	1	2	2	....	....	....	....	....
	Yaroslavl	Russia	8	0	2	2	12	1	0	0	0	0
002-03	Yaroslavl	Russia	20	3	4	7	20	2	0	0	0	0
003-04	Yaroslavl 2	Russia-3	4	4	2	6	4	....	....	....	....	....
	Yaroslavl	Russia	43	10	12	22	18	3	0	0	0	0
004-05	Yaroslavl 2	Russia-3	20	13	14	27	42	....	....	....	....	....
	Yaroslavl	Russia	21	1	0	1	8	2	0	0	0	0
005-06	Yaroslavl	Russia	49	11	17	28	55	11	1	2	3	0
006-07	Yaroslavl	Russia	35	11	8	19	30	7	2	2	4	6
007-08	Yaroslavl	Russia	46	6	16	22	28	7	0	1	1	8
008-09	Yaroslavl	Rus-KHL	48	10	18	28	26	19	4	8	12	24
009-10	Yaroslavl	Rus-KHL	31	3	7	10	4	17	5	6	11	24

UEGSEGGER, Tyler (ROOG-suh-guhr, TIGH-luhr) TOR.

enter. Shoots right. 6', 185 lbs. Born, Denver, CO, January 19, 1988.
'oronto's 6th choice, 166th overall, in 2006 Entry Draft).

			Regular Season					Playoffs				
eason	Club	League	GP	G	A	Pts	PIM	GP	G	A	Pts	PIM
004-05	Shat.-St. Mary's	High-MN	69	26	54	80	30	....	....	....	....	....
005-06	Shat.-St. Mary's	High-MN	60	38	51	89	70	....	....	....	....	....
006-07	U. of Denver	WCHA	40	15	19	34	25	....	....	....	....	....
007-08	U. of Denver	WCHA	31	10	12	22	39	....	....	....	....	....
008-09	U. of Denver	WCHA	35	15	11	26	40	....	....	....	....	....
009-10	U. of Denver	WCHA	41	16	25	41	30	....	....	....	....	....

/CHA Second All-Star Team (2010)

UFENACH, Bryan (RUHF-ehn-ak, BRIGH-uhn) DET.

efense. Shoots left. 5'11", 184 lbs. Born, Cameron, Ont., April 15, 1989.
)etroit's 5th choice, 208th overall, in 2007 Entry Draft).

			Regular Season					Playoffs				
eason	Club	League	GP	G	A	Pts	PIM	GP	G	A	Pts	PIM
005-06	Lindsay Muskies	OPJHL	48	11	15	26	50	4	1	1	2	6
006-07	Lindsay Muskies	OPJHL	31	11	21	32	28	5	1	2	3	8
007-08	Clarkson Knights	ECAC	35	3	3	6	12	....	....	....	....	....
008-09	Clarkson Knights	ECAC	34	9	9	18	32	....	....	....	....	....
009-10	Clarkson Knights	ECAC	34	5	15	20	49	....	....	....	....	....

UNDBLAD, David (RUHND-blahd, DAY-vihd) OTT.

efense. Shoots right. 6'2", 189 lbs. Born, Lycksele, Sweden, October 8, 1990.
t. Louis' 1st choice, 17th overall, in 2009 Entry Draft).

			Regular Season					Playoffs				
eason	Club	League	GP	G	A	Pts	PIM	GP	G	A	Pts	PIM
004-05	Lycksele SK	Sweden-4	1	0	0	0	0	....	....	....	....	....
005-06	Lycksele SK	Sweden-4	11	5	2	7	2	....	....	....	....	....
006-07	Skelleftea U18	Swe-U18	4	1	1	2	0	....	....	....	....	....
	Skelleftea Jr.	Swe-Jr.	14	3	4	7	12	2	0	0	0	2
007-08	Skelleftea U18	Swe-U18	4	3	2	5	29	....	....	....	....	....
	Skelleftea Jr.	Swe-Jr.	35	11	15	26	44	2	1	3	4	6
	Skelleftea AIK HK	Sweden	6	0	0	0	2	....	....	....	....	....
008-09	Skelleftea AIK Jr.	Swe-Jr.	10	8	7	15	2	....	....	....	....	....
	Skelleftea AIK	Sweden	45	0	10	10	8	10	1	1	2	2
009-10	Skelleftea AIK Jr.	Swe-Jr.	3	2	2	4	4	....	....	....	....	....
	Skelleftea AIK	Sweden	47	1	12	13	14	12	0	1	1	2

'aded to **Ottawa** by **St. Louis** for Ottawa's 1st round choice (Vladimir Tarasenko) in 2010 Entry 'aft, June 25, 2010.

USSELL, Ryan (RUH-sehl, RIGH-uhn) MTL.

enter. Shoots left. 5'10", 174 lbs. Born, Caroline, Alta., May 2, 1987.
Y Rangers' 9th choice, 211th overall, in 2005 Entry Draft).

			Regular Season					Playoffs				
ason	Club	League	GP	G	A	Pts	PIM	GP	G	A	Pts	PIM
003-04	Kootenay Ice	WHL	67	3	9	12	27	4	0	0	0	0
004-05	Kootenay Ice	WHL	66	32	21	53	18	16	6	7	13	12
005-06	Kootenay Ice	WHL	72	33	42	75	30	6	3	5	8	2
006-07	Kootenay Ice	WHL	58	30	46	76	40	7	3	6	9	2
007-08	Hamilton Bulldogs	AHL	25	2	1	3	4	....	....	....	....	....
	Cincinnati	ECHL	12	6	4	10	4	15	3	4	7	0
008-09	Hamilton Bulldogs	AHL	79	20	19	39	24	6	1	3	4	2
009-10	Hamilton Bulldogs	AHL	74	19	18	37	8	19	7	5	12	0

aded to **Montreal** by **NY Rangers** for Montreal's 7th round choice (David Skokan) in 2007 ntry Draft, May 31, 2007.

UST, Bryan (RUHST, BRIGH-uhn) PIT.

ght wing. Shoots right. 6', 191 lbs. Born, Pontiac, MI, May 11, 1992.
ittsburgh's 2nd choice, 80th overall, in 2010 Entry Draft).

			Regular Season					Playoffs				
ason	Club	League	GP	G	A	Pts	PIM	GP	G	A	Pts	PIM
007-08	Det. Honeybaked	MWEHL	31	17	28	45	6	....	....	....	....	....
	Det. Honeybaked	Minor-MI	37	27	20	47	....	....	....	....	....	....
008-09	USNTDP	NAHL	42	6	9	15	18	9	0	2	2	4
	USNTDP	U-17	16	3	2	5	4	....	....	....	....	....
009-10	USNTDP	USHL	27	10	13	23	6	....	....	....	....	....
	USNTDP	U-17	1	0	0	0	0	....	....	....	....	....
	USNTDP	U-18	38	16	13	29	18	....	....	....	....	....

Signed Letter of Intent to attend **University of Notre Dame** (CCHA) in fall of 2010.

RUST, Matt (RUHST, MAT) CBJ

Center. Shoots left. 5'10", 192 lbs. Born, Bloomfield Hills, MI, March 23, 1989.
(Florida's 4th choice, 101st overall, in 2007 Entry Draft).

			Regular Season					Playoffs				
Season	Club	League	GP	G	A	Pts	PIM	GP	G	A	Pts	PIM
2004-05	Det. Honeybaked	MWEHL	50	16	24	40	....	....	....	....	....	....
2005-06	USNTDP	U-17	20	5	5	10	22	....	....	....	....	....
	USNTDP	NAHL	36	9	8	17	36	12	2	0	2	0
2006-07	USNTDP	U-18	36	3	16	19	34	....	....	....	....	....
	USNTDP	NAHL	15	9	6	15	31	....	....	....	....	....
2007-08	U. of Michigan	CCHA	38	12	11	23	69	....	....	....	....	....
2008-09	U. of Michigan	CCHA	37	11	11	22	39	....	....	....	....	....
2009-10	U. of Michigan	CCHA	45	13	27	40	24	....	....	....	....	....

Traded to **Columbus** by **Florida** for Mathieu Roy, March 3, 2010.

RUTH, Theo (ROOTH, THEE-oh) CBJ

Defense. Shoots right. 6'1", 210 lbs. Born, Naperville, IL, February 14, 1989.
(Washington's 3rd choice, 46th overall, in 2007 Entry Draft).

			Regular Season					Playoffs				
Season	Club	League	GP	G	A	Pts	PIM	GP	G	A	Pts	PIM
2004-05	Chicago Mission	MAHL	46	8	8	16	....	....	....	....	....	....
2005-06	USNTDP	U-17	18	2	3	5	22	....	....	....	....	....
	USNTDP	NAHL	36	1	2	3	33	12	0	2	2	8
2006-07	USNTDP	U-18	39	2	6	8	52	....	....	....	....	....
	USNTDP	NAHL	9	3	6	9	14	....	....	....	....	....
2007-08	U. of Notre Dame	CCHA	42	2	3	5	36	....	....	....	....	....
2008-09	U. of Notre Dame	CCHA	36	2	5	7	42	....	....	....	....	....
2009-10	U. of Notre Dame	CCHA	22	0	5	5	52	....	....	....	....	....

Traded to **Columbus** by **Washington** for Sergei Fedorov, February 26, 2008.

RUTKOWSKI, Troy (ruht-KOW-skee, TROI) COL.

Defense. Shoots right. 6'2", 208 lbs. Born, Edmonton, Alta., April 29, 1992.
(Colorado's 6th choice, 137th overall, in 2010 Entry Draft).

			Regular Season					Playoffs				
Season	Club	League	GP	G	A	Pts	PIM	GP	G	A	Pts	PIM
2007-08	SSAC Athletics	AMHL	36	6	16	22	28	....	....	....	....	....
2008-09	Portland	WHL	64	6	9	15	34	....	....	....	....	....
2009-10	Portland	WHL	71	12	31	43	70	13	4	3	7	8

RUZICKA, Vladimir (roo-ZHEECH-kuh, vla-DIH-meer) PHX.

Center. Shoots left. 6'1", 196 lbs. Born, Most, Czech., February 17, 1989.
(Phoenix's 5th choice, 103rd overall, in 2007 Entry Draft).

			Regular Season					Playoffs				
Season	Club	League	GP	G	A	Pts	PIM	GP	G	A	Pts	PIM
2002-03	Slavia U17	CzR-U17	20	1	5	6	2	1	0	0	0	0
2003-04	Slavia U17	CzR-U17	51	18	35	53	24	7	5	8	13	4
2004-05	Slavia U17	CzR-U17	38	22	39	61	38	6	4	4	8	10
2005-06	Slavia U17	CzR-U17	3	3	6	9	22	6	5	7	12	14
	HC Slavia Praha Jr.	CzRep-Jr.	37	15	26	41	42	1	0	1	1	0
	HC Slavia Praha	CzRep	13	1	1	2	4	....	....	....	....	....
2006-07	HC Slavia Praha Jr.	CzRep-Jr.	37	24	34	58	54	4	1	2	3	4
	HC Slavia Praha	CzRep	3	0	0	0	0	....	....	....	....	....
2007-08	HC Slavia Praha Jr.	CzRep-Jr.	1	0	0	0	4	1	0	0	0	2
	HC Slavia Praha	CzRep	42	7	8	15	18	19	1	0	1	4
2008-09	HC Slavia Praha	CzRep	36	5	6	11	14	14	2	1	3	6
2009-10	HC Slavia Praha	CzRep	47	6	10	16	22	15	3	1	4	4
	Havl. Brod	CzRep-2	3	1	2	3	0	....	....	....	....	....

RYAN, Ben (RIGH-uhn, BEHN) NSH.

Center. Shoots right. 5'11", 193 lbs. Born, Detroit, MI, October 16, 1988.
(Nashville's 5th choice, 114th overall, in 2007 Entry Draft).

			Regular Season					Playoffs				
Season	Club	League	GP	G	A	Pts	PIM	GP	G	A	Pts	PIM
2005-06	Des Moines	USHL	60	14	23	37	38	11	4	1	5	4
2006-07	Des Moines	USHL	59	22	42	64	66	8	3	5	8	8
2007-08	U. of Notre Dame	CCHA	47	10	16	26	22	....	....	....	....	....
2008-09	U. of Notre Dame	CCHA	39	12	15	27	30	....	....	....	....	....
2009-10	U. of Notre Dame	CCHA	29	7	12	19	24	....	....	....	....	....

RYAN, Ken (RIGH-uhn, KEHN) TOR.

Right wing. Shoots right. 6', 204 lbs. Born, Franklin Village, MI, July 10, 1991.
(Toronto's 2nd choice, 50th overall, in 2009 Entry Draft).

			Regular Season					Playoffs				
Season	Club	League	GP	G	A	Pts	PIM	GP	G	A	Pts	PIM
2006-07	Det. Honeybaked	MWEHL	31	16	17	33	34	....	....	....	....	....
	Det. Honeybaked	Exhib.	34	17	24	41	....	....	....	....	....	....
2007-08	USNTDP	NAHL	36	10	8	18	53	....	....	....	....	....
	USNTDP	U-17	13	0	5	5	12	....	....	....	....	....
2008-09	USNTDP	NAHL	16	4	9	13	12	....	....	....	....	....
	USNTDP	U-18	46	23	13	36	38	....	....	....	....	....
2009-10	Windsor Spitfires	OHL	52	14	21	35	33	19	3	2	5	14

SACCHETTI, Nico (SA-sheh-tee, NEE-koh) DAL.

Center. Shoots left. 5'11", 189 lbs. Born, Virginia, MN, August 21, 1989.
(Dallas' 1st choice, 50th overall, in 2007 Entry Draft).

			Regular Season					Playoffs				
Season	Club	League	GP	G	A	Pts	PIM	GP	G	A	Pts	PIM
2004-05	Virginia Blue Devils	High-MN	29	25	29	54	....	....	....	....	....	....
2005-06	Virginia Blue Devils	High-MN	27	29	45	74	....	....	....	....	....	....
2006-07	Virginia Blue Devils	High-MN	25	38	52	90	22	....	....	....	....	....
2007-08	Omaha Lancers	USHL	56	10	14	24	51	14	1	2	3	10
2008-09	U. of Minnesota	WCHA	36	4	3	7	43	....	....	....	....	....
2009-10	U. of Minnesota	WCHA	38	4	11	15	12	....	....	....	....	....

SACKRISON, Andy (sak-RIH-suhn, AN-dee) ST.L.

Center. Shoots left. 6'1", 197 lbs. Born, St. Louis Park, MN, November 12, 1987.
(St. Louis' 7th choice, 124th overall, in 2006 Entry Draft).

			Regular Season					Playoffs				
Season	Club	League	GP	G	A	Pts	PIM	GP	G	A	Pts	PIM
2004-05	St. Louis Park	High-MN	26	18	15	33	....	....	....	....	....	....
2005-06	St. Louis Park	High-MN	25	42	27	69	....	....	....	....	....	....
2006-07	Tri-City Storm	USHL	59	12	15	27	19	9	2	0	2	6
2007-08	Minnesota State	WCHA	36	6	14	20	4	....	....	....	....	....
2008-09	Minnesota State	WCHA	31	3	5	8	18	....	....	....	....	....
2009-10	Minnesota State	WCHA	21	3	2	5	4	....	....	....	....	....

ST. DENIS, Frederic (SAINT-deh-nee, FREHD-uhr-ihk) **MTL.**

Defense. Shoots left. 5'11", 192 lbs. Born, Greenfield Park, Que., January 23, 1986.

			Regular Season					Playoffs				
Season	Club	League	GP	G	A	Pts	PIM	GP	G	A	Pts	PIM
2001-02	C.C. Lemoyne	QAAA	42	4	6	10	4	....	....	....	....	....
2002-03	C.C. Lemoyne	QAAA	31	8	15	23	6	....	....	....	....	....
	Drummondville	QMJHL	14	0	0	0	0	....	....	....	....	....
2003-04	Drummondville	QMJHL	67	7	10	17	30	5	0	1	1	2
2004-05	Drummondville	QMJHL	70	11	22	33	36	6	2	3	5	0
2005-06	Drummondville	QMJHL	69	17	50	67	74	....	....	....	....	....
2006-07	Drummondville	QMJHL	65	9	29	38	59	12	1	7	8	8
2007-08	U. Quebec T-R	OUAA	28	4	14	18	4	....	....	....	....	....
2008-09	Hamilton Bulldogs	AHL	7	1	1	2	6	....	....	....	....	....
	Cincinnati	ECHL	41	1	22	23	22	15	0	5	5	14
2009-10	Hamilton Bulldogs	AHL	59	3	14	17	38	19	0	1	1	20

QMJHL Second All-Star Team (2006)

Signed as a free agent by **Hamilton** (AHL), September 27, 2008. Signed as a free agent by **Montreal**. July 5, 2010.

SALLINEN, Jere (sa-LIGH-nehn, YAIR-ray) **MIN.**

Right wing. Shoots left. 6'1", 203 lbs. Born, Espoo, Finland, October 26, 1990.
(Minnesota's 6th choice, 163rd overall, in 2009 Entry Draft).

			Regular Season					Playoffs				
Season	Club	League	GP	G	A	Pts	PIM	GP	G	A	Pts	PIM
2006-07	Blues Espoo U18	Fin-U18	26	9	3	12	44	7	2	2	4	16
2007-08	Blues Espoo U18	Fin-U18	13	8	10	18	16	4	1	5	6	12
	Blues Espoo Jr.	Fin-Jr.	36	11	19	30	94	3	0	2	2	8
	Blues Espoo	Finland	6	0	0	0	2	....	....	....	....	....
2008-09	Blues Espoo Jr.	Fin-Jr.	9	1	2	3	31	....	....	....	....	....
2009-10	Blues Espoo	Finland	38	5	6	11	18	3	0	2	2	2
	Suomi U20	Finland-2	3	0	0	0	2	....	....	....	....	....
	Blues Espoo Jr.	Fin-Jr.	6	5	3	8	10	....	....	....	....	....

SALMONSSON, Johannes (sal-MUHN-suhn, yoh-HA-nuhs) **PIT.**

Left wing. Shoots left. 6'2", 183 lbs. Born, Uppsala, Sweden, February 7, 1986.
(Pittsburgh's 2nd choice, 31st overall, in 2004 Entry Draft).

			Regular Season					Playoffs				
Season	Club	League	GP	G	A	Pts	PIM	GP	G	A	Pts	PIM
2002-03	Almtuna	Sweden-2	26	10	14	24	4	....	....	....	....	....
2003-04	Djurgarden Jr.	Swe-Jr.	6	4	9	13	6	....	....	....	....	....
	Djurgarden	Sweden	25	0	3	3	4	....	....	....	....	....
	Almtuna	Sweden-2	2	0	0	0	0	....	....	....	....	....
2004-05	Almtuna	Sweden-2	8	0	2	2	6	....	....	....	....	....
	Djurgarden Jr.	Swe-Jr.	4	2	0	2	4	....	....	....	....	....
	Djurgarden	Sweden	30	2	2	4	6	9	0	0	0	0
2005-06	Spokane Chiefs	WHL	54	12	15	27	30	....	....	....	....	....
2006-07	Brynas IF Gavle Jr.	Swe-Jr.	2	0	7	7	0	....	....	....	....	....
	Brynas IF Gavle	Sweden	45	8	3	11	28	....	....	....	....	....
2007-08	Brynas IF Gavle Jr.	Swe-Jr.	2	0	2	2	2	....	....	....	....	....
	Brynas IF Gavle	Sweden	9	0	1	1	2	....	....	....	....	....
	Rogle	Sweden-2	34	15	9	24	36	....	....	....	....	....
2008-09	Rogle	Sweden	33	5	4	9	12	....	....	....	....	....
2009-10	EHC Biel-Bienne	Swiss	6	2	3	5	0	....	....	....	....	....
	HC Davos	Swiss	23	5	6	11	4	1	0	0	0	0

Signed as a free agent by **Gavle** (Sweden), September 18, 2006.

SAMUELSSON, Jesper (SAM-yuhl-suhn, YEHS-puhr) **DET.**

Center. Shoots left. 5'11", 178 lbs. Born, Stockholm, Sweden, June 13, 1988.
(Detroit's 6th choice, 211th overall, in 2008 Entry Draft).

			Regular Season					Playoffs				
Season	Club	League	GP	G	A	Pts	PIM	GP	G	A	Pts	PIM
2004-05	Hasten	Sweden-3	1	0	0	0	0	....	....	....	....	....
2005-06	Hasten	Sweden-3	36	8	11	19	67	....	....	....	....	....
2006-07	Hasten	Sweden-3	36	15	29	44	38	....	....	....	....	....
2007-08	HC Vita Hasten	Sweden-3	40	20	42	62	73	....	....	....	....	....
2008-09	Timra IK Jr.	Swe-Jr.	4	2	0	2	2	....	....	....	....	....
	Sundsvall	Sweden-2	13	1	5	6	38	....	....	....	....	....
	Timra IK	Sweden	40	2	1	3	10	3	0	0	0	0
2009-10	Timra IK	Sweden	23	0	1	1	8	....	....	....	....	....
	Sundsvall	Sweden-2	45	5	13	18	65	9	2	0	2	29

SAMUELSSON, Philip (SAM-yuhl-suhn, FIHL-ihp) **PIT.**

Defense. Shoots left. 6'3", 198 lbs. Born, Leksand, Sweden, July 26, 1991.
(Pittsburgh's 2nd choice, 61st overall, in 2009 Entry Draft).

			Regular Season					Playoffs				
Season	Club	League	GP	G	A	Pts	PIM	GP	G	A	Pts	PIM
2006-07	P.F. Chang's	Minor-AZ	54	9	31	40	70	....	....	....	....	....
2007-08	P.F. Chang's	Minor-AZ	41	8	25	33	48	....	....	....	....	....
2008-09	Chicago Steel	USHL	54	0	22	22	60	....	....	....	....	....
	USNTDP	U-18	4	0	0	0	6	....	....	....	....	....
2009-10	Boston College	H-East	42	1	13	14	36	....	....	....	....	....

SAMUELS-THOMAS, Jordan (SAM-yewlz-TAW-muhs, JOHR-dahn) **ATL.**

Left wing. Shoots left. 6'3", 200 lbs. Born, Hartford, CT, May 28, 1990.
(Atlanta's 9th choice, 203rd overall, in 2009 Entry Draft).

			Regular Season					Playoffs				
Season	Club	League	GP	G	A	Pts	PIM	GP	G	A	Pts	PIM
2006-07	Hartford	AtJHL	43	21	37	58	44	....	....	....	....	....
2007-08	Waterloo	USHL	56	8	3	11	65	11	0	2	2	10
2008-09	Waterloo	USHL	59	32	22	54	59	3	2	1	3	2
2009-10	Bowling Green	CCHA	35	11	14	25	30	....	....	....	....	....

SANDIN, Emil (san-DEEN, eh-MIHL) **OTT.**

Left wing. Shoots left. 5'10", 178 lbs. Born, Uppsala, Sweden, February 28, 1988.
(Ottawa's 7th choice, 199th overall, in 2008 Entry Draft).

			Regular Season					Playoffs				
Season	Club	League	GP	G	A	Pts	PIM	GP	G	A	Pts	PIM
2004-05	Brynas IF Gavle Jr.	Swe-Jr.	2	0	0	0	0	....	....	....	....	....
2005-06	Brynas U18	Swe-U18	4	2	3	5	14	....	....	....	....	....
	Brynas IF Gavle Jr.	Swe-Jr.	31	9	9	18	8	2	2	0	2	0
2006-07	Brynas IF Gavle Jr.	Swe-Jr.	39	10	20	30	40	4	1	0	1	4
2007-08	Brynas IF Gavle Jr.	Swe-Jr.	28	10	25	35	50	7	1	4	5	8
	Brynas IF Gavle	Sweden	19	0	4	4	0	....	....	....	....	....
	Brynas IF Gavle	Sweden-Q	2	0	0	0	0	....	....	....	....	....
2008-09	Brynas IF Gavle	Sweden	53	6	11	17	6	4	0	0	0	4
2009-10	Brynas IF Gavle	Sweden	51	2	10	12	10	5	0	1	1	0
	Brynas IF Gavle Jr.	Swe-Jr.	2	0	1	1	0	....	....	....	....	....

SANTORELLI, Mark (san-toh-REHL-ee, MAHRK) **NSH**

Center. Shoots right. 6'1", 191 lbs. Born, Edmonton, Alta., August 6, 1988.
(Nashville's 6th choice, 119th overall, in 2007 Entry Draft).

			Regular Season					Playoffs				
Season	Club	League	GP	G	A	Pts	PIM	GP	G	A	Pts	PIM
2003-04	Abbotsford Pilots	PIJHL	40	12	19	31	33	....	....	....	....	....
	Chilliwack Chiefs	BCHL	1	0	1	1	0	....	....	....	....	....
2004-05	Salmon Arm	BCHL	59	9	16	25	10	11	2	3	5	[illegible]
2005-06	Salmon Arm	BCHL	20	2	10	12	11	....	....	....	....	....
	Burnaby Express	BCHL	39	15	28	43	16	20	2	14	16	[illegible]
2006-07	Chilliwack Bruins	WHL	72	29	53	82	46	5	2	3	5	[illegible]
2007-08	Chilliwack Bruins	WHL	72	27	*74	*101	40	4	1	4	5	[illegible]
	Milwaukee	AHL	1	0	0	0	0	2	0	0	0	[illegible]
2008-09	Milwaukee	AHL	53	1	6	7	8	....	....	....	....	....
	Cincinnati	ECHL	6	1	2	3	0	15	1	6	7	[illegible]
2009-10	Milwaukee	AHL	68	11	13	24	6	6	1	2	3	[illegible]

WHL West Second All-Star Team (2008)

SAPONARI, Vinny (sa-pawn-AIR-ee, VIH-nee) **ATL**

Right wing. Shoots right. 6'1", 190 lbs. Born, Powder Springs, GA, February 15, 1990.
(Atlanta's 4th choice, 94th overall, in 2008 Entry Draft).

			Regular Season					Playoffs				
Season	Club	League	GP	G	A	Pts	PIM	GP	G	A	Pts	PIM
2006-07	USNTDP	U-17	4	11	6	17	....	....	....	....	....	....
	USNTDP	U-18	21	4	3	7	6	....	....	....	....	....
	USNTDP	NAHL	35	9	10	19	43	....	....	....	....	....
2007-08	USNTDP	U-18	42	12	16	28	42	....	....	....	....	....
	USNTDP	NAHL	15	1	7	8	0	....	....	....	....	....
2008-09	Boston University	H-East	44	8	9	17	39	....	....	....	....	....
2009-10	Boston University	H-East	38	12	18	30	32	....	....	....	....	....

SAUVE, Maxime (soh-VAY, max-EEM) **BOS**

Center. Shoots left. 6', 185 lbs. Born, Tours, France, January 30, 1990.
(Boston's 2nd choice, 47th overall, in 2008 Entry Draft).

			Regular Season					Playoffs				
Season	Club	League	GP	G	A	Pts	PIM	GP	G	A	Pts	PIM
2005-06	Laval-Laurentides	QAAA	41	16	30	46	54	5	1	3	4	[illegible]
2006-07	Quebec Remparts	QMJHL	60	10	6	16	24	2	0	0	0	[illegible]
2007-08	Quebec Remparts	QMJHL	38	12	20	32	22	....	....	....	....	....
	Val-d'Or Foreurs	QMJHL	32	14	19	33	8	4	2	3	5	[illegible]
2008-09	Val-d'Or Foreurs	QMJHL	64	27	49	76	43	....	....	....	....	....
2009-10	Val-d'Or Foreurs	QMJHL	25	13	22	35	26	6	5	2	7	[illegible]
	Providence Bruins	AHL	6	2	0	2	2	....	....	....	....	....

SAUVE, Yann (soh-VAY, YAHN) **VAN**

Defense. Shoots left. 6'3", 220 lbs. Born, Montreal, Que., February 18, 1990.
(Vancouver's 2nd choice, 41st overall, in 2008 Entry Draft).

			Regular Season					Playoffs				
Season	Club	League	GP	G	A	Pts	PIM	GP	G	A	Pts	PIM
2005-06	Chateauguay	QAAA	42	14	15	29	63	19	2	12	14	[illegible]
2006-07	Saint John	QMJHL	60	2	13	15	75	....	....	....	....	....
2007-08	Saint John	QMJHL	69	6	15	21	92	14	1	2	3	[illegible]
2008-09	Saint John	QMJHL	61	5	25	30	64	4	0	2	2	[illegible]
2009-10	Saint John	QMJHL	61	7	29	36	65	21	5	10	15	[illegible]

SAVARD, David (suh-VAHRD, DAY-vihd) **CB**

Defense. Shoots right. 6'2", 214 lbs. Born, St. Hyacinthe, Que., October 22, 1990.
(Columbus' 3rd choice, 94th overall, in 2009 Entry Draft).

			Regular Season					Playoffs				
Season	Club	League	GP	G	A	Pts	PIM	GP	G	A	Pts	PIM
2006-07	Sem. St-Francois	QAAA	44	10	16	26	52	18	1	12	13	[illegible]
2007-08	Baie-Comeau	QMJHL	35	1	6	7	22	....	....	....	....	....
	Moncton Wildcats	QMJHL	32	0	5	5	18	....	....	....	....	....
2008-09	Moncton Wildcats	QMJHL	68	9	35	44	33	10	5	5	10	[illegible]
2009-10	Moncton Wildcats	QMJHL	64	13	*64	77	36	21	1	14	15	[illegible]

QMJHL First All-Star Team (2010) • Canadian Major Junior First All-Star Team (2010) • Canadian Major Junior Defenseman of the Year (2010)

SCANDELLA, Marco (skan-DEHL-a, MAHR-koh) **MI**

Defense. Shoots left. 6'2", 213 lbs. Born, Montreal, Que., February 23, 1990.
(Minnesota's 2nd choice, 55th overall, in 2008 Entry Draft).

			Regular Season					Playoffs				
Season	Club	League	GP	G	A	Pts	PIM	GP	G	A	Pts	PIM
2005-06	Ecole Montpetit	QAAA	42	3	4	7	40	3	0	0	0	[illegible]
2006-07	Mtl. Predators	QAAA	42	7	13	20	66	3	0	1	1	[illegible]
2007-08	Val-d'Or Foreurs	QMJHL	65	4	10	14	35	4	0	1	1	[illegible]
2008-09	Val-d'Or Foreurs	QMJHL	58	10	27	37	64	....	....	....	....	....
	Houston Aeros	AHL	2	0	0	0	0	6	0	0	0	[illegible]
2009-10	Val-d'Or Foreurs	QMJHL	31	9	22	31	41	6	2	4	6	[illegible]
	Houston Aeros	AHL	7	0	1	1	7	....	....	....	....	....

SCEVIOUR, Colton (SEE-vee-yuhr, KOHL-tuhn) **DA**

Center/Right wing. Shoots right. 6', 201 lbs. Born, Red Deer, Alta., April 20, 1989.
(Dallas' 3rd choice, 112th overall, in 2007 Entry Draft).

			Regular Season					Playoffs				
Season	Club	League	GP	G	A	Pts	PIM	GP	G	A	Pts	PIM
2004-05	Red Deer	AMHL	36	15	22	37	32	....	....	....	....	....
	Portland	WHL	6	1	0	1	6	4	0	0	0	[illegible]
2005-06	Portland	WHL	58	3	6	9	25	12	0	1	1	[illegible]
2006-07	Portland	WHL	49	12	26	38	38	....	....	....	....	....
2007-08	Portland	WHL	17	2	8	10	9	....	....	....	....	....
	Lethbridge	WHL	52	31	23	54	36	19	3	10	13	[illegible]
2008-09	Lethbridge	WHL	69	29	51	80	48	11	4	3	7	[illegible]
2009-10	Texas Stars	AHL	80	9	22	31	19	24	1	7	8	[illegible]

SCHAUS, Nick (SHAWS, NIHK) S.J.

Defense. Shoots right. 5'11", 200 lbs. Born, Orchard Park, NY, July 3, 1986.

			Regular Season					Playoffs				
Season	Club	League	GP	G	A	Pts	PIM	GP	G	A	Pts	PIM
2002-03	River City Lancers	USHL	60	4	9	13	60	11	0	0	0	10
2003-04	River City Lancers	USHL	57	1	12	13	144	3	0	0	0	6
2004-05	Omaha Lancers	USHL	58	1	21	22	141	5	0	0	0	8
2005-06	Omaha Lancers	USHL	60	9	44	53	80	5	0	2	2	6
2006-07	U. Mass-Lowell	H-East	36	1	13	14	56	....	....	....	....	....
2007-08	U. Mass-Lowell	H-East	37	0	6	6	83	....	....	....	....	....
2008-09	U. Mass-Lowell	H-East	38	5	17	22	65	....	....	....	....	....
2009-10	U. Mass-Lowell	H-East	37	4	19	23	16	....	....	....	....	....
	Worcester Sharks	AHL	4	0	3	3	2	11	0	3	3	14

Signed as a free agent by **San Jose**, March 22, 2010.

SCHEMITSCH, Geoffrey (SHEHM-ihtsch, JEHF-ree) T.B.

Defense. Shoots right. 6'1", 180 lbs. Born, Toronto, Ont., April 1, 1992.
(Tampa Bay's 5th choice, 96th overall, in 2010 Entry Draft).

			Regular Season					Playoffs				
Season	Club	League	GP	G	A	Pts	PIM	GP	G	A	Pts	PIM
2008-09	Mississauga Reps	GTHL	33	9	22	31	20	....	....	....	....	....
2009-10	Owen Sound	OHL	62	4	36	40	24	....	....	....	....	....

SCHIESTEL, Drew (SHIGHS-tuhl, DROO) BUF.

Defense. Shoots right. 6'1", 193 lbs. Born, Hamilton, Ont., March 9, 1989.
(Buffalo's 2nd choice, 59th overall, in 2007 Entry Draft).

			Regular Season					Playoffs				
Season	Club	League	GP	G	A	Pts	PIM	GP	G	A	Pts	PIM
2004-05	Hamilton Reps	Minor-ON	68	21	27	46	....	....	....	....	....	....
2005-06	Mississauga	OHL	40	1	4	5	42	....	....	....	....	....
2006-07	Mississauga	OHL	66	6	15	21	40	5	0	6	6	2
2007-08	Niagara Ice Dogs	OHL	68	8	29	37	40	10	1	6	7	10
2008-09	Niagara Ice Dogs	OHL	63	10	38	48	75	12	2	6	8	14
2009-10	Portland Pirates	AHL	52	1	11	12	19	4	0	0	0	0

SCHIRA, Craig (SHIH-rah, KRAYG) OTT.

Defense. Shoots right. 6', 196 lbs. Born, Spiritwood, Sask., April 21, 1988.

			Regular Season					Playoffs				
Season	Club	League	GP	G	A	Pts	PIM	GP	G	A	Pts	PIM
2003-04	Saskatoon Blazers	SMHL	39	2	10	12	20	....	....	....	....	....
	Regina Pats	WHL	2	0	0	0	2	....	....	....	....	....
2004-05	Regina Pats	WHL	60	1	7	8	25	....	....	....	....	....
2005-06	Regina Pats	WHL	71	5	28	33	72	6	1	1	2	2
2006-07	Regina Pats	WHL	71	3	23	26	74	10	0	0	0	4
2007-08	Regina Pats	WHL	2	0	1	1	0	....	....	....	....	....
	Vancouver Giants	WHL	63	8	22	30	58	10	0	1	1	0
2008-09	Vancouver Giants	WHL	71	16	43	59	46	17	2	4	6	4
2009-10	Binghamton	AHL	68	8	13	21	27	....	....	....	....	....

Signed as a free agent by **Ottawa**, March 9, 2009.

SCHROEDER, Jordan (SHRAY-duhr, JOHR-dahn) VAN.

Center. Shoots right. 5'8", 182 lbs. Born, Burnsville, MN, September 29, 1990.
(Vancouver's 1st choice, 22nd overall, in 2009 Entry Draft).

			Regular Season					Playoffs				
Season	Club	League	GP	G	A	Pts	PIM	GP	G	A	Pts	PIM
2005-06	Saint Thomas	High-MN	31	27	35	62	....	....	....	....	....	....
	Team Southeast	UMHSEL	....	7	14	21	....	....	....	....	....	....
2006-07	USNTDP	NAHL	31	12	11	23	10	....	....	....	....	....
	USNTDP	U-17	8	2	8	10	2	....	....	....	....	....
	USNTDP	U-18	17	6	13	19	4	....	....	....	....	....
2007-08	USNTDP	NAHL	14	1	8	9	4	....	....	....	....	....
	USNTDP	U-18	41	21	23	44	12	....	....	....	....	....
2008-09	U. of Minnesota	WCHA	35	13	32	45	29	....	....	....	....	....
2009-10	U. of Minnesota	WCHA	37	9	19	28	14	....	....	....	....	....
	Manitoba Moose	AHL	11	4	5	9	0	6	3	3	6	4

WCHA All-Rookie Team (2009) • WCHA Second All-Star Team (2009) • WCHA Rookie of the Year (2009)

SCHULTZ, Ian (SHUHLTZ, EE-an) MTL.

Right wing. Shoots right. 6'1", 208 lbs. Born, Calgary, Alta., February 4, 1990.
(St. Louis' 6th choice, 87th overall, in 2008 Entry Draft).

			Regular Season					Playoffs				
Season	Club	League	GP	G	A	Pts	PIM	GP	G	A	Pts	PIM
2006-07	Calgary Buffaloes	AMHL	32	13	25	38	92	7	2	7	9	26
	Calgary Hitmen	WHL	1	1	0	1	0	....	....	....	....	....
2007-08	Calgary Hitmen	WHL	67	15	15	30	128	16	2	7	9	19
2008-09	Calgary Hitmen	WHL	58	15	26	41	127	18	5	7	12	24
2009-10	Calgary Hitmen	WHL	70	24	31	55	150	23	8	7	15	26

Traded to **Montreal** by **St. Louis** with Lars Eller for Jaroslav Halak, June 17, 2010.

SCHULTZ, Justin (SHUHLTZ, JUHS-tihn) ANA.

Defense. Shoots right. 6'2", 180 lbs. Born, Kelowna, B.C., July 6, 1990.
(Anaheim's 4th choice, 43rd overall, in 2008 Entry Draft).

			Regular Season					Playoffs				
Season	Club	League	GP	G	A	Pts	PIM	GP	G	A	Pts	PIM
2006-07	Westside Warriors	Minor-BC	....	29	29	58	29	....	....	....	....	....
2007-08	Westside Warriors	BCHL	57	9	31	40	28	11	3	5	8	4
2008-09	Westside Warriors	BCHL	49	15	35	50	29	6	1	2	3	2
2009-10	U. of Wisconsin	WCHA	43	6	16	22	12	....	....	....	....	....

WCHA All-Rookie Team (2010)

SCHUTZ, Felix (SCHUTZ, FEEL-ihx) BUF.

Center. Shoots left. 5'11", 191 lbs. Born, Erding, West Germany, November 3, 1987.
(Buffalo's 4th choice, 117th overall, in 2006 Entry Draft).

			Regular Season					Playoffs				
Season	Club	League	GP	G	A	Pts	PIM	GP	G	A	Pts	PIM
2003-04	Mannheim Jr.	Ger-Jr.	30	22	22	44	12	....	....	....	....	....
2004-05	EV Landshut Jr.	Ger-Jr.	9	6	8	14	33	2	2	3	5	0
	Landshut Cann.	German-2	24	1	2	3	8	5	0	0	0	2
2005-06	Saint John	QMJHL	65	21	31	52	61	....	....	....	....	....
2006-07	Saint John	QMJHL	18	4	7	11	16	....	....	....	....	....
	Val-d'Or Foreurs	QMJHL	27	15	18	33	28	20	5	10	15	22
2007-08	ERC Ingolstadt	Germany	46	12	13	25	76	3	0	1	1	2
2008-09	Portland Pirates	AHL	78	15	27	42	61	5	1	1	2	2
2009-10	Portland Pirates	AHL	67	13	14	27	61	3	0	0	0	10

QMJHL All-Rookie Team (2006)

SCHWARTZ, Jaden (SHWOHRTZ, JAY-duhn) ST.L.

Center. Shoots left. 5'10", 180 lbs. Born, Melfort, Sask., June 25, 1992.
(St. Louis' 1st choice, 14th overall, in 2010 Entry Draft).

			Regular Season					Playoffs				
Season	Club	League	GP	G	A	Pts	PIM	GP	G	A	Pts	PIM
2008-09	Notre Dame	SJHL	46	34	42	76	15	....	....	....	....	....
2009-10	Tri-City Storm	USHL	60	33	50	*83	18	3	3	0	3	0

USHL First All-Star Team (2010)

• Signed Letter of Intent to attend **Colorado College** (WCHA) in fall of 2010.

SCOTT, Greg (SKAWT, GREHG) TOR.

Right wing. Shoots right. 6', 188 lbs. Born, Victoria, B.C., June 3, 1988.

			Regular Season					Playoffs				
Season	Club	League	GP	G	A	Pts	PIM	GP	G	A	Pts	PIM
2004-05	Peninsula Panthers	VIJHL	48	34	40	74	65	....	....	....	....	....
	Victoria Salsa	BCHL	7	1	1	2	0	....	....	....	....	....
2005-06	Seattle	WHL	69	8	14	22	37	7	1	3	4	4
2006-07	Seattle	WHL	72	18	14	32	62	11	0	2	2	2
2007-08	Seattle	WHL	72	38	37	75	56	12	5	4	9	9
2008-09	Seattle	WHL	65	32	44	76	39	5	0	6	6	2
2009-10	Toronto Marlies	AHL	71	10	22	32	28	....	....	....	....	....
	Reading Royals	ECHL	5	1	1	2	2	13	1	9	10	0

Signed as a free agent by **Toronto**, July 3, 2008.

SDAO, Michael (S'DAY-oh, MIGH-kuhl) OTT.

Defense. Shoots left. 6'4", 207 lbs. Born, Bloomington, MN, July 3, 1989.
(Ottawa's 9th choice, 191st overall, in 2009 Entry Draft).

			Regular Season					Playoffs				
Season	Club	League	GP	G	A	Pts	PIM	GP	G	A	Pts	PIM
2005-06	Culver Academy	High-IN	40	1	6	7	38	....	....	....	....	....
2006-07	Culver Academy	High-IN	43	1	6	7	85	....	....	....	....	....
2007-08	Lincoln Stars	USHL	53	3	6	9	178	8	0	1	1	20
2008-09	Lincoln Stars	USHL	51	3	7	10	162	7	0	0	0	*33
2009-10	Princeton	ECAC	30	5	4	9	48	....	....	....	....	....

SEABROOK, Keith (SEE-bruk, KEETH) CGY.

Defense. Shoots right. 6', 200 lbs. Born, Delta, B.C., August 2, 1988.
(Washington's 5th choice, 52nd overall, in 2006 Entry Draft).

			Regular Season					Playoffs				
Season	Club	League	GP	G	A	Pts	PIM	GP	G	A	Pts	PIM
2004-05	Coquitlam Express	BCHL	58	8	20	28	70	....	....	....	....	....
2005-06	Burnaby Express	BCHL	57	10	24	34	81	....	....	....	....	....
2006-07	U. of Denver	WCHA	37	2	11	13	24	....	....	....	....	....
2007-08	Calgary Hitmen	WHL	59	4	13	17	47	14	0	5	5	13
2008-09	Calgary Hitmen	WHL	64	15	40	55	58	18	4	11	15	26
2009-10	Abbotsford Heat	AHL	78	10	18	28	53	12	2	1	3	30

• Left **University of Denver** (WCHA) and signed with **Calgary** (WHL), July 30, 2007. Traded to **Calgary** by **Washington** for future considerations, July 17, 2009.

SEDOV, Pavel (se-DAHF, PAH-vehl) T.B.

Right wing. Shoots left. 6'3", 200 lbs. Born, Voskresensk, USSR, January 12, 1982.
(Tampa Bay's 5th choice, 161st overall, in 2000 Entry Draft).

			Regular Season					Playoffs				
Season	Club	League	GP	G	A	Pts	PIM	GP	G	A	Pts	PIM
99-2000	Voskresensk	Russia-2	10	0	0	0	2	....	....	....	....	....
	Voskresensk 2	Russia-3	21	5	5	10	26	....	....	....	....	....
2000-01	Voskresensk	Russia-2	38	2	1	3	10	....	....	....	....	....
2001-02	Voskresensk 2	Russia-3	12	4	1	5	0	....	....	....	....	....
	Voskresensk	Russia-2	18	3	1	4	0	....	....	....	....	....
2002-03	Voskresensk 2	Russia-3	7	2	4	6	4	....	....	....	....	....
	Voskresensk	Russia-2	25	1	5	6	6	....	....	....	....	....
2003-04	THK Tver	Russia-2	26	2	6	8	6	....	....	....	....	....
	Voskresensk	Russia	10	1	0	1	2	....	....	....	....	....
	Voskresensk 2	Russia-3	STATISTICS NOT AVAILABLE									
2004-05	HK Tver	Russia-3	STATISTICS NOT AVAILABLE									
	HK Dmitrov	Russia-3	STATISTICS NOT AVAILABLE									
	HK Ryazan	Russia-4	STATISTICS NOT AVAILABLE									
2005-06			DID NOT PLAY									
2006-07	HK Ryazan	Russia-3	70	24	29	53	16	....	....	....	....	....
2007-08	HK Ryazan	Russia-2	50	6	10	16	14	....	....	....	....	....
2008-09	HK Ryazan	Russia-2	63	13	13	26	18	8	3	4	7	2
2009-10	HK Ryazan	Russia-2	44	14	8	22	14	8	0	1	1	4

SEGUIN, Tyler (SAY-gihn, TIGH-luhr) BOS.

Center. Shoots right. 6'1", 186 lbs. Born, Brampton, Ont., January 31, 1992.
(Boston's 1st choice, 2nd overall, in 2010 Entry Draft).

			Regular Season					Playoffs				
Season	Club	League	GP	G	A	Pts	PIM	GP	G	A	Pts	PIM
2007-08	Tor. Young Nats	GTHL	51	39	47	86	56	....	....	....	....	....
2008-09	Plymouth Whalers	OHL	61	21	46	67	28	11	5	11	16	8
2009-10	Plymouth Whalers	OHL	63	48	58	*106	54	9	5	5	10	8

OHL First All-Star Team (2010) • OHL Player of the Year (2010) • Canadian Major Junior First All-Star Team (2010)

SELLECK, Eric (SEHL-ehk, AIR-ihk) FLA.

Left wing. Shoots left. 6'2", 210 lbs. Born, Spencerville, Ont., October 20, 1987.

			Regular Season					Playoffs				
Season	Club	League	GP	G	A	Pts	PIM	GP	G	A	Pts	PIM
2006-07	Pembroke	CJHL	53	23	24	47	137	15	4	8	12	29
2007-08	Pembroke	CJHL	49	43	38	81	120	14	8	21	29	28
2008-09	Oswego State	NCAA-3	26	13	13	26	45	....	....	....	....	....
2009-10	Oswego State	NCAA-3	28	21	33	54	48	....	....	....	....	....

SUNYAC (NCAA-3) Rookie of the Year (2009) • SUNYAC (NCAA-3) Player of the Year (2010) • NCAA-3 East All-American Team (2010)

Signed as a free agent by **Florida**, April 21, 2010.

SEMIN, Dmitri (SEH-min, dih-MEE-tree) ST.L.

Center. Shoots left. 5'10", 185 lbs. Born, Moscow, USSR, August 14, 1983.
(St. Louis' 4th choice, 159th overall, in 2001 Entry Draft).

			Regular Season					Playoffs				
Season	Club	League	GP	G	A	Pts	PIM	GP	G	A	Pts	PIM
99-2000	Spartak Moscow 2	Russia-3	27	9	10	19	10	....	....	....	....	....
	Spartak Moscow	Russia-2	1	0	0	0	0	....	....	....	....	....
2000-01	Spartak Moscow	Russia-2	21	6	3	9	4	11	2	3	5	4
2001-02	Spartak Moscow 2	Russia-3	4	5	0	5	4	....	....	....	....	....
	Spartak Moscow	Russia	44	2	6	8	14	....	....	....	....	....
2002-03	Spartak Moscow	Russia	51	9	13	22	30	....	....	....	....	....
2003-04	Spartak Moscow	Russia-2	60	15	23	38	34	13	2	2	4	2
2004-05	Spartak Moscow	Russia	53	7	7	14	34	....	....	....	....	....
2005-06	Spartak Moscow	Russia	51	12	14	26	38	3	0	1	1	0
2006-07	Yaroslavl	Russia	41	13	13	26	30	7	3	2	5	2
2007-08	Yaroslavl	Russia	54	9	14	23	46	16	1	2	3	10
2008-09	Yaroslavl	Rus-KHL	53	7	13	20	28	16	4	5	9	33
2009-10	Mytischi	Rus-KHL	55	5	21	26	46	4	1	0	1	4

SERSEN, Michal (suhr-SEHN, MEE-khahl) T.B.

Defense. Shoots left. 6'2", 200 lbs. Born, Celnica, Czech., December 28, 1985.
(Pittsburgh's 7th choice, 130th overall, in 2004 Entry Draft).

			Regular Season					Playoffs				
Season	Club	League	GP	G	A	Pts	PIM	GP	G	A	Pts	PIM
2002-03	Bratislava Jr.	Slovak-Jr.	33	5	4	9	51	....	....	....	....	....
	Bratislava	Slovakia	17	0	0	0	0	....	....	....	....	....
2003-04	Rimouski Oceanic	QMJHL	45	7	18	25	30	9	1	5	6	6
2004-05	Rimouski Oceanic	QMJHL	67	9	33	42	74	13	0	8	8	18
2005-06	Quebec Remparts	QMJHL	63	22	57	79	76	23	3	18	21	36
2006-07	Bratislava	Slovakia	42	1	4	5	28	14	0	1	1	2
2007-08	Bratislava	Slovakia	54	9	9	18	58	18	1	2	3	6
2008-09	Bratislava	Slovakia	40	4	12	16	49	....	....	....	....	....
2009-10	Bratislava	Slovakia	41	3	8	11	34	15	2	8	10	28

QMJHL Second All-Star Team (2006) • Memorial Cup Tournament All-Star Team (2006)

Signed as a free agent by **Bratislava** (Slovakia), October 14, 2006. Traded to **Tampa Bay** by **Pittsburgh** for Tampa Bay's 5th round choice (Alex Velischek) in 2009 Entry Draft, October 1, 2008.

SERTICH, Marty (SUHR-tihch, MAHR-tee)

Center. Shoots left. 5'9", 165 lbs. Born, Roseville, MN, October 13, 1982.

			Regular Season					Playoffs				
Season	Club	League	GP	G	A	Pts	PIM	GP	G	A	Pts	PIM
2001-02	Sioux Falls	USHL	61	19	33	52	30	3	1	0	1	0
2002-03	Colorado College	WCHA	42	9	20	29	26	....	....	....	....	....
2003-04	Colorado College	WCHA	39	11	28	39	12	....	....	....	....	....
2004-05	Colorado College	WCHA	42	27	37	*64	26	....	....	....	....	....
2005-06	Colorado College	WCHA	42	14	36	50	55	....	....	....	....	....
2006-07	Iowa Stars	AHL	44	13	20	33	24	2	0	1	1	0
2007-08	Iowa Stars	AHL	79	27	25	52	42	....	....	....	....	....
2008-09	Lake Erie Monsters	AHL	24	7	8	15	22	....	....	....	....	....
2009-10	Lake Erie Monsters	AHL	53	9	19	28	22	....	....	....	....	....

WCHA Second All-Star Team (2006)

Signed as a free agent by **Dallas**, July 10, 2006. Traded to **Colorado** by **Dallas** for future considerations, June 10, 2008.

SEVERYN, C.J. (SEH-vuhr-ihn, SEE-JAY) CGY.

Left wing. Shoots left. 6'1", 195 lbs. Born, Beaver, PA, June 2, 1989.
(Calgary's 5th choice, 186th overall, in 2007 Entry Draft).

			Regular Season					Playoffs				
Season	Club	League	GP	G	A	Pts	PIM	GP	G	A	Pts	PIM
2004-05	Pittsburgh Hornets	MWEHL	65	27	44	71	....	....	....	....	....	....
2005-06	USNTDP	U-17	19	2	3	5	40	....	....	....	....	....
	USNTDP	NAHL	32	2	13	15	77	12	1	0	1	12
2006-07	USNTDP	U-18	42	8	8	16	32	....	....	....	....	....
	USNTDP	NAHL	15	0	3	3	22	....	....	....	....	....
2007-08	Ohio State	CCHA	32	0	2	2	20	....	....	....	....	....
2008-09	Ohio State	CCHA	33	9	3	12	24	....	....	....	....	....
2009-10	Ohio State	CCHA	38	9	6	15	40	....	....	....	....	....

SEXTON, Ben (SEHKS-tuhn, BEHN) BOS.

Center. Shoots right. 5'11", 192 lbs. Born, Ottawa, Ont., June 6, 1991.
(Boston's 5th choice, 206th overall, in 2009 Entry Draft).

			Regular Season					Playoffs				
Season	Club	League	GP	G	A	Pts	PIM	GP	G	A	Pts	PIM
2007-08	Nepean Raiders	CJHL	48	15	15	30	71	6	1	5	6	4
2008-09	Nepean Raiders	CJHL	38	14	21	35	54	11	3	9	12	22
2009-10	Penticton Vees	BCHL	50	13	29	42	83	5	1	2	3	4

• Signed Letter of Intent to attend **Clarkson University** (ECAC) in fall of 2010.

SHADILOV, Igor (sha-DEE-lahf, EE-gohr) WSH.

Defense. Shoots left. 6'2", 189 lbs. Born, Moscow, USSR, June 7, 1980.
(Washington's 10th choice, 249th overall, in 1999 Entry Draft).

			Regular Season					Playoffs				
Season	Club	League	GP	G	A	Pts	PIM	GP	G	A	Pts	PIM
1996-97	Dyn'o Moscow 2	Russia-3	30	3	7	10	30	....	....	....	....	....
1997-98	Dynamo Moscow	Russia	38	1	0	1	6	....	....	....	....	....
1998-99	Dyn'o Moscow 2	Russia-3	28	2	9	11	15	....	....	....	....	....
	Dynamo Moscow	Russia	2	0	0	0	0	....	....	....	....	....
	Krylja Sovetov	Russia	9	0	0	0	0	....	....	....	....	....
99-2000	THK Tver	Russia-2	14	0	3	3	6	....	....	....	....	....
	Dynamo Moscow	Russia	26	0	2	2	8	16	0	0	0	2
2000-01	Dynamo Moscow	Russia	34	1	5	6	12	....	....	....	....	....
2001-02	Cherepovets	Russia	33	7	3	10	10	4	0	0	0	2
2002-03	Cherepovets	Russia	32	3	3	6	28	12	1	3	4	4
2003-04	Dynamo Moscow	Russia	56	4	8	12	16	3	0	1	1	2
2004-05	Dynamo Moscow	Russia	34	0	5	5	12	....	....	....	....	....
2005-06	Ak Bars Kazan	Russia	49	3	9	12	20	13	1	1	2	6
2006-07	Ak Bars Kazan	Russia	49	5	10	15	32	16	1	1	2	41
2007-08	Ufa	Russia	45	5	11	16	18	16	0	2	2	8
2008-09	Ufa	Rus-KHL	29	5	9	14	10	....	....	....	....	....
2009-10	Ak Bars Kazan	Rus-KHL	17	0	0	0	8	....	....	....	....	....

SHAFIGULIN, Grigory (sha-fih-GOO-lihn, grih-GOH-ree) NSH.

Center. Shoots left. 6'2", 185 lbs. Born, Chelyabinsk, USSR, January 13, 1985.
(Nashville's 8th choice, 98th overall, in 2003 Entry Draft).

			Regular Season					Playoffs				
Season	Club	League	GP	G	A	Pts	PIM	GP	G	A	Pts	PIM
2000-01	Chelyabinsk 2	Russia-3	6	3	2	5	8	....	....	....	....	....
2001-02	Yaroslavl 2	Russia-3	19	2	2	4	12	....	....	....	....	....
2002-03	Yaroslavl 2	Russia-3	33	18	12	30	46	7	0	4	4	31
	Yaroslavl	Russia	11	0	1	1	4	8	0	0	0	4
2003-04	Yaroslavl 2	Russia-3	11	3	8	11	22	....	....	....	....	....
	Yaroslavl	Russia	29	3	0	3	4	2	0	0	0	0
2004-05	Yaroslavl 2	Russia-3	1	0	2	2	0	....	....	....	....	....
	Yaroslavl	Russia	46	5	6	11	49	9	0	0	0	10
2005-06	Yaroslavl	Russia	32	3	6	9	20	3	0	0	0	6
	Yaroslavl 2	Russia-3	7	1	3	4	18	....	....	....	....	....
2006-07	Yaroslavl	Russia	54	5	16	21	46	7	3	0	3	14
2007-08	Ak Bars Kazan	Russia	39	5	5	10	112	8	1	0	1	4
2008-09	Ak Bars Kazan	Rus-KHL	28	4	5	9	18	....	....	....	....	....
	Vityaz Chekhov	Rus-KHL	14	3	5	8	6	....	....	....	....	....
2009-10	Nizhny Novgorod	Rus-KHL	40	5	12	17	62	....	....	....	....	....

SHATTENKIRK, Kevin (SHAH-tehn-kuhrk, KEH-vihn) COL.

Defense. Shoots right. 5'11", 193 lbs. Born, Greenwich, CT, January 29, 1989.
(Colorado's 1st choice, 14th overall, in 2007 Entry Draft).

			Regular Season					Playoffs				
Season	Club	League	GP	G	A	Pts	PIM	GP	G	A	Pts	PIM
2004-05	Brunswick Bruins	High-CT	22	10	18	28	....	....	....	....	....	....
2005-06	USNTDP	U-17	13	4	4	8	4	....	....	....	....	....
	USNTDP	NAHL	28	6	9	15	17	12	3	7	10	10
2006-07	USNTDP	U-18	43	8	19	27	36	....	....	....	....	....
	USNTDP	NAHL	14	5	8	13	26	....	....	....	....	....
2007-08	Boston University	H-East	40	4	17	21	38	....	....	....	....	....
2008-09	Boston University	H-East	43	7	21	28	40	....	....	....	....	....
2009-10	Boston University	H-East	38	7	22	29	38	....	....	....	....	....
	Lake Erie Monsters	AHL	3	0	2	2	0	....	....	....	....	....

Hockey East All-Rookie Team (2008) • Hockey East Second All-Star Team (2009) • NCAA East Second All-American Team (2009)

SHATTOCK, Tyler (SHA-tuhk, TIGH-luhr) ST.L.

Right wing. Shoots right. 6'3", 200 lbs. Born, Vernon, B.C., February 10, 1990.
(St. Louis' 4th choice, 108th overall, in 2009 Entry Draft).

			Regular Season					Playoffs				
Season	Club	League	GP	G	A	Pts	PIM	GP	G	A	Pts	PIM
2005-06	Thompson Blazers	BCMML	STATISTICS NOT AVAILABLE									
	Kamloops Blazers	WHL	2	0	1	1	2	....	....	....	....	....
2006-07	Kamloops Blazers	WHL	58	7	9	16	51	4	0	0	0	0
2007-08	Kamloops Blazers	WHL	48	9	14	23	45	4	1	1	2	4
2008-09	Kamloops Blazers	WHL	68	30	39	69	82	4	0	1	1	6
2009-10	Kamloops Blazers	WHL	42	22	28	50	65	....	....	....	....	....
	Calgary Hitmen	WHL	30	8	20	28	26	21	5	12	17	24

SHEAHAN, Riley (SHEE-huhn, RIGH-lee) DET.

Center. Shoots left. 6'2", 202 lbs. Born, St. Catharines, Ont., December 7, 1991.
(Detroit's 1st choice, 21st overall, in 2010 Entry Draft).

			Regular Season					Playoffs				
Season	Club	League	GP	G	A	Pts	PIM	GP	G	A	Pts	PIM
2007-08	St. Catharines	OJHL-B	45	22	39	61	39	16	5	10	15	14
2008-09	St. Catharines	OJHL-B	40	27	46	73	55	11	8	5	13	30
2009-10	U. of Notre Dame	CCHA	37	6	11	17	22	....	....	....	....	....

SHEFER, Andrei (SHEH-fuhr, AWN-dray) L.A.

Left wing. Shoots left. 6'1", 198 lbs. Born, Yekaterinburg, USSR, July 26, 1981.
(Los Angeles' 1st choice, 43rd overall, in 1999 Entry Draft).

			Regular Season					Playoffs				
Season	Club	League	GP	G	A	Pts	PIM	GP	G	A	Pts	PIM
1997-98	Yekaterinburg 2	Russia-3	16	3	3	6	18	....	....	....	....	....
1998-99	Cherepovets 3	Russia-4	6	2	2	4	18	....	....	....	....	....
	Cherepovets 2	Russia-3	21	6	5	11	20	....	....	....	....	....
	Cherepovets	Russia	8	1	0	1	4	....	....	....	....	....
99-2000	Halifax	QMJHL	72	34	42	76	30	10	0	5	5	4
2000-01	SKA St. Petersburg	Russia	11	6	1	7	4	....	....	....	....	....
	Cherepovets	Russia	20	1	1	2	10	6	1	0	1	0
2001-02	Cherepovets 2	Russia-3	3	1	2	3	2	....	....	....	....	....
	Cherepovets	Russia	8	0	0	0	6	....	....	....	....	....
	SKA St. Petersburg	Russia	28	4	4	8	10	....	....	....	....	....
2002-03	Cherepovets	Russia	37	2	4	6	10	10	0	0	0	0
	Cherepovets 2	Russia-3	3	1	2	3	2	....	....	....	....	....
2003-04	Cherepovets	Russia	55	4	6	10	46	....	....	....	....	....
2004-05	Cherepovets	Russia	46	1	11	12	18	....	....	....	....	....
2005-06	Cherepovets	Russia	45	2	1	3	32	4	0	1	1	0
2006-07	CSKA Moscow	Russia	45	7	7	14	48	2	0	0	0	2
2007-08	CSKA Moscow	Russia	53	3	14	17	34	6	1	1	2	0
2008-09	Cherepovets	Rus-KHL	37	3	5	8	16	....	....	....	....	....
2009-10	Cherepovets	Rus-KHL	51	5	12	17	26	....	....	....	....	....

SHELAST, Tyler (SHEE-last, TIGH-luhr)

Wing. Shoots right. 6'1", 210 lbs. Born, Edmonton, Alta., December 26, 1984.

			Regular Season					Playoffs				
Season	Club	League	GP	G	A	Pts	PIM	GP	G	A	Pts	PIM
2003-04	Powell River Kings	BCHL	58	25	42	67	131	7	1	3	4	6
2004-05	Michigan Tech	WCHA	37	11	8	19	42	....	....	....	....	....
2005-06	Michigan Tech	WCHA	37	9	9	18	44	....	....	....	....	....
2006-07	Michigan Tech	WCHA	38	15	9	24	18	....	....	....	....	....
2007-08	Michigan Tech	WCHA	39	16	10	26	26	....	....	....	....	....
	Iowa Stars	AHL	11	1	1	2	0	....	....	....	....	....
2008-09	Hamilton Bulldogs	AHL	17	2	1	3	4	....	....	....	....	....
	Idaho Steelheads	ECHL	31	9	12	21	23	4	0	0	0	4
2009-10	Texas Stars	AHL	32	2	3	5	20	....	....	....	....	....
	Allen Americans	CHL	5	2	1	3	2	....	....	....	....	....

Signed as a free agent by **Dallas**, March 19, 2008.

SHIELDS, David (SHEELDZ, DAY-vihd) ST.L.

Defense. Shoots right. 6'3", 216 lbs. Born, Buffalo, NY, January 27, 1991.
(St. Louis' 5th choice, 168th overall, in 2009 Entry Draft).

			Regular Season					Playoffs				
Season	Club	League	GP	G	A	Pts	PIM	GP	G	A	Pts	PIM
2006-07	Maksymum	Minor-NY	37	4	16	20	60	....	....	....	....	....
2007-08	Erie Otters	OHL	60	1	3	4	31	....	....	....	....	....
2008-09	Erie Otters	OHL	61	1	16	17	28	5	0	0	0	5
2009-10	Erie Otters	OHL	68	7	12	19	42	4	0	0	0	12

SHIPLEY, Steven (SHIHP-lee, STEE-vehn) **BUF.**

Center. Shoots left. 6'3", 210 lbs. Born, London, Ont., April 22, 1992.
(Buffalo's 5th choice, 98th overall, in 2010 Entry Draft).

					Regular Season					Playoffs		
Season	Club	League	GP	G	A	Pts	PIM	GP	G	A	Pts	PIM
2007-08	Elgin-Mid. Chiefs	Minor-ON	65	53	51	104	....	....	....	....	....	....
2008-09	Owen Sound	OHL	63	16	23	39	19	4	0	0	0	0
2009-10	Owen Sound	OHL	68	23	40	63	32	....	....	....	....	....

SHORE, Drew (SHOHR, DROO) **FLA.**

Center. Shoots right. 6'3", 190 lbs. Born, Denver, CO, January 29, 1991.
(Florida's 2nd choice, 44th overall, in 2009 Entry Draft).

					Regular Season					Playoffs		
Season	Club	League	GP	G	A	Pts	PIM	GP	G	A	Pts	PIM
2006-07	Det. Honeybaked	MWEHL	31	9	25	34	20	....	....	....	....	....
	Det. Honeybaked	Exhib.	34	17	23	40	....	....	....	....	....	....
2007-08	USNTDP	NAHL	35	9	16	25	12	3	0	1	1	0
	USNTDP	U-17	16	4	8	12	6	....	....	....	....	....
2008-09	USNTDP	NAHL	15	7	7	14	16	....	....	....	....	....
	USNTDP	U-18	47	10	25	35	30	....	....	....	....	....
2009-10	U. of Denver	WCHA	41	5	14	19	18	....	....	....	....	....

SHUGG, Justin (SHUHG, JUHS-tihn) **CAR.**

Left wing. Shoots right. 5'11", 194 lbs. Born, Niagara Falls, Ont., December 24, 1991.
(Carolina's 6th choice, 105th overall, in 2010 Entry Draft).

					Regular Season					Playoffs		
Season	Club	League	GP	G	A	Pts	PIM	GP	G	A	Pts	PIM
2006-07	Niagara Falls	Minor-ON	70	65	46	111	42	....	....	....	....	....
2007-08	Oshawa Generals	OHL	38	4	10	14	10	....	....	....	....	....
	Windsor Spitfires	OHL	23	0	3	3	2	3	0	0	0	0
2008-09	Windsor Spitfires	OHL	68	17	16	33	48	20	5	4	9	16
2009-10	Windsor Spitfires	OHL	67	39	40	79	43	18	5	10	15	10

SIDORENKO, Kirill (sih-dohr-EHN-koh, kih-RIHL) **DAL.**

Center. Shoots left. 6'3", 187 lbs. Born, Omsk, USSR, March 30, 1983.
(Dallas' 9th choice, 180th overall, in 2002 Entry Draft).

					Regular Season					Playoffs		
Season	Club	League	GP	G	A	Pts	PIM	GP	G	A	Pts	PIM
1998-99	Omsk 2	Russia-4	2	0	0	0	2	....	....	....	....	....
99-2000	Omsk 2	Russia-3	26	2	11	13	14	....	....	....	....	....
2000-01	Omsk 2	Russia-3	30	8	7	15	44	....	....	....	....	....
2001-02	Mostovik Kurgan	Russia-2	50	11	6	17	64	....	....	....	....	....
2002-03	Sibir Novosibirsk	Russia	30	1	1	2	2	....	....	....	....	....
2003-04	Energiya Kemerovo	Russia-2	14	1	1	2	6	....	....	....	....	....
	Zauralje Kurgan	Russia-2	32	3	3	6	6	4	0	0	0	27
2004-05	Omsk 2	Russia-3	18	7	4	11	12	....	....	....	....	....
	CSK VVS Samara	Russia-2	16	2	2	4	0	....	....	....	....	....
2005-06	CSK VVS Samara	Russia-2	47	8	11	19	62	....	....	....	....	....
	Krylja Sovetov	Russia-2	6	3	3	6	8	17	1	3	4	4
2006-07	Krylja Sovetov 2	Russia-3	4	2	1	3	6	....	....	....	....	....
	Krylja Sovetov	Russia	35	5	4	9	22	....	....	....	....	....
2007-08	Titan Klin	Russia-2	53	6	12	18	43	....	....	....	....	....
2008-09	Kristall Saratov	Russia-2	56	17	9	26	54	....	....	....	....	....
2009-10	Zauralje Kurgan	Russia-2	40	4	8	12	10	4	0	2	2	2

SILAS, Stephen (SIGH-luhs, STEE-vehn) **COL.**

Defense. Shoots left. 6'1", 183 lbs. Born, Brampton, Ont., June 26, 1992.
(Colorado's 4th choice, 95th overall, in 2010 Entry Draft).

					Regular Season					Playoffs		
Season	Club	League	GP	G	A	Pts	PIM	GP	G	A	Pts	PIM
2007-08	Halton Hurricanes	Minor-ON	73	25	52	77	69	....	....	....	....	....
2008-09	Belleville Bulls	OHL	63	3	14	17	18	17	0	0	0	10
2009-10	Belleville Bulls	OHL	66	4	45	49	61	....	....	....	....	....

SILFVERBERG, Jakob (SIHL-vuhr-buhrg, YA-kuhb) **OTT.**

Left wing. Shoots right. 6'2", 190 lbs. Born, Gavle, Sweden, October 13, 1990.
(Ottawa's 2nd choice, 39th overall, in 2009 Entry Draft).

					Regular Season					Playoffs		
Season	Club	League	GP	G	A	Pts	PIM	GP	G	A	Pts	PIM
2005-06	Brynas U18	Swe-U18	8	0	0	0	0	....	....	....	....	....
2006-07	Brynas U18	Swe-U18	14	3	8	11	6	3	0	0	0	0
	Brynas IF Gavle Jr.	Swe-Jr.	6	1	3	4	0	....	....	....	....	....
2007-08	Brynas U18	Swe-U18	5	5	3	8	2	5	3	4	7	2
	Brynas IF Gavle Jr.	Swe-Jr.	30	8	12	20	8	7	3	0	3	2
2008-09	Brynas IF Gavle Jr.	Swe-Jr.	30	14	24	38	6	....	....	....	....	....
	Brynas IF Gavle	Sweden	16	3	1	4	2	4	0	0	0	2
2009-10	Brynas IF Gavle	Sweden	48	8	8	16	4	5	1	1	2	2
	Brynas IF Gavle Jr.	Swe-Jr.	1	1	1	2	0	3	3	2	5	0

SIMEK, Juraj (SEE-mehk, YUHR-ay) **T.B.**

Wing. Shoots left. 6'1", 190 lbs. Born, Presov, Czech., September 29, 1987.
(Vancouver's 4th choice, 167th overall, in 2006 Entry Draft).

					Regular Season					Playoffs		
Season	Club	League	GP	G	A	Pts	PIM	GP	G	A	Pts	PIM
2002-03	SC Bern Jr.	Swiss-Jr.	2	1	0	1	0	2	0	0	0	0
2003-04	Kloten Flyers Jr.	Swiss-Jr.	36	8	6	14	28	....	....	....	....	....
2004-05	Kloten Flyers Jr.	Swiss-Jr.	39	17	13	30	62	9	2	3	5	10
	Kloten Flyers	Swiss	18	0	0	0	0	....	....	....	....	....
	Kloten Flyers	Swiss	18	0	0	0	0	....	....	....	....	....
2005-06	Kloten Flyers Jr.	Swiss-Jr.	45	24	44	68	202	....	....	....	....	....
	Kloten Flyers	Swiss	8	0	1	1	4	....	....	....	....	....
	EHC Biel-Bienne	Swiss-2	3	0	0	0	2	....	....	....	....	....
2006-07	Brandon	WHL	58	28	29	57	41	9	1	5	6	6
2007-08	Manitoba Moose	AHL	66	7	10	17	30	1	1	0	1	0
2008-09	Norfolk Admirals	AHL	63	9	13	22	49	....	....	....	....	....
2009-10	Norfolk Admirals	AHL	75	21	15	36	31	....	....	....	....	....

Traded to **Tampa Bay** by **Vancouver** with Lukas Krajicek for Shane O'Brien and Michel Ouellet, October 6, 2008.

SIMS, Shane (SIHMZ, SHAYN) **NYI**

Defense. Shoots right. 6'1", 195 lbs. Born, East Amherst, NY, April 30, 1988.
(NY Islanders' 8th choice, 126th overall, in 2006 Entry Draft).

					Regular Season					Playoffs		
Season	Club	League	GP	G	A	Pts	PIM	GP	G	A	Pts	PIM
2004-05	Buffalo Lightning	OPJHL	48	14	26	40	47	....	....	....	....	....
2005-06	Des Moines	USHL	59	10	12	22	80	11	2	0	2	12
2006-07	Des Moines	USHL	59	10	19	29	137	8	1	3	4	8
2007-08	Ohio State	CCHA	39	1	10	11	45	....	....	....	....	....
2008-09	Ohio State	CCHA	42	7	17	24	42	....	....	....	....	....
2009-10	Ohio State	CCHA	34	5	12	17	22	....	....	....	....	....

USHL All-Rookie Team (2006)

SINDEL, Jakub (SHIHN-dehl, YA-kuhb) **CHI.**

Center. Shoots right. 6', 172 lbs. Born, Jihlava, Czech., January 24, 1986.
(Chicago's 5th choice, 54th overall, in 2004 Entry Draft).

					Regular Season					Playoffs		
Season	Club	League	GP	G	A	Pts	PIM	GP	G	A	Pts	PIM
99-2000	Slavia U17	CzR-U17	32	10	6	16	6	....	....	....	....	....
2000-01	Slavia U17	CzR-U17	26	12	15	27	2	6	1	0	1	0
2001-02	Slavia U17	CzR-U17	34	32	14	46	34	2	0	1	1	2
	HC Slavia Praha Jr.	CzRep-Jr.	14	7	4	11	10	....	....	....	....	....
2002-03	HC Slavia Praha Jr.	CzRep-Jr.	35	12	11	23	39	2	0	1	1	0
2003-04	HC Sparta Praha	CzRep	34	5	1	6	14	13	1	1	2	2
	Sparta Jr.	CzRep-Jr.	13	8	14	22	4	....	....	....	....	....
	HC Dukla Jihlava	CzRep-2	1	0	0	0	0	....	....	....	....	....
2004-05	Sparta Jr.	CzRep-Jr.	9	5	16	21	16	....	....	....	....	....
	HC Sparta Praha	CzRep	10	0	2	2	0	....	....	....	....	....
	Trebic	CzRep-2	5	0	0	0	0	....	....	....	....	....
	Brandon	WHL	35	16	13	29	12	24	7	4	11	22
2005-06	HC Sparta Praha	CzRep	12	1	1	2	6	....	....	....	....	....
	Plzen	CzRep	31	11	8	19	18	....	....	....	....	....
2006-07	Plzen	CzRep	50	16	10	26	30	....	....	....	....	....
	BK Mlada Boleslav	CzRep-2	4	1	0	1	4	8	5	5	10	20
2007-08	Plzen	CzRep	45	19	4	23	16	4	0	2	2	4
	BK Mlada Boleslav	CzRep-2	....	....	....	....	....	11	5	2	7	8
2008-09	Plzen	CzRep	22	4	4	8	12	....	....	....	....	....
	Pelicans Lahti	Finland	23	7	8	15	12	8	2	2	4	8
2009-10	HC Kometa Brno	CzRep	56	16	10	26	44	....	....	....	....	....

SIPOTZ, Brian (SIHP-awtz, BRIGH-uhn)

Defense. Shoots right. 6'7", 235 lbs. Born, South Bend, IN, September 16, 1981.
(Atlanta's 3rd choice, 100th overall, in 2001 Entry Draft).

					Regular Season					Playoffs		
Season	Club	League	GP	G	A	Pts	PIM	GP	G	A	Pts	PIM
99-2000	Culver Academy	High-IN	45	14	22	36	56	....	....	....	....	....
2000-01	Miami U.	CCHA	32	0	1	1	48	....	....	....	....	....
2001-02	Miami U.	CCHA	25	0	1	1	28	....	....	....	....	....
2002-03	Miami U.	CCHA	26	0	0	0	24	....	....	....	....	....
2003-04	Miami U.	CCHA	36	0	3	3	39	....	....	....	....	....
2004-05	Chicago Wolves	AHL	75	2	6	8	31	18	1	2	3	6
	Gwinnett	ECHL	2	0	0	0	0	....	....	....	....	....
2005-06	Chicago Wolves	AHL	57	2	12	14	41	....	....	....	....	....
2006-07	Chicago Wolves	AHL	73	2	10	12	36	8	0	0	0	2
2007-08	Chicago Wolves	AHL	54	1	4	5	22	21	0	4	4	14
2008-09	Chicago Wolves	AHL	66	2	5	7	36	....	....	....	....	....
2009-10	Chicago Wolves	AHL	44	0	8	8	51	8	0	0	0	4
	Gwinnett	ECHL	3	0	0	0	0	....	....	....	....	....

SKACHKOV, Evgeny (skatch-KAWF, yehv-GEH-nee) **ST.L.**

Left wing. Shoots right. 6', 187 lbs. Born, Penza, USSR, July 14, 1984.
(St. Louis' 10th choice, 221st overall, in 2003 Entry Draft).

					Regular Season					Playoffs		
Season	Club	League	GP	G	A	Pts	PIM	GP	G	A	Pts	PIM
2000-01	Dizelist Penza	Russia-2	9	0	0	0	0	....	....	....	....	....
2001-02	Kapitan Stupino	Russia-3		Statistics Not Available								
2002-03	Stupino	Russia-3		Statistics Not Available								
	Kapitan Stupino	EEHL	34	4	4	8	2	....	....	....	....	....
2003-04	CSKA Moscow 2	Russia-3		Did Not Play – Injured								
	CSKA Moscow	Russia	1	0	0	0	2	....	....	....	....	....
2004-05	Spartak Moscow	Russia	9	0	2	2	0	....	....	....	....	....
2005-06	Spartak Moscow 2	Russia-3	55	25	31	56	98	....	....	....	....	....
	Spartak Moscow	Russia	2	0	0	0	6	....	....	....	....	....
2006-07	Chelyabinsk	Russia	52	13	9	22	52	....	....	....	....	....
2007-08	Chelyabinsk	Russia	53	14	13	27	58	3	1	0	1	6
2008-09	Chelyabinsk	Rus-KHL	54	14	18	32	56	3	0	0	0	14
2009-10	Chelyabinsk	Rus-KHL	51	22	14	36	143	....	....	....	....	....

SKINNER, Jeff (SKIH-nuhr, JEHF) **CAR.**

Center. Shoots left. 5'10", 193 lbs. Born, Markham, Ont., May 16, 1992.
(Carolina's 1st choice, 7th overall, in 2010 Entry Draft).

					Regular Season					Playoffs		
Season	Club	League	GP	G	A	Pts	PIM	GP	G	A	Pts	PIM
2007-08	Tor. Young Nats	GTHL	50	62	35	97	139	....	....	....	....	....
2008-09	Kitchener Rangers	OHL	63	27	24	51	34	....	....	....	....	....
2009-10	Kitchener Rangers	OHL	64	50	40	90	72	20	*20	13	33	14

SKOKAN, David (SKOH-kahn, DAY-vihd) **NYR**

Center. Shoots left. 6', 191 lbs. Born, Poprad, Czech., December 6, 1988.
(NY Rangers' 5th choice, 193rd overall, in 2007 Entry Draft).

					Regular Season					Playoffs		
Season	Club	League	GP	G	A	Pts	PIM	GP	G	A	Pts	PIM
2003-04	Poprad U18	Svk-U18	38	17	28	45	110	6	1	5	6	37
	HK SKP Poprad Jr.	Slovak-Jr.	7	2	0	2	7	....	....	....	....	....
2004-05	Poprad U18	Svk-U18	4	4	6	10	37	....	....	....	....	....
	HK SKP Poprad Jr.	Slovak-Jr.	24	5	19	24	52	....	....	....	....	....
	HK SKP Poprad	Slovakia	8	0	0	0	6	2	0	0	0	25
2005-06	Rimouski Oceanic	QMJHL	53	6	15	21	143	....	....	....	....	....
2006-07	Rimouski Oceanic	QMJHL	52	14	21	35	62	....	....	....	....	....
2007-08	Rimouski Oceanic	QMJHL	53	19	21	40	92	8	0	5	5	10
2008-09	HK Poprad	Slovakia	33	9	9	18	115	....	....	....	....	....
	HK Poprad	Slovak-Q	1	0	0	0	25	....	....	....	....	....
2009-10	Bratislava	Slovakia	32	11	4	15	70	15	3	3	6	14

SLANEY, Robert (SLAY-nee, RAW-buhrt) TOR.

Left wing. Shoots left. 6'2", 203 lbs. Born, Upper Island Cove, Nfld., October 13, 1988.

			Regular Season					Playoffs				
Season	Club	League	GP	G	A	Pts	PIM	GP	G	A	Pts	PIM
2005-06	Cape Breton	QMJHL	54	3	4	7	21	7	0	3	3	4
2006-07	Cape Breton	QMJHL	58	13	12	25	67	15	5	5	10	8
2007-08	Cape Breton	QMJHL	64	26	29	55	63	11	6	3	9	10
2008-09	Cape Breton	QMJHL	63	36	45	81	78	7	5	4	9	18
2009-10	Toronto Marlies	AHL	34	0	6	6	15	....	....	....	....	....
	Reading Royals	ECHL	22	1	10	11	22	....	....	....	....	....

Canadian Major Junior Scholastic Player of the Year (2008)

Signed as a free agent by **Toronto**, April 14, 2009.

SMITH, Austin (SMIHTH, AUZ-tihn) DAL.

Right wing. Shoots right. 5'11", 160 lbs. Born, Dallas, TX, November 7, 1988.
(Dallas' 4th choice, 128th overall, in 2007 Entry Draft).

			Regular Season					Playoffs				
Season	Club	League	GP	G	A	Pts	PIM	GP	G	A	Pts	PIM
2003-04	Dallas Jesuit Prep	High-TX	STATISTICS NOT AVAILABLE									
2004-05	Dallas Jesuit Prep	High-TX	STATISTICS NOT AVAILABLE									
	Alliance Bulldogs	NTHL	53	29	46	75	24	....	....	....	....	....
2005-06	The Gunnery	High-CT	31	23	20	43	22	....	....	....	....	....
2006-07	The Gunnery	High-CT	30	25	38	63	36	....	....	....	....	....
2007-08	Penticton Vees	BCHL	60	32	35	67	42	15	11	11	22	12
2008-09	Colgate	ECAC	37	17	14	31	24	....	....	....	....	....
2009-10	Colgate	ECAC	36	16	25	41	20	....	....	....	....	....

SMITH, Barron (SMIHTH, BAIR-uhn) TOR.

Defense. Shoots right. 6'5", 205 lbs. Born, Hinsdale, IL, April 2, 1991.
(Toronto's 7th choice, 188th overall, in 2009 Entry Draft).

			Regular Season					Playoffs				
Season	Club	League	GP	G	A	Pts	PIM	GP	G	A	Pts	PIM
2006-07	Chicago Mission	MWEHL	30	1	5	6	58	....	....	....	....	....
2007-08	Chicago Steel	USHL	41	1	4	5	65	7	0	0	0	20
2008-09	London Knights	OHL	14	0	0	0	21	....	....	....	....	....
	Peterborough	OHL	20	0	2	2	36	....	....	....	....	....
2009-10	Peterborough	OHL	36	0	4	4	62	3	0	0	0	2

SMITH, Ben (SMIHTH, BEHN) CHI.

Right wing. Shoots right. 5'11", 205 lbs. Born, Winston-Salem, NC, July 11, 1988.
(Chicago's 5th choice, 169th overall, in 2008 Entry Draft).

			Regular Season					Playoffs				
Season	Club	League	GP	G	A	Pts	PIM	GP	G	A	Pts	PIM
2006-07	Boston College	H-East	42	10	8	18	10	....	....	....	....	....
2007-08	Boston College	H-East	44	25	25	50	12	....	....	....	....	....
2008-09	Boston College	H-East	37	6	11	17	6	....	....	....	....	....
2009-10	Rockford IceHogs	AHL	....	....	....	....	....	3	1	0	1	0
	Boston College	H-East	42	16	21	37	8	....	....	....	....	....

NCAA Championship All-Tournament Team (2008, 2010) • NCAA Championship Tournament MVP (2010)

SMITH, Brendan (SMIHTH, BREHN-duhn) DET.

Defense. Shoots left. 6'2", 190 lbs. Born, Toronto, Ont., February 8, 1989.
(Detroit's 1st choice, 27th overall, in 2007 Entry Draft).

			Regular Season					Playoffs				
Season	Club	League	GP	G	A	Pts	PIM	GP	G	A	Pts	PIM
2004-05	Toronto Marlboros	GTHL	66	22	63	85	120	....	....	....	....	....
2005-06	St. Michael's	OPJHL	39	5	21	26	55	17	1	5	6	44
2006-07	St. Michael's	OPJHL	39	12	24	36	90	16	6	14	20	30
2007-08	U. of Wisconsin	WCHA	22	2	10	12	26	....	....	....	....	....
2008-09	U. of Wisconsin	WCHA	31	9	14	23	75	....	....	....	....	....
2009-10	U. of Wisconsin	WCHA	42	15	37	52	76	....	....	....	....	....

WCHA First All-Star Team (2010) • NCAA West First All-American Team (2010) • NCAA Championship All-Tournament Team (2010)

SMITH, Craig (SMIHTH, KRAYG) NSH.

Center. Shoots right. 6'1", 197 lbs. Born, Madison, WI, September 5, 1989.
(Nashville's 6th choice, 98th overall, in 2009 Entry Draft).

			Regular Season					Playoffs				
Season	Club	League	GP	G	A	Pts	PIM	GP	G	A	Pts	PIM
2004-05	Madison Lancers	High-WI	20	16	24	40	....	....	....	....	....	....
2005-06	Madison Lancers	High-WI	20	35	26	61	....	....	....	....	....	....
2006-07	Waterloo	USHL	45	8	10	18	28	4	0	1	1	8
2007-08	Waterloo	USHL	58	13	10	23	90	11	2	3	5	8
2008-09	Waterloo	USHL	54	28	48	76	108	3	1	3	4	26
2009-10	U. of Wisconsin	WCHA	41	8	25	33	72	....	....	....	....	....

USHL First All-Star Team (2009) • WCHA All-Rookie Team (2010)

SMITH, Dalton (SMIHTH, DAHL-tuhn) CBJ

Left wing. Shoots left. 6'2", 201 lbs. Born, Markham, Ont., June 30, 1992.
(Columbus' 2nd choice, 34th overall, in 2010 Entry Draft).

			Regular Season					Playoffs				
Season	Club	League	GP	G	A	Pts	PIM	GP	G	A	Pts	PIM
2007-08	Osh. Generals	Minor-ON	62	22	38	60	192	....	....	....	....	....
2008-09	Whitby Fury	OJHL	40	10	13	23	109	4	2	1	3	12
	Ottawa 67's	OHL	17	2	5	7	8	7	0	0	0	0
2009-10	Ottawa 67's	OHL	62	21	23	44	129	12	3	3	6	27

SMITH, Reilly (SMIHTH, RIGH-lee) DAL.

Right wing. Shoots left. 6', 157 lbs. Born, Toronto, Ont., April 1, 1991.
(Dallas' 3rd choice, 69th overall, in 2009 Entry Draft).

			Regular Season					Playoffs				
Season	Club	League	GP	G	A	Pts	PIM	GP	G	A	Pts	PIM
2007-08	Tor. Young Nats	GTHL	70	80	77	157	56	....	....	....	....	....
	St. Michael's	OPJHL	13	2	7	9	22	1	0	0	0	2
2008-09	St. Michael's	OJHL	49	27	48	75	44	6	9	6	15	10
2009-10	Miami U.	CCHA	44	8	12	20	24	....	....	....	....	....

SMITH-PELLY, Devante (SMITH-PEH-lee, deh-VAHN-tay) ANA.

Right wing. Shoots right. 6', 211 lbs. Born, Scarborough, Ont., June 14, 1992.
(Anaheim's 3rd choice, 42nd overall, in 2010 Entry Draft).

			Regular Season					Playoffs				
Season	Club	League	GP	G	A	Pts	PIM	GP	G	A	Pts	PIM
2007-08	Tor. Jr. Canadiens	GTHL	85	38	39	77	159	....	....	....	....	....
2008-09	St. Michael's	OHL	57	13	12	25	24	11	2	3	5	4
2009-10	St. Michael's	OHL	60	29	33	62	35	16	8	6	14	20

SMOLYANINOV, Vitali (smoh-LEE-ya-NEE-nohv, vih-TAL-ee) T.B.

Left wing. Shoots left. 6'3", 205 lbs. Born, Nizhnekamsk, USSR, August 5, 1983.
(Tampa Bay's 12th choice, 261st overall, in 2001 Entry Draft).

			Regular Season					Playoffs				
Season	Club	League	GP	G	A	Pts	PIM	GP	G	A	Pts	PIM
1998-99	Nizhnekamsk 2	Russia-4	12	1	0	1	0	....	....	....	....	....
99-2000	Nizhnekamsk 2	Russia-3	54	7	7	14	28	....	....	....	....	....
2000-01	Nizhnekamsk 2	Russia-3	STATISTICS NOT AVAILABLE									
2001-02	Nizhnekamsk	Russia	1	0	0	0	0	....	....	....	....	....
2002-03	HK Voronezh	Russia-2	14	1	1	2	12	....	....	....	....	....
2003-04	Karaganda	Kazakh.	9	2	3	5	0	....	....	....	....	....
	Karaganda	Russia-2	19	0	1	1	32	....	....	....	....	....
2004-05	Karaganda	Kazakh.	7	5	3	8	2	....	....	....	....	....
	Karaganda	Russia-2	20	1	5	6	10	....	....	....	....	....
2005-06	Irtysh Pavlodar	Kazakh.	14	8	6	14	12	....	....	....	....	....
	Irtysh Pavlodar	Russia-3	STATISTICS NOT AVAILABLE									
2006-07	Barys Astana	Russia-3	42	8	19	27	36	....	....	....	....	....
	Barys Astana	Kazakh.	22	10	6	16	52	....	....	....	....	....
2007-08	Barys Astana	Russia-2	51	18	21	39	54	7	1	1	2	2
2008-09	Barys Astana	Rus-KHL	14	1	2	3	10	....	....	....	....	....
	Khanty-Mansiisk	Russia-2	2	0	1	1	2	....	....	....	....	....
	Gazovik Tyumen	Russia-2	20	7	7	14	12	8	3	0	3	6
2009-10	Gazovik Tyumen	Russia-2	36	5	18	23	24	7	3	1	4	2

SNEEP, Carl (SNEEP, KAHRL) PIT.

Defense. Shoots right. 6'4", 210 lbs. Born, St. Louis Park, MN, November 5, 1987.
(Pittsburgh's 2nd choice, 32nd overall, in 2006 Entry Draft).

			Regular Season					Playoffs				
Season	Club	League	GP	G	A	Pts	PIM	GP	G	A	Pts	PIM
2004-05	Brainerd	High-MN	26	20	21	41	25	....	....	....	....	....
2005-06	Brainerd	High-MN	26	14	23	37	34	....	....	....	....	....
	Lincoln Stars	USHL	13	1	3	4	9	9	0	1	1	6
2006-07	Boston College	H-East	38	1	9	10	8	....	....	....	....	....
2007-08	Boston College	H-East	44	3	12	15	15	....	....	....	....	....
2008-09	Boston College	H-East	33	2	9	11	26	....	....	....	....	....
2009-10	Boston College	H-East	42	11	17	28	26	....	....	....	....	....

SNETSINGER, Brad (SNEHT-sihng-uhr, BRAD)

Left wing. Shoots left. 6'2", 195 lbs. Born, Ajax, Ont., April 8, 1987.

			Regular Season					Playoffs				
Season	Club	League	GP	G	A	Pts	PIM	GP	G	A	Pts	PIM
2003-04	Milton IceHawks	OPJHL	40	10	9	19	30	....	....	....	....	....
	Mississauga	OHL	8	2	1	3	2	1	0	0	0	0
2004-05	Mississauga	OHL	54	8	5	13	30	5	0	0	0	0
2005-06	Windsor Spitfires	OHL	60	29	15	44	29	7	2	3	5	8
2006-07	Windsor Spitfires	OHL	63	29	33	62	86	....	....	....	....	....
2007-08	Windsor Spitfires	OHL	68	37	52	89	45	2	0	0	0	5
2008-09	Lowell Devils	AHL	8	1	0	1	6	....	....	....	....	....
	Trenton Devils	ECHL	49	21	28	49	22	7	0	2	2	10
2009-10	Lowell Devils	AHL	57	5	13	18	14	4	0	1	1	0

Signed as a free agent by **New Jersey**, December 20, 2007.

SODERBERG, Carl (SOH-dehr-buhrg, KAHRL) BOS.

Center. Shoots left. 6'3", 198 lbs. Born, Malmo, Sweden, October 12, 1985.
(St. Louis' 2nd choice, 49th overall, in 2004 Entry Draft).

			Regular Season					Playoffs				
Season	Club	League	GP	G	A	Pts	PIM	GP	G	A	Pts	PIM
2000-01	Skane	Exhib.	8	1	2	3	2	....	....	....	....	....
	Malmo U18	Swe-U18	3	1	1	2	0	....	....	....	....	....
2001-02	Malmo U18	Swe-U18	13	9	20	29	18	....	....	....	....	....
	Malmo Jr.	Swe-Jr.	4	0	2	2	2	7	0	2	2	4
2002-03	Malmo U18	Swe-U18	4	6	3	9	25	....	....	....	....	....
	Malmo Jr.	Swe-Jr.	28	17	18	35	22	6	2	4	6	8
2003-04	Malmo	Sweden	24	1	1	2	8	....	....	....	....	....
	Malmo U18	Swe-U18	27	23	25	48	30	6	1	2	3	10
	Malmo	Sweden-Q	8	1	1	2	4	....	....	....	....	....
2004-05	Morrums GoIS IK	Sweden-2	14	5	6	11	8	....	....	....	....	....
	Malmo Jr.	Swe-Jr.	12	13	6	19	43	3	2	1	3	12
	Malmo	Sweden	38	0	5	5	8	....	....	....	....	....
	Malmo	Sweden-Q	7	0	0	0	0	....	....	....	....	....
2005-06	Malmo	Sweden-2	49	20	27	47	47	....	....	....	....	....
2006-07	Malmo	Sweden	31	12	18	30	14	....	....	....	....	....
2007-08	Malmo	Sweden-2	42	22	36	58	18	....	....	....	....	....
2008-09	Malmo	Sweden-2	45	18	41	59	26	....	....	....	....	....
2009-10	Malmo	Sweden-2	51	20	31	51	53	5	0	1	1	0

Traded to **Boston** by **St. Louis** for Hannu Toivonen, July 23, 2007.

SOIN, Sergei (SOY-ihn, SAIR-gay) NSH.

Center/Left wing. Shoots left. 6', 185 lbs. Born, Moscow, USSR, March 31, 1982.
(Colorado's 3rd choice, 50th overall, in 2000 Entry Draft).

			Regular Season					Playoffs				
Season	Club	League	GP	G	A	Pts	PIM	GP	G	A	Pts	PIM
1997-98	Krylja Sovetov 2	Russia-3	2	0	0	0	0	....	....	....	....	....
1998-99	Krylja Sovetov	Russia	34	1	4	5	12	....	....	....	....	....
99-2000	Krylja Sovetov 2	Russia-3	8	2	3	5	12	....	....	....	....	....
	Krylja Sovetov	Russia-2	32	8	8	16	28	14	0	2	2	6
2000-01	Krylja Sovetov 2	Russia-3	8	2	3	5	12	....	....	....	....	....
	Krylja Sovetov	Russia-2	19	6	3	9	8	11	2	2	4	2
2001-02	Krylja Sovetov 2	Russia-3	5	2	6	8	20	....	....	....	....	....
	Krylja Sovetov	Russia	41	5	7	12	8	....	....	....	....	....
2002-03	Krylja Sovetov	Russia	49	8	6	14	40	....	....	....	....	....
2003-04	CSKA Moscow	Russia	49	1	6	7	32	....	....	....	....	....
2004-05	CSKA Moscow	Russia	19	3	3	6	10	....	....	....	....	....
2005-06	Cherepovets	Russia	48	5	12	17	36	4	1	1	2	0
2006-07	Cherepovets	Russia	52	12	12	24	78	5	2	1	3	0
2007-08	Cherepovets	Russia	52	9	11	20	22	7	1	1	2	4
2008-09	Cherepovets	Rus-KHL	51	7	19	26	38	....	....	....	....	....
2009-10	Cherepovets	Rus-KHL	52	7	13	20	30	....	....	....	....	....

Traded to **Nashville** by **Colorado** for Tomas Slovak, June 21, 2003.

SOL, Cody (SAWL, KOH-dee) ATL.

Defense. Shoots left. 6'4", 245 lbs. Born, Woodstock, Ont., February 11, 1991.
(Atlanta's 6th choice, 125th overall, in 2009 Entry Draft).

			Regular Season					Playoffs				
Season	Club	League	GP	G	A	Pts	PIM	GP	G	A	Pts	PIM
2007-08	St. Mary's Lincolns	OJHL-B	20	2	2	4	30	....	....	....	....	....
	Saginaw Spirit	OHL	12	0	0	0	4	1	0	0	0	0
2008-09	Saginaw Spirit	OHL	66	1	6	7	128	8	0	2	2	14
2009-10	Saginaw Spirit	OHL	55	7	8	15	151	6	0	0	0	8
	Chicago Wolves	AHL	1	0	0	0	0	....	....	....	....	....

SOLAREV, Ilja (SOH-luh-rehv, IHL-yuh) T.B.

Left wing. Shoots left. 6'3", 176 lbs. Born, Perm, USSR, August 2, 1982.
(Tampa Bay's 13th choice, 281st overall, in 2001 Entry Draft).

			Regular Season					Playoffs				
Season	Club	League	GP	G	A	Pts	PIM	GP	G	A	Pts	PIM
1997-98	Perm 2	Russia-3	4	1	0	1	0	....	....	....	....	....
1998-99	Perm 2	Russia-4	20	2	6	8	10	....	....	....	....	....
99-2000	Perm 2	Russia-3	35	3	2	5	24	....	....	....	....	....
2000-01	Perm 2	Russia-3	STATISTICS NOT AVAILABLE									
	Perm	Russia	5	0	1	1	0	....	....	....	....	....
2001-02	Leninogorsk	Russia-2	31	3	5	8	20	....	....	....	....	....
	HK Tambov	Russia-3	2	0	0	0	0	....	....	....	....	....
2002-03	Perm 2	Russia-3	STATISTICS NOT AVAILABLE									
	HK Brest	Belarus	STATISTICS NOT AVAILABLE									
2003-04	Motor Barnaul	Russia-2	34	6	6	12	20	1	0	0	0	0
2004-05	Energiya Kemerovo	Russia-2	36	3	2	5	28	....	....	....	....	....
2005-06	HK Lipetsk	Russia-2	49	4	6	10	30	3	0	0	0	0
2006-07	Satpayev	Russia-2	44	17	16	33	24	....	....	....	....	....
	Satpayev	Kazakh.	21	7	2	9	12	....	....	....	....	....
2007-08	Satpayev	Russia-2	29	10	10	20	24	....	....	....	....	....
	Barys Astana	Russia-2	22	4	9	13	26	7	2	1	3	6
2008-09	Barys Astana	Rus-KHL	46	8	7	15	24	....	....	....	....	....
2009-10	Barys Astana	Rus-KHL	37	5	4	9	20	3	0	1	1	4

SONNE, Brett (SOHNE, BREHT) ST.L.

Center/Left wing. Shoots left. 6', 190 lbs. Born, Chilliwack, B.C., March 16, 1989.
(St. Louis' 6th choice, 85th overall, in 2007 Entry Draft).

			Regular Season					Playoffs				
Season	Club	League	GP	G	A	Pts	PIM	GP	G	A	Pts	PIM
2004-05	Port Coquitlam	PIJHL	47	21	34	55	125	....	....	....	....	....
	Calgary Hitmen	WHL	6	0	0	0	2	....	....	....	....	....
2005-06	Calgary Hitmen	WHL	64	12	9	21	38	13	1	2	3	8
2006-07	Calgary Hitmen	WHL	71	21	9	30	65	18	5	1	6	22
2007-08	Calgary Hitmen	WHL	29	8	12	20	12	16	3	1	4	14
2008-09	Calgary Hitmen	WHL	62	48	52	100	58	14	7	9	16	18
2009-10	Peoria Rivermen	AHL	77	11	13	24	33	....	....	....	....	....

WHL East First All-Star Team (2009) • WHL Player of the Year (2009) • Canadian Major Junior Second All-Star Team (2009)

SORENSEN, Marcus (SOHR-ehn-suhn, MAHR-kuhs) OTT.

Right wing. Shoots left. 5'11", 161 lbs. Born, Sodertalje, Sweden, April 7, 1992.
(Ottawa's 2nd choice, 106th overall, in 2010 Entry Draft).

			Regular Season					Playoffs				
Season	Club	League	GP	G	A	Pts	PIM	GP	G	A	Pts	PIM
2008-09	Sodertalje SK U18	Swe-U18	32	16	12	28	92	4	2	3	5	6
2009-10	Sodertalje SK U18	Swe-U18	15	15	27	42	61	2	1	1	2	2
	Sodertalje SK Jr.	Swe-Jr.	27	7	10	17	54	....	....	....	....	....

SORYAL, Justin (SOHR-yahl, JUHS-tihn) NYR

Left wing. Shoots left. 6'3", 209 lbs. Born, Newmarket, Ont., June 29, 2007.

			Regular Season					Playoffs				
Season	Club	League	GP	G	A	Pts	PIM	GP	G	A	Pts	PIM
2003-04	Aurora Tigers	OPJHL	3	0	0	0	2	....	....	....	....	....
2004-05	Peterborough	OHL	29	0	1	1	54	14	0	1	1	21
2005-06	Peterborough	OHL	53	3	3	6	136	17	0	1	1	16
2006-07	Peterborough	OHL	60	26	27	53	125	....	....	....	....	....
2007-08	Peterborough	OHL	59	17	22	39	140	5	2	0	2	8
2008-09	Hartford Wolf Pack	AHL	43	3	7	10	114	....	....	....	....	....
2009-10	Hartford Wolf Pack	AHL	67	5	4	9	159	....	....	....	....	....

Signed as a free agent by **NY Rangers**, March 12, 2008.

SPINA, David (SPEE-nuh, DAY-vihd)

Left wing. Shoots left. 5'10", 186 lbs. Born, Mesa, AZ, June 5, 1983.

			Regular Season					Playoffs				
Season	Club	League	GP	G	A	Pts	PIM	GP	G	A	Pts	PIM
99-2000	Texas Tornado	NAHL	54	15	26	41	31	....	....	....	....	....
2000-01	USNTDP	USHL	23	3	7	10	28	....	....	....	....	....
2001-02	Boston College	H-East	36	13	13	26	39	....	....	....	....	....
2002-03	Boston College	H-East	37	17	20	37	34	....	....	....	....	....
2003-04	Boston College	H-East	25	6	6	12	20	....	....	....	....	....
2004-05	Boston College	H-East	40	13	15	28	42	....	....	....	....	....
	Utah Grizzlies	AHL	9	0	0	0	2	....	....	....	....	....
2005-06	Springfield Falcons	AHL	54	11	13	24	36	....	....	....	....	....
	South Carolina	ECHL	11	7	0	7	6	....	....	....	....	....
2006-07	Springfield Falcons	AHL	73	15	20	35	80	....	....	....	....	....
	Johnstown Chiefs	ECHL	6	4	2	6	4	....	....	....	....	....
2007-08	San Antonio	AHL	76	21	29	50	35	7	3	0	3	2
2008-09	San Antonio	AHL	63	16	38	54	55	....	....	....	....	....
2009-10	San Antonio	AHL	26	6	11	17	29	....	....	....	....	....

Signed as a free agent by **Phoenix**, July 2, 2008.

SPOONER, Ryan (SPOO-nuhr, RIGH-uhn) BOS.

Center. Shoots left. 5'10", 182 lbs. Born, Ottawa, Ont., January 30, 1992.
(Boston's 3rd choice, 45th overall, in 2010 Entry Draft).

			Regular Season					Playoffs				
Season	Club	League	GP	G	A	Pts	PIM	GP	G	A	Pts	PIM
2007-08	Ott. Senators	Minor-ON	53	52	45	97	16	....	....	....	....	....
2008-09	Peterborough	OHL	62	30	28	58	8	4	0	1	1	0
2009-10	Peterborough	OHL	47	19	35	54	12	3	0	1	1	2

SPURGEON, Tyler (SPUHR-juhn, TIGH-luhr)

Center. Shoots left. 5'11", 188 lbs. Born, Edmonton, Alta., April 10, 1986.
(Edmonton's 9th choice, 242nd overall, in 2004 Entry Draft).

			Regular Season					Playoffs				
Season	Club	League	GP	G	A	Pts	PIM	GP	G	A	Pts	PIM
2001-02	Edmonton MLAC	AMHL	35	39	36	75	12	....	....	....	....	....
	Kelowna Rockets	WHL	2	0	1	1	0	....	....	....	....	....
2002-03	Kelowna Rockets	WHL	50	7	6	13	21	19	2	5	7	6
2003-04	Kelowna Rockets	WHL	49	8	16	24	24	17	4	5	9	9
2004-05	Kelowna Rockets	WHL	72	21	41	62	32	24	11	6	17	12
2005-06	Kelowna Rockets	WHL	39	7	17	24	22	12	0	3	3	14
2006-07	Wilkes-Barre	AHL	34	5	10	15	10	6	1	0	1	4
	Stockton Thunder	ECHL	39	12	17	29	26	....	....	....	....	....
2007-08	Springfield Falcons	AHL	12	1	7	8	2	....	....	....	....	....
2008-09	Springfield Falcons	AHL	73	6	14	20	35	....	....	....	....	....
2009-10	Wilkes-Barre	AHL	20	1	2	3	9	....	....	....	....	....
	Idaho Steelheads	ECHL	48	26	39	65	14	....	....	....	....	....
	Abbotsford Heat	AHL	8	1	4	5	0	9	0	2	2	17

STAAL, Jared (STAWL, JAIR-uhd) CAR.

Right wing. Shoots right. 6'4", 210 lbs. Born, Thunder Bay, Ont., August 21, 1990.
(Phoenix's 3rd choice, 49th overall, in 2008 Entry Draft).

			Regular Season					Playoffs				
Season	Club	League	GP	G	A	Pts	PIM	GP	G	A	Pts	PIM
2005-06	Thunder Bay Kings	Minor-ON	64	24	25	49	72	....	....	....	....	....
2006-07	Sudbury Wolves	OHL	63	2	1	3	18	21	1	0	1	2
2007-08	Sudbury Wolves	OHL	60	21	28	49	44	....	....	....	....	....
2008-09	Sudbury Wolves	OHL	67	19	33	52	38	6	0	1	1	2
	San Antonio	AHL	5	0	0	0	0	....	....	....	....	....
2009-10	Sudbury Wolves	OHL	59	12	37	49	57	3	0	0	0	4
	San Antonio	AHL	5	0	1	1	2	....	....	....	....	....

Traded to **Carolina** by **Phoenix** for Nashville's 5th round choice (previously acquired, Phoenix selected Louis Domingue) in 2010 Entry Draft, May 13, 2010.

STAHL, Tyler (STAHL, TIGH-luhr) CAR.

Defense. Shoots right. 6'1", 196 lbs. Born, Drumheller, Alta., January 29, 1992.
(Carolina's 7th choice, 167th overall, in 2010 Entry Draft).

			Regular Season					Playoffs				
Season	Club	League	GP	G	A	Pts	PIM	GP	G	A	Pts	PIM
2007-08	Caronport	Minor-SK	36	6	11	17	104	....	....	....	....	....
	Chilliwack Bruins	WHL	1	0	0	0	0	....	....	....	....	....
2008-09	Drumheller	AJHL	1	0	0	0	2	....	....	....	....	....
	Caronport	Minor-SK	35	23	21	44	182	....	....	....	....	....
2009-10	Chilliwack Bruins	WHL	59	0	6	6	146	6	0	0	0	18

STANTON, Ryan CHI.

Defense. Shoots left. 6'2", 205 lbs. Born, St. Albert, Alta., July 20, 1989.

			Regular Season					Playoffs				
Season	Club	League	GP	G	A	Pts	PIM	GP	G	A	Pts	PIM
2005-06	Moose Jaw	WHL	2	0	0	0	2	....	....	....	....	....
2006-07	Moose Jaw	WHL	54	0	8	8	75	....	....	....	....	....
2007-08	Moose Jaw	WHL	58	4	16	20	68	6	0	0	0	2
2008-09	Moose Jaw	WHL	69	5	29	34	111	....	....	....	....	....
2009-10	Moose Jaw	WHL	59	10	30	40	81	7	0	6	6	4
	Rockford IceHogs	AHL	2	0	1	1	0	2	0	0	0	0

Signed as a free agent by **Chicago**, March 12, 2010.

STASYUK, Denis (stah-S'YUHK, DEH-nihs) FLA.

Center. Shoots left. 6'1", 165 lbs. Born, Novokuznetsk, USSR, September 2, 1985.
(Florida's 9th choice, 171st overall, in 2003 Entry Draft).

			Regular Season					Playoffs				
Season	Club	League	GP	G	A	Pts	PIM	GP	G	A	Pts	PIM
2002-03	Novokuznetsk 2	Russia-3	STATISTICS NOT AVAILABLE									
	Novokuznetsk	Russia	11	1	0	1	0	....	....	....	....	....
2003-04	Novokuznetsk	Russia	5	0	0	0	0	....	....	....	....	....
	Novokuznetsk 2	Russia-3	STATISTICS NOT AVAILABLE									
2004-05	Amur Khabarovsk	Russia-2	44	11	10	21	12	10	1	2	3	6
2005-06	Novokuznetsk	Russia	41	7	2	9	18	3	0	0	0	0
2006-07	Novokuznetsk	Russia	26	0	1	1	16	3	0	0	0	0
2007-08	Novokuznetsk	Russia	33	4	2	6	14	....	....	....	....	....
2008-09	Novokuznetsk	Rus-KHL	44	2	8	10	12	....	....	....	....	....
2009-10	Novokuznetsk	Rus-KHL	55	8	5	13	12	....	....	....	....	....

STEFANOVICH, Mikhail (steh-fan-AWV-ihch, mih-kigh-EHL) TOR.

Right wing. Shoots right. 6'2", 202 lbs. Born, Minsk, USSR, November 27, 1989.
(Toronto's 3rd choice, 98th overall, in 2008 Entry Draft).

			Regular Season					Playoffs				
Season	Club	League	GP	G	A	Pts	PIM	GP	G	A	Pts	PIM
2004-05	Dynamo Minsk 2	Belarus-2	19	3	7	10	8	....	....	....	....	....
	HK Gomel 2	Belarus-2	14	3	0	3	6	....	....	....	....	....
2005-06	HK Gomel 2	Belarus-2	37	18	12	30	64	....	....	....	....	....
2006-07	HK Gomel 2	Belarus-2	3	3	1	4	4	....	....	....	....	....
	HK Gomel	Belarus	41	16	9	25	43	5	1	0	1	2
2007-08	HK Gomel	Belarus	1	0	0	0	0	....	....	....	....	....
	Quebec Remparts	QMJHL	62	32	34	66	32	11	4	4	8	10
2008-09	Quebec Remparts	QMJHL	56	49	27	76	17	17	11	5	16	6
2009-10	Quebec Remparts	QMJHL	53	25	43	68	24	8	3	9	12	10

STEFISHEN, Taylor (STEH-fih-shehn, TAY-luhr) NSH.

Left wing. Shoots right. 5'11", 191 lbs. Born, North Vancouver, B.C., August 15, 1990.
(Nashville's 4th choice, 136th overall, in 2008 Entry Draft).

			Regular Season					Playoffs				
Season	Club	League	GP	G	A	Pts	PIM	GP	G	A	Pts	PIM
2006-07	Langley Chiefs	BCHL	59	25	31	56	73	7	5	1	6	8
2007-08	Langley Chiefs	BCHL	57	33	48	81	71	12	6	10	16	19
2008-09	Ohio State	CCHA	15	3	5	8	2	....	....	....	....	....
2009-10	Ohio State	CCHA	27	5	8	13	12	....	....	....	....	....

STEJSKAL, Joe (STAY-kuhl, JOH) MTL.

Defense. Shoots right. 6'2", 186 lbs. Born, Grand Rapids, MN, April 30, 1988.
(Montreal's 6th choice, 133rd overall, in 2007 Entry Draft).

			Regular Season					Playoffs				
Season	Club	League	GP	G	A	Pts	PIM	GP	G	A	Pts	PIM
2003-04	Grand Rapids	High-MN	....	1	7	8	....	....	....	....	....	....
2004-05	Grand Rapids	High-MN	....	2	8	10	....	....	....	....	....	....
2005-06	Grand Rapids	High-MN	....	7	18	25	....	....	....	....	....	....
2006-07	Grand Rapids	High-MN	24	11	17	28	42	....	....	....	....	....
2007-08	Dartmouth	ECAC	32	1	4	5	46	....	....	....	....	....
2008-09	Dartmouth	ECAC	29	7	5	12	53	....	....	....	....	....
2009-10	Dartmouth	ECAC	32	3	7	10	26	....	....	....	....	....

STEPAN, Derek (STEH-pan, DAIR-ihk) NYR

Center. Shoots right. 6', 187 lbs. Born, Hastings, MN, June 18, 1990.
(NY Rangers' 2nd choice, 51st overall, in 2008 Entry Draft).

			Regular Season					Playoffs				
Season	Club	League	GP	G	A	Pts	PIM	GP	G	A	Pts	PIM
2006-07	Shat.-St. Mary's	High-MN	63	38	32	70	22	....	....	....	....	....
2007-08	Shat.-St. Mary's	High-MN	60	44	67	111	22	....	....	....	....	....
2008-09	U. of Wisconsin	WCHA	40	9	24	33	6	....	....	....	....	....
2009-10	U. of Wisconsin	WCHA	41	12	*42	*54	8	....	....	....	....	....

STEPHENSON, Logan (STEE-vehn-suhn, LOH-guhn)

Defense. Shoots left. 6'3", 197 lbs. Born, Saskatoon, Sask., February 19, 1986.
(Phoenix's 2nd choice, 35th overall, in 2004 Entry Draft).

			Regular Season					Playoffs				
Season	Club	League	GP	G	A	Pts	PIM	GP	G	A	Pts	PIM
2001-02	Notre Dame	SMHL	37	4	2	6	74	....	....	....	....	....
	Tri-City Americans	WHL	....	....	....	....	....	3	0	0	0	0
2002-03	Tri-City Americans	WHL	50	0	6	6	121	....	....	....	....	....
2003-04	Tri-City Americans	WHL	69	3	8	11	112	11	1	1	2	10
2004-05	Tri-City Americans	WHL	59	6	9	15	86	5	0	0	0	2
2005-06	Tri-City Americans	WHL	71	10	43	53	162	5	1	0	1	18
2006-07	San Antonio	AHL	73	3	5	8	90	....	....	....	....	....
2007-08	San Antonio	AHL	74	1	7	8	94	7	0	1	1	6
2008-09	San Antonio	AHL	19	1	1	2	40	....	....	....	....	....
	Iowa Chops	AHL	25	0	2	2	21	....	....	....	....	....
	Rockford IceHogs	AHL	16	1	2	3	31	4	0	0	0	14
2009-10	Adirondack	AHL	62	1	7	8	140	....	....	....	....	....

WHL West Second All-Star Team (2006)

Traded to **Anaheim** by **Phoenix** for Joakim Lindstrom, December 3, 2008. Traded to **Chicago** by **Anaheim** with Samuel Pahlsson and future considerations for James Wisniewski and Petri Kontiola, March 4, 2009. Signed as a free agent by **Adirondack** (AHL), December 13, 2009.

STEVENSON, Dustin (STEE-vehn-suhn, DUHS-tihn) WSH.

Defense. Shoots left. 6'5", 220 lbs. Born, Gull Lake, Sask., August 12, 1989.

			Regular Season					Playoffs				
Season	Club	League	GP	G	A	Pts	PIM	GP	G	A	Pts	PIM
2007-08	La Ronge	SJHL	53	2	11	13	63	6	0	2	2	2
2008-09	La Ronge	SJHL	53	15	24	39	124	....	....	....	....	....
2009-10	La Ronge	SJHL	56	11	36	47	134	....	....	....	....	....

Signed as a free agent by **Washington**, April 5, 2010.

STOESZ, Myles (STOHZ, MIGH-uhlz)

Left wing. Shoots right. 6'2", 210 lbs. Born, Steinbach, Man., February 15, 1987.
(Atlanta's 8th choice, 207th overall, in 2005 Entry Draft).

			Regular Season					Playoffs				
Season	Club	League	GP	G	A	Pts	PIM	GP	G	A	Pts	PIM
2003-04	Spokane Chiefs	WHL	43	1	1	2	133	0	0	0	0	0
2004-05	Spokane Chiefs	WHL	67	1	8	9	238	....	....	....	....	....
2005-06	Spokane Chiefs	WHL	56	0	2	2	260	....	....	....	....	....
2006-07	Chilliwack Bruins	WHL	40	3	2	5	135	....	....	....	....	....
	Regina Pats	WHL	29	4	2	6	89	9	0	0	0	21
2007-08	Gwinnett	ECHL	64	4	2	6	*291	1	0	0	0	0
2008-09	Gwinnett	ECHL	43	4	3	7	158	....	....	....	....	....
	Trenton Devils	ECHL	10	0	0	0	30	3	0	0	0	9
2009-10	Lowell Devils	AHL	35	1	1	2	148	....	....	....	....	....
	Trenton Devils	ECHL	19	4	2	6	97	....	....	....	....	....

Traded to **New Jersey** by **Atlanta** with Niclas Havelid for Anssi Salmela, March 1, 2009.

STONE, Mark (STOHN, MAHRK) OTT.

Right wing. Shoots right. 6'2", 182 lbs. Born, Winnipeg, Man., May 13, 1992.
(Ottawa's 3rd choice, 178th overall, in 2010 Entry Draft).

			Regular Season					Playoffs				
Season	Club	League	GP	G	A	Pts	PIM	GP	G	A	Pts	PIM
2007-08	Wpg. Thrashers	MMHL	40	22	31	53	28	9	7	7	14	2
2008-09	Brandon	WHL	56	17	22	39	27	12	1	3	4	4
2009-10	Brandon	WHL	39	11	17	28	25	15	1	3	4	4

STONE, Michael (STOHN, MIGH-kuhl) PHX.

Defense. Shoots right. 6'3", 200 lbs. Born, Winnipeg, Man., June 7, 1990.
(Phoenix's 4th choice, 69th overall, in 2008 Entry Draft).

			Regular Season					Playoffs				
Season	Club	League	GP	G	A	Pts	PIM	GP	G	A	Pts	PIM
2005-06	Wpg. Thrashers	MMHL	40	14	18	32	14	....	....	....	....	....
2006-07	Calgary Hitmen	WHL	55	2	18	20	32	17	0	3	3	14
2007-08	Calgary Hitmen	WHL	71	10	25	35	28	14	3	4	7	10
2008-09	Calgary Hitmen	WHL	69	19	42	61	87	18	2	11	13	16
2009-10	Calgary Hitmen	WHL	69	21	44	65	91	23	5	15	20	26

WHL East Second All-Star Team (2009) • WHL East First All-Star Team (2010)

STOYKEWYCH, Peter (STOY-kuh-wihch, PEE-tuhr) ATL.

Defense. Shoots left. 6'2", 190 lbs. Born, Winnipeg, Man., July 14, 1992.
(Atlanta's 9th choice, 199th overall, in 2010 Entry Draft).

			Regular Season					Playoffs				
Season	Club	League	GP	G	A	Pts	PIM	GP	G	A	Pts	PIM
2007-08	Winnipeg Wild	MMHL	39	1	21	22	22	....	....	....	....	....
2008-09	Wpg. South Blues	MJHL	28	2	7	9	....	....	....	....	....	....
2009-10	Wpg. South Blues	MJHL	56	6	25	31	63	4	1	0	1	16

• Signed Letter of Intent to attend **Colorado College** (WCHA) in fall of 2010.

STRAIT, Brian (STRAYT, BRIGH-uhn) PIT.

Defense. Shoots left. 6'1", 200 lbs. Born, Boston, MA, January 4, 1988.
(Pittsburgh's 3rd choice, 65th overall, in 2006 Entry Draft).

			Regular Season					Playoffs				
Season	Club	League	GP	G	A	Pts	PIM	GP	G	A	Pts	PIM
2003-04	NMH School	High-MA	30	5	15	20	....	....	....	....	....	....
2004-05	USNTDP	U-17	18	1	5	6	8	....	....	....	....	....
	USNTDP	NAHL	42	4	8	12	42	10	0	2	2	2
2005-06	USNTDP	U-18	40	2	7	9	31	....	....	....	....	....
	USNTDP	NAHL	15	0	5	5	41	....	....	....	....	....
2006-07	Boston University	H-East	36	3	3	6	47	....	....	....	....	....
2007-08	Boston University	H-East	37	0	10	10	20	....	....	....	....	....
2008-09	Boston University	H-East	38	2	5	7	67	....	....	....	....	....
2009-10	Wilkes-Barre	AHL	78	2	12	14	73	4	0	1	1	0

STRAKA, Petr (STRAH-kuh, PEH-tuhr) CBJ

Right wing. Shoots left. 6'1", 191 lbs. Born, Plzen, Czechoslovakia, June 15, 1992.
(Columbus' 3rd choice, 55th overall, in 2010 Entry Draft).

			Regular Season					Playoffs				
Season	Club	League	GP	G	A	Pts	PIM	GP	G	A	Pts	PIM
2006-07	HC Plzen U17	CzR-U17	22	5	6	11	14	7	0	0	0	0
2007-08	HC Plzen U17	CzR-U17	46	40	34	74	42	8	5	9	14	4
2008-09	HC Plzen U17	CzR-U17	1	1	2	3	4	1	0	2	2	2
	HC Plzen Jr.	CzRep-Jr.	27	13	10	23	6	5	3	1	4	2
2009-10	Rimouski Oceanic	QMJHL	62	28	36	64	54	12	5	9	14	10

QMJHL All-Rookie Team (2010) • Canadian Major Junior All-Rookie Team (2010)

SUCHARSKI, Nick (soo-CHAR-skee, NIHK) CBJ

Left wing. Shoots left. 6'1", 195 lbs. Born, Toronto, Ont., November 15, 1987.
(Columbus' 6th choice, 136th overall, in 2006 Entry Draft).

			Regular Season					Playoffs				
Season	Club	League	GP	G	A	Pts	PIM	GP	G	A	Pts	PIM
2003-04	Wexford Raiders	OPJHL	43	15	29	44	48	....	....	....	....	....
2004-05	Wexford Raiders	OPJHL	46	26	27	53	78	13	6	10	16	20
2005-06	Michigan State	CCHA	36	2	5	7	18	....	....	....	....	....
2006-07	Michigan State	CCHA	41	9	15	24	32	....	....	....	....	....
2007-08	Michigan State	CCHA	41	9	17	26	32	....	....	....	....	....
2008-09	Michigan State	CCHA	6	0	1	1	6	....	....	....	....	....
2009-10	Michigan State	CCHA	37	9	10	19	47	....	....	....	....	....

SULLIVAN, Sean (SUHL-ih-vuhn, SHAWN) S.J.

Defense. Shoots left. 6', 190 lbs. Born, Boston, MA, March 29, 1984.
(Phoenix's 7th choice, 272nd overall, in 2003 Entry Draft).

			Regular Season					Playoffs				
Season	Club	League	GP	G	A	Pts	PIM	GP	G	A	Pts	PIM
2001-02	St. Sebastian's	High-MA	31	3	11	14	4	....	....	....	....	....
2002-03	St. Sebastian's	High-MA	41	9	30	39	59	....	....	....	....	....
2003-04	Boston University	H-East	36	2	5	7	14	....	....	....	....	....
2004-05	Boston University	H-East	41	1	3	4	10	....	....	....	....	....
2005-06	Boston University	H-East	40	3	14	17	32	....	....	....	....	....
2006-07	Boston University	H-East	38	3	12	15	12	....	....	....	....	....
	San Antonio	AHL	7	0	0	0	0	....	....	....	....	....
2007-08	San Antonio	AHL	34	0	8	8	13	1	0	0	0	4
	Arizona Sundogs	CHL	22	9	16	25	19	....	....	....	....	....
2008-09	San Antonio	AHL	65	9	23	32	24	....	....	....	....	....
2009-10	San Antonio	AHL	77	12	37	49	32	....	....	....	....	....

NCAA East Second All-American Team (2007)

Signed as a free agent by **San Jose**, July 15, 2010.

SUMMERS, Chris (SUHM-mehrs, KRIHS) PHX.

Defense. Shoots left. 6'2", 180 lbs. Born, Ann Arbor, MI, February 5, 1988.
(Phoenix's 2nd choice, 29th overall, in 2006 Entry Draft).

			Regular Season					Playoffs				
Season	Club	League	GP	G	A	Pts	PIM	GP	G	A	Pts	PIM
2004-05	USNTDP	U-17	13	2	2	4	10	....	....	....	....	....
	USNTDP	NAHL	31	2	5	7	20	7	1	0	1	0
2005-06	USNTDP	U-18	42	4	9	13	67	....	....	....	....	....
	USNTDP	NAHL	17	2	2	4	20	....	....	....	....	....
2006-07	U. of Michigan	CCHA	41	6	8	14	58	....	....	....	....	....
2007-08	U. of Michigan	CCHA	41	2	11	13	65	....	....	....	....	....
2008-09	U. of Michigan	CCHA	41	4	13	17	40	....	....	....	....	....
2009-10	U. of Michigan	CCHA	40	4	12	16	28	....	....	....	....	....
	San Antonio	AHL	6	1	0	1	0	....	....	....	....	....

SUNDHER, Kevin (SUHND-hurh, KEH-vihn) BUF.

Center. Shoots left. 6', 192 lbs. Born, Surrey, B.C., January 18, 1992.
(Buffalo's 3rd choice, 75th overall, in 2010 Entry Draft).

			Regular Season					Playoffs				
Season	Club	League	GP	G	A	Pts	PIM	GP	G	A	Pts	PIM
2007-08	Valley West Hawks	BCMML	40	20	34	54	86	....	....	....	....	....
	Chilliwack Bruins	WHL	6	0	1	1	2	....	....	....	....	....
2008-09	Chilliwack Bruins	WHL	67	19	20	39	68	....	....	....	....	....
2009-10	Chilliwack Bruins	WHL	72	25	36	61	101	6	3	2	5	4

SUTCH, Gregg (SUHCH, GREHG) BUF.

Right wing. Shoots right. 6'2", 198 lbs. Born, Scarborough, Ont., February 9, 1992.
(Buffalo's 6th choice, 143rd overall, in 2010 Entry Draft).

			Regular Season					Playoffs				
Season	Club	League	GP	G	A	Pts	PIM	GP	G	A	Pts	PIM
2007-08	York Simcoe	Minor-ON	69	52	29	81	74	....	....	....	....	....
2008-09	Sarnia Sting	OHL	60	7	8	15	53	5	0	1	1	2
2009-10	St. Michael's	OHL	43	3	5	8	55	16	4	1	5	10

SWEATT, Bill (SWEHT, BIHL)

Left wing. Shoots left. 6', 190 lbs. Born, Elburn, IL, September 21, 1988.
(Chicago's 2nd choice, 38th overall, in 2007 Entry Draft).

			Regular Season					Playoffs				
Season	Club	League	GP	G	A	Pts	PIM	GP	G	A	Pts	PIM
2003-04	Team Illinois	MWEHL	74	33	37	70	....	....	....	....	....	....
2004-05	USNTDP	U-17	11	5	10	15	54	....	....	....	....	....
	USNTDP	NAHL	41	7	9	16	12	10	4	3	7	6
2005-06	USNTDP	U-18	42	19	11	30	24	....	....	....	....	....
	USNTDP	NAHL	17	10	15	25	4	....	....	....	....	....
2006-07	Colorado College	WCHA	30	9	17	26	18	....	....	....	....	....
2007-08	Colorado College	WCHA	37	10	17	27	38	....	....	....	....	....
2008-09	Colorado College	WCHA	37	12	11	23	28	....	....	....	....	....
2009-10	Colorado College	WCHA	39	15	18	33	18	....	....	....	....	....

Traded to **Toronto** by **Chicago** with Kris Versteeg for Viktor Stalberg, Christopher Didomenico and Phillipe Paradis, June 30, 2010.

SWEATT, Lee (SWEHT, LEE) VAN.

Defense. Shoots right. 5'9", 195 lbs. Born, Elburn, IL, August 13, 1985.

			Regular Season					Playoffs				
Season	Club	League	GP	G	A	Pts	PIM	GP	G	A	Pts	PIM
2003-04	Colorado College	WCHA	37	4	12	16	20	....	....	....	....	....
2004-05	Colorado College	WCHA	42	3	25	28	34	....	....	....	....	....
2005-06	Colorado College	WCHA	41	5	16	21	36	....	....	....	....	....
2006-07	Colorado College	WCHA	37	9	15	24	51	....	....	....	....	....
	San Antonio	AHL	11	0	1	1	8	....	....	....	....	....
2007-08	TPS Turku	Finland	56	15	18	33	42	2	0	0	0	2
2008-09	Salzburg	Austria	52	10	26	36	99	12	2	4	6	14
2009-10	Dynamo Riga	Rus-KHL	37	2	5	7	18	....	....	....	....	....
	TPS Turku	Finland	21	9	7	16	8	15	*7	6	13	8

Signed as a free agent by **Vancouver**, May 31, 2010.

SWEETLAND, Andrew (SWEET-land, AN-droo)

Left wing. Shoots left. 6'2", 204 lbs. Born, Bonavista, Nfld., October 21, 1986.

			Regular Season					Playoffs				
Season	Club	League	GP	G	A	Pts	PIM	GP	G	A	Pts	PIM
2004-05	Couchiching	OPJHL	42	34	24	58	8	....	....	....	....	....
2005-06	Couchiching	OPJHL	30	18	15	33	6	....	....	....	....	....
2006-07	Amherst Ramblers	MJAHL	54	56	61	117	20	6	3	8	11	0
2007-08	U. of Maine	H-East	28	8	9	17	2	....	....	....	....	....
2008-09	Rochester	AHL	48	1	2	3	12	....	....	....	....	....
	Florida Everblades	ECHL	23	10	13	23	8	11	2	4	6	2
2009-10	Rochester	AHL	51	5	8	13	10	....	....	....	....	....

Signed as a free agent by **Florida**, March 31, 2008.

SWIFT, Michael (SWIHFT, MIGH-kuhl) **N.J.**

Center. Shoots left. 5'8", 170 lbs. Born, Peterborough, Ont., March 26, 1987.

			Regular Season					Playoffs				
Season	Club	League	GP	G	A	Pts	PIM	GP	G	A	Pts	PIM
2003-04	Mississauga	OHL	9	2	2	4	6	....	....	....	....	....
2004-05	Mississauga	OHL	67	15	17	32	46	5	0	0	0	4
2005-06	Mississauga	OHL	65	22	32	54	46	....	....	....	....	....
2006-07	Mississauga	OHL	67	34	59	93	76	5	0	1	1	6
	Laredo Bucks	CHL	....	....	....	....	....	12	1	3	4	8
2007-08	Niagara Ice Dogs	OHL	68	38	62	100	130	10	9	9	18	22
2008-09	Lowell Devils	AHL	52	12	15	27	50	....	....	....	....	....
2009-10	Lowell Devils	AHL	76	24	31	55	71	4	0	1	1	4

Signed as a free agent by **New Jersey**, April 19, 2008.

SZWARZ, Jordan (SWAWRZ, JOHR-dahn) **PHX.**

Right wing. Shoots right. 5'11", 189 lbs. Born, Burlington, Ont., May 14, 1991.
(Phoenix's 4th choice, 97th overall, in 2009 Entry Draft).

			Regular Season					Playoffs				
Season	Club	League	GP	G	A	Pts	PIM	GP	G	A	Pts	PIM
2006-07	Burlington Eagles	Minor-ON	66	56	54	110	88	....	....	....	....	....
2007-08	Saginaw Spirit	OHL	65	12	21	33	56	4	0	0	0	2
2008-09	Saginaw Spirit	OHL	67	17	34	51	76	8	1	5	6	10
2009-10	Saginaw Spirit	OHL	65	26	28	54	82	6	1	2	3	0
	San Antonio	AHL	1	0	0	0	0	....	....	....	....	....

TALBOT, Julian (TAL-buht, JOO-lee-uhn) **COL.**

Center. Shoots left. 6', 185 lbs. Born, Wahnapitae, Ont., March 24, 1985.

			Regular Season					Playoffs				
Season	Club	League	GP	G	A	Pts	PIM	GP	G	A	Pts	PIM
2002-03	Ottawa 67's	OHL	62	10	18	28	13	23	1	7	8	2
2003-04	Ottawa 67's	OHL	68	18	31	49	56	7	1	4	5	6
2004-05	Ottawa 67's	OHL	68	25	41	66	50	21	8	12	20	31
2005-06	Ottawa 67's	OHL	65	30	47	77	70	3	1	2	3	8
2006-07	Providence Bruins	AHL	7	1	2	3	0	....	....	....	....	....
	Alaska Aces	ECHL	66	20	33	53	54	15	9	11	20	8
2007-08	Peoria Rivermen	AHL	78	24	26	50	53	....	....	....	....	....
2008-09	Peoria Rivermen	AHL	65	20	23	43	43	7	0	1	1	4
2009-10	Peoria Rivermen	AHL	76	17	15	32	34	....	....	....	....	....

Signed as a free agent by **St. Louis**, March 19, 2008. Traded to **Colorado** by **St. Louis** for T.J. Hensick, June 17, 2010.

TANEV, Chris (TA-nehv, KRIHS) **VAN.**

Defense. Shoots right. 6'2", 183 lbs. Born, Toronto, Ont., December 20, 1989.

			Regular Season					Playoffs				
Season	Club	League	GP	G	A	Pts	PIM	GP	G	A	Pts	PIM
2006-07	Durham Fury	OPJHL	40	0	9	9	8	....	....	....	....	....
2007-08	Durham Fury	OPJHL	19	1	6	7	12	....	....	....	....	....
	Stouffville Spirit	OPJHL	4	0	0	0	0	....	....	....	....	....
	Markham Waxers	OPJHL	26	1	9	10	12	....	....	....	....	....
2008-09	Markham Waxers	OJHL	50	4	37	41	33	....	....	....	....	....
2009-10	RIT Tigers	AH	41	10	18	28	4	....	....	....	....	....

Signed as a free agent by **Vancouver**, May 31, 2010.

TAORMINA, Matt (tah'ohr-MEE-nah, MAT) **N.J.**

Defense. Shoots left. 5'10", 185 lbs. Born, Washington Township, MI, October 20, 1986.

			Regular Season					Playoffs				
Season	Club	League	GP	G	A	Pts	PIM	GP	G	A	Pts	PIM
2004-05	Texarkana Bandits	NAHL	52	14	30	44	44	....	....	....	....	....
2005-06	Providence College	H-East	36	1	10	11	16	....	....	....	....	....
2006-07	Providence College	H-East	35	5	2	7	6	....	....	....	....	....
2007-08	Providence College	H-East	36	9	18	27	12	....	....	....	....	....
2008-09	Providence College	H-East	34	5	15	20	16	....	....	....	....	....
	Binghamton	AHL	11	2	3	5	4	....	....	....	....	....
2009-10	Lowell Devils	AHL	75	10	40	50	45	5	1	3	4	4

Signed as a free agent by **Lowell** (AHL), August 20, 2009. Signed as a free agent by **New Jersey**, February 26, 2010.

TARASENKO, Vladimir (ta-rah-SEHN-koh, vla-DIH-meer) **ST.L.**

Right wing. Shoots left. 5'11", 185 lbs. Born, Yaroslavl, USSR, December 13, 1991.
(St. Louis' 2nd choice, 16th overall, in 2010 Entry Draft).

			Regular Season					Playoffs				
Season	Club	League	GP	G	A	Pts	PIM	GP	G	A	Pts	PIM
2007-08	Sibir Novosibirsk 2	Russia-3	17	6	4	10	2	....	....	....	....	....
2008-09	Sibir Novosibirsk 2	Russia-3	STATISTICS NOT AVAILABLE									
	Sibir Novosibirsk	Rus-KHL	38	7	3	10	2	....	....	....	....	....
2009-10	Novosibirsk Jr.	Russia-Jr.	1	1	0	1	0	....	....	....	....	....
	Sibir Novosibirsk	Rus-KHL	42	13	11	24	18	....	....	....	....	....

TARDY, Maxwell (TAHR-dee, MAX-wehl) **ST.L.**

Center. Shoots right. 6', 168 lbs. Born, Duluth, MN, October 27, 1990.
(St. Louis' 6th choice, 202nd overall, in 2009 Entry Draft).

			Regular Season					Playoffs				
Season	Club	League	GP	G	A	Pts	PIM	GP	G	A	Pts	PIM
2007-08	Duluth East	High-MN	9	1	3	4	8	....	....	....	....	....
2008-09	Duluth East	High-MN	30	35	25	60	24	....	....	....	....	....
	Team North	UMHSEL	24	19	20	39	....	....	....	....	....	....
2009-10	Tri-City Storm	USHL	52	12	24	36	34	3	0	1	1	4

• Signed Letter of Intent to attend **University of Minnesota-Duluth** (WCHA) in fall of 2010.

TATAR, Tomas (TAH-tahr, TAW-mahsh) **DET.**

Center. Shoots left. 5'10", 179 lbs. Born, Ilava, Czechoslovakia, December 1, 1990.
(Detroit's 2nd choice, 60th overall, in 2009 Entry Draft).

			Regular Season					Playoffs				
Season	Club	League	GP	G	A	Pts	PIM	GP	G	A	Pts	PIM
2004-05	Dubnica U18	Svk-U18	1	0	0	0	0	....	....	....	....	....
2005-06	Dubnica U18	Svk-U18	43	11	15	26	18	....	....	....	....	....
2006-07	Dubnica Jr.	Slovak-Jr.	6	3	0	3	2	....	....	....	....	....
	Dukla Trencin U18	Svk-U18	48	33	44	77	42	....	....	....	....	....
2007-08	Dukla Trencin U18	Svk-U18	4	9	4	13	0	....	....	....	....	....
	Dukla Trencin Jr.	Slovak-Jr.	42	41	35	76	32	....	....	....	....	....
2008-09	HC 07 Detva	Slovak-2	1	1	1	2	2	....	....	....	....	....
	HKm Zvolen	Slovakia	48	7	8	15	20	13	5	3	8	4
2009-10	Grand Rapids	AHL	58	16	16	32	12	....	....	....	....	....

TEDENBY, Mattias (TEH-dehn-bew, muh-TIGH-uhs) **N.J.**

Left wing. Shoots left. 5'10", 175 lbs. Born, Vetlanda, Sweden, February 21, 1990.
(New Jersey's 1st choice, 24th overall, in 2008 Entry Draft).

			Regular Season					Playoffs				
Season	Club	League	GP	G	A	Pts	PIM	GP	G	A	Pts	PIM
2005-06	HV 71 U18	Swe-U18	13	8	7	15	24	5	1	0	1	10
2006-07	HV 71 U18	Swe-U18	2	4	0	4	2	5	7	2	9	14
	HV 71 Jr.	Swe-Jr.	27	10	10	20	43	4	3	1	4	2
2007-08	HV 71 U18	Swe-U18	1	1	0	1	0	....	....	....	....	....
	HV 71 Jr.	Swe-Jr.	25	14	16	30	14	2	0	0	0	0
	HV 71 Jonkoping	Sweden	23	3	3	6	6	5	0	0	0	0
2008-09	IK Oskarshamn	Sweden-2	13	2	9	11	6	....	....	....	....	....
	HV 71 Jonkoping	Sweden	32	3	1	4	6	18	6	3	9	6
2009-10	HV 71 Jonkoping	Sweden	44	12	7	19	30	16	2	3	5	6

TELEGIN, Ivan (tuh-LEH-gihn, ih-VUHN) **ATL.**

Left wing. Shoots left. 6'3", 185 lbs. Born, Novokuznetsk, Russia, February 28, 1992.
(Atlanta's 3rd choice, 101st overall, in 2010 Entry Draft).

			Regular Season					Playoffs				
Season	Club	League	GP	G	A	Pts	PIM	GP	G	A	Pts	PIM
2008-09	Novokuznetsk 2	Russia-3	STATISTICS NOT AVAILABLE									
2009-10	Saginaw Spirit	OHL	51	26	18	44	20	6	1	1	2	6

TERESCHENKO, Alexei (teh-reh-SHEHN-koh, al-EHX-ay) **DAL.**

Center. Shoots left. 5'11", 176 lbs. Born, Mozhaisk, USSR, December 16, 1980.
(Dallas' 4th choice, 91st overall, in 2000 Entry Draft).

			Regular Season					Playoffs				
Season	Club	League	GP	G	A	Pts	PIM	GP	G	A	Pts	PIM
1996-97	Dyn'o Moscow 2	Russia-3	9	0	0	0	2	....	....	....	....	....
1997-98	Dynamo Moscow	Russia	26	6	7	13	30	....	....	....	....	....
1998-99	Dyn'o Moscow 2	Russia-3	28	4	17	21	20	....	....	....	....	....
	THK Tver	Russia-2	12	3	4	7	4	....	....	....	....	....
	Dynamo Moscow	Russia	1	0	1	1	0	2	0	0	0	0
99-2000	Dynamo Moscow	Russia	27	1	1	2	10	17	1	1	2	8
2000-01	Dynamo Moscow	Russia	39	3	2	5	18	....	....	....	....	....
2001-02	Yaroslavl 2	Russia-3	1	0	0	0	0	....	....	....	....	....
	Dynamo Moscow	Russia	40	3	6	9	20	3	0	0	0	0
2002-03	Dynamo Moscow	Russia	40	7	9	16	14	5	1	0	1	2
2003-04	Dynamo Moscow	Russia	47	8	12	20	26	3	0	0	0	4
2004-05	Dynamo Moscow	Russia	31	3	6	9	8	10	0	1	1	2
2005-06	Ak Bars Kazan	Russia	36	3	12	15	12	10	0	4	4	12
2006-07	Ak Bars Kazan	Russia	53	8	22	30	38	16	3	6	9	6
2007-08	Ufa	Russia	51	16	24	40	22	16	5	4	9	6
2008-09	Ufa	Rus-KHL	55	29	29	58	22	4	0	1	1	8
2009-10	Ak Bars Kazan	Rus-KHL	52	12	13	25	18	22	2	5	7	6

TERNAVSKY, Artem (tuhr-NAV-skee, AHR-tehm) **WSH.**

Defense. Shoots left. 6'2", 208 lbs. Born, Magnitogorsk, USSR, June 2, 1983.
(Washington's 4th choice, 160th overall, in 2001 Entry Draft).

			Regular Season					Playoffs				
Season	Club	League	GP	G	A	Pts	PIM	GP	G	A	Pts	PIM
99-2000	CSKA Moscow 2	Russia-3	2	0	1	1	0	....	....	....	....	....
	HK Moscow 2	Russia-3	25	0	4	4	42	....	....	....	....	....
2000-01	Sherbrooke	QMJHL	65	3	15	18	143	....	....	....	....	....
2001-02	Mostovik Kurgan	Russia-2	25	0	0	0	46	....	....	....	....	....
2002-03	Sibir Novosibirsk	Russia	42	1	1	2	20	....	....	....	....	....
2003-04	Ufa	Russia	12	0	0	0	4	....	....	....	....	....
	Magnitogorsk 2	Russia-3	7	1	0	1	0	....	....	....	....	....
2004-05	Nizhny Novgorod	Russia-2	16	0	1	1	18	....	....	....	....	....
	Motor Barnaul	Russia-2	8	0	1	1	14	....	....	....	....	....
2005-06	Karaganda	Kazakh.	17	1	1	2	12	....	....	....	....	....
	Karaganda	Russia-2	39	3	2	5	26	6	0	1	1	2
2006-07	Gazovik Tyumen	Russia-2	56	3	12	15	78	3	1	0	1	4
	Ust-Kamenogorsk	Kazakh.	14	3	2	5	12	....	....	....	....	....
2007-08	Novokuznetsk	Russia	56	6	7	13	46	....	....	....	....	....
2008-09	CSKA Moscow	Rus-KHL	53	4	3	7	40	8	0	0	0	8
2009-10	Novokuznetsk	Rus-KHL	14	0	1	1	8	....	....	....	....	....
	Dynamo Minsk	Rus-KHL	2	0	0	0	0	....	....	....	....	....
	Vityaz Chekhov	Rus-KHL	11	0	1	1	10	....	....	....	....	....

TERRY, Chris (TAIR-ee, KRIHS) **CAR.**

Left wing. Shoots left. 5'10", 190 lbs. Born, Brampton, Ont., April 7, 1989.
(Carolina's 4th choice, 132nd overall, in 2007 Entry Draft).

			Regular Season					Playoffs				
Season	Club	League	GP	G	A	Pts	PIM	GP	G	A	Pts	PIM
2003-04	Markham	GTHL	66	39	50	89	....	....	....	....	....	....
2004-05	Markham	GTHL	60	42	53	95	113	9	0	9	9	14
2005-06	Plymouth Whalers	OHL	64	9	19	28	72	11	3	2	5	4
2006-07	Plymouth Whalers	OHL	68	22	44	66	98	20	8	10	18	21
2007-08	Plymouth Whalers	OHL	68	44	57	101	107	4	4	3	7	6
	Albany River Rats	AHL	1	0	0	0	0	....	....	....	....	....
2008-09	Plymouth Whalers	OHL	53	39	55	94	75	11	7	9	16	18
2009-10	Albany River Rats	AHL	80	17	30	47	47	8	2	4	6	0

TESTWUIDE, Mike (TEHST-wud, MIGHK) **PHI.**

Right wing. Shoots right. 6'3", 220 lbs. Born, Vail, CO, February 5, 1987.

			Regular Season					Playoffs				
Season	Club	League	GP	G	A	Pts	PIM	GP	G	A	Pts	PIM
2004-05	Waterloo	USHL	46	2	8	10	43	....	....	....	....	....
2005-06	Waterloo	USHL	54	18	13	31	88	....	....	....	....	....
2006-07	Colorado College	WCHA	29	8	2	10	25	....	....	....	....	....
2007-08	Colorado College	WCHA	33	11	10	21	31	....	....	....	....	....
2008-09	Colorado College	WCHA	36	4	5	9	20	....	....	....	....	....
2009-10	Colorado College	WCHA	36	21	10	31	26	....	....	....	....	....

Signed as a free agent by **Philadelphia**, March 19, 2010.

TEUBERT, Colten (TEW-buhrt, KOHL-tuhn) L.A.

Defense. Shoots right. 6'4", 194 lbs. Born, White Rock, B.C., March 8, 1990.
(Los Angeles' 2nd choice, 13th overall, in 2008 Entry Draft).

			Regular Season					Playoffs				
Season	Club	League	GP	G	A	Pts	PIM	GP	G	A	Pts	PIM
2005-06	South West Hawks	Minor-BC	29	8	12	20	122	....	....	....	....	....
	Regina Pats	WHL	14	0	2	2	16	6	0	1	1	4
2006-07	Regina Pats	WHL	63	3	8	11	91	10	0	1	1	13
2007-08	Regina Pats	WHL	66	7	16	23	135	6	1	4	5	6
2008-09	Regina Pats	WHL	60	12	25	37	136	....	....	....	....	....
	Ontario Reign	ECHL	8	0	1	1	10	6	0	1	1	19
2009-10	Regina Pats	WHL	60	10	30	40	115	....	....	....	....	....
	Ontario Reign	ECHL	10	1	2	3	10	....	....	....	....	....

THANG, Ryan (THAYNG, RIGH-uhn) NSH.

Left wing. Shoots right. 5'11", 189 lbs. Born, Chicago, IL, May 11, 1987.
(Nashville's 4th choice, 81st overall, in 2007 Entry Draft).

			Regular Season					Playoffs				
Season	Club	League	GP	G	A	Pts	PIM	GP	G	A	Pts	PIM
2004-05	Sioux Falls	USHL	58	9	22	31	45	....	....	....	....	....
2005-06	Sioux Falls	USHL	32	8	14	22	52	....	....	....	....	....
	Omaha Lancers	USHL	25	15	15	30	26	5	2	1	3	2
2006-07	U. of Notre Dame	CCHA	42	20	21	41	22	....	....	....	....	....
2007-08	U. of Notre Dame	CCHA	47	18	14	32	48	....	....	....	....	....
2008-09	U. of Notre Dame	CCHA	33	10	9	19	36	....	....	....	....	....
2009-10	U. of Notre Dame	CCHA	37	9	14	23	55	....	....	....	....	....
	Milwaukee	AHL	12	3	3	6	4	7	1	3	4	2

CCHA All-Rookie Team (2007)

THERIAU, Alex (TAIR-ee-oh, Al-ehx) DAL.

Defense. Shoots left. 6'2", 189 lbs. Born, Duncan, B.C., February 14, 1992.
(Dallas' 4th choice, 109th overall, in 2010 Entry Draft).

			Regular Season					Playoffs				
Season	Club	League	GP	G	A	Pts	PIM	GP	G	A	Pts	PIM
2007-08	Valley West Hawks	BCMML	37	7	22	29	77	....	....	....	....	....
	Lethbridge	WHL	4	0	0	0	2	....	....	....	....	....
2008-09	Lethbridge	WHL	29	0	4	4	17	....	....	....	....	....
	Everett Silvertips	WHL	26	1	0	1	11	1	0	0	0	0
2009-10	Everett Silvertips	WHL	70	4	20	24	68	7	0	2	2	4

THOMAS, Christian (TAW-mas, KRIHS-ch'yehn) NYR

Right wing. Shoots right. 5'9", 164 lbs. Born, Toronto, Ont., May 26, 1992.
(NY Rangers' 2nd choice, 40th overall, in 2010 Entry Draft).

			Regular Season					Playoffs				
Season	Club	League	GP	G	A	Pts	PIM	GP	G	A	Pts	PIM
2007-08	Toronto Marlboros	GTHL	52	32	34	66	36	....	....	....	....	....
2008-09	London Knights	OHL	32	4	7	11	4	....	....	....	....	....
	Oshawa Generals	OHL	27	4	10	14	10	....	....	....	....	....
2009-10	Oshawa Generals	OHL	64	41	25	66	27	....	....	....	....	....

TIMMINS, Scott (TIHM-mihnz, SKAWT) FLA.

Center. Shoots left. 5'11", 191 lbs. Born, Hamilton, Ont., September 11, 1989.
(Florida's 7th choice, 165th overall, in 2009 Entry Draft).

			Regular Season					Playoffs				
Season	Club	League	GP	G	A	Pts	PIM	GP	G	A	Pts	PIM
2005-06	Burlington	OPJHL	31	8	4	12	8	4	1	1	2	0
2006-07	Kitchener Rangers	OHL	42	2	5	7	8	....	....	....	....	....
2007-08	Kitchener Rangers	OHL	62	17	12	29	46	20	3	5	8	10
2008-09	Kitchener Rangers	OHL	38	25	24	49	28	....	....	....	....	....
	Windsor Spitfires	OHL	28	10	14	24	33	20	6	10	16	26
2009-10	Windsor Spitfires	OHL	56	30	24	54	47	19	11	11	22	18

TINORDI, Jarred (tih-NOHR-dee, JAIR-uhd) MTL.

Defense. Shoots left. 6'6", 205 lbs. Born, Millersville, MD, February 20, 1992.
(Montreal's 1st choice, 22nd overall, in 2010 Entry Draft).

			Regular Season					Playoffs				
Season	Club	League	GP	G	A	Pts	PIM	GP	G	A	Pts	PIM
2008-09	USNTDP	NAHL	42	2	13	15	53	9	1	0	1	6
	USNTDP	U-17	16	3	1	4	12	....	....	....	....	....
	USNTDP	U-18	1	0	1	1	0	....	....	....	....	....
2009-10	USNTDP	USHL	26	4	5	9	68	....	....	....	....	....
	USNTDP	U-18	39	2	6	8	37	....	....	....	....	....

• Signed Letter of Intent to attend **University of Notre Dame** (CCHA) in fall of 2010.

TKACHENKO, Ivan (t'kuh-CHEHN-koh, ee-VAHN) CBJ

Left wing. Shoots left. 5'10", 187 lbs. Born, Yaroslavl, USSR, November 9, 1979.
(Columbus' 5th choice, 98th overall, in 2002 Entry Draft).

			Regular Season					Playoffs				
Season	Club	League	GP	G	A	Pts	PIM	GP	G	A	Pts	PIM
1997-98	Yaroslavl 2	Russia-2	STATISTICS NOT AVAILABLE									
	Torpedo Yaroslavl	Russia	....	....	....	....	....	1	0	0	0	0
1998-99	Yaroslavl 2	Russia-3	28	15	13	28	26	....	....	....	....	....
99-2000	Yaroslavl 2	Russia-3	1	1	0	1	0	....	....	....	....	....
	Motor Zavolzhje	Russia-2	43	15	14	29	22	....	....	....	....	....
	Nizhnekamsk 2	Russia-3	8	6	3	9	24	....	....	....	....	....
	Nizhnekamsk	Russia	5	1	0	1	0	4	0	1	1	0
2000-01	Nizhnekamsk	Russia	28	2	2	4	14	4	0	1	1	0
2001-02	Yaroslavl 2	Russia-3	1	0	1	1	2	....	....	....	....	....
	Yaroslavl	Russia	44	13	20	33	57	9	5	2	7	4
2002-03	Yaroslavl	Russia	44	11	6	17	57	10	2	3	5	6
2003-04	Yaroslavl	Russia	56	7	11	18	22	3	0	0	0	0
2004-05	Yaroslavl	Russia	59	15	15	30	30	9	2	3	5	8
2005-06	Yaroslavl	Russia	45	10	21	31	30	11	1	2	3	16
	Yaroslavl 2	Russia-3	1	0	1	1	2	....	....	....	....	....
2006-07	Yaroslavl	Russia	52	9	24	33	30	7	1	2	3	6
2007-08	Yaroslavl	Russia	56	14	15	29	34	16	1	3	4	6
2008-09	Yaroslavl	Rus-KHL	56	14	13	27	40	19	3	5	8	10
2009-10	Yaroslavl	Rus-KHL	56	6	16	22	34	17	3	4	7	8

TOCHKIN, Kellan (TAWCH-kihn, KEHL-uhn) VAN.

Right wing. Shoots right. 5'10", 170 lbs. Born, Abbotsford, B.C., February 15, 1991.

			Regular Season					Playoffs				
Season	Club	League	GP	G	A	Pts	PIM	GP	G	A	Pts	PIM
2006-07	Fraser Valley	BCMML	37	34	34	68	48	....	....	....	....	....
	Everett Silvertips	WHL	3	0	0	0	2	....	....	....	....	....
2007-08	Ridge Meadow	PIJHL	32	24	35	59	56	10	3	8	11	2
	Langley Chiefs	BCHL	1	0	1	1	0	....	....	....	....	....
2008-09	Everett Silvertips	WHL	72	20	54	74	37	2	1	0	1	2
2009-10	Everett Silvertips	WHL	72	28	40	68	64	7	1	1	2	11

Signed as a free agent by **Vancouver**, July 27, 2009.

TOEWS, David (TAYVZ, DAY-vihd) NYI

Center. Shoots right. 5'10", 191 lbs. Born, Winnipeg, Man., June 7, 1990.
(NY Islanders' 5th choice, 66th overall, in 2008 Entry Draft).

			Regular Season					Playoffs				
Season	Club	League	GP	G	A	Pts	PIM	GP	G	A	Pts	PIM
2005-06	Colorado Outlaws	Minor-CO	STATISTICS NOT AVAILABLE									
2006-07	Shat.-St. Mary's	High-MN	61	34	47	81	52	....	....	....	....	....
2007-08	Shat.-St. Mary's	High-MN	51	44	56	100	20	....	....	....	....	....
2008-09	North Dakota	WCHA	23	5	6	11	4	....	....	....	....	....
2009-10	North Dakota	WCHA	32	4	11	15	12	....	....	....	....	....

TOFFOLI, Tyler (TAW-foh-lee, TIGH-luhr) L.A.

Center. Shoots right. 6', 178 lbs. Born, Scarborough, Ont., April 24, 1992.
(Los Angeles' 2nd choice, 47th overall, in 2010 Entry Draft).

			Regular Season					Playoffs				
Season	Club	League	GP	G	A	Pts	PIM	GP	G	A	Pts	PIM
2007-08	Tor. Jr. Canadiens	GTHL	83	68	106	174	72	....	....	....	....	....
2008-09	Ottawa 67's	OHL	54	17	29	46	16	7	2	6	8	4
2009-10	Ottawa 67's	OHL	65	37	42	79	54	12	7	6	13	10

TOPOL, Sergei (TOH-puhl, SAIR-gay) VAN.

Center. Shoots left. 6'1", 183 lbs. Born, Omsk, USSR, February 15, 1985.
(Vancouver's 8th choice, 252nd overall, in 2003 Entry Draft).

			Regular Season					Playoffs				
Season	Club	League	GP	G	A	Pts	PIM	GP	G	A	Pts	PIM
2002-03	Omsk 2	Russia-3	45	16	5	21	18	....	....	....	....	....
2003-04	Avangard Omsk	Russia	9	0	0	0	2	....	....	....	....	....
	Omsk 2	Russia-3	39	25	14	39	10	....	....	....	....	....
2004-05	Mechel	Russia-2	19	1	0	1	6	....	....	....	....	....
	Mechel 2	Russia-3	5	2	1	3	8	....	....	....	....	....
	Omsk 2	Russia-3	18	6	4	10	4	....	....	....	....	....
	Avangard Omsk	Russia	2	1	0	1	0	....	....	....	....	....
2005-06	Omsk 2	Russia-3	33	24	15	39	26	....	....	....	....	....
	Avangard Omsk	Russia	17	1	0	1	12	....	....	....	....	....
2006-07	Avangard Omsk 2	Russia-3	26	18	14	32	30	....	....	....	....	....
	Avangard Omsk	Russia	27	0	1	1	12	1	0	0	0	2
2007-08	Avtomobilist	Russia-2	16	0	7	7	10	....	....	....	....	....
	Avtomobilist 2	Russia-3	6	6	4	10	14	....	....	....	....	....
	Nizhny Tagil	Russia-2	6	1	0	1	0	....	....	....	....	....
2008-09	Yermak Angarsk	Russia-2	50	17	8	25	38	4	0	1	1	2
2009-10	Novokuznetsk	Rus-KHL	22	3	3	6	4	....	....	....	....	....

TORQUATO, Zack (tohr-KAH-toh, ZAK)

Center. Shoots right. 6', 195 lbs. Born, Sault Ste Marie, Ont., June 8, 1989.
(Detroit's 4th choice, 178th overall, in 2007 Entry Draft).

			Regular Season					Playoffs				
Season	Club	League	GP	G	A	Pts	PIM	GP	G	A	Pts	PIM
2004-05	Stratford Cullitons	OJHL-B	47	34	41	75	52	....	....	....	....	....
2005-06	Saginaw Spirit	OHL	65	19	18	37	56	4	1	0	1	6
2006-07	Saginaw Spirit	OHL	22	10	13	23	24	....	....	....	....	....
	Erie Otters	OHL	43	20	26	46	69	....	....	....	....	....
2007-08	Erie Otters	OHL	66	25	42	67	112	....	....	....	....	....
	Grand Rapids	AHL	11	1	0	1	8	....	....	....	....	....
2008-09	Erie Otters	OHL	66	29	34	63	78	5	2	4	6	11
	Grand Rapids	AHL	1	0	0	0	0	....	....	....	....	....
2009-10	Erie Otters	OHL	68	31	62	93	72	4	1	2	3	0
	Idaho Steelheads	ECHL	2	0	0	0	0	....	....	....	....	....

Signed as a free agent by **Rockford** (AHL), August 2, 2010.

TOUSIGNANT, Mathieu (TOO-saynt, ma-t'yoo) DAL.

Center. Shoots left. 6', 185 lbs. Born, St-Etienne De Lauzon, Que., November 21, 1989.

			Regular Season					Playoffs				
Season	Club	League	GP	G	A	Pts	PIM	GP	G	A	Pts	PIM
2004-05	Magog	QAAA	8	2	1	3	0	....	....	....	....	....
2005-06	Magog	QAAA	43	22	36	58	50	13	6	9	15	26
	Baie-Comeau	QMJHL	1	0	1	1	2	....	....	....	....	....
2006-07	Baie-Comeau	QMJHL	70	8	25	33	93	9	2	2	4	9
2007-08	Baie-Comeau	QMJHL	36	14	20	34	68	....	....	....	....	....
	P.E.I. Rocket	QMJHL	27	8	14	22	61	4	2	4	6	14
2008-09	P.E.I. Rocket	QMJHL	35	14	24	38	72	....	....	....	....	....
	Chicoutimi	QMJHL	33	15	24	39	73	4	1	1	2	11
2009-10	Texas Stars	AHL	45	4	3	7	62	....	....	....	....	....
	Idaho Steelheads	ECHL	20	6	11	17	53	13	1	2	3	27

Signed as a free agent by **Dallas**, March 24, 2010.

TREMBLAY, Nick (TRAWM-blay, NIHK-oh-las) BOS.

Center. Shoots left. 5'11", 190 lbs. Born, Ottawa, Ont., April 5, 1988.
(Boston's 5th choice, 173rd overall, in 2008 Entry Draft).

			Regular Season					Playoffs				
Season	Club	League	GP	G	A	Pts	PIM	GP	G	A	Pts	PIM
2005-06	Champlain College	QJHL	48	13	22	35	36	9	1	1	2	8
2006-07	Champlain College	QJHL	53	26	26	52	58	7	1	2	3	2
2007-08	Smiths Falls Bears	CJHL	57	*51	59	*110	12	9	5	8	13	10
2008-09	Clarkson Knights	ECAC	36	4	7	11	22	....	....	....	....	....
2009-10	Clarkson Knights	ECAC	37	3	17	20	12	....	....	....	....	....

TREVELYAN, T.J. (truh-VEHL-yuhn, TEE-JAY) **S.J.**

Left wing. Shoots left. 5'9", 180 lbs. Born, Mississauga, Ont., March 6, 1984.

			Regular Season					Playoffs				
Season	Club	League	GP	G	A	Pts	PIM	GP	G	A	Pts	PIM
2002-03	St. Lawrence	ECAC	34	10	12	22	38	....	....	....	....	....
2003-04	St. Lawrence	ECAC	38	*23	16	39	62	....	....	....	....	....
2004-05	St. Lawrence	ECAC	38	*25	20	45	61	....	....	....	....	....
2005-06	St. Lawrence	ECAC	40	20	28	*48	43	....	....	....	....	....
2006-07	Providence Bruins	AHL	60	28	24	52	41	13	3	6	9	12
	Long Beach	ECHL	15	9	8	17	16	....	....	....	....	....
2007-08	Providence Bruins	AHL	72	18	20	38	23	10	5	3	8	6
2008-09	Iowa Chops	AHL	76	23	24	47	18	....	....	....	....	....
2009-10	Worcester Sharks	AHL	63	28	16	44	16	8	4	2	6	2

ECAC First All-Star Team (2005, 2006) • ECAC Player of the Year (2006) • NCAA East First All-American Team (2006)

Signed as a free agent by **Boston**, August 17, 2006. Signed as a free agent by **San Jose**, May 28, 2010.

TRIVINO, Corey (trih-VEE-noh, KOH-ree) **NYI**

Center. Shoots left. 6'1", 170 lbs. Born, Etobicoke, Ont., January 12, 1990.
(NY Islanders' 2nd choice, 36th overall, in 2008 Entry Draft).

			Regular Season					Playoffs				
Season	Club	League	GP	G	A	Pts	PIM	GP	G	A	Pts	PIM
2005-06	Toronto Marlboros	GTHL	30	17	22	39	4	....	....	....	....	....
2006-07	Stouffville Spirit	OPJHL	49	24	34	58	24	9	1	6	7	16
2007-08	Stouffville Spirit	OPJHL	39	19	50	69	22	15	5	17	22	10
2008-09	Boston University	H-East	32	6	7	13	14	....	....	....	....	....
2009-10	Boston University	H-East	28	4	11	15	2	....	....	....	....	....

TROPP, Corey (TROHP, KOHR-ee) **BUF.**

Right wing. Shoots right. 6', 183 lbs. Born, Grosse Pointe, MI, July 25, 1989.
(Buffalo's 3rd choice, 89th overall, in 2007 Entry Draft).

			Regular Season					Playoffs				
Season	Club	League	GP	G	A	Pts	PIM	GP	G	A	Pts	PIM
2005-06	Sioux Falls	USHL	46	7	8	15	21	14	2	3	5	8
2006-07	Sioux Falls	USHL	54	26	36	62	76	8	4	9	*13	0
2007-08	Michigan State	CCHA	42	6	11	17	16	....	....	....	....	....
2008-09	Michigan State	CCHA	21	3	8	11	45	....	....	....	....	....
2009-10	Michigan State	CCHA	37	20	22	42	50	....	....	....	....	....

CCHA Second All-Star Team (2010)

TROTMAN, Zach (TRAWT-muhn, ZAK) **BOS.**

Defense. Shoots right. 6'3", 211 lbs. Born, Novi, MI, August 26, 1990.
(Boston's 8th choice, 210th overall, in 2010 Entry Draft).

			Regular Season					Playoffs				
Season	Club	League	GP	G	A	Pts	PIM	GP	G	A	Pts	PIM
2008-09	Wichita Falls	NAHL	47	2	4	6	79	5	0	1	1	8
2009-10	Lake Superior	CCHA	36	2	6	8	18	....	....	....	....	....

TRUKHNO, Vyacheslav (trookh-NOH, V'YTACH-ih-slav)

Left wing. Shoots left. 6'1", 197 lbs. Born, Khimki, USSR, February 22, 1987.
(Edmonton's 6th choice, 120th overall, in 2005 Entry Draft).

			Regular Season					Playoffs				
Season	Club	League	GP	G	A	Pts	PIM	GP	G	A	Pts	PIM
2002-03	Rungstead IK	Den-2	1	2	3	5	0	....	....	....	....	....
	Rungstead	Denmark	27	7	4	11	8	12	0	1	1	8
2003-04	Rungstead	Denmark	35	12	11	23	18	7	0	0	0	8
2004-05	P.E.I. Rocket	QMJHL	64	25	34	59	57	....	....	....	....	....
2005-06	P.E.I. Rocket	QMJHL	60	28	68	96	81	3	2	2	4	0
2006-07	Gatineau	QMJHL	60	25	77	102	67	5	0	6	6	19
2007-08	Springfield Falcons	AHL	64	14	21	35	44	....	....	....	....	....
2008-09	Springfield Falcons	AHL	56	7	19	26	35	....	....	....	....	....
2009-10	Springfield Falcons	AHL	73	12	14	26	57	....	....	....	....	....

QMJHL All-Rookie Team (2005) • Canadian Major Junior All-Rookie Team (2005) • QMJHL First All-Star Team (2007)

TRUNEV, Maxim (troo-NAWF, max-EEM) **MTL.**

Right wing. Shoots right. 5'11", 174 lbs. Born, Kirovo-Chepetsk, USSR, September 7, 1990.
(Montreal's 4th choice, 138th overall, in 2008 Entry Draft).

			Regular Season					Playoffs				
Season	Club	League	GP	G	A	Pts	PIM	GP	G	A	Pts	PIM
2005-06	Cherepovets 2	Russia-3	Statistics Not Available									
2006-07	Cherepovets 2	Russia-3	Statistics Not Available									
2007-08	Cherepovets 2	Russia-3	Statistics Not Available									
	Cherepovets	Russia	1	0	0	0	0	....	....	....	....	....
2008-09	Cherepovets	Rus-KHL	32	4	1	5	8	....	....	....	....	....
2009-10	Cherepovets	Rus-KHL	30	3	1	4	12	....	....	....	....	....
	Cherepovets Jr.	Russia-Jr.	14	10	14	24	58	3	1	0	1	2

TURNBULL, Joshua (TUHRN-buhl, JAWSH-oo-uh) **L.A.**

Center. Shoots right. 5'11", 172 lbs. Born, Hayward, WI, July 12, 1988.
(Los Angeles' 8th choice, 137th overall, in 2007 Entry Draft).

			Regular Season					Playoffs				
Season	Club	League	GP	G	A	Pts	PIM	GP	G	A	Pts	PIM
2005-06	Duluth East	High-MN	Statistics Not Available									
2006-07	Waterloo	USHL	60	25	29	54	66	9	3	1	4	12
2007-08	U. of Wisconsin	WCHA	37	4	7	11	44	....	....	....	....	....
2008-09	U. of Wisconsin	WCHA	24	4	2	6	26	....	....	....	....	....
2009-10	U. of Wisconsin	WCHA	12	2	0	2	10	....	....	....	....	....

USHL All-Rookie Team (2007)

TURNBULL, Travis (TUHRN-buhl, TRA-vihs) **BUF.**

Forward. Shoots right. 6', 197 lbs. Born, Chesterfield, MO, July 7, 1986.

			Regular Season					Playoffs				
Season	Club	League	GP	G	A	Pts	PIM	GP	G	A	Pts	PIM
2003-04	Sioux City	USHL	56	7	12	19	73	7	0	0	0	9
2004-05	Sioux City	USHL	44	17	21	38	103	13	4	2	6	61
2005-06	U. of Michigan	CCHA	41	9	9	18	67	....	....	....	....	....
2006-07	U. of Michigan	CCHA	41	8	9	17	54	....	....	....	....	....
2007-08	U. of Michigan	CCHA	43	15	12	27	48	....	....	....	....	....
2008-09	U. of Michigan	CCHA	41	8	20	28	74	....	....	....	....	....
	Portland Pirates	AHL	3	0	0	0	5	5	0	0	0	4
2009-10	Portland Pirates	AHL	57	9	9	18	98	4	0	0	0	2

Signed as a free agent by **Buffalo**, April 6, 2009.

TYRELL, Dana (TIH-rehl, DAY-nuh) **T.B.**

Center/Right wing. Shoots left. 5'11", 185 lbs. Born, Airdrie, Alta., April 23, 1989.
(Tampa Bay's 1st choice, 47th overall, in 2007 Entry Draft).

			Regular Season					Playoffs				
Season	Club	League	GP	G	A	Pts	PIM	GP	G	A	Pts	PIM
2003-04	Airdrie Xtreme	AMBHL	35	21	47	68	28	7	6	4	10	....
2004-05	UFA Bisons	AMHL	34	16	23	39	32	16	8	9	*17	....
	Prince George	WHL	1	0	0	0	2	....	....	....	....	....
2005-06	Prince George	WHL	69	7	11	18	44	5	0	0	0	2
2006-07	Prince George	WHL	72	30	26	56	51	15	1	6	7	4
2007-08	Prince George	WHL	68	25	40	65	47	....	....	....	....	....
	Norfolk Admirals	AHL	11	1	5	6	6	....	....	....	....	....
2008-09	Prince George	WHL	30	19	21	40	27	....	....	....	....	....
2009-10	Norfolk Admirals	AHL	74	9	27	36	22	....	....	....	....	....

ULLSTROM, David (UHL-struhm, DAY-vihd) **NYI**

Center. Shoots left. 6'3", 198 lbs. Born, Jonkoping, Sweden, April 22, 1989.
(NY Islanders' 9th choice, 102nd overall, in 2008 Entry Draft).

			Regular Season					Playoffs				
Season	Club	League	GP	G	A	Pts	PIM	GP	G	A	Pts	PIM
2005-06	HV 71 U18	Swe-U18	13	5	8	13	14	5	4	1	5	14
	HV 71 Jr.	Swe-Jr.	1	0	0	0	0	....	....	....	....	....
2006-07	HV 71 U18	Swe-U18	1	0	0	0	2	5	2	6	8	10
	HV 71 Jr.	Swe-Jr.	39	16	14	30	30	4	0	2	2	0
2007-08	HV 71 Jr.	Swe-Jr.	40	27	27	54	86	3	2	2	4	0
	HV 71 Jonkoping	Sweden	7	0	0	0	0	....	....	....	....	....
2008-09	HV 71 Jr.	Swe-Jr.	2	0	0	0	0	....	....	....	....	....
	Boras HC	Sweden-2	15	9	7	16	22	....	....	....	....	....
	HV 71 Jonkoping	Sweden	19	1	3	4	6	14	1	0	1	4
2009-10	HV 71 Jonkoping	Sweden	47	5	11	16	27	16	2	0	2	0
	HV 71 Jr.	Swe-Jr.	1	1	0	1	2	....	....	....	....	....

URBOM, Alexander (OOR-bohm, al-ehx-AN-duhr) **N.J.**

Defense. Shoots left. 6'5", 210 lbs. Born, Stockholm, Sweden, December 20, 1990.
(New Jersey's 3rd choice, 73rd overall, in 2009 Entry Draft).

			Regular Season					Playoffs				
Season	Club	League	GP	G	A	Pts	PIM	GP	G	A	Pts	PIM
2005-06	Djurgarden U18	Swe-U18	2	0	0	0	0	....	....	....	....	....
2006-07	Djurgarden U18	Swe-U18	31	6	11	17	36	3	0	1	1	2
2007-08	Djurgarden U18	Swe-U18	7	2	6	8	6	5	1	0	1	2
	Djurgarden Jr.	Swe-Jr.	39	3	8	11	54	7	0	1	1	2
2008-09	Djurgarden Jr.	Swe-Jr.	16	5	6	11	45	....	....	....	....	....
	Djurgarden	Sweden	28	0	0	0	2	....	....	....	....	....
	Djurgarden U18	Swe-U18	....	....	....	....	....	5	1	0	1	2
2009-10	Brandon	WHL	66	12	21	33	87	15	4	3	7	17

UTKIN, Dmitri (OOT-kihn, dih-MEE-tree) **BOS.**

Left wing. Shoots left. 6', 170 lbs. Born, Yaroslavl, USSR, June 10, 1984.
(Boston's 5th choice, 228th overall, in 2002 Entry Draft).

			Regular Season					Playoffs				
Season	Club	League	GP	G	A	Pts	PIM	GP	G	A	Pts	PIM
2000-01	Yaroslavl 2	Russia-3	49	12	1	13	10	....	....	....	....	....
2001-02	Yaroslavl 2	Russia-3	32	15	7	22	33	....	....	....	....	....
2002-03	Yaroslavl	Russia	4	0	1	1	0	....	....	....	....	....
2003-04	Spartak Moscow	Russia-2	57	10	10	20	8	13	3	3	6	2
2004-05	Keramin Minsk	BelOpen	8	2	0	2	31	....	....	....	....	....
	HK Brest	BelOpen	20	4	12	16	4	....	....	....	....	....
	HK Riga 2000	BelOpen	....	....	....	....	....	3	0	0	0	0
	HK Riga 2000	Latvia	....	....	....	....	....	6	3	2	5	0
2005-06	Spartak Moscow	Russia	33	3	1	4	4	2	0	0	0	0
	Spartak Moscow 2	Russia-3	10	5	2	7	8	....	....	....	....	....
2006-07	Chelyabinsk	Russia	50	6	8	14	20	....	....	....	....	....
2007-08	Chelyabinsk 2	Russia-3	16	4	3	7	2	....	....	....	....	....
	Chelyabinsk	Russia	5	1	0	1	2	....	....	....	....	....
	Avtomobilist	Russia-2	11	2	0	2	0	6	1	0	1	0
2008-09	Mechel	Russia-2	40	13	8	21	40	....	....	....	....	....
	Khanty-Mansiisk	Russia-2	8	4	3	7	0	16	2	7	9	4
2009-10	Khanty-Mansiisk	Russia-2	22	3	5	8	4	....	....	....	....	....
	Toros Neftekamsk	Russia-2	18	2	1	3	0	13	3	3	6	2

VAIVE, Justin (VIGHV, JUHS-tihn) **ANA.**

Left wing. Shoots left. 6'5", 213 lbs. Born, Buffalo, NY, July 8, 1989.
(Anaheim's 4th choice, 92nd overall, in 2007 Entry Draft).

			Regular Season					Playoffs				
Season	Club	League	GP	G	A	Pts	PIM	GP	G	A	Pts	PIM
2004-05	Toronto Marlboros	GTHL	72	38	64	102	....	....	....	....	....	....
2005-06	USNTDP	U-17	13	3	5	8	18	....	....	....	....	....
	USNTDP	NAHL	24	4	8	12	34	5	1	1	2	6
2006-07	USNTDP	U-18	43	7	8	15	49	....	....	....	....	....
	USNTDP	NAHL	15	4	1	5	22	....	....	....	....	....
2007-08	Miami U.	CCHA	41	3	7	10	65	....	....	....	....	....
2008-09	Miami U.	CCHA	37	6	6	12	44	....	....	....	....	....
2009-10	Miami U.	CCHA	43	5	3	8	51	....	....	....	....	....

VALENTENKO, Pavel (val-ehn-TEHN-koh, PAH-vehl) **NYR**

Defense. Shoots left. 6'2", 220 lbs. Born, Nizhnekamsk, USSR, October 20, 1987.
(Montreal's 5th choice, 139th overall, in 2006 Entry Draft).

			Regular Season					Playoffs				
Season	Club	League	GP	G	A	Pts	PIM	GP	G	A	Pts	PIM
2002-03	Lada Togliatti 2	Russia-3	6	0	0	0	4	....	....	....	....	....
2003-04	Nizhnekamsk 2	Russia-3	26	0	1	1	28	....	....	....	....	....
2004-05	Nizhnekamsk 2	Russia-3	Statistics Not Available									
2005-06	Nizhnekamsk 2	Russia-3	Statistics Not Available									
	Nizhnekamsk	Russia	2	0	0	0	2	....	....	....	....	....
2006-07	Nizhnekamsk	Russia	50	0	2	2	62	4	0	0	0	2
2007-08	Hamilton Bulldogs	AHL	57	1	15	16	58	....	....	....	....	....
2008-09	Hamilton Bulldogs	AHL	4	0	2	2	2	....	....	....	....	....
	Dynamo Moscow	Rus-KHL	8	0	1	1	8	1	0	0	0	2
2009-10	Dynamo Moscow	Rus-KHL	7	0	0	0	2	....	....	....	....	....

• Missed majority of 2008-09 season for personal reasons. Signed as a free agent by **Dynamo Moscow** (Russia-KHL), October 31, 2008. Traded to **NY Rangers** by **Montreal** with Christopher Higgins and Ryan McDonagh for Scott Gomez, Tom Pyatt and Michael Busto, June 30, 2009.

VALENTINE, Scott (VAL-ehn-tighn, SKAWT) ANA.

Defense. Shoots left. 6', 196 lbs. Born, Ottawa, Ont., May 2, 1991.
(Anaheim's 7th choice, 166th overall, in 2009 Entry Draft).

			Regular Season					Playoffs				
Season	Club	League	GP	G	A	Pts	PIM	GP	G	A	Pts	PIM
2007-08	Hawkesbury	CJHL	51	2	15	17	81	11	3	4	7	18
	London Knights	OHL	3	0	0	0	2	....	....	....	....	....
2008-09	London Knights	OHL	17	0	0	0	20	....	....	....	....	....
	Oshawa Generals	OHL	26	1	8	9	51	....	....	....	....	....
2009-10	Oshawa Generals	OHL	63	5	14	19	82	....	....	....	....	....

VANDE VELDE, Chris (VAN-deh VEHLD, KRIHS) EDM.

Center. Shoots left. 6'2", 190 lbs. Born, Moorhead, MN, March 15, 1987.
(Edmonton's 5th choice, 97th overall, in 2005 Entry Draft).

			Regular Season					Playoffs				
Season	Club	League	GP	G	A	Pts	PIM	GP	G	A	Pts	PIM
2003-04	Moorhead Spuds	High-MN	29	19	24	43	....	....	....	....	....	....
2004-05	Moorhead Spuds	High-MN	30	35	32	67	28	....	....	....	....	....
	Lincoln Stars	USHL	7	1	4	5	0	4	0	2	2	0
2005-06	Lincoln Stars	USHL	56	16	20	36	70	9	1	3	4	10
2006-07	North Dakota	WCHA	38	3	6	9	37	....	....	....	....	....
2007-08	North Dakota	WCHA	43	15	17	32	38	....	....	....	....	....
2008-09	North Dakota	WCHA	43	18	17	35	69	....	....	....	....	....
2009-10	North Dakota	WCHA	42	16	25	41	22	....	....	....	....	....

VARONE, Philip (vah-ROHN, FIHL-ihp) S.J.

Center. Shoots left. 5'10", 186 lbs. Born, Vaughan, Ont., December 4, 1990.
(San Jose's 3rd choice, 147th overall, in 2009 Entry Draft).

			Regular Season					Playoffs				
Season	Club	League	GP	G	A	Pts	PIM	GP	G	A	Pts	PIM
2006-07	Kitchener	OJHL-B	20	10	11	21	21	....	....	....	....	....
	Kitchener Rangers	OHL	13	1	3	4	2	....	....	....	....	....
2007-08	Kitchener Rangers	OHL	35	5	20	25	12	....	....	....	....	....
	London Knights	OHL	31	10	26	36	14	5	1	1	2	7
2008-09	London Knights	OHL	58	19	33	52	32	14	10	9	19	19
2009-10	London Knights	OHL	31	9	22	31	17	....	....	....	....	....

VASYUNOV, Alexander (vahs-YUH-nawv, al-EHX-AN-duhr) N.J.

Left wing. Shoots right. 6'1", 210 lbs. Born, Yaroslavl, USSR, April 22, 1988.
(New Jersey's 2nd choice, 58th overall, in 2006 Entry Draft).

			Regular Season					Playoffs				
Season	Club	League	GP	G	A	Pts	PIM	GP	G	A	Pts	PIM
2004-05	Yaroslavl 2	Russia-3	28	10	2	12	6	....	....	....	....	....
2005-06	Yaroslavl 2	Russia-3	29	29	6	35	14	....	....	....	....	....
	Yaroslavl	Russia	2	0	0	0	2	....	....	....	....	....
2006-07	Yaroslavl 2	Russia-3	30	16	9	25	52	....	....	....	....	....
	Yaroslavl	Russia	17	0	0	0	4	....	....	....	....	....
2007-08	Yaroslavl	Russia	22	4	0	4	4	16	2	0	2	2
2008-09	Yaroslavl	Rus-KHL	2	0	0	0	0	....	....	....	....	....
	Lowell Devils	AHL	69	15	13	28	12	....	....	....	....	....
2009-10	Lowell Devils	AHL	68	16	22	38	10	5	2	2	4	0

VATANEN, Sami (VAH-ta-nehn, SA-mee) ANA.

Defense. Shoots right. 5'9", 163 lbs. Born, Jyvaskyla, Finland, June 3, 1991.
(Anaheim's 5th choice, 106th overall, in 2009 Entry Draft).

			Regular Season					Playoffs				
Season	Club	League	GP	G	A	Pts	PIM	GP	G	A	Pts	PIM
2006-07	JyP Jyvaskyla U18	Fin-U18	....	....	....	....	....	7	1	0	1	2
2007-08	JyP Jyvaskyla U18	Fin-U18	35	9	29	38	30	1	0	0	0	0
	JyP Jyvaskyla Jr.	Fin-Jr.	....	....	....	....	....	2	0	0	0	0
2008-09	JyP Jyvaskyla U18	Fin-U18	2	0	0	0	0	1	1	1	2	14
	Suomi U20	Finland-2	2	0	0	0	2	....	....	....	....	....
	D Team Jyvaskyla	Finland-2	5	1	1	2	8	....	....	....	....	....
	JyP Jyvaskyla Jr.	Fin-Jr.	20	3	7	10	22	....	....	....	....	....
2009-10	JYP Jyvaskyla	Finland	55	7	23	30	44	14	3	4	7	6
	Suomi U20	Finland-2	1	0	0	0	2	....	....	....	....	....

VEILLEUX, Keven (VAY-oo, KEH-vihn) PIT.

Center. Shoots right. 6'5", 202 lbs. Born, Saint-Renee, Que., June 27, 1989.
(Pittsburgh's 2nd choice, 51st overall, in 2007 Entry Draft).

			Regular Season					Playoffs				
Season	Club	League	GP	G	A	Pts	PIM	GP	G	A	Pts	PIM
2004-05	Levis	QAAA	11	1	0	1	0	2	0	1	1	0
2005-06	Levis	QAAA	26	12	23	35	53	....	....	....	....	....
	Victoriaville Tigres	QMJHL	33	2	13	15	4	5	0	1	1	2
2006-07	Victoriaville Tigres	QMJHL	70	20	35	55	53	6	1	5	6	4
2007-08	Victoriaville Tigres	QMJHL	42	10	32	42	54	....	....	....	....	....
	Rimouski Oceanic	QMJHL	19	7	15	22	22	9	3	4	7	2
2008-09	Rimouski Oceanic	QMJHL	29	15	33	48	47	13	7	12	19	31
2009-10	Wilkes-Barre	AHL	9	2	1	3	12	....	....	....	....	....

• Missed majority of 2009-10 season recovering from shoulder injury.

VELISCHEK, Alex (VEHL-ih-shehk, Al-ehx) PIT.

Defense. Shoots left. 6', 200 lbs. Born, Quebec City, Que., December 17, 1990.
(Pittsburgh's 5th choice, 123rd overall, in 2009 Entry Draft).

			Regular Season					Playoffs				
Season	Club	League	GP	G	A	Pts	PIM	GP	G	A	Pts	PIM
2005-06	Delbarton	High-NJ	26	8	14	22	18	....	....	....	....	....
2006-07	Delbarton	High-NJ	24	12	14	26	26	....	....	....	....	....
2007-08	Delbarton	High-NJ	27	9	14	23	36	....	....	....	....	....
2008-09	Delbarton	High-NJ	30	16	35	51	42	....	....	....	....	....
2009-10	Providence College	H-East	34	1	11	12	44	....	....	....	....	....

VEY, Linden (VAY, LIHN-duhn) L.A.

Right wing. Shoots right. 6', 189 lbs. Born, Wakaw, Sask., July 17, 1991.
(Los Angeles' 5th choice, 96th overall, in 2009 Entry Draft).

			Regular Season					Playoffs				
Season	Club	League	GP	G	A	Pts	PIM	GP	G	A	Pts	PIM
2006-07	Beardy's	SMHL	44	28	44	72	26	....	....	....	....	....
	Medicine Hat	WHL	2	0	0	0	2	....	....	....	....	....
2007-08	Medicine Hat	WHL	48	8	9	17	21	5	0	1	1	2
2008-09	Medicine Hat	WHL	71	24	48	72	20	11	2	5	7	2
2009-10	Medicine Hat	WHL	72	24	51	75	34	12	2	6	8	8

VIEDENSKY, Marek (vee-ehd-EHN-skee, MAR-ehk) S.J.

Center. Shoots right. 6'4", 195 lbs. Born, Handlova, Czechoslovakia, August 18, 1990.
(San Jose's 4th choice, 189th overall, in 2009 Entry Draft).

			Regular Season					Playoffs				
Season	Club	League	GP	G	A	Pts	PIM	GP	G	A	Pts	PIM
2004-05	Prievidza U18	Svk-U18	10	2	1	3	2	....	....	....	....	....
2005-06	Prievidza U18	Svk-U18	31	18	18	36	18	....	....	....	....	....
2006-07	Dukla Trencin U18	Svk-U18	12	6	12	18	6	....	....	....	....	....
	Dukla Trencin Jr.	Slovak-Jr.	30	5	3	8	8	7	1	1	2	16
2007-08	Dukla Trencin U18	Svk-U18	2	0	1	1	0	....	....	....	....	....
	Dukla Trencin Jr.	Slovak-Jr.	33	11	15	26	24	7	1	1	2	6
2008-09	Prince George	WHL	59	16	24	40	34	4	2	0	2	2
2009-10	Prince George	WHL	31	4	21	25	37	....	....	....	....	....
	Saskatoon Blades	WHL	30	16	18	34	27	10	7	3	10	0

VIGILANTE, John (vih-jih-LAN-tee, JAWN)

Left wing. Shoots left. 6', 190 lbs. Born, Dearborn, MI, May 24, 1985.

			Regular Season					Playoffs				
Season	Club	League	GP	G	A	Pts	PIM	GP	G	A	Pts	PIM
2002-03	Plymouth Whalers	OHL	65	15	24	39	31	18	6	3	9	8
2003-04	Plymouth Whalers	OHL	66	30	38	68	25	9	1	7	8	8
2004-05	Plymouth Whalers	OHL	68	24	38	62	17	4	0	0	0	0
2005-06	Plymouth Whalers	OHL	55	24	53	77	34	13	4	12	16	0
2006-07	Milwaukee	AHL	62	8	19	27	10	2	0	0	0	2
2007-08	Milwaukee	AHL	73	15	31	46	12	6	0	1	1	0
2008-09	Syracuse Crunch	AHL	52	7	8	15	14	....	....	....	....	....
	Quad City Flames	AHL	24	7	8	15	2	....	....	....	....	....
2009-10	Grand Rapids	AHL	79	11	14	25	31	....	....	....	....	....

Signed as a free agent by **Nashville**, December 7, 2005. Signed as a free agent by **Columbus**, July 8, 2008. Signed as a free agent by **Grand Rapids** (AHL), September 11, 2009.

VINCOUR, Tomas (VIHN-tsoh-oor, TAW-mahsh) DAL.

Center. Shoots right. 6'2", 199 lbs. Born, Brno, Czechoslovakia, November 19, 1990.
(Dallas' 4th choice, 129th overall, in 2009 Entry Draft).

			Regular Season					Playoffs				
Season	Club	League	GP	G	A	Pts	PIM	GP	G	A	Pts	PIM
2004-05	Brno U17	CzR-U17	42	23	13	36	36	....	....	....	....	....
2005-06	Brno U17	CzR-U17	21	13	14	27	77	....	....	....	....	....
	Brno Jr.	CzRep-Jr.	28	8	10	18	61	....	....	....	....	....
	Brno	CzRep-2	1	0	0	0	0	....	....	....	....	....
2006-07	Brno U17	CzR-U17	1	0	0	0	0	2	0	2	2	0
	Brno Jr.	CzRep-Jr.	41	15	24	39	58	....	....	....	....	....
	Brno	CzRep-2	4	0	1	1	0	....	....	....	....	....
2007-08	Edmonton	WHL	65	16	23	39	36	....	....	....	....	....
2008-09	Edmonton	WHL	49	17	19	36	23	....	....	....	....	....
2009-10	Edmonton	WHL	33	17	9	26	31	....	....	....	....	....
	Vancouver Giants	WHL	24	12	10	22	17	15	7	6	13	8

VISHNYAKOV, Albert (vihsh-nyeh-KAWF, al-BAIRT) T.B.

Left wing. Shoots right. 6', 185 lbs. Born, Almyetevsk, USSR, December 30, 1983.
(Tampa Bay's 9th choice, 273rd overall, in 2003 Entry Draft).

			Regular Season					Playoffs				
Season	Club	League	GP	G	A	Pts	PIM	GP	G	A	Pts	PIM
99-2000	Almetjevsk 2	Russia-3	41	11	5	16	68	....	....	....	....	....
2000-01	Almetjevsk	Russia-2	29	0	0	0	2	....	....	....	....	....
2001-02	Ak Bars Kazan	Russia	9	0	1	1	2	....	....	....	....	....
	Nizhny Novgorod	Russia	6	1	0	1	0	....	....	....	....	....
	Nizh. Novgorod 2	Russia-3	4	2	2	4	10	....	....	....	....	....
2002-03	Ak Bars Kazan	Russia	47	7	6	13	47	5	1	0	1	0
2003-04	Nizhnekamsk	Russia	10	2	3	5	10	....	....	....	....	....
	Ak Bars Kazan 2	Russia-3	STATISTICS NOT AVAILABLE									
	Ak Bars Kazan	Russia	10	1	1	2	8	....	....	....	....	....
2004-05	Dynamo Moscow	Russia	28	1	2	3	10	....	....	....	....	....
2005-06	Dynamo Moscow	Russia	48	9	3	12	78	3	0	0	0	0
2006-07	Dynamo Moscow	Russia	33	9	6	15	36	1	0	0	0	0
2007-08	Spartak Moscow	Russia	8	2	0	2	14	....	....	....	....	....
	Novokuznetsk	Russia	19	1	7	8	12	....	....	....	....	....
2008-09	Novokuznetsk	Rus-KHL	50	6	9	15	28	....	....	....	....	....
2009-10	Novokuznetsk	Rus-KHL	52	11	9	20	42	....	....	....	....	....

VITALE, Joe (vih-TA-lee, JOH) PIT.

Center. Shoots right. 6', 205 lbs. Born, St. Louis, MO, August 20, 1985.
(Pittsburgh's 7th choice, 195th overall, in 2005 Entry Draft).

			Regular Season					Playoffs				
Season	Club	League	GP	G	A	Pts	PIM	GP	G	A	Pts	PIM
2003-04	St. Louis Jr. Blues	CSJHL	43	21	29	50	42	....	....	....	....	....
2004-05	Sioux Falls	USHL	53	11	20	31	62	....	....	....	....	....
2005-06	Northeastern	H-East	31	8	8	16	71	....	....	....	....	....
2006-07	Northeastern	H-East	35	7	9	16	54	....	....	....	....	....
2007-08	Northeastern	H-East	37	12	23	35	75	....	....	....	....	....
2008-09	Northeastern	H-East	40	7	20	27	68	....	....	....	....	....
	Wilkes-Barre	AHL	5	2	2	4	2	12	0	0	0	12
2009-10	Wilkes-Barre	AHL	74	6	26	32	70	4	0	2	2	0

Hockey East Second All-Star Team (2008)

VOGELHUBER, Trent (VOH-guhl-hew-buhr, TREHNT) CBJ

Right wing. Shoots right. 6'1", 197 lbs. Born, Cleveland, OH, July 13, 1988.
(Columbus' 7th choice, 211th overall, in 2007 Entry Draft).

			Regular Season					Playoffs				
Season	Club	League	GP	G	A	Pts	PIM	GP	G	A	Pts	PIM
2004-05	Ohio AAA	Ind.	67	32	30	62	77	....	....	....	....	....
2005-06	Ohio AAA	GLHL	44	27	52	79	28	....	....	....	....	....
2006-07	St. Louis Bandits	NAHL	31	10	16	26	24	....	....	....	....	....
2007-08	Des Moines	USHL	2	0	1	1	0	....	....	....	....	....
2008-09	Miami U.	CCHA	29	2	2	4	22	....	....	....	....	....
2009-10	Miami U.	CCHA	42	8	4	12	30	....	....	....	....	....

VOLPATTI, Aaron (vohl-PA-tee, AIR-uhn) VAN.

Left wing. Shoots left. 6'1", 201 lbs. Born, Revelstoke, B.C., May 30, 1985.

			Regular Season					Playoffs				
Season	Club	League	GP	G	A	Pts	PIM	GP	G	A	Pts	PIM
2003-04	Vernon Vipers	BCHL	55	1	4	5	134	....	....	....	....	....
2004-05	Vernon Vipers	BCHL	57	6	12	18	106	....	....	....	....	....
2005-06	Vernon Vipers	BCHL	25	6	8	14	39	....	....	....	....	....
2006-07	Brown U.	ECAC	23	5	2	7	39	....	....	....	....	....
2007-08	Brown U.	ECAC	31	4	6	10	28	....	....	....	....	....
2008-09	Brown U.	ECAC	32	6	6	12	54	....	....	....	....	....
2009-10	Brown U.	ECAC	37	17	15	32	*115	....	....	....	....	....
	Manitoba Moose	AHL	8	1	1	2	17	5	1	0	1	21

Signed as a free agent by **Vancouver**, March 22, 2010.

VOROSHNIN, Pavel (vo-rohsh-NIHN, PAH-vehl) BUF.

Defense. Shoots left. 6'2", 183 lbs. Born, Chelyabinsk, USSR, March 23, 1984.
(Buffalo's 7th choice, 172nd overall, in 2003 Entry Draft).

			Regular Season					Playoffs				
Season	Club	League	GP	G	A	Pts	PIM	GP	G	A	Pts	PIM
2001-02	Chelyabinsk	Russia-2	32	0	2	2	10	....	....	....	....	....
2002-03	Mississauga	OHL	68	9	27	36	81	1	0	0	0	2
2003-04	Mississauga	OHL	18	0	4	4	6	....	....	....	....	....
	Owen Sound	OHL	40	3	18	21	36	7	0	2	2	4
2004-05	Metallurg Serov	Russia-2	34	0	1	1	12	....	....	....	....	....
2005-06	Lada Togliatti	Russia	33	0	1	1	18	8	0	1	1	0
2006-07	Lada Togliatti	Russia	3	0	0	0	2	....	....	....	....	....
	Mytischi	Russia	9	0	1	1	0	....	....	....	....	....
2007-08	Mytischi	Russia	18	0	0	0	12	....	....	....	....	....
2008-09	Khimik	Rus-KHL	41	1	5	6	28	....	....	....	....	....
2009-10	Gazovik Tyumen	Russia-2	19	0	2	2	16	....	....	....	....	....
	Khanty-Mansiisk	Russia-2	2	0	0	0	4	....	....	....	....	....
	Mechel 2	Russia-3	2	0	3	3	0	....	....	....	....	....
	Mechel	Russia-2	4	0	0	0	0	8	1	0	1	6

VOYNOV, Viatcheslav (VOY-nawf, v'ya-cheh-SLAV) L.A.

Defense. Shoots right. 5'11", 202 lbs. Born, Chelyabinsk, USSR, January 15, 1990.
(Los Angeles' 3rd choice, 32nd overall, in 2008 Entry Draft).

			Regular Season					Playoffs				
Season	Club	League	GP	G	A	Pts	PIM	GP	G	A	Pts	PIM
2005-06	Chelyabinsk 2	Russia-3	2	0	0	0	0	....	....	....	....	....
2006-07	Chelyabinsk	Russia	31	0	0	0	12	....	....	....	....	....
2007-08	Chelyabinsk 2	Russia-3	2	1	0	1	0	....	....	....	....	....
	Chelyabinsk	Russia	36	1	3	4	20	2	0	0	0	0
2008-09	Manchester	AHL	61	8	15	23	46	....	....	....	....	....
2009-10	Manchester	AHL	79	10	19	29	43	9	1	3	4	0

WAGNER, Chris (WAG-nuhr, KRIHS) ANA.

Right wing. Shoots right. 6', 200 lbs. Born, Wellesley, MA, May 27, 1991.
(Anaheim's 4th choice, 122nd overall, in 2010 Entry Draft).

			Regular Season					Playoffs				
Season	Club	League	GP	G	A	Pts	PIM	GP	G	A	Pts	PIM
2008-09	South Shore	EJHL	38	20	14	34	72	2	2	0	2	0
2009-10	South Shore	EJHL	44	34	49	*83	70	4	3	6	9	8

• Signed Letter of Intent to attend **Colgate University** (ECAC) in fall of 2010.

WAHL, Mitch (WAWL, MIHTCH) CGY.

Center. Shoots right. 6', 200 lbs. Born, Long Beach, CA, January 22, 1990.
(Calgary's 2nd choice, 48th overall, in 2008 Entry Draft).

			Regular Season					Playoffs				
Season	Club	League	GP	G	A	Pts	PIM	GP	G	A	Pts	PIM
2005-06	L.A. Jr. Kings	Minor-CA	64	40	50	90	95	....	....	....	....	....
	Spokane Chiefs	WHL	2	0	0	0	0	....	....	....	....	....
2006-07	Spokane Chiefs	WHL	69	16	32	48	50	4	0	1	1	5
2007-08	Spokane Chiefs	WHL	67	20	53	73	63	21	6	8	14	20
2008-09	Spokane Chiefs	WHL	63	32	35	67	78	12	2	11	13	6
2009-10	Spokane Chiefs	WHL	72	30	66	96	96	7	4	5	9	8
	Abbotsford Heat	AHL	4	1	3	4	0	12	2	4	6	4

Memorial Cup All-Star Team (2008) • WHL West First All-Star Team (2010)

WALKER, Luke (WAW-kuhr, LEWK) COL.

Right wing. Shoots right. 6'1", 174 lbs. Born, New Haven, CT, February 19, 1990.
(Colorado's 7th choice, 139th overall, in 2010 Entry Draft).

			Regular Season					Playoffs				
Season	Club	League	GP	G	A	Pts	PIM	GP	G	A	Pts	PIM
2006-07	Okanagan Prep	Minor-BC	52	50	42	92	87	....	....	....	....	....
2007-08	Portland	WHL	70	9	12	21	84	....	....	....	....	....
2008-09	Portland	WHL	71	29	23	52	84	....	....	....	....	....
2009-10	Portland	WHL	61	27	30	57	103	13	6	4	10	17

WALSH, Dustin (WAWLSH, DUHS-tihn) MTL.

Center. Shoots left. 6'2", 175 lbs. Born, Shannonville, Ont., March 20, 1991.
(Montreal's 6th choice, 169th overall, in 2009 Entry Draft).

			Regular Season					Playoffs				
Season	Club	League	GP	G	A	Pts	PIM	GP	G	A	Pts	PIM
2007-08	Quinte West Pack	OPJHL	22	11	7	18	10	....	....	....	....	....
2008-09	Trenton Hercs	OJHL	32	22	20	42	20	....	....	....	....	....
	Kingston	OJHL	12	10	11	21	8	25	13	11	24	10
2009-10	Dartmouth	ECAC	22	8	2	10	6	....	....	....	....	....

WANNSTROM, Sebastian (VAN-strohm, seh-BAS-t'yehn) ST.L.

Right wing. Shoots right. 6'1", 180 lbs. Born, Gavle, Sweden, March 3, 1991.
(St. Louis' 3rd choice, 44th overall, in 2010 Entry Draft).

			Regular Season					Playoffs				
Season	Club	League	GP	G	A	Pts	PIM	GP	G	A	Pts	PIM
2006-07	Brynas U18	Swe-U18	11	0	4	4	4	3	0	0	0	4
2007-08	Brynas U18	Swe-U18	5	0	1	1	4	5	1	3	4	2
	Brynas IF Gavle Jr.	Swe-Jr.	15	0	4	4	8	....	....	....	....	....
2008-09	Brynas U18	Swe-U18	9	6	12	18	12	2	0	3	3	0
	Brynas IF Gavle Jr.	Swe-Jr.	32	11	9	20	4	6	0	0	0	0
2009-10	Brynas IF Gavle Jr.	Swe-Jr.	35	30	27	57	55	5	2	3	5	0
	Brynas IF Gavle	Sweden	18	0	0	0	2	1	0	0	0	0

WARG, Stefan (WAHRG, STEH-fan) ANA.

Defense. Shoots right. 6'3", 204 lbs. Born, Stockholm, Sweden, February 6, 1990.
(Anaheim's 9th choice, 143rd overall, in 2008 Entry Draft).

			Regular Season					Playoffs				
Season	Club	League	GP	G	A	Pts	PIM	GP	G	A	Pts	PIM
2006-07	Vasteras U18	Swe-U18	14	0	6	6	14	5	0	0	0	6
2007-08	Vasteras U18	Swe-U18	1	0	0	0	12	....	....	....	....	....
	Vasteras Jr.	Swe-Jr.	33	2	6	8	61	3	0	0	0	14
	VIK Vasteras HK	Sweden-2	3	0	0	0	0	....	....	....	....	....
2008-09	Seattle	WHL	70	1	16	17	80	5	0	0	0	2
2009-10	Seattle	WHL	37	0	13	13	53	....	....	....	....	....
	Prince Albert	WHL	27	0	7	7	42	....	....	....	....	....

WARSOFSKY, David (wawr-SAWF-skee, DAY-vihd) BOS.

Defense. Shoots left. 5'8", 170 lbs. Born, Marshfield, MA, May 30, 1990.
(St. Louis' 7th choice, 95th overall, in 2008 Entry Draft).

			Regular Season					Playoffs				
Season	Club	League	GP	G	A	Pts	PIM	GP	G	A	Pts	PIM
2005-06	Cushing	High-MA	....	8	26	34	....	....	....	....	....	....
2006-07	Cushing	High-MA	29	15	34	49	55	....	....	....	....	....
2007-08	USNTDP	U-18	41	5	29	34	26	....	....	....	....	....
	USNTDP	NAHL	15	4	2	6	8	....	....	....	....	....
2008-09	Boston University	H-East	45	3	20	23	28	....	....	....	....	....
2009-10	Boston University	H-East	34	12	11	23	48	....	....	....	....	....

Traded to **Boston** by **St. Louis** for Vladimir Sobotka, June 26, 2010.

WATKINS, Matt (WAHT-kihns, MAT) PHX.

Right wing. Shoots left. 5'10", 180 lbs. Born, Aylesbury, Sask., November 22, 1986.
(Dallas' 6th choice, 160th overall, in 2005 Entry Draft).

			Regular Season					Playoffs				
Season	Club	League	GP	G	A	Pts	PIM	GP	G	A	Pts	PIM
2003-04	Tisdale Trojans	SMHL	44	34	37	71	52	....	....	....	....	....
2004-05	Vernon Vipers	BCHL	60	36	38	74	53	....	....	....	....	....
2005-06	North Dakota	WCHA	46	5	4	9	45	....	....	....	....	....
2006-07	North Dakota	WCHA	38	6	11	17	31	....	....	....	....	....
2007-08	North Dakota	WCHA	43	8	10	18	34	....	....	....	....	....
2008-09	North Dakota	WCHA	41	7	7	14	40	....	....	....	....	....
2009-10	Las Vegas	ECHL	14	4	7	11	12	....	....	....	....	....
	San Antonio	AHL	51	12	10	22	17	....	....	....	....	....

Signed as a free agent by **Phoenix**, September 30, 2009.

WATSON, Austin (WAWT-suhn, AW-stuhn) NSH.

Left wing. Shoots right. 6'4", 188 lbs. Born, Ann Arbor, MI, January 13, 1992.
(Nashville's 1st choice, 18th overall, in 2010 Entry Draft).

			Regular Season					Playoffs				
Season	Club	League	GP	G	A	Pts	PIM	GP	G	A	Pts	PIM
2007-08	Det. Compuware	Minor-MI	....	45	104	149	....	....	....	....	....	....
2008-09	Windsor Spitfires	OHL	63	10	19	29	41	20	0	3	3	15
2009-10	Windsor Spitfires	OHL	42	11	23	34	14	....	....	....	....	....
	Peterborough	OHL	10	9	11	20	8	4	2	0	2	2

WATSON, Ryan (WAWT-suhn, RIGH-uhn) FLA.

Left wing. Shoots left. 6'1", 175 lbs. Born, Cambridge, Ont., March 1, 1988.
(Florida's 7th choice, 191st overall, in 2007 Entry Draft).

			Regular Season					Playoffs				
Season	Club	League	GP	G	A	Pts	PIM	GP	G	A	Pts	PIM
2005-06	Cambridge	OJHL-B	46	7	19	26	58	16	5	5	10	14
2006-07	Cambridge	OJHL-B	37	27	29	56	55	9	2	7	9	18
2007-08	Western Mich.	CCHA	34	4	4	8	16	....	....	....	....	....
2008-09	Western Mich.	CCHA	35	4	2	6	22	....	....	....	....	....
2009-10	Western Mich.	CCHA	20	2	0	2	10	....	....	....	....	....

WATT, J.D. (WAHT , JAY-DEE) CGY.

Right wing. Shoots right. 6'2", 200 lbs. Born, Calgary, Alta., May 25, 1987.
(Calgary's 4th choice, 111th overall, in 2005 Entry Draft).

			Regular Season					Playoffs				
Season	Club	League	GP	G	A	Pts	PIM	GP	G	A	Pts	PIM
2003-04	Drumheller	AJHL	59	20	17	37	245	....	....	....	....	....
	Vancouver Giants	WHL	3	1	0	1	0	10	0	3	3	14
2004-05	Vancouver Giants	WHL	66	6	7	13	213	....	....	....	....	....
2005-06	Vancouver Giants	WHL	58	8	29	37	199	18	4	3	7	42
2006-07	Vancouver Giants	WHL	70	34	19	53	182	21	2	3	5	72
2007-08	Red Deer Rebels	WHL	29	7	8	15	87	....	....	....	....	....
	Regina Pats	WHL	29	6	16	22	82	6	2	6	8	19
2008-09	Quad City Flames	AHL	42	0	2	2	146	....	....	....	....	....
	Las Vegas	ECHL	18	5	9	14	51	16	3	4	7	70
2009-10	Abbotsford Heat	AHL	70	8	5	13	267	2	0	0	0	9
	Utah Grizzlies	ECHL	1	0	0	0	5	....	....	....	....	....

WEAL, Jordan (WEEL, JOHR-dahn) L.A.

Center. Shoots right. 5'10", 162 lbs. Born, North Vancouver, B.C., April 15, 1992.
(Los Angeles' 3rd choice, 70th overall, in 2010 Entry Draft).

			Regular Season					Playoffs				
Season	Club	League	GP	G	A	Pts	PIM	GP	G	A	Pts	PIM
2007-08	Van. NW Giants	BCMML	40	*39	*61	*100	44	2	0	2	2	2
	Regina Pats	WHL	3	0	1	1	0	4	0	0	0	0
2008-09	Regina Pats	WHL	65	16	54	70	26	....	....	....	....	....
2009-10	Regina Pats	WHL	72	35	67	102	54	....	....	....	....	....

WEBER, Will (WEH-buhr, WIHL) CBJ

Defense. Shoots left. 6'4", 219 lbs. Born, Gaylord, MI, October 28, 1988.
(Columbus' 3rd choice, 53rd overall, in 2007 Entry Draft).

			Regular Season					Playoffs				
Season	Club	League	GP	G	A	Pts	PIM	GP	G	A	Pts	PIM
2003-04	Gaylord	High-MI	STATISTICS NOT AVAILABLE									
2004-05	Gaylord	High-MI	STATISTICS NOT AVAILABLE									
2005-06	Gaylord	High-MI	STATISTICS NOT AVAILABLE									
2006-07	Gaylord	High-MI	25	18	20	38	104	....	....	....	....	....
2007-08	Chicago Steel	USHL	46	8	10	18	137	....	....	....	....	....
2008-09	Miami U.	CCHA	38	3	2	5	75	....	....	....	....	....
2009-10	Miami U.	CCHA	43	1	9	10	62	....	....	....	....	....

WEISE, Dale (WIHGS, DAYL) **NYR**

Right wing. Shoots right. 6'2", 202 lbs. Born, Winnipeg, Man., August 5, 1988.
(NY Rangers' 5th choice, 111th overall, in 2008 Entry Draft).

			Regular Season					Playoffs				
Season	**Club**	**League**	**GP**	**G**	**A**	**Pts**	**PIM**	**GP**	**G**	**A**	**Pts**	**PIM**
2005-06	Swift Current	WHL	53	4	14	18	57	4	0	0	0	2
2006-07	Swift Current	WHL	67	18	25	43	94	6	0	1	1	8
2007-08	Swift Current	WHL	53	29	22	51	84	12	7	6	13	20
2008-09	Hartford Wolf Pack	AHL	74	11	12	23	64	6	3	1	4	2
2009-10	Hartford Wolf Pack	AHL	73	28	22	50	114	....	....	....	....	....

WELLER, Justin (WEHL-uhr, JUHS-tihn) **PHX.**

Defense. Shoots right. 6'2", 205 lbs. Born, Daysland, Alta., July 26, 1991.
(Phoenix's 5th choice, 105th overall, in 2009 Entry Draft).

			Regular Season					Playoffs				
Season	**Club**	**League**	**GP**	**G**	**A**	**Pts**	**PIM**	**GP**	**G**	**A**	**Pts**	**PIM**
2006-07	Sherwood Park	AMHL	35	0	8	8	46	9	3	2	5	10
2007-08	Red Deer Rebels	WHL	49	0	3	3	40	....	....	....	....	....
2008-09	Red Deer Rebels	WHL	32	0	4	4	30	....	....	....	....	....
2009-10	Red Deer Rebels	WHL	71	2	7	9	88	4	0	1	1	16

WELLER, Shawn (WEHL-uhr, SHAWN)

Left wing. Shoots left. 6'2", 205 lbs. Born, Glens Falls, NY, July 8, 1986.
(Ottawa's 3rd choice, 77th overall, in 2004 Entry Draft).

			Regular Season					Playoffs				
Season	**Club**	**League**	**GP**	**G**	**A**	**Pts**	**PIM**	**GP**	**G**	**A**	**Pts**	**PIM**
2001-02	South Glen Falls	High-NY	25	32	21	53	....	....	....	....	....	....
2002-03	Capital District	EJHL	STATISTICS NOT AVAILABLE									
2003-04	Capital District	EJHL	37	18	25	43	110	3	3	3	6	6
	Capital District	Exhib.	30	16	19	35	78	....	....	....	....	....
2004-05	Clarkson Knights	ECAC	33	3	11	14	72	....	....	....	....	....
2005-06	Clarkson Knights	ECAC	37	14	10	24	*103	....	....	....	....	....
2006-07	Clarkson Knights	ECAC	39	19	21	40	62	....	....	....	....	....
	Binghamton	AHL	5	0	0	0	4	....	....	....	....	....
2007-08	Binghamton	AHL	59	8	8	16	40	....	....	....	....	....
	Elmira Jackals	ECHL	10	4	5	9	11	....	....	....	....	....
2008-09	Binghamton	AHL	70	4	5	9	57	....	....	....	....	....
	Elmira Jackals	ECHL	4	1	1	2	2	....	....	....	....	....
2009-10	Abbotsford Heat	AHL	31	8	4	12	19	3	1	1	2	14
	Bakersfield	ECHL	42	18	28	46	55	....	....	....	....	....

Traded to **Anaheim** by **Ottawa** for Jason Bailey, September 4, 2009.

WELLWOOD, Eric (WEHL-wud, AIR-ihk) **PHI.**

Left wing. Shoots left. 5'11", 180 lbs. Born, Windsor, Ont., March 6, 1990.
(Philadelphia's 5th choice, 172nd overall, in 2009 Entry Draft).

			Regular Season					Playoffs				
Season	**Club**	**League**	**GP**	**G**	**A**	**Pts**	**PIM**	**GP**	**G**	**A**	**Pts**	**PIM**
2006-07	Tecumseh Chiefs	OJHL-B	34	10	10	20	33	....	....	....	....	....
	Windsor Spitfires	OHL	23	2	5	7	0	....	....	....	....	....
2007-08	Windsor Spitfires	OHL	68	9	7	16	12	5	0	0	0	2
2008-09	Windsor Spitfires	OHL	61	16	18	34	12	20	10	11	21	12
2009-10	Windsor Spitfires	OHL	65	31	37	68	36	19	4	6	10	6

WEREK, Ethan (WAIR-ehk, EE-thuhn) **NYR**

Center. Shoots left. 6'1", 195 lbs. Born, Markham, Ont., June 7, 1991.
(NY Rangers' 2nd choice, 47th overall, in 2009 Entry Draft).

			Regular Season					Playoffs				
Season	**Club**	**League**	**GP**	**G**	**A**	**Pts**	**PIM**	**GP**	**G**	**A**	**Pts**	**PIM**
2006-07	Toronto Marlboros	GTHL	55	59	69	128	72	....	....	....	....	....
2007-08	Stouffville Spirit	OPJHL	37	29	41	70	76	15	6	13	19	44
2008-09	Kingston	OHL	66	32	32	64	83	....	....	....	....	....
2009-10	Kingston	OHL	57	30	34	64	68	6	3	2	5	9

WESTGARTH, Brett (WEHST-garth, BREHT)

Defense. Shoots right. 6'2", 215 lbs. Born, Amherstburg, Ont., February 4, 1982.

			Regular Season					Playoffs				
Season	**Club**	**League**	**GP**	**G**	**A**	**Pts**	**PIM**	**GP**	**G**	**A**	**Pts**	**PIM**
2002-03	Princeton	ECAC	27	1	0	1	30	....	....	....	....	....
2003-04	Princeton	ECAC	23	0	1	1	18	....	....	....	....	....
2004-05			DID NOT PLAY									
2005-06	Princeton	ECAC	31	3	8	11	30	....	....	....	....	....
2006-07	Princeton	ECAC	33	0	11	11	32	....	....	....	....	....
	Syracuse Crunch	AHL	5	0	1	1	6	....	....	....	....	....
2007-08	Iowa Stars	AHL	37	2	3	5	89	....	....	....	....	....
	Flint Generals	IHL	27	2	10	12	39	....	....	....	....	....
2008-09	Worcester Sharks	AHL	77	2	7	9	137	9	0	0	0	42
2009-10	Bridgeport	AHL	46	3	5	8	68	....	....	....	....	....
	Worcester Sharks	AHL	18	0	3	3	27	2	0	1	1	0

Signed as a free agent by **San Jose**, July 17, 2008. Signed as a free agent by **NY Islanders**, July 2, 2009. Traded to **San Joses** by **NY Islanders** for future considerations, March 2, 2010.

WESTIN, John (WEHS-tihn, JAWN) **MTL.**

Left wing. Shoots left. 6', 183 lbs. Born, Kramfors, Sweden, May 19, 1992.
(Montreal's 5th choice, 207th overall, in 2010 Entry Draft).

			Regular Season					Playoffs				
Season	**Club**	**League**	**GP**	**G**	**A**	**Pts**	**PIM**	**GP**	**G**	**A**	**Pts**	**PIM**
2007-08	Kramfors U18	Swe-U18	21	24	17	41	40	....	....	....	....	....
2008-09	MODO U18	Swe-U18	30	7	14	21	40	5	6	2	8	33
	MODO Jr.	Swe-Jr.	5	0	2	2	2	2	0	0	0	0
2009-10	MODO U18	Swe-U18	13	8	7	15	12	1	1	0	1	0
	MODO Jr.	Swe-Jr.	31	16	10	26	18	3	1	1	2	0

WEY, Patrick (WAY, PAT-rihk) **WSH.**

Defense. Shoots right. 6'2", 209 lbs. Born, Pittsburgh, PA, March 21, 1991.
(Washington's 4th choice, 115th overall, in 2009 Entry Draft).

			Regular Season					Playoffs				
Season	**Club**	**League**	**GP**	**G**	**A**	**Pts**	**PIM**	**GP**	**G**	**A**	**Pts**	**PIM**
2006-07	Pittsburgh Hornets	MWEHL	18	0	5	5	14	....	....	....	....	....
2007-08	Waterloo	USHL	35	1	5	6	30	8	1	0	1	2
2008-09	Waterloo	USHL	58	7	27	34	75	3	0	0	0	0
2009-10	Boston College	H-East	27	0	5	5	24	....	....	....	....	....

WHITE, Patrick (WIGHT, PAT-rihk) **S.J.**

Center. Shoots right. 6'1", 186 lbs. Born, Grand Rapids, MN, January 20, 1989.
(Vancouver's 1st choice, 25th overall, in 2007 Entry Draft).

			Regular Season					Playoffs				
Season	**Club**	**League**	**GP**	**G**	**A**	**Pts**	**PIM**	**GP**	**G**	**A**	**Pts**	**PIM**
2003-04	Grand Rapids	High-MN	....	3	6	9	....	....	....	....	....	....
2004-05	Grand Rapids	High-MN	....	17	15	32	....	....	....	....	....	....
2005-06	Grand Rapids	High-MN	....	24	28	52	....	....	....	....	....	....
2006-07	Grand Rapids	High-MN	....	19	35	54	....	....	....	....	....	....
	Tri-City Storm	USHL	12	8	1	9	4	....	....	....	....	....
2007-08	U. of Minnesota	WCHA	45	6	4	10	20	....	....	....	....	....
2008-09	U. of Minnesota	WCHA	36	7	9	16	18	....	....	....	....	....
2009-10	U. of Minnesota	WCHA	39	9	8	17	20	....	....	....	....	....

Traded to **San Jose** by **Vancouver** with Daniel Rahimi for Christian Ehrhoff and Brad Lukowich, August 28, 2009.

WHITMORE, Derek (WHIHT-mohr, DAIR-ihk) **BUF.**

Forward. Shoots left. 5'11", 185 lbs. Born, Rochester, NY, December 17, 1984.

			Regular Season					Playoffs				
Season	**Club**	**League**	**GP**	**G**	**A**	**Pts**	**PIM**	**GP**	**G**	**A**	**Pts**	**PIM**
2002-03	Waterloo	USHL	58	15	13	28	51	6	1	0	1	0
2003-04	Waterloo	USHL	10	2	0	2	6	....	....	....	....	....
	Lincoln Stars	USHL	45	19	23	42	22	....	....	....	....	....
2004-05	Bowling Green	CCHA	33	11	6	17	14	....	....	....	....	....
2005-06	Bowling Green	CCHA	34	13	6	19	17	....	....	....	....	....
2006-07	Bowling Green	CCHA	38	19	10	29	20	....	....	....	....	....
2007-08	Bowling Green	CCHA	38	27	10	37	33	....	....	....	....	....
	Rochester	AHL	8	1	0	1	2	....	....	....	....	....
2008-09	Portland Pirates	AHL	77	11	11	22	17	5	1	1	2	2
2009-10	Portland Pirates	AHL	78	18	16	34	24	4	2	1	3	0

CCHA Second All-Star Team (2008)

Signed as a free agent by **Buffalo**, March 26, 2008.

WICK, Roman (WIHK, ROH-muhn) **OTT.**

Right wing. Shoots left. 6'2", 192 lbs. Born, Kloten, Switz., December 30, 1985.
(Ottawa's 8th choice, 156th overall, in 2004 Entry Draft).

			Regular Season					Playoffs				
Season	**Club**	**League**	**GP**	**G**	**A**	**Pts**	**PIM**	**GP**	**G**	**A**	**Pts**	**PIM**
2000-01	Kloten Flyers Jr.	Swiss-Jr.	26	4	1	5	6	5	1	0	1	2
2001-02	Kloten Flyers Jr.	Swiss-Jr.	34	19	27	46	32	8	1	2	3	4
2002-03	Kloten Flyers Jr.	Swiss-Jr.	28	29	22	51	68	2	0	1	1	0
	Kloten Flyers	Swiss	9	1	0	1	4	1	0	0	0	0
2003-04	Kloten Flyers	Swiss	20	1	1	2	6	....	....	....	....	....
	Kloten Flyers	Swiss-Q	7	3	1	4	0	....	....	....	....	....
	GCK Lions Zurich	Swiss-2	6	4	0	4	6	....	....	....	....	....
2004-05	Red Deer Rebels	WHL	66	32	38	70	25	7	1	2	3	6
2005-06	Red Deer Rebels	WHL	23	7	10	17	8	....	....	....	....	....
	Lethbridge	WHL	38	14	17	31	20	6	4	3	7	6
2006-07	Kloten Flyers	Swiss	44	12	11	23	20	11	1	1	2	2
2007-08	Kloten Flyers	Swiss	50	12	15	27	46	4	1	2	3	2
2008-09	Kloten Flyers	Swiss	45	24	13	37	38	15	5	*10	*15	12
2009-10	Kloten Flyers	Swiss	37	15	16	31	8	10	4	6	10	8
	Switzerland	Olympics	5	2	3	5	2	....	....	....	....	....

WIDEMAN, Chris (WIGHD-muhn, KRIHS) **OTT.**

Defense. Shoots right. 5'10", 177 lbs. Born, St. Louis, MO, January 7, 1990.
(Ottawa's 4th choice, 100th overall, in 2009 Entry Draft).

			Regular Season					Playoffs				
Season	**Club**	**League**	**GP**	**G**	**A**	**Pts**	**PIM**	**GP**	**G**	**A**	**Pts**	**PIM**
2006-07	St.L. AAA Blues	Minor-MO	62	9	21	30	122	....	....	....	....	....
	St. Louis Bandits	NAHL	1	0	0	0	0	7	0	1	1	4
2007-08	Cedar Rapids	USHL	53	2	12	14	51	1	0	0	0	0
2008-09	Miami U.	CCHA	39	0	26	26	56	....	....	....	....	....
2009-10	Miami U.	CCHA	44	5	17	22	63	....	....	....	....	....

CCHA All-Rookie Team (2009)

WIERCIOCH, Patrick (WEER-kawsh, PAT-rihk) **OTT.**

Defense. Shoots left. 6'4", 192 lbs. Born, Burnaby, B.C., September 12, 1990.
(Ottawa's 2nd choice, 42nd overall, in 2008 Entry Draft).

			Regular Season					Playoffs				
Season	**Club**	**League**	**GP**	**G**	**A**	**Pts**	**PIM**	**GP**	**G**	**A**	**Pts**	**PIM**
2006-07	Burnaby Express	BCHL	42	9	16	25	46	14	3	4	7	10
2007-08	Omaha Lancers	USHL	40	3	18	21	24	14	2	9	11	22
2008-09	U. of Denver	WCHA	36	12	23	35	26	....	....	....	....	....
2009-10	U. of Denver	WCHA	39	6	21	27	34	....	....	....	....	....

WCHA All-Rookie Team (2009) • WCHA Second All-Star Team (2009) • WCHA First All-Star Team (2010) • NCAA West First All-American Team (2010)

WILD, Cody (WIGHLD, KOH-dee) **BOS.**

Defense. Shoots left. 6'1", 205 lbs. Born, Limestone, ME, June 5, 1987.
(Edmonton's 4th choice, 140th overall, in 2006 Entry Draft).

			Regular Season					Playoffs				
Season	**Club**	**League**	**GP**	**G**	**A**	**Pts**	**PIM**	**GP**	**G**	**A**	**Pts**	**PIM**
2003-04	Bos. Jr. Bruins	EJHL	53	5	24	29	12	....	....	....	....	....
2004-05	Bos. Jr. Bruins	EJHL	64	16	36	52	44	....	....	....	....	....
2005-06	Providence College	H-East	36	6	15	21	24	....	....	....	....	....
2006-07	Providence College	H-East	32	6	8	14	28	....	....	....	....	....
2007-08	Providence College	H-East	32	4	18	22	28	....	....	....	....	....
	Springfield Falcons	AHL	13	1	2	3	8	....	....	....	....	....
2008-09	Springfield Falcons	AHL	59	4	14	18	42	....	....	....	....	....
	Stockton Thunder	ECHL	6	1	2	3	8	....	....	....	....	....
2009-10	Springfield Falcons	AHL	37	0	14	14	24	....	....	....	....	....
	Providence Bruins	AHL	18	0	3	3	10	....	....	....	....	....
	Stockton Thunder	ECHL	4	0	1	1	4	....	....	....	....	....

Hockey East All-Rookie Team (2006)

Traded to **Boston** by **Edmonton** for Matt Marquardt, March 2, 2010.

WILLIAMS, Nigel (WIHL-yuhms, NIGH-juhl) NYR

Defense. Shoots left. 6'4", 226 lbs. Born, Aurora, IL, April 18, 1988.
(Colorado's 2nd choice, 51st overall, in 2006 Entry Draft).

			Regular Season					Playoffs				
Season	Club	League	GP	G	A	Pts	PIM	GP	G	A	Pts	PIM
2004-05	Team Illinois	MWEHL	60	14	18	32	....	....	....	....	....	....
	USNTDP	U-17	3	2	1	3	4	....	....	....	....	....
2005-06	USNTDP	U-18	40	3	6	9	40	....	....	....	....	....
	USNTDP	NAHL	19	3	4	7	23	....	....	....	....	....
2006-07	U. of Wisconsin	WCHA	1	0	0	0	2	....	....	....	....	....
	Saginaw Spirit	OHL	46	17	19	36	92	6	2	1	3	10
2007-08	Saginaw Spirit	OHL	29	5	19	24	60	....	....	....	....	....
	Belleville Bulls	OHL	38	10	12	22	40	21	7	11	18	20
2008-09	Lake Erie Monsters	AHL	70	7	14	21	55	....	....	....	....	....
2009-10	Hartford Wolf Pack	AHL	56	4	16	20	50	....	....	....	....	....

Traded to **NY Rangers** by **Colorado** for Brian Fahey, July 16, 2009.

WILSON, Garrett (WIHL-suhn, GAIR-reht) FLA.

Left wing. Shoots left. 6'2", 199 lbs. Born, Barrie, Ont., March 16, 1991.
(Florida's 4th choice, 107th overall, in 2009 Entry Draft).

			Regular Season					Playoffs				
Season	Club	League	GP	G	A	Pts	PIM	GP	G	A	Pts	PIM
2007-08	Tecumseh Chiefs	OJHL-B	46	11	26	37	40	14	13	8	21	22
	Windsor Spitfires	OHL	7	1	0	1	2	3	0	0	0	0
2008-09	Owen Sound	OHL	53	17	18	35	44	4	1	3	4	7
2009-10	Owen Sound	OHL	65	36	26	62	80	....	....	....	....	....

WILSON, Jason (WIHL-suhn, JAY-suhn) NYR

Left wing. Shoots left. 6'2", 206 lbs. Born, Toronto, Ont., April 15, 1990.
(NY Rangers' 4th choice, 130th overall, in 2010 Entry Draft).

			Regular Season					Playoffs				
Season	Club	League	GP	G	A	Pts	PIM	GP	G	A	Pts	PIM
2007-08	Tor. Canadiens	OPJHL	37	7	10	17	69	11	1	1	2	4
2008-09	London Knights	OHL	52	12	5	17	104	14	0	2	2	8
2009-10	Owen Sound	OHL	46	17	18	35	101	....	....	....	....	....

WILSON, Kelsey (WIHL-suhn, KEHL-see) NSH.

Left wing. Shoots left. 6'1", 214 lbs. Born, Sault Ste. Marie, Ont., January 22, 1986.

			Regular Season					Playoffs				
Season	Club	League	GP	G	A	Pts	PIM	GP	G	A	Pts	PIM
2003-04	Sarnia Sting	OHL	62	5	11	16	106	5	0	0	0	4
2004-05	Sarnia Sting	OHL	37	0	3	3	118	....	....	....	....	....
	Guelph Storm	OHL	23	7	4	11	78	4	0	0	0	9
2005-06	Guelph Storm	OHL	67	38	31	69	196	15	12	6	18	33
2006-07	Milwaukee	AHL	74	9	10	19	215	4	0	0	0	6
2007-08	Milwaukee	AHL	66	8	11	19	179	6	1	0	1	22
2008-09	Milwaukee	AHL	80	15	17	32	160	10	1	2	3	20
2009-10	Salzburg	Austria	64	19	24	43	265	....	....	....	....	....

Signed as a free agent by **Nashville**, October 6, 2006.

WINGELS, Tommy (WIHN-guhls, TAW-mee) S.J.

Center. Shoots right. 6', 195 lbs. Born, Evanston, IL, April 12, 1988.
(San Jose's 5th choice, 177th overall, in 2008 Entry Draft).

			Regular Season					Playoffs				
Season	Club	League	GP	G	A	Pts	PIM	GP	G	A	Pts	PIM
2006-07	Cedar Rapids	USHL	47	10	18	28	52	6	3	0	3	6
2007-08	Miami U.	CCHA	42	15	14	29	22	....	....	....	....	....
2008-09	Miami U.	CCHA	41	11	17	28	66	....	....	....	....	....
2009-10	Miami U.	CCHA	44	17	25	42	49	....	....	....	....	....

NCAA Championship All-Tournament Team (2009) • CCHA Second All-Star Team (2010)

WINKLER, Scott (WIHNK-luhr, SKAWT) DAL.

Center. Shoots right. 6'2", 195 lbs. Born, Asker, Norway, February 22, 1990.
(Dallas' 2nd choice, 89th overall, in 2008 Entry Draft).

			Regular Season					Playoffs				
Season	Club	League	GP	G	A	Pts	PIM	GP	G	A	Pts	PIM
2005-06	Frisk Asker IF/NTG	Norway-Jr.	3	1	0	1	0	....	....	....	....	....
2006-07	Frisk Asker IF/NTG	Norway-Jr.	26	34	30	64	20	8	5	3	8	2
	Asker 2	Norway-2	25	6	6	12	2	....	....	....	....	....
2007-08	Russell Stover	Minor-MO	70	40	52	92	36	....	....	....	....	....
2008-09	Cedar Rapids	USHL	55	10	26	36	35	5	0	2	2	0
2009-10	Colorado College	WCHA	21	1	1	2	4	....	....	....	....	....

WINNETT, Ben (wih-NEHT, BEHN) TOR.

Left wing. Shoots right. 6'1", 185 lbs. Born, New Westminster, B.C., April 3, 1989.
(Toronto's 3rd choice, 104th overall, in 2007 Entry Draft).

			Regular Season					Playoffs				
Season	Club	League	GP	G	A	Pts	PIM	GP	G	A	Pts	PIM
2005-06	Salmon Arm	BCHL	60	18	31	49	31	1	1	1	2	6
2006-07	Salmon Arm	BCHL	39	27	30	57	58	11	3	7	10	12
2007-08	U. of Michigan	CCHA	41	6	5	11	12	....	....	....	....	....
2008-09	U. of Michigan	CCHA	32	4	7	11	16	....	....	....	....	....
2009-10	U. of Michigan	CCHA	44	6	8	14	22	....	....	....	....	....

WITKOWSKI, Luke (wiht-KOW-skee, LEWK) T.B.

Defense. Shoots right. 6'2", 200 lbs. Born, Holland, MI, April 14, 1990.
(Tampa Bay's 6th choice, 160th overall, in 2008 Entry Draft).

			Regular Season					Playoffs				
Season	Club	League	GP	G	A	Pts	PIM	GP	G	A	Pts	PIM
2006-07	Team nXi Majors	Minor-MI	59	18	22	40	172	....	....	....	....	....
2007-08	Ohio	USHL	58	3	10	13	139	....	....	....	....	....
2008-09	Fargo Force	USHL	55	6	16	22	118	10	2	1	3	29
2009-10	Western Mich.	CCHA	32	2	4	6	67	....	....	....	....	....

WOHLBERG, David (WOHL-buhrg, DAY-vihd) N.J.

Center. Shoots left. 6'1", 190 lbs. Born, South Lyon, MI, July 18, 1990.
(New Jersey's 7th choice, 172nd overall, in 2008 Entry Draft).

			Regular Season					Playoffs				
Season	Club	League	GP	G	A	Pts	PIM	GP	G	A	Pts	PIM
2006-07	USNTDP	U-17	12	2	6	8	42	....	....	....	....	....
	USNTDP	NAHL	45	10	10	20	99	6	3	0	3	6
2007-08	USNTDP	U-18	37	9	7	16	48	....	....	....	....	....
	USNTDP	NAHL	22	10	5	15	27	....	....	....	....	....
2008-09	U. of Michigan	CCHA	40	15	15	30	51	....	....	....	....	....
2009-10	U. of Michigan	CCHA	44	10	17	27	76	....	....	....	....	....

CCHA All-Rookie Team (2009) • CCHA Rookie of the Year (2009)

WRENN, William (REHN, WILL-yuhm) S.J.

Defense. Shoots right. 6'1", 190 lbs. Born, Anchorage, AK, March 16, 1991.
(San Jose's 1st choice, 43rd overall, in 2009 Entry Draft).

			Regular Season					Playoffs				
Season	Club	League	GP	G	A	Pts	PIM	GP	G	A	Pts	PIM
2007-08	USNTDP	NAHL	43	0	5	5	36	3	0	0	0	15
	USNTDP	U-17	17	0	2	2	14	....	....	....	....	....
2008-09	USNTDP	NAHL	13	1	4	5	37	....	....	....	....	....
	USNTDP	U-18	47	5	7	12	46	....	....	....	....	....
2009-10	U. of Denver	WCHA	23	0	7	7	36	....	....	....	....	....

YACHMENEV, Denis (YATCH-muh-nehv, DEH-nihs) FLA.

Left wing. Shoots left. 6'1", 185 lbs. Born, Chelyabinsk, USSR, June 4, 1984.
(Florida's 9th choice, 200th overall, in 2002 Entry Draft).

			Regular Season					Playoffs				
Season	Club	League	GP	G	A	Pts	PIM	GP	G	A	Pts	PIM
2000-01	Chelyabinsk 2	Russia-3	36	40	27	67	....	....	....	....	....	....
2001-02	North Bay	OHL	65	17	12	29	32	5	2	0	2	0
2002-03	Saginaw Spirit	OHL	68	17	28	45	69	....	....	....	....	....
2003-04	Omsk 2	Russia-3	13	12	4	16	10	....	....	....	....	....
	Amur Khabarovsk	Russia	25	0	1	1	4	....	....	....	....	....
2004-05	Amur Khabarovsk	Russia-2	42	7	14	21	28	13	3	1	4	8
2005-06	Amur Khabarovsk	Russia-2	46	9	14	23	43	11	2	3	5	6
2006-07	Sibir Novosibirsk	Russia	16	0	0	0	8	1	0	0	0	0
	Sibir Novosibirsk 2	Russia-3	6	0	3	3	8	....	....	....	....	....
2007-08	Chelyabinsk	Russia	40	2	7	9	22	2	0	0	0	0
2008-09	Chelyabinsk	Rus-KHL	8	0	0	0	2	....	....	....	....	....
	Chelyabinsk 2	Russia-3	49	29	20	49	48	....	....	....	....	....
2009-10	Gazovik Tyumen	Russia-2	40	11	5	16	12	7	0	4	4	6

YEMELIN, Alexei (yeh-MUH-lehn, al-EHX-ay) MTL.

Defense. Shoots left. 6', 187 lbs. Born, Togliatti, USSR, April 25, 1986.
(Montreal's 2nd choice, 84th overall, in 2004 Entry Draft).

			Regular Season					Playoffs				
Season	Club	League	GP	G	A	Pts	PIM	GP	G	A	Pts	PIM
2002-03	Lada Togliatti 2	Russia-3	31	1	1	2	20	....	....	....	....	....
2003-04	Lada Togliatti 2	Russia-3	2	0	0	0	10	....	....	....	....	....
	CSK VVS Samara	Russia-2	52	2	4	6	180	1	0	0	0	18
2004-05	Lada Togliatti	Russia	12	0	1	1	24	2	0	0	0	2
2005-06	Lada Togliatti	Russia	44	6	6	12	131	6	0	1	1	*47
2006-07	Lada Togliatti	Russia	43	2	5	7	74	3	0	0	0	4
2007-08	Ak Bars Kazan	Russia	56	0	5	5	123	10	0	1	1	10
2008-09	Ak Bars Kazan	Rus-KHL	51	0	3	3	58	7	1	0	1	20
2009-10	Ak Bars Kazan	Rus-KHL	46	1	6	7	50	22	5	8	13	24

YOGAN, Andrew (YOH-guhn, An-DROO) NYR

Center/Left wing. Shoots left. 6'3", 203 lbs. Born, Coral Springs, FL, December 4, 1991.
(NY Rangers' 3rd choice, 100th overall, in 2010 Entry Draft).

			Regular Season					Playoffs				
Season	Club	League	GP	G	A	Pts	PIM	GP	G	A	Pts	PIM
2006-07	Fla. Jr. Panthers	Minor-FL	52	45	36	81	34	....	....	....	....	....
2007-08	Windsor Spitfires	OHL	50	5	2	7	32	5	0	0	0	6
2008-09	Windsor Spitfires	OHL	16	5	3	8	24	....	....	....	....	....
	Erie Otters	OHL	35	17	17	34	32	....	....	....	....	....
2009-10	Erie Otters	OHL	63	25	30	55	97	....	....	....	....	....

YOUNG, Gus (YUHNG, GUHS) COL.

Defense. Shoots left. 6'2", 190 lbs. Born, Dedham, MA, July 10, 1991.
(Colorado's 7th choice, 184th overall, in 2009 Entry Draft).

			Regular Season					Playoffs				
Season	Club	League	GP	G	A	Pts	PIM	GP	G	A	Pts	PIM
2006-07	Nobles	High-MA	31	3	10	13	14	....	....	....	....	....
2007-08	Little Bruins	Minor-MA	11	0	6	6	....	....	....	....	....	....
	Nobles	High-MA	29	6	9	15	....	....	....	....	....	....
2008-09	Cape Cod Whalers	Minor-MA	14	3	11	14	....	....	....	....	....	....
	Nobles	High-MA	29	5	29	34	16	....	....	....	....	....
2009-10	Cape Cod Whalers	Minor-MA	33	13	27	40	....	....	....	....	....	....
	Nobles	High-MA	29	12	26	38	10	....	....	....	....	....

• Signed Letter of Intent to attend **Yale University** (ECAC) in fall of 2011.

YOUNG, Harry (YUHNG, HAIR-ee) N.J.

Defense. Shoots left. 6'4", 210 lbs. Born, Windsor, Ont., November 12, 1989.
(New Jersey's 8th choice, 202nd overall, in 2008 Entry Draft).

			Regular Season					Playoffs				
Season	Club	League	GP	G	A	Pts	PIM	GP	G	A	Pts	PIM
2005-06	Guelph Storm	OHL	44	0	4	4	20	....	....	....	....	....
2006-07	Guelph Storm	OHL	7	0	2	2	11	....	....	....	....	....
	Windsor Spitfires	OHL	47	0	3	3	72	....	....	....	....	....
2007-08	Windsor Spitfires	OHL	68	2	12	14	155	5	0	1	1	8
2008-09	Windsor Spitfires	OHL	46	8	4	12	138	20	1	4	5	*41
2009-10	Windsor Spitfires	OHL	65	9	11	20	153	19	0	1	1	24

YUNKOV, Mikhail (yuhn-KAWF, mih-kigh-EHL) WSH.

Center. Shoots left. 6', 180 lbs. Born, Voskresensk, USSR, February 16, 1986.
(Washington's 5th choice, 62nd overall, in 2004 Entry Draft).

			Regular Season					Playoffs				
Season	Club	League	GP	G	A	Pts	PIM	GP	G	A	Pts	PIM
2001-02	Krylja Sovetov 2	Russia-3	4	0	1	1	0	....	....	....	....	....
2002-03	Krylja Sovetov	Russia	7	1	0	1	2	....	....	....	....	....
	Krylja Sovetov 2	Russia-3	3	0	1	1	0	....	....	....	....	....
2003-04	Krylja Sovetov	Russia-2	38	5	10	15	12	4	0	1	1	0
	Krylja Sovetov 2	Russia-3	STATISTICS NOT AVAILABLE									
2004-05	Krylja Sovetov 2	Russia-3	1	0	0	0	0	....	....	....	....	....
	Krylja Sovetov	Russia-2	38	9	14	23	22	3	0	1	1	4
2005-06	Ak Bars Kazan	Russia	33	3	4	7	35	11	0	1	1	6
2006-07	Ak Bars Kazan	Russia	47	3	6	9	12	16	1	2	3	8
2007-08	Spartak Moscow	Russia	57	4	6	10	20	5	1	0	1	6
2008-09	Spartak Moscow	Rus-KHL	54	7	14	21	30	6	0	2	2	6
2009-10	Ak Bars Kazan	Rus-KHL	32	0	3	3	12	4	0	1	1	2

ZABORSKY, Tomas (za-BOHR-skee, TAW-mahsh) ANA.

Wing. Shoots left. 6'1", 188 lbs. Born, Banska Bystrica, Czech., November 14, 1987.
(NY Rangers' 5th choice, 137th overall, in 2006 Entry Draft).

			Regular Season					Playoffs				
Season	Club	League	GP	G	A	Pts	PIM	GP	G	A	Pts	PIM
2003-04	Dukla Trencin U18	Svk-U18	46	20	12	32	8	7	4	2	6	4
2004-05	Dukla Trencin U18	Svk-U18	46	44	25	69	53	7	4	4	8	39
	Dukla Trencin Jr.	Slovak-Jr.	7	1	2	3	0	1	0	1	1	0
2005-06	Dukla Trencin Jr.	Slovak-Jr.	42	39	22	61	18	7	10	5	15	2
	Dukla Trencin	Slovakia	4	0	0	0	2	....	....	....	....	....
	P. Bystrica	Slovak-2	5	0	1	1	2	....	....	....	....	....
2006-07	Saginaw Spirit	OHL	59	19	24	43	18	6	1	2	3	4
2007-08	Saginaw Spirit	OHL	68	31	39	70	42	4	2	1	3	2
	Hartford Wolf Pack	AHL	2	0	1	1	0	....	....	....	....	....
2008-09	Hartford Wolf Pack	AHL	8	1	2	3	2	....	....	....	....	....
	Charlotte	ECHL	28	4	8	12	14	....	....	....	....	....
	Dayton Bombers	ECHL	19	10	6	16	14	....	....	....	....	....
2009-10	Assat Pori	Finland	43	9	17	26	67	....	....	....	....	....

Signed as a free agent by **Pori** (Finland), October 22, 2009. Traded to **Anaheim** by **NY Rangers** for Matt McCue, July 19, 2010.

ZAGRAPAN, Marek (ZAG-rah-pahn, MAIR-ehk) BUF.

Center. Shoots left. 6'1", 195 lbs. Born, Presov, Czech., December 6, 1986.
(Buffalo's 1st choice, 13th overall, in 2005 Entry Draft).

			Regular Season					Playoffs				
Season	Club	League	GP	G	A	Pts	PIM	GP	G	A	Pts	PIM
2001-02	HC Zlin U17	CzR-U17	48	23	14	37	24	6	1	0	1	2
2002-03	HC Zlin U17	CzR-U17	15	18	16	34	14	3	1	0	1	6
	HC Zlin Jr.	CzRep-Jr.	25	9	13	22	10	....	....	....	....	....
	HC Hame Zlin	CzRep	13	1	1	2	10	....	....	....	....	....
2003-04	HC Zlin Jr.	CzRep-Jr.	42	23	12	35	40	7	1	3	4	4
	HC Hame Zlin	CzRep	5	0	0	0	0	....	....	....	....	....
	HC Kometa Brno	CzRep-2	5	0	1	1	0	....	....	....	....	....
2004-05	Chicoutimi	QMJHL	59	32	50	82	50	17	11	6	17	28
2005-06	Chicoutimi	QMJHL	59	35	52	87	63	8	4	6	10	4
2006-07	Rochester	AHL	71	17	21	38	39	6	1	0	1	2
2007-08	Rochester	AHL	76	18	22	40	66	....	....	....	....	....
2008-09	Portland Pirates	AHL	80	21	28	49	44	5	2	1	3	2
2009-10	Cherepovets	Rus-KHL	51	10	6	16	40	....	....	....	....	....

Signed as a free agent by **Cherepovets** (Russia-KHL), May 29, 2009.

ZAHN, Teigan (ZAWN, TEE-guhn) T.B.

Defense. Shoots left. 6'2", 222 lbs. Born, Regina, Sask., January 4, 1990.
(Tampa Bay's 8th choice, 186th overall, in 2010 Entry Draft).

			Regular Season					Playoffs				
Season	Club	League	GP	G	A	Pts	PIM	GP	G	A	Pts	PIM
2005-06	Moose Jaw	SMHL	STATISTICS NOT AVAILABLE									
	Saskatoon Blades	WHL	1	0	0	0	2	....	....	....	....	....
2006-07	Saskatoon Blades	WHL	39	0	3	3	68	....	....	....	....	....
2007-08	Saskatoon Blades	WHL	69	4	15	19	104	....	....	....	....	....
2008-09	Saskatoon Blades	WHL	62	5	11	16	160	7	1	2	3	12
2009-10	Saskatoon Blades	WHL	44	0	3	3	84	10	0	2	2	8

• Re-entered NHL Entry Draft. Originally Chicago's 3rd choice, 132nd overall, in 2008 Entry Draft.

ZAPLETAL, Jan (ZAH-pleht-tuhl, YAHN) T.B.

Defense. Shoots right. 6'3", 190 lbs. Born, Brno, Czech., August 21, 1986.
(Tampa Bay's 6th choice, 188th overall, in 2004 Entry Draft).

			Regular Season					Playoffs				
Season	Club	League	GP	G	A	Pts	PIM	GP	G	A	Pts	PIM
2001-02	HC Ytong Brno Jr.	CzRep-Jr.	27	3	0	3	8	....	....	....	....	....
2002-03	HC Vsetin Jr.	CzRep-Jr.	39	5	7	12	10	10	0	0	0	2
2003-04	HC Vsetin Jr.	CzRep-Jr.	51	2	4	6	26	4	0	0	0	0
2004-05	Regina Pats	WHL	55	3	2	5	20	....	....	....	....	....
2005-06	HC Vsetin Jr.	CzRep-Jr.	9	0	3	3	2	....	....	....	....	....
	HC Vsetin	CzRep	16	0	0	0	10	....	....	....	....	....
	Jind. Hradec	CzRep-2	20	0	0	0	16	....	....	....	....	....
2006-07	VSK Technika Brno	CzRep-3	22	1	5	6	32	....	....	....	....	....
2007-08	HC Olomouc	CzRep-2	10	0	0	0	10	....	....	....	....	....
	HC TJ Sternberk	CzRep-3	11	2	3	5	12	....	....	....	....	....
	SHK Hodonin	CzRep-3	16	2	2	4	22	3	0	1	1	2
2008-09	HC TJ Sternberk	CzRep-3	39	5	7	12	48	5	2	0	2	6
2009-10	HC Breclav	CzRep-3	12	0	1	1	6	....	....	....	....	....
	Blansko	CzRep-3	5	0	0	0	2	....	....	....	....	....

ZELISKA, Lukas (zeh-LIHS-kah, LOO-kahsh) NYR

Center. Shoots right. 5'11", 175 lbs. Born, Martin, Czech., January 8, 1988.
(NY Rangers' 7th choice, 204th overall, in 2006 Entry Draft).

			Regular Season					Playoffs				
Season	Club	League	GP	G	A	Pts	PIM	GP	G	A	Pts	PIM
2003-04	HC Trinec U17	CzR-U17	48	39	41	80	166	5	2	2	4	4
	HC Trinec Jr.	CzRep-Jr.	7	1	1	2	2	....	....	....	....	....
2004-05	HC Trinec U17	CzR-U17	11	7	11	18	40	....	....	....	....	....
	HC Trinec Jr.	CzRep-Jr.	13	1	2	3	6	....	....	....	....	....
2005-06	HC Trinec Jr.	CzRep-Jr.	29	8	3	11	81	7	4	1	5	22
	HC Ocelari Trinec	CzRep	1	0	0	0	0	....	....	....	....	....
2006-07	Prince Albert	WHL	61	4	25	29	77	5	1	4	5	4
2007-08	Prostejov	CzRep-2	2	0	0	0	0	....	....	....	....	....
	HC Trinec Jr.	CzRep-Jr.	38	23	29	52	236	7	2	4	6	10
2008-09	HC Ocelari Trinec	CzRep	14	0	0	0	0	....	....	....	....	....
	HC Havirov	CzRep-2	32	10	5	15	52	4	0	1	1	6
2009-10	MHC Martin	Slovakia	13	1	0	1	2	12	0	0	0	0
	Havirov	CzRep-2	28	4	5	9	26	....	....	....	....	....
	MHK Dolny Kubin	Slovak-2	1	1	1	2	0	....	....	....	....	....

ZIMAKOV, Sergei (zih-MAH-kahv, SAIR-gay) WSH.

Defense. Shoots left. 6'1", 194 lbs. Born, Moscow, USSR, January 15, 1978.
(Washington's 4th choice, 58th overall, in 1996 Entry Draft).

			Regular Season					Playoffs				
Season	Club	League	GP	G	A	Pts	PIM	GP	G	A	Pts	PIM
1994-95	Omaha Lancers	USHL	48	14	46	60	22	....	....	....	....	....
1995-96	Krylja Sovetov	CIS	49	2	7	9	36	....	....	....	....	....
1996-97	Krylja Sovetov	Russia	39	4	3	7	57	2	0	0	0	0
1997-98	Krylja Sovetov	Russia	42	4	1	5	48	....	....	....	....	....
1998-99	Ak Bars Kazan	Russia	28	1	0	1	6	8	0	1	1	6
99-2000	Perm	Russia	31	1	2	3	34	3	0	1	1	0
2000-01	CSKA Moscow 2	Russia-3	3	2	2	4	2	....	....	....	....	....
	CSKA Moscow	Russia	26	1	5	6	28	....	....	....	....	....
2001-02	CSKA Moscow	Russia	42	3	10	13	74	....	....	....	....	....
2002-03	Ufa	Russia	11	0	0	0	8	....	....	....	....	....
	Ufa 2	Russia-3	STATISTICS NOT AVAILABLE									
2003-04	Spartak Moscow	Russia-2	60	11	17	28	38	12	0	1	1	10
2004-05	Spartak Moscow	Russia	23	2	2	4	20	....	....	....	....	....
2005-06	Spartak Moscow	Russia	46	3	11	14	55	3	0	0	0	4
2006-07	Vityaz Chekhov	Russia	36	3	2	5	38	3	0	0	0	0
2007-08	Spartak Moscow	Russia	11	1	1	2	10	....	....	....	....	....
	Krylja Sovetov	Russia-2	17	7	5	12	34	....	....	....	....	....
2008-09	MHK Krylja Sov.	Russia-2	55	6	10	16	75	15	2	6	8	16
2009-10			DID NOT PLAY									

ZIMMERMAN, Sean (ZIH-mehr-man, SHAWN) VAN.

Defense. Shoots right. 6'3", 205 lbs. Born, Denver, CO, May 24, 1987.
(New Jersey's 6th choice, 170th overall, in 2005 Entry Draft).

			Regular Season					Playoffs				
Season	Club	League	GP	G	A	Pts	PIM	GP	G	A	Pts	PIM
2002-03	Spokane Braves	KIJHL	45	3	5	8	70	....	....	....	....	....
2003-04	Spokane Chiefs	WHL	67	4	4	8	16	4	0	0	0	0
2004-05	Spokane Chiefs	WHL	71	2	14	16	36	....	....	....	....	....
2005-06	Spokane Chiefs	WHL	72	2	19	21	44	....	....	....	....	....
	Albany River Rats	AHL	6	0	0	0	4	....	....	....	....	....
2006-07	Spokane Chiefs	WHL	60	2	12	14	69	6	0	2	2	2
	Lowell Devils	AHL	1	0	0	0	2	....	....	....	....	....
2007-08	Lowell Devils	AHL	66	0	6	6	47	....	....	....	....	....
	Trenton Devils	ECHL	8	0	1	1	10	....	....	....	....	....
2008-09	San Antonio	AHL	36	2	0	2	30	....	....	....	....	....
	Arizona Sundogs	CHL	20	0	3	3	20	....	....	....	....	....
2009-10	San Antonio	AHL	72	2	7	9	105	....	....	....	....	....

Traded to **Phoenix** by **New Jersey** for Kevin Cormier, September 12, 2008. Traded to **Vancouver** by **Phoenix** with Phoenix's 6th round choice (Alex Friesen) in 2010 Entry Draft for Mathieu Schneider, March 3, 2010.

ZUBAREV, Andrei (ZOO-bah-rehv, AWN-dray) ATL.

Defense. Shoots left. 6'1", 205 lbs. Born, Ufa, USSR, March 3, 1987.
(Atlanta's 7th choice, 187th overall, in 2005 Entry Draft).

			Regular Season					Playoffs				
Season	Club	League	GP	G	A	Pts	PIM	GP	G	A	Pts	PIM
2003-04	Ufa 2	Russia-3	STATISTICS NOT AVAILABLE									
	Ufa	Russia	6	0	1	1	4	....	....	....	....	....
2004-05	Ufa 2	Russia-3	28	2	4	6	32	....	....	....	....	....
	Ufa	Russia	5	0	0	0	4	....	....	....	....	....
2005-06	Ak Bars Kazan	Russia	40	2	11	13	40	....	....	....	....	....
2006-07	Ak Bars Kazan	Russia	20	0	0	0	32	....	....	....	....	....
2007-08	Ak Bars Kazan	Russia	39	4	3	7	86	2	0	0	0	0
2008-09	Mytischi	Rus-KHL	35	0	4	4	65	7	2	3	5	29
2009-10	Mytischi	Rus-KHL	55	7	9	16	58	4	0	0	0	2

ZUCCARELLO-AASEN, Mats (zoo-ka-REHL-oh-AH-suhn, MATS) NYR

Left wing. Shoots left. 5'9", 170 lbs. Born, Oslo, Norway, September 1, 1987.

			Regular Season					Playoffs				
Season	Club	League	GP	G	A	Pts	PIM	GP	G	A	Pts	PIM
2003-04	Frisk-Asker U18	Nor-U18	24	23	14	37	44	2	3	1	4	0
	Frisk-Asker Jr.	Norway-Jr.	20	7	14	21	14	3	0	2	2	0
2004-05	Frisk-Asker U18	Nor-U18	12	11	18	29	50	....	....	....	....	....
	Frisk-Asker Jr.	Norway-Jr.	27	19	17	36	16	5	3	3	6	6
	Frisk-Asker IF	Norway	1	0	0	0	0	....	....	....	....	....
2005-06	Frisk Asker IF/NTG	Norway-Jr.	2	7	0	7	0	2	2	3	5	0
	Frisk-Asker Tigers	Norway	21	5	3	8	12	4	0	0	0	2
2006-07	Frisk Asker IF/NTG	Norway-Jr.	....	....	....	....	....	1	3	4	7	2
	Frisk-Asker IF	Norway	43	34	25	59	36	7	4	4	8	2
2007-08	Frisk-Asker IF	Norway	33	24	40	64	48	15	12	15	27	24
2008-09	MODO	Sweden	35	12	28	40	38	....	....	....	....	....
2009-10	MODO	Sweden	55	23	41	*64	62	....	....	....	....	....
	Norway	Olympics	4	1	2	3	4	....	....	....	....	....

Signed as a free agent by **NY Rangers**, May 26, 2010.

ZUCKER, Jason (ZOO-kuhr, JAY-suhn) MIN.

Left wing. Shoots left. 5'11", 177 lbs. Born, Las Vegas, NV, January 16, 1992.
(Minnesota's 4th choice, 59th overall, in 2010 Entry Draft).

			Regular Season					Playoffs				
Season	Club	League	GP	G	A	Pts	PIM	GP	G	A	Pts	PIM
2007-08	Det. Compuware	MWEHL	30	17	21	38	30	....	....	....	....	....
	Det. Compuware	Minor-MI	42	29	35	64	....	....	....	....	....	....
2008-09	USNTDP	NAHL	36	11	5	16	55	....	....	....	....	....
	USNTDP	U-17	12	8	6	14	....	....	....	....	....	....
	USNTDP	U-18	16	2	6	8	8	....	....	....	....	....
2009-10	USNTDP	USHL	22	11	7	18	23	....	....	....	....	....
	USNTDP	U-18	38	18	17	35	24	....	....	....	....	....

• Signed Letter of Intent to attend **University of Denver** (WCHA) in fall of 2010.

2010-11 NHL Player Register

Note: The 2010-11 NHL Player Register lists forwards and defensemen only. Goaltenders are listed separately. The NHL Player Register lists every active skater who played in the NHL in 2009-10 plus additional players with NHL experience. Trades and roster changes are current as of August 15, 2010.

Abbreviations: GP – games played; **G** – goals; **A** – assists; **Pts** – points; **PIM** – penalties in minutes; **PP** – power-play goals; **SH** – shorthanded goals; **GW** – game-winning goals; **S** – shots; **%** – shooting percentage; **+/–** – plus/minus; **TF** – total faceoffs taken; **F%** – faceoff winning percentage; **Min** – average time on ice per game; ***** – league-leading total **♦** – member of Stanley Cup-winning team.
Prospect Register begins on page 275.
Goaltender Register begins on page 583.
League abbreviations are listed on page 662.

ABDELKADER, Justin

(abdehl-KAY-duhr, JUHS-tihn) **DET.**

Left wing. Shoots left. 6'2", 215 lbs.   Born, Muskegon, MI, February 25, 1987. Detroit's 2nd choice, 42nd overall, in 2005 Entry Draft.

							Regular Season										Playoffs						
Season	Club	League	GP	G	A	Pts	PIM	PP	SH	GW	S	%	+/–	TF	F%	Min	GP	G	A	Pts	PIM	PP	SH	GW	Min
2003-04	Muskegon M.S.	High-MI	28	37	43	80	....	....	....	....	....	....	....	....	....	....	....	....	....	....	....	....	....	....	....
2004-05	Cedar Rapids	USHL	60	27	25	52	86	....	....	....	....	....	....	....	....	....	11	0	4	4	8	....	....	....	....
2005-06	Michigan State	CCHA	44	10	12	22	83	....	....	....	....	....	....	....	....	....	....	....	....	....	....	....	....	....	....
2006-07	Michigan State	CCHA	38	15	18	33	91	....	....	....	....	....	....	....	....	....	....	....	....	....	....	....	....	....	....
2007-08	Michigan State	CCHA	42	19	21	40	107	....	....	....	....	....	....	....	....	....	....	....	....	....	....	....	....	....	....
	Detroit	**NHL**	2	0	0	0	2	0	0	0	6	0.0	0	12	41.7	12:13									
2008-09	**Detroit**	**NHL**	2	0	0	0	0	0	0	0	2	0.0	0	7	57.1	9:18	10	2	1	3	0	0	0	0	6:58
	Grand Rapids	AHL	76	24	28	52	102										10	6	2	8	23				
2009-10	**Detroit**	**NHL**	50	3	3	6	35	0	0	0	79	3.8	–11	318	46.5	10:35	11	1	1	2	*36	0	0	0	7:30
	Grand Rapids	AHL	33	11	13	24	86																		
	NHL Totals		54	3	3	6	37	0	0	0	87	3.4		337	46.6	10:36	21	3	2	5	36	0	0	0	7:15

NCAA Championship All-Tournament Team (2007) • NCAA Championship Tournament MVP (2007) • AHL All-Rookie Team (2009)

ADAMS, Craig

(A-duhmz, KRAYG) **PIT.**

Right wing. Shoots right. 6', 197 lbs.   Born, Seria, Brunei, April 26, 1977. Hartford's 9th choice, 223rd overall, in 1996 Entry Draft.

							Regular Season										Playoffs						
Season	Club	League	GP	G	A	Pts	PIM	PP	SH	GW	S	%	+/–	TF	F%	Min	GP	G	A	Pts	PIM	PP	SH	GW	Min
1995-96	Harvard Crimson	ECAC	34	8	9	17	56	....	....	....	....	....	....	....	....	....	....	....	....	....	....	....	....	....	....
1996-97	Harvard Crimson	ECAC	32	6	4	10	36	....	....	....	....	....	....	....	....	....	....	....	....	....	....	....	....	....	....
1997-98	Harvard Crimson	ECAC	12	6	6	12	12	....	....	....	....	....	....	....	....	....	....	....	....	....	....	....	....	....	....
1998-99	Harvard Crimson	ECAC	31	9	14	23	53	....	....	....	....	....	....	....	....	....	....	....	....	....	....	....	....	....	....
99-2000	Cincinnati	IHL	73	12	12	24	124	....	....	....	....	....	....	....	....	....	8	0	1	1	14	....	....	....	....
2000-01	**Carolina**	**NHL**	44	1	0	1	20	0	0	0	15	6.7	–7	4	25.0	4:30	3	0	0	0	0	0	0	0	3:45
	Cincinnati	IHL	4	0	1	1	9										1	0	0	0	2				
2001-02	**Carolina**	**NHL**	33	0	1	1	38	0	0	0	17	0.0	2	9	33.3	5:54	1	0	0	0	0	0	0	0	7:41
	Lowell	AHL	22	5	4	9	51																		
2002-03	**Carolina**	**NHL**	81	6	12	18	71	1	0	1	107	5.6	–11	20	35.0	12:12									
2003-04	**Carolina**	**NHL**	80	7	10	17	69	0	1	0	110	6.4	–5	20	45.0	13:41									
2004-05	HC Milano	Italy	30	15	14	29	57	....	....	....	....	....	....	....	....	....	15	4	7	11	26	....	....	....	....
2005-06♦	**Carolina**	**NHL**	67	10	11	21	51	1	1	2	68	14.7	1	13	53.9	12:18	25	0	0	0	10	0	0	0	8:16
	Lowell	AHL	13	4	3	7	20																		
2006-07	**Carolina**	**NHL**	82	7	7	14	54	0	1	1	71	9.9	–9	36	30.6	10:04									
2007-08	**Carolina**	**NHL**	40	2	3	5	34	0	0	0	31	6.5	–8	11	27.3	9:48									
	Chicago	**NHL**	35	2	4	6	24	0	1	1	32	6.3	–8	30	53.3	11:56									
2008-09	**Chicago**	**NHL**	36	2	4	6	22	1	0	0	38	5.3	–3	16	37.5	8:43									
	♦ **Pittsburgh**	**NHL**	9	0	1	1	0	0	0	0	9	0.0	0	5	40.0	8:34	24	3	2	5	16	0	0	0	9:45
2009-10	**Pittsburgh**	**NHL**	82	0	10	10	72	0	0	0	84	0.0	–5	562	43.8	11:06	13	2	1	3	15	0	0	1	10:38
	NHL Totals		589	37	63	100	455	3	4	5	582	6.4		726	42.8	10:35	66	5	3	8	41	0	0	3	9:03

• Rights transferred to **Carolina** after **Hartford** franchise relocated, June 25, 1997. • Missed majority of 1997-98 season recovering from shoulder injury suffered in game vs. University of Wisconsin (WCHA), December 27, 1997. Signed as a free agent by **Milano**, (Italy), July 28, 2004. Signed as a free agent by **Anaheim**, August 25, 2005. Traded to **Carolina** by **Anaheim** for Bruno St. Jacques, October 3, 2005. Traded to **Chicago** by **Carolina** for future considerations, January 17, 2008. Claimed on waivers by **Pittsburgh** from **Chicago**, March 4, 2009.

AFINOGENOV, Maxim

(ah-fihn-ah-GEHN-ahf, max-IHM)

Right wing. Shoots left. 6', 190 lbs.   Born, Moscow, USSR, September 4, 1979. Buffalo's 3rd choice, 69th overall, in 1997 Entry Draft.

Season	Club	League	GP	G	A	Pts	PIM	PP	SH	GW	S	%	+/–	TF	F%	Min	GP	G	A	Pts	PIM	PP	SH	GW	Min
1996-97	Dynamo Moscow	Russia	29	6	5	11	10	....	....	....	....	....	....	....	....	....	4	0	2	2	0	....	....	....	....
	Dynamo Moscow	EuroHL	3	0	0	0	0	....	....	....	....	....	....	....	....	....	3	1	0	1	4	....	....	....	....
1997-98	Dynamo Moscow	Russia	35	10	5	15	53	....	....	....	....	....	....	....	....	....	....	....	....	....	....	....	....	....	....
	Dynamo Moscow	EuroHL	6	3	1	4	27	....	....	....	....	....	....	....	....	....	....	....	....	....	....	....	....	....	....
1998-99	Dynamo Moscow	Russia	38	8	13	21	24	....	....	....	....	....	....	....	....	....	16	*10	6	*16	14	....	....	....	....
	Dynamo Moscow	EuroHL	5	3	5	8	29	....	....	....	....	....	....	....	....	....	4	2	1	3	27	....	....	....	....
99-2000	**Buffalo**	**NHL**	65	16	18	34	41	2	0	2	128	12.5	–4	0	0.0	13:09	5	0	1	1	2	0	0	0	12:53
	Rochester	AHL	15	6	12	18	8										8	3	1	4	4				
2000-01	**Buffalo**	**NHL**	78	14	22	36	40	3	0	5	190	7.4	1	2	0.0	14:32	11	2	3	5	4	0	0	0	10:56
2001-02	**Buffalo**	**NHL**	81	21	19	40	69	3	1	0	234	9.0	–9	1	100.0	15:22									
	Russia	Olympics	6	2	2	4	4	....	....	....	....	....	....	....	....	....	....	....	....	....	....	....	....	....	....
2002-03	**Buffalo**	**NHL**	35	5	6	11	21	2	0	2	77	6.5	–12	4	50.0	13:24									
2003-04	**Buffalo**	**NHL**	73	17	14	31	57	3	0	4	148	11.5	–4	9	22.2	13:46									
2004-05	Dynamo Moscow	Russia	36	13	14	27	91	....	....	....	....	....	....	....	....	....	10	4	4	8	8	....	....	....	....
2005-06	**Buffalo**	**NHL**	77	22	51	73	84	11	0	3	241	9.1	6	17	17.7	16:20	18	3	5	8	10	0	0	0	16:53
	Russia	Olympics	8	0	1	1	10	....	....	....	....	....	....	....	....	....	....	....	....	....	....	....	....	....	....
2006-07	**Buffalo**	**NHL**	56	23	38	61	66	7	0	3	151	15.2	19	3	66.7	17:03	15	5	4	9	6	3	0	2	15:24
2007-08	**Buffalo**	**NHL**	56	10	18	28	42	1	0	1	114	8.8	–16	5	20.0	16:03									
2008-09	**Buffalo**	**NHL**	48	6	14	20	20	0	0	0	93	6.5	–7	3	0.0	12:36									

Season	Club	League	GP	G	A	Pts	PIM	PP	SH	GW	S	%	+/-	TF	F%	Min	GP	G	A	Pts	PIM	PP	SH	GW	Min
			Regular Season														Playoffs								
2009-10	**Atlanta**	**NHL**	**82**	**24**	**37**	**61**	**46**	**6**	**0**	**3**	**181**	**13.3**	**−17**	**3**	**33.3**	**17:24**	....	....	....	....	....	....	....	....	....
	Russia	Olympics	4	1	1	2	0	....	....	....	....	....	....	....	....	....	....	....	....	....	....	....	....	....	....
	NHL Totals		**651**	**158**	**237**	**395**	**486**	**38**	**1**	**23**	**1557**	**10.1**		**47**	**25.5**	**15:08**	**49**	**10**	**13**	**23**	**22**	**3**	**0**	**2**	**14:41**

• Missed majority of 2002-03 season recovering from head injury suffered prior to training camp, August, 2002. Signed as a free agent by **Dynamo Moscow** (Russia), June 19, 2004. Signed as a free agent by **Atlanta**, September 29, 2009. Signed as a free agent by **St. Petersburg** (Russia-KHL), August 6, 2010.

ALBERTS, Andrew

(AL-buhrts, AN-droo) **VAN.**

Defense. Shoots left. 6'5", 218 lbs. Born, Minneapolis, MN, June 30, 1981. Boston's 5th choice, 179th overall, in 2001 Entry Draft.

Season	Club	League	GP	G	A	Pts	PIM	PP	SH	GW	S	%	+/-	TF	F%	Min	GP	G	A	Pts	PIM	PP	SH	GW	Min
1998-99	Benide	High-MN	26	10	25	35	....	....	....	....	....	....	....	....	....	....	....	....	....	....	....	....	....	....	....
99-2000	Waterloo	USHL	49	2	2	4	55	....	....	....	....	....	....	....	....	....	4	0	0	0	12	....	....	....	....
2000-01	Waterloo	USHL	54	4	10	14	128	....	....	....	....	....	....	....	....	....	....	....	....	....	....	....	....	....	....
2001-02	Boston College	H-East	38	2	10	12	52	....	....	....	....	....	....	....	....	....	....	....	....	....	....	....	....	....	....
2002-03	Boston College	H-East	39	6	16	22	60	....	....	....	....	....	....	....	....	....	....	....	....	....	....	....	....	....	....
2003-04	Boston College	H-East	42	4	12	16	64	....	....	....	....	....	....	....	....	....	....	....	....	....	....	....	....	....	....
2004-05	Boston College	H-East	30	4	12	16	67	....	....	....	....	....	....	....	....	....	....	....	....	....	....	....	....	....	....
	Providence Bruins	AHL	8	0	0	0	16	....	....	....	....	....	....	....	....	....	16	1	4	5	40	....	....	....	....
2005-06	**Boston**	**NHL**	**73**	**1**	**6**	**7**	**68**	**0**	**1**	**0**	**30**	**3.3**	**3**	**2**	**50.0**	**12:50**	....	....	....	....	....	....	....	....	....
	Providence Bruins	AHL	6	0	1	1	7	....	....	....	....	....	....	....	....	....	....	....	....	....	....	....	....	....	....
2006-07	**Boston**	**NHL**	**76**	**0**	**10**	**10**	**124**	**0**	**0**	**0**	**41**	**0.0**	**−15**	**1**	**0.0**	**19:40**	....	....	....	....	....	....	....	....	....
2007-08	**Boston**	**NHL**	**35**	**0**	**2**	**2**	**39**	**0**	**0**	**0**	**25**	**0.0**	**4**	**2**	**50.0**	**20:37**	**2**	**0**	**0**	**0**	**0**	**0**	**0**	**0**	**11:07**
2008-09	**Philadelphia**	**NHL**	**79**	**1**	**12**	**13**	**61**	**0**	**0**	**0**	**46**	**2.2**	**6**	**0**	**0.0**	**15:48**	**6**	**0**	**1**	**1**	**10**	**0**	**0**	**0**	**13:40**
2009-10	**Carolina**	**NHL**	**62**	**2**	**8**	**10**	**74**	**0**	**0**	**0**	**38**	**5.3**	**7**	**0**	**0.0**	**15:04**	....	....	....	....	....	....	....	....	....
	Vancouver	**NHL**	**14**	**1**	**1**	**2**	**13**	**0**	**0**	**0**	**12**	**8.3**	**−1**	**1**	**0.0**	**16:45**	**10**	**0**	**1**	**1**	**27**	**0**	**0**	**0**	**12:27**
	NHL Totals		**339**	**5**	**39**	**44**	**379**	**0**	**1**	**0**	**192**	**2.6**		**6**	**33.3**	**16:26**	**18**	**0**	**2**	**2**	**37**	**0**	**0**	**0**	**12:42**

Hockey East Second All-Star Team (2004) • NCAA East First All-American Team (2004, 2005) • Hockey East First All-Star Team (2005)

• Missed majority of 2007-08 season recovering from post-concussion symptoms. Traded to **Philadelphia** by **Boston** for Ned Lukacevic and Philadelphia's 4th round choice (Lane MacDermid) in 2009 Entry Draft, October 14, 2008. Signed as a free agent by **Carolina**, July 15, 2009. Traded to **Vancouver** by **Carolina** for Vancouver's 3rd round choice (Austin Levi) in 2010 Entry Draft, March 3, 2010.

ALFREDSSON, Daniel

(AHL-frehd-suhn, DAN-yehl) **OTT.**

Right wing. Shoots right. 5'11", 200 lbs. Born, Gothenburg, Sweden, December 11, 1972. Ottawa's 5th choice, 133rd overall, in 1994 Entry Draft.

Season	Club	League	GP	G	A	Pts	PIM	PP	SH	GW	S	%	+/-	TF	F%	Min	GP	G	A	Pts	PIM	PP	SH	GW	Min
1990-91	Molndal Hockey	Sweden-2	3	0	0	0	2	....	....	....	....	....	....	....	....	....	8	4	4	8	4	....	....	....	....
1991-92	Molndal	Sweden-2	32	12	8	20	43	....	....	....	....	....	....	....	....	....	....	....	....	....	....	....	....	....	....
1992-93	V.Frolunda	Sweden	20	1	5	6	8	....	....	....	....	....	....	....	....	....	....	....	....	....	....	....	....	....	....
1993-94	V.Frolunda	Sweden	39	20	10	30	18	....	....	....	....	....	....	....	....	....	4	1	1	2	....	....	....	....	....
1994-95	V.Frolunda	Sweden	22	7	11	18	22	....	....	....	....	....	....	....	....	....	....	....	....	....	....	....	....	....	....
1995-96	**Ottawa**	**NHL**	**82**	**26**	**35**	**61**	**28**	**8**	**2**	**3**	**212**	**12.3**	**−18**	....	....	....	....	....	....	....	....	....	....	....	....
1996-97	**Ottawa**	**NHL**	**76**	**24**	**47**	**71**	**30**	**11**	**1**	**1**	**247**	**9.7**	**5**	....	....	....	**7**	**5**	**2**	**7**	**6**	**3**	**0**	**2**	....
1997-98	**Ottawa**	**NHL**	**55**	**17**	**28**	**45**	**18**	**7**	**0**	**7**	**149**	**11.4**	**7**	....	....	....	**11**	**7**	**2**	**9**	**20**	**2**	**1**	**1**	....
	Sweden	Olympics	4	2	3	5	2	....	....	....	....	....	....	....	....	....	....	....	....	....	....	....	....	....	....
1998-99	**Ottawa**	**NHL**	**58**	**11**	**22**	**33**	**14**	**3**	**0**	**5**	**163**	**6.7**	**8**	**7**	**57.1**	**17:22**	**4**	**1**	**2**	**3**	**4**	**1**	**0**	**0**	**22:23**
99-2000	**Ottawa**	**NHL**	**57**	**21**	**38**	**59**	**28**	**4**	**2**	**0**	**164**	**12.8**	**11**	**3**	**66.7**	**18:45**	**6**	**1**	**3**	**4**	**2**	**1**	**0**	**0**	**20:22**
2000-01	**Ottawa**	**NHL**	**68**	**24**	**46**	**70**	**30**	**10**	**0**	**3**	**206**	**11.7**	**11**	**8**	**50.0**	**18:47**	**4**	**1**	**0**	**1**	**2**	**0**	**0**	**0**	**21:20**
2001-02	**Ottawa**	**NHL**	**78**	**37**	**34**	**71**	**45**	**9**	**1**	**4**	**243**	**15.2**	**3**	**30**	**30.0**	**20:19**	**12**	**7**	**6**	**13**	**4**	**3**	**0**	**3**	**21:43**
	Sweden	Olympics	4	1	4	5	2	....	....	....	....	....	....	....	....	....	....	....	....	....	....	....	....	....	....
2002-03	**Ottawa**	**NHL**	**78**	**27**	**51**	**78**	**42**	**9**	**0**	**6**	**240**	**11.3**	**15**	**40**	**40.0**	**19:32**	**18**	**4**	**4**	**8**	**12**	**4**	**0**	**1**	**18:00**
2003-04	**Ottawa**	**NHL**	**77**	**32**	**48**	**80**	**24**	**9**	**0**	**5**	**230**	**13.9**	**12**	**33**	**24.2**	**19:24**	**7**	**1**	**2**	**3**	**2**	**0**	**0**	**0**	**20:03**
2004-05	Frolunda	Sweden	15	8	9	17	10	....	....	....	....	....	....	....	....	....	14	*12	6	*18	8	....	....	....	....
2005-06	**Ottawa**	**NHL**	**77**	**43**	**60**	**103**	**50**	**16**	**5**	**8**	**249**	**17.3**	**29**	**44**	**20.5**	**21:41**	**10**	**2**	**8**	**10**	**4**	**1**	**0**	**0**	**21:10**
	Sweden	Olympics	8	5	5	10	4	....	....	....	....	....	....	....	....	....	....	....	....	....	....	....	....	....	....
2006-07	**Ottawa**	**NHL**	**77**	**29**	**58**	**87**	**42**	**7**	**2**	**7**	**240**	**12.1**	**42**	**43**	**34.9**	**21:35**	**20**	***14**	**8**	***22**	**10**	***6**	**1**	***4**	**23:20**
2007-08	**Ottawa**	**NHL**	**70**	**40**	**49**	**89**	**34**	**9**	***7**	**5**	**217**	**18.4**	**15**	**39**	**53.9**	**22:17**	**2**	**0**	**0**	**0**	**0**	**0**	**0**	**0**	**19:20**
2008-09	**Ottawa**	**NHL**	**79**	**24**	**50**	**74**	**24**	**8**	**1**	**3**	**204**	**11.8**	**7**	**17**	**23.5**	**20:53**	....	....	....	....	....	....	....	....	....
2009-10	**Ottawa**	**NHL**	**70**	**20**	**51**	**71**	**22**	**4**	**1**	**5**	**168**	**11.9**	**8**	**40**	**35.0**	**19:40**	**6**	**2**	**6**	**8**	**2**	**0**	**0**	**0**	**22:54**
	Sweden	Olympics	4	3	0	3	0	....	....	....	....	....	....	....	....	....	....	....	....	....	....	....	....	....	....
	NHL Totals		**1002**	**375**	**617**	**992**	**431**	**114**	**22**	**62**	**2932**	**12.8**		**304**	**34.9**	**20:07**	**107**	**45**	**43**	**88**	**68**	**21**	**2**	**11**	**21:05**

NHL All-Rookie Team (1996) • Calder Memorial Trophy (1996) • NHL Second All-Star Team (2006)

Played in NHL All-Star Game (1996, 1997, 1998, 2004, 2008)

Signed as a free agent by **Frolunda** (Sweden), November 10, 2004.

ALLEN, Bryan

(AHL-lehn, BRIGH-uhn) **FLA.**

Defense. Shoots left. 6'4", 220 lbs. Born, Kingston, Ont., August 21, 1980. Vancouver's 1st choice, 4th overall, in 1998 Entry Draft.

Season	Club	League	GP	G	A	Pts	PIM	PP	SH	GW	S	%	+/-	TF	F%	Min	GP	G	A	Pts	PIM	PP	SH	GW	Min
1995-96	Ernestown Jets	OHA-C	36	1	16	17	71	....	....	....	....	....	....	....	....	....	....	....	....	....	....	....	....	....	....
1996-97	Oshawa Generals	OHL	60	2	4	6	76	....	....	....	....	....	....	....	....	....	18	1	3	4	26	....	....	....	....
1997-98	Oshawa Generals	OHL	48	6	13	19	126	....	....	....	....	....	....	....	....	....	5	0	5	5	18	....	....	....	....
1998-99	Oshawa Generals	OHL	37	7	15	22	77	....	....	....	....	....	....	....	....	....	15	0	3	3	26	....	....	....	....
99-2000	Oshawa Generals	OHL	3	0	2	2	12	....	....	....	....	....	....	....	....	....	3	0	0	0	13	....	....	....	....
	Syracuse Crunch	AHL	9	1	1	2	11	....	....	....	....	....	....	....	....	....	2	0	0	0	2	....	....	....	....
2000-01	**Vancouver**	**NHL**	**6**	**0**	**0**	**0**	**0**	**0**	**0**	**0**	**2**	**0.0**	**0**	**0**	**0.0**	**9:20**	**2**	**0**	**0**	**0**	**2**	**0**	**0**	**0**	**13:47**
	Kansas City	IHL	75	5	20	25	99	....	....	....	....	....	....	....	....	....	....	....	....	....	....	....	....	....	....
2001-02	**Vancouver**	**NHL**	**11**	**0**	**0**	**0**	**6**	**0**	**0**	**0**	**4**	**0.0**	**1**	**0**	**0.0**	**10:47**	....	....	....	....	....	....	....	....	....
	Manitoba Moose	AHL	68	7	18	25	121	....	....	....	....	....	....	....	....	....	5	0	1	1	8	....	....	....	....
2002-03	**Vancouver**	**NHL**	**48**	**5**	**3**	**8**	**73**	**0**	**0**	**1**	**43**	**11.6**	**8**	**0**	**0.0**	**12:56**	**1**	**0**	**0**	**0**	**2**	**0**	**0**	**0**	**10:35**
	Manitoba Moose	AHL	7	0	1	1	4	....	....	....	....	....	....	....	....	....	....	....	....	....	....	....	....	....	....
2003-04	**Vancouver**	**NHL**	**74**	**2**	**5**	**7**	**94**	**0**	**0**	**0**	**70**	**2.9**	**−10**	**0**	**0.0**	**16:51**	**4**	**0**	**0**	**0**	**2**	**0**	**0**	**0**	**14:37**
2004-05	Voskresensk	Russia	19	0	3	3	34	....	....	....	....	....	....	....	....	....	....	....	....	....	....	....	....	....	....
2005-06	**Vancouver**	**NHL**	**77**	**7**	**10**	**17**	**115**	**1**	**0**	**0**	**88**	**8.0**	**4**	**0**	**0.0**	**20:27**	....	....	....	....	....	....	....	....	....
2006-07	**Florida**	**NHL**	**82**	**4**	**21**	**25**	**112**	**0**	**0**	**0**	**99**	**4.0**	**7**	**1**	**0.0**	**21:36**	....	....	....	....	....	....	....	....	....
2007-08	**Florida**	**NHL**	**73**	**2**	**14**	**16**	**67**	**0**	**0**	**0**	**67**	**3.0**	**5**	**0**	**0.0**	**21:17**	....	....	....	....	....	....	....	....	....
2008-09	**Florida**	**NHL**	**2**	**0**	**1**	**1**	**0**	**0**	**0**	**0**	**5**	**0.0**	**2**	**0**	**0.0**	**27:11**	....	....	....	....	....	....	....	....	....
2009-10	**Florida**	**NHL**	**74**	**4**	**9**	**13**	**99**	**0**	**1**	**2**	**78**	**5.1**	**−8**	**0**	**0.0**	**19:10**	....	....	....	....	....	....	....	....	....
	NHL Totals		**447**	**24**	**63**	**87**	**566**	**1**	**1**	**3**	**456**	**5.3**		**1**	**0.0**	**18:49**	**7**	**0**	**0**	**0**	**6**	**0**	**0**	**0**	**13:48**

OHL First All-Star Team (1999)

• Missed majority of 1999-2000 season recovering from knee injury suffered during training camp, September 21, 1999. Signed as a free agent by **Voskresensk** (Russia), December 20, 2004. Traded to **Florida** by **Vancouver** with Todd Bertuzzi and Alex Auld for Roberto Luongo, Lukas Krajicek and Florida's 6th round choice (Sergei Shirokov) in 2006 Entry Draft, June 23, 2006. • Missed majority of 2008-09 season recovering from off-season arthroscopic knee surgery and follow-up cartilage surgery (October 27, 2008).

ALMOND, Cody

(al-MUHND, KOH-dee) **MIN.**

Center. Shoots left. 6'2", 215 lbs. Born, Calgary, Alta., July 24, 1989. Minnesota's 3rd choice, 140th overall, in 2007 Entry Draft.

Season	Club	League	GP	G	A	Pts	PIM	PP	SH	GW	S	%	+/-	TF	F%	Min	GP	G	A	Pts	PIM	PP	SH	GW	Min
2004-05	Cgy. Stampeders	SAMHL	30	28	15	43	108	....	....	....	....	....	....	....	....	....	....	....	....	....	....	....	....	....	....
2005-06	Kelowna Rockets	WHL	23	2	1	3	7	....	....	....	....	....	....	....	....	....	8	0	0	0	0	....	....	....	....
2006-07	Kelowna Rockets	WHL	68	15	28	43	72	....	....	....	....	....	....	....	....	....	....	....	....	....	....	....	....	....	....
2007-08	Kelowna Rockets	WHL	69	22	34	56	114	....	....	....	....	....	....	....	....	....	7	1	2	3	2	....	....	....	....
2008-09	Kelowna Rockets	WHL	70	33	33	66	105	....	....	....	....	....	....	....	....	....	22	10	17	27	*51	....	....	....	....
2009-10	**Minnesota**	**NHL**	**7**	**1**	**0**	**1**	**9**	**0**	**0**	**0**	**6**	**16.7**	**−3**	**30**	**60.0**	**7:45**	....	....	....	....	....	....	....	....	....
	Houston Aeros	AHL	48	7	11	18	77	....	....	....	....	....	....	....	....	....	....	....	....	....	....	....	....	....	....
	NHL Totals		**7**	**1**	**0**	**1**	**9**	**0**	**0**	**0**	**6**	**16.7**		**30**	**60.0**	**7:45**	....	....	....	....	....	....	....	....	....

			Regular Season														Playoffs								
Season	Club	League	GP	G	A	Pts	PIM	PP	SH	GW	S	%	+/-	TF	F%	Min	GP	G	A	Pts	PIM	PP	SH	GW	Min

ALZNER, Karl

(ALZ-nuhr, KARL) **WSH.**

Defense. Shoots left. 6'2", 210 lbs. Born, Burnaby, B.C., September 24, 1988. Washington's 1st choice, 5th overall, in 2007 Entry Draft.

2002-03	Burnaby W.C.	Minor-BC	64	17	31	48	24	....	....	....	....	....	....	....	....	....	....	....	....	....	....	....	....	....	....
2003-04	Richmond	PIJHL	41	3	9	12	8	....	....	....	....	....	....	....	....	....	13	0	2	2	0	....	....	....	....
	Calgary Hitmen	WHL	1	0	0	0	0	....	....	....	....	....	....	....	....	....	....	....	....	....	....	....	....	....	....
2004-05	Calgary Hitmen	WHL	66	0	10	10	19	....	....	....	....	....	....	....	....	....	12	0	3	3	9	....	....	....	....
2005-06	Calgary Hitmen	WHL	70	4	20	24	28	....	....	....	....	....	....	....	....	....	13	1	3	4	4	....	....	....	....
2006-07	Calgary Hitmen	WHL	63	8	39	47	32	....	....	....	....	....	....	....	....	....	18	1	12	13	4	....	....	....	....
2007-08	Calgary Hitmen	WHL	60	7	29	36	15	....	....	....	....	....	....	....	....	....	16	6	2	8	4	....	....	....	....
2008-09	**Washington**	**NHL**	**30**	**1**	**4**	**5**	**2**	**0**	**0**	**0**	**31**	**3.2**	**–1**	**0**	**0.0**	**19:25**	....	....	....	....	....	....	....	....	....
	Hershey Bears	AHL	48	4	16	20	10	....	....	....	....	....	....	....	....	....	10	0	2	2	2	....	....	....	....
2009-10	**Washington**	**NHL**	**21**	**0**	**5**	**5**	**8**	**0**	**0**	**0**	**16**	**0.0**	**–2**	**0**	**0.0**	**16:24**	**1**	**0**	**0**	**0**	**0**	**0**	**0**	**0**	**15:09**
	Hershey Bears	AHL	56	3	18	21	10	....	....	....	....	....	....	....	....	....	20	3	7	10	4	....	....	....	....
	NHL Totals		**51**	**1**	**9**	**10**	**10**	**0**	**0**	**0**	**47**	**2.1**		**0**	**0.0**	**18:11**	**1**	**0**	**0**	**0**	**0**	**0**	**0**	**0**	**15:09**

WHL East Second All-Star Team (2007) • Canadian Major Junior Second All-Star Team (2007) • WHL East First All-Star Team (2008) • WHL Defenseman of the Year (2008) • WHL Player of the Year (2008) • Canadian Major Junior First All-Star Team (2008) • Canadian Major Junior Defenseman of the Year (2008)

ANDERSSON, Jonas

(AN-duhr-suhn, YOH-nuhs) **NSH.**

Right wing. Shoots left. 6'3", 204 lbs. Born, Stockholm, Sweden, February 24, 1981. Nashville's 2nd choice, 33rd overall, in 1999 Entry Draft.

1997-98	AIK Solna Jr.	Swe-Jr.	33	14	16	30	32	....	....	....	....	....	....	....	....	....	....	....	....	....	....	....	....	....	....
1998-99	AIK Solna Jr.	Swe-Jr.	16	3	7	10	18	....	....	....	....	....	....	....	....	....	....	....	....	....	....	....	....	....	....
99-2000	North Bay	OHL	67	31	36	67	27	....	....	....	....	....	....	....	....	....	6	2	2	4	2	....	....	....	....
	Milwaukee	IHL	2	1	0	1	0	....	....	....	....	....	....	....	....	....	2	0	0	0	2	....	....	....	....
2000-01	Milwaukee	IHL	52	6	7	13	44	....	....	....	....	....	....	....	....	....	5	0	0	0	2	....	....	....	....
2001-02	**Nashville**	**NHL**	**5**	**0**	**0**	**0**	**2**	**0**	**0**	**0**	**4**	**0.0**	**–2**	**0**	**0.0**	**9:06**	....	....	....	....	....	....	....	....	....
	Milwaukee	AHL	71	13	17	30	19	....	....	....	....	....	....	....	....	....	....	....	....	....	....	....	....	....	....
2002-03	Milwaukee	AHL	49	7	4	11	12	....	....	....	....	....	....	....	....	....	5	0	1	1	4	....	....	....	....
2003-04			DID NOT PLAY – INJURED																						
2004-05	Sodertalje SK	Sweden	34	0	4	4	8	....	....	....	....	....	....	....	....	....	....	....	....	....	....	....	....	....	....
	Brynas IF Gavle	Sweden	7	2	0	2	2	....	....	....	....	....	....	....	....	....	....	....	....	....	....	....	....	....	....
2005-06	Ilves Tampere	Finland	48	8	10	18	26	....	....	....	....	....	....	....	....	....	4	2	0	2	0	....	....	....	....
2006-07	HPK Hameenlinna	Finland	23	6	7	13	20	....	....	....	....	....	....	....	....	....	9	0	1	1	8	....	....	....	....
2007-08	HPK Hameenlinna	Finland	42	11	13	24	42	....	....	....	....	....	....	....	....	....	....	....	....	....	....	....	....	....	....
	Karpat Oulu	Finland	13	1	7	8	4	....	....	....	....	....	....	....	....	....	10	3	7	10	4	....	....	....	....
2008-09	Karpat Oulu	Finland	55	24	33	57	54	....	....	....	....	....	....	....	....	....	15	6	4	10	10	....	....	....	....
2009-10	Dynamo Minsk	Rus-KHL	30	7	13	20	12	....	....	....	....	....	....	....	....	....	....	....	....	....	....	....	....	....	....
	NHL Totals		**5**	**0**	**0**	**0**	**2**	**0**	**0**	**0**	**4**	**0.0**		**0**	**0.0**	**9:06**	....	....	....	....	....	....	....	....	....

• Missed entire 2003-04 season recovering from wrist injury suffered in training camp, September 30, 2003. Signed as a free agent by **Sodertalje** (Sweden), April 28, 2004. Signed as a free agent by **Gavle** (Sweden), January 22, 2005. Signed as a free agent by **Ilves Tampere** (Finland), August 22, 2005. Signed as a free agent by **Hameenlinna** (Finland), April 23, 2006. Signed as a free agent by **Oulu** (Finland), January 23, 2008. Signed as a free agent by **Minsk** (Russia-KHL), April 16, 2009.

ANISIMOV, Artem

(a-NEE-see-mawv, AHR-tehm) **NYR**

Center. Shoots left. 6'4", 197 lbs. Born, Yaroslavl, USSR, May 24, 1988. NY Rangers' 2nd choice, 54th overall, in 2006 Entry Draft.

2004-05	Yaroslavl 2	Russia-3	24	3	5	8	10	....	....	....	....	....	....	....	....	....	....	....	....	....	....	....	....	....	....
2005-06	Yaroslavl	Russia	10	0	1	1	4	....	....	....	....	....	....	....	....	....	....	....	....	....	....	....	....	....	....
	Yaroslavl 2	Russia-3	32	15	12	27	28	....	....	....	....	....	....	....	....	....	....	....	....	....	....	....	....	....	....
2006-07	Yaroslavl 2	Russia-3	2	2	0	2	0	....	....	....	....	....	....	....	....	....	....	....	....	....	....	....	....	....	....
	Yaroslavl	Russia	39	2	8	10	26	....	....	....	....	....	....	....	....	....	7	3	2	5	4	....	....	....	....
2007-08	Hartford	AHL	74	16	27	43	30	....	....	....	....	....	....	....	....	....	5	1	0	1	2	....	....	....	....
2008-09	**NY Rangers**	**NHL**	**1**	**0**	**0**	**0**	**0**	**0**	**0**	**0**	**1**	**0.0**	**0**	**5**	**40.0**	**9:27**	**1**	**0**	**0**	**0**	**0**	**0**	**0**	**0**	**5:35**
	Hartford	AHL	80	37	44	81	50	....	....	....	....	....	....	....	....	....	6	2	0	2	0	....	....	....	....
2009-10	**NY Rangers**	**NHL**	**82**	**12**	**16**	**28**	**32**	**1**	**0**	**2**	**124**	**9.7**	**–2**	**690**	**44.9**	**12:54**	....	....	....	....	....	....	....	....	....
	NHL Totals		**83**	**12**	**16**	**28**	**32**	**1**	**0**	**2**	**125**	**9.6**		**695**	**44.9**	**12:52**	**1**	**0**	**0**	**0**	**0**	**0**	**0**	**0**	**5:35**

ANTROPOV, Nik

(an-TROH-pahv, NIHK) **ATL.**

Center. Shoots left. 6'6", 240 lbs. Born, Ust-Kamenogorsk, USSR, February 18, 1980. Toronto's 1st choice, 10th overall, in 1998 Entry Draft.

1996-97	Ust-Kamenogorsk	Russia-2	8	2	1	3	6	....	....	....	....	....	....	....	....	....	....	....	....	....	....	....	....	....	....
1997-98	Ust-Kamenogorsk	Russia-2	42	15	24	39	62	....	....	....	....	....	....	....	....	....	....	....	....	....	....	....	....	....	....
1998-99	Dynamo Moscow	Russia	30	5	9	14	30	....	....	....	....	....	....	....	....	....	11	0	1	1	4	....	....	....	....
99-2000	**Toronto**	**NHL**	**66**	**12**	**18**	**30**	**41**	**0**	**0**	**2**	**89**	**13.5**	**14**	**501**	**46.3**	**12:48**	**3**	**0**	**0**	**0**	**4**	**0**	**0**	**0**	**10:14**
	St. John's	AHL	2	0	0	0	4	....	....	....	....	....	....	....	....	....	....	....	....	....	....	....	....	....	....
2000-01	**Toronto**	**NHL**	**52**	**6**	**11**	**17**	**30**	**0**	**0**	**1**	**71**	**8.5**	**5**	**431**	**44.3**	**10:02**	**9**	**2**	**1**	**3**	**12**	**1**	**0**	**1**	**11:04**
2001-02	**Toronto**	**NHL**	**11**	**1**	**1**	**2**	**4**	**0**	**0**	**0**	**12**	**8.3**	**–1**	**31**	**38.7**	**8:57**	....	....	....	....	....	....	....	....	....
	St. John's	AHL	34	11	24	35	47	....	....	....	....	....	....	....	....	....	....	....	....	....	....	....	....	....	....
2002-03	**Toronto**	**NHL**	**72**	**16**	**29**	**45**	**124**	**2**	**1**	**6**	**102**	**15.7**	**11**	**621**	**40.1**	**15:00**	**3**	**0**	**0**	**0**	**0**	**0**	**0**	**0**	**19:17**
2003-04	**Toronto**	**NHL**	**62**	**13**	**18**	**31**	**62**	**1**	**1**	**2**	**89**	**14.6**	**7**	**309**	**40.8**	**15:18**	**13**	**0**	**2**	**2**	**18**	**0**	**0**	**0**	**15:56**
2004-05	Ak Bars Kazan	Russia	10	2	3	5	6	....	....	....	....	....	....	....	....	....	....	....	....	....	....	....	....	....	....
	Yaroslavl	Russia	26	4	15	19	44	....	....	....	....	....	....	....	....	....	9	3	4	7	18	....	....	....	....
2005-06	**Toronto**	**NHL**	**57**	**12**	**19**	**31**	**56**	**2**	**1**	**0**	**113**	**10.6**	**13**	**172**	**34.3**	**15:34**	....	....	....	....	....	....	....	....	....
	Kazakhstan	Olympics	5	1	0	1	4	....	....	....	....	....	....	....	....	....	....	....	....	....	....	....	....	....	....
2006-07	**Toronto**	**NHL**	**54**	**18**	**15**	**33**	**44**	**4**	**0**	**4**	**125**	**14.4**	**8**	**34**	**35.3**	**16:36**	....	....	....	....	....	....	....	....	....
2007-08	**Toronto**	**NHL**	**72**	**26**	**30**	**56**	**92**	**12**	**0**	**5**	**165**	**15.8**	**10**	**271**	**42.1**	**20:07**	....	....	....	....	....	....	....	....	....
2008-09	**Toronto**	**NHL**	**63**	**21**	**25**	**46**	**24**	**6**	**0**	**2**	**171**	**12.3**	**–13**	**195**	**41.0**	**17:13**	....	....	....	....	....	....	....	....	....
	NY Rangers	**NHL**	**18**	**7**	**6**	**13**	**6**	**2**	**0**	**2**	**53**	**13.2**	**–1**	**4**	**0.0**	**17:05**	**7**	**2**	**1**	**3**	**6**	**1**	**0**	**0**	**16:42**
2009-10	**Atlanta**	**NHL**	**76**	**24**	**43**	**67**	**44**	**8**	**0**	**4**	**126**	**19.0**	**13**	**1108**	**43.4**	**18:14**	....	....	....	....	....	....	....	....	....
	NHL Totals		**603**	**156**	**215**	**371**	**527**	**37**	**3**	**28**	**1116**	**14.0**		**3677**	**42.3**	**15:45**	**35**	**4**	**4**	**8**	**40**	**2**	**0**	**1**	**14:38**

Signed as a free agent by **Kazan** (Russia), October 27, 2004. Signed as a free agent by **Yaroslavl** (Russia), December 20, 2004. Traded to **NY Rangers** by **Toronto** for NY Ranger's 2nd round choice (Kenny Ryan) in 2009 Entry Draft, March 4, 2009. Signed as a free agent by **Atlanta**, July 2, 2009.

ARMSTRONG, Colby

(AHRM-strawng, KOHL-bee) **TOR.**

Right wing. Shoots right. 6'2", 195 lbs. Born, Lloydminster, Sask., November 23, 1982. Pittsburgh's 1st choice, 21st overall, in 2001 Entry Draft.

1998-99	Sask. Contacts	SMHL	33	21	19	40	103	....	....	....	....	....	....	....	....	....	....	....	....	....	....	....	....	....	....
	Red Deer Rebels	WHL	1	0	1	1	0	....	....	....	....	....	....	....	....	....	....	....	....	....	....	....	....	....	....
99-2000	Red Deer Rebels	WHL	68	13	25	38	122	....	....	....	....	....	....	....	....	....	2	0	1	1	11	....	....	....	....
2000-01	Red Deer Rebels	WHL	72	36	42	78	156	....	....	....	....	....	....	....	....	....	21	6	6	12	29	....	....	....	....
2001-02	Red Deer Rebels	WHL	64	27	41	68	115	....	....	....	....	....	....	....	....	....	23	6	10	16	32	....	....	....	....
2002-03	Wilkes-Barre	AHL	73	7	11	18	76	....	....	....	....	....	....	....	....	....	3	0	0	0	4	....	....	....	....
2003-04	Wilkes-Barre	AHL	67	10	17	27	71	....	....	....	....	....	....	....	....	....	24	3	1	4	45	....	....	....	....
2004-05	Wilkes-Barre	AHL	80	18	37	55	89	....	....	....	....	....	....	....	....	....	10	4	2	6	14	....	....	....	....
2005-06	**Pittsburgh**	**NHL**	**47**	**16**	**24**	**40**	**58**	**7**	**2**	**3**	**86**	**18.6**	**15**	**44**	**27.3**	**19:04**	....	....	....	....	....	....	....	....	....
	Wilkes-Barre	AHL	31	11	18	29	44	....	....	....	....	....	....	....	....	....	....	....	....	....	....	....	....	....	....
2006-07	**Pittsburgh**	**NHL**	**80**	**12**	**22**	**34**	**67**	**1**	**1**	**3**	**145**	**8.3**	**2**	**13**	**15.4**	**16:50**	**5**	**0**	**1**	**1**	**11**	**0**	**0**	**0**	**15:18**
2007-08	**Pittsburgh**	**NHL**	**54**	**9**	**15**	**24**	**50**	**0**	**0**	**2**	**84**	**10.7**	**6**	**12**	**25.0**	**15:24**	....	....	....	....	....	....	....	....	....
	Atlanta	**NHL**	**18**	**4**	**7**	**11**	**6**	**1**	**0**	**1**	**29**	**13.8**	**–2**	**3**	**0.0**	**18:02**	....	....	....	....	....	....	....	....	....
2008-09	**Atlanta**	**NHL**	**82**	**22**	**18**	**40**	**75**	**3**	**0**	**2**	**141**	**15.6**	**5**	**28**	**28.6**	**15:09**	....	....	....	....	....	....	....	....	....
2009-10	**Atlanta**	**NHL**	**79**	**15**	**14**	**29**	**61**	**0**	**1**	**1**	**101**	**14.9**	**6**	**20**	**50.0**	**14:48**	....	....	....	....	....	....	....	....	....
	NHL Totals		**360**	**78**	**100**	**178**	**317**	**12**	**4**	**12**	**586**	**13.3**		**120**	**29.2**	**16:08**	**5**	**0**	**1**	**1**	**11**	**0**	**0**	**0**	**15:18**

Traded to **Atlanta** by **Pittsburgh** with Erik Christensen, Angelo Esposito and Pittsburgh's 1st round choice (Daultan Leveille) in 2008 Entry Draft for Marian Hossa and Pascal Dupuis, February 26, 2008. Signed as a free agent by **Toronto**, July 1, 2010.

ARMSTRONG, Derek

(AHRM-strawng, DAIR-ihk)

Center. Shoots right. 6', 197 lbs. Born, Ottawa, Ont., April 23, 1973. NY Islanders' 5th choice, 128th overall, in 1992 Entry Draft.

			Regular Season														Playoffs								
Season	Club	League	GP	G	A	Pts	PIM	PP	SH	GW	S	%	+/-	TF	F%	Min	GP	G	A	Pts	PIM	PP	SH	GW	Min
1989-90	Hawkesbury	CJHL	48	8	10	18	30																		
1990-91	Hawkesbury	CJHL	54	27	45	72	49																		
	Sudbury Wolves	OHL	2	0	2	2	0																		
1991-92	Sudbury Wolves	OHL	66	31	54	85	22										9	2	2	4	2				
1992-93	Sudbury Wolves	OHL	66	44	62	106	56										14	9	10	19	26				
1993-94	**NY Islanders**	**NHL**	**1**	**0**	**0**	**0**	**0**	**0**	**0**	**0**	**2**	**0.0**	**0**												
	Salt Lake	IHL	76	23	35	58	61																		
1994-95	Denver Grizzlies	IHL	59	13	18	31	65										6	0	2	2	0				
1995-96	**NY Islanders**	**NHL**	**19**	**1**	**3**	**4**	**14**	**0**	**0**	**0**	**23**	**4.3**	**-6**												
	Worcester IceCats	AHL	51	11	15	26	33										4	2	1	3	0				
1996-97	**NY Islanders**	**NHL**	**50**	**6**	**7**	**13**	**33**	**0**	**0**	**2**	**36**	**16.7**	**-8**												
	Utah Grizzlies	IHL	17	4	8	12	10										6	0	4	4	4				
1997-98	**Ottawa**	**NHL**	**9**	**2**	**0**	**2**	**9**	**0**	**0**	**1**	**8**	**25.0**	**1**												
	Detroit Vipers	IHL	10	0	1	1	2																		
	Hartford	AHL	54	16	30	46	40										15	2	6	8	22				
1998-99	**NY Rangers**	**NHL**	**3**	**0**	**0**	**0**	**0**	**0**	**0**	**0**	**1**	**0.0**	**0**	**0**	**0.0**	**2:50**									
	Hartford	AHL	59	29	51	80	73										7	5	4	9	10				
99-2000	**NY Rangers**	**NHL**	**1**	**0**	**0**	**0**	**0**	**0**	**0**	**0**	**1**	**0.0**	**0**	**3**	**33.3**	**3:10**									
	Hartford	AHL	77	28	54	82	101										23	7	16	23	24				
2000-01	**NY Rangers**	**NHL**	**3**	**0**	**0**	**0**	**0**	**0**	**0**	**0**	**6**	**0.0**	**0**	**30**	**50.0**	**11:22**									
	Hartford	AHL	75	32	*69	*101	73										5	0	6	6	6				
2001-02	SC Bern	Swiss	44	17	36	53	62										6	3	5	8	8				
2002-03	**Los Angeles**	**NHL**	**66**	**12**	**26**	**38**	**30**	**2**	**0**	**1**	**106**	**11.3**	**5**	**708**	**50.0**	**15:40**									
	Manchester	AHL	2	3	0	3	4																		
2003-04	**Los Angeles**	**NHL**	**57**	**14**	**21**	**35**	**33**	**5**	**0**	**1**	**101**	**13.9**	**4**	**912**	**52.0**	**17:00**									
2004-05	Geneve	Swiss	9	6	7	13	18																		
	Rapperswil	Swiss	3	1	3	4	4																		
2005-06	**Los Angeles**	**NHL**	**62**	**13**	**28**	**41**	**46**	**7**	**0**	**1**	**100**	**13.0**	**-2**	**546**	**50.7**	**15:31**									
2006-07	**Los Angeles**	**NHL**	**67**	**11**	**33**	**44**	**62**	**3**	**0**	**0**	**109**	**10.1**	**13**	**842**	**47.9**	**15:04**									
2007-08	**Los Angeles**	**NHL**	**77**	**8**	**27**	**35**	**63**	**1**	**0**	**2**	**118**	**6.8**	**4**	**750**	**50.7**	**13:17**									
2008-09	**Los Angeles**	**NHL**	**56**	**5**	**4**	**9**	**63**	**1**	**0**	**1**	**42**	**11.9**	**-11**	**240**	**47.9**	**8:29**									
2009-10	**St. Louis**	**NHL**	**6**	**0**	**0**	**0**	**2**	**0**	**0**	**0**	**6**	**0.0**	**-2**	**15**	**46.7**	**6:59**									
	Peoria Rivermen	AHL	46	17	19	36	21																		
	NHL Totals		**477**	**72**	**149**	**221**	**355**	**19**	**0**	**9**	**659**	**10.9**		**4046**	**50.1**	**13:58**									

AHL Second All-Star Team (2000) • Jack A. Butterfield Trophy (AHL – Playoff MVP) (2000) • AHL First All-Star Team (2001) • John P. Sollenberger Trophy (AHL – Leading Scorer) (2001) • Les Cunningham Award (AHL – MVP) (2001)

Signed as a free agent by **Ottawa**, July 28, 1997. • Loaned to **Hartford** (AHL) by **Ottawa**, October 28, 1997. Signed as a free agent by **NY Rangers**, August 10, 1998. Signed as a free agent by **Bern** (Swiss) with NY Rangers retaining NHL rights, July 18, 2001. Traded to **Los Angeles** by **NY Rangers** for Los Angeles' 6th round choice (Chris Holt) in 2003 Entry Draft, July 16, 2002. Signed as a free agent by **Geneve** (Swiss), October 12, 2004. Signed as a free agent by **Rapperswil** (Swiss), February 13, 2005. Signed as a free agent by **St. Louis**, September 8, 2009.

ARMSTRONG, Riley

(AHRM-strawng, RIGH-lee)

Right wing. Shoots right. 5'11", 185 lbs. Born, Saskatoon, Sask., November 8, 1984.

Season	Club	League	GP	G	A	Pts	PIM	PP	SH	GW	S	%	+/-	TF	F%	Min	GP	G	A	Pts	PIM	PP	SH	GW	Min
2001-02	Yorkton Terriers	SMHL	42	43	34	77	....																		
2002-03	Kootenay Ice	WHL	65	6	10	16	69										10	0	1	1	14				
2003-04	Everett Silvertips	WHL	69	18	26	44	119										21	5	4	9	46				
2004-05	Cleveland Barons	AHL	70	8	11	19	117																		
2005-06	Cleveland Barons	AHL	64	4	5	9	67																		
2006-07	Worcester Sharks	AHL	73	19	17	36	108										6	0	1	1	12				
2007-08	Worcester Sharks	AHL	64	15	19	34	91																		
2008-09	**San Jose**	**NHL**	**2**	**0**	**0**	**0**	**2**	**0**	**0**	**0**	**1**	**0.0**	**-1**	**0**	**0.0**	**7:26**									
	Worcester Sharks	AHL	71	25	17	42	101										12	3	10	13	46				
2009-10	Abbotsford Heat	AHL	38	11	8	19	55																		
	Grand Rapids	AHL	17	3	2	5	14																		
	NHL Totals		**2**	**0**	**0**	**0**	**2**	**0**	**0**	**0**	**1**	**0.0**		**0**	**0.0**	**7:26**									

Signed as a free agent by **San Jose**, September 15, 2004. Signed as a free agent by **Calgary**, July 2, 2009. Traded to **Detroit** by **Calgary** for Andy Delmore, March 3, 2010.

ARNASON, Tyler

(AHR-na-suhn, TIGH-luhr)

Center. Shoots left. 5'11", 204 lbs. Born, Oklahoma City, OK, March 16, 1979. Chicago's 6th choice, 183rd overall, in 1998 Entry Draft.

Season	Club	League	GP	G	A	Pts	PIM	PP	SH	GW	S	%	+/-	TF	F%	Min	GP	G	A	Pts	PIM	PP	SH	GW	Min
1996-97	Wpg. South Blues	MJHL	50	35	50	85	15										6	3	3	6	18				
1997-98	Fargo-Moorhead	USHL	52	37	45	82	16										4	1	1	2	2				
1998-99	St. Cloud State	WCHA	38	14	17	31	16																		
99-2000	St. Cloud State	WCHA	39	19	30	49	18																		
2000-01	St. Cloud State	WCHA	41	28	28	56	14																		
2001-02	**Chicago**	**NHL**	**21**	**3**	**1**	**4**	**4**	**0**	**0**	**0**	**19**	**15.8**	**-3**	**112**	**41.1**	**9:28**	**3**	**0**	**0**	**0**	**0**	**0**	**0**	**0**	**7:43**
	Norfolk Admirals	AHL	60	26	30	56	42																		
2002-03	**Chicago**	**NHL**	**82**	**19**	**20**	**39**	**20**	**3**	**0**	**6**	**178**	**10.7**	**7**	**626**	**40.3**	**14:30**									
2003-04	**Chicago**	**NHL**	**82**	**22**	**33**	**55**	**16**	**6**	**0**	**2**	**222**	**9.9**	**-13**	**904**	**43.1**	**16:34**									
2004-05	Brynas IF Gavle	Sweden	4	0	0	0	0																		
2005-06	**Chicago**	**NHL**	**60**	**13**	**28**	**41**	**40**	**5**	**0**	**1**	**161**	**8.1**	**5**	**492**	**44.7**	**14:58**									
	Ottawa	**NHL**	**19**	**0**	**4**	**4**	**4**	**0**	**0**	**0**	**42**	**0.0**	**-4**	**172**	**51.7**	**12:19**									
2006-07	**Colorado**	**NHL**	**82**	**16**	**33**	**49**	**26**	**1**	**0**	**3**	**211**	**7.6**	**-8**	**422**	**43.8**	**14:20**									
2007-08	**Colorado**	**NHL**	**70**	**10**	**21**	**31**	**16**	**3**	**0**	**1**	**179**	**5.6**	**-1**	**792**	**47.4**	**15:16**	**10**	**2**	**3**	**5**	**2**	**1**	**0**	**0**	**14:12**
2008-09	**Colorado**	**NHL**	**71**	**5**	**17**	**22**	**14**	**2**	**0**	**1**	**108**	**4.6**	**-16**	**721**	**46.1**	**13:19**									
2009-10	Hartford	AHL	11	0	3	3	2																		
	Dynamo Riga	Rus-KHL	26	4	7	11	6										3	0	1	1	0				
	NHL Totals		**487**	**88**	**157**	**245**	**140**	**20**	**0**	**14**	**1120**	**7.9**		**4241**	**44.5**	**14:31**	**13**	**2**	**3**	**5**	**2**	**1**	**0**	**0**	**12:42**

USHL First All-Star Team (1998) • WCHA All-Rookie Team (1999) • WCHA Second All-Star Team (2000) • AHL All-Rookie Team (2002) • Dudley "Red" Garrett Memorial Award (AHL – Rookie of the Year) (2002) • NHL All-Rookie Team (2003)

Signed as a free agent by **Gavle** (Sweden), October 29, 2004. Traded to **Ottawa** by **Chicago** for Brandon Bochenski and Ottawa's 2nd round choice (Simon Danis-Pepin) in 2006 Entry Draft, March 9, 2006. Signed as a free agent by **Colorado**, July 1, 2006. Signed as a free agent by **NY Rangers**, July 3, 2009. Signed as a free agent by **Riga** (Russia-KHL), November 10, 2009.

ARNOTT, Jason

(AHR-nawt, JAY-suhn) **N.J.**

Center. Shoots right. 6'5", 220 lbs. Born, Collingwood, Ont., October 11, 1974. Edmonton's 1st choice, 7th overall, in 1993 Entry Draft.

Season	Club	League	GP	G	A	Pts	PIM	PP	SH	GW	S	%	+/-	TF	F%	Min	GP	G	A	Pts	PIM	PP	SH	GW	Min
1989-90	Stayner Siskins	OHA-C	34	21	31	52	12																		
1990-91	Lindsay Bears	OHA-B	42	17	44	61	10										8	9	8	17	6				
1991-92	Oshawa Generals	OHL	57	9	15	24	12																		
1992-93	Oshawa Generals	OHL	56	41	57	98	74										13	9	9	18	20				
1993-94	**Edmonton**	**NHL**	**78**	**33**	**35**	**68**	**104**	**10**	**0**	**4**	**194**	**17.0**	**1**												
1994-95	**Edmonton**	**NHL**	**42**	**15**	**22**	**37**	**128**	**7**	**0**	**1**	**156**	**9.6**	**-14**												
1995-96	**Edmonton**	**NHL**	**64**	**28**	**31**	**59**	**87**	**8**	**0**	**5**	**244**	**11.5**	**-6**												
1996-97	**Edmonton**	**NHL**	**67**	**19**	**38**	**57**	**92**	**10**	**1**	**2**	**248**	**7.7**	**-21**				**12**	**3**	**6**	**9**	**18**	**1**	**0**	**0**	
1997-98	**Edmonton**	**NHL**	**35**	**5**	**13**	**18**	**78**	**1**	**0**	**0**	**100**	**5.0**	**-16**												
	New Jersey	**NHL**	**35**	**5**	**10**	**15**	**21**	**3**	**0**	**2**	**99**	**5.1**	**-8**				**5**	**0**	**2**	**2**	**0**	**0**	**0**	**0**	
1998-99	**New Jersey**	**NHL**	**74**	**27**	**27**	**54**	**79**	**8**	**0**	**3**	**200**	**13.5**	**10**	**872**	**49.3**	**15:24**	**7**	**2**	**2**	**4**	**4**	**1**	**0**	**0**	**16:48**
99-2000 ♦	**New Jersey**	**NHL**	**76**	**22**	**34**	**56**	**51**	**7**	**0**	**4**	**244**	**9.0**	**22**	**1172**	**46.9**	**17:05**	**23**	**8**	**12**	**20**	**18**	**3**	**0**	**1**	**16:29**
2000-01	**New Jersey**	**NHL**	**54**	**21**	**34**	**55**	**75**	**8**	**0**	**3**	**138**	**15.2**	**23**	**760**	**49.6**	**16:12**	**23**	**8**	**7**	**15**	**16**	***5**	**0**	**0**	**15:49**
2001-02	**New Jersey**	**NHL**	**63**	**22**	**19**	**41**	**59**	**8**	**0**	**1**	**169**	**13.0**	**3**	**934**	**47.8**	**17:13**									
	Dallas	**NHL**	**10**	**3**	**1**	**4**	**6**	**2**	**0**	**2**	**28**	**10.7**	**-1**	**77**	**52.0**	**18:13**									
2002-03	**Dallas**	**NHL**	**72**	**23**	**24**	**47**	**51**	**7**	**0**	**6**	**169**	**13.6**	**9**	**1130**	**53.3**	**16:12**	**11**	**3**	**2**	**5**	**6**	**1**	**0**	**0**	**15:35**
2003-04	**Dallas**	**NHL**	**73**	**21**	**36**	**57**	**66**	**5**	**0**	**5**	**143**	**14.7**	**23**	**1203**	**53.0**	**17:00**	**5**	**1**	**1**	**2**	**2**	**1**	**0**	**0**	**17:23**
2004-05			DID NOT PLAY																						
2005-06	**Dallas**	**NHL**	**81**	**32**	**44**	**76**	**102**	**11**	**1**	**5**	**167**	**19.2**	**13**	**1306**	**51.2**	**17:12**	**5**	**0**	**3**	**3**	**4**	**0**	**0**	**0**	**20:04**
2006-07	**Nashville**	**NHL**	**68**	**27**	**27**	**54**	**48**	**12**	**0**	**6**	**190**	**14.2**	**15**	**1145**	**50.6**	**17:59**	**5**	**2**	**1**	**3**	**2**	**1**	**0**	**0**	**19:17**
2007-08	**Nashville**	**NHL**	**79**	**28**	**44**	**72**	**54**	**13**	**0**	**3**	**248**	**11.3**	**19**	**1260**	**48.7**	**18:59**	**4**	**1**	**0**	**1**	**4**	**0**	**0**	**1**	**18:29**

			Regular Season														Playoffs								
Season	Club	League	GP	G	A	Pts	PIM	PP	SH	GW	S	%	+/-	TF	F%	Min	GP	G	A	Pts	PIM	PP	SH	GW	Min
2008-09	Nashville	NHL	65	33	24	57	49	9	0	5	196	16.8	2	1037	50.6	18:55	....	....	....	....	....	....	....	....	....
2009-10	Nashville	NHL	63	19	27	46	26	6	0	3	216	8.8	0	1077	48.8	18:42	6	2	0	2	0	1	0	0	17:51
	NHL Totals		**1099**	**383**	**490**	**873**	**1176**	**135**	**2**	**60**	**3149**	**12.2**		**11973**	**50.1**	**17:22**	**106**	**30**	**36**	**66**	**74**	**14**	**0**	**2**	**16:49**

NHL All-Rookie Team (1994)

Played in NHL All-Star Game (1997, 2008)

Traded to **New Jersey** by **Edmonton** with Bryan Muir for Valeri Zelepukin and Bill Guerin, January 4, 1998. Traded to **Dallas** by **New Jersey** with Randy McKay and New Jersey's 1st round choice (later traded to Columbus, later traded to Buffalo – Buffalo selected Daniel Paille) in 2002 Entry Draft for Joe Nieuwendyk and Jamie Langenbrunner, March 19, 2002. Signed as a free agent by **Nashville**, July 2, 2006. Traded to **New Jersey** by **Nashville** for Matt Halischuk and New Jersey's 2nd round choice in 2011 Entry Draft, June 19, 2010.

ARTYUKHIN, Evgeny

(ahr-TYEW-khin, ehv-GEH-nee)

Right wing. Shoots left. 6'4", 255 lbs. Born, Moscow, USSR, April 4, 1983. Tampa Bay's 4th choice, 94th overall, in 2001 Entry Draft.

Season	Club	League	GP	G	A	Pts	PIM	PP	SH	GW	S	%	+/-	TF	F%	Min	GP	G	A	Pts	PIM	PP	SH	GW	Min
99-2000	Vityaz Podolsk 2	Russia-3	26	9	8	17	46	....	....	....	....	....	....	....	....	....	....	....	....	....	....	....	....	....	....
	Vityaz Podolsk	Russia-2	3	0	0	0	2	....	....	....	....	....	....	....	....	....	....	....	....	....	....	....	....	....	....
2000-01	Vityaz Podolsk	Russia	24	0	1	1	14	....	....	....	....	....	....	....	....	....	....	....	....	....	....	....	....	....	....
2001-02	Vityaz Podolsk 2	Russia-3	4	3	1	4	6	....	....	....	....	....	....	....	....	....	....	....	....	....	....	....	....	....	....
	Vityaz Podolsk	Russia-2	49	15	7	22	94	....	....	....	....	....	....	....	....	....	12	0	1	1	18	....	....	....	....
2002-03	Moncton Wildcats	QMJHL	53	13	27	40	204	....	....	....	....	....	....	....	....	....	6	1	2	3	29	....	....	....	....
2003-04	Hershey Bears	AHL	36	3	3	6	111	....	....	....	....	....	....	....	....	....	....	....	....	....	....	....	....	....	....
	Pensacola	ECHL	6	1	0	1	14	....	....	....	....	....	....	....	....	....	....	....	....	....	....	....	....	....	....
2004-05	Springfield	AHL	62	9	19	28	142	....	....	....	....	....	....	....	....	....	....	....	....	....	....	....	....	....	....
2005-06	**Tampa Bay**	**NHL**	**72**	**4**	**13**	**17**	**90**	**1**	**0**	**0**	**79**	**5.1**	**-4**	**0**	**0.0**	**8:43**	**5**	**1**	**0**	**1**	**6**	**0**	**0**	**0**	**8:14**
	Springfield	AHL	4	2	1	3	4	....	....	....	....	....	....	....	....	....	....	....	....	....	....	....	....	....	....
2006-07	Yaroslavl	Russia	44	5	8	13	183	....	....	....	....	....	....	....	....	....	1	0	0	0	0	....	....	....	....
2007-08	Avangard Omsk	Russia	19	3	2	5	40	....	....	....	....	....	....	....	....	....	....	....	....	....	....	....	....	....	....
	CSKA Moscow	Russia	23	3	5	8	99	....	....	....	....	....	....	....	....	....	6	4	0	4	6	....	....	....	....
2008-09	**Tampa Bay**	**NHL**	**73**	**6**	**10**	**16**	**151**	**1**	**0**	**0**	**100**	**6.0**	**1**	**2**	**0.0**	**10:40**	....	....	....	....	....	....	....	....	....
2009-10	**Anaheim**	**NHL**	**37**	**4**	**5**	**9**	**41**	**0**	**0**	**0**	**21**	**19.0**	**0**	**1**	**0.0**	**9:04**	....	....	....	....	....	....	....	....	....
	Atlanta	**NHL**	**17**	**5**	**2**	**7**	**31**	**0**	**0**	**0**	**21**	**23.8**	**-4**	**1**	**100.0**	**8:39**	....	....	....	....	....	....	....	....	....
	NHL Totals		**199**	**19**	**30**	**49**	**313**	**2**	**0**	**0**	**221**	**8.6**		**4**	**25.0**	**9:30**	**5**	**1**	**0**	**1**	**6**	**0**	**0**	**0**	**8:14**

Signed as a free agent by **Yaroslavl** (Russia), August 5, 2006. Signede as a free agent by **Omsk** (Russia), July 26, 2007. • Transferred to **CSKA Moscow** (Russia) from **Omsk** (Russia), October 24 2007. Traded to **Anaheim** by **Tampa Bay** for Drew Miller and Anaheim's 3rd round choice (Adam Janosik) in 2010 Entry Draft, August 13, 2009. Traded to **Atlanta** by **Anaheim** for Nathan Oystrick and future considerations, March 1, 2010.

ASHAM, Arron

(ASH-uhm, AIR-ruhn)

Right wing. Shoots right. 5'11", 205 lbs. Born, Portage La Prairie, Man., April 13, 1978. Montreal's 3rd choice, 71st overall, in 1996 Entry Draft.

Season	Club	League	GP	G	A	Pts	PIM	PP	SH	GW	S	%	+/-	TF	F%	Min	GP	G	A	Pts	PIM	PP	SH	GW	Min
1993-94	Portage	MAHA	21	18	19	37	82	....	....	....	....	....	....	....	....	....	....	....	....	....	....	....	....	....	....
1994-95	Red Deer Rebels	WHL	62	11	16	27	126	....	....	....	....	....	....	....	....	....	....	....	....	....	....	....	....	....	....
1995-96	Red Deer Rebels	WHL	70	32	45	77	174	....	....	....	....	....	....	....	....	....	10	6	3	9	20	....	....	....	....
1996-97	Red Deer Rebels	WHL	67	45	51	96	149	....	....	....	....	....	....	....	....	....	16	12	14	26	36	....	....	....	....
1997-98	Red Deer Rebels	WHL	67	43	49	92	153	....	....	....	....	....	....	....	....	....	5	0	2	2	8	....	....	....	....
	Fredericton	AHL	2	1	1	2	0	....	....	....	....	....	....	....	....	....	2	0	1	1	0	....	....	....	....
1998-99	**Montreal**	**NHL**	**7**	**0**	**0**	**0**	**0**	**0**	**0**	**0**	**5**	**0.0**	**-4**	**0**	**0.0**	**7:27**	....	....	....	....	....	....	....	....	....
	Fredericton	AHL	60	16	18	34	118	....	....	....	....	....	....	....	....	....	13	8	6	14	11	....	....	....	....
99-2000	**Montreal**	**NHL**	**33**	**4**	**2**	**6**	**24**	**0**	**1**	**1**	**29**	**13.8**	**-7**	**1**	**0.0**	**10:14**	....	....	....	....	....	....	....	....	....
	Quebec Citadelles	AHL	13	4	5	9	32	....	....	....	....	....	....	....	....	....	2	0	0	0	2	....	....	....	....
2000-01	**Montreal**	**NHL**	**46**	**2**	**3**	**5**	**59**	**0**	**0**	**0**	**32**	**6.3**	**-9**	**3**	**100.0**	**8:28**	....	....	....	....	....	....	....	....	....
	Quebec Citadelles	AHL	15	7	9	16	51	....	....	....	....	....	....	....	....	....	7	1	2	3	2	....	....	....	....
2001-02	**Montreal**	**NHL**	**35**	**5**	**4**	**9**	**55**	**0**	**0**	**0**	**30**	**16.7**	**7**	**4**	**25.0**	**8:13**	**3**	**0**	**1**	**1**	**0**	**0**	**0**	**0**	**5:39**
	Quebec Citadelles	AHL	24	9	14	23	35	....	....	....	....	....	....	....	....	....	....	....	....	....	....	....	....	....	....
2002-03	**NY Islanders**	**NHL**	**78**	**15**	**19**	**34**	**57**	**4**	**0**	**1**	**114**	**13.2**	**1**	**17**	**41.2**	**12:13**	**5**	**0**	**0**	**0**	**16**	**0**	**0**	**0**	**15:09**
2003-04	**NY Islanders**	**NHL**	**79**	**12**	**12**	**24**	**92**	**1**	**0**	**0**	**108**	**11.1**	**-12**	**23**	**34.8**	**13:13**	**5**	**0**	**1**	**1**	**4**	**0**	**0**	**0**	**8:44**
2004-05	EHC Visp	Swiss-2	5	2	4	6	6	....	....	....	....	....	....	....	....	....	4	1	1	2	8	....	....	....	....
2005-06	**NY Islanders**	**NHL**	**63**	**9**	**15**	**24**	**103**	**2**	**1**	**0**	**99**	**9.1**	**-5**	**63**	**41.3**	**13:33**	....	....	....	....	....	....	....	....	....
2006-07	**NY Islanders**	**NHL**	**80**	**11**	**12**	**23**	**63**	**0**	**0**	**2**	**85**	**12.9**	**3**	**10**	**60.0**	**9:20**	**5**	**1**	**0**	**1**	**0**	**0**	**0**	**0**	**10:08**
2007-08	**New Jersey**	**NHL**	**77**	**6**	**4**	**10**	**84**	**0**	**0**	**2**	**68**	**8.8**	**-6**	**3**	**0.0**	**8:33**	**5**	**0**	**1**	**1**	**2**	**0**	**0**	**0**	**5:04**
2008-09	**Philadelphia**	**NHL**	**78**	**8**	**12**	**20**	**155**	**0**	**0**	**1**	**74**	**10.8**	**0**	**15**	**46.7**	**8:45**	**6**	**1**	**1**	**2**	**6**	**0**	**0**	**1**	**7:55**
2009-10	**Philadelphia**	**NHL**	**72**	**10**	**14**	**24**	**126**	**0**	**0**	**2**	**91**	**11.0**	**-2**	**13**	**15.4**	**10:04**	**23**	**4**	**3**	**7**	**10**	**0**	**0**	**0**	**11:14**
	NHL Totals		**648**	**82**	**97**	**179**	**818**	**7**	**2**	**9**	**735**	**11.2**		**152**	**39.5**	**10:23**	**52**	**6**	**7**	**13**	**38**	**0**	**0**	**1**	**9:58**

Traded to **NY Islanders** by **Montreal** with Montreal's 5th round choice (Marcus Paulsson) in 2002 Entry Draft for Mariusz Czerkawski, June 22, 2002. Signed as a free agent by **Visp** (Swiss-2), January 19, 2005. Signed as a free agent by **New Jersey**, August 7, 2007. Signed as a free agent by **Philadelphia**, July 7, 2008.

AUCOIN, Adrian

(oh-KOIN, AY-dree-uhn) **PHX.**

Defense. Shoots right. 6'2", 213 lbs. Born, Ottawa, Ont., July 3, 1973. Vancouver's 7th choice, 117th overall, in 1992 Entry Draft.

Season	Club	League	GP	G	A	Pts	PIM	PP	SH	GW	S	%	+/-	TF	F%	Min	GP	G	A	Pts	PIM	PP	SH	GW	Min
1989-90	Nepean Raiders	CJHL	54	2	14	16	95	....	....	....	....	....	....	....	....	....	4	0	1	1		....	....	....	....
1990-91	Nepean Raiders	CJHL	56	17	33	50	125	....	....	....	....	....	....	....	....	....	....	....	....	....	....	....	....	....	....
1991-92	Boston University	H-East	32	2	10	12	60	....	....	....	....	....	....	....	....	....	....	....	....	....	....	....	....	....	....
1992-93	Canada	Nat-Tm	42	8	10	18	71	....	....	....	....	....	....	....	....	....	....	....	....	....	....	....	....	....	....
1993-94	Canada	Nat-Tm	59	5	12	17	80	....	....	....	....	....	....	....	....	....	....	....	....	....	....	....	....	....	....
	Canada	Olympics	4	0	0	0	2	....	....	....	....	....	....	....	....	....	....	....	....	....	....	....	....	....	....
	Hamilton	AHL	13	1	2	3	19	....	....	....	....	....	....	....	....	....	4	0	2	2	6	....	....	....	....
1994-95	Syracuse Crunch	AHL	71	13	18	31	52	....	....	....	....	....	....	....	....	....	....	....	....	....	....	....	....	....	....
	Vancouver	**NHL**	**1**	**1**	**0**	**1**	**0**	**0**	**0**	**0**	**2**	**50.0**	**1**	....	....	....	**4**	**1**	**0**	**1**	**0**	**1**	**0**	**0**	....
1995-96	**Vancouver**	**NHL**	**49**	**4**	**14**	**18**	**34**	**2**	**0**	**0**	**85**	**4.7**	**8**	....	....	....	**6**	**0**	**0**	**0**	**2**	**0**	**0**	**0**	....
	Syracuse Crunch	AHL	29	5	13	18	47	....	....	....	....	....	....	....	....	....	....	....	....	....	....	....	....	....	....
1996-97	**Vancouver**	**NHL**	**70**	**5**	**16**	**21**	**63**	**1**	**0**	**0**	**116**	**4.3**	**0**	....	....	....	....	....	....	....	....	....	....	....	....
1997-98	**Vancouver**	**NHL**	**35**	**3**	**3**	**6**	**21**	**1**	**0**	**1**	**44**	**6.8**	**-4**	....	....	....	....	....	....	....	....	....	....	....	....
1998-99	**Vancouver**	**NHL**	**82**	**23**	**11**	**34**	**77**	**18**	**2**	**3**	**174**	**13.2**	**-14**	**1**	**100.0**	**23:52**	....	....	....	....	....	....	....	....	....
99-2000	**Vancouver**	**NHL**	**57**	**10**	**14**	**24**	**30**	**4**	**0**	**1**	**126**	**7.9**	**7**	**0**	**0.0**	**23:06**	....	....	....	....	....	....	....	....	....
2000-01	**Vancouver**	**NHL**	**47**	**3**	**13**	**16**	**20**	**1**	**0**	**0**	**99**	**3.0**	**13**	**0**	**0.0**	**18:21**	....	....	....	....	....	....	....	....	....
	Tampa Bay	**NHL**	**26**	**1**	**11**	**12**	**25**	**1**	**0**	**0**	**60**	**1.7**	**-8**	**0**	**0.0**	**23:34**	....	....	....	....	....	....	....	....	....
2001-02	**NY Islanders**	**NHL**	**81**	**12**	**22**	**34**	**62**	**7**	**0**	**1**	**232**	**5.2**	**23**	**0**	**0.0**	**28:54**	**7**	**2**	**5**	**7**	**4**	**2**	**0**	**0**	**32:19**
2002-03	**NY Islanders**	**NHL**	**73**	**8**	**27**	**35**	**70**	**5**	**0**	**1**	**175**	**4.6**	**-5**	**0**	**0.0**	**29:01**	**5**	**1**	**2**	**3**	**4**	**0**	**0**	**0**	**31:43**
2003-04	**NY Islanders**	**NHL**	**81**	**13**	**31**	**44**	**54**	**4**	**0**	**2**	**213**	**6.1**	**29**	**0**	**0.0**	**26:38**	**5**	**0**	**0**	**0**	**6**	**0**	**0**	**0**	**28:21**
2004-05	MODO	Sweden	14	2	4	6	32	....	....	....	....	....	....	....	....	....	6	1	0	1	16	....	....	....	....
2005-06	**Chicago**	**NHL**	**33**	**1**	**5**	**6**	**38**	**1**	**0**	**0**	**59**	**1.7**	**-13**	**0**	**0.0**	**22:58**	....	....	....	....	....	....	....	....	....
2006-07	**Chicago**	**NHL**	**59**	**4**	**12**	**16**	**50**	**2**	**0**	**3**	**96**	**4.2**	**-22**	**0**	**0.0**	**20:50**	....	....	....	....	....	....	....	....	....
2007-08	**Calgary**	**NHL**	**76**	**10**	**25**	**35**	**37**	**5**	**0**	**1**	**121**	**8.3**	**13**	**0**	**0.0**	**20:58**	**7**	**0**	**3**	**3**	**4**	**0**	**0**	**0**	**18:13**
2008-09	**Calgary**	**NHL**	**81**	**10**	**24**	**34**	**46**	**3**	**0**	**3**	**126**	**7.9**	**-8**	**0**	**0.0**	**22:18**	**6**	**2**	**1**	**3**	**2**	**0**	**0**	**0**	**21:10**
2009-10	**Phoenix**	**NHL**	**82**	**8**	**20**	**28**	**56**	**1**	**0**	**2**	**144**	**5.6**	**2**	**1**	**100.0**	**22:33**	**7**	**0**	**2**	**2**	**10**	**0**	**0**	**0**	**21:16**
	NHL Totals		**933**	**116**	**248**	**364**	**683**	**56**	**2**	**18**	**1872**	**6.2**		**2**	**100.0**	**23:54**	**47**	**6**	**13**	**19**	**32**	**3**	**0**	**0**	**25:08**

Played in NHL All-Star Game (2004)

• Missed majority of 1997-98 season recovering from ankle (October 4, 1997 vs. Anaheim) and groin (November 1, 1997 vs. Pittsburgh) injuries. Traded to **Tampa Bay** by **Vancouver** with Vancouver's 2nd round choice (Alexander Polushin) in 2001 Entry Draft for Dan Cloutier, February 7, 2001. Traded to **NY Islanders** by **Tampa Bay** with Alexander Kharitonov for Mathieu Biron and NY Islanders' 2nd round choice (later traded to Washington, later traded to Vancouver – Vancouver selected Denis Grot) in 2002 Entry Draft, June 22, 2001. Signed as a free agent by **MODO** (Sweden), December 21, 2004. Signed as a free agent by **Chicago**, August 2, 2005. Traded to **Calgary** by **Chicago** with Chicago's 7th round choice (C.J. Severyn) in 2007 Entry Draft for Andrei Zyuzin and Steve Marr, June 22, 2007. Signed as a free agent by **Phoenix**, July 2, 2009.

AUCOIN, Keith

(oh-KOIN, KEETH) **WSH.**

Center. Shoots right. 5'9", 187 lbs. Born, Waltham, MA, November 6, 1978.

Season	Club	League	GP	G	A	Pts	PIM	PP	SH	GW	S	%	+/-	TF	F%	Min	GP	G	A	Pts	PIM	PP	SH	GW	Min
1997-98	Norwich U.	ECAC-3	26	19	14	33	....	....	....	....	....	....	....	....	....	....	....	....	....	....	....	....	....	....	....
1998-99	Norwich U.	ECAC-3	31	33	39	72	....	....	....	....	....	....	....	....	....	....	....	....	....	....	....	....	....	....	....
99-2000	Norwich U.	ECAC-3	31	36	41	77	14	....	....	....	....	....	....	....	....	....	....	....	....	....	....	....	....	....	....
2000-01	Norwich U.	ECAC-3	28	26	30	56	26	....	....	....	....	....	....	....	....	....	....	....	....	....	....	....	....	....	....
2001-02	Lowell	AHL	30	6	10	16	8	....	....	....	....	....	....	....	....	....	....	....	....	....	....	....	....	....	....
	Florida Everblades	ECHL	1	0	2	2	0	....	....	....	....	....	....	....	....	....	....	....	....	....	....	....	....	....	....
	BC Icemen	UHL	44	23	35	58	42	....	....	....	....	....	....	....	....	....	10	3	5	8	4	....	....	....	....

Season	Club	League	GP	G	A	Pts	PIM	PP	SH	GW	S	%	+/-	TF	F%	Min	GP	G	A	Pts	PIM	PP	SH	GW	Min
			Regular Season														Playoffs								
2002-03	Providence Bruins	AHL	78	25	49	74	71	....	....	....	....	....	....	....	....	....	4	0	1	1	6	....	....	....	....
2003-04	Cincinnati	AHL	80	18	30	48	64	....	....	....	....	....	....	....	....	....	9	0	3	3	4	....	....	....	....
2004-05	Memphis	CHL	5	4	5	9	10	....	....	....	....	....	....	....	....	....	....	....	....	....	....	....	....	....	....
	Providence Bruins	AHL	72	21	45	66	49	....	....	....	....	....	....	....	....	....	17	4	*14	18	18	....	....	....	....
2005-06	**Carolina**	**NHL**	**7**	**0**	**1**	**1**	**4**	**0**	**0**	**0**	**3**	**0.0**	**–4**	**4**	**100.0**	**5:19**	....	....	....	....	....	....	....	....	....
	Lowell	AHL	72	29	56	85	68	....	....	....	....	....	....	....	....	....	....	....	....	....	....	....	....	....	....
2006-07	**Carolina**	**NHL**	**8**	**0**	**1**	**1**	**0**	**0**	**0**	**0**	**6**	**0.0**	**1**	**29**	**65.5**	**6:17**	....	....	....	....	....	....	....	....	....
	Albany River Rats	AHL	65	27	72	99	108	....	....	....	....	....	....	....	....	....	5	1	3	4	7	....	....	....	....
2007-08	**Carolina**	**NHL**	**38**	**5**	**8**	**13**	**10**	**0**	**0**	**0**	**65**	**7.7**	**3**	**327**	**37.9**	**13:28**	....	....	....	....	....	....	....	....	....
	Albany River Rats	AHL	38	8	37	45	38	....	....	....	....	....	....	....	....	....	....	....	....	....	....	....	....	....	....
2008-09	**Washington**	**NHL**	**12**	**2**	**4**	**6**	**4**	**1**	**0**	**0**	**15**	**13.3**	**5**	**83**	**39.8**	**10:19**	....	....	....	....	....	....	....	....	....
	Hershey Bears	AHL	70	25	*71	96	73	....	....	....	....	....	....	....	....	....	21	5	*18	23	16	....	....	....	....
2009-10	**Washington**	**NHL**	**9**	**1**	**4**	**5**	**0**	**0**	**0**	**0**	**4**	**25.0**	**–2**	**56**	**55.4**	**8:48**	....	....	....	....	....	....	....	....	....
	Hershey Bears	AHL	72	35	*71	*106	49	....	....	....	....	....	....	....	....	....	21	2	*23	25	2	....	....	....	....
	NHL Totals		**74**	**8**	**18**	**26**	**18**	**1**	**0**	**0**	**93**	**8.6**		**499**	**42.3**	**10:50**	....	....	....	....	....	....	....	....	....

ECAC-3 First All-Star Team (2000, 2001) • ECAC-3 Player of the Year (2000, 2001) • AHL Second All-Star Team (2006, 2007) • AHL First All-Star Team (2009) • John B. Sollenberger Trophy (AHL – Leading Scorer) (2010) • Les Cunningham Award (AHL – MVP) (2010)

Signed as a free agent by **Lowell** (AHL), June 19, 2001. Signed as a free agent by **Providence** (AHL), August 2, 2002. Signed as a free agent by **Anaheim**, August 29, 2003. Signed to a PTO (professional tryout) contract by **Providence** (AHL), November 4, 2004, Signed as a free agent by **Providence** (AHL), December 9, 2004. Signed as a free agent by **Carolina**, August 4, 2005. Signed as a free agent by **Washington**, July 3, 2008.

AVERY, Sean

(AY-vuhr-ee, SHAWN) **NYR**

Center. Shoots left. 5'11", 195 lbs. Born, Pickering, Ont., April 10, 1980.

Season	Club	League	GP	G	A	Pts	PIM	PP	SH	GW	S	%	+/-	TF	F%	Min	GP	G	A	Pts	PIM	PP	SH	GW	Min
1995-96	Markham	Minor-ON	70	34	81	115	180	....	....	....	....	....	....	....	....	....	....	....	....	....	....	....	....	....	....
	Markham Waxers	MTJHL	1	0	0	0	4	....	....	....	....	....	....	....	....	....	....	....	....	....	....	....	....	....	....
1996-97	Owen Sound	OHL	58	10	21	31	86	....	....	....	....	....	....	....	....	....	4	1	0	1	4	....	....	....	....
1997-98	Owen Sound	OHL	47	13	41	54	105	....	....	....	....	....	....	....	....	....	....	....	....	....	....	....	....	....	....
1998-99	Owen Sound	OHL	28	22	23	45	70	....	....	....	....	....	....	....	....	....	....	....	....	....	....	....	....	....	....
	Kingston	OHL	33	14	25	39	88	....	....	....	....	....	....	....	....	....	5	1	3	4	13	....	....	....	....
99-2000	Kingston	OHL	55	28	56	84	215	....	....	....	....	....	....	....	....	....	5	2	2	4	26	....	....	....	....
2000-01	Cincinnati	AHL	58	8	15	23	304	....	....	....	....	....	....	....	....	....	4	1	0	1	19	....	....	....	....
2001-02	**Detroit**	**NHL**	**36**	**2**	**2**	**4**	**68**	**0**	**0**	**1**	**30**	**6.7**	**1**	**299**	**51.8**	**7:51**	....	....	....	....	....	....	....	....	....
	Cincinnati	AHL	36	14	7	21	106	....	....	....	....	....	....	....	....	....	....	....	....	....	....	....	....	....	....
2002-03	**Detroit**	**NHL**	**39**	**5**	**6**	**11**	**120**	**0**	**0**	**2**	**40**	**12.5**	**7**	**224**	**58.0**	**7:03**	....	....	....	....	....	....	....	....	....
	Grand Rapids	AHL	15	6	6	12	82	....	....	....	....	....	....	....	....	....	....	....	....	....	....	....	....	....	....
	Los Angeles	**NHL**	**12**	**1**	**3**	**4**	**33**	**0**	**0**	**0**	**19**	**5.3**	**0**	**49**	**46.9**	**13:50**	....	....	....	....	....	....	....	....	....
	Manchester	AHL	....	....	....	....	....	....	....	....	....	....	....	....	....	....	3	2	1	3	8	....	....	....	....
2003-04	**Los Angeles**	**NHL**	**76**	**9**	**19**	**28**	***261**	**0**	**0**	**2**	**125**	**7.2**	**2**	**124**	**54.8**	**11:41**	....	....	....	....	....	....	....	....	....
2004-05	Pelicans Lahti	Finland	2	3	0	3	26	....	....	....	....	....	....	....	....	....	....	....	....	....	....	....	....	....	....
	Motor City	UHL	16	15	11	26	149	....	....	....	....	....	....	....	....	....	....	....	....	....	....	....	....	....	....
2005-06	**Los Angeles**	**NHL**	**75**	**15**	**24**	**39**	***257**	**1**	**3**	**1**	**189**	**7.9**	**–5**	**226**	**44.3**	**13:37**	....	....	....	....	....	....	....	....	....
2006-07	**Los Angeles**	**NHL**	**55**	**10**	**18**	**28**	**116**	**1**	**1**	**2**	**160**	**6.3**	**–10**	**180**	**47.2**	**16:52**	....	....	....	....	....	....	....	....	....
	NY Rangers	**NHL**	**29**	**8**	**12**	**20**	**58**	**1**	**0**	**0**	**89**	**9.0**	**11**	**110**	**52.7**	**17:49**	**10**	**1**	**4**	**5**	**27**	**0**	**0**	**0**	**19:27**
2007-08	**NY Rangers**	**NHL**	**57**	**15**	**18**	**33**	**154**	**2**	**0**	**4**	**125**	**12.0**	**6**	**28**	**39.3**	**15:50**	**8**	**4**	**3**	**7**	**6**	**1**	**0**	**1**	**14:14**
2008-09	**Dallas**	**NHL**	**23**	**3**	**7**	**10**	**77**	**0**	**0**	**0**	**49**	**6.1**	**2**	**12**	**41.7**	**14:59**	....	....	....	....	....	....	....	....	....
	Hartford	AHL	8	2	1	3	8	....	....	....	....	....	....	....	....	....	....	....	....	....	....	....	....	....	....
	NY Rangers	**NHL**	**18**	**5**	**7**	**12**	**34**	**2**	**0**	**0**	**50**	**10.0**	**4**	**6**	**66.7**	**16:44**	**6**	**0**	**2**	**2**	**24**	**0**	**0**	**0**	**17:38**
2009-10	**NY Rangers**	**NHL**	**69**	**11**	**20**	**31**	**160**	**3**	**0**	**1**	**139**	**7.9**	**0**	**14**	**28.6**	**13:23**	....	....	....	....	....	....	....	....	....
	NHL Totals		**489**	**84**	**136**	**220**	**1338**	**10**	**4**	**13**	**1015**	**8.3**		**1272**	**50.6**	**13:24**	**24**	**5**	**9**	**14**	**57**	**1**	**0**	**1**	**17:15**

Signed as a free agent by **Detroit**, September 21, 1999. Traded to **Los Angeles** by **Detroit** with Maxim Kuznetsov, Detroit's 1st round choice (Jeff Tambellini) in 2003 Entry Draft and Detroit's 2nd round choice (later traded to Boston – Boston selected Martins Karsums) in 2004 Entry Draft for Mathieu Schneider, March 11, 2003. Signed as a free agent by **Lahti** (Finland), November 24, 2004. Signed as a free agent by **Motor City** (UHL), February 11, 2005. Traded to **NY Rangers** by **Los Angeles** with John Seymour for Jason Ward, Jan Marek, Marc-Andre Cliche and NY Rangers' 3rd round choice (later traded to Buffalo - Buffalo selected Corey Fienhage) in 2008 Entry Draft, February 5, 2007. Signed as a free agent by **Dallas**, July 2, 2008. Claimed on waivers by **NY Rangers** from **Dallas**, March 3, 2009.

AXELSSON, P.J.

(AHX-ehl-suhn, PEE-JAY)

Left wing. Shoots left. 6'1", 188 lbs. Born, Kungalv, Sweden, February 26, 1975. Boston's 7th choice, 177th overall, in 1995 Entry Draft.

Season	Club	League	GP	G	A	Pts	PIM	PP	SH	GW	S	%	+/-	TF	F%	Min	GP	G	A	Pts	PIM	PP	SH	GW	Min
1992-93	V.Frolunda Jr.	Swe-Jr.	16	9	5	14	12	....	....	....	....	....	....	....	....	....	....	....	....	....	....	....	....	....	....
	V.Frolunda	Sweden	1	0	0	0	0	....	....	....	....	....	....	....	....	....	....	....	....	....	....	....	....	....	....
1993-94	V.Frolunda	Sweden	11	0	0	0	4	....	....	....	....	....	....	....	....	....	4	0	0	0	0	....	....	....	....
1994-95	V.Frolunda Jr.	Swe-Jr.	19	16	9	25	22	....	....	....	....	....	....	....	....	....	....	....	....	....	....	....	....	....	....
	V.Frolunda	Sweden	11	2	1	3	6	....	....	....	....	....	....	....	....	....	5	0	0	0	0	....	....	....	....
1995-96	V.Frolunda	Sweden	36	15	5	20	10	....	....	....	....	....	....	....	....	....	13	3	0	3	10	....	....	....	....
1996-97	V.Frolunda	Sweden	50	19	15	34	34	....	....	....	....	....	....	....	....	....	3	0	2	2	0	....	....	....	....
	V.Frolunda	EuroHL	3	1	1	2	0	....	....	....	....	....	....	....	....	....	3	0	0	0	2	....	....	....	....
1997-98	**Boston**	**NHL**	**82**	**8**	**19**	**27**	**38**	**2**	**0**	**1**	**144**	**5.6**	**–14**	....	....	....	**6**	**1**	**0**	**1**	**0**	**0**	**0**	**0**	
1998-99	**Boston**	**NHL**	**77**	**7**	**10**	**17**	**18**	**0**	**0**	**2**	**146**	**4.8**	**–14**	**8**	**75.0**	**16:38**	**12**	**1**	**1**	**2**	**4**	**0**	**0**	**0**	**15:11**
99-2000	**Boston**	**NHL**	**81**	**10**	**16**	**26**	**24**	**0**	**0**	**4**	**186**	**5.4**	**1**	**22**	**27.3**	**16:43**	....	....	....	....	....	....	....	....	....
2000-01	**Boston**	**NHL**	**81**	**8**	**15**	**23**	**27**	**0**	**0**	**2**	**146**	**5.5**	**–12**	**41**	**36.6**	**12:30**	....	....	....	....	....	....	....	....	....
2001-02	**Boston**	**NHL**	**78**	**7**	**17**	**24**	**16**	**0**	**2**	**0**	**127**	**5.5**	**6**	**17**	**35.3**	**14:42**	**6**	**2**	**1**	**3**	**6**	**0**	**1**	**1**	**16:48**
	Sweden	Olympics	4	0	0	0	2	....	....	....	....	....	....	....	....	....	....	....	....	....	....	....	....	....	....
2002-03	**Boston**	**NHL**	**66**	**17**	**19**	**36**	**24**	**2**	**2**	**1**	**122**	**13.9**	**8**	**17**	**23.5**	**16:37**	**5**	**0**	**0**	**0**	**6**	**0**	**0**	**0**	**13:23**
2003-04	**Boston**	**NHL**	**68**	**6**	**14**	**20**	**42**	**0**	**0**	**1**	**107**	**5.6**	**2**	**13**	**15.4**	**16:19**	**7**	**0**	**0**	**0**	**4**	**0**	**0**	**0**	**14:43**
2004-05	Frolunda	Sweden	45	8	9	17	95	....	....	....	....	....	....	....	....	....	14	1	*10	11	18	....	....	....	....
2005-06	**Boston**	**NHL**	**59**	**10**	**18**	**28**	**4**	**1**	**2**	**1**	**113**	**8.8**	**–3**	**27**	**40.7**	**17:36**	....	....	....	....	....	....	....	....	....
	Sweden	Olympics	8	3	3	6	0	....	....	....	....	....	....	....	....	....	....	....	....	....	....	....	....	....	....
2006-07	**Boston**	**NHL**	**55**	**11**	**16**	**27**	**52**	**3**	**2**	**0**	**81**	**13.6**	**–10**	**38**	**34.2**	**19:34**	....	....	....	....	....	....	....	....	....
2007-08	**Boston**	**NHL**	**75**	**13**	**16**	**29**	**15**	**0**	**2**	**2**	**100**	**13.0**	**11**	**45**	**37.8**	**17:36**	**7**	**0**	**0**	**0**	**2**	**0**	**0**	**0**	**16:57**
2008-09	**Boston**	**NHL**	**75**	**6**	**24**	**30**	**16**	**2**	**0**	**0**	**87**	**6.9**	**–1**	**47**	**34.0**	**16:14**	**11**	**0**	**1**	**1**	**2**	**0**	**0**	**0**	**14:03**
2009-10	Frolunda	Sweden	47	10	16	26	51	....	....	....	....	....	....	....	....	....	....	....	....	....	....	....	....	....	....
	NHL Totals		**797**	**103**	**184**	**287**	**276**	**10**	**10**	**14**	**1359**	**7.6**		**275**	**34.9**	**16:18**	**54**	**4**	**3**	**7**	**24**	**0**	**1**	**1**	**15:08**

Signed as a free agent by **Frolunda** (Sweden), September 15, 2004. Signed as a free agent by **Frolunda** (Sweden), July 28, 2009.

BABCHUK, Anton

(bab-CHUHK, AN-tawn) **CAR.**

Defense. Shoots right. 6'5", 212 lbs. Born, Kiev, USSR, May 6, 1984. Chicago's 1st choice, 21st overall, in 2002 Entry Draft.

Season	Club	League	GP	G	A	Pts	PIM	PP	SH	GW	S	%	+/-	TF	F%	Min	GP	G	A	Pts	PIM	PP	SH	GW	Min
99-2000	Elektrostal 2	Russia-3	6	0	0	0	8	....	....	....	....	....	....	....	....	....	....	....	....	....	....	....	....	....	....
	Elektrostal 2	Russia-3	18	0	1	1	18	....	....	....	....	....	....	....	....	....	....	....	....	....	....	....	....	....	....
2000-01	Elektrostal	Russia-2	7	0	0	0	12	....	....	....	....	....	....	....	....	....	....	....	....	....	....	....	....	....	....
	Russia 17	Nat-Tm	15	1	3	4	12	....	....	....	....	....	....	....	....	....	....	....	....	....	....	....	....	....	....
2001-02	Elektrostal	Russia-2	40	7	8	15	90	....	....	....	....	....	....	....	....	....	....	....	....	....	....	....	....	....	....
	Elektrostal 2	Russia-3	3	0	0	0	8	....	....	....	....	....	....	....	....	....	....	....	....	....	....	....	....	....	....
2002-03	Ak Bars Kazan	Russia	10	0	0	0	4	....	....	....	....	....	....	....	....	....	....	....	....	....	....	....	....	....	....
	St. Petersburg	Russia	20	3	0	3	10	....	....	....	....	....	....	....	....	....	....	....	....	....	....	....	....	....	....
	Spartak St. Pet.	Russia-2	1	1	0	1	0	....	....	....	....	....	....	....	....	....	....	....	....	....	....	....	....	....	....
2003-04	**Chicago**	**NHL**	**5**	**0**	**2**	**2**	**2**	**0**	**0**	**0**	**11**	**0.0**	**–1**	**0**	**0.0**	**12:43**	....	....	....	....	....	....	....	....	....
	Norfolk Admirals	AHL	73	8	14	22	89	....	....	....	....	....	....	....	....	....	8	0	2	2	6	....	....	....	....
2004-05	Norfolk Admirals	AHL	66	8	16	24	88	....	....	....	....	....	....	....	....	....	2	0	0	0	2	....	....	....	....
2005-06	**Chicago**	**NHL**	**17**	**2**	**3**	**5**	**16**	**1**	**0**	**0**	**24**	**8.3**	**–5**	**0**	**0.0**	**16:38**	....	....	....	....	....	....	....	....	....
	Norfolk Admirals	AHL	24	5	7	12	22	....	....	....	....	....	....	....	....	....	....	....	....	....	....	....	....	....	....
	♦ **Carolina**	**NHL**	**22**	**3**	**2**	**5**	**6**	**2**	**0**	**0**	**32**	**9.4**	**–2**	**0**	**0.0**	**13:22**	....	....	....	....	....	....	....	....	....
	Lowell	AHL	5	1	3	4	0	....	....	....	....	....	....	....	....	....	....	....	....	....	....	....	....	....	....
2006-07	**Carolina**	**NHL**	**52**	**2**	**12**	**14**	**30**	**0**	**0**	**2**	**63**	**3.2**	**–6**	**0**	**0.0**	**17:26**	....	....	....	....	....	....	....	....	....
	Albany River Rats	AHL	9	1	6	7	2	....	....	....	....	....	....	....	....	....	....	....	....	....	....	....	....	....	....
2007-08	Avangard Omsk	Russia	57	9	17	26	30	....	....	....	....	....	....	....	....	....	4	1	1	2	6	....	....	....	....
2008-09	**Carolina**	**NHL**	**72**	**16**	**19**	**35**	**16**	**9**	**0**	**4**	**127**	**12.6**	**13**	**0**	**0.0**	**18:04**	**13**	**0**	**1**	**1**	**10**	**0**	**0**	**0**	**16:03**
2009-10	Omsk	Rus-KHL	49	9	13	22	36	....	....	....	....	....	....	....	....	....	2	0	0	0	0	....	....	....	....
	NHL Totals		**168**	**23**	**38**	**61**	**70**	**12**	**0**	**6**	**257**	**8.9**		**0**	**0.0**	**16:57**	**13**	**0**	**1**	**1**	**10**	**0**	**0**	**0**	**16:03**

Traded to **Carolina** by **Chicago** for Danny Richmond and Columbus' 4th round choice (previously acquired, later traded to Toronto - Toronto selected James Reimer) in 2006 Entry Draft, January 20, 2006.
Signed as a free agent by **Omsk** (Russia-KHL), September 20, 2009.

BACKES, David
(BA-kuhs, DAY-vihd) **ST.L.**

Center. Shoots right. 6'3", 225 lbs. Born, Blaine, MN, May 1, 1984. St. Louis' 2nd choice, 62nd overall, in 2003 Entry Draft.

			Regular Season														Playoffs								
Season	Club	League	GP	G	A	Pts	PIM	PP	SH	GW	S	%	+/-	TF	F%	Min	GP	G	A	Pts	PIM	PP	SH	GW	Min
99-2000	Spring Lake Park	High-MN	24	17	20	37	....	....	....	....	....	....	....	....	....	....	....	....	....	....	....	....	....	....	....
2000-01	Spring Lake Park	High-MN	24	29	46	75	....	....	....	....	....	....	....	....	....	....	....	....	....	....	....	....	....	....	....
2001-02	Chicago Steel	USHL	25	31	36	67	....	....	....	....	....	....	....	....	....	....	2	1	1	2	....	....	....	....	....
	Lincoln Stars	USHL	30	11	10	21	54	....	....	....	....	....	....	....	....	....	3	0	0	0	2	....	....	....	....
2002-03	Lincoln Stars	USHL	57	28	41	69	126	....	....	....	....	....	....	....	....	....	7	4	1	5	17	....	....	....	....
2003-04	Minnesota State	WCHA	39	16	21	37	66	....	....	....	....	....	....	....	....	....	....	....	....	....	....	....	....	....	....
2004-05	Minnesota State	WCHA	38	17	23	40	55	....	....	....	....	....	....	....	....	....	....	....	....	....	....	....	....	....	....
2005-06	Minnesota State	WCHA	38	13	29	42	91	....	....	....	....	....	....	....	....	....	....	....	....	....	....	....	....	....	....
	Peoria Rivermen	AHL	12	5	5	10	10	....	....	....	....	....	....	....	....	....	3	1	1	2	8	....	....	....	....
2006-07	**St. Louis**	**NHL**	**49**	**10**	**13**	**23**	**37**	**2**	**0**	**2**	**89**	**11.2**	**6**	**26**	**46.2**	**13:25**	....	....	....	....	....	....	....	....	....
	Peoria Rivermen	AHL	31	10	3	13	47	....	....	....	....	....	....	....	....	....	....	....	....	....	....	....	....	....	....
2007-08	**St. Louis**	**NHL**	**72**	**13**	**18**	**31**	**99**	**3**	**0**	**2**	**129**	**10.1**	**-11**	**67**	**44.8**	**14:41**	....	....	....	....	....	....	....	....	....
2008-09	**St. Louis**	**NHL**	**82**	**31**	**23**	**54**	**165**	**6**	**2**	**1**	**208**	**14.9**	**-3**	**477**	**44.4**	**17:41**	**4**	**1**	**2**	**3**	**10**	**0**	**0**	**0**	**22:56**
2009-10	**St. Louis**	**NHL**	**79**	**17**	**31**	**48**	**106**	**5**	**0**	**3**	**163**	**10.4**	**-4**	**1065**	**47.3**	**18:18**	....	....	....	....	....	....	....	....	....
	United States	Olympics	6	1	2	3	2	....	....	....	....	....	....	....	....	....	....	....	....	....	....	....	....	....	....
	NHL Totals		**282**	**71**	**85**	**156**	**407**	**16**	**2**	**8**	**589**	**12.1**		**1635**	**46.4**	**16:21**	**4**	**1**	**2**	**3**	**10**	**0**	**0**	**0**	**22:56**

USHL First All-Star Team (2003) • WCHA All-Rookie Team (2004) • WCHA Second All-Star Team (2006) • NCAA West Second All-American Team (2006)

BACKLUND, Mikael
(BAHK-luhnd, mih-KIGH-ehl) **CGY.**

Center. Shoots left. 6', 200 lbs. Born, Vasteras, Sweden, March 17, 1989. Calgary's 1st choice, 24th overall, in 2007 Entry Draft.

Season	Club	League	GP	G	A	Pts	PIM	PP	SH	GW	S	%	+/-	TF	F%	Min	GP	G	A	Pts	PIM	PP	SH	GW	Min
2004-05	Vasteras U18	Swe-U18	14	5	6	11	14	....	....	....	....	....	....	....	....	....	4	2	1	3	2	....	....	....	....
2005-06	Vasteras Jr.	Swe-Jr.	25	15	16	31	30	....	....	....	....	....	....	....	....	....	....	....	....	....	....	....	....	....	....
	VIK Vasteras HK	Sweden-2	12	2	2	4	14	....	....	....	....	....	....	....	....	....	....	....	....	....	....	....	....	....	....
2006-07	Vasteras U18	Swe-U18	2	2	1	3	2	....	....	....	....	....	....	....	....	....	1	0	0	0	10	....	....	....	....
	Vasteras Jr.	Swe-Jr.	7	5	4	9	8	....	....	....	....	....	....	....	....	....	5	1	0	1	4	....	....	....	....
	VIK Vasteras HK	Sweden-2	18	1	2	3	14	....	....	....	....	....	....	....	....	....	....	....	....	....	....	....	....	....	....
2007-08	Vasteras Jr.	Swe-Jr.	9	7	6	13	20	....	....	....	....	....	....	....	....	....	....	....	....	....	....	....	....	....	....
	VIK Vasteras HK	Sweden-2	46	11	4	15	28	....	....	....	....	....	....	....	....	....	5	4	3	7	0	....	....	....	....
2008-09	Vasteras Jr.	Swe-Jr.	2	3	2	5	0	....	....	....	....	....	....	....	....	....	....	....	....	....	....	....	....	....	....
	VIK Vasteras HK	Sweden-2	17	4	4	8	39	....	....	....	....	....	....	....	....	....	....	....	....	....	....	....	....	....	....
	Calgary	**NHL**	**1**	**0**	**0**	**0**	**0**	**0**	**0**	**0**	**1**	**0.0**	**0**	**7**	**28.6**	**10:44**	....	....	....	....	....	....	....	....	....
	Kelowna Rockets	WHL	28	12	18	30	26	....	....	....	....	....	....	....	....	....	19	*13	10	23	26	....	....	....	....
2009-10	**Calgary**	**NHL**	**23**	**1**	**9**	**10**	**6**	**0**	**0**	**0**	**47**	**2.1**	**5**	**191**	**53.4**	**12:36**	....	....	....	....	....	....	....	....	....
	Abbotsford Heat	AHL	54	15	17	32	26	....	....	....	....	....	....	....	....	....	13	1	8	9	14	....	....	....	....
	NHL Totals		**24**	**1**	**9**	**10**	**6**	**0**	**0**	**0**	**48**	**2.1**		**198**	**52.5**	**12:31**	....	....	....	....	....	....	....	....	....

• Assigned to **Vasteras** (Sweden-2) by **Calgary**, October 4, 2008.

BACKMAN, Christian
(BAK-man, KRIH-stan)

Defense. Shoots left. 6'4", 210 lbs. Born, Alingsas, Sweden, April 28, 1980. St. Louis' 1st choice, 24th overall, in 1998 Entry Draft.

Season	Club	League	GP	G	A	Pts	PIM	PP	SH	GW	S	%	+/-	TF	F%	Min	GP	G	A	Pts	PIM	PP	SH	GW	Min
1996-97	V.Frolunda Jr.	Swe-Jr.	26	2	5	7	16	....	....	....	....	....	....	....	....	....	....	....	....	....	....	....	....	....	....
1997-98	V.Frolunda U18	Swe-U18	4	4	1	5	2	....	....	....	....	....	....	....	....	....	5	2	2	4	2	....	....	....	....
	V.Frolunda Jr.	Swe-Jr.	28	5	14	19	12	....	....	....	....	....	....	....	....	....	2	0	1	1	4	....	....	....	....
1998-99	V.Frolunda Jr.	Swe-Jr.	4	0	2	2	4	....	....	....	....	....	....	....	....	....	....	....	....	....	....	....	....	....	....
	V.Frolunda	Sweden	49	0	4	4	4	....	....	....	....	....	....	....	....	....	4	0	0	0	0	....	....	....	....
99-2000	V.Frolunda Jr.	Swe-Jr.	5	1	1	2	0	....	....	....	....	....	....	....	....	....	3	1	1	2	0	....	....	....	....
	Gislaveds SK	Sweden-2	21	5	2	7	8	....	....	....	....	....	....	....	....	....	....	....	....	....	....	....	....	....	....
	V.Frolunda	Sweden	27	1	0	1	14	....	....	....	....	....	....	....	....	....	5	0	0	0	0	....	....	....	....
2000-01	V.Frolunda	Sweden	50	1	10	11	32	....	....	....	....	....	....	....	....	....	3	0	2	2	2	....	....	....	....
2001-02	V.Frolunda	Sweden	44	7	4	11	38	....	....	....	....	....	....	....	....	....	10	0	0	0	8	....	....	....	....
2002-03	**St. Louis**	**NHL**	**4**	**0**	**0**	**0**	**0**	**0**	**0**	**0**	**4**	**0.0**	**-3**	**0**	**0.0**	**12:22**	....	....	....	....	....	....	....	....	....
	Worcester IceCats	AHL	72	8	19	27	66	....	....	....	....	....	....	....	....	....	3	0	1	1	5	....	....	....	....
2003-04	**St. Louis**	**NHL**	**66**	**5**	**13**	**18**	**16**	**1**	**0**	**0**	**92**	**5.4**	**3**	**0**	**0.0**	**19:20**	**5**	**0**	**2**	**2**	**4**	**0**	**0**	**0**	**23:06**
	Worcester IceCats	AHL	4	1	2	3	2	....	....	....	....	....	....	....	....	....	....	....	....	....	....	....	....	....	....
2004-05	Frolunda	Sweden	50	4	15	19	40	....	....	....	....	....	....	....	....	....	14	2	7	9	10	....	....	....	....
2005-06	**St. Louis**	**NHL**	**52**	**6**	**12**	**18**	**48**	**3**	**0**	**1**	**70**	**8.6**	**-15**	**0**	**0.0**	**24:49**	....	....	....	....	....	....	....	....	....
	Sweden	Olympics	8	1	2	3	6	....	....	....	....	....	....	....	....	....	....	....	....	....	....	....	....	....	....
2006-07	**St. Louis**	**NHL**	**61**	**7**	**11**	**18**	**36**	**1**	**0**	**0**	**80**	**8.8**	**13**	**0**	**0.0**	**22:10**	....	....	....	....	....	....	....	....	....
2007-08	**St. Louis**	**NHL**	**45**	**1**	**9**	**10**	**30**	**0**	**0**	**0**	**30**	**3.3**	**-4**	**0**	**0.0**	**19:22**	....	....	....	....	....	....	....	....	....
	NY Rangers	**NHL**	**18**	**2**	**6**	**8**	**20**	**1**	**0**	**0**	**21**	**9.5**	**2**	**0**	**0.0**	**18:49**	**8**	**0**	**0**	**0**	**12**	**0**	**0**	**0**	**18:16**
2008-09	**Columbus**	**NHL**	**56**	**2**	**5**	**7**	**32**	**1**	**0**	**1**	**54**	**3.7**	**5**	**1**	**0.0**	**15:39**	....	....	....	....	....	....	....	....	....
2009-10	Frolunda	Sweden	47	10	18	28	46	....	....	....	....	....	....	....	....	....	7	1	2	3	6	....	....	....	....
	NHL Totals		**302**	**23**	**56**	**79**	**182**	**7**	**0**	**2**	**351**	**6.6**		**1**	**0.0**	**20:03**	**13**	**0**	**2**	**2**	**16**	**0**	**0**	**0**	**20:07**

Signed as a free agent by **Frolunda** (Sweden), September 15, 2004. Traded to **NY Rangers** by **St. Louis** for NY Rangers' 4th round choice (later traded back to NY Rangers - NY Rangers selected Dale Weise) in 2008 Entry Draft, February 26, 2008. Traded to **Columbus** by **NY Rangers** with Fedor Tyutin for Nikolai Zherdev and Dan Fritsche, July 2, 2008. Signed as a free agent by **Frolunda** (Sweden), October 9, 2009.

BACKSTROM, Nicklas
(BAK-struhm, NIHK-luhs) **WSH.**

Center. Shoots left. 6'1", 210 lbs. Born, Gavle, Sweden, November 23, 1987. Washington's 1st choice, 4th overall, in 2006 Entry Draft.

Season	Club	League	GP	G	A	Pts	PIM	PP	SH	GW	S	%	+/-	TF	F%	Min	GP	G	A	Pts	PIM	PP	SH	GW	Min
2001-02	Brynas U18	Swe-U18	2	0	0	0	0	....	....	....	....	....	....	....	....	....	....	....	....	....	....	....	....	....	....
2002-03	Brynas U18	Swe-U18	STATISTICS NOT AVAILABLE																						
2003-04	Brynas U18	Swe-U18	6	9	5	14	4	....	....	....	....	....	....	....	....	....	3	0	3	3	0	....	....	....	....
	Brynas IF Gavle Jr.	Swe-Jr.	21	2	6	8	2	....	....	....	....	....	....	....	....	....	5	0	0	0	4	....	....	....	....
2004-05	Brynas IF Gavle Jr.	Swe-Jr.	29	17	17	34	24	....	....	....	....	....	....	....	....	....	....	....	....	....	....	....	....	....	....
	Brynas IF Gavle	Sweden	19	0	0	0	2	....	....	....	....	....	....	....	....	....	....	....	....	....	....	....	....	....	....
2005-06	Brynas IF Gavle	Sweden	46	10	16	26	30	....	....	....	....	....	....	....	....	....	4	1	0	1	2	....	....	....	....
	Brynas IF Gavle Jr.	Swe-Jr.	....	....	....	....	....	....	....	....	....	....	....	....	....	....	1	0	0	0	2	....	....	....	....
2006-07	Brynas IF Gavle	Sweden	45	12	28	40	46	....	....	....	....	....	....	....	....	....	7	3	3	6	6	....	....	....	....
2007-08	**Washington**	**NHL**	**82**	**14**	**55**	**69**	**24**	**3**	**0**	**4**	**153**	**9.2**	**13**	**874**	**46.3**	**19:00**	**7**	**4**	**2**	**6**	**2**	**3**	**0**	**0**	**20:26**
2008-09	**Washington**	**NHL**	**82**	**22**	**66**	**88**	**46**	**14**	**0**	**1**	**174**	**12.6**	**16**	**1171**	**48.7**	**19:57**	**14**	**3**	**12**	**15**	**8**	**2**	**0**	**0**	**21:40**
2009-10	**Washington**	**NHL**	**82**	**33**	**68**	**101**	**50**	**11**	**0**	**4**	**222**	**14.9**	**37**	**1336**	**49.9**	**20:27**	**7**	**5**	**4**	**9**	**4**	**0**	**0**	**1**	**21:03**
	Sweden	Olympics	4	1	5	6	0	....	....	....	....	....	....	....	....	....	....	....	....	....	....	....	....	....	....
	NHL Totals		**246**	**69**	**189**	**258**	**120**	**28**	**0**	**9**	**549**	**12.6**		**3381**	**48.6**	**19:48**	**28**	**12**	**18**	**30**	**14**	**5**	**0**	**1**	**21:12**

NHL All-Rookie Team (2008)

BAILEY, Josh
(BAY-lee, JAWSH) **NYI**

Center. Shoots left. 6'1", 188 lbs. Born, Bowmanville, Ont., October 2, 1989. NY Islanders' 1st choice, 9th overall, in 2008 Entry Draft.

Season	Club	League	GP	G	A	Pts	PIM	PP	SH	GW	S	%	+/-	TF	F%	Min	GP	G	A	Pts	PIM	PP	SH	GW	Min
2004-05	Clarington	Minor-ON	69	53	59	112	38	....	....	....	....	....	....	....	....	....	....	....	....	....	....	....	....	....	....
2005-06	Owen Sound	OHL	55	7	19	26	8	....	....	....	....	....	....	....	....	....	11	0	0	0	0	....	....	....	....
2006-07	Owen Sound	OHL	27	11	15	26	8	....	....	....	....	....	....	....	....	....	....	....	....	....	....	....	....	....	....
	Windsor Spitfires	OHL	42	11	24	35	16	....	....	....	....	....	....	....	....	....	....	....	....	....	....	....	....	....	....
2007-08	Windsor Spitfires	OHL	67	29	67	96	32	....	....	....	....	....	....	....	....	....	5	1	5	6	2	....	....	....	....
2008-09	**NY Islanders**	**NHL**	**68**	**7**	**18**	**25**	**16**	**3**	**0**	**0**	**74**	**9.5**	**-14**	**807**	**41.1**	**15:29**	....	....	....	....	....	....	....	....	....
2009-10	**NY Islanders**	**NHL**	**73**	**16**	**19**	**35**	**18**	**3**	**1**	**2**	**112**	**14.3**	**5**	**426**	**40.1**	**15:09**	....	....	....	....	....	....	....	....	....
	NHL Totals		**141**	**23**	**37**	**60**	**34**	**6**	**1**	**2**	**186**	**12.4**		**1233**	**40.8**	**15:18**	....	....	....	....	....	....	....	....	....

BALLARD, Keith
(BAL-uhrd, KEETH) **VAN.**

Defense. Shoots left. 5'11", 208 lbs. Born, Baudette, MN, November 26, 1982. Buffalo's 1st choice, 11th overall, in 2002 Entry Draft.

Season	Club	League	GP	G	A	Pts	PIM	PP	SH	GW	S	%	+/-	TF	F%	Min	Playoffs GP	G	A	Pts	PIM	PP	SH	GW	Min
99-2000	USNTDP	U-18	6	1	1	2	4																		
	USNTDP	USHL	58	12	21	33	119																		
2000-01	Omaha Lancers	USHL	56	22	29	51	168										10	1	6	7	8				
2001-02	U. of Minnesota	WCHA	41	10	13	23	42																		
2002-03	U. of Minnesota	WCHA	41	12	29	41	78																		
2003-04	U. of Minnesota	WCHA	37	11	25	36	83																		
2004-05	Utah Grizzlies	AHL	60	2	18	20	88																		
2005-06	Phoenix	NHL	82	8	31	39	99	1	3	1	102	7.8	–18	0	0.0	19:59									
2006-07	Phoenix	NHL	69	5	22	27	59	2	0	0	79	6.3	–7	0	0.0	22:00									
2007-08	Phoenix	NHL	82	6	15	21	85	2	1	1	105	5.7	7	0	0.0	21:16									
2008-09	Florida	NHL	82	6	28	34	72	1	0	1	106	5.7	14	1	0.0	22:23									
2009-10	Florida	NHL	82	8	20	28	88	1	0	1	90	8.9	–7	0	0.0	22:24									
	NHL Totals		397	33	116	149	403	7	4	4	482	6.8		1	0.0	21:36									

USHL First All-Star Team (2001) • WCHA All-Rookie Team (2002) • WCHA First All-Star Team (2003, 2004) • NCAA West First All-American Team (2004)

Traded to **Colorado** by **Buffalo** for Steve Reinprecht, July 3, 2003. Traded to **Phoenix** by **Colorado** with Derek Morris for Ossi Vaananen, Chris Gratton and Phoenix's 2nd round choice (Paul Stastny) in 2005 Entry Draft, March 9, 2004. Traded to **Florida** by **Phoenix** with Nick Boynton and Ottawa's 2nd round choice (previously acquired, later traded back to Phoenix - Phoenix selected Jared Staal) in 2008 Entry Draft for Olli Jokinen, June 20, 2008. Traded to **Vancouver** by **Florida** with Victor Oreskovich for Steve Bernier, Michael Grabner and Vancouver's 1st round choice (Quinton Howden) in 2010 Entry Draft, June 25, 2010.

BANNISTER, Drew
(BAN-nihs-stuhr, DROO)

Defense. Shoots right. 6'2", 198 lbs. Born, Belleville, Ont., September 4, 1974. Tampa Bay's 2nd choice, 26th overall, in 1992 Entry Draft.

Season	Club	League	GP	G	A	Pts	PIM	PP	SH	GW	S	%	+/-	TF	F%	Min	Playoffs GP	G	A	Pts	PIM	PP	SH	GW	Min
1989-90	Sudbury Legion	NOHA	26	13	14	27	98																		
1990-91	Sault Ste. Marie	OHL	41	2	8	10	51										4	0	0	0	0				
1991-92	Sault Ste. Marie	OHL	64	4	21	25	122										16	3	10	13	36				
1992-93	Sault Ste. Marie	OHL	59	5	28	33	114										18	2	7	9	12				
1993-94	Sault Ste. Marie	OHL	58	7	43	50	108										14	6	9	15	20				
1994-95	Atlanta Knights	IHL	72	5	7	12	74										5	0	2	2	22				
1995-96	Tampa Bay	NHL	13	0	1	1	4	0	0	0	10	0.0	–1												
	Atlanta Knights	IHL	61	3	13	16	105										3	0	0	0	4				
1996-97	Tampa Bay	NHL	64	4	13	17	44	1	0	0	57	7.0	–21												
	Edmonton	NHL	1	0	1	1	0	0	0	0	2	0.0	–2				12	0	0	0	30	0	0	0	
1997-98	Edmonton	NHL	34	0	2	2	42	0	0	0	27	0.0	–7												
	Anaheim	NHL	27	0	6	6	47	0	0	0	23	0.0	–2												
1998-99	Las Vegas	IHL	16	2	1	3	73																		
	Tampa Bay	NHL	21	1	2	3	24	0	0	0	29	3.4	–4	0	0.0	15:49									
99-2000	Hartford	AHL	44	6	14	20	121										18	2	9	11	53				
2000-01	NY Rangers	NHL	3	0	0	0	0	0	0	0	3	0.0	–1	0	0.0	10:47									
	Hartford	AHL	73	9	30	39	143										5	0	2	2	6				
2001-02	Anaheim	NHL	1	0	0	0	0	0	0	0	1	0.0	0	0	0.0	13:19									
	Cincinnati	AHL	30	1	10	11	57										3	0	1	1	6				
2002-03	Karpat Oulu	Finland	41	2	12	14	81										14	2	0	2	*42				
2003-04	Blues Espoo	Finland	36	2	8	10	42										9	0	3	3	26				
	Cherepovets	Russia	3	0	0	0	4																		
2004-05	Nurnberg	Germany	46	1	12	13	97																		
2005-06	Kassel Huskies	Germany	44	9	12	21	79										5	2	6	8	8				
2006-07	Kassel Huskies	German-2	43	9	32	41																			
2007-08	Kassel Huskies	German-2	41	11	27	38	73										15	4	12	16	28				
2008-09	Kassel Huskies	Germany	34	2	15	17	84																		
2009-10	Binghamton	AHL	57	4	10	14	77																		
	NHL Totals		164	5	25	30	161	1	0	0	152	3.3		0	0.0	15:07	12	0	0	0	30	0	0	0	

Memorial Cup Tournament All-Star Team (1992, 1993) • OHL Second All-Star Team (1994)

Traded to **Edmonton** by **Tampa Bay** with Tampa Bay's 6th round choice (Peter Sarno) in 1997 Entry Draft for Jeff Norton, March 18, 1997. Traded to **Anaheim** by **Edmonton** for Bobby Dollas, January 9, 1998. Traded to **Tampa Bay** by **Anaheim** for Tampa Bay's 5th round choice (Peter Podhradsky) in 2000 Entry Draft, December 10, 1998. Signed as a free agent by **NY Rangers**, October 3, 1999. Signed as a free agent by **Anaheim**, July 27, 2001. • Missed majority of 2001-02 season recovering from shoulder injury suffered in game vs. Utah (AHL), November 30, 2001. Signed as a free agent by **Oulu** (Finland), October 20, 2002. Signed as a free agent by **Ottawa**, August 6, 2009.

BARANKA, Ivan
(ba-RAN-kuh, IGH-vuhn) **NYR**

Defense. Shoots left. 6'3", 205 lbs. Born, Ilava, Czech., May 19, 1985. NY Rangers' 2nd choice, 50th overall, in 2003 Entry Draft.

Season	Club	League	GP	G	A	Pts	PIM	PP	SH	GW	S	%	+/-	TF	F%	Min	Playoffs GP	G	A	Pts	PIM	PP	SH	GW	Min
2002-03	Dubnica Jr.	Slovak-Jr.	27	1	7	8	44																		
	Dubnica	Slovak-2	2	0	0	0	0																		
2003-04	Everett Silvertips	WHL	58	3	12	15	69										20	3	5	8	26				
2004-05	Everett Silvertips	WHL	64	7	16	23	64										11	3	1	4	6				
	Hartford	AHL															1	0	0	0	0				
2005-06	Hartford	AHL	59	5	16	21	87																		
2006-07	Hartford	AHL	54	3	20	23	50																		
2007-08	NY Rangers	NHL	1	0	1	1	0	0	0	0	1	0.0	1	0	0.0	12:44									
	Hartford	AHL	61	5	21	26	53										5	0	2	2	2				
2008-09	Spartak Moscow	Rus-KHL	47	2	8	10	50										6	1	2	3	6				
2009-10	Spartak Moscow	Rus-KHL	55	10	22	32	56										10	2	2	4	12				
	Slovakia	Olympics	7	1	0	1	0																		
	NHL Totals		1	0	1	1	0	0	0	0	1	0.0		0	0.0	12:44									

Signed as a free agent by **Spartak Moscow** (Russia-KHL), May 13, 2008.

BARCH, Krys
(BAHRCH, KRIHS) **DAL.**

Right wing. Shoots left. 6'1", 222 lbs. Born, Hamilton, Ont., March 26, 1980. Washington's 3rd choice, 106th overall, in 1998 Entry Draft.

Season	Club	League	GP	G	A	Pts	PIM	PP	SH	GW	S	%	+/-	TF	F%	Min	Playoffs GP	G	A	Pts	PIM	PP	SH	GW	Min
1995-96	Georgetown	OPJHL	41	6	8	14	10																		
1996-97	Georgetown	OPJHL	51	18	26	44	58																		
1997-98	London Knights	OHL	65	9	27	36	62										16	4	3	7	16				
1998-99	London Knights	OHL	66	18	20	38	66										25	9	17	26	15				
99-2000	London Knights	OHL	56	23	26	49	78																		
	Portland Pirates	AHL															4	0	2	2	2				
2000-01	Portland Pirates	AHL	76	10	15	25	91										2	0	0	0	0				
2001-02	Portland Pirates	AHL	29	3	8	11	28																		
	Richmond	ECHL	25	6	4	10	43																		
2002-03	Portland Pirates	AHL	36	1	7	8	49																		
2003-04			DID NOT PLAY																						
2004-05	Norfolk Admirals	AHL	9	1	0	1	37																		
	Greenville	ECHL	55	11	19	30	154										3	0	0	0	36				
2005-06	Iowa Stars	AHL	43	7	6	13	129										7	0	1	1	37				
	Greenville	ECHL	14	10	4	14	75																		
2006-07	Dallas	NHL	26	3	2	5	107	0	0	2	12	25.0	2	1	0.0	5:38									
	Iowa Stars	AHL	31	3	5	8	110																		
2007-08	Dallas	NHL	48	1	2	3	105	0	0	0	23	4.3	–3	2	0.0	6:30	3	0	0	0	2	0	0	0	2:21
2008-09	Dallas	NHL	72	4	5	9	133	0	0	1	27	14.8	1	7	28.6	6:27									
2009-10	Dallas	NHL	63	0	6	6	130	0	0	0	29	0.0	0	3	0.0	7:03									
	NHL Totals		209	8	15	23	475	0	0	3	91	8.8		13	15.4	6:33	3	0	0	0	2	0	0	0	2:21

Signed as a free agent by **Dallas**, July 18, 2006.

			Regular Season														Playoffs								
Season	Club	League	GP	G	A	Pts	PIM	PP	SH	GW	S	%	+/-	TF	F%	Min	GP	G	A	Pts	PIM	PP	SH	GW	Min

BARKER, Cam
(BAR-kuhr, KAM) **MIN.**

Defense. Shoots left. 6'3", 215 lbs. Born, Winnipeg, Man., April 4, 1986. Chicago's 1st choice, 3rd overall, in 2004 Entry Draft.

2001-02	Cornwall Colts	CJHL	72	6	23	29	132	....	....	....	....	....	....	....	....	....	....	....	....	....	....	....	....	....	....
	Medicine Hat	WHL	3	0	1	1	0	....	....	....	....	....	....	....	....	....	....	....	....	....	....	....	....	....	....
2002-03	Medicine Hat	WHL	64	10	37	47	79	....	....	....	....	....	....	....	....	....	11	3	4	7	17	....	....	....	....
2003-04	Medicine Hat	WHL	69	21	44	65	105	....	....	....	....	....	....	....	....	....	20	3	9	12	18	....	....	....	....
2004-05	Medicine Hat	WHL	52	15	33	48	99	....	....	....	....	....	....	....	....	....	12	3	3	6	16	....	....	....	....
2005-06	**Chicago**	**NHL**	**1**	**0**	**0**	**0**	**0**	**0**	**0**	**0**	**1**	**0.0**	**0**	**0**	**0.0**	**11:02**	....	....	....	....	....	....	....	....	....
	Medicine Hat	WHL	26	5	13	18	63	....	....	....	....	....	....	....	....	....	13	4	8	12	*59	....	....	....	....
2006-07	**Chicago**	**NHL**	**35**	**1**	**7**	**8**	**44**	**1**	**0**	**0**	**38**	**2.6**	**–12**	**0**	**0.0**	**19:19**	....	....	....	....	....	....	....	....	....
	Norfolk Admirals	AHL	34	5	10	15	53	....	....	....	....	....	....	....	....	....	6	1	3	4	13	....	....	....	....
2007-08	**Chicago**	**NHL**	**45**	**6**	**12**	**18**	**52**	**2**	**0**	**0**	**42**	**14.3**	**–3**	**0**	**0.0**	**17:12**	....	....	....	....	....	....	....	....	....
	Rockford IceHogs	AHL	29	8	11	19	67	....	....	....	....	....	....	....	....	....	....	....	....	....	....	....	....	....	....
2008-09	**Chicago**	**NHL**	**68**	**6**	**34**	**40**	**65**	**5**	**0**	**1**	**101**	**5.9**	**–6**	**1**	**0.0**	**18:20**	**17**	**3**	**6**	**9**	**2**	**0**	**0**	**0**	**16:39**
	Rockford IceHogs	AHL	7	3	2	5	6	....	....	....	....	....	....	....	....	....	....	....	....	....	....	....	....	....	....
2009-10	**Chicago**	**NHL**	**51**	**4**	**10**	**14**	**58**	**3**	**0**	**1**	**74**	**5.4**	**7**	**0**	**0.0**	**13:06**	....	....	....	....	....	....	....	....	....
	Minnesota	**NHL**	**19**	**1**	**6**	**7**	**10**	**1**	**0**	**0**	**31**	**3.2**	**–2**	**0**	**0.0**	**22:02**	....	....	....	....	....	....	....	....	....
	NHL Totals		**219**	**18**	**69**	**87**	**229**	**12**	**0**	**2**	**287**	**6.3**		**1**	**0.0**	**17:20**	**17**	**3**	**6**	**9**	**2**	**0**	**0**	**0**	**16:39**

Traded to **Minnesota** by **Chicago** for Kim Johnsson and Nick Leddy, February 12, 2010.

BARTULIS, Oskars
(bahr-TEW-lihs, AWZ-kahrz) **PHI.**

Defense. Shoots left. 6'2", 184 lbs. Born, Ogre, Latvia, January 21, 1987. Philadelphia's 2nd choice, 91st overall, in 2005 Entry Draft.

2001-02	Prizma '83 Riga	EEHL-B	3	1	0	1	2	....	....	....	....	....	....	....	....	....	....	....	....	....	....	....	....	....	....
	Prizma '83 Riga	Latvia	6	0	1	1	2	....	....	....	....	....	....	....	....	....	....	....	....	....	....	....	....	....	....
2002-03	Prizma '83 Riga	EEHL-B	12	5	5	10	12	....	....	....	....	....	....	....	....	....	....	....	....	....	....	....	....	....	....
	Vilki Riga	Latvia	....	0	1	1	12	....	....	....	....	....	....	....	....	....	....	....	....	....	....	....	....	....	....
2003-04	CSKA Moscow 2	Russia-3	65	3	9	12	....	....	....	....	....	....	....	....	....	....	....	....	....	....	....	....	....	....	....
2004-05	Moncton Wildcats	QMJHL	62	5	19	24	55	....	....	....	....	....	....	....	....	....	12	1	1	2	16	....	....	....	....
2005-06	Moncton Wildcats	QMJHL	54	6	25	31	84	....	....	....	....	....	....	....	....	....	21	1	9	10	22	....	....	....	....
2006-07	Cape Breton	QMJHL	55	13	35	48	52	....	....	....	....	....	....	....	....	....	16	3	9	12	24	....	....	....	....
2007-08	Philadelphia	AHL	57	1	20	21	42	....	....	....	....	....	....	....	....	....	....	....	....	....	....	....	....	....	....
2008-09	Philadelphia	AHL	80	2	11	13	59	....	....	....	....	....	....	....	....	....	4	0	0	0	4	....	....	....	....
2009-10	**Philadelphia**	**NHL**	**53**	**1**	**8**	**9**	**28**	**0**	**0**	**0**	**26**	**3.8**	**–12**	**0**	**0.0**	**13:59**	**7**	**0**	**0**	**0**	**4**	**0**	**0**	**0**	**6:44**
	Adirondack	AHL	12	2	2	4	14	....	....	....	....	....	....	....	....	....	....	....	....	....	....	....	....	....	....
	Latvia	Olympics	4	0	0	0	2	....	....	....	....	....	....	....	....	....	....	....	....	....	....	....	....	....	....
	NHL Totals		**53**	**1**	**8**	**9**	**28**	**0**	**0**	**0**	**26**	**3.8**		**0**	**0.0**	**13:59**	**7**	**0**	**0**	**0**	**4**	**0**	**0**	**0**	**6:44**

QMJHL All-Rookie Team (2005) • Canadian Major Junior All-Rookie Team (2005) • QMJHL Second All-Star Team (2007)

BASS, Cody
(BAS, KOH-dee) **OTT.**

Center. Shoots right. 6'1", 211 lbs. Born, Owen Sound, Ont., January 7, 1987. Ottawa's 3rd choice, 95th overall, in 2005 Entry Draft.

2003-04	Mississauga	OHL	61	3	7	10	30	....	....	....	....	....	....	....	....	....	24	2	3	5	21	....	....	....	....
2004-05	Mississauga	OHL	66	11	17	28	103	....	....	....	....	....	....	....	....	....	5	1	1	2	8	....	....	....	....
2005-06	Mississauga	OHL	67	16	25	41	152	....	....	....	....	....	....	....	....	....	....	....	....	....	....	....	....	....	....
	Binghamton	AHL	9	1	0	1	2	....	....	....	....	....	....	....	....	....	....	....	....	....	....	....	....	....	....
2006-07	Mississauga	OHL	23	5	11	16	37	....	....	....	....	....	....	....	....	....	....	....	....	....	....	....	....	....	....
	Saginaw Spirit	OHL	30	5	24	29	49	....	....	....	....	....	....	....	....	....	6	1	2	3	10	....	....	....	....
	Binghamton	AHL	5	0	2	2	9	....	....	....	....	....	....	....	....	....	....	....	....	....	....	....	....	....	....
2007-08	**Ottawa**	**NHL**	**21**	**2**	**2**	**4**	**19**	**0**	**1**	**1**	**12**	**16.7**	**–1**	**73**	**43.8**	**5:19**	**4**	**1**	**0**	**1**	**6**	**0**	**0**	**0**	**8:21**
	Binghamton	AHL	24	3	5	8	44	....	....	....	....	....	....	....	....	....	....	....	....	....	....	....	....	....	....
2008-09	**Ottawa**	**NHL**	**12**	**0**	**0**	**0**	**15**	**0**	**0**	**0**	**5**	**0.0**	**–2**	**50**	**42.0**	**5:41**	....	....	....	....	....	....	....	....	....
	Binghamton	AHL	18	1	1	2	41	....	....	....	....	....	....	....	....	....	....	....	....	....	....	....	....	....	....
2009-10	Binghamton	AHL	57	5	6	11	109	....	....	....	....	....	....	....	....	....	....	....	....	....	....	....	....	....	....
	NHL Totals		**33**	**2**	**2**	**4**	**34**	**0**	**1**	**1**	**17**	**11.8**		**123**	**43.1**	**5:27**	**4**	**1**	**0**	**1**	**6**	**0**	**0**	**0**	**8:21**

• Missed remainder of 2008-09 season recovering from shoulder injury suffered in game at Calgary, December 27, 2008.

BATTAGLIA, Bates
(buh-TAG-lee-ah, BAYTS)

Left wing. Shoots left. 6'2", 205 lbs. Born, Chicago, IL, December 13, 1975. Anaheim's 6th choice, 132nd overall, in 1994 Entry Draft.

1992-93	Team Illinois	MEHL	60	42	42	84	68	....	....	....	....	....	....	....	....	....	....	....	....	....	....	....	....	....	....
1993-94	Caledon	MTJHL	44	15	33	48	104	....	....	....	....	....	....	....	....	....	....	....	....	....	....	....	....	....	....
1994-95	Lake Superior	CCHA	38	6	14	20	34	....	....	....	....	....	....	....	....	....	....	....	....	....	....	....	....	....	....
1995-96	Lake Superior	CCHA	40	13	22	35	48	....	....	....	....	....	....	....	....	....	....	....	....	....	....	....	....	....	....
1996-97	Lake Superior	CCHA	38	12	27	39	80	....	....	....	....	....	....	....	....	....	....	....	....	....	....	....	....	....	....
1997-98	**Carolina**	**NHL**	**33**	**2**	**4**	**6**	**10**	**0**	**0**	**1**	**21**	**9.5**	**–1**	....	....	....	....	....	....	....	....	....	....	....	....
	New Haven	AHL	48	15	21	36	48	....	....	....	....	....	....	....	....	....	1	0	0	0	0	....	....	....	....
1998-99	**Carolina**	**NHL**	**60**	**7**	**11**	**18**	**22**	**0**	**0**	**0**	**52**	**13.5**	**7**	**144**	**39.6**	**9:53**	**6**	**0**	**3**	**3**	**8**	**0**	**0**	**0**	**15:22**
99-2000	**Carolina**	**NHL**	**77**	**16**	**18**	**34**	**39**	**3**	**0**	**3**	**86**	**18.6**	**20**	**23**	**26.1**	**15:12**	....	....	....	....	....	....	....	....	....
2000-01	**Carolina**	**NHL**	**80**	**12**	**15**	**27**	**76**	**2**	**0**	**3**	**133**	**9.0**	**–14**	**5**	**60.0**	**14:28**	**6**	**0**	**2**	**2**	**2**	**0**	**0**	**1**	**11:25**
2001-02	**Carolina**	**NHL**	**82**	**21**	**25**	**46**	**44**	**5**	**1**	**2**	**167**	**12.6**	**–6**	**12**	**33.3**	**19:05**	**23**	**5**	**9**	**14**	**14**	**1**	**0**	**1**	**20:42**
2002-03	**Carolina**	**NHL**	**70**	**5**	**14**	**19**	**90**	**0**	**1**	**1**	**96**	**5.2**	**–17**	**16**	**25.0**	**18:39**	....	....	....	....	....	....	....	....	....
	Colorado	**NHL**	**13**	**1**	**5**	**6**	**10**	**1**	**0**	**1**	**27**	**3.7**	**–2**	**3**	**0.0**	**15:19**	**7**	**0**	**2**	**2**	**4**	**0**	**0**	**0**	**14:39**
2003-04	**Colorado**	**NHL**	**4**	**0**	**1**	**1**	**4**	**0**	**0**	**0**	**1**	**0.0**	**–1**	**1**	**100.0**	**11:04**	....	....	....	....	....	....	....	....	....
	Washington	**NHL**	**66**	**4**	**6**	**10**	**38**	**0**	**0**	**1**	**69**	**5.8**	**–23**	**116**	**32.8**	**13:37**	....	....	....	....	....	....	....	....	....
2004-05	Mississippi	ECHL	25	6	11	17	24	....	....	....	....	....	....	....	....	....	4	0	0	0	10	....	....	....	....
2005-06	Toronto Marlies	AHL	79	20	47	67	86	....	....	....	....	....	....	....	....	....	5	1	1	2	6	....	....	....	....
2006-07	**Toronto**	**NHL**	**82**	**12**	**19**	**31**	**45**	**0**	**0**	**0**	**94**	**12.8**	**9**	**4**	**0.0**	**12:27**	....	....	....	....	....	....	....	....	....
2007-08	**Toronto**	**NHL**	**13**	**0**	**0**	**0**	**7**	**0**	**0**	**0**	**6**	**0.0**	**–6**	**1**	**0.0**	**4:46**	....	....	....	....	....	....	....	....	....
	Toronto Marlies	AHL	56	12	14	26	42	....	....	....	....	....	....	....	....	....	19	6	2	8	28	....	....	....	....
2008-09	Toronto Marlies	AHL	59	17	34	51	55	....	....	....	....	....	....	....	....	....	6	2	3	5	4	....	....	....	....
2009-10	Syracuse Crunch	AHL	29	6	16	22	15	....	....	....	....	....	....	....	....	....	....	....	....	....	....	....	....	....	....
	Jokerit Helsinki	Finland	17	1	0	1	12	....	....	....	....	....	....	....	....	....	2	1	0	1	0	....	....	....	....
	NHL Totals		**580**	**80**	**118**	**198**	**385**	**11**	**2**	**12**	**752**	**10.6**		**325**	**34.8**	**14:39**	**42**	**5**	**16**	**21**	**28**	**1**	**0**	**1**	**17:36**

Traded to **Hartford** by **Anaheim** with Anaheim's 4th round choice (Josef Vasicek) in 1998 Entry Draft for Mark Janssens, March 18, 1997. • Rights transferred to **Carolina** after **Hartford** franchise relocated, June 25, 1997. Traded to **Colorado** by **Carolina** for Radim Vrbata, March 11, 2003. Traded to **Washington** by **Colorado** with Jonas Johansson for Steve Konowalchuk and Washington's 3rd round choice (later traded to Carolina – Carolina selected Casey Borer) in 2004 Entry Draft, October 22, 2003. Signed as a free agent by **Mississippi** (ECHL), February 21, 2005. Signed to a PTO (professional tryout) contract by **Toronto** (AHL), October 2, 2005. Signed as a free agent by **Toronto**, July 8, 2006. Signed as a free agent by **Syracuse** (AHL), November 18, 2009. Signed as a free agent by **Jokerit Helsinki** (Finland), February 3, 2010.

BAUMGARTNER, Nolan
(BAWM-gahrt-nuhr, NOH-luhn) **VAN.**

Defense. Shoots right. 6'2", 195 lbs. Born, Calgary, Alta., March 23, 1976. Washington's 1st choice, 10th overall, in 1994 Entry Draft.

1991-92	Cgy. AAA Flames	AMHL	39	11	29	40	40	....	....	....	....	....	....	....	....	....	....	....	....	....	....	....	....	....	....
1992-93	Kamloops Blazers	WHL	43	0	5	5	30	....	....	....	....	....	....	....	....	....	11	1	1	2	0	....	....	....	....
1993-94	Kamloops Blazers	WHL	69	13	42	55	109	....	....	....	....	....	....	....	....	....	19	3	14	17	33	....	....	....	....
1994-95	Kamloops Blazers	WHL	62	8	36	44	71	....	....	....	....	....	....	....	....	....	21	4	13	17	16	....	....	....	....
1995-96	Kamloops Blazers	WHL	28	13	15	28	45	....	....	....	....	....	....	....	....	....	16	1	9	10	26	....	....	....	....
	Washington	**NHL**	**1**	**0**	**0**	**0**	**0**	**0**	**0**	**0**	**0**	**0.0**	**–1**	....	....	....	**1**	**0**	**0**	**0**	**10**	**0**	**0**	**0**	....
1996-97	Portland Pirates	AHL	8	2	2	4	4	....	....	....	....	....	....	....	....	....	....	....	....	....	....	....	....	....	....
1997-98	**Washington**	**NHL**	**4**	**0**	**1**	**1**	**0**	**0**	**0**	**0**	**4**	**0.0**	**0**	....	....	....	....	....	....	....	....	....	....	....	....
	Portland Pirates	AHL	70	2	24	26	70	....	....	....	....	....	....	....	....	....	10	1	4	5	10	....	....	....	....
1998-99	**Washington**	**NHL**	**5**	**0**	**0**	**0**	**0**	**0**	**0**	**0**	**1**	**0.0**	**–3**	**0**	**0.0**	**8:41**	....	....	....	....	....	....	....	....	....
	Portland Pirates	AHL	38	5	14	19	62	....	....	....	....	....	....	....	....	....	....	....	....	....	....	....	....	....	....
99-2000	**Washington**	**NHL**	**8**	**0**	**1**	**1**	**2**	**0**	**0**	**0**	**6**	**0.0**	**1**	**0**	**0.0**	**10:31**	....	....	....	....	....	....	....	....	....
	Portland Pirates	AHL	71	5	18	23	56	....	....	....	....	....	....	....	....	....	4	1	2	3	10	....	....	....	....
2000-01	**Chicago**	**NHL**	**8**	**0**	**0**	**0**	**6**	**0**	**0**	**0**	**7**	**0.0**	**–4**	**2**	**50.0**	**12:40**	....	....	....	....	....	....	....	....	....
	Norfolk Admirals	AHL	63	5	28	33	75	....	....	....	....	....	....	....	....	....	9	2	3	5	11	....	....	....	....
2001-02	Norfolk Admirals	AHL	76	10	24	34	72	....	....	....	....	....	....	....	....	....	4	0	1	1	2	....	....	....	....

			Regular Season														Playoffs								
Season	Club	League	GP	G	A	Pts	PIM	PP	SH	GW	S	%	+/-	TF	F%	Min	GP	G	A	Pts	PIM	PP	SH	GW	M
2002-03	**Vancouver**	**NHL**	**8**	**1**	**2**	**3**	**4**	**1**	**0**	**0**	**7**	**14.3**	**4**	**0**	**0.0**	**11:36**	2	0	0	0	0	0	0	0	11:0
	Manitoba Moose	AHL	59	8	31	39	82	....	....	....	....	....	....	....	....	....	1	0	0	0	4	....	....	....	....
2003-04	**Pittsburgh**	**NHL**	**5**	**0**	**0**	**0**	**2**	**0**	**0**	**0**	**6**	**0.0**	**–7**	**0**	**0.0**	**19:20**	....	....	....	....	....	....	....	....	....
	Vancouver	**NHL**	**9**	**0**	**3**	**3**	**2**	**0**	**0**	**0**	**9**	**0.0**	**3**	**0**	**0.0**	**11:52**	....	....	....	....	....	....	....	....	....
	Manitoba Moose	AHL	55	6	21	27	101	....	....	....	....	....	....	....	....	....	....	....	....	....	....	....	....	....	....
2004-05	Manitoba Moose	AHL	78	9	30	39	51	....	....	....	....	....	....	....	....	....	14	0	4	4	10	....	....	....	....
2005-06	**Vancouver**	**NHL**	**70**	**5**	**29**	**34**	**30**	**4**	**1**	**1**	**73**	**6.8**	**11**	**1**	**0.0**	**16:29**	....	....	....	....	....	....	....	....	....
2006-07	**Philadelphia**	**NHL**	**6**	**0**	**1**	**1**	**21**	**0**	**0**	**0**	**4**	**0.0**	**0**	**0**	**0.0**	**15:00**	....	....	....	....	....	....	....	....	....
	Philadelphia	AHL	51	6	20	26	46	....	....	....	....	....	....	....	....	....	....	....	....	....	....	....	....	....	....
	Dallas	**NHL**	**7**	**0**	**2**	**2**	**0**	**0**	**0**	**0**	**4**	**0.0**	**0**	**0**	**0.0**	**12:14**	....	....	....	....	....	....	....	....	....
2007-08	Iowa Stars	AHL	56	5	13	18	47	....	....	....	....	....	....	....	....	....	....	....	....	....	....	....	....	....	....
	Manitoba Moose	AHL	18	0	6	6	10	....	....	....	....	....	....	....	....	....	3	0	1	1	4	....	....	....	....
2008-09	Manitoba Moose	AHL	72	11	22	33	50	....	....	....	....	....	....	....	....	....	22	0	5	5	22	....	....	....	....
2009-10	**Vancouver**	**NHL**	**12**	**1**	**1**	**2**	**2**	**0**	**0**	**0**	**12**	**8.3**	**7**	**0**	**0.0**	**14:12**	**1**	**0**	**0**	**0**	**0**	**0**	**0**	**0**	**9:2**
	Manitoba Moose	AHL	37	3	9	12	22	....	....	....	....	....	....	....	....	....	....	....	....	....	....	....	....	....	....
	NHL Totals		**143**	**7**	**40**	**47**	**69**	**5**	**1**	**1**	**133**	**5.3**		**3**	**33.3**	**14:41**	**4**	**0**	**0**	**0**	**10**	**0**	**0**	**0**	**10:3**

Memorial Cup Tournement All-Star Team (1994, 1995) • WHL West First All-Star Team (1995, 1996) • Canadian Major Junior First All-Star Team (1995) • Canadian Major Junior Defenseman of the Year (1995)

Traded to **Chicago** by **Washington** for Remi Royer, July 20, 2000. Signed as a free agent by **Vancouver**, July 11, 2002. Claimed by **Pittsburgh** from **Vancouver** in Waiver Draft, October 3, 2003. Claimed on waivers by **Vancouver** from **Pittsburgh**, November 1, 2003. Signed as a free agent by **Philadelphia**, July 1, 2006. Claimed on waivers by **Dallas** from **Philadelphia**, February 24, 2007. Signed as a free agent by **Vancouver**, July 2, 2008.

BAYDA, Ryan

(BAY-duh, RIGH-uhn)

Left wing. Shoots left. 5'11", 185 lbs. Born, Saskatoon, Sask., December 9, 1980. Carolina's 2nd choice, 80th overall, in 2000 Entry Draft.

Season	Club	League	GP	G	A	Pts	PIM	PP	SH	GW	S	%	+/-	TF	F%	Min	GP	G	A	Pts	PIM	PP	SH	GW	M
1995-96	Saskatoon Flyers	SMHL	60	85	74	159	85	....	....	....	....	....	....	....	....	....	....	....	....	....	....	....	....	....	....
1996-97	Sask. Contacts	SMHL	44	22	23	45	18	....	....	....	....	....	....	....	....	....	....	....	....	....	....	....	....	....	....
1997-98	Sask. Contacts	SMHL	41	29	49	78	103	....	....	....	....	....	....	....	....	....	....	....	....	....	....	....	....	....	....
1998-99	Vernon Vipers	BCHL	45	24	58	82	15	....	....	....	....	....	....	....	....	....	....	....	....	....	....	....	....	....	....
99-2000	North Dakota	WCHA	44	17	23	40	30	....	....	....	....	....	....	....	....	....	....	....	....	....	....	....	....	....	....
2000-01	North Dakota	WCHA	46	25	34	59	48	....	....	....	....	....	....	....	....	....	....	....	....	....	....	....	....	....	....
2001-02	North Dakota	WCHA	37	19	28	47	52	....	....	....	....	....	....	....	....	....	....	....	....	....	....	....	....	....	....
	Lowell	AHL	3	1	1	2	0	....	....	....	....	....	....	....	....	....	5	3	0	3	0	....	....	....	....
2002-03	**Carolina**	**NHL**	**25**	**4**	**10**	**14**	**16**	**0**	**0**	**1**	**49**	**8.2**	**–5**	**2**	**100.0**	**17:15**	....	....	....	....	....	....	....	....	....
	Lowell	AHL	53	11	32	43	32	....	....	....	....	....	....	....	....	....	....	....	....	....	....	....	....	....	....
2003-04	**Carolina**	**NHL**	**44**	**3**	**3**	**6**	**22**	**0**	**0**	**1**	**65**	**4.6**	**–14**	**4**	**0.0**	**10:57**	....	....	....	....	....	....	....	....	....
	Lowell	AHL	34	7	15	22	28	....	....	....	....	....	....	....	....	....	....	....	....	....	....	....	....	....	....
2004-05	Lowell	AHL	80	13	27	40	91	....	....	....	....	....	....	....	....	....	9	3	3	6	4	....	....	....	....
2005-06	Manitoba Moose	AHL	59	13	25	38	52	....	....	....	....	....	....	....	....	....	13	1	6	7	27	....	....	....	....
2006-07	**Carolina**	**NHL**	**9**	**1**	**1**	**2**	**2**	**0**	**0**	**0**	**10**	**10.0**	**–1**	**0**	**0.0**	**8:41**	....	....	....	....	....	....	....	....	....
	Albany River Rats	AHL	55	29	25	54	66	....	....	....	....	....	....	....	....	....	5	3	2	5	4	....	....	....	....
2007-08	**Carolina**	**NHL**	**31**	**3**	**3**	**6**	**28**	**0**	**0**	**0**	**58**	**5.2**	**–2**	**2**	**0.0**	**12:36**	....	....	....	....	....	....	....	....	....
	Albany River Rats	AHL	21	7	10	17	6	....	....	....	....	....	....	....	....	....	....	....	....	....	....	....	....	....	....
2008-09	**Carolina**	**NHL**	**70**	**5**	**7**	**12**	**26**	**0**	**0**	**0**	**62**	**8.1**	**2**	**18**	**44.4**	**10:27**	**15**	**2**	**2**	**4**	**18**	**0**	**0**	**0**	**6:2**
2009-10	Wilkes-Barre	AHL	21	8	3	11	14	....	....	....	....	....	....	....	....	....	....	....	....	....	....	....	....	....	....
	NHL Totals		**179**	**16**	**24**	**40**	**94**	**0**	**0**	**2**	**244**	**6.6**		**26**	**38.5**	**11:48**	**15**	**2**	**2**	**4**	**18**	**0**	**0**	**0**	**6:2**

BCHL Rookie of the Year (1999) • WCHA All-Rookie Team (2000) • WCHA Second All-Star Team (2001, 2002)

Signed as a free agent by **Nurnberg** (Germany), July 18, 2010.

BEAGLE, Jay

(BEE-guhl, JAY) **WSH**

Right wing. Shoots right. 6'3", 200 lbs. Born, Calgary, Alta., October 16, 1985.

Season	Club	League	GP	G	A	Pts	PIM	PP	SH	GW	S	%	+/-	TF	F%	Min	GP	G	A	Pts	PIM	PP	SH	GW	M
2003-04	Calgary Royals	AJHL	58	10	27	37	100	....	....	....	....	....	....	....	....	....	....	....	....	....	....	....	....	....	....
2004-05	Calgary Royals	AJHL	64	28	42	70	114	....	....	....	....	....	....	....	....	....	....	....	....	....	....	....	....	....	....
2005-06	Alaska Anchorage	WCHA	31	4	6	10	40	....	....	....	....	....	....	....	....	....	....	....	....	....	....	....	....	....	....
2006-07	Alaska Anchorage	WCHA	36	10	10	20	93	....	....	....	....	....	....	....	....	....	....	....	....	....	....	....	....	....	....
	Idaho Steelheads	ECHL	8	2	8	10	4	....	....	....	....	....	....	....	....	....	18	1	2	3	22	....	....	....	....
2007-08	Hershey Bears	AHL	64	19	18	37	41	....	....	....	....	....	....	....	....	....	5	0	1	1	2	....	....	....	....
2008-09	**Washington**	**NHL**	**3**	**0**	**0**	**0**	**2**	**0**	**0**	**0**	**5**	**0.0**	**–3**	**13**	**38.5**	**7:36**	**4**	**0**	**0**	**0**	**0**	**0**	**0**	**0**	**3:33**
	Hershey Bears	AHL	47	4	5	9	37	....	....	....	....	....	....	....	....	....	18	1	3	4	16	....	....	....	....
2009-10	**Washington**	**NHL**	**7**	**1**	**1**	**2**	**2**	**0**	**0**	**0**	**10**	**10.0**	**–1**	**31**	**54.8**	**9:16**	....	....	....	....	....	....	....	....	....
	Hershey Bears	AHL	66	16	19	35	25	....	....	....	....	....	....	....	....	....	21	2	6	8	0	....	....	....	....
	NHL Totals		**10**	**1**	**1**	**2**	**4**	**0**	**0**	**0**	**15**	**6.7**		**44**	**50.0**	**8:46**	**4**	**0**	**0**	**0**	**0**	**0**	**0**	**0**	**3:33**

Signed as a free agent by **Washington**, March 26, 2008.

BEAUCHEMIN, Francois

(boh-sheh-MEH, frahn-SWUH) **TOR**

Defense. Shoots left. 6', 213 lbs. Born, Sorel, Que., June 4, 1980. Montreal's 3rd choice, 75th overall, in 1998 Entry Draft.

Season	Club	League	GP	G	A	Pts	PIM	PP	SH	GW	S	%	+/-	TF	F%	Min	GP	G	A	Pts	PIM	PP	SH	GW	M
1995-96	Richelieu Riverains	QAAA	40	9	23	32	59	....	....	....	....	....	....	....	....	....	....	....	....	....	....	....	....	....	....
1996-97	Laval Titan	QMJHL	66	7	21	28	132	....	....	....	....	....	....	....	....	....	3	0	0	0	2	....	....	....	....
1997-98	Laval Titan	QMJHL	70	12	35	47	132	....	....	....	....	....	....	....	....	....	16	1	3	4	23	....	....	....	....
1998-99	Acadie-Bathurst	QMJHL	31	4	17	21	53	....	....	....	....	....	....	....	....	....	23	2	16	18	55	....	....	....	....
99-2000	Acadie-Bathurst	QMJHL	38	11	36	47	64	....	....	....	....	....	....	....	....	....	....	....	....	....	....	....	....	....	....
	Moncton Wildcats	QMJHL	33	8	31	39	35	....	....	....	....	....	....	....	....	....	16	2	11	13	14	....	....	....	....
2000-01	Quebec Citadelles	AHL	56	3	6	9	44	....	....	....	....	....	....	....	....	....	....	....	....	....	....	....	....	....	....
2001-02	Quebec Citadelles	AHL	56	8	11	19	88	....	....	....	....	....	....	....	....	....	3	0	1	1	0	....	....	....	....
	Mississippi	ECHL	7	1	3	4	2	....	....	....	....	....	....	....	....	....	....	....	....	....	....	....	....	....	....
2002-03	**Montreal**	**NHL**	**1**	**0**	**0**	**0**	**0**	**0**	**0**	**0**	**1**	**0.0**	**–1**	**0**	**0.0**	**17:11**	....	....	....	....	....	....	....	....	....
	Hamilton	AHL	75	7	21	28	92	....	....	....	....	....	....	....	....	....	23	1	9	10	16	....	....	....	....
2003-04	Hamilton	AHL	77	9	27	36	57	....	....	....	....	....	....	....	....	....	10	2	4	6	18	....	....	....	....
2004-05	Syracuse Crunch	AHL	72	3	27	30	55	....	....	....	....	....	....	....	....	....	....	....	....	....	....	....	....	....	....
2005-06	**Columbus**	**NHL**	**11**	**0**	**2**	**2**	**11**	**0**	**0**	**0**	**16**	**0.0**	**–6**	**0**	**0.0**	**17:16**	....	....	....	....	....	....	....	....	....
	Anaheim	**NHL**	**61**	**8**	**26**	**34**	**41**	**4**	**0**	**3**	**121**	**6.6**	**8**	**1**	**0.0**	**24:14**	**16**	**3**	**6**	**9**	**11**	**3**	**0**	**0**	**27:26**
2006-07 ♦	**Anaheim**	**NHL**	**71**	**7**	**21**	**28**	**49**	**2**	**0**	**0**	**128**	**5.5**	**7**	**1**	**0.0**	**25:28**	**20**	**4**	**4**	**8**	**16**	**4**	**0**	**0**	**30:33**
2007-08	**Anaheim**	**NHL**	**82**	**2**	**19**	**21**	**59**	**0**	**0**	**2**	**144**	**1.4**	**–9**	**1**	**0.0**	**25:32**	**6**	**0**	**0**	**0**	**26**	**0**	**0**	**0**	**21:02**
2008-09	**Anaheim**	**NHL**	**20**	**4**	**1**	**5**	**12**	**0**	**0**	**2**	**45**	**8.9**	**–3**	**0**	**0.0**	**24:54**	**13**	**1**	**0**	**1**	**15**	**0**	**0**	**0**	**21:25**
2009-10	**Toronto**	**NHL**	**82**	**5**	**21**	**26**	**33**	**4**	**0**	**1**	**170**	**2.9**	**–13**	**4**	**75.0**	**25:28**	....	....	....	....	....	....	....	....	....
	NHL Totals		**328**	**26**	**90**	**116**	**205**	**10**	**0**	**8**	**625**	**4.2**		**7**	**42.9**	**24:55**	**55**	**8**	**10**	**18**	**68**	**7**	**0**	**0**	**26:27**

QMJHL All-Rookie Team (1997) • QMJHL Second All-Star Team (2000)

Claimed on waivers by **Columbus** from **Montreal**, September 15, 2004. Traded to **Anaheim** by **Columbus** with Tyler Wright for Sergei Fedorov and Anaheim's 5th round choice (Maxime Frechette) in 2006 Entry Draft, November 15, 2005. • Missed remainder of 2008-09 regular season recovering from knee injury suffered in game vs. Nashville, November 14, 2008. Signed as a free agent by **Toronto**, July 6, 2009.

BEGIN, Steve

(bay-ZHIN, STEEV)

Center. Shoots left. 6', 192 lbs. Born, Trois-Rivieres, Que., June 14, 1978. Calgary's 3rd choice, 40th overall, in 1996 Entry Draft.

Season	Club	League	GP	G	A	Pts	PIM	PP	SH	GW	S	%	+/-	TF	F%	Min	GP	G	A	Pts	PIM	PP	SH	GW	M
1993-94	Cap-d-Madelaine	QAAA	8	0	1	1	6	....	....	....	....	....	....	....	....	....	2	0	0	0	0	....	....	....	....
1994-95	Cap-d-Madelaine	QAAA	35	9	15	24	48	....	....	....	....	....	....	....	....	....	3	0	0	0	2	....	....	....	....
1995-96	Val-d'Or Foreurs	QMJHL	64	13	23	36	218	....	....	....	....	....	....	....	....	....	13	1	3	4	33	....	....	....	....
1996-97	Val-d'Or Foreurs	QMJHL	58	13	33	46	229	....	....	....	....	....	....	....	....	....	10	0	3	3	8	....	....	....	....
	Saint John Flames	AHL	....	....	....	....	....	....	....	....	....	....	....	....	....	....	4	0	2	2	6	....	....	....	....
1997-98	**Calgary**	**NHL**	**5**	**0**	**0**	**0**	**23**	**0**	**0**	**0**	**2**	**0.0**	**0**	....	....	....	....	....	....	....	....	....	....	....	....
	Val-d'Or Foreurs	QMJHL	35	18	17	35	73	....	....	....	....	....	....	....	....	....	15	2	12	14	34	....	....	....	....
1998-99	Saint John Flames	AHL	73	11	9	20	156	....	....	....	....	....	....	....	....	....	7	2	0	2	18	....	....	....	....
99-2000	**Calgary**	**NHL**	**13**	**1**	**1**	**2**	**18**	**0**	**0**	**0**	**3**	**33.3**	**–3**	**19**	**47.4**	**7:13**	....	....	....	....	....	....	....	....	....
	Saint John Flames	AHL	47	13	12	25	99	....	....	....	....	....	....	....	....	....	....	....	....	....	....	....	....	....	....
2000-01	**Calgary**	**NHL**	**4**	**0**	**0**	**0**	**21**	**0**	**0**	**0**	**3**	**0.0**	**0**	**0**	**0.0**	**6:04**	....	....	....	....	....	....	....	....	....
	Saint John Flames	AHL	58	14	14	28	109	....	....	....	....	....	....	....	....	....	19	10	7	17	18	....	....	....	....
2001-02	**Calgary**	**NHL**	**51**	**7**	**5**	**12**	**79**	**1**	**0**	**0**	**65**	**10.8**	**–3**	**129**	**53.5**	**9:25**	....	....	....	....	....	....	....	....	....
2002-03	**Calgary**	**NHL**	**50**	**3**	**1**	**4**	**51**	**0**	**0**	**1**	**59**	**5.1**	**–7**	**50**	**60.0**	**9:13**	....	....	....	....	....	....	....	....	....

Season	Club	League	GP	G	A	Pts	PIM	PP	SH	GW	S	%	+/-	TF	F%	Min	GP	G	A	Pts	PIM	PP	SH	GW	Min
			Regular Season														Playoffs								
2003-04	**Montreal**	**NHL**	**52**	**10**	**5**	**15**	**41**	**0**	**1**	**1**	**91**	**11.0**	**6**	**436**	**48.6**	**12:32**	**9**	**0**	**1**	**1**	**10**	**0**	**0**	**0**	**12:26**
2004-05	Hamilton	AHL	21	10	3	13	20	....	....	....	....	....	....	....	....	....	4	0	2	2	8	....	....	....	....
2005-06	**Montreal**	**NHL**	**76**	**11**	**12**	**23**	**113**	**1**	**2**	**2**	**134**	**8.2**	**9**	**573**	**50.1**	**14:19**	**2**	**0**	**0**	**0**	**2**	**0**	**0**	**0**	**13:42**
2006-07	**Montreal**	**NHL**	**52**	**5**	**5**	**10**	**46**	**0**	**0**	**0**	**64**	**7.8**	**-6**	**159**	**49.7**	**11:55**	....	....	....	....	....	....	....	....	....
2007-08	**Montreal**	**NHL**	**44**	**3**	**5**	**8**	**48**	**0**	**0**	**0**	**67**	**4.5**	**0**	**69**	**34.8**	**11:38**	**12**	**0**	**3**	**3**	**8**	**0**	**0**	**0**	**12:45**
2008-09	**Montreal**	**NHL**	**42**	**6**	**4**	**10**	**27**	**0**	**0**	**1**	**65**	**9.2**	**-5**	**78**	**53.9**	**10:51**	....	....	....	....	....	....	....	....	....
	Dallas	**NHL**	**20**	**1**	**1**	**2**	**15**	**0**	**0**	**0**	**25**	**4.0**	**-1**	**55**	**41.8**	**10:26**	....	....	....	....	....	....	....	....	....
2009-10	**Boston**	**NHL**	**77**	**5**	**9**	**14**	**53**	**0**	**1**	**2**	**110**	**4.5**	**-7**	**694**	**53.5**	**12:50**	**13**	**1**	**0**	**1**	**10**	**0**	**0**	**0**	**11:57**
	NHL Totals		**486**	**52**	**48**	**100**	**535**	**2**	**4**	**7**	**688**	**7.6**		**2262**	**50.7**	**11:36**	**36**	**1**	**4**	**5**	**30**	**0**	**0**	**0**	**12:26**

ck A. Butterfield Trophy (AHL – Playoff MVP) (2001)

aded to **Buffalo** by **Calgary** with Chris Drury for Steve Reinprecht and Rhett Warrener, July 3, 2003. Claimed by **Montreal** from **Buffalo** in Waiver Draft, October 3, 2003. Traded to **Dallas** by **Montreal** r Doug Janik, February 26, 2009. Signed as a free agent by **Boston**, July 1, 2009.

BELAK, Wade

(BEE-lak, WAYD) **NSH.**

Right wing. Shoots right. 6'5", 222 lbs. Born, Saskatoon, Sask., July 3, 1976. Quebec's 1st choice, 12th overall, in 1994 Entry Draft.

Season	Club	League	GP	G	A	Pts	PIM	PP	SH	GW	S	%	+/-	TF	F%	Min	GP	G	A	Pts	PIM	PP	SH	GW	Min
1991-92	North Battleford	SMBHL	57	6	20	26	186	....	....	....	....	....	....	....	....	....	....	....	....	....	....	....	....	....	....
1992-93	North Battleford	SJHL	50	5	15	20	146	....	....	....	....	....	....	....	....	....	....	....	....	....	....	....	....	....	....
	Saskatoon Blades	WHL	7	0	0	0	23	....	....	....	....	....	....	....	....	....	7	0	0	0	0	....	....	....	....
1993-94	Saskatoon Blades	WHL	69	4	13	17	226	....	....	....	....	....	....	....	....	....	16	2	2	4	43	....	....	....	....
1994-95	Saskatoon Blades	WHL	72	4	14	18	290	....	....	....	....	....	....	....	....	....	9	0	0	0	36	....	....	....	....
	Cornwall Aces	AHL	....	....	....	....	....	....	....	....	....	....	....	....	....	....	11	1	2	3	40	....	....	....	....
1995-96	Saskatoon Blades	WHL	63	3	15	18	207	....	....	....	....	....	....	....	....	....	4	0	0	0	9	....	....	....	....
	Cornwall Aces	AHL	5	0	0	0	18	....	....	....	....	....	....	....	....	....	2	0	0	0	2	....	....	....	....
1996-97	**Colorado**	**NHL**	**5**	**0**	**0**	**0**	**11**	**0**	**0**	**0**	**1**	**0.0**	**-1**	....	....	....	....	....	....	....	....	....	....	....	....
	Hershey Bears	AHL	65	1	7	8	320	....	....	....	....	....	....	....	....	....	16	0	1	1	61	....	....	....	....
1997-98	**Colorado**	**NHL**	**8**	**1**	**1**	**2**	**27**	**0**	**0**	**1**	**2**	**50.0**	**-3**	....	....	....	....	....	....	....	....	....	....	....	....
	Hershey Bears	AHL	11	0	0	0	30	....	....	....	....	....	....	....	....	....	....	....	....	....	....	....	....	....	....
1998-99	**Colorado**	**NHL**	**22**	**0**	**0**	**0**	**71**	**0**	**0**	**0**	**5**	**0.0**	**-2**	**0**	**0.0**	**6:48**	....	....	....	....	....	....	....	....	....
	Hershey Bears	AHL	17	0	1	1	49	....	....	....	....	....	....	....	....	....	....	....	....	....	....	....	....	....	....
	Calgary	**NHL**	**9**	**0**	**1**	**1**	**23**	**0**	**0**	**0**	**2**	**0.0**	**3**	**0**	**0.0**	**10:46**	....	....	....	....	....	....	....	....	....
	Saint John Flames	AHL	12	0	2	2	43	....	....	....	....	....	....	....	....	....	6	0	1	1	23	....	....	....	....
99-2000	**Calgary**	**NHL**	**40**	**0**	**2**	**2**	**122**	**0**	**0**	**0**	**11**	**0.0**	**-4**	**1**	**0.0**	**7:33**	....	....	....	....	....	....	....	....	....
2000-01	**Calgary**	**NHL**	**23**	**0**	**0**	**0**	**79**	**0**	**0**	**0**	**8**	**0.0**	**-2**	**0**	**0.0**	**6:54**	....	....	....	....	....	....	....	....	....
	Toronto	**NHL**	**16**	**1**	**1**	**2**	**31**	**0**	**0**	**0**	**8**	**12.5**	**-4**	**0**	**0.0**	**13:38**	....	....	....	....	....	....	....	....	....
2001-02	**Toronto**	**NHL**	**63**	**1**	**3**	**4**	**142**	**0**	**0**	**0**	**47**	**2.1**	**2**	**0**	**0.0**	**9:14**	**16**	**1**	**0**	**1**	**18**	**0**	**0**	**0**	**7:28**
2002-03	**Toronto**	**NHL**	**55**	**3**	**6**	**9**	**196**	**0**	**0**	**0**	**33**	**9.1**	**-2**	**0**	**0.0**	**10:50**	**2**	**0**	**0**	**0**	**4**	**0**	**0**	**0**	**8:22**
2003-04	**Toronto**	**NHL**	**34**	**1**	**1**	**2**	**109**	**0**	**0**	**0**	**15**	**6.7**	**0**	**0**	**0.0**	**7:00**	**4**	**0**	**0**	**0**	**14**	**0**	**0**	**0**	**9:59**
2004-05	Coventry Blaze	Britain	20	3	5	8	109	....	....	....	....	....	....	....	....	....	8	1	1	2	16	....	....	....	....
2005-06	**Toronto**	**NHL**	**55**	**0**	**3**	**3**	**109**	**0**	**0**	**0**	**16**	**0.0**	**-13**	**0**	**0.0**	**9:59**	....	....	....	....	....	....	....	....	....
2006-07	**Toronto**	**NHL**	**65**	**0**	**3**	**3**	**110**	**0**	**0**	**0**	**16**	**0.0**	**-8**	**0**	**0.0**	**5:02**	....	....	....	....	....	....	....	....	....
2007-08	**Toronto**	**NHL**	**30**	**1**	**0**	**1**	**66**	**0**	**0**	**0**	**13**	**7.7**	**-2**	**1**	**0.0**	**4:02**	....	....	....	....	....	....	....	....	....
	Florida	**NHL**	**17**	**0**	**0**	**0**	**12**	**0**	**0**	**0**	**4**	**0.0**	**0**	**0**	**0.0**	**4:09**	....	....	....	....	....	....	....	....	....
2008-09	**Florida**	**NHL**	**15**	**0**	**0**	**0**	**25**	**0**	**0**	**0**	**4**	**0.0**	**0**	**0**	**0.0**	**4:25**	....	....	....	....	....	....	....	....	....
	Nashville	**NHL**	**38**	**0**	**2**	**2**	**54**	**0**	**0**	**0**	**15**	**0.0**	**-1**	**0**	**0.0**	**5:35**	....	....	....	....	....	....	....	....	....
2009-10	**Nashville**	**NHL**	**39**	**0**	**2**	**2**	**58**	**0**	**0**	**0**	**8**	**0.0**	**0**	**0**	**0.0**	**4:21**	....	....	....	....	....	....	....	....	....
	NHL Totals		**534**	**8**	**25**	**33**	**1245**	**0**	**0**	**1**	**208**	**3.8**		**2**	**0.0**	**7:24**	**22**	**1**	**0**	**1**	**36**	**0**	**0**	**0**	**8:00**

Rights transferred to **Colorado** after **Quebec** franchise relocated, June 21, 1995. Traded to **Calgary** by **Colorado** with Rene Corbet, Robyn Regehr and Colorado's 2nd round compensatory choice (Jarret toll) in 2000 Entry Draft for Theoren Fleury and Chris Dingman, February 28, 1999. • Missed majority of 1999-2000 and 2000-01 seasons recovering from shoulder injury suffered in game vs. Colorado, ebruary 10, 2000. Claimed on waivers by **Toronto** from **Calgary**, February 16, 2001. • Missed majority of 2003-04 season recovering from abdomen (November 20, 2003 vs. Edmonton) and knee anuary 6, 2004 vs. Nashville) injuries. Signed as a free agent by **Coventry** (Britain), November 8, 2004. Traded to **Florida** by **Toronto** for Florida's 5th round choice (Jerome Flaake) in 2008 Entry Draft, ebruary 26, 2008. Traded to **Nashville** by **Florida** for Nick Tarnasky, November 27, 2008.

BELANGER, Eric

(buh-LAWN-zhay, AIR-ihk)

Center. Shoots left. 5'11", 187 lbs. Born, Sherbrooke, Que., December 16, 1977. Los Angeles' 5th choice, 96th overall, in 1996 Entry Draft.

Season	Club	League	GP	G	A	Pts	PIM	PP	SH	GW	S	%	+/-	TF	F%	Min	GP	G	A	Pts	PIM	PP	SH	GW	Min
1993-94	Magog	QAAA	32	19	24	43	24	....	....	....	....	....	....	....	....	....	13	5	6	11	36	....	....	....	....
1994-95	Beauport	QMJHL	71	12	28	40	24	....	....	....	....	....	....	....	....	....	18	5	9	14	25	....	....	....	....
1995-96	Beauport	QMJHL	59	35	48	83	18	....	....	....	....	....	....	....	....	....	20	13	14	27	6	....	....	....	....
1996-97	Beauport	QMJHL	31	13	37	50	30	....	....	....	....	....	....	....	....	....	....	....	....	....	....	....	....	....	....
	Rimouski Oceanic	QMJHL	31	26	41	67	36	....	....	....	....	....	....	....	....	....	4	2	3	5	10	....	....	....	....
1997-98	Fredericton	AHL	56	17	34	51	28	....	....	....	....	....	....	....	....	....	4	2	1	3	2	....	....	....	....
1998-99	Springfield	AHL	33	8	18	26	10	....	....	....	....	....	....	....	....	....	3	0	1	1	2	....	....	....	....
	Long Beach	IHL	1	0	0	0	0	....	....	....	....	....	....	....	....	....	....	....	....	....	....	....	....	....	....
99-2000	Lowell	AHL	65	15	25	40	20	....	....	....	....	....	....	....	....	....	7	3	3	6	2	....	....	....	....
2000-01	**Los Angeles**	**NHL**	**62**	**9**	**12**	**21**	**16**	**1**	**2**	**1**	**80**	**11.3**	**14**	**849**	**56.4**	**13:25**	**13**	**1**	**4**	**5**	**2**	**0**	**0**	**1**	**13:47**
	Lowell	AHL	13	8	10	18	4	....	....	....	....	....	....	....	....	....	....	....	....	....	....	....	....	....	....
2001-02	**Los Angeles**	**NHL**	**53**	**8**	**16**	**24**	**21**	**2**	**1**	**1**	**67**	**11.9**	**2**	**882**	**57.7**	**14:33**	**7**	**0**	**0**	**0**	**4**	**0**	**0**	**0**	**12:57**
2002-03	**Los Angeles**	**NHL**	**62**	**16**	**19**	**35**	**26**	**0**	**3**	**1**	**114**	**14.0**	**-5**	**1143**	**51.8**	**17:42**	....	....	....	....	....	....	....	....	....
2003-04	**Los Angeles**	**NHL**	**81**	**13**	**20**	**33**	**44**	**0**	**1**	**2**	**132**	**9.8**	**-16**	**1418**	**53.7**	**17:01**	....	....	....	....	....	....	....	....	....
2004-05	HC Forst Bolzano	Italy	12	13	10	23	20	....	....	....	....	....	....	....	....	....	9	3	7	10	33	....	....	....	....
2005-06	**Los Angeles**	**NHL**	**65**	**17**	**20**	**37**	**62**	**5**	**0**	**1**	**119**	**14.3**	**-5**	**1179**	**49.0**	**17:33**	....	....	....	....	....	....	....	....	....
2006-07	**Carolina**	**NHL**	**56**	**8**	**12**	**20**	**14**	**3**	**0**	**1**	**100**	**8.0**	**-2**	**689**	**53.4**	**14:51**	....	....	....	....	....	....	....	....	....
	Atlanta	**NHL**	**24**	**9**	**6**	**15**	**12**	**1**	**0**	**0**	**49**	**18.4**	**0**	**517**	**52.6**	**19:29**	**4**	**1**	**0**	**1**	**12**	**1**	**0**	**0**	**16:47**
2007-08	**Minnesota**	**NHL**	**75**	**13**	**24**	**37**	**30**	**7**	**1**	**3**	**115**	**11.3**	**-6**	**1195**	**49.1**	**17:13**	**6**	**0**	**0**	**0**	**4**	**0**	**0**	**0**	**18:34**
2008-09	**Minnesota**	**NHL**	**79**	**13**	**23**	**36**	**26**	**4**	**0**	**4**	**147**	**8.8**	**-5**	**1205**	**52.0**	**17:50**	....	....	....	....	....	....	....	....	....
2009-10	**Minnesota**	**NHL**	**60**	**13**	**22**	**35**	**28**	**3**	**0**	**3**	**120**	**10.8**	**-1**	**722**	**57.6**	**15:45**	....	....	....	....	....	....	....	....	....
	Washington	**NHL**	**17**	**2**	**4**	**6**	**4**	**0**	**0**	**0**	**31**	**6.5**	**3**	**202**	**52.0**	**14:40**	**7**	**0**	**1**	**1**	**4**	**0**	**0**	**0**	**14:05**
	NHL Totals		**634**	**121**	**178**	**299**	**283**	**26**	**8**	**17**	**1074**	**11.3**		**10001**	**52.9**	**16:26**	**37**	**2**	**5**	**7**	**26**	**1**	**0**	**1**	**14:47**

igned as a free agent by **Bolzano** (Italy), December 22, 2004. Traded to **Carolina** by **Los Angeles** with Tim Gleason for Oleg Tverdovsky and Jack Johnson, September 29, 2006. Traded to **Nashville** by **Carolina** for Josef Vasicek, February 9, 2007. Traded to **Atlanta** by **Nashville** for Vitaly Vishnevski, February 10, 2007. Signed as a free agent by **Minnesota**, July 3, 2007. Traded to **Washington** by **Minnesota** for Washington's 2nd round choice (Johan Larsson) in 2010 Entry Draft, March 3, 2010.

BELESKEY, Matt

(beh-LEH-skee, MAT) **ANA.**

Left wing. Shoots left. 6', 204 lbs. Born, Windsor, Ont., June 7, 1988. Anaheim's 4th choice, 112th overall, in 2006 Entry Draft.

Season	Club	League	GP	G	A	Pts	PIM	PP	SH	GW	S	%	+/-	TF	F%	Min	GP	G	A	Pts	PIM	PP	SH	GW	Min
2004-05	Belleville Bulls	OHL	68	10	13	23	118	....	....	....	....	....	....	....	....	....	5	0	0	0	18	....	....	....	....
2005-06	Belleville Bulls	OHL	61	20	20	40	119	....	....	....	....	....	....	....	....	....	6	1	2	3	10	....	....	....	....
2006-07	Belleville Bulls	OHL	66	27	41	68	124	....	....	....	....	....	....	....	....	....	15	4	10	14	18	....	....	....	....
2007-08	Belleville Bulls	OHL	62	41	49	90	106	....	....	....	....	....	....	....	....	....	21	12	21	33	23	....	....	....	....
2008-09	**Anaheim**	**NHL**	**2**	**0**	**0**	**0**	**0**	**0**	**0**	**0**	**0**	**0.0**	**0**	**2**	**0.0**	**11:10**	....	....	....	....	....	....	....	....	....
	Iowa Chops	AHL	58	11	24	35	58	....	....	....	....	....	....	....	....	....	....	....	....	....	....	....	....	....	....
2009-10	**Anaheim**	**NHL**	**60**	**11**	**7**	**18**	**35**	**0**	**0**	**3**	**123**	**8.9**	**-10**	**20**	**40.0**	**13:59**	....	....	....	....	....	....	....	....	....
	San Antonio	AHL	12	1	4	5	19	....	....	....	....	....	....	....	....	....	....	....	....	....	....	....	....	....	....
	Toronto Marlies	AHL	3	1	1	2	2	....	....	....	....	....	....	....	....	....	....	....	....	....	....	....	....	....	....
	NHL Totals		**62**	**11**	**7**	**18**	**35**	**0**	**0**	**3**	**123**	**8.9**		**22**	**36.4**	**13:54**									

BELL, Brendan

(BEHL, BREHN-duhn)

Defense. Shoots left. 6'2", 211 lbs. Born, Ottawa, Ont., March 31, 1983. Toronto's 3rd choice, 65th overall, in 2001 Entry Draft.

Season	Club	League	GP	G	A	Pts	PIM	PP	SH	GW	S	%	+/-	TF	F%	Min	GP	G	A	Pts	PIM	PP	SH	GW	Min
1998-99	Ott. Jr. Senators	CJHL	54	7	20	27	46	....	....	....	....	....	....	....	....	....	....	....	....	....	....	....	....	....	....
99-2000	Ottawa 67's	OHL	48	1	32	33	34	....	....	....	....	....	....	....	....	....	5	0	1	1	4	....	....	....	....
2000-01	Ottawa 67's	OHL	68	7	32	39	59	....	....	....	....	....	....	....	....	....	20	1	11	12	22	....	....	....	....
2001-02	Ottawa 67's	OHL	67	10	36	46	56	....	....	....	....	....	....	....	....	....	13	2	5	7	25	....	....	....	....
2002-03	Ottawa 67's	OHL	55	14	39	53	46	....	....	....	....	....	....	....	....	....	23	8	19	27	25	....	....	....	....
2003-04	St. John's	AHL	74	7	18	25	72	....	....	....	....	....	....	....	....	....	....	....	....	....	....	....	....	....	....
2004-05	St. John's	AHL	75	6	25	31	57	....	....	....	....	....	....	....	....	....	5	0	1	1	2	....	....	....	....
2005-06	**Toronto**	**NHL**	**1**	**0**	**0**	**0**	**0**	**0**	**0**	**0**	**2**	**0.0**	**0**	**0**	**0.0**	**14:00**	....	....	....	....	....	....	....	....	....
	Toronto Marlies	AHL	70	6	37	43	99	....	....	....	....	....	....	....	....	....	5	0	4	4	10	....	....	....	....
2006-07	**Toronto**	**NHL**	**31**	**1**	**4**	**5**	**19**	**1**	**0**	**0**	**29**	**3.4**	**-3**	**1**	**0.0**	**12:08**	....	....	....	....	....	....	....	....	....
	Phoenix	**NHL**	**14**	**0**	**2**	**2**	**8**	**0**	**0**	**0**	**18**	**0.0**	**-8**	**0**	**0.0**	**17:07**	....	....	....	....	....	....	....	....	....

Season	Club	League	GP	G	A	Pts	PIM	PP	SH	GW	S	%	+/-	TF	F%	Min	GP	G	A	Pts	PIM	PP	SH	GW	M
										Regular Season										Playoffs					
2007-08	Phoenix	NHL	2	0	0	0	0	0	0	0	0	0.0	-2	0	0.0	14:49									
	San Antonio	AHL	69	7	24	31	80																		
2008-09	Ottawa	NHL	53	6	15	21	24	5	0	1	76	7.9	-5	0	0.0	17:44	7	2	5	7	10				
	Binghamton	AHL	15	6	9	15	12																		
2009-10	Peoria Rivermen	AHL	22	4	13	17	26																		
	Syracuse Crunch	AHL	49	10	25	35	30																		
	NHL Totals		101	7	21	28	51	6	0	1	125	5.6		1	0.0	15:50									

OHL First All-Star Team (2003) • Canadian Major Junior First All-Star Team (2003) • Canadian Major Junior Defenseman of the Year (2003)
Traded to **Phoenix** by **Toronto** with Toronto's 2nd round choice (later traded to Nashville - Nashville selected Roman Josi in 2008 Entry Draft for Yanic Perreault and Phoenix's 5th round choice (Joel Champagne) in 2008 Entry Draft, February 27, 2007. Signed as a free agent by **Ottawa**, July 11, 2008. Signed as a free agent by **St. Louis**, July 31, 2009. Traded to **Columbus** by **St. Louis** with Tomas Kana for Pascal Pelletier, December 8, 2009. Signed as a free agent by **Omsk** (Russia-KHL), May 20, 2010.

BELLE, Shawn

Defense. Shoots left. 6'1", 240 lbs.   Born, Edmonton, Alta., January 3, 1985. St. Louis' 1st choice, 30th overall, in 2003 Entry Draft.   (BEHL, SHAWN)   EDM

Season	Club	League	GP	G	A	Pts	PIM	PP	SH	GW	S	%	+/-	TF	F%	Min	GP	G	A	Pts	PIM
99-2000	K of C Squires	AMBHL	34	7	20	27	36														
2000-01	K of C Squires	AMBHL	39	18	30	48	69														
	Regina Pats	WHL	4	0	3	3	0														
	Tri-City	WHL	2	0	1	1	0														
2001-02	Tri-City	WHL	64	1	17	18	51														
2002-03	Tri-City	WHL	66	7	14	21	79										5	2	1	3	2
2003-04	Tri-City	WHL	55	9	20	29	68														
2004-05	Tri-City	WHL	62	13	32	45	76										11	3	5	8	15
2005-06	Iowa Stars	AHL	45	1	2	3	63										5	1	1	2	6
	Houston Aeros	AHL	16	1	1	2	18														
2006-07	Minnesota	NHL	9	0	1	1	0	0	0	0	3	0.0	4	0	0.0	9:56	8	0	1	1	4
	Houston Aeros	AHL	57	4	14	18	73														
2007-08	Houston Aeros	AHL	63	1	2	3	74										3	0	0	0	2
2008-09	Hamilton	AHL	60	3	10	13	93										6	1	0	1	16
2009-10	Montreal	NHL	2	0	0	0	0	0	0	0	0	0.0	-2	0	0.0	10:38					
	Hamilton	AHL	70	3	16	19	69										19	1	6	7	20
	NHL Totals		11	0	1	1	0	0	0	0	4	0.0		0	0.0	10:04					

• Rights traded to **Dallas** by **St. Louis** for Jason Bacashihua, June 25, 2004. Traded to **Minnesota** by **Dallas** with Martin Skoula for Willie Mitchell and Minnesota's 2nd round choice (Nico Saccheti) in 2007 Entry Draft, March 9, 2006. Traded to **Montreal** by **Minnesota** for Cory Locke, July 11, 2008. Signed as a free agent by **Edmonton**, July 12. 2010.

BENN, Jamie

Left wing. Shoots left. 6'2", 207 lbs.   Born, Victoria, B.C., July 18, 1989. Dallas' 5th choice, 129th overall, in 2007 Entry Draft.   (BEHN, JAY-mee)   DAL.

Season	Club	League	GP	G	A	Pts	PIM	PP	SH	GW	S	%	+/-	TF	F%	Min	GP	G	A	Pts	PIM
2004-05	Peninsula Eagles	Minor-BC	STATISTICS NOT AVAILABLE																		
	Peninsula	VIJHL	4	1	2	3	2														
2005-06	Peninsula	VIJHL	38	31	24	55	92										2	0	0	0	0
2006-07	Victoria Grizzlies	BCHL	53	42	23	65	78										7	5	7	10	20
2007-08	Kelowna Rockets	WHL	51	33	32	65	68										11	5	4	9	12
2008-09	Kelowna Rockets	WHL	56	46	36	82	71										7	3	8	11	4
2009-10	Dallas	NHL	82	22	19	41	45	2	0	3	182	12.1	-1	236	46.2	14:42	19	*13	*20	*33	18
	Texas Stars	AHL															24	*14	12	26	22
	NHL Totals		82	22	19	41	45	2	0	3	182	12.1		236	46.2	14:42					

WHL West First All-Star Team (2009)

BENTIVOGLIO, Sean

Left wing. Shoots left. 5'10", 190 lbs.   Born, Thorold, Ont., October 16, 1985.   (behn-tih-VOHG-lee-oh, SHAWN)

Season	Club	League	GP	G	A	Pts	PIM	PP	SH	GW	S	%	+/-	TF	F%	Min	GP	G	A	Pts	PIM
2003-04	Niagara University	CHA	39	2	19	21	14														
2004-05	Niagara University	CHA	36	9	18	27	20														
2005-06	Niagara University	CHA	33	16	22	38	55														
2006-07	Niagara University	CHA	37	16	30	46	53														
	Providence Bruins	AHL	15	3	11	14	8														
2007-08	Bridgeport	AHL	68	9	23	32	28										13	3	6	9	14
2008-09	NY Islanders	NHL	1	0	0	0	2	0	0	0	2	0.0		1	0.0	11:31					
	Bridgeport	AHL	78	13	19	32	47										4	1	1	2	4
2009-10	Bridgeport	AHL	80	19	26	45	64										5	1	1	2	12
	NHL Totals		1	0	0	0	2	0	0	0	2	0.0		1	0.0	11:31					

Signed as a free agent by **NY Islanders**, May 19, 2007.

BERGENHEIM, Sean

Left wing. Shoots left. 5'10", 205 lbs.   Born, Helsinki, Finland, February 8, 1984. NY Islanders' 1st choice, 22nd overall, in 2002 Entry Draft.   (BUHR-gehn-highm, SHAWN)

Season	Club	League	GP	G	A	Pts	PIM	PP	SH	GW	S	%	+/-	TF	F%	Min	GP	G	A	Pts	PIM
99-2000	Jokerit U18	Fin-U18	30	22	11	33	34										3	1	0	1	0
2000-01	Jokerit U18	Fin-U18	17	10	8	18	14										3	1	0	1	2
	Jokerit Helsinki Jr.	Fin-Jr.	18	6	4	10	26										6	9	5	14	8
2001-02	Jokerit U18	Fin-U18															2	0	0	0	4
	Jokerit Helsinki Jr.	Fin-Jr.	23	11	19	30	36										5	6	2	8	18
	Kiekko-Vantaa	Finland-2	4	0	0	0	52										1	0	0	0	0
	Jokerit Helsinki	Finland	28	2	2	4	4														
2002-03	Jokerit Helsinki Jr.	Fin-Jr.	2	3	0	3	2														
	Jokerit Helsinki	Finland	38	3	3	6	4														
2003-04	NY Islanders	NHL	18	1	1	2	4	0	1	0	12	8.3	-4	2	50.0	8:55	2	0	0	0	0
	Jokerit Helsinki	Finland	20	2	2	4	18										3	1	2	3	0
	Bridgeport	AHL															7	2	3	5	10
2004-05	Bridgeport	AHL	61	15	14	29	69														
2005-06	NY Islanders	NHL	28	4	5	9	20	0	0	1	63	6.3	-11	14	28.6	13:17					
	Bridgeport	AHL	55	25	22	47	112										7	0	2	2	24
2006-07	Yaroslavl	Russia	9	1	4	5	26														
	Frolunda	Sweden	36	16	17	33	80														
2007-08	NY Islanders	NHL	78	10	12	22	62	1	0	1	155	6.5	-3	15	60.0	11:15					
2008-09	NY Islanders	NHL	59	15	9	24	64	0	4	5	152	9.9	-2	22	40.9	14:15					
2009-10	NY Islanders	NHL	63	10	13	23	45	0	2	0	133	7.5	1	17	29.4	14:04					
	NHL Totals		246	40	40	80	195	1	7	7	515	7.8		70	40.0	12:45					

Signed as a free agent by **Yaroslavl** (Russia), August 5, 2006. Signed as a free agent by **Frolunda** (Sweden), November 3, 2006.

BERGERON, Marc-Andre

Defense. Shoots left. 5'9", 198 lbs.   Born, St-Louis-de-France, Que., October 13, 1980.   (BAIR-zhur-uhn, MAHRK-AWN-dray)

Season	Club	League	GP	G	A	Pts	PIM	PP	SH	GW	S	%	+/-	TF	F%	Min	GP	G	A	Pts	PIM	PP	SH	GW	M
1996-97	Cap-d-Madeleine	QAAA	4	0	1	1	0																		
1997-98	Baie-Comeau	QMJHL	40	6	14	20	48										2	0	0	0	0				
1998-99	Baie-Comeau	QMJHL	46	8	14	22	57																		
	Shawinigan	QMJHL	24	6	7	13	66																		
99-2000	Shawinigan	QMJHL	70	24	50	74	173										5	2	2	4	24				
2000-01	Shawinigan	QMJHL	69	42	59	101	185										13	4	7	11	45				
2001-02	Hamilton	AHL	50	2	13	15	61										10	4	11	15	24				
2002-03	Edmonton	NHL	5	1	1	2	9	0	0	0	5	20.0	2	0	0.0	16:30	9	1	4	5	8				
	Hamilton	AHL	66	8	31	39	73										1	0	1	1	0				19:20
2003-04	Edmonton	NHL	54	9	17	26	26	3	0	0	105	8.6	13	0	0.0	17:39	20	1	6	7	25				
	Toronto	AHL	17	4	3	7	23																		
2004-05	Brynas IF Gavle	Sweden	10	3	2	5	72																		
	Brynas IF Gavle	Sweden-Q	9	1	2	3	8																		
2005-06	Edmonton	NHL	75	15	20	35	38	8	0	1	144	10.4	3	0	0.0	21:14	18	2	1	3	14	2	0	0	14:56

			Regular Season														Playoffs								
Season	Club	League	GP	G	A	Pts	PIM	PP	SH	GW	S	%	+/-	TF	F%	Min	GP	G	A	Pts	PIM	PP	SH	GW	Min
2006-07	Edmonton	NHL	55	8	17	25	28	6	0	3	111	7.2	–9	0	0.0	17:27	....	....	....	....	....	....	....	....	....
	NY Islanders	NHL	23	6	15	21	10	4	0	1	55	10.9	5	0	0.0	23:07	5	1	1	2	6	1	0	1	27:21
2007-08	NY Islanders	NHL	46	9	9	18	16	8	0	1	96	9.4	–14	0	0.0	18:17	....	....	....	....	....	....	....	....	....
	Anaheim	NHL	9	0	1	1	4	0	0	0	12	0.0	–2	0	0.0	12:50	....	....	....	....	....	....	....	....	....
2008-09	Minnesota	NHL	72	14	18	32	30	7	0	3	140	10.0	5	0	0.0	16:54	....	....	....	....	....	....	....	....	....
2009-10	Montreal	NHL	60	13	21	34	16	7	0	4	123	10.6	–7	0	0.0	15:04	19	2	4	6	10	2	0	0	16:27
	Hamilton	AHL	3	0	6	6	0	....	....	....	....	....	....	....	....	....	....	....	....	....	....	....	....	....	....
	NHL Totals		399	75	119	194	177	43	0	13	791	9.5		0	0.0	18:02	43	5	7	12	30	5	0	1	17:09

QMJHL First All-Star Team (2001) • Canadian Major Junior First All-Star Team (2001) • Canadian Major Junior Defenseman of the Year (2001) • AHL Second All-Star Team (2003)

Signed as a free agent by **Edmonton**, July 20, 2001. Signed as a free agent by **Gavle** (Sweden), January 23, 2005. Traded to **NY Islanders** by **Edmonton** with Edmonton's 3rd round choice (later traded back to Edmonton, later traded to Anaheim, later traded back to NY Islanders - NY Islanders selected Kirill Petrov) in 2008 Entry Draft for Denis Grebeshkov, February 18, 2007. Traded to **Anaheim** by **NY Islanders** for Edmonton's 3rd round choice (previously acquired, NY Islanders selected Kirill Petrov) in 2008 Entry Draft, February 26, 2008. Traded to **Minnesota** by **Anaheim** for Minnesota's 3rd round choice (Brandon McMillan) in 2008 Entry Draft, June 10, 2008. Signed as a free agent by **Montreal**, October 6, 2009.

BERGERON, Patrice

(BUHR-zhuhr-uhn, pa-TREES) **BOS.**

Center. Shoots right. 6'2", 194 lbs. Born, Ancienne-Lorette, Que., July 24, 1985. Boston's 2nd choice, 45th overall, in 2003 Entry Draft.

Season	Club	League	GP	G	A	Pts	PIM	PP	SH	GW	S	%	+/-	TF	F%	Min	GP	G	A	Pts	PIM	PP	SH	GW	Min
2000-01	Ste-Foy	QAAA	5	1	2	3	0	....	....	....	....	....	....	....	....	....	....	....	....	....	....	....	....	....	....
2001-02	St-Francois	QAAA	38	25	37	62	18	....	....	....	....	....	....	....	....	....	8	6	4	10	10	....	....	....	....
	Acadie-Bathurst	QMJHL	4	0	1	1	0	....	....	....	....	....	....	....	....	....	....	....	....	....	....	....	....	....	....
2002-03	Acadie-Bathurst	QMJHL	70	23	50	73	62	....	....	....	....	....	....	....	....	....	11	6	9	15	6	....	....	....	....
2003-04	Boston	NHL	71	16	23	39	22	7	0	2	133	12.0	5	699	49.4	16:21	7	1	3	4	0	0	0	1	17:13
2004-05	Providence Bruins	AHL	68	21	40	61	59	....	....	....	....	....	....	....	....	....	16	5	7	12	4	....	....	....	....
2005-06	Boston	NHL	81	31	42	73	22	12	1	6	310	10.0	3	1447	54.7	20:36	....	....	....	....	....	....	....	....	....
2006-07	Boston	NHL	77	22	48	70	26	14	0	6	224	9.8	–28	1560	51.2	20:49	....	....	....	....	....	....	....	....	....
2007-08	Boston	NHL	10	3	4	7	2	2	0	0	24	12.5	2	175	50.3	18:10	....	....	....	....	....	....	....	....	....
2008-09	Boston	NHL	64	8	31	39	16	1	1	1	155	5.2	2	1025	54.5	17:59	11	0	5	5	11	0	0	0	17:56
2009-10	Boston	NHL	73	19	33	52	28	0	1	4	184	10.3	6	1342	58.0	18:54	13	4	7	11	2	0	0	1	20:23
	Canada	Olympics	7	0	1	1	2	....	....	....	....	....	....	....	....	....	....	....	....	....	....	....	....	....	....
	NHL Totals		376	99	181	280	116	36	3	19	1030	9.6		6248	53.8	19:00	31	5	15	20	13	0	0	2	18:48

QAAA Second All-Star Team (2002)

• Missed majority of 2007-08 season recovering from concussion suffered in game vs. Philadelphia, October 27, 2007.

BERGFORS, Niclas

(BUHRG-fohrs, NIHK-luhs) **ATL.**

Right wing. Shoots right. 5'11", 195 lbs. Born, Sodertalje, Sweden, March 7, 1987. New Jersey's 1st choice, 23rd overall, in 2005 Entry Draft.

Season	Club	League	GP	G	A	Pts	PIM	PP	SH	GW	S	%	+/-	TF	F%	Min	GP	G	A	Pts	PIM	PP	SH	GW	Min
2002-03	Sodertalje SK U18	Swe-U18	4	4	4	8	0	....	....	....	....	....	....	....	....	....	....	....	....	....	....	....	....	....	....
	Sodertalje SK Jr.	Swe-Jr.	13	1	5	6	4	....	....	....	....	....	....	....	....	....	....	....	....	....	....	....	....	....	....
2003-04	Sodertalje SK U18	Swe-U18	5	14	4	18	4	....	....	....	....	....	....	....	....	....	2	0	1	1	6	....	....	....	....
	Sodertalje SK Jr.	Swe-Jr.	31	13	17	30	22	....	....	....	....	....	....	....	....	....	2	1	1	2	0	....	....	....	....
2004-05	Sodertalje SK Jr.	Swe-Jr.	21	18	16	34	25	....	....	....	....	....	....	....	....	....	3	0	3	3	4	....	....	....	....
	Sodertalje SK	Sweden	25	1	0	1	2	....	....	....	....	....	....	....	....	....	2	0	0	0	0	....	....	....	....
2005-06	Albany River Rats	AHL	65	17	23	40	10	....	....	....	....	....	....	....	....	....	....	....	....	....	....	....	....	....	....
2006-07	Lowell Devils	AHL	60	13	19	32	8	....	....	....	....	....	....	....	....	....	....	....	....	....	....	....	....	....	....
2007-08	New Jersey	NHL	1	0	0	0	0	0	0	0	3	0.0	–1	1	0.0	11:17	....	....	....	....	....	....	....	....	....
	Lowell Devils	AHL	66	12	15	27	22	....	....	....	....	....	....	....	....	....	....	....	....	....	....	....	....	....	....
2008-09	New Jersey	NHL	8	1	0	1	0	0	0	0	6	16.7	–1	0	0.0	5:48	....	....	....	....	....	....	....	....	....
	Lowell Devils	AHL	66	22	29	51	14	....	....	....	....	....	....	....	....	....	....	....	....	....	....	....	....	....	....
2009-10	New Jersey	NHL	54	13	14	27	10	8	0	4	134	9.7	–7	7	71.4	14:53	....	....	....	....	....	....	....	....	....
	Atlanta	NHL	27	8	9	17	0	1	0	2	83	9.6	–3	12	33.3	16:30	....	....	....	....	....	....	....	....	....
	NHL Totals		90	22	23	45	10	9	0	6	226	9.7		20	45.0	14:31	....	....	....	....	....	....	....	....	....

NHL All-Rookie Team (2010)

Traded to **Atlanta** by **New Jersey** with Johnny Oduya, Patrice Cormier and New Jersey's 1st (later traded to Chicago - Chicago selected Kevin Hayes) and 2nd (later traded to Chicago - Chicago selected Justin Holl) round choices in 2010 Entry Draft for Ilya Kovalchuk, Anssi Salmela and Atlanta's 2nd round choice (Jonathon Merrill) in 2010 Entry Draft, February 4, 2010.

BERGLUND, Patrik

(BUHRG-luhnd, PAT-rihk) **ST.L.**

Center. Shoots left. 6'4", 215 lbs. Born, Vasteras, Sweden, June 2, 1988. St. Louis' 2nd choice, 25th overall, in 2006 Entry Draft.

Season	Club	League	GP	G	A	Pts	PIM	PP	SH	GW	S	%	+/-	TF	F%	Min	GP	G	A	Pts	PIM	PP	SH	GW	Min
2002-03	Vasteras U18	Swe-U18	1	0	1	1	0	....	....	....	....	....	....	....	....	....	....	....	....	....	....	....	....	....	....
2003-04	Vasteras U18	Swe-U18	10	4	1	5	18	....	....	....	....	....	....	....	....	....	....	....	....	....	....	....	....	....	....
2004-05	Vasteras U18	Swe-U18	5	2	1	3	4	....	....	....	....	....	....	....	....	....	3	0	1	1	6	....	....	....	....
	Vasteras Jr.	Swe-Jr.	25	5	5	10	14	....	....	....	....	....	....	....	....	....	....	....	....	....	....	....	....	....	....
2005-06	Vasteras Jr.	Swe-Jr.	27	17	12	29	38	....	....	....	....	....	....	....	....	....	....	....	....	....	....	....	....	....	....
	VIK Vasteras HK	Sweden-2	21	3	1	4	4	....	....	....	....	....	....	....	....	....	....	....	....	....	....	....	....	....	....
2006-07	VIK Vasteras HK	Sweden-2	35	21	27	48	30	....	....	....	....	....	....	....	....	....	1	0	0	0	2	....	....	....	....
	Vasteras Jr.	Swe-Jr.	....	....	....	....	....	....	....	....	....	....	....	....	....	....	5	4	5	9	6	....	....	....	....
2007-08	VIK Vasteras HK	Sweden-2	46	22	32	54	26	....	....	....	....	....	....	....	....	....	5	1	2	3	6	....	....	....	....
2008-09	St. Louis	NHL	76	21	26	47	16	7	0	1	143	14.7	19	540	39.8	14:43	4	0	0	0	2	0	0	0	10:11
2009-10	St. Louis	NHL	71	13	13	26	16	6	0	4	129	10.1	–5	504	43.7	13:30	....	....	....	....	....	....	....	....	....
	NHL Totals		147	34	39	73	32	13	0	5	272	12.5		1044	41.7	14:08	4	0	0	0	2	0	0	0	10:11

NHL All-Rookie Team (2009)

BERNIER, Steve

(BAIRN-yay, STEEV) **FLA.**

Right wing. Shoots right. 6'2", 216 lbs. Born, Quebec City, Que., March 31, 1985. San Jose's 2nd choice, 16th overall, in 2003 Entry Draft.

Season	Club	League	GP	G	A	Pts	PIM	PP	SH	GW	S	%	+/-	TF	F%	Min	GP	G	A	Pts	PIM	PP	SH	GW	Min
1998-99	Quebec AA Aces	QAHA	28	33	23	56	24	....	....	....	....	....	....	....	....	....	....	....	....	....	....	....	....	....	....
99-2000	Quebec AA Aces	QAHA	26	12	23	35	42	....	....	....	....	....	....	....	....	....	....	....	....	....	....	....	....	....	....
2000-01	Ste-Foy	QAAA	39	17	35	52	48	....	....	....	....	....	....	....	....	....	16	9	17	26	8	....	....	....	....
2001-02	Moncton Wildcats	QMJHL	66	31	28	59	51	....	....	....	....	....	....	....	....	....	....	....	....	....	....	....	....	....	....
2002-03	Moncton Wildcats	QMJHL	71	49	52	101	90	....	....	....	....	....	....	....	....	....	2	1	0	1	2	....	....	....	....
2003-04	Moncton Wildcats	QMJHL	66	36	46	82	80	....	....	....	....	....	....	....	....	....	20	7	10	17	17	....	....	....	....
2004-05	Moncton Wildcats	QMJHL	68	35	36	71	114	....	....	....	....	....	....	....	....	....	12	6	13	19	22	....	....	....	....
2005-06	San Jose	NHL	39	14	13	27	35	2	1	1	75	18.7	4	8	62.5	14:08	11	1	5	6	8	1	0	1	15:17
	Cleveland Barons	AHL	49	20	23	43	33	....	....	....	....	....	....	....	....	....	....	....	....	....	....	....	....	....	....
2006-07	San Jose	NHL	62	15	16	31	29	6	0	4	104	14.4	5	18	27.8	13:35	11	0	1	1	2	0	0	0	10:39
	Worcester Sharks	AHL	10	3	4	7	2	....	....	....	....	....	....	....	....	....	....	....	....	....	....	....	....	....	....
2007-08	San Jose	NHL	59	13	10	23	62	4	0	0	96	13.5	–2	10	50.0	13:07	....	....	....	....	....	....	....	....	....
	Buffalo	NHL	17	3	6	9	2	0	0	0	35	8.6	1	5	20.0	14:06	....	....	....	....	....	....	....	....	....
2008-09	Vancouver	NHL	81	15	17	32	27	2	0	4	137	10.9	4	21	23.8	13:50	10	2	2	4	7	2	0	2	15:00
2009-10	Vancouver	NHL	59	11	11	22	21	3	0	0	95	11.6	0	34	20.6	14:10	12	4	1	5	0	2	0	0	9:59
	NHL Totals		317	71	73	144	176	17	1	9	542	13.1		96	29.2	13:46	44	7	9	16	17	5	0	3	12:37

QMJHL All-Rookie Team (2002) • QMJHL Second All-Star Team (2003, 2004) • Canadian Major Junior Second All-Star Team (2003)

Traded to **Buffalo** by **San Jose** with San Jose's 1st round choice (Tyler Ennis) in 2008 Entry Draft for Brian Campbell and Buffalo's 7th round choice (Drew Daniels) in 2008 Entry Draft, February 26, 2008. Traded to **Vancouver** by **Buffalo** for Los Angeles' 3rd round choice (previously acquired, Buffalo selected Brayden McNabb) in 2009 Entry Draft and Vancouver's 2nd round choice (later traded to Columbus – Columbus selected Petr Straka) in 2010 Entry Draft, July 4, 2008. Traded to **Florida** by **Vancouver** with Michael Grabner and Vancouver's 1st round choice (Quinton Howden) in 2010 Entry Draft for Keith Ballard and Victor Oreskovich, June 25, 2010.

BERTUZZI, Todd

(buhr-TOO-zee, TAWD) **DET.**

Right wing. Shoots left. 6'3", 225 lbs. Born, Sudbury, Ont., February 2, 1975. NY Islanders' 1st choice, 23rd overall, in 1993 Entry Draft.

Season	Club	League	GP	G	A	Pts	PIM	PP	SH	GW	S	%	+/-	TF	F%	Min	GP	G	A	Pts	PIM	PP	SH	GW	Min
1990-91	Sudbury Legion	NOHA	48	25	46	71	247	....	....	....	....	....	....	....	....	....	....	....	....	....	....	....	....	....	....
	Sudbury Cubs	NOJHA	3	3	2	5	10	....	....	....	....	....	....	....	....	....	....	....	....	....	....	....	....	....	....
1991-92	Guelph Storm	OHL	47	7	14	21	145	....	....	....	....	....	....	....	....	....	....	....	....	....	....	....	....	....	....
1992-93	Guelph Storm	OHL	59	27	32	59	164	....	....	....	....	....	....	....	....	....	5	2	2	4	6	....	....	....	....
1993-94	Guelph Storm	OHL	61	28	54	82	165	....	....	....	....	....	....	....	....	....	9	2	6	8	30	....	....	....	....
1994-95	Guelph Storm	OHL	62	54	65	119	58	....	....	....	....	....	....	....	....	....	14	*15	18	33	41	....	....	....	....
1995-96	NY Islanders	NHL	76	18	21	39	83	4	0	2	127	14.2	–14	....	....	....	....	....	....	....	....	....	....	....	....

			Regular Season														Playoffs								
Season	Club	League	GP	G	A	Pts	PIM	PP	SH	GW	S	%	+/-	TF	F%	Min	GP	G	A	Pts	PIM	PP	SH	GW	Min
1996-97	**NY Islanders**	**NHL**	**64**	**10**	**13**	**23**	**68**	**3**	**0**	**1**	**79**	**12.7**	**-3**	....	....	....	....	....	....	....	....	....	....	....	....
	Utah Grizzlies	IHL	13	5	5	10	16	....	....	....	....	....	....	....	....	....	....	....	....	....	....	....	....	....	....
1997-98	**NY Islanders**	**NHL**	**52**	**7**	**11**	**18**	**58**	**1**	**0**	**1**	**63**	**11.1**	**-19**	....	....	....	....	....	....	....	....	....	....	....	....
	Vancouver	**NHL**	**22**	**6**	**9**	**15**	**63**	**1**	**1**	**1**	**39**	**15.4**	**2**	....	....	....	....	....	....	....	....	....	....	....	....
1998-99	**Vancouver**	**NHL**	**32**	**8**	**8**	**16**	**44**	**1**	**0**	**3**	**72**	**11.1**	**-6**	**191**	**43.5**	**18:28**	....	....	....	....	....	....	....	....	....
99-2000	**Vancouver**	**NHL**	**80**	**25**	**25**	**50**	**126**	**4**	**0**	**2**	**173**	**14.5**	**-2**	**476**	**46.6**	**15:24**	....	....	....	....	....	....	....	....	....
2000-01	**Vancouver**	**NHL**	**79**	**25**	**30**	**55**	**93**	**14**	**0**	**3**	**203**	**12.3**	**-18**	**84**	**45.2**	**17:13**	**4**	**2**	**2**	**4**	**8**	**0**	**0**	**0**	**19:01**
2001-02	**Vancouver**	**NHL**	**72**	**36**	**49**	**85**	**110**	**14**	**0**	**3**	**203**	**17.7**	**21**	**151**	**49.0**	**19:40**	**6**	**2**	**2**	**4**	**14**	**1**	**0**	**0**	**21:50**
2002-03	**Vancouver**	**NHL**	**82**	**46**	**51**	**97**	**144**	***25**	**0**	**7**	**243**	**18.9**	**2**	**208**	**47.1**	**20:34**	**14**	**2**	**4**	**6**	***60**	**0**	**0**	**0**	**21:05**
2003-04	**Vancouver**	**NHL**	**69**	**17**	**43**	**60**	**122**	**8**	**0**	**2**	**156**	**10.9**	**21**	**111**	**45.1**	**21:00**	....	....	....	....	....	....	....	....	....
2004-05		DID NOT PLAY – SUSPENDED																							
2005-06	**Vancouver**	**NHL**	**82**	**25**	**46**	**71**	**120**	**12**	**0**	**3**	**200**	**12.5**	**-17**	**363**	**43.8**	**19:08**	....	....	....	....	....	....	....	....	....
	Canada	Olympics	6	0	3	3	6	....	....	....	....	....	....	....	....	....	....	....	....	....	....	....	....	....	....
2006-07	**Florida**	**NHL**	**7**	**1**	**6**	**7**	**13**	**1**	**0**	**0**	**8**	**12.5**	**-4**	**0**	**0.0**	**16:32**	....	....	....	....	....	....	....	....	....
	Detroit	**NHL**	**8**	**2**	**2**	**4**	**6**	**0**	**0**	**0**	**15**	**13.3**	**3**	**2**	**50.0**	**15:32**	**16**	**3**	**4**	**7**	**15**	**1**	**0**	**0**	**14:25**
2007-08	**Anaheim**	**NHL**	**68**	**14**	**26**	**40**	**97**	**4**	**0**	**2**	**121**	**11.6**	**8**	**110**	**45.5**	**16:27**	**6**	**0**	**2**	**2**	**14**	**0**	**0**	**0**	**14:15**
2008-09	**Calgary**	**NHL**	**66**	**15**	**29**	**44**	**74**	**6**	**0**	**4**	**127**	**11.8**	**-13**	**45**	**46.7**	**18:36**	**6**	**1**	**1**	**2**	**8**	**0**	**0**	**0**	**17:25**
2009-10	**Detroit**	**NHL**	**82**	**18**	**26**	**44**	**80**	**4**	**0**	**4**	**216**	**8.3**	**-7**	**23**	**47.8**	**16:46**	**12**	**2**	**9**	**11**	**12**	**1**	**0**	**0**	**17:08**
	NHL Totals		**941**	**273**	**395**	**668**	**1301**	**102**	**1**	**38**	**2045**	**13.3**		**1764**	**45.7**	**18:15**	**64**	**12**	**24**	**36**	**131**	**3**	**0**	**0**	**17:38**

OHL Second All-Star Team (1995) • NHL First All-Star Team (2003)

Played in NHL All-Star Game (2003, 2004)

Traded to **Vancouver** by **NY Islanders** with Bryan McCabe and NY Islanders' 3rd round choice (Jarkko Ruutu) in 1998 Entry Draft for Trevor Linden, February 6, 1998. • Missed majority of 1998-99 season recovering from leg injury suffered in game vs. Washington, November 1, 1998. • Suspended indefinitely by NHL for deliberate injury to Steve Moore in game vs. Colorado, March 8, 2004. • Reinstated by NHL on August 8, 2005. Traded to **Florida** by **Vancouver** with Bryan Allen and Alex Auld for Roberto Luongo, Lukas Krajicek and Florida's 6th round choice (Sergei Shirokov) in 2006 Entry Draft, June 23, 2006. Traded to **Detroit** by **Florida** for Shawn Matthias and Detroit's 2nd round choice (later traded to Nashville - Nashville selected Nick Spaling) in 2007 Entry Draft, February 27, 2007. • Missed majority of 2006-07 season recovering from recurring back injury. Signed as a free agent by **Anaheim**, July 2, 2007. Signed as a free agent by **Calgary**, July 7, 2008. Signed as a free agent by **Detroit**, August 18, 2009.

BETTS, Blair (BEHTS, BLAIR) PHI.

Center. Shoots left. 6'3", 210 lbs. Born, Edmonton, Alta., February 16, 1980. Calgary's 2nd choice, 33rd overall, in 1998 Entry Draft.

1995-96	Sherwood Park	AMHL	34	22	19	41	69	....	....	....	....	....	....	....	....	....	....	....	....	....	....	....	....	....	....
1996-97	Prince George	WHL	58	12	18	30	19	....	....	....	....	....	....	....	....	....	15	2	2	4	6	....	....	....	....
1997-98	Prince George	WHL	71	35	41	76	38	....	....	....	....	....	....	....	....	....	11	4	6	10	8	....	....	....	....
1998-99	Prince George	WHL	42	20	22	42	39	....	....	....	....	....	....	....	....	....	7	3	2	5	8	....	....	....	....
99-2000	Prince George	WHL	44	24	35	59	38	....	....	....	....	....	....	....	....	....	13	11	11	22	6	....	....	....	....
2000-01	Saint John Flames	AHL	75	13	15	28	28	....	....	....	....	....	....	....	....	....	19	2	3	5	4	....	....	....	....
2001-02	**Calgary**	**NHL**	**6**	**1**	**0**	**1**	**2**	**0**	**0**	**1**	**4**	**25.0**	**-1**	**39**	**48.7**	**7:05**	....	....	....	....	....	....	....	....	....
	Saint John Flames	AHL	67	20	29	49	10	....	....	....	....	....	....	....	....	....	....	....	....	....	....	....	....	....	....
2002-03	**Calgary**	**NHL**	**9**	**1**	**3**	**4**	**0**	**0**	**0**	**0**	**16**	**6.3**	**3**	**71**	**53.5**	**11:33**	....	....	....	....	....	....	....	....	....
	Saint John Flames	AHL	19	6	7	13	6	....	....	....	....	....	....	....	....	....	....	....	....	....	....	....	....	....	....
2003-04	**Calgary**	**NHL**	**20**	**1**	**2**	**3**	**10**	**1**	**0**	**1**	**21**	**4.8**	**-1**	**248**	**54.0**	**12:46**	....	....	....	....	....	....	....	....	....
2004-05	Hartford	AHL	16	5	4	9	4	....	....	....	....	....	....	....	....	....	....	....	....	....	....	....	....	....	....
2005-06	**NY Rangers**	**NHL**	**66**	**8**	**2**	**10**	**24**	**0**	**1**	**0**	**94**	**8.5**	**-10**	**817**	**53.4**	**12:55**	**4**	**1**	**1**	**2**	**2**	**0**	**0**	**0**	**16:12**
2006-07	**NY Rangers**	**NHL**	**82**	**9**	**4**	**13**	**24**	**1**	**1**	**0**	**120**	**7.5**	**-4**	**1186**	**52.3**	**14:02**	**10**	**0**	**0**	**0**	**4**	**0**	**0**	**0**	**11:15**
2007-08	**NY Rangers**	**NHL**	**75**	**2**	**5**	**7**	**20**	**0**	**0**	**0**	**85**	**2.4**	**-4**	**771**	**50.3**	**11:52**	**8**	**0**	**0**	**0**	**2**	**0**	**0**	**0**	**7:16**
2008-09	**NY Rangers**	**NHL**	**81**	**6**	**4**	**10**	**16**	**0**	**2**	**1**	**83**	**7.2**	**-5**	**884**	**49.3**	**10:37**	**6**	**0**	**0**	**0**	**0**	**0**	**0**	**0**	**9:08**
2009-10	**Philadelphia**	**NHL**	**63**	**8**	**10**	**18**	**14**	**1**	**1**	**2**	**63**	**12.7**	**7**	**855**	**50.9**	**12:37**	**23**	**1**	**1**	**2**	**4**	**0**	**0**	**0**	**11:19**
	NHL Totals		**402**	**36**	**30**	**66**	**110**	**3**	**5**	**5**	**486**	**7.4**		**4871**	**51.4**	**12:19**	**51**	**2**	**2**	**4**	**12**	**0**	**0**	**0**	**10:48**

• Missed majority of 2002-03 season recovering from shoulder injury suffered in training camp, September 27, 2002. • Missed majority of 2003-04 season recovering from shoulder injuries suffered in games vs. Chicago (November 22, 2003) and Colorado (December 31, 2003). Traded to **NY Rangers** by **Calgary** with Jamie McLennan and Greg Moore for Chris Simon and NY Rangers' 7th round choice (Matt Schneider) in 2004 Entry Draft, March 6, 2004. Signed as a free agent by **Philadelphia**, October 1, 2009.

BICKELL, Bryan (BIH-kuhl, BRIGH-uhn) CHI.

Left wing. Shoots left. 6'4", 223 lbs. Born, Bowmanville, Ont., March 9, 1986. Chicago's 3rd choice, 41st overall, in 2004 Entry Draft.

2000-01	Tor. Red Wings	GTHL	68	24	26	50	20	....	....	....	....	....	....	....	....	....	5	3	1	4	4	....	....	....	....
2001-02	Tor. Red Wings	GTHL	65	31	41	72	76	....	....	....	....	....	....	....	....	....	2	2	2	4	0	....	....	....	....
2002-03	Ottawa 67's	OHL	50	7	10	17	4	....	....	....	....	....	....	....	....	....	20	5	3	8	12	....	....	....	....
2003-04	Ottawa 67's	OHL	59	20	16	36	76	....	....	....	....	....	....	....	....	....	7	3	0	3	11	....	....	....	....
2004-05	Ottawa 67's	OHL	66	22	32	54	95	....	....	....	....	....	....	....	....	....	21	5	12	17	32	....	....	....	....
2005-06	Ottawa 67's	OHL	41	28	22	50	41	....	....	....	....	....	....	....	....	....	....	....	....	....	....	....	....	....	....
	Windsor Spitfires	OHL	26	17	16	33	19	....	....	....	....	....	....	....	....	....	7	5	5	10	10	....	....	....	....
2006-07	**Chicago**	**NHL**	**3**	**2**	**0**	**2**	**0**	**0**	**0**	**0**	**10**	**20.0**	**1**	**0**	**0.0**	**11:49**	....	....	....	....	....	....	....	....	....
	Norfolk Admirals	AHL	48	10	15	25	66	....	....	....	....	....	....	....	....	....	2	0	0	0	0	....	....	....	....
2007-08	**Chicago**	**NHL**	**4**	**0**	**0**	**0**	**2**	**0**	**0**	**0**	**3**	**0.0**	**-1**	**0**	**0.0**	**9:08**	....	....	....	....	....	....	....	....	....
	Rockford IceHogs	AHL	73	19	20	39	52	....	....	....	....	....	....	....	....	....	12	2	3	5	11	....	....	....	....
2008-09	Rockford IceHogs	AHL	42	6	8	14	60	....	....	....	....	....	....	....	....	....	4	0	2	2	4	....	....	....	....
2009-10	**Chicago**	**NHL**	**16**	**3**	**1**	**4**	**5**	**0**	**0**	**1**	**20**	**15.0**	**4**	**2**	**0.0**	**9:36**	**4**	**0**	**1**	**1**	**2**	**0**	**0**	**0**	**13:14**
	Rockford IceHogs	AHL	65	16	15	31	58	....	....	....	....	....	....	....	....	....	6	0	1	1	0	....	....	....	....
	NHL Totals		**23**	**5**	**1**	**6**	**7**	**0**	**0**	**1**	**33**	**15.2**		**2**	**0.0**	**9:48**	**4**	**0**	**1**	**1**	**2**	**0**	**0**	**0**	**13:14**

BIEKSA, Kevin (BEE-ehks-ah, KEH-vihn) VAN.

Defense. Shoots right. 6'1", 198 lbs. Born, Grimsby, Ont., June 16, 1981. Vancouver's 4th choice, 151st overall, in 2001 Entry Draft.

1997-98	Burlington	OPJHL	27	0	3	3	10	....	....	....	....	....	....	....	....	....	....	....	....	....	....	....	....	....	....
1998-99	Burlington	OPJHL	49	8	29	37	83	....	....	....	....	....	....	....	....	....	....	....	....	....	....	....	....	....	....
99-2000	Burlington	OPJHL	49	6	27	33	139	....	....	....	....	....	....	....	....	....	....	....	....	....	....	....	....	....	....
2000-01	Bowling Green	CCHA	35	4	9	13	90	....	....	....	....	....	....	....	....	....	....	....	....	....	....	....	....	....	....
2001-02	Bowling Green	CCHA	40	5	10	15	68	....	....	....	....	....	....	....	....	....	....	....	....	....	....	....	....	....	....
2002-03	Bowling Green	CCHA	34	8	17	25	92	....	....	....	....	....	....	....	....	....	....	....	....	....	....	....	....	....	....
2003-04	Bowling Green	CCHA	38	7	15	22	66	....	....	....	....	....	....	....	....	....	....	....	....	....	....	....	....	....	....
	Manitoba Moose	AHL	4	0	2	2	2	....	....	....	....	....	....	....	....	....	....	....	....	....	....	....	....	....	....
2004-05	Manitoba Moose	AHL	80	12	27	39	192	....	....	....	....	....	....	....	....	....	14	1	1	2	52	....	....	....	....
2005-06	**Vancouver**	**NHL**	**39**	**0**	**6**	**6**	**77**	**0**	**0**	**0**	**38**	**0.0**	**-1**	**0**	**0.0**	**16:06**	....	....	....	....	....	....	....	....	....
	Manitoba Moose	AHL	23	3	17	20	71	....	....	....	....	....	....	....	....	....	13	0	10	10	38	....	....	....	....
2006-07	**Vancouver**	**NHL**	**81**	**12**	**30**	**42**	**134**	**6**	**0**	**2**	**203**	**5.9**	**1**	**0**	**0.0**	**24:16**	**9**	**0**	**0**	**0**	**20**	**0**	**0**	**0**	**28:01**
2007-08	**Vancouver**	**NHL**	**34**	**2**	**10**	**12**	**90**	**1**	**0**	**1**	**64**	**3.1**	**-11**	**0**	**0.0**	**23:24**	....	....	....	....	....	....	....	....	....
	Manitoba Moose	AHL	1	0	1	1	2	....	....	....	....	....	....	....	....	....	....	....	....	....	....	....	....	....	....
2008-09	**Vancouver**	**NHL**	**72**	**11**	**32**	**43**	**97**	**5**	**0**	**2**	**153**	**7.2**	**-4**	**0**	**0.0**	**23:29**	**10**	**0**	**5**	**5**	**14**	**0**	**0**	**0**	**24:08**
2009-10	**Vancouver**	**NHL**	**55**	**3**	**19**	**22**	**85**	**1**	**0**	**0**	**95**	**3.2**	**-5**	**0**	**0.0**	**21:49**	**12**	**3**	**5**	**8**	**14**	**1**	**0**	**1**	**22:37**
	NHL Totals		**281**	**28**	**97**	**125**	**483**	**13**	**0**	**5**	**553**	**5.1**		**0**	**0.0**	**22:21**	**31**	**3**	**10**	**13**	**48**	**1**	**0**	**1**	**24:40**

AHL All-Rookie Team (2005)

BISSONNETTE, Paul (bih-sawn-EHT, PAWL) PHX.

Left wing. Shoots left. 6'3", 220 lbs. Born, Welland, Ont., March 11, 1985. Pittsburgh's 5th choice, 121st overall, in 2003 Entry Draft.

2001-02	North Bay	OHL	57	3	3	6	21	....	....	....	....	....	....	....	....	....	5	0	0	0	2	....	....	....	....
2002-03	Saginaw Spirit	OHL	67	7	16	23	57	....	....	....	....	....	....	....	....	....	....	....	....	....	....	....	....	....	....
2003-04	Saginaw Spirit	OHL	67	5	14	19	96	....	....	....	....	....	....	....	....	....	....	....	....	....	....	....	....	....	....
2004-05	Saginaw Spirit	OHL	28	1	6	7	46	....	....	....	....	....	....	....	....	....	....	....	....	....	....	....	....	....	....
	Owen Sound	OHL	35	2	11	13	46	....	....	....	....	....	....	....	....	....	8	1	3	4	2	....	....	....	....
2005-06	Wilkes-Barre	AHL	55	1	5	6	60	....	....	....	....	....	....	....	....	....	11	0	1	1	4	....	....	....	....
	Wheeling Nailers	ECHL	14	3	7	10	4	....	....	....	....	....	....	....	....	....	....	....	....	....	....	....	....	....	....
2006-07	Wilkes-Barre	AHL	3	0	0	0	6	....	....	....	....	....	....	....	....	....	....	....	....	....	....	....	....	....	....
	Wheeling Nailers	ECHL	65	10	32	42	115	....	....	....	....	....	....	....	....	....	....	....	....	....	....	....	....	....	....
2007-08	Wilkes-Barre	AHL	46	3	5	8	145	....	....	....	....	....	....	....	....	....	7	0	0	0	11	....	....	....	....
	Wheeling Nailers	ECHL	22	3	14	17	43	....	....	....	....	....	....	....	....	....	....	....	....	....	....	....	....	....	....

			Regular Season														Playoffs								
Season	Club	League	GP	G	A	Pts	PIM	PP	SH	GW	S	%	+/-	TF	F%	Min	GP	G	A	Pts	PIM	PP	SH	GW	Min
2008-09	Pittsburgh	NHL	15	0	1	1	22	0	0	0	4	0.0	–1	0	0.0	3:31	....	....	....	....	....	....	....	....	....
	Wilkes-Barre	AHL	57	9	7	16	176	....	....	....	....	....	....	....	....	....	8	0	2	2	9	....	....	....	....
2009-10	Phoenix	NHL	41	3	2	5	117	0	0	1	25	12.0	–2	0	0.0	5:52	....	....	....	....	....	....	....	....	....
	NHL Totals		56	3	3	6	139	0	0	1	29	10.3		0	0.0	5:14	....	....	....	....	....	....	....	....	....

Claimed on waivers by **Phoenix** from **Pittsburgh**, September 30, 2009.

BITZ, Byron

(BIHTZ, BIGH-ruhn) **FLA.**

Right wing. Shoots right. 6'5", 215 lbs. Born, Saskatoon, Sask., July 21, 1984. Boston's 4th choice, 107th overall, in 2003 Entry Draft.

2000-01	Saskatoon	SMBHL	40	17	35	52	....	....	....	....	....	....	....	....	....	....	....	....	....	....	....	....	....	....	....
2001-02	Saskatoon	SMHL	41	25	48	73	69	....	....	....	....	....	....	....	....	....	11	12	10	22	9	....	....	....	....
2002-03	Nanaimo Clippers	BCHL	58	27	46	73	59	....	....	....	....	....	....	....	....	....	....	....	....	....	....	....	....	....	....
2003-04	Cornell Big Red	ECAC	31	5	16	21	36	....	....	....	....	....	....	....	....	....	....	....	....	....	....	....	....	....	....
2004-05	Cornell Big Red	ECAC	29	5	10	15	20	....	....	....	....	....	....	....	....	....	....	....	....	....	....	....	....	....	....
2005-06	Cornell Big Red	ECAC	35	10	18	28	52	....	....	....	....	....	....	....	....	....	....	....	....	....	....	....	....	....	....
2006-07	Cornell Big Red	ECAC	29	8	16	24	49	....	....	....	....	....	....	....	....	....	....	....	....	....	....	....	....	....	....
2007-08	Providence Bruins	AHL	61	13	14	27	70	....	....	....	....	....	....	....	....	....	10	1	1	2	6	....	....	....	....
2008-09	Boston	NHL	35	4	3	7	18	0	0	0	31	12.9	0	50	42.0	10:22	5	1	1	2	2	0	0	0	11:27
	Providence Bruins	AHL	37	3	7	10	68	....	....	....	....	....	....	....	....	....	....	....	....	....	....	....	....	....	....
2009-10	Boston	NHL	45	4	5	9	31	0	0	2	51	7.8	–9	17	41.2	10:57	....	....	....	....	....	....	....	....	....
	Florida	NHL	7	1	1	2	2	0	0	0	7	14.3	1	1	0.0	11:37	....	....	....	....	....	....	....	....	....
	NHL Totals		87	9	9	18	51	0	0	2	89	10.1		68	41.2	10:46	5	1	1	2	2	0	0	0	11:27

Traded to **Florida** by **Boston** with Craig Weller and Tampa Bay's 2nd round choice (previously acquired, Florida selected Alexander Petrovic) in 2010 Entry Draft for Dennis Seidenberg and Matt Bartkowski, March 3, 2010.

BLAKE, Jason

(BLAYK, JAY-suhn) **ANA.**

Left wing. Shoots left. 5'10", 186 lbs. Born, Moorhead, MN, September 2, 1973.

1991-92	Moorhead Spuds	High-MN	25	30	30	60	....	....	....	....	....	....	....	....	....	....	....	....	....	....	....	....	....	....	....
1992-93	Waterloo	USHL	45	24	27	51	107	....	....	....	....	....	....	....	....	....	....	....	....	....	....	....	....	....	....
1993-94	Waterloo	USHL	47	50	50	100	76	....	....	....	....	....	....	....	....	....	....	....	....	....	....	....	....	....	....
1994-95	Ferris State	CCHA	36	16	16	32	46	....	....	....	....	....	....	....	....	....	....	....	....	....	....	....	....	....	....
1995-96	North Dakota	WCHA	DID NOT PLAY – TRANSFERRED COLLEGES																						
1996-97	North Dakota	WCHA	43	19	32	51	44	....	....	....	....	....	....	....	....	....	....	....	....	....	....	....	....	....	....
1997-98	North Dakota	WCHA	38	24	27	51	62	....	....	....	....	....	....	....	....	....	....	....	....	....	....	....	....	....	....
1998-99	North Dakota	WCHA	38	*28	*41	*69	49	....	....	....	....	....	....	....	....	....	....	....	....	....	....	....	....	....	....
	Los Angeles	NHL	1	1	0	1	0	0	0	0	5	20.0	1	14	35.7	17:13	....	....	....	....	....	....	....	....	....
	Orlando	IHL	5	3	5	8	6	....	....	....	....	....	....	....	....	....	13	3	4	7	20	....	....	....	....
99-2000	Los Angeles	NHL	64	5	18	23	26	0	0	1	131	3.8	4	269	43.9	11:17	3	0	0	0	0	0	0	0	9:35
	Long Beach	IHL	7	3	6	9	2	....	....	....	....	....	....	....	....	....	....	....	....	....	....	....	....	....	....
2000-01	Los Angeles	NHL	17	1	3	4	10	0	0	0	27	3.7	–8	13	61.5	10:03	....	....	....	....	....	....	....	....	....
	Lowell	AHL	2	0	1	1	2	....	....	....	....	....	....	....	....	....	....	....	....	....	....	....	....	....	....
	NY Islanders	NHL	30	4	8	12	24	1	1	0	73	5.5	–12	118	44.1	15:43	....	....	....	....	....	....	....	....	....
2001-02	NY Islanders	NHL	82	8	10	18	36	0	0	1	136	5.9	–11	23	43.5	12:54	7	0	1	1	13	0	0	0	12:13
2002-03	NY Islanders	NHL	81	25	30	55	58	3	1	4	253	9.9	16	22	18.2	17:38	5	0	1	1	2	0	0	0	19:39
2003-04	NY Islanders	NHL	75	22	25	47	56	1	4	3	243	9.1	11	70	41.4	18:49	4	2	0	2	2	0	0	0	18:09
2004-05	HC Lugano	Swiss	7	2	2	4	4	....	....	....	....	....	....	....	....	....	....	....	....	....	....	....	....	....	....
2005-06	NY Islanders	NHL	76	28	29	57	60	12	2	2	304	9.2	0	152	42.8	18:47	....	....	....	....	....	....	....	....	....
	United States	Olympics	6	0	0	0	2	....	....	....	....	....	....	....	....	....	....	....	....	....	....	....	....	....	....
2006-07	NY Islanders	NHL	82	40	29	69	34	14	0	7	305	13.1	1	117	57.3	18:09	5	1	2	3	2	0	0	0	17:04
2007-08	Toronto	NHL	82	15	37	52	28	2	0	0	332	4.5	–4	28	50.0	17:49	....	....	....	....	....	....	....	....	....
2008-09	Toronto	NHL	78	25	38	63	40	5	1	5	302	8.3	–2	77	46.8	18:21	....	....	....	....	....	....	....	....	....
2009-10	Toronto	NHL	56	10	16	26	26	2	0	2	170	5.9	–4	53	35.9	15:50	....	....	....	....	....	....	....	....	....
	Anaheim	NHL	26	6	9	15	10	4	0	0	69	8.7	–6	28	42.9	16:02	....	....	....	....	....	....	....	....	....
	NHL Totals		750	190	252	442	408	44	9	25	2350	8.1		984	44.6	16:31	24	3	4	7	19	0	0	0	15:26

USHL Player of the Year (1994) • WCHA First All-Star Team (1997, 1998, 1999) • NCAA West Second All-American Team (1998) • WCHA Player of the Year (1999) • NCAA West First All-American Team (1999) • Bill Masterton Memorial Trophy (2008)

Played in NHL All-Star Game (2007)

Signed as a free agent by **Los Angeles**, April 20, 1999. Traded to **NY Islanders** by **Los Angeles** for NY Islanders' 5th round choice (Joel Andresen) in 2002 Entry Draft, January 3, 2001. Signed as a free agent by **Lugano** (Swiss), December 1, 2004. Signed as a free agent by **Toronto**, July 1, 2007. Traded to **Anaheim** by **Toronto** with Vesa Toskala for Jean-Sebastien Giguere, January 31, 2010.

BLAKE, Rob

(BLAYK, RAWB)

Defense. Shoots right. 6'4", 220 lbs. Born, Simcoe, Ont., December 10, 1969. Los Angeles' 4th choice, 70th overall, in 1988 Entry Draft.

1985-86	Brantford Classics	OHA-B	39	3	13	16	43	....	....	....	....	....	....	....	....	....	....	....	....	....	....	....	....	....	....
1986-87	Stratford Cullitons	OHA-B	31	11	20	31	115	....	....	....	....	....	....	....	....	....	....	....	....	....	....	....	....	....	....
1987-88	Bowling Green	CCHA	43	5	8	13	88	....	....	....	....	....	....	....	....	....	....	....	....	....	....	....	....	....	....
1988-89	Bowling Green	CCHA	46	11	21	32	140	....	....	....	....	....	....	....	....	....	....	....	....	....	....	....	....	....	....
1989-90	Bowling Green	CCHA	42	23	36	59	140	....	....	....	....	....	....	....	....	....	....	....	....	....	....	....	....	....	....
	Los Angeles	NHL	4	0	0	0	4	0	0	0	3	0.0	0	....	....	....	8	1	3	4	4	1	0	0	....
1990-91	Los Angeles	NHL	75	12	34	46	125	9	0	2	150	8.0	3	....	....	....	12	1	4	5	26	1	0	0	....
1991-92	Los Angeles	NHL	57	7	13	20	102	5	0	0	131	5.3	–5	....	....	....	6	2	1	3	12	0	0	0	....
1992-93	Los Angeles	NHL	76	16	43	59	152	10	0	4	243	6.6	18	....	....	....	23	4	6	10	46	1	1	0	....
1993-94	Los Angeles	NHL	84	20	48	68	137	7	0	6	304	6.6	–7	....	....	....	....	....	....	....	....	....	....	....	....
1994-95	Los Angeles	NHL	24	4	7	11	38	4	0	1	76	5.3	–16	....	....	....	....	....	....	....	....	....	....	....	....
1995-96	Los Angeles	NHL	6	1	2	3	8	0	0	0	13	7.7	0	....	....	....	....	....	....	....	....	....	....	....	....
1996-97	Los Angeles	NHL	62	8	23	31	82	4	0	1	169	4.7	–28	....	....	....	....	....	....	....	....	....	....	....	....
1997-98	Los Angeles	NHL	81	23	27	50	94	11	0	4	261	8.8	–3	....	....	....	4	0	0	0	6	0	0	0	....
	Canada	Olympics	6	1	1	2	2	....	....	....	....	....	....	....	....	....	....	....	....	....	....	....	....	....	....
1998-99	Los Angeles	NHL	62	12	23	35	128	5	1	2	216	5.6	–7	0	0.0	24:52	....	....	....	....	....	....	....	....	....
99-2000	Los Angeles	NHL	77	18	39	57	112	12	0	5	327	5.5	10	0	0.0	28:30	4	0	2	2	4	0	0	0	30:10
2000-01	Los Angeles	NHL	54	17	32	49	69	9	0	1	223	7.6	–8	0	0.0	28:11	....	....	....	....	....	....	....	....	....
	♦ Colorado	NHL	13	2	8	10	8	1	0	1	44	4.5	11	0	0.0	26:03	23	6	13	19	16	3	0	0	29:26
2001-02	Colorado	NHL	75	16	40	56	58	10	0	2	229	7.0	16	0	0.0	27:35	20	6	6	12	16	1	0	0	26:38
	Canada	Olympics	6	1	2	3	2	....	....	....	....	....	....	....	....	....	....	....	....	....	....	....	....	....	....
2002-03	Colorado	NHL	79	17	28	45	57	8	2	3	269	6.3	20	0	0.0	26:21	7	1	2	3	8	0	0	0	27:28
2003-04	Colorado	NHL	74	13	33	46	61	8	0	3	242	5.4	6	1	0.0	24:23	9	0	5	5	6	0	0	0	20:17
2004-05			DID NOT PLAY																						
2005-06	Colorado	NHL	81	14	37	51	94	7	1	1	264	5.3	2	2	0.0	24:22	9	3	1	4	8	2	0	1	28:19
	Canada	Olympics	6	0	1	1	2	....	....	....	....	....	....	....	....	....	....	....	....	....	....	....	....	....	....
2006-07	Los Angeles	NHL	72	14	20	34	82	11	0	1	208	6.7	–26	3	33.3	24:24	....	....	....	....	....	....	....	....	....
2007-08	Los Angeles	NHL	71	9	22	31	98	5	0	2	144	6.3	–19	8	50.0	22:44	....	....	....	....	....	....	....	....	....
2008-09	San Jose	NHL	73	10	35	45	110	6	0	1	198	5.1	15	0	0.0	21:16	6	1	3	4	4	0	0	0	21:50
2009-10	San Jose	NHL	70	7	23	30	60	4	0	1	182	3.8	14	0	0.0	21:21	15	1	1	2	10	0	0	0	23:20
	NHL Totals		1270	240	537	777	1679	136	4	41	3896	6.2		14	35.7	24:54	146	26	47	73	166	9	1	1	26:15

CCHA Second All-Star Team (1989) • CCHA First All-Star Team (1990) • NCAA West First All-American Team (1990) • NHL All-Rookie Team (1991) • NHL First All-Star Team (1998) • James Norris Memorial Trophy (1998) • NHL Second All-Star Team (2000, 2001, 2002)

Played in NHL All-Star Game (1994, 1999, 2000, 2001, 2002, 2003, 2004)

• Missed majority of 1995-96 season recovering from knee injury suffered in game vs. Washington, October 20, 1995. Traded to **Colorado** by **Los Angeles** with Steve Reinprecht for Adam Deadmarsh, Aaron Miller, a player to be named later (Jared Aulin, March 22, 2001) and Colorado's 1st round choices in 2001 (Dave Steckel) and 2003 (Brian Boyle) Entry Drafts, February 21, 2001. Signed as a free agent by **Los Angeles**, July 1, 2006. Signed as a free agent by **San Jose**, July 3, 2008. • Officially announced his retirement, June 18, 2010.

BLIZNAK, Mario (BLIZH-nak, MAHR-ee-oh) VAN.

Center. Shoots left. 6', 185 lbs. Born, Trencin, Czech., March 6, 1987. Vancouver's 6th choice, 205th overall, in 2005 Entry Draft.

			Regular Season														Playoffs								
Season	Club	League	GP	G	A	Pts	PIM	PP	SH	GW	S	%	+/-	TF	F%	Min	GP	G	A	Pts	PIM	PP	SH	GW	Min
2003-04	Dubnica U18	Svk-U18	46	25	26	51	62	....	....	....	....	....	....	....	....	....	....	....	....	....	....	....	....	....	....
	Dubnica Jr.	Slovak-Jr.	2	1	0	1	2	....	....	....	....	....	....	....	....	....	....	....	....	....	....	....	....	....	....
2004-05	Dubnica U18	Svk-U18	14	5	8	13	45	....	....	....	....	....	....	....	....	....	....	....	....	....	....	....	....	....	....
	Dubnica Jr.	Slovak-Jr.	36	22	17	39	38	....	....	....	....	....	....	....	....	....	....	....	....	....	....	....	....	....	....
	Dubnica	Slovakia	19	0	0	0	14	....	....	....	....	....	....	....	....	....	....	....	....	....	....	....	....	....	....
2005-06	Vancouver Giants	WHL	69	9	12	21	29	....	....	....	....	....	....	....	....	....	18	4	1	5	14	....	....	....	....
2006-07	Vancouver Giants	WHL	47	8	14	22	20	....	....	....	....	....	....	....	....	....	22	6	6	12	14	....	....	....	....
2007-08	Vancouver Giants	WHL	67	19	32	51	36	....	....	....	....	....	....	....	....	....	10	3	5	8	2	....	....	....	....
2008-09	Manitoba Moose	AHL	64	7	9	16	24	....	....	....	....	....	....	....	....	....	21	3	2	5	8	....	....	....	....
2009-10	**Vancouver**	**NHL**	**2**	**0**	**0**	**0**	**0**	**0**	**0**	**0**	**1**	**0.0**	**–2**	**14**	**64.3**	**8:31**	....	....	....	....	....	....	....	....	....
	Manitoba Moose	AHL	76	13	15	28	40	....	....	....	....	....	....	....	....	....	6	2	1	3	2	....	....	....	....
	NHL Totals		**2**	**0**	**0**	**0**	**0**	**0**	**0**	**0**	**1**	**0.0**		**14**	**64.3**	**8:31**	....	....	....	....	....	....	....	....	....

BLUNDEN, Michael (BLUHN-dehn, MIGH-kuhl) CBJ

Right wing. Shoots right. 6'4", 211 lbs. Born, Toronto, Ont., December 15, 1986. Chicago's 2nd choice, 43rd overall, in 2005 Entry Draft.

Season	Club	League	GP	G	A	Pts	PIM	PP	SH	GW	S	%	+/-	TF	F%	Min	GP	G	A	Pts	PIM	PP	SH	GW	Min
2002-03	Erie Otters	OHL	63	10	7	17	55	....	....	....	....	....	....	....	....	....	....	....	....	....	....	....	....	....	....
2003-04	Erie Otters	OHL	52	22	17	39	53	....	....	....	....	....	....	....	....	....	3	0	0	0	0	....	....	....	....
2004-05	Erie Otters	OHL	61	22	19	41	75	....	....	....	....	....	....	....	....	....	2	0	0	0	2	....	....	....	....
2005-06	Erie Otters	OHL	60	46	38	84	63	....	....	....	....	....	....	....	....	....	....	....	....	....	....	....	....	....	....
	Norfolk Admirals	AHL	11	1	5	6	2	....	....	....	....	....	....	....	....	....	1	0	0	0	0	....	....	....	....
2006-07	**Chicago**	**NHL**	**9**	**0**	**0**	**0**	**10**	**0**	**0**	**0**	**10**	**0.0**	**–5**	**1**	**0.0**	**11:23**	....	....	....	....	....	....	....	....	....
	Norfolk Admirals	AHL	17	4	5	9	15	....	....	....	....	....	....	....	....	....	....	....	....	....	....	....	....	....	....
2007-08	**Chicago**	**NHL**	**1**	**0**	**0**	**0**	**0**	**0**	**0**	**0**	**1**	**0.0**	**–1**	**0**	**0.0**	**7:51**	....	....	....	....	....	....	....	....	....
	Rockford IceHogs	AHL	74	16	21	37	83	....	....	....	....	....	....	....	....	....	12	1	3	4	35	....	....	....	....
2008-09	Rockford IceHogs	AHL	37	3	7	10	42	....	....	....	....	....	....	....	....	....	....	....	....	....	....	....	....	....	....
	Syracuse Crunch	AHL	39	9	12	21	68	....	....	....	....	....	....	....	....	....	....	....	....	....	....	....	....	....	....
2009-10	Syracuse Crunch	AHL	25	7	9	16	43	....	....	....	....	....	....	....	....	....	....	....	....	....	....	....	....	....	....
	Columbus	**NHL**	**40**	**2**	**2**	**4**	**59**	**0**	**0**	**0**	**40**	**5.0**	**3**	**90**	**32.2**	**8:07**	....	....	....	....	....	....	....	....	....
	NHL Totals		**50**	**2**	**2**	**4**	**69**	**0**	**0**	**0**	**51**	**3.9**		**91**	**31.9**	**8:42**	....	....	....	....	....	....	....	....	....

• Missed majority of 2006-07 season recovering from shoulder injury sufffered in game vs. Hershey (AHL), December 10, 2006. Traded to **Columbus** by **Chicago** for Adam Pineault, January 10, 2008.

BOCHENSKI, Brandon (boh-CHEHN-skee, BRAN-duhn)

Right wing. Shoots right. 6'1", 187 lbs. Born, Blaine, MN, April 4, 1982. Ottawa's 9th choice, 223rd overall, in 2001 Entry Draft.

Season	Club	League	GP	G	A	Pts	PIM	PP	SH	GW	S	%	+/-	TF	F%	Min	GP	G	A	Pts	PIM	PP	SH	GW	Min
99-2000	Blaine Bengals	High-MN	28	32	30	62	....	....	....	....	....	....	....	....	....	....	....	....	....	....	....	....	....	....	....
2000-01	Lincoln Stars	USHL	55	*47	33	80	22	....	....	....	....	....	....	....	....	....	11	5	7	12	4	....	....	....	....
2001-02	North Dakota	WCHA	36	17	15	32	36	....	....	....	....	....	....	....	....	....	....	....	....	....	....	....	....	....	....
2002-03	North Dakota	WCHA	43	35	27	62	42	....	....	....	....	....	....	....	....	....	....	....	....	....	....	....	....	....	....
2003-04	North Dakota	WCHA	41	27	33	60	40	....	....	....	....	....	....	....	....	....	....	....	....	....	....	....	....	....	....
2004-05	Binghamton	AHL	75	34	36	70	16	....	....	....	....	....	....	....	....	....	6	1	0	1	2	....	....	....	....
2005-06	**Ottawa**	**NHL**	**20**	**6**	**7**	**13**	**14**	**2**	**0**	**0**	**39**	**15.4**	**7**	**4**	**50.0**	**12:17**	....	....	....	....	....	....	....	....	....
	Binghamton	AHL	33	22	24	46	36	....	....	....	....	....	....	....	....	....	....	....	....	....	....	....	....	....	....
	Chicago	**NHL**	**20**	**2**	**2**	**4**	**8**	**0**	**0**	**0**	**23**	**8.7**	**–9**	**8**	**37.5**	**8:53**	....	....	....	....	....	....	....	....	....
	Norfolk Admirals	AHL	....	....	....	....	....	....	....	....	....	....	....	....	....	....	3	1	1	2	0	....	....	....	....
2006-07	**Chicago**	**NHL**	**10**	**2**	**0**	**2**	**2**	**0**	**0**	**0**	**20**	**10.0**	**–2**	**1**	**0.0**	**9:59**	....	....	....	....	....	....	....	....	....
	Norfolk Admirals	AHL	35	33	33	66	31	....	....	....	....	....	....	....	....	....	....	....	....	....	....	....	....	....	....
	Boston	**NHL**	**31**	**11**	**11**	**22**	**14**	**3**	**0**	**2**	**72**	**15.3**	**3**	**4**	**25.0**	**14:59**	....	....	....	....	....	....	....	....	....
2007-08	**Boston**	**NHL**	**20**	**0**	**6**	**6**	**6**	**0**	**0**	**0**	**30**	**0.0**	**2**	**6**	**33.3**	**12:48**	....	....	....	....	....	....	....	....	....
	Providence Bruins	AHL	2	1	0	1	0	....	....	....	....	....	....	....	....	....	....	....	....	....	....	....	....	....	....
	Anaheim	**NHL**	**12**	**2**	**2**	**4**	**6**	**1**	**0**	**0**	**17**	**11.8**	**2**	**1**	**0.0**	**12:28**	....	....	....	....	....	....	....	....	....
	Nashville	**NHL**	**8**	**1**	**2**	**3**	**0**	**0**	**0**	**0**	**9**	**11.1**	**2**	**0**	**0.0**	**9:01**	**3**	**0**	**0**	**0**	**0**	**0**	**0**	**0**	**6:36**
2008-09	**Tampa Bay**	**NHL**	**7**	**0**	**1**	**1**	**2**	**0**	**0**	**0**	**11**	**0.0**	**–3**	**0**	**0.0**	**10:47**	....	....	....	....	....	....	....	....	....
	Norfolk Admirals	AHL	69	27	26	53	48	....	....	....	....	....	....	....	....	....	....	....	....	....	....	....	....	....	....
2009-10	**Tampa Bay**	**NHL**	**28**	**4**	**9**	**13**	**2**	**1**	**0**	**0**	**43**	**9.3**	**–1**	**5**	**40.0**	**12:16**	....	....	....	....	....	....	....	....	....
	Norfolk Admirals	AHL	42	21	19	40	16	....	....	....	....	....	....	....	....	....	....	....	....	....	....	....	....	....	....
	NHL Totals		**156**	**28**	**40**	**68**	**54**	**7**	**0**	**2**	**264**	**10.6**		**29**	**34.5**	**12:05**	**3**	**0**	**0**	**0**	**0**	**0**	**0**	**0**	**6:36**

USHL First All-Star Team (2001) • USHL Rookie of the Year (2001) • WCHA All-Rookie Team (2002) • WCHA Rookie of the Year (2002) • WCHA Second All-Star Team (2003) • WCHA First All-Star Team (2004) • NCAA West First All-American Team (2004) • AHL All-Rookie Team (2005)

Traded to **Chicago** by **Ottawa** with Ottawa's 2nd round choice (Simon Danis-Pepin) in 2006 Entry Draft for Tyler Arnason, March 9, 2006. Traded to **Boston** by **Chicago** for Kris Versteeg and future considerations, February 3, 2007. Traded to **Anaheim** by **Boston** for Shane Hnidy and Anaheim's 6th round choice (Nicholas Tremblay) in 2008 Entry Draft, January 2, 2008. Traded to **Nashville** by **Anaheim** for future considerations, February 26, 2008. Signed as a free agent by **Tampa Bay**, July 8, 2008.

BODIE, Troy (BOH-dee, TROI) ANA.

Right wing. Shoots right. 6'4", 214 lbs. Born, Portage La Prairie, Man., January 25, 1985. Edmonton's 12th choice, 278th overall, in 2003 Entry Draft.

Season	Club	League	GP	G	A	Pts	PIM	PP	SH	GW	S	%	+/-	TF	F%	Min	GP	G	A	Pts	PIM	PP	SH	GW	Min
2001-02	Central Plains	MMMHL	40	22	21	43	10	....	....	....	....	....	....	....	....	....	....	....	....	....	....	....	....	....	....
2002-03	Kelowna Rockets	WHL	35	4	4	8	36	....	....	....	....	....	....	....	....	....	11	1	1	2	2	....	....	....	....
2003-04	Kelowna Rockets	WHL	71	8	12	20	112	....	....	....	....	....	....	....	....	....	17	7	3	10	6	....	....	....	....
2004-05	Kelowna Rockets	WHL	72	24	24	48	96	....	....	....	....	....	....	....	....	....	24	4	13	17	26	....	....	....	....
2005-06	Kelowna Rockets	WHL	72	28	25	53	117	....	....	....	....	....	....	....	....	....	12	5	4	9	8	....	....	....	....
2006-07	Hamilton	AHL	20	0	1	1	29	....	....	....	....	....	....	....	....	....	....	....	....	....	....	....	....	....	....
	Stockton Thunder	ECHL	46	21	17	38	80	....	....	....	....	....	....	....	....	....	6	0	2	2	6	....	....	....	....
2007-08	Springfield	AHL	62	9	6	15	108	....	....	....	....	....	....	....	....	....	....	....	....	....	....	....	....	....	....
2008-09	**Anaheim**	**NHL**	**4**	**0**	**0**	**0**	**0**	**0**	**0**	**0**	**5**	**0.0**	**0**	**2**	**50.0**	**8:09**	....	....	....	....	....	....	....	....	....
	Iowa Chops	AHL	71	15	12	27	105	....	....	....	....	....	....	....	....	....	....	....	....	....	....	....	....	....	....
2009-10	**Anaheim**	**NHL**	**44**	**5**	**2**	**7**	**80**	**0**	**1**	**1**	**58**	**8.6**	**–8**	**1**	**0.0**	**11:15**	....	....	....	....	....	....	....	....	....
	San Antonio	AHL	16	2	1	3	43	....	....	....	....	....	....	....	....	....	....	....	....	....	....	....	....	....	....
	Toronto Marlies	AHL	16	6	4	10	13	....	....	....	....	....	....	....	....	....	....	....	....	....	....	....	....	....	....
	NHL Totals		**48**	**5**	**2**	**7**	**80**	**0**	**1**	**1**	**63**	**7.9**		**3**	**33.3**	**10:59**	....	....	....	....	....	....	....	....	....

Signed as a free agent by **Anaheim**, July 22, 2008.

BODNARCHUK, Andrew (BAWD-nahr-chuhk, AN-droo) BOS.

Defense. Shoots left. 5'11", 185 lbs. Born, Drumheller, Alta., July 11, 1988. Boston's 5th choice, 128th overall, in 2006 Entry Draft.

Season	Club	League	GP	G	A	Pts	PIM	PP	SH	GW	S	%	+/-	TF	F%	Min	GP	G	A	Pts	PIM	PP	SH	GW	Min
2003-04	Dartmouth	NSMHL	58	16	23	39	81	....	....	....	....	....	....	....	....	....	....	....	....	....	....	....	....	....	....
2004-05	St. Paul's School	High-NH	36	3	15	18	....	....	....	....	....	....	....	....	....	....	....	....	....	....	....	....	....	....	....
2005-06	Halifax	QMJHL	68	6	17	23	136	....	....	....	....	....	....	....	....	....	11	0	2	2	22	....	....	....	....
2006-07	Halifax	QMJHL	63	16	41	57	96	....	....	....	....	....	....	....	....	....	12	1	10	11	25	....	....	....	....
	Providence Bruins	AHL	....	....	....	....	....	....	....	....	....	....	....	....	....	....	1	0	0	0	0	....	....	....	....
2007-08	Halifax	QMJHL	65	10	33	43	89	....	....	....	....	....	....	....	....	....	14	0	9	9	16	....	....	....	....
2008-09	Providence Bruins	AHL	62	1	8	9	33	....	....	....	....	....	....	....	....	....	15	0	2	2	22	....	....	....	....
2009-10	**Boston**	**NHL**	**5**	**0**	**0**	**0**	**2**	**0**	**0**	**0**	**0**	**0.0**	**–2**	**0**	**0.0**	**7:19**	....	....	....	....	....	....	....	....	....
	Providence Bruins	AHL	70	5	10	15	51	....	....	....	....	....	....	....	....	....	....	....	....	....	....	....	....	....	....
	NHL Totals		**5**	**0**	**0**	**0**	**2**	**0**	**0**	**0**	**0**	**0.0**		**0**	**0.0**	**7:19**	....	....	....	....	....	....	....	....	....

QMJHL All-Rookie Team (2006)

BOEDKER, Mikkel (BAWD-kuhr, MIH-kehl) PHX.

Right wing. Shoots left. 5'11", 202 lbs. Born, Brondby, Denmark, December 16, 1989. Phoenix's 1st choice, 8th overall, in 2008 Entry Draft.

Season	Club	League	GP	G	A	Pts	PIM	PP	SH	GW	S	%	+/-	TF	F%	Min	GP	G	A	Pts	PIM	PP	SH	GW	Min
2004-05	Rodovre IK	Den-2	1	0	1	1	0	....	....	....	....	....	....	....	....	....	....	....	....	....	....	....	....	....	....
2005-06	Frolunda U18	Swe-U18	5	2	0	2	0	....	....	....	....	....	....	....	....	....	2	0	1	1	0	....	....	....	....
	Frolunda Jr.	Swe-Jr.	37	9	8	17	22	....	....	....	....	....	....	....	....	....	2	1	2	3	0	....	....	....	....
2006-07	Frolunda U18	Swe-U18	3	3	2	5	2	....	....	....	....	....	....	....	....	....	6	5	4	9	2	....	....	....	....
	Frolunda Jr.	Swe-Jr.	39	19	30	49	14	....	....	....	....	....	....	....	....	....	8	6	5	11	6	....	....	....	....
	Frolunda	Sweden	2	0	0	0	0	....	....	....	....	....	....	....	....	....	....	....	....	....	....	....	....	....	....

Season	Club	League	GP	G	A	Pts	PIM	PP	SH	GW	S	%	+/-	TF	F%	Min	GP	G	A	Pts	PIM	PP	SH	GW	Min
			Regular Season														Playoffs								
2007-08	Kitchener Rangers	OHL	62	29	44	73	14	....	....	....	....	....	....	....	....	....	20	9	*26	35	2	....	....	....	....
2008-09	**Phoenix**	**NHL**	**78**	**11**	**17**	**28**	**18**	**2**	**0**	**3**	**116**	**9.5**	**–6**	**8**	**12.5**	**15:32**	....	....	....	....	....	....	....	....	....
2009-10	**Phoenix**	**NHL**	**14**	**1**	**2**	**3**	**0**	**0**	**0**	**0**	**7**	**14.3**	**2**	**0**	**0.0**	**8:43**	....	....	....	....	....	....	....	....	....
	San Antonio	AHL	64	11	27	38	4	....	....	....	....	....	....	....	....	....	....	....	....	....	....	....	....	....	....
	NHL Totals		**92**	**12**	**19**	**31**	**18**	**2**	**0**	**3**	**123**	**9.8**		**8**	**12.5**	**14:30**	....	....	....	....	....	....	....	....	....

BOGOSIAN, Zach

(buh-GOH-zhuhn, ZAK) **ATL.**

Defense. Shoots right. 6'3", 205 lbs. Born, Massena, NY, July 15, 1990. Atlanta's 1st choice, 3rd overall, in 2008 Entry Draft.

Season	Club	League	GP	G	A	Pts	PIM	PP	SH	GW	S	%	+/-	TF	F%	Min	GP	G	A	Pts	PIM	PP	SH	GW	Min
2005-06	Cushing	High-MA	36	1	16	17	....	....	....	....	....	....	....	....	....	....	....	....	....	....	....	....	....	....	....
2006-07	Peterborough	OHL	67	7	26	33	63	....	....	....	....	....	....	....	....	....	....	....	....	....	....	....	....	....	....
2007-08	Peterborough	OHL	60	11	50	61	72	....	....	....	....	....	....	....	....	....	5	0	3	3	8	....	....	....	....
2008-09	**Atlanta**	**NHL**	**47**	**9**	**10**	**19**	**47**	**2**	**1**	**1**	**90**	**10.0**	**11**	**0**	**0.0**	**18:06**	....	....	....	....	....	....	....	....	....
	Chicago Wolves	AHL	5	1	0	1	0	....	....	....	....	....	....	....	....	....	....	....	....	....	....	....	....	....	....
2009-10	**Atlanta**	**NHL**	**81**	**10**	**13**	**23**	**61**	**3**	**1**	**0**	**155**	**6.5**	**–18**	**0**	**0.0**	**21:25**	....	....	....	....	....	....	....	....	....
	NHL Totals		**128**	**19**	**23**	**42**	**108**	**5**	**2**	**1**	**245**	**7.8**		**0**	**0.0**	**20:12**	....	....	....	....	....	....	....	....	....

OHL First All-Star Team (2008)

BOIS, Danny

(BOIZ, DA-nee)

Right wing. Shoots right. 6', 196 lbs. Born, Thunder Bay, Ont., June 1, 1983. Colorado's 2nd choice, 97th overall, in 2001 Entry Draft.

Season	Club	League	GP	G	A	Pts	PIM	PP	SH	GW	S	%	+/-	TF	F%	Min	GP	G	A	Pts	PIM	PP	SH	GW	Min
1998-99	T. Bay Kings	TBMHL	15	7	12	19	28	....	....	....	....	....	....	....	....	....	....	....	....	....	....	....	....	....	....
99-2000	Wellington Dukes	OPJHL	37	15	20	35	115	....	....	....	....	....	....	....	....	....	....	....	....	....	....	....	....	....	....
2000-01	London Knights	OHL	66	21	16	37	218	....	....	....	....	....	....	....	....	....	5	2	1	3	19	....	....	....	....
2001-02	London Knights	OHL	62	16	14	30	256	....	....	....	....	....	....	....	....	....	12	2	2	4	47	....	....	....	....
2002-03	London Knights	OHL	56	19	13	32	207	....	....	....	....	....	....	....	....	....	13	4	6	10	38	....	....	....	....
2003-04	London Knights	OHL	52	14	25	39	242	....	....	....	....	....	....	....	....	....	7	4	4	8	29	....	....	....	....
2004-05	Binghamton	AHL	72	2	4	6	287	....	....	....	....	....	....	....	....	....	6	0	1	1	2	....	....	....	....
2005-06	Binghamton	AHL	79	18	17	35	224	....	....	....	....	....	....	....	....	....	....	....	....	....	....	....	....	....	....
2006-07	**Ottawa**	**NHL**	**1**	**0**	**0**	**0**	**7**	**0**	**0**	**0**	**1**	**0.0**	**0**	**2**	**50.0**	**3:53**	....	....	....	....	....	....	....	....	....
	Binghamton	AHL	65	14	13	27	153	....	....	....	....	....	....	....	....	....	....	....	....	....	....	....	....	....	....
2007-08	Binghamton	AHL	54	8	13	21	153	....	....	....	....	....	....	....	....	....	....	....	....	....	....	....	....	....	....
2008-09	Binghamton	AHL	66	12	12	24	149	....	....	....	....	....	....	....	....	....	....	....	....	....	....	....	....	....	....
2009-10	Rockford IceHogs	AHL	73	10	12	22	156	....	....	....	....	....	....	....	....	....	4	0	0	0	20	....	....	....	....
	NHL Totals		**1**	**0**	**0**	**0**	**7**	**0**	**0**	**0**	**1**	**0.0**		**2**	**50.0**	**3:53**	....	....	....	....	....	....	....	....	....

Signed as a free agent by **Ottawa**, April 30, 2004. Signed as a free agent by **Chicago**, July 20, 2009.

BOLDUC, Alexandre

(bohl-DUHK, ahl-ehx-AHN-druh) **VAN.**

Center. Shoots left. 6'1", 197 lbs. Born, Montreal, Que., June 26, 1985. St. Louis' 6th choice, 127th overall, in 2003 Entry Draft.

Season	Club	League	GP	G	A	Pts	PIM	PP	SH	GW	S	%	+/-	TF	F%	Min	GP	G	A	Pts	PIM	PP	SH	GW	Min
2000-01	Notre Dame	SMHL	61	17	35	52	....	....	....	....	....	....	....	....	....	....	....	....	....	....	....	....	....	....	....
2001-02	Rouyn-Noranda	QMJHL	64	6	14	20	69	....	....	....	....	....	....	....	....	....	4	1	1	2	4	....	....	....	....
2002-03	Rouyn-Noranda	QMJHL	66	14	29	43	131	....	....	....	....	....	....	....	....	....	4	0	2	2	2	....	....	....	....
2003-04	Rouyn-Noranda	QMJHL	65	23	35	58	115	....	....	....	....	....	....	....	....	....	11	3	4	7	18	....	....	....	....
2004-05	Rouyn-Noranda	QMJHL	33	7	10	17	46	....	....	....	....	....	....	....	....	....	....	....	....	....	....	....	....	....	....
	Shawinigan	QMJHL	29	7	11	18	14	....	....	....	....	....	....	....	....	....	3	0	0	0	0	....	....	....	....
2005-06	Manitoba Moose	AHL	29	3	7	10	35	....	....	....	....	....	....	....	....	....	....	....	....	....	....	....	....	....	....
	Bakersfield	ECHL	24	10	6	16	56	....	....	....	....	....	....	....	....	....	11	4	4	8	28	....	....	....	....
2006-07	Manitoba Moose	AHL	32	4	5	9	35	....	....	....	....	....	....	....	....	....	5	0	0	0	8	....	....	....	....
	Bakersfield	ECHL	16	7	17	24	42	....	....	....	....	....	....	....	....	....	6	2	4	6	9	....	....	....	....
2007-08	Manitoba Moose	AHL	70	18	19	37	93	....	....	....	....	....	....	....	....	....	6	1	0	1	6	....	....	....	....
2008-09	**Vancouver**	**NHL**	**7**	**0**	**1**	**1**	**4**	**0**	**0**	**0**	**7**	**0.0**	**1**	**13**	**38.5**	**7:20**	....	....	....	....	....	....	....	....	....
	Manitoba Moose	AHL	63	12	21	33	116	....	....	....	....	....	....	....	....	....	13	5	4	9	14	....	....	....	....
2009-10	**Vancouver**	**NHL**	**15**	**0**	**0**	**0**	**13**	**0**	**0**	**0**	**14**	**0.0**	**–3**	**87**	**54.0**	**9:58**	....	....	....	....	....	....	....	....	....
	Manitoba Moose	AHL	13	2	1	3	20	....	....	....	....	....	....	....	....	....	....	....	....	....	....	....	....	....	....
	NHL Totals		**22**	**0**	**1**	**1**	**17**	**0**	**0**	**0**	**21**	**0.0**		**100**	**52.0**	**9:08**	....	....	....	....	....	....	....	....	....

Signed as a free agent by **Vancouver**, July 2, 2008. • Missed majority of 2009-10 season recovering from shoulder injury.

BOLL, Jared

(BOWL, JAIR-ehd) **CBJ**

Right wing. Shoots right. 6'3", 210 lbs. Born, Charlotte, NC, May 13, 1986. Columbus' 4th choice, 101st overall, in 2005 Entry Draft.

Season	Club	League	GP	G	A	Pts	PIM	PP	SH	GW	S	%	+/-	TF	F%	Min	GP	G	A	Pts	PIM	PP	SH	GW	Min
2003-04	Lincoln Stars	USHL	57	6	8	14	*176	....	....	....	....	....	....	....	....	....	....	....	....	....	....	....	....	....	....
2004-05	Lincoln Stars	USHL	59	23	24	47	*294	....	....	....	....	....	....	....	....	....	4	1	3	4	25	....	....	....	....
2005-06	Plymouth Whalers	OHL	65	19	22	41	205	....	....	....	....	....	....	....	....	....	13	2	4	6	21	....	....	....	....
2006-07	Plymouth Whalers	OHL	66	28	27	55	198	....	....	....	....	....	....	....	....	....	20	6	4	10	*66	....	....	....	....
2007-08	**Columbus**	**NHL**	**75**	**5**	**5**	**10**	**226**	**0**	**0**	**3**	**63**	**7.9**	**–4**	**6**	**33.3**	**8:01**	....	....	....	....	....	....	....	....	....
2008-09	**Columbus**	**NHL**	**75**	**4**	**10**	**14**	**180**	**1**	**0**	**0**	**73**	**5.5**	**–6**	**4**	**0.0**	**8:54**	**1**	**0**	**0**	**0**	**0**	**0**	**0**	**0**	**5:17**
2009-10	**Columbus**	**NHL**	**68**	**4**	**3**	**7**	**149**	**0**	**0**	**0**	**56**	**7.1**	**–8**	**3**	**0.0**	**7:12**	....	....	....	....	....	....	....	....	....
	NHL Totals		**218**	**13**	**18**	**31**	**555**	**1**	**0**	**3**	**192**	**6.8**		**13**	**15.4**	**8:04**	**1**	**0**	**0**	**0**	**0**	**0**	**0**	**0**	**5:17**

BOLLAND, Dave

(BOHL-uhnd, DAYV) **CHI.**

Center. Shoots right. 6', 181 lbs. Born, Toronto, Ont., June 5, 1986. Chicago's 2nd choice, 32nd overall, in 2004 Entry Draft.

Season	Club	League	GP	G	A	Pts	PIM	PP	SH	GW	S	%	+/-	TF	F%	Min	GP	G	A	Pts	PIM	PP	SH	GW	Min
2000-01	Tor. Red Wings	GTHL	95	79	67	146	....	....	....	....	....	....	....	....	....	....	....	....	....	....	....	....	....	....	....
2001-02	Tor. Red Wings	GTHL	36	35	35	70	40	....	....	....	....	....	....	....	....	....	....	....	....	....	....	....	....	....	....
2002-03	London Knights	OHL	64	7	10	17	21	....	....	....	....	....	....	....	....	....	14	2	1	3	2	....	....	....	....
2003-04	London Knights	OHL	65	37	30	67	58	....	....	....	....	....	....	....	....	....	15	3	10	13	18	....	....	....	....
2004-05	London Knights	OHL	66	34	51	85	97	....	....	....	....	....	....	....	....	....	18	11	14	25	30	....	....	....	....
2005-06	London Knights	OHL	59	*57	73	130	104	....	....	....	....	....	....	....	....	....	15	*15	9	24	41	....	....	....	....
2006-07	**Chicago**	**NHL**	**1**	**0**	**0**	**0**	**0**	**0**	**0**	**0**	**1**	**0.0**	**–1**	**11**	**36.4**	**11:17**	....	....	....	....	....	....	....	....	....
	Norfolk Admirals	AHL	65	17	32	49	53	....	....	....	....	....	....	....	....	....	6	0	4	4	17	....	....	....	....
2007-08	**Chicago**	**NHL**	**39**	**4**	**13**	**17**	**28**	**0**	**0**	**0**	**49**	**8.2**	**6**	**385**	**46.5**	**13:43**	....	....	....	....	....	....	....	....	....
	Rockford IceHogs	AHL	16	6	4	10	22	....	....	....	....	....	....	....	....	....	7	0	0	0	8	....	....	....	....
2008-09	**Chicago**	**NHL**	**81**	**19**	**28**	**47**	**52**	**2**	**2**	**4**	**111**	**17.1**	**19**	**1177**	**44.4**	**16:27**	**17**	**4**	**8**	**12**	**24**	**1**	**1**	**1**	**18:43**
2009-10 ♦	**Chicago**	**NHL**	**39**	**6**	**10**	**16**	**28**	**1**	**0**	**0**	**52**	**11.5**	**5**	**555**	**49.4**	**17:22**	**22**	**8**	**8**	**16**	**30**	**2**	**2**	**1**	**18:40**
	NHL Totals		**160**	**29**	**51**	**80**	**108**	**3**	**2**	**4**	**213**	**13.6**		**2128**	**46.0**	**15:59**	**39**	**12**	**16**	**28**	**54**	**3**	**3**	**2**	**18:41**

OHL First All-Star Team (2006) • Canadian Major Junior First All-Star Team (2006)
• Missed majority of 2009-10 season recovering from recurring back injury and resulting surgery, November 10, 2009.

BONINO, Nick

(boh-NEE-noh, NIHK) **ANA.**

Center. Shoots left. 6'1", 190 lbs. Born, Hartford, CT, April 20, 1988. San Jose's 6th choice, 173rd overall, in 2007 Entry Draft.

Season	Club	League	GP	G	A	Pts	PIM	PP	SH	GW	S	%	+/-	TF	F%	Min	GP	G	A	Pts	PIM	PP	SH	GW	Min
2003-04	Farmington	High-CT	24	44	23	67	10	....	....	....	....	....	....	....	....	....	....	....	....	....	....	....	....	....	....
2004-05	Farmington	High-CT	24	68	23	91	12	....	....	....	....	....	....	....	....	....	....	....	....	....	....	....	....	....	....
2005-06	Avon Old Farms	High-CT	25	26	30	56	10	....	....	....	....	....	....	....	....	....	....	....	....	....	....	....	....	....	....
2006-07	Avon Old Farms	High-CT	26	24	42	66	14	....	....	....	....	....	....	....	....	....	....	....	....	....	....	....	....	....	....
2007-08	Boston University	H-East	39	16	13	29	10	....	....	....	....	....	....	....	....	....	....	....	....	....	....	....	....	....	....
2008-09	Boston University	H-East	44	18	32	50	30	....	....	....	....	....	....	....	....	....	....	....	....	....	....	....	....	....	....
2009-10	Boston University	H-East	33	11	27	38	12	....	....	....	....	....	....	....	....	....	....	....	....	....	....	....	....	....	....
	Anaheim	**NHL**	**9**	**1**	**1**	**2**	**6**	**1**	**0**	**0**	**14**	**7.1**	**0**	**78**	**43.6**	**14:13**	....	....	....	....	....	....	....	....	....
	NHL Totals		**9**	**1**	**1**	**2**	**6**	**1**	**0**	**0**	**14**	**7.1**		**78**	**43.6**	**14:13**	....	....	....	....	....	....	....	....	....

NCAA Championship All-Tournament Team (2009)
Traded to **Anaheim** by **San Jose** with Timo Pielmeier and future considerations for Travis Moen and Kent Huskins, March 4, 2009.

BOOGAARD, Derek

(BOO-gard, DAIR-ihk) **NYR**

Left wing. Shoots right. 6'7", 260 lbs. Born, Saskatoon, Sask., June 23, 1982. Minnesota's 6th choice, 202nd overall, in 2001 Entry Draft.

Season	Club	League	GP	G	A	Pts	PIM	PP	SH	GW	S	%	+/-	TF	F%	Min	GP	G	A	Pts	PIM	PP	SH	GW	Min
			Regular Season														Playoffs								
1998-99	Regina Caps	SJHL	35	2	3	5	166																		
99-2000	Regina Pats	WHL	5	0	0	0	17																		
	Prince George	WHL	33	0	0	0	149																		
2000-01	Prince George	WHL	61	1	8	9	245										6	1	0	1	31				
2001-02	Prince George	WHL	2	0	0	0	16																		
	Medicine Hat	WHL	46	1	8	9	178																		
2002-03	Medicine Hat	WHL	27	1	2	3	65																		
	Louisiana	ECHL	33	1	2	3	240										2	0	0	0	0				
2003-04	Houston Aeros	AHL	53	0	4	4	207										2	0	1	1	16				
2004-05	Houston Aeros	AHL	56	1	4	5	259										5	0	0	0	38				
2005-06	**Minnesota**	**NHL**	**65**	**2**	**4**	**6**	**158**	**0**	**0**	**1**	**15**	**13.3**	**2**	**0**	**0.0**	**5:23**									
2006-07	**Minnesota**	**NHL**	**48**	**0**	**1**	**1**	**120**	**0**	**0**	**0**	**11**	**0.0**	**0**	**0**	**0.0**	**4:38**	**4**	**0**	**1**	**1**	**20**	**0**	**0**	**0**	**5:59**
2007-08	**Minnesota**	**NHL**	**34**	**0**	**0**	**0**	**74**	**0**	**0**	**0**	**6**	**0.0**	**–5**	**0**	**0.0**	**3:56**	**6**	**0**	**0**	**0**	**24**	**0**	**0**	**0**	**4:48**
2008-09	**Minnesota**	**NHL**	**51**	**0**	**3**	**3**	**87**	**0**	**0**	**0**	**13**	**0.0**	**3**	**0**	**0.0**	**5:00**									
2009-10	**Minnesota**	**NHL**	**57**	**0**	**4**	**4**	**105**	**0**	**0**	**0**	**26**	**0.0**	**–12**	**0**	**0.0**	**6:09**									
	NHL Totals		**255**	**2**	**12**	**14**	**544**	**0**	**0**	**1**	**71**	**2.8**		**0**	**0.0**	**5:09**	**10**	**0**	**1**	**1**	**44**	**0**	**0**	**0**	**5:16**

Signed as a free agent by **NY Rangers**, July 1, 2010.

BOOTH, David

(BOOTH, DAY-vihd) **FLA.**

Left wing. Shoots left. 6', 212 lbs. Born, Detroit, MI, November 24, 1984. Florida's 3rd choice, 53rd overall, in 2004 Entry Draft.

Season	Club	League	GP	G	A	Pts	PIM	PP	SH	GW	S	%	+/-	TF	F%	Min	GP	G	A	Pts	PIM	PP	SH	GW	Min
2000-01	Det. Compuware	NAHL	42	17	13	30	44										2	1	0	1	2				
2001-02	USNTDP	U-18	40	12	6	18	17																		
	USNTDP	USHL	12	4	3	7	6																		
	USNTDP	NAHL	6	1	3	4	18																		
2002-03	Michigan State	CCHA	39	17	19	36	53																		
2003-04	Michigan State	CCHA	30	8	10	18	30																		
2004-05	Michigan State	CCHA	29	7	9	16	30																		
2005-06	Michigan State	CCHA	37	13	22	35	50																		
2006-07	**Florida**	**NHL**	**48**	**3**	**7**	**10**	**12**	**0**	**0**	**1**	**86**	**3.5**	**0**	**11**	**36.4**	**9:34**									
	Rochester	AHL	25	7	7	14	26										6	0	2	2	4				
2007-08	**Florida**	**NHL**	**73**	**22**	**18**	**40**	**26**	**1**	**0**	**6**	**228**	**9.6**	**13**	**38**	**34.2**	**16:10**									
2008-09	**Florida**	**NHL**	**72**	**31**	**29**	**60**	**38**	**11**	**0**	**5**	**246**	**12.6**	**10**	**17**	**41.2**	**17:05**									
2009-10	**Florida**	**NHL**	**28**	**8**	**8**	**16**	**23**	**0**	**0**	**1**	**95**	**8.4**	**–3**	**10**	**20.0**	**18:08**									
	NHL Totals		**221**	**64**	**62**	**126**	**99**	**12**	**0**	**13**	**655**	**9.8**		**76**	**34.2**	**15:17**									

CCHA All-Rookie Team (2003)

• Missed majority of 2009-10 season recovering from head injury suffered in game at Philadelphia, October 24, 2009.

BOOTLAND, Darryl

(BOOT-land, DAIR-uhl)

Right wing. Shoots right. 6'1", 197 lbs. Born, Toronto, Ont., November 2, 1981. Colorado's 12th choice, 252nd overall, in 2000 Entry Draft.

Season	Club	League	GP	G	A	Pts	PIM	PP	SH	GW	S	%	+/-	TF	F%	Min	GP	G	A	Pts	PIM	PP	SH	GW	Min
1997-98	Orangeville	OHA-B	44	22	26	48	177																		
1998-99	Barrie Colts	OHL	38	18	11	29	89																		
	St. Michael's	OHL	28	12	6	18	80																		
99-2000	St. Michael's	OHL	65	24	30	54	166																		
2000-01	St. Michael's	OHL	56	32	33	65	136										11	3	1	4	20				
2001-02	St. Michael's	OHL	61	41	56	97	137										15	8	10	18	50				
2002-03	Toledo Storm	ECHL	54	17	19	36	322																		
	Grand Rapids	AHL	16	1	4	5	41										15	3	2	5	46				
2003-04	**Detroit**	**NHL**	**22**	**1**	**1**	**2**	**74**	**0**	**0**	**1**	**13**	**7.7**	**–3**	**1**	**100.0**	**6:07**									
	Grand Rapids	AHL	54	12	2	14	175										4	0	1	1	2				
2004-05	Grand Rapids	AHL	78	14	20	34	336																		
2005-06	Grand Rapids	AHL	77	27	29	56	392										16	5	7	12	50				
2006-07	**Detroit**	**NHL**	**6**	**0**	**0**	**0**	**9**	**0**	**0**	**0**	**4**	**0.0**	**0**	**2**	**100.0**	**4:08**									
	Grand Rapids	AHL	68	18	13	31	222										6	1	0	1	32				
2007-08	**NY Islanders**	**NHL**	**4**	**0**	**1**	**1**	**2**	**0**	**0**	**0**	**3**	**0.0**	**0**	**0**	**0.0**	**4:42**									
	Bridgeport	AHL	28	2	8	10	93																		
	Portland Pirates	AHL	35	2	5	7	132										16	1	1	2	21				
2008-09	Manitoba Moose	AHL	14	5	4	9	42																		
	Salzburg	Austria	14	4	8	12	89										14	4	6	10	62				
2009-10	Kalamazoo Wings	ECHL	25	10	9	19	90																		
	Manitoba Moose	AHL	12	1	1	2	49																		
	Vienna Capitals	Austria	4	1	2	3	6										12	5	0	5	22				
	NHL Totals		**32**	**1**	**2**	**3**	**85**	**0**	**0**	**1**	**20**	**5.0**		**3**	**100.0**	**5:34**									

Signed as a free agent by **Detroit**, July 25, 2002. Signed as a free agent by **NY Islanders**, July 9, 2007. Traded to **Anaheim** by **NY Islanders** for Matt Keith, January 9, 2008. Signed as a free agent by **Kalamazoo** (ECHL), September 2, 2009. Signed to a PTO (professional tryout) contract by **Manitoba** (AHL), November 4, 2009. Signed as a free agent by **Vienna** (Austria), February 1, 2010.

BORER, Casey

(BOHR-uhr, KAY-see) **CAR.**

Defense. Shoots left. 6'2", 205 lbs. Born, Minneapolis, MN, July 28, 1985. Carolina's 3rd choice, 69th overall, in 2004 Entry Draft.

Season	Club	League	GP	G	A	Pts	PIM	PP	SH	GW	S	%	+/-	TF	F%	Min	GP	G	A	Pts	PIM	PP	SH	GW	Min
2002-03	USNTDP	U-18	46	2	2	4	36																		
	USNTDP	NAHL	10	1	2	3	10																		
2003-04	St. Cloud State	WCHA	31	0	8	8	18																		
2004-05	St. Cloud State	WCHA	35	0	11	11	40																		
2005-06	St. Cloud State	WCHA	42	3	8	11	24																		
2006-07	St. Cloud State	WCHA	40	2	9	11	30																		
	Albany River Rats	AHL	1	0	0	0	0																		
2007-08	**Carolina**	**NHL**	**11**	**1**	**2**	**3**	**4**	**0**	**0**	**0**	**5**	**20.0**	**–3**	**0**	**0.0**	**15:17**									
	Albany River Rats	AHL	61	6	13	19	58																		
2008-09	**Carolina**	**NHL**	**3**	**0**	**0**	**0**	**5**	**0**	**0**	**0**	**0**	**0.0**	**0**	**0**	**0.0**	**11:05**									
	Albany River Rats	AHL	51	4	6	10	26																		
2009-10	**Carolina**	**NHL**	**2**	**0**	**0**	**0**	**0**	**0**	**0**	**0**	**0**	**0.0**	**–1**	**0**	**0.0**	**10:46**									
	Albany River Rats	AHL	30	1	8	9	13										6	0	1	1	0				
	NHL Totals		**16**	**1**	**2**	**3**	**9**	**0**	**0**	**0**	**5**	**20.0**		**0**	**0.0**	**13:56**									

Fred T. Hunt Memorial Award (AHL – Sportsmanship) (2010)

• Missed remainder of 2008-09 season and majority of 2009-10 season recovering from neck injury suffered in Albany River Rats bus accident, February 19, 2009, and resulting surgery, September 23, 2009.

BOUCHARD, Pierre-Marc

(BOO-shahrd, PEE-air- MAHRK) **MIN.**

Center. Shoots left. 5'10", 173 lbs. Born, Sherbrooke, Que., April 27, 1984. Minnesota's 1st choice, 8th overall, in 2002 Entry Draft.

Season	Club	League	GP	G	A	Pts	PIM	PP	SH	GW	S	%	+/-	TF	F%	Min	GP	G	A	Pts	PIM	PP	SH	GW	Min
1998-99	Mtl.-Bourassa	QAHA	28	23	41	64																			
99-2000	Charles-Lemoyne	QAAA	42	28	*45	*74	20										9	4	8	12	6				
2000-01	Chicoutimi	QMJHL	67	38	57	95	20										6	5	8	13	0				
2001-02	Chicoutimi	QMJHL	69	46	*94	*140	54										4	2	3	5	4				
2002-03	**Minnesota**	**NHL**	**50**	**7**	**13**	**20**	**18**	**5**	**0**	**1**	**53**	**13.2**	**1**	**474**	**40.7**	**13:16**	**5**	**0**	**1**	**1**	**2**	**0**	**0**	**0**	**13:15**
2003-04	**Minnesota**	**NHL**	**61**	**4**	**18**	**22**	**22**	**2**	**0**	**0**	**60**	**6.7**	**–7**	**60**	**50.0**	**14:00**									
2004-05	Houston Aeros	AHL	67	12	42	54	46										5	0	1	1	0				
2005-06	**Minnesota**	**NHL**	**80**	**17**	**42**	**59**	**28**	**7**	**0**	**3**	**118**	**14.4**	**3**	**15**	**46.7**	**15:15**									
2006-07	**Minnesota**	**NHL**	**82**	**20**	**37**	**57**	**14**	**5**	**0**	**3**	**173**	**11.6**	**13**	**18**	**33.3**	**15:59**	**5**	**1**	**1**	**2**	**0**	**0**	**0**	**0**	**14:48**
2007-08	**Minnesota**	**NHL**	**81**	**13**	**50**	**63**	**34**	**6**	**0**	**4**	**129**	**10.1**	**11**	**10**	**40.0**	**16:51**	**6**	**2**	**2**	**4**	**2**	**1**	**0**	**1**	**17:47**
2008-09	**Minnesota**	**NHL**	**71**	**16**	**30**	**46**	**20**	**2**	**0**	**1**	**142**	**11.3**	**–5**	**19**	**57.9**	**16:59**									
2009-10	**Minnesota**	**NHL**	**1**	**0**	**0**	**0**	**2**	**0**	**0**	**0**	**0**	**0.0**	**0**	**3**	**33.3**	**10:44**									
	NHL Totals		**426**	**77**	**190**	**267**	**138**	**27**	**0**	**12**	**675**	**11.4**		**599**	**42.1**	**15:34**	**16**	**3**	**4**	**7**	**4**	**1**	**0**	**1**	**15:26**

QMJHL Rookie of the Year (2001) • QMJHL First All-Star Team (2002) • Canadian Major Junior First All-Star Team (2002) • Canadian Major Junior Player of the Year (2002)

• Missed majority of 2009-10 season recovering from recurring head injury.

			Regular Season															Playoffs								
Season	Club	League	GP	G	A	Pts	PIM	PP	SH	GW	S	%	+/-	TF	F%	Min	GP	G	A	Pts	PIM	PP	SH	GW	Min

BOUILLON, Francis

(BOO-liawn, FRAN-sihs) **NSH.**

Defense. Shoots left. 5'8", 198 lbs. Born, New York, NY, October 17, 1975.

Season	Club	League	GP	G	A	Pts	PIM	PP	SH	GW	S	%	+/-	TF	F%	Min	GP	G	A	Pts	PIM	PP	SH	GW	Min
1991-92	Mtl-Bourassa	QAAA	42	2	5	7	28	....	....	....	....	....	....	....	....	....	9	1	0	1	6	....	....	....	....
1992-93	Laval Titan	QMJHL	46	0	7	7	45	....	....	....	....	....	....	....	....	....	....	....	....	....	....	....	....	....	....
1993-94	Laval Titan	QMJHL	68	3	15	18	129	....	....	....	....	....	....	....	....	....	19	2	9	11	48	....	....	....	....
1994-95	Laval Titan	QMJHL	72	8	25	33	115	....	....	....	....	....	....	....	....	....	20	3	11	14	21	....	....	....	....
1995-96	Granby	QMJHL	68	11	35	46	156	....	....	....	....	....	....	....	....	....	21	2	12	14	30	....	....	....	....
1996-97	Wheeling Nailers	ECHL	69	10	32	42	77	....	....	....	....	....	....	....	....	....	3	0	2	2	10	....	....	....	....
1997-98	Quebec Rafales	IHL	71	8	27	35	76	....	....	....	....	....	....	....	....	....	....	....	....	....	....	....	....	....	....
1998-99	Fredericton	AHL	79	19	36	55	174	....	....	....	....	....	....	....	....	....	5	2	1	3	0	....	....	....	....
99-2000	**Montreal**	**NHL**	74	3	13	16	38	2	0	1	76	3.9	−7	1	0.0	15:52	....	....	....	....	....	....	....	....	....
2000-01	**Montreal**	**NHL**	29	0	6	6	26	0	0	0	24	0.0	3	0	0.0	13:24	....	....	....	....	....	....	....	....	....
	Quebec Citadelles	AHL	4	0	0	0	0	....	....	....	....	....	....	....	....	....	....	....	....	....	....	....	....	....	....
2001-02	**Montreal**	**NHL**	28	0	5	5	33	0	0	0	24	0.0	−5	0	0.0	18:47	....	....	....	....	....	....	....	....	....
	Quebec Citadelles	AHL	38	8	14	22	30	....	....	....	....	....	....	....	....	....	....	....	....	....	....	....	....	....	....
2002-03	**Nashville**	**NHL**	4	0	0	0	2	0	0	0	0	0.0	−1	0	0.0	12:52	....	....	....	....	....	....	....	....	....
	Montreal	**NHL**	20	3	1	4	2	0	1	0	30	10.0	−1	0	0.0	20:24	....	....	....	....	....	....	....	....	....
	Hamilton	AHL	29	1	12	13	31	....	....	....	....	....	....	....	....	....	....	....	....	....	....	....	....	....	....
2003-04	**Montreal**	**NHL**	73	2	16	18	70	0	0	0	86	2.3	1	0	0.0	19:39	11	0	0	0	7	0	0	0	18:00
2004-05	Leksands IF	Sweden-2	31	10	21	31	46	....	....	....	....	....	....	....	....	....	....	....	....	....	....	....	....	....	....
2005-06	**Montreal**	**NHL**	67	3	19	22	34	3	0	1	75	4.0	−6	0	0.0	20:47	6	1	2	3	10	1	0	0	22:24
2006-07	**Montreal**	**NHL**	62	3	11	14	52	1	0	1	56	5.4	−10	0	0.0	18:19	....	....	....	....	....	....	....	....	....
2007-08	**Montreal**	**NHL**	74	2	6	8	61	0	0	0	60	3.3	9	0	0.0	17:22	7	1	2	3	4	0	0	0	15:55
2008-09	**Montreal**	**NHL**	54	5	4	9	53	0	0	1	51	9.8	−7	0	0.0	16:30	1	0	0	0	0	0	0	0	1:46
2009-10	**Nashville**	**NHL**	81	3	8	11	50	1	0	1	86	3.5	5	0	0.0	19:18	6	0	0	0	6	0	0	0	19:37
	NHL Totals		566	24	89	113	421	7	1	5	568	4.2		1	0.0	18:06	31	2	4	6	27	1	0	0	18:10

Signed as a free agent by **Montreal**, August 18, 1998. • Missed majority of 2000-01 season recovering from ankle injury suffered in game vs. Calgary, December 31, 2000. Claimed by **Nashville** from **Montreal** in Waiver Draft, October 4, 2002. Claimed on waivers by **Montreal** from **Nashville**, October 25, 2002. Signed as a free agent by **Leksands** (Sweden-2), November 15, 2004. Signed as a free agent by **Nashville**, September 30, 2009.

BOULERICE, Jesse

(BOO-luhr-ighs, JEH-see)

Right wing. Shoots right. 6'2", 215 lbs. Born, Plattsburgh, NY, August 10, 1978. Philadelphia's 4th choice, 133rd overall, in 1996 Entry Draft.

Season	Club	League	GP	G	A	Pts	PIM	PP	SH	GW	S	%	+/-	TF	F%	Min	GP	G	A	Pts	PIM	PP	SH	GW	Min
1994-95	Hawkesbury	CJHL	46	1	8	9	160	....	....	....	....	....	....	....	....	....	....	....	....	....	....	....	....	....	....
1995-96	Detroit	OHL	64	2	5	7	150	....	....	....	....	....	....	....	....	....	16	0	0	0	12	....	....	....	....
1996-97	Detroit	OHL	33	10	14	24	209	....	....	....	....	....	....	....	....	....	....	....	....	....	....	....	....	....	....
1997-98	Plymouth Whalers	OHL	53	20	23	43	170	....	....	....	....	....	....	....	....	....	13	2	4	6	35	....	....	....	....
1998-99	Philadelphia	AHL	24	1	2	3	82	....	....	....	....	....	....	....	....	....	....	....	....	....	....	....	....	....	....
	New Orleans	ECHL	12	0	1	1	38	....	....	....	....	....	....	....	....	....	....	....	....	....	....	....	....	....	....
99-2000	Philadelphia	AHL	40	3	4	7	85	....	....	....	....	....	....	....	....	....	4	0	2	2	4	....	....	....	....
	Trenton Titans	ECHL	25	8	8	16	90	....	....	....	....	....	....	....	....	....	....	....	....	....	....	....	....	....	....
2000-01	Philadelphia	AHL	60	3	4	7	256	....	....	....	....	....	....	....	....	....	10	1	1	2	28	....	....	....	....
2001-02	**Philadelphia**	**NHL**	3	0	0	0	5	0	0	0	1	0.0	−1	0	0.0	4:18	....	....	....	....	....	....	....	....	....
	Philadelphia	AHL	41	2	5	7	204	....	....	....	....	....	....	....	....	....	....	....	....	....	....	....	....	....	....
	Lowell	AHL	15	2	4	6	80	....	....	....	....	....	....	....	....	....	5	0	2	2	6	....	....	....	....
2002-03	**Carolina**	**NHL**	48	2	1	3	108	0	0	0	12	16.7	−2	0	0.0	3:54	....	....	....	....	....	....	....	....	....
2003-04	**Carolina**	**NHL**	76	6	1	7	127	0	0	0	46	13.0	−5	0	0.0	6:32	....	....	....	....	....	....	....	....	....
2004-05				DID NOT PLAY																					
2005-06	**Carolina**	**NHL**	26	0	0	0	51	0	0	0	3	0.0	−3	0	0.0	2:30	....	....	....	....	....	....	....	....	....
	St. Louis	**NHL**	12	0	0	0	13	0	0	0	2	0.0	−4	0	0.0	2:39	....	....	....	....	....	....	....	....	....
2006-07	Albany River Rats	AHL	16	4	3	7	36	....	....	....	....	....	....	....	....	....	....	....	....	....	....	....	....	....	....
2007-08	**Philadelphia**	**NHL**	5	0	0	0	29	0	0	0	1	0.0	−2	0	0.0	3:52	....	....	....	....	....	....	....	....	....
	Philadelphia	AHL	36	2	4	6	101	....	....	....	....	....	....	....	....	....	7	0	0	0	2	....	....	....	....
2008-09	**Lake Erie**	AHL	41	4	3	7	97	....	....	....	....	....	....	....	....	....	....	....	....	....	....	....	....	....	....
	Edmonton	**NHL**	2	0	0	0	0	0	0	0	0	0.0	0	0	0.0	3:43	....	....	....	....	....	....	....	....	....
2009-10	Wilkes-Barre	AHL	54	4	3	7	124	....	....	....	....	....	....	....	....	....	4	0	0	0	6	....	....	....	....
	NHL Totals		172	8	2	10	333	0	0	0	65	12.3		0	0.0	4:46									

Traded to **Carolina** by **Philadelphia** for Greg Koehler, February 13, 2002. Traded to **St. Louis** by **Carolina** with Mike Zigomanis, the rights to Magnus Kahnberg, Carolina's 1st round choice (later traded to New Jersey - New Jersey selected Matthew Corrente) in 2006 Entry Draft, Toronto's 4th round choice (previously acquired, St. Louis selected Reto Berra) in 2006 Entry Draft and Chicago's 4th round choice (previously acquired, St. Louis selected Cade Fairchild) in 2007 Entry Draft for Doug Weight and Erkki Rajamaki, January 30, 2006. Signed as a free agent by **Carolina**, August 2, 2006. Signed as a free agent by **Philadelphia**, October 3, 2007. Signed to a PTO (professional tryout) contract by **Lake Erie** (AHL), October 8, 2008. Signed as a free agent by **Colorado**, November 8, 2008. Claimed on waivers by **Edmonton** from **Colorado**, November 11, 2008.

BOULTON, Eric

(BOHL-tuhn, AIR-ihk) **ATL.**

Left wing. Shoots left. 6'1", 225 lbs. Born, Halifax, N.S., August 17, 1976. NY Rangers' 12th choice, 234th overall, in 1994 Entry Draft.

Season	Club	League	GP	G	A	Pts	PIM	PP	SH	GW	S	%	+/-	TF	F%	Min	GP	G	A	Pts	PIM	PP	SH	GW	Min
1992-93	Cole Harbour	MJrHL	44	12	15	27	212	....	....	....	....	....	....	....	....	....	....	....	....	....	....	....	....	....	....
1993-94	Oshawa Generals	OHL	45	4	3	7	149	....	....	....	....	....	....	....	....	....	5	0	0	0	16	....	....	....	....
1994-95	Oshawa Generals	OHL	27	7	5	12	125	....	....	....	....	....	....	....	....	....	....	....	....	....	....	....	....	....	....
	Sarnia Sting	OHL	24	3	7	10	134	....	....	....	....	....	....	....	....	....	4	0	1	1	10	....	....	....	....
1995-96	Sarnia Sting	OHL	66	14	29	43	243	....	....	....	....	....	....	....	....	....	9	0	3	3	29	....	....	....	....
1996-97	Binghamton	AHL	23	2	3	5	67	....	....	....	....	....	....	....	....	....	3	0	0	0	4	....	....	....	....
	Charlotte	ECHL	44	14	11	25	325	....	....	....	....	....	....	....	....	....	3	0	1	1	6	....	....	....	....
1997-98	Charlotte	ECHL	53	11	16	27	202	....	....	....	....	....	....	....	....	....	4	1	0	1	0	....	....	....	....
	Fort Wayne	IHL	8	0	2	2	42	....	....	....	....	....	....	....	....	....	....	....	....	....	....	....	....	....	....
1998-99	Kentucky	AHL	34	3	3	6	154	....	....	....	....	....	....	....	....	....	10	0	1	1	36	....	....	....	....
	Florida Everblades	ECHL	26	9	13	22	143	....	....	....	....	....	....	....	....	....	....	....	....	....	....	....	....	....	....
	Houston Aeros	IHL	7	1	0	1	41	....	....	....	....	....	....	....	....	....	....	....	....	....	....	....	....	....	....
99-2000	Rochester	AHL	76	2	2	4	276	....	....	....	....	....	....	....	....	....	18	2	1	3	53	....	....	....	....
2000-01	**Buffalo**	**NHL**	35	1	2	3	94	0	0	0	20	5.0	−1	2	0.0	5:42	....	....	....	....	....	....	....	....	....
2001-02	**Buffalo**	**NHL**	35	2	3	5	129	0	0	1	21	9.5	−1	0	0.0	6:08	....	....	....	....	....	....	....	....	....
2002-03	**Buffalo**	**NHL**	58	1	5	6	178	0	0	0	33	3.0	1	6	33.3	6:35	....	....	....	....	....	....	....	....	....
2003-04	**Buffalo**	**NHL**	44	1	2	3	110	0	0	0	20	5.0	−2	1	0.0	4:52	....	....	....	....	....	....	....	....	....
2004-05	Columbia Inferno	ECHL	48	23	16	39	124	....	....	....	....	....	....	....	....	....	4	2	3	5	8	....	....	....	....
2005-06	**Atlanta**	**NHL**	51	4	5	9	87	0	0	0	28	14.3	−4	2	50.0	4:54	....	....	....	....	....	....	....	....	....
2006-07	**Atlanta**	**NHL**	45	3	4	7	49	0	0	0	42	7.1	2	2	50.0	6:16	4	0	0	0	24	0	0	0	5:04
2007-08	**Atlanta**	**NHL**	74	4	5	9	127	0	0	0	64	6.3	−10	4	25.0	7:27	....	....	....	....	....	....	....	....	....
2008-09	**Atlanta**	**NHL**	76	3	10	13	176	0	0	0	71	4.2	−3	4	25.0	7:33	....	....	....	....	....	....	....	....	....
2009-10	**Atlanta**	**NHL**	62	2	6	8	113	1	0	0	39	5.1	−1	4	50.0	6:51	....	....	....	....	....	....	....	....	....
	NHL Totals		480	21	42	63	1063	1	0	1	338	6.2		25	32.0	6:26	4	0	0	0	24	0	0	0	5:04

Signed as a free agent by **Buffalo**, September 14, 1999. Signed as a free agent by **Columbia** (ECHL), November 24, 2004. Signed as a free agent by **Atlanta**, August 8, 2005.

BOURQUE, Chris

(BOHRK, KRIHS) **WSH.**

Center. Shoots left. 5'8", 180 lbs. Born, Boston, MA, January 29, 1986. Washington's 4th choice, 33rd overall, in 2004 Entry Draft.

Season	Club	League	GP	G	A	Pts	PIM	PP	SH	GW	S	%	+/-	TF	F%	Min	GP	G	A	Pts	PIM	PP	SH	GW	Min
2002-03	Cushing	High-MA	28	31	26	57	49	....	....	....	....	....	....	....	....	....	....	....	....	....	....	....	....	....	....
2003-04	Cushing	High-MA	31	37	53	90	96	....	....	....	....	....	....	....	....	....	....	....	....	....	....	....	....	....	....
2004-05	Boston University	H-East	35	10	13	23	50	....	....	....	....	....	....	....	....	....	....	....	....	....	....	....	....	....	....
	Portland Pirates	AHL	6	1	1	2	2	....	....	....	....	....	....	....	....	....	....	....	....	....	....	....	....	....	....
2005-06	Hershey Bears	AHL	52	8	28	36	40	....	....	....	....	....	....	....	....	....	1	0	0	0	0	....	....	....	....
2006-07	Hershey Bears	AHL	76	25	33	58	49	....	....	....	....	....	....	....	....	....	19	2	6	8	18	....	....	....	....
2007-08	**Washington**	**NHL**	4	0	0	0	2	0	0	0	4	0.0	0	1	0.0	8:42	....	....	....	....	....	....	....	....	....
	Hershey Bears	AHL	73	28	35	63	56	....	....	....	....	....	....	....	....	....	5	1	3	4	8	....	....	....	....
2008-09	**Washington**	**NHL**	8	1	0	1	0	0	0	0	11	9.1	0	0	0.0	9:46	....	....	....	....	....	....	....	....	....
	Hershey Bears	AHL	69	21	52	73	57	....	....	....	....	....	....	....	....	....	22	5	16	21	30	....	....	....	....

Season	Club	League	GP	G	A	Pts	PIM	PP	SH	GW	S	%	+/-	TF	F%	Min	GP	G	A	Pts	PIM	PP	SH	GW	Min
2009-10	Pittsburgh	NHL	20	0	3	3	10	0	0	0	20	0.0	−4	0	0.0	9:35	....	....	....	....	....	....	....	....	....
	Washington	NHL	1	0	0	0	0	0	0	0	1	0.0	−2	0	0.0	9:37	....	....	....	....	....	....	....	....	....
	Hershey Bears	AHL	49	22	48	70	26										21	7	20	*27	10				
	NHL Totals		33	1	3	4	12	0	0	0	36	2.8		1	0.0	9:31	....								

Hockey East All-Rookie Team (2005)
Claimed on waivers by **Pittsburgh** from **Washington**, September 30, 2009. Claimed on waivers by **Washington** from **Pittsburgh**, December 5, 2009. Signed as a free agent by **Mytischi** (Russia-KHL), June 23, 2010.

BOURQUE, Rene
(BOHRK, reh-NAY) **CGY.**

Left wing. Shoots left. 6'2", 213 lbs. Born, Lac La Biche, Alta., December 10, 1981.

Season	Club	League	GP	G	A	Pts	PIM	PP	SH	GW	S	%	+/-	TF	F%	Min	GP	G	A	Pts	PIM	PP	SH	GW	Min
2000-01	U. of Wisconsin	WCHA	32	10	5	15	18																		
2001-02	U. of Wisconsin	WCHA	38	12	7	19	26																		
2002-03	U. of Wisconsin	WCHA	40	19	8	27	54																		
2003-04	U. of Wisconsin	WCHA	42	16	20	36	74																		
2004-05	Norfolk Admirals	AHL	78	33	27	60	105										6	1	0	1	8				
2005-06	Chicago	NHL	77	16	18	34	56	4	0	2	180	8.9	3	11	36.4	15:20									
2006-07	Chicago	NHL	44	7	10	17	38	2	1	1	82	8.5	−4	9	22.2	16:01									
	Norfolk Admirals	AHL	1	0	0	0	0																		
2007-08	Chicago	NHL	62	10	14	24	42	0	5	2	103	9.7	6	8	25.0	15:16									
2008-09	Calgary	NHL	58	21	19	40	70	0	1	0	149	14.1	18	18	50.0	16:05	5	1	0	1	22	0	0	0	17:06
2009-10	Calgary	NHL	73	27	31	58	88	6	4	5	215	12.6	7	25	32.0	18:19									
	NHL Totals		314	81	92	173	294	12	11	10	729	11.1		71	35.2	16:15	5	1	0	1	22	0	0	0	17:06

AHL All-Rookie Team (2005) • Dudley "Red" Garrett Memorial Trophy (AHL - Top Rookie) (2005)
Signed as a free agent by **Chicago**, July 29, 2004. Traded to **Calgary** by **Chicago** for Calgary's 2nd round choice (later traded to Toronto – Toronto selected Brad Ross) in 2010 Entry Draft, July 1, 2008.

BOUWMEESTER, Jay
(BOW-mee-stuhr, JAY) **CGY.**

Defense. Shoots left. 6'4", 212 lbs. Born, Edmonton, Alta., September 27, 1983. Florida's 1st choice, 3rd overall, in 2002 Entry Draft.

Season	Club	League	GP	G	A	Pts	PIM	PP	SH	GW	S	%	+/-	TF	F%	Min	GP	G	A	Pts	PIM	PP	SH	GW	Min
1998-99	Edmonton SSAC	AMHL	32	14	29	43	36																		
	Medicine Hat	WHL	8	2	1	3	2																		
99-2000	Medicine Hat	WHL	64	13	21	34	26																		
2000-01	Medicine Hat	WHL	61	14	39	53	44																		
2001-02	Medicine Hat	WHL	61	11	50	61	42																		
2002-03	Florida	NHL	82	4	12	16	14	2	0	0	110	3.6	−29	0	0.0	20:09									
2003-04	Florida	NHL	61	2	18	20	30	0	0	0	85	2.4	−15	0	0.0	23:02									
	San Antonio	AHL	2	0	1	1	2																		
2004-05	San Antonio	AHL	64	4	13	17	50																		
	Chicago Wolves	AHL	18	6	3	9	12										18	0	14	14					
2005-06	Florida	NHL	82	5	41	46	79	0	0	0	189	2.6	1	1	0.0	25:29									
	Canada	Olympics	6	0	0	0	0																		
2006-07	Florida	NHL	82	12	30	42	66	3	0	3	174	6.9	23	0	0.0	26:09									
2007-08	Florida	NHL	82	15	22	37	72	4	0	0	182	8.2	−5	0	0.0	27:28									
2008-09	Florida	NHL	82	15	27	42	68	9	0	2	182	8.2	−2	0	0.0	26:59									
2009-10	Calgary	NHL	82	3	26	29	48	1	0	0	130	2.3	−4	0	0.0	25:55									
	NHL Totals		553	56	176	232	377	19	0	5	1052	5.3		1	0.0	25:06									

WHL East First All-Star Team (2002) • NHL All-Rookie Team (2003)
Played in NHL All-Star Game (2007, 2009)
• Loaned to **Chicago** (AHL) by **Florida** (San Antonio-AHL) for cash, March 8, 2005. Traded to **Calgary** by **Florida** for Jordan Leopold and Phoenix's 3rd round choice (previously acquired, Florida selected Josh Birkholz) in 2009 Entry Draft, June 27, 2009.

BOWMAN, Drayson
(BOH-muhn, DRAY-suhn) **CAR.**

Center/Left wing. Shoots left. 6'1", 190 lbs. Born, Grand Rapids, MI, March 8, 1989. Carolina's 2nd choice, 72nd overall, in 2007 Entry Draft.

Season	Club	League	GP	G	A	Pts	PIM	PP	SH	GW	S	%	+/-	TF	F%	Min	GP	G	A	Pts	PIM	PP	SH	GW	Min
2004-05	Kimberley	KIJHL	47	29	30	59	108																		
	Spokane Chiefs	WHL	4	0	0	0	0																		
2005-06	Spokane Chiefs	WHL	72	17	17	34	51																		
2006-07	Spokane Chiefs	WHL	61	24	19	43	55										6	2	5	7	4				
2007-08	Spokane Chiefs	WHL	66	42	40	82	62										21	11	9	20	8				
2008-09	Spokane Chiefs	WHL	62	47	36	83	107										12	8	5	13	8				
2009-10	Carolina	NHL	9	2	0	2	4	1	0	0	17	11.8	−1	0	0.0	12:01									
	Albany River Rats	AHL	56	17	15	32	29										8	3	6	9	12				
	NHL Totals		9	2	0	2	4	1	0	0	17	11.8		0	0.0	12:01									

WHL West Second All-Star Team (2008, 2009) • Memorial Cup All-Star Team (2008)

BOYCE, Darryl
(BOIS, DAIR-uhl) **TOR.**

Center. Shoots left. 6', 200 lbs. Born, Summerside, P.E.I., July 7, 1984.

Season	Club	League	GP	G	A	Pts	PIM	PP	SH	GW	S	%	+/-	TF	F%	Min	GP	G	A	Pts	PIM	PP	SH	GW	Min
2001-02	St. Michael's	OHL	67	10	11	21	71										15	2	5	7	46				
2002-03	St. Michael's	OHL	64	16	21	37	119										19	1	3	4	28				
2003-04	St. Michael's	OHL	64	13	24	37	110										18	1	3	4	23				
2004-05	St. Michael's	OHL	67	15	35	50	152										10	2	5	7	28				
2005-06	New Brunswick	AUAA	28	15	17	32	50																		
2006-07	New Brunswick	AUAA	25	14	19	33	63																		
2007-08	Toronto Marlies	AHL	41	8	16	24	71																		
	Toronto	NHL	1	0	0	0	0	0	0	0	0	0.0	0	2100.0		3:20									
2008-09	Toronto Marlies	AHL	73	12	18	30	131										6	2	0	2	27				
2009-10	Toronto Marlies	AHL	20	2	9	11	48																		
	NHL Totals		1	0	0	0	0	0	0	0	0	0.0		2100.0		3:20									

Signed as a free agent by **Toronto** (AHL), April, 2007. Signed as a free agent by **Toronto**, January 1, 2008. • Missed majority of 2009-10 season recovering from various injuries.

BOYCHUK, Johnny
(BOY-chuhk, JAW-nee) **BOS.**

Defense. Shoots right. 6'2", 225 lbs. Born, Edmonton, Alta., January 19, 1984. Colorado's 2nd choice, 61st overall, in 2002 Entry Draft.

Season	Club	League	GP	G	A	Pts	PIM	PP	SH	GW	S	%	+/-	TF	F%	Min	GP	G	A	Pts	PIM	PP	SH	GW	Min
1998-99	Edm. Cycle	AMBHL	36	8	20	28	59																		
99-2000	Edm. Cycle	AMHL	35	6	17	23	59																		
2000-01	Calgary Hitmen	WHL	66	4	8	12	61										12	1	1	2	17				
2001-02	Calgary Hitmen	WHL	70	8	32	40	85										7	1	1	2	6				
2002-03	Calgary Hitmen	WHL	40	8	18	26	58																		
	Moose Jaw	WHL	27	5	17	22	32										13	2	6	8	29				
2003-04	Moose Jaw	WHL	62	13	20	33	71										10	1	9	10	9				
2004-05	Hershey Bears	AHL	80	3	12	15	69																		
2005-06	Lowell	AHL	74	6	26	32	73																		
2006-07	Albany River Rats	AHL	80	10	18	28	125										5	1	1	2	4				
2007-08	Colorado	NHL	4	0	0	0	0	0	0	0	3	0.0	1	1	0.0	8:57									
	Lake Erie	AHL	60	8	18	26	63																		
2008-09	Boston	NHL	1	0	0	0	0	0	0	0	0	0.0	0	0	0.0	14:48									
	Providence Bruins	AHL	78	20	46	66	61										16	3	5	8	19				
2009-10	Boston	NHL	51	5	10	15	43	0	0	0	96	5.2	10	0	0.0	17:39	13	2	4	6	6	1	0	0	26:10
	Providence Bruins	AHL	2	1	0	1	0																		
	NHL Totals		56	5	10	15	43	0	0	0	99	5.1		1	0.0	16:59	13	2	4	6	6	1	0	0	26:10

AHL First All-Star Team (2009) • Eddie Shore Award (AHL – Outstanding Defenseman) (2009)
Traded to **Boston** by **Colorado** for Matt Hendricks, June 24, 2008.

			Regular Season														Playoffs								
Season	Club	League	GP	G	A	Pts	PIM	PP	SH	GW	S	%	+/-	TF	F%	Min	GP	G	A	Pts	PIM	PP	SH	GW	Min

BOYCHUK, Zach

(BOY-chuhk, ZAK) **CAR.**

Center. Shoots left. 5'10", 185 lbs. Born, Airdrie, Alta., October 4, 1989. Carolina's 1st choice, 14th overall, in 2008 Entry Draft.

Season	Club	League	GP	G	A	Pts	PIM	PP	SH	GW	S	%	+/-	TF	F%	Min	GP	G	A	Pts	PIM	PP	SH	GW	Min
2004-05	UFA Bisons	AMHL	36	13	14	27	18	....	....	....	....	....	....	....	....	....	16	10	5	15	....	....	....	....	....
2005-06	Lethbridge	WHL	64	18	33	51	30	....	....	....	....	....	....	....	....	....	6	0	5	5	2	....	....	....	....
2006-07	Lethbridge	WHL	69	31	60	91	52	....	....	....	....	....	....	....	....	....	....	....	....	....	....	....	....	....	....
2007-08	Lethbridge	WHL	61	33	39	72	80	....	....	....	....	....	....	....	....	....	18	*13	8	21	6	....	....	....	....
2008-09	**Carolina**	**NHL**	**2**	**0**	**0**	**0**	**0**	**0**	**0**	**0**	**0**	**0.0**	**0**	**1**	**0.0**	**12:03**	....	....	....	....	....	....	....	....	....
	Lethbridge	WHL	43	28	29	57	22	....	....	....	....	....	....	....	....	....	11	7	6	13	12	....	....	....	....
	Albany River Rats	AHL	2	0	1	1	2	....	....	....	....	....	....	....	....	....	....	....	....	....	....	....	....	....	....
2009-10	**Carolina**	**NHL**	**31**	**3**	**6**	**9**	**2**	**0**	**0**	**0**	**37**	**8.1**	**1**	**9**	**55.6**	**10:45**	....	....	....	....	....	....	....	....	....
	Albany River Rats	AHL	52	15	21	36	24	....	....	....	....	....	....	....	....	....	8	2	3	5	4	....	....	....	....
	NHL Totals		**33**	**3**	**6**	**9**	**2**	**0**	**0**	**0**	**37**	**8.1**		**10**	**50.0**	**10:50**	....	....	....	....	....	....	....	....	....

VHL East Second All-Star Team (2007, 2008)

BOYD, Dustin

(BOID, DUHS-tihn) **MTL.**

Center. Shoots left. 6', 187 lbs. Born, Winnipeg, Man., July 16, 1986. Calgary's 3rd choice, 98th overall, in 2004 Entry Draft.

Season	Club	League	GP	G	A	Pts	PIM	PP	SH	GW	S	%	+/-	TF	F%	Min	GP	G	A	Pts	PIM	PP	SH	GW	Min
2001-02	Wpg. Warriors	MMMHL	40	50	57	107	16	....	....	....	....	....	....	....	....	....	....	....	....	....	....	....	....	....	....
2002-03	Moose Jaw	WHL	63	11	17	28	15	....	....	....	....	....	....	....	....	....	13	0	3	3	2	....	....	....	....
2003-04	Moose Jaw	WHL	72	18	20	38	40	....	....	....	....	....	....	....	....	....	10	2	2	4	8	....	....	....	....
2004-05	Moose Jaw	WHL	66	26	35	61	57	....	....	....	....	....	....	....	....	....	5	1	2	3	2	....	....	....	....
2005-06	Moose Jaw	WHL	64	48	42	90	34	....	....	....	....	....	....	....	....	....	22	7	11	18	10	....	....	....	....
2006-07	**Calgary**	**NHL**	**13**	**2**	**2**	**4**	**4**	**0**	**0**	**1**	**8**	**25.0**	**5**	**16**	**50.0**	**10:09**	....	....	....	....	....	....	....	....	....
	Omaha	AHL	66	27	33	60	34	....	....	....	....	....	....	....	....	....	6	1	1	2	0	....	....	....	....
2007-08	**Calgary**	**NHL**	**48**	**7**	**5**	**12**	**6**	**0**	**0**	**1**	**46**	**15.2**	**–11**	**129**	**50.4**	**9:49**	....	....	....	....	....	....	....	....	....
	Quad City Flames	AHL	18	2	7	9	4	....	....	....	....	....	....	....	....	....	....	....	....	....	....	....	....	....	....
2008-09	**Calgary**	**NHL**	**71**	**11**	**11**	**22**	**10**	**1**	**1**	**3**	**74**	**14.9**	**–11**	**477**	**45.5**	**12:52**	**5**	**1**	**0**	**1**	**0**	**0**	**0**	**0**	**9:52**
	Quad City Flames	AHL	5	2	0	2	2	....	....	....	....	....	....	....	....	....	....	....	....	....	....	....	....	....	....
2009-10	**Calgary**	**NHL**	**60**	**8**	**11**	**19**	**15**	**0**	**0**	**2**	**80**	**10.0**	**5**	**368**	**49.7**	**12:14**	....	....	....	....	....	....	....	....	....
	Nashville	**NHL**	**18**	**3**	**2**	**5**	**4**	**0**	**0**	**1**	**32**	**9.4**	**1**	**105**	**58.1**	**12:11**	**4**	**0**	**0**	**0**	**0**	**0**	**0**	**0**	**7:03**
	NHL Totals		**210**	**31**	**31**	**62**	**39**	**1**	**1**	**8**	**240**	**12.9**		**1095**	**48.8**	**11:46**	**9**	**1**	**0**	**1**	**0**	**0**	**0**	**0**	**8:37**

VHL East First All-Star Team (2006)

'raded to **Nashville** by **Calgary** for Nashville's 4th round choice (Bill Arnold) in 2010 Entry Draft, March 3, 2010. Traded to **Montreal** by **Nashville** with Dan Ellis and future considerations for Sergei
Kostitsyn and future considerations, June 29, 2010.

BOYES, Brad

(BOIZ, BRAD) **ST.L.**

Center. Shoots right. 6', 200 lbs. Born, Mississauga, Ont., April 17, 1982. Toronto's 1st choice, 24th overall, in 2000 Entry Draft.

Season	Club	League	GP	G	A	Pts	PIM	PP	SH	GW	S	%	+/-	TF	F%	Min	GP	G	A	Pts	PIM	PP	SH	GW	Min
1997-98	Mississauga Reps	MTHL	44	27	50	77	....	....	....	....	....	....	....	....	....	....	....	....	....	....	....	....	....	....	....
1998-99	Erie Otters	OHL	59	24	36	60	30	....	....	....	....	....	....	....	....	....	5	1	2	3	10	....	....	....	....
99-2000	Erie Otters	OHL	68	36	46	82	38	....	....	....	....	....	....	....	....	....	13	6	8	14	10	....	....	....	....
2000-01	Erie Otters	OHL	59	45	45	90	42	....	....	....	....	....	....	....	....	....	15	10	13	23	8	....	....	....	....
2001-02	Erie Otters	OHL	47	36	41	77	42	....	....	....	....	....	....	....	....	....	21	22	*19	41	27	....	....	....	....
2002-03	St. John's	AHL	65	23	28	51	45	....	....	....	....	....	....	....	....	....	....	....	....	....	....	....	....	....	....
	Cleveland Barons	AHL	15	7	6	13	21	....	....	....	....	....	....	....	....	....	....	....	....	....	....	....	....	....	....
2003-04	**San Jose**	**NHL**	**1**	**0**	**0**	**0**	**2**	**0**	**0**	**0**	**0**	**0.0**	**–2**	**0**	**0.0**	**13:03**	....	....	....	....	....	....	....	....	....
	Cleveland Barons	AHL	61	25	35	60	38	....	....	....	....	....	....	....	....	....	....	....	....	....	....	....	....	....	....
	Providence Bruins	AHL	17	6	6	12	13	....	....	....	....	....	....	....	....	....	2	1	0	1	0	....	....	....	....
2004-05	Providence Bruins	AHL	80	33	42	75	58	....	....	....	....	....	....	....	....	....	16	8	7	15	23	....	....	....	....
2005-06	**Boston**	**NHL**	**82**	**26**	**43**	**69**	**30**	**8**	**0**	**3**	**203**	**12.8**	**11**	**265**	**53.6**	**15:46**	....	....	....	....	....	....	....	....	....
2006-07	**Boston**	**NHL**	**62**	**13**	**21**	**34**	**25**	**1**	**1**	**1**	**139**	**9.4**	**–17**	**220**	**44.1**	**16:04**	....	....	....	....	....	....	....	....	....
	St. Louis	**NHL**	**19**	**4**	**8**	**12**	**4**	**0**	**0**	**1**	**43**	**9.3**	**0**	**93**	**58.1**	**17:25**	....	....	....	....	....	....	....	....	....
2007-08	**St. Louis**	**NHL**	**82**	**43**	**22**	**65**	**20**	**11**	**0**	**9**	**207**	**20.8**	**1**	**236**	**44.5**	**17:57**	....	....	....	....	....	....	....	....	....
2008-09	**St. Louis**	**NHL**	**82**	**33**	**39**	**72**	**26**	**16**	**0**	**11**	**220**	**15.0**	**–20**	**315**	**49.2**	**19:08**	**4**	**2**	**1**	**3**	**0**	**1**	**0**	**0**	**21:34**
2009-10	**St. Louis**	**NHL**	**82**	**14**	**28**	**42**	**26**	**2**	**0**	**3**	**197**	**7.1**	**1**	**311**	**44.4**	**16:47**	....	....	....	....	....	....	....	....	....
	NHL Totals		**410**	**133**	**161**	**294**	**133**	**38**	**1**	**28**	**1009**	**13.2**		**1440**	**48.0**	**17:12**	**4**	**2**	**1**	**3**	**0**	**1**	**0**	**0**	**21:34**

:anadian Major Junior Scholastic Player of the Year (2000) • OHL Second All-Star Team (2001) • OHL First All-Star Team (2002) • Canadian Major Junior Second All-Star Team (2002) • Canadian Major
unior Sportsman of the Year (2002) • AHL All-Rookie Team (2003) • AHL Second All-Star Team (2004) • NHL All-Rookie Team (2006)

'raded to **San Jose** by **Toronto** with Alyn McCauley and Toronto's 1st round choice (later traded to Boston – Boston selected Mark Stuart) in 2003 Entry Draft for Owen Nolan, March 5, 2003. Traded to
Boston by **San Jose** for Jeff Jillson, March 9, 2004. Traded to **St. Louis** by **Boston** for Dennis Wideman, February 27, 2007.

BOYLE, Brian

(BOIL, BRIGH-uhn) **NYR**

Center. Shoots left. 6'7", 252 lbs. Born, Hingham, MA, December 18, 1984. Los Angeles' 2nd choice, 26th overall, in 2003 Entry Draft.

Season	Club	League	GP	G	A	Pts	PIM	PP	SH	GW	S	%	+/-	TF	F%	Min	GP	G	A	Pts	PIM	PP	SH	GW	Min
2000-01	St. Sebastian's	High-MA	25	20	19	39		....	....	....	....	....	....	....	....	....	....	....	....	....	....	....	....	....	....
2001-02	St. Sebastian's	High-MA	28	21	26	47	22	....	....	....	....	....	....	....	....	....	....	....	....	....	....	....	....	....	....
2002-03	St. Sebastian's	High-MA	31	32	31	62	46	....	....	....	....	....	....	....	....	....	....	....	....	....	....	....	....	....	....
2003-04	Boston College	H-East	35	5	3	8	36	....	....	....	....	....	....	....	....	....	....	....	....	....	....	....	....	....	....
2004-05	Boston College	H-East	40	19	8	27	64	....	....	....	....	....	....	....	....	....	....	....	....	....	....	....	....	....	....
2005-06	Boston College	H-East	42	22	*30	52	90	....	....	....	....	....	....	....	....	....	....	....	....	....	....	....	....	....	....
2006-07	Boston College	H-East	42	19	*34	*53	*104	....	....	....	....	....	....	....	....	....	....	....	....	....	....	....	....	....	....
	Manchester	AHL	2	0	0	0	2	....	....	....	....	....	....	....	....	....	16	3	5	8	13	....	....	....	....
2007-08	**Los Angeles**	**NHL**	**8**	**4**	**1**	**5**	**4**	**0**	**0**	**0**	**19**	**21.1**	**4**	**80**	**46.3**	**13:38**	....	....	....	....	....	....	....	....	....
	Manchester	AHL	70	31	31	62	87	....	....	....	....	....	....	....	....	....	....	....	....	....	....	....	....	....	....
2008-09	**Los Angeles**	**NHL**	**28**	**4**	**1**	**5**	**42**	**0**	**0**	**1**	**36**	**11.1**	**–9**	**225**	**45.3**	**10:08**	....	....	....	....	....	....	....	....	....
	Manchester	AHL	42	10	11	21	73	....	....	....	....	....	....	....	....	....	....	....	....	....	....	....	....	....	....
2009-10	**NY Rangers**	**NHL**	**71**	**4**	**2**	**6**	**47**	**0**	**0**	**1**	**73**	**5.5**	**–6**	**323**	**38.7**	**8:25**	....	....	....	....	....	....	....	....	....
	NHL Totals		**107**	**12**	**4**	**16**	**93**	**0**	**0**	**2**	**128**	**9.4**		**628**	**42.0**	**9:16**	....	....	....	....	....	....	....	....	....

lockey East First All-Star Team (2006, 2007) • NCAA East Second All-American Team (2006) • NCAA East First All-American Team (2007) • NCAA Championship All-Tournament Team (2007)

'raded to **NY Rangers** by **Los Angeles** for NY Rangers' 3rd round choice (Jordan Weal) in 2010 Entry Draft, June 27, 2009.

BOYLE, Dan

(BOIL, DAN) **S.J.**

Defense. Shoots right. 5'11", 190 lbs. Born, Ottawa, Ont., July 12, 1976.

Season	Club	League	GP	G	A	Pts	PIM	PP	SH	GW	S	%	+/-	TF	F%	Min	GP	G	A	Pts	PIM	PP	SH	GW	Min
1992-93	Gloucester	CJHL	55	22	51	73	60	....	....	....	....	....	....	....	....	....	....	....	....	....	....	....	....	....	....
1993-94	Gloucester	CJHL	53	27	54	81	155	....	....	....	....	....	....	....	....	....	....	....	....	....	....	....	....	....	....
1994-95	Miami U.	CCHA	35	8	18	26	24	....	....	....	....	....	....	....	....	....	....	....	....	....	....	....	....	....	....
1995-96	Miami U.	CCHA	36	7	20	27	70	....	....	....	....	....	....	....	....	....	....	....	....	....	....	....	....	....	....
1996-97	Miami U.	CCHA	40	11	43	54	52	....	....	....	....	....	....	....	....	....	....	....	....	....	....	....	....	....	....
1997-98	Miami U.	CCHA	37	14	26	40	58	....	....	....	....	....	....	....	....	....	....	....	....	....	....	....	....	....	....
1998-99	**Florida**	**NHL**	**22**	**3**	**5**	**8**	**6**	**1**	**0**	**1**	**31**	**9.7**	**0**	**1**	**100.0**	**18:50**	....	....	....	....	....	....	....	....	....
	Kentucky	AHL	53	8	34	42	87	....	....	....	....	....	....	....	....	....	12	3	5	8	16	....	....	....	....
99-2000	**Florida**	**NHL**	**13**	**0**	**3**	**3**	**4**	**0**	**0**	**0**	**9**	**0.0**	**–2**	**0**	**0.0**	**16:57**	....	....	....	....	....	....	....	....	....
	Louisville Panthers	AHL	58	14	38	52	75	....	....	....	....	....	....	....	....	....	4	0	2	2	8	....	....	....	....
2000-01	**Florida**	**NHL**	**69**	**4**	**18**	**22**	**28**	**1**	**0**	**0**	**83**	**4.8**	**–14**	**0**	**0.0**	**16:56**	....	....	....	....	....	....	....	....	....
	Louisville Panthers	AHL	6	0	5	5	12	....	....	....	....	....	....	....	....	....	....	....	....	....	....	....	....	....	....
2001-02	**Florida**	**NHL**	**25**	**3**	**3**	**6**	**12**	**1**	**0**	**0**	**31**	**9.7**	**–1**	**2**	**50.0**	**15:40**	....	....	....	....	....	....	....	....	....
	Tampa Bay	**NHL**	**41**	**5**	**15**	**20**	**27**	**2**	**0**	**1**	**68**	**7.4**	**–15**	**0**	**0.0**	**22:28**	....	....	....	....	....	....	....	....	....
2002-03	**Tampa Bay**	**NHL**	**77**	**13**	**40**	**53**	**44**	**8**	**0**	**1**	**136**	**9.6**	**9**	**2**	**0.0**	**24:31**	**11**	**0**	**7**	**7**	**6**	**0**	**0**	**0**	**27:45**
2003-04♦	**Tampa Bay**	**NHL**	**78**	**9**	**30**	**39**	**60**	**3**	**0**	**2**	**137**	**6.6**	**23**	**0**	**0.0**	**22:46**	**23**	**2**	**8**	**10**	**16**	**1**	**0**	**0**	**21:27**
2004-05	Djurgarden	Sweden	32	9	9	18	47	....	....	....	....	....	....	....	....	....	12	2	3	5	26	....	....	....	....
2005-06	**Tampa Bay**	**NHL**	**79**	**15**	**38**	**53**	**38**	**6**	**0**	**4**	**153**	**9.8**	**–8**	**1**	**0.0**	**23:26**	**5**	**1**	**3**	**4**	**6**	**0**	**0**	**0**	**25:54**
	Canada	Olympics	DID NOT PLAY																						
2006-07	**Tampa Bay**	**NHL**	**82**	**20**	**43**	**63**	**62**	**10**	**1**	**4**	**203**	**9.9**	**–5**	**1**	**0.0**	**27:03**	**6**	**0**	**1**	**1**	**2**	**0**	**0**	**0**	**28:03**
2007-08	**Tampa Bay**	**NHL**	**37**	**4**	**21**	**25**	**57**	**2**	**0**	**1**	**74**	**5.4**	**–29**	**0**	**0.0**	**27:24**	....	....	....	....	....	....	....	....	....
2008-09	**San Jose**	**NHL**	**77**	**16**	**41**	**57**	**52**	**8**	**0**	**4**	**213**	**7.5**	**6**	**1**	**0.0**	**24:46**	**6**	**2**	**2**	**4**	**8**	**1**	**0**	**0**	**23:17**

			Regular Season														Playoffs								
Season	Club	League	GP	G	A	Pts	PIM	PP	SH	GW	S	%	+/-	TF	F%	Min	GP	G	A	Pts	PIM	PP	SH	GW	Min
2009-10	San Jose	NHL	76	15	43	58	70	6	0	3	180	8.3	6	3	0.0	26:13	15	2	12	14	8	1	0	0	27:11
	Canada	Olympics	7	1	5	6	2	....	....	....	....	....	....	....	....	....	....	....	....	....	....	....	....	....	....
	NHL Totals		676	107	300	407	460	48	1	21	1318	8.1		11	18.2	23:19	66	7	33	40	46	3	0	0	24:54

CCHA First All-Star Team (1997, 1998) • NCAA West First All-American Team (1997, 1998) • AHL All-Rookie Team (1999 • AHL Second All-Star Team (1999, 2000) • NHL Second All-Star Team (2007, 2009)

Played in NHL All-Star Game (2009)

Signed as a free agent by **Florida**, March 30, 1998. Traded to **Tampa Bay** by **Florida** for Tampa Bay's 5th round choice (Martin Tuma) in 2003 Entry Draft, January 7, 2002. Signed as a free agent by **Djurgarden** (Sweden), November 14, 2004. • Missed majority of 2007-08 season recovering from off-ice wrist injury, September 22, 2007 and follow-up surgery, November 6, 2007. Traded to **San Jose** by **Tampa Bay** with Brad Lukowich for Matt Carle, Ty Wishart, San Jose's 1st round choice (later traded to Ottawa, later traded to NY Islanders, later traded to Columbus, later traded to Anaheim - Anaheim selected Kyle Palmieri) in 2009 Entry Draft and San Jose's 4th round choice (James Mullin) in 2010 Entry Draft, July 4, 2008.

BOYNTON, Nick

(BOIN-tuhn, NIHK) **CHI.**

Defense. Shoots right. 6'1", 218 lbs. Born, Nobleton, Ont., January 14, 1979. Boston's 1st choice, 21st overall, in 1999 Entry Draft.

Season	Club	League	GP	G	A	Pts	PIM	PP	SH	GW	S	%	+/-	TF	F%	Min	GP	G	A	Pts	PIM	PP	SH	GW	Min
1993-94	Caledon	MTJHL	4	0	1	1	0	....	....	....	....	....	....	....	....	....	....	....	....	....	....	....	....	....	....
1994-95	Caledon	MTJHL	44	10	35	45	139	....	....	....	....	....	....	....	....	....	....	....	....	....	....	....	....	....	....
1995-96	Ottawa 67's	OHL	64	10	14	24	90	....	....	....	....	....	....	....	....	....	4	0	3	3	10	....	....	....	....
1996-97	Ottawa 67's	OHL	63	13	51	64	143	....	....	....	....	....	....	....	....	....	24	4	*24	28	38	....	....	....	....
1997-98	Ottawa 67's	OHL	40	7	31	38	94	....	....	....	....	....	....	....	....	....	13	0	4	4	24	....	....	....	....
1998-99	Ottawa 67's	OHL	51	11	48	59	83	....	....	....	....	....	....	....	....	....	9	1	9	10	18	....	....	....	....
99-2000	Boston	NHL	5	0	0	0	0	0	0	0	6	0.0	–5	0	0.0	21:21	....	....	....	....	....	....	....	....	....
	Providence Bruins	AHL	53	5	14	19	66	....	....	....	....	....	....	....	....	....	12	1	0	1	6	....	....	....	....
2000-01	Boston	NHL	1	0	0	0	0	0	0	0	1	0.0	–1	0	0.0	14:27	....	....	....	....	....	....	....	....	....
	Providence Bruins	AHL	78	6	27	33	105	....	....	....	....	....	....	....	....	....	17	0	2	2	35	....	....	....	....
2001-02	Boston	NHL	80	4	14	18	107	0	0	1	136	2.9	18	0	0.0	18:30	6	1	2	3	8	0	0	0	21:30
2002-03	Boston	NHL	78	7	17	24	99	0	1	2	160	4.4	8	1	0.0	22:41	5	0	1	1	4	0	0	0	23:22
2003-04	Boston	NHL	81	6	24	30	98	1	1	1	178	3.4	17	0	0.0	22:32	7	0	2	2	2	0	0	0	24:44
2004-05	Nottingham	Britain	9	1	3	4	4	....	....	....	....	....	....	....	....	....	6	1	2	3	22	....	....	....	....
2005-06	Boston	NHL	54	5	7	12	93	1	1	0	89	5.6	–7	1	100.0	20:39	....	....	....	....	....	....	....	....	....
2006-07	Phoenix	NHL	59	2	9	11	138	1	0	0	53	3.8	–13	1	0.0	16:48	....	....	....	....	....	....	....	....	....
2007-08	Phoenix	NHL	79	3	9	12	125	0	1	0	94	3.2	–9	0	0.0	17:01	....	....	....	....	....	....	....	....	....
2008-09	Florida	NHL	68	5	16	21	91	0	0	1	104	4.8	7	0	0.0	16:36	....	....	....	....	....	....	....	....	....
2009-10	Anaheim	NHL	42	1	6	7	59	1	0	0	39	2.6	1	0	0.0	16:45	....	....	....	....	....	....	....	....	....
	Manitoba Moose	AHL	9	0	4	4	4	....	....	....	....	....	....	....	....	....	....	....	....	....	....	....	....	....	....
	♦ Chicago	NHL	7	0	1	1	12	0	0	0	11	0.0	4	0	0.0	15:56	3	0	0	0	2	0	0	0	8:23
	Rockford IceHogs	AHL	6	0	1	1	18	....	....	....	....	....	....	....	....	....	....	....	....	....	....	....	....	....	....
	NHL Totals		554	33	103	136	822	4	4	5	871	3.8		3	33.3	19:07	21	1	5	6	16	0	0	0	21:09

• Re-entered NHL Entry Draft. Originally Washington's 1st choice, 9th overall, in 1997 Entry Draft.

OHL All-Rookie Team (1996) • Memorial Cup Tournament All-Star Team (1999) • Stafford Smythe Memorial Trophy (Memorial Cup Tournament - MVP) (1999) • NHL All-Rookie Team (2002)

Played in NHL All-Star Game (2004)

Signed as a free agent by **Nottingham** (Britain), January 26, 2005. Traded to **Phoenix** by **Boston** with Boston's 4th round choice (later traded to Toronto – Toronto selected Matt Frattin) in 2007 Entry Draft for Paul Mara and Phoenix's 3rd round choice (later traded to Anaheim - Anaheim selected Maxime Macenauer) in 2007 Entry Draft, June 26, 2006. Traded to **Florida** by **Phoenix** with Keith Ballard and Ottawa's 2nd round choice (previously acquired, later traded back to Phoenix – Phoenix selected Jared Staal) in 2008 Entry Draft for Olli Jokinen, June 20, 2008. Signed as a free agent by **Anaheim**, July 9, 2009. Traded to **Chicago** by **Anaheim** for future considerations, March 2, 2010.

BOZAK, Tyler

(BOH-zak, TIGH-luhr) **TOR.**

Center. Shoots right. 6'1", 183 lbs. Born, Regina, Sask., March 19, 1986.

Season	Club	League	GP	G	A	Pts	PIM	PP	SH	GW	S	%	+/-	TF	F%	Min	GP	G	A	Pts	PIM	PP	SH	GW	Min
2003-04	Reg. Pat Cdns.	SMHL	42	17	19	36	40	....	....	....	....	....	....	....	....	....	....	....	....	....	....	....	....	....	....
2004-05	Victoria Salsa	BCHL	55	15	16	31	24	....	....	....	....	....	....	....	....	....	5	0	2	2	2	....	....	....	....
2005-06	Victoria Salsa	BCHL	56	31	38	69	26	....	....	....	....	....	....	....	....	....	16	8	8	16	14	....	....	....	....
2006-07	Victoria Grizzlies	BCHL	59	45	83	128	45	....	....	....	....	....	....	....	....	....	....	....	....	....	....	....	....	....	....
2007-08	U. of Denver	WCHA	41	18	16	34	22	....	....	....	....	....	....	....	....	....	....	....	....	....	....	....	....	....	....
2008-09	U. of Denver	WCHA	19	8	15	23	10	....	....	....	....	....	....	....	....	....	....	....	....	....	....	....	....	....	....
2009-10	Toronto	NHL	37	8	19	27	6	2	0	1	51	15.7	–5	648	55.3	19:14	....	....	....	....	....	....	....	....	....
	Toronto Marlies	AHL	32	4	16	20	6	....	....	....	....	....	....	....	....	....	....	....	....	....	....	....	....	....	....
	NHL Totals		37	8	19	27	6	2	0	1	51	15.7		648	55.2	19:14	....	....	....	....	....	....	....	....	....

WCHA All-Rookie Team (2008)

Signed as a free agent by **Toronto**, April 3, 2009.

BRADLEY, Matt

(BRAD-lee, MAT) **WSH.**

Right wing. Shoots right. 6'3", 201 lbs. Born, Stittsville, Ont., June 13, 1978. San Jose's 4th choice, 102nd overall, in 1996 Entry Draft.

Season	Club	League	GP	G	A	Pts	PIM	PP	SH	GW	S	%	+/-	TF	F%	Min	GP	G	A	Pts	PIM	PP	SH	GW	Min
1994-95	Cumberland	CJHL	49	13	20	33	18	....	....	....	....	....	....	....	....	....	....	....	....	....	....	....	....	....	....
1995-96	Kingston	OHL	55	10	14	24	17	....	....	....	....	....	....	....	....	....	6	0	1	1	6	....	....	....	....
1996-97	Kingston	OHL	65	24	24	48	41	....	....	....	....	....	....	....	....	....	5	0	4	4	2	....	....	....	....
	Kentucky	AHL	1	0	1	1	0	....	....	....	....	....	....	....	....	....	....	....	....	....	....	....	....	....	....
1997-98	Kingston	OHL	55	33	50	83	24	....	....	....	....	....	....	....	....	....	8	3	4	7	7	....	....	....	....
1998-99	Kentucky	AHL	79	23	20	43	57	....	....	....	....	....	....	....	....	....	10	1	4	5	4	....	....	....	....
99-2000	Kentucky	AHL	80	22	19	41	81	....	....	....	....	....	....	....	....	....	9	6	3	9	9	....	....	....	....
2000-01	San Jose	NHL	21	1	1	2	19	0	0	0	16	6.3	0	0	0.0	6:58	....	....	....	....	....	....	....	....	....
	Kentucky	AHL	22	5	8	13	16	....	....	....	....	....	....	....	....	....	1	1	0	1	5	....	....	....	....
2001-02	San Jose	NHL	54	9	13	22	43	0	0	2	63	14.3	22	2	0.0	8:27	10	0	0	0	0	0	0	0	5:16
2002-03	San Jose	NHL	46	2	3	5	37	0	0	0	21	9.5	–1	1	0.0	7:54	....	....	....	....	....	....	....	....	....
2003-04	Pittsburgh	NHL	82	7	9	16	65	0	0	1	85	8.2	–27	29	41.4	12:48	....	....	....	....	....	....	....	....	....
2004-05	Bulldogs Dornbirn	Austria-2	6	5	2	7	18	....	....	....	....	....	....	....	....	....	....	....	....	....	....	....	....	....	....
2005-06	Washington	NHL	74	7	12	19	72	0	0	1	87	8.0	–8	25	52.0	12:36	....	....	....	....	....	....	....	....	....
2006-07	Washington	NHL	57	4	9	13	47	0	0	0	77	5.2	–5	20	45.0	11:55	....	....	....	....	....	....	....	....	....
2007-08	Washington	NHL	77	7	11	18	74	1	1	2	111	6.3	1	32	43.8	10:00	7	0	2	2	2	0	0	0	11:40
2008-09	Washington	NHL	81	5	6	11	59	0	0	1	98	5.1	–1	24	41.7	10:37	14	2	4	6	0	0	1	1	12:45
2009-10	Washington	NHL	77	10	14	24	47	0	1	5	98	10.2	6	28	39.3	11:02	7	1	2	3	2	0	0	0	10:36
	NHL Totals		569	52	78	130	463	1	2	12	656	7.9		161	42.9	10:44	38	3	8	11	4	0	1	1	10:11

Traded to **Pittsburgh** by **San Jose** for Wayne Primeau, March 11, 2003. Signed as a free agent by **Dornbirn** (Austria-2), November 14, 2004. Signed as a free agent by **Washington**, August 18, 2005.

BRASHEAR, Donald

(bra-SHEER, DAWN-uohld)

Left wing. Shoots left. 6'3", 237 lbs. Born, Bedford, IN, January 7, 1972.

Season	Club	League	GP	G	A	Pts	PIM	PP	SH	GW	S	%	+/-	TF	F%	Min	GP	G	A	Pts	PIM	PP	SH	GW	Min
1988-89	Ste-Foy	QAAA	10	1	2	3	10	....	....	....	....	....	....	....	....	....	....	....	....	....	....	....	....	....	....
1989-90	Longueuil	QMJHL	64	12	14	26	169	....	....	....	....	....	....	....	....	....	7	0	0	0	11	....	....	....	....
1990-91	Longueuil	QMJHL	68	12	26	38	195	....	....	....	....	....	....	....	....	....	8	0	3	3	33	....	....	....	....
1991-92	Verdun	QMJHL	65	18	24	42	283	....	....	....	....	....	....	....	....	....	18	4	2	6	98	....	....	....	....
1992-93	Fredericton	AHL	76	11	3	14	261	....	....	....	....	....	....	....	....	....	5	0	0	0	8	....	....	....	....
1993-94	Montreal	NHL	14	2	2	4	34	0	0	0	15	13.3	0	....	....	....	2	0	0	0	0	0	0	0	....
	Fredericton	AHL	62	38	28	66	250	....	....	....	....	....	....	....	....	....	....	....	....	....	....	....	....	....	....
1994-95	Fredericton	AHL	29	10	9	19	182	....	....	....	....	....	....	....	....	....	17	7	5	12	77	....	....	....	....
	Montreal	NHL	20	1	1	2	63	0	0	1	10	10.0	–5	....	....	....	....	....	....	....	....	....	....	....	....
1995-96	Montreal	NHL	67	0	4	4	223	0	0	0	25	0.0	–10	....	....	....	6	0	0	0	2	0	0	0	....
1996-97	Montreal	NHL	10	0	0	0	38	0	0	0	6	0.0	–2	....	....	....	....	....	....	....	....	....	....	....	....
	Vancouver	NHL	59	8	5	13	207	0	0	2	55	14.5	–6	....	....	....	....	....	....	....	....	....	....	....	....
1997-98	Vancouver	NHL	77	9	9	18	*372	0	0	1	64	14.1	–9	....	....	....	....	....	....	....	....	....	....	....	....
1998-99	Vancouver	NHL	82	8	10	18	209	2	0	1	112	7.1	–25	6	16.7	13:25	....	....	....	....	....	....	....	....	....
99-2000	Vancouver	NHL	60	11	2	13	136	1	0	3	83	13.3	–9	11	36.4	13:07	....	....	....	....	....	....	....	....	....
2000-01	Vancouver	NHL	79	9	19	28	145	0	0	1	127	7.1	0	6	16.7	13:27	4	0	0	0	0	0	0	0	14:47
2001-02	Vancouver	NHL	31	5	8	13	90	1	0	0	45	11.1	–8	4	25.0	13:58	....	....	....	....	....	....	....	....	....
	Philadelphia	NHL	50	4	15	19	109	0	0	2	62	6.5	0	1	0.0	13:00	5	0	0	0	19	0	0	0	9:55
2002-03	Philadelphia	NHL	80	8	17	25	161	0	0	1	99	8.1	5	27	33.3	13:23	13	1	2	3	21	0	0	0	11:09
2003-04	Philadelphia	NHL	64	6	7	13	212	0	0	0	72	8.3	–1	18	38.9	11:02	18	1	3	4	61	1	0	0	8:56
2004-05	Quebec RadioX	QNAHL	47	18	32	50	260	....	....	....	....	....	....	....	....	....	8	4	6	10	42	....	....	....	....
2005-06	Philadelphia	NHL	76	4	5	9	166	0	0	0	73	5.5	–2	7	28.6	8:36	1	0	0	0	0	0	0	0	4:20

			Regular Season														Playoffs								
Season	Club	League	GP	G	A	Pts	PIM	PP	SH	GW	S	%	+/-	TF	F%	Min	GP	G	A	Pts	PIM	PP	SH	GW	Min
2006-07	**Washington**	**NHL**	77	4	9	13	156	0	0	0	47	8.5	1	8	25.0	7:58	....	....	....	....	....	....	....	....	....
2007-08	**Washington**	**NHL**	80	5	3	8	119	0	0	0	59	8.5	−7	1	0.0	7:52	7	1	1	2	0	0	0	0	7:30
2008-09	**Washington**	**NHL**	63	1	3	4	121	0	0	1	43	2.3	−6	0	0.0	8:15	4	0	0	0	18	0	0	0	3:25
2009-10	**NY Rangers**	**NHL**	36	0	1	1	73	0	0	0	18	0.0	−9	0	0.0	6:15	....	....	....	....	....	....	....	....	....
	Hartford	AHL	27	2	4	6	25	....	....	....	....	....	....	....	....	....	....	....	....	....	....	....	....	....	....
	NHL Totals		**1025**	**85**	**120**	**205**	**2634**	**4**	**0**	**13**	**1015**	**8.4**		**89**	**30.3**	**10:52**	**60**	**3**	**6**	**9**	**121**	**1**	**0**	**0**	**9:19**

igned as a free agent by **Montreal**, July 28, 1992. Traded to **Vancouver** by **Montreal** for Jassen Cullimore, November 13, 1996. Traded to **Philadelphia** by **Vancouver** with Vancouver's 6th round hoice (later traded to Columbus – Columbus selected Jaroslav Balastik) in 2002 Entry Draft for Jan Hlavac and Tampa Bay's 3rd round choice (previously acquired, Vancouver selected Brett Skinner) in 2002 ntry Draft, December 17, 2001. Signed as a free agent by **Quebec** (QNAHL), September 21, 2004. Signed as a free agent by **Washington**, July 14, 2006. Signed as a free agent by **NY Rangers**, July 1, 009. Traded to **Atlanta** by **NY Rangers** with Patrick Rissmiller for Todd White, August 2, 2010.

BRASSARD, Derick

(bruh-SAHRD, DAIR-ihk) **CBJ**

Center. Shoots left. 6'1", 190 lbs. Born, Hull, Que., September 22, 1987. Columbus' 1st choice, 6th overall, in 2006 Entry Draft.

2004-05	Drummondville	QMJHL	69	25	51	76	25	....	....	....	....	....	....	....	....	....	6	1	5	6	6	....	....	....	....
2005-06	Drummondville	QMJHL	58	44	72	116	92	....	....	....	....	....	....	....	....	....	7	5	4	9	10	....	....	....	....
2006-07	Drummondville	QMJHL	14	6	19	25	24	....	....	....	....	....	....	....	....	....	12	9	15	24	12	....	....	....	....
2007-08	**Columbus**	**NHL**	17	1	1	2	6	0	0	0	13	7.7	−4	80	42.5	9:03	....	....	....	....	....	....	....	....	....
	Syracuse Crunch	AHL	42	15	36	51	51	....	....	....	....	....	....	....	....	....	13	4	9	13	10	....	....	....	....
2008-09	**Columbus**	**NHL**	31	10	15	25	17	3	0	1	59	16.9	12	332	48.5	14:25	....	....	....	....	....	....	....	....	....
2009-10	**Columbus**	**NHL**	79	9	27	36	48	4	0	0	125	7.2	−17	503	41.8	14:57	....	....	....	....	....	....	....	....	....
	NHL Totals		**127**	**20**	**43**	**63**	**71**	**7**	**0**	**1**	**197**	**10.2**		**915**	**44.3**	**14:02**	....	....	....	....	....	....	....	....	....

MJHL First All-Star Team (2006) • Canadian Major Junior Second All-Star Team (2006)

Missed majority of 2006-07 season recovering from recurring shoulder injury. • Missed majority of 2008-09 season recovering from shoulder injury suffered in game at Dallas, December 18, 2008.

BRENNAN, Kip

(BREH-nan, KIHP)

Left wing. Shoots left. 6'4", 230 lbs. Born, Kingston, Ont., August 27, 1980. Los Angeles' 4th choice, 103rd overall, in 1998 Entry Draft.

1995-96	St. Mike's B's	OPJHL	40	0	11	11	155	....	....	....	....	....	....	....	....	....	7	0	1	1	20	....	....	....	....
1996-97	Windsor Spitfires	OHL	42	0	10	10	156	....	....	....	....	....	....	....	....	....	5	0	1	1	16	....	....	....	....
1997-98	Windsor Spitfires	OHL	24	0	7	7	103	....	....	....	....	....	....	....	....	....	....	....	....	....	....	....	....	....	....
	Sudbury Wolves	OHL	24	0	3	3	85	....	....	....	....	....	....	....	....	....	....	....	....	....	....	....	....	....	....
1998-99	Sudbury Wolves	OHL	38	9	12	21	160	....	....	....	....	....	....	....	....	....	....	....	....	....	....	....	....	....	....
99-2000	Sudbury Wolves	OHL	55	16	16	32	228	....	....	....	....	....	....	....	....	....	12	3	3	6	67	....	....	....	....
2000-01	Lowell	AHL	23	2	3	5	117	....	....	....	....	....	....	....	....	....	....	....	....	....	....	....	....	....	....
	Sudbury Wolves	OHL	27	7	14	21	94	....	....	....	....	....	....	....	....	....	12	5	6	11	*92	....	....	....	....
2001-02	**Los Angeles**	**NHL**	4	0	0	0	22	0	0	0	0	0.0	1	0	0.0	4:40	....	....	....	....	....	....	....	....	....
	Manchester	AHL	44	4	1	5	269	....	....	....	....	....	....	....	....	....	4	0	1	1	26	....	....	....	....
2002-03	**Los Angeles**	**NHL**	19	0	0	0	57	0	0	0	6	0.0	0	2	0.0	4:52	....	....	....	....	....	....	....	....	....
	Manchester	AHL	35	3	2	5	195	....	....	....	....	....	....	....	....	....	3	0	0	0	0	....	....	....	....
2003-04	**Los Angeles**	**NHL**	18	1	0	1	79	0	0	0	6	16.7	−1	0	0.0	5:01	....	....	....	....	....	....	....	....	....
	Manchester	AHL	2	0	0	0	6	....	....	....	....	....	....	....	....	....	....	....	....	....	....	....	....	....	....
	Atlanta	**NHL**	5	0	0	0	17	0	0	0	2	0.0	0	0	0.0	3:37	....	....	....	....	....	....	....	....	....
2004-05	Chicago Wolves	AHL	48	7	6	13	267	....	....	....	....	....	....	....	....	....	18	1	1	2	*105	....	....	....	....
2005-06	**Anaheim**	**NHL**	12	0	1	1	35	0	0	0	5	0.0	−2	1	0.0	4:16	....	....	....	....	....	....	....	....	....
	Portland Pirates	AHL	9	2	1	3	22	....	....	....	....	....	....	....	....	....	....	....	....	....	....	....	....	....	....
2006-07	Hershey Bears	AHL	26	4	2	6	67	....	....	....	....	....	....	....	....	....	6	0	1	1	30	....	....	....	....
	Toronto Marlies	AHL	1	0	0	0	6	....	....	....	....	....	....	....	....	....	....	....	....	....	....	....	....	....	....
	Long Beach	ECHL	11	2	3	5	74	....	....	....	....	....	....	....	....	....	....	....	....	....	....	....	....	....	....
2007-08	**NY Islanders**	**NHL**	3	0	0	0	12	0	0	0	0	0.0	0	0	0.0	4:21	....	....	....	....	....	....	....	....	....
	Bridgeport	AHL	49	2	1	3	247	....	....	....	....	....	....	....	....	....	....	....	....	....	....	....	....	....	....
2008-09	HIFK Helsinki	Finland	22	0	3	3	118	....	....	....	....	....	....	....	....	....	....	....	....	....	....	....	....	....	....
	Hershey Bears	AHL	22	1	3	4	88	....	....	....	....	....	....	....	....	....	1	0	0	0	4	....	....	....	....
	South Carolina	ECHL	3	0	0	0	16	....	....	....	....	....	....	....	....	....	....	....	....	....	....	....	....	....	....
2009-10	Springfield	AHL	53	0	3	3	263	....	....	....	....	....	....	....	....	....	....	....	....	....	....	....	....	....	....
	NHL Totals		**61**	**1**	**1**	**2**	**222**	**0**	**0**	**0**	**19**	**5.3**		**3**	**0.0**	**4:39**	....	....	....	....	....	....	....	....	....

aded to **Atlanta** by **Los Angeles** for Jeff Cowan, March 9, 2004. • Missed majority of the 2003-04 season as a healthy reserve. Signed as a free agent by **Chicago** (AHL), September 27, 2004. Traded to **naheim** by **Atlanta** for Mark Popovic, August 23, 2005. Signed as a free agent by **NY Islanders**, July 3, 2007. Signed as a free agent by **HIFK Helsinki** (Finland), August 15, 2008. Signed as a free agent **Hershey** (AHL), December 16, 2008. Signed as a free agent by **Springfield** (AHL), August 27, 2009.

BRENT, Tim

(BREHNT, TIHM) **TOR.**

Center. Shoots right. 6', 197 lbs. Born, Cambridge, Ont., March 10, 1984. Anaheim's 3rd choice, 75th overall, in 2004 Entry Draft.

99-2000	Cambridge	OHA-B	40	19	16	35	42	....	....	....	....	....	....	....	....	....	....	....	....	....	....	....	....	....	....
2000-01	St. Michael's	OHL	64	9	19	28	31	....	....	....	....	....	....	....	....	....	18	2	8	10	6	....	....	....	....
2001-02	St. Michael's	OHL	61	19	40	59	52	....	....	....	....	....	....	....	....	....	14	7	12	19	20	....	....	....	....
2002-03	St. Michael's	OHL	60	24	42	66	74	....	....	....	....	....	....	....	....	....	19	7	17	24	14	....	....	....	....
2003-04	St. Michael's	OHL	53	26	41	67	105	....	....	....	....	....	....	....	....	....	18	4	13	17	24	....	....	....	....
2004-05	Cincinnati	AHL	46	5	13	18	42	....	....	....	....	....	....	....	....	....	12	0	1	1	6	....	....	....	....
2005-06	Portland Pirates	AHL	37	15	9	24	32	....	....	....	....	....	....	....	....	....	15	4	4	8	16	....	....	....	....
2006-07	**Anaheim**	**NHL**	15	1	0	1	6	0	0	0	14	7.1	−5	86	48.8	6:55	....	....	....	....	....	....	....	....	....
	Portland Pirates	AHL	48	16	14	30	40	....	....	....	....	....	....	....	....	....	....	....	....	....	....	....	....	....	....
2007-08	**Pittsburgh**	**NHL**	1	0	0	0	0	0	0	0	0	0.0	−1	5	60.0	4:34	....	....	....	....	....	....	....	....	....
	Wilkes-Barre	AHL	74	18	43	61	79	....	....	....	....	....	....	....	....	....	23	*12	15	27	10	....	....	....	....
2008-09	**Chicago**	**NHL**	2	0	0	0	2	0	0	0	0	0.0	0	10	50.0	8:21	....	....	....	....	....	....	....	....	....
	Rockford IceHogs	AHL	64	20	42	62	59	....	....	....	....	....	....	....	....	....	4	0	1	1	2	....	....	....	....
2009-10	**Toronto**	**NHL**	1	0	0	0	0	0	0	0	3	0.0	0	8	50.0	13:21	....	....	....	....	....	....	....	....	....
	Toronto Marlies	AHL	33	13	15	28	19	....	....	....	....	....	....	....	....	....	....	....	....	....	....	....	....	....	....
	NHL Totals		**19**	**1**	**0**	**1**	**8**	**0**	**0**	**0**	**17**	**5.9**		**109**	**49.5**	**7:17**	....	....	....	....	....	....	....	....	....

Re-entered NHL Entry Draft. Originally Anaheim's 2nd choice, 37th overall, in 2002 Entry Draft.

aded to **Pittsburgh** by **Anaheim** for Stephen Dixon, June 23, 2007. Traded to **Chicago** by **Pittsburgh** for Danny Richmond, July 17, 2008. Signed as a free agent by **Toronto**, July 6, 2009. • Missed ajority of 2009-10 season recovering from recurring chest injury.

BREWER, Eric

(BREW-uhr, AIR-ihk) **ST.L.**

Defense. Shoots left. 6'3", 222 lbs. Born, Vernon, B.C., April 17, 1979. NY Islanders' 2nd choice, 5th overall, in 1997 Entry Draft.

1994-95	Kamloops	Minor-BC	40	19	19	38	62	....	....	....	....	....	....	....	....	....	....	....	....	....	....	....	....	....	....
1995-96	Prince George	WHL	63	4	10	14	25	....	....	....	....	....	....	....	....	....	....	....	....	....	....	....	....	....	....
1996-97	Prince George	WHL	71	5	24	29	81	....	....	....	....	....	....	....	....	....	15	2	4	6	16	....	....	....	....
1997-98	Prince George	WHL	34	5	28	33	45	....	....	....	....	....	....	....	....	....	11	4	2	6	19	....	....	....	....
1998-99	**NY Islanders**	**NHL**	63	5	6	11	32	2	0	0	63	7.9	−14	0	0.0	15:28	....	....	....	....	....	....	....	....	....
99-2000	**NY Islanders**	**NHL**	26	0	2	2	20	0	0	0	30	0.0	−11	0	0.0	18:33	....	....	....	....	....	....	....	....	....
	Lowell	AHL	25	2	2	4	26	....	....	....	....	....	....	....	....	....	7	0	0	0	0	....	....	....	....
2000-01	**Edmonton**	**NHL**	77	7	14	21	53	2	0	2	91	7.7	15	0	0.0	18:31	6	1	5	6	2	1	0	0	28:12
2001-02	**Edmonton**	**NHL**	81	7	18	25	45	6	0	2	165	4.2	−5	0	0.0	23:56	....	....	....	....	....	....	....	....	....
	Canada	Olympics	6	2	0	2	0	....	....	....	....	....	....	....	....	....	....	....	....	....	....	....	....	....	....
2002-03	**Edmonton**	**NHL**	80	8	21	29	45	1	0	1	147	5.4	−11	1	100.0	24:56	6	1	3	4	6	0	0	0	25:31
2003-04	**Edmonton**	**NHL**	77	7	18	25	67	3	0	1	135	5.2	−6	0	0.0	24:40	....	....	....	....	....	....	....	....	....
2004-05			DID NOT PLAY																						
2005-06	**St. Louis**	**NHL**	32	6	3	9	45	1	0	1	64	9.4	−17	0	0.0	23:28	....	....	....	....	....	....	....	....	....
2006-07	**St. Louis**	**NHL**	82	6	23	29	69	2	0	1	111	5.4	−10	0	0.0	24:32	....	....	....	....	....	....	....	....	....
2007-08	**St. Louis**	**NHL**	77	1	21	22	91	0	0	0	101	1.0	−18	0	0.0	24:38	....	....	....	....	....	....	....	....	....

			Regular Season														Playoffs								
Season	Club	League	GP	G	A	Pts	PIM	PP	SH	GW	S	%	+/-	TF	F%	Min	GP	G	A	Pts	PIM	PP	SH	GW	Min
2008-09	**St. Louis**	**NHL**	**28**	**1**	**5**	**6**	**24**	**1**	**0**	**0**	**49**	**2.0**	**–14**	**0**	**0.0**	**25:07**									
2009-10	**St. Louis**	**NHL**	**59**	**8**	**7**	**15**	**46**	**0**	**0**	**0**	**84**	**9.5**	**–17**	**0**	**0.0**	**21:27**									
	NHL Totals		**682**	**56**	**138**	**194**	**537**	**18**	**0**	**8**	**1040**	**5.4**		**1**	**100.0**	**22:30**	**12**	**2**	**8**	**10**	**8**	**1**	**0**	**0**	**26:51**

WHL West Second All-Star Team (1998)

Played in NHL All-Star Game (2003)

Traded to **Edmonton** by **NY Islanders** with Josh Green and NY Islanders' 2nd round choice (Brad Winchester) in 2000 Entry Draft for Roman Hamrlik, June 24, 2000. Traded to **St. Louis** by **Edmonton** with Doug Lynch and Jeff Woywitka for Chris Pronger, August 2, 2005. • Missed majority of 2005-06 season recovering from shoulder injuries suffered in games at Columbus (November 16, 2005) and Atlanta (January 13, 2006). • Missed majority of 2008-09 season recovering from back injury suffered in game at Los Angeles, December 11, 2008.

BRIERE, Danny

(bree-AIR, DA-nee) **PHI.**

Center. Shoots right. 5'10", 179 lbs. Born, Gatineau, Que., October 6, 1977. Phoenix's 2nd choice, 24th overall, in 1996 Entry Draft.

			Regular Season														Playoffs								
Season	Club	League	GP	G	A	Pts	PIM	PP	SH	GW	S	%	+/-	TF	F%	Min	GP	G	A	Pts	PIM	PP	SH	GW	Min
1992-93	Abitibi Regents	QAAA	42	24	30	54	28										3	0	3	3	8				
1993-94	Gatineau	QAAA	44	56	47	103	56																		
1994-95	Drummondville	QMJHL	72	51	72	123	54										4	2	3	5	2				
1995-96	Drummondville	QMJHL	67	*67	*96	*163	84										6	6	12	18	8				
1996-97	Drummondville	QMJHL	59	52	78	130	94										8	7	7	14	14				
1997-98	**Phoenix**	**NHL**	**5**	**1**	**0**	**1**	**2**	**0**	**0**	**0**	**4**	**25.0**	**1**												
	Springfield	AHL	68	36	56	92	42										4	1	2	3	4				
1998-99	**Phoenix**	**NHL**	**64**	**8**	**14**	**22**	**30**	**2**	**0**	**2**	**90**	**8.9**	**–3**	**484**	**47.5**	**11:13**									
	Las Vegas	IHL	1	1	1	2	0																		
	Springfield	AHL	13	2	6	8	20										3	0	1	1	2				
99-2000	**Phoenix**	**NHL**	**13**	**1**	**1**	**2**	**0**	**0**	**0**	**0**	**9**	**11.1**	**0**	**65**	**49.2**	**7:41**	**1**	**0**	**0**	**0**	**0**	**0**	**0**	**0**	**6:16**
	Springfield	AHL	58	29	42	71	56																		
2000-01	**Phoenix**	**NHL**	**30**	**11**	**4**	**15**	**12**	**9**	**0**	**1**	**43**	**25.6**	**–2**	**210**	**50.0**	**10:50**									
	Springfield	AHL	30	21	25	46	30																		
2001-02	**Phoenix**	**NHL**	**78**	**32**	**28**	**60**	**52**	**12**	**0**	**5**	**149**	**21.5**	**6**	**951**	**51.8**	**15:44**	**5**	**2**	**1**	**3**	**2**	**1**	**0**	**1**	**16:25**
2002-03	**Phoenix**	**NHL**	**68**	**17**	**29**	**46**	**50**	**4**	**0**	**3**	**142**	**12.0**	**–21**	**1108**	**52.5**	**17:02**									
	Buffalo	**NHL**	**14**	**7**	**5**	**12**	**12**	**5**	**0**	**1**	**39**	**17.9**	**1**	**206**	**50.0**	**17:49**									
2003-04	**Buffalo**	**NHL**	**82**	**28**	**37**	**65**	**70**	**11**	**0**	**3**	**194**	**14.4**	**–7**	**1066**	**47.1**	**18:20**									
2004-05	SC Bern	Swiss	36	16	29	45	26										11	1	6	7	2				
2005-06	**Buffalo**	**NHL**	**48**	**25**	**33**	**58**	**48**	**11**	**0**	**4**	**147**	**17.0**	**3**	**517**	**50.7**	**19:04**	**18**	**8**	**11**	**19**	**12**	**3**	**0**	**2**	**18:48**
2006-07	**Buffalo**	**NHL**	**81**	**32**	**63**	**95**	**89**	**9**	**0**	**6**	**234**	**13.7**	**17**	**1089**	**49.6**	**19:19**	**16**	**3**	**12**	**15**	**16**	**2**	**0**	**1**	**20:53**
2007-08	**Philadelphia**	**NHL**	**79**	**31**	**41**	**72**	**68**	**14**	**0**	**3**	**182**	**17.0**	**–22**	**1250**	**50.5**	**18:52**	**17**	**9**	**7**	**16**	**20**	***6**	**0**	**3**	**18:26**
2008-09	**Philadelphia**	**NHL**	**29**	**11**	**14**	**25**	**26**	**4**	**0**	**0**	**54**	**20.4**	**–1**	**147**	**46.3**	**15:39**	**6**	**1**	**3**	**4**	**8**	**1**	**0**	**0**	**16:41**
2009-10	**Philadelphia**	**NHL**	**75**	**26**	**27**	**53**	**71**	**8**	**0**	**1**	**193**	**13.5**	**–2**	**120**	**44.2**	**16:35**	**23**	**12**	**18**	***30**	**18**	**4**	**0**	**4**	**19:37**
	NHL Totals		**666**	**230**	**296**	**526**	**530**	**89**	**0**	**29**	**1480**	**15.5**		**7213**	**49.9**	**16:34**	**86**	**35**	**52**	**87**	**76**	**17**	**0**	**11**	**18:54**

QMJHL All-Rookie Team (1995) • QMJHL Offensive Rookie of the Year (1995) • QMJHL Second All-Star Team (1996, 1997) • AHL All-Rookie Team (1998) • AHL First All-Star Team (1998) • Dudley "Red" Garrett Memorial Award (AHL – Rookie of the Year) (1998)

Played in NHL All-Star Game (2007)

Traded to **Buffalo** by **Phoenix** with Phoenix's 3rd round choice (Andrej Sekera) in 2004 Entry Draft for Chris Gratton and Buffalo's 4th round choice (later traded to Edmonton – Edmonton selected Liam Reddox) in 2004 Entry Draft, March 10, 2003. Signed as a free agent by **Bern** (Swiss), September 28, 2004. Signed as a free agent by **Philadelphia**, July 1, 2007. • Missed majority of 2008-09 season recovering from abdominal surgery (October 25, 2008) and groin surgery (January 22, 2009).

BRIND'AMOUR, Rod

(BRIHND-uh-MOHR, RAWD)

Center. Shoots left. 6'1", 205 lbs. Born, Ottawa, Ont., August 9, 1970. St. Louis' 1st choice, 9th overall, in 1988 Entry Draft.

			Regular Season														Playoffs								
Season	Club	League	GP	G	A	Pts	PIM	PP	SH	GW	S	%	+/-	TF	F%	Min	GP	G	A	Pts	PIM	PP	SH	GW	Min
1986-87	Notre Dame	SMHL	33	38	50	88	66																		
1987-88	Notre Dame	SJHL	56	46	61	107	136																		
1988-89	Michigan State	CCHA	42	27	32	59	63																		
	St. Louis	**NHL**															**5**	**2**	**0**	**2**	**4**	**0**	**0**	**0**	
1989-90	**St. Louis**	**NHL**	**79**	**26**	**35**	**61**	**46**	**10**	**0**	**1**	**160**	**16.3**	**23**				**12**	**5**	**8**	**13**	**6**	**1**	**0**	**0**	
1990-91	**St. Louis**	**NHL**	**78**	**17**	**32**	**49**	**93**	**4**	**0**	**3**	**169**	**10.1**	**2**				**13**	**2**	**5**	**7**	**10**	**1**	**0**	**0**	
1991-92	**Philadelphia**	**NHL**	**80**	**33**	**44**	**77**	**100**	**8**	**4**	**5**	**202**	**16.3**	**–3**												
1992-93	**Philadelphia**	**NHL**	**81**	**37**	**49**	**86**	**89**	**13**	**4**	**4**	**206**	**18.0**	**–8**												
1993-94	**Philadelphia**	**NHL**	**84**	**35**	**62**	**97**	**85**	**14**	**1**	**4**	**230**	**15.2**	**–9**												
1994-95	**Philadelphia**	**NHL**	**48**	**12**	**27**	**39**	**33**	**4**	**1**	**2**	**86**	**14.0**	**–4**				**15**	**6**	**9**	**15**	**8**	**2**	**1**	**1**	
1995-96	**Philadelphia**	**NHL**	**82**	**26**	**61**	**87**	**110**	**4**	**4**	**5**	**213**	**12.2**	**20**				**12**	**2**	**5**	**7**	**6**	**1**	**0**	**0**	
1996-97	**Philadelphia**	**NHL**	**82**	**27**	**32**	**59**	**41**	**8**	**2**	**3**	**205**	**13.2**	**2**				**19**	***13**	**8**	**21**	**10**	**4**	**2**	**1**	
1997-98	**Philadelphia**	**NHL**	**82**	**36**	**38**	**74**	**54**	**10**	**2**	**8**	**205**	**17.6**	**–2**				**5**	**2**	**2**	**4**	**7**	**0**	**0**	**0**	
	Canada	Olympics	6	1	2	3	0																		
1998-99	**Philadelphia**	**NHL**	**82**	**24**	**50**	**74**	**47**	**10**	**0**	**3**	**191**	**12.6**	**3**	**1773**	**56.5**	**21:29**	**6**	**1**	**3**	**4**	**0**	**0**	**0**	**0**	**25:08**
99-2000	**Philadelphia**	**NHL**	**12**	**5**	**3**	**8**	**4**	**4**	**0**	**0**	**26**	**19.2**	**–1**	**291**	**60.5**	**20:50**									
	Carolina	**NHL**	**33**	**4**	**10**	**14**	**22**	**0**	**1**	**1**	**61**	**6.6**	**–12**	**704**	**55.5**	**20:35**									
2000-01	**Carolina**	**NHL**	**79**	**20**	**36**	**56**	**47**	**5**	**1**	**5**	**163**	**12.3**	**–7**	**1907**	**60.4**	**22:07**	**6**	**1**	**3**	**4**	**6**	**0**	**0**	**1**	**23:27**
2001-02	**Carolina**	**NHL**	**81**	**23**	**32**	**55**	**40**	**5**	**2**	**5**	**162**	**14.2**	**3**	**2058**	**59.2**	**22:07**	**23**	**4**	**8**	**12**	**16**	**2**	**1**	**1**	**24:52**
2002-03	**Carolina**	**NHL**	**48**	**14**	**23**	**37**	**37**	**7**	**1**	**0**	**110**	**12.7**	**–9**	**1242**	**56.5**	**23:46**									
2003-04	**Carolina**	**NHL**	**78**	**12**	**26**	**38**	**28**	**1**	**0**	**1**	**141**	**8.5**	**0**	**1817**	**61.1**	**21:23**									
2004-05	Kloten Flyers	Swiss	2	2	1	3	0										5	2	4	6	6				
2005-06♦	**Carolina**	**NHL**	**78**	**31**	**39**	**70**	**68**	**19**	**2**	**5**	**198**	**15.7**	**8**	**2145**	**59.1**	**24:18**	**25**	**12**	**6**	**18**	**16**	**6**	**0**	**4**	**23:52**
2006-07	**Carolina**	**NHL**	**78**	**26**	**56**	**82**	**46**	**9**	**2**	**5**	**181**	**14.4**	**7**	**2047**	**59.3**	**23:19**									
2007-08	**Carolina**	**NHL**	**59**	**19**	**32**	**51**	**38**	**6**	**0**	**4**	**151**	**12.6**	**0**	**1460**	**58.3**	**22:27**									
2008-09	**Carolina**	**NHL**	**80**	**16**	**35**	**51**	**36**	**6**	**1**	**1**	**135**	**11.9**	**–23**	**1488**	**61.0**	**18:58**	**18**	**1**	**3**	**4**	**8**	**0**	**0**	**0**	**15:23**
2009-10	**Carolina**	**NHL**	**80**	**9**	**10**	**19**	**36**	**2**	**0**	**2**	**95**	**9.5**	**–29**	**849**	**58.8**	**12:43**									
	NHL Totals		**1484**	**452**	**732**	**1184**	**1100**	**149**	**28**	**67**	**3290**	**13.7**		**17781**	**59.0**	**21:05**	**159**	**51**	**60**	**111**	**97**	**17**	**4**	**8**	**22:16**

CCHA Rookie of the Year (1989) • NHL All-Rookie Team (1990) • Frank J. Selke Trophy (2006, 2007)

Played in NHL All-Star Game (1992)

Traded to **Philadelphia** by **St. Louis** with Dan Quinn for Ron Sutter and Murray Baron, September 22, 1991. Traded to **Carolina** by **Philadelphia** with Jean-Marc Pelletier and Philadelphia's 2nd round choice (later traded to Colorado – Colorado selected Agris Saviels) in 2000 Entry Draft for Keith Primeau and Carolina's 5th round choice (later traded to NY Islanders – NY Islanders selected Kristofer Ottosson) in 2000 Entry Draft, January 23, 2000. Signed as a free agent by **Kloten** (Swiss), February 16, 2005. • Officially announced his retirement, June 30, 2010.

BRINE, David

(BRIGHN, DAY-vihd)

Center. Shoots left. 6'1", 201 lbs. Born, Truro, N.S., January 6, 1985.

			Regular Season														Playoffs								
Season	Club	League	GP	G	A	Pts	PIM	PP	SH	GW	S	%	+/-	TF	F%	Min	GP	G	A	Pts	PIM	PP	SH	GW	Min
2002-03	Truro Bearcats	MJrHL	52	21	32	53	29																		
2003-04	Halifax	QMJHL	70	22	25	47	20																		
2004-05	Halifax	QMJHL	67	14	37	51	36										13	6	7	13	8				
2005-06	Halifax	QMJHL	70	34	66	100	80										11	1	5	6	23				
	Manitoba Moose	AHL															9	0	1	1	2				
2006-07	Rochester	AHL	22	4	4	8	4																		
	Florida Everblades	ECHL	52	9	21	30	22										15	6	4	10	22				
2007-08	**Florida**	**NHL**	**9**	**0**	**1**	**1**	**4**	**0**	**0**	**0**	**3**	**0.0**	**–1**	**44**	**38.6**	**6:02**									
	Rochester	AHL	66	9	11	20	26																		
2008-09	Rochester	AHL	79	8	23	31	35																		
2009-10	Rochester	AHL	69	14	18	32	14										7	0	1	1	2				
	NHL Totals		**9**	**0**	**1**	**1**	**4**	**0**	**0**	**0**	**3**	**0.0**		**44**	**38.6**	**6:02**									

Signed as a free agent by **Florida**, September 14, 2006.

BRODZIAK, Kyle

(brohd-ZEE-ak, KIGHL) **MIN.**

Center. Shoots right. 6'2", 209 lbs. Born, St. Paul, Alta., May 25, 1984. Edmonton's 9th choice, 214th overall, in 2003 Entry Draft.

			Regular Season														Playoffs								
Season	Club	League	GP	G	A	Pts	PIM	PP	SH	GW	S	%	+/-	TF	F%	Min	GP	G	A	Pts	PIM	PP	SH	GW	Min
99-2000	Ft. Saskatchewan	AMBHL	36	23	33	56	57																		
	Moose Jaw	WHL	2	0	0	0	0																		
2000-01	Moose Jaw	WHL	57	2	8	10	49										3	0	0	0	0				
2001-02	Moose Jaw	WHL	72	8	12	20	56										12	0	3	3	11				
2002-03	Moose Jaw	WHL	72	32	30	62	84										13	5	3	8	16				
2003-04	Moose Jaw	WHL	70	39	54	93	58										10	5	4	9	10				
2004-05	Edmonton	AHL	56	6	26	32	49																		

			Regular Season														Playoffs								
Season	Club	League	GP	G	A	Pts	PIM	PP	SH	GW	S	%	+/-	TF	F%	Min	GP	G	A	Pts	PIM	PP	SH	GW	Min
2005-06	Edmonton	NHL	10	0	0	0	4	0	0	0	7	0.0	–4	75	52.0	11:02	....	....	....	....	....	....	....	....	....
	Iowa Stars	AHL	55	12	19	31	41	....	....	....	....	....	....	....	....	....	7	1	3	4	2	....	....	....	....
2006-07	Edmonton	NHL	6	1	0	1	2	0	0	0	11	9.1	0	48	52.1	17:08	....	....	....	....	....	....	....	....	....
	Wilkes-Barre	AHL	62	24	32	56	44	....	....	....	....	....	....	....	....	....	11	1	5	6	14	....	....	....	....
2007-08	Edmonton	NHL	80	14	17	31	33	0	1	3	125	11.2	–6	297	51.5	12:55	....	....	....	....	....	....	....	....	....
2008-09	Edmonton	NHL	79	11	16	27	21	1	1	3	99	11.1	4	947	51.6	12:43	....	....	....	....	....	....	....	....	....
2009-10	Minnesota	NHL	82	9	23	32	22	0	0	3	140	6.4	–3	1001	48.4	15:20	....	....	....	....	....	....	....	....	....
	NHL Totals		257	35	56	91	82	1	2	9	382	9.2		2368	50.3	13:39	....	....	....	....	....	....	....	....	....

VHL East First All-Star Team (2004) • Canadian Major Junior Second All-Star Team (2004)

raded to **Minnesota** by **Edmonton** with Edmonton's 6th round choice (Darcy Kuemper) in 2009 Entry Draft for Dallas's 4th round choice (previously acquired, Edmonton selected Kyle Bigos) in 2009 Entry)raft and Minnesota's 5th round choice (Olivier Roy) in 2009 Entry Draft, June 27, 2009.

BROOKBANK, Sheldon

(BRUK-bank, SHEHL-duhn) **ANA.**

Defense. Shoots right. 6'1", 200 lbs. Born, Lanigan, Sask., October 3, 1980.

Season	Club	League	GP	G	A	Pts	PIM	PP	SH	GW	S	%	+/-	TF	F%	Min	GP	G	A	Pts	PIM	PP	SH	GW	Min
2000-01	Humboldt	SJHL	59	14	35	49	281	....	....	....	....	....	....	....	....	....	....	....	....	....	....	....	....	....	....
2001-02	Grand Rapids	AHL	6	0	1	1	24	....	....	....	....	....	....	....	....	....	....	....	....	....	....	....	....	....	....
	Mississippi	ECHL	62	8	21	29	137	....	....	....	....	....	....	....	....	....	10	1	4	5	27	....	....	....	....
2002-03	Grand Rapids	AHL	69	2	11	13	136	....	....	....	....	....	....	....	....	....	15	1	3	4	28	....	....	....	....
2003-04	Cincinnati	AHL	74	2	9	11	216	....	....	....	....	....	....	....	....	....	9	0	2	2	20	....	....	....	....
2004-05	Cincinnati	AHL	60	1	11	12	181	....	....	....	....	....	....	....	....	....	11	0	0	0	40	....	....	....	....
2005-06	Milwaukee	AHL	73	9	26	35	232	....	....	....	....	....	....	....	....	....	21	1	8	9	49	....	....	....	....
2006-07	Nashville	NHL	3	0	1	1	12	0	0	0	3	0.0	0	0	0.0	8:16	....	....	....	....	....	....	....	....	....
	Milwaukee	AHL	78	15	38	53	176	....	....	....	....	....	....	....	....	....	4	0	0	0	6	....	....	....	....
2007-08	New Jersey	NHL	44	0	8	8	63	0	0	0	43	0.0	0	0	0.0	15:08	....	....	....	....	....	....	....	....	....
	Lowell Devils	AHL	1	0	0	0	5	....	....	....	....	....	....	....	....	....	....	....	....	....	....	....	....	....	....
2008-09	New Jersey	NHL	15	0	0	0	25	0	0	0	6	0.0	1	0	0.0	8:51	....	....	....	....	....	....	....	....	....
	Anaheim	NHL	29	1	3	4	51	0	0	0	24	4.2	3	0	0.0	13:50	13	0	0	0	18	0	0	0	11:13
2009-10	Anaheim	NHL	66	0	9	9	114	0	0	0	60	0.0	10	0	0.0	14:58	....	....	....	....	....	....	....	....	....
	NHL Totals		157	1	21	22	265	0	0	0	136	0.7		0	0.0	14:05	13	0	0	0	18	0	0	0	11:13

HL First All-Star Team (2007) • Eddie Shore Award (AHL - Outstanding Defenseman) (2007)

igned as a free agent by **Anaheim**, July 21, 2003. Signed as a free agent by **Nashville**, August 4, 2005. Signed as a free agent by **Columbus**, July 1, 2007. Claimed on waivers by **New Jersey** from **olumbus**, October 2, 2007. Traded to **Anaheim** by **New Jersey** for David McIntyre, February 3, 2009.

BROOKBANK, Wade

(BRUK-bank, WAYD)

Left wing. Shoots left. 6'4", 225 lbs. Born, Lanigan, Sask., September 29, 1977.

Season	Club	League	GP	G	A	Pts	PIM	PP	SH	GW	S	%	+/-	TF	F%	Min	GP	G	A	Pts	PIM	PP	SH	GW	Min
1997-98	Melville	SJHL	58	8	21	29	330	....	....	....	....	....	....	....	....	....	....	....	....	....	....	....	....	....	....
	Anchorage Aces	WCHL	7	0	0	0	46	....	....	....	....	....	....	....	....	....	4	0	0	0	20	....	....	....	....
1998-99	Anchorage Aces	WCHL	56	0	4	4	337	....	....	....	....	....	....	....	....	....	....	....	....	....	....	....	....	....	....
99-2000	Oklahoma City	CHL	68	3	9	12	354	....	....	....	....	....	....	....	....	....	7	1	1	2	29	....	....	....	....
2000-01	Orlando	IHL	29	0	1	1	122	....	....	....	....	....	....	....	....	....	4	0	0	0	6	....	....	....	....
	Oklahoma City	CHL	46	1	13	14	267	....	....	....	....	....	....	....	....	....	5	0	0	0	24	....	....	....	....
2001-02	Grand Rapids	AHL	73	1	6	7	337	....	....	....	....	....	....	....	....	....	3	0	1	1	14	....	....	....	....
2002-03	Binghamton	AHL	8	0	0	0	28	....	....	....	....	....	....	....	....	....	....	....	....	....	....	....	....	....	....
2003-04	Nashville	NHL	9	0	0	0	38	0	0	0	1	0.0	–4	0	0.0	3:28	....	....	....	....	....	....	....	....	....
	Milwaukee	AHL	6	0	0	0	6	....	....	....	....	....	....	....	....	....	....	....	....	....	....	....	....	....	....
	Binghamton	AHL	4	0	0	0	31	....	....	....	....	....	....	....	....	....	....	....	....	....	....	....	....	....	....
	Vancouver	NHL	20	2	0	2	95	0	0	1	6	33.3	3	0	0.0	3:50	....	....	....	....	....	....	....	....	....
	Manitoba Moose	AHL	4	0	0	0	12	....	....	....	....	....	....	....	....	....	....	....	....	....	....	....	....	....	....
2004-05	Manitoba Moose	AHL	68	0	10	10	285	....	....	....	....	....	....	....	....	....	9	0	0	0	10	....	....	....	....
2005-06	Vancouver	NHL	32	1	2	3	81	0	0	0	10	10.0	3	0	0.0	4:56	....	....	....	....	....	....	....	....	....
2006-07	Boston	NHL	7	1	0	1	15	0	0	0	1	100.0	–1	1	0.0	4:25	....	....	....	....	....	....	....	....	....
	Providence Bruins	AHL	4	0	0	0	15	....	....	....	....	....	....	....	....	....	....	....	....	....	....	....	....	....	....
	Wilkes-Barre	AHL	39	1	0	1	116	....	....	....	....	....	....	....	....	....	5	0	0	0	6	....	....	....	....
2007-08	Carolina	NHL	32	1	1	2	76	0	0	0	12	8.3	4	4	25.0	3:48	....	....	....	....	....	....	....	....	....
	Albany River Rats	AHL	25	0	2	2	28	....	....	....	....	....	....	....	....	....	....	....	....	....	....	....	....	....	....
2008-09	Carolina	NHL	27	1	0	1	40	0	0	0	8	12.5	0	0	0.0	2:30	....	....	....	....	....	....	....	....	....
	Norfolk Admirals	AHL	24	0	1	1	46	....	....	....	....	....	....	....	....	....	....	....	....	....	....	....	....	....	....
2009-10	Wilkes-Barre	AHL	68	3	4	7	168	....	....	....	....	....	....	....	....	....	4	0	0	0	6	....	....	....	....
	NHL Totals		127	6	3	9	345	0	0	1	38	15.8		5	20.0	3:50	....	....	....	....	....	....	....	....	....

igned as a free agent by **Orlando** (IHL), September 1, 2000. Signed as a free agent by **Ottawa**, July 27, 2001. • Missed majority of 2002-03 season recovering from knee injury suffered in game vs. Vilkes-Barre (AHL), November 2, 2002. Claimed by **Nashville** from **Ottawa** in Waiver Draft, October 3, 2003. Traded to **Vancouver** by **Nashville** for future considerations, December 17, 2003. Claimed n waivers by **Ottawa** from **Vancouver**, December 19, 2003. Traded to **Florida** by **Ottawa** for future considerations, December 29, 2003. Claimed on waivers by **Vancouver** from **Florida**, January 3, 004. • Missed majority of 2005-06 season recovering from two head injuries suffered during the season and as a healthy reserve. Signed as a free agent by **Boston**, July 21, 2006. Traded to **Pittsburgh** by **oston** for future considerations, December 19, 2006. Signed as a free agent by **Carolina**, July 1, 2007. Traded to **Tampa Bay** by **Carolina** with Josef Melichar and future considerations for Jussi Jokinen, ebruary 7, 2009. Signed as a free agent by **Pittsburgh**, July 31, 2009.

BROUWER, Troy

(BROW-uhr, TROI) **CHI.**

Right wing. Shoots right. 6'2", 214 lbs. Born, Vancouver, B.C., August 17, 1985. Chicago's 13th choice, 214th overall, in 2004 Entry Draft.

Season	Club	League	GP	G	A	Pts	PIM	PP	SH	GW	S	%	+/-	TF	F%	Min	GP	G	A	Pts	PIM	PP	SH	GW	Min
2001-02	Moose Jaw	WHL	13	0	0	0	7	....	....	....	....	....	....	....	....	....	....	....	....	....	....	....	....	....	....
2002-03	Moose Jaw	WHL	59	9	12	21	54	....	....	....	....	....	....	....	....	....	13	1	2	3	14	....	....	....	....
2003-04	Moose Jaw	WHL	72	23	26	49	111	....	....	....	....	....	....	....	....	....	10	3	0	3	12	....	....	....	....
2004-05	Moose Jaw	WHL	71	22	25	47	132	....	....	....	....	....	....	....	....	....	5	1	2	3	8	....	....	....	....
2005-06	Moose Jaw	WHL	72	49	53	*102	122	....	....	....	....	....	....	....	....	....	17	10	4	14	34	....	....	....	....
2006-07	Chicago	NHL	10	0	0	0	7	0	0	0	7	0.0	–7	0	0.0	9:55	....	....	....	....	....	....	....	....	....
	Norfolk Admirals	AHL	66	41	38	79	70	....	....	....	....	....	....	....	....	....	6	1	0	1	4	....	....	....	....
2007-08	Chicago	NHL	2	0	1	1	0	0	0	0	0	0.0	1	0	0.0	11:56	....	....	....	....	....	....	....	....	....
	Rockford IceHogs	AHL	75	35	19	54	154	....	....	....	....	....	....	....	....	....	12	5	4	9	16	....	....	....	....
2008-09	Chicago	NHL	69	10	16	26	50	4	1	0	126	7.9	7	20	45.0	15:05	17	0	2	2	12	0	0	0	11:51
	Rockford IceHogs	AHL	5	2	6	8	20	....	....	....	....	....	....	....	....	....	....	....	....	....	....	....	....	....	....
2009-10♦	Chicago	NHL	78	22	18	40	66	7	1	7	116	19.0	9	9	55.6	16:22	19	4	4	8	8	0	0	0	11:01
	NHL Totals		159	32	35	67	123	11	2	7	249	12.9		29	48.3	15:21	36	4	6	10	20	0	0	0	11:25

/HL East First All-Star Team (2006) • Canadian Major Junior Second All-Star Team (2006) • AHL All-Rookie Team (2007) • AHL Second All-Star Team (2007)

BROWN, Dustin

(BROWN, DUHS-tihn) **L.A.**

Left wing. Shoots right. 6', 208 lbs. Born, Ithaca, NY, November 4, 1984. Los Angeles' 1st choice, 13th overall, in 2003 Entry Draft.

Season	Club	League	GP	G	A	Pts	PIM	PP	SH	GW	S	%	+/-	TF	F%	Min	GP	G	A	Pts	PIM	PP	SH	GW	Min
1998-99	Ithaca	High-NY	18	4	13	17	....	....	....	....	....	....	....	....	....	....	....	....	....	....	....	....	....	....	....
99-2000	Ithaca	High-NY	24	33	21	53	....	....	....	....	....	....	....	....	....	....	....	....	....	....	....	....	....	....	....
2000-01	Guelph Storm	OHL	53	23	22	45	45	....	....	....	....	....	....	....	....	....	4	0	0	0	10	....	....	....	....
2001-02	Guelph Storm	OHL	63	41	32	73	56	....	....	....	....	....	....	....	....	....	9	8	5	13	14	....	....	....	....
2002-03	Guelph Storm	OHL	58	34	42	76	89	....	....	....	....	....	....	....	....	....	11	7	8	15	6	....	....	....	....
2003-04	Los Angeles	NHL	31	1	4	5	16	0	0	0	40	2.5	0	1	0.0	10:29	....	....	....	....	....	....	....	....	....
2004-05	Manchester	AHL	79	29	45	74	96	....	....	....	....	....	....	....	....	....	6	5	2	7	10	....	....	....	....
2005-06	Los Angeles	NHL	79	14	14	28	80	6	0	2	159	8.8	–10	15	66.7	13:59	....	....	....	....	....	....	....	....	....
2006-07	Los Angeles	NHL	81	17	29	46	54	13	0	1	195	8.7	–21	77	49.4	18:43	....	....	....	....	....	....	....	....	....
2007-08	Los Angeles	NHL	78	33	27	60	55	12	2	4	219	15.1	–13	40	50.0	20:18	....	....	....	....	....	....	....	....	....
2008-09	Los Angeles	NHL	80	24	29	53	64	7	0	6	292	8.2	–15	54	46.3	19:24	....	....	....	....	....	....	....	....	....
2009-10	Los Angeles	NHL	82	24	32	56	41	7	0	3	248	9.7	–6	39	43.6	19:15	6	1	4	5	6	1	0	0	18:53
	United States	Olympics	6	0	0	0	0	....	....	....	....	....	....	....	....	....	....	....	....	....	....	....	....	....	....
	NHL Totals		431	113	135	248	310	45	2	16	1153	9.8		226	48.7	17:46	6	1	4	5	6	1	0	0	18:53

HL All-Rookie Team (2001) • Canadian Major Junior Scholastic Player of the Year (2003)

ayed in NHL All-Star Game (2009)

Missed majority of 2003-04 season recovering from ankle injury suffered in game vs. Chicago, November 29, 2003.

BROWN, Mike

(BROWN, MIGHK) **TOR.**

Right wing. Shoots right. 5'11", 201 lbs. Born, Northbrook, IL, June 24, 1985. Vancouver's 4th choice, 159th overall, in 2004 Entry Draft.

Season	Club	League	GP	G	A	Pts	PIM	PP	SH	GW	S	%	+/-	TF	F%	Min	Playoffs GP	G	A	Pts	PIM	PP	SH	GW	Min
						Regular Season																			
2000-01	Chicago Chill	USAHA	66	27	23	50	....	....	....	....	....	....	....	....	....	....	....	....	....	....	....	....	....	....	....
2001-02	USNTDP	U-17	17	6	4	10	13	....	....	....	....	....	....	....	....	....	....	....	....	....	....	....	....	....	....
	USNTDP	NAHL	46	5	11	16	56	....	....	....	....	....	....	....	....	....	....	....	....	....	....	....	....	....	....
2002-03	USNTDP	U-18	34	5	3	8	16	....	....	....	....	....	....	....	....	....	....	....	....	....	....	....	....	....	....
	USNTDP	NAHL	9	0	3	3	29	....	....	....	....	....	....	....	....	....	....	....	....	....	....	....	....	....	....
2003-04	U. of Michigan	CCHA	42	8	5	13	51	....	....	....	....	....	....	....	....	....	....	....	....	....	....	....	....	....	....
2004-05	U. of Michigan	CCHA	35	3	5	8	95	....	....	....	....	....	....	....	....	....	....	....	....	....	....	....	....	....	....
2005-06	Manitoba Moose	AHL	73	7	8	15	139	....	....	....	....	....	....	....	....	....	13	1	2	3	17	....	....	....	....
2006-07	Manitoba Moose	AHL	62	3	0	3	194	....	....	....	....	....	....	....	....	....	13	0	2	2	16	....	....	....	....
2007-08	**Vancouver**	**NHL**	**19**	**1**	**0**	**1**	**55**	**0**	**0**	**0**	**9**	**11.1**	**–2**	**0**	**0.0**	**6:19**	....	....	....	....	....	....	....	....	....
	Manitoba Moose	AHL	54	10	3	13	201	....	....	....	....	....	....	....	....	....	6	2	0	2	11	....	....	....	....
2008-09	**Vancouver**	**NHL**	**20**	**0**	**1**	**1**	**85**	**0**	**0**	**0**	**6**	**0.0**	**–5**	**2**	**0.0**	**5:29**	....	....	....	....	....	....	....	....	....
	Anaheim	**NHL**	**28**	**2**	**1**	**3**	**60**	**0**	**0**	**2**	**38**	**5.3**	**–2**	**4**	**0.0**	**10:02**	**13**	**0**	**2**	**2**	**25**	**0**	**0**	**0**	**8:28**
2009-10	**Anaheim**	**NHL**	**75**	**6**	**1**	**7**	**106**	**0**	**1**	**2**	**82**	**7.3**	**1**	**7**	**0.0**	**8:21**	....	....	....	....	....	....	....	....	....
	NHL Totals		**142**	**9**	**3**	**12**	**306**	**0**	**1**	**4**	**135**	**6.7**		**13**	**0.0**	**8:00**	**13**	**0**	**2**	**2**	**25**	**0**	**0**	**0**	**8:28**

Traded to **Anaheim** by **Vancouver** for Nathan McIver, February 4, 2009. Traded to **Toronto** by **Anaheim** for Toronto's 5th round choice (Chris Wagner) in 2010 Entry Draft, June 25, 2010.

BRULE, Gilbert

(broo-LAY, zhihl-BAIR) **EDM.**

Center. Shoots right. 5'10", 180 lbs. Born, Edmonton, Alta., January 1, 1987. Columbus' 1st choice, 6th overall, in 2005 Entry Draft.

Season	Club	League	GP	G	A	Pts	PIM	PP	SH	GW	S	%	+/-	TF	F%	Min	Playoffs GP	G	A	Pts	PIM	PP	SH	GW	Min
2002-03	Quesnel	BCHL	48	32	25	57	71	....	....	....	....	....	....	....	....	....	....	....	....	....	....	....	....	....	....
	Vancouver Giants	WHL	1	0	0	0	0	....	....	....	....	....	....	....	....	....	4	1	0	1	0	....	....	....	....
2003-04	Vancouver Giants	WHL	67	25	35	60	100	....	....	....	....	....	....	....	....	....	11	4	5	9	10	....	....	....	....
2004-05	Vancouver Giants	WHL	70	39	48	87	169	....	....	....	....	....	....	....	....	....	6	1	3	4	8	....	....	....	....
2005-06	**Columbus**	**NHL**	**7**	**2**	**2**	**4**	**0**	**0**	**0**	**0**	**11**	**18.2**	**–2**	**60**	**43.3**	**13:11**	....	....	....	....	....	....	....	....	....
	Vancouver Giants	WHL	27	23	15	38	40	....	....	....	....	....	....	....	....	....	18	*16	14	*30	44	....	....	....	....
2006-07	**Columbus**	**NHL**	**78**	**9**	**10**	**19**	**28**	**3**	**0**	**0**	**98**	**9.2**	**–21**	**268**	**45.9**	**10:39**	....	....	....	....	....	....	....	....	....
2007-08	**Columbus**	**NHL**	**61**	**1**	**8**	**9**	**24**	**0**	**0**	**1**	**74**	**1.4**	**–4**	**78**	**51.3**	**9:54**	....	....	....	....	....	....	....	....	....
	Syracuse Crunch	AHL	16	5	5	10	44	....	....	....	....	....	....	....	....	....	13	2	3	5	16	....	....	....	....
2008-09	**Edmonton**	**NHL**	**11**	**2**	**1**	**3**	**12**	**0**	**0**	**1**	**13**	**15.4**	**–3**	**5**	**80.0**	**9:52**	....	....	....	....	....	....	....	....	....
	Springfield	AHL	39	13	11	24	58	....	....	....	....	....	....	....	....	....	....	....	....	....	....	....	....	....	....
2009-10	**Edmonton**	**NHL**	**65**	**17**	**20**	**37**	**38**	**2**	**0**	**3**	**121**	**14.0**	**–8**	**274**	**52.6**	**14:14**	....	....	....	....	....	....	....	....	....
	NHL Totals		**222**	**31**	**41**	**72**	**102**	**5**	**0**	**5**	**317**	**9.8**		**685**	**49.2**	**11:32**	....	....	....	....	....	....	....	....	....

WHL West First All-Star Team (2005) • Canadian Major Junior Second All-Star Team (2005) • Canadian Major Junior Scholastic Player of the Year (2005) • WHL West Second All-Star Team (2006) • Memorial Cup Tournament All-Star Team (2006) • Ed Chynoweth Trophy (Memorial Cup Tournament - Leading Scorer) (2006)

• Missed majority of 2005-06 season recovering from sternum (October 7, 2005 vs. Calgary) and leg (November 30, 2005 at Minnesota) injuries. Traded to **Edmonton** by **Columbus** for Raffi Torres, July 1, 2008.

BRUNETTE, Andrew

(broo-NEHT, AN-droo) **MIN.**

Left wing. Shoots left. 6'1", 210 lbs. Born, Sudbury, Ont., August 24, 1973. Washington's 6th choice, 174th overall, in 1993 Entry Draft.

Season	Club	League	GP	G	A	Pts	PIM	PP	SH	GW	S	%	+/-	TF	F%	Min	Playoffs GP	G	A	Pts	PIM	PP	SH	GW	Min
1989-90	Rayside-Balfour	NOHA	32	38	*65	*103	....	....	....	....	....	....	....	....	....	....	....	....	....	....	....	....	....	....	....
	Rayside-Balfour	NOJHA	4	1	1	2	0	....	....	....	....	....	....	....	....	....	....	....	....	....	....	....	....	....	....
1990-91	Owen Sound	OHL	63	15	20	35	15	....	....	....	....	....	....	....	....	....	....	....	....	....	....	....	....	....	....
1991-92	Owen Sound	OHL	66	51	47	98	42	....	....	....	....	....	....	....	....	....	5	5	0	5	8	....	....	....	....
1992-93	Owen Sound	OHL	66	*62	*100	*162	91	....	....	....	....	....	....	....	....	....	8	8	6	14	16	....	....	....	....
1993-94	Portland Pirates	AHL	23	9	11	20	10	....	....	....	....	....	....	....	....	....	2	0	1	1	0	....	....	....	....
	Providence Bruins	AHL	3	0	0	0	0	....	....	....	....	....	....	....	....	....	....	....	....	....	....	....	....	....	....
	Hampton Roads	ECHL	20	12	18	30	32	....	....	....	....	....	....	....	....	....	7	7	6	13	18	....	....	....	....
1994-95	Portland Pirates	AHL	79	30	50	80	53	....	....	....	....	....	....	....	....	....	7	3	3	6	10	....	....	....	....
1995-96	**Washington**	**NHL**	**11**	**3**	**3**	**6**	**0**	**0**	**0**	**1**	**16**	**18.8**	**5**	....	....	....	**6**	**1**	**3**	**4**	**0**	**0**	**0**	**0**	....
	Portland Pirates	AHL	69	28	66	94	125	....	....	....	....	....	....	....	....	....	20	11	18	29	15	....	....	....	....
1996-97	**Washington**	**NHL**	**23**	**4**	**7**	**11**	**12**	**2**	**0**	**0**	**23**	**17.4**	**–3**	....	....	....	....	....	....	....	....	....	....	....	....
	Portland Pirates	AHL	50	22	51	73	48	....	....	....	....	....	....	....	....	....	5	1	2	3	0	....	....	....	....
1997-98	**Washington**	**NHL**	**28**	**11**	**12**	**23**	**12**	**4**	**0**	**2**	**42**	**26.2**	**2**	....	....	....	....	....	....	....	....	....	....	....	....
	Portland Pirates	AHL	43	21	46	67	64	....	....	....	....	....	....	....	....	....	10	1	11	12	12	....	....	....	....
1998-99	**Nashville**	**NHL**	**77**	**11**	**20**	**31**	**26**	**7**	**0**	**1**	**65**	**16.9**	**–10**	**8**	**50.0**	**13:13**	....	....	....	....	....	....	....	....	....
99-2000	**Atlanta**	**NHL**	**81**	**23**	**27**	**50**	**30**	**9**	**0**	**2**	**107**	**21.5**	**–32**	**8**	**25.0**	**15:42**	....	....	....	....	....	....	....	....	....
2000-01	**Atlanta**	**NHL**	**77**	**15**	**44**	**59**	**26**	**6**	**0**	**4**	**104**	**14.4**	**–5**	**11**	**54.6**	**16:58**	....	....	....	....	....	....	....	....	....
2001-02	**Minnesota**	**NHL**	**81**	**21**	**48**	**69**	**18**	**10**	**0**	**2**	**106**	**19.8**	**–4**	**111**	**58.6**	**16:02**	....	....	....	....	....	....	....	....	....
2002-03	**Minnesota**	**NHL**	**82**	**18**	**28**	**46**	**30**	**9**	**0**	**2**	**97**	**18.6**	**–10**	**59**	**44.1**	**14:29**	**18**	**7**	**6**	**13**	**4**	**4**	**0**	**1**	**15:00**
2003-04	**Minnesota**	**NHL**	**82**	**15**	**34**	**49**	**12**	**7**	**0**	**3**	**90**	**16.7**	**3**	**49**	**46.9**	**15:32**	....	....	....	....	....	....	....	....	....
2004-05			DID NOT PLAY																						
2005-06	**Colorado**	**NHL**	**82**	**24**	**39**	**63**	**48**	**11**	**0**	**2**	**129**	**18.6**	**9**	**18**	**33.3**	**15:01**	**9**	**3**	**6**	**9**	**8**	**1**	**0**	**1**	**17:47**
2006-07	**Colorado**	**NHL**	**82**	**27**	**56**	**83**	**36**	**9**	**0**	**2**	**173**	**15.6**	**–8**	**8**	**62.5**	**17:31**	....	....	....	....	....	....	....	....	....
2007-08	**Colorado**	**NHL**	**82**	**19**	**40**	**59**	**14**	**7**	**0**	**2**	**125**	**15.2**	**5**	**8**	**37.5**	**15:33**	**10**	**5**	**3**	**8**	**2**	**3**	**0**	**0**	**17:02**
2008-09	**Minnesota**	**NHL**	**80**	**22**	**28**	**50**	**18**	**9**	**0**	**3**	**118**	**18.6**	**–5**	**9**	**22.2**	**16:57**	....	....	....	....	....	....	....	....	....
2009-10	**Minnesota**	**NHL**	**82**	**25**	**36**	**61**	**12**	**12**	**0**	**3**	**129**	**19.4**	**–5**	**10**	**50.0**	**17:02**	....	....	....	....	....	....	....	....	....
	NHL Totals		**950**	**238**	**422**	**660**	**294**	**102**	**0**	**29**	**1324**	**18.0**		**299**	**49.2**	**15:49**	**43**	**16**	**18**	**34**	**14**	**8**	**0**	**2**	**16:13**

OHL First All-Star Team (1993) • Canadian Major Junior Second All-Star Team (1993) • AHL Second All-Star Team (1995)

Claimed by **Nashville** from **Washington** in Expansion Draft, June 26, 1998. Traded to **Atlanta** by **Nashville** for Atlanta's 5th round choice (Matt Hendricks) in 2000 Entry Draft, June 21, 1999. Signed as a free agent by **Minnesota**, July 17, 2001. Signed as a free agent by **Colorado**, August 6, 2005. Signed as a free agent by **Minnesota**, July 1, 2008.

BRUNNSTROM, Fabian

{BRUHN-struhm, FAY-bee-yehn) **DAL.**

Left wing. Shoots left. 6'2", 212 lbs. Born, Jonstorp, Sweden, February 6, 1985.

Season	Club	League	GP	G	A	Pts	PIM	PP	SH	GW	S	%	+/-	TF	F%	Min	Playoffs GP	G	A	Pts	PIM	PP	SH	GW	Min
2002-03	Jonstorps IF	Sweden-3	STATISTICS NOT AVAILABLE																						
2003-04	Helsingborgs HC	Sweden-4	....	6	7	13	....	....	....	....	....	....	....	....	....	....	....	....	....	....	....	....	....	....	....
2004-05	Helsingborgs HC	Sweden-4	....	18	11	29	....	....	....	....	....	....	....	....	....	....	....	....	....	....	....	....	....	....	....
2005-06	Jonstorps IF	Sweden-3	38	21	23	44	8	....	....	....	....	....	....	....	....	....	....	....	....	....	....	....	....	....	....
	Rogle	Sweden-2	3	0	0	0	2	....	....	....	....	....	....	....	....	....	....	....	....	....	....	....	....	....	....
2006-07	Boras HC	Sweden-3	49	38	41	79	32	....	....	....	....	....	....	....	....	....	2	1	3	4	0	....	....	....	....
2007-08	Farjestad	Sweden	54	9	28	37	16	....	....	....	....	....	....	....	....	....	12	1	0	1	6	....	....	....	....
2008-09	**Dallas**	**NHL**	**55**	**17**	**12**	**29**	**8**	**4**	**0**	**5**	**81**	**21.0**	**–8**	**0**	**0.0**	**11:37**	....	....	....	....	....	....	....	....	....
	Manitoba Moose	AHL	1	0	0	0	0	....	....	....	....	....	....	....	....	....	....	....	....	....	....	....	....	....	....
2009-10	**Dallas**	**NHL**	**44**	**2**	**9**	**11**	**10**	**0**	**0**	**0**	**38**	**5.3**	**–3**	**3**	**33.3**	**10:40**	....	....	....	....	....	....	....	....	....
	Texas Stars	AHL	8	1	4	5	2	....	....	....	....	....	....	....	....	....	....	....	....	....	....	....	....	....	....
	NHL Totals		**99**	**19**	**21**	**40**	**18**	**4**	**0**	**5**	**119**	**16.0**		**3**	**33.3**	**11:12**	....	....	....	....	....	....	....	....	....

Signed as a free agent by **Dallas**, May 8, 2008.

BURISH, Adam

(BUHR-ish, A-duhm) **DAL.**

Right wing. Shoots right. 6', 189 lbs. Born, Madison, WI, January 6, 1983. Chicago's 9th choice, 282nd overall, in 2002 Entry Draft.

Season	Club	League	GP	G	A	Pts	PIM	PP	SH	GW	S	%	+/-	TF	F%	Min	Playoffs GP	G	A	Pts	PIM	PP	SH	GW	Min
2000-01	Edgewood	High-WI	22	25	30	55	22	....	....	....	....	....	....	....	....	....	....	....	....	....	....	....	....	....	....
2001-02	Green Bay	USHL	61	24	33	57	122	....	....	....	....	....	....	....	....	....	1	0	0	0	0	....	....	....	....
2002-03	U. of Wisconsin	WCHA	19	0	6	6	32	....	....	....	....	....	....	....	....	....	....	....	....	....	....	....	....	....	....
2003-04	U. of Wisconsin	WCHA	43	6	13	19	63	....	....	....	....	....	....	....	....	....	....	....	....	....	....	....	....	....	....
2004-05	U. of Wisconsin	WCHA	41	13	7	20	41	....	....	....	....	....	....	....	....	....	....	....	....	....	....	....	....	....	....
2005-06	U. of Wisconsin	WCHA	42	9	24	33	67	....	....	....	....	....	....	....	....	....	....	....	....	....	....	....	....	....	....
2006-07	**Chicago**	**NHL**	**9**	**0**	**0**	**0**	**2**	**0**	**0**	**0**	**12**	**0.0**	**–4**	**6**	**50.0**	**11:08**	....	....	....	....	....	....	....	....	....
	Norfolk Admirals	AHL	64	11	10	21	146	....	....	....	....	....	....	....	....	....	6	1	1	2	4	....	....	....	....
2007-08	**Chicago**	**NHL**	**81**	**4**	**4**	**8**	**214**	**0**	**1**	**1**	**69**	**5.8**	**–13**	**264**	**42.1**	**11:45**	....	....	....	....	....	....	....	....	....

Season	Club	League	GP	G	A	Pts	PIM	PP	SH	GW	S	%	+/-	TF	F%	Min	GP	G	A	Pts	PIM	PP	SH	GW	Min
2008-09	Chicago	NHL	66	6	3	9	93	0	0	2	83	7.2	3	124	39.5	9:12	17	3	2	5	30	0	0	1	11:02
2009-10 ♦	Chicago	NHL	13	1	3	4	14	0	0	0	9	11.1	2	21	33.3	8:46	15	0	0	0	2	0	0	0	5:35
	NHL Totals		169	11	10	21	323	0	1	3	173	6.4		415	41.0	10:30	32	3	2	5	32	0	0	1	8:29

NCAA Championship All-Tournament Team (2006)
Missed majority of 2009-10 season recovering from knee injury, suffered in pre-season game at Minnesota, September 20, 2009. Signed as a free agent by **Dallas**, July 1, 2010.

BURNS, Brent
(BUHRNZ, BREHNT)   **MIN.**

Defense. Shoots right. 6'5", 219 lbs.   Born, Ajax, Ont., March 9, 1985. Minnesota's 1st choice, 20th overall, in 2003 Entry Draft.

Season	Club	League	GP	G	A	Pts	PIM	PP	SH	GW	S	%	+/-	TF	F%	Min	GP	G	A	Pts	PIM	PP	SH	GW	Min
2000-01	North York	MTHL	46	4	7	11	16																		
2001-02	Couchiching	OPJHL	68	15	25	40	14																		
2002-03	Brampton	OHL	68	15	25	40	14											11	5	6	11	6				
2003-04	**Minnesota**	**NHL**	36	1	5	6	12	0	0	0	34	2.9	−10	7	28.6	13:29									
	Houston Aeros	AHL	1	0	1	1	2																		
2004-05	Houston Aeros	AHL	73	11	16	27	57										5	0	0	0	4				
2005-06	**Minnesota**	**NHL**	72	4	12	16	32	1	0	1	73	5.5	−7	11	54.6	14:07									
2006-07	**Minnesota**	**NHL**	77	7	18	25	26	3	0	3	108	6.5	16	4	25.0	15:48	5	0	1	1	14	0	0	0	18:59
2007-08	**Minnesota**	**NHL**	82	15	28	43	80	8	0	4	158	9.5	12	1100.0		23:06	6	0	2	2	6	0	0	0	27:35
2008-09	**Minnesota**	**NHL**	59	8	19	27	45	4	0	2	147	5.4	−7	5	60.0	22:22									
2009-10	**Minnesota**	**NHL**	47	3	17	20	32	2	0	0	104	2.9	−15	0	0.0	22:22									
	NHL Totals		373	38	99	137	227	18	0	10	624	6.1		28	46.4	18:44	11	0	3	3	20	0	0	0	23:40

Missed majority of 2003-04 season on assignment to Team Canada and as a healthy reserve. • Missed majority of 2009-10 season recovering from head injury suffered in game vs. Phoenix, November 18, 2009.

BURROWS, Alexandre
(BUHR-ohz, al-ehx-AHN-druh)   **VAN.**

Left wing. Shoots left. 6'1", 188 lbs.   Born, Pincourt, Que., April 11, 1981.

Season	Club	League	GP	G	A	Pts	PIM	PP	SH	GW	S	%	+/-	TF	F%	Min	GP	G	A	Pts	PIM	PP	SH	GW	Min
2000-01	Shawinigan	QMJHL	63	16	14	30	105										10	2	1	3	8				
2001-02	Shawinigan	QMJHL	64	35	35	70	184										10	9	10	19	20				
2002-03	Greenville	ECHL	53	9	17	26	201																		
	Baton Rouge	ECHL	13	4	2	6	64																		
2003-04	Manitoba Moose	AHL	2	0	0	0	0																		
	Columbia Inferno	ECHL	64	29	44	73	194										4	2	0	2	28				
2004-05	Manitoba Moose	AHL	72	9	17	26	107										14	0	3	3	37				
	Columbia Inferno	ECHL	4	5	1	6	4																		
2005-06	**Vancouver**	**NHL**	43	7	5	12	61	0	1	1	49	14.3	5	19	47.4	10:24									
	Manitoba Moose	AHL	33	12	18	30	57										13	6	7	13	27				
2006-07	**Vancouver**	**NHL**	81	3	6	9	93	0	0	1	70	4.3	−7	16	43.8	11:26	11	1	0	1	14	0	0	0	10:34
2007-08	**Vancouver**	**NHL**	82	12	19	31	179	1	3	3	126	9.5	11	37	35.1	15:06									
2008-09	**Vancouver**	**NHL**	82	28	23	51	150	0	4	3	175	16.0	23	80	46.3	16:51	10	3	1	4	20	0	0	1	18:48
2009-10	**Vancouver**	**NHL**	82	35	32	67	121	4	5	3	209	16.7	34	34	41.2	17:52	12	3	3	6	22	0	0	0	18:51
	NHL Totals		370	85	85	170	604	5	13	11	629	13.5		186	43.0	14:45	33	7	4	11	56	0	0	1	16:04

Signed as a free agent by **Manitoba** (AHL), October 21, 2003. Signed as a free agent by **Vancouver**, November 8, 2005.

BUTLER, Bobby
(BUHT-luhr, BAW-bee)   **OTT.**

Right wing. Shoots right. 6', 185 lbs.   Born, Marlborough, MA, April 26, 1987.

Season	Club	League	GP	G	A	Pts	PIM	PP	SH	GW	S	%	+/-	TF	F%	Min	GP	G	A	Pts	PIM	PP	SH	GW	Min
2002-03	Bos. Little Bruins	Minor-MA	35	21	27	48	12																		
2003-04	Bos. Jr. Bruins	EJHL	13	1	3	4	0																		
2004-05	Bos. Jr. Bruins	EJHL	59	15	18	33	28																		
2005-06	Bos. Jr. Bruins	EJHL	56	19	20	39	20																		
	Bos. Jr. Bruins	EJHL	61	28	30	58	48																		
2006-07	New Hampshire	H-East	38	9	3	12	12																		
2007-08	New Hampshire	H-East	38	14	12	26	20																		
2008-09	New Hampshire	H-East	38	9	21	30	36																		
2009-10	New Hampshire	H-East	39	29	24	53	20																		
	Ottawa	**NHL**	2	0	0	0	0	0	0	0	2	0.0	−1	0	0.0	8:21									
	NHL Totals		2	0	0	0	0	0	0	0	2	0.0		0	0.0	8:21									

Hockey East First All-Star Team (2010) • Hockey East Player of the Year (2010) • NCAA East First All-American Team (2010)
Signed as a free agent by **Ottawa**, March 29, 2010.

BUTLER, Chris
(BUHT-luhr, KRIHS)   **BUF.**

Defense. Shoots left. 6'2", 205 lbs.   Born, St. Louis, MO, October 27, 1986. Buffalo's 4th choice, 96th overall, in 2005 Entry Draft.

Season	Club	League	GP	G	A	Pts	PIM	PP	SH	GW	S	%	+/-	TF	F%	Min	GP	G	A	Pts	PIM	PP	SH	GW	Min
2003-04	Sioux City	USHL	55	3	6	9	37										7	0	1	1	6				
2004-05	Sioux City	USHL	60	6	22	28	90										13	1	6	7	10				
2005-06	U. of Denver	WCHA	35	7	15	22	28																		
2006-07	U. of Denver	WCHA	39	10	17	27	42																		
2007-08	U. of Denver	WCHA	41	3	14	17	38																		
2008-09	**Buffalo**	**NHL**	47	2	4	6	18	0	0	1	36	5.6	11	0	0.0	16:43									
	Portland Pirates	AHL	27	2	10	12	14										4	0	0	0	0				
2009-10	**Buffalo**	**NHL**	59	1	20	21	22	0	0	0	61	1.6	−15	0	0.0	20:01									
	NHL Totals		106	3	24	27	40	0	0	1	97	3.1		0	0.0	18:33									

USHL First All-Star Team (2005) • WCHA All-Rookie Team (2006) • WCHA Second All-Star Team (2008) • NCAA West Second All-American Team (2008)

BYERS, Dane
(BIGH-uhrs, DAYN)   **NYR**

Left wing. Shoots left. 6'3", 204 lbs.   Born, Nipawin, Sask., February 21, 1986. NY Rangers' 4th choice, 48th overall, in 2004 Entry Draft.

Season	Club	League	GP	G	A	Pts	PIM	PP	SH	GW	S	%	+/-	TF	F%	Min	GP	G	A	Pts	PIM	PP	SH	GW	Min
2002-03	Prince Albert	WHL	49	8	6	14	46																		
2003-04	Prince Albert	WHL	51	9	8	17	134										6	1	2	3	17				
2004-05	Prince Albert	WHL	65	11	9	20	181										17	4	6	10	18				
2005-06	Prince Albert	WHL	71	21	27	48	157																		
	Hartford	AHL	5	0	2	2	6																		
2006-07	Hartford	AHL	78	17	30	47	213										7	2	0	2	16				
2007-08	**NY Rangers**	**NHL**	1	0	0	0	0	0	0	0	0	0.0	−1	0	0.0	5:05									
	Hartford	AHL	73	23	23	46	184										5	2	1	3	2				
2008-09	Hartford	AHL	9	4	3	7	18										6	3	1	4	7				
2009-10	**NY Rangers**	**NHL**	5	1	0	1	31	0	0	0	3	33.3	1	0	0.0	6:21									
	Hartford	AHL	74	25	27	52	100																		
	NHL Totals		6	1	0	1	31	0	0	0	3	33.3		0	0.0	6:09									

Missed majority of 2008-09 season recovering from knee injury, suffered in game vs. Worcester (AHL), October 31, 2008..

BYFUGLIEN, Dustin
(BUHF-lihn, DUHS-tihn)   **ATL.**

Right wing. Shoots right. 6'4", 255 lbs.   Born, Minneapolis, MN, March 27, 1985. Chicago's 8th choice, 245th overall, in 2003 Entry Draft.

Season	Club	League	GP	G	A	Pts	PIM	PP	SH	GW	S	%	+/-	TF	F%	Min	GP	G	A	Pts	PIM	PP	SH	GW	Min
2001-02	Chicago Mission	MAHL	52	32	30	62	40																		
	Brandon	WHL	3	0	0	0	0																		
2002-03	Brandon	WHL	8	1	1	2	4																		
	Prince George	WHL	48	9	28	37	74										5	1	3	4	12·				
2003-04	Prince George	WHL	66	16	29	45	137																		
2004-05	Prince George	WHL	64	22	36	58	184																		
2005-06	**Chicago**	**NHL**	25	3	2	5	24	0	0	1	45	6.7	−6	0	0.0	17:19									
	Norfolk Admirals	AHL	53	8	15	23	75										4	1	2	3	4				
2006-07	**Chicago**	**NHL**	9	1	2	3	10	0	0	0	18	5.6	−2	0	0.0	17:18									
	Norfolk Admirals	AHL	63	16	28	44	146										6	0	2	2	18				
2007-08	**Chicago**	**NHL**	67	19	17	36	59	7	0	4	163	11.7	−7	1	0.0	17:02									
	Rockford IceHogs	AHL	8	2	5	7	25																		

			Regular Season														Playoffs								
Season	Club	League	GP	G	A	Pts	PIM	PP	SH	GW	S	%	+/-	TF	F%	Min	GP	G	A	Pts	PIM	PP	SH	GW	Min
2008-09	Chicago	NHL	77	15	16	31	81	3	0	4	202	7.4	7	11	18.2	14:52	17	3	6	9	26	1	0	0	17:11
2009-10♦	Chicago	NHL	82	17	17	34	94	6	0	3	211	8.1	-7	2	50.0	16:25	22	11	5	16	20	5	0	5	16:16
	NHL Totals		260	55	54	109	268	16	0	12	639	8.6		14	21.4	16:14	39	14	11	25	46	6	0	5	16:40

AHL Second All-Star Team (2007)

Traded to **Atlanta** by **Chicago** with Brent Sopel, Ben Eager and Akim Aliu for Marty Reasoner, Joey Crabb, Jeremy Morin and New Jersey's 1st (previously acquired, Chicago selected Kevin Hayes) and 2nd (previously acquired, Chicago selected Justin Holl) round choices in 2010 Entry Draft, June 24, 2010.

CALDER, Kyle

(KAWL-duhr, KIGHL)

Left wing. Shoots left. 5'11", 177 lbs. Born, Mannville, Alta., January 5, 1979. Chicago's 7th choice, 130th overall, in 1997 Entry Draft.

Season	Club	League	GP	G	A	Pts	PIM	PP	SH	GW	S	%	+/-	TF	F%	Min	GP	G	A	Pts	PIM	PP	SH	GW	Min
1994-95	Leduc Oil Barons	AMHL	27	25	32	57	22	....	....	....	....	....	....	....	....	....	....	....	....	....	....	....	....	....	....
1995-96	Regina Pats	WHL	27	1	7	8	10	....	....	....	....	....	....	....	....	....	11	0	0	0	0	....	....	....	....
1996-97	Regina Pats	WHL	62	25	34	59	17	....	....	....	....	....	....	....	....	....	5	3	0	3	6	....	....	....	....
1997-98	Regina Pats	WHL	62	27	50	77	58	....	....	....	....	....	....	....	....	....	2	0	1	1	0	....	....	....	....
1998-99	Regina Pats	WHL	34	23	28	51	29	....	....	....	....	....	....	....	....	....	....	....	....	....	....	....	....	....	....
	Kamloops Blazers	WHL	27	19	18	37	30	....	....	....	....	....	....	....	....	....	15	6	10	16	6	....	....	....	....
99-2000	**Chicago**	**NHL**	**8**	**1**	**1**	**2**	**2**	**0**	**0**	**0**	**5**	**20.0**	**-3**	**2**	**0.0**	**9:59**	....	....	....	....	....	....	....	....	....
	Cleveland	IHL	74	14	22	36	43	....	....	....	....	....	....	....	....	....	9	2	2	4	14	....	....	....	....
2000-01	**Chicago**	**NHL**	**43**	**5**	**10**	**15**	**14**	**0**	**0**	**1**	**63**	**7.9**	**-4**	**2**	**0.0**	**12:43**	....	....	....	....	....	....	....	....	....
	Norfolk Admirals	AHL	37	12	15	27	21	....	....	....	....	....	....	....	....	....	9	2	6	8	2	....	....	....	....
2001-02	**Chicago**	**NHL**	**81**	**17**	**36**	**53**	**47**	**6**	**0**	**3**	**133**	**12.8**	**8**	**0**	**0.0**	**16:33**	**5**	**2**	**0**	**2**	**2**	**1**	**0**	**0**	**16:45**
2002-03	**Chicago**	**NHL**	**82**	**15**	**27**	**42**	**40**	**7**	**0**	**2**	**164**	**9.1**	**-6**	**4**	**25.0**	**16:43**	....	....	....	....	....	....	....	....	....
2003-04	**Chicago**	**NHL**	**66**	**21**	**18**	**39**	**29**	**10**	**0**	**1**	**144**	**14.6**	**-18**	**13**	**30.8**	**17:08**	....	....	....	....	....	....	....	....	....
2004-05	Sodertalje SK	Sweden	12	5	1	6	6	....	....	....	....	....	....	....	....	....	10	5	1	6	2	....	....	....	....
2005-06	**Chicago**	**NHL**	**79**	**26**	**33**	**59**	**52**	**6**	**2**	**6**	**183**	**14.2**	**-4**	**13**	**46.2**	**18:23**	....	....	....	....	....	....	....	....	....
2006-07	**Philadelphia**	**NHL**	**59**	**9**	**12**	**21**	**36**	**2**	**2**	**0**	**88**	**10.2**	**-31**	**10**	**30.0**	**15:02**	....	....	....	....	....	....	....	....	....
	Detroit	**NHL**	**19**	**5**	**9**	**14**	**22**	**1**	**0**	**2**	**42**	**11.9**	**6**	**2**	**50.0**	**17:05**	**13**	**0**	**1**	**1**	**8**	**0**	**0**	**0**	**8:59**
2007-08	**Los Angeles**	**NHL**	**65**	**7**	**13**	**20**	**18**	**3**	**0**	**0**	**70**	**10.0**	**-11**	**18**	**38.9**	**13:00**	....	....	....	....	....	....	....	....	....
2008-09	**Los Angeles**	**NHL**	**74**	**8**	**19**	**27**	**41**	**2**	**0**	**1**	**93**	**8.6**	**-1**	**3**	**33.3**	**13:10**	....	....	....	....	....	....	....	....	....
2009-10	**Anaheim**	**NHL**	**14**	**0**	**2**	**2**	**8**	**0**	**0**	**0**	**20**	**0.0**	**-7**	**4**	**25.0**	**14:07**	....	....	....	....	....	....	....	....	....
	Toronto Marlies	AHL	40	14	16	30	18	....	....	....	....	....	....	....	....	....	....	....	....	....	....	....	....	....	....
	Bakersfield	ECHL	5	3	3	6	0	....	....	....	....	....	....	....	....	....	10	5	5	10	4	....	....	....	....
	NHL Totals		**590**	**114**	**180**	**294**	**309**	**37**	**4**	**16**	**1005**	**11.3**		**71**	**33.8**	**15:31**	**18**	**2**	**1**	**3**	**10**	**1**	**0**	**0**	**11:09**

Signed as a free agent by **Sodertalje** (Sweden), January 20, 2005. Traded to **Philadelphia** by **Chicago** for Michael Handzus, August 4, 2006. Traded to **Chicago** by **Philadelphia** for Lasse Kukkonen and Chicago's 3rd round choice (Garrett Klotz) in 2007 Entry Draft, February 26, 2007. Traded to **Detroit** by **Chicago** for Jason Williams, February 26, 2007. Signed as a free agent by **Los Angeles**, July 2, 2007. Signed as a free agent by **Anaheim**, October 27, 2009.

CALDWELL, Ryan

(KAWLD-wehl, RIGH-uhn)

Defense. Shoots left. 6'2", 174 lbs. Born, Deloraine, Man., June 15, 1981. NY Islanders' 7th choice, 202nd overall, in 2000 Entry Draft.

Season	Club	League	GP	G	A	Pts	PIM	PP	SH	GW	S	%	+/-	TF	F%	Min	GP	G	A	Pts	PIM	PP	SH	GW	Min
1998-99	Shat.-St. Mary's	High-MN	29	24	55	79	22	....	....	....	....	....	....	....	....	....	....	....	....	....	....	....	....	....	....
99-2000	Thunder Bay	USHL	46	3	20	23	152	....	....	....	....	....	....	....	....	....	....	....	....	....	....	....	....	....	....
2000-01	U. of Denver	WCHA	36	3	20	23	76	....	....	....	....	....	....	....	....	....	....	....	....	....	....	....	....	....	....
2001-02	U. of Denver	WCHA	40	3	16	19	76	....	....	....	....	....	....	....	....	....	....	....	....	....	....	....	....	....	....
2002-03	U. of Denver	WCHA	38	5	14	19	58	....	....	....	....	....	....	....	....	....	....	....	....	....	....	....	....	....	....
2003-04	U. of Denver	WCHA	42	15	12	27	96	....	....	....	....	....	....	....	....	....	....	....	....	....	....	....	....	....	....
2004-05	Bridgeport	AHL	73	2	19	21	65	....	....	....	....	....	....	....	....	....	....	....	....	....	....	....	....	....	....
2005-06	**NY Islanders**	**NHL**	**2**	**0**	**0**	**0**	**2**	**0**	**0**	**0**	**2**	**0.0**	**-2**	**0**	**0.0**	**16:33**	....	....	....	....	....	....	....	....	....
	Bridgeport	AHL	61	2	13	15	38	....	....	....	....	....	....	....	....	....	7	1	1	2	2	....	....	....	....
2006-07	Syracuse Crunch	AHL	61	7	23	30	94	....	....	....	....	....	....	....	....	....	....	....	....	....	....	....	....	....	....
2007-08	**Phoenix**	**NHL**	**2**	**0**	**0**	**0**	**2**	**0**	**0**	**0**	**1**	**0.0**	**0**	**0**	**0.0**	**6:08**	....	....	....	....	....	....	....	....	....
	San Antonio	AHL	71	3	18	21	94	....	....	....	....	....	....	....	....	....	7	0	0	0	4	....	....	....	....
2008-09	Dusseldorf	Germany	47	4	14	18	132	....	....	....	....	....	....	....	....	....	15	3	7	10	33	....	....	....	....
2009-10	Dusseldorf	Germany	55	5	16	21	75	....	....	....	....	....	....	....	....	....	3	0	0	0	6	....	....	....	....
	NHL Totals		**4**	**0**	**0**	**0**	**4**	**0**	**0**	**0**	**3**	**0.0**		**0**	**0.0**	**11:20**	....	....	....	....	....	....	....	....	....

WCHA All-Rookie Team (2001) • WCHA Second All-Star Team (2004) • NCAA West First All-American Team (2004) • NCAA Championship All-Tournament Team (2004)

Traded to **Columbus** by **NY Islanders** for Eric Boguniecki, October 25, 2006. Signed as a free agent by **Phoenix**, July 23, 2007. Signed as a free agent by **Dusseldorf** (Germany), July 31, 2008.

CALLAHAN, Joe

(kal-AH-han, JOH) **FLA**

Defense. Shoots right. 6'3", 220 lbs. Born, Brockton, MA, December 20, 1982. Phoenix's 4th choice, 70th overall, in 2002 Entry Draft.

Season	Club	League	GP	G	A	Pts	PIM	PP	SH	GW	S	%	+/-	TF	F%	Min	GP	G	A	Pts	PIM	PP	SH	GW	Min
2001-02	Yale	ECAC	31	3	8	11	20	....	....	....	....	....	....	....	....	....	....	....	....	....	....	....	....	....	....
2002-03	Yale	ECAC	32	2	11	13	38	....	....	....	....	....	....	....	....	....	....	....	....	....	....	....	....	....	....
2003-04	Yale	ECAC	31	6	14	20	38	....	....	....	....	....	....	....	....	....	....	....	....	....	....	....	....	....	....
	Springfield	AHL	13	0	4	4	12	....	....	....	....	....	....	....	....	....	....	....	....	....	....	....	....	....	....
2004-05	Utah Grizzlies	AHL	75	4	7	11	66	....	....	....	....	....	....	....	....	....	....	....	....	....	....	....	....	....	....
2005-06	San Antonio	AHL	80	1	5	6	88	....	....	....	....	....	....	....	....	....	....	....	....	....	....	....	....	....	....
2006-07	San Antonio	AHL	78	1	13	14	65	....	....	....	....	....	....	....	....	....	....	....	....	....	....	....	....	....	....
2007-08	Portland Pirates	AHL	65	1	23	24	59	....	....	....	....	....	....	....	....	....	18	1	11	12	25	....	....	....	....
2008-09	**NY Islanders**	**NHL**	**18**	**0**	**2**	**2**	**4**	**0**	**0**	**0**	**6**	**0.0**	**5**	**1**	**0.0**	**15:00**	....	....	....	....	....	....	....	....	....
	Bridgeport	AHL	56	4	9	13	38	....	....	....	....	....	....	....	....	....	5	1	2	3	4	....	....	....	....
2009-10	**San Jose**	**NHL**	**1**	**0**	**1**	**1**	**0**	**0**	**0**	**0**	**0**	**0.0**	**1**	**0**	**0.0**	**9:34**	....	....	....	....	....	....	....	....	....
	Worcester Sharks	AHL	35	4	11	15	19	....	....	....	....	....	....	....	....	....	2	0	0	0	2	....	....	....	....
	NHL Totals		**19**	**0**	**3**	**3**	**4**	**0**	**0**	**0**	**6**	**0.0**		**1**	**0.0**	**14:43**	....	....	....	....	....	....	....	....	....

Signed as a free agent by **Anaheim**, July 12, 2007. Signed as a free agent by **NY Islanders**, July 8, 2008. Signed as a free agent by **San Jose**, July 16, 2009. • Missed majority of 2009-10 season recovering from upper body injury and resulting surgery, February 11, 2010. Signed as a free agent by **Florida**, August 3, 2010.

CALLAHAN, Ryan

(kal-AH-han, RIGH-uhn) **NY**

Right wing. Shoots right. 5'11", 188 lbs. Born, Rochester, NY, March 21, 1985. NY Rangers' 9th choice, 127th overall, in 2004 Entry Draft.

Season	Club	League	GP	G	A	Pts	PIM	PP	SH	GW	S	%	+/-	TF	F%	Min	GP	G	A	Pts	PIM	PP	SH	GW	Min
2002-03	Guelph Storm	OHL	59	14	17	31	47	....	....	....	....	....	....	....	....	....	11	0	3	3	2	....	....	....	....
2003-04	Guelph Storm	OHL	68	36	32	68	86	....	....	....	....	....	....	....	....	....	22	*13	8	21	20	....	....	....	....
2004-05	Guelph Storm	OHL	60	28	26	54	108	....	....	....	....	....	....	....	....	....	4	1	1	2	6	....	....	....	....
2005-06	Guelph Storm	OHL	62	52	32	84	126	....	....	....	....	....	....	....	....	....	13	7	17	24	20	....	....	....	....
2006-07	**NY Rangers**	**NHL**	**14**	**4**	**2**	**6**	**9**	**0**	**0**	**1**	**40**	**10.0**	**5**	**3**	**66.7**	**10:31**	**10**	**2**	**1**	**3**	**6**	**1**	**0**	**0**	**12:1**
	Hartford	AHL	60	35	20	55	74	....	....	....	....	....	....	....	....	....	....	....	....	....	....	....	....	....	....
2007-08	**NY Rangers**	**NHL**	**52**	**8**	**5**	**13**	**31**	**0**	**1**	**1**	**92**	**8.7**	**7**	**5**	**20.0**	**12:22**	**10**	**2**	**2**	**4**	**10**	**0**	**1**	**1**	**15:5**
	Hartford	AHL	11	7	8	15	27	....	....	....	....	....	....	....	....	....	....	....	....	....	....	....	....	....	....
2008-09	**NY Rangers**	**NHL**	**81**	**22**	**18**	**40**	**45**	**2**	**1**	**1**	**237**	**9.3**	**7**	**10**	**70.0**	**17:04**	**7**	**2**	**0**	**2**	**4**	**1**	**0**	**1**	**19:4**
2009-10	**NY Rangers**	**NHL**	**77**	**19**	**18**	**37**	**48**	**9**	**0**	**3**	**204**	**9.3**	**-12**	**35**	**48.6**	**19:24**	....	....	....	....	....	....	....	....	....
	United States	Olympics	6	0	1	1	2	....	....	....	....	....	....	....	....	....	....	....	....	....	....	....	....	....	....
	NHL Totals		**224**	**53**	**43**	**96**	**133**	**11**	**2**	**6**	**573**	**9.2**		**53**	**50.9**	**16:22**	**27**	**6**	**3**	**9**	**20**	**2**	**1**	**2**	**15:3**

OHL Second All-Star Team (2006) • AHL All-Rookie Team (2007)

CAMMALLERI, Michael

(kam-UH-LAIR-ee, MIGH-kuhl) **MTL**

Center. Shoots left. 5'9", 182 lbs. Born, Richmond Hill, Ont., June 8, 1982. Los Angeles' 3rd choice, 49th overall, in 2001 Entry Draft.

Season	Club	League	GP	G	A	Pts	PIM	PP	SH	GW	S	%	+/-	TF	F%	Min	GP	G	A	Pts	PIM	PP	SH	GW	Min
1997-98	Bramalea Blues	OPJHL	46	36	52	88	30	....	....	....	....	....	....	....	....	....	....	....	....	....	....	....	....	....	....
1998-99	Bramalea Blues	OPJHL	41	31	72	103	51	....	....	....	....	....	....	....	....	....	....	....	....	....	....	....	....	....	....
99-2000	U. of Michigan	CCHA	39	13	13	26	32	....	....	....	....	....	....	....	....	....	....	....	....	....	....	....	....	....	....
2000-01	U. of Michigan	CCHA	42	*29	32	61	24	....	....	....	....	....	....	....	....	....	....	....	....	....	....	....	....	....	....
2001-02	U. of Michigan	CCHA	29	23	21	44	28	....	....	....	....	....	....	....	....	....	....	....	....	....	....	....	....	....	....
2002-03	**Los Angeles**	**NHL**	**28**	**5**	**3**	**8**	**22**	**2**	**0**	**2**	**40**	**12.5**	**-4**	**253**	**51.4**	**14:05**	....	....	....	....	....	....	....	....	....
	Manchester	AHL	13	5	15	20	12	....	....	....	....	....	....	....	....	....	....	....	....	....	....	....	....	....	....
2003-04	**Los Angeles**	**NHL**	**31**	**9**	**6**	**15**	**20**	**2**	**0**	**2**	**53**	**17.0**	**1**	**280**	**53.6**	**13:18**	....	....	....	....	....	....	....	....	....
	Manchester	AHL	41	20	19	39	28	....	....	....	....	....	....	....	....	....	1	0	1	1	0	....	....	....	....
2004-05	Manchester	AHL	79	*46	63	109	60	....	....	....	....	....	....	....	....	....	6	1	5	6	0	....	....	....	....
2005-06	**Los Angeles**	**NHL**	**80**	**26**	**29**	**55**	**50**	**15**	**0**	**4**	**206**	**12.6**	**-14**	**578**	**53.5**	**16:45**	....	....	....	....	....	....	....	....	....
2006-07	**Los Angeles**	**NHL**	**81**	**34**	**46**	**80**	**48**	**16**	**0**	**5**	**299**	**11.4**	**5**	**301**	**54.2**	**18:03**	....	....	....	....	....	....	....	....	....

Season	Club	League	Regular Season GP	G	A	Pts	PIM	PP	SH	GW	S	%	+/-	TF	F%	Min	Playoffs GP	G	A	Pts	PIM	PP	SH	GW	Min
2007-08	Los Angeles	NHL	63	19	28	47	30	10	0	1	210	9.0	-16	380	54.2	18:35	....	....	....	....	....	....	....	....	....
2008-09	Calgary	NHL	81	39	43	82	44	19	0	6	255	15.3	-2	368	60.3	17:33	6	1	2	3	2	0	0	0	18:02
2009-10	Montreal	NHL	65	26	24	50	16	4	0	4	218	11.9	7	51	51.0	19:31	19	*13	6	19	6	4	0	3	20:40
	NHL Totals		429	158	179	337	230	68	0	24	1281	12.3		2211	54.5	17:25	25	14	8	22	8	4	0	3	20:02

CCHA First All-Star Team (2001) • NCAA West Second All-American Team (2001) • CCHA Second All-Star Team (2002) • NCAA West First All-American Team (2002) • AHL Second All-Star Team (2005) • Willie Marshall Award (AHL - Top Goal-scorer) (2005)

• Missed majority of 2002-03 season recovering from head injury suffered in game vs. San Jose, January 28, 2003. Traded to **Calgary** by **Los Angeles** with Calgary's 2nd round choice (previously acquired, Calgary selected Mitch Wahl) in 2008 Entry Draft for Calgary's 1st round choice (later traded to Anaheim – Anaheim selected Jake Gardiner) in 2008 Entry Draft and Calgary's 2nd round choice (later traded to Carolina – Carolina selected Brian Dumoulin) in 2009 Entry Draft, June 20, 2008. Signed as a free agent by **Montreal**, July 1, 2009.

CAMPBELL, Brian
(KAM-behl, BRIGH-uhn) **CHI.**

Defense. Shoots left. 6', 189 lbs. Born, Strathroy, Ont., May 23, 1979. Buffalo's 7th choice, 156th overall, in 1997 Entry Draft.

1994-95	Petrolia Oil Barons	OHA-B	49	11	27	38	43	....	....	....	....	....	....	....	....	....	....	....	....	....	....	....	....	....	....
1995-96	Ottawa 67's	OHL	66	5	22	27	23	....	....	....	....	....	....	....	....	....	4	0	1	1	2	....	....	....	....
1996-97	Ottawa 67's	OHL	66	7	36	43	12	....	....	....	....	....	....	....	....	....	24	2	11	13	8	....	....	....	....
1997-98	Ottawa 67's	OHL	66	14	39	53	31	....	....	....	....	....	....	....	....	....	13	1	14	15	0	....	....	....	....
1998-99	Ottawa 67's	OHL	62	12	75	87	27	....	....	....	....	....	....	....	....	....	9	2	10	12	6	....	....	....	....
	Rochester	AHL	....	....	....	....	....	....	....	....	....	....	....	....	....	....	2	0	0	0	0	....	....	....	....
99-2000	Buffalo	NHL	12	1	4	5	4	0	0	0	10	10.0	-2	0	0.0	15:48	....	....	....	....	....	....	....	....	....
	Rochester	AHL	67	2	24	26	22	....	....	....	....	....	....	....	....	....	21	0	3	3	0	....	....	....	....
2000-01	Buffalo	NHL	8	0	0	0	2	0	0	0	7	0.0	-2	0	0.0	15:40	....	....	....	....	....	....	....	....	....
	Rochester	AHL	65	7	25	32	24	....	....	....	....	....	....	....	....	....	4	0	1	1	0	....	....	....	....
2001-02	Buffalo	NHL	29	3	3	6	12	0	0	0	30	10.0	0	1	0.0	15:18	....	....	....	....	....	....	....	....	....
	Rochester	AHL	45	2	35	37	13	....	....	....	....	....	....	....	....	....	....	....	....	....	....	....	....	....	....
2002-03	Buffalo	NHL	65	2	17	19	20	0	0	1	90	2.2	-8	1	0.0	18:40	....	....	....	....	....	....	....	....	....
2003-04	Buffalo	NHL	53	3	8	11	12	0	0	0	45	6.7	-8	0	0.0	16:02	....	....	....	....	....	....	....	....	....
2004-05	Jokerit Helsinki	Finland	44	12	13	25	12	....	....	....	....	....	....	....	....	....	12	3	4	7	6	....	....	....	....
2005-06	Buffalo	NHL	79	12	32	44	16	5	0	5	105	11.4	-14	0	0.0	17:43	18	0	6	6	12	0	0	0	20:29
2006-07	Buffalo	NHL	82	6	42	48	35	1	0	1	92	6.5	28	0	0.0	21:53	16	3	4	7	14	2	0	0	21:39
2007-08	Buffalo	NHL	63	5	38	43	12	3	0	0	102	4.9	-1	0	0.0	25:06	....	....	....	....	....	....	....	....	....
	San Jose	NHL	20	3	16	19	8	2	0	0	40	7.5	9	0	0.0	25:07	13	1	6	7	4	0	0	0	29:19
2008-09	Chicago	NHL	82	7	45	52	22	4	0	1	108	6.5	5	0	0.0	22:34	17	2	8	10	0	2	0	0	20:29
2009-10♦	Chicago	NHL	68	7	31	38	18	3	0	2	131	5.3	18	0	0.0	23:13	19	1	4	5	2	0	0	0	19:35
	NHL Totals		561	49	236	285	161	18	0	10	760	6.4		2	0.0	20:33	83	7	28	35	32	4	0	0	21:53

OHL First All-Star Team (1999) • OHL MVP (1999) • Canadian Major Junior First All-Star Team (1999) • Canadian Major Junior Player of the Year (1999) • George Parsons Trophy (Memorial Cup Tournament - Most Sportsmanlike Player) (1999) • NHL Second All-Star Team (2008)

Played in NHL All-Star Game (2007, 2008, 2009)

Signed as a free agent by **Jokerit Helsinki** (Finland), October 19, 2004. Traded to **San Jose** by **Buffalo** with Buffalo's 7th round choice (Drew Daniels) in 2008 Entry Draft for Steve Bernier and San Jose's 1st round choice (Tyler Ennis) in 2008 Entry Draft, February 26, 2008. Signed as a free agent by **Chicago**, July 1, 2008.

CAMPBELL, Darcy
(KAM-behl, DAHR-see)

Defense. Shoots left. 6'1", 180 lbs. Born, Airdrie, Alta., May 12, 1984.

2002-03	Canmore Eagles	AJHL	62	10	37	47	112	....	....	....	....	....	....	....	....	....	9	2	2	4	6	....	....	....	....
2003-04	Canmore Eagles	AJHL	24	6	15	21	25	....	....	....	....	....	....	....	....	....	14	2	7	9	2	....	....	....	....
	Olds Grizzlys	AJHL	36	9	19	28	40	....	....	....	....	....	....	....	....	....	....	....	....	....	....	....	....	....	....
2004-05	Alaska	CCHA	37	2	10	12	56	....	....	....	....	....	....	....	....	....	....	....	....	....	....	....	....	....	....
2005-06	Alaska	CCHA	38	5	9	14	67	....	....	....	....	....	....	....	....	....	....	....	....	....	....	....	....	....	....
2006-07	Alaska	CCHA	39	4	20	24	54	....	....	....	....	....	....	....	....	....	....	....	....	....	....	....	....	....	....
	Columbus	NHL	1	0	0	0	0	0	0	0	0	0.0	0	0	0.0	5:41	....	....	....	....	....	....	....	....	....
2007-08	Syracuse Crunch	AHL	28	1	5	6	26	....	....	....	....	....	....	....	....	....	....	....	....	....	....	....	....	....	....
	Lake Erie	AHL	8	1	0	1	2	....	....	....	....	....	....	....	....	....	....	....	....	....	....	....	....	....	....
2008-09	Lake Erie	AHL	74	7	8	15	61	....	....	....	....	....	....	....	....	....	....	....	....	....	....	....	....	....	....
2009-10	TPS Turku	Finland	33	2	9	11	38	....	....	....	....	....	....	....	....	....	....	....	....	....	....	....	....	....	....
	HC Slavia Praha	CzRep	12	0	1	1	14	....	....	....	....	....	....	....	....	....	16	1	3	4	10	....	....	....	....
	NHL Totals		1	0	0	0	0	0	0	0	0	0.0		0	0.0	5:41	....	....	....	....	....	....	....	....	....

AJHL South All-Rookie Team (2003) • AJHL South First All-Star Team (2004)

Signed as a free agent by **Columbus**, March 24, 2007. Traded to **Colorado** by **Columbus** with Phillipe Dupuis for Mark Rycroft, January 22, 2008. Signed as a free agent by **Turku** (Finland), June 10, 2009. • Transferred to **Slavia Praha** (CzRep) from **Turku** (Finland), January 16. 2010..

CAMPBELL, Gregory
(KAM-behl, GREH-goh-ree) **BOS.**

Left wing. Shoots left. 6', 197 lbs. Born, London, Ont., December 17, 1983. Florida's 4th choice, 67th overall, in 2002 Entry Draft.

1998-99	Aylmer Aces	OHA-B	49	5	9	14	44	....	....	....	....	....	....	....	....	....	....	....	....	....	....	....	....	....	....
99-2000	St. Thomas Stars	OHA-B	51	12	8	20	51	....	....	....	....	....	....	....	....	....	....	....	....	....	....	....	....	....	....
2000-01	Plymouth Whalers	OHL	65	2	12	14	40	....	....	....	....	....	....	....	....	....	10	0	0	0	7	....	....	....	....
2001-02	Plymouth Whalers	OHL	65	17	36	53	105	....	....	....	....	....	....	....	....	....	6	0	2	2	13	....	....	....	....
2002-03	Kitchener Rangers	OHL	55	23	33	56	116	....	....	....	....	....	....	....	....	....	21	15	4	19	34	....	....	....	....
2003-04	Florida	NHL	2	0	0	0	5	0	0	0	0	0.0	-1	1	0.0	9:09	....	....	....	....	....	....	....	....	....
	San Antonio	AHL	76	13	16	29	73	....	....	....	....	....	....	....	....	....	....	....	....	....	....	....	....	....	....
2004-05	San Antonio	AHL	70	12	16	28	113	....	....	....	....	....	....	....	....	....	....	....	....	....	....	....	....	....	....
2005-06	Florida	NHL	64	3	6	9	40	0	0	0	59	5.1	-11	38	34.2	8:38	....	....	....	....	....	....	....	....	....
	Rochester	AHL	11	3	3	6	30	....	....	....	....	....	....	....	....	....	....	....	....	....	....	....	....	....	....
2006-07	Florida	NHL	79	6	3	9	66	0	1	0	103	5.8	-10	588	45.2	10:34	....	....	....	....	....	....	....	....	....
2007-08	Florida	NHL	81	5	13	18	72	0	2	1	113	4.4	-12	460	51.1	12:27	....	....	....	....	....	....	....	....	....
2008-09	Florida	NHL	77	13	19	32	76	1	0	1	135	9.6	0	1018	50.0	16:47	....	....	....	....	....	....	....	....	....
2009-10	Florida	NHL	60	2	15	17	53	1	0	1	84	2.4	-5	341	46.3	15:24	....	....	....	....	....	....	....	....	....
	NHL Totals		363	29	56	85	312	1	3	3	494	5.9		2446	48.3	12:45	....	....	....	....	....	....	....	....	....

Memorial Cup Tournament All-Star Team (2003) • George Parsons Trophy (Memorial Cup Tournament - Most Sportsmanlike Player) (2003) • Ed Chynoweth Trophy (Memorial Cup Tournament - Leading Scorer) (2003)

Traded to **Boston** by **Florida** with Nathan Horton for Dennis Wideman, Boston's 1st round choice (later traded to Los Angeles – Los Angeles selected Derek Forbert) in 2010 Entry Draft and Boston's 3rd round choice in 2011 Entry Draft, June 22, 2010.

CAMPOLI, Chris
(kam-POH-lee, KRIHS) **OTT.**

Defense. Shoots left. 6', 190 lbs. Born, North York, Ont., July 9, 1984. NY Islanders' 8th choice, 227th overall, in 2004 Entry Draft.

2001-02	Erie Otters	OHL	68	2	24	26	117	....	....	....	....	....	....	....	....	....	20	0	5	5	18	....	....	....	....
2002-03	Erie Otters	OHL	60	8	40	48	82	....	....	....	....	....	....	....	....	....	....	....	....	....	....	....	....	....	....
2003-04	Erie Otters	OHL	67	20	46	66	66	....	....	....	....	....	....	....	....	....	8	0	6	6	16	....	....	....	....
2004-05	Bridgeport	AHL	79	15	34	49	78	....	....	....	....	....	....	....	....	....	....	....	....	....	....	....	....	....	....
2005-06	NY Islanders	NHL	80	9	25	34	46	2	0	2	123	7.3	-16	0	0.0	18:32	....	....	....	....	....	....	....	....	....
2006-07	NY Islanders	NHL	51	1	13	14	23	0	0	0	41	2.4	-3	0	0.0	14:50	5	1	1	2	2	0	0	0	13:30
	Bridgeport	AHL	15	3	3	6	8	....	....	....	....	....	....	....	....	....	....	....	....	....	....	....	....	....	....
2007-08	NY Islanders	NHL	46	4	14	18	16	2	1	0	68	5.9	-1	0	0.0	19:09	....	....	....	....	....	....	....	....	....
2008-09	NY Islanders	NHL	51	6	11	17	43	0	1	2	53	11.3	-20	0	0.0	19:50	....	....	....	....	....	....	....	....	....
	Ottawa	NHL	25	5	8	13	12	2	0	2	38	13.2	4	0	0.0	18:58	....	....	....	....	....	....	....	....	....
2009-10	Ottawa	NHL	67	4	14	18	16	1	0	1	71	5.6	-3	1	0.0	17:51	6	0	2	2	4	0	0	0	19:48
	NHL Totals		320	29	85	114	156	7	2	7	394	7.4		1	0.0	18:08	11	1	3	4	6	0	0	0	16:56

OHL Humanitarian Player of the Year (2004) • Canadian Major Junior Humanitarian Player of the Year (2004) • AHL All-Rookie Team (2005)

Traded to **Ottawa** by **NY Islanders** with Mike Comrie for Dean McAmmond and San Jose's 1st round choice (previously acquired, later traded to Columbus, later traded to Anaheim – Anaheim selected Kyle Palmieri) in 2009 Entry Draft, February 20, 2009.

			Regular Season														Playoffs								
Season	Club	League	GP	G	A	Pts	PIM	PP	SH	GW	S	%	+/-	TF	F%	Min	GP	G	A	Pts	PIM	PP	SH	GW	Min

CAPUTI, Luca

(ka-POO-tee, LOO-ka) **TOR.**

Left wing. Shoots left. 6'3", 200 lbs. Born, Toronto, Ont., October 1, 1988. Pittsburgh's 5th choice, 111th overall, in 2007 Entry Draft.

Season	Club	League	GP	G	A	Pts	PIM	PP	SH	GW	S	%	+/-	TF	F%	Min	GP	G	A	Pts	PIM	PP	SH	GW	Min
2003-04	Tor. Jr. Canadiens	GTHL	53	52	55	107	127	....	....	....	....	....	....	....	....	....	....	....	....	....	....	....	....	....	....
2004-05	Mississauga	OHL	48	5	1	6	25	....	....	....	....	....	....	....	....	....	....	....	....	....	....	....	....	....	....
2005-06	Mississauga	OHL	32	3	0	3	43	....	....	....	....	....	....	....	....	....	....	....	....	....	....	....	....	....	....
2006-07	Mississauga	OHL	68	27	38	65	66	....	....	....	....	....	....	....	....	....	5	2	1	3	0	....	....	....	....
2007-08	Niagara Ice Dogs	OHL	66	51	60	111	107	....	....	....	....	....	....	....	....	....	10	8	9	17	14	....	....	....	....
	Wilkes-Barre	AHL	....	....	....	....	....	....	....	....	....	....	....	....	....	....	19	4	4	8	8	....	....	....	....
2008-09	**Pittsburgh**	**NHL**	**5**	**1**	**0**	**1**	**4**	**0**	**0**	**0**	**7**	**14.3**	**–1**	**0**	**0.0**	**10:16**	....	....	....	....	....	....	....	....	....
	Wilkes-Barre	AHL	66	18	27	45	45	....	....	....	....	....	....	....	....	....	12	3	5	8	10	....	....	....	....
	Wheeling Nailers	ECHL	3	2	1	3	0	....	....	....	....	....	....	....	....	....	....	....	....	....	....	....	....	....	....
2009-10	**Pittsburgh**	**NHL**	**4**	**1**	**1**	**2**	**2**	**0**	**0**	**0**	**4**	**25.0**	**–1**	**0**	**0.0**	**11:46**	....	....	....	....	....	....	....	....	....
	Wilkes-Barre	AHL	54	23	24	47	61	....	....	....	....	....	....	....	....	....	....	....	....	....	....	....	....	....	....
	Toronto	**NHL**	**19**	**1**	**5**	**6**	**10**	**0**	**0**	**0**	**32**	**3.1**	**0**	**23**	**43.5**	**14:38**	....	....	....	....	....	....	....	....	....
	NHL Totals		**28**	**3**	**6**	**9**	**16**	**0**	**0**	**0**	**43**	**7.0**		**23**	**43.5**	**13:26**	....	....	....	....	....	....	....	....	....

OHL Second All-Star Team (2008)

Traded to **Toronto** by **Pittsburgh** with Martin Skoula for Alexei Ponikarovsky, March 2, 2010.

CARCILLO, Daniel

(KAR-sihl-oh, DAN-yuhl) **PHI.**

Left wing. Shoots left. 6', 205 lbs. Born, King City, Ont., January 28, 1985. Pittsburgh's 4th choice, 73rd overall, in 2003 Entry Draft.

Season	Club	League	GP	G	A	Pts	PIM	PP	SH	GW	S	%	+/-	TF	F%	Min	GP	G	A	Pts	PIM	PP	SH	GW	Min
2001-02	Milton Merchants	OHA-B	47	15	16	31	162	....	....	....	....	....	....	....	....	....	....	....	....	....	....	....	....	....	....
2002-03	Sarnia Sting	OHL	68	29	37	66	157	....	....	....	....	....	....	....	....	....	6	0	4	4	14	....	....	....	....
2003-04	Sarnia Sting	OHL	61	30	29	59	148	....	....	....	....	....	....	....	....	....	4	1	2	3	12	....	....	....	....
2004-05	Sarnia Sting	OHL	12	2	7	9	40	....	....	....	....	....	....	....	....	....	....	....	....	....	....	....	....	....	....
	Mississauga	OHL	20	8	10	18	75	....	....	....	....	....	....	....	....	....	5	3	1	4	18	....	....	....	....
2005-06	Wilkes-Barre	AHL	51	11	13	24	311	....	....	....	....	....	....	....	....	....	11	1	0	1	47	....	....	....	....
	Wheeling Nailers	ECHL	6	3	2	5	32	....	....	....	....	....	....	....	....	....	....	....	....	....	....	....	....	....	....
2006-07	Wilkes-Barre	AHL	52	21	9	30	183	....	....	....	....	....	....	....	....	....	....	....	....	....	....	....	....	....	....
	Phoenix	**NHL**	**18**	**4**	**3**	**7**	**74**	**3**	**0**	**0**	**32**	**12.5**	**–7**	**0**	**0.0**	**14:56**	....	....	....	....	....	....	....	....	....
2007-08	**Phoenix**	**NHL**	**57**	**13**	**11**	**24**	***324**	**3**	**0**	**1**	**106**	**12.3**	**1**	**5**	**80.0**	**12:43**	....	....	....	....	....	....	....	....	....
	San Antonio	AHL	5	2	1	3	16	....	....	....	....	....	....	....	....	....	....	....	....	....	....	....	....	....	....
2008-09	**Phoenix**	**NHL**	**54**	**3**	**7**	**10**	***174**	**2**	**0**	**0**	**95**	**3.2**	**–13**	**18**	**55.6**	**11:59**	....	....	....	....	....	....	....	....	....
	Philadelphia	**NHL**	**20**	**0**	**4**	**4**	***80**	**0**	**0**	**0**	**35**	**0.0**	**–2**	**2**	**100.0**	**10:16**	**5**	**1**	**1**	**2**	**5**	**0**	**0**	**0**	**8:11**
2009-10	**Philadelphia**	**NHL**	**76**	**12**	**10**	**22**	**207**	**1**	**0**	**1**	**105**	**11.4**	**5**	**3**	**33.3**	**11:15**	**17**	**2**	**4**	**6**	**34**	**0**	**0**	**1**	**10:32**
	NHL Totals		**225**	**32**	**35**	**67**	**859**	**9**	**0**	**2**	**373**	**8.6**		**28**	**60.7**	**12:00**	**22**	**3**	**5**	**8**	**39**	**0**	**0**	**1**	**10:00**

Traded to **Phoenix** by **Pittsburgh** with Pittsburgh's 3rd round choice (later traded to NY Rangers - NY Rangers selected Tomas Kundratek) in 2008 Entry Draft for Georges Laraque, February 27, 2007. Traded to **Philadelphia** by **Phoenix** for Scottie Upshall and Philadelphia's 2nd round choice in 2011 Entry Draft, March 4, 2009.

CARKNER, Matt

(KARK-nehr, MAT) **OTT.**

Defense. Shoots right. 6'4", 231 lbs. Born, Winchester, Ont., November 3, 1980. Montreal's 2nd choice, 58th overall, in 1999 Entry Draft.

Season	Club	League	GP	G	A	Pts	PIM	PP	SH	GW	S	%	+/-	TF	F%	Min	GP	G	A	Pts	PIM	PP	SH	GW	Min
1996-97	Winchester	OHA-B	29	1	18	19	....	....	....	....	....	....	....	....	....	....	....	....	....	....	....	....	....	....	....
1997-98	Peterborough	OHL	57	0	6	6	121	....	....	....	....	....	....	....	....	....	4	0	0	0	2	....	....	....	....
1998-99	Peterborough	OHL	60	2	16	18	173	....	....	....	....	....	....	....	....	....	5	0	0	0	20	....	....	....	....
99-2000	Peterborough	OHL	62	3	13	16	177	....	....	....	....	....	....	....	....	....	5	0	1	1	6	....	....	....	....
2000-01	Peterborough	OHL	53	8	8	16	128	....	....	....	....	....	....	....	....	....	7	0	3	3	25	....	....	....	....
2001-02	Cleveland Barons	AHL	74	0	3	3	335	....	....	....	....	....	....	....	....	....	....	....	....	....	....	....	....	....	....
2002-03	Cleveland Barons	AHL	39	1	4	5	104	....	....	....	....	....	....	....	....	....	....	....	....	....	....	....	....	....	....
2003-04	Cleveland Barons	AHL	60	2	11	13	115	....	....	....	....	....	....	....	....	....	9	0	3	3	39	....	....	....	....
2004-05	Cleveland Barons	AHL	73	0	10	10	192	....	....	....	....	....	....	....	....	....	....	....	....	....	....	....	....	....	....
2005-06	**San Jose**	**NHL**	**1**	**0**	**1**	**1**	**2**	**0**	**0**	**0**	**0**	**0.0**	**0**	**0**	**0.0**	**6:01**	....	....	....	....	....	....	....	....	....
	Cleveland Barons	AHL	69	10	21	31	202	....	....	....	....	....	....	....	....	....	....	....	....	....	....	....	....	....	....
2006-07	Wilkes-Barre	AHL	75	6	24	30	167	....	....	....	....	....	....	....	....	....	8	1	0	1	19	....	....	....	....
2007-08	Binghamton	AHL	67	10	15	25	218	....	....	....	....	....	....	....	....	....	....	....	....	....	....	....	....	....	....
2008-09	**Ottawa**	**NHL**	**1**	**0**	**0**	**0**	**0**	**0**	**0**	**0**	**0**	**0.0**	**0**	**0**	**0.0**	**4:08**	....	....	....	....	....	....	....	....	....
	Binghamton	AHL	67	3	18	21	210	....	....	....	....	....	....	....	....	....	....	....	....	....	....	....	....	....	....
2009-10	**Ottawa**	**NHL**	**81**	**2**	**9**	**11**	**190**	**0**	**0**	**0**	**87**	**2.3**	**0**	**0**	**0.0**	**16:55**	**6**	**1**	**0**	**1**	**12**	**0**	**0**	**1**	**18:38**
	NHL Totals		**83**	**2**	**10**	**12**	**192**	**0**	**0**	**0**	**87**	**2.3**		**0**	**0.0**	**16:38**	**6**	**1**	**0**	**1**	**12**	**0**	**0**	**1**	**18:38**

Yanick Dupre Memorial Award (AHL - Outstanding Humanitarian Contribution) (2007)

Signed as a free agent by **San Jose**, June 6, 2001. • Missed majority of 2002-03 season recovering from knee injury suffered in game vs. Utah (AHL), January 4, 2003. Signed as a free agent by **Pittsburgh**, July 23, 2006. Signed as a free agent by **Ottawa**, July 3, 2007.

CARLE, Mathieu

(KAHRL, MA-tyew) **MTL.**

Defense. Shoots right. 6', 203 lbs. Born, Gatineau, Que., September 30, 1987. Montreal's 3rd choice, 53rd overall, in 2006 Entry Draft.

Season	Club	League	GP	G	A	Pts	PIM	PP	SH	GW	S	%	+/-	TF	F%	Min	GP	G	A	Pts	PIM	PP	SH	GW	Min
2004-05	Acadie-Bathurst	QMJHL	69	4	29	33	53	....	....	....	....	....	....	....	....	....	....	....	....	....	....	....	....	....	....
2005-06	Acadie-Bathurst	QMJHL	67	18	51	69	122	....	....	....	....	....	....	....	....	....	17	1	14	15	29	....	....	....	....
2006-07	Acadie-Bathurst	QMJHL	38	12	39	51	52	....	....	....	....	....	....	....	....	....	....	....	....	....	....	....	....	....	....
	Rouyn-Noranda	QMJHL	25	4	15	19	27	....	....	....	....	....	....	....	....	....	16	6	10	16	16	....	....	....	....
2007-08	Hamilton	AHL	64	7	17	24	43	....	....	....	....	....	....	....	....	....	....	....	....	....	....	....	....	....	....
2008-09	Hamilton	AHL	59	7	22	29	43	....	....	....	....	....	....	....	....	....	6	0	2	2	4	....	....	....	....
2009-10	**Montreal**	**NHL**	**3**	**0**	**0**	**0**	**4**	**0**	**0**	**0**	**2**	**0.0**	**1**	**0**	**0.0**	**14:28**	....	....	....	....	....	....	....	....	....
	Hamilton	AHL	31	5	10	15	26	....	....	....	....	....	....	....	....	....	1	0	0	0	0	....	....	....	....
	NHL Totals		**3**	**0**	**0**	**0**	**4**	**0**	**0**	**0**	**2**	**0.0**		**0**	**0.0**	**14:28**	....	....	....	....	....	....	....	....	....

QMJHL All-Rookie Team (2004)

• Missed majority of 2009-10 season recovering from head injury suffered in pre-season game vs. Chicago, September 24, 2009.

CARLE, Matt

(KAHRL, MAT) **PHI.**

Defense. Shoots left. 6', 205 lbs. Born, Anchorage, AK, September 25, 1984. San Jose's 4th choice, 47th overall, in 2003 Entry Draft.

Season	Club	League	GP	G	A	Pts	PIM	PP	SH	GW	S	%	+/-	TF	F%	Min	GP	G	A	Pts	PIM	PP	SH	GW	Min
99-2000	Alaska All-Stars	AASHA	42	14	28	42	....	....	....	....	....	....	....	....	....	....	....	....	....	....	....	....	....	....	....
2000-01	USNTDP	U-17	13	0	1	1	....	....	....	....	....	....	....	....	....	....	....	....	....	....	....	....	....	....	....
	USNTDP	NAHL	55	1	4	5	33	....	....	....	....	....	....	....	....	....	....	....	....	....	....	....	....	....	....
2001-02	USNTDP	U-18	45	3	13	16	30	....	....	....	....	....	....	....	....	....	....	....	....	....	....	....	....	....	....
	USNTDP	NAHL	7	1	2	3	0	....	....	....	....	....	....	....	....	....	....	....	....	....	....	....	....	....	....
	USNTDP	USHL	12	0	0	0	21	....	....	....	....	....	....	....	....	....	....	....	....	....	....	....	....	....	....
2002-03	River City Lancers	USHL	59	12	30	42	98	....	....	....	....	....	....	....	....	....	11	2	2	4	20	....	....	....	....
2003-04	U. of Denver	WCHA	30	5	20	25	33	....	....	....	....	....	....	....	....	....	....	....	....	....	....	....	....	....	....
2004-05	U. of Denver	WCHA	43	13	31	44	68	....	....	....	....	....	....	....	....	....	....	....	....	....	....	....	....	....	....
2005-06	U. of Denver	WCHA	39	11	*42	53	58	....	....	....	....	....	....	....	....	....	....	....	....	....	....	....	....	....	....
	San Jose	**NHL**	**12**	**3**	**3**	**6**	**14**	**2**	**0**	**1**	**11**	**27.3**	**–2**	**0**	**0.0**	**16:07**	**11**	**0**	**3**	**3**	**4**	**0**	**0**	**0**	**15:17**
2006-07	**San Jose**	**NHL**	**77**	**11**	**31**	**42**	**30**	**8**	**0**	**1**	**111**	**9.9**	**9**	**1**	**0.0**	**18:08**	**11**	**2**	**3**	**5**	**0**	**1**	**0**	**1**	**14:51**
	Worcester Sharks	AHL	3	0	2	2	0	....	....	....	....	....	....	....	....	....	....	....	....	....	....	....	....	....	....
2007-08	**San Jose**	**NHL**	**62**	**2**	**13**	**15**	**26**	**2**	**0**	**1**	**63**	**3.2**	**–8**	**1**	**100.0**	**16:33**	**11**	**0**	**1**	**1**	**4**	**0**	**0**	**0**	**13:56**
2008-09	**Tampa Bay**	**NHL**	**12**	**1**	**1**	**2**	**6**	**0**	**0**	**0**	**13**	**7.7**	**1**	**0**	**0.0**	**21:58**	....	....	....	....	....	....	....	....	....
	Philadelphia	**NHL**	**64**	**4**	**20**	**24**	**16**	**0**	**0**	**2**	**72**	**5.6**	**2**	**0**	**0.0**	**21:17**	**6**	**0**	**3**	**3**	**4**	**0**	**0**	**0**	**22:15**
2009-10	**Philadelphia**	**NHL**	**80**	**6**	**29**	**35**	**16**	**2**	**0**	**1**	**137**	**4.4**	**19**	**0**	**0.0**	**23:23**	**23**	**1**	**12**	**13**	**8**	**0**	**0**	**0**	**25:54**
	NHL Totals		**307**	**27**	**97**	**124**	**108**	**14**	**0**	**6**	**407**	**6.6**		**2**	**50.0**	**19:55**	**62**	**3**	**22**	**25**	**20**	**1**	**0**	**1**	**19:35**

USHL First All-Star Team (2003) • USHL Defenseman of the Year (2003) • WCHA All-Rookie Team (2004) • WCHA First All-Star Team (2005, 2006) • NCAA West First All-American Team (2005, 2006) • NCAA Championship All-Tournament Team (2005) • WCHA Player of the Year (2006) • Hobey Baker Memorial Award (Top U.S. Collegiate Player) (2006) • NHL All-Rookie Team (2007)

Traded to **Tampa Bay** by **San Jose** with Ty Wishart, San Jose's 1st round choice (later traded to Ottawa, later traded to NY Islanders, later traded to Columbus, later traded to Anaheim – Anaheim selected Kyle Palmieri) in 2009 Entry Draft and San Jose's 4th round choice (James Mullin) in 2010 Entry Draft for Dan Boyle and Brad Lukowich, July 4, 2008. Traded to **Philadelphia** by **Tampa Bay** with San Jose's 3rd round choice (previously acquired, Philadelphia selected Simon Bertilsson) in 2009 Entry Draft for Steve Eminger, Steve Downie and Tampa Bay's 4th round choice (previously acquired, Tampa Bay selected Alex Hutchings) in 2009 Entry Draft, November 7, 2008.

			Regular Season														Playoffs							
Season	Club	League	GP	G	A	Pts	PIM	PP	SH	GW	S	%	+/-	TF	F%	Min	GP	G	A	Pts	PIM	PP	SH	GW	Min

CARLSON, John (KAHRL-suhn, JAWN) **WSH.**

Defense. Shoots right. 6'3", 208 lbs. Born, Natick, MA, January 10, 1990. Washington's 2nd choice, 27th overall, in 2008 Entry Draft.

Season	Club	League	GP	G	A	Pts	PIM	PP	SH	GW	S	%	+/-	TF	F%	Min	GP	G	A	Pts	PIM	PP	SH	GW	Min
2005-06	N.J. Rockets	AtJHL	38	2	10	12	42	....	....	....	....	....	....	....	....	....	....	....	....	....	....	....	....	....	....
2006-07	N.J. Rockets	AtJHL	44	12	38	50	96	....	....	....	....	....	....	....	....	....	....	....	....	....	....	....	....	....	....
	Indiana Ice	USHL	2	0	0	0	6	....	....	....	....	....	....	....	....	....	....	....	....	....	....	....	....	....	....
2007-08	Indiana Ice	USHL	59	12	31	43	72	....	....	....	....	....	....	....	....	....	4	1	0	1	0	....	....	....	....
2008-09	London Knights	OHL	59	16	60	76	65	....	....	....	....	....	....	....	....	....	14	7	15	22	16	....	....	....	....
	Hershey Bears	AHL	....	....	....	....	....	....	....	....	....	....	....	....	....	....	16	2	1	3	0	....	....	....	....
2009-10	**Washington**	**NHL**	22	1	5	6	8	0	0	0	21	4.8	11	0	0.0	15:15	7	1	3	4	0	0	0	0	20:14
	Hershey Bears	AHL	48	4	35	39	26	....	....	....	....	....	....	....	....	....	13	2	4	6	8	....	....	....	....
	NHL Totals		22	1	5	6	8	0	0	0	21	4.8		0	0.0	15:15	7	1	3	4	0	0	0	0	20:14

USHL All-Rookie Team (2008) • USHL Second All-Star Team (2008) • OHL Second All-Star Team (2009) • Canadian Major Junior All-Rookie Team (2009)

CARSON, Brett (KAR-suhn, BREHT) **CAR.**

Defense. Shoots right. 6'4", 210 lbs. Born, Regina, Sask., November 29, 1985. Carolina's 4th choice, 109th overall, in 2004 Entry Draft.

Season	Club	League	GP	G	A	Pts	PIM	PP	SH	GW	S	%	+/-	TF	F%	Min	GP	G	A	Pts	PIM	PP	SH	GW	Min
99-2000	Pipestone Valley	SSMHL	8	0	0	0	0	....	....	....	....	....	....	....	....	....	....	....	....	....	....	....	....	....	....
2000-01	Pipestone Valley	SSMHL	31	5	17	22	20	....	....	....	....	....	....	....	....	....	....	....	....	....	....	....	....	....	....
2001-02	Yorkton Terriers	SMHL	41	16	37	53	32	....	....	....	....	....	....	....	....	....	....	....	....	....	....	....	....	....	....
	Moose Jaw	WHL	6	0	0	0	0	....	....	....	....	....	....	....	....	....	12	2	0	2	0	....	....	....	....
2002-03	Moose Jaw	WHL	28	1	4	5	28	....	....	....	....	....	....	....	....	....	....	....	....	....	....	....	....	....	....
	Calgary Hitmen	WHL	30	3	6	9	4	....	....	....	....	....	....	....	....	....	5	2	1	3	0	....	....	....	....
2003-04	Calgary Hitmen	WHL	71	5	27	32	49	....	....	....	....	....	....	....	....	....	7	0	0	0	6	....	....	....	....
2004-05	Calgary Hitmen	WHL	61	8	16	24	61	....	....	....	....	....	....	....	....	....	8	2	2	4	8	....	....	....	....
2005-06	Calgary Hitmen	WHL	72	11	29	40	62	....	....	....	....	....	....	....	....	....	13	1	6	7	20	....	....	....	....
2006-07	Albany River Rats	AHL	63	2	16	18	26	....	....	....	....	....	....	....	....	....	5	0	2	2	0	....	....	....	....
	Florida Everblades	ECHL	3	1	1	2	0	....	....	....	....	....	....	....	....	....	....	....	....	....	....	....	....	....	....
2007-08	Albany River Rats	AHL	77	2	22	24	32	....	....	....	....	....	....	....	....	....	7	1	3	4	11	....	....	....	....
2008-09	**Carolina**	**NHL**	5	0	0	0	4	0	0	0	2	0.0	-3	0	0.0	15:44	....	....	....	....	....	....	....	....	....
	Albany River Rats	AHL	69	6	29	35	34	....	....	....	....	....	....	....	....	....	....	....	....	....	....	....	....	....	....
2009-10	**Carolina**	**NHL**	54	2	10	12	12	0	0	0	42	4.8	5	0	0.0	17:22	....	....	....	....	....	....	....	....	....
	Albany River Rats	AHL	14	3	8	11	0	....	....	....	....	....	....	....	....	....	....	....	....	....	....	....	....	....	....
	NHL Totals		59	2	10	12	16	0	0	0	44	4.5		0	0.0	17:14	....	....	....	....	....	....	....	....	....

WHL East First All-Star Team (2006)

CARTER, Jeff (KAHR-tuhr, JEHF) **PHI.**

Center. Shoots right. 6'3", 200 lbs. Born, London, Ont., January 1, 1985. Philadelphia's 1st choice, 11th overall, in 2003 Entry Draft.

Season	Club	League	GP	G	A	Pts	PIM	PP	SH	GW	S	%	+/-	TF	F%	Min	GP	G	A	Pts	PIM	PP	SH	GW	Min
2000-01	Strathroy Rockets	OHA-B	49	27	20	47	10	....	....	....	....	....	....	....	....	....	....	....	....	....	....	....	....	....	....
2001-02	Sault Ste. Marie	OHL	63	18	17	35	12	....	....	....	....	....	....	....	....	....	4	0	0	0	2	....	....	....	....
2002-03	Sault Ste. Marie	OHL	61	35	36	71	55	....	....	....	....	....	....	....	....	....	4	0	2	2	2	....	....	....	....
2003-04	Sault Ste. Marie	OHL	57	36	30	66	26	....	....	....	....	....	....	....	....	....	....	....	....	....	....	....	....	....	....
	Philadelphia	AHL	....	....	....	....	....	....	....	....	....	....	....	....	....	....	12	4	1	5	0	....	....	....	....
2004-05	Sault Ste. Marie	OHL	55	34	40	74	40	....	....	....	....	....	....	....	....	....	7	5	5	10	6	....	....	....	....
	Philadelphia	AHL	3	0	1	1	4	....	....	....	....	....	....	....	....	....	21	12	11	23	12	....	....	....	....
2005-06	**Philadelphia**	**NHL**	81	23	19	42	40	6	2	7	189	12.2	10	683	48.2	12:04	6	0	0	0	10	0	0	0	13:04
2006-07	**Philadelphia**	**NHL**	62	14	23	37	48	3	2	1	215	6.5	-17	1062	45.4	19:00	....	....	....	....	....	....	....	....	....
2007-08	**Philadelphia**	**NHL**	82	29	24	53	55	7	2	5	260	11.2	6	1378	47.7	18:51	17	6	5	11	12	3	0	1	20:08
2008-09	**Philadelphia**	**NHL**	82	46	38	84	68	13	4	*12	342	13.5	23	1725	48.3	20:57	6	1	0	1	8	0	0	0	20:21
2009-10	**Philadelphia**	**NHL**	74	33	28	61	38	11	2	6	319	10.3	2	1314	52.4	19:18	12	5	2	7	2	2	0	1	17:57
	NHL Totals		381	145	132	277	249	40	12	31	1325	10.9		6162	48.5	17:58	41	12	7	19	32	5	0	2	18:29

OHL Second All-Star Team (2004) • OHL First All-Star Team (2005) • Canadian Major Junior Sportsman of the Year (2005) • Canadian Major Junior First All-Star Team (2005) • Played in NHL All-Star Game (2009)

CARTER, Ryan (KAHR-tuhr, RIGH-uhn) **ANA.**

Center. Shoots left. 6'2", 200 lbs. Born, White Bear Lake, MN, August 3, 1983.

Season	Club	League	GP	G	A	Pts	PIM	PP	SH	GW	S	%	+/-	TF	F%	Min	GP	G	A	Pts	PIM	PP	SH	GW	Min
2002-03	Green Bay	USHL	55	19	17	36	94	....	....	....	....	....	....	....	....	....	....	....	....	....	....	....	....	....	....
2003-04	Green Bay	USHL	59	22	23	45	131	....	....	....	....	....	....	....	....	....	....	....	....	....	....	....	....	....	....
2004-05	Minnesota State	WCHA	37	15	8	23	44	....	....	....	....	....	....	....	....	....	....	....	....	....	....	....	....	....	....
2005-06	Minnesota State	WCHA	39	19	16	35	71	....	....	....	....	....	....	....	....	....	....	....	....	....	....	....	....	....	....
2006-07	Portland Pirates	AHL	76	16	20	36	85	....	....	....	....	....	....	....	....	....	4	0	0	0	0	0	0	0	3:12
	♦ **Anaheim**	**NHL**	....	....	....	....	....	....	....	....	....	....	....	....	....	....	....	....	....	....	....	....	....	....	....
2007-08	**Anaheim**	**NHL**	34	4	4	8	36	0	0	1	56	7.1	-2	299	61.5	10:29	6	0	0	0	6	0	0	0	11:03
	Portland Pirates	AHL	13	3	2	5	38	....	....	....	....	....	....	....	....	....	....	....	....	....	....	....	....	....	....
2008-09	**Anaheim**	**NHL**	48	3	6	9	52	0	0	1	40	7.5	3	304	48.0	9:06	10	2	3	5	0	1	0	0	12:14
2009-10	**Anaheim**	**NHL**	38	4	5	9	31	0	0	1	38	10.5	0	221	52.5	9:51	....	....	....	....	....	....	....	....	....
	NHL Totals		120	11	15	26	119	0	0	3	134	8.2		824	54.1	9:44	20	2	3	5	6	1	0	0	10:04

Signed as a free agent by **Anaheim**, July 12, 2006. • Missed majority of 2009-10 season recovering from foot injury suffered in pre-game skate at Columbus, November 13, 2009.

CAVANAGH, Tom (KAV-a-naw, TAWM) **SAN JOSE**

Left wing. Shoots left. 6', 200 lbs. Born, Warwick, RI, March 24, 1982. San Jose's 6th choice, 182nd overall, in 2001 Entry Draft.

Season	Club	League	GP	G	A	Pts	PIM	PP	SH	GW	S	%	+/-	TF	F%	Min	GP	G	A	Pts	PIM	PP	SH	GW	Min
1997-98	Toll Gate Titans	High-RI	15	5	17	22	·6	....	....	....	....	....	....	....	....	....	4	2	8	10	4	....	....	....	....
1998-99	Toll Gate Titans	High-RI	15	9	20	29	26	....	....	....	....	....	....	....	....	....	5	5	4	9	6	....	....	....	....
99-2000	Toll Gate Titans	High-RI	18	25	29	*54	28	....	....	....	....	....	....	....	....	....	5	0	12	12	9	....	....	....	....
2000-01	Exeter	High-NH	31	*42	40	82	34	....	....	....	....	....	....	....	....	....	....	....	....	....	....	....	....	....	....
2001-02	Harvard Crimson	ECAC	34	8	17	25	4	....	....	....	....	....	....	....	....	....	....	....	....	....	....	....	....	....	....
2002-03	Harvard Crimson	ECAC	34	14	13	27	31	....	....	....	....	....	....	....	....	....	....	....	....	....	....	....	....	....	....
2003-04	Harvard Crimson	ECAC	36	16	20	36	26	....	....	....	....	....	....	....	....	....	....	....	....	....	....	....	....	....	....
2004-05	Harvard Crimson	ECAC	34	10	19	29	22	....	....	....	....	....	....	....	....	....	....	....	....	....	....	....	....	....	....
2005-06	Cleveland Barons	AHL	62	10	11	21	36	....	....	....	....	....	....	....	....	....	....	....	....	....	....	....	....	....	....
2006-07	Worcester Sharks	AHL	74	12	32	44	56	....	....	....	....	....	....	....	....	....	6	1	0	1	6	....	....	....	....
2007-08	**San Jose**	**NHL**	1	0	1	1	0	0	0	0	0	0.0	1	3	33.3	13:54	....	....	....	....	....	....	....	....	....
	Worcester Sharks	AHL	77	19	36	55	55	....	....	....	....	....	....	....	....	....	....	....	....	....	....	....	....	....	....
2008-09	**San Jose**	**NHL**	17	1	1	2	4	0	0	0	9	11.1	-2	57	45.6	7:44	....	....	....	....	....	....	....	....	....
	Worcester Sharks	AHL	51	15	24	39	37	....	....	....	....	....	....	....	....	....	12	3	2	5	8	....	....	....	....
2009-10	Manchester	AHL	17	3	5	8	10	....	....	....	....	....	....	....	....	....	....	....	....	....	....	....	....	....	....
	NHL Totals		18	1	2	3	4	0	0	0	9	11.1		60	45.0	8:04	....	....	....	....	....	....	....	....	....

ECAC Second All-Star Team (2005)
Signed as a free agent by **Manchester** (AHL), January 2, 2010.

CHARA, Zdeno (CHAH-rah, z'DEHN-oh) **BOS.**

Defense. Shoots left. 6'9", 255 lbs. Born, Trencin, Czechoslovakia, March 18, 1977. NY Islanders' 3rd choice, 56th overall, in 1996 Entry Draft.

Season	Club	League	GP	G	A	Pts	PIM	PP	SH	GW	S	%	+/-	TF	F%	Min	GP	G	A	Pts	PIM	PP	SH	GW	Min
1994-95	Dukla Trencin U18	Svk-U18	30	22	22	44	113	....	....	....	....	....	....	....	....	....	....	....	....	....	....	....	....	....	....
	Dukla Trencin Jr.	Slovak-Jr.	2	0	0	0	0	....	....	....	....	....	....	....	....	....	....	....	....	....	....	....	....	....	....
1995-96	Dukla Trencin Jr.	Slovak-Jr.	22	1	13	14	80	....	....	....	....	....	....	....	....	....	....	....	....	....	....	....	....	....	....
	HK VTJ Piestany	Slovak-2	10	1	3	4	10	....	....	....	....	....	....	....	....	....	....	....	....	....	....	....	....	....	....
	Sparta Jr.	CzRep-Jr.	15	1	2	3	42	....	....	....	....	....	....	....	....	....	....	....	....	....	....	....	....	....	....
	HC Sparta Praha	CzRep	1	0	0	0	0	....	....	....	....	....	....	....	....	....	....	....	....	....	....	....	....	....	....
1996-97	Prince George	WHL	49	3	19	22	120	....	....	....	....	....	....	....	....	....	15	1	7	8	45	....	....	....	....
1997-98	**NY Islanders**	**NHL**	25	0	1	1	50	0	0	0	10	0.0	1	....	....	....	....	....	....	....	....	....	....	....	....
	Kentucky	AHL	48	4	9	13	125	....	....	....	....	....	....	....	....	....	1	0	0	0	4	....	....	....	....
1998-99	**NY Islanders**	**NHL**	59	2	6	8	83	0	1	0	56	3.6	-8	0	0.0	18:54	....	....	....	....	....	....	....	....	....
	Lowell	AHL	23	2	2	4	47	....	....	....	....	....	....	....	....	....	....	....	....	....	....	....	....	....	....
99-2000	**NY Islanders**	**NHL**	65	2	9	11	57	0	0	1	47	4.3	-27	0	0.0	22:52	....	....	....	....	....	....	....	....	....

			Regular Season														Playoffs								
Season	Club	League	GP	G	A	Pts	PIM	PP	SH	GW	S	%	+/-	TF	F%	Min	GP	G	A	Pts	PIM	PP	SH	GW	Min
2000-01	**NY Islanders**	**NHL**	**82**	**2**	**7**	**9**	**157**	**0**	**1**	**0**	**83**	**2.4**	**–27**	**0**	**0.0**	**22:20**	....	....	....	....	....	....	....	....	....
2001-02	Dukla Trencin	Slovakia	8	2	2	4	32	....	....	....	....	....	....	....	....	....	....	....	....	....	....	....	....	....	....
	Ottawa	**NHL**	**75**	**10**	**13**	**23**	**156**	**4**	**1**	**2**	**105**	**9.5**	**30**	**0**	**0.0**	**22:16**	**10**	**0**	**1**	**1**	**12**	**0**	**0**	**0**	**26:07**
2002-03	**Ottawa**	**NHL**	**74**	**9**	**30**	**39**	**116**	**3**	**0**	**2**	**168**	**5.4**	**29**	**0**	**0.0**	**24:57**	**18**	**1**	**6**	**7**	**14**	**0**	**0**	**0**	**25:07**
2003-04	**Ottawa**	**NHL**	**79**	**16**	**25**	**41**	**147**	**7**	**0**	**3**	**185**	**8.6**	**33**	**0**	**0.0**	**24:38**	**7**	**1**	**1**	**2**	**8**	**0**	**0**	**0**	**24:38**
2004-05	Farjestad	Sweden	33	10	15	25	132	....	....	....	....	....	....	....	....	....	13	3	5	8	82	....	....	....	....
2005-06	**Ottawa**	**NHL**	**71**	**16**	**27**	**43**	**135**	**10**	**1**	**3**	**212**	**7.5**	**17**	**24**	**41.7**	**27:11**	**10**	**1**	**3**	**4**	**23**	**1**	**0**	**0**	**27:32**
	Slovakia	Olympics	6	1	1	2	2	....	....	....	....	....	....	....	....	....	....	....	....	....	....	....	....	....	....
2006-07	**Boston**	**NHL**	**80**	**11**	**32**	**43**	**100**	**9**	**0**	**3**	**204**	**5.4**	**–21**	**1**	**0.0**	**27:58**	....	....	....	....	....	....	....	....	....
2007-08	**Boston**	**NHL**	**77**	**17**	**34**	**51**	**114**	**9**	**1**	**0**	**207**	**8.2**	**14**	**0**	**0.0**	**26:50**	**7**	**1**	**1**	**2**	**12**	**1**	**0**	**0**	**25:52**
2008-09	**Boston**	**NHL**	**80**	**19**	**31**	**50**	**95**	**11**	**0**	**3**	**216**	**8.8**	**23**	**4**	**25.0**	**26:04**	**11**	**1**	**3**	**4**	**12**	**1**	**0**	**1**	**25:11**
2009-10	**Boston**	**NHL**	**80**	**7**	**37**	**44**	**87**	**4**	**0**	**1**	**242**	**2.9**	**19**	**2**	**50.0**	**25:22**	**13**	**2**	**5**	**7**	**29**	**0**	**0**	**1**	**28:08**
	Slovakia	Olympics	7	0	3	3	6	....	....	....	....	....	....	....	....	....	....	....	....	....	....	....	....	....	....
	NHL Totals		**847**	**111**	**252**	**363**	**1297**	**57**	**5**	**18**	**1735**	**6.4**		**31**	**38.7**	**24:38**	**76**	**7**	**20**	**27**	**110**	**3**	**0**	**2**	**26:07**

AHL All-Rookie Team (1998) • NHL First All-Star Team (2004, 2009) • NHL Second All-Star Team (2006, 2008) • James Norris Memorial Trophy (2009)

Played in NHL All-Star Game (2003, 2007, 2008, 2009)

Traded to **Ottawa** by **NY Islanders** with Bill Muckalt and NY Islanders' 1st round choice (Jason Spezza) in 2001 Entry Draft for Alexei Yashin, June 23, 2001. Signed as a free agent by **Farjestad** (Sweden), September 24, 2004. Signed as a free agent by **Boston**, July 1, 2006.

CHEECHOO, Jonathan

(CHEE-choo, JAWN-ah-thuhn)

Right wing. Shoots right. 6'1", 200 lbs. Born, Moose Factory, Ont., July 15, 1980. San Jose's 2nd choice, 29th overall, in 1998 Entry Draft.

Season	Club	League	GP	G	A	Pts	PIM	PP	SH	GW	S	%	+/-	TF	F%	Min	GP	G	A	Pts	PIM	PP	SH	GW	Min
1996-97	Kitchener	OHA-B	43	35	41	76	33	....	....	....	....	....	....	....	....	....	....	....	....	....	....	....	....	....	....
1997-98	Belleville Bulls	OHL	64	31	45	76	62	....	....	....	....	....	....	....	....	....	10	4	2	6	10	....	....	....	....
1998-99	Belleville Bulls	OHL	63	35	47	82	74	....	....	....	....	....	....	....	....	....	21	15	15	30	27	....	....	....	....
99-2000	Belleville Bulls	OHL	66	45	46	91	102	....	....	....	....	....	....	....	....	....	16	5	12	17	16	....	....	....	....
2000-01	Kentucky	AHL	75	32	34	66	63	....	....	....	....	....	....	....	....	....	3	0	0	0	0	....	....	....	....
2001-02	Cleveland Barons	AHL	53	21	25	46	54	....	....	....	....	....	....	....	....	....	....	....	....	....	....	....	....	....	....
2002-03	**San Jose**	**NHL**	**66**	**9**	**7**	**16**	**39**	**0**	**0**	**3**	**94**	**9.6**	**–5**	**8**	**37.5**	**10:43**	....	....	....	....	....	....	....	....	....
	Cleveland Barons	AHL	9	3	4	7	16	....	....	....	....	....	....	....	....	....	....	....	....	....	....	....	....	....	....
2003-04	**San Jose**	**NHL**	**81**	**28**	**19**	**47**	**33**	**8**	**0**	**9**	**175**	**16.0**	**5**	**7**	**14.3**	**16:12**	**17**	**4**	**6**	**10**	**10**	**1**	**0**	**0**	**17:37**
2004-05	HV 71 Jonkoping	Sweden	20	5	0	5	10	....	....	....	....	....	....	....	....	....	....	....	....	....	....	....	....	....	....
2005-06	**San Jose**	**NHL**	**82**	***56**	**37**	**93**	**58**	**24**	**2**	***11**	**317**	**17.7**	**23**	**20**	**20.0**	**19:57**	**11**	**4**	**5**	**9**	**8**	**1**	**0**	**1**	**24:00**
2006-07	**San Jose**	**NHL**	**76**	**37**	**32**	**69**	**69**	**15**	**0**	**5**	**250**	**14.8**	**11**	**32**	**31.3**	**17:34**	**11**	**3**	**3**	**6**	**6**	**1**	**0**	**1**	**16:25**
2007-08	**San Jose**	**NHL**	**69**	**23**	**14**	**37**	**46**	**10**	**0**	**4**	**220**	**10.5**	**11**	**20**	**20.0**	**16:36**	**13**	**4**	**4**	**8**	**4**	**0**	**0**	**1**	**18:21**
2008-09	**San Jose**	**NHL**	**66**	**12**	**17**	**29**	**59**	**5**	**1**	**4**	**152**	**7.9**	**–3**	**4**	**25.0**	**15:19**	**6**	**1**	**1**	**2**	**4**	**0**	**0**	**0**	**10:10**
2009-10	**Ottawa**	**NHL**	**61**	**5**	**9**	**14**	**20**	**0**	**0**	**0**	**117**	**4.3**	**–13**	**10**	**40.0**	**11:57**	**1**	**0**	**0**	**0**	**0**	**0**	**0**	**0**	**7:13**
	Binghamton	AHL	25	8	6	14	37	....	....	....	....	....	....	....	....	....	....	....	....	....	....	....	....	....	....
	NHL Totals		**501**	**170**	**135**	**305**	**324**	**62**	**3**	**36**	**1325**	**12.8**		**101**	**26.7**	**15:43**	**59**	**16**	**19**	**35**	**32**	**3**	**0**	**3**	**17:49**

OHL All-Rookie Team (1998) • AHL All-Rookie Team (2001) • Maurice "Rocket" Richard Trophy (2006)

Played in NHL All-Star Game (2007)

Signed as a free agent by **Jonkoping** (Sweden), December 21, 2004. Traded to **Ottawa** by **San Jose** with Milan Michalek and San Jose's 2nd round choice (later traded to NY Islanders, later traded to Chicago - Chicago selected Kent Simpson) in 2010 Entry Draft for Dany Heatley and Ottawa's 5th round choice (Isaac MacLeod) in 2010 Entry Draft, September 12, 2009.

CHELIOS, Chris

(CHELL-EE-ohs, KRIHS)

Defense. Shoots right. 6', 191 lbs. Born, Chicago, IL, January 25, 1962. Montreal's 5th choice, 40th overall, in 1981 Entry Draft.

Season	Club	League	GP	G	A	Pts	PIM	PP	SH	GW	S	%	+/-	TF	F%	Min	GP	G	A	Pts	PIM	PP	SH	GW	Min
1979-80	Moose Jaw	SJHL	53	12	31	43	118	....	....	....	....	....	....	....	....	....	....	....	....	....	....	....	....	....	....
1980-81	Moose Jaw	SJHL	54	23	64	87	175	....	....	....	....	....	....	....	....	....	....	....	....	....	....	....	....	....	....
1981-82	U. of Wisconsin	WCHA	43	6	43	49	50	....	....	....	....	....	....	....	....	....	....	....	....	....	....	....	....	....	....
1982-83	U. of Wisconsin	WCHA	26	9	17	26	50	....	....	....	....	....	....	....	....	....	....	....	....	....	....	....	....	....	....
1983-84	United States	Nat-Tm	60	14	35	49	58	....	....	....	....	....	....	....	....	....	....	....	....	....	....	....	....	....	....
	United States	Olympics	6	0	4	4	8	....	....	....	....	....	....	....	....	....	....	....	....	....	....	....	....	....	....
	Montreal	**NHL**	**12**	**0**	**2**	**2**	**12**	**0**	**0**	**0**	**23**	**0.0**	**–5**	....	....	....	**15**	**1**	**9**	**10**	**17**	**1**	**0**	**0**	....
1984-85	**Montreal**	**NHL**	**74**	**9**	**55**	**64**	**87**	**2**	**1**	**0**	**199**	**4.5**	**11**	....	....	....	**9**	**2**	**8**	**10**	**17**	**2**	**0**	**0**	....
1985-86♦	**Montreal**	**NHL**	**41**	**8**	**26**	**34**	**67**	**2**	**0**	**0**	**101**	**7.9**	**4**	....	....	....	**20**	**2**	**9**	**11**	**49**	**1**	**0**	**0**	....
1986-87	**Montreal**	**NHL**	**71**	**11**	**33**	**44**	**124**	**6**	**0**	**2**	**141**	**7.8**	**–5**	....	....	....	**17**	**4**	**9**	**13**	**38**	**2**	**1**	**0**	....
1987-88	**Montreal**	**NHL**	**71**	**20**	**41**	**61**	**172**	**10**	**1**	**5**	**199**	**10.1**	**14**	....	....	....	**11**	**3**	**1**	**4**	**29**	**1**	**0**	**0**	....
1988-89	**Montreal**	**NHL**	**80**	**15**	**58**	**73**	**185**	**8**	**0**	**6**	**206**	**7.3**	**35**	....	....	....	**21**	**4**	**15**	**19**	**28**	**1**	**0**	**2**	....
1989-90	**Montreal**	**NHL**	**53**	**9**	**22**	**31**	**136**	**1**	**2**	**1**	**123**	**7.3**	**20**	....	....	....	**5**	**0**	**1**	**1**	**8**	**0**	**0**	**0**	....
1990-91	**Chicago**	**NHL**	**77**	**12**	**52**	**64**	**192**	**5**	**2**	**2**	**187**	**6.4**	**23**	....	....	....	**6**	**1**	**7**	**8**	**46**	**1**	**0**	**0**	....
1991-92	**Chicago**	**NHL**	**80**	**9**	**47**	**56**	**245**	**2**	**2**	**2**	**239**	**3.8**	**24**	....	....	....	**18**	**6**	**15**	**21**	**37**	**3**	**0**	**1**	....
1992-93	**Chicago**	**NHL**	**84**	**15**	**58**	**73**	**282**	**8**	**0**	**2**	**290**	**5.2**	**14**	....	....	....	**4**	**0**	**2**	**2**	**14**	**0**	**0**	**0**	....
1993-94	**Chicago**	**NHL**	**76**	**16**	**44**	**60**	**212**	**7**	**1**	**2**	**219**	**7.3**	**12**	....	....	....	**6**	**1**	**1**	**2**	**8**	**1**	**0**	**0**	....
1994-95	EHC Biel-Bienne	Swiss	3	0	3	3	4	....	....	....	....	....	....	....	....	....	....	....	....	....	....	....	....	....	....
	Chicago	**NHL**	**48**	**5**	**33**	**38**	**72**	**3**	**1**	**0**	**166**	**3.0**	**17**	....	....	....	**16**	**4**	**7**	**11**	**12**	**0**	**1**	**3**	....
1995-96	**Chicago**	**NHL**	**81**	**14**	**58**	**72**	**140**	**7**	**0**	**3**	**219**	**6.4**	**25**	....	....	....	**9**	**0**	**3**	**3**	**8**	**0**	**0**	**0**	....
1996-97	**Chicago**	**NHL**	**72**	**10**	**38**	**48**	**112**	**2**	**0**	**2**	**194**	**5.2**	**16**	....	....	....	**6**	**0**	**1**	**1**	**8**	**0**	**0**	**0**	....
1997-98	**Chicago**	**NHL**	**81**	**3**	**39**	**42**	**151**	**1**	**0**	**0**	**205**	**1.5**	**–7**	....	....	....	....	....	....	....	....	....	....	....	....
	United States	Olympics	4	2	0	2	2	....	....	....	....	....	....	....	....	....	....	....	....	....	....	....	....	....	....
1998-99	**Chicago**	**NHL**	**65**	**8**	**26**	**34**	**89**	**2**	**1**	**0**	**172**	**4.7**	**–4**	**4**	**25.0**	**27:19**	....	....	....	....	....	....	....	....	....
	Detroit	**NHL**	**10**	**1**	**1**	**2**	**4**	**1**	**0**	**1**	**15**	**6.7**	**5**	**0**	**0.0**	**22:21**	**10**	**0**	**4**	**4**	**14**	**0**	**0**	**0**	**27:15**
99-2000	**Detroit**	**NHL**	**81**	**3**	**31**	**34**	**103**	**0**	**0**	**0**	**135**	**2.2**	**48**	**0**	**0.0**	**25:16**	**9**	**0**	**1**	**1**	**8**	**0**	**0**	**0**	**24:06**
2000-01	**Detroit**	**NHL**	**24**	**0**	**3**	**3**	**45**	**0**	**0**	**0**	**26**	**0.0**	**4**	**0**	**0.0**	**22:51**	**5**	**1**	**0**	**1**	**2**	**0**	**0**	**0**	**19:41**
2001-02♦	**Detroit**	**NHL**	**79**	**6**	**33**	**39**	**126**	**1**	**0**	**1**	**128**	**4.7**	***40**	**0**	**0.0**	**25:18**	**23**	**1**	**13**	**14**	**44**	**1**	**0**	**0**	**26:22**
	United States	Olympics	6	1	0	1	4	....	....	....	....	....	....	....	....	....	....	....	....	....	....	....	....	....	....
2002-03	**Detroit**	**NHL**	**66**	**2**	**17**	**19**	**78**	**0**	**1**	**1**	**92**	**2.2**	**4**	**0**	**0.0**	**24:15**	**4**	**0**	**0**	**0**	**2**	**0**	**0**	**0**	**25:43**
2003-04	**Detroit**	**NHL**	**69**	**2**	**19**	**21**	**61**	**0**	**0**	**0**	**113**	**1.8**	**12**	**0**	**0.0**	**21:21**	**8**	**0**	**1**	**1**	**4**	**0**	**0**	**0**	**21:13**
2004-05	Motor City	UHL	23	5	19	24	25	....	....	....	....	....	....	....	....	....	....	....	....	....	....	....	....	....	....
2005-06	**Detroit**	**NHL**	**81**	**4**	**7**	**11**	**108**	**1**	**1**	**0**	**83**	**4.8**	**22**	**4**	**25.0**	**18:29**	**6**	**0**	**0**	**0**	**6**	**0**	**0**	**0**	**19:25**
	United States	Olympics	6	0	1	1	2	....	....	....	....	....	....	....	....	....	....	....	....	....	....	....	....	....	....
2006-07	**Detroit**	**NHL**	**71**	**0**	**11**	**11**	**34**	**0**	**0**	**0**	**72**	**0.0**	**11**	**1**	**0.0**	**18:08**	**18**	**1**	**6**	**7**	**12**	**0**	**1**	**0**	**20:07**
2007-08♦	**Detroit**	**NHL**	**69**	**3**	**9**	**12**	**36**	**0**	**0**	**1**	**60**	**5.0**	**11**	**0**	**0.0**	**16:58**	**14**	**0**	**0**	**0**	**10**	**0**	**0**	**0**	**12:54**
2008-09	**Detroit**	**NHL**	**28**	**0**	**0**	**0**	**18**	**0**	**0**	**0**	**14**	**0.0**	**1**	**0**	**0.0**	**11:40**	**6**	**0**	**0**	**0**	**2**	**0**	**0**	**0**	**7:21**
	Grand Rapids	AHL	2	0	1	1	2	....	....	....	....	....	....	....	....	....	....	....	....	....	....	....	....	....	....
2009-10	Chicago Wolves	AHL	46	5	17	22	24	....	....	....	....	....	....	....	....	....	14	0	0	0	12	....	....	....	....
	Atlanta	**NHL**	**7**	**0**	**0**	**0**	**0**	**0**	**0**	**0**	**5**	**0.0**	**–2**	**0**	**0.0**	**11:10**	....	....	....	....	....	....	....	....	....
	NHL Totals		**1651**	**185**	**763**	**948**	**2891**	**69**	**13**	**31**	**3626**	**5.1**		**9**	**22.2**	**21:35**	**266**	**31**	**113**	**144**	**423**	**14**	**3**	**6**	**21:04**

WCHA Second All-Star Team (1983) • NCAA Championship All-Tournament Team (1983) • NHL All-Rookie Team (1985) • NHL First All-Star Team (1989, 1993, 1995, 1996, 2002) • James Norris Memorial Trophy (1989, 1993, 1996) • NHL Second All-Star Team (1991, 1997) • Bud Light Plus/Minus Award (2002) • Mark Messier NHL Leadership Award (2007)

Played in NHL All-Star Game (1985, 1990, 1991, 1992, 1993, 1994, 1996, 1997, 1998, 2000, 2002)

Traded to **Chicago** by **Montreal** with Montreal's 2nd round choice (Michael Pomichter) in 1991 Entry Draft for Denis Savard, June 29, 1990. Traded to **Detroit** by **Chicago** for Anders Eriksson and Detroit's 1st round choices in 1999 (Steve McCarthy) and 2001 (Adam Munro) Entry Drafts, March 23, 1999. • Missed majority of 2000-01 season recovering from knee injury suffered in game vs. Dallas, November 17, 2000. Signed as a free agent by **Motor City** (UHL), February 1, 2005. • Missed majority of 2008-09 season recovering from leg injury suffered during pre-season game at Montreal, September 30, 2008. Signed as a free agent by **Chicago** (AHL), October 20, 2009. Signed as a free agent by **Atlanta**, March 2, 2010.

CHIMERA, Jason

(shih-MAIR-uh, JAY-suhn) **WSH.**

Left wing. Shoots left. 6'2", 216 lbs. Born, Edmonton, Alta., May 2, 1979. Edmonton's 5th choice, 121st overall, in 1997 Entry Draft.

Season	Club	League	GP	G	A	Pts	PIM	PP	SH	GW	S	%	+/-	TF	F%	Min	GP	G	A	Pts	PIM	PP	SH	GW	Min
1994-95	Edmonton Pats	AMHL	33	27	31	58	42	....	....	....	....	....	....	....	....	....	....	....	....	....	....	....	....	....	....
1995-96	Edmonton Pats	AMHL	34	23	24	47	44	....	....	....	....	....	....	....	....	....	....	....	....	....	....	....	....	....	....
1996-97	Medicine Hat	WHL	71	16	23	39	64	....	....	....	....	....	....	....	....	....	4	0	1	1	4	....	....	....	....
1997-98	Medicine Hat	WHL	72	34	32	66	93	....	....	....	....	....	....	....	....	....	....	....	....	....	....	....	....	....	....
	Hamilton	AHL	4	0	0	0	8	....	....	....	....	....	....	....	....	....	....	....	....	....	....	....	....	....	....
1998-99	Medicine Hat	WHL	37	18	22	40	84	....	....	....	....	....	....	....	....	....	....	....	....	....	....	....	....	....	....
	Brandon	WHL	21	14	12	26	32	....	....	....	....	....	....	....	....	....	5	4	1	5	8	....	....	....	....
99-2000	Hamilton	AHL	78	15	13	28	77	....	....	....	....	....	....	....	....	....	10	0	2	2	12	....	....	....	....
2000-01	**Edmonton**	**NHL**	**1**	**0**	**0**	**0**	**0**	**0**	**0**	**0**	**0**	**0.0**	**0**	**0**	**0.0**	**6:58**	....	....	....	....	....	....	....	....	....
	Hamilton	AHL	78	29	25	54	93	....	....	....	....	....	....	....	....	....	....	....	....	....	....	....	....	....	....

Season	Club	League	Regular Season														Playoffs								
			GP	G	A	Pts	PIM	PP	SH	GW	S	%	+/-	TF	F%	Min	GP	G	A	Pts	PIM	PP	SH	GW	Min
2001-02	Edmonton	NHL	3	1	0	1	0	0	0	0	3	33.3	–3	0	0.0	12:44	....	....	....	....	....	....	....	....	....
	Hamilton	AHL	77	26	51	77	158	....	....	....	....	....	....	....	....	....	15	4	6	10	10	....	....	....	....
2002-03	Edmonton	NHL	66	14	9	23	36	0	1	4	90	15.6	–2	11	54.6	10:46	2	0	2	2	0	0	0	0	10:55
2003-04	Edmonton	NHL	60	4	8	12	57	0	0	1	79	5.1	–1	22	31.8	10:07	....	....	....	....	....	....	....	....	....
2004-05	AS Varese Hockey	Italy	15	7	3	10	34	....	....	....	....	....	....	....	....	....	5	2	1	3	31	....	....	....	....
2005-06	Columbus	NHL	80	17	13	30	95	1	1	5	127	13.4	–10	16	50.0	12:41	....	....	....	....	....	....	....	....	....
2006-07	Columbus	NHL	82	15	21	36	91	2	2	2	151	9.9	2	38	36.8	15:22	....	....	....	....	....	....	....	....	....
2007-08	Columbus	NHL	81	14	17	31	98	1	1	3	198	7.1	–5	35	45.7	17:30	....	....	....	....	....	....	....	....	....
2008-09	Columbus	NHL	49	8	14	22	41	1	0	1	115	7.0	8	42	42.9	16:15	4	0	1	1	2	0	0	0	13:21
2009-10	Columbus	NHL	39	8	9	17	47	1	0	1	92	8.7	–7	23	65.2	14:47	....	....	....	....	....	....	....	....	....
	Washington	NHL	39	7	10	17	51	0	0	0	68	10.3	6	17	41.2	12:36	7	1	2	3	2	0	0	1	11:46
	NHL Totals		500	88	101	189	516	6	5	17	923	9.5		204	44.6	13:50	13	1	5	6	4	0	0	1	12:07

AHL First All-Star Team (2002)

Traded to **Phoenix** by **Edmonton** with Edmonton's 3rd round choice (later traded to Carolina, later traded to NY Rangers – NY Rangers selected Billy Ryan) in 2004 Entry Draft for New Jersey's 2nd round choice (previously acquired, Edmonton selected Geoff Paukovich) in 2004 Entry Draft and Buffalo's 4th round choice (previously acquired, Edmonton selected Liam Reddox) in 2004 Entry Draft, June 26, 2004. Signed as a free agent by **Varese** (Italy), December 15, 2004. Traded to **Columbus** by **Phoenix** with Cale Hulse and Mike Rupp for Geoff Sanderson and Tim Jackman, October 8, 2005. Traded to **Washington** by **Columbus** for Chris Clark and Milan Jurcina, December 28, 2009.

CHIPCHURA, Kyle

(chip-CHUHR-a, KIGHL) **ANA.**

Center. Shoots left. 6'2", 206 lbs. Born, Westlock, Alta., February 19, 1986. Montreal's 1st choice, 18th overall, in 2004 Entry Draft.

Season	Club	League	GP	G	A	Pts	PIM	PP	SH	GW	S	%	+/-	TF	F%	Min	GP	G	A	Pts	PIM	PP	SH	GW	Min
2000-01	Spruce Grove	AMBHL	36	26	34	60	48	....	....	....	....	....	....	....	....	....	....	....	....	....	....	....	....	....	....
2001-02	Ft. Saskatchewan	AMBHL	33	15	36	51	78	....	....	....	....	....	....	....	....	....	17	16	20	36	....	....	....	....	....
2002-03	Prince Albert	WHL	63	9	21	30	89	....	....	....	....	....	....	....	....	....	....	....	....	....	....	....	....	....	....
2003-04	Prince Albert	WHL	64	15	33	48	118	....	....	....	....	....	....	....	....	....	6	2	4	6	12	....	....	....	....
2004-05	Prince Albert	WHL	28	14	18	32	32	....	....	....	....	....	....	....	....	....	14	4	7	11	25	....	....	....	....
2005-06	Prince Albert	WHL	59	21	34	55	81	....	....	....	....	....	....	....	....	....	....	....	....	....	....	....	....	....	....
	Hamilton	AHL	8	1	2	3	6	....	....	....	....	....	....	....	....	....	....	....	....	....	....	....	....	....	....
2006-07	Hamilton	AHL	80	12	27	39	56	....	....	....	....	....	....	....	....	....	22	6	7	13	20	....	....	....	....
2007-08	**Montreal**	NHL	36	4	7	11	10	0	0	0	36	11.1	–1	317	43.9	11:22	....	....	....	....	....	....	....	....	....
	Hamilton	AHL	39	10	11	21	27	....	....	....	....	....	....	....	....	....	....	....	....	....	....	....	....	....	....
2008-09	**Montreal**	NHL	13	0	3	3	5	0	0	0	5	0.0	–6	107	43.9	10:18	....	....	....	....	....	....	....	....	....
	Hamilton	AHL	51	14	21	35	65	....	....	....	....	....	....	....	....	....	6	3	0	3	2	....	....	....	....
2009-10	**Montreal**	NHL	19	0	0	0	16	0	0	0	11	0.0	–10	106	53.8	8:38	....	....	....	....	....	....	....	....	....
	Anaheim	NHL	55	6	6	12	56	0	1	1	43	14.0	–2	670	47.9	12:29	....	....	....	....	....	....	....	....	....
	NHL Totals		123	10	16	26	87	0	1	1	95	10.5		1200	47.0	11:20	....	....	....	....	....	....	....	....	....

WHL East Second All-Star Team (2006)

Traded to **Anaheim** by **Montreal** for a 4th round choice in 2011 Entry Draft, December 1, 2009.

CHORNEY, Taylor

(CHOHR-nee, TAY-luhr) **EDM.**

Defense. Shoots left. 5'11", 182 lbs. Born, Thunder Bay, Ont., April 27, 1987. Edmonton's 2nd choice, 36th overall, in 2005 Entry Draft.

Season	Club	League	GP	G	A	Pts	PIM	PP	SH	GW	S	%	+/-	TF	F%	Min	GP	G	A	Pts	PIM	PP	SH	GW	Min
2003-04	Shat.-St. Mary's	High-MN	74	12	44	56	58	....	....	....	....	....	....	....	....	....	....	....	....	....	....	....	....	....	....
2004-05	Shat.-St. Mary's	High-MN	50	4	30	34	52	....	....	....	....	....	....	....	....	....	....	....	....	....	....	....	....	....	....
2005-06	North Dakota	WCHA	44	3	15	18	54	....	....	....	....	....	....	....	....	....	....	....	....	....	....	....	....	....	....
2006-07	North Dakota	WCHA	39	8	23	31	48	....	....	....	....	....	....	....	....	....	....	....	....	....	....	....	....	....	....
2007-08	North Dakota	WCHA	43	3	21	24	24	....	....	....	....	....	....	....	....	....	....	....	....	....	....	....	....	....	....
2008-09	**Edmonton**	NHL	2	0	0	0	0	0	0	0	0	0.0	–4	0	0.0	15:43	....	....	....	....	....	....	....	....	....
	Springfield	AHL	68	5	16	21	22	....	....	....	....	....	....	....	....	....	....	....	....	....	....	....	....	....	....
2009-10	**Edmonton**	NHL	42	0	3	3	12	0	0	0	35	0.0	–21	0	0.0	17:24	....	....	....	....	....	....	....	....	....
	Springfield	AHL	32	4	9	13	14	....	....	....	....	....	....	....	....	....	....	....	....	....	....	....	....	....	....
	NHL Totals		44	0	3	3	12	0	0	0	35	0.0		0	0.0	17:19	....	....	....	....	....	....	....	....	....

WCHA Second All-Star Team (2007) • NCAA West Second All-American Team (2007) • WCHA First All-Star Team (2008)

CHRISTENSEN, Erik

(KRIHS-tehn-suhn, AIR-ihk) **NYR**

Center. Shoots left. 6'1", 203 lbs. Born, Edmonton, Alta., December 17, 1983. Pittsburgh's 3rd choice, 69th overall, in 2002 Entry Draft.

Season	Club	League	GP	G	A	Pts	PIM	PP	SH	GW	S	%	+/-	TF	F%	Min	GP	G	A	Pts	PIM	PP	SH	GW	Min
1998-99	Leduc Oil Kings	AMBHL	36	34	42	76	70	....	....	....	....	....	....	....	....	....	....	....	....	....	....	....	....	....	....
99-2000	Kamloops Blazers	WHL	66	9	5	14	41	....	....	....	....	....	....	....	....	....	4	0	0	0	2	....	....	....	....
2000-01	Kamloops Blazers	WHL	72	21	23	44	36	....	....	....	....	....	....	....	....	....	4	1	1	2	0	....	....	....	....
2001-02	Kamloops Blazers	WHL	70	22	36	58	68	....	....	....	....	....	....	....	....	....	4	0	0	0	4	....	....	....	....
2002-03	Kamloops Blazers	WHL	67	*54	54	*108	60	....	....	....	....	....	....	....	....	....	6	1	7	8	14	....	....	....	....
2003-04	Kamloops Blazers	WHL	29	10	14	24	40	....	....	....	....	....	....	....	....	....	....	....	....	....	....	....	....	....	....
	Brandon	WHL	34	17	21	38	20	....	....	....	....	....	....	....	....	....	11	8	4	12	8	....	....	....	....
2004-05	Wilkes-Barre	AHL	77	14	13	27	33	....	....	....	....	....	....	....	....	....	11	1	6	7	4	....	....	....	....
2005-06	**Pittsburgh**	NHL	33	6	7	13	34	2	0	0	85	7.1	–3	381	53.0	14:17	....	....	....	....	....	....	....	....	....
	Wilkes-Barre	AHL	48	24	22	46	50	....	....	....	....	....	....	....	....	....	11	2	2	4	2	....	....	....	....
2006-07	**Pittsburgh**	NHL	61	18	15	33	26	6	0	1	133	13.5	–3	240	56.3	11:38	4	0	0	0	6	0	0	0	8:15
	Wilkes-Barre	AHL	16	12	12	24	8	....	....	....	....	....	....	....	....	....	....	....	....	....	....	....	....	....	....
2007-08	**Pittsburgh**	NHL	49	9	11	20	28	2	0	0	109	8.3	–3	314	58.6	12:37	....	....	....	....	....	....	....	....	....
	Atlanta	NHL	10	2	2	4	2	0	0	0	23	8.7	–7	160	58.1	16:57	....	....	....	....	....	....	....	....	....
2008-09	**Atlanta**	NHL	47	5	14	19	14	1	0	0	90	5.6	–7	427	54.6	11:55	....	....	....	....	....	....	....	....	....
	Anaheim	NHL	17	2	7	9	6	1	0	0	32	6.3	–2	70	62.9	11:55	8	0	2	2	0	0	0	0	10:37
2009-10	**Anaheim**	NHL	9	0	0	0	2	0	0	0	9	0.0	–3	51	41.2	11:27	....	....	....	....	....	....	....	....	....
	Manitoba Moose	AHL	6	2	0	2	0	....	....	....	....	....	....	....	....	....	....	....	....	....	....	....	....	....	....
	NY Rangers	NHL	49	8	18	26	24	1	0	1	77	10.4	14	623	49.4	15:28	....	....	....	....	....	....	....	....	....
	NHL Totals		275	50	74	124	136	13	0	2	558	9.0		2266	53.8	13:28	12	0	2	2	6	0	0	0	9:50

WHL West First All-Star Team (2003) • Canadian Major Junior Second All-Star Team (2003)

Traded to **Atlanta** by **Pittsburgh** with Colby Armstrong, Angelo Esposito and Pittsburgh's 1st round choice (Daultan Leveille) in 2008 Entry Draft for Marian Hossa and Pascal Dupuis, February 26, 2008. Traded to **Anaheim** by **Atlanta** for Eric O'Dell, March 4, 2009. Claimed on waivers by **NY Rangers** from **Anaheim**, December 2, 2009.

CHUCKO, Kris

(CHUH-koh, KRIHS) **CGY.**

Left wing. Shoots right. 6'2", 190 lbs. Born, Burnaby, B.C., March 13, 1986. Calgary's 1st choice, 24th overall, in 2004 Entry Draft.

Season	Club	League	GP	G	A	Pts	PIM	PP	SH	GW	S	%	+/-	TF	F%	Min	GP	G	A	Pts	PIM	PP	SH	GW	Min
2002-03	Salmon Arm	BCHL	59	14	19	33	80	....	....	....	....	....	....	....	....	....	11	5	3	8	12	....	....	....	....
2003-04	Salmon Arm	BCHL	53	32	55	87	161	....	....	....	....	....	....	....	....	....	14	10	9	19	36	....	....	....	....
2004-05	U. of Minnesota	WCHA	44	10	11	21	61	....	....	....	....	....	....	....	....	....	....	....	....	....	....	....	....	....	....
2005-06	U. of Minnesota	WCHA	33	4	9	13	40	....	....	....	....	....	....	....	....	....	....	....	....	....	....	....	....	....	....
2006-07	Omaha	AHL	80	14	14	28	72	....	....	....	....	....	....	....	....	....	6	0	0	0	2	....	....	....	....
2007-08	Quad City Flames	AHL	80	15	15	30	38	....	....	....	....	....	....	....	....	....	....	....	....	....	....	....	....	....	....
2008-09	**Calgary**	NHL	2	0	0	0	2	0	0	0	0	0.0	0	1	0.0	7:02	....	....	....	....	....	....	....	....	....
	Quad City Flames	AHL	74	28	23	51	59	....	....	....	....	....	....	....	....	....	....	....	....	....	....	....	....	....	....
2009-10	Abbotsford Heat	AHL	41	9	9	18	56	....	....	....	....	....	....	....	....	....	....	....	....	....	....	....	....	....	....
	NHL Totals		2	0	0	0	2	0	0	0	0	0.0		1	0.0	7:02	....	....	....	....	....	....	....	....	....

CLARK, Brett

(KLAHRK, BREHT) **T.B.**

Defense. Shoots left. 6', 195 lbs. Born, Wapella, Sask., December 23, 1976. Montreal's 7th choice, 154th overall, in 1996 Entry Draft.

Season	Club	League	GP	G	A	Pts	PIM	PP	SH	GW	S	%	+/-	TF	F%	Min	GP	G	A	Pts	PIM	PP	SH	GW	Min
1994-95	Melville	SJHL	62	19	32	51	77	....	....	....	....	....	....	....	....	....	....	....	....	....	....	....	....	....	....
1995-96	U. of Maine	H-East	39	7	31	38	22	....	....	....	....	....	....	....	....	....	....	....	....	....	....	....	....	....	....
1996-97	Canada	Nat-Tm	57	6	21	27	52	....	....	....	....	....	....	....	....	....	....	....	....	....	....	....	....	....	....
1997-98	**Montreal**	NHL	41	1	0	1	20	0	0	0	26	3.8	–3	....	....	....	4	0	1	1	4	....	....	....	....
	Fredericton	AHL	20	0	6	6	6	....	....	....	....	....	....	....	....	....	....	....	....	....	....	....	....	....	....
1998-99	**Montreal**	NHL	61	2	2	4	16	0	0	0	36	5.6	–3	0	0.0	13:11	....	....	....	....	....	....	....	....	....
	Fredericton	AHL	3	1	0	1	0	....	....	....	....	....	....	....	....	....	....	....	....	....	....	....	....	....	....
99-2000	**Atlanta**	NHL	14	0	1	1	4	0	0	0	13	0.0	–12	0	0.0	16:51	....	....	....	....	....	....	....	....	....
	Orlando	IHL	63	9	17	26	31	....	....	....	....	....	....	....	....	....	6	0	1	1	0	....	....	....	....
2000-01	**Atlanta**	NHL	28	1	2	3	14	0	0	0	35	2.9	–12	0	0.0	18:02	....	....	....	....	....	....	....	....	....
	Orlando	IHL	43	2	9	11	32	....	....	....	....	....	....	....	....	....	15	1	6	7	2	....	....	....	....

Season	Club	League	GP	G	A	Pts	PIM	PP	SH	GW	S	%	+/-	TF	F%	Min	GP	G	A	Pts	PIM	PP	SH	GW	Min
2001-02	Atlanta	NHL	2	0	0	0	0	0	0	0	0	0.0	-3		1100.0	15:32									
	Chicago Wolves	AHL	42	3	17	20	18																		
	Hershey Bears	AHL	32	7	9	16	12										8	0	2	2	6				
2002-03	Hershey Bears	AHL	80	8	27	35	26										5	0	4	4	4				
2003-04	Colorado	NHL	12	1	1	2	6	0	0	0	14	7.1	3	0	0.0	10:26									
	Hershey Bears	AHL	64	11	21	32	37																		
2004-05	Hershey Bears	AHL	67	7	37	44	54																		
2005-06	Colorado	NHL	80	9	27	36	56	4	0	1	148	6.1	3	1	0.0	19:39	9	2	2	4	2	0	1	0	24:17
2006-07	Colorado	NHL	82	10	29	39	50	4	0	1	140	7.1	5		1100.0	23:41									
2007-08	Colorado	NHL	57	5	16	21	33	1	0	0	87	5.7	5	0	0.0	23:09									
2008-09	Colorado	NHL	76	2	10	12	32	0	0	1	97	2.1	-16	0	0.0	22:20									
2009-10	Colorado	NHL	64	3	17	20	28	2	0	1	75	4.0	6	0	0.0	19:08	1	0	0	0	0	0	0	0	17:55
	NHL Totals		517	34	105	139	259	11	0	4	671	5.1		3	66.7	19:52	10	2	2	4	2	0	1	0	23:39

Claimed by **Atlanta** from **Montreal** in Expansion Draft, June 25, 1999. Traded to **Colorado** by **Atlanta** for Frederic Cassivi, January 24, 2002. Signed as a free agent by **Tampa Bay**, July 5, 2010.

CLARK, Chris (KLAHRK, KRIHS) CBJ

Right wing. Shoots right. 6', 196 lbs. Born, South Windsor, CT, March 8, 1976. Calgary's 3rd choice, 77th overall, in 1994 Entry Draft.

Season	Club	League	GP	G	A	Pts	PIM	PP	SH	GW	S	%	+/-	TF	F%	Min	GP	G	A	Pts	PIM	PP	SH	GW	Min
1990-91	South Windsor	High-CT	23	16	15	31	24																		
1991-92	Spring. Olympics	NEJHL	49	21	29	50	56																		
1992-93	Spring. Olympics	NEJHL	43	17	60	77	120																		
1993-94	Spring. Olympics	NEJHL	35	31	26	57	185																		
1994-95	Clarkson Knights	ECAC	32	12	11	23	92																		
1995-96	Clarkson Knights	ECAC	38	10	8	18	108																		
1996-97	Clarkson Knights	ECAC	37	23	25	48	*86																		
1997-98	Clarkson Knights	ECAC	35	18	21	39	*106										7	2	4	6	15				
1998-99	Saint John Flames	AHL	73	13	27	40	123																		
99-2000	Calgary	NHL	22	0	1	1	14	0	0	0	17	0.0	-3	0	0.0	9:02									
	Saint John Flames	AHL	48	16	17	33	134																		
2000-01	Calgary	NHL	29	5	1	6	38	1	0	0	43	11.6	0	3	33.3	11:56	18	4	10	14	49				
	Saint John Flames	AHL	48	18	17	35	131																		
2001-02	Calgary	NHL	64	10	7	17	79	2	1	4	109	9.2	-12	21	33.3	13:57									
2002-03	Calgary	NHL	81	10	12	22	126	2	0	2	156	6.4	-11	40	32.5	14:24									
2003-04	Calgary	NHL	82	10	15	25	106	4	0	2	137	7.3	-3	97	36.1	14:05	26	3	3	6	30	1	0	0	14:3
2004-05	SC Bern	Swiss	3	0	0	0	6																		
	Storhamar	Norway	15	10	4	14	86										7	4	4	8	14				
2005-06	Washington	NHL	78	20	19	39	110	1	3	0	144	13.9	9	209	49.3	15:24									
2006-07	Washington	NHL	74	30	24	54	66	9	4	2	164	18.3	-10	118	50.9	18:25									
2007-08	Washington	NHL	18	5	4	9	43	1	0	1	29	17.2	0	13	46.2	16:54									
2008-09	Washington	NHL	32	1	5	6	32	0	0	0	36	2.8	-3	6	50.0	11:34	8	1	0	1	8	0	0	0	6:3
2009-10	Washington	NHL	38	4	11	15	27	0	0	1	59	6.8	-4	10	30.0	11:39									
	Columbus	NHL	36	3	2	5	21	0	0	0	46	6.5	-8	10	40.0	12:06									
	NHL Totals		554	98	101	199	662	20	8	12	940	10.4		527	44.6	14:13	34	4	3	7	38	1	0	0	12:4

ECAC Second All-Star Team (1998)
Signed as a free agent by **Bern** (Swiss), October 3, 2004. Signed as a free agent by **Storhamar** (Norway), December 29, 2004. Traded to **Washington** by **Calgary** with Calgary's 7th round choice (Andrew Glass) in 2007 Entry Draft for Washington's 7th round choice (Devin Didiomete) in 2006 Entry Draft and Washington's 6th round choice (later traded to Colorado - Colorado selected Jens Hellgren) in 2007 Entry Draft, August 4, 2005. • Missed majority of 2007-08 season recovering from recurring groin injury. • Missed majority of 2008-09 season recovering from wrist surgery, February 4, 2009. Traded to **Columbus** by **Washington** with Milan Jurcina for Jason Chimera, December 28, 2009.

CLARKSON, David (KLAHRK-suhn, DAYV-ihd) N.J

Right wing. Shoots right. 6'1", 200 lbs. Born, Toronto, Ont., March 31, 1984.

Season	Club	League	GP	G	A	Pts	PIM	PP	SH	GW	S	%	+/-	TF	F%	Min	GP	G	A	Pts	PIM	PP	SH	GW	Min
2001-02	Belleville Bulls	OHL	22	2	7	9	34										8	1	1	2	6				
2002-03	Belleville Bulls	OHL	3	0	0	0	11										21	4	3	7	23				
	Kitchener Rangers	OHL	54	17	11	28	122																		
2003-04	Kitchener Rangers	OHL	55	22	17	39	173										15	6	2	8	40				
2004-05	Kitchener Rangers	OHL	51	33	21	54	145																		
2005-06	Albany River Rats	AHL	56	13	21	34	233																		
2006-07	New Jersey	NHL	7	3	1	4	6	2	0	1	18	16.7	-1	1	0.0	17:02	3	0	0	0	2	0	0	0	6:4
	Lowell Devils	AHL	67	20	18	38	150																		
2007-08	New Jersey	NHL	81	9	13	22	183	0	0	1	151	6.0	1	15	40.0	12:02	5	0	0	0	4	0	0	0	12:2
2008-09	New Jersey	NHL	82	17	15	32	164	4	0	3	158	10.8	-1	7	28.6	12:03	7	2	0	2	19	1	0	1	8:3
2009-10	New Jersey	NHL	46	11	13	24	85	3	0	2	106	10.4	3	20	30.0	14:27	5	0	0	0	22	0	0	0	12:2
	NHL Totals		216	40	42	82	438	9	0	7	433	9.2		43	32.6	12:43	20	2	0	2	47	1	0	1	10:1

Signed as a free agent by **New Jersey**, August 12, 2005.

CLEARY, Daniel (KLIH-ree, DAN-yehl) DET

Right wing. Shoots left. 6', 205 lbs. Born, Carbonear, Nfld., December 18, 1978. Chicago's 1st choice, 13th overall, in 1997 Entry Draft.

Season	Club	League	GP	G	A	Pts	PIM	PP	SH	GW	S	%	+/-	TF	F%	Min	GP	G	A	Pts	PIM	PP	SH	GW	Min
1993-94	Kingston	MTJHL	41	18	28	46	33										2	0	1	1	0				
1994-95	Belleville Bulls	OHL	62	26	55	81	62										16	7	10	17	23				
1995-96	Belleville Bulls	OHL	64	53	62	115	74										14	10	17	27	40				
1996-97	Belleville Bulls	OHL	64	32	48	80	88										6	3	4	7	6				
1997-98	Chicago	NHL	6	0	0	0	0	0	0	0	4	0.0	-2												
	Belleville Bulls	OHL	30	16	31	47	14										10	6	*17	*23	10				
	Indianapolis Ice	IHL	4	2	1	3	6																		
1998-99	Chicago	NHL	35	4	5	9	24	0	0	0	49	8.2	-1	13	46.2	14:21									
	Portland Pirates	AHL	30	9	17	26	74										3	0	0	0	0				
	Hamilton	AHL	9	0	1	1	7										4	0	1	1	2	0	0	0	8:4
99-2000	Edmonton	NHL	17	3	2	5	8	0	0	1	18	16.7	-1		1100.0	9:44	5	2	3	5	18				
	Hamilton	AHL	58	22	52	74	108										6	1	1	2	8	1	0	0	14:4
2000-01	Edmonton	NHL	81	14	21	35	37	2	0	2	107	13.1	5	13	23.1	12:58									
2001-02	Edmonton	NHL	65	10	19	29	51	2	1	1	75	13.3	-1	5	60.0	12:43									
2002-03	Edmonton	NHL	57	4	13	17	31	0	0	0	89	4.5	5	5	40.0	11:58									
2003-04	Phoenix	NHL	68	6	11	17	42	0	3	0	83	7.2	-8	51	39.2	13:12									
2004-05	Mora IK	Sweden	47	11	26	37	138																		
2005-06	Detroit	NHL	77	3	12	15	40	0	0	1	106	2.8	5	286	45.8	10:30	6	0	1	1	6	0	0	0	16:3
2006-07	Detroit	NHL	71	20	20	40	24	6	2	5	135	14.8	6	411	51.1	15:28	18	4	8	12	30	1	*2	0	16:2
2007-08♦	Detroit	NHL	63	20	22	42	33	5	0	3	177	11.3	21	110	50.9	17:23	22	2	1	3	4	0	1	0	17:5
2008-09	Detroit	NHL	74	14	26	40	46	3	0	3	163	8.6	0	121	55.4	16:56	23	9	6	15	12	0	0	*3	16:5
2009-10	Detroit	NHL	64	15	19	34	29	2	0	2	140	10.7	-3	119	49.6	17:14	12	2	0	2	4	0	0	0	14:
	NHL Totals		678	113	170	283	365	20	6	19	1146	9.9		1135	49.2	14:07	91	18	18	36	66	2	3	3	15:

OHL All-Rookie Team (1995) • OHL First All-Star Team (1996, 1997) • AHL Second All-Star Team (2000)
Traded to **Edmonton** by **Chicago** with Chad Kilger, Ethan Moreau and Christian Laflamme for Boris Mironov, Dean McAmmond and Jonas Elofsson, March 20, 1999. Signed as a free agent by **Phoenix**, July 15, 2003. Signed as a free agent by **Mora** (Sweden), September 6, 2004. Signed as a free agent by **Detroit**, October 4, 2005.

CLICHE, Marc-Andre (KLEESH, MAHRK-AWN-dray) L.A

Center. Shoots right. 6', 198 lbs. Born, Rouyn-Noranda, Que., March 23, 1987. NY Rangers' 3rd choice, 56th overall, in 2005 Entry Draft.

Season	Club	League	GP	G	A	Pts	PIM	PP	SH	GW	S	%	+/-	TF	F%	Min	GP	G	A	Pts	PIM	PP	SH	GW	Min
2003-04	Lewiston	QMJHL	52	8	10	18	17										7	1	2	3	0				
2004-05	Lewiston	QMJHL	19	4	4	8	8																		
2005-06	Lewiston	QMJHL	66	37	45	82	60										6	2	2	4	0				
2006-07	Lewiston	QMJHL	52	24	30	54	42										16	6	16	22	10				
2007-08	Manchester	AHL	52	11	10	21	25										4	0	1	1	2				
2008-09	Manchester	AHL	31	5	4	9	19																		

Season	Club	League	GP	G	A	Pts	PIM	PP	SH	GW	S	%	+/-	TF	F%	Min	GP	G	A	Pts	PIM	PP	SH	GW	Min
			Regular Season														**Playoffs**								
2009-10	**Los Angeles**	**NHL**	**1**	**0**	**0**	**0**	**0**	**0**	**0**	**0**	**0**	**0.0**	**1**	**6**	**66.7**	**7:23**	....	....	....	....	....	....	....	....	....
	Manchester	AHL	66	11	14	25	45	....	....	....	....	....	....	....	....	....	12	1	1	2	8	....	....	....	....
	NHL Totals		**1**	**0**	**0**	**0**	**0**	**0**	**0**	**0**	**0**	**0.0**		**6**	**66.7**	**7:23**	....	....	....	....	....	....	....	....	....

Traded to **Los Angeles** by **NY Rangers** with Jason Ward, Jan Marek and NY Rangers' 3rd round choice (later traded to Buffalo - Buffalo selected Corey Fienhage) in 2008 Entry Draft for Sean Avery and John Seymour, February 5, 2007. • Missed majority of 2008-09 season recovering from shoulder injury suffered in training camp.

CLITSOME, Grant

(KLIHT-suhm, GRANT) **CBJ**

Defense. Shoots left. 6', 210 lbs. Born, Gloucester, Ont., April 14, 1985. Columbus' 12th choice, 271st overall, in 2004 Entry Draft.

Season	Club	League	GP	G	A	Pts	PIM	PP	SH	GW	S	%	+/-	TF	F%	Min	GP	G	A	Pts	PIM	PP	SH	GW	Min
2003-04	Nepean Raiders	CJHL	55	13	26	39	67	....	....	....	....	....	....	....	....	....	17	1	10	11	6	....	....	....	....
2004-05	Clarkson Knights	ECAC	39	2	11	13	36	....	....	....	....	....	....	....	....	....	....	....	....	....	....	....	....	....	....
2005-06	Clarkson Knights	ECAC	34	2	17	19	20	....	....	....	....	....	....	....	....	....	....	....	....	....	....	....	....	....	....
2006-07	Clarkson Knights	ECAC	38	7	12	19	38	....	....	....	....	....	....	....	....	....	....	....	....	....	....	....	....	....	....
2007-08	Clarkson Knights	ECAC	39	5	17	22	28	....	....	....	....	....	....	....	....	....	....	....	....	....	....	....	....	....	....
	Syracuse Crunch	AHL	....	....	....	....	....	....	....	....	....	....	....	....	....	....	1	0	0	0	0	....	....	....	....
2008-09	Syracuse Crunch	AHL	73	4	15	19	74	....	....	....	....	....	....	....	....	....	....	....	....	....	....	....	....	....	....
2009-10	**Columbus**	**NHL**	**11**	**1**	**2**	**3**	**6**	**0**	**0**	**0**	**7**	**14.3**	**0**	**0**	**0.0**	**14:44**	....	....	....	....	....	....	....	....	....
	Syracuse Crunch	AHL	64	5	15	20	42	....	....	....	....	....	....	....	....	....	....	....	....	....	....	....	....	....	....
	NHL Totals		**11**	**1**	**2**	**3**	**6**	**0**	**0**	**0**	**7**	**14.3**		**0**	**0.0**	**14:44**	....	....	....	....	....	....	....	....	....

ECAC First All-Star Team (2008) • NCAA East Second All-American Team (2008)

CLOWE, Ryane

(KLOH, RIGH-uhn) **S.J.**

Right wing. Shoots left. 6'2", 225 lbs. Born, St. John's, Nfld., September 30, 1982. San Jose's 5th choice, 175th overall, in 2001 Entry Draft.

Season	Club	League	GP	G	A	Pts	PIM	PP	SH	GW	S	%	+/-	TF	F%	Min	GP	G	A	Pts	PIM	PP	SH	GW	Min
2000-01	Rimouski Oceanic	QMJHL	32	15	10	25	43	....	....	....	....	....	....	....	....	....	11	8	1	9	12	....	....	....	....
2001-02	Rimouski Oceanic	QMJHL	53	28	45	73	120	....	....	....	....	....	....	....	....	....	7	1	6	7	2	....	....	....	....
2002-03	Rimouski Oceanic	QMJHL	17	8	19	27	44	....	....	....	....	....	....	....	....	....	....	....	....	....	....	....	....	....	....
	Montreal Rocket	QMJHL	43	18	30	48	60	....	....	....	....	....	....	....	....	....	7	3	7	10	6	....	....	....	....
2003-04	Cleveland Barons	AHL	72	11	29	40	97	....	....	....	....	....	....	....	....	....	8	3	1	4	9	....	....	....	....
2004-05	Cleveland Barons	AHL	74	27	35	62	101	....	....	....	....	....	....	....	....	....	....	....	....	....	....	....	....	....	....
2005-06	**San Jose**	**NHL**	**18**	**0**	**2**	**2**	**9**	**0**	**0**	**0**	**14**	**0.0**	**–2**	**2**	**0.0**	**9:40**	**1**	**0**	**0**	**0**	**0**	**0**	**0**	**0**	**5:06**
	Cleveland Barons	AHL	35	13	21	34	35	....	....	....	....	....	....	....	....	....	....	....	....	....	....	....	....	....	....
2006-07	**San Jose**	**NHL**	**58**	**16**	**18**	**34**	**78**	**4**	**0**	**3**	**93**	**17.2**	**4**	**5**	**60.0**	**13:11**	**11**	**4**	**2**	**6**	**17**	**0**	**0**	**1**	**15:19**
2007-08	**San Jose**	**NHL**	**15**	**3**	**5**	**8**	**22**	**2**	**0**	**0**	**22**	**13.6**	**–1**	**14**	**35.7**	**14:17**	**13**	**5**	**4**	**9**	**12**	**2**	**0**	**0**	**19:00**
2008-09	**San Jose**	**NHL**	**71**	**22**	**30**	**52**	**51**	**11**	**0**	**1**	**161**	**13.7**	**8**	**120**	**40.8**	**17:47**	**6**	**1**	**1**	**2**	**8**	**0**	**0**	**0**	**18:22**
2009-10	**San Jose**	**NHL**	**82**	**19**	**38**	**57**	**131**	**2**	**0**	**2**	**189**	**10.1**	**0**	**73**	**48.0**	**17:10**	**15**	**2**	**8**	**10**	**28**	**0**	**0**	**0**	**20:11**
	NHL Totals		**244**	**60**	**93**	**153**	**291**	**19**	**0**	**6**	**479**	**12.5**		**214**	**43.0**	**15:40**	**46**	**12**	**15**	**27**	**65**	**2**	**0**	**1**	**18:07**

• Missed majority of 2007-08 season recovering from knee injury suffered in game at Columbus, October 27, 2007.

CLUNE, Rich

(KLOON, RITCH) **L.A.**

Left wing. Shoots left. 5'10", 198 lbs. Born, Toronto, Ont., April 25, 1987. Dallas' 3rd choice, 71st overall, in 2005 Entry Draft.

Season	Club	League	GP	G	A	Pts	PIM	PP	SH	GW	S	%	+/-	TF	F%	Min	GP	G	A	Pts	PIM	PP	SH	GW	Min
2003-04	Sarnia Sting	OHL	58	3	13	16	72	....	....	....	....	....	....	....	....	....	5	0	1	1	0	....	....	....	....
2004-05	Sarnia Sting	OHL	68	21	13	34	103	....	....	....	....	....	....	....	....	....	....	....	....	....	....	....	....	....	....
2005-06	Sarnia Sting	OHL	61	20	32	52	126	....	....	....	....	....	....	....	....	....	....	....	....	....	....	....	....	....	....
2006-07	Barrie Colts	OHL	67	32	46	78	151	....	....	....	....	....	....	....	....	....	8	3	4	7	8	....	....	....	....
	Iowa Stars	AHL	1	0	0	0	2	....	....	....	....	....	....	....	....	....	....	....	....	....	....	....	....	....	....
2007-08	Iowa Stars	AHL	38	3	5	8	137	....	....	....	....	....	....	....	....	....	....	....	....	....	....	....	....	....	....
	Idaho Steelheads	ECHL	19	1	9	10	41	....	....	....	....	....	....	....	....	....	....	....	....	....	....	....	....	....	....
2008-09	Manchester	AHL	35	3	6	9	87	....	....	....	....	....	....	....	....	....	....	....	....	....	....	....	....	....	....
2009-10	**Los Angeles**	**NHL**	**14**	**0**	**2**	**2**	**26**	**0**	**0**	**0**	**7**	**0.0**	**1**	**5**	**40.0**	**7:17**	**4**	**0**	**0**	**0**	**5**	**0**	**0**	**0**	**5:12**
	NHL Totals		**14**	**0**	**2**	**2**	**26**	**0**	**0**	**0**	**7**	**0.0**		**5**	**40.0**	**7:17**	**4**	**0**	**0**	**0**	**5**	**0**	**0**	**0**	**5:12**

Traded to **Los Angeles** by **Dallas** for Lauri Tukonen, July 21, 2008.

CLUTTERBUCK, Cal

(KLUH-tuhr-buhck, KAL) **MIN.**

Right wing. Shoots right. 5'11", 213 lbs. Born, Welland, Ont., November 18, 1987. Minnesota's 3rd choice, 72nd overall, in 2006 Entry Draft.

Season	Club	League	GP	G	A	Pts	PIM	PP	SH	GW	S	%	+/-	TF	F%	Min	GP	G	A	Pts	PIM	PP	SH	GW	Min
2004-05	St. Michael's	OHL	38	10	6	16	55	....	....	....	....	....	....	....	....	....	....	....	....	....	....	....	....	....	....
	Oshawa Generals	OHL	27	9	9	18	42	....	....	....	....	....	....	....	....	....	....	....	....	....	....	....	....	....	....
2005-06	Oshawa Generals	OHL	66	35	33	68	139	....	....	....	....	....	....	....	....	....	....	....	....	....	....	....	....	....	....
2006-07	Oshawa Generals	OHL	65	35	54	89	153	....	....	....	....	....	....	....	....	....	9	8	5	13	21	....	....	....	....
2007-08	**Minnesota**	**NHL**	**2**	**0**	**0**	**0**	**0**	**0**	**0**	**0**	**0**	**0.0**	**0**	**1**	**100.0**	**7:05**	....	....	....	....	....	....	....	....	....
	Houston Aeros	AHL	73	11	13	24	97	....	....	....	....	....	....	....	....	....	5	0	0	0	14	....	....	....	....
2008-09	**Minnesota**	**NHL**	**78**	**11**	**7**	**18**	**76**	**1**	**0**	**1**	**136**	**8.1**	**–5**	**17**	**11.8**	**13:00**	....	....	....	....	....	....	....	....	....
	Houston Aeros	AHL	2	0	0	0	0	....	....	....	....	....	....	....	....	....	....	....	....	....	....	....	....	....	....
2009-10	**Minnesota**	**NHL**	**74**	**13**	**8**	**21**	**52**	**1**	**2**	**1**	**136**	**9.6**	**–8**	**10**	**30.0**	**14:17**	....	....	....	....	....	....	....	....	....
	NHL Totals		**154**	**24**	**15**	**39**	**128**	**2**	**2**	**2**	**272**	**8.8**		**28**	**21.4**	**13:32**	....	....	....	....	....	....	....	....	....

COBURN, Braydon

(KOH-buhrn, BRAY-duhn) **PHI.**

Defense. Shoots left. 6'5", 220 lbs. Born, Calgary, Alta., February 27, 1985. Atlanta's 1st choice, 8th overall, in 2003 Entry Draft.

Season	Club	League	GP	G	A	Pts	PIM	PP	SH	GW	S	%	+/-	TF	F%	Min	GP	G	A	Pts	PIM	PP	SH	GW	Min
2000-01	Notre Dame	SMHL	32	3	19	22	70	....	....	....	....	....	....	....	....	....	....	....	....	....	....	....	....	....	....
	Portland	WHL	2	0	1	1	0	....	....	....	....	....	....	....	....	....	14	0	4	4	2	....	....	....	....
2001-02	Portland	WHL	68	4	33	37	100	....	....	....	....	....	....	....	....	....	7	1	1	2	9	....	....	....	....
2002-03	Portland	WHL	53	3	16	19	147	....	....	....	....	....	....	....	....	....	7	0	1	1	8	....	....	....	....
2003-04	Portland	WHL	55	10	20	30	92	....	....	....	....	....	....	....	....	....	5	0	1	1	10	....	....	....	....
2004-05	Portland	WHL	60	12	32	44	144	....	....	....	....	....	....	....	....	....	7	1	5	6	6	....	....	....	....
	Chicago Wolves	AHL	3	0	1	1	5	....	....	....	....	....	....	....	....	....	18	0	1	1	36	....	....	....	....
2005-06	**Atlanta**	**NHL**	**9**	**0**	**1**	**1**	**4**	**0**	**0**	**0**	**4**	**0.0**	**–2**	**0**	**0.0**	**7:43**	....	....	....	....	....	....	....	....	....
	Chicago Wolves	AHL	73	6	20	26	134	....	....	....	....	....	....	....	....	....	....	....	....	....	....	....	....	....	....
2006-07	**Atlanta**	**NHL**	**29**	**0**	**4**	**4**	**30**	**0**	**0**	**0**	**21**	**0.0**	**1**	**0**	**0.0**	**11:41**	....	....	....	....	....	....	....	....	....
	Chicago Wolves	AHL	15	1	10	11	36	....	....	....	....	....	....	....	....	....	....	....	....	....	....	....	....	....	....
	Philadelphia	**NHL**	**20**	**3**	**4**	**7**	**16**	**1**	**0**	**0**	**33**	**9.1**	**–2**	**0**	**0.0**	**20:58**	....	....	....	....	....	....	....	....	....
2007-08	**Philadelphia**	**NHL**	**78**	**9**	**27**	**36**	**74**	**5**	**0**	**2**	**113**	**8.0**	**17**	**0**	**0.0**	**21:14**	**14**	**0**	**6**	**6**	**14**	**0**	**0**	**0**	**22:25**
2008-09	**Philadelphia**	**NHL**	**80**	**7**	**21**	**28**	**97**	**3**	**0**	**0**	**130**	**5.4**	**7**	**0**	**0.0**	**24:37**	**6**	**0**	**3**	**3**	**7**	**0**	**0**	**0**	**26:29**
2009-10	**Philadelphia**	**NHL**	**81**	**5**	**14**	**19**	**54**	**1**	**0**	**0**	**122**	**4.1**	**–6**	**0**	**0.0**	**21:08**	**23**	**1**	**3**	**4**	**22**	**1**	**0**	**1**	**25:09**
	NHL Totals		**297**	**24**	**71**	**95**	**275**	**10**	**0**	**2**	**423**	**5.7**		**0**	**0.0**	**20:46**	**43**	**1**	**12**	**13**	**43**	**1**	**0**	**1**	**24:27**

WHL Rookie of the Year (2002) • WHL West First All-Star Team (2004, 2005) • Canadian Major Junior Second All-Star Team (2005)
Traded to **Philadelphia** by **Atlanta** for Alexei Zhitnik, February 24, 2007.

COGLIANO, Andrew

(kawg-lee-A-noh, AN-droo) **EDM.**

Center. Shoots left. 5'10", 184 lbs. Born, Toronto, Ont., June 14, 1987. Edmonton's 1st choice, 25th overall, in 2005 Entry Draft.

Season	Club	League	GP	G	A	Pts	PIM	PP	SH	GW	S	%	+/-	TF	F%	Min	GP	G	A	Pts	PIM	PP	SH	GW	Min
2002-03	Vaughan	GTHL	58	39	54	93	122	....	....	....	....	....	....	....	....	....	....	....	....	....	....	....	....	....	....
2003-04	St. Mike's B's	OPJHL	36	26	47	73	14	....	....	....	....	....	....	....	....	....	24	11	20	31	12	....	....	....	....
2004-05	St. Mike's B's	OPJHL	49	36	*66	*102	33	....	....	....	....	....	....	....	....	....	25	*22	*24	*46	20	....	....	....	....
2005-06	U. of Michigan	CCHA	39	12	16	28	38	....	....	....	....	....	....	....	....	....	....	....	....	....	....	....	....	....	....
2006-07	U. of Michigan	CCHA	38	24	26	50	12	....	....	....	....	....	....	....	....	....	....	....	....	....	....	....	....	....	....
2007-08	**Edmonton**	**NHL**	**82**	**18**	**27**	**45**	**20**	**1**	**2**	**5**	**98**	**18.4**	**1**	**542**	**39.5**	**13:40**	....	....	....	....	....	....	....	....	....
2008-09	**Edmonton**	**NHL**	**82**	**18**	**20**	**38**	**22**	**4**	**0**	**4**	**116**	**15.5**	**–6**	**702**	**37.2**	**14:24**	....	....	....	....	....	....	....	....	....
2009-10	**Edmonton**	**NHL**	**82**	**10**	**18**	**28**	**31**	**1**	**0**	**1**	**139**	**7.2**	**–5**	**379**	**43.0**	**14:11**	....	....	....	....	....	....	....	....	....
	NHL Totals		**246**	**46**	**65**	**111**	**73**	**6**	**2**	**10**	**353**	**13.0**		**1623**	**39.3**	**14:05**	....	....	....	....	....	....	....	....	....

CCHA All-Rookie Team (2006)

			Regular Season														Playoffs								
Season	Club	League	GP	G	A	Pts	PIM	PP	SH	GW	S	%	+/-	TF	F%	Min	GP	G	A	Pts	PIM	PP	SH	GW	Min

COLAIACOVO, Carlo

(koh-lee-A-KOH-voh, KAHR-loh) **ST.L.**

Defense. Shoots left. 6'1", 200 lbs. Born, Toronto, Ont., January 27, 1983. Toronto's 1st choice, 17th overall, in 2001 Entry Draft.

Season	Club	League	GP	G	A	Pts	PIM	PP	SH	GW	S	%	+/-	TF	F%	Min	GP	G	A	Pts	PIM	PP	SH	GW	Min
1998-99	Mississauga Reps	GTHL	44	10	12	23	28	....	....	....	....	....	....	....	....	....	....	....	....	....	....	....	....	....	....
99-2000	Erie Otters	OHL	52	4	18	22	12	....	....	....	....	....	....	....	....	....	13	2	4	6	9	....	....	....	....
2000-01	Erie Otters	OHL	62	12	27	39	59	....	....	....	....	....	....	....	....	....	14	4	7	11	16	....	....	....	....
2001-02	Erie Otters	OHL	60	13	27	40	49	....	....	....	....	....	....	....	....	....	21	7	10	17	20	....	....	....	....
2002-03	**Toronto**	**NHL**	**2**	**0**	**1**	**1**	**0**	**0**	**0**	**0**	**1**	**0.0**	**0**	**0**	**0.0**	**13:43**	....	....	....	....	....	....	....	....	....
	Erie Otters	OHL	35	14	21	35	12	....	....	....	....	....	....	....	....	....	....	....	....	....	....	....	....	....	....
2003-04	**Toronto**	**NHL**	**2**	**0**	**1**	**1**	**2**	**0**	**0**	**0**	**0**	**0.0**	**1**	**0**	**0.0**	**13:56**	....	....	....	....	....	....	....	....	....
	St. John's	AHL	62	6	25	31	50	....	....	....	....	....	....	....	....	....	....	....	....	....	....	....	....	....	....
2004-05	St. John's	AHL	49	4	20	24	59	....	....	....	....	....	....	....	....	....	5	0	1	1	2	....	....	....	....
2005-06	**Toronto**	**NHL**	**21**	**2**	**5**	**7**	**17**	**1**	**0**	**0**	**21**	**9.5**	**0**	**1**	**0.0**	**15:26**	....	....	....	....	....	....	....	....	....
	Toronto Marlies	AHL	14	5	6	11	14	....	....	....	....	....	....	....	....	....	....	....	....	....	....	....	....	....	....
2006-07	**Toronto**	**NHL**	**48**	**8**	**9**	**17**	**22**	**0**	**0**	**1**	**60**	**13.3**	**5**	**0**	**0.0**	**17:57**	....	....	....	....	....	....	....	....	....
	Toronto Marlies	AHL	5	1	5	6	4	....	....	....	....	....	....	....	....	....	....	....	....	....	....	....	....	....	....
2007-08	**Toronto**	**NHL**	**28**	**2**	**4**	**6**	**10**	**0**	**0**	**1**	**30**	**6.7**	**-4**	**0**	**0.0**	**17:26**	....	....	....	....	....	....	....	....	....
	Toronto Marlies	AHL	2	0	0	0	0	....	....	....	....	....	....	....	....	....	....	....	....	....	....	....	....	....	....
2008-09	**Toronto**	**NHL**	**10**	**0**	**1**	**1**	**6**	**0**	**0**	**0**	**9**	**0.0**	**-2**	**0**	**0.0**	**16:52**	....	....	....	....	....	....	....	....	....
	St. Louis	**NHL**	**63**	**3**	**26**	**29**	**29**	**0**	**0**	**0**	**78**	**3.8**	**2**	**0**	**0.0**	**18:29**	**4**	**0**	**0**	**0**	**2**	**0**	**0**	**0**	**22:19**
2009-10	**St. Louis**	**NHL**	**67**	**7**	**25**	**32**	**60**	**4**	**1**	**1**	**74**	**9.5**	**8**	**1**	**100.0**	**17:18**	....	....	....	....	....	....	....	....	....
	NHL Totals		**241**	**22**	**72**	**94**	**146**	**5**	**1**	**3**	**273**	**8.1**		**2**	**50.0**	**17:31**	**4**	**0**	**0**	**0**	**2**	**0**	**0**	**0**	**22:19**

OHL Second All-Star Team (2002, 2003)

• Missed remainder of 2005-06 season recovering from head injury suffered in game at Ottawa, January 23, 2006. • Missed majority of 2007-08 season recovering from recurring knee injury. Traded to **St. Louis** by **Toronto** with Alex Steen for Lee Stempniak, November 24, 2008.

COLE, Erik

(KOHL, AIR-ihk) **CAR.**

Left wing. Shoots left. 6'2", 205 lbs. Born, Oswego, NY, November 6, 1978. Carolina's 3rd choice, 71st overall, in 1998 Entry Draft.

Season	Club	League	GP	G	A	Pts	PIM	PP	SH	GW	S	%	+/-	TF	F%	Min	GP	G	A	Pts	PIM	PP	SH	GW	Min
1995-96	Oswego	High-NY	40	49	41	90	....	....	....	....	....	....	....	....	....	....	....	....	....	....	....	....	....	....	....
1996-97	Des Moines	USHL	48	30	34	64	140	....	....	....	....	....	....	....	....	....	5	2	0	2	6	....	....	....	....
1997-98	Clarkson Knights	ECAC	34	11	20	31	55	....	....	....	....	....	....	....	....	....	....	....	....	....	....	....	....	....	....
1998-99	Clarkson Knights	ECAC	36	*22	20	42	50	....	....	....	....	....	....	....	....	....	....	....	....	....	....	....	....	....	....
99-2000	Clarkson Knights	ECAC	33	19	11	30	46	....	....	....	....	....	....	....	....	....	....	....	....	....	....	....	....	....	....
	Cincinnati	IHL	9	4	3	7	2	....	....	....	....	....	....	....	....	....	7	1	1	2	2	....	....	....	....
2000-01	Cincinnati	IHL	69	23	20	43	28	....	....	....	....	....	....	....	....	....	5	1	0	1	2	....	....	....	....
2001-02	**Carolina**	**NHL**	**81**	**16**	**24**	**40**	**35**	**3**	**0**	**2**	**159**	**10.1**	**-10**	**17**	**47.1**	**16:04**	**23**	**6**	**3**	**9**	**30**	**1**	**0**	**1**	**18:27**
2002-03	**Carolina**	**NHL**	**53**	**14**	**13**	**27**	**72**	**6**	**2**	**3**	**125**	**11.2**	**1**	**56**	**39.3**	**17:08**	....	....	....	....	....	....	....	....	....
2003-04	**Carolina**	**NHL**	**80**	**18**	**24**	**42**	**93**	**2**	**2**	**3**	**172**	**10.5**	**-4**	**15**	**46.7**	**18:06**	....	....	....	....	....	....	....	....	....
2004-05	Eisbaren Berlin	Germany	39	6	21	27	76	....	....	....	....	....	....	....	....	....	8	5	1	6	37	....	....	....	....
2005-06 ♦	**Carolina**	**NHL**	**60**	**30**	**29**	**59**	**54**	**3**	**3**	**8**	**164**	**18.3**	**19**	**19**	**36.8**	**19:18**	**2**	**0**	**0**	**0**	**0**	**0**	**0**	**0**	**15:29**
	United States	Olympics	6	1	2	3	0	....	....	....	....	....	....	....	....	....	....	....	....	....	....	....	....	....	....
2006-07	**Carolina**	**NHL**	**71**	**29**	**32**	**61**	**76**	**9**	**0**	**4**	**166**	**17.5**	**2**	**27**	**40.7**	**18:01**	....	....	....	....	....	....	....	....	....
2007-08	**Carolina**	**NHL**	**73**	**22**	**29**	**51**	**76**	**10**	**0**	**4**	**216**	**10.2**	**5**	**38**	**23.7**	**19:22**	....	....	....	....	....	....	....	....	....
2008-09	**Edmonton**	**NHL**	**63**	**16**	**11**	**27**	**63**	**5**	**0**	**1**	**145**	**11.0**	**-3**	**48**	**39.6**	**17:05**	....	....	....	....	....	....	....	....	....
	Carolina	**NHL**	**17**	**2**	**13**	**15**	**10**	**0**	**0**	**0**	**33**	**6.1**	**3**	**1**	**100.0**	**19:36**	**18**	**0**	**5**	**5**	**22**	**0**	**0**	**0**	**17:17**
2009-10	**Carolina**	**NHL**	**40**	**11**	**5**	**16**	**29**	**2**	**0**	**1**	**81**	**13.6**	**-9**	**15**	**26.7**	**16:23**	....	....	....	....	....	....	....	....	....
	NHL Totals		**538**	**158**	**180**	**338**	**508**	**40**	**7**	**26**	**1261**	**12.5**		**236**	**37.3**	**17:48**	**43**	**6**	**8**	**14**	**52**	**1**	**0**	**1**	**17:50**

USHL Second All-Star Team (1997) • ECAC Rookie of the Year (1998) (co-winner - Willie Mitchell) • ECAC First All-Star Team (1999) • NCAA East Second All-American Team (1999) • ECAC Second All-Star Team (2000)

Signed as a free agent by **Berlin** (Germany), October 24, 2004. Traded to **Edmonton** by **Carolina** for Joni Pitkanen, July 1, 2008. Traded to **Carolina** by **Edmonton** with Edmonton's 5th round choice (Matt Kennedy) in 2009 Entry Draft for Patrick O'Sullivan and Carolina's 2nd round choice (later traded to Buffalo, later traded to Toronto – Toronto selected Jesse Blacker) in 2009 Entry Draft, March 4, 2009. • Missed majority of 2009-10 season recovering from leg and upper body injuries.

COLLINS, Sean

(KAW-lihnz, SHAWN) **WSH.**

Defense. Shoots right. 6'1", 215 lbs. Born, Troy, MI, October 30, 1983.

Season	Club	League	GP	G	A	Pts	PIM	PP	SH	GW	S	%	+/-	TF	F%	Min	GP	G	A	Pts	PIM	PP	SH	GW	Min
2002-03	Sioux City	USHL	59	6	22	28	89	....	....	....	....	....	....	....	....	....	4	0	1	1	2	....	....	....	....
2003-04	Ohio State	CCHA	41	3	12	15	57	....	....	....	....	....	....	....	....	....	....	....	....	....	....	....	....	....	....
2004-05	Ohio State	CCHA	40	9	17	26	40	....	....	....	....	....	....	....	....	....	....	....	....	....	....	....	....	....	....
2005-06	Ohio State	CCHA	39	7	11	18	63	....	....	....	....	....	....	....	....	....	....	....	....	....	....	....	....	....	....
2006-07	Ohio State	CCHA	37	9	19	28	50	....	....	....	....	....	....	....	....	....	....	....	....	....	....	....	....	....	....
	Hershey Bears	AHL	3	0	0	0	2	....	....	....	....	....	....	....	....	....	....	....	....	....	....	....	....	....	....
2007-08	Hershey Bears	AHL	12	0	0	0	11	....	....	....	....	....	....	....	....	....	....	....	....	....	....	....	....	....	....
	South Carolina	ECHL	31	1	13	14	16	....	....	....	....	....	....	....	....	....	20	1	8	9	24	....	....	....	....
2008-09	**Washington**	**NHL**	**15**	**1**	**1**	**2**	**12**	**0**	**0**	**0**	**14**	**7.1**	**1**	**0**	**0.0**	**14:32**	....	....	....	....	....	....	....	....	....
	Hershey Bears	AHL	39	1	7	8	38	....	....	....	....	....	....	....	....	....	6	0	2	2	2	....	....	....	....
2009-10	Hershey Bears	AHL	63	1	17	18	55	....	....	....	....	....	....	....	....	....	15	1	2	3	16	....	....	....	....
	NHL Totals		**15**	**1**	**1**	**2**	**12**	**0**	**0**	**0**	**14**	**7.1**		**0**	**0.0**	**14:32**	....	....	....	....	....	....	....	....	....

Signed as a free agent by **Washington**, March 19, 2007.

COLLITON, Jeremy

(KAW-lih-tuhn, JAIR-eh-mee) **NYI**

Center. Shoots right. 6'2", 195 lbs. Born, Blackie, Alta., January 13, 1985. NY Islanders' 4th choice, 58th overall, in 2003 Entry Draft.

Season	Club	League	GP	G	A	Pts	PIM	PP	SH	GW	S	%	+/-	TF	F%	Min	GP	G	A	Pts	PIM	PP	SH	GW	Min
99-2000	Airdrie Express	AMHL	33	16	25	41	28	....	....	....	....	....	....	....	....	....	....	....	....	....	....	....	....	....	....
2000-01	Crowsnest Pass	AJHL	63	18	30	48	98	....	....	....	....	....	....	....	....	....	....	....	....	....	....	....	....	....	....
2001-02	Prince Albert	WHL	68	11	21	32	53	....	....	....	....	....	....	....	....	....	....	....	....	....	....	....	....	....	....
2002-03	Prince Albert	WHL	58	20	28	48	76	....	....	....	....	....	....	....	....	....	....	....	....	....	....	....	....	....	....
2003-04	Prince Albert	WHL	62	24	26	50	73	....	....	....	....	....	....	....	....	....	6	5	5	10	8	....	....	....	....
2004-05	Prince Albert	WHL	41	16	30	46	25	....	....	....	....	....	....	....	....	....	17	3	4	7	21	....	....	....	....
2005-06	**NY Islanders**	**NHL**	**19**	**1**	**1**	**2**	**6**	**0**	**0**	**0**	**9**	**11.1**	**2**	**76**	**40.8**	**6:18**	....	....	....	....	....	....	....	....	....
	Bridgeport	AHL	66	20	32	52	44	....	....	....	....	....	....	....	....	....	6	0	1	1	2	....	....	....	....
2006-07	**NY Islanders**	**NHL**	**1**	**0**	**0**	**0**	**0**	**0**	**0**	**0**	**0**	**0.0**	**-1**	**0**	**0.0**	**4:40**	....	....	....	....	....	....	....	....	....
	Bridgeport	AHL	45	10	12	22	32	....	....	....	....	....	....	....	....	....	....	....	....	....	....	....	....	....	....
2007-08	**NY Islanders**	**NHL**	**16**	**0**	**0**	**0**	**8**	**0**	**0**	**0**	**16**	**0.0**	**-4**	**104**	**51.9**	**8:46**	....	....	....	....	....	....	....	....	....
	Bridgeport	AHL	65	9	11	20	44	....	....	....	....	....	....	....	....	....	....	....	....	....	....	....	....	....	....
2008-09	**NY Islanders**	**NHL**	**6**	**0**	**1**	**1**	**2**	**0**	**0**	**0**	**4**	**0.0**	**-2**	**70**	**64.3**	**11:03**	....	....	....	....	....	....	....	....	....
	Bridgeport	AHL	56	8	28	36	36	....	....	....	....	....	....	....	....	....	2	0	1	1	0	....	....	....	....
2009-10	Rogle	Sweden	46	11	10	21	24	....	....	....	....	....	....	....	....	....	....	....	....	....	....	....	....	....	....
	Rogle	Sweden-Q	10	3	3	6	8	....	....	....	....	....	....	....	....	....	....	....	....	....	....	....	....	....	....
	NHL Totals		**42**	**1**	**2**	**3**	**16**	**0**	**0**	**0**	**29**	**3.4**		**250**	**52.0**	**7:53**	....	....	....	....	....	....	....	....	....

Signed as a free agent by **Rogle** (Sweden), June 19, 2009.

COMEAU, Blake

(KOH-moh, BLAYK) **NYI**

Right wing. Shoots right. 6'1", 207 lbs. Born, Meadow Lake, Sask., February 18, 1986. NY Islanders' 2nd choice, 47th overall, in 2004 Entry Draft.

Season	Club	League	GP	G	A	Pts	PIM	PP	SH	GW	S	%	+/-	TF	F%	Min	GP	G	A	Pts	PIM	PP	SH	GW	Min
2001-02	Sask. Contacts	SMHL	42	27	33	60	72	....	....	....	....	....	....	....	....	....	....	....	....	....	....	....	....	....	....
	Kelowna Rockets	WHL	3	0	0	0	4	....	....	....	....	....	....	....	....	....	....	....	....	....	....	....	....	....	....
2002-03	Kelowna Rockets	WHL	54	5	18	23	77	....	....	....	....	....	....	....	....	....	19	2	1	3	20	....	....	....	....
2003-04	Kelowna Rockets	WHL	71	10	23	33	123	....	....	....	....	....	....	....	....	....	17	4	2	6	23	....	....	....	....
2004-05	Kelowna Rockets	WHL	65	24	23	47	108	....	....	....	....	....	....	....	....	....	24	6	12	18	34	....	....	....	....
2005-06	Kelowna Rockets	WHL	60	21	53	74	85	....	....	....	....	....	....	....	....	....	12	4	9	13	22	....	....	....	....
	Bridgeport	AHL	....	....	....	....	....	....	....	....	....	....	....	....	....	....	7	0	3	3	0	....	....	....	....
2006-07	**NY Islanders**	**NHL**	**3**	**0**	**0**	**0**	**0**	**0**	**0**	**0**	**1**	**0.0**	**0**	**0**	**0.0**	**9:25**	....	....	....	....	....	....	....	....	....
	Bridgeport	AHL	61	12	31	43	46	....	....	....	....	....	....	....	....	....	....	....	....	....	....	....	....	....	....
2007-08	**NY Islanders**	**NHL**	**51**	**8**	**7**	**15**	**22**	**1**	**0**	**1**	**67**	**11.9**	**1**	**27**	**29.6**	**11:40**	....	....	....	....	....	....	....	....	....
	Bridgeport	AHL	31	4	15	19	30	....	....	....	....	....	....	....	....	....	....	....	....	....	....	....	....	....	....

			Regular Season														Playoffs								
Season	Club	League	GP	G	A	Pts	PIM	PP	SH	GW	S	%	+/-	TF	F%	Min	GP	G	A	Pts	PIM	PP	SH	GW	Min
2008-09	NY Islanders	NHL	53	7	18	25	32	2	0	0	78	9.0	–17	45	31.1	16:17	....	....	....	....	....	....	....	....	....
	Bridgeport	AHL	19	4	15	19	22	....	....	....	....	....	....	....	....	....	2	0	0	0	0	....	....	....	....
2009-10	NY Islanders	NHL	61	17	18	35	40	0	1	2	133	12.8	–2	21	47.6	15:25	....	....	....	....	....	....	....	....	....
	NHL Totals		168	32	43	75	94	3	1	3	279	11.5		93	34.4	14:27	....	....	....	....	....	....	....	....	....

VHL West First All-Star Team (2006)

COMMODORE, Mike

(KAWM-uh-dohr, MIGHK) **CBJ**

Defense. Shoots right. 6'5", 235 lbs. Born, Fort Saskatchewan, Alta., November 7, 1979. New Jersey's 2nd choice, 42nd overall, in 1999 Entry Draft.

Season	Club	League	GP	G	A	Pts	PIM	PP	SH	GW	S	%	+/-	TF	F%	Min	GP	G	A	Pts	PIM	PP	SH	GW	Min
1996-97	Ft. Saskatchewan	AJHL	51	3	8	11	244	....	....	....	....	....	....	....	....	....	....	....	....	....	....	....	....	....	....
1997-98	North Dakota	WCHA	29	0	5	5	74	....	....	....	....	....	....	....	....	....	....	....	....	....	....	....	....	....	....
1998-99	North Dakota	WCHA	39	5	8	13	154	....	....	....	....	....	....	....	....	....	....	....	....	....	....	....	....	....	....
99-2000	North Dakota	WCHA	38	5	7	12	*154	....	....	....	....	....	....	....	....	....	....	....	....	....	....	....	....	....	....
2000-01	New Jersey	NHL	20	1	4	5	14	0	0	0	11	9.1	5	0	0.0	12:46	....	....	....	....	....	....	....	....	....
	Albany River Rats	AHL	41	2	5	7	59	....	....	....	....	....	....	....	....	....	....	....	....	....	....	....	....	....	....
2001-02	New Jersey	NHL	37	0	1	1	30	0	0	0	22	0.0	–12	0	0.0	12:37	....	....	....	....	....	....	....	....	....
	Albany River Rats	AHL	14	0	3	3	31	....	....	....	....	....	....	....	....	....	....	....	....	....	....	....	....	....	....
2002-03	Cincinnati	AHL	61	2	9	11	210	....	....	....	....	....	....	....	....	....	....	....	....	....	....	....	....	....	....
	Calgary	NHL	6	0	1	1	19	0	0	0	5	0.0	2	0	0.0	11:35	....	....	....	....	....	....	....	....	....
	Saint John Flames	AHL	7	0	3	3	18	....	....	....	....	....	....	....	....	....	....	....	....	....	....	....	....	....	....
2003-04	Calgary	NHL	12	0	0	0	25	0	0	0	10	0.0	–4	0	0.0	15:17	20	0	2	2	19	0	0	0	11:34
	Lowell	AHL	37	5	11	16	75	....	....	....	....	....	....	....	....	....	....	....	....	....	....	....	....	....	....
2004-05	Lowell	AHL	73	6	29	35	175	....	....	....	....	....	....	....	....	....	11	1	2	3	18	....	....	....	....
2005-06♦	Carolina	NHL	72	3	10	13	138	0	0	2	72	4.2	12	1	0.0	15:30	25	2	2	4	33	0	1	0	19:27
2006-07	Carolina	NHL	82	7	22	29	113	0	2	1	136	5.1	0	0	0.0	19:54	....	....	....	....	....	....	....	....	....
2007-08	Carolina	NHL	41	3	9	12	74	0	0	0	67	4.5	2	0	0.0	19:16	....	....	....	....	....	....	....	....	....
	Ottawa	NHL	26	0	2	2	26	0	0	0	30	0.0	–9	0	0.0	16:33	4	0	2	2	0	0	0	0	20:14
2008-09	Columbus	NHL	81	5	19	24	100	0	0	0	103	4.9	11	3	66.7	22:54	4	0	0	0	18	0	0	0	21:32
2009-10	Columbus	NHL	57	2	9	11	62	0	0	1	54	3.7	–9	0	0.0	19:00	....	....	....	....	....	....	....	....	....
	NHL Totals		434	21	77	98	601	0	2	4	510	4.1		4	50.0	18:09	53	2	6	8	70	0	1	0	16:42

CAA Championship All-Tournament Team (2000)

aded to **Anaheim** by **New Jersey** with Petr Sykora, Jean-Francois Damphousse and Igor Pohanka for Jeff Friesen, Oleg Tverdovsky and Maxim Balmochnykh, July 6, 2002. Traded to **Calgary** by **Anaheim** ith Jean-Francois Damphousse for Rob Niedermayer, March 11, 2003. Traded to **Carolina** by **Calgary** for Atlanta's 3rd round choice (previously acquired, Calgary selected Gord Baldwin) in 2005 Entry raft, July 29, 2005. Traded to **Ottawa** by **Carolina** with Cory Stillman for Joe Corvo and Patrick Eaves, February 11, 2008. Signed as a free agent by **Columbus**, July 1, 2008.

COMRIE, Mike

(KAWM-ree, MIGHK)

Center. Shoots left. 5'10", 185 lbs. Born, Edmonton, Alta., September 11, 1980. Edmonton's 5th choice, 91st overall, in 1999 Entry Draft.

Season	Club	League	GP	G	A	Pts	PIM	PP	SH	GW	S	%	+/-	TF	F%	Min	GP	G	A	Pts	PIM	PP	SH	GW	Min
1995-96	Edmonton SSAC	AMHL	33	51	52	103	....	....	....	....	....	....	....	....	....	....	....	....	....	....	....	....	....	....	....
1996-97	St. Albert Saints	AJHL	63	37	41	78	44	....	....	....	....	....	....	....	....	....	....	....	....	....	....	....	....	....	....
1997-98	St. Albert Saints	AJHL	58	*60	*78	*138	134	....	....	....	....	....	....	....	....	....	19	*24	*24	*48	51	....	....	....	....
1998-99	U. of Michigan	CCHA	42	19	25	44	38	....	....	....	....	....	....	....	....	....	....	....	....	....	....	....	....	....	....
99-2000	U. of Michigan	CCHA	40	24	35	59	95	....	....	....	....	....	....	....	....	....	....	....	....	....	....	....	....	....	....
2000-01	Kootenay Ice	WHL	37	39	40	79	79	....	....	....	....	....	....	....	....	....	....	....	....	....	....	....	....	....	....
	Edmonton	NHL	41	8	14	22	14	3	0	1	62	12.9	6	372	43.3	11:23	6	1	2	3	0	1	0	1	15:00
2001-02	Edmonton	NHL	82	33	27	60	45	8	0	5	170	19.4	16	1198	47.3	17:32	....	....	....	....	....	....	....	....	....
2002-03	Edmonton	NHL	69	20	31	51	90	8	0	6	170	11.8	–18	1069	47.1	17:51	6	1	0	1	10	0	0	0	13:07
2003-04	Philadelphia	NHL	21	4	5	9	12	0	0	1	36	11.1	2	165	50.9	12:51	....	....	....	....	....	....	....	....	....
	Phoenix	NHL	28	8	7	15	16	1	1	1	65	12.3	–8	304	50.3	17:50	....	....	....	....	....	....	....	....	....
2004-05	Farjestad	Sweden	10	1	6	7	10	....	....	....	....	....	....	....	....	....	....	....	....	....	....	....	....	....	....
2005-06	Phoenix	NHL	80	30	30	60	55	10	0	4	190	15.8	2	781	52.8	16:01	....	....	....	....	....	....	....	....	....
2006-07	Phoenix	NHL	24	7	13	20	20	4	0	1	38	18.4	1	210	48.6	16:36	....	....	....	....	....	....	....	....	....
	Ottawa	NHL	41	13	12	25	24	3	0	2	87	14.9	–1	244	50.0	14:27	20	2	4	6	17	0	0	0	12:41
2007-08	NY Islanders	NHL	76	21	28	49	87	4	0	3	194	10.8	–21	1227	46.0	19:11	....	....	....	....	....	....	....	....	....
2008-09	NY Islanders	NHL	41	7	13	20	26	2	0	0	80	8.8	–8	390	41.3	16:28	....	....	....	....	....	....	....	....	....
	Ottawa	NHL	22	3	4	7	6	0	0	1	41	7.3	–7	27	37.0	14:17	....	....	....	....	....	....	....	....	....
2009-10	Edmonton	NHL	43	13	8	21	30	5	0	0	97	13.4	–9	47	53.2	14:14	....	....	....	....	....	....	....	....	....
	NHL Totals		568	167	192	359	425	48	1	25	1230	13.6		6034	47.5	16:16	32	4	6	10	27	1	0	1	13:12

CHA All-Rookie Team (1999) • CCHA First All-Star Team (1999) • CCHA Rookie of the Year (1999) • CCHA First All-Star Team (2000) • NCAA West Second All-American Team (2000)

Left **University of Michigan** (CCHA) and signed as a free agent by **Kootenay** (WHL), August 23, 2000. • Left **Kootenay** (WHL) and signed with **Edmonton**, December 30, 2000. Traded to **iladelphia** by **Edmonton** for Jeff Woywitka, Philadelphia's 1st round choice (Rob Schremp) in 2004 Entry Draft and Philadelphia's 3rd round choice (Danny Syvret) in 2005 Entry Draft, December 16, 03. Traded to **Phoenix** by **Philadelphia** for Sean Burke, Branko Radivojevic and Ben Eager, February 9, 2004. Signed as a free agent by **Farjestad** (Sweden), October 30, 2004. Traded to **Ottawa** by **oenix** for Alexei Kaigorodov, January 3, 2007. Signed as a free agent by **NY Islanders**, July 5, 2007. Traded to **Ottawa** by **NY Islanders** with Chris Campoli for Dean McAmmond and San Jose's 1st und choice (previously acquired, later traded to Columbus, later traded to Anaheim – Anaheim selected Kyle Palmieri) in 2009 Entry Draft, February 20, 2009. Signed as a free agent by **Edmonton**, ptember 10, 2009.

CONBOY, Tim

(KAWN-boi, TIHM) **BUF.**

Defense. Shoots right. 6'2", 210 lbs. Born, Farmington, MN, March 22, 1982. San Jose's 6th choice, 217th overall, in 2002 Entry Draft.

Season	Club	League	GP	G	A	Pts	PIM	PP	SH	GW	S	%	+/-	TF	F%	Min	GP	G	A	Pts	PIM	PP	SH	GW	Min
99-2000	Brainerd	High-MN	22	20	26	46	....	....	....	....	....	....	....	....	....	....	....	....	....	....	....	....	....	....	....
2000-01	Rochester	USHL	51	5	9	14	256	....	....	....	....	....	....	....	....	....	....	....	....	....	....	....	....	....	....
2001-02	Rochester	USHL	14	1	6	7	65	....	....	....	....	....	....	....	....	....	....	....	....	....	....	....	....	....	....
	Topeka	USHL	29	4	15	19	128	....	....	....	....	....	....	....	....	....	....	....	....	....	....	....	....	....	....
2002-03	St. Cloud State	WCHA	31	3	12	15	48	....	....	....	....	....	....	....	....	....	....	....	....	....	....	....	....	....	....
2003-04	St. Cloud State	WCHA	32	5	5	10	68	....	....	....	....	....	....	....	....	....	....	....	....	....	....	....	....	....	....
	Cleveland Barons	AHL	....	....	....	....	....	....	....	....	....	....	....	....	....	....	3	0	3	3	4	....	....	....	....
2004-05	Cleveland Barons	AHL	61	4	11	15	134	....	....	....	....	....	....	....	....	....	....	....	....	....	....	....	....	....	....
2005-06	Cleveland Barons	AHL	78	6	14	20	124	....	....	....	....	....	....	....	....	....	....	....	....	....	....	....	....	....	....
2006-07	Albany River Rats	AHL	75	3	7	10	163	....	....	....	....	....	....	....	....	....	5	0	1	1	6	....	....	....	....
2007-08	Carolina	NHL	19	0	5	5	60	0	0	0	16	0.0	1	0	0.0	6:58	....	....	....	....	....	....	....	....	....
	Albany River Rats	AHL	52	2	2	4	191	....	....	....	....	....	....	....	....	....	1	0	0	0	21	....	....	....	....
2008-09	Carolina	NHL	28	0	1	1	37	0	0	0	13	0.0	–1	0	0.0	5:21	3	0	0	0	9	0	0	0	4:22
	Albany River Rats	AHL	39	1	5	6	127	....	....	....	....	....	....	....	....	....	....	....	....	....	....	....	....	....	....
2009-10	Carolina	NHL	12	0	0	0	24	0	0	0	5	0.0	–5	0	0.0	4:18	....	....	....	....	....	....	....	....	....
	Albany River Rats	AHL	37	0	3	3	87	....	....	....	....	....	....	....	....	....	8	0	1	1	18	....	....	....	....
	NHL Totals		59	0	6	6	121	0	0	0	34	0.0		0	0.0	5:40	3	0	0	0	9	0	0	0	4:22

ned as a free agent by **Carolina**, July 21, 2006. Signed as a free agent by **Buffalo**, July 16, 2010.

CONNER, Chris

(KAWN-uhr, KRIHS) **PIT.**

Wing. Shoots left. 5'8", 180 lbs. Born, Westland, MI, December 23, 1983.

Season	Club	League	GP	G	A	Pts	PIM	PP	SH	GW	S	%	+/-	TF	F%	Min	GP	G	A	Pts	PIM	PP	SH	GW	Min
2002-03	Michigan Tech	WCHA	38	13	24	37	8	....	....	....	....	....	....	....	....	....	....	....	....	....	....	....	....	....	....
2003-04	Michigan Tech	WCHA	38	25	14	39	12	....	....	....	....	....	....	....	....	....	....	....	....	....	....	....	....	....	....
2004-05	Michigan Tech	WCHA	37	14	10	24	6	....	....	....	....	....	....	....	....	....	....	....	....	....	....	....	....	....	....
2005-06	Michigan Tech	WCHA	38	17	12	29	18	....	....	....	....	....	....	....	....	....	....	....	....	....	....	....	....	....	....
	Iowa Stars	AHL	15	2	3	5	0	....	....	....	....	....	....	....	....	....	7	1	1	2	2	....	....	....	....
2006-07	Dallas	NHL	11	1	2	3	4	0	0	0	18	5.6	–3	1	100.0	11:15	....	....	....	....	....	....	....	....	....
	Iowa Stars	AHL	48	19	18	37	24	....	....	....	....	....	....	....	....	....	12	2	5	7	2	....	....	....	....
2007-08	Dallas	NHL	22	3	2	5	6	0	0	0	27	11.1	0	1	100.0	12:00	1	0	0	0	0	0	0	0	4:17
	Iowa Stars	AHL	55	13	26	39	17	....	....	....	....	....	....	....	....	....	....	....	....	....	....	....	....	....	....
2008-09	Dallas	NHL	38	3	10	13	10	0	0	1	34	8.8	–5	1	0.0	10:56	....	....	....	....	....	....	....	....	....
	Peoria Rivermen	AHL	30	16	12	28	10	....	....	....	....	....	....	....	....	....	....	....	....	....	....	....	....	....	....
2009-10	Pittsburgh	NHL	8	2	1	3	0	0	0	1	11	18.2	–1	1	0.0	9:36	1	0	0	0	0	0	0	0	11:03
	Wilkes-Barre	AHL	59	19	37	56	21	....	....	....	....	....	....	....	....	....	4	2	2	4	2	....	....	....	....
	NHL Totals		79	9	15	24	20	0	0	2	90	10.0		4	50.0	11:08	2	0	0	0	0	0	0	0	7:40

CHA Second All-Star Team (2004)

ned as a free agent by **Dallas**, July 13, 2006. Signed as a free agent by **Pittsburgh**, July 5. 2009.

CONNOLLY, Tim (KAW-nuhl-lee, TIHM) BUF.

Center. Shoots right. 6'1", 191 lbs. Born, Syracuse, NY, May 7, 1981. NY Islanders' 1st choice, 5th overall, in 1999 Entry Draft.

			Regular Season														Playoffs								
Season	Club	League	GP	G	A	Pts	PIM	PP	SH	GW	S	%	+/-	TF	F%	Min	GP	G	A	Pts	PIM	PP	SH	GW	Min
1996-97	Syracuse	MTJHL	50	42	62	104	34	....	....	....	....	....	....	....	....	....	....	....	....	....	....	....	....	....	....
1997-98	Erie Otters	OHL	59	30	32	62	32	....	....	....	....	....	....	....	....	....	7	1	6	7	6	....	....	....	....
1998-99	Erie Otters	OHL	46	34	34	68	50	....	....	....	....	....	....	....	....	....	....	....	....	....	....	....	....	....	....
99-2000	**NY Islanders**	**NHL**	**81**	**14**	**20**	**34**	**44**	**2**	**1**	**1**	**114**	**12.3**	**–25**	**786**	**36.3**	**16:18**	....	....	....	....	....	....	....	....	....
2000-01	**NY Islanders**	**NHL**	**82**	**10**	**31**	**41**	**42**	**5**	**0**	**0**	**171**	**5.8**	**–14**	**989**	**41.7**	**20:02**	....	....	....	....	....	....	....	....	....
2001-02	**Buffalo**	**NHL**	**82**	**10**	**35**	**45**	**34**	**3**	**0**	**3**	**126**	**7.9**	**4**	**1074**	**39.6**	**16:58**	....	....	....	....	....	....	....	....	....
2002-03	**Buffalo**	**NHL**	**80**	**12**	**13**	**25**	**32**	**6**	**0**	**2**	**159**	**7.5**	**–28**	**845**	**42.8**	**16:00**	....	....	....	....	....	....	....	....	....
2003-04	**Buffalo**	**NHL**	DID NOT PLAY – INJURED																						
2004-05	Langnau	Swiss	16	7	3	10	14	....	....	....	....	....	....	....	....	....	....	....	....	....	....	....	....	....	....
2005-06	**Buffalo**	**NHL**	**63**	**16**	**39**	**55**	**28**	**7**	**0**	**3**	**99**	**16.2**	**5**	**844**	**42.5**	**18:00**	**8**	**5**	**6**	**11**	**0**	**1**	**1**	**1**	**17:29**
2006-07	**Buffalo**	**NHL**	**2**	**1**	**0**	**1**	**2**	**0**	**0**	**0**	**2**	**50.0**	**1**	**13**	**53.9**	**13:07**	**16**	**0**	**9**	**9**	**4**	**0**	**0**	**0**	**16:56**
2007-08	**Buffalo**	**NHL**	**48**	**7**	**33**	**40**	**8**	**3**	**1**	**3**	**111**	**6.3**	**4**	**463**	**48.0**	**18:41**	....	....	....	....	....	....	....	....	....
2008-09	**Buffalo**	**NHL**	**48**	**18**	**29**	**47**	**22**	**5**	**1**	**5**	**126**	**14.3**	**12**	**544**	**42.1**	**19:07**	....	....	....	....	....	....	....	....	....
2009-10	**Buffalo**	**NHL**	**73**	**17**	**48**	**65**	**28**	**7**	**1**	**5**	**206**	**8.3**	**10**	**764**	**46.9**	**18:37**	**6**	**0**	**1**	**1**	**2**	**0**	**0**	**0**	**17:49**
	NHL Totals		**559**	**105**	**248**	**353**	**240**	**38**	**4**	**22**	**1114**	**9.4**		**6322**	**42.1**	**17:50**	**30**	**5**	**16**	**21**	**6**	**1**	**1**	**1**	**17:16**

Traded to **Buffalo** by **NY Islanders** with Taylor Pyatt for Michael Peca, June 24, 2001. • Missed entire 2003-04 season recovering from head injury suffered in pre-season game vs. Chicago, October 2, 2003. Signed as a free agent by **Langnau** (Swiss), October 10, 2004. • Missed majority of 2006-07 season recovering from concussion suffered in playoff game vs. Ottawa, May 8, 2006.

CONROY, Craig (KAWN-roi, KRAYG) CGY

Center. Shoots right. 6'2", 193 lbs. Born, Potsdam, NY, September 4, 1971. Montreal's 7th choice, 123rd overall, in 1990 Entry Draft.

			Regular Season														Playoffs								
Season	Club	League	GP	G	A	Pts	PIM	PP	SH	GW	S	%	+/-	TF	F%	Min	GP	G	A	Pts	PIM	PP	SH	GW	Min
1989-90	Northwood	High-NY	31	33	43	76	....	....	....	....	....	....	....	....	....	....	....	....	....	....	....	....	....	....	....
1990-91	Clarkson Knights	ECAC	40	8	21	29	24	....	....	....	....	....	....	....	....	....	....	....	....	....	....	....	....	....	....
1991-92	Clarkson Knights	ECAC	31	19	17	36	36	....	....	....	....	....	....	....	....	....	....	....	....	....	....	....	....	....	....
1992-93	Clarkson Knights	ECAC	35	10	23	33	26	....	....	....	....	....	....	....	....	....	....	....	....	....	....	....	....	....	....
1993-94	Clarkson Knights	ECAC	34	26	*40	*66	46	....	....	....	....	....	....	....	....	....	....	....	....	....	....	....	....	....	....
1994-95	Fredericton	AHL	55	26	18	44	29	....	....	....	....	....	....	....	....	....	11	7	3	10	6	....	....	....	....
	Montreal	**NHL**	**6**	**1**	**0**	**1**	**0**	**0**	**0**	**0**	**4**	**25.0**	**–1**	....	....	....	....	....	....	....	....	....	....	....	....
1995-96	**Montreal**	**NHL**	**7**	**0**	**0**	**0**	**2**	**0**	**0**	**0**	**1**	**0.0**	**–4**	....	....	....	....	....	....	....	....	....	....	....	....
	Fredericton	AHL	67	31	38	69	65	....	....	....	....	....	....	....	....	....	10	5	7	12	6	....	....	....	....
1996-97	Fredericton	AHL	9	10	6	16	10	....	....	....	....	....	....	....	....	....	....	....	....	....	....	....	....	....	....
	St. Louis	**NHL**	**61**	**6**	**11**	**17**	**43**	**0**	**0**	**1**	**74**	**8.1**	**0**	....	....	....	**6**	**0**	**0**	**0**	**8**	**0**	**0**	**0**	....
	Worcester IceCats	AHL	5	5	6	11	2	....	....	....	....	....	....	....	....	....	....	....	....	....	....	....	....	....	....
1997-98	**St. Louis**	**NHL**	**81**	**14**	**29**	**43**	**46**	**0**	**3**	**1**	**118**	**11.9**	**20**	....	....	....	**10**	**1**	**2**	**3**	**8**	**0**	**0**	**1**	....
1998-99	**St. Louis**	**NHL**	**69**	**14**	**25**	**39**	**38**	**0**	**1**	**1**	**134**	**10.4**	**14**	**1190**	**54.6**	**16:39**	**13**	**2**	**1**	**3**	**6**	**0**	**0**	**0**	**15:0**
99-2000	**St. Louis**	**NHL**	**79**	**12**	**15**	**27**	**36**	**1**	**2**	**3**	**98**	**12.2**	**5**	**1339**	**53.6**	**14:48**	**7**	**0**	**2**	**2**	**2**	**0**	**0**	**0**	**13:1**
2000-01	**St. Louis**	**NHL**	**69**	**11**	**14**	**25**	**46**	**0**	**3**	**2**	**101**	**10.9**	**2**	**729**	**55.1**	**14:01**	....	....	....	....	....	....	....	....	....
	Calgary	**NHL**	**14**	**3**	**4**	**7**	**14**	**0**	**1**	**0**	**32**	**9.4**	**0**	**264**	**52.7**	**18:08**	....	....	....	....	....	....	....	....	....
2001-02	**Calgary**	**NHL**	**81**	**27**	**48**	**75**	**32**	**7**	**2**	**4**	**146**	**18.5**	**24**	**1654**	**54.3**	**20:56**	....	....	....	....	....	....	....	....	....
2002-03	**Calgary**	**NHL**	**79**	**22**	**37**	**59**	**36**	**5**	**0**	**2**	**143**	**15.4**	**–4**	**1579**	**57.0**	**19:47**	....	....	....	....	....	....	....	....	....
2003-04	**Calgary**	**NHL**	**63**	**8**	**39**	**47**	**44**	**2**	**0**	**0**	**112**	**7.1**	**13**	**1402**	**53.9**	**19:13**	**26**	**6**	**11**	**17**	**12**	**2**	**0**	**1**	**20:2**
2004-05			DID NOT PLAY																						
2005-06	**Los Angeles**	**NHL**	**78**	**22**	**44**	**66**	**78**	**5**	**3**	**3**	**154**	**14.3**	**13**	**1429**	**51.2**	**19:13**	....	....	....	....	....	....	....	....	....
	United States	Olympics	6	1	4	5	2	....	....	....	....	....	....	....	....	....	....	....	....	....	....	....	....	....	....
2006-07	**Los Angeles**	**NHL**	**52**	**5**	**11**	**16**	**38**	**4**	**0**	**2**	**73**	**6.8**	**–13**	**802**	**51.5**	**15:29**	....	....	....	....	....	....	....	....	....
	Calgary	**NHL**	**28**	**8**	**13**	**21**	**18**	**0**	**1**	**0**	**39**	**20.5**	**10**	**443**	**50.3**	**16:00**	**6**	**1**	**1**	**2**	**8**	**0**	**0**	**0**	**15:3**
2007-08	**Calgary**	**NHL**	**79**	**12**	**22**	**34**	**71**	**1**	**0**	**4**	**116**	**10.3**	**6**	**1411**	**51.5**	**17:09**	**7**	**0**	**2**	**2**	**8**	**0**	**0**	**0**	**16:4**
2008-09	**Calgary**	**NHL**	**82**	**12**	**36**	**48**	**28**	**0**	**1**	**1**	**104**	**11.5**	**20**	**1382**	**52.8**	**15:22**	**6**	**0**	**1**	**1**	**0**	**0**	**0**	**0**	**12:3**
2009-10	**Calgary**	**NHL**	**63**	**3**	**12**	**15**	**25**	**0**	**0**	**1**	**52**	**5.8**	**–6**	**879**	**51.5**	**13:34**	....	....	....	....	....	....	....	....	....
	NHL Totals		**991**	**180**	**360**	**540**	**595**	**25**	**17**	**25**	**1501**	**12.0**		**14503**	**53.4**	**17:01**	**81**	**10**	**20**	**30**	**52**	**2**	**0**	**2**	**17:0**

ECAC First All-Star Team (1994) • NCAA East First All-American Team (1994) • NCAA Final Four All-Tournament Team (1994)

Traded to **St. Louis** by **Montreal** with Pierre Turgeon and Rory Fitzpatrick for Murray Baron, Shayne Corson and St. Louis' 5th round choice (Gennady Razin) in 1997 Entry Draft, October 29, 1996. Traded to **Calgary** by **St. Louis** with St. Louis' 7th round choice (David Moss) in 2001 Entry Draft for Cory Stillman, March 13, 2001. Signed as a free agent by **Los Angeles**, July 6, 2004. Traded to **Calgary** by **Lo Angeles** for Jamie Lundmark, Calgary's 4th round choice (Dwight King) in 2007 Entry Draft and Calgary's 2nd round choice (later traded back to Calgary - Calgary selected Mitch Wahl) in 2008 Entry Draft, January 29, 2007.

COOKE, Matt (KUK, MAT) PIT

Center. Shoots left. 5'11", 205 lbs. Born, Belleville, Ont., September 7, 1978. Vancouver's 8th choice, 144th overall, in 1997 Entry Draft.

			Regular Season														Playoffs								
Season	Club	League	GP	G	A	Pts	PIM	PP	SH	GW	S	%	+/-	TF	F%	Min	GP	G	A	Pts	PIM	PP	SH	GW	Min
1994-95	Wellington Dukes	MTJHL	46	9	23	32	62	....	....	....	....	....	....	....	....	....	....	....	....	....	....	....	....	....	....
1995-96	Windsor Spitfires	OHL	61	8	11	19	102	....	....	....	....	....	....	....	....	....	7	1	3	4	6	....	....	....	....
1996-97	Windsor Spitfires	OHL	65	45	50	95	146	....	....	....	....	....	....	....	....	....	5	5	5	10	10	....	....	....	....
1997-98	Windsor Spitfires	OHL	23	14	19	33	50	....	....	....	....	....	....	....	....	....	....	....	....	....	....	....	....	....	....
	Kingston	OHL	25	8	13	21	49	....	....	....	....	....	....	....	....	....	12	8	8	16	20	....	....	....	....
1998-99	**Vancouver**	**NHL**	**30**	**0**	**2**	**2**	**27**	**0**	**0**	**0**	**22**	**0.0**	**–12**	**189**	**40.2**	**8:07**	....	....	....	....	....	....	....	....	....
	Syracuse Crunch	AHL	37	15	18	33	119	....	....	....	....	....	....	....	....	....	....	....	....	....	....	....	....	....	....
99-2000	**Vancouver**	**NHL**	**51**	**5**	**7**	**12**	**39**	**0**	**1**	**1**	**58**	**8.6**	**3**	**71**	**39.4**	**11:48**	....	....	....	....	....	....	....	....	....
	Syracuse Crunch	AHL	18	5	8	13	27	....	....	....	....	....	....	....	....	....	....	....	....	....	....	....	....	....	....
2000-01	**Vancouver**	**NHL**	**81**	**14**	**13**	**27**	**94**	**0**	**2**	**0**	**121**	**11.6**	**5**	**321**	**43.0**	**14:35**	**4**	**0**	**0**	**0**	**4**	**0**	**0**	**0**	**12:0**
2001-02	**Vancouver**	**NHL**	**82**	**13**	**20**	**33**	**111**	**1**	**0**	**2**	**103**	**12.6**	**4**	**28**	**32.1**	**14:03**	**6**	**3**	**2**	**5**	**0**	**1**	**0**	**0**	**15:0**
2002-03	**Vancouver**	**NHL**	**82**	**15**	**27**	**42**	**82**	**1**	**4**	**0**	**118**	**12.7**	**21**	**31**	**35.5**	**13:24**	**14**	**2**	**1**	**3**	**12**	**0**	**0**	**0**	**14:0**
2003-04	**Vancouver**	**NHL**	**53**	**11**	**12**	**23**	**73**	**1**	**1**	**4**	**79**	**13.9**	**5**	**34**	**52.9**	**14:06**	**7**	**3**	**1**	**4**	**12**	**0**	**0**	**1**	**18:2**
2004-05			DID NOT PLAY																						
2005-06	**Vancouver**	**NHL**	**45**	**8**	**10**	**18**	**71**	**0**	**0**	**2**	**67**	**11.9**	**–8**	**25**	**24.0**	**13:57**	....	....	....	....	....	....	....	....	....
2006-07	**Vancouver**	**NHL**	**81**	**10**	**20**	**30**	**64**	**1**	**0**	**3**	**133**	**7.5**	**0**	**19**	**47.4**	**15:37**	**1**	**0**	**0**	**0**	**2**	**0**	**0**	**0**	**9:5**
2007-08	**Vancouver**	**NHL**	**61**	**7**	**9**	**16**	**64**	**0**	**0**	**1**	**68**	**10.3**	**–4**	**26**	**42.3**	**13:24**	....	....	....	....	....	....	....	....	....
	Washington	**NHL**	**17**	**3**	**4**	**7**	**27**	**0**	**1**	**0**	**18**	**16.7**	**5**	**2**	**50.0**	**12:19**	**7**	**0**	**0**	**0**	**4**	**0**	**0**	**0**	**13:5**
2008-09♦	**Pittsburgh**	**NHL**	**76**	**13**	**18**	**31**	**101**	**0**	**0**	**1**	**86**	**15.1**	**0**	**19**	**36.8**	**14:13**	**24**	**1**	**6**	**7**	**22**	**0**	**0**	**0**	**15:0**
2009-10	**Pittsburgh**	**NHL**	**79**	**15**	**15**	**30**	**106**	**2**	**0**	**1**	**105**	**14.3**	**17**	**24**	**54.2**	**14:47**	**13**	**4**	**2**	**6**	**22**	**0**	**0**	**0**	**15:1**
	NHL Totals		**738**	**114**	**157**	**271**	**859**	**6**	**9**	**15**	**978**	**11.7**		**789**	**41.4**	**13:49**	**76**	**13**	**12**	**25**	**78**	**1**	**0**	**1**	**14:5**

Traded to **Washington** by **Vancouver** for Matt Pettinger, February 26, 2008. Signed as a free agent by **Pittsburgh**, July 6, 2008.

CORRENTE, Matthew (kohr-REHN-tay, MA-thew) N.

Defense. Shoots right. 6', 205 lbs. Born, Mississauga, Ont., March 17, 1988. New Jersey's 1st choice, 30th overall, in 2006 Entry Draft.

			Regular Season														Playoffs								
Season	Club	League	GP	G	A	Pts	PIM	PP	SH	GW	S	%	+/-	TF	F%	Min	GP	G	A	Pts	PIM	PP	SH	GW	Min
2004-05	Saginaw Spirit	OHL	62	6	9	15	89	....	....	....	....	....	....	....	....	....	....	....	....	....	....	....	....	....	....
2005-06	Saginaw Spirit	OHL	61	6	24	30	172	....	....	....	....	....	....	....	....	....	4	1	1	2	8	....	....	....	....
2006-07	Saginaw Spirit	OHL	29	2	13	15	67	....	....	....	....	....	....	....	....	....	....	....	....	....	....	....	....	....	....
	Mississauga	OHL	14	1	10	11	27	....	....	....	....	....	....	....	....	....	5	0	1	1	8	....	....	....	....
2007-08	Niagara Ice Dogs	OHL	21	2	13	15	64	....	....	....	....	....	....	....	....	....	10	0	5	5	33	....	....	....	....
2008-09	Lowell Devils	AHL	67	6	12	18	161	....	....	....	....	....	....	....	....	....	....	....	....	....	....	....	....	....	....
2009-10	**New Jersey**	**NHL**	**12**	**0**	**0**	**0**	**24**	**0**	**0**	**0**	**6**	**0.0**	**0**	**0**	**0.0**	**8:51**	**2**	**0**	**0**	**0**	**2**	**0**	**0**	**0**	**5:**
	Lowell Devils	AHL	43	5	15	20	74	....	....	....	....	....	....	....	....	....	....	....	....	....	....	....	....	....	....
	NHL Totals		**12**	**0**	**0**	**0**	**24**	**0**	**0**	**0**	**6**	**0.0**		**0**	**0.0**	**8:51**	**2**	**0**	**0**	**0**	**2**	**0**	**0**	**0**	**5:5**

CORVO, Joe (KOHR-voh, JOH) CA

Defense. Shoots right. 6', 204 lbs. Born, Oak Park, IL, June 20, 1977. Los Angeles' 4th choice, 83rd overall, in 1997 Entry Draft.

			Regular Season														Playoffs								
Season	Club	League	GP	G	A	Pts	PIM	PP	SH	GW	S	%	+/-	TF	F%	Min	GP	G	A	Pts	PIM	PP	SH	GW	Min
1995-96	Western Mich.	CCHA	41	5	25	30	38	....	....	....	....	....	....	....	....	....	....	....	....	....	....	....	....	....	....
1996-97	Western Mich.	CCHA	32	12	21	33	85	....	....	....	....	....	....	....	....	....	....	....	....	....	....	....	....	....	....
1997-98	Western Mich.	CCHA	32	5	12	17	93	....	....	....	....	....	....	....	....	....	....	....	....	....	....	....	....	....	....
1998-99	Springfield	AHL	50	5	15	20	32	....	....	....	....	....	....	....	....	....	....	....	....	....	....	....	....	....	....
	Hampton Roads	ECHL	5	0	0	0	15	....	....	....	....	....	....	....	....	....	4	0	1	1	0	....	....	....	....
99-2000			DID NOT PLAY																						
2000-01	Lowell	AHL	77	10	23	33	31	....	....	....	....	....	....	....	....	....	4	3	1	4	0	....	....	....	....
2001-02	Manchester	AHL	80	13	37	50	30	....	....	....	....	....	....	....	....	....	5	0	5	5	0	....	....	....	....

			Regular Season														Playoffs								
Season	Club	League	GP	G	A	Pts	PIM	PP	SH	GW	S	%	+/-	TF	F%	Min	GP	G	A	Pts	PIM	PP	SH	GW	Min
2002-03	Los Angeles	NHL	50	5	7	12	14	2	0	0	84	6.0	2	0	0.0	18:37	....	....	....	....	....	....	....	....	....
	Manchester	AHL	26	8	18	26	8	....	....	....	....	....	....	....	....	....	3	0	0	0	0	....	....	....	....
2003-04	Los Angeles	NHL	72	8	17	25	36	0	0	3	150	5.3	7	1	0.0	21:09	....	....	....	....	....	....	....	....	....
2004-05	Chicago Wolves	AHL	23	7	7	14	14	....	....	....	....	....	....	....	....	....	18	4	5	9	12	....	....	....	....
2005-06	Los Angeles	NHL	81	14	26	40	38	7	0	3	190	7.4	16	0	0.0	19:59	....	....	....	....	....	....	....	....	....
2006-07	Ottawa	NHL	76	8	29	37	42	3	0	2	160	5.0	8	0	0.0	18:04	20	2	7	9	6	1	0	1	17:18
2007-08	Ottawa	NHL	51	6	21	27	18	1	0	1	111	5.4	13	0	0.0	17:41	....	....	....	....	....	....	....	....	....
	Carolina	NHL	23	7	14	21	8	5	0	2	56	12.5	4	0	0.0	20:46	....	....	....	....	....	....	....	....	....
2008-09	Carolina	NHL	81	14	24	38	18	8	1	6	213	6.6	–1	0	0.0	24:19	18	2	5	7	4	1	0	1	25:27
2009-10	Carolina	NHL	34	4	8	12	10	4	0	0	76	5.3	–6	0	0.0	25:13	....	....	....	....	....	....	....	....	....
	Washington	NHL	18	2	4	6	2	1	0	0	23	8.7	–4	0	0.0	19:41	7	1	1	2	4	0	0	0	16:53
	NHL Totals		486	68	150	218	186	31	1	17	1063	6.4		1	0.0	20:35	45	5	13	18	14	2	0	2	20:30

CCHA All-Rookie Team (1996) • CCHA Second All-Star Team (1997)

• Missed entire 1999-2000 season after failing to come to contract terms with **Los Angeles.** Signed as a free agent by **Chicago** (AHL), February 24, 2005. Signed as a free agent by **Ottawa**, July 1, 2006. Traded to **Carolina** by **Ottawa** with Patrick Eaves for Cory Stillman and Mike Commodore, February 11, 2008. • Missed majority of 2009-10 season recovering from leg injury suffered in game vs. Washington, November 30, 2009. Traded to **Washington** by **Carolina** for Brian Pothier, Oskar Osala and Washington's 2nd round choice (later traded to NY Rangers) in 2011 Entry Draft, March 3, 2010. Signed as a free agent by **Carolina**, July 7, 2010.

COTE, Riley

(KOH-tay, RIGH-lee)

Right wing. Shoots left. 6'2", 220 lbs. Born, Winnipeg, Man., March 16, 1982.

Season	Club	League	GP	G	A	Pts	PIM	PP	SH	GW	S	%	+/-	TF	F%	Min	GP	G	A	Pts	PIM	PP	SH	GW	Min
1998-99	Prince Albert	WHL	37	3	2	5	63	....	....	....	....	....	....	....	....	....	9	0	0	0	9	....	....	....	....
99-2000	Prince Albert	WHL	67	6	7	13	71	....	....	....	....	....	....	....	....	....	3	1	0	1	2	....	....	....	....
2000-01	Prince Albert	WHL	64	17	35	52	114	....	....	....	....	....	....	....	....	....	....	....	....	....	....	....	....	....	....
2001-02	Prince Albert	WHL	67	28	23	51	134	....	....	....	....	....	....	....	....	....	....	....	....	....	....	....	....	....	....
2002-03	St. John's	AHL	6	0	0	0	5	....	....	....	....	....	....	....	....	....	....	....	....	....	....	....	....	....	....
	Memphis	CHL	51	8	6	14	241	....	....	....	....	....	....	....	....	....	14	1	0	1	54	....	....	....	....
2003-04	Syracuse Crunch	AHL	9	0	0	0	19	....	....	....	....	....	....	....	....	....	....	....	....	....	....	....	....	....	....
	Dayton Bombers	ECHL	57	6	11	17	258	....	....	....	....	....	....	....	....	....	....	....	....	....	....	....	....	....	....
2004-05	Philadelphia	AHL	61	4	7	11	280	....	....	....	....	....	....	....	....	....	13	0	0	0	6	....	....	....	....
2005-06	Philadelphia	AHL	70	3	1	4	259	....	....	....	....	....	....	....	....	....	....	....	....	....	....	....	....	....	....
2006-07	Philadelphia	NHL	8	0	0	0	11	0	0	0	3	0.0	0	0	0.0	4:30	....	....	....	....	....	....	....	....	....
	Philadelphia	AHL	37	1	4	5	125	....	....	....	....	....	....	....	....	....	....	....	....	....	....	....	....	....	....
2007-08	Philadelphia	NHL	70	1	3	4	202	0	0	0	17	5.9	2	2	50.0	4:17	3	0	0	0	0	0	0	0	4:08
2008-09	Philadelphia	NHL	63	0	3	3	174	0	0	0	24	0.0	–7	0	0.0	4:10	....	....	....	....	....	....	....	....	....
2009-10	Philadelphia	NHL	15	0	0	0	24	0	0	0	7	0.0	0	0	0.0	3:02	....	....	....	....	....	....	....	....	....
	NHL Totals		156	1	6	7	411	0	0	0	51	2.0		2	50.0	4:07	3	0	0	0	0	0	0	0	4:08

Signed as a free agent by **Philadelphia**, August 23, 2005. • Missed majority of 2009-10 season as a healthy reserve. • Officially announced his retirement, August 9, 2010.

COUTURE, Logan

(koh-TYOOR, LOH-guhn) **S.J.**

Center. Shoots left. 6'1", 195 lbs. Born, Guelph, Ont., March 28, 1989. San Jose's 1st choice, 9th overall, in 2007 Entry Draft.

Season	Club	League	GP	G	A	Pts	PIM	PP	SH	GW	S	%	+/-	TF	F%	Min	GP	G	A	Pts	PIM	PP	SH	GW	Min
2004-05	St. Thomas Stars	OJHL-B	48	24	22	46	....	....	....	....	....	....	....	....	....	....	....	....	....	....	....	....	....	....	....
2005-06	Ottawa 67's	OHL	65	25	39	64	52	....	....	....	....	....	....	....	....	....	6	3	4	7	0	....	....	....	....
2006-07	Ottawa 67's	OHL	54	26	52	78	24	....	....	....	....	....	....	....	....	....	5	1	7	8	4	....	....	....	....
2007-08	Ottawa 67's	OHL	51	21	37	58	37	....	....	....	....	....	....	....	....	....	4	2	1	3	0	....	....	....	....
2008-09	Ottawa 67's	OHL	62	39	48	87	46	....	....	....	....	....	....	....	....	....	7	3	7	10	6	....	....	....	....
	Worcester Sharks	AHL	4	0	0	0	7	....	....	....	....	....	....	....	....	....	12	2	1	3	11	....	....	....	....
2009-10	San Jose	NHL	25	5	4	9	6	1	0	1	42	11.9	4	143	52.5	10:16	15	4	0	4	4	0	0	1	11:23
	Worcester Sharks	AHL	42	20	33	53	12	....	....	....	....	....	....	....	....	....	....	....	....	....	....	....	....	....	....
	NHL Totals		25	5	4	9	6	1	0	1	42	11.9		143	52.4	10:16	15	4	0	4	4	0	0	1	11:23

COWAN, Jeff

(KOW-an, JEHF)

Left wing. Shoots left. 6'2", 205 lbs. Born, Scarborough, Ont., September 27, 1976.

Season	Club	League	GP	G	A	Pts	PIM	PP	SH	GW	S	%	+/-	TF	F%	Min	GP	G	A	Pts	PIM	PP	SH	GW	Min
1992-93	Guelph Platers	OHA-B	45	8	8	16	22	....	....	....	....	....	....	....	....	....	....	....	....	....	....	....	....	....	....
1993-94	Guelph Platers	OHA-B	43	30	26	56	96	....	....	....	....	....	....	....	....	....	....	....	....	....	....	....	....	....	....
	Guelph Storm	OHL	17	1	0	1	5	....	....	....	....	....	....	....	....	....	....	....	....	....	....	....	....	....	....
1994-95	Guelph Storm	OHL	51	10	7	17	14	....	....	....	....	....	....	....	....	....	14	1	1	2	0	....	....	....	....
1995-96	Barrie Colts	OHL	66	38	14	52	29	....	....	....	....	....	....	....	....	....	5	1	2	3	6	....	....	....	....
1996-97	Saint John Flames	AHL	22	5	5	10	8	....	....	....	....	....	....	....	....	....	....	....	....	....	....	....	....	....	....
	Roanoke Express	ECHL	47	21	13	34	42	....	....	....	....	....	....	....	....	....	....	....	....	....	....	....	....	....	....
1997-98	Saint John Flames	AHL	69	15	13	28	23	....	....	....	....	....	....	....	....	....	13	4	1	5	14	....	....	....	....
1998-99	Saint John Flames	AHL	71	7	12	19	117	....	....	....	....	....	....	....	....	....	4	0	1	1	10	....	....	....	....
99-2000	Calgary	NHL	13	4	1	5	16	0	0	0	26	15.4	2	0	0.0	10:22	....	....	....	....	....	....	....	....	....
	Saint John Flames	AHL	47	15	10	25	77	....	....	....	....	....	....	....	....	....	....	....	....	....	....	....	....	....	....
2000-01	Calgary	NHL	51	9	4	13	74	2	0	1	48	18.8	–8	5	20.0	9:06	....	....	....	....	....	....	....	....	....
2001-02	Calgary	NHL	19	1	0	1	40	0	0	1	13	7.7	–3	2	50.0	7:44	....	....	....	....	....	....	....	....	....
	Atlanta	NHL	38	4	1	5	50	0	0	1	51	7.8	–11	5	20.0	12:27	....	....	....	....	....	....	....	....	....
2002-03	Atlanta	NHL	66	3	5	8	115	0	0	0	52	5.8	–15	10	30.0	8:24	....	....	....	....	....	....	....	....	....
2003-04	Atlanta	NHL	58	9	15	24	68	1	0	1	74	12.2	2	9	22.2	10:04	....	....	....	....	....	....	....	....	....
	Los Angeles	NHL	13	2	1	3	24	1	0	0	15	13.3	–1	2	50.0	11:43	....	....	....	....	....	....	....	....	....
2004-05	DID NOT PLAY																								
2005-06	Los Angeles	NHL	46	8	1	9	73	0	0	0	53	15.1	–8	4	25.0	8:26	....	....	....	....	....	....	....	....	....
2006-07	Los Angeles	NHL	21	0	2	2	32	0	0	0	28	0.0	–1	1	0.0	7:37	....	....	....	....	....	....	....	....	....
	Vancouver	NHL	42	7	3	10	93	0	1	0	46	15.2	4	0	0.0	8:15	10	2	0	2	22	0	0	1	11:38
2007-08	Vancouver	NHL	46	0	1	1	110	0	0	0	35	0.0	–5	1	0.0	8:45	....	....	....	....	....	....	....	....	....
2008-09	Peoria Rivermen	AHL	71	5	10	15	94	....	....	....	....	....	....	....	....	....	7	1	1	2	0	....	....	....	....
2009-10	Portland Pirates	AHL	62	18	13	31	57	....	....	....	....	....	....	....	....	....	4	0	0	0	0	....	....	....	....
	NHL Totals		413	47	34	81	695	4	1	4	441	10.7		39	25.6	9:13	10	2	0	2	22	0	0	1	11:38

Signed as a free agent by **Calgary**, October 2, 1995. Traded to **Atlanta** by **Calgary** with the rights to Kurtis Foster for Petr Buzek and Atlanta's 6th round choice (Adam Pardy) in 2004 Entry Draft, December 18, 2001. Traded to **Los Angeles** by **Atlanta** for Kip Brennan, March 9, 2004. Claimed on waivers by **Vancouver** from **Los Angeles**, December 30, 2006. Signed as a free agent by **Buffalo**, August 20, 2009.

COWEN, Jared

(KOW-ehn, JAIR-ehd) **OTT.**

Defense. Shoots left. 6'5", 228 lbs. Born, Saskatoon, Sask., January 25, 1991. Ottawa's 1st choice, 9th overall, in 2009 Entry Draft.

Season	Club	League	GP	G	A	Pts	PIM	PP	SH	GW	S	%	+/-	TF	F%	Min	GP	G	A	Pts	PIM	PP	SH	GW	Min
2006-07	Sask. Contacts	SMHL	41	6	22	28	103	....	....	....	....	....	....	....	....	....	....	....	....	....	....	....	....	....	....
	Spokane Chiefs	WHL	6	0	2	2	2	....	....	....	....	....	....	....	....	....	6	0	1	1	6	....	....	....	....
2007-08	Spokane Chiefs	WHL	68	4	14	18	62	....	....	....	....	....	....	....	....	....	21	1	3	4	17	....	....	....	....
2008-09	Spokane Chiefs	WHL	48	7	14	21	45	....	....	....	....	....	....	....	....	....	....	....	....	....	....	....	....	....	....
2009-10	Ottawa	NHL	1	0	0	0	2	0	0	0	0	0.0	0	0	0.0	6:46	....	....	....	....	....	....	....	....	....
	Spokane Chiefs	WHL	59	8	22	30	74	....	....	....	....	....	....	....	....	....	7	1	1	2	8	....	....	....	....
	NHL Totals		1	0	0	0	2	0	0	0	0	0.0		0	0.0	6:46	....	....	....	....	....	....	....	....	....

WHL West Second All-Star Team (2010)

CRABB, Joey

(KRAB, JOH-ee) **TOR.**

Right wing. Shoots right. 6'1", 190 lbs. Born, Anchorage, AK, April 3, 1983. NY Rangers' 7th choice, 226th overall, in 2002 Entry Draft.

Season	Club	League	GP	G	A	Pts	PIM	PP	SH	GW	S	%	+/-	TF	F%	Min	GP	G	A	Pts	PIM	PP	SH	GW	Min
99-2000	USNTDP	NAHL	55	13	10	23	69	....	....	....	....	....	....	....	....	....	3	1	0	1	4	....	....	....	....
2000-01	USNTDP	U-18	39	10	10	20	22	....	....	....	....	....	....	....	....	....	....	....	....	....	....	....	....	....	....
	USNTDP	USHL	21	2	3	5	18	....	....	....	....	....	....	....	....	....	....	....	....	....	....	....	....	....	....
2001-02	Green Bay	USHL	61	15	27	42	94	....	....	....	....	....	....	....	....	....	7	4	8	12	21	....	....	....	....
2002-03	Colorado College	WCHA	35	4	4	8	40	....	....	....	....	....	....	....	....	....	....	....	....	....	....	....	....	....	....
2003-04	Colorado College	WCHA	39	15	12	27	20	....	....	....	....	....	....	....	....	....	....	....	....	....	....	....	....	....	....
2004-05	Colorado College	WCHA	43	16	16	32	44	....	....	....	....	....	....	....	....	....	....	....	....	....	....	....	....	....	....
2005-06	Colorado College	WCHA	42	18	25	43	45	....	....	....	....	....	....	....	....	....	....	....	....	....	....	....	....	....	....
2006-07	Chicago Wolves	AHL	63	7	15	22	25	....	....	....	....	....	....	....	....	....	6	0	0	0	0	....	....	....	....
2007-08	Chicago Wolves	AHL	72	9	26	35	78	....	....	....	....	....	....	....	....	....	24	1	4	5	20	....	....	....	....

			Regular Season														Playoffs								
Season	Club	League	GP	G	A	Pts	PIM	PP	SH	GW	S	%	+/-	TF	F%	Min	GP	G	A	Pts	PIM	PP	SH	GW	Min
2008-09	**Atlanta**	**NHL**	**29**	**4**	**5**	**9**	**28**	**0**	**1**	**1**	**33**	**12.1**	**–2**	**33**	**39.4**	**12:13**	....	....	....	....	....	....	....	....	....
	Chicago Wolves	AHL	42	15	14	29	62	....	....	....	....	....	....	....	....	....	....	....	....	....	....	....	....	....	....
2009-10	Chicago Wolves	AHL	79	24	29	53	59	....	....	....	....	....	....	....	....	....	14	6	5	11	12	....	....	....	....
	NHL Totals		**29**	**4**	**5**	**9**	**28**	**0**	**1**	**1**	**33**	**12.1**		**33**	**39.4**	**12:13**	....	....	....	....	....	....	....	....	....

Signed as a free agent by **Atlanta**, August 31, 2006. Traded to **Chicago** by **Atlanta** with Marty Reasoner, Jeremy Morin and New Jersey's 1st (previously acquired, Chicago selected Kevin Hayes) and 2nd (previously acquired, Chicago selected Justin Holl) round choices in 2010 Entry Draft for Brent Sopel, Dustin Byfuglien, Ben Eager and Akim Aliu, June 24, 2010. Signed as a free agent by **Toronto**, July 15, 2010.

CRAIG, Ryan

(KRAIG, RIGH-uhn) **PIT.**

Center. Shoots left. 6'2", 212 lbs. Born, Abbotsford, B.C., January 6, 1982. Tampa Bay's 10th choice, 255th overall, in 2002 Entry Draft.

1997-98	Abbotsford	Minor-BC	80	118	120	238	110	....	....	....	....	....	....	....	....	....	....	....	....	....	....	....	....	....	....
	Brandon	WHL	1	0	0	0	0	....	....	....	....	....	....	....	....	....	....	....	....	....	....	....	....	....	....
1998-99	Brandon	WHL	54	11	12	23	46	....	....	....	....	....	....	....	....	....	5	0	0	0	4	....	....	....	....
99-2000	Brandon	WHL	65	17	19	36	40	....	....	....	....	....	....	....	....	....	....	....	....	....	....	....	....	....	....
2000-01	Brandon	WHL	70	38	33	71	49	....	....	....	....	....	....	....	....	....	6	3	0	3	7	....	....	....	....
2001-02	Brandon	WHL	52	29	35	64	52	....	....	....	....	....	....	....	....	....	19	11	10	21	13	....	....	....	....
2002-03	Brandon	WHL	60	42	32	74	69	....	....	....	....	....	....	....	....	....	17	5	8	13	29	....	....	....	....
2003-04	Hershey Bears	AHL	61	4	8	12	24	....	....	....	....	....	....	....	....	....	....	....	....	....	....	....	....	....	....
	Pensacola	ECHL	5	3	5	8	0	....	....	....	....	....	....	....	....	....	2	0	1	1	0	....	....	....	....
2004-05	Springfield	AHL	80	27	14	41	50	....	....	....	....	....	....	....	....	....	....	....	....	....	....	....	....	....	....
2005-06	**Tampa Bay**	**NHL**	**48**	**15**	**13**	**28**	**6**	**6**	**0**	**0**	**81**	**18.5**	**–4**	**95**	**46.3**	**15:21**	**5**	**0**	**0**	**0**	**10**	**0**	**0**	**0**	**12:59**
	Springfield	AHL	28	12	10	22	14	....	....	....	....	....	....	....	....	....	....	....	....	....	....	....	....	....	....
2006-07	**Tampa Bay**	**NHL**	**72**	**14**	**13**	**27**	**55**	**4**	**0**	**2**	**130**	**10.8**	**–11**	**110**	**40.0**	**15:20**	**6**	**0**	**0**	**0**	**12**	**0**	**0**	**0**	**7:02**
2007-08	**Tampa Bay**	**NHL**	**7**	**1**	**1**	**2**	**0**	**1**	**0**	**0**	**8**	**12.5**	**–1**	**1**	**100.0**	**13:04**	....	....	....	....	....	....	....	....	....
	Norfolk Admirals	AHL	2	1	2	3	2	....	....	....	....	....	....	....	....	....	....	....	....	....	....	....	....	....	....
2008-09	**Tampa Bay**	**NHL**	**54**	**2**	**4**	**6**	**60**	**0**	**0**	**0**	**64**	**3.1**	**–7**	**222**	**49.6**	**10:16**	....	....	....	....	....	....	....	....	....
2009-10	**Tampa Bay**	**NHL**	**3**	**0**	**0**	**0**	**5**	**0**	**0**	**0**	**5**	**0.0**	**0**	**1**	**0.0**	**9:47**	....	....	....	....	....	....	....	....	....
	Norfolk Admirals	AHL	73	23	22	45	64	....	....	....	....	....	....	....	....	....	....	....	....	....	....	....	....	....	....
	NHL Totals		**184**	**32**	**31**	**63**	**126**	**11**	**0**	**2**	**288**	**11.1**		**429**	**46.4**	**13:41**	**11**	**0**	**0**	**0**	**22**	**0**	**0**	**0**	**9:44**

WHL East First All-Star Team (2003) • Canadian Major Junior Humanitarian Player of the Year (2003)

• Missed majority of 2007-08 season recovering from back and knee injuries.

CROMBEEN, B.J.

(KRAWM-been, BEE-JAY) **ST.L.**

Right wing. Shoots right. 6'2", 210 lbs. Born, Denver, CO, July 10, 1985. Dallas' 3rd choice, 54th overall, in 2003 Entry Draft.

2000-01	Newmarket	OPJHL	35	14	14	28	63	....	....	....	....	....	....	....	....	....	....	....	....	....	....	....	....	....	....
2001-02	Barrie Colts	OHL	60	12	13	25	118	....	....	....	....	....	....	....	....	....	20	1	1	2	31	....	....	....	....
2002-03	Barrie Colts	OHL	63	22	24	46	133	....	....	....	....	....	....	....	....	....	6	1	0	1	8	....	....	....	....
2003-04	Barrie Colts	OHL	62	21	29	50	154	....	....	....	....	....	....	....	....	....	12	5	7	12	35	....	....	....	....
2004-05	Barrie Colts	OHL	63	31	18	49	111	....	....	....	....	....	....	....	....	....	6	2	4	6	35	....	....	....	....
2005-06	Iowa Stars	AHL	52	5	7	12	97	....	....	....	....	....	....	....	....	....	5	1	0	1	9	....	....	....	....
	Idaho Steelheads	ECHL	8	5	3	8	5	....	....	....	....	....	....	....	....	....	....	....	....	....	....	....	....	....	....
2006-07	Assat Pori	Finland	55	13	9	22	152	....	....	....	....	....	....	....	....	....	....	....	....	....	....	....	....	....	....
	Idaho Steelheads	ECHL	13	7	4	11	43	....	....	....	....	....	....	....	....	....	22	5	5	10	45	....	....	....	....
2007-08	**Dallas**	**NHL**	**8**	**0**	**2**	**2**	**39**	**0**	**0**	**0**	**9**	**0.0**	**1**	**1**	**0.0**	**6:38**	**5**	**0**	**0**	**0**	**0**	**0**	**0**	**0**	**4:16**
	Iowa Stars	AHL	65	14	14	28	158	....	....	....	....	....	....	....	....	....	....	....	....	....	....	....	....	....	....
2008-09	**Dallas**	**NHL**	**15**	**1**	**4**	**5**	**26**	**0**	**0**	**0**	**12**	**8.3**	**–1**	**0**	**0.0**	**8:14**	....	....	....	....	....	....	....	....	....
	St. Louis	**NHL**	**66**	**11**	**6**	**17**	**122**	**0**	**1**	**3**	**112**	**9.8**	**–8**	**7**	**42.9**	**13:45**	**4**	**0**	**0**	**0**	**12**	**0**	**0**	**0**	**9:46**
2009-10	**St. Louis**	**NHL**	**79**	**7**	**8**	**15**	**168**	**0**	**1**	**1**	**120**	**5.8**	**–5**	**51**	**35.3**	**13:05**	....	....	....	....	....	....	....	....	....
	NHL Totals		**168**	**19**	**20**	**39**	**355**	**0**	**2**	**4**	**253**	**7.5**		**59**	**35.6**	**12:36**	**9**	**0**	**0**	**0**	**12**	**0**	**0**	**0**	**6:43**

Signed as a free agent by **Pori** (Finland), August 2, 2006. Claimed on waivers by **St. Louis** from **Dallas**, November 18, 2008.

CROSBY, Sidney

(KRAWZ-bee, SIHD-nee) **PIT.**

Center. Shoots left. 5'11", 200 lbs. Born, Cole Harbour, N.S., August 7, 1987. Pittsburgh's 1st choice, 1st overall, in 2005 Entry Draft.

2001-02	Dartmouth	NSMHL	74	95	98	193	114	....	....	....	....	....	....	....	....	....	....	....	....	....	....	....	....	....	....
2002-03	Shat.-St. Mary's	High-MN	57	72	90	162	....	....	....	....	....	....	....	....	....	....	....	....	....	....	....	....	....	....	....
2003-04	Rimouski Oceanic	QMJHL	59	54	*81	*135	74	....	....	....	....	....	....	....	....	....	9	7	9	16	10	....	....	....	....
2004-05	Rimouski Oceanic	QMJHL	62	*66	*102	*168	84	....	....	....	....	....	....	....	....	....	13	*14	*17	*31	16	....	....	....	....
2005-06	**Pittsburgh**	**NHL**	**81**	**39**	**63**	**102**	**110**	**16**	**0**	**5**	**278**	**14.0**	**–1**	**1174**	**45.5**	**20:08**	....	....	....	....	....	....	....	....	....
2006-07	**Pittsburgh**	**NHL**	**79**	**36**	**84**	***120**	**60**	**13**	**0**	**4**	**250**	**14.4**	**10**	**1686**	**49.8**	**20:46**	**5**	**3**	**2**	**5**	**4**	**1**	**0**	**1**	**21:40**
2007-08	**Pittsburgh**	**NHL**	**53**	**24**	**48**	**72**	**39**	**6**	**0**	**4**	**173**	**13.9**	**18**	**1103**	**51.4**	**20:51**	**20**	**6**	***21**	***27**	**12**	**2**	**0**	**1**	**20:42**
2008-09 ♦	**Pittsburgh**	**NHL**	**77**	**33**	**70**	**103**	**76**	**7**	**0**	**3**	**238**	**13.9**	**3**	**1615**	**51.3**	**21:57**	**24**	***15**	**16**	**31**	**14**	**5**	**0**	**2**	**20:49**
2009-10	**Pittsburgh**	**NHL**	**81**	***51**	**58**	**109**	**71**	**13**	**2**	**6**	**298**	**17.1**	**15**	**1791**	**55.9**	**21:57**	**13**	**6**	**13**	**19**	**6**	**1**	**0**	**1**	**23:32**
	Canada	Olympics	7	4	3	7	4	....	....	....	....	....	....	....	....	....	....	....	....	....	....	....	....	....	....
	NHL Totals		**371**	**183**	**323**	**506**	**356**	**55**	**2**	**22**	**1237**	**14.8**		**7369**	**51.2**	**21:08**	**62**	**30**	**52**	**82**	**36**	**9**	**0**	**5**	**21:25**

QMJHL All-Rookie Team (2004) • QMJHL First All-Star Team (2004, 2005) • QMJHL Player of the Year (2004, 2005) • Canadian Major Junior First All-Star Team (2004, 2005) • Canadian Major Junior Rookie of the Year (2004) • Canadian Major Junior Player of the Year (2004, 2005) • Memorial Cup All-Star Team (2005) • Ed Chynoweth Trophy (Memorial Cup Tournament - Leading Scorer) (2005) • NHL All-Rookie Team (2006) • NHL First All-Star Team (2007) • Art Ross Trophy (2007) • Lester B. Pearson Award (2007) • Hart Memorial Trophy (2007) • NHL Second All-Star Team (2010) • Mark Messier NHL Leadership Award (2010) • Maurice "Rocket" Richard Trophy (2010) (tied with Steven Stamkos)

Played in NHL All-Star Game (2007)

CULLEN, Mark

(KUH-lehn, MAHRK) **FLA.**

Center. Shoots left. 5'11", 182 lbs. Born, Moorhead, MN, October 28, 1978.

1996-97	Fargo High	High-ND	30	20	45	65	....	....	....	....	....	....	....	....	....	....	....	....	....	....	....	....	....	....	....
1997-98	Fargo-Moorhead	USHL	30	17	37	54	16	....	....	....	....	....	....	....	....	....	4	3	0	3	25	....	....	....	....
1998-99	Colorado College	WCHA	42	8	25	33	22	....	....	....	....	....	....	....	....	....	....	....	....	....	....	....	....	....	....
99-2000	Colorado College	WCHA	37	11	20	31	22	....	....	....	....	....	....	....	....	....	....	....	....	....	....	....	....	....	....
2000-01	Colorado College	WCHA	31	20	33	53	26	....	....	....	....	....	....	....	....	....	....	....	....	....	....	....	....	....	....
2001-02	Colorado College	WCHA	43	14	36	50	14	....	....	....	....	....	....	....	....	....	....	....	....	....	....	....	....	....	....
2002-03	Houston Aeros	AHL	72	22	25	47	20	....	....	....	....	....	....	....	....	....	15	3	7	10	4	....	....	....	....
2003-04	Houston Aeros	AHL	53	10	28	38	28	....	....	....	....	....	....	....	....	....	2	0	0	0	0	....	....	....	....
2004-05	Houston Aeros	AHL	64	10	24	34	26	....	....	....	....	....	....	....	....	....	5	1	1	2	0	....	....	....	....
2005-06	**Chicago**	**NHL**	**29**	**7**	**9**	**16**	**2**	**0**	**0**	**0**	**45**	**15.6**	**7**	**281**	**48.8**	**13:15**	....	....	....	....	....	....	....	....	....
	Norfolk Admirals	AHL	54	29	39	68	48	....	....	....	....	....	....	....	....	....	4	2	2	4	0	....	....	....	....
2006-07	**Philadelphia**	**NHL**	**3**	**0**	**0**	**0**	**0**	**0**	**0**	**0**	**4**	**0.0**	**–3**	**14**	**50.0**	**6:15**	....	....	....	....	....	....	....	....	....
	Philadelphia	AHL	56	16	36	52	34	....	....	....	....	....	....	....	....	....	....	....	....	....	....	....	....	....	....
2007-08	Grand Rapids	AHL	59	16	31	47	61	....	....	....	....	....	....	....	....	....	....	....	....	....	....	....	....	....	....
2008-09	Manitoba Moose	AHL	56	14	25	39	22	....	....	....	....	....	....	....	....	....	20	4	9	13	0	....	....	....	....
2009-10	Rockford IceHogs	AHL	62	21	32	53	16	....	....	....	....	....	....	....	....	....	4	0	2	2	2	....	....	....	....
	NHL Totals		**32**	**7**	**9**	**16**	**2**	**0**	**0**	**0**	**49**	**14.3**		**295**	**48.8**	**12:36**	....	....	....	....	....	....	....	....	....

USHL All-Rookie Team (1998) • USHL Rookie of the Year (1998) • WCHA First All-Star Team (2001, 2002) • NCAA West Second All-American Team (2001) • Fred Hunt Memorial Trophy (AHL - Sportsmanship) (2006)

Signed as a free agent by **Minnesota**, April 8, 2002. Signed as a free agent by **Chicago**, August 4, 2005. Signed as a free agent by **Philadelphia**, July 5, 2006. Signed as a free agent by **Detroit**, July 16, 2007. Signed as a free agent by **Vancouver**, July 4, 2008. Signed as a free agent by **Chicago**, July 13, 2009. Signed as a free agent by **Florida**, July 24, 2010.

CULLEN, Matt

(KUH-lehn, MAT) **MIN.**

Center. Shoots left. 6'1", 200 lbs. Born, Virginia, MN, November 2, 1976. Anaheim's 2nd choice, 35th overall, in 1996 Entry Draft.

1994-95	Moorhead Spuds	High-MN	28	47	42	89	78	....	....	....	....	....	....	....	....	....	....	....	....	....	....	....	....	....	....
1995-96	St. Cloud State	WCHA	39	12	29	41	28	....	....	....	....	....	....	....	....	....	....	....	....	....	....	....	....	....	....
1996-97	St. Cloud State	WCHA	36	15	30	45	70	....	....	....	....	....	....	....	....	....	....	....	....	....	....	....	....	....	....
	Baltimore Bandits	AHL	6	3	3	6	7	....	....	....	....	....	....	....	....	....	3	0	2	2	0	....	....	....	....
1997-98	**Anaheim**	**NHL**	**61**	**6**	**21**	**27**	**23**	**2**	**0**	**0**	**75**	**8.0**	**–4**	....	....	....	....	....	....	....	....	....	....	....	....
	Cincinnati	AHL	18	15	12	27	2	....	....	....	....	....	....	....	....	....	....	....	....	....	....	....	....	....	....
1998-99	**Anaheim**	**NHL**	**75**	**11**	**14**	**25**	**47**	**5**	**1**	**1**	**112**	**9.8**	**–12**	**1047**	**47.7**	**15:31**	**4**	**0**	**0**	**0**	**0**	**0**	**0**	**0**	**15:30**
	Cincinnati	AHL	3	1	2	3	8	....	....	....	....	....	....	....	....	....	....	....	....	....	....	....	....	....	....

			Regular Season														Playoffs								
Season	Club	League	GP	G	A	Pts	PIM	PP	SH	GW	S	%	+/-	TF	F%	Min	GP	G	A	Pts	PIM	PP	SH	GW	Min
99-2000	Anaheim	NHL	80	13	26	39	24	1	0	1	137	9.5	5	1247	44.6	16:54	....	....	....	....	....	....	....	....	....
2000-01	Anaheim	NHL	82	10	30	40	38	4	0	1	159	6.3	–23	1478	48.0	18:15	....	....	....	....	....	....	....	....	....
2001-02	Anaheim	NHL	79	18	30	48	24	3	1	4	164	11.0	–1	1283	51.4	17:01	....	....	....	....	....	....	....	....	....
2002-03	Anaheim	NHL	50	7	14	21	12	1	0	1	77	9.1	–4	271	50.6	14:18	....	....	....	....	....	....	....	....	....
	Florida	NHL	30	6	6	12	22	2	1	1	54	11.1	–4	423	47.3	14:43	....	....	....	....	....	....	....	....	....
2003-04	Florida	NHL	56	6	13	19	24	1	0	2	75	8.0	–2	735	50.6	14:12	....	....	....	....	....	....	....	....	....
2004-05	SG Cortina	Italy	36	*27	33	60	64	....	....	....	....	....	....	....	....	....	18	8	14	22	32	....	....	....	....
2005-06 ♦	Carolina	NHL	78	25	24	49	40	8	0	5	214	11.7	4	583	52.1	16:26	25	4	14	18	12	2	0	1	15:37
2006-07	NY Rangers	NHL	80	16	25	41	52	2	3	2	217	7.4	0	1134	54.6	17:10	10	1	3	4	6	0	0	1	16:55
2007-08	Carolina	NHL	59	13	36	49	32	8	0	1	137	9.5	2	649	56.1	16:52	....	....	....	....	....	....	....	....	....
2008-09	Carolina	NHL	69	22	21	43	20	4	2	2	139	15.8	11	884	51.7	16:48	18	3	3	6	14	0	1	0	16:41
2009-10	Carolina	NHL	60	12	28	40	26	1	2	1	137	8.8	0	898	49.1	19:02	....	....	....	....	....	....	....	....	....
	Ottawa	NHL	21	4	4	8	8	1	0	1	58	6.9	–7	223	58.7	17:59	6	3	5	8	0	2	0	0	23:14
	NHL Totals		880	169	292	461	392	43	10	23	1755	9.6		10855	50.2	16:39	63	11	25	36	32	4	1	2	16:51

VCHA Second All-Star Team (1997)

raded to **Florida** by **Anaheim** with Pavel Trnka and Anaheim's 4th round choice (James Pemberton) in 2003 Entry Draft for Sandis Ozolinsh and Lance Ward, January 30, 2003. Signed as a free agent by **arolina**, August 5, 2004. Signed as a free agent by **Cortina** (Italy), September 18, 2004. Signed as a free agent by **NY Rangers**, July 1, 2006. Traded to **Carolina** by **NY Rangers** for Andrew Hutchinson, e Barnes and Carolina's 3rd round choice (Evgeny Grachev) in 2008 Entry Draft, July 17, 2007. Traded to **Ottawa** by **Carolina** for Alexandre Picard and Ottawa's 2nd round choice (later traded to dmonton - Edmonton selected Martin Marincin) in 2010 Entry Draft, February 12, 2010. Signed as a free agent by **Minnesota**, July 1, 2010.

CULLIMORE, Jassen

(KUHL-ih-mohr, JAY-suhn) **CHI.**

Defense. Shoots left. 6'5", 235 lbs. Born, Simcoe, Ont., December 4, 1972. Vancouver's 2nd choice, 29th overall, in 1991 Entry Draft.

1986-87	Caledonia	OHA-C	18	2	0	2	9	....	....	....	....	....	....	....	....	....	....	....	....	....	....	....	....	....	....
1987-88	Simcoe Rams	OHA-C	35	11	14	25	92	....	....	....	....	....	....	....	....	....	....	....	....	....	....	....	....	....	....
1988-89	Peterborough	OHA-B	29	11	17	28	88	....	....	....	....	....	....	....	....	....	....	....	....	....	....	....	....	....	....
	Peterborough	OHL	20	2	1	3	6	....	....	....	....	....	....	....	....	....	....	....	....	....	....	....	....	....	....
1989-90	Peterborough	OHL	59	2	6	8	61	....	....	....	....	....	....	....	....	....	11	0	2	2	8	....	....	....	....
1990-91	Peterborough	OHL	62	8	16	24	74	....	....	....	....	....	....	....	....	....	4	1	0	1	7	....	....	....	....
1991-92	Peterborough	OHL	54	9	37	46	65	....	....	....	....	....	....	....	....	....	10	3	6	9	8	....	....	....	....
1992-93	Hamilton	AHL	56	5	7	12	60	....	....	....	....	....	....	....	....	....	....	....	....	....	....	....	....	....	....
1993-94	Hamilton	AHL	71	8	20	28	86	....	....	....	....	....	....	....	....	....	3	0	1	1	2	....	....	....	....
1994-95	Syracuse Crunch	AHL	33	2	7	9	66	....	....	....	....	....	....	....	....	....	....	....	....	....	....	....	....	....	....
	Vancouver	NHL	34	1	2	3	39	0	0	0	30	3.3	–2	....	....	....	11	0	0	0	12	0	0	0	....
1995-96	Vancouver	NHL	27	1	1	2	21	0	0	1	12	8.3	4	....	....	....	....	....	....	....	....	....	....	....	....
1996-97	Vancouver	NHL	3	0	0	0	2	0	0	0	2	0.0	–2	....	....	....	....	....	....	....	....	....	....	....	....
	Montreal	NHL	49	2	6	8	42	0	1	1	52	3.8	4	....	....	....	2	0	0	0	2	0	0	0	....
1997-98	Montreal	NHL	3	0	0	0	4	0	0	0	1	0.0	0	....	....	....	....	....	....	....	....	....	....	....	....
	Fredericton	AHL	5	1	0	1	8	....	....	....	....	....	....	....	....	....	....	....	....	....	....	....	....	....	....
	Tampa Bay	NHL	25	1	2	3	22	1	0	0	17	5.9	–4	....	....	....	....	....	....	....	....	....	....	....	....
1998-99	Tampa Bay	NHL	78	5	12	17	81	1	1	1	73	6.8	–22	0	0.0	20:14	....	....	....	....	....	....	....	....	....
99-2000	Providence Bruins	AHL	16	5	10	15	31	....	....	....	....	....	....	....	....	....	....	....	....	....	....	....	....	....	....
	Tampa Bay	NHL	46	1	1	2	66	0	0	0	23	4.3	–12	2	0.0	15:38	....	....	....	....	....	....	....	....	....
2000-01	Tampa Bay	NHL	74	1	6	7	80	0	0	0	56	1.8	–6	0	0.0	19:43	....	....	....	....	....	....	....	....	....
2001-02	Tampa Bay	NHL	78	4	9	13	58	0	0	1	84	4.8	–1	0	0.0	20:07	....	....	....	....	....	....	....	....	....
2002-03	Tampa Bay	NHL	28	1	3	4	31	0	0	0	23	4.3	3	0	0.0	18:25	11	1	1	2	4	0	0	0	22:11
2003-04 ♦	Tampa Bay	NHL	79	2	5	7	58	0	0	1	78	2.6	8	0	0.0	19:02	11	0	2	2	6	0	0	0	15:15
2004-05		DID NOT PLAY																							
2005-06	Chicago	NHL	54	1	6	7	53	1	0	1	23	4.3	–24	0	0.0	16:58	....	....	....	....	....	....	....	....	....
2006-07	Chicago	NHL	65	1	6	7	64	0	0	0	17	5.9	–6	0	0.0	16:17	....	....	....	....	....	....	....	....	....
2007-08	Florida	NHL	65	3	10	13	38	0	0	1	55	5.5	21	1	100.0	18:04	....	....	....	....	....	....	....	....	....
	Rochester	AHL	3	0	1	1	4	....	....	....	....	....	....	....	....	....	....	....	....	....	....	....	....	....	....
2008-09	Florida	NHL	68	2	8	10	37	0	0	0	52	3.8	–10	0	0.0	16:48	....	....	....	....	....	....	....	....	....
2009-10	Rockford IceHogs	AHL	59	2	6	8	52	....	....	....	....	....	....	....	....	....	....	....	....	....	....	....	....	....	....
	NHL Totals		776	26	77	103	696	3	2	7	598	4.3		3	33.3	18:19	35	1	3	4	24	0	0	0	18:43

HL Second All-Star Team (1992)

aded to **Montreal** by **Vancouver** for Donald Brashear, November 13, 1996. Claimed on waivers by **Tampa Bay** from **Montreal**, January 22, 1998. • Loaned to **Providence** (AHL) by **Tampa Bay**, ctober 1, 1999. • Missed majority of 2002-03 season recovering from elbow injury suffered in game vs. Vancouver, November 29, 2002. Signed as a free agent by **Chicago**, July 22, 2004. Traded to **ontreal** by **Chicago** with Tony Salmelainen for Sergei Samsonov, June 16, 2007. Signed as a free agent by **Florida**, October 26, 2007. Signed to a PTO (professional tryout) contract by **Rockford** (AHL), ctober 22, 2009. Signed as a free agent by **Chicago**, February 17, 2010.

CUMISKEY, Kyle

(kuh-MIHS-kee, KIGHL) **COL.**

Defense. Shoots left. 5'10", 185 lbs. Born, Abbotsford, B.C., December 2, 1986. Colorado's 9th choice, 222nd overall, in 2005 Entry Draft.

2002-03	Penticton	BCHL	59	10	11	21	36	....	....	....	....	....	....	....	....	....	....	....	....	....	....	....	....	....	....
2003-04	Kelowna Rockets	WHL	54	2	7	9	20	....	....	....	....	....	....	....	....	....	17	0	0	0	0	....	....	....	....
2004-05	Kelowna Rockets	WHL	72	4	36	40	47	....	....	....	....	....	....	....	....	....	24	0	13	13	12	....	....	....	....
2005-06	Kelowna Rockets	WHL	51	6	24	30	52	....	....	....	....	....	....	....	....	....	12	0	6	6	8	....	....	....	....
2006-07	Colorado	NHL	9	1	1	2	2	0	0	0	8	12.5	0	0	0.0	13:28	....	....	....	....	....	....	....	....	....
	Albany River Rats	AHL	63	7	26	33	32	....	....	....	....	....	....	....	....	....	5	0	2	2	6	....	....	....	....
2007-08	Colorado	NHL	38	0	5	5	16	0	0	0	19	0.0	–3	0	0.0	12:08	....	....	....	....	....	....	....	....	....
	Lake Erie	AHL	5	1	1	2	4	....	....	....	....	....	....	....	....	....	....	....	....	....	....	....	....	....	....
2008-09	Colorado	NHL	6	0	0	0	0	0	0	0	2	0.0	–2	0	0.0	8:32	....	....	....	....	....	....	....	....	....
	Lake Erie	AHL	28	5	12	17	16	....	....	....	....	....	....	....	....	....	....	....	....	....	....	....	....	....	....
2009-10	Colorado	NHL	61	7	13	20	20	2	0	1	74	9.5	0	0	0.0	19:48	6	1	1	2	2	0	0	0	22:37
	NHL Totals		114	8	19	27	38	2	0	1	103	7.8		0	0.0	16:09	6	1	1	2	2	0	0	0	22:37

DADONOV, Evgeny

(do-DON-nauv, ehv-GEH-nee) **FLA.**

Right wing. Shoots left. 5'10", 178 lbs. Born, Chelyabinsk, USSR, March 12, 1989. Florida's 3rd choice, 71st overall, in 2007 Entry Draft.

2005-06	Chelyabinsk 2	Russia-3	12	1	4	5	2	....	....	....	....	....	....	....	....	....	....	....	....	....	....	....	....	....	....
	Chelyabinsk	Russia-2	....	....	....	....	....	....	....	....	....	....	....	....	....	....	1	0	0	0	0	....	....	....	....
2006-07	Chelyabinsk 2	Russia-3	4	2	0	2	14	....	....	....	....	....	....	....	....	....	....	....	....	....	....	....	....	....	....
	Chelyabinsk	Russia	24	1	1	2	8	....	....	....	....	....	....	....	....	....	....	....	....	....	....	....	....	....	....
2007-08	Chelyabinsk 2	Russia-3	12	4	7	11	32	....	....	....	....	....	....	....	....	....	....	....	....	....	....	....	....	....	....
	Chelyabinsk	Russia	43	7	13	20	20	....	....	....	....	....	....	....	....	....	2	0	0	0	0	....	....	....	....
2008-09	Chelyabinsk	Rus-KHL	40	11	4	15	8	....	....	....	....	....	....	....	....	....	3	0	0	0	2	....	....	....	....
2009-10	Florida	NHL	4	0	0	0	0	0	0	0	4	0.0	–1	0	0.0	13:14	....	....	....	....	....	....	....	....	....
	Rochester	AHL	76	17	23	40	36	....	....	....	....	....	....	....	....	....	7	0	1	1	0	....	....	....	....
	NHL Totals		4	0	0	0	0	0	0	0	4	0.0		0	0.0	13:14	....	....	....	....	....	....	....	....	....

D'AGOSTINI, Matt

(DAG-uh-stee-noh, MAT) **ST.L.**

Right wing. Shoots right. 6', 200 lbs. Born, Sault Ste. Marie, Ont., October 23, 1986. Montreal's 5th choice, 190th overall, in 2005 Entry Draft.

2003-04	Soo North Stars	GNML	36	36	23	59	41	....	....	....	....	....	....	....	....	....	....	....	....	....	....	....	....	....	....
2004-05	Guelph Storm	OHL	59	24	22	46	29	....	....	....	....	....	....	....	....	....	4	0	2	2	8	....	....	....	....
2005-06	Guelph Storm	OHL	66	25	54	79	81	....	....	....	....	....	....	....	....	....	15	8	20	28	16	....	....	....	....
2006-07	Hamilton	AHL	63	21	28	49	33	....	....	....	....	....	....	....	....	....	22	4	9	13	18	....	....	....	....
2007-08	Montreal	NHL	1	0	0	0	2	0	0	0	0	0.0	0	0	0.0	8:49	....	....	....	....	....	....	....	....	....
	Hamilton	AHL	76	23	30	53	38	....	....	....	....	....	....	....	....	....	....	....	....	....	....	....	....	....	....
2008-09	Montreal	NHL	53	12	9	21	16	3	0	1	116	10.3	–17	9	33.3	13:25	3	0	0	0	0	0	0	0	11:49
	Hamilton	AHL	20	14	11	25	16	....	....	....	....	....	....	....	....	....	....	....	....	....	....	....	....	....	....
2009-10	Montreal	NHL	40	2	2	4	26	0	0	0	48	4.2	–12	3	66.7	9:53	....	....	....	....	....	....	....	....	....
	Hamilton	AHL	3	0	1	1	2	....	....	....	....	....	....	....	....	....	....	....	....	....	....	....	....	....	....
	St. Louis	NHL	7	0	0	0	2	0	0	0	6	0.0	–3	7	71.4	9:13	....	....	....	....	....	....	....	....	....
	NHL Totals		101	14	11	25	46	3	0	1	170	8.2		19	52.6	11:41	3	0	0	0	0	0	0	0	11:49

ded to **St. Louis** by **Montreal** for Aaron Palushaj, March 2, 2010.

DALEY, Trevor
(DAY-lee, TREH-vuhr) **DAL**

Defense. Shoots left. 5'11", 199 lbs. Born, Toronto, Ont., October 9, 1983. Dallas' 5th choice, 43rd overall, in 2002 Entry Draft.

			Regular Season														Playoffs								
Season	Club	League	GP	G	A	Pts	PIM	PP	SH	GW	S	%	+/-	TF	F%	Min	GP	G	A	Pts	PIM	PP	SH	GW	Min
1998-99	Vaughan Vipers	OPJHL	44	10	36	46	79	....	....	....	....	....	....	....	....	....	....	....	....	....	....	....	....	....	....
99-2000	Sault Ste. Marie	OHL	54	16	30	46	77	....	....	....	....	....	....	....	....	....	15	3	7	10	12	....	....	....	....
2000-01	Sault Ste. Marie	OHL	58	14	27	41	105	....	....	....	....	....	....	....	....	....	....	....	....	....	....	....	....	....	....
2001-02	Sault Ste. Marie	OHL	47	9	39	48	38	....	....	....	....	....	....	....	....	....	6	2	2	4	4	....	....	....	....
2002-03	Sault Ste. Marie	OHL	57	20	33	53	128	....	....	....	....	....	....	....	....	....	1	0	0	0	2	....	....	....	....
2003-04	**Dallas**	**NHL**	**27**	**1**	**5**	**6**	**14**	**1**	**0**	**0**	**34**	**2.9**	**–6**	**0**	**0.0**	**16:02**	**1**	**0**	**0**	**0**	**0**	**0**	**0**	**0**	**10:21**
	Utah Grizzlies	AHL	40	8	6	14	76	....	....	....	....	....	....	....	....	....	....	....	....	....	....	....	....	....	....
2004-05	Hamilton	AHL	78	7	27	34	109	....	....	....	....	....	....	....	....	....	4	0	1	1	2	....	....	....	....
2005-06	**Dallas**	**NHL**	**81**	**3**	**11**	**14**	**87**	**0**	**0**	**1**	**91**	**3.3**	**–2**	**0**	**0.0**	**18:40**	**3**	**0**	**0**	**0**	**0**	**0**	**0**	**0**	**11:30**
2006-07	**Dallas**	**NHL**	**74**	**4**	**8**	**12**	**63**	**0**	**0**	**1**	**68**	**5.9**	**2**	**0**	**0.0**	**19:23**	**7**	**1**	**0**	**1**	**4**	**0**	**0**	**0**	**22:26**
2007-08	**Dallas**	**NHL**	**82**	**5**	**19**	**24**	**85**	**0**	**0**	**1**	**87**	**5.7**	**–1**	**1**	**100.0**	**19:48**	**18**	**1**	**0**	**1**	**20**	**0**	**0**	**0**	**18:52**
2008-09	**Dallas**	**NHL**	**75**	**7**	**18**	**25**	**73**	**0**	**0**	**2**	**104**	**6.7**	**2**	**1**	**0.0**	**22:00**	....	....	....	....	....	....	....	....	....
2009-10	**Dallas**	**NHL**	**77**	**6**	**16**	**22**	**25**	**2**	**0**	**2**	**107**	**5.6**	**3**	**0**	**0.0**	**22:11**	....	....	....	....	....	....	....	....	....
	NHL Totals		**416**	**26**	**77**	**103**	**347**	**3**	**0**	**7**	**491**	**5.3**		**2**	**50.0**	**20:06**	**29**	**2**	**0**	**2**	**24**	**0**	**0**	**0**	**18:40**

DARCHE, Mathieu
(DAHRSH, MA-thew) **MTL.**

Left wing. Shoots left. 6'1", 215 lbs. Born, St. Laurent, Que., November 26, 1976.

Season	Club	League	GP	G	A	Pts	PIM	PP	SH	GW	S	%	+/-	TF	F%	Min	GP	G	A	Pts	PIM	PP	SH	GW	Min
1995-96	Choate-Rosemary	High-CT	STATISTICS NOT AVAILABLE																						
1996-97	McGill Redmen	OUAA	23	1	2	3	27	....	....	....	....	....	....	....	....	....	....	....	....	....	....	....	....	....	....
1997-98	McGill Redmen	OUAA	40	28	17	45	69	....	....	....	....	....	....	....	....	....	....	....	....	....	....	....	....	....	....
1998-99	McGill Redmen	OUAA	32	16	24	40	60	....	....	....	....	....	....	....	....	....	....	....	....	....	....	....	....	....	....
99-2000	McGill Redmen	OUAA	33	31	41	*72	38	....	....	....	....	....	....	....	....	....	5	2	8	10	16	....	....	....	....
2000-01	**Columbus**	**NHL**	**9**	**0**	**0**	**0**	**0**	**0**	**0**	**0**	**9**	**0.0**	**–4**	**1**	**0.0**	**10:07**	....	....	....	....	....	....	....	....	....
	Syracuse Crunch	AHL	66	16	24	40	21	....	....	....	....	....	....	....	....	....	5	0	1	1	4	....	....	....	....
2001-02	**Columbus**	**NHL**	**14**	**1**	**1**	**2**	**6**	**0**	**0**	**0**	**15**	**6.7**	**–5**	**3**	**33.3**	**9:49**	....	....	....	....	....	....	....	....	....
	Syracuse Crunch	AHL	63	22	23	45	26	....	....	....	....	....	....	....	....	....	10	2	5	7	2	....	....	....	....
2002-03	**Columbus**	**NHL**	**1**	**0**	**0**	**0**	**0**	**0**	**0**	**0**	**0**	**0.0**	**–1**	**0**	**0.0**	**6:57**	....	....	....	....	....	....	....	....	....
	Syracuse Crunch	AHL	76	32	32	64	38	....	....	....	....	....	....	....	....	....	....	....	....	....	....	....	....	....	....
2003-04	**Nashville**	**NHL**	**2**	**0**	**0**	**0**	**0**	**0**	**0**	**0**	**1**	**0.0**	**–1**	**0**	**0.0**	**6:39**	....	....	....	....	....	....	....	....	....
	Milwaukee	AHL	76	28	31	59	41	....	....	....	....	....	....	....	....	....	22	6	8	14	8	....	....	....	....
2004-05	Hershey Bears	AHL	79	29	25	54	49	....	....	....	....	....	....	....	....	....	....	....	....	....	....	....	....	....	....
2005-06	Fuchse Duisburg	Germany	52	12	13	25	88	....	....	....	....	....	....	....	....	....	5	1	3	4	4	....	....	....	....
2006-07	**San Jose**	**NHL**	**2**	**0**	**0**	**0**	**0**	**0**	**0**	**0**	**3**	**0.0**	**0**	**0**	**0.0**	**9:13**	....	....	....	....	....	....	....	....	....
	Worcester Sharks	AHL	76	35	45	80	72	....	....	....	....	....	....	....	....	....	5	2	2	4	2	....	....	....	....
2007-08	**Tampa Bay**	**NHL**	**73**	**7**	**15**	**22**	**20**	**1**	**1**	**0**	**120**	**5.8**	**–14**	**89**	**48.3**	**14:26**	....	....	....	....	....	....	....	....	....
	Norfolk Admirals	AHL	4	3	7	10	2	....	....	....	....	....	....	....	....	....	....	....	....	....	....	....	....	....	....
2008-09	Portland Pirates	AHL	80	31	35	66	37	....	....	....	....	....	....	....	....	....	5	0	0	0	4	....	....	....	....
2009-10	**Montreal**	**NHL**	**29**	**5**	**5**	**10**	**4**	**0**	**0**	**3**	**43**	**11.6**	**2**	**5**	**60.0**	**10:51**	**11**	**0**	**1**	**1**	**2**	**0**	**0**	**0**	**6:14**
	Hamilton	AHL	32	16	9	25	4	....	....	....	....	....	....	....	....	....	....	....	....	....	....	....	....	....	....
	NHL Totals		**130**	**13**	**21**	**34**	**30**	**1**	**1**	**3**	**191**	**6.8**		**98**	**48.0**	**12:35**	**11**	**0**	**1**	**1**	**2**	**0**	**0**	**0**	**6:14**

OUAA East Second All-Star Team (1998) • OUAA East First All-Star Team (1999) • OUAA First All-Star Team (2000) • CIAU All-Canadian Team (2000)

Signed as a free agent by **Columbus**, May 16, 2000. Signed as a free agent by **Nashville**, September 10, 2003. Signed as a free agent by **Colorado**, July 26, 2004. Signed as a free agent by **San Jose**, July 10, 2006. Signed as a free agent by **Tampa Bay**, July 2, 2007. Signed as a free agent by **Buffalo**, July 24, 2008. Signed as a free agent by **Montreal**, July 2, 2009.

DATSYUK, Pavel
(daht-SOOK, PAH-vehl) **DET.**

Center. Shoots left. 5'11", 194 lbs. Born, Sverdlovsk, USSR, July 20, 1978. Detroit's 8th choice, 171st overall, in 1998 Entry Draft.

Season	Club	League	GP	G	A	Pts	PIM	PP	SH	GW	S	%	+/-	TF	F%	Min	GP	G	A	Pts	PIM	PP	SH	GW	Min
1996-97	Yekaterinburg 2	Russia-3	18	2	2	4	4	....	....	....	....	....	....	....	....	....	....	....	....	....	....	....	....	....	....
	Yekaterinburg	Russia	36	12	10	22	12	....	....	....	....	....	....	....	....	....	....	....	....	....	....	....	....	....	....
1997-98	Yekaterinburg	Russia	24	3	5	8	4	....	....	....	....	....	....	....	....	....	....	....	....	....	....	....	....	....	....
	Yekaterinburg 2	Russia-3	22	7	8	15	4	....	....	....	....	....	....	....	....	....	....	....	....	....	....	....	....	....	....
1998-99	Yekaterinburg 2	Russia-4	10	14	14	28	4	....	....	....	....	....	....	....	....	....	....	....	....	....	....	....	....	....	....
	Yekaterinburg	Russia-2	35	21	23	44	14	....	....	....	....	....	....	....	....	....	9	3	7	10	10	....	....	....	....
99-2000	Yekaterinburg	Russia	15	1	3	4	4	....	....	....	....	....	....	....	....	....	....	....	....	....	....	....	....	....	....
2000-01	Ak Bars Kazan	Russia	42	9	18	27	10	....	....	....	....	....	....	....	....	....	4	0	1	1	2	....	....	....	....
2001-02♦	**Detroit**	**NHL**	**70**	**11**	**24**	**35**	**4**	**2**	**0**	**1**	**79**	**13.9**	**4**	**794**	**47.7**	**13:39**	**21**	**3**	**3**	**6**	**2**	**1**	**0**	**1**	**10:40**
	Russia	Olympics	6	1	2	3	0	....	....	....	....	....	....	....	....	....	....	....	....	....	....	....	....	....	....
2002-03	**Detroit**	**NHL**	**64**	**12**	**39**	**51**	**16**	**1**	**0**	**1**	**82**	**14.6**	**20**	**778**	**48.2**	**15:28**	**4**	**0**	**0**	**0**	**0**	**0**	**0**	**0**	**18:48**
2003-04	**Detroit**	**NHL**	**75**	**30**	**38**	**68**	**35**	**8**	**1**	**4**	**136**	**22.1**	**–2**	**1314**	**54.0**	**18:16**	**12**	**0**	**6**	**6**	**2**	**0**	**0**	**0**	**17:23**
2004-05	Dynamo Moscow	Russia	47	15	17	32	16	....	....	....	....	....	....	....	....	....	10	*6	3	9	4	....	....	....	....
2005-06	**Detroit**	**NHL**	**75**	**28**	**59**	**87**	**22**	**11**	**0**	**4**	**145**	**19.3**	**26**	**1059**	**53.1**	**17:53**	**5**	**0**	**3**	**3**	**0**	**0**	**0**	**0**	**20:05**
	Russia	Olympics	8	1	7	8	10	....	....	....	....	....	....	....	....	....	....	....	....	....	....	....	....	....	....
2006-07	**Detroit**	**NHL**	**79**	**27**	**60**	**87**	**20**	**5**	**2**	**5**	**207**	**13.0**	**36**	**845**	**56.2**	**19:57**	**18**	**8**	**8**	**16**	**8**	**4**	**0**	**2**	**22:03**
2007-08♦	**Detroit**	**NHL**	**82**	**31**	**66**	**97**	**20**	**10**	**1**	**6**	**264**	**11.7**	***41**	**833**	**54.4**	**21:23**	**22**	**10**	**13**	**23**	**6**	**4**	**0**	**1**	**21:40**
2008-09	**Detroit**	**NHL**	**81**	**32**	**65**	**97**	**22**	**11**	**1**	**3**	**248**	**12.9**	**34**	**1135**	**56.0**	**19:13**	**16**	**1**	**8**	**9**	**9**	**1**	**0**	**0**	**20:05**
2009-10	**Detroit**	**NHL**	**80**	**27**	**43**	**70**	**18**	**9**	**0**	**3**	**203**	**13.3**	**17**	**1070**	**55.1**	**20:21**	**12**	**6**	**7**	**13**	**8**	**1**	**0**	**1**	**18:49**
	Russia	Olympics	4	1	2	3	2	....	....	....	....	....	....	....	....	....	....	....	....	....	....	....	....	....	....
	NHL Totals		**606**	**198**	**394**	**592**	**157**	**57**	**5**	**27**	**1364**	**14.5**		**7828**	**53.4**	**18:26**	**110**	**28**	**48**	**76**	**35**	**11**	**0**	**5**	**18:27**

Lady Byng Memorial Trophy (2006, 2007, 2008, 2009) • Frank J. Selke Trophy (2008, 2009, 2010) • NHL Second All-Star Team (2009)

Played in NHL All-Star Game (2004, 2008)

• Spent majority of 1999-2000 season on **Kazan** (Russia) reserve squad. Signed as a free agent by **Dynamo Moscow** (Russia), June 19, 2004.

DAUGAVINS, Kaspars
(DAH-gah-vihnsh, KAS-purz) **OTT.**

Left wing. Shoots left. 5'11", 209 lbs. Born, Riga, Latvia, May 18, 1988. Ottawa's 3rd choice, 91st overall, in 2006 Entry Draft.

Season	Club	League	GP	G	A	Pts	PIM	PP	SH	GW	S	%	+/-	TF	F%	Min	GP	G	A	Pts	PIM	PP	SH	GW	Min
2003-04	HK Riga 2000	EEHL	2	0	1	1	0	....	....	....	....	....	....	....	....	....	....	....	....	....	....	....	....	....	....
	Prizma/Riga 86	Latvia	14	6	6	12	10	....	....	....	....	....	....	....	....	....	2	1	1	2	4	....	....	....	....
2004-05	CSKA Moscow 2	Russia-3	STATISTICS NOT AVAILABLE																						
2005-06	HK Riga 2000	Latvia	....	4	6	10	16	....	....	....	....	....	....	....	....	....	....	....	....	....	....	....	....	....	....
	HK Riga 2000	BelOpen	45	4	11	15	16	....	....	....	....	....	....	....	....	....	....	....	....	....	....	....	....	....	....
2006-07	St. Michael's	OHL	61	18	42	60	64	....	....	....	....	....	....	....	....	....	....	....	....	....	....	....	....	....	....
	Binghamton	AHL	11	2	0	2	9	....	....	....	....	....	....	....	....	....	....	....	....	....	....	....	....	....	....
2007-08	St. Michael's	OHL	62	40	34	74	42	....	....	....	....	....	....	....	....	....	4	2	1	3	4	....	....	....	....
	Binghamton	AHL	3	0	1	1	0	....	....	....	....	....	....	....	....	....	....	....	....	....	....	....	....	....	....
2008-09	Binghamton	AHL	23	2	1	3	9	....	....	....	....	....	....	....	....	....	....	....	....	....	....	....	....	....	....
	St. Michael's	OHL	30	11	17	28	35	....	....	....	....	....	....	....	....	....	11	2	7	9	14	....	....	....	....
2009-10	**Ottawa**	**NHL**	**1**	**0**	**0**	**0**	**0**	**0**	**0**	**0**	**2**	**0.0**	**0**	**0**	**0.0**	**8:26**	....	....	....	....	....	....	....	....	....
	Binghamton	AHL	72	21	25	46	16	....	....	....	....	....	....	....	....	....	....	....	....	....	....	....	....	....	....
	Latvia	Olympics	4	0	0	0	2	....	....	....	....	....	....	....	....	....	....	....	....	....	....	....	....	....	....
	NHL Totals		**1**	**0**	**0**	**0**	**0**	**0**	**0**	**0**	**2**	**0.0**		**0**	**0.0**	**8:26**	....	....	....	....	....	....	....	....	....

OHL All-Rookie Team (2007)

DAVIS, Patrick
(DAY-vihs, PAT-rihk) **N.J.**

Right wing. Shoots right. 6'2", 195 lbs. Born, Sterling, MI, December 28, 1986. New Jersey's 4th choice, 99th overall, in 2005 Entry Draft.

Season	Club	League	GP	G	A	Pts	PIM	PP	SH	GW	S	%	+/-	TF	F%	Min	GP	G	A	Pts	PIM	PP	SH	GW	Min
2002-03	Detroit Belle Tire	MWEHL	STATISTICS NOT AVAILABLE																						
	Sioux City	USHL	16	3	2	5	8	....	....	....	....	....	....	....	....	....	1	0	0	0	2	....	....	....	....
2003-04	Kitchener Rangers	OHL	27	8	10	18	21	....	....	....	....	....	....	....	....	....	....	....	....	....	....	....	....	....	....
2004-05	Kitchener Rangers	OHL	59	20	30	50	41	....	....	....	....	....	....	....	....	....	14	3	4	7	20	....	....	....	....
2005-06	Kitchener Rangers	OHL	22	13	4	17	30	....	....	....	....	....	....	....	....	....	....	....	....	....	....	....	....	....	....
	Windsor Spitfires	OHL	38	22	29	51	64	....	....	....	....	....	....	....	....	....	7	2	6	8	12	....	....	....	....
	Albany River Rats	AHL	3	0	0	0	2	....	....	....	....	....	....	....	....	....	....	....	....	....	....	....	....	....	....
2006-07	Lowell Devils	AHL	41	5	13	18	26	....	....	....	....	....	....	....	....	....	....	....	....	....	....	....	....	....	....
2007-08	Lowell Devils	AHL	60	7	12	19	58	....	....	....	....	....	....	....	....	....	....	....	....	....	....	....	....	....	....
2008-09	**New Jersey**	**NHL**	**1**	**0**	**0**	**0**	**0**	**0**	**0**	**0**	**0**	**0.0**	**0**	**0**	**0.0**	**4:30**	....	....	....	....	....	....	....	....	....
	Lowell Devils	AHL	74	13	17	30	45	....	....	....	....	....	....	....	....	....	....	....	....	....	....	....	....	....	....

			Regular Season														Playoffs								
Season	Club	League	GP	G	A	Pts	PIM	PP	SH	GW	S	%	+/-	TF	F%	Min	GP	G	A	Pts	PIM	PP	SH	GW	Min
2009-10	**New Jersey**	**NHL**	**8**	**1**	**0**	**1**	**0**	**0**	**0**	**0**	**8**	**12.5**	**–2**	**6**	**66.7**	**12:37**									
	Lowell Devils	AHL	73	15	20	35	39										5	2	0	2	2				
	NHL Totals		**9**	**1**	**0**	**1**	**0**	**0**	**0**	**0**	**8**	**12.5**		**6**	**66.7**	**11:42**									

DAVISON, Rob

(DAY-vihs-ohn, RAWB) **N.J.**

Defense. Shoots left. 6'3", 215 lbs. Born, St. Catharines, Ont., May 1, 1980. San Jose's 4th choice, 98th overall, in 1998 Entry Draft.

Season	Club	League	GP	G	A	Pts	PIM	PP	SH	GW	S	%	+/-	TF	F%	Min	GP	G	A	Pts	PIM	PP	SH	GW	Min
1996-97	St. Mike's B's	OPJHL	45	2	6	8	93										6	0	0	0	9				
1997-98	North Bay	OHL	59	0	11	11	200																		
1998-99	North Bay	OHL	59	2	17	19	150										4	0	1	1	12				
99-2000	North Bay	OHL	67	4	6	10	194										6	0	1	1	8				
2000-01	Kentucky	AHL	72	0	4	4	230										3	0	0	0	0				
2001-02	Cleveland Barons	AHL	70	1	3	4	206																		
2002-03	**San Jose**	**NHL**	**15**	**1**	**2**	**3**	**22**	**0**	**0**	**0**	**15**	**6.7**	**4**	**0**	**0.0**	**17:53**									
	Cleveland Barons	AHL	42	1	3	4	82																		
2003-04	**San Jose**	**NHL**	**55**	**0**	**3**	**3**	**92**	**0**	**0**	**0**	**33**	**0.0**	**–3**	**0**	**0.0**	**14:22**	**5**	**0**	**2**	**2**	**4**	**0**	**0**	**0**	**9:01**
2004-05	Cardiff Devils	Britain	24	2	3	5	114										8	0	1	1	12				
2005-06	**San Jose**	**NHL**	**69**	**1**	**5**	**6**	**76**	**0**	**0**	**0**	**36**	**2.8**	**6**	**0**	**0.0**	**13:50**	**1**	**0**	**0**	**0**	**0**	**0**	**0**	**0**	**8:00**
2006-07	**San Jose**	**NHL**	**22**	**0**	**2**	**2**	**27**	**0**	**0**	**0**	**14**	**0.0**	**–2**	**0**	**0.0**	**9:19**									
2007-08	**San Jose**	**NHL**	**15**	**0**	**0**	**0**	**21**	**0**	**0**	**0**	**10**	**0.0**	**–3**	**0**	**0.0**	**7:47**									
	NY Islanders	**NHL**	**19**	**1**	**1**	**2**	**32**	**0**	**1**	**0**	**22**	**4.5**	**–3**	**0**	**0.0**	**18:40**									
2008-09	**Vancouver**	**NHL**	**23**	**0**	**2**	**2**	**51**	**0**	**0**	**0**	**15**	**0.0**	**–4**	**0**	**0.0**	**10:05**									
2009-10	**New Jersey**	**NHL**	**1**	**0**	**0**	**0**	**0**	**0**	**0**	**0**	**0**	**0.0**	**0**	**0**	**0.0**	**3:59**									
	Lowell Devils	AHL	70	4	13	17	182										5	0	1	1	12				
	NHL Totals		**219**	**3**	**15**	**18**	**321**	**0**	**1**	**0**	**145**	**2.1**		**0**	**0.0**	**13:22**	**6**	**0**	**2**	**2**	**4**	**0**	**0**	**0**	**8:51**

gned as a free agent by **Cardiff** (Britain), October 5, 2004. Traded to **NY Islanders** by **San Jose** for NY Islanders' 7th round choice (Jason Demers) in 2008 Entry Draft, February 26, 2008. Signed as a free gent by **Vancouver**, July 10, 2008. • Missed majority of 2006-07, 2007-08 and 2008-09 seasons recovering from various injuries and as a healthy reserve. Signed as a free agent by **New Jersey**, July 31, 009.

DAWES, Nigel

(DAWZ, NIGH-juhl)

Left wing. Shoots left. 5'9", 193 lbs. Born, Winnipeg, Man., February 9, 1985. NY Rangers' 5th choice, 149th overall, in 2003 Entry Draft.

Season	Club	League	GP	G	A	Pts	PIM	PP	SH	GW	S	%	+/-	TF	F%	Min	GP	G	A	Pts	PIM	PP	SH	GW	Min
2000-01	Wpg. Warriors	MMMHL	36	55	41	96	74																		
2001-02	Kootenay Ice	WHL	54	15	19	34	14										22	9	6	15	8				
2002-03	Kootenay Ice	WHL	72	47	45	92	54										11	4	8	12	6				
2003-04	Kootenay Ice	WHL	56	47	23	70	31										4	1	2	3	10				
	Hartford	AHL	4	0	0	0	0																		
2004-05	Kootenay Ice	WHL	63	50	26	76	30										12	5	10	15	5				
2005-06	Hartford	AHL	77	35	31	66	21										13	6	6	12	9				
2006-07	**NY Rangers**	**NHL**	**8**	**1**	**0**	**1**	**0**	**0**	**0**	**0**	**7**	**14.3**	**–4**	**1**	**0.0**	**6:44**	**1**	**0**	**0**	**0**	**0**	**0**	**0**	**0**	**9:02**
	Hartford	AHL	65	27	33	60	29										7	5	6	11	9				
2007-08	**NY Rangers**	**NHL**	**61**	**14**	**15**	**29**	**10**	**3**	**0**	**4**	**121**	**11.6**	**11**	**2**	**50.0**	**12:59**	**10**	**2**	**2**	**4**	**0**	**0**	**0**	**0**	**12:31**
	Hartford	AHL	20	14	20	34	2																		
2008-09	**NY Rangers**	**NHL**	**52**	**10**	**9**	**19**	**15**	**3**	**0**	**4**	**96**	**10.4**	**–2**	**0**	**0.0**	**13:03**									
	Phoenix	**NHL**	**12**	**0**	**2**	**2**	**0**	**0**	**0**	**0**	**19**	**0.0**	**–4**	**0**	**0.0**	**14:09**									
2009-10	**Calgary**	**NHL**	**66**	**14**	**18**	**32**	**18**	**4**	**0**	**2**	**96**	**14.6**	**1**	**1**	**0.0**	**14:32**									
	NHL Totals		**199**	**39**	**44**	**83**	**43**	**10**	**0**	**10**	**339**	**11.5**		**4**	**25.0**	**13:20**	**11**	**2**	**2**	**4**	**0**	**0**	**0**	**0**	**12:12**

'HL West Second All-Star Team (2003) • WHL West First All-Star Team (2004, 2005)

aded to **Phoenix** by **NY Rangers** with Dmitri Kalinin and Petr Prucha for Derek Morris, March 4, 2009. Claimed on waivers by **Calgary**, July 15, 2009.

DEL ZOTTO, Michael

(DEHL ZAW-toh, MIGH-kuhl) **NYR**

Defense. Shoots left. 6'1", 195 lbs. Born, Stouffville, Ont., June 24, 1990. NY Rangers' 1st choice, 20th overall, in 2008 Entry Draft.

Season	Club	League	GP	G	A	Pts	PIM	PP	SH	GW	S	%	+/-	TF	F%	Min	GP	G	A	Pts	PIM	PP	SH	GW	Min
2005-06	Markham Waxers	Minor-ON	73	30	90	120	90																		
2006-07	Oshawa Generals	OHL	64	10	47	57	78										9	3	9	12	14				
2007-08	Oshawa Generals	OHL	64	16	47	63	82										15	2	6	8	38				
2008-09	Oshawa Generals	OHL	34	7	26	33	48																		
	London Knights	OHL	28	6	24	30	30										14	3	16	19	18				
2009-10	**NY Rangers**	**NHL**	**80**	**9**	**28**	**37**	**32**	**4**	**0**	**1**	**81**	**11.1**	**–20**	**0**	**0.0**	**18:58**									
	NHL Totals		**80**	**9**	**28**	**37**	**32**	**4**	**0**	**1**	**81**	**11.1**		**0**	**0.0**	**18:58**									

HL All-Rookie Team (2010)

DELMORE, Andy

(DEHL-mohr, AN-dee)

Defense. Shoots right. 6'1", 200 lbs. Born, LaSalle, Ont., December 26, 1976.

Season	Club	League	GP	G	A	Pts	PIM	PP	SH	GW	S	%	+/-	TF	F%	Min	GP	G	A	Pts	PIM	PP	SH	GW	Min
1992-93	Chatham	OHA-B	47	4	21	25	38																		
1993-94	North Bay	OHL	45	2	7	9	33										17	0	0	0	2				
1994-95	North Bay	OHL	40	2	14	16	21																		
	Sarnia Sting	OHL	27	5	13	18	27										3	0	0	0	2				
1995-96	Sarnia Sting	OHL	64	21	38	59	45										10	3	7	10	2				
1996-97	Sarnia Sting	OHL	64	18	60	78	39										12	2	10	12	10				
	Fredericton	AHL	4	0	1	1	0																		
1997-98	Philadelphia	AHL	73	9	30	39	46										18	4	4	8	21				
1998-99	**Philadelphia**	**NHL**	**2**	**0**	**1**	**1**	**0**	**0**	**0**	**0**	**2**	**0.0**	**–1**	**0**	**0.0**	**20:42**									
	Philadelphia	AHL	70	5	18	23	51										15	1	4	5	6				
99-2000	**Philadelphia**	**NHL**	**27**	**2**	**5**	**7**	**8**	**0**	**0**	**1**	**55**	**3.6**	**–1**	**0**	**0.0**	**17:17**	**18**	**5**	**2**	**7**	**14**	**1**	**0**	**1**	**17:33**
	Philadelphia	AHL	39	12	14	26	31																		
2000-01	**Philadelphia**	**NHL**	**66**	**5**	**9**	**14**	**16**	**2**	**0**	**0**	**119**	**4.2**	**2**	**0**	**0.0**	**17:39**	**2**	**1**	**0**	**1**	**2**	**0**	**0**	**1**	**15:20**
2001-02	**Nashville**	**NHL**	**73**	**16**	**22**	**38**	**22**	**11**	**0**	**3**	**175**	**9.1**	**–13**	**0**	**0.0**	**19:40**									
2002-03	**Nashville**	**NHL**	**71**	**18**	**16**	**34**	**28**	**14**	**0**	**6**	**149**	**12.1**	**–17**	**0**	**0.0**	**17:05**									
2003-04	**Buffalo**	**NHL**	**37**	**2**	**5**	**7**	**29**	**2**	**0**	**0**	**40**	**5.0**	**–5**	**0**	**0.0**	**15:11**									
	Rochester	AHL	8	0	2	2	2																		
2004-05	Adler Mannheim	Germany	50	7	16	23	59										14	1	6	7	12				
2005-06	**Columbus**	**NHL**	**7**	**0**	**0**	**0**	**2**	**0**	**0**	**0**	**7**	**0.0**	**–1**	**0**	**0.0**	**15:24**									
	Syracuse Crunch	AHL	66	17	55	72	46										6	0	1	1	19				
2006-07	Springfield	AHL	47	12	12	24	22																		
	Chicago Wolves	AHL	28	5	11	16	10										15	0	6	6	2				
2007-08	Hamburg Freezers	Germany	51	10	25	35	90										8	0	1	1	12				
2008-09	Hamburg Freezers	Germany	52	9	22	31	70										9	1	3	4	8				
2009-10	Grand Rapids	AHL	54	5	15	20	32																		
	Abbotsford Heat	AHL	9	1	3	4	4										5	0	3	3	0				
	NHL Totals		**283**	**43**	**58**	**101**	**105**	**29**	**0**	**10**	**547**	**7.9**		**0**	**0.0**	**17:38**	**20**	**6**	**2**	**8**	**16**	**1**	**0**	**2**	**17:19**

ıL First All-Star Team (1997) • AHL First All-Star Team (2006) • Eddie Shore Award (AHL - Outstanding Defenseman) (2006)

ıned as a free agent by **Philadelphia**, June 9, 1997. Traded to **Nashville** by **Philadelphia** for Nashville's 3rd round choice (later traded to Phoenix – Phoenix selected Joe Callahan) in 2002 Entry Draft, y 31, 2001. Traded to **Buffalo** by **Nashville** for Buffalo's 3rd round choice (later traded to Minnesota – Minnesota selected Clayton Stoner) in 2004 Entry Draft, June 27, 2003. Traded to **San Jose** by **ffalo** with Curtis Brown for Jeff Jillson and San Jose's compensatory 7th round choice (Andrew Orpik) in 2005 Entry Draft, March 9, 2004. Traded to **Boston** by **San Jose** for future considerations, March 2004. Signed as a free agent by **Mannheim** (Germany), July 21, 2004. Signed as a free agent by **Detroit**, August 16, 2005. Claimed on waivers by **Columbus** from **Detroit**, October 4, 2005. Signed as ree agent by **Tampa Bay**, July 1, 2006. Traded to **Atlanta** by **Tampa Bay** with Andre Deveaux for Stephen Baby and Kyle Wanvig, February 1, 2007. Signed as a free agent by **Hamburg** (Germany), ıe 13, 2007. Signed as a free agent by **Detroit**, July 28, 2009. Traded to **Calgary** by **Detroit** for Riley Armstrong, March 3, 2010.

DEMERS, Jason

(duh-MAIRZ, JAY-suhn) **S.J.**

Defense. Shoots right. 6'1", 195 lbs. Born, Dorval, Que., June 9, 1988. San Jose's 6th choice, 186th overall, in 2008 Entry Draft.

Season	Club	League	GP	G	A	Pts	PIM	PP	SH	GW	S	%	+/-	TF	F%	Min	GP	G	A	Pts	PIM	PP	SH	GW	Min
2004-05	Moncton Wildcats	QMJHL	25	0	1	1	10																		
2005-06	Moncton Wildcats	QMJHL	21	1	3	4	15																		
	Victoriaville Tigres	QMJHL	33	2	13	15	58										5	0	2	2	10				
2006-07	Victoriaville Tigres	QMJHL	69	5	19	24	98										6	0	0	0	2				
2007-08	Victoriaville Tigres	QMJHL	67	9	55	64	91										6	1	5	6	6				
2008-09	Worcester Sharks	AHL	78	2	31	33	54										12	0	4	4	6				

			Regular Season														Playoffs								
Season	Club	League	GP	G	A	Pts	PIM	PP	SH	GW	S	%	+/-	TF	F%	Min	GP	G	A	Pts	PIM	PP	SH	GW	Min
2009-10	San Jose	NHL	51	4	17	21	21	3	0	1	52	7.7	5	0	0.0	15:26	15	1	4	5	8	1	0	0	11:10
	Worcester Sharks	AHL	25	4	13	17	24	....	....	....	....	....	....	....	....	....	....	....	....	....	....	....	....	....	....
	NHL Totals		51	4	17	21	21	3	0	1	52	7.7		0	0.0	15:26	15	1	4	5	8	1	0	0	11:10

DEMITRA, Pavol

(deh-MEET-rah, PAH-vohl)

Left wing. Shoots left. 6', 200 lbs. Born, Dubnica, Czech., November 29, 1974. Ottawa's 9th choice, 227th overall, in 1993 Entry Draft.

Season	Club	League	GP	G	A	Pts	PIM	PP	SH	GW	S	%	+/-	TF	F%	Min	GP	G	A	Pts	PIM	PP	SH	GW	Min
1991-92	Dubnica	Czech-2	28	13	10	23	12	....	....	....	....	....	....	....	....	....	....	....	....	....	....	....	....	....	....
1992-93	Dubnica	Czech-2	4	3	0	3	....	....	....	....	....	....	....	....	....	....	....	....	....	....	....	....	....	....	....
	Dukla Trencin	Czech	46	11	17	28	0	....	....	....	....	....	....	....	....	....	....	....	....	....	....	....	....	....	....
1993-94	Ottawa	NHL	12	1	1	2	4	1	0	0	10	10.0	–7	....	....	....	....	....	....	....	....	....	....	....	....
	P.E.I. Senators	AHL	41	18	23	41	8	....	....	....	....	....	....	....	....	....	....	....	....	....	....	....	....	....	....
1994-95	P.E.I. Senators	AHL	61	26	48	74	23	....	....	....	....	....	....	....	....	....	5	0	7	7	0	....	....	....	....
	Ottawa	NHL	16	4	3	7	0	1	0	0	21	19.0	–4	....	....	....	....	....	....	....	....	....	....	....	....
1995-96	Ottawa	NHL	31	7	10	17	6	2	0	1	66	10.6	–3	....	....	....	....	....	....	....	....	....	....	....	....
	P.E.I. Senators	AHL	48	28	53	81	44	....	....	....	....	....	....	....	....	....	....	....	....	....	....	....	....	....	....
1996-97	Dukla Trencin	Slovakia	1	1	1	2	....	....	....	....	....	....	....	....	....	....	....	....	....	....	....	....	....	....	....
	Las Vegas	IHL	22	8	13	21	10	....	....	....	....	....	....	....	....	....	....	....	....	....	....	....	....	....	....
	St. Louis	NHL	8	3	0	3	2	2	0	1	15	20.0	0	....	....	....	6	1	3	4	6	0	0	0	....
	Grand Rapids	IHL	42	20	30	50	24	....	....	....	....	....	....	....	....	....	....	....	....	....	....	....	....	....	....
1997-98	St. Louis	NHL	61	22	30	52	22	4	4	6	147	15.0	11	....	....	....	10	3	3	6	2	0	0	0	....
1998-99	St. Louis	NHL	82	37	52	89	16	14	0	10	259	14.3	13	250	44.0	20:10	13	5	4	9	4	3	0	1	19:1
99-2000	St. Louis	NHL	71	28	47	75	8	8	0	4	241	11.6	34	41	39.0	19:13	....	....	....	....	....	....	....	....	....
2000-01	St. Louis	NHL	44	20	25	45	16	5	0	5	124	16.1	27	8	37.5	18:03	15	2	4	6	2	0	0	1	18:1
2001-02	St. Louis	NHL	82	35	43	78	46	11	0	*10	212	16.5	13	1224	48.1	19:11	10	4	7	11	6	2	1	1	19:4
	Slovakia	Olympics	2	1	2	3	2	....	....	....	....	....	....	....	....	....	....	....	....	....	....	....	....	....	....
2002-03	St. Louis	NHL	78	36	57	93	32	11	0	4	205	17.6	0	1253	46.1	19:47	7	2	4	6	2	1	0	0	18:2
2003-04	St. Louis	NHL	68	23	35	58	18	8	0	5	179	12.8	1	770	47.3	20:30	5	1	0	1	4	0	0	0	18:0
2004-05	Dukla Trencin	Slovakia	54	*28	*54	*82	39	....	....	....	....	....	....	....	....	....	12	4	13	17	14	....	....	....	....
2005-06	Los Angeles	NHL	58	25	37	62	42	7	5	7	184	13.6	21	114	49.1	21:04	....	....	....	....	....	....	....	....	....
	Slovakia	Olympics	6	2	5	7	2	....	....	....	....	....	....	....	....	....	....	....	....	....	....	....	....	....	....
2006-07	Minnesota	NHL	71	25	39	64	28	9	1	4	175	14.3	0	513	47.8	20:39	5	1	3	4	0	0	0	0	19:4
2007-08	Minnesota	NHL	68	15	39	54	24	2	0	1	126	11.9	9	890	45.3	19:42	6	1	2	3	2	1	0	0	21:0
2008-09	Vancouver	NHL	69	20	33	53	20	4	0	1	143	14.0	6	242	54.6	17:29	6	1	2	3	2	1	0	0	17:3
2009-10	Vancouver	NHL	28	3	13	16	0	1	0	0	53	5.7	3	86	53.5	16:13	11	2	4	6	4	0	0	0	14:2
	Slovakia	Olympics	7	3	*7	*10	2	....	....	....	....	....	....	....	....	....	....	....	....	....	....	....	....	....	....
	NHL Totals		847	304	464	768	284	90	10	59	2160	14.1		5391	47.2	19:29	94	23	36	59	34	8	1	3	18:1

Lady Byng Memorial Trophy (2000) • Olympic Tournament All-Star Team (2010)

Played in NHL All-Star Game (1999, 2000, 2002)

Traded to **St. Louis** by **Ottawa** for Christer Olsson, November 27, 1996. Signed as a free agent by **Trencin** (Slovakia), September 17, 2004. Signed as a free agent by **Los Angeles**, August 2, 2005. Traded to **Minnesota** by **Los Angeles** for Patrick O'Sullivan and Edmonton's 1st round choice (previously acquired, Los Angeles selected Trevor Lewis) in 2006 Entry Draft, June 24, 2006. Signed as a free agent by **Vancouver**, July 10, 2008. • Missed majority of 2009-10 season recovering from shoulder injury suffered during playoff game vs. Chicago, May 2, 2009. Signed as a free agent by **Yaroslavl** (Russia-KHL), July 15, 2010.

DESBIENS, Guillaume

(deh-BYEHN, GEE-OHM) **VAN**

Right wing. Shoots right. 6'2", 210 lbs. Born, Alma, Que., April 20, 1985. Atlanta's 3rd choice, 116th overall, in 2003 Entry Draft.

Season	Club	League	GP	G	A	Pts	PIM	PP	SH	GW	S	%	+/-	TF	F%	Min	GP	G	A	Pts	PIM	PP	SH	GW	Min
2001-02	Rouyn-Noranda	QMJHL	65	14	10	24	115	....	....	....	....	....	....	....	....	....	4	1	1	2	9	....	....	....	....
2002-03	Rouyn-Noranda	QMJHL	64	15	18	33	233	....	....	....	....	....	....	....	....	....	4	0	0	0	4	....	....	....	....
2003-04	Rouyn-Noranda	QMJHL	58	20	21	41	199	....	....	....	....	....	....	....	....	....	11	2	2	4	24	....	....	....	....
2004-05	Rouyn-Noranda	QMJHL	56	27	16	43	206	....	....	....	....	....	....	....	....	....	10	1	4	5	25	....	....	....	....
2005-06	Chicago Wolves	AHL	3	0	0	0	7	....	....	....	....	....	....	....	....	....	....	....	....	....	....	....	....	....	....
	Gwinnett	ECHL	65	33	27	60	187	....	....	....	....	....	....	....	....	....	17	10	6	16	38	....	....	....	....
2006-07	Chicago Wolves	AHL	54	3	6	9	118	....	....	....	....	....	....	....	....	....	6	0	1	1	2	....	....	....	....
2007-08	Chicago Wolves	AHL	23	2	1	3	30	....	....	....	....	....	....	....	....	....	1	0	1	1	0	....	....	....	....
	Gwinnett	ECHL	10	2	5	7	46	....	....	....	....	....	....	....	....	....	8	3	6	9	10	....	....	....	....
2008-09	Manitoba Moose	AHL	78	21	26	47	158	....	....	....	....	....	....	....	....	....	22	4	8	12	18	....	....	....	....
2009-10	Vancouver	NHL	1	0	0	0	2	0	0	0	0	0.0	0	0	0.0	9:25	....	....	....	....	....	....	....	....	....
	Manitoba Moose	AHL	67	19	15	34	144	....	....	....	....	....	....	....	....	....	6	3	6	9	17	....	....	....	....
	NHL Totals		1	0	0	0	2	0	0	0	0	0.0		0	0.0	9:25	....	....	....	....	....	....	....	....	....

Signed as a free agent by **Manitoba** (AHL), December 15, 2008. Signed as a free agent by **Vancouver**, July 22, 2009.

DESHARNAIS, David

(day-hahr-NAY, DAY-vihd) **MTL**

Center. Shoots left. 5'7", 177 lbs. Born, Quebec, Que., September 14, 1986.

Season	Club	League	GP	G	A	Pts	PIM	PP	SH	GW	S	%	+/-	TF	F%	Min	GP	G	A	Pts	PIM	PP	SH	GW	Min
2003-04	Chicoutimi	QMJHL	70	23	28	51	12	....	....	....	....	....	....	....	....	....	18	4	7	11	8	....	....	....	....
2004-05	Chicoutimi	QMJHL	68	32	65	97	39	....	....	....	....	....	....	....	....	....	17	5	10	15	8	....	....	....	....
2005-06	Chicoutimi	QMJHL	63	33	85	118	44	....	....	....	....	....	....	....	....	....	9	2	9	11	4	....	....	....	....
2006-07	Chicoutimi	QMJHL	61	38	70	108	32	....	....	....	....	....	....	....	....	....	4	1	5	6	2	....	....	....	....
	Bridgeport	AHL	7	1	1	2	4	....	....	....	....	....	....	....	....	....	....	....	....	....	....	....	....	....	....
2007-08	Hamilton	AHL	4	0	1	1	6	....	....	....	....	....	....	....	....	....	....	....	....	....	....	....	....	....	....
	Cincinnati	ECHL	68	29	*77	*106	18	....	....	....	....	....	....	....	....	....	22	9	*24	*33	18	....	....	....	....
2008-09	Hamilton	AHL	77	24	34	58	20	....	....	....	....	....	....	....	....	....	6	1	3	4	4	....	....	....	....
2009-10	Montreal	NHL	6	0	1	1	0	0	0	0	2	0.0	–1	28	57.1	8:27	....	....	....	....	....	....	....	....	....
	Hamilton	AHL	60	27	51	78	34	....	....	....	....	....	....	....	....	....	19	10	13	23	16	....	....	....	....
	NHL Totals		6	0	1	1	0	0	0	0	2	0.0		28	57.1	8:27	....	....	....	....	....	....	....	....	....

ECHL Rookie of the Year (2008) • ECHL Leading Scorer (2008) • ECHL MVP (2008)

Signed as a free agent by **Montreal**, November 5, 2008.

DEVEAUX, Andre

(de-VOH, AWN-dray)

Center. Shoots right. 6'3", 220 lbs. Born, Welland, Ont., February 23, 1984. Montreal's 4th choice, 182nd overall, in 2002 Entry Draft.

Season	Club	League	GP	G	A	Pts	PIM	PP	SH	GW	S	%	+/-	TF	F%	Min	GP	G	A	Pts	PIM	PP	SH	GW	Min
2000-01	Belleville Bulls	OHL	58	3	6	9	65	....	....	....	....	....	....	....	....	....	10	3	6	9	6	....	....	....	....
2001-02	Belleville Bulls	OHL	64	8	13	21	89	....	....	....	....	....	....	....	....	....	11	1	2	3	30	....	....	....	....
2002-03	Belleville Bulls	OHL	34	6	12	18	93	....	....	....	....	....	....	....	....	....	....	....	....	....	....	....	....	....	....
	Owen Sound	OHL	29	9	10	19	33	....	....	....	....	....	....	....	....	....	4	2	2	4	6	....	....	....	....
2003-04	Owen Sound	OHL	64	16	30	46	151	....	....	....	....	....	....	....	....	....	7	3	3	6	21	....	....	....	....
2004-05	Springfield	AHL	73	4	8	12	210	....	....	....	....	....	....	....	....	....	....	....	....	....	....	....	....	....	....
2005-06	Springfield	AHL	59	6	5	11	135	....	....	....	....	....	....	....	....	....	....	....	....	....	....	....	....	....	....
	Johnstown Chiefs	ECHL	11	4	7	11	36	....	....	....	....	....	....	....	....	....	5	1	1	2	2	....	....	....	....
2006-07	Springfield	AHL	8	1	2	3	8	....	....	....	....	....	....	....	....	....	....	....	....	....	....	....	....	....	....
	Johnstown Chiefs	ECHL	21	6	8	14	51	....	....	....	....	....	....	....	....	....	....	....	....	....	....	....	....	....	....
	Chicago Wolves	AHL	28	4	4	8	105	....	....	....	....	....	....	....	....	....	14	3	2	5	48	....	....	....	....
2007-08	Chicago Wolves	AHL	66	7	11	18	232	....	....	....	....	....	....	....	....	....	24	0	2	2	67	....	....	....	....
2008-09	Toronto	NHL	21	0	1	1	75	0	0	0	15	0.0	–3	7	28.6	7:14	....	....	....	....	....	....	....	....	....
	Toronto Marlies	AHL	38	14	11	25	114	....	....	....	....	....	....	....	....	....	6	0	3	3	14	....	....	....	....
2009-10	Toronto	NHL	1	0	0	0	0	0	0	0	1	0.0	–1	1	100.0	6:09	....	....	....	....	....	....	....	....	....
	Toronto Marlies	AHL	72	16	25	41	216	....	....	....	....	....	....	....	....	....	....	....	....	....	....	....	....	....	....
	NHL Totals		22	0	1	1	75	0	0	0	16	0.0		8	37.5	7:11	....	....	....	....	....	....	....	....	....

Signed as a free agent by **Tampa Bay**, September 15, 2004. Traded to **Atlanta** by **Tampa Bay** with Andy Delmore for and Stephen Baby and Kyle Wanvig, February 1, 2007. Signed as a free agent by **Toronto**, July 21, 2008.

			Regular Season														Playoffs								
Season	Club	League	GP	G	A	Pts	PIM	PP	SH	GW	S	%	+/-	TF	F%	Min	GP	G	A	Pts	PIM	PP	SH	GW	Min

DEVEREAUX, Boyd

(DEH-vuhr-oh, BOID)

Center. Shoots left. 6'2", 195 lbs. Born, Seaforth, Ont., April 16, 1978. Edmonton's 1st choice, 6th overall, in 1996 Entry Draft.

Season	Club	League	GP	G	A	Pts	PIM	PP	SH	GW	S	%	+/-	TF	F%	Min	GP	G	A	Pts	PIM	PP	SH	GW	Min
1992-93	Seaforth Sailors	OHA-D	34	7	20	27	13	....	....	....	....	....	....	....	....	....	....	....	....	....	....	....	....	....	....
1993-94	Stratford Cullitons	OHA-B	46	12	27	39	8	....	....	....	....	....	....	....	....	....	....	....	....	....	....	....	....	....	....
1994-95	Stratford Cullitons	OHA-B	45	31	74	105	21	....	....	....	....	....	....	....	....	....	....	....	....	....	....	....	....	....	....
1995-96	Kitchener Rangers	OHL	66	20	38	58	35	....	....	....	....	....	....	....	....	....	12	3	7	10	4	....	....	....	....
1996-97	Kitchener Rangers	OHL	54	28	41	69	37	....	....	....	....	....	....	....	....	....	13	4	11	15	8	....	....	....	....
	Hamilton	AHL	....	....	....	....	....	....	....	....	....	....	....	....	....	....	1	0	1	1	0	....	....	....	....
1997-98	**Edmonton**	**NHL**	**38**	**1**	**4**	**5**	**6**	**0**	**0**	**0**	**27**	**3.7**	**-5**	....	....	....	....	....	....	....	....	....	....	....	....
	Hamilton	AHL	14	5	6	11	6	....	....	....	....	....	....	....	....	....	9	1	1	2	8	....	....	....	....
1998-99	**Edmonton**	**NHL**	**61**	**6**	**8**	**14**	**23**	**0**	**1**	**4**	**39**	**15.4**	**2**	**409**	**42.8**	**10:09**	**1**	**0**	**0**	**0**	**0**	**0**	**0**	**0**	**32:46**
	Hamilton	AHL	7	4	6	10	2	....	....	....	....	....	....	....	....	....	8	0	3	3	4	....	....	....	....
99-2000	**Edmonton**	**NHL**	**76**	**8**	**19**	**27**	**20**	**0**	**1**	**2**	**108**	**7.4**	**7**	**241**	**34.9**	**12:36**	....	....	....	....	....	....	....	....	....
2000-01	**Detroit**	**NHL**	**55**	**5**	**6**	**11**	**14**	**0**	**0**	**0**	**66**	**7.6**	**1**	**124**	**37.1**	**10:08**	**2**	**0**	**0**	**0**	**0**	**0**	**0**	**0**	**10:39**
2001-02 ♦	**Detroit**	**NHL**	**79**	**9**	**16**	**25**	**24**	**0**	**0**	**2**	**116**	**7.8**	**9**	**12**	**33.3**	**11:30**	**21**	**2**	**4**	**6**	**4**	**0**	**0**	**0**	**10:58**
2002-03	**Detroit**	**NHL**	**61**	**3**	**9**	**12**	**16**	**0**	**0**	**1**	**72**	**4.2**	**4**	**7**	**42.9**	**9:26**	....	....	....	....	....	....	....	....	....
2003-04	**Detroit**	**NHL**	**61**	**6**	**9**	**15**	**20**	**0**	**0**	**2**	**62**	**9.7**	**-1**	**14**	**50.0**	**9:58**	**3**	**1**	**0**	**1**	**0**	**0**	**0**	**0**	**6:36**
2004-05			DID NOT PLAY																						
2005-06	**Phoenix**	**NHL**	**78**	**8**	**14**	**22**	**44**	**1**	**0**	**1**	**76**	**10.5**	**-13**	**281**	**36.7**	**12:47**	....	....	....	....	....	....	....	....	....
2006-07	**Toronto**	**NHL**	**33**	**8**	**11**	**19**	**12**	**0**	**0**	**0**	**57**	**14.0**	**4**	**42**	**26.2**	**15:17**	....	....	....	....	....	....	....	....	....
	Toronto Marlies	AHL	30	6	8	14	14	....	....	....	....	....	....	....	....	....	....	....	....	....	....	....	....	....	....
2007-08	**Toronto**	**NHL**	**62**	**7**	**11**	**18**	**24**	**0**	**1**	**1**	**81**	**8.6**	**-6**	**6**	**33.3**	**13:58**	....	....	....	....	....	....	....	....	....
2008-09	**Toronto**	**NHL**	**23**	**6**	**5**	**11**	**2**	**0**	**3**	**0**	**41**	**14.6**	**3**	**9**	**44.4**	**13:42**	....	....	....	....	....	....	....	....	....
	Toronto Marlies	AHL	45	9	7	16	14	....	....	....	....	....	....	....	....	....	....	....	....	....	....	....	....	....	....
2009-10	HC Lugano	Swiss	16	2	2	4	8	....	....	....	....	....	....	....	....	....	....	....	....	....	....	....	....	....	....
	NHL Totals		**627**	**67**	**112**	**179**	**205**	**1**	**6**	**13**	**745**	**9.0**		**1145**	**38.3**	**11:44**	**27**	**3**	**4**	**7**	**4**	**0**	**0**	**0**	**11:16**

Canadian Major Junior Scholastic Player of the Year (1996)

Signed as a free agent by **Detroit**, August 23, 2000. Signed as a free agent by **Phoenix**, July 5, 2004. Signed as a free agent by **Toronto**, October 7, 2006. Signed as a free agent by **Lugano** (Swiss), November 3, 2009.

DiPENTA, Joe

(DIH-pehn-tah, JOH)

Defense. Shoots left. 6'2", 199 lbs. Born, Barrie, Ont., February 25, 1979. Florida's 2nd choice, 61st overall, in 1998 Entry Draft.

Season	Club	League	GP	G	A	Pts	PIM	PP	SH	GW	S	%	+/-	TF	F%	Min	GP	G	A	Pts	PIM	PP	SH	GW	Min
1996-97	Smiths Falls Bears	CJHL	54	13	22	35	92	....	....	....	....	....	....	....	....	....	....	....	....	....	....	....	....	....	....
1997-98	Boston University	H-East	38	2	16	18	50	....	....	....	....	....	....	....	....	....	....	....	....	....	....	....	....	....	....
1998-99	Boston University	H-East	36	2	15	17	72	....	....	....	....	....	....	....	....	....	....	....	....	....	....	....	....	....	....
99-2000	Halifax	QMJHL	63	13	43	56	83	....	....	....	....	....	....	....	....	....	10	3	4	7	26	....	....	....	....
2000-01	Philadelphia	AHL	71	3	5	8	65	....	....	....	....	....	....	....	....	....	10	1	2	3	15	....	....	....	....
2001-02	Philadelphia	AHL	61	2	4	6	71	....	....	....	....	....	....	....	....	....	....	....	....	....	....	....	....	....	....
	Chicago Wolves	AHL	15	0	2	2	15	....	....	....	....	....	....	....	....	....	25	1	3	4	22	....	....	....	....
2002-03	**Atlanta**	**NHL**	**3**	**1**	**1**	**2**	**0**	**0**	**0**	**0**	**2**	**50.0**	**3**	**0**	**0.0**	**15:47**	....	....	....	....	....	....	....	....	....
	Chicago Wolves	AHL	76	2	17	19	107	....	....	....	....	....	....	....	....	....	9	0	1	1	7	....	....	....	....
2003-04	Chicago Wolves	AHL	73	0	6	6	105	....	....	....	....	....	....	....	....	....	10	1	0	1	13	....	....	....	....
2004-05	Manitoba Moose	AHL	73	2	10	12	48	....	....	....	....	....	....	....	....	....	14	0	5	5	2	....	....	....	....
2005-06	**Anaheim**	**NHL**	**72**	**2**	**6**	**8**	**46**	**0**	**0**	**0**	**27**	**7.4**	**8**	**0**	**0.0**	**13:31**	**16**	**0**	**0**	**0**	**13**	**0**	**0**	**0**	**11:34**
2006-07 ♦	**Anaheim**	**NHL**	**76**	**2**	**6**	**8**	**48**	**0**	**0**	**1**	**33**	**6.1**	**1**	**1**	**0.0**	**12:09**	**16**	**0**	**0**	**0**	**4**	**0**	**0**	**0**	**8:12**
2007-08	**Anaheim**	**NHL**	**23**	**1**	**4**	**5**	**16**	**0**	**0**	**0**	**5**	**20.0**	**3**	**0**	**0.0**	**10:39**	....	....	....	....	....	....	....	....	....
2008-09	Frolunda	Sweden	47	1	5	6	71	....	....	....	....	....	....	....	....	....	11	0	1	1	12	....	....	....	....
2009-10	Portland Pirates	AHL	65	2	5	7	83	....	....	....	....	....	....	....	....	....	4	0	0	0	4	....	....	....	....
	NHL Totals		**174**	**6**	**17**	**23**	**110**	**0**	**0**	**1**	**67**	**9.0**		**1**	**0.0**	**12:35**	**32**	**0**	**0**	**0**	**17**	**0**	**0**	**0**	**9:53**

• Left **Boston University** (Hockey East) and signed with **Halifax** (QMJHL), May 2, 1999. Signed as a free agent by **Philadelphia**, July 12, 2000. Traded to **Atlanta** by **Philadelphia** for Jarrod Skalde, March 5, 2002. Signed as a free agent by **Vancouver**, August 19, 2004. Signed as a free agent by **Anaheim**, August 11, 2005. • Missed majority of 2007-08 season as a healthy reserve. Signed as a free agent by **Frolunda** (Sweden), July 15, 2008. Signed as a free agent by **Buffalo**, July 11, 2009.

DiSALVATORE, Jon

(dih-SAL-vuh-tohr, JAWN) **MIN.**

Right wing. Shoots right. 6'1", 200 lbs. Born, Bangor, ME, March 30, 1981. San Jose's 2nd choice, 104th overall, in 2000 Entry Draft.

Season	Club	League	GP	G	A	Pts	PIM	PP	SH	GW	S	%	+/-	TF	F%	Min	GP	G	A	Pts	PIM	PP	SH	GW	Min
1997-98	N.E. Jr. Coyotes	EJHL	38	24	41	65	....	....	....	....	....	....	....	....	....	....	....	....	....	....	....	....	....	....	....
1998-99	N.E. Jr. Coyotes	EJHL	48	44	76	*120	38	....	....	....	....	....	....	....	....	....	....	....	....	....	....	....	....	....	....
99-2000	Providence	H-East	38	15	12	27	12	....	....	....	....	....	....	....	....	....	....	....	....	....	....	....	....	....	....
2000-01	Providence	H-East	36	9	16	25	29	....	....	....	....	....	....	....	....	....	....	....	....	....	....	....	....	....	....
2001-02	Providence	H-East	38	16	26	42	6	....	....	....	....	....	....	....	....	....	....	....	....	....	....	....	....	....	....
2002-03	Providence	H-East	36	19	29	48	12	....	....	....	....	....	....	....	....	....	....	....	....	....	....	....	....	....	....
2003-04	Cleveland Barons	AHL	74	22	24	46	30	....	....	....	....	....	....	....	....	....	8	1	1	2	2	....	....	....	....
2004-05	Worcester IceCats	AHL	79	22	23	45	42	....	....	....	....	....	....	....	....	....	....	....	....	....	....	....	....	....	....
2005-06	**St. Louis**	**NHL**	**5**	**0**	**0**	**0**	**2**	**0**	**0**	**0**	**3**	**0.0**	**-1**	**0**	**0.0**	**8:27**	....	....	....	....	....	....	....	....	....
	Peoria Rivermen	AHL	72	22	45	67	42	....	....	....	....	....	....	....	....	....	4	0	0	0	0	....	....	....	....
2006-07	Peoria Rivermen	AHL	76	21	39	60	50	....	....	....	....	....	....	....	....	....	....	....	....	....	....	....	....	....	....
2007-08	San Antonio	AHL	66	22	24	46	46	....	....	....	....	....	....	....	....	....	7	2	1	3	9	....	....	....	....
2008-09	Lowell Devils	AHL	76	20	33	53	32	....	....	....	....	....	....	....	....	....	....	....	....	....	....	....	....	....	....
2009-10	Houston Aeros	AHL	79	21	31	52	28	....	....	....	....	....	....	....	....	....	....	....	....	....	....	....	....	....	....
	NHL Totals		**5**	**0**	**0**	**0**	**2**	**0**	**0**	**0**	**3**	**0.0**		**0**	**0.0**	**8:27**	....	....	....	....	....	....	....	....	....

Signed as a free agent by **St. Louis**, June 30, 2004. Signed as a free agent by **Phoenix**, July 9, 2007. Signed as a free agent by **New Jersey**, July 17, 2008. Signed as a free agent by **Minnesota**, July 17, 2009.

DOAN, Shane

(DOHN, SHAYN) **PHX.**

Right wing. Shoots right. 6'2", 224 lbs. Born, Halkirk, Alta., October 10, 1976. Winnipeg's 1st choice, 7th overall, in 1995 Entry Draft.

Season	Club	League	GP	G	A	Pts	PIM	PP	SH	GW	S	%	+/-	TF	F%	Min	GP	G	A	Pts	PIM	PP	SH	GW	Min
1991-92	Killam Selects	AAHA	56	80	84	164	74	....	....	....	....	....	....	....	....	....	....	....	....	....	....	....	....	....	....
1992-93	Kamloops Blazers	WHL	51	7	12	19	65	....	....	....	....	....	....	....	....	....	13	0	1	1	8	....	....	....	....
1993-94	Kamloops Blazers	WHL	52	24	24	48	88	....	....	....	....	....	....	....	....	....	....	....	....	....	....	....	....	....	....
1994-95	Kamloops Blazers	WHL	71	37	57	94	106	....	....	....	....	....	....	....	....	....	21	6	10	16	16	....	....	....	....
1995-96	**Winnipeg**	**NHL**	**74**	**7**	**10**	**17**	**101**	**1**	**0**	**3**	**106**	**6.6**	**-9**	....	....	....	**6**	**0**	**0**	**0**	**6**	**0**	**0**	**0**	....
1996-97	**Phoenix**	**NHL**	**63**	**4**	**8**	**12**	**49**	**0**	**0**	**0**	**100**	**4.0**	**-3**	....	....	....	**4**	**0**	**0**	**0**	**2**	**0**	**0**	**0**	....
1997-98	**Phoenix**	**NHL**	**33**	**5**	**6**	**11**	**35**	**0**	**0**	**3**	**42**	**11.9**	**-3**	....	....	....	**6**	**1**	**0**	**1**	**6**	**0**	**0**	**0**	....
	Springfield	AHL	39	21	21	42	64	....	....	....	....	....	....	....	....	....	....	....	....	....	....	....	....	....	....
1998-99	**Phoenix**	**NHL**	**79**	**6**	**16**	**22**	**54**	**0**	**0**	**0**	**156**	**3.8**	**-5**	**6**	**16.7**	**12:42**	**7**	**2**	**2**	**4**	**6**	**0**	**0**	**2**	**17:58**
99-2000	**Phoenix**	**NHL**	**81**	**26**	**25**	**51**	**66**	**1**	**1**	**4**	**221**	**11.8**	**6**	**25**	**36.0**	**16:51**	**4**	**1**	**2**	**3**	**8**	**1**	**0**	**0**	**18:11**
2000-01	**Phoenix**	**NHL**	**76**	**26**	**37**	**63**	**89**	**6**	**1**	**6**	**220**	**11.8**	**0**	**15**	**40.0**	**19:32**	....	....	....	....	....	....	....	....	....
2001-02	**Phoenix**	**NHL**	**81**	**20**	**29**	**49**	**61**	**6**	**0**	**2**	**205**	**9.8**	**11**	**52**	**44.2**	**18:10**	**5**	**2**	**2**	**4**	**6**	**0**	**0**	**0**	**17:21**
2002-03	**Phoenix**	**NHL**	**82**	**21**	**37**	**58**	**86**	**7**	**0**	**2**	**225**	**9.3**	**3**	**623**	**39.8**	**18:47**	....	....	....	....	....	....	....	....	....
2003-04	**Phoenix**	**NHL**	**79**	**27**	**41**	**68**	**47**	**9**	**2**	**1**	**254**	**10.6**	**-11**	**55**	**40.0**	**21:46**	....	....	....	....	....	....	....	....	....
2004-05			DID NOT PLAY																						
2005-06	**Phoenix**	**NHL**	**82**	**30**	**36**	**66**	**123**	**17**	**0**	**7**	**254**	**11.8**	**-9**	**126**	**43.7**	**19:08**	....	....	....	....	....	....	....	....	....
	Canada	Olympics	6	2	1	3	2	....	....	....	....	....	....	....	....	....	....	....	....	....	....	....	....	....	....
2006-07	**Phoenix**	**NHL**	**73**	**27**	**28**	**55**	**73**	**11**	**0**	**7**	**209**	**12.9**	**-14**	**174**	**39.1**	**20:27**	....	....	....	....	....	....	....	....	....
2007-08	**Phoenix**	**NHL**	**80**	**28**	**50**	**78**	**59**	**9**	**2**	**5**	**243**	**11.5**	**4**	**187**	**41.2**	**20:46**	....	....	....	....	....	....	....	....	....
2008-09	**Phoenix**	**NHL**	**82**	**31**	**42**	**73**	**72**	**10**	**0**	**4**	**230**	**13.5**	**5**	**362**	**44.2**	**20:15**	....	....	....	....	....	....	....	....	....
2009-10	**Phoenix**	**NHL**	**82**	**18**	**37**	**55**	**41**	**5**	**0**	**4**	**234**	**7.7**	**3**	**153**	**45.8**	**19:10**	**3**	**1**	**1**	**2**	**4**	**0**	**0**	**0**	**13:22**
	NHL Totals		**1047**	**276**	**402**	**678**	**956**	**82**	**6**	**48**	**2699**	**10.2**		**1778**	**41.6**	**18:51**	**35**	**7**	**7**	**14**	**38**	**1**	**0**	**2**	**17:07**

Memorial Cup Tournament All-Star Team (1995) • Stafford Smythe Memorial Trophy (Memorial Cup Tournament - MVP) (1995) • King Clancy Memorial Trophy (2010)

Played in NHL All-Star Game (2004, 2009)

• Transferred to **Phoenix** after **Winnipeg** franchise relocated, July 1, 1996.

DOELL, Kevin

(DOH-ehl, KEH-vihn)

Center. Shoots left. 5'11", 190 lbs. Born, Saskatoon, Sask., July 15, 1979.

			Regular Season														Playoffs								
Season	Club	League	GP	G	A	Pts	PIM	PP	SH	GW	S	%	+/-	TF	F%	Min	GP	G	A	Pts	PIM	PP	SH	GW	Min
99-2000	U. of Denver	WCHA	40	8	15	23	18																		
2000-01	U. of Denver	WCHA	36	9	10	19	26																		
2001-02	U. of Denver	WCHA	41	20	23	43	28																		
2002-03	U. of Denver	WCHA	41	25	26	51	34																		
2003-04	Chicago Wolves	AHL	8	1	1	2	6										1	0	0	0	0				
	Gwinnett	ECHL	63	33	41	74	88										13	1	6	7	12				
2004-05	Chicago Wolves	AHL	45	4	8	12	69																		
	Gwinnett	ECHL	11	6	9	15	14										8	2	1	3	14				
2005-06	Chicago Wolves	AHL	78	17	34	51	72																		
2006-07	Chicago Wolves	AHL	80	14	19	33	107										15	2	4	6	14				
2007-08	**Atlanta**	**NHL**	**8**	**0**	**1**	**1**	**4**	**0**	**0**	**0**	**6**	**0.0**	**–2**	**53**	**47.2**	**9:40**									
	Chicago Wolves	AHL	68	16	17	33	75										24	4	5	9	41				
2008-09	Leksands IF	Sweden-2	37	22	27	49	105																		
2009-10	Chicago Wolves	AHL	79	16	21	37	69										9	3	0	3	2				
	NHL Totals		**8**	**0**	**1**	**1**	**4**	**0**	**0**	**0**	**6**	**0.0**		**53**	**47.2**	**9:40**									

ECHL All-Rookie Team (2004) • ECHL Rookie of the Year (2004)

Signed as a free agent by **Atlanta**, June 30, 2004. Signed as a free agent by **Leksands** (Sweden-2), July 31, 2008. Signed as a free agent by **Chicago** (AHL), July 29, 2009.

DONOVAN, Shean

(DAW-nuh-vuhn, SHAWN)

Right wing. Shoots right. 6'3", 218 lbs. Born, Timmins, Ont., January 22, 1975. San Jose's 2nd choice, 28th overall, in 1993 Entry Draft.

			Regular Season														Playoffs								
Season	Club	League	GP	G	A	Pts	PIM	PP	SH	GW	S	%	+/-	TF	F%	Min	GP	G	A	Pts	PIM	PP	SH	GW	Min
1990-91	Kanata Valley	CJHL	44	8	5	13	8																		
1991-92	Ottawa 67's	OHL	58	11	8	19	14										11	1	0	1	5				
1992-93	Ottawa 67's	OHL	66	29	23	52	33																		
1993-94	Ottawa 67's	OHL	62	35	49	84	63										17	10	11	21	14				
1994-95	Ottawa 67's	OHL	29	22	19	41	41																		
	San Jose	**NHL**	**14**	**0**	**0**	**0**	**6**	**0**	**0**	**0**	**13**	**0.0**	**–6**				**7**	**0**	**1**	**1**	**6**	**0**	**0**	**0**	
	Kansas City	IHL	5	0	2	2	7										14	5	3	8	23				
1995-96	**San Jose**	**NHL**	**74**	**13**	**8**	**21**	**39**	**0**	**1**	**2**	**73**	**17.8**	**–17**												
	Kansas City	IHL	4	0	0	0	8										5	0	0	0	8				
1996-97	**San Jose**	**NHL**	**73**	**9**	**6**	**15**	**42**	**0**	**1**	**0**	**115**	**7.8**	**–18**												
	Kentucky	AHL	3	1	3	4	18																		
1997-98	**San Jose**	**NHL**	**20**	**3**	**3**	**6**	**22**	**0**	**0**	**0**	**24**	**12.5**	**3**												
	Colorado	**NHL**	**47**	**5**	**7**	**12**	**48**	**0**	**0**	**0**	**57**	**8.8**	**3**												
1998-99	**Colorado**	**NHL**	**68**	**7**	**12**	**19**	**37**	**1**	**0**	**1**	**81**	**8.6**	**4**	**9**	**22.2**	**8:46**	**5**	**0**	**0**	**0**	**2**	**0**	**0**	**0**	**4:55**
99-2000	**Colorado**	**NHL**	**18**	**1**	**0**	**1**	**8**	**0**	**0**	**0**	**13**	**7.7**	**–4**	**1**	**0.0**	**5:20**									
	Atlanta	**NHL**	**33**	**4**	**7**	**11**	**18**	**1**	**0**	**1**	**53**	**7.5**	**–13**	**22**	**31.8**	**14:19**									
2000-01	**Atlanta**	**NHL**	**63**	**12**	**11**	**23**	**47**	**1**	**3**	**1**	**93**	**12.9**	**–14**	**218**	**45.9**	**14:03**									
2001-02	**Atlanta**	**NHL**	**48**	**6**	**6**	**12**	**40**	**1**	**0**	**2**	**64**	**9.4**	**–16**	**12**	**50.0**	**13:30**									
	Pittsburgh	**NHL**	**13**	**2**	**1**	**3**	**4**	**0**	**0**	**0**	**18**	**11.1**	**–5**	**4**	**0.0**	**14:34**									
2002-03	**Pittsburgh**	**NHL**	**52**	**4**	**5**	**9**	**30**	**0**	**1**	**0**	**66**	**6.1**	**–6**	**37**	**24.3**	**13:01**									
	Calgary	**NHL**	**13**	**1**	**2**	**3**	**7**	**0**	**0**	**1**	**22**	**4.5**	**–2**	**3**	**66.7**	**15:39**									
2003-04	**Calgary**	**NHL**	**82**	**18**	**24**	**42**	**72**	**3**	**3**	**8**	**138**	**13.0**	**14**	**53**	**39.6**	**14:55**	**24**	**5**	**5**	**10**	**23**	**0**	**0**	**2**	**15:27**
2004-05	Geneve	Swiss	12	5	3	8	30																		
2005-06	**Calgary**	**NHL**	**80**	**9**	**11**	**20**	**82**	**0**	**1**	**0**	**132**	**6.8**	**9**	**26**	**30.8**	**11:47**	**7**	**0**	**0**	**0**	**6**	**0**	**0**	**0**	**11:24**
2006-07	**Boston**	**NHL**	**76**	**6**	**11**	**17**	**56**	**0**	**0**	**0**	**108**	**5.6**	**–13**	**41**	**43.9**	**14:09**									
2007-08	**Ottawa**	**NHL**	**82**	**5**	**7**	**12**	**73**	**0**	**0**	**3**	**91**	**5.5**	**–3**	**29**	**37.9**	**9:35**	**4**	**1**	**0**	**1**	**2**	**0**	**0**	**0**	**14:00**
2008-09	**Ottawa**	**NHL**	**65**	**5**	**5**	**10**	**34**	**0**	**0**	**1**	**58**	**8.6**	**–2**	**9**	**44.4**	**7:50**									
2009-10	**Ottawa**	**NHL**	**30**	**2**	**3**	**5**	**40**	**0**	**0**	**0**	**24**	**8.3**	**–4**	**5**	**0.0**	**7:26**	**2**	**0**	**0**	**0**	**0**	**0**	**0**	**0**	**6:55**
	NHL Totals		**951**	**112**	**129**	**241**	**705**	**7**	**10**	**20**	**1243**	**9.0**		**469**	**40.1**	**11:48**	**49**	**6**	**6**	**12**	**39**	**0**	**0**	**2**	**12:58**

Traded to **Colorado** by **San Jose** with San Jose's 1st round choice (Alex Tanguay) in 1998 Entry Draft for Mike Ricci and Colorado's 2nd round choice (later traded to Buffalo – Buffalo selected Jaroslav Kristek) in 1998 Entry Draft, November 21, 1997. Traded to **Atlanta** by **Colorado** for Rick Tabaracci, December 8, 1999. Claimed on waivers by **Pittsburgh** from **Atlanta**, March 15, 2002. Traded to **Calgary** by **Pittsburgh** for Micki Dupont and Mathias Johansson, March 11, 2003. Signed as a free agent by **Geneve** (Swiss), November 13, 2004. Signed as a free agent by **Boston**, July 2, 2006. Traded to **Ottawa** by **Boston** for Peter Schaefer, July 17, 2007. • Missed majority of 2009-10 season recovering from knee injury suffered in game vs. Pittsburgh, November 19, 2009 and as a healthy reserve.

DORSETT, Derek

(DOHRS-iht, DAIR-ihk) **CBJ**

Right wing. Shoots right. 5'11", 187 lbs. Born, Kindersley, Sask., December 20, 1986. Columbus' 9th choice, 189th overall, in 2006 Entry Draft.

			Regular Season														Playoffs								
Season	Club	League	GP	G	A	Pts	PIM	PP	SH	GW	S	%	+/-	TF	F%	Min	GP	G	A	Pts	PIM	PP	SH	GW	Min
2004-05	Medicine Hat	WHL	51	5	11	16	108										13	5	1	6	35				
2005-06	Medicine Hat	WHL	68	25	23	48	*279										13	8	4	12	53				
2006-07	Medicine Hat	WHL	61	19	45	64	206										17	8	8	16	56				
2007-08	Syracuse Crunch	AHL	64	10	8	18	289										12	0	1	1	56				
2008-09	**Columbus**	**NHL**	**52**	**4**	**1**	**5**	**150**	**0**	**0**	**1**	**59**	**6.8**	**–1**	**9**	**44.4**	**8:53**	**3**	**0**	**0**	**0**	**2**	**0**	**0**	**0**	**9:11**
	Syracuse Crunch	AHL	7	1	5	6	35																		
2009-10	**Columbus**	**NHL**	**51**	**4**	**10**	**14**	**105**	**0**	**0**	**0**	**57**	**7.0**	**6**	**33**	**27.3**	**10:53**									
	NHL Totals		**103**	**8**	**11**	**19**	**255**	**0**	**0**	**1**	**116**	**6.9**		**42**	**31.0**	**9:53**	**3**	**0**	**0**	**0**	**2**	**0**	**0**	**0**	**9:11**

DOUGHTY, Drew

(DOW-tee, DROO) **L.A.**

Defense. Shoots right. 6', 211 lbs. Born, London, Ont., December 8, 1989. Los Angeles' 1st choice, 2nd overall, in 2008 Entry Draft.

			Regular Season														Playoffs								
Season	Club	League	GP	G	A	Pts	PIM	PP	SH	GW	S	%	+/-	TF	F%	Min	GP	G	A	Pts	PIM	PP	SH	GW	Min
2004-05	Lon. Jr. Knights	Minor-ON	55	19	30	49	31																		
2005-06	Guelph Storm	OHL	65	5	28	33	40										14	0	13	13	18				
2006-07	Guelph Storm	OHL	67	21	53	74	76										4	2	3	5	8				
2007-08	Guelph Storm	OHL	58	13	37	50	68										10	3	6	9	14				
2008-09	**Los Angeles**	**NHL**	**81**	**6**	**21**	**27**	**56**	**3**	**0**	**1**	**126**	**4.8**	**–17**	**0**	**0.0**	**23:50**									
2009-10	**Los Angeles**	**NHL**	**82**	**16**	**43**	**59**	**54**	**9**	**0**	**5**	**142**	**11.3**	**20**	**0**	**0.0**	**24:59**	**6**	**3**	**4**	**7**	**4**	**2**	**0**	**0**	**27:26**
	Canada	Olympics	7	0	2	2	2																		
	NHL Totals		**163**	**22**	**64**	**86**	**110**	**12**	**0**	**6**	**268**	**8.2**		**0**	**0.0**	**24:24**	**6**	**3**	**4**	**7**	**4**	**2**	**0**	**0**	**27:26**

OHL All-Rookie Team (2006) • OHL First All-Star Team (2007, 2008) • Canadian Major Junior First All-Star Team (2008) • NHL All-Rookie Team (2009) • NHL Second All-Star Team (2010)

DOWELL, Jake

(DOW-uhl, JAYK) **CHI.**

Center. Shoots left. 6', 199 lbs. Born, Eau Claire, WI, March 4, 1985. Chicago's 10th choice, 140th overall, in 2004 Entry Draft.

			Regular Season														Playoffs								
Season	Club	League	GP	G	A	Pts	PIM	PP	SH	GW	S	%	+/-	TF	F%	Min	GP	G	A	Pts	PIM	PP	SH	GW	Min
2000-01	Eau Claire Mem.	High-WI	24	25	30	55																			
2001-02	USNTDP	U-17	11	5	1	6	14																		
	USNTDP	NAHL	44	5	12	17	51																		
2002-03	USNTDP	U-18	54	8	17	25	54																		
	USNTDP	NAHL	9	2	2	4	13																		
2003-04	U. of Wisconsin	WCHA	37	6	13	19	48																		
2004-05	U. of Wisconsin	WCHA	38	12	14	26	74																		
2005-06	U. of Wisconsin	WCHA	43	5	15	20	42																		
2006-07	U. of Wisconsin	WCHA	41	19	6	25	54																		
	Norfolk Admirals	AHL	9	2	3	5	8										6	0	3	3	4				
2007-08	**Chicago**	**NHL**	**19**	**2**	**1**	**3**	**10**	**0**	**1**	**0**	**19**	**10.5**	**1**	**170**	**46.5**	**11:56**									
	Rockford IceHogs	AHL	49	7	10	17	64										12	1	1	2	6				
2008-09	**Chicago**	**NHL**	**1**	**0**	**0**	**0**	**2**	**0**	**0**	**0**	**0**	**0.0**	**1**	**12**	**66.7**	**13:37**									
	Rockford IceHogs	AHL	75	6	14	20	128										4	0	0	0	0				
2009-10	**Chicago**	**NHL**	**3**	**1**	**1**	**2**	**5**	**0**	**0**	**0**	**4**	**25.0**	**1**	**4**	**50.0**	**6:56**									
	Rockford IceHogs	AHL	78	7	16	23	96										4	0	0	0	0				
	NHL Totals		**23**	**3**	**2**	**5**	**17**	**0**	**1**	**0**	**23**	**13.0**		**186**	**47.8**	**11:21**									

DOWNIE, Steve
(DOW-nee, STEEV) **T.B.**

Right wing. Shoots right. 6', 200 lbs. Born, Newmarket, Ont., April 3, 1987. Philadelphia's 1st choice, 29th overall, in 2005 Entry Draft.

			Regular Season															Playoffs								
Season	Club	League	GP	G	A	Pts	PIM	PP	SH	GW	S	%	+/-	TF	F%	Min	GP	G	A	Pts	PIM	PP	SH	GW	Min
2002-03	Aurora Tigers	OPJHL	34	12	13	25	55																		
2003-04	Windsor Spitfires	OHL	49	7	9	16	90										4	0	1	1	27				
2004-05	Windsor Spitfires	OHL	61	21	52	73	179										11	4	5	9	49				
2005-06	Windsor Spitfires	OHL	1	3	0	3	4																		
	Peterborough	OHL	34	16	34	50	109										19	6	15	21	38				
2006-07	Peterborough	OHL	28	23	36	59	92																		
	Kitchener Rangers	OHL	17	12	21	33	32										9	8	14	22	15				
	Philadelphia	AHL	1	0	0	0	0																		
2007-08	**Philadelphia**	**NHL**	**32**	**6**	**6**	**12**	**73**	**0**	**1**	**1**	**25**	**24.0**	**2**	**15**	**33.3**	**9:51**	**6**	**0**	**1**	**1**	**10**	**0**	**0**	**0**	**6:04**
	Philadelphia	AHL	21	5	12	17	114																		
2008-09	**Philadelphia**	**NHL**	**6**	**0**	**0**	**0**	**11**	**0**	**0**	**0**	**1**	**0.0**	**–4**	**13**	**15.4**	**5:57**									
	Philadelphia	AHL	4	1	7	8	23																		
	Tampa Bay	**NHL**	**23**	**3**	**3**	**6**	**54**	**0**	**0**	**1**	**25**	**12.0**	**2**	**7**	**42.9**	**9:04**									
	Norfolk Admirals	AHL	23	8	17	25	107																		
2009-10	**Tampa Bay**	**NHL**	**79**	**22**	**24**	**46**	**208**	**7**	**0**	**1**	**116**	**19.0**	**14**	**34**	**50.0**	**14:43**									
	NHL Totals		**140**	**31**	**33**	**64**	**346**	**7**	**1**	**3**	**167**	**18.6**		**69**	**39.1**	**12:18**	**6**	**0**	**1**	**1**	**10**	**0**	**0**	**0**	**6:04**

raded to **Tampa Bay** by **Philadelphia** with Steve Eminger and Tampa Bay's 4th round choice (previously acquired, Tampa Bay selected Alex Hutchings) in 2009 Entry Draft for Matt Carle and San Jose's rd round choice (previously acquired, Philadelphia selected Simon Bertilsson) in 2009 Entry Draft, November 7, 2008.

DRAPER, Kris
(DRAY-puhr, KRIHS) **DET.**

Center. Shoots left. 5'10", 188 lbs. Born, Toronto, Ont., May 24, 1971. Winnipeg's 4th choice, 62nd overall, in 1989 Entry Draft.

Season	Club	League	GP	G	A	Pts	PIM	PP	SH	GW	S	%	+/-	TF	F%	Min	GP	G	A	Pts	PIM	PP	SH	GW	Min
1987-88	Don Mills Flyers	MTHL	40	35	32	67	46																		
1988-89	Canada	Nat-Tm	60	11	15	26	16																		
1989-90	Canada	Nat-Tm	61	12	22	34	44																		
1990-91	Ottawa 67's	OHL	39	19	42	61	35										17	8	11	19	20				
	Winnipeg	**NHL**	**3**	**1**	**0**	**1**	**5**	**0**	**0**	**0**	**1**	**100.0**	**0**												
	Moncton Hawks	AHL	7	2	1	3	2																		
1991-92	**Winnipeg**	**NHL**	**10**	**2**	**0**	**2**	**2**	**0**	**0**	**0**	**19**	**10.5**	**0**				**2**	**0**	**0**	**0**	**0**	**0**	**0**	**0**	
	Moncton Hawks	AHL	61	11	18	29	113										4	0	1	1	6				
1992-93	**Winnipeg**	**NHL**	**7**	**0**	**0**	**0**	**2**	**0**	**0**	**0**	**5**	**0.0**	**–6**												
	Moncton Hawks	AHL	67	12	23	35	40										5	2	2	4	18				
1993-94	**Detroit**	**NHL**	**39**	**5**	**8**	**13**	**31**	**0**	**1**	**0**	**55**	**9.1**	**11**				**7**	**2**	**2**	**4**	**4**	**0**	**1**	**0**	
	Adirondack	AHL	46	20	23	43	49																		
1994-95	**Detroit**	**NHL**	**36**	**2**	**6**	**8**	**22**	**0**	**0**	**0**	**44**	**4.5**	**1**				**18**	**4**	**1**	**5**	**12**	**0**	**1**	**1**	
1995-96	**Detroit**	**NHL**	**52**	**7**	**9**	**16**	**32**	**0**	**1**	**0**	**51**	**13.7**	**2**				**18**	**4**	**2**	**6**	**18**	**0**	**1**	**0**	
1996-97 ♦	**Detroit**	**NHL**	**76**	**8**	**5**	**13**	**73**	**1**	**0**	**1**	**85**	**9.4**	**–11**				**20**	**2**	**4**	**6**	**12**	**0**	**1**	**0**	
1997-98 ♦	**Detroit**	**NHL**	**64**	**13**	**10**	**23**	**45**	**1**	**0**	**4**	**96**	**13.5**	**5**				**19**	**1**	**3**	**4**	**12**	**0**	**0**	**1**	
1998-99	**Detroit**	**NHL**	**80**	**4**	**14**	**18**	**79**	**0**	**1**	**1**	**78**	**5.1**	**2**	**887**	**54.6**	**12:43**	**10**	**0**	**1**	**1**	**6**	**0**	**0**	**0**	**11:35**
99-2000	**Detroit**	**NHL**	**51**	**5**	**7**	**12**	**28**	**0**	**0**	**3**	**76**	**6.6**	**3**	**380**	**57.6**	**13:33**	**9**	**2**	**0**	**2**	**6**	**0**	**0**	**0**	**12:26**
2000-01	**Detroit**	**NHL**	**75**	**8**	**17**	**25**	**38**	**0**	**1**	**1**	**123**	**6.5**	**17**	**997**	**56.5**	**13:26**	**6**	**0**	**1**	**1**	**2**	**0**	**0**	**0**	**16:08**
2001-02 ♦	**Detroit**	**NHL**	**82**	**15**	**15**	**30**	**56**	**0**	**2**	**3**	**137**	**10.9**	**26**	**756**	**53.2**	**15:35**	**23**	**2**	**3**	**5**	**20**	**0**	**0**	**0**	**17:00**
2002-03	**Detroit**	**NHL**	**82**	**14**	**21**	**35**	**82**	**0**	**1**	**2**	**142**	**9.9**	**6**	**1059**	**56.9**	**16:12**	**4**	**0**	**0**	**0**	**4**	**0**	**0**	**0**	**17:29**
2003-04	**Detroit**	**NHL**	**67**	**24**	**16**	**40**	**31**	**2**	**5**	**1**	**149**	**16.1**	**22**	**1058**	**56.9**	**17:44**	**12**	**1**	**3**	**4**	**6**	**0**	**0**	**0**	**18:29**
2004-05			DID NOT PLAY																						
2005-06	**Detroit**	**NHL**	**80**	**10**	**22**	**32**	**58**	**0**	**1**	**1**	**153**	**6.5**	**3**	**1287**	**57.7**	**17:46**	**6**	**0**	**0**	**0**	**6**	**0**	**0**	**0**	**19:58**
	Canada	Olympics	6	0	0	0	0																		
2006-07	**Detroit**	**NHL**	**81**	**14**	**15**	**29**	**58**	**0**	**5**	**1**	**157**	**8.9**	**7**	**1242**	**57.3**	**16:45**	**18**	**2**	**0**	**2**	**24**	**0**	**0**	**0**	**16:36**
2007-08 ♦	**Detroit**	**NHL**	**65**	**9**	**8**	**17**	**68**	**0**	**2**	**2**	**97**	**9.3**	**–2**	**944**	**58.6**	**15:38**	**22**	**3**	**1**	**4**	**10**	**0**	**0**	**1**	**15:27**
2008-09	**Detroit**	**NHL**	**79**	**7**	**10**	**17**	**40**	**0**	**1**	**2**	**93**	**7.5**	**–13**	**1000**	**60.3**	**11:59**	**8**	**1**	**0**	**1**	**0**	**0**	**0**	**0**	**8:37**
2009-10	**Detroit**	**NHL**	**81**	**7**	**15**	**22**	**28**	**1**	**0**	**0**	**98**	**7.1**	**–2**	**319**	**52.0**	**11:32**	**12**	**0**	**0**	**0**	**16**	**0**	**0**	**0**	**7:24**
	NHL Totals		**1110**	**155**	**198**	**353**	**778**	**5**	**21**	**22**	**1659**	**9.3**		**9929**	**56.9**	**14:48**	**214**	**24**	**21**	**45**	**158**	**0**	**4**	**3**	**14:48**

rank J. Selke Trophy (2004)

raded to **Detroit** by **Winnipeg** for future considerations, June 30, 1993.

DREWISKE, Davis
(droo-WIHS-kee, DAY-vihs) **L.A.**

Defense. Shoots left. 6'2", 222 lbs. Born, Hudson, WI, November 22, 1984.

Season	Club	League	GP	G	A	Pts	PIM	PP	SH	GW	S	%	+/-	TF	F%	Min	GP	G	A	Pts	PIM	PP	SH	GW	Min
2003-04	Des Moines	USHL	60	4	19	23	63										3	0	0	0	4				
2004-05	U. of Wisconsin	WCHA	34	1	5	6	20																		
2005-06	U. of Wisconsin	WCHA	35	2	2	4	22																		
2006-07	U. of Wisconsin	WCHA	41	4	6	10	46																		
2007-08	U. of Wisconsin	WCHA	40	5	16	21	46																		
	Manchester	AHL	5	0	0	0	6										4	0	1	1	6				
2008-09	**Los Angeles**	**NHL**	**17**	**0**	**3**	**3**	**18**	**0**	**0**	**0**	**21**	**0.0**	**1**	**0**	**0.0**	**17:19**									
	Manchester	AHL	61	1	13	14	95																		
2009-10	**Los Angeles**	**NHL**	**42**	**1**	**7**	**8**	**14**	**0**	**0**	**0**	**32**	**3.1**	**–4**	**0**	**0.0**	**15:15**									
	NHL Totals		**59**	**1**	**10**	**11**	**32**	**0**	**0**	**0**	**53**	**1.9**		**0**	**0.0**	**15:51**									

gned as a free agent by **Los Angeles**, April 1, 2008.

DRURY, Chris
(DROO-ree, KRIHS) **NYR**

Center. Shoots right. 5'10", 190 lbs. Born, Trumbull, CT, August 20, 1976. Quebec's 5th choice, 72nd overall, in 1994 Entry Draft.

Season	Club	League	GP	G	A	Pts	PIM	PP	SH	GW	S	%	+/-	TF	F%	Min	GP	G	A	Pts	PIM	PP	SH	GW	Min
1991-92	Fairfield Prep	High-CT	25	22	27	49	....																		
1992-93	Fairfield Prep	High-CT	24	25	32	57	15																		
1993-94	Fairfield Prep	High-CT	24	37	18	55	....																		
1994-95	Boston University	H-East	39	12	15	27	38																		
1995-96	Boston University	H-East	37	35	33	*68	46																		
1996-97	Boston University	H-East	41	*38	24	62	64																		
1997-98	Boston University	H-East	38	28	29	57	88																		
1998-99	**Colorado**	**NHL**	**79**	**20**	**24**	**44**	**62**	**6**	**0**	**3**	**138**	**14.5**	**9**	**418**	**46.9**	**13:15**	**19**	**6**	**2**	**8**	**4**	**0**	**0**	**4**	**11:28**
99-2000	**Colorado**	**NHL**	**82**	**20**	**47**	**67**	**42**	**7**	**0**	**2**	**213**	**9.4**	**8**	**1321**	**53.1**	**18:33**	**17**	**4**	**10**	**14**	**4**	**1**	**0**	**2**	**18:30**
2000-01 ♦	**Colorado**	**NHL**	**71**	**24**	**41**	**65**	**47**	**11**	**0**	**5**	**204**	**11.8**	**6**	**552**	**55.1**	**18:03**	**23**	**11**	**5**	**16**	**4**	**2**	**0**	**2**	**19:06**
2001-02	**Colorado**	**NHL**	**82**	**21**	**25**	**46**	**38**	**5**	**0**	**6**	**236**	**8.9**	**1**	**1139**	**53.2**	**17:57**	**21**	**5**	**7**	**12**	**10**	**1**	**0**	**3**	**17:01**
	United States	Olympics	6	0	0	0	0																		
2002-03	**Calgary**	**NHL**	**80**	**23**	**30**	**53**	**33**	**5**	**1**	**5**	**224**	**10.3**	**–9**	**942**	**53.8**	**18:33**									
2003-04	**Buffalo**	**NHL**	**76**	**18**	**35**	**53**	**68**	**5**	**1**	**2**	**152**	**11.8**	**8**	**1491**	**54.9**	**18:04**									
2004-05			DID NOT PLAY																						
2005-06	**Buffalo**	**NHL**	**81**	**30**	**37**	**67**	**32**	**16**	**2**	**5**	**172**	**17.4**	**–11**	**1641**	**55.5**	**18:06**	**18**	**9**	**9**	**18**	**10**	**5**	**1**	**1**	**19:20**
	United States	Olympics	6	0	3	3	2																		
2006-07	**Buffalo**	**NHL**	**77**	**37**	**32**	**69**	**30**	**17**	**3**	**9**	**199**	**18.6**	**1**	**1613**	**58.8**	**18:47**	**16**	**8**	**5**	**13**	**2**	**3**	**0**	**3**	**20:45**
2007-08	**NY Rangers**	**NHL**	**82**	**25**	**33**	**58**	**45**	**12**	**0**	**7**	**220**	**11.4**	**–3**	**1359**	**54.9**	**19:48**	**10**	**3**	**3**	**6**	**8**	**0**	**0**	**1**	**18:27**
2008-09	**NY Rangers**	**NHL**	**81**	**22**	**34**	**56**	**32**	**10**	**1**	**2**	**219**	**10.0**	**–8**	**1183**	**51.0**	**20:15**	**6**	**1**	**0**	**1**	**2**	**0**	**0**	**1**	**13:32**
2009-10	**NY Rangers**	**NHL**	**77**	**14**	**18**	**32**	**31**	**2**	**0**	**1**	**148**	**9.5**	**–10**	**1206**	**52.9**	**17:47**									
	United States	Olympics	6	2	0	2	0																		
	NHL Totals		**868**	**254**	**356**	**610**	**460**	**96**	**8**	**47**	**2125**	**12.0**		**12865**	**54.2**	**18:07**	**130**	**47**	**41**	**88**	**44**	**12**	**1**	**17**	**17:30**

ockey East Second All-Star Team (1996, 1997) • NCAA East Second All-American Team (1996) • Hockey East Player of the Year (1997, 1998) • NCAA East First All-American Team (1997, 1998) • NCAA hampionship All-Tournament Team (1997) • Hockey East First All-Star Team (1998) • Hobey Baker Memorial Award (Top U.S. Collegiate Player) (1998) • NHL All-Rookie Team (1999) • Calder Memorial rophy (1999)

Rights transferred to **Colorado** after **Quebec** franchise relocated, June 21, 1995. Traded to **Calgary** by **Colorado** with Stephane Yelle for Derek Morris, Jeff Shantz and Dean McAmmond, October 1, 002. Traded to **Buffalo** by **Calgary** with Steve Begin for Steve Reinprecht and Rhett Warrener, July 3, 2003. Signed as a free agent by **NY Rangers**, July 1, 2007.

DUBINSKY, Brandon

(DOO-bihn-skee, BRAN-duhn) **NYR**

Center. Shoots left. 6'1", 205 lbs. Born, Anchorage, AK, April 29, 1986. NY Rangers' 6th choice, 60th overall, in 2004 Entry Draft.

			Regular Season														Playoffs								
Season	Club	League	GP	G	A	Pts	PIM	PP	SH	GW	S	%	+/-	TF	F%	Min	GP	G	A	Pts	PIM	PP	SH	GW	Min
2001-02	Alaska All-Stars	AASHA	37	14	24	38	....	....	....	....	....	....	....	....	....	....	....	....	....	....	....	....	....	....	....
2002-03	Portland	WHL	44	8	18	26	35	....	....	....	....	....	....	....	....	....	7	2	2	4	10	....	....	....	....
2003-04	Portland	WHL	71	30	48	78	137	....	....	....	....	....	....	....	....	....	5	0	2	2	6	....	....	....	....
2004-05	Portland	WHL	68	23	36	59	160	....	....	....	....	....	....	....	....	....	7	4	5	9	8	....	....	....	....
2005-06	Portland	WHL	51	21	46	67	98	....	....	....	....	....	....	....	....	....	12	5	10	15	24	....	....	....	....
	Hartford	AHL	....	....	....	....	....	....	....	....	....	....	....	....	....	....	11	5	5	10	14	....	....	....	....
2006-07	**NY Rangers**	**NHL**	**6**	**0**	**0**	**0**	**2**	**0**	**0**	**0**	**9**	**0.0**	**0**	**26**	**46.2**	**8:10**	....	....	....	....	....	....	....	....	....
	Hartford	AHL	71	21	22	43	115	....	....	....	....	....	....	....	....	....	7	1	3	4	12	....	....	....	....
2007-08	**NY Rangers**	**NHL**	**82**	**14**	**26**	**40**	**79**	**1**	**0**	**0**	**157**	**8.9**	**8**	**995**	**51.5**	**14:30**	**10**	**4**	**4**	**8**	**12**	**2**	**0**	**0**	**18:59**
2008-09	**NY Rangers**	**NHL**	**82**	**13**	**28**	**41**	**112**	**3**	**1**	**7**	**188**	**6.9**	**–6**	**870**	**53.6**	**16:38**	**7**	**1**	**3**	**4**	**18**	**0**	**0**	**1**	**18:14**
2009-10	**NY Rangers**	**NHL**	**69**	**20**	**24**	**44**	**54**	**6**	**2**	**5**	**165**	**12.1**	**9**	**675**	**51.4**	**19:33**	....	....	....	....	....	....	....	....	....
	NHL Totals		**239**	**47**	**78**	**125**	**247**	**10**	**3**	**12**	**519**	**9.1**		**2566**	**52.1**	**16:32**	**17**	**5**	**7**	**12**	**30**	**2**	**0**	**1**	**18:41**

WHL West Second All-Star Team (2004, 2006)

DUCHENE, Matt

(DOO-shayn, MAT) **COL.**

Center. Shoots left. 5'11", 200 lbs. Born, Haliburton, Ont., January 16, 1991. Colorado's 1st choice, 3rd overall, in 2009 Entry Draft.

Season	Club	League	GP	G	A	Pts	PIM	PP	SH	GW	S	%	+/-	TF	F%	Min	GP	G	A	Pts	PIM	PP	SH	GW	Min
2006-07	Cent. Ont. Wolves	Minor-ON	52	69	37	106	36	....	....	....	....	....	....	....	....	....	....	....	....	....	....	....	....	....	....
2007-08	Brampton	OHL	64	30	20	50	22	....	....	....	....	....	....	....	....	....	5	1	1	2	10	....	....	....	....
2008-09	Brampton	OHL	57	31	48	79	42	....	....	....	....	....	....	....	....	....	21	14	12	26	21	....	....	....	....
2009-10	**Colorado**	**NHL**	**81**	**24**	**31**	**55**	**16**	**10**	**1**	**2**	**180**	**13.3**	**1**	**1088**	**44.0**	**17:44**	**6**	**0**	**3**	**3**	**0**	**0**	**0**	**0**	**19:20**
	NHL Totals		**81**	**24**	**31**	**55**	**16**	**10**	**1**	**2**	**180**	**13.3**		**1088**	**44.0**	**17:44**	**6**	**0**	**3**	**3**	**0**	**0**	**0**	**0**	**19:20**

NHL All-Rookie Team (2010)

DUCO, Mike

(DOO-koh, MIGHK) **FLA.**

Left wing. Shoots left. 5'10", 200 lbs. Born, Toronto, Ont., July 8, 1987.

Season	Club	League	GP	G	A	Pts	PIM	PP	SH	GW	S	%	+/-	TF	F%	Min	GP	G	A	Pts	PIM	PP	SH	GW	Min
2003-04	Kitchener Rangers	OHL	5	1	2	3	4	....	....	....	....	....	....	....	....	....	4	0	1	1	4	....	....	....	....
2004-05	Kitchener Rangers	OHL	62	24	26	50	78	....	....	....	....	....	....	....	....	....	15	0	0	0	11	....	....	....	....
2005-06	Kitchener Rangers	OHL	59	22	22	44	113	....	....	....	....	....	....	....	....	....	5	2	1	3	10	....	....	....	....
2006-07	Kitchener Rangers	OHL	54	20	20	40	121	....	....	....	....	....	....	....	....	....	9	1	1	2	12	....	....	....	....
2007-08	Kitchener Rangers	OHL	62	32	22	54	173	....	....	....	....	....	....	....	....	....	20	*16	6	22	37	....	....	....	....
2008-09	Rochester	AHL	68	14	14	28	147	....	....	....	....	....	....	....	....	....	....	....	....	....	....	....	....	....	....
2009-10	**Florida**	**NHL**	**10**	**0**	**0**	**0**	**50**	**0**	**0**	**0**	**6**	**0.0**	**–3**	**0**	**0.0**	**7:43**	....	....	....	....	....	....	....	....	....
	Rochester	AHL	59	9	10	19	111	....	....	....	....	....	....	....	....	....	7	1	0	1	18	....	....	....	....
	NHL Totals		**10**	**0**	**0**	**0**	**50**	**0**	**0**	**0**	**6**	**0.0**		**0**	**0.0**	**7:43**	....	....	....	....	....	....	....	....	....

Signed as a free agent by **Florida**, October 8, 2007.

DUMONT, J.P.

(DOO-mawnt, JAY-PEE) **NSH.**

Right wing. Shoots left. 6'1", 205 lbs. Born, Montreal, Que., April 1, 1978. NY Islanders' 1st choice, 3rd overall, in 1996 Entry Draft.

Season	Club	League	GP	G	A	Pts	PIM	PP	SH	GW	S	%	+/-	TF	F%	Min	GP	G	A	Pts	PIM	PP	SH	GW	Min
1993-94	Mtl-Bourassa	QAAA	44	27	20	47	44	....	....	....	....	....	....	....	....	....	4	2	3	5	4	....	....	....	....
1994-95	Mtl-Bourassa	QAAA	10	2	7	9	12	....	....	....	....	....	....	....	....	....	....	....	....	....	....	....	....	....	....
	Val-d'Or Foreurs	QMJHL	48	5	14	19	24	....	....	....	....	....	....	....	....	....	....	....	....	....	....	....	....	....	....
1995-96	Val-d'Or Foreurs	QMJHL	66	48	57	105	109	....	....	....	....	....	....	....	....	....	13	12	8	20	22	....	....	....	....
1996-97	Val-d'Or Foreurs	QMJHL	62	44	64	108	86	....	....	....	....	....	....	....	....	....	13	9	7	16	12	....	....	....	....
1997-98	Val-d'Or Foreurs	QMJHL	55	57	42	99	63	....	....	....	....	....	....	....	....	....	19	31	15	46	18	....	....	....	....
1998-99	**Chicago**	**NHL**	**25**	**9**	**6**	**15**	**10**	**0**	**0**	**2**	**42**	**21.4**	**7**	**10**	**50.0**	**14:14**	....	....	....	....	....	....	....	....	....
	Portland Pirates	AHL	50	32	14	46	39	....	....	....	....	....	....	....	....	....	....	....	....	....	....	....	....	....	....
	Chicago Wolves	IHL	....	....	....	....	....	....	....	....	....	....	....	....	....	....	10	4	1	5	6	....	....	....	....
99-2000	**Chicago**	**NHL**	**47**	**10**	**8**	**18**	**18**	**0**	**0**	**1**	**86**	**11.6**	**–6**	**12**	**33.3**	**12:54**	....	....	....	....	....	....	....	....	....
	Cleveland	IHL	7	5	2	7	8	....	....	....	....	....	....	....	....	....	....	....	....	....	....	....	....	....	....
	Rochester	AHL	13	7	10	17	18	....	....	....	....	....	....	....	....	....	21	14	7	21	32	....	....	....	....
2000-01	**Buffalo**	**NHL**	**79**	**23**	**28**	**51**	**54**	**9**	**0**	**5**	**156**	**14.7**	**1**	**3**	**33.3**	**15:01**	**13**	**4**	**3**	**7**	**8**	**0**	**0**	**0**	**14:32**
2001-02	**Buffalo**	**NHL**	**76**	**23**	**21**	**44**	**42**	**7**	**0**	**3**	**154**	**14.9**	**–10**	**4**	**50.0**	**15:14**	....	....	....	....	....	....	....	....	....
2002-03	**Buffalo**	**NHL**	**76**	**14**	**21**	**35**	**44**	**2**	**0**	**2**	**135**	**10.4**	**–14**	**15**	**20.0**	**15:04**	....	....	....	....	....	....	....	....	....
2003-04	**Buffalo**	**NHL**	**77**	**22**	**31**	**53**	**40**	**10**	**0**	**1**	**156**	**14.1**	**–9**	**32**	**43.8**	**17:00**	....	....	....	....	....	....	....	....	....
2004-05	SC Bern	Swiss	3	2	2	4	6	....	....	....	....	....	....	....	....	....	10	4	1	5	16	....	....	....	....
2005-06	**Buffalo**	**NHL**	**54**	**20**	**20**	**40**	**38**	**9**	**0**	**4**	**116**	**17.2**	**–1**	**9**	**11.1**	**16:00**	**18**	**7**	**7**	**14**	**14**	**3**	**0**	**1**	**16:39**
2006-07	**Nashville**	**NHL**	**82**	**21**	**45**	**66**	**28**	**5**	**0**	**3**	**143**	**14.7**	**14**	**6**	**16.7**	**16:12**	**5**	**4**	**2**	**6**	**0**	**1**	**1**	**1**	**21:03**
2007-08	**Nashville**	**NHL**	**80**	**29**	**43**	**72**	**34**	**7**	**0**	**8**	**192**	**15.1**	**5**	**13**	**23.1**	**18:30**	**6**	**0**	**2**	**2**	**4**	**0**	**0**	**0**	**17:23**
2008-09	**Nashville**	**NHL**	**82**	**16**	**49**	**65**	**20**	**5**	**0**	**4**	**176**	**9.1**	**1**	**6**	**50.0**	**17:30**	....	....	....	....	....	....	....	....	....
2009-10	**Nashville**	**NHL**	**74**	**17**	**28**	**45**	**20**	**3**	**1**	**3**	**112**	**15.2**	**8**	**0**	**0.0**	**14:46**	**6**	**2**	**2**	**4**	**0**	**0**	**0**	**1**	**14:18**
	NHL Totals		**752**	**204**	**300**	**504**	**348**	**57**	**1**	**36**	**1468**	**13.9**		**110**	**33.6**	**15:54**	**48**	**17**	**16**	**33**	**26**	**4**	**1**	**3**	**16:20**

QMJHL Second All-Star Team (1997) • AHL All-Rookie Team (1999)

• Rights traded to **Chicago** by **NY Islanders** with NY Islanders' 5th round choice (later traded to Philadelphia – Philadelphia selected Francis Belanger) in 1998 Entry Draft for Dmitri Nabokov, May 30, 1998. Traded to **Buffalo** by **Chicago** with Doug Gilmour for Michal Grosek, March 10, 2000. Signed as a free agent by **Bern** (Swiss), February 9, 2005. Signed as a free agent by **Nashville**, August 29, 2006.

DUPUIS, Pascal

(doo-PWEE, pas-KAL) **PIT.**

Left wing. Shoots left. 6'1", 205 lbs. Born, Laval, Que., April 7, 1979.

Season	Club	League	GP	G	A	Pts	PIM	PP	SH	GW	S	%	+/-	TF	F%	Min	GP	G	A	Pts	PIM	PP	SH	GW	Min
1995-96	Laval-Laurentides	QAAA	41	10	15	25	....	....	....	....	....	....	....	....	....	....	14	11	11	22	....	....	....	....	....
1996-97	Rouyn-Noranda	QMJHL	44	9	15	24	20	....	....	....	....	....	....	....	....	....	....	....	....	....	....	....	....	....	....
1997-98	Rouyn-Noranda	QMJHL	39	9	17	26	36	....	....	....	....	....	....	....	....	....	....	....	....	....	....	....	....	....	....
	Shawinigan	QMJHL	28	7	13	20	10	....	....	....	....	....	....	....	....	....	6	2	0	2	4	....	....	....	....
1998-99	Shawinigan	QMJHL	57	30	42	72	118	....	....	....	....	....	....	....	....	....	6	1	8	9	18	....	....	....	....
99-2000	Shawinigan	QMJHL	61	50	55	105	99	....	....	....	....	....	....	....	....	....	13	*15	7	22	4	....	....	....	....
2000-01	**Minnesota**	**NHL**	**4**	**1**	**0**	**1**	**4**	**1**	**0**	**0**	**8**	**12.5**	**0**	**0**	**0.0**	**15:36**	....	....	....	....	....	....	....	....	....
	Cleveland	IHL	70	19	24	43	37	....	....	....	....	....	....	....	....	....	4	0	0	0	0	....	....	....	....
2001-02	**Minnesota**	**NHL**	**76**	**15**	**12**	**27**	**16**	**3**	**2**	**0**	**154**	**9.7**	**–10**	**40**	**32.5**	**15:08**	....	....	....	....	....	....	....	....	....
2002-03	**Minnesota**	**NHL**	**80**	**20**	**28**	**48**	**44**	**6**	**0**	**4**	**183**	**10.9**	**17**	**186**	**40.9**	**17:30**	**16**	**4**	**4**	**8**	**8**	**2**	**0**	**1**	**16:58**
2003-04	**Minnesota**	**NHL**	**59**	**11**	**15**	**26**	**20**	**2**	**0**	**1**	**127**	**8.7**	**5**	**129**	**45.7**	**15:48**	....	....	....	....	....	....	....	....	....
2004-05	HC Ajoie	Swiss-2	8	5	5	10	26	....	....	....	....	....	....	....	....	....	6	6	8	14	8	....	....	....	....
2005-06	**Minnesota**	**NHL**	**67**	**10**	**16**	**26**	**40**	**4**	**0**	**2**	**151**	**6.6**	**–10**	**93**	**29.0**	**16:30**	....	....	....	....	....	....	....	....	....
2006-07	**Minnesota**	**NHL**	**48**	**10**	**3**	**13**	**38**	**2**	**2**	**0**	**106**	**9.4**	**–7**	**110**	**27.3**	**15:07**	....	....	....	....	....	....	....	....	....
	NY Rangers	**NHL**	**6**	**1**	**0**	**1**	**0**	**0**	**0**	**0**	**10**	**10.0**	**–4**	**2**	**50.0**	**15:30**	....	....	....	....	....	....	....	....	....
	Atlanta	**NHL**	**17**	**3**	**2**	**5**	**4**	**0**	**0**	**1**	**40**	**7.5**	**–6**	**19**	**52.6**	**16:44**	**4**	**1**	**2**	**3**	**4**	**0**	**0**	**0**	**20:28**
2007-08	**Atlanta**	**NHL**	**62**	**10**	**5**	**15**	**24**	**0**	**3**	**1**	**111**	**9.0**	**–4**	**13**	**38.5**	**14:46**	....	....	....	....	....	....	....	....	....
	Pittsburgh	**NHL**	**16**	**2**	**10**	**12**	**8**	**0**	**0**	**0**	**32**	**6.3**	**4**	**3**	**0.0**	**16:50**	**20**	**2**	**5**	**7**	**18**	**0**	**0**	**0**	**16:14**
2008-09♦	**Pittsburgh**	**NHL**	**71**	**12**	**16**	**28**	**30**	**0**	**0**	**2**	**145**	**8.3**	**1**	**16**	**18.8**	**14:13**	**16**	**0**	**0**	**0**	**8**	**0**	**0**	**0**	**8:23**
2009-10	**Pittsburgh**	**NHL**	**81**	**18**	**20**	**38**	**16**	**0**	**0**	**5**	**157**	**11.5**	**5**	**33**	**39.4**	**14:11**	**13**	**2**	**6**	**8**	**4**	**0**	**0**	**1**	**16:51**
	NHL Totals		**587**	**113**	**127**	**240**	**244**	**18**	**7**	**16**	**1224**	**9.2**		**644**	**36.8**	**15:30**	**69**	**9**	**17**	**26**	**42**	**2**	**0**	**2**	**14:57**

Signed as a free agent by **Minnesota**, August 18, 2000. Signed as a free agent by **Ajoie** (Swiss-2), January 14, 2005. Traded to **NY Rangers** by **Minnesota** for Adam Hall, February 9, 2007. Traded to **Atlanta** by **NY Rangers** with NY Rangers' 3rd round choice (later traded to Pittsburgh - Pittsburgh selected Robert Bortuzzo) in 2007 Entry Draft for Alex Bourret, February 27, 2007. Traded to **Pittsburgh** by **Atlanta** with Marian Hossa for Colby Armstrong, Erik Christensen, Angelo Esposito and Pittsburgh's 1st round choice (Daulton Leveille) in 2008 Entry Draft, February 26, 2008.

DUPUIS, Philippe

(doo-PWEE, fihl-EEP) **COL.**

Center. Shoots right. 6', 196 lbs. Born, Laval, Que., April 24, 1985. Columbus' 5th choice, 104th overall, in 2003 Entry Draft.

Season	Club	League	GP	G	A	Pts	PIM	PP	SH	GW	S	%	+/-	TF	F%	Min	GP	G	A	Pts	PIM	PP	SH	GW	Min
2000-01	Laval-Laurentides	QAAA	46	16	27	43	74	....	....	....	....	....	....	....	....	....	8	1	5	6	30	....	....	....	....
2001-02	Hull Olympiques	QMJHL	67	7	14	21	59	....	....	....	....	....	....	....	....	....	12	6	5	11	14	....	....	....	....
2002-03	Hull Olympiques	QMJHL	68	22	34	56	89	....	....	....	....	....	....	....	....	....	20	2	4	6	22	....	....	....	....
2003-04	Gatineau	QMJHL	60	18	37	55	77	....	....	....	....	....	....	....	....	....	15	6	10	16	14	....	....	....	....
2004-05	Rouyn-Noranda	QMJHL	62	34	50	84	60	....	....	....	....	....	....	....	....	....	10	5	3	8	8	....	....	....	....
2005-06	Moncton Wildcats	QMJHL	56	32	76	108	52	....	....	....	....	....	....	....	....	....	19	14	18	32	14	....	....	....	....

			Regular Season														Playoffs								
Season	Club	League	GP	G	A	Pts	PIM	PP	SH	GW	S	%	+/-	TF	F%	Min	GP	G	A	Pts	PIM	PP	SH	GW	Min
2006-07	Syracuse Crunch	AHL	51	11	11	22	18	....	....	....	....	....	....	....	....	....	....	....	....	....	....	....	....	....	....
	Dayton Bombers	ECHL	8	3	2	5	8	....	....	....	....	....	....	....	....	....	19	6	9	15	28	....	....	....	....
2007-08	Syracuse Crunch	AHL	29	7	4	11	2	....	....	....	....	....	....	....	....	....	....	....	....	....	....	....	....	....	....
	Lake Erie	AHL	17	5	3	8	12	....	....	....	....	....	....	....	....	....	....	....	....	....	....	....	....	....	....
2008-09	**Colorado**	**NHL**	**8**	**0**	**0**	**0**	**4**	**0**	**0**	**0**	**11**	**0.0**	**–1**	**50**	**52.0**	**9:34**	....	....	....	....	....	....	....	....	....
	Lake Erie	AHL	67	17	29	46	42	....	....	....	....	....	....	....	....	....	....	....	....	....	....	....	....	....	....
2009-10	**Colorado**	**NHL**	**4**	**0**	**1**	**1**	**2**	**0**	**0**	**0**	**4**	**0.0**	**1**	**20**	**45.0**	**8:14**	....	....	....	....	....	....	....	....	....
	Lake Erie	AHL	68	16	19	35	47	....	....	....	....	....	....	....	....	....	....	....	....	....	....	....	....	....	....
	NHL Totals		**12**	**0**	**1**	**1**	**6**	**0**	**0**	**0**	**15**	**0.0**		**70**	**50.0**	**9:07**	....	....	....	....	....	....	....	....	....

Traded to **Colorado** by **Columbus** with Darcy Campbell for Mark Rycroft, January 22, 2008.

DURNO, Chris

(DUHR-noh, KRIHS) **T.B.**

Center. Shoots left. 6'4", 205 lbs. Born, Scarborough, Ont., October 31, 1980.

			Regular Season														Playoffs								
Season	Club	League	GP	G	A	Pts	PIM	PP	SH	GW	S	%	+/-	TF	F%	Min	GP	G	A	Pts	PIM	PP	SH	GW	Min
99-2000	Michigan Tech	WCHA	24	1	1	2	30	....	....	....	....	....	....	....	....	....	....	....	....	....	....	....	....	....	....
2000-01	Michigan Tech	WCHA	35	9	6	15	46	....	....	....	....	....	....	....	....	....	....	....	....	....	....	....	....	....	....
2001-02	Michigan Tech	WCHA	36	7	8	15	48	....	....	....	....	....	....	....	....	....	....	....	....	....	....	....	....	....	....
2002-03	Michigan Tech	WCHA	35	5	11	16	60	....	....	....	....	....	....	....	....	....	....	....	....	....	....	....	....	....	....
2003-04	Gwinnett	ECHL	68	20	26	46	46	....	....	....	....	....	....	....	....	....	13	7	5	12	10	....	....	....	....
2004-05	Gwinnett	ECHL	66	20	36	56	101	....	....	....	....	....	....	....	....	....	8	5	2	7	8	....	....	....	....
2005-06	Gwinnett	ECHL	13	12	10	22	19	....	....	....	....	....	....	....	....	....	....	....	....	....	....	....	....	....	....
	Milwaukee	AHL	57	20	20	40	52	....	....	....	....	....	....	....	....	....	21	2	2	4	18	....	....	....	....
2006-07	Norfolk Admirals	AHL	22	4	1	5	61	....	....	....	....	....	....	....	....	....	....	....	....	....	....	....	....	....	....
	Portland Pirates	AHL	12	1	1	2	2	....	....	....	....	....	....	....	....	....	....	....	....	....	....	....	....	....	....
	Milwaukee	AHL	29	13	3	16	24	....	....	....	....	....	....	....	....	....	4	1	2	3	10	....	....	....	....
2007-08	San Antonio	AHL	80	23	26	49	109	....	....	....	....	....	....	....	....	....	7	0	2	2	26	....	....	....	....
2008-09	**Colorado**	**NHL**	**2**	**0**	**0**	**0**	**0**	**0**	**0**	**0**	**3**	**0.0**	**0**	**0**	**0.0**	**6:02**	....	....	....	....	....	....	....	....	....
	Lake Erie	AHL	76	18	27	45	131	....	....	....	....	....	....	....	....	....	....	....	....	....	....	....	....	....	....
2009-10	**Colorado**	**NHL**	**41**	**4**	**4**	**8**	**47**	**0**	**0**	**0**	**27**	**14.8**	**3**	**40**	**52.5**	**7:28**	**1**	**0**	**0**	**0**	**0**	**0**	**0**	**0**	**6:09**
	Lake Erie	AHL	17	10	8	18	20	....	....	....	....	....	....	....	....	....	....	....	....	....	....	....	....	....	....
	NHL Totals		**43**	**4**	**4**	**8**	**47**	**0**	**0**	**0**	**30**	**13.3**		**40**	**52.5**	**7:24**	**1**	**0**	**0**	**0**	**0**	**0**	**0**	**0**	**6:09**

Signed as a free agent by **Chicago**, September 25, 2006. Traded to **Anaheim** by **Chicago** with Sebastiien Caron and Matt Keith for P.A. Parenteau and Bruno St. Jacques, December 28, 2006. Traded to **Nashville** by **Anaheim** for Shane Endicott, January 26, 2007. Signed as a free agent by **Colorado**, July 3, 2008. Signed as a free agent by **Tampa Bay**, July 25, 2010.

DVORAK, Radek

(duh-VOHR-ak, RA-dehk) **FLA.**

Right wing. Shoots right. 6'2", 200 lbs. Born, Tabor, Czech., March 9, 1977. Florida's 1st choice, 10th overall, in 1995 Entry Draft.

			Regular Season														Playoffs								
Season	Club	League	GP	G	A	Pts	PIM	PP	SH	GW	S	%	+/-	TF	F%	Min	GP	G	A	Pts	PIM	PP	SH	GW	Min
1992-93	C. Budejovice Jr.	Czech-Jr.	35	44	46	90	....	....	....	....	....	....	....	....	....	....	....	....	....	....	....	....	....	....	....
1993-94	C. Budejovice Jr.	CzRep-Jr.	20	17	18	35	....	....	....	....	....	....	....	....	....	....	....	....	....	....	....	....	....	....	....
	C. Budejovice	CzRep	8	0	0	0	0	....	....	....	....	....	....	....	....	....	....	....	....	....	....	....	....	....	....
1994-95	C. Budejovice	CzRep	10	3	5	8	2	....	....	....	....	....	....	....	....	....	9	5	1	6					
1995-96	**Florida**	**NHL**	**77**	**13**	**14**	**27**	**20**	**0**	**0**	**4**	**126**	**10.3**	**5**	....	....	....	**16**	**1**	**3**	**4**	**0**	**0**	**0**	**0**	....
1996-97	**Florida**	**NHL**	**78**	**18**	**21**	**39**	**30**	**2**	**0**	**1**	**139**	**12.9**	**–2**	....	....	....	**3**	**0**	**0**	**0**	**0**	**0**	**0**	**0**	....
1997-98	**Florida**	**NHL**	**64**	**12**	**24**	**36**	**33**	**2**	**3**	**0**	**112**	**10.7**	**–1**	....	....	....	....	....	....	....	....	....	....	....	....
1998-99	**Florida**	**NHL**	**82**	**19**	**24**	**43**	**29**	**0**	**4**	**0**	**182**	**10.4**	**7**	**98**	**46.9**	**16:13**	....	....	....	....	....	....	....	....	....
99-2000	**Florida**	**NHL**	**35**	**7**	**10**	**17**	**6**	**0**	**0**	**1**	**67**	**10.4**	**5**	**16**	**37.5**	**15:25**	....	....	....	....	....	....	....	....	....
	NY Rangers	**NHL**	**46**	**11**	**22**	**33**	**10**	**0**	**1**	**0**	**90**	**12.2**	**0**	**34**	**35.3**	**18:24**	....	....	....	....	....	....	....	....	....
2000-01	**NY Rangers**	**NHL**	**82**	**31**	**36**	**67**	**20**	**2**	**1**	**3**	**230**	**13.5**	**9**	**20**	**30.0**	**19:04**	....	....	....	....	....	....	....	....	....
2001-02	**NY Rangers**	**NHL**	**65**	**17**	**20**	**37**	**14**	**3**	**3**	**1**	**210**	**8.1**	**–20**	**5**	**0.0**	**19:44**	....	....	....	....	....	....	....	....	....
	Czech Republic	Olympics	4	0	0	0	0	....	....	....	....	....	....	....	....	....	....	....	....	....	....	....	....	....	....
2002-03	**NY Rangers**	**NHL**	**63**	**6**	**21**	**27**	**16**	**2**	**0**	**0**	**134**	**4.5**	**–3**	**9**	**44.4**	**15:42**	....	....	....	....	....	....	....	....	....
	Edmonton	**NHL**	**12**	**4**	**4**	**8**	**14**	**1**	**0**	**0**	**32**	**12.5**	**–3**	**1**	**0.0**	**16:07**	**4**	**1**	**0**	**1**	**0**	**0**	**0**	**1**	**15:05**
2003-04	**Edmonton**	**NHL**	**78**	**15**	**35**	**50**	**26**	**6**	**0**	**0**	**188**	**8.0**	**18**	**24**	**29.2**	**16:56**	....	....	....	....	....	....	....	....	....
2004-05	C. Budejovice	CzRep-2	32	23	35	58	18	....	....	....	....	....	....	....	....	....	16	5	13	18	20	....	....	....	....
2005-06	**Edmonton**	**NHL**	**64**	**8**	**20**	**28**	**26**	**2**	**0**	**2**	**131**	**6.1**	**–2**	**14**	**28.6**	**16:34**	**16**	**0**	**2**	**2**	**4**	**0**	**0**	**0**	**13:29**
2006-07	**St. Louis**	**NHL**	**82**	**10**	**27**	**37**	**48**	**1**	**1**	**1**	**139**	**7.2**	**–6**	**26**	**38.5**	**15:38**	....	....	....	....	....	....	....	....	....
2007-08	**Florida**	**NHL**	**67**	**8**	**9**	**17**	**16**	**0**	**1**	**1**	**146**	**5.5**	**–1**	**12**	**16.7**	**15:07**	....	....	....	....	....	....	....	....	....
2008-09	**Florida**	**NHL**	**81**	**15**	**21**	**36**	**42**	**0**	**4**	**3**	**136**	**11.0**	**0**	**17**	**35.3**	**16:26**	....	....	....	....	....	....	....	....	....
2009-10	**Florida**	**NHL**	**76**	**14**	**18**	**32**	**20**	**1**	**3**	**1**	**140**	**10.0**	**–7**	**17**	**17.7**	**17:26**	....	....	....	....	....	....	....	....	....
	NHL Totals		**1052**	**208**	**326**	**534**	**370**	**27**	**22**	**18**	**2202**	**9.4**		**293**	**36.2**	**16:54**	**39**	**2**	**5**	**7**	**4**	**0**	**0**	**1**	**13:48**

Traded to **San Jose** by **Florida** for Mike Vernon and San Jose's 3rd round choice (Sean O'Connor) in 2000 Entry Draft, December 30, 1999. Traded to **NY Rangers** by **San Jose** for Todd Harvey and NY Rangers' 4th round choice (Dimitri Patzold) in 2001 Entry Draft, December 30, 1999. Traded to **Edmonton** by **NY Rangers** with Cory Cross for Anson Carter and Ales Pisa, March 11, 2003. Signed as a free agent by **Ceske Budejovice** (CzRep-2), September 15, 2004. Signed as a free agent by **St. Louis**, September 14, 2006. Signed as a free agent by **Florida**, July 1, 2007.

DWYER, Patrick

(DWIGH-uhr, PAT-rihk) **CAR.**

Right wing. Shoots right. 5'11", 175 lbs. Born, Spokane, WA, June 22, 1983. Atlanta's 3rd choice, 116th overall, in 2002 Entry Draft.

			Regular Season														Playoffs								
Season	Club	League	GP	G	A	Pts	PIM	PP	SH	GW	S	%	+/-	TF	F%	Min	GP	G	A	Pts	PIM	PP	SH	GW	Min
2000-01	Great Falls	NWJHL	40	33	57	90	106	....	....	....	....	....	....	....	....	....	12	10	12	22	....	....	....	....	....
2001-02	Western Mich.	CCHA	38	17	17	34	26	....	....	....	....	....	....	....	....	....	....	....	....	....	....	....	....	....	....
2002-03	Western Mich.	CCHA	33	9	10	19	20	....	....	....	....	....	....	....	....	....	....	....	....	....	....	....	....	....	....
2003-04	Western Mich.	CCHA	35	13	13	26	22	....	....	....	....	....	....	....	....	....	....	....	....	....	....	....	....	....	....
2004-05	Western Mich.	CCHA	36	6	16	22	56	....	....	....	....	....	....	....	....	....	....	....	....	....	....	....	....	....	....
2005-06	Chicago Wolves	AHL	73	16	29	45	49	....	....	....	....	....	....	....	....	....	....	....	....	....	....	....	....	....	....
2006-07	Albany River Rats	AHL	79	16	25	41	39	....	....	....	....	....	....	....	....	....	5	0	1	1	5	....	....	....	....
2007-08	Albany River Rats	AHL	59	13	12	25	29	....	....	....	....	....	....	....	....	....	7	0	2	2	0	....	....	....	....
2008-09	**Carolina**	**NHL**	**13**	**1**	**0**	**1**	**0**	**0**	**0**	**0**	**9**	**11.1**	**–2**	**12**	**41.7**	**8:34**	**2**	**0**	**1**	**1**	**0**	**0**	**0**	**0**	**4:48**
	Albany River Rats	AHL	62	24	16	40	29	....	....	....	....	....	....	....	....	....	....	....	....	....	....	....	....	....	....
2009-10	**Carolina**	**NHL**	**58**	**7**	**5**	**12**	**6**	**0**	**0**	**2**	**80**	**8.8**	**–3**	**224**	**34.8**	**12:30**	....	....	....	....	....	....	....	....	....
	NHL Totals		**71**	**8**	**5**	**13**	**6**	**0**	**0**	**2**	**89**	**9.0**		**236**	**35.2**	**11:47**	**2**	**0**	**1**	**1**	**0**	**0**	**0**	**0**	**4:48**

CCHA All-Rookie Team (2002) • CCHA Rookie of the Year (2002)

Signed as a free agent by **Carolina**, July 7, 2006.

EAGER, Ben

(EE-guhr, BEHN) **ATL.**

Left wing. Shoots left. 6'2", 230 lbs. Born, Ottawa, Ont., January 22, 1984. Phoenix's 2nd choice, 23rd overall, in 2002 Entry Draft.

			Regular Season														Playoffs								
Season	Club	League	GP	G	A	Pts	PIM	PP	SH	GW	S	%	+/-	TF	F%	Min	GP	G	A	Pts	PIM	PP	SH	GW	Min
99-2000	Ott. Jr. Senators	CJHL	50	8	11	19	119	....	....	....	....	....	....	....	....	....	....	....	....	....	....	....	....	....	....
2000-01	Oshawa Generals	OHL	61	4	6	10	120	....	....	....	....	....	....	....	....	....	....	....	....	....	....	....	....	....	....
2001-02	Oshawa Generals	OHL	63	14	23	37	255	....	....	....	....	....	....	....	....	....	5	0	1	1	13	....	....	....	....
2002-03	Oshawa Generals	OHL	58	16	24	40	216	....	....	....	....	....	....	....	....	....	8	0	4	4	8	....	....	....	....
2003-04	Oshawa Generals	OHL	61	25	27	52	204	....	....	....	....	....	....	....	....	....	7	2	3	5	31	....	....	....	....
	Philadelphia	AHL	5	0	0	0	0	....	....	....	....	....	....	....	....	....	3	0	1	1	8	....	....	....	....
2004-05	Philadelphia	AHL	66	7	10	17	232	....	....	....	....	....	....	....	....	....	16	1	1	2	71	....	....	....	....
2005-06	**Philadelphia**	**NHL**	**25**	**3**	**5**	**8**	**18**	**0**	**0**	**0**	**21**	**14.3**	**0**	**0**	**0.0**	**7:24**	**2**	**0**	**0**	**0**	**26**	**0**	**0**	**0**	**7:06**
	Philadelphia	AHL	49	6	12	18	256	....	....	....	....	....	....	....	....	....	....	....	....	....	....	....	....	....	....
2006-07	**Philadelphia**	**NHL**	**63**	**6**	**5**	**11**	***233**	**0**	**0**	**0**	**48**	**12.5**	**–13**	**1**	**100.0**	**8:14**	....	....	....	....	....	....	....	....	....
	Philadelphia	AHL	3	0	0	0	21	....	....	....	....	....	....	....	....	....	....	....	....	....	....	....	....	....	....
2007-08	**Philadelphia**	**NHL**	**23**	**0**	**0**	**0**	**62**	**0**	**0**	**0**	**11**	**0.0**	**–8**	**5**	**20.0**	**5:29**	....	....	....	....	....	....	....	....	....
	Chicago	**NHL**	**9**	**0**	**2**	**2**	**27**	**0**	**0**	**0**	**5**	**0.0**	**–1**	**0**	**0.0**	**6:37**	....	....	....	....	....	....	....	....	....
2008-09	**Chicago**	**NHL**	**75**	**11**	**4**	**15**	**161**	**0**	**0**	**0**	**80**	**13.8**	**1**	**0**	**0.0**	**8:31**	**17**	**1**	**1**	**2**	***61**	**0**	**0**	**1**	**8:32**
2009-10 ♦	**Chicago**	**NHL**	**60**	**7**	**9**	**16**	**120**	**0**	**0**	**2**	**68**	**10.3**	**9**	**1**	**0.0**	**8:20**	**18**	**1**	**2**	**3**	**20**	**0**	**0**	**1**	**6:02**
	NHL Totals		**255**	**27**	**25**	**52**	**621**	**0**	**0**	**2**	**233**	**11.6**		**7**	**28.6**	**7:57**	**37**	**2**	**3**	**5**	**107**	**0**	**0**	**2**	**7:14**

Traded to **Philadelphia** by **Phoenix** with Sean Burke and Branko Radivojevic for Mike Comrie, February 9, 2004. Traded to **Chicago** by **Philadelphia** for Jim Vandermeer, December 18, 2007. Traded to **Atlanta** by **Chicago** with Brent Sopel, Dustin Byfuglien and Akim Aliu for Marty Reasoner, Joey Crabb, Jeremy Morin and New Jersey's 1st (previously acquired, Chicago selected Kevin Hayes) and 2nd (previously acquired, Chicago selected Justin Holl) round choices in 2010 Entry Draft, June 24, 2010.

EARL, Robbie
(UHRL, RAW-bee) **MIN.**

Left wing. Shoots left. 5'11", 197 lbs. Born, Chicago, IL, June 6, 1985. Toronto's 4th choice, 187th overall, in 2004 Entry Draft.

			Regular Season														Playoffs								
Season	Club	League	GP	G	A	Pts	PIM	PP	SH	GW	S	%	+/-	TF	F%	Min	GP	G	A	Pts	PIM	PP	SH	GW	Min
2000-01	L.A. Jr. Kings	Minor-CA	29	48	22	70	....	....	....	....	....	....	....	....	....	....	....	....	....	....	....	....	....	....	....
2001-02	USNTDP	U-17	15	8	9	17	....	....	....	....	....	....	....	....	....	....	....	....	....	....	....	....	....	....	....
	USNTDP	NAHL	43	14	7	21	43	....	....	....	....	....	....	....	....	....	....	....	....	....	....	....	....	....	....
2002-03	USNTDP	U-18	43	16	8	24	58	....	....	....	....	....	....	....	....	....	....	....	....	....	....	....	....	....	....
	USNTDP	NAHL	10	4	5	9	18	....	....	....	....	....	....	....	....	....	....	....	....	....	....	....	....	....	....
2003-04	U. of Wisconsin	WCHA	42	14	13	27	46	....	....	....	....	....	....	....	....	....	....	....	....	....	....	....	....	....	....
2004-05	U. of Wisconsin	WCHA	41	20	24	44	62	....	....	....	....	....	....	....	....	....	....	....	....	....	....	....	....	....	....
2005-06	U. of Wisconsin	WCHA	42	24	26	50	56	....	....	....	....	....	....	....	....	....	....	....	....	....	....	....	....	....	....
	Toronto Marlies	AHL	1	0	0	0	0	....	....	....	....	....	....	....	....	....	3	0	0	0	0	....	....	....	....
2006-07	Toronto Marlies	AHL	67	12	18	30	50	....	....	....	....	....	....	....	....	....	....	....	....	....	....	....	....	....	....
2007-08	**Toronto**	**NHL**	**9**	**0**	**1**	**1**	**0**	**0**	**0**	**0**	**9**	**0.0**	**-2**	**2**	**100.0**	**9:14**	....	....	....	....	....	....	....	....	....
	Toronto Marlies	AHL	66	14	33	47	56	....	....	....	....	....	....	....	....	....	....	....	....	....	....	....	....	....	....
2008-09	Toronto Marlies	AHL	36	2	8	10	28	....	....	....	....	....	....	....	....	....	....	....	....	....	....	....	....	....	....
	Houston Aeros	AHL	33	4	5	9	26	....	....	....	....	....	....	....	....	....	20	5	4	9	14	....	....	....	....
2009-10	**Minnesota**	**NHL**	**32**	**6**	**0**	**6**	**6**	**0**	**0**	**0**	**29**	**20.7**	**1**	**2**	**0.0**	**8:56**	....	....	....	....	....	....	....	....	....
	Houston Aeros	AHL	41	10	8	18	16	....	....	....	....	....	....	....	....	....	....	....	....	....	....	....	....	....	....
	NHL Totals		**41**	**6**	**1**	**7**	**6**	**0**	**0**	**0**	**38**	**15.8**		**4**	**50.0**	**9:00**	....	....	....	....	....	....	....	....	....

WCHA All-Rookie Team (2004) • WCHA Second All-Star Team (2005) • NCAA Championship All-Tournament Team (2006) • NCAA Championship Tournament MVP (2006)

Traded to **Minnesota** by **Toronto** for Ryan Hamilton, January 21, 2009.

EATON, Mark
(EE-tohn, MAHRK) **NYI**

Defense. Shoots left. 6'2", 204 lbs. Born, Wilmington, DE, May 6, 1977.

Season	Club	League	GP	G	A	Pts	PIM	PP	SH	GW	S	%	+/-	TF	F%	Min	GP	G	A	Pts	PIM	PP	SH	GW	Min
1995-96	Waterloo	USHL	50	4	21	25	....	....	....	....	....	....	....	....	....	....	....	....	....	....	....	....	....	....	....
1996-97	Waterloo	USHL	50	6	32	38	62	....	....	....	....	....	....	....	....	....	....	....	....	....	....	....	....	....	....
1997-98	U. of Notre Dame	CCHA	41	12	17	29	32	....	....	....	....	....	....	....	....	....	....	....	....	....	....	....	....	....	....
1998-99	Philadelphia	AHL	74	9	27	36	38	....	....	....	....	....	....	....	....	....	16	4	8	12	0	....	....	....	....
99-2000	**Philadelphia**	**NHL**	**27**	**1**	**1**	**2**	**8**	**0**	**0**	**1**	**25**	**4.0**	**1**	**0**	**0.0**	**18:17**	**7**	**0**	**0**	**0**	**0**	**0**	**0**	**0**	**13:36**
	Philadelphia	AHL	47	9	17	26	6	....	....	....	....	....	....	....	....	....	....	....	....	....	....	....	....	....	....
2000-01	**Nashville**	**NHL**	**34**	**3**	**8**	**11**	**14**	**1**	**0**	**1**	**32**	**9.4**	**7**	**0**	**0.0**	**17:13**	....	....	....	....	....	....	....	....	....
	Milwaukee	IHL	34	3	12	15	27	....	....	....	....	....	....	....	....	....	....	....	....	....	....	....	....	....	....
2001-02	**Nashville**	**NHL**	**58**	**3**	**5**	**8**	**24**	**0**	**0**	**0**	**52**	**5.8**	**-12**	**0**	**0.0**	**17:12**	....	....	....	....	....	....	....	....	....
2002-03	**Nashville**	**NHL**	**50**	**2**	**7**	**9**	**22**	**0**	**0**	**0**	**52**	**3.8**	**1**	**0**	**0.0**	**15:45**	....	....	....	....	....	....	....	....	....
	Milwaukee	AHL	3	1	0	1	2	....	....	....	....	....	....	....	....	....	....	....	....	....	....	....	....	....	....
2003-04	**Nashville**	**NHL**	**75**	**4**	**9**	**13**	**26**	**0**	**0**	**1**	**82**	**4.9**	**16**	**0**	**0.0**	**20:56**	**6**	**0**	**0**	**0**	**2**	**0**	**0**	**0**	**19:51**
2004-05	Grand Rapids	AHL	29	3	3	6	21	....	....	....	....	....	....	....	....	....	....	....	....	....	....	....	....	....	....
2005-06	**Nashville**	**NHL**	**69**	**3**	**1**	**4**	**44**	**0**	**0**	**0**	**28**	**10.7**	**-2**	**0**	**0.0**	**19:43**	**5**	**0**	**0**	**0**	**8**	**0**	**0**	**0**	**17:49**
2006-07	**Pittsburgh**	**NHL**	**35**	**0**	**3**	**3**	**16**	**0**	**0**	**0**	**22**	**0.0**	**-6**	**0**	**0.0**	**19:12**	**5**	**0**	**0**	**0**	**0**	**0**	**0**	**0**	**18:31**
2007-08	**Pittsburgh**	**NHL**	**36**	**0**	**3**	**3**	**4**	**0**	**0**	**0**	**28**	**0.0**	**6**	**0**	**0.0**	**19:40**	....	....	....	....	....	....	....	....	....
2008-09•	**Pittsburgh**	**NHL**	**68**	**4**	**5**	**9**	**36**	**1**	**0**	**0**	**34**	**11.8**	**3**	**1**	**100.0**	**17:46**	**24**	**4**	**3**	**7**	**10**	**1**	**0**	**0**	**18:07**
2009-10	**Pittsburgh**	**NHL**	**79**	**3**	**13**	**16**	**26**	**0**	**0**	**1**	**65**	**4.6**	**5**	**0**	**0.0**	**19:45**	**13**	**0**	**3**	**3**	**4**	**0**	**0**	**0**	**20:43**
	NHL Totals		**531**	**23**	**55**	**78**	**220**	**2**	**0**	**4**	**420**	**5.5**		**1**	**100.0**	**18:44**	**60**	**4**	**6**	**10**	**24**	**1**	**0**	**0**	**18:20**

USHL Second All-Star Team (1997) • Curt Hammer Award (USHL – Most Gentlemanly Player) (1997) • CCHA Rookie of the Year (1998)

Signed as a free agent by **Philadelphia**, August 4, 1998. Traded to **Nashville** by **Philadelphia** for Detroit's 3rd round choice (previously acquired, Philadelphia selected Patrick Sharp) in 2001 Entry Draft, September 29, 2000. Signed as a free agent by **Grand Rapids** (AHL), February 16, 2005. Signed as a free agent by **Pittsburgh**, July 3, 2006. Signed as a free agent by **NY Islanders**, July 2, 2010.

EAVES, Patrick
(EEVZ, PAT-rihk) **DET.**

Right wing. Shoots right. 6', 191 lbs. Born, Calgary, Alta., May 1, 1984. Ottawa's 1st choice, 29th overall, in 2003 Entry Draft.

Season	Club	League	GP	G	A	Pts	PIM	PP	SH	GW	S	%	+/-	TF	F%	Min	GP	G	A	Pts	PIM	PP	SH	GW	Min
99-2000	Shat.-St. Mary's	High-MN	50	23	24	47	....	....	....	....	....	....	....	....	....	....	....	....	....	....	....	....	....	....	....
2000-01	USNTDP	U-17	13	7	8	15	3	....	....	....	....	....	....	....	....	....	....	....	....	....	....	....	....	....	....
	USNTDP	NAHL	34	12	11	23	75	....	....	....	....	....	....	....	....	....	....	....	....	....	....	....	....	....	....
2001-02	USNTDP	U-18	32	19	21	40	87	....	....	....	....	....	....	....	....	....	....	....	....	....	....	....	....	....	....
	USNTDP	USHL	9	1	4	5	18	....	....	....	....	....	....	....	....	....	....	....	....	....	....	....	....	....	....
	USNTDP	NAHL	8	5	3	8	37	....	....	....	....	....	....	....	....	....	....	....	....	....	....	....	....	....	....
2002-03	Boston College	H-East	14	10	8	18	61	....	....	....	....	....	....	....	....	....	....	....	....	....	....	....	....	....	....
2003-04	Boston College	H-East	34	18	23	41	66	....	....	....	....	....	....	....	....	....	....	....	....	....	....	....	....	....	....
2004-05	Boston College	H-East	36	19	29	48	36	....	....	....	....	....	....	....	....	....	....	....	....	....	....	....	....	....	....
2005-06	**Ottawa**	**NHL**	**58**	**20**	**9**	**29**	**22**	**5**	**1**	**4**	**100**	**20.0**	**7**	**14**	**21.4**	**12:29**	**10**	**1**	**0**	**1**	**10**	**0**	**0**	**0**	**11:40**
	Binghamton	AHL	18	5	8	13	10	....	....	....	....	....	....	....	....	....	....	....	....	....	....	....	....	....	....
2006-07	**Ottawa**	**NHL**	**73**	**14**	**18**	**32**	**36**	**3**	**1**	**1**	**130**	**10.8**	**1**	**9**	**11.1**	**12:13**	**7**	**0**	**2**	**2**	**2**	**0**	**0**	**0**	**7:23**
2007-08	**Ottawa**	**NHL**	**26**	**4**	**6**	**10**	**6**	**1**	**0**	**1**	**59**	**6.8**	**0**	**1**	**100.0**	**12:44**	....	....	....	....	....	....	....	....	....
	Carolina	**NHL**	**11**	**1**	**4**	**5**	**4**	**1**	**0**	**0**	**22**	**4.5**	**-2**	**2**	**0.0**	**12:51**	....	....	....	....	....	....	....	....	....
2008-09	**Carolina**	**NHL**	**74**	**6**	**8**	**14**	**31**	**1**	**1**	**1**	**115**	**5.2**	**7**	**12**	**41.7**	**11:15**	**18**	**1**	**2**	**3**	**13**	**0**	**0**	**0**	**9:29**
2009-10	**Detroit**	**NHL**	**65**	**12**	**10**	**22**	**26**	**0**	**1**	**1**	**120**	**10.0**	**0**	**14**	**28.6**	**13:26**	**8**	**0**	**0**	**0**	**2**	**0**	**0**	**0**	**11:58**
	NHL Totals		**307**	**57**	**55**	**112**	**125**	**11**	**4**	**8**	**546**	**10.4**		**52**	**26.9**	**12:22**	**43**	**2**	**4**	**6**	**27**	**0**	**0**	**0**	**10:07**

Hockey East Second All-Star Team (2004) • NCAA East Second All-American Team (2004) • Hockey East First All-Star Team (2005) • NCAA East First All-American Team (2005)

• Missed majority of 2002-03 season recovering from neck injury suffered in game vs. University of Maine (Hockey East), December 7, 2002. Traded to **Carolina** by **Ottawa** with Joe Corvo for Cory Stillman and Mike Commodore, February 11, 2008. • Missed majority of 2007-08 season recovering from shoulder injury suffered in game at Buffalo, November 21, 2007. Traded to **Boston** by **Carolina** with Carolina's 4th round choice (Craig Cunningham) in 2010 Entry Draft for Aaron Ward, July 24, 2009. Signed as a free agent by **Detroit**, August 4, 2009.

EBBETT, Andrew
(EH-beht, AN-droo) **PHX.**

Center. Shoots left. 5'9", 174 lbs. Born, Calgary, Alta., January 2, 1983.

Season	Club	League	GP	G	A	Pts	PIM	PP	SH	GW	S	%	+/-	TF	F%	Min	GP	G	A	Pts	PIM	PP	SH	GW	Min
2002-03	U. of Michigan	CCHA	43	9	18	27	22	....	....	....	....	....	....	....	....	....	....	....	....	....	....	....	....	....	....
2003-04	U. of Michigan	CCHA	43	9	28	37	56	....	....	....	....	....	....	....	....	....	....	....	....	....	....	....	....	....	....
2004-05	U. of Michigan	CCHA	40	6	31	37	28	....	....	....	....	....	....	....	....	....	....	....	....	....	....	....	....	....	....
2005-06	U. of Michigan	CCHA	41	14	28	42	25	....	....	....	....	....	....	....	....	....	....	....	....	....	....	....	....	....	....
2006-07	Binghamton	AHL	71	26	39	65	44	....	....	....	....	....	....	....	....	....	....	....	....	....	....	....	....	....	....
2007-08	**Anaheim**	**NHL**	**3**	**0**	**0**	**0**	**2**	**0**	**0**	**0**	**3**	**0.0**	**3**	**29**	**58.6**	**13:18**	....	....	....	....	....	....	....	....	....
	Portland Pirates	AHL	74	18	54	72	66	....	....	....	....	....	....	....	....	....	18	6	11	17	4	....	....	....	....
2008-09	**Anaheim**	**NHL**	**48**	**8**	**24**	**32**	**24**	**6**	**0**	**0**	**100**	**8.0**	**8**	**455**	**48.6**	**13:52**	**13**	**1**	**2**	**3**	**8**	**0**	**0**	**0**	**13:11**
	Iowa Chops	AHL	28	10	19	29	6	....	....	....	....	....	....	....	....	....	....	....	....	....	....	....	....	....	....
2009-10	**Anaheim**	**NHL**	**2**	**0**	**0**	**0**	**0**	**0**	**0**	**0**	**1**	**0.0**	**-1**	**17**	**35.3**	**12:55**	....	....	....	....	....	....	....	....	....
	Chicago	**NHL**	**10**	**1**	**0**	**1**	**2**	**0**	**0**	**0**	**14**	**7.1**	**1**	**72**	**50.0**	**10:43**	....	....	....	....	....	....	....	....	....
	Minnesota	**NHL**	**49**	**8**	**6**	**14**	**6**	**2**	**0**	**2**	**57**	**14.0**	**-8**	**464**	**50.0**	**13:06**	....	....	....	....	....	....	....	....	....
	NHL Totals		**112**	**17**	**30**	**47**	**34**	**8**	**0**	**2**	**175**	**9.7**		**1037**	**49.4**	**13:13**	**13**	**1**	**2**	**3**	**8**	**0**	**0**	**0**	**13:11**

Signed as a free agent by **Anaheim**, May 16, 2007. Claimed on waivers by **Chicago** from **Anaheim**, October 17, 2009. Claimed on waivers by **Minnesota** from **Chicago**, November 21, 2009. Signed as a free agent by **Phoenix**, July 2, 2010.

ECKFORD, Tyler
(EHK-fuhrd, TIGH-luhr) **N.J.**

Defense. Shoots left. 6'1", 205 lbs. Born, Vancouver, B.C., September 8, 1985. New Jersey's 5th choice, 217th overall, in 2004 Entry Draft.

Season	Club	League	GP	G	A	Pts	PIM	PP	SH	GW	S	%	+/-	TF	F%	Min	GP	G	A	Pts	PIM	PP	SH	GW	Min
2003-04	South Surrey	BCHL	58	7	30	37	101	....	....	....	....	....	....	....	....	....	13	2	8	10	34	....	....	....	....
2004-05	South Surrey	BCHL	60	22	43	65	93	....	....	....	....	....	....	....	....	....	25	4	15	19	46	....	....	....	....
2005-06	Alaska	CCHA	38	3	15	18	43	....	....	....	....	....	....	....	....	....	....	....	....	....	....	....	....	....	....
2006-07	Alaska	CCHA	39	5	17	22	54	....	....	....	....	....	....	....	....	....	....	....	....	....	....	....	....	....	....
2007-08	Alaska	CCHA	35	8	23	31	55	....	....	....	....	....	....	....	....	....	....	....	....	....	....	....	....	....	....
2008-09	Lowell Devils	AHL	72	2	25	27	59	....	....	....	....	....	....	....	....	....	....	....	....	....	....	....	....	....	....
2009-10	**New Jersey**	**NHL**	**3**	**0**	**1**	**1**	**4**	**0**	**0**	**0**	**1**	**0.0**	**0**	**0**	**0.0**	**7:23**	....	....	....	....	....	....	....	....	....
	Lowell Devils	AHL	61	8	23	31	26	....	....	....	....	....	....	....	....	....	5	1	0	1	2	....	....	....	....
	NHL Totals		**3**	**0**	**1**	**1**	**4**	**0**	**0**	**0**	**1**	**0.0**		**0**	**0.0**	**7:23**	....	....	....	....	....	....	....	....	....

CCHA All-Rookie Team (2006) • CCHA First All-Star Team (2008) • NCAA West First All-American Team (2008)

			Regular Season															Playoffs							
Season	Club	League	GP	G	A	Pts	PIM	PP	SH	GW	S	%	+/-	TF	F%	Min	GP	G	A	Pts	PIM	PP	SH	GW	Min

EDLER, Alexander   (EHD-luhr, al-EHX-AN-duhr)   VAN.

Defense. Shoots left. 6'3", 215 lbs.   Born, Ostersund, Sweden, April 21, 1986. Vancouver's 2nd choice, 91st overall, in 2004 Entry Draft.

Season	Club	League	GP	G	A	Pts	PIM	PP	SH	GW	S	%	+/-	TF	F%	Min	GP	G	A	Pts	PIM	PP	SH	GW	Min
2001-02	Jamtland	Exhib.	8	0	1	1	2	....	....	....	....	....	....	....	....	....	....	....	....	....	....	....	....	....	....
2002-03	Jamtland	Exhib.	8	2	1	3	0	....	....	....	....	....	....	....	....	....	....	....	....	....	....	....	....	....	....
2003-04	Jamtland Jr.	Swe-Jr.	6	0	3	3	6	....	....	....	....	....	....	....	....	....	....	....	....	....	....	....	....	....	....
	Jamtland	Sweden-3	24	3	6	9	20	....	....	....	....	....	....	....	....	....	....	....	....	....	....	....	....	....	....
2004-05	MODO Jr.	Swe-Jr.	33	8	15	23	40	....	....	....	....	....	....	....	....	....	....	5	1	0	1	6	....	....	....	....
2005-06	Kelowna Rockets	WHL	62	13	40	53	44	....	....	....	....	....	....	....	....	....	....	12	3	5	8	12	....	....	....	....
2006-07	**Vancouver**	**NHL**	22	1	2	3	6	0	0	0	10	10.0	3	0	0.0	11:27	3	0	0	0	2	0	0	0	11:51
	Manitoba Moose	AHL	49	5	21	26	28	....	....	....	....	....	....	....	....	....	8	0	0	0	2	....	....	....	....
2007-08	**Vancouver**	**NHL**	75	8	12	20	42	4	0	0	124	6.5	6	1	100.0	21:20	....	....	....	....	....	....	....	....	....
	Manitoba Moose	AHL	2	0	1	1	0	....	....	....	....	....	....	....	....	....	....	....	....	....	....	....	....	....	....
2008-09	**Vancouver**	**NHL**	80	10	27	37	54	5	0	1	145	6.9	11	1	100.0	21:08	10	1	7	8	6	1	0	0	22:09
2009-10	**Vancouver**	**NHL**	76	5	37	42	40	2	0	0	161	3.1	0	2	0.0	22:39	12	2	4	6	10	1	0	0	23:07
	NHL Totals		253	24	78	102	142	11	0	1	440	5.5		4	50.0	20:48	25	3	11	14	18	2	0	0	21:22

EHRHOFF, Christian   (AIR-hawf, KRIHS-tyehn)   VAN.

Defense. Shoots left. 6'2", 203 lbs.   Born, Moers, West Germany, July 6, 1982. San Jose's 2nd choice, 106th overall, in 2001 Entry Draft.

Season	Club	League	GP	G	A	Pts	PIM	PP	SH	GW	S	%	+/-	TF	F%	Min	GP	G	A	Pts	PIM	PP	SH	GW	Min
1998-99	Krefelder EV Jr.	Ger-Jr.	22	10	14	24	46	....	....	....	....	....	....	....	....	....	....	....	....	....	....	....	....	....	....
99-2000	EV Duisburg	German-3	41	3	12	15	50	....	....	....	....	....	....	....	....	....	3	0	0	0	0	....	....	....	....
	Krefeld Pinguine	Germany	9	1	0	1	6	....	....	....	....	....	....	....	....	....	....	....	....	....	....	....	....	....	....
2000-01	EV Duisburg	German-3	6	1	2	3	12	....	....	....	....	....	....	....	....	....	3	0	0	0	0	....	....	....	....
	Krefeld Pinguine	Germany	58	3	11	14	73	....	....	....	....	....	....	....	....	....	....	....	....	....	....	....	....	....	....
2001-02	Krefeld Pinguine	Germany	46	7	17	24	81	....	....	....	....	....	....	....	....	....	14	3	6	9	24	....	....	....	....
	Germany	Olympics	7	0	0	0	8	....	....	....	....	....	....	....	....	....	....	....	....	....	....	....	....	....	....
2002-03	Krefeld Pinguine	Germany	48	10	17	27	54	....	....	....	....	....	....	....	....	....	14	3	6	9	24	....	....	....	....
2003-04	**San Jose**	**NHL**	41	1	11	12	14	0	0	1	58	1.7	4	0	0.0	15:23	....	....	....	....	....	....	....	....	....
	Cleveland Barons	AHL	27	4	10	14	43	....	....	....	....	....	....	....	....	....	9	2	6	8	11	....	....	....	....
2004-05	Cleveland Barons	AHL	79	12	23	35	103	....	....	....	....	....	....	....	....	....	....	....	....	....	....	....	....	....	....
2005-06	**San Jose**	**NHL**	64	5	18	23	32	2	0	2	124	4.0	10	0	0.0	17:48	11	2	6	8	18	1	0	1	19:47
	Germany	Olympics	5	1	1	2	4	....	....	....	....	....	....	....	....	....	....	....	....	....	....	....	....	....	....
2006-07	**San Jose**	**NHL**	82	10	23	33	63	6	0	2	164	6.1	8	1	0.0	18:34	11	0	4	4	6	0	0	0	17:47
2007-08	**San Jose**	**NHL**	77	1	21	22	72	1	0	0	97	1.0	9	0	0.0	21:44	10	0	5	5	14	0	0	0	23:04
2008-09	**San Jose**	**NHL**	77	8	34	42	63	5	0	2	165	4.8	-12	0	0.0	21:14	6	0	0	0	2	0	0	0	24:47
2009-10	**Vancouver**	**NHL**	80	14	30	44	42	6	0	3	181	7.7	36	0	0.0	22:47	12	3	4	7	8	1	0	0	24:09
	Germany	Olympics	4	0	0	0	4	....	....	....	....	....	....	....	....	....	....	....	....	....	....	....	....	....	....
	NHL Totals		421	39	137	176	286	20	0	11	789	4.9		0	0.0	20:01	50	5	17	22	48	2	0	1	21:39

Traded to **Vancouver** by **San Jose** with Brad Lukowich for Patrick White and Daniel Rahimi, August 28, 2009.

ELIAS, Patrik   (ehl-EE-ahsh, PAT-rihk)   N.J.

Left wing. Shoots left. 6'1", 195 lbs.   Born, Trebic, Czech., April 13, 1976. New Jersey's 2nd choice, 51st overall, in 1994 Entry Draft.

Season	Club	League	GP	G	A	Pts	PIM	PP	SH	GW	S	%	+/-	TF	F%	Min	GP	G	A	Pts	PIM	PP	SH	GW	Min
1992-93	Poldi Kladno	Czech	2	0	0	0	....	....	....	....	....	....	....	....	....	....	....	....	....	....	....	....	....	....	....	....
1993-94	HC Kladno	CzRep	15	1	2	3	....	....	....	....	....	....	....	....	....	....	....	11	2	2	4	....	....	....	....	....
1994-95	HC Kladno	CzRep	28	4	3	7	37	....	....	....	....	....	....	....	....	....	7	1	2	3	12	....	....	....	....
1995-96	**New Jersey**	**NHL**	1	0	0	0	0	0	0	0	2	0.0	-1	....	....	....	....	....	....	....	....	....	....	....	....
	Albany River Rats	AHL	74	27	36	63	83	....	....	....	....	....	....	....	....	....	4	1	1	2	2	....	....	....	....
1996-97	**New Jersey**	**NHL**	17	2	3	5	2	0	0	0	23	8.7	-4	....	....	....	8	2	3	5	4	1	0	0	....
	Albany River Rats	AHL	57	24	43	67	76	....	....	....	....	....	....	....	....	....	6	1	2	3	8	....	....	....	....
1997-98	**New Jersey**	**NHL**	74	18	19	37	28	5	0	6	147	12.2	18	....	....	....	4	0	1	1	0	0	0	0	....
	Albany River Rats	AHL	3	3	0	3	2	....	....	....	....	....	....	....	....	....	....	....	....	....	....	....	....	....	....
1998-99	**New Jersey**	**NHL**	74	17	33	50	34	3	0	2	157	10.8	19	99	38.4	15:50	7	0	5	5	6	0	0	0	18:07
99-2000	Trebic	CzRep-2	2	2	1	3	2	....	....	....	....	....	....	....	....	....	....	....	....	....	....	....	....	....	....
	Pardubice	CzRep	5	1	4	5	31	....	....	....	....	....	....	....	....	....	....	....	....	....	....	....	....	....	....
♦	**New Jersey**	**NHL**	72	35	37	72	58	9	0	9	183	19.1	16	134	45.5	17:28	23	7	*13	20	9	2	1	1	17:44
2000-01	**New Jersey**	**NHL**	82	40	56	96	51	8	3	6	220	18.2	*45	155	41.3	18:44	25	9	14	23	10	3	1	2	18:14
2001-02	**New Jersey**	**NHL**	75	29	32	61	36	8	1	8	199	14.6	4	128	45.3	18:57	6	2	4	6	2	0	0	0	20:33
	Czech Republic	Olympics	4	1	1	2	0	....	....	....	....	....	....	....	....	....	....	....	....	....	....	....	....	....	....
2002-03 ♦	**New Jersey**	**NHL**	81	28	29	57	22	6	0	4	255	11.0	17	427	43.8	18:05	24	5	8	13	26	2	0	2	17:14
2003-04	**New Jersey**	**NHL**	82	38	43	81	44	9	3	3	300	12.7	26	49	36.7	18:46	5	3	2	5	2	1	0	1	18:59
2004-05	Znojmo	CzRep	28	8	20	28	65	....	....	....	....	....	....	....	....	....	....	....	....	....	....	....	....	....	....
	Magnitogorsk	Russia	17	5	9	14	28	....	....	....	....	....	....	....	....	....	....	....	....	....	....	....	....	....	....
2005-06	**New Jersey**	**NHL**	38	16	29	45	20	6	0	3	142	11.3	11	10	20.0	18:34	9	6	10	16	4	4	0	0	18:43
	Czech Republic	Olympics	1	0	0	0	2	....	....	....	....	....	....	....	....	....	....	....	....	....	....	....	....	....	....
2006-07	**New Jersey**	**NHL**	75	21	48	69	38	8	0	5	267	7.9	1	18	38.9	18:37	10	1	9	10	4	1	0	0	19:13
2007-08	**New Jersey**	**NHL**	74	20	35	55	38	7	0	8	263	7.6	10	776	45.6	18:28	5	4	2	6	4	3	0	0	20:30
2008-09	**New Jersey**	**NHL**	77	31	47	78	32	12	2	6	247	12.6	18	87	29.9	18:34	7	1	2	3	2	0	0	0	17:53
2009-10	**New Jersey**	**NHL**	58	19	29	48	40	3	1	4	145	13.1	18	457	44.9	17:37	5	0	4	4	2	0	0	0	18:41
	Czech Republic	Olympics	5	2	2	4	2	....	....	....	....	....	....	....	....	....	....	....	....	....	....	....	....	....	....
	NHL Totals		880	314	440	754	443	84	10	70	2550	12.3		2340	43.6	18:10	138	40	77	117	79	19	2	6	18:17

NHL All-Rookie Team (1998) • NHL First All-Star Team (2001) • Bud Light Plus/Minus Award (2001) (tied with Joe Sakic)
Played in NHL All-Star Game (2000, 2002)
Signed as a free agent by **Znojmo** (CzRep), September 6, 2004. Signed as a free agent by **Magnitogorsk** (Russia), December 9, 2004. • Missed majority of 2005-06 season recovering from Hepatitis-A.

ELKINS, Corey   (EHL-kihns, KOH-ree)   L.A.

Left wing. Shoots left. 6'3", 216 lbs.   Born, West Bloomfield, MI, February 23, 1985.

Season	Club	League	GP	G	A	Pts	PIM	PP	SH	GW	S	%	+/-	TF	F%	Min	GP	G	A	Pts	PIM	PP	SH	GW	Min
2002-03	Det. Compuware	NAHL	49	8	11	19	37	....	....	....	....	....	....	....	....	....	....	....	....	....	....	....	....	....	....
2003-04	St. Louis	USHL	57	12	17	29	36	....	....	....	....	....	....	....	....	....	....	....	....	....	....	....	....	....	....
2004-05	Sioux City	USHL	58	19	23	42	27	....	....	....	....	....	....	....	....	....	13	4	1	5	8	....	....	....	....
2005-06	Ohio State	CCHA	9	0	0	0	0	....	....	....	....	....	....	....	....	....	....	....	....	....	....	....	....	....	....
2006-07	Ohio State	CCHA	26	7	7	14	10	....	....	....	....	....	....	....	....	....	....	....	....	....	....	....	....	....	....
2007-08	Ohio State	CCHA	25	2	3	5	12	....	....	....	....	....	....	....	....	....	....	....	....	....	....	....	....	....	....
2008-09	Ohio State	CCHA	42	18	23	41	18	....	....	....	....	....	....	....	....	....	....	....	....	....	....	....	....	....	....
2009-10	**Los Angeles**	**NHL**	3	1	0	1	0	0	0	0	5	20.0	-2	18	33.3	11:54	....	....	....	....	....	....	....	....	....
	Manchester	AHL	73	21	22	43	24	....	....	....	....	....	....	....	....	....	14	3	5	8	0	....	....	....	....
	NHL Totals		3	1	0	1	0	0	0	0	5	20.0		18	33.3	11:54	....	....	....	....	....	....	....	....	....

Signed as a free agent by **Los Angeles**, March 31, 2009.

ELLER, Lars   (EHL-uhr, LARZ)   MTL.

Center. Shoots left. 6'1", 198 lbs.   Born, Herlev, Denmark, May 8, 1989. St. Louis' 1st choice, 13th overall, in 2007 Entry Draft.

Season	Club	League	GP	G	A	Pts	PIM	PP	SH	GW	S	%	+/-	TF	F%	Min	GP	G	A	Pts	PIM	PP	SH	GW	Min
2004-05	Rodovre IK Jr.	Den-Jr.	28	21	26	47	20	....	....	....	....	....	....	....	....	....	....	....	....	....	....	....	....	....	....
	Rodovre	Denmark	1	3	1	4	0	....	....	....	....	....	....	....	....	....	2	0	0	0	0	....	....	....	....
2005-06	Frolunda U18	Swe-U18	8	2	4	6	10	....	....	....	....	....	....	....	....	....	2	0	0	0	0	....	....	....	....
	Frolunda Jr.	Swe-Jr.	36	7	7	14	6	....	....	....	....	....	....	....	....	....	6	3	2	5	8	....	....	....	....
2006-07	Frolunda U18	Swe-U18	3	1	4	5	6	....	....	....	....	....	....	....	....	....	8	4	5	9	24	....	....	....	....
	Frolunda Jr.	Swe-Jr.	39	18	37	55	58	....	....	....	....	....	....	....	....	....	....	....	....	....	....	....	....	....	....
2007-08	Boras HC	Sweden-2	19	2	6	8	8	....	....	....	....	....	....	....	....	....	7	5	6	11	14	....	....	....	....
	Frolunda Jr.	Swe-Jr.	9	4	4	8	10	....	....	....	....	....	....	....	....	....	7	0	1	1	2	....	....	....	....
	Frolunda	Sweden	14	0	2	2	4	....	....	....	....	....	....	....	....	....	10	3	1	4	12	....	....	....	....
2008-09	Frolunda	Sweden	48	12	17	29	28	....	....	....	....	....	....	....	....	....	....	....	....	....	....	....	....	....	....
2009-10	**St. Louis**	**NHL**	7	2	0	2	4	1	0	0	8	25.0	2	19	47.4	10:49	....	....	....	....	....	....	....	....	....
	Peoria Rivermen	AHL	70	18	39	57	84	....	....	....	....	....	....	....	....	....	....	....	....	....	....	....	....	....	....
	NHL Totals		7	2	0	2	4	1	0	0	8	25.0		19	47.4	10:49	....	....	....	....	....	....	....	....	....

Traded to **Montreal** by **St. Louis** with Ian Schultz for Jaroslav Halak, June 17, 2010.

			Regular Season														Playoffs								
Season	Club	League	GP	G	A	Pts	PIM	PP	SH	GW	S	%	+/-	TF	F%	Min	GP	G	A	Pts	PIM	PP	SH	GW	Min

ELLERBY, Keaton

(EHL-uhr-bee, KEE-tuhn) **FLA**

Defense. Shoots left. 6'4", 186 lbs. Born, Strathmore, Alta., November 5, 1988. Florida's 1st choice, 10th overall, in 2007 Entry Draft.

Season	Club	League	GP	G	A	Pts	PIM	PP	SH	GW	S	%	+/-	TF	F%	Min	GP	G	A	Pts	PIM	PP	SH	GW	Min
2003-04	Okotoks Oilers	AMHA	30	7	32	39	69	....	....	....	....	....	....	....	....	....	....	....	....	....	....	....	....	....	....
2004-05	Kamloops Blazers	WHL	60	0	1	1	77	....	....	....	....	....	....	....	....	....	6	0	0	0	16	....	....	....	....
2005-06	Kamloops Blazers	WHL	68	2	6	8	121	....	....	....	....	....	....	....	....	....	....	....	....	....	....	....	....	....	....
2006-07	Kamloops Blazers	WHL	69	2	23	25	120	....	....	....	....	....	....	....	....	....	4	1	2	3	12	....	....	....	....
2007-08	Kamloops Blazers	WHL	16	0	3	3	29	....	....	....	....	....	....	....	....	....	....	....	....	....	....	....	....	....	....
	Moose Jaw	WHL	53	2	21	23	81	....	....	....	....	....	....	....	....	....	5	0	2	2	15	....	....	....	....
2008-09	Rochester	AHL	75	3	20	23	44	....	....	....	....	....	....	....	....	....	....	....	....	....	....	....	....	....	....
2009-10	**Florida**	**NHL**	**22**	**0**	**0**	**0**	**2**	**0**	**0**	**0**	**5**	**0.0**	**–1**	**0**	**0.0**	**5:26**	....	....	....	....	....	....	....	....	....
	Rochester	AHL	58	6	13	19	34	....	....	....	....	....	....	....	....	....	7	1	0	1	4	....	....	....	....
	NHL Totals		**22**	**0**	**0**	**0**	**2**	**0**	**0**	**0**	**5**	**0.0**		**0**	**0.0**	**5:26**	....	....	....	....	....	....	....	....	....

ELLIS, Matt

(EHL-ihs, MAT)

Left wing. Shoots left. 6', 212 lbs. Born, Welland, Ont., August 31, 1981.

Season	Club	League	GP	G	A	Pts	PIM	PP	SH	GW	S	%	+/-	TF	F%	Min	GP	G	A	Pts	PIM	PP	SH	GW	Min
1998-99	St. Michael's	OHL	47	10	8	18	6	....	....	....	....	....	....	....	....	....	....	....	....	....	....	....	....	....	....
99-2000	St. Michael's	OHL	59	15	20	35	20	....	....	....	....	....	....	....	....	....	....	....	....	....	....	....	....	....	....
2000-01	St. Michael's	OHL	68	21	24	45	19	....	....	....	....	....	....	....	....	....	18	4	8	12	6	....	....	....	....
2001-02	St. Michael's	OHL	66	38	51	89	20	....	....	....	....	....	....	....	....	....	15	8	6	14	6	....	....	....	....
2002-03	Toledo Storm	ECHL	71	27	32	59	34	....	....	....	....	....	....	....	....	....	7	3	5	8	0	....	....	....	....
2003-04	Grand Rapids	AHL	64	5	10	15	23	....	....	....	....	....	....	....	....	....	4	0	0	0	2	....	....	....	....
2004-05	Grand Rapids	AHL	79	18	23	41	59	....	....	....	....	....	....	....	....	....	....	....	....	....	....	....	....	....	....
2005-06	Grand Rapids	AHL	74	20	28	48	61	....	....	....	....	....	....	....	....	....	16	4	1	5	20	....	....	....	....
2006-07	**Detroit**	**NHL**	**16**	**0**	**0**	**0**	**6**	**0**	**0**	**0**	**22**	**0.0**	**–1**	**48**	**47.9**	**5:35**	....	....	....	....	....	....	....	....	....
	Grand Rapids	AHL	65	26	23	49	44	....	....	....	....	....	....	....	....	....	7	4	3	7	4	....	....	....	....
2007-08	**Detroit**	**NHL**	**35**	**2**	**4**	**6**	**12**	**0**	**0**	**1**	**28**	**7.1**	**1**	**87**	**49.4**	**5:23**	....	....	....	....	....	....	....	....	....
	Los Angeles	**NHL**	**19**	**1**	**1**	**2**	**14**	**0**	**1**	**0**	**38**	**2.6**	**2**	**27**	**37.0**	**12:41**	....	....	....	....	....	....	....	....	....
2008-09	**Buffalo**	**NHL**	**45**	**7**	**5**	**12**	**12**	**0**	**0**	**2**	**73**	**9.6**	**4**	**239**	**46.9**	**8:50**	....	....	....	....	....	....	....	....	....
	Portland Pirates	AHL	12	2	2	4	4	....	....	....	....	....	....	....	....	....	....	....	....	....	....	....	....	....	....
2009-10	**Buffalo**	**NHL**	**72**	**3**	**10**	**13**	**12**	**0**	**0**	**1**	**112**	**2.7**	**–1**	**282**	**50.0**	**9:03**	**3**	**1**	**0**	**1**	**0**	**0**	**0**	**0**	**9:44**
	NHL Totals		**187**	**13**	**20**	**33**	**56**	**0**	**1**	**4**	**273**	**4.8**		**683**	**48.2**	**8:23**	**3**	**1**	**0**	**1**	**0**	**0**	**0**	**0**	**9:44**

Signed as a free agent by **Detroit**, May 10, 2002. Claimed on waivers by **Los Angeles** from **Detroit**, February 21, 2008. Claimed on waivers by **Buffalo** from **Los Angeles**, October 1, 2008.

ELLISON, Matt

(EHL-ih-suhn, MAT) **NSH**

Right wing. Shoots right. 6', 192 lbs. Born, Duncan, B.C., December 8, 1983. Chicago's 4th choice, 128th overall, in 2002 Entry Draft.

Season	Club	League	GP	G	A	Pts	PIM	PP	SH	GW	S	%	+/-	TF	F%	Min	GP	G	A	Pts	PIM	PP	SH	GW	Min
1997-98	Cowichan Valley	Minor-BC	24	27	31	58	10	....	....	....	....	....	....	....	....	....	....	....	....	....	....	....	....	....	....
1998-99	Kerry Park	VIJHL	38	40	47	87	110	....	....	....	....	....	....	....	....	....	....	....	....	....	....	....	....	....	....
99-2000	Cowichan Valley	BCHL	60	11	23	34	95	....	....	....	....	....	....	....	....	....	....	....	....	....	....	....	....	....	....
2000-01	Cowichan Valley	BCHL	60	22	44	66	102	....	....	....	....	....	....	....	....	....	....	....	....	....	....	....	....	....	....
2001-02	Cowichan Valley	BCHL	60	42	*75	*117	76	....	....	....	....	....	....	....	....	....	10	5	6	11	8	....	....	....	....
2002-03	Red Deer Rebels	WHL	72	40	56	96	80	....	....	....	....	....	....	....	....	....	22	7	13	20	28	....	....	....	....
2003-04	**Chicago**	**NHL**	**10**	**0**	**1**	**1**	**0**	**0**	**0**	**0**	**4**	**0.0**	**–3**	**46**	**39.1**	**12:40**	....	....	....	....	....	....	....	....	....
	Norfolk Admirals	AHL	71	14	21	35	115	....	....	....	....	....	....	....	....	....	7	0	1	1	4	....	....	....	....
2004-05	Norfolk Admirals	AHL	71	14	37	51	44	....	....	....	....	....	....	....	....	....	5	0	1	1	2	....	....	....	....
2005-06	**Chicago**	**NHL**	**26**	**3**	**9**	**12**	**17**	**1**	**0**	**0**	**47**	**6.4**	**–4**	**76**	**43.4**	**14:45**	....	....	....	....	....	....	....	....	....
	Philadelphia	**NHL**	**5**	**0**	**1**	**1**	**2**	**0**	**0**	**0**	**2**	**0.0**	**2**	**10**	**50.0**	**6:28**	....	....	....	....	....	....	....	....	....
	Philadelphia	AHL	48	12	13	25	35	....	....	....	....	....	....	....	....	....	....	....	....	....	....	....	....	....	....
2006-07	**Philadelphia**	**NHL**	**2**	**0**	**0**	**0**	**0**	**0**	**0**	**0**	**1**	**0.0**	**0**	**8**	**37.5**	**5:58**	....	....	....	....	....	....	....	....	....
	Philadelphia	AHL	62	12	27	39	43	....	....	....	....	....	....	....	....	....	....	....	....	....	....	....	....	....	....
2007-08	Milwaukee	AHL	75	26	32	58	55	....	....	....	....	....	....	....	....	....	5	0	0	0	2	....	....	....	....
2008-09	Dynamo Riga	Rus-KHL	55	15	22	37	84	....	....	....	....	....	....	....	....	....	3	0	1	1	0	....	....	....	....
2009-10	MVD	Rus-KHL	52	16	18	34	102	....	....	....	....	....	....	....	....	....	22	4	5	9	10	....	....	....	....
	NHL Totals		**43**	**3**	**11**	**14**	**19**	**1**	**0**	**0**	**54**	**5.6**		**140**	**42.1**	**12:53**	....	....	....	....	....	....	....	....	....

WHL East Second All-Star Team (2003) • WHL Rookie of the Year (2003) • Canadian Major Junior Rookie of the Year (2003)

Traded to **Philadelphia** by **Chicago** with Chicago's 3rd round choice (later traded to Montreal - Montreal selected Ryan White) in 2006 Entry Draft for Patrick Sharp and Eric Meloche, December 5, 2005. Traded to **Nashville** by **Philadlephia** for future considerations, June 4, 2007. Signed as a free agent by **Riga** (Russia-KHL), July 4, 2008. Signed as a free agent by **MVD Moscow** (Russia-KHL), August 4, 2009. Signed as a free agent by **Nizhny Novgorod** (Russia-KHL), May 30, 2010.

EMINGER, Steve

(EH-mihn-juhr, STEEV) **NYR**

Defense. Shoots right. 6'2", 210 lbs. Born, Woodbridge, Ont., October 31, 1983. Washington's 1st choice, 12th overall, in 2002 Entry Draft.

Season	Club	League	GP	G	A	Pts	PIM	PP	SH	GW	S	%	+/-	TF	F%	Min	GP	G	A	Pts	PIM	PP	SH	GW	Min
1998-99	Bramalea Blues	OPJHL	47	6	9	15	81	....	....	....	....	....	....	....	....	....	....	....	....	....	....	....	....	....	....
99-2000	Kitchener Rangers	OHL	50	2	14	16	74	....	....	....	....	....	....	....	....	....	5	0	0	0	0	....	....	....	....
2000-01	Kitchener Rangers	OHL	54	6	26	32	66	....	....	....	....	....	....	....	....	....	....	....	....	....	....	....	....	....	....
2001-02	Kitchener Rangers	OHL	64	19	39	58	93	....	....	....	....	....	....	....	....	....	4	0	2	2	10	....	....	....	....
2002-03	**Washington**	**NHL**	**17**	**0**	**2**	**2**	**24**	**0**	**0**	**0**	**6**	**0.0**	**–3**	**0**	**0.0**	**10:08**	....	....	....	....	....	....	....	....	....
	Kitchener Rangers	OHL	23	2	27	29	40	....	....	....	....	....	....	....	....	....	21	3	8	11	44	....	....	....	....
2003-04	**Washington**	**NHL**	**41**	**0**	**4**	**4**	**45**	**0**	**0**	**0**	**12**	**0.0**	**–11**	**0**	**0.0**	**17:32**	....	....	....	....	....	....	....	....	....
	Portland Pirates	AHL	41	0	4	4	40	....	....	....	....	....	....	....	....	....	7	0	1	1	2	....	....	....	....
2004-05	Portland Pirates	AHL	62	3	17	20	40	....	....	....	....	....	....	....	....	....	....	....	....	....	....	....	....	....	....
2005-06	**Washington**	**NHL**	**66**	**5**	**13**	**18**	**81**	**1**	**0**	**0**	**50**	**10.0**	**–12**	**1**	**100.0**	**21:21**	....	....	....	....	....	....	....	....	....
2006-07	**Washington**	**NHL**	**68**	**1**	**16**	**17**	**63**	**0**	**0**	**0**	**27**	**3.7**	**–14**	**1**	**100.0**	**18:56**	....	....	....	....	....	....	....	....	....
2007-08	**Washington**	**NHL**	**20**	**0**	**2**	**2**	**8**	**0**	**0**	**0**	**14**	**0.0**	**–4**	**0**	**0.0**	**11:08**	**5**	**1**	**0**	**1**	**2**	**0**	**0**	**0**	**16:06**
2008-09	**Philadelphia**	**NHL**	**12**	**0**	**2**	**2**	**8**	**0**	**0**	**0**	**9**	**0.0**	**0**	**0**	**0.0**	**17:53**	....	....	....	....	....	....	....	....	....
	Tampa Bay	**NHL**	**50**	**4**	**19**	**23**	**36**	**2**	**0**	**0**	**63**	**6.3**	**–4**	**1**	**0.0**	**23:33**	....	....	....	....	....	....	....	....	....
	Florida	**NHL**	**9**	**1**	**0**	**1**	**6**	**0**	**0**	**1**	**13**	**7.7**	**1**	**0**	**0.0**	**15:49**	....	....	....	....	....	....	....	....	....
2009-10	**Anaheim**	**NHL**	**63**	**4**	**12**	**16**	**30**	**0**	**0**	**1**	**45**	**8.9**	**1**	**0**	**0.0**	**19:29**	....	....	....	....	....	....	....	....	....
	NHL Totals		**346**	**15**	**70**	**85**	**301**	**3**	**0**	**2**	**239**	**6.3**		**3**	**66.7**	**19:00**	**5**	**1**	**0**	**1**	**2**	**0**	**0**	**0**	**16:06**

OHL Second All-Star Team (2002, 2003) • Canadian Major Junior Second All-Star Team (2002) • Memorial Cup Tournament All-Star Team (2003)

Traded to **Philadelphia** by **Washington** with Washington's 3rd round choice (Jacob Deserres) in 2008 Entry Draft for Philadelphia's 1st round choice (John Carlson) in 2008 Entry Draft, June 20, 2008. Traded to **Tampa Bay** by **Philadelphia** with Steve Downie and Tampa Bay's 4th round choice (previously acquired, Tampa Bay selected Alex Hutchings) in 2009 Entry Draft for Matt Carle and San Jose's 3rd round choice (previously acquired, Philadelphia selected Simon Bertilsson) in 2009 Entry Draft, November 7, 2008. Traded to **Florida** by **Tampa Bay** for Noah Welch and Florida's 3rd round choice (later traded to Detroit – Detroit selected Andrej Nestrasil) in 2009 Entry Draft, March 4, 2009. Signed as a free agent by **Anaheim**, September 4, 2009. Traded to **NY Rangers** by **Anaheim** for Aaron Voros and Ryan Hillier, July 9, 2010.

ENGELLAND, Deryk

(ehn-GUHL-uhnd, DEH-rihk) **PIT**

Defense. Shoots right. 6'2", 202 lbs. Born, Edmonton, Alta., April 5, 1982. New Jersey's 11th choice, 194th overall, in 2000 Entry Draft.

Season	Club	League	GP	G	A	Pts	PIM	PP	SH	GW	S	%	+/-	TF	F%	Min	GP	G	A	Pts	PIM	PP	SH	GW	Min
1998-99	Moose Jaw	WHL	2	0	0	0	0	....	....	....	....	....	....	....	....	....	....	....	....	....	....	....	....	....	....
99-2000	Moose Jaw	WHL	55	0	5	5	62	....	....	....	....	....	....	....	....	....	4	0	0	0	0	....	....	....	....
2000-01	Moose Jaw	WHL	65	4	11	15	157	....	....	....	....	....	....	....	....	....	4	0	0	0	10	....	....	....	....
2001-02	Moose Jaw	WHL	56	7	10	17	102	....	....	....	....	....	....	....	....	....	12	0	2	2	27	....	....	....	....
2002-03	Moose Jaw	WHL	65	3	8	11	199	....	....	....	....	....	....	....	....	....	13	1	1	2	20	....	....	....	....
2003-04	Lowell	AHL	26	0	0	0	34	....	....	....	....	....	....	....	....	....	....	....	....	....	....	....	....	....	....
	Las Vegas	ECHL	35	2	11	13	63	....	....	....	....	....	....	....	....	....	2	0	0	0	0	....	....	....	....
2004-05	Las Vegas	ECHL	72	5	16	21	138	....	....	....	....	....	....	....	....	....	....	....	....	....	....	....	....	....	....
2005-06	Hershey Bears	AHL	37	0	4	4	77	....	....	....	....	....	....	....	....	....	1	0	0	0	0	....	....	....	....
	South Carolina	ECHL	35	3	13	16	20	....	....	....	....	....	....	....	....	....	....	....	....	....	....	....	....	....	....
2006-07	Hershey Bears	AHL	44	4	6	10	95	....	....	....	....	....	....	....	....	....	14	0	0	0	14	....	....	....	....
	Reading Royals	ECHL	6	0	3	3	8	....	....	....	....	....	....	....	....	....	....	....	....	....	....	....	....	....	....
2007-08	Wilkes-Barre	AHL	80	2	15	17	141	....	....	....	....	....	....	....	....	....	23	1	3	4	14	....	....	....	....
2008-09	Wilkes-Barre	AHL	80	3	11	14	143	....	....	....	....	....	....	....	....	....	12	0	2	2	6	....	....	....	....
2009-10	**Pittsburgh**	**NHL**	**9**	**0**	**2**	**2**	**17**	**0**	**0**	**0**	**4**	**0.0**	**–2**	**0**	**0.0**	**16:08**	....	....	....	....	....	....	....	....	....
	Wilkes-Barre	AHL	71	5	6	11	121	....	....	....	....	....	....	....	....	....	4	0	1	1	7	....	....	....	....
	NHL Totals		**9**	**0**	**2**	**2**	**17**	**0**	**0**	**0**	**4**	**0.0**		**0**	**0.0**	**16:08**	....	....	....	....	....	....	....	....	....

Signed as a free agent by **Calgary**, July, 2003. Signed as a free agent by **Pittsburgh**, July 16, 2007.

ENNIS, Tyler

(EH-nihs, TIGH-luhr) **BUF.**

Center. Shoots left. 5'9", 163 lbs. Born, Edmonton, Alta., October 6, 1989. Buffalo's 2nd choice, 26th overall, in 2008 Entry Draft.

Season	Club	League	GP	G	A	Pts	PIM	PP	SH	GW	S	%	+/-	TF	F%	Min	GP	G	A	Pts	PIM	PP	SH	GW	Min
			Regular Season														Playoffs								
2004-05	K of C Pats	AMHL	36	15	17	32	10																		
2005-06	Medicine Hat	WHL	43	3	7	10	10										7	0	0	0	0				
2006-07	Medicine Hat	WHL	71	26	24	50	30										22	8	4	12	6				
2007-08	Medicine Hat	WHL	70	43	48	91	42										5	0	4	4	6				
2008-09	Medicine Hat	WHL	61	43	42	85	21										11	8	11	19	10				
2009-10	**Buffalo**	**NHL**	**10**	**3**	**6**	**9**	**6**	**0**	**0**	**0**	**23**	**13.0**	**1**	**31**	**41.9**	**15:20**	**6**	**1**	**3**	**4**	**0**	**0**	**0**	**0**	**17:09**
	Portland Pirates	AHL	69	23	42	65	12																		
	NHL Totals		**10**	**3**	**6**	**9**	**6**	**0**	**0**	**0**	**23**	**13.0**		**31**	**41.9**	**15:20**	**6**	**1**	**3**	**4**	**0**	**0**	**0**	**0**	**17:09**

WHL East First All-Star Team (2008, 2009) • Dudley "Red" Garrett Memorial Award (AHL – Rookie of the Year) (2010)

ENSTROM, Tobias

(EHN-struhm, toh-BYE-uhs) **ATL.**

Defense. Shoots left. 5'10", 180 lbs. Born, Nordingra, Sweden, November 5, 1984. Atlanta's 8th choice, 239th overall, in 2003 Entry Draft.

Season	Club	League	GP	G	A	Pts	PIM	PP	SH	GW	S	%	+/-	TF	F%	Min	GP	G	A	Pts	PIM	PP	SH	GW	Min
99-2000	MoDo U18	Swe-U18	3	0	0	0	0																		
2000-01	MoDo U18	Swe-U18	16	7	6	13	18																		
	MoDo Jr.	Swe-Jr.	1	0	0	0	0																		
2001-02	MODO Jr.	Swe-Jr.	21	1	7	8	10										2	1	1	2	2				
2002-03	MODO Jr.	Swe-Jr.	7	4	6	10	31																		
	MODO	Sweden	42	1	5	6	16										6	0	1	1	4				
2003-04	MODO	Sweden	33	1	4	5	6										6	1	1	2	2				
2004-05	MODO	Sweden	49	4	10	14	24										2	0	0	0	0				
2005-06	MODO	Sweden	47	4	7	11	48										4	0	1	1	25				
2006-07	MODO	Sweden	55	7	21	28	52										20	1	11	12	37				
2007-08	**Atlanta**	**NHL**	**82**	**5**	**33**	**38**	**42**	**4**	**0**	**0**	**105**	**4.8**	**–5**	**0**	**0.0**	**24:28**									
2008-09	**Atlanta**	**NHL**	**82**	**5**	**27**	**32**	**52**	**2**	**1**	**1**	**86**	**5.8**	**14**	**2**	**50.0**	**23:32**									
2009-10	**Atlanta**	**NHL**	**82**	**6**	**44**	**50**	**30**	**2**	**0**	**0**	**109**	**5.5**	**–5**	**0**	**0.0**	**22:16**									
	Sweden	Olympics	4	0	2	2	4																		
	NHL Totals		**246**	**16**	**104**	**120**	**124**	**8**	**1**	**1**	**300**	**5.3**		**2**	**50.0**	**23:25**									

NHL All-Rookie Team (2008)

ERAT, Martin

(EE-rat, MAHR-tihn) **NSH.**

Right wing. Shoots left. 6', 200 lbs. Born, Trebic, Czech., August 29, 1981. Nashville's 12th choice, 191st overall, in 1999 Entry Draft.

Season	Club	League	GP	G	A	Pts	PIM	PP	SH	GW	S	%	+/-	TF	F%	Min	GP	G	A	Pts	PIM	PP	SH	GW	Min
1997-98	HC ZPS Zlin Jr.	CzRep-Jr.	46	35	30	65																			
1998-99	HC ZPS Zlin Jr.	CzRep-Jr.	35	21	23	44																			
	Zlin	CzRep	5	0	0	0	2																		
99-2000	Saskatoon Blades	WHL	66	27	26	53	82										11	4	8	12	16				
2000-01	Saskatoon Blades	WHL	31	19	35	54	48																		
	Red Deer Rebels	WHL	17	4	24	28	24										22	*15	*21	*36	32				
2001-02	**Nashville**	**NHL**	**80**	**9**	**24**	**33**	**32**	**2**	**0**	**2**	**84**	**10.7**	**–11**	**3**	**66.7**	**13:10**									
2002-03	**Nashville**	**NHL**	**27**	**1**	**7**	**8**	**14**	**1**	**0**	**0**	**39**	**2.6**	**–9**	**1**	**0.0**	**12:47**									
	Milwaukee	AHL	45	10	22	32	41										6	5	4	9	4				
2003-04	**Nashville**	**NHL**	**76**	**16**	**33**	**49**	**38**	**4**	**0**	**2**	**137**	**11.7**	**10**	**31**	**29.0**	**15:00**	**6**	**0**	**1**	**1**	**6**	**0**	**0**	**0**	**14:09**
2004-05	HC Hame Zlin	CzRep	48	20	23	43	129										16	*7	5	12	12				
2005-06	**Nashville**	**NHL**	**80**	**20**	**29**	**49**	**76**	**5**	**0**	**1**	**143**	**14.0**	**0**	**25**	**16.0**	**14:45**	**5**	**1**	**1**	**2**	**6**	**1**	**0**	**0**	**19:31**
	Czech Republic	Olympics	8	1	1	2	4																		
2006-07	**Nashville**	**NHL**	**68**	**16**	**41**	**57**	**50**	**5**	**1**	**3**	**132**	**12.1**	**13**	**43**	**44.2**	**18:59**	**3**	**0**	**1**	**1**	**0**	**0**	**0**	**0**	**14:13**
2007-08	**Nashville**	**NHL**	**76**	**23**	**34**	**57**	**40**	**4**	**0**	**6**	**163**	**14.1**	**–3**	**41**	**36.6**	**18:39**	**6**	**1**	**3**	**4**	**8**	**0**	**0**	**0**	**20:56**
2008-09	**Nashville**	**NHL**	**71**	**17**	**33**	**50**	**48**	**3**	**0**	**3**	**149**	**11.4**	**–7**	**38**	**29.0**	**18:34**									
2009-10	**Nashville**	**NHL**	**74**	**21**	**28**	**49**	**50**	**5**	**0**	**2**	**168**	**12.5**	**–7**	**73**	**32.9**	**17:59**	**6**	**4**	**1**	**5**	**4**	**0**	**0**	**0**	**18:56**
	Czech Republic	Olympics	5	0	1	1	2																		
	NHL Totals		**552**	**123**	**229**	**352**	**348**	**29**	**1**	**19**	**1015**	**12.1**		**255**	**32.9**	**16:27**	**26**	**6**	**7**	**13**	**24**	**1**	**0**	**0**	**17:51**

Signed as a free agent by **Zlin** (CzRep), September 5, 2004.

ERICSSON, Jonathan

(AIR-ihk-suhn, JAWN-ah-thuhn) **DET.**

Defense. Shoots left. 6'4", 220 lbs. Born, Karlskrona, Sweden, March 2, 1984. Detroit's 10th choice, 291st overall, in 2002 Entry Draft.

Season	Club	League	GP	G	A	Pts	PIM	PP	SH	GW	S	%	+/-	TF	F%	Min	GP	G	A	Pts	PIM	PP	SH	GW	Min
2001-02	Hasten Jr.	Swe-Jr.	STATISTICS NOT AVAILABLE																						
2002-03	Vita Hasten	Sweden-3	40	2	4	6	36																		
2003-04	Sodertalje SK	Sweden	42	1	0	1	12																		
2004-05	Sodertalje SK	Sweden	15	0	0	0	4										1	0	0	0	0				
2005-06	Sodertalje SK Jr.	Swe-Jr.	1	0	0	0	2																		
	Almtuna	Sweden-2	19	2	3	5	44																		
	Sodertalje SK	Sweden	24	0	0	0	20																		
	Sodertalje SK	Sweden-Q	7	0	1	1	4																		
2006-07	Grand Rapids	AHL	67	5	24	29	102										7	0	0	0	8				
2007-08	**Detroit**	**NHL**	**8**	**1**	**0**	**1**	**4**	**1**	**0**	**0**	**19**	**5.3**	**–3**	**0**	**0.0**	**15:58**									
	Grand Rapids	AHL	69	10	24	34	83																		
2008-09	**Detroit**	**NHL**	**19**	**1**	**3**	**4**	**15**	**0**	**0**	**0**	**25**	**4.0**	**–1**	**0**	**0.0**	**17:40**	**22**	**4**	**4**	**8**	**25**	**0**	**0**	**1**	**18:44**
	Grand Rapids	AHL	40	2	13	15	48																		
2009-10	**Detroit**	**NHL**	**62**	**4**	**9**	**13**	**44**	**0**	**1**	**1**	**55**	**7.3**	**–15**	**0**	**0.0**	**16:42**	**12**	**0**	**2**	**2**	**8**	**0**	**0**	**0**	**14:17**
	NHL Totals		**89**	**6**	**12**	**18**	**63**	**1**	**1**	**1**	**99**	**6.1**		**0**	**0.0**	**16:51**	**34**	**4**	**6**	**10**	**33**	**0**	**0**	**1**	**17:10**

ERIKSSON, Anders

(AIR-ihk-suhn, AND-uhrs)

Defense. Shoots left. 6'3", 224 lbs. Born, Bollnas, Sweden, January 9, 1975. Detroit's 1st choice, 22nd overall, in 1993 Entry Draft.

Season	Club	League	GP	G	A	Pts	PIM	PP	SH	GW	S	%	+/-	TF	F%	Min	GP	G	A	Pts	PIM	PP	SH	GW	Min
1992-93	MoDo Jr.	Swe-Jr.	10	5	3	8	14																		
	MoDo	Sweden	20	0	2	2	2										1	0	0	0	0				
1993-94	MoDo	Sweden	38	2	8	10	42										11	0	0	0	8				
	MoDo Jr.	Swe-Jr.	3	1	2	3	34																		
1994-95	MoDo	Sweden	39	3	6	9	54																		
1995-96	**Detroit**	**NHL**	**1**	**0**	**0**	**0**	**2**	**0**	**0**	**0**	**0**	**0.0**	**1**				**3**	**0**	**0**	**0**	**0**	**0**	**0**	**0**	
	Adirondack	AHL	75	6	36	42	64										3	0	0	0	0				
1996-97	**Detroit**	**NHL**	**23**	**0**	**6**	**6**	**10**	**0**	**0**	**0**	**27**	**0.0**	**5**												
	Adirondack	AHL	44	3	25	28	36										4	0	1	1	4				
1997-98♦	**Detroit**	**NHL**	**66**	**7**	**14**	**21**	**32**	**1**	**0**	**2**	**91**	**7.7**	**21**				**18**	**0**	**5**	**5**	**16**	**0**	**0**	**0**	
1998-99	**Detroit**	**NHL**	**61**	**2**	**10**	**12**	**34**	**0**	**0**	**1**	**67**	**3.0**	**5**	**0**	**0.0**	**15:54**									
	Chicago	**NHL**	**11**	**0**	**8**	**8**	**0**	**0**	**0**	**0**	**12**	**0.0**	**6**	**0**	**0.0**	**22:51**									
99-2000	**Chicago**	**NHL**	**73**	**3**	**25**	**28**	**20**	**0**	**0**	**1**	**86**	**3.5**	**4**	**1**	**100.0**	**21:03**									
2000-01	**Chicago**	**NHL**	**13**	**2**	**3**	**5**	**2**	**1**	**0**	**0**	**19**	**10.5**	**–4**	**0**	**0.0**	**21:20**									
	Florida	**NHL**	**60**	**0**	**21**	**21**	**28**	**0**	**0**	**0**	**80**	**0.0**	**2**	**1**	**0.0**	**21:02**									
2001-02	**Toronto**	**NHL**	**34**	**0**	**2**	**2**	**12**	**0**	**0**	**0**	**31**	**0.0**	**–1**	**0**	**0.0**	**15:55**	**10**	**0**	**0**	**0**	**0**	**0**	**0**	**0**	**17:24**
	St. John's	AHL	25	4	6	10	14										11	0	5	5	6				
2002-03	**Toronto**	**NHL**	**4**	**0**	**0**	**0**	**0**	**0**	**0**	**0**	**7**	**0.0**	**1**	**0**	**0.0**	**19:02**									
	St. John's	AHL	72	5	34	39	133																		
2003-04	**Columbus**	**NHL**	**66**	**7**	**20**	**27**	**18**	**2**	**0**	**1**	**84**	**8.3**	**–6**	**0**	**0.0**	**20:42**									
	Syracuse Crunch	AHL	9	1	3	4	12																		
2004-05	HV 71 Jonkoping	Sweden	32	1	9	10	54																		
2005-06	Magnitogorsk	Russia	17	2	7	9	10										11	3	2	5	16				
	Springfield	AHL	12	1	8	9	10																		
2006-07	**Columbus**	**NHL**	**79**	**0**	**23**	**23**	**46**	**0**	**0**	**0**	**78**	**0.0**	**12**	**1**	**100.0**	**20:12**									
2007-08	**Calgary**	**NHL**	**61**	**1**	**17**	**18**	**36**	**1**	**0**	**0**	**50**	**2.0**	**–5**	**0**	**0.0**	**20:47**	**3**	**0**	**1**	**1**	**2**	**0**	**0**	**0**	**18:16**
2008-09	Quad City Flames	AHL	64	4	45	49	60																		
	Calgary	**NHL**															**2**	**0**	**0**	**0**	**0**	**0**	**0**	**0**	**18:42**

Season	Club	League	GP	G	A	Pts	PIM	PP	SH	GW	S	%	+/-	TF	F%	Min	GP	G	A	Pts	PIM	PP	SH	GW	Min
			Regular Season														Playoffs								
2009-10	San Antonio	AHL	10	1	3	4	2																		
	Phoenix	**NHL**	**12**	**0**	**3**	**3**	**2**	**0**	**0**	**0**	**4**	**0.0**	**0**	**0**	**0.0**	**15:45**									
	NY Rangers	**NHL**	**8**	**0**	**2**	**2**	**0**	**0**	**0**	**0**	**2**	**0.0**	**2**	**0**	**0.0**	**14:30**									
	Hartford	AHL	8	0	3	3	4																		
	NHL Totals		**572**	**22**	**154**	**176**	**242**	**5**	**0**	**5**	**638**	**3.4**		**3**	**66.7**	**19:36**	**36**	**0**	**6**	**6**	**18**	**0**	**0**	**0**	**17:45**

Traded to **Chicago** by **Detroit** with Detroit's 1st round choices in 1999 (Steve McCarthy) and 2001 (Adam Munro) Entry Drafts for Chris Chelios, March 23, 1999. Traded to **Florida** by **Chicago** for Jaroslav Spacek, November 6, 2000. Signed as a free agent by **Toronto**, July 4, 2001. Signed as a free agent by **Columbus**, October 10, 2003. Signed as a free agent by **Calgary**, September 16, 2004. Signed as a free agent by **Jonkoping** (Sweden), October 29, 2004. Signed as a fee agent by **Columbus**, July 1, 2006. Signed as a free agent by **Calgary**, July 5, 2007. Signed as a free agent by **San Antonio** (AHL), December 4, 2009. Signed as a free agent by **Phoenix**, December 21, 2009. Traded to **NY Rangers** by **Phoenix** for Miika Wiikman and NY Rangers' 7th round choice in 2011 Entry Draft, March 3, 2010.

ERIKSSON, Loui

(AIR-ihk-suhn, LOO-ee) **DAL.**

Left wing. Shoots left. 6'1", 189 lbs. Born, Goteborg, Sweden, July 17, 1985. Dallas' 1st choice, 33rd overall, in 2003 Entry Draft.

Season	Club	League	GP	G	A	Pts	PIM	PP	SH	GW	S	%	+/-	TF	F%	Min	GP	G	A	Pts	PIM	PP	SH	GW	Min
2000-01	V.Frolunda U18	Swe-U18	9	5	3	8	4																		
	V.Frolunda Jr.	Swe-Jr.	1	0	0	0	0																		
2001-02	V.Frolunda U18	Swe-U18	1	1	0	1	0																		
	V.Frolunda Jr.	Swe-Jr.	35	7	15	22	2										8	2	3	5	2				
2002-03	V.Frolunda Jr.	Swe-Jr.	30	16	15	31	10										8	4	6	10	4				
2003-04	V.Frolunda	Sweden	46	8	5	13	4										10	1	5	6	0				
2004-05	Frolunda	Sweden	39	5	9	14	4										12	0	0	0	0				
2005-06	Iowa Stars	AHL	78	31	29	60	27										7	2	5	7	0				
2006-07	**Dallas**	**NHL**	**59**	**6**	**13**	**19**	**18**	**2**	**0**	**0**	**78**	**7.7**	**–3**	**9**	**44.4**	**13:11**	**4**	**0**	**1**	**1**	**0**	**0**	**0**	**0**	**15:47**
	Iowa Stars	AHL	15	5	3	8	13										9	2	5	7	0				
2007-08	**Dallas**	**NHL**	**69**	**14**	**17**	**31**	**28**	**4**	**0**	**0**	**120**	**11.7**	**5**	**13**	**15.4**	**14:02**	**18**	**4**	**4**	**8**	**8**	**1**	**0**	**0**	**18:12**
	Iowa Stars	AHL	2	1	2	3	2																		
2008-09	**Dallas**	**NHL**	**82**	**36**	**27**	**63**	**14**	**7**	**1**	**4**	**178**	**20.2**	**14**	**11**	**18.2**	**19:50**									
2009-10	**Dallas**	**NHL**	**82**	**29**	**42**	**71**	**26**	**6**	**2**	**4**	**214**	**13.6**	**–4**	**11**	**36.4**	**19:46**									
	Sweden	Olympics	4	3	1	4	0																		
	NHL Totals		**292**	**85**	**99**	**184**	**86**	**19**	**3**	**8**	**590**	**14.4**		**44**	**27.3**	**17:06**	**22**	**4**	**5**	**9**	**8**	**1**	**0**	**0**	**17:46**

ERSKINE, John

(UHR-skihn, JAWN) **WSH.**

Defense. Shoots left. 6'4", 220 lbs. Born, Kingston, Ont., June 26, 1980. Dallas' 1st choice, 39th overall, in 1998 Entry Draft.

Season	Club	League	GP	G	A	Pts	PIM	PP	SH	GW	S	%	+/-	TF	F%	Min	GP	G	A	Pts	PIM	PP	SH	GW	Min
1996-97	Quinte Hawks	MTJHL	48	4	16	20	241																		
1997-98	London Knights	OHL	55	0	9	9	205										16	0	5	5	25				
1998-99	London Knights	OHL	57	8	12	20	208										25	5	10	15	38				
99-2000	London Knights	OHL	58	12	31	43	177																		
2000-01	Utah Grizzlies	IHL	77	1	8	9	284																		
2001-02	**Dallas**	**NHL**	**33**	**0**	**1**	**1**	**62**	**0**	**0**	**0**	**16**	**0.0**	**–8**	**0**	**0.0**	**10:44**									
	Utah Grizzlies	AHL	39	2	6	8	118										3	0	0	0	10				
2002-03	**Dallas**	**NHL**	**16**	**2**	**0**	**2**	**29**	**0**	**0**	**0**	**12**	**16.7**	**1**	**0**	**0.0**	**10:45**									
	Utah Grizzlies	AHL	52	2	8	10	274										1	0	1	1	15				
2003-04	**Dallas**	**NHL**	**32**	**0**	**1**	**1**	**84**	**0**	**0**	**0**	**23**	**0.0**	**–9**	**0**	**0.0**	**12:36**									
	Utah Grizzlies	AHL	5	0	0	0	18																		
2004-05	Houston Aeros	AHL	61	3	7	10	238										5	0	1	1	20				
2005-06	**Dallas**	**NHL**	**26**	**0**	**0**	**0**	**62**	**0**	**0**	**0**	**9**	**0.0**	**–3**	**0**	**0.0**	**11:00**									
	NY Islanders	**NHL**	**34**	**1**	**0**	**1**	**99**	**0**	**0**	**0**	**23**	**4.3**	**–12**	**0**	**0.0**	**14:37**									
2006-07	**Washington**	**NHL**	**29**	**1**	**6**	**7**	**69**	**0**	**0**	**0**	**14**	**7.1**	**–13**	**0**	**0.0**	**18:03**									
	Hershey Bears	AHL	4	0	2	2	9																		
2007-08	**Washington**	**NHL**	**51**	**2**	**7**	**9**	**96**	**0**	**0**	**1**	**48**	**4.2**	**1**	**0**	**0.0**	**15:43**	**7**	**0**	**2**	**2**	**6**	**0**	**0**	**0**	**17:07**
2008-09	**Washington**	**NHL**	**52**	**0**	**4**	**4**	**63**	**0**	**0**	**0**	**50**	**0.0**	**1**	**0**	**0.0**	**16:48**	**12**	**0**	**1**	**1**	**16**	**0**	**0**	**0**	**19:06**
2009-10	**Washington**	**NHL**	**50**	**1**	**5**	**6**	**66**	**0**	**0**	**0**	**50**	**2.0**	**16**	**0**	**0.0**	**15:59**									
	NHL Totals		**323**	**7**	**24**	**31**	**630**	**0**	**0**	**1**	**245**	**2.9**		**0**	**0.0**	**14:35**	**19**	**0**	**3**	**3**	**22**	**0**	**0**	**0**	**18:22**

OHL First All-Star Team (2000)

• Missed majority of 2003-04 season recovering from ankle (December 27, 2003 vs. Columbus) and hernia (January 24, 2004 vs. St. Louis) injuries. Traded to **NY Islanders** by **Dallas** with Dallas' 2nd round choice (Jesse Joensuu) in 2006 Entry Draft for Janne Niinimaa and NY Islanders' 5th round choice (Ondrej Roman) in 2007 Entry Draft, January 10, 2005. Signed as a free agent by **Washington**, September 14, 2006. • Missed majority of 2006-07 season recovering from foot (December 16, 2006 vs. Philadelphia) and thumb (March 9, 2007 vs. Carolina) injuries.

EVANS, Brennan

(EH-vans, BREH-nuhn) **ST.L.**

Defense. Shoots left. 6'3", 220 lbs. Born, North Battleford, Sask., January 6, 1982.

Season	Club	League	GP	G	A	Pts	PIM	PP	SH	GW	S	%	+/-	TF	F%	Min	GP	G	A	Pts	PIM	PP	SH	GW	Min
1998-99	Camrose Kodiaks	AJHL	47	1	6	7	98										5	0	2	2	0				
	Seattle	WHL															1	0	0	0	0				
99-2000	Seattle	WHL	52	1	2	3	40										1	0	0	0	0				
2000-01	Seattle	WHL	11	1	0	1	25																		
	Kootenay Ice	WHL	55	2	7	9	105										11	0	0	0	25				
2001-02	Kootenay Ice	WHL	72	2	3	5	121										22	0	6	6	38				
2002-03	Kootenay Ice	WHL	67	6	17	23	182										11	1	1	2	24				
2003-04	Lowell	AHL	64	1	9	10	65																		
	Calgary	**NHL**															**2**	**0**	**0**	**0**	**0**	**0**	**0**	**0**	**2:52**
2004-05	Lowell	AHL	51	0	7	7	79										5	0	0	0	2				
2005-06	Binghamton	AHL	70	3	6	9	198																		
2006-07	Worcester Sharks	AHL	75	2	14	16	170										5	0	1	1	21				
2007-08	Worcester Sharks	AHL	80	1	13	14	211																		
2008-09	Iowa Chops	AHL	75	1	14	15	189																		
2009-10	Toronto Marlies	AHL	79	1	7	8	199																		
	NHL Totals																**2**	**0**	**0**	**0**	**0**	**0**	**0**	**0**	**2:52**

Signed as a free agent by **Calgary**, September 30, 2003. Signed as a free agent by **San Jose**, July 18, 2007. Signed as a free agent by **Anaheim**, July 11, 2008. • Assigned to **Toronto** (AHL) by **Anaheim**, October 2, 2009. Signed as a free agent by **St. Louis**, July 12, 2010.

EXELBY, Garnet

(EHX-uhl-bee, GAHR-neht)

Defense. Shoots left. 6'1", 215 lbs. Born, Ste. Anne, Man., August 16, 1981. Atlanta's 9th choice, 217th overall, in 1999 Entry Draft.

Season	Club	League	GP	G	A	Pts	PIM	PP	SH	GW	S	%	+/-	TF	F%	Min	GP	G	A	Pts	PIM	PP	SH	GW	Min
1997-98	Wpg. South Blues	MJHL	46	5	11	16	110																		
1998-99	Saskatoon Blades	WHL	61	5	3	8	91																		
99-2000	Saskatoon Blades	WHL	63	1	8	9	79										11	0	2	2	21				
2000-01	Saskatoon Blades	WHL	43	5	10	15	110																		
	Regina Pats	WHL	22	2	8	10	51										6	0	2	2	2				
2001-02	Chicago Wolves	AHL	75	3	4	7	257										25	0	4	4	49				
2002-03	**Atlanta**	**NHL**	**15**	**0**	**2**	**2**	**41**	**0**	**0**	**0**	**9**	**0.0**	**0**	**0**	**0.0**	**18:04**									
	Chicago Wolves	AHL	53	3	6	9	140										9	0	1	1	27				
2003-04	**Atlanta**	**NHL**	**71**	**1**	**9**	**10**	**134**	**0**	**0**	**0**	**42**	**2.4**	**–10**	**0**	**0.0**	**19:32**									
2004-05			DID NOT PLAY																						
2005-06	**Atlanta**	**NHL**	**75**	**1**	**9**	**10**	**75**	**0**	**0**	**0**	**44**	**2.3**	**11**	**0**	**0.0**	**15:41**									
2006-07	**Atlanta**	**NHL**	**58**	**2**	**8**	**10**	**56**	**0**	**1**	**0**	**57**	**3.5**	**2**	**0**	**0.0**	**18:00**	**4**	**0**	**0**	**0**	**6**	**0**	**0**	**0**	**15:38**
2007-08	**Atlanta**	**NHL**	**79**	**2**	**5**	**7**	**85**	**0**	**0**	**0**	**37**	**5.4**	**–21**	**0**	**0.0**	**18:53**									
2008-09	**Atlanta**	**NHL**	**59**	**0**	**7**	**7**	**120**	**0**	**0**	**0**	**42**	**0.0**	**–2**	**0**	**0.0**	**16:43**									
2009-10	**Toronto**	**NHL**	**51**	**1**	**3**	**4**	**73**	**0**	**0**	**0**	**14**	**7.1**	**–8**	**0**	**0.0**	**10:06**									
	NHL Totals		**408**	**7**	**43**	**50**	**584**	**0**	**1**	**0**	**245**	**2.9**		**0**	**0.0**	**16:51**	**4**	**0**	**0**	**0**	**6**	**0**	**0**	**0**	**15:38**

Traded to **Toronto** by **Atlanta** with Colin Stuart for Pavel Kubina and Tim Stapleton, July 1, 2009.

FALK, Justin

(FAWLK, JUHS-tihn) **MIN.**

Defense. Shoots left. 6'5", 217 lbs. Born, Snowflake, Man., October 11, 1988. Minnesota's 2nd choice, 110th overall, in 2007 Entry Draft.

Season	Club	League	GP	G	A	Pts	PIM	PP	SH	GW	S	%	+/-	TF	F%	Min	GP	G	A	Pts	PIM	PP	SH	GW	Min
2004-05	Swan Valley	MJHL	56	0	8	8	46																		
	Calgary Hitmen	WHL	4	0	0	0	2										5	0	0	0	0				
2005-06	Calgary Hitmen	WHL	5	0	2	2	0																		
	Spokane Chiefs	WHL	48	0	8	8	35																		
2006-07	Spokane Chiefs	WHL	62	3	12	15	88										6	0	0	0	8				
2007-08	Spokane Chiefs	WHL	72	4	22	26	98										21	1	4	5	12				

			Regular Season														Playoffs								
Season	Club	League	GP	G	A	Pts	PIM	PP	SH	GW	S	%	+/-	TF	F%	Min	GP	G	A	Pts	PIM	PP	SH	GW	Min
2008-09	Houston Aeros	AHL	65	0	3	3	44	....	....	....	....	....	....	....	....	....	20	0	2	2	4	....	....	....	....
2009-10	**Minnesota**	**NHL**	**3**	**0**	**0**	**0**	**0**	**0**	**0**	**0**	**1**	**0.0**	**-2**	**0**	**0.0**	**7:33**	....	....	....	....	....	....	....	....	....
	Houston Aeros	AHL	69	3	6	9	87	....	....	....	....	....	....	....	....	....	....	....	....	....	....	....	....	....	....
	NHL Totals		**3**	**0**	**0**	**0**	**0**	**0**	**0**	**0**	**1**	**0.0**		**0**	**0.0**	**7:33**	....	....	....	....	....	....	....	....	....

emorial Cup All-Star Team (2008)

FATA, Drew
(FA-tuh, DROO)

Defense. Shoots left. 6'1", 220 lbs. Born, Sault Ste. Marie, Ont., July 28, 1983. Pittsburgh's 3rd choice, 86th overall, in 2001 Entry Draft.

			Regular Season														Playoffs								
Season	Club	League	GP	G	A	Pts	PIM	PP	SH	GW	S	%	+/-	TF	F%	Min	GP	G	A	Pts	PIM	PP	SH	GW	Min
1998-99	S.S. Marie AA	NOHA	46	4	16	20	55	....	....	....	....	....	....	....	....	....	....	....	....	....	....	....	....	....	....
99-2000	St. Mike's B's	OPJHL	49	9	18	27	144	....	....	....	....	....	....	....	....	....	....	....	....	....	....	....	....	....	....
2000-01	St. Michael's	OHL	58	5	15	20	134	....	....	....	....	....	....	....	....	....	18	1	3	4	26	....	....	....	....
2001-02	St. Michael's	OHL	67	7	21	28	175	....	....	....	....	....	....	....	....	....	15	1	9	10	38	....	....	....	....
2002-03	St. Michael's	OHL	35	6	13	19	66	....	....	....	....	....	....	....	....	....	....	....	....	....	....	....	....	....	....
	Kingston	OHL	34	2	17	19	64	....	....	....	....	....	....	....	....	....	....	....	....	....	....	....	....	....	....
2003-04	Wilkes-Barre	AHL	23	1	2	3	26	....	....	....	....	....	....	....	....	....	....	....	....	....	....	....	....	....	....
	Wheeling Nailers	ECHL	28	6	10	16	61	....	....	....	....	....	....	....	....	....	4	0	0	0	8	....	....	....	....
2004-05	Wilkes-Barre	AHL	32	1	1	2	88	....	....	....	....	....	....	....	....	....	5	0	1	1	37	....	....	....	....
	Wheeling Nailers	ECHL	22	0	1	1	55	....	....	....	....	....	....	....	....	....	....	....	....	....	....	....	....	....	....
2005-06	Wilkes-Barre	AHL	28	1	12	13	98	....	....	....	....	....	....	....	....	....	11	0	0	0	16	....	....	....	....
	Wheeling Nailers	ECHL	34	10	8	18	145	....	....	....	....	....	....	....	....	....	....	....	....	....	....	....	....	....	....
2006-07	Bridgeport	AHL	64	3	7	10	185	....	....	....	....	....	....	....	....	....	....	....	....	....	....	....	....	....	....
	NY Islanders	**NHL**	**3**	**1**	**0**	**1**	**5**	**0**	**0**	**0**	**1**	**100.0**	**-2**	**0**	**0.0**	**10:17**	**1**	**0**	**0**	**0**	**0**	**0**	**0**	**0**	**6:04**
2007-08	**NY Islanders**	**NHL**	**5**	**0**	**1**	**1**	**4**	**0**	**0**	**0**	**4**	**0.0**	**-1**	**0**	**0.0**	**17:30**	....	....	....	....	....	....	....	....	....
	Bridgeport	AHL	71	3	11	14	197	....	....	....	....	....	....	....	....	....	....	....	....	....	....	....	....	....	....
2008-09	San Antonio	AHL	7	0	0	0	6	....	....	....	....	....	....	....	....	....	....	....	....	....	....	....	....	....	....
	Binghamton	AHL	68	7	9	16	135	....	....	....	....	....	....	....	....	....	....	....	....	....	....	....	....	....	....
2009-10	Providence Bruins	AHL	27	1	3	4	47	....	....	....	....	....	....	....	....	....	....	....	....	....	....	....	....	....	....
	NHL Totals		**8**	**1**	**1**	**2**	**9**	**0**	**0**	**0**	**5**	**20.0**		**0**	**0.0**	**14:48**	**1**	**0**	**0**	**0**	**0**	**0**	**0**	**0**	**6:04**

gned as a free agent by **NY Islanders**, December 21, 2006. Signed as a free agent by **Phoenix**, July 2, 2008. Traded to **Ottawa** by **Phoenix** for Alexander Nikulin, November 3, 2008. Signed as a free gent by **Boston**, July 7, 2009.

FEDORUK, Todd
(FEH-duh-ruhk, TAWD)

Left wing. Shoots left. 6'2", 232 lbs. Born, Redwater, Alta., February 13, 1979. Philadelphia's 6th choice, 164th overall, in 1997 Entry Draft.

			Regular Season														Playoffs								
Season	Club	League	GP	G	A	Pts	PIM	PP	SH	GW	S	%	+/-	TF	F%	Min	GP	G	A	Pts	PIM	PP	SH	GW	Min
1994-95	Ft. Saskatchewan	AMHL	STATISTICS NOT AVAILABLE																						
1995-96	Kelowna Rockets	WHL	44	1	1	2	83	....	....	....	....	....	....	....	....	....	4	0	0	0	6	....	....	....	....
1996-97	Kelowna Rockets	WHL	31	1	5	6	87	....	....	....	....	....	....	....	....	....	6	0	0	0	13	....	....	....	....
1997-98	Kelowna Rockets	WHL	31	3	5	8	120	....	....	....	....	....	....	....	....	....	....	....	....	....	....	....	....	....	....
	Regina Pats	WHL	21	4	3	7	80	....	....	....	....	....	....	....	....	....	9	1	2	3	23	....	....	....	....
1998-99	Regina Pats	WHL	39	12	12	24	107	....	....	....	....	....	....	....	....	....	....	....	....	....	....	....	....	....	....
	Prince Albert	WHL	28	6	4	10	75	....	....	....	....	....	....	....	....	....	13	1	6	7	49	....	....	....	....
99-2000	Trenton Titans	ECHL	18	2	5	7	118	....	....	....	....	....	....	....	....	....	....	....	....	....	....	....	....	....	....
	Philadelphia	AHL	19	1	2	3	40	....	....	....	....	....	....	....	....	....	5	0	1	1	2	....	....	....	....
2000-01	**Philadelphia**	**NHL**	**53**	**5**	**5**	**10**	**109**	**0**	**0**	**0**	**28**	**17.9**	**0**	**0**	**0.0**	**7:02**	**2**	**0**	**0**	**0**	**20**	**0**	**0**	**0**	**5:57**
	Philadelphia	AHL	14	0	1	1	49	....	....	....	....	....	....	....	....	....	....	....	....	....	....	....	....	....	....
2001-02	**Philadelphia**	**NHL**	**55**	**3**	**4**	**7**	**141**	**0**	**0**	**0**	**21**	**14.3**	**-2**	**5**	**0.0**	**6:21**	**3**	**0**	**0**	**0**	**0**	**0**	**0**	**0**	**2:46**
	Philadelphia	AHL	7	0	1	1	54	....	....	....	....	....	....	....	....	....	....	....	....	....	....	....	....	....	....
2002-03	**Philadelphia**	**NHL**	**63**	**1**	**5**	**6**	**105**	**0**	**0**	**0**	**33**	**3.0**	**1**	**1**	**0.0**	**6:30**	**1**	**0**	**0**	**0**	**0**	**0**	**0**	**0**	**4:52**
2003-04	**Philadelphia**	**NHL**	**49**	**1**	**4**	**5**	**136**	**0**	**0**	**1**	**33**	**3.0**	**-4**	**0**	**0.0**	**6:47**	**1**	**0**	**0**	**0**	**2**	**0**	**0**	**0**	**6:42**
	Philadelphia	AHL	2	0	2	2	2	....	....	....	....	....	....	....	....	....	....	....	....	....	....	....	....	....	....
2004-05	Philadelphia	AHL	42	4	12	16	142	....	....	....	....	....	....	....	....	....	16	2	2	4	33	....	....	....	....
2005-06	**Anaheim**	**NHL**	**76**	**4**	**19**	**23**	**174**	**0**	**0**	**1**	**69**	**5.8**	**6**	**8**	**37.5**	**8:24**	**12**	**0**	**0**	**0**	**16**	**0**	**0**	**0**	**8:19**
2006-07	**Anaheim**	**NHL**	**10**	**0**	**3**	**3**	**36**	**0**	**0**	**0**	**2**	**0.0**	**2**	**1**	**0.0**	**7:30**	....	....	....	....	....	....	....	....	....
	Philadelphia	**NHL**	**48**	**3**	**8**	**11**	**84**	**0**	**0**	**0**	**28**	**10.7**	**-11**	**2**	**0.0**	**9:03**	....	....	....	....	....	....	....	....	....
2007-08	**Dallas**	**NHL**	**11**	**0**	**2**	**2**	**33**	**0**	**0**	**0**	**6**	**0.0**	**2**	**0**	**0.0**	**6:50**	....	....	....	....	....	....	....	....	....
	Minnesota	**NHL**	**58**	**6**	**5**	**11**	**106**	**2**	**0**	**0**	**51**	**11.8**	**0**	**4**	**0.0**	**10:59**	**6**	**1**	**1**	**2**	**16**	**1**	**0**	**0**	**13:38**
2008-09	**Phoenix**	**NHL**	**72**	**6**	**7**	**13**	**72**	**0**	**0**	**0**	**56**	**10.7**	**-9**	**15**	**26.7**	**10:36**	....	....	....	....	....	....	....	....	....
2009-10	**Tampa Bay**	**NHL**	**50**	**3**	**3**	**6**	**54**	**0**	**0**	**0**	**22**	**13.6**	**-12**	**2**	**100.0**	**7:31**	....	....	....	....	....	....	....	....	....
	NHL Totals		**545**	**32**	**65**	**97**	**1050**	**2**	**0**	**2**	**349**	**9.2**		**38**	**23.7**	**8:11**	**25**	**1**	**1**	**2**	**54**	**1**	**0**	**0**	**8:32**

raded to **Anaheim** by **Philadelphia** for Anaheim's 2nd round choice (later traded to Phoenix - Phoenix selected Pier-Olivier Pelletier) in 2005 Entry Draft, July 29, 2005. Traded to **Philadelphia** by **naheim** for Philadelphia's 4th round choice (Justin Vaive) in 2007 Entry Draft, November 13, 2006. Signed as a free agent by **Dallas**, July 9, 2007. Claimed on waivers by **Minnesota** from **Dallas**, ovember 22, 2007. Signed as a free agent by **Phoenix**, July 1, 2008. Traded to **Tampa Bay** by **Phoenix** with David Hale for Radim Vrbata, July 21, 2009.

FEDOTENKO, Ruslan
(feh-doh-TEHN-koh, roos-LAHN)

Left wing. Shoots left. 6'2", 195 lbs. Born, Kiev, USSR, January 18, 1979.

			Regular Season														Playoffs								
Season	Club	League	GP	G	A	Pts	PIM	PP	SH	GW	S	%	+/-	TF	F%	Min	GP	G	A	Pts	PIM	PP	SH	GW	Min
1995-96	Kiev 2	EEHL	33	9	11	20	12	....	....	....	....	....	....	....	....	....	....	....	....	....	....	....	....	....	....
	Sokol Kiev	CIS	2	0	0	0	0	....	....	....	....	....	....	....	....	....	....	....	....	....	....	....	....	....	....
1996-97	TPS Turku U18	Fin-U18	3	3	2	5	2	....	....	....	....	....	....	....	....	....	....	....	....	....	....	....	....	....	....
	TPS Turku Jr.	Fin-Jr.	11	1	1	2	2	....	....	....	....	....	....	....	....	....	....	....	....	....	....	....	....	....	....
	Kiekko-67 Turku	Finland-2	22	4	3	7	16	....	....	....	....	....	....	....	....	....	....	....	....	....	....	....	....	....	....
	Kiekko Turku	Finland-3	....	....	....	....	....	....	....	....	....	....	....	....	....	....	3	1	0	1	2	....	....	....	....
1997-98	Melfort Mustangs	SJHL	68	35	31	66	55	....	....	....	....	....	....	....	....	....	....	....	....	....	....	....	....	....	....
1998-99	Sioux City	USHL	55	43	34	77	139	....	....	....	....	....	....	....	....	....	5	5	1	6	9	....	....	....	....
99-2000	Trenton Titans	ECHL	8	5	3	8	9	....	....	....	....	....	....	....	....	....	....	....	....	....	....	....	....	....	....
	Philadelphia	AHL	67	16	34	50	42	....	....	....	....	....	....	....	....	....	2	0	0	0	0	....	....	....	....
2000-01	**Philadelphia**	**NHL**	**74**	**16**	**20**	**36**	**72**	**3**	**0**	**4**	**119**	**13.4**	**8**	**7**	**71.4**	**14:38**	**6**	**0**	**1**	**1**	**4**	**0**	**0**	**0**	**11:18**
	Philadelphia	AHL	8	1	0	1	8	....	....	....	....	....	....	....	....	....	....	....	....	....	....	....	....	....	....
2001-02	**Philadelphia**	**NHL**	**78**	**17**	**9**	**26**	**43**	**0**	**1**	**3**	**121**	**14.0**	**15**	**41**	**43.9**	**13:56**	**5**	**1**	**0**	**1**	**2**	**0**	**0**	**1**	**14:11**
	Ukraine	Olympics	1	1	0	1	4	....	....	....	....	....	....	....	....	....	....	....	....	....	....	....	....	....	....
2002-03	**Tampa Bay**	**NHL**	**76**	**19**	**13**	**32**	**44**	**6**	**0**	**6**	**114**	**16.7**	**-7**	**90**	**48.9**	**16:01**	**11**	**0**	**1**	**1**	**2**	**0**	**0**	**0**	**13:58**
2003-04♦	**Tampa Bay**	**NHL**	**77**	**17**	**22**	**39**	**30**	**0**	**0**	**3**	**116**	**14.7**	**14**	**58**	**55.2**	**14:39**	**22**	**12**	**2**	**14**	**14**	**5**	**0**	**3**	**16:40**
2004-05			DID NOT PLAY																						
2005-06	**Tampa Bay**	**NHL**	**80**	**26**	**15**	**41**	**44**	**4**	**0**	**6**	**164**	**15.9**	**-4**	**28**	**42.9**	**15:21**	**5**	**0**	**0**	**0**	**20**	**0**	**0**	**0**	**14:38**
2006-07	**Tampa Bay**	**NHL**	**80**	**12**	**20**	**32**	**52**	**2**	**0**	**1**	**154**	**7.8**	**-3**	**8**	**25.0**	**16:15**	**4**	**0**	**0**	**0**	**4**	**0**	**0**	**0**	**17:27**
2007-08	**NY Islanders**	**NHL**	**67**	**16**	**17**	**33**	**40**	**8**	**0**	**2**	**121**	**13.2**	**-9**	**28**	**39.3**	**16:42**	....	....	....	....	....	....	....	....	....
2008-09♦	**Pittsburgh**	**NHL**	**65**	**16**	**23**	**39**	**44**	**1**	**0**	**3**	**117**	**13.7**	**18**	**18**	**22.2**	**14:06**	**24**	**7**	**7**	**14**	**4**	**0**	**0**	**0**	**14:31**
2009-10	**Pittsburgh**	**NHL**	**80**	**11**	**19**	**30**	**50**	**3**	**0**	**3**	**158**	**7.0**	**-17**	**28**	**35.7**	**14:39**	**6**	**0**	**0**	**0**	**4**	**0**	**0**	**0**	**12:31**
	NHL Totals		**677**	**150**	**158**	**308**	**419**	**27**	**1**	**31**	**1184**	**12.7**		**306**	**45.1**	**15:08**	**83**	**20**	**11**	**31**	**54**	**5**	**0**	**4**	**14:46**

JSHL First All-Star Team (1999)

igned as a free agent by **Philadelphia**, August 3, 1999. Traded to **Tampa Bay** by **Philadelphia** with Tampa Bay's 2nd round choice (previously acquired, later traded to Dallas – Dallas selected Tobias tephan) in 2002 Entry Draft and Phoenix's 2nd round choice (previously acquired, later traded to San Jose – San Jose selected Dan Spang) in 2002 Entry Draft for Tampa Bay's 1st round choice (Joni itkanen) in 2002 Entry Draft, June 21, 2002. Signed as a free agent by **NY Islanders**, July 4, 2007. Signed as a free agent by **Pittsburgh**, July 3, 2008.

FEHR, Eric
(FAIR, AIR-ihk) **WSH.**

Right wing. Shoots right. 6'4", 212 lbs. Born, Winkler, Man., September 7, 1985. Washington's 1st choice, 18th overall, in 2003 Entry Draft.

			Regular Season														Playoffs								
Season	Club	League	GP	G	A	Pts	PIM	PP	SH	GW	S	%	+/-	TF	F%	Min	GP	G	A	Pts	PIM	PP	SH	GW	Min
2000-01	Pembina Valley	MMMHL	36	45	13	58	30	....	....	....	....	....	....	....	....	....	....	....	....	....	....	....	....	....	....
	Brandon	WHL	4	0	0	0	0	....	....	....	....	....	....	....	....	....	....	....	....	....	....	....	....	....	....
2001-02	Brandon	WHL	63	11	16	27	29	....	....	....	....	....	....	....	....	....	12	1	1	2	0	....	....	....	....
2002-03	Brandon	WHL	70	26	29	55	76	....	....	....	....	....	....	....	....	....	17	4	8	12	26	....	....	....	....
2003-04	Brandon	WHL	71	50	34	84	129	....	....	....	....	....	....	....	....	....	7	5	0	5	16	....	....	....	....
2004-05	Brandon	WHL	71	*59	52	*111	91	....	....	....	....	....	....	....	....	....	24	16	16	*32	47	....	....	....	....
2005-06	**Washington**	**NHL**	**11**	**0**	**0**	**0**	**2**	**0**	**0**	**0**	**10**	**0.0**	**0**	**4**	**25.0**	**5:45**	....	....	....	....	....	....	....	....	....
	Hershey Bears	AHL	70	25	28	53	70	....	....	....	....	....	....	....	....	....	19	8	3	11	8	....	....	....	....
2006-07	**Washington**	**NHL**	**14**	**2**	**1**	**3**	**8**	**0**	**0**	**1**	**25**	**8.0**	**3**	**6**	**16.7**	**10:43**	....	....	....	....	....	....	....	....	....
	Hershey Bears	AHL	40	22	19	41	63	....	....	....	....	....	....	....	....	....	....	....	....	....	....	....	....	....	....
2007-08	**Washington**	**NHL**	**23**	**1**	**5**	**6**	**6**	**0**	**0**	**0**	**40**	**2.5**	**4**	**2**	**0.0**	**10:31**	**5**	**1**	**0**	**1**	**0**	**0**	**0**	**0**	**9:41**
	Hershey Bears	AHL	11	3	4	7	4	....	....	....	....	....	....	....	....	....	2	1	3	4	2	....	....	....	....

Season	Club	League	GP	G	A	Pts	PIM	PP	SH	GW	S	%	+/-	TF	F%	Min	GP	G	A	Pts	PIM	PP	SH	GW	M
2008-09	Washington	NHL	61	12	13	25	22	1	0	2	134	9.0	8	3	33.3	11:15	9	0	0	0	0	0	0	0	7:2
2009-10	Washington	NHL	69	21	18	39	24	3	0	3	145	14.5	18	2	50.0	12:08	7	3	1	4	4	0	0	0	11:2
	NHL Totals		178	36	37	73	62	4	0	6	354	10.2		17	23.5	11:07	21	4	1	5	4	0	0	0	9:1

WHL East First All-Star Team (2005) • WHL Player of the Year (2005) • Canadian Major Junior Second All-Star Team (2005)

FERENCE, Andrew

Defense. Shoots left. 5'11", 189 lbs.   Born, Edmonton, Alta., March 17, 1979. Pittsburgh's 8th choice, 208th overall, in 1997 Entry Draft.

(FAIR-ehns, AN-droo)   BOS

Season	Club	League	GP	G	A	Pts	PIM	PP	SH	GW	S	%	+/-	TF	F%	Min	GP	G	A	Pts	PIM	PP	SH	GW	M
1994-95	Sherwood Park	AMHL	31	4	14	18	74																		
	Portland	WHL	2	0	0	0	4																		
1995-96	Portland	WHL	72	9	31	40	159																		
1996-97	Portland	WHL	72	12	32	44	163										7	1	3	4	12				
1997-98	Portland	WHL	72	11	57	68	142										6	1	2	3	12				
1998-99	Portland	WHL	40	11	21	32	104										16	2	18	20	28				
	Kansas City	IHL	5	1	2	3	4										4	1	4	5	10				
99-2000	Pittsburgh	NHL	30	2	4	6	20	0	0	1	26	7.7	3	0	0.0	16:19	3	0	0	0	9				
	Wilkes-Barre	AHL	44	8	20	28	58																		
2000-01	Pittsburgh	NHL	36	4	11	15	28	1	0	1	47	8.5	6	0	0.0	18:51	18	3	7	10	16	1	0	1	22:02
	Wilkes-Barre	AHL	43	6	18	24	95										3	1	0	1	12				
2001-02	Pittsburgh	NHL	75	4	7	11	73	1	0	0	82	4.9	-12	2	0.0	18:34									
2002-03	Pittsburgh	NHL	22	1	3	4	36	1	0	0	22	4.5	-16	1	100.0	19:33									
	Wilkes-Barre	AHL	1	0	0	0	2																		
	Calgary	NHL	16	0	4	4	6	0	0	0	17	0.0	1	0	0.0	17:38									
2003-04	Calgary	NHL	72	4	12	16	53	1	0	0	86	4.7	5	0	0.0	18:40	26	0	3	3	25			0	24:13
2004-05	C. Budejovice	CzRep-2	19	5	6	11	45										12	2	7	9	10				
2005-06	Calgary	NHL	82	4	27	31	85	2	0	0	111	3.6	-12	1	0.0	20:08	7	0	4	4	12			0	23:09
2006-07	Calgary	NHL	54	2	10	12	66	1	0	0	51	3.9	7	3	33.3	18:29									
	Boston	NHL	26	1	2	3	31	0	0	0	29	3.4	-2	0	0.0	22:22									
2007-08	Boston	NHL	59	1	14	15	50	0	0	0	71	1.4	-14	1	100.0	22:15	7	0	4	4	6	0	0	0	21:39
2008-09	Boston	NHL	47	1	15	16	40	1	0	0	72	1.4	7	0	0.0	21:32	3	0	0	0	4	0	0	0	15:30
2009-10	Boston	NHL	51	0	8	8	16	0	0	0	60	0.0	-7	0	0.0	19:42	13	0	1	1	18	0	0	0	14:58
	NHL Totals		570	24	117	141	504	8	0	2	674	3.6		8	37.5	19:37	74	3	19	22	81	1	0	1	21:22

WHL West First All-Star Team (1998) • WHL West Second All-Star Team (1999)

• Missed majority of 2002-03 season recovering from groin (November 18, 2002 vs. Montreal) and ankle (March 20, 2003 vs. Los Angeles) injuries. Traded to **Calgary** by **Pittsburgh** for Calgary's 3rd round choice (Brian Gifford) in 2004 Entry Draft, February 9, 2003. Signed as a free agent by **Ceske Budejovice** (CzRep-2), December 1, 2004. Traded to **Boston** by **Calgary** with Chuck Kobasew for Brad Stuart, Wayne Primeau and Washington's 4th round choice (previously acquired, Calgary selected T.J. Brodie) in 2008 Entry Draft, February 10, 2007.

FERRIERO, Benn

Center. Shoots right. 5'11", 195 lbs.   Born, Boston, MA, April 29, 1987. Phoenix's 8th choice, 196th overall, in 2006 Entry Draft.

(fuh-RAIR-oh, BEHN)   S.J.

Season	Club	League	GP	G	A	Pts	PIM	PP	SH	GW	S	%	+/-	TF	F%	Min	GP	G	A	Pts	PIM	PP	SH	GW	M
2001-02	Gov. Dummer	High-MA	STATISTICS NOT AVAILABLE																						
2002-03	Gov. Dummer	High-MA		8	10	18																			
2003-04	Gov. Dummer	High-MA	28	19	24	43																			
2004-05	Gov. Dummer	High-MA	28	15	27	42																			
2005-06	Boston College	H-East	42	16	9	25	36																		
2006-07	Boston College	H-East	42	23	23	46	43																		
2007-08	Boston College	H-East	44	17	25	42	71																		
2008-09	Boston College	H-East	37	8	18	26	44																		
2009-10	San Jose	NHL	24	2	3	5	8	0	0	0	42	4.8	4	4	75.0	11:08									
	Worcester Sharks	AHL	58	19	31	50	20										11	4	2	6	4				
	NHL Totals		24	2	3	5	8	0	0	0	42	4.8		4	75.0	11:08									

Hockey East All-Rookie Team (2006)
Signed as a free agent by **San Jose**, August 23, 2009.

FESTERLING, Brett

Defense. Shoots left. 6'1", 210 lbs.   Born, Quesnel, B.C., March 3, 1986.

(FEHS-tuhr-lihng, BREHT)   ANA.

Season	Club	League	GP	G	A	Pts	PIM	PP	SH	GW	S	%	+/-	TF	F%	Min	GP	G	A	Pts	PIM	PP	SH	GW	M
2001-02	Quesnel Thunder	Minor-BC	40	18	26	44	44																		
	Quesnel	BCHL	7	0	0	0	0																		
	Tri-City	WHL	3	0	0	0	0																		
2002-03	Tri-City	WHL	55	3	8	11	26																		
2003-04	Tri-City	WHL	54	1	9	10	34																		
2004-05	Tri-City	WHL	33	3	11	14	20										11	1	1	2	2				
	Vancouver Giants	WHL	32	2	4	6	10																		
2005-06	Vancouver Giants	WHL	67	1	6	7	35										5	0	0	0	6				
2006-07	Vancouver Giants	WHL	70	5	16	21	80										18	0	1	1	10				
2007-08	Portland Pirates	AHL	74	3	11	14	64										22	1	6	7	24				
2008-09	Anaheim	NHL	40	0	5	5	18	0	0	0	15	0.0	5	0	0.0	16:40	1	0	0	0	0	0	0	0	14:34
	Iowa Chops	AHL	34	0	7	7	31										15	1	3	4	6				
2009-10	Anaheim	NHL	42	0	3	3	15	0	0	0	25	0.0	1	0	0.0	12:30									
	San Antonio	AHL	17	0	1	1	19																		
	Toronto Marlies	AHL	11	0	4	4	8																		
	NHL Totals		82	0	8	8	33	0	0	0	40	0.0		0	0.0	14:32	1	0	0	0	0	0	0	0	14:34

Signed as a free agent by **Anaheim**, September 14, 2005.

FIDDLER, Vernon

Center. Shoots left. 5'11", 201 lbs.   Born, Edmonton, Alta., May 9, 1980.

(FIHD-luhr, VUHR-nuhn)   PHX.

Season	Club	League	GP	G	A	Pts	PIM	PP	SH	GW	S	%	+/-	TF	F%	Min	GP	G	A	Pts	PIM	PP	SH	GW	M
1997-98	Kelowna Rockets	WHL	65	10	11	21	31										7	0	1	1	4				
1998-99	Kelowna Rockets	WHL	68	22	21	43	82										6	2	0	2	8				
99-2000	Kelowna Rockets	WHL	64	20	28	48	60										5	1	3	4	4				
2000-01	Kelowna Rockets	WHL	3	0	2	2	0																		
	Medicine Hat	WHL	67	33	38	71	100																		
	Arkansas	ECHL	3	0	1	1	2																		
2001-02	Roanoke Express	ECHL	44	27	28	55	71										5	3	0	3	5				
	Norfolk Admirals	AHL	38	8	5	13	28										4	1	3	4	2				
2002-03	Nashville	NHL	19	4	2	6	14	0	0	1	20	20.0	2	171	53.8	9:40									
	Milwaukee	AHL	54	8	16	24	70										6	1	2	3	14				
2003-04	Nashville	NHL	10	0	0	0	23	0	0	0	8	0.0	-6	123	49.6	8:06									
	Milwaukee	AHL	47	9	15	24	72										22	5	3	8	36				
2004-05	Milwaukee	AHL	73	20	22	42	70										7	0	0	0	18				
2005-06	Nashville	NHL	40	8	4	12	42	3	0	2	46	17.4	-2	464	52.6	13:49	2	0	1	1	0	0	0	0	8:48
	Milwaukee	AHL	11	1	6	7	20																		
2006-07	Nashville	NHL	72	11	15	26	40	0	1	1	90	12.2	11	680	51.6	13:38	5	1	1	2	4	0	0	0	12:21
2007-08	Nashville	NHL	79	11	21	32	47	2	1	1	97	11.3	-4	384	50.3	13:56	6	0	0	0	0	0	0	0	16:48
2008-09	Nashville	NHL	78	11	6	17	24	1	2	2	114	9.6	-13	612	54.1	13:58									
2009-10	Phoenix	NHL	76	8	22	30	46	0	3	1	119	6.7	13	1121	52.5	14:21	6	1	1	2	14	0	0	0	14:04
	NHL Totals		381	53	70	123	236	6	7	8	494	10.7		3555	52.3	13:29	19	2	3	5	18	0	0	0	13:55

ECHL All-Rookie Team (2002)
Signed as a free agent by **Arkansas** (ECHL), March 31, 2001. Traded to **Roanoke** (ECHL) by **Arkansas** (ECHL) for Calvin Elfring, August 11, 2001. Signed as a free agent by **Nashville**, May 6, 2002. Signed as a free agent by **Phoenix**, July 1, 2009.

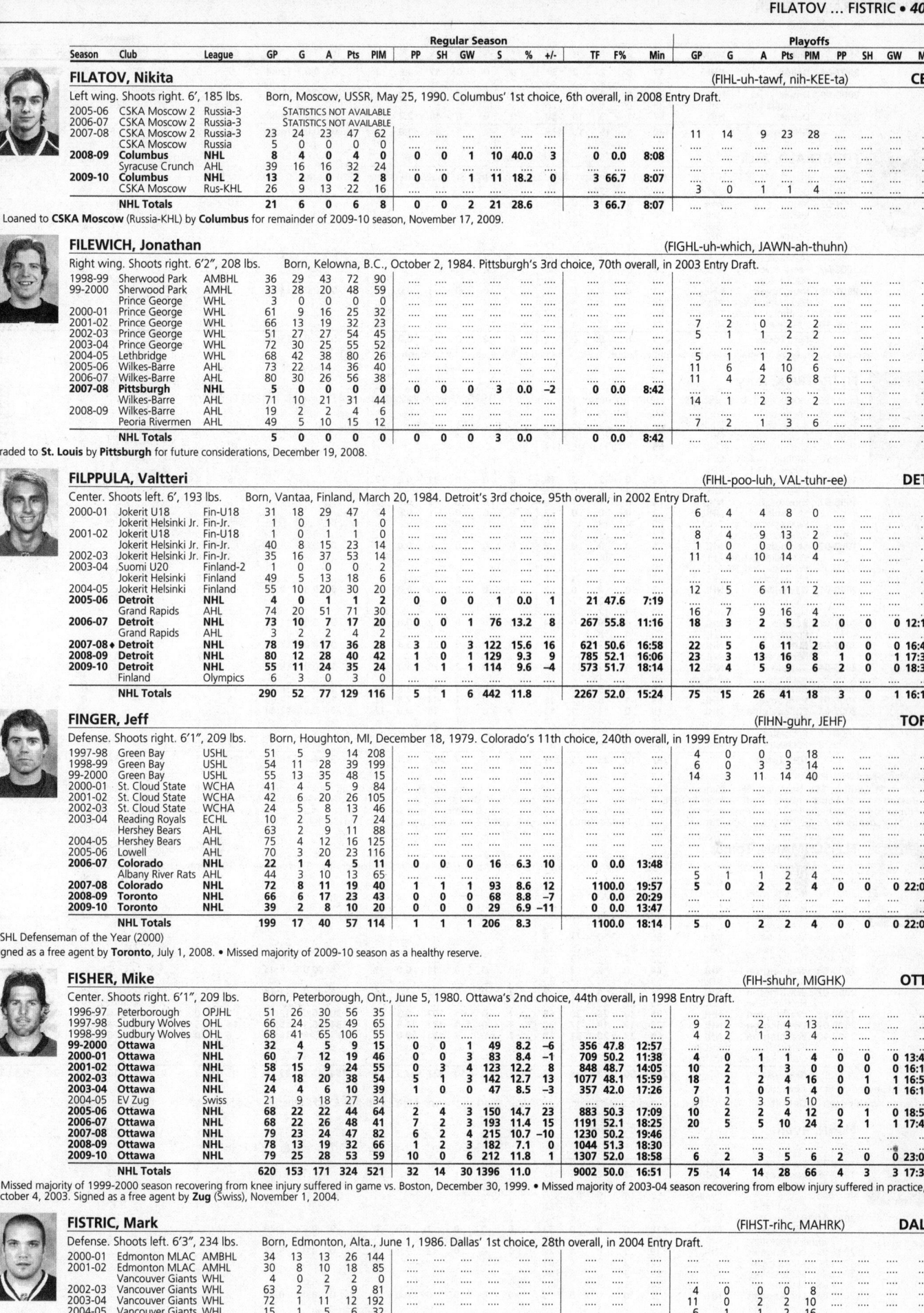

			Regular Season														Playoffs								
Season	Club	League	GP	G	A	Pts	PIM	PP	SH	GW	S	%	+/-	TF	F%	Min	GP	G	A	Pts	PIM	PP	SH	GW	Min

FILATOV, Nikita

(FIHL-uh-tawf, nih-KEE-ta) **CBJ**

Left wing. Shoots right. 6', 185 lbs. Born, Moscow, USSR, May 25, 1990. Columbus' 1st choice, 6th overall, in 2008 Entry Draft.

2005-06	CSKA Moscow 2	Russia-3	STATISTICS NOT AVAILABLE																						
2006-07	CSKA Moscow 2	Russia-3	STATISTICS NOT AVAILABLE																						
2007-08	CSKA Moscow 2	Russia-3	23	24	23	47	62	....	....	....	....	....	....	....	....	....	11	14	9	23	28	....	....	....	....
	CSKA Moscow	Russia	5	0	0	0	0	....	....	....	....	....	....	....	....	....	....	....	....	....	....	....	....	....	....
2008-09	**Columbus**	**NHL**	**8**	**4**	**0**	**4**	**0**	**0**	**0**	**1**	**10**	**40.0**	**3**	**0**	**0.0**	**8:08**	....	....	....	....	....	....	....	....	....
	Syracuse Crunch	AHL	39	16	16	32	24	....	....	....	....	....	....	....	....	....	....	....	....	....	....	....	....	....	....
2009-10	**Columbus**	**NHL**	**13**	**2**	**0**	**2**	**8**	**0**	**0**	**1**	**11**	**18.2**	**0**	**3**	**66.7**	**8:07**	....	....	....	....	....	....	....	....	....
	CSKA Moscow	Rus-KHL	26	9	13	22	16	....	....	....	....	....	....	....	....	....	3	0	1	1	4	....	....	....	....
	NHL Totals		**21**	**6**	**0**	**6**	**8**	**0**	**0**	**2**	**21**	**28.6**		**3**	**66.7**	**8:07**	....	....	....	....	....	....	....	....	....

• Loaned to **CSKA Moscow** (Russia-KHL) by **Columbus** for remainder of 2009-10 season, November 17, 2009.

FILEWICH, Jonathan

(FIGHL-uh-which, JAWN-ah-thuhn)

Right wing. Shoots right. 6'2", 208 lbs. Born, Kelowna, B.C., October 2, 1984. Pittsburgh's 3rd choice, 70th overall, in 2003 Entry Draft.

1998-99	Sherwood Park	AMBHL	36	29	43	72	90	....	....	....	....	....	....	....	....	....	....	....	....	....	....	....	....	....	....
99-2000	Sherwood Park	AMHL	33	28	20	48	59	....	....	....	....	....	....	....	....	....	....	....	....	....	....	....	....	....	....
	Prince George	WHL	3	0	0	0	0	....	....	....	....	....	....	....	....	....	....	....	....	....	....	....	....	....	....
2000-01	Prince George	WHL	61	9	16	25	32	....	....	....	....	....	....	....	....	....	....	....	....	....	....	....	....	....	....
2001-02	Prince George	WHL	66	13	19	32	23	....	....	....	....	....	....	....	....	....	7	2	0	2	2	....	....	....	....
2002-03	Prince George	WHL	51	27	27	54	45	....	....	....	....	....	....	....	....	....	5	1	1	2	2	....	....	....	....
2003-04	Prince George	WHL	72	30	25	55	52	....	....	....	....	....	....	....	....	....	....	....	....	....	....	....	....	....	....
2004-05	Lethbridge	WHL	68	42	38	80	26	....	....	....	....	....	....	....	....	....	5	1	1	2	2	....	....	....	....
2005-06	Wilkes-Barre	AHL	73	22	14	36	40	....	....	....	....	....	....	....	....	....	11	6	4	10	6	....	....	....	....
2006-07	Wilkes-Barre	AHL	80	30	26	56	38	....	....	....	....	....	....	....	....	....	11	4	2	6	8	....	....	....	....
2007-08	**Pittsburgh**	**NHL**	**5**	**0**	**0**	**0**	**0**	**0**	**0**	**0**	**3**	**0.0**	**–2**	**0**	**0.0**	**8:42**	....	....	....	....	....	....	....	....	....
	Wilkes-Barre	AHL	71	10	21	31	44	....	....	....	....	....	....	....	....	....	14	1	2	3	2	....	....	....	....
2008-09	Wilkes-Barre	AHL	19	2	2	4	6	....	....	....	....	....	....	....	....	....	....	....	....	....	....	....	....	....	....
	Peoria Rivermen	AHL	49	5	10	15	12	....	....	....	....	....	....	....	....	....	7	2	1	3	6	....	....	....	....
	NHL Totals		**5**	**0**	**0**	**0**	**0**	**0**	**0**	**0**	**3**	**0.0**		**0**	**0.0**	**8:42**	....	....	....	....	....	....	....	....	....

Traded to **St. Louis** by **Pittsburgh** for future considerations, December 19, 2008.

FILPPULA, Valtteri

(FIHL-poo-luh, VAL-tuhr-ee) **DET.**

Center. Shoots left. 6', 193 lbs. Born, Vantaa, Finland, March 20, 1984. Detroit's 3rd choice, 95th overall, in 2002 Entry Draft.

2000-01	Jokerit U18	Fin-U18	31	18	29	47	4	....	....	....	....	....	....	....	....	....	6	4	4	8	0	....	....	....	....
	Jokerit Helsinki Jr.	Fin-Jr.	1	0	1	1	0	....	....	....	....	....	....	....	....	....	....	....	....	....	....	....	....	....	....
2001-02	Jokerit U18	Fin-U18	1	0	1	1	0	....	....	....	....	....	....	....	....	....	8	4	9	13	2	....	....	....	....
	Jokerit Helsinki Jr.	Fin-Jr.	40	8	15	23	14	....	....	....	....	....	....	....	....	....	1	0	0	0	0	....	....	....	....
2002-03	Jokerit Helsinki Jr.	Fin-Jr.	35	16	37	53	14	....	....	....	....	....	....	....	....	....	11	4	10	14	4	....	....	....	....
2003-04	Suomi U20	Finland-2	1	0	0	0	2	....	....	....	....	....	....	....	....	....	....	....	....	....	....	....	....	....	....
	Jokerit Helsinki	Finland	49	5	13	18	6	....	....	....	....	....	....	....	....	....	....	....	....	....	....	....	....	....	....
2004-05	Jokerit Helsinki	Finland	55	10	20	30	20	....	....	....	....	....	....	....	....	....	12	5	6	11	2	....	....	....	....
2005-06	**Detroit**	**NHL**	**4**	**0**	**1**	**1**	**2**	**0**	**0**	**0**	**1**	**0.0**	**1**	**21**	**47.6**	**7:19**	....	....	....	....	....	....	....	....	....
	Grand Rapids	AHL	74	20	51	71	30	....	....	....	....	....	....	....	....	....	16	7	9	16	4	....	....	....	....
2006-07	**Detroit**	**NHL**	**73**	**10**	**7**	**17**	**20**	**0**	**0**	**1**	**76**	**13.2**	**8**	**267**	**55.8**	**11:16**	**18**	**3**	**2**	**5**	**2**	**0**	**0**	**0**	**12:12**
	Grand Rapids	AHL	3	2	2	4	2	....	....	....	....	....	....	....	....	....	....	....	....	....	....	....	....	....	....
2007-08♦	**Detroit**	**NHL**	**78**	**19**	**17**	**36**	**28**	**3**	**0**	**3**	**122**	**15.6**	**16**	**621**	**50.6**	**16:58**	**22**	**5**	**6**	**11**	**2**	**0**	**0**	**0**	**16:40**
2008-09	**Detroit**	**NHL**	**80**	**12**	**28**	**40**	**42**	**1**	**0**	**1**	**129**	**9.3**	**9**	**785**	**52.1**	**16:06**	**23**	**3**	**13**	**16**	**8**	**1**	**0**	**1**	**17:38**
2009-10	**Detroit**	**NHL**	**55**	**11**	**24**	**35**	**24**	**1**	**1**	**1**	**114**	**9.6**	**–4**	**573**	**51.7**	**18:14**	**12**	**4**	**5**	**9**	**6**	**2**	**0**	**0**	**18:34**
	Finland	Olympics	6	3	0	3	0	....	....	....	....	....	....	....	....	....	....	....	....	....	....	....	....	....	....
	NHL Totals		**290**	**52**	**77**	**129**	**116**	**5**	**1**	**6**	**442**	**11.8**		**2267**	**52.0**	**15:24**	**75**	**15**	**26**	**41**	**18**	**3**	**0**	**1**	**16:12**

FINGER, Jeff

(FIHN-guhr, JEHF) **TOR.**

Defense. Shoots right. 6'1", 209 lbs. Born, Houghton, MI, December 18, 1979. Colorado's 11th choice, 240th overall, in 1999 Entry Draft.

1997-98	Green Bay	USHL	51	5	9	14	208	....	....	....	....	....	....	....	....	....	4	0	0	0	18	....	....	....	....
1998-99	Green Bay	USHL	54	11	28	39	199	....	....	....	....	....	....	....	....	....	6	0	3	3	14	....	....	....	....
99-2000	Green Bay	USHL	55	13	35	48	15	....	....	....	....	....	....	....	....	....	14	3	11	14	40	....	....	....	....
2000-01	St. Cloud State	WCHA	41	4	5	9	84	....	....	....	....	....	....	....	....	....	....	....	....	....	....	....	....	....	....
2001-02	St. Cloud State	WCHA	42	6	20	26	105	....	....	....	....	....	....	....	....	....	....	....	....	....	....	....	....	....	....
2002-03	St. Cloud State	WCHA	24	5	8	13	46	....	....	....	....	....	....	....	....	....	....	....	....	....	....	....	....	....	....
2003-04	Reading Royals	ECHL	10	2	5	7	24	....	....	....	....	....	....	....	....	....	....	....	....	....	....	....	....	....	....
	Hershey Bears	AHL	63	2	9	11	88	....	....	....	....	....	....	....	....	....	....	....	....	....	....	....	....	....	....
2004-05	Hershey Bears	AHL	75	4	12	16	125	....	....	....	....	....	....	....	....	....	....	....	....	....	....	....	....	....	....
2005-06	Lowell	AHL	70	3	20	23	116	....	....	....	....	....	....	....	....	....	....	....	....	....	....	....	....	....	....
2006-07	**Colorado**	**NHL**	**22**	**1**	**4**	**5**	**11**	**0**	**0**	**0**	**16**	**6.3**	**10**	**0**	**0.0**	**13:48**	....	....	....	....	....	....	....	....	....
	Albany River Rats	AHL	44	3	10	13	65	....	....	....	....	....	....	....	....	....	5	1	1	2	4	....	....	....	....
2007-08	**Colorado**	**NHL**	**72**	**8**	**11**	**19**	**40**	**1**	**1**	**1**	**93**	**8.6**	**12**	**1**	**100.0**	**19:57**	**5**	**0**	**2**	**2**	**4**	**0**	**0**	**0**	**22:05**
2008-09	**Toronto**	**NHL**	**66**	**6**	**17**	**23**	**43**	**0**	**0**	**0**	**68**	**8.8**	**–7**	**0**	**0.0**	**20:29**	....	....	....	....	....	....	....	....	....
2009-10	**Toronto**	**NHL**	**39**	**2**	**8**	**10**	**20**	**0**	**0**	**0**	**29**	**6.9**	**–11**	**0**	**0.0**	**13:47**	....	....	....	....	....	....	....	....	....
	NHL Totals		**199**	**17**	**40**	**57**	**114**	**1**	**1**	**1**	**206**	**8.3**		**1**	**100.0**	**18:14**	**5**	**0**	**2**	**2**	**4**	**0**	**0**	**0**	**22:05**

USHL Defenseman of the Year (2000)

Signed as a free agent by **Toronto**, July 1, 2008. • Missed majority of 2009-10 season as a healthy reserve.

FISHER, Mike

(FIH-shuhr, MIGHK) **OTT.**

Center. Shoots right. 6'1", 209 lbs. Born, Peterborough, Ont., June 5, 1980. Ottawa's 2nd choice, 44th overall, in 1998 Entry Draft.

1996-97	Peterborough	OPJHL	51	26	30	56	35	....	....	....	....	....	....	....	....	....	....	....	....	....	....	....	....	....	....
1997-98	Sudbury Wolves	OHL	66	24	25	49	65	....	....	....	....	....	....	....	....	....	9	2	2	4	13	....	....	....	....
1998-99	Sudbury Wolves	OHL	68	41	65	106	55	....	....	....	....	....	....	....	....	....	4	2	1	3	4	....	....	....	....
99-2000	**Ottawa**	**NHL**	**32**	**4**	**5**	**9**	**15**	**0**	**0**	**1**	**49**	**8.2**	**–6**	**356**	**47.8**	**12:57**	....	....	....	....	....	....	....	....	....
2000-01	**Ottawa**	**NHL**	**60**	**7**	**12**	**19**	**46**	**0**	**0**	**3**	**83**	**8.4**	**–1**	**709**	**50.2**	**11:38**	**4**	**0**	**1**	**1**	**4**	**0**	**0**	**0**	**13:41**
2001-02	**Ottawa**	**NHL**	**58**	**15**	**9**	**24**	**55**	**0**	**3**	**4**	**123**	**12.2**	**8**	**848**	**48.7**	**14:05**	**10**	**2**	**1**	**3**	**0**	**0**	**0**	**0**	**16:17**
2002-03	**Ottawa**	**NHL**	**74**	**18**	**20**	**38**	**54**	**5**	**1**	**3**	**142**	**12.7**	**13**	**1077**	**48.1**	**15:59**	**18**	**2**	**2**	**4**	**16**	**0**	**1**	**1**	**16:58**
2003-04	**Ottawa**	**NHL**	**24**	**4**	**6**	**10**	**39**	**1**	**0**	**0**	**47**	**8.5**	**–3**	**357**	**42.0**	**17:26**	**7**	**1**	**0**	**1**	**4**	**0**	**0**	**1**	**16:11**
2004-05	EV Zug	Swiss	21	9	18	27	34	....	....	....	....	....	....	....	....	....	9	2	3	5	10	....	....	....	....
2005-06	**Ottawa**	**NHL**	**68**	**22**	**22**	**44**	**64**	**2**	**4**	**3**	**150**	**14.7**	**23**	**883**	**50.3**	**17:09**	**10**	**2**	**2**	**4**	**12**	**0**	**1**	**0**	**18:50**
2006-07	**Ottawa**	**NHL**	**68**	**22**	**26**	**48**	**41**	**7**	**2**	**3**	**193**	**11.4**	**15**	**1191**	**52.1**	**18:25**	**20**	**5**	**5**	**10**	**24**	**2**	**1**	**1**	**17:43**
2007-08	**Ottawa**	**NHL**	**79**	**23**	**24**	**47**	**82**	**6**	**2**	**4**	**215**	**10.7**	**–10**	**1230**	**50.2**	**19:46**	....	....	....	....	....	....	....	....	....
2008-09	**Ottawa**	**NHL**	**78**	**13**	**19**	**32**	**66**	**1**	**2**	**3**	**182**	**7.1**	**0**	**1044**	**51.3**	**18:30**	....	....	....	....	....	....	....	....	....
2009-10	**Ottawa**	**NHL**	**79**	**25**	**28**	**53**	**59**	**10**	**0**	**6**	**212**	**11.8**	**1**	**1307**	**52.0**	**18:58**	**6**	**2**	**3**	**5**	**6**	**2**	**0**	**0**	**23:04**
	NHL Totals		**620**	**153**	**171**	**324**	**521**	**32**	**14**	**30**	**1396**	**11.0**		**9002**	**50.0**	**16:51**	**75**	**14**	**14**	**28**	**66**	**4**	**3**	**3**	**17:34**

Missed majority of 1999-2000 season recovering from knee injury suffered in game vs. Boston, December 30, 1999. • Missed majority of 2003-04 season recovering from elbow injury suffered in practice, October 4, 2003. Signed as a free agent by **Zug** (Swiss), November 1, 2004.

FISTRIC, Mark

(FIHST-rihc, MAHRK) **DAL.**

Defense. Shoots left. 6'3", 234 lbs. Born, Edmonton, Alta., June 1, 1986. Dallas' 1st choice, 28th overall, in 2004 Entry Draft.

2000-01	Edmonton MLAC	AMBHL	34	13	13	26	144	....	....	....	....	....	....	....	....	....	....	....	....	....	....	....	....	....	....
2001-02	Edmonton MLAC	AMHL	30	8	10	18	85	....	....	....	....	....	....	....	....	....	....	....	....	....	....	....	....	....	....
	Vancouver Giants	WHL	4	0	2	2	0	....	....	....	....	....	....	....	....	....	....	....	....	....	....	....	....	....	....
2002-03	Vancouver Giants	WHL	63	2	7	9	81	....	....	....	....	....	....	....	....	....	4	0	0	0	8	....	....	....	....
2003-04	Vancouver Giants	WHL	72	1	11	12	192	....	....	....	....	....	....	....	....	....	11	0	2	2	10	....	....	....	....
2004-05	Vancouver Giants	WHL	15	1	5	6	32	....	....	....	....	....	....	....	....	....	6	1	1	2	16	....	....	....	....
2005-06	Vancouver Giants	WHL	60	7	22	29	148	....	....	....	....	....	....	....	....	....	18	1	9	10	30	....	....	....	....
2006-07	Iowa Stars	AHL	80	2	22	24	83	....	....	....	....	....	....	....	....	....	12	0	0	0	16	....	....	....	....

			Regular Season														Playoffs								
Season	Club	League	GP	G	A	Pts	PIM	PP	SH	GW	S	%	+/-	TF	F%	Min	GP	G	A	Pts	PIM	PP	SH	GW	Min
2007-08	**Dallas**	**NHL**	**37**	**0**	**2**	**2**	**24**	**0**	**0**	**0**	**17**	**0.0**	**3**	**0**	**0.0**	**12:44**	**9**	**0**	**0**	**0**	**6**	**0**	**0**	**0**	**14:51**
	Iowa Stars	AHL	30	1	4	5	48	....	....	....	....	....	....	....	....	....	....	....	....	....	....	....	....	....	....
2008-09	**Dallas**	**NHL**	**36**	**0**	**4**	**4**	**42**	**0**	**0**	**0**	**35**	**0.0**	**–1**	**0**	**0.0**	**15:57**	....	....	....	....	....	....	....	....	....
	Manitoba Moose	AHL	35	0	8	8	26	....	....	....	....	....	....	....	....	....	22	2	5	7	26	....	....	....	....
2009-10	**Dallas**	**NHL**	**67**	**1**	**9**	**10**	**69**	**0**	**0**	**0**	**46**	**2.2**	**27**	**0**	**0.0**	**14:56**	....	....	....	....	....	....	....	....	....
	NHL Totals		**140**	**1**	**15**	**16**	**135**	**0**	**0**	**0**	**98**	**1.0**		**0**	**0.0**	**14:37**	**9**	**0**	**0**	**0**	**6**	**0**	**0**	**0**	**14:51**

FITZGERALD, Zack

(fihtz-JAIR-uhld, ZAK) **CAR.**

Defense. Shoots left. 6'2", 205 lbs. Born, Two Harbors, MN, June 16, 1985. St. Louis' 4th choice, 88th overall, in 2003 Entry Draft.

Season	Club	League	GP	G	A	Pts	PIM	PP	SH	GW	S	%	+/-	TF	F%	Min	GP	G	A	Pts	PIM	PP	SH	GW	Min
2000-01	Duluth East	High-MN	26	1	7	8	44	....	....	....	....	....	....	....	....	....	....	....	....	....	....	....	....	....	....
2001-02	Seattle	WHL	61	3	7	10	214	....	....	....	....	....	....	....	....	....	10	0	2	2	19	....	....	....	....
2002-03	Seattle	WHL	64	8	14	22	232	....	....	....	....	....	....	....	....	....	15	0	4	4	33	....	....	....	....
2003-04	Seattle	WHL	58	4	15	19	163	....	....	....	....	....	....	....	....	....	....	....	....	....	....	....	....	....	....
2004-05	Seattle	WHL	65	7	18	25	*244	....	....	....	....	....	....	....	....	....	9	0	3	3	24	....	....	....	....
2005-06	Peoria Rivermen	AHL	13	1	1	2	47	....	....	....	....	....	....	....	....	....	....	....	....	....	....	....	....	....	....
	Alaska Aces	ECHL	12	1	1	2	108	....	....	....	....	....	....	....	....	....	....	....	....	....	....	....	....	....	....
2006-07	Peoria Rivermen	AHL	29	0	2	2	86	....	....	....	....	....	....	....	....	....	....	....	....	....	....	....	....	....	....
	Alaska Aces	ECHL	10	0	1	1	48	....	....	....	....	....	....	....	....	....	14	2	3	5	*82	....	....	....	....
2007-08	**Vancouver**	**NHL**	**1**	**0**	**0**	**0**	**0**	**0**	**0**	**0**	**1**	**0.0**	**0**	**0**	**0.0**	**13:20**	....	....	....	....	....	....	....	....	....
	Manitoba Moose	AHL	48	5	3	8	158	....	....	....	....	....	....	....	....	....	3	0	0	0	14	....	....	....	....
2008-09	Manitoba Moose	AHL	56	0	8	8	209	....	....	....	....	....	....	....	....	....	16	0	1	1	14	....	....	....	....
2009-10	Albany River Rats	AHL	77	2	12	14	*311	....	....	....	....	....	....	....	....	....	2	0	0	0	0	....	....	....	....
	NHL Totals		**1**	**0**	**0**	**0**	**0**	**0**	**0**	**0**	**1**	**0.0**		**0**	**0.0**	**13:20**	....	....	....	....	....	....	....	....	....

Traded to **Vancouver** by **St. Louis** for Francois-Pierre Guenette, August 1, 2007. Signed as a free agent by **Carolina**, July 15, 2009.

FITZPATRICK, Rory

(FIHTZ-pa-trihk, ROHR-ee)

Defense. Shoots right. 6'2", 208 lbs. Born, Rochester, NY, January 11, 1975. Montreal's 2nd choice, 47th overall, in 1993 Entry Draft.

Season	Club	League	GP	G	A	Pts	PIM	PP	SH	GW	S	%	+/-	TF	F%	Min	GP	G	A	Pts	PIM	PP	SH	GW	Min
1990-91	Rochester	EmJHL	40	0	5	5	....	....	....	....	....	....	....	....	....	....	....	....	....	....	....	....	....	....	....
1991-92	Rochester	EmJHL	28	8	28	36	141	....	....	....	....	....	....	....	....	....	....	....	....	....	....	....	....	....	....
1992-93	Sudbury Wolves	OHL	58	4	20	24	68	....	....	....	....	....	....	....	....	....	14	0	0	0	17	....	....	....	....
1993-94	Sudbury Wolves	OHL	65	12	34	46	112	....	....	....	....	....	....	....	....	....	10	2	5	7	10	....	....	....	....
1994-95	Sudbury Wolves	OHL	56	12	36	48	72	....	....	....	....	....	....	....	....	....	18	3	15	18	21	....	....	....	....
	Fredericton	AHL	....	....	....	....	....	....	....	....	....	....	....	....	....	....	10	1	2	3	5	....	....	....	....
1995-96	**Montreal**	**NHL**	**42**	**0**	**2**	**2**	**18**	**0**	**0**	**0**	**31**	**0.0**	**–7**	....	....	....	**6**	**1**	**1**	**2**	**0**	**0**	**0**	**0**	
	Fredericton	AHL	18	4	6	10	36	....	....	....	....	....	....	....	....	....	....	....	....	....	....	....	....	....	....
1996-97	**Montreal**	**NHL**	**6**	**0**	**1**	**1**	**6**	**0**	**0**	**0**	**5**	**0.0**	**–2**	....	....	....	....	....	....	....	....	....	....	....	....
	St. Louis	**NHL**	**2**	**0**	**0**	**0**	**2**	**0**	**0**	**0**	**1**	**0.0**	**–2**	....	....	....	....	....	....	....	....	....	....	....	....
	Worcester IceCats	AHL	49	4	13	17	78	....	....	....	....	....	....	....	....	....	5	1	2	3	0	....	....	....	....
1997-98	Worcester IceCats	AHL	62	8	22	30	111	....	....	....	....	....	....	....	....	....	11	0	3	3	26	....	....	....	....
1998-99	**St. Louis**	**NHL**	**1**	**0**	**0**	**0**	**2**	**0**	**0**	**0**	**0**	**0.0**	**–3**	**0**	**0.0**	**4:49**	....	....	....	....	....	....	....	....	....
	Worcester IceCats	AHL	53	5	16	21	82	....	....	....	....	....	....	....	....	....	4	0	1	1	17	....	....	....	....
99-2000	Worcester IceCats	AHL	28	0	5	5	48	....	....	....	....	....	....	....	....	....	....	....	....	....	....	....	....	....	....
	Milwaukee	IHL	27	2	1	3	27	....	....	....	....	....	....	....	....	....	3	0	2	2	2	....	....	....	....
2000-01	**Nashville**	**NHL**	**2**	**0**	**0**	**0**	**2**	**0**	**0**	**0**	**0**	**0.0**	**–2**	**0**	**0.0**	**9:47**	....	....	....	....	....	....	....	....	....
	Milwaukee	IHL	22	0	2	2	32	....	....	....	....	....	....	....	....	....	....	....	....	....	....	....	....	....	....
	Hamilton	AHL	34	3	17	20	29	....	....	....	....	....	....	....	....	....	....	....	....	....	....	....	....	....	....
2001-02	**Buffalo**	**NHL**	**5**	**0**	**0**	**0**	**4**	**0**	**0**	**0**	**2**	**0.0**	**–2**	**0**	**0.0**	**11:54**	....	....	....	....	....	....	....	....	....
	Rochester	AHL	60	4	8	12	83	....	....	....	....	....	....	....	....	....	2	0	1	1	0	....	....	....	....
2002-03	**Buffalo**	**NHL**	**36**	**1**	**3**	**4**	**16**	**0**	**0**	**0**	**29**	**3.4**	**–7**	**0**	**0.0**	**17:02**	....	....	....	....	....	....	....	....	....
	Rochester	AHL	41	5	11	16	65	....	....	....	....	....	....	....	....	....	....	....	....	....	....	....	....	....	....
2003-04	**Buffalo**	**NHL**	**60**	**4**	**7**	**11**	**44**	**2**	**0**	**2**	**78**	**5.1**	**–5**	**1**	**100.0**	**19:02**	....	....	....	....	....	....	....	....	....
2004-05	Rochester	AHL	20	1	1	2	18	....	....	....	....	....	....	....	....	....	9	0	1	1	12	....	....	....	....
2005-06	**Buffalo**	**NHL**	**56**	**4**	**5**	**9**	**50**	**2**	**0**	**1**	**45**	**8.9**	**–18**	**1**	**0.0**	**16:22**	**11**	**0**	**4**	**4**	**16**	**0**	**0**	**0**	**17:12**
2006-07	**Vancouver**	**NHL**	**58**	**1**	**6**	**7**	**46**	**0**	**0**	**1**	**41**	**2.4**	**12**	**1**	**100.0**	**14:06**	**3**	**0**	**0**	**0**	**6**	**0**	**0**	**0**	**21:08**
2007-08	**Philadelphia**	**NHL**	**19**	**0**	**1**	**1**	**11**	**0**	**0**	**0**	**10**	**0.0**	**–12**	**0**	**0.0**	**12:44**	....	....	....	....	....	....	....	....	....
	Philadelphia	AHL	19	1	4	5	24	....	....	....	....	....	....	....	....	....	12	0	2	2	11	....	....	....	....
2008-09	Rochester	AHL	46	4	10	14	37	....	....	....	....	....	....	....	....	....	....	....	....	....	....	....	....	....	....
2009-10	Rochester	AHL	44	0	6	6	37	....	....	....	....	....	....	....	....	....	2	0	0	0	0	....	....	....	....
	NHL Totals		**287**	**10**	**25**	**35**	**201**	**4**	**0**	**4**	**242**	**4.1**		**3**	**66.7**	**16:06**	**20**	**1**	**5**	**6**	**22**	**0**	**0**	**0**	**18:02**

OHL All-Rookie Team (1993)

Traded to **St. Louis** by **Montreal** with Pierre Turgeon and Craig Conroy for Murray Baron, Shayne Corson and St. Louis' 5th round choice (Gennady Razin) in 1997 Entry Draft, October 29, 1996. Claimed by **Boston** from **St. Louis** in Waiver Draft, October 5, 1998. Claimed on waivers by **St. Louis** from **Boston**, October 7, 1998. Traded to **Nashville** by **St. Louis** for Dan Keczmer, February 9, 2000. Traded to **Edmonton** by **Nashville** for future considerations, January 12, 2001. Signed as a free agent by **Buffalo**, August 14, 2001. Signed as a free agent by **Rochester** (AHL), March 2, 2005. Signed as a free agent by **Vancouver**, August 18, 2006. Signed as a free agent by **Philadelphia**, October 9, 2007. Signed as a free agent by **Florida**, July 3, 2008.

FLEISCHMANN, Tomas

(FLIGHSH-muhn, TAW-mahsh) **WSH**

Left wing/Center. Shoots left. 6'1", 192 lbs. Born, Koprivnice, Czech., May 16, 1984. Detroit's 2nd choice, 63rd overall, in 2002 Entry Draft.

Season	Club	League	GP	G	A	Pts	PIM	PP	SH	GW	S	%	+/-	TF	F%	Min	GP	G	A	Pts	PIM	PP	SH	GW	Min
99-2000	HC Vitkovice Jr.	CzRep-Jr.	46	9	13	22	6	....	....	....	....	....	....	....	....	....	....	....	....	....	....	....	....	....	....
2000-01	HC Vitkovice U17	CzR-U17	30	28	34	62	8	....	....	....	....	....	....	....	....	....	....	....	....	....	....	....	....	....	....
	HC Vitkovice Jr.	CzRep-Jr.	21	4	9	13	8	....	....	....	....	....	....	....	....	....	....	....	....	....	....	....	....	....	....
2001-02	HC Vitkovice Jr.	CzRep-Jr.	46	26	35	51	16	....	....	....	....	....	....	....	....	....	....	....	....	....	....	....	....	....	....
	TJ Novy Jicin	CzRep-3	8	3	2	5	8	....	....	....	....	....	....	....	....	....	7	3	4	7	35	....	....	....	....
2002-03	Moose Jaw	WHL	65	21	50	71	36	....	....	....	....	....	....	....	....	....	12	4	11	15	6	....	....	....	....
2003-04	Moose Jaw	WHL	60	33	42	75	32	....	....	....	....	....	....	....	....	....	10	3	4	7	10	....	....	....	....
2004-05	Portland Pirates	AHL	53	7	12	19	14	....	....	....	....	....	....	....	....	....	....	....	....	....	....	....	....	....	....
2005-06	**Washington**	**NHL**	**14**	**0**	**2**	**2**	**0**	**0**	**0**	**0**	**11**	**0.0**	**–7**	**5**	**40.0**	**6:45**	....	....	....	....	....	....	....	....	....
	Hershey Bears	AHL	57	30	33	63	32	....	....	....	....	....	....	....	....	....	20	11	*21	32	15	....	....	....	....
2006-07	**Washington**	**NHL**	**29**	**4**	**4**	**8**	**8**	**1**	**0**	**1**	**52**	**7.7**	**–6**	**14**	**35.7**	**11:38**	....	....	....	....	....	....	....	....	....
	Hershey Bears	AHL	45	22	29	51	22	....	....	....	....	....	....	....	....	....	19	5	16	21	10	....	....	....	....
2007-08	**Washington**	**NHL**	**75**	**10**	**20**	**30**	**18**	**1**	**0**	**1**	**107**	**9.3**	**–7**	**30**	**50.0**	**12:37**	**2**	**0**	**0**	**0**	**0**	**0**	**0**	**0**	**9:49**
2008-09	**Washington**	**NHL**	**73**	**19**	**18**	**37**	**20**	**7**	**0**	**4**	**131**	**14.5**	**–3**	**34**	**26.5**	**15:05**	**14**	**3**	**1**	**4**	**4**	**1**	**0**	**1**	**14:19**
2009-10	**Washington**	**NHL**	**69**	**23**	**28**	**51**	**28**	**7**	**0**	**4**	**121**	**19.0**	**9**	**371**	**43.1**	**16:02**	**6**	**0**	**1**	**1**	**6**	**1**	**0**	**0**	**13:21**
	Hershey Bears	AHL	2	0	1	1	0	....	....	....	....	....	....	....	....	....	....	....	....	....	....	....	....	....	....
	Czech Republic	Olympics	5	1	2	3	2	....	....	....	....	....	....	....	....	....	....	....	....	....	....	....	....	....	....
	NHL Totals		**260**	**56**	**72**	**128**	**74**	**16**	**0**	**10**	**422**	**13.3**		**454**	**42.1**	**13:48**	**22**	**3**	**2**	**5**	**10**	**1**	**0**	**1**	**13:39**

WHL East Second All-Star Team (2004)

Traded to **Washington** by **Detroit** with Detroit's 1st round choice (Mike Green) in 2004 Entry Draft and Detroit's 4th round choice (Luke Lynes) in 2006 Entry Draft for Robert Lang, February 27, 2004.

FLINN, Ryan

(FLIHN, RIGH-yan)

Left wing. Shoots left. 6'5", 248 lbs. Born, Halifax, N.S., April 20, 1980. New Jersey's 8th choice, 143rd overall, in 1998 Entry Draft.

Season	Club	League	GP	G	A	Pts	PIM	PP	SH	GW	S	%	+/-	TF	F%	Min	GP	G	A	Pts	PIM	PP	SH	GW	Min
1996-97	Laval Titan	QMJHL	23	3	2	5	56	....	....	....	....	....	....	....	....	....	2	0	0	0	0	....	....	....	....
1997-98	Laval Titan	QMJHL	59	4	12	16	217	....	....	....	....	....	....	....	....	....	15	1	0	1	63	....	....	....	....
1998-99	Acadie-Bathurst	QMJHL	44	3	4	7	195	....	....	....	....	....	....	....	....	....	23	2	0	2	37	....	....	....	....
99-2000	Halifax	QMJHL	67	14	19	33	365	....	....	....	....	....	....	....	....	....	....	....	....	....	....	....	....	....	....
2000-01	Cape Breton	QMJHL	57	16	17	33	280	....	....	....	....	....	....	....	....	....	9	1	1	2	43	....	....	....	....
2001-02	Reading Royals	ECHL	20	1	3	4	130	....	....	....	....	....	....	....	....	....	....	....	....	....	....	....	....	....	....
	Los Angeles	**NHL**	**10**	**0**	**0**	**0**	**51**	**0**	**0**	**0**	**2**	**0.0**	**0**	**0**	**0.0**	**3:29**	....	....	....	....	....	....	....	....	....
	Manchester	AHL	37	0	1	1	113	....	....	....	....	....	....	....	....	....	1	0	0	0	0	....	....	....	....
2002-03	**Los Angeles**	**NHL**	**19**	**1**	**0**	**1**	**28**	**0**	**0**	**0**	**13**	**7.7**	**0**	**0**	**0.0**	**5:28**	....	....	....	....	....	....	....	....	....
	Manchester	AHL	27	2	2	4	95	....	....	....	....	....	....	....	....	....	....	....	....	....	....	....	....	....	....
2003-04	Manchester	AHL	59	3	5	8	164	....	....	....	....	....	....	....	....	....	6	0	0	0	4	....	....	....	....
2004-05	Manchester	AHL	14	1	1	2	112	....	....	....	....	....	....	....	....	....	....	....	....	....	....	....	....	....	....
2005-06	**Los Angeles**	**NHL**	**2**	**0**	**0**	**0**	**5**	**0**	**0**	**0**	**0**	**0.0**	**0**	**0**	**0.0**	**0:25**	....	....	....	....	....	....	....	....	....
	Manchester	AHL	6	0	1	1	38	....	....	....	....	....	....	....	....	....	....	....	....	....	....	....	....	....	....
2006-07	San Antonio	AHL	61	2	4	6	166	....	....	....	....	....	....	....	....	....	....	....	....	....	....	....	....	....	....
2007-08	Springfield	AHL	24	0	1	1	82	....	....	....	....	....	....	....	....	....	....	....	....	....	....	....	....	....	....
	Hershey Bears	AHL	17	3	0	3	53	....	....	....	....	....	....	....	....	....	2	0	0	0	2	....	....	....	....

			Regular Season														Playoffs								
Season	Club	League	GP	G	A	Pts	PIM	PP	SH	GW	S	%	+/-	TF	F%	Min	GP	G	A	Pts	PIM	PP	SH	GW	Min
2008-09	Hamilton	AHL	52	2	2	4	122										4	0	0	0	0				
2009-10	Rockford IceHogs	AHL	20	2	2	4	74																		
	NHL Totals		**31**	**1**	**0**	**1**	**84**	**0**	**0**	**0**	**15**	**6.7**		**0**	**0.0**	**4:30**									

igned as a free agent by **Los Angeles**, January 8, 2002. • Missed majority of 2004-05 season recovering from foot and leg injuries. • Missed majority of 2005-06 season recovering from head injury uffered in game vs. Chicago, November 26, 2005. Signed as a free agent by **Edmonton**, July 17, 2007. Signed as a free agent by **Montreal**, July 7, 2008. Signed as a free agent by **Rockford** (AHL), anuary 13, 2009.

FLOOD, Mark

(FLUD, MAHRK)

Defense. Shoots right. 6'1", 190 lbs. Born, Charlottetown, P.E.I., September 29, 1984. Montreal's 8th choice, 188th overall, in 2003 Entry Draft.

Season	Club	League	GP	G	A	Pts	PIM	PP	SH	GW	S	%	+/-	TF	F%	Min	GP	G	A	Pts	PIM	PP	SH	GW	Min
2000-01	Charlotwn AAA	PEIHA	STATISTICS NOT AVAILABLE																						
	Charlotwn Abbies	MJrHL	11	0	2	2	2																		
2001-02	Peterborough	OHL	57	1	4	5	21										6	0	0	0	2				
2002-03	Peterborough	OHL	68	5	24	29	18										7	1	2	3	0				
2003-04	Peterborough	OHL	68	15	29	44	30																		
2004-05	Peterborough	OHL	60	4	38	42	14										14	2	7	9	0				
2005-06	Syracuse Crunch	AHL	9	1	1	2	2																		
	Dayton Bombers	ECHL	50	11	14	25	20																		
2006-07	Syracuse Crunch	AHL	8	1	1	2	2																		
	Albany River Rats	AHL	36	3	7	10	20																		
2007-08	Albany River Rats	AHL	53	10	12	22	18																		
2008-09	Albany River Rats	AHL	76	6	25	31	27																		
2009-10	**NY Islanders**	**NHL**	**6**	**0**	**1**	**1**	**0**	**0**	**0**	**0**	**5**	**0.0**	**–4**	**0**	**0.0**	**12:43**									
	Bridgeport	AHL	61	10	23	33	39										5	0	2	2	6				
	NHL Totals		**6**	**0**	**1**	**1**	**0**	**0**	**0**	**0**	**5**	**0.0**		**0**	**0.0**	**12:43**									

gned as a free agent by **Columbus**, August 22, 2005. Traded to **Carolina** by **Columbus** for Derrick Walser, November 29, 2006. Signed as a free agent by **NY Islanders**, July 6, 2009.

FOLIGNO, Nick

(foh-LEE-noh, NIHK) **OTT.**

Left wing. Shoots left. 6', 209 lbs. Born, Buffalo, NY, October 31, 1987. Ottawa's 1st choice, 28th overall, in 2006 Entry Draft.

Season	Club	League	GP	G	A	Pts	PIM	PP	SH	GW	S	%	+/-	TF	F%	Min	GP	G	A	Pts	PIM	PP	SH	GW	Min
2003-04	USNTDP	U-17	18	7	9	16	28																		
	USNTDP	NAHL	43	8	12	20	44										7	2	1	3	8				
2004-05	USNTDP	U-18	4	2	1	3	0																		
	Sudbury Wolves	OHL	65	10	28	38	111										12	5	5	10	16				
2005-06	Sudbury Wolves	OHL	65	24	46	70	146										10	1	3	4	28				
2006-07	Sudbury Wolves	OHL	66	31	57	88	135										21	12	17	29	36				
2007-08	**Ottawa**	**NHL**	**45**	**6**	**3**	**9**	**20**	**0**	**0**	**0**	**44**	**13.6**	**0**	**49**	**44.9**	**9:10**	**4**	**1**	**0**	**1**	**2**	**0**	**0**	**0**	**12:50**
	Binghamton	AHL	28	6	13	19	16																		
2008-09	**Ottawa**	**NHL**	**81**	**17**	**15**	**32**	**59**	**7**	**0**	**2**	**145**	**11.7**	**–10**	**47**	**44.7**	**13:41**									
2009-10	**Ottawa**	**NHL**	**61**	**9**	**17**	**26**	**53**	**2**	**0**	**2**	**83**	**10.8**	**6**	**50**	**34.0**	**14:19**	**6**	**0**	**1**	**1**	**2**	**0**	**0**	**0**	**17:07**
	NHL Totals		**187**	**32**	**35**	**67**	**132**	**9**	**0**	**4**	**272**	**11.8**		**146**	**41.1**	**12:48**	**10**	**1**	**1**	**2**	**4**	**0**	**0**	**0**	**15:24**

FOOTE, Adam

(FUT, A-duhm) **COL.**

Defense. Shoots right. 6'2", 220 lbs. Born, Toronto, Ont., July 10, 1971. Quebec's 2nd choice, 22nd overall, in 1989 Entry Draft.

Season	Club	League	GP	G	A	Pts	PIM	PP	SH	GW	S	%	+/-	TF	F%	Min	GP	G	A	Pts	PIM	PP	SH	GW	Min
1987-88	Whitby Midgets	Minor-ON	65	25	43	68	108																		
1988-89	Sault Ste. Marie	OHL	66	7	32	39	120																		
1989-90	Sault Ste. Marie	OHL	61	12	43	55	199																		
1990-91	Sault Ste. Marie	OHL	59	18	51	69	93										14	5	12	17	28				
1991-92	**Quebec**	**NHL**	**46**	**2**	**5**	**7**	**44**	**0**	**0**	**0**	**55**	**3.6**	**–4**												
	Halifax Citadels	AHL	6	0	1	1	2																		
1992-93	**Quebec**	**NHL**	**81**	**4**	**12**	**16**	**168**	**0**	**1**	**0**	**54**	**7.4**	**6**				**6**	**0**	**1**	**1**	**2**	**0**	**0**	**0**	
1993-94	**Quebec**	**NHL**	**45**	**2**	**6**	**8**	**67**	**0**	**0**	**0**	**42**	**4.8**	**3**												
1994-95	**Quebec**	**NHL**	**35**	**0**	**7**	**7**	**52**	**0**	**0**	**0**	**24**	**0.0**	**17**				**6**	**0**	**1**	**1**	**14**	**0**	**0**	**0**	
1995-96♦	**Colorado**	**NHL**	**73**	**5**	**11**	**16**	**88**	**1**	**0**	**1**	**49**	**10.2**	**27**				**22**	**1**	**3**	**4**	**36**	**0**	**0**	**0**	
1996-97	**Colorado**	**NHL**	**78**	**2**	**19**	**21**	**135**	**0**	**0**	**0**	**60**	**3.3**	**16**				**17**	**0**	**4**	**4**	**62**	**0**	**0**	**0**	
1997-98	**Colorado**	**NHL**	**77**	**3**	**14**	**17**	**124**	**0**	**0**	**1**	**64**	**4.7**	**–3**				**7**	**0**	**0**	**0**	**23**	**0**	**0**	**0**	
	Canada	Olympics	6	0	1	1	4																		
1998-99	**Colorado**	**NHL**	**64**	**5**	**16**	**21**	**92**	**3**	**0**	**0**	**83**	**6.0**	**20**	**0**	**0.0**	**24:50**	**19**	**2**	**3**	**5**	**24**	**1**	**0**	**0**	**28:34**
99-2000	**Colorado**	**NHL**	**59**	**5**	**13**	**18**	**98**	**1**	**0**	**2**	**63**	**7.9**	**5**	**0**	**0.0**	**25:51**	**16**	**0**	**7**	**7**	**28**	**0**	**0**	**0**	**26:05**
2000-01♦	**Colorado**	**NHL**	**35**	**3**	**12**	**15**	**42**	**1**	**1**	**1**	**59**	**5.1**	**6**	**0**	**0.0**	**25:22**	**23**	**3**	**4**	**7**	***47**	**1**	**0**	**1**	**28:22**
2001-02	**Colorado**	**NHL**	**55**	**5**	**22**	**27**	**55**	**1**	**1**	**0**	**85**	**5.9**	**7**	**0**	**0.0**	**25:59**	**21**	**1**	**6**	**7**	**28**	**0**	**0**	**0**	**27:46**
	Canada	Olympics	6	1	0	1	2																		
2002-03	**Colorado**	**NHL**	**78**	**11**	**20**	**31**	**88**	**3**	**0**	**2**	**106**	**10.4**	**30**	**0**	**0.0**	**25:43**	**6**	**0**	**1**	**1**	**8**	**0**	**0**	**0**	**24:12**
2003-04	**Colorado**	**NHL**	**73**	**8**	**22**	**30**	**87**	**5**	**0**	**1**	**105**	**7.6**	**13**	**0**	**0.0**	**24:03**	**11**	**0**	**4**	**4**	**10**	**0**	**0**	**0**	**25:06**
2004-05			DID NOT PLAY																						
2005-06	**Columbus**	**NHL**	**65**	**6**	**16**	**22**	**89**	**2**	**2**	**1**	**67**	**9.0**	**–16**	**0**	**0.0**	**24:34**									
	Canada	Olympics	6	0	1	1	6																		
2006-07	**Columbus**	**NHL**	**59**	**3**	**9**	**12**	**71**	**2**	**0**	**0**	**78**	**3.8**	**–17**	**0**	**0.0**	**24:44**									
2007-08	**Columbus**	**NHL**	**63**	**1**	**14**	**15**	**95**	**0**	**1**	**0**	**57**	**1.8**	**3**	**0**	**0.0**	**24:02**									
	Colorado	**NHL**	**12**	**0**	**1**	**1**	**12**	**0**	**0**	**0**	**9**	**0.0**	**–1**	**0**	**0.0**	**20:01**	**10**	**0**	**0**	**0**	**6**	**0**	**0**	**0**	**21:14**
2008-09	**Colorado**	**NHL**	**42**	**1**	**6**	**7**	**30**	**0**	**0**	**1**	**19**	**5.3**	**–12**	**0**	**0.0**	**19:41**									
2009-10	**Colorado**	**NHL**	**67**	**0**	**9**	**9**	**64**	**0**	**0**	**0**	**26**	**0.0**	**8**	**0**	**0.0**	**19:22**	**6**	**0**	**1**	**1**	**10**	**0**	**0**	**0**	**21:23**
	NHL Totals		**1107**	**66**	**234**	**300**	**1501**	**19**	**6**	**10**	**1105**	**6.0**		**0**	**0.0**	**24:00**	**170**	**7**	**35**	**42**	**298**	**2**	**0**	**1**	**26:24**

HL First All-Star Team (1991)

Transferred to **Colorado** after **Quebec** franchise relocated, June 21, 1995. • Missed majority of 2000-01 season recovering from shoulder injury suffered in game vs. Carolina, January 6, 2001. Signed as free agent by **Columbus**, August 2, 2005. Traded to **Colorado** by **Columbus** for Colorado's 1st round choice (later traded to Philadelphia - Philadelphia selected Luca Sbisa) in 2008 Entry Draft and olorado's 4th round choice (David Savard) in 2009 Entry Draft, February 26, 2008.

FORTUNUS, Maxime

(fohr-TOON-uhs, MAX-eem) **DAL.**

Defense. Shoots right. 6'1", 198 lbs. Born, La Prairie, Que., July 28, 1983.

Season	Club	League	GP	G	A	Pts	PIM	PP	SH	GW	S	%	+/-	TF	F%	Min	GP	G	A	Pts	PIM	PP	SH	GW	Min
99-2000	Baie-Comeau	QMJHL	68	6	15	21	36										6	0	0	0	2				
2000-01	Baie-Comeau	QMJHL	71	10	31	41	106										11	2	4	6	6				
2001-02	Baie-Comeau	QMJHL	72	11	30	41	76										5	0	1	1	2				
2002-03	Baie-Comeau	QMJHL	69	12	32	44	44										12	2	4	6	6				
2003-04	Baie-Comeau	QMJHL	5	1	0	1	15																		
	Houston Aeros	AHL	12	0	2	2	2										1	0	0	0	0				
	Louisiana	ECHL	64	3	15	18	27										4	1	1	2	0				
2004-05	Houston Aeros	AHL	13	0	0	0	4																		
	Louisiana	ECHL	59	8	16	24	26																		
2005-06	Manitoba Moose	AHL	76	3	10	13	36										13	0	0	0	10				
2006-07	Manitoba Moose	AHL	72	2	18	20	64										13	1	4	5	10				
2007-08	Manitoba Moose	AHL	65	8	13	21	28										6	0	1	1	4				
2008-09	Manitoba Moose	AHL	58	7	12	19	18										22	3	7	10	2				
2009-10	**Dallas**	**NHL**	**8**	**0**	**0**	**0**	**4**	**0**	**0**	**0**	**5**	**0.0**	**–6**	**0**	**0.0**	**15:09**									
	Texas Stars	AHL	72	11	12	23	28										24	2	7	9	14				
	NHL Totals		**8**	**0**	**0**	**0**	**4**	**0**	**0**	**0**	**5**	**0.0**		**0**	**0.0**	**15:09**									

gned as a free agent by **Dallas**, July 3, 2008.

FOSTER, Alex

(FAW-stuhr, AL-ehx) **TOR.**

Center. Shoots left. 6', 200 lbs. Born, Canton, MI, August 26, 1984.

Season	Club	League	GP	G	A	Pts	PIM	PP	SH	GW	S	%	+/-	TF	F%	Min	GP	G	A	Pts	PIM	PP	SH	GW	Min
2002-03	Sioux Falls	USHL	57	6	15	21	72										3	0	1	1	8				
2003-04	Sioux Falls	USHL	5	0	1	1	0																		
	Danville Wings	USHL	55	23	30	53	91										6	1	2	3	6				
2004-05	Bowling Green	CCHA	34	8	23	31	31																		
2005-06	Bowling Green	CCHA	38	11	40	51	40																		
2006-07	Toronto Marlies	AHL	57	8	9	17	31																		
	Columbia Inferno	ECHL	9	1	10	11	6																		

Season	Club	League	Regular Season GP	G	A	Pts	PIM	PP	SH	GW	S	%	+/-	TF	F%	Min	Playoffs GP	G	A	Pts	PIM	PP	SH	GW	Mi
2007-08	**Toronto**	**NHL**	**3**	**0**	**0**	**0**	**0**	**0**	**0**	**0**	**1**	**0.0**	**0**	**1**	**0.0**	**3:32**	....	....	....	....	....	....	....	....	....
	Toronto Marlies	AHL	67	18	28	46	30	....	....	....	....	....	....	....	....	....	19	2	6	8	12	....	....	....	....
2008-09	Toronto Marlies	AHL	80	12	23	35	88	....	....	....	....	....	....	....	....	....	6	2	3	5	8	....	....	....	....
2009-10	Toronto Marlies	AHL	30	9	8	17	20	....	....	....	....	....	....	....	....	....	....	....	....	....	....	....	....	....	....
	NHL Totals		**3**	**0**	**0**	**0**	**0**	**0**	**0**	**0**	**1**	**0.0**		**1**	**0.0**	**3:32**	....	....	....	....	....	....	....	....	....

CCHA Second All-Star Team (2006)

Signed as a free agent by **Toronto**, March 8, 2006. • Missed majority of 2009-10 season recovering from various injuries.

FOSTER, Kurtis

(FAW-stuhr, KUHR-this) **EDM**

Defense. Shoots right. 6'5", 223 lbs. Born, Carp, Ont., November 24, 1981. Calgary's 2nd choice, 40th overall, in 2000 Entry Draft.

Season	Club	League	GP	G	A	Pts	PIM	PP	SH	GW	S	%	+/-	TF	F%	Min	GP	G	A	Pts	PIM	PP	SH	GW	Mi
1996-97	Ottawa Valley	ODMHA	36	7	18	25	88	....	....	....	....	....	....	....	....	....	....	....	....	....	....	....	....	....	....
1997-98	Peterborough	OHL	39	1	1	2	45	....	....	....	....	....	....	....	....	....	4	0	0	0	2	....	....	....	....
1998-99	Peterborough	OHL	54	2	13	15	59	....	....	....	....	....	....	....	....	....	5	0	0	0	6	....	....	....	....
99-2000	Peterborough	OHL	68	6	18	24	116	....	....	....	....	....	....	....	....	....	5	1	2	3	4	....	....	....	....
2000-01	Peterborough	OHL	62	17	24	41	78	....	....	....	....	....	....	....	....	....	7	1	1	2	10	....	....	....	....
2001-02	Peterborough	OHL	33	10	4	14	58	....	....	....	....	....	....	....	....	....	....	....	....	....	....	....	....	....	....
	Chicago Wolves	AHL	39	6	9	15	59	....	....	....	....	....	....	....	....	....	14	1	1	2	21	....	....	....	....
2002-03	**Atlanta**	**NHL**	**2**	**0**	**0**	**0**	**0**	**0**	**0**	**0**	**1**	**0.0**	**–2**	**0**	**0.0**	**11:06**	....	....	....	....	....	....	....	....	....
	Chicago Wolves	AHL	75	15	27	42	159	....	....	....	....	....	....	....	....	....	9	1	3	4	14	....	....	....	....
2003-04	**Atlanta**	**NHL**	**3**	**0**	**1**	**1**	**0**	**0**	**0**	**0**	**1**	**0.0**	**0**	**0**	**0.0**	**6:58**	....	....	....	....	....	....	....	....	....
	Chicago Wolves	AHL	67	11	19	30	95	....	....	....	....	....	....	....	....	....	10	0	3	3	12	....	....	....	....
2004-05	Cincinnati	AHL	78	17	25	42	71	....	....	....	....	....	....	....	....	....	9	2	3	5	28	....	....	....	....
2005-06	**Minnesota**	**NHL**	**58**	**10**	**18**	**28**	**60**	**6**	**0**	**2**	**124**	**8.1**	**–3**	**0**	**0.0**	**19:13**	....	....	....	....	....	....	....	....	....
	Houston Aeros	AHL	19	4	11	15	32	....	....	....	....	....	....	....	....	....	....	....	....	....	....	....	....	....	....
2006-07	**Minnesota**	**NHL**	**57**	**3**	**20**	**23**	**52**	**0**	**0**	**0**	**135**	**2.2**	**–3**	**1**	**100.0**	**17:59**	**3**	**0**	**2**	**2**	**0**	**0**	**0**	**0**	**18:3**
2007-08	**Minnesota**	**NHL**	**56**	**7**	**12**	**19**	**37**	**3**	**0**	**2**	**118**	**5.9**	**0**	**3**	**66.7**	**16:24**	....	....	....	....	....	....	....	....	....
2008-09	**Minnesota**	**NHL**	**10**	**1**	**5**	**6**	**6**	**0**	**0**	**0**	**10**	**10.0**	**7**	**0**	**0.0**	**13:35**	....	....	....	....	....	....	....	....	....
	Houston Aeros	AHL	6	1	5	6	6	....	....	....	....	....	....	....	....	....	....	....	....	....	....	....	....	....	....
2009-10	**Tampa Bay**	**NHL**	**71**	**8**	**34**	**42**	**48**	**3**	**0**	**1**	**165**	**4.8**	**–5**	**0**	**0.0**	**17:11**	....	....	....	....	....	....	....	....	....
	NHL Totals		**257**	**29**	**90**	**119**	**203**	**12**	**0**	**5**	**554**	**5.2**		**4**	**75.0**	**17:21**	**3**	**0**	**2**	**2**	**0**	**0**	**0**	**0**	**18:3**

Yanick Dupre Memorial Award (AHL - Outstanding Humanitarian Contribution) (2004)

• Rights traded to **Atlanta** by **Calgary** with Jeff Cowan for Petr Buzek and Atlanta's 6th round choice (Adam Pardy) in 2004 Entry Draft, December 18, 2001. Traded to **Anaheim** by **Atlanta** for Niclas Havelid, June 26, 2004. Signed as a free agent by **Minnesota**, August 4, 2005. • Missed majority of 2008-09 season recovering from leg injury suffered in game vs. San Jose, March 20, 2008. Signed as a free agent by **Tampa Bay**, July 8, 2009. Signed as a free agent by **Edmonton**, July 1, 2010.

FRANSON, Cody

(FRAN-suhn, KOH-dee) **NSH**

Defense. Shoots right. 6'5", 213 lbs. Born, Salmon Arm, B.C., August 8, 1987. Nashville's 3rd choice, 79th overall, in 2005 Entry Draft.

Season	Club	League	GP	G	A	Pts	PIM	PP	SH	GW	S	%	+/-	TF	F%	Min	GP	G	A	Pts	PIM	PP	SH	GW	Mi
2002-03	Sicamous	Minor-BC	65	44	82	126	42	....	....	....	....	....	....	....	....	....	....	....	....	....	....	....	....	....	....
	Vancouver Giants	WHL	3	0	0	0	0	....	....	....	....	....	....	....	....	....	....	....	....	....	....	....	....	....	....
2003-04	Beaver Valley	KIJHL	48	10	22	32	70	....	....	....	....	....	....	....	....	....	....	....	....	....	....	....	....	....	....
	Trail	BCHL	2	0	1	1	0	....	....	....	....	....	....	....	....	....	....	....	....	....	....	....	....	....	....
	Vancouver Giants	WHL	2	0	0	0	0	....	....	....	....	....	....	....	....	....	....	....	....	....	....	....	....	....	....
2004-05	Vancouver Giants	WHL	64	2	11	13	44	....	....	....	....	....	....	....	....	....	4	0	1	1	0	....	....	....	....
2005-06	Vancouver Giants	WHL	71	15	40	55	61	....	....	....	....	....	....	....	....	....	18	5	15	20	12	....	....	....	....
2006-07	Vancouver Giants	WHL	59	17	34	51	88	....	....	....	....	....	....	....	....	....	19	3	4	7	10	....	....	....	....
2007-08	Milwaukee	AHL	76	11	25	36	40	....	....	....	....	....	....	....	....	....	6	0	2	2	2	....	....	....	....
2008-09	Milwaukee	AHL	76	11	41	52	47	....	....	....	....	....	....	....	....	....	11	3	5	8	8	....	....	....	....
2009-10	**Nashville**	**NHL**	**61**	**6**	**15**	**21**	**16**	**1**	**0**	**3**	**90**	**6.7**	**15**	**0**	**0.0**	**14:12**	**4**	**0**	**1**	**1**	**2**	**0**	**0**	**0**	**9:0**
	Milwaukee	AHL	6	2	5	7	4	....	....	....	....	....	....	....	....	....	....	....	....	....	....	....	....	....	....
	NHL Totals		**61**	**6**	**15**	**21**	**16**	**1**	**0**	**3**	**90**	**6.7**		**0**	**0.0**	**14:12**	**4**	**0**	**1**	**1**	**2**	**0**	**0**	**0**	**9:0**

WHL West Second All-Star Team (2006) • WHL West First All-Star Team (2007) • Memorial Cup Tournament All-Star Team (2007) • AHL Second All-Star Team (2009)

FRANZEN, Johan

(FRAN-zehn, YOH-han) **DET**

Left wing. Shoots left. 6'3", 222 lbs. Born, Landsbro, Sweden, December 23, 1979. Detroit's 1st choice, 97th overall, in 2004 Entry Draft.

Season	Club	League	GP	G	A	Pts	PIM	PP	SH	GW	S	%	+/-	TF	F%	Min	GP	G	A	Pts	PIM	PP	SH	GW	Mi
2001-02	Linkopings HC	Sweden	36	2	6	8	64	....	....	....	....	....	....	....	....	....	....	....	....	....	....	....	....	....	....
2002-03	Linkopings HC	Sweden	37	2	4	6	14	....	....	....	....	....	....	....	....	....	....	....	....	....	....	....	....	....	....
2003-04	Linkopings HC	Sweden	49	12	18	30	26	....	....	....	....	....	....	....	....	....	5	0	1	1	8	....	....	....	....
2004-05	Linkopings HC	Sweden	43	7	7	14	45	....	....	....	....	....	....	....	....	....	6	2	0	2	16	....	....	....	....
2005-06	**Detroit**	**NHL**	**80**	**12**	**4**	**16**	**36**	**0**	**2**	**2**	**119**	**10.1**	**4**	**171**	**41.5**	**12:27**	**6**	**1**	**2**	**3**	**4**	**0**	**0**	**0**	**12:0**
2006-07	**Detroit**	**NHL**	**69**	**10**	**20**	**30**	**37**	**0**	**1**	**2**	**151**	**6.6**	**20**	**45**	**40.0**	**15:35**	**18**	**3**	**4**	**7**	**10**	**0**	**0**	**2**	**16:4**
2007-08♦	**Detroit**	**NHL**	**72**	**27**	**11**	**38**	**51**	**14**	**0**	**8**	**199**	**13.6**	**12**	**390**	**48.5**	**17:44**	**16**	***13**	**5**	**18**	**14**	***6**	***2**	***5**	**18:4**
2008-09	**Detroit**	**NHL**	**71**	**34**	**25**	**59**	**44**	**11**	**1**	**8**	**246**	**13.8**	**21**	**241**	**56.0**	**18:06**	**23**	**12**	**11**	**23**	**12**	**4**	**0**	**3**	**19:4**
2009-10	**Detroit**	**NHL**	**27**	**10**	**11**	**21**	**22**	**6**	**0**	**1**	**91**	**11.0**	**1**	**27**	**55.6**	**18:42**	**12**	**6**	**12**	**18**	**16**	**1**	**0**	**1**	**17:3**
	Sweden	Olympics	4	1	1	2	2	....	....	....	....	....	....	....	....	....	....	....	....	....	....	....	....	....	....
	NHL Totals		**319**	**93**	**71**	**164**	**190**	**31**	**4**	**21**	**806**	**11.5**		**874**	**49.0**	**16:06**	**75**	**35**	**34**	**69**	**56**	**11**	**2**	**11**	**17:5**

• Missed majority of 2009-10 season recovering from knee injury suffered in game vs. Chicago, October 8, 2009.

FRASER, Colin

(FRAY-zuhr, KAW-lihn) **EDM**

Center. Shoots left. 6'1", 190 lbs. Born, Surrey, B.C., January 28, 1985. Philadelphia's 3rd choice, 69th overall, in 2003 Entry Draft.

Season	Club	League	GP	G	A	Pts	PIM	PP	SH	GW	S	%	+/-	TF	F%	Min	GP	G	A	Pts	PIM	PP	SH	GW	Mi
2000-01	Port Coquitlam	PIJHL	38	16	24	40	90	....	....	....	....	....	....	....	....	....	8	2	2	4	21	....	....	....	....
2001-02	Red Deer Rebels	WHL	67	11	31	42	126	....	....	....	....	....	....	....	....	....	23	2	1	3	39	....	....	....	....
2002-03	Red Deer Rebels	WHL	69	15	37	52	192	....	....	....	....	....	....	....	....	....	22	7	6	13	40	....	....	....	....
2003-04	Red Deer Rebels	WHL	70	24	29	53	174	....	....	....	....	....	....	....	....	....	19	5	9	14	24	....	....	....	....
2004-05	Red Deer Rebels	WHL	63	24	43	67	148	....	....	....	....	....	....	....	....	....	7	2	5	7	8	....	....	....	....
	Norfolk Admirals	AHL	3	0	0	0	20	....	....	....	....	....	....	....	....	....	6	1	0	1	2	....	....	....	....
2005-06	Norfolk Admirals	AHL	75	12	13	25	145	....	....	....	....	....	....	....	....	....	4	0	0	0	7	....	....	....	....
2006-07	**Chicago**	**NHL**	**1**	**0**	**0**	**0**	**2**	**0**	**0**	**0**	**0**	**0.0**	**–1**	**2**	**0.0**	**3:18**	....	....	....	....	....	....	....	....	....
	Norfolk Admirals	AHL	67	12	24	36	158	....	....	....	....	....	....	....	....	....	6	1	0	1	21	....	....	....	....
2007-08	**Chicago**	**NHL**	**5**	**0**	**0**	**0**	**7**	**0**	**0**	**0**	**4**	**0.0**	**–2**	**38**	**36.8**	**10:19**	....	....	....	....	....	....	....	....	....
	Rockford IceHogs	AHL	75	17	24	41	165	....	....	....	....	....	....	....	....	....	12	1	2	3	28	....	....	....	....
2008-09	**Chicago**	**NHL**	**81**	**6**	**11**	**17**	**55**	**0**	**1**	**0**	**67**	**9.0**	**3**	**787**	**47.8**	**10:54**	**2**	**0**	**0**	**0**	**2**	**0**	**0**	**0**	**11:3**
2009-10♦	**Chicago**	**NHL**	**70**	**7**	**12**	**19**	**44**	**0**	**0**	**0**	**92**	**7.6**	**6**	**445**	**48.8**	**9:36**	**3**	**0**	**0**	**0**	**0**	**0**	**0**	**0**	**8:2**
	NHL Totals		**157**	**13**	**23**	**36**	**108**	**0**	**1**	**0**	**163**	**8.0**		**1272**	**47.7**	**10:15**	**5**	**0**	**0**	**0**	**2**	**0**	**0**	**0**	**9:3**

Canadian Major Junior Humanitarian Player of the Year (2005)

Traded to **Chicago** by **Philadelphia** with Jim Vandermeer and Los Angeles' 2nd round choice (previously acquired, Chicago selected Bryan Bickell) in 2004 Entry Draft for Alex Zhamnov and Washington's 4th round choice (previously acquired, Philadelphia selected R.J. Anderson) in 2004 Entry Draft, February 19, 2004. Traded to **Edmonton** by **Chicago** for Edmonton's 6th round choice (Mirko Hoefflin) in 2010 Entry Draft, June 24, 2010.

FRASER, Jamie

(FRAY-zuhr, JAY-mee) **MIN**

Defense. Shoots left. 6', 198 lbs. Born, Sarnia, Ont., November 17, 1985.

Season	Club	League	GP	G	A	Pts	PIM	PP	SH	GW	S	%	+/-	TF	F%	Min	GP	G	A	Pts	PIM	PP	SH	GW	Mi
2002-03	Brampton	OHL	57	3	11	14	13	....	....	....	....	....	....	....	....	....	10	0	2	2	2	....	....	....	....
2003-04	Brampton	OHL	61	4	13	17	36	....	....	....	....	....	....	....	....	....	12	3	1	4	6	....	....	....	....
2004-05	Sarnia Sting	OHL	66	10	21	31	22	....	....	....	....	....	....	....	....	....	....	....	....	....	....	....	....	....	....
2005-06	Sarnia Sting	OHL	65	16	26	42	68	....	....	....	....	....	....	....	....	....	....	....	....	....	....	....	....	....	....
	South Carolina	ECHL	3	1	0	1	2	....	....	....	....	....	....	....	....	....	6	1	1	2	2	....	....	....	....
2006-07	Syracuse Crunch	AHL	2	0	0	0	0	....	....	....	....	....	....	....	....	....	....	....	....	....	....	....	....	....	....
	South Carolina	ECHL	27	5	23	28	6	....	....	....	....	....	....	....	....	....	....	....	....	....	....	....	....	....	....
	Bridgeport	AHL	43	3	11	14	16	....	....	....	....	....	....	....	....	....	....	....	....	....	....	....	....	....	....
2007-08	Bridgeport	AHL	70	11	13	24	20	....	....	....	....	....	....	....	....	....	....	....	....	....	....	....	....	....	....

Season	Club	League	GP	G	A	Pts	PIM	PP	SH	GW	S	%	+/-	TF	F%	Min	GP	G	A	Pts	PIM	PP	SH	GW	Min
								Regular Season									Playoffs								
2008-09	**NY Islanders**	**NHL**	1	0	0	0	0	0	0	0	0	0.0	0	0	0.0	11:00	....								
	Bridgeport	AHL	66	7	14	21	30										....								
2009-10	Houston Aeros	AHL	59	6	16	22	36										....								
	NHL Totals		1	0	0	0	0	0	0	0	0	0.0		0	0.0	11:00	....								

Signed as a free agent by **NY Islanders**, February 22, 2007. Signed as a free agent by **Minnesota**, July 8, 2009.

FRASER, Mark (FRAY-zuhr, MAHRK) N.J.

Defense. Shoots left. 6'3", 220 lbs. Born, Ottawa, Ont., September 29, 1986. New Jersey's 3rd choice, 84th overall, in 2005 Entry Draft.

Season	Club	League	GP	G	A	Pts	PIM	PP	SH	GW	S	%	+/-	TF	F%	Min	GP	G	A	Pts	PIM	PP	SH	GW	Min
2004-05	Gloucester	CJHL	STATISTICS NOT AVAILABLE																					
	Kitchener Rangers	OHL	58	0	8	8	96										15	0	3	3	26				
2005-06	Kitchener Rangers	OHL	59	0	5	5	129										5	0	1	1	4				
	Albany River Rats	AHL	4	0	0	0	2																		
2006-07	**New Jersey**	**NHL**	7	0	0	0	7	0	0	0	1	0.0	-1	0	0.0	3:34									
	Lowell Devils	AHL	71	1	8	9	73																		
2007-08	Lowell Devils	AHL	79	1	17	18	96																		
2008-09	Lowell Devils	AHL	74	3	14	17	152																		
2009-10	**New Jersey**	**NHL**	61	3	3	6	36	0	0	0	24	12.5	3	0	0.0	12:23	1	0	0	0	0	0	0	0	5:52
	NHL Totals		68	3	3	6	43	0	0	0	25	12.0		0	0.0	11:28	1	0	0	0	0	0	0	0	5:52

FRISCHMON, Trevor (FRIHCH-muhn, TREH-vuhr) CBJ

Center. Shoots left. 6', 202 lbs. Born, Ham Lake, MN, August 5, 1981.

Season	Club	League	GP	G	A	Pts	PIM	PP	SH	GW	S	%	+/-	TF	F%	Min	GP	G	A	Pts	PIM	PP	SH	GW	Min
99-2000	Lincoln Stars	USHL	4	1	1	2	48										8	0	2	2	0				
2000-01	Lincoln Stars	USHL	55	13	18	31	49										11	4	1	5	0				
2001-02	Lincoln Stars	USHL	58	17	28	45	38										4	0	2	2	2				
2002-03	Colorado College	WCHA	38	3	4	7	22																		
2003-04	Colorado College	WCHA	39	10	7	17	34																		
2004-05	Colorado College	WCHA	42	10	16	26	24																		
2005-06	Colorado College	WCHA	41	7	9	16	41																		
2006-07	Syracuse Crunch	AHL	33	0	7	7	10																		
	Dayton Bombers	ECHL	24	5	8	13	14										20	3	5	8	24				
2007-08	Syracuse Crunch	AHL	59	5	11	16	38										13	1	2	3	10				
	Charlotte	ECHL	7	1	4	5	2																		
2008-09	Syracuse Crunch	AHL	80	5	20	25	57																		
2009-10	**Columbus**	**NHL**	3	0	0	0	4	0	0	0	1	0.0	0	6	66.7	6:06									
	Syracuse Crunch	AHL	75	7	18	25	34																		
	NHL Totals		3	0	0	0	4	0	0	0	1	0.0		6	66.7	6:06									

Signed as a free agent by **Columbus**, July 3, 2009.

FRITSCHE, Dan (FRIH-tchee, DAN)

Center. Shoots right. 6'1", 204 lbs. Born, Parma, OH, July 13, 1985. Columbus' 2nd choice, 46th overall, in 2003 Entry Draft.

Season	Club	League	GP	G	A	Pts	PIM	PP	SH	GW	S	%	+/-	TF	F%	Min	GP	G	A	Pts	PIM	PP	SH	GW	Min
2000-01	Cleveland Barons	NAHL	49	23	29	52	47										1	1	1	2	0				
2001-02	Sarnia Sting	OHL	17	5	13	18	20																		
2002-03	Sarnia Sting	OHL	61	32	39	71	79										5	2	2	4	4				
2003-04	Sarnia Sting	OHL	27	16	13	29	26										5	1	5	6	0				
	Columbus	**NHL**	19	1	0	1	12	0	0	0	19	5.3	-5	139	38.1	8:24									
	Syracuse Crunch	AHL	4	2	0	2	0										4	0	1	1	4				
2004-05	Sarnia Sting	OHL	2	1	1	2	0																		
	London Knights	OHL	28	17	18	35	18										17	9	13	22	12				
2005-06	**Columbus**	**NHL**	59	6	7	13	22	0	0	0	93	6.5	-14	270	48.9	10:17									
	Syracuse Crunch	AHL	19	5	4	9	12										6	2	2	4	8				
2006-07	**Columbus**	**NHL**	59	12	15	27	35	5	1	4	81	14.8	3	296	49.3	14:02									
2007-08	**Columbus**	**NHL**	69	10	12	22	22	1	1	4	109	9.2	2	121	48.8	12:21									
2008-09	**NY Rangers**	**NHL**	16	1	3	4	2	0	0	0	20	5.0	-2	7	71.4	9:33									
	Minnesota	**NHL**	34	4	5	9	10	1	1	0	34	11.8	-3	87	41.4	11:09									
2009-10	Syracuse Crunch	AHL	67	13	29	42	12																		
	NHL Totals		256	34	42	76	103	7	3	8	356	9.6		920	46.8	11:38									

Memorial Cup Tournament All-Star Team (2005)
• Missed majority of 2001-02 season recovering from shoulder surgery, December 12, 2001. Traded to **NY Rangers** by **Columbus** with Nikolai Zherdev for Fedor Tyutin and Christian Backman, July 2, 2008. Traded to **Minnesota** by **NY Rangers** for Erik Reitz, January 29, 2009. Signed as a free agent by **Syracuse** (AHL), October 6, 2009.

FRITZ, Mitch (FRIHTZ, MIHTCH) T.B.

Left wing. Shoots left. 6'7", 242 lbs. Born, Osoyoos, B.C., November 24, 1980.

Season	Club	League	GP	G	A	Pts	PIM	PP	SH	GW	S	%	+/-	TF	F%	Min	GP	G	A	Pts	PIM	PP	SH	GW	Min
1998-99	Kelowna Rockets	WHL	52	9	0	9	156										2	0	0	0	0				
99-2000	Kelowna Rockets	WHL	58	4	2	6	204										5	0	0	0	0				
2000-01	Lowell	AHL	5	0	0	0	20																		
	Tallahassee	ECHL	42	5	3	8	79																		
2001-02	Hamilton	AHL	13	0	0	0	37																		
	Saint John Flames	AHL	11	0	0	0	34																		
	Columbus	ECHL	45	3	7	10	284																		
2002-03	Milwaukee	AHL	13	1	2	3	33																		
	Columbus	ECHL	33	2	4	6	144																		
2003-04	Worcester IceCats	AHL	4	0	0	0	10										4	0	0	0	4				
	Columbus	ECHL	64	3	9	12	149																		
2004-05	Springfield	AHL	45	3	1	4	179																		
2005-06	Springfield	AHL	69	6	5	11	212																		
2006-07	Springfield	AHL	63	0	1	1	144																		
2007-08	Hartford	AHL	11	1	4	5	34										2	0	0	0	4				
2008-09	**NY Islanders**	**NHL**	20	0	0	0	42	0	0	0	2	0.0	-4	1	100.0	2:41									
	Bridgeport	AHL	36	0	2	2	58																		
2009-10	Norfolk Admirals	AHL	73	2	4	6	157																		
	NHL Totals		20	0	0	0	42	0	0	0	2	0.0		1	100.0	2:41									

Yanick Dupre Memorial Award (AHL - Outstanding Humanitarian Contribution) (2006)
Signed as a free agent by **Tampa Bay**, August 5, 2005. • Rights traded to **NY Rangers** by **Tampa Bay** for the rights to Bryce Lampman, July 4, 2007. • Missed majority of 2007-08 season recovering from shoulder surgery. Signed as a free agent by **NY Islanders**, July 3, 2008. Signed as a free agent by **Tampa Bay**, September 30, 2009.

FROGREN, Jonas (FREW-grehn, YOH-nuhs)

Defense. Shoots left. 6'1", 189 lbs. Born, Falun, Sweden, August 28, 1980. Calgary's 8th choice, 206th overall, in 1998 Entry Draft.

Season	Club	League	GP	G	A	Pts	PIM	PP	SH	GW	S	%	+/-	TF	F%	Min	GP	G	A	Pts	PIM	PP	SH	GW	Min
1996-97	Farjestad Jr.	Swe-Jr.	20	2	7	9	4																		
1997-98	Farjestad Jr.	Swe-Jr.	28	5	6	11	12										2	1	0	1	0				
1998-99	Farjestad Jr.	Swe-Jr.	28	10	8	18	16										6	0	2	2	10				
	Farjestad	Sweden	22	0	0	0	2																		
	Farjestad	EuroHL	5	0	0	0	0										2	0	0	0	0				
99-2000	Bofors	Sweden-2	43	2	7	9	40																		
2000-01	Farjestad	Sweden	49	3	0	3	10										16	0	0	0	4				
	Farjestad Jr.	Swe-Jr.	1	0	0	0	0																		
2001-02	Farjestad	Sweden	50	3	6	9	18										10	0	0	0	4				
2002-03	Farjestad	Sweden	50	1	7	8	48										14	0	0	0	16				
2003-04	Farjestad	Sweden	47	5	5	10	38										17	2	0	2	6				
2004-05	Farjestad	Sweden	34	1	0	1	26										15	0	2	2	2				
2005-06	Farjestad	Sweden	46	3	3	6	84										17	1	1	2	6				
2006-07	Farjestad	Sweden	53	4	4	8	40										7	1	0	1	0				
2007-08	Farjestad	Sweden	47	0	1	1	38										12	0	1	1	12				

			Regular Season														Playoffs								
Season	Club	League	GP	G	A	Pts	PIM	PP	SH	GW	S	%	+/-	TF	F%	Min	GP	G	A	Pts	PIM	PP	SH	GW	Min
2008-09	Toronto	NHL	41	1	6	7	28	0	0	0	12	8.3	0	1	0.0	13:26									
	Toronto Marlies	AHL															3	0	0	0	0				
2009-10	Toronto Marlies	AHL	56	3	8	11	41																		
	NHL Totals		41	1	6	7	28	0	0	0	12	8.3		1	0.0	13:26									

Signed as a free agent by **Toronto**, July 9, 2008. Signed as a free agent by **Farjestad** (Sweden), April 20, 2010.

FROLIK, Michael

(FROH-lihk, MIGH-kuhl) **FLA.**

Center. Shoots left. 6'1", 185 lbs. Born, Kladno, Czech., February 17, 1988. Florida's 1st choice, 10th overall, in 2006 Entry Draft.

2002-03	HC Kladno U17	CzR-U17	46	37	21	58	36										9	9	1	10	18				
	HC Kladno Jr.	CzRep-Jr.															1	0	0	0	2				
2003-04	HC Kladno U17	CzR-U17	1	0	1	1	2																		
	HC Kladno Jr.	CzRep-Jr.	53	21	23	44	22										7	3	1	4	6				
2004-05	HC Kladno U17	CzR-U17															1	1	0	1	0				
	HC Kladno Jr.	CzRep-Jr.	15	9	11	20	18										5	1	0	1	0				
	HC Rabat Kladno	CzRep	27	3	1	4	6										1	0	0	0	0				
2005-06	HC Kladno Jr.	CzRep-Jr.	3	1	2	3	0										6	3	9	12	6				
	HC Rabat Kladno	CzRep	48	2	7	9	32																		
2006-07	Rimouski Oceanic	QMJHL	52	31	42	73	40																		
2007-08	Rimouski Oceanic	QMJHL	45	24	41	65	22										9	2	4	6	12				
2008-09	Florida	NHL	79	21	24	45	22	1	0	2	158	13.3	10	67	40.3	14:48									
2009-10	Florida	NHL	82	21	22	43	43	5	0	1	219	9.6	-4	35	37.1	17:29									
	NHL Totals		161	42	46	88	65	6	0	3	377	11.1		102	39.2	16:10									

QMJHL All-Rookie Team (2007)

FROLOV, Alexander

(FROH-lawf, Alehx-AN-duhr) **NYR**

Left wing. Shoots right. 6'2", 210 lbs. Born, Moscow, USSR, June 19, 1982. Los Angeles' 1st choice, 20th overall, in 2000 Entry Draft.

1998-99	Spartak Moscow	Russia	1	0	0	0	0																		
99-2000	Yaroslavl 2	Russia-3	36	27	13	40	30																		
2000-01	Krylja Sovetov	Russia-2	44	20	19	39	8																		
2001-02	Krylja Sovetov	Russia	43	18	12	30	16										3	1	0	1	0				
	Krylja Sovetov 2	Russia-3	2	0	0	0	4																		
2002-03	Los Angeles	NHL	79	14	17	31	34	1	0	3	141	9.9	12	9	22.2	14:23									
2003-04	Los Angeles	NHL	77	24	24	48	24	5	2	3	168	14.3	8	34	32.4	17:13									
	Nizhny Novgorod	Russia	1	0	0	0	0																		
2004-05	CSKA Moscow	Russia	42	20	17	37	10																		
	Dynamo Moscow	Russia	6	2	1	3	2										6	2	1	3	0				
2005-06	Los Angeles	NHL	69	21	33	54	40	4	3	4	174	12.1	17	4	50.0	19:18									
	Russia	Olympics	3	0	1	1	0																		
2006-07	Los Angeles	NHL	82	35	36	71	34	10	1	6	195	17.9	-8	19	36.8	19:56									
2007-08	Los Angeles	NHL	71	23	44	67	22	5	0	7	160	14.4	1	11	18.2	18:48									
2008-09	Los Angeles	NHL	77	32	27	59	30	12	1	1	176	18.2	-6	11	45.5	19:55									
2009-10	Los Angeles	NHL	81	19	32	51	26	5	0	1	182	10.4	-1	12	58.3	18:26	6	1	3	4	0	0	0	0	16:49
	NHL Totals		536	168	213	381	210	42	7	25	1196	14.0		100	36.0	18:16	6	1	3	4	0	0	0	0	16:49

Signed as a free agent by **CSKA Moscow** (Russia), July 14, 2004. Signed as a free agent by **Dynamo Moscow** (Russia), February 17, 2005. Signed as a free agent by **NY Rangers**, July 27, 2010.

FUNK, Michael

(FUHNK, MIGH-kuhl)

Defense. Shoots left. 6'4", 199 lbs. Born, Abbotsford, B.C., August 15, 1986. Buffalo's 2nd choice, 43rd overall, in 2004 Entry Draft.

2001-02	Abbotsford	Minor-BC	72	9	24	33	84																		
2002-03	Portland	WHL	68	1	15	16	54										7	0	1	1	15				
2003-04	Portland	WHL	71	3	25	28	86										5	0	1	1	6				
2004-05	Portland	WHL	71	8	22	30	84										7	1	1	2	4				
2005-06	Portland	WHL	70	11	36	47	88										5	0	0	0	8				
2006-07	Buffalo	NHL	5	0	2	2	0	0	0	0	1	0.0	2	0	0.0	3:26									
	Rochester	AHL	61	2	5	7	57										6	0	1	1	4				
2007-08	Buffalo	NHL	4	0	0	0	0	0	0	0	1	0.0	-3	0	0.0	11:37									
	Rochester	AHL	58	0	10	10	104																		
2008-09	Portland Pirates	AHL	13	1	2	3	8																		
2009-10	Manitoba Moose	AHL	19	1	6	7	14																		
	NHL Totals		9	0	2	2	0	0	0	0	2	0.0		0	0.0	7:04									

• Missed majority of 2008-09 season recovering from head injury suffered in training camp. Signed as a free agent by **Vancouver**, July 22, 2009.

GABORIK, Marian

(GAB-rihk, MAIR-ee-uhn) **NYR**

Right wing. Shoots left. 6'1", 200 lbs. Born, Trencin, Czech., February 14, 1982. Minnesota's 1st choice, 3rd overall, in 2000 Entry Draft.

1997-98	Dukla Trencin Jr.	Slovak-Jr.	36	37	22	59	28																		
	Dukla Trencin	Slovakia	1	1	0	1	0																		
1998-99	Dukla Trencin	Slovakia	33	11	9	20	6										3	1	0	1	2				
99-2000	Dukla Trencin	Slovakia	50	25	21	46	34										5	1	2	3	2				
2000-01	Minnesota	NHL	71	18	18	36	32	6	0	3	179	10.1	-6	3	33.3	15:26									
2001-02	Minnesota	NHL	78	30	37	67	34	10	0	4	221	13.6	0	4	25.0	16:47									
2002-03	Minnesota	NHL	81	30	35	65	46	5	1	8	280	10.7	12	16	25.0	17:24	18	9	8	17	6	4	0	0	18:12
2003-04	Dukla Trencin	Slovakia	9	10	3	13	10																		
	Minnesota	NHL	65	18	22	40	20	3	0	4	220	8.2	10	11	45.5	18:17									
2004-05	Dukla Trencin	Slovakia	29	25	27	52	46										12	8	9	17	26				
	Farjestad	Sweden	12	6	4	10	45																		
2005-06	Minnesota	NHL	65	38	28	66	64	10	2	7	252	15.1	6	11	27.3	18:26									
	Slovakia	Olympics	6	3	4	7	4																		
2006-07	Minnesota	NHL	48	30	27	57	40	12	1	7	196	15.3	12	4	0.0	19:38	5	3	1	4	8	1	1	1	19:32
2007-08	Minnesota	NHL	77	42	41	83	63	11	1	8	278	15.1	17	21	28.6	19:36	6	0	1	1	4	0	0	0	21:51
2008-09	Minnesota	NHL	17	13	10	23	2	2	1	2	68	19.1	3	5	0.0	20:00									
2009-10	NY Rangers	NHL	76	42	44	86	37	14	1	4	272	15.4	15	7	28.6	21:15									
	Slovakia	Olympics	7	4	1	5	6																		
	NHL Totals		578	261	262	523	338	73	7	47	1966	13.3		82	26.8	18:21	29	12	10	22	18	5	1	1	19:11

Played in NHL All-Star Game (2003, 2008)

Signed as a free agent by **Trencin** (Slovakia), July 5, 2004. Signed as a free agent by **Farjestad** (Sweden), December 21, 2004. • Missed majority of 2008-09 season recovering from hip surgery, January 5, 2009. Signed as a free agent by **NY Rangers**, July 1, 2009.

GAGNE, Simon

(gah-N'YAY, see-MOHN) **T.B.**

Left wing. Shoots left. 6', 195 lbs. Born, Ste-Foy, Que., February 29, 1980. Philadelphia's 1st choice, 22nd overall, in 1998 Entry Draft.

1995-96	Ste-Foy	QAAA	27	13	9	22	18										15	7	8	15	8				
1996-97	Beauport	QMJHL	51	9	22	31	49																		
1997-98	Quebec Remparts	QMJHL	53	30	39	69	26										12	11	5	16	23				
1998-99	Quebec Remparts	QMJHL	61	50	*70	*120	42										13	9	8	17	4				
99-2000	Philadelphia	NHL	80	20	28	48	22	8	1	4	159	12.6	11	443	42.2	14:59	17	5	5	10	2	2	0	1	16:46
2000-01	Philadelphia	NHL	69	27	32	59	18	6	0	7	191	14.1	24	21	28.6	18:05	6	3	0	3	0	2	0	0	19:09
2001-02	Philadelphia	NHL	79	33	33	66	32	4	1	7	199	16.6	31	6	83.3	18:09	5	0	0	0	2	0	0	0	19:16
	Canada	Olympics	6	1	3	4	0																		
2002-03	Philadelphia	NHL	46	9	18	27	16	1	1	3	115	7.8	20	70	42.9	17:24	13	4	1	5	6	0	1	1	18:13
2003-04	Philadelphia	NHL	80	24	21	45	29	6	0	6	211	11.4	12	104	39.4	16:27	18	5	4	9	12	0	0	1	16:48
2004-05			DID NOT PLAY																					
2005-06	Philadelphia	NHL	72	47	32	79	38	12	2	7	334	14.1	31	18	38.9	20:46	6	3	1	4	2	1	0	0	21:45
	Canada	Olympics	6	1	2	3	6																		
2006-07	Philadelphia	NHL	76	41	27	68	30	13	2	4	291	14.1	2	49	42.9	21:02									
2007-08	Philadelphia	NHL	25	7	11	18	4	5	0	2	76	9.2	-8	2	50.0	18:09									

			Regular Season														Playoffs								
Season	Club	League	GP	G	A	Pts	PIM	PP	SH	GW	S	%	+/-	TF	F%	Min	GP	G	A	Pts	PIM	PP	SH	GW	Min
2008-09	**Philadelphia**	**NHL**	**79**	**34**	**40**	**74**	**42**	**12**	**4**	**3**	**221**	**15.4**	**21**	**10**	**30.0**	**19:01**	**6**	**3**	**1**	**4**	**2**	**1**	**1**	**1**	**20:29**
2009-10	**Philadelphia**	**NHL**	**58**	**17**	**23**	**40**	**47**	**5**	**0**	**4**	**183**	**9.3**	**–1**	**4**	**25.0**	**18:37**	**19**	**9**	**3**	**12**	**0**	**5**	**0**	**2**	**17:35**
	NHL Totals		**664**	**259**	**265**	**524**	**278**	**72**	**11**	**47**	**1980**	**13.1**		**727**	**41.5**	**18:16**	**90**	**32**	**15**	**47**	**26**	**11**	**2**	**6**	**18:02**

QMJHL Second All-Star Team (1999) • NHL All-Rookie Team (2000)
Played in NHL ALL-Star Game (2001, 2007)
• Missed majority of 2007-08 season recovering from head injury suffered in game at Pittsburgh, February 10, 2008. Traded to **Tampa Bay** by **Philadelphia** for Matt Walker and Tampa Bay's 4th round choice in 2011 Entry Draft, July 19, 2010.

GAGNER, Sam
(GAH-n'yay, SAM) **EDM.**

Center/Wing. Shoots right. 5'11", 191 lbs. Born, London, Ont., August 10, 1989. Edmonton's 1st choice, 6th overall, in 2007 Entry Draft.

Season	Club	League	GP	G	A	Pts	PIM	PP	SH	GW	S	%	+/-	TF	F%	Min	GP	G	A	Pts	PIM	PP	SH	GW	Min
2001-02	Tor. Marlboros	GTHL	68	56	61	117	42	....	....	....	....	....	....	....	....	....	....	....	....	....	....	....	....	....	....
2002-03	Tor. Marlboros	GTHL	72	68	86	154	35	....	....	....	....	....	....	....	....	....	....	....	....	....	....	....	....	....	....
2003-04	Tor. Marlboros	GTHL	85	64	108	171	36	....	....	....	....	....	....	....	....	....	....	....	....	....	....	....	....	....	....
2004-05	Tor. Marlboros	GTHL	70	62	118	180	56	....	....	....	....	....	....	....	....	....	....	....	....	....	....	....	....	....	....
	Milton Icehawks	OPJHL	13	5	10	15	10	....	....	....	....	....	....	....	....	....	....	....	....	....	....	....	....	....	....
2005-06	Sioux City	USHL	56	11	35	46	60	....	....	....	....	....	....	....	....	....	....	....	....	....	....	....	....	....	....
2006-07	London Knights	OHL	53	35	83	118	36	....	....	....	....	....	....	....	....	....	16	7	*22	29	22	....	....	....	....
2007-08	**Edmonton**	**NHL**	**79**	**13**	**36**	**49**	**23**	**4**	**0**	**1**	**135**	**9.6**	**–21**	**299**	**41.8**	**15:41**	....	....	....	....	....	....	....	....	....
2008-09	**Edmonton**	**NHL**	**76**	**16**	**25**	**41**	**51**	**6**	**0**	**1**	**156**	**10.3**	**–1**	**690**	**42.0**	**16:46**	....	....	....	....	....	....	....	....	....
2009-10	**Edmonton**	**NHL**	**68**	**15**	**26**	**41**	**33**	**6**	**0**	**1**	**170**	**8.8**	**–8**	**709**	**47.4**	**16:17**	....	....	....	....	....	....	....	....	....
	NHL Totals		**223**	**44**	**87**	**131**	**107**	**16**	**0**	**3**	**461**	**9.5**		**1698**	**44.2**	**16:14**	....	....	....	....	....	....	....	....	....

USHL All-Rookie Team (2006) • OHL All-Rookie Team (2007)

GAGNON, Aaron
(GAN-YAWN, AIR-ruhn) **DAL.**

Center. Shoots right. 5'11", 186 lbs. Born, Quesnel, B.C., April 24, 1986. Phoenix's 8th choice, 240th overall, in 2004 Entry Draft.

Season	Club	League	GP	G	A	Pts	PIM	PP	SH	GW	S	%	+/-	TF	F%	Min	GP	G	A	Pts	PIM	PP	SH	GW	Min
2001-02	North Okanoghan	Minor-BC	41	59	59	118	60	....	....	....	....	....	....	....	....	....	....	....	....	....	....	....	....	....	....
	Seattle	WHL	2	0	0	0	0	....	....	....	....	....	....	....	....	....	....	....	....	....	....	....	....	....	....
2002-03	Seattle	WHL	60	5	13	18	14	....	....	....	....	....	....	....	....	....	15	3	2	5	4	....	....	....	....
2003-04	Seattle	WHL	63	21	15	36	29	....	....	....	....	....	....	....	....	....	....	....	....	....	....	....	....	....	....
2004-05	Seattle	WHL	72	31	34	65	29	....	....	....	....	....	....	....	....	....	12	4	5	9	16	....	....	....	....
2005-06	Seattle	WHL	62	24	21	45	40	....	....	....	....	....	....	....	....	....	7	5	3	8	6	....	....	....	....
2006-07	Seattle	WHL	59	42	38	80	58	....	....	....	....	....	....	....	....	....	11	6	2	8	10	....	....	....	....
2007-08	Iowa Stars	AHL	25	0	1	1	8	....	....	....	....	....	....	....	....	....	....	....	....	....	....	....	....	....	....
	Idaho Steelheads	ECHL	22	7	14	21	4	....	....	....	....	....	....	....	....	....	4	1	1	2	2	....	....	....	....
2008-09	Grand Rapids	AHL	61	8	11	19	28	....	....	....	....	....	....	....	....	....	10	1	2	3	2	....	....	....	....
2009-10	**Dallas**	**NHL**	**2**	**0**	**0**	**0**	**0**	**0**	**0**	**0**	**2**	**0.0**	**0**	**11**	**72.7**	**8:49**	....	....	....	....	....	....	....	....	....
	Texas Stars	AHL	78	27	31	58	42	....	....	....	....	....	....	....	....	....	24	8	4	12	18	....	....	....	....
	NHL Totals		**2**	**0**	**0**	**0**	**0**	**0**	**0**	**0**	**2**	**0.0**		**11**	**72.7**	**8:49**	....	....	....	....	....	....	....	....	....

WHL West First All-Star Team (2005, 2007)
Signed as a free agent by **Dallas**, February 2, 2007.

GALIARDI, T.J.
(gal-ee-AR-dee, TEE-JAY) **COL.**

Left wing. Shoots left. 6'2", 190 lbs. Born, Calgary, Alta., April 22, 1988. Colorado's 4th choice, 55th overall, in 2007 Entry Draft.

Season	Club	League	GP	G	A	Pts	PIM	PP	SH	GW	S	%	+/-	TF	F%	Min	GP	G	A	Pts	PIM	PP	SH	GW	Min
2004-05	Cgy. North Stars	AMHL	36	14	16	30	32	....	....	....	....	....	....	....	....	....	....	....	....	....	....	....	....	....	....
2005-06	Calgary Royals	AJHL	56	19	37	56	60	....	....	....	....	....	....	....	....	....	....	....	....	....	....	....	....	....	....
2006-07	Dartmouth	ECAC	33	14	17	31	30	....	....	....	....	....	....	....	....	....	....	....	....	....	....	....	....	....	....
2007-08	Calgary Hitmen	WHL	72	18	52	70	77	....	....	....	....	....	....	....	....	....	16	5	*19	*24	20	....	....	....	....
2008-09	**Colorado**	**NHL**	**11**	**3**	**1**	**4**	**6**	**0**	**0**	**0**	**14**	**21.4**	**–4**	**133**	**42.1**	**16:21**	....	....	....	....	....	....	....	....	....
	Lake Erie	AHL	66	10	17	27	32	....	....	....	....	....	....	....	....	....	....	....	....	....	....	....	....	....	....
2009-10	**Colorado**	**NHL**	**70**	**15**	**24**	**39**	**28**	**2**	**1**	**3**	**120**	**12.5**	**6**	**327**	**50.5**	**18:11**	**6**	**0**	**2**	**2**	**6**	**0**	**0**	**0**	**20:50**
	NHL Totals		**81**	**18**	**25**	**43**	**34**	**2**	**1**	**3**	**134**	**13.4**		**460**	**48.0**	**17:56**	**6**	**0**	**2**	**2**	**6**	**0**	**0**	**0**	**20:50**

ECAC All-Rookie Team (2007)

GARRISON, Jason
(GAIR-ih-suhn, JAY-suhn) **FLA.**

Defense. Shoots left. 6'2", 220 lbs. Born, White Rock, B.C., November 13, 1984.

Season	Club	League	GP	G	A	Pts	PIM	PP	SH	GW	S	%	+/-	TF	F%	Min	GP	G	A	Pts	PIM	PP	SH	GW	Min
2003-04	Nanaimo Clippers	BCHL	52	7	20	27	31	....	....	....	....	....	....	....	....	....	24	3	10	13	12	....	....	....	....
2004-05	Nanaimo Clippers	BCHL	57	22	40	62	42	....	....	....	....	....	....	....	....	....	....	....	....	....	....	....	....	....	....
2005-06	U. Minn-Duluth	WCHA	40	3	9	12	26	....	....	....	....	....	....	....	....	....	....	....	....	....	....	....	....	....	....
2006-07	U. Minn-Duluth	WCHA	21	1	2	3	16	....	....	....	....	....	....	....	....	....	....	....	....	....	....	....	....	....	....
2007-08	U. Minn-Duluth	WCHA	26	5	9	14	26	....	....	....	....	....	....	....	....	....	....	....	....	....	....	....	....	....	....
2008-09	**Florida**	**NHL**	**1**	**0**	**0**	**0**	**0**	**0**	**0**	**0**	**0**	**0.0**	**0**	**0**	**0.0**	**11:57**	....	....	....	....	....	....	....	....	....
	Rochester	AHL	75	8	27	35	68	....	....	....	....	....	....	....	....	....	....	....	....	....	....	....	....	....	....
2009-10	**Florida**	**NHL**	**39**	**2**	**6**	**8**	**23**	**0**	**0**	**0**	**24**	**8.3**	**5**	**0**	**0.0**	**15:08**	....	....	....	....	....	....	....	....	....
	Rochester	AHL	38	3	16	19	33	....	....	....	....	....	....	....	....	....	7	2	7	9	0	....	....	....	....
	NHL Totals		**40**	**2**	**6**	**8**	**23**	**0**	**0**	**0**	**24**	**8.3**		**0**	**0.0**	**15:03**	....	....	....	....	....	....	....	....	....

Signed as a free agent by **Florida**, April 2, 2008.

GAUSTAD, Paul
(GAW-stad, PAWL) **BUF.**

Center. Shoots left. 6'4", 224 lbs. Born, Fargo, ND, February 3, 1982. Buffalo's 6th choice, 220th overall, in 2000 Entry Draft.

Season	Club	League	GP	G	A	Pts	PIM	PP	SH	GW	S	%	+/-	TF	F%	Min	GP	G	A	Pts	PIM	PP	SH	GW	Min
1998-99	Portland Hawks	USAHA	45	47	53	100	81	....	....	....	....	....	....	....	....	....	....	....	....	....	....	....	....	....	....
99-2000	Portland	WHL	56	6	8	14	110	....	....	....	....	....	....	....	....	....	....	....	....	....	....	....	....	....	....
2000-01	Portland	WHL	70	11	30	41	168	....	....	....	....	....	....	....	....	....	16	10	6	16	59	....	....	....	....
2001-02	Portland	WHL	72	36	44	80	202	....	....	....	....	....	....	....	....	....	6	3	1	4	16	....	....	....	....
2002-03	**Buffalo**	**NHL**	**1**	**0**	**0**	**0**	**0**	**0**	**0**	**0**	**0**	**0.0**	**0**	**7**	**42.9**	**5:48**	....	....	....	....	....	....	....	....	....
	Rochester	AHL	80	14	39	53	137	....	....	....	....	....	....	....	....	....	3	0	0	0	4	....	....	....	....
2003-04	Rochester	AHL	78	9	22	31	169	....	....	....	....	....	....	....	....	....	16	3	10	13	30	....	....	....	....
2004-05	Rochester	AHL	76	18	25	43	192	....	....	....	....	....	....	....	....	....	9	6	5	11	16	....	....	....	....
2005-06	**Buffalo**	**NHL**	**78**	**9**	**15**	**24**	**65**	**0**	**0**	**0**	**113**	**8.0**	**4**	**829**	**52.2**	**12:08**	**18**	**0**	**4**	**4**	**14**	**0**	**0**	**0**	**12:21**
2006-07	**Buffalo**	**NHL**	**54**	**9**	**13**	**22**	**74**	**3**	**0**	**0**	**75**	**12.0**	**11**	**386**	**52.9**	**13:19**	**7**	**0**	**1**	**1**	**2**	**0**	**0**	**0**	**11:00**
2007-08	**Buffalo**	**NHL**	**82**	**10**	**26**	**36**	**85**	**5**	**0**	**2**	**136**	**7.4**	**–4**	**1165**	**54.9**	**17:10**	....	....	....	....	....	....	....	....	....
2008-09	**Buffalo**	**NHL**	**62**	**12**	**17**	**29**	**108**	**3**	**1**	**1**	**122**	**9.8**	**4**	**858**	**52.7**	**16:06**	....	....	....	....	....	....	....	....	....
2009-10	**Buffalo**	**NHL**	**65**	**12**	**10**	**22**	**82**	**3**	**0**	**1**	**111**	**10.8**	**–7**	**1043**	**57.4**	**15:45**	**6**	**0**	**1**	**1**	**8**	**0**	**0**	**0**	**18:40**
	NHL Totals		**342**	**52**	**81**	**133**	**414**	**14**	**1**	**4**	**557**	**9.3**		**4288**	**54.4**	**14:55**	**31**	**0**	**6**	**6**	**24**	**0**	**0**	**0**	**13:16**

GAUTHIER, Gabe
(GOH-tyay, GAYB)

Left wing. Shoots left. 5'8", 199 lbs. Born, Torrance, CA, January 20, 1984.

Season	Club	League	GP	G	A	Pts	PIM	PP	SH	GW	S	%	+/-	TF	F%	Min	GP	G	A	Pts	PIM	PP	SH	GW	Min
2002-03	U. of Denver	WCHA	41	8	8	16	30	....	....	....	....	....	....	....	....	....	....	....	....	....	....	....	....	....	....
2003-04	U. of Denver	WCHA	42	18	25	43	32	....	....	....	....	....	....	....	....	....	....	....	....	....	....	....	....	....	....
2004-05	U. of Denver	WCHA	41	23	29	52	44	....	....	....	....	....	....	....	....	....	....	....	....	....	....	....	....	....	....
2005-06	U. of Denver	WCHA	38	15	24	39	35	....	....	....	....	....	....	....	....	....	....	....	....	....	....	....	....	....	....
2006-07	**Los Angeles**	**NHL**	**5**	**0**	**0**	**0**	**2**	**0**	**0**	**0**	**6**	**0.0**	**–1**	**23**	**47.8**	**9:57**	....	....	....	....	....	....	....	....	....
	Manchester	AHL	69	14	28	42	54	....	....	....	....	....	....	....	....	....	16	1	4	5	14	....	....	....	....
2007-08	**Los Angeles**	**NHL**	**3**	**0**	**0**	**0**	**0**	**0**	**0**	**0**	**2**	**0.0**	**0**	**17**	**47.1**	**7:08**	....	....	....	....	....	....	....	....	....
	Manchester	AHL	61	23	37	60	43	....	....	....	....	....	....	....	....	....	3	0	0	0	4	....	....	....	....
2008-09	Manchester	AHL	69	12	30	42	32	....	....	....	....	....	....	....	....	....	....	....	....	....	....	....	....	....	....
2009-10	Manchester	AHL	71	8	27	35	36	....	....	....	....	....	....	....	....	....	16	7	4	11	8	....	....	....	....
	NHL Totals		**8**	**0**	**0**	**0**	**2**	**0**	**0**	**0**	**8**	**0.0**		**40**	**47.5**	**8:53**	....	....	....	....	....	....	....	....	....

NCAA Championship All-Tournament Team (2005)
Signed as a free agent by **Los Angeles**, July 12, 2006.

			Regular Season														Playoffs								
Season	Club	League	GP	G	A	Pts	PIM	PP	SH	GW	S	%	+/-	TF	F%	Min	GP	G	A	Pts	PIM	PP	SH	GW	M

GERBE, Nathan

(GUHR-bee, NAY-thuhn) **BUF**

Center. Shoots left. 5'6", 178 lbs. Born, Oxford, MI, July 24, 1987. Buffalo's 5th choice, 142nd overall, in 2005 Entry Draft.

Season	Club	League	GP	G	A	Pts	PIM	PP	SH	GW	S	%	+/-	TF	F%	Min	GP	G	A	Pts	PIM	PP	SH	GW	M
2002-03	River City Lancers	USHL	25	3	3	6	49	....	....	....	....	....	....	....	....	....	7	1	1	2	2	....	....	....	....
2003-04	USNTDP	U-17	32	14	12	26	66	....	....	....	....	....	....	....	....	....	....	....	....	....	....	....	....	....	....
	USNTDP	NAHL	26	11	7	18	87	....	....	....	....	....	....	....	....	....	....	....	....	....	....	....	....	....	....
2004-05	USNTDP	U-18	26	6	11	17	48	....	....	....	....	....	....	....	....	....	....	....	....	....	....	....	....	....	....
	USNTDP	NAHL	12	7	5	12	25	....	....	....	....	....	....	....	....	....	....	....	....	....	....	....	....	....	....
2005-06	Boston College	H-East	39	11	7	18	75	....	....	....	....	....	....	....	....	....	....	....	....	....	....	....	....	....	....
2006-07	Boston College	H-East	41	*25	22	47	76	....	....	....	....	....	....	....	....	....	....	....	....	....	....	....	....	....	....
2007-08	Boston College	H-East	43	*35	33	*68	65	....	....	....	....	....	....	....	....	....	....	....	....	....	....	....	....	....	....
2008-09	**Buffalo**	**NHL**	**10**	**0**	**1**	**1**	**4**	**0**	**0**	**0**	**24**	**0.0**	**3**	**1**	**100.0**	**13:37**	....	....	....	....	....	....	....	....	....
	Portland Pirates	AHL	57	30	26	56	63	....	....	....	....	....	....	....	....	....	5	0	0	0	4	....	....	....	....
2009-10	**Buffalo**	**NHL**	**10**	**2**	**3**	**5**	**4**	**2**	**0**	**1**	**29**	**6.9**	**1**	**3**	**33.3**	**14:39**	**2**	**1**	**1**	**2**	**0**	**0**	**0**	**0**	**14:3**
	Portland Pirates	AHL	44	11	27	38	46	....	....	....	....	....	....	....	....	....	4	1	1	2	4	....	....	....	....
	NHL Totals		**20**	**2**	**4**	**6**	**8**	**2**	**0**	**1**	**53**	**3.8**		**4**	**50.0**	**14:08**	**2**	**1**	**1**	**2**	**0**	**0**	**0**	**0**	**14:3**

Hockey East Second Alll-Star Team (2007) • NCAA Championship All-Tournament Team (2007, 2008) • Hockey East First All-Star Team (2008) • NCAA East First All-American Team (2008) • NCAA Championship Tournament MVP (2008) • AHL All-Rookie Team (2009) • Dudley "Red" Garrett Memorial Award (AHL – Rookie of the Year) (2009)

GERMYN, Carsen

(JUHR-mihn, KAHR-sehn)

Right wing. Shoots right. 5'11", 190 lbs. Born, Campbell River, B.C., February 22, 1982.

Season	Club	League	GP	G	A	Pts	PIM	PP	SH	GW	S	%	+/-	TF	F%	Min	GP	G	A	Pts	PIM	PP	SH	GW	M
1998-99	Kelowna Rockets	WHL	59	6	10	16	61	....	....	....	....	....	....	....	....	....	5	0	0	0	2	....	....	....	....
99-2000	Kelowna Rockets	WHL	71	16	29	45	111	....	....	....	....	....	....	....	....	....	5	3	3	6	4	....	....	....	....
2000-01	Kelowna Rockets	WHL	71	35	52	87	102	....	....	....	....	....	....	....	....	....	6	2	6	8	10	....	....	....	....
2001-02	Kelowna Rockets	WHL	23	10	18	28	43	....	....	....	....	....	....	....	....	....	....	....	....	....	....	....	....	....	....
	Red Deer Rebels	WHL	37	23	25	48	83	....	....	....	....	....	....	....	....	....	23	4	12	16	24	....	....	....	....
2002-03	Red Deer Rebels	WHL	63	26	33	59	108	....	....	....	....	....	....	....	....	....	23	4	9	13	25	....	....	....	....
2003-04	Norfolk Admirals	AHL	77	11	16	27	104	....	....	....	....	....	....	....	....	....	6	1	0	1	2	....	....	....	....
2004-05	Lowell	AHL	60	9	11	20	115	....	....	....	....	....	....	....	....	....	10	0	0	0	25	....	....	....	....
2005-06	**Calgary**	**NHL**	**2**	**0**	**0**	**0**	**0**	**0**	**0**	**0**	**2**	**0.0**	**–1**	**0**	**0.0**	**5:00**	....	....	....	....	....	....	....	....	....
	Omaha	AHL	77	24	31	55	127	....	....	....	....	....	....	....	....	....	....	....	....	....	....	....	....	....	....
2006-07	**Calgary**	**NHL**	**2**	**0**	**0**	**0**	**0**	**0**	**0**	**0**	**3**	**0.0**	**0**	**2**	**50.0**	**8:26**	....	....	....	....	....	....	....	....	....
	Omaha	AHL	77	28	32	60	124	....	....	....	....	....	....	....	....	....	6	1	1	2	2	....	....	....	....
2007-08	Quad City Flames	AHL	77	19	29	48	133	....	....	....	....	....	....	....	....	....	....	....	....	....	....	....	....	....	....
2008-09	Quad City Flames	AHL	75	13	47	60	57	....	....	....	....	....	....	....	....	....	....	....	....	....	....	....	....	....	....
2009-10	Abbotsford Heat	AHL	21	5	10	15	8	....	....	....	....	....	....	....	....	....	....	....	....	....	....	....	....	....	....
	NHL Totals		**4**	**0**	**0**	**0**	**0**	**0**	**0**	**0**	**5**	**0.0**		**2**	**50.0**	**6:43**	....	....	....	....	....	....	....	....	....

Signed as a free agent by **Calgary**, July 6, 2004.

GERVAIS, Bruno

(ZHUR-vay, BROO-noh) **NYI**

Defense. Shoots right. 6'1", 205 lbs. Born, Longueuil, Que., October 3, 1984. NY Islanders' 6th choice, 182nd overall, in 2003 Entry Draft.

Season	Club	League	GP	G	A	Pts	PIM	PP	SH	GW	S	%	+/-	TF	F%	Min	GP	G	A	Pts	PIM	PP	SH	GW	M
99-2000	Antoine-Girouard	QAAA	6	0	0	0	0	....	....	....	....	....	....	....	....	....	4	0	0	0	0	....	....	....	....
2000-01	Antoine-Girouard	QAAA	40	8	27	35	46	....	....	....	....	....	....	....	....	....	7	4	2	6	8	....	....	....	....
2001-02	Acadie-Bathurst	QMJHL	65	4	12	16	42	....	....	....	....	....	....	....	....	....	16	3	1	4	8	....	....	....	....
2002-03	Acadie-Bathurst	QMJHL	72	22	28	50	73	....	....	....	....	....	....	....	....	....	11	3	5	8	14	....	....	....	....
2003-04	Acadie-Bathurst	QMJHL	23	4	6	10	28	....	....	....	....	....	....	....	....	....	....	....	....	....	....	....	....	....	....
2004-05	Bridgeport	AHL	76	8	22	30	58	....	....	....	....	....	....	....	....	....	....	....	....	....	....	....	....	....	....
2005-06	**NY Islanders**	**NHL**	**27**	**3**	**4**	**7**	**8**	**1**	**0**	**0**	**21**	**14.3**	**–1**	**0**	**0.0**	**16:47**	....	....	....	....	....	....	....	....	....
	Bridgeport	AHL	55	17	25	42	70	....	....	....	....	....	....	....	....	....	7	1	2	3	0	....	....	....	....
2006-07	**NY Islanders**	**NHL**	**51**	**0**	**6**	**6**	**28**	**0**	**0**	**0**	**47**	**0.0**	**–10**	**0**	**0.0**	**15:23**	**5**	**1**	**1**	**2**	**2**	**0**	**0**	**0**	**15:36**
	Bridgeport	AHL	3	0	0	0	6	....	....	....	....	....	....	....	....	....	....	....	....	....	....	....	....	....	....
2007-08	**NY Islanders**	**NHL**	**60**	**0**	**13**	**13**	**34**	**0**	**0**	**0**	**59**	**0.0**	**–5**	**0**	**0.0**	**20:00**	....	....	....	....	....	....	....	....	....
2008-09	**NY Islanders**	**NHL**	**69**	**3**	**16**	**19**	**33**	**0**	**0**	**1**	**82**	**3.7**	**–15**	**1**	**0.0**	**21:36**	....	....	....	....	....	....	....	....	....
2009-10	**NY Islanders**	**NHL**	**71**	**3**	**14**	**17**	**31**	**1**	**0**	**1**	**83**	**3.6**	**–15**	**0**	**0.0**	**20:01**	....	....	....	....	....	....	....	....	....
	NHL Totals		**278**	**9**	**53**	**62**	**134**	**2**	**0**	**2**	**292**	**3.1**		**1**	**0.0**	**19:14**	**5**	**1**	**1**	**2**	**2**	**0**	**0**	**0**	**15:36**

QMJHL Second All-Star Team (2003)

• Missed majority of 2003-04 season recovering from knee injury suffered during Team Canada Jr. training camp, December 12, 2003.

GETZLAF, Ryan

(GEHTZ-laf, RIGH-uhn) **ANA.**

Center. Shoots right. 6'4", 220 lbs. Born, Regina, Sask., May 10, 1985. Anaheim's 1st choice, 19th overall, in 2003 Entry Draft.

Season	Club	League	GP	G	A	Pts	PIM	PP	SH	GW	S	%	+/-	TF	F%	Min	GP	G	A	Pts	PIM	PP	SH	GW	M
2000-01	Regina Rangers	SBHL	41	33	41	74	189	....	....	....	....	....	....	....	....	....	....	....	....	....	....	....	....	....	....
	Reg. Pat Cdns.	SMHL	8	4	3	7	8	....	....	....	....	....	....	....	....	....	....	....	....	....	....	....	....	....	....
2001-02	Calgary Hitmen	WHL	63	9	9	18	34	....	....	....	....	....	....	....	....	....	7	2	1	3	4	....	....	....	....
2002-03	Calgary Hitmen	WHL	70	29	39	68	121	....	....	....	....	....	....	....	....	....	5	1	1	2	6	....	....	....	....
2003-04	Calgary Hitmen	WHL	49	28	47	75	97	....	....	....	....	....	....	....	....	....	7	5	1	6	12	....	....	....	....
2004-05	Calgary Hitmen	WHL	51	29	25	54	102	....	....	....	....	....	....	....	....	....	12	4	13	17	18	....	....	....	....
	Cincinnati	AHL	....	....	....	....	....	....	....	....	....	....	....	....	....	....	10	1	4	5	4	....	....	....	....
2005-06	**Anaheim**	**NHL**	**57**	**14**	**25**	**39**	**22**	**10**	**0**	**1**	**116**	**12.1**	**6**	**534**	**44.0**	**12:35**	**16**	**3**	**4**	**7**	**13**	**2**	**0**	**1**	**15:49**
	Portland Pirates	AHL	17	8	25	33	36	....	....	....	....	....	....	....	....	....	1	0	0	0	4	....	....	....	....
2006-07 ♦	**Anaheim**	**NHL**	**82**	**25**	**33**	**58**	**66**	**11**	**1**	**6**	**203**	**12.3**	**17**	**888**	**49.4**	**15:04**	**21**	**7**	**10**	**17**	**32**	**3**	**1**	**3**	**21:43**
2007-08	**Anaheim**	**NHL**	**77**	**24**	**58**	**82**	**94**	**4**	**1**	**2**	**185**	**13.0**	**32**	**1152**	**47.3**	**19:39**	**6**	**2**	**3**	**5**	**6**	**1**	**0**	**0**	**20:29**
2008-09	**Anaheim**	**NHL**	**81**	**25**	**66**	**91**	**121**	**9**	**0**	**2**	**227**	**11.0**	**5**	**1128**	**50.2**	**20:08**	**13**	**4**	**14**	**18**	**25**	**1**	**0**	**0**	**24:08**
2009-10	**Anaheim**	**NHL**	**66**	**19**	**50**	**69**	**79**	**8**	**0**	**5**	**149**	**12.8**	**4**	**1124**	**47.4**	**21:40**	....	....	....	....	....	....	....	....	....
	Canada	Olympics	7	3	4	7	2	....	....	....	....	....	....	....	....	....	....	....	....	....	....	....	....	....	....
	NHL Totals		**363**	**107**	**232**	**339**	**382**	**42**	**2**	**16**	**880**	**12.2**		**4826**	**48.0**	**17:59**	**56**	**16**	**31**	**47**	**76**	**7**	**1**	**4**	**20:28**

WHL East First All-Star Team (2004) • WHL East Second All-Star Team (2005)

Played in NHL All-Star Game (2008, 2009)

GILBERT, Tom

(GIHL-buhrt, TAWM) **EDM.**

Defense. Shoots right. 6'3", 206 lbs. Born, Bloomington, MN, January 10, 1983. Colorado's 5th choice, 129th overall, in 2002 Entry Draft.

Season	Club	League	GP	G	A	Pts	PIM	PP	SH	GW	S	%	+/-	TF	F%	Min	GP	G	A	Pts	PIM	PP	SH	GW	M
99-2000	Bloomington-Jeff.	High-MN	18	7	18	25	....	....	....	....	....	....	....	....	....	....	....	....	....	....	....	....	....	....	....
2000-01	Bloomington-Jeff.	High-MN	23	20	18	38	....	....	....	....	....	....	....	....	....	....	....	....	....	....	....	....	....	....	....
	Chicago Steel	USHL	1	0	0	0	0	....	....	....	....	....	....	....	....	....	....	....	....	....	....	....	....	....	....
2001-02	Chicago Steel	USHL	57	13	15	28	62	....	....	....	....	....	....	....	....	....	4	0	0	0	4	....	....	....	....
2002-03	U. of Wisconsin	WCHA	39	7	13	20	36	....	....	....	....	....	....	....	....	....	....	....	....	....	....	....	....	....	....
2003-04	U. of Wisconsin	WCHA	39	6	15	21	36	....	....	....	....	....	....	....	....	....	....	....	....	....	....	....	....	....	....
2004-05	U. of Wisconsin	WCHA	41	8	9	17	48	....	....	....	....	....	....	....	....	....	....	....	....	....	....	....	....	....	....
2005-06	U. of Wisconsin	WCHA	43	12	19	31	32	....	....	....	....	....	....	....	....	....	....	....	....	....	....	....	....	....	....
2006-07	**Edmonton**	**NHL**	**12**	**1**	**5**	**6**	**0**	**0**	**0**	**0**	**13**	**7.7**	**–1**	**0**	**0.0**	**20:05**	....	....	....	....	....	....	....	....	....
	Wilkes-Barre	AHL	48	4	26	30	32	....	....	....	....	....	....	....	....	....	10	1	7	8	10	....	....	....	....
2007-08	**Edmonton**	**NHL**	**82**	**13**	**20**	**33**	**20**	**3**	**0**	**1**	**98**	**13.3**	**–6**	**0**	**0.0**	**22:12**	....	....	....	....	....	....	....	....	....
2008-09	**Edmonton**	**NHL**	**82**	**5**	**40**	**45**	**26**	**2**	**0**	**1**	**107**	**4.7**	**6**	**0**	**0.0**	**21:58**	....	....	....	....	....	....	....	....	....
2009-10	**Edmonton**	**NHL**	**82**	**5**	**26**	**31**	**16**	**1**	**1**	**0**	**98**	**5.1**	**–10**	**0**	**0.0**	**22:25**	....	....	....	....	....	....	....	....	....
	NHL Totals		**258**	**24**	**91**	**115**	**62**	**6**	**1**	**2**	**316**	**7.6**		**0**	**0.0**	**22:06**	....	....	....	....	....	....	....	....	....

WCHA First All-Star Team (2006) • NCAA West Second All-American Team (2006) • NCAA Championship All-Tournament Team (2006) • NHL All-Rookie Team (2008)

Traded to **Edmonton** by **Colorado** for Tommy Salo and Edmonton's 6th round choice (Justin Mercier) in 2005 Entry Draft, March 8, 2004.

GILL, Hal

(GIHL, HAL) **MTL.**

Defense. Shoots left. 6'7", 241 lbs. Born, Concord, MA, April 6, 1975. Boston's 8th choice, 207th overall, in 1993 Entry Draft.

			Regular Season														Playoffs								
Season	Club	League	GP	G	A	Pts	PIM	PP	SH	GW	S	%	+/-	TF	F%	Min	GP	G	A	Pts	PIM	PP	SH	GW	Min
1992-93	Nashoba	High-MA	20	25	25	50	....	....	....	....	....	....	....	....	....	....	....	....	....	....	....	....	....	....	....
1993-94	Providence	H-East	31	1	2	3	26	....	....	....	....	....	....	....	....	....	....	....	....	....	....	....	....	....	....
1994-95	Providence	H-East	26	1	3	4	22	....	....	....	....	....	....	....	....	....	....	....	....	....	....	....	....	....	....
1995-96	Providence	H-East	39	5	12	17	54	....	....	....	....	....	....	....	....	....	....	....	....	....	....	....	....	....	....
1996-97	Providence	H-East	35	5	16	21	52	....	....	....	....	....	....	....	....	....	....	....	....	....	....	....	....	....	....
1997-98	**Boston**	**NHL**	**68**	**2**	**4**	**6**	**47**	**0**	**0**	**0**	**56**	**3.6**	**4**	....	....	....	**6**	**0**	**0**	**0**	**4**	**0**	**0**	**0**	....
	Providence Bruins	AHL	4	1	0	1	23	....	....	....	....	....	....	....	....	....	....	....	....	....	....	....	....	....	....
1998-99	**Boston**	**NHL**	**80**	**3**	**7**	**10**	**63**	**0**	**0**	**2**	**102**	**2.9**	**-10**	**1**	**100.0**	**20:54**	**12**	**0**	**0**	**0**	**14**	**0**	**0**	**0**	**20:41**
99-2000	**Boston**	**NHL**	**81**	**3**	**9**	**12**	**51**	**0**	**0**	**0**	**120**	**2.5**	**0**	**0**	**0.0**	**17:15**	....	....	....	....	....	....	....	....	....
2000-01	**Boston**	**NHL**	**80**	**1**	**10**	**11**	**71**	**0**	**0**	**0**	**79**	**1.3**	**-2**	**0**	**0.0**	**18:21**	....	....	....	....	....	....	....	....	....
2001-02	**Boston**	**NHL**	**79**	**4**	**18**	**22**	**77**	**0**	**0**	**0**	**137**	**2.9**	**16**	**0**	**0.0**	**24:13**	**6**	**0**	**1**	**1**	**2**	**0**	**0**	**0**	**23:04**
2002-03	**Boston**	**NHL**	**76**	**4**	**13**	**17**	**56**	**0**	**0**	**0**	**114**	**3.5**	**21**	**0**	**0.0**	**20:42**	**5**	**0**	**0**	**0**	**4**	**0**	**0**	**0**	**20:19**
2003-04	**Boston**	**NHL**	**82**	**2**	**7**	**9**	**99**	**0**	**0**	**0**	**104**	**1.9**	**16**	**0**	**0.0**	**18:24**	**7**	**0**	**1**	**1**	**4**	**0**	**0**	**0**	**19:03**
2004-05	Lukko Rauma	Finland	31	2	8	10	110	....	....	....	....	....	....	....	....	....	8	0	0	0	*57	....	....	....	....
2005-06	**Boston**	**NHL**	**80**	**1**	**9**	**10**	**124**	**0**	**0**	**0**	**68**	**1.5**	**-4**	**0**	**0.0**	**18:37**	....	....	....	....	....	....	....	....	....
2006-07	**Toronto**	**NHL**	**82**	**6**	**14**	**20**	**91**	**0**	**0**	**1**	**79**	**7.6**	**11**	**1**	**0.0**	**18:53**	....	....	....	....	....	....	....	....	....
2007-08	**Toronto**	**NHL**	**63**	**2**	**18**	**20**	**52**	**0**	**0**	**0**	**69**	**2.9**	**0**	**0**	**0.0**	**20:42**	....	....	....	....	....	....	....	....	....
	Pittsburgh	**NHL**	**18**	**1**	**3**	**4**	**16**	**0**	**0**	**0**	**17**	**5.9**	**6**	**0**	**0.0**	**17:31**	**20**	**0**	**1**	**1**	**12**	**0**	**0**	**0**	**19:17**
2008-09 ♦	**Pittsburgh**	**NHL**	**62**	**2**	**8**	**10**	**53**	**0**	**0**	**0**	**40**	**5.0**	**11**	**0**	**0.0**	**17:54**	**24**	**0**	**2**	**2**	**6**	**0**	**0**	**0**	**19:26**
2009-10	**Montreal**	**NHL**	**68**	**2**	**9**	**11**	**68**	**0**	**0**	**0**	**41**	**4.9**	**-10**	**1**	**0.0**	**18:21**	**18**	**0**	**1**	**1**	**20**	**0**	**0**	**0**	**19:54**
	NHL Totals		**919**	**33**	**129**	**162**	**868**	**0**	**0**	**3**	**1026**	**3.2**		**3**	**33.3**	**19:27**	**98**	**0**	**6**	**6**	**66**	**0**	**0**	**0**	**19:55**

Signed as a free agent by **Rauma** (Finland), November 25, 2004. Signed as a free agent by **Toronto**, July 1, 2006. Traded to **Pittsburgh** by **Toronto** for Pittsburgh's 2nd round choice (Jimmy Hayes) in 2008 Entry Draft and Pittsburgh's 5th round choice (later traded to NY Rangers, later traded back to Pittsburgh – Pittsburgh selected Andy Bathgate) in 2009 Entry Draft, February 26, 2008. Signed as a free agent by **Montreal**, July 1, 2009.

GILLIES, Colton

(GIHL-eez, KOHL-tuhn) **MIN.**

Center. Shoots left. 6'4", 207 lbs. Born, White Rock, B.C., February 12, 1989. Minnesota's 1st choice, 16th overall, in 2007 Entry Draft.

Season	Club	League	GP	G	A	Pts	PIM	PP	SH	GW	S	%	+/-	TF	F%	Min	GP	G	A	Pts	PIM	PP	SH	GW	Min
2004-05	North Delta Flyers	PIJHL	44	9	17	26	....	....	....	....	....	....	....	....	....	....	6	2	1	3	....	....	....	....	....
	South Surrey	BCHL	3	1	0	1	0	....	....	....	....	....	....	....	....	....	....	....	....	....	....	....	....	....	....
	Saskatoon Blades	WHL	9	1	1	2	8	....	....	....	....	....	....	....	....	....	2	0	0	0	0	....	....	....	....
2005-06	Saskatoon Blades	WHL	63	6	6	12	57	....	....	....	....	....	....	....	....	....	8	0	0	0	4	....	....	....	....
2006-07	Saskatoon Blades	WHL	65	13	17	30	148	....	....	....	....	....	....	....	....	....	....	....	....	....	....	....	....	....	....
2007-08	Saskatoon Blades	WHL	58	24	23	47	97	....	....	....	....	....	....	....	....	....	....	....	....	....	....	....	....	....	....
	Houston Aeros	AHL	11	1	7	8	4	....	....	....	....	....	....	....	....	....	5	0	0	0	2	....	....	....	....
2008-09	**Minnesota**	**NHL**	**45**	**2**	**5**	**7**	**18**	**0**	**0**	**1**	**22**	**9.1**	**-2**	**2**	**50.0**	**8:14**	....	....	....	....	....	....	....	....	....
2009-10	Houston Aeros	AHL	72	7	13	20	73	....	....	....	....	....	....	....	....	....	....	....	....	....	....	....	....	....	....
	NHL Totals		**45**	**2**	**5**	**7**	**18**	**0**	**0**	**1**	**22**	**9.1**		**2**	**50.0**	**8:14**	....	....	....	....	....	....	....	....	....

GILLIES, Trevor

(GIHL-eez, TREH-vuhr) **NYI**

Left wing. Shoots left. 6'3", 215 lbs. Born, Cambridge, Ont., January 30, 1979.

Season	Club	League	GP	G	A	Pts	PIM	PP	SH	GW	S	%	+/-	TF	F%	Min	GP	G	A	Pts	PIM	PP	SH	GW	Min
1996-97	North Bay	OHL	26	0	3	3	72	....	....	....	....	....	....	....	....	....	....	....	....	....	....	....	....	....	....
1997-98	North Bay	OHL	2	0	0	0	4	....	....	....	....	....	....	....	....	....	....	....	....	....	....	....	....	....	....
	Sarnia Sting	OHL	17	0	1	1	33	....	....	....	....	....	....	....	....	....	....	....	....	....	....	....	....	....	....
	Oshawa Generals	OHL	45	1	2	3	184	....	....	....	....	....	....	....	....	....	7	0	1	1	12	....	....	....	....
1998-99	Oshawa Generals	OHL	66	6	9	15	270	....	....	....	....	....	....	....	....	....	11	0	2	2	28	....	....	....	....
99-2000	Lowell	AHL	8	0	0	0	38	....	....	....	....	....	....	....	....	....	....	....	....	....	....	....	....	....	....
	Mississippi	ECHL	53	0	6	6	202	....	....	....	....	....	....	....	....	....	....	....	....	....	....	....	....	....	....
2000-01	Greensboro	ECHL	63	1	6	7	303	....	....	....	....	....	....	....	....	....	....	....	....	....	....	....	....	....	....
	Worcester IceCats	AHL	....	....	....	....	....	....	....	....	....	....	....	....	....	....	6	0	0	0	24	....	....	....	....
2001-02	Providence Bruins	AHL	5	0	0	0	21	....	....	....	....	....	....	....	....	....	....	....	....	....	....	....	....	....	....
	Augusta Lynx	ECHL	46	0	1	1	*269	....	....	....	....	....	....	....	....	....	....	....	....	....	....	....	....	....	....
	Richmond	ECHL	18	0	1	1	*51	....	....	....	....	....	....	....	....	....	....	....	....	....	....	....	....	....	....
2002-03	Lowell	AHL	25	0	1	1	132	....	....	....	....	....	....	....	....	....	....	....	....	....	....	....	....	....	....
	Richmond	ECHL	6	0	0	0	20	....	....	....	....	....	....	....	....	....	....	....	....	....	....	....	....	....	....
	Peoria Rivermen	ECHL	24	0	1	1	180	....	....	....	....	....	....	....	....	....	....	....	....	....	....	....	....	....	....
2003-04	Springfield	AHL	61	2	1	3	277	....	....	....	....	....	....	....	....	....	....	....	....	....	....	....	....	....	....
2004-05	Hartford	AHL	49	0	2	2	277	....	....	....	....	....	....	....	....	....	....	....	....	....	....	....	....	....	....
2005-06	**Anaheim**	**NHL**	**1**	**0**	**0**	**0**	**21**	**0**	**0**	**0**	**1**	**0.0**	**0**	**0**	**0.0**	**2:40**	....	....	....	....	....	....	....	....	....
	Portland Pirates	AHL	50	2	3	5	169	....	....	....	....	....	....	....	....	....	4	0	0	0	0	....	....	....	....
2006-07	Portland Pirates	AHL	51	1	6	7	151	....	....	....	....	....	....	....	....	....	....	....	....	....	....	....	....	....	....
	Augusta Lynx	ECHL	7	0	2	2	23	....	....	....	....	....	....	....	....	....	....	....	....	....	....	....	....	....	....
2007-08	Albany River Rats	AHL	51	1	1	2	112	....	....	....	....	....	....	....	....	....	7	0	0	0	19	....	....	....	....
2008-09	Albany River Rats	AHL	30	0	0	0	125	....	....	....	....	....	....	....	....	....	....	....	....	....	....	....	....	....	....
2009-10	Bridgeport	AHL	24	1	0	1	169	....	....	....	....	....	....	....	....	....	....	....	....	....	....	....	....	....	....
	NY Islanders	**NHL**	**14**	**0**	**1**	**1**	**75**	**0**	**0**	**0**	**6**	**0.0**	**-2**	**0**	**0.0**	**3:49**	....	....	....	....	....	....	....	....	....
	NHL Totals		**15**	**0**	**1**	**1**	**96**	**0**	**0**	**0**	**7**	**0.0**		**0**	**0.0**	**3:45**	....	....	....	....	....	....	....	....	....

Signed as a free agent by **NY Rangers**, July 20, 2004. Traded to **Anaheim** by **NY Rangers** with NY Rangers' 4th round choice (later traded back to NY Rangers, later traded to Washington - Washington selected Brett Bruneteau) in 2007 Entry Draft for Steve Rucchin, August 23, 2005. Signed as a free agent by **Carolina**, July 2, 2007. • Missed majority of 2008-09 season recovering from injury suffered in game at Wilkes-Barre (AHL), December 20, 2008. Signed as a free agent by **Bridgeport** (AHL), October 2, 2009. Signed as a free agent by **NY Islanders**, January 29, 2010.

GILROY, Matt

(GIHL-roy, MAT) **NYR**

Defense. Shoots right. 6'1", 201 lbs. Born, North Bellmore, NY, July 30, 1984.

Season	Club	League	GP	G	A	Pts	PIM	PP	SH	GW	S	%	+/-	TF	F%	Min	GP	G	A	Pts	PIM	PP	SH	GW	Min
2000-01	St. Mary's Gaels	High-NY	STATISTICS NOT AVAILABLE																						
2001-02	St. Mary's Gaels	High-NY	STATISTICS NOT AVAILABLE																						
2002-03	St. Mary's Gaels	High-NY	STATISTICS NOT AVAILABLE																						
2003-04	NY Apple Core	EJHL	STATISTICS NOT AVAILABLE																						
2004-05	Walpole Stars	EJHL	55	24	29	53	20	....	....	....	....	....	....	....	....	....	....	....	....	....	....	....	....	....	....
2005-06	Boston University	H-East	36	2	6	8	10	....	....	....	....	....	....	....	....	....	....	....	....	....	....	....	....	....	....
2006-07	Boston University	H-East	39	9	17	26	14	....	....	....	....	....	....	....	....	....	....	....	....	....	....	....	....	....	....
2007-08	Boston University	H-East	40	6	15	21	12	....	....	....	....	....	....	....	....	....	....	....	....	....	....	....	....	....	....
2008-09	Boston University	H-East	45	8	29	37	12	....	....	....	....	....	....	....	....	....	....	....	....	....	....	....	....	....	....
2009-10	**NY Rangers**	**NHL**	**69**	**4**	**11**	**15**	**23**	**0**	**0**	**1**	**82**	**4.9**	**0**	**1**	**100.0**	**16:19**	....	....	....	....	....	....	....	....	....
	Hartford	AHL	5	0	4	4	4	....	....	....	....	....	....	....	....	....	....	....	....	....	....	....	....	....	....
	NHL Totals		**69**	**4**	**11**	**15**	**23**	**0**	**0**	**1**	**82**	**4.9**		**1**	**100.0**	**16:19**	....	....	....	....	....	....	....	....	....

Hockey East First All-Star Team (2008, 2009) • NCAA East First All-American Team (2008, 2009) • Hobey Baker Memorial Award (Top U.S. Collegiate Player) (2009)

Signed as a free agent by **NY Rangers**, April 17, 2009.

GIONTA, Brian

(jee-OHN-tuh, BRIGH-uhn) **MTL.**

Right wing. Shoots right. 5'7", 173 lbs. Born, Rochester, NY, January 18, 1979. New Jersey's 4th choice, 82nd overall, in 1998 Entry Draft.

Season	Club	League	GP	G	A	Pts	PIM	PP	SH	GW	S	%	+/-	TF	F%	Min	GP	G	A	Pts	PIM	PP	SH	GW	Min
1994-95	Rochester	EmJHL	28	*52	37	*89	....	....	....	....	....	....	....	....	....	....	....	....	....	....	....	....	....	....	....
1995-96	Niagara Scenic	MTJHL	51	47	44	91	59	....	....	....	....	....	....	....	....	....	....	....	....	....	....	....	....	....	....
1996-97	Niagara Scenic	MTJHL	50	57	70	127	101	....	....	....	....	....	....	....	....	....	6	6	11	17	21	....	....	....	....
1997-98	Boston College	H-East	40	30	32	62	44	....	....	....	....	....	....	....	....	....	....	....	....	....	....	....	....	....	....
1998-99	Boston College	H-East	39	27	33	60	46	....	....	....	....	....	....	....	....	....	....	....	....	....	....	....	....	....	....
99-2000	Boston College	H-East	42	*33	23	56	66	....	....	....	....	....	....	....	....	....	....	....	....	....	....	....	....	....	....
2000-01	Boston College	H-East	43	*33	21	*54	47	....	....	....	....	....	....	....	....	....	....	....	....	....	....	....	....	....	....
2001-02	**New Jersey**	**NHL**	**33**	**4**	**7**	**11**	**8**	**0**	**0**	**0**	**58**	**6.9**	**10**	**36**	**44.4**	**13:25**	**6**	**2**	**2**	**4**	**0**	**0**	**1**	**2**	**17:08**
	Albany River Rats	AHL	37	9	16	25	18	....	....	....	....	....	....	....	....	....	....	....	....	....	....	....	....	....	....
2002-03 ♦	**New Jersey**	**NHL**	**58**	**12**	**13**	**25**	**23**	**2**	**0**	**3**	**129**	**9.3**	**5**	**14**	**57.1**	**14:48**	**24**	**1**	**8**	**9**	**6**	**0**	**0**	**0**	**14:31**
2003-04	**New Jersey**	**NHL**	**75**	**21**	**8**	**29**	**36**	**0**	**0**	**8**	**174**	**12.1**	**19**	**60**	**58.3**	**14:44**	**5**	**2**	**3**	**5**	**0**	**1**	**0**	**0**	**15:41**
2004-05	Albany River Rats	AHL	15	5	7	12	10	....	....	....	....	....	....	....	....	....	....	....	....	....	....	....	....	....	....
2005-06	**New Jersey**	**NHL**	**82**	**48**	**41**	**89**	**46**	**24**	**1**	**10**	**291**	**16.5**	**18**	**73**	**38.4**	**19:49**	**9**	**3**	**4**	**7**	**2**	**1**	**1**	**2**	**20:06**
	United States	Olympics	6	4	0	4	2	....	....	....	....	....	....	....	....	....	....	....	....	....	....	....	....	....	....

			Regular Season														Playoffs								
Season	Club	League	GP	G	A	Pts	PIM	PP	SH	GW	S	%	+/-	TF	F%	Min	GP	G	A	Pts	PIM	PP	SH	GW	Min
2006-07	**New Jersey**	**NHL**	**62**	**25**	**20**	**45**	**36**	**11**	**0**	**4**	**194**	**12.9**	**–3**	**31**	**38.7**	**18:49**	**11**	**8**	**1**	**9**	**4**	**3**	**0**	**1**	**19:15**
2007-08	**New Jersey**	**NHL**	**82**	**22**	**31**	**53**	**46**	**8**	**1**	**4**	**257**	**8.6**	**1**	**55**	**54.6**	**18:16**	**5**	**1**	**0**	**1**	**2**	**0**	**0**	**0**	**17:52**
2008-09	**New Jersey**	**NHL**	**81**	**20**	**40**	**60**	**32**	**3**	**3**	**1**	**248**	**8.1**	**12**	**132**	**38.6**	**16:58**	**7**	**2**	**3**	**5**	**4**	**0**	**0**	**0**	**17:49**
2009-10	**Montreal**	**NHL**	**61**	**28**	**18**	**46**	**26**	**10**	**0**	**3**	**237**	**11.8**	**3**	**13**	**53.9**	**20:45**	**19**	**9**	**6**	**15**	**14**	**4**	**0**	**1**	**22:11**
	NHL Totals		**534**	**180**	**178**	**358**	**253**	**58**	**5**	**33**	**1588**	**11.3**		**414**	**45.2**	**17:29**	**86**	**28**	**27**	**55**	**32**	**9**	**2**	**6**	**18:07**

Hockey East Rookie of the Year (1998) • Hockey East Second All-Star Team (1998) • NCAA East Second All-American Team (1998) • Hockey East First All-Star Team (1999, 2000, 2001) • NCAA East First All-American Team (1999, 2000, 2001) • Hockey East Player of the Year (2001)

Signed as a free agent by **Montreal**, July 1, 2009.

GIORDANO, Mark

(jee-ohr-DAN-oh, MAHRK) **CGY.**

Defense. Shoots left. 6', 203 lbs. Born, Toronto, Ont., October 3, 1983.

Season	Club	League	GP	G	A	Pts	PIM	PP	SH	GW	S	%	+/-	TF	F%	Min	GP	G	A	Pts	PIM	PP	SH	GW	Min
2002-03	Owen Sound	OHL	68	18	30	48	109	....	....	....	....	....	....	....	....	....	4	1	3	4	2	....	....	....	....
2003-04	Owen Sound	OHL	65	14	35	49	72	....	....	....	....	....	....	....	....	....	7	1	3	4	5	....	....	....	....
2004-05	Lowell	AHL	66	6	10	16	85	....	....	....	....	....	....	....	....	....	11	0	1	1	41	....	....	....	....
2005-06	**Calgary**	**NHL**	**7**	**0**	**1**	**1**	**8**	**0**	**0**	**0**	**5**	**0.0**	**2**	**0**	**0.0**	**12:05**	....	....	....	....	....	....	....	....	....
	Omaha	AHL	73	16	42	58	141	....	....	....	....	....	....	....	....	....	....	....	....	....	....	....	....	....	....
2006-07	**Calgary**	**NHL**	**48**	**7**	**8**	**15**	**36**	**3**	**0**	**2**	**49**	**14.3**	**7**	**0**	**0.0**	**13:27**	**4**	**1**	**0**	**1**	**0**	**1**	**0**	**0**	**12:16**
	Omaha	AHL	5	0	2	2	8	....	....	....	....	....	....	....	....	....	3	0	1	1	2	....	....	....	....
2007-08	Dynamo Moscow	Russia	50	4	8	12	89	....	....	....	....	....	....	....	....	....	9	1	5	6	35	....	....	....	....
2008-09	**Calgary**	**NHL**	**58**	**2**	**17**	**19**	**59**	**2**	**0**	**0**	**82**	**2.4**	**2**	**0**	**0.0**	**16:13**	....	....	....	....	....	....	....	....	....
2009-10	**Calgary**	**NHL**	**82**	**11**	**19**	**30**	**81**	**5**	**0**	**1**	**111**	**9.9**	**17**	**0**	**0.0**	**20:50**	....	....	....	....	....	....	....	....	....
	NHL Totals		**195**	**20**	**45**	**65**	**184**	**10**	**0**	**3**	**247**	**8.1**		**0**	**0.0**	**17:20**	**4**	**1**	**0**	**1**	**0**	**1**	**0**	**0**	**12:16**

Signed as a free agent by **Calgary**, July 6, 2004. Signed as a free agent by **Dynamo Moscow** (Russia) August 28, 2007. Signed as a free agent by **Calgary**, July 1, 2008.

GIRARDI, Dan

(jih-RAHR-dee, DAN) **NYR**

Defense. Shoots right. 6'2", 215 lbs. Born, Welland, Ont., April 29, 1984.

Season	Club	League	GP	G	A	Pts	PIM	PP	SH	GW	S	%	+/-	TF	F%	Min	GP	G	A	Pts	PIM	PP	SH	GW	Min
2000-01	Barrie Colts	OHL	6	0	0	0	0	....	....	....	....	....	....	....	....	....	....	....	....	....	....	....	....	....	....
2001-02	Barrie Colts	OHL	21	0	1	1	0	....	....	....	....	....	....	....	....	....	20	0	0	0	0	....	....	....	....
2002-03	Barrie Colts	OHL	31	3	13	16	24	....	....	....	....	....	....	....	....	....	....	....	....	....	....	....	....	....	....
	Guelph Storm	OHL	36	1	13	14	20	....	....	....	....	....	....	....	....	....	11	0	9	9	14	....	....	....	....
2003-04	Guelph Storm	OHL	68	8	39	47	55	....	....	....	....	....	....	....	....	....	22	2	17	19	10	....	....	....	....
2004-05	Guelph Storm	OHL	38	5	20	25	24	....	....	....	....	....	....	....	....	....	....	....	....	....	....	....	....	....	....
	London Knights	OHL	31	4	10	14	14	....	....	....	....	....	....	....	....	....	18	0	6	6	10	....	....	....	....
2005-06	Hartford	AHL	66	8	31	39	44	....	....	....	....	....	....	....	....	....	13	4	5	9	8	....	....	....	....
	Charlotte	ECHL	7	1	4	5	6	....	....	....	....	....	....	....	....	....	....	....	....	....	....	....	....	....	....
2006-07	**NY Rangers**	**NHL**	**34**	**0**	**6**	**6**	**8**	**0**	**0**	**0**	**33**	**0.0**	**7**	**0**	**0.0**	**15:50**	**10**	**0**	**0**	**0**	**4**	**0**	**0**	**0**	**19:52**
	Hartford	AHL	45	2	22	24	16	....	....	....	....	....	....	....	....	....	....	....	....	....	....	....	....	....	....
2007-08	**NY Rangers**	**NHL**	**82**	**10**	**18**	**28**	**14**	**5**	**0**	**1**	**147**	**6.8**	**0**	**1**	**0.0**	**21:12**	**10**	**0**	**3**	**3**	**6**	**0**	**0**	**0**	**20:42**
2008-09	**NY Rangers**	**NHL**	**82**	**4**	**18**	**22**	**53**	**2**	**0**	**1**	**122**	**3.3**	**–14**	**0**	**0.0**	**21:32**	**7**	**0**	**0**	**0**	**6**	**0**	**0**	**0**	**21:04**
2009-10	**NY Rangers**	**NHL**	**82**	**6**	**18**	**24**	**53**	**1**	**1**	**1**	**108**	**5.6**	**–2**	**0**	**0.0**	**21:29**	....	....	....	....	....	....	....	....	....
	NHL Totals		**280**	**20**	**60**	**80**	**128**	**8**	**1**	**3**	**410**	**4.9**		**1**	**0.0**	**20:44**	**27**	**0**	**3**	**3**	**16**	**0**	**0**	**0**	**20:29**

AHL All-Rookie Team (2006)

Signed as a free agent by **NY Rangers**, July 1, 2006.

GIROUX, Alexandre

(ZHIH-roo, al-ehx-AHN-druh) **EDM.**

Center/Left wing. Shoots left. 6'2", 200 lbs. Born, Quebec City, Que., June 16, 1981. Ottawa's 9th choice, 213th overall, in 1999 Entry Draft.

Season	Club	League	GP	G	A	Pts	PIM	PP	SH	GW	S	%	+/-	TF	F%	Min	GP	G	A	Pts	PIM	PP	SH	GW	Min
1997-98	Ste-Foy	QAAA	42	28	30	58	96	....	....	....	....	....	....	....	....	....	....	....	....	....	....	....	....	....	....
1998-99	Hull Olympiques	QMJHL	67	15	22	37	124	....	....	....	....	....	....	....	....	....	22	2	2	4	8	....	....	....	....
99-2000	Hull Olympiques	QMJHL	72	52	47	99	117	....	....	....	....	....	....	....	....	....	15	12	6	18	30	....	....	....	....
2000-01	Hull Olympiques	QMJHL	38	31	32	63	62	....	....	....	....	....	....	....	....	....	....	....	....	....	....	....	....	....	....
	Rouyn-Noranda	QMJHL	25	13	14	27	56	....	....	....	....	....	....	....	....	....	9	2	6	8	22	....	....	....	....
2001-02	Grand Rapids	AHL	70	11	16	27	74	....	....	....	....	....	....	....	....	....	....	....	....	....	....	....	....	....	....
2002-03	Binghamton	AHL	67	19	16	35	101	....	....	....	....	....	....	....	....	....	10	1	0	1	10	....	....	....	....
2003-04	Binghamton	AHL	59	19	23	42	79	....	....	....	....	....	....	....	....	....	....	....	....	....	....	....	....	....	....
	Hartford	AHL	16	6	3	9	13	....	....	....	....	....	....	....	....	....	16	3	4	7	28	....	....	....	....
2004-05	Hartford	AHL	78	32	22	54	128	....	....	....	....	....	....	....	....	....	6	3	3	6	23	....	....	....	....
2005-06	**NY Rangers**	**NHL**	**1**	**0**	**0**	**0**	**0**	**0**	**0**	**0**	**0**	**0.0**	**–1**	**0**	**0.0**	**2:50**	....	....	....	....	....	....	....	....	....
	Hartford	AHL	73	36	31	67	102	....	....	....	....	....	....	....	....	....	13	7	9	16	17	....	....	....	....
2006-07	**Washington**	**NHL**	**9**	**2**	**2**	**4**	**2**	**0**	**0**	**0**	**11**	**18.2**	**–4**	**2**	**50.0**	**10:11**	....	....	....	....	....	....	....	....	....
	Hershey Bears	AHL	67	42	28	70	82	....	....	....	....	....	....	....	....	....	19	4	7	11	27	....	....	....	....
2007-08	Chicago Wolves	AHL	44	19	22	41	47	....	....	....	....	....	....	....	....	....	....	....	....	....	....	....	....	....	....
	Hershey Bears	AHL	24	14	13	27	30	....	....	....	....	....	....	....	....	....	5	3	1	4	2	....	....	....	....
2008-09	**Washington**	**NHL**	**12**	**1**	**1**	**2**	**10**	**0**	**0**	**1**	**20**	**5.0**	**4**	**1**	**0.0**	**10:34**	....	....	....	....	....	....	....	....	....
	Hershey Bears	AHL	69	*60	37	*97	84	....	....	....	....	....	....	....	....	....	22	*15	13	*28	22	....	....	....	....
2009-10	**Washington**	**NHL**	**9**	**1**	**2**	**3**	**4**	**0**	**0**	**0**	**17**	**5.9**	**3**	**0**	**0.0**	**10:22**	....	....	....	....	....	....	....	....	....
	Hershey Bears	AHL	69	*50	53	103	34	....	....	....	....	....	....	....	....	....	21	*14	13	*27	22	....	....	....	....
	NHL Totals		**31**	**4**	**5**	**9**	**16**	**0**	**0**	**1**	**48**	**8.3**		**3**	**33.3**	**10:09**	....	....	....	....	....	....	....	....	....

AHL First All-Star Team (2009) • Willie Marshall Award (AHL – Top Goal-scorer) (2009, 2010) • John B. Sollenberger Trophy (AHL – Leading Scorer) (2009) • Les Cunningham Award (AHL – MVP) (2009)

Traded to **NY Rangers** by **Ottawa** with Karel Rachunek for Greg De Vries, March 9, 2004. Signed as a free agent by **Washington**, July 14, 2006. Signed as a free agent by **Atlanta**, July 13, 2007. Traded to **Washington** by **Atlanta** for Joe Motzko, February 26, 2008. Signed as a free agent by **Edmonton**, July 2, 2010.

GIROUX, Claude

(zhih-ROO, KLOHD) **PHI.**

Right wing. Shoots right. 5'11", 172 lbs. Born, Hearst, Ont., January 12, 1988. Philadelphia's 1st choice, 22nd overall, in 2006 Entry Draft.

Season	Club	League	GP	G	A	Pts	PIM	PP	SH	GW	S	%	+/-	TF	F%	Min	GP	G	A	Pts	PIM	PP	SH	GW	Min
2004-05	Cumberland	CJHL	48	13	27	40	30	....	....	....	....	....	....	....	....	....	....	....	....	....	....	....	....	....	....
2005-06	Gatineau	QMJHL	69	39	64	103	64	....	....	....	....	....	....	....	....	....	17	5	15	20	24	....	....	....	....
2006-07	Gatineau	QMJHL	63	48	64	112	49	....	....	....	....	....	....	....	....	....	5	2	5	7	2	....	....	....	....
	Philadelphia	AHL	5	1	1	2	6	....	....	....	....	....	....	....	....	....	....	....	....	....	....	....	....	....	....
2007-08	**Philadelphia**	**NHL**	**2**	**0**	**0**	**0**	**0**	**0**	**0**	**0**	**2**	**0.0**	**–2**	**0**	**0.0**	**9:35**	....	....	....	....	....	....	....	....	....
	Gatineau	QMJHL	55	38	68	106	37	....	....	....	....	....	....	....	....	....	19	17	*34	*51	6	....	....	....	....
2008-09	**Philadelphia**	**NHL**	**42**	**9**	**18**	**27**	**14**	**2**	**0**	**0**	**67**	**13.4**	**10**	**309**	**47.3**	**15:10**	**6**	**2**	**3**	**5**	**6**	**0**	**0**	**0**	**15:57**
	Philadelphia	AHL	33	17	17	34	22	....	....	....	....	....	....	....	....	....	....	....	....	....	....	....	....	....	....
2009-10	**Philadelphia**	**NHL**	**82**	**16**	**31**	**47**	**23**	**8**	**0**	**2**	**145**	**11.0**	**–9**	**600**	**49.5**	**16:37**	**23**	**10**	**11**	**21**	**4**	**3**	**0**	**2**	**18:45**
	NHL Totals		**126**	**25**	**49**	**74**	**37**	**10**	**0**	**2**	**214**	**11.7**		**909**	**48.7**	**16:01**	**29**	**12**	**14**	**26**	**10**	**3**	**0**	**2**	**18:10**

QMJHL All-Rookie Team (2006) • QMJHL First All-Star Team (2008) • Canadian Major Junior First All-Star Team (2008)

GLASS, Tanner

(GLAS, TA-nuhr) **VAN.**

Forward. Shoots left. 6'1", 210 lbs. Born, Regina, Sask., November 29, 1983. Florida's 13th choice, 265th overall, in 2003 Entry Draft.

Season	Club	League	GP	G	A	Pts	PIM	PP	SH	GW	S	%	+/-	TF	F%	Min	GP	G	A	Pts	PIM	PP	SH	GW	Min
2000-01	Yorkton Mallers	SMHL	39	31	29	60	120	....	....	....	....	....	....	....	....	....	4	3	1	4	10	....	....	....	....
2001-02	Penticton	BCHL	57	11	28	39	171	....	....	....	....	....	....	....	....	....	....	....	....	....	....	....	....	....	....
2002-03	Penticton	BCHL	32	15	25	40	108	....	....	....	....	....	....	....	....	....	....	....	....	....	....	....	....	....	....
	Nanaimo Clippers	BCHL	18	8	14	22	46	....	....	....	....	....	....	....	....	....	....	....	....	....	....	....	....	....	....
2003-04	Dartmouth	ECAC	26	4	7	11	18	....	....	....	....	....	....	....	....	....	....	....	....	....	....	....	....	....	....
2004-05	Dartmouth	ECAC	33	7	8	15	32	....	....	....	....	....	....	....	....	....	....	....	....	....	....	....	....	....	....
2005-06	Dartmouth	ECAC	33	12	16	28	56	....	....	....	....	....	....	....	....	....	....	....	....	....	....	....	....	....	....
2006-07	Dartmouth	ECAC	32	8	20	28	92	....	....	....	....	....	....	....	....	....	....	....	....	....	....	....	....	....	....
	Rochester	AHL	4	0	1	1	5	....	....	....	....	....	....	....	....	....	....	....	....	....	....	....	....	....	....
2007-08	**Florida**	**NHL**	**41**	**1**	**1**	**2**	**39**	**0**	**0**	**0**	**11**	**9.1**	**–5**	**2**	**0.0**	**4:25**	....	....	....	....	....	....	....	....	....
	Rochester	AHL	43	6	5	11	84	....	....	....	....	....	....	....	....	....	....	....	....	....	....	....	....	....	....
2008-09	**Florida**	**NHL**	**3**	**0**	**0**	**0**	**7**	**0**	**0**	**0**	**1**	**0.0**	**0**	**1**	**100.0**	**6:45**	....	....	....	....	....	....	....	....	....
	Rochester	AHL	44	4	9	13	100	....	....	....	....	....	....	....	....	....	....	....	....	....	....	....	....	....	....
2009-10	**Vancouver**	**NHL**	**67**	**4**	**7**	**11**	**115**	**0**	**0**	**0**	**52**	**7.7**	**5**	**18**	**16.7**	**10:28**	**4**	**0**	**0**	**0**	**0**	**0**	**0**	**0**	**3:08**
	NHL Totals		**111**	**5**	**8**	**13**	**161**	**0**	**0**	**0**	**64**	**7.8**		**21**	**19.0**	**8:08**	**4**	**0**	**0**	**0**	**0**	**0**	**0**	**0**	**3:08**

Signed as a free aget by **Vancouver**, July 22, 2009.

GLEASON, Tim

(GLEE-suhn, TIHM) **CAR.**

Defense. Shoots left. 6', 217 lbs. Born, Clawson, MI, January 29, 1983. Ottawa's 2nd choice, 23rd overall, in 2001 Entry Draft.

			Regular Season														Playoffs								
Season	Club	League	GP	G	A	Pts	PIM	PP	SH	GW	S	%	+/-	TF	F%	Min	GP	G	A	Pts	PIM	PP	SH	GW	Min
1998-99	Leamington Flyers	OHA-B	52	5	26	31	76	....	....	....	....	....	....	....	....	....	....	....	....	....	....	....	....	....	....
99-2000	Windsor Spitfires	OHL	55	5	13	18	101	....	....	....	....	....	....	....	....	....	12	2	4	6	14	....	....	....	....
2000-01	Windsor Spitfires	OHL	47	8	28	36	124	....	....	....	....	....	....	....	....	....	9	1	2	3	23	....	....	....	....
2001-02	Windsor Spitfires	OHL	67	17	42	59	109	....	....	....	....	....	....	....	....	....	16	7	13	20	40	....	....	....	....
2002-03	Windsor Spitfires	OHL	45	7	31	38	75	....	....	....	....	....	....	....	....	....	7	5	2	7	17	....	....	....	....
2003-04	**Los Angeles**	**NHL**	**47**	**0**	**7**	**7**	**21**	**0**	**0**	**0**	**45**	**0.0**	**1**	**0**	**0.0**	**14:59**	....	....	....	....	....	....	....	....	....
	Manchester	AHL	22	0	8	8	19	....	....	....	....	....	....	....	....	....	6	0	1	1	4	....	....	....	....
2004-05	Manchester	AHL	67	10	14	24	112	....	....	....	....	....	....	....	....	....	5	0	0	0	4	....	....	....	....
2005-06	**Los Angeles**	**NHL**	**78**	**2**	**19**	**21**	**77**	**0**	**0**	**0**	**72**	**2.8**	**0**	**0**	**0.0**	**17:41**	....	....	....	....	....	....	....	....	....
2006-07	**Carolina**	**NHL**	**57**	**2**	**4**	**6**	**57**	**1**	**0**	**0**	**72**	**2.8**	**–10**	**0**	**0.0**	**18:53**	....	....	....	....	....	....	....	....	....
2007-08	**Carolina**	**NHL**	**80**	**3**	**16**	**19**	**84**	**0**	**0**	**0**	**98**	**3.1**	**5**	**0**	**0.0**	**18:38**	....	....	....	....	....	....	....	....	....
2008-09	**Carolina**	**NHL**	**70**	**0**	**12**	**12**	**68**	**0**	**0**	**0**	**61**	**0.0**	**3**	**0**	**0.0**	**20:40**	**18**	**1**	**4**	**5**	**32**	**0**	**0**	**1**	**20:29**
2009-10	**Carolina**	**NHL**	**61**	**5**	**14**	**19**	**78**	**1**	**1**	**0**	**76**	**6.6**	**0**	**0**	**0.0**	**21:12**	....	....	....	....	....	....	....	....	....
	United States	Olympics	6	0	0	0	0	....	....	....	....	....	....	....	....	....	....	....	....	....	....	....	....	....	....
	NHL Totals		**393**	**12**	**72**	**84**	**385**	**2**	**1**	**0**	**424**	**2.8**		**0**	**0.0**	**18:48**	**18**	**1**	**4**	**5**	**32**	**0**	**0**	**1**	**20:29**

• Rights traded to **Los Angeles** by **Ottawa** for Bryan Smolinski, March 11, 2003. Traded to **Carolina** by **Los Angeles** with Eric Belanger for Oleg Tverdovsky and Jack Johnson, September 29, 2006.

GLENCROSS, Curtis

(GLEHN-kraws, KUHR-tihs) **CGY.**

Center. Shoots left. 6'1", 195 lbs. Born, Kindersley, Sask., December 28, 1982.

Season	Club	League	GP	G	A	Pts	PIM	PP	SH	GW	S	%	+/-	TF	F%	Min	GP	G	A	Pts	PIM	PP	SH	GW	Min
2001-02	Brooks Bandits	AJHL	....	42	26	68	....	....	....	....	....	....	....	....	....	....	....	....	....	....	....	....	....	....	....
2002-03	Alaska Anchorage	WCHA	35	11	12	23	79	....	....	....	....	....	....	....	....	....	....	....	....	....	....	....	....	....	....
2003-04	Alaska Anchorage	WCHA	37	21	13	34	79	....	....	....	....	....	....	....	....	....	....	....	....	....	....	....	....	....	....
	Cincinnati	AHL	7	2	1	3	6	....	....	....	....	....	....	....	....	....	9	1	6	7	10	....	....	....	....
2004-05	Cincinnati	AHL	51	6	3	9	63	....	....	....	....	....	....	....	....	....	12	2	0	2	10	....	....	....	....
2005-06	Portland Pirates	AHL	41	15	10	25	85	....	....	....	....	....	....	....	....	....	19	4	6	10	37	....	....	....	....
2006-07	**Anaheim**	**NHL**	**2**	**1**	**0**	**1**	**2**	**0**	**0**	**0**	**5**	**20.0**	**–1**	**0**	**0.0**	**10:43**	....	....	....	....	....	....	....	....	....
	Portland Pirates	AHL	31	6	10	16	74	....	....	....	....	....	....	....	....	....	....	....	....	....	....	....	....	....	....
	Columbus	**NHL**	**7**	**0**	**0**	**0**	**0**	**0**	**0**	**0**	**3**	**0.0**	**–4**	**2**	**0.0**	**8:43**	....	....	....	....	....	....	....	....	....
	Syracuse Crunch	AHL	29	19	16	35	53	....	....	....	....	....	....	....	....	....	....	....	....	....	....	....	....	....	....
2007-08	**Columbus**	**NHL**	**36**	**6**	**6**	**12**	**25**	**1**	**0**	**1**	**63**	**9.5**	**3**	**14**	**57.1**	**12:07**	....	....	....	....	....	....	....	....	....
	Edmonton	**NHL**	**26**	**9**	**4**	**13**	**28**	**0**	**0**	**0**	**41**	**22.0**	**5**	**11**	**45.5**	**10:19**	....	....	....	....	....	....	....	....	....
2008-09	**Calgary**	**NHL**	**74**	**13**	**27**	**40**	**42**	**1**	**1**	**3**	**152**	**8.6**	**14**	**62**	**48.4**	**14:41**	**6**	**0**	**3**	**3**	**12**	**0**	**0**	**0**	**15:00**
2009-10	**Calgary**	**NHL**	**67**	**15**	**18**	**33**	**58**	**2**	**3**	**2**	**117**	**12.8**	**11**	**24**	**37.5**	**15:43**	....	....	....	....	....	....	....	....	....
	NHL Totals		**212**	**44**	**55**	**99**	**155**	**4**	**4**	**6**	**381**	**11.5**		**113**	**46.0**	**13:48**	**6**	**0**	**3**	**3**	**12**	**0**	**0**	**0**	**15:00**

Signed as a free agent by **Anaheim**, March 25, 2004. Traded to **Columbus** by **Anaheim** with Zenon Konopka and Anaheim's 7th round choice (Trent Vogelhuber) in 2007 Entry Draft for Mark Hartigan, Joe Motzko and Columbus' 4th round choice (Sebastian Stefaniszin) in 2007 Entry Draft, January 26, 2007. Traded to **Edmonton** by **Columbus** for Dick Tarnstrom, February 1, 2008. Signed as a free agent by **Calgary**, July 2, 2008.

GLUMAC, Mike

(GLOO-kmak, MIGHK)

Right wing. Shoots right. 6'2", 209 lbs. Born, Niagara Falls, Ont., April 5, 1980.

Season	Club	League	GP	G	A	Pts	PIM	PP	SH	GW	S	%	+/-	TF	F%	Min	GP	G	A	Pts	PIM	PP	SH	GW	Min
1996-97	St. Mike's B's	OPJHL	50	13	25	38	33	....	....	....	....	....	....	....	....	....	6	1	0	1	2	....	....	....	....
1997-98	Newmarket	OPJHL	36	16	16	32	57	....	....	....	....	....	....	....	....	....	....	....	....	....	....	....	....	....	....
1998-99	Miami U.	CCHA	35	2	0	2	44	....	....	....	....	....	....	....	....	....	....	....	....	....	....	....	....	....	....
99-2000	Miami U.	CCHA	36	8	5	13	52	....	....	....	....	....	....	....	....	....	....	....	....	....	....	....	....	....	....
2000-01	Miami U.	CCHA	37	9	10	19	46	....	....	....	....	....	....	....	....	....	....	....	....	....	....	....	....	....	....
2001-02	Miami U.	CCHA	36	15	8	23	28	....	....	....	....	....	....	....	....	....	....	....	....	....	....	....	....	....	....
2002-03	Pee Dee Pride	ECHL	69	37	32	69	49	....	....	....	....	....	....	....	....	....	....	....	....	....	....	....	....	....	....
	Cleveland Barons	AHL	2	0	0	0	0	....	....	....	....	....	....	....	....	....	....	....	....	....	....	....	....	....	....
2003-04	Worcester IceCats	AHL	80	28	24	52	74	....	....	....	....	....	....	....	....	....	10	3	3	6	11	....	....	....	....
2004-05	Worcester IceCats	AHL	45	12	17	29	27	....	....	....	....	....	....	....	....	....	....	....	....	....	....	....	....	....	....
2005-06	**St. Louis**	**NHL**	**33**	**7**	**5**	**12**	**33**	**5**	**0**	**0**	**55**	**12.7**	**–8**	**5**	**40.0**	**12:25**	....	....	....	....	....	....	....	....	....
	Peoria Rivermen	AHL	49	25	32	57	64	....	....	....	....	....	....	....	....	....	4	1	1	2	5	....	....	....	....
2006-07	**St. Louis**	**NHL**	**3**	**0**	**1**	**1**	**0**	**0**	**0**	**0**	**4**	**0.0**	**1**	**0**	**0.0**	**8:24**	....	....	....	....	....	....	....	....	....
	Peoria Rivermen	AHL	72	27	30	57	115	....	....	....	....	....	....	....	....	....	....	....	....	....	....	....	....	....	....
2007-08	**St. Louis**	**NHL**	**4**	**0**	**0**	**0**	**5**	**0**	**0**	**0**	**3**	**0.0**	**–1**	**3**	**33.3**	**10:08**	....	....	....	....	....	....	....	....	....
	Peoria Rivermen	AHL	75	21	28	49	99	....	....	....	....	....	....	....	....	....	....	....	....	....	....	....	....	....	....
2008-09	Hamilton	AHL	66	33	19	52	60	....	....	....	....	....	....	....	....	....	6	1	3	4	4	....	....	....	....
2009-10	Hamilton	AHL	75	20	20	40	70	....	....	....	....	....	....	....	....	....	19	11	3	14	11	....	....	....	....
	NHL Totals		**40**	**7**	**6**	**13**	**38**	**5**	**0**	**0**	**62**	**11.3**		**8**	**37.5**	**11:53**	....	....	....	....	....	....	....	....	....

ECHL All-Rookie Team (2003)

Signed as a free agent by **Pee Dee** (ECHL), August 28, 2002. Signed as a free agent by **Worcester** (AHL), October 6, 2003. Signed as a free agent by **St. Louis**, June 29, 2004. Signed as a free agent by **Montreal**, July 16, 2008.

GOC, Marcel

(GAWCH, MAHR-sehl) **NSH.**

Center. Shoots left. 6'1", 202 lbs. Born, Calw, West Germany, August 24, 1983. San Jose's 1st choice, 20th overall, in 2001 Entry Draft.

Season	Club	League	GP	G	A	Pts	PIM	PP	SH	GW	S	%	+/-	TF	F%	Min	GP	G	A	Pts	PIM	PP	SH	GW	Min
1998-99	Schwenningen Jr.	Ger-Jr.	12	23	10	33	12	....	....	....	....	....	....	....	....	....	....	....	....	....	....	....	....	....	....
99-2000	Schwenningen	Germany	51	0	3	3	4	....	....	....	....	....	....	....	....	....	11	1	1	2	2	....	....	....	....
2000-01	Schwenningen	Germany	58	13	28	41	12	....	....	....	....	....	....	....	....	....	....	....	....	....	....	....	....	....	....
2001-02	Schwenningen	Germany	45	8	9	17	24	....	....	....	....	....	....	....	....	....	....	....	....	....	....	....	....	....	....
	Adler Mannheim	Germany	8	0	2	2	0	....	....	....	....	....	....	....	....	....	....	....	....	....	....	....	....	....	....
2002-03	Adler Mannheim	Germany	36	6	14	20	16	....	....	....	....	....	....	....	....	....	8	1	2	3	0	....	....	....	....
2003-04	Cleveland Barons	AHL	78	16	21	37	24	....	....	....	....	....	....	....	....	....	....	....	....	....	....	....	....	....	....
	San Jose	**NHL**	....	....	....	....	....	....	....	....	....	....	....	....	....	....	**5**	**1**	**1**	**2**	**0**	**0**	**0**	**1**	**7:08**
2004-05	Cleveland Barons	AHL	76	16	34	50	28	....	....	....	....	....	....	....	....	....	....	....	....	....	....	....	....	....	....
2005-06	**San Jose**	**NHL**	**81**	**8**	**14**	**22**	**22**	**2**	**0**	**2**	**96**	**8.3**	**–7**	**808**	**47.9**	**11:42**	**11**	**0**	**3**	**3**	**0**	**0**	**0**	**0**	**12:38**
	Germany	Olympics	5	1	0	1	0	....	....	....	....	....	....	....	....	....	....	....	....	....	....	....	....	....	....
2006-07	**San Jose**	**NHL**	**78**	**5**	**8**	**13**	**24**	**0**	**1**	**0**	**96**	**5.2**	**–2**	**659**	**55.2**	**12:01**	**11**	**2**	**1**	**3**	**4**	**0**	**0**	**0**	**14:49**
2007-08	**San Jose**	**NHL**	**51**	**5**	**3**	**8**	**12**	**0**	**0**	**0**	**87**	**5.7**	**–15**	**208**	**51.4**	**10:41**	**4**	**0**	**0**	**0**	**2**	**0**	**0**	**0**	**8:03**
2008-09	**San Jose**	**NHL**	**55**	**2**	**9**	**11**	**18**	**0**	**0**	**1**	**104**	**1.9**	**–6**	**570**	**58.3**	**13:55**	**6**	**0**	**0**	**0**	**2**	**0**	**0**	**0**	**10:33**
2009-10	**Nashville**	**NHL**	**73**	**12**	**18**	**30**	**14**	**0**	**0**	**1**	**118**	**10.2**	**10**	**912**	**52.1**	**14:41**	**6**	**0**	**1**	**1**	**2**	**0**	**0**	**0**	**16:07**
	Germany	Olympics	4	2	1	3	0	....	....	....	....	....	....	....	....	....	....	....	....	....	....	....	....	....	....
	NHL Totals		**338**	**32**	**52**	**84**	**90**	**2**	**1**	**4**	**501**	**6.4**		**3157**	**52.7**	**12:38**	**43**	**3**	**6**	**9**	**10**	**0**	**0**	**1**	**12:19**

Signed as a free agent by **Nashville**, August 21, 2009.

GODARD, Eric

(GAW-duhrd, AIR-ihk) **PIT.**

Right wing. Shoots right. 6'4", 214 lbs. Born, Vernon, B.C., March 7, 1980.

Season	Club	League	GP	G	A	Pts	PIM	PP	SH	GW	S	%	+/-	TF	F%	Min	GP	G	A	Pts	PIM	PP	SH	GW	Min
1997-98	Lethbridge	WHL	7	0	0	0	26	....	....	....	....	....	....	....	....	....	2	0	0	0	0	....	....	....	....
1998-99	Lethbridge	WHL	66	2	5	7	213	....	....	....	....	....	....	....	....	....	4	0	0	0	14	....	....	....	....
99-2000	Lethbridge	WHL	60	3	5	8	*310	....	....	....	....	....	....	....	....	....	....	....	....	....	....	....	....	....	....
	Louisville Panthers	AHL	4	0	1	1	16	....	....	....	....	....	....	....	....	....	....	....	....	....	....	....	....	....	....
2000-01	Louisville Panthers	AHL	45	0	0	0	132	....	....	....	....	....	....	....	....	....	....	....	....	....	....	....	....	....	....
2001-02	Bridgeport	AHL	67	1	4	5	198	....	....	....	....	....	....	....	....	....	20	0	4	4	30	....	....	....	....
2002-03	**NY Islanders**	**NHL**	**19**	**0**	**0**	**0**	**48**	**0**	**0**	**0**	**6**	**0.0**	**–3**	**0**	**0.0**	**4:32**	**2**	**0**	**1**	**1**	**4**	**0**	**0**	**0**	**1:09**
	Bridgeport	AHL	46	2	2	4	199	....	....	....	....	....	....	....	....	....	6	0	0	0	16	....	....	....	....
2003-04	**NY Islanders**	**NHL**	**31**	**0**	**1**	**1**	**97**	**0**	**0**	**0**	**5**	**0.0**	**–2**	**1**	**0.0**	**3:46**	....	....	....	....	....	....	....	....	....
	Bridgeport	AHL	7	0	0	0	13	....	....	....	....	....	....	....	....	....	....	....	....	....	....	....	....	....	....
2004-05	Bridgeport	AHL	75	7	11	18	295	....	....	....	....	....	....	....	....	....	....	....	....	....	....	....	....	....	....
2005-06	**NY Islanders**	**NHL**	**57**	**2**	**2**	**4**	**115**	**0**	**0**	**0**	**17**	**11.8**	**–2**	**1**	**0.0**	**3:34**	....	....	....	....	....	....	....	....	....
2006-07	**Calgary**	**NHL**	**19**	**0**	**1**	**1**	**50**	**0**	**0**	**0**	**3**	**0.0**	**0**	**0**	**0.0**	**3:47**	....	....	....	....	....	....	....	....	....
	Omaha	AHL	36	5	4	9	94	....	....	....	....	....	....	....	....	....	....	....	....	....	....	....	....	....	....
2007-08	**Calgary**	**NHL**	**74**	**1**	**1**	**2**	**171**	**0**	**0**	**1**	**14**	**7.1**	**–8**	**1**	**0.0**	**4:43**	**5**	**0**	**0**	**0**	**2**	**0**	**0**	**0**	**3:31**

			Regular Season														Playoffs								
Season	Club	League	GP	G	A	Pts	PIM	PP	SH	GW	S	%	+/-	TF	F%	Min	GP	G	A	Pts	PIM	PP	SH	GW	Min
2008-09♦	Pittsburgh	NHL	71	2	2	4	171	0	0	0	20	10.0	–3	1	100.0	4:04	....	....	....	....	....	....	....	....	....
2009-10	Pittsburgh	NHL	45	1	2	3	76	0	0	0	17	5.9	2	1	100.0	4:11	....	....	....	....	....	....	....	....	....
	NHL Totals		316	6	9	15	728	0	0	1	82	7.3		5	40.0	4:08	7	0	1	1	6	0	0	0	2:50

Signed as a free agent by **Florida**, September 24, 1999. Traded to **NY Islanders** by **Florida** for Florida's 3rd round choice (previously acquired, Florida selected Gregory Campbell) in 2002 Entry Draft, June 22, 2002. • Missed majority of 2003-04 season as a healthy reserve. Signed as a free agent by **Calgary**, August 14, 2006. Signed as a free agent by **Pittsburgh**, July 1, 2008.

GOERTZEN, Steven

(GUHRT-sehn, STEE-vehn)

Right wing. Shoots right. 6'2", 216 lbs. Born, Stony Plain, Alta., May 26, 1984. Columbus' 11th choice, 225th overall, in 2002 Entry Draft.

99-2000	Spruce Grove	AMBHL	36	16	17	33	30	....	....	....	....	....	....	....	....	....	....	....	....	....	....	....	....	....	....
2000-01	St. Albert Raiders	AMHL	34	11	19	30	70	....	....	....	....	....	....	....	....	....	....	....	....	....	....	....	....	....	....
	St. Albert Saints	AJHL	1	0	0	0	0	....	....	....	....	....	....	....	....	....	....	....	....	....	....	....	....	....	....
2001-02	Seattle	WHL	66	6	9	15	45	....	....	....	....	....	....	....	....	....	....	....	....	....	....	....	....	....	....
2002-03	Seattle	WHL	71	12	19	31	95	....	....	....	....	....	....	....	....	....	11	2	0	2	4	....	....	....	....
2003-04	Seattle	WHL	69	15	18	33	115	....	....	....	....	....	....	....	....	....	14	4	3	7	9	....	....	....	....
	Syracuse Crunch	AHL	8	0	3	3	4	....	....	....	....	....	....	....	....	....	1	0	0	0	0	....	....	....	....
2004-05	Syracuse Crunch	AHL	57	2	7	9	100	....	....	....	....	....	....	....	....	....	....	....	....	....	....	....	....	....	....
	Dayton Bombers	ECHL	11	0	3	3	2	....	....	....	....	....	....	....	....	....	....	....	....	....	....	....	....	....	....
2005-06	**Columbus**	**NHL**	**39**	**0**	**0**	**0**	**44**	**0**	**0**	**0**	**23**	**0.0**	**–17**	**11**	**54.6**	**8:32**	....	....	....	....	....	....	....	....	....
	Syracuse Crunch	AHL	40	7	8	15	55	....	....	....	....	....	....	....	....	....	6	0	1	1	34	....	....	....	....
2006-07	**Columbus**	**NHL**	**7**	**0**	**0**	**0**	**10**	**0**	**0**	**0**	**1**	**0.0**	**0**	**0**	**0.0**	**5:21**	....	....	....	....	....	....	....	....	....
	Syracuse Crunch	AHL	60	9	7	16	120	....	....	....	....	....	....	....	....	....	....	....	....	....	....	....	....	....	....
2007-08	Syracuse Crunch	AHL	59	8	5	13	72	....	....	....	....	....	....	....	....	....	....	....	....	....	....	....	....	....	....
	San Antonio	AHL	22	1	3	4	34	....	....	....	....	....	....	....	....	....	7	1	0	1	5	....	....	....	....
2008-09	**Phoenix**	**NHL**	**16**	**2**	**2**	**4**	**24**	**0**	**0**	**0**	**18**	**11.1**	**–2**	**2**	**50.0**	**9:42**	....	....	....	....	....	....	....	....	....
	San Antonio	AHL	57	6	8	14	90	....	....	....	....	....	....	....	....	....	....	....	....	....	....	....	....	....	....
2009-10	**Carolina**	**NHL**	**6**	**0**	**0**	**0**	**5**	**0**	**0**	**0**	**1**	**0.0**	**–2**	**0**	**0.0**	**7:44**	....	....	....	....	....	....	....	....	....
	Albany River Rats	AHL	71	8	15	23	85	....	....	....	....	....	....	....	....	....	8	0	1	1	7	....	....	....	....
	NHL Totals		**68**	**2**	**2**	**4**	**83**	**0**	**0**	**0**	**43**	**4.7**		**13**	**53.8**	**8:24**	....	....	....	....	....	....	....	....	....

Traded to **Phoenix** by **Columbus** for Nat DiCasmirro, February 28, 2008. Signed as a free agent by **Carolina**, July 8, 2009.

GOLIGOSKI, Alex

(goh-lih-GAW-skee, AL-ehx) **PIT.**

Defense. Shoots left. 5'11", 180 lbs. Born, Grand Rapids, MN, July 30, 1985. Pittsburgh's 3rd choice, 61st overall, in 2004 Entry Draft.

2002-03	Grand Rapids	High-MN	28	14	20	34	22	....	....	....	....	....	....	....	....	....	....	....	....	....	....	....	....	....	....
2003-04	Grand Rapids	High-MN	26	25	31	56	16	....	....	....	....	....	....	....	....	....	....	....	....	....	....	....	....	....	....
	Sioux Falls	USHL	10	0	2	2	6	....	....	....	....	....	....	....	....	....	....	....	....	....	....	....	....	....	....
2004-05	U. of Minnesota	WCHA	33	5	15	20	44	....	....	....	....	....	....	....	....	....	....	....	....	....	....	....	....	....	....
2005-06	U. of Minnesota	WCHA	41	11	28	39	63	....	....	....	....	....	....	....	....	....	....	....	....	....	....	....	....	....	....
2006-07	U. of Minnesota	WCHA	44	9	30	39	51	....	....	....	....	....	....	....	....	....	....	....	....	....	....	....	....	....	....
2007-08	**Pittsburgh**	**NHL**	**3**	**0**	**2**	**2**	**2**	**0**	**0**	**0**	**2**	**0.0**	**2**	**0**	**0.0**	**13:56**	....	....	....	....	....	....	....	....	....
	Wilkes-Barre	AHL	70	10	28	38	53	....	....	....	....	....	....	....	....	....	23	4	24	28	18	....	....	....	....
2008-09♦	**Pittsburgh**	**NHL**	**45**	**6**	**14**	**20**	**16**	**4**	**0**	**0**	**61**	**9.8**	**5**	**0**	**0.0**	**18:18**	**2**	**0**	**1**	**1**	**0**	**0**	**0**	**0**	**10:22**
	Wilkes-Barre	AHL	26	2	16	18	16	....	....	....	....	....	....	....	....	....	9	1	5	6	10	....	....	....	....
2009-10	**Pittsburgh**	**NHL**	**69**	**8**	**29**	**37**	**22**	**2**	**0**	**0**	**98**	**8.2**	**7**	**0**	**0.0**	**21:25**	**13**	**2**	**7**	**9**	**2**	**1**	**0**	**0**	**20:34**
	NHL Totals		**117**	**14**	**45**	**59**	**40**	**6**	**0**	**0**	**161**	**8.7**		**0**	**0.0**	**20:02**	**15**	**2**	**8**	**10**	**2**	**1**	**0**	**0**	**19:13**

WCHA All-Rookie Team (2005) • WCHA Second All-Star Team (2006) • WCHA First All-Star Team (2007) • NCAA West First All-American Team (2007)

GOMEZ, Scott

(GOH-mehz, SKAWT) **MTL.**

Center. Shoots left. 5'11", 202 lbs. Born, Anchorage, AK, December 23, 1979. New Jersey's 2nd choice, 27th overall, in 1998 Entry Draft.

1994-95	East High	High-AK	28	30	48	78	....	....	....	....	....	....	....	....	....	....	....	....	....	....	....	....	....	....	....
1995-96	East High	High-AK	27	*56	49	*101	....	....	....	....	....	....	....	....	....	....	....	....	....	....	....	....	....	....	....
	Anchorage	AAHL	40	*70	*67	*137	44	....	....	....	....	....	....	....	....	....	....	....	....	....	....	....	....	....	....
1996-97	South Surrey	BCHL	56	48	76	124	94	....	....	....	....	....	....	....	....	....	21	18	23	41	57	....	....	....	....
1997-98	Tri-City	WHL	45	12	37	49	57	....	....	....	....	....	....	....	....	....	....	....	....	....	....	....	....	....	....
1998-99	Tri-City	WHL	58	30	*78	108	55	....	....	....	....	....	....	....	....	....	10	6	13	19	31	....	....	....	....
99-2000♦	**New Jersey**	**NHL**	**82**	**19**	**51**	**70**	**78**	**7**	**0**	**1**	**204**	**9.3**	**14**	**341**	**44.6**	**16:21**	**23**	**4**	**6**	**10**	**4**	**1**	**0**	**2**	**14:08**
2000-01	**New Jersey**	**NHL**	**76**	**14**	**49**	**63**	**46**	**2**	**0**	**4**	**155**	**9.0**	**–1**	**1010**	**44.6**	**15:46**	**25**	**5**	**9**	**14**	**24**	**0**	**0**	**0**	**16:06**
2001-02	**New Jersey**	**NHL**	**76**	**10**	**38**	**48**	**36**	**1**	**0**	**1**	**156**	**6.4**	**–4**	**628**	**48.7**	**16:46**	....	....	....	....	....	....	....	....	....
2002-03♦	**New Jersey**	**NHL**	**80**	**13**	**42**	**55**	**48**	**2**	**0**	**4**	**205**	**6.3**	**17**	**864**	**47.5**	**16:01**	**24**	**3**	**9**	**12**	**2**	**0**	**0**	**0**	**13:45**
2003-04	**New Jersey**	**NHL**	**80**	**14**	***56**	**70**	**70**	**3**	**0**	**1**	**189**	**7.4**	**18**	**1129**	**46.2**	**16:00**	**5**	**0**	**6**	**6**	**0**	**0**	**0**	**0**	**17:14**
2004-05	Alaska Aces	ECHL	61	13	*73	*86	69	....	....	....	....	....	....	....	....	....	4	1	3	4	4	....	....	....	....
2005-06	**New Jersey**	**NHL**	**82**	**33**	**51**	**84**	**42**	**9**	**0**	**5**	**244**	**13.5**	**8**	**1434**	**52.6**	**18:47**	**9**	**5**	**4**	**9**	**6**	**4**	**0**	**1**	**18:14**
	United States	Olympics	6	1	4	5	10	....	....	....	....	....	....	....	....	....	....	....	....	....	....	....	....	....	....
2006-07	**New Jersey**	**NHL**	**72**	**13**	**47**	**60**	**42**	**4**	**0**	**1**	**248**	**5.2**	**7**	**1204**	**52.2**	**18:56**	**11**	**4**	**10**	**14**	**14**	**0**	**0**	**1**	**20:01**
2007-08	**NY Rangers**	**NHL**	**81**	**16**	**54**	**70**	**36**	**7**	**0**	**3**	**242**	**6.6**	**3**	**1165**	**52.5**	**19:54**	**10**	**4**	**7**	**11**	**8**	**1**	**0**	**0**	**20:53**
2008-09	**NY Rangers**	**NHL**	**77**	**16**	**42**	**58**	**60**	**3**	**1**	**7**	**271**	**5.9**	**–2**	**1312**	**52.4**	**21:04**	**7**	**2**	**3**	**5**	**4**	**1**	**0**	**0**	**19:58**
2009-10	**Montreal**	**NHL**	**78**	**12**	**47**	**59**	**60**	**5**	**0**	**1**	**180**	**6.7**	**1**	**1375**	**50.8**	**19:56**	**19**	**2**	**12**	**14**	**25**	**0**	**0**	**0**	**21:10**
	NHL Totals		**784**	**160**	**477**	**637**	**518**	**43**	**1**	**28**	**2094**	**7.6**		**10462**	**49.9**	**17:56**	**133**	**29**	**66**	**95**	**87**	**7**	**0**	**4**	**17:08**

WHL West First All-Star Team (1999) • NHL All-Rookie Team (2000) • Calder Memorial Trophy (2000) • ECHL First All-Star Team (2005) • ECHL Leading Scorer (2005) • ECHL MVP (2005)

Played in NHL All-Star Game (2000, 2008)

Signed as a free agent by **Alaska** (ECHL), October 25, 2004. Signed as a free agent by **NY Rangers**, July 1, 2007. Traded to **Montreal** by **NY Rangers** with Tom Pyatt and Michael Busto for Christopher Higgins, Ryan McDonagh and Pavel Valentenko, June 30, 2009.

GONCHAR, Sergei

(gohn-CHAR, SAIR-gay) **OTT.**

Defense. Shoots left. 6'2", 211 lbs. Born, Chelyabinsk, USSR, April 13, 1974. Washington's 1st choice, 14th overall, in 1992 Entry Draft.

1990-91	Mechel	USSR-2	2	0	0	0	0	....	....	....	....	....	....	....	....	....	....	....	....	....	....	....	....	....	....
	Chelyabinsk	USSR-Q	11	0	0	0	4	....	....	....	....	....	....	....	....	....	....	....	....	....	....	....	....	....	....
1991-92	Chelyabinsk	CIS	31	1	0	1	6	....	....	....	....	....	....	....	....	....	....	....	....	....	....	....	....	....	....
1992-93	Dynamo Moscow	CIS	31	1	3	4	70	....	....	....	....	....	....	....	....	....	10	0	0	0	12	....	....	....	....
1993-94	Dynamo Moscow	CIS	44	4	5	9	36	....	....	....	....	....	....	....	....	....	....	....	....	....	....	....	....	....	....
	Portland Pirates	AHL	....	....	....	....	....	....	....	....	....	....	....	....	....	....	2	0	0	0	0	....	....	....	....
1994-95	Portland Pirates	AHL	61	10	32	42	67	....	....	....	....	....	....	....	....	....	....	....	....	....	....	....	....	....	....
	Washington	**NHL**	**31**	**2**	**5**	**7**	**22**	**0**	**0**	**0**	**38**	**5.3**	**4**	....	....	....	**7**	**2**	**2**	**4**	**2**	**0**	**0**	**1**	....
1995-96	**Washington**	**NHL**	**78**	**15**	**26**	**41**	**60**	**4**	**0**	**4**	**139**	**10.8**	**25**	....	....	....	**6**	**2**	**4**	**6**	**4**	**1**	**0**	**0**	....
1996-97	**Washington**	**NHL**	**57**	**13**	**17**	**30**	**36**	**3**	**0**	**3**	**129**	**10.1**	**–11**	....	....	....	....	....	....	....	....	....	....	....	....
1997-98	Lada Togliatti	Russia	7	3	2	5	4	....	....	....	....	....	....	....	....	....	....	....	....	....	....	....	....	....	....
	Washington	**NHL**	**72**	**5**	**16**	**21**	**66**	**2**	**0**	**0**	**134**	**3.7**	**2**	....	....	....	**21**	**7**	**4**	**11**	**30**	**3**	**1**	**2**	....
	Russia	Olympics	6	0	2	2	0	....	....	....	....	....	....	....	....	....	....	....	....	....	....	....	....	....	....
1998-99	**Washington**	**NHL**	**53**	**21**	**10**	**31**	**57**	**13**	**1**	**3**	**180**	**11.7**	**1**	**0**	**0.0**	**23:55**	....	....	....	....	....	....	....	....	....
99-2000	**Washington**	**NHL**	**73**	**18**	**36**	**54**	**52**	**5**	**0**	**3**	**181**	**9.9**	**26**	**0**	**0.0**	**21:46**	**5**	**1**	**0**	**1**	**6**	**0**	**0**	**0**	**19:58**
2000-01	**Washington**	**NHL**	**76**	**19**	**38**	**57**	**70**	**8**	**0**	**2**	**241**	**7.9**	**12**	**1**	**100.0**	**22:26**	**6**	**1**	**3**	**4**	**2**	**1**	**0**	**0**	**19:45**
2001-02	**Washington**	**NHL**	**76**	**26**	**33**	**59**	**58**	**7**	**0**	**2**	**216**	**12.0**	**–1**	**1**	**100.0**	**23:51**	....	....	....	....	....	....	....	....	....
	Russia	Olympics	6	0	0	0	2	....	....	....	....	....	....	....	....	....	....	....	....	....	....	....	....	....	....
2002-03	**Washington**	**NHL**	**82**	**18**	**49**	**67**	**52**	**7**	**0**	**2**	**224**	**8.0**	**13**	**0**	**0.0**	**26:35**	**6**	**0**	**5**	**5**	**4**	**0**	**0**	**0**	**29:00**
2003-04	**Washington**	**NHL**	**56**	**7**	**42**	**49**	**44**	**4**	**0**	**0**	**127**	**5.5**	**–20**	**0**	**0.0**	**27:57**	....	....	....	....	....	....	....	....	....
	Boston	**NHL**	**15**	**4**	**5**	**9**	**12**	**2**	**0**	**0**	**34**	**11.8**	**6**	**0**	**0.0**	**25:32**	**7**	**1**	**4**	**5**	**4**	**1**	**0**	**1**	**27:51**
2004-05	Magnitogorsk	Russia	40	2	17	19	54	....	....	....	....	....	....	....	....	....	4	1	1	2	6	....	....	....	....
2005-06	**Pittsburgh**	**NHL**	**75**	**12**	**46**	**58**	**100**	**8**	**0**	**2**	**192**	**6.3**	**–13**	**0**	**0.0**	**24:40**	....	....	....	....	....	....	....	....	....
	Russia	Olympics	8	0	2	2	8	....	....	....	....	....	....	....	....	....	....	....	....	....	....	....	....	....	....
2006-07	**Pittsburgh**	**NHL**	**82**	**13**	**54**	**67**	**72**	**10**	**1**	**3**	**191**	**6.8**	**–5**	**0**	**0.0**	**26:34**	**5**	**1**	**3**	**4**	**2**	**1**	**0**	**0**	**26:53**
2007-08	**Pittsburgh**	**NHL**	**78**	**12**	**53**	**65**	**66**	**8**	**0**	**2**	**173**	**6.9**	**13**	**0**	**0.0**	**25:55**	**20**	**1**	**13**	**14**	**8**	**1**	**0**	**0**	**25:13**
2008-09♦	**Pittsburgh**	**NHL**	**25**	**6**	**13**	**19**	**26**	**5**	**0**	**1**	**71**	**8.5**	**6**	**0**	**0.0**	**25:11**	**22**	**3**	**11**	**14**	**12**	**2**	**0**	**2**	**23:03**

			Regular Season														Playoffs								
Season	Club	League	GP	G	A	Pts	PIM	PP	SH	GW	S	%	+/-	TF	F%	Min	GP	G	A	Pts	PIM	PP	SH	GW	Min
2009-10	**Pittsburgh**	**NHL**	**62**	**11**	**39**	**50**	**49**	**6**	**0**	**3**	**138**	**8.0**	**–4**	**0**	**0.0**	**24:24**	**13**	**2**	**10**	**12**	**4**	**1**	**0**	**1**	**26:27**
	Russia	Olympics	4	1	0	1	2	....	....	....	....	....	....	....	....	....	....	....	....	....	....	....	....	....	....
	NHL Totals		**991**	**202**	**482**	**684**	**842**	**92**	**2**	**30**	**2408**	**8.4**		**2**	**100.0**	**24:50**	**118**	**21**	**59**	**80**	**78**	**11**	**1**	**7**	**24:43**

NHL Second All-Star Team (2002, 2003)

Played in NHL All-Star Game (2001, 2002, 2003, 2008)

Traded to **Boston** by **Washington** for Shaonne Morrisonn and Boston's 1st (Jeff Schultz) and 2nd (Michail Yunkov) round choices in 2004 Entry Draft, March 3, 2004. Signed as a free agent by **Magnitogorsk** (Russia), September 21, 2004. Signed as a free agent by **Pittsburgh**, August 3, 2005. Signed as a free agent by **Ottawa**, July 1, 2010.

GORDON, Andrew
(GOHR-duhn, AN-droo) **WSH.**

Right wing. Shoots right. 5'11", 180 lbs. Born, Halifax, N.S., December 13, 1985. Washington's 11th choice, 197th overall, in 2004 Entry Draft.

2002-03	Notre Dame	SJHL	58	20	27	47	12	....	....	....	....	....	....	....	....	....	....	....	....	....	....	....	....	....	....
2003-04	Notre Dame	SJHL	55	20	44	64	12	....	....	....	....	....	....	....	....	....	....	....	....	....	....	....	....	....	....
2004-05	St. Cloud State	WCHA	38	9	8	17	6	....	....	....	....	....	....	....	....	....	....	....	....	....	....	....	....	....	....
2005-06	St. Cloud State	WCHA	42	20	20	40	22	....	....	....	....	....	....	....	....	....	....	....	....	....	....	....	....	....	....
2006-07	St. Cloud State	WCHA	40	22	23	45	16	....	....	....	....	....	....	....	....	....	....	....	....	....	....	....	....	....	....
2007-08	Hershey Bears	AHL	58	16	35	51	39	....	....	....	....	....	....	....	....	....	5	3	2	5	2	....	....	....	....
	South Carolina	ECHL	11	8	6	14	6	....	....	....	....	....	....	....	....	....	9	5	3	8	8	....	....	....	....
2008-09	**Washington**	**NHL**	**1**	**0**	**0**	**0**	**0**	**0**	**0**	**0**	**1**	**0.0**	**0**	**0**	**0.0**	**7:12**	....	....	....	....	....	....	....	....	....
	Hershey Bears	AHL	80	21	24	45	47	....	....	....	....	....	....	....	....	....	22	6	4	10	6	....	....	....	....
2009-10	**Washington**	**NHL**	**2**	**0**	**0**	**0**	**0**	**0**	**0**	**0**	**0**	**0.0**	**–2**	**0**	**0.0**	**6:41**	....	....	....	....	....	....	....	....	....
	Hershey Bears	AHL	79	37	34	71	57	....	....	....	....	....	....	....	....	....	17	13	7	20	2	....	....	....	....
	NHL Totals		**3**	**0**	**0**	**0**	**0**	**0**	**0**	**0**	**1**	**0.0**		**0**	**0.0**	**6:51**	....	....	....	....	....	....	....	....	....

WCHA First All-Star Team (2007)

GORDON, Boyd
(GOHR-duhn, BOID) **WSH.**

Center. Shoots right. 6'1", 200 lbs. Born, Unity, Sask., October 19, 1983. Washington's 3rd choice, 17th overall, in 2002 Entry Draft.

1997-98	Regina Flyers	SMHA	60	70	102	172	53	....	....	....	....	....	....	....	....	....	....	....	....	....	....	....	....	....	....
1998-99	Regina Rangers	SMBHL	60	70	102	172	53	....	....	....	....	....	....	....	....	....	....	....	....	....	....	....	....	....	....
99-2000	Red Deer Rebels	WHL	66	10	26	36	24	....	....	....	....	....	....	....	....	....	4	0	1	1	16	....	....	....	....
2000-01	Red Deer Rebels	WHL	72	12	27	39	39	....	....	....	....	....	....	....	....	....	22	3	6	9	2	....	....	....	....
2001-02	Red Deer Rebels	WHL	66	22	29	51	19	....	....	....	....	....	....	....	....	....	23	10	12	22	8	....	....	....	....
2002-03	Red Deer Rebels	WHL	56	33	48	81	28	....	....	....	....	....	....	....	....	....	23	8	12	20	14	....	....	....	....
2003-04	**Washington**	**NHL**	**41**	**1**	**5**	**6**	**8**	**0**	**0**	**0**	**42**	**2.4**	**–9**	**328**	**43.0**	**13:11**	....	....	....	....	....	....	....	....	....
	Portland Pirates	AHL	43	5	17	22	16	....	....	....	....	....	....	....	....	....	7	2	1	3	0	....	....	....	....
2004-05	Portland Pirates	AHL	80	17	22	39	35	....	....	....	....	....	....	....	....	....	....	....	....	....	....	....	....	....	....
2005-06	**Washington**	**NHL**	**25**	**0**	**1**	**1**	**4**	**0**	**0**	**0**	**12**	**0.0**	**–4**	**216**	**46.3**	**11:40**	....	....	....	....	....	....	....	....	....
	Hershey Bears	AHL	58	16	22	38	23	....	....	....	....	....	....	....	....	....	21	3	5	8	10	....	....	....	....
2006-07	**Washington**	**NHL**	**71**	**7**	**22**	**29**	**14**	**0**	**2**	**0**	**104**	**6.7**	**10**	**1214**	**52.1**	**15:53**	....	....	....	....	....	....	....	....	....
2007-08	**Washington**	**NHL**	**67**	**7**	**9**	**16**	**12**	**0**	**1**	**0**	**100**	**7.0**	**5**	**904**	**55.8**	**15:44**	**7**	**0**	**0**	**0**	**0**	**0**	**0**	**0**	**13:23**
2008-09	**Washington**	**NHL**	**63**	**5**	**9**	**14**	**16**	**0**	**1**	**2**	**69**	**7.2**	**–4**	**667**	**56.1**	**13:28**	**14**	**0**	**3**	**3**	**4**	**0**	**0**	**0**	**11:17**
2009-10	**Washington**	**NHL**	**36**	**4**	**6**	**10**	**12**	**0**	**0**	**0**	**40**	**10.0**	**4**	**205**	**61.0**	**10:17**	**6**	**1**	**1**	**2**	**0**	**0**	**1**	**0**	**11:02**
	Hershey Bears	AHL	2	0	2	2	0	....	....	....	....	....	....	....	....	....	....	....	....	....	....	....	....	....	....
	NHL Totals		**303**	**24**	**52**	**76**	**66**	**0**	**4**	**2**	**367**	**6.5**		**3534**	**53.1**	**13:58**	**27**	**1**	**4**	**5**	**4**	**0**	**1**	**0**	**11:46**

WHL East First All-Star Team (2003)

• Missed majority of 2009-10 season recovering from recurring back injury.

GORGES, Josh
(GOHR-juhz, JAWSH) **MTL.**

Defense. Shoots left. 6'1", 200 lbs. Born, Kelowna, B.C., August 14, 1984.

2000-01	Kelowna Rockets	WHL	57	4	6	10	24	....	....	....	....	....	....	....	....	....	6	1	1	2	4	....	....	....	....
2001-02	Kelowna Rockets	WHL	72	7	34	41	74	....	....	....	....	....	....	....	....	....	15	1	7	8	8	....	....	....	....
2002-03	Kelowna Rockets	WHL	54	11	48	59	76	....	....	....	....	....	....	....	....	....	19	3	17	20	16	....	....	....	....
2003-04	Kelowna Rockets	WHL	62	11	31	42	38	....	....	....	....	....	....	....	....	....	17	2	13	15	6	....	....	....	....
2004-05	Cleveland Barons	AHL	74	4	8	12	37	....	....	....	....	....	....	....	....	....	....	....	....	....	....	....	....	....	....
2005-06	**San Jose**	**NHL**	**49**	**0**	**6**	**6**	**31**	**0**	**0**	**0**	**25**	**0.0**	**5**	**0**	**0.0**	**17:38**	**11**	**0**	**1**	**1**	**4**	**0**	**0**	**0**	**18:56**
	Cleveland Barons	AHL	18	2	3	5	12	....	....	....	....	....	....	....	....	....	....	....	....	....	....	....	....	....	....
2006-07	**San Jose**	**NHL**	**47**	**1**	**3**	**4**	**26**	**0**	**0**	**0**	**37**	**2.7**	**–3**	**0**	**0.0**	**17:48**	....	....	....	....	....	....	....	....	....
	Worcester Sharks	AHL	7	0	1	1	2	....	....	....	....	....	....	....	....	....	....	....	....	....	....	....	....	....	....
	Montreal	**NHL**	**7**	**0**	**0**	**0**	**0**	**0**	**0**	**0**	**3**	**0.0**	**–1**	**0**	**0.0**	**12:28**	....	....	....	....	....	....	....	....	....
2007-08	**Montreal**	**NHL**	**62**	**0**	**9**	**9**	**32**	**0**	**0**	**0**	**41**	**0.0**	**0**	**0**	**0.0**	**16:20**	**12**	**0**	**3**	**3**	**0**	**0**	**0**	**0**	**18:20**
2008-09	**Montreal**	**NHL**	**81**	**4**	**19**	**23**	**37**	**2**	**0**	**0**	**63**	**6.3**	**12**	**1**	**0.0**	**20:08**	**4**	**0**	**1**	**1**	**7**	**0**	**0**	**0**	**23:46**
2009-10	**Montreal**	**NHL**	**82**	**3**	**7**	**10**	**39**	**0**	**0**	**1**	**52**	**5.8**	**2**	**0**	**0.0**	**21:01**	**19**	**0**	**2**	**2**	**14**	**0**	**0**	**0**	**22:42**
	NHL Totals		**328**	**8**	**44**	**52**	**165**	**2**	**0**	**1**	**221**	**3.6**		**1**	**0.0**	**18:46**	**46**	**0**	**7**	**7**	**25**	**0**	**0**	**0**	**20:45**

WHL West Second All-Star Team (2003) • WHL West First All-Star Team (2004) • George Parsons Trophy (Memorial Cup Tournament - Most Sportsmanlike Player) (2004)

Signed as a free agent by **San Jose**, September 20, 2002. Traded to **Montreal** by **San Jose** with San Jose's 1st round choice (Max Pacioretty) in 2007 Entry Draft for Craig Rivet and Montreal's 5th round choice (Julien Demers) in 2008 Entry Draft, February 25, 2007.

GRABNER, Michael
(GRAB-nuhr, MIGH-kuhl) **FLA.**

Right wing. Shoots left. 6', 170 lbs. Born, Villach, Austria, October 5, 1987. Vancouver's 1st choice, 14th overall, in 2006 Entry Draft.

2002-03	EC Villacher SV Jr.	Austria-Jr.	13	6	4	10	4	....	....	....	....	....	....	....	....	....	....	....	....	....	....	....	....	....	....
2003-04	EC Villacher SV Jr.	Austria-Jr.	23	32	5	37	58	....	....	....	....	....	....	....	....	....	....	....	....	....	....	....	....	....	....
	EC Villacher SV	Austria	18	2	1	3	0	....	....	....	....	....	....	....	....	....	....	....	....	....	....	....	....	....	....
	Austria	WJ18-B	5	3	1	4	4	....	....	....	....	....	....	....	....	....	....	....	....	....	....	....	....	....	....
2004-05	Spokane Chiefs	WHL	58	13	11	24	18	....	....	....	....	....	....	....	....	....	....	....	....	....	....	....	....	....	....
2005-06	Spokane Chiefs	WHL	67	36	14	50	28	....	....	....	....	....	....	....	....	....	....	....	....	....	....	....	....	....	....
2006-07	Spokane Chiefs	WHL	55	39	16	55	34	....	....	....	....	....	....	....	....	....	6	0	1	1	2	....	....	....	....
	Manitoba Moose	AHL	2	1	1	2	0	....	....	....	....	....	....	....	....	....	6	0	0	0	0	....	....	....	....
2007-08	Manitoba Moose	AHL	74	22	22	44	8	....	....	....	....	....	....	....	....	....	6	3	0	3	2	....	....	....	....
2008-09	Manitoba Moose	AHL	66	30	18	48	20	....	....	....	....	....	....	....	....	....	20	10	7	17	2	....	....	....	....
2009-10	**Vancouver**	**NHL**	**20**	**5**	**6**	**11**	**8**	**2**	**0**	**1**	**63**	**7.9**	**2**	**2**	**50.0**	**13:54**	**9**	**1**	**0**	**1**	**0**	**0**	**0**	**0**	**9:06**
	Manitoba Moose	AHL	38	15	11	26	6	....	....	....	....	....	....	....	....	....	....	....	....	....	....	....	....	....	....
	NHL Totals		**20**	**5**	**6**	**11**	**8**	**2**	**0**	**1**	**63**	**7.9**		**2**	**50.0**	**13:54**	**9**	**1**	**0**	**1**	**0**	**0**	**0**	**0**	**9:06**

Traded to **Florida** by **Vancouver** with Steve Bernier and Vancouver's 1st round choice (Quinton Howden) in 2010 Entry Draft for Keith Ballard and Victor Oreskovich, June 25, 2010.

GRABOVSKI, Mikhail
(gra-BAWV-skee, mih-kigh-EHL) **TOR.**

Center. Shoots left. 5'11", 183 lbs. Born, Potsdam, East Germany, January 31, 1984. Montreal's 4th choice, 150th overall, in 2004 Entry Draft.

2001-02	HC Minsk	Belarus	26	10	7	17	16	....	....	....	....	....	....	....	....	....	....	....	....	....	....	....	....	....	....
2002-03	HC Minsk	Belarus	STATISTICS NOT AVAILABLE																						
2003-04	Nizhnekamsk	Russia	45	6	11	17	26	....	....	....	....	....	....	....	....	....	5	0	0	0	4	....	....	....	....
2004-05	Nizhnekamsk	Russia	60	16	20	36	32	....	....	....	....	....	....	....	....	....	3	2	0	2	2	....	....	....	....
	Yunost-Minsk	BelOpen	....	....	....	....	....	....	....	....	....	....	....	....	....	....	5	2	4	6	6	....	....	....	....
2005-06	Dynamo Moscow	Russia	48	10	17	27	28	....	....	....	....	....	....	....	....	....	4	0	0	0	4	....	....	....	....
	Yunost-Minsk	BelOpen	8	6	8	14	10	....	....	....	....	....	....	....	....	....	....	....	....	....	....	....	....	....	....
2006-07	**Montreal**	**NHL**	**3**	**0**	**0**	**0**	**0**	**0**	**0**	**0**	**5**	**0.0**	**–2**	**31**	**41.9**	**13:18**	....	....	....	....	....	....	....	....	....
	Hamilton	AHL	66	17	37	54	34	....	....	....	....	....	....	....	....	....	20	4	7	11	21	....	....	....	....
2007-08	**Montreal**	**NHL**	**24**	**3**	**6**	**9**	**8**	**0**	**0**	**1**	**23**	**13.0**	**–4**	**154**	**33.1**	**11:14**	....	....	....	....	....	....	....	....	....
	Hamilton	AHL	12	8	12	20	6	....	....	....	....	....	....	....	....	....	....	....	....	....	....	....	....	....	....
2008-09	**Toronto**	**NHL**	**78**	**20**	**28**	**48**	**92**	**6**	**0**	**2**	**120**	**16.7**	**–8**	**957**	**44.5**	**16:13**	....	....	....	....	....	....	....	....	....
2009-10	**Toronto**	**NHL**	**59**	**10**	**25**	**35**	**10**	**2**	**1**	**3**	**126**	**7.9**	**3**	**735**	**49.8**	**16:48**	....	....	....	....	....	....	....	....	....
	NHL Totals		**164**	**33**	**59**	**92**	**110**	**8**	**1**	**6**	**274**	**12.0**		**1877**	**45.6**	**15:39**									

Traded to **Toronto** by **Montreal** for Greg Pateryn and Toronto's 2nd round choice (later traded to Chicago, later traded back to Toronto, later traded to Boston - Boston selected Jared Knight) in 2010 Entry Draft, July 3, 2008.

					Regular Season														Playoffs							
Season	Club	League	GP	G	A	Pts	PIM	PP	SH	GW	S	%	+/-	TF	F%	Min	GP	G	A	Pts	PIM	PP	SH	GW	Min

GRAGNANI, Marc-Andre
(GRUH-na-nee, MAHRK-AWN-dray) **BUF.**

Defense. Shoots left. 6'2", 201 lbs.   Born, Montreal, Que., March 11, 1987. Buffalo's 3rd choice, 87th overall, in 2005 Entry Draft.

Season	Club	League	GP	G	A	Pts	PIM	PP	SH	GW	S	%	+/-	TF	F%	Min	GP	G	A	Pts	PIM
2002-03	West Island Lions	QAAA	34	3	15	18	22														
2003-04	P.E.I. Rocket	QMJHL	61	2	13	15	42										11	0	0	0	4
2004-05	P.E.I. Rocket	QMJHL	68	10	29	39	48														
2005-06	P.E.I. Rocket	QMJHL	62	16	55	71	75										6	1	4	5	14
2006-07	P.E.I. Rocket	QMJHL	65	22	46	68	58										7	5	8	13	4
2007-08	**Buffalo**	**NHL**	2	0	0	0	4	0	0	0	1	0.0	−2	0	0.0	6:18					
	Rochester	AHL	78	14	38	52	38														
2008-09	**Buffalo**	**NHL**	4	0	0	0	2	0	0	0	3	0.0	2	0	0.0	15:23	5	0	2	2	4
	Portland Pirates	AHL	76	9	42	51	59														
2009-10	Portland Pirates	AHL	66	12	31	43	37										4	0	2	2	0
	NHL Totals		6	0	0	0	6	0	0	0	4	0.0		0	0.0	12:21					

GRANT, Triston
(GRANT, TRIHS-tuhn) **FLA.**

Left wing. Shoots left. 6'1", 211 lbs.   Born, Neepawa, Man., February 2, 1984. Philadelphia's 10th choice, 286th overall, in 2004 Entry Draft.

Season	Club	League	GP	G	A	Pts	PIM	PP	SH	GW	S	%	+/-	TF	F%	Min	GP	G	A	Pts	PIM
2000-01	Neepawa Natives	MJHL	STATISTICS NOT AVAILABLE																		
	Lethbridge	WHL	23	2	0	2	75										5	0	0	0	11
2001-02	Lethbridge	WHL	36	8	1	9	110														
	Vancouver Giants	WHL	21	2	4	6	53														
2002-03	Vancouver Giants	WHL	72	10	10	20	200										4	0	0	0	10
2003-04	Vancouver Giants	WHL	69	10	8	18	267										11	1	1	2	33
2004-05	Vancouver Giants	WHL	70	20	12	32	193										6	1	0	1	8
2005-06	Philadelphia	AHL	64	2	3	5	190														
2006-07	**Philadelphia**	**NHL**	8	0	1	1	10	0	0	0	3	0.0	−1	0	0.0	4:32					
	Philadelphia	AHL	61	5	6	11	199										12	0	2	2	34
2007-08	Philadelphia	AHL	72	10	11	21	181										11	1	1	2	12
2008-09	Milwaukee	AHL	55	3	8	11	153														
2009-10	**Nashville**	**NHL**	3	0	0	0	9	0	0	0	2	0.0	−1	0	0.0	7:14					
	Milwaukee	AHL	74	12	13	25	236										5	0	2	2	16
	NHL Totals		11	0	1	1	19	0	0	0	5	0.0		0	0.0	5:16					

Traded to **Nashville** by **Philadelphia** with Philadelphia's 7th round choice (later traded to St. Louis – St. Louis selected Maxwell Tardy) in 2009 Entry Draft for Janne Niskala, June 24, 2008. Signed as a free agent by **Florida**, July 2, 2010.

GRATTON, Josh
(GRAHT-uhn, JAWSH)

Left wing. Shoots left. 6'2", 215 lbs.   Born, Brantford, Ont., September 9, 1982.

Season	Club	League	GP	G	A	Pts	PIM	PP	SH	GW	S	%	+/-	TF	F%	Min	GP	G	A	Pts	PIM
2000-01	Sudbury Wolves	OHL	44	5	13	18	110										9	1	1	2	25
2001-02	Sudbury Wolves	OHL	14	5	4	9	47										1	1	0	1	7
	Kingston	OHL	46	14	14	28	140										6	2	1	3	8
2002-03	Windsor Spitfires	OHL	62	26	30	56	192										8	0	0	0	35
2003-04	Cincinnati	AHL	21	2	2	4	69														
	San Diego Gulls	ECHL	30	4	6	10	239										21	3	3	6	78
2004-05	Philadelphia	AHL	57	9	5	14	246														
	Trenton Titans	ECHL	1	0	0	0	0														
2005-06	**Philadelphia**	**NHL**	3	0	0	0	14	0	0	0	3	0.0	0	0	0.0	5:00					
	Philadelphia	AHL	53	9	10	19	265														
	Phoenix	**NHL**	11	1	0	1	30	0	0	0	14	7.1	−3	0	0.0	8:00					
2006-07	**Phoenix**	**NHL**	52	1	1	2	188	0	0	0	29	3.4	−9	1	0.0	5:54					
	San Antonio	AHL	3	1	1	2	8														
2007-08	**Phoenix**	**NHL**	1	0	0	0	5	0	0	0	0	0.0	1	0	0.0	9:40					
	San Antonio	AHL	38	5	9	14	124										4	0	1	1	11
	Hartford	AHL	20	6	6	12	72														
2008-09	Milwaukee	AHL	7	2	3	5	10														
	Philadelphia	**NHL**	19	1	2	3	57	0	0	0	14	7.1	−2	0	0.0	6:14					
	Philadelphia	AHL	14	1	0	1	46										2	0	0	0	2
2009-10	Chicago Wolves	AHL	21	0	2	2	60														
	Vityaz Chekhov	Rus-KHL	11	2	3	5	112														
	NHL Totals		86	3	3	6	294	0	0	0	60	5.0		1	0.0	6:16					

Signed as a free agent by **Philadelphia**, July 27, 2004. Traded to **Phoenix** by **Philadelphia** with Florida's 2nd round choice (previously acquired, later traded to Detroit - Detroit selected Cory Emerton) in 2006 Entry Draft and Tampa Bay's 2nd round choice (previously acquired, later traded to Detroit - Detroit selected Shawn Matthias) in 2006 Entry Draft for Denis Gauthier, March 9, 2006. Traded to **NY Rangers** by **Phoenix** with David LeNeveu, Fredrik Sjostrom and Phoenix's 5th round choice (Roman Horak) in 2009 Entry Draft for Marcel Hossa and Al Montoya, February 26, 2008. Signed as a free agent by **Nashville**, July 9, 2008. Traded to **Philadelphia** by **Nashville** for Tim Ramholt, October 31, 2008. Signed as a free agent by **Atlanta**, July 30, 2009. Signed as a free agent by **Chekhov** (Russia-KHL), January 18, 2010.

GREBESHKOV, Denis
(greh-behsh-KAHV, DEH-nihs)

Defense. Shoots left. 6', 209 lbs.   Born, Yaroslavl, USSR, October 11, 1983. Los Angeles' 1st choice, 18th overall, in 2002 Entry Draft.

Season	Club	League	GP	G	A	Pts	PIM	PP	SH	GW	S	%	+/-	TF	F%	Min	GP	G	A	Pts	PIM	PP	SH	GW	Min
99-2000	Yaroslavl 2	Russia-3	42	2	1	3	12										6	0	0	0	2				
2000-01	Yaroslavl 2	Russia-3	34	7	2	9	20																		
2001-02	Yaroslavl 2	Russia-3	7	1	1	2	2																		
	Yaroslavl	Russia	27	1	2	3	10																		
2002-03	Yaroslavl	Russia	48	0	7	7	26										10	0	1	1	2				
2003-04	**Los Angeles**	**NHL**	4	0	1	1	0	0	0	0	5	0.0	−4	0	0.0	18:29									
	Manchester	AHL	43	2	7	9	34										6	0	1	1	6				
2004-05	Manchester	AHL	75	5	44	49	87										6	0	4	4	2				
2005-06	**Los Angeles**	**NHL**	8	0	2	2	12	0	0	0	10	0.0	−4	0	0.0	15:16									
	Manchester	AHL	48	2	25	27	59										7	1	1	2	8				
	NY Islanders	**NHL**	21	0	3	3	8	0	0	0	14	0.0	−8	0	0.0	17:11									
	Bridgeport	AHL															7	0	2	2	6				
2006-07	Yaroslavl	Russia	47	8	9	17	79																		
2007-08	**Edmonton**	**NHL**	71	3	15	18	22	1	0	0	34	8.8	0	0	0.0	16:53									
2008-09	**Edmonton**	**NHL**	72	7	32	39	38	2	0	0	62	11.3	12	0	0.0	21:10									
2009-10	**Edmonton**	**NHL**	47	6	13	19	26	1	0	0	43	14.0	−16	1100.0		21:49									
	Russia	Olympics	4	0	1	1	2																		
	Nashville	**NHL**	4	1	1	2	6	0	0	0	4	25.0	0	0	0.0	16:28	2	0	2	2	0	0	0	0	0 11:22
	NHL Totals		227	17	67	84	112	4	0	0	172	9.9		1100.0		19:15	2	0	2	2	0	0	0	0	0 11:22

Traded to **NY Islanders** by **Los Angeles** with Jeff Tambellini for Mark Parrish and Brent Sopel, March 8, 2006. Signed as a free agent by **Yaroslavl** (Russia), July 10, 2006. Traded to **Edmonton** by **NY Islanders** for Marc-Andre Bergeron and Edmonton's 3rd round choice (later traded back to Edmonton, later traded to Anaheim, later traded back to NY Islanders - NY Islanders selected Kirill Petrov) in 2008 Entry Draft, February 18, 2007. Traded to **Nashville** by **Edmonton** for Nashville's 2nd round choice (Curtis Hamilton) in 2010 Entry Draft, March 1, 2010. Signed as a free agent by **St. Petersburg** (Russia-KHL), July 28, 2010.

GREEN, Josh
(GREEN, JAWSH) **ANA**

Left wing. Shoots left. 6'4", 225 lbs.   Born, Camrose, Alta., November 16, 1977. Los Angeles' 1st choice, 30th overall, in 1996 Entry Draft.

Season	Club	League	GP	G	A	Pts	PIM	PP	SH	GW	S	%	+/-	TF	F%	Min	GP	G	A	Pts	PIM
1992-93	Camrose Kodiaks	Minor-AB	60	55	45	100	80														
1993-94	Medicine Hat	WHL	63	22	22	44	43										3	0	0	0	4
1994-95	Medicine Hat	WHL	68	32	23	55	64										5	5	1	6	2
1995-96	Medicine Hat	WHL	46	18	25	43	55										5	2	2	4	4
1996-97	Medicine Hat	WHL	51	25	32	57	61														
	Swift Current	WHL	23	15	10	25	33										10	9	7	16	19
1997-98	Swift Current	WHL	5	9	1	10	9														
	Portland	WHL	26	12	16	28	44										4	1	3	4	6
	Fredericton	AHL	43	16	15	31	14														
1998-99	**Los Angeles**	**NHL**	27	1	3	4	8	1	0	0	35	2.9	−5	2	50.0	11:44					
	Springfield	AHL	41	15	15	30	29														
99-2000	**NY Islanders**	**NHL**	49	12	14	26	41	2	0	3	109	11.0	−7	12	50.0	13:36					
	Lowell	AHL	17	6	2	8	19														

			Regular Season														Playoffs								
Season	Club	League	GP	G	A	Pts	PIM	PP	SH	GW	S	%	+/-	TF	F%	Min	GP	G	A	Pts	PIM	PP	SH	GW	Min
2000-01	Hamilton	AHL	2	2	0	2	2																		
	Edmonton	**NHL**															**3**	**0**	**0**	**0**	**0**	**0**	**0**	**0**	**7:55**
2001-02	**Edmonton**	**NHL**	**61**	**10**	**5**	**15**	**52**	**1**	**0**	**1**	**78**	**12.8**	**9**	**18**	**38.9**	**10:05**									
2002-03	**Edmonton**	**NHL**	**20**	**0**	**2**	**2**	**12**	**0**	**0**	**0**	**20**	**0.0**	**–3**	**5**	**0.0**	**10:22**									
	NY Rangers	**NHL**	**4**	**0**	**0**	**0**	**2**	**0**	**0**	**0**	**3**	**0.0**	**–1**	**0**	**0.0**	**9:07**									
	Washington	**NHL**	**21**	**1**	**2**	**3**	**7**	**0**	**0**	**0**	**20**	**5.0**	**1**	**3**	**0.0**	**8:07**									
2003-04	**Calgary**	**NHL**	**36**	**2**	**4**	**6**	**24**	**0**	**0**	**0**	**47**	**4.3**	**–3**	**39**	**30.8**	**11:18**									
	Lowell	AHL	22	6	9	15	46																		
	NY Rangers	**NHL**	**14**	**3**	**2**	**5**	**8**	**0**	**0**	**1**	**29**	**10.3**	**0**	**9**	**55.6**	**14:16**									
2004-05	Manitoba Moose	AHL	67	21	19	40	72										14	9	5	14	26				
2005-06	**Vancouver**	**NHL**	**33**	**4**	**2**	**6**	**14**	**0**	**0**	**0**	**35**	**11.4**	**2**	**146**	**40.4**	**8:35**									
	Manitoba Moose	AHL	35	7	24	31	33										10	5	5	10	23				
2006-07	**Vancouver**	**NHL**	**57**	**2**	**5**	**7**	**25**	**0**	**0**	**2**	**74**	**2.7**	**0**	**266**	**40.6**	**11:25**	**9**	**0**	**1**	**1**	**12**	**0**	**0**	**0**	**10:13**
2007-08	Salzburg	Austria	43	20	22	42	100																		
2008-09	Iowa Chops	AHL	39	10	14	24	52																		
	Anaheim	**NHL**															**5**	**0**	**0**	**0**	**0**	**0**	**0**	**0**	**5:53**
2009-10	MODO	Sweden	47	12	8	20	79																		
	NHL Totals		**322**	**35**	**39**	**74**	**193**	**4**	**0**	**7**	**450**	**7.8**		**500**	**39.6**	**11:02**	**17**	**0**	**1**	**1**	**12**	**0**	**0**	**0**	**8:32**

Traded to **NY Islanders** by **Los Angeles** with Olli Jokinen, Mathieu Biron and Los Angeles' 1st round choice (Taylor Pyatt) in 1999 Entry Draft for Ziggy Palffy, Brian Smolinski, Marcel Cousineau and New Jersey's 4th round choice (previously acquired, Los Angeles selected Daniel Johansson) in 1999 Entry Draft, June 20, 1999. Traded to **Edmonton** by **NY Islanders** with Eric Brewer and NY Islanders' 2nd round choice (Brad Winchester) in 2000 Entry Draft for Roman Hamrlik, June 24, 2000. • Missed majority of 2000-01 season recovering from shoulder injury suffered in game vs. Detroit, October 10, 2000. Traded to **NY Rangers** by **Edmonton** for future considerations, December 12, 2002. Claimed on waivers by **Washington** from **NY Rangers**, January 15, 2003. Signed as a free agent by **Calgary**, July 17, 2003. Claimed on waivers by **NY Rangers** from **Calgary**, March 6, 2004. Signed to a PTO (professional tryout) contract by **Manitoba** (AHL), September 27, 2004. Signed as a free agent by **Vancouver**, August 23, 2005. Signed as a free agent by **Salzburg** (Austria), July 30, 2007. Signed as a free agent by **Anaheim**, July 22, 2008. Signed as a free agent by **MODO** (Sweden). July 9, 2009.

GREEN, Mike

(GREEN, MIGHK) **WSH.**

Defense. Shoots right. 6'1", 204 lbs. Born, Calgary, Alta., October 12, 1985. Washington's 3rd choice, 29th overall, in 2004 Entry Draft.

Season	Club	League	GP	G	A	Pts	PIM	PP	SH	GW	S	%	+/-	TF	F%	Min	GP	G	A	Pts	PIM	PP	SH	GW	Min
2000-01	Cgy. North Stars	AMHL	36	4	23	27	34																		
	Saskatoon Blades	WHL	7	0	2	2	0																		
2001-02	Saskatoon Blades	WHL	62	3	20	23	57										7	0	1	1	2				
2002-03	Saskatoon Blades	WHL	72	6	36	42	70										6	0	2	2	6				
2003-04	Saskatoon Blades	WHL	59	14	25	39	92																		
2004-05	Saskatoon Blades	WHL	67	14	52	66	105										4	0	0	0	6				
2005-06	**Washington**	**NHL**	**22**	**1**	**2**	**3**	**18**	**0**	**0**	**0**	**13**	**7.7**	**–8**	**0**	**0.0**	**14:54**									
	Hershey Bears	AHL	56	9	34	43	79										21	3	15	18	30				
2006-07	**Washington**	**NHL**	**70**	**2**	**10**	**12**	**36**	**0**	**0**	**0**	**68**	**2.9**	**–10**	**0**	**0.0**	**15:29**									
2007-08	**Washington**	**NHL**	**82**	**18**	**38**	**56**	**62**	**8**	**0**	**4**	**234**	**7.7**	**6**	**1**	**0.0**	**23:38**	**7**	**3**	**4**	**7**	**15**	**2**	**0**	**0**	**26:59**
2008-09	**Washington**	**NHL**	**68**	**31**	**42**	**73**	**68**	**18**	**1**	**4**	**243**	**12.8**	**24**	**0**	**0.0**	**25:46**	**14**	**1**	**8**	**9**	**12**	**1**	**0**	**0**	**24:59**
2009-10	**Washington**	**NHL**	**75**	**19**	**57**	**76**	**54**	**10**	**0**	**4**	**205**	**9.3**	**39**	**0**	**0.0**	**25:29**	**7**	**0**	**3**	**3**	**12**	**0**	**0**	**0**	**26:01**
	NHL Totals		**317**	**71**	**149**	**220**	**238**	**36**	**1**	**12**	**763**	**9.3**		**1**	**0.0**	**22:07**	**28**	**4**	**15**	**19**	**39**	**3**	**0**	**0**	**25:45**

WHL East First All-Star Team (2005) • AHL All-Rookie Team (2006) • NHL First All-Star Team (2009, 2010)

GREENE, Andy

(GREEN, AN-dee) **N.J.**

Defense. Shoots left. 5'11", 190 lbs. Born, Trenton, MI, October 30, 1982.

Season	Club	League	GP	G	A	Pts	PIM	PP	SH	GW	S	%	+/-	TF	F%	Min	GP	G	A	Pts	PIM	PP	SH	GW	Min
2002-03	Miami U.	CCHA	41	4	19	23	64																		
2003-04	Miami U.	CCHA	41	7	19	26	78																		
2004-05	Miami U.	CCHA	38	7	27	34	66																		
2005-06	Miami U.	CCHA	39	9	22	31	48																		
2006-07	**New Jersey**	**NHL**	**23**	**1**	**5**	**6**	**6**	**1**	**0**	**0**	**23**	**4.3**	**–1**	**0**	**0.0**	**14:15**	**11**	**2**	**1**	**3**	**2**	**0**	**0**	**1**	**17:04**
	Lowell Devils	AHL	52	5	16	21	28																		
2007-08	**New Jersey**	**NHL**	**59**	**2**	**8**	**10**	**22**	**2**	**0**	**0**	**50**	**4.0**	**0**	**0**	**0.0**	**19:30**	**2**	**0**	**0**	**0**	**0**	**0**	**0**	**0**	**15:11**
2008-09	**New Jersey**	**NHL**	**49**	**2**	**7**	**9**	**22**	**0**	**0**	**0**	**38**	**5.3**	**3**	**0**	**0.0**	**16:17**	**3**	**0**	**1**	**1**	**0**	**0**	**0**	**0**	**15:18**
2009-10	**New Jersey**	**NHL**	**78**	**6**	**31**	**37**	**14**	**4**	**0**	**4**	**86**	**7.0**	**9**	**0**	**0.0**	**23:32**	**5**	**1**	**1**	**2**	**6**	**1**	**0**	**0**	**19:42**
	NHL Totals		**209**	**11**	**51**	**62**	**64**	**7**	**0**	**4**	**197**	**5.6**		**0**	**0.0**	**19:41**	**21**	**3**	**3**	**6**	**8**	**1**	**0**	**1**	**17:16**

CCHA All-Rookie Team (2003) • CCHA First All-Star Team (2004, 2005, 2006) • NCAA West First All-American Team (2006)

Signed as a free agent by **New Jersey**, April 4, 2006.

GREENE, Matt

(GREEN, MAT) **L.A.**

Defense. Shoots right. 6'3", 237 lbs. Born, Grand Ledge, MI, May 13, 1983. Edmonton's 4th choice, 44th overall, in 2002 Entry Draft.

Season	Club	League	GP	G	A	Pts	PIM	PP	SH	GW	S	%	+/-	TF	F%	Min	GP	G	A	Pts	PIM	PP	SH	GW	Min
2000-01	USNTDP	U-18	34	0	9	9	8																		
	USNTDP	USHL	20	0	1	1	51																		
2001-02	Green Bay	USHL	55	4	20	24	150										7	0	1	1	31				
2002-03	North Dakota	WCHA	39	0	4	4	*135																		
2003-04	North Dakota	WCHA	40	1	16	17	86																		
2004-05	North Dakota	WCHA	43	2	8	10	*126																		
2005-06	**Edmonton**	**NHL**	**27**	**0**	**2**	**2**	**43**	**0**	**0**	**0**	**10**	**0.0**	**–6**	**0**	**0.0**	**11:13**	**18**	**0**	**1**	**1**	**34**	**0**	**0**	**0**	**10:03**
	Iowa Stars	AHL	26	2	5	7	47																		
2006-07	**Edmonton**	**NHL**	**78**	**1**	**9**	**10**	**109**	**0**	**0**	**0**	**52**	**1.9**	**–22**	**0**	**0.0**	**17:36**									
2007-08	**Edmonton**	**NHL**	**46**	**0**	**1**	**1**	**53**	**0**	**0**	**0**	**28**	**0.0**	**–3**	**0**	**0.0**	**16:42**									
2008-09	**Los Angeles**	**NHL**	**82**	**2**	**12**	**14**	**111**	**0**	**0**	**0**	**76**	**2.6**	**1**	**1**	**100.0**	**19:44**									
2009-10	**Los Angeles**	**NHL**	**75**	**2**	**7**	**9**	**83**	**0**	**0**	**1**	**57**	**3.5**	**4**	**0**	**0.0**	**17:29**	**6**	**0**	**1**	**1**	**0**	**0**	**0**	**0**	**18:45**
	NHL Totals		**308**	**5**	**31**	**36**	**399**	**0**	**0**	**1**	**223**	**2.2**		**1**	**100.0**	**17:27**	**24**	**0**	**2**	**2**	**34**	**0**	**0**	**0**	**12:14**

USHL Second All-Star Team (2002)

Traded to **Los Angeles** by **Edmonton** with Jarret Stoll for Lubomir Visnovsky, June 29, 2008.

GREENTREE, Kyle

(GREEN-TREE, KIGHL) **WSH.**

Left wing. Shoots left. 6'3", 215 lbs. Born, Victoria, B.C., November 15, 1983.

Season	Club	League	GP	G	A	Pts	PIM	PP	SH	GW	S	%	+/-	TF	F%	Min	GP	G	A	Pts	PIM	PP	SH	GW	Min
99-2000	Victoria Salsa	BCHL	28	7	6	13	11																		
2000-01	Victoria Salsa	BCHL	59	27	38	65	50																		
2001-02	Victoria Salsa	BCHL	57	42	43	85	125																		
2002-03	Victoria Salsa	BCHL	52	46	53	99	110																		
2003-04	Victoria Salsa	BCHL	59	62	53	115	170										5	4	5	9	29				
2004-05	Alaska	CCHA	37	12	20	32	31																		
2005-06	Alaska	CCHA	39	8	19	27	58																		
2006-07	Alaska	CCHA	39	21	21	42	78																		
	Philadelphia	AHL	8	2	0	2	2																		
2007-08	**Philadelphia**	**NHL**	**2**	**0**	**0**	**0**	**0**	**0**	**0**	**0**	**3**	**0.0**	**–1**	**0**	**0.0**	**9:12**									
	Philadelphia	AHL	72	24	24	48	83										12	1	3	4	11				
2008-09	**Calgary**	**NHL**	**2**	**0**	**0**	**0**	**0**	**0**	**0**	**0**	**3**	**0.0**	**–1**	**0**	**0.0**	**9:18**									
	Quad City Flames	AHL	79	39	37	76	63																		
2009-10	Rockford IceHogs	AHL	64	25	20	45	57										3	0	0	0	19				
	NHL Totals		**4**	**0**	**0**	**0**	**0**	**0**	**0**	**0**	**6**	**0.0**		**0**	**0.0**	**9:15**									

Signed as a free agent by **Philadelphia**, March 14, 2007. Traded to **Calgary** by **Philadelphia** for Tim Ramholt, June 30, 2008. Traded to **Chicago** by **Calgary** for Aaron Johnson, October 7, 2009. Signed as a free agent by **Washington**, July 7, 2010.

GRIER, Mike

(GREER, MIGHK) **BUF.**

Right wing. Shoots right. 6'1", 227 lbs. Born, Detroit, MI, January 5, 1975. St. Louis' 7th choice, 219th overall, in 1993 Entry Draft.

Season	Club	League	GP	G	A	Pts	PIM	PP	SH	GW	S	%	+/-	TF	F%	Min	GP	G	A	Pts	PIM	PP	SH	GW	Min
1992-93	St. Sebastian's	High-MA	22	16	27	43	32																		
1993-94	Boston University	H-East	39	9	9	18	56																		
1994-95	Boston University	H-East	37	*29	26	55	85																		
1995-96	Boston University	H-East	38	21	25	46	82																		
1996-97	**Edmonton**	**NHL**	**79**	**15**	**17**	**32**	**45**	**4**	**0**	**2**	**89**	**16.9**	**7**				**12**	**3**	**1**	**4**	**4**	**1**	**0**	**1**	
1997-98	**Edmonton**	**NHL**	**66**	**9**	**6**	**15**	**73**	**1**	**0**	**1**	**90**	**10.0**	**–3**				**12**	**2**	**2**	**4**	**13**	**0**	**0**	**1**	
1998-99	**Edmonton**	**NHL**	**82**	**20**	**24**	**44**	**54**	**3**	**2**	**1**	**143**	**14.0**	**5**	**34**	**20.6**	**15:57**	**4**	**1**	**1**	**2**	**6**	**0**	**0**	**0**	**23:26**

			Regular Season														Playoffs								
Season	Club	League	GP	G	A	Pts	PIM	PP	SH	GW	S	%	+/-	TF	F%	Min	GP	G	A	Pts	PIM	PP	SH	GW	Min
99-2000	Edmonton	NHL	65	9	22	31	68	0	3	2	115	7.8	9	32	46.8	15:45	....	....	....	....	....	....	....	....	....
2000-01	Edmonton	NHL	74	20	16	36	20	2	3	2	124	16.1	11	36	38.9	16:44	6	0	0	0	8	0	0	0	21:23
2001-02	Edmonton	NHL	82	8	17	25	32	0	2	3	112	7.1	1	38	47.4	15:01	....	....	....	....	....	....	....	....	....
2002-03	Washington	NHL	82	15	17	32	36	2	2	2	133	11.3	–14	98	43.9	17:48	6	1	1	2	2	0	0	0	17:59
2003-04	Washington	NHL	68	8	12	20	32	1	1	0	115	7.0	–19	54	44.4	17:25	....	....	....	....	....	....	....	....	....
	Buffalo	NHL	14	1	8	9	4	0	0	0	18	5.6	10	11	63.6	17:29	....	....	....	....	....	....	....	....	....
2004-05			DID NOT PLAY																						
2005-06	Buffalo	NHL	81	7	16	23	28	0	0	4	109	6.4	–7	9	22.2	14:22	18	3	5	8	2	0	1	0	16:17
2006-07	San Jose	NHL	81	16	17	33	43	2	3	1	125	12.8	–5	46	41.3	16:26	11	2	2	4	27	0	0	0	17:16
2007-08	San Jose	NHL	78	9	13	22	24	1	3	4	132	6.8	–8	86	25.6	16:13	13	0	1	1	2	0	0	0	15:20
2008-09	San Jose	NHL	62	10	13	23	25	0	1	2	108	9.3	8	43	34.9	15:00	6	0	0	0	6	0	0	0	10:33
2009-10	Buffalo	NHL	73	10	12	22	14	0	0	2	123	8.1	–4	52	38.5	15:48	6	2	0	2	2	0	0	0	18:34
	NHL Totals		987	157	210	367	498	16	20	26	1536	10.2		539	38.2	16:04	94	14	13	27	72	1	1	2	16:57

Hockey East First All-Star Team (1995) • NCAA East First All-American Team (1995)

• Rights traded to **Edmonton** by **St. Louis** with Curtis Joseph for St. Louis' 1st round choices in 1996 (previously acquired, St. Louis selected Marty Reasoner) and 1997 (previously acquired, later traded to Los Angeles – Los Angeles selected Matt Zultek) Entry Drafts, August 4, 1995. Traded to **Washington** by **Edmonton** for Washington's 2nd round choice (later traded to NY Islanders – NY Islanders selected Evgeni Tunik) in 2003 Entry Draft and Vancouver's 3rd round choice (previously acquired, Edmonton selected Zachery Stortini) in 2003 Entry Draft, October 7, 2002. Traded to **Buffalo** by **Washington** for Jakub Klepis, March 9, 2004. Signed as a free agent by **San Jose**, July 3, 2006. Signed as a free agent by **Buffalo**, August 10, 2009.

GROSSMAN, Nicklas

(GROHS-man, NIHK-luhs) **DAL.**

Defense. Shoots left. 6'4", 226 lbs. Born, Stockholm, Sweden, January 22, 1985. Dallas' 4th choice, 56th overall, in 2004 Entry Draft.

			Regular Season														Playoffs								
Season	Club	League	GP	G	A	Pts	PIM	PP	SH	GW	S	%	+/-	TF	F%	Min	GP	G	A	Pts	PIM	PP	SH	GW	Min
2002-03	Sodertalje SK Jr.	Swe-Jr.	34	1	1	2	32	....	....	....	....	....	....	....	....	....	....	....	....	....	....	....	....	....	....
2003-04	Sodertalje SK Jr.	Swe-Jr.	33	1	2	3	32	....	....	....	....	....	....	....	....	....	2	0	0	0	0	....	....	....	....
	Sodertalje SK	Sweden	1	0	0	0	0	....	....	....	....	....	....	....	....	....	....	....	....	....	....	....	....	....	....
2004-05	Sodertalje SK Jr.	Swe-Jr.	12	3	6	9	8	....	....	....	....	....	....	....	....	....	1	0	0	0	0	....	....	....	....
	Sodertalje SK	Sweden	31	0	2	2	14	....	....	....	....	....	....	....	....	....	9	0	0	0	0	....	....	....	....
2005-06	Iowa Stars	AHL	61	2	3	5	49	....	....	....	....	....	....	....	....	....	7	0	1	1	4	....	....	....	....
2006-07	Dallas	NHL	8	0	0	0	4	0	0	0	8	0.0	–1	0	0.0	12:49	....	....	....	....	....	....	....	....	....
	Iowa Stars	AHL	67	2	8	10	40	....	....	....	....	....	....	....	....	....	8	0	0	0	10	....	....	....	....
2007-08	Dallas	NHL	62	0	7	7	22	0	0	0	34	0.0	10	0	0.0	15:33	18	1	1	2	6	0	0	0	18:37
	Iowa Stars	AHL	10	0	0	0	10	....	....	....	....	....	....	....	....	....	....	....	....	....	....	....	....	....	....
2008-09	Dallas	NHL	81	2	10	12	51	0	0	1	60	3.3	–8	0	0.0	17:39	....	....	....	....	....	....	....	....	....
2009-10	Dallas	NHL	71	0	7	7	32	0	0	0	58	0.0	–3	1	0.0	19:11	....	....	....	....	....	....	....	....	....
	NHL Totals		222	2	24	26	109	0	0	1	160	1.3		1	0.0	17:23	18	1	1	2	6	0	0	0	18:37

GUENIN, Nate

(GEH-nihn, NAYT) **CBJ**

Defense. Shoots right. 6'2", 210 lbs. Born, Sewickley, PA, December 10, 1982. NY Rangers' 3rd choice, 127th overall, in 2002 Entry Draft.

			Regular Season														Playoffs								
Season	Club	League	GP	G	A	Pts	PIM	PP	SH	GW	S	%	+/-	TF	F%	Min	GP	G	A	Pts	PIM	PP	SH	GW	Min
99-2000	Pittsburgh	AAHA	40	3	10	13	122	....	....	....	....	....	....	....	....	....	....	....	....	....	....	....	....	....	....
2000-01	Green Bay	USHL	54	2	11	13	70	....	....	....	....	....	....	....	....	....	4	1	1	2	6	....	....	....	....
2001-02	Green Bay	USHL	56	4	11	15	150	....	....	....	....	....	....	....	....	....	7	3	3	6	10	....	....	....	....
2002-03	Ohio State	CCHA	42	2	9	11	85	....	....	....	....	....	....	....	....	....	....	....	....	....	....	....	....	....	....
2003-04	Ohio State	CCHA	29	2	15	17	92	....	....	....	....	....	....	....	....	....	....	....	....	....	....	....	....	....	....
2004-05	Ohio State	CCHA	41	2	12	14	136	....	....	....	....	....	....	....	....	....	....	....	....	....	....	....	....	....	....
2005-06	Ohio State	CCHA	39	0	11	11	87	....	....	....	....	....	....	....	....	....	....	....	....	....	....	....	....	....	....
2006-07	Philadelphia	NHL	9	0	2	2	4	0	0	0	0	0.0	0	0	0.0	8:40	....	....	....	....	....	....	....	....	....
	Philadelphia	AHL	68	3	9	12	92	....	....	....	....	....	....	....	....	....	....	....	....	....	....	....	....	....	....
2007-08	Philadelphia	NHL	2	0	0	0	2	0	0	0	0	0.0	2	0	0.0	9:57	....	....	....	....	....	....	....	....	....
	Philadelphia	AHL	77	4	13	17	146	....	....	....	....	....	....	....	....	....	12	0	1	1	18	....	....	....	....
2008-09	Philadelphia	NHL	1	0	0	0	0	0	0	0	0	0.0	0	0	0.0	13:25	....	....	....	....	....	....	....	....	....
	Philadelphia	AHL	62	0	14	14	95	....	....	....	....	....	....	....	....	....	4	0	0	0	10	....	....	....	....
2009-10	Pittsburgh	NHL	2	0	0	0	0	0	0	0	1	0.0	–2	0	0.0	13:32	....	....	....	....	....	....	....	....	....
	Wilkes-Barre	AHL	41	3	2	5	63	....	....	....	....	....	....	....	....	....	....	....	....	....	....	....	....	....	....
	Peoria Rivermen	AHL	27	2	11	13	35	....	....	....	....	....	....	....	....	....	....	....	....	....	....	....	....	....	....
	NHL Totals		14	0	2	2	6	0	0	0	1	0.0		0	0.0	9:53	....	....	....	....	....	....	....	....	....

USHL All-Rookie Team (2001) • CCHA Second All-Star Team (2005)

Signed as a free agent by **Philadelphia**, August 16, 2006. Signed as a free agent by **Pittsburgh**, July 3, 2009. Traded to **St. Louis** by **Pittsburgh** for Steve Wagner, February 11, 2010. Signed as a free agent by **Columbus**, July 2, 2010.

GUERIN, Bill

(GAIR-ihn, BIHL)

Right wing. Shoots right. 6'2", 220 lbs. Born, Worcester, MA, November 9, 1970. New Jersey's 1st choice, 5th overall, in 1989 Entry Draft.

			Regular Season														Playoffs								
Season	Club	League	GP	G	A	Pts	PIM	PP	SH	GW	S	%	+/-	TF	F%	Min	GP	G	A	Pts	PIM	PP	SH	GW	Min
1985-86	Spring. Olympics	NEJHL	48	26	19	45	71	....	....	....	....	....	....	....	....	....	....	....	....	....	....	....	....	....	....
1986-87	Spring. Olympics	NEJHL	32	34	20	54	40	....	....	....	....	....	....	....	....	....	....	....	....	....	....	....	....	....	....
1987-88	Spring. Olympics	NEJHL	38	31	44	75	146	....	....	....	....	....	....	....	....	....	....	....	....	....	....	....	....	....	....
1988-89	Spring. Olympics	NEJHL	31	32	35	67	90	....	....	....	....	....	....	....	....	....	....	....	....	....	....	....	....	....	....
1989-90	Boston College	H-East	39	14	11	25	54	....	....	....	....	....	....	....	....	....	....	....	....	....	....	....	....	....	....
1990-91	Boston College	H-East	38	26	19	45	102	....	....	....	....	....	....	....	....	....	....	....	....	....	....	....	....	....	....
1991-92	United States	Nat-Tm	46	12	15	27	67	....	....	....	....	....	....	....	....	....	....	....	....	....	....	....	....	....	....
	New Jersey	NHL	5	0	1	1	9	0	0	0	8	0.0	1	....	....	....	6	3	0	3	4	0	0	0	....
	Utica Devils	AHL	22	13	10	23	6	....	....	....	....	....	....	....	....	....	4	1	3	4	14	....	....	....	....
1992-93	New Jersey	NHL	65	14	20	34	63	0	0	2	123	11.4	14	....	....	....	5	1	1	2	4	0	0	0	....
	Utica Devils	AHL	18	10	7	17	47	....	....	....	....	....	....	....	....	....	....	....	....	....	....	....	....	....	....
1993-94	New Jersey	NHL	81	25	19	44	101	2	0	3	195	12.8	14	....	....	....	17	2	1	3	35	0	0	1	....
1994-95 ♦	New Jersey	NHL	48	12	13	25	72	4	0	3	96	12.5	6	....	....	....	20	3	8	11	30	1	0	0	....
1995-96	New Jersey	NHL	80	23	30	53	116	8	0	6	216	10.6	7	....	....	....	....	....	....	....	....	....	....	....	....
1996-97	New Jersey	NHL	82	29	18	47	95	7	0	9	177	16.4	–2	....	....	....	8	2	1	3	18	1	0	1	....
1997-98	New Jersey	NHL	19	5	5	10	13	1	0	2	48	10.4	0	....	....	....	....	....	....	....	....	....	....	....	....
	Edmonton	NHL	40	13	16	29	80	8	0	2	130	10.0	1	....	....	....	12	7	1	8	17	*4	0	0	....
	United States	Olympics	4	0	3	3	2	....	....	....	....	....	....	....	....	....	....	....	....	....	....	....	....	....	....
1998-99	Edmonton	NHL	80	30	34	64	133	13	0	2	261	11.5	7	74	40.5	19:42	3	0	2	2	2	0	0	0	26:14
99-2000	Edmonton	NHL	70	24	22	46	123	11	0	2	188	12.8	4	13	46.2	18:01	5	3	2	5	9	1	0	0	17:55
2000-01	Edmonton	NHL	21	12	10	22	18	4	0	1	64	18.8	11	0	0.0	19:49	....	....	....	....	....	....	....	....	....
	Boston	NHL	64	28	35	63	122	7	1	4	225	12.4	–4	36	41.7	22:43	....	....	....	....	....	....	....	....	....
2001-02	Boston	NHL	78	41	25	66	91	10	1	7	355	11.5	–1	17	52.9	20:45	6	4	2	6	6	3	0	0	21:17
	United States	Olympics	6	4	0	4	4	....	....	....	....	....	....	....	....	....	....	....	....	....	....	....	....	....	....
2002-03	Dallas	NHL	64	25	25	50	113	11	0	2	229	10.9	5	20	25.0	18:33	4	0	0	0	4	0	0	0	8:34
2003-04	Dallas	NHL	82	34	35	69	109	9	0	*10	263	12.9	14	16	18.8	18:42	5	0	1	1	4	0	0	0	20:09
2004-05			DID NOT PLAY																						
2005-06	Dallas	NHL	70	13	27	40	115	3	0	2	210	6.2	0	16	50.0	16:25	5	3	1	4	0	1	0	0	16:14
	United States	Olympics	6	1	0	1	0	....	....	....	....	....	....	....	....	....	....	....	....	....	....	....	....	....	....
2006-07	St. Louis	NHL	61	28	19	47	52	7	0	6	189	14.8	8	10	50.0	17:26	....	....	....	....	....	....	....	....	....
	San Jose	NHL	16	8	1	9	14	2	0	1	36	22.2	2	2	50.0	15:22	9	0	2	2	12	0	0	0	17:06
2007-08	NY Islanders	NHL	81	23	21	44	65	7	0	5	227	10.1	–15	18	66.7	17:23	....	....	....	....	....	....	....	....	....
2008-09	NY Islanders	NHL	61	16	20	36	63	5	0	3	181	8.8	–15	61	44.3	17:13	....	....	....	....	....	....	....	....	....
	♦ Pittsburgh	NHL	17	5	7	12	18	0	0	1	45	11.1	3	3	100.0	14:44	24	7	8	15	15	2	0	2	17:01
2009-10	Pittsburgh	NHL	78	21	24	45	75	11	0	4	227	9.3	–9	28	50.0	17:32	11	4	5	9	2	1	0	0	18:17
	NHL Totals		1263	429	427	856	1660	130	2	77	3693	11.6		314	43.9	18:29	140	39	35	74	162	14	0	4	17:43

NHL Second All-Star Team (2002)

Played in NHL All-Star Game (2001, 2003, 2004, 2007)

Traded to **Edmonton** by **New Jersey** with Valeri Zelepukin for Jason Arnott and Bryan Muir, January 4, 1998. Traded to **Boston** by **Edmonton** for Anson Carter, Boston's 1st (Ales Hemsky) and 2nd (Doug Lynch) round choices in 2001 Entry Draft and future considerations, November 15, 2000. Signed as a free agent by **Dallas**, July 3, 2002. Signed as a free agent by **St. Louis**, July 3, 2006. Traded to **San Jose** by **St. Louis** for Ville Nieminen, Jay Barriball and New Jersey's 1st round choice (previously acquired, St. Louis selected David Perron) in 2007 Entry Draft, February 27, 2007. Signed as a free agent by **NY Islanders**, July 5, 2007. Traded to **Pittsburgh** by **NY Islanders** for Pittsburgh's 3rd round choice (later traded to Phoenix – Phoenix selected Michael Lee) in 2009 Entry Draft, March 4, 2009.

GUITE, Ben

(GEE-tay, BEHN)

Right wing. Shoots right. 6'1", 211 lbs. Born, Montreal, Que., July 17, 1978. Montreal's 8th choice, 172nd overall, in 1997 Entry Draft.

Season	Club	League	Regular Season GP	G	A	Pts	PIM	PP	SH	GW	S	%	+/-	TF	F%	Min	Playoffs GP	G	A	Pts	PIM	PP	SH	GW	Min
1994-95	Lac St-Louis Lions	QAAA	40	9	12	21											4	0	0	0	0				
1995-96	Capital District	Exhib.	STATISTICS NOT AVAILABLE																						
1996-97	U. of Maine	H-East	34	7	7	14	21																		
1997-98	U. of Maine	H-East	32	6	12	18	20																		
1998-99	U. of Maine	H-East	40	12	16	28	30																		
99-2000	U. of Maine	H-East	40	22	14	36	36																		
2000-01	Tallahassee	ECHL	68	11	18	29	34																		
2001-02	Bridgeport	AHL	68	12	18	30	39																		
	Cincinnati	AHL	10	2	5	7	4										3	0	0	0	2				
2002-03	Cincinnati	AHL	80	13	16	29	44																		
2003-04	Bridgeport	AHL	79	6	18	24	73										7	0	0	0	6				
2004-05	Providence Bruins	AHL	77	9	15	24	69										17	3	4	7	34				
2005-06	**Boston**	**NHL**	**1**	**0**	**0**	**0**	**0**	**0**	**0**	**0**	**2**	**0.0**	**0**	**11**	**18.2**	**8:53**									
	Providence Bruins	AHL	73	22	30	52	87										6	1	3	4	14				
2006-07	**Colorado**	**NHL**	**39**	**3**	**8**	**11**	**16**	**0**	**1**	**1**	**63**	**4.8**	**–4**	**388**	**49.5**	**12:17**									
	Albany River Rats	AHL	36	10	19	29	22																		
2007-08	**Colorado**	**NHL**	**79**	**11**	**11**	**22**	**47**	**0**	**0**	**2**	**103**	**10.7**	**1**	**805**	**48.0**	**13:05**	**10**	**1**	**0**	**1**	**14**	**0**	**1**	**0**	**12:02**
2008-09	**Colorado**	**NHL**	**50**	**5**	**7**	**12**	**30**	**0**	**0**	**1**	**63**	**7.9**	**2**	**555**	**51.5**	**12:43**									
2009-10	**Nashville**	**NHL**	**6**	**0**	**0**	**0**	**4**	**0**	**0**	**0**	**5**	**0.0**	**–3**	**34**	**44.1**	**8:30**									
	Milwaukee	AHL	64	8	13	21	56										7	3	1	4	6				
	NHL Totals		**175**	**19**	**26**	**45**	**97**	**0**	**1**	**4**	**236**	**8.1**		**1793**	**49.1**	**12:37**	**10**	**1**	**0**	**1**	**14**	**0**	**1**	**0**	**12:02**

gned as a free agent by **NY Islanders**, August, 2001. Traded to **Anaheim** by **NY Islanders** with the rights to Bjorn Mellin for Dave Roche, March 19, 2002. Signed as a free agent by **NY Rangers**, eptember 16, 2003. Signed as a free agent by **Bridgeport** (AHL), October 10, 2003. Signed to a PTO (professional tryout) contract by **Providence** (AHL), September 28, 2004. Signed as a free agent by oston, August 15, 2005. Signed as a free agent by **Colorado**, July 12, 2006. Signed as a free agent by **Nashville**, July 14, 2009.

GUNNARSSON, Carl

(GUHN-nuhr-suhn, KARL) **TOR.**

Defense. Shoots left. 6'2", 196 lbs. Born, Orebro, Sweden, November 9, 1986. Toronto's 6th choice, 194th overall, in 2007 Entry Draft.

Season	Club	League	Regular Season GP	G	A	Pts	PIM	PP	SH	GW	S	%	+/-	TF	F%	Min	Playoffs GP	G	A	Pts	PIM	PP	SH	GW	Min
2003-04	HC Orebro 90	Sweden-2	43	0	4	4	16																		
2004-05	Linkoping U18	Swe-U18	1	0	1	1	2																		
	Linkopings HC Jr.	Swe-Jr.	22	2	5	7	24																		
2005-06	Linkopings HC Jr.	Swe-Jr.	30	7	6	13	26										4	1	0	1	4				
	IFK Arboga IK	Sweden-2	12	1	5	6	8																		
	Linkopings HC	Sweden	14	0	0	0	0																		
2006-07	Linkopings HC Jr.	Swe-Jr.	6	0	5	5	6																		
	VIK Vasteras HK	Sweden-2	15	2	3	5	14																		
	Linkopings HC	Sweden	30	2	2	4	8										15	0	4	4	4				
2007-08	Linkopings HC	Sweden	53	2	7	9	26										16	0	4	4	10				
2008-09	Linkopings HC	Sweden	53	6	10	16	26										7	0	1	1	2				
2009-10	**Toronto**	**NHL**	**43**	**3**	**12**	**15**	**10**	**0**	**0**	**0**	**45**	**6.7**	**8**	**1**	**0.0**	**21:26**									
	Toronto Marlies	AHL	12	0	2	2	2																		
	NHL Totals		**43**	**3**	**12**	**15**	**10**	**0**	**0**	**0**	**45**	**6.7**		**1**	**0.0**	**21:26**									

HAGMAN, Niklas

(HAG-muhn, NIHK-luhs) **CGY.**

Left wing. Shoots left. 6', 209 lbs. Born, Espoo, Finland, December 5, 1979. Florida's 3rd choice, 70th overall, in 1999 Entry Draft.

Season	Club	League	Regular Season GP	G	A	Pts	PIM	PP	SH	GW	S	%	+/-	TF	F%	Min	Playoffs GP	G	A	Pts	PIM	PP	SH	GW	Min
1995-96	HIFK Helsinki U18	Fin-U18	26	12	21	33	32										4	3	0	3	2				
	HIFK Helsinki Jr.	Fin-Jr.	12	3	1	4	0																		
1996-97	HIFK Helsinki Jr.	Fin-Jr.	30	13	12	25	30																		
	HIFK Helsinki U18	Fin-U18	21	19	12	31	46										4	1	1	2	0				
1997-98	HIFK Helsinki U18	Fin-U18	1	0	1	1	0																		
	HIFK Helsinki Jr.	Fin-Jr.	26	9	5	14	16																		
	HIFK Helsinki	Finland	8	1	0	1	0																		
1998-99	HIFK Helsinki	Finland	17	1	1	2	14																		
	HIFK Helsinki Jr.	Fin-Jr.	15	4	10	14	43																		
	HIFK Helsinki	EuroHL	1	0	1	1	0																		
	Blues Espoo	Finland	14	1	1	2	2										4	1	0	1	0				
99-2000	Karpat Oulu Jr.	Fin-Jr.	4	7	3	10	0																		
	Karpat Oulu	Finland-2	41	17	18	35	12										7	4	2	6	0				
2000-01	Karpat Oulu	Finland	56	28	18	46	32										8	3	1	4	0				
2001-02	**Florida**	**NHL**	**78**	**10**	**18**	**28**	**8**	**0**	**1**	**2**	**134**	**7.5**	**–6**	**32**	**28.1**	**13:50**									
	Finland	Olympics	4	1	2	3	0																		
2002-03	**Florida**	**NHL**	**80**	**8**	**15**	**23**	**20**	**2**	**0**	**0**	**132**	**6.1**	**–8**	**17**	**11.8**	**13:31**									
2003-04	**Florida**	**NHL**	**75**	**10**	**13**	**23**	**22**	**0**	**1**	**2**	**122**	**8.2**	**–5**	**19**	**21.1**	**14:47**									
2004-05	HC Davos	Swiss	44	17	22	39	20										15	10	7	17	6				
2005-06	**Florida**	**NHL**	**30**	**2**	**4**	**6**	**2**	**0**	**0**	**0**	**52**	**3.8**	**–8**	**10**	**10.0**	**14:00**									
	Dallas	**NHL**	**54**	**6**	**9**	**15**	**16**	**0**	**1**	**0**	**74**	**8.1**	**–2**	**6**	**66.7**	**11:17**	**5**	**2**	**1**	**3**	**4**	**0**	**0**	**1**	**10:50**
	Finland	Olympics	8	0	1	1	2																		
2006-07	**Dallas**	**NHL**	**82**	**17**	**12**	**29**	**34**	**2**	**1**	**2**	**152**	**11.2**	**3**	**15**	**20.0**	**14:26**	**7**	**0**	**1**	**1**	**10**	**0**	**0**	**0**	**16:26**
2007-08	**Dallas**	**NHL**	**82**	**27**	**14**	**41**	**51**	**4**	**4**	**8**	**178**	**15.2**	**4**	**19**	**10.5**	**15:36**	**18**	**2**	**1**	**3**	**14**	**0**	**0**	**0**	**13:25**
2008-09	**Toronto**	**NHL**	**65**	**22**	**20**	**42**	**4**	**6**	**0**	**3**	**168**	**13.1**	**–5**	**1**	**0.0**	**17:05**									
2009-10	**Toronto**	**NHL**	**55**	**20**	**13**	**33**	**23**	**4**	**0**	**1**	**148**	**13.5**	**–3**	**31**	**32.3**	**16:09**									
	Calgary	**NHL**	**27**	**5**	**6**	**11**	**2**	**0**	**0**	**1**	**68**	**7.4**	**–1**	**7**	**28.6**	**16:05**									
	Finland	Olympics	6	4	2	6	2																		
	NHL Totals		**628**	**127**	**124**	**251**	**182**	**18**	**8**	**19**	**1228**	**10.3**		**157**	**23.6**	**14:38**	**30**	**4**	**3**	**7**	**28**	**0**	**0**	**1**	**13:41**

gned as a free agent by **Davos** (Swiss), July 23, 2004. Traded to **Dallas** by **Florida** for Dallas' 7th round choice (Sergei Gayduchenko) in 2007 Entry Draft, December 12, 2005. Signed as a free agent by ronto, July 1, 2008. Traded to **Calgary** by **Toronto** with Matt Stajan, Jamal Mayers and Ian White for Dion Phaneuf, Fredrik Sjostrom and Keith Aulie, January 31, 2010.

HAINSEY, Ron

(HAYN-zee, RAWN) **ATL.**

Defense. Shoots left. 6'3", 210 lbs. Born, Bolton, CT, March 24, 1981. Montreal's 1st choice, 13th overall, in 2000 Entry Draft.

Season	Club	League	Regular Season GP	G	A	Pts	PIM	PP	SH	GW	S	%	+/-	TF	F%	Min	Playoffs GP	G	A	Pts	PIM	PP	SH	GW	Min
1997-98	USNTDP	U-17	18	2	7	9	28																		
	USNTDP	USHL	3	0	0	0	0																		
	USNTDP	NAHL	40	4	7	11	16										5	0	1	1	0				
1998-99	USNTDP	USHL	48	5	12	17	45																		
99-2000	U. Mass-Lowell	H-East	30	3	8	11	20																		
2000-01	U. Mass-Lowell	H-East	33	10	26	36	51																		
	Quebec Citadelles	AHL	4	1	0	1	0										1	0	0	0	0				
2001-02	Quebec Citadelles	AHL	63	7	24	31	26										3	0	0	0	0				
2002-03	**Montreal**	**NHL**	**21**	**0**	**0**	**0**	**2**	**0**	**0**	**0**	**12**	**0.0**	**–1**	**0**	**0.0**	**12:25**									
	Hamilton	AHL	33	2	11	13	26										23	1	10	11	20				
2003-04	**Montreal**	**NHL**	**11**	**1**	**1**	**2**	**4**	**0**	**0**	**0**	**11**	**9.1**	**3**	**0**	**0.0**	**13:15**									
	Hamilton	AHL	54	7	24	31	35										10	0	5	5	6				
2004-05	Hamilton	AHL	68	9	14	23	45										4	1	1	2	0				
2005-06	Hamilton	AHL	22	3	14	17	19																		
	Columbus	**NHL**	**55**	**2**	**15**	**17**	**43**	**1**	**0**	**0**	**81**	**2.5**	**13**	**1**	**0.0**	**17:47**									
2006-07	**Columbus**	**NHL**	**80**	**9**	**25**	**34**	**69**	**7**	**0**	**0**	**136**	**6.6**	**–19**	**2**	**50.0**	**22:53**									
2007-08	**Columbus**	**NHL**	**78**	**8**	**24**	**32**	**25**	**8**	**0**	**0**	**161**	**5.0**	**–7**	**0**	**0.0**	**22:34**									
2008-09	**Atlanta**	**NHL**	**81**	**6**	**33**	**39**	**32**	**4**	**0**	**0**	**148**	**4.1**	**–16**	**0**	**0.0**	**22:22**									
2009-10	**Atlanta**	**NHL**	**80**	**5**	**21**	**26**	**39**	**0**	**0**	**0**	**121**	**4.1**	**–6**	**0**	**0.0**	**22:08**									
	NHL Totals		**406**	**31**	**119**	**150**	**214**	**20**	**0**	**0**	**670**	**4.6**		**3**	**33.3**	**21:05**									

ckey East First All-Star Team (2001) • NCAA East Second All-American Team (2001) • AHL All-Rookie Team (2002)

aimed on waivers by **Columbus** from **Montreal**, November 29, 2005. Signed as a free agent by **Atlanta**, July 2, 2008.

HALE, David

(HAYL, DAY-vihd) **OTT.**

Defense. Shoots left. 6'1", 218 lbs. Born, Colorado Springs, CO, June 18, 1981. New Jersey's 1st choice, 22nd overall, in 2000 Entry Draft.

			Regular Season														Playoffs								
Season	Club	League	GP	G	A	Pts	PIM	PP	SH	GW	S	%	+/-	TF	F%	Min	GP	G	A	Pts	PIM	PP	SH	GW	Min
1997-98	Colorado North	High-CO	25	11	33	44	154	....	....	....	....	....	....	....	....	....	....	....	....	....	....	....	....	....	....
1998-99	Sioux City	USHL	56	3	15	18	127	....	....	....	....	....	....	....	....	....	5	0	0	0	18	....	....	....	....
99-2000	Sioux City	USHL	54	6	18	24	187	....	....	....	....	....	....	....	....	....	5	0	2	2	6	....	....	....	....
2000-01	North Dakota	WCHA	44	4	5	9	79	....	....	....	....	....	....	....	....	....	....	....	....	....	....	....	....	....	....
2001-02	North Dakota	WCHA	34	4	5	9	63	....	....	....	....	....	....	....	....	....	....	....	....	....	....	....	....	....	....
2002-03	North Dakota	WCHA	26	2	6	8	49	....	....	....	....	....	....	....	....	....	....	....	....	....	....	....	....	....	....
2003-04	**New Jersey**	**NHL**	**65**	**0**	**4**	**4**	**72**	**0**	**0**	**0**	**45**	**0.0**	**12**	**0**	**0.0**	**15:01**	**1**	**0**	**0**	**0**	**0**	**0**	**0**	**0**	**8:5**
2004-05	Albany River Rats	AHL	30	2	3	5	39	....	....	....	....	....	....	....	....	....	....	....	....	....	....	....	....	....	....
2005-06	**New Jersey**	**NHL**	**38**	**0**	**4**	**4**	**21**	**0**	**0**	**0**	**19**	**0.0**	**5**	**0**	**0.0**	**12:03**	**8**	**0**	**2**	**2**	**12**	**0**	**0**	**0**	**12:06**
	Albany River Rats	AHL	30	2	5	7	64	....	....	....	....	....	....	....	....	....	....	....	....	....	....	....	....	....	....
2006-07	**New Jersey**	**NHL**	**43**	**0**	**1**	**1**	**26**	**0**	**0**	**0**	**21**	**0.0**	**2**	**0**	**0.0**	**9:41**	....	....	....	....	....	....	....	....	....
	Lowell Devils	AHL	2	0	1	1	0	....	....	....	....	....	....	....	....	....	....	....	....	....	....	....	....	....	....
	Calgary	**NHL**	**11**	**0**	**0**	**0**	**10**	**0**	**0**	**0**	**12**	**0.0**	**-2**	**0**	**0.0**	**15:47**	**2**	**0**	**0**	**0**	**6**	**0**	**0**	**0**	**12:4**
2007-08	**Calgary**	**NHL**	**58**	**0**	**2**	**2**	**46**	**0**	**0**	**0**	**35**	**0.0**	**0**	**0**	**0.0**	**13:53**	**6**	**0**	**0**	**0**	**2**	**0**	**0**	**0**	**12:4**
2008-09	**Phoenix**	**NHL**	**48**	**3**	**6**	**9**	**36**	**0**	**0**	**0**	**22**	**13.6**	**-11**	**0**	**0.0**	**15:08**	....	....	....	....	....	....	....	....	....
2009-10	**Tampa Bay**	**NHL**	**39**	**0**	**4**	**4**	**25**	**0**	**0**	**0**	**25**	**0.0**	**-2**	**0**	**0.0**	**14:03**	....	....	....	....	....	....	....	....	....
	Norfolk Admirals	AHL	4	1	1	2	0	....	....	....	....	....	....	....	....	....	....	....	....	....	....	....	....	....	....
	NHL Totals		**302**	**3**	**21**	**24**	**236**	**0**	**0**	**0**	**179**	**1.7**		**0**	**0.0**	**13:35**	**17**	**0**	**2**	**2**	**20**	**0**	**0**	**0**	**12:1**

USHL First All-Star Team (2000)

Traded to **Calgary** by **New Jersey** with New Jersey's 5th round choice (later traded to Buffalo - Buffalo selected Jean-Simon Allard) in 2007 Entry Draft for Calgary's 3rd round choice (Nick Palmieri) in 2007 Entry Draft, February 27, 2007. Signed as a free agent by **Phoenix**, July 3, 2008. Traded to **Tampa Bay** by **Phoenix** with Todd Fedoruk for Radim Vrbata, July 21, 2009. Signed as a free agent by **Ottawa**, August 4, 2010.

HALEY, Michael

(HAY-lee, MIGH-kuhl) **NY**

Center. Shoots left. 5'11", 198 lbs. Born, Guelph, Ont., March 30, 1986.

Season	Club	League	GP	G	A	Pts	PIM	PP	SH	GW	S	%	+/-	TF	F%	Min	GP	G	A	Pts	PIM	PP	SH	GW	Min
2002-03	Sarnia Sting	OHL	43	3	3	6	32	....	....	....	....	....	....	....	....	....	6	0	0	0	2	....	....	....	....
2003-04	Sarnia Sting	OHL	51	8	8	16	69	....	....	....	....	....	....	....	....	....	....	....	....	....	....	....	....	....	....
2004-05	Sarnia Sting	OHL	61	14	16	30	122	....	....	....	....	....	....	....	....	....	....	....	....	....	....	....	....	....	....
2005-06	Sarnia Sting	OHL	23	2	6	8	83	....	....	....	....	....	....	....	....	....	....	....	....	....	....	....	....	....	....
	St. Michael's	OHL	30	12	0	12	78	....	....	....	....	....	....	....	....	....	4	0	1	1	11	....	....	....	....
2006-07	St. Michael's	OHL	68	30	24	54	174	....	....	....	....	....	....	....	....	....	....	....	....	....	....	....	....	....	....
	South Carolina	ECHL	7	5	1	6	13	....	....	....	....	....	....	....	....	....	....	....	....	....	....	....	....	....	....
2007-08	Bridgeport	AHL	36	2	2	4	75	....	....	....	....	....	....	....	....	....	....	....	....	....	....	....	....	....	....
	Utah Grizzlies	ECHL	28	11	8	19	115	....	....	....	....	....	....	....	....	....	14	7	6	13	49	....	....	....	....
2008-09	Bridgeport	AHL	45	5	3	8	99	....	....	....	....	....	....	....	....	....	5	1	0	1	10	....	....	....	....
2009-10	**NY Islanders**	**NHL**	**2**	**0**	**0**	**0**	**9**	**0**	**0**	**0**	**0**	**0.0**	**-3**	**5**	**20.0**	**7:37**	....	....	....	....	....	....	....	....	....
	Bridgeport	AHL	65	6	8	14	196	....	....	....	....	....	....	....	....	....	3	0	0	0	4	....	....	....	....
	NHL Totals		**2**	**0**	**0**	**0**	**9**	**0**	**0**	**0**	**0**	**0.0**		**5**	**20.0**	**7:37**	....	....	....	....	....	....	....	....	....

Signed as a free agent by **NY Islanders**, May 19, 2008.

HALISCHUK, Matt

(huh-LIHS-chuhk, MAT) **NSH**

Right wing. Shoots right. 6', 186 lbs. Born, Toronto, Ont., June 1, 1988. New Jersey's 4th choice, 117th overall, in 2007 Entry Draft.

Season	Club	League	GP	G	A	Pts	PIM	PP	SH	GW	S	%	+/-	TF	F%	Min	GP	G	A	Pts	PIM	PP	SH	GW	Min
2003-04	Tor. Jr. Canadiens	GTHL	53	37	48	85	27	....	....	....	....	....	....	....	....	....	....	....	....	....	....	....	....	....	....
2004-05	St. Michael's	OHL	30	3	3	6	4	....	....	....	....	....	....	....	....	....	....	....	....	....	....	....	....	....	....
	St. Mike's B's	OPJHL	17	5	11	16	8	....	....	....	....	....	....	....	....	....	32	10	15	25	4	....	....	....	....
2005-06	St. Michael's	OHL	61	13	18	31	16	....	....	....	....	....	....	....	....	....	4	1	1	2	0	....	....	....	....
2006-07	Kitchener Rangers	OHL	67	33	33	66	20	....	....	....	....	....	....	....	....	....	9	4	1	5	10	....	....	....	....
2007-08	Kitchener Rangers	OHL	40	13	46	59	16	....	....	....	....	....	....	....	....	....	20	*16	16	32	0	....	....	....	....
2008-09	**New Jersey**	**NHL**	**1**	**0**	**1**	**1**	**0**	**0**	**0**	**0**	**0**	**0.0**	**-1**	**0**	**0.0**	**9:47**	....	....	....	....	....	....	....	....	....
	Lowell Devils	AHL	47	14	15	29	10	....	....	....	....	....	....	....	....	....	....	....	....	....	....	....	....	....	....
2009-10	**New Jersey**	**NHL**	**20**	**1**	**1**	**2**	**2**	**0**	**0**	**0**	**22**	**4.5**	**-4**	**4**	**25.0**	**11:18**	....	....	....	....	....	....	....	....	....
	Lowell Devils	AHL	32	11	11	22	2	....	....	....	....	....	....	....	....	....	1	0	0	0	0	....	....	....	....
	NHL Totals		**21**	**1**	**2**	**3**	**2**	**0**	**0**	**0**	**22**	**4.5**		**4**	**25.0**	**11:14**	....	....	....	....	....	....	....	....	....

OHL First All-Star Team (2008) • George Parsons Trophy (Memorial Cup Tournament - Most Sportsmanlike Player) (2008)

Traded to **Nashville** by **New Jersey** with New Jersey's 2nd round choice in 2011 Entry Draft for Jason Arnott, June 19, 2010.

HALL, Adam

(HAWL, A-duhm) **T.B**

Right wing. Shoots right. 6'3", 206 lbs. Born, Kalamazoo, MI, August 14, 1980. Nashville's 3rd choice, 52nd overall, in 1999 Entry Draft.

Season	Club	League	GP	G	A	Pts	PIM	PP	SH	GW	S	%	+/-	TF	F%	Min	GP	G	A	Pts	PIM	PP	SH	GW	Min
1996-97	Bramalea Blues	OPJHL	43	9	14	23	92	....	....	....	....	....	....	....	....	....	....	....	....	....	....	....	....	....	....
1997-98	USNTDP	U-18	29	18	9	27	19	....	....	....	....	....	....	....	....	....	....	....	....	....	....	....	....	....	....
	USNTDP	USHL	21	9	11	20	20	....	....	....	....	....	....	....	....	....	....	....	....	....	....	....	....	....	....
	USNTDP	NAHL	15	12	1	13	20	....	....	....	....	....	....	....	....	....	6	3	2	5	4	....	....	....	....
1998-99	Michigan State	CCHA	36	16	7	23	74	....	....	....	....	....	....	....	....	....	....	....	....	....	....	....	....	....	....
99-2000	Michigan State	CCHA	40	*26	13	39	38	....	....	....	....	....	....	....	....	....	....	....	....	....	....	....	....	....	....
2000-01	Michigan State	CCHA	42	18	12	30	42	....	....	....	....	....	....	....	....	....	....	....	....	....	....	....	....	....	....
2001-02	Michigan State	CCHA	41	19	15	34	36	....	....	....	....	....	....	....	....	....	....	....	....	....	....	....	....	....	....
	Nashville	**NHL**	**1**	**0**	**1**	**1**	**0**	**0**	**0**	**0**	**2**	**0.0**	**0**	**0**	**0.0**	**14:04**	....	....	....	....	....	....	....	....	....
	Milwaukee	AHL	6	2	2	4	4	....	....	....	....	....	....	....	....	....	....	....	....	....	....	....	....	....	....
2002-03	**Nashville**	**NHL**	**79**	**16**	**12**	**28**	**31**	**8**	**0**	**2**	**146**	**11.0**	**-8**	**17**	**52.9**	**14:09**	....	....	....	....	....	....	....	....	....
	Milwaukee	AHL	1	0	0	0	2	....	....	....	....	....	....	....	....	....	....	....	....	....	....	....	....	....	....
2003-04	**Nashville**	**NHL**	**79**	**13**	**14**	**27**	**37**	**6**	**0**	**1**	**151**	**8.6**	**-8**	**348**	**56.3**	**16:14**	**6**	**2**	**1**	**3**	**2**	**0**	**0**	**1**	**18:2**
2004-05	KalPa Kuopio	Finland-2	36	23	17	40	28	....	....	....	....	....	....	....	....	....	9	2	3	5	4	....	....	....	....
2005-06	**Nashville**	**NHL**	**75**	**14**	**15**	**29**	**40**	**10**	**0**	**5**	**122**	**11.5**	**0**	**470**	**48.9**	**16:47**	**5**	**1**	**0**	**1**	**0**	**1**	**0**	**1**	**12:1**
2006-07	**NY Rangers**	**NHL**	**49**	**4**	**8**	**12**	**18**	**3**	**0**	**0**	**61**	**6.6**	**-13**	**59**	**45.8**	**12:27**	....	....	....	....	....	....	....	....	....
	Minnesota	**NHL**	**23**	**2**	**3**	**5**	**8**	**0**	**0**	**0**	**42**	**4.8**	**2**	**11**	**72.7**	**12:13**	**3**	**0**	**0**	**0**	**7**	**0**	**0**	**0**	**10:0**
2007-08	**Pittsburgh**	**NHL**	**46**	**2**	**4**	**6**	**24**	**0**	**0**	**0**	**39**	**5.1**	**-2**	**290**	**50.3**	**11:52**	**17**	**3**	**1**	**4**	**8**	**0**	**0**	**1**	**10:5**
2008-09	**Tampa Bay**	**NHL**	**74**	**5**	**5**	**10**	**29**	**1**	**0**	**0**	**90**	**5.6**	**-9**	**338**	**50.0**	**11:12**	....	....	....	....	....	....	....	....	....
2009-10	Norfolk Admirals	AHL	79	16	25	41	47	....	....	....	....	....	....	....	....	....	....	....	....	....	....	....	....	....	....
	NHL Totals		**426**	**56**	**62**	**118**	**187**	**28**	**0**	**8**	**653**	**8.6**		**1533**	**51.2**	**13:56**	**31**	**6**	**2**	**8**	**17**	**1**	**0**	**3**	**12:3**

CCHA Second All-Star Team (2000)

Signed as a free agent by **Kuopio** (Finland-2), October 11, 2004. Traded to **NY Rangers** by **Nashville** for Dominic Moore, July 19, 2006. Traded to **Minnesota** by **NY Rangers** for Pascal Dupuis, February 9, 2007. Signed as a free agent by **Pittsburgh**, October 1, 2007. Signed as a free agent by **Tampa Bay**, July 1, 2008.

HALPERN, Jeff

(HAL-pehrn, JEHF)

Center. Shoots right. 5'11", 198 lbs. Born, Potomac, MD, May 3, 1976.

Season	Club	League	GP	G	A	Pts	PIM	PP	SH	GW	S	%	+/-	TF	F%	Min	GP	G	A	Pts	PIM	PP	SH	GW	Min
1994-95	Stratford Cullitons	OHA-B	44	29	54	83	43	....	....	....	....	....	....	....	....	....	....	....	....	....	....	....	....	....	....
1995-96	Princeton	ECAC	29	3	11	14	30	....	....	....	....	....	....	....	....	....	....	....	....	....	....	....	....	....	....
1996-97	Princeton	ECAC	33	7	24	31	35	....	....	....	....	....	....	....	....	....	....	....	....	....	....	....	....	....	....
1997-98	Princeton	ECAC	36	*28	25	*53	46	....	....	....	....	....	....	....	....	....	....	....	....	....	....	....	....	....	....
1998-99	Princeton	ECAC	33	*22	22	44	32	....	....	....	....	....	....	....	....	....	....	....	....	....	....	....	....	....	....
	Portland Pirates	AHL	6	2	1	3	4	....	....	....	....	....	....	....	....	....	....	....	....	....	....	....	....	....	....
99-2000	**Washington**	**NHL**	**79**	**18**	**11**	**29**	**39**	**4**	**4**	**1**	**108**	**16.7**	**21**	**812**	**51.1**	**13:14**	**5**	**2**	**1**	**3**	**0**	**1**	**0**	**1**	**15:1**
2000-01	**Washington**	**NHL**	**80**	**21**	**21**	**42**	**60**	**2**	**1**	**5**	**110**	**19.1**	**13**	**1293**	**52.4**	**16:08**	**6**	**2**	**3**	**5**	**17**	**1**	**0**	**1**	**20:0**
2001-02	**Washington**	**NHL**	**48**	**5**	**14**	**19**	**29**	**0**	**0**	**4**	**74**	**6.8**	**-9**	**661**	**56.0**	**15:19**	....	....	....	....	....	....	....	....	....
2002-03	**Washington**	**NHL**	**82**	**13**	**21**	**34**	**88**	**1**	**2**	**2**	**126**	**10.3**	**6**	**1492**	**54.1**	**17:25**	**6**	**0**	**1**	**1**	**2**	**0**	**0**	**0**	**19:5**
2003-04	**Washington**	**NHL**	**79**	**19**	**27**	**46**	**56**	**7**	**0**	**2**	**114**	**16.7**	**-21**	**1509**	**54.3**	**19:03**	....	....	....	....	....	....	....	....	....
2004-05	HC Ajoie	Swiss-2	15	5	12	17	52	....	....	....	....	....	....	....	....	....	....	....	....	....	....	....	....	....	....
	Kloten Flyers	Swiss	9	7	4	11	6	....	....	....	....	....	....	....	....	....	....	....	....	....	....	....	....	....	....
2005-06	**Washington**	**NHL**	**70**	**11**	**33**	**44**	**79**	**6**	**0**	**1**	**151**	**7.3**	**-8**	**1454**	**55.2**	**20:00**	....	....	....	....	....	....	....	....	....
2006-07	**Dallas**	**NHL**	**76**	**8**	**17**	**25**	**78**	**1**	**0**	**4**	**106**	**7.5**	**-7**	**1135**	**51.8**	**16:48**	**7**	**2**	**1**	**3**	**4**	**0**	**0**	**1**	**18:5**
2007-08	**Dallas**	**NHL**	**64**	**10**	**14**	**24**	**40**	**1**	**1**	**0**	**86**	**11.6**	**-2**	**548**	**54.0**	**16:21**	....	....	....	....	....	....	....	....	....
	Tampa Bay	**NHL**	**19**	**10**	**8**	**18**	**14**	**3**	**0**	**2**	**46**	**21.7**	**2**	**185**	**46.0**	**18:12**	....	....	....	....	....	....	....	....	....

			Regular Season														Playoffs								
Season	Club	League	GP	G	A	Pts	PIM	PP	SH	GW	S	%	+/-	TF	F%	Min	GP	G	A	Pts	PIM	PP	SH	GW	Min
2008-09	Tampa Bay	NHL	52	7	9	16	32	1	1	1	60	11.7	−13	822	52.8	17:01									
2009-10	Tampa Bay	NHL	55	9	8	17	27	2	0	1	65	13.8	−13	479	52.0	15:39									
	Los Angeles	NHL	16	0	2	2	12	0	0	0	6	0.0	−1	91	49.5	10:41	6	0	0	0	4	0	0	0	10:12
	NHL Totals		720	131	185	316	554	28	9	23	1052	12.5		10481	53.3	16:39	30	6	6	12	27	2	0	3	17:01

ECAC Second All-Star Team (1998, 1999)

Signed as a free agent by **Washington**, March 29, 1999. Signed as a free agent by **Ajoie** (Swiss-2), October 8, 2004. Signed as a free agent by **Kloten** (Swiss), December 30, 2004. Signed as a free agent by **Dallas**, July 5, 2006. Traded to **Tampa Bay** by **Dallas** with Jussi Jokinen, Mike Smith and Dallas' 4th round choice (later traded to Minnesota, later traded to Edmonton – Edmonton selected Kyle Bigos) in 2009 Entry Draft for Brad Richards and Johan Holmqvist, February 26, 2008. Traded to **Los Angeles** by **Tampa Bay** for Teddy Purcell and Florida's 3rd round choice (previously acquired, Tampa Bay selected Brock Beukeboom) in 2010 Entry Draft, March 3, 2010.

HAMEL, Denis

(ha-MEHL, deh-NEE)

Left wing. Shoots left. 6'1", 201 lbs. Born, Lachute, Que., May 10, 1977. St. Louis' 5th choice, 153rd overall, in 1995 Entry Draft.

Season	Club	League	GP	G	A	Pts	PIM	PP	SH	GW	S	%	+/-	TF	F%	Min	GP	G	A	Pts	PIM	PP	SH	GW	Min
1992-93	Lachute Regents	QAAA	32	18	24	42																			
1993-94	Lac St-Louis Lions	QAAA	28	10	11	21	50																		
	Abitibi Foresters	QAAA	15	5	7	12	29										5	0	3	3	16				
1994-95	Chicoutimi	QMJHL	66	15	12	27	155										12	2	0	2	27				
1995-96	Chicoutimi	QMJHL	65	40	49	89	199										17	10	14	24	64				
1996-97	Chicoutimi	QMJHL	70	50	50	100	357										20	15	10	25	58				
1997-98	Rochester	AHL	74	10	15	25	98										4	1	2	3	0				
1998-99	Rochester	AHL	74	16	17	33	121										20	3	4	7	10				
99-2000	Buffalo	NHL	3	1	0	1	0	0	0	0	3	33.3	−1	0	0.0	9:45									
	Rochester	AHL	76	34	24	58	122										21	6	7	13	49				
2000-01	Buffalo	NHL	41	8	3	11	22	1	1	3	55	14.5	−2	171	33.9	10:58									
2001-02	Buffalo	NHL	61	2	6	8	28	0	0	0	80	2.5	−1	94	39.4	11:00									
2002-03	Buffalo	NHL	25	2	0	2	17	0	0	1	41	4.9	−4	4	25.0	12:40									
	Rochester	AHL	48	27	20	47	64										3	3	2	5	4				
2003-04	Ottawa	NHL	5	0	0	0	0	0	0	0	6	0.0	−3	1	100.0	6:16									
	Binghamton	AHL	78	29	38	67	116										2	0	0	0	2				
2004-05	Binghamton	AHL	80	39	39	78	75										5	1	0	1	4				
2005-06	Ottawa	NHL	4	1	0	1	0	0	0	0	9	11.1	1	1	0.0	9:10									
	Binghamton	AHL	77	*56	35	91	65																		
2006-07	Ottawa	NHL	43	4	3	7	10	0	0	0	36	11.1	4	9	33.3	5:38									
	Atlanta	NHL	3	1	0	1	0	0	0	0	3	33.3	0	2	0.0	10:25									
	Philadelphia	NHL	7	0	0	0	0	0	0	0	3	0.0	−4	0	0.0	6:58									
2007-08	Binghamton	AHL	67	32	23	55	60																		
2008-09	Binghamton	AHL	63	25	25	50	36																		
2009-10	Binghamton	AHL	73	22	29	51	45																		
	NHL Totals		192	19	12	31	77	1	1	4	236	8.1		282	35.5	9:40									

QMJHL All-Rookie Team (1995) • AHL First All-Star Team (2004) • Willie Marshall Award (AHL - Top Goal-scorer) (2006) (tied with Don MacLean) • Yanick Dupre Memorial Award (AHL - Outstanding Humanitarian Contribution) (2008)

Traded to **Buffalo** by **St. Louis** for Charlie Huddy and Buffalo's 7th round choice (Daniel Corso) in 1996 Entry Draft, March 19, 1996. • Missed majority of 2000-01 season recovering from knee injury suffered in game vs. NY Islanders, January 27, 2001. Signed as a free agent by **Ottawa**, July 5, 2003. Claimed by **Washington** from **Ottawa** in Waiver Draft, October 3, 2003. Traded to **Ottawa** by **Washington** for future considerations, October 5, 2003. Claimed on waivers by **Atlanta** from **Ottawa**, February 10, 2007. Claimed on waivers by **Philadelphia** from **Atlanta**, February 27, 2007. Signed as a free agent by **Ottawa** , July 6, 2007.

HAMHUIS, Dan

(HAM-HOOS, DAN) **VAN.**

Defense. Shoots left. 6'1", 209 lbs. Born, Smithers, B.C., December 13, 1982. Nashville's 1st choice, 12th overall, in 2001 Entry Draft.

Season	Club	League	GP	G	A	Pts	PIM	PP	SH	GW	S	%	+/-	TF	F%	Min	GP	G	A	Pts	PIM	PP	SH	GW	Min
1997-98	Smithers A's	Minor-BC	59	59	72	131	59																		
1998-99	Prince George	WHL	56	1	3	4	45										7	1	2	3	8				
99-2000	Prince George	WHL	70	10	23	33	140										13	2	3	5	35				
2000-01	Prince George	WHL	62	13	47	60	125										6	2	3	5	15				
2001-02	Prince George	WHL	59	10	50	60	135										7	0	5	5	16				
2002-03	Milwaukee	AHL	68	6	21	27	81										6	0	3	3	2				
2003-04	Nashville	NHL	80	7	19	26	57	2	0	4	115	6.1	−12	0	0.0	22:08	6	0	2	2	6	0	0	0	20:29
2004-05	Milwaukee	AHL	76	13	38	51	85										7	0	2	2	10				
2005-06	Nashville	NHL	82	7	31	38	70	4	1	1	135	5.2	11	0	0.0	22:34	5	0	2	2	2	0	0	0	19:41
2006-07	Nashville	NHL	81	6	14	20	66	0	0	1	84	7.1	8	1	0.0	21:20	5	0	1	1	2	0	0	0	21:36
2007-08	Nashville	NHL	80	4	23	27	66	1	0	1	127	3.1	−4	0	0.0	22:44	6	1	1	2	6	1	0	0	22:47
2008-09	Nashville	NHL	82	3	23	26	67	1	1	1	135	2.2	−4	0	0.0	22:50									
2009-10	Nashville	NHL	78	5	19	24	49	0	0	0	115	4.3	4	0	0.0	21:15	6	0	2	2	2	0	0	0	22:25
	NHL Totals		483	32	129	161	375	8	2	8	711	4.5		1	0.0	22:09	28	1	8	9	18	1	0	0	21:27

WHL West First All-Star Team (2001, 2002) • WHL Player of the Year (2002) • Canadian Major Junior First All-Star Team (2002) • Canadian Major Junior Defenseman of the Year (2002) • AHL Second All-Star Team (2005)

Traded to **Philadelphia** by **Nashville** for Ryan Parent and future considerations, June 19, 2010. Traded to **Pittsburgh** by **Philadelphia** for Pittsburgh's 3rd round choice in 2011 Entry Draft, June 25, 2010. Signed as a free agent by **Vancouver**, July 1, 2010.

HAMILL, Zach

(HA-mihl, ZAK) **BOS.**

Center. Shoots right. 5'11", 180 lbs. Born, Vancouver, B.C., September 23, 1988. Boston's 1st choice, 8th overall, in 2007 Entry Draft.

Season	Club	League	GP	G	A	Pts	PIM	PP	SH	GW	S	%	+/-	TF	F%	Min	GP	G	A	Pts	PIM	PP	SH	GW	Min
2002-03	Port Coquitlam	Minor-BC	61	120	83	203																			
2003-04	Port Coquitlam	PIJHL	39	30	31	51	50																		
	Everett Silvertips	WHL	4	0	2	2	0										20	3	2	5	2				
2004-05	Everett Silvertips	WHL	57	8	25	33	29										11	2	3	5	8				
2005-06	Everett Silvertips	WHL	53	21	38	59	28										15	3	11	14	4				
2006-07	Everett Silvertips	WHL	69	32	*61	*93	90										12	2	8	10	16				
2007-08	Everett Silvertips	WHL	67	26	49	75	88										4	0	3	3	2				
	Providence Bruins	AHL	7	0	5	5	6										9	1	3	4	0				
2008-09	Providence Bruins	AHL	65	13	13	26	40										16	1	5	6	4				
2009-10	Boston	NHL	1	0	1	1	0	0	0	0	1	0.0	1	4	25.0	12:08									
	Providence Bruins	AHL	75	14	30	44	24																		
	NHL Totals		1	0	1	1	0	0	0	0	1	0.0		4	25.0	12:08									

WHL West First All-Star Team (2007) • Canadian Major Junior First All-Star Team (2007)

HAMILTON, Jeff

(HAM-ihl-tuhn, JEHF)

Center. Shoots right. 5'10", 185 lbs. Born, Englewood, OH, September 4, 1977.

Season	Club	League	GP	G	A	Pts	PIM	PP	SH	GW	S	%	+/-	TF	F%	Min	GP	G	A	Pts	PIM	PP	SH	GW	Min
1995-96	Avon Old Farms	High-CT	24	29	23	52																			
1996-97	Yale	ECAC	31	10	13	23	26																		
1997-98	Yale	ECAC	33	27	20	47	28																		
1998-99	Yale	ECAC	30	20	28	48	51																		
99-2000	Yale	ECAC	2	0	1	1	0																		
2000-01	Yale	ECAC	31	23	32	55	39																		
2001-02	Karpat Oulu	Finland	39	18	15	33	16										3	0	0	0	0				
2002-03	Bridgeport	AHL	67	22	16	38	35										9	3	3	6	0				
2003-04	NY Islanders	NHL	1	0	0	0	0	0	0	0	1	0.0	0	0	0.0	10:00									
	Bridgeport	AHL	67	*43	25	68	26										7	4	0	4	4				
2004-05	Hartford	AHL	60	23	30	53	32										6	4	3	7	0				
2005-06	Ak Bars Kazan	Russia	8	0	1	1	16																		
	NY Islanders	NHL	13	2	6	8	8	1	0	0	29	6.9	0	6	16.7	10:33									
	Bridgeport	AHL	39	24	26	50	28																		
2006-07	Chicago	NHL	70	18	21	39	22	3	0	4	138	13.0	−4	55	36.4	12:56									
2007-08	Carolina	NHL	58	9	15	24	10	7	0	1	116	7.8	−8	79	48.1	10:48									
	Albany River Rats	AHL	9	3	6	9	6																		

Season	Club	League	GP	G	A	Pts	PIM	PP	SH	GW	S	%	+/-	TF	F%	Min	GP	G	A	Pts	PIM	PP	SH	GW	Min
			Regular Season														Playoffs								
2008-09	Chicago Wolves	AHL	50	16	37	53	18	....	....	....	....	....	....	....	....	....	....	....	....	....	....	....	....	....	....
	Toronto	**NHL**	**15**	**3**	**3**	**6**	**4**	**0**	**0**	**1**	**30**	**10.0**	**2**	**11**	**27.3**	**12:57**	....	....	....	....	....	....	....	....	....
2009-10	HC Lugano	Swiss	46	22	24	46	28	....	....	....	....	....	....	....	....	....	4	0	0	0	4	....	....	....	....
	NHL Totals		**157**	**32**	**45**	**77**	**44**	**11**	**0**	**6**	**314**	**10.2**		**151**	**41.1**	**11:56**	....	....	....	....	....	....	....	....	....

ECAC All-Rookie Team (1997) • ECAC First All-Star Team (1998, 1999, 2001) • NCAA East Second All-American Team (1998, 1999) • NCAA East First All-American Team (2001) • AHL First All-Star Team (2004) • Willie Marshall Award (AHL - Top Goal-scorer) (2004)

• Missed majority of 1999-2000 season recovering from abdominal injury suffered in game vs. University of Michigan (CCHA), October 30, 1999. Signed as a free agent by **Oulu** (Finland), October 4, 2001. Signed as a free agent by **NY Islanders**, August 6, 2002. Signed as a free agent by **Hartford** (AHL), October 10, 2004. Signed as a free agent by **Kazan** (Russia), September 5, 2005. Signed as a free agent by **Chicago**, September 29, 2006. Signed as a free agent by **Carolina**, July 1, 2007. Signed as a free agent by **Toronto**, March 5, 2009. Signed as a free agent by **Lugano** (Swiss), August 5, 2009.

HAMRLIK, Roman

(HAHM-reh-lik, ROH-muhn) **MTL.**

Defense. Shoots left. 6'2", 207 lbs. Born, Zlin, Czech., April 12, 1974. Tampa Bay's 1st choice, 1st overall, in 1992 Entry Draft.

Season	Club	League	GP	G	A	Pts	PIM	PP	SH	GW	S	%	+/-	TF	F%	Min	GP	G	A	Pts	PIM	PP	SH	GW	Min
1990-91	AC ZPS Zlin	Czech	14	2	2	4	18	....	....	....	....	....	....	....	....	....	....	....	....	....	....	....	....	....	....
1991-92	AC ZPS Zlin	Czech	34	5	5	10	50	....	....	....	....	....	....	....	....	....	....	....	....	....	....	....	....	....	....
1992-93	**Tampa Bay**	**NHL**	**67**	**6**	**15**	**21**	**71**	**1**	**0**	**1**	**113**	**5.3**	**–21**	....	....	....	....	....	....	....	....	....	....	....	....
	Atlanta Knights	IHL	2	1	1	2	2	....	....	....	....	....	....	....	....	....	....	....	....	....	....	....	....	....	....
1993-94	**Tampa Bay**	**NHL**	**64**	**3**	**18**	**21**	**135**	**0**	**0**	**0**	**158**	**1.9**	**–14**	....	....	....	....	....	....	....	....	....	....	....	....
1994-95	AC ZPS Zlin	CzRep	2	1	0	1	10	....	....	....	....	....	....	....	....	....	....	....	....	....	....	....	....	....	....
	Tampa Bay	**NHL**	**48**	**12**	**11**	**23**	**86**	**7**	**1**	**2**	**134**	**9.0**	**–18**	....	....	....	....	....	....	....	....	....	....	....	....
1995-96	**Tampa Bay**	**NHL**	**82**	**16**	**49**	**65**	**103**	**12**	**0**	**2**	**281**	**5.7**	**–24**	....	....	....	**5**	**0**	**1**	**1**	**4**	**0**	**0**	**0**	....
1996-97	**Tampa Bay**	**NHL**	**79**	**12**	**28**	**40**	**57**	**6**	**0**	**0**	**238**	**5.0**	**–29**	....	....	....	....	....	....	....	....	....	....	....	....
1997-98	**Tampa Bay**	**NHL**	**37**	**3**	**12**	**15**	**22**	**1**	**0**	**0**	**86**	**3.5**	**–18**	....	....	....	....	....	....	....	....	....	....	....	....
	Edmonton	**NHL**	**41**	**6**	**20**	**26**	**48**	**4**	**1**	**3**	**112**	**5.4**	**3**	....	....	....	**12**	**0**	**6**	**6**	**12**	**0**	**0**	**0**	....
	Czech Republic	Olympics	6	1	0	1	2	....	....	....	....	....	....	....	....	....	....	....	....	....	....	....	....	....	....
1998-99	**Edmonton**	**NHL**	**75**	**8**	**24**	**32**	**70**	**3**	**0**	**0**	**172**	**4.7**	**9**	**0**	**0.0**	**23:49**	**3**	**0**	**0**	**0**	**2**	**0**	**0**	**0**	**16:23**
99-2000	Zlin	CzRep	6	0	3	3	4	....	....	....	....	....	....	....	....	....	....	....	....	....	....	....	....	....	....
	Edmonton	**NHL**	**80**	**8**	**37**	**45**	**68**	**5**	**0**	**0**	**180**	**4.4**	**1**	**0**	**0.0**	**25:18**	**5**	**0**	**1**	**1**	**4**	**0**	**0**	**0**	**24:44**
2000-01	**NY Islanders**	**NHL**	**76**	**16**	**30**	**46**	**92**	**5**	**1**	**4**	**232**	**6.9**	**–20**	**1**	**100.0**	**25:12**	....	....	....	....	....	....	....	....	....
2001-02	**NY Islanders**	**NHL**	**70**	**11**	**26**	**37**	**78**	**4**	**1**	**1**	**169**	**6.5**	**7**	**1**	**0.0**	**25:32**	**7**	**1**	**6**	**7**	**6**	**0**	**0**	**0**	**29:09**
	Czech Republic	Olympics	4	0	1	1	2	....	....	....	....	....	....	....	....	....	....	....	....	....	....	....	....	....	....
2002-03	**NY Islanders**	**NHL**	**73**	**9**	**32**	**41**	**87**	**3**	**0**	**2**	**151**	**6.0**	**21**	**0**	**0.0**	**26:34**	**5**	**0**	**2**	**2**	**2**	**0**	**0**	**0**	**29:24**
2003-04	**NY Islanders**	**NHL**	**81**	**7**	**22**	**29**	**68**	**2**	**0**	**2**	**182**	**3.8**	**2**	**0**	**0.0**	**24:35**	**5**	**0**	**1**	**1**	**2**	**0**	**0**	**0**	**25:30**
2004-05	HC Hame Zlin	CzRep	45	2	14	16	70	....	....	....	....	....	....	....	....	....	17	1	3	4	24	....	....	....	....
2005-06	**Calgary**	**NHL**	**51**	**7**	**19**	**26**	**56**	**1**	**1**	**0**	**89**	**7.9**	**8**	**0**	**0.0**	**21:51**	**7**	**0**	**2**	**2**	**2**	**0**	**0**	**0**	**19:44**
2006-07	**Calgary**	**NHL**	**75**	**7**	**31**	**38**	**88**	**1**	**0**	**1**	**125**	**5.6**	**22**	**0**	**0.0**	**24:52**	**6**	**0**	**1**	**1**	**8**	**0**	**0**	**0**	**26:53**
2007-08	**Montreal**	**NHL**	**77**	**5**	**21**	**26**	**38**	**3**	**0**	**3**	**129**	**3.9**	**7**	**0**	**0.0**	**23:08**	**12**	**1**	**2**	**3**	**8**	**0**	**0**	**0**	**22:55**
2008-09	**Montreal**	**NHL**	**81**	**6**	**27**	**33**	**62**	**0**	**0**	**0**	**143**	**4.2**	**4**	**0**	**0.0**	**21:55**	**4**	**0**	**0**	**0**	**2**	**0**	**0**	**0**	**25:19**
2009-10	**Montreal**	**NHL**	**75**	**6**	**20**	**26**	**56**	**2**	**0**	**1**	**100**	**6.0**	**–2**	**0**	**0.0**	**23:26**	**19**	**0**	**9**	**9**	**15**	**0**	**0**	**0**	**20:08**
	NHL Totals		**1232**	**148**	**442**	**590**	**1285**	**60**	**5**	**22**	**2794**	**5.3**		**2**	**50.0**	**24:15**	**90**	**2**	**31**	**33**	**67**	**0**	**0**	**0**	**23:25**

Played in NHL All-Star Game (1996, 1999, 2003)

Traded to **Edmonton** by **Tampa Bay** with Paul Comrie for Bryan Marchment, Steve Kelly and Jason Bonsignore, December 30, 1997. Traded to **NY Islanders** by **Edmonton** for Eric Brewer, Josh Green and NY Islanders' 2nd round choice (Brad Winchester) in 2000 Entry Draft, June 24, 2000. Signed as a free agent by **Zlin** (CzRep), August 4, 2004. Signed as a free agent by **Calgary**, August 14, 2005 Signed as a free agent by **Montreal**, July 2, 2007.

HANDZUS, Michal

(HAHND-zoos, MIGH-kuhl) **L.A.**

Center. Shoots left. 6'4", 216 lbs. Born, Banska Bystrica, Czech., March 11, 1977. St. Louis' 3rd choice, 101st overall, in 1995 Entry Draft.

Season	Club	League	GP	G	A	Pts	PIM	PP	SH	GW	S	%	+/-	TF	F%	Min	GP	G	A	Pts	PIM	PP	SH	GW	Min
1993-94	B. Bystrica Jr.	Slovak-Jr.	40	23	36	59	....	....	....	....	....	....	....	....	....	....	....	....	....	....	....	....	....	....	....
1994-95	B. Bystrica	Slovak-2	22	15	14	29	10	....	....	....	....	....	....	....	....	....	....	....	....	....	....	....	....	....	....
1995-96	B. Bystrica	Slovakia	19	3	1	4	8	....	....	....	....	....	....	....	....	....	....	....	....	....	....	....	....	....	....
1996-97	HC SKP PS Poprad	Slovakia	44	15	18	33	....	....	....	....	....	....	....	....	....	....	....	....	....	....	....	....	....	....	....
1997-98	Worcester IceCats	AHL	69	27	36	63	54	....	....	....	....	....	....	....	....	....	11	2	6	8	10	....	....	....	....
1998-99	**St. Louis**	**NHL**	**66**	**4**	**12**	**16**	**30**	**0**	**0**	**0**	**78**	**5.1**	**–9**	**794**	**49.9**	**14:48**	**11**	**0**	**2**	**2**	**8**	**0**	**0**	**0**	**16:52**
99-2000	**St. Louis**	**NHL**	**81**	**25**	**28**	**53**	**44**	**3**	**4**	**5**	**166**	**15.1**	**19**	**1243**	**51.5**	**17:43**	**7**	**0**	**3**	**3**	**6**	**0**	**0**	**0**	**16:35**
2000-01	**St. Louis**	**NHL**	**36**	**10**	**14**	**24**	**12**	**3**	**2**	**2**	**58**	**17.2**	**11**	**581**	**50.6**	**18:00**	....	....	....	....	....	....	....	....	....
	Phoenix	**NHL**	**10**	**4**	**4**	**8**	**21**	**0**	**1**	**0**	**14**	**28.6**	**5**	**111**	**60.4**	**15:26**	....	....	....	....	....	....	....	....	....
2001-02	**Phoenix**	**NHL**	**79**	**15**	**30**	**45**	**34**	**3**	**1**	**1**	**94**	**16.0**	**–8**	**1227**	**48.7**	**16:09**	**5**	**0**	**0**	**0**	**2**	**0**	**0**	**0**	**15:01**
	Slovakia	Olympics	2	1	0	1	6	....	....	....	....	....	....	....	....	....	....	....	....	....	....	....	....	....	....
2002-03	**Philadelphia**	**NHL**	**82**	**23**	**21**	**44**	**46**	**1**	**1**	**9**	**133**	**17.3**	**13**	**1350**	**52.3**	**17:33**	**13**	**2**	**6**	**8**	**6**	**0**	**0**	**1**	**18:23**
2003-04	**Philadelphia**	**NHL**	**82**	**20**	**38**	**58**	**82**	**7**	**1**	**2**	**135**	**14.8**	**18**	**1457**	**49.9**	**18:43**	**18**	**5**	**5**	**10**	**10**	**0**	**0**	**0**	**18:33**
2004-05	HKm Zvolen	Slovakia	33	14	24	38	34	....	....	....	....	....	....	....	....	....	17	5	10	15	6	....	....	....	....
2005-06	**Philadelphia**	**NHL**	**73**	**11**	**33**	**44**	**38**	**2**	**1**	**1**	**113**	**9.7**	**–2**	**1143**	**53.2**	**18:28**	**6**	**0**	**2**	**2**	**2**	**0**	**0**	**0**	**15:56**
2006-07	**Chicago**	**NHL**	**8**	**3**	**5**	**8**	**6**	**1**	**0**	**0**	**9**	**33.3**	**4**	**173**	**51.5**	**20:59**	....	....	....	....	....	....	....	....	....
2007-08	**Los Angeles**	**NHL**	**82**	**7**	**14**	**21**	**45**	**0**	**3**	**0**	**89**	**7.9**	**–21**	**1167**	**45.6**	**15:14**	....	....	....	....	....	....	....	....	....
2008-09	**Los Angeles**	**NHL**	**82**	**18**	**24**	**42**	**32**	**7**	**1**	**4**	**143**	**12.6**	**–7**	**1320**	**54.5**	**18:54**	....	....	....	....	....	....	....	....	....
2009-10	**Los Angeles**	**NHL**	**81**	**20**	**22**	**42**	**38**	**5**	**1**	**6**	**117**	**17.1**	**4**	**1363**	**50.9**	**18:18**	**6**	**3**	**2**	**5**	**4**	**3**	**0**	**0**	**19:31**
	Slovakia	Olympics	7	3	3	6	0	....	....	....	....	....	....	....	....	....	....	....	....	....	....	....	....	....	....
	NHL Totals		**762**	**160**	**245**	**405**	**428**	**32**	**16**	**30**	**1149**	**13.9**		**11929**	**50.9**	**17:24**	**66**	**10**	**20**	**30**	**38**	**3**	**0**	**1**	**17:37**

Traded to **Phoenix** by **St. Louis** with Ladislav Nagy, the rights to Jeff Taffe and St. Louis' 1st round choice (Ben Eager) in 2002 Entry Draft for Keith Tkachuk, March 13, 2001. Traded to **Philadelphia** by **Phoenix** with Robert Esche for Brian Boucher and Nashville's 3rd round choice (previously acquired, Phoenix selected Joe Callahan) in 2002 Entry Draft, June 12, 2002. Signed as a free agent by **Zvolen** (Slovakia), October 27, 2004. Traded to **Chicago** by **Philadelphia** for Kyle Calder, August 4, 2006. • Missed remainder of 2006-07 season recovering from knee injury suffered in game vs. St. Louis, October 21, 2006. Signed as a free agent by **Los Angeles**, July 2, 2007.

HANNAN, Scott

(HAN-nan, SKAWT) **COL.**

Defense. Shoots left. 6'1", 225 lbs. Born, Richmond, B.C., January 23, 1979. San Jose's 2nd choice, 23rd overall, in 1997 Entry Draft.

Season	Club	League	GP	G	A	Pts	PIM	PP	SH	GW	S	%	+/-	TF	F%	Min	GP	G	A	Pts	PIM	PP	SH	GW	Min
1994-95	Surrey Wolves	Minor-BC	70	54	54	108	200	....	....	....	....	....	....	....	....	....	....	....	....	....	....	....	....	....	....
	Tacoma Rockets	WHL	2	0	0	0	0	....	....	....	....	....	....	....	....	....	....	....	....	....	....	....	....	....	....
1995-96	Kelowna Rockets	WHL	69	4	5	9	76	....	....	....	....	....	....	....	....	....	6	0	1	1	4	....	....	....	....
1996-97	Kelowna Rockets	WHL	70	17	26	43	101	....	....	....	....	....	....	....	....	....	6	0	0	0	8	....	....	....	....
1997-98	Kelowna Rockets	WHL	47	10	30	40	70	....	....	....	....	....	....	....	....	....	7	2	7	9	14	....	....	....	....
1998-99	**San Jose**	**NHL**	**5**	**0**	**2**	**2**	**6**	**0**	**0**	**0**	**4**	**0.0**	**0**	**0**	**0.0**	**7:15**	....	....	....	....	....	....	....	....	....
	Kelowna Rockets	WHL	47	15	30	45	92	....	....	....	....	....	....	....	....	....	6	1	2	3	14	....	....	....	....
	Kentucky	AHL	2	0	0	0	2	....	....	....	....	....	....	....	....	....	12	0	2	2	10	....	....	....	....
99-2000	**San Jose**	**NHL**	**30**	**1**	**2**	**3**	**10**	**0**	**0**	**0**	**28**	**3.6**	**7**	**1**	**0.0**	**17:09**	**1**	**0**	**1**	**1**	**0**	**0**	**0**	**0**	**18:14**
	Kentucky	AHL	41	5	12	17	40	....	....	....	....	....	....	....	....	....	....	....	....	....	....	....	....	....	....
2000-01	**San Jose**	**NHL**	**75**	**3**	**14**	**17**	**51**	**0**	**0**	**1**	**96**	**3.1**	**10**	**0**	**0.0**	**19:02**	**6**	**0**	**1**	**1**	**6**	**0**	**0**	**0**	**25:10**
2001-02	**San Jose**	**NHL**	**75**	**2**	**12**	**14**	**57**	**0**	**0**	**1**	**68**	**2.9**	**10**	**1**	**100.0**	**20:19**	**12**	**0**	**2**	**2**	**12**	**0**	**0**	**0**	**20:46**
2002-03	**San Jose**	**NHL**	**81**	**3**	**19**	**22**	**61**	**1**	**0**	**0**	**103**	**2.9**	**0**	**3**	**33.3**	**24:16**	....	....	....	....	....	....	....	....	....
2003-04	**San Jose**	**NHL**	**82**	**6**	**15**	**21**	**48**	**0**	**0**	**0**	**114**	**5.3**	**10**	**0**	**0.0**	**23:41**	**17**	**1**	**5**	**6**	**22**	**1**	**0**	**1**	**26:38**
2004-05			DID NOT PLAY																						
2005-06	**San Jose**	**NHL**	**81**	**6**	**18**	**24**	**58**	**2**	**0**	**1**	**104**	**5.8**	**7**	**0**	**0.0**	**24:34**	**11**	**0**	**1**	**1**	**6**	**0**	**0**	**0**	**25:16**
2006-07	**San Jose**	**NHL**	**79**	**4**	**20**	**24**	**38**	**0**	**1**	**1**	**79**	**5.1**	**1**	**0**	**0.0**	**22:49**	**11**	**0**	**2**	**2**	**33**	**0**	**0**	**0**	**21:42**
2007-08	**Colorado**	**NHL**	**82**	**2**	**19**	**21**	**55**	**0**	**0**	**0**	**79**	**2.5**	**–5**	**1**	**100.0**	**22:41**	**9**	**0**	**1**	**1**	**4**	**0**	**0**	**0**	**19:15**
2008-09	**Colorado**	**NHL**	**81**	**1**	**9**	**10**	**26**	**0**	**0**	**0**	**70**	**1.4**	**–21**	**1**	**0.0**	**22:22**	....	....	....	....	....	....	....	....	....
2009-10	**Colorado**	**NHL**	**81**	**2**	**14**	**16**	**40**	**0**	**0**	**0**	**53**	**3.8**	**2**	**2**	**100.0**	**21:56**	**6**	**0**	**0**	**0**	**4**	**0**	**0**	**0**	**22:33**
	NHL Totals		**752**	**30**	**144**	**174**	**450**	**3**	**1**	**4**	**798**	**3.8**		**9**	**55.6**	**22:09**	**73**	**1**	**13**	**14**	**87**	**1**	**0**	**1**	**23:14**

WHL West First All-Star Team (1999)

Signed as a free agent by **Colorado**, July 1, 2007.

HANSEN, Jannik

(HAHN-suhn, YAH-nihk) **VAN**

Left wing. Shoots right. 6'1", 195 lbs. Born, Herlev, Denmark, March 15, 1986. Vancouver's 7th choice, 287th overall, in 2004 Entry Draft.

Season	Club	League	GP	G	A	Pts	PIM	PP	SH	GW	S	%	+/-	TF	F%	Min	GP	G	A	Pts	PIM	PP	SH	GW	Min
2002-03	Rodovre	Denmark	15	0	0	0	0	....	....	....	....	....	....	....	....	....	....	....	....	....	....	....	....	....	....
	Malmo U18	Swe-U18	12	8	7	15	2	....	....	....	....	....	....	....	....	....	3	2	0	2	0	....	....	....	....
	Denmark	WJ18-B	5	2	5	7	14	....	....	....	....	....	....	....	....	....	....	....	....	....	....	....	....	....	....
2003-04	Rodovre	Denmark	35	12	7	19	48	....	....	....	....	....	....	....	....	....	....	....	....	....	....	....	....	....	....
2004-05	Rodovre	Denmark	32	17	17	34	40	....	....	....	....	....	....	....	....	....	5	3	1	4	24	....	....	....	....
2005-06	Portland	WHL	64	24	40	64	67	....	....	....	....	....	....	....	....	....	12	7	6	13	16	....	....	....	....

			Regular Season														Playoffs								
Season	Club	League	GP	G	A	Pts	PIM	PP	SH	GW	S	%	+/-	TF	F%	Min	GP	G	A	Pts	PIM	PP	SH	GW	Min
2006-07	Manitoba Moose	AHL	72	12	22	34	38	....	....	....	....	....	....	....	....	....	6	0	0	0	2	....	....	....	....
	Vancouver	**NHL**	....	....	....	....	....	....	....	....	....	....	....	....	....	....	**10**	**0**	**1**	**1**	**4**	**0**	**0**	**0**	**12:41**
2007-08	**Vancouver**	**NHL**	**5**	**0**	**0**	**0**	**2**	**0**	**0**	**0**	**3**	**0.0**	**0**	**1**	**100.0**	**11:34**	....	....	....	....	....	....	....	....	....
	Manitoba Moose	AHL	50	21	22	43	22	....	....	....	....	....	....	....	....	....	6	2	2	4	0	....	....	....	....
2008-09	**Vancouver**	**NHL**	**55**	**6**	**15**	**21**	**37**	**0**	**0**	**1**	**64**	**9.4**	**5**	**12**	**16.7**	**12:31**	**2**	**0**	**0**	**0**	**0**	**0**	**0**	**0**	**10:16**
	Manitoba Moose	AHL	2	1	0	1	2	....	....	....	....	....	....	....	....	....	....	....	....	....	....	....	....	....	....
2009-10	**Vancouver**	**NHL**	**47**	**9**	**6**	**15**	**18**	**0**	**1**	**3**	**67**	**13.4**	**–5**	**14**	**42.9**	**12:20**	**12**	**1**	**2**	**3**	**4**	**0**	**0**	**0**	**10:05**
	Manitoba Moose	AHL	5	0	2	2	5	....	....	....	....	....	....	....	....	....	....	....	....	....	....	....	....	....	....
	NHL Totals		**107**	**15**	**21**	**36**	**57**	**0**	**1**	**4**	**134**	**11.2**		**27**	**33.3**	**12:24**	**24**	**1**	**3**	**4**	**8**	**0**	**0**	**0**	**11:11**

HANSON, Christian

(HAN-suhn, KRIHST-chehn) **TOR.**

Center. Shoots right. 6'3", 228 lbs. Born, Venetia, PA, March 10, 1986.

Season	Club	League	GP	G	A	Pts	PIM	PP	SH	GW	S	%	+/-	TF	F%	Min	GP	G	A	Pts	PIM	PP	SH	GW	Min
2003-04	Tri-City Storm	USHL	58	11	8	19	35	....	....	....	....	....	....	....	....	....	11	2	2	4	4	....	....	....	....
2004-05	Tri-City Storm	USHL	60	19	33	52	23	....	....	....	....	....	....	....	....	....	9	1	2	3	8	....	....	....	....
2005-06	U. of Notre Dame	CCHA	23	1	2	3	14	....	....	....	....	....	....	....	....	....	....	....	....	....	....	....	....	....	....
2006-07	U. of Notre Dame	CCHA	33	6	2	8	24	....	....	....	....	....	....	....	....	....	....	....	....	....	....	....	....	....	....
2007-08	U. of Notre Dame	CCHA	47	13	9	22	57	....	....	....	....	....	....	....	....	....	....	....	....	....	....	....	....	....	....
2008-09	U. of Notre Dame	CCHA	37	16	15	31	28	....	....	....	....	....	....	....	....	....	....	....	....	....	....	....	....	....	....
	Toronto	**NHL**	**5**	**1**	**1**	**2**	**2**	**0**	**0**	**0**	**9**	**11.1**	**–1**	**4**	**25.0**	**16:19**	....	....	....	....	....	....	....	....	....
2009-10	**Toronto**	**NHL**	**31**	**2**	**5**	**7**	**16**	**0**	**1**	**0**	**45**	**4.4**	**–2**	**177**	**55.4**	**13:22**	....	....	....	....	....	....	....	....	....
	Toronto Marlies	AHL	38	12	19	31	35	....	....	....	....	....	....	....	....	....	....	....	....	....	....	....	....	....	....
	NHL Totals		**36**	**3**	**6**	**9**	**18**	**0**	**1**	**0**	**54**	**5.6**		**181**	**54.7**	**13:47**	....	....	....	....	....	....	....	....	....

CCHA Second All-Star Team (2009)

Signed as a free agent by **Toronto**, March 31, 2009.

HANZAL, Martin

(HAHN-zuhl, MAHR-tihn) **PHX.**

Center. Shoots left. 6'5", 218 lbs. Born, Pisek, Czech., February 20, 1987. Phoenix's 1st choice, 17th overall, in 2005 Entry Draft.

Season	Club	League	GP	G	A	Pts	PIM	PP	SH	GW	S	%	+/-	TF	F%	Min	GP	G	A	Pts	PIM	PP	SH	GW	Min
2002-03	C. Budejovice U17	CzR-U17	47	24	30	54	28	....	....	....	....	....	....	....	....	....	7	1	3	4	25	....	....	....	....
2003-04	C. Budejovice U17	CzR-U17	2	0	2	2	2	....	....	....	....	....	....	....	....	....	2	1	0	1	4	....	....	....	....
	C. Budejovice Jr.	CzRep-Jr.	53	15	7	22	32	....	....	....	....	....	....	....	....	....	....	....	....	....	....	....	....	....	....
2004-05	C. Budejovice Jr.	CzRep-Jr.	37	22	22	44	80	....	....	....	....	....	....	....	....	....	2	1	2	3	2	....	....	....	....
	C. Budejovice	CzRep-2	15	1	2	3	2	....	....	....	....	....	....	....	....	....	6	0	0	0	6	....	....	....	....
2005-06	C. Budejovice Jr.	CzRep-Jr.	7	3	5	8	20	....	....	....	....	....	....	....	....	....	....	....	....	....	....	....	....	....	....
	C. Budejovice	CzRep	19	0	1	1	10	....	....	....	....	....	....	....	....	....	....	....	....	....	....	....	....	....	....
	BK Mlada Boleslav	CzRep-2	5	2	0	2	0	....	....	....	....	....	....	....	....	....	....	....	....	....	....	....	....	....	....
	Omaha Lancers	USHL	19	4	15	19	30	....	....	....	....	....	....	....	....	....	5	1	0	1	4	....	....	....	....
2006-07	Red Deer Rebels	WHL	60	26	59	85	94	....	....	....	....	....	....	....	....	....	6	2	7	9	19	....	....	....	....
2007-08	**Phoenix**	**NHL**	**72**	**8**	**27**	**35**	**28**	**1**	**1**	**3**	**111**	**7.2**	**–7**	**1019**	**46.1**	**16:45**	....	....	....	....	....	....	....	....	....
2008-09	**Phoenix**	**NHL**	**74**	**11**	**20**	**31**	**40**	**0**	**2**	**2**	**97**	**11.3**	**–4**	**1078**	**48.3**	**16:21**	....	....	....	....	....	....	....	....	....
2009-10	**Phoenix**	**NHL**	**81**	**11**	**22**	**33**	**104**	**2**	**0**	**0**	**147**	**7.5**	**0**	**1104**	**50.6**	**18:29**	**7**	**0**	**3**	**3**	**10**	**0**	**0**	**0**	**18:58**
	NHL Totals		**227**	**30**	**69**	**99**	**172**	**3**	**3**	**5**	**355**	**8.5**		**3201**	**48.4**	**17:14**	**7**	**0**	**3**	**3**	**10**	**0**	**0**	**0**	**18:58**

WHL East Second All-Star Team (2007)

HARRISON, Jay

(HAIR-ih-suhn, JAY) **CAR.**

Defense. Shoots left. 6'4", 211 lbs. Born, Oshawa, Ont., November 3, 1982. Toronto's 4th choice, 82nd overall, in 2001 Entry Draft.

Season	Club	League	GP	G	A	Pts	PIM	PP	SH	GW	S	%	+/-	TF	F%	Min	GP	G	A	Pts	PIM	PP	SH	GW	Min
1997-98	Oshawa	OHA-B	42	1	11	12	143	....	....	....	....	....	....	....	....	....	....	....	....	....	....	....	....	....	....
1998-99	Brampton	OHL	63	1	14	15	108	....	....	....	....	....	....	....	....	....	....	....	....	....	....	....	....	....	....
99-2000	Brampton	OHL	68	2	18	20	139	....	....	....	....	....	....	....	....	....	6	0	2	2	15	....	....	....	....
2000-01	Brampton	OHL	53	4	15	19	112	....	....	....	....	....	....	....	....	....	9	1	1	2	17	....	....	....	....
2001-02	Brampton	OHL	61	12	31	43	116	....	....	....	....	....	....	....	....	....	....	....	....	....	....	....	....	....	....
	St. John's	AHL	7	0	1	1	2	....	....	....	....	....	....	....	....	....	10	0	0	0	4	....	....	....	....
	Memphis	CHL	....	....	....	....	....	....	....	....	....	....	....	....	....	....	1	0	0	0	2	....	....	....	....
2002-03	St. John's	AHL	72	2	8	10	72	....	....	....	....	....	....	....	....	....	....	....	....	....	....	....	....	....	....
2003-04	St. John's	AHL	70	4	5	9	141	....	....	....	....	....	....	....	....	....	....	....	....	....	....	....	....	....	....
2004-05	St. John's	AHL	60	0	4	4	108	....	....	....	....	....	....	....	....	....	4	0	1	1	14	....	....	....	....
2005-06	**Toronto**	**NHL**	**8**	**0**	**1**	**1**	**2**	**0**	**0**	**0**	**7**	**0.0**	**5**	**0**	**0.0**	**18:50**	....	....	....	....	....	....	....	....	....
	Toronto Marlies	AHL	57	9	20	29	100	....	....	....	....	....	....	....	....	....	5	1	3	4	8	....	....	....	....
2006-07	**Toronto**	**NHL**	**5**	**0**	**0**	**0**	**6**	**0**	**0**	**0**	**3**	**0.0**	**–5**	**0**	**0.0**	**8:22**	....	....	....	....	....	....	....	....	....
	Toronto Marlies	AHL	41	4	14	18	68	....	....	....	....	....	....	....	....	....	....	....	....	....	....	....	....	....	....
2007-08	Toronto Marlies	AHL	69	13	14	27	73	....	....	....	....	....	....	....	....	....	18	2	10	12	35	....	....	....	....
2008-09	EV Zug	Swiss	41	6	9	15	96	....	....	....	....	....	....	....	....	....	7	1	2	3	33	....	....	....	....
	Toronto	**NHL**	**7**	**0**	**1**	**1**	**10**	**0**	**0**	**0**	**6**	**0.0**	**–2**	**0**	**0.0**	**17:16**	....	....	....	....	....	....	....	....	....
2009-10	**Carolina**	**NHL**	**38**	**1**	**5**	**6**	**50**	**0**	**0**	**0**	**30**	**3.3**	**–8**	**0**	**0.0**	**14:43**	....	....	....	....	....	....	....	....	....
	Albany River Rats	AHL	32	2	12	14	22	....	....	....	....	....	....	....	....	....	8	0	3	3	23	....	....	....	....
	NHL Totals		**58**	**1**	**7**	**8**	**68**	**0**	**0**	**0**	**46**	**2.2**		**0**	**0.0**	**15:03**	....	....	....	....	....	....	....	....	....

OHL All-Rookie Team (1999)

gned as a free agent by **Zug** (Swiss), June 16, 2008. Signed as a free agent by **Toronto**, March 27, 2009. Signed as a free agent by **Carolina**, July 9, 2009.

HARROLD, Peter

(HAIR-ohld, PEE-tuhr) **L.A.**

Defense. Shoots right. 6', 185 lbs. Born, Kirtland Hills, OH, June 8, 1983.

Season	Club	League	GP	G	A	Pts	PIM	PP	SH	GW	S	%	+/-	TF	F%	Min	GP	G	A	Pts	PIM	PP	SH	GW	Min
2003-04	Boston College	H-East	40	2	12	14	12	....	....	....	....	....	....	....	....	....	....	....	....	....	....	....	....	....	....
2004-05	Boston College	H-East	35	4	10	14	22	....	....	....	....	....	....	....	....	....	....	....	....	....	....	....	....	....	....
2005-06	Boston College	H-East	42	7	23	30	32	....	....	....	....	....	....	....	....	....	....	....	....	....	....	....	....	....	....
2006-07	**Los Angeles**	**NHL**	**12**	**0**	**2**	**2**	**8**	**0**	**0**	**0**	**11**	**0.0**	**0**	**1**	**0.0**	**15:12**	....	....	....	....	....	....	....	....	....
	Manchester	AHL	62	7	27	34	43	....	....	....	....	....	....	....	....	....	16	3	8	11	18	....	....	....	....
2007-08	**Los Angeles**	**NHL**	**25**	**2**	**3**	**5**	**2**	**0**	**0**	**0**	**16**	**12.5**	**3**	**2**	**50.0**	**16:23**	....	....	....	....	....	....	....	....	....
	Manchester	AHL	49	7	36	43	25	....	....	....	....	....	....	....	....	....	4	0	1	1	4	....	....	....	....
2008-09	**Los Angeles**	**NHL**	**69**	**4**	**8**	**12**	**28**	**1**	**0**	**1**	**95**	**4.2**	**–13**	**16**	**37.5**	**13:10**	....	....	....	....	....	....	....	....	....
2009-10	**Los Angeles**	**NHL**	**39**	**1**	**2**	**3**	**8**	**0**	**0**	**0**	**23**	**4.3**	**–2**	**14**	**14.3**	**9:15**	**2**	**0**	**0**	**0**	**0**	**0**	**0**	**0**	**11:58**
	NHL Totals		**145**	**7**	**15**	**22**	**46**	**1**	**0**	**1**	**145**	**4.8**		**33**	**27.3**	**12:50**	**2**	**0**	**0**	**0**	**0**	**0**	**0**	**0**	**11:58**

ockey East First All-Star Team (2006) • NCAA East First All-American Team (2006)

gned as a free agent by **Los Angeles**, April 12, 2006. • Missed majority of 2009-10 season as a healthy reserve.

HARTNELL, Scott

(HAHRT-nuhl, SKAWT) **PHI.**

Left wing. Shoots left. 6'2", 210 lbs. Born, Regina, Sask., April 18, 1982. Nashville's 1st choice, 6th overall, in 2000 Entry Draft.

Season	Club	League	GP	G	A	Pts	PIM	PP	SH	GW	S	%	+/-	TF	F%	Min	GP	G	A	Pts	PIM	PP	SH	GW	Min
1997-98	Lloydminster	AJHL	56	9	25	34	82	....	....	....	....	....	....	....	....	....	4	2	1	3	8	....	....	....	....
	Prince Albert	WHL	1	0	1	1	2	....	....	....	....	....	....	....	....	....	....	....	....	....	....	....	....	....	....
1998-99	Prince Albert	WHL	65	10	34	44	104	....	....	....	....	....	....	....	....	....	14	0	5	5	22	....	....	....	....
99-2000	Prince Albert	WHL	62	27	55	82	124	....	....	....	....	....	....	....	....	....	6	3	2	5	6	....	....	....	....
2000-01	**Nashville**	**NHL**	**75**	**2**	**14**	**16**	**48**	**0**	**0**	**0**	**92**	**2.2**	**–8**	**3**	**33.3**	**10:54**	....	....	....	....	....	....	....	....	....
2001-02	**Nashville**	**NHL**	**75**	**14**	**27**	**41**	**111**	**3**	**0**	**4**	**162**	**8.6**	**5**	**12**	**25.0**	**16:58**	....	....	....	....	....	....	....	....	....
2002-03	**Nashville**	**NHL**	**82**	**12**	**22**	**34**	**101**	**2**	**0**	**2**	**221**	**5.4**	**–3**	**23**	**30.4**	**15:17**	....	....	....	....	....	....	....	....	....
2003-04	**Nashville**	**NHL**	**59**	**18**	**15**	**33**	**87**	**5**	**0**	**3**	**154**	**11.7**	**–5**	**48**	**37.5**	**16:16**	**6**	**1**	**2**	**3**	**2**	**0**	**0**	**0**	**15:37**
2004-05	Valerengen	Norway	28	17	12	29	103	....	....	....	....	....	....	....	....	....	11	12	7	19	24	....	....	....	....
2005-06	**Nashville**	**NHL**	**81**	**25**	**23**	**48**	**101**	**10**	**2**	**8**	**211**	**11.8**	**8**	**58**	**37.9**	**16:05**	**5**	**1**	**0**	**1**	**4**	**0**	**0**	**0**	**12:12**
2006-07	**Nashville**	**NHL**	**64**	**22**	**17**	**39**	**96**	**10**	**0**	**2**	**150**	**14.7**	**19**	**134**	**47.0**	**15:43**	**5**	**1**	**1**	**2**	**28**	**1**	**0**	**0**	**14:23**
2007-08	**Philadelphia**	**NHL**	**80**	**24**	**19**	**43**	**159**	**10**	**1**	**6**	**176**	**13.6**	**2**	**32**	**40.6**	**16:11**	**17**	**3**	**4**	**7**	**20**	**0**	**0**	**0**	**15:28**
2008-09	**Philadelphia**	**NHL**	**82**	**30**	**30**	**60**	**143**	**6**	**1**	**5**	**210**	**14.3**	**14**	**36**	**50.0**	**17:48**	**6**	**1**	**1**	**2**	**23**	**1**	**0**	**0**	**18:36**
2009-10	**Philadelphia**	**NHL**	**81**	**14**	**30**	**44**	**155**	**8**	**0**	**4**	**171**	**8.2**	**–6**	**5**	**20.0**	**15:43**	**23**	**8**	**9**	**17**	**25**	**3**	**0**	**0**	**16:14**
	NHL Totals		**679**	**161**	**197**	**358**	**1001**	**54**	**4**	**34**	**1547**	**10.4**		**351**	**41.6**	**15:40**	**62**	**15**	**17**	**32**	**102**	**5**	**0**	**0**	**15:43**

gned as a free agent by **Oslo** (Norway), October 21, 2004. Traded to **Philadelphia** by **Nashville** with Kimmo Timmonen for Nashville's 1st round choice (previously acquired, Nashville selected Jonathon
um) in 2007 Entry Draft, June 18, 2007.

HAVELID, Niclas
(HAHV-lihd, NIHK-luhs)

Defense. Shoots left. 6', 200 lbs. Born, Stockholm, Sweden, April 12, 1973. Anaheim's 2nd choice, 83rd overall, in 1999 Entry Draft.

			Regular Season														Playoffs								
Season	Club	League	GP	G	A	Pts	PIM	PP	SH	GW	S	%	+/-	TF	F%	Min	GP	G	A	Pts	PIM	PP	SH	GW	Min
1988-89	Enkopings SK	Sweden-3	7	0	1	1	0																		
1989-90	Enkopings SK	Sweden-3	24	1	2	3	28																		
1990-91	Arlanda	Sweden-2	30	2	3	5	22																		
1991-92	AIK Solna	Sweden	10	0	0	0	2																		
1992-93	AIK Solna	Sweden	30	1	2	3	22										3	0	0	0	2				
1993-94	AIK Solna	Sweden-2	22	3	9	12	14																		
1994-95	AIK Solna	Sweden	40	3	7	10	38																		
1995-96	AIK Solna	Sweden	40	5	6	11	30																		
1996-97	AIK Solna	Sweden	49	3	6	9	42										7	1	2	3	8				
1997-98	AIK Solna	Sweden	43	8	4	12	42										10	1	3	4	39				
1998-99	Malmo	Sweden	50	10	12	22	42										8	0	4	4	10				
99-2000	**Anaheim**	**NHL**	**50**	**2**	**7**	**9**	**20**	**0**	**0**	**2**	**70**	**2.9**	**0**	**1**	**0.0**	**19:10**									
	Cincinnati	AHL	2	0	0	0	0																		
2000-01	**Anaheim**	**NHL**	**47**	**4**	**10**	**14**	**34**	**2**	**0**	**1**	**69**	**5.8**	**–6**	**4**	**0.0**	**21:51**									
2001-02	**Anaheim**	**NHL**	**52**	**1**	**2**	**3**	**40**	**0**	**0**	**0**	**45**	**2.2**	**–13**	**1**	**0.0**	**17:01**									
2002-03	**Anaheim**	**NHL**	**82**	**11**	**22**	**33**	**30**	**4**	**0**	**5**	**169**	**6.5**	**5**	**3**	**0.0**	**22:30**	**21**	**0**	**4**	**4**	**2**	**0**	**0**	**0**	**25:41**
2003-04	**Anaheim**	**NHL**	**79**	**6**	**20**	**26**	**28**	**5**	**0**	**3**	**122**	**4.9**	**–28**	**0**	**0.0**	**22:39**									
2004-05	Sodertalje SK	Sweden	46	2	2	4	60										10	1	1	2	18				
2005-06	**Atlanta**	**NHL**	**82**	**4**	**28**	**32**	**48**	**2**	**0**	**0**	**84**	**4.8**	**9**	**0**	**0.0**	**24:25**									
	Sweden	Olympics	7	0	0	0	4																		
2006-07	**Atlanta**	**NHL**	**77**	**3**	**18**	**21**	**52**	**1**	**0**	**1**	**82**	**3.7**	**–2**	**1**	**0.0**	**25:16**	**4**	**0**	**2**	**2**	**0**	**0**	**0**	**0**	**24:14**
2007-08	**Atlanta**	**NHL**	**81**	**1**	**13**	**14**	**42**	**0**	**0**	**0**	**54**	**1.9**	**2**	**0**	**0.0**	**20:30**									
2008-09	**Atlanta**	**NHL**	**63**	**2**	**13**	**15**	**42**	**0**	**1**	**0**	**41**	**4.9**	**4**	**0**	**0.0**	**20:54**									
	New Jersey	**NHL**	**15**	**0**	**4**	**4**	**6**	**0**	**0**	**0**	**15**	**0.0**	**–2**	**0**	**0.0**	**19:43**	**7**	**0**	**1**	**1**	**2**	**0**	**0**	**0**	**17:31**
2009-10	Linkopings HC	Sweden	53	3	10	13	28										12	0	5	5	18				
	NHL Totals		**628**	**34**	**137**	**171**	**342**	**14**	**1**	**12**	**751**	**4.5**		**10**	**0.0**	**21:51**	**32**	**0**	**7**	**7**	**4**	**0**	**0**	**0**	**23:43**

Traded to **Atlanta** by **Anaheim** for Kurtis Foster, June 26, 2004. Signed as a free agent by **Sodertalje** (Sweden), August 9, 2004. Traded to **New Jersey** by **Atlanta** with Myles Stoesz for Anssi Salmela, March 1, 2009. Signed as a free agent by **Linkopings** (Sweden), May 15, 2009.

HAVLAT, Martin
(HAV-lat, MAHR-tihn) **MIN.**

Right wing. Shoots left. 6'2", 217 lbs. Born, Mlada Boleslav, Czech., April 19, 1981. Ottawa's 1st choice, 26th overall, in 1999 Entry Draft.

			Regular Season														Playoffs								
Season	Club	League	GP	G	A	Pts	PIM	PP	SH	GW	S	%	+/-	TF	F%	Min	GP	G	A	Pts	PIM	PP	SH	GW	Min
1997-98	Ytong Brno Jr.	CzRep-Jr.	32	38	29	67	....																		
1998-99	HC Trinec Jr.	CzRep-Jr.	31	28	23	51	....																		
	Trinec	CzRep	24	2	3	5	4										8	0	0	0	....				
99-2000	HC Ocelari Trinec	CzRep	46	13	29	42	42										4	0	2	2	8				
2000-01	**Ottawa**	**NHL**	**73**	**19**	**23**	**42**	**20**	**7**	**0**	**5**	**133**	**14.3**	**8**	**40**	**30.0**	**13:47**	**4**	**0**	**0**	**0**	**2**	**0**	**0**	**0**	**14:04**
2001-02	**Ottawa**	**NHL**	**72**	**22**	**28**	**50**	**66**	**9**	**0**	**6**	**145**	**15.2**	**–7**	**15**	**40.0**	**14:46**	**12**	**2**	**5**	**7**	**14**	**2**	**0**	**2**	**16:19**
	Czech Republic	Olympics	4	3	1	4	27																		
2002-03	**Ottawa**	**NHL**	**67**	**24**	**35**	**59**	**30**	**9**	**0**	**4**	**179**	**13.4**	**20**	**7**	**14.3**	**16:27**	**18**	**5**	**6**	**11**	**14**	**1**	**0**	**2**	**16:27**
2003-04	HC Sparta Praha	CzRep	5	1	3	4	8																		
	Ottawa	**NHL**	**68**	**31**	**37**	**68**	**46**	**13**	**0**	**7**	**175**	**17.7**	**12**	**11**	**36.4**	**16:44**	**7**	**0**	**3**	**3**	**2**	**0**	**0**	**0**	**16:10**
2004-05	Znojmo	CzRep	12	10	4	14	16																		
	Dynamo Moscow	Russia	10	2	0	2	14																		
	HC Sparta Praha	CzRep	9	5	4	9	37										5	0	0	0	20				
2005-06	**Ottawa**	**NHL**	**18**	**9**	**7**	**16**	**4**	**2**	**1**	**1**	**57**	**15.8**	**6**	**25**	**36.0**	**18:11**	**10**	**7**	**6**	**13**	**4**	**3**	**0**	**1**	**17:13**
2006-07	**Chicago**	**NHL**	**56**	**25**	**32**	**57**	**28**	**5**	**0**	**1**	**176**	**14.2**	**15**	**12**	**33.3**	**21:24**									
2007-08	**Chicago**	**NHL**	**35**	**10**	**17**	**27**	**22**	**3**	**0**	**2**	**87**	**11.5**	**4**	**3**	**0.0**	**18:35**									
2008-09	**Chicago**	**NHL**	**81**	**29**	**48**	**77**	**30**	**5**	**0**	**5**	**249**	**11.6**	**29**	**8**	**25.0**	**17:25**	**16**	**5**	**10**	**15**	**8**	**0**	**0**	**1**	**15:34**
2009-10	**Minnesota**	**NHL**	**73**	**18**	**36**	**54**	**34**	**4**	**0**	**3**	**169**	**10.7**	**–19**	**12**	**50.0**	**17:56**									
	Czech Republic	Olympics	5	0	2	2	0																		
	NHL Totals		**543**	**187**	**263**	**450**	**280**	**57**	**1**	**34**	**1370**	**13.6**		**133**	**33.1**	**16:57**	**67**	**19**	**30**	**49**	**44**	**6**	**0**	**6**	**16:10**

NHL All-Rookie Team (2001)

Played in NHL All-Star Game (2007)

Signed as a free agent by **Znojmo** (CzRep), September 24, 2004. Signed as a free agent by **Dynamo Moscow** (Russia), November 10, 2004. Signed as a free agent by **Sparta Praha** (CzRep), January 31, 2005. • Missed majority of 2005-06 season recovering from shoulder injury suffered in game vs. Montreal, November 29, 2005. Traded to **Chicago** by **Ottawa** with Bryan Smolinski for Tom Preissing, Josh Hennessy, Michal Barinka and Chicago's 2nd round choice (Patrick Wiercioch) in 2008 Entry Draft, July 10, 2006. • Missed majority of 2007-08 season recovering from shoulder (October 4, 2007 at Minnesota) and groin (December 22, 2007 at Ottawa) injuries. Signed as a free agent by **Minnesota**, July 1, 2009.

HAYDAR, Darren
(HAY-duhr, DAIR-ehn)

Right wing. Shoots right. 5'9", 170 lbs. Born, Toronto, Ont., October 22, 1979. Nashville's 15th choice, 248th overall, in 1999 Entry Draft.

			Regular Season														Playoffs								
Season	Club	League	GP	G	A	Pts	PIM	PP	SH	GW	S	%	+/-	TF	F%	Min	GP	G	A	Pts	PIM	PP	SH	GW	Min
1995-96	Milton Merchants	OPJHL	6	1	2	3	4																		
1996-97	Milton Merchants	OPJHL	51	32	68	100	68																		
1997-98	Milton Merchants	OPJHL	51	*71	*69	*140	65																		
1998-99	New Hampshire	H-East	41	31	30	61	34																		
99-2000	New Hampshire	H-East	38	22	19	41	42																		
2000-01	New Hampshire	H-East	39	18	23	41	38																		
2001-02	New Hampshire	H-East	40	31	*45	*76	28																		
2002-03	**Nashville**	**NHL**	**2**	**0**	**0**	**0**	**0**	**0**	**0**	**0**	**1**	**0.0**	**–1**	**0**	**0.0**	**8:54**									
	Milwaukee	AHL	75	29	46	75	36										6	1	4	5	2				
2003-04	Milwaukee	AHL	79	22	37	59	35										22	*11	15	*26	10				
2004-05	Milwaukee	AHL	59	24	26	50	42										7	3	4	7	14				
2005-06	Milwaukee	AHL	80	35	57	92	50										21	*18	17	*35	18				
2006-07	**Atlanta**	**NHL**	**4**	**0**	**0**	**0**	**0**	**0**	**0**	**0**	**4**	**0.0**	**0**	**3**	**66.7**	**8:01**									
	Chicago Wolves	AHL	73	41	*81	*122	55										15	*10	*14	*24	14				
2007-08	**Atlanta**	**NHL**	**16**	**1**	**7**	**8**	**2**	**0**	**0**	**0**	**14**	**7.1**	**4**	**2**	**0.0**	**11:46**									
	Chicago Wolves	AHL	51	19	39	58	52										24	*12	15	27	8				
2008-09	Grand Rapids	AHL	79	31	49	80	26										10	4	7	11	4				
2009-10	**Colorado**	**NHL**	**1**	**0**	**0**	**0**	**0**	**0**	**0**	**0**	**2**	**0.0**	**0**	**0**	**0.0**	**5:22**									
	Lake Erie	AHL	66	23	41	64	60																		
	NHL Totals		**23**	**1**	**7**	**8**	**2**	**0**	**0**	**0**	**21**	**4.8**		**5**	**40.0**	**10:35**									

Hockey East Second All-Star Team (1999, 2000) • Hockey East Rookie of the Year (1999) • Hockey East First All-Star Team (2002) • Hockey East Player of the Year (2002) • AHL All-Rookie Team (2003) • Dudley "Red" Garrett Memorial Award (AHL – Rookie of the Year) (2003) • AHL First All-Star Team (2007) • John P. Sollenberger Trophy (AHL - Top Scorer) (2007) • Les Cunningham Award (AHL - MVP) (2007) • AHL Second All-Star Team (2009)

Signed as a free agent by **Atlanta**, July 4, 2006. Signed as a free agent by **Detroit**, July 23, 2008. Signed as a free agent by **Colorado**, July 6, 2009.

HEATLEY, Dany
(HEET-lee, DA-nee) **S.J.**

Left wing. Shoots left. 6'4", 220 lbs. Born, Freiburg, West Germany, January 21, 1981. Atlanta's 1st choice, 2nd overall, in 2000 Entry Draft.

			Regular Season														Playoffs								
Season	Club	League	GP	G	A	Pts	PIM	PP	SH	GW	S	%	+/-	TF	F%	Min	GP	G	A	Pts	PIM	PP	SH	GW	Min
1996-97	Calgary Blazers	AMHL	25	30	42	72	26																		
1997-98	Calgary Buffaloes	AMHL	36	39	42	*81	34										10	10	12	*22	30				
1998-99	Calgary Canucks	AJHL	60	*70	56	*126	91										13	*22	13	*35	6				
99-2000	U. of Wisconsin	WCHA	38	28	28	56	32																		
2000-01	U. of Wisconsin	WCHA	39	24	33	57	74																		
2001-02	**Atlanta**	**NHL**	**82**	**26**	**41**	**67**	**56**	**7**	**0**	**4**	**202**	**12.9**	**–19**	**116**	**32.8**	**19:53**									
2002-03	**Atlanta**	**NHL**	**77**	**41**	**48**	**89**	**58**	**19**	**1**	**6**	**252**	**16.3**	**–8**	**49**	**36.7**	**21:57**									
2003-04	**Atlanta**	**NHL**	**31**	**13**	**12**	**25**	**18**	**5**	**0**	**3**	**83**	**15.7**	**–8**	**41**	**24.4**	**19:53**									
2004-05	SC Bern	Swiss	16	14	10	24	58																		
	Ak Bars Kazan	Russia	11	3	1	4	22										4	2	1	3	4				
2005-06	**Ottawa**	**NHL**	**82**	**50**	**53**	**103**	**86**	**23**	**2**	**7**	**300**	**16.7**	**29**	**166**	**53.6**	**21:09**	**10**	**3**	**9**	**12**	**11**	**3**	**0**	**1**	**18:56**
	Canada	Olympics	6	2	1	3	8																		
2006-07	**Ottawa**	**NHL**	**82**	**50**	**55**	**105**	**74**	**17**	**3**	***10**	**310**	**16.1**	**31**	**60**	**38.3**	**21:02**	**20**	**7**	***15**	***22**	**14**	**2**	**0**	**2**	**21:18**
2007-08	**Ottawa**	**NHL**	**71**	**41**	**41**	**82**	**76**	**13**	**0**	**8**	**224**	**18.3**	**33**	**26**	**57.7**	**21:44**	**4**	**0**	**1**	**1**	**6**	**0**	**0**	**0**	**21:41**
2008-09	**Ottawa**	**NHL**	**82**	**39**	**33**	**72**	**88**	**15**	**0**	**6**	**258**	**15.1**	**–11**	**30**	**46.7**	**20:07**									

			Regular Season														Playoffs								
Season	Club	League	GP	G	A	Pts	PIM	PP	SH	GW	S	%	+/-	TF	F%	Min	GP	G	A	Pts	PIM	PP	SH	GW	Min
2009-10	**San Jose**	**NHL**	**82**	**39**	**43**	**82**	**54**	**18**	**1**	**9**	**280**	**13.9**	**14**	**35**	**40.0**	**20:14**	**14**	**2**	**11**	**13**	**16**	**1**	**0**	**0**	**20:41**
	Canada	Olympics	7	4	3	7	4	....	....	....	....	....	....	....	....	....	....	....	....	....	....	....	....	....	....
	NHL Totals		**589**	**299**	**326**	**625**	**510**	**117**	**7**	**53**	**1909**	**15.7**		**523**	**42.3**	**20:48**	**48**	**12**	**36**	**48**	**47**	**6**	**0**	**3**	**20:40**

WCHA First All-Star Team (2000) • WCHA Rookie of the Year (2000) • NCAA West Second All-American Team (2000) • WCHA Second All-Star Team (2001) • NCAA West First All-American Team (2001) • NHL All-Rookie Team (2002) • Calder Memorial Trophy (2002) • NHL Second All-Star Team (2006) • NHL First All-Star Team (2007)

Played in NHL All-Star Game (2003, 2007, 2009)

• Missed majority of 2003-04 season recovering from injuries suffered in automobile accident, September 29, 2003. Signed as a free agent by **Bern** (Swiss), October 13, 2004. Signed as a free agent by **Kazan** (Russia), February 9, 2005. Traded to **Ottawa** by **Atlanta** for Marian Hossa and Greg de Vries, August 23, 2005. Traded to **San Jose** by **Ottawa** with Ottawa's 5th round choice (Isaac MacLeod) in 2010 Entry Draft for Milan Michalek, Jonathan Cheechoo and San Jose's 2nd round choice (later traded to NY Islanders, later traded to Chicago - Chicago selected Kent Simpson) in 2010 Entry Draft, September 12, 2009.

HECHT, Jochen

(HEHSHT, YOH-khehn) **BUF.**

Left wing. Shoots left. 6'1", 196 lbs. Born, Mannheim, West Germany, June 21, 1977. St. Louis' 1st choice, 49th overall, in 1995 Entry Draft.

1993-94	Mannheim Jr.	Ger-Jr.	28	27	13	40	103	....	....	....	....	....	....	....	....	....	....	....	....	....	....	....	....	....	....
1994-95	Adler Mannheim	Germany	43	11	12	23	68	....	....	....	....	....	....	....	....	....	10	5	4	9	12	....	....	....	....
1995-96	Adler Mannheim	Germany	44	12	16	28	68	....	....	....	....	....	....	....	....	....	8	3	2	5	6	....	....	....	....
1996-97	Adler Mannheim	Germany	46	21	21	42	36	....	....	....	....	....	....	....	....	....	9	3	3	6	4	....	....	....	....
1997-98	Adler Mannheim	Germany	44	7	19	26	42	....	....	....	....	....	....	....	....	....	10	1	1	2	14	....	....	....	....
	Adler Mannheim	EuroHL	5	0	4	4	8	....	....	....	....	....	....	....	....	....	....	....	....	....	....	....	....	....	....
	Germany	Olympics	4	1	0	1	6	....	....	....	....	....	....	....	....	....	....	....	....	....	....	....	....	....	....
1998-99	**St. Louis**	**NHL**	**3**	**0**	**0**	**0**	**0**	**0**	**0**	**0**	**4**	**0.0**	**–2**	**19**	**21.1**	**13:16**	**5**	**2**	**0**	**2**	**0**	**0**	**0**	**0**	**16:40**
	Worcester IceCats	AHL	74	21	35	56	48	....	....	....	....	....	....	....	....	....	4	1	1	2	2	....	....	....	....
99-2000	**St. Louis**	**NHL**	**63**	**13**	**21**	**34**	**28**	**5**	**0**	**1**	**140**	**9.3**	**20**	**75**	**49.3**	**15:25**	**7**	**4**	**6**	**10**	**2**	**1**	**0**	**1**	**17:02**
2000-01	**St. Louis**	**NHL**	**72**	**19**	**25**	**44**	**48**	**8**	**3**	**1**	**208**	**9.1**	**11**	**160**	**43.8**	**17:56**	**15**	**2**	**4**	**6**	**4**	**0**	**0**	**0**	**17:19**
2001-02	**Edmonton**	**NHL**	**82**	**16**	**24**	**40**	**60**	**5**	**0**	**3**	**211**	**7.6**	**4**	**26**	**53.9**	**15:00**	....	....	....	....	....	....	....	....	....
	Germany	Olympics	4	1	1	2	2	....	....	....	....	....	....	....	....	....	....	....	....	....	....	....	....	....	....
2002-03	**Buffalo**	**NHL**	**49**	**10**	**16**	**26**	**30**	**2**	**0**	**2**	**145**	**6.9**	**4**	**33**	**30.3**	**17:55**	....	....	....	....	....	....	....	....	....
2003-04	**Buffalo**	**NHL**	**64**	**15**	**37**	**52**	**49**	**2**	**1**	**0**	**174**	**8.6**	**17**	**141**	**43.3**	**19:00**	....	....	....	....	....	....	....	....	....
2004-05	Adler Mannheim	Germany	48	16	34	50	151	....	....	....	....	....	....	....	....	....	14	10	10	*20	14	....	....	....	....
2005-06	**Buffalo**	**NHL**	**64**	**18**	**24**	**42**	**34**	**4**	**2**	**4**	**179**	**10.1**	**10**	**156**	**39.7**	**18:07**	**15**	**2**	**6**	**8**	**8**	**0**	**0**	**1**	**17:29**
2006-07	**Buffalo**	**NHL**	**76**	**19**	**37**	**56**	**39**	**3**	**0**	**1**	**197**	**9.6**	**19**	**145**	**39.3**	**18:51**	**16**	**4**	**1**	**5**	**10**	**0**	**0**	**1**	**17:41**
2007-08	**Buffalo**	**NHL**	**75**	**22**	**27**	**49**	**38**	**3**	**1**	**2**	**229**	**9.6**	**1**	**905**	**42.0**	**19:19**	....	....	....	....	....	....	....	....	....
2008-09	**Buffalo**	**NHL**	**70**	**12**	**15**	**27**	**33**	**3**	**1**	**1**	**173**	**6.9**	**–9**	**538**	**43.7**	**17:24**	....	....	....	....	....	....	....	....	....
2009-10	**Buffalo**	**NHL**	**79**	**21**	**21**	**42**	**35**	**3**	**0**	**2**	**224**	**9.4**	**14**	**322**	**45.3**	**17:11**	....	....	....	....	....	....	....	....	....
	Germany	Olympics	4	0	1	1	2	....	....	....	....	....	....	....	....	....	....	....	....	....	....	....	....	....	....
	NHL Totals		**697**	**165**	**247**	**412**	**394**	**38**	**8**	**17**	**1884**	**8.8**		**2520**	**42.7**	**17:34**	**58**	**14**	**17**	**31**	**24**	**1**	**0**	**3**	**17:22**

Traded to **Edmonton** by **St. Louis** with Marty Reasoner and Jan Horacek for Doug Weight and Michel Riesen, July 1, 2001. Traded to **Buffalo** by **Edmonton** for Atlanta's 2nd round choice (previously acquired, Edmonton selected Jeff Deslauriers) in 2002 Entry Draft and Nashville's 2nd round choice (previously acquired, Edmonton selected Jarret Stoll) in 2002 Entry Draft, June 22, 2002. Signed as a free agent by **Mannheim** (Germany), August 2, 2004.

HEDMAN, Victor

(HEHD-muhn, VIHK-tohr) **T.B.**

Defense. Shoots left. 6'6", 230 lbs. Born, Ornskoldsvik, Sweden, December 18, 1990. Tampa Bay's 1st choice, 2nd overall, in 2009 Entry Draft.

2005-06	MODO U18	Swe-U18	8	3	3	6	14	....	....	....	....	....	....	....	....	....	2	0	0	0	0	....	....	....	....
	MODO Jr.	Swe-Jr.	10	0	1	1	8	....	....	....	....	....	....	....	....	....	....	....	....	....	....	....	....	....	....
2006-07	MODO U18	Swe-U18	3	3	0	3	29	....	....	....	....	....	....	....	....	....	....	....	....	....	....	....	....	....	....
	MODO Jr.	Swe-Jr.	34	13	12	25	30	....	....	....	....	....	....	....	....	....	5	1	1	2	44	....	....	....	....
2007-08	MODO Jr.	Swe-Jr.	6	2	1	3	26	....	....	....	....	....	....	....	....	....	3	2	0	2	4	....	....	....	....
	MODO	Sweden	39	2	2	4	44	....	....	....	....	....	....	....	....	....	5	1	0	1	4	....	....	....	....
2008-09	MODO Jr.	Swe-Jr.	2	0	2	2	10	....	....	....	....	....	....	....	....	....	5	0	1	1	2	....	....	....	....
	MODO	Sweden	43	7	14	21	52	....	....	....	....	....	....	....	....	....	....	....	....	....	....	....	....	....	....
2009-10	**Tampa Bay**	**NHL**	**74**	**4**	**16**	**20**	**79**	**0**	**0**	**0**	**90**	**4.4**	**–3**	**0**	**0.0**	**20:51**	....	....	....	....	....	....	....	....	....
	NHL Totals		**74**	**4**	**16**	**20**	**79**	**0**	**0**	**0**	**90**	**4.4**		**0**	**0.0**	**20:51**	....	....	....	....	....	....	....	....	....

HEIKKINEN, Ilkka

(HAY-kih-nehn, IHL-ka) **NYR**

Defense. Shoots left. 6'2", 205 lbs. Born, Rauma, Finland, November 13, 1984.

2004-05	Lukko Rauma	Finland	48	0	2	2	8	....	....	....	....	....	....	....	....	....	9	0	0	0	0	....	....	....	....
2005-06	Lukko Rauma	Finland	55	5	10	15	46	....	....	....	....	....	....	....	....	....	....	....	....	....	....	....	....	....	....
2006-07	Lukko Rauma	Finland	55	7	17	24	71	....	....	....	....	....	....	....	....	....	3	0	0	0	0	....	....	....	....
2007-08	HIFK Helsinki	Finland	51	11	26	37	96	....	....	....	....	....	....	....	....	....	7	0	2	2	6	....	....	....	....
2008-09	HIFK Helsinki	Finland	54	8	26	34	22	....	....	....	....	....	....	....	....	....	2	0	1	1	0	....	....	....	....
2009-10	**NY Rangers**	**NHL**	**7**	**0**	**0**	**0**	**0**	**0**	**0**	**0**	**4**	**0.0**	**2**	**0**	**0.0**	**8:52**	....	....	....	....	....	....	....	....	....
	Hartford	AHL	72	8	30	38	27	....	....	....	....	....	....	....	....	....	....	....	....	....	....	....	....	....	....
	NHL Totals		**7**	**0**	**0**	**0**	**0**	**0**	**0**	**0**	**4**	**0.0**		**0**	**0.0**	**8:52**	....	....	....	....	....	....	....	....	....

Signed as a free agent by **NY Rangers**, May 20, 2009. Signed as a free agent by **Novosibirsk** (Russia-KHL), May 21, 2010.

HEJDA, Jan

(HAY-dah, YAHN) **CBJ**

Defense. Shoots left. 6'3", 229 lbs. Born, Prague, Czech., June 18, 1978. Buffalo's 4th choice, 106th overall, in 2003 Entry Draft.

1997-98	HC Slavia Praha	CzRep	44	2	5	7	51	....	....	....	....	....	....	....	....	....	5	0	0	0	6	....	....	....	....
1998-99	HC Slavia Praha	CzRep	34	1	2	3	38	....	....	....	....	....	....	....	....	....	....	....	....	....	....	....	....	....	....
99-2000	HC Slavia Praha	CzRep	26	1	2	3	14	....	....	....	....	....	....	....	....	....	....	....	....	....	....	....	....	....	....
	HC Femax Havirov	CzRep	7	0	2	2	6	....	....	....	....	....	....	....	....	....	....	....	....	....	....	....	....	....	....
	Liberec	CzRep-2	1	0	0	0	4	....	....	....	....	....	....	....	....	....	....	....	....	....	....	....	....	....	....
2000-01	HC Slavia Praha	CzRep	38	2	6	8	70	....	....	....	....	....	....	....	....	....	11	3	0	3	12	....	....	....	....
	SK Kadan	CzRep-2	8	1	0	1	6	....	....	....	....	....	....	....	....	....	....	....	....	....	....	....	....	....	....
2001-02	HC Slavia Praha	CzRep	42	9	8	17	52	....	....	....	....	....	....	....	....	....	9	1	1	2	14	....	....	....	....
2002-03	HC Slavia Praha	CzRep	52	6	11	17	44	....	....	....	....	....	....	....	....	....	17	5	8	13	12	....	....	....	....
2003-04	CSKA Moscow	Russia	60	1	5	6	26	....	....	....	....	....	....	....	....	....	....	....	....	....	....	....	....	....	....
2004-05	CSKA Moscow	Russia	60	2	11	13	59	....	....	....	....	....	....	....	....	....	....	....	....	....	....	....	....	....	....
2005-06	Mytischi	Russia	50	3	12	15	56	....	....	....	....	....	....	....	....	....	9	2	3	5	24	....	....	....	....
2006-07	**Edmonton**	**NHL**	**39**	**1**	**8**	**9**	**20**	**0**	**0**	**1**	**33**	**3.0**	**–6**	**0**	**0.0**	**20:23**	....	....	....	....	....	....	....	....	....
	Hamilton	AHL	5	0	3	3	21	....	....	....	....	....	....	....	....	....	....	....	....	....	....	....	....	....	....
2007-08	**Columbus**	**NHL**	**81**	**0**	**13**	**13**	**61**	**0**	**0**	**0**	**71**	**0.0**	**20**	**0**	**0.0**	**21:08**	....	....	....	....	....	....	....	....	....
2008-09	**Columbus**	**NHL**	**82**	**3**	**18**	**21**	**38**	**0**	**0**	**1**	**66**	**4.5**	**23**	**1**	**0.0**	**22:23**	**3**	**0**	**0**	**0**	**2**	**0**	**0**	**0**	**16:53**
2009-10	**Columbus**	**NHL**	**62**	**3**	**10**	**13**	**36**	**1**	**0**	**0**	**63**	**4.8**	**–14**	**2**	**50.0**	**20:39**	....	....	....	....	....	....	....	....	....
	Czech Republic	Olympics	5	0	0	0	4	....	....	....	....	....	....	....	....	....	....	....	....	....	....	....	....	....	....
	NHL Totals		**264**	**7**	**49**	**56**	**155**	**1**	**0**	**2**	**233**	**3.0**		**3**	**33.3**	**21:18**	**3**	**0**	**0**	**0**	**2**	**0**	**0**	**0**	**16:53**

Rights traded to **Edmonton** by **Buffalo** for Edmonton's 7th round choice (Nick Eno) in 2007 Entry Draft, July 10, 2006. Signed as a free agent by **Columbus**, July 5, 2007.

HEJDUK, Milan

(HAY-dook, MEE-lan) **COL.**

Right wing. Shoots right. 6', 190 lbs. Born, Usti nad Labem, Czech., February 14, 1976. Quebec's 6th choice, 87th overall, in 1994 Entry Draft.

1993-94	HC Pardubice	CzRep	22	6	3	9	....	....	....	....	....	....	....	....	....	....	10	5	1	6	....	....	....	....	....
1994-95	HC Pardubice	CzRep	43	11	13	24	6	....	....	....	....	....	....	....	....	....	6	3	1	4	0	....	....	....	....
1995-96	Pardubice	CzRep	37	13	7	20	....	....	....	....	....	....	....	....	....	....	....	....	....	....	....	....	....	....	....
1996-97	Pardubice	CzRep	51	27	11	38	10	....	....	....	....	....	....	....	....	....	10	6	0	6	27	....	....	....	....
1997-98	Pardubice	CzRep	48	26	19	45	20	....	....	....	....	....	....	....	....	....	3	0	0	0	2	....	....	....	....
	Czech Republic	Olympics	4	0	0	0	2	....	....	....	....	....	....	....	....	....	....	....	....	....	....	....	....	....	....
1998-99	**Colorado**	**NHL**	**82**	**14**	**34**	**48**	**26**	**4**	**0**	**5**	**178**	**7.9**	**8**	**2**	**50.0**	**15:45**	**16**	**6**	**6**	**12**	**4**	**1**	**0**	**3**	**15:53**
99-2000	**Colorado**	**NHL**	**82**	**36**	**36**	**72**	**16**	**13**	**0**	**9**	**228**	**15.8**	**14**	**3**	**100.0**	**19:58**	**17**	**5**	**4**	**9**	**6**	**3**	**0**	**1**	**19:56**
2000-01 ♦	**Colorado**	**NHL**	**80**	**41**	**38**	**79**	**36**	**12**	**1**	**9**	**213**	**19.2**	**32**	**3**	**33.3**	**19:52**	**23**	**7**	***16**	**23**	**6**	**4**	**0**	**1**	**21:33**
2001-02	**Colorado**	**NHL**	**62**	**21**	**23**	**44**	**24**	**7**	**1**	**5**	**139**	**15.1**	**0**	**5**	**40.0**	**20:11**	**16**	**3**	**3**	**6**	**4**	**1**	**0**	**0**	**18:24**
	Czech Republic	Olympics	4	1	0	1	0	....	....	....	....	....	....	....	....	....	....	....	....	....	....	....	....	....	....
2002-03	**Colorado**	**NHL**	**82**	***50**	**48**	**98**	**32**	**18**	**0**	**4**	**244**	**20.5**	***52**	**43**	**44.2**	**19:50**	**7**	**2**	**2**	**4**	**2**	**1**	**0**	**0**	**20:42**
2003-04	**Colorado**	**NHL**	**82**	**35**	**40**	**75**	**20**	**16**	**0**	**6**	**237**	**14.8**	**19**	**69**	**47.8**	**18:46**	**11**	**5**	**2**	**7**	**0**	**2**	**0**	**0**	**18:40**
2004-05	Pardubice	CzRep	48	25	26	51	14	....	....	....	....	....	....	....	....	....	16	6	2	8	6	....	....	....	....

			Regular Season														Playoffs								
Season	Club	League	GP	G	A	Pts	PIM	PP	SH	GW	S	%	+/-	TF	F%	Min	GP	G	A	Pts	PIM	PP	SH	GW	Min
2005-06	**Colorado**	**NHL**	**74**	**24**	**34**	**58**	**24**	**14**	**1**	**2**	**221**	**10.9**	**13**	**23**	**17.4**	**18:33**	**9**	**2**	**6**	**8**	**2**	**0**	**0**	**0**	**20:56**
	Czech Republic	Olympics	8	2	1	3	2	....	....	....	....	....	....	....	....	....	....	....	....	....	....	....	....	....	....
2006-07	**Colorado**	**NHL**	**80**	**35**	**35**	**70**	**44**	**12**	**1**	**6**	**257**	**13.6**	**10**	**109**	**45.0**	**17:53**	....	....	....	....	....	....	....	....	....
2007-08	**Colorado**	**NHL**	**77**	**29**	**25**	**54**	**36**	**8**	**1**	**4**	**205**	**14.1**	**8**	**136**	**39.7**	**19:21**	**10**	**3**	**3**	**6**	**4**	**2**	**0**	**0**	**19:05**
2008-09	**Colorado**	**NHL**	**82**	**27**	**32**	**59**	**16**	**10**	**1**	**2**	**211**	**12.8**	**–19**	**160**	**45.0**	**19:56**	....	....	....	....	....	....	....	....	....
2009-10	**Colorado**	**NHL**	**56**	**23**	**21**	**44**	**10**	**8**	**0**	**4**	**153**	**15.0**	**6**	**14**	**28.6**	**19:01**	**3**	**1**	**0**	**1**	**0**	**0**	**0**	**0**	**12:58**
	NHL Totals		**839**	**335**	**366**	**701**	**284**	**122**	**6**	**56**	**2286**	**14.7**		**567**	**42.7**	**18:59**	**112**	**34**	**42**	**76**	**28**	**14**	**0**	**5**	**19:13**

NHL All-Rookie Team (1999) • NHL Second All-Star Team (2003) • Bud Light Plus/Minus Award (2003) (tied with Peter Forsberg) • Maurice "Rocket" Richard Trophy (2003)
Played in NHL All-Star Game (2000, 2001, 2009)

• Rights transferred to **Colorado** after **Quebec** franchise relocated, June 21, 1995. Signed as a free agent by **Pardubice** (CzRep), September 18, 2004.

HELM, Darren

(HEHLM, DAIR-ehn) **DET.**

Center/Left wing. Shoots left. 5'11", 195 lbs. Born, Winnipeg, Man., January 21, 1987. Detroit's 5th choice, 132nd overall, in 2005 Entry Draft.

2003-04	Selkirk Fishermen	MJBHL	34	39	32	71	34	....	....	....	....	....	....	....	....	....	....	....	....	....	....	....	....	....	....
2004-05	Medicine Hat	WHL	72	10	14	24	27	....	....	....	....	....	....	....	....	....	13	2	6	8	10	....	....	....	....
2005-06	Medicine Hat	WHL	70	41	38	79	37	....	....	....	....	....	....	....	....	....	13	5	4	9	2	....	....	....	....
2006-07	Medicine Hat	WHL	59	25	39	64	53	....	....	....	....	....	....	....	....	....	23	10	12	22	14	....	....	....	....
2007-08♦	**Detroit**	**NHL**	**7**	**0**	**0**	**0**	**2**	**0**	**0**	**0**	**7**	**0.0**	**–2**	**23**	**21.7**	**7:00**	**18**	**2**	**2**	**4**	**2**	**0**	**0**	**0**	**7:30**
	Grand Rapids	AHL	67	16	15	31	30	....	....	....	....	....	....	....	....	....	....	....	....	....	....	....	....	....	....
2008-09	**Detroit**	**NHL**	**16**	**0**	**1**	**1**	**4**	**0**	**0**	**0**	**29**	**0.0**	**–7**	**132**	**56.1**	**12:26**	**23**	**4**	**1**	**5**	**4**	**0**	**0**	**1**	**12:06**
	Grand Rapids	AHL	55	13	24	37	24	....	....	....	....	....	....	....	....	....	....	....	....	....	....	....	....	....	....
2009-10	**Detroit**	**NHL**	**75**	**11**	**13**	**24**	**18**	**0**	**3**	**3**	**165**	**6.7**	**–2**	**875**	**51.1**	**14:30**	**12**	**1**	**0**	**1**	**4**	**0**	**0**	**0**	**13:56**
	NHL Totals		**98**	**11**	**14**	**25**	**24**	**0**	**3**	**3**	**201**	**5.5**		**1030**	**51.1**	**13:37**	**53**	**7**	**3**	**10**	**10**	**0**	**0**	**1**	**10:57**

WHL East First All-Star Team (2006) • WHL East Second All-Star Team (2007) • Memorial Cup Tournament All-Star Team (2007)

HELMER, Bryan

(HEHL-muhr, BRIGH-uhn)

Defense. Shoots right. 6'2", 208 lbs. Born, Sault Ste. Marie, Ont., July 15, 1972.

1989-90	Wellington Dukes	OHA-B	44	4	20	24	204	....	....	....	....	....	....	....	....	....	....	....	....	....	....	....	....	....	....
	Belleville Bulls	OHL	6	0	1	1	0	....	....	....	....	....	....	....	....	....	....	....	....	....	....	....	....	....	....
1990-91	Wellington Dukes	OHA-B	50	11	14	25	109	....	....	....	....	....	....	....	....	....	....	....	....	....	....	....	....	....	....
1991-92	Wellington Dukes	MTJHL	42	17	31	48	66	....	....	....	....	....	....	....	....	....	3	2	1	3	0	....	....	....	....
1992-93	Wellington Dukes	MTJHL	48	21	54	75	84	....	....	....	....	....	....	....	....	....	9	4	8	12	22	....	....	....	....
1993-94	Albany River Rats	AHL	65	4	19	23	79	....	....	....	....	....	....	....	....	....	5	0	0	0	9	....	....	....	....
1994-95	Albany River Rats	AHL	77	7	36	43	101	....	....	....	....	....	....	....	....	....	7	1	0	1	0	....	....	....	....
1995-96	Albany River Rats	AHL	80	14	30	44	107	....	....	....	....	....	....	....	....	....	4	2	0	2	6	....	....	....	....
1996-97	Albany River Rats	AHL	77	12	27	39	113	....	....	....	....	....	....	....	....	....	16	1	7	8	10	....	....	....	....
1997-98	Albany River Rats	AHL	80	14	49	63	101	....	....	....	....	....	....	....	....	....	13	4	9	13	18	....	....	....	....
1998-99	**Phoenix**	**NHL**	**11**	**0**	**0**	**0**	**23**	**0**	**0**	**0**	**11**	**0.0**	**2**	**0**	**0.0**	**7:43**	....	....	....	....	....	....	....	....	....
	Las Vegas	IHL	8	1	3	4	28	....	....	....	....	....	....	....	....	....	....	....	....	....	....	....	....	....	....
	St. Louis	**NHL**	**29**	**0**	**4**	**4**	**19**	**0**	**0**	**0**	**38**	**0.0**	**3**	**1**	**100.0**	**19:08**	....	....	....	....	....	....	....	....	....
	Worcester IceCats	AHL	16	7	8	15	18	....	....	....	....	....	....	....	....	....	4	0	0	0	12	....	....	....	....
99-2000	**St. Louis**	**NHL**	**15**	**1**	**1**	**2**	**10**	**1**	**0**	**1**	**19**	**5.3**	**–3**	**0**	**0.0**	**16:15**	....	....	....	....	....	....	....	....	....
	Worcester IceCats	AHL	54	10	25	35	124	....	....	....	....	....	....	....	....	....	9	1	4	5	10	....	....	....	....
2000-01	**Vancouver**	**NHL**	**20**	**2**	**4**	**6**	**18**	**0**	**0**	**0**	**28**	**7.1**	**0**	**0**	**0.0**	**16:51**	....	....	....	....	....	....	....	....	....
	Kansas City	IHL	42	4	15	19	76	....	....	....	....	....	....	....	....	....	....	....	....	....	....	....	....	....	....
2001-02	**Vancouver**	**NHL**	**40**	**5**	**5**	**10**	**53**	**2**	**0**	**1**	**43**	**11.6**	**10**	**0**	**0.0**	**12:04**	**6**	**0**	**0**	**0**	**0**	**0**	**0**	**0**	**9:09**
	Manitoba Moose	AHL	34	6	18	24	69	....	....	....	....	....	....	....	....	....	....	....	....	....	....	....	....	....	....
2002-03	**Vancouver**	**NHL**	**2**	**0**	**0**	**0**	**0**	**0**	**0**	**0**	**2**	**0.0**	**1**	**0**	**0.0**	**13:24**	....	....	....	....	....	....	....	....	....
	Manitoba Moose	AHL	60	7	24	31	82	....	....	....	....	....	....	....	....	....	14	0	4	4	20	....	....	....	....
2003-04	**Phoenix**	**NHL**	**17**	**0**	**1**	**1**	**10**	**0**	**0**	**0**	**10**	**0.0**	**–5**	**0**	**0.0**	**12:46**	....	....	....	....	....	....	....	....	....
	Springfield	AHL	9	1	6	7	6	....	....	....	....	....	....	....	....	....	....	....	....	....	....	....	....	....	....
2004-05	Grand Rapids	AHL	80	7	18	25	64	....	....	....	....	....	....	....	....	....	....	....	....	....	....	....	....	....	....
2005-06	Grand Rapids	AHL	80	12	44	56	138	....	....	....	....	....	....	....	....	....	16	1	8	9	24	....	....	....	....
2006-07	San Antonio	AHL	70	6	23	29	81	....	....	....	....	....	....	....	....	....	....	....	....	....	....	....	....	....	....
2007-08	San Antonio	AHL	66	5	15	20	53	....	....	....	....	....	....	....	....	....	7	0	0	0	6	....	....	....	....
2008-09	**Washington**	**NHL**	**12**	**0**	**3**	**3**	**2**	**0**	**0**	**0**	**8**	**0.0**	**–1**	**0**	**0.0**	**16:36**	....	....	....	....	....	....	....	....	....
	Hershey Bears	AHL	63	2	25	27	59	....	....	....	....	....	....	....	....	....	22	3	5	8	24	....	....	....	....
2009-10	Hershey Bears	AHL	71	6	26	32	95	....	....	....	....	....	....	....	....	....	21	0	5	5	33	....	....	....	....
	NHL Totals		**146**	**8**	**18**	**26**	**135**	**3**	**0**	**2**	**159**	**5.0**		**1**	**100.0**	**14:42**	**6**	**0**	**0**	**0**	**0**	**0**	**0**	**0**	**9:09**

AHL First All-Star Team (1998) • AHL Second All-Star Team (2006)

Signed as a free agent by **New Jersey**, July 10, 1994. Signed as a free agent by **Phoenix**, July 17, 1998. Claimed on waivers by **St. Louis** from **Phoenix**, December 19, 1998. Signed as a free agent by **Vancouver**, August 21, 2000. Traded to **Phoenix** by **Vancouver** for Martin Grenier, July 25, 2003. • Missed majority of 2003-04 season recovering from shoulder injury suffered during training camp, September 29, 2003. Signed as a free agent by **Detroit**, July 21, 2004. Signed as a free agent by **Phoenix**, July 19, 2006. Signed as a free agent by **Washington**, November 28, 2008.

HELMINEN, Dwight

(HEHL-mih-nehn, DWIGHT)

Center. Shoots left. 5'10", 190 lbs. Born, Hancock, MI, June 22, 1983. Edmonton's 12th choice, 244th overall, in 2002 Entry Draft.

1998-99	Det. Compuware	MNHL	32	9	7	16	....	....	....	....	....	....	....	....	....	....	....	....	....	....	....	....	....	....	....
99-2000	USNTDP	USHL	30	5	7	12	10	....	....	....	....	....	....	....	....	....	....	....	....	....	....	....	....	....	....
	USNTDP	NAHL	30	7	10	17	8	....	....	....	....	....	....	....	....	....	....	....	....	....	....	....	....	....	....
2000-01	USNTDP	U-18	42	9	36	45	20	....	....	....	....	....	....	....	....	....	....	....	....	....	....	....	....	....	....
	USNTDP	USHL	24	12	7	19	8	....	....	....	....	....	....	....	....	....	....	....	....	....	....	....	....	....	....
	USNTDP	NAHL	1	0	1	1	2	....	....	....	....	....	....	....	....	....	....	....	....	....	....	....	....	....	....
2001-02	U. of Michigan	CCHA	39	10	8	18	10	....	....	....	....	....	....	....	....	....	....	....	....	....	....	....	....	....	....
2002-03	U. of Michigan	CCHA	39	17	16	33	34	....	....	....	....	....	....	....	....	....	....	....	....	....	....	....	....	....	....
2003-04	U. of Michigan	CCHA	41	17	11	28	4	....	....	....	....	....	....	....	....	....	....	....	....	....	....	....	....	....	....
2004-05	Hartford	AHL	41	2	7	9	10	....	....	....	....	....	....	....	....	....	....	....	....	....	....	....	....	....	....
	Charlotte	ECHL	28	5	16	21	10	....	....	....	....	....	....	....	....	....	15	7	3	10	2	....	....	....	....
2005-06	Hartford	AHL	77	32	24	56	40	....	....	....	....	....	....	....	....	....	13	3	5	8	10	....	....	....	....
2006-07	Hartford	AHL	80	15	24	39	32	....	....	....	....	....	....	....	....	....	7	1	1	2	2	....	....	....	....
2007-08	JYP Jyvaskyla	Finland	52	20	25	45	10	....	....	....	....	....	....	....	....	....	6	3	3	6	0	....	....	....	....
2008-09	**Carolina**	**NHL**	**23**	**1**	**1**	**2**	**0**	**0**	**0**	**0**	**15**	**6.7**	**–2**	**131**	**46.6**	**6:50**	**1**	**0**	**0**	**0**	**0**	**0**	**0**	**0**	**3:08**
	Albany River Rats	AHL	54	15	15	30	26	....	....	....	....	....	....	....	....	....	....	....	....	....	....	....	....	....	....
2009-10	**San Jose**	**NHL**	**4**	**1**	**0**	**1**	**0**	**0**	**0**	**0**	**1**	**100.0**	**–1**	**9**	**22.2**	**10:59**	**7**	**1**	**0**	**1**	**4**	**0**	**0**	**0**	**6:01**
	Worcester Sharks	AHL	74	12	10	22	16	....	....	....	....	....	....	....	....	....	2	0	0	0	0	....	....	....	....
	NHL Totals		**27**	**2**	**1**	**3**	**0**	**0**	**0**	**0**	**16**	**12.5**		**140**	**45.0**	**7:27**	**8**	**1**	**0**	**1**	**4**	**0**	**0**	**0**	**5:40**

Traded to **NY Rangers** by **Edmonton** with Steve Valiquette and Edmonton's 2nd round compensatory choice (Dane Byers) in 2004 Entry Draft for Petr Nedved and Jussi Markkanen, March 3, 2004. Signed as a free agent by **Jyvaskyla** (Finland), July 7, 2007. Signed as a free agent by **Carolina**, July 3, 2008. Signed as a free agent by **San Jose**, July 16, 2009. Signed as a free agent by **Lahti** (Finland), June 21, 2010.

HEMSKY, Ales

(HEHM-skee, ahl-EHSH) **EDM.**

Right wing. Shoots right. 6', 192 lbs. Born, Pardubice, Czech., August 13, 1983. Edmonton's 1st choice, 13th overall, in 2001 Entry Draft.

99-2000	HC Pardubice Jr.	CzRep-Jr.	45	20	36	56	54	....	....	....	....	....	....	....	....	....	7	4	14	18	36	....	....	....	....
	Pardubice	CzRep	4	0	1	1	0	....	....	....	....	....	....	....	....	....	....	....	....	....	....	....	....	....	....
2000-01	Hull Olympiques	QMJHL	68	36	64	100	67	....	....	....	....	....	....	....	....	....	5	2	3	5	2	....	....	....	....
2001-02	Hull Olympiques	QMJHL	53	27	70	97	86	....	....	....	....	....	....	....	....	....	10	6	10	16	6	....	....	....	....
2002-03	**Edmonton**	**NHL**	**59**	**6**	**24**	**30**	**14**	**0**	**0**	**1**	**50**	**12.0**	**5**	**3**	**33.3**	**12:04**	**6**	**0**	**0**	**0**	**0**	**0**	**0**	**0**	**12:46**
2003-04	**Edmonton**	**NHL**	**71**	**12**	**22**	**34**	**14**	**4**	**0**	**3**	**87**	**13.8**	**–7**	**3**	**33.3**	**14:26**	....	....	....	....	....	....	....	....	....
2004-05	Pardubice	CzRep	47	13	18	31	28	....	....	....	....	....	....	....	....	....	16	4	*10	*14	26	....	....	....	....
2005-06	**Edmonton**	**NHL**	**81**	**19**	**58**	**77**	**64**	**7**	**1**	**4**	**178**	**10.7**	**–5**	**7**	**42.9**	**16:59**	**24**	**6**	**11**	**17**	**14**	**4**	**0**	**2**	**16:06**
	Czech Republic	Olympics	8	1	2	3	2	....	....	....	....	....	....	....	....	....	....	....	....	....	....	....	....	....	....
2006-07	**Edmonton**	**NHL**	**64**	**13**	**40**	**53**	**40**	**5**	**0**	**1**	**122**	**10.7**	**–7**	**10**	**30.0**	**16:59**	....	....	....	....	....	....	....	....	....
2007-08	**Edmonton**	**NHL**	**74**	**20**	**51**	**71**	**34**	**8**	**0**	**2**	**184**	**10.9**	**–9**	**5**	**20.0**	**18:35**	....	....	....	....	....	....	....	....	....

			Regular Season														Playoffs								
Season	Club	League	GP	G	A	Pts	PIM	PP	SH	GW	S	%	+/-	TF	F%	Min	GP	G	A	Pts	PIM	PP	SH	GW	Min
2008-09	**Edmonton**	**NHL**	72	23	43	66	32	4	0	2	185	12.4	1	4	0.0	18:39	....	....	....	....	....	....	....	....	....
2009-10	**Edmonton**	**NHL**	22	7	15	22	8	3	0	0	57	12.3	7	1	100.0	17:56	....	....	....	....	....	....	....	....	....
	NHL Totals		443	100	253	353	206	31	1	13	863	11.6		33	30.3	16:30	30	6	11	17	14	4	0	2	15:26

QMJHL Second All-Star Team (2002)

Signed as a free agent by **Pardubice** (CzRep), September 18, 2004. • Missed majority of 2009-10 season recovering from shoulder injury suffered during game vs. Los Angeles, November 25, 2009.

HENDRICKS, Matt

(HEHN-drihks, MAT)

Center. Shoots left. 6', 215 lbs. Born, Blaine, MN, June 17, 1981. Nashville's 5th choice, 131st overall, in 2000 Entry Draft.

1998-99	Blaine Bengals	High-MN	22	23	34	57	42	....	....	....	....	....	....	....	....	....	....	....	....	....	....	....	....	....	....
99-2000	Blaine Bengals	High-MN	21	23	30	53	28	....	....	....	....	....	....	....	....	....	....	....	....	....	....	....	....	....	....
2000-01	St. Cloud State	WCHA	37	3	9	12	23	....	....	....	....	....	....	....	....	....	....	....	....	....	....	....	....	....	....
2001-02	St. Cloud State	WCHA	42	19	20	39	74	....	....	....	....	....	....	....	....	....	....	....	....	....	....	....	....	....	....
2002-03	St. Cloud State	WCHA	37	18	18	36	64	....	....	....	....	....	....	....	....	....	....	....	....	....	....	....	....	....	....
2003-04	St. Cloud State	WCHA	36	13	11	24	32	....	....	....	....	....	....	....	....	....	....	....	....	....	....	....	....	....	....
	Milwaukee	AHL	1	0	0	0	2	....	....	....	....	....	....	....	....	....	....	....	....	....	....	....	....	....	....
2004-05	Lowell	AHL	15	1	2	3	10	....	....	....	....	....	....	....	....	....	....	....	....	....	....	....	....	....	....
	Florida Everblades	ECHL	54	24	26	50	94	....	....	....	....	....	....	....	....	....	4	0	0	0	4	....	....	....	....
2005-06	Rochester	AHL	56	13	14	27	84	....	....	....	....	....	....	....	....	....	....	....	....	....	....	....	....	....	....
2006-07	Hershey Bears	AHL	65	18	26	44	105	....	....	....	....	....	....	....	....	....	19	8	4	12	18	....	....	....	....
2007-08	Providence Bruins	AHL	67	22	30	52	121	....	....	....	....	....	....	....	....	....	10	0	3	3	6	....	....	....	....
2008-09	**Colorado**	**NHL**	4	0	0	0	13	0	0	0	5	0.0	1	1	0.0	8:30	....	....	....	....	....	....	....	....	....
	Lake Erie	AHL	43	14	15	29	71	....	....	....	....	....	....	....	....	....	....	....	....	....	....	....	....	....	....
2009-10	**Colorado**	**NHL**	56	9	7	16	74	0	1	1	63	14.3	1	83	39.8	9:16	6	0	0	0	0	0	0	0	9:52
	NHL Totals		60	9	7	16	87	0	1	1	68	13.2		84	39.3	9:13	6	0	0	0	0	0	0	0	9:52

igned as a free agent by **Boston**, July 9, 2007. Traded to **Colorado** by **Boston** for Johnny Boychuk, June 24, 2008.

HENDRY, Jordan

(HEHN-dree, JOHR-dahn) **CHI.**

Defense. Shoots left. 6', 197 lbs. Born, Nokomis, Sask., February 23, 1984.

2002-03	Alaska	CCHA	35	3	5	8	10	....	....	....	....	....	....	....	....	....	....	....	....	....	....	....	....	....	....
2003-04	Alaska	CCHA	36	4	9	13	38	....	....	....	....	....	....	....	....	....	....	....	....	....	....	....	....	....	....
2004-05	Alaska	CCHA	3	0	1	1	21	....	....	....	....	....	....	....	....	....	....	....	....	....	....	....	....	....	....
2005-06	Alaska	CCHA	38	4	10	14	74	....	....	....	....	....	....	....	....	....	....	....	....	....	....	....	....	....	....
	Norfolk Admirals	AHL	13	1	4	5	13	....	....	....	....	....	....	....	....	....	3	0	0	0	2	....	....	....	....
2006-07	Norfolk Admirals	AHL	80	4	12	16	84	....	....	....	....	....	....	....	....	....	6	0	2	2	6	....	....	....	....
2007-08	**Chicago**	**NHL**	40	1	3	4	22	0	0	0	32	3.1	0	0	0.0	17:13	....	....	....	....	....	....	....	....	....
	Rockford IceHogs	AHL	45	3	4	7	58	....	....	....	....	....	....	....	....	....	1	0	0	0	2	....	....	....	....
2008-09	**Chicago**	**NHL**	9	0	0	0	4	0	0	0	1	0.0	–1	0	0.0	10:06	....	....	....	....	....	....	....	....	....
	Rockford IceHogs	AHL	53	3	6	9	45	....	....	....	....	....	....	....	....	....	4	0	0	0	2	....	....	....	....
2009-10♦	**Chicago**	**NHL**	43	2	6	8	10	0	0	1	42	4.8	5	0	0.0	11:51	15	0	0	0	2	0	0	0	8:09
	NHL Totals		92	3	9	12	36	0	0	1	75	4.0		0	0.0	14:01	15	0	0	0	2	0	0	0	8:09

gned as a free agent by **Chicago**, July 17, 2006.

HENNESSY, Josh

(HEHN-eh-see, JAWSH)

Center. Shoots left. 6', 192 lbs. Born, Brockton, MA, February 7, 1985. San Jose's 3rd choice, 43rd overall, in 2003 Entry Draft.

2000-01	Milton Academy	High-MA	28	20	30	50	20	....	....	....	....	....	....	....	....	....	....	....	....	....	....	....	....	....	....
2001-02	Quebec Remparts	QMJHL	70	20	20	40	24	....	....	....	....	....	....	....	....	....	9	3	9	12	8	....	....	....	....
2002-03	Quebec Remparts	QMJHL	72	33	51	84	44	....	....	....	....	....	....	....	....	....	11	6	9	15	10	....	....	....	....
2003-04	Quebec Remparts	QMJHL	59	40	42	82	55	....	....	....	....	....	....	....	....	....	....	....	....	....	....	....	....	....	....
2004-05	Quebec Remparts	QMJHL	68	35	50	85	39	....	....	....	....	....	....	....	....	....	12	2	9	11	6	....	....	....	....
2005-06	Cleveland Barons	AHL	80	24	39	63	60	....	....	....	....	....	....	....	....	....	....	....	....	....	....	....	....	....	....
2006-07	**Ottawa**	**NHL**	10	1	0	1	4	0	0	0	6	16.7	0	43	37.2	5:39	....	....	....	....	....	....	....	....	....
	Binghamton	AHL	76	27	30	57	54	....	....	....	....	....	....	....	....	....	....	....	....	....	....	....	....	....	....
2007-08	**Ottawa**	**NHL**	5	0	0	0	0	0	0	0	2	0.0	–1	12	41.7	3:46	....	....	....	....	....	....	....	....	....
	Binghamton	AHL	76	22	29	51	49	....	....	....	....	....	....	....	....	....	....	....	....	....	....	....	....	....	....
2008-09	**Ottawa**	**NHL**	1	0	0	0	0	0	0	0	0	0.0	0	7	28.6	13:40	....	....	....	....	....	....	....	....	....
	Binghamton	AHL	59	20	17	37	26	....	....	....	....	....	....	....	....	....	....	....	....	....	....	....	....	....	....
2009-10	**Ottawa**	**NHL**	4	0	0	0	0	0	0	0	2	0.0	–1	13	61.5	5:59	....	....	....	....	....	....	....	....	....
	Binghamton	AHL	78	30	38	68	26	....	....	....	....	....	....	....	....	....	....	....	....	....	....	....	....	....	....
	NHL Totals		20	1	0	1	4	0	0	0	10	10.0		75	41.3	5:39	....	....	....	....	....	....	....	....	....

aded to **Chicago** by **San Jose** with Tom Preissing for Mark Bell, July 9, 2006. Traded to **Ottawa** by **Chicago** with Tom Preissing, Michal Barinka and Chicago's 2nd round choice (Patrick Wiercioch) in 008 Entry Draft for Martin Havlat and Bryan Smolinski, July 10, 2006.

HENRY, Alex

(HEHN-ree, AL-ehx) **MTL.**

Defense. Shoots left. 6'6", 231 lbs. Born, Elliot Lake, Ont., October 18, 1979. Edmonton's 2nd choice, 67th overall, in 1998 Entry Draft.

1995-96	Timmins Majors	NOHA	30	4	11	15	6	....	....	....	....	....	....	....	....	....	....	....	....	....	....	....	....	....	....
	Timmins	NOJHA	2	0	0	0	0	....	....	....	....	....	....	....	....	....	....	....	....	....	....	....	....	....	....
1996-97	London Knights	OHL	61	1	10	11	65	....	....	....	....	....	....	....	....	....	....	....	....	....	....	....	....	....	....
1997-98	London Knights	OHL	62	5	9	14	97	....	....	....	....	....	....	....	....	....	16	0	3	3	14	....	....	....	....
1998-99	London Knights	OHL	68	5	23	28	105	....	....	....	....	....	....	....	....	....	25	3	10	13	22	....	....	....	....
99-2000	Hamilton	AHL	60	1	0	1	69	....	....	....	....	....	....	....	....	....	....	....	....	....	....	....	....	....	....
2000-01	Hamilton	AHL	56	2	3	5	87	....	....	....	....	....	....	....	....	....	....	....	....	....	....	....	....	....	....
2001-02	Hamilton	AHL	69	4	8	12	143	....	....	....	....	....	....	....	....	....	15	1	2	3	16	....	....	....	....
2002-03	**Edmonton**	**NHL**	3	0	0	0	0	0	0	0	0	0.0	–1	0	0.0	7:02	....	....	....	....	....	....	....	....	....
	Washington	**NHL**	38	0	0	0	80	0	0	0	8	0.0	–4	1	0.0	3:39	....	....	....	....	....	....	....	....	....
	Portland Pirates	AHL	3	0	1	1	0	....	....	....	....	....	....	....	....	....	....	....	....	....	....	....	....	....	....
2003-04	**Minnesota**	**NHL**	71	2	4	6	106	0	0	0	37	5.4	4	2	0.0	14:53	....	....	....	....	....	....	....	....	....
2004-05	ESV Kaufbeuren	German-2	26	6	6	12	32	....	....	....	....	....	....	....	....	....	....	....	....	....	....	....	....	....	....
2005-06	**Minnesota**	**NHL**	63	0	5	5	73	0	0	0	41	0.0	–4	2	50.0	11:26	....	....	....	....	....	....	....	....	....
2006-07	Milwaukee	AHL	64	1	6	7	66	....	....	....	....	....	....	....	....	....	2	0	0	0	7	....	....	....	....
2007-08	Milwaukee	AHL	80	3	13	16	142	....	....	....	....	....	....	....	....	....	6	0	1	1	10	....	....	....	....
2008-09	**Montreal**	**NHL**	2	0	0	0	10	0	0	0	0	0.0	–2	0	0.0	6:34	....	....	....	....	....	....	....	....	....
	Hamilton	AHL	79	3	7	10	127	....	....	....	....	....	....	....	....	....	6	0	0	0	8	....	....	....	....
2009-10	Hamilton	AHL	68	0	13	13	154	....	....	....	....	....	....	....	....	....	19	2	2	4	22	....	....	....	....
	NHL Totals		177	2	9	11	269	0	0	0	86	2.3		5	20.0	11:01	....	....	....	....	....	....	....	....	....

aimed on waivers by **Washington** from **Edmonton**, October 24, 2002. Claimed on waivers by **Minnesota** from **Washington**, October 9, 2003. Signed as a free agent by **Kaufbeuren** (German-2), nuary 15, 2005. Signed as a free agent by **Nashville**, August 22, 2006. Signed as a free agent by **Montreal**, July 3, 2008.

HENSICK, T.J.

(HEHN-sihk, TEE-JAY) **ST.L.**

Center. Shoots right. 5'10", 185 lbs. Born, Lansing, MI, December 10, 1985. Colorado's 5th choice, 88th overall, in 2005 Entry Draft.

2001-02	USNTDP	U-17	17	10	5	15	....	....	....	....	....	....	....	....	....	....	....	....	....	....	....	....	....	....	....
	USNTDP	NAHL	46	15	25	40	10	....	....	....	....	....	....	....	....	....	....	....	....	....	....	....	....	....	....
2002-03	USNTDP	U-18	48	24	24	48	11	....	....	....	....	....	....	....	....	....	....	....	....	....	....	....	....	....	....
	USNTDP	NAHL	10	6	7	13	0	....	....	....	....	....	....	....	....	....	....	....	....	....	....	....	....	....	....
2003-04	U. of Michigan	CCHA	43	12	*34	46	38	....	....	....	....	....	....	....	....	....	....	....	....	....	....	....	....	....	....
2004-05	U. of Michigan	CCHA	39	23	32	55	24	....	....	....	....	....	....	....	....	....	....	....	....	....	....	....	....	....	....
2005-06	U. of Michigan	CCHA	41	17	35	52	44	....	....	....	....	....	....	....	....	....	....	....	....	....	....	....	....	....	....
2006-07	U. of Michigan	CCHA	41	23	*46	*69	38	....	....	....	....	....	....	....	....	....	....	....	....	....	....	....	....	....	....
2007-08	**Colorado**	**NHL**	31	6	5	11	2	4	0	1	52	11.5	–4	256	42.2	11:59	2	0	1	1	0	0	0	0	15:29
	Lake Erie	AHL	50	12	33	45	18	....	....	....	....	....	....	....	....	....	....	....	....	....	....	....	....	....	....
2008-09	**Colorado**	**NHL**	61	4	17	21	14	1	0	0	116	3.4	–7	510	47.3	12:54	....	....	....	....	....	....	....	....	....
	Lake Erie	AHL	12	7	9	16	2	....	....	....	....	....	....	....	....	....	....	....	....	....	....	....	....	....	....

			Regular Season														Playoffs								
Season	Club	League	GP	G	A	Pts	PIM	PP	SH	GW	S	%	+/-	TF	F%	Min	GP	G	A	Pts	PIM	PP	SH	GW	Min
2009-10	**Colorado**	**NHL**	**7**	**1**	**2**	**3**	**0**	**0**	**0**	**0**	**13**	**7.7**	**0**	**14**	**42.9**	**9:27**	....	....	....	....	....	....	....	....	....
	Lake Erie	AHL	58	20	50	70	25	....	....	....	....	....	....	....	....	....	....	....	....	....	....	....	....	....	....
	NHL Totals		**99**	**11**	**24**	**35**	**16**	**5**	**0**	**1**	**181**	**6.1**		**780**	**45.5**	**12:22**	**2**	**0**	**1**	**1**	**0**	**0**	**0**	**0**	**15:29**

CCHA All-Rookie Team (2004) • CCHA First All-Star Team (2004, 2005, 2007) • CCHA Rookie of the Year (2004) • NCAA West First All-American Team (2005, 2007) • CCHA Second All-Star Team (2006)
Traded to **St. Louis** by **Colorado** for Julian Talbot, June 17, 2010.

HESHKA, Shaun

(HEHSH-kah, SHAWN) **PHX.**

Defense. Shoots right. 6'1", 208 lbs. Born, Melville, Sask., July 30, 1985.

			Regular Season														Playoffs								
Season	Club	League	GP	G	A	Pts	PIM	PP	SH	GW	S	%	+/-	TF	F%	Min	GP	G	A	Pts	PIM	PP	SH	GW	Min
2002-03	Melville	SJHL	53	6	14	20	53	....	....	....	....	....	....	....	....	....	....	....	....	....	....	....	....	....	....
2003-04	Everett Silvertips	WHL	66	3	7	10	25	....	....	....	....	....	....	....	....	....	21	0	2	2	8	....	....	....	....
2004-05	Everett Silvertips	WHL	72	12	26	38	21	....	....	....	....	....	....	....	....	....	11	2	0	2	6	....	....	....	....
2005-06	Everett Silvertips	WHL	66	10	49	59	91	....	....	....	....	....	....	....	....	....	14	3	10	13	10	....	....	....	....
2006-07	Manitoba Moose	AHL	57	2	4	6	14	....	....	....	....	....	....	....	....	....	7	0	0	0	8	....	....	....	....
	Victoria	ECHL	3	0	1	1	4	....	....	....	....	....	....	....	....	....	....	....	....	....	....	....	....	....	....
2007-08	Manitoba Moose	AHL	77	9	21	30	59	....	....	....	....	....	....	....	....	....	6	0	1	1	4	....	....	....	....
2008-09	Manitoba Moose	AHL	77	3	23	26	25	....	....	....	....	....	....	....	....	....	22	0	5	5	12	....	....	....	....
2009-10	**Phoenix**	**NHL**	**8**	**0**	**2**	**2**	**4**	**0**	**0**	**0**	**3**	**0.0**	**0**	**0**	**0.0**	**13:19**	....	....	....	....	....	....	....	....	....
	San Antonio	AHL	73	7	26	33	34	....	....	....	....	....	....	....	....	....	....	....	....	....	....	....	....	....	....
	NHL Totals		**8**	**0**	**2**	**2**	**4**	**0**	**0**	**0**	**3**	**0.0**		**0**	**0.0**	**13:19**	....	....	....	....	....	....	....	....	....

WHL West First All-Star Team (2006)

Signed as a free agent by **Vancouver**, July 24, 2006. Traded to **Phoenix** by **Vancouver** for Phoenix's 7th round choice (Steven Anthony) in 2009 Entry Draft, June 27, 2009.

HIGGINS, Christopher

(HIH-gihns, KRIHS-toh-fuhr) **FLA.**

Left wing. Shoots left. 6', 205 lbs. Born, Smithtown, NY, June 2, 1983. Montreal's 1st choice, 14th overall, in 2002 Entry Draft.

			Regular Season														Playoffs								
Season	Club	League	GP	G	A	Pts	PIM	PP	SH	GW	S	%	+/-	TF	F%	Min	GP	G	A	Pts	PIM	PP	SH	GW	Min
99-2000	Avon Old Farms	High-CT	27	19	20	39	10	....	....	....	....	....	....	....	....	....	....	....	....	....	....	....	....	....	....
2000-01	Avon Old Farms	High-CT	24	22	14	36	29	....	....	....	....	....	....	....	....	....	....	....	....	....	....	....	....	....	....
2001-02	Yale	ECAC	27	14	17	31	32	....	....	....	....	....	....	....	....	....	....	....	....	....	....	....	....	....	....
2002-03	Yale	ECAC	28	20	21	41	41	....	....	....	....	....	....	....	....	....	....	....	....	....	....	....	....	....	....
2003-04	**Montreal**	**NHL**	**2**	**0**	**0**	**0**	**0**	**0**	**0**	**0**	**0**	**0.0**	**0**	**9**	**22.2**	**6:18**	....	....	....	....	....	....	....	....	....
	Hamilton	AHL	67	21	27	48	18	....	....	....	....	....	....	....	....	....	10	3	2	5	0	....	....	....	....
2004-05	Hamilton	AHL	76	28	23	51	33	....	....	....	....	....	....	....	....	....	4	3	3	6	4	....	....	....	....
2005-06	**Montreal**	**NHL**	**80**	**23**	**15**	**38**	**26**	**7**	**3**	**3**	**148**	**15.5**	**–1**	**45**	**51.1**	**14:25**	**6**	**1**	**3**	**4**	**0**	**0**	**0**	**0**	**17:04**
2006-07	**Montreal**	**NHL**	**61**	**22**	**16**	**38**	**26**	**8**	**3**	**3**	**159**	**13.8**	**–11**	**53**	**34.0**	**17:54**	....	....	....	....	....	....	....	....	....
2007-08	**Montreal**	**NHL**	**82**	**27**	**25**	**52**	**22**	**12**	**0**	**5**	**241**	**11.2**	**0**	**62**	**35.5**	**17:57**	**12**	**3**	**2**	**5**	**2**	**0**	**0**	**0**	**18:27**
2008-09	**Montreal**	**NHL**	**57**	**12**	**11**	**23**	**22**	**2**	**2**	**1**	**151**	**7.9**	**–1**	**57**	**50.9**	**17:00**	**4**	**2**	**0**	**2**	**2**	**0**	**0**	**0**	**17:35**
2009-10	**NY Rangers**	**NHL**	**55**	**6**	**8**	**14**	**32**	**0**	**0**	**1**	**137**	**4.4**	**–9**	**63**	**41.3**	**17:55**	....	....	....	....	....	....	....	....	....
	Calgary	**NHL**	**12**	**2**	**1**	**3**	**0**	**0**	**0**	**0**	**28**	**7.1**	**0**	**7**	**28.6**	**15:52**	....	....	....	....	....	....	....	....	....
	NHL Totals		**349**	**92**	**76**	**168**	**128**	**29**	**8**	**13**	**864**	**10.6**		**296**	**41.2**	**16:50**	**22**	**6**	**5**	**11**	**4**	**0**	**0**	**0**	**17:55**

ECAC All-Rookie Team (2002) • ECAC Second All-Star Team (2002) • ECAC Rookie of the Year (2002) • ECAC First All-Star Team (2003) • ECAC Player of the Year (2003) (co-winner - David LeNeveu)
• NCAA East First All-American Team (2003)

Traded to **NY Rangers** by **Montreal** with Ryan McDonagh and Pavel Valentenko for Scott Gomez, Tom Pyatt and Michael Busto, June 30, 2009. Traded to **Calgary** by **NY Rangers** with Ales Kotalik for Olli Jokinen and Brandon Prust, February 2, 2010. Signed as a free agent by **Florida**, July 2, 2010.

HILBERT, Andy

(HIHL-buhrt, AN-dee)

Center/Left wing. Shoots left. 5'11", 198 lbs. Born, Lansing, MI, February 6, 1981. Boston's 3rd choice, 37th overall, in 2000 Entry Draft.

			Regular Season														Playoffs								
Season	Club	League	GP	G	A	Pts	PIM	PP	SH	GW	S	%	+/-	TF	F%	Min	GP	G	A	Pts	PIM	PP	SH	GW	Min
1997-98	USNTDP	U-17	29	14	10	24	34	....	....	....	....	....	....	....	....	....	....	....	....	....	....	....	....	....	....
	USNTDP	NAHL	39	19	16	35	102	....	....	....	....	....	....	....	....	....	7	1	4	5	12	....	....	....	....
1998-99	USNTDP	U-18	6	6	1	7	4	....	....	....	....	....	....	....	....	....	....	....	....	....	....	....	....	....	....
	USNTDP	USHL	46	23	35	58	140	....	....	....	....	....	....	....	....	....	....	....	....	....	....	....	....	....	....
99-2000	U. of Michigan	CCHA	35	17	15	32	39	....	....	....	....	....	....	....	....	....	....	....	....	....	....	....	....	....	....
2000-01	U. of Michigan	CCHA	42	26	38	64	72	....	....	....	....	....	....	....	....	....	....	....	....	....	....	....	....	....	....
2001-02	**Boston**	**NHL**	**6**	**1**	**0**	**1**	**2**	**0**	**0**	**0**	**11**	**9.1**	**–2**	**4**	**50.0**	**11:34**	....	....	....	....	....	....	....	....	....
	Providence Bruins	AHL	72	26	27	53	74	....	....	....	....	....	....	....	....	....	2	0	0	0	2	....	....	....	....
2002-03	**Boston**	**NHL**	**14**	**0**	**3**	**3**	**7**	**0**	**0**	**0**	**22**	**0.0**	**–1**	**34**	**44.1**	**11:30**	....	....	....	....	....	....	....	....	....
	Providence Bruins	AHL	64	35	35	70	119	....	....	....	....	....	....	....	....	....	4	0	1	1	4	....	....	....	....
2003-04	**Boston**	**NHL**	**18**	**2**	**0**	**2**	**9**	**0**	**0**	**0**	**27**	**7.4**	**1**	**11**	**54.6**	**8:57**	**5**	**1**	**0**	**1**	**0**	**0**	**0**	**0**	**5:32**
	Providence Bruins	AHL	19	3	5	8	20	....	....	....	....	....	....	....	....	....	....	....	....	....	....	....	....	....	....
2004-05	Providence Bruins	AHL	79	37	42	79	83	....	....	....	....	....	....	....	....	....	17	7	*14	*21	27	....	....	....	....
2005-06	**Chicago**	**NHL**	**28**	**5**	**4**	**9**	**22**	**0**	**0**	**1**	**50**	**10.0**	**–4**	**21**	**38.1**	**10:05**	....	....	....	....	....	....	....	....	....
	Norfolk Admirals	AHL	5	3	4	7	2	....	....	....	....	....	....	....	....	....	....	....	....	....	....	....	....	....	....
	Pittsburgh	**NHL**	**19**	**7**	**11**	**18**	**16**	**3**	**0**	**1**	**51**	**13.7**	**8**	**146**	**38.4**	**17:27**	....	....	....	....	....	....	....	....	....
2006-07	**NY Islanders**	**NHL**	**81**	**8**	**20**	**28**	**34**	**0**	**0**	**1**	**164**	**4.9**	**10**	**128**	**52.3**	**11:30**	**5**	**0**	**0**	**0**	**2**	**0**	**0**	**0**	**8:08**
2007-08	**NY Islanders**	**NHL**	**70**	**8**	**8**	**16**	**18**	**0**	**0**	**0**	**127**	**6.3**	**2**	**220**	**45.0**	**13:29**	....	....	....	....	....	....	....	....	....
2008-09	**NY Islanders**	**NHL**	**67**	**11**	**16**	**27**	**22**	**1**	**1**	**0**	**167**	**6.6**	**–3**	**186**	**38.2**	**16:09**	....	....	....	....	....	....	....	....	....
2009-10	**Minnesota**	**NHL**	**4**	**0**	**0**	**0**	**2**	**0**	**0**	**0**	**6**	**0.0**	**–2**	**2**	**0.0**	**9:43**	....	....	....	....	....	....	....	....	....
	Houston Aeros	AHL	33	9	16	25	8	....	....	....	....	....	....	....	....	....	....	....	....	....	....	....	....	....	....
	NHL Totals		**307**	**42**	**62**	**104**	**132**	**4**	**1**	**3**	**625**	**6.7**		**752**	**43.1**	**13:02**	**10**	**1**	**0**	**1**	**2**	**0**	**0**	**0**	**6:50**

CCHA First All-Star Team (2001) • NCAA West First All-American Team (2001) • AHL All-Rookie Team (2002) • AHL Second All-Star Team (2005)

• Missed majority of 2003-04 season recovering from groin injury suffered in pre-season game vs. Detroit, September 15, 2003. Traded to **Chicago** by **Boston** for Chicago's 5th round choice (later traded to NY Islanders - NY Islanders selected Shane Sims) in 2006 Entry Draft, November 6, 2005. Claimed on waivers by **Pittsburgh** from **Chicago**, March 9, 2006. Signed as a free agent by **NY Islanders**, July 4, 2006. Signed as a free agent by **Minnesota**, September 30, 2009.

HILLEN, Jack

(HIHL-uhn, JAK) **NYI**

Defense. Shoots left. 5'11", 200 lbs. Born, Minnetonka, MN, January 24, 1986.

			Regular Season														Playoffs								
Season	Club	League	GP	G	A	Pts	PIM	PP	SH	GW	S	%	+/-	TF	F%	Min	GP	G	A	Pts	PIM	PP	SH	GW	Min
2003-04	Tri-City Storm	USHL	31	12	32	44	18	....	....	....	....	....	....	....	....	....	....	....	....	....	....	....	....	....	....
2004-05	Colorado College	WCHA	30	2	9	11	20	....	....	....	....	....	....	....	....	....	....	....	....	....	....	....	....	....	....
2005-06	Colorado College	WCHA	42	4	9	13	48	....	....	....	....	....	....	....	....	....	....	....	....	....	....	....	....	....	....
2006-07	Colorado College	WCHA	38	7	8	15	38	....	....	....	....	....	....	....	....	....	....	....	....	....	....	....	....	....	....
2007-08	Colorado College	WCHA	41	6	*31	37	60	....	....	....	....	....	....	....	....	....	....	....	....	....	....	....	....	....	....
	NY Islanders	**NHL**	**2**	**0**	**1**	**1**	**4**	**0**	**0**	**0**	**3**	**0.0**	**1**	**0**	**0.0**	**15:32**	....	....	....	....	....	....	....	....	....
2008-09	**NY Islanders**	**NHL**	**40**	**1**	**5**	**6**	**16**	**0**	**0**	**0**	**47**	**2.1**	**–9**	**0**	**0.0**	**15:13**	....	....	....	....	....	....	....	....	....
	Bridgeport	AHL	33	4	13	17	31	....	....	....	....	....	....	....	....	....	5	0	2	2	2	....	....	....	....
2009-10	**NY Islanders**	**NHL**	**69**	**3**	**18**	**21**	**44**	**1**	**0**	**0**	**78**	**3.8**	**–5**	**1**	**100.0**	**20:42**	....	....	....	....	....	....	....	....	....
	NHL Totals		**111**	**4**	**24**	**28**	**64**	**1**	**0**	**0**	**128**	**3.1**		**1**	**100.0**	**18:37**	....	....	....	....	....	....	....	....	....

WCHA First All-Star Team (2008) • NCAA West First All-American Team (2008)
Signed as a free agent by **NY Islanders**, April 1, 2008.

HINOTE, Dan

(HIGH-noht, DAN)

Right wing. Shoots right. 6', 187 lbs. Born, Leesburg, FL, January 30, 1977. Colorado's 9th choice, 167th overall, in 1996 Entry Draft.

			Regular Season														Playoffs								
Season	Club	League	GP	G	A	Pts	PIM	PP	SH	GW	S	%	+/-	TF	F%	Min	GP	G	A	Pts	PIM	PP	SH	GW	Min
1993-94	Elk River Elks	High-MN	STATISTICS NOT AVAILABLE																						
1994-95	Army	NCAA	33	20	24	44	20	....	....	....	....	....	....	....	....	....	....	....	....	....	....	....	....	....	....
1995-96	Army	NCAA	34	21	24	45	22	....	....	....	....	....	....	....	....	....	....	....	....	....	....	....	....	....	....
1996-97	Oshawa Generals	OHL	60	15	13	28	58	....	....	....	....	....	....	....	....	....	18	4	5	9	8	....	....	....	....
1997-98	Oshawa Generals	OHL	35	12	15	27	39	....	....	....	....	....	....	....	....	....	5	2	2	4	7	....	....	....	....
	Hershey Bears	AHL	24	1	4	5	25	....	....	....	....	....	....	....	....	....	....	....	....	....	....	....	....	....	....
1998-99	Hershey Bears	AHL	65	4	16	20	95	....	....	....	....	....	....	....	....	....	5	3	1	4	6	....	....	....	....
99-2000	**Colorado**	**NHL**	**27**	**1**	**3**	**4**	**10**	**0**	**0**	**0**	**14**	**7.1**	**0**	**132**	**51.5**	**7:51**	....	....	....	....	....	....	....	....	....
	Hershey Bears	AHL	55	28	31	59	96	....	....	....	....	....	....	....	....	....	14	4	5	9	19	....	....	....	....
2000-01♦	**Colorado**	**NHL**	**76**	**5**	**10**	**15**	**51**	**1**	**0**	**1**	**69**	**7.2**	**1**	**506**	**49.8**	**10:21**	**23**	**2**	**4**	**6**	**21**	**0**	**0**	**0**	**8:22**
2001-02	**Colorado**	**NHL**	**58**	**6**	**6**	**12**	**39**	**0**	**1**	**3**	**75**	**8.0**	**8**	**267**	**51.3**	**12:27**	**19**	**1**	**2**	**3**	**9**	**0**	**0**	**0**	**10:46**
2002-03	**Colorado**	**NHL**	**60**	**6**	**4**	**10**	**49**	**0**	**0**	**3**	**65**	**9.2**	**4**	**218**	**46.8**	**10:36**	**7**	**1**	**2**	**3**	**2**	**0**	**0**	**0**	**14:19**
2003-04	**Colorado**	**NHL**	**59**	**4**	**7**	**11**	**57**	**0**	**2**	**0**	**53**	**7.5**	**–6**	**151**	**48.3**	**12:42**	**11**	**1**	**0**	**1**	**0**	**0**	**1**	**0**	**13:04**
2004-05	MODO	Sweden	18	2	1	3	106	....	....	....	....	....	....	....	....	....	5	0	0	0	56	....	....	....	....

			Regular Season														Playoffs								
Season	Club	League	GP	G	A	Pts	PIM	PP	SH	GW	S	%	+/-	TF	F%	Min	GP	G	A	Pts	PIM	PP	SH	GW	Min
2005-06	Colorado	NHL	73	5	8	13	48	0	1	2	70	7.1	-5	335	42.1	10:41	9	1	1	2	31	0	0	0	13:27
2006-07	St. Louis	NHL	41	5	5	10	23	0	0	1	37	13.5	-8	173	49.1	13:04	....	....	....	....	....	....	....	....	....
2007-08	St. Louis	NHL	58	5	5	10	42	0	0	0	42	11.9	-3	33	42.4	10:31	....	....	....	....	....	....	....	....	....
2008-09	St. Louis	NHL	51	1	4	5	64	0	0	0	24	4.2	-7	74	47.3	10:55	3	0	0	0	4	0	0	0	8:50
2009-10	MODO	Sweden	26	4	4	8	28	....	....	....	....	....	....	....	....	....	....	....	....	....	....	....	....	....	....
	NHL Totals		503	38	52	90	383	1	4	10	449	8.5		1889	48.0	11:07	72	6	9	15	67	0	1	0	10:57

Signed as a free agent by **MODO** (Sweden), December 22, 2004. Signed as a free agent by **St. Louis**, July 3, 2006. Signed as a free agent by **MODO** (Sweden), November 18, 2009.

HJALMARSSON, Niklas

(JAHL-muhr-suhn, NIHK-luhs) **CHI.**

Defense. Shoots left. 6'3", 205 lbs. Born, Eksjo, Sweden, June 6, 1987. Chicago's 5th choice, 108th overall, in 2005 Entry Draft.

Season	Club	League	GP	G	A	Pts	PIM	PP	SH	GW	S	%	+/-	TF	F%	Min	GP	G	A	Pts	PIM	PP	SH	GW	Min
2003-04	HV 71 Jr.	Swe-Jr.	15	1	3	4	14	....	....	....	....	....	....	....	....	....	2	0	0	0	8	....	....	....	....
2004-05	HV 71 U18	Swe-U18	3	0	2	2	4	....	....	....	....	....	....	....	....	....	....	....	....	....	....	....	....	....	....
	HV 71 Jr.	Swe-Jr.	31	4	11	15	87	....	....	....	....	....	....	....	....	....	....	....	....	....	....	....	....	....	....
	HV 71 Jonkoping	Sweden	14	0	0	0	0	....	....	....	....	....	....	....	....	....	....	....	....	....	....	....	....	....	....
2005-06	HV 71 Jr.	Swe-Jr.	7	3	2	5	12	....	....	....	....	....	....	....	....	....	....	....	....	....	....	....	....	....	....
	HV 71 Jonkoping	Sweden	4	1	2	3	0	....	....	....	....	....	....	....	....	....	12	0	1	1	4	....	....	....	....
2006-07	HV 71 Jonkoping	Sweden	37	2	0	2	24	....	....	....	....	....	....	....	....	....	14	1	1	2	0	....	....	....	....
	HV 71 Jr.	Swe-Jr.	7	0	2	2	14	....	....	....	....	....	....	....	....	....	....	....	....	....	....	....	....	....	....
	IK Oskarshamn	Sweden-2	8	1	2	3	6	....	....	....	....	....	....	....	....	....	....	....	....	....	....	....	....	....	....
2007-08	**Chicago**	**NHL**	**13**	**0**	**1**	**1**	**13**	**0**	**0**	**0**	**5**	**0.0**	**-2**	**0**	**0.0**	**13:37**	....	....	....	....	....	....	....	....	....
	Rockford IceHogs	AHL	47	4	9	13	31	....	....	....	....	....	....	....	....	....	12	0	4	4	8	....	....	....	....
2008-09	**Chicago**	**NHL**	**21**	**1**	**2**	**3**	**0**	**0**	**0**	**0**	**15**	**6.7**	**4**	**0**	**0.0**	**14:59**	**17**	**0**	**1**	**1**	**6**	**0**	**0**	**0**	**16:37**
	Rockford IceHogs	AHL	52	2	16	18	53	....	....	....	....	....	....	....	....	....	....	....	....	....	....	....	....	....	....
2009-10♦	**Chicago**	**NHL**	**77**	**2**	**15**	**17**	**20**	**0**	**0**	**1**	**62**	**3.2**	**9**	**0**	**0.0**	**19:40**	**22**	**1**	**7**	**8**	**6**	**0**	**0**	**0**	**21:01**
	NHL Totals		**111**	**3**	**18**	**21**	**33**	**0**	**0**	**1**	**82**	**3.7**		**0**	**0.0**	**18:04**	**39**	**1**	**8**	**9**	**12**	**0**	**0**	**0**	**19:06**

HNIDY, Shane

(NIGH-dee, SHAYN)

Defense. Shoots right. 6'2", 204 lbs. Born, Neepawa, Man., November 8, 1975. Buffalo's 7th choice, 173rd overall, in 1994 Entry Draft.

Season	Club	League	GP	G	A	Pts	PIM	PP	SH	GW	S	%	+/-	TF	F%	Min	GP	G	A	Pts	PIM	PP	SH	GW	Min
1990-91	Yellowhead	MMMHL	36	9	11	20	92	....	....	....	....	....	....	....	....	....	....	....	....	....	....	....	....	....	....
1991-92	Swift Current	WHL	56	1	3	4	11	....	....	....	....	....	....	....	....	....	4	0	0	0	0	....	....	....	....
1992-93	Swift Current	WHL	45	5	12	17	62	....	....	....	....	....	....	....	....	....	....	....	....	....	....	....	....	....	....
	Prince Albert	WHL	27	2	10	12	43	....	....	....	....	....	....	....	....	....	....	....	....	....	....	....	....	....	....
1993-94	Prince Albert	WHL	69	7	26	33	113	....	....	....	....	....	....	....	....	....	....	....	....	....	....	....	....	....	....
1994-95	Prince Albert	WHL	72	5	29	34	169	....	....	....	....	....	....	....	....	....	15	4	7	11	29	....	....	....	....
1995-96	Prince Albert	WHL	58	11	42	53	100	....	....	....	....	....	....	....	....	....	18	4	11	15	34	....	....	....	....
1996-97	Baton Rouge	ECHL	21	3	10	13	50	....	....	....	....	....	....	....	....	....	....	....	....	....	....	....	....	....	....
	Saint John Flames	AHL	44	2	12	14	112	....	....	....	....	....	....	....	....	....	....	....	....	....	....	....	....	....	....
1997-98	Grand Rapids	IHL	77	6	12	18	210	....	....	....	....	....	....	....	....	....	3	0	2	2	23	....	....	....	....
1998-99	Adirondack	AHL	68	9	20	29	121	....	....	....	....	....	....	....	....	....	3	0	1	1	0	....	....	....	....
99-2000	Cincinnati	AHL	68	9	19	28	153	....	....	....	....	....	....	....	....	....	....	....	....	....	....	....	....	....	....
2000-01	**Ottawa**	**NHL**	**52**	**3**	**2**	**5**	**84**	**0**	**0**	**1**	**47**	**6.4**	**8**	**0**	**0.0**	**13:05**	**1**	**0**	**0**	**0**	**0**	**0**	**0**	**0**	**13:23**
	Grand Rapids	IHL	2	0	0	0	2	....	....	....	....	....	....	....	....	....	....	....	....	....	....	....	....	....	....
2001-02	**Ottawa**	**NHL**	**33**	**1**	**1**	**2**	**57**	**0**	**0**	**0**	**34**	**2.9**	**-10**	**0**	**0.0**	**16:56**	**12**	**1**	**1**	**2**	**12**	**0**	**0**	**0**	**16:00**
2002-03	**Ottawa**	**NHL**	**67**	**0**	**8**	**8**	**130**	**0**	**0**	**0**	**58**	**0.0**	**-1**	**1**	**0.0**	**13:55**	**1**	**0**	**0**	**0**	**0**	**0**	**0**	**0**	**9:38**
2003-04	**Ottawa**	**NHL**	**37**	**0**	**5**	**5**	**72**	**0**	**0**	**0**	**16**	**0.0**	**2**	**0**	**0.0**	**11:19**	....	....	....	....	....	....	....	....	....
	Nashville	**NHL**	**9**	**0**	**2**	**2**	**10**	**0**	**0**	**0**	**12**	**0.0**	**3**	**0**	**0.0**	**18:11**	**5**	**0**	**0**	**0**	**6**	**0**	**0**	**0**	**12:31**
2004-05	Florida Everblades	ECHL	19	1	4	5	56	....	....	....	....	....	....	....	....	....	17	0	4	4	6	....	....	....	....
2005-06	**Atlanta**	**NHL**	**66**	**0**	**3**	**3**	**33**	**0**	**0**	**0**	**50**	**0.0**	**1**	**0**	**0.0**	**10:14**	....	....	....	....	....	....	....	....	....
2006-07	**Atlanta**	**NHL**	**72**	**5**	**7**	**12**	**63**	**0**	**1**	**1**	**86**	**5.8**	**15**	**0**	**0.0**	**15:38**	**4**	**1**	**0**	**1**	**0**	**0**	**0**	**0**	**15:48**
2007-08	**Anaheim**	**NHL**	**33**	**1**	**2**	**3**	**30**	**0**	**0**	**0**	**21**	**4.8**	**2**	**0**	**0.0**	**13:08**	....	....	....	....	....	....	....	....	....
	Boston	**NHL**	**43**	**1**	**4**	**5**	**41**	**0**	**1**	**0**	**28**	**3.6**	**-4**	**0**	**0.0**	**14:42**	**7**	**1**	**1**	**2**	**9**	**0**	**0**	**0**	**17:11**
2008-09	**Boston**	**NHL**	**65**	**3**	**9**	**12**	**45**	**1**	**0**	**1**	**49**	**6.1**	**6**	**0**	**0.0**	**15:38**	**7**	**1**	**0**	**1**	**0**	**0**	**0**	**0**	**14:06**
2009-10	**Minnesota**	**NHL**	**70**	**2**	**12**	**14**	**66**	**0**	**0**	**0**	**49**	**4.1**	**-6**	**0**	**0.0**	**13:32**	....	....	....	....	....	....	....	....	....
	NHL Totals		**547**	**16**	**55**	**71**	**631**	**1**	**2**	**3**	**450**	**3.6**		**1**	**0.0**	**13:52**	**37**	**4**	**2**	**6**	**27**	**0**	**0**	**0**	**15:08**

Signed as a free agent by **Detroit**, August 6, 1998. Traded to **Ottawa** by **Detroit** for Ottawa's 8th round choice (Todd Jackson) in 2000 Entry Draft, June 25, 2000. • Missed majority of 2001-02 season recovering from ankle injury suffered in game vs. Boston, December 26, 2001. Traded to **Nashville** by **Ottawa** for Colorado's 3rd round choice (previously acquired, Ottawa selected Peter Regin) in 2004 Entry Draft, March 9, 2004. Signed as a free agent by **Florida** (ECHL), December 6, 2004. Traded to **Atlanta** by **Nashville** for Atlanta's 4th round choice (Niko Snellman) in 2006 Entry Draft, July 30, 2005. Signed as a free agent by **Anaheim**, July 5, 2007. Traded to **Boston** by **Anaheim** with Anaheim's 6th round choice (Nicholas Tremblay) in 2008 Entry Draft for Brandon Bochenski, January 2, 2008. Signed as a free agent by **Minnesota**, July 3, 2009.

HOGGAN, Jeff

(HOH-guhn, JEHF)

Left wing. Shoots left. 6'1", 193 lbs. Born, Hope, B.C., February 1, 1978.

Season	Club	League	GP	G	A	Pts	PIM	PP	SH	GW	S	%	+/-	TF	F%	Min	GP	G	A	Pts	PIM	PP	SH	GW	Min
1998-99	Powell River Kings	BCHL	STATISTICS NOT AVAILABLE																						
99-2000	Nebraska-Omaha	CCHA	34	16	9	25	82	....	....	....	....	....	....	....	....	....	....	....	....	....	....	....	....	....	....
2000-01	Nebraska-Omaha	CCHA	42	12	17	29	78	....	....	....	....	....	....	....	....	....	....	....	....	....	....	....	....	....	....
2001-02	Nebraska-Omaha	CCHA	41	24	21	45	92	....	....	....	....	....	....	....	....	....	....	....	....	....	....	....	....	....	....
	Houston Aeros	AHL	....	....	....	....	....	....	....	....	....	....	....	....	....	....	4	0	0	0	2	....	....	....	....
2002-03	Houston Aeros	AHL	65	6	5	11	45	....	....	....	....	....	....	....	....	....	14	1	2	3	23	....	....	....	....
2003-04	Houston Aeros	AHL	77	21	15	36	88	....	....	....	....	....	....	....	....	....	2	0	1	1	4	....	....	....	....
2004-05	Worcester IceCats	AHL	47	16	9	25	55	....	....	....	....	....	....	....	....	....	....	....	....	....	....	....	....	....	....
2005-06	**St. Louis**	**NHL**	**52**	**2**	**6**	**8**	**34**	**0**	**0**	**0**	**60**	**3.3**	**-16**	**4**	**25.0**	**8:47**	....	....	....	....	....	....	....	....	....
2006-07	**Boston**	**NHL**	**46**	**0**	**2**	**2**	**33**	**0**	**0**	**0**	**53**	**0.0**	**-8**	**3**	**33.3**	**7:04**	....	....	....	....	....	....	....	....	....
	Providence Bruins	AHL	22	4	7	11	27	....	....	....	....	....	....	....	....	....	13	4	3	7	17	....	....	....	....
2007-08	**Boston**	**NHL**	**1**	**0**	**0**	**0**	**0**	**0**	**0**	**0**	**0**	**0.0**	**0**	**0**	**0.0**	**7:57**	....	....	....	....	....	....	....	....	....
	Providence Bruins	AHL	71	29	31	60	59	....	....	....	....	....	....	....	....	....	5	3	4	7	4	....	....	....	....
2008-09	**Phoenix**	**NHL**	**4**	**0**	**1**	**1**	**7**	**0**	**0**	**0**	**7**	**0.0**	**-1**	**2**	**0.0**	**12:00**	....	....	....	....	....	....	....	....	....
	San Antonio	AHL	60	22	13	35	64	....	....	....	....	....	....	....	....	....	....	....	....	....	....	....	....	....	....
2009-10	**Phoenix**	**NHL**	**4**	**0**	**0**	**0**	**2**	**0**	**0**	**0**	**5**	**0.0**	**-1**	**2**	**0.0**	**7:07**	....	....	....	....	....	....	....	....	....
	San Antonio	AHL	70	13	20	33	44	....	....	....	....	....	....	....	....	....	....	....	....	....	....	....	....	....	....
	NHL Totals		**107**	**2**	**9**	**11**	**76**	**0**	**0**	**0**	**125**	**1.6**		**11**	**18.2**	**8:06**	....	....	....	....	....	....	....	....	....

CCHA First All-Star Team (2002) • NCAA West Second All-American Team (2002)

Signed to a PTO (professional tryout) contract by **Houston** (AHL), April 4, 2002. Signed as a free agent by **Minnesota**, August 20, 2002. Signed as a free agent by **Worcester** (AHL), September, 2004. Signed as a free agent by **St. Louis**, August 2, 2005. Signed as a free agent by **Boston**, July 21, 2006. Signed as a free agent by **Phoenix**, July 15, 2008. Signed as a free agent by **Wolfsburg** (Germany), July 29, 2010.

HOLLWEG, Ryan

(HOHL-wehg, RIGH-uhn) **PHX.**

Center. Shoots left. 5'10", 212 lbs. Born, Downey, CA, April 23, 1983. NY Rangers' 10th choice, 238th overall, in 2001 Entry Draft.

Season	Club	League	GP	G	A	Pts	PIM	PP	SH	GW	S	%	+/-	TF	F%	Min	GP	G	A	Pts	PIM	PP	SH	GW	Min
1998-99	Langley Hornets	BCHL	58	14	40	54	187	....	....	....	....	....	....	....	....	....	....	....	....	....	....	....	....	....	....
99-2000	Medicine Hat	WHL	54	19	27	46	107	....	....	....	....	....	....	....	....	....	....	....	....	....	....	....	....	....	....
2000-01	Medicine Hat	WHL	65	19	39	58	125	....	....	....	....	....	....	....	....	....	....	....	....	....	....	....	....	....	....
2001-02	Medicine Hat	WHL	58	30	40	70	121	....	....	....	....	....	....	....	....	....	....	....	....	....	....	....	....	....	....
	Hartford	AHL	8	1	1	2	2	....	....	....	....	....	....	....	....	....	9	0	2	2	19	....	....	....	....
2002-03	Medicine Hat	WHL	4	1	1	2	8	....	....	....	....	....	....	....	....	....	....	....	....	....	....	....	....	....	....
2003-04	Medicine Hat	WHL	52	25	32	57	117	....	....	....	....	....	....	....	....	....	20	6	9	15	22	....	....	....	....
2004-05	Hartford	AHL	73	8	6	14	239	....	....	....	....	....	....	....	....	....	6	1	0	1	9	....	....	....	....
2005-06	**NY Rangers**	**NHL**	**52**	**2**	**3**	**5**	**84**	**0**	**0**	**0**	**32**	**6.3**	**-3**	**19**	**57.9**	**7:15**	**4**	**0**	**1**	**1**	**19**	**0**	**0**	**0**	**10:26**
	Hartford	AHL	7	2	1	3	11	....	....	....	....	....	....	....	....	....	....	....	....	....	....	....	....	....	....
2006-07	**NY Rangers**	**NHL**	**78**	**1**	**2**	**3**	**131**	**0**	**0**	**0**	**63**	**1.6**	**-11**	**86**	**39.5**	**8:14**	**2**	**0**	**0**	**0**	**2**	**0**	**0**	**0**	**5:19**
2007-08	**NY Rangers**	**NHL**	**70**	**2**	**2**	**4**	**96**	**0**	**0**	**0**	**59**	**3.4**	**-12**	**39**	**46.2**	**8:18**	**8**	**0**	**0**	**0**	**2**	**0**	**0**	**0**	**4:50**
2008-09	**Toronto**	**NHL**	**25**	**0**	**2**	**2**	**38**	**0**	**0**	**0**	**12**	**0.0**	**-7**	**3**	**33.3**	**6:28**	....	....	....	....	....	....	....	....	....
	Toronto Marlies	AHL	28	2	1	3	34	....	....	....	....	....	....	....	....	....	6	0	0	0	20	....	....	....	....
2009-10	San Antonio	AHL	53	4	6	10	93	....	....	....	....	....	....	....	....	....	....	....	....	....	....	....	....	....	....
	NHL Totals		**225**	**5**	**9**	**14**	**349**	**0**	**0**	**0**	**166**	**3.0**		**147**	**43.5**	**7:50**	**14**	**0**	**1**	**1**	**23**	**0**	**0**	**0**	**6:30**

Missed majority of 2002-03 season recovering from head injury suffered in game vs. Vancouver (WHL), October 8, 2002. Traded to **Toronto** by **NY Rangers** for Pittsburgh's 5th round choice (previously acquired, later traded back to Pittsburgh – Pittsburgh selected Andy Bathgate) in 2009 Entry Draft, July 14, 2008. Signed as a free agent by **Phoenix**, September 28, 2009.

HOLMSTROM, Tomas
(HOHLM-struhm, TAW-mas) **DET.**

Left wing. Shoots left. 6', 198 lbs. Born, Pitea, Sweden, January 23, 1973. Detroit's 9th choice, 257th overall, in 1994 Entry Draft.

			Regular Season														Playoffs								
Season	Club	League	GP	G	A	Pts	PIM	PP	SH	GW	S	%	+/-	TF	F%	Min	GP	G	A	Pts	PIM	PP	SH	GW	Min
1989-90	Pitea HC	Sweden-2	9	1	0	1	4																		
1990-91	Pitea HC	Sweden-2	26	5	4	9	16																		
1991-92	Pitea HC	Sweden-2	31	15	12	27	44																		
1992-93	Pitea HC	Sweden-2	32	17	15	32	30																		
1993-94	Bodens IK	Sweden-2	34	23	16	39	86										9	3	3	6	24				
1994-95	Lulea HF	Sweden	40	14	14	28	56										8	1	2	3	20				
1995-96	Lulea HF	Sweden	34	12	11	23	78										11	6	2	8	22				
1996-97 ♦	**Detroit**	**NHL**	**47**	**6**	**3**	**9**	**33**	**3**	**0**	**0**	**53**	**11.3**	**–10**				**1**	**0**	**0**	**0**	**0**	**0**	**0**	**0**	
	Adirondack	AHL	6	3	1	4	7																		
1997-98 ♦	**Detroit**	**NHL**	**57**	**5**	**17**	**22**	**44**	**1**	**0**	**1**	**48**	**10.4**	**6**				**22**	**7**	**12**	**19**	**16**	**2**	**0**	**0**	
1998-99	**Detroit**	**NHL**	**82**	**13**	**21**	**34**	**69**	**5**	**0**	**4**	**100**	**13.0**	**–11**	**0**	**0.0**	**12:22**	**10**	**4**	**3**	**7**	**4**	**2**	**0**	**1**	**12:32**
99-2000	**Detroit**	**NHL**	**72**	**13**	**22**	**35**	**43**	**4**	**0**	**1**	**71**	**18.3**	**4**	**0**	**0.0**	**12:06**	**9**	**3**	**1**	**4**	**16**	**1**	**0**	**1**	**11:42**
2000-01	**Detroit**	**NHL**	**73**	**16**	**24**	**40**	**40**	**9**	**0**	**2**	**74**	**21.6**	**–12**	**2**	**50.0**	**11:41**	**6**	**1**	**3**	**4**	**8**	**1**	**0**	**0**	**14:23**
2001-02 ♦	**Detroit**	**NHL**	**69**	**8**	**18**	**26**	**58**	**6**	**0**	**1**	**79**	**10.1**	**–12**	**2**	**0.0**	**12:23**	**23**	**8**	**3**	**11**	**8**	**3**	**0**	**2**	**11:31**
	Sweden	Olympics	4	1	0	1	0																		
2002-03	**Detroit**	**NHL**	**74**	**20**	**20**	**40**	**62**	**12**	**0**	**2**	**109**	**18.3**	**11**	**2**	**0.0**	**12:28**	**4**	**1**	**1**	**2**	**4**	**1**	**0**	**0**	**14:37**
2003-04	**Detroit**	**NHL**	**67**	**15**	**15**	**30**	**38**	**6**	**0**	**0**	**74**	**20.3**	**8**	**3**	**0.0**	**12:23**	**12**	**2**	**2**	**4**	**10**	**1**	**0**	**1**	**11:27**
2004-05	Lulea HF	Sweden	47	14	16	30	50										4	0	0	0	18				
2005-06	**Detroit**	**NHL**	**81**	**29**	**30**	**59**	**66**	**11**	**0**	**8**	**140**	**20.7**	**14**	**0**	**0.0**	**13:59**	**6**	**1**	**2**	**3**	**12**	**1**	**0**	**0**	**17:04**
	Sweden	Olympics	8	1	3	4	10																		
2006-07	**Detroit**	**NHL**	**77**	**30**	**22**	**52**	**58**	**13**	**0**	**5**	**176**	**17.0**	**13**	**0**	**0.0**	**15:13**	**15**	**5**	**3**	**8**	**14**	**4**	**0**	**1**	**16:15**
2007-08 ♦	**Detroit**	**NHL**	**59**	**20**	**20**	**40**	**58**	**11**	**0**	**5**	**137**	**14.6**	**9**	**1**	**0.0**	**17:33**	**21**	**4**	**8**	**12**	**26**	**1**	**0**	**0**	**17:10**
2008-09	**Detroit**	**NHL**	**53**	**14**	**23**	**37**	**38**	**8**	**0**	**1**	**75**	**18.7**	**18**	**8**	**37.5**	**15:16**	**23**	**2**	**5**	**7**	**22**	**0**	**0**	**0**	**13:45**
2009-10	**Detroit**	**NHL**	**68**	**25**	**20**	**45**	**60**	**13**	**0**	**5**	**131**	**19.1**	**5**	**1**	**0.0**	**15:49**	**12**	**4**	**3**	**7**	**12**	**1**	**0**	**1**	**13:27**
	NHL Totals		**879**	**214**	**255**	**469**	**667**	**102**	**0**	**35**	**1267**	**16.9**		**19**	**21.1**	**13:38**	**164**	**42**	**46**	**88**	**152**	**18**	**0**	**7**	**13:55**

Signed as a free agent by **Lulea** (Sweden), September 16, 2004.

HORCOFF, Shawn
(hohr-KAWF, SHAWN) **EDM.**

Center. Shoots left. 6'1", 208 lbs. Born, Trail, B.C., September 17, 1978. Edmonton's 3rd choice, 99th overall, in 1998 Entry Draft.

Season	Club	League	GP	G	A	Pts	PIM	PP	SH	GW	S	%	+/-	TF	F%	Min	GP	G	A	Pts	PIM	PP	SH	GW	Min
1994-95	Trail Smokies	RMJHL	47	50	46	96	26																		
1995-96	Chilliwack Chiefs	BCHL	58	49	96	*145	44										9	5	19	24	12				
1996-97	Michigan State	CCHA	40	10	13	23	20																		
1997-98	Michigan State	CCHA	34	14	13	27	50																		
1998-99	Michigan State	CCHA	39	12	25	37	70																		
99-2000	Michigan State	CCHA	42	14	*51	*65	50																		
2000-01	**Edmonton**	**NHL**	**49**	**9**	**7**	**16**	**10**	**0**	**0**	**2**	**42**	**21.4**	**8**	**122**	**41.8**	**9:14**	**5**	**0**	**0**	**0**	**0**	**0**	**0**	**0**	**6:31**
	Hamilton	AHL	24	10	18	28	19																		
2001-02	**Edmonton**	**NHL**	**61**	**8**	**14**	**22**	**18**	**0**	**0**	**0**	**57**	**14.0**	**3**	**454**	**46.3**	**11:20**									
	Hamilton	AHL	2	1	2	3	6																		
2002-03	**Edmonton**	**NHL**	**78**	**12**	**21**	**33**	**55**	**2**	**0**	**3**	**98**	**12.2**	**10**	**301**	**42.9**	**13:30**	**6**	**3**	**1**	**4**	**6**	**0**	**0**	**1**	**15:27**
2003-04	**Edmonton**	**NHL**	**80**	**15**	**25**	**40**	**73**	**0**	**2**	**3**	**110**	**13.6**	**0**	**1378**	**50.7**	**17:31**									
2004-05	Mora IK	Sweden	50	19	27	46	117																		
2005-06	**Edmonton**	**NHL**	**79**	**22**	**51**	**73**	**85**	**3**	**3**	**5**	**167**	**13.2**	**0**	**1421**	**52.7**	**19:59**	**24**	**7**	**12**	**19**	**12**	**1**	**1**	**2**	**21:37**
2006-07	**Edmonton**	**NHL**	**80**	**16**	**35**	**51**	**56**	**5**	**0**	**5**	**168**	**9.5**	**–22**	**1422**	**50.6**	**20:50**									
2007-08	**Edmonton**	**NHL**	**53**	**21**	**29**	**50**	**30**	**6**	**0**	**2**	**115**	**18.3**	**1**	**963**	**50.6**	**22:13**									
2008-09	**Edmonton**	**NHL**	**80**	**17**	**36**	**53**	**39**	**8**	**0**	**2**	**178**	**9.6**	**7**	**1756**	**53.9**	**21:22**									
2009-10	**Edmonton**	**NHL**	**77**	**13**	**23**	**36**	**51**	**4**	**0**	**1**	**123**	**10.6**	**–29**	**1337**	**46.5**	**19:26**									
	NHL Totals		**637**	**133**	**241**	**374**	**417**	**28**	**5**	**23**	**1058**	**12.6**		**9154**	**50.4**	**17:37**	**35**	**10**	**13**	**23**	**18**	**1**	**1**	**3**	**18:24**

CCHA First All-Star Team (2000) • CCHA Player of the Year (2000) • NCAA West First All-American Team (2000)
Played in NHL All-Star Game (2008)
Signed as a free agent by **Mora** (Sweden), September 6, 2004.

HORDICHUK, Darcy
(HOHR-dih-chuhk, DAHR-see) **VAN.**

Left wing. Shoots left. 6'1", 211 lbs. Born, Kamsack, Sask., August 10, 1980. Atlanta's 9th choice, 180th overall, in 2000 Entry Draft.

Season	Club	League	GP	G	A	Pts	PIM	PP	SH	GW	S	%	+/-	TF	F%	Min	GP	G	A	Pts	PIM	PP	SH	GW	Min
1996-97	Yorkton Mallers	SMHL	57	6	15	21	230																		
	Calgary Hitmen	WHL	3	0	0	0	2																		
1997-98	Dauphin Kings	MJHL	58	12	21	33	279																		
1998-99	Saskatoon Blades	WHL	66	3	2	5	246																		
99-2000	Saskatoon Blades	WHL	63	6	8	14	269										11	4	2	6	43				
2000-01	**Atlanta**	**NHL**	**11**	**0**	**0**	**0**	**38**	**0**	**0**	**0**	**6**	**0.0**	**–3**	**0**	**0.0**	**7:18**									
	Orlando	IHL	69	7	3	10	*369										16	3	3	6	*41				
2001-02	**Atlanta**	**NHL**	**33**	**1**	**1**	**2**	**127**	**0**	**0**	**0**	**8**	**12.5**	**–5**	**4**	**25.0**	**6:03**									
	Chicago Wolves	AHL	34	5	4	9	127																		
	Phoenix	**NHL**	**1**	**0**	**0**	**0**	**14**	**0**	**0**	**0**	**0**	**0.0**	**0**	**0**	**0.0**	**7:18**									
2002-03	**Phoenix**	**NHL**	**25**	**0**	**0**	**0**	**82**	**0**	**0**	**0**	**5**	**0.0**	**–1**	**0**	**0.0**	**4:47**									
	Springfield	AHL	22	1	3	4	38																		
	Florida	**NHL**	**3**	**0**	**0**	**0**	**15**	**0**	**0**	**0**	**2**	**0.0**	**–1**	**0**	**0.0**	**9:45**									
2003-04	**Florida**	**NHL**	**57**	**3**	**1**	**4**	**158**	**0**	**0**	**1**	**27**	**11.1**	**–10**	**4**	**50.0**	**6:46**									
2004-05			Did not play																						
2005-06	**Nashville**	**NHL**	**74**	**7**	**6**	**13**	**163**	**0**	**0**	**1**	**52**	**13.5**	**9**	**1**	**0.0**	**6:09**									
2006-07	**Nashville**	**NHL**	**53**	**1**	**3**	**4**	**90**	**0**	**0**	**0**	**22**	**4.5**	**–2**	**0**	**0.0**	**4:48**	**2**	**0**	**0**	**0**	**0**	**0**	**0**	**0**	**3:38**
2007-08	**Nashville**	**NHL**	**45**	**1**	**2**	**3**	**60**	**0**	**0**	**1**	**18**	**5.6**	**–1**	**0**	**0.0**	**5:09**	**5**	**0**	**0**	**0**	**2**	**0**	**0**	**0**	**3:32**
2008-09	**Vancouver**	**NHL**	**73**	**4**	**1**	**5**	**109**	**0**	**0**	**0**	**26**	**15.4**	**1**	**1**	**100.0**	**5:32**	**10**	**1**	**0**	**1**	**14**	**0**	**0**	**0**	**5:20**
2009-10	**Vancouver**	**NHL**	**56**	**1**	**1**	**2**	**142**	**0**	**0**	**0**	**21**	**4.8**	**–7**	**1**	**0.0**	**6:02**									
	NHL Totals		**431**	**18**	**15**	**33**	**998**	**0**	**0**	**3**	**187**	**9.6**		**11**	**36.4**	**5:49**	**17**	**1**	**0**	**1**	**16**	**0**	**0**	**0**	**4:36**

Traded to **Phoenix** by **Atlanta** with Atlanta's 4th (Lance Monych) and 5th (John Zeiler) round choices in 2002 Entry Draft for Kiril Safronov, the rights to Ruslan Zainullin and Phoenix's 4th round choice (Patrick Dwyer) in 2002 Entry Draft, March 19, 2002. Traded to **Florida** by **Phoenix** with Phoenix's 2nd round choice (later traded to Tampa Bay – Tampa Bay selected Matt Smaby) in 2003 Entry Draft for Brad Ference, March 8, 2003. Traded to **Nashville** by **Florida** for Nashville's 4th round choice (Matt Duffy) in 2005 Entry Draft, July 27, 2005. Traded to **Carolina** by **Nashville** with Nashville's 5th round choice (later traded to Phoenix – Phoenix selected Louis Domingue) in 2010 Entry Draft for Carolina's 5th round choice (later traded to Tampa Bay – Tampa Bay selected Michael Zador) in 2009 Entry Draft, June 19, 2008. Signed as a free agent by **Vancouver**, July 1, 2008.

HORNQVIST, Patric
(HOHRN-kwihst, PAT-rihk) **NSH.**

Right wing. Shoots left. 5'11", 188 lbs. Born, Sollentuna, Sweden, January 1, 1987. Nashville's 7th choice, 230th overall, in 2005 Entry Draft.

Season	Club	League	GP	G	A	Pts	PIM	PP	SH	GW	S	%	+/-	TF	F%	Min	GP	G	A	Pts	PIM	PP	SH	GW	Min
2003-04	Vasby Jr.	Swe-Jr.	10	7	10	17	30																		
	Vasby	Sweden-3	32	8	5	13	26																		
2004-05	Vasby	Sweden-3	28	12	12	24	36																		
	Djurgarden Jr.	Swe-Jr.	5	3	0	3	2																		
2005-06	Djurgarden Jr.	Swe-Jr.	4	2	1	3	2										4	1	2	3	2				
	Djurgarden	Sweden	47	5	2	7	36																		
2006-07	Djurgarden	Sweden	49	23	11	34	38																		
	Djurgarden Jr.	Swe-Jr.															7	2	5	7	14				
2007-08	Djurgarden	Sweden	53	18	12	30	58										5	0	1	1	6				
2008-09	**Nashville**	**NHL**	**28**	**2**	**5**	**7**	**16**	**0**	**0**	**0**	**54**	**3.7**	**–3**	**5**	**20.0**	**11:24**									
	Milwaukee	AHL	49	17	18	35	44										11	4	4	8	6				
2009-10	**Nashville**	**NHL**	**80**	**30**	**21**	**51**	**40**	**10**	**0**	**8**	**275**	**10.9**	**18**	**18**	**27.8**	**15:41**	**2**	**0**	**1**	**1**	**4**	**0**	**0**	**0**	**13:10**
	Sweden	Olympics	4	1	0	1	4																		
	NHL Totals		**108**	**32**	**26**	**58**	**56**	**10**	**0**	**8**	**329**	**9.7**		**23**	**26.1**	**14:35**	**2**	**0**	**1**	**1**	**4**	**0**	**0**	**0**	**13:10**

HORTON, Nathan

(HOHR-tuhn, NAY-thuhn) **BOS.**

Center. Shoots right. 6'2", 229 lbs. Born, Welland, Ont., May 29, 1985. Florida's 1st choice, 3rd overall, in 2003 Entry Draft.

Season	Club	League	GP	G	A	Pts	PIM	PP	SH	GW	S	%	+/-	TF	F%	Min	GP	G	A	Pts	PIM	PP	SH	GW	Min
			Regular Season														Playoffs								
2000-01	Thorold	OHA-B	41	16	31	47	75	....	....	....	....	....	....	....	....	....	....	....	....	....	....	....	....	....	....
2001-02	Oshawa Generals	OHL	64	31	36	67	84	....	....	....	....	....	....	....	....	....	5	1	2	3	10	....	....	....	....
2002-03	Oshawa Generals	OHL	54	33	35	68	111	....	....	....	....	....	....	....	....	....	13	9	6	15	10	....	....	....	....
2003-04	**Florida**	**NHL**	**55**	**14**	**8**	**22**	**57**	**6**	**1**	**0**	**81**	**17.3**	**–5**	**270**	**41.9**	**13:20**	....	....	....	....	....	....	....	....	....
2004-05	San Antonio	AHL	21	5	4	9	21	....	....	....	....	....	....	....	....	....	....	....	....	....	....	....	....	....	....
2005-06	**Florida**	**NHL**	**71**	**28**	**19**	**47**	**89**	**3**	**0**	**1**	**162**	**17.3**	**8**	**24**	**45.8**	**16:53**	....	....	....	....	....	....	....	....	....
2006-07	**Florida**	**NHL**	**82**	**31**	**31**	**62**	**61**	**7**	**1**	**3**	**217**	**14.3**	**15**	**31**	**48.4**	**18:04**	....	....	....	....	....	....	....	....	....
2007-08	**Florida**	**NHL**	**82**	**27**	**35**	**62**	**85**	**9**	**0**	**3**	**212**	**12.7**	**15**	**73**	**39.7**	**18:44**	....	....	....	....	....	....	....	....	....
2008-09	**Florida**	**NHL**	**67**	**22**	**23**	**45**	**48**	**5**	**1**	**5**	**131**	**16.8**	**–5**	**863**	**43.7**	**17:51**	....	....	....	....	....	....	....	....	....
2009-10	**Florida**	**NHL**	**65**	**20**	**37**	**57**	**42**	**7**	**2**	**4**	**159**	**12.6**	**–1**	**85**	**56.5**	**20:53**	....	....	....	....	....	....	....	....	....
	NHL Totals		**422**	**142**	**153**	**295**	**382**	**37**	**5**	**16**	**962**	**14.8**		**1346**	**44.1**	**17:47**	....	....	....	....	....	....	....	....	....

OHL All-Rookie Team (2002)

igned as a free agent by **San Antonio** (AHL), October 28, 2004. Traded to **Boston** by **Florida** with Gregory Campbell for Dennis Wideman, Boston's 1st round choice (later traded to Los Angeles – Los ngeles selected Derek Forbort) in 2010 Entry Draft and Boston's 3rd round choice in 2011 Entry Draft, June 22, 2010.

HOSSA, Marcel

(HOH-sa, MAHR-sehl)

Left wing. Shoots left. 6'3", 220 lbs. Born, Ilava, Czech., October 12, 1981. Montreal's 2nd choice, 16th overall, in 2000 Entry Draft.

Season	Club	League	GP	G	A	Pts	PIM	PP	SH	GW	S	%	+/-	TF	F%	Min	GP	G	A	Pts	PIM	PP	SH	GW	Min
			Regular Season														Playoffs								
1996-97	Dukla Trencin Jr.	Slovak-Jr.	45	30	21	51	30	....	....	....	....	....	....	....	....	....	....	....	....	....	....	....	....	....	....
1997-98	Dukla Trencin Jr.	Slovak-Jr.	39	11	38	49	44	....	....	....	....	....	....	....	....	....	....	....	....	....	....	....	....	....	....
1998-99	Portland	WHL	70	7	14	21	66	....	....	....	....	....	....	....	....	....	2	0	0	0	2	....	....	....	....
99-2000	Portland	WHL	60	24	29	53	58	....	....	....	....	....	....	....	....	....	....	....	....	....	....	....	....	....	....
2000-01	Portland	WHL	58	34	56	90	58	....	....	....	....	....	....	....	....	....	16	5	7	12	14	....	....	....	....
2001-02	**Montreal**	**NHL**	**10**	**3**	**1**	**4**	**2**	**0**	**0**	**0**	**20**	**15.0**	**2**	**0**	**0.0**	**11:09**	....	....	....	....	....	....	....	....	....
	Quebec Citadelles	AHL	50	17	15	32	24	....	....	....	....	....	....	....	....	....	3	0	0	0	4	....	....	....	....
2002-03	**Montreal**	**NHL**	**34**	**6**	**7**	**13**	**14**	**2**	**0**	**1**	**51**	**11.8**	**3**	**4**	**50.0**	**13:58**	....	....	....	....	....	....	....	....	....
	Hamilton	AHL	37	19	13	32	18	....	....	....	....	....	....	....	....	....	21	4	7	11	12	....	....	....	....
2003-04	**Montreal**	**NHL**	**15**	**1**	**1**	**2**	**8**	**0**	**0**	**0**	**19**	**5.3**	**–3**	**5**	**40.0**	**14:50**	....	....	....	....	....	....	....	....	....
	Hamilton	AHL	57	18	22	40	45	....	....	....	....	....	....	....	....	....	10	2	3	5	8	....	....	....	....
2004-05	Mora IK	Sweden	48	18	6	24	69	....	....	....	....	....	....	....	....	....	....	....	....	....	....	....	....	....	....
2005-06	**NY Rangers**	**NHL**	**64**	**10**	**6**	**16**	**28**	**3**	**0**	**0**	**105**	**9.5**	**–6**	**7**	**28.6**	**10:45**	**4**	**0**	**0**	**0**	**6**	**0**	**0**	**0**	**13:18**
	Slovakia	Olympics	6	0	0	0	0	....	....	....	....	....	....	....	....	....	....	....	....	....	....	....	....	....	....
2006-07	**NY Rangers**	**NHL**	**64**	**10**	**8**	**18**	**26**	**3**	**0**	**2**	**83**	**12.0**	**–4**	**18**	**16.7**	**12:27**	**10**	**2**	**2**	**4**	**4**	**0**	**0**	**0**	**15:58**
2007-08	**NY Rangers**	**NHL**	**36**	**1**	**7**	**8**	**24**	**0**	**0**	**0**	**54**	**1.9**	**8**	**5**	**20.0**	**14:36**	....	....	....	....	....	....	....	....	....
	Hartford	AHL	5	1	0	1	2	....	....	....	....	....	....	....	....	....	....	....	....	....	....	....	....	....	....
	Phoenix	**NHL**	**14**	**0**	**0**	**0**	**4**	**0**	**0**	**0**	**12**	**0.0**	**–6**	**10**	**20.0**	**11:39**	....	....	....	....	....	....	....	....	....
2008-09	Dynamo Riga	Rus-KHL	52	22	22	44	118	....	....	....	....	....	....	....	....	....	3	2	0	2	0	....	....	....	....
2009-10	Dynamo Riga	Rus-KHL	56	*35	20	55	44	....	....	....	....	....	....	....	....	....	9	4	1	5	4	....	....	....	....
	Slovakia	Olympics	7	0	1	1	0	....	....	....	....	....	....	....	....	....	....	....	....	....	....	....	....	....	....
	NHL Totals		**237**	**31**	**30**	**61**	**106**	**8**	**0**	**3**	**344**	**9.0**		**49**	**24.5**	**12:35**	**14**	**2**	**2**	**4**	**10**	**0**	**0**	**0**	**15:12**

WHL West Second All-Star Team (2001)

gned as a free agent by **Mora** (Sweden), September 25, 2004. Traded to **NY Rangers** by **Montreal** for Garth Murray, September 30, 2005. Traded to **Phoenix** by **NY Rangers** with Al Montoya for Josh ratton, David LeNeveu, Fredrik Sjostrom and Phoenix's 5th round choice (Roman Horak) in 2009 Entry Draft, February 26, 2008. Signed as a free agent by **Riga** (Russia-KHL), July 30, 2008.

HOSSA, Marian

(HOH-sa, MAIR-ee-uhn) **CHI.**

Right wing. Shoots left. 6'1", 210 lbs. Born, Stara Lubovna, Czech., January 12, 1979. Ottawa's 1st choice, 12th overall, in 1997 Entry Draft.

Season	Club	League	GP	G	A	Pts	PIM	PP	SH	GW	S	%	+/-	TF	F%	Min	GP	G	A	Pts	PIM	PP	SH	GW	Min
			Regular Season														Playoffs								
1995-96	Dukla Trencin Jr.	Slovak-Jr.	53	42	49	91	26	....	....	....	....	....	....	....	....	....	....	....	....	....	....	....	....	....	....
1996-97	Dukla Trencin	Slovakia	46	25	19	44	33	....	....	....	....	....	....	....	....	....	7	5	5	10		....	....	....	....
1997-98	Portland	WHL	53	45	40	85	50	....	....	....	....	....	....	....	....	....	16	13	6	19	6	....	....	....	....
	Ottawa	**NHL**	**7**	**0**	**1**	**1**	**0**	**0**	**0**	**0**	**10**	**0.0**	**–1**	....	....	....	....	....	....	....	....	....	....	....	....
1998-99	**Ottawa**	**NHL**	**60**	**15**	**15**	**30**	**37**	**1**	**0**	**2**	**124**	**12.1**	**18**	**4**	**25.0**	**13:59**	**4**	**0**	**2**	**2**	**4**	**0**	**0**	**0**	**16:46**
99-2000	**Ottawa**	**NHL**	**78**	**29**	**27**	**56**	**32**	**5**	**0**	**4**	**240**	**12.1**	**5**	**7**	**57.1**	**17:12**	**6**	**0**	**0**	**0**	**2**	**0**	**0**	**0**	**15:22**
2000-01	**Ottawa**	**NHL**	**81**	**32**	**43**	**75**	**44**	**11**	**2**	**7**	**249**	**12.9**	**19**	**14**	**42.9**	**18:01**	**4**	**1**	**1**	**2**	**4**	**0**	**0**	**0**	**19:02**
2001-02	Dukla Trencin	Slovakia	8	3	4	7	16	....	....	....	....	....	....	....	....	....	....	....	....	....	....	....	....	....	....
	Ottawa	**NHL**	**80**	**31**	**35**	**66**	**50**	**9**	**1**	**4**	**278**	**11.2**	**11**	**12**	**33.3**	**18:29**	**12**	**4**	**6**	**10**	**2**	**1**	**0**	**0**	**19:04**
	Slovakia	Olympics	2	4	2	6	0	....	....	....	....	....	....	....	....	....	....	....	....	....	....	....	....	....	....
2002-03	**Ottawa**	**NHL**	**80**	**45**	**35**	**80**	**34**	**14**	**0**	**10**	**229**	**19.7**	**8**	**19**	**36.8**	**18:31**	**18**	**5**	**11**	**16**	**6**	**3**	**0**	**1**	**18:41**
2003-04	**Ottawa**	**NHL**	**81**	**36**	**46**	**82**	**46**	**14**	**1**	**5**	**233**	**15.5**	**4**	**25**	**40.0**	**18:37**	**7**	**3**	**1**	**4**	**0**	**1**	**0**	**2**	**21:24**
2004-05	Mora IK	Sweden	24	18	14	32	22	....	....	....	....	....	....	....	....	....	....	....	....	....	....	....	....	....	....
	Dukla Trencin	Slovakia	25	22	20	42	38	....	....	....	....	....	....	....	....	....	5	4	5	9	14	....	....	....	....
2005-06	**Atlanta**	**NHL**	**80**	**39**	**53**	**92**	**67**	**14**	***7**	**7**	**341**	**11.4**	**17**	**15**	**26.7**	**21:41**	....	....	....	....	....	....	....	....	....
	Slovakia	Olympics	6	5	5	10	4	....	....	....	....	....	....	....	....	....	....	....	....	....	....	....	....	....	....
2006-07	**Atlanta**	**NHL**	**82**	**43**	**57**	**100**	**49**	**17**	**3**	**5**	**340**	**12.6**	**18**	**18**	**22.2**	**21:41**	**4**	**0**	**1**	**1**	**6**	**0**	**0**	**0**	**18:55**
2007-08	**Atlanta**	**NHL**	**60**	**26**	**30**	**56**	**30**	**8**	**2**	**4**	**229**	**11.4**	**–14**	**14**	**28.6**	**21:55**	....	....	....	....	....	....	....	....	....
	Pittsburgh	**NHL**	**12**	**3**	**7**	**10**	**6**	**0**	**0**	**0**	**35**	**8.6**	**0**	**1**	**0.0**	**18:34**	**20**	**12**	**14**	**26**	**12**	**5**	**0**	**2**	**21:00**
2008-09	**Detroit**	**NHL**	**74**	**40**	**31**	**71**	**63**	**10**	**0**	**8**	**307**	**13.0**	**27**	**19**	**21.1**	**17:48**	**23**	**6**	**9**	**15**	**10**	**2**	**1**	**1**	**18:38**
2009-10 ♦	**Chicago**	**NHL**	**57**	**24**	**27**	**51**	**18**	**2**	**5**	**2**	**199**	**12.1**	**24**	**1**	**0.0**	**18:44**	**22**	**3**	**12**	**15**	**25**	**0**	**0**	**1**	**18:25**
	Slovakia	Olympics	7	3	6	9	6	....	....	....	....	....	....	....	....	....	....	....	....	....	....	....	....	....	....
	NHL Totals		**832**	**363**	**407**	**770**	**476**	**105**	**21**	**58**	**2814**	**12.9**		**149**	**32.2**	**18:50**	**120**	**34**	**57**	**91**	**71**	**12**	**1**	**7**	**19:00**

WHL West First All-Star Team (1998) • WHL Rookie of the Year (1998) • Canadian Major Junior First All-Star Team (1998) • Memorial Cup Tournament All-Star Team (1998) • NHL All-Rookie Team (1999) • HL Second All-Star Team (2009)

ayed in NHL All-Star Game (2001, 2003, 2007, 2008)

gned as a free agent by **Trencin** (Slovakia), September 16, 2004. Signed as a free agent by **Mora** (Sweden), November 11, 2004. Signed as a free agent by **Trencin** (Slovakia), January 31, 2005. Traded to lanta by **Ottawa** with Greg de Vries for Dany Heatley, August 23, 2005. Traded to **Pittsburgh** by **Atlanta** with Pascal Dupuis for Colby Armstrong, Erik Christensen, Angelo Esposito and Pittsburgh's 1st und choice (Daulton Leveille) in 2008 Entry Draft , February 26, 2008. Signed as a free agent by **Detroit**, July 2, 2008. Signed as a free agent by **Chicago**, July 1, 2009.

HUDLER, Jiri

(HOOD-luhr, YIH-ree) **DET.**

Center. Shoots left. 5'10", 182 lbs. Born, Olomouc, Czech., January 4, 1984. Detroit's 1st choice, 58th overall, in 2002 Entry Draft.

Season	Club	League	GP	G	A	Pts	PIM	PP	SH	GW	S	%	+/-	TF	F%	Min	GP	G	A	Pts	PIM	PP	SH	GW	Min
			Regular Season														Playoffs								
1998-99	HC Vsetin U17	CzR-U17	46	57	57	114	....	....	....	....	....	....	....	....	....	....	....	....	....	....	....	....	....	....	....
99-2000	HC Vsetin Jr.	CzRep-Jr.	53	29	31	60	75	....	....	....	....	....	....	....	....	....	....	....	....	....	....	....	....	....	....
	Vsetin	CzRep	2	0	1	1	0	....	....	....	....	....	....	....	....	....	....	....	....	....	....	....	....	....	....
2000-01	HC Vsetin Jr.	CzRep-Jr.	16	8	14	22	16	....	....	....	....	....	....	....	....	....	....	....	....	....	....	....	....	....	....
	HC Slovnaft Vsetin	CzRep	22	1	4	5	10	....	....	....	....	....	....	....	....	....	....	....	....	....	....	....	....	....	....
	HC Femax Havirov	CzRep	15	5	1	6	12	....	....	....	....	....	....	....	....	....	....	....	....	....	....	....	....	....	....
2001-02	HC Vsetin	CzRep	46	15	31	46	54	....	....	....	....	....	....	....	....	....	....	....	....	....	....	....	....	....	....
	Liberec	CzRep-2	13	9	7	16	10	....	....	....	....	....	....	....	....	....	....	....	....	....	....	....	....	....	....
	HC Olomouc	CzRep-3	1	0	2	2	4	....	....	....	....	....	....	....	....	....	....	....	....	....	....	....	....	....	....
2002-03	HC Vsetin	CzRep	30	19	27	46	22	....	....	....	....	....	....	....	....	....	....	....	....	....	....	....	....	....	....
	Ak Bars Kazan	Russia	11	1	5	6	12	....	....	....	....	....	....	....	....	....	1	0	0	0	0	....	....	....	....
2003-04	**Detroit**	**NHL**	**12**	**1**	**2**	**3**	**10**	**1**	**0**	**0**	**8**	**12.5**	**–1**	**50**	**30.0**	**8:10**	....	....	....	....	....	....	....	....	....
	Grand Rapids	AHL	57	17	32	49	46	....	....	....	....	....	....	....	....	....	4	1	5	6	2	....	....	....	....
2004-05	Grand Rapids	AHL	52	12	22	34	10	....	....	....	....	....	....	....	....	....	....	....	....	....	....	....	....	....	....
	HC Vsetin	CzRep	7	5	2	7	10	....	....	....	....	....	....	....	....	....	....	....	....	....	....	....	....	....	....
2005-06	**Detroit**	**NHL**	**4**	**0**	**0**	**0**	**2**	**0**	**0**	**0**	**3**	**0.0**	**0**	**0**	**0.0**	**7:13**	....	....	....	....	....	....	....	....	....
	Grand Rapids	AHL	76	36	61	97	56	....	....	....	....	....	....	....	....	....	16	6	16	22	20	....	....	....	....
2006-07	**Detroit**	**NHL**	**76**	**15**	**10**	**25**	**36**	**3**	**0**	**4**	**107**	**14.0**	**16**	**20**	**30.0**	**10:02**	**6**	**0**	**2**	**2**	**4**	**0**	**0**	**0**	**9:09**
2007-08 ♦	**Detroit**	**NHL**	**81**	**13**	**29**	**42**	**26**	**3**	**0**	**2**	**131**	**9.9**	**11**	**26**	**38.5**	**13:10**	**22**	**5**	**9**	**14**	**14**	**2**	**0**	**2**	**11:36**
2008-09	**Detroit**	**NHL**	**82**	**23**	**34**	**57**	**16**	**6**	**0**	**2**	**155**	**14.8**	**7**	**29**	**44.8**	**13:39**	**23**	**4**	**8**	**12**	**6**	**2**	**0**	**1**	**13:28**
2009-10	Dynamo Moscow	Rus-KHL	54	19	35	54	18	....	....	....	....	....	....	....	....	....	4	0	1	1	4	....	....	....	....
	NHL Totals		**255**	**52**	**75**	**127**	**90**	**13**	**0**	**8**	**404**	**12.9**		**125**	**35.2**	**12:04**	**51**	**9**	**19**	**28**	**24**	**4**	**0**	**3**	**12:09**

L Second All-Star Team (2006)

ned as a free agent by **Vsetin** (CzRep), December 2, 2004. Signed as a free agent by **Dynamo Moscow** (Russia-KHL), July 10, 2009.

HUNT, Jamie

(HUHNT, JAY-mee)

Defense. Shoots left. 6'2", 200 lbs. Born, Calgary, Alta., April 20, 1984.

Season	Club	League	Regular Season GP	G	A	Pts	PIM	PP	SH	GW	S	%	+/-	TF	F%	Min	Playoffs GP	G	A	Pts	PIM	PP	SH	GW	Min
2002-03	Calgary Canucks	AJHL	63	8	20	28	35	....	....	....	....	....	....	....	....	....	....	....	....	....	....	....	....	....	....
2003-04	Mercyhurst	AH	27	3	16	19	4	....	....	....	....	....	....	....	....	....	....	....	....	....	....	....	....	....	....
2004-05	Mercyhurst	AH	38	5	12	17	36	....	....	....	....	....	....	....	....	....	....	....	....	....	....	....	....	....	....
2005-06	Mercyhurst	AH	33	12	33	45	49	....	....	....	....	....	....	....	....	....	....	....	....	....	....	....	....	....	....
2006-07	Washington	NHL	1	0	0	0	0	0	0	0	0	0.0	–1	0	0.0	6:01	....	....	....	....	....	....	....	....	....
	Hershey Bears	AHL	36	2	10	12	33	....	....	....	....	....	....	....	....	....	....	....	....	....	....	....	....	....	....
2007-08	Hershey Bears	AHL	60	4	9	13	30	....	....	....	....	....	....	....	....	....	4	0	0	0	0	....	....	....	....
2008-09	Augsburg	Germany	50	4	21	25	57	....	....	....	....	....	....	....	....	....	4	1	0	1	4	....	....	....	....
2009-10	Chicago Wolves	AHL	42	6	11	17	17	....	....	....	....	....	....	....	....	....	....	....	....	....	....	....	....	....	....
	NHL Totals		1	0	0	0	0	0	0	0	0	0.0		0	0.0	6:01	....	....	....	....	....	....	....	....	....

AH All-Rookie Team (2004) • AH First All-Star Team (2006)

Signed as a free agent by **Washington**, March 31, 2006. • Missed majority of 2006-07 season recovering from wrist injury suffered in game vs. Philadelphia (AHL), January 24, 2007. Signed as a free agent by **Chicago** (AHL), August 18, 2009.

HUNTER, Trent

(HUHN-tuhr, TREHNT) **NY**

Right wing. Shoots right. 6'3", 210 lbs. Born, Red Deer, Alta., July 5, 1980. Anaheim's 4th choice, 150th overall, in 1998 Entry Draft.

Season	Club	League	Regular Season GP	G	A	Pts	PIM	PP	SH	GW	S	%	+/-	TF	F%	Min	Playoffs GP	G	A	Pts	PIM	PP	SH	GW	Min
1996-97	Red Deer	AMHL	42	30	25	55	50	....	....	....	....	....	....	....	....	....	....	....	....	....	....	....	....	....	....
1997-98	Prince George	WHL	60	13	14	27	34	....	....	....	....	....	....	....	....	....	8	1	0	1	4	....	....	....	....
1998-99	Prince George	WHL	50	18	20	38	34	....	....	....	....	....	....	....	....	....	7	2	5	7	2	....	....	....	....
99-2000	Prince George	WHL	67	46	49	95	47	....	....	....	....	....	....	....	....	....	13	7	15	22	6	....	....	....	....
2000-01	Springfield	AHL	57	18	17	35	14	....	....	....	....	....	....	....	....	....	....	....	....	....	....	....	....	....	....
2001-02	Bridgeport	AHL	80	30	35	65	30	....	....	....	....	....	....	....	....	....	17	8	11	19	6	....	....	....	....
	NY Islanders	NHL	....	....	....	....	....	....	....	....	....	....	....	....	....	....	4	1	1	2	2	0	0	0	11:13
2002-03	NY Islanders	NHL	8	0	4	4	4	0	0	0	19	0.0	5	1	0.0	12:13	....	....	....	....	....	....	....	....	....
	Bridgeport	AHL	70	30	41	71	39	....	....	....	....	....	....	....	....	....	9	7	4	11	10	....	....	....	....
2003-04	NY Islanders	NHL	77	25	26	51	16	4	0	7	187	13.4	23	19	36.8	15:39	5	0	0	0	4	0	0	0	11:38
2004-05	Nykoping	Sweden-2	33	13	12	25	73	....	....	....	....	....	....	....	....	....	4	5	3	8	2	....	....	....	....
2005-06	NY Islanders	NHL	82	16	19	35	34	5	0	3	221	7.2	–9	32	28.1	17:50	....	....	....	....	....	....	....	....	....
2006-07	NY Islanders	NHL	77	20	15	35	22	5	1	2	168	11.9	5	14	42.9	16:00	5	3	0	3	0	0	0	0	15:05
2007-08	NY Islanders	NHL	82	12	29	41	43	2	0	1	222	5.4	–17	29	20.7	18:13	....	....	....	....	....	....	....	....	....
2008-09	NY Islanders	NHL	55	14	17	31	41	5	0	2	154	9.1	–8	20	25.0	16:23	....	....	....	....	....	....	....	....	....
2009-10	NY Islanders	NHL	61	11	17	28	18	3	0	1	159	6.9	3	9	22.2	15:11	....	....	....	....	....	....	....	....	....
	NHL Totals		442	98	127	225	178	24	1	16	1130	8.7		124	28.2	16:33	14	4	1	5	6	0	0	0	12:45

WHL West First All-Star Team (2000) • NHL All-Rookie Team (2004)

Traded to **NY Islanders** by **Anaheim** for Columbus' 4th round choice (previously acquired, Anaheim selected Jonas Ronnqvist) in 2000 Entry Draft, May 23, 2000. Signed as a free agent by **Nykoping** (Sweden-2), November 8, 2004.

HUNWICK, Matt

(HUHN-wihk, MAT) **BOS**

Defense. Shoots left. 5'11", 193 lbs. Born, Warren, MI, May 21, 1985. Boston's 6th choice, 224th overall, in 2004 Entry Draft.

Season	Club	League	Regular Season GP	G	A	Pts	PIM	PP	SH	GW	S	%	+/-	TF	F%	Min	Playoffs GP	G	A	Pts	PIM	PP	SH	GW	Min
2001-02	USNTDP	U-17	14	3	4	7	6	....	....	....	....	....	....	....	....	....	....	....	....	....	....	....	....	....	....
	USNTDP	NAHL	29	2	1	3	30	....	....	....	....	....	....	....	....	....	....	....	....	....	....	....	....	....	....
2002-03	USNTDP	U-18	40	6	16	22	40	....	....	....	....	....	....	....	....	....	....	....	....	....	....	....	....	....	....
	USNTDP	NAHL	8	2	2	4	23	....	....	....	....	....	....	....	....	....	....	....	....	....	....	....	....	....	....
2003-04	U. of Michigan	CCHA	41	1	14	15	62	....	....	....	....	....	....	....	....	....	....	....	....	....	....	....	....	....	....
2004-05	U. of Michigan	CCHA	40	6	19	25	60	....	....	....	....	....	....	....	....	....	....	....	....	....	....	....	....	....	....
2005-06	U. of Michigan	CCHA	41	11	19	30	70	....	....	....	....	....	....	....	....	....	....	....	....	....	....	....	....	....	....
2006-07	U. of Michigan	CCHA	41	6	21	27	64	....	....	....	....	....	....	....	....	....	....	....	....	....	....	....	....	....	....
2007-08	Boston	NHL	13	0	1	1	4	0	0	0	6	0.0	–1	0	0.0	10:36	....	....	....	....	....	....	....	....	....
	Providence Bruins	AHL	55	2	21	23	49	....	....	....	....	....	....	....	....	....	10	0	5	5	8	....	....	....	....
2008-09	Boston	NHL	53	6	21	27	31	0	0	1	58	10.3	15	0	0.0	16:59	1	0	0	0	0	0	0	0	15:5
	Providence Bruins	AHL	3	0	3	3	0	....	....	....	....	....	....	....	....	....	....	....	....	....	....	....	....	....	....
2009-10	Boston	NHL	76	6	8	14	32	1	1	1	60	10.0	–16	1	0.0	17:58	13	0	6	6	2	0	0	0	21:5
	NHL Totals		142	12	30	42	67	1	1	2	124	9.7		1	0.0	16:56	14	0	6	6	2	0	0	0	21:3

CCHA All-Rookie Team (2004) • CCHA Second All-Star Team (2005, 2006) • CCHA First All-Star Team (2007) • NCAA West Second All-American Team (2007)

HUSELIUS, Kristian

(hoo-SAY-lee-uhs, KRIHST-yan) **CB**

Left wing. Shoots left. 6'2", 184 lbs. Born, Osterhaninge, Sweden, November 10, 1978. Florida's 2nd choice, 47th overall, in 1997 Entry Draft.

Season	Club	League	Regular Season GP	G	A	Pts	PIM	PP	SH	GW	S	%	+/-	TF	F%	Min	Playoffs GP	G	A	Pts	PIM	PP	SH	GW	Min
1994-95	Hammarby Jr.	Swe-Jr.	17	6	2	8	2	....	....	....	....	....	....	....	....	....	....	....	....	....	....	....	....	....	....
1995-96	Hammarby Jr.	Swe-Jr.	25	13	8	21	14	....	....	....	....	....	....	....	....	....	....	....	....	....	....	....	....	....	....
	Hammarby	Sweden-2	6	1	0	1	0	....	....	....	....	....	....	....	....	....	....	....	....	....	....	....	....	....	....
1996-97	Farjestad	Sweden	13	2	0	2	4	....	....	....	....	....	....	....	....	....	5	1	0	1	0	....	....	....	....
1997-98	Farjestad	Sweden	34	2	1	3	2	....	....	....	....	....	....	....	....	....	11	0	0	0	0	....	....	....	....
	Farjestad	EuroHL	5	2	3	5	0	....	....	....	....	....	....	....	....	....	....	....	....	....	....	....	....	....	....
1998-99	Farjestad	Sweden	28	4	4	8	4	....	....	....	....	....	....	....	....	....	....	....	....	....	....	....	....	....	....
	Farjestad	EuroHL	6	2	2	4	8	....	....	....	....	....	....	....	....	....	1	0	0	0	0	....	....	....	....
	V.Frolunda	Sweden	20	2	2	4	2	....	....	....	....	....	....	....	....	....	4	1	0	1	0	....	....	....	....
99-2000	V.Frolunda	Sweden	50	21	23	44	20	....	....	....	....	....	....	....	....	....	5	2	2	4	8	....	....	....	....
2000-01	V.Frolunda	Sweden	49	*32	*35	*67	26	....	....	....	....	....	....	....	....	....	5	4	5	9	14	....	....	....	....
2001-02	Florida	NHL	79	23	22	45	14	6	1	3	169	13.6	–4	14	21.4	16:55	....	....	....	....	....	....	....	....	....
2002-03	Florida	NHL	78	20	23	43	20	3	0	3	187	10.7	–6	6	33.3	17:20	....	....	....	....	....	....	....	....	....
2003-04	Florida	NHL	76	10	21	31	24	2	0	2	168	6.0	–6	185	37.8	14:14	....	....	....	....	....	....	....	....	....
2004-05	Linkopings HC	Sweden	34	14	*35	49	10	....	....	....	....	....	....	....	....	....	....	....	....	....	....	....	....	....	....
	Rapperswil	Swiss	....	....	....	....	....	....	....	....	....	....	....	....	....	....	4	1	3	4	2	....	....	....	....
2005-06	Florida	NHL	24	5	3	8	4	2	0	0	57	8.8	–11	3	66.7	14:44	....	....	....	....	....	....	....	....	....
	Calgary	NHL	54	15	24	39	36	6	0	4	107	14.0	2	3	33.3	14:55	7	2	4	6	4	2	0	0	15:3
2006-07	Calgary	NHL	81	34	43	77	26	14	2	6	173	19.7	21	14	28.6	17:23	6	0	2	2	4	0	0	0	15:0
2007-08	Calgary	NHL	81	25	41	66	40	6	0	5	202	12.4	10	4	25.0	17:42	7	0	4	4	6	0	0	0	13:4
2008-09	Columbus	NHL	74	21	35	56	44	5	0	2	212	9.9	1	45	28.9	19:31	4	1	1	2	4	1	0	0	17:5
2009-10	Columbus	NHL	74	23	40	63	36	8	1	5	162	14.2	–4	14	28.6	18:24	....	....	....	....	....	....	....	....	....
	NHL Totals		621	176	252	428	244	52	4	30	1437	12.2		288	34.7	17:02	24	3	11	14	18	3	0	0	15:1

NHL All-Rookie Team (2002)

Signed as a free agent by **Linkopings** (Sweden), July 29, 2004. Signed as a free agent by **Rapperswil** (Swiss), February 23, 2005. Traded to **Calgary** by **Florida** for Steve Montador and Dustin Johner, December 2, 2005. Signed as a free agent by **Columbus**, July 2, 2008.

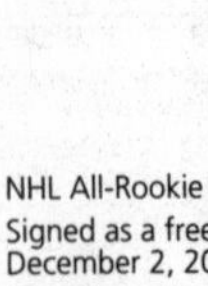

HUSKINS, Kent

(HUHS-kihnz, KEHNT) **S.**

Defense. Shoots left. 6'4", 205 lbs. Born, Ottawa, Ont., May 4, 1979. Chicago's 3rd choice, 156th overall, in 1998 Entry Draft.

Season	Club	League	Regular Season GP	G	A	Pts	PIM	PP	SH	GW	S	%	+/-	TF	F%	Min	Playoffs GP	G	A	Pts	PIM	PP	SH	GW	Min
1995-96	Kanata Valley	CJHL	49	6	21	27	18	....	....	....	....	....	....	....	....	....	....	....	....	....	....	....	....	....	....
1996-97	Kanata Valley	CJHL	53	11	36	47	89	....	....	....	....	....	....	....	....	....	....	....	....	....	....	....	....	....	....
1997-98	Clarkson Knights	ECAC	35	2	8	10	46	....	....	....	....	....	....	....	....	....	....	....	....	....	....	....	....	....	....
1998-99	Clarkson Knights	ECAC	37	5	11	16	28	....	....	....	....	....	....	....	....	....	....	....	....	....	....	....	....	....	....
99-2000	Clarkson Knights	ECAC	28	2	16	18	30	....	....	....	....	....	....	....	....	....	....	....	....	....	....	....	....	....	....
2000-01	Clarkson Knights	ECAC	35	6	28	34	22	....	....	....	....	....	....	....	....	....	....	....	....	....	....	....	....	....	....
2001-02	Norfolk Admirals	AHL	65	4	11	15	44	....	....	....	....	....	....	....	....	....	4	0	1	1	0	....	....	....	....
2002-03	Norfolk Admirals	AHL	80	5	22	27	48	....	....	....	....	....	....	....	....	....	9	2	2	4	4	....	....	....	....
2003-04	San Antonio	AHL	79	5	14	19	42	....	....	....	....	....	....	....	....	....	....	....	....	....	....	....	....	....	....
2004-05	Manitoba Moose	AHL	65	5	11	16	41	....	....	....	....	....	....	....	....	....	14	0	2	2	12	....	....	....	....
2005-06	Portland Pirates	AHL	80	8	23	31	64	....	....	....	....	....	....	....	....	....	18	3	6	9	14	....	....	....	....
2006-07 ♦	Anaheim	NHL	33	0	3	3	14	0	0	0	16	0.0	–3	0	0.0	14:04	21	0	1	1	11	0	0	0	11:
	Portland Pirates	AHL	39	3	12	15	23	....	....	....	....	....	....	....	....	....	....	....	....	....	....	....	....	....	....
2007-08	Anaheim	NHL	76	4	15	19	59	1	0	2	46	8.7	23	0	0.0	16:05	6	0	1	1	2	0	0	0	14:

Season	Club	League	Regular Season GP	G	A	Pts	PIM	PP	SH	GW	S	%	+/-	TF	F%	Min	Playoffs GP	G	A	Pts	PIM	PP	SH	GW	Min
2008-09	Anaheim	NHL	33	2	4	6	27	0	0	0	20	10.0	6	1	0.0	18:47									
2009-10	San Jose	NHL	82	3	19	22	47	0	0	0	47	6.4	6	0	0.0	17:29	15	0	0	0	6	0	0	0	12:48
	NHL Totals		224	9	41	50	147	1	0	2	129	7.0		1	0.0	16:42	42	0	2	2	19	0	0	0	12:32

ECAC First All-Star Team (2000, 2001) • NCAA East First All-American Team (2001)

Signed as a free agent by **Florida**, August 14, 2003. Signed as a free agent by **Manitoba** (AHL), September 16, 2004. Signed as a free agent by **Anaheim**, August 30, 2005. Traded to **San Jose** by **Anaheim** with Travis Moen for Timo Pielmeier, Nick Bonino and future considerations, March 4, 2009.

HUTCHINSON, Andrew

(HUHT-chihn-suhn, AN-droo) **PIT.**

Defense. Shoots right. 6'2", 206 lbs. Born, Evanston, IL, March 24, 1980. Nashville's 4th choice, 54th overall, in 1999 Entry Draft.

Season	Club	League	GP	G	A	Pts	PIM	PP	SH	GW	S	%	+/-	TF	F%	Min	GP	G	A	Pts	PIM	PP	SH	GW	Min
1996-97	Det. Caesars	MNHL	82	15	41	56																			
1997-98	USNTDP	U-18	27	3	11	14	35																		
	USNTDP	USHL	15	0	7	7	8																		
	USNTDP	NAHL	12	2	0	2	8										5	2	3	5	2				
1998-99	Michigan State	CCHA	37	3	12	15	26																		
99-2000	Michigan State	CCHA	42	5	12	17	64																		
2000-01	Michigan State	CCHA	42	5	19	24	46																		
2001-02	Michigan State	CCHA	39	6	16	22	24																		
	Milwaukee	AHL	5	0	1	1	0																		
2002-03	Milwaukee	AHL	63	9	17	26	40																		
	Toledo Storm	ECHL	10	2	5	7	4										3	1	0	1	0				
2003-04	Nashville	NHL	18	4	4	8	4	2	0	1	24	16.7	1	0	0.0	16:43									
	Milwaukee	AHL	46	12	12	24	39										22	5	11	16	33				
2004-05	Milwaukee	AHL	76	10	35	45	79										7	1	3	4	8				
2005-06 ♦	Carolina	NHL	36	3	8	11	18	2	0	0	33	9.1	–2	0	0.0	10:22									
2006-07	Carolina	NHL	41	3	11	14	30	2	0	0	45	6.7	0	0	0.0	12:13									
2007-08	Hartford	AHL	67	18	46	64	66										5	2	2	4	4				
2008-09	Tampa Bay	NHL	2	0	0	0	0	0	0	0	2	0.0	–5	0	0.0	14:44									
	Norfolk Admirals	AHL	20	1	12	13	14																		
	Dallas	NHL	38	2	3	5	12	0	0	0	56	3.6	–4	0	0.0	14:20									
2009-10	Texas Stars	AHL	78	9	29	38	50										21	5	11	16	14				
	NHL Totals		135	12	26	38	64	6	0	1	160	7.5		0	0.0	12:58									

CHA Second All-Star Team (2001, 2002) • NCAA West Second All-American Team (2002) • AHL First All-Star Team (2008) • Eddie Shore Award (AHL – Outstanding Defenseman) (2008)

raded to **Carolina** by **Nashville** for Phoenix's 3rd round choice (previously acquired, Nashville selected Teemu Laakso) in 2005 Entry Draft, July 29, 2005. Traded to **NY Rangers** by **Carolina** with Joe arnes and Carolina's 3rd round choice (Evgeny Grachev) in 2008 Entry Draft for Matt Cullen, July 17, 2007. Signed as a free agent by **Tampa Bay**, July 9, 2008. Traded to **Dallas** by **Tampa Bay** for Lauri ukonen, November 30, 2008. Signed as a free agent by **Pittsburgh**, July 7, 2010.

IGGULDEN, Mike

(IHG-gul-den, MIGHK)

Right wing. Shoots right. 6'3", 215 lbs. Born, St. Catharines, Ont., November 9, 1982.

Season	Club	League	GP	G	A	Pts	PIM	PP	SH	GW	S	%	+/-	TF	F%	Min	GP	G	A	Pts	PIM	PP	SH	GW	Min
2001-02	Cornell Big Red	ECAC	30	1	3	4	6																		
2002-03	Cornell Big Red	ECAC	15	0	2	2	19																		
2003-04	Cornell Big Red	ECAC	30	2	8	10	10																		
2004-05	Cornell Big Red	ECAC	35	10	8	18	8																		
	Rochester	AHL	6	1	0	1	7																		
2005-06	Cleveland Barons	AHL	77	22	26	48	57																		
2006-07	Worcester Sharks	AHL	73	30	27	57	55										6	3	3	6	0				
2007-08	San Jose	NHL	1	0	0	0	0	0	0	0	1	0.0	–1	0	0.0	6:40									
	Worcester Sharks	AHL	78	29	37	66	63																		
2008-09	NY Islanders	NHL	11	1	4	5	4	0	0	0	16	6.3	–3	2	50.0	12:08									
	Bridgeport	AHL	72	25	40	65	42										2	1	2	3	0				
2009-10	Dynamo Riga	Rus-KHL	55	13	20	33	44										5	0	0	0	2				
	NHL Totals		12	1	4	5	4	0	0	0	17	5.9		2	50.0	11:40									

igned to an ATO (amateur tryout) contract by **Rochester** (AHL), April 5, 2004. Signed to a PTO (professional tryout) contract by **Cleveland** (AHL), September 19, 2005. Signed as a free agent by **San Jose**, anuary 16, 2006. Signed as a free agent by **NY Islanders**, July 3, 2008. Signed as a free agent by **Riga** (Russia-KHL), July 10, 2009.

IGINLA, Jarome

(ih-GIHN-lah, jah-ROHM) **CGY.**

Right wing. Shoots right. 6'1", 207 lbs. Born, Edmonton, Alta., July 1, 1977. Dallas' 1st choice, 11th overall, in 1995 Entry Draft.

Season	Club	League	GP	G	A	Pts	PIM	PP	SH	GW	S	%	+/-	TF	F%	Min	GP	G	A	Pts	PIM	PP	SH	GW	Min
1991-92	St. Albert Raiders	AMHL	36	26	30	56	22																		
1992-93	St. Albert Raiders	AMHL	36	34	53	*87	20																		
1993-94	Kamloops Blazers	WHL	48	6	23	29	33										19	3	6	9	10				
1994-95	Kamloops Blazers	WHL	72	33	38	71	111										21	7	11	18	34				
1995-96	Kamloops Blazers	WHL	63	63	73	136	120										16	16	13	29	44				
	Calgary	NHL															2	1	1	2	0	0	0	0	
1996-97	Calgary	NHL	82	21	29	50	37	8	1	3	169	12.4	–4												
1997-98	Calgary	NHL	70	13	19	32	29	0	2	1	154	8.4	–10												
1998-99	Calgary	NHL	82	28	23	51	58	7	0	4	211	13.3	1	111	51.4	16:30									
99-2000	Calgary	NHL	77	29	34	63	26	12	0	4	256	11.3	0	278	52.9	18:24									
2000-01	Calgary	NHL	77	31	40	71	62	10	0	4	229	13.5	–2	638	51.7	19:58									
2001-02	Calgary	NHL	82	*52	44	*96	77	16	1	7	311	16.7	27	308	55.2	22:22									
	Canada	Olympics	6	3	1	4	0																		
2002-03	Calgary	NHL	75	35	32	67	49	11	3	6	316	11.1	–10	90	43.3	21:26									
2003-04	Calgary	NHL	81	*41	32	73	84	8	4	*10	265	15.5	21	305	54.4	21:18	26	*13	9	22	45	4	*2	3	23:18
2004-05			Did not play																						
2005-06	Calgary	NHL	82	35	32	67	86	17	1	6	293	11.9	5	541	54.2	21:42	7	5	3	8	11	1	1	1	24:14
	Canada	Olympics	6	2	1	3	4																		
2006-07	Calgary	NHL	70	39	55	94	40	13	1	7	264	14.8	12	406	53.0	22:04	6	2	2	4	12	0	0	1	23:45
2007-08	Calgary	NHL	82	50	48	98	83	15	0	9	338	14.8	27	445	55.1	21:26	7	4	5	9	2	3	0	0	22:43
2008-09	Calgary	NHL	82	35	54	89	37	10	0	4	289	12.1	–2	501	52.5	21:37	6	3	1	4	0	2	0	0	20:56
2009-10	Calgary	NHL	82	32	37	69	58	10	0	5	257	12.5	–2	323	47.1	20:36									
	Canada	Olympics	7	*5	2	7	0																		
	NHL Totals		1024	441	479	920	726	137	13	70	3352	13.2		3946	52.6	20:40	54	28	21	49	70	10	3	5	23:08

eorge Parsons Trophy (Memorial Cup Tournament - Most Sportsmanlike Player) (1995) • WHL West First All-Star Team (1996) • WHL Player of the Year (1996) • Canadian Major Junior First All-Star Team 996) • NHL All-Rookie Team (1997) • NHL First All-Star Team (2002, 2008, 2009) • Maurice "Rocket" Richard Trophy (2002) • Art Ross Trophy (2002) • Lester B. Pearson Award (2002) • NHL Second l-Star Team (2004) • King Clancy Memorial Trophy (2004) • Maurice "Rocket" Richard Trophy (2004) (tied with Ilya Kovalchuk and Rick Nash) • Mark Messier NHL Leadership Award (2009)

ayed in NHL All-Star Game (2002, 2003, 2004, 2008, 2009)

aded to **Calgary** by **Dallas** with Corey Millen for Joe Nieuwendyk, December 19, 1995.

IRMEN, Danny

(UHR-mehn, DA-nee)

Center. Shoots right. 6', 190 lbs. Born, Fargo, ND, September 6, 1984. Minnesota's 3rd choice, 78th overall, in 2003 Entry Draft.

Season	Club	League	GP	G	A	Pts	PIM	PP	SH	GW	S	%	+/-	TF	F%	Min	GP	G	A	Pts	PIM	PP	SH	GW	Min
2001-02	Lincoln Stars	USHL	61	17	36	53																			
2002-03	Lincoln Stars	USHL	45	21	34	55	78										10	8	6	14	17				
2003-04	U. of Minnesota	WCHA	44	14	8	22	40																		
2004-05	U. of Minnesota	WCHA	44	24	19	43	66																		
2005-06	U. of Minnesota	WCHA	30	16	22	38	40																		
	Houston Aeros	AHL	4	0	2	2	0										7	0	0	0	4				
2006-07	Houston Aeros	AHL	80	17	20	37	45																		
2007-08	Houston Aeros	AHL	77	10	13	23	51										5	0	1	1	0				
2008-09	Houston Aeros	AHL	69	7	11	18	39										20	2	0	2	8				
2009-10	Minnesota	NHL	2	0	0	0	0	0	0	0	0	0.0	–1	0	0.0	4:38									
	Houston Aeros	AHL	74	13	17	30	52																		
	NHL Totals		2	0	0	0	0	0	0	0	0	0.0		0	0.0	4:38									

SHL Second All-Star Team (2003) • USHL Playoff MVP (2003)

IRWIN, Brayden
(UHR-wihn, BRAY-duhn) **TOR.**

Right wing. Shoots right. 6'5", 215 lbs. Born, Toronto, Ont., March 24, 1987.

Season	Club	League	Regular Season GP	G	A	Pts	PIM	PP	SH	GW	S	%	+/-	TF	F%	Min	Playoffs GP	G	A	Pts	PIM	PP	SH	GW	Min
2005-06	St. Michael's	OPJHL	21	8	12	20	44	....	....	....	....	....	....	....	....	....	20	11	10	21	22	....	....	....	....
2006-07	U. of Vermont	H-East	33	7	12	19	14	....	....	....	....	....	....	....	....	....	....	....	....	....	....	....	....	....	....
2007-08	U. of Vermont	H-East	39	10	8	18	48	....	....	....	....	....	....	....	....	....	....	....	....	....	....	....	....	....	....
2008-09	U. of Vermont	H-East	33	6	5	11	60	....	....	....	....	....	....	....	....	....	....	....	....	....	....	....	....	....	....
2009-10	U. of Vermont	H-East	39	15	19	34	72	....	....	....	....	....	....	....	....	....	....	....	....	....	....	....	....	....	....
	Toronto	**NHL**	**2**	**0**	**0**	**0**	**2**	**0**	**0**	**0**	**3**	**0.0**	**0**	**6**	**50.0**	**10:06**	....	....	....	....	....	....	....	....	....
	NHL Totals		**2**	**0**	**0**	**0**	**2**	**0**	**0**	**0**	**3**	**0.0**		**6**	**50.0**	**10:06**	....	....	....	....	....	....	....	....	....

Signed as a free agent by **Toronto**, March 30, 2010.

IVANANS, Raitis
(EE-vahn-ahns, RIGHT-uhs) **CGY.**

Left wing. Shoots left. 6'4", 240 lbs. Born, Riga, Latvia, January 3, 1979.

Season	Club	League	GP	G	A	Pts	PIM	PP	SH	GW	S	%	+/-	TF	F%	Min	GP	G	A	Pts	PIM	PP	SH	GW	Min
1997-98	Flint Generals	UHL	18	0	1	1	20	....	....	....	....	....	....	....	....	....	....	....	....	....	....	....	....	....	....
1998-99	Macon Whoopee	CHL	16	1	1	2	20	....	....	....	....	....	....	....	....	....	....	....	....	....	....	....	....	....	....
	Tulsa Oilers	CHL	32	2	7	9	39	....	....	....	....	....	....	....	....	....	....	....	....	....	....	....	....	....	....
99-2000	Pensacola	ECHL	59	3	7	10	146	....	....	....	....	....	....	....	....	....	2	0	0	0	0	....	....	....	....
2000-01	Hershey Bears	AHL	2	0	0	0	0	....	....	....	....	....	....	....	....	....	....	....	....	....	....	....	....	....	....
	New Haven	UHL	66	4	10	14	270	....	....	....	....	....	....	....	....	....	8	1	0	1	4	....	....	....	....
2001-02	Toledo Storm	ECHL	16	2	2	4	59	....	....	....	....	....	....	....	....	....	....	....	....	....	....	....	....	....	....
	Baton Rouge	ECHL	40	4	5	9	180	....	....	....	....	....	....	....	....	....	....	....	....	....	....	....	....	....	....
2002-03	Milwaukee	AHL	17	0	0	0	38	....	....	....	....	....	....	....	....	....	1	0	0	0	15	....	....	....	....
	Rockford IceHogs	UHL	50	4	2	6	208	....	....	....	....	....	....	....	....	....	....	....	....	....	....	....	....	....	....
2003-04	Milwaukee	AHL	54	1	7	8	166	....	....	....	....	....	....	....	....	....	7	0	1	1	17	....	....	....	....
	Rockford IceHogs	UHL	1	0	0	0	0	....	....	....	....	....	....	....	....	....	....	....	....	....	....	....	....	....	....
2004-05	Hamilton	AHL	75	2	5	7	259	....	....	....	....	....	....	....	....	....	2	0	1	1	0	....	....	....	....
2005-06	**Montreal**	**NHL**	**4**	**0**	**0**	**0**	**9**	**0**	**0**	**0**	**0**	**0.0**	**-1**	**0**	**0.0**	**2:58**	....	....	....	....	....	....	....	....	....
	Hamilton	AHL	43	2	0	2	120	....	....	....	....	....	....	....	....	....	....	....	....	....	....	....	....	....	....
2006-07	**Los Angeles**	**NHL**	**66**	**4**	**4**	**8**	**140**	**0**	**0**	**0**	**37**	**10.8**	**-12**	**1**	**0.0**	**6:59**	....	....	....	....	....	....	....	....	....
2007-08	**Los Angeles**	**NHL**	**73**	**6**	**2**	**8**	**134**	**0**	**0**	**0**	**48**	**12.5**	**-10**	**0**	**0.0**	**7:30**	....	....	....	....	....	....	....	....	....
2008-09	**Los Angeles**	**NHL**	**76**	**2**	**0**	**2**	**145**	**0**	**0**	**2**	**25**	**8.0**	**-8**	**0**	**0.0**	**6:22**	....	....	....	....	....	....	....	....	....
2009-10	**Los Angeles**	**NHL**	**61**	**0**	**0**	**0**	**136**	**0**	**0**	**0**	**18**	**0.0**	**-8**	**0**	**0.0**	**4:54**	**1**	**0**	**0**	**0**	**0**	**0**	**0**	**0**	**5:48**
	NHL Totals		**280**	**12**	**6**	**18**	**564**	**0**	**0**	**2**	**128**	**9.4**		**1**	**0.0**	**6:26**	**1**	**0**	**0**	**0**	**0**	**0**	**0**	**0**	**5:48**

Signed as a free agent by **Montreal**, July 16, 2004. Signed as a free agent by **Los Angeles**, July 13, 2006. Signed as a free agent by **Calgary**, July 1, 2010.

JACKMAN, Barret
(JAK-man, BAIR-reht) **ST.L**

Defense. Shoots left. 6', 210 lbs. Born, Trail, B.C., March 5, 1981. St. Louis' 1st choice, 17th overall, in 1999 Entry Draft.

Season	Club	League	GP	G	A	Pts	PIM	PP	SH	GW	S	%	+/-	TF	F%	Min	GP	G	A	Pts	PIM	PP	SH	GW	Min
1996-97	Beaver Valley	VIJHL	32	22	25	47	180	....	....	....	....	....	....	....	....	....	....	....	....	....	....	....	....	....	....
1997-98	Regina Pats	WHL	68	2	11	13	224	....	....	....	....	....	....	....	....	....	9	0	3	3	32	....	....	....	....
1998-99	Regina Pats	WHL	70	8	36	44	259	....	....	....	....	....	....	....	....	....	....	....	....	....	....	....	....	....	....
99-2000	Regina Pats	WHL	53	9	37	46	175	....	....	....	....	....	....	....	....	....	6	1	1	2	19	....	....	....	....
	Worcester IceCats	AHL	....	....	....	....	....	....	....	....	....	....	....	....	....	....	2	0	0	0	13	....	....	....	....
2000-01	Regina Pats	WHL	43	9	27	36	138	....	....	....	....	....	....	....	....	....	6	0	3	3	8	....	....	....	....
2001-02	**St. Louis**	**NHL**	**1**	**0**	**0**	**0**	**0**	**0**	**0**	**0**	**1**	**0.0**	**0**	**0**	**0.0**	**18:56**	**1**	**0**	**0**	**0**	**2**	**0**	**0**	**0**	**18:2**
	Worcester IceCats	AHL	75	2	12	14	266	....	....	....	....	....	....	....	....	....	3	0	1	1	4	....	....	....	....
2002-03	**St. Louis**	**NHL**	**82**	**3**	**16**	**19**	**190**	**0**	**0**	**0**	**66**	**4.5**	**23**	**0**	**0.0**	**20:03**	**7**	**0**	**0**	**0**	**14**	**0**	**0**	**0**	**21:5**
2003-04	**St. Louis**	**NHL**	**15**	**1**	**2**	**3**	**41**	**0**	**0**	**0**	**11**	**9.1**	**-1**	**0**	**0.0**	**18:16**	....	....	....	....	....	....	....	....	....
2004-05	Missouri	UHL	28	3	17	20	61	....	....	....	....	....	....	....	....	....	3	0	0	0	4	....	....	....	....
2005-06	**St. Louis**	**NHL**	**63**	**4**	**6**	**10**	**156**	**0**	**0**	**2**	**56**	**7.1**	**-6**	**0**	**0.0**	**18:46**	....	....	....	....	....	....	....	....	....
2006-07	**St. Louis**	**NHL**	**70**	**3**	**24**	**27**	**82**	**1**	**0**	**1**	**86**	**3.5**	**20**	**0**	**0.0**	**21:30**	....	....	....	....	....	....	....	....	....
	Peoria Rivermen	AHL	1	0	0	0	0	....	....	....	....	....	....	....	....	....	....	....	....	....	....	....	....	....	....
2007-08	**St. Louis**	**NHL**	**78**	**2**	**14**	**16**	**93**	**1**	**0**	**0**	**80**	**2.5**	**-12**	**0**	**0.0**	**22:24**	....	....	....	....	....	....	....	....	....
2008-09	**St. Louis**	**NHL**	**82**	**4**	**17**	**21**	**86**	**1**	**1**	**0**	**89**	**4.5**	**-17**	**0**	**0.0**	**23:26**	**4**	**0**	**1**	**1**	**5**	**0**	**0**	**0**	**25:1**
2009-10	**St. Louis**	**NHL**	**66**	**2**	**15**	**17**	**81**	**0**	**1**	**0**	**73**	**2.7**	**3**	**1**	**0.0**	**22:41**	....	....	....	....	....	....	....	....	....
	NHL Totals		**457**	**19**	**94**	**113**	**729**	**3**	**2**	**3**	**462**	**4.1**		**1**	**0.0**	**21:25**	**12**	**0**	**1**	**1**	**21**	**0**	**0**	**0**	**22:4**

WHL East Second All-Star Team (2000) • AHL All-Rookie Team (2002) • NHL All-Rookie Team (2003) • Calder Memorial Trophy (2003)

• Missed majority of 2003-04 season recovering from shoulder injury suffered in game vs. Vancouver, October 22, 2003. Signed as a free agent by **Missouri** (UHL), February 3, 2005.

JACKMAN, Tim
(JAK-man, TIHM) **CGY**

Right wing. Shoots right. 6'4", 210 lbs. Born, Minot, ND, November 14, 1981. Columbus' 2nd choice, 38th overall, in 2001 Entry Draft.

Season	Club	League	GP	G	A	Pts	PIM	PP	SH	GW	S	%	+/-	TF	F%	Min	GP	G	A	Pts	PIM	PP	SH	GW	Min
1998-99	Park Center	High-MN	22	22	22	44		....	....	....	....	....	....	....	....	....	....	....	....	....	....	....	....	....	....
99-2000	Park Center	High-MN	19	34	22	56		....	....	....	....	....	....	....	....	....	....	....	....	....	....	....	....	....	....
	Twin Cities	USHL	25	11	9	20	58	....	....	....	....	....	....	....	....	....	13	8	5	13	12	....	....	....	....
2000-01	Minnesota State	WCHA	37	11	14	25	92	....	....	....	....	....	....	....	....	....	....	....	....	....	....	....	....	....	....
2001-02	Minnesota State	WCHA	36	14	14	28	86	....	....	....	....	....	....	....	....	....	....	....	....	....	....	....	....	....	....
2002-03	Syracuse Crunch	AHL	77	9	7	16	48	....	....	....	....	....	....	....	....	....	....	....	....	....	....	....	....	....	....
2003-04	**Columbus**	**NHL**	**19**	**1**	**2**	**3**	**16**	**0**	**0**	**0**	**18**	**5.6**	**-7**	**1**	**100.0**	**9:56**	....	....	....	....	....	....	....	....	....
	Syracuse Crunch	AHL	64	23	13	36	61	....	....	....	....	....	....	....	....	....	7	2	3	5	12	....	....	....	....
2004-05	Syracuse Crunch	AHL	73	14	21	35	98	....	....	....	....	....	....	....	....	....	....	....	....	....	....	....	....	....	....
2005-06	**Phoenix**	**NHL**	**8**	**0**	**0**	**0**	**21**	**0**	**0**	**0**	**4**	**0.0**	**1**	**1**	**0.0**	**7:13**	....	....	....	....	....	....	....	....	....
	San Antonio	AHL	50	7	13	20	127	....	....	....	....	....	....	....	....	....	....	....	....	....	....	....	....	....	....
	Manchester	AHL	18	2	3	5	33	....	....	....	....	....	....	....	....	....	7	0	3	3	20	....	....	....	....
2006-07	**Los Angeles**	**NHL**	**5**	**0**	**0**	**0**	**10**	**0**	**0**	**0**	**3**	**0.0**	**-1**	**0**	**0.0**	**6:36**	....	....	....	....	....	....	....	....	....
	Manchester	AHL	69	19	14	33	143	....	....	....	....	....	....	....	....	....	16	3	3	6	26	....	....	....	....
2007-08	**NY Islanders**	**NHL**	**36**	**1**	**3**	**4**	**57**	**0**	**0**	**0**	**36**	**2.8**	**-3**	**2**	**100.0**	**6:37**	....	....	....	....	....	....	....	....	....
	Bridgeport	AHL	44	15	21	36	67	....	....	....	....	....	....	....	....	....	....	....	....	....	....	....	....	....	....
2008-09	**NY Islanders**	**NHL**	**69**	**5**	**7**	**12**	**155**	**0**	**1**	**0**	**99**	**5.1**	**-17**	**22**	**31.8**	**11:45**	....	....	....	....	....	....	....	....	....
	Bridgeport	AHL	12	6	1	7	35	....	....	....	....	....	....	....	....	....	....	....	....	....	....	....	....	....	....
2009-10	**NY Islanders**	**NHL**	**54**	**4**	**5**	**9**	**98**	**0**	**0**	**0**	**51**	**7.8**	**-4**	**7**	**42.9**	**9:39**	....	....	....	....	....	....	....	....	....
	NHL Totals		**191**	**11**	**17**	**28**	**357**	**0**	**1**	**0**	**211**	**5.2**		**33**	**39.4**	**9:41**	....	....	....	....	....	....	....	....	....

Traded to **Phoenix** by **Columbus** with Geoff Sanderson for Cale Hulse, Mike Rupp and Jason Chimera, October 8, 2005. Traded to **Los Angeles** by **Phoenix** for Yanick Lehoux, March 9, 2006. Signed as free agent by **NY Islanders**, July 5, 2007. Signed as a free agent by **Calgary**, July 1, 2010.

JACKSON, Scott
(JAK-suhn, SKAWT) **T.B.**

Defense. Shoots left. 6'4", 215 lbs. Born, Salmon Arm, B.C., February 5, 1987. St. Louis' 2nd choice, 37th overall, in 2005 Entry Draft.

Season	Club	League	GP	G	A	Pts	PIM	PP	SH	GW	S	%	+/-	TF	F%	Min	GP	G	A	Pts	PIM	PP	SH	GW	Min
2002-03	Sicamous Eagles	KIJHL	45	2	20	22	20	....	....	....	....	....	....	....	....	....	....	....	....	....	....	....	....	....	....
	Seattle	WHL	2	0	0	0	2	....	....	....	....	....	....	....	....	....	....	....	....	....	....	....	....	....	....
2003-04	Seattle	WHL	66	4	9	13	17	....	....	....	....	....	....	....	....	....	....	....	....	....	....	....	....	....	....
2004-05	Seattle	WHL	72	6	16	22	46	....	....	....	....	....	....	....	....	....	12	1	2	3	4	....	....	....	....
2005-06	Seattle	WHL	57	3	23	26	48	....	....	....	....	....	....	....	....	....	7	1	4	5	12	....	....	....	....
2006-07	Seattle	WHL	71	4	31	35	52	....	....	....	....	....	....	....	....	....	11	0	5	5	9	....	....	....	....
2007-08	Seattle	WHL	58	6	17	23	44	....	....	....	....	....	....	....	....	....	12	2	2	4	8	....	....	....	....
2008-09	Norfolk Admirals	AHL	34	0	4	4	14	....	....	....	....	....	....	....	....	....	....	....	....	....	....	....	....	....	....
	Mississippi	ECHL	3	1	0	1	2	....	....	....	....	....	....	....	....	....	....	....	....	....	....	....	....	....	....
2009-10	**Tampa Bay**	**NHL**	**1**	**0**	**0**	**0**	**0**	**0**	**0**	**0**	**0**	**0.0**	**0**	**0**	**0.0**	**13:44**	....	....	....	....	....	....	....	....	....
	Norfolk Admirals	AHL	72	1	14	15	32	....	....	....	....	....	....	....	....	....	....	....	....	....	....	....	....	....	....
	NHL Totals		**1**	**0**	**0**	**0**	**0**	**0**	**0**	**0**	**0**	**0.0**		**0**	**0.0**	**13:44**	....	....	....	....	....	....	....	....	....

Signed as a free agent by **Tampa Bay**, July 3, 2008.

			Regular Season														Playoffs								
Season	Club	League	GP	G	A	Pts	PIM	PP	SH	GW	S	%	+/-	TF	F%	Min	GP	G	A	Pts	PIM	PP	SH	GW	Min

JACQUES, Jean-Francois (ZHAWK, ZHAWN-fran-SWUH) **EDM.**

Left wing. Shoots left. 6'4", 217 lbs. Born, Montreal, Que., April 29, 1985. Edmonton's 3rd choice, 68th overall, in 2003 Entry Draft.

Season	Club	League	GP	G	A	Pts	PIM	PP	SH	GW	S	%	+/-	TF	F%	Min	GP	G	A	Pts	PIM	PP	SH	GW	Min
2000-01	Cap-d-Madeleine	QAAA	39	22	13	35	28	....	....	....	....	....	....	....	....	....	10	5	8	13	14	....	....	....	....
2001-02	Baie-Comeau	QMJHL	66	10	14	24	136	....	....	....	....	....	....	....	....	....	5	1	0	1	2	....	....	....	....
2002-03	Baie-Comeau	QMJHL	67	12	21	33	123	....	....	....	....	....	....	....	....	....	12	4	2	6	13	....	....	....	....
2003-04	Baie-Comeau	QMJHL	59	20	24	44	70	....	....	....	....	....	....	....	....	....	4	1	0	1	4	....	....	....	....
2004-05	Baie-Comeau	QMJHL	69	36	42	78	56	....	....	....	....	....	....	....	....	....	6	3	5	8	6	....	....	....	....
	Edmonton	AHL	6	0	0	0	5	....	....	....	....	....	....	....	....	....	....	....	....	....	....	....	....	....	....
2005-06	**Edmonton**	**NHL**	7	0	0	0	0	0	0	0	8	0.0	–3	0	0.0	6:43	....	....	....	....	....	....	....	....	....
	Hamilton	AHL	65	24	19	43	131	....	....	....	....	....	....	....	....	....	....	....	....	....	....	....	....	....	....
2006-07	**Edmonton**	**NHL**	37	0	0	0	33	0	0	0	23	0.0	–11	2	0.0	7:55	....	....	....	....	....	....	....	....	....
	Wilkes-Barre	AHL	29	10	17	27	53	....	....	....	....	....	....	....	....	....	11	1	2	3	43	....	....	....	....
2007-08	**Edmonton**	**NHL**	9	0	0	0	2	0	0	0	2	0.0	–3	0	0.0	6:10	....	....	....	....	....	....	....	....	....
	Springfield	AHL	38	11	14	25	63	....	....	....	....	....	....	....	....	....	....	....	....	....	....	....	....	....	....
2008-09	**Edmonton**	**NHL**	7	1	0	1	9	0	0	0	3	33.3	0	0	0.0	7:22	....	....	....	....	....	....	....	....	....
	Springfield	AHL	8	1	5	6	13	....	....	....	....	....	....	....	....	....	....	....	....	....	....	....	....	....	....
2009-10	**Edmonton**	**NHL**	49	4	7	11	78	0	0	0	49	8.2	–15	5	40.0	11:12	....	....	....	....	....	....	....	....	....
	NHL Totals		109	5	7	12	122	0	0	0	85	5.9		7	28.6	9:08	....	....	....	....	....	....	....	....	....

• Missed majority of 2008-09 season recovering from off-season back surgery.

JAFFRAY, Jason (JAF-ray, JAY-suhn) **ANA.**

Left wing. Shoots left. 6'1", 195 lbs. Born, Rimbey, Alta., June 30, 1981.

Season	Club	League	GP	G	A	Pts	PIM	PP	SH	GW	S	%	+/-	TF	F%	Min	GP	G	A	Pts	PIM	PP	SH	GW	Min
1997-98	Edmonton Ice	WHL	6	0	1	1	0	....	....	....	....	....	....	....	....	....	....	....	....	....	....	....	....	....	....
1998-99	Kootenay Ice	WHL	57	14	12	26	50	....	....	....	....	....	....	....	....	....	7	1	2	3	6	....	....	....	....
99-2000	Kootenay Ice	WHL	71	24	28	52	104	....	....	....	....	....	....	....	....	....	21	10	9	19	17	....	....	....	....
2000-01	Kootenay Ice	WHL	70	31	42	73	108	....	....	....	....	....	....	....	....	....	11	5	7	12	10	....	....	....	....
2001-02	Kootenay Ice	WHL	32	15	19	34	38	....	....	....	....	....	....	....	....	....	....	....	....	....	....	....	....	....	....
	Swift Current	WHL	41	23	26	49	44	....	....	....	....	....	....	....	....	....	12	4	5	9	25	....	....	....	....
2002-03	Norfolk Admirals	AHL	2	0	0	0	0	....	....	....	....	....	....	....	....	....	....	....	....	....	....	....	....	....	....
	Roanoke Express	ECHL	64	34	51	85	89	....	....	....	....	....	....	....	....	....	4	0	3	3	4	....	....	....	....
2003-04	Wilkes-Barre	AHL	5	0	1	1	0	....	....	....	....	....	....	....	....	....	....	....	....	....	....	....	....	....	....
	Wheeling Nailers	ECHL	54	37	37	74	81	....	....	....	....	....	....	....	....	....	2	1	1	2	2	....	....	....	....
2004-05	Cleveland Barons	AHL	30	10	6	16	23	....	....	....	....	....	....	....	....	....	....	....	....	....	....	....	....	....	....
	Manitoba Moose	AHL	14	4	4	8	6	....	....	....	....	....	....	....	....	....	1	0	0	0	0	....	....	....	....
	Wheeling Nailers	ECHL	23	6	6	12	22	....	....	....	....	....	....	....	....	....	....	....	....	....	....	....	....	....	....
2005-06	Manitoba Moose	AHL	73	12	35	47	58	....	....	....	....	....	....	....	....	....	13	6	1	7	11	....	....	....	....
2006-07	Manitoba Moose	AHL	77	35	46	81	75	....	....	....	....	....	....	....	....	....	13	6	7	13	6	....	....	....	....
2007-08	**Vancouver**	**NHL**	19	2	4	6	19	1	0	1	15	13.3	4	176	47.7	12:35	....	....	....	....	....	....	....	....	....
	Manitoba Moose	AHL	43	21	27	48	51	....	....	....	....	....	....	....	....	....	3	1	4	5	9	....	....	....	....
2008-09	**Vancouver**	**NHL**	14	2	2	4	14	0	0	2	11	18.2	–2	65	47.7	9:04	....	....	....	....	....	....	....	....	....
	Manitoba Moose	AHL	56	23	26	49	52	....	....	....	....	....	....	....	....	....	22	9	10	19	12	....	....	....	....
2009-10	**Calgary**	**NHL**	3	0	0	0	0	0	0	0	4	0.0	–1	14	35.7	6:39	....	....	....	....	....	....	....	....	....
	Abbotsford Heat	AHL	72	25	29	54	70	....	....	....	....	....	....	....	....	....	9	2	1	3	8	....	....	....	....
	NHL Totals		36	4	6	10	33	1	0	3	30	13.3		255	47.1	10:43	....	....	....	....	....	....	....	....	....

ECHL Rookie of the Year (2003) • AHL Second All-Star Team (2007)

Signed as a free agent by **Vancouver**, July 3, 2007. Signed as a free agent by **Calgary**, July 7, 2009. Traded to **Anaheim** by **Calgary** with future considerations for Logan MacMillan and future considerations, June 30, 2010.

JAMES, Connor (JAYMZ, KAW-nuhr)

Right wing. Shoots right. 5'10", 180 lbs. Born, Calgary, Alta., August 25, 1982. Los Angeles' 11th choice, 279th overall, in 2002 Entry Draft.

Season	Club	League	GP	G	A	Pts	PIM	PP	SH	GW	S	%	+/-	TF	F%	Min	GP	G	A	Pts	PIM	PP	SH	GW	Min
1998-99	Calgary Buffaloes	AMHL	36	33	53	86	20	....	....	....	....	....	....	....	....	....	....	....	....	....	....	....	....	....	....
99-2000	Calgary Royals	AJHL	64	36	57	93	41	....	....	....	....	....	....	....	....	....	....	....	....	....	....	....	....	....	....
2000-01	U. of Denver	WCHA	38	8	19	27	14	....	....	....	....	....	....	....	....	....	....	....	....	....	....	....	....	....	....
2001-02	U. of Denver	WCHA	41	16	26	42	18	....	....	....	....	....	....	....	....	....	....	....	....	....	....	....	....	....	....
2002-03	U. of Denver	WCHA	41	20	23	43	12	....	....	....	....	....	....	....	....	....	....	....	....	....	....	....	....	....	....
2003-04	U. of Denver	WCHA	40	13	25	38	16	....	....	....	....	....	....	....	....	....	....	....	....	....	....	....	....	....	....
2004-05	Bakersfield	ECHL	51	21	25	46	34	....	....	....	....	....	....	....	....	....	5	3	1	4	0	....	....	....	....
	Manchester	AHL	14	2	1	3	10	....	....	....	....	....	....	....	....	....	3	0	0	0	0	....	....	....	....
2005-06	**Los Angeles**	**NHL**	2	0	0	0	0	0	0	0	1	0.0	–1	6	33.3	7:19	....	....	....	....	....	....	....	....	....
	Manchester	AHL	77	17	25	42	43	....	....	....	....	....	....	....	....	....	7	0	0	0	2	....	....	....	....
2006-07	Wilkes-Barre	AHL	70	12	20	32	29	....	....	....	....	....	....	....	....	....	11	4	8	8	8	....	....	....	....
2007-08	**Pittsburgh**	**NHL**	13	1	0	1	2	1	0	0	9	11.1	–2	0	0.0	7:26	....	....	....	....	....	....	....	....	....
	Wilkes-Barre	AHL	64	9	28	37	30	....	....	....	....	....	....	....	....	....	23	8	5	13	6	....	....	....	....
2008-09	**Pittsburgh**	**NHL**	1	0	0	0	0	0	0	0	0	0.0	0	0	0.0	8:15	....	....	....	....	....	....	....	....	....
	Wilkes-Barre	AHL	76	19	30	49	24	....	....	....	....	....	....	....	....	....	9	0	2	2	2	....	....	....	....
2009-10	Augsburg	Germany	55	15	38	53	28	....	....	....	....	....	....	....	....	....	14	4	8	12	6	....	....	....	....
	NHL Totals		16	1	0	1	2	1	0	0	10	10.0		6	33.3	7:28	....	....	....	....	....	....	....	....	....

NCAA Championship All-Tournament Team (2004)

Signed as a free agent by **Pittsburgh**, August 9, 2006. Signed as a free agent by **Augsburg** (Germany), July 31, 2009.

JANCEVSKI, Dan (jan-SEHV-skee, DAN) **PHI.**

Defense. Shoots left. 6'3", 222 lbs. Born, Windsor, Ont., June 15, 1981. Dallas' 2nd choice, 66th overall, in 1999 Entry Draft.

Season	Club	League	GP	G	A	Pts	PIM	PP	SH	GW	S	%	+/-	TF	F%	Min	GP	G	A	Pts	PIM	PP	SH	GW	Min
1995-96	Riverside Selects	Minor-ON	59	9	22	31	67	....	....	....	....	....	....	....	....	....	....	....	....	....	....	....	....	....	....
1996-97	Windsor Lions	Minor-ON	47	6	20	26	99	....	....	....	....	....	....	....	....	....	....	....	....	....	....	....	....	....	....
1997-98	Tecumseh	OHA-B	49	3	11	14	145	....	....	....	....	....	....	....	....	....	....	....	....	....	....	....	....	....	....
1998-99	London Knights	OHL	68	2	12	14	115	....	....	....	....	....	....	....	....	....	25	1	7	8	24	....	....	....	....
99-2000	London Knights	OHL	59	8	15	23	138	....	....	....	....	....	....	....	....	....	....	....	....	....	....	....	....	....	....
2000-01	London Knights	OHL	39	4	23	27	95	....	....	....	....	....	....	....	....	....	....	....	....	....	....	....	....	....	....
	Sudbury Wolves	OHL	31	3	14	17	42	....	....	....	....	....	....	....	....	....	12	0	9	9	17	....	....	....	....
2001-02	Utah Grizzlies	AHL	77	0	13	13	147	....	....	....	....	....	....	....	....	....	5	0	0	0	4	....	....	....	....
2002-03	Utah Grizzlies	AHL	76	1	10	11	172	....	....	....	....	....	....	....	....	....	2	0	1	1	12	....	....	....	....
2003-04	Utah Grizzlies	AHL	80	5	17	22	171	....	....	....	....	....	....	....	....	....	....	....	....	....	....	....	....	....	....
2004-05	Hamilton	AHL	80	6	20	26	163	....	....	....	....	....	....	....	....	....	4	0	0	0	2	....	....	....	....
2005-06	**Dallas**	**NHL**	2	0	0	0	0	0	0	0	0	0.0	1	0	0.0	9:13	....	....	....	....	....	....	....	....	....
	Iowa Stars	AHL	77	9	29	38	91	....	....	....	....	....	....	....	....	....	7	1	1	2	6	....	....	....	....
2006-07	Hamilton	AHL	80	7	24	31	87	....	....	....	....	....	....	....	....	....	22	3	11	14	16	....	....	....	....
2007-08	**Tampa Bay**	**NHL**	2	0	0	0	2	0	0	0	0	0.0	–1	0	0.0	2:23	....	....	....	....	....	....	....	....	....
	Norfolk Admirals	AHL	37	4	16	20	52	....	....	....	....	....	....	....	....	....	....	....	....	....	....	....	....	....	....
	Dallas	**NHL**	2	0	0	0	0	0	0	0	3	0.0	0	0	0.0	9:19	....	....	....	....	....	....	....	....	....
	Iowa Stars	AHL	33	3	7	10	36	....	....	....	....	....	....	....	....	....	....	....	....	....	....	....	....	....	....
2008-09	**Dallas**	**NHL**	3	0	0	0	0	0	0	0	4	0.0	0	0	0.0	15:20	....	....	....	....	....	....	....	....	....
	Hamilton	AHL	76	1	27	28	76	....	....	....	....	....	....	....	....	....	6	0	3	3	6	....	....	....	....
2009-10	Texas Stars	AHL	78	3	20	23	71	....	....	....	....	....	....	....	....	....	24	1	11	12	20	....	....	....	....
	NHL Totals		9	0	0	0	2	0	0	0	7	0.0		0	0.0	9:45	....	....	....	....	....	....	....	....	....

Signed as a free agent by **Montreal**, July 13, 2006. Signed as a free agent by **Tampa Bay**, July 6, 2007. Traded to **Dallas** by **Tampa Bay** for Junior Lessard, January 15, 2008. Signed as a free agent by **Philadelphia**, July 22, 2010.

JANIK, Doug (JAN-nihk, DUHG) **DET.**

Defense. Shoots left. 6'1", 215 lbs. Born, Agawam, MA, March 26, 1980. Buffalo's 3rd choice, 55th overall, in 1999 Entry Draft.

Season	Club	League	GP	G	A	Pts	PIM	PP	SH	GW	S	%	+/-	TF	F%	Min	GP	G	A	Pts	PIM	PP	SH	GW	Min
1995-96	N.E. Jr. Whalers	EJHL	48	16	38	54		....	....	....	....	....	....	....	....	....	....	....	....	....	....	....	....	....	....
1996-97	N.E. Jr. Whalers	EJHL	39	12	24	36	22	....	....	....	....	....	....	....	....	....	11	5	9	14	10	....	....	....	....
1997-98	USNTDP	U-18	29	6	13	19	43	....	....	....	....	....	....	....	....	....	....	....	....	....	....	....	....	....	....
	USNTDP	USHL	19	1	6	7	34	....	....	....	....	....	....	....	....	....	....	....	....	....	....	....	....	....	....
	USNTDP	NAHL	10	0	4	4	10	....	....	....	....	....	....	....	....	....	7	1	3	4	18	....	....	....	....
1998-99	U. of Maine	H-East	35	3	13	16	44	....	....	....	....	....	....	....	....	....	....	....	....	....	....	....	....	....	....

			Regular Season														Playoffs								
Season	Club	League	GP	G	A	Pts	PIM	PP	SH	GW	S	%	+/-	TF	F%	Min	GP	G	A	Pts	PIM	PP	SH	GW	Min
99-2000	U. of Maine	H-East	36	6	14	20	54	....	....	....	....	....	....	....	....	....	....	....	....	....	....	....	....	....	....
2000-01	U. of Maine	H-East	39	3	15	18	52	....	....	....	....	....	....	....	....	....	....	....	....	....	....	....	....	....	....
2001-02	Rochester	AHL	80	6	17	23	100	....	....	....	....	....	....	....	....	....	2	0	0	0	0	....	....	....	....
2002-03	**Buffalo**	**NHL**	**6**	**0**	**0**	**0**	**2**	**0**	**0**	**0**	**1**	**0.0**	**1**	**0**	**0.0**	**7:42**	....	....	....	....	....	....	....	....	....
	Rochester	AHL	75	3	13	16	120	....	....	....	....	....	....	....	....	....	3	0	0	0	6	....	....	....	....
2003-04	**Buffalo**	**NHL**	**4**	**0**	**0**	**0**	**19**	**0**	**0**	**0**	**3**	**0.0**	**0**	**0**	**0.0**	**8:26**	....	....	....	....	....	....	....	....	....
	Rochester	AHL	74	2	14	16	109	....	....	....	....	....	....	....	....	....	16	1	2	3	22	....	....	....	....
2004-05	Rochester	AHL	76	2	10	12	196	....	....	....	....	....	....	....	....	....	9	0	2	2	10	....	....	....	....
2005-06	Rochester	AHL	71	5	19	24	161	....	....	....	....	....	....	....	....	....	....	....	....	....	....	....	....	....	....
	Buffalo	**NHL**	....	....	....	....	....	....	....	....	....	....	....	....	....	....	**5**	**1**	**0**	**1**	**2**	**0**	**0**	**0**	**10:30**
2006-07	**Tampa Bay**	**NHL**	**75**	**2**	**9**	**11**	**53**	**0**	**0**	**0**	**49**	**4.1**	**–11**	**0**	**0.0**	**14:28**	**1**	**0**	**0**	**0**	**0**	**0**	**0**	**0**	**3:42**
2007-08	**Tampa Bay**	**NHL**	**61**	**1**	**3**	**4**	**45**	**0**	**0**	**0**	**23**	**4.3**	**–3**	**0**	**0.0**	**9:20**	....	....	....	....	....	....	....	....	....
2008-09	**Dallas**	**NHL**	**13**	**0**	**1**	**1**	**2**	**0**	**0**	**0**	**1**	**0.0**	**–2**	**0**	**0.0**	**9:45**	....	....	....	....	....	....	....	....	....
	Rockford IceHogs	AHL	4	0	2	2	4	....	....	....	....	....	....	....	....	....	....	....	....	....	....	....	....	....	....
	Montreal	**NHL**	**2**	**0**	**0**	**0**	**2**	**0**	**0**	**0**	**0**	**0.0**	**–1**	**0**	**0.0**	**13:54**	....	....	....	....	....	....	....	....	....
	Hamilton	AHL	18	0	5	5	10	....	....	....	....	....	....	....	....	....	6	0	0	0	7	....	....	....	....
2009-10	**Detroit**	**NHL**	**13**	**0**	**2**	**2**	**18**	**0**	**0**	**0**	**5**	**0.0**	**–3**	**0**	**0.0**	**13:28**	....	....	....	....	....	....	....	....	....
	Grand Rapids	AHL	66	6	31	37	84	....	....	....	....	....	....	....	....	....	....	....	....	....	....	....	....	....	....
	NHL Totals		**174**	**3**	**15**	**18**	**141**	**0**	**0**	**0**	**82**	**3.7**		**0**	**0.0**	**11:52**	**6**	**1**	**0**	**1**	**2**	**0**	**0**	**0**	**9:22**

Signed as a free agent by **Tampa Bay**, July 6, 2006. Signed as a free agent by **Chicago**, July 15, 2008. Claimed on waivers by **Dallas** from **Chicago**, October 2, 2008. Claimed on waivers by **Chicago** from **Dallas**, October 8, 2008. Traded to **Dallas** by **Chicago** for Dallas's 7th round choice (Mac Carruth) in 2010 Entry Draft, October 8, 2008. Traded to **Montreal** by **Dallas** for Steve Begin, February 26, 2009. Signed as a free agent by **Detroit**, July 8, 2009.

JANSSEN, Cam

(JAN-suhn, KAM) **ST.L.**

Right wing. Shoots right. 6', 215 lbs. Born, St. Louis, MO, April 15, 1984. New Jersey's 6th choice, 117th overall, in 2002 Entry Draft.

Season	Club	League	GP	G	A	Pts	PIM	PP	SH	GW	S	%	+/-	TF	F%	Min	GP	G	A	Pts	PIM	PP	SH	GW	Min
2000-01	St. Louis Jr. Blues	CSJHL	45	1	2	3	244	....	....	....	....	....	....	....	....	....	....	....	....	....	....	....	....	....	....
2001-02	Windsor Spitfires	OHL	64	5	17	22	*268	....	....	....	....	....	....	....	....	....	10	0	0	0	13	....	....	....	....
2002-03	Windsor Spitfires	OHL	50	1	12	13	211	....	....	....	....	....	....	....	....	....	7	0	1	1	22	....	....	....	....
2003-04	Windsor Spitfires	OHL	35	4	9	13	144	....	....	....	....	....	....	....	....	....	....	....	....	....	....	....	....	....	....
	Guelph Storm	OHL	29	7	4	11	125	....	....	....	....	....	....	....	....	....	22	3	3	6	49	....	....	....	....
2004-05	Albany River Rats	AHL	70	1	3	4	337	....	....	....	....	....	....	....	....	....	....	....	....	....	....	....	....	....	....
2005-06	**New Jersey**	**NHL**	**47**	**0**	**0**	**0**	**91**	**0**	**0**	**0**	**10**	**0.0**	**–3**	**2**	**100.0**	**4:44**	**9**	**0**	**0**	**0**	**26**	**0**	**0**	**0**	**3:43**
	Albany River Rats	AHL	26	1	3	4	117	....	....	....	....	....	....	....	....	....	....	....	....	....	....	....	....	....	....
2006-07	**New Jersey**	**NHL**	**48**	**1**	**0**	**1**	**114**	**0**	**0**	**0**	**9**	**11.1**	**–2**	**1**	**100.0**	**4:06**	....	....	....	....	....	....	....	....	....
	Lowell Devils	AHL	9	0	1	1	29	....	....	....	....	....	....	....	....	....	....	....	....	....	....	....	....	....	....
2007-08	**St. Louis**	**NHL**	**12**	**0**	**1**	**1**	**18**	**0**	**0**	**0**	**9**	**0.0**	**–1**	**0**	**0.0**	**7:07**	....	....	....	....	....	....	....	....	....
	Lowell Devils	AHL	3	0	0	0	4	....	....	....	....	....	....	....	....	....	....	....	....	....	....	....	....	....	....
2008-09	**St. Louis**	**NHL**	**56**	**1**	**3**	**4**	**131**	**0**	**0**	**0**	**22**	**4.5**	**–5**	**2**	**0.0**	**5:01**	**1**	**0**	**0**	**0**	**0**	**0**	**0**	**0**	**3:59**
2009-10	**St. Louis**	**NHL**	**43**	**0**	**0**	**0**	**190**	**0**	**0**	**0**	**11**	**0.0**	**–3**	**1**	**0.0**	**4:43**	....	....	....	....	....	....	....	....	....
	NHL Totals		**206**	**2**	**4**	**6**	**544**	**0**	**0**	**0**	**61**	**3.3**		**6**	**50.0**	**4:48**	**10**	**0**	**0**	**0**	**26**	**0**	**0**	**0**	**3:45**

Traded to **St. Louis** by **New Jersey** for Bryce Salvador, February 26, 2008.

JEFFREY, Dustin

(JEHF-ree, DUHS-tihn) **PIT.**

Center. Shoots left. 6'1", 205 lbs. Born, Sarnia, Ont., February 27, 1988. Pittsburgh's 8th choice, 171st overall, in 2007 Entry Draft.

Season	Club	League	GP	G	A	Pts	PIM	PP	SH	GW	S	%	+/-	TF	F%	Min	GP	G	A	Pts	PIM	PP	SH	GW	Min
2003-04	Lambton Sting	Minor-ON	40	44	23	67	22	....	....	....	....	....	....	....	....	....	....	....	....	....	....	....	....	....	....
2004-05	Mississauga	OHL	53	10	15	25	20	....	....	....	....	....	....	....	....	....	....	....	....	....	....	....	....	....	....
2005-06	Mississauga	OHL	30	6	9	15	26	....	....	....	....	....	....	....	....	....	....	....	....	....	....	....	....	....	....
	Sault Ste. Marie	OHL	39	12	11	23	10	....	....	....	....	....	....	....	....	....	4	1	2	3	2	....	....	....	....
2006-07	Sault Ste. Marie	OHL	68	34	58	92	40	....	....	....	....	....	....	....	....	....	13	6	12	18	11	....	....	....	....
2007-08	Sault Ste. Marie	OHL	56	38	59	97	30	....	....	....	....	....	....	....	....	....	14	3	8	11	12	....	....	....	....
	Wilkes-Barre	AHL	....	....	....	....	....	....	....	....	....	....	....	....	....	....	15	2	1	3	4	....	....	....	....
2008-09	**Pittsburgh**	**NHL**	**14**	**1**	**2**	**3**	**0**	**0**	**0**	**0**	**18**	**5.6**	**4**	**103**	**41.8**	**10:47**	....	....	....	....	....	....	....	....	....
	Wilkes-Barre	AHL	63	11	26	37	31	....	....	....	....	....	....	....	....	....	12	5	5	10	8	....	....	....	....
2009-10	**Pittsburgh**	**NHL**	**1**	**0**	**0**	**0**	**0**	**0**	**0**	**0**	**0**	**0.0**	**0**	**0**	**0.0**	**8:35**	....	....	....	....	....	....	....	....	....
	Wilkes-Barre	AHL	77	24	47	71	16	....	....	....	....	....	....	....	....	....	4	0	1	1	6	....	....	....	....
	NHL Totals		**15**	**1**	**2**	**3**	**0**	**0**	**0**	**0**	**18**	**5.6**		**103**	**41.7**	**10:38**	....	....	....	....	....	....	....	....	....

JOENSUU, Jesse

(YOH-ehn-soo, JEH-see) **NYI**

Wing. Shoots left. 6'4", 212 lbs. Born, Pori, Finland, October 5, 1987. NY Islanders' 2nd choice, 60th overall, in 2006 Entry Draft.

Season	Club	League	GP	G	A	Pts	PIM	PP	SH	GW	S	%	+/-	TF	F%	Min	GP	G	A	Pts	PIM	PP	SH	GW	Min
2002-03	Assat Pori U18	Fin-U18	26	8	10	18	53	....	....	....	....	....	....	....	....	....	3	1	2	3	0	....	....	....	....
	Assat Pori Jr.	Fin-Jr.	3	0	1	1	2	....	....	....	....	....	....	....	....	....	....	....	....	....	....	....	....	....	....
2003-04	Assat Pori U18	Fin-U18	6	7	2	9	8	....	....	....	....	....	....	....	....	....	....	....	....	....	....	....	....	....	....
	Assat Pori Jr.	Fin-Jr.	28	7	9	16	18	....	....	....	....	....	....	....	....	....	3	0	1	1	2	....	....	....	....
	Assat Pori	Finland	6	0	0	0	0	....	....	....	....	....	....	....	....	....	....	....	....	....	....	....	....	....	....
2004-05	Assat Pori Jr.	Fin-Jr.	17	7	13	20	20	....	....	....	....	....	....	....	....	....	2	1	1	2	2	....	....	....	....
	Assat Pori	Finland	39	1	1	2	4	....	....	....	....	....	....	....	....	....	....	....	....	....	....	....	....	....	....
2005-06	Suomi U20	Finland-2	2	1	0	1	12	....	....	....	....	....	....	....	....	....	....	....	....	....	....	....	....	....	....
	Assat Pori	Finland	51	4	8	12	57	....	....	....	....	....	....	....	....	....	14	0	2	2	12	....	....	....	....
2006-07	Assat Pori Jr.	Fin-Jr.	5	2	1	3	6	....	....	....	....	....	....	....	....	....	....	....	....	....	....	....	....	....	....
	Suomi U20	Finland-2	2	0	2	2	6	....	....	....	....	....	....	....	....	....	....	....	....	....	....	....	....	....	....
	Assat Pori	Finland	52	9	17	26	74	....	....	....	....	....	....	....	....	....	....	....	....	....	....	....	....	....	....
2007-08	Assat Pori	Finland	56	17	18	35	89	....	....	....	....	....	....	....	....	....	....	....	....	....	....	....	....	....	....
	Bridgeport	AHL	1	0	0	0	0	....	....	....	....	....	....	....	....	....	....	....	....	....	....	....	....	....	....
2008-09	**NY Islanders**	**NHL**	**7**	**1**	**2**	**3**	**4**	**0**	**0**	**0**	**9**	**11.1**	**–1**	**0**	**0.0**	**12:06**	....	....	....	....	....	....	....	....	....
	Bridgeport	AHL	71	20	19	39	58	....	....	....	....	....	....	....	....	....	5	2	1	3	4	....	....	....	....
2009-10	**NY Islanders**	**NHL**	**11**	**1**	**0**	**1**	**4**	**0**	**0**	**0**	**13**	**7.7**	**4**	**1**	**0.0**	**11:09**	....	....	....	....	....	....	....	....	....
	Bridgeport	AHL	70	14	34	48	66	....	....	....	....	....	....	....	....	....	5	0	2	2	6	....	....	....	....
	NHL Totals		**18**	**2**	**2**	**4**	**8**	**0**	**0**	**0**	**22**	**9.1**		**1**	**0.0**	**11:31**	....	....	....	....	....	....	....	....	....

JOHNSON, Aaron

(JAWN-suhn, AIR-ruhn)

Defense. Shoots left. 6'1", 208 lbs. Born, Port Hawkesbury, N.S., April 30, 1983. Columbus' 4th choice, 85th overall, in 2001 Entry Draft.

Season	Club	League	GP	G	A	Pts	PIM	PP	SH	GW	S	%	+/-	TF	F%	Min	GP	G	A	Pts	PIM	PP	SH	GW	Min
1998-99	Cape Breton	NSAHA	56	28	42	70	98	....	....	....	....	....	....	....	....	....	....	....	....	....	....	....	....	....	....
99-2000	Rimouski Oceanic	QMJHL	63	1	14	15	57	....	....	....	....	....	....	....	....	....	8	0	0	0	0	....	....	....	....
2000-01	Rimouski Oceanic	QMJHL	64	12	41	53	128	....	....	....	....	....	....	....	....	....	11	2	4	6	35	....	....	....	....
2001-02	Rimouski Oceanic	QMJHL	68	17	49	66	172	....	....	....	....	....	....	....	....	....	7	1	2	3	12	....	....	....	....
2002-03	Rimouski Oceanic	QMJHL	25	4	20	24	41	....	....	....	....	....	....	....	....	....	....	....	....	....	....	....	....	....	....
	Quebec Remparts	QMJHL	32	6	31	37	41	....	....	....	....	....	....	....	....	....	11	4	4	8	25	....	....	....	....
2003-04	**Columbus**	**NHL**	**29**	**2**	**6**	**8**	**32**	**0**	**0**	**1**	**33**	**6.1**	**–2**	**0**	**0.0**	**15:02**	....	....	....	....	....	....	....	....	....
	Syracuse Crunch	AHL	49	6	15	21	83	....	....	....	....	....	....	....	....	....	7	2	3	5	27	....	....	....	....
2004-05	Syracuse Crunch	AHL	77	6	17	23	140	....	....	....	....	....	....	....	....	....	....	....	....	....	....	....	....	....	....
2005-06	**Columbus**	**NHL**	**26**	**2**	**6**	**8**	**23**	**1**	**0**	**1**	**28**	**7.1**	**9**	**0**	**0.0**	**14:12**	....	....	....	....	....	....	....	....	....
	Syracuse Crunch	AHL	49	5	24	29	122	....	....	....	....	....	....	....	....	....	6	1	3	4	19	....	....	....	....
2006-07	**Columbus**	**NHL**	**61**	**3**	**7**	**10**	**38**	**0**	**0**	**0**	**52**	**5.8**	**–9**	**0**	**0.0**	**12:44**	....	....	....	....	....	....	....	....	....
2007-08	**NY Islanders**	**NHL**	**30**	**0**	**2**	**2**	**30**	**0**	**0**	**0**	**16**	**0.0**	**2**	**0**	**0.0**	**13:52**	....	....	....	....	....	....	....	....	....
	Bridgeport	AHL	2	0	0	0	0	....	....	....	....	....	....	....	....	....	....	....	....	....	....	....	....	....	....
2008-09	**Chicago**	**NHL**	**38**	**3**	**5**	**8**	**33**	**0**	**0**	**1**	**27**	**11.1**	**19**	**0**	**0.0**	**14:09**	....	....	....	....	....	....	....	....	....
	Rockford IceHogs	AHL	2	0	1	1	4	....	....	....	....	....	....	....	....	....	....	....	....	....	....	....	....	....	....
2009-10	**Calgary**	**NHL**	**22**	**1**	**2**	**3**	**19**	**0**	**0**	**0**	**13**	**7.7**	**0**	**0**	**0.0**	**12:11**	....	....	....	....	....	....	....	....	....
	Edmonton	**NHL**	**19**	**3**	**4**	**7**	**16**	**1**	**0**	**0**	**23**	**13.0**	**–6**	**0**	**0.0**	**19:40**	....	....	....	....	....	....	....	....	....
	NHL Totals		**225**	**14**	**32**	**46**	**191**	**2**	**0**	**3**	**192**	**7.3**		**0**	**0.0**	**14:07**	....	....	....	....	....	....	....	....	....

Signed as a free agent by **NY Islanders**, July 12, 2007. • Missed majority of 2007-08 season recovering from recurring knee injury and as a healthy reserve. Signed as a free agent by **Chicago**, July 15, 2008. Traded to **Calgary** by **Chicago** for Kyle Greentree, October 7, 2009. Traded to **Edmonton** by **Calgary** with Calgary's 3rd round choice in 2011 Entry Draft for Steve Staios, March 3, 2010.

JOHNSON, Erik

(JAWN-suhn, AIR-ihk) **ST.L.**

Defense. Shoots right. 6'4", 236 lbs. Born, Bloomington, MN, March 21, 1988. St. Louis' 1st choice, 1st overall, in 2006 Entry Draft.

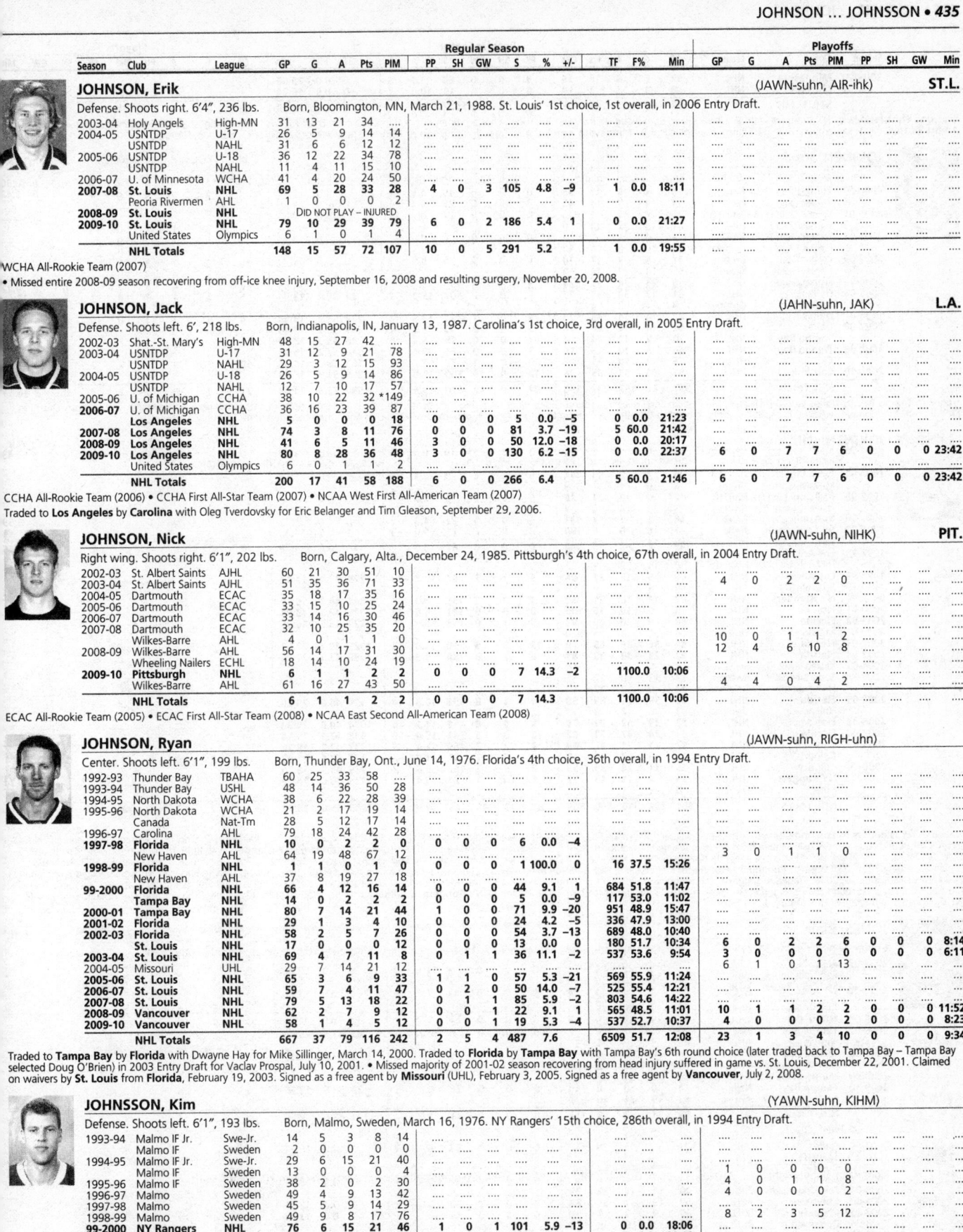

			Regular Season														Playoffs								
Season	Club	League	GP	G	A	Pts	PIM	PP	SH	GW	S	%	+/-	TF	F%	Min	GP	G	A	Pts	PIM	PP	SH	GW	Min
2003-04	Holy Angels	High-MN	31	13	21	34	....																		
2004-05	USNTDP	U-17	26	5	9	14	14																		
	USNTDP	NAHL	31	6	6	12	12																		
2005-06	USNTDP	U-18	36	12	22	34	78																		
	USNTDP	NAHL	11	4	11	15	10																		
2006-07	U. of Minnesota	WCHA	41	4	20	24	50																		
2007-08	**St. Louis**	**NHL**	**69**	**5**	**28**	**33**	**28**	**4**	**0**	**3**	**105**	**4.8**	**–9**	**1**	**0.0**	**18:11**									
	Peoria Rivermen	AHL	1	0	0	0	2																		
2008-09	**St. Louis**	**NHL**	DID NOT PLAY – INJURED																						
2009-10	**St. Louis**	**NHL**	**79**	**10**	**29**	**39**	**79**	**6**	**0**	**2**	**186**	**5.4**	**1**	**0**	**0.0**	**21:27**									
	United States	Olympics	6	1	0	1	4																		
	NHL Totals		**148**	**15**	**57**	**72**	**107**	**10**	**0**	**5**	**291**	**5.2**		**1**	**0.0**	**19:55**									

WCHA All-Rookie Team (2007)
• Missed entire 2008-09 season recovering from off-ice knee injury, September 16, 2008 and resulting surgery, November 20, 2008.

JOHNSON, Jack

(JAHN-suhn, JAK) **L.A.**

Defense. Shoots left. 6', 218 lbs. Born, Indianapolis, IN, January 13, 1987. Carolina's 1st choice, 3rd overall, in 2005 Entry Draft.

Season	Club	League	GP	G	A	Pts	PIM	PP	SH	GW	S	%	+/-	TF	F%	Min	GP	G	A	Pts	PIM	PP	SH	GW	Min
2002-03	Shat.-St. Mary's	High-MN	48	15	27	42	....																		
2003-04	USNTDP	U-17	31	12	9	21	78																		
	USNTDP	NAHL	29	3	12	15	93																		
2004-05	USNTDP	U-18	26	5	9	14	86																		
	USNTDP	NAHL	12	7	10	17	57																		
2005-06	U. of Michigan	CCHA	38	10	22	32	*149																		
2006-07	U. of Michigan	CCHA	36	16	23	39	87																		
	Los Angeles	**NHL**	**5**	**0**	**0**	**0**	**18**	**0**	**0**	**0**	**5**	**0.0**	**–5**	**0**	**0.0**	**21:23**									
2007-08	**Los Angeles**	**NHL**	**74**	**3**	**8**	**11**	**76**	**0**	**0**	**0**	**81**	**3.7**	**–19**	**5**	**60.0**	**21:42**									
2008-09	**Los Angeles**	**NHL**	**41**	**6**	**5**	**11**	**46**	**3**	**0**	**0**	**50**	**12.0**	**–18**	**0**	**0.0**	**20:17**									
2009-10	**Los Angeles**	**NHL**	**80**	**8**	**28**	**36**	**48**	**3**	**0**	**0**	**130**	**6.2**	**–15**	**0**	**0.0**	**22:37**	**6**	**0**	**7**	**7**	**6**	**0**	**0**	**0**	**23:42**
	United States	Olympics	6	0	1	1	2																		
	NHL Totals		**200**	**17**	**41**	**58**	**188**	**6**	**0**	**0**	**266**	**6.4**		**5**	**60.0**	**21:46**	**6**	**0**	**7**	**7**	**6**	**0**	**0**	**0**	**23:42**

CCHA All-Rookie Team (2006) • CCHA First All-Star Team (2007) • NCAA West First All-American Team (2007)
Traded to **Los Angeles** by **Carolina** with Oleg Tverdovsky for Eric Belanger and Tim Gleason, September 29, 2006.

JOHNSON, Nick

(JAWN-suhn, NIHK) **PIT.**

Right wing. Shoots right. 6'1", 202 lbs. Born, Calgary, Alta., December 24, 1985. Pittsburgh's 4th choice, 67th overall, in 2004 Entry Draft.

Season	Club	League	GP	G	A	Pts	PIM	PP	SH	GW	S	%	+/-	TF	F%	Min	GP	G	A	Pts	PIM	PP	SH	GW	Min
2002-03	St. Albert Saints	AJHL	60	21	30	51	10																		
2003-04	St. Albert Saints	AJHL	51	35	36	71	33										4	0	2	2	0				
2004-05	Dartmouth	ECAC	35	18	17	35	16																		
2005-06	Dartmouth	ECAC	33	15	10	25	24																		
2006-07	Dartmouth	ECAC	33	14	16	30	46																		
2007-08	Dartmouth	ECAC	32	10	25	35	20																		
	Wilkes-Barre	AHL	4	0	1	1	0										10	0	1	1	2				
2008-09	Wilkes-Barre	AHL	56	14	17	31	30										12	4	6	10	8				
	Wheeling Nailers	ECHL	18	14	10	24	19																		
2009-10	**Pittsburgh**	**NHL**	**6**	**1**	**1**	**2**	**2**	**0**	**0**	**0**	**7**	**14.3**	**–2**	**1**	**100.0**	**10:06**									
	Wilkes-Barre	AHL	61	16	27	43	50										4	4	0	4	2				
	NHL Totals		**6**	**1**	**1**	**2**	**2**	**0**	**0**	**0**	**7**	**14.3**		**1**	**100.0**	**10:06**									

ECAC All-Rookie Team (2005) • ECAC First All-Star Team (2008) • NCAA East Second All-American Team (2008)

JOHNSON, Ryan

(JAWN-suhn, RIGH-uhn)

Center. Shoots left. 6'1", 199 lbs. Born, Thunder Bay, Ont., June 14, 1976. Florida's 4th choice, 36th overall, in 1994 Entry Draft.

Season	Club	League	GP	G	A	Pts	PIM	PP	SH	GW	S	%	+/-	TF	F%	Min	GP	G	A	Pts	PIM	PP	SH	GW	Min
1992-93	Thunder Bay	TBAHA	60	25	33	58	....																		
1993-94	Thunder Bay	USHL	48	14	36	50	28																		
1994-95	North Dakota	WCHA	38	6	22	28	39																		
1995-96	North Dakota	WCHA	21	2	17	19	14																		
	Canada	Nat-Tm	28	5	12	17	14																		
1996-97	Carolina	AHL	79	18	24	42	28																		
1997-98	**Florida**	**NHL**	**10**	**0**	**2**	**2**	**0**	**0**	**0**	**0**	**6**	**0.0**	**–4**												
	New Haven	AHL	64	19	48	67	12										3	0	1	1	0				
1998-99	**Florida**	**NHL**	**1**	**1**	**0**	**1**	**0**	**0**	**0**	**0**	**1**	**100.0**	**0**	**16**	**37.5**	**15:26**									
	New Haven	AHL	37	8	19	27	18																		
99-2000	**Florida**	**NHL**	**66**	**4**	**12**	**16**	**14**	**0**	**0**	**0**	**44**	**9.1**	**1**	**684**	**51.8**	**11:47**									
	Tampa Bay	**NHL**	**14**	**0**	**2**	**2**	**2**	**0**	**0**	**0**	**5**	**0.0**	**–9**	**117**	**53.0**	**11:02**									
2000-01	**Tampa Bay**	**NHL**	**80**	**7**	**14**	**21**	**44**	**1**	**0**	**0**	**71**	**9.9**	**–20**	**951**	**48.9**	**15:47**									
2001-02	**Florida**	**NHL**	**29**	**1**	**3**	**4**	**10**	**0**	**0**	**0**	**24**	**4.2**	**–5**	**336**	**47.9**	**13:00**									
2002-03	**Florida**	**NHL**	**58**	**2**	**5**	**7**	**26**	**0**	**0**	**0**	**54**	**3.7**	**–13**	**689**	**48.0**	**10:40**									
	St. Louis	**NHL**	**17**	**0**	**0**	**0**	**12**	**0**	**0**	**0**	**13**	**0.0**	**0**	**180**	**51.7**	**10:34**	**6**	**0**	**2**	**2**	**6**	**0**	**0**	**0**	**8:14**
2003-04	**St. Louis**	**NHL**	**69**	**4**	**7**	**11**	**8**	**0**	**1**	**1**	**36**	**11.1**	**–2**	**537**	**53.6**	**9:54**	**3**	**0**	**0**	**0**	**0**	**0**	**0**	**0**	**6:11**
2004-05	Missouri	UHL	29	7	14	21	12										6	1	0	1	13				
2005-06	**St. Louis**	**NHL**	**65**	**3**	**6**	**9**	**33**	**1**	**1**	**0**	**57**	**5.3**	**–21**	**569**	**55.9**	**11:24**									
2006-07	**St. Louis**	**NHL**	**59**	**7**	**4**	**11**	**47**	**0**	**2**	**0**	**50**	**14.0**	**–7**	**525**	**55.4**	**12:21**									
2007-08	**St. Louis**	**NHL**	**79**	**5**	**13**	**18**	**22**	**0**	**1**	**1**	**85**	**5.9**	**–2**	**803**	**54.6**	**14:22**									
2008-09	**Vancouver**	**NHL**	**62**	**2**	**7**	**9**	**12**	**0**	**0**	**1**	**22**	**9.1**	**1**	**565**	**48.5**	**11:01**	**10**	**1**	**1**	**2**	**2**	**0**	**0**	**0**	**11:52**
2009-10	**Vancouver**	**NHL**	**58**	**1**	**4**	**5**	**12**	**0**	**0**	**1**	**19**	**5.3**	**–4**	**537**	**52.7**	**10:37**	**4**	**0**	**0**	**0**	**2**	**0**	**0**	**0**	**8:23**
	NHL Totals		**667**	**37**	**79**	**116**	**242**	**2**	**5**	**4**	**487**	**7.6**		**6509**	**51.7**	**12:08**	**23**	**1**	**3**	**4**	**10**	**0**	**0**	**0**	**9:34**

Traded to **Tampa Bay** by **Florida** with Dwayne Hay for Mike Sillinger, March 14, 2000. Traded to **Florida** by **Tampa Bay** with Tampa Bay's 6th round choice (later traded back to Tampa Bay – Tampa Bay selected Doug O'Brien) in 2003 Entry Draft for Vaclav Prospal, July 10, 2001. • Missed majority of 2001-02 season recovering from head injury suffered in game vs. St. Louis, December 22, 2001. Claimed on waivers by **St. Louis** from **Florida**, February 19, 2003. Signed as a free agent by **Missouri** (UHL), February 3, 2005. Signed as a free agent by **Vancouver**, July 2, 2008.

JOHNSSON, Kim

(YAWN-suhn, KIHM)

Defense. Shoots left. 6'1", 193 lbs. Born, Malmo, Sweden, March 16, 1976. NY Rangers' 15th choice, 286th overall, in 1994 Entry Draft.

Season	Club	League	GP	G	A	Pts	PIM	PP	SH	GW	S	%	+/-	TF	F%	Min	GP	G	A	Pts	PIM	PP	SH	GW	Min
1993-94	Malmo IF Jr.	Swe-Jr.	14	5	3	8	14																		
	Malmo IF	Sweden	2	0	0	0	0																		
1994-95	Malmo IF Jr.	Swe-Jr.	29	6	15	21	40																		
	Malmo IF	Sweden	13	0	0	0	4										1	0	0	0	0				
1995-96	Malmo IF	Sweden	38	2	0	2	30										4	0	1	1	8				
1996-97	Malmo	Sweden	49	4	9	13	42										4	0	0	0	2				
1997-98	Malmo	Sweden	45	5	9	14	29																		
1998-99	Malmo	Sweden	49	9	8	17	76										8	2	3	5	12				
99-2000	**NY Rangers**	**NHL**	**76**	**6**	**15**	**21**	**46**	**1**	**0**	**1**	**101**	**5.9**	**–13**	**0**	**0.0**	**18:06**									
2000-01	**NY Rangers**	**NHL**	**75**	**5**	**21**	**26**	**40**	**4**	**0**	**0**	**104**	**4.8**	**–3**	**0**	**0.0**	**21:16**									
2001-02	**Philadelphia**	**NHL**	**82**	**11**	**30**	**41**	**42**	**5**	**0**	**1**	**150**	**7.3**	**12**	**0**	**0.0**	**23:02**	**5**	**0**	**0**	**0**	**2**	**0**	**0**	**0**	**22:48**
	Sweden	Olympics	4	1	1	2	0																		
2002-03	**Philadelphia**	**NHL**	**82**	**10**	**29**	**39**	**38**	**5**	**0**	**2**	**159**	**6.3**	**11**	**0**	**0.0**	**24:05**	**13**	**0**	**3**	**3**	**8**	**0**	**0**	**0**	**26:07**
2003-04	**Philadelphia**	**NHL**	**80**	**13**	**29**	**42**	**26**	**4**	**0**	**3**	**189**	**6.9**	**16**	**0**	**0.0**	**24:27**	**15**	**2**	**6**	**8**	**8**	**0**	**0**	**1**	**26:11**
2004-05	HC Ambri-Piotta	Swiss	24	4	10	14	61																		
2005-06	**Philadelphia**	**NHL**	**47**	**6**	**19**	**25**	**34**	**3**	**0**	**0**	**97**	**6.2**	**5**	**0**	**0.0**	**23:17**									
	Sweden	Olympics	DID NOT PLAY																						
2006-07	**Minnesota**	**NHL**	**76**	**3**	**19**	**22**	**64**	**3**	**0**	**0**	**98**	**3.1**	**–4**	**0**	**0.0**	**23:33**	**4**	**0**	**0**	**0**	**2**	**0**	**0**	**0**	**23:06**
2007-08	**Minnesota**	**NHL**	**80**	**4**	**23**	**27**	**42**	**2**	**0**	**0**	**87**	**4.6**	**–4**	**0**	**0.0**	**23:27**	**6**	**0**	**1**	**1**	**18**	**0**	**0**	**0**	**28:08**
2008-09	**Minnesota**	**NHL**	**81**	**2**	**22**	**24**	**44**	**1**	**0**	**0**	**93**	**2.2**	**–3**	**0**	**0.0**	**24:32**									

			Regular Season														Playoffs								
Season	Club	League	GP	G	A	Pts	PIM	PP	SH	GW	S	%	+/-	TF	F%	Min	GP	G	A	Pts	PIM	PP	SH	GW	Min
2009-10	Minnesota	NHL	52	6	8	14	26	3	0	0	84	7.1	3	0	0.0	23:46	....	....	....	....	....	....	....	....	....
	Chicago	NHL	8	1	2	3	4	0	0	0	10	10.0	7	0	0.0	16:24	....	....	....	....	....	....	....	....	....
	NHL Totals		**739**	**67**	**217**	**284**	**406**	**31**	**0**	**7**	**1172**	**5.7**		**0**	**0.0**	**22:53**	**43**	**2**	**10**	**12**	**38**	**0**	**0**	**1**	**25:45**

Traded to **Philadelphia** by **NY Rangers** with Jan Hlavac, Pavel Brendl and NY Rangers' 3rd round choice (Stefan Ruzicka) in 2003 Entry Draft for Eric Lindros, August 20, 2001. Signed as a free agent by **Ambri-Piotta** (Swiss), September 18, 2004. Signed as a free agent by **Minnesota**, July 1, 2006. Traded to **Chicago** by **Minnesota** with Nick Leddy for Cam Barker, February 12, 2010.

JOKINEN, Jussi

(YOH-kih-nihn, YEW-see) **CAR**

Center. Shoots left. 5'11", 198 lbs. Born, Kalajoki, Finland, April 1, 1983. Dallas' 7th choice, 192nd overall, in 2001 Entry Draft.

Season	Club	League	GP	G	A	Pts	PIM	PP	SH	GW	S	%	+/-	TF	F%	Min	GP	G	A	Pts	PIM	PP	SH	GW	Min
99-2000	Karpat Oulu U18	Fin-U18	15	6	25	31	14	....	....	....	....	....	....	....	....	....	6	2	3	5	0	....	....	....	....
	Karpat Oulu Jr.	Fin-Jr.	28	4	7	11	14	....	....	....	....	....	....	....	....	....	....	....	....	....	....	....	....	....	....
2000-01	Karpat Oulu U18	Fin-U18	1	2	1	3	0	....	....	....	....	....	....	....	....	....	....	....	....	....	....	....	....	....	....
	Karpat Oulu Jr.	Fin-Jr.	41	18	31	49	69	....	....	....	....	....	....	....	....	....	6	2	1	3	0	....	....	....	....
2001-02	Karpat Oulu Jr.	Fin-Jr.	2	4	1	5	2	....	....	....	....	....	....	....	....	....	1	1	1	2	0	....	....	....	....
	Karpat Oulu	Finland	54	10	6	16	38	....	....	....	....	....	....	....	....	....	4	1	0	1	0	....	....	....	....
2002-03	Karpat Oulu	Finland	51	14	23	37	10	....	....	....	....	....	....	....	....	....	15	2	1	3	33	....	....	....	....
2003-04	Karpat Oulu	Finland	55	15	23	38	20	....	....	....	....	....	....	....	....	....	15	3	4	7	6	....	....	....	....
2004-05	Karpat Oulu	Finland	56	23	24	47	24	....	....	....	....	....	....	....	....	....	12	3	4	7	2	....	....	....	....
2005-06	**Dallas**	**NHL**	**81**	**17**	**38**	**55**	**30**	**8**	**0**	**2**	**107**	**15.9**	**2**	**23**	**30.4**	**13:34**	**5**	**2**	**1**	**3**	**0**	**1**	**0**	**0**	**13:4**
	Finland	Olympics	8	1	3	4	2	....	....	....	....	....	....	....	....	....	....	....	....	....	....	....	....	....	....
2006-07	**Dallas**	**NHL**	**82**	**14**	**34**	**48**	**18**	**6**	**0**	**1**	**121**	**11.6**	**8**	**278**	**52.2**	**13:54**	**4**	**0**	**1**	**1**	**0**	**0**	**0**	**0**	**13:2**
2007-08	**Dallas**	**NHL**	**52**	**14**	**14**	**28**	**14**	**5**	**0**	**2**	**93**	**15.1**	**2**	**295**	**53.2**	**12:44**	....	....	....	....	....	....	....	....	....
	Tampa Bay	**NHL**	**20**	**2**	**12**	**14**	**4**	**1**	**0**	**0**	**38**	**5.3**	**–16**	**46**	**45.7**	**18:57**	....	....	....	....	....	....	....	....	....
2008-09	**Tampa Bay**	**NHL**	**46**	**6**	**10**	**16**	**16**	**2**	**0**	**0**	**64**	**9.4**	**–8**	**510**	**52.2**	**15:38**	....	....	....	....	....	....	....	....	....
	Carolina	**NHL**	**25**	**1**	**10**	**11**	**12**	**0**	**0**	**1**	**37**	**2.7**	**–2**	**163**	**58.3**	**14:43**	**18**	**7**	**4**	**11**	**2**	**2**	**0**	***3**	**15:3**
2009-10	**Carolina**	**NHL**	**81**	**30**	**35**	**65**	**36**	**10**	**0**	**6**	**160**	**18.8**	**3**	**265**	**51.3**	**16:49**	....	....	....	....	....	....	....	....	....
	NHL Totals		**387**	**84**	**153**	**237**	**130**	**32**	**0**	**12**	**620**	**13.5**		**1580**	**52.3**	**14:48**	**27**	**9**	**6**	**15**	**2**	**3**	**0**	**3**	**14:5**

Traded to **Tampa Bay** by **Dallas** with Jeff Halpern, Mike Smith and Dallas' 4th round choice (later traded to Minnesota, later traded to Edmonton – Edmonton selected Kyle Bigos) in 2009 Entry Draft for Brad Richards and Johan Holmqvist, February 26, 2008. Traded to **Carolina** by **Tampa Bay** for Wade Brookbank, Josef Melichar and future considerations, February 7, 2009.

JOKINEN, Olli

(YOH-kih-nihn, OH-lee) **CGY**

Center. Shoots left. 6'3", 215 lbs. Born, Kuopio, Finland, December 5, 1978. Los Angeles' 1st choice, 3rd overall, in 1997 Entry Draft.

Season	Club	League	GP	G	A	Pts	PIM	PP	SH	GW	S	%	+/-	TF	F%	Min	GP	G	A	Pts	PIM	PP	SH	GW	Min
1994-95	KalPa Kuopio U18	Fin-U18	30	22	28	50	92	....	....	....	....	....	....	....	....	....	....	....	....	....	....	....	....	....	....
	KalPa Kuopio Jr.	Fin-Jr.	6	0	1	1	6	....	....	....	....	....	....	....	....	....	....	....	....	....	....	....	....	....	....
1995-96	KalPa Kuopio U18	Fin-U18	9	9	13	22	4	....	....	....	....	....	....	....	....	....	....	....	....	....	....	....	....	....	....
	KalPa Kuopio Jr.	Fin-Jr.	25	20	14	34	47	....	....	....	....	....	....	....	....	....	7	4	4	8	20	....	....	....	....
	KalPa Kuopio	Finland	15	1	1	2	2	....	....	....	....	....	....	....	....	....	....	....	....	....	....	....	....	....	....
1996-97	HIFK Helsinki Jr.	Fin-Jr.	2	1	0	1	6	....	....	....	....	....	....	....	....	....	....	....	....	....	....	....	....	....	....
	HIFK Helsinki	Finland	50	14	27	41	88	....	....	....	....	....	....	....	....	....	....	....	....	....	....	....	....	....	....
1997-98	**Los Angeles**	**NHL**	**8**	**0**	**0**	**0**	**6**	**0**	**0**	**0**	**12**	**0.0**	**–5**	....	....	....	....	....	....	....	....	....	....	....	....
	HIFK Helsinki	Finland	30	11	28	39	32	....	....	....	....	....	....	....	....	....	9	7	2	9	2	....	....	....	....
1998-99	**Los Angeles**	**NHL**	**66**	**9**	**12**	**21**	**44**	**3**	**1**	**1**	**87**	**10.3**	**–10**	**779**	**43.9**	**14:42**	....	....	....	....	....	....	....	....	....
	Springfield	AHL	9	3	6	9	6	....	....	....	....	....	....	....	....	....	....	....	....	....	....	....	....	....	....
99-2000	**NY Islanders**	**NHL**	**82**	**11**	**10**	**21**	**80**	**1**	**2**	**3**	**138**	**8.0**	**0**	**841**	**46.1**	**16:15**	....	....	....	....	....	....	....	....	....
2000-01	**Florida**	**NHL**	**78**	**6**	**10**	**16**	**106**	**0**	**0**	**0**	**121**	**5.0**	**–22**	**638**	**42.3**	**13:23**	....	....	....	....	....	....	....	....	....
2001-02	**Florida**	**NHL**	**80**	**9**	**20**	**29**	**98**	**3**	**1**	**0**	**153**	**5.9**	**–16**	**1222**	**45.2**	**18:05**	....	....	....	....	....	....	....	....	....
	Finland	Olympics	4	2	1	3	0	....	....	....	....	....	....	....	....	....	....	....	....	....	....	....	....	....	....
2002-03	**Florida**	**NHL**	**81**	**36**	**29**	**65**	**79**	**13**	**3**	**6**	**240**	**15.0**	**–17**	**1925**	**46.7**	**22:02**	....	....	....	....	....	....	....	....	....
2003-04	**Florida**	**NHL**	**82**	**26**	**32**	**58**	**81**	**8**	**2**	**8**	**280**	**9.3**	**–16**	**1986**	**47.1**	**22:35**	....	....	....	....	....	....	....	....	....
2004-05	Kloten Flyers	Swiss	8	6	1	7	14	....	....	....	....	....	....	....	....	....	....	....	....	....	....	....	....	....	....
	Sodertalje SK	Sweden	23	13	9	22	52	....	....	....	....	....	....	....	....	....	....	....	....	....	....	....	....	....	....
	HIFK Helsinki	Finland	14	9	8	17	10	....	....	....	....	....	....	....	....	....	5	2	0	2	24	....	....	....	....
2005-06	**Florida**	**NHL**	**82**	**38**	**51**	**89**	**88**	**14**	**1**	**9**	**351**	**10.8**	**14**	**955**	**46.9**	**20:29**	....	....	....	....	....	....	....	....	....
	Finland	Olympics	8	6	2	8	2	....	....	....	....	....	....	....	....	....	....	....	....	....	....	....	....	....	....
2006-07	**Florida**	**NHL**	**82**	**39**	**52**	**91**	**78**	**9**	**1**	**8**	**351**	**11.1**	**18**	**1074**	**44.3**	**20:32**	....	....	....	....	....	....	....	....	....
2007-08	**Florida**	**NHL**	**82**	**34**	**37**	**71**	**67**	**18**	**0**	**5**	**341**	**10.0**	**–19**	**938**	**43.1**	**19:54**	....	....	....	....	....	....	....	....	....
2008-09	**Phoenix**	**NHL**	**57**	**21**	**21**	**42**	**49**	**6**	**2**	**2**	**169**	**12.4**	**–5**	**737**	**42.2**	**18:10**	....	....	....	....	....	....	....	....	....
	Calgary	**NHL**	**19**	**8**	**7**	**15**	**18**	**3**	**0**	**1**	**67**	**11.9**	**–7**	**215**	**47.4**	**21:03**	**6**	**2**	**3**	**5**	**4**	**0**	**0**	**0**	**19:2**
2009-10	**Calgary**	**NHL**	**56**	**11**	**24**	**35**	**53**	**2**	**0**	**2**	**162**	**6.8**	**2**	**739**	**49.3**	**18:30**	....	....	....	....	....	....	....	....	....
	NY Rangers	**NHL**	**26**	**4**	**11**	**15**	**22**	**1**	**0**	**1**	**74**	**5.4**	**1**	**234**	**49.6**	**16:29**	....	....	....	....	....	....	....	....	....
	Finland	Olympics	6	3	1	4	2	....	....	....	....	....	....	....	....	....	....	....	....	....	....	....	....	....	....
	NHL Totals		**881**	**252**	**316**	**568**	**869**	**81**	**13**	**46**	**2546**	**9.9**		**12283**	**45.6**	**18:42**	**6**	**2**	**3**	**5**	**4**	**0**	**0**	**0**	**19:2**

Played in NHL All-Star Game (2003)

Traded to **NY Islanders** by **Los Angeles** with Josh Green, Mathieu Biron and Los Angeles' 1st round choice (Taylor Pyatt) in 1999 Entry Draft for Ziggy Palffy, Bryan Smolinski, Marcel Cousineau and New Jersey's 4th round choice (previously acquired, Los Angeles selected Daniel Johansson) in 1999 Entry Draft, June 20, 1999. Traded to **Florida** by **NY Islanders** with Roberto Luongo for Mark Parrish and Oleg Kvasha, June 24, 2000. Signed as a free agent by **Kloten** (Swiss), September 15, 2004. Signed as a free agent by **Sodertalje** (Sweden), November, 2004. Signed as a free agent by **HIFK Helsinki** (Finland), January 30, 2005.Traded to **Phoenix** by **Florida** for Keith Ballard, Nick Boynton and Ottawa's 2nd round choice (previously acquired, later traded back to Phoenix - Phoenix selected Jared Staal) i 2008 Entry Draft, June 20, 2008. Traded to **Calgary** by **Phoenix** with Phoenix's 3rd round choice (later traded to Florida – Florida selected Josh Birkholz) in 2009 Entry Draft for Matthew Lombardi, Brando Prust and Calgary's 1st round choice (Brandon Gormley) in 2010 Entry Draft, March 4, 2009. Traded to **NY Rangers** by **Calgary** with Brandon Prust for Christopher Higgins and Ales Kotalik, February 2, 2010. Signed as a free agent by **Calgary**, July 1, 2010.

JONES, Blair

(JOHNZ, BLAYR) **T.**

Center. Shoots right. 6'3", 215 lbs. Born, Central Butte, Sask., September 27, 1986. Tampa Bay's 5th choice, 102nd overall, in 2005 Entry Draft.

Season	Club	League	GP	G	A	Pts	PIM	PP	SH	GW	S	%	+/-	TF	F%	Min	GP	G	A	Pts	PIM	PP	SH	GW	Min
2002-03	Bethune	SBHL	STATISTICS NOT AVAILABLE																						
	Red Deer Rebels	WHL	37	3	4	7	17	....	....	....	....	....	....	....	....	....	10	1	0	1	0	....	....	....	....
2003-04	Red Deer Rebels	WHL	72	9	22	31	55	....	....	....	....	....	....	....	....	....	19	1	5	6	24	....	....	....	....
2004-05	Red Deer Rebels	WHL	39	7	18	25	48	....	....	....	....	....	....	....	....	....	....	....	....	....	....	....	....	....	....
	Moose Jaw	WHL	29	7	18	25	30	....	....	....	....	....	....	....	....	....	5	2	5	7	8	....	....	....	....
2005-06	Moose Jaw	WHL	72	35	50	85	85	....	....	....	....	....	....	....	....	....	22	9	12	21	45	....	....	....	....
2006-07	**Tampa Bay**	**NHL**	**20**	**1**	**2**	**3**	**2**	**0**	**0**	**0**	**6**	**16.7**	**0**	**65**	**41.5**	**5:46**	....	....	....	....	....	....	....	....	....
	Springfield	AHL	45	5	16	21	36	....	....	....	....	....	....	....	....	....	....	....	....	....	....	....	....	....	....
2007-08	**Tampa Bay**	**NHL**	**4**	**0**	**0**	**0**	**0**	**0**	**0**	**0**	**1**	**0.0**	**0**	**8**	**12.5**	**1:55**	....	....	....	....	....	....	....	....	....
	Norfolk Admirals	AHL	75	14	28	42	50	....	....	....	....	....	....	....	....	....	....	....	....	....	....	....	....	....	....
2008-09	Norfolk Admirals	AHL	80	20	34	54	61	....	....	....	....	....	....	....	....	....	....	....	....	....	....	....	....	....	....
2009-10	**Tampa Bay**	**NHL**	**14**	**0**	**0**	**0**	**10**	**0**	**0**	**0**	**26**	**0.0**	**–5**	**28**	**53.6**	**12:50**	....	....	....	....	....	....	....	....	....
	Norfolk Admirals	AHL	63	9	21	30	27	....	....	....	....	....	....	....	....	....	....	....	....	....	....	....	....	....	....
	NHL Totals		**38**	**1**	**2**	**3**	**12**	**0**	**0**	**0**	**33**	**3.0**		**101**	**42.6**	**7:58**	....	....	....	....	....	....	....	....	....

WHL East Second All-Star Team (2006)

JONES, David

(JOHNZ, DAY-vihd) **CO**

Right wing. Shoots right. 6'2", 210 lbs. Born, Guelph, Ont., August 10, 1984. Colorado's 8th choice, 288th overall, in 2003 Entry Draft.

Season	Club	League	GP	G	A	Pts	PIM	PP	SH	GW	S	%	+/-	TF	F%	Min	GP	G	A	Pts	PIM	PP	SH	GW	Min
2000-01	Port Coquitlam	PIJHL	40	18	11	29	33	....	....	....	....	....	....	....	....	....	....	....	....	....	....	....	....	....	....
2001-02	Coquitlam	BCHL	59	19	32	51	62	....	....	....	....	....	....	....	....	....	....	....	....	....	....	....	....	....	....
2002-03	Coquitlam	BCHL	35	9	19	28	55	....	....	....	....	....	....	....	....	....	7	2	6	8	8	....	....	....	....
2003-04	Coquitlam	BCHL	53	33	60	93	78	....	....	....	....	....	....	....	....	....	7	3	6	9	4	....	....	....	....
2004-05	Dartmouth	ECAC	34	9	5	14	26	....	....	....	....	....	....	....	....	....	....	....	....	....	....	....	....	....	....
2005-06	Dartmouth	ECAC	33	17	17	34	38	....	....	....	....	....	....	....	....	....	....	....	....	....	....	....	....	....	....
2006-07	Dartmouth	ECAC	33	18	26	*44	22	....	....	....	....	....	....	....	....	....	....	....	....	....	....	....	....	....	....
2007-08	**Colorado**	**NHL**	**27**	**2**	**4**	**6**	**8**	**1**	**0**	**0**	**37**	**5.4**	**–5**	**8**	**37.5**	**11:22**	**10**	**0**	**1**	**1**	**6**	**0**	**0**	**0**	**11:**
	Lake Erie	AHL	45	14	16	30	16	....	....	....	....	....	....	....	....	....	....	....	....	....	....	....	....	....	....
2008-09	**Colorado**	**NHL**	**40**	**8**	**5**	**13**	**8**	**1**	**0**	**1**	**47**	**17.0**	**–8**	**8**	**50.0**	**12:44**	....	....	....	....	....	....	....	....	....
2009-10	**Colorado**	**NHL**	**23**	**10**	**6**	**16**	**2**	**1**	**2**	**3**	**39**	**25.6**	**1**	**7**	**28.6**	**17:56**	....	....	....	....	....	....	....	....	....
	NHL Totals		**90**	**20**	**15**	**35**	**18**	**3**	**2**	**4**	**123**	**16.3**		**23**	**39.1**	**13:39**	**10**	**0**	**1**	**1**	**6**	**0**	**0**	**0**	**11:**

ECAC Second All-Star Team (2006) • ECAC First All-Star Tearm (2007) • NCAA East First All-American Team (2007)

• Missed majority of 2008-09 season recovering from shoulder injury suffered in game vs. San Jose, January 27, 2009. • Missed remainder of 2009-10 season recovering from knee injury suffered in game vs. Minnesota, November 28, 2009.

JONES, Randy

(JOHNZ, RAN-dee)

Defense. Shoots left. 6'2", 200 lbs. Born, Quispamsis, N.B., July 23, 1981.

Season	Club	League	GP	G	A	Pts	PIM	PP	SH	GW	S	%	+/-	TF	F%	Min	GP	G	A	Pts	PIM	PP	SH	GW	Min
			Regular Season														Playoffs								
99-2000	Cobourg Cougars	OPJHL	44	20	36	56	51																		
2000-01	Cobourg Cougars	OPJHL	28	15	21	36	46																		
2001-02	Clarkson Knights	ECAC	34	9	11	20	32																		
2002-03	Clarkson Knights	ECAC	33	13	20	33	65																		
2003-04	**Philadelphia**	**NHL**	**5**	**0**	**0**	**0**	**0**	**0**	**0**	**0**	**5**	**0.0**	**1**	**0**	**0.0**	**12:00**									
	Philadelphia	AHL	55	8	24	32	63										12	0	1	1	17				
2004-05	Philadelphia	AHL	69	5	19	24	32										18	0	5	5	10				
2005-06	**Philadelphia**	**NHL**	**28**	**0**	**8**	**8**	**16**	**0**	**0**	**0**	**21**	**0.0**	**–6**	**1**	**100.0**	**14:58**									
	Philadelphia	AHL	21	2	3	5	53																		
2006-07	**Philadelphia**	**NHL**	**66**	**4**	**18**	**22**	**38**	**0**	**0**	**0**	**67**	**6.0**	**–14**	**1**	**0.0**	**16:06**									
2007-08	**Philadelphia**	**NHL**	**71**	**5**	**26**	**31**	**58**	**1**	**0**	**0**	**103**	**4.9**	**8**	**0**	**0.0**	**19:24**	**16**	**0**	**2**	**2**	**4**	**0**	**0**	**0**	**21:24**
2008-09	**Philadelphia**	**NHL**	**47**	**4**	**4**	**8**	**22**	**1**	**0**	**2**	**45**	**8.9**	**8**	**0**	**0.0**	**19:07**	**6**	**0**	**1**	**1**	**0**	**0**	**0**	**0**	**14:38**
	Philadelphia	AHL	2	0	2	2	0																		
2009-10	Adirondack	AHL	6	0	1	1	6																		
	Los Angeles	**NHL**	**48**	**5**	**16**	**21**	**28**	**1**	**1**	**1**	**54**	**9.3**	**–3**	**0**	**0.0**	**18:10**	**4**	**0**	**0**	**0**	**2**	**0**	**0**	**0**	**17:42**
	NHL Totals		**265**	**18**	**72**	**90**	**162**	**3**	**1**	**3**	**295**	**6.1**		**2**	**50.0**	**17:42**	**26**	**0**	**3**	**3**	**6**	**0**	**0**	**0**	**19:16**

ECAC First All-Star Team (2003)

Signed as a free agent by **Philadelphia**, July 24, 2003. Claimed on waivers by **Los Angeles** from **Philadelphia**, October 29, 2009.

JONES, Ryan

(JOHNZ, RIGH-uhn) **EDM.**

Right wing. Shoots left. 6'1", 202 lbs. Born, Chatham, Ont., June 14, 1984. Minnesota's 5th choice, 111th overall, in 2004 Entry Draft.

Season	Club	League	GP	G	A	Pts	PIM	PP	SH	GW	S	%	+/-	TF	F%	Min	GP	G	A	Pts	PIM	PP	SH	GW	Min
2002-03	Chatham	OHA-B	38	12	11	23	42																		
2003-04	Chatham	OHA-B	46	39	30	69	64										17	17	9	26	25				
2004-05	Miami U.	CCHA	38	8	7	15	79																		
2005-06	Miami U.	CCHA	39	22	13	35	72																		
2006-07	Miami U.	CCHA	42	29	19	48	88																		
2007-08	Miami U.	CCHA	42	31	18	49	83																		
	Houston Aeros	AHL	4	0	0	0	2										4	1	1	2	2				
2008-09	**Nashville**	**NHL**	**46**	**7**	**10**	**17**	**22**	**2**	**0**	**1**	**63**	**11.1**	**1**	**10**	**10.0**	**11:26**									
	Milwaukee	AHL	25	13	9	22	30										11	4	3	7	10				
2009-10	**Nashville**	**NHL**	**41**	**7**	**4**	**11**	**18**	**2**	**0**	**0**	**53**	**13.2**	**3**	**1**	**0.0**	**10:43**									
	Milwaukee	AHL	15	4	1	5	15																		
	Edmonton	**NHL**	**8**	**1**	**0**	**1**	**8**	**0**	**0**	**0**	**9**	**11.1**	**–3**	**0**	**0.0**	**10:21**									
	NHL Totals		**95**	**15**	**14**	**29**	**48**	**4**	**0**	**1**	**125**	**12.0**		**11**	**9.1**	**11:02**									

CCHA Second All-Star Team (2006, 2007) • CCHA First All-Star Team (2008) • NCAA West First All-American Team (2008)

Traded to **Nashville** by **Minnesota** with Minnesota's 2nd round choice (Charles-Olivier Roussel) in 2009 Entry Draft for Marek Zidlicky, July 1, 2008. Claimed on waivers by **Edmonton** from **Nashville**, March 3, 2010.

JOSLIN, Derek

(JAWS-lihn, DAIR-ihk) **S.J.**

Defense. Shoots left. 6'1", 200 lbs. Born, Richmond Hill, Ont., March 17, 1987. San Jose's 5th choice, 149th overall, in 2005 Entry Draft.

Season	Club	League	GP	G	A	Pts	PIM	PP	SH	GW	S	%	+/-	TF	F%	Min	GP	G	A	Pts	PIM	PP	SH	GW	Min
2002-03	Vaughan	GTHL	60	9	18	27	72																		
2003-04	Aurora Tigers	OPJHL	36	4	12	16	....																		
	Ottawa 67's	OHL	7	0	0	0	4																		
2004-05	Ottawa 67's	OHL	68	6	24	30	44										21	0	3	3	24				
2005-06	Ottawa 67's	OHL	68	11	37	48	40										6	1	5	6	10				
	Cleveland Barons	AHL	2	0	0	0	0																		
2006-07	Ottawa 67's	OHL	68	11	38	49	66										5	1	4	5	4				
	Worcester Sharks	AHL	3	0	0	0	0										4	0	0	0	2				
2007-08	Worcester Sharks	AHL	80	10	24	34	44																		
2008-09	**San Jose**	**NHL**	**12**	**0**	**0**	**0**	**6**	**0**	**0**	**0**	**9**	**0.0**	**–3**	**0**	**0.0**	**11:22**									
	Worcester Sharks	AHL	63	11	19	30	40										12	0	2	2	8				
2009-10	**San Jose**	**NHL**	**24**	**0**	**3**	**3**	**12**	**0**	**0**	**0**	**19**	**0.0**	**1**	**0**	**0.0**	**13:53**									
	Worcester Sharks	AHL	55	5	27	32	29										11	4	1	5	4				
	NHL Totals		**36**	**0**	**3**	**3**	**18**	**0**	**0**	**0**	**28**	**0.0**		**0**	**0.0**	**13:02**									

JOVANOVSKI, Ed

(joh-van-OHV-skee, EHD) **PHX.**

Defense. Shoots left. 6'3", 218 lbs. Born, Windsor, Ont., June 26, 1976. Florida's 1st choice, 1st overall, in 1994 Entry Draft.

Season	Club	League	GP	G	A	Pts	PIM	PP	SH	GW	S	%	+/-	TF	F%	Min	GP	G	A	Pts	PIM	PP	SH	GW	Min
1991-92	Windsor	Minor-ON	50	25	40	65	88																		
1992-93	Windsor Bulldogs	OHA-B	48	7	46	53	88																		
1993-94	Windsor Spitfires	OHL	62	15	36	51	221										4	0	0	0	15				
1994-95	Windsor Spitfires	OHL	50	23	42	65	198										9	2	7	9	39				
1995-96	**Florida**	**NHL**	**70**	**10**	**11**	**21**	**137**	**2**	**0**	**2**	**116**	**8.6**	**–3**				**22**	**1**	**8**	**9**	**52**	**0**	**0**	**0**	
1996-97	**Florida**	**NHL**	**61**	**7**	**16**	**23**	**172**	**3**	**0**	**1**	**80**	**8.8**	**–1**				**5**	**0**	**0**	**0**	**4**	**0**	**0**	**0**	
1997-98	**Florida**	**NHL**	**81**	**9**	**14**	**23**	**158**	**2**	**1**	**3**	**142**	**6.3**	**–12**												
1998-99	**Florida**	**NHL**	**41**	**3**	**13**	**16**	**82**	**1**	**0**	**1**	**68**	**4.4**	**–4**	**0**	**0.0**	**22:35**									
	Vancouver	**NHL**	**31**	**2**	**9**	**11**	**44**	**0**	**0**	**0**	**41**	**4.9**	**–5**	**0**	**0.0**	**21:16**									
99-2000	**Vancouver**	**NHL**	**75**	**5**	**21**	**26**	**54**	**1**	**0**	**1**	**109**	**4.6**	**–3**	**0**	**0.0**	**24:03**									
2000-01	**Vancouver**	**NHL**	**79**	**12**	**35**	**47**	**102**	**4**	**0**	**2**	**193**	**6.2**	**–1**	**0**	**0.0**	**24:57**	**4**	**1**	**1**	**2**	**0**	**0**	**0**	**0**	**25:54**
2001-02	**Vancouver**	**NHL**	**82**	**17**	**31**	**48**	**101**	**7**	**1**	**3**	**202**	**8.4**	**–7**	**0**	**0.0**	**25:11**	**6**	**1**	**4**	**5**	**8**	**1**	**0**	**0**	**25:48**
	Canada	Olympics	6	0	3	3	4																		
2002-03	**Vancouver**	**NHL**	**67**	**6**	**40**	**46**	**113**	**2**	**0**	**1**	**145**	**4.1**	**19**	**0**	**0.0**	**24:15**	**14**	**7**	**1**	**8**	**22**	**4**	**1**	**2**	**23:40**
2003-04	**Vancouver**	**NHL**	**56**	**7**	**16**	**23**	**64**	**2**	**0**	**1**	**143**	**4.9**	**2**	**0**	**0.0**	**23:11**	**7**	**0**	**4**	**4**	**6**	**0**	**0**	**0**	**26:36**
2004-05			DID NOT PLAY																						
2005-06	**Vancouver**	**NHL**	**44**	**8**	**25**	**33**	**58**	**6**	**0**	**2**	**87**	**9.2**	**–8**	**0**	**0.0**	**24:26**									
	Canada	Olympics	DID NOT PLAY – INJURED																						
2006-07	**Phoenix**	**NHL**	**54**	**11**	**18**	**29**	**63**	**6**	**0**	**1**	**135**	**8.1**	**–6**	**0**	**0.0**	**23:09**									
2007-08	**Phoenix**	**NHL**	**80**	**12**	**39**	**51**	**73**	**8**	**0**	**2**	**240**	**5.0**	**–13**	**0**	**0.0**	**22:33**									
2008-09	**Phoenix**	**NHL**	**82**	**9**	**27**	**36**	**106**	**6**	**0**	**3**	**194**	**4.6**	**–15**	**1**	**0.0**	**22:10**									
2009-10	**Phoenix**	**NHL**	**66**	**10**	**24**	**34**	**55**	**5**	**0**	**2**	**117**	**8.5**	**–12**	**1**	**0.0**	**21:38**	**7**	**1**	**0**	**1**	**4**	**0**	**0**	**0**	**21:13**
	NHL Totals		**969**	**128**	**339**	**467**	**1382**	**55**	**2**	**25**	**2012**	**6.4**		**2**	**0.0**	**23:25**	**65**	**11**	**18**	**29**	**96**	**5**	**1**	**2**	**24:20**

OHL All-Rookie Team (1994) • OHL Second All-Star Team (1994) • OHL First All-Star Team (1995) • NHL All-Rookie Team (1996)

Played in NHL All-Star Game (2001, 2002, 2003, 2007, 2008)

Traded to **Vancouver** by **Florida** with Dave Gagner, Mike Brown, Kevin Weekes and Florida's 1st round choice (Nathan Smith) in 2000 Entry Draft for Pavel Bure, Bret Hedican, Brad Ference and Vancouver's 3rd round choice (Robert Fried) in 2000 Entry Draft, January 17, 1999. Signed as a free agent by **Phoenix**, July 1, 2006.

JUNLAND, Jonas

(YUHN-land, YOH-nuhs) **ST.L.**

Defense. Shoots left. 6'2", 198 lbs. Born, Linkoping, Sweden, November 15, 1987. St. Louis' 4th choice, 64th overall, in 2006 Entry Draft.

Season	Club	League	GP	G	A	Pts	PIM	PP	SH	GW	S	%	+/-	TF	F%	Min	GP	G	A	Pts	PIM	PP	SH	GW	Min
2002-03	Linkoping U18	Swe-U18	7	0	0	0	6																		
2003-04	Linkoping U18	Swe-U18	4	0	0	0	4																		
	Linkopings HC Jr.	Swe-Jr.	19	1	0	1	12																		
2004-05	Linkoping U18	Swe-U18	11	6	5	11	35																		
	Linkopings HC Jr.	Swe-Jr.	32	3	5	8	96																		
2005-06	Linkopings HC Jr.	Swe-Jr.	32	17	23	40	44																		
	Linkoping U18	Swe-U18	1	5	0	5	2																		
	Linkopings HC	Sweden	4	0	0	0	0																		
2006-07	Linkopings HC Jr.	Swe-Jr.	9	6	7	13	26																		
	IK Oskarshamn	Sweden-2	4	0	3	3	4																		
	Linkopings HC	Sweden	41	1	4	5	22										15	0	5	5	20				
2007-08	Linkopings HC	Sweden	52	3	17	20	42										16	4	3	7	18				
2008-09	**St. Louis**	**NHL**	**1**	**0**	**0**	**0**	**2**	**0**	**0**	**0**	**0**	**0.0**	**0**	**0**	**0.0**	**12:28**									
	Peoria Rivermen	AHL	70	13	18	31	52										5	0	1	1	6				

			Regular Season														Playoffs								
Season	**Club**	**League**	**GP**	**G**	**A**	**Pts**	**PIM**	**PP**	**SH**	**GW**	**S**	**%**	**+/-**	**TF**	**F%**	**Min**	**GP**	**G**	**A**	**Pts**	**PIM**	**PP**	**SH**	**GW**	**Min**
2009-10	**St. Louis**	**NHL**	**3**	**0**	**2**	**2**	**0**	**0**	**0**	**0**	**7**	**0.0**	**–3**	**0**	**0.0**	**17:11**	....	....	....	....	....	....	....	....	....
	Peoria Rivermen	AHL	74	14	30	44	49	....	....	....	....	....	....	....	....	....	....	....	....	....	....	....	....	....	....
	NHL Totals		**4**	**0**	**2**	**2**	**2**	**0**	**0**	**0**	**7**	**0.0**		**0**	**0.0**	**16:00**	....	....	....	....	....	....	....	....	....

Signed as a free agent by **Farjestad** (Sweden), May 1, 2010

JURCINA, Milan

(YEWR-chee-nah, MEE-lan) **NYI**

Defense. Shoots right. 6'4", 236 lbs. Born, Liptovsky Mikulas, Czech., June 7, 1983. Boston's 7th choice, 241st overall, in 2001 Entry Draft.

99-2000	L. Mikulas Jr.	Slovak-Jr.	STATISTICS NOT AVAILABLE																						
2000-01	Halifax	QMJHL	68	0	5	5	56	....	....	....	....	....	....	....	....	....	6	0	2	2	12	....	....	....	....
2001-02	Halifax	QMJHL	61	4	16	20	58	....	....	....	....	....	....	....	....	....	13	5	3	8	10	....	....	....	....
2002-03	Halifax	QMJHL	51	15	13	28	102	....	....	....	....	....	....	....	....	....	25	6	6	12	40	....	....	....	....
2003-04	Providence Bruins	AHL	73	5	12	17	52	....	....	....	....	....	....	....	....	....	2	0	1	1	2	....	....	....	....
2004-05	Providence Bruins	AHL	79	6	17	23	92	....	....	....	....	....	....	....	....	....	17	1	3	4	30	....	....	....	....
2005-06	**Boston**	**NHL**	**51**	**6**	**5**	**11**	**54**	**2**	**0**	**0**	**64**	**9.4**	**3**	**1**	**0.0**	**16:28**	....	....	....	....	....	....	....	....	....
	Providence Bruins	AHL	7	0	3	3	8	....	....	....	....	....	....	....	....	....	....	....	....	....	....	....	....	....	....
	Slovakia	Olympics	6	0	1	1	8	....	....	....	....	....	....	....	....	....	....	....	....	....	....	....	....	....	....
2006-07	**Boston**	**NHL**	**40**	**2**	**1**	**3**	**20**	**0**	**0**	**1**	**29**	**6.9**	**–5**	**0**	**0.0**	**10:42**	....	....	....	....	....	....	....	....	....
	Washington	**NHL**	**30**	**2**	**7**	**9**	**24**	**0**	**0**	**0**	**42**	**4.8**	**5**	**0**	**0.0**	**23:09**	....	....	....	....	....	....	....	....	....
2007-08	**Washington**	**NHL**	**75**	**1**	**8**	**9**	**30**	**1**	**0**	**0**	**58**	**1.7**	**4**	**0**	**0.0**	**16:38**	**7**	**0**	**0**	**0**	**6**	**0**	**0**	**0**	**16:26**
2008-09	**Washington**	**NHL**	**79**	**3**	**11**	**14**	**68**	**0**	**0**	**1**	**95**	**3.2**	**1**	**0**	**0.0**	**16:09**	**14**	**2**	**0**	**2**	**12**	**0**	**1**	**0**	**16:46**
2009-10	**Washington**	**NHL**	**27**	**0**	**4**	**4**	**14**	**0**	**0**	**0**	**32**	**0.0**	**0**	**0**	**0.0**	**17:26**	....	....	....	....	....	....	....	....	....
	Columbus	**NHL**	**17**	**1**	**2**	**3**	**10**	**0**	**0**	**1**	**17**	**5.9**	**2**	**0**	**0.0**	**18:02**	....	....	....	....	....	....	....	....	....
	Slovakia	Olympics	7	0	0	0	2	....	....	....	....	....	....	....	....	....	....	....	....	....	....	....	....	....	....
	NHL Totals		**319**	**15**	**38**	**53**	**220**	**3**	**0**	**3**	**337**	**4.5**		**1**	**0.0**	**16:30**	**21**	**2**	**0**	**2**	**18**	**0**	**1**	**0**	**16:40**

Traded to **Washington** by **Boston** for Washington's 4th round choice (later traded to Calgary - Calgary selected T. J. Brodie) in 2008 Entry Draft, February 1, 2007. Traded to **Columbus** by **Washington** with Chris Clark for Jason Chimera, December 28, 2009. Traded to **Washington** by **Columbus** for future considerations, March 3, 2010. Signed as a free agent by **NY Islanders**, July 2, 2010.

KABERLE, Frantisek

(KA-buhr-lay, FRAN-tih-sehk)

Defense. Shoots left. 6', 190 lbs. Born, Kladno, Czech., November 8, 1973. Los Angeles' 3rd choice, 76th overall, in 1999 Entry Draft.

1991-92	Poldi Kladno	Czech	37	1	4	5	8	....	....	....	....	....	....	....	....	....	8	0	1	1	0	....	....	....	....
1992-93	Poldi Kladno	Czech	40	4	5	9	....	....	....	....	....	....	....	....	....	....	9	2	4	6	....	....	....	....	....
1993-94	HC Kladno	CzRep	41	4	16	20	....	....	....	....	....	....	....	....	....	....	11	1	1	2	....	....	....	....	....
1994-95	HC Kladno	CzRep	40	7	17	24	20	....	....	....	....	....	....	....	....	....	8	0	3	3	12	....	....	....	....
1995-96	MoDo	Sweden	40	5	7	12	34	....	....	....	....	....	....	....	....	....	8	0	1	1	0	....	....	....	....
1996-97	MoDo	Sweden	50	3	11	14	28	....	....	....	....	....	....	....	....	....	....	....	....	....	....	....	....	....	....
1997-98	MoDo	Sweden	46	5	4	9	22	....	....	....	....	....	....	....	....	....	9	1	1	2	4	....	....	....	....
1998-99	MoDo	Sweden	45	15	18	33	4	....	....	....	....	....	....	....	....	....	13	2	5	7	8	....	....	....	....
99-2000	**Los Angeles**	**NHL**	**37**	**0**	**9**	**9**	**4**	**0**	**0**	**0**	**41**	**0.0**	**3**	**0**	**0.0**	**17:04**	....	....	....	....	....	....	....	....	....
	Long Beach	IHL	18	2	8	10	8	....	....	....	....	....	....	....	....	....	....	....	....	....	....	....	....	....	....
	Atlanta	**NHL**	**14**	**1**	**6**	**7**	**6**	**0**	**1**	**0**	**35**	**2.9**	**–13**	**0**	**0.0**	**24:39**	....	....	....	....	....	....	....	....	....
	Lowell	AHL	4	0	2	2	0	....	....	....	....	....	....	....	....	....	....	....	....	....	....	....	....	....	....
2000-01	**Atlanta**	**NHL**	**51**	**4**	**11**	**15**	**18**	**1**	**0**	**1**	**99**	**4.0**	**11**	**1**	**0.0**	**22:17**	....	....	....	....	....	....	....	....	....
2001-02	**Atlanta**	**NHL**	**61**	**5**	**20**	**25**	**24**	**1**	**0**	**0**	**82**	**6.1**	**–11**	**0**	**0.0**	**21:35**	....	....	....	....	....	....	....	....	....
2002-03	**Atlanta**	**NHL**	**79**	**7**	**19**	**26**	**32**	**3**	**1**	**2**	**105**	**6.7**	**–19**	**0**	**0.0**	**21:57**	....	....	....	....	....	....	....	....	....
2003-04	**Atlanta**	**NHL**	**67**	**3**	**26**	**29**	**30**	**2**	**0**	**1**	**94**	**3.2**	**2**	**2**	**50.0**	**23:20**	....	....	....	....	....	....	....	....	....
2004-05	HC Rabat Kladno	CzRep	22	5	11	16	34	....	....	....	....	....	....	....	....	....	....	....	....	....	....	....	....	....	....
	MODO	Sweden	8	2	2	4	0	....	....	....	....	....	....	....	....	....	6	1	0	1	27	....	....	....	....
2005-06 ♦	**Carolina**	**NHL**	**77**	**6**	**38**	**44**	**46**	**1**	**0**	**3**	**126**	**4.8**	**8**	**0**	**0.0**	**19:37**	**25**	**4**	**9**	**13**	**8**	**3**	**0**	**1**	**18:25**
	Czech Republic	Olympics	8	0	1	1	6	....	....	....	....	....	....	....	....	....	....	....	....	....	....	....	....	....	....
2006-07	**Carolina**	**NHL**	**27**	**2**	**6**	**8**	**20**	**1**	**0**	**1**	**33**	**6.1**	**8**	**0**	**0.0**	**15:32**	....	....	....	....	....	....	....	....	....
2007-08	**Carolina**	**NHL**	**80**	**0**	**22**	**22**	**30**	**0**	**0**	**0**	**89**	**0.0**	**–4**	**0**	**0.0**	**17:09**	....	....	....	....	....	....	....	....	....
2008-09	**Carolina**	**NHL**	**30**	**1**	**7**	**8**	**8**	**1**	**0**	**0**	**28**	**3.6**	**–4**	**0**	**0.0**	**14:03**	**7**	**0**	**1**	**1**	**2**	**0**	**0**	**0**	**12:14**
2009-10	Kladno	CzRep	64	4	17	21	74	....	....	....	....	....	....	....	....	....	....	....	....	....	....	....	....	....	....
	NHL Totals		**523**	**29**	**164**	**193**	**218**	**10**	**2**	**8**	**732**	**4.0**		**3**	**33.3**	**19:59**	**32**	**4**	**10**	**14**	**10**	**3**	**0**	**1**	**17:04**

Traded to **Atlanta** by **Los Angeles** with Donald Audette for Kelly Buchberger and Nelson Emerson, March 13, 2000. Signed as a free agent by **Carolina**, July 15, 2004. Signed as a free agent by **Kladno** (CzRep), September 17, 2004. Signed as a free agent by **MODO** (Sweden), January 31, 2005. • Missed majority of 2006-07 season recovering from off-season shoulder surgery. • Missed majority of 2008-09 season recovering from various injuries. Signed as a free agent by **Kladno** (CzRep), August 28, 2009.

KABERLE, Tomas

(KA-buhr-lay, TAW-mas) **TOR.**

Defense. Shoots left. 6'1", 214 lbs. Born, Rakovnik, Czech., March 2, 1978. Toronto's 13th choice, 204th overall, in 1996 Entry Draft.

1994-95	HC Kladno Jr.	CzRep-Jr.	37	7	10	17	....	....	....	....	....	....	....	....	....	....	....	....	....	....	....	....	....	....	....
	HC Kladno	CzRep	4	0	1	1	0	....	....	....	....	....	....	....	....	....	....	....	....	....	....	....	....	....	....
1995-96	Kladno Jr.	CzRep-Jr.	23	6	13	19	....	....	....	....	....	....	....	....	....	....	....	....	....	....	....	....	....	....	....
	HC Poldi Kladno	CzRep	23	0	1	1	2	....	....	....	....	....	....	....	....	....	2	0	0	0	0	....	....	....	....
1996-97	HC Poldi Kladno	CzRep	49	0	5	5	26	....	....	....	....	....	....	....	....	....	3	0	0	0	0	....	....	....	....
1997-98	Kladno	CzRep	47	4	19	23	12	....	....	....	....	....	....	....	....	....	....	....	....	....	....	....	....	....	....
	St. John's	AHL	2	0	0	0	0	....	....	....	....	....	....	....	....	....	....	....	....	....	....	....	....	....	....
1998-99	**Toronto**	**NHL**	**57**	**4**	**18**	**22**	**12**	**0**	**0**	**2**	**71**	**5.6**	**3**	**0**	**0.0**	**18:42**	**14**	**0**	**3**	**3**	**2**	**0**	**0**	**0**	**17:10**
99-2000	**Toronto**	**NHL**	**82**	**7**	**33**	**40**	**24**	**2**	**0**	**0**	**82**	**8.5**	**3**	**0**	**0.0**	**22:55**	**12**	**1**	**4**	**5**	**0**	**0**	**0**	**1**	**23:01**
2000-01	**Toronto**	**NHL**	**82**	**6**	**39**	**45**	**24**	**0**	**0**	**1**	**96**	**6.3**	**10**	**2**	**0.0**	**22:41**	**11**	**1**	**3**	**4**	**0**	**0**	**0**	**1**	**21:33**
2001-02	Kladno	CzRep	9	1	7	8	4	....	....	....	....	....	....	....	....	....	....	....	....	....	....	....	....	....	....
	Toronto	**NHL**	**69**	**10**	**29**	**39**	**2**	**5**	**0**	**3**	**85**	**11.8**	**5**	**2**	**100.0**	**25:00**	**20**	**2**	**8**	**10**	**16**	**0**	**0**	**0**	**28:40**
	Czech Republic	Olympics	4	0	1	1	2	....	....	....	....	....	....	....	....	....	....	....	....	....	....	....	....	....	....
2002-03	**Toronto**	**NHL**	**82**	**11**	**36**	**47**	**30**	**4**	**1**	**2**	**119**	**9.2**	**20**	**3**	**66.7**	**24:50**	**7**	**2**	**1**	**3**	**0**	**1**	**0**	**1**	**30:04**
2003-04	**Toronto**	**NHL**	**71**	**3**	**28**	**31**	**18**	**0**	**0**	**1**	**88**	**3.4**	**16**	**2**	**0.0**	**23:12**	**13**	**0**	**3**	**3**	**6**	**0**	**0**	**0**	**20:16**
2004-05	HC Rabat Kladno	CzRep	49	8	31	39	38	....	....	....	....	....	....	....	....	....	7	1	0	1	0	....	....	....	....
2005-06	**Toronto**	**NHL**	**82**	**9**	**58**	**67**	**46**	**6**	**0**	**2**	**163**	**5.5**	**–1**	**0**	**0.0**	**28:10**	....	....	....	....	....	....	....	....	....
	Czech Republic	Olympics	8	2	2	4	2	....	....	....	....	....	....	....	....	....	....	....	....	....	....	....	....	....	....
2006-07	**Toronto**	**NHL**	**74**	**11**	**47**	**58**	**20**	**2**	**0**	**1**	**128**	**8.6**	**3**	**0**	**0.0**	**25:52**	....	....	....	....	....	....	....	....	....
2007-08	**Toronto**	**NHL**	**82**	**8**	**45**	**53**	**22**	**6**	**0**	**1**	**155**	**5.2**	**–8**	**2**	**50.0**	**24:52**	....	....	....	....	....	....	....	....	....
2008-09	**Toronto**	**NHL**	**57**	**4**	**27**	**31**	**8**	**3**	**0**	**1**	**93**	**4.3**	**–8**	**0**	**0.0**	**23:28**	....	....	....	....	....	....	....	....	....
2009-10	**Toronto**	**NHL**	**82**	**7**	**42**	**49**	**24**	**3**	**0**	**1**	**158**	**4.4**	**–16**	**0**	**0.0**	**22:21**	....	....	....	....	....	....	....	....	....
	Czech Republic	Olympics	5	1	2	3	0	....	....	....	....	....	....	....	....	....	....	....	....	....	....	....	....	....	....
	NHL Totals		**820**	**80**	**402**	**482**	**230**	**31**	**1**	**15**	**1238**	**6.5**		**11**	**45.5**	**23:58**	**77**	**6**	**22**	**28**	**24**	**1**	**0**	**3**	**23:23**

Played in NHL All-Star Game (2002, 2007, 2008, 2009)

Signed as a restricted free agent by **Kladno** (CzRep) with **Toronto** retaining NHL rights, September 29, 2001. Signed as a free agent by **Kladno** (CzRep), September 17, 2004.

KADRI, Nazem

(KAH-dree, NA-zihm) **TOR.**

Center. Shoots left. 6', 177 lbs. Born, London, Ont., October 6, 1990. Toronto's 1st choice, 7th overall, in 2009 Entry Draft.

2005-06	Lon. Jr. Knights	Minor-ON	62	49	43	92	82	....	....	....	....	....	....	....	....	....	....	....	....	....	....	....	....	....	....
2006-07	Kitchener Rangers	OHL	62	7	15	22	30	....	....	....	....	....	....	....	....	....	9	0	2	2	4	....	....	....	....
2007-08	Kitchener Rangers	OHL	68	25	40	65	57	....	....	....	....	....	....	....	....	....	20	9	17	26	26	....	....	....	....
2008-09	London Knights	OHL	56	25	53	78	31	....	....	....	....	....	....	....	....	....	14	9	12	21	22	....	....	....	....
2009-10	London Knights	OHL	56	35	58	93	105	....	....	....	....	....	....	....	....	....	12	9	18	27	26	....	....	....	....
	Toronto	**NHL**	**1**	**0**	**0**	**0**	**0**	**0**	**0**	**0**	**0**	**0.0**	**–1**	**13**	**15.4**	**17:26**	....	....	....	....	....	....	....	....	....
	NHL Totals		**1**	**0**	**0**	**0**	**0**	**0**	**0**	**0**	**0**	**0.0**		**13**	**15.4**	**17:26**	....	....	....	....	....	....	....	....	....

OHL Second All-Star Team (2010)

KAIGORODOV, Alexei

(kay-goh-ROH-dahv, al-EHX-ay) **PHX.**

Center. Shoots left. 6'1", 194 lbs. Born, Magnitogorsk, USSR, July 29, 1983. Ottawa's 2nd choice, 47th overall, in 2002 Entry Draft.

			Regular Season														Playoffs								
Season	Club	League	GP	G	A	Pts	PIM	PP	SH	GW	S	%	+/-	TF	F%	Min	GP	G	A	Pts	PIM	PP	SH	GW	Min
1998-99	Magnitogorsk 2	Russia-4	10	6	4	10	2	....	....	....	....	....	....	....	....	....	....	....	....	....	....	....	....	....	....
99-2000	Magnitogorsk 2	Russia-3	19	2	3	5	8	....	....	....	....	....	....	....	....	....	....	....	....	....	....	....	....	....	....
2000-01	Magnitogorsk 2	Russia-3	45	12	30	42	26	....	....	....	....	....	....	....	....	....	....	....	....	....	....	....	....	....	....
2001-02	Magnitogorsk	Russia	46	4	12	16	20	....	....	....	....	....	....	....	....	....	9	0	3	3	2	....	....	....	....
2002-03	Magnitogorsk	Russia	46	8	14	22	20	....	....	....	....	....	....	....	....	....	3	0	1	1	0	....	....	....	....
2003-04	Magnitogorsk	Russia	49	4	12	16	24	....	....	....	....	....	....	....	....	....	14	2	2	4	4	....	....	....	....
2004-05	Magnitogorsk	Russia	57	15	34	49	40	....	....	....	....	....	....	....	....	....	5	0	3	3	2	....	....	....	....
2005-06	Magnitogorsk	Russia	50	9	21	30	42	....	....	....	....	....	....	....	....	....	11	0	1	1	6	....	....	....	....
2006-07	**Ottawa**	**NHL**	**6**	**0**	**1**	**1**	**0**	**0**	**0**	**0**	**3**	**0.0**	**1**	**24**	**20.8**	**4:53**	....	....	....	....	....	....	....	....	....
	Magnitogorsk	Russia	32	6	12	18	18	....	....	....	....	....	....	....	....	....	15	2	8	10	14	....	....	....	....
2007-08	Magnitogorsk	Russia	56	6	33	39	30	....	....	....	....	....	....	....	....	....	13	1	4	5	4	....	....	....	....
2008-09	Magnitogorsk	Rus-KHL	56	10	29	39	26	....	....	....	....	....	....	....	....	....	12	4	4	8	10	....	....	....	....
2009-10	Magnitogorsk	Rus-KHL	52	4	11	15	16	....	....	....	....	....	....	....	....	....	8	0	0	0	4	....	....	....	....
	NHL Totals		**6**	**0**	**1**	**1**	**0**	**0**	**0**	**0**	**3**	**0.0**		**24**	**20.8**	**4:53**	....	....	....	....	....	....	....	....	....

Traded to **Phoenix** by **Ottawa** for Mike Comrie, January 3, 2007.

KALETA, Patrick

(ka-LEH-tuh, PAT-rihk) **BUF.**

Right wing. Shoots right. 5'11", 198 lbs. Born, Buffalo, NY, June 8, 1986. Buffalo's 5th choice, 176th overall, in 2004 Entry Draft.

Season	Club	League	GP	G	A	Pts	PIM	PP	SH	GW	S	%	+/-	TF	F%	Min	GP	G	A	Pts	PIM	PP	SH	GW	Min
2002-03	Peterborough	OHL	67	7	9	16	67	....	....	....	....	....	....	....	....	....	7	0	0	0	6	....	....	....	....
2003-04	Peterborough	OHL	67	14	14	28	124	....	....	....	....	....	....	....	....	....	....	....	....	....	....	....	....	....	....
2004-05	Peterborough	OHL	62	24	28	52	146	....	....	....	....	....	....	....	....	....	14	3	3	6	30	....	....	....	....
2005-06	Peterborough	OHL	68	16	35	51	121	....	....	....	....	....	....	....	....	....	19	8	10	18	43	....	....	....	....
2006-07	**Buffalo**	**NHL**	**7**	**0**	**2**	**2**	**21**	**0**	**0**	**0**	**6**	**0.0**	**3**	**0**	**0.0**	**6:49**	....	....	....	....	....	....	....	....	....
	Rochester	AHL	58	5	10	15	133	....	....	....	....	....	....	....	....	....	5	0	0	0	12	....	....	....	....
2007-08	**Buffalo**	**NHL**	**40**	**3**	**2**	**5**	**41**	**0**	**0**	**0**	**26**	**11.5**	**1**	**6**	**16.7**	**6:19**	....	....	....	....	....	....	....	....	....
	Rochester	AHL	29	1	3	4	109	....	....	....	....	....	....	....	....	....	....	....	....	....	....	....	....	....	....
2008-09	**Buffalo**	**NHL**	**51**	**4**	**5**	**9**	**89**	**0**	**0**	**0**	**35**	**11.4**	**1**	**5**	**20.0**	**8:55**	....	....	....	....	....	....	....	....	....
2009-10	**Buffalo**	**NHL**	**55**	**10**	**5**	**15**	**89**	**0**	**2**	**4**	**64**	**15.6**	**2**	**2**	**0.0**	**10:09**	**6**	**1**	**1**	**2**	**22**	**0**	**0**	**0**	**10:04**
	NHL Totals		**153**	**17**	**14**	**31**	**240**	**0**	**2**	**4**	**131**	**13.0**		**13**	**15.4**	**8:35**	**6**	**1**	**1**	**2**	**22**	**0**	**0**	**0**	**10:04**

KALININ, Dmitri

(kah-LIHN-ihn, dih-MEE-tree)

Defense. Shoots left. 6'3", 210 lbs. Born, Chelyabinsk, USSR, July 22, 1980. Buffalo's 1st choice, 18th overall, in 1998 Entry Draft.

Season	Club	League	GP	G	A	Pts	PIM	PP	SH	GW	S	%	+/-	TF	F%	Min	GP	G	A	Pts	PIM	PP	SH	GW	Min
1995-96	Chelyabinsk	CIS	20	0	3	3	10	....	....	....	....	....	....	....	....	....	....	....	....	....	....	....	....	....	....
1996-97	Yunior-T Kurgan	Russia-3	20	0	0	0	10	....	....	....	....	....	....	....	....	....	....	....	....	....	....	....	....	....	....
	Chelyabinsk	Russia	2	0	0	0	0	....	....	....	....	....	....	....	....	....	2	0	0	0	0	....	....	....	....
1997-98	Chelyabinsk	Russia	26	0	2	2	24	....	....	....	....	....	....	....	....	....	....	....	....	....	....	....	....	....	....
1998-99	Moncton Wildcats	QMJHL	39	7	18	25	44	....	....	....	....	....	....	....	....	....	4	1	1	2	0	....	....	....	....
	Rochester	AHL	3	0	1	1	14	....	....	....	....	....	....	....	....	....	7	0	0	0	6	....	....	....	....
99-2000	**Buffalo**	**NHL**	**4**	**0**	**0**	**0**	**4**	**0**	**0**	**0**	**3**	**0.0**	**0**	**0**	**0.0**	**16:53**	....	....	....	....	....	....	....	....	....
	Rochester	AHL	75	2	19	21	52	....	....	....	....	....	....	....	....	....	21	2	9	11	8	....	....	....	....
2000-01	**Buffalo**	**NHL**	**79**	**4**	**18**	**22**	**38**	**2**	**0**	**0**	**88**	**4.5**	**−2**	**1**	**100.0**	**19:50**	**13**	**0**	**2**	**2**	**4**	**0**	**0**	**0**	**20:05**
2001-02	**Buffalo**	**NHL**	**58**	**2**	**11**	**13**	**26**	**0**	**0**	**0**	**67**	**3.0**	**−6**	**0**	**0.0**	**18:03**	....	....	....	....	....	....	....	....	....
2002-03	**Buffalo**	**NHL**	**65**	**8**	**13**	**21**	**57**	**3**	**1**	**0**	**83**	**9.6**	**−7**	**0**	**0.0**	**21:41**	....	....	....	....	....	....	....	....	....
	Rochester	AHL	1	0	0	0	0	....	....	....	....	....	....	....	....	....	....	....	....	....	....	....	....	....	....
2003-04	**Buffalo**	**NHL**	**77**	**10**	**24**	**34**	**42**	**2**	**1**	**4**	**118**	**8.5**	**0**	**0**	**0.0**	**23:06**	....	....	....	....	....	....	....	....	....
2004-05	Magnitogorsk	Russia	48	2	8	10	14	....	....	....	....	....	....	....	....	....	5	0	0	0	2	....	....	....	....
2005-06	**Buffalo**	**NHL**	**55**	**2**	**16**	**18**	**54**	**0**	**0**	**0**	**47**	**4.3**	**14**	**0**	**0.0**	**16:45**	**8**	**0**	**2**	**2**	**2**	**0**	**0**	**0**	**16:53**
2006-07	**Buffalo**	**NHL**	**82**	**7**	**22**	**29**	**36**	**0**	**1**	**0**	**86**	**8.1**	**19**	**1**	**100.0**	**19:31**	**16**	**2**	**3**	**5**	**14**	**0**	**0**	**0**	**18:11**
2007-08	**Buffalo**	**NHL**	**46**	**1**	**7**	**8**	**32**	**1**	**0**	**0**	**60**	**1.7**	**−7**	**0**	**0.0**	**17:20**	....	....	....	....	....	....	....	....	....
2008-09	**NY Rangers**	**NHL**	**58**	**1**	**12**	**13**	**26**	**0**	**0**	**0**	**51**	**2.0**	**−7**	**0**	**0.0**	**17:01**	....	....	....	....	....	....	....	....	....
	Phoenix	**NHL**	**15**	**1**	**3**	**4**	**6**	**1**	**0**	**0**	**16**	**6.3**	**−2**	**0**	**0.0**	**20:12**	....	....	....	....	....	....	....	....	....
2009-10	Ufa	Rus-KHL	53	12	10	22	32	....	....	....	....	....	....	....	....	....	15	2	3	5	*58	....	....	....	....
	Russia	Olympics	4	1	1	2	0	....	....	....	....	....	....	....	....	....	....	....	....	....	....	....	....	....	....
	NHL Totals		**539**	**36**	**126**	**162**	**321**	**9**	**3**	**4**	**619**	**5.8**		**2**	**100.0**	**19:26**	**37**	**2**	**7**	**9**	**20**	**0**	**0**	**0**	**18:34**

AHL All-Rookie Team (2000)

Signed as a free agent by **Magnitogorsk** (Russia), September 25, 2004. Signed as a free agent by **NY Rangers**, July 3, 2008. Traded to **Phoenix** by **NY Rangers** with Nigel Dawes and Petr Prucha for Derek Morris, March 4, 2009. Signed as a free agent by **Ufa** (Russia-KHL), July 21, 2009.

KALINSKI, Jon

(kuh-LIHN-skee, JAWN) **PHI.**

Left wing. Shoots left. 6'1", 175 lbs. Born, Bonnyville , Alta., May 25, 1987. Philadelphia's 5th choice, 152nd overall, in 2007 Entry Draft.

Season	Club	League	GP	G	A	Pts	PIM	PP	SH	GW	S	%	+/-	TF	F%	Min	GP	G	A	Pts	PIM	PP	SH	GW	Min
2003-04	Bonnyville	AJHL	52	13	13	26	68	....	....	....	....	....	....	....	....	....	5	0	0	0	8	....	....	....	....
2004-05	Bonnyville	AJHL	58	16	25	41	195	....	....	....	....	....	....	....	....	....	4	2	0	2	6	....	....	....	....
2005-06	Minnesota State	WCHA	30	4	7	11	73	....	....	....	....	....	....	....	....	....	....	....	....	....	....	....	....	....	....
2006-07	Minnesota State	WCHA	37	17	10	27	74	....	....	....	....	....	....	....	....	....	....	....	....	....	....	....	....	....	....
2007-08	Minnesota State	WCHA	39	8	10	18	56	....	....	....	....	....	....	....	....	....	....	....	....	....	....	....	....	....	....
	Philadelphia	AHL	5	0	3	3	4	....	....	....	....	....	....	....	....	....	10	1	2	3	14	....	....	....	....
2008-09	**Philadelphia**	**NHL**	**12**	**1**	**2**	**3**	**0**	**0**	**0**	**1**	**7**	**14.3**	**−2**	**46**	**45.7**	**7:37**	....	....	....	....	....	....	....	....	....
	Philadelphia	AHL	46	10	7	17	49	....	....	....	....	....	....	....	....	....	4	1	2	3	4	....	....	....	....
2009-10	**Philadelphia**	**NHL**	**10**	**0**	**2**	**2**	**0**	**0**	**0**	**0**	**9**	**0.0**	**−2**	**30**	**36.7**	**6:57**	....	....	....	....	....	....	....	....	....
	NHL Totals		**22**	**1**	**4**	**5**	**0**	**0**	**0**	**1**	**16**	**6.3**		**76**	**42.1**	**7:19**	....	....	....	....	....	....	....	....	....

KALUS, Petr

(KAY-lihs, PEE-tuhr) **MIN.**

Left wing. Shoots left. 6'1", 197 lbs. Born, Ostrava, Czech., June 29, 1987. Boston's 2nd choice, 39th overall, in 2005 Entry Draft.

Season	Club	League	GP	G	A	Pts	PIM	PP	SH	GW	S	%	+/-	TF	F%	Min	GP	G	A	Pts	PIM	PP	SH	GW	Min
2002-03	HC Ostrava U17	CzR-U17	18	3	19	22	14	....	....	....	....	....	....	....	....	....	....	....	....	....	....	....	....	....	....
	HC Vitkovice U17	CzR-U17	10	3	1	4	37	....	....	....	....	....	....	....	....	....	....	....	....	....	....	....	....	....	....
	HC Vitkovice Jr.	CzRep-Jr.	11	0	0	0	4	....	....	....	....	....	....	....	....	....	....	....	....	....	....	....	....	....	....
2003-04	HC Vitkovice U17	CzR-U17	9	7	5	12	60	....	....	....	....	....	....	....	....	....	7	3	5	8	2	....	....	....	....
	HC Vitkovice Jr.	CzRep-Jr.	41	8	8	16	67	....	....	....	....	....	....	....	....	....	....	....	....	....	....	....	....	....	....
2004-05	HC Vitkovice Jr.	CzRep-Jr.	39	20	11	31	161	....	....	....	....	....	....	....	....	....	2	2	0	2	25	....	....	....	....
	Vitkovice	CzRep	1	0	0	0	0	....	....	....	....	....	....	....	....	....	....	....	....	....	....	....	....	....	....
2005-06	Regina Pats	WHL	60	36	22	58	87	....	....	....	....	....	....	....	....	....	6	4	1	5	6	....	....	....	....
2006-07	**Boston**	**NHL**	**9**	**4**	**1**	**5**	**6**	**1**	**0**	**0**	**8**	**50.0**	**0**	**0**	**0.0**	**11:16**	....	....	....	....	....	....	....	....	....
	Providence Bruins	AHL	43	13	17	30	110	....	....	....	....	....	....	....	....	....	9	1	0	1	12	....	....	....	....
2007-08	Houston Aeros	AHL	58	8	10	18	57	....	....	....	....	....	....	....	....	....	....	....	....	....	....	....	....	....	....
2008-09	MVD	Rus-KHL	17	0	2	2	106	....	....	....	....	....	....	....	....	....	....	....	....	....	....	....	....	....	....
	Houston Aeros	AHL	2	0	0	0	0	....	....	....	....	....	....	....	....	....	....	....	....	....	....	....	....	....	....
2009-10	**Minnesota**	**NHL**	**2**	**0**	**0**	**0**	**0**	**0**	**0**	**0**	**0**	**0.0**	**0**	**1**	**0.0**	**7:44**	....	....	....	....	....	....	....	....	....
	Houston Aeros	AHL	66	12	11	23	77	....	....	....	....	....	....	....	....	....	....	....	....	....	....	....	....	....	....
	NHL Totals		**11**	**4**	**1**	**5**	**6**	**1**	**0**	**0**	**8**	**50.0**		**1**	**0.0**	**10:38**	....	....	....	....	....	....	....	....	....

Traded to **Minnesota** by **Boston** with Boston's 4th round choice (Alexander Fallstrom) in 2009 Entry Draft for Manny Fernandez, July 1, 2007.

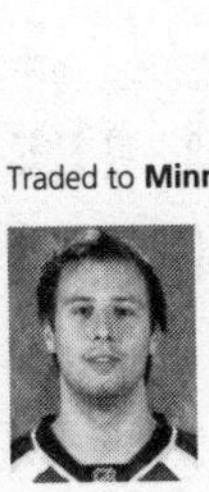

KANA, Tomas

(KA-nah, TAW-mahsh) **CBJ**

Center. Shoots right. 6', 208 lbs. Born, Opava, Czech., November 29, 1987. St. Louis' 3rd choice, 31st overall, in 2006 Entry Draft.

Season	Club	League	GP	G	A	Pts	PIM	PP	SH	GW	S	%	+/-	TF	F%	Min	GP	G	A	Pts	PIM	PP	SH	GW	Min
2002-03	HC Vitkovice U17	CzR-U17	44	20	14	34	72	....	....	....	....	....	....	....	....	....	2	2	0	2	4	....	....	....	....
	HC Vitkovice Jr.	CzRep-Jr.	3	2	0	2	4	....	....	....	....	....	....	....	....	....	....	....	....	....	....	....	....	....	....
2003-04	HC Vitkovice U17	CzR-U17	8	2	9	11	33	....	....	....	....	....	....	....	....	....	7	4	5	9	18	....	....	....	....
	HC Vitkovice Jr.	CzRep-Jr.	50	12	7	19	78	....	....	....	....	....	....	....	....	....	....	....	....	....	....	....	....	....	....
2004-05	HC Vitkovice Jr.	CzRep-Jr.	46	12	22	34	155	....	....	....	....	....	....	....	....	....	2	0	0	0	2	....	....	....	....
	Vitkovice	CzRep	1	0	0	0	0	....	....	....	....	....	....	....	....	....	....	....	....	....	....	....	....	....	....
2005-06	Vitkovice	CzRep	42	5	9	14	50	....	....	....	....	....	....	....	....	....	6	0	1	1	2	....	....	....	....
	HC Vitkovice Jr.	CzRep-Jr.	5	4	3	7	16	....	....	....	....	....	....	....	....	....	....	....	....	....	....	....	....	....	....

			Regular Season													Playoffs								
Season	Club	League	GP	G	A	Pts	PIM	PP	SH	GW	S	%	+/-	TF	F%	Min	GP	G	A	Pts	PIM	PP	SH	GW	Min
2006-07	Vitkovice	CzRep	44	9	7	16	54	....	....	....	....	....	....	....	....	....	....	....	....	....	....	....	....	....	....
	BK Mlada Boleslav	CzRep-2	6	2	1	3	16	....	....	....	....	....	....	....	....	....	6	1	0	1	16	....	....	....	....
2007-08	Alaska Aces	ECHL	12	2	0	2	4	....	....	....	....	....	....	....	....	....	....	....	....	....	....	....	....	....	....
	HC Sareza Ostrava	CzRep-2	8	3	0	3	6	....	....	....	....	....	....	....	....	....	....	....	....	....	....	....	....	....	....
	Vitkovice	CzRep	8	1	1	2	6	....	....	....	....	....	....	....	....	....	....	....	....	....	....	....	....	....	....
	Usti n. L.	CzRep	17	4	4	8	18	....	....	....	....	....	....	....	....	....	....	....	....	....	....	....	....	....	....
	Usti n. L.	CzRep-Q	....	....	....	....	....	....	....	....	....	....	....	....	....	....	3	0	0	0	2	....	....	....	....
2008-09	Peoria Rivermen	AHL	18	1	0	1	15	....	....	....	....	....	....	....	....	....	....	....	....	....	....	....	....	....	....
	Alaska Aces	ECHL	30	6	14	20	65	....	....	....	....	....	....	....	....	....	21	1	2	3	10	....	....	....	....
2009-10	Alaska Aces	ECHL	11	0	6	6	10	....	....	....	....	....	....	....	....	....	....	....	....	....	....	....	....	....	....
	Columbus	NHL	6	0	2	2	2	0	0	0	4	0.0	2	0	0.0	8:41	....	....	....	....	....	....	....	....	....
	Syracuse Crunch	AHL	50	15	13	28	47	....	....	....	....	....	....	....	....	....	....	....	....	....	....	....	....	....	....
	NHL Totals		6	0	2	2	2	0	0	0	4	0.0		0	0.0	8:41	....	....	....	....	....	....	....	....	....

Traded to **Columbus** by **St. Louis** with Brendan Bell for Pascal Pelletier, December 8, 2009.

KANE, Boyd

(KAYN, BOID)

Left wing. Shoots left. 6'2", 225 lbs. Born, Swift Current, Sask., April 18, 1978. NY Rangers' 4th choice, 114th overall, in 1998 Entry Draft.

1994-95	Regina Pats	WHL	25	6	5	11	6	....	....	....	....	....	....	....	....	....	4	0	0	0	0	....	....	....	....
1995-96	Regina Pats	WHL	72	21	42	63	155	....	....	....	....	....	....	....	....	....	11	5	7	12	12	....	....	....	....
1996-97	Regina Pats	WHL	66	25	50	75	154	....	....	....	....	....	....	....	....	....	5	1	1	2	15	....	....	....	....
1997-98	Regina Pats	WHL	68	48	45	93	133	....	....	....	....	....	....	....	....	....	9	5	7	12	29	....	....	....	....
1998-99	Hartford	AHL	56	3	5	8	23	....	....	....	....	....	....	....	....	....	....	....	....	....	....	....	....	....	....
	Charlotte	ECHL	12	5	6	11	14	....	....	....	....	....	....	....	....	....	....	....	....	....	....	....	....	....	....
99-2000	Hartford	AHL	8	0	0	0	9	....	....	....	....	....	....	....	....	....	....	....	....	....	....	....	....	....	....
	Charlotte	ECHL	47	10	19	29	110	....	....	....	....	....	....	....	....	....	....	....	....	....	....	....	....	....	....
	Binghamton	UHL	3	0	2	2	4	....	....	....	....	....	....	....	....	....	1	0	0	0	0	....	....	....	....
2000-01	Charlotte	ECHL	12	9	8	17	6	....	....	....	....	....	....	....	....	....	....	....	....	....	....	....	....	....	....
	Hartford	AHL	56	11	17	28	81	....	....	....	....	....	....	....	....	....	5	2	0	2	2	....	....	....	....
2001-02	Hartford	AHL	78	17	22	39	193	....	....	....	....	....	....	....	....	....	10	1	2	3	50	....	....	....	....
2002-03	Springfield	AHL	72	15	22	37	121	....	....	....	....	....	....	....	....	....	6	3	1	4	8	....	....	....	....
2003-04	Philadelphia	NHL	7	0	0	0	7	0	0	0	6	0.0	-4	3	33.3	9:56	....	....	....	....	....	....	....	....	....
	Philadelphia	AHL	73	13	22	35	177	....	....	....	....	....	....	....	....	....	12	0	1	1	39	....	....	....	....
2004-05	Philadelphia	AHL	58	9	15	24	112	....	....	....	....	....	....	....	....	....	21	0	7	7	28	....	....	....	....
2005-06	Washington	NHL	5	0	1	1	2	0	0	0	1	0.0	1	0	0.0	4:04	....	....	....	....	....	....	....	....	....
	Hershey Bears	AHL	74	20	29	49	185	....	....	....	....	....	....	....	....	....	21	4	9	13	14	....	....	....	....
2006-07	Philadelphia	NHL	15	0	2	2	28	0	0	0	7	0.0	-4	4	25.0	6:58	....	....	....	....	....	....	....	....	....
	Philadelphia	AHL	57	10	22	32	98	....	....	....	....	....	....	....	....	....	....	....	....	....	....	....	....	....	....
2007-08	Philadelphia	AHL	57	18	26	44	102	....	....	....	....	....	....	....	....	....	12	4	4	8	25	....	....	....	....
2008-09	Philadelphia	NHL	1	0	0	0	0	0	0	0	0	0.0	0	0	0.0	8:12	....	....	....	....	....	....	....	....	....
	Philadelphia	AHL	58	17	26	43	74	....	....	....	....	....	....	....	....	....	4	1	1	2	6	....	....	....	....
2009-10	Washington	NHL	3	0	0	0	2	0	0	0	2	0.0	-1	0	0.0	8:13	....	....	....	....	....	....	....	....	....
	Hershey Bears	AHL	76	24	20	44	77	....	....	....	....	....	....	....	....	....	21	1	6	7	34	....	....	....	....
	NHL Totals		31	0	3	3	39	0	0	0	16	0.0		7	28.6	7:20	....	....	....	....	....	....	....	....	....

• Re-entered NHL Entry Draft. Originally Pittsburgh's 3rd choice, 72nd overall, in 1996 Entry Draft.

Traded to **Tampa Bay** by **NY Rangers** for Gordie Dwyer, October 10, 2002. Signed as a free agent by **Philadelphia**, July 14, 2003. Signed as a free agent by **Washington**, August 12, 2005. Signed as a free agent by **Philadelphia**, July 13, 2006. Signed as a free agent by **Washington**, July 13, 2009.

KANE, Evander

(KAYN, ee-VAN-duhr) **ATL.**

Left wing. Shoots left. 6'2", 190 lbs. Born, Vancouver, B.C., August 2, 1991. Atlanta's 1st choice, 4th overall, in 2009 Entry Draft.

2006-07	Greater Van.	BCMML	30	22	32	54	150	....	....	....	....	....	....	....	....	....	....	....	....	....	....	....	....	....	....
	Vancouver Giants	WHL	8	1	0	1	11	....	....	....	....	....	....	....	....	....	5	0	0	0	0	....	....	....	....
2007-08	Vancouver Giants	WHL	65	24	17	41	66	....	....	....	....	....	....	....	....	....	10	1	2	3	8	....	....	....	....
2008-09	Vancouver Giants	WHL	61	48	48	96	89	....	....	....	....	....	....	....	....	....	17	7	8	15	45	....	....	....	....
2009-10	Atlanta	NHL	66	14	12	26	62	0	1	3	127	11.0	2	26	53.9	14:00	....	....	....	....	....	....	....	....	....
	NHL Totals		66	14	12	26	62	0	1	3	127	11.0		26	53.8	14:00	....	....	....	....	....	....	....	....	....

WHL West First All-Star Team (2009)

KANE, Patrick

(KAYN, PAT-rihk) **CHI.**

Right wing. Shoots left. 5'10", 178 lbs. Born, Buffalo, NY, November 19, 1988. Chicago's 1st choice, 1st overall, in 2007 Entry Draft.

2003-04	Det. Honeybaked	MWEHL	70	83	77	160	....	....	....	....	....	....	....	....	....	....	....	....	....	....	....	....	....	....	....
2004-05	USNTDP	U-17	23	16	17	33	8	....	....	....	....	....	....	....	....	....	....	....	....	....	....	....	....	....	....
	USNTDP	NAHL	40	16	21	37	8	....	....	....	....	....	....	....	....	....	9	7	8	15	2	....	....	....	....
2005-06	USNTDP	U-18	43	35	33	68	10	....	....	....	....	....	....	....	....	....	....	....	....	....	....	....	....	....	....
	USNTDP	NAHL	15	17	17	34	12	....	....	....	....	....	....	....	....	....	....	....	....	....	....	....	....	....	....
2006-07	London Knights	OHL	58	62	83	*145	52	....	....	....	....	....	....	....	....	....	16	10	21	*31	16	....	....	....	....
2007-08	Chicago	NHL	82	21	51	72	52	7	0	4	191	11.0	-5	26	61.5	18:22	....	....	....	....	....	....	....	....	....
2008-09	Chicago	NHL	80	25	45	70	42	13	0	4	254	9.8	-2	31	41.9	18:40	16	9	5	14	12	2	0	0	16:36
2009-10 ♦	Chicago	NHL	82	30	58	88	20	9	0	6	261	11.5	16	22	40.9	19:12	22	10	18	28	6	1	1	1	18:55
	United States	Olympics	6	3	2	5	2	....	....	....	....	....	....	....	....	....	....	....	....	....	....	....	....	....	....
	NHL Totals		244	76	154	230	114	29	0	14	706	10.8		79	48.1	18:44	38	19	23	42	18	3	1	1	17:56

OHL All-Rookie Team (2007) • OHL First All-Star Team (2007) • OHL Rookie of the Year (2007) • Canadian Major Junior First All-Star Team (2007) • Canadian Major Junior Rookie of the Year (2007) • NHL All-Rookie Team (2008) • Calder Memorial Trophy (2008) • NHL First All-Star Team (2010)

Played in NHL All-Star Game (2009)

KARIYA, Paul

(kah-REE-ah, PAWL)

Left wing. Shoots left. 5'10", 185 lbs. Born, Vancouver, B.C., October 16, 1974. Anaheim's 1st choice, 4th overall, in 1993 Entry Draft.

1990-91	Penticton	BCJHL	54	45	67	112	8	....	....	....	....	....	....	....	....	....	....	....	....	....	....	....	....	....	....
1991-92	Penticton	BCJHL	40	46	86	132	18	....	....	....	....	....	....	....	....	....	....	....	....	....	....	....	....	....	....
1992-93	U. of Maine	H-East	39	25	*75	*100	12	....	....	....	....	....	....	....	....	....	....	....	....	....	....	....	....	....	....
1993-94	U. of Maine	H-East	12	8	16	24	4	....	....	....	....	....	....	....	....	....	....	....	....	....	....	....	....	....	....
	Canada	Nat-Tm	23	7	34	41	2	....	....	....	....	....	....	....	....	....	....	....	....	....	....	....	....	....	....
	Canada	Olympics	8	3	4	7	2	....	....	....	....	....	....	....	....	....	....	....	....	....	....	....	....	....	....
1994-95	Anaheim	NHL	47	18	21	39	4	7	1	3	134	13.4	-17	....	....	....	....	....	....	....	....	....	....	....	....
1995-96	Anaheim	NHL	82	50	58	108	20	20	3	9	349	14.3	9	....	....	....	....	....	....	....	....	....	....	....	....
1996-97	Anaheim	NHL	69	44	55	99	6	15	3	*10	340	12.9	36	....	....	....	11	7	6	13	4	4	0	1	....
1997-98	Anaheim	NHL	22	17	14	31	23	3	0	2	103	16.5	12	....	....	....	....	....	....	....	....	....	....	....	....
1998-99	Anaheim	NHL	82	39	62	101	40	11	2	4	429	9.1	17	91	48.4	25:32	3	1	3	4	0	0	0	0	26:03
99-2000	Anaheim	NHL	74	42	44	86	24	11	3	3	324	13.0	22	99	39.4	24:22	....	....	....	....	....	....	....	....	....
2000-01	Anaheim	NHL	66	33	34	67	20	18	3	3	230	14.3	-9	149	44.3	23:02	....	....	....	....	....	....	....	....	....
2001-02	Anaheim	NHL	82	32	25	57	28	11	0	8	289	11.1	-15	94	41.5	22:13	....	....	....	....	....	....	....	....	....
	Canada	Olympics	6	3	1	4	0	....	....	....	....	....	....	....	....	....	....	....	....	....	....	....	....	....	....
2002-03	Anaheim	NHL	82	25	56	81	48	11	1	2	257	9.7	-3	39	30.8	20:17	21	6	6	12	6	0	0	1	21:15
2003-04	Colorado	NHL	51	11	25	36	22	5	1	1	110	10.0	-5	18	27.8	18:37	1	0	1	1	0	0	0	0	16:00
2004-05			DID NOT PLAY																						
2005-06	Nashville	NHL	82	31	54	85	40	14	0	3	245	12.7	-6	9	11.1	19:05	5	2	5	7	0	2	0	0	20:47
2006-07	Nashville	NHL	82	24	52	76	36	5	0	2	224	10.7	6	3	0.0	20:23	5	0	2	2	2	0	0	0	19:36
2007-08	St. Louis	NHL	82	16	49	65	50	5	0	1	223	7.2	-10	6	0.0	18:44	....	....	....	....	....	....	....	....	....

			Regular Season														Playoffs								
Season	Club	League	GP	G	A	Pts	PIM	PP	SH	GW	S	%	+/-	TF	F%	Min	GP	G	A	Pts	PIM	PP	SH	GW	Min
2008-09	**St. Louis**	**NHL**	**11**	**2**	**13**	**15**	**2**	**0**	**0**	**0**	**31**	**6.5**	**1**	**0**	**0.0**	**18:06**	....	....	....	....	....	....	....	....	....
2009-10	**St. Louis**	**NHL**	**75**	**18**	**25**	**43**	**36**	**3**	**0**	**2**	**221**	**8.1**	**–7**	**10**	**40.0**	**17:09**	....	....	....	....	....	....	....	....	....
	NHL Totals		**989**	**402**	**587**	**989**	**399**	**139**	**17**	**53**	**3509**	**11.5**		**518**	**40.5**	**20:57**	**46**	**16**	**23**	**39**	**12**	**6**	**0**	**2**	**21:12**

Hockey East First All-Star Team (1993) • Hockey East Rookie of the Year (1993) • Hockey East Player of the Year (1993) • NCAA East First All-American Team (1993) • NCAA Championship All-Tournament Team (1993) • Hobey Baker Memorial Award (Top U.S. Collegiate Player) (1993) • NHL All-Rookie Team (1995) • Lady Byng Memorial Trophy (1996, 1997) • NHL First All-Star Team (1996, 1997, 1999) • NHL Second All-Star Team (2000, 2003)

Played in NHL All-Star Game (1996, 1997, 1999, 2000, 2001, 2002, 2003)

• Missed majority of 1997-98 season after failing to come to contract terms with **Anaheim** and recovering from head injury suffered in game vs. San Jose, February 1, 1998. Signed as a free agent by **Colorado**, July 3, 2003. Signed as a free agent by **Nashville**, August 5, 2005. Signed as a free agent by **St. Louis**, July 1, 2007. • Missed majority of 2008-09 season recovering from lower body injury suffered in game at Anaheim, November 5, 2008.

KARLSSON, Erik

(KAHRL-suhn, AIR-ihk) **OTT.**

Defense. Shoots right. 5'11", 175 lbs. Born, Landsbro, Sweden, May 31, 1990. Ottawa's 1st choice, 15th overall, in 2008 Entry Draft.

Season	Club	League	GP	G	A	Pts	PIM	PP	SH	GW	S	%	+/-	TF	F%	Min	GP	G	A	Pts	PIM	PP	SH	GW	Min
2006-07	Sodertalje SK U18	Swe-U18	2	0	1	1	33	....	....	....	....	....	....	....	....	....	....	....	....	....	....	....	....	....	....
	Sodertalje SK Jr.	Swe-Jr.	10	2	8	10	8	....	....	....	....	....	....	....	....	....	....	....	....	....	....	....	....	....	....
2007-08	Frolunda U18	Swe-U18	3	1	2	3	2	....	....	....	....	....	....	....	....	....	2	0	1	1	10	....	....	....	....
	Frolunda Jr.	Swe-Jr.	38	13	24	37	68	....	....	....	....	....	....	....	....	....	5	1	0	1	4	....	....	....	....
	Frolunda	Sweden	7	1	0	1	0	....	....	....	....	....	....	....	....	....	6	0	0	0	0	....	....	....	....
2008-09	Frolunda Jr.	Swe-Jr.	1	0	2	2	2	....	....	....	....	....	....	....	....	....	....	....	....	....	....	....	....	....	....
	Boras HC	Sweden-2	7	0	1	1	14	....	....	....	....	....	....	....	....	....	....	....	....	....	....	....	....	....	....
	Frolunda	Sweden	45	5	5	10	10	....	....	....	....	....	....	....	....	....	11	1	2	3	24	....	....	....	....
2009-10	**Ottawa**	**NHL**	**60**	**5**	**21**	**26**	**24**	**1**	**0**	**0**	**112**	**4.5**	**–5**	**0**	**0.0**	**20:07**	**6**	**1**	**5**	**6**	**4**	**1**	**0**	**0**	**25:52**
	Binghamton	AHL	12	0	11	11	22	....	....	....	....	....	....	....	....	....	....	....	....	....	....	....	....	....	....
	NHL Totals		**60**	**5**	**21**	**26**	**24**	**1**	**0**	**0**	**112**	**4.5**		**0**	**0.0**	**20:07**	**6**	**1**	**5**	**6**	**4**	**1**	**0**	**0**	**25:52**

KARSUMS, Martins

(KAHR-suhmz, MAHR-tihnsh) **T.B.**

Right wing. Shoots right. 5'10", 198 lbs. Born, Riga, Latvia, February 26, 1986. Boston's 2nd choice, 64th overall, in 2004 Entry Draft.

Season	Club	League	GP	G	A	Pts	PIM	PP	SH	GW	S	%	+/-	TF	F%	Min	GP	G	A	Pts	PIM	PP	SH	GW	Min
2000-01	Prizma '83 Riga Jr.	Latvia-Jr.	2	0	0	0	0	....	....	....	....	....	....	....	....	....	....	....	....	....	....	....	....	....	....
	Lido Nafta Jr.	Latvia-Jr.	18	8	6	14	....	....	....	....	....	....	....	....	....	....	....	....	....	....	....	....	....	....	....
2001-02	Prizma '83 Riga	EEHL-B	16	7	8	15	4	....	....	....	....	....	....	....	....	....	....	....	....	....	....	....	....	....	....
	Prizma '83 Riga	Latvia	6	4	1	5	4	....	....	....	....	....	....	....	....	....	....	....	....	....	....	....	....	....	....
2002-03	HK Riga 2000	EEHL	2	0	0	0	0	....	....	....	....	....	....	....	....	....	....	....	....	....	....	....	....	....	....
	Vilki Riga	Latvia	....	7	5	12	14	....	....	....	....	....	....	....	....	....	....	....	....	....	....	....	....	....	....
2003-04	Moncton Wildcats	QMJHL	60	30	23	53	76	....	....	....	....	....	....	....	....	....	20	8	9	17	14	....	....	....	....
2004-05	Moncton Wildcats	QMJHL	30	14	12	26	31	....	....	....	....	....	....	....	....	....	2	0	0	0	0	....	....	....	....
2005-06	Moncton Wildcats	QMJHL	49	34	31	65	89	....	....	....	....	....	....	....	....	....	21	15	11	26	22	....	....	....	....
2006-07	Providence Bruins	AHL	54	13	22	35	41	....	....	....	....	....	....	....	....	....	12	3	1	4	2	....	....	....	....
2007-08	Providence Bruins	AHL	79	20	43	63	57	....	....	....	....	....	....	....	....	....	10	7	3	10	6	....	....	....	....
2008-09	**Boston**	**NHL**	**6**	**0**	**1**	**1**	**0**	**0**	**0**	**0**	**6**	**0.0**	**–3**	**1**	**0.0**	**9:45**	....	....	....	....	....	....	....	....	....
	Providence Bruins	AHL	43	17	24	41	20	....	....	....	....	....	....	....	....	....	....	....	....	....	....	....	....	....	....
	Tampa Bay	**NHL**	**18**	**1**	**4**	**5**	**6**	**0**	**0**	**0**	**22**	**4.5**	**–5**	**2**	**100.0**	**11:40**	....	....	....	....	....	....	....	....	....
2009-10	Norfolk Admirals	AHL	36	4	12	16	6	....	....	....	....	....	....	....	....	....	....	....	....	....	....	....	....	....	....
	Dynamo Riga	Rus-KHL	12	4	4	8	16	....	....	....	....	....	....	....	....	....	9	2	1	3	4	....	....	....	....
	Latvia	Olympics	4	0	2	2	2	....	....	....	....	....	....	....	....	....	....	....	....	....	....	....	....	....	....
	NHL Totals		**24**	**1**	**5**	**6**	**6**	**0**	**0**	**0**	**28**	**3.6**		**3**	**66.7**	**11:11**	....	....	....	....	....	....	....	....	....

QMJHL All-Rookie Team (2004)

Traded to **Tampa Bay** by **Boston** with Matt Lashoff for Mark Recchi and Tampa Bay's 2nd round choice (later traded to Florida - Florida selected Alexander Petrovic) in 2010 Entry Draft, March 4, 2009. Signed as a free agent by **Riga** (Russia-KHL), January 17, 2010.

KASPAR, Lukas

(kash-PAR, LOO-kahsh)

Right wing. Shoots left. 6'2", 220 lbs. Born, Most, Czech., September 23, 1985. San Jose's 1st choice, 22nd overall, in 2004 Entry Draft.

Season	Club	League	GP	G	A	Pts	PIM	PP	SH	GW	S	%	+/-	TF	F%	Min	GP	G	A	Pts	PIM	PP	SH	GW	Min
2000-01	Litvinov U17	CzR-U17	48	27	19	46	64	....	....	....	....	....	....	....	....	....	6	2	3	5	0	....	....	....	....
2001-02	Litvinov U17	CzR-U17	48	35	41	76	143	....	....	....	....	....	....	....	....	....	2	1	1	2	0	....	....	....	....
2002-03	Litvinov Jr.	CzRep-Jr.	26	14	14	28	40	....	....	....	....	....	....	....	....	....	....	....	....	....	....	....	....	....	....
	Litvinov	CzRep	9	1	1	2	2	....	....	....	....	....	....	....	....	....	....	....	....	....	....	....	....	....	....
2003-04	Litvinov Jr.	CzRep-Jr.	23	21	14	35	56	....	....	....	....	....	....	....	....	....	1	0	0	0	0	....	....	....	....
	Litvinov	CzRep	37	4	2	6	10	....	....	....	....	....	....	....	....	....	....	....	....	....	....	....	....	....	....
	Usti n. L.	CzRep-2	1	1	0	1	0	....	....	....	....	....	....	....	....	....	....	....	....	....	....	....	....	....	....
	Most	CzRep-3	....	....	....	....	....	....	....	....	....	....	....	....	....	....	1	0	0	0	2	....	....	....	....
2004-05	Ottawa 67's	OHL	59	21	30	51	45	....	....	....	....	....	....	....	....	....	21	6	14	20	8	....	....	....	....
2005-06	Cleveland Barons	AHL	76	14	22	36	88	....	....	....	....	....	....	....	....	....	....	....	....	....	....	....	....	....	....
2006-07	Worcester Sharks	AHL	78	12	28	40	64	....	....	....	....	....	....	....	....	....	6	0	2	2	6	....	....	....	....
2007-08	**San Jose**	**NHL**	**3**	**0**	**0**	**0**	**0**	**0**	**0**	**0**	**5**	**0.0**	**–2**	**1**	**0.0**	**12:15**	....	....	....	....	....	....	....	....	....
	Worcester Sharks	AHL	73	17	24	41	44	....	....	....	....	....	....	....	....	....	....	....	....	....	....	....	....	....	....
2008-09	**San Jose**	**NHL**	**13**	**2**	**2**	**4**	**8**	**0**	**0**	**1**	**14**	**14.3**	**0**	**4**	**0.0**	**9:08**	....	....	....	....	....	....	....	....	....
	Worcester Sharks	AHL	65	17	27	44	40	....	....	....	....	....	....	....	....	....	12	2	2	4	0	....	....	....	....
2009-10	Adirondack	AHL	8	1	2	3	4	....	....	....	....	....	....	....	....	....	....	....	....	....	....	....	....	....	....
	Karpat Oulu	Finland	39	14	17	31	20	....	....	....	....	....	....	....	....	....	10	1	4	5	12	....	....	....	....
	NHL Totals		**16**	**2**	**2**	**4**	**8**	**0**	**0**	**1**	**19**	**10.5**		**5**	**0.0**	**9:43**	....	....	....	....	....	....	....	....	....

Signed as a free agent by **Philadelphia**, July 23, 2009. Signed as a free agent by **Oulu** (Finland), November 4, 2009.

KEITH, Duncan

(KEETH, DUHN-kuhn) **CHI.**

Defense. Shoots left. 6'1", 196 lbs. Born, Winnipeg, Man., July 16, 1983. Chicago's 2nd choice, 54th overall, in 2002 Entry Draft.

Season	Club	League	GP	G	A	Pts	PIM	PP	SH	GW	S	%	+/-	TF	F%	Min	GP	G	A	Pts	PIM	PP	SH	GW	Min
1998-99	Penticton	Minor-BC	44	51	57	108	45	....	....	....	....	....	....	....	....	....	....	....	....	....	....	....	....	....	....
99-2000	Penticton	BCHL	59	9	27	36	37	....	....	....	....	....	....	....	....	....	....	....	....	....	....	....	....	....	....
2000-01	Penticton	BCHL	60	18	64	82	61	....	....	....	....	....	....	....	....	....	9	4	6	10	18	....	....	....	....
2001-02	Michigan State	CCHA	41	3	12	15	18	....	....	....	....	....	....	....	....	....	....	....	....	....	....	....	....	....	....
2002-03	Michigan State	CCHA	15	3	6	9	8	....	....	....	....	....	....	....	....	....	....	....	....	....	....	....	....	....	....
	Kelowna Rockets	WHL	37	11	35	46	60	....	....	....	....	....	....	....	....	....	19	3	11	14	12	....	....	....	....
2003-04	Norfolk Admirals	AHL	75	7	18	25	44	....	....	....	....	....	....	....	....	....	8	1	1	2	6	....	....	....	....
2004-05	Norfolk Admirals	AHL	79	9	17	26	78	....	....	....	....	....	....	....	....	....	6	0	0	0	14	....	....	....	....
2005-06	**Chicago**	**NHL**	**81**	**9**	**12**	**21**	**79**	**1**	**1**	**0**	**134**	**6.7**	**–11**	**0**	**0.0**	**23:26**	....	....	....	....	....	....	....	....	....
2006-07	**Chicago**	**NHL**	**82**	**2**	**29**	**31**	**76**	**0**	**0**	**0**	**122**	**1.6**	**0**	**0**	**0.0**	**23:36**	....	....	....	....	....	....	....	....	....
2007-08	**Chicago**	**NHL**	**82**	**12**	**20**	**32**	**56**	**1**	**1**	**0**	**148**	**8.1**	**30**	**0**	**0.0**	**25:34**	....	....	....	....	....	....	....	....	....
2008-09	**Chicago**	**NHL**	**77**	**8**	**36**	**44**	**60**	**1**	**1**	**1**	**173**	**4.6**	**33**	**0**	**0.0**	**25:34**	**17**	**0**	**6**	**6**	**10**	**0**	**0**	**0**	**24:39**
2009-10♦	**Chicago**	**NHL**	**82**	**14**	**55**	**69**	**51**	**3**	**1**	**1**	**213**	**6.6**	**21**	**0**	**0.0**	**26:36**	**22**	**2**	**15**	**17**	**10**	**0**	**0**	**0**	**28:11**
	Canada	Olympics	7	0	6	6	2	....	....	....	....	....	....	....	....	....	....	....	....	....	....	....	....	....	....
	NHL Totals		**404**	**45**	**152**	**197**	**322**	**7**	**4**	**2**	**790**	**5.7**		**0**	**0.0**	**24:57**	**39**	**2**	**21**	**23**	**20**	**0**	**0**	**0**	**26:38**

NHL First All-Star Team (2010) • James Norris Memorial Trophy (2010)

Played in NHL All-Star Game (2008)

• Left **Michigan State** (CCHA) and signed as a free agent by **Kelowna** (WHL), December 27, 2002.

KEITH, Matt

(KEETH, MAT)

Right wing. Shoots right. 6'2", 200 lbs. Born, Edmonton, Alta., April 11, 1983. Chicago's 3rd choice, 59th overall, in 2001 Entry Draft.

Season	Club	League	GP	G	A	Pts	PIM	PP	SH	GW	S	%	+/-	TF	F%	Min	GP	G	A	Pts	PIM	PP	SH	GW	Min
1998-99	Banff Icemen	HJHL	STATISTICS NOT AVAILABLE																						
	Spokane Chiefs	WHL	7	1	0	1	4	....	....	....	....	....	....	....	....	....	....	....	....	....	....	....	....	....	....
99-2000	Spokane Chiefs	WHL	39	1	3	4	37	....	....	....	....	....	....	....	....	....	15	1	2	3	11	....	....	....	....
2000-01	Spokane Chiefs	WHL	33	13	14	27	63	....	....	....	....	....	....	....	....	....	12	1	3	4	14	....	....	....	....
2001-02	Spokane Chiefs	WHL	68	34	33	67	71	....	....	....	....	....	....	....	....	....	11	5	5	10	16	....	....	....	....
2002-03	Spokane Chiefs	WHL	7	2	2	4	11	....	....	....	....	....	....	....	....	....	....	....	....	....	....	....	....	....	....
	Red Deer Rebels	WHL	49	25	26	51	32	....	....	....	....	....	....	....	....	....	23	6	7	13	30	....	....	....	....
2003-04	**Chicago**	**NHL**	**20**	**2**	**3**	**5**	**10**	**1**	**0**	**0**	**21**	**9.5**	**–5**	**2**	**100.0**	**11:58**	....	....	....	....	....	....	....	....	....
	Norfolk Admirals	AHL	66	13	13	26	57	....	....	....	....	....	....	....	....	....	8	1	2	3	10	....	....	....	....

Season	Club	League	GP	G	A	Pts	PIM	PP	SH	GW	S	%	+/-	TF	F%	Min	GP	G	A	Pts	PIM	PP	SH	GW	Min
2004-05	Norfolk Admirals	AHL	80	18	31	49	74										6	0	1	1	0				
2005-06	Chicago	NHL	2	0	0	0	0	0	0	0	6	0.0	0	0	0.0	11:42									
	Norfolk Admirals	AHL	72	26	19	45	61										3	0	1	1	0				
2006-07	Chicago	NHL	2	0	0	0	4	0	0	0	0	0.0	-2	0	0.0	9:33									
	Norfolk Admirals	AHL	19	2	8	10	15																		
	Portland Pirates	AHL	44	10	12	22	22																		
2007-08	Portland Pirates	AHL	34	5	5	10	13																		
	NY Islanders	NHL	3	0	0	0	0	0	0	0	3	0.0	-1	0	0.0	10:41									
	Bridgeport	AHL	42	8	9	17	22																		
2008-09	ERC Ingolstadt	Germany	46	15	13	28	60																		
2009-10	Rockford IceHogs	AHL	69	21	20	41	27										4	0	0	0	2				
NHL Totals			27	2	3	5	14	1	0	0	30	6.7		2	100.0	11:37									

• Missed majority of 2000-01 season recovering from shoulder injury suffered in game vs. Tri-City (WHL), September 22, 2000. Traded to **Anaheim** by **Chicago** with Sebastien Caron and Chris Durno for P.A. Parenteau and Bruno St. Jacques, December 28, 2006. Traded to **NY Islanders** by **Anaheim** for Darryl Bootland, January 9, 2008. Signed as a free agent by **Rockford** (AHL), October 1, 2009.

KELLER, Ryan
Center. Shoots right. 5'10", 196 lbs. Born, Saskatoon, Sask., January 6, 1984. (KEHL-uhr, RIGH-uhn) **OTT.**

Season	Club	League	GP	G	A	Pts	PIM	PP	SH	GW	S	%	+/-	TF	F%	Min	GP	G	A	Pts	PIM	PP	SH	GW	Min
2001-02	Saskatoon Blades	WHL	52	18	23	41	58										7	1	2	3	14				
2002-03	Saskatoon Blades	WHL	66	38	41	79	101										6	7	1	8	8				
2003-04	Saskatoon Blades	WHL	72	24	20	44	59																		
2004-05	Saskatoon Blades	WHL	67	40	33	73	63																		
2005-06	Grand Rapids	AHL	10	1	0	1	14										4	1	1	2	9				
	Muskegon Fury	UHL	65	41	40	81	79										13	0	0	0	0				
2006-07	Grand Rapids	AHL	38	9	8	17	26										3	2	2	4	0				
	Syracuse Crunch	AHL	22	5	9	14	14																		
2007-08	Blues Espoo	Finland	47	22	22	44	24										17	3	6	9	22				
2008-09	Blues Espoo	Finland	54	21	34	55	38										14	*9	7	16	4				
2009-10	Ottawa	NHL	6	0	0	0	0	0	0	0	5	0.0	-1	0	0.0	6:13									
	Binghamton	AHL	72	34	34	68	48																		
NHL Totals			6	0	0	0	0	0	0	0	5	0.0		0	0.0	6:13									

Signed as a free agent by **Ottawa**, June 1, 2009.

KELLY, Chris
Center/Left wing. Shoots left. 6', 198 lbs. Born, Toronto, Ont., November 11, 1980. Ottawa's 4th choice, 94th overall, in 1999 Entry Draft. (KEHL-lee, KRIHS) **OTT.**

Season	Club	League	GP	G	A	Pts	PIM	PP	SH	GW	S	%	+/-	TF	F%	Min	GP	G	A	Pts	PIM	PP	SH	GW	Min
1995-96	Toronto Marlies	MTHL	42	25	45	70	25																		
1996-97	Aurora Tigers	MTJHL	49	14	20	34	11																		
1997-98	London Knights	OHL	54	15	14	29	4										16	4	5	9	12				
1998-99	London Knights	OHL	68	36	41	77	60										25	9	17	26	22				
99-2000	London Knights	OHL	63	29	43	72	57																		
2000-01	London Knights	OHL	31	21	34	55	46																		
	Sudbury Wolves	OHL	19	5	16	21	17																		
2001-02	Grand Rapids	AHL	31	3	3	6	20										12	11	5	16	14				
	Muskegon Fury	UHL	4	1	2	3	0										5	1	1	2	5				
2002-03	Binghamton	AHL	77	17	14	31	73										14	2	3	5	8				
2003-04	Ottawa	NHL	4	0	0	0	0	0	0	0	4	0.0	-2	5	40.0	9:29									
	Binghamton	AHL	54	15	19	34	40										2	0	0	0	4				
2004-05	Binghamton	AHL	77	24	36	60	57										6	1	2	3	11				
2005-06	Ottawa	NHL	82	10	20	30	76	1	0	2	112	8.9	21	808	45.8	12:20	10	0	0	0	2	0	0	0	11:49
2006-07	Ottawa	NHL	82	15	23	38	40	1	2	0	131	11.5	28	564	49.8	15:18	20	3	4	7	4	0	0	0	15:28
2007-08	Ottawa	NHL	75	11	19	30	30	0	1	1	124	8.9	3	162	53.1	16:36									
2008-09	Ottawa	NHL	82	12	11	23	38	0	1	1	118	10.2	-10	494	47.4	15:36									
2009-10	Ottawa	NHL	81	15	17	32	38	0	0	3	112	13.4	-7	894	45.6	14:58	6	1	5	6	2	1	0	0	18:46
NHL Totals			406	63	90	153	222	2	4	7	601	10.5		2927	47.2	14:53	36	4	9	13	8	1	0	0	15:00

KENNEDY, Tim
Left wing. Shoots left. 5'10", 173 lbs. Born, Buffalo, NY, April 30, 1986. Washington's 6th choice, 181st overall, in 2005 Entry Draft. (KEH-nuh-dee, TIHM)

Season	Club	League	GP	G	A	Pts	PIM	PP	SH	GW	S	%	+/-	TF	F%	Min	GP	G	A	Pts	PIM	PP	SH	GW	Min
2003-04	Sioux City	USHL	56	9	10	19	42										7	2	2	4	6				
2004-05	Sioux City	USHL	54	30	31	61	112										13	*6	*11	*17	18				
2005-06	Michigan State	CCHA	29	4	15	19	31																		
2006-07	Michigan State	CCHA	42	18	25	43	49																		
2007-08	Michigan State	CCHA	42	20	23	43	50																		
2008-09	Buffalo	NHL	1	0	0	0	0	0	0	0	1	0.0	0	1	0.0	11:04									
	Portland Pirates	AHL	73	18	49	67	51										5	0	1	1	2				
2009-10	Buffalo	NHL	78	10	16	26	50	1	0	3	98	10.2	-3	397	33.5	12:57	6	1	2	3	4	0	0	0	14:25
NHL Totals			79	10	16	26	50	1	0	3	99	10.1		398	33.4	12:56	6	1	2	3	4	0	0	0	14:25

USHL Second All-Star Team (2005) • NCAA Championship All-Tournament Team (2007) • CCHA Second All-Star Team (2008) • AHL All-Rookie Team (2009)
Traded to **Buffalo** by **Washington** for Buffalo's 6th round choice (Mathieu Perreault) in 2006 Entry Draft, July 30, 2005.

KENNEDY, Tyler
Center. Shoots right. 5'11", 183 lbs. Born, Sault Ste. Marie, Ont., July 15, 1986. Pittsburgh's 6th choice, 99th overall, in 2004 Entry Draft. (KEH-nuh-dee, TIGH-luhr) **PIT.**

Season	Club	League	GP	G	A	Pts	PIM	PP	SH	GW	S	%	+/-	TF	F%	Min	GP	G	A	Pts	PIM	PP	SH	GW	Min
2002-03	Sault Ste. Marie	OHL	61	5	10	15	28										4	0	0	0	0				
2003-04	Sault Ste. Marie	OHL	63	16	26	42	28																		
2004-05	Sault Ste. Marie	OHL	61	21	36	57	37										4	1	3	4	4				
2005-06	Sault Ste. Marie	OHL	64	22	48	70	60										4	1	2	3	2				
2006-07	Wilkes-Barre	AHL	40	12	25	37	20																		
2007-08	Pittsburgh	NHL	55	10	9	19	35	1	0	4	104	9.6	2	8	25.0	12:13	20	0	4	4	13	0	0	0	10:18
	Wilkes-Barre	AHL	10	5	4	9	10																		
2008-09	Pittsburgh	NHL	67	15	20	35	30	0	0	3	171	8.8	15	78	53.9	13:46	24	5	4	9	4	0	0	3	13:40
2009-10	Pittsburgh	NHL	64	13	12	25	31	1	0	4	175	7.4	10	64	42.2	12:35	10	0	0	0	2	0	0	0	11:57
NHL Totals			186	38	41	79	96	2	0	11	450	8.4		150	47.3	12:54	54	5	8	13	19	0	0	3	12:06

KESLER, Ryan
Center. Shoots right. 6'2", 202 lbs. Born, Livonia, MI, August 31, 1984. Vancouver's 1st choice, 23rd overall, in 2003 Entry Draft. (KEHZ-luhr, RIGH-uhn) **VAN.**

Season	Club	League	GP	G	A	Pts	PIM	PP	SH	GW	S	%	+/-	TF	F%	Min	GP	G	A	Pts	PIM	PP	SH	GW	Min
99-2000	Det. Honeybaked	MWEHL	72	44	73	117																			
2000-01	USNTDP	U-18	26	8	20	28	24																		
	USNTDP	NAHL	56	7	21	28	40																		
2001-02	USNTDP	U-18	46	11	33	44	23																		
	USNTDP	USHL	13	5	5	10	10																		
	USNTDP	NAHL	10	5	6	11	4																		
2002-03	Ohio State	CCHA	40	11	20	31	44																		
2003-04	Vancouver	NHL	28	2	3	5	16	0	0	0	23	8.7	-2	194	40.2	10:42									
	Manitoba Moose	AHL	33	3	8	11	29																		
2004-05	Manitoba Moose	AHL	78	30	27	57	105										14	4	5	9	8				
2005-06	Vancouver	NHL	82	10	13	23	79	1	0	2	119	8.4	1	984	46.8	14:03									
2006-07	Vancouver	NHL	48	6	10	16	40	0	0	0	88	6.8	1	690	46.1	16:26	1	0	0	0	0	0	0	0	27:51
2007-08	Vancouver	NHL	80	21	16	37	79	4	2	2	177	11.9	1	1358	53.0	19:03									
2008-09	Vancouver	NHL	82	26	33	59	61	10	2	2	179	14.5	8	976	54.0	19:28	10	2	3	5	14	1	0	0	20:29
2009-10	Vancouver	NHL	82	25	50	75	104	12	1	5	214	11.7	7	1401	55.1	19:38	12	1	9	10	4	0	0	0	21:19
	United States	Olympics	6	2	0	2																			
NHL Totals			402	90	125	215	379	27	5	11	800	11.3		5603	51.3	17:20	23	3	11	14	18	1	0	0	21:14

			Regular Season															Playoffs							
Season	Club	League	GP	G	A	Pts	PIM	PP	SH	GW	S	%	+/-	TF	F%	Min	GP	G	A	Pts	PIM	PP	SH	GW	Min

KESSEL, Phil   (KEH-suhl, FIHL)   **TOR.**

Center. Shoots right. 5'11", 180 lbs.   Born, Madison, WI, October 2, 1987. Boston's 1st choice, 5th overall, in 2006 Entry Draft.

Season	Club	League	GP	G	A	Pts	PIM	PP	SH	GW	S	%	+/-	TF	F%	Min	GP	G	A	Pts	PIM	PP	SH	GW	Min
2003-04	USNTDP	U-17	32	31	18	49	8	....	....	....	....	....	....	....	....	....									
	USNTDP	NAHL	30	21	12	33	18	....	....	....	....	....	....	....	....	....									
2004-05	USNTDP	U-18	31	41	32	73	16	....	....	....	....	....	....	....	....	....									
	USNTDP	NAHL	14	11	14	25	21	....	....	....	....	....	....	....	....	....									
2005-06	U. of Minnesota	WCHA	39	18	33	51	28	....	....	....	....	....	....	....	....	....									
2006-07	**Boston**	**NHL**	70	11	18	29	12	1	0	0	170	6.5	–12	373	40.8	14:04									
	Providence Bruins	AHL	2	1	0	1	2	....	....	....	....	....	....	....	....	....									
2007-08	**Boston**	**NHL**	82	19	18	37	28	5	0	3	213	8.9	–6	326	42.3	15:14	4	3	1	4	2	1	0	0	14:31
2008-09	**Boston**	**NHL**	70	36	24	60	16	8	0	6	232	15.5	23	87	48.3	16:34	11	6	5	11	4	0	0	0	15:55
2009-10	**Toronto**	**NHL**	70	30	25	55	21	8	0	5	297	10.1	–8	122	48.4	19:33									
	United States	Olympics	6	1	1	2	0	....	....	....	....	....	....	....	....	....									
	NHL Totals		**292**	**96**	**85**	**181**	**77**	**22**	**0**	**14**	**912**	**10.5**		**908**	**43.1**	**16:18**	**15**	**9**	**6**	**15**	**6**	**1**	**0**	**0**	**15:33**

WCHA All-Rookie Team (2006) • WCHA Rookie of the Year (2006) • Bill Masterton Memorial Trophy (2007)
Traded to **Toronto** by **Boston** for Toronto's 1st (Tyler Seguin) and 2nd (Jared Knight) round choices in 2010 Entry Draft and Toronto's 1st round choice in 2011 Entry Draft, September 18, 2009.

KINDL, Jakub   (KEEHN-duhl, YA-kuhb)   **DET.**

Defense. Shoots left. 6'3", 210 lbs.   Born, Sumperk, Czech., February 10, 1987. Detroit's 1st choice, 19th overall, in 2005 Entry Draft.

Season	Club	League	GP	G	A	Pts	PIM	PP	SH	GW	S	%	+/-	TF	F%	Min	GP	G	A	Pts	PIM	PP	SH	GW	Min
2002-03	HC Pardubice U17	CzR-U17	3	0	3	3	10	....	....	....	....	....	....	....	....	....									
	HC Pardubice Jr.	CzRep-Jr.	27	0	3	3	46	....	....	....	....	....	....	....	....	....									
	Pardubice	CzRep	1	0	0	0	0	....	....	....	....	....	....	....	....	....									
2003-04	HC Pardubice U17	CzR-U17	2	0	1	1	6	....	....	....	....	....	....	....	....	....									
	HC Pardubice Jr.	CzRep-Jr.	48	4	14	18	108	....	....	....	....	....	....	....	....	....									
	Hr. Kralove	CzRep-2	1	0	0	0	0	....	....	....	....	....	....	....	....	....									
2004-05	Kitchener Rangers	OHL	62	3	11	14	92	....	....	....	....	....	....	....	....	....	12	0	0	0	22				
2005-06	Kitchener Rangers	OHL	60	12	46	58	112	....	....	....	....	....	....	....	....	....	5	1	0	1	10				
	Grand Rapids	AHL	3	0	1	1	2	....	....	....	....	....	....	....	....	....									
2006-07	Kitchener Rangers	OHL	54	11	44	55	142	....	....	....	....	....	....	....	....	....	9	2	9	11	8				
	Grand Rapids	AHL						....	....	....	....	....	....	....	....	....	7	0	2	2	0				
2007-08	Grand Rapids	AHL	75	3	14	17	82	....	....	....	....	....	....	....	....	....									
2008-09	Grand Rapids	AHL	78	6	27	33	76	....	....	....	....	....	....	....	....	....	10	2	1	3	2				
2009-10	**Detroit**	**NHL**	3	0	0	0	0	0	0	0	1	0.0	–2	0	0.0	10:50	....	....	....	....	....				
	Grand Rapids	AHL	73	3	30	33	59	....	....	....	....	....	....	....	....	....									
	NHL Totals		**3**	**0**	**0**	**0**	**0**	**0**	**0**	**0**	**1**	**0.0**		**0**	**0.0**	**10:50**	....	....	....	....	....				

OHL Second All-Star Team (2007)

KING, D.J.   (KIHNG, DEE-JAY)   **WSH.**

Center. Shoots left. 6'3", 230 lbs.   Born, Meadow Lake, Sask., January 27, 1984. St. Louis' 6th choice, 190th overall, in 2002 Entry Draft.

Season	Club	League	GP	G	A	Pts	PIM	PP	SH	GW	S	%	+/-	TF	F%	Min	GP	G	A	Pts	PIM	PP	SH	GW	Min
2000-01	Beardy's	SMHL	52	30	28	58	120	....	....	....	....	....	....	....	....	....									
2001-02	Lethbridge	WHL	65	10	14	24	104	....	....	....	....	....	....	....	....	....									
2002-03	Lethbridge	WHL	55	15	17	32	139	....	....	....	....	....	....	....	....	....									
2003-04	Lethbridge	WHL	35	8	15	23	102	....	....	....	....	....	....	....	....	....									
	Kelowna Rockets	WHL	28	5	2	7	80	....	....	....	....	....	....	....	....	....	17	1	6	7	16				
2004-05	Worcester IceCats	AHL	74	6	8	14	178	....	....	....	....	....	....	....	....	....									
2005-06	Peoria Rivermen	AHL	67	5	6	11	160	....	....	....	....	....	....	....	....	....	2	0	0	0	2				
	Alaska Aces	ECHL	5	0	4	4	4	....	....	....	....	....	....	....	....	....									
2006-07	**St. Louis**	**NHL**	27	1	1	2	52	0	0	0	12	8.3	–3	2	50.0	5:31	....	....	....	....	....				
	Peoria Rivermen	AHL	38	5	4	9	102	....	....	....	....	....	....	....	....	....									
2007-08	**St. Louis**	**NHL**	61	3	3	6	100	0	0	1	36	8.3	–4	7	28.6	5:36	....	....	....	....	....				
2008-09	**St. Louis**	**NHL**	1	0	1	1	0	0	0	0	0	0.0		0	0.0	8:20	....	....	....	....	....				
2009-10	**St. Louis**	**NHL**	12	0	0	0	33	0	0	0	5	0.0	–4	0	0.0	4:30	....	....	....	....	....				
	Peoria Rivermen	AHL	10	0	1	1	13	....	....	....	....	....	....	....	....	....									
	NHL Totals		**101**	**4**	**5**	**9**	**185**	**0**	**0**	**1**	**53**	**7.5**		**9**	**33.3**	**5:29**	....	....	....	....	....				

• Missed majority of 2008-09 season recovering from recurring shoulder injury. • Missed majority of 2009-10 season recovering from hand injury and as a healthy reserve. Traded to **Washigton** by **St. Louis** for Stefan Della Rovere, July 28, 2010.

KING, Jason   (KIHNG, JAY-suhn)

Center. Shoots left. 6'1", 195 lbs.   Born, Corner Brook, Nfld., September 14, 1981. Vancouver's 5th choice, 212th overall, in 2001 Entry Draft.

Season	Club	League	GP	G	A	Pts	PIM	PP	SH	GW	S	%	+/-	TF	F%	Min	GP	G	A	Pts	PIM	PP	SH	GW	Min
99-2000	Halifax	QMJHL	53	3	7	10	8	....	....	....	....	....	....	....	....	....	10	0	0	0	2				
2000-01	Halifax	QMJHL	72	48	41	89	78	....	....	....	....	....	....	....	....	....	6	3	2	5	16				
2001-02	Halifax	QMJHL	61	*63	36	99	39	....	....	....	....	....	....	....	....	....	13	9	8	17	13				
2002-03	**Vancouver**	**NHL**	8	0	2	2	0	0	0	0	12	0.0	0	0	0.0	11:17	....	....	....	....	....				
	Manitoba Moose	AHL	67	20	20	40	15	....	....	....	....	....	....	....	....	....	14	4	3	7	14				
2003-04	**Vancouver**	**NHL**	47	12	9	21	8	6	0	1	107	11.2	0	3	66.7	12:43	1	0	0	0	0	0	0	0	6:21
	Manitoba Moose	AHL	29	12	11	23	6	....	....	....	....	....	....	....	....	....									
2004-05	Manitoba Moose	AHL	59	26	27	53	22	....	....	....	....	....	....	....	....	....	13	3	4	7	8				
2005-06	Manitoba Moose	AHL	36	20	14	34	34	....	....	....	....	....	....	....	....	....									
2006-07	Skelleftea AIK HK	Sweden	55	15	4	19	20	....	....	....	....	....	....	....	....	....									
	Skelleftea AIK HK	Sweden-Q	9	3	2	5	6	....	....	....	....	....	....	....	....	....									
2007-08	**Anaheim**	**NHL**	4	0	0	0	0	0	0	0	2	0.0	–3	1100.0		10:57	....	....	....	....	....				
	Portland Pirates	AHL	65	29	30	59	42	....	....	....	....	....	....	....	....	....	13	6	3	9	12				
2008-09	Adler Mannheim	Germany	37	7	10	17	70	....	....	....	....	....	....	....	....	....	7	3	1	4	2				
2009-10	Hamburg Freezers	Germany	53	25	23	48	42	....	....	....	....	....	....	....	....	....									
	NHL Totals		**59**	**12**	**11**	**23**	**8**	**6**	**0**	**1**	**121**	**9.9**		**4**	**75.0**	**12:24**	**1**	**0**	**0**	**0**	**0**	**0**	**0**	**0**	**6:21**

QMJHL Second All-Star Team (2001)
• Missed majority of 2005-06 season recovering from head injury suffered in game vs. Grand Rapids (AHL), March 9, 2005. Traded to **Anaheim** by **Vancouver** for Ryan Shannon and future considerations, June 23, 2007. Signed as a free agent by **Skelleftea** (Sweden), September 13, 2006. Signed as a free agent by **Mannheim** (Germany), June 2, 2008. Signed as a free agent by **Hamburg** (Germany), May 15, 2009.

KINRADE, Geoff   (KIHN-rayd, JEHF)   **OTT.**

Defense. Shoots left. 6', 195 lbs.   Born, Nelson, B.C., July 29, 1985.

Season	Club	League	GP	G	A	Pts	PIM	PP	SH	GW	S	%	+/-	TF	F%	Min	GP	G	A	Pts	PIM	PP	SH	GW	Min
2003-04	Cowichan Valley	BCHL	48	2	3	5	34	....	....	....	....	....	....	....	....	....	6	1	2	3	4				
2004-05	Cowichan Valley	BCHL	60	13	21	34	49	....	....	....	....	....	....	....	....	....									
2005-06	Michigan Tech	WCHA	33	1	6	7	46	....	....	....	....	....	....	....	....	....									
2006-07	Michigan Tech	WCHA	40	5	14	19	30	....	....	....	....	....	....	....	....	....									
2007-08	Michigan Tech	WCHA	39	5	14	19	30	....	....	....	....	....	....	....	....	....									
2008-09	Michigan Tech	WCHA	38	3	13	16	18	....	....	....	....	....	....	....	....	....									
	Tampa Bay	**NHL**	1	0	0	0	0	0	0	0	1	0.0	–1	0	0.0	17:32	....	....	....	....	....				
	Norfolk Admirals	AHL	10	1	4	5	12	....	....	....	....	....	....	....	....	....									
2009-10	Binghamton	AHL	76	7	20	27	59	....	....	....	....	....	....	....	....	....									
	NHL Totals		**1**	**0**	**0**	**0**	**0**	**0**	**0**	**0**	**1**	**0.0**		**0**	**0.0**	**17:32**	....	....	....	....	....				

Signed to an ATO (amateur tryout) contract by **Tampa Bay**, April 9, 2009. Signed as a free agent by **Ottawa**, July 10, 2009.

KLEIN, Kevin   (KLIGHN, KEH-vihn)   **NSH.**

Defense. Shoots right. 6'1", 201 lbs.   Born, Kitchener, Ont., December 13, 1984. Nashville's 3rd choice, 37th overall, in 2003 Entry Draft.

Season	Club	League	GP	G	A	Pts	PIM	PP	SH	GW	S	%	+/-	TF	F%	Min	GP	G	A	Pts	PIM	PP	SH	GW	Min
99-2000	Kitchener Midgets	Minor-ON	54	12	29	41	40	....	....	....	....	....	....	....	....	....									
2000-01	St. Michael's	OHL	58	3	16	19	21	....	....	....	....	....	....	....	....	....	18	0	5	5	17				
2001-02	St. Michael's	OHL	68	5	22	27	35	....	....	....	....	....	....	....	....	....	15	2	7	9	17				
2002-03	St. Michael's	OHL	67	11	33	44	88	....	....	....	....	....	....	....	....	....	17	1	9	10	8				
2003-04	St. Michael's	OHL	5	0	1	1	2	....	....	....	....	....	....	....	....	....									
	Guelph Storm	OHL	46	6	23	29	40	....	....	....	....	....	....	....	....	....	22	10	11	21	12				

			Regular Season														Playoffs								
Season	Club	League	GP	G	A	Pts	PIM	PP	SH	GW	S	%	+/-	TF	F%	Min	GP	G	A	Pts	PIM	PP	SH	GW	Min
2004-05	Milwaukee	AHL	65	4	12	16	22	....	....	....	....	....	....	....	....	....	7	0	0	0	11	....	....	....	....
	Rockford IceHogs	UHL	3	2	1	3	0	....	....	....	....	....	....	....	....	....	....	....	....	....	....	....	....	....	....
2005-06	**Nashville**	**NHL**	**2**	**0**	**0**	**0**	**0**	**0**	**0**	**0**	**0**	**0.0**	**–1**	**0**	**0.0**	**13:40**	....	....	....	....	....	....	....	....	....
	Milwaukee	AHL	76	10	33	43	31	....	....	....	....	....	....	....	....	....	21	3	7	10	31	....	....	....	....
2006-07	**Nashville**	**NHL**	**3**	**1**	**0**	**1**	**0**	**0**	**0**	**0**	**2**	**50.0**	**3**	**0**	**0.0**	**16:37**	....	....	....	....	....	....	....	....	....
	Milwaukee	AHL	70	5	15	20	67	....	....	....	....	....	....	....	....	....	4	1	0	1	0	....	....	....	....
2007-08	**Nashville**	**NHL**	**13**	**0**	**2**	**2**	**6**	**0**	**0**	**0**	**14**	**0.0**	**–3**	**0**	**0.0**	**14:24**	....	....	....	....	....	....	....	....	....
	Milwaukee	AHL	9	0	3	3	2	....	....	....	....	....	....	....	....	....	....	....	....	....	....	....	....	....	....
2008-09	**Nashville**	**NHL**	**63**	**4**	**8**	**12**	**19**	**1**	**0**	**0**	**41**	**9.8**	**–2**	**0**	**0.0**	**12:40**	....	....	....	....	....	....	....	....	....
2009-10	**Nashville**	**NHL**	**81**	**1**	**10**	**11**	**27**	**0**	**0**	**0**	**67**	**1.5**	**–13**	**0**	**0.0**	**19:55**	**6**	**0**	**2**	**2**	**4**	**0**	**0**	**0**	**17:43**
	NHL Totals		**162**	**6**	**20**	**26**	**52**	**1**	**0**	**0**	**124**	**4.8**		**0**	**0.0**	**16:31**	**6**	**0**	**2**	**2**	**4**	**0**	**0**	**0**	**17:43**

KLEMENTYEV, Anton

(kluh-MEHN-tee-ehv, AN-tawn) **NYI**

Defense. Shoots right. 6'1", 200 lbs. Born, Togliatti, USSR, March 25, 1990. NY Islanders' 6th choice, 122nd overall, in 2009 Entry Draft.

Season	Club	League	GP	G	A	Pts	PIM	PP	SH	GW	S	%	+/-	TF	F%	Min	GP	G	A	Pts	PIM	PP	SH	GW	Min
2006-07	Yaroslavl 2	Russia-3	36	2	6	8	69	....	....	....	....	....	....	....	....	....	....	....	....	....	....	....	....	....	....
2007-08	Yaroslavl 2	Russia-3	STATISTICS NOT AVAILABLE																						
2008-09	Yaroslavl 2	Russia-3	STATISTICS NOT AVAILABLE																						
	Yaroslavl	Rus-KHL	1	0	0	0	0										....	....	....	....	....	....	....	....	....
2009-10	**NY Islanders**	**NHL**	**1**	**0**	**0**	**0**	**0**	**0**	**0**	**0**	**0**	**0.0**	**0**	**0**	**0.0**	**6:20**	....	....	....	....	....	....	....	....	....
	Bridgeport	AHL	28	1	2	3	14	....	....	....	....	....	....	....	....	....	....	....	....	....	....	....	....	....	....
	NHL Totals		**1**	**0**	**0**	**0**	**0**	**0**	**0**	**0**	**0**	**0.0**		**0**	**0.0**	**6:20**	....	....	....	....	....	....	....	....	....

KLEPIS, Jakub

(KLEH-pihsh, YA-kuhb) **WSH.**

Center. Shoots right. 6'1", 198 lbs. Born, Prague, Czech., June 5, 1984. Ottawa's 1st choice, 16th overall, in 2002 Entry Draft.

Season	Club	League	GP	G	A	Pts	PIM	PP	SH	GW	S	%	+/-	TF	F%	Min	GP	G	A	Pts	PIM	PP	SH	GW	Min
99-2000	Slavia Jr.	CzRep-Jr.	48	14	26	40	30	....	....	....	....	....	....	....	....	....	....	....	....	....	....	....	....	....	....
2000-01	Slavia Jr.	CzRep-Jr.	52	21	25	46	82	....	....	....	....	....	....	....	....	....	....	....	....	....	....	....	....	....	....
2001-02	Portland	WHL	70	14	50	64	111	....	....	....	....	....	....	....	....	....	7	0	3	3	22	....	....	....	....
2002-03	HC Slavia Praha	CzRep	38	2	6	8	22	....	....	....	....	....	....	....	....	....	4	0	0	0	6	....	....	....	....
	Slavia Jr.	CzRep-Jr.	11	4	5	9	59	....	....	....	....	....	....	....	....	....	3	0	3	3	4	....	....	....	....
2003-04	HC Slavia Praha	CzRep	44	4	9	13	43	....	....	....	....	....	....	....	....	....	17	5	3	8	10	....	....	....	....
2004-05	Portland Pirates	AHL	78	13	14	27	76	....	....	....	....	....	....	....	....	....	....	....	....	....	....	....	....	....	....
2005-06	**Washington**	**NHL**	**25**	**1**	**3**	**4**	**8**	**0**	**0**	**0**	**26**	**3.8**	**–11**	**22**	**40.9**	**7:25**	....	....	....	....	....	....	....	....	....
	Hershey Bears	AHL	54	11	20	31	49	....	....	....	....	....	....	....	....	....	15	2	6	8	4	....	....	....	....
2006-07	**Washington**	**NHL**	**41**	**3**	**7**	**10**	**28**	**0**	**0**	**0**	**38**	**7.9**	**–2**	**184**	**41.3**	**9:58**	....	....	....	....	....	....	....	....	....
	Hershey Bears	AHL	31	6	26	32	24	....	....	....	....	....	....	....	....	....	19	7	7	14	14	....	....	....	....
2007-08	Hershey Bears	AHL	19	5	6	11	9	....	....	....	....	....	....	....	....	....	....	....	....	....	....	....	....	....	....
	HC Slavia Praha	CzRep	24	5	7	12	22	....	....	....	....	....	....	....	....	....	19	*10	7	17	24	....	....	....	....
2008-09	Omsk	Rus-KHL	55	18	17	35	51	....	....	....	....	....	....	....	....	....	9	2	4	6	0	....	....	....	....
2009-10	Omsk	Rus-KHL	56	10	12	22	50	....	....	....	....	....	....	....	....	....	3	0	2	2	2	....	....	....	....
	NHL Totals		**66**	**4**	**10**	**14**	**36**	**0**	**0**	**0**	**64**	**6.3**		**206**	**41.3**	**9:00**	....	....	....	....	....	....	....	....	....

Traded to **Buffalo** by **Ottawa** for Vaclav Varada and Buffalo's 5th round choice (Tim Cook) in 2003 Entry Draft, February 25, 2003. Traded to **Washington** by **Buffalo** for Mike Grier, March 9, 2004. Signed as a free agent by **Omsk** (Russia-KHL), April 22, 2008.

KLESLA, Rostislav

(KLEHS-luh, RAHS-tih-slav) **CBJ**

Defense. Shoots left. 6'3", 220 lbs. Born, Novy Jicin, Czech., March 21, 1982. Columbus' 1st choice, 4th overall, in 2000 Entry Draft.

Season	Club	League	GP	G	A	Pts	PIM	PP	SH	GW	S	%	+/-	TF	F%	Min	GP	G	A	Pts	PIM	PP	SH	GW	Min
1997-98	HC Opava Jr.	CzRep-Jr.	38	11	18	29	87	....	....	....	....	....	....	....	....	....	8	2	2	4	0	....	....	....	....
1998-99	Sioux City	USHL	54	4	12	16	100	....	....	....	....	....	....	....	....	....	5	2	0	2	2	....	....	....	....
99-2000	Brampton	OHL	67	16	29	45	174	....	....	....	....	....	....	....	....	....	6	1	1	2	21	....	....	....	....
2000-01	**Columbus**	**NHL**	**8**	**2**	**0**	**2**	**6**	**0**	**0**	**0**	**10**	**20.0**	**–1**	**0**	**0.0**	**18:25**	....	....	....	....	....	....	....	....	....
	Brampton	OHL	45	18	36	54	59	....	....	....	....	....	....	....	....	....	9	2	9	11	26	....	....	....	....
2001-02	**Columbus**	**NHL**	**75**	**8**	**8**	**16**	**74**	**1**	**0**	**0**	**102**	**7.8**	**–6**	**0**	**0.0**	**18:52**	....	....	....	....	....	....	....	....	....
2002-03	**Columbus**	**NHL**	**72**	**2**	**14**	**16**	**71**	**0**	**0**	**0**	**89**	**2.2**	**–22**	**0**	**0.0**	**18:45**	....	....	....	....	....	....	....	....	....
2003-04	**Columbus**	**NHL**	**47**	**2**	**11**	**13**	**27**	**0**	**0**	**1**	**74**	**2.7**	**–16**	**0**	**0.0**	**18:19**	....	....	....	....	....	....	....	....	....
2004-05	HC Vsetin	CzRep	41	7	17	24	136	....	....	....	....	....	....	....	....	....	....	....	....	....	....	....	....	....	....
	HPK Hameenlinna	Finland	9	1	2	3	12	....	....	....	....	....	....	....	....	....	10	0	2	2	12	....	....	....	....
2005-06	**Columbus**	**NHL**	**51**	**6**	**13**	**19**	**75**	**2**	**0**	**1**	**84**	**7.1**	**–4**	**2**	**100.0**	**21:27**	....	....	....	....	....	....	....	....	....
2006-07	**Columbus**	**NHL**	**75**	**9**	**13**	**22**	**105**	**2**	**0**	**0**	**159**	**5.7**	**–13**	**0**	**0.0**	**22:54**	....	....	....	....	....	....	....	....	....
2007-08	**Columbus**	**NHL**	**82**	**6**	**12**	**18**	**60**	**3**	**0**	**1**	**130**	**4.6**	**7**	**5**	**80.0**	**23:13**	....	....	....	....	....	....	....	....	....
2008-09	**Columbus**	**NHL**	**34**	**1**	**8**	**9**	**38**	**0**	**0**	**0**	**30**	**3.3**	**2**	**1**	**0.0**	**20:59**	**4**	**0**	**1**	**1**	**0**	**0**	**0**	**0**	**21:22**
2009-10	**Columbus**	**NHL**	**26**	**2**	**6**	**8**	**26**	**0**	**0**	**1**	**24**	**8.3**	**–7**	**0**	**0.0**	**20:07**	....	....	....	....	....	....	....	....	....
	NHL Totals		**470**	**38**	**85**	**123**	**482**	**8**	**0**	**4**	**702**	**5.4**		**8**	**75.0**	**20:41**	**4**	**0**	**1**	**1**	**0**	**0**	**0**	**0**	**21:22**

OHL All-Rookie Team (2000) • Canadian Major Junior All-Rookie Team (2000) • OHL First All-Star Team (2001) • NHL All-Rookie Team (2002)

Signed as a free agent by **Vsetin** (CzRep), September 17, 2004. Signed as a free agent by **Hameenlinna** (Finland), January 29, 2005. • Missed majority of 2008-09 season recovering from various injuries. • Missed majority of 2009-10 season recovering from injury suffered in game vs. St.Louis, November 30, 2009.

KNUBLE, Mike

(kuh-NOO-buhl, MIGHK) **WSH.**

Right wing. Shoots right. 6'3", 223 lbs. Born, Toronto, Ont., July 4, 1972. Detroit's 4th choice, 76th overall, in 1991 Entry Draft.

Season	Club	League	GP	G	A	Pts	PIM	PP	SH	GW	S	%	+/-	TF	F%	Min	GP	G	A	Pts	PIM	PP	SH	GW	Min
1988-89	East Kentwood	High-MI	28	52	37	89	60	....	....	....	....	....	....	....	....	....	....	....	....	....	....	....	....	....	....
1989-90	East Kentwood	High-MI	29	63	40	103	40	....	....	....	....	....	....	....	....	....	....	....	....	....	....	....	....	....	....
1990-91	Kalamazoo	NAHL	36	18	24	42	30	....	....	....	....	....	....	....	....	....	....	....	....	....	....	....	....	....	....
1991-92	U. of Michigan	CCHA	43	7	8	15	48	....	....	....	....	....	....	....	....	....	....	....	....	....	....	....	....	....	....
1992-93	U. of Michigan	CCHA	39	26	16	42	57	....	....	....	....	....	....	....	....	....	....	....	....	....	....	....	....	....	....
1993-94	U. of Michigan	CCHA	41	32	26	58	71	....	....	....	....	....	....	....	....	....	....	....	....	....	....	....	....	....	....
1994-95	U. of Michigan	CCHA	34	*38	22	60	62	....	....	....	....	....	....	....	....	....	....	....	....	....	....	....	....	....	....
	Adirondack	AHL	....	....	....	....	....	....	....	....	....	....	....	....	....	....	3	0	0	0	0	....	....	....	....
1995-96	Adirondack	AHL	80	22	23	45	59	....	....	....	....	....	....	....	....	....	3	1	0	1	0	....	....	....	....
1996-97	**Detroit**	**NHL**	**9**	**1**	**0**	**1**	**0**	**0**	**0**	**0**	**10**	**10.0**	**–1**	....	....	....	....	....	....	....	....	....	....	....	....
	Adirondack	AHL	68	28	35	63	54	....	....	....	....	....	....	....	....	....	....	....	....	....	....	....	....	....	....
1997-98 ♦	**Detroit**	**NHL**	**53**	**7**	**6**	**13**	**16**	**0**	**0**	**0**	**54**	**13.0**	**2**	....	....	....	**3**	**0**	**1**	**1**	**0**	**0**	**0**	**0**	....
1998-99	**NY Rangers**	**NHL**	**82**	**15**	**20**	**35**	**26**	**3**	**0**	**1**	**113**	**13.3**	**–7**	**1**	**100.0**	**14:52**	....	....	....	....	....	....	....	....	....
99-2000	**NY Rangers**	**NHL**	**59**	**9**	**5**	**14**	**18**	**1**	**0**	**1**	**50**	**18.0**	**–5**	**9**	**55.6**	**10:39**	....	....	....	....	....	....	....	....	....
	Boston	**NHL**	**14**	**3**	**3**	**6**	**8**	**1**	**0**	**1**	**28**	**10.7**	**–2**	**3**	**0.0**	**19:29**	....	....	....	....	....	....	....	....	....
2000-01	**Boston**	**NHL**	**82**	**7**	**13**	**20**	**37**	**0**	**1**	**1**	**92**	**7.6**	**0**	**115**	**31.3**	**10:34**	....	....	....	....	....	....	....	....	....
2001-02	**Boston**	**NHL**	**54**	**8**	**6**	**14**	**42**	**0**	**0**	**2**	**77**	**10.4**	**9**	**27**	**44.4**	**9:45**	**2**	**0**	**0**	**0**	**0**	**0**	**0**	**0**	**3:30**
2002-03	**Boston**	**NHL**	**75**	**30**	**29**	**59**	**45**	**9**	**0**	**4**	**185**	**16.2**	**18**	**34**	**44.1**	**17:24**	**5**	**0**	**2**	**2**	**2**	**0**	**0**	**0**	**17:35**
2003-04	**Boston**	**NHL**	**82**	**21**	**25**	**46**	**32**	**4**	**0**	**3**	**192**	**10.9**	**19**	**54**	**31.5**	**18:47**	**7**	**2**	**0**	**2**	**0**	**1**	**0**	**0**	**19:45**
2004-05	Linkopings HC	Sweden	49	*26	13	39	40	....	....	....	....	....	....	....	....	....	6	0	1	1	2	....	....	....	....
2005-06	**Philadelphia**	**NHL**	**82**	**34**	**31**	**65**	**80**	**13**	**2**	**6**	**217**	**15.7**	**25**	**161**	**32.3**	**20:21**	**6**	**1**	**3**	**4**	**8**	**0**	**0**	**0**	**19:17**
	United States	Olympics	6	1	1	2	4	....	....	....	....	....	....	....	....	....	....	....	....	....	....	....	....	....	....
2006-07	**Philadelphia**	**NHL**	**64**	**24**	**30**	**54**	**56**	**10**	**0**	**1**	**160**	**15.0**	**2**	**62**	**37.1**	**19:38**	....	....	....	....	....	....	....	....	....
2007-08	**Philadelphia**	**NHL**	**82**	**29**	**26**	**55**	**72**	**15**	**1**	**3**	**177**	**16.4**	**–3**	**25**	**40.0**	**18:55**	**12**	**3**	**4**	**7**	**6**	**0**	**0**	**1**	**18:34**
2008-09	**Philadelphia**	**NHL**	**82**	**27**	**20**	**47**	**62**	**11**	**0**	**6**	**173**	**15.6**	**5**	**51**	**35.3**	**18:10**	**6**	**2**	**1**	**3**	**2**	**0**	**0**	**0**	**18:26**
2009-10	**Washington**	**NHL**	**69**	**29**	**24**	**53**	**59**	**6**	**0**	**5**	**151**	**19.2**	**23**	**6**	**0.0**	**16:53**	**7**	**2**	**4**	**6**	**6**	**0**	**1**	**0**	**17:50**
	NHL Totals		**889**	**244**	**238**	**482**	**553**	**73**	**4**	**34**	**1679**	**14.5**		**548**	**34.5**	**16:19**	**48**	**10**	**15**	**25**	**24**	**1**	**1**	**1**	**17:56**

CCHA Second All-Star Team (1994, 1995) • NCAA West Second All-American Team (1995)

Traded to **NY Rangers** by **Detroit** for NY Rangers' 2nd round choice (Tomas Kopecky) in 2000 Entry Draft, October 1, 1998. Traded to **Boston** by **NY Rangers** for Rob DiMaio, March 10, 2000. Signed as a free agent by **Philadelphia**, July 3, 2004. Signed as a free agent by **Linkopings** (Sweden), August 2, 2004. Signed as a free agent by **Washington**, July 1, 2009.

			Regular Season														Playoffs							
Season	Club	League	GP	G	A	Pts	PIM	PP	SH	GW	S	%	+/-	TF	F%	Min	GP	G	A	Pts	PIM	PP	SH	GW	Min

KOBASEW, Chuck (KOH-buh-soo, CHUHK) MIN.

Right wing. Shoots left. 6', 192 lbs.   Born, Vancouver, B.C., April 17, 1982. Calgary's 1st choice, 14th overall, in 2001 Entry Draft.

Season	Club	League	GP	G	A	Pts	PIM	PP	SH	GW	S	%	+/-	TF	F%	Min	GP	G	A	Pts	PIM	PP	SH	GW	Min
1997-98	Osoyoos Heat	KIJHL	6	2	2	4	2	....	....	....	....	....	....	....	....	....	....	....	....	....	....	....	....	....	....
1998-99	Osoyoos Heat	KIJHL	23	25	24	49	....	....	....	....	....	....	....	....	....	....	....	....	....	....	....	....	....	....	....
	Penticton	BCHL	30	11	17	28	18	....	....	....	....	....	....	....	....	....	....	....	....	....	....	....	....	....	....
99-2000	Penticton	BCHL	58	*54	52	106	83	....	....	....	....	....	....	....	....	....	....	....	....	....	....	....	....	....	....
2000-01	Boston College	H-East	43	27	22	49	38	....	....	....	....	....	....	....	....	....	....	....	....	....	....	....	....	....	....
2001-02	Kelowna Rockets	WHL	55	41	21	62	114	....	....	....	....	....	....	....	....	....	15	10	5	15	22	....	....	....	....
2002-03	**Calgary**	**NHL**	23	4	2	6	8	1	0	1	29	13.8	-3	5	0.0	11:48	....	....	....	....	....	....	....	....	....
	Saint John Flames	AHL	48	21	12	33	61	....	....	....	....	....	....	....	....	....	....	....	....	....	....	....	....	....	....
2003-04	**Calgary**	**NHL**	70	6	11	17	51	3	0	0	78	7.7	-12	91	42.9	10:22	26	0	1	1	24	0	0	0	9:02
2004-05	Lowell	AHL	79	38	37	75	110	....	....	....	....	....	....	....	....	....	11	6	3	9	27	....	....	....	....
2005-06	**Calgary**	**NHL**	77	20	11	31	64	10	0	4	143	14.0	-10	47	25.5	12:16	7	1	0	1	0	0	0	1	12:29
2006-07	**Calgary**	**NHL**	40	4	13	17	37	1	0	1	69	5.8	7	26	30.8	13:13	....	....	....	....	....	....	....	....	....
	Boston	**NHL**	10	1	1	2	25	1	0	0	24	4.2	-6	6	16.7	18:51	....	....	....	....	....	....	....	....	....
2007-08	**Boston**	**NHL**	73	22	17	39	29	6	3	5	147	15.0	6	70	40.0	17:41	....	....	....	....	....	....	....	....	....
2008-09	**Boston**	**NHL**	68	21	21	42	56	6	0	3	129	16.3	5	26	23.1	14:41	11	3	3	6	14	0	0	1	16:09
2009-10	**Boston**	**NHL**	7	0	1	1	2	0	0	0	13	0.0	-2	0	0.0	14:22	....	....	....	....	....	....	....	....	....
	Minnesota	**NHL**	42	9	5	14	16	2	0	2	58	15.5	-9	8	25.0	13:50	....	....	....	....	....	....	....	....	....
	NHL Totals		410	87	82	169	288	30	3	14	690	12.6		279	34.4	13:44	44	4	4	8	38	0	0	2	11:21

Hockey East Second All-Star Team (2001) • Hockey East Rookie of the Year (2001) • NCAA Championship All-Tournament Team (2001) • NCAA Championship Tournament MVP (2001) • AHL First All-Star Team (2005)

Left **Boston College** (Hockey East) and signed with **Kelowna** (WHL), August 13, 2001. Traded to **Boston** by **Calgary** with Andrew Ference for Brad Stuart, Wayne Primeau and Washington's 4th round choice (previously acquired, Calgary selected T.J. Brodie) in 2008 Entry Draft, February 10, 2007. Traded to **Minnesota** by **Boston** for Craig Weller, Alexander Fallstrom and Minnesota's 2nd round choice in 2011 Entry Draft, October 18, 2009.

KOCI, David (KOH-chee, DAY-vihd) COL.

Left wing. Shoots left. 6'6", 238 lbs.   Born, Prague, Czech., May 12, 1981. Pittsburgh's 5th choice, 146th overall, in 2000 Entry Draft.

Season	Club	League	GP	G	A	Pts	PIM	PP	SH	GW	S	%	+/-	TF	F%	Min	GP	G	A	Pts	PIM	PP	SH	GW	Min
1997-98	Sparta Jr.	CzRep-Jr.	41	2	9	11	105	....	....	....	....	....	....	....	....	....	....	....	....	....	....	....	....	....	....
1998-99	Hvezda Praha Jr.	CzRep-Jr.	22	1	3	4	36	....	....	....	....	....	....	....	....	....	....	....	....	....	....	....	....	....	....
	Sparta Jr.	CzRep-Jr.	7	0	0	0	4	....	....	....	....	....	....	....	....	....	....	....	....	....	....	....	....	....	....
99-2000	Sparta Jr.	CzRep-Jr.	47	0	6	6	124	....	....	....	....	....	....	....	....	....	....	....	....	....	....	....	....	....	....
2000-01	Prince George	WHL	70	2	7	9	155	....	....	....	....	....	....	....	....	....	6	0	0	0	20	....	....	....	....
2001-02	Wilkes-Barre	AHL	26	1	3	4	98	....	....	....	....	....	....	....	....	....	....	....	....	....	....	....	....	....	....
	Wheeling Nailers	ECHL	33	2	4	6	105	....	....	....	....	....	....	....	....	....	....	....	....	....	....	....	....	....	....
2002-03	Wilkes-Barre	AHL	9	0	0	0	4	....	....	....	....	....	....	....	....	....	....	....	....	....	....	....	....	....	....
	Wheeling Nailers	ECHL	48	0	1	1	103	....	....	....	....	....	....	....	....	....	....	....	....	....	....	....	....	....	....
2003-04	Wilkes-Barre	AHL	78	1	7	8	298	....	....	....	....	....	....	....	....	....	10	0	0	0	24	....	....	....	....
2004-05	Wilkes-Barre	AHL	68	1	8	9	311	....	....	....	....	....	....	....	....	....	....	....	....	....	....	....	....	....	....
2005-06	Wilkes-Barre	AHL	13	0	0	0	59	....	....	....	....	....	....	....	....	....	....	....	....	....	....	....	....	....	....
2006-07	**Chicago**	**NHL**	9	0	0	0	88	0	0	0	3	0.0	-3	0	0.0	4:44	....	....	....	....	....	....	....	....	....
	Norfolk Admirals	AHL	44	0	1	1	223	....	....	....	....	....	....	....	....	....	....	....	....	....	....	....	....	....	....
2007-08	**Chicago**	**NHL**	18	0	0	0	68	0	0	0	2	0.0	-4	0	0.0	3:38	....	....	....	....	....	....	....	....	....
	Rockford IceHogs	AHL	7	0	0	0	25	....	....	....	....	....	....	....	....	....	....	....	....	....	....	....	....	....	....
	Norfolk Admirals	AHL	21	0	2	2	57	....	....	....	....	....	....	....	....	....	....	....	....	....	....	....	....	....	....
2008-09	**Tampa Bay**	**NHL**	33	1	1	2	132	0	0	0	8	12.5	3	0	0.0	6:14	....	....	....	....	....	....	....	....	....
	St. Louis	**NHL**	4	0	0	0	9	0	0	0	5	0.0	-2	0	0.0	3:37	....	....	....	....	....	....	....	....	....
2009-10	**Colorado**	**NHL**	43	1	0	1	84	0	0	0	6	16.7	-2	0	0.0	3:03	....	....	....	....	....	....	....	....	....
	NHL Totals		107	2	1	3	381	0	0	0	24	8.3		0	0.0	4:18	....	....	....	....	....	....	....	....	....

Missed majority of 2005-06 season recovering from knee injury, November, 2006. Signed as a free agent by **Chicago**, July 17, 2006. Signed as a free agent by **Tampa Bay**, July 3, 2008. Claimed on waivers by **St. Louis** from **Tampa Bay**, October 21, 2008. Claimed on waivers by **Tampa Bay** from **St. Louis**, November 20, 2008. Signed as a free agent by **Colorado**, July 1, 2009.

KOHN, Dustin (KOHN, DUHS-tihn) NYI

Defense. Shoots left. 6'2", 200 lbs.   Born, Edmonton, Alta., February 2, 1987. NY Islanders' 2nd choice, 46th overall, in 2005 Entry Draft.

Season	Club	League	GP	G	A	Pts	PIM	PP	SH	GW	S	%	+/-	TF	F%	Min	GP	G	A	Pts	PIM	PP	SH	GW	Min
2003-04	Calgary Hitmen	WHL	52	3	6	9	13	....	....	....	....	....	....	....	....	....	7	0	1	1	2	....	....	....	....
2004-05	Calgary Hitmen	WHL	71	8	35	43	61	....	....	....	....	....	....	....	....	....	12	0	4	4	6	....	....	....	....
2005-06	Calgary Hitmen	WHL	38	2	12	14	20	....	....	....	....	....	....	....	....	....	....	....	....	....	....	....	....	....	....
	Brandon	WHL	31	2	13	15	30	....	....	....	....	....	....	....	....	....	6	0	4	4	10	....	....	....	....
	Bridgeport	AHL	2	0	0	0	0	....	....	....	....	....	....	....	....	....	....	....	....	....	....	....	....	....	....
2006-07	Brandon	WHL	61	5	45	50	77	....	....	....	....	....	....	....	....	....	11	1	8	9	18	....	....	....	....
2007-08	Bridgeport	AHL	62	3	9	12	28	....	....	....	....	....	....	....	....	....	....	....	....	....	....	....	....	....	....
2008-09	Bridgeport	AHL	58	4	13	17	45	....	....	....	....	....	....	....	....	....	5	0	0	0	4	....	....	....	....
2009-10	**NY Islanders**	**NHL**	22	0	4	4	4	0	0	0	7	0.0	-2	0	0.0	11:36	....	....	....	....	....	....	....	....	....
	Bridgeport	AHL	45	2	15	17	53	....	....	....	....	....	....	....	....	....	5	2	2	4	2	....	....	....	....
	NHL Totals		22	0	4	4	4	0	0	0	7	0.0		0	0.0	11:36	....	....	....	....	....	....	....	....	....

KOISTINEN, Ville (KOIS-tih-nehn, VIHL-ee)

Defense. Shoots left. 5'11", 187 lbs.   Born, Oulu, Finland, June 17, 1982.

Season	Club	League	GP	G	A	Pts	PIM	PP	SH	GW	S	%	+/-	TF	F%	Min	GP	G	A	Pts	PIM	PP	SH	GW	Min
1998-99	Ilves Tampere U18	Fin-U18	34	4	10	14	86	....	....	....	....	....	....	....	....	....	....	....	....	....	....	....	....	....	....
	Ilves Tampere Jr.	Fin-Jr.	1	0	0	0	2	....	....	....	....	....	....	....	....	....	....	....	....	....	....	....	....	....	....
99-2000	Ilves Tampere U18	Fin-U18	14	4	6	10	69	....	....	....	....	....	....	....	....	....	....	....	....	....	....	....	....	....	....
	Ilves Tampere Jr.	Fin-Jr.	34	4	2	6	40	....	....	....	....	....	....	....	....	....	....	....	....	....	....	....	....	....	....
2000-01	Ilves Tampere	Finland	6	0	0	0	0	....	....	....	....	....	....	....	....	....	5	0	1	1	0	....	....	....	....
	Ilves Tampere Jr.	Fin-Jr.	26	1	8	9	101	....	....	....	....	....	....	....	....	....	....	....	....	....	....	....	....	....	....
2001-02	Ilves Tampere	Finland	53	1	8	9	42	....	....	....	....	....	....	....	....	....	....	....	....	....	....	....	....	....	....
	Ilves Tampere Jr.	Fin-Jr.	6	2	2	4	16	....	....	....	....	....	....	....	....	....	....	....	....	....	....	....	....	....	....
2002-03	Ilves Tampere	Finland	18	4	1	5	8	....	....	....	....	....	....	....	....	....	....	....	....	....	....	....	....	....	....
	Ilves Tampere Jr.	Fin-Jr.	1	0	0	0	10	....	....	....	....	....	....	....	....	....	....	....	....	....	....	....	....	....	....
2003-04	Ilves Tampere	Finland	54	7	16	23	51	....	....	....	....	....	....	....	....	....	7	0	2	2	0	....	....	....	....
2004-05	Ilves Tampere	Finland	52	6	14	20	69	....	....	....	....	....	....	....	....	....	3	0	0	0	0	....	....	....	....
2005-06	Ilves Tampere	Finland	56	8	26	34	70	....	....	....	....	....	....	....	....	....	4	0	1	1	2	....	....	....	....
2006-07	Milwaukee	AHL	59	9	32	41	44	....	....	....	....	....	....	....	....	....	4	0	2	2	4	....	....	....	....
2007-08	**Nashville**	**NHL**	48	4	13	17	18	2	0	1	60	6.7	13	0	0.0	16:48	....	....	....	....	....	....	....	....	....
2008-09	**Nashville**	**NHL**	38	3	8	11	14	1	0	2	42	7.1	0	1	0.0	14:42	....	....	....	....	....	....	....	....	....
2009-10	**Florida**	**NHL**	17	1	3	4	8	0	0	0	12	8.3	1	0	0.0	7:50	....	....	....	....	....	....	....	....	....
	Rochester	AHL	8	1	1	2	4	....	....	....	....	....	....	....	....	....	....	....	....	....	....	....	....	....	....
	NHL Totals		103	8	24	32	40	3	0	3	114	7.0		1	0.0	14:33	....	....	....	....	....	....	....	....	....

Signed as a free agent by **Nashville**, May 11, 2006. • Missed majority of 2008-09 season as a healthy reserve. • Missed majority of 2009-10 season recovering from knee injury and resulting surgery, December 28, 2010.

KOIVU, Mikko (KOI-voo, MEE-koh) MIN.

Center. Shoots left. 6'2", 214 lbs.   Born, Turku, Finland, March 12, 1983. Minnesota's 1st choice, 6th overall, in 2001 Entry Draft.

Season	Club	League	GP	G	A	Pts	PIM	PP	SH	GW	S	%	+/-	TF	F%	Min	GP	G	A	Pts	PIM	PP	SH	GW	Min
99-2000	TPS Turku U18	Fin-U18	11	4	9	13	18	....	....	....	....	....	....	....	....	....	13	1	4	5	8	....	....	....	....
	TPS Turku Jr.	Fin-Jr.	30	4	8	12	22	....	....	....	....	....	....	....	....	....	7	2	10	12	2	....	....	....	....
2000-01	TPS Turku U18	Fin-U18	4	0	0	0	0	....	....	....	....	....	....	....	....	....	3	1	1	2	6	....	....	....	....
	TPS Turku Jr.	Fin-Jr.	26	9	36	45	26	....	....	....	....	....	....	....	....	....	....	....	....	....	....	....	....	....	....
	TPS Turku	Finland	21	0	1	1	2	....	....	....	....	....	....	....	....	....	....	....	....	....	....	....	....	....	....
2001-02	TPS Turku Jr.	Fin-Jr.	2	0	1	1	12	....	....	....	....	....	....	....	....	....	....	....	....	....	....	....	....	....	....
	TPS Turku	Finland	48	4	3	7	34	....	....	....	....	....	....	....	....	....	8	0	3	3	4	....	....	....	....
2002-03	TPS Turku	Finland	37	7	13	20	20	....	....	....	....	....	....	....	....	....	7	2	2	4	6	....	....	....	....
2003-04	TPS Turku	Finland	45	6	24	30	36	....	....	....	....	....	....	....	....	....	13	1	7	8	8	....	....	....	....
2004-05	Houston Aeros	AHL	67	20	28	48	47	....	....	....	....	....	....	....	....	....	5	1	0	1	2	....	....	....	....
2005-06	**Minnesota**	**NHL**	64	6	15	21	40	3	0	0	96	6.3	-9	724	47.4	13:17	....	....	....	....	....	....	....	....	....
	Finland	Olympics	8	0	0	0	6	....	....	....	....	....	....	....	....	....	....	....	....	....	....	....	....	....	....
2006-07	**Minnesota**	**NHL**	82	20	34	54	58	9	2	2	162	12.3	6	1165	50.9	17:29	5	1	0	1	4	0	0	0	17:43

			Regular Season														Playoffs								
Season	Club	League	GP	G	A	Pts	PIM	PP	SH	GW	S	%	+/-	TF	F%	Min	GP	G	A	Pts	PIM	PP	SH	GW	Min
2007-08	**Minnesota**	**NHL**	**57**	**11**	**31**	**42**	**42**	**2**	**0**	**2**	**144**	**7.6**	**13**	**1032**	**52.5**	**20:53**	**6**	**4**	**1**	**5**	**4**	**0**	**1**	**0**	**21:56**
2008-09	**Minnesota**	**NHL**	**79**	**20**	**47**	**67**	**66**	**5**	**4**	**3**	**236**	**8.5**	**2**	**1625**	**52.7**	**21:29**	....	....	....	....	....	....	....	....	....
2009-10	**Minnesota**	**NHL**	**80**	**22**	**49**	**71**	**50**	**8**	**1**	**2**	**246**	**8.9**	**–2**	**1518**	**56.9**	**20:45**	....	....	....	....	....	....	....	....	....
	Finland	Olympics	6	0	4	4	2	....	....	....	....	....	....	....	....	....	....	....	....	....	....	....	....	....	....
	NHL Totals		**362**	**79**	**176**	**255**	**256**	**27**	**7**	**9**	**884**	**8.9**		**6064**	**52.8**	**18:52**	**11**	**5**	**1**	**6**	**8**	**0**	**1**	**0**	**20:01**

KOIVU, Saku

(KOI-voo, SA-koo) **ANA**

Center. Shoots left. 5'10", 178 lbs. Born, Turku, Finland, November 23, 1974. Montreal's 1st choice, 21st overall, in 1993 Entry Draft.

Season	Club	League	GP	G	A	Pts	PIM	PP	SH	GW	S	%	+/-	TF	F%	Min	GP	G	A	Pts	PIM	PP	SH	GW	Min
1990-91	TPS Turku U18	Fin-U18	24	20	28	48	26	....	....	....	....	....	....	....	....	....	....	....	....	....	....	....	....	....	....
	TPS Turku Jr.	Fin-Jr.	13	3	7	10	6	....	....	....	....	....	....	....	....	....	....	....	....	....	....	....	....	....	....
1991-92	TPS Turku U18	Fin-U18	12	3	7	10	6	....	....	....	....	....	....	....	....	....	....	....	....	....	....	....	....	....	....
	TPS Turku Jr.	Fin-Jr.	34	25	28	53	57	....	....	....	....	....	....	....	....	....	8	5	9	14	6	....	....	....	....
1992-93	TPS Turku	Finland	46	3	7	10	28	....	....	....	....	....	....	....	....	....	11	3	2	5	2	....	....	....	....
1993-94	TPS Turku	Finland	47	23	30	53	42	....	....	....	....	....	....	....	....	....	11	4	8	12	16	....	....	....	....
	Finland	Olympics	8	4	3	7	12	....	....	....	....	....	....	....	....	....	....	....	....	....	....	....	....	....	....
1994-95	TPS Turku	Finland	45	27	47	74	73	....	....	....	....	....	....	....	....	....	13	7	10	17	16	....	....	....	....
1995-96	**Montreal**	**NHL**	**82**	**20**	**25**	**45**	**40**	**8**	**3**	**2**	**136**	**14.7**	**–7**	....	....	....	**6**	**3**	**1**	**4**	**8**	**0**	**0**	**0**	....
1996-97	**Montreal**	**NHL**	**50**	**17**	**39**	**56**	**38**	**5**	**0**	**3**	**135**	**12.6**	**7**	....	....	....	**5**	**1**	**3**	**4**	**10**	**0**	**0**	**0**	....
1997-98	**Montreal**	**NHL**	**69**	**14**	**43**	**57**	**48**	**2**	**2**	**3**	**145**	**9.7**	**8**	....	....	....	**6**	**2**	**3**	**5**	**2**	**1**	**0**	**0**	....
	Finland	Olympics	6	2	8	10	4	....	....	....	....	....	....	....	....	....	....	....	....	....	....	....	....	....	....
1998-99	**Montreal**	**NHL**	**65**	**14**	**30**	**44**	**38**	**4**	**2**	**0**	**145**	**9.7**	**–7**	**1427**	**52.6**	**20:02**	....	....	....	....	....	....	....	....	....
99-2000	**Montreal**	**NHL**	**24**	**3**	**18**	**21**	**14**	**1**	**0**	**0**	**53**	**5.7**	**7**	**495**	**52.9**	**19:13**	....	....	....	....	....	....	....	....	....
2000-01	**Montreal**	**NHL**	**54**	**17**	**30**	**47**	**40**	**7**	**0**	**3**	**113**	**15.0**	**2**	**1092**	**47.6**	**21:23**	....	....	....	....	....	....	....	....	....
2001-02	**Montreal**	**NHL**	**3**	**0**	**2**	**2**	**0**	**0**	**0**	**0**	**2**	**0.0**	**0**	**13**	**61.5**	**13:57**	**12**	**4**	**6**	**10**	**4**	**1**	**0**	**1**	**15:54**
2002-03	**Montreal**	**NHL**	**82**	**21**	**50**	**71**	**72**	**5**	**1**	**5**	**147**	**14.3**	**5**	**1566**	**49.6**	**19:14**	....	....	....	....	....	....	....	....	....
2003-04	**Montreal**	**NHL**	**68**	**14**	**41**	**55**	**52**	**5**	**0**	**3**	**112**	**12.5**	**–5**	**1194**	**53.9**	**19:18**	**11**	**3**	**8**	**11**	**10**	**2**	**0**	**0**	**20:34**
2004-05	TPS Turku	Finland	20	8	8	16	28	....	....	....	....	....	....	....	....	....	6	3	2	5	30	....	....	....	....
2005-06	**Montreal**	**NHL**	**72**	**17**	**45**	**62**	**70**	**5**	**0**	**4**	**138**	**12.3**	**1**	**1412**	**53.8**	**18:31**	**3**	**0**	**2**	**2**	**2**	**0**	**0**	**0**	**14:24**
	Finland	Olympics	8	3	*8	*11	12	....	....	....	....	....	....	....	....	....	....	....	....	....	....	....	....	....	....
2006-07	**Montreal**	**NHL**	**81**	**22**	**53**	**75**	**74**	**11**	**1**	**4**	**154**	**14.3**	**–21**	**1453**	**54.9**	**18:07**	....	....	....	....	....	....	....	....	....
2007-08	**Montreal**	**NHL**	**77**	**16**	**40**	**56**	**93**	**8**	**0**	**3**	**150**	**10.7**	**–4**	**1341**	**52.3**	**18:07**	**7**	**3**	**6**	**9**	**4**	**2**	**0**	**0**	**19:33**
2008-09	**Montreal**	**NHL**	**65**	**16**	**34**	**50**	**44**	**5**	**0**	**5**	**123**	**13.0**	**4**	**1122**	**54.1**	**17:03**	**4**	**0**	**3**	**3**	**2**	**0**	**0**	**0**	**17:45**
2009-10	**Anaheim**	**NHL**	**71**	**19**	**33**	**52**	**36**	**5**	**1**	**6**	**124**	**15.3**	**14**	**1110**	**51.4**	**18:35**	....	....	....	....	....	....	....	....	....
	Finland	Olympics	6	0	2	2	6	....	....	....	....	....	....	....	....	....	....	....	....	....	....	....	....	....	....
	NHL Totals		**863**	**210**	**483**	**693**	**659**	**71**	**10**	**41**	**1677**	**12.5**		**12225**	**52.3**	**18:51**	**54**	**16**	**32**	**48**	**42**	**6**	**0**	**1**	**18:03**

Bill Masterton Memorial Trophy (2002) • Olympic Tournament All-Star Team (2006) • King Clancy Memorial Trophy (2007)

Played in NHL All-Star Game (1998)

• Missed majority of 1999-2000 season recovering from shoulder injury suffered in game vs. NY Rangers, October 30, 1999. • Missed majority of 2001-02 season recovering from non-Hodgkin 's lymphoma, September 6, 2001. Signed as a free agent by **Turku** (Finland), October 21, 2004. Signed as a free agent by **Anaheim**, July 8, 2009.

KOLANOS, Krys

(koh-LA-nohs, KRIHS)

Center. Shoots right. 6'3", 206 lbs. Born, Calgary, Alta., July 27, 1981. Phoenix's 1st choice, 19th overall, in 2000 Entry Draft.

Season	Club	League	GP	G	A	Pts	PIM	PP	SH	GW	S	%	+/-	TF	F%	Min	GP	G	A	Pts	PIM	PP	SH	GW	Min
1996-97	Calgary Flames	AAHA	24	24	35	59		....	....	....	....	....	....	....	....	....	....	....	....	....	....	....	....	....	....
1997-98	Calgary Buffaloes	AMHL	34	34	43	77	29	....	....	....	....	....	....	....	....	....	....	....	....	....	....	....	....	....	....
1998-99	Calgary Royals	AJHL	58	43	67	110	98	....	....	....	....	....	....	....	....	....	....	....	....	....	....	....	....	....	....
99-2000	Boston College	H-East	42	16	16	32	48	....	....	....	....	....	....	....	....	....	....	....	....	....	....	....	....	....	....
2000-01	Boston College	H-East	41	25	25	50	54	....	....	....	....	....	....	....	....	....	....	....	....	....	....	....	....	....	....
2001-02	**Phoenix**	**NHL**	**57**	**11**	**11**	**22**	**48**	**0**	**0**	**5**	**81**	**13.6**	**6**	**703**	**46.4**	**13:05**	**2**	**0**	**0**	**0**	**6**	**0**	**0**	**0**	**11:12**
2002-03	**Phoenix**	**NHL**	**2**	**0**	**0**	**0**	**0**	**0**	**0**	**0**	**8**	**0.0**	**0**	**16**	**31.3**	**14:06**	....	....	....	....	....	....	....	....	....
2003-04	**Phoenix**	**NHL**	**41**	**4**	**6**	**10**	**24**	**1**	**0**	**1**	**61**	**6.6**	**–9**	**283**	**43.8**	**13:31**	....	....	....	....	....	....	....	....	....
	Springfield	AHL	32	10	11	21	38	....	....	....	....	....	....	....	....	....	....	....	....	....	....	....	....	....	....
2004-05	Blues Espoo	Finland	15	7	9	16	40	....	....	....	....	....	....	....	....	....	....	....	....	....	....	....	....	....	....
	Krefeld Pinguine	Germany	7	3	2	5	16	....	....	....	....	....	....	....	....	....	....	....	....	....	....	....	....	....	....
2005-06	**Phoenix**	**NHL**	**9**	**2**	**1**	**3**	**2**	**1**	**0**	**0**	**15**	**13.3**	**2**	**75**	**53.3**	**11:30**	....	....	....	....	....	....	....	....	....
	San Antonio	AHL	3	0	1	1	0	....	....	....	....	....	....	....	....	....	....	....	....	....	....	....	....	....	....
	Edmonton	**NHL**	**6**	**0**	**0**	**0**	**2**	**0**	**0**	**0**	**7**	**0.0**	**–1**	**32**	**50.0**	**7:39**	....	....	....	....	....	....	....	....	....
	Lowell	AHL	19	10	11	21	40	....	....	....	....	....	....	....	....	....	....	....	....	....	....	....	....	....	....
	Wilkes-Barre	AHL	18	10	8	18	19	....	....	....	....	....	....	....	....	....	11	2	0	2	16	....	....	....	....
2006-07	Grand Rapids	AHL	17	6	6	12	8	....	....	....	....	....	....	....	....	....	....	....	....	....	....	....	....	....	....
	Langnau	Swiss	14	2	9	11	48	....	....	....	....	....	....	....	....	....	....	....	....	....	....	....	....	....	....
	EV Zug	Swiss	....	....	....	....	....	....	....	....	....	....	....	....	....	....	8	6	0	6	8	....	....	....	....
2007-08	Quad City Flames	AHL	65	30	33	63	84	....	....	....	....	....	....	....	....	....	....	....	....	....	....	....	....	....	....
2008-09	**Minnesota**	**NHL**	**21**	**3**	**3**	**6**	**16**	**1**	**0**	**0**	**30**	**10.0**	**3**	**115**	**51.3**	**10:36**	....	....	....	....	....	....	....	....	....
	Houston Aeros	AHL	45	31	20	51	42	....	....	....	....	....	....	....	....	....	18	6	8	14	18	....	....	....	....
2009-10	Adirondack	AHL	27	9	6	15	22	....	....	....	....	....	....	....	....	....	....	....	....	....	....	....	....	....	....
	NHL Totals		**136**	**20**	**21**	**41**	**92**	**3**	**0**	**6**	**202**	**9.9**		**1224**	**46.6**	**12:30**	**2**	**0**	**0**	**0**	**6**	**0**	**0**	**0**	**11:12**

Hockey East All-Rookie Team (2000) • Hockey East Second All-Star Team (2001) • NCAA East Second All-American Team (2001) • NCAA Championship All-Tournament Team (2001)

• Missed majority of 2002-03 season recovering from head injury suffered in game vs. Pittsburgh, March 20, 2002. Signed as a free agent by **Espoo** (Finland), October 25, 2004. Signed as a free agent by **Krefeld** (Germany), February 16, 2005. Claimed on waivers by **Edmonton** from **Phoenix**, November 11, 2005. Claimed on waivers by **Phoenix** from **Edmonton**, December 19, 2005. Traded to **Carolina** by **Phoenix** for Pavel Brendl, December 28, 2005. Traded to **Pittsburgh** by **Carolina** with Niklas Nordgren and Carolina's 2nd round choice (later traded to San Jose, later traded to Philadelphia - Philadelphia selected Kevin Marshall) in 2007 Entry Draft for Mark Recchi, March 9, 2006. Signed as a free agent by **Detroit**, July 15, 2006. Signed as a free agent by **Minnesota**, July 11, 2008. Signed as a free agent by **Philadelphia**, July 23, 2009.

KOLARIK, Chad

(kah-LOHR-ihk, CHAD) **CBJ**

Center. Shoots right. 5'10", 175 lbs. Born, Abington, PA, January 26, 1986. Phoenix's 7th choice, 199th overall, in 2004 Entry Draft.

Season	Club	League	GP	G	A	Pts	PIM	PP	SH	GW	S	%	+/-	TF	F%	Min	GP	G	A	Pts	PIM	PP	SH	GW	Min
2002-03	USNTDP	U-17	21	14	10	24	4	....	....	....	....	....	....	....	....	....	....	....	....	....	....	....	....	....	....
	USNTDP	NAHL	44	16	22	38	43	....	....	....	....	....	....	....	....	....	....	....	....	....	....	....	....	....	....
2003-04	USNTDP	U-18	45	18	20	38	16	....	....	....	....	....	....	....	....	....	....	....	....	....	....	....	....	....	....
	USNTDP	NAHL	10	3	4	7	4	....	....	....	....	....	....	....	....	....	....	....	....	....	....	....	....	....	....
2004-05	U. of Michigan	CCHA	42	18	17	35	53	....	....	....	....	....	....	....	....	....	....	....	....	....	....	....	....	....	....
2005-06	U. of Michigan	CCHA	41	12	26	38	30	....	....	....	....	....	....	....	....	....	....	....	....	....	....	....	....	....	....
2006-07	U. of Michigan	CCHA	41	18	27	45	24	....	....	....	....	....	....	....	....	....	....	....	....	....	....	....	....	....	....
2007-08	U. of Michigan	CCHA	39	30	26	56	24	....	....	....	....	....	....	....	....	....	....	....	....	....	....	....	....	....	....
	San Antonio	AHL	....	....	....	....	....	....	....	....	....	....	....	....	....	....	7	4	2	6	0	....	....	....	....
2008-09	San Antonio	AHL	76	20	30	50	47	....	....	....	....	....	....	....	....	....	....	....	....	....	....	....	....	....	....
2009-10	San Antonio	AHL	59	17	18	35	41	....	....	....	....	....	....	....	....	....	....	....	....	....	....	....	....	....	....
	Columbus	**NHL**	**2**	**0**	**0**	**0**	**0**	**0**	**0**	**0**	**2**	**0.0**	**–1**	**0**	**0.0**	**6:29**	....	....	....	....	....	....	....	....	....
	Syracuse Crunch	AHL	17	9	6	15	14	....	....	....	....	....	....	....	....	....	....	....	....	....	....	....	....	....	....
	NHL Totals		**2**	**0**	**0**	**0**	**0**	**0**	**0**	**0**	**2**	**0.0**		**0**	**0.0**	**6:29**	....	....	....	....	....	....	....	....	....

CCHA First All-Star Team (2008) • NCAA West Second All-American Team (2008)

Traded to **Columbus** by **Phoenix** for Alexandre Picard, March 3, 2010.

KOMISAREK, Mike

(koh-mih-SAIR-ehk, MIGHK) **TOR.**

Defense. Shoots right. 6'4", 243 lbs. Born, West Islip, NY, January 19, 1982. Montreal's 1st choice, 7th overall, in 2001 Entry Draft.

Season	Club	League	GP	G	A	Pts	PIM	PP	SH	GW	S	%	+/-	TF	F%	Min	GP	G	A	Pts	PIM	PP	SH	GW	Min
1998-99	N.E. Jr. Coyotes	EJHL	53	17	24	51	....	....	....	....	....	....	....	....	....	....	....	....	....	....	....	....	....	....	....
99-2000	USNTDP	U-18	6	0	0	0	12	....	....	....	....	....	....	....	....	....	....	....	....	....	....	....	....	....	....
	USNTDP	USHL	51	5	8	13	124	....	....	....	....	....	....	....	....	....	....	....	....	....	....	....	....	....	....
	USNTDP	NAHL	1	0	0	0	16	....	....	....	....	....	....	....	....	....	....	....	....	....	....	....	....	....	....
2000-01	U. of Michigan	CCHA	41	4	12	16	77	....	....	....	....	....	....	....	....	....	....	....	....	....	....	....	....	....	....
2001-02	U. of Michigan	CCHA	40	11	19	30	70	....	....	....	....	....	....	....	....	....	....	....	....	....	....	....	....	....	....
2002-03	**Montreal**	**NHL**	**21**	**0**	**1**	**1**	**28**	**0**	**0**	**0**	**26**	**0.0**	**–6**	**0**	**0.0**	**16:42**	....	....	....	....	....	....	....	....	....
	Hamilton	AHL	56	5	25	30	79	....	....	....	....	....	....	....	....	....	23	1	5	6	60	....	....	....	....
2003-04	**Montreal**	**NHL**	**46**	**0**	**4**	**4**	**34**	**0**	**0**	**0**	**40**	**0.0**	**4**	**0**	**0.0**	**12:00**	**7**	**0**	**0**	**0**	**8**	**0**	**0**	**0**	**14:09**
	Hamilton	AHL	18	2	7	9	47	....	....	....	....	....	....	....	....	....	....	....	....	....	....	....	....	....	....
2004-05	Hamilton	AHL	20	1	4	5	49	....	....	....	....	....	....	....	....	....	4	0	1	1	8	....	....	....	....
2005-06	**Montreal**	**NHL**	**71**	**2**	**4**	**6**	**116**	**0**	**0**	**0**	**66**	**3.0**	**–1**	**0**	**0.0**	**14:40**	**6**	**0**	**0**	**0**	**10**	**0**	**0**	**0**	**18:35**

			Regular Season														Playoffs								
Season	Club	League	GP	G	A	Pts	PIM	PP	SH	GW	S	%	+/-	TF	F%	Min	GP	G	A	Pts	PIM	PP	SH	GW	Min
2006-07	**Montreal**	**NHL**	**82**	**4**	**15**	**19**	**96**	**0**	**2**	**1**	**78**	**5.1**	**7**	**0**	**0.0**	**19:16**	....	....	....	....	....	....	....	....	....
2007-08	**Montreal**	**NHL**	**75**	**4**	**13**	**17**	**101**	**0**	**0**	**1**	**75**	**5.3**	**9**	**1**	**0.0**	**21:09**	**12**	**1**	**2**	**3**	**18**	**0**	**0**	**1**	**20:02**
2008-09	**Montreal**	**NHL**	**66**	**2**	**9**	**11**	**121**	**0**	**0**	**0**	**56**	**3.6**	**0**	**0**	**0.0**	**20:37**	**4**	**0**	**0**	**0**	**20**	**0**	**0**	**0**	**19:00**
2009-10	**Toronto**	**NHL**	**34**	**0**	**4**	**4**	**40**	**0**	**0**	**0**	**35**	**0.0**	**-9**	**0**	**0.0**	**19:56**	....	....	....	....	....	....	....	....	....
	NHL Totals		**395**	**12**	**50**	**62**	**536**	**0**	**2**	**2**	**376**	**3.2**		**1**	**0.0**	**18:06**	**29**	**1**	**2**	**3**	**56**	**0**	**0**	**1**	**18:10**

CHA First All-Star Team (2002) • NCAA West First All-American Team (2002) • AHL All-Rookie Team (2003)
ayed in NHL All-Star Game (2009)
gned as a free agent by **Toronto**, July 1, 2009. • Missed majority of 2009-10 season recovering from recurrring shoulder injury and resulting surgery, February 10, 2010.

KONOPKA, Zenon (kuh-NOHP-kah, ZEH-nohn) NYI

Center. Shoots left. 6', 211 lbs. Born, Niagara on the Lake, Ont., January 2, 1981.

Season	Club	League	GP	G	A	Pts	PIM	PP	SH	GW	S	%	+/-	TF	F%	Min	GP	G	A	Pts	PIM	PP	SH	GW	Min
1998-99	Ottawa 67's	OHL	56	7	8	15	62	....	....	....	....	....	....	....	....	....	7	0	0	0	2	....	....	....	....
99-2000	Ottawa 67's	OHL	59	8	11	19	107	....	....	....	....	....	....	....	....	....	11	1	2	3	8	....	....	....	....
2000-01	Ottawa 67's	OHL	66	20	45	65	120	....	....	....	....	....	....	....	....	....	20	7	13	20	47	....	....	....	....
2001-02	Ottawa 67's	OHL	61	18	68	86	100	....	....	....	....	....	....	....	....	....	13	8	6	14	49	....	....	....	....
2002-03	Wilkes-Barre	AHL	4	0	1	1	9	....	....	....	....	....	....	....	....	....	....	....	....	....	....	....	....	....	....
	Wheeling Nailers	ECHL	68	22	48	70	231	....	....	....	....	....	....	....	....	....	....	....	....	....	....	....	....	....	....
2003-04	Utah Grizzlies	AHL	43	7	4	11	198	....	....	....	....	....	....	....	....	....	....	....	....	....	....	....	....	....	....
	Idaho Steelheads	ECHL	23	6	22	28	82	....	....	....	....	....	....	....	....	....	17	9	8	17	30	....	....	....	....
2004-05	Cincinnati	AHL	75	17	29	46	212	....	....	....	....	....	....	....	....	....	12	3	3	6	26	....	....	....	....
2005-06	**Anaheim**	**NHL**	**23**	**4**	**3**	**7**	**48**	**2**	**0**	**0**	**18**	**22.2**	**-4**	**142**	**53.5**	**7:19**	....	....	....	....	....	....	....	....	....
	Portland Pirates	AHL	34	18	26	44	57	....	....	....	....	....	....	....	....	....	19	11	18	29	46	....	....	....	....
2006-07	Lada Togliatti	Russia	4	0	0	0	8	....	....	....	....	....	....	....	....	....	....	....	....	....	....	....	....	....	....
	Columbus	**NHL**	**6**	**0**	**0**	**0**	**20**	**0**	**0**	**0**	**2**	**0.0**	**-2**	**22**	**63.6**	**5:00**	....	....	....	....	....	....	....	....	....
	Portland Pirates	AHL	42	11	24	35	97	....	....	....	....	....	....	....	....	....	....	....	....	....	....	....	....	....	....
	Syracuse Crunch	AHL	20	9	11	20	70	....	....	....	....	....	....	....	....	....	....	....	....	....	....	....	....	....	....
2007-08	**Columbus**	**NHL**	**3**	**0**	**0**	**0**	**15**	**0**	**0**	**0**	**4**	**0.0**	**0**	**21**	**52.4**	**7:54**	....	....	....	....	....	....	....	....	....
	Syracuse Crunch	AHL	62	24	31	55	194	....	....	....	....	....	....	....	....	....	13	3	7	10	42	....	....	....	....
2008-09	**Tampa Bay**	**NHL**	**7**	**0**	**1**	**1**	**29**	**0**	**0**	**0**	**6**	**0.0**	**-1**	**25**	**68.0**	**7:01**	....	....	....	....	....	....	....	....	....
	Norfolk Admirals	AHL	70	17	40	57	186	....	....	....	....	....	....	....	....	....	....	....	....	....	....	....	....	....	....
2009-10	**Tampa Bay**	**NHL**	**74**	**2**	**3**	**5**	***265**	**0**	**0**	**1**	**41**	**4.9**	**-11**	**462**	**62.3**	**8:08**	....	....	....	....	....	....	....	....	....
	NHL Totals		**113**	**6**	**7**	**13**	**377**	**2**	**0**	**1**	**71**	**8.5**		**672**	**60.4**	**7:44**	....	....	....	....	....	....	....	....	....

CHL All-Rookie Team (2003)
gned as a free agent by **Utah** (AHL), September 10, 2003. Signed as a free agent by **Anaheim**, September 1, 2004. Signed as a free agent by **Togliatti** (Russia), July 26, 2006. Traded to **Columbus** by **naheim** with Curtis Glencross and Anaheim's 7th round choice (Trent Vogelhuber) in 2007 Entry Draft for Mark Hartigan, Joe Motzko and Columbus' 4th round choice (Sebastian Stefaniszin) in 2007 ntry Draft, January 26, 2007. Signed as a free agent by **Tampa Bay**, July 10, 2008. Signed as a free agent by **NY Islanders**, July 2, 2010.

KONTIOLA, Petri (KAWN-tee-oh-la, PEH-tree) ANA.

Center. Shoots right. 6', 204 lbs. Born, Seinajoki, Finland, October 4, 1984. Chicago's 12th choice, 196th overall, in 2004 Entry Draft.

Season	Club	League	GP	G	A	Pts	PIM	PP	SH	GW	S	%	+/-	TF	F%	Min	GP	G	A	Pts	PIM	PP	SH	GW	Min
2001-02	Tappara U18	Fin-U18	22	5	3	8	8	....	....	....	....	....	....	....	....	....	2	1	0	1	2	....	....	....	....
2002-03	Tappara Jr.	Fin-Jr.	36	7	10	17	12	....	....	....	....	....	....	....	....	....	8	3	3	6	0	....	....	....	....
2003-04	Suomi U20	Finland-2	6	1	1	2	4	....	....	....	....	....	....	....	....	....	....	....	....	....	....	....	....	....	....
	Tappara Jr.	Fin-Jr.	12	3	12	15	8	....	....	....	....	....	....	....	....	....	10	4	4	8	10	....	....	....	....
	Tappara Tampere	Finland	39	4	9	13	29	....	....	....	....	....	....	....	....	....	3	1	1	2	0	....	....	....	....
2004-05	Tappara Jr.	Fin-Jr.	1	1	0	1	0	....	....	....	....	....	....	....	....	....	....	....	....	....	....	....	....	....	....
	Tappara Tampere	Finland	54	8	17	25	24	....	....	....	....	....	....	....	....	....	8	2	2	4	2	....	....	....	....
2005-06	Tappara Tampere	Finland	56	9	*35	44	55	....	....	....	....	....	....	....	....	....	6	1	3	4	0	....	....	....	....
2006-07	Tappara Tampere	Finland	51	12	35	47	50	....	....	....	....	....	....	....	....	....	5	1	3	4	8	....	....	....	....
2007-08	**Chicago**	**NHL**	**12**	**0**	**5**	**5**	**6**	**0**	**0**	**0**	**13**	**0.0**	**5**	**45**	**68.9**	**14:33**	....	....	....	....	....	....	....	....	....
	Rockford IceHogs	AHL	66	18	50	68	32	....	....	....	....	....	....	....	....	....	12	5	5	10	4	....	....	....	....
2008-09	Rockford IceHogs	AHL	61	15	38	53	22	....	....	....	....	....	....	....	....	....	....	....	....	....	....	....	....	....	....
	Iowa Chops	AHL	20	4	5	9	8	....	....	....	....	....	....	....	....	....	....	....	....	....	....	....	....	....	....
2009-10	Magnitogorsk	Rus-KHL	54	7	15	22	24	....	....	....	....	....	....	....	....	....	10	2	2	4	0	....	....	....	....
	NHL Totals		**12**	**0**	**5**	**5**	**6**	**0**	**0**	**0**	**13**	**0.0**		**45**	**68.9**	**14:33**	....	....	....	....	....	....	....	....	....

raded to **Anaheim** by **Chicago** with James Wisniewski for Samuel Pahlsson, Logan Stephenson and future considerations, March 4, 2009. Signed as a free agent by **Magnitogorsk** (Russia-KHL), May 26, 009.

KOPECKY, Tomas (koh-PEHTS-kee, TAW-mahsh) CHI.

Center. Shoots left. 6'3", 203 lbs. Born, Ilava, Czech., February 5, 1982. Detroit's 2nd choice, 38th overall, in 2000 Entry Draft.

Season	Club	League	GP	G	A	Pts	PIM	PP	SH	GW	S	%	+/-	TF	F%	Min	GP	G	A	Pts	PIM	PP	SH	GW	Min
1997-98	Dukla Trencin Jr.	Slovak-Jr.	41	19	22	41	....	....	....	....	....	....	....	....	....	....	....	....	....	....	....	....	....	....	....
1998-99	Dukla Trencin Jr.	Slovak-Jr.	44	13	16	29	18	....	....	....	....	....	....	....	....	....	....	....	....	....	....	....	....	....	....
99-2000	Dukla Trencin Jr.	Slovak-Jr.	14	8	9	17	36	....	....	....	....	....	....	....	....	....	....	....	....	....	....	....	....	....	....
	Dukla Trencin	Slovakia	52	3	4	7	24	....	....	....	....	....	....	....	....	....	5	0	0	0	0	....	....	....	....
2000-01	Lethbridge	WHL	49	22	28	50	52	....	....	....	....	....	....	....	....	....	5	1	1	2	6	....	....	....	....
	Cincinnati	AHL	1	0	0	0	0	....	....	....	....	....	....	....	....	....	....	....	....	....	....	....	....	....	....
2001-02	Lethbridge	WHL	60	34	42	76	94	....	....	....	....	....	....	....	....	....	4	2	1	3	15	....	....	....	....
	Cincinnati	AHL	2	1	1	2	6	....	....	....	....	....	....	....	....	....	2	0	0	0	0	....	....	....	....
2002-03	Grand Rapids	AHL	70	17	21	38	32	....	....	....	....	....	....	....	....	....	14	0	0	0	6	....	....	....	....
2003-04	Grand Rapids	AHL	48	6	6	12	28	....	....	....	....	....	....	....	....	....	1	0	0	0	2	....	....	....	....
2004-05	Grand Rapids	AHL	48	8	8	16	35	....	....	....	....	....	....	....	....	....	....	....	....	....	....	....	....	....	....
2005-06	**Detroit**	**NHL**	**1**	**0**	**0**	**0**	**2**	**0**	**0**	**0**	**1**	**0.0**	**1**	**0**	**0.0**	**9:41**	....	....	....	....	....	....	....	....	....
	Grand Rapids	AHL	77	32	37	69	108	....	....	....	....	....	....	....	....	....	16	3	4	7	25	....	....	....	....
2006-07	**Detroit**	**NHL**	**26**	**1**	**0**	**1**	**22**	**0**	**0**	**0**	**27**	**3.7**	**-2**	**5**	**40.0**	**7:15**	**4**	**0**	**0**	**0**	**6**	**0**	**0**	**0**	**3:38**
2007-08♦	**Detroit**	**NHL**	**77**	**5**	**7**	**12**	**43**	**0**	**0**	**1**	**87**	**5.7**	**2**	**109**	**40.4**	**9:37**	....	....	....	....	....	....	....	....	....
2008-09	**Detroit**	**NHL**	**79**	**6**	**13**	**19**	**46**	**1**	**1**	**2**	**110**	**5.5**	**-7**	**79**	**45.6**	**10:25**	**8**	**0**	**1**	**1**	**7**	**0**	**0**	**0**	**9:32**
2009-10♦	**Chicago**	**NHL**	**74**	**10**	**11**	**21**	**28**	**1**	**0**	**2**	**95**	**10.5**	**0**	**118**	**44.1**	**9:29**	**17**	**4**	**2**	**6**	**8**	**1**	**0**	**1**	**13:35**
	Slovakia	Olympics	7	1	0	1	2	....	....	....	....	....	....	....	....	....	....	....	....	....	....	....	....	....	....
	NHL Totals		**257**	**22**	**31**	**53**	**141**	**2**	**1**	**5**	**320**	**6.9**		**311**	**43.1**	**9:35**	**29**	**4**	**3**	**7**	**21**	**1**	**0**	**1**	**11:05**

Missed majority of 2006-07 season recovering from broken collarbone suffered in game vs. Chicago, December 14, 2006. Signed as a free agent by **Chicago**, July 1, 2009.

KOPITAR, Anze (KOH-pih-tahr, AHN-zheh) L.A.

Center. Shoots left. 6'3", 222 lbs. Born, Jesenice, Yugoslavia, August 24, 1987. Los Angeles' 1st choice, 11th overall, in 2005 Entry Draft.

Season	Club	League	GP	G	A	Pts	PIM	PP	SH	GW	S	%	+/-	TF	F%	Min	GP	G	A	Pts	PIM	PP	SH	GW	Min
2002-03	Jesenice U18	Sloven-U18	14	38	38	76	10	....	....	....	....	....	....	....	....	....	....	....	....	....	....	....	....	....	....
	Jesenice Jr.	Sloven-Jr.	20	15	12	27	8	....	....	....	....	....	....	....	....	....	....	....	....	....	....	....	....	....	....
	Kranjska Gora	Slovenia	11	4	4	8	4	....	....	....	....	....	....	....	....	....	....	....	....	....	....	....	....	....	....
2003-04	Jesenice Jr.	Sloven-Jr.	25	32	28	60	16	....	....	....	....	....	....	....	....	....	....	....	....	....	....	....	....	....	....
	Kranjska Gora	Slovenia	21	14	11	25	10	....	....	....	....	....	....	....	....	....	4	1	1	2	0	....	....	....	....
2004-05	Sodertalje SK U18	Swe-U18	1	1	2	3	0	....	....	....	....	....	....	....	....	....	1	0	0	0	2	....	....	....	....
	Sodertalje SK Jr.	Swe-Jr.	30	28	21	49	26	....	....	....	....	....	....	....	....	....	2	1	1	2	0	....	....	....	....
	Sodertalje SK	Sweden	5	0	0	0	0	....	....	....	....	....	....	....	....	....	10	0	0	0	0	....	....	....	....
2005-06	Sodertalje SK	Sweden	47	8	12	20	28	....	....	....	....	....	....	....	....	....	....	....	....	....	....	....	....	....	....
	Sodertalje SK	Sweden-Q	10	7	4	11	6	....	....	....	....	....	....	....	....	....	....	....	....	....	....	....	....	....	....
2006-07	**Los Angeles**	**NHL**	**72**	**20**	**41**	**61**	**24**	**7**	**2**	**1**	**193**	**10.4**	**-12**	**1204**	**46.1**	**20:32**	....	....	....	....	....	....	....	....	....
2007-08	**Los Angeles**	**NHL**	**82**	**32**	**45**	**77**	**22**	**12**	**2**	**3**	**201**	**15.9**	**-15**	**1150**	**49.2**	**20:41**	....	....	....	....	....	....	....	....	....
2008-09	**Los Angeles**	**NHL**	**82**	**27**	**39**	**66**	**32**	**7**	**1**	**3**	**234**	**11.5**	**-17**	**1355**	**49.5**	**20:27**	....	....	....	....	....	....	....	....	....
2009-10	**Los Angeles**	**NHL**	**82**	**34**	**47**	**81**	**16**	**14**	**1**	**2**	**259**	**13.1**	**6**	**1211**	**49.7**	**21:47**	**6**	**2**	**3**	**5**	**2**	**1**	**0**	**1**	**21:13**
	NHL Totals		**318**	**113**	**172**	**285**	**94**	**40**	**6**	**9**	**887**	**12.7**		**4920**	**48.7**	**20:53**	**6**	**2**	**3**	**5**	**2**	**1**	**0**	**1**	**21:13**

layed in NHL All-Star Game (2008)

KORPIKOSKI, Lauri

(kohr-pih-KAWS-kee, LOW-ree) **PHX**

Left wing. Shoots left. 6'1", 195 lbs. Born, Turku, Finland, July 28, 1986. NY Rangers' 2nd choice, 19th overall, in 2004 Entry Draft.

			Regular Season														Playoffs								
Season	Club	League	GP	G	A	Pts	PIM	PP	SH	GW	S	%	+/-	TF	F%	Min	GP	G	A	Pts	PIM	PP	SH	GW	Min
2002-03	TPS Turku U18	Fin-U18	21	7	4	11	10	....	....	....	....	....	....	....	....	....	....	....	....	....	....	....	....	....	....
2003-04	TPS Turku U18	Fin-U18	....	....	....	....	....	....	....	....	....	....	....	....	....	....	4	5	3	8	16	....	....	....	....
	TPS Turku Jr.	Fin-Jr.	36	12	8	20	20	....	....	....	....	....	....	....	....	....	4	0	2	2	4	....	....	....	....
2004-05	TPS Turku Jr.	Fin-Jr.	3	3	0	3	0	....	....	....	....	....	....	....	....	....	....	....	....	....	....	....	....	....	....
	TPS Turku	Finland	41	0	6	6	12	....	....	....	....	....	....	....	....	....	6	1	0	1	0	....	....	....	....
2005-06	TPS Turku Jr.	Fin-Jr.	1	1	0	1	2	....	....	....	....	....	....	....	....	....	....	....	....	....	....	....	....	....	....
	Suomi U20	Finland-2	3	1	3	4	0	....	....	....	....	....	....	....	....	....	....	....	....	....	....	....	....	....	....
	TPS Turku	Finland	51	3	4	7	16	....	....	....	....	....	....	....	....	....	2	0	1	1	0	....	....	....	....
	Hartford	AHL	5	2	1	3	0	....	....	....	....	....	....	....	....	....	11	1	0	1	2	....	....	....	....
2006-07	Hartford	AHL	78	11	27	38	23	....	....	....	....	....	....	....	....	....	7	0	0	0	0	....	....	....	....
2007-08	Hartford	AHL	79	23	27	50	71	....	....	....	....	....	....	....	....	....	5	1	1	2	0	....	....	....	....
	NY Rangers	**NHL**	....	....	....	....	....	....	....	....	....	....	....	....	....	....	**1**	**1**	**0**	**1**	**0**	**0**	**0**	**0**	**7:1**
2008-09	**NY Rangers**	**NHL**	**68**	**6**	**8**	**14**	**14**	**0**	**0**	**1**	**63**	**9.5**	**−10**	**220**	**40.0**	**10:55**	**7**	**0**	**2**	**2**	**0**	**0**	**0**	**0**	**13:1**
	Hartford	AHL	4	4	2	6	0	....	....	....	....	....	....	....	....	....	....	....	....	....	....	....	....	....	....
2009-10	**Phoenix**	**NHL**	**71**	**5**	**6**	**11**	**16**	**0**	**0**	**1**	**68**	**7.4**	**−10**	**49**	**28.6**	**12:18**	**7**	**1**	**0**	**1**	**2**	**0**	**1**	**0**	**16:16**
	NHL Totals		**139**	**11**	**14**	**25**	**30**	**0**	**0**	**2**	**131**	**8.4**		**269**	**37.9**	**11:37**	**15**	**2**	**2**	**4**	**2**	**0**	**1**	**0**	**14:13**

Traded to **Phoenix** by **NY Rangers** for Enver Lisin, July 13, 2009.

KOSTITSYN, Andrei

(kaws-TIHT-sihn, AWN-dray) **MTL**

Left wing. Shoots left. 6', 214 lbs. Born, Novopolotsk, USSR, February 3, 1985. Montreal's 1st choice, 10th overall, in 2003 Entry Draft.

			Regular Season														Playoffs								
Season	Club	League	GP	G	A	Pts	PIM	PP	SH	GW	S	%	+/-	TF	F%	Min	GP	G	A	Pts	PIM	PP	SH	GW	Min
99-2000	Belarus	WJ18-A	6	0	0	0	4	....	....	....	....	....	....	....	....	....	....	....	....	....	....	....	....	....	....
2000-01	Novopolotsk	Belarus	1	2	1	3	2	....	....	....	....	....	....	....	....	....	....	....	....	....	....	....	....	....	....
	Novopolotsk	EEHL	5	1	0	1	0	....	....	....	....	....	....	....	....	....	....	....	....	....	....	....	....	....	....
	Yunost Minsk	Belarus	3	1	4	5	8	....	....	....	....	....	....	....	....	....	....	....	....	....	....	....	....	....	....
	HC Vitebsk	Belarus	17	17	6	23	42	....	....	....	....	....	....	....	....	....	....	....	....	....	....	....	....	....	....
	Belarus	WJ18-B	5	7	7	*14	8	....	....	....	....	....	....	....	....	....	....	....	....	....	....	....	....	....	....
2001-02	Novopolotsk	Belarus	17	9	6	15	28	....	....	....	....	....	....	....	....	....	....	....	....	....	....	....	....	....	....
	Novopolotsk	EEHL	29	9	8	17	16	....	....	....	....	....	....	....	....	....	....	....	....	....	....	....	....	....	....
	Yunost Minsk	Belarus	6	2	0	2	8	....	....	....	....	....	....	....	....	....	....	....	....	....	....	....	....	....	....
2002-03	CSKA Moscow	Russia	6	0	0	0	2	....	....	....	....	....	....	....	....	....	....	....	....	....	....	....	....	....	....
	Voskresensk	Russia-2	2	1	1	2	0	....	....	....	....	....	....	....	....	....	....	....	....	....	....	....	....	....	....
	Yunost Minsk	Belarus	4	6	4	10	43	....	....	....	....	....	....	....	....	....	....	....	....	....	....	....	....	....	....
	CSKA Moscow 2	Russia-3	3	2	2	4	25	....	....	....	....	....	....	....	....	....	....	....	....	....	....	....	....	....	....
	Belarus	WC-A	2	1	0	1	2	....	....	....	....	....	....	....	....	....	....	....	....	....	....	....	....	....	....
2003-04	CSKA Moscow 2	Russia-3	STATISTICS NOT AVAILABLE																						
	CSKA Moscow	Russia	12	0	1	1	2	....	....	....	....	....	....	....	....	....	....	....	....	....	....	....	....	....	....
	Yunost Minsk	Belarus	STATISTICS NOT AVAILABLE																						
2004-05	Hamilton	AHL	66	12	11	23	24	....	....	....	....	....	....	....	....	....	3	0	0	0	0	....	....	....	....
2005-06	**Montreal**	**NHL**	**12**	**2**	**1**	**3**	**2**	**0**	**0**	**0**	**9**	**22.2**	**1**	**1**	**0.0**	**7:32**	....	....	....	....	....	....	....	....	....
	Hamilton	AHL	64	18	29	47	76	....	....	....	....	....	....	....	....	....	....	....	....	....	....	....	....	....	....
2006-07	**Montreal**	**NHL**	**22**	**1**	**10**	**11**	**6**	**0**	**0**	**0**	**38**	**2.6**	**3**	**1**	**0.0**	**13:17**	....	....	....	....	....	....	....	....	....
	Hamilton	AHL	50	21	31	52	50	....	....	....	....	....	....	....	....	....	....	....	....	....	....	....	....	....	....
2007-08	**Montreal**	**NHL**	**78**	**26**	**27**	**53**	**29**	**12**	**0**	**5**	**156**	**16.7**	**15**	**6**	**66.7**	**15:41**	**12**	**5**	**3**	**8**	**2**	**1**	**0**	**1**	**16:01**
2008-09	**Montreal**	**NHL**	**74**	**23**	**18**	**41**	**50**	**6**	**0**	**2**	**169**	**13.6**	**−7**	**6**	**50.0**	**15:35**	**4**	**1**	**0**	**1**	**2**	**0**	**0**	**0**	**14:15**
2009-10	**Montreal**	**NHL**	**59**	**15**	**18**	**33**	**32**	**6**	**0**	**2**	**136**	**11.0**	**1**	**6**	**16.7**	**15:59**	**19**	**3**	**5**	**8**	**12**	**1**	**0**	**0**	**14:15**
	NHL Totals		**245**	**67**	**74**	**141**	**119**	**24**	**0**	**9**	**508**	**13.2**		**20**	**40.0**	**15:07**	**35**	**9**	**8**	**17**	**16**	**2**	**0**	**1**	**14:51**

KOSTITSYN, Sergei

(kaws-TIHT-sihn, SAIR-gay) **NSH.**

Left wing. Shoots left. 6', 210 lbs. Born, Novopolotsk, USSR, March 20, 1987. Montreal's 6th choice, 200th overall, in 2005 Entry Draft.

			Regular Season														Playoffs								
Season	Club	League	GP	G	A	Pts	PIM	PP	SH	GW	S	%	+/-	TF	F%	Min	GP	G	A	Pts	PIM	PP	SH	GW	Min
2003-04	HK Gomel	EEHL	6	0	1	1	0	....	....	....	....	....	....	....	....	....	....	....	....	....	....	....	....	....	....
	HK Gomel 2	EEHL-B	6	7	2	9	14	....	....	....	....	....	....	....	....	....	....	....	....	....	....	....	....	....	....
	Yunior Minsk	EEHL-B	STATISTICS NOT AVAILABLE																						
	Yunior Minsk	Belarus	3	0	0	0	0	....	....	....	....	....	....	....	....	....	....	....	....	....	....	....	....	....	....
	HK Gomel	Belarus	22	5	4	9	4	....	....	....	....	....	....	....	....	....	11	1	2	3	8	....	....	....	....
2004-05	HK Gomel	BelOpen	40	4	10	14	24	....	....	....	....	....	....	....	....	....	4	2	0	2	12	....	....	....	....
2005-06	London Knights	OHL	63	26	52	78	78	....	....	....	....	....	....	....	....	....	19	13	24	37	*44	....	....	....	....
2006-07	London Knights	OHL	59	40	*91	131	76	....	....	....	....	....	....	....	....	....	16	9	12	21	39	....	....	....	....
2007-08	**Montreal**	**NHL**	**52**	**9**	**18**	**27**	**51**	**3**	**1**	**0**	**49**	**18.4**	**9**	**23**	**34.8**	**14:21**	**12**	**3**	**5**	**8**	**14**	**0**	**0**	**0**	**15:09**
	Hamilton	AHL	22	6	16	22	18	....	....	....	....	....	....	....	....	....	....	....	....	....	....	....	....	....	....
2008-09	**Montreal**	**NHL**	**56**	**8**	**15**	**23**	**64**	**5**	**0**	**1**	**74**	**10.8**	**−3**	**9**	**33.3**	**14:08**	**1**	**0**	**0**	**0**	**2**	**0**	**0**	**0**	**12:10**
	Hamilton	AHL	16	5	8	13	18	....	....	....	....	....	....	....	....	....	....	....	....	....	....	....	....	....	....
2009-10	**Montreal**	**NHL**	**47**	**7**	**11**	**18**	**8**	**0**	**0**	**2**	**59**	**11.9**	**4**	**7**	**14.3**	**14:10**	**5**	**0**	**0**	**0**	**0**	**0**	**0**	**0**	**7:59**
	Hamilton	AHL	16	4	9	13	2	....	....	....	....	....	....	....	....	....	....	....	....	....	....	....	....	....	....
	Belarus	Olympics	4	2	3	5	0	....	....	....	....	....	....	....	....	....	....	....	....	....	....	....	....	....	....
	NHL Totals		**155**	**24**	**44**	**68**	**123**	**8**	**1**	**3**	**182**	**13.2**		**39**	**30.8**	**14:13**	**18**	**3**	**5**	**8**	**16**	**0**	**0**	**0**	**12:59**

OHL All-Rookie Team (2006)

Traded to **Nashville** by **Montreal** with future considerations for Dan Ellis, Dustin Boyd and future considerations, June 29, 2010.

KOSTOPOULOS, Tom

(kaw-STAWP-oh-lihs, TAWM) **CAR.**

Right wing. Shoots right. 6', 200 lbs. Born, Mississauga, Ont., January 24, 1979. Pittsburgh's 9th choice, 204th overall, in 1999 Entry Draft.

			Regular Season														Playoffs								
Season	Club	League	GP	G	A	Pts	PIM	PP	SH	GW	S	%	+/-	TF	F%	Min	GP	G	A	Pts	PIM	PP	SH	GW	Min
1995-96	Brampton	OPJHL	24	9	9	18	28	....	....	....	....	....	....	....	....	....	....	....	....	....	....	....	....	....	....
1996-97	London Knights	OHL	64	13	12	25	67	....	....	....	....	....	....	....	....	....	....	....	....	....	....	....	....	....	....
1997-98	London Knights	OHL	66	24	26	50	108	....	....	....	....	....	....	....	....	....	16	6	4	10	26	....	....	....	....
1998-99	London Knights	OHL	66	27	60	87	114	....	....	....	....	....	....	....	....	....	25	19	16	35	32	....	....	....	....
99-2000	Wilkes-Barre	AHL	76	26	32	58	121	....	....	....	....	....	....	....	....	....	....	....	....	....	....	....	....	....	....
2000-01	Wilkes-Barre	AHL	80	16	36	52	120	....	....	....	....	....	....	....	....	....	21	3	9	12	6	....	....	....	....
2001-02	**Pittsburgh**	**NHL**	**11**	**1**	**2**	**3**	**9**	**0**	**0**	**0**	**8**	**12.5**	**−1**	**0**	**0.0**	**12:03**	....	....	....	....	....	....	....	....	....
	Wilkes-Barre	AHL	70	27	26	53	112	....	....	....	....	....	....	....	....	....	....	....	....	....	....	....	....	....	....
2002-03	**Pittsburgh**	**NHL**	**8**	**0**	**1**	**1**	**0**	**0**	**0**	**0**	**6**	**0.0**	**−4**	**2**	**0.0**	**4:33**	....	....	....	....	....	....	....	....	....
	Wilkes-Barre	AHL	71	21	42	63	131	....	....	....	....	....	....	....	....	....	6	1	2	3	7	....	....	....	....
2003-04	**Pittsburgh**	**NHL**	**60**	**9**	**13**	**22**	**67**	**2**	**1**	**1**	**101**	**8.9**	**−14**	**10**	**30.0**	**14:26**	....	....	....	....	....	....	....	....	....
	Wilkes-Barre	AHL	21	7	13	20	43	....	....	....	....	....	....	....	....	....	24	7	16	23	32	....	....	....	....
2004-05	Manchester	AHL	64	25	46	71	99	....	....	....	....	....	....	....	....	....	6	0	7	7	10	....	....	....	....
2005-06	**Los Angeles**	**NHL**	**76**	**8**	**14**	**22**	**100**	**0**	**0**	**1**	**74**	**10.8**	**−8**	**30**	**36.7**	**12:56**	....	....	....	....	....	....	....	....	....
2006-07	**Los Angeles**	**NHL**	**76**	**7**	**15**	**22**	**73**	**0**	**0**	**0**	**90**	**7.8**	**−2**	**62**	**29.0**	**11:34**	....	....	....	....	....	....	....	....	....
2007-08	**Montreal**	**NHL**	**67**	**7**	**6**	**13**	**113**	**0**	**3**	**1**	**98**	**7.1**	**−3**	**28**	**28.6**	**11:16**	**12**	**3**	**1**	**4**	**6**	**0**	**0**	**1**	**13:35**
2008-09	**Montreal**	**NHL**	**78**	**8**	**14**	**22**	**106**	**0**	**1**	**0**	**121**	**6.6**	**−1**	**16**	**31.3**	**14:09**	**4**	**0**	**1**	**1**	**4**	**0**	**0**	**0**	**14:01**
2009-10	**Carolina**	**NHL**	**82**	**8**	**13**	**21**	**106**	**0**	**2**	**0**	**103**	**7.8**	**4**	**21**	**47.6**	**12:31**	....	....	....	....	....	....	....	....	....
	NHL Totals		**458**	**48**	**78**	**126**	**574**	**2**	**7**	**3**	**601**	**8.0**		**169**	**32.5**	**12:37**	**16**	**3**	**2**	**5**	**10**	**0**	**0**	**1**	**13:41**

Signed as a free agent by **Manchester** (AHL), July 12, 2004. Signed as a free agent by **Los Angeles**, August 1, 2005. Signed as a free agent by **Montreal**, July 4, 2007. Signed as a free agent by **Carolina**, July 14, 2009.

KOTALIK, Ales

(KOH-tahl-eek, ahl-EHSH) **CGY.**

Right wing. Shoots right. 6'1", 225 lbs. Born, Jindrichuv Hradec, Czech., December 23, 1978. Buffalo's 7th choice, 164th overall, in 1998 Entry Draft.

			Regular Season														Playoffs								
Season	Club	League	GP	G	A	Pts	PIM	PP	SH	GW	S	%	+/-	TF	F%	Min	GP	G	A	Pts	PIM	PP	SH	GW	Min
1993-94	C. Budejovice Jr.	CzRep-Jr.	28	12	12	24	....	....	....	....	....	....	....	....	....	....	....	....	....	....	....	....	....	....	....
1994-95	C. Budejovice Jr.	CzRep-Jr.	36	26	17	43	....	....	....	....	....	....	....	....	....	....	....	....	....	....	....	....	....	....	....
1995-96	C. Budejovice Jr.	CzRep-Jr.	28	6	7	13	....	....	....	....	....	....	....	....	....	....	....	....	....	....	....	....	....	....	....
1996-97	C. Budejovice Jr.	CzRep-Jr.	36	15	16	31	24	....	....	....	....	....	....	....	....	....	....	....	....	....	....	....	....	....	....
1997-98	C. Budejovice	CzRep	47	9	7	16	14	....	....	....	....	....	....	....	....	....	....	....	....	....	....	....	....	....	....
1998-99	C. Budejovice	CzRep	41	8	13	21	16	....	....	....	....	....	....	....	....	....	3	0	0	0	....	....	....	....	....
99-2000	C. Budejovice	CzRep	43	7	12	19	34	....	....	....	....	....	....	....	....	....	3	0	1	1	6	....	....	....	....
2000-01	C. Budejovice	CzRep	52	19	29	48	54	....	....	....	....	....	....	....	....	....	....	....	....	....	....	....	....	....	....

			Regular Season														Playoffs								
Season	Club	League	GP	G	A	Pts	PIM	PP	SH	GW	S	%	+/-	TF	F%	Min	GP	G	A	Pts	PIM	PP	SH	GW	Min
2001-02	**Buffalo**	**NHL**	**13**	**1**	**3**	**4**	**2**	**0**	**0**	**0**	**21**	**4.8**	**–1**	**11**	**27.3**	**12:35**	....	....	....	....	....	....	....	....	....
	Rochester	AHL	68	18	25	43	55	....	....	....	....	....	....	....	....	....	1	0	0	0	0	....	....	....	....
2002-03	**Buffalo**	**NHL**	**68**	**21**	**14**	**35**	**30**	**4**	**0**	**2**	**138**	**15.2**	**–2**	**37**	**51.4**	**15:15**	....	....	....	....	....	....	....	....	....
	Rochester	AHL	8	0	2	2	4	....	....	....	....	....	....	....	....	....	....	....	....	....	....	....	....	....	....
2003-04	**Buffalo**	**NHL**	**62**	**15**	**11**	**26**	**41**	**2**	**0**	**3**	**142**	**10.6**	**–1**	**14**	**50.0**	**15:11**	....	....	....	....	....	....	....	....	....
2004-05	Liberec	CzRep	25	8	8	16	46	....	....	....	....	....	....	....	....	....	12	2	5	7	12	....	....	....	....
2005-06	**Buffalo**	**NHL**	**82**	**25**	**37**	**62**	**62**	**10**	**0**	**5**	**261**	**9.6**	**–3**	**29**	**41.4**	**15:34**	**18**	**4**	**7**	**11**	**8**	**0**	**0**	**3**	**15:15**
	Czech Republic	Olympics	4	0	0	0	0	....	....	....	....	....	....	....	....	....	....	....	....	....	....	....	....	....	....
2006-07	**Buffalo**	**NHL**	**66**	**16**	**22**	**38**	**46**	**3**	**0**	**4**	**162**	**9.9**	**–5**	**35**	**48.6**	**14:31**	**16**	**2**	**2**	**4**	**8**	**0**	**0**	**0**	**12:29**
2007-08	**Buffalo**	**NHL**	**79**	**23**	**20**	**43**	**58**	**12**	**0**	**1**	**207**	**11.1**	**–5**	**220**	**44.6**	**15:21**	....	....	....	....	....	....	....	....	....
2008-09	**Buffalo**	**NHL**	**56**	**13**	**19**	**32**	**28**	**8**	**0**	**1**	**153**	**8.5**	**–7**	**77**	**39.0**	**15:14**	....	....	....	....	....	....	....	....	....
	Edmonton	**NHL**	**19**	**7**	**4**	**11**	**6**	**1**	**0**	**0**	**55**	**12.7**	**2**	**8**	**75.0**	**16:06**	....	....	....	....	....	....	....	....	....
2009-10	**NY Rangers**	**NHL**	**45**	**8**	**14**	**22**	**38**	**4**	**0**	**3**	**100**	**8.0**	**–18**	**2**	**0.0**	**13:56**	....	....	....	....	....	....	....	....	....
	Calgary	**NHL**	**26**	**3**	**2**	**5**	**29**	**1**	**0**	**1**	**72**	**4.2**	**1**	**8**	**62.5**	**14:36**	....	....	....	....	....	....	....	....	....
	NHL Totals		**516**	**132**	**146**	**278**	**340**	**45**	**0**	**20**	**1311**	**10.1**		**441**	**44.7**	**15:02**	**34**	**6**	**9**	**15**	**16**	**0**	**0**	**3**	**13:57**

Signed as a free agent by **Liberec** (CzRep), September 6, 2004. Traded to **Edmonton** by **Buffalo** for Carolina's 2nd round choice (previously acquired, later traded to Toronto – Toronto selected Jesse Blacker) in 2009 Entry Draft, March 4, 2009. Signed as a free agent by **NY Rangers**, July 9, 2009. Traded to **Calgary** by **NY Rangers** with Christopher Higgins for Olli Jokinen and Brandon Prust, February 2, 2010.

KOVALCHUK, Ilya

(koh-vuhl-CHUHK, IHL-yah)

Left wing. Shoots right. 6'2", 230 lbs. Born, Tver, USSR, April 15, 1983. Atlanta's 1st choice, 1st overall, in 2001 Entry Draft.

99-2000	Spartak Moscow	Russia-2	49	12	5	17	75	....	....	....	....	....	....	....	....	....	....	....	....	....	....	....	....	....	....
	Spartak 2	Russia-3	2	2	1	3	14	....	....	....	....	....	....	....	....	....	....	....	....	....	....	....	....	....	....
2000-01	Spartak Moscow	Russia-2	40	28	18	46	78	....	....	....	....	....	....	....	....	....	12	14	4	18	38	....	....	....	....
2001-02	**Atlanta**	**NHL**	**65**	**29**	**22**	**51**	**28**	**7**	**0**	**4**	**184**	**15.8**	**–19**	**6**	**16.7**	**18:32**	....	....	....	....	....	....	....	....	....
	Russia	Olympics	6	1	2	3	14	....	....	....	....	....	....	....	....	....	....	....	....	....	....	....	....	....	....
2002-03	**Atlanta**	**NHL**	**81**	**38**	**29**	**67**	**57**	**9**	**0**	**3**	**257**	**14.8**	**–24**	**15**	**40.0**	**19:27**	....	....	....	....	....	....	....	....	....
2003-04	**Atlanta**	**NHL**	**81**	***41**	**46**	**87**	**63**	**16**	**1**	**6**	**341**	**12.0**	**–10**	**28**	**32.1**	**23:41**	....	....	....	....	....	....	....	....	....
2004-05	Ak Bars Kazan	Russia	53	19	23	42	72	....	....	....	....	....	....	....	....	....	4	0	1	1	0	....	....	....	....
2005-06	**Atlanta**	**NHL**	**78**	**52**	**46**	**98**	**68**	***27**	**0**	**7**	**323**	**16.1**	**–6**	**47**	**40.4**	**22:23**	....	....	....	....	....	....	....	....	....
	Russia	Olympics	8	4	1	5	31	....	....	....	....	....	....	....	....	....	....	....	....	....	....	....	....	....	....
2006-07	**Atlanta**	**NHL**	**82**	**42**	**34**	**76**	**66**	**18**	**0**	**7**	**336**	**12.5**	**–2**	**66**	**39.4**	**21:32**	**4**	**1**	**1**	**2**	**19**	**0**	**0**	**0**	**18:42**
2007-08	**Atlanta**	**NHL**	**79**	**52**	**35**	**87**	**52**	**16**	**2**	**4**	**283**	**18.4**	**–12**	**32**	**43.8**	**21:30**	....	....	....	....	....	....	....	....	....
2008-09	**Atlanta**	**NHL**	**79**	**43**	**48**	**91**	**50**	**12**	**0**	**6**	**275**	**15.6**	**–12**	**14**	**35.7**	**21:48**	....	....	....	....	....	....	....	....	....
2009-10	**Atlanta**	**NHL**	**49**	**31**	**27**	**58**	**45**	**10**	**0**	**3**	**179**	**17.3**	**1**	**23**	**21.7**	**22:14**	....	....	....	....	....	....	....	....	....
	New Jersey	**NHL**	**27**	**10**	**17**	**27**	**8**	**2**	**0**	**1**	**111**	**9.0**	**9**	**7**	**28.6**	**21:40**	**5**	**2**	**4**	**6**	**6**	**1**	**0**	**0**	**23:38**
	Russia	Olympics	4	1	2	3	0	....	....	....	....	....	....	....	....	....	....	....	....	....	....	....	....	....	....
	NHL Totals		**621**	**338**	**304**	**642**	**437**	**117**	**3**	**41**	**2289**	**14.8**		**238**	**36.6**	**21:26**	**9**	**3**	**5**	**8**	**25**	**1**	**0**	**0**	**21:26**

NHL All-Rookie Team (2002) • NHL Second All-Star Team (2004) • Maurice "Rocket" Richard Trophy (2004) (tied with Jarome Iginla and Rick Nash)

Played in NHL All-Star Game (2004, 2008, 2009)

Signed as a free agent by **Kazan** (Russia) August 22, 2004. Traded to **New Jersey** by **Atlanta** with Anssi Salmela and Atlanta's 2nd round choice (Jonathon Merrill) in 2010 Entry Draft for Johnny Oduya, Niclas Bergfors, Patrice Cormier and New Jersey's 1st (later traded to Chicago - Chicago selected Kevin Hayes) and 2nd (later traded to Chicago - Chicago selected Justin Holl) round choices in 2010 Entry Draft, February 4, 2010.

KOVALEV, Alex

(koh-VAH-lehv, AL-ehx) **OTT.**

Right wing. Shoots left. 6'2", 222 lbs. Born, Togliatti, USSR, February 24, 1973. NY Rangers' 1st choice, 15th overall, in 1991 Entry Draft.

1989-90	Dynamo Moscow	USSR	1	0	0	0	0	....	....	....	....	....	....	....	....	....	....	....	....	....	....	....	....	....	....
1990-91	Dyn'o Moscow 2	USSR-3	21	16	....	....	....	....	....	....	....	....	....	....	....	....	....	....	....	....	....	....	....	....	....
	Dynamo Moscow	USSR	18	1	2	3	4	....	....	....	....	....	....	....	....	....	....	....	....	....	....	....	....	....	....
	Dynamo Moscow	Super-S	1	0	0	0	0	....	....	....	....	....	....	....	....	....	....	....	....	....	....	....	....	....	....
1991-92	Dynamo Moscow	CIS	33	16	9	25	20	....	....	....	....	....	....	....	....	....	....	....	....	....	....	....	....	....	....
	Dyn'o Moscow 2	CIS-3	4	5	0	5	12	....	....	....	....	....	....	....	....	....	....	....	....	....	....	....	....	....	....
	Russia	Olympics	8	1	2	3	14	....	....	....	....	....	....	....	....	....	....	....	....	....	....	....	....	....	....
1992-93	**NY Rangers**	**NHL**	**65**	**20**	**18**	**38**	**79**	**3**	**0**	**3**	**134**	**14.9**	**–10**	....	....	....	....	....	....	....	....	....	....	....	....
	Binghamton	AHL	13	13	11	24	35	....	....	....	....	....	....	....	....	....	9	3	5	8	14	....	....	....	....
1993-94 ♦	**NY Rangers**	**NHL**	**76**	**23**	**33**	**56**	**154**	**7**	**0**	**3**	**184**	**12.5**	**18**	....	....	....	**23**	**9**	**12**	**21**	**18**	**5**	**0**	**2**	....
1994-95	Lada Togliatti	CIS	12	8	8	16	49	....	....	....	....	....	....	....	....	....	....	....	....	....	....	....	....	....	....
	NY Rangers	**NHL**	**48**	**13**	**15**	**28**	**30**	**1**	**1**	**1**	**103**	**12.6**	**–6**	....	....	....	**10**	**4**	**7**	**11**	**10**	**0**	**0**	**0**	....
1995-96	**NY Rangers**	**NHL**	**81**	**24**	**34**	**58**	**98**	**8**	**1**	**7**	**206**	**11.7**	**5**	....	....	....	**11**	**3**	**4**	**7**	**14**	**0**	**0**	**1**	....
1996-97	**NY Rangers**	**NHL**	**45**	**13**	**22**	**35**	**42**	**1**	**0**	**0**	**110**	**11.8**	**11**	....	....	....	....	....	....	....	....	....	....	....	....
1997-98	**NY Rangers**	**NHL**	**73**	**23**	**30**	**53**	**44**	**8**	**0**	**3**	**173**	**13.3**	**–22**	....	....	....	....	....	....	....	....	....	....	....	....
1998-99	**NY Rangers**	**NHL**	**14**	**3**	**4**	**7**	**12**	**1**	**0**	**1**	**35**	**8.6**	**–6**	**18**	**44.4**	**19:53**	....	....	....	....	....	....	....	....	....
	Pittsburgh	**NHL**	**63**	**20**	**26**	**46**	**37**	**5**	**1**	**4**	**156**	**12.8**	**8**	**226**	**43.4**	**20:30**	**10**	**5**	**7**	**12**	**14**	**0**	**0**	**1**	**20:24**
99-2000	**Pittsburgh**	**NHL**	**82**	**26**	**40**	**66**	**94**	**9**	**2**	**4**	**254**	**10.2**	**–3**	**306**	**47.4**	**22:53**	**11**	**1**	**5**	**6**	**10**	**0**	**0**	**0**	**26:35**
2000-01	**Pittsburgh**	**NHL**	**79**	**44**	**51**	**95**	**96**	**12**	**2**	**9**	**307**	**14.3**	**12**	**255**	**40.0**	**23:35**	**18**	**5**	**5**	**10**	**16**	**1**	**0**	**0**	**20:57**
2001-02	**Pittsburgh**	**NHL**	**67**	**32**	**44**	**76**	**80**	**8**	**1**	**3**	**266**	**12.0**	**2**	**179**	**45.3**	**24:03**	....	....	....	....	....	....	....	....	....
	Russia	Olympics	6	3	1	4	4	....	....	....	....	....	....	....	....	....	....	....	....	....	....	....	....	....	....
2002-03	**Pittsburgh**	**NHL**	**54**	**27**	**37**	**64**	**50**	**8**	**0**	**1**	**212**	**12.7**	**–11**	**19**	**31.6**	**24:03**	....	....	....	....	....	....	....	....	....
	NY Rangers	**NHL**	**24**	**10**	**3**	**13**	**20**	**3**	**0**	**2**	**59**	**16.9**	**2**	**19**	**42.1**	**20:09**	....	....	....	....	....	....	....	....	....
2003-04	**NY Rangers**	**NHL**	**66**	**13**	**29**	**42**	**54**	**3**	**0**	**0**	**178**	**7.3**	**–5**	**29**	**48.3**	**19:37**	....	....	....	....	....	....	....	....	....
	Montreal	**NHL**	**12**	**1**	**2**	**3**	**12**	**0**	**0**	**1**	**29**	**3.4**	**–4**	**2**	**50.0**	**15:36**	**11**	**6**	**4**	**10**	**8**	**1**	**0**	**1**	**20:11**
2004-05	Ak Bars Kazan	Russia	35	10	12	22	80	....	....	....	....	....	....	....	....	....	4	0	0	0	8	....	....	....	....
2005-06	**Montreal**	**NHL**	**69**	**23**	**42**	**65**	**76**	**9**	**0**	**5**	**206**	**11.2**	**–1**	**47**	**48.9**	**19:28**	**6**	**4**	**3**	**7**	**4**	**1**	**0**	**0**	**19:21**
	Russia	Olympics	8	4	2	6	4	....	....	....	....	....	....	....	....	....	....	....	....	....	....	....	....	....	....
2006-07	**Montreal**	**NHL**	**73**	**18**	**29**	**47**	**78**	**8**	**0**	**5**	**197**	**9.1**	**–19**	**162**	**46.3**	**18:15**	....	....	....	....	....	....	....	....	....
2007-08	**Montreal**	**NHL**	**82**	**35**	**49**	**84**	**70**	**17**	**0**	**5**	**230**	**15.2**	**18**	**58**	**55.2**	**19:33**	**12**	**5**	**6**	**11**	**8**	**2**	**1**	**1**	**21:41**
2008-09	**Montreal**	**NHL**	**78**	**26**	**39**	**65**	**74**	**11**	**1**	**4**	**209**	**12.4**	**–5**	**50**	**32.0**	**19:26**	**4**	**2**	**1**	**3**	**2**	**0**	**0**	**0**	**19:54**
2009-10	**Ottawa**	**NHL**	**77**	**18**	**31**	**49**	**54**	**4**	**0**	**5**	**165**	**10.9**	**–8**	**3**	**33.3**	**18:10**	....	....	....	....	....	....	....	....	....
	NHL Totals		**1228**	**412**	**578**	**990**	**1254**	**126**	**9**	**66**	**3413**	**12.1**		**1373**	**44.4**	**20:41**	**116**	**44**	**54**	**98**	**104**	**10**	**1**	**6**	**21:33**

NHL Second All-Star Team (2008)

Played in NHL All-Star Game (2001, 2003, 2009)

Traded to **Pittsburgh** by **NY Rangers** with Harry York for Petr Nedved, Chris Tamer and Sean Pronger, November 25, 1998. Traded to **NY Rangers** by **Pittsburgh** with Mike Wilson, Janne Laukkanen and Dan LaCouture for Joel Bouchard, Richard Lintner, Rico Fata and Mikael Samuelsson, February 10, 2003. Traded to **Montreal** by **NY Rangers** for Jozef Balej and Montreal's 2nd round choice (Bruce Graham) in 2004 Entry Draft, March 2, 2004. Signed as a free agent by **Kazan** (Russia), November 3, 2004. Signed as a free agent by **Ottawa**, July 6, 2009.

KOZLOV, Viktor

(KAWZ-lahf, VIHK-tohr)

Center. Shoots right. 6'4", 232 lbs. Born, Togliatti, USSR, February 14, 1975. San Jose's 1st choice, 6th overall, in 1993 Entry Draft.

1990-91	Lada Togliatti	USSR-2	2	2	0	2	0	....	....	....	....	....	....	....	....	....	....	....	....	....	....	....	....	....	....
1991-92	Lada Togliatti	CIS	3	0	0	0	0	....	....	....	....	....	....	....	....	....	....	....	....	....	....	....	....	....	....
1992-93	Dynamo Moscow	CIS	30	6	5	11	4	....	....	....	....	....	....	....	....	....	10	3	0	3	0	....	....	....	....
1993-94	Dynamo Moscow	CIS	42	16	9	25	14	....	....	....	....	....	....	....	....	....	....	....	....	....	....	....	....	....	....
1994-95	Dynamo Moscow	CIS	3	1	1	2	2	....	....	....	....	....	....	....	....	....	....	....	....	....	....	....	....	....	....
	San Jose	**NHL**	**16**	**2**	**0**	**2**	**2**	**0**	**0**	**0**	**23**	**8.7**	**–5**	....	....	....	....	....	....	....	....	....	....	....	....
	Kansas City	IHL	4	1	1	2	0	....	....	....	....	....	....	....	....	....	13	4	5	9	12	....	....	....	....
1995-96	**San Jose**	**NHL**	**62**	**6**	**13**	**19**	**6**	**1**	**0**	**0**	**107**	**5.6**	**–15**	....	....	....	....	....	....	....	....	....	....	....	....
	Kansas City	IHL	15	4	7	11	12	....	....	....	....	....	....	....	....	....	....	....	....	....	....	....	....	....	....
1996-97	**San Jose**	**NHL**	**78**	**16**	**25**	**41**	**40**	**4**	**0**	**4**	**184**	**8.7**	**–16**	....	....	....	....	....	....	....	....	....	....	....	....
1997-98	**San Jose**	**NHL**	**18**	**5**	**2**	**7**	**2**	**2**	**0**	**0**	**51**	**9.8**	**–2**	....	....	....	....	....	....	....	....	....	....	....	....
	Florida	**NHL**	**46**	**12**	**11**	**23**	**14**	**3**	**2**	**0**	**114**	**10.5**	**–1**	....	....	....	....	....	....	....	....	....	....	....	....
1998-99	**Florida**	**NHL**	**65**	**16**	**35**	**51**	**24**	**5**	**1**	**1**	**209**	**7.7**	**13**	**985**	**41.2**	**19:03**	....	....	....	....	....	....	....	....	....
99-2000	**Florida**	**NHL**	**80**	**17**	**53**	**70**	**16**	**6**	**0**	**2**	**223**	**7.6**	**24**	**1616**	**42.9**	**19:27**	**4**	**0**	**1**	**1**	**0**	**0**	**0**	**0**	**16:06**
2000-01	**Florida**	**NHL**	**51**	**14**	**23**	**37**	**10**	**6**	**0**	**2**	**139**	**10.1**	**–4**	**817**	**41.6**	**18:23**	....	....	....	....	....	....	....	....	....
2001-02	**Florida**	**NHL**	**50**	**9**	**18**	**27**	**20**	**6**	**0**	**1**	**143**	**6.3**	**–16**	**840**	**43.1**	**19:54**	....	....	....	....	....	....	....	....	....
2002-03	**Florida**	**NHL**	**74**	**22**	**34**	**56**	**18**	**7**	**1**	**1**	**232**	**9.5**	**–8**	**404**	**42.8**	**22:35**	....	....	....	....	....	....	....	....	....
2003-04	**Florida**	**NHL**	**48**	**11**	**16**	**27**	**16**	**3**	**1**	**1**	**117**	**9.4**	**–4**	**200**	**49.0**	**19:30**	....	....	....	....	....	....	....	....	....
	New Jersey	**NHL**	**11**	**2**	**4**	**6**	**2**	**0**	**0**	**0**	**26**	**7.7**	**0**	**112**	**56.3**	**13:26**	**2**	**0**	**0**	**0**	**0**	**0**	**0**	**0**	**8:55**
2004-05	Lada Togliatti	Russia	52	15	22	37	22	....	....	....	....	....	....	....	....	....	10	3	3	6	6	....	....	....	....

			Regular Season														Playoffs								
Season	Club	League	GP	G	A	Pts	PIM	PP	SH	GW	S	%	+/-	TF	F%	Min	GP	G	A	Pts	PIM	PP	SH	GW	Min
2005-06	New Jersey	NHL	69	12	13	25	16	2	0	1	122	9.8	0	185	47.0	13:32	3	0	0	0	0	0	0	0	14:05
	Russia	Olympics	8	2	3	5	2	....	....	....	....	....	....	....	....	....	....	....	....	....	....	....	....	....	....
2006-07	NY Islanders	NHL	81	25	26	51	28	5	0	4	165	15.2	12	462	39.0	16:25	5	0	2	2	2	0	0	0	16:34
2007-08	Washington	NHL	81	16	38	54	18	2	0	2	219	7.3	28	442	45.9	17:35	7	0	3	3	2	0	0	0	17:58
2008-09	Washington	NHL	67	13	28	41	16	2	0	0	153	8.5	-9	33	30.3	15:40	14	4	2	6	6	0	0	1	15:54
2009-10	Ufa	Rus-KHL	48	10	18	28	43	....	....	....	....	....	....	....	....	....	16	3	4	7	0	....	....	....	....
	Russia	Olympics	4	1	0	1	0	....	....	....	....	....	....	....	....	....	....	....	....	....	....	....	....	....	....
	NHL Totals		897	198	339	537	248	54	5	19	2227	8.9		6096	42.9	18:03	35	4	8	12	10	0	0	1	15:52

Played in NHL All-Star Game (2000)

Traded to **Florida** by **San Jose** with Florida's 5th round choice (previously acquired, Florida selected Jaroslav Spacek) in 1998 Entry Draft for Dave Lowry and Florida's 1st round choice (later traded to Tampa Bay – Tampa Bay selected Vincent Lecavalier) in 1998 Entry Draft, November 13, 1997. Traded to **New Jersey** by **Florida** for Christian Berglund and Victor Uchevatov, March 1, 2004. Signed as a free agent by **Togliatti** (Russia), July 11, 2004. Signed as a free agent by **NY Islanders**, September 13, 2006. Signed as a free agent by **Washington**, July 1, 2007. Signed as a free agent by **Ufa** (Russia-KHL), May 26, 2009.

KOZLOV, Vyacheslav

(KAWZ-lahf, V'YTACH-ih-slav)

Left wing. Shoots left. 5'10", 190 lbs. Born, Voskresensk, USSR, May 3, 1972. Detroit's 2nd choice, 45th overall, in 1990 Entry Draft.

Season	Club	League	GP	G	A	Pts	PIM	PP	SH	GW	S	%	+/-	TF	F%	Min	GP	G	A	Pts	PIM	PP	SH	GW	Min
1987-88	Voskresensk	USSR	2	0	0	0	0	....	....	....	....	....	....	....	....	....	....	....	....	....	....	....	....	....	....
1988-89	Voskresensk	USSR	14	0	1	1	2	....	....	....	....	....	....	....	....	....	....	....	....	....	....	....	....	....	....
1989-90	Voskresensk	USSR	45	14	12	26	38	....	....	....	....	....	....	....	....	....	....	....	....	....	....	....	....	....	....
1990-91	Voskresensk	USSR	45	11	13	24	46	....	....	....	....	....	....	....	....	....	....	....	....	....	....	....	....	....	....
1991-92	CSKA Moscow	CIS	11	6	5	11	12	....	....	....	....	....	....	....	....	....	....	....	....	....	....	....	....	....	....
	Detroit	NHL	7	0	2	2	2	0	0	0	9	0.0	-2	....	....	....	....	....	....	....	....	....	....	....	....
1992-93	Detroit	NHL	17	4	1	5	14	0	0	0	26	15.4	-1	....	....	....	4	0	2	2	2	0	0	0	....
	Adirondack	AHL	45	23	36	59	54	....	....	....	....	....	....	....	....	....	4	1	1	2	4	....	....	....	....
1993-94	Detroit	NHL	77	34	39	73	50	8	2	6	202	16.8	27	....	....	....	7	2	5	7	12	0	0	0	....
	Adirondack	AHL	3	0	1	1	15	....	....	....	....	....	....	....	....	....	....	....	....	....	....	....	....	....	....
1994-95	CSKA Moscow	CIS	10	3	4	7	14	....	....	....	....	....	....	....	....	....	....	....	....	....	....	....	....	....	....
	Detroit	NHL	46	13	20	33	45	5	0	3	97	13.4	12	....	....	....	18	9	7	16	10	1	0	*4	....
1995-96	Detroit	NHL	82	36	37	73	70	9	0	7	237	15.2	33	....	....	....	19	5	7	12	10	2	0	1	....
1996-97 ◆	Detroit	NHL	75	23	22	45	46	3	0	6	211	10.9	21	....	....	....	20	8	5	13	14	4	0	2	....
1997-98 ◆	Detroit	NHL	80	25	27	52	46	6	0	1	221	11.3	14	....	....	....	22	6	8	14	10	1	0	*4	....
1998-99	Detroit	NHL	79	29	29	58	45	6	1	4	209	13.9	10	38	36.8	16:02	10	6	1	7	4	3	0	0	14:44
99-2000	Detroit	NHL	72	18	18	36	28	4	0	3	165	10.9	11	28	35.7	15:30	8	2	1	3	12	1	0	1	12:20
2000-01	Detroit	NHL	72	20	18	38	30	4	0	5	187	10.7	9	51	47.1	14:43	6	4	1	5	2	2	0	0	16:27
2001-02	Buffalo	NHL	38	9	13	22	16	3	0	1	68	13.2	0	24	41.7	16:31	....	....	....	....	....	....	....	....	....
2002-03	Atlanta	NHL	79	21	49	70	66	9	1	2	185	11.4	-10	67	34.3	20:01	....	....	....	....	....	....	....	....	....
2003-04	Atlanta	NHL	76	20	32	52	74	6	0	1	191	10.5	-12	164	32.3	20:20	....	....	....	....	....	....	....	....	....
2004-05	Voskresensk	Russia	38	12	18	30	69	....	....	....	....	....	....	....	....	....	....	....	....	....	....	....	....	....	....
	Ak Bars Kazan	Russia	8	2	4	6	0	....	....	....	....	....	....	....	....	....	4	1	0	1	8	....	....	....	....
2005-06	Atlanta	NHL	82	25	46	71	33	8	0	1	206	12.1	14	317	39.8	17:47	....	....	....	....	....	....	....	....	....
2006-07	Atlanta	NHL	81	28	52	80	36	8	0	8	190	14.7	9	326	46.9	20:29	4	0	0	0	6	0	0	0	17:33
2007-08	Atlanta	NHL	82	17	24	41	26	5	0	4	161	10.6	-10	68	45.6	15:56	....	....	....	....	....	....	....	....	....
2008-09	Atlanta	NHL	82	26	50	76	44	12	0	3	165	15.8	-14	8	37.5	17:14	....	....	....	....	....	....	....	....	....
2009-10	Atlanta	NHL	55	8	18	26	33	3	0	1	113	7.1	-15	15	40.0	15:16	....	....	....	....	....	....	....	....	....
	NHL Totals		1182	356	497	853	704	99	4	56	2843	12.5		1106	41.0	17:23	118	42	37	79	82	14	0	12	14:49

Traded to **Buffalo** by **Detroit** with Detroit's 1st round choice (later traded to Columbus, later traded to Atlanta – Atlanta selected Jim Slater) in 2002 Entry Draft for Dominik Hasek, July 1, 2001. • Missed majority of 2001-02 season recovering from Achilles tendon injury suffered in game vs. Columbus, December 31, 2001. Traded to **Atlanta** by **Buffalo** with Buffalo's 2nd round choice (later traded to Columbus – Columbus selected Joakim Lindstrom) in 2003 Entry Draft for Atlanta's 2nd round choice (later traded to Edmonton – Edmonton selected Jeff Deslauriers) in 2003 Entry Draft and Vancouver's 3rd round choice (previously acquired, Buffalo selected John Adams) in 2003 Entry Draft, June 22, 2002. Signed as a free agent by **Voskresensk** (Russia), September 15, 2004. Signed as a free agent by **Kazan** (Russia), February 17, 2005.

KRAJICEK, Lukas

(KRIGH-ih-chehk, LOO-kahsh)

Defense. Shoots left. 6'3", 205 lbs. Born, Prostejov, Czech., March 11, 1983. Florida's 2nd choice, 24th overall, in 2001 Entry Draft.

Season	Club	League	GP	G	A	Pts	PIM	PP	SH	GW	S	%	+/-	TF	F%	Min	GP	G	A	Pts	PIM	PP	SH	GW	Min
1998-99	HC ZPS Zlin Jr.	CzRep-Jr.	48	8	18	26	40	....	....	....	....	....	....	....	....	....	....	....	....	....	....	....	....	....	....
99-2000	Det. Compuware	NAHL	53	5	22	27	61	....	....	....	....	....	....	....	....	....	5	0	1	1	18	....	....	....	....
2000-01	Peterborough	OHL	61	8	27	35	53	....	....	....	....	....	....	....	....	....	7	0	5	5	0	....	....	....	....
2001-02	Florida	NHL	5	0	0	0	0	0	0	0	3	0.0	0	0	0.0	13:23	....	....	....	....	....	....	....	....	....
	Peterborough	OHL	55	10	32	42	56	....	....	....	....	....	....	....	....	....	6	0	5	5	6	....	....	....	....
2002-03	Peterborough	OHL	52	11	42	53	42	....	....	....	....	....	....	....	....	....	7	0	3	3	0	....	....	....	....
	San Antonio	AHL	3	0	1	1	0	....	....	....	....	....	....	....	....	....	3	0	0	0	0	....	....	....	....
2003-04	Florida	NHL	18	1	6	7	12	1	0	0	16	6.3	-2	0	0.0	13:32	....	....	....	....	....	....	....	....	....
	San Antonio	AHL	54	5	12	17	24	....	....	....	....	....	....	....	....	....	....	....	....	....	....	....	....	....	....
2004-05	San Antonio	AHL	78	2	22	24	57	....	....	....	....	....	....	....	....	....	....	....	....	....	....	....	....	....	....
2005-06	Florida	NHL	67	2	14	16	50	2	0	0	89	2.2	1	0	0.0	18:30	....	....	....	....	....	....	....	....	....
2006-07	Vancouver	NHL	78	3	13	16	64	1	0	2	105	2.9	-4	0	0.0	18:31	12	0	2	2	12	0	0	0	18:50
2007-08	Vancouver	NHL	39	2	9	11	36	1	0	0	28	7.1	-3	0	0.0	18:10	....	....	....	....	....	....	....	....	....
2008-09	Tampa Bay	NHL	71	2	17	19	48	0	0	0	66	3.0	-8	0	0.0	19:37	....	....	....	....	....	....	....	....	....
2009-10	Tampa Bay	NHL	23	0	1	1	21	0	0	0	17	0.0	-4	0	0.0	17:32	....	....	....	....	....	....	....	....	....
	Norfolk Admirals	AHL	15	0	6	6	8	....	....	....	....	....	....	....	....	....	....	....	....	....	....	....	....	....	....
	Philadelphia	NHL	27	1	1	2	14	0	0	0	25	4.0	-10	0	0.0	16:58	22	0	3	3	8	0	0	0	10:01
	NHL Totals		328	11	61	72	245	5	0	2	349	3.2		0	0.0	18:10	34	0	5	5	20	0	0	0	13:08

OHL All-Rookie Team (2001) • OHL First All-Star Team (2003) • Canadian Major Junior Second All-Star Team (2003)

Traded to **Vancouver** by **Florida** with Roberto Luongo and Florida's 6th round choice (Sergei Shirokov) in 2006 Entry Draft for Todd Bertuzzi, Bryan Allen and Alex Auld, June 23, 2006. Traded to **Tampa Bay** by **Vancouver** with Juraj Simek for Shane O'Brien and Michel Ouellet, October 6, 2008. Signed as a free agent by **Philadelphia**, January 31, 2010.

KREJCI, David

(KRAY-chee, DAY-vihd) **BOS.**

Center. Shoots right. 6', 177 lbs. Born, Sternberk, Czech., April 28, 1986. Boston's 1st choice, 63rd overall, in 2004 Entry Draft.

Season	Club	League	GP	G	A	Pts	PIM	PP	SH	GW	S	%	+/-	TF	F%	Min	GP	G	A	Pts	PIM	PP	SH	GW	Min
2000-01	HC Olomouc U17	CzR-U17	26	2	6	8	4	....	....	....	....	....	....	....	....	....	3	1	1	2	0	....	....	....	....
2001-02	HC Trinec U17	CzR-U17	48	32	27	59	30	....	....	....	....	....	....	....	....	....	6	2	4	6	2	....	....	....	....
2002-03	HC Trinec U17	CzR-U17	22	12	24	36	42	....	....	....	....	....	....	....	....	....	....	....	....	....	....	....	....	....	....
	HC Trinec Jr.	CzRep-Jr.	12	4	5	9	2	....	....	....	....	....	....	....	....	....	12	5	5	10	8	....	....	....	....
2003-04	HC Kladno Jr.	CzRep-Jr.	50	23	37	60	37	....	....	....	....	....	....	....	....	....	7	3	6	9	4	....	....	....	....
2004-05	Gatineau	QMJHL	62	22	41	63	31	....	....	....	....	....	....	....	....	....	10	2	7	9	10	....	....	....	....
2005-06	Gatineau	QMJHL	55	27	54	81	54	....	....	....	....	....	....	....	....	....	17	10	22	32	24	....	....	....	....
2006-07	Boston	NHL	6	0	0	0	2	0	0	0	2	0.0	-3	14	28.6	4:24	....	....	....	....	....	....	....	....	....
	Providence Bruins	AHL	69	31	43	74	47	....	....	....	....	....	....	....	....	....	13	3	13	16	22	....	....	....	....
2007-08	Boston	NHL	56	6	21	27	20	1	1	0	73	8.2	-3	635	48.2	14:55	7	1	4	5	2	1	0	0	19:09
	Providence Bruins	AHL	25	7	21	28	19	....	....	....	....	....	....	....	....	....	....	....	....	....	....	....	....	....	....
2008-09	Boston	NHL	82	22	51	73	26	5	2	6	146	15.1	*37	1048	50.3	16:52	11	2	6	8	2	0	0	1	17:18
2009-10	Boston	NHL	79	17	35	52	26	6	0	3	156	10.9	8	1104	50.7	18:15	9	4	4	8	2	2	0	0	19:06
	Czech Republic	Olympics	5	2	1	3	6	....	....	....	....	....	....	....	....	....	....	....	....	....	....	....	....	....	....
	NHL Totals		223	45	107	152	74	12	3	9	377	11.9		2801	49.9	16:32	27	7	14	21	6	3	0	1	18:23

KREPS, Kamil

(KREHPS, KA-mihl)

Center. Shoots right. 6'2", 194 lbs. Born, Litomerice, Czech., November 18, 1984. Florida's 3rd choice, 38th overall, in 2003 Entry Draft.

Season	Club	League	GP	G	A	Pts	PIM	PP	SH	GW	S	%	+/-	TF	F%	Min	GP	G	A	Pts	PIM	PP	SH	GW	Min
99-2000	Litvinov Jr.	CzRep-Jr.	48	18	16	34	10	....	....	....	....	....	....	....	....	....	....	....	....	....	....	....	....	....	....
2000-01	Litvinov Jr.	CzRep-Jr.	47	16	23	39	6	....	....	....	....	....	....	....	....	....	6	2	6	8	10	....	....	....	....
2001-02	Brampton	OHL	68	19	24	43	14	....	....	....	....	....	....	....	....	....	....	....	....	....	....	....	....	....	....
2002-03	Brampton	OHL	53	19	42	61	12	....	....	....	....	....	....	....	....	....	11	3	5	8	4	....	....	....	....
2003-04	Brampton	OHL	57	19	27	46	19	....	....	....	....	....	....	....	....	....	12	7	8	15	2	....	....	....	....
2004-05	San Antonio	AHL	58	5	6	11	11	....	....	....	....	....	....	....	....	....	....	....	....	....	....	....	....	....	....
	Texas Wildcatters	ECHL	12	5	6	11	6	....	....	....	....	....	....	....	....	....	....	....	....	....	....	....	....	....	....
2005-06	Rochester	AHL	61	13	19	32	20	....	....	....	....	....	....	....	....	....	....	....	....	....	....	....	....	....	....
2006-07	Florida	NHL	14	1	1	2	6	0	0	0	20	5.0	-1	113	48.7	11:13	....	....	....	....	....	....	....	....	....
	Rochester	AHL	50	14	21	35	16	....	....	....	....	....	....	....	....	....	6	1	0	1	0	....	....	....	....

			Regular Season														Playoffs								
Season	Club	League	GP	G	A	Pts	PIM	PP	SH	GW	S	%	+/-	TF	F%	Min	GP	G	A	Pts	PIM	PP	SH	GW	Min
2007-08	Florida	NHL	76	8	17	25	29	1	0	2	99	8.1	10	763	53.9	12:59									
	Rochester	AHL	6	1	5	6	6																		
2008-09	Florida	NHL	66	4	15	19	18	0	1	1	77	5.2	2	870	50.5	13:58									
2009-10	Florida	NHL	76	5	9	14	18	1	0	1	83	6.0	–7	737	51.8	12:42									
	NHL Totals		232	18	42	60	71	2	1	4	279	6.5		2483	51.8	13:04									

gned as a free agent by **Oulu** (Finland), June 1, 2010.

KROG, Jason

(KROHG, JAY-suhn) **ATL.**

Center. Shoots right. 5'11", 185 lbs. Born, Fernie, B.C., October 9, 1975.

Season	Club	League	GP	G	A	Pts	PIM	PP	SH	GW	S	%	+/-	TF	F%	Min	GP	G	A	Pts	PIM	PP	SH	GW	Min
1992-93	Chilliwack Chiefs	BCJHL	52	30	27	57	52																		
1993-94	Chilliwack Chiefs	BCJHL	42	19	36	55	20																		
1994-95	Chilliwack Chiefs	BCJHL	60	47	81	128	36																		
1995-96	New Hampshire	H-East	34	4	16	20	20																		
1996-97	New Hampshire	H-East	39	23	*44	*67	28																		
1997-98	New Hampshire	H-East	38	*33	33	66	44																		
1998-99	New Hampshire	H-East	41	*34	*51	*85	38																		
99-2000	NY Islanders	NHL	17	2	4	6	6	1	0	0	22	9.1	–1	81	53.1	10:03									
	Lowell	AHL	45	6	21	27	22																		
	Providence Bruins	AHL	11	9	8	17	4										6	2	2	4	0				
2000-01	NY Islanders	NHL	9	0	3	3	0	0	0	0	7	0.0	4	60	48.3	10:32									
	Lowell	AHL	26	11	16	27	6																		
	Springfield	AHL	24	7	23	30	4																		
2001-02	NY Islanders	NHL	2	0	0	0	0	0	0	0	0	0.0	0	13	46.2	6:40									
	Bridgeport	AHL	64	26	36	62	13										20	10	13	23	8				
2002-03	Anaheim	NHL	67	10	15	25	12	0	1	1	92	10.9	1	634	60.4	13:47	21	3	1	4	4	0	0	0	12:10
	Cincinnati	AHL	9	3	4	7	6																		
2003-04	Anaheim	NHL	80	6	12	18	16	1	0	1	111	5.4	–4	769	58.5	11:58									
2004-05	EC Villacher SV	Austria	48	27	33	60	38										3	0	1	1	4				
2005-06	Geneve	Swiss	29	15	14	29	32																		
	Frolunda	Sweden	7	5	1	6	6										17	5	3	8	10				
2006-07	Atlanta	NHL	14	1	3	4	6	0	0	0	14	7.1	3	165	55.2	13:58									
	Chicago Wolves	AHL	44	26	54	80	20										15	5	14	19	17				
	NY Rangers	NHL	9	2	0	2	4	0	0	1	8	25.0	2	66	56.1	9:58									
2007-08	Chicago Wolves	AHL	80	*39	*73	*112	30										24	*12	*26	*38	2				
2008-09	Vancouver	NHL	4	1	0	1	2	1	0	0	5	20.0	0	24	58.3	10:14									
	Manitoba Moose	AHL	74	30	56	86	30										22	8	15	23	0				
2009-10	Chicago Wolves	AHL	78	14	61	75	34										14	5	6	11	6				
	NHL Totals		202	22	37	59	46	3	1	3	259	8.5		1812	58.1	12:19	21	3	1	4	4	0	0	0	12:10

Hockey East First All-Star Team (1997, 1998, 1999) • NCAA East Second All-American Team (1997) • Hockey East Player of the Year (1999) • NCAA East First All-American Team (1999) • NCAA Championship All-Tournament Team (1999) • Hobey Baker Memorial Award (Top U.S. Collegiate Player) (1999) • AHL First All-Star Team (2008) • Willie Marshall Award (AHL – Top Goal-scorer) (2008) • John B. Sollenberger Trophy (AHL – Leading Scorer) (2008) • Les Cunningham Award (AHL – MVP) (2008) • AHL Second All-Star Team (2009)

Signed as a free agent by **NY Islanders**, May 14, 1999. • Loaned to **Providence** (AHL) by **NY Islanders**, March 1, 2000. Signed as a free agent by **Anaheim**, July 17, 2002. Signed as a free agent by **Villacher** (Austria), August 24, 2004. Signed as a free agent by **Geneve** (Swiss), May 19, 2005. Signed as a free agent by **Frolunda** (Sweden), January 31, 2006. Signed as a free agent by **Atlanta**, July 4, 2006. Claimed on waivers by **NY Rangers** from **Atlanta**, January 12, 2007. Claimed on waivers by **Atlanta** from **NY Rangers**, February 27, 2007. Signed as a free agent by **Vancouver**, July 14, 2008. Signed as a free agent by **Atlanta**, July 6, 2009.

KRONWALL, Niklas

(KRAWN-wahl, NIHK-luhs) **DET.**

Defense. Shoots left. 6', 192 lbs. Born, Stockholm, Sweden, January 12, 1981. Detroit's 1st choice, 29th overall, in 2000 Entry Draft.

Season	Club	League	GP	G	A	Pts	PIM	PP	SH	GW	S	%	+/-	TF	F%	Min	GP	G	A	Pts	PIM	PP	SH	GW	Min
1996-97	Djurgarden Jr.	Swe-Jr.	1	0	0	0	0																		
1997-98	Djurgarden Jr.	Swe-Jr.	27	4	3	7	71										2	0	0	0	2				
1998-99	Huddinge IK	Sweden-2	14	0	1	1	10																		
	Huddinge IK Jr.	Swe-Jr.	2	0	0	0	6																		
99-2000	Djurgarden	Sweden	37	1	4	5	16										8	0	0	0	8				
2000-01	Djurgarden	Sweden	31	1	9	10	32										15	0	1	1	8				
2001-02	Djurgarden	Sweden	48	5	7	12	34										5	0	0	0	0				
2002-03	Djurgarden	Sweden	50	5	13	18	46										12	3	2	5	18				
2003-04	Detroit	NHL	20	1	4	5	16	0	0	1	18	5.6	5	0	0.0	13:51									
	Grand Rapids	AHL	25	2	11	13	20																		
2004-05	Grand Rapids	AHL	76	13	40	53	53																		
2005-06	Detroit	NHL	27	1	8	9	28	1	0	0	28	3.6	11	0	0.0	20:31	6	0	3	3	2	0	0	0	22:43
	Grand Rapids	AHL	1	0	0	0	0																		
	Sweden	Olympics	2	1	1	2	8																		
2006-07	Detroit	NHL	68	1	21	22	54	1	0	0	104	1.0	0	0	0.0	20:39									
2007-08 ♦	Detroit	NHL	65	7	28	35	44	0	0	0	108	6.5	25	0	0.0	21:06	22	0	15	15	18	0	0	0	23:20
2008-09	Detroit	NHL	80	6	45	51	50	4	0	1	121	5.0	2	1	100.0	22:54	23	2	7	9	33	2	0	0	23:24
2009-10	Detroit	NHL	48	7	15	22	32	3	0	0	68	10.3	5	0	0.0	21:55	12	0	5	5	12	0	0	0	23:15
	Sweden	Olympics	4	0	0	0	2																		
	NHL Totals		308	23	121	144	224	9	0	2	447	5.1		1	100.0	21:05	63	2	30	32	65	2	0	0	23:17

AHL First All-Star Team (2005) • Eddie Shore Award (AHL – Outstanding Defenseman) (2005)

• Missed majority of 2005-06 season recovering from knee surgery.

KRONWALL, Staffan

(KRAWN-wahl, STAH-fuhn) **CGY.**

Defense. Shoots left. 6'4", 209 lbs. Born, Jarfalla, Sweden, September 10, 1982. Toronto's 9th choice, 285th overall, in 2002 Entry Draft.

Season	Club	League	GP	G	A	Pts	PIM	PP	SH	GW	S	%	+/-	TF	F%	Min	GP	G	A	Pts	PIM	PP	SH	GW	Min
99-2000	Huddinge IK Jr.	Swe-Jr.	34	2	0	2	38																		
	Huddinge IK U18	Swe-U18	7	0	3	3	0																		
2000-01	Huddinge IK Jr.	Swe-Jr.	23	6	1	7	16																		
	Huddinge IK	Sweden-3	1	0	0	0	0																		
2001-02	Huddinge IK	Sweden-2	42	4	7	11	30																		
	Huddinge IK Jr.	Swe-Jr.	1	0	0	0	0										4	2	1	3	27				
2002-03	Djurgarden	Sweden	48	4	6	10	65										12	1	1	2	8				
2003-04	Djurgarden	Sweden	44	1	5	6	54										4	0	1	1	2				
2004-05	Brynas IF Gavle	Sweden	3	0	1	1	4																		
	Djurgarden Jr.	Swe-Jr.	5	2	4	6	0																		
	Djurgarden	Sweden	35	1	4	5	43										12	2	0	2	10				
2005-06	Toronto	NHL	34	0	1	1	14	0	0	0	18	0.0	–3	0	0.0	12:57									
	Toronto Marlies	AHL	16	1	10	11	12										4	0	2	2	2				
2006-07	Toronto Marlies	AHL	47	3	14	17	32																		
2007-08	Toronto	NHL	18	0	0	0	7	0	0	0	9	0.0	–2	0	0.0	11:07									
	Toronto Marlies	AHL	26	3	7	10	14										19	1	1	2	11				
2008-09	Toronto Marlies	AHL	42	7	18	25	46																		
	Washington	NHL	3	0	0	0	0	0	0	0	4	0.0	–1	0	0.0	13:13									
	Hershey Bears	AHL	17	2	7	9	13										21	3	9	12	6				
2009-10	Calgary	NHL	11	1	2	3	2	0	0	1	6	16.7	–1	0	0.0	9:54									
	Abbotsford Heat	AHL	44	5	23	28	24										9	0	2	2	0				
	NHL Totals		66	1	3	4	23	0	0	1	37	2.7		0	0.0	11:57									

Claimed on waivers by **Washington** from **Toronto**, February 6, 2009. Signed as a free agent by **Calgary**, July 14, 2009.

KUBA, Filip

(KOO-bah, FIHL-ihp) **OTT.**

Defense. Shoots left. 6'4", 229 lbs. Born, Ostrava, Czech., December 29, 1976. Florida's 8th choice, 192nd overall, in 1995 Entry Draft.

Season	Club	League	GP	G	A	Pts	PIM	PP	SH	GW	S	%	+/-	TF	F%	Min	GP	G	A	Pts	PIM	PP	SH	GW	Min
1994-95	HC Vitkovice Jr.	CzRep-Jr.	35	10	15	25																			
	HC Vitkovice	CzRep															4	0	0	0	2				
1995-96	HC Vitkovice	CzRep	19	0	1	1																			
1996-97	Carolina	AHL	51	0	12	12	38																		
1997-98	New Haven	AHL	77	4	13	17	58										3	1	1	2	0				
1998-99	Florida	NHL	5	0	1	1	0	0	0	0	5	0.0	2	0	0.0	22:29									
	Kentucky	AHL	45	2	8	10	33										10	0	1	1	4				

			Regular Season															Playoffs								
Season	Club	League	GP	G	A	Pts	PIM	PP	SH	GW	S	%	+/-	TF	F%	Min	GP	G	A	Pts	PIM	PP	SH	GW	M
99-2000	**Florida**	**NHL**	**13**	**1**	**5**	**6**	**2**	**1**	**0**	**1**	**16**	**6.3**	**-3**	**0**	**0.0**	**13:52**									
	Houston Aeros	IHL	27	3	6	9	13										11	1	2	3	4				
2000-01	**Minnesota**	**NHL**	**75**	**9**	**21**	**30**	**28**	**4**	**0**	**4**	**141**	**6.4**	**-6**	**1**	**0.0**	**24:16**									
2001-02	**Minnesota**	**NHL**	**62**	**5**	**19**	**24**	**32**	**3**	**0**	**1**	**101**	**5.0**	**-6**	**0**	**0.0**	**25:30**									
2002-03	**Minnesota**	**NHL**	**78**	**8**	**21**	**29**	**29**	**4**	**2**	**1**	**129**	**6.2**	**0**	**1**	**0.0**	**23:56**	**18**	**3**	**5**	**8**	**24**	**3**	**0**	**0**	**26:4**
2003-04	**Minnesota**	**NHL**	**77**	**5**	**19**	**24**	**28**	**2**	**1**	**2**	**114**	**4.4**	**-7**	**2**	**0.0**	**24:06**									
2004-05			DID NOT PLAY																						
2005-06	**Minnesota**	**NHL**	**65**	**6**	**19**	**25**	**44**	**1**	**1**	**1**	**69**	**8.7**	**0**	**2**	**0.0**	**21:46**									
	Czech Republic	Olympics	8	1	0	1	0																		
2006-07	**Tampa Bay**	**NHL**	**81**	**15**	**22**	**37**	**36**	**5**	**1**	**2**	**106**	**14.2**	**-9**	**0**	**0.0**	**20:12**	**6**	**1**	**4**	**5**	**4**	**0**	**1**	**0**	**20:4**
2007-08	**Tampa Bay**	**NHL**	**75**	**6**	**25**	**31**	**40**	**2**	**0**	**0**	**113**	**5.3**	**-8**	**2**	**0.0**	**24:57**									
2008-09	**Ottawa**	**NHL**	**71**	**3**	**37**	**40**	**28**	**2**	**0**	**0**	**111**	**2.7**	**4**	**0**	**0.0**	**23:17**									
2009-10	**Ottawa**	**NHL**	**53**	**3**	**25**	**28**	**28**	**2**	**0**	**0**	**90**	**3.3**	**-5**	**1**	**0.0**	**22:51**									
	Czech Republic	Olympics	5	0	1	1	0																		
	NHL Totals		**655**	**61**	**214**	**275**	**295**	**26**	**5**	**12**	**995**	**6.1**		**9**	**0.0**	**23:13**	**24**	**4**	**9**	**13**	**28**	**3**	**1**	**0**	**25:1**

Played in NHL All-Star Game (2004)

Traded to **Calgary** by **Florida** for Rocky Thompson, March 16, 2000. Claimed by **Minnesota** from **Calgary** in Expansion Draft, June 23, 2000. Signed as a free agent by **Tampa Bay**, July 1, 2006. Traded to **Ottawa** by **Tampa Bay** with Alexandre Picard and San Jose's 1st round choice (previously acquired, later traded to NY Islanders, later traded to Columbus, later traded to Anaheim - Anaheim selected Kyle Palmieri) in 2009 Entry Draft for Andrej Meszaros, August 29, 2008.

KUBINA, Pavel
(koo-BEE-nuh, PAH-vehl) **T.B.**

Defense. Shoots right. 6'4", 250 lbs. Born, Celadna, Czech., April 15, 1977. Tampa Bay's 6th choice, 179th overall, in 1996 Entry Draft.

Season	Club	League	GP	G	A	Pts	PIM	PP	SH	GW	S	%	+/-	TF	F%	Min	GP	G	A	Pts	PIM	PP	SH	GW	M
1993-94	HC Vitkovice Jr.	CzRep-Jr.	35	4	3	7																			
	HC Vitkovice	CzRep	1	0	0	0																			
1994-95	HC Vitkovice Jr.	CzRep-Jr.	20	6	10	16																			
	HC Vitkovice	CzRep	8	2	0	2	10										4	0	0	0	0				
1995-96	HC Vitkovice Jr.	CzRep-Jr.	16	5	10	15																			
	HC Vitkovice	CzRep	33	3	4	7	32										4	0	0	0	0				
1996-97	HC Vitkovice	CzRep	1	0	0	0	0																		
	Moose Jaw	WHL	61	12	32	44	116										11	2	5	7	27				
1997-98	**Tampa Bay**	**NHL**	**10**	**1**	**2**	**3**	**22**	**0**	**0**	**0**	**8**	**12.5**	**-1**												
	Adirondack	AHL	55	4	8	12	86										1	1	0	1	14				
1998-99	**Tampa Bay**	**NHL**	**68**	**9**	**12**	**21**	**80**	**3**	**1**	**1**	**119**	**7.6**	**-33**	**2**	**0.0**	**22:47**									
	Cleveland	IHL	6	2	2	4	16																		
99-2000	**Tampa Bay**	**NHL**	**69**	**8**	**18**	**26**	**93**	**6**	**0**	**3**	**128**	**6.3**	**-19**	**0**	**0.0**	**22:32**									
2000-01	**Tampa Bay**	**NHL**	**70**	**11**	**19**	**30**	**103**	**6**	**1**	**1**	**128**	**8.6**	**-14**	**2**	**0.0**	**24:06**									
2001-02	**Tampa Bay**	**NHL**	**82**	**11**	**23**	**34**	**106**	**5**	**2**	**3**	**189**	**5.8**	**-22**	**1**	**100.0**	**23:39**									
	Czech Republic	Olympics	4	0	1	1	0																		
2002-03	**Tampa Bay**	**NHL**	**75**	**3**	**19**	**22**	**78**	**0**	**0**	**0**	**139**	**2.2**	**-7**	**1**	**0.0**	**21:24**	**11**	**0**	**0**	**0**	**12**	**0**	**0**	**0**	**24:5**
2003-04♦	**Tampa Bay**	**NHL**	**81**	**17**	**18**	**35**	**85**	**8**	**1**	**4**	**153**	**11.1**	**9**	**1**	**0.0**	**21:09**	**22**	**0**	**4**	**4**	**50**	**0**	**0**	**0**	**22:5**
2004-05	Vitkovice	CzRep	28	6	5	11	46										12	4	6	10	34				
2005-06	**Tampa Bay**	**NHL**	**76**	**5**	**33**	**38**	**96**	**4**	**0**	**3**	**155**	**3.2**	**-12**	**2**	**0.0**	**22:25**	**5**	**1**	**1**	**2**	**26**	**1**	**0**	**0**	**20:0**
	Czech Republic	Olympics	8	1	1	2	12																		
2006-07	**Toronto**	**NHL**	**61**	**7**	**14**	**21**	**48**	**4**	**0**	**1**	**97**	**7.2**	**7**	**0**	**0.0**	**21:19**									
2007-08	**Toronto**	**NHL**	**72**	**11**	**29**	**40**	**116**	**6**	**0**	**4**	**136**	**8.1**	**5**	**1**	**0.0**	**23:55**									
2008-09	**Toronto**	**NHL**	**82**	**14**	**26**	**40**	**94**	**9**	**0**	**4**	**184**	**7.6**	**-15**	**0**	**0.0**	**22:03**									
2009-10	**Atlanta**	**NHL**	**76**	**6**	**32**	**38**	**66**	**2**	**0**	**1**	**159**	**3.8**	**0**	**0**	**0.0**	**22:38**									
	Czech Republic	Olympics	5	0	0	0	2																		
	NHL Totals		**822**	**103**	**245**	**348**	**987**	**53**	**5**	**25**	**1595**	**6.5**		**10**	**10.0**	**22:32**	**38**	**1**	**5**	**6**	**88**	**1**	**0**	**0**	**23:0**

Played in NHL All-Star Game (2004)

Signed as a free agent by **Vitkovice** (CzRep), September 17, 2004. Signed as a free agent by **Toronto**, July 1, 2006. Traded to **Atlanta** by **Toronto** with Tim Stapleton for Garnet Exelby and Colin Stuart, July 1, 2009. Signed as a free agent by **Tampa Bay**, July 2, 2010.

KUKKONEN, Lasse
(koo-KOH-nuhn, LAH-say)

Defense. Shoots left. 6'1", 190 lbs. Born, Oulu, Finland, September 18, 1981. Chicago's 4th choice, 151st overall, in 2003 Entry Draft.

Season	Club	League	GP	G	A	Pts	PIM	PP	SH	GW	S	%	+/-	TF	F%	Min	GP	G	A	Pts	PIM	PP	SH	GW	M
1997-98	Karpat Oulu U18	Fin-U18	36	5	16	21	46																		
1998-99	Karpat Oulu U18	Fin-U18	2	1	2	3	0																		
	Karpat Oulu Jr.	Fin-Jr.	34	2	13	15	24																		
99-2000	Karpat Oulu Jr.	Fin-Jr.	27	9	11	20	26																		
	Karpat Oulu	Finland-2	22	0	4	4	14																		
2000-01	Karpat Oulu	Finland	47	1	5	6	46										9	0	2	2	4				
2001-02	Karpat Oulu	Finland	55	2	6	8	42										4	0	3	3	4				
	Karpat Oulu Jr.	Fin-Jr.															1	1	0	1	0				
2002-03	Karpat Oulu	Finland	56	6	12	18	67										15	1	4	5	16				
2003-04	**Chicago**	**NHL**	**10**	**0**	**1**	**1**	**4**	**0**	**0**	**0**	**9**	**0.0**	**-2**	**0**	**0.0**	**13:37**									
	Norfolk Admirals	AHL	59	3	11	14	58										8	0	0	0	8				
2004-05	Karpat Oulu	Finland	55	5	13	18	68										12	0	2	2	6				
2005-06	Karpat Oulu	Finland	56	11	16	27	38										11	5	7	12	8				
	Finland	Olympics	2	0	0	0	0																		
2006-07	**Chicago**	**NHL**	**54**	**5**	**9**	**14**	**30**	**1**	**0**	**2**	**45**	**11.1**	**5**	**0**	**0.0**	**16:35**									
	Philadelphia	**NHL**	**20**	**0**	**0**	**0**	**8**	**0**	**0**	**0**	**9**	**0.0**	**-1**	**0**	**0.0**	**18:29**									
2007-08	**Philadelphia**	**NHL**	**53**	**1**	**4**	**5**	**38**	**0**	**0**	**0**	**31**	**3.2**	**3**	**0**	**0.0**	**15:44**	**14**	**0**	**2**	**2**	**6**	**0**	**0**	**0**	**15:2**
2008-09	**Philadelphia**	**NHL**	**22**	**0**	**2**	**2**	**10**	**0**	**0**	**0**	**10**	**0.0**	**-2**	**1**	**0.0**	**10:43**									
	Philadelphia	AHL	26	0	11	11	20										4	2	0	2	6				
2009-10	Omsk	Rus-KHL	53	6	6	12	34										3	0	1	1	0				
	Finland	Olympics	6	0	1	1	4																		
	NHL Totals		**159**	**6**	**16**	**22**	**90**	**1**	**0**	**2**	**104**	**5.8**		**1**	**0.0**	**15:33**	**14**	**0**	**2**	**2**	**6**	**0**	**0**	**0**	**15:2**

Signed as a free agent by **Oulu** (Finland), September 11, 2004. Traded to **Philadelphia** by **Chicago** with Chicago's 3rd round choice (Garrett Klotz) in 2007 Entry Draft for Kyle Calder, February 26, 2007. Signed as a free agent by **Omsk** (Russia-KHL), June 24, 2009.

KULDA , Arturs
(KOOL-da, AHR-tuhrs) **ATL**

Defense. Shoots left. 6'2", 210 lbs. Born, Riga, Latvia, July 25, 1988. Atlanta's 7th choice, 200th overall, in 2006 Entry Draft.

Season	Club	League	GP	G	A	Pts	PIM	PP	SH	GW	S	%	+/-	TF	F%	Min	GP	G	A	Pts	PIM	PP	SH	GW	M
2003-04	Prizma/Riga 86	Latvia	11	0	0	0	8										2	0	0	0	0				
2004-05	CSKA Moscow 2	Russia-3	STATISTICS NOT AVAILABLE																						
2005-06	CSKA Moscow 2	Russia-3	44	5	12	17																			
2006-07	Peterborough	OHL	58	2	9	11	83																		
2007-08	Peterborough	OHL	55	7	27	34	87										5	1	3	4	6				
	Chicago Wolves	AHL	5	0	1	1	10										22	1	5	6	32				
2008-09	Chicago Wolves	AHL	57	1	14	15	59																		
2009-10	**Atlanta**	**NHL**	**4**	**0**	**2**	**2**	**2**	**0**	**0**	**0**	**5**	**0.0**	**2**	**0**	**0.0**	**11:59**									
	Chicago Wolves	AHL	66	6	19	25	46										14	1	4	5	8				
	NHL Totals		**4**	**0**	**2**	**2**	**2**	**0**	**0**	**0**	**5**	**0.0**		**0**	**0.0**	**11:59**									

KULEMIN, Nikolai
(KOOL-ay-mihn, NIH-koh-ligh) **TOR**

Wing. Shoots left. 6'1", 225 lbs. Born, Magnitogorsk, USSR, July 14, 1986. Toronto's 2nd choice, 44th overall, in 2006 Entry Draft.

Season	Club	League	GP	G	A	Pts	PIM	PP	SH	GW	S	%	+/-	TF	F%	Min	GP	G	A	Pts	PIM	PP	SH	GW	M
2003-04	Magnitogorsk 2	Russia-3	43	8	18	26	91																		
2004-05	Magnitogorsk 2	Russia-3	43	9	13	22	44																		
2005-06	Magnitogorsk	Russia	31	5	7	12	8										11	2	4	6	6				
	Magnitogorsk 2	Russia-3	4	3	1	4	6																		
2006-07	Magnitogorsk	Russia	54	27	12	39	42										15	10	1	11	10				
2007-08	Magnitogorsk	Russia	57	21	12	33	63										11	2	2	4	29				
2008-09	**Toronto**	**NHL**	**73**	**15**	**16**	**31**	**18**	**2**	**0**	**1**	**129**	**11.6**	**-8**	**66**	**53.0**	**13:48**									
	Toronto Marlies	AHL	5	0	0	0	0																		
2009-10	**Toronto**	**NHL**	**78**	**16**	**20**	**36**	**16**	**0**	**1**	**3**	**145**	**11.0**	**0**	**66**	**40.9**	**16:22**									
	NHL Totals		**151**	**31**	**36**	**67**	**34**	**2**	**1**	**4**	**274**	**11.3**		**132**	**47.0**	**15:08**									

KULIKOV, Dmitry
(kool-YIH-kawf, dih-MEE-tree) **FLA.**

Defense. Shoots left. 6'1", 183 lbs. Born, Lipetsk, USSR, October 29, 1990. Florida's 1st choice, 14th overall, in 2009 Entry Draft.

Season	Club	League	GP	G	A	Pts	PIM	PP	SH	GW	S	%	+/-	TF	F%	Min	GP	G	A	Pts	PIM	PP	SH	GW	Min
			Regular Season														Playoffs								
2007-08	Yaroslavl 2	Russia-3	STATISTICS NOT AVAILABLE																						
2008-09	Drummondville	QMJHL	57	12	50	62	46	....	....	....	....	....	....	....	....	....	19	2	18	20	16	....	....	....	....
2009-10	**Florida**	**NHL**	**68**	**3**	**13**	**16**	**32**	**1**	**0**	**0**	**87**	**3.4**	**–5**	**0**	**0.0**	**17:56**	....	....	....	....	....	....	....	....	....
	NHL Totals		**68**	**3**	**13**	**16**	**32**	**1**	**0**	**0**	**87**	**3.4**		**0**	**0.0**	**17:56**	....	....	....	....	....	....	....	....	....

QMJHL All-Rookie Team (2009) • QMJHL First All-Star Team (2009) • QMJHL Rookie of the Year (2009) • Canadian Major Junior Second All-Star Team (2009) • Canadian Major Junior All-Rookie Team (2009)

KUNITZ, Chris
(KOO-nihtz, KRIHS) **PIT.**

Left wing. Shoots left. 6', 193 lbs. Born, Regina, Sask., September 26, 1979.

Season	Club	League	GP	G	A	Pts	PIM	PP	SH	GW	S	%	+/-	TF	F%	Min	GP	G	A	Pts	PIM	PP	SH	GW	Min
1996-97	Yorkton Mallers	SMHL	64	38	38	76	233	....	....	....	....	....	....	....	....	....	....	....	....	....	....	....	....	....	....
1997-98	Melville	SJHL	STATISTICS NOT AVAILABLE																						
1998-99	Melville	SJHL	63	57	32	89	222	....	....	....	....	....	....	....	....	....	....	....	....	....	....	....	....	....	....
99-2000	Ferris State	CCHA	38	20	9	29	70	....	....	....	....	....	....	....	....	....	....	....	....	....	....	....	....	....	....
2000-01	Ferris State	CCHA	37	16	13	29	81	....	....	....	....	....	....	....	....	....	....	....	....	....	....	....	....	....	....
2001-02	Ferris State	CCHA	35	*28	10	38	68	....	....	....	....	....	....	....	....	....	....	....	....	....	....	....	....	....	....
2002-03	Ferris State	CCHA	42	*35	*44	*79	56	....	....	....	....	....	....	....	....	....	....	....	....	....	....	....	....	....	....
2003-04	**Anaheim**	**NHL**	**21**	**0**	**6**	**6**	**12**	**0**	**0**	**0**	**31**	**0.0**	**1**	**7**	**14.3**	**9:07**	....	....	....	....	....	....	....	....	....
	Cincinnati	AHL	59	19	25	44	101	....	....	....	....	....	....	....	....	....	9	3	2	5	24	....	....	....	....
2004-05	Cincinnati	AHL	54	22	17	39	71	....	....	....	....	....	....	....	....	....	12	1	7	8	20	....	....	....	....
2005-06	**Atlanta**	**NHL**	**2**	**0**	**0**	**0**	**2**	**0**	**0**	**0**	**0**	**0.0**	**–3**	**0**	**0.0**	**5:43**	....	....	....	....	....	....	....	....	....
	Anaheim	**NHL**	**67**	**19**	**22**	**41**	**69**	**5**	**1**	**2**	**149**	**12.8**	**19**	**15**	**46.7**	**14:08**	**16**	**3**	**5**	**8**	**8**	**0**	**0**	**0**	**12:30**
	Portland Pirates	AHL	5	0	4	4	12	....	....	....	....	....	....	....	....	....	....	....	....	....	....	....	....	....	....
2006-07 ♦	**Anaheim**	**NHL**	**81**	**25**	**35**	**60**	**81**	**11**	**0**	**5**	**180**	**13.9**	**23**	**13**	**30.8**	**17:03**	**13**	**1**	**5**	**6**	**19**	**0**	**0**	**0**	**17:47**
2007-08	**Anaheim**	**NHL**	**82**	**21**	**29**	**50**	**80**	**7**	**1**	**6**	**196**	**10.7**	**8**	**49**	**32.7**	**16:54**	**6**	**0**	**2**	**2**	**8**	**0**	**0**	**0**	**18:30**
2008-09	**Anaheim**	**NHL**	**62**	**16**	**19**	**35**	**55**	**3**	**0**	**2**	**139**	**11.5**	**9**	**22**	**45.5**	**16:29**	....	....	....	....	....	....	....	....	....
	♦ **Pittsburgh**	**NHL**	**20**	**7**	**11**	**18**	**16**	**3**	**0**	**1**	**39**	**17.9**	**3**	**5**	**60.0**	**16:17**	**24**	**1**	**13**	**14**	**19**	**0**	**0**	**0**	**16:55**
2009-10	**Pittsburgh**	**NHL**	**50**	**13**	**19**	**32**	**39**	**2**	**1**	**0**	**131**	**9.9**	**3**	**15**	**40.0**	**16:26**	**13**	**4**	**7**	**11**	**8**	**1**	**0**	**0**	**17:26**
	NHL Totals		**385**	**101**	**141**	**242**	**354**	**31**	**3**	**16**	**865**	**11.7**		**126**	**37.3**	**15:49**	**72**	**9**	**32**	**41**	**62**	**1**	**0**	**0**	**16:19**

CCHA First All-Star Team (2002, 2003) • CCHA Player of the Year (2003) • NCAA West First All-American Team (2003)

Signed as a free agent by **Anaheim**, April 1, 2003. Claimed on waivers by **Atlanta** from **Anaheim**, October 4, 2005. Claimed on waivers by **Anaheim** from **Atlanta**, October 18, 2005. Traded to **Pittsburgh** by **Anaheim** with Eric Tangradi for Ryan Whitney, February 26, 2009.

LAAKSO, Teemu
(LAK-soh, TEE-moo) **NSH.**

Defense. Shoots right. 6'1", 209 lbs. Born, Tuusula, Finland, August 27, 1987. Nashville's 2nd choice, 78th overall, in 2005 Entry Draft.

Season	Club	League	GP	G	A	Pts	PIM	PP	SH	GW	S	%	+/-	TF	F%	Min	GP	G	A	Pts	PIM	PP	SH	GW	Min
2002-03	KJT U18	Fin-U18	18	2	5	7	24	....	....	....	....	....	....	....	....	....	....	....	....	....	....	....	....	....	....
2003-04	HIFK Helsinki Jr.	Fin-Jr.	41	3	6	9	20	....	....	....	....	....	....	....	....	....	3	0	1	1	0	....	....	....	....
2004-05	HIFK Helsinki U18	Fin-U18	....	....	....	....	....	....	....	....	....	....	....	....	....	....	1	0	0	0	0	....	....	....	....
	HIFK Helsinki Jr.	Fin-Jr.	20	5	4	9	18	....	....	....	....	....	....	....	....	....	....	....	....	....	....	....	....	....	....
	HIFK Helsinki	Finland	15	0	2	2	2	....	....	....	....	....	....	....	....	....	....	....	....	....	....	....	....	....	....
2005-06	HIFK Helsinki Jr.	Fin-Jr.	6	1	2	3	32	....	....	....	....	....	....	....	....	....	....	....	....	....	....	....	....	....	....
	Suomi U20	Finland-2	6	2	0	2	10	....	....	....	....	....	....	....	....	....	....	....	....	....	....	....	....	....	....
	HIFK Helsinki	Finland	47	2	1	3	20	....	....	....	....	....	....	....	....	....	8	1	0	1	0	....	....	....	....
2006-07	Suomi U20	Finland-2	2	0	1	1	4	....	....	....	....	....	....	....	....	....	....	....	....	....	....	....	....	....	....
	HIFK Helsinki	Finland	50	3	6	9	70	....	....	....	....	....	....	....	....	....	5	0	1	1	0	....	....	....	....
2007-08	HIFK Helsinki	Finland	53	3	7	10	40	....	....	....	....	....	....	....	....	....	7	0	0	0	2	....	....	....	....
2008-09	Milwaukee	AHL	42	2	7	9	50	....	....	....	....	....	....	....	....	....	....	....	....	....	....	....	....	....	....
2009-10	**Nashville**	**NHL**	**7**	**0**	**0**	**0**	**2**	**0**	**0**	**0**	**5**	**0.0**	**–2**	**0**	**0.0**	**10:48**	....	....	....	....	....	....	....	....	....
	Milwaukee	AHL	46	4	9	13	42	....	....	....	....	....	....	....	....	....	7	1	2	3	4	....	....	....	....
	NHL Totals		**7**	**0**	**0**	**0**	**2**	**0**	**0**	**0**	**5**	**0.0**		**0**	**0.0**	**10:48**	....	....	....	....	....	....	....	....	....

LaCOUTURE, Dan
(LA-koo-TUHR, DAN)

Left wing. Shoots left. 6'2", 215 lbs. Born, Hyannis, MA, April 18, 1977. NY Islanders' 2nd choice, 29th overall, in 1996 Entry Draft.

Season	Club	League	GP	G	A	Pts	PIM	PP	SH	GW	S	%	+/-	TF	F%	Min	GP	G	A	Pts	PIM	PP	SH	GW	Min
1992-93	Natick Redmen	High-MA	20	38	34	72	46	....	....	....	....	....	....	....	....	....	....	....	....	....	....	....	....	....	....
1993-94	Natick Redmen	High-MA	21	52	49	101	58	....	....	....	....	....	....	....	....	....	....	....	....	....	....	....	....	....	....
1994-95	Spring. Olympics	NEJHL	52	44	56	100	98	....	....	....	....	....	....	....	....	....	....	....	....	....	....	....	....	....	....
1995-96	Spring. Olympics	NEJHL	29	24	35	59	79	....	....	....	....	....	....	....	....	....	13	12	13	25	23	....	....	....	....
1996-97	Boston University	H-East	31	13	12	25	18	....	....	....	....	....	....	....	....	....	....	....	....	....	....	....	....	....	....
1997-98	Hamilton	AHL	77	15	10	25	31	....	....	....	....	....	....	....	....	....	5	1	0	1	0	....	....	....	....
1998-99	**Edmonton**	**NHL**	**3**	**0**	**0**	**0**	**0**	**0**	**0**	**0**	**0**	**0.0**	**1**	**0**	**0.0**	**6:30**	....	....	....	....	....	....	....	....	....
	Hamilton	AHL	72	17	14	31	73	....	....	....	....	....	....	....	....	....	9	2	1	3	2	....	....	....	....
99-2000	**Edmonton**	**NHL**	**5**	**0**	**0**	**0**	**10**	**0**	**0**	**0**	**2**	**0.0**	**0**	**0**	**0.0**	**7:02**	**1**	**0**	**0**	**0**	**0**	**0**	**0**	**0**	**2:05**
	Hamilton	AHL	70	23	17	40	85	....	....	....	....	....	....	....	....	....	6	2	1	3	0	....	....	....	....
2000-01	**Edmonton**	**NHL**	**37**	**2**	**4**	**6**	**29**	**0**	**0**	**1**	**22**	**9.1**	**–2**	**5**	**20.0**	**7:06**	....	....	....	....	....	....	....	....	....
	Pittsburgh	**NHL**	**11**	**0**	**0**	**0**	**14**	**0**	**0**	**0**	**1**	**0.0**	**0**	**1**	**100.0**	**5:57**	**5**	**0**	**0**	**0**	**2**	**0**	**0**	**0**	**5:46**
2001-02	**Pittsburgh**	**NHL**	**82**	**6**	**11**	**17**	**71**	**0**	**1**	**0**	**77**	**7.8**	**–19**	**21**	**38.1**	**13:16**	....	....	....	....	....	....	....	....	....
2002-03	**Pittsburgh**	**NHL**	**44**	**2**	**2**	**4**	**72**	**0**	**0**	**0**	**30**	**6.7**	**–8**	**5**	**80.0**	**9:13**	....	....	....	....	....	....	....	....	....
	NY Rangers	**NHL**	**24**	**1**	**4**	**5**	**0**	**0**	**0**	**0**	**17**	**5.9**	**4**	**1**	**0.0**	**10:18**	....	....	....	....	....	....	....	....	....
2003-04	**NY Rangers**	**NHL**	**59**	**5**	**2**	**7**	**82**	**1**	**0**	**1**	**39**	**12.8**	**–13**	**8**	**50.0**	**9:29**	....	....	....	....	....	....	....	....	....
2004-05	Providence Bruins	AHL	64	12	15	27	52	....	....	....	....	....	....	....	....	....	6	1	1	2	4	....	....	....	....
2005-06	HC Davos	Swiss	4	2	1	3	4	....	....	....	....	....	....	....	....	....	....	....	....	....	....	....	....	....	....
	Boston	**NHL**	**55**	**2**	**2**	**4**	**53**	**0**	**1**	**0**	**37**	**5.4**	**–6**	**0**	**0.0**	**6:15**	....	....	....	....	....	....	....	....	....
2006-07	**New Jersey**	**NHL**	**6**	**0**	**0**	**0**	**7**	**0**	**0**	**0**	**0**	**0.0**	**0**	**0**	**0.0**	**4:57**	....	....	....	....	....	....	....	....	....
	Lowell Devils	AHL	39	8	3	11	33	....	....	....	....	....	....	....	....	....	....	....	....	....	....	....	....	....	....
2007-08	HC Lugano	Swiss	15	1	1	2	18	....	....	....	....	....	....	....	....	....	....	....	....	....	....	....	....	....	....
2008-09	**Carolina**	**NHL**	**11**	**2**	**0**	**2**	**10**	**0**	**0**	**1**	**4**	**50.0**	**–1**	**10**	**40.0**	**4:16**	....	....	....	....	....	....	....	....	....
	Albany River Rats	AHL	12	1	5	6	4	....	....	....	....	....	....	....	....	....	....	....	....	....	....	....	....	....	....
	Barys Astana	Rus-KHL	12	2	1	3	51	....	....	....	....	....	....	....	....	....	3	0	0	0	0	....	....	....	....
2009-10	Providence Bruins	AHL	9	1	0	1	2	....	....	....	....	....	....	....	....	....	....	....	....	....	....	....	....	....	....
	NHL Totals		**337**	**20**	**25**	**45**	**348**	**1**	**2**	**3**	**229**	**8.7**		**51**	**43.1**	**9:13**	**6**	**0**	**0**	**0**	**2**	**0**	**0**	**0**	**5:09**

Traded to **Edmonton** by **NY Islanders** for Mariusz Czerkawski, August 25, 1997. Traded to **Pittsburgh** by **Edmonton** for Sven Butenschon, March 13, 2001. Traded to **NY Rangers** by **Pittsburgh** with Mike Wilson, Alex Kovalev and Janne Laukkanen for Joel Bouchard, Richard Lintner, Rico Fata and Mikael Samuelsson, February 10, 2003. Signed to a PTO (professional tryout) contract by **Providence** (AHL), November 2, 2004. Signed as a free agent by **Boston**, November 24, 2005. Signed as a free agent by **New Jersey**, October 4, 2006. Signed as a free agent by **Anaheim**, July 18, 2007. Signed as a free agent by **Lugano** (Swiss), January 22, 2008. Signed as a free agent by **Carolina**, October 6, 2008. • Suspended by **Carolina**, December 29, 2008. Signed as a free agent by **Astana** (Russia-KHL), January 4, 2009. Signed to a PTO (professional tryout) contract by **Providence** (AHL), November 19, 2009.

LADD, Andrew
(LAD, AN-droo) **ATL.**

Left wing. Shoots left. 6'2", 200 lbs. Born, Maple Ridge, B.C., December 12, 1985. Carolina's 1st choice, 4th overall, in 2004 Entry Draft.

Season	Club	League	GP	G	A	Pts	PIM	PP	SH	GW	S	%	+/-	TF	F%	Min	GP	G	A	Pts	PIM	PP	SH	GW	Min
2000-01	Okanagan Chiefs	Minor-BC	6	4	8	12	10	....	....	....	....	....	....	....	....	....	....	....	....	....	....	....	....	....	....
2001-02	Port Coquitlam	Minor-BC	50	50	41	91	49	....	....	....	....	....	....	....	....	....	....	....	....	....	....	....	....	....	....
	Vancouver Giants	WHL	1	0	0	0	0	....	....	....	....	....	....	....	....	....	....	....	....	....	....	....	....	....	....
2002-03	Coquitlam	BCHL	58	15	40	55	61	....	....	....	....	....	....	....	....	....	....	....	....	....	....	....	....	....	....
2003-04	Calgary Hitmen	WHL	71	30	45	75	119	....	....	....	....	....	....	....	....	....	7	1	6	7	10	....	....	....	....
2004-05	Calgary Hitmen	WHL	65	19	26	45	167	....	....	....	....	....	....	....	....	....	12	7	4	11	18	....	....	....	....
2005-06 ♦	**Carolina**	**NHL**	**29**	**6**	**5**	**11**	**4**	**3**	**0**	**0**	**43**	**14.0**	**0**	**0**	**0.0**	**11:10**	**17**	**2**	**3**	**5**	**4**	**0**	**0**	**1**	**9:27**
	Lowell	AHL	25	11	8	19	28	....	....	....	....	....	....	....	....	....	....	....	....	....	....	....	....	....	....
2006-07	**Carolina**	**NHL**	**65**	**11**	**10**	**21**	**46**	**2**	**0**	**3**	**109**	**10.1**	**1**	**1**	**0.0**	**11:12**	....	....	....	....	....	....	....	....	....
2007-08	**Carolina**	**NHL**	**43**	**9**	**9**	**18**	**31**	**0**	**0**	**1**	**76**	**11.8**	**9**	**5**	**60.0**	**11:45**	....	....	....	....	....	....	....	....	....
	Albany River Rats	AHL	2	1	0	1	4	....	....	....	....	....	....	....	....	....	....	....	....	....	....	....	....	....	....
	Chicago	**NHL**	**20**	**5**	**7**	**12**	**4**	**1**	**0**	**0**	**55**	**9.1**	**4**	**3**	**33.3**	**14:58**	....	....	....	....	....	....	....	....	....

			Regular Season														Playoffs								
Season	Club	League	GP	G	A	Pts	PIM	PP	SH	GW	S	%	+/-	TF	F%	Min	GP	G	A	Pts	PIM	PP	SH	GW	M
2008-09	**Chicago**	**NHL**	82	15	34	49	28	0	0	2	195	7.7	26	42	23.8	14:24	17	3	1	4	12	0	0	1	12:5
2009-10♦	**Chicago**	**NHL**	82	17	21	38	67	0	0	1	148	11.5	2	12	41.7	13:42	19	3	3	6	12	0	0	0	12:4
	NHL Totals		321	63	86	149	180	6	0	7	626	10.1		63	30.2	12:57	53	8	7	15	28	0	0	2	11:4

Traded to **Chicago** by **Carolina** for Tuomo Ruutu, February 26, 2008. Traded to **Atlanta** by **Chicago** for Ivan Vishnevskiy and a 2nd round choice in 2011 Entry Draft, July 1, 2010.

LAICH, Brooks

(LIGHK, BRUKS) **WSH**

Center. Shoots left. 6'2", 200 lbs. Born, Wawota, Sask., June 23, 1983. Ottawa's 7th choice, 193rd overall, in 2001 Entry Draft.

99-2000	Tisdale Trojans	SMHL	57	51	52	103	....	....	....	....	....	....	....	....	....	....	....	....	....	....	....	....	....	....	
2000-01	Moose Jaw	WHL	71	9	21	30	28	....	....	....	....	....	....	....	....	....	4	0	0	0	5	....	....	....	
2001-02	Moose Jaw	WHL	28	6	14	20	12	....	....	....	....	....	....	....	....	....	....	....	....	....	....	....	....	....	
	Seattle	WHL	47	22	36	58	42	....	....	....	....	....	....	....	....	....	11	5	3	8	11	....	....	....	
2002-03	Seattle	WHL	60	41	53	94	65	....	....	....	....	....	....	....	....	....	15	5	14	19	24	....	....	....	
2003-04	**Ottawa**	**NHL**	1	0	0	0	2	0	0	0	1	0.0	0	7	42.9	9:34	....	....	....	....	....	....	....	....	
	Binghamton	AHL	44	15	18	33	16	....	....	....	....	....	....	....	....	....	....	....	....	....	....	....	....	....	
	Washington	**NHL**	4	0	1	1	0	0	0	0	2	0.0	–1	49	51.0	10:50	....	....	....	....	....	....	....	....	
	Portland Pirates	AHL	22	1	3	4	12	....	....	....	....	....	....	....	....	....	6	0	0	0	0	....	....	....	
2004-05	Portland Pirates	AHL	68	16	10	26	33	....	....	....	....	....	....	....	....	....	....	....	....	....	....	....	....	....	
2005-06	**Washington**	**NHL**	73	7	14	21	26	1	0	1	118	5.9	–9	666	49.7	11:13	....	....	....	....	....	....	....	....	
	Hershey Bears	AHL	10	7	6	13	8	....	....	....	....	....	....	....	....	....	21	8	7	15	29	....	....	....	
2006-07	**Washington**	**NHL**	73	8	10	18	29	2	3	0	119	6.7	–2	563	51.9	13:36	....	....	....	....	....	....	....	....	
2007-08	**Washington**	**NHL**	82	21	16	37	35	8	2	4	122	17.2	–3	596	47.2	14:03	7	1	5	6	4	0	0	0	18:3
2008-09	**Washington**	**NHL**	82	23	30	53	31	9	1	3	185	12.4	–1	511	51.1	17:17	14	3	4	7	10	2	0	0	17:2
2009-10	**Washington**	**NHL**	78	25	34	59	34	12	1	4	222	11.3	16	337	45.1	18:17	7	2	1	3	4	0	0	1	19:5
	NHL Totals		393	84	105	189	157	32	7	12	769	10.9		2729	49.3	14:55	28	6	10	16	18	2	0	1	18:2

WHL West First All-Star Team (2003)

Traded to **Washington** by **Ottawa** with Ottawa's 2nd round choice (later traded to Colorado - Colorado selected Chris Durand) in 2005 Entry Draft for Peter Bondra, February 18, 2004.

LAING, Quintin

(LANG, QUIHN-tihn)

Left wing. Shoots left. 6'3", 183 lbs. Born, Rosetown, Sask., June 8, 1979. Detroit's 3rd choice, 102nd overall, in 1997 Entry Draft.

1993-94	Delisle Contacts	SAHA	30	25	50	75	25	....	....	....	....	....	....	....	....	....	....	....	....	....	....	....	....	....	
1994-95	Delisle Contacts	SAHA	30	30	45	75	15	....	....	....	....	....	....	....	....	....	....	....	....	....	....	....	....	....	
1995-96	Sask. Contacts	SMHL	44	18	12	30	20	....	....	....	....	....	....	....	....	....	....	....	....	....	....	....	....	....	
1996-97	Kelowna Rockets	WHL	63	13	24	37	54	....	....	....	....	....	....	....	....	....	1	0	0	0	0	....	....	....	
1997-98	Kelowna Rockets	WHL	59	11	24	35	47	....	....	....	....	....	....	....	....	....	7	0	1	1	8	....	....	....	
1998-99	Kelowna Rockets	WHL	70	11	10	21	107	....	....	....	....	....	....	....	....	....	6	3	0	3	0	....	....	....	
99-2000	Kelowna Rockets	WHL	68	22	30	52	61	....	....	....	....	....	....	....	....	....	5	1	1	2	8	....	....	....	
2000-01	Norfolk Admirals	AHL	10	0	1	1	10	....	....	....	....	....	....	....	....	....	....	....	....	....	....	....	....	....	
	Jackson Bandits	ECHL	60	13	24	37	39	....	....	....	....	....	....	....	....	....	5	0	0	0	0	....	....	....	
2001-02	Jackson Bandits	ECHL	16	4	6	10	12	....	....	....	....	....	....	....	....	....	....	....	....	....	....	....	....	....	
	Norfolk Admirals	AHL	61	6	15	21	32	....	....	....	....	....	....	....	....	....	4	0	0	0	2	....	....	....	
2002-03	Norfolk Admirals	AHL	69	5	12	17	33	....	....	....	....	....	....	....	....	....	8	2	2	4	0	....	....	....	
2003-04	**Chicago**	**NHL**	3	0	1	1	0	0	0	0	3	0.0	1	0	0.0	11:57	....	....	....	....	....	....	....	....	
	Norfolk Admirals	AHL	78	12	10	22	74	....	....	....	....	....	....	....	....	....	8	5	1	6	4	....	....	....	
2004-05	Norfolk Admirals	AHL	66	10	13	23	54	....	....	....	....	....	....	....	....	....	4	0	0	0	0	....	....	....	
2005-06	Norfolk Admirals	AHL	73	14	31	45	70	....	....	....	....	....	....	....	....	....	4	0	0	0	0	....	....	....	
2006-07	Hershey Bears	AHL	75	15	28	43	44	....	....	....	....	....	....	....	....	....	19	2	5	7	21	....	....	....	
2007-08	**Washington**	**NHL**	39	1	5	6	10	0	0	1	48	2.1	4	6	33.3	11:33	....	....	....	....	....	....	....	....	
	Hershey Bears	AHL	20	2	6	8	28	....	....	....	....	....	....	....	....	....	....	....	....	....	....	....	....	....	
2008-09	**Washington**	**NHL**	1	0	0	0	0	0	0	0	2	0.0	1	0	0.0	10:19	....	....	....	....	....	....	....	....	
	Hershey Bears	AHL	55	9	16	25	21	....	....	....	....	....	....	....	....	....	9	2	2	4	0	....	....	....	
2009-10	**Washington**	**NHL**	36	2	2	4	21	0	0	0	38	5.3	2	7	57.1	9:38	....	....	....	....	....	....	....	....	
	Hershey Bears	AHL	2	0	0	0	0	....	....	....	....	....	....	....	....	....	....	....	....	....	....	....	....	....	
	NHL Totals		79	3	8	11	31	0	0	1	91	3.3		13	46.2	10:41	....	....	....	....	....	....	....	....	

Signed as a free agent by **Chicago**, June 4, 2003. Signed as a free agent by **Washington**, July 18, 2006. • Missed majority of 2009-10 season recovering from broken jaw suffered in game at NY Rangers, November 17, 2009 and as a healthy reserve.

LALIBERTE, David

(la-lih-BUHR-tee, DAY-vihd) **PHI**

Right wing. Shoots right. 6'1", 194 lbs. Born, St-Jean-Sur-Richelieu, Que., March 17, 1986. Philadelphia's 3rd choice, 124th overall, in 2004 Entry Draft.

2001-02	Antoine-Girouard	QAAA	41	21	21	42	14	....	....	....	....	....	....	....	....	....	15	8	9	17	6	....	....	....	
2002-03	Montreal Rocket	QMJHL	66	15	14	29	10	....	....	....	....	....	....	....	....	....	6	3	0	3	2	....	....	....	
2003-04	P.E.I. Rocket	QMJHL	70	21	22	43	51	....	....	....	....	....	....	....	....	....	11	1	3	4	6	....	....	....	
2004-05	P.E.I. Rocket	QMJHL	41	23	13	36	36	....	....	....	....	....	....	....	....	....	....	....	....	....	....	....	....	....	
2005-06	P.E.I. Rocket	QMJHL	34	12	11	23	41	....	....	....	....	....	....	....	....	....	6	3	1	4	6	....	....	....	
2006-07	P.E.I. Rocket	QMJHL	68	50	48	98	86	....	....	....	....	....	....	....	....	....	7	5	4	9	4	....	....	....	
2007-08	Philadelphia	AHL	27	3	6	9	13	....	....	....	....	....	....	....	....	....	....	....	....	....	....	....	....	....	
	Wheeling Nailers	ECHL	27	10	14	24	16	....	....	....	....	....	....	....	....	....	....	....	....	....	....	....	....	....	
2008-09	Philadelphia	AHL	70	28	20	48	43	....	....	....	....	....	....	....	....	....	4	0	1	1	4	....	....	....	
2009-10	**Philadelphia**	**NHL**	11	2	1	3	6	0	0	1	8	25.0	1	1	100.0	7:47	1	0	0	0	2	0	0	0	5:3
	Adirondack	AHL	66	18	28	46	39	....	....	....	....	....	....	....	....	....	....	....	....	....	....	....	....	....	
	NHL Totals		11	2	1	3	6	0	0	1	8	25.0		1	100.0	7:47	1	0	0	0	2	0	0	0	5:3

LAMPMAN, Bryce

(LAMP-man, BRIGHS)

Defense. Shoots left. 6'1", 205 lbs. Born, Rochester, MN, August 31, 1982. NY Rangers' 4th choice, 113th overall, in 2001 Entry Draft.

1998-99	Rochester	USHL	53	3	8	11	33	....	....	....	....	....	....	....	....	....	....	....	....	....	....	....	....	....	
99-2000	Rochester	USHL	10	0	0	0	14	....	....	....	....	....	....	....	....	....	....	....	....	....	....	....	....	....	
	Omaha Lancers	USHL	11	1	2	3	38	....	....	....	....	....	....	....	....	....	4	0	0	0	0	....	....	....	
2000-01	Omaha Lancers	USHL	55	10	11	21	77	....	....	....	....	....	....	....	....	....	12	1	4	5	12	....	....	....	
2001-02	Nebraska-Omaha	CCHA	26	0	4	4	28	....	....	....	....	....	....	....	....	....	....	....	....	....	....	....	....	....	
2002-03	Kamloops Blazers	WHL	29	1	17	18	32	....	....	....	....	....	....	....	....	....	....	....	....	....	....	....	....	....	
	Hartford	AHL	45	0	6	6	32	....	....	....	....	....	....	....	....	....	2	0	1	1	0	....	....	....	
2003-04	**NY Rangers**	**NHL**	8	0	0	0	0	0	0	0	7	0.0	–4	0	0.0	19:34	....	....	....	....	....	....	....	....	
	Hartford	AHL	68	4	11	15	50	....	....	....	....	....	....	....	....	....	16	1	3	4	14	....	....	....	
2004-05	Hartford	AHL	74	7	18	25	74	....	....	....	....	....	....	....	....	....	4	0	0	0	4	....	....	....	
2005-06	**NY Rangers**	**NHL**	1	0	0	0	2	0	0	0	1	0.0	–1	0	0.0	13:40	....	....	....	....	....	....	....	....	
	Hartford	AHL	11	2	3	5	16	....	....	....	....	....	....	....	....	....	....	....	....	....	....	....	....	....	
2006-07	**NY Rangers**	**NHL**	1	0	0	0	0	0	0	0	0	0.0	0	0	0.0	12:08	....	....	....	....	....	....	....	....	
	Hartford	AHL	60	6	19	25	62	....	....	....	....	....	....	....	....	....	7	2	0	2	2	....	....	....	
2007-08	Norfolk Admirals	AHL	16	3	3	6	4	....	....	....	....	....	....	....	....	....	....	....	....	....	....	....	....	....	
	Iowa Stars	AHL	53	4	11	15	32	....	....	....	....	....	....	....	....	....	....	....	....	....	....	....	....	....	
2008-09	Amur Khabarovsk	Rus-KHL	9	0	0	0	4	....	....	....	....	....	....	....	....	....	....	....	....	....	....	....	....	....	
2009-10	Peoria Rivermen	AHL	54	7	13	20	22	....	....	....	....	....	....	....	....	....	....	....	....	....	....	....	....	....	
	NHL Totals		10	0	0	0	2	0	0	0	8	0.0		0	0.0	18:14	....	....	....	....	....	....	....	....	

• Left **University of Nebraska-Omaha** (CCHA) and signed as a free agent by **Kamloops** (WHL), August 1, 2002. • Missed majority of 2005-06 season recovering from shoulder injury. • Rights traded to **Tampa Bay** by **NY Rangers** for the rights to Mitch Fritz, July 4, 2007. Traded to **Dallas** by **Tampa Bay** for Mario Scalzo, November 19, 2007. Signed as a free agent by **Khabarovsk** (Russia-KHL), June 7, 2008. • Missed majority of 2008-09 season recovering from various injuries. Signed as a free agent by **St. Louis** July 29, 2009.

LANG, Robert

(LANG, RAW-buhrt)

Center. Shoots right. 6'3", 217 lbs. Born, Teplice, Czech., December 19, 1970. Los Angeles' 6th choice, 133rd overall, in 1990 Entry Draft.

1988-89	CHZ Litvinov	Czech	7	3	2	5	0	....	....	....	....	....	....	....	....	....	....	....	....	....	....	....	....	....	
1989-90	CHZ Litvinov	Czech	32	8	7	15	....	....	....	....	....	....	....	....	....	....	8	3	3	6	....	....	....	....	
1990-91	HC CHZ Litvinov	Czech	56	26	26	52	38	....	....	....	....	....	....	....	....	....	....	....	....	....	....	....	....	....	
1991-92	Litvinov	Czech	43	12	31	43	34	....	....	....	....	....	....	....	....	....	....	....	....	....	....	....	....	....	
	Czechoslovakia	Olympics	8	5	8	13	8	....	....	....	....	....	....	....	....	....	....	....	....	....	....	....	....	....	
1992-93	**Los Angeles**	**NHL**	11	0	5	5	2	0	0	0	3	0.0	–3	....	....	....	....	....	....	....	....	....	....	....	
	Phoenix	IHL	38	9	21	30	20	....	....	....	....	....	....	....	....	....	....	....	....	....	....	....	....	....	

Season	Club	League	GP	G	A	Pts	PIM	PP	SH	GW	S	%	+/-	TF	F%	Min	GP	G	A	Pts	PIM	PP	SH	GW	Min
			Regular Season														Playoffs								
1993-94	Los Angeles	NHL	32	9	10	19	10	0	0	0	41	22.0	7												
	Phoenix	IHL	44	11	24	35	34																		
1994-95	Litvinov	CzRep	16	4	19	23	28																		
	Los Angeles	NHL	36	4	8	12	4	0	0	0	38	10.5	–7												
1995-96	Los Angeles	NHL	68	6	16	22	10	0	2	0	71	8.5	–15												
1996-97	HC Sparta Praha	CzRep	38	14	27	41	30										5	1	2	3	4				
	HC Sparta Praha	EuroHL	4	2	2	4	0										4	2	1	3	2				
1997-98	Boston	NHL	3	0	0	0	2	0	0	0	2	0.0	1												
	Pittsburgh	NHL	51	9	13	22	14	1	1	2	64	14.1	6				6	0	3	3	2	0	0	0	
	Czech Republic	Olympics	6	0	3	3	0																		
	Houston Aeros	IHL	9	1	7	8	4																		
1998-99	Pittsburgh	NHL	72	21	23	44	24	7	0	3	137	15.3	–10	964	44.8	16:24	12	0	2	2	0	0	0	0	13:58
99-2000	Pittsburgh	NHL	78	23	42	65	14	13	0	5	142	16.2	–9	1433	50.7	19:22	11	3	3	6	0	2	0	0	21:42
2000-01	Pittsburgh	NHL	82	32	48	80	28	10	0	2	177	18.1	20	1348	43.9	20:24	16	4	4	8	4	0	0	0	19:21
2001-02	Pittsburgh	NHL	62	18	32	50	16	5	1	3	175	10.3	9	1172	46.3	22:56									
	Czech Republic	Olympics	4	1	2	3	2																		
2002-03	Washington	NHL	82	22	47	69	22	10	0	2	146	15.1	12	1069	45.9	18:47	6	2	1	3	2	0	0	1	21:55
2003-04	Washington	NHL	63	29	45	74	24	10	0	2	149	19.5	2	744	44.1	21:46									
	Detroit	NHL	6	1	4	5	0	0	0	1	14	7.1	2	96	57.3	16:20	12	4	5	9	6	0	0	0	18:10
2004-05		DID NOT PLAY																							
2005-06	Detroit	NHL	72	20	42	62	72	8	0	3	171	11.7	17	861	50.3	16:15	6	3	3	6	2	2	0	0	19:12
	Czech Republic	Olympics	8	0	4	4	4																		
2006-07	Detroit	NHL	81	19	33	52	66	6	0	4	166	11.4	12	812	49.4	16:49	18	2	6	8	8	0	0	0	15:10
2007-08	Chicago	NHL	76	21	33	54	50	7	0	3	172	12.2	9	1117	53.1	18:25									
2008-09	Montreal	NHL	50	18	21	39	36	8	1	3	101	17.8	6	768	48.8	16:53									
2009-10	Phoenix	NHL	64	9	20	29	28	3	0	1	84	10.7	–4	734	51.1	15:05	4	0	1	1	0	0	0	0	9:03
	NHL Totals		989	261	442	703	422	88	5	34	1853	14.1		11118	48.1	18:27	91	18	28	46	24	4	0	1	17:32

ayed in NHL All-Star Game (2004)

gned as a free agent by **Pittsburgh**, September 2, 1997. Claimed by **Boston** from **Pittsburgh** in Waiver Draft, September 28, 1997. Claimed on waivers by **Pittsburgh** from **Boston**, October 25, 1997. gned as a free agent by **Washington**, July 1, 2002. Traded to **Detroit** by **Washington** for Tomas Fleischmann, Detroit's 1st round choice (Mike Green) in 2004 Entry Draft and Detroit's 4th round choice uke Lynes) in 2006 Entry Draft, February 27, 2004. Signed as a free agent by **Chicago**, July 2, 2007. Traded to **Montreal** by **Chicago** for Toronto's 2nd round choice (previously acquired, later traded back Toronto, later traded to Boston - Boston selected Jared Knight) in 2010 Entry Draft, September 12, 2008. Signed as a free agent by **Phoenix**, September 29, 2009.

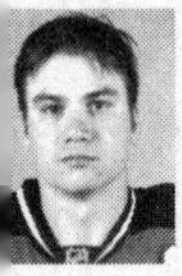

LANGENBRUNNER, Jamie

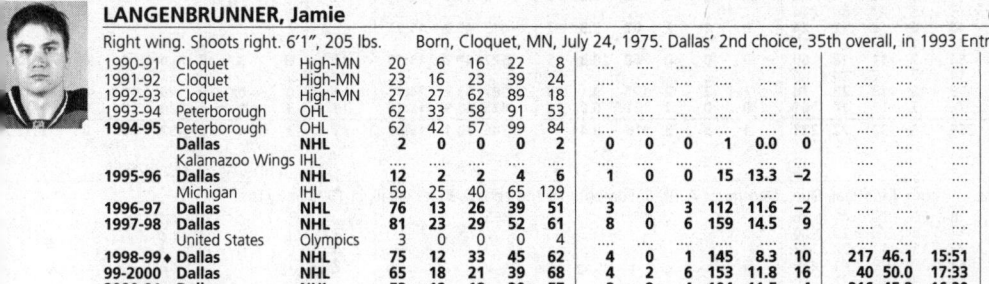

(lan-gehn-BRUH-nuhr, JAY-mee) **N.J.**

Right wing. Shoots right. 6'1", 205 lbs. Born, Cloquet, MN, July 24, 1975. Dallas' 2nd choice, 35th overall, in 1993 Entry Draft.

Season	Club	League	GP	G	A	Pts	PIM	PP	SH	GW	S	%	+/-	TF	F%	Min	GP	G	A	Pts	PIM	PP	SH	GW	Min
1990-91	Cloquet	High-MN	20	6	16	22	8																		
1991-92	Cloquet	High-MN	23	16	23	39	24																		
1992-93	Cloquet	High-MN	27	27	62	89	18																		
1993-94	Peterborough	OHL	62	33	58	91	53										7	4	6	10	2				
1994-95	Peterborough	OHL	62	42	57	99	84										11	8	14	22	12				
	Dallas	NHL	2	0	0	0	2	0	0	0	1	0.0	0												
	Kalamazoo Wings	IHL															11	1	3	4	2				
1995-96	Dallas	NHL	12	2	2	4	6	1	0	0	15	13.3	–2												
	Michigan	IHL	59	25	40	65	129										10	3	10	13	8				
1996-97	Dallas	NHL	76	13	26	39	51	3	0	3	112	11.6	–2				5	1	1	2	14	0	0	1	
1997-98	Dallas	NHL	81	23	29	52	61	8	0	6	159	14.5	9				16	1	4	5	14	0	0	1	
	United States	Olympics	3	0	0	0	4																		
1998-99♦	Dallas	NHL	75	12	33	45	62	4	0	1	145	8.3	10	217	46.1	15:51	23	10	7	17	16	*4	0	3	17:43
99-2000	Dallas	NHL	65	18	21	39	68	4	2	6	153	11.8	16	40	50.0	17:33	15	1	7	8	18	1	0	0	15:28
2000-01	Dallas	NHL	53	12	18	30	57	3	2	4	104	11.5	4	316	45.3	16:30	10	2	2	4	6	0	0	1	19:26
2001-02	Dallas	NHL	68	10	16	26	54	0	1	2	132	7.6	–11	120	45.0	15:45									
	New Jersey	NHL	14	3	3	6	23	0	0	2	31	9.7	2	2	50.0	15:27	5	0	1	1	8	0	0	0	14:57
2002-03♦	New Jersey	NHL	78	22	33	55	65	5	1	5	197	11.2	17	72	47.2	17:48	24	*11	7	*18	16	1	0	*4	17:34
2003-04	New Jersey	NHL	53	10	16	26	43	1	2	2	130	7.7	9	31	51.6	16:01	5	0	2	2	2	0	0	0	15:04
2004-05	ERC Ingolstadt	Germany	11	2	2	4	22										11	1	6	7	6				
2005-06	New Jersey	NHL	80	19	34	53	74	8	1	1	243	7.8	–1	41	43.9	18:36	9	3	10	13	16	1	0	1	19:46
2006-07	New Jersey	NHL	82	23	37	60	64	12	0	7	243	9.5	–9	23	34.8	18:33	11	2	6	8	7	1	0	1	19:16
2007-08	New Jersey	NHL	64	13	28	41	30	5	1	2	152	8.6	–1	18	55.6	18:18	5	0	4	4	4	0	0	0	18:30
2008-09	New Jersey	NHL	81	29	40	69	56	6	3	7	229	12.7	25	25	40.0	18:06	4	2	1	3	2	0	0	0	16:13
2009-10	New Jersey	NHL	81	19	42	61	44	6	2	4	228	8.3	6	60	48.3	19:33	5	0	1	1	4	0	0	0	18:38
	United States	Olympics	6	1	3	4	0																		
	NHL Totals		965	228	378	606	760	66	15	52	2274	10.0		965	45.9	17:35	137	33	53	86	127	8	0	12	17:38

raded to **New Jersey** by **Dallas** with Joe Nieuwendyk for Jason Arnott, Randy McKay and New Jersey's 1st round choice (later traded to Columbus, later traded to Buffalo – Buffalo selected Daniel Paille) in 002 Entry Draft, March 19, 2002. Signed as a free agent by **Ingolstadt** (Germany), January 24, 2005.

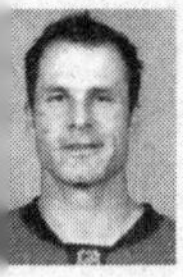

LANGKOW, Daymond

(LANG-kow, DAY-muhn) **CGY.**

Center. Shoots left. 5'10", 183 lbs. Born, Edmonton, Alta., September 27, 1976. Tampa Bay's 1st choice, 5th overall, in 1995 Entry Draft.

Season	Club	League	GP	G	A	Pts	PIM	PP	SH	GW	S	%	+/-	TF	F%	Min	GP	G	A	Pts	PIM	PP	SH	GW	Min
1991-92	Edmonton Pats	AMHL	35	36	45	81	100																		
	Tri-City	WHL	1	0	0	0	0																		
1992-93	Tri-City	WHL	64	22	42	64	100										4	1	0	1	4				
1993-94	Tri-City	WHL	61	40	43	83	174										4	2	2	4	15				
1994-95	Tri-City	WHL	72	*67	73	*140	142										17	12	15	27	52				
1995-96	Tri-City	WHL	48	30	61	91	103										11	14	13	27	20				
	Tampa Bay	NHL	4	0	1	1	0	0	0	0	4	0.0	–1												
1996-97	Tampa Bay	NHL	79	15	13	28	35	3	1	1	170	8.8	1												
	Adirondack	AHL	2	1	1	2	0																		
1997-98	Tampa Bay	NHL	68	8	14	22	62	2	0	1	156	5.1	–9												
1998-99	Tampa Bay	NHL	22	4	6	10	15	1	0	1	40	10.0	0	399	48.4	17:10									
	Cleveland	IHL	4	1	1	2	18																		
	Philadelphia	NHL	56	10	13	23	24	3	1	1	109	9.2	–8	738	48.0	15:12	6	0	2	2	2	0	0	0	16:50
99-2000	Philadelphia	NHL	82	18	32	50	56	5	0	7	222	8.1	1	1263	45.1	16:57	16	5	5	10	23	1	1	2	20:03
2000-01	Philadelphia	NHL	71	13	41	54	50	3	0	2	190	6.8	12	1181	47.2	18:38	6	2	4	6	2	1	0	0	20:17
2001-02	Phoenix	NHL	80	27	35	62	36	6	3	2	171	15.8	18	1379	46.2	19:11	5	1	0	1	0	0	0	0	21:06
2002-03	Phoenix	NHL	82	20	32	52	56	4	2	2	196	10.2	20	1972	46.5	21:00									
2003-04	Phoenix	NHL	81	21	31	52	40	4	1	2	174	12.1	4	1472	43.1	21:07									
2004-05		DID NOT PLAY																							
2005-06	Calgary	NHL	82	25	34	59	46	11	0	7	171	14.6	2	1130	47.4	18:07	7	1	5	6	6	1	0	0	19:42
2006-07	Calgary	NHL	81	33	44	77	44	10	1	6	247	13.4	23	1173	45.9	20:07	6	2	2	4	4	2	0	1	20:06
2007-08	Calgary	NHL	80	30	35	65	19	14	1	4	201	14.9	16	817	43.7	18:50	7	3	2	5	0	2	0	0	18:21
2008-09	Calgary	NHL	73	21	28	49	20	4	0	3	161	13.0	1	753	46.9	17:11	6	0	3	3	2	0	0	0	17:06
2009-10	Calgary	NHL	72	14	23	37	30	1	1	2	126	11.1	2	1130	43.5	18:55									
	NHL Totals		1013	259	382	641	533	71	11	41	2338	11.1		13407	45.8	18:44	59	14	23	37	39	7	1	3	19:18

/HL West First All-Star Team (1995) • Canadian Major Junior First All-Star Team (1995) • WHL West Second All-Star Team (1996)

raded to **Philadelphia** by **Tampa Bay** with Mikael Renberg for Chris Gratton and Mike Sillinger, December 12, 1998. Traded to **Phoenix** by **Philadelphia** for Phoenix's 2nd round choice (later traded to ampa Bay, later traded to San Jose – San Jose selected Dan Spang) in 2002 Entry Draft and Phoenix's 1st round choice (Jeff Carter) in 2003 Entry Draft, July 2, 2001. Traded to **Calgary** by **Phoenix** for enis Gauthier and Oleg Saprykin, August 26, 2004.

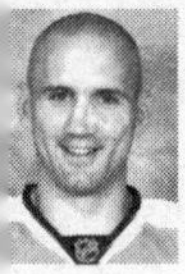

LAPERRIERE, Ian

(luh-PAIR-ee-YAIR, EE-an) **PHI.**

Right wing. Shoots right. 6'1", 200 lbs. Born, Montreal, Que., January 19, 1974. St. Louis' 6th choice, 158th overall, in 1992 Entry Draft.

Season	Club	League	GP	G	A	Pts	PIM	PP	SH	GW	S	%	+/-	TF	F%	Min	GP	G	A	Pts	PIM	PP	SH	GW	Min
1989-90	Mtl-Bourassa	QAAA	22	4	10	14	10										3	0	1	1	6				
1990-91	Drummondville	QMJHL	65	19	29	48	117										14	2	9	11	48				
1991-92	Drummondville	QMJHL	70	28	49	77	160										4	2	2	4	9				
1992-93	Drummondville	QMJHL	60	44	*96	140	188										10	6	13	19	20				
1993-94	Drummondville	QMJHL	62	41	72	113	150										9	4	6	10	35				
	St. Louis	NHL	1	0	0	0	0	0	0	0	1	0.0	0												
	Peoria Rivermen	IHL															5	1	3	4	2				
1994-95	Peoria Rivermen	IHL	51	16	32	48	111																		
	St. Louis	NHL	37	13	14	27	85	1	0	1	53	24.5	12				7	0	4	4	21	0	0	0	

Season	Club	League	GP	G	A	Pts	PIM	PP	SH	GW	S	%	+/-	TF	F%	Min	GP	G	A	Pts	PIM	PP	SH	GW	Min
			Regular Season														Playoffs								
1995-96	**St. Louis**	**NHL**	**33**	**3**	**6**	**9**	**87**	**1**	**0**	**1**	**31**	**9.7**	**–4**												
	Worcester IceCats	AHL	3	2	1	3	22																		
	NY Rangers	**NHL**	**28**	**1**	**2**	**3**	**53**	**0**	**0**	**0**	**21**	**4.8**	**–5**												
	Los Angeles	**NHL**	**10**	**2**	**3**	**5**	**15**	**0**	**0**	**0**	**18**	**11.1**	**–2**												
1996-97	**Los Angeles**	**NHL**	**62**	**8**	**15**	**23**	**102**	**0**	**1**	**2**	**84**	**9.5**	**–25**												
1997-98	**Los Angeles**	**NHL**	**77**	**6**	**15**	**21**	**131**	**0**	**1**	**1**	**74**	**8.1**	**0**				**4**	**1**	**0**	**1**	**6**	**0**	**0**	**0**	
1998-99	**Los Angeles**	**NHL**	**72**	**3**	**10**	**13**	**138**	**0**	**0**	**1**	**62**	**4.8**	**–5**	**643**	**47.3**	**11:47**									
99-2000	**Los Angeles**	**NHL**	**79**	**9**	**13**	**22**	**185**	**0**	**0**	**1**	**87**	**10.3**	**–14**	**1111**	**53.7**	**13:15**	**4**	**0**	**0**	**0**	**2**	**0**	**0**	**0**	**10:2**
2000-01	**Los Angeles**	**NHL**	**79**	**8**	**10**	**18**	**141**	**0**	**0**	**0**	**60**	**13.3**	**5**	**297**	**51.9**	**12:02**	**13**	**1**	**2**	**3**	**12**	**0**	**0**	**0**	**14:0**
2001-02	**Los Angeles**	**NHL**	**81**	**8**	**14**	**22**	**125**	**0**	**0**	**3**	**89**	**9.0**	**5**	**134**	**49.3**	**13:45**	**7**	**0**	**1**	**1**	**9**	**0**	**0**	**0**	**14:1**
2002-03	**Los Angeles**	**NHL**	**73**	**7**	**12**	**19**	**122**	**1**	**1**	**1**	**85**	**8.2**	**–9**	**317**	**49.2**	**15:46**									
2003-04	**Los Angeles**	**NHL**	**62**	**10**	**12**	**22**	**58**	**1**	**0**	**3**	**59**	**16.9**	**–4**	**446**	**54.0**	**15:50**									
2004-05		DID NOT PLAY																							
2005-06	**Colorado**	**NHL**	**82**	**21**	**24**	**45**	**116**	**1**	**1**	**3**	**133**	**15.8**	**3**	**963**	**45.9**	**17:10**	**9**	**0**	**1**	**1**	**27**	**0**	**0**	**0**	**13:4**
2006-07	**Colorado**	**NHL**	**81**	**8**	**21**	**29**	**133**	**0**	**0**	**0**	**118**	**6.8**	**5**	**389**	**46.8**	**13:51**									
2007-08	**Colorado**	**NHL**	**70**	**4**	**15**	**19**	**140**	**0**	**0**	**1**	**68**	**5.9**	**–5**	**141**	**45.4**	**13:39**	**10**	**1**	**1**	**2**	**19**	**0**	**0**	**0**	**12:5**
2008-09	**Colorado**	**NHL**	**74**	**7**	**12**	**19**	**163**	**0**	**0**	**0**	**61**	**11.5**	**0**	**446**	**44.0**	**13:50**									
2009-10	**Philadelphia**	**NHL**	**82**	**3**	**17**	**20**	**162**	**0**	**0**	**0**	**53**	**5.7**	**–1**	**66**	**42.4**	**12:30**	**13**	**0**	**1**	**1**	**6**	**0**	**0**	**0**	**9:3**
	NHL Totals		**1083**	**121**	**215**	**336**	**1956**	**5**	**4**	**18**	**1157**	**10.5**		**4953**	**49.0**	**13:55**	**67**	**3**	**10**	**13**	**102**	**0**	**0**	**0**	**12:2**

QMJHL Second All-Star Team (1993)

Traded to **NY Rangers** by **St. Louis** for Stephane Matteau, December 28, 1995. Traded to **Los Angeles** by **NY Rangers** with Ray Ferraro, Mattias Norstrom, Nathan LaFayette and NY Rangers' 4th round choice (Sean Blanchard) in 1997 Entry Draft for Marty McSorley, Jari Kurri and Shane Churla, March 14, 1996. Signed as a free agent by **Colorado**, July 2, 2004. Signed as a free agent by **Philadelphia**, Jul 1, 2009.

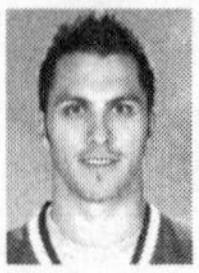

LAPIERRE, Maxim

(la-PEE-air, max-EEM) **MTL**

Center. Shoots right. 6'2", 207 lbs. Born, St. Leonard, Que., March 29, 1985. Montreal's 3rd choice, 61st overall, in 2003 Entry Draft.

Season	Club	League	GP	G	A	Pts	PIM	PP	SH	GW	S	%	+/-	TF	F%	Min	GP	G	A	Pts	PIM	PP	SH	GW	Min
2001-02	Cap-d-Madeleine	QAAA	42	14	27	41	44										10	3	5	8	16				
	Montreal Rocket	QMJHL	9	2	0	2	2																		
2002-03	Montreal Rocket	QMJHL	72	22	21	43	55										7	1	3	4	6				
2003-04	P.E.I. Rocket	QMJHL	67	25	36	61	138										11	7	2	9	14				
2004-05	P.E.I. Rocket	QMJHL	69	25	27	52	139																		
2005-06	**Montreal**	**NHL**	**1**	**0**	**0**	**0**	**0**	**0**	**0**	**0**	**0**	**0.0**	**–1**	**2**	**50.0**	**3:04**									
	Hamilton	AHL	73	13	23	36	214																		
2006-07	**Montreal**	**NHL**	**46**	**6**	**6**	**12**	**24**	**0**	**1**	**2**	**82**	**7.3**	**–7**	**425**	**45.2**	**11:25**									
	Hamilton	AHL	37	11	13	24	59										22	6	6	12	41				
2007-08	**Montreal**	**NHL**	**53**	**7**	**11**	**18**	**60**	**0**	**0**	**0**	**68**	**10.3**	**5**	**527**	**49.2**	**13:10**	**12**	**0**	**3**	**3**	**6**	**0**	**0**	**0**	**11:3**
	Hamilton	AHL	19	7	7	14	63																		
2008-09	**Montreal**	**NHL**	**79**	**15**	**13**	**28**	**76**	**1**	**2**	**2**	**165**	**9.1**	**9**	**987**	**53.2**	**14:48**	**4**	**0**	**0**	**0**	**26**	**0**	**0**	**0**	**14:5**
2009-10	**Montreal**	**NHL**	**76**	**7**	**7**	**14**	**61**	**0**	**0**	**1**	**101**	**6.9**	**–14**	**425**	**48.9**	**12:16**	**19**	**3**	**1**	**4**	**20**	**0**	**0**	**1**	**12:2**
	NHL Totals		**255**	**35**	**37**	**72**	**221**	**1**	**3**	**5**	**416**	**8.4**		**2366**	**50.1**	**13:03**	**35**	**3**	**4**	**7**	**52**	**0**	**0**	**1**	**12:2**

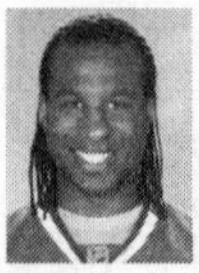

LARAQUE, Georges

(luh-RAK, ZHAWRZH)

Right wing. Shoots right. 6'3", 253 lbs. Born, Montreal, Que., December 7, 1976. Edmonton's 2nd choice, 31st overall, in 1995 Entry Draft.

Season	Club	League	GP	G	A	Pts	PIM	PP	SH	GW	S	%	+/-	TF	F%	Min	GP	G	A	Pts	PIM	PP	SH	GW	Min
1991-92	Mtl-Bourassa	QAHA	28	20	20	40	30																		
1992-93	Mtl-Bourassa	QAAA	37	8	20	28	50										3	1	2	3	2				
1993-94	St-Jean Lynx	QMJHL	70	11	11	22	142										4	0	0	0	7				
1994-95	St-Jean Lynx	QMJHL	62	19	22	41	259										7	1	1	2	42				
1995-96	Laval Titan	QMJHL	11	8	13	21	76																		
	St-Hyacinthe	QMJHL	8	3	4	7	59																		
	Granby	QMJHL	22	9	7	16	125										18	7	6	13	104				
1996-97	Hamilton	AHL	73	14	20	34	179										15	1	3	4	12				
1997-98	**Edmonton**	**NHL**	**11**	**0**	**0**	**0**	**59**	**0**	**0**	**0**	**4**	**0.0**	**–4**												
	Hamilton	AHL	46	10	20	30	154										3	0	0	0	11				
1998-99	**Edmonton**	**NHL**	**39**	**3**	**2**	**5**	**57**	**0**	**0**	**0**	**17**	**17.6**	**–1**	**0**	**0.0**	**5:31**	**4**	**0**	**0**	**0**	**2**	**0**	**0**	**0**	**7:3**
	Hamilton	AHL	25	6	8	14	93																		
99-2000	**Edmonton**	**NHL**	**76**	**8**	**8**	**16**	**123**	**0**	**0**	**0**	**56**	**14.3**	**5**	**0**	**0.0**	**8:28**	**5**	**0**	**1**	**1**	**6**	**0**	**0**	**0**	**9:1**
2000-01	**Edmonton**	**NHL**	**82**	**13**	**16**	**29**	**148**	**1**	**0**	**1**	**73**	**17.8**	**5**	**0**	**0.0**	**9:03**	**6**	**1**	**1**	**2**	**8**	**0**	**0**	**0**	**9:5**
2001-02	**Edmonton**	**NHL**	**80**	**5**	**14**	**19**	**157**	**1**	**0**	**1**	**95**	**5.3**	**6**	**0**	**0.0**	**9:48**									
2002-03	**Edmonton**	**NHL**	**64**	**6**	**7**	**13**	**110**	**0**	**0**	**2**	**46**	**13.0**	**–4**	**0**	**0.0**	**9:15**	**6**	**1**	**3**	**4**	**4**	**0**	**0**	**0**	**12:1**
2003-04	**Edmonton**	**NHL**	**66**	**6**	**11**	**17**	**99**	**1**	**0**	**1**	**54**	**11.1**	**7**	**0**	**0.0**	**9:22**									
2004-05	AIK Solna	Sweden-3	16	11	5	16	24																		
2005-06	**Edmonton**	**NHL**	**72**	**2**	**10**	**12**	**73**	**0**	**0**	**0**	**50**	**4.0**	**–5**	**3**	**33.3**	**6:35**	**15**	**1**	**1**	**2**	***44**	**0**	**0**	**0**	**5:3**
2006-07	**Phoenix**	**NHL**	**56**	**5**	**17**	**22**	**52**	**1**	**0**	**0**	**34**	**14.7**	**7**	**14**	**28.6**	**10:17**									
	Pittsburgh	**NHL**	**17**	**0**	**2**	**2**	**18**	**0**	**0**	**0**	**10**	**0.0**	**–3**	**3**	**33.3**	**7:34**	**2**	**0**	**0**	**0**	**0**	**0**	**0**	**0**	**4:2**
2007-08	**Pittsburgh**	**NHL**	**71**	**4**	**9**	**13**	**141**	**0**	**0**	**2**	**29**	**13.8**	**0**	**1**	**0.0**	**7:42**	**15**	**1**	**2**	**3**	**4**	**0**	**0**	**0**	**6:0**
2008-09	**Montreal**	**NHL**	**33**	**0**	**2**	**2**	**61**	**0**	**0**	**0**	**15**	**0.0**	**–6**	**1**	**0.0**	**7:39**	**4**	**0**	**0**	**0**	**4**	**0**	**0**	**0**	**10:5**
2009-10	**Montreal**	**NHL**	**28**	**1**	**2**	**3**	**28**	**0**	**0**	**0**	**2**	**50.0**	**–6**	**0**	**0.0**	**5:46**									
	NHL Totals		**695**	**53**	**100**	**153**	**1126**	**4**	**0**	**7**	**485**	**10.9**		**22**	**27.3**	**8:23**	**57**	**4**	**8**	**12**	**72**	**0**	**0**	**0**	**7:3**

Signed as a free agent by **Solna** (Sweden-3), January 31, 2005. Signed as a free agent by **Phoenix**, July 5, 2006. Traded to **Pittsburgh** by **Phoenix** for Daniel Carcillo and Pittsburgh's 3rd round choice (later traded to NY Rangers - NY Rangers selected Tomas Kundratek) in 2008 Entry Draft, February 27, 2007. Signed as a free agent by **Montreal**, July 3, 2008. • Missed majority of 2008-09 season recovering from various injuries and as a healthy reserve.

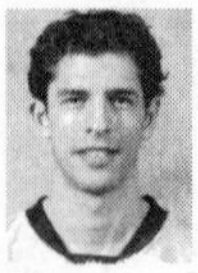

LARMAN, Drew

(LAHR-man, DROO)

Center. Shoots right. 6'3", 195 lbs. Born, Canton, MI, May 15, 1985.

Season	Club	League	GP	G	A	Pts	PIM	PP	SH	GW	S	%	+/-	TF	F%	Min	GP	G	A	Pts	PIM	PP	SH	GW	Min
2002-03	Sarnia Sting	OHL	67	4	14	18	25																		
2003-04	Sarnia Sting	OHL	68	9	18	27	13										5	0	1	1	0				
2004-05	Sarnia Sting	OHL	12	2	0	2	6																		
	London Knights	OHL	58	11	10	21	28										18	3	4	7	8				
2005-06	Rochester	AHL	44	7	8	15	24																		
	Florida Everblades	ECHL	6	0	0	0	4										8	4	2	6	4				
2006-07	**Florida**	**NHL**	**16**	**2**	**0**	**2**	**2**	**0**	**0**	**0**	**15**	**13.3**	**–3**	**97**	**46.4**	**7:23**									
	Rochester	AHL	54	17	11	28	35																		
2007-08	**Florida**	**NHL**	**6**	**0**	**1**	**1**	**2**	**0**	**0**	**0**	**1**	**0.0**	**1**	**26**	**38.5**	**6:00**									
	Rochester	AHL	54	10	12	22	44																		
2008-09	Rochester	AHL	61	10	13	23	40																		
2009-10	**Boston**	**NHL**	**4**	**0**	**0**	**0**	**0**	**0**	**0**	**0**	**5**	**0.0**	**–1**	**2**	**50.0**	**8:05**									
	Providence Bruins	AHL	55	6	6	12	26																		
	NHL Totals		**26**	**2**	**1**	**3**	**4**	**0**	**0**	**0**	**21**	**9.5**		**125**	**44.8**	**7:10**									

Signed as a free agent by **Florida**, September 28, 2005. Signed as a free agent by **Boston** July 13, 2009.

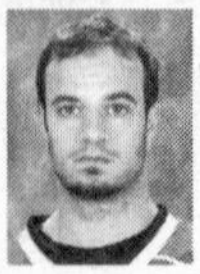

LaROSE, Chad

(lah-ROHZ, CHAD) **CAR**

Right wing. Shoots right. 5'10", 181 lbs. Born, Fraser, MI, March 27, 1982.

Season	Club	League	GP	G	A	Pts	PIM	PP	SH	GW	S	%	+/-	TF	F%	Min	GP	G	A	Pts	PIM	PP	SH	GW	Min
99-2000	Sioux Falls	USHL	54	29	26	55	28										3	0	1	1	0				
2000-01	Sioux Falls	USHL	24	11	22	33	50																		
	Plymouth Whalers	OHL	32	18	7	25	24										19	10	10	20	22				
2001-02	Plymouth Whalers	OHL	53	32	27	59	40										6	3	4	7	16				
2002-03	Plymouth Whalers	OHL	67	61	56	117	52										15	9	8	17	25				
2003-04	Lowell	AHL	36	7	9	16	29																		
	Florida Everblades	ECHL	41	16	19	35	16										14	3	4	7	20				
2004-05	Lowell	AHL	66	20	22	42	32										11	3	5	8	10				
2005-06♦	**Carolina**	**NHL**	**49**	**1**	**12**	**13**	**35**	**0**	**0**	**1**	**62**	**1.6**	**7**	**5**	**40.0**	**10:35**	**21**	**0**	**1**	**1**	**10**	**0**	**0**	**0**	**8:5**
	Lowell	AHL	23	14	11	25	10																		
2006-07	**Carolina**	**NHL**	**80**	**6**	**12**	**18**	**10**	**0**	**2**	**0**	**94**	**6.4**	**–2**	**50**	**30.0**	**10:13**									
2007-08	**Carolina**	**NHL**	**58**	**11**	**12**	**23**	**46**	**0**	**1**	**2**	**117**	**9.4**	**6**	**19**	**31.6**	**14:03**									

			Regular Season														Playoffs								
Season	Club	League	GP	G	A	Pts	PIM	PP	SH	GW	S	%	+/-	TF	F%	Min	GP	G	A	Pts	PIM	PP	SH	GW	Min
2008-09	**Carolina**	**NHL**	**81**	**19**	**12**	**31**	**35**	**0**	**2**	**4**	**171**	**11.1**	**6**	**18**	**27.8**	**15:08**	**18**	**4**	**7**	**11**	**16**	**0**	**0**	**0**	**17:48**
2009-10	**Carolina**	**NHL**	**56**	**11**	**17**	**28**	**24**	**0**	**1**	**0**	**138**	**8.0**	**–2**	**12**	**16.7**	**15:42**	....	....	....	....	....	....	....	....	....
	NHL Totals		**324**	**48**	**65**	**113**	**150**	**0**	**6**	**7**	**582**	**8.2**		**104**	**28.8**	**13:08**	**39**	**4**	**8**	**12**	**26**	**0**	**0**	**0**	**13:02**

HL Second All-Star Team (2003)

igned as a free agent by **Carolina**, August 6, 2003.

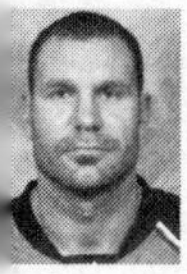

LARSEN, Brad

(LAR-suhn, BRAD)

Left wing. Shoots left. 6', 210 lbs. Born, Nakusp, B.C., June 28, 1977. Colorado's 5th choice, 87th overall, in 1997 Entry Draft.

Season	Club	League	GP	G	A	Pts	PIM	PP	SH	GW	S	%	+/-	TF	F%	Min	GP	G	A	Pts	PIM	PP	SH	GW	Min
1992-93	Nelson	RMJHL	42	31	37	68	164	....	....	....	....	....	....	....	....	....	....	....	....	....	....	....	....	....	....
1993-94	Swift Current	WHL	64	15	18	33	32	....	....	....	....	....	....	....	....	....	7	1	2	3	4	....	....	....	....
1994-95	Swift Current	WHL	62	24	33	57	73	....	....	....	....	....	....	....	....	....	6	0	1	1	2	....	....	....	....
1995-96	Swift Current	WHL	51	30	47	77	67	....	....	....	....	....	....	....	....	....	6	3	2	5	13	....	....	....	....
1996-97	Swift Current	WHL	61	36	46	82	61	....	....	....	....	....	....	....	....	....	....	....	....	....	....	....	....	....	....
1997-98	**Colorado**	**NHL**	**1**	**0**	**0**	**0**	**0**	**0**	**0**	**0**	**0**	**0.0**	**0**	....	....	....	....	....	....	....	....	....	....	....	....
	Hershey Bears	AHL	65	12	10	22	80	....	....	....	....	....	....	....	....	....	7	3	2	5	2	....	....	....	....
1998-99	Hershey Bears	AHL	18	3	4	7	11	....	....	....	....	....	....	....	....	....	5	0	1	1	6	....	....	....	....
99-2000	Hershey Bears	AHL	52	13	26	39	66	....	....	....	....	....	....	....	....	....	14	5	2	7	29	....	....	....	....
2000-01	**Colorado**	**NHL**	**9**	**0**	**0**	**0**	**0**	**0**	**0**	**0**	**3**	**0.0**	**1**	**14**	**57.1**	**9:17**	....	....	....	....	....	....	....	....	....
	Hershey Bears	AHL	67	21	25	46	93	....	....	....	....	....	....	....	....	....	10	1	3	4	6	....	....	....	....
2001-02	**Colorado**	**NHL**	**50**	**2**	**7**	**9**	**47**	**1**	**0**	**0**	**38**	**5.3**	**4**	**71**	**54.9**	**8:07**	**21**	**1**	**1**	**2**	**13**	**0**	**0**	**0**	**7:07**
2002-03	**Colorado**	**NHL**	**6**	**0**	**3**	**3**	**2**	**0**	**0**	**0**	**6**	**0.0**	**3**	**31**	**41.9**	**8:17**	....	....	....	....	....	....	....	....	....
	Hershey Bears	AHL	25	3	6	9	25	....	....	....	....	....	....	....	....	....	4	1	1	2	8	....	....	....	....
2003-04	**Colorado**	**NHL**	**26**	**2**	**2**	**4**	**11**	**0**	**0**	**0**	**17**	**11.8**	**2**	**9**	**44.4**	**7:41**	....	....	....	....	....	....	....	....	....
	Hershey Bears	AHL	21	4	13	17	40	....	....	....	....	....	....	....	....	....	....	....	....	....	....	....	....	....	....
	Atlanta	**NHL**	**6**	**0**	**0**	**0**	**2**	**0**	**0**	**0**	**6**	**0.0**	**–2**	**6**	**66.7**	**13:39**	....	....	....	....	....	....	....	....	....
2004-05	Chicago Wolves	AHL	75	26	23	49	112	....	....	....	....	....	....	....	....	....	18	4	7	11	22	....	....	....	....
2005-06	**Atlanta**	**NHL**	**62**	**7**	**8**	**15**	**21**	**0**	**3**	**1**	**48**	**14.6**	**–3**	**81**	**34.6**	**10:59**	....	....	....	....	....	....	....	....	....
	Chicago Wolves	AHL	6	1	0	1	8	....	....	....	....	....	....	....	....	....	....	....	....	....	....	....	....	....	....
2006-07	**Atlanta**	**NHL**	**72**	**7**	**6**	**13**	**39**	**0**	**2**	**0**	**61**	**11.5**	**–11**	**82**	**39.0**	**12:22**	**4**	**0**	**2**	**2**	**0**	**0**	**0**	**0**	**16:57**
2007-08	**Atlanta**	**NHL**	**62**	**1**	**3**	**4**	**12**	**0**	**0**	**0**	**35**	**2.9**	**–17**	**81**	**42.0**	**9:02**	....	....	....	....	....	....	....	....	....
2008-09	**Anaheim**	**NHL**	DID NOT PLAY – INJURED																						
2009-10	Portland Pirates	AHL	55	13	13	26	40	....	....	....	....	....	....	....	....	....	4	0	0	0	0	....	....	....	....
	NHL Totals		**294**	**19**	**29**	**48**	**134**	**1**	**5**	**1**	**214**	**8.9**		**375**	**43.2**	**10:05**	**25**	**1**	**3**	**4**	**13**	**0**	**0**	**0**	**8:41**

Re-entered NHL Entry Draft. Originally Ottawa's 3rd choice, 53rd overall, in 1995 Entry Draft.

VHL East Second All-Star Team (1997)

Rights traded to **Colorado** by **Ottawa** for Janne Laukkanen, January 26, 1996. • Missed majority of 1998-99 season recovering from abdominal injury suffered in game vs. Albany (AHL), November 20, 998. • Missed majority of 2002-03 season recovering from groin (October 27, 2002 vs. Minnesota) and back (December 11, 2002 vs. Vancouver) injuries. Claimed on waivers by **Atlanta** from **Colorado**, ebruary 25, 2004. Traded to **Anaheim** by **Atlanta** with Ken Klee and Chad Painchaud for Mathieu Schneider, September 26, 2008. • Missed entire 2008-09 season recovering from surgery to repair sports ernia injury, October 3, 2008. Signed as a free agent by **Portland** (AHL), September 12, 2009.

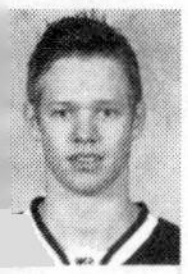

LARSEN, Philip

(LAHR-suhn, FIHL-ihp) **DAL.**

Defense. Shoots right. 6'1", 183 lbs. Born, Esbjerg, Denmark, December 7, 1989. Dallas' 3rd choice, 149th overall, in 2008 Entry Draft.

Season	Club	League	GP	G	A	Pts	PIM	PP	SH	GW	S	%	+/-	TF	F%	Min	GP	G	A	Pts	PIM	PP	SH	GW	Min
2004-05	Esbjerg IK Jr.	Den-Jr.	10	1	0	1	2	....	....	....	....	....	....	....	....	....	....	....	....	....	....	....	....	....	....
2005-06	Rogle Jr.	Swe-Jr.	32	1	4	5	24	....	....	....	....	....	....	....	....	....	....	....	....	....	....	....	....	....	....
	Rogle	Sweden-2	13	0	0	0	0	....	....	....	....	....	....	....	....	....	....	....	....	....	....	....	....	....	....
2006-07	Frolunda U18	Swe-U18	3	1	2	3	2	....	....	....	....	....	....	....	....	....	4	2	1	3	8	....	....	....	....
	Frolunda Jr.	Swe-Jr.	37	3	15	18	50	....	....	....	....	....	....	....	....	....	8	0	1	1	6	....	....	....	....
	Frolunda	Sweden	5	0	0	0	0	....	....	....	....	....	....	....	....	....	....	....	....	....	....	....	....	....	....
2007-08	Frolunda Jr.	Swe-Jr.	8	1	4	5	12	....	....	....	....	....	....	....	....	....	7	0	4	4	6	....	....	....	....
	Boras HC	Sweden-2	24	5	5	10	32	....	....	....	....	....	....	....	....	....	....	....	....	....	....	....	....	....	....
	Frolunda	Sweden	16	0	0	0	2	....	....	....	....	....	....	....	....	....	....	....	....	....	....	....	....	....	....
2008-09	Frolunda Jr.	Swe-Jr.	1	1	0	1	0	....	....	....	....	....	....	....	....	....	....	....	....	....	....	....	....	....	....
	Frolunda	Sweden	53	2	15	17	18	....	....	....	....	....	....	....	....	....	11	2	1	3	4	....	....	....	....
2009-10	**Dallas**	**NHL**	**2**	**0**	**1**	**1**	**0**	**0**	**0**	**0**	**1**	**0.0**	**1**	**0**	**0.0**	**12:27**	....	....	....	....	....	....	....	....	....
	Frolunda	Sweden	42	1	9	10	20	....	....	....	....	....	....	....	....	....	7	0	0	0	4	....	....	....	....
	NHL Totals		**2**	**0**	**1**	**1**	**0**	**0**	**0**	**0**	**1**	**0.0**		**0**	**0.0**	**12:27**	....	....	....	....	....	....	....	....	....

Assigned to **Frolunda** (Sweden) by **Dallas**, September 20. 2009.

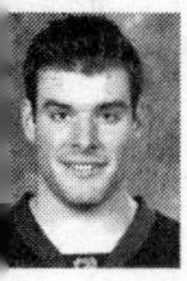

LASHOFF, Matt

(LASH-awf, MAT) **T.B.**

Defense. Shoots left. 6'2", 205 lbs. Born, Albany, NY, September 29, 1986. Boston's 1st choice, 22nd overall, in 2005 Entry Draft.

Season	Club	League	GP	G	A	Pts	PIM	PP	SH	GW	S	%	+/-	TF	F%	Min	GP	G	A	Pts	PIM	PP	SH	GW	Min
2002-03	USNTDP	U-17	16	1	3	4	14	....	....	....	....	....	....	....	....	....	....	....	....	....	....	....	....	....	....
	USNTDP	NAHL	46	2	5	7	53	....	....	....	....	....	....	....	....	....	....	....	....	....	....	....	....	....	....
2003-04	Kitchener Rangers	OHL	62	5	19	24	94	....	....	....	....	....	....	....	....	....	5	0	1	1	0	....	....	....	....
2004-05	Kitchener Rangers	OHL	44	4	18	22	44	....	....	....	....	....	....	....	....	....	13	0	3	3	18	....	....	....	....
2005-06	Kitchener Rangers	OHL	56	7	40	47	146	....	....	....	....	....	....	....	....	....	5	1	1	2	12	....	....	....	....
	Providence Bruins	AHL	7	1	1	2	6	....	....	....	....	....	....	....	....	....	6	0	0	0	6	....	....	....	....
2006-07	**Boston**	**NHL**	**12**	**0**	**2**	**2**	**12**	**0**	**0**	**0**	**8**	**0.0**	**–6**	**0**	**0.0**	**14:55**	....	....	....	....	....	....	....	....	....
	Providence Bruins	AHL	64	11	26	37	60	....	....	....	....	....	....	....	....	....	....	....	....	....	....	....	....	....	....
2007-08	**Boston**	**NHL**	**18**	**1**	**4**	**5**	**0**	**1**	**0**	**0**	**11**	**9.1**	**–2**	**0**	**0.0**	**13:35**	....	....	....	....	....	....	....	....	....
	Providence Bruins	AHL	60	9	27	36	79	....	....	....	....	....	....	....	....	....	9	0	4	4	6	....	....	....	....
2008-09	**Boston**	**NHL**	**16**	**0**	**1**	**1**	**10**	**0**	**0**	**0**	**6**	**0.0**	**1**	**0**	**0.0**	**13:07**	....	....	....	....	....	....	....	....	....
	Providence Bruins	AHL	33	5	16	21	36	....	....	....	....	....	....	....	....	....	....	....	....	....	....	....	....	....	....
	Tampa Bay	**NHL**	**12**	**0**	**7**	**7**	**10**	**0**	**0**	**0**	**19**	**0.0**	**–7**	**0**	**0.0**	**23:46**	....	....	....	....	....	....	....	....	....
	Norfolk Admirals	AHL	2	0	0	0	2	....	....	....	....	....	....	....	....	....	....	....	....	....	....	....	....	....	....
2009-10	**Tampa Bay**	**NHL**	**5**	**0**	**0**	**0**	**21**	**0**	**0**	**0**	**2**	**0.0**	**–2**	**0**	**0.0**	**8:53**	....	....	....	....	....	....	....	....	....
	Norfolk Admirals	AHL	68	8	16	24	105	....	....	....	....	....	....	....	....	....	....	....	....	....	....	....	....	....	....
	NHL Totals		**63**	**1**	**14**	**15**	**53**	**1**	**0**	**0**	**46**	**2.2**		**0**	**0.0**	**15:17**	....	....	....	....	....	....	....	....	....

HL All-Rookie Team (2007)

raded to **Tampa Bay** by **Boston** with Martins Karsums for Mark Recchi and Tampa Bay's 2nd round choice (later traded to Florida - Florida selected Alexander Petrovic) in 2010 Entry Draft, March 4, 2009.

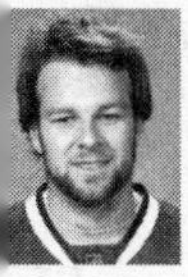

LATENDRESSE, Guillaume

(lah-TEHN-drehs, GEE-OHM) **MIN.**

Left wing. Shoots left. 6'2", 230 lbs. Born, Ste-Catherine, Que., May 24, 1987. Montreal's 2nd choice, 45th overall, in 2005 Entry Draft.

Season	Club	League	GP	G	A	Pts	PIM	PP	SH	GW	S	%	+/-	TF	F%	Min	GP	G	A	Pts	PIM	PP	SH	GW	Min
2003-04	Drummondville	QMJHL	53	24	25	49	66	....	....	....	....	....	....	....	....	....	....	....	....	....	....	....	....	....	....
2004-05	Drummondville	QMJHL	65	29	49	78	76	....	....	....	....	....	....	....	....	....	6	6	4	10	7	....	....	....	....
2005-06	Drummondville	QMJHL	51	43	40	83	105	....	....	....	....	....	....	....	....	....	5	3	2	5	8	....	....	....	....
2006-07	**Montreal**	**NHL**	**80**	**16**	**13**	**29**	**47**	**5**	**0**	**3**	**121**	**13.2**	**–20**	**16**	**12.5**	**12:36**	....	....	....	....	....	....	....	....	....
2007-08	**Montreal**	**NHL**	**73**	**16**	**11**	**27**	**41**	**2**	**0**	**3**	**116**	**13.8**	**–2**	**8**	**25.0**	**12:15**	**8**	**0**	**1**	**1**	**19**	**0**	**0**	**0**	**10:43**
2008-09	**Montreal**	**NHL**	**56**	**14**	**12**	**26**	**45**	**1**	**0**	**2**	**117**	**12.0**	**4**	**2**	**50.0**	**13:37**	**4**	**0**	**0**	**0**	**12**	**0**	**0**	**0**	**11:44**
2009-10	**Montreal**	**NHL**	**23**	**2**	**1**	**3**	**4**	**0**	**0**	**0**	**27**	**7.4**	**–4**	**0**	**0.0**	**11:21**	....	....	....	....	....	....	....	....	....
	Minnesota	**NHL**	**55**	**25**	**12**	**37**	**12**	**7**	**0**	**4**	**133**	**18.8**	**1**	**9**	**11.1**	**16:28**	....	....	....	....	....	....	....	....	....
	NHL Totals		**287**	**73**	**49**	**122**	**149**	**15**	**0**	**12**	**514**	**14.2**		**35**	**17.1**	**13:21**	**12**	**0**	**1**	**1**	**31**	**0**	**0**	**0**	**11:03**

raded to **Minnesota** by **Montreal** for Benoit Pouliot, November 23, 2009.

MJHL All-Rookie Team (2004)

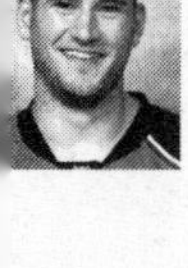

LaVALLEE, Jordan

(LA-VA-lee, JOHR-dahn)

Left wing. Shoots left. 6'3", 225 lbs. Born, Corvallis, OR, May 11, 1986. Atlanta's 5th choice, 116th overall, in 2005 Entry Draft.

Season	Club	League	GP	G	A	Pts	PIM	PP	SH	GW	S	%	+/-	TF	F%	Min	GP	G	A	Pts	PIM	PP	SH	GW	Min
2002-03	Quebec Remparts	QMJHL	55	3	6	9	54	....	....	....	....	....	....	....	....	....	11	0	1	1	0	....	....	....	....
2003-04	Quebec Remparts	QMJHL	69	11	16	27	111	....	....	....	....	....	....	....	....	....	5	2	0	2	6	....	....	....	....
2004-05	Quebec Remparts	QMJHL	64	40	26	66	108	....	....	....	....	....	....	....	....	....	13	5	2	7	26	....	....	....	....
2005-06	Quebec Remparts	QMJHL	37	18	19	37	34	....	....	....	....	....	....	....	....	....	23	7	8	15	30	....	....	....	....
2006-07	Chicago Wolves	AHL	79	16	18	34	90	....	....	....	....	....	....	....	....	....	14	7	1	8	8	....	....	....	....
2007-08	**Atlanta**	**NHL**	**2**	**1**	**1**	**2**	**0**	**0**	**0**	**0**	**1**	**100.0**	**2**	**0**	**0.0**	**11:28**	....	....	....	....	....	....	....	....	....
	Chicago Wolves	AHL	76	20	22	42	73	....	....	....	....	....	....	....	....	....	24	3	5	8	16	....	....	....	....

Season	Club	League	GP	G	A	Pts	PIM	PP	SH	GW	S	%	+/-	TF	F%	Min	GP	G	A	Pts	PIM	PP	SH	GW	Min
			Regular Season														Playoffs								
2008-09	**Atlanta**	**NHL**	**2**	**0**	**0**	**0**	**0**	**0**	**0**	**0**	**1**	**0.0**	**–1**	**0**	**0.0**	**6:40**									
	Chicago Wolves	AHL	64	19	12	31	94																		
2009-10	Syracuse Crunch	AHL	78	10	22	32	75																		
	NHL Totals		**4**	**1**	**1**	**2**	**0**	**0**	**0**	**0**	**2**	**50.0**		**0**	**0.0**	**9:04**									

Traded to **Columbus** by **Atlanta** for future considerations, October 8, 2009.

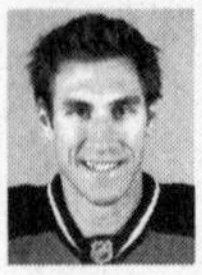

LEACH, Jay

(LEECH, JAY) **S.J.**

Defense. Shoots left. 6'4", 220 lbs. Born, Syracuse, NY, September 2, 1979. Phoenix's 5th choice, 115th overall, in 1998 Entry Draft.

Season	Club	League	GP	G	A	Pts	PIM	PP	SH	GW	S	%	+/-	TF	F%	Min	GP	G	A	Pts	PIM	PP	SH	GW	Min
1994-95	John Marshall	High-MN	10	0	0	0	14																		
1995-96	John Marshall	High-MN	11	1	2	3	8										4	0	0	0	0				
	Capital District	Exhib.	53	3	8	11	33																		
1996-97	Capital District	Exhib.	57	8	50	58	140																		
1997-98	Providence	H-East	32	0	8	8	29																		
1998-99	Providence	H-East	33	1	8	9	42																		
99-2000	Providence	H-East	37	1	9	10	101																		
2000-01	Providence	H-East	40	4	21	25	104																		
2001-02	Mississippi	ECHL	70	3	13	16	116										10	1	1	2	8				
2002-03	Springfield	AHL	9	0	0	0	0																		
	Augusta Lynx	ECHL	65	8	11	19	162																		
2003-04	Providence Bruins	AHL	3	0	0	0	4																		
	Long Beach	ECHL	3	0	1	1	4																		
	Bridgeport	AHL	23	0	1	1	33										7	0	1	1	10				
	Trenton Titans	ECHL	31	2	11	13	45																		
2004-05	Providence Bruins	AHL	62	4	5	9	92										17	0	0	0	28				
	Trenton Titans	ECHL	11	0	2	2	17																		
2005-06	**Boston**	**NHL**	**2**	**0**	**0**	**0**	**7**	**0**	**0**	**0**	**0**	**0.0**	**1**	**0**	**0.0**	**6:20**									
	Providence Bruins	AHL	72	5	11	16	100										6	0	1	1	15				
2006-07	Providence Bruins	AHL	73	2	5	7	128										13	0	4	4	13				
2007-08	**Tampa Bay**	**NHL**	**2**	**0**	**0**	**0**	**0**	**0**	**0**	**0**	**0**	**0.0**	**–1**	**0**	**0.0**	**4:37**									
	Norfolk Admirals	AHL	55	3	8	11	54																		
	Portland Pirates	AHL	20	3	6	9	30										18	1	0	1	7				
2008-09	**New Jersey**	**NHL**	**24**	**0**	**1**	**1**	**21**	**0**	**0**	**0**	**5**	**0.0**	**0**	**0**	**0.0**	**14:50**									
	Lowell Devils	AHL	24	2	4	6	29																		
2009-10	Lowell Devils	AHL	12	0	3	3	10																		
	Montreal	**NHL**	**7**	**0**	**0**	**0**	**5**	**0**	**0**	**0**	**4**	**0.0**	**0**	**0**	**0.0**	**13:02**									
	San Jose	**NHL**	**28**	**1**	**1**	**2**	**20**	**0**	**0**	**0**	**26**	**3.8**	**3**	**0**	**0.0**	**15:11**									
	NHL Totals		**63**	**1**	**2**	**3**	**53**	**0**	**0**	**0**	**35**	**2.9**		**0**	**0.0**	**14:12**									

Signed as a free agent by **Boston**, September 26, 2003. Signed as a free agent by **Tampa Bay**, July 3, 2007. Traded to **Anaheim** by **Tampa Bay** for Brandon Segal and Anaheim's 7th round choice (David Carle) in 2008 Entry Draft, February 26, 2008. Signed as a free agent by **New Jersey**, July 17, 2008. Claimed on waivers by **Montreal** from **New Jersey**, November 6, 2009. Claimed on waivers by **San Jose** from **Montreal**, December 1, 2009.

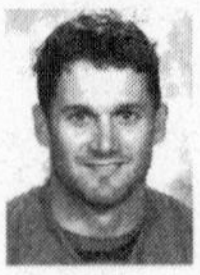

LEBDA, Brett

(LEHB-dah, BREHT) **TOR.**

Defense. Shoots left. 5'9", 195 lbs. Born, Buffalo Grove, IL, January 15, 1982.

Season	Club	League	GP	G	A	Pts	PIM	PP	SH	GW	S	%	+/-	TF	F%	Min	GP	G	A	Pts	PIM	PP	SH	GW	Min
1998-99	USNTDP	U-17	11	1	7	8	4																		
	USNTDP	USHL	3	0	0	0	0																		
	USNTDP	NAHL	52	11	17	28	56																		
99-2000	USNTDP	U-18	4	0	0	0	6																		
	USNTDP	USHL	22	6	7	13	28																		
2000-01	U. of Notre Dame	CCHA	39	7	19	26	109																		
2001-02	U. of Notre Dame	CCHA	34	6	8	14	54																		
2002-03	U. of Notre Dame	CCHA	40	7	14	21	48																		
2003-04	U. of Notre Dame	CCHA	39	6	18	24	42																		
	Grand Rapids	AHL	6	0	1	1	0										4	0	0	0	2				
2004-05	Grand Rapids	AHL	80	2	10	12	34																		
2005-06	**Detroit**	**NHL**	**46**	**3**	**9**	**12**	**20**	**1**	**0**	**1**	**50**	**6.0**	**9**	**2**	**0.0**	**12:38**	**6**	**0**	**0**	**0**	**4**	**0**	**0**	**0**	**13:09**
	Grand Rapids	AHL	25	4	14	18	42										11	1	4	5	8				
2006-07	**Detroit**	**NHL**	**74**	**5**	**13**	**18**	**61**	**1**	**0**	**2**	**107**	**4.7**	**16**	**0**	**0.0**	**14:54**	**12**	**0**	**2**	**2**	**8**	**0**	**0**	**0**	**16:23**
2007-08♦	**Detroit**	**NHL**	**78**	**3**	**11**	**14**	**48**	**0**	**0**	**1**	**110**	**2.7**	**–1**	**1**	**0.0**	**16:29**	**19**	**0**	**2**	**2**	**6**	**0**	**0**	**0**	**12:33**
2008-09	**Detroit**	**NHL**	**65**	**6**	**10**	**16**	**48**	**0**	**0**	**1**	**69**	**8.7**	**9**	**1**	**100.0**	**13:39**	**23**	**0**	**6**	**6**	**22**	**0**	**0**	**0**	**13:21**
2009-10	**Detroit**	**NHL**	**63**	**1**	**7**	**8**	**24**	**0**	**0**	**0**	**61**	**1.6**	**–2**	**0**	**0.0**	**14:59**	**2**	**0**	**0**	**0**	**0**	**0**	**0**	**0**	**5:56**
	NHL Totals		**326**	**18**	**50**	**68**	**201**	**2**	**0**	**5**	**397**	**4.5**		**4**	**25.0**	**14:44**	**62**	**0**	**10**	**10**	**40**	**0**	**0**	**0**	**13:26**

CCHA All-Rookie Team (2001) • CCHA Second All-Star Team (2004)

Signed as a free agent by **Detroit**, April 3, 2004. Signed as a free agent by **Toronto**, July 7, 2010.

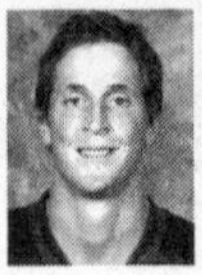

LECAVALIER, Vincent

(luh-KAV-uhl-YAY, VIHN-sihnt) **T.B.**

Center. Shoots left. 6'4", 223 lbs. Born, Ile Bizard, Que., April 21, 1980. Tampa Bay's 1st choice, 1st overall, in 1998 Entry Draft.

Season	Club	League	GP	G	A	Pts	PIM	PP	SH	GW	S	%	+/-	TF	F%	Min	GP	G	A	Pts	PIM	PP	SH	GW	Min
1995-96	Notre Dame	SMHL	22	52	52	104																			
1996-97	Rimouski Oceanic	QMJHL	64	42	61	103	38										4	4	3	7	2				
1997-98	Rimouski Oceanic	QMJHL	58	44	71	115	117										18	*15	*26	*41	46				
1998-99	**Tampa Bay**	**NHL**	**82**	**13**	**15**	**28**	**23**	**2**	**0**	**2**	**125**	**10.4**	**–19**	**953**	**40.3**	**13:40**									
99-2000	**Tampa Bay**	**NHL**	**80**	**25**	**42**	**67**	**43**	**6**	**0**	**3**	**166**	**15.1**	**–25**	**1288**	**44.4**	**19:18**									
2000-01	**Tampa Bay**	**NHL**	**68**	**23**	**28**	**51**	**66**	**7**	**0**	**3**	**165**	**13.9**	**–26**	**1278**	**44.9**	**19:57**									
2001-02	**Tampa Bay**	**NHL**	**76**	**20**	**17**	**37**	**61**	**5**	**0**	**3**	**164**	**12.2**	**–18**	**931**	**41.5**	**17:09**									
2002-03	**Tampa Bay**	**NHL**	**80**	**33**	**45**	**78**	**39**	**11**	**2**	**3**	**274**	**12.0**	**0**	**1200**	**43.9**	**19:33**	**11**	**3**	**3**	**6**	**22**	**1**	**0**	**1**	**22:36**
2003-04♦	**Tampa Bay**	**NHL**	**81**	**32**	**34**	**66**	**52**	**5**	**2**	**6**	**242**	**13.2**	**24**	**1119**	**41.4**	**18:04**	**23**	**9**	**7**	**16**	**25**	**2**	**0**	**0**	**19:39**
2004-05	Ak Bars Kazan	Russia	30	7	9	16	78										4	1	0	1	6				
2005-06	**Tampa Bay**	**NHL**	**80**	**35**	**40**	**75**	**90**	**13**	**2**	**7**	**309**	**11.3**	**0**	**1366**	**51.2**	**20:08**	**5**	**1**	**3**	**4**	**7**	**1**	**0**	**0**	**22:17**
	Canada	Olympics	6	0	3	3	16																		
2006-07	**Tampa Bay**	**NHL**	**82**	***52**	**56**	**108**	**44**	**16**	**5**	**7**	**339**	**15.3**	**2**	**1653**	**46.6**	**22:36**	**6**	**5**	**2**	**7**	**10**	**1**	**0**	**1**	**26:29**
2007-08	**Tampa Bay**	**NHL**	**81**	**40**	**52**	**92**	**89**	**10**	**1**	**7**	**318**	**12.6**	**–17**	**1671**	**48.8**	**22:57**									
2008-09	**Tampa Bay**	**NHL**	**77**	**29**	**38**	**67**	**54**	**10**	**1**	**6**	**291**	**10.0**	**–9**	**1395**	**50.9**	**20:15**									
2009-10	**Tampa Bay**	**NHL**	**82**	**24**	**46**	**70**	**63**	**5**	**0**	**3**	**295**	**8.1**	**–16**	**1449**	**53.2**	**19:47**									
	NHL Totals		**869**	**326**	**413**	**739**	**624**	**90**	**13**	**50**	**2688**	**12.1**		**14303**	**46.6**	**19:24**	**45**	**18**	**15**	**33**	**64**	**5**	**0**	**2**	**21:34**

QMJHL All-Rookie Team (1997) • QMJHL Offensive Rookie of the Year (1997) • Canadian Major Junior Rookie of the Year (1997) • QMJHL First All-Star Team (1998) • Canadian Major Junior First All-Star Team (1998) • NHL Second All-Star Team (2007) • Maurice "Rocket" Richard Trophy (2007) • King Clancy Memorial Trophy (2008)

Played in NHL All-Star Game (2003, 2007, 2008, 2009)

Signed as a free agent by **Kazan** (Russia), November 4, 2004.

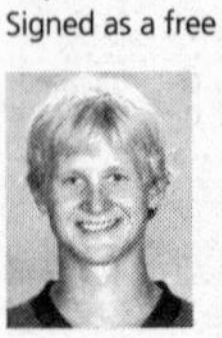

LEE, Brian

(LEE, BRIGH-uhn) **OTT.**

Defense. Shoots right. 6'3", 206 lbs. Born, Moorhead, MN, March 26, 1987. Ottawa's 1st choice, 9th overall, in 2005 Entry Draft.

Season	Club	League	GP	G	A	Pts	PIM	PP	SH	GW	S	%	+/-	TF	F%	Min	GP	G	A	Pts	PIM	PP	SH	GW	Min
2003-04	Moorhead Spuds	High-MN	29	10	38	48																			
2004-05	Moorhead Spuds	High-MN	25	12	26	38																			
	Lincoln Stars	USHL	12	0	3	3	4										4	2	3	5	2				
2005-06	North Dakota	WCHA	44	4	23	27	44																		
2006-07	North Dakota	WCHA	38	2	24	26	69																		
2007-08	**Ottawa**	**NHL**	**6**	**0**	**1**	**1**	**4**	**0**	**0**	**0**	**6**	**0.0**	**1**	**0**	**0.0**	**16:49**	**4**	**0**	**0**	**0**	**2**	**0**	**0**	**0**	**14:31**
	Binghamton	AHL	55	3	22	25	51																		
2008-09	**Ottawa**	**NHL**	**53**	**2**	**11**	**13**	**33**	**1**	**0**	**1**	**51**	**3.9**	**–2**	**0**	**0.0**	**18:53**									
	Binghamton	AHL	27	2	10	12	41																		
2009-10	**Ottawa**	**NHL**	**23**	**2**	**1**	**3**	**12**	**0**	**0**	**0**	**22**	**9.1**	**–5**	**0**	**0.0**	**15:33**									
	Binghamton	AHL	41	3	12	15	52																		
	NHL Totals		**82**	**4**	**13**	**17**	**49**	**1**	**0**	**1**	**79**	**5.1**		**0**	**0.0**	**17:48**	**4**	**0**	**0**	**0**	**2**	**0**	**0**	**0**	**14:31**

WCHA All-Rookie Team (2006)

			Regular Season														Playoffs							
Season	Club	League	GP	G	A	Pts	PIM	PP	SH	GW	S	%	+/-	TF	F%	Min	GP	G	A	Pts	PIM	PP	SH	GW	Min

LEGWAND, David
(LEHG-wawnd, DAY-vihd)   **NSH.**

Center. Shoots left. 6'2", 204 lbs.   Born, Detroit, MI, August 17, 1980. Nashville's 1st choice, 2nd overall, in 1998 Entry Draft.

Season	Club	League	GP	G	A	Pts	PIM	PP	SH	GW	S	%	+/-	TF	F%	Min	GP	G	A	Pts	PIM	PP	SH	GW	Min
1996-97	Det. Compuware	MNHL	44	21	41	62	58	....	....	....	....	....	....	....	....	....	....	....	....	....	....	....	....	....	....
1997-98	Plymouth Whalers	OHL	59	54	51	105	56	....	....	....	....	....	....	....	....	....	15	8	12	20	24	....	....	....	....
1998-99	Plymouth Whalers	OHL	55	31	49	80	65	....	....	....	....	....	....	....	....	....	11	3	8	11	8	....	....	.:.	....
	Nashville	**NHL**	**1**	**0**	**0**	**0**	**0**	0	0	0	2	0.0	0	9	55.6	12:50	....	....	....	....	....	....	....	....	....
99-2000	**Nashville**	**NHL**	71	13	15	28	30	4	0	2	111	11.7	-6	637	41.6	14:43	....	....	....	....	....	....	....	....	....
2000-01	Nashville	NHL	81	13	28	41	38	3	0	3	172	7.6	1	888	40.3	15:14	....	....	....	....	....	....	....	....	....
2001-02	Nashville	NHL	63	11	19	30	54	1	1	1	121	9.1	1	843	40.5	16:25	....	....	....	....	....	....	....	....	....
2002-03	Nashville	NHL	64	17	31	48	34	3	1	4	167	10.2	-2	1095	46.6	19:14	....	....	....	....	....	....	....	....	....
2003-04	Nashville	NHL	82	18	29	47	46	5	1	5	165	10.9	9	1109	45.1	17:17	6	1	0	1	8	0	1	0	15:41
2004-05	EHC Basel	Swiss-2	3	6	2	8	2	....	....	....	....	....	....	....	....	....	19	16	23	39	20	....	....	....	....
2005-06	**Nashville**	**NHL**	44	7	19	26	34	0	0	5	109	6.4	3	580	44.7	16:50	5	0	1	1	8	0	0	0	17:21
	Milwaukee	AHL	3	0	0	0	0	....	....	....	....	....	....	....	....	....	....	....	....	....	....	....	....	....	....
2006-07	Nashville	NHL	78	27	36	63	44	3	1	7	153	17.6	23	1108	45.3	18:22	5	0	3	3	2	0	0	0	22:23
2007-08	Nashville	NHL	65	15	29	44	38	4	0	1	144	10.4	-4	700	43.6	18:01	3	1	0	1	2	0	0	0	18:15
2008-09	Nashville	NHL	73	20	22	42	32	1	3	1	175	11.4	-3	1023	49.8	19:27	....	....	....	....	....	....	....	....	....
2009-10	Nashville	NHL	82	11	27	38	24	0	1	3	151	7.3	-5	1124	47.9	18:42	6	2	5	7	8	0	0	1	19:16
	NHL Totals		704	152	255	407	374	24	8	32	1470	10.3		9116	44.9	17:26	25	4	9	13	28	0	1	1	18:32

OHL All-Rookie Team (1998) • OHL First All-Star Team (1998) • OHL Rookie of the Year (1998) • OHL MVP (1998) • Canadian Major Junior Rookie of the Year (1998)
Signed as a free agent by **Basel** (Swiss-2), January 27, 2005.

LEHMAN, Scott
(LAY-man, SKAWT)

Defense. Shoots left. 6'1", 194 lbs.   Born, Fort McMurray, Alta., January 6, 1986. Atlanta's 3rd choice, 76th overall, in 2004 Entry Draft.

Season	Club	League	GP	G	A	Pts	PIM	PP	SH	GW	S	%	+/-	TF	F%	Min	GP	G	A	Pts	PIM	PP	SH	GW	Min
2002-03	St. Michael's	OHL	53	3	10	13	50	....	....	....	....	....	....	....	....	....	19	1	3	4	34	....	....	....	....
2003-04	St. Michael's	OHL	66	5	27	32	189	....	....	....	....	....	....	....	....	....	18	2	2	4	38	....	....	....	....
2004-05	St. Michael's	OHL	57	2	19	21	189	....	....	....	....	....	....	....	....	....	10	2	2	4	31	....	....	....	....
2005-06	St. Michael's	OHL	68	5	50	55	175	....	....	....	....	....	....	....	....	....	4	0	2	2	15	....	....	....	....
2006-07	Chicago Wolves	AHL	3	0	0	0	14	....	....	....	....	....	....	....	....	....	....	....	....	....	....	....	....	....	....
	Gwinnett	ECHL	72	2	12	14	86	....	....	....	....	....	....	....	....	....	4	0	0	0	11	....	....	....	....
2007-08	Chicago Wolves	AHL	40	2	5	7	109	....	....	....	....	....	....	....	....	....	....	....	....	....	....	....	....	....	....
	Gwinnett	ECHL	6	0	2	2	18	....	....	....	....	....	....	....	....	....	....	....	....	....	....	....	....	....	....
2008-09	**Atlanta**	**NHL**	**1**	**0**	**0**	**0**	**0**	0	0	0	0	0.0	0	0	0.0	3:03	....	....	....	....	....	....	....	....	....
	Chicago Wolves	AHL	50	2	3	5	86	....	....	....	....	....	....	....	....	....	....	....	....	....	....	....	....	....	....
2009-10	Chicago Wolves	AHL	11	0	2	2	16	....	....	....	....	....	....	....	....	....	....	....	....	....	....	....	....	....	....
	NHL Totals		1	0	0	0	0	0	0	0	0	0.0	0	0	0.0	3:03	....	....	....	....	....	....	....	....	....

Missed majority of 2009-10 season recovering from shoulder injury suffered in game at Rockford (AHL), December 2, 2009. Signed as a free agent by **Milwaukee** (AHL), July 21, 2010.

LEHOUX, Yanick
(luh-HOO, YAH-nihk)

Center. Shoots right. 6'1", 200 lbs.   Born, Montreal, Que., April 8, 1982. Los Angeles' 3rd choice, 86th overall, in 2000 Entry Draft.

Season	Club	League	GP	G	A	Pts	PIM	PP	SH	GW	S	%	+/-	TF	F%	Min	GP	G	A	Pts	PIM	PP	SH	GW	Min
1997-98	Cap-d-Madeleine	QAAA	42	29	50	79	26	....	....	....	....	....	....	....	....	....	....	....	....	....	....	....	....	....	....
1998-99	Baie-Comeau	QMJHL	63	10	20	30	31	....	....	....	....	....	....	....	....	....	....	....	....	....	....	....	....	....	....
99-2000	Baie-Comeau	QMJHL	67	31	61	92	14	....	....	....	....	....	....	....	....	....	6	1	2	3	2	....	....	....	....
2000-01	Baie-Comeau	QMJHL	70	67	68	135	62	....	....	....	....	....	....	....	....	....	11	8	16	24	0	....	....	....	....
2001-02	Baie-Comeau	QMJHL	66	56	69	125	63	....	....	....	....	....	....	....	....	....	5	5	4	9	0	....	....	....	....
	Manchester	AHL	....	....	....	....	....	....	....	....	....	....	....	....	....	....	1	0	0	0	0	....	....	....	....
2002-03	Manchester	AHL	78	16	21	37	26	....	....	....	....	....	....	....	....	....	1	0	0	0	0	....	....	....	....
2003-04	Manchester	AHL	66	14	28	42	22	....	....	....	....	....	....	....	....	....	5	2	3	5	16	....	....	....	....
2004-05	Manchester	AHL	38	23	31	54	16	....	....	....	....	....	....	....	....	....	....	....	....	....	....	....	....	....	....
2005-06	Geneve	Swiss	7	5	2	7	6	....	....	....	....	....	....	....	....	....	....	....	....	....	....	....	....	....	....
	EHC Basel	Swiss	4	0	2	2	4	....	....	....	....	....	....	....	....	....	....	....	....	....	....	....	....	....	....
	Phoenix	**NHL**	**3**	**1**	**0**	**1**	**2**	0	0	0	5	20.0	1	24	33.3	9:50	....	....	....	....	....	....	....	....	....
	San Antonio	AHL	23	8	6	14	13	....	....	....	....	....	....	....	....	....	....	....	....	....	....	....	....	....	....
	Manchester	AHL	31	10	6	16	23	....	....	....	....	....	....	....	....	....	....	....	....	....	....	....	....	....	....
2006-07	**Phoenix**	**NHL**	**7**	**1**	**2**	**3**	**4**	1	0	0	10	10.0	-1	10	60.0	12:32	....	....	....	....	....	....	....	....	....
	San Antonio	AHL	72	31	42	73	26	....	....	....	....	....	....	....	....	....	....	....	....	....	....	....	....	....	....
2007-08	San Antonio	AHL	7	1	3	4	2	....	....	....	....	....	....	....	....	....	....	....	....	....	....	....	....	....	....
	Mytischi	Russia	17	2	5	7	8	....	....	....	....	....	....	....	....	....	....	....	....	....	....	....	....	....	....
2008-09	Hamilton	AHL	80	19	41	60	38	....	....	....	....	....	....	....	....	....	6	1	1	2	4	....	....	....	....
2009-10	Sodertalje SK	Sweden	39	12	19	31	18	....	....	....	....	....	....	....	....	....	....	....	....	....	....	....	....	....	....
	Sodertalje SK	Sweden-Q	10	6	3	9	2	....	....	....	....	....	....	....	....	....	....	....	....	....	....	....	....	....	....
	NHL Totals		10	2	2	4	6	1	0	0	15	13.3		34	41.2	11:44	....	....	....	....	....	....	....	....	....

QMJHL Second All-Star Team (2002)
Signed as a free agent by **Geneve** (Swiss), September 5 2005. Claimed on waivers by **Phoenix** from **Los Angeles**, November 5, 2005. Claimed on waivers by **Los Angeles** from **Phoenix**, November 25, 2005. Traded to **Phoenix** by **Los Angeles** for Tim Jackman, March 9, 2006. Signed as a free agent by **Mytischi** (Russia), November 10, 2007. Signed as a free agent by **Montreal**, July 25, 2008. Signed as a free agent by **Sodertalje** (Sweden), July 6, 2009.

LEHTINEN, Jere
(LEH-tih-nehn, YUH-ree)

Right wing. Shoots right. 6', 194 lbs.   Born, Espoo, Finland, June 24, 1973. Minnesota's 3rd choice, 88th overall, in 1992 Entry Draft.

Season	Club	League	GP	G	A	Pts	PIM	PP	SH	GW	S	%	+/-	TF	F%	Min	GP	G	A	Pts	PIM	PP	SH	GW	Min
1989-90	Kiekko-Espoo Jr.	Fin-Jr.	32	23	23	46	6	....	....	....	....	....	....	....	....	....	5	0	3	3	0	....	....	....	....
1990-91	K-Espoo U18	Fin-U18	11	18	14	32	0	....	....	....	....	....	....	....	....	....	....	....	....	....	....	....	....	....	....
	Kiekko-Espoo Jr.	Fin-Jr.	10	8	6	14	4	....	....	....	....	....	....	....	....	....	....	....	....	....	....	....	....	....	....
	Kiekko-Espoo	Finland-2	32	15	9	24	12	....	....	....	....	....	....	....	....	....	....	....	....	....	....	....	....	....	....
1991-92	Kiekko-Espoo Jr.	Fin-Jr.	8	5	4	9	2	....	....	....	....	....	....	....	....	....	....	....	....	....	....	....	....	....	....
	Kiekko-Espoo	Finland-2	43	32	17	49	6	....	....	....	....	....	....	....	....	....	5	2	4	6	2	....	....	....	....
1992-93	Kiekko-Espoo Jr.	Fin-Jr.	4	5	3	8	8	....	....	....	....	....	....	....	....	....	....	....	....	....	....	....	....	....	....
	Kiekko-Espoo	Finland	45	13	14	27	6	....	....	....	....	....	....	....	....	....	....	....	....	....	....	....	....	....	....
1993-94	TPS Turku	Finland	42	19	20	39	6	....	....	....	....	....	....	....	....	....	11	11	2	13	2	....	....	....	....
	Finland	Olympics	8	3	0	3	0	....	....	....	....	....	....	....	....	....	....	....	....	....	....	....	....	....	....
1994-95	TPS Turku	Finland	39	19	23	42	33	....	....	....	....	....	....	....	....	....	13	8	6	14	4	....	....	....	....
1995-96	**Dallas**	**NHL**	57	6	22	28	16	0	0	1	109	5.5	5	....	....	....	....	....	....	....	....	....	....	....	....
	Michigan	IHL	1	1	0	1	0	....	....	....	....	....	....	....	....	....	....	....	....	....	....	....	....	....	....
1996-97	Dallas	NHL	63	16	27	43	2	3	1	2	134	11.9	26	....	....	....	7	2	2	4	0	0	0	0	....
1997-98	Dallas	NHL	72	23	19	42	20	7	2	6	201	11.4	19	....	....	....	12	3	5	8	2	1	0	0	....
	Finland	Olympics	6	4	2	6	2	....	....	....	....	....	....	....	....	....	....	....	....	....	....	....	....	....	....
1998-99 ♦	**Dallas**	**NHL**	74	20	32	52	18	7	1	2	173	11.6	29	9	33.3	19:36	23	10	3	13	2	1	1	0	21:09
99-2000	Dallas	NHL	17	3	5	8	0	0	0	1	29	10.3	1	0	0.0	17:31	13	1	5	6	2	0	0	0	21:15
2000-01	Dallas	NHL	74	20	25	45	24	7	0	1	148	13.5	14	7	28.6	19:17	10	1	0	1	2	0	0	0	20:13
2001-02	Dallas	NHL	73	25	24	49	14	7	1	4	198	12.6	27	18	22.2	19:50	....	....	....	....	....	....	....	....	....
	Finland	Olympics	4	1	2	3	2	....	....	....	....	....	....	....	....	....	....	....	....	....	....	....	....	....	....
2002-03	Dallas	NHL	80	31	17	48	20	5	0	3	238	13.0	39	36	22.2	18:47	12	3	2	5	0	1	0	0	21:12
2003-04	Dallas	NHL	58	13	13	26	20	4	1	4	138	9.4	0	10	40.0	19:27	5	0	0	0	0	0	0	0	19:19
2004-05					DID NOT PLAY																				
2005-06	**Dallas**	**NHL**	80	33	19	52	30	14	1	6	216	15.3	9	28	21.4	18:42	5	3	1	4	0	1	0	0	22:10
	Finland	Olympics	8	3	5	8	0	....	....	....	....	....	....	....	....	....	....	....	....	....	....	....	....	....	....
2006-07	Dallas	NHL	73	26	17	43	16	11	1	5	194	13.4	5	36	13.9	19:26	7	0	0	0	2	0	0	0	24:02
2007-08	Dallas	NHL	48	15	22	37	14	9	0	1	118	12.7	9	11	9.1	18:55	14	4	4	8	2	3	0	0	20:34
2008-09	Dallas	NHL	48	8	16	24	8	2	0	1	119	6.7	1	7	28.6	19:00	....	....	....	....	....	....	....	....	....
2009-10	Dallas	NHL	58	4	13	17	8	1	1	0	87	4.6	-8	11	18.2	14:45	....	....	....	....	....	....	....	....	....
	Finland	Olympics	6	0	0	0	0	....	....	....	....	....	....	....	....	....	....	....	....	....	....	....	....	....	....
	NHL Totals		875	243	271	514	210	77	9	37	2102	11.6		173	21.4	18:48	108	27	22	49	12	7	1	1	21:09

Frank J. Selke Trophy (1998, 1999, 2003)
Played in NHL All-Star Game (1998)
Rights transferred to **Dallas** after **Minnesota** franchise relocated, June 9, 1993. • Missed majority of 1999-2000 season recovering from leg injury suffered in game vs. Nashville, October 16, 1999.

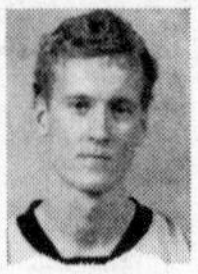

LEHTONEN, Mikko
(LEH-tuh-nehn, MEE-koh) **BOS**

Right wing. Shoots right. 6'5", 196 lbs. Born, Espoo, Finland, April 1, 1987. Boston's 3rd choice, 83rd overall, in 2005 Entry Draft.

			Regular Season														Playoffs								
Season	Club	League	GP	G	A	Pts	PIM	PP	SH	GW	S	%	+/-	TF	F%	Min	GP	G	A	Pts	PIM	PP	SH	GW	Min
2002-03	Blues Espoo U18	Fin-U18	11	1	3	4	2	....	....	....	....	....	....	....	....	....	1	0	0	0	0	....	....	....	....
2003-04	Blues Espoo U18	Fin-U18	20	8	7	15	22	....	....	....	....	....	....	....	....	....	....	....	....	....	....	....	....	....	....
	Blues Espoo Jr.	Fin-Jr.	19	3	0	3	0	....	....	....	....	....	....	....	....	....	5	0	0	0	0	....	....	....	....
2004-05	Blues Espoo U18	Fin-U18	2	0	2	2	0	....	....	....	....	....	....	....	....	....	....	....	....	....	....	....	....	....	....
	Blues Espoo Jr.	Fin-Jr.	37	6	9	15	38	....	....	....	....	....	....	....	....	....	6	3	1	4	0	....	....	....	....
	Blues Espoo	Finland	1	0	0	0	0	....	....	....	....	....	....	....	....	....	....	....	....	....	....	....	....	....	....
2005-06	Blues Espoo Jr.	Fin-Jr.	15	3	4	7	12	....	....	....	....	....	....	....	....	....	10	5	2	7	6	....	....	....	....
	Suomi U20	Finland-2	3	1	0	1	2	....	....	....	....	....	....	....	....	....	....	....	....	....	....	....	....	....	....
	Blues Espoo	Finland	25	4	0	4	0	....	....	....	....	....	....	....	....	....	....	....	....	....	....	....	....	....	....
2006-07	Suomi U20	Finland-2	3	0	3	3	0	....	....	....	....	....	....	....	....	....	....	....	....	....	....	....	....	....	....
	Blues Espoo	Finland	39	6	9	15	24	....	....	....	....	....	....	....	....	....	9	1	1	2	4	....	....	....	....
2007-08	Blues Espoo	Finland	42	8	12	20	12	....	....	....	....	....	....	....	....	....	17	1	8	9	4	....	....	....	....
2008-09	**Boston**	**NHL**	**1**	**0**	**0**	**0**	**0**	**0**	**0**	**0**	**1**	**0.0**	**0**	**0**	**0.0**	**16:14**	....	....	....	....	....	....	....	....	....
	Providence Bruins	AHL	72	28	25	53	39	....	....	....	....	....	....	....	....	....	14	2	5	7	4	....	....	....	....
2009-10	**Boston**	**NHL**	**1**	**0**	**0**	**0**	**0**	**0**	**0**	**0**	**1**	**0.0**	**–1**	**0**	**0.0**	**7:08**	....	....	....	....	....	....	....	....	....
	Providence Bruins	AHL	78	23	27	50	58	....	....	....	....	....	....	....	....	....	....	....	....	....	....	....	....	....	....
	NHL Totals		**2**	**0**	**0**	**0**	**0**	**0**	**0**	**0**	**2**	**0.0**		**0**	**0.0**	**11:41**	....	....	....	....	....	....	....	....	....

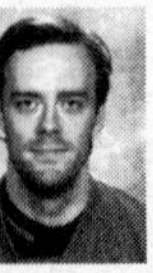

LEINO, Ville
(LAY-noh, VIHL-ee) **PHI**

Left wing. Shoots left. 6'1", 190 lbs. Born, Savonlinna, Finland, October 6, 1983.

			Regular Season														Playoffs								
Season	Club	League	GP	G	A	Pts	PIM	PP	SH	GW	S	%	+/-	TF	F%	Min	GP	G	A	Pts	PIM	PP	SH	GW	Min
2002-03	Ilves Tampere Jr.	Fin-Jr.	26	14	21	35	24	....	....	....	....	....	....	....	....	....	....	....	....	....	....	....	....	....	....
	Ilves Tampere	Finland	23	1	1	2	0	....	....	....	....	....	....	....	....	....	....	....	....	....	....	....	....	....	....
2003-04	Ilves Tampere Jr.	Fin-Jr.	5	4	6	10	6	....	....	....	....	....	....	....	....	....	....	....	....	....	....	....	....	....	....
	Ilves Tampere	Finland	54	9	15	24	26	....	....	....	....	....	....	....	....	....	7	1	1	2	4	....	....	....	....
2004-05	Ilves Tampere	Finland	56	8	11	19	32	....	....	....	....	....	....	....	....	....	7	1	0	1	2	....	....	....	....
2005-06	HPK Hameenlinna	Finland	56	12	31	43	65	....	....	....	....	....	....	....	....	....	13	3	*9	12	4	....	....	....	....
2006-07	HPK Hameenlinna	Finland	50	11	29	40	73	....	....	....	....	....	....	....	....	....	8	1	9	10	31	....	....	....	....
2007-08	Jokerit Helsinki	Finland	55	28	*49	77	18	....	....	....	....	....	....	....	....	....	14	8	11	19	8	....	....	....	....
2008-09	**Detroit**	**NHL**	**13**	**5**	**4**	**9**	**6**	**0**	**0**	**1**	**17**	**29.4**	**5**	**12**	**58.3**	**12:42**	**7**	**0**	**2**	**2**	**0**	**0**	**0**	**0**	**8:4**
	Grand Rapids	AHL	57	15	31	46	18	....	....	....	....	....	....	....	....	....	10	3	10	13	10	....	....	....	....
2009-10	**Detroit**	**NHL**	**42**	**4**	**3**	**7**	**6**	**1**	**0**	**1**	**54**	**7.4**	**–10**	**5**	**20.0**	**13:13**	....	....	....	....	....	....	....	....	....
	Philadelphia	**NHL**	**13**	**2**	**2**	**4**	**4**	**0**	**0**	**1**	**23**	**8.7**	**2**	**9**	**55.6**	**12:40**	**19**	**7**	**14**	**21**	**6**	**0**	**0**	**2**	**16:1**
	NHL Totals		**68**	**11**	**9**	**20**	**16**	**1**	**0**	**3**	**94**	**11.7**		**26**	**50.0**	**13:01**	**26**	**7**	**16**	**23**	**6**	**0**	**0**	**2**	**14:1**

Signed as a free agent by **Detroit**, May 10, 2008. Traded to **Philadelpia** by **Detroit** for Ole-Kristian Tollefsen and Philadelphia's 5th round choice in 2011 Entry Draft, February 6, 2010.

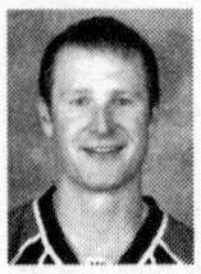

LEOPOLD, Jordan
(LEE-oh-pohld, JOHR-dahn) **BUF**

Defense. Shoots left. 6'1", 200 lbs. Born, Golden Valley, MN, August 3, 1980. Anaheim's 1st choice, 44th overall, in 1999 Entry Draft.

			Regular Season														Playoffs								
Season	Club	League	GP	G	A	Pts	PIM	PP	SH	GW	S	%	+/-	TF	F%	Min	GP	G	A	Pts	PIM	PP	SH	GW	Min
1995-96	Armstrong	High-MN	19	11	14	25	30	....	....	....	....	....	....	....	....	....	....	....	....	....	....	....	....	....	....
1996-97	Armstrong	High-MN	30	24	36	60	....	....	....	....	....	....	....	....	....	....	....	....	....	....	....	....	....	....	....
1997-98	USNTDP	U-18	25	7	3	10	2	....	....	....	....	....	....	....	....	....	....	....	....	....	....	....	....	....	....
	USNTDP	USHL	19	2	4	6	6	....	....	....	....	....	....	....	....	....	....	....	....	....	....	....	....	....	....
	USNTDP	NAHL	16	2	5	7	8	....	....	....	....	....	....	....	....	....	....	....	....	....	....	....	....	....	....
1998-99	U. of Minnesota	WCHA	39	7	16	23	20	....	....	....	....	....	....	....	....	....	....	....	....	....	....	....	....	....	....
99-2000	U. of Minnesota	WCHA	39	6	18	24	20	....	....	....	....	....	....	....	....	....	....	....	....	....	....	....	....	....	....
2000-01	U. of Minnesota	WCHA	42	12	37	49	38	....	....	....	....	....	....	....	....	....	....	....	....	....	....	....	....	....	....
2001-02	U. of Minnesota	WCHA	44	20	28	48	28	....	....	....	....	....	....	....	....	....	....	....	....	....	....	....	....	....	....
2002-03	**Calgary**	**NHL**	**58**	**4**	**10**	**14**	**12**	**3**	**0**	**0**	**78**	**5.1**	**–15**	**0**	**0.0**	**20:36**	....	....	....	....	....	....	....	....	....
	Saint John Flames	AHL	3	1	2	3	0	....	....	....	....	....	....	....	....	....	....	....	....	....	....	....	....	....	....
2003-04	**Calgary**	**NHL**	**82**	**9**	**24**	**33**	**24**	**6**	**0**	**1**	**138**	**6.5**	**8**	**0**	**0.0**	**22:14**	**26**	**0**	**10**	**10**	**6**	**0**	**0**	**0**	**25:4**
2004-05		DID NOT PLAY																							
2005-06	**Calgary**	**NHL**	**74**	**2**	**18**	**20**	**68**	**2**	**0**	**1**	**87**	**2.3**	**6**	**0**	**0.0**	**22:20**	**7**	**0**	**1**	**1**	**4**	**0**	**0**	**0**	**19:1**
	United States	Olympics	6	1	0	1	4	....	....	....	....	....	....	....	....	....	....	....	....	....	....	....	....	....	....
2006-07	**Colorado**	**NHL**	**15**	**2**	**3**	**5**	**14**	**1**	**1**	**0**	**19**	**10.5**	**–4**	**0**	**0.0**	**19:47**	....	....	....	....	....	....	....	....	....
2007-08	**Colorado**	**NHL**	**43**	**5**	**8**	**13**	**20**	**2**	**0**	**1**	**35**	**14.3**	**5**	**0**	**0.0**	**15:59**	**7**	**0**	**3**	**3**	**0**	**0**	**0**	**0**	**17:0**
2008-09	**Colorado**	**NHL**	**64**	**6**	**14**	**20**	**18**	**1**	**0**	**1**	**82**	**7.3**	**–10**	**0**	**0.0**	**18:10**	....	....	....	....	....	....	....	....	....
	Calgary	**NHL**	**19**	**1**	**3**	**4**	**6**	**0**	**0**	**0**	**25**	**4.0**	**–5**	**0**	**0.0**	**20:58**	**6**	**0**	**1**	**1**	**8**	**0**	**0**	**0**	**23:1**
2009-10	**Florida**	**NHL**	**61**	**7**	**11**	**18**	**22**	**1**	**0**	**1**	**69**	**10.1**	**–7**	**0**	**0.0**	**22:25**	....	....	....	....	....	....	....	....	....
	Pittsburgh	**NHL**	**20**	**4**	**4**	**8**	**6**	**0**	**0**	**2**	**26**	**15.4**	**5**	**0**	**0.0**	**20:27**	**8**	**0**	**0**	**0**	**2**	**0**	**0**	**0**	**16:3**
	NHL Totals		**436**	**40**	**95**	**135**	**190**	**16**	**1**	**7**	**559**	**7.2**		**0**	**0.0**	**20:37**	**54**	**0**	**15**	**15**	**20**	**0**	**0**	**0**	**22:0**

WCHA All-Rookie Team (1999) • WCHA Second All-Star Team (2000) • WCHA First All-Star Team (2001, 2002) • NCAA West First All-American Team (2001) • Hobey Baker Memorial Award (Top U.S. Collegiate Player) (2002)

Traded to **Calgary** by **Anaheim** for Andrei Nazarov and Calgary's 2nd round choice (later traded to Phoenix, later traded back to Calgary – Calgary selected Andrei Taratukhin) in 2001 Entry Draft, September 26, 2000. Traded to **Colorado** by **Calgary** with Calgary's 2nd round choice (Codey Burki) in 2006 Entry Draft and Calgary's 2nd round choice (Trevor Cann) in 2007 Entry Draft for Alex Tanguay, June 24, 2006. • Missed majority of 2006-07 season recovering from off-season hernia surgery, groin injury and wrist injury suffered in game vs. Calgary, February 15, 2007. Traded to **Calgary** by **Colorado** for Ryan Wilson, Lawrence Nycholat and Montreal's 2nd round choice (previously acquired, Colorado selected Stefan Elliott) in 2009 Entry Draft, March 4, 2009. Traded to **Florida** by **Calgary** with Phoenix's 3rd round choice (previously acquired, Florida selected Josh Birkholz) in 2009 Entry Draft for Jay Bouwmeester, June 27, 2009. Traded to **Pittsburgh** by **Florida** for Pittsburgh's 2nd round choice (Connor Brickley) in 2010 Entry Draft, March 1, 2010. Signed as a free agent by **Buffalo**, July 1, 2010.

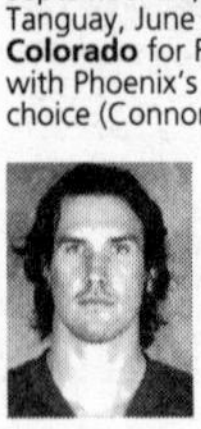

LEPISTO, Sami
(LEH-pihs-toh, SA-mee) **PHX**

Defense. Shoots left. 6', 190 lbs. Born, Espoo, Finland, October 17, 1984. Washington's 6th choice, 66th overall, in 2004 Entry Draft.

			Regular Season														Playoffs								
Season	Club	League	GP	G	A	Pts	PIM	PP	SH	GW	S	%	+/-	TF	F%	Min	GP	G	A	Pts	PIM	PP	SH	GW	Min
2001-02	Jokerit U18	Fin-U18	20	8	14	22	36	....	....	....	....	....	....	....	....	....	8	4	8	12	12	....	....	....	....
	Jokerit Helsinki Jr.	Fin-Jr.	14	0	5	5	2	....	....	....	....	....	....	....	....	....	....	....	....	....	....	....	....	....	....
2002-03	Jokerit Helsinki Jr.	Fin-Jr.	36	5	14	19	34	....	....	....	....	....	....	....	....	....	11	1	5	6	8	....	....	....	....
2003-04	Suomi U20	Finland-2	1	0	0	0	0	....	....	....	....	....	....	....	....	....	....	....	....	....	....	....	....	....	....
	Jokerit Helsinki	Finland	53	3	4	7	20	....	....	....	....	....	....	....	....	....	8	0	1	1	4	....	....	....	....
2004-05	Jokerit Helsinki	Finland	55	7	18	25	44	....	....	....	....	....	....	....	....	....	12	1	7	8	12	....	....	....	....
2005-06	Jokerit Helsinki	Finland	56	8	21	29	68	....	....	....	....	....	....	....	....	....	....	....	....	....	....	....	....	....	....
2006-07	Jokerit Helsinki	Finland	26	1	9	10	32	....	....	....	....	....	....	....	....	....	10	2	2	4	4	....	....	....	....
2007-08	**Washington**	**NHL**	**7**	**0**	**1**	**1**	**12**	**0**	**0**	**0**	**8**	**0.0**	**–1**	**0**	**0.0**	**13:17**	....	....	....	....	....	....	....	....	....
	Hershey Bears	AHL	55	4	41	45	51	....	....	....	....	....	....	....	....	....	5	0	1	1	4	....	....	....	....
2008-09	**Washington**	**NHL**	**7**	**0**	**4**	**4**	**6**	**0**	**0**	**0**	**7**	**0.0**	**–3**	**0**	**0.0**	**19:36**	....	....	....	....	....	....	....	....	....
	Hershey Bears	AHL	70	4	38	42	80	....	....	....	....	....	....	....	....	....	....	....	....	....	....	....	....	....	....
2009-10	**Phoenix**	**NHL**	**66**	**1**	**10**	**11**	**60**	**0**	**0**	**1**	**68**	**1.5**	**14**	**1**	**100.0**	**18:14**	**7**	**1**	**0**	**1**	**6**	**0**	**0**	**0**	**15:5**
	Finland	Olympics	6	0	1	1	6	....	....	....	....	....	....	....	....	....	....	....	....	....	....	....	....	....	....
	NHL Totals		**80**	**1**	**15**	**16**	**78**	**0**	**0**	**1**	**83**	**1.2**		**1**	**100.0**	**17:55**	**7**	**1**	**0**	**1**	**6**	**0**	**0**	**0**	**15:5**

Traded to **Phoenix** by **Washington** for Phoenix's 5th round choice (Caleb Herbert) in 2010 Entry Draft, June 27, 2009.

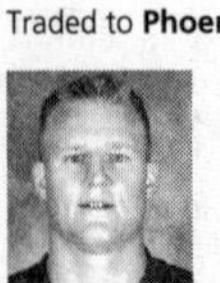

LESSARD, Francis
(leh-SAHR, FRAN-sihs) **OTT**

Right wing. Shoots right. 6'3", 235 lbs. Born, Montreal, Que., May 30, 1979. Carolina's 3rd choice, 80th overall, in 1997 Entry Draft.

			Regular Season														Playoffs								
Season	Club	League	GP	G	A	Pts	PIM	PP	SH	GW	S	%	+/-	TF	F%	Min	GP	G	A	Pts	PIM	PP	SH	GW	Min
1994-95	Laval-Laurentides	QAAA	1	0	0	0	0	....	....	....	....	....	....	....	....	....	....	....	....	....	....	....	....	....	....
1995-96	Laval-Laurentides	QAAA	41	5	7	12	73	....	....	....	....	....	....	....	....	....	13	1	3	4	....	....	....	....	....
1996-97	Val-d'Or Foreurs	QMJHL	66	1	9	10	287	....	....	....	....	....	....	....	....	....	....	....	....	....	....	....	....	....	....
1997-98	Val-d'Or Foreurs	QMJHL	63	3	20	23	338	....	....	....	....	....	....	....	....	....	19	1	6	7	*101	....	....	....	....
1998-99	Drummondville	QMJHL	53	12	36	48	295	....	....	....	....	....	....	....	....	....	....	....	....	....	....	....	....	....	....
99-2000	Philadelphia	AHL	78	4	8	12	416	....	....	....	....	....	....	....	....	....	5	0	1	1	7	....	....	....	....
2000-01	Philadelphia	AHL	64	3	7	10	330	....	....	....	....	....	....	....	....	....	10	0	0	0	33	....	....	....	....
2001-02	Philadelphia	AHL	60	0	6	6	251	....	....	....	....	....	....	....	....	....	....	....	....	....	....	....	....	....	....
	Atlanta	**NHL**	**5**	**0**	**0**	**0**	**26**	**0**	**0**	**0**	**2**	**0.0**	**0**	**0**	**0.0**	**12:45**	....	....	....	....	....	....	....	....	....
	Chicago Wolves	AHL	7	2	1	3	34	....	....	....	....	....	....	....	....	....	15	0	1	1	40	....	....	....	....
2002-03	**Atlanta**	**NHL**	**18**	**0**	**2**	**2**	**61**	**0**	**0**	**0**	**7**	**0.0**	**1**	**0**	**0.0**	**5:40**	....	....	....	....	....	....	....	....	....
	Chicago Wolves	AHL	50	2	5	7	194	....	....	....	....	....	....	....	....	....	1	0	0	0	0	....	....	....	....
2003-04	**Atlanta**	**NHL**	**62**	**1**	**1**	**2**	**181**	**0**	**0**	**0**	**19**	**5.3**	**–5**	**1**	**0.0**	**4:28**	....	....	....	....	....	....	....	....	....

Season	Club	League	GP	G	A	Pts	PIM	PP	SH	GW	S	%	+/-	TF	F%	Min	GP	G	A	Pts	PIM	PP	SH	GW	Min
			Regular Season														Playoffs								
2004-05			DID NOT PLAY																						
2005-06	**Atlanta**	**NHL**	**6**	**0**	**0**	**0**	**0**	**0**	**0**	**0**	**0**	**0.0**	**–2**	**0**	**0.0**	**2:33**	....	....	....	....	....	....	....	....	....
	Chicago Wolves	AHL	36	2	3	5	163	....	....	....	....	....	....	....	....	....	....	....	....	....	....	....	....	....	....
2006-07	Hartford	AHL	58	3	6	9	*309	....	....	....	....	....	....	....	....	....	....	....	....	....	....	....	....	....	....
2007-08	Hartford	AHL	14	4	1	5	49	....	....	....	....	....	....	....	....	....	....	....	....	....	....	....	....	....	....
2008-09	San Antonio	AHL	59	2	2	4	*324	....	....	....	....	....	....	....	....	....	....	....	....	....	....	....	....	....	....
2009-10	San Antonio	AHL	61	2	2	4	289	....	....	....	....	....	....	....	....	....	....	....	....	....	....	....	....	....	....
	NHL Totals		**91**	**1**	**3**	**4**	**268**	**0**	**0**	**0**	**28**	**3.6**		**1**	**0.0**	**5:02**	....	....	....	....	....	....	....	....	....

Memorial Cup Tournament All-Star Team (1998)

Traded to **Philadelphia** by **Carolina** for Philadelphia's 8th round choice (Antti Jokella) in 1999 Entry Draft, May 25, 1999. Traded to **Atlanta** by **Philadelphia** for David Harlock and Atlanta's 3rd (later traded to Phoenix – Phoenix selected Tyler Redenbach) and 7th (later traded to San Jose – San Jose selected Joe Pavelski) round choices in 2003 Entry Draft, March 15, 2002. Signed as a free agent by **Phoenix**, July 31, 2008. Signed as a free agent by **Ottawa**, August 4, 2010.

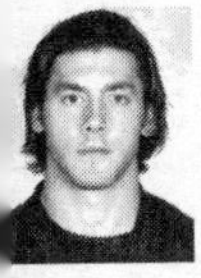

LETANG, Kris

(leh-TANG, KRIHS) **PIT.**

Defense. Shoots right. 6', 201 lbs. Born, Montreal, Que., April 24, 1987. Pittsburgh's 3rd choice, 62nd overall, in 2005 Entry Draft.

Season	Club	League	GP	G	A	Pts	PIM	PP	SH	GW	S	%	+/-	TF	F%	Min	GP	G	A	Pts	PIM	PP	SH	GW	Min
2002-03	Antoine-Girouard	QAAA	42	2	10	12	34	....	....	....	....	....	....	....	....	....	....	....	....	....	....	....	....	....	....
2003-04	Antoine-Girouard	QAAA	39	12	41	53	94	....	....	....	....	....	....	....	....	....	13	7	9	16	38	....	....	....	....
2004-05	Val-d'Or Foreurs	QMJHL	70	13	19	32	79	....	....	....	....	....	....	....	....	....	....	....	....	....	....	....	....	....	....
2005-06	Val-d'Or Foreurs	QMJHL	60	25	43	68	156	....	....	....	....	....	....	....	....	....	5	1	5	6	20	....	....	....	....
2006-07	**Pittsburgh**	**NHL**	**7**	**2**	**0**	**2**	**4**	**2**	**0**	**0**	**8**	**25.0**	**–3**	**0**	**0.0**	**11:33**	....	....	....	....	....	....	....	....	....
	Val-d'Or Foreurs	QMJHL	40	14	38	52	74	....	....	....	....	....	....	....	....	....	19	12	19	31	48	....	....	....	....
	Wilkes-Barre	AHL	....	....	....	....	....	....	....	....	....	....	....	....	....	....	1	0	1	1	2	....	....	....	....
2007-08	**Pittsburgh**	**NHL**	**63**	**6**	**11**	**17**	**23**	**1**	**0**	**3**	**68**	**8.8**	**–1**	**0**	**0.0**	**18:10**	**16**	**0**	**2**	**2**	**12**	**0**	**0**	**0**	**17:07**
	Wilkes-Barre	AHL	10	1	6	7	4	....	....	....	....	....	....	....	....	....	....	....	....	....	....	....	....	....	....
2008-09 ♦	**Pittsburgh**	**NHL**	**74**	**10**	**23**	**33**	**24**	**4**	**1**	**3**	**138**	**7.2**	**–7**	**1**	**0.0**	**21:09**	**23**	**4**	**9**	**13**	**26**	**2**	**0**	**1**	**19:18**
2009-10	**Pittsburgh**	**NHL**	**73**	**3**	**24**	**27**	**51**	**0**	**0**	**0**	**174**	**1.7**	**1**	**0**	**0.0**	**21:34**	**13**	**5**	**2**	**7**	**6**	**4**	**0**	**1**	**23:15**
	NHL Totals		**217**	**21**	**58**	**79**	**102**	**7**	**1**	**6**	**388**	**5.4**		**1**	**0.0**	**20:07**	**52**	**9**	**13**	**22**	**44**	**6**	**0**	**2**	**19:37**

QMJHL All-Rookie Team (2005) • Canadian Major Junior All-Rookie Team (2005) • QMJHL First All-Star Team (2006, 2007) • Canadian Major Junior Second All-Star Team (2006. 2007)

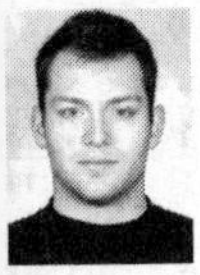

LETESTU, Mark

(luh-TEHS- too, MAHRK) **PIT.**

Center. Shoots right. 5'11", 195 lbs. Born, Elk Point, Alta., February 4, 1985.

Season	Club	League	GP	G	A	Pts	PIM	PP	SH	GW	S	%	+/-	TF	F%	Min	GP	G	A	Pts	PIM	PP	SH	GW	Min
2003-04	Bonnyville	AJHL	58	22	27	49	24	....	....	....	....	....	....	....	....	....	....	....	....	....	....	....	....	....	....
2004-05	Bonnyville	AJHL	63	39	47	86	32	....	....	....	....	....	....	....	....	....	....	....	....	....	....	....	....	....	....
2005-06	Bonnyville	AJHL	58	50	55	105	59	....	....	....	....	....	....	....	....	....	....	....	....	....	....	....	....	....	....
2006-07	Western Mich.	CCHA	37	24	22	46	14	....	....	....	....	....	....	....	....	....	....	....	....	....	....	....	....	....	....
	Wilkes-Barre	AHL	3	0	0	0	0	....	....	....	....	....	....	....	....	....	2	0	0	0	2	....	....	....	....
2007-08	Wilkes-Barre	AHL	52	6	12	18	28	....	....	....	....	....	....	....	....	....	13	0	3	3	0	....	....	....	....
	Wheeling Nailers	ECHL	6	1	2	3	4	....	....	....	....	....	....	....	....	....	....	....	....	....	....	....	....	....	....
2008-09	Wilkes-Barre	AHL	73	24	37	61	6	....	....	....	....	....	....	....	....	....	12	2	8	10	4	....	....	....	....
2009-10	**Pittsburgh**	**NHL**	**10**	**1**	**0**	**1**	**2**	**0**	**0**	**0**	**9**	**11.1**	**–2**	**74**	**55.4**	**9:38**	**4**	**0**	**1**	**1**	**0**	**0**	**0**	**0**	**9:39**
	Wilkes-Barre	AHL	63	21	34	55	21	....	....	....	....	....	....	....	....	....	4	0	3	3	0	....	....	....	....
	NHL Totals		**10**	**1**	**0**	**1**	**2**	**0**	**0**	**0**	**9**	**11.1**		**74**	**55.4**	**9:38**	**4**	**0**	**1**	**1**	**0**	**0**	**0**	**0**	**9:39**

Signed as a free agent by **Pittsburgh**, March 22, 2007.

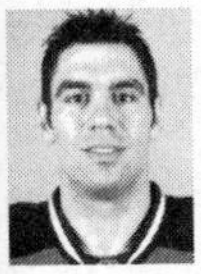

LETOURNEAU-LEBLOND, Pierre-Luc

(leh-TOOR-noh-leh-BLAWN) **N.J.**

Left wing. Shoots left. 6'2", 215 lbs. Born, Levis, Que., June 4, 1985. New Jersey's 4th choice, 216th overall, in 2004 Entry Draft.

Season	Club	League	GP	G	A	Pts	PIM	PP	SH	GW	S	%	+/-	TF	F%	Min	GP	G	A	Pts	PIM	PP	SH	GW	Min
2003-04	Baie-Comeau	QMJHL	62	2	3	5	198	....	....	....	....	....	....	....	....	....	4	0	0	0	6	....	....	....	....
2004-05	Baie-Comeau	QMJHL	67	1	6	7	229	....	....	....	....	....	....	....	....	....	6	0	1	1	10	....	....	....	....
2005-06	Albany River Rats	AHL	27	1	1	2	130	....	....	....	....	....	....	....	....	....	....	....	....	....	....	....	....	....	....
	Adirondack	UHL	31	3	6	9	165	....	....	....	....	....	....	....	....	....	6	0	1	1	29	....	....	....	....
2006-07	Trenton Titans	ECHL	52	4	9	13	183	....	....	....	....	....	....	....	....	....	4	0	0	0	15	....	....	....	....
2007-08	Lowell Devils	AHL	36	3	3	6	98	....	....	....	....	....	....	....	....	....	....	....	....	....	....	....	....	....	....
	Trenton Devils	ECHL	6	0	1	1	46	....	....	....	....	....	....	....	....	....	....	....	....	....	....	....	....	....	....
2008-09	**New Jersey**	**NHL**	**8**	**0**	**1**	**1**	**22**	**0**	**0**	**0**	**3**	**0.0**	**3**	**0**	**0.0**	**4:51**	....	....	....	....	....	....	....	....	....
	Lowell Devils	AHL	60	5	5	10	216	....	....	....	....	....	....	....	....	....	....	....	....	....	....	....	....	....	....
2009-10	**New Jersey**	**NHL**	**27**	**0**	**2**	**2**	**48**	**0**	**0**	**0**	**9**	**0.0**	**–4**	**2**	**50.0**	**5:31**	**5**	**0**	**0**	**0**	**10**	**0**	**0**	**0**	**4:34**
	Lowell Devils	AHL	5	0	2	2	18	....	....	....	....	....	....	....	....	....	....	....	....	....	....	....	....	....	....
	NHL Totals		**35**	**0**	**3**	**3**	**70**	**0**	**0**	**0**	**12**	**0.0**		**2**	**50.0**	**5:22**	**5**	**0**	**0**	**0**	**10**	**0**	**0**	**0**	**4:34**

• Missed majority of 2009-10 season recovering from recurring upper body injury and as a healthy reserve.

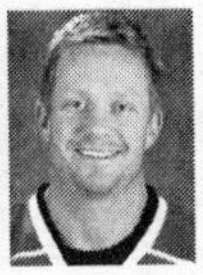

LETOWSKI, Trevor

(leh-TOW-skee, TREH-vuhr)

Right wing. Shoots right. 5'10", 180 lbs. Born, Thunder Bay, Ont., April 5, 1977. Phoenix's 6th choice, 174th overall, in 1996 Entry Draft.

Season	Club	League	GP	G	A	Pts	PIM	PP	SH	GW	S	%	+/-	TF	F%	Min	GP	G	A	Pts	PIM	PP	SH	GW	Min
1993-94	T. Bay Kings	TBMHL	64	41	60	101	48	....	....	....	....	....	....	....	....	....	....	....	....	....	....	....	....	....	....
1994-95	Sarnia Sting	OHL	66	22	19	41	33	....	....	....	....	....	....	....	....	....	4	0	1	1	9	....	....	....	....
1995-96	Sarnia Sting	OHL	66	36	63	99	66	....	....	....	....	....	....	....	....	....	10	9	5	14	10	....	....	....	....
1996-97	Sarnia Sting	OHL	55	35	73	108	51	....	....	....	....	....	....	....	....	....	12	9	12	21	20	....	....	....	....
1997-98	Springfield	AHL	75	11	20	31	26	....	....	....	....	....	....	....	....	....	4	1	0	1	2	....	....	....	....
1998-99	**Phoenix**	**NHL**	**14**	**2**	**2**	**4**	**2**	**0**	**0**	**0**	**8**	**25.0**	**1**	**49**	**55.1**	**6:01**	....	....	....	....	....	....	....	....	....
	Springfield	AHL	67	32	35	67	46	....	....	....	....	....	....	....	....	....	3	1	0	1	2	....	....	....	....
99-2000	**Phoenix**	**NHL**	**82**	**19**	**20**	**39**	**20**	**3**	**4**	**3**	**125**	**15.2**	**2**	**692**	**47.7**	**16:03**	**5**	**1**	**1**	**2**	**4**	**0**	**0**	**0**	**15:52**
2000-01	**Phoenix**	**NHL**	**77**	**7**	**15**	**22**	**32**	**0**	**1**	**3**	**110**	**6.4**	**–2**	**726**	**46.1**	**16:20**	....	....	....	....	....	....	....	....	....
2001-02	**Phoenix**	**NHL**	**33**	**2**	**6**	**8**	**4**	**0**	**0**	**0**	**43**	**4.7**	**2**	**250**	**52.4**	**14:27**	....	....	....	....	....	....	....	....	....
	Vancouver	**NHL**	**42**	**7**	**10**	**17**	**15**	**1**	**0**	**0**	**65**	**10.8**	**2**	**111**	**44.1**	**12:47**	**6**	**0**	**1**	**1**	**8**	**0**	**0**	**0**	**11:50**
2002-03	**Vancouver**	**NHL**	**78**	**11**	**14**	**25**	**36**	**1**	**1**	**2**	**136**	**8.1**	**8**	**70**	**41.4**	**12:26**	**6**	**0**	**1**	**1**	**0**	**0**	**0**	**0**	**9:40**
2003-04	**Columbus**	**NHL**	**73**	**15**	**17**	**32**	**16**	**4**	**0**	**1**	**126**	**11.9**	**–12**	**146**	**43.8**	**16:19**	....	....	....	....	....	....	....	....	....
2004-05	Fribourg	Swiss	9	4	5	9	6	....	....	....	....	....	....	....	....	....	11	7	9	16	8	....	....	....	....
2005-06	**Columbus**	**NHL**	**81**	**10**	**18**	**28**	**36**	**1**	**1**	**1**	**135**	**7.4**	**–2**	**284**	**45.8**	**16:32**	....	....	....	....	....	....	....	....	....
2006-07	**Carolina**	**NHL**	**61**	**2**	**6**	**8**	**18**	**0**	**0**	**0**	**69**	**2.9**	**–8**	**208**	**48.6**	**9:41**	....	....	....	....	....	....	....	....	....
2007-08	**Carolina**	**NHL**	**75**	**9**	**9**	**18**	**30**	**0**	**1**	**1**	**67**	**13.4**	**–10**	**602**	**44.7**	**10:16**	....	....	....	....	....	....	....	....	....
2008-09	Barys Astana	Rus-KHL	37	9	7	16	30	....	....	....	....	....	....	....	....	....	3	1	0	1	2	....	....	....	....
2009-10	Barys Astana	Rus-KHL	54	3	10	13	24	....	....	....	....	....	....	....	....	....	3	0	0	0	0	....	....	....	....
	NHL Totals		**616**	**84**	**117**	**201**	**209**	**10**	**8**	**11**	**884**	**9.5**		**3138**	**46.7**	**13:51**	**17**	**1**	**3**	**4**	**12**	**0**	**0**	**0**	**12:15**

Traded to **Vancouver** by **Phoenix** with Todd Warriner, Tyler Bouck and Phoenix's 3rd round choice (later traded back to Phoenix – Phoenix selected Dimitri Pestunov) in 2003 Entry Draft for Drake Berehowsky and Denis Pederson, December 28, 2001. Signed as a free agent by **Columbus**, July 3, 2003. Signed as a free agent by **Fribourg** (Swiss), January 7, 2005. Signed as a free agent by **Carolina**, July 6, 2006. Signed as a free agent by **Astana** (Russia-KHL), August 3, 2008.

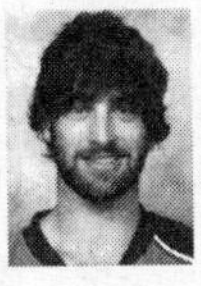

LEWIS, Grant

(LOO-ihs, GRANT) **ATL.**

Defense. Shoots right. 6'3", 205 lbs. Born, Pittsburgh, PA, January 20, 1985. Atlanta's 2nd choice, 40th overall, in 2004 Entry Draft.

Season	Club	League	GP	G	A	Pts	PIM	PP	SH	GW	S	%	+/-	TF	F%	Min	GP	G	A	Pts	PIM	PP	SH	GW	Min
2002-03	Pittsburgh Forge	NAHL	50	2	7	9	59	....	....	....	....	....	....	....	....	....	....	....	....	....	....	....	....	....	....
2003-04	Dartmouth	ECAC	34	3	22	25	57	....	....	....	....	....	....	....	....	....	....	....	....	....	....	....	....	....	....
2004-05	Dartmouth	ECAC	33	5	17	22	32	....	....	....	....	....	....	....	....	....	....	....	....	....	....	....	....	....	....
2005-06	Dartmouth	ECAC	29	4	11	15	53	....	....	....	....	....	....	....	....	....	....	....	....	....	....	....	....	....	....
2006-07	Dartmouth	ECAC	24	1	14	15	30	....	....	....	....	....	....	....	....	....	....	....	....	....	....	....	....	....	....
2007-08	Chicago Wolves	AHL	43	2	14	16	44	....	....	....	....	....	....	....	....	....	2	0	0	0	2	....	....	....	....
2008-09	**Atlanta**	**NHL**	**1**	**0**	**0**	**0**	**0**	**0**	**0**	**0**	**1**	**0.0**	**0**	**0**	**0.0**	**15:29**	....	....	....	....	....	....	....	....	....
	Chicago Wolves	AHL	54	0	22	22	72	....	....	....	....	....	....	....	....	....	....	....	....	....	....	....	....	....	....
2009-10	Chicago Wolves	AHL	26	1	2	3	23	....	....	....	....	....	....	....	....	....	....	....	....	....	....	....	....	....	....
	Hershey Bears	AHL	10	0	3	3	6	....	....	....	....	....	....	....	....	....	1	0	0	0	0	....	....	....	....
	NHL Totals		**1**	**0**	**0**	**0**	**0**	**0**	**0**	**0**	**1**	**0.0**		**0**	**0.0**	**15:29**	....	....	....	....	....	....	....	....	....

ECAC All-Rookie Team (2004) • ECAC First All-Star Team (2004) • ECAC Second All-Star Team (2006)

LEWIS, Trevor

(LOO-ihs, TREH-vuhr) **L.A**

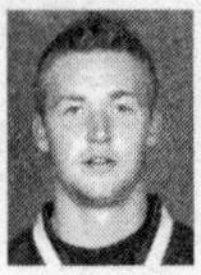

Center. Shoots right. 6', 199 lbs. Born, Salt Lake City, UT, January 8, 1987. Los Angeles' 2nd choice, 17th overall, in 2006 Entry Draft.

			Regular Season														Playoffs								
Season	Club	League	GP	G	A	Pts	PIM	PP	SH	GW	S	%	+/-	TF	F%	Min	GP	G	A	Pts	PIM	PP	SH	GW	Mi
2004-05	Des Moines	USHL	52	10	12	22	70	....	....	....	....	....	....	....	....	....	....	....	....	....	....	....	....	....	..
2005-06	Des Moines	USHL	56	35	40	75	69	....	....	....	....	....	....	....	....	....	11	3	*13	*16	16	....	....	....	..
2006-07	Owen Sound	OHL	62	29	44	73	51	....	....	....	....	....	....	....	....	....	4	1	2	3	0	....	....	....	..
	Manchester	AHL	8	4	2	6	2	....	....	....	....	....	....	....	....	....	2	0	0	0	0	....	....	....	..
2007-08	Manchester	AHL	76	12	16	28	43	....	....	....	....	....	....	....	....	....	4	0	0	0	2	....	....	....	..
2008-09	**Los Angeles**	**NHL**	**6**	**1**	**2**	**3**	**0**	**0**	**0**	**0**	**10**	**10.0**	**0**	**4**	**25.0**	**11:36**	....	....	....	....	....	....	....	....	..
	Manchester	AHL	75	20	31	51	30	....	....	....	....	....	....	....	....	....	....	....	....	....	....	....	....	....	..
2009-10	**Los Angeles**	**NHL**	**5**	**0**	**0**	**0**	**0**	**0**	**0**	**0**	**4**	**0.0**	**–3**	**5**	**0.0**	**9:08**	....	....	....	....	....	....	....	....	..
	Manchester	AHL	23	5	2	7	6	....	....	....	....	....	....	....	....	....	16	5	4	9	10	....	....	....	..
	NHL Totals		**11**	**1**	**2**	**3**	**0**	**0**	**0**	**0**	**14**	**7.1**		**9**	**11.1**	**10:28**	....	....	....	....	....	....	....	....	..

USHL Player of the Year (2006)

• Missed majority of 2009-10 season recovering from upper body injury and as a healthy reserve.

LIDSTROM, Nicklas

(LID-struhm, NIHK-luhs) **DET**

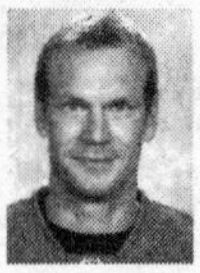

Defense. Shoots left. 6'1", 190 lbs. Born, Vasteras, Sweden, April 28, 1970. Detroit's 3rd choice, 53rd overall, in 1989 Entry Draft.

			Regular Season														Playoffs								
Season	Club	League	GP	G	A	Pts	PIM	PP	SH	GW	S	%	+/-	TF	F%	Min	GP	G	A	Pts	PIM	PP	SH	GW	Mi
1987-88	Vasteras	Sweden-2	3	0	0	0	0	....	....	....	....	....	....	....	....	....	5	0	0	0	6	....	....	....	..
1988-89	Vasteras IK	Sweden	34	1	6	7	4	....	....	....	....	....	....	....	....	....	5	0	2	2	0	....	....	....	..
1989-90	Vasteras IK	Sweden	39	8	8	16	14	....	....	....	....	....	....	....	....	....	2	0	1	1	2	....	....	....	..
1990-91	Vasteras IK	Sweden	38	4	19	23	2	....	....	....	....	....	....	....	....	....	4	0	0	0	4	....	....	....	..
1991-92	**Detroit**	**NHL**	**80**	**11**	**49**	**60**	**22**	**5**	**0**	**1**	**168**	**6.5**	**36**	....	....	....	**11**	**1**	**2**	**3**	**0**	**1**	**0**	**0**	..
1992-93	**Detroit**	**NHL**	**84**	**7**	**34**	**41**	**28**	**3**	**0**	**2**	**156**	**4.5**	**7**	....	....	....	**7**	**1**	**0**	**1**	**0**	**1**	**0**	**0**	..
1993-94	**Detroit**	**NHL**	**84**	**10**	**46**	**56**	**26**	**4**	**0**	**3**	**200**	**5.0**	**43**	....	....	....	**7**	**3**	**2**	**5**	**0**	**1**	**1**	**0**	..
1994-95	Vasteras IK	Sweden	13	2	10	12	4	....	....	....	....	....	....	....	....	....	....	....	....	....	....	....	....	....	..
	Detroit	**NHL**	**43**	**10**	**16**	**26**	**6**	**7**	**0**	**0**	**90**	**11.1**	**15**	....	....	....	**18**	**4**	**12**	**16**	**8**	**3**	**0**	**2**	..
1995-96	**Detroit**	**NHL**	**81**	**17**	**50**	**67**	**20**	**8**	**1**	**1**	**211**	**8.1**	**29**	....	....	....	**19**	**5**	**9**	**14**	**10**	**1**	**0**	**0**	..
1996-97♦	**Detroit**	**NHL**	**79**	**15**	**42**	**57**	**30**	**8**	**0**	**1**	**214**	**7.0**	**11**	....	....	....	**20**	**2**	**6**	**8**	**2**	**0**	**0**	**0**	..
1997-98♦	**Detroit**	**NHL**	**80**	**17**	**42**	**59**	**18**	**7**	**1**	**1**	**205**	**8.3**	**22**	....	....	....	**22**	**6**	**13**	**19**	**8**	**2**	**0**	**2**	..
	Sweden	Olympics	4	1	1	2	2	....	....	....	....	....	....	....	....	....	....	....	....	....	....	....	....	....	..
1998-99	**Detroit**	**NHL**	**81**	**14**	**43**	**57**	**14**	**6**	**2**	**3**	**205**	**6.8**	**14**	**0**	**0.0**	**26:31**	**10**	**2**	**9**	**11**	**4**	**2**	**0**	**0**	**30:2**
99-2000	**Detroit**	**NHL**	**81**	**20**	**53**	**73**	**18**	**9**	**4**	**3**	**218**	**9.2**	**19**	**0**	**0.0**	**28:45**	**9**	**2**	**4**	**6**	**4**	**1**	**0**	**0**	**30:2**
2000-01	**Detroit**	**NHL**	**82**	**15**	**56**	**71**	**18**	**8**	**0**	**0**	**272**	**5.5**	**9**	**0**	**0.0**	**28:27**	**6**	**1**	**7**	**8**	**0**	**0**	**0**	**0**	**29:1**
2001-02♦	**Detroit**	**NHL**	**78**	**9**	**50**	**59**	**20**	**6**	**0**	**0**	**215**	**4.2**	**13**	**0**	**0.0**	**28:49**	**23**	**5**	**11**	**16**	**2**	**2**	**1**	**2**	**31:1**
	Sweden	Olympics	4	1	5	6	0	....	....	....	....	....	....	....	....	....	....	....	....	....	....	....	....	....	..
2002-03	**Detroit**	**NHL**	**82**	**18**	**44**	**62**	**38**	**8**	**1**	**4**	**175**	**10.3**	**40**	**0**	**0.0**	**29:20**	**4**	**0**	**2**	**2**	**0**	**0**	**0**	**0**	**33:3**
2003-04	**Detroit**	**NHL**	**81**	**10**	**28**	**38**	**18**	**3**	**1**	**3**	**194**	**5.2**	**19**	**0**	**0.0**	**27:39**	**12**	**2**	**5**	**7**	**4**	**2**	**0**	**0**	**27:0**
2004-05			DID NOT PLAY																						
2005-06	**Detroit**	**NHL**	**80**	**16**	**64**	**80**	**50**	**9**	**0**	**2**	**243**	**6.6**	**21**	**0**	**0.0**	**28:07**	**6**	**1**	**1**	**2**	**2**	**1**	**0**	**1**	**31:5**
	Sweden	Olympics	8	2	4	6	2	....	....	....	....	....	....	....	....	....	....	....	....	....	....	....	....	....	..
2006-07	**Detroit**	**NHL**	**80**	**13**	**49**	**62**	**46**	**10**	**0**	**1**	**224**	**5.8**	**40**	**0**	**0.0**	**27:29**	**18**	**4**	**14**	**18**	**6**	**4**	**0**	**2**	**30:3**
2007-08♦	**Detroit**	**NHL**	**76**	**10**	**60**	**70**	**40**	**5**	**0**	**4**	**188**	**5.3**	**40**	**0**	**0.0**	**26:43**	**22**	**3**	**10**	**13**	**14**	**1**	**1**	**1**	**26:4**
2008-09	**Detroit**	**NHL**	**78**	**16**	**43**	**59**	**30**	**10**	**0**	**4**	**180**	**8.9**	**31**	**0**	**0.0**	**24:49**	**21**	**4**	**12**	**16**	**6**	**3**	**0**	**1**	**25:3**
2009-10	**Detroit**	**NHL**	**82**	**9**	**40**	**49**	**24**	**5**	**0**	**1**	**194**	**4.6**	**22**	**0**	**0.0**	**25:26**	**12**	**4**	**6**	**10**	**2**	**3**	**0**	**0**	**26:2**
	Sweden	Olympics	4	0	0	0	2	....	....	....	....	....	....	....	....	....	....	....	....	....	....	....	....	....	..
	NHL Totals		**1412**	**237**	**809**	**1046**	**466**	**121**	**10**	**34**	**3552**	**6.7**		**0**	**0.0**	**27:28**	**247**	**50**	**125**	**175**	**72**	**28**	**3**	**11**	**28:4**

NHL All-Rookie Team (1992) • NHL First All-Star Team (1998, 1999, 2000, 2001, 2002, 2003, 2006, 2007, 2008) • James Norris Memorial Trophy (2001, 2002, 2003, 2006, 2007, 2008) • Conn Smythe Trophy (2002) • Olympic Tournament All-Star Team (2006) • NHL Second All-Star Team (2009, 2010)

Played in NHL All-Star Game (1996, 1998, 1999, 2000, 2001, 2002, 2003, 2004, 2007, 2008)

LIFFITON, David

(LIH-fih-tuhn, DAY-vihd) **COL**

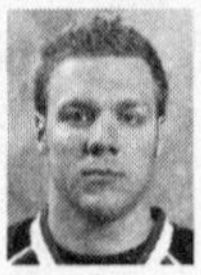

Defense. Shoots left. 6'2", 210 lbs. Born, Windsor, Ont., October 18, 1984. Colorado's 1st choice, 63rd overall, in 2003 Entry Draft.

			Regular Season														Playoffs								
Season	Club	League	GP	G	A	Pts	PIM	PP	SH	GW	S	%	+/-	TF	F%	Min	GP	G	A	Pts	PIM	PP	SH	GW	Mi
2000-01	Aylmer Aces	OHA-B	51	1	9	10	51	....	....	....	....	....	....	....	....	....	....	....	....	....	....	....	....	....	..
2001-02	Plymouth Whalers	OHL	62	3	9	12	65	....	....	....	....	....	....	....	....	....	6	0	0	0	0	....	....	....	..
2002-03	Plymouth Whalers	OHL	64	5	11	16	139	....	....	....	....	....	....	....	....	....	18	1	3	4	29	....	....	....	..
2003-04	Plymouth Whalers	OHL	44	2	9	11	85	....	....	....	....	....	....	....	....	....	9	0	0	0	12	....	....	....	..
2004-05	Hartford	AHL	33	0	1	1	74	....	....	....	....	....	....	....	....	....	....	....	....	....	....	....	....	....	..
	Charlotte	ECHL	16	0	2	2	18	....	....	....	....	....	....	....	....	....	15	1	4	5	27	....	....	....	..
2005-06	**NY Rangers**	**NHL**	**1**	**0**	**0**	**0**	**2**	**0**	**0**	**0**	**0**	**0.0**	**0**	**0**	**0.0**	**8:42**	....	....	....	....	....	....	....	....	..
	Hartford	AHL	50	2	7	9	158	....	....	....	....	....	....	....	....	....	....	....	....	....	....	....	....	....	..
2006-07	**NY Rangers**	**NHL**	**2**	**0**	**0**	**0**	**7**	**0**	**0**	**0**	**2**	**0.0**	**1**	**0**	**0.0**	**11:31**	....	....	....	....	....	....	....	....	..
	Hartford	AHL	72	2	11	13	189	....	....	....	....	....	....	....	....	....	7	1	1	2	18	....	....	....	..
2007-08	Hartford	AHL	21	0	2	2	52	....	....	....	....	....	....	....	....	....	....	....	....	....	....	....	....	....	..
2008-09	Esbjerg	Denmark	25	3	6	9	84	....	....	....	....	....	....	....	....	....	4	0	0	0	4	....	....	....	..
2009-10	Syracuse Crunch	AHL	72	5	15	20	118	....	....	....	....	....	....	....	....	....	....	....	....	....	....	....	....	....	..
	NHL Totals		**3**	**0**	**0**	**0**	**9**	**0**	**0**	**0**	**2**	**0.0**		**0**	**0.0**	**10:35**	....	....	....	....	....	....	....	....	..

Traded to **NY Rangers** by **Colorado** with Chris McAllister and Florida's 2nd round choice (previously acquired, later traded back to Florida – Florida selected David Shantz) in 2004 Entry Draft for Matthew Barnaby and NY Rangers' 3rd round choice (Denis Parshin) in 2004 Entry Draft, March 8, 2004. • Missed majority of 2007-08 season recovering from post-concussion symptoms. Signed as a free agent by **New Jersey**, September 29, 2009. Signed as a free agent by **Colorado**, July 2, 2010.

LILES, John-Michael

(LIGH-uhls, JAWN-MIGHK-uhl) **COL**

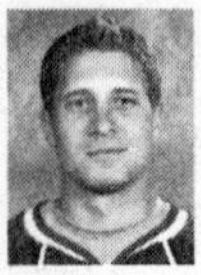

Defense. Shoots left. 5'10", 185 lbs. Born, Indianapolis, IN, November 25, 1980. Colorado's 8th choice, 159th overall, in 2000 Entry Draft.

			Regular Season														Playoffs								
Season	Club	League	GP	G	A	Pts	PIM	PP	SH	GW	S	%	+/-	TF	F%	Min	GP	G	A	Pts	PIM	PP	SH	GW	Mi
1997-98	USNTDP	U-17	15	0	6	6	4	....	....	....	....	....	....	....	....	....	....	....	....	....	....	....	....	....	..
	USNTDP	USHL	5	0	1	1	0	....	....	....	....	....	....	....	....	....	....	....	....	....	....	....	....	....	..
	USNTDP	NAHL	42	4	7	11	40	....	....	....	....	....	....	....	....	....	5	2	0	2	0	....	....	....	..
1998-99	USNTDP	USHL	46	4	14	18	47	....	....	....	....	....	....	....	....	....	....	....	....	....	....	....	....	....	..
	USNTDP	NAHL	13	2	5	7	6	....	....	....	....	....	....	....	....	....	....	....	....	....	....	....	....	....	..
99-2000	Michigan State	CCHA	40	8	20	28	26	....	....	....	....	....	....	....	....	....	....	....	....	....	....	....	....	....	..
2000-01	Michigan State	CCHA	42	7	18	25	28	....	....	....	....	....	....	....	....	....	....	....	....	....	....	....	....	....	..
2001-02	Michigan State	CCHA	41	13	22	35	18	....	....	....	....	....	....	....	....	....	....	....	....	....	....	....	....	....	..
2002-03	Michigan State	CCHA	39	16	34	50	46	....	....	....	....	....	....	....	....	....	....	....	....	....	....	....	....	....	..
	Hershey Bears	AHL	5	0	1	1	4	....	....	....	....	....	....	....	....	....	5	0	0	0	2	....	....	....	..
2003-04	**Colorado**	**NHL**	**79**	**10**	**24**	**34**	**28**	**2**	**0**	**1**	**115**	**8.7**	**7**	**0**	**0.0**	**16:14**	**11**	**0**	**1**	**1**	**4**	**0**	**0**	**0**	**16:4**
2004-05	Iserlohn Roosters	Germany	17	5	6	11	24	....	....	....	....	....	....	....	....	....	....	....	....	....	....	....	....	....	..
2005-06	**Colorado**	**NHL**	**82**	**14**	**35**	**49**	**44**	**6**	**0**	**1**	**154**	**9.1**	**5**	**1**	**100.0**	**18:31**	**9**	**1**	**2**	**3**	**6**	**1**	**0**	**0**	**17:3**
	United States	Olympics	6	0	2	2	2	....	....	....	....	....	....	....	....	....	....	....	....	....	....	....	....	....	..
2006-07	**Colorado**	**NHL**	**71**	**14**	**30**	**44**	**24**	**8**	**0**	**3**	**128**	**10.9**	**0**	**0**	**0.0**	**17:46**	....	....	....	....	....	....	....	....	..
2007-08	**Colorado**	**NHL**	**81**	**6**	**26**	**32**	**26**	**5**	**0**	**1**	**163**	**3.7**	**2**	**0**	**0.0**	**19:40**	**10**	**2**	**3**	**5**	**2**	**1**	**0**	**0**	**19:0**
2008-09	**Colorado**	**NHL**	**75**	**12**	**27**	**39**	**31**	**6**	**0**	**1**	**146**	**8.2**	**–19**	**0**	**0.0**	**21:33**	....	....	....	....	....	....	....	....	..
2009-10	**Colorado**	**NHL**	**59**	**6**	**25**	**31**	**30**	**3**	**0**	**2**	**96**	**6.3**	**–2**	**0**	**0.0**	**18:28**	**6**	**1**	**1**	**2**	**4**	**1**	**0**	**0**	**19:0**
	NHL Totals		**447**	**62**	**167**	**229**	**183**	**30**	**0**	**9**	**802**	**7.7**		**1**	**100.0**	**18:42**	**36**	**4**	**7**	**11**	**16**	**3**	**0**	**0**	**17:5**

CCHA Second All-Star Team (2001) • CCHA First All-Star Team (2002, 2003) • NCAA West Second All-American Team (2002) • NCAA West First All-American Team (2003) • NHL All-Rookie Team (2004)

Signed as a free agent by **Iserlohn** (Germany), December 29, 2004.

LILJA, Andreas

(LIHL-yuh, awn-DRAY-uhs)

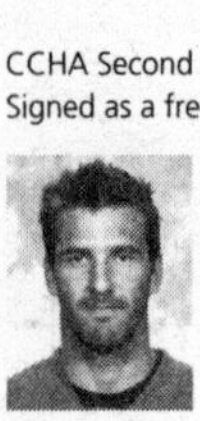

Defense. Shoots left. 6'3", 220 lbs. Born, Helsingborg, Sweden, July 13, 1975. Los Angeles' 2nd choice, 54th overall, in 2000 Entry Draft.

			Regular Season														Playoffs								
Season	Club	League	GP	G	A	Pts	PIM	PP	SH	GW	S	%	+/-	TF	F%	Min	GP	G	A	Pts	PIM	PP	SH	GW	Mi
1993-94	Malmo IF Jr.	Swe-Jr.	14	3	7	10	38	....	....	....	....	....	....	....	....	....	....	....	....	....	....	....	....	....	..
1994-95	Malmo IF Jr.	Swe-Jr.	30	7	13	20	82	....	....	....	....	....	....	....	....	....	....	....	....	....	....	....	....	....	..
	Malmo IF	Sweden	3	0	0	0	2	....	....	....	....	....	....	....	....	....	....	....	....	....	....	....	....	....	..
1995-96	Malmo IF Jr.	Swe-Jr.	3	0	1	1	6	....	....	....	....	....	....	....	....	....	....	....	....	....	....	....	....	....	..
	Malmo IF	Sweden	40	1	5	6	63	....	....	....	....	....	....	....	....	....	5	0	1	1	2	....	....	....	..
1996-97	Malmo	Sweden	47	1	0	1	22	....	....	....	....	....	....	....	....	....	4	0	0	0	10	....	....	....	..
1997-98	Malmo	Sweden	10	0	0	0	0	....	....	....	....	....	....	....	....	....	....	....	....	....	....	....	....	....	..
	Mora IK	Sweden-2	13	1	4	5	30	....	....	....	....	....	....	....	....	....	4	1	0	1	14	....	....	....	..

			Regular Season														Playoffs								
Season	Club	League	GP	G	A	Pts	PIM	PP	SH	GW	S	%	+/-	TF	F%	Min	GP	G	A	Pts	PIM	PP	SH	GW	Min
1998-99	Malmo	Sweden	41	0	3	3	44	....	....	....	....	....	....	....	....	....	1	0	0	0	4	....	....	....	....
99-2000	Malmo	Sweden	49	8	11	19	88	....	....	....	....	....	....	....	....	....	6	0	0	0	8	....	....	....	....
2000-01	**Los Angeles**	**NHL**	**2**	**0**	**0**	**0**	**4**	**0**	**0**	**0**	**1**	**0.0**	**−2**	**0**	**0.0**	**12:22**	**1**	**0**	**0**	**0**	**0**	**0**	**0**	**0**	**6:56**
	Lowell	AHL	61	7	29	36	149	....	....	....	....	....	....	....	....	....	4	0	6	6	6	....	....	....	....
2001-02	**Los Angeles**	**NHL**	**26**	**1**	**4**	**5**	**22**	**1**	**0**	**0**	**12**	**8.3**	**3**	**0**	**0.0**	**11:27**	**5**	**0**	**0**	**0**	**6**	**0**	**0**	**0**	**10:26**
	Manchester	AHL	4	0	1	1	4	....	....	....	....	....	....	....	....	....	....	....	....	....	....	....	....	....	....
2002-03	**Los Angeles**	**NHL**	**17**	**0**	**3**	**3**	**14**	**0**	**0**	**0**	**13**	**0.0**	**5**	**0**	**0.0**	**20:04**	....	....	....	....	....	....	....	....	....
	Florida	**NHL**	**56**	**4**	**8**	**12**	**56**	**0**	**0**	**0**	**59**	**6.8**	**8**	**0**	**0.0**	**19:11**	....	....	....	....	....	....	....	....	....
2003-04	**Florida**	**NHL**	**79**	**3**	**4**	**7**	**90**	**0**	**0**	**0**	**79**	**3.8**	**−8**	**1**	**0.0**	**19:34**	....	....	....	....	....	....	....	....	....
2004-05	Mora IK	Sweden	44	3	8	11	67	....	....	....	....	....	....	....	....	....	....	....	....	....	....	....	....	....	....
	HC Ambri-Piotta	Swiss	....	....	....	....	....	....	....	....	....	....	....	....	....	....	5	0	2	2	6	....	....	....	....
2005-06	**Detroit**	**NHL**	**82**	**2**	**13**	**15**	**98**	**0**	**0**	**1**	**78**	**2.6**	**18**	**1**	**0.0**	**19:01**	**6**	**0**	**1**	**1**	**6**	**0**	**0**	**0**	**19:21**
2006-07	**Detroit**	**NHL**	**57**	**0**	**5**	**5**	**54**	**0**	**0**	**0**	**37**	**0.0**	**6**	**1**	**0.0**	**15:25**	**18**	**1**	**0**	**1**	**10**	**0**	**0**	**0**	**19:02**
2007-08◆	**Detroit**	**NHL**	**79**	**2**	**10**	**12**	**93**	**0**	**0**	**2**	**72**	**2.8**	**−2**	**1**	**0.0**	**18:14**	**12**	**0**	**1**	**1**	**16**	**0**	**0**	**0**	**14:05**
2008-09	**Detroit**	**NHL**	**60**	**2**	**11**	**13**	**66**	**0**	**0**	**0**	**60**	**3.3**	**13**	**1**	**0.0**	**17:00**	....	....	....	....	....	....	....	....	....
2009-10	**Detroit**	**NHL**	**20**	**1**	**1**	**2**	**4**	**0**	**0**	**0**	**19**	**5.3**	**−2**	**0**	**0.0**	**14:08**	**11**	**0**	**0**	**0**	**14**	**0**	**0**	**0**	**11:00**
	Grand Rapids	AHL	4	0	0	0	6	....	....	....	....	....	....	....	....	....	....	....	....	....	....	....	....	....	....
	NHL Totals		**478**	**15**	**59**	**74**	**501**	**1**	**0**	**3**	**430**	**3.5**		**5**	**0.0**	**17:42**	**53**	**1**	**2**	**3**	**52**	**0**	**0**	**0**	**15:15**

• Missed majority of 2001-02 season as a healthy reserve. Traded to **Florida** by **Los Angeles** with Jaroslav Bednar for Dmitry Yushkevich and Florida's 5th round choice (previously acquired, Los Angeles selected Brady Murray) in 2003 Entry Draft, November 26, 2002. Signed as a free agent by **Nashville**, July 26, 2004. Signed as a free agent by **Mora** (Sweden), September 15, 2004. Signed as a free agent by **Ambri-Piotta** (Swiss), February 25, 2005. Signed as a free agent by **Detroit**, August 24, 2005. • Missed remainder of 2008-09 season and majority of 2009-10 season recovering from head injury suffered in game at Nashville, February 28, 2009.

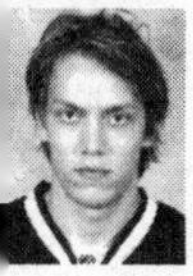

LINDGREN, Perttu

(LIHND-gruhn, PUHR-too) **DAL.**

Center. Shoots left. 6', 185 lbs. Born, Tampere, Finland, August 26, 1987. Dallas' 4th choice, 75th overall, in 2005 Entry Draft.

Season	Club	League	GP	G	A	Pts	PIM	PP	SH	GW	S	%	+/-	TF	F%	Min	GP	G	A	Pts	PIM	PP	SH	GW	Min
2003-04	Ilves Tampere U18	Fin-U18	24	11	17	28	26	....	....	....	....	....	....	....	....	....	....	....	....	....	....	....	....	....	....
	Ilves Tampere Jr.	Fin-Jr.	2	0	0	0	0	....	....	....	....	....	....	....	....	....	....	....	....	....	....	....	....	....	....
2004-05	Ilves Tampere Jr.	Fin-Jr.	38	12	29	41	2	....	....	....	....	....	....	....	....	....	10	7	10	17	4	....	....	....	....
	Ilves Tampere	Finland	2	0	0	0	0	....	....	....	....	....	....	....	....	....	....	....	....	....	....	....	....	....	....
2005-06	Ilves Tampere Jr.	Fin-Jr.	2	1	0	1	0	....	....	....	....	....	....	....	....	....	....	....	....	....	....	....	....	....	....
	Suomi U20	Finland-2	3	0	3	3	0	....	....	....	....	....	....	....	....	....	....	....	....	....	....	....	....	....	....
	Ilves Tampere	Finland	51	13	24	37	16	....	....	....	....	....	....	....	....	....	4	0	0	0	0	....	....	....	....
2006-07	Suomi U20	Finland-2	2	1	1	2	2	....	....	....	....	....	....	....	....	....	....	....	....	....	....	....	....	....	....
	Ilves Tampere	Finland	43	4	22	26	38	....	....	....	....	....	....	....	....	....	7	4	2	6	2	....	....	....	....
2007-08	Iowa Stars	AHL	69	10	24	34	6	....	....	....	....	....	....	....	....	....	....	....	....	....	....	....	....	....	....
2008-09	Lukko Rauma	Finland	49	5	19	24	16	....	....	....	....	....	....	....	....	....	7	1	0	1	6	....	....	....	....
2009-10	**Dallas**	**NHL**	**1**	**0**	**0**	**0**	**0**	**0**	**0**	**0**	**0**	**0.0**	**0**	**5**	**40.0**	**8:33**	....	....	....	....	....	....	....	....	....
	Texas Stars	AHL	74	14	33	47	14	....	....	....	....	....	....	....	....	....	24	7	10	17	2	....	....	....	....
	NHL Totals		**1**	**0**	**0**	**0**	**0**	**0**	**0**	**0**	**0**	**0.0**		**5**	**40.0**	**8:33**	....	....	....	....	....	....	....	....	....

• Assigned to **Rauma** (Finland) by **Dallas**, October 2, 2008.

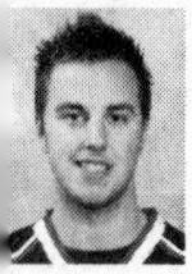

LINDSTROM, Joakim

(LIHND-struhm, YOH-ah-kihm)

Center. Shoots left. 6', 187 lbs. Born, Skelleftea, Sweden, December 5, 1983. Columbus' 2nd choice, 41st overall, in 2002 Entry Draft.

Season	Club	League	GP	G	A	Pts	PIM	PP	SH	GW	S	%	+/-	TF	F%	Min	GP	G	A	Pts	PIM	PP	SH	GW	Min
99-2000	MoDo U18	Swe-U18	17	6	*14	20	32	....	....	....	....	....	....	....	....	....	....	....	....	....	....	....	....	....	....
	Malmo Jr.	Swe-Jr.	10	4	4	8	2	....	....	....	....	....	....	....	....	....	....	....	....	....	....	....	....	....	....
2000-01	Malmo Jr.	Swe-Jr.	12	7	14	21	46	....	....	....	....	....	....	....	....	....	4	2	3	5	24	....	....	....	....
	MoDo	Sweden	10	2	3	5	2	....	....	....	....	....	....	....	....	....	7	0	1	1	0	....	....	....	....
2001-02	Malmo Jr.	Swe-Jr.	10	9	6	15	67	....	....	....	....	....	....	....	....	....	....	....	....	....	....	....	....	....	....
	IF Troja-Ljungby	Sweden-2	3	0	0	0	12	....	....	....	....	....	....	....	....	....	....	....	....	....	....	....	....	....	....
	MODO	Sweden	42	4	3	7	20	....	....	....	....	....	....	....	....	....	14	3	5	8	8	....	....	....	....
2002-03	MODO	Sweden	29	4	2	6	14	....	....	....	....	....	....	....	....	....	6	1	1	2	2	....	....	....	....
	Malmo Jr.	Swe-Jr.	2	5	1	6	8	....	....	....	....	....	....	....	....	....	....	....	....	....	....	....	....	....	....
	Ornskoldsviks SK	Sweden-2	2	1	1	2	4	....	....	....	....	....	....	....	....	....	....	....	....	....	....	....	....	....	....
2003-04	MODO	Sweden	15	0	2	2	0	....	....	....	....	....	....	....	....	....	....	....	....	....	....	....	....	....	....
	Sundsvall	Sweden-2	2	0	5	5	0	....	....	....	....	....	....	....	....	....	....	....	....	....	....	....	....	....	....
2004-05	MODO Jr.	Swe-Jr.	2	4	1	5	0	....	....	....	....	....	....	....	....	....	....	....	....	....	....	....	....	....	....
	MODO	Sweden	37	2	3	5	24	....	....	....	....	....	....	....	....	....	....	....	....	....	....	....	....	....	....
	Syracuse Crunch	AHL	13	4	4	8	0	....	....	....	....	....	....	....	....	....	....	....	....	....	....	....	....	....	....
2005-06	**Columbus**	**NHL**	**3**	**0**	**0**	**0**	**0**	**0**	**0**	**0**	**4**	**0.0**	**0**	**0**	**0.0**	**5:11**	....	....	....	....	....	....	....	....	....
	Syracuse Crunch	AHL	64	14	29	43	52	....	....	....	....	....	....	....	....	....	6	1	1	2	0	....	....	....	....
2006-07	**Columbus**	**NHL**	**9**	**1**	**0**	**1**	**4**	**0**	**0**	**0**	**9**	**11.1**	**−3**	**0**	**0.0**	**8:28**	....	....	....	....	....	....	....	....	....
	Syracuse Crunch	AHL	50	22	26	48	34	....	....	....	....	....	....	....	....	....	....	....	....	....	....	....	....	....	....
2007-08	**Columbus**	**NHL**	**25**	**3**	**4**	**7**	**14**	**2**	**0**	**1**	**25**	**12.0**	**0**	**7**	**28.6**	**9:26**	....	....	....	....	....	....	....	....	....
	Syracuse Crunch	AHL	49	25	35	60	68	....	....	....	....	....	....	....	....	....	13	4	3	7	6	....	....	....	....
2008-09	Iowa Chops	AHL	21	7	14	21	33	....	....	....	....	....	....	....	....	....	....	....	....	....	....	....	....	....	....
	Phoenix	**NHL**	**44**	**9**	**11**	**20**	**28**	**3**	**0**	**2**	**77**	**11.7**	**−6**	**14**	**35.7**	**14:52**	....	....	....	....	....	....	....	....	....
	San Antonio	AHL	3	1	1	2	2	....	....	....	....	....	....	....	....	....	....	....	....	....	....	....	....	....	....
2009-10	Nizhny Novgorod	Rus-KHL	55	10	20	30	62	....	....	....	....	....	....	....	....	....	....	....	....	....	....	....	....	....	....
	NHL Totals		**81**	**13**	**15**	**28**	**46**	**5**	**0**	**3**	**115**	**11.3**		**21**	**33.3**	**12:07**	....	....	....	....	....	....	....	....	....

Traded to **Anaheim** by **Columbus** for Anaheim's 4th round choice (Mathieu Corbeil-Theriault) in 2010 Entry Draft, July 14, 2008. Claimed on waivers by **Chicago** from **Anaheim**, October 3, 2008. Claimed on waivers by **Anaheim** from **Chicago**, October 7, 2008. Traded to **Phoenix** by **Anaheim** for Logan Stephenson, December 3, 2008. Signed as a free agent by **Novgorod** (Russia-KHL). June 30, 2009.

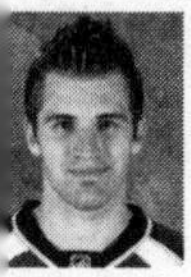

LINGLET, Charles

(LIHNG-leht, CHAHR-uhlz)

Left wing. Shoots left. 6'2", 205 lbs. Born, Montreal, Que., June 22, 1982.

Season	Club	League	GP	G	A	Pts	PIM	PP	SH	GW	S	%	+/-	TF	F%	Min	GP	G	A	Pts	PIM	PP	SH	GW	Min
99-2000	Baie-Comeau	QMJHL	64	14	20	34	13	....	....	....	....	....	....	....	....	....	6	3	3	6	4	....	....	....	....
2000-01	Baie-Comeau	QMJHL	70	21	34	55	61	....	....	....	....	....	....	....	....	....	11	2	2	4	10	....	....	....	....
2001-02	Baie-Comeau	QMJHL	72	52	71	123	34	....	....	....	....	....	....	....	....	....	5	1	3	4	2	....	....	....	....
2002-03	Baie-Comeau	QMJHL	47	21	27	48	35	....	....	....	....	....	....	....	....	....	12	3	8	11	18	....	....	....	....
2003-04	Utah Grizzlies	AHL	7	0	0	0	2	....	....	....	....	....	....	....	....	....	....	....	....	....	....	....	....	....	....
	Alaska Aces	ECHL	62	20	35	55	61	....	....	....	....	....	....	....	....	....	7	2	5	7	4	....	....	....	....
2004-05	Alaska Aces	ECHL	72	28	34	62	44	....	....	....	....	....	....	....	....	....	15	6	10	16	14	....	....	....	....
2005-06	Peoria Rivermen	AHL	38	14	7	21	10	....	....	....	....	....	....	....	....	....	....	....	....	....	....	....	....	....	....
	Las Vegas	ECHL	16	5	9	14	15	....	....	....	....	....	....	....	....	....	12	5	4	9	20	....	....	....	....
2006-07	Peoria Rivermen	AHL	73	31	29	60	30	....	....	....	....	....	....	....	....	....	....	....	....	....	....	....	....	....	....
2007-08	Peoria Rivermen	AHL	80	24	42	66	65	....	....	....	....	....	....	....	....	....	....	....	....	....	....	....	....	....	....
2008-09	Peoria Rivermen	AHL	37	1	8	9	23	....	....	....	....	....	....	....	....	....	....	....	....	....	....	....	....	....	....
	Springfield	AHL	21	7	9	16	6	....	....	....	....	....	....	....	....	....	....	....	....	....	....	....	....	....	....
2009-10	Springfield	AHL	75	19	55	74	36	....	....	....	....	....	....	....	....	....	....	....	....	....	....	....	....	....	....
	Edmonton	**NHL**	**5**	**0**	**0**	**0**	**2**	**0**	**0**	**0**	**7**	**0.0**	**−5**	**1**	**0.0**	**10:16**	....	....	....	....	....	....	....	....	....
	NHL Totals		**5**	**0**	**0**	**0**	**2**	**0**	**0**	**0**	**7**	**0.0**		**1**	**0.0**	**10:16**	....	....	....	....	....	....	....	....	....

QMJHL First All-Star Team (2002)

Signed as a free agent by **St. Louis**, January 1, 2007. • Loaned to **Springfield** (AHL) by **St. Louis** (Peoria-AHL), February 18, 2009. Signed as a free agent by **Springfield** (AHL), September, 2009. Signed as a free agent by **Edmonton**, March 31, 2010. Signed as a free agent by **Novgorod** (Russia-KHL), June 28, 2010.

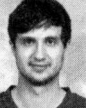

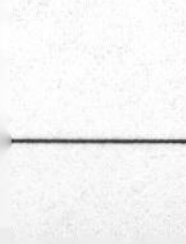

LISIN, Enver

(LEE-sihn, EHN-vuhr)

Right wing. Shoots left. 6'2", 200 lbs. Born, Moscow, USSR, April 22, 1986. Phoenix's 3rd choice, 50th overall, in 2004 Entry Draft.

Season	Club	League	GP	G	A	Pts	PIM	PP	SH	GW	S	%	+/-	TF	F%	Min	GP	G	A	Pts	PIM	PP	SH	GW	Min
2001-02	Dyn'o Moscow 2	Russia-3	6	3	0	3	14	....	....	....	....	....	....	....	....	....	....	....	....	....	....	....	....	....	....
2002-03	Dyn'o Moscow 2	Russia-3	STATISTICS NOT AVAILABLE					....	....	....	....	....	....	....	....	....	....	....	....	....	....	....	....	....	....
2003-04	Dyn'o Moscow 2	Russia-3	STATISTICS NOT AVAILABLE					....	....	....	....	....	....	....	....	....	....	....	....	....	....	....	....	....	....
	Kristall Saratov	Russia-2	35	10	6	16	30	....	....	....	....	....	....	....	....	....	4	1	0	1	0	....	....	....	....
2004-05	Ak Bars Kazan 2	Russia-3	....	4	3	7	....	....	....	....	....	....	....	....	....	....	....	....	....	....	....	....	....	....	....
	Ak Bars Kazan	Russia	53	8	4	12	4	....	....	....	....	....	....	....	....	....	3	0	0	0	0	....	....	....	....
2005-06	Ak Bars Kazan	Russia	43	7	5	12	26	....	....	....	....	....	....	....	....	....	13	3	1	4	6	....	....	....	....

			Regular Season														Playoffs								
Season	Club	League	GP	G	A	Pts	PIM	PP	SH	GW	S	%	+/-	TF	F%	Min	GP	G	A	Pts	PIM	PP	SH	GW	Min
2006-07	**Phoenix**	**NHL**	17	1	1	2	16	1	0	0	35	2.9	–18	7	28.6	15:02	....	....	....	....	....	....	....	....	....
	San Antonio	AHL	2	2	0	2	4	....	....	....	....	....	....	....	....	....	....	....	....	....	....	....	....	....	....
	Ak Bars Kazan	Russia	20	6	2	8	18	....	....	....	....	....	....	....	....	....	1	0	0	0	0	....	....	....	....
2007-08	**Phoenix**	**NHL**	13	4	1	5	6	1	0	0	27	14.8	–5	2	50.0	14:27	....	....	....	....	....	....	....	....	....
	San Antonio	AHL	58	16	19	35	26	....	....	....	....	....	....	....	....	....	6	1	2	3	0	....	....	....	....
2008-09	**Phoenix**	**NHL**	48	13	8	21	24	1	0	2	105	12.4	–13	6	33.3	14:50	....	....	....	....	....	....	....	....	....
	San Antonio	AHL	10	2	4	6	6	....	....	....	....	....	....	....	....	....	....	....	....	....	....	....	....	....	....
2009-10	**NY Rangers**	**NHL**	57	6	8	14	18	0	0	0	91	6.6	–1	3	66.7	11:11	....	....	....	....	....	....	....	....	....
	NHL Totals		135	24	18	42	64	3	0	2	258	9.3		18	38.9	13:17	....	....	....	....	....	....	....	....	....

Traded to **NY Rangers** by **Phoenix** for Lauri Korpikoski, July 13, 2009.

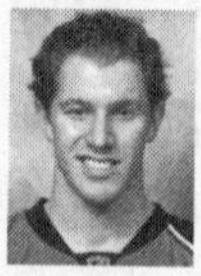

LITTLE, Bryan

(LIH-tuhl, BRIGH-uhn) **ATL.**

Right wing. Shoots right. 5'11", 185 lbs. Born, Edmonton, Alta., November 12, 1987. Atlanta's 1st choice, 12th overall, in 2006 Entry Draft.

Season	Club	League	GP	G	A	Pts	PIM	PP	SH	GW	S	%	+/-	TF	F%	Min	GP	G	A	Pts	PIM	PP	SH	GW	Min
2003-04	Barrie Colts	OHL	64	34	24	58	18	....	....	....	....	....	....	....	....	....	12	5	5	10	7	....	....	....	....
2004-05	Barrie Colts	OHL	62	36	32	68	34	....	....	....	....	....	....	....	....	....	4	5	1	6	2	....	....	....	....
2005-06	Barrie Colts	OHL	64	42	67	109	99	....	....	....	....	....	....	....	....	....	14	8	15	23	19	....	....	....	....
2006-07	Barrie Colts	OHL	57	41	66	107	77	....	....	....	....	....	....	....	....	....	8	4	5	9	8	....	....	....	....
	Chicago Wolves	AHL	....	....	....	....	....	....	....	....	....	....	....	....	....	....	2	0	0	0	0	....	....	....	....
2007-08	**Atlanta**	**NHL**	48	6	10	16	18	2	0	1	76	7.9	–2	505	45.2	15:37	....	....	....	....	....	....	....	....	....
	Chicago Wolves	AHL	34	9	16	25	10	....	....	....	....	....	....	....	....	....	24	8	5	13	10	....	....	....	....
2008-09	**Atlanta**	**NHL**	79	31	20	51	24	12	0	4	172	18.0	–5	214	43.5	16:55	....	....	....	....	....	....	....	....	....
2009-10	**Atlanta**	**NHL**	79	13	21	34	20	3	0	1	165	7.9	–6	154	44.2	15:45	....	....	....	....	....	....	....	....	....
	NHL Totals		206	50	51	101	62	17	0	6	413	12.1		873	44.6	16:10	....	....	....	....	....	....	....	....	....

OHL Second All-Star Team (2007)

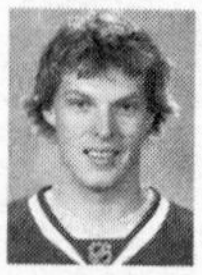

LOCKE, Corey

(LAWK, KOH-ree) **OTT.**

Center. Shoots left. 5'9", 189 lbs. Born, Toronto, Ont., May 8, 1984. Montreal's 5th choice, 113th overall, in 2003 Entry Draft.

Season	Club	League	GP	G	A	Pts	PIM	PP	SH	GW	S	%	+/-	TF	F%	Min	GP	G	A	Pts	PIM	PP	SH	GW	Min
2000-01	Newmarket	OPJHL	49	34	51	85	16	....	....	....	....	....	....	....	....	....	16	10	12	22	14	....	....	....	....
2001-02	Ottawa 67's	OHL	55	18	25	43	18	....	....	....	....	....	....	....	....	....	13	6	7	13	10	....	....	....	....
2002-03	Ottawa 67's	OHL	66	*63	*88	*151	83	....	....	....	....	....	....	....	....	....	23	*19	19	*38	30	....	....	....	....
2003-04	Ottawa 67's	OHL	65	*51	67	*118	82	....	....	....	....	....	....	....	....	....	7	7	3	10	10	....	....	....	....
2004-05	Hamilton	AHL	78	16	27	43	20	....	....	....	....	....	....	....	....	....	4	0	0	0	2	....	....	....	....
2005-06	Hamilton	AHL	77	19	40	59	67	....	....	....	....	....	....	....	....	....	....	....	....	....	....	....	....	....	....
2006-07	Hamilton	AHL	80	20	35	55	54	....	....	....	....	....	....	....	....	....	22	*10	12	22	10	....	....	....	....
2007-08	**Montreal**	**NHL**	1	0	0	0	0	0	0	0	1	0.0	–1	5	40.0	5:59	....	....	....	....	....	....	....	....	....
	Hamilton	AHL	78	30	42	72	50	....	....	....	....	....	....	....	....	....	....	....	....	....	....	....	....	....	....
2008-09	Houston Aeros	AHL	77	25	54	79	60	....	....	....	....	....	....	....	....	....	20	12	11	23	32	....	....	....	....
2009-10	**NY Rangers**	**NHL**	3	0	0	0	0	0	0	0	2	0.0	1	7	14.3	6:18	....	....	....	....	....	....	....	....	....
	Hartford	AHL	76	31	54	85	44	....	....	....	....	....	....	....	....	....	....	....	....	....	....	....	....	....	....
	NHL Totals		4	0	0	0	0	0	0	0	3	0.0		12	25.0	6:13	....	....	....	....	....	....	....	....	....

OHL First All-Star Team (2003, 2004) • OHL Player of the Year (2003, 2004) • Canadian Major Junior First All-Star Team (2003, 2004) • Canadian Major Junior Player of the Year (2003)

Traded to **Minnesota** by **Montreal** for Shawn Belle, July 11, 2008. Signed as a free agent by **NY Rangers**, July 3, 2009. Signed as a free agent by **Ottawa**, July 7, 2010.

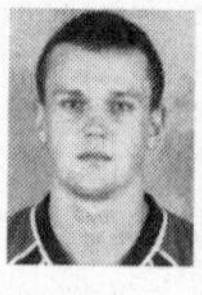

LOJEK, Martin

(LOI-yehk, MAHR-tihn)

Defense. Shoots right. 6'4", 220 lbs. Born, Brno, Czech., August 19, 1985. Florida's 5th choice, 105th overall, in 2003 Entry Draft.

Season	Club	League	GP	G	A	Pts	PIM	PP	SH	GW	S	%	+/-	TF	F%	Min	GP	G	A	Pts	PIM	PP	SH	GW	Min
2000-01	HC Pardubice Jr.	CzRep-Jr.	48	2	2	4	42	....	....	....	....	....	....	....	....	....	7	0	0	0	6	....	....	....	....
2001-02	HC Pardubice Jr.	CzRep-Jr.	40	2	4	6	24	....	....	....	....	....	....	....	....	....	7	1	0	1	2	....	....	....	....
2002-03	Brampton	OHL	65	1	13	14	47	....	....	....	....	....	....	....	....	....	11	0	1	1	6	....	....	....	....
2003-04	Brampton	OHL	68	3	17	20	37	....	....	....	....	....	....	....	....	....	12	0	4	4	2	....	....	....	....
2004-05	Brampton	OHL	58	1	12	13	58	....	....	....	....	....	....	....	....	....	6	0	0	0	6	....	....	....	....
2005-06	Rochester	AHL	15	1	1	2	16	....	....	....	....	....	....	....	....	....	....	....	....	....	....	....	....	....	....
	Florida Everblades	ECHL	45	3	11	14	40	....	....	....	....	....	....	....	....	....	2	0	0	0	0	....	....	....	....
2006-07	**Florida**	**NHL**	3	0	1	1	0	0	0	0	0	0.0	2	0	0.0	8:23	....	....	....	....	....	....	....	....	....
	Rochester	AHL	69	6	13	19	87	....	....	....	....	....	....	....	....	....	....	....	....	....	....	....	....	....	....
2007-08	**Florida**	**NHL**	2	0	0	0	0	0	0	0	2	0.0	–1	0	0.0	6:08	....	....	....	....	....	....	....	....	....
	Rochester	AHL	72	6	5	11	97	....	....	....	....	....	....	....	....	....	....	....	....	....	....	....	....	....	....
2008-09	HC Ocelari Trinec	CzRep	9	0	1	1	6	....	....	....	....	....	....	....	....	....	....	....	....	....	....	....	....	....	....
	Pardubice	CzRep	12	0	0	0	0	....	....	....	....	....	....	....	....	....	7	2	1	3	4	....	....	....	....
2009-10	HC Ocelari Trinec	CzRep	47	1	3	4	28	....	....	....	....	....	....	....	....	....	5	0	0	0	10	....	....	....	....
	NHL Totals		5	0	1	1	0	0	0	0	2	0.0		0	0.0	7:29	....	....	....	....	....	....	....	....	....

Signed as a free agent by **Trinec** (CzRep), May 1, 2008. • Loaned to **Pardubice** (CzRep) by **Trinec** (CzRep), December 19, 2008.

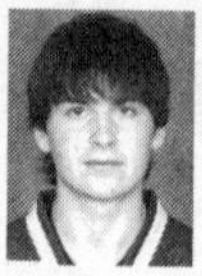

LOKTIONOV, Andrei

(lawk-too-OH-nawf, ahn-DRAY) **L.A.**

Center. Shoots left. 5'10", 179 lbs. Born, Voskresensk, USSR, May 30, 1990. Los Angeles' 7th choice, 123rd overall, in 2008 Entry Draft.

Season	Club	League	GP	G	A	Pts	PIM	PP	SH	GW	S	%	+/-	TF	F%	Min	GP	G	A	Pts	PIM	PP	SH	GW	Min
2005-06	Spartak 2	Russia-3	4	1	1	2	2	....	....	....	....	....	....	....	....	....	....	....	....	....	....	....	....	....	....
2006-07	Yaroslavl 2	Russia-3	31	7	21	28	26	....	....	....	....	....	....	....	....	....	....	....	....	....	....	....	....	....	....
2007-08	Yaroslavl 2	Russia-3	STATISTICS NOT AVAILABLE																						
	Yaroslavl	Russia	5	0	1	1	0										1	0	0	0	0	....	....	....	....
2008-09	Windsor Spitfires	OHL	51	24	42	66	16	....	....	....	....	....	....	....	....	....	20	11	22	33	2	....	....	....	....
2009-10	**Los Angeles**	**NHL**	1	0	0	0	0	0	0	0	1	0.0	0	8	12.5	11:52	....	....	....	....	....	....	....	....	....
	Manchester	AHL	29	9	15	24	12	....	....	....	....	....	....	....	....	....	16	1	8	9	2	....	....	....	....
	NHL Totals		1	0	0	0	0	0	0	0	1	0.0		8	12.5	11:52	....	....	....	....	....	....	....	....	....

• Missed majority of 2009-10 season recovering from shoulder injury suffered in game at Vancouver, November 26, 2009 and resulting surgery, November 29, 2009.

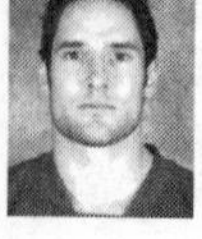

LOMBARDI, Matthew

(lawm-BAHR-dee, MA-thew) **NSH.**

Center. Shoots left. 6', 198 lbs. Born, Montreal, Que., March 18, 1982. Calgary's 3rd choice, 90th overall, in 2002 Entry Draft.

Season	Club	League	GP	G	A	Pts	PIM	PP	SH	GW	S	%	+/-	TF	F%	Min	GP	G	A	Pts	PIM	PP	SH	GW	Min
1997-98	Gatineau	QAAA	42	10	13	23	....	....	....	....	....	....	....	....	....	....	13	4	7	11	....	....	....	....	....
1998-99	Victoriaville Tigres	QMJHL	47	6	10	16	8	....	....	....	....	....	....	....	....	....	5	0	0	0	0	....	....	....	....
99-2000	Victoriaville Tigres	QMJHL	65	18	26	44	28	....	....	....	....	....	....	....	....	....	6	0	0	0	6	....	....	....	....
2000-01	Victoriaville Tigres	QMJHL	72	28	39	67	66	....	....	....	....	....	....	....	....	....	13	12	6	18	10	....	....	....	....
2001-02	Victoriaville Tigres	QMJHL	66	57	73	130	70	....	....	....	....	....	....	....	....	....	22	*17	18	35	18	....	....	....	....
2002-03	Saint John Flames	AHL	76	25	21	46	41	....	....	....	....	....	....	....	....	....	....	....	....	....	....	....	....	....	....
2003-04	**Calgary**	**NHL**	79	16	13	29	32	3	2	4	130	12.3	4	992	47.9	14:26	13	1	5	6	4	0	0	1	14:46
2004-05	Lowell	AHL	9	3	1	4	9	....	....	....	....	....	....	....	....	....	11	0	3	3	16	....	....	....	....
2005-06	**Calgary**	**NHL**	55	6	20	26	48	1	2	2	72	8.3	–1	499	52.9	14:09	7	0	2	2	2	0	0	0	15:51
	Omaha	AHL	1	1	1	2	0	....	....	....	....	....	....	....	....	....	....	....	....	....	....	....	....	....	....
2006-07	**Calgary**	**NHL**	81	20	26	46	48	5	4	5	176	11.4	10	965	49.1	16:22	6	1	1	2	0	1	0	0	15:19
2007-08	**Calgary**	**NHL**	82	14	22	36	67	2	2	4	181	7.7	–6	955	47.6	17:19	7	0	0	0	4	0	0	0	17:14
2008-09	**Calgary**	**NHL**	50	9	21	30	30	0	1	2	119	7.6	11	459	53.4	16:27	....	....	....	....	....	....	....	....	....
	Phoenix	**NHL**	19	5	11	16	14	1	0	0	58	8.6	2	384	50.3	20:54	....	....	....	....	....	....	....	....	....
2009-10	**Phoenix**	**NHL**	78	19	34	53	36	4	0	2	174	10.9	8	910	49.7	17:56	7	1	5	6	2	0	0	0	17:36
	NHL Totals		444	89	147	236	275	16	11	19	910	9.8		5164	49.5	16:24	40	3	13	16	12	1	0	1	15:58

• Re-entered NHL Entry Draft. Originally Edmonton's 7th choice, 215th overall, in 2000 Entry Draft.

Memorial Cup Tournament All-Star Team (2002) • Ed Chynoweth Trophy (Memorial Cup Tournament - Leading Scorer) (2002)

Traded to **Phoenix** by **Calgary** with Brandon Prust and Calgary's 1st round choice (Brandon Gormley) in 2010 Entry Draft for Olli Jokinen and Phoenix's 3rd round choice (later traded to Florida – Florida selected Josh Birkholz) in 2009 Entry Draft, March 4, 2009. Signed as a free agent by **Nashville**, July 2, 2010.

			Regular Season														Playoffs								
Season	Club	League	GP	G	A	Pts	PIM	PP	SH	GW	S	%	+/-	TF	F%	Min	GP	G	A	Pts	PIM	PP	SH	GW	Min

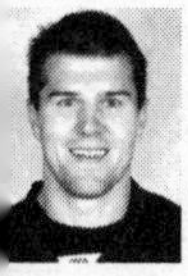

LOVEJOY, Ben (LUHV-joi, BEHN) PIT.

Defense. Shoots right. 6'2", 215 lbs. Born, Concord, NH, February 20, 1984.

Season	Club	League	GP	G	A	Pts	PIM	PP	SH	GW	S	%	+/-	TF	F%	Min	GP	G	A	Pts	PIM	PP	SH	GW	Min
2002-03	Boston College	H-East	22	0	6	6	6	....	....	....	....	....	....	....	....	....	....	....	....	....	....	....	....	....	....
2003-04	Dartmouth	ECAC	DID NOT PLAY – TRANSFERRED COLLEGES																						
2004-05	Dartmouth	ECAC	32	2	11	13	28	....	....	....	....	....	....	....	....	....	....	....	....	....	....	....	....	....	....
2005-06	Dartmouth	ECAC	32	2	16	18	24	....	....	....	....	....	....	....	....	....	....	....	....	....	....	....	....	....	....
2006-07	Dartmouth	ECAC	32	7	16	23	28	....	....	....	....	....	....	....	....	....	....	....	....	....	....	....	....	....	....
	Norfolk Admirals	AHL	5	0	0	0	6	....	....	....	....	....	....	....	....	....	....	....	....	....	....	....	....	....	....
2007-08	Wilkes-Barre	AHL	72	2	18	20	63	....	....	....	....	....	....	....	....	....	23	2	8	10	18	....	....	....	....
2008-09	**Pittsburgh**	**NHL**	**2**	**0**	**0**	**0**	**0**	**0**	**0**	**0**	**1**	**0.0**	**0**	**0**	**0.0**	**11:53**	....	....	....	....	....	....	....	....	....
	Wilkes-Barre	AHL	76	7	24	31	84	....	....	....	....	....	....	....	....	....	12	1	1	2	14	....	....	....	....
2009-10	**Pittsburgh**	**NHL**	**12**	**0**	**3**	**3**	**2**	**0**	**0**	**0**	**14**	**0.0**	**8**	**0**	**0.0**	**16:37**	....	....	....	....	....	....	....	....	....
	Wilkes-Barre	AHL	65	9	20	29	92	....	....	....	....	....	....	....	....	....	2	0	2	2	2	....	....	....	....
	NHL Totals		**14**	**0**	**3**	**3**	**2**	**0**	**0**	**0**	**15**	**0.0**		**0**	**0.0**	**15:56**	....	....	....	....	....	....	....	....	....

HL Second All-Star Team (2009)

igned as a free agent by **Wilkes-Barre** (AHL), June 14, 2007. Signed as a free agent by **Pittsburgh**, July 7, 2008.

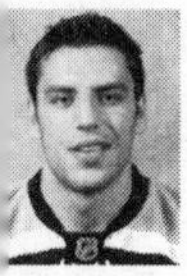

LUCIC, Milan (LOO-cheech, MEE-lahn) BOS.

Left wing. Shoots left. 6'3", 228 lbs. Born, Vancouver, B.C., June 7, 1988. Boston's 3rd choice, 50th overall, in 2006 Entry Draft.

Season	Club	League	GP	G	A	Pts	PIM	PP	SH	GW	S	%	+/-	TF	F%	Min	GP	G	A	Pts	PIM	PP	SH	GW	Min
2004-05	Coquitlam	BCHL	50	9	14	23	100	....	....	....	....	....	....	....	....	....	....	....	....	....	....	....	....	....	....
	Vancouver Giants	WHL	1	0	0	0	2	....	....	....	....	....	....	....	....	....	2	0	0	0	0	....	....	....	....
2005-06	Vancouver Giants	WHL	62	9	10	19	149	....	....	....	....	....	....	....	....	....	18	3	4	7	23	....	....	....	....
2006-07	Vancouver Giants	WHL	70	30	38	68	147	....	....	....	....	....	....	....	....	....	22	7	12	19	26	....	....	....	....
2007-08	**Boston**	**NHL**	**77**	**8**	**19**	**27**	**89**	**1**	**0**	**4**	**88**	**9.1**	**–2**	**8**	**50.0**	**12:07**	**7**	**2**	**0**	**2**	**4**	**0**	**0**	**0**	**16:24**
2008-09	**Boston**	**NHL**	**72**	**17**	**25**	**42**	**136**	**2**	**0**	**3**	**97**	**17.5**	**17**	**10**	**60.0**	**14:57**	**10**	**3**	**6**	**9**	**43**	**0**	**0**	**0**	**15:14**
2009-10	**Boston**	**NHL**	**50**	**9**	**11**	**20**	**44**	**0**	**0**	**2**	**72**	**12.5**	**–7**	**14**	**21.4**	**14:21**	**13**	**5**	**4**	**9**	**19**	**2**	**0**	**1**	**16:27**
	NHL Totals		**199**	**34**	**55**	**89**	**269**	**3**	**0**	**9**	**257**	**13.2**		**32**	**40.6**	**13:42**	**30**	**10**	**10**	**20**	**66**	**2**	**0**	**1**	**16:02**

Memorial Cup Tournament All-Star Team (2007) • Stafford Smythe Memorial Trophy (Memorial Cup Tournament - MVP) (2007)

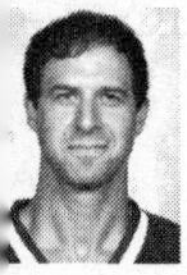

LUKOWICH, Brad (loo-KUH-which, BRAD) DAL.

Defense. Shoots left. 6'1", 200 lbs. Born, Cranbrook, B.C., August 12, 1976. NY Islanders' 4th choice, 90th overall, in 1994 Entry Draft.

Season	Club	League	GP	G	A	Pts	PIM	PP	SH	GW	S	%	+/-	TF	F%	Min	GP	G	A	Pts	PIM	PP	SH	GW	Min
1992-93	Cranbrook Colts	RMJHL	54	21	41	62	162	....	....	....	....	....	....	....	....	....	....	....	....	....	....	....	....	....	....
	Kamloops Blazers	WHL	1	0	0	0	0	....	....	....	....	....	....	....	....	....	....	....	....	....	....	....	....	....	....
1993-94	Kamloops Blazers	WHL	42	5	11	16	166	....	....	....	....	....	....	....	....	....	16	0	1	1	35	....	....	....	....
1994-95	Kamloops Blazers	WHL	63	10	35	45	125	....	....	....	....	....	....	....	....	....	18	0	7	7	21	....	....	....	....
1995-96	Kamloops Blazers	WHL	65	14	55	69	114	....	....	....	....	....	....	....	....	....	13	2	10	12	29	....	....	....	....
1996-97	Michigan	IHL	69	2	6	8	77	....	....	....	....	....	....	....	....	....	4	0	1	1	2	....	....	....	....
1997-98	**Dallas**	**NHL**	**4**	**0**	**1**	**1**	**2**	**0**	**0**	**0**	**2**	**0.0**	**–2**	....	....	....	....	....	....	....	....	....	....	....	....
	Michigan	IHL	60	6	27	33	104	....	....	....	....	....	....	....	....	....	4	0	4	4	14	....	....	....	....
1998-99	**Dallas**	**NHL**	**14**	**1**	**2**	**3**	**19**	**0**	**0**	**0**	**8**	**12.5**	**3**	**0**	**0.0**	**16:18**	**8**	**0**	**1**	**1**	**4**	**0**	**0**	**0**	**10:00**
	Michigan	IHL	67	8	21	29	95	....	....	....	....	....	....	....	....	....	....	....	....	....	....	....	....	....	....
99-2000	**Dallas**	**NHL**	**60**	**3**	**1**	**4**	**50**	**0**	**0**	**1**	**33**	**9.1**	**–14**	**1**	**0.0**	**11:44**	....	....	....	....	....	....	....	....	....
2000-01	**Dallas**	**NHL**	**80**	**4**	**10**	**14**	**76**	**0**	**0**	**2**	**43**	**9.3**	**28**	**1**	**100.0**	**14:48**	**10**	**1**	**0**	**1**	**4**	**0**	**0**	**0**	**17:28**
2001-02	**Dallas**	**NHL**	**66**	**1**	**6**	**7**	**40**	**0**	**0**	**0**	**56**	**1.8**	**–1**	**0**	**0.0**	**13:14**	....	....	....	....	....	....	....	....	....
2002-03	**Tampa Bay**	**NHL**	**70**	**1**	**14**	**15**	**46**	**0**	**0**	**0**	**52**	**1.9**	**4**	**1**	**0.0**	**17:34**	**9**	**0**	**1**	**1**	**2**	**0**	**0**	**0**	**17:48**
2003-04♦	**Tampa Bay**	**NHL**	**79**	**5**	**14**	**19**	**24**	**0**	**0**	**1**	**86**	**5.8**	**29**	**3**	**0.0**	**18:45**	**18**	**0**	**2**	**2**	**6**	**0**	**0**	**0**	**15:51**
2004-05	Fort Worth	CHL	16	3	5	8	33	....	....	....	....	....	....	....	....	....	....	....	....	....	....	....	....	....	....
2005-06	**NY Islanders**	**NHL**	**57**	**1**	**12**	**13**	**32**	**0**	**0**	**1**	**36**	**2.8**	**–3**	**0**	**0.0**	**19:15**	....	....	....	....	....	....	....	....	....
	New Jersey	**NHL**	**18**	**1**	**7**	**8**	**8**	**0**	**0**	**0**	**13**	**7.7**	**3**	**0**	**0.0**	**19:11**	**9**	**0**	**0**	**0**	**4**	**0**	**0**	**0**	**21:28**
2006-07	**New Jersey**	**NHL**	**75**	**4**	**8**	**12**	**36**	**0**	**1**	**2**	**50**	**8.0**	**1**	**0**	**0.0**	**20:13**	**11**	**0**	**1**	**1**	**2**	**0**	**0**	**0**	**19:57**
2007-08	**Tampa Bay**	**NHL**	**59**	**1**	**6**	**7**	**20**	**0**	**0**	**0**	**28**	**3.6**	**–15**	**0**	**0.0**	**16:36**	....	....	....	....	....	....	....	....	....
2008-09	**San Jose**	**NHL**	**58**	**0**	**8**	**8**	**12**	**0**	**0**	**0**	**43**	**0.0**	**5**	**0**	**0.0**	**16:13**	**6**	**0**	**0**	**0**	**0**	**0**	**0**	**0**	**14:30**
2009-10	Texas Stars	AHL	29	3	15	18	10	....	....	....	....	....	....	....	....	....	....	....	....	....	....	....	....	....	....
	Vancouver	**NHL**	**13**	**1**	**1**	**2**	**4**	**0**	**0**	**1**	**1**	**100.0**	**5**	**0**	**0.0**	**11:13**	....	....	....	....	....	....	....	....	....
	NHL Totals		**653**	**23**	**90**	**113**	**369**	**0**	**1**	**8**	**451**	**5.1**		**6**	**16.7**	**16:32**	**71**	**1**	**5**	**6**	**22**	**0**	**0**	**0**	**16:54**

raded to **Dallas** by **NY Islanders** for Dallas' 3rd round choice (Robert Schnabel) in 1997 Entry Draft, June 1, 1996. Traded to **Minnesota** by **Dallas** with Manny Fernandez for Minnesota's 3rd round hoice (Joel Lundqvist) in 2000 Entry Draft and Minnesota's 4th round choice (later traded back to Minnesota, later traded to Los Angeles – Los Angeles selected Aaron Rome) in 2002 Entry Draft, June 12, 000. Traded to **Dallas** by **Minnesota** with Minnesota's 3rd (Yared Hagos) and 9th (Dale Sullivan) round choices in 2001 Entry Draft for Aaron Gavey, Pavel Patera, Dallas' 8th round choice (Eric Johansson) n 2000 Entry Draft and Minnesota's 4th round choice (previously acquired, later traded to Los Angeles – Los Angeles selected Aaron Rome) in 2002 Entry Draft, June 25, 2000. Traded to **Tampa Bay** by **allas** with Dallas' 7th round choice (Jay Rosehill) in 2003 Entry Draft for Tampa Bay's 2nd round choice (previously acquired, later traded back to Tampa Bay, later traded to Dallas – Dallas selected Tobias tephan) in 2002 Entry Draft, June 22, 2002. Signed as a free agent by **Fort Worth** (CHL), September 21, 2004. Signed as a free agent by **NY Islanders**, August 11, 2005. Traded to **New Jersey** by **NY slanders** for New Jersey's 3rd round choice (later traded to Phoenix - Phoenix selected Jonas Ahnelov) in 2006 Entry Draft, March 9, 2006. Signed as a free agent by **Tampa Bay**, July 3, 2007. Traded to **an Jose** by **Tampa Bay** with Dan Boyle for Matt Carle, Ty Wishart, San Jose's 1st round choice (later traded to Ottawa, later traded to NY Islanders, later traded to Columbus, later traded to Anaheim - naheim selected Kyle Palmieri) in 2009 Entry Draft and San Jose's 4th round choice (James Mullin) in 2010 Entry Draft, July 4, 2008. Traded to **Vancouver** by **San Jose** with Christian Ehrhoff for Patrick Vhite and Daniel Rahimi, August 28, 2009. • Assigned to **Texas** (AHL) by **Vancouver**, October 1, 2009. Signed as a free agent by **Dallas**, July 15, 2010.

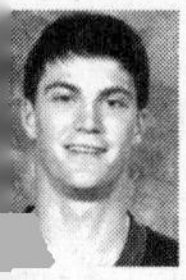

LUNDIN, Mike (LUHN-dihn, MIGHK) T.B.

Defense. Shoots left. 6'2", 197 lbs. Born, Burnsville, MN, September 24, 1984. Tampa Bay's 3rd choice, 102nd overall, in 2004 Entry Draft.

Season	Club	League	GP	G	A	Pts	PIM	PP	SH	GW	S	%	+/-	TF	F%	Min	GP	G	A	Pts	PIM	PP	SH	GW	Min
2002-03	Apple Valley	High-MN	27	8	20	27	....	....	....	....	....	....	....	....	....	....	....	....	....	....	....	....	....	....	....
2003-04	U. of Maine	H-East	44	3	16	19	34	....	....	....	....	....	....	....	....	....	....	....	....	....	....	....	....	....	....
2004-05	U. of Maine	H-East	40	1	13	14	2	....	....	....	....	....	....	....	....	....	....	....	....	....	....	....	....	....	....
2005-06	U. of Maine	H-East	36	3	13	16	4	....	....	....	....	....	....	....	....	....	....	....	....	....	....	....	....	....	....
2006-07	U. of Maine	H-East	40	6	14	20	2	....	....	....	....	....	....	....	....	....	....	....	....	....	....	....	....	....	....
2007-08	**Tampa Bay**	**NHL**	**81**	**0**	**6**	**6**	**16**	**0**	**0**	**0**	**33**	**0.0**	**3**	**0**	**0.0**	**13:48**	....	....	....	....	....	....	....	....	....
2008-09	**Tampa Bay**	**NHL**	**25**	**0**	**2**	**2**	**4**	**0**	**0**	**0**	**8**	**0.0**	**–4**	**1**	**0.0**	**16:39**	....	....	....	....	....	....	....	....	....
	Norfolk Admirals	AHL	51	4	25	29	18	....	....	....	....	....	....	....	....	....	....	....	....	....	....	....	....	....	....
2009-10	**Tampa Bay**	**NHL**	**49**	**3**	**10**	**13**	**18**	**0**	**0**	**0**	**42**	**7.1**	**–4**	**0**	**0.0**	**21:57**	....	....	....	....	....	....	....	....	....
	Norfolk Admirals	AHL	27	2	14	16	4	....	....	....	....	....	....	....	....	....	....	....	....	....	....	....	....	....	....
	NHL Totals		**155**	**3**	**18**	**21**	**38**	**0**	**0**	**0**	**83**	**3.6**		**1**	**0.0**	**16:50**	....	....	....	....	....	....	....	....	....

ockey East Second All-Star Team (2007)

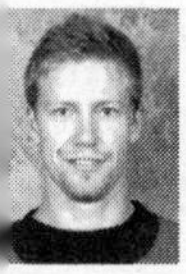

LUNDMARK, Jamie (LUHND-mahrk, JAY-mee) NSH.

Center. Shoots right. 6', 197 lbs. Born, Edmonton, Alta., January 16, 1981. NY Rangers' 2nd choice, 9th overall, in 1999 Entry Draft.

Season	Club	League	GP	G	A	Pts	PIM	PP	SH	GW	S	%	+/-	TF	F%	Min	GP	G	A	Pts	PIM	PP	SH	GW	Min
1996-97	St. Albert Saints	AJHL	35	10	9	19	8	....	....	....	....	....	....	....	....	....	....	....	....	....	....	....	....	....	....
1997-98	St. Albert Saints	AJHL	57	33	58	91	171	....	....	....	....	....	....	....	....	....	19	13	18	31	5	....	....	....	....
1998-99	Moose Jaw	WHL	70	40	51	91	121	....	....	....	....	....	....	....	....	....	11	5	4	9	24	....	....	....	....
99-2000	Moose Jaw	WHL	37	21	27	48	33	....	....	....	....	....	....	....	....	....	....	....	....	....	....	....	....	....	....
2000-01	Seattle	WHL	52	35	42	77	49	....	....	....	....	....	....	....	....	....	9	4	4	8	16	....	....	....	....
2001-02	Hartford	AHL	79	27	32	59	56	....	....	....	....	....	....	....	....	....	10	3	4	7	16	....	....	....	....
2002-03	**NY Rangers**	**NHL**	**55**	**8**	**11**	**19**	**16**	**0**	**0**	**0**	**78**	**10.3**	**–3**	**62**	**43.6**	**12:04**	....	....	....	....	....	....	....	....	....
	Hartford	AHL	22	9	9	18	18	....	....	....	....	....	....	....	....	....	2	0	0	0	0	....	....	....	....
2003-04	**NY Rangers**	**NHL**	**56**	**2**	**8**	**10**	**33**	**0**	**0**	**1**	**68**	**2.9**	**–8**	**379**	**40.4**	**12:46**	....	....	....	....	....	....	....	....	....
2004-05	HC Forst Bolzano	Italy	14	9	9	18	22	....	....	....	....	....	....	....	....	....	....	....	....	....	....	....	....	....	....
	Hartford	AHL	64	14	27	41	146	....	....	....	....	....	....	....	....	....	6	2	4	6	8	....	....	....	....
2005-06	**NY Rangers**	**NHL**	**3**	**1**	**0**	**1**	**6**	**0**	**0**	**0**	**1**	**100.0**	**–2**	**2**	**0.0**	**9:49**	....	....	....	....	....	....	....	....	....
	Phoenix	**NHL**	**38**	**5**	**13**	**18**	**36**	**1**	**0**	**0**	**61**	**8.2**	**–1**	**366**	**58.7**	**12:37**	....	....	....	....	....	....	....	....	....
	San Antonio	AHL	4	1	2	3	2	....	....	....	....	....	....	....	....	....	....	....	....	....	....	....	....	....	....
	Calgary	**NHL**	**12**	**4**	**6**	**10**	**20**	**1**	**0**	**1**	**16**	**25.0**	**2**	**103**	**53.4**	**12:32**	**4**	**0**	**1**	**1**	**7**	**0**	**0**	**0**	**9:44**
2006-07	**Calgary**	**NHL**	**39**	**0**	**4**	**4**	**31**	**0**	**0**	**0**	**28**	**0.0**	**–4**	**233**	**55.4**	**8:37**	....	....	....	....	....	....	....	....	....
	Los Angeles	**NHL**	**29**	**7**	**2**	**9**	**25**	**0**	**0**	**0**	**53**	**13.2**	**–8**	**410**	**47.6**	**16:03**	....	....	....	....	....	....	....	....	....
2007-08	Dynamo Moscow	Russia	17	2	1	3	31	....	....	....	....	....	....	....	....	....	....	....	....	....	....	....	....	....	....
	Lake Erie	AHL	51	13	20	33	71	....	....	....	....	....	....	....	....	....	....	....	....	....	....	....	....	....	....
2008-09	**Calgary**	**NHL**	**27**	**8**	**8**	**16**	**17**	**0**	**0**	**0**	**50**	**16.0**	**2**	**120**	**51.7**	**13:59**	**2**	**0**	**0**	**0**	**0**	**0**	**0**	**0**	**7:06**
	Quad City Flames	AHL	54	15	37	52	31	....	....	....	....	....	....	....	....	....	....	....	....	....	....	....	....	....	....

			Regular Season														Playoffs								
Season	Club	League	GP	G	A	Pts	PIM	PP	SH	GW	S	%	+/-	TF	F%	Min	GP	G	A	Pts	PIM	PP	SH	GW	Min
2009-10	**Calgary**	**NHL**	**21**	**4**	**5**	**9**	**4**	**1**	**0**	**1**	**36**	**11.1**	**–6**	**62**	**48.4**	**15:22**	....	....	....	....	....	....	....	....	....
	Abbotsford Heat	AHL	32	9	12	21	64	....	....	....	....	....	....	....	....	....	....	....	....	....	....	....	....	....	....
	Toronto	**NHL**	**15**	**1**	**2**	**3**	**16**	**0**	**0**	**0**	**16**	**6.3**	**–1**	**30**	**50.0**	**11:34**	....	....	....	....	....	....	....	....	....
	NHL Totals		**295**	**40**	**59**	**99**	**204**	**3**	**0**	**3**	**407**	**9.8**		**1767**	**49.9**	**12:35**	**6**	**0**	**1**	**1**	**7**	**0**	**0**	**0**	**8:51**

WHL All-Rookie Team (1999) • WHL East Second All-Star Team (1999) • WHL West First All-Star Team (2001)

Signed as a free agent by **Bolzano** (Italy), September 21, 2004. Signed as a free agent by **Hartford** (AHL), November 16, 2004. Traded to **Phoenix** by **NY Rangers** for Jeff Taffe, October 18, 2005. Traded to **Calgary** by **Phoenix** for Calgary's 4th round choice (later traded to NY Islanders - NY Islanders selected Doug Rogers) in 2006 Entry Draft, March 9, 2006. Traded to **Los Angeles** by **Calgary** with Calgary's 4th round choice (Dwight King) in 2007 Entry Draft and Calgary's 2nd round choice (later traded back to Calgary - Calgary selected Mitch Wahl) in 2008 Entry Draft for Craig Conroy, January 29, 2007. Signed as a free agent by **Dynamo Moscow** (Russia), July 27, 2007. Signed as a free agent by **Lake Erie** (AHL), December 8, 2007. Signed as a free agent by **Calgary**, July 16, 2008. Claimed on waivers by **Toronto** from **Calgary**, February 16, 2010. Signed as a free agent by **Nashville**, July 16, 2010.

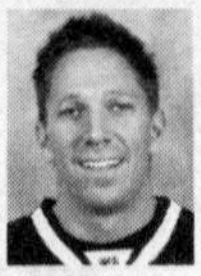

LUNDQVIST, Joel

(LUHND-kvihst, JOHL)

Center. Shoots left. 6'1", 194 lbs. Born, Are, Sweden, March 2, 1982. Dallas' 3rd choice, 68th overall, in 2000 Entry Draft.

Season	Club	League	GP	G	A	Pts	PIM	PP	SH	GW	S	%	+/-	TF	F%	Min	GP	G	A	Pts	PIM	PP	SH	GW	Min
1997-98	Rogle Jr.	Swe-Jr.	59	36	40	76	....	....	....	....	....	....	....	....	....	....	....	....	....	....	....	....	....	....	....
1998-99	V.Frolunda U18	Swe-U18	32	26	38	64	37	....	....	....	....	....	....	....	....	....	4	3	1	4	2	....	....	....	....
99-2000	V.Frolunda U18	Swe-U18	4	2	4	6	4	....	....	....	....	....	....	....	....	....	....	....	....	....	....	....	....	....	....
	V.Frolunda Jr.	Swe-Jr.	25	7	12	19	2	....	....	....	....	....	....	....	....	....	6	2	3	5	2	....	....	....	....
2000-01	V.Frolunda Jr.	Swe-Jr.	18	14	27	41	12	....	....	....	....	....	....	....	....	....	....	....	....	....	....	....	....	....	....
	Molndal	Sweden-2	26	18	13	31	22	....	....	....	....	....	....	....	....	....	....	....	....	....	....	....	....	....	....
	V.Frolunda	Sweden	9	0	0	0	0	....	....	....	....	....	....	....	....	....	....	....	....	....	....	....	....	....	....
2001-02	V.Frolunda	Sweden	46	12	14	26	28	....	....	....	....	....	....	....	....	....	10	1	3	4	8	....	....	....	....
	V.Frolunda Jr.	Swe-Jr.	....	....	....	....	....	....	....	....	....	....	....	....	....	....	1	0	0	0	0	....	....	....	....
2002-03	V.Frolunda	Sweden	50	17	20	37	113	....	....	....	....	....	....	....	....	....	16	6	3	9	12	....	....	....	....
2003-04	V.Frolunda	Sweden	49	9	14	23	48	....	....	....	....	....	....	....	....	....	10	2	2	4	8	....	....	....	....
2004-05	Frolunda	Sweden	50	7	12	19	38	....	....	....	....	....	....	....	....	....	13	2	5	7	57	....	....	....	....
2005-06	Frolunda	Sweden	49	10	22	32	87	....	....	....	....	....	....	....	....	....	17	3	4	7	34	....	....	....	....
2006-07	**Dallas**	**NHL**	**36**	**3**	**3**	**6**	**14**	**0**	**0**	**0**	**36**	**8.3**	**–5**	**91**	**62.6**	**11:20**	**7**	**2**	**0**	**2**	**6**	**0**	**0**	**0**	**13:58**
	Iowa Stars	AHL	40	16	22	38	30	....	....	....	....	....	....	....	....	....	9	6	4	10	10	....	....	....	....
2007-08	**Dallas**	**NHL**	**55**	**3**	**11**	**14**	**22**	**0**	**0**	**0**	**48**	**6.3**	**–3**	**224**	**47.8**	**10:52**	**18**	**2**	**5**	**7**	**8**	**0**	**0**	**1**	**14:0**
	Iowa Stars	AHL	8	2	4	6	2	....	....	....	....	....	....	....	....	....	....	....	....	....	....	....	....	....	....
2008-09	**Dallas**	**NHL**	**43**	**1**	**5**	**6**	**20**	**0**	**0**	**1**	**32**	**3.1**	**–9**	**76**	**38.2**	**10:49**	....	....	....	....	....	....	....	....	....
2009-10	Frolunda	Sweden	49	11	20	31	34	....	....	....	....	....	....	....	....	....	1	0	0	0	0	....	....	....	....
	NHL Totals		**134**	**7**	**19**	**26**	**56**	**0**	**0**	**1**	**116**	**6.0**		**391**	**49.4**	**10:59**	**25**	**4**	**5**	**9**	**14**	**0**	**0**	**1**	**14:04**

Signed as a free agent by **Frolunda** (Sweden), October 9, 2009.

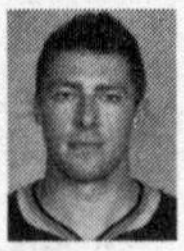

LUPUL, Joffrey

(LOO-puhl, JAWF-ree) **ANA**

Right wing. Shoots right. 6'1", 206 lbs. Born, Fort Saskatchewan, Alta., September 23, 1983. Anaheim's 1st choice, 7th overall, in 2002 Entry Draft.

Season	Club	League	GP	G	A	Pts	PIM	PP	SH	GW	S	%	+/-	TF	F%	Min	GP	G	A	Pts	PIM	PP	SH	GW	Min
1998-99	Ft. Saskatchewan	Minor-AB	36	40	50	90	40	....	....	....	....	....	....	....	....	....	....	....	....	....	....	....	....	....	....
99-2000	Ft. Saskatchewan	AMHL	34	43	30	*73	47	....	....	....	....	....	....	....	....	....	4	0	1	1	2	....	....	....	....
2000-01	Medicine Hat	WHL	69	30	26	56	39	....	....	....	....	....	....	....	....	....	22	3	6	9	2	....	....	....	....
2001-02	Medicine Hat	WHL	72	*56	50	106	95	....	....	....	....	....	....	....	....	....	....	....	....	....	....	....	....	....	....
2002-03	Medicine Hat	WHL	50	41	37	78	82	....	....	....	....	....	....	....	....	....	11	4	11	15	20	....	....	....	....
2003-04	**Anaheim**	**NHL**	**75**	**13**	**21**	**34**	**28**	**4**	**0**	**2**	**137**	**9.5**	**–6**	**11**	**9.1**	**13:37**	....	....	....	....	....	....	....	....	....
	Cincinnati	AHL	3	3	2	5	2	....	....	....	....	....	....	....	....	....	....	....	....	....	....	....	....	....	....
2004-05	Cincinnati	AHL	65	30	26	56	58	....	....	....	....	....	....	....	....	....	12	3	9	12	27	....	....	....	....
2005-06	**Anaheim**	**NHL**	**81**	**28**	**25**	**53**	**48**	**12**	**2**	**2**	**296**	**9.5**	**–13**	**101**	**37.6**	**16:38**	**16**	**9**	**2**	**11**	**31**	**1**	**0**	**1**	**16:4**
2006-07	**Edmonton**	**NHL**	**81**	**16**	**12**	**28**	**45**	**5**	**0**	**1**	**172**	**9.3**	**–29**	**14**	**35.7**	**15:36**	....	....	....	....	....	....	....	....	....
2007-08	**Philadelphia**	**NHL**	**56**	**20**	**26**	**46**	**35**	**7**	**0**	**3**	**176**	**11.4**	**2**	**4**	**75.0**	**18:13**	**17**	**4**	**6**	**10**	**2**	**2**	**0**	**1**	**16:1**
2008-09	**Philadelphia**	**NHL**	**79**	**25**	**25**	**50**	**58**	**6**	**0**	**4**	**194**	**12.9**	**1**	**21**	**47.6**	**15:41**	**6**	**1**	**1**	**2**	**2**	**0**	**0**	**0**	**17:0**
2009-10	**Anaheim**	**NHL**	**23**	**10**	**4**	**14**	**18**	**0**	**0**	**0**	**66**	**15.2**	**3**	**5**	**20.0**	**15:58**	....	....	....	....	....	....	....	....	....
	NHL Totals		**395**	**112**	**113**	**225**	**232**	**34**	**2**	**12**	**1041**	**10.8**		**156**	**37.2**	**15:50**	**39**	**14**	**9**	**23**	**35**	**3**	**0**	**2**	**16:3**

WHL East First All-Star Team (2002) • Canadian Major Junior First All-Star Team (2002)

Traded to **Edmonton** by **Anaheim** with Ladislav Smid, Anaheim's 1st round choice (later traded to Phoenix - Phoenix selected Nick Ross) in 2007 Entry Draft and Anaheim's 1st (Jordan Eberle) and 2nd (later traded to NY Islanders - NY Islanders selected Travis Hamonic) round choices in 2008 Entry Draft for Chris Pronger, July 3, 2006. Traded to **Philadelphia** by **Edmonton** with Jason Smith for Joni Pitkanen, Geoff Sanderson and Philadelphia's 3rd round choice (Cameron Abney) in 2009 Entry Draft, July 1, 2007. Traded to **Anaheim** by **Philadelphia** with Luca Sbisa, Philadelphia's 1st round choices in 2009 (later traded to Columbus - Columbus selected John Moore) and 2010 (Emerson Etem) Entry Drafts and future considerations for Chris Pronger and Ryan Dingle, June 26, 2009. • Missed majority of 2009-10 season recovering from recurring back injury and resulting surgery, December 16, 2009.

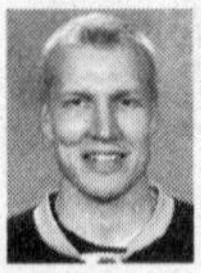

LYDMAN, Toni

(LEWD-man, TOH-nee) **ANA**

Defense. Shoots left. 6'1", 210 lbs. Born, Lahti, Finland, September 25, 1977. Calgary's 5th choice, 89th overall, in 1996 Entry Draft.

Season	Club	League	GP	G	A	Pts	PIM	PP	SH	GW	S	%	+/-	TF	F%	Min	GP	G	A	Pts	PIM	PP	SH	GW	Min
1993-94	K-Reipas U18	Fin-U18	9	3	1	4	4	....	....	....	....	....	....	....	....	....	....	....	....	....	....	....	....	....	....
	K-Reipas Jr.	Fin-Jr.	1	0	0	0	0	....	....	....	....	....	....	....	....	....	....	....	....	....	....	....	....	....	....
1994-95	K-Reipas U18	Fin-U18	9	7	4	11	12	....	....	....	....	....	....	....	....	....	....	....	....	....	....	....	....	....	....
	K-Reipas Jr.	Fin-Jr.	26	6	4	10	10	....	....	....	....	....	....	....	....	....	....	....	....	....	....	....	....	....	....
1995-96	Reipas Lahti Jr.	Fin-Jr.	9	2	2	4	6	....	....	....	....	....	....	....	....	....	....	....	....	....	....	....	....	....	....
	Reipas Lahti	Finland-2	39	5	2	7	30	....	....	....	....	....	....	....	....	....	3	0	1	1	0	....	....	....	....
1996-97	Tappara Tampere	Finland	49	1	2	3	65	....	....	....	....	....	....	....	....	....	3	0	0	0	6	....	....	....	....
1997-98	Tappara Tampere	Finland	48	4	10	14	48	....	....	....	....	....	....	....	....	....	4	0	2	2	0	....	....	....	....
1998-99	HIFK Helsinki	Finland	42	4	7	11	36	....	....	....	....	....	....	....	....	....	11	0	3	3	2	....	....	....	....
	HIFK Helsinki	EuroHL	6	0	2	2	29	....	....	....	....	....	....	....	....	....	4	1	....	....	....	....	....	....	....
99-2000	HIFK Helsinki	Finland	46	4	18	22	36	....	....	....	....	....	....	....	....	....	9	0	4	4	6	....	....	....	....
2000-01	**Calgary**	**NHL**	**62**	**3**	**16**	**19**	**30**	**1**	**0**	**0**	**80**	**3.8**	**–7**	**0**	**0.0**	**20:36**	....	....	....	....	....	....	....	....	....
2001-02	**Calgary**	**NHL**	**79**	**6**	**22**	**28**	**52**	**1**	**0**	**0**	**126**	**4.8**	**–8**	**0**	**0.0**	**21:10**	....	....	....	....	....	....	....	....	....
2002-03	**Calgary**	**NHL**	**81**	**6**	**20**	**26**	**28**	**3**	**0**	**0**	**143**	**4.2**	**–7**	**0**	**0.0**	**25:47**	....	....	....	....	....	....	....	....	....
2003-04	**Calgary**	**NHL**	**67**	**4**	**16**	**20**	**30**	**2**	**0**	**1**	**93**	**4.3**	**6**	**0**	**0.0**	**21:13**	**6**	**0**	**1**	**1**	**2**	**0**	**0**	**0**	**14:3**
2004-05	HIFK Helsinki	Finland	8	1	2	3	2	....	....	....	....	....	....	....	....	....	5	0	3	3	0	....	....	....	....
2005-06	**Buffalo**	**NHL**	**75**	**1**	**16**	**17**	**82**	**0**	**0**	**0**	**68**	**1.5**	**9**	**0**	**0.0**	**21:38**	**18**	**1**	**4**	**5**	**18**	**0**	**0**	**0**	**23:0**
	Finland	Olympics	8	1	0	1	10	....	....	....	....	....	....	....	....	....	....	....	....	....	....	....	....	....	....
2006-07	**Buffalo**	**NHL**	**67**	**2**	**17**	**19**	**55**	**0**	**0**	**1**	**44**	**4.5**	**10**	**0**	**0.0**	**20:36**	**16**	**2**	**2**	**4**	**14**	**0**	**0**	**0**	**23:4**
2007-08	**Buffalo**	**NHL**	**82**	**4**	**22**	**26**	**74**	**3**	**0**	**0**	**86**	**4.7**	**1**	**1**	**0.0**	**21:40**	....	....	....	....	....	....	....	....	....
2008-09	**Buffalo**	**NHL**	**80**	**3**	**20**	**23**	**70**	**0**	**0**	**0**	**99**	**3.0**	**0**	**0**	**0.0**	**21:47**	....	....	....	....	....	....	....	....	....
2009-10	**Buffalo**	**NHL**	**67**	**4**	**16**	**20**	**30**	**0**	**0**	**1**	**77**	**5.2**	**10**	**0**	**0.0**	**18:52**	**6**	**0**	**1**	**1**	**6**	**0**	**0**	**0**	**26:1**
	Finland	Olympics	6	0	0	0	2	....	....	....	....	....	....	....	....	....	....	....	....	....	....	....	....	....	....
	NHL Totals		**660**	**33**	**165**	**198**	**451**	**10**	**0**	**3**	**816**	**4.0**		**1**	**0.0**	**21:35**	**46**	**3**	**8**	**11**	**40**	**0**	**0**	**0**	**22:3**

Signed as a free agent by **HIFK Helsinki** (Finland), January 31, 2005. Traded to **Buffalo** by **Calgary** for Buffalo's 3rd round choice (John Armstrong) in 2006 Entry Draft, August 25, 2005. Signed as a free agent by **Anaheim**, July 1, 2010.

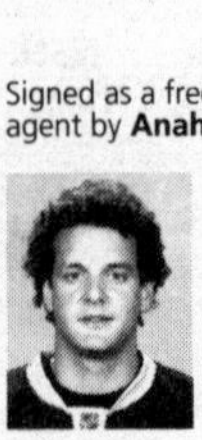

MacARTHUR, Clarke

(muh-KAR-thuhr, KLAHRK)

Left wing. Shoots left. 5'11", 191 lbs. Born, Lloydminster, Alta., April 6, 1985. Buffalo's 3rd choice, 74th overall, in 2003 Entry Draft.

Season	Club	League	GP	G	A	Pts	PIM	PP	SH	GW	S	%	+/-	TF	F%	Min	GP	G	A	Pts	PIM	PP	SH	GW	Min
99-2000	Lloydminster	CABHL	24	19	45	64	51	....	....	....	....	....	....	....	....	....	5	9	6	15	4	....	....	....	....
2000-01	Strathcona	AMBHL	38	36	63	99	44	....	....	....	....	....	....	....	....	....	8	6	2	8	10	....	....	....	....
2001-02	Drayton Valley	AJHL	61	22	40	62	33	....	....	....	....	....	....	....	....	....	16	5	8	13	34	....	....	....	....
2002-03	Medicine Hat	WHL	70	23	52	75	104	....	....	....	....	....	....	....	....	....	11	3	6	9	8	....	....	....	....
2003-04	Medicine Hat	WHL	62	35	40	75	93	....	....	....	....	....	....	....	....	....	20	8	10	18	16	....	....	....	....
2004-05	Medicine Hat	WHL	58	30	44	74	100	....	....	....	....	....	....	....	....	....	13	3	8	11	18	....	....	....	....
	Rochester	AHL	....	....	....	....	....	....	....	....	....	....	....	....	....	....	3	0	1	1	0	....	....	....	....
2005-06	Rochester	AHL	69	21	32	53	71	....	....	....	....	....	....	....	....	....	....	....	....	....	....	....	....	....	....
2006-07	**Buffalo**	**NHL**	**19**	**3**	**4**	**7**	**4**	**0**	**0**	**0**	**16**	**18.8**	**4**	**50**	**46.0**	**8:54**	....	....	....	....	....	....	....	....	....
	Rochester	AHL	51	21	42	63	57	....	....	....	....	....	....	....	....	....	6	2	4	6	4	....	....	....	....
2007-08	**Buffalo**	**NHL**	**37**	**8**	**7**	**15**	**20**	**0**	**0**	**1**	**51**	**15.7**	**3**	**14**	**28.6**	**14:34**	....	....	....	....	....	....	....	....	....
	Rochester	AHL	43	14	28	42	26	....	....	....	....	....	....	....	....	....	....	....	....	....	....	....	....	....	....
2008-09	**Buffalo**	**NHL**	**71**	**17**	**14**	**31**	**56**	**5**	**0**	**0**	**108**	**15.7**	**–4**	**218**	**34.9**	**13:50**	....	....	....	....	....	....	....	....	....

			Regular Season														Playoffs								
Season	Club	League	GP	G	A	Pts	PIM	PP	SH	GW	S	%	+/-	TF	F%	Min	GP	G	A	Pts	PIM	PP	SH	GW	Min
2009-10	Buffalo	NHL	60	13	13	26	47	3	0	3	99	13.1	-14	143	43.4	14:22	....	....	....	....	....	....	....	....	....
	Atlanta	NHL	21	3	6	9	2	1	1	0	30	10.0	-2	10	50.0	15:37	....	....	....	....	....	....	....	....	....
	NHL Totals		208	44	44	88	129	9	1	4	304	14.5		435	39.1	13:51	....	....	....	....	....	....	....	....	....

Memorial Cup Tournament All-Star Team (2004) • WHL East First All-Star Team (2005)

Traded to **Atlanta** by **Buffalo** for Atlanta's 3rd (Jerome Gauthier-Leduc) and 4th (Steven Shipley) round choices in 2010 Entry Draft, March 3, 2010.

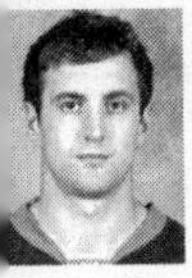

MacDONALD, Andrew

(MAK-DAWN-uhld, AN-droo) **NYI**

Defense. Shoots left. 6'1", 188 lbs. Born, Judique, N.S., September 7, 1986. NY Islanders' 10th choice, 160th overall, in 2006 Entry Draft.

Season	Club	League	GP	G	A	Pts	PIM	PP	SH	GW	S	%	+/-	TF	F%	Min	GP	G	A	Pts	PIM	PP	SH	GW	Min
2003-04	Truro Bearcats	MJrHL	50	8	20	28	43	....	....	....	....	....	....	....	....	....	10	0	0	0	....	....	....	....	....
2004-05	Truro Bearcats	MJrHL	56	11	22	33	60	....	....	....	....	....	....	....	....	....	17	6	7	13	....	....	....	....	....
2005-06	Moncton Wildcats	QMJHL	68	6	40	46	62	....	....	....	....	....	....	....	....	....	21	2	11	13	10	....	....	....	....
2006-07	Moncton Wildcats	QMJHL	65	14	44	58	81	....	....	....	....	....	....	....	....	....	7	1	5	6	4	....	....	....	....
	Bridgeport	AHL	3	0	0	0	0	....	....	....	....	....	....	....	....	....	....	....	....	....	....	....	....	....	....
2007-08	Bridgeport	AHL	21	2	3	5	10	....	....	....	....	....	....	....	....	....	....	....	....	....	....	....	....	....	....
	Utah Grizzlies	ECHL	37	1	11	12	39	....	....	....	....	....	....	....	....	....	15	3	9	12	12	....	....	....	....
2008-09	**NY Islanders**	**NHL**	**3**	**0**	**0**	**0**	**2**	0	0	0	1	0.0	2	0	0.0	10:10	....	....	....	....	....	....	....	....	....
	Bridgeport	AHL	69	9	24	33	46	....	....	....	....	....	....	....	....	....	5	1	1	2	4	....	....	....	....
2009-10	**NY Islanders**	**NHL**	**46**	**1**	**6**	**7**	**20**	0	0	0	43	2.3	4	1	0.0	20:05	....	....	....	....	....	....	....	....	....
	Bridgeport	AHL	21	2	6	8	29	....	....	....	....	....	....	....	....	....	5	3	1	4	10	....	....	....	....
	NHL Totals		**49**	**1**	**6**	**7**	**22**	0	0	0	44	2.3		1	0.0	19:29	....	....	....	....	....	....	....	....	....

QMJHL First All-Star Team (2007)

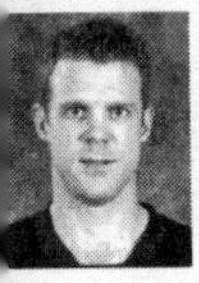

MacDONALD, Craig

(MAK-DAWN-uhld, KRAYG)

Left wing. Shoots left. 6'1", 201 lbs. Born, Antigonish, N.S., April 7, 1977. Hartford's 3rd choice, 88th overall, in 1996 Entry Draft.

Season	Club	League	GP	G	A	Pts	PIM	PP	SH	GW	S	%	+/-	TF	F%	Min	GP	G	A	Pts	PIM	PP	SH	GW	Min
1994-95	Lawrence	High-MA	30	25	52	77	10	....	....	....	....	....	....	....	....	....	....	....	....	....	....	....	....	....	....
1995-96	Harvard Crimson	ECAC	34	7	10	17	10	....	....	....	....	....	....	....	....	....	....	....	....	....	....	....	....	....	....
1996-97	Harvard Crimson	ECAC	32	6	10	16	20	....	....	....	....	....	....	....	....	....	....	....	....	....	....	....	....	....	....
1997-98	Canada	Nat-Tm	58	18	29	47	38	....	....	....	....	....	....	....	....	....	....	....	....	....	....	....	....	....	....
1998-99	**Carolina**	**NHL**	**11**	**0**	**0**	**0**	**0**	0	0	0	5	0.0	0	2	100.0	2:29	1	0	0	0	0	0	0	0	2:46
	New Haven	AHL	62	17	31	48	77	....	....	....	....	....	....	....	....	....	....	....	....	....	....	....	....	....	....
99-2000	Cincinnati	IHL	78	12	24	36	76	....	....	....	....	....	....	....	....	....	11	4	1	5	8	....	....	....	....
2000-01	Cincinnati	IHL	82	20	28	48	104	....	....	....	....	....	....	....	....	....	5	0	1	1	6	....	....	....	....
2001-02	**Carolina**	**NHL**	**12**	**1**	**1**	**2**	**0**	0	0	0	15	6.7	-1	19	47.4	10:11	4	0	0	0	2	0	0	0	4:42
	Lowell	AHL	64	19	22	41	61	....	....	....	....	....	....	....	....	....	....	....	....	....	....	....	....	....	....
2002-03	**Carolina**	**NHL**	**35**	**1**	**3**	**4**	**20**	0	0	0	43	2.3	-3	72	55.6	9:21	....	....	....	....	....	....	....	....	....
	Lowell	AHL	27	7	20	27	38	....	....	....	....	....	....	....	....	....	....	....	....	....	....	....	....	....	....
2003-04	**Florida**	**NHL**	**34**	**0**	**3**	**3**	**25**	0	0	0	42	0.0	-5	398	45.7	12:31	....	....	....	....	....	....	....	....	....
	San Antonio	AHL	2	0	0	0	4	....	....	....	....	....	....	....	....	....	....	....	....	....	....	....	....	....	....
	Boston	**NHL**	**18**	**0**	**3**	**3**	**8**	0	0	0	17	0.0	0	155	47.1	8:42	1	0	0	0	0	0	0	0	2:11
2004-05	Lowell	AHL	71	10	18	28	104	....	....	....	....	....	....	....	....	....	2	0	0	0	0	....	....	....	....
2005-06	**Calgary**	**NHL**	**25**	**3**	**2**	**5**	**8**	1	0	0	27	11.1	5	33	45.5	10:16	1	0	0	0	0	0	0	0	7:50
	Omaha	AHL	37	8	19	27	57	....	....	....	....	....	....	....	....	....	....	....	....	....	....	....	....	....	....
2006-07	**Chicago**	**NHL**	**25**	**3**	**2**	**5**	**14**	0	1	0	30	10.0	-2	178	47.8	11:12	....	....	....	....	....	....	....	....	....
	Norfolk Admirals	AHL	50	15	25	40	45	....	....	....	....	....	....	....	....	....	6	2	3	5	8	....	....	....	....
2007-08	**Tampa Bay**	**NHL**	**65**	**2**	**9**	**11**	**16**	0	0	0	84	2.4	-10	406	49.8	10:52	....	....	....	....	....	....	....	....	....
	Norfolk Admirals	AHL	7	3	8	11	8	....	....	....	....	....	....	....	....	....	....	....	....	....	....	....	....	....	....
2008-09	**Columbus**	**NHL**	**8**	**1**	**1**	**2**	**0**	0	0	1	6	16.7	1	11	36.4	10:39	....	....	....	....	....	....	....	....	....
	Syracuse Crunch	AHL	70	15	25	40	71	....	....	....	....	....	....	....	....	....	....	....	....	....	....	....	....	....	....
2009-10	Dusseldorf	Germany	56	19	23	42	76	....	....	....	....	....	....	....	....	....	3	2	0	2	0	....	....	....	....
	NHL Totals		**233**	**11**	**24**	**35**	**91**	1	1	1	269	4.1		1274	48.0	10:15	7	0	0	0	2	0	0	0	4:31

• Rights transferred to **Carolina** after **Hartford** franchise relocated, June 25, 1997. Signed as a free agent by **Florida**, August 14, 2003. Claimed on waivers by **Boston** from **Florida**, January 20, 2004. Signed as a free agent by **Calgary**, August 11, 2005. Signed as a free agent by **Chicago**, August 1, 2006. Signed as a free agent by **Tampa Bay**, July 2, 2007. Signed as a free agent by **Columbus**, July 14, 2008. Signed as a free agent by **Dusseldorf** (Germany), June 30, 2009.

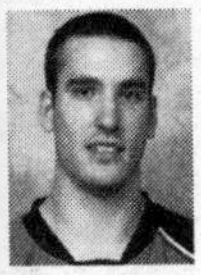

MACHACEK, Spencer

(muh-HA-chehk, SPEHN-suhr) **ATL.**

Right wing. Shoots right. 6'1", 195 lbs. Born, Lethbridge, Alta., October 14, 1988. Atlanta's 1st choice, 67th overall, in 2007 Entry Draft.

Season	Club	League	GP	G	A	Pts	PIM	PP	SH	GW	S	%	+/-	TF	F%	Min	GP	G	A	Pts	PIM	PP	SH	GW	Min
2004-05	Brooks Bandits	AJHL	59	16	20	36	41	....	....	....	....	....	....	....	....	....	10	2	2	4	8	....	....	....	....
2005-06	Vancouver Giants	WHL	70	23	22	45	53	....	....	....	....	....	....	....	....	....	18	6	8	14	8	....	....	....	....
2006-07	Vancouver Giants	WHL	63	21	24	45	32	....	....	....	....	....	....	....	....	....	22	9	11	20	14	....	....	....	....
2007-08	Vancouver Giants	WHL	70	33	45	78	69	....	....	....	....	....	....	....	....	....	10	5	2	7	6	....	....	....	....
2008-09	**Atlanta**	**NHL**	**2**	**0**	**0**	**0**	**0**	0	0	0	1	0.0	0	0	0.0	8:12	....	....	....	....	....	....	....	....	....
	Chicago Wolves	AHL	77	23	25	48	23	....	....	....	....	....	....	....	....	....	....	....	....	....	....	....	....	....	....
2009-10	Chicago Wolves	AHL	79	20	29	49	68	....	....	....	....	....	....	....	....	....	13	7	4	11	8	....	....	....	....
	NHL Totals		**2**	**0**	**0**	**0**	**0**	0	0	0	1	0.0		0	0.0	8:12	....	....	....	....	....	....	....	....	....

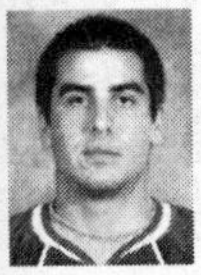

MACIAS, Ray

(mah-CHEE-ahs, RAY) **COL.**

Defense. Shoots right. 6'2", 195 lbs. Born, Long Beach, CA, September 18, 1986. Colorado's 6th choice, 124th overall, in 2005 Entry Draft.

Season	Club	League	GP	G	A	Pts	PIM	PP	SH	GW	S	%	+/-	TF	F%	Min	GP	G	A	Pts	PIM	PP	SH	GW	Min
2002-03	L.A. Jr. Kings	Minor-CA	49	37	26	63	100	....	....	....	....	....	....	....	....	....	....	....	....	....	....	....	....	....	....
	Kamloops Blazers	WHL	4	0	0	0	0	....	....	....	....	....	....	....	....	....	2	0	0	0	0	....	....	....	....
2003-04	Kamloops Blazers	WHL	69	12	17	29	14	....	....	....	....	....	....	....	....	....	5	2	0	2	0	....	....	....	....
2004-05	Kamloops Blazers	WHL	69	12	35	47	18	....	....	....	....	....	....	....	....	....	2	0	0	0	0	....	....	....	....
2005-06	Kamloops Blazers	WHL	68	12	26	38	34	....	....	....	....	....	....	....	....	....	....	....	....	....	....	....	....	....	....
2006-07	Kamloops Blazers	WHL	70	30	40	70	58	....	....	....	....	....	....	....	....	....	....	....	....	....	....	....	....	....	....
2007-08	Lake Erie	AHL	42	4	9	13	18	....	....	....	....	....	....	....	....	....	....	....	....	....	....	....	....	....	....
	Johnstown Chiefs	ECHL	5	0	5	5	0	....	....	....	....	....	....	....	....	....	6	1	3	4	2	....	....	....	....
2008-09	**Colorado**	**NHL**	**6**	**0**	**1**	**1**	**0**	0	0	0	4	0.0	0	0	0.0	17:59	....	....	....	....	....	....	....	....	....
	Lake Erie	AHL	36	3	15	18	20	....	....	....	....	....	....	....	....	....	....	....	....	....	....	....	....	....	....
	Johnstown Chiefs	ECHL	8	1	5	6	4	....	....	....	....	....	....	....	....	....	....	....	....	....	....	....	....	....	....
2009-10	Lake Erie	AHL	52	7	10	17	16	....	....	....	....	....	....	....	....	....	....	....	....	....	....	....	....	....	....
	NHL Totals		**6**	**0**	**1**	**1**	**0**	0	0	0	4	0.0		0	0.0	17:59	....	....	....	....	....	....	....	....	....

WHL West First All-Star Team (2007)

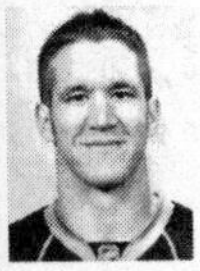

MacINTYRE, Steve

(MAK-ihn-tighr, STEEV) **EDM.**

Left wing. Shoots left. 6'5", 250 lbs. Born, Brock, Sask., August 8, 1980.

Season	Club	League	GP	G	A	Pts	PIM	PP	SH	GW	S	%	+/-	TF	F%	Min	GP	G	A	Pts	PIM	PP	SH	GW	Min
2002-03	St. Jean Mission	QSPHL	10	1	1	2	68	....	....	....	....	....	....	....	....	....	....	....	....	....	....	....	....	....	....
	Muskegon Fury	UHL	54	2	1	3	279	....	....	....	....	....	....	....	....	....	5	0	0	0	24	....	....	....	....
2003-04	Hartford	AHL	3	0	0	0	0	....	....	....	....	....	....	....	....	....	....	....	....	....	....	....	....	....	....
	Charlotte	ECHL	61	1	4	5	217	....	....	....	....	....	....	....	....	....	....	....	....	....	....	....	....	....	....
	Jacksonville	WHA2	6	0	2	2	18	....	....	....	....	....	....	....	....	....	5	0	1	1	17	....	....	....	....
2004-05	Hartford	AHL	27	1	1	2	207	....	....	....	....	....	....	....	....	....	....	....	....	....	....	....	....	....	....
	Charlotte	ECHL	46	1	4	5	214	....	....	....	....	....	....	....	....	....	11	0	4	4	17	....	....	....	....
2005-06	Charlotte	ECHL	61	3	2	5	238	....	....	....	....	....	....	....	....	....	1	0	0	0	4	....	....	....	....
2006-07	Quad City	UHL	46	2	1	3	168	....	....	....	....	....	....	....	....	....	5	0	0	0	6	....	....	....	....
2007-08	Providence Bruins	AHL	62	2	3	5	213	....	....	....	....	....	....	....	....	....	5	0	0	0	9	....	....	....	....
2008-09	**Edmonton**	**NHL**	**22**	**2**	**0**	**2**	**40**	0	0	1	6	33.3	-2	0	0.0	3:55	....	....	....	....	....	....	....	....	....
2009-10	**Edmonton**	**NHL**	**4**	**0**	**0**	**0**	**7**	0	0	0	0	0.0	0	0	0.0	1:35	....	....	....	....	....	....	....	....	....
	Florida	**NHL**	**18**	**0**	**1**	**1**	**17**	0	0	0	3	0.0	-3	0	0.0	3:10	....	....	....	....	....	....	....	....	....
	Rochester	AHL	34	0	2	2	86	....	....	....	....	....	....	....	....	....	6	0	0	0	23	....	....	....	....
	NHL Totals		**44**	**2**	**1**	**3**	**64**	0	0	1	9	22.2		0	0.0	3:24	....	....	....	....	....	....	....	....	....

Signed as a free agent by **NY Rangers**, August 15, 2005. Signed as a free agent by **Quad City** (UHL), August 24, 2006. Signed as a free agent by **Florida**, July 3, 2008. Claimed on waivers by **Edmonton** from **Florida**, September 30, 2008. • Missed majority of 2008-09 season recovering from facial injury and as a healthy reserve. Claimed on waivers by **Florida** from **Edmonton**, November 10, 2009.

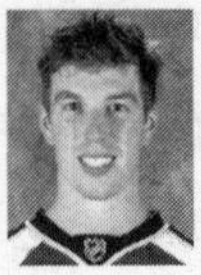

MacKENZIE, Aaron

(muh-KEHN-zee, AIR-ruhn)

Defense. Shoots left. 6'1", 195 lbs. Born, Terrace Bay, Ont., March 7, 1981.

Season	Club	League	Regular Season GP	G	A	Pts	PIM	PP	SH	GW	S	%	+/-	TF	F%	Min	Playoffs GP	G	A	Pts	PIM	PP	SH	GW	Min
1998-99	Thunder Bay	USHL	49	8	12	20	123	....	....	....	....	....	....	....	....	....	3	0	1	1	0	....	....	....	....
99-2000	U. of Denver	WCHA	40	1	9	10	56	....	....	....	....	....	....	....	....	....	....	....	....	....	....	....	....	....	....
2000-01	U. of Denver	WCHA	37	2	6	8	45	....	....	....	....	....	....	....	....	....	....	....	....	....	....	....	....	....	....
2001-02	U. of Denver	WCHA	39	5	18	23	30	....	....	....	....	....	....	....	....	....	....	....	....	....	....	....	....	....	....
2002-03	U. of Denver	WCHA	41	11	21	32	33	....	....	....	....	....	....	....	....	....	....	....	....	....	....	....	....	....	....
2003-04	Worcester IceCats	AHL	66	5	9	14	108	....	....	....	....	....	....	....	....	....	10	0	2	2	10	....	....	....	....
2004-05	Worcester IceCats	AHL	75	2	13	15	106	....	....	....	....	....	....	....	....	....	....	....	....	....	....	....	....	....	....
2005-06	Peoria Rivermen	AHL	51	2	7	9	35	....	....	....	....	....	....	....	....	....	4	0	0	0	6	....	....	....	....
2006-07	Peoria Rivermen	AHL	67	1	6	7	46	....	....	....	....	....	....	....	....	....	....	....	....	....	....	....	....	....	....
2007-08	Peoria Rivermen	AHL	55	0	5	5	20	....	....	....	....	....	....	....	....	....	....	....	....	....	....	....	....	....	....
2008-09	**Colorado**	**NHL**	**5**	**0**	**0**	**0**	**0**	**0**	**0**	**0**	**3**	**0.0**	**1**	**0**	**0.0**	**14:38**	....	....	....	....	....	....	....	....	....
	Lake Erie	AHL	52	3	9	12	50	....	....	....	....	....	....	....	....	....	....	....	....	....	....	....	....	....	....
2009-10	Idaho Steelheads	ECHL	3	0	0	0	2	....	....	....	....	....	....	....	....	....	....	....	....	....	....	....	....	....	....
	Pardubice	CzRep	29	0	1	1	24	....	....	....	....	....	....	....	....	....	6	0	1	1	8	....	....	....	....
	NHL Totals		**5**	**0**	**0**	**0**	**0**	**0**	**0**	**0**	**3**	**0.0**		**0**	**0.0**	**14:38**	....	....	....	....	....	....	....	....	....

WCHA First All-Star Team (2003)

Signed as a free agent by **Worcester** (AHL), October 6, 2003. Signed as a free agent by **St. Louis**, June 29, 2004. Signed as a free agent by **Peoria** (AHL), August 24, 2007. Signed as a free agent by **Colorado**, July 14, 2008. Signed as a free agent by **Idaho** (ECHL), October 19, 2009. Signed as a free agent by **Pardubice** (CzRep), November 2, 2009.

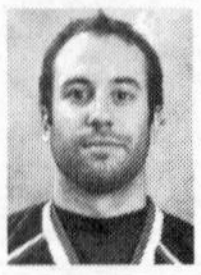

MacKENZIE, Derek

(muh-KEHN-zee, DAIR-ihk) **CB**

Center. Shoots left. 5'11", 182 lbs. Born, Sudbury, Ont., June 11, 1981. Atlanta's 6th choice, 128th overall, in 1999 Entry Draft.

Season	Club	League	Regular Season GP	G	A	Pts	PIM	PP	SH	GW	S	%	+/-	TF	F%	Min	Playoffs GP	G	A	Pts	PIM	PP	SH	GW	Min
1996-97	Rayside-Balfour	NOJHA	40	23	32	55	40	....	....	....	....	....	....	....	....	....	....	....	....	....	....	....	....	....	....
1997-98	Sudbury Wolves	OHL	59	9	11	20	26	....	....	....	....	....	....	....	....	....	....	....	....	....	....	....	....	....	....
1998-99	Sudbury Wolves	OHL	68	22	65	87	74	....	....	....	....	....	....	....	....	....	4	2	4	6	2	....	....	....	....
99-2000	Sudbury Wolves	OHL	68	24	33	57	110	....	....	....	....	....	....	....	....	....	12	5	9	14	16	....	....	....	....
2000-01	Sudbury Wolves	OHL	62	40	49	89	89	....	....	....	....	....	....	....	....	....	12	6	8	14	16	....	....	....	....
2001-02	**Atlanta**	**NHL**	**1**	**0**	**0**	**0**	**2**	**0**	**0**	**0**	**1**	**0.0**	**-1**	**16**	**56.3**	**13:51**	....	....	....	....	....	....	....	....	....
	Chicago Wolves	AHL	68	13	12	25	80	....	....	....	....	....	....	....	....	....	25	4	2	6	20	....	....	....	....
2002-03	Chicago Wolves	AHL	80	14	18	32	97	....	....	....	....	....	....	....	....	....	9	0	0	0	4	....	....	....	....
2003-04	**Atlanta**	**NHL**	**12**	**0**	**1**	**1**	**10**	**0**	**0**	**0**	**7**	**0.0**	**0**	**63**	**46.0**	**6:38**	....	....	....	....	....	....	....	....	....
	Chicago Wolves	AHL	63	19	16	35	67	....	....	....	....	....	....	....	....	....	10	7	1	8	13	....	....	....	....
2004-05	Chicago Wolves	AHL	78	13	20	33	87	....	....	....	....	....	....	....	....	....	18	5	6	11	33	....	....	....	....
2005-06	**Atlanta**	**NHL**	**11**	**0**	**1**	**1**	**8**	**0**	**0**	**0**	**11**	**0.0**	**0**	**59**	**55.9**	**6:33**	....	....	....	....	....	....	....	....	....
	Chicago Wolves	AHL	36	10	12	22	48	....	....	....	....	....	....	....	....	....	....	....	....	....	....	....	....	....	....
2006-07	**Atlanta**	**NHL**	**4**	**0**	**0**	**0**	**0**	**0**	**0**	**0**	**3**	**0.0**	**1**	**16**	**56.3**	**5:00**	....	....	....	....	....	....	....	....	....
	Chicago Wolves	AHL	52	14	23	37	62	....	....	....	....	....	....	....	....	....	....	....	....	....	....	....	....	....	....
2007-08	**Columbus**	**NHL**	**17**	**2**	**0**	**2**	**8**	**0**	**0**	**0**	**19**	**10.5**	**-2**	**73**	**34.3**	**7:47**	....	....	....	....	....	....	....	....	....
	Syracuse Crunch	AHL	62	25	24	49	46	....	....	....	....	....	....	....	....	....	13	6	8	14	22	....	....	....	....
2008-09	**Columbus**	**NHL**	**1**	**0**	**0**	**0**	**2**	**0**	**0**	**0**	**1**	**0.0**	**-1**	**4**	**50.0**	**7:15**	....	....	....	....	....	....	....	....	....
	Syracuse Crunch	AHL	64	22	30	52	50	....	....	....	....	....	....	....	....	....	....	....	....	....	....	....	....	....	....
2009-10	**Columbus**	**NHL**	**18**	**1**	**3**	**4**	**0**	**0**	**0**	**0**	**14**	**7.1**	**3**	**104**	**54.8**	**8:42**	....	....	....	....	....	....	....	....	....
	Syracuse Crunch	AHL	47	17	30	47	30	....	....	....	....	....	....	....	....	....	....	....	....	....	....	....	....	....	....
	NHL Totals		**64**	**3**	**5**	**8**	**30**	**0**	**0**	**0**	**56**	**5.4**		**335**	**49.0**	**7:31**	....	....	....	....	....	....	....	....	....

Signed as a free agent by **Columbus**, July 11, 2007.

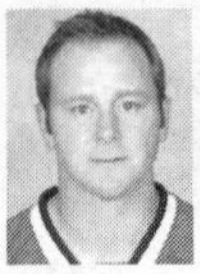

MADDEN, John

(MA-dehn, JAWN) **MIN**

Center. Shoots left. 5'11", 190 lbs. Born, Barrie, Ont., May 4, 1973.

Season	Club	League	Regular Season GP	G	A	Pts	PIM	PP	SH	GW	S	%	+/-	TF	F%	Min	Playoffs GP	G	A	Pts	PIM	PP	SH	GW	Min
1989-90	Alliston Hornets	OHA-C	31	24	25	49	26	....	....	....	....	....	....	....	....	....	....	....	....	....	....	....	....	....	....
1990-91	Alliston Hornets	OHA-C	14	15	21	36	10	....	....	....	....	....	....	....	....	....	....	....	....	....	....	....	....	....	....
	Barrie Colts	OHA-B	1	0	0	0	0	....	....	....	....	....	....	....	....	....	....	....	....	....	....	....	....	....	....
1991-92	Barrie Colts	OHA-B	42	50	54	104	46	....	....	....	....	....	....	....	....	....	13	10	9	19	14	....	....	....	....
1992-93	Barrie Colts	COJHL	43	49	75	124	62	....	....	....	....	....	....	....	....	....	....	....	....	....	....	....	....	....	....
1993-94	U. of Michigan	CCHA	36	6	11	17	14	....	....	....	....	....	....	....	....	....	....	....	....	....	....	....	....	....	....
1994-95	U. of Michigan	CCHA	39	21	22	43	8	....	....	....	....	....	....	....	....	....	....	....	....	....	....	....	....	....	....
1995-96	U. of Michigan	CCHA	43	27	30	57	45	....	....	....	....	....	....	....	....	....	....	....	....	....	....	....	....	....	....
1996-97	U. of Michigan	CCHA	42	26	37	63	56	....	....	....	....	....	....	....	....	....	....	....	....	....	....	....	....	....	....
1997-98	Albany River Rats	AHL	74	20	36	56	40	....	....	....	....	....	....	....	....	....	13	3	13	16	14	....	....	....	....
1998-99	**New Jersey**	**NHL**	**4**	**0**	**1**	**1**	**0**	**0**	**0**	**0**	**4**	**0.0**	**-2**	**0**	**0.0**	**9:13**	....	....	....	....	....	....	....	....	....
	Albany River Rats	AHL	75	38	60	98	44	....	....	....	....	....	....	....	....	....	5	2	2	4	6	....	....	....	....
99-2000◆	**New Jersey**	**NHL**	**74**	**16**	**9**	**25**	**6**	**0**	***6**	**3**	**115**	**13.9**	**7**	**770**	**47.5**	**11:40**	**20**	**3**	**4**	**7**	**0**	**0**	**1**	**2**	**15:3**
2000-01	**New Jersey**	**NHL**	**80**	**23**	**15**	**38**	**12**	**0**	**3**	**4**	**163**	**14.1**	**24**	**974**	**46.6**	**15:35**	**25**	**4**	**3**	**7**	**6**	**0**	**0**	**0**	**15:1**
2001-02	**New Jersey**	**NHL**	**82**	**15**	**8**	**23**	**25**	**0**	**0**	**2**	**170**	**8.8**	**6**	**1001**	**47.0**	**15:36**	**6**	**0**	**0**	**0**	**0**	**0**	**0**	**0**	**17:2**
2002-03◆	**New Jersey**	**NHL**	**80**	**19**	**22**	**41**	**26**	**2**	**2**	**3**	**207**	**9.2**	**13**	**1502**	**50.9**	**18:18**	**24**	**6**	**10**	**16**	**2**	**2**	**1**	**1**	**19:3**
2003-04	**New Jersey**	**NHL**	**80**	**12**	**23**	**35**	**22**	**1**	**1**	**1**	**210**	**5.7**	**7**	**1377**	**53.3**	**17:17**	**5**	**0**	**0**	**0**	**0**	**0**	**0**	**0**	**14:5**
2004-05	HIFK Helsinki	Finland	3	0	0	0	0	....	....	....	....	....	....	....	....	....	....	....	....	....	....	....	....	....	....
2005-06	**New Jersey**	**NHL**	**82**	**16**	**20**	**36**	**36**	**0**	**1**	**0**	**194**	**8.2**	**-7**	**1613**	**51.5**	**18:59**	**9**	**4**	**1**	**5**	**8**	**0**	***2**	**0**	**18:5**
2006-07	**New Jersey**	**NHL**	**74**	**12**	**20**	**32**	**14**	**0**	**0**	**1**	**153**	**7.8**	**-7**	**1366**	**49.8**	**18:53**	**11**	**1**	**1**	**2**	**2**	**0**	**0**	**0**	**21:1**
2007-08	**New Jersey**	**NHL**	**80**	**20**	**23**	**43**	**26**	**3**	**3**	**3**	**185**	**10.8**	**1**	**1463**	**53.7**	**19:27**	**5**	**2**	**1**	**3**	**2**	**0**	**0**	**1**	**21:1**
2008-09	**New Jersey**	**NHL**	**76**	**7**	**16**	**23**	**26**	**0**	**1**	**2**	**132**	**5.3**	**-7**	**1160**	**51.6**	**16:25**	**7**	**0**	**1**	**1**	**4**	**0**	**0**	**0**	**18:2**
2009-10◆	**Chicago**	**NHL**	**79**	**10**	**13**	**23**	**12**	**0**	**0**	**0**	**127**	**7.9**	**-2**	**1156**	**53.0**	**15:25**	**22**	**1**	**1**	**2**	**2**	**0**	**0**	**0**	**11:3**
	NHL Totals		**791**	**150**	**170**	**320**	**205**	**6**	**17**	**19**	**1660**	**9.0**		**12382**	**50.9**	**16:45**	**134**	**21**	**22**	**43**	**26**	**2**	**4**	**4**	**16:4**

CCHA First All-Star Team (1997) • NCAA West First All-American Team (1997) • Frank J. Selke Trophy (2001)

Signed as a free agent by **New Jersey**, June 26, 1997. Signed as a free agent by **HIFK Helsinki** (Finland), November 29, 2004. Signed as a free agent by **Chicago**, July 2, 2009. Signed as a free agent by **Minnesota**, August 6, 2010.

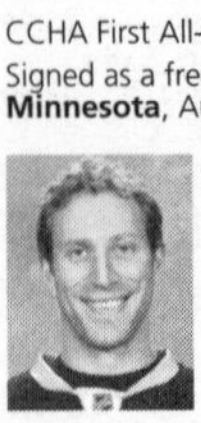

MAIR, Adam

(MAIR, A-duhm)

Center. Shoots right. 6'1", 208 lbs. Born, Hamilton, Ont., February 15, 1979. Toronto's 2nd choice, 84th overall, in 1997 Entry Draft.

Season	Club	League	Regular Season GP	G	A	Pts	PIM	PP	SH	GW	S	%	+/-	TF	F%	Min	Playoffs GP	G	A	Pts	PIM	PP	SH	GW	Min
1994-95	Ohsweken	OHA-B	39	21	23	44	91	....	....	....	....	....	....	....	....	....	....	....	....	....	....	....	....	....	....
1995-96	Owen Sound	OHL	62	12	15	27	63	....	....	....	....	....	....	....	....	....	6	0	0	0	2	....	....	....	....
1996-97	Owen Sound	OHL	65	16	35	51	113	....	....	....	....	....	....	....	....	....	4	1	0	1	2	....	....	....	....
1997-98	Owen Sound	OHL	56	25	27	52	179	....	....	....	....	....	....	....	....	....	11	6	3	9	31	....	....	....	....
1998-99	Owen Sound	OHL	43	23	41	64	109	....	....	....	....	....	....	....	....	....	16	10	10	20	*47	....	....	....	....
	Toronto	**NHL**	....	....	....	....	....	....	....	....	....	....	....	....	....	....	**5**	**1**	**0**	**1**	**14**	**0**	**0**	**0**	**5:3**
	St. John's	AHL	....	....	....	....	....	....	....	....	....	....	....	....	....	....	3	1	0	1	6	....	....	....	....
99-2000	**Toronto**	**NHL**	**8**	**1**	**0**	**1**	**6**	**0**	**0**	**0**	**7**	**14.3**	**-1**	**9**	**33.3**	**11:33**	**5**	**0**	**0**	**0**	**8**	**0**	**0**	**0**	**10:1**
	St. John's	AHL	66	22	27	49	124	....	....	....	....	....	....	....	....	....	....	....	....	....	....	....	....	....	....
2000-01	**Toronto**	**NHL**	**16**	**0**	**2**	**2**	**14**	**0**	**0**	**0**	**17**	**0.0**	**3**	**56**	**51.8**	**9:01**	....	....	....	....	....	....	....	....	....
	St. John's	AHL	47	18	27	45	69	....	....	....	....	....	....	....	....	....	....	....	....	....	....	....	....	....	....
	Los Angeles	**NHL**	**10**	**0**	**0**	**0**	**6**	**0**	**0**	**0**	**5**	**0.0**	**-3**	**21**	**61.9**	**6:14**	....	....	....	....	....	....	....	....	....
2001-02	**Los Angeles**	**NHL**	**18**	**1**	**1**	**2**	**57**	**0**	**0**	**0**	**10**	**10.0**	**1**	**31**	**58.1**	**7:11**	....	....	....	....	....	....	....	....	....
	Manchester	AHL	27	10	9	19	48	....	....	....	....	....	....	....	....	....	5	5	1	6	10	....	....	....	....
2002-03	**Buffalo**	**NHL**	**79**	**6**	**11**	**17**	**146**	**0**	**1**	**1**	**83**	**7.2**	**-4**	**572**	**51.2**	**10:37**	....	....	....	....	....	....	....	....	....
2003-04	**Buffalo**	**NHL**	**81**	**6**	**14**	**20**	**146**	**1**	**0**	**1**	**82**	**7.3**	**-3**	**340**	**45.9**	**9:38**	....	....	....	....	....	....	....	....	....
2004-05			DID NOT PLAY																						
2005-06	**Buffalo**	**NHL**	**40**	**2**	**5**	**7**	**47**	**0**	**0**	**0**	**40**	**5.0**	**-2**	**12**	**41.7**	**7:59**	**3**	**0**	**0**	**0**	**0**	**0**	**0**	**0**	**9:1**
2006-07	**Buffalo**	**NHL**	**82**	**2**	**9**	**11**	**128**	**0**	**0**	**0**	**73**	**2.7**	**-1**	**130**	**46.2**	**7:33**	**16**	**1**	**4**	**5**	**10**	**0**	**0**	**0**	**7:3**
2007-08	**Buffalo**	**NHL**	**72**	**5**	**12**	**17**	**66**	**0**	**0**	**2**	**62**	**8.1**	**-2**	**361**	**45.4**	**8:52**	....	....	....	....	....	....	....	....	....
2008-09	**Buffalo**	**NHL**	**75**	**8**	**11**	**19**	**95**	**0**	**0**	**1**	**75**	**10.7**	**4**	**414**	**48.3**	**10:35**	....	....	....	....	....	....	....	....	....
2009-10	**Buffalo**	**NHL**	**69**	**6**	**8**	**14**	**73**	**0**	**0**	**0**	**67**	**9.0**	**-2**	**178**	**52.3**	**9:14**	**6**	**1**	**1**	**2**	**4**	**0**	**0**	**0**	**12:0**
	NHL Totals		**550**	**37**	**73**	**110**	**784**	**1**	**1**	**5**	**521**	**7.1**		**2124**	**48.7**	**9:11**	**35**	**3**	**5**	**8**	**36**	**0**	**0**	**0**	**8:3**

Traded to **Los Angeles** by **Toronto** with Toronto's 2nd round choice (Michael Cammalleri) in 2001 Entry Draft for Aki Berg, March 13, 2001. Traded to **Buffalo** by **Los Angeles** with Los Angeles' 5th round choice (Thomas Morrow) in 2003 Entry Draft for Erik Rasmussen, July 24, 2002. • Missed majority of 2005-06 season recovering from groin (training camp) and head (January 12, 2006 vs. Phoenix) injuries.

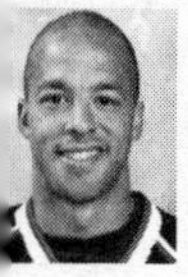

MALHOTRA, Manny
(mal-HOH-truh, MAN-ee) **VAN.**

Center. Shoots left. 6'2", 220 lbs. Born, Mississauga, Ont., May 18, 1980. NY Rangers' 1st choice, 7th overall, in 1998 Entry Draft.

Season	Club	League	GP	G	A	Pts	PIM	PP	SH	GW	S	%	+/-	TF	F%	Min	GP	G	A	Pts	PIM	PP	SH	GW	Min
			Regular Season														Playoffs								
1995-96	Mississauga Reps	MTHL	54	27	44	71	62	....	....	....	....	....	....	....	....	....	....	....	....	....	....	....	....	....	....
1996-97	Guelph Storm	OHL	61	16	28	44	26	....	....	....	....	....	....	....	....	....	18	7	7	14	11	....	....	....	....
1997-98	Guelph Storm	OHL	57	16	35	51	29	....	....	....	....	....	....	....	....	....	12	7	6	13	8	....	....	....	....
1998-99	**NY Rangers**	**NHL**	**73**	**8**	**8**	**16**	**13**	**1**	**0**	**2**	**61**	**13.1**	**-2**	**588**	**43.9**	**8:36**	....	....	....	....	....	....	....	....	....
99-2000	**NY Rangers**	**NHL**	**27**	**0**	**0**	**0**	**4**	**0**	**0**	**0**	**18**	**0.0**	**-6**	**132**	**44.7**	**6:42**	....	....	....	....	....	....	....	....	....
	Guelph Storm	OHL	5	2	2	4	4	....	....	....	....	....	....	....	....	....	6	0	2	2	4	....	....	....	....
	Hartford	AHL	12	1	5	6	2	....	....	....	....	....	....	....	....	....	23	1	2	3	10	....	....	....	....
2000-01	**NY Rangers**	**NHL**	**50**	**4**	**8**	**12**	**31**	**0**	**0**	**2**	**46**	**8.7**	**-10**	**248**	**44.4**	**9:03**	....	....	....	....	....	....	....	....	....
	Hartford	AHL	28	5	6	11	69	....	....	....	....	....	....	....	....	....	5	0	0	0	0	....	....	....	....
2001-02	**NY Rangers**	**NHL**	**56**	**7**	**6**	**13**	**42**	**0**	**1**	**1**	**41**	**17.1**	**-1**	**310**	**42.9**	**10:14**	....	....	....	....	....	....	....	....	....
	Dallas	**NHL**	**16**	**1**	**0**	**1**	**5**	**0**	**0**	**0**	**19**	**5.3**	**-3**	**121**	**48.8**	**10:37**	....	....	....	....	....	....	....	....	....
2002-03	**Dallas**	**NHL**	**59**	**3**	**7**	**10**	**42**	**0**	**0**	**1**	**62**	**4.8**	**-2**	**447**	**47.0**	**9:22**	**5**	**1**	**0**	**1**	**0**	**0**	**0**	**0**	**8:13**
2003-04	**Dallas**	**NHL**	**9**	**0**	**0**	**0**	**4**	**0**	**0**	**0**	**4**	**0.0**	**-2**	**13**	**61.5**	**7:48**	....	....	....	....	....	....	....	....	....
	Columbus	**NHL**	**56**	**12**	**13**	**25**	**24**	**1**	**0**	**2**	**103**	**11.7**	**-5**	**840**	**53.8**	**14:47**	....	....	....	....	....	....	....	....	....
2004-05	Ljubljana	Slovenia	13	6	7	13	20	....	....	....	....	....	....	....	....	....	....	....	....	....	....	....	....	....	....
	Ljubljana	Interliga	13	7	7	14	16	....	....	....	....	....	....	....	....	....	....	....	....	....	....	....	....	....	....
	HV 71 Jonkoping	Sweden	20	5	2	7	16	....	....	....	....	....	....	....	....	....	....	....	....	....	....	....	....	....	....
2005-06	**Columbus**	**NHL**	**58**	**10**	**21**	**31**	**41**	**1**	**1**	**0**	**102**	**9.8**	**1**	**827**	**56.4**	**16:21**	....	....	....	....	....	....	....	....	....
2006-07	**Columbus**	**NHL**	**82**	**9**	**16**	**25**	**76**	**2**	**0**	**3**	**109**	**8.3**	**-8**	**1127**	**55.1**	**14:48**	....	....	....	....	....	....	....	....	....
2007-08	**Columbus**	**NHL**	**71**	**11**	**18**	**29**	**34**	**2**	**0**	**2**	**112**	**9.8**	**-3**	**1158**	**59.0**	**16:28**	....	....	....	....	....	....	....	....	....
2008-09	**Columbus**	**NHL**	**77**	**11**	**24**	**35**	**28**	**0**	**0**	**3**	**116**	**9.5**	**9**	**1380**	**58.0**	**18:01**	**4**	**0**	**0**	**0**	**0**	**0**	**0**	**0**	**17:54**
2009-10	**San Jose**	**NHL**	**71**	**14**	**19**	**33**	**41**	**2**	**0**	**4**	**111**	**12.6**	**17**	**664**	**62.5**	**15:37**	**15**	**1**	**0**	**1**	**0**	**1**	**0**	**0**	**16:55**
	NHL Totals		**705**	**90**	**140**	**230**	**385**	**9**	**2**	**20**	**904**	**10.0**		**7855**	**54.4**	**13:10**	**24**	**2**	**0**	**2**	**0**	**1**	**0**	**0**	**15:16**

emorial Cup Tournament All-Star Team (1998) • George Parsons Trophy (Memorial Cup Tournament - Most Sportsmanlike Player) (1998)

raded to **Dallas** by **NY Rangers** with Barrett Heisten for Martin Rucinsky and Roman Lyashenko, March 12, 2002. Claimed on waivers by **Columbus** from **Dallas**, November 21, 2003. Signed as a free gent by **Ljubljana** (Slovenia), October 8, 2004. Signed as a free agent by **Jonkoping** (Sweden), December 20, 2004. Signed as a free agent by **San Jose**, September 23, 2009. Signed as a free agent by **ancouver**, July 1, 2010.

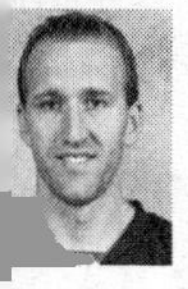

MALIK, Marek
(MAW-leck, MAIR-ehk)

Defense. Shoots left. 6'6", 235 lbs. Born, Ostrava, Czech., June 24, 1975. Hartford's 2nd choice, 72nd overall, in 1993 Entry Draft.

Season	Club	League	GP	G	A	Pts	PIM	PP	SH	GW	S	%	+/-	TF	F%	Min	GP	G	A	Pts	PIM	PP	SH	GW	Min
1992-93	TJ Vitkovice Jr.	Czech-Jr.	20	5	10	15	16	....	....	....	....	....	....	....	....	....	....	....	....	....	....	....	....	....	....
1993-94	HC Vitkovice	CzRep	38	3	3	6	0	....	....	....	....	....	....	....	....	....	3	0	1	1	0	....	....	....	....
1994-95	Springfield	AHL	58	11	30	41	91	....	....	....	....	....	....	....	....	....	....	....	....	....	....	....	....	....	....
	Hartford	**NHL**	**1**	**0**	**1**	**1**	**0**	**0**	**0**	**0**	**0**	**0.0**	**1**	....	....	....	....	....	....	....	....	....	....	....	....
1995-96	**Hartford**	**NHL**	**7**	**0**	**0**	**0**	**4**	**0**	**0**	**0**	**2**	**0.0**	**-3**	....	....	....	....	....	....	....	....	....	....	....	....
	Springfield	AHL	68	8	14	22	135	....	....	....	....	....	....	....	....	....	8	1	3	4	20	....	....	....	....
1996-97	**Hartford**	**NHL**	**47**	**1**	**5**	**6**	**50**	**0**	**0**	**1**	**33**	**3.0**	**5**	....	....	....	....	....	....	....	....	....	....	....	....
	Springfield	AHL	3	0	3	3	4	....	....	....	....	....	....	....	....	....	....	....	....	....	....	....	....	....	....
1997-98	Malmo	Sweden	37	1	5	6	21	....	....	....	....	....	....	....	....	....	....	....	....	....	....	....	....	....	....
1998-99	HC Vitkovice	CzRep	1	1	0	1	6	....	....	....	....	....	....	....	....	....	....	....	....	....	....	....	....	....	....
	Carolina	**NHL**	**52**	**2**	**9**	**11**	**36**	**1**	**0**	**0**	**36**	**5.6**	**-6**	**0**	**0.0**	**21:14**	**4**	**0**	**0**	**0**	**4**	**0**	**0**	**0**	**11:26**
	New Haven	AHL	21	2	8	10	28	....	....	....	....	....	....	....	....	....	....	....	....	....	....	....	....	....	....
99-2000	**Carolina**	**NHL**	**57**	**4**	**10**	**14**	**63**	**0**	**0**	**1**	**57**	**7.0**	**13**	**0**	**0.0**	**18:00**	....	....	....	....	....	....	....	....	....
2000-01	**Carolina**	**NHL**	**61**	**6**	**14**	**20**	**34**	**1**	**0**	**1**	**72**	**8.3**	**-4**	**0**	**0.0**	**19:36**	**3**	**0**	**0**	**0**	**6**	**0**	**0**	**0**	**19:37**
2001-02	**Carolina**	**NHL**	**82**	**4**	**19**	**23**	**88**	**0**	**0**	**0**	**91**	**4.4**	**8**	**0**	**0.0**	**20:29**	**23**	**0**	**3**	**3**	**18**	**0**	**0**	**0**	**18:09**
2002-03	**Carolina**	**NHL**	**10**	**0**	**2**	**2**	**16**	**0**	**0**	**0**	**9**	**0.0**	**-3**	**0**	**0.0**	**17:02**	....	....	....	....	....	....	....	....	....
	Vancouver	**NHL**	**69**	**7**	**11**	**18**	**52**	**1**	**1**	**2**	**68**	**10.3**	**23**	**1**	**0.0**	**18:06**	**14**	**1**	**1**	**2**	**10**	**1**	**0**	**0**	**16:06**
2003-04	**Vancouver**	**NHL**	**78**	**3**	**16**	**19**	**45**	**0**	**0**	**0**	**61**	**4.9**	***35**	**1**	**0.0**	**18:05**	**7**	**0**	**0**	**0**	**10**	**0**	**0**	**0**	**20:03**
2004-05	Vitkovice	CzRep	42	1	9	10	50	....	....	....	....	....	....	....	....	....	7	0	0	0	37	....	....	....	....
2005-06	**NY Rangers**	**NHL**	**74**	**2**	**16**	**18**	**78**	**0**	**0**	**2**	**70**	**2.9**	**28**	**0**	**0.0**	**20:26**	**4**	**0**	**1**	**1**	**6**	**0**	**0**	**0**	**20:43**
	Czech Republic	Olympics	8	0	0	0	8	....	....	....	....	....	....	....	....	....	....	....	....	....	....	....	....	....	....
2006-07	**NY Rangers**	**NHL**	**69**	**2**	**19**	**21**	**70**	**0**	**0**	**0**	**57**	**3.5**	**32**	**2**	**0.0**	**19:16**	**10**	**1**	**3**	**4**	**10**	**0**	**0**	**0**	**21:25**
2007-08	**NY Rangers**	**NHL**	**42**	**2**	**8**	**10**	**48**	**0**	**0**	**0**	**34**	**5.9**	**7**	**0**	**0.0**	**19:14**	....	....	....	....	....	....	....	....	....
2008-09	**Tampa Bay**	**NHL**	**42**	**0**	**5**	**5**	**36**	**0**	**0**	**0**	**22**	**0.0**	**-3**	**0**	**0.0**	**19:10**	....	....	....	....	....	....	....	....	....
2009-10	Vitkovice	CzRep	8	0	4	4	6	....	....	....	....	....	....	....	....	....	....	....	....	....	....	....	....	....	....
	Geneve	Swiss	25	0	4	4	10	....	....	....	....	....	....	....	....	....	20	2	8	10	12	....	....	....	....
	NHL Totals		**691**	**33**	**135**	**168**	**620**	**3**	**1**	**7**	**612**	**5.4**		**4**	**0.0**	**19:19**	**65**	**2**	**8**	**10**	**64**	**1**	**0**	**0**	**18:14**

Transferred to **Carolina** after **Hartford** franchise relocated, June 25, 1997. Traded to **Vancouver** by **Carolina** with Darren Langdon for Jan Hlavac and Harold Druken, November 1, 2002. Signed as a free gent by **Vitkovice** (CzRep), September 17, 2004. Signed as a free agent by **NY Rangers**, August 2, 2005. Signed as a free agent by **Tampa Bay**, October 23, 2008. Signed as a free agent by **Vitkovice** zRep), October 13, 2009. Signed as a free agent by **Geneve** (Swiss), November 23, 2009.

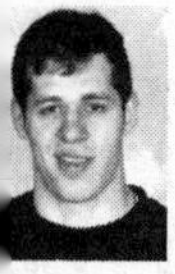

MALKIN, Evgeni
(MAHL-kihn, ehv-GEH-nee) **PIT.**

Center. Shoots left. 6'3", 195 lbs. Born, Magnitogorsk, USSR, July 31, 1986. Pittsburgh's 1st choice, 2nd overall, in 2004 Entry Draft.

Season	Club	League	GP	G	A	Pts	PIM	PP	SH	GW	S	%	+/-	TF	F%	Min	GP	G	A	Pts	PIM	PP	SH	GW	Min
2003-04	Magnitogorsk 2	Russia-3	2	1	0	1	8	....	....	....	....	....	....	....	....	....	....	....	....	....	....	....	....	....	....
	Magnitogorsk	Russia	34	3	9	12	12	....	....	....	....	....	....	....	....	....	....	....	....	....	....	....	....	....	....
2004-05	Magnitogorsk 2	Russia-3	2	1	1	2	2	....	....	....	....	....	....	....	....	....	....	....	....	....	....	....	....	....	....
	Magnitogorsk	Russia	52	12	20	32	24	....	....	....	....	....	....	....	....	....	5	0	4	4	0	....	....	....	....
2005-06	Magnitogorsk	Russia	46	21	26	47	46	....	....	....	....	....	....	....	....	....	11	5	10	15	41	....	....	....	....
	Russia	Olympics	7	2	4	6	31	....	....	....	....	....	....	....	....	....	....	....	....	....	....	....	....	....	....
2006-07	**Pittsburgh**	**NHL**	**78**	**33**	**52**	**85**	**80**	**16**	**0**	**6**	**242**	**13.6**	**2**	**728**	**43.3**	**19:10**	**5**	**0**	**4**	**4**	**8**	**0**	**0**	**0**	**19:34**
2007-08	**Pittsburgh**	**NHL**	**82**	**47**	**59**	**106**	**78**	**17**	**0**	**5**	**272**	**17.3**	**16**	**890**	**39.3**	**21:19**	**20**	**10**	**12**	**22**	**24**	**5**	**1**	**3**	**20:48**
2008-09♦	**Pittsburgh**	**NHL**	**82**	**35**	***78**	***113**	**80**	**14**	**2**	**4**	**290**	**12.1**	**17**	**668**	**42.4**	**22:31**	**24**	**14**	***22**	***36**	**51**	***7**	**0**	***3**	**20:57**
2009-10	**Pittsburgh**	**NHL**	**67**	**28**	**49**	**77**	**100**	**13**	**2**	**7**	**268**	**10.4**	**-6**	**498**	**40.0**	**20:51**	**13**	**5**	**6**	**11**	**6**	**4**	**0**	**1**	**21:54**
	Russia	Olympics	4	3	3	6	0	....	....	....	....	....	....	....	....	....	....	....	....	....	....	....	....	....	....
	NHL Totals		**309**	**143**	**238**	**381**	**338**	**60**	**4**	**22**	**1072**	**13.3**		**2784**	**41.2**	**20:59**	**62**	**29**	**44**	**73**	**89**	**16**	**1**	**7**	**20:59**

HL All-Rookie Team (2007) • Calder Memorial Trophy (2007) • NHL First All-Star Team (2008, 2009) • Art Ross Trophy (2009) • Conn Smythe Trophy (2009)
ayed in NHL All-Star Game (2008, 2009)

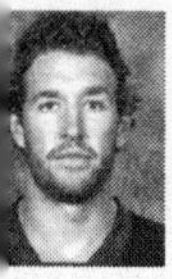

MALONE, Ryan
(MA-lohn, RIGH-uhn) **T.B.**

Left wing. Shoots left. 6'4", 220 lbs. Born, Pittsburgh, PA, December 1, 1979. Pittsburgh's 5th choice, 115th overall, in 1999 Entry Draft.

Season	Club	League	GP	G	A	Pts	PIM	PP	SH	GW	S	%	+/-	TF	F%	Min	GP	G	A	Pts	PIM	PP	SH	GW	Min
1997-98	Shat.-St. Mary's	High-MN	50	41	44	85	69	....	....	....	....	....	....	....	....	....	....	....	....	....	....	....	....	....	....
1998-99	Omaha Lancers	USHL	51	14	22	36	81	....	....	....	....	....	....	....	....	....	12	2	4	6	23	....	....	....	....
99-2000	St. Cloud State	WCHA	38	9	21	30	68	....	....	....	....	....	....	....	....	....	....	....	....	....	....	....	....	....	....
2000-01	St. Cloud State	WCHA	36	7	18	25	52	....	....	....	....	....	....	....	....	....	....	....	....	....	....	....	....	....	....
2001-02	St. Cloud State	WCHA	41	24	25	49	76	....	....	....	....	....	....	....	....	....	....	....	....	....	....	....	....	....	....
2002-03	St. Cloud State	WCHA	27	16	20	36	85	....	....	....	....	....	....	....	....	....	....	....	....	....	....	....	....	....	....
	Wilkes-Barre	AHL	3	0	1	1	2	....	....	....	....	....	....	....	....	....	....	....	....	....	....	....	....	....	....
2003-04	**Pittsburgh**	**NHL**	**81**	**22**	**21**	**43**	**64**	**5**	**3**	**4**	**139**	**15.8**	**-23**	**230**	**27.4**	**18:54**	....	....	....	....	....	....	....	....	....
2004-05	Blues Espoo	Finland	9	2	1	3	36	....	....	....	....	....	....	....	....	....	....	....	....	....	....	....	....	....	....
	SV Renon	Italy	10	6	2	8	20	....	....	....	....	....	....	....	....	....	6	4	4	8	36	....	....	....	....
	HC Ambri-Piotta	Swiss	....	....	....	....	....	....	....	....	....	....	....	....	....	....	1	0	0	0	2	....	....	....	....
2005-06	**Pittsburgh**	**NHL**	**77**	**22**	**22**	**44**	**63**	**10**	**5**	**1**	**153**	**14.4**	**-22**	**728**	**39.6**	**18:06**	....	....	....	....	....	....	....	....	....
2006-07	**Pittsburgh**	**NHL**	**64**	**16**	**15**	**31**	**71**	**1**	**1**	**0**	**125**	**12.8**	**4**	**109**	**44.0**	**16:15**	**5**	**0**	**0**	**0**	**0**	**0**	**0**	**0**	**13:48**
2007-08	**Pittsburgh**	**NHL**	**77**	**27**	**24**	**51**	**103**	**11**	**2**	**6**	**159**	**17.0**	**14**	**38**	**31.6**	**19:05**	**20**	**6**	**10**	**16**	**25**	**3**	**0**	**2**	**18:43**
2008-09	**Tampa Bay**	**NHL**	**70**	**26**	**19**	**45**	**98**	**7**	**0**	**3**	**124**	**21.0**	**4**	**47**	**29.8**	**17:45**	....	....	....	....	....	....	....	....	....
2009-10	**Tampa Bay**	**NHL**	**69**	**21**	**26**	**47**	**68**	**7**	**0**	**7**	**172**	**12.2**	**-8**	**97**	**39.2**	**18:46**	....	....	....	....	....	....	....	....	....
	United States	Olympics	6	3	2	5	6	....	....	....	....	....	....	....	....	....	....	....	....	....	....	....	....	....	....
	NHL Totals		**438**	**134**	**127**	**261**	**467**	**41**	**11**	**21**	**872**	**15.4**		**1249**	**37.1**	**18:12**	**25**	**6**	**10**	**16**	**25**	**3**	**0**	**2**	**17:44**

HL All-Rookie Team (2004)

ned as a free agent by **Espoo** (Finland), September 29, 2004. Signed as a free agent by **Renon** (Italy), January 3, 2005. Signed as a free agent by **Ambri-Piotta** (Swiss), February 25, 2005. Traded to **mpa Bay** by **Pittsburgh** with Gary Roberts for Tampa Bay's 3rd round choice (Ben Hanowski) in 2009 Entry Draft, June 28, 2008.

Season	Club	League	GP	G	A	Pts	PIM	PP	SH	GW	S	%	+/-	TF	F%	Min	GP	G	A	Pts	PIM	PP	SH	GW	Mi
			Regular Season														Playoffs								

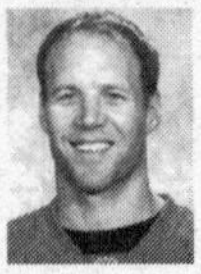

MALTBY, Kirk

(MAHLT-bee, KUHRK)

Right wing. Shoots right. 6', 195 lbs. Born, Guelph, Ont., December 22, 1972. Edmonton's 4th choice, 65th overall, in 1992 Entry Draft.

Season	Club	League	GP	G	A	Pts	PIM	PP	SH	GW	S	%	+/-	TF	F%	Min	GP	G	A	Pts	PIM	PP	SH	GW	Mi
1988-89	Cambridge	OHA-B	48	28	18	46	138	....	....	....	....	....	....	....	....	....	....	....	....	....	....	....	....	....	
1989-90	Owen Sound	OHL	61	12	15	27	90	....	....	....	....	....	....	....	....	....	12	1	6	7	15	....	....	....	
1990-91	Owen Sound	OHL	66	34	32	66	100	....	....	....	....	....	....	....	....	....	....	....	....	....	....	....	....	....	
1991-92	Owen Sound	OHL	66	50	41	91	99	....	....	....	....	....	....	....	....	....	5	3	3	6	18	....	....	....	
1992-93	Cape Breton	AHL	73	22	23	45	130	....	....	....	....	....	....	....	....	....	16	3	3	6	45	....	....	....	
1993-94	**Edmonton**	**NHL**	**68**	**11**	**8**	**19**	**74**	**0**	**1**	**1**	**89**	**12.4**	**–2**	....	....	....	....	....	....	....	....	....	....	....	
1994-95	**Edmonton**	**NHL**	**47**	**8**	**3**	**11**	**49**	**0**	**2**	**1**	**73**	**11.0**	**–11**	....	....	....	....	....	....	....	....	....	....	....	
1995-96	**Edmonton**	**NHL**	**49**	**2**	**6**	**8**	**61**	**0**	**0**	**1**	**51**	**3.9**	**–16**	....	....	....	....	....	....	....	....	....	....	....	
	Cape Breton	AHL	4	1	2	3	6	....	....	....	....	....	....	....	....	....	....	....	....	....	....	....	....	....	
	Detroit	**NHL**	**6**	**1**	**0**	**1**	**6**	**0**	**0**	**0**	**4**	**25.0**	**0**	....	....	....	**8**	**0**	**1**	**1**	**4**	**0**	**0**	**0**	
1996-97♦	**Detroit**	**NHL**	**66**	**3**	**5**	**8**	**75**	**0**	**0**	**0**	**62**	**4.8**	**3**	....	....	....	**20**	**5**	**2**	**7**	**24**	**0**	**1**	**1**	
1997-98♦	**Detroit**	**NHL**	**65**	**14**	**9**	**23**	**89**	**2**	**1**	**3**	**106**	**13.2**	**11**	....	....	....	**22**	**3**	**1**	**4**	**30**	**0**	**1**	**0**	
1998-99	**Detroit**	**NHL**	**53**	**8**	**6**	**14**	**34**	**0**	**1**	**2**	**76**	**10.5**	**–6**	**10**	**40.0**	**13:13**	**10**	**1**	**0**	**1**	**8**	**0**	**0**	**1**	**11:3**
99-2000	**Detroit**	**NHL**	**41**	**6**	**8**	**14**	**24**	**0**	**2**	**1**	**71**	**8.5**	**1**	**2**	**50.0**	**13:30**	**8**	**0**	**1**	**1**	**4**	**0**	**0**	**0**	**13:4**
2000-01	**Detroit**	**NHL**	**79**	**12**	**7**	**19**	**22**	**1**	**3**	**3**	**119**	**10.1**	**16**	**14**	**35.7**	**14:17**	**6**	**0**	**0**	**0**	**6**	**0**	**0**	**0**	**15:2**
2001-02♦	**Detroit**	**NHL**	**82**	**9**	**15**	**24**	**40**	**0**	**1**	**5**	**108**	**8.3**	**15**	**38**	**47.4**	**13:23**	**23**	**3**	**3**	**6**	**32**	**0**	***2**	**0**	**16:3**
2002-03	**Detroit**	**NHL**	**82**	**14**	**23**	**37**	**91**	**0**	**4**	**1**	**116**	**12.1**	**17**	**43**	**37.2**	**16:10**	**4**	**0**	**0**	**0**	**4**	**0**	**0**	**0**	**17:1**
2003-04	**Detroit**	**NHL**	**79**	**14**	**19**	**33**	**80**	**1**	**4**	**4**	**123**	**11.4**	**24**	**30**	**43.3**	**16:16**	**12**	**1**	**3**	**4**	**11**	**0**	**0**	**0**	**17:3**
2004-05			DID NOT PLAY																						
2005-06	**Detroit**	**NHL**	**82**	**5**	**6**	**11**	**80**	**0**	**1**	**0**	**115**	**4.3**	**–9**	**22**	**50.0**	**13:44**	**6**	**2**	**1**	**3**	**4**	**0**	**0**	**1**	**13:0**
2006-07	**Detroit**	**NHL**	**82**	**6**	**5**	**11**	**50**	**0**	**0**	**0**	**113**	**5.3**	**–9**	**14**	**28.6**	**13:11**	**18**	**1**	**1**	**2**	**10**	**0**	**1**	**0**	**10:4**
2007-08♦	**Detroit**	**NHL**	**61**	**6**	**4**	**10**	**32**	**0**	**0**	**1**	**70**	**8.6**	**–8**	**7**	**42.9**	**12:04**	**12**	**0**	**1**	**1**	**10**	**0**	**0**	**0**	**9:4**
2008-09	**Detroit**	**NHL**	**78**	**5**	**6**	**11**	**28**	**0**	**0**	**1**	**58**	**8.6**	**–9**	**10**	**40.0**	**9:08**	**20**	**0**	**1**	**1**	**2**	**0**	**0**	**0**	**9:0**
2009-10	**Detroit**	**NHL**	**52**	**4**	**2**	**6**	**32**	**0**	**1**	**0**	**43**	**9.3**	**1**	**13**	**53.9**	**10:06**	....	....	....	....	....	....	....	....	
	NHL Totals		**1072**	**128**	**132**	**260**	**867**	**4**	**21**	**24**	**1397**	**9.2**		**203**	**42.4**	**13:19**	**169**	**16**	**15**	**31**	**149**	**0**	**5**	**3**	**13:0**

Traded to **Detroit** by **Edmonton** for Dan McGillis, March 20, 1996. • Missed majority of 1999-2000 season recovering from hernia injury suffered in game vs. Dallas, October 5, 1999.

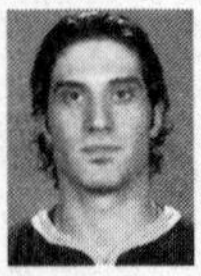

MANCARI, Mark

(man-KAH-ree, MAHRK) **BU**

Right wing. Shoots right. 6'3", 225 lbs. Born, London, Ont., July 11, 1985. Buffalo's 6th choice, 207th overall, in 2004 Entry Draft.

Season	Club	League	GP	G	A	Pts	PIM	PP	SH	GW	S	%	+/-	TF	F%	Min	GP	G	A	Pts	PIM	PP	SH	GW	Mi
2001-02	Ottawa 67's	OHL	34	3	3	6	10	....	....	....	....	....	....	....	....	....	2	0	1	1	0	....	....	....	
2002-03	Ottawa 67's	OHL	61	8	11	19	20	....	....	....	....	....	....	....	....	....	11	2	1	3	2	....	....	....	
2003-04	Ottawa 67's	OHL	67	29	36	65	56	....	....	....	....	....	....	....	....	....	7	5	3	8	11	....	....	....	
2004-05	Ottawa 67's	OHL	64	36	32	68	86	....	....	....	....	....	....	....	....	....	21	*14	10	24	24	....	....	....	
2005-06	Rochester	AHL	71	18	24	42	80	....	....	....	....	....	....	....	....	....	....	....	....	....	....	....	....	....	
2006-07	**Buffalo**	**NHL**	**3**	**0**	**1**	**1**	**2**	**0**	**0**	**0**	**1**	**0.0**	**–1**	**0**	**0.0**	**6:12**	....	....	....	....	....	....	....	....	
	Rochester	AHL	64	23	34	57	49	....	....	....	....	....	....	....	....	....	6	1	5	6	6	....	....	....	
2007-08	Rochester	AHL	80	21	36	57	78	....	....	....	....	....	....	....	....	....	....	....	....	....	....	....	....	....	
2008-09	**Buffalo**	**NHL**	**7**	**1**	**1**	**2**	**4**	**0**	**0**	**0**	**21**	**4.8**	**–4**	**7**	**57.1**	**13:16**	....	....	....	....	....	....	....	....	
	Portland Pirates	AHL	73	29	38	67	61	....	....	....	....	....	....	....	....	....	5	1	2	3	2	....	....	....	
2009-10	**Buffalo**	**NHL**	**6**	**1**	**1**	**2**	**4**	**0**	**0**	**0**	**19**	**5.3**	**3**	**3**	**0.0**	**14:04**	....	....	....	....	....	....	....	....	
	Portland Pirates	AHL	74	28	46	74	55	....	....	....	....	....	....	....	....	....	4	1	1	2	2	....	....	....	
	NHL Totals		**16**	**2**	**3**	**5**	**10**	**0**	**0**	**0**	**41**	**4.9**		**10**	**40.0**	**12:15**	....	....	....	....	....	....	....	....	

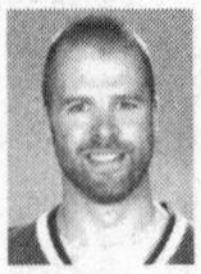

MARA, Paul

(MAIR-uh, PAWL)

Defense. Shoots left. 6'4", 207 lbs. Born, Ridgewood, NJ, September 7, 1979. Tampa Bay's 1st choice, 7th overall, in 1997 Entry Draft.

Season	Club	League	GP	G	A	Pts	PIM	PP	SH	GW	S	%	+/-	TF	F%	Min	GP	G	A	Pts	PIM	PP	SH	GW	Mi
1994-95	Belmont Hill	High-MA	28	5	17	22	28	....	....	....	....	....	....	....	....	....	....	....	....	....	....	....	....	....	
1995-96	Belmont Hill	High-MA	28	18	20	38	40	....	....	....	....	....	....	....	....	....	....	....	....	....	....	....	....	....	
1996-97	Sudbury Wolves	OHL	44	9	34	43	61	....	....	....	....	....	....	....	....	....	....	....	....	....	....	....	....	....	
1997-98	Sudbury Wolves	OHL	25	8	18	26	79	....	....	....	....	....	....	....	....	....	....	....	....	....	....	....	....	....	
	Plymouth Whalers	OHL	25	8	15	23	30	....	....	....	....	....	....	....	....	....	15	3	14	17	30	....	....	....	
1998-99	Plymouth Whalers	OHL	52	13	41	54	95	....	....	....	....	....	....	....	....	....	11	5	7	12	28	....	....	....	
	Tampa Bay	**NHL**	**1**	**1**	**1**	**2**	**0**	**1**	**0**	**0**	**1**	**100.0**	**–3**	**0**	**0.0**	**19:34**	....	....	....	....	....	....	....	....	
99-2000	**Tampa Bay**	**NHL**	**54**	**7**	**11**	**18**	**73**	**4**	**0**	**1**	**78**	**9.0**	**–27**	**0**	**0.0**	**22:13**	....	....	....	....	....	....	....	....	
	Detroit Vipers	IHL	15	3	5	8	22	....	....	....	....	....	....	....	....	....	....	....	....	....	....	....	....	....	
2000-01	**Tampa Bay**	**NHL**	**46**	**6**	**10**	**16**	**40**	**2**	**0**	**1**	**58**	**10.3**	**–17**	**0**	**0.0**	**23:06**	....	....	....	....	....	....	....	....	
	Detroit Vipers	IHL	10	3	3	6	22	....	....	....	....	....	....	....	....	....	....	....	....	....	....	....	....	....	
	Phoenix	**NHL**	**16**	**0**	**4**	**4**	**14**	**0**	**0**	**0**	**20**	**0.0**	**1**	**0**	**0.0**	**19:22**	....	....	....	....	....	....	....	....	
2001-02	**Phoenix**	**NHL**	**75**	**7**	**17**	**24**	**58**	**2**	**0**	**0**	**112**	**6.3**	**–6**	**2**	**100.0**	**21:34**	**5**	**0**	**0**	**0**	**4**	**0**	**0**	**0**	**22:5**
2002-03	**Phoenix**	**NHL**	**73**	**10**	**15**	**25**	**78**	**1**	**0**	**0**	**95**	**10.5**	**–7**	**1**	**0.0**	**21:06**	....	....	....	....	....	....	....	....	
2003-04	**Phoenix**	**NHL**	**81**	**6**	**36**	**42**	**48**	**1**	**0**	**0**	**140**	**4.3**	**–11**	**2**	**0.0**	**23:37**	....	....	....	....	....	....	....	....	
2004-05	Hannover	Germany	35	5	13	18	89	....	....	....	....	....	....	....	....	....	....	....	....	....	....	....	....	....	
2005-06	**Phoenix**	**NHL**	**78**	**15**	**32**	**47**	**70**	**8**	**0**	**0**	**157**	**9.6**	**–12**	**1**	**0.0**	**21:29**	....	....	....	....	....	....	....	....	
2006-07	**Boston**	**NHL**	**59**	**3**	**15**	**18**	**95**	**0**	**0**	**0**	**60**	**5.0**	**–22**	**0**	**0.0**	**21:53**	....	....	....	....	....	....	....	....	
	NY Rangers	**NHL**	**19**	**2**	**3**	**5**	**18**	**1**	**0**	**0**	**40**	**5.0**	**6**	**0**	**0.0**	**22:56**	**10**	**2**	**2**	**4**	**18**	**2**	**0**	**0**	**19:4**
2007-08	**NY Rangers**	**NHL**	**61**	**1**	**16**	**17**	**52**	**0**	**0**	**0**	**80**	**1.3**	**1**	**1**	**0.0**	**17:53**	**10**	**0**	**1**	**1**	**20**	**0**	**0**	**0**	**17:4**
2008-09	**NY Rangers**	**NHL**	**76**	**5**	**16**	**21**	**94**	**1**	**0**	**0**	**102**	**4.9**	**2**	**2**	**50.0**	**18:58**	**7**	**1**	**1**	**2**	**8**	**0**	**0**	**0**	**14:4**
2009-10	**Montreal**	**NHL**	**42**	**0**	**8**	**8**	**48**	**0**	**0**	**0**	**30**	**0.0**	**–16**	**0**	**0.0**	**18:44**	....	....	....	....	....	....	....	....	
	NHL Totals		**681**	**63**	**184**	**247**	**688**	**21**	**0**	**2**	**973**	**6.5**		**9**	**33.3**	**21:07**	**32**	**3**	**4**	**7**	**50**	**2**	**0**	**0**	**18:3**

Traded to **Phoenix** by **Tampa Bay** with Mike Johnson, Ruslan Zainullin and NY Islanders' 2nd round choice (previously acquired, Phoenix selected Matthew Spiller) in 2001 Entry Draft for Nikolai Khabibuli and Stan Neckar, March 5, 2001. Signed as a free agent by **Hannover** (Germany), October 29, 2004. Traded to **Boston** by **Phoenix** with Phoenix's 3rd round choice (later traded to Anaheim - Anaheim selected Maxime Macenauer) in 2007 Entry Draft for Nick Boynton and Boston's 4th round choice (later traded to Toronto - Toronto selected Matt Frattin) in 2007 Entry Draft, June 26, 2006. Traded to **NY Rangers** by **Boston** for Aaron Ward, February 27, 2007. Signed as a free agent by **Montreal**, July 10, 2009.

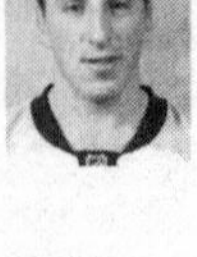

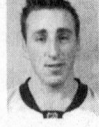

MARCHAND, Brad

(mahr-SHAND, BRAD) **BO**

Center. Shoots left. 5'9", 183 lbs. Born, Halifax, N.S., May 11, 1988. Boston's 4th choice, 71st overall, in 2006 Entry Draft.

Season	Club	League	GP	G	A	Pts	PIM	PP	SH	GW	S	%	+/-	TF	F%	Min	GP	G	A	Pts	PIM	PP	SH	GW	Mi
2003-04	Dartmouth	NSMHL	60	47	47	94	104	....	....	....	....	....	....	....	....	....	....	....	....	....	....	....	....	....	
2004-05	Moncton Wildcats	QMJHL	61	9	20	29	52	....	....	....	....	....	....	....	....	....	11	1	0	1	7	....	....	....	
2005-06	Moncton Wildcats	QMJHL	68	29	37	66	83	....	....	....	....	....	....	....	....	....	20	5	14	19	34	....	....	....	
2006-07	Val-d'Or Foreurs	QMJHL	57	33	47	80	108	....	....	....	....	....	....	....	....	....	20	*16	*24	*40	36	....	....	....	
2007-08	Val-d'Or Foreurs	QMJHL	33	21	23	44	36	....	....	....	....	....	....	....	....	....	....	....	....	....	....	....	....	....	
	Halifax	QMJHL	26	10	19	29	40	....	....	....	....	....	....	....	....	....	14	3	16	19	18	....	....	....	
2008-09	Providence Bruins	AHL	79	18	41	59	67	....	....	....	....	....	....	....	....	....	16	7	8	15	26	....	....	....	
2009-10	**Boston**	**NHL**	**20**	**0**	**1**	**1**	**20**	**0**	**0**	**0**	**32**	**0.0**	**–3**	**11**	**27.3**	**11:58**	....	....	....	....	....	....	....	....	
	Providence Bruins	AHL	34	13	19	32	51	....	....	....	....	....	....	....	....	....	....	....	....	....	....	....	....	....	
	NHL Totals		**20**	**0**	**1**	**1**	**20**	**0**	**0**	**0**	**32**	**0.0**		**11**	**27.3**	**11:58**	....	....	....	....	....	....	....	....	

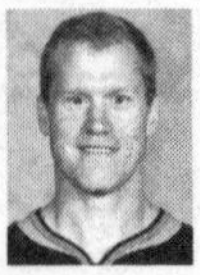

MARCHANT, Todd

(mahr-SHAHNT, TAWD) **AN**

Center. Shoots left. 5'10", 179 lbs. Born, Buffalo, NY, August 12, 1973. NY Rangers' 8th choice, 164th overall, in 1993 Entry Draft.

Season	Club	League	GP	G	A	Pts	PIM	PP	SH	GW	S	%	+/-	TF	F%	Min	GP	G	A	Pts	PIM	PP	SH	GW	Mi
1990-91	Niagara Scenics	NAHL	37	31	47	78	....	....	....	....	....	....	....	....	....	....	....	....	....	....	....	....	....	....	
1991-92	Clarkson Knights	ECAC	32	20	12	32	32	....	....	....	....	....	....	....	....	....	....	....	....	....	....	....	....	....	
1992-93	Clarkson Knights	ECAC	33	18	28	46	38	....	....	....	....	....	....	....	....	....	....	....	....	....	....	....	....	....	
1993-94	United States	Nat-Tm	59	28	39	67	48	....	....	....	....	....	....	....	....	....	....	....	....	....	....	....	....	....	
	United States	Olympics	8	1	1	2	6	....	....	....	....	....	....	....	....	....	....	....	....	....	....	....	....	....	
	NY Rangers	**NHL**	**1**	**0**	**0**	**0**	**0**	**0**	**0**	**0**	**1**	**0.0**	**–1**	....	....	....	....	....	....	....	....	....	....	....	
	Binghamton	AHL	8	2	7	9	6	....	....	....	....	....	....	....	....	....	....	....	....	....	....	....	....	....	
	Edmonton	**NHL**	**3**	**0**	**1**	**1**	**2**	**0**	**0**	**0**	**5**	**0.0**	**–1**	....	....	....	....	....	....	....	....	....	....	....	
	Cape Breton	AHL	3	1	4	5	2	....	....	....	....	....	....	....	....	....	5	1	1	2	0	....	....	....	
1994-95	Cape Breton	AHL	38	22	25	47	25	....	....	....	....	....	....	....	....	....	....	....	....	....	....	....	....	....	
	Edmonton	**NHL**	**45**	**13**	**14**	**27**	**32**	**3**	**2**	**2**	**95**	**13.7**	**–3**	....	....	....	....	....	....	....	....	....	....	....	
1995-96	**Edmonton**	**NHL**	**81**	**19**	**19**	**38**	**66**	**2**	**3**	**2**	**221**	**8.6**	**–19**	....	....	....	....	....	....	....	....	....	....	....	
1996-97	**Edmonton**	**NHL**	**79**	**14**	**19**	**33**	**44**	**0**	**4**	**3**	**202**	**6.9**	**11**	....	....	....	**12**	**4**	**2**	**6**	**12**	**0**	***3**	**1**	
1997-98	**Edmonton**	**NHL**	**76**	**14**	**21**	**35**	**71**	**2**	**1**	**3**	**194**	**7.2**	**9**	....	....	....	**12**	**1**	**1**	**2**	**10**	**0**	**0**	**0**	
1998-99	**Edmonton**	**NHL**	**82**	**14**	**22**	**36**	**65**	**3**	**1**	**2**	**183**	**7.7**	**3**	**1449**	**50.0**	**16:47**	**4**	**1**	**1**	**2**	**12**	**0**	**0**	**0**	**24:**
99-2000	**Edmonton**	**NHL**	**82**	**17**	**23**	**40**	**70**	**0**	**1**	**0**	**170**	**10.0**	**7**	**1593**	**52.9**	**17:08**	**3**	**1**	**0**	**1**	**2**	**0**	**0**	**0**	**18:**

			Regular Season														Playoffs								
Season	Club	League	GP	G	A	Pts	PIM	PP	SH	GW	S	%	+/-	TF	F%	Min	GP	G	A	Pts	PIM	PP	SH	GW	Min
2000-01	Edmonton	NHL	71	13	26	39	51	0	4	2	113	11.5	1	1549	53.8	17:54	6	0	0	0	4	0	0	0	22:57
2001-02	Edmonton	NHL	82	12	22	34	41	0	3	1	124	9.7	7	1523	52.4	16:58	....	....	....	....	....	....	....	....	....
2002-03	Edmonton	NHL	77	20	40	60	48	7	1	3	146	13.7	13	1336	58.0	19:54	6	0	2	2	2	0	0	0	20:03
2003-04	Columbus	NHL	77	9	25	34	34	4	0	2	163	5.5	−17	1412	50.9	20:39	....	....	....	....	....	....	....	....	....
2004-05			DID NOT PLAY																						
2005-06	Columbus	NHL	18	3	6	9	20	0	0	0	42	7.1	−1	289	50.2	20:05	....	....	....	....	....	....	....	....	....
	Anaheim	NHL	61	6	19	25	46	0	0	0	90	6.7	3	743	51.7	16:25	16	3	10	13	14	0	0	0	17:34
2006-07 ♦	Anaheim	NHL	56	8	15	23	44	0	3	2	115	7.0	7	647	54.3	15:10	11	0	3	3	12	0	0	0	15:44
2007-08	Anaheim	NHL	75	9	7	16	48	0	0	0	93	9.7	−3	673	49.2	14:49	6	2	0	2	0	0	0	0	17:40
2008-09	Anaheim	NHL	72	5	13	18	34	0	2	0	101	5.0	−2	593	50.3	14:32	13	1	1	2	16	0	0	1	19:56
2009-10	Anaheim	NHL	78	9	13	22	32	0	3	1	83	10.8	−16	569	49.9	15:49	....	....	....	....	....	....	....	....	....
	NHL Totals		1116	185	305	490	748	21	28	23	2141	8.6		12376	52.4	17:03	89	13	20	33	84	0	3	2	18:54

ECAC Second All-Star Team (1993)

Traded to **Edmonton** by **NY Rangers** for Craig MacTavish, March 21, 1994. Signed as a free agent by **Columbus**, July 3, 2003. Claimed on waivers by **Anaheim** from **Columbus**, November 21, 2005.

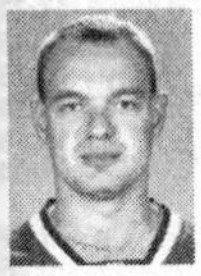

MARKOV, Andrei
(MAHR-kahf, AHN-dray) **MTL.**

Defense. Shoots left. 6', 207 lbs. Born, Voskresensk, USSR, December 20, 1978. Montreal's 6th choice, 162nd overall, in 1998 Entry Draft.

Season	Club	League	GP	G	A	Pts	PIM	PP	SH	GW	S	%	+/-	TF	F%	Min	GP	G	A	Pts	PIM	PP	SH	GW	Min
1995-96	Voskresensk	CIS	38	0	0	0	14	....	....	....	....	....	....	....	....	....	....	....	....	....	....	....	....	....	....
1996-97	Voskresensk	Russia	43	8	4	12	32	....	....	....	....	....	....	....	....	....	2	1	1	2	0	....	....	....	....
1997-98	Voskresensk	Russia	43	10	5	15	83	....	....	....	....	....	....	....	....	....	....	....	....	....	....	....	....	....	....
1998-99	Dynamo Moscow	Russia	38	10	11	21	32	....	....	....	....	....	....	....	....	....	16	3	6	9	6	....	....	....	....
	Dynamo Moscow	EuroHL	12	7	5	12	12	....	....	....	....	....	....	....	....	....	6	2	2	4	4	....	....	....	....
99-2000	Dynamo Moscow	Russia	29	11	12	23	28	....	....	....	....	....	....	....	....	....	17	4	3	7	8	....	....	....	....
2000-01	Montreal	NHL	63	6	17	23	18	2	0	0	82	7.3	−6	2	50.0	16:53	....	....	....	....	....	....	....	....	....
	Quebec Citadelles	AHL	14	0	5	5	4	....	....	....	....	....	....	....	....	....	7	1	1	2	2	....	....	....	....
2001-02	Montreal	NHL	56	5	19	24	24	2	0	1	73	6.8	−1	0	0.0	17:15	12	1	3	4	8	0	0	1	15:53
	Quebec Citadelles	AHL	12	4	6	10	7	....	....	....	....	....	....	....	....	....	....	....	....	....	....	....	....	....	....
2002-03	Montreal	NHL	79	13	24	37	34	3	0	2	159	8.2	13	1	0.0	23:17	....	....	....	....	....	....	....	....	....
2003-04	Montreal	NHL	69	6	22	28	20	2	0	0	105	5.7	−2	2	50.0	21:29	11	1	4	5	8	0	0	1	22:52
2004-05	Dynamo Moscow	Russia	42	7	16	23	76	....	....	....	....	....	....	....	....	....	10	2	0	2	22	....	....	....	....
2005-06	Montreal	NHL	67	10	36	46	74	6	1	1	88	11.4	13	1	0.0	23:33	6	0	1	1	4	0	0	0	25:29
	Russia	Olympics	8	1	2	3	6	....	....	....	....	....	....	....	....	....	....	....	....	....	....	....	....	....	....
2006-07	Montreal	NHL	77	6	43	49	56	5	0	2	128	4.7	2	1	0.0	24:29	....	....	....	....	....	....	....	....	....
2007-08	Montreal	NHL	82	16	42	58	63	10	1	2	145	11.0	1	0	0.0	24:58	12	1	3	4	8	0	0	0	24:54
2008-09	Montreal	NHL	78	12	52	64	36	7	0	3	165	7.3	−2	0	0.0	24:38	....	....	....	....	....	....	....	....	....
2009-10	Montreal	NHL	45	6	28	34	32	4	0	1	85	7.1	11	0	0.0	23:48	8	0	4	4	0	0	0	0	23:47
	Russia	Olympics	4	0	2	2	0	....	....	....	....	....	....	....	....	....	....	....	....	....	....	....	....	....	....
	NHL Totals		616	80	283	363	357	41	2	12	1030	7.8		7	28.6	22:29	49	3	15	18	28	0	0	2	22:07

Played in NHL All-Star Game (2008, 2009)

Signed as a free agent by **Dynamo Moscow** (Russia), June 19, 2004.

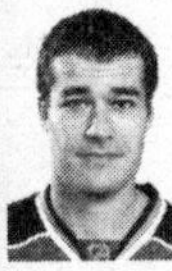

MARLEAU, Patrick
(mahr-LOH, PAT-rihk) **S.J.**

Center. Shoots left. 6'2", 220 lbs. Born, Aneroid, Sask., September 15, 1979. San Jose's 1st choice, 2nd overall, in 1997 Entry Draft.

Season	Club	League	GP	G	A	Pts	PIM	PP	SH	GW	S	%	+/-	TF	F%	Min	GP	G	A	Pts	PIM	PP	SH	GW	Min
1993-94	Swift Current	SMHL	53	72	95	167	....	....	....	....	....	....	....	....	....	....	....	....	....	....	....	....	....	....	....
1994-95	Swift Current	SMHL	31	30	22	52	18	....	....	....	....	....	....	....	....	....	....	....	....	....	....	....	....	....	....
1995-96	Seattle	WHL	72	32	42	74	22	....	....	....	....	....	....	....	....	....	5	3	4	7	4	....	....	....	....
1996-97	Seattle	WHL	71	51	74	125	37	....	....	....	....	....	....	....	....	....	15	7	16	23	12	....	....	....	....
1997-98	San Jose	NHL	74	13	19	32	14	1	0	2	90	14.4	5	....	....	....	5	0	1	1	0	0	0	0	....
1998-99	San Jose	NHL	81	21	24	45	24	4	0	4	134	15.7	10	1121	43.4	15:11	6	2	1	3	4	2	0	0	11:08
99-2000	San Jose	NHL	81	17	23	40	36	3	0	3	161	10.6	−9	851	42.0	14:11	5	1	1	2	2	1	0	0	11:51
2000-01	San Jose	NHL	81	25	27	52	22	5	0	6	146	17.1	7	1088	44.8	16:17	6	2	0	2	4	0	0	0	14:50
2001-02	San Jose	NHL	79	21	23	44	40	3	0	5	121	17.4	9	897	47.3	14:04	12	6	5	11	6	1	0	3	15:50
2002-03	San Jose	NHL	82	28	29	57	33	8	1	3	172	16.3	−10	1403	47.3	18:31	....	....	....	....	....	....	....	....	....
2003-04	San Jose	NHL	80	28	29	57	24	9	0	5	220	12.7	−5	1014	41.6	18:12	17	8	4	12	6	4	1	2	19:16
2004-05			DID NOT PLAY																						
2005-06	San Jose	NHL	82	34	52	86	26	20	1	4	260	13.1	−12	1216	46.8	19:56	11	9	5	14	8	4	0	2	21:07
2006-07	San Jose	NHL	77	32	46	78	33	14	0	9	180	17.8	9	693	50.5	18:34	11	3	3	6	2	1	0	1	18:59
2007-08	San Jose	NHL	78	19	29	48	33	7	0	2	185	10.3	−19	605	52.4	18:14	13	4	4	8	2	0	*2	0	23:04
2008-09	San Jose	NHL	76	38	33	71	18	11	5	10	251	15.1	16	591	52.5	21:21	6	2	1	3	8	1	0	2	20:29
2009-10	San Jose	NHL	82	44	39	83	22	12	4	6	274	16.1	21	615	51.4	21:13	14	8	5	13	8	3	1	2	22:07
	Canada	Olympics	7	2	3	5	0	....	....	....	....	....	....	....	....	....	....	....	....	....	....	....	....	....	....
	NHL Totals		953	320	373	693	325	97	11	59	2194	14.6		10094	46.6	17:47	106	45	30	75	50	17	4	12	18:52

WHL West First All-Star Team (1997)

Played in NHL All-Star Game (2004, 2007, 2009)

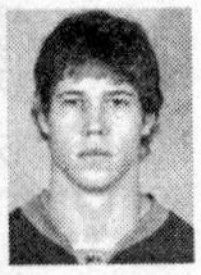

MARTIN, Matthew
(MAHR-tihn, MA-thew) **NYI**

Left wing. Shoots left. 6'2", 192 lbs. Born, Windsor, Ont., May 8, 1989. NY Islanders' 11th choice, 148th overall, in 2008 Entry Draft.

Season	Club	League	GP	G	A	Pts	PIM	PP	SH	GW	S	%	+/-	TF	F%	Min	GP	G	A	Pts	PIM	PP	SH	GW	Min
2005-06	Blenheim Blast	OHA-C	40	11	12	23	102	....	....	....	....	....	....	....	....	....	....	....	....	....	....	....	....	....	....
2006-07	Sarnia Blast	OJHL-B	9	2	5	7	16	....	....	....	....	....	....	....	....	....	....	....	....	....	....	....	....	....	....
	Sarnia Sting	OHL	39	3	3	6	52	....	....	....	....	....	....	....	....	....	4	0	0	0	0	....	....	....	....
2007-08	Sarnia Sting	OHL	66	25	13	38	155	....	....	....	....	....	....	....	....	....	9	3	3	6	16	....	....	....	....
2008-09	Sarnia Sting	OHL	61	35	30	65	142	....	....	....	....	....	....	....	....	....	5	3	0	3	10	....	....	....	....
2009-10	NY Islanders	NHL	5	0	2	2	26	0	0	0	10	0.0	−1	0	0.0	13:14	....	....	....	....	....	....	....	....	....
	Bridgeport	AHL	76	12	19	31	113	....	....	....	....	....	....	....	....	....	5	1	2	3	4	....	....	....	....
	NHL Totals		5	0	2	2	26	0	0	0	10	0.0		0	0.0	13:14	....	....	....	....	....	....	....	....	....

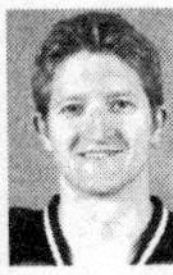

MARTIN, Paul
(MAHR-tihn, PAWL) **PIT.**

Defense. Shoots left. 6'1", 200 lbs. Born, Minneapolis, MN, March 5, 1981. New Jersey's 5th choice, 62nd overall, in 2000 Entry Draft.

Season	Club	League	GP	G	A	Pts	PIM	PP	SH	GW	S	%	+/-	TF	F%	Min	GP	G	A	Pts	PIM	PP	SH	GW	Min
1998-99	Elk River Elks	High-MN	24	9	11	20	....	....	....	....	....	....	....	....	....	....	....	....	....	....	....	....	....	....	....
99-2000	Elk River Elks	High-MN	24	15	35	50	26	....	....	....	....	....	....	....	....	....	....	....	....	....	....	....	....	....	....
2000-01	U. of Minnesota	WCHA	38	3	17	20	8	....	....	....	....	....	....	....	....	....	....	....	....	....	....	....	....	....	....
2001-02	U. of Minnesota	WCHA	44	8	30	38	22	....	....	....	....	....	....	....	....	....	....	....	....	....	....	....	....	....	....
2002-03	U. of Minnesota	WCHA	45	9	30	39	32	....	....	....	....	....	....	....	....	....	....	....	....	....	....	....	....	....	....
2003-04	New Jersey	NHL	70	6	18	24	4	2	0	2	82	7.3	12	0	0.0	20:08	5	1	1	2	4	1	0	0	23:40
2004-05	Fribourg	Swiss	11	3	4	7	2	....	....	....	....	....	....	....	....	....	....	....	....	....	....	....	....	....	....
2005-06	New Jersey	NHL	80	5	32	37	32	3	0	0	97	5.2	1	0	0.0	23:37	9	0	3	3	4	0	0	0	24:17
2006-07	New Jersey	NHL	82	3	23	26	18	1	0	0	84	3.6	−9	0	0.0	25:13	11	0	4	4	6	0	0	0	25:09
2007-08	New Jersey	NHL	73	5	27	32	22	2	0	2	93	5.4	20	0	0.0	23:53	5	1	2	3	2	1	0	0	25:35
2008-09	New Jersey	NHL	73	5	28	33	36	2	0	1	107	4.7	21	0	0.0	24:22	7	0	4	4	2	0	0	0	26:20
2009-10	New Jersey	NHL	22	2	9	11	2	1	0	0	21	9.5	10	0	0.0	22:30	5	0	0	0	0	0	0	0	22:24
	NHL Totals		400	26	137	163	114	11	0	5	484	5.4		0	0.0	23:28	42	2	14	16	18	2	0	0	24:42

Minnesota High School Player of the Year (1999) • WCHA All-Rookie Team (2001) • WCHA Second All-Star Team (2002, 2003) • NCAA West Second All-American Team (2003) • NCAA Championship All-Tournament Team (2003)

Signed as a free agent by **Fribourg** (Swiss), November 4, 2004. • Missed majority of 2009-10 season recovering from arm injury suffered in game at Pittsburgh, October 24, 2009. Signed as a free agent by **Pittsburgh**, July 1, 2010.

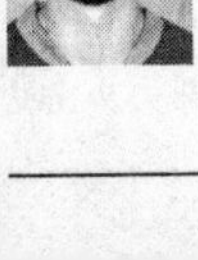

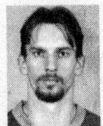

MARTINEK, Radek
(MAHR-tee-nihk, RA-dehk) **NYI**

Defense. Shoots right. 6'1", 203 lbs. Born, Havlicko Brod, Czech., August 31, 1976. NY Islanders' 12th choice, 228th overall, in 1999 Entry Draft.

Season	Club	League	GP	G	A	Pts	PIM	PP	SH	GW	S	%	+/-	TF	F%	Min	GP	G	A	Pts	PIM	PP	SH	GW	Min
1996-97	C. Budejovice	CzRep	52	3	5	8	40	....	....	....	....	....	....	....	....	....	5	0	1	1	2	....	....	....	....
	C. Budejovice	EuroHL	6	0	0	0	0	....	....	....	....	....	....	....	....	....	2	0	0	0	0	....	....	....	....
1997-98	C. Budejovice	CzRep	42	2	7	9	36	....	....	....	....	....	....	....	....	....	....	....	....	....	....	....	....	....	....
1998-99	C. Budejovice	CzRep	52	12	13	25	50	....	....	....	....	....	....	....	....	....	3	0	2	2	....	....	....	....	....
99-2000	C. Budejovice	CzRep	45	5	18	23	24	....	....	....	....	....	....	....	....	....	3	0	0	0	6	....	....	....	....
2000-01	C. Budejovice	CzRep	44	8	10	18	45	....	....	....	....	....	....	....	....	....	....	....	....	....	....	....	....	....	....

			Regular Season														Playoffs								
Season	Club	League	GP	G	A	Pts	PIM	PP	SH	GW	S	%	+/-	TF	F%	Min	GP	G	A	Pts	PIM	PP	SH	GW	Min
2001-02	NY Islanders	NHL	23	1	4	5	16	0	0	1	25	4.0	5	0	0.0	21:07	....	....	....	....	....	....	....	....	....
2002-03	NY Islanders	NHL	66	2	11	13	26	0	0	1	67	3.0	15	0	0.0	17:15	4	0	0	0	4	0	0	0	10:16
	Bridgeport	AHL	3	0	3	3	2	....	....	....	....	....	....	....	....	....	....	....	....	....	....	....	....	....	....
2003-04	NY Islanders	NHL	47	4	3	7	43	0	0	1	48	8.3	−9	0	0.0	13:03	5	0	1	1	0	0	0	0	12:12
2004-05	C. Budejovice	CzRep-2	30	12	18	30	80	....	....	....	....	....	....	....	....	....	12	2	3	5	6	....	....	....	....
2005-06	NY Islanders	NHL	74	1	16	17	32	0	0	0	79	1.3	−9	1	0.0	18:16	....	....	....	....	....	....	....	....	....
2006-07	NY Islanders	NHL	43	2	15	17	40	0	0	0	44	4.5	19	1	100.0	19:54	....	....	....	....	....	....	....	....	....
2007-08	NY Islanders	NHL	69	0	15	15	40	0	0	0	98	0.0	−9	0	0.0	22:52	....	....	....	....	....	....	....	....	....
2008-09	NY Islanders	NHL	51	6	4	10	28	1	0	1	54	11.1	−16	0	0.0	21:34	....	....	....	....	....	....	....	....	....
2009-10	NY Islanders	NHL	16	2	1	3	12	0	1	0	24	8.3	−1	0	0.0	22:48	....	....	....	....	....	....	....	....	....
	NHL Totals		389	18	69	87	237	1	1	4	439	4.1		2	50.0	19:15	9	0	1	1	4	0	0	0	11:20

• Missed majority of 2001-02 season recovering from knee injury suffered in game vs. NY Rangers, November 11, 2001. Signed as a free agent by **Ceske Budejovice** (CzRep-2), September 17, 2004. • Missed majority of 2009-10 season recovering from knee injury suffered in game at New Jersey, November 7, 2009.

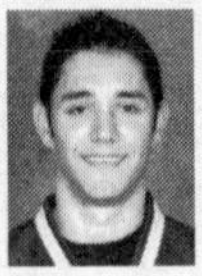

MARTINEZ, Alec

(mar-TEE-nehz, AL-ehk) **L.A.**

Defense. Shoots left. 6'1", 208 lbs. Born, Rochester Hills, MI, July 26, 1987. Los Angeles' 5th choice, 95th overall, in 2007 Entry Draft.

Season	Club	League	GP	G	A	Pts	PIM	PP	SH	GW	S	%	+/-	TF	F%	Min	GP	G	A	Pts	PIM	PP	SH	GW	Min
2004-05	Cedar Rapids	USHL	58	10	11	21	30	....	....	....	....	....	....	....	....	....	11	1	2	3	8	....	....	....	....
2005-06	Miami U.	CCHA	39	3	8	11	31	....	....	....	....	....	....	....	....	....	....	....	....	....	....	....	....	....	....
2006-07	Miami U.	CCHA	42	9	15	24	40	....	....	....	....	....	....	....	....	....	....	....	....	....	....	....	....	....	....
2007-08	Miami U.	CCHA	42	9	23	32	42	....	....	....	....	....	....	....	....	....	....	....	....	....	....	....	....	....	....
2008-09	Manchester	AHL	72	8	15	23	42	....	....	....	....	....	....	....	....	....	....	....	....	....	....	....	....	....	....
2009-10	Los Angeles	NHL	4	0	0	0	2	0	0	0	6	0.0	−2	0	0.0	15:25	....	....	....	....	....	....	....	....	....
	Manchester	AHL	55	7	23	30	26	....	....	....	....	....	....	....	....	....	16	0	3	3	10	....	....	....	....
	NHL Totals		4	0	0	0	2	0	0	0	6	0.0		0	0.0	15:25	....	....	....	....	....	....	....	....	....

CCHA First All-Star Team (2008) • NCAA West Second All-American Team (2008)

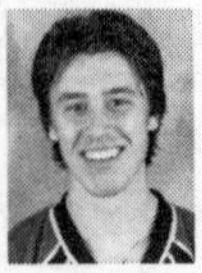

MATTHIAS, Shawn

(muh-TIGH-uhs, SHAWN) **FLA**

Center. Shoots left. 6'2", 213 lbs. Born, Mississauga, Ont., February 19, 1988. Detroit's 2nd choice, 47th overall, in 2006 Entry Draft.

Season	Club	League	GP	G	A	Pts	PIM	PP	SH	GW	S	%	+/-	TF	F%	Min	GP	G	A	Pts	PIM	PP	SH	GW	Min
2004-05	Belleville Bulls	OHL	37	1	1	2	15	....	....	....	....	....	....	....	....	....	3	0	0	0	0	....	....	....	....
2005-06	Belleville Bulls	OHL	67	13	21	34	42	....	....	....	....	....	....	....	....	....	6	3	0	3	2	....	....	....	....
2006-07	Belleville Bulls	OHL	64	38	35	73	61	....	....	....	....	....	....	....	....	....	15	13	5	18	10	....	....	....	....
2007-08	Florida	NHL	4	2	0	2	2	1	0	0	5	40.0	−2	38	44.7	13:08	....	....	....	....	....	....	....	....	....
	Belleville Bulls	OHL	53	32	47	79	50	....	....	....	....	....	....	....	....	....	1	1	0	1	0	....	....	....	....
2008-09	Florida	NHL	16	0	2	2	2	0	0	0	11	0.0	−3	91	50.6	9:10	....	....	....	....	....	....	....	....	....
	Rochester	AHL	61	10	10	20	16	....	....	....	....	....	....	....	....	....	....	....	....	....	....	....	....	....	....
2009-10	Florida	NHL	55	7	9	16	10	0	0	2	67	10.4	−3	313	38.0	10:48	....	....	....	....	....	....	....	....	....
	Rochester	AHL	27	6	7	13	12	....	....	....	....	....	....	....	....	....	7	2	5	7	7	....	....	....	....
	NHL Totals		75	9	11	20	14	1	0	2	83	10.8		442	41.2	10:34	....	....	....	....	....	....	....	....	....

Traded to **Florida** by **Detroit** with Detroit's 2nd round choice (later traded to Nashville - Nashville selected Nick Spaling) in 2007 Entry Draft for Todd Bertuzzi, February 27, 2007.

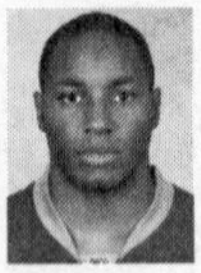

MAULDIN, Greg

(MAWL-dihn, GREHG) **COL**

Center. Shoots right. 5'11", 195 lbs. Born, Boston, MA, June 10, 1982. Columbus' 10th choice, 199th overall, in 2002 Entry Draft.

Season	Club	League	GP	G	A	Pts	PIM	PP	SH	GW	S	%	+/-	TF	F%	Min	GP	G	A	Pts	PIM	PP	SH	GW	Min
99-2000	Bos. Jr. Bruins	EJHL	58	45	42	87	14	....	....	....	....	....	....	....	....	....	....	....	....	....	....	....	....	....	....
2000-01	Bos. Jr. Bruins	EJHL	53	48	58	106	73	....	....	....	....	....	....	....	....	....	....	....	....	....	....	....	....	....	....
2001-02	Massachusetts	H-East	33	12	12	24	10	....	....	....	....	....	....	....	....	....	....	....	....	....	....	....	....	....	....
2002-03	Massachusetts	H-East	36	21	20	41	26	....	....	....	....	....	....	....	....	....	....	....	....	....	....	....	....	....	....
2003-04	Massachusetts	H-East	29	15	14	29	15	....	....	....	....	....	....	....	....	....	....	....	....	....	....	....	....	....	....
	Columbus	NHL	6	0	0	0	4	0	0	0	6	0.0	−2	0	0.0	8:47	....	....	....	....	....	....	....	....	....
	Syracuse Crunch	AHL	2	0	0	0	0	....	....	....	....	....	....	....	....	....	1	0	0	0	0	....	....	....	....
2004-05	Syracuse Crunch	AHL	66	7	20	27	49	....	....	....	....	....	....	....	....	....	....	....	....	....	....	....	....	....	....
2005-06	Syracuse Crunch	AHL	56	12	17	29	53	....	....	....	....	....	....	....	....	....	....	....	....	....	....	....	....	....	....
	Houston Aeros	AHL	11	1	3	4	0	....	....	....	....	....	....	....	....	....	8	1	1	2	2	....	....	....	....
2006-07	Bloomington	UHL	2	0	0	0	2	....	....	....	....	....	....	....	....	....	....	....	....	....	....	....	....	....	....
	Huddinge IK	Sweden-2	6	1	2	3	0	....	....	....	....	....	....	....	....	....	....	....	....	....	....	....	....	....	....
	IK Oskarshamn	Sweden-2	26	5	8	13	31	....	....	....	....	....	....	....	....	....	....	....	....	....	....	....	....	....	....
2007-08	Binghamton	AHL	71	15	18	33	37	....	....	....	....	....	....	....	....	....	....	....	....	....	....	....	....	....	....
2008-09	Binghamton	AHL	80	24	27	51	41	....	....	....	....	....	....	....	....	....	....	....	....	....	....	....	....	....	....
2009-10	NY Islanders	NHL	1	0	0	0	0	0	0	0	2	0.0	−1	11	72.7	10:02	....	....	....	....	....	....	....	....	....
	Bridgeport	AHL	77	25	29	54	35	....	....	....	....	....	....	....	....	....	5	1	2	3	0	....	....	....	....
	NHL Totals		7	0	0	0	4	0	0	0	8	0.0		11	72.7	8:58	....	....	....	....	....	....	....	....	....

EJHL First All-Star Team (2000, 2001) • EJHL MVP (2000)

Signed as a free agent by **Oskarshamn** (Sweden-2), October 23, 2006. Signed as a free agent by **Binghamton** (AHL), August 9, 2007. Signed as a free agent by **Ottawa**, July 7, 2008. Signed as a free agent by **NY Islanders**, July 6, 2009. Signed as a free agent by **Colorado**, July 2, 2010.

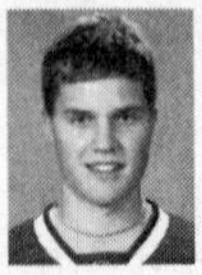

MAXWELL, Ben

(MAX-wehl, BEHN) **MTL**

Center. Shoots left. 6'1", 195 lbs. Born, North Vancouver, B.C., March 30, 1988. Montreal's 2nd choice, 49th overall, in 2006 Entry Draft.

Season	Club	League	GP	G	A	Pts	PIM	PP	SH	GW	S	%	+/-	TF	F%	Min	GP	G	A	Pts	PIM	PP	SH	GW	Min
2003-04	North Delta Ice	PIJHL	40	17	28	45	46	....	....	....	....	....	....	....	....	....	5	3	6	9	0	....	....	....	....
	South Surrey	BCHL	2	0	0	0	0	....	....	....	....	....	....	....	....	....	....	....	....	....	....	....	....	....	....
	Kootenay Ice	WHL	3	0	1	1	2	....	....	....	....	....	....	....	....	....	1	0	0	0	0	....	....	....	....
2004-05	Kootenay Ice	WHL	68	8	10	18	37	....	....	....	....	....	....	....	....	....	16	0	1	1	6	....	....	....	....
2005-06	Kootenay Ice	WHL	69	28	32	60	52	....	....	....	....	....	....	....	....	....	6	3	5	8	0	....	....	....	....
2006-07	Kootenay Ice	WHL	39	19	34	53	42	....	....	....	....	....	....	....	....	....	7	1	4	5	21	....	....	....	....
2007-08	Kootenay Ice	WHL	31	9	18	27	26	....	....	....	....	....	....	....	....	....	10	6	3	9	14	....	....	....	....
2008-09	Montreal	NHL	7	0	0	0	2	0	0	0	2	0.0	−1	53	37.7	9:55	....	....	....	....	....	....	....	....	....
	Hamilton	AHL	73	22	36	58	58	....	....	....	....	....	....	....	....	....	6	3	1	4	4	....	....	....	....
2009-10	Montreal	NHL	13	0	0	0	6	0	0	0	6	0.0	−2	16	50.0	8:47	1	0	0	0	0	0	0	0	1:0
	Hamilton	AHL	57	16	28	44	22	....	....	....	....	....	....	....	....	....	1	0	0	0	0	....	....	....	....
	NHL Totals		20	0	0	0	8	0	0	0	8	0.0		69	40.6	9:11	1	0	0	0	0	0	0	0	1:0

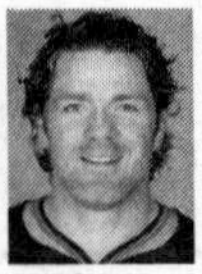

MAY, Brad

(MAY, BRAD)

Left wing. Shoots left. 6'1", 213 lbs. Born, Toronto, Ont., November 29, 1971. Buffalo's 1st choice, 14th overall, in 1990 Entry Draft.

Season	Club	League	GP	G	A	Pts	PIM	PP	SH	GW	S	%	+/-	TF	F%	Min	GP	G	A	Pts	PIM	PP	SH	GW	Min
1987-88	Markham	Minor-ON	31	22	37	59	58	....	....	....	....	....	....	....	....	....	....	....	....	....	....	....	....	....	....
	Markham	OHA-B	6	1	1	2	21	....	....	....	....	....	....	....	....	....	....	....	....	....	....	....	....	....	....
1988-89	Niagara Falls	OHL	65	8	14	22	304	....	....	....	....	....	....	....	....	....	17	0	1	1	55	....	....	....	....
1989-90	Niagara Falls	OHL	61	32	58	90	223	....	....	....	....	....	....	....	....	....	16	9	13	22	64	....	....	....	....
1990-91	Niagara Falls	OHL	34	37	32	69	93	....	....	....	....	....	....	....	....	....	14	11	14	25	53	....	....	....	....
1991-92	Buffalo	NHL	69	11	6	17	309	1	0	3	82	13.4	−12	....	....	....	7	1	4	5	2	0	0	1	....
1992-93	Buffalo	NHL	82	13	13	26	242	0	0	1	114	11.4	3	....	....	....	8	1	1	2	14	0	0	1	....
1993-94	Buffalo	NHL	84	18	27	45	171	3	0	3	166	10.8	−6	....	....	....	7	0	2	2	9	0	0	0	....
1994-95	Buffalo	NHL	33	3	3	6	87	1	0	0	42	7.1	5	....	....	....	4	0	0	0	2	0	0	0	....
1995-96	Buffalo	NHL	79	15	29	44	295	3	0	4	168	8.9	6	....	....	....	....	....	....	....	....	....	....	....	....
1996-97	Buffalo	NHL	42	3	4	7	106	1	0	1	75	4.0	−8	....	....	....	10	1	1	2	32	0	0	0	....
1997-98	Buffalo	NHL	36	4	7	11	113	0	0	0	41	9.8	2	....	....	....	....	....	....	....	....	....	....	....	....
	Vancouver	NHL	27	9	3	12	41	4	0	2	56	16.1	0	....	....	....	....	....	....	....	....	....	....	....	....
1998-99	Vancouver	NHL	66	6	11	17	102	1	0	1	91	6.6	−14	8	12.5	13:04	....	....	....	....	....	....	....	....	....
99-2000	Vancouver	NHL	59	9	7	16	90	0	0	3	66	13.6	−2	3	0.0	10:24	....	....	....	....	....	....	....	....	....
2000-01	Phoenix	NHL	62	11	14	25	107	0	0	0	83	13.3	10	3	33.3	11:11	....	....	....	....	....	....	....	....	....
2001-02	Phoenix	NHL	72	10	12	22	95	1	0	3	105	9.5	11	3	0.0	12:04	5	0	0	0	0	0	0	0	10:1
2002-03	Phoenix	NHL	20	3	4	7	32	0	0	0	24	12.5	3	0	0.0	9:56	....	....	....	....	....	....	....	....	....
	Vancouver	NHL	3	0	0	0	10	0	0	0	1	0.0	1	0	0.0	7:48	14	0	0	0	15	0	0	0	7:2
2003-04	Vancouver	NHL	70	5	6	11	137	0	0	0	75	6.7	−2	8	50.0	8:56	6	1	0	1	6	0	0	0	7:0
2004-05			DID NOT PLAY																						
2005-06	Colorado	NHL	54	3	3	6	82	0	0	0	55	5.5	−14	6	33.3	8:23	3	0	0	0	0	0	0	0	9:2
2006-07	Colorado	NHL	10	0	3	3	8	0	0	0	11	0.0	0	0	0.0	11:28	....	....	....	....	....	....	....	....	....
	♦ Anaheim	NHL	14	0	1	1	13	0	0	0	11	0.0	−1	0	0.0	8:39	18	0	1	1	28	0	0	0	7:2

			Regular Season														Playoffs								
Season	Club	League	GP	G	A	Pts	PIM	PP	SH	GW	S	%	+/-	TF	F%	Min	GP	G	A	Pts	PIM	PP	SH	GW	Min
2007-08	Anaheim	NHL	61	3	1	4	53	0	0	2	34	8.8	2	3	0.0	6:37	6	0	0	0	4	0	0	0	6:56
2008-09	Anaheim	NHL	20	0	5	5	28	0	0	0	5	0.0	5	3	33.3	6:22	....	....	....	....	....	....	....	....	....
	Toronto	NHL	38	1	1	2	61	0	0	0	27	3.7	–5	1	0.0	7:44	....	....	....	....	....	....	....	....	....
2009-10	Detroit	NHL	40	0	1	1	66	0	0	0	26	0.0	–5	1	0.0	6:58	....	....	....	....	....	....	....	....	....
	Grand Rapids	AHL	17	5	5	10	40	....	....	....	....	....	....	....	....	....	....	....	....	....	....	....	....	....	....
	NHL Totals		1041	127	161	288	2248	15	0	23	1358	9.4		39	23.1	9:38	88	4	9	13	112	0	0	2	7:42

OHL Second All-Star Team (1990, 1991)

• Missed majority of 1990-91 season recovering from knee injury suffered at Team Canada Juniors evaluation camp, August 21, 1990. Traded to **Vancouver** by **Buffalo** with Buffalo's 3rd round choice (later traded to Tampa Bay – Tampa Bay selected Jimmie Olvestad) in 1999 Entry Draft for Geoff Sanderson, February 4, 1998. Traded to **Phoenix** by **Vancouver** for future considerations, June 24, 2000. • Missed majority of 2002-03 season recovering from shoulder injury suffered in pre-season game vs. Detroit, October 6, 2002. Traded to **Vancouver** by **Phoenix** for Phoenix's 3rd round choice (previously acquired, Phoenix selected Dimitri Pestunov) in 2003 Entry Draft, March 11, 2003. Signed as a free agent by **Colorado**, August 5, 2005. Traded to **Anaheim** by **Colorado** for Michael Wall, February 27, 2007. • Missed majority of 2006-07 season recovering from shoulder injury suffered in pre-season game vs. Detroit, September 25, 2006. Traded to **Toronto** by **Anaheim** for future considerations, January 7, 2009. Signed as a free agent by **Detroit**, October 8, 2009.

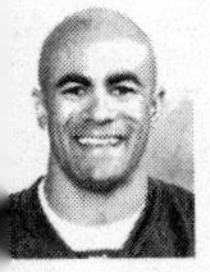

MAYERS, Jamal

(MAI-uhrz, JUH-MAHL) **S.J.**

Right wing. Shoots right. 6'1", 215 lbs. Born, Toronto, Ont., October 24, 1974. St. Louis' 3rd choice, 89th overall, in 1993 Entry Draft.

			Regular Season														Playoffs								
Season	Club	League	GP	G	A	Pts	PIM	PP	SH	GW	S	%	+/-	TF	F%	Min	GP	G	A	Pts	PIM	PP	SH	GW	Min
1990-91	Thornhill	MTJHL	44	12	24	36	78	....	....	....	....	....	....	....	....	....	....	....	....	....	....	....	....	....	....
1991-92	Thornhill	MTJHL	56	38	69	107	36	....	....	....	....	....	....	....	....	....	....	....	....	....	....	....	....	....	....
1992-93	Western Mich.	CCHA	38	8	17	25	26	....	....	....	....	....	....	....	....	....	....	....	....	....	....	....	....	....	....
1993-94	Western Mich.	CCHA	40	17	32	49	40	....	....	....	....	....	....	....	....	....	....	....	....	....	....	....	....	....	....
1994-95	Western Mich.	CCHA	39	13	32	45	40	....	....	....	....	....	....	....	....	....	....	....	....	....	....	....	....	....	....
1995-96	Western Mich.	CCHA	38	17	22	39	75	....	....	....	....	....	....	....	....	....	....	....	....	....	....	....	....	....	....
1996-97	St. Louis	NHL	6	0	1	1	2	0	0	0	7	0.0	–3	....	....	....	....	....	....	....	....	....	....	....	....
	Worcester IceCats	AHL	62	12	14	26	104	....	....	....	....	....	....	....	....	....	5	4	5	9	4	....	....	....	....
1997-98	Worcester IceCats	AHL	61	19	24	43	117	....	....	....	....	....	....	....	....	....	11	3	4	7	10	....	....	....	....
1998-99	St. Louis	NHL	34	4	5	9	40	0	0	0	48	8.3	–3	2	50.0	8:08	11	0	1	1	8	0	0	0	8:34
	Worcester IceCats	AHL	20	9	7	16	34	....	....	....	....	....	....	....	....	....	....	....	....	....	....	....	....	....	....
99-2000	St. Louis	NHL	79	7	10	17	90	0	0	0	99	7.1	0	77	52.0	9:46	7	0	4	4	2	0	0	0	10:42
2000-01	St. Louis	NHL	77	8	13	21	117	0	0	0	132	6.1	–3	273	51.3	11:04	15	2	3	5	8	0	0	0	11:28
2001-02	St. Louis	NHL	77	9	8	17	99	0	1	0	105	8.6	9	761	52.6	11:36	10	3	0	3	2	0	0	2	11:14
2002-03	St. Louis	NHL	15	2	5	7	8	0	0	0	26	7.7	1	111	51.4	14:21	....	....	....	....	....	....	....	....	....
2003-04	St. Louis	NHL	80	6	5	11	91	0	1	3	130	4.6	–19	681	48.6	13:01	5	0	0	0	0	0	0	0	12:55
2004-05	Hammarby	Sweden-2	19	9	13	22	36	....	....	....	....	....	....	....	....	....	....	....	....	....	....	....	....	....	....
	Missouri	UHL	13	5	2	7	68	....	....	....	....	....	....	....	....	....	....	....	....	....	....	....	....	....	....
2005-06	St. Louis	NHL	67	15	11	26	129	0	2	1	111	13.5	–22	363	48.5	15:07	....	....	....	....	....	....	....	....	....
2006-07	St. Louis	NHL	80	8	14	22	89	0	2	0	129	6.2	–19	432	57.4	14:37	....	....	....	....	....	....	....	....	....
2007-08	St. Louis	NHL	80	12	15	27	91	0	1	3	153	7.8	–19	683	56.2	15:56	....	....	....	....	....	....	....	....	....
2008-09	Toronto	NHL	71	7	9	16	82	0	0	1	72	9.7	–7	429	57.3	10:33	....	....	....	....	....	....	....	....	....
2009-10	Toronto	NHL	44	2	6	8	78	0	0	0	47	4.3	–5	264	56.8	8:55	....	....	....	....	....	....	....	....	....
	Calgary	NHL	27	1	5	6	53	0	0	1	28	3.6	2	115	55.7	9:11	....	....	....	....	....	....	....	....	....
	NHL Totals		737	81	107	188	969	0	7	9	1087	7.5		4191	53.4	12:10	48	5	8	13	20	0	0	2	10:47

• Missed majority of 2002-03 season recovering from knee injury suffered in game vs. Calgary, November 16, 2002. Signed as a free agent by **Hammarby** (Sweden-2), November 16, 2004. Signed as a free agent by **Missouri** (UHL), March 11, 2005. Traded to **Toronto** by **St. Louis** for Florida's 3rd round choice (previously acquired, St. Louis selected James Livingston) in 2008 Entry Draft, June 19, 2008. Traded to **Calgary** by **Toronto** with Matt Stajan, Niklas Hagman and Ian White for Dion Phaneuf, Fredrik Sjostrom and Keith Aulie, January 31, 2010. Signed as a free agent by **San Jose**, August 4, 2010.

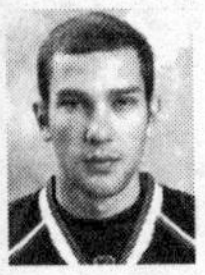

MAYOROV, Maksim

(may-YOHR-ahv, mahx-EEM) **CBJ**

Left wing. Shoots left. 6'2", 213 lbs. Born, Andizhan, USSR, March 26, 1989. Columbus' 5th choice, 94th overall, in 2007 Entry Draft.

			Regular Season														Playoffs								
Season	Club	League	GP	G	A	Pts	PIM	PP	SH	GW	S	%	+/-	TF	F%	Min	GP	G	A	Pts	PIM	PP	SH	GW	Min
2005-06	Ak Bars Kazan 2	Russia-3	STATISTICS NOT AVAILABLE																						
2006-07	Leninogorsk	Russia-2	28	6	4	10	6	....	....	....	....	....	....	....	....	....	....	....	....	....	....	....	....	....	....
	Almetjevsk	Russia-2	6	1	1	2	0	....	....	....	....	....	....	....	....	....	4	0	0	0	2	....	....	....	....
2007-08	Ak Bars Kazan	Russia	11	1	0	1	16	....	....	....	....	....	....	....	....	....	....	....	....	....	....	....	....	....	....
2008-09	Columbus	NHL	3	0	0	0	0	0	0	0	1	0.0	0	0	0.0	5:44	....	....	....	....	....	....	....	....	....
	Syracuse Crunch	AHL	71	17	14	31	30	....	....	....	....	....	....	....	....	....	....	....	....	....	....	....	....	....	....
2009-10	Columbus	NHL	4	0	0	0	0	0	0	0	4	0.0	–1	0	0.0	7:40	....	....	....	....	....	....	....	....	....
	Syracuse Crunch	AHL	74	17	15	32	24	....	....	....	....	....	....	....	....	....	....	....	....	....	....	....	....	....	....
	NHL Totals		7	0	0	0	0	0	0	0	5	0.0		0	0.0	6:50	....	....	....	....	....	....	....	....	....

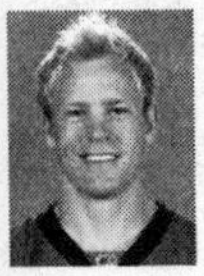

McAMMOND, Dean

(muh-KAM-uhnd, DEEN)

Center. Shoots left. 5'11", 195 lbs. Born, Grand Cache, Alta., June 15, 1973. Chicago's 1st choice, 22nd overall, in 1991 Entry Draft.

			Regular Season														Playoffs								
Season	Club	League	GP	G	A	Pts	PIM	PP	SH	GW	S	%	+/-	TF	F%	Min	GP	G	A	Pts	PIM	PP	SH	GW	Min
1988-89	St. Albert Raiders	AMHL	36	33	44	77	132	....	....	....	....	....	....	....	....	....	....	....	....	....	....	....	....	....	....
1989-90	Prince Albert	WHL	53	11	11	22	49	....	....	....	....	....	....	....	....	....	14	2	3	5	18	....	....	....	....
1990-91	Prince Albert	WHL	71	33	35	68	108	....	....	....	....	....	....	....	....	....	2	0	1	1	6	....	....	....	....
1991-92	Prince Albert	WHL	63	37	54	91	189	....	....	....	....	....	....	....	....	....	10	12	11	23	26	....	....	....	....
	Chicago	NHL	5	0	2	2	0	0	0	0	4	0.0	–2	....	....	....	3	0	0	0	2	0	0	0	....
1992-93	Prince Albert	WHL	30	19	29	48	44	....	....	....	....	....	....	....	....	....	....	....	....	....	....	....	....	....	....
	Swift Current	WHL	18	10	13	23	24	....	....	....	....	....	....	....	....	....	17	*16	19	35	20	....	....	....	....
1993-94	Edmonton	NHL	45	6	21	27	16	2	0	0	52	11.5	12	....	....	....	....	....	....	....	....	....	....	....	....
	Cape Breton	AHL	28	9	12	21	38	....	....	....	....	....	....	....	....	....	....	....	....	....	....	....	....	....	....
1994-95	Edmonton	NHL	6	0	0	0	0	0	0	0	3	0.0	–1	....	....	....	....	....	....	....	....	....	....	....	....
1995-96	Edmonton	NHL	53	15	15	30	23	4	0	0	79	19.0	6	....	....	....	....	....	....	....	....	....	....	....	....
	Cape Breton	AHL	22	9	15	24	55	....	....	....	....	....	....	....	....	....	....	....	....	....	....	....	....	....	....
1996-97	Edmonton	NHL	57	12	17	29	28	4	0	6	106	11.3	–15	....	....	....	....	....	....	....	....	....	....	....	....
1997-98	Edmonton	NHL	77	19	31	50	46	8	0	3	128	14.8	9	....	....	....	12	1	4	5	12	0	0	0	....
1998-99	Edmonton	NHL	65	9	16	25	36	1	0	0	122	7.4	5	26	38.5	14:15	....	....	....	....	....	....	....	....	....
	Chicago	NHL	12	1	4	5	2	0	0	1	16	6.3	3	37	48.6	15:43	....	....	....	....	....	....	....	....	....
99-2000	Chicago	NHL	76	14	18	32	72	1	0	1	118	11.9	11	257	39.7	16:25	....	....	....	....	....	....	....	....	....
2000-01	Chicago	NHL	61	10	16	26	43	1	0	1	95	10.5	4	23	43.5	15:30	....	....	....	....	....	....	....	....	....
	Philadelphia	NHL	10	1	1	2	0	1	0	0	17	5.9	–1	65	46.2	12:00	4	0	0	0	2	0	0	0	9:25
2001-02	Calgary	NHL	73	21	30	51	60	7	0	4	152	13.8	2	143	55.2	18:56	....	....	....	....	....	....	....	....	....
2002-03	Colorado	NHL	41	10	8	18	10	2	0	2	72	13.9	1	9	55.6	14:24	....	....	....	....	....	....	....	....	....
2003-04	Calgary	NHL	64	17	13	30	18	4	1	5	101	16.8	9	768	49.1	16:52	....	....	....	....	....	....	....	....	....
2004-05	Albany River Rats	AHL	79	19	42	61	72	....	....	....	....	....	....	....	....	....	....	....	....	....	....	....	....	....	....
2005-06	St. Louis	NHL	78	15	22	37	32	4	0	0	116	12.9	–25	289	47.4	16:02	....	....	....	....	....	....	....	....	....
2006-07	Ottawa	NHL	81	14	15	29	28	0	2	1	86	16.3	11	677	44.2	11:08	18	5	3	8	11	0	1	1	11:27
2007-08	Ottawa	NHL	68	9	13	22	12	0	3	1	67	13.4	1	259	43.2	11:32	4	0	0	0	4	0	0	0	13:30
2008-09	Ottawa	NHL	44	3	4	7	16	0	1	2	40	7.5	2	276	42.0	9:40	....	....	....	....	....	....	....	....	....
	NY Islanders	NHL	18	2	7	9	8	0	0	0	19	10.5	5	267	47.2	15:09	....	....	....	....	....	....	....	....	....
2009-10	Lowell Devils	AHL	6	1	2	3	6	....	....	....	....	....	....	....	....	....	....	....	....	....	....	....	....	....	....
	New Jersey	NHL	62	8	9	17	40	1	1	2	87	9.2	–1	556	45.5	12:51	5	0	0	0	4	0	0	0	11:19
	NHL Totals		996	186	262	448	490	40	8	29	1480	12.6		3652	45.8	14:30	46	6	7	13	35	0	1	1	11:26

Traded to **Edmonton** by **Chicago** with Igor Kravchuk for Joe Murphy, February 24, 1993. Traded to **Chicago** by **Edmonton** with Boris Mironov and Jonas Elofsson for Chad Kilger, Daniel Cleary, Ethan Moreau and Christian Laflamme, March 20, 1999. Traded to **Philadelphia** by **Chicago** for Philadelphia's 3rd round choice (later traded to Toronto – Toronto selected Nicolas Corbeil) in 2001 Entry Draft, March 13, 2001. Traded to **Calgary** by **Philadelphia** for Calgary's 4th round choice (Rosario Ruggeri) in 2002 Entry Draft, June 24, 2001. Traded to **Colorado** by **Calgary** with Derek Morris and Jeff Shantz for Chris Drury and Stephane Yelle, October 1, 2002. Traded to **Calgary** by **Colorado** for Calgary's 5th round choice (Mark McCutcheon) in 2003 Entry Draft, March 11, 2003. • Ruled ineligible to play remainder of 2002-03 season by NHL due to transaction violation by Calgary, March 15, 2003. Signed as a free agent by **New Jersey**, October 5, 2004. Signed as a free agent by **St. Louis**, August 9, 2005. Signed as a free agent by **Ottawa**, August 2, 2006. Traded to **NY Islanders** by **Ottawa** with San Jose's 1st round choice (previously acquired, later traded to Columbus, later traded to Anaheim – Anaheim selected Kyle Palmieri) in 2009 Entry Draft for Mike Comrie and Chris Campoli, February 20. 2009. Signed as a free agent by **Lowell** (AHL), October 20, 2009. Signed as a free agent by **New Jersey**, November 6, 2009.

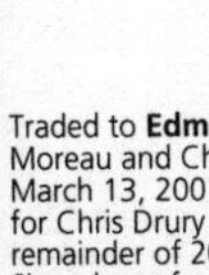

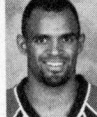

McARDLE, Kenndal

(muh-KAHR-duhl, KEHN-dahl) **FLA.**

Left wing. Shoots left. 5'11", 190 lbs. Born, Toronto, Ont., January 4, 1987. Florida's 1st choice, 20th overall, in 2005 Entry Draft.

			Regular Season														Playoffs								
Season	Club	League	GP	G	A	Pts	PIM	PP	SH	GW	S	%	+/-	TF	F%	Min	GP	G	A	Pts	PIM	PP	SH	GW	Min
2002-03	Burnaby W.C.	Minor-BC	30	1	9	10	131	....	....	....	....	....	....	....	....	....	....	....	....	....	....	....	....	....	....
	Moose Jaw	WHL	2	0	0	0	0	....	....	....	....	....	....	....	....	....	....	....	....	....	....	....	....	....	....
2003-04	Moose Jaw	WHL	54	8	8	16	57	....	....	....	....	....	....	....	....	....	10	3	2	5	6	....	....	....	....
2004-05	Moose Jaw	WHL	70	37	37	74	122	....	....	....	....	....	....	....	....	....	5	1	0	1	16	....	....	....	....
2005-06	Moose Jaw	WHL	72	28	43	71	135	....	....	....	....	....	....	....	....	....	22	6	10	16	43	....	....	....	....

Season	Club	League	GP	G	A	Pts	PIM	PP	SH	GW	S	%	+/-	TF	F%	Min	GP	G	A	Pts	PIM	PP	SH	GW	M
			Regular Season														Playoffs								
2006-07	Moose Jaw	WHL	26	10	10	20	75																		
	Vancouver Giants	WHL	37	9	13	22	54										22	*11	9	20	49				
2007-08	Rochester	AHL	36	5	5	10	31																		
	Florida Everblades	ECHL	6	3	1	4	26										3	0	0	0	2				
2008-09	**Florida**	**NHL**	**3**	**0**	**0**	**0**	**2**	**0**	**0**	**0**	**1**	**0.0**	**–1**	**0**	**0.0**	**7:30**									
	Rochester	AHL	58	12	12	24	79																		
2009-10	**Florida**	**NHL**	**19**	**1**	**2**	**3**	**29**	**0**	**0**	**0**	**10**	**10.0**	**–4**	**0**	**0.0**	**8:54**									
	Rochester	AHL	18	3	5	8	63																		
	NHL Totals		**22**	**1**	**2**	**3**	**31**	**0**	**0**	**0**	**11**	**9.1**		**0**	**0.0**	**8:42**									

• Missed majority of 2009-10 season recovering from shoulder injury suffered in game at Nashville, November 28, 2010.

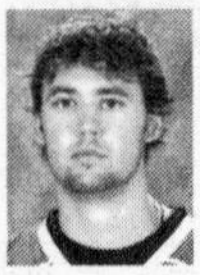

McBAIN, Jamie

(muhk-BAYN, JAY-mee) **CAR**

Defense. Shoots right. 6'2", 200 lbs. Born, Edina, MN, February 25, 1988. Carolina's 1st choice, 63rd overall, in 2006 Entry Draft.

Season	Club	League	GP	G	A	Pts	PIM	PP	SH	GW	S	%	+/-	TF	F%	Min	GP	G	A	Pts	PIM	PP	SH	GW	M
2003-04	Shat.-St. Mary's	High-MN	73	6	27	33																			
2004-05	USNTDP	U-17	14	1	6	7	16																		
	USNTDP	NAHL	38	2	7	9	22										10	0	3	3	4				
2005-06	USNTDP	U-18	41	9	16	25	35																		
	USNTDP	NAHL	14	0	5	5	6																		
2006-07	U. of Wisconsin	WCHA	36	3	15	18	36																		
2007-08	U. of Wisconsin	WCHA	35	5	19	24	18																		
2008-09	U. of Wisconsin	WCHA	40	7	30	37	30																		
	Albany River Rats	AHL	10	1	1	2	2																		
2009-10	**Carolina**	**NHL**	**14**	**3**	**7**	**10**	**0**	**1**	**0**	**1**	**29**	**10.3**	**6**	**0**	**0.0**	**25:47**									
	Albany River Rats	AHL	68	7	33	40	10										8	4	2	6	8				
	NHL Totals		**14**	**3**	**7**	**10**	**0**	**1**	**0**	**1**	**29**	**10.3**		**0**	**0.0**	**25:47**									

WCHA All-Rookie Team (2007) • WCHA First All-Star Team (2009) • WCHA Player of the Year (2009) • NCAA West First All-American Team (2009)

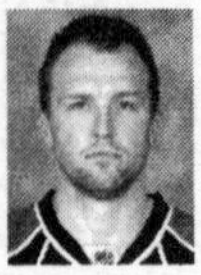

McCABE, Bryan

(muh-KAYB, BRIGH-uhn) **FLA**

Defense. Shoots left. 6'2", 220 lbs. Born, St. Catharines, Ont., June 8, 1975. NY Islanders' 2nd choice, 40th overall, in 1993 Entry Draft.

Season	Club	League	GP	G	A	Pts	PIM	PP	SH	GW	S	%	+/-	TF	F%	Min	GP	G	A	Pts	PIM	PP	SH	GW	M
1990-91	Calgary Canucks	AMHL	33	14	34	48	55																		
1991-92	Medicine Hat	WHL	68	6	24	30	157										4	0	0	0	6				
1992-93	Medicine Hat	WHL	14	0	13	13	83																		
	Spokane Chiefs	WHL	46	3	44	47	134										6	1	5	6	28				
1993-94	Spokane Chiefs	WHL	64	22	62	84	218										3	0	4	4	4				
1994-95	Spokane Chiefs	WHL	42	14	39	53	115																		
	Brandon	WHL	20	6	10	16	38										18	4	13	17	59				
1995-96	**NY Islanders**	**NHL**	**82**	**7**	**16**	**23**	**156**	**3**	**0**	**1**	**130**	**5.4**	**–24**												
1996-97	**NY Islanders**	**NHL**	**82**	**8**	**20**	**28**	**165**	**2**	**1**	**2**	**117**	**6.8**	**–2**												
1997-98	**NY Islanders**	**NHL**	**56**	**3**	**9**	**12**	**145**	**1**	**0**	**0**	**81**	**3.7**	**9**												
	Vancouver	**NHL**	**26**	**1**	**11**	**12**	**64**	**0**	**1**	**0**	**42**	**2.4**	**10**												
1998-99	**Vancouver**	**NHL**	**69**	**7**	**14**	**21**	**120**	**1**	**2**	**0**	**98**	**7.1**	**–11**	**1**	**0.0**	**24:13**									
99-2000	**Chicago**	**NHL**	**79**	**6**	**19**	**25**	**139**	**2**	**0**	**2**	**119**	**5.0**	**–8**	**1**	**0.0**	**23:23**									
2000-01	**Toronto**	**NHL**	**82**	**5**	**24**	**29**	**123**	**3**	**0**	**2**	**159**	**3.1**	**16**	**0**	**0.0**	**23:49**	**11**	**2**	**3**	**5**	**16**	**1**	**0**	**0**	**23:5**
2001-02	**Toronto**	**NHL**	**82**	**17**	**26**	**43**	**129**	**8**	**0**	**1**	**157**	**10.8**	**16**	**1**	**0.0**	**24:34**	**20**	**5**	**5**	**10**	**30**	**3**	**0**	**1**	**29:3**
2002-03	**Toronto**	**NHL**	**75**	**6**	**18**	**24**	**135**	**3**	**0**	**1**	**149**	**4.0**	**9**	**1**	**0.0**	**23:39**	**7**	**0**	**3**	**3**	**10**	**0**	**0**	**0**	**27:2**
2003-04	**Toronto**	**NHL**	**75**	**16**	**37**	**53**	**86**	**8**	**0**	**2**	**168**	**9.5**	**22**	**2**	**50.0**	**25:44**	**13**	**3**	**5**	**8**	**14**	**2**	**0**	**0**	**28:4**
2004-05	HV 71 Jonkoping	Sweden	10	1	0	1	30																		
2005-06	**Toronto**	**NHL**	**73**	**19**	**49**	**68**	**116**	**13**	**0**	**6**	**207**	**9.2**	**–1**	**1**	**0.0**	**28:18**									
	Canada	Olympics	6	0	0	0	18																		
2006-07	**Toronto**	**NHL**	**82**	**15**	**42**	**57**	**115**	**11**	**0**	**1**	**207**	**7.2**	**3**	**0**	**0.0**	**26:50**									
2007-08	**Toronto**	**NHL**	**54**	**5**	**18**	**23**	**81**	**4**	**0**	**2**	**107**	**4.7**	**–2**	**0**	**0.0**	**25:55**									
2008-09	**Florida**	**NHL**	**69**	**15**	**24**	**39**	**41**	**8**	**0**	**3**	**153**	**9.8**	**–1**	**0**	**0.0**	**23:08**									
2009-10	**Florida**	**NHL**	**82**	**8**	**35**	**43**	**83**	**3**	**0**	**1**	**169**	**4.7**	**–4**	**0**	**0.0**	**23:20**									
	NHL Totals		**1068**	**138**	**362**	**500**	**1698**	**70**	**4**	**24**	**2063**	**6.7**		**7**	**14.3**	**24:46**	**51**	**10**	**16**	**26**	**70**	**6**	**0**	**1**	**27:5**

WHL West Second All-Star Team (1993) • WHL West First All-Star Team (1994) • WHL East First All-Star Team (1995) • Memorial Cup Tournament All-Star Team (1995) • NHL Second All-Star Team (2004)

Traded to **Vancouver** by **NY Islanders** with Todd Bertuzzi and NY Islanders' 3rd round choice (Jarkko Ruutu) in 1998 Entry Draft for Trevor Linden, February 6, 1998. Traded to **Chicago** by **Vancouver** with Vancouver's 1st round choice (Pavel Vorobiev) in 2000 Entry Draft for Chicago's 1st round choice (later traded to Tampa Bay, later traded to NY Rangers – NY Rangers selected Pavel Brendl) in 1999 Entry Draft, June 25, 1999. Traded to **Toronto** by **Chicago** for Alexander Karpovtsev and Toronto's 4th round choice (Vladimir Gusev) in 2001 Entry Draft, October 2, 2000. Signed as a free agent by **Jonkoping** (Sweden), October 29, 2004. Traded to **Florida** by **Toronto** with Toronto's 4th round choice (Sam Brittain) in 2010 Entry Draft for Mike Van Ryn, September 2, 2008.

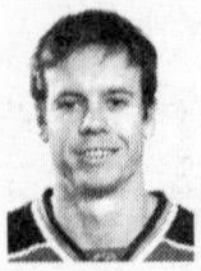

McCARTHY, John

(muh-KAHR-thee, JAWN) **S.**

Left wing. Shoots left. 6'1", 200 lbs. Born, Boston, MA, August 9, 1986. San Jose's 5th choice, 202nd overall, in 2006 Entry Draft.

Season	Club	League	GP	G	A	Pts	PIM	PP	SH	GW	S	%	+/-	TF	F%	Min	GP	G	A	Pts	PIM	PP	SH	GW	M
2004-05	Des Moines	USHL	60	8	10	18	32																		
2005-06	Boston University	H-East	33	2	2	4	12																		
2006-07	Boston University	H-East	39	2	3	5	18																		
2007-08	Boston University	H-East	38	4	3	7	24																		
2008-09	Boston University	H-East	45	6	23	29	24																		
2009-10	**San Jose**	**NHL**	**4**	**0**	**0**	**0**	**0**	**0**	**0**	**0**	**3**	**0.0**	**–3**	**0**	**0.0**	**9:08**									
	Worcester Sharks	AHL	74	15	27	42	39										11	2	3	5	10				
	NHL Totals		**4**	**0**	**0**	**0**	**0**	**0**	**0**	**0**	**3**	**0.0**		**0**	**0.0**	**9:08**									

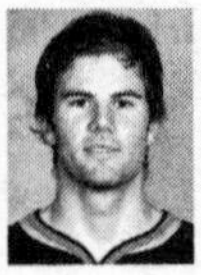

McCARTHY, Steve

(muh-KAHR-thee, STEEV)

Defense. Shoots left. 6'1", 210 lbs. Born, Trail, B.C., February 3, 1981. Chicago's 1st choice, 23rd overall, in 1999 Entry Draft.

Season	Club	League	GP	G	A	Pts	PIM	PP	SH	GW	S	%	+/-	TF	F%	Min	GP	G	A	Pts	PIM	PP	SH	GW	M
1996-97	Trail	BCHL	57	25	52	77	81																		
	Edmonton Ice	WHL	2	0	0	0	0																		
1997-98	Edmonton Ice	WHL	58	11	29	40	59																		
1998-99	Kootenay Ice	WHL	57	19	33	52	79										6	0	5	5	8				
99-2000	**Chicago**	**NHL**	**5**	**1**	**1**	**2**	**4**	**1**	**0**	**0**	**4**	**25.0**	**0**	**0**	**0.0**	**15:09**									
	Kootenay Ice	WHL	37	13	23	36	36																		
2000-01	**Chicago**	**NHL**	**44**	**0**	**5**	**5**	**8**	**0**	**0**	**0**	**32**	**0.0**	**–7**	**0**	**0.0**	**14:47**									
	Norfolk Admirals	AHL	7	0	4	4	2																		
2001-02	**Chicago**	**NHL**	**3**	**0**	**0**	**0**	**2**	**0**	**0**	**0**	**2**	**0.0**	**–1**	**0**	**0.0**	**11:48**									
	Norfolk Admirals	AHL	77	7	21	28	37										2	0	3	3	2				
2002-03	**Chicago**	**NHL**	**57**	**1**	**4**	**5**	**23**	**0**	**0**	**0**	**55**	**1.8**	**–1**	**0**	**0.0**	**16:25**									
	Norfolk Admirals	AHL	19	1	6	7	14										9	0	4	4	0				
2003-04	**Chicago**	**NHL**	**25**	**1**	**3**	**4**	**8**	**0**	**0**	**0**	**29**	**3.4**	**–9**	**0**	**0.0**	**19:21**									
2004-05			DID NOT PLAY																						
2005-06	**Vancouver**	**NHL**	**51**	**2**	**4**	**6**	**43**	**0**	**0**	**0**	**46**	**4.3**	**3**	**0**	**0.0**	**13:17**									
	Atlanta	**NHL**	**16**	**7**	**3**	**10**	**8**	**2**	**0**	**0**	**20**	**35.0**	**0**	**0**	**0.0**	**16:44**									
2006-07	**Atlanta**	**NHL**	**46**	**4**	**12**	**16**	**24**	**3**	**0**	**0**	**51**	**7.8**	**4**	**0**	**0.0**	**15:17**									
2007-08	**Atlanta**	**NHL**	**55**	**1**	**6**	**7**	**48**	**0**	**0**	**0**	**41**	**2.4**	**–23**	**0**	**0.0**	**15:47**									
2008-09	Ufa	Rus-KHL	18	0	0	0	16																		
2009-10	Chicago Wolves	AHL	25	2	5	7	28																		
	NHL Totals		**302**	**17**	**38**	**55**	**168**	**6**	**0**	**0**	**280**	**6.1**		**0**	**0.0**	**15:33**									

• Missed majority of 2003-04 season recovering from groin injury suffered in game vs. Calgary, November 22, 2003. Traded to **Vancouver** by **Chicago** for Vancouver's 3rd round choice (Josh Unice) in 2007 Entry Draft, August 22, 2005. Traded to **Atlanta** by **Vancouver** for Atlanta's 4th round choice (later traded back to Atlanta - Atlanta selected Niklas Lucenius) in 2007 Entry Draft, March 9, 2006. Signed as a free agent by **Ufa** (Russia-KHL), July 12, 2008. Signed as a free agent by **Anaheim**, July 10, 2009. Traded to **Atlanta** by **Anaheim** for future considerations, September 24, 2009. • Missed majority of 2009-10 season recovering from recurring knee injury.

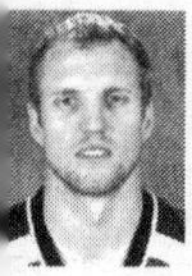

McCLEMENT, Jay
(muh-KLEHM-ehnt, JAY) **ST.L.**

Center. Shoots left. 6'1", 200 lbs. Born, Kingston, Ont., March 2, 1983. St. Louis' 1st choice, 57th overall, in 2001 Entry Draft.

			Regular Season														Playoffs								
Season	Club	League	GP	G	A	Pts	PIM	PP	SH	GW	S	%	+/-	TF	F%	Min	GP	G	A	Pts	PIM	PP	SH	GW	Min
1997-98	Kingston	OPJHL	48	3	8	11	15	....	....	....	....	....	....	....	....	....	....	....	....	....	....	....	....	....	....
1998-99	Kingston	OPJHL	51	25	28	53	34	....	....	....	....	....	....	....	....	....	....	....	....	....	....	....	....	....	....
99-2000	Brampton	OHL	63	13	16	29	34	....	....	....	....	....	....	....	....	....	6	0	4	4	8	....	....	....	....
2000-01	Brampton	OHL	66	30	19	49	61	....	....	....	....	....	....	....	....	....	9	4	2	6	10	....	....	....	....
2001-02	Brampton	OHL	61	26	29	55	43	....	....	....	....	....	....	....	....	....	....	....	....	....	....	....	....	....	....
2002-03	Brampton	OHL	45	22	27	49	37	....	....	....	....	....	....	....	....	....	11	3	4	7	11	....	....	....	....
	Worcester IceCats	AHL	....	....	....	....	....	....	....	....	....	....	....	....	....	....	1	0	0	0	0	....	....	....	....
2003-04	Worcester IceCats	AHL	69	12	13	25	20	....	....	....	....	....	....	....	....	....	10	0	3	3	0	....	....	....	....
2004-05	Worcester IceCats	AHL	79	17	34	51	45	....	....	....	....	....	....	....	....	....	....	....	....	....	....	....	....	....	....
2005-06	**St. Louis**	**NHL**	**67**	**6**	**21**	**27**	**30**	**1**	**0**	**2**	**76**	**7.9**	**–23**	**691**	**46.9**	**13:56**	....	....	....	....	....	....	....	....	....
	Peoria Rivermen	AHL	11	4	5	9	4	....	....	....	....	....	....	....	....	....	4	0	2	2	2	....	....	....	....
2006-07	**St. Louis**	**NHL**	**81**	**8**	**28**	**36**	**55**	**0**	**0**	**0**	**104**	**7.7**	**3**	**839**	**52.7**	**13:53**	....	....	....	....	....	....	....	....	....
2007-08	**St. Louis**	**NHL**	**81**	**9**	**13**	**22**	**26**	**0**	**0**	**2**	**110**	**8.2**	**–17**	**700**	**52.3**	**13:55**	....	....	....	....	....	....	....	....	....
2008-09	**St. Louis**	**NHL**	**82**	**12**	**14**	**26**	**29**	**0**	**3**	**3**	**137**	**8.8**	**–10**	**1451**	**52.1**	**16:36**	**4**	**0**	**0**	**0**	**4**	**0**	**0**	**0**	**16:28**
2009-10	**St. Louis**	**NHL**	**82**	**11**	**18**	**29**	**22**	**0**	**0**	**3**	**109**	**10.1**	**0**	**1412**	**49.7**	**16:44**	....	....	....	....	....	....	....	....	....
	NHL Totals		**393**	**46**	**94**	**140**	**162**	**1**	**3**	**10**	**536**	**8.6**		**5093**	**50.8**	**15:04**	**4**	**0**	**0**	**0**	**4**	**0**	**0**	**0**	**16:28**

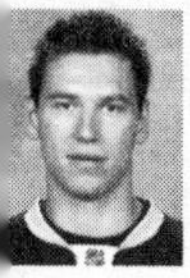

McCORMICK, Cody
(muh-KOHR-mihk, KOH-dee) **BUF.**

Center/Right wing. Shoots right. 6'3", 215 lbs. Born, London, Ont., April 18, 1983. Colorado's 5th choice, 144th overall, in 2001 Entry Draft.

1998-99	Elgin-Middlesex	MHAO	58	22	40	62	81	....	....	....	....	....	....	....	....	....	....	....	....	....	....	....	....	....	....
99-2000	Belleville Bulls	OHL	45	3	4	7	42	....	....	....	....	....	....	....	....	....	9	1	0	1	10	....	....	....	....
2000-01	Belleville Bulls	OHL	66	7	16	23	135	....	....	....	....	....	....	....	....	....	10	1	1	2	23	....	....	....	....
2001-02	Belleville Bulls	OHL	63	10	17	27	118	....	....	....	....	....	....	....	....	....	11	2	4	6	24	....	....	....	....
2002-03	Belleville Bulls	OHL	61	36	33	69	166	....	....	....	....	....	....	....	....	....	7	4	7	11	11	....	....	....	....
2003-04	**Colorado**	**NHL**	**44**	**2**	**3**	**5**	**73**	**0**	**0**	**1**	**33**	**6.1**	**–4**	**110**	**32.7**	**8:07**	....	....	....	....	....	....	....	....	....
	Hershey Bears	AHL	32	3	6	9	60	....	....	....	....	....	....	....	....	....	....	....	....	....	....	....	....	....	....
2004-05	Hershey Bears	AHL	40	5	6	11	68	....	....	....	....	....	....	....	....	....	....	....	....	....	....	....	....	....	....
2005-06	**Colorado**	**NHL**	**45**	**4**	**4**	**8**	**29**	**0**	**0**	**1**	**43**	**9.3**	**1**	**16**	**25.0**	**7:42**	....	....	....	....	....	....	....	....	....
	Lowell	AHL	13	1	6	7	34	....	....	....	....	....	....	....	....	....	....	....	....	....	....	....	....	....	....
2006-07	**Colorado**	**NHL**	**6**	**0**	**1**	**1**	**6**	**0**	**0**	**0**	**6**	**0.0**	**1**	**3**	**33.3**	**6:44**	....	....	....	....	....	....	....	....	....
	Albany River Rats	AHL	42	8	8	16	64	....	....	....	....	....	....	....	....	....	5	1	0	1	4	....	....	....	....
2007-08	**Colorado**	**NHL**	**40**	**2**	**2**	**4**	**50**	**0**	**0**	**1**	**45**	**4.4**	**5**	**17**	**35.3**	**10:58**	**4**	**0**	**1**	**1**	**7**	**0**	**0**	**0**	**11:53**
	Lake Erie	AHL	13	2	4	6	16	....	....	....	....	....	....	....	....	....	....	....	....	....	....	....	....	....	....
2008-09	**Colorado**	**NHL**	**55**	**1**	**11**	**12**	**92**	**0**	**0**	**0**	**66**	**1.5**	**–5**	**107**	**35.5**	**9:36**	....	....	....	....	....	....	....	....	....
2009-10	Portland Pirates	AHL	66	17	12	29	168	....	....	....	....	....	....	....	....	....	3	0	0	0	9	....	....	....	....
	Buffalo	**NHL**	....	....	....	....	....	....	....	....	....	....	....	....	....	....	**3**	**0**	**2**	**2**	**14**	**0**	**0**	**0**	**10:41**
	NHL Totals		**190**	**9**	**21**	**30**	**250**	**0**	**0**	**3**	**193**	**4.7**		**253**	**33.6**	**9:00**	**7**	**0**	**3**	**3**	**21**	**0**	**0**	**0**	**11:22**

HL First All-Star Team (2003)

igned as a free agent by **Buffalo**, August 1, 2009.

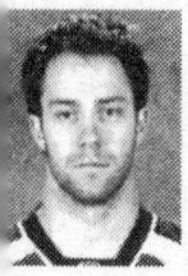

McDONALD, Andy
(muhk-DAWN-uhld, AN-dee) **ST.L.**

Center. Shoots left. 5'11", 190 lbs. Born, Strathroy, Ont., August 25, 1977.

1993-94	Strathroy Rockets	OHA-B	7	2	2	4	0	....	....	....	....	....	....	....	....	....	....	....	....	....	....	....	....	....	....
1994-95	Strathroy Rockets	OHA-B	50	32	41	73	24	....	....	....	....	....	....	....	....	....	....	....	....	....	....	....	....	....	....
1995-96	Strathroy Rockets	OHA-B	52	31	56	87	103	....	....	....	....	....	....	....	....	....	....	....	....	....	....	....	....	....	....
1996-97	Colgate	ECAC	33	9	10	19	16	....	....	....	....	....	....	....	....	....	....	....	....	....	....	....	....	....	....
1997-98	Colgate	ECAC	35	13	19	32	26	....	....	....	....	....	....	....	....	....	....	....	....	....	....	....	....	....	....
1998-99	Colgate	ECAC	35	20	26	46	42	....	....	....	....	....	....	....	....	....	....	....	....	....	....	....	....	....	....
99-2000	Colgate	ECAC	34	25	*33	*58	49	....	....	....	....	....	....	....	....	....	....	....	....	....	....	....	....	....	....
2000-01	**Anaheim**	**NHL**	**16**	**1**	**0**	**1**	**6**	**0**	**0**	**0**	**21**	**4.8**	**0**	**139**	**48.9**	**11:11**	....	....	....	....	....	....	....	....	....
	Cincinnati	AHL	46	15	25	40	21	....	....	....	....	....	....	....	....	....	3	0	1	1	2	....	....	....	....
2001-02	**Anaheim**	**NHL**	**53**	**7**	**21**	**28**	**10**	**2**	**0**	**3**	**79**	**8.9**	**2**	**818**	**53.7**	**15:59**	....	....	....	....	....	....	....	....	....
	Cincinnati	AHL	21	7	25	32	6	....	....	....	....	....	....	....	....	....	....	....	....	....	....	....	....	....	....
2002-03	**Anaheim**	**NHL**	**46**	**10**	**11**	**21**	**14**	**3**	**0**	**1**	**92**	**10.9**	**–1**	**604**	**56.0**	**18:31**	....	....	....	....	....	....	....	....	....
2003-04	**Anaheim**	**NHL**	**79**	**9**	**21**	**30**	**24**	**2**	**1**	**1**	**162**	**5.6**	**–13**	**282**	**54.3**	**16:34**	....	....	....	....	....	....	....	....	....
2004-05	ERC Ingolstadt	Germany	36	13	17	30	26	....	....	....	....	....	....	....	....	....	10	5	2	7	35	....	....	....	....
2005-06	**Anaheim**	**NHL**	**82**	**34**	**51**	**85**	**32**	**13**	**0**	**7**	**229**	**14.8**	**24**	**1095**	**56.3**	**16:48**	**16**	**2**	**7**	**9**	**10**	**2**	**0**	**0**	**16:33**
2006-07 ♦	**Anaheim**	**NHL**	**82**	**27**	**51**	**78**	**46**	**8**	**0**	**3**	**252**	**10.7**	**16**	**908**	**55.4**	**17:35**	**21**	**10**	**4**	**14**	**10**	**5**	**0**	**0**	**18:37**
2007-08	**Anaheim**	**NHL**	**33**	**4**	**12**	**16**	**30**	**0**	**0**	**0**	**79**	**5.1**	**–4**	**392**	**55.4**	**16:41**	....	....	....	....	....	....	....	....	....
	St. Louis	**NHL**	**49**	**14**	**22**	**36**	**32**	**3**	**0**	**1**	**103**	**13.6**	**–17**	**556**	**55.8**	**18:40**	....	....	....	....	....	....	....	....	....
2008-09	**St. Louis**	**NHL**	**46**	**15**	**29**	**44**	**24**	**6**	**1**	**1**	**128**	**11.7**	**–13**	**367**	**58.0**	**19:05**	**4**	**1**	**3**	**4**	**0**	**0**	**0**	**0**	**23:35**
2009-10	**St. Louis**	**NHL**	**79**	**24**	**33**	**57**	**18**	**6**	**0**	**3**	**191**	**12.6**	**–9**	**447**	**53.9**	**18:08**	....	....	....	....	....	....	....	....	....
	NHL Totals		**565**	**145**	**251**	**396**	**236**	**43**	**2**	**20**	**1336**	**10.9**		**5608**	**55.2**	**17:19**	**41**	**13**	**14**	**27**	**20**	**7**	**0**	**0**	**18:18**

CAC Second All-Star Team (1999) • ECAC First All-Star Team (2000) • ECAC Player of the Year (2000) • NCAA East First All-American Team (2000)

layed in NHL All-Star Game (2007)

igned as a free agent by **Anaheim**, April 3, 2000. Signed as a free agent by **Ingolstadt** (Germany), September 17, 2004. Traded to **St. Louis** by **Anaheim** for Doug Weight, Michal Birner and St. Louis' th round choice (later traded to Los Angeles, later traded back to St. Louis - St. Louis selected Paul Karpowich) in 2008 Entry Draft, December 14, 2007.

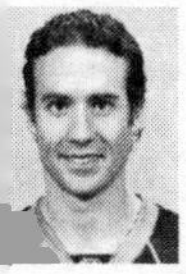

McDONALD, Colin
(muhk-DAWN-uhld, KAW-lihn)

Right wing. Shoots right. 6'2", 190 lbs. Born, New Haven, CT, September 30, 1984. Edmonton's 2nd choice, 51st overall, in 2003 Entry Draft.

2001-02	N.E. Jr. Coyotes	EJHL	39	16	20	36	50	....	....	....	....	....	....	....	....	....	....	....	....	....	....	....	....	....	....
2002-03	N.E. Jr. Coyotes	EJHL	44	28	40	*68	59	....	....	....	....	....	....	....	....	....	....	....	....	....	....	....	....	....	....
2003-04	Providence	H-East	37	10	6	16	47	....	....	....	....	....	....	....	....	....	....	....	....	....	....	....	....	....	....
2004-05	Providence	H-East	26	11	5	16	14	....	....	....	....	....	....	....	....	....	....	....	....	....	....	....	....	....	....
2005-06	Providence	H-East	36	9	19	28	29	....	....	....	....	....	....	....	....	....	....	....	....	....	....	....	....	....	....
2006-07	Providence	H-East	36	13	4	17	30	....	....	....	....	....	....	....	....	....	....	....	....	....	....	....	....	....	....
2007-08	Springfield	AHL	73	12	11	23	46	....	....	....	....	....	....	....	....	....	....	....	....	....	....	....	....	....	....
2008-09	Springfield	AHL	77	10	12	22	65	....	....	....	....	....	....	....	....	....	....	....	....	....	....	....	....	....	....
	Stockton Thunder	ECHL	3	0	2	2	0	....	....	....	....	....	....	....	....	....	....	....	....	....	....	....	....	....	....
2009-10	**Edmonton**	**NHL**	**2**	**1**	**0**	**1**	**0**	**0**	**0**	**0**	**3**	**33.3**	**1**	**0**	**0.0**	**6:42**	....	....	....	....	....	....	....	....	....
	Springfield	AHL	76	12	11	23	38	....	....	....	....	....	....	....	....	....	....	....	....	....	....	....	....	....	....
	NHL Totals		**2**	**1**	**0**	**1**	**0**	**0**	**0**	**0**	**3**	**33.3**		**0**	**0.0**	**6:42**	....	....	....	....	....	....	....	....	....

ockey East All-Rookie Team (2004)

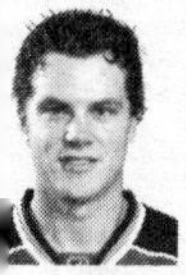

McGINN, Jamie
(muh-GIHN, JAY-mee) **S.J.**

Left wing. Shoots left. 6'1", 200 lbs. Born, Fergus, Ont., August 5, 1988. San Jose's 2nd choice, 36th overall, in 2006 Entry Draft.

2003-04	Tor. Jr. Canadiens	GTHL	31	....	....	48	....										18	14	18	32		....	....	....	....
2004-05	Ottawa 67's	OHL	59	10	12	22	35	....	....	....	....	....	....	....	....	....	18	4	7	11	0	....	....	....	....
2005-06	Ottawa 67's	OHL	65	26	31	57	113	....	....	....	....	....	....	....	....	....	6	2	2	4	4	....	....	....	....
2006-07	Ottawa 67's	OHL	68	46	43	89	49	....	....	....	....	....	....	....	....	....	5	5	1	6	2	....	....	....	....
	Worcester Sharks	AHL	4	1	1	2	4	....	....	....	....	....	....	....	....	....	6	0	0	0	8	....	....	....	....
2007-08	Ottawa 67's	OHL	51	29	29	58	54	....	....	....	....	....	....	....	....	....	4	2	2	4	4	....	....	....	....
	Worcester Sharks	AHL	8	0	2	2	0	....	....	....	....	....	....	....	....	....	....	....	....	....	....	....	....	....	....
2008-09	**San Jose**	**NHL**	**35**	**4**	**2**	**6**	**2**	**1**	**0**	**1**	**27**	**14.8**	**–6**	**7**	**85.7**	**8:55**	....	....	....	....	....	....	....	....	....
	Worcester Sharks	AHL	47	19	11	30	52	....	....	....	....	....	....	....	....	....	6	4	0	4	19	....	....	....	....
2009-10	**San Jose**	**NHL**	**59**	**10**	**3**	**13**	**38**	**0**	**0**	**2**	**76**	**13.2**	**–3**	**16**	**43.8**	**10:00**	**15**	**0**	**0**	**0**	**8**	**0**	**0**	**0**	**7:45**
	Worcester Sharks	AHL	27	7	14	21	15	....	....	....	....	....	....	....	....	....	....	....	....	....	....	....	....	....	....
	NHL Totals		**94**	**14**	**5**	**19**	**40**	**1**	**0**	**3**	**103**	**13.6**		**23**	**56.5**	**9:36**	**15**	**0**	**0**	**0**	**8**	**0**	**0**	**0**	**7:45**

			Regular Season														Playoffs							
Season	Club	League	GP	G	A	Pts	PIM	PP	SH	GW	S	%	+/-	TF	F%	Min	GP	G	A	Pts	PIM	PP	SH	GW	Mi

McGRATTAN, Brian

(muh-GRA-tuhn, BRIGH-uhn)

Right wing. Shoots right. 6'4", 235 lbs.   Born, Hamilton, Ont., September 2, 1981. Los Angeles' 5th choice, 104th overall, in 1999 Entry Draft.

Season	Club	League	GP	G	A	Pts	PIM	PP	SH	GW	S	%	+/-	TF	F%	Min	GP	G	A	Pts	PIM
1997-98	Guelph Fire	OHA-B	15	4	3	7	94														
	Guelph Storm	OHL	25	3	2	5	11														
1998-99	Guelph Storm	OHL	6	1	3	4	15														
	Sudbury Wolves	OHL	53	7	10	17	153										4	0	0	0	8
99-2000	Sudbury Wolves	OHL	25	2	8	10	79														
	Mississauga	OHL	42	9	13	22	166														
2000-01	Mississauga	OHL	31	20	9	29	83														
2001-02	Mississauga	OHL	7	2	3	5	16														
	Owen Sound	OHL	2	0	0	0	0														
	Oshawa Generals	OHL	25	10	5	15	72										6	2	0	2	20
	Sault Ste. Marie	OHL	26	8	7	15	71										1	0	0	0	0
2002-03	Binghamton	AHL	59	9	10	19	173										1	0	0	0	0
2003-04	Binghamton	AHL	66	9	11	20	327														
2004-05	Binghamton	AHL	71	7	1	8	*551										6	1	2	2	28
2005-06	Ottawa	NHL	60	2	3	5	141	0	0	0	36	5.6	0	0	0.0	4:14					
2006-07	Ottawa	NHL	45	0	2	2	100	0	0	0	22	0.0	-1	1100.0		3:51					
2007-08	Ottawa	NHL	38	0	3	3	46	0	0	0	11	0.0	0	0	0.0	2:52					
2008-09	Phoenix	NHL	5	0	0	0	22	0	0	0	2	0.0	-2	0	0.0	5:31					
	San Antonio	AHL	1	0	0	0	2														
2009-10	Calgary	NHL	34	1	3	4	86	0	0	0	19	5.3	3	0	0.0	3:26					
	NHL Totals		182	3	11	14	395	0	0	0	90	3.3		1100.0		3:45					

• Missed majority of 2000-01 season recovering from knee injury suffered in game vs. Kingston (OHL), January 1, 2001. Signed as a free agent by **Ottawa**, June 2, 2002. • Missed majority of 2007-08 season as a healthy reserve. Traded to **Phoenix** by **Ottawa** for Boston's 5th round choice (previously acquired, Ottawa selected Jeff Costello) in 2009 Entry Draft, June 25, 2008. Signed as a free agent by **Calgary**, July 11, 2009. • Missed majority of 2009-10 season as a healthy reserve.

McIVER, Nathan

(muh-KEE-vuhr, NAY-thuhn)   **BOS.**

Defense. Shoots left. 6'2", 211 lbs.   Born, Summerside, P.E.I., January 6, 1985. Vancouver's 9th choice, 254th overall, in 2003 Entry Draft.

Season	Club	League	GP	G	A	Pts	PIM	PP	SH	GW	S	%	+/-	TF	F%	Min	GP	G	A	Pts	PIM
2001-02	Summerside	MJrHL	47	4	4	8	91										5	0	0	0	9
2002-03	St. Michael's	OHL	68	5	10	15	121										19	0	4	4	41
2003-04	St. Michael's	OHL	57	4	11	15	183										16	0	1	1	22
2004-05	St. Michael's	OHL	67	4	22	26	160										3	0	1	1	13
2005-06	Manitoba Moose	AHL	66	1	6	7	155										12	0	0	0	28
2006-07	Vancouver	NHL	1	0	0	0	7	0	0	0	0	0.0	-3	0	0.0	11:20					
	Manitoba Moose	AHL	63	1	2	3	139										2	0	0	0	0
2007-08	Vancouver	NHL	17	0	0	0	52	0	0	0	9	0.0	-8	0	0.0	10:28					
	Manitoba Moose	AHL	43	3	3	6	108										6	0	1	1	11
2008-09	Anaheim	NHL	18	0	1	1	36	0	0	0	5	0.0	2	0	0.0	9:24					
	Manitoba Moose	AHL	28	0	2	2	59														
2009-10	Manitoba Moose	AHL	44	1	4	5	109										10	0	0	0	0
	NHL Totals		36	0	1	1	95	0	0	0	14	0.0		0	0.0	9:57					

Claimed on waivers by **Anaheim** from **Vancouver**, October 4, 2008. Traded to **Vancouver** by **Anaheim** for Mike Brown, February 4, 2009. Signed as a free agent by **Boston**, July 5, 2010.

McKEE, Jay

(muh-KEE, JAY)

Defense. Shoots left. 6'4", 203 lbs.   Born, Kingston, Ont., September 8, 1977. Buffalo's 1st choice, 14th overall, in 1995 Entry Draft.

Season	Club	League	GP	G	A	Pts	PIM	PP	SH	GW	S	%	+/-	TF	F%	Min	GP	G	A	Pts	PIM	PP	SH	GW	Mi
1992-93	Ernestown Jets	OHA-C	36	0	17	17	37																		
	Kingston	MTJHL	2	0	0	0	0																		
1993-94	Sudbury Wolves	OHL	51	0	1	1	51										3	0	0	0	0				
1994-95	Sudbury Wolves	OHL	39	6	6	12	91																		
	Niagara Falls	OHL	26	3	13	16	60										6	2	3	5	10				
1995-96	Niagara Falls	OHL	64	5	41	46	129										10	1	5	6	16				
	Buffalo	NHL	1	0	1	1	2	0	0	0	2	0.0	1												
	Rochester	AHL	4	0	1	1	15																		
1996-97	Buffalo	NHL	43	1	9	10	35	0	0	0	29	3.4	3				3	0	0	0	0	0	0	0	
	Rochester	AHL	7	2	5	7	4																		
1997-98	Buffalo	NHL	56	1	13	14	42	0	0	0	55	1.8	-1				1	0	0	0	0	0	0	0	
	Rochester	AHL	13	1	7	8	11																		
1998-99	Buffalo	NHL	72	0	6	6	75	0	0	0	57	0.0	20	0	0.0	20:28	21	0	3	3	24	0	0	0	22:31
99-2000	Buffalo	NHL	78	5	12	17	50	1	0	1	84	6.0	5	0	0.0	20:58	1	0	0	0	0	0	0	0	17:57
2000-01	Buffalo	NHL	74	1	10	11	76	0	0	0	62	1.6	9	2	0.0	19:24	8	1	0	1	6	0	0	1	19:23
2001-02	Buffalo	NHL	81	2	11	13	43	0	0	0	50	4.0	18	0	0.0	19:26									
2002-03	Buffalo	NHL	59	0	5	5	49	0	0	0	44	0.0	-16	0	0.0	18:45									
2003-04	Buffalo	NHL	43	2	3	5	41	0	0	0	29	6.9	6	0	0.0	17:44									
2004-05			DID NOT PLAY																						
2005-06	Buffalo	NHL	75	5	11	16	57	0	1	0	50	10.0	0	1	0.0	18:03	17	2	3	5	30	0	0	1	20:17
2006-07	St. Louis	NHL	23	0	0	0	12	0	0	0	19	0.0	-9	0	0.0	20:14									
2007-08	St. Louis	NHL	66	2	7	9	44	0	0	2	42	4.8	2	0	0.0	17:54									
2008-09	St. Louis	NHL	69	1	7	8	44	0	0	0	43	2.3	11	2	0.0	17:19	4	0	0	0	4	0	0	0	14:56
2009-10	Pittsburgh	NHL	62	1	9	10	54	0	0	0	42	2.4	6	1	0.0	15:26	5	0	0	0	2	0	0	0	14:56
	NHL Totals		802	21	104	125	622	1	1	6	608	3.5		6	0.0	18:43	60	3	6	9	66	0	0	2	20:06

OHL Second All-Star Team (1996)

Signed as a free agent by **St. Louis**, July 1, 2006. • Missed majority of 2006-07 season recovering from hand injury suffered in game vs. Vancouver, October 20, 2006. Signed as a free agent by **Pittsburgh**, July 10, 2009.

McLAREN, Frazer

(muh-KLAIR-uhn, FRAY-zuhr)   **S.J.**

Left wing. Shoots left. 6'5", 250 lbs.   Born, Winnipeg, Man., October 29, 1987. San Jose's 8th choice, 203rd overall, in 2007 Entry Draft.

Season	Club	League	GP	G	A	Pts	PIM	PP	SH	GW	S	%	+/-	TF	F%	Min	GP	G	A	Pts	PIM
2002-03	Kelvin	High-MB	56	27	24	51	136														
2003-04	Portland	WHL	50	0	3	3	44										1	0	0	0	0
2004-05	Portland	WHL	71	6	5	11	124										7	0	0	0	10
2005-06	Portland	WHL	70	12	6	18	194										12	0	2	2	27
2006-07	Portland	WHL	61	19	12	31	186														
2007-08	Portland	WHL	18	4	3	7	45														
	Moose Jaw	WHL	48	15	18	33	119										6	1	1	2	8
	Worcester Sharks	AHL	4	0	1	1	17														
2008-09	Worcester Sharks	AHL	75	7	1	8	181										12	1	4	5	*50
2009-10	San Jose	NHL	23	1	5	6	54	0	0	0	13	7.7	6	0	0.0	6:02					
	Worcester Sharks	AHL	52	4	11	15	148										11	0	0	0	37
	NHL Totals		23	1	5	6	54	0	0	0	13	7.7		0	0.0	6:02					

McLEAN, Brett

(muh-KLAYN, BREHT)

Center. Shoots left. 5'11", 185 lbs.   Born, Comox, B.C., August 14, 1978. Dallas' 9th choice, 242nd overall, in 1997 Entry Draft.

Season	Club	League	GP	G	A	Pts	PIM	PP	SH	GW	S	%	+/-	TF	F%	Min	GP	G	A	Pts	PIM
1993-94	Notre Dame	SMBHL	71	109	124	233	70														
1994-95	Tacoma Rockets	WHL	67	11	23	34	33										4	0	1	1	0
1995-96	Kelowna Rockets	WHL	71	37	42	79	60										6	2	2	4	6
1996-97	Kelowna Rockets	WHL	72	44	60	104	98										6	4	2	6	12
1997-98	Kelowna Rockets	WHL	54	42	45	87	91										7	4	5	9	17
1998-99	Kelowna Rockets	WHL	44	32	38	70	46														
	Brandon	WHL	21	15	16	31	20										5	1	6	7	8
	Cincinnati	AHL	7	0	3	3	6														
99-2000	Johnstown Chiefs	ECHL	8	4	7	11	6														
	Saint John Flames	AHL	72	15	23	38	115										3	0	1	1	2
2000-01	Cleveland	IHL	74	20	24	44	54										4	0	0	0	18
2001-02	Houston Aeros	AHL	78	24	21	45	71										14	1	6	7	12

			Regular Season														Playoffs								
Season	Club	League	GP	G	A	Pts	PIM	PP	SH	GW	S	%	+/-	TF	F%	Min	GP	G	A	Pts	PIM	PP	SH	GW	Min
2002-03	**Chicago**	**NHL**	**2**	**0**	**0**	**0**	**0**	**0**	**0**	**0**	**1**	**0.0**	**-1**	**19**	**26.3**	**10:47**	....	....	....	....	....	....	....	....	....
	Norfolk Admirals	AHL	77	23	38	61	60	....	....	....	....	....	....	....	....	....	9	2	6	8	9	....	....	....	....
2003-04	**Chicago**	**NHL**	**76**	**11**	**20**	**31**	**54**	**5**	**1**	**0**	**125**	**8.8**	**-11**	**1135**	**51.1**	**17:33**	....	....	....	....	....	....	....	....	....
	Norfolk Admirals	AHL	4	3	3	6	6	....	....	....	....	....	....	....	....	....	....	....	....	....	....	....	....	....	....
2004-05	Malmo	Sweden	38	7	6	13	102	....	....	....	....	....	....	....	....	....	....	....	....	....	....	....	....	....	....
	Malmo	Sweden-Q	9	1	1	2	16	....	....	....	....	....	....	....	....	....	....	....	....	....	....	....	....	....	....
2005-06	**Colorado**	**NHL**	**82**	**9**	**31**	**40**	**51**	**1**	**0**	**0**	**115**	**7.8**	**-7**	**770**	**50.7**	**12:12**	**8**	**0**	**1**	**1**	**4**	**0**	**0**	**0**	**10:40**
2006-07	**Colorado**	**NHL**	**78**	**15**	**20**	**35**	**36**	**0**	**0**	**3**	**134**	**11.2**	**8**	**413**	**50.1**	**13:38**	....	....	....	....	....	....	....	....	....
2007-08	**Florida**	**NHL**	**67**	**14**	**23**	**37**	**34**	**3**	**1**	**1**	**140**	**10.0**	**-5**	**624**	**47.4**	**16:14**	....	....	....	....	....	....	....	....	....
2008-09	**Florida**	**NHL**	**80**	**7**	**12**	**19**	**29**	**0**	**0**	**2**	**114**	**6.1**	**-12**	**456**	**43.2**	**12:26**	....	....	....	....	....	....	....	....	....
2009-10	SC Bern	Swiss	34	13	20	33	24	....	....	....	....	....	....	....	....	....	15	5	7	12	8	....	....	....	....
	NHL Totals		**385**	**56**	**106**	**162**	**204**	**9**	**2**	**6**	**629**	**8.9**		**3417**	**49.0**	**14:17**	**8**	**0**	**1**	**1**	**4**	**0**	**0**	**0**	**10:40**

HL West Second All-Star Team (1998)

gned as a free agent by **Calgary**, September 1, 1999. Signed as a free agent by **Minnesota**, July 13, 2000. Signed as a free agent by **Chicago**, July 23, 2002. Signed as a free agent by **Colorado**, July 22, 004. Signed as a free agent by **Malmo** (Sweden), September 24, 2004. Signed as a free agent by **Florida**, July 1, 2007. Signed as a free agent by **Bern** (Swiss), October 10, 2009.

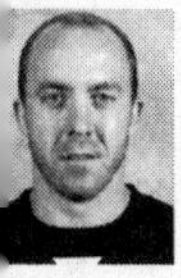

McLEAN, Kurtis

(muh-KLAYN, KUHR-this)

Center. Shoots right. 5'11", 175 lbs. Born, Kirkland Lake, Ont., November 2, 1980.

Season	Club	League	GP	G	A	Pts	PIM	PP	SH	GW	S	%	+/-	TF	F%	Min	GP	G	A	Pts	PIM	PP	SH	GW	Min
2005-06	Wilkes-Barre	AHL	32	4	11	15	8	....	....	....	....	....	....	....	....	....	....	....	....	....	....	....	....	....	....
	Wheeling Nailers	ECHL	41	31	25	56	32	....	....	....	....	....	....	....	....	....	5	4	4	8	4	....	....	....	....
2006-07	Wilkes-Barre	AHL	55	16	16	32	24	....	....	....	....	....	....	....	....	....	10	4	3	7	4	....	....	....	....
	Wheeling Nailers	ECHL	16	11	12	23	21	....	....	....	....	....	....	....	....	....	....	....	....	....	....	....	....	....	....
2007-08	Wilkes-Barre	AHL	76	22	32	54	58	....	....	....	....	....	....	....	....	....	23	4	15	19	8	....	....	....	....
2008-09	**NY Islanders**	**NHL**	**4**	**1**	**0**	**1**	**0**	**0**	**0**	**1**	**5**	**20.0**	**1**	**1**	**0.0**	**10:34**	....	....	....	....	....	....	....	....	....
	Bridgeport	AHL	62	15	37	52	30	....	....	....	....	....	....	....	....	....	....	....	....	....	....	....	....	....	....
2009-10	Lukko Rauma	Finland	42	18	25	43	28	....	....	....	....	....	....	....	....	....	4	0	1	1	10	....	....	....	....
	NHL Totals		**4**	**1**	**0**	**1**	**0**	**0**	**0**	**1**	**5**	**20.0**		**1**	**0.0**	**10:34**	....	....	....	....	....	....	....	....	....

gned as a free agent by **Wilkes-Barre** (AHL), September 29, 2005. Signed as a free agent by **Pittsburgh**, September 7, 2006. Signed as a free agent by **NY Islanders**, July 3, 2008. Signed as a free agent **Rauma** (Finland), May 29, 2009.

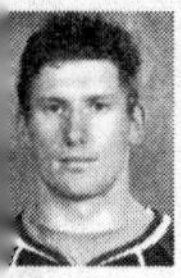

McLEOD, Cody

(muh-KLOWD, KOH-dee) **COL.**

Left wing. Shoots left. 6'2", 210 lbs. Born, Binscarth, Man., June 26, 1984.

Season	Club	League	GP	G	A	Pts	PIM	PP	SH	GW	S	%	+/-	TF	F%	Min	GP	G	A	Pts	PIM	PP	SH	GW	Min
2001-02	Portland	WHL	47	10	3	13	86	....	....	....	....	....	....	....	....	....	5	0	0	0	0	....	....	....	....
2002-03	Portland	WHL	71	15	18	33	153	....	....	....	....	....	....	....	....	....	7	1	1	2	13	....	....	....	....
2003-04	Portland	WHL	69	13	18	31	227	....	....	....	....	....	....	....	....	....	5	2	2	4	6	....	....	....	....
2004-05	Portland	WHL	70	31	29	60	195	....	....	....	....	....	....	....	....	....	7	0	3	3	8	....	....	....	....
	Adirondack	UHL	1	0	0	0	0	....	....	....	....	....	....	....	....	....	5	0	0	0	11	....	....	....	....
2005-06	Lowell	AHL	33	4	5	9	87	....	....	....	....	....	....	....	....	....	....	....	....	....	....	....	....	....	....
	San Diego Gulls	ECHL	16	4	5	9	48	....	....	....	....	....	....	....	....	....	2	2	1	3	14	....	....	....	....
2006-07	Albany River Rats	AHL	73	11	8	19	180	....	....	....	....	....	....	....	....	....	5	0	0	0	4	....	....	....	....
2007-08	**Colorado**	**NHL**	**49**	**4**	**5**	**9**	**120**	**0**	**0**	**0**	**60**	**6.7**	**-6**	**3**	**0.0**	**10:07**	**10**	**1**	**1**	**2**	**26**	**0**	**0**	**0**	**12:23**
	Lake Erie	AHL	27	6	7	13	101	....	....	....	....	....	....	....	....	....	....	....	....	....	....	....	....	....	....
2008-09	**Colorado**	**NHL**	**79**	**15**	**5**	**20**	**162**	**0**	**0**	**3**	**118**	**12.7**	**-11**	**5**	**40.0**	**11:35**	....	....	....	....	....	....	....	....	....
2009-10	**Colorado**	**NHL**	**74**	**7**	**11**	**18**	**138**	**0**	**0**	**1**	**117**	**6.0**	**-13**	**13**	**30.8**	**12:56**	**6**	**0**	**0**	**0**	**5**	**0**	**0**	**0**	**11:03**
	NHL Totals		**202**	**26**	**21**	**47**	**420**	**0**	**0**	**4**	**295**	**8.8**		**21**	**28.6**	**11:43**	**16**	**1**	**1**	**2**	**31**	**0**	**0**	**0**	**11:53**

gned as a free agent by **Colorado**, July 6, 2006.

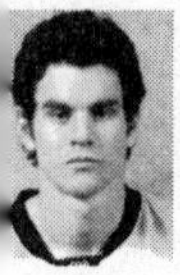

McQUAID, Adam

(muh-KWAYD, A-duhm) **BOS.**

Defense. Shoots right. 6'5", 209 lbs. Born, Charlottetown, P.E.I., October 12, 1986. Columbus' 2nd choice, 55th overall, in 2005 Entry Draft.

Season	Club	League	GP	G	A	Pts	PIM	PP	SH	GW	S	%	+/-	TF	F%	Min	GP	G	A	Pts	PIM	PP	SH	GW	Min
2003-04	Sudbury Wolves	OHL	47	3	6	9	25	....	....	....	....	....	....	....	....	....	7	0	1	1	2	....	....	....	....
2004-05	Sudbury Wolves	OHL	66	3	16	19	98	....	....	....	....	....	....	....	....	....	8	0	2	2	10	....	....	....	....
2005-06	Sudbury Wolves	OHL	68	3	14	17	107	....	....	....	....	....	....	....	....	....	10	0	1	1	16	....	....	....	....
2006-07	Sudbury Wolves	OHL	65	9	22	31	110	....	....	....	....	....	....	....	....	....	21	1	5	6	24	....	....	....	....
2007-08	Providence Bruins	AHL	68	1	8	9	73	....	....	....	....	....	....	....	....	....	10	0	0	0	9	....	....	....	....
2008-09	Providence Bruins	AHL	78	4	11	15	141	....	....	....	....	....	....	....	....	....	16	0	3	3	26	....	....	....	....
2009-10	**Boston**	**NHL**	**19**	**1**	**0**	**1**	**21**	**0**	**0**	**1**	**10**	**10.0**	**-5**	**0**	**0.0**	**10:44**	**9**	**0**	**0**	**0**	**6**	**0**	**0**	**0**	**10:12**
	Providence Bruins	AHL	32	3	7	10	66	....	....	....	....	....	....	....	....	....	....	....	....	....	....	....	....	....	....
	NHL Totals		**19**	**1**	**0**	**1**	**21**	**0**	**0**	**1**	**10**	**10.0**		**0**	**0.0**	**10:44**	**9**	**0**	**0**	**0**	**6**	**0**	**0**	**0**	**10:12**

aded to **Boston** by **Columbus** for Boston's 5th round choice (later traded to Dallas - Dallas selected Jamie Benn) in 2007 Entry Draft, May 16, 2007.

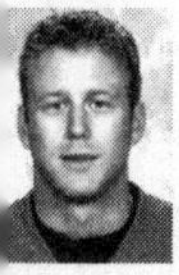

MEECH, Derek

(MEECH, DAIR-ihk) **DET.**

Defense. Shoots left. 5'11", 200 lbs. Born, Winnipeg, Man., April 21, 1984. Detroit's 7th choice, 229th overall, in 2002 Entry Draft.

Season	Club	League	GP	G	A	Pts	PIM	PP	SH	GW	S	%	+/-	TF	F%	Min	GP	G	A	Pts	PIM	PP	SH	GW	Min
99-2000	Wpg. Warriors	MMMHL	36	15	40	55	24	....	....	....	....	....	....	....	....	....	....	....	....	....	....	....	....	....	....
	Red Deer Rebels	WHL	5	1	0	1	2	....	....	....	....	....	....	....	....	....	....	....	....	....	....	....	....	....	....
2000-01	Red Deer Rebels	WHL	60	2	7	9	40	....	....	....	....	....	....	....	....	....	22	0	0	0	9	....	....	....	....
2001-02	Red Deer Rebels	WHL	71	8	19	27	33	....	....	....	....	....	....	....	....	....	13	1	1	2	6	....	....	....	....
2002-03	Red Deer Rebels	WHL	65	6	16	22	53	....	....	....	....	....	....	....	....	....	12	1	1	2	12	....	....	....	....
2003-04	Red Deer Rebels	WHL	62	10	28	38	40	....	....	....	....	....	....	....	....	....	19	4	7	11	10	....	....	....	....
2004-05	Grand Rapids	AHL	78	6	8	14	40	....	....	....	....	....	....	....	....	....	....	....	....	....	....	....	....	....	....
2005-06	Grand Rapids	AHL	79	4	16	20	85	....	....	....	....	....	....	....	....	....	16	0	2	2	4	....	....	....	....
2006-07	**Detroit**	**NHL**	**4**	**0**	**0**	**0**	**2**	**0**	**0**	**0**	**3**	**0.0**	**1**	**0**	**0.0**	**5:47**	....	....	....	....	....	....	....	....	....
	Grand Rapids	AHL	67	6	23	29	40	....	....	....	....	....	....	....	....	....	7	0	1	1	4	....	....	....	....
2007-08	**Detroit**	**NHL**	**32**	**0**	**3**	**3**	**6**	**0**	**0**	**0**	**44**	**0.0**	**-5**	**0**	**0.0**	**12:08**	....	....	....	....	....	....	....	....	....
	Grand Rapids	AHL	6	1	1	2	0	....	....	....	....	....	....	....	....	....	....	....	....	....	....	....	....	....	....
2008-09	**Detroit**	**NHL**	**41**	**2**	**5**	**7**	**12**	**0**	**0**	**0**	**44**	**4.5**	**-12**	**2**	**0.0**	**10:03**	**2**	**0**	**0**	**0**	**0**	**0**	**0**	**0**	**4:04**
2009-10	**Detroit**	**NHL**	**49**	**2**	**4**	**6**	**19**	**1**	**0**	**2**	**57**	**3.5**	**-12**	**0**	**0.0**	**11:55**	....	....	....	....	....	....	....	....	....
	NHL Totals		**126**	**4**	**12**	**16**	**39**	**1**	**0**	**2**	**148**	**2.7**		**2**	**0.0**	**11:10**	**2**	**0**	**0**	**0**	**0**	**0**	**0**	**0**	**4:04**

HL East Second All-Star Team (2004)

Missed majority of 2007-08 season as a healthy reserve.

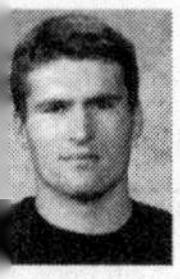

MELICHAR, Josef

(mehl-ee-KHAHR, YOH-sehf)

Defense. Shoots left. 6'2", 220 lbs. Born, Ceske Budejovice, Czech., January 20, 1979. Pittsburgh's 3rd choice, 71st overall, in 1997 Entry Draft.

Season	Club	League	GP	G	A	Pts	PIM	PP	SH	GW	S	%	+/-	TF	F%	Min	GP	G	A	Pts	PIM	PP	SH	GW	Min
1995-96	C. Budejovice Jr.	CzRep-Jr.	38	3	4	7	....	....	....	....	....	....	....	....	....	....	....	....	....	....	....	....	....	....	....
1996-97	C. Budejovice Jr.	CzRep-Jr.	41	2	3	5	10	....	....	....	....	....	....	....	....	....	....	....	....	....	....	....	....	....	....
1997-98	Tri-City	WHL	67	9	24	33	154	....	....	....	....	....	....	....	....	....	....	....	....	....	....	....	....	....	....
1998-99	Tri-City	WHL	65	8	28	36	125	....	....	....	....	....	....	....	....	....	11	1	0	1	15	....	....	....	....
99-2000	Wilkes-Barre	AHL	80	3	9	12	126	....	....	....	....	....	....	....	....	....	....	....	....	....	....	....	....	....	....
2000-01	**Pittsburgh**	**NHL**	**18**	**0**	**2**	**2**	**21**	**0**	**0**	**0**	**9**	**0.0**	**-5**	**0**	**0.0**	**14:54**	....	....	....	....	....	....	....	....	....
	Wilkes-Barre	AHL	46	2	5	7	69	....	....	....	....	....	....	....	....	....	21	0	5	5	6	....	....	....	....
2001-02	**Pittsburgh**	**NHL**	**60**	**0**	**3**	**3**	**68**	**0**	**0**	**0**	**46**	**0.0**	**-1**	**0**	**0.0**	**16:46**	....	....	....	....	....	....	....	....	....
2002-03	**Pittsburgh**	**NHL**	**8**	**0**	**0**	**0**	**2**	**0**	**0**	**0**	**6**	**0.0**	**-2**	**0**	**0.0**	**15:19**	....	....	....	....	....	....	....	....	....
2003-04	**Pittsburgh**	**NHL**	**82**	**3**	**5**	**8**	**62**	**0**	**0**	**0**	**78**	**3.8**	**-17**	**0**	**0.0**	**19:01**	....	....	....	....	....	....	....	....	....
2004-05	HC Sparta Praha	CzRep	13	0	4	4	8	....	....	....	....	....	....	....	....	....	5	0	0	0	6	....	....	....	....
2005-06	**Pittsburgh**	**NHL**	**72**	**3**	**12**	**15**	**66**	**0**	**1**	**0**	**53**	**5.7**	**-2**	**0**	**0.0**	**17:26**	....	....	....	....	....	....	....	....	....
2006-07	**Pittsburgh**	**NHL**	**70**	**1**	**11**	**12**	**44**	**0**	**0**	**0**	**57**	**1.8**	**1**	**0**	**0.0**	**18:49**	**5**	**0**	**0**	**0**	**2**	**0**	**0**	**0**	**17:21**
2007-08	C. Budejovice	CzRep	6	0	0	0	4	....	....	....	....	....	....	....	....	....	....	....	....	....	....	....	....	....	....
	Linkopings HC	Sweden	50	0	8	8	74	....	....	....	....	....	....	....	....	....	16	1	1	2	39	....	....	....	....

Season	Club	League	GP	G	A	Pts	PIM	PP	SH	GW	S	%	+/-	TF	F%	Min	GP	G	A	Pts	PIM	PP	SH	GW	Min
			Regular Season														Playoffs								
2008-09	**Carolina**	**NHL**	**15**	**0**	**4**	**4**	**8**	**0**	**0**	**0**	**3**	**0.0**	**−1**	**0**	**0.0**	**8:40**									
	Albany River Rats	AHL	25	1	4	5	35																		
	Tampa Bay	**NHL**	**24**	**0**	**5**	**5**	**29**	**0**	**0**	**0**	**16**	**0.0**	**1**	**0**	**0.0**	**16:58**									
	Norfolk Admirals	AHL	1	0	0	0	0																		
2009-10	C. Budejovice	CzRep	52	5	9	14	80										5	0	0	0	6				
	NHL Totals		**349**	**7**	**42**	**49**	**300**	**0**	**1**	**0**	**268**	**2.6**		**0**	**0.0**	**17:23**	**5**	**0**	**0**	**0**	**2**	**0**	**0**	**0**	**17:2**

• Missed majority of 2002-03 season recovering from shoulder injury suffered in game vs. Boston, October 13, 2002. Signed as a free agent by **Sparta Praha** (CzRep), September 17, 2004. Signed as a free agent by **Linkopings** (Sweden), October 3, 2007. Signed as a free agent by **Carolina**, July 2, 2008. Traded to **Tampa Bay** by **Carolina** with Wade Brookbank and future considerations for Jussi Jokinen, February 7, 2009. Signed as a free agent by **Ceske Budejovice** (CzRep), July 25, 2009.

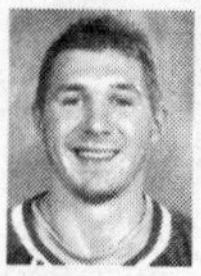

MERCIER, Justin

(MUHR-see-uhr, JUHS-tihn) **COL.**

Forward. Shoots left. 5'11", 190 lbs. Born, Erie, PA, June 25, 1987. Colorado's 8th choice, 168th overall, in 2005 Entry Draft.

Season	Club	League	GP	G	A	Pts	PIM	PP	SH	GW	S	%	+/-	TF	F%	Min	GP	G	A	Pts	PIM	PP	SH	GW	Min
2003-04	St. Louis	USHL	60	12	9	21																			
2004-05	USNTDP	U-18	26	1	7	8	31																		
	USNTDP	NAHL	16	4	3	7	33																		
2005-06	Miami U.	CCHA	35	3	7	10	32																		
2006-07	Miami U.	CCHA	40	10	15	25	59																		
2007-08	Miami U.	CCHA	42	25	15	40	42																		
2008-09	Miami U.	CCHA	40	14	15	29	58																		
2009-10	**Colorado**	**NHL**	**9**	**1**	**1**	**2**	**0**	**0**	**0**	**0**	**5**	**20.0**	**2**	**1**	**100.0**	**7:11**									
	Lake Erie	AHL	64	13	10	23	54																		
	NHL Totals		**9**	**1**	**1**	**2**	**0**	**0**	**0**	**0**	**5**	**20.0**		**1**	**100.0**	**7:11**									

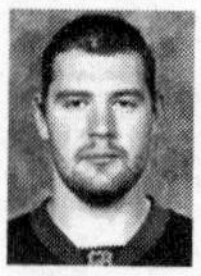

MESZAROS, Andrej

(MEHT-zahr-ohsh, AWN-dray) **PHI.**

Defense. Shoots left. 6'2", 223 lbs. Born, Povazska Bystrica, Czech., October 13, 1985. Ottawa's 1st choice, 23rd overall, in 2004 Entry Draft.

Season	Club	League	GP	G	A	Pts	PIM	PP	SH	GW	S	%	+/-	TF	F%	Min	GP	G	A	Pts	PIM	PP	SH	GW	Min
2002-03	Dukla Trencin Jr.	Slovak-Jr.	33	6	10	16	12																		
	Dukla Trencin	Slovakia	23	0	1	1	4																		
2003-04	Dukla Trencin	Slovakia	44	3	3	6	8										14	3	1	4	2				
	Dukla Trencin Jr.	Slovak-Jr.	5	2	2	4	0																		
2004-05	Vancouver Giants	WHL	59	11	30	41	94										6	1	3	4	14				
2005-06	**Ottawa**	**NHL**	**82**	**10**	**29**	**39**	**61**	**5**	**0**	**2**	**137**	**7.3**	**34**	**1**	**0.0**	**18:11**	**10**	**1**	**0**	**1**	**18**	**0**	**0**	**0**	**17:50**
	Slovakia	Olympics	6	0	2	2	4																		
2006-07	**Ottawa**	**NHL**	**82**	**7**	**28**	**35**	**102**	**0**	**0**	**1**	**147**	**4.8**	**−15**	**0**	**0.0**	**21:41**	**20**	**1**	**6**	**7**	**12**	**0**	**0**	**0**	**20:29**
2007-08	**Ottawa**	**NHL**	**82**	**9**	**27**	**36**	**50**	**6**	**1**	**1**	**160**	**5.6**	**5**	**1**	**0.0**	**21:02**	**4**	**0**	**1**	**1**	**6**	**0**	**0**	**0**	**18:59**
2008-09	**Tampa Bay**	**NHL**	**52**	**2**	**14**	**16**	**36**	**1**	**0**	**1**	**87**	**2.3**	**−4**	**1**	**0.0**	**24:11**									
2009-10	**Tampa Bay**	**NHL**	**81**	**6**	**11**	**17**	**50**	**2**	**0**	**1**	**145**	**4.1**	**−14**	**0**	**0.0**	**20:11**									
	Slovakia	Olympics	7	0	0	0	4																		
	NHL Totals		**379**	**34**	**109**	**143**	**299**	**14**	**1**	**6**	**676**	**5.0**		**3**	**0.0**	**20:48**	**34**	**2**	**7**	**9**	**36**	**0**	**0**	**0**	**19:32**

WHL West Second All-Star Team (2005) • NHL All-Rookie Team (2006)

Traded to **Tampa Bay** by **Ottawa** for Filip Kuba, Alexandre Picard and San Jose's 1st round choice (previously acquired, later traded to NY Islanders, later traded to Columbus, later traded to Anaheim - Anaheim selected Kyle Palmieri) in 2009 Entry Draft, August 29, 2008. Traded to **Philadelphia** by **Tampa Bay** for a 2nd round choice in 2011 Entry Draft, July 1, 2010.

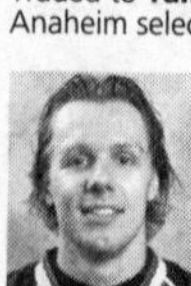

METHOT, Marc

(meh-THAWT, MAHRK) **CBJ**

Defense. Shoots left. 6'3", 230 lbs. Born, Ottawa, Ont., June 21, 1985. Columbus' 7th choice, 168th overall, in 2003 Entry Draft.

Season	Club	League	GP	G	A	Pts	PIM	PP	SH	GW	S	%	+/-	TF	F%	Min	GP	G	A	Pts	PIM	PP	SH	GW	Min
2001-02	Kanata Laser	CJHL	50	3	10	13	22																		
2002-03	London Knights	OHL	68	2	13	15	46										14	2	4	6	6				
2003-04	London Knights	OHL	63	2	9	11	66										15	0	3	3	18				
2004-05	London Knights	OHL	67	4	12	16	88										18	2	1	3	32				
2005-06	Syracuse Crunch	AHL	70	1	12	13	75										5	0	0	0	8				
2006-07	**Columbus**	**NHL**	**20**	**0**	**4**	**4**	**12**	**0**	**0**	**0**	**11**	**0.0**	**5**	**0**	**0.0**	**14:38**									
	Syracuse Crunch	AHL	59	1	15	16	58																		
2007-08	**Columbus**	**NHL**	**9**	**0**	**0**	**0**	**8**	**0**	**0**	**0**	**9**	**0.0**	**−1**	**0**	**0.0**	**14:14**									
	Syracuse Crunch	AHL	66	7	6	13	130										13	0	6	6	14				
2008-09	**Columbus**	**NHL**	**66**	**4**	**13**	**17**	**55**	**0**	**0**	**0**	**58**	**6.9**	**7**	**0**	**0.0**	**17:57**	**4**	**0**	**0**	**0**	**2**	**0**	**0**	**0**	**16:15**
2009-10	**Columbus**	**NHL**	**60**	**2**	**6**	**8**	**51**	**0**	**0**	**0**	**42**	**4.8**	**−8**	**0**	**0.0**	**19:31**									
	NHL Totals		**155**	**6**	**23**	**29**	**126**	**0**	**0**	**0**	**120**	**5.0**		**0**	**0.0**	**17:55**	**4**	**0**	**0**	**0**	**2**	**0**	**0**	**0**	**16:15**

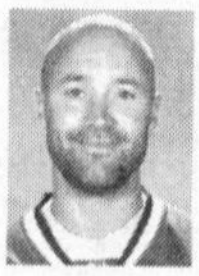

METROPOLIT, Glen

(meh-troh-PAW-liht, GLEHN)

Center. Shoots right. 5'10", 196 lbs. Born, Toronto, Ont., June 25, 1974.

Season	Club	League	GP	G	A	Pts	PIM	PP	SH	GW	S	%	+/-	TF	F%	Min	GP	G	A	Pts	PIM	PP	SH	GW	Min
1992-93	Richmond Hill	MTJHL	43	27	36	63	36																		
1993-94	Richmond Hill	MTJHL	49	38	62	100	83																		
1994-95	Vernon Vipers	BCJHL	60	43	74	117	92																		
1995-96	Nashville Knights	ECHL	58	30	31	61	62										5	3	8	11	2				
	Atlanta Knights	IHL	1	0	0	0	0																		
1996-97	Pensacola	ECHL	54	35	47	82	45										12	9	16	25	28				
	Quebec Rafales	IHL	22	5	4	9	14										5	0	0	0	2				
1997-98	Grand Rapids	IHL	79	20	35	55	90										3	1	1	2	0				
1998-99	Grand Rapids	IHL	77	28	53	81	92																		
99-2000	**Washington**	**NHL**	**30**	**6**	**13**	**19**	**4**	**1**	**0**	**1**	**57**	**10.5**	**5**	**37**	**46.0**	**13:17**	**2**	**0**	**0**	**0**	**2**	**0**	**0**	**0**	**7:07**
	Portland Pirates	AHL	48	18	42	60	73										1	1	0	1	0				
2000-01	**Washington**	**NHL**	**15**	**1**	**5**	**6**	**10**	**0**	**0**	**0**	**20**	**5.0**	**−2**	**3**	**33.3**	**11:50**	**1**	**0**	**0**	**0**	**0**	**0**	**0**	**0**	**7:03**
	Portland Pirates	AHL	51	25	42	67	59																		
2001-02	**Tampa Bay**	**NHL**	**2**	**0**	**0**	**0**	**0**	**0**	**0**	**0**	**1**	**0.0**	**−2**	**2**	**50.0**	**10:26**									
	Washington	**NHL**	**33**	**1**	**16**	**17**	**6**	**0**	**0**	**0**	**51**	**2.0**	**3**	**145**	**49.7**	**14:24**									
	Portland Pirates	AHL	32	17	22	39	20																		
2002-03	**Washington**	**NHL**	**23**	**2**	**3**	**5**	**6**	**0**	**0**	**1**	**22**	**9.1**	**4**	**99**	**49.5**	**10:07**									
	Portland Pirates	AHL	33	7	23	30	23										3	1	1	2	0				
2003-04	Jokerit Helsinki	Finland	55	15	35	50	77										7	6	1	7	33				
2004-05	Jokerit Helsinki	Finland	51	16	31	47	42										12	5	6	11	20				
2005-06	HC Lugano	Swiss	44	24	*39	*63	60										17	9	18	27	8				
2006-07	**Atlanta**	**NHL**	**57**	**12**	**16**	**28**	**20**	**4**	**0**	**2**	**92**	**13.0**	**9**	**206**	**49.0**	**11:47**									
	St. Louis	**NHL**	**20**	**2**	**3**	**5**	**14**	**1**	**0**	**0**	**31**	**6.5**	**0**	**154**	**50.0**	**12:58**									
2007-08	**Boston**	**NHL**	**82**	**11**	**22**	**33**	**36**	**1**	**0**	**5**	**141**	**7.8**	**−3**	**1242**	**49.4**	**16:26**	**7**	**1**	**0**	**1**	**4**	**0**	**0**	**1**	**16:27**
2008-09	**Philadelphia**	**NHL**	**55**	**4**	**10**	**14**	**15**	**1**	**0**	**0**	**63**	**6.3**	**−1**	**562**	**50.2**	**12:59**									
	Montreal	**NHL**	**21**	**2**	**1**	**3**	**13**	**0**	**0**	**0**	**19**	**10.5**	**−4**	**215**	**46.5**	**11:37**	**4**	**0**	**2**	**2**	**2**	**0**	**0**	**0**	**16:04**
2009-10	**Montreal**	**NHL**	**69**	**16**	**13**	**29**	**24**	**10**	**0**	**1**	**115**	**13.9**	**−1**	**661**	**49.5**	**13:34**	**16**	**0**	**2**	**2**	**4**	**0**	**0**	**0**	**6:43**
	NHL Totals		**407**	**57**	**102**	**159**	**148**	**18**	**0**	**10**	**612**	**9.3**		**3326**	**49.3**	**13:27**	**30**	**1**	**4**	**5**	**12**	**0**	**0**	**1**	**10:16**

Signed as a free agent by **Washington**, July 19, 1999. Claimed by **Tampa Bay** from **Washington** in Waiver Draft, September 28, 2001. Claimed on waivers by **Washington** from **Tampa Bay**, October 20, 2001. Signed as a free agent by **Jokerit Helsinki** (Finland), April 22, 2003. Claimed by **Ottawa** from **Washington** in Waiver Draft, October 3, 2003. Signed as a free agent by **Atlanta**, July 3, 2006. Traded to **St. Louis** by **Atlanta** with Atlanta's 1st (later traded to Calgary - Calgary selected Mikael Backlund) and 3rd (Brett Sonne) round choices in 2007 Entry Draft and Atlanta's 1st (later traded back to Atlanta - Atlanta selected Zach Bogosian) and 2nd (Philip McRae) round choices in 2008 Entry Draft for Keith Tkachuk, February 25, 2007. Signed as a free agent by **Boston**, October 3, 2007. Signed as a free agent by **Philadelphia**, July 1, 2008. Claimed on waivers by **Montreal** from **Philadelphia**, February 27, 2009. Signed as a free agent by **Zug** (Swiss), August 2, 2010.

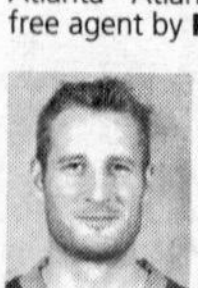

MEYER, Freddy

(MAY-uhr, FREH-dee)

Defense. Shoots left. 5'10", 192 lbs. Born, Sanbornville, NH, January 4, 1981.

Season	Club	League	GP	G	A	Pts	PIM	PP	SH	GW	S	%	+/-	TF	F%	Min	GP	G	A	Pts	PIM	PP	SH	GW	Min
1996-97	Cardigan Mtn.	High-NH	STATISTICS NOT AVAILABLE																						
1997-98	USNTDP	NAHL															2	1	0	1	37				
1998-99	USNTDP	U-18	6	1	4	5	8																		
	USNTDP	USHL	54	10	23	33	151																		
99-2000	USNTDP	USHL	28	3	8	11	60																		
	USNTDP	NAHL	3	0	2	2	0																		
	Boston University	H-East	25	1	11	12	52																		
2000-01	Boston University	H-East	28	6	13	19	82																		
2001-02	Boston University	H-East	37	5	15	20	78																		
2002-03	Boston University	H-East	36	5	16	21	76																		

Season	Club	League	GP	G	A	Pts	PIM	PP	SH	GW	S	%	+/-	TF	F%	Min	GP	G	A	Pts	PIM	PP	SH	GW	Min
			Regular Season														Playoffs								
2003-04	**Philadelphia**	**NHL**	1	0	0	0	0	0	0	0	1	0.0	0	0	0.0	15:24	....	....	....	....	....	....	....	....	....
	Philadelphia	AHL	59	14	14	28	50	....	....	....	....	....	....	....	....	....	12	0	3	3	8	....	....	....	....
2004-05	Philadelphia	AHL	59	6	9	15	71	....	....	....	....	....	....	....	....	....	21	3	9	12	34	....	....	....	....
2005-06	**Philadelphia**	**NHL**	57	6	21	27	33	2	0	0	68	8.8	10	0	0.0	17:56	6	0	1	1	8	0	0	0	18:23
	Philadelphia	AHL	11	3	3	6	22	....	....	....	....	....	....	....	....	....	....	....	....	....	....	....	....	....	....
2006-07	**Philadelphia**	**NHL**	25	2	3	5	14	1	0	0	27	7.4	–4	0	0.0	18:36	....	....	....	....	....	....	....	....	....
	NY Islanders	**NHL**	35	0	3	3	24	0	0	0	14	0.0	0	0	0.0	16:39	....	....	....	....	....	....	....	....	....
2007-08	**Phoenix**	**NHL**	5	0	0	0	0	0	0	0	2	0.0	–4	0	0.0	6:43	....	....	....	....	....	....	....	....	....
	San Antonio	AHL	8	0	2	2	12	....	....	....	....	....	....	....	....	....	....	....	....	....	....	....	....	....	....
	NY Islanders	**NHL**	52	3	9	12	22	0	0	2	49	6.1	6	0	0.0	19:54	....	....	....	....	....	....	....	....	....
2008-09	**NY Islanders**	**NHL**	27	4	5	9	14	0	0	1	36	11.1	–19	0	0.0	21:00	....	....	....	....	....	....	....	....	....
2009-10	**NY Islanders**	**NHL**	64	4	11	15	40	0	0	0	56	7.1	–2	0	0.0	16:46	....	....	....	....	....	....	....	....	....
	NHL Totals		266	19	52	71	147	3	0	3	253	7.5		0	0.0	18:01	6	0	1	1	8	0	0	0	18:23

ockey East All-Rookie Team (2000) • Hockey East First All-Star Team (2003) • NCAA East First All-American Team (2003)

gned as a free agent by **Philadelphia**, May 21, 2003. Traded to **NY Islanders** by **Philadelphia** with Philadelphia's 3rd round choice (Mark Katic) in 2007 Entry Draft for Alexei Zhitnik, December 16, 006. Claimed on waivers by **Phoenix** from **NY Islanders**, October 8, 2007. Claimed on waivers by **NY Islanders** from **Phoenix**, November 10, 2007. • Missed majority of 2008-09 season recovering from odominal and groin injuries.

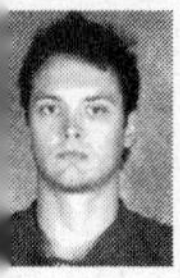

MEYER, Stefan
(MAY-uhr, STEH-fan) **CGY.**

Left wing. Shoots left. 6'2", 195 lbs. Born, Medicine Hat, Alta., July 20, 1985. Florida's 4th choice, 55th overall, in 2003 Entry Draft.

Season	Club	League	GP	G	A	Pts	PIM	PP	SH	GW	S	%	+/-	TF	F%	Min	GP	G	A	Pts	PIM	PP	SH	GW	Min
2000-01	Notre Dame	SBHL	50	36	52	88	71	....	....	....	....	....	....	....	....	....	....	....	....	....	....	....	....	....	....
2001-02	Medicine Hat	WHL	67	18	22	40	48	....	....	....	....	....	....	....	....	....	....	....	....	....	....	....	....	....	....
2002-03	Medicine Hat	WHL	70	36	16	52	90	....	....	....	....	....	....	....	....	....	11	3	3	6	14	....	....	....	....
2003-04	Medicine Hat	WHL	72	34	41	75	69	....	....	....	....	....	....	....	....	....	19	7	10	17	27	....	....	....	....
2004-05	Medicine Hat	WHL	69	34	43	77	104	....	....	....	....	....	....	....	....	....	13	2	4	6	8	....	....	....	....
2005-06	Rochester	AHL	68	12	16	28	139	....	....	....	....	....	....	....	....	....	....	....	....	....	....	....	....	....	....
2006-07	Rochester	AHL	63	13	9	22	90	....	....	....	....	....	....	....	....	....	6	0	2	2	8	....	....	....	....
2007-08	**Florida**	**NHL**	4	0	0	0	0	0	0	0	0	0.0	–1	6	50.0	2:26	....	....	....	....	....	....	....	....	....
	Rochester	AHL	70	21	19	40	77	....	....	....	....	....	....	....	....	....	....	....	....	....	....	....	....	....	....
2008-09	Rochester	AHL	65	18	22	40	57	....	....	....	....	....	....	....	....	....	....	....	....	....	....	....	....	....	....
2009-10	San Antonio	AHL	67	10	8	18	86	....	....	....	....	....	....	....	....	....	....	....	....	....	....	....	....	....	....
	NHL Totals		4	0	0	0	0	0	0	0	0	0.0		6	50.0	2:26	....	....	....	....	....	....	....	....	....

aded to **Phoenix** by **Florida** for Steve Reinprecht, June 19, 2009. Signed as a free agent by **Calgary**, July 20, 2010.

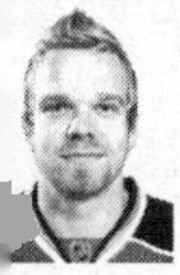

MICHALEK, Milan
(mih-KHAL-ihk, MEE-lan) **OTT.**

Right wing. Shoots left. 6'2", 225 lbs. Born, Jindrichuv Hradec, Czech., December 7, 1984. San Jose's 1st choice, 6th overall, in 2003 Entry Draft.

Season	Club	League	GP	G	A	Pts	PIM	PP	SH	GW	S	%	+/-	TF	F%	Min	GP	G	A	Pts	PIM	PP	SH	GW	Min
99-2000	C. Budejovice Jr.	CzRep-Jr.	48	16	26	42	42	....	....	....	....	....	....	....	....	....	6	3	1	4	4	....	....	....	....
2000-01	C. Budejovice Jr.	CzRep-Jr.	30	10	13	23	30	....	....	....	....	....	....	....	....	....	4	1	3	4	2	....	....	....	....
	C. Budejovice	CzRep	5	0	0	0	0	....	....	....	....	....	....	....	....	....	....	....	....	....	....	....	....	....	....
2001-02	C. Budejovice	CzRep	47	6	11	17	12	....	....	....	....	....	....	....	....	....	....	....	....	....	....	....	....	....	....
	C. Budejovice Jr.	CzRep-Jr.	5	3	2	5	4	....	....	....	....	....	....	....	....	....	7	5	4	9	14	....	....	....	....
2002-03	C. Budejovice	CzRep	46	3	5	8	14	....	....	....	....	....	....	....	....	....	4	1	0	1	2	....	....	....	....
	Kladno	CzRep-2	....	....	....	....	....	....	....	....	....	....	....	....	....	....	6	2	2	4	16	....	....	....	....
2003-04	**San Jose**	**NHL**	2	1	0	1	4	0	0	0	1	100.0	1	0	0.0	9:05	....	....	....	....	....	....	....	....	....
	Cleveland Barons	AHL	7	2	2	4	4	....	....	....	....	....	....	....	....	....	....	....	....	....	....	....	....	....	....
2004-05			DID NOT PLAY																						
2005-06	**San Jose**	**NHL**	81	17	18	35	45	4	0	2	159	10.7	1	4	0.0	15:46	9	1	4	5	8	1	0	0	15:11
2006-07	**San Jose**	**NHL**	78	26	40	66	36	11	0	9	191	13.6	17	11	18.2	16:46	11	4	2	6	4	0	0	1	18:50
2007-08	**San Jose**	**NHL**	79	24	31	55	47	5	1	8	233	10.3	19	10	60.0	18:05	13	4	0	4	4	1	0	1	17:34
2008-09	**San Jose**	**NHL**	77	23	34	57	52	6	0	6	179	12.8	11	30	46.7	18:27	6	1	0	1	2	1	0	0	19:22
2009-10	**Ottawa**	**NHL**	66	22	12	34	18	8	2	3	163	13.5	–12	8	50.0	18:15	1	0	0	0	0	0	0	0	12:08
	Czech Republic	Olympics	5	2	0	2	0	....	....	....	....	....	....	....	....	....	....	....	....	....	....	....	....	....	....
	NHL Totals		383	113	135	248	202	34	3	28	926	12.2		63	41.3	17:23	40	10	6	16	18	3	0	2	17:31

Missed majority of 2003-04 season recovering from knee injury suffered in game vs. Calgary, October 11, 2003. Traded to **Ottawa** by **San Jose** with Jonathan Cheechoo and San Jose's 2nd round choice ater traded to NY Islanders, later traded to Chicago - Chicago selected Kent Simpson) in 2010 Entry Draft for Dany Heatley and Ottawa's 5th round choice (Isaac MacLeod) in 2010 Entry Draft, September 2, 2009.

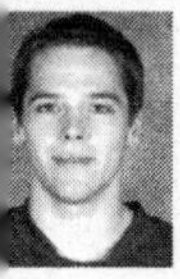

MICHALEK, Zbynek
(mih-KHAL-ihk, z'BIGH-nehk) **PIT.**

Defense. Shoots right. 6'2", 210 lbs. Born, Jindrichuv Hradec, Czech., December 23, 1982.

Season	Club	League	GP	G	A	Pts	PIM	PP	SH	GW	S	%	+/-	TF	F%	Min	GP	G	A	Pts	PIM	PP	SH	GW	Min
99-2000	Karlovy Vary Jr.	CzRep-Jr.	40	2	10	12	20	....	....	....	....	....	....	....	....	....	....	....	....	....	....	....	....	....	....
2000-01	Shawinigan	QMJHL	69	10	29	39	52	....	....	....	....	....	....	....	....	....	3	0	0	0	0	....	....	....	....
2001-02	Shawinigan	QMJHL	68	16	35	51	54	....	....	....	....	....	....	....	....	....	12	8	9	17	17	....	....	....	....
2002-03	Houston Aeros	AHL	62	4	10	14	26	....	....	....	....	....	....	....	....	....	23	1	1	2	6	....	....	....	....
2003-04	**Minnesota**	**NHL**	22	1	1	2	4	0	0	0	17	5.9	–7	0	0.0	14:13	....	....	....	....	....	....	....	....	....
	Houston Aeros	AHL	55	5	16	21	32	....	....	....	....	....	....	....	....	....	2	1	0	1	0	....	....	....	....
2004-05	Houston Aeros	AHL	76	7	17	24	48	....	....	....	....	....	....	....	....	....	5	1	2	3	4	....	....	....	....
2005-06	**Phoenix**	**NHL**	82	9	15	24	62	5	0	2	105	8.6	4	0	0.0	22:50	....	....	....	....	....	....	....	....	....
2006-07	**Phoenix**	**NHL**	82	4	24	28	34	3	0	0	144	2.8	–20	1	100.0	23:40	....	....	....	....	....	....	....	....	....
2007-08	**Phoenix**	**NHL**	75	4	13	17	34	0	0	2	92	4.3	9	0	0.0	21:36	....	....	....	....	....	....	....	....	....
2008-09	**Phoenix**	**NHL**	82	6	21	27	28	0	0	0	106	5.7	–13	0	0.0	22:43	....	....	....	....	....	....	....	....	....
2009-10	**Phoenix**	**NHL**	72	3	14	17	30	2	0	1	104	2.9	5	0	0.0	22:39	7	0	2	2	2	0	0	0	20:28
	Czech Republic	Olympics	5	0	0	0	2	....	....	....	....	....	....	....	....	....	....	....	....	....	....	....	....	....	....
	NHL Totals		415	27	88	115	192	10	0	5	568	4.8		1	100.0	22:16	7	0	2	2	2	0	0	0	20:28

gned as a free agent by **Minnesota**, September 29, 2001. Traded to **Phoenix** by **Minnesota** for Erik Westrum and Dustin Wood, August 26, 2005. Signed as a free agent by **Pittsburgh**, July 1, 2010.

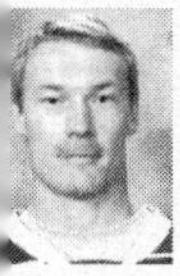

MIETTINEN, Antti
(mih-EHT-tih-nehn, AN-tee) **MIN.**

Right wing. Shoots right. 6', 190 lbs. Born, Hameenlinna, Finland, July 3, 1980. Dallas' 10th choice, 224th overall, in 2000 Entry Draft.

Season	Club	League	GP	G	A	Pts	PIM	PP	SH	GW	S	%	+/-	TF	F%	Min	GP	G	A	Pts	PIM	PP	SH	GW	Min
1996-97	HPK U18	Fin-U18	36	24	29	53	34	....	....	....	....	....	....	....	....	....	....	....	....	....	....	....	....	....	....
1997-98	HPK U18	Fin-U18	34	13	28	41	63	....	....	....	....	....	....	....	....	....	....	....	....	....	....	....	....	....	....
	HPK Jr.	Fin-Jr.	8	1	0	1	2	....	....	....	....	....	....	....	....	....	....	....	....	....	....	....	....	....	....
1998-99	HPK Jr.	Fin-Jr.	35	17	22	39	28	....	....	....	....	....	....	....	....	....	3	2	3	5	2	....	....	....	....
	FPS Forssa	Finland-2	4	3	1	4	6	....	....	....	....	....	....	....	....	....	....	....	....	....	....	....	....	....	....
	HPK Hameenlinna	Finland	13	0	0	0	2	....	....	....	....	....	....	....	....	....	4	0	0	0	0	....	....	....	....
99-2000	HPK Jr.	Fin-Jr.	31	24	53	77	28	....	....	....	....	....	....	....	....	....	2	1	6	7	2	....	....	....	....
	HPK Hameenlinna	Finland	39	2	1	3	8	....	....	....	....	....	....	....	....	....	7	1	0	1	0	....	....	....	....
2000-01	HPK Jr.	Fin-Jr.	4	3	10	13	2	....	....	....	....	....	....	....	....	....	....	....	....	....	....	....	....	....	....
	HPK Hameenlinna	Finland	55	13	11	24	20	....	....	....	....	....	....	....	....	....	....	....	....	....	....	....	....	....	....
2001-02	HPK Hameenlinna	Finland	56	19	37	56	50	....	....	....	....	....	....	....	....	....	8	2	4	6	8	....	....	....	....
2002-03	HPK Hameenlinna	Finland	53	25	25	50	54	....	....	....	....	....	....	....	....	....	10	1	7	8	29	....	....	....	....
2003-04	**Dallas**	**NHL**	16	1	0	1	0	0	0	1	17	5.9	–9	1	0.0	9:51	....	....	....	....	....	....	....	....	....
	Utah Grizzlies	AHL	48	7	23	30	20	....	....	....	....	....	....	....	....	....	....	....	....	....	....	....	....	....	....
2004-05	Hamilton	AHL	35	8	20	28	21	....	....	....	....	....	....	....	....	....	4	1	1	2	6	....	....	....	....
2005-06	**Dallas**	**NHL**	79	11	20	31	46	4	0	1	107	10.3	0	1	100.0	12:06	5	0	1	1	8	0	0	0	12:10
2006-07	**Dallas**	**NHL**	74	11	14	25	38	6	0	1	141	7.8	–5	11	18.2	14:20	4	1	1	2	2	0	0	0	12:16
2007-08	**Dallas**	**NHL**	69	15	19	34	34	5	0	3	136	11.0	4	23	60.9	13:59	15	1	1	2	0	0	0	0	9:33
2008-09	**Minnesota**	**NHL**	82	15	29	44	32	4	2	3	186	8.1	–1	60	46.7	18:17	....	....	....	....	....	....	....	....	....
2009-10	**Minnesota**	**NHL**	79	20	22	42	44	5	0	4	175	11.4	–2	83	42.2	18:03	....	....	....	....	....	....	....	....	....
	Finland	Olympics	6	1	0	1	0	....	....	....	....	....	....	....	....	....	....	....	....	....	....	....	....	....	....
	NHL Totals		399	73	104	177	194	24	2	13	762	9.6		179	44.7	15:12	24	2	3	5	10	0	0	0	10:33

gned as a free agent by **Minnesota**, July 3, 2008.

							Regular Season											Playoffs						
Season	Club	League	GP	G	A	Pts	PIM	PP	SH	GW	S	%	+/-	TF	F%	Min	GP	G	A	Pts	PIM	PP	SH	GW	M

MIHALIK, Vladimir

(mih-HAHL-ihk, vla-DIH-meer)   T.B

Defense. Shoots left. 6'7", 240 lbs.   Born, Presov, Czech., January 29, 1987. Tampa Bay's 1st choice, 30th overall, in 2005 Entry Draft.

Season	Club	League	GP	G	A	Pts	PIM	PP	SH	GW	S	%	+/-	TF	F%	Min	GP	G	A	Pts	PIM	PP	SH	GW	M
2003-04	Presov	Svk-U18	6	4	4	8	4	....	....	....	....	....	....	....	....	....	....	....	....	....	....	....	....	....	
	Presov Jr.	Slovak-Jr.	23	6	10	16	44	....	....	....	....	....	....	....	....	....	....	....	....	....	....	....	....	....	
2004-05	PHK Presov Jr.	Slovak-Jr.	23	6	10	16	44	....	....	....	....	....	....	....	....	....	....	....	....	....	....	....	....	....	
	PHK Presov	Slovak-2	32	3	1	4	24	....	....	....	....	....	....	....	....	....	....	....	....	....	....	....	....	....	
2005-06	Red Deer Rebels	WHL	62	3	9	12	86	....	....	....	....	....	....	....	....	....	6	0	1	1	2	....	....	....	
2006-07	Prince George	WHL	53	7	19	26	91	....	....	....	....	....	....	....	....	....	15	1	2	3	17	....	....	....	
2007-08	Norfolk Admirals	AHL	68	1	15	16	68	....	....	....	....	....	....	....	....	....	....	....	....	....	....	....	....	....	
2008-09	**Tampa Bay**	**NHL**	**11**	**0**	**3**	**3**	**6**	0	0	0	7	0.0	-3	0	0.0	13:24	....	....	....	....	....	....	....	....	
	Norfolk Admirals	AHL	61	2	13	15	58	....	....	....	....	....	....	....	....	....	....	....	....	....	....	....	....	....	
2009-10	**Tampa Bay**	**NHL**	**4**	**0**	**0**	**0**	**2**	0	0	0	1	0.0	-4	0	0.0	11:32	....	....	....	....	....	....	....	....	
	Norfolk Admirals	AHL	75	2	16	18	67	....	....	....	....	....	....	....	....	....	....	....	....	....	....	....	....	....	
	NHL Totals		**15**	**0**	**3**	**3**	**8**	0	0	0	8	0.0		0	0.0	12:54	....	....	....	....	....	....	....	....	

MIKKELSON, Brendan

(MIGHK-ehl-sohn, BREHN-duhn)   ANA

Defense. Shoots left. 6'3", 205 lbs.   Born, Regina, Sask., June 22, 1987. Anaheim's 2nd choice, 31st overall, in 2005 Entry Draft.

Season	Club	League	GP	G	A	Pts	PIM	PP	SH	GW	S	%	+/-	TF	F%	Min	GP	G	A	Pts	PIM	PP	SH	GW	M
2003-04	Portland	WHL	65	3	12	15	43	....	....	....	....	....	....	....	....	....	5	1	0	1	0	....	....	....	
2004-05	Portland	WHL	70	5	10	15	60	....	....	....	....	....	....	....	....	....	7	1	2	3	0	....	....	....	
2005-06	Portland	WHL	3	1	1	2	4	....	....	....	....	....	....	....	....	....	....	....	....	....	....	....	....	....	
	Vancouver Giants	WHL	19	1	8	9	37	....	....	....	....	....	....	....	....	....	....	....	....	....	....	....	....	....	
2006-07	Vancouver Giants	WHL	69	6	23	29	60	....	....	....	....	....	....	....	....	....	21	3	7	10	10	....	....	....	
2007-08	Portland Pirates	AHL	66	6	10	16	50	....	....	....	....	....	....	....	....	....	14	2	6	8	2	....	....	....	
2008-09	**Anaheim**	**NHL**	**34**	**0**	**2**	**2**	**17**	0	0	0	19	0.0	0	0	0.0	13:56	....	....	....	....	....	....	....	....	
	Iowa Chops	AHL	31	2	8	10	18	....	....	....	....	....	....	....	....	....	....	....	....	....	....	....	....	....	
2009-10	**Anaheim**	**NHL**	**28**	**0**	**2**	**2**	**14**	0	0	0	21	0.0	-5	0	0.0	15:00	....	....	....	....	....	....	....	....	
	Toronto Marlies	AHL	49	7	15	22	43	....	....	....	....	....	....	....	....	....	....	....	....	....	....	....	....	....	
	NHL Totals		**62**	**0**	**4**	**4**	**31**	0	0	0	40	0.0		0	0.0	14:25	....	....	....	....	....	....	....	....	

Memorial Cup Tournament All-Star Team (2007)

• Missed majority of 2005-06 season recovering from shoulder and knee injuries.

MILLER, Drew

(MIH-luhr, DROO)   DET.

Left wing. Shoots left. 6'2", 178 lbs.   Born, Dover, NJ, February 17, 1984. Anaheim's 6th choice, 186th overall, in 2003 Entry Draft.

Season	Club	League	GP	G	A	Pts	PIM	PP	SH	GW	S	%	+/-	TF	F%	Min	GP	G	A	Pts	PIM	PP	SH	GW	M
2000-01	Capital Centre	NAHL	37	4	3	7	22	....	....	....	....	....	....	....	....	....	....	....	....	....	....	....	....	....	
2001-02	Capital Centre	NAHL	54	18	16	34	56	....	....	....	....	....	....	....	....	....	....	....	....	....	....	....	....	....	
2002-03	Capital Centre	NAHL	11	10	9	19		....	....	....	....	....	....	....	....	....	....	....	....	....	....	....	....	....	
	River City Lancers	USHL	49	14	11	25	22	....	....	....	....	....	....	....	....	....	11	5	4	9	6	....	....	....	
2003-04	Michigan State	CCHA	41	4	6	10	39	....	....	....	....	....	....	....	....	....	....	....	....	....	....	....	....	....	
2004-05	Michigan State	CCHA	40	17	16	33	20	....	....	....	....	....	....	....	....	....	....	....	....	....	....	....	....	....	
2005-06	Michigan State	CCHA	44	18	25	43	30	....	....	....	....	....	....	....	....	....	....	....	....	....	....	....	....	....	
2006-07	Portland Pirates	AHL	79	16	20	36	51	....	....	....	....	....	....	....	....	....	....	....	....	....	....	....	....	....	
◆	**Anaheim**	**NHL**						....	....	....	....	....	....	....	....	....	3	0	0	0	2	0	0	0	7:00
2007-08	**Anaheim**	**NHL**	**26**	**2**	**3**	**5**	**6**	0	0	0	30	6.7	-1	9	33.3	11:11	....	....	....	....	....	....	....	....	
	Portland Pirates	AHL	31	16	20	36	12	....	....	....	....	....	....	....	....	....	16	1	7	8	12	....	....	....	
2008-09	**Anaheim**	**NHL**	**27**	**4**	**6**	**10**	**17**	0	0	0	45	8.9	0	14	21.4	12:59	13	2	1	3	2	0	0	1	16:09
	Iowa Chops	AHL	53	23	15	38	10	....	....	....	....	....	....	....	....	....	....	....	....	....	....	....	....	....	
2009-10	**Tampa Bay**	**NHL**	**14**	**0**	**0**	**0**	**2**	0	0	0	10	0.0	-3	2	0.0	12:14	....	....	....	....	....	....	....	....	
	Detroit	**NHL**	**66**	**10**	**9**	**19**	**10**	1	1	3	93	10.8	5	41	34.2	12:42	12	1	1	2	4	0	0	0	12:35
	NHL Totals		**133**	**16**	**18**	**34**	**35**	1	1	3	178	9.0		66	30.3	12:25	28	3	2	5	8	0	0	1	13:38

Traded to **Tampa Bay** by **Anaheim** with Anaheim's 3rd round choice (Adam Janosik) in 2010 Entry Draft for Evgeny Artyukhin, August 13, 2009. Claimed on waivers by **Detroit** from **Tampa Bay**, November 11, 2009.

MILROY, Duncan

(MIHL-roi, DUHN-kuhn)

Right wing. Shoots right. 6', 198 lbs.   Born, Edmonton, Alta., February 8, 1983. Montreal's 3rd choice, 37th overall, in 2001 Entry Draft.

Season	Club	League	GP	G	A	Pts	PIM	PP	SH	GW	S	%	+/-	TF	F%	Min	GP	G	A	Pts	PIM	PP	SH	GW	M
1998-99	Edm. Maple Leafs	AMHL	34	34	36	70	73	....	....	....	....	....	....	....	....	....	....	....	....	....	....	....	....	....	
	Swift Current	WHL	3	0	0	0	0	....	....	....	....	....	....	....	....	....	....	....	....	....	....	....	....	....	
99-2000	Swift Current	WHL	68	15	15	30	20	....	....	....	....	....	....	....	....	....	12	3	5	8	12	....	....	....	
2000-01	Swift Current	WHL	68	38	54	92	51	....	....	....	....	....	....	....	....	....	19	9	12	21	6	....	....	....	
2001-02	Swift Current	WHL	26	20	11	31	20	....	....	....	....	....	....	....	....	....	....	....	....	....	....	....	....	....	
	Kootenay Ice	WHL	38	25	31	56	24	....	....	....	....	....	....	....	....	....	22	*17	*20	*37	26	....	....	....	
2002-03	Kootenay Ice	WHL	61	34	44	78	40	....	....	....	....	....	....	....	....	....	11	5	3	8	8	....	....	....	
2003-04	Hamilton	AHL	50	4	10	14	14	....	....	....	....	....	....	....	....	....	10	3	1	4	4	....	....	....	
2004-05	Hamilton	AHL	76	15	18	33	18	....	....	....	....	....	....	....	....	....	3	0	0	0	4	....	....	....	
2005-06	Hamilton	AHL	77	16	19	35	63	....	....	....	....	....	....	....	....	....	....	....	....	....	....	....	....	....	
2006-07	**Montreal**	**NHL**	**5**	**0**	**1**	**1**	**0**	0	0	0	6	0.0	-2	1	0.0	12:56	....	....	....	....	....	....	....	....	
	Hamilton	AHL	64	25	33	58	24	....	....	....	....	....	....	....	....	....	22	2	11	13	10	....	....	....	
2007-08	Hamilton	AHL	79	15	24	39	37	....	....	....	....	....	....	....	....	....	....	....	....	....	....	....	....	....	
2008-09	ERC Ingolstadt	Germany	49	14	34	48	16	....	....	....	....	....	....	....	....	....	....	....	....	....	....	....	....	....	
2009-10	Houston Aeros	AHL	74	12	24	36	28	....	....	....	....	....	....	....	....	....	....	....	....	....	....	....	....	....	
	NHL Totals		**5**	**0**	**1**	**1**	**0**	0	0	0	6	0.0		1	0.0	12:56	....	....	....	....	....	....	....	....	

Yanick Dupre Memorial Award (AHL - Outstanding Humanitarian Contribution) (2005)

Signed as a free agent by **Ingolstadt** (Germany), July 31, 2008. Signed as a free agent by **Minnesota**, July 17, 2009.

MINARD, Chris

(mih-NAHRD, KRIHS)   DET.

Center. Shoots left. 6'1", 190 lbs.   Born, Thompson, Man., November 18, 1981.

Season	Club	League	GP	G	A	Pts	PIM	PP	SH	GW	S	%	+/-	TF	F%	Min	GP	G	A	Pts	PIM	PP	SH	GW	M
1997-98	Owen Sound	OHL	9	0	1	1	1	....	....	....	....	....	....	....	....	....	1	0	0	0	2	....	....	....	
1998-99	Owen Sound	OHL	43	6	9	15	18	....	....	....	....	....	....	....	....	....	....	....	....	....	....	....	....	....	
99-2000	Owen Sound	OHL	38	12	14	26	39	....	....	....	....	....	....	....	....	....	....	....	....	....	....	....	....	....	
	St. Michael's	OHL	28	5	14	19	6	....	....	....	....	....	....	....	....	....	....	....	....	....	....	....	....	....	
2000-01	St. Michael's	OHL	40	11	8	19	28	....	....	....	....	....	....	....	....	....	....	....	....	....	....	....	....	....	
	Oshawa Generals	OHL	28	12	12	24	18	....	....	....	....	....	....	....	....	....	....	....	....	....	....	....	....	....	
2001-02	Oshawa Generals	OHL	67	36	35	71	20	....	....	....	....	....	....	....	....	....	5	2	3	5	6	....	....	....	
2002-03	Pensacola	ECHL	72	15	17	32	71	....	....	....	....	....	....	....	....	....	4	0	0	0	6	....	....	....	
2003-04	San Angelo Saints	CHL	64	39	36	75	51	....	....	....	....	....	....	....	....	....	5	1	1	2	2	....	....	....	
2004-05	Alaska Aces	ECHL	69	*49	29	78	54	....	....	....	....	....	....	....	....	....	15	4	4	8	12	....	....	....	
	Milwaukee	AHL	1	0	0	0	0	....	....	....	....	....	....	....	....	....	....	....	....	....	....	....	....	....	
2005-06	Albany River Rats	AHL	37	7	12	19	26	....	....	....	....	....	....	....	....	....	....	....	....	....	....	....	....	....	
	Alaska Aces	ECHL	33	26	16	42	38	....	....	....	....	....	....	....	....	....	....	....	....	....	....	....	....	....	
2006-07	Lowell Devils	AHL	65	32	17	49	30	....	....	....	....	....	....	....	....	....	22	*14	5	19	*54	....	....	....	
2007-08	**Pittsburgh**	**NHL**	**15**	**1**	**1**	**2**	**10**	0	0	0	9	11.1	-1	0	0.0	3:53	....	....	....	....	....	....	....	....	
	Wilkes-Barre	AHL	56	25	17	42	33	....	....	....	....	....	....	....	....	....	23	11	6	17	10	....	....	....	
2008-09	**Pittsburgh**	**NHL**	**20**	**1**	**2**	**3**	**4**	0	0	1	33	3.0	0	2100.0		9:25	....	....	....	....	....	....	....	....	
	Wilkes-Barre	AHL	54	34	23	57	38	....	....	....	....	....	....	....	....	....	12	6	3	9	12	....	....	....	
2009-10	**Edmonton**	**NHL**	**5**	**0**	**1**	**1**	**0**	0	0	0	4	0.0	-3	0	0.0	9:44	....	....	....	....	....	....	....	....	
	Springfield	AHL	40	22	16	38	18	....	....	....	....	....	....	....	....	....	....	....	....	....	....	....	....	....	
	NHL Totals		**40**	**2**	**4**	**6**	**14**	0	0	1	46	4.3		2100.0		7:23	....	....	....	....	....	....	....	....	

Signed as a free agent by **Albany** (AHL), August 16, 2005. Signed as a free agent by **Pittsburgh**, July 12, 2007. Signed as a free agent by **Edmonton**, July 13, 2009. Signed as a free agent by **Detroit**, July 6, 2010.

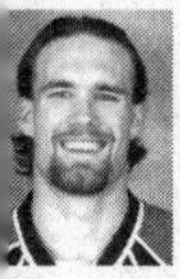

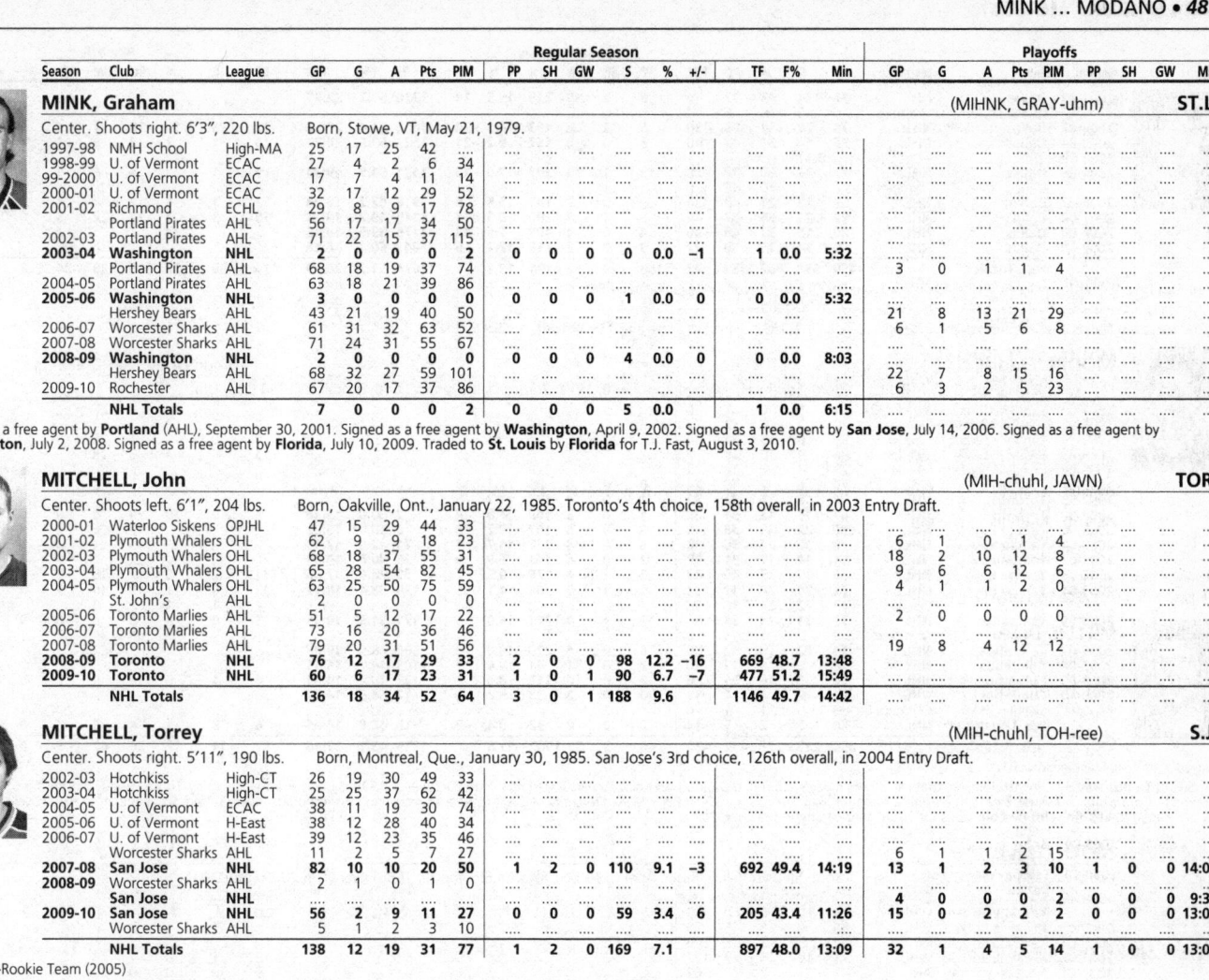

MINK, Graham

(MIHNK, GRAY-uhm) **ST.L.**

Center. Shoots right. 6'3", 220 lbs. Born, Stowe, VT, May 21, 1979.

Season	Club	League	GP	G	A	Pts	PIM	PP	SH	GW	S	%	+/-	TF	F%	Min	GP	G	A	Pts	PIM	PP	SH	GW	Min
			Regular Season														Playoffs								
1997-98	NMH School	High-MA	25	17	25	42	....	....	....	....	....	....	....	....	....	....	....	....	....	....	....	....	....	....	....
1998-99	U. of Vermont	ECAC	27	4	2	6	34	....	....	....	....	....	....	....	....	....	....	....	....	....	....	....	....	....	....
99-2000	U. of Vermont	ECAC	17	7	4	11	14	....	....	....	....	....	....	....	....	....	....	....	....	....	....	....	....	....	....
2000-01	U. of Vermont	ECAC	32	17	12	29	52	....	....	....	....	....	....	....	....	....	....	....	....	....	....	....	....	....	....
2001-02	Richmond	ECHL	29	8	9	17	78	....	....	....	....	....	....	....	....	....	....	....	....	....	....	....	....	....	....
	Portland Pirates	AHL	56	17	17	34	50	....	....	....	....	....	....	....	....	....	....	....	....	....	....	....	....	....	....
2002-03	Portland Pirates	AHL	71	22	15	37	115	....	....	....	....	....	....	....	....	....	....	....	....	....	....	....	....	....	....
2003-04	**Washington**	**NHL**	**2**	**0**	**0**	**0**	**2**	**0**	**0**	**0**	**0**	**0.0**	**-1**	**1**	**0.0**	**5:32**	....	....	....	....	....	....	....	....	....
	Portland Pirates	AHL	68	18	19	37	74	....	....	....	....	....	....	....	....	....	3	0	1	1	4	....	....	....	....
2004-05	Portland Pirates	AHL	63	18	21	39	86	....	....	....	....	....	....	....	....	....	....	....	....	....	....	....	....	....	....
2005-06	**Washington**	**NHL**	**3**	**0**	**0**	**0**	**0**	**0**	**0**	**0**	**1**	**0.0**	**0**	**0**	**0.0**	**5:32**	....	....	....	....	....	....	....	....	....
	Hershey Bears	AHL	43	21	19	40	50	....	....	....	....	....	....	....	....	....	21	8	13	21	29	....	....	....	....
2006-07	Worcester Sharks	AHL	61	31	32	63	52	....	....	....	....	....	....	....	....	....	6	1	5	6	8	....	....	....	....
2007-08	Worcester Sharks	AHL	71	24	31	55	67	....	....	....	....	....	....	....	....	....	....	....	....	....	....	....	....	....	....
2008-09	**Washington**	**NHL**	**2**	**0**	**0**	**0**	**0**	**0**	**0**	**0**	**4**	**0.0**	**0**	**0**	**0.0**	**8:03**	....	....	....	....	....	....	....	....	....
	Hershey Bears	AHL	68	32	27	59	101	....	....	....	....	....	....	....	....	....	22	7	8	15	16	....	....	....	....
2009-10	Rochester	AHL	67	20	17	37	86	....	....	....	....	....	....	....	....	....	6	3	2	5	23	....	....	....	....
	NHL Totals		**7**	**0**	**0**	**0**	**2**	**0**	**0**	**0**	**5**	**0.0**		**1**	**0.0**	**6:15**	....	....	....	....	....	....	....	....	....

gned as a free agent by **Portland** (AHL), September 30, 2001. Signed as a free agent by **Washington**, April 9, 2002. Signed as a free agent by **San Jose**, July 14, 2006. Signed as a free agent by **ashington**, July 2, 2008. Signed as a free agent by **Florida**, July 10, 2009. Traded to **St. Louis** by **Florida** for T.J. Fast, August 3, 2010.

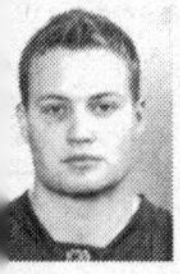

MITCHELL, John

(MIH-chuhl, JAWN) **TOR.**

Center. Shoots left. 6'1", 204 lbs. Born, Oakville, Ont., January 22, 1985. Toronto's 4th choice, 158th overall, in 2003 Entry Draft.

Season	Club	League	GP	G	A	Pts	PIM	PP	SH	GW	S	%	+/-	TF	F%	Min	GP	G	A	Pts	PIM	PP	SH	GW	Min
2000-01	Waterloo Siskens	OPJHL	47	15	29	44	33	....	....	....	....	....	....	....	....	....	....	....	....	....	....	....	....	....	....
2001-02	Plymouth Whalers	OHL	62	9	9	18	23	....	....	....	....	....	....	....	....	....	6	1	0	1	4	....	....	....	....
2002-03	Plymouth Whalers	OHL	68	18	37	55	31	....	....	....	....	....	....	....	....	....	18	2	10	12	8	....	....	....	....
2003-04	Plymouth Whalers	OHL	65	28	54	82	45	....	....	....	....	....	....	....	....	....	9	6	6	12	6	....	....	....	....
2004-05	Plymouth Whalers	OHL	63	25	50	75	59	....	....	....	....	....	....	....	....	....	4	1	1	2	0	....	....	....	....
	St. John's	AHL	2	0	0	0	0	....	....	....	....	....	....	....	....	....	....	....	....	....	....	....	....	....	....
2005-06	Toronto Marlies	AHL	51	5	12	17	22	....	....	....	....	....	....	....	....	....	2	0	0	0	0	....	....	....	....
2006-07	Toronto Marlies	AHL	73	16	20	36	46	....	....	....	....	....	....	....	....	....	....	....	....	....	....	....	....	....	....
2007-08	Toronto Marlies	AHL	79	20	31	51	56	....	....	....	....	....	....	....	....	....	19	8	4	12	12	....	....	....	....
2008-09	**Toronto**	**NHL**	**76**	**12**	**17**	**29**	**33**	**2**	**0**	**0**	**98**	**12.2**	**-16**	**669**	**48.7**	**13:48**	....	....	....	....	....	....	....	....	....
2009-10	**Toronto**	**NHL**	**60**	**6**	**17**	**23**	**31**	**1**	**0**	**1**	**90**	**6.7**	**-7**	**477**	**51.2**	**15:49**	....	....	....	....	....	....	....	....	....
	NHL Totals		**136**	**18**	**34**	**52**	**64**	**3**	**0**	**1**	**188**	**9.6**		**1146**	**49.7**	**14:42**	....	....	....	....	....	....	....	....	....

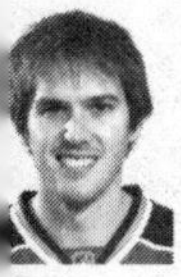

MITCHELL, Torrey

(MIH-chuhl, TOH-ree) **S.J.**

Center. Shoots right. 5'11", 190 lbs. Born, Montreal, Que., January 30, 1985. San Jose's 3rd choice, 126th overall, in 2004 Entry Draft.

Season	Club	League	GP	G	A	Pts	PIM	PP	SH	GW	S	%	+/-	TF	F%	Min	GP	G	A	Pts	PIM	PP	SH	GW	Min
2002-03	Hotchkiss	High-CT	26	19	30	49	33	....	....	....	....	....	....	....	....	....	....	....	....	....	....	....	....	....	....
2003-04	Hotchkiss	High-CT	25	25	37	62	42	....	....	....	....	....	....	....	....	....	....	....	....	....	....	....	....	....	....
2004-05	U. of Vermont	ECAC	38	11	19	30	74	....	....	....	....	....	....	....	....	....	....	....	....	....	....	....	....	....	....
2005-06	U. of Vermont	H-East	38	12	28	40	34	....	....	....	....	....	....	....	....	....	....	....	....	....	....	....	....	....	....
2006-07	U. of Vermont	H-East	39	12	23	35	46	....	....	....	....	....	....	....	....	....	....	....	....	....	....	....	....	....	....
	Worcester Sharks	AHL	11	2	5	7	27	....	....	....	....	....	....	....	....	....	6	1	1	2	15	....	....	....	....
2007-08	**San Jose**	**NHL**	**82**	**10**	**10**	**20**	**50**	**1**	**2**	**0**	**110**	**9.1**	**-3**	**692**	**49.4**	**14:19**	**13**	**1**	**2**	**3**	**10**	**1**	**0**	**0**	**14:00**
2008-09	Worcester Sharks	AHL	2	1	0	1	0	....	....	....	....	....	....	....	....	....	....	....	....	....	....	....	....	....	....
	San Jose	**NHL**	....	....	....	....	....	....	....	....	....	....	....	....	....	....	**4**	**0**	**0**	**0**	**2**	**0**	**0**	**0**	**9:38**
2009-10	**San Jose**	**NHL**	**56**	**2**	**9**	**11**	**27**	**0**	**0**	**0**	**59**	**3.4**	**6**	**205**	**43.4**	**11:26**	**15**	**0**	**2**	**2**	**2**	**0**	**0**	**0**	**13:05**
	Worcester Sharks	AHL	5	1	2	3	10	....	....	....	....	....	....	....	....	....	....	....	....	....	....	....	....	....	....
	NHL Totals		**138**	**12**	**19**	**31**	**77**	**1**	**2**	**0**	**169**	**7.1**		**897**	**48.0**	**13:09**	**32**	**1**	**4**	**5**	**14**	**1**	**0**	**0**	**13:02**

CAC All-Rookie Team (2005)

Missed majority of 2008-09 season recovering from leg injury suffered during training camp, September 18, 2008.

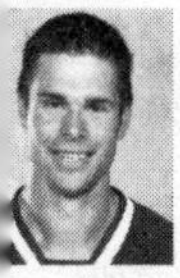

MITCHELL, Willie

(MIH-chuhl, WIH-lee)

Defense. Shoots left. 6'3", 208 lbs. Born, Port McNeill, B.C., April 23, 1977. New Jersey's 12th choice, 199th overall, in 1996 Entry Draft.

Season	Club	League	GP	G	A	Pts	PIM	PP	SH	GW	S	%	+/-	TF	F%	Min	GP	G	A	Pts	PIM	PP	SH	GW	Min
1993-94	Notre Dame	SMHL	31	4	11	15	81	....	....	....	....	....	....	....	....	....	....	....	....	....	....	....	....	....	....
1994-95	Kelowna Spartans	BCHL	42	3	8	11	71	....	....	....	....	....	....	....	....	....	....	....	....	....	....	....	....	....	....
1995-96	Melfort Mustangs	SJHL	19	2	6	8	....	....	....	....	....	....	....	....	....	....	14	0	2	2	12	....	....	....	....
1996-97	Melfort Mustangs	SJHL	64	14	42	56	227	....	....	....	....	....	....	....	....	....	4	0	1	1	23	....	....	....	....
1997-98	Clarkson Knights	ECAC	34	9	17	26	105	....	....	....	....	....	....	....	....	....	....	....	....	....	....	....	....	....	....
1998-99	Clarkson Knights	ECAC	34	10	19	29	40	....	....	....	....	....	....	....	....	....	....	....	....	....	....	....	....	....	....
	Albany River Rats	AHL	6	1	3	4	29	....	....	....	....	....	....	....	....	....	....	....	....	....	....	....	....	....	....
99-2000	**New Jersey**	**NHL**	**2**	**0**	**0**	**0**	**0**	**0**	**0**	**0**	**2**	**0.0**	**1**	**0**	**0.0**	**16:04**	....	....	....	....	....	....	....	....	....
	Albany River Rats	AHL	63	5	14	19	71	....	....	....	....	....	....	....	....	....	5	1	2	3	4	....	....	....	....
2000-01	**New Jersey**	**NHL**	**16**	**0**	**2**	**2**	**29**	**0**	**0**	**0**	**14**	**0.0**	**0**	**0**	**0.0**	**14:52**	....	....	....	....	....	....	....	....	....
	Albany River Rats	AHL	41	3	13	16	94	....	....	....	....	....	....	....	....	....	....	....	....	....	....	....	....	....	....
	Minnesota	**NHL**	**17**	**1**	**7**	**8**	**11**	**0**	**0**	**0**	**16**	**6.3**	**4**	**0**	**0.0**	**20:49**	....	....	....	....	....	....	....	....	....
2001-02	**Minnesota**	**NHL**	**68**	**3**	**10**	**13**	**68**	**0**	**0**	**1**	**67**	**4.5**	**-16**	**0**	**0.0**	**21:25**	....	....	....	....	....	....	....	....	....
2002-03	**Minnesota**	**NHL**	**69**	**2**	**12**	**14**	**84**	**0**	**1**	**1**	**67**	**3.0**	**13**	**0**	**0.0**	**21:28**	**18**	**1**	**3**	**4**	**14**	**0**	**0**	**0**	**24:48**
2003-04	**Minnesota**	**NHL**	**70**	**1**	**13**	**14**	**83**	**0**	**0**	**0**	**58**	**1.7**	**12**	**2**	**50.0**	**22:36**	....	....	....	....	....	....	....	....	....
2004-05			DID NOT PLAY																						
2005-06	**Minnesota**	**NHL**	**64**	**2**	**6**	**8**	**87**	**0**	**0**	**0**	**48**	**4.2**	**15**	**0**	**0.0**	**20:52**	....	....	....	....	....	....	....	....	....
	Dallas	**NHL**	**16**	**0**	**2**	**2**	**26**	**0**	**0**	**0**	**10**	**0.0**	**4**	**0**	**0.0**	**20:46**	**5**	**0**	**0**	**0**	**2**	**0**	**0**	**0**	**23:21**
2006-07	**Vancouver**	**NHL**	**62**	**1**	**10**	**11**	**45**	**0**	**0**	**0**	**54**	**1.9**	**1**	**0**	**0.0**	**22:13**	**12**	**0**	**1**	**1**	**12**	**0**	**0**	**0**	**27:14**
2007-08	**Vancouver**	**NHL**	**72**	**2**	**10**	**12**	**81**	**0**	**0**	**1**	**65**	**3.1**	**6**	**0**	**0.0**	**23:12**	....	....	....	....	....	....	....	....	....
2008-09	**Vancouver**	**NHL**	**82**	**3**	**20**	**23**	**59**	**0**	**0**	**1**	**88**	**3.4**	**29**	**1**	**0.0**	**22:55**	**10**	**0**	**2**	**2**	**22**	**0**	**0**	**0**	**24:13**
2009-10	**Vancouver**	**NHL**	**48**	**4**	**8**	**12**	**48**	**0**	**0**	**1**	**47**	**8.5**	**13**	**0**	**0.0**	**22:37**	....	....	....	....	....	....	....	....	....
	NHL Totals		**586**	**19**	**100**	**119**	**621**	**0**	**1**	**5**	**536**	**3.5**		**3**	**33.3**	**21:53**	**45**	**1**	**6**	**7**	**50**	**0**	**0**	**0**	**25:09**

HL First All-Star Team (1997) • SJHL Top Defenseman Award (1997) • ECAC Second All-Star Team (1998) • ECAC Rookie of the Year (1998) (co-winner - Erik Cole) • ECAC First All-Star Team (1999)
NCAA East Second All-American Team (1999)

raded to **Minnesota** by **New Jersey** for Sean O'Donnell, March 4, 2001. Traded to **Dallas** by **Minnesota** with Minnesota's 2nd round choice (Nico Saccheti) in 2007 Entry Draft for Martin Skoula and hawn Belle, March 9, 2006. Signed as a free agent by **Vancouver**, July 1, 2006.

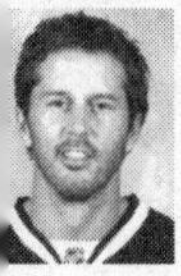

MODANO, Mike

(moh-DA-noh, MIGHK) **DET.**

Center. Shoots left. 6'3", 212 lbs. Born, Livonia, MI, June 7, 1970. Minnesota's 1st choice, 1st overall, in 1988 Entry Draft.

Season	Club	League	GP	G	A	Pts	PIM	PP	SH	GW	S	%	+/-	TF	F%	Min	GP	G	A	Pts	PIM	PP	SH	GW	Min
1985-86	Det. Compuware	MNHL	69	66	65	131	32	....	....	....	....	....	....	....	....	....	....	....	....	....	....	....	....	....	....
1986-87	Prince Albert	WHL	70	32	30	62	96	....	....	....	....	....	....	....	....	....	8	1	4	5	4	....	....	....	....
1987-88	Prince Albert	WHL	65	47	80	127	80	....	....	....	....	....	....	....	....	....	9	7	11	18	18	....	....	....	....
1988-89	Prince Albert	WHL	41	39	66	105	74	....	....	....	....	....	....	....	....	....	....	....	....	....	....	....	....	....	....
	Minnesota	**NHL**	....	....	....	....	....	....	....	....	....	....	....	....	....	....	**2**	**0**	**0**	**0**	**0**	**0**	**0**	**0**	....
1989-90	**Minnesota**	**NHL**	**80**	**29**	**46**	**75**	**63**	**12**	**0**	**2**	**172**	**16.9**	**-7**	....	....	....	**7**	**1**	**1**	**2**	**12**	**0**	**0**	**0**	....
1990-91	**Minnesota**	**NHL**	**79**	**28**	**36**	**64**	**65**	**9**	**0**	**2**	**232**	**12.1**	**2**	....	....	....	**23**	**8**	**12**	**20**	**16**	**3**	**0**	**1**	....
1991-92	**Minnesota**	**NHL**	**76**	**33**	**44**	**77**	**46**	**5**	**0**	**8**	**256**	**12.9**	**-9**	....	....	....	**7**	**3**	**2**	**5**	**4**	**1**	**0**	**0**	....
1992-93	**Minnesota**	**NHL**	**82**	**33**	**60**	**93**	**83**	**9**	**0**	**7**	**307**	**10.7**	**-7**	....	....	....	....	....	....	....	....	....	....	....	....
1993-94	**Dallas**	**NHL**	**76**	**50**	**43**	**93**	**54**	**18**	**0**	**4**	**281**	**17.8**	**-8**	....	....	....	**9**	**7**	**3**	**10**	**16**	**2**	**0**	**2**	....
1994-95	**Dallas**	**NHL**	**30**	**12**	**17**	**29**	**8**	**4**	**1**	**0**	**100**	**12.0**	**7**	....	....	....	....	....	....	....	....	....	....	....	....
1995-96	**Dallas**	**NHL**	**78**	**36**	**45**	**81**	**63**	**8**	**4**	**4**	**320**	**11.3**	**-12**	....	....	....	....	....	....	....	....	....	....	....	....
1996-97	**Dallas**	**NHL**	**80**	**35**	**48**	**83**	**42**	**9**	**5**	**9**	**291**	**12.0**	**43**	....	....	....	**7**	**4**	**1**	**5**	**0**	**1**	**1**	**2**	....
1997-98	**Dallas**	**NHL**	**52**	**21**	**38**	**59**	**32**	**7**	**5**	**2**	**191**	**11.0**	**25**	....	....	....	**17**	**4**	**10**	**14**	**12**	**1**	**0**	**1**	....
	United States	Olympics	4	2	0	2	0	....	....	....	....	....	....	....	....	....	....	....	....	....	....	....	....	....	....
1998-99 ♦	**Dallas**	**NHL**	**77**	**34**	**47**	**81**	**44**	**6**	**4**	**7**	**224**	**15.2**	**29**	**1572**	**51.1**	**20:50**	**23**	**5**	***18**	**23**	**16**	**1**	**1**	**1**	**24:40**
99-2000	**Dallas**	**NHL**	**77**	**38**	**43**	**81**	**48**	**11**	**1**	**8**	**188**	**20.2**	**0**	**1763**	**51.4**	**22:55**	**23**	**10**	***13**	**23**	**10**	***4**	**0**	**2**	**25:26**
2000-01	**Dallas**	**NHL**	**81**	**33**	**51**	**84**	**52**	**8**	**3**	**7**	**208**	**15.9**	**26**	**1791**	**52.0**	**22:24**	**9**	**3**	**4**	**7**	**0**	**2**	**0**	**0**	**25:43**

Season	Club	League	GP	G	A	Pts	PIM	PP	SH	GW	S	%	+/-	TF	F%	Min	GP	G	A	Pts	PIM	PP	SH	GW	M
			Regular Season														Playoffs								
2001-02	**Dallas**	**NHL**	**78**	**34**	**43**	**77**	**38**	**6**	**2**	**5**	**219**	**15.5**	**14**	**1710**	**53.7**	**22:27**	....	....	....	....	....	....	....	....	....
	United States	Olympics	6	0	*6	6	4	....	....	....	....	....	....	....	....	....	....	....	....	....	....	....	....	....	....
2002-03	**Dallas**	**NHL**	**79**	**28**	**57**	**85**	**30**	**5**	**2**	**6**	**193**	**14.5**	**34**	**1808**	**51.4**	**20:53**	**12**	**5**	**10**	**15**	**4**	**1**	**0**	**2**	**23:5**
2003-04	**Dallas**	**NHL**	**76**	**14**	**30**	**44**	**46**	**6**	**0**	**0**	**152**	**9.2**	**–21**	**1523**	**52.6**	**20:27**	**5**	**1**	**2**	**3**	**8**	**1**	**0**	**0**	**23:1**
2004-05			DID NOT PLAY																						
2005-06	**Dallas**	**NHL**	**78**	**27**	**50**	**77**	**58**	**12**	**1**	**4**	**207**	**13.0**	**23**	**1421**	**51.1**	**19:34**	**5**	**1**	**3**	**4**	**4**	**1**	**0**	**0**	**22:1**
	United States	Olympics	6	2	0	2	6	....	....	....	....	....	....	....	....	....	....	....	....	....	....	....	....	....	....
2006-07	**Dallas**	**NHL**	**59**	**22**	**21**	**43**	**34**	**9**	**0**	**7**	**141**	**15.6**	**9**	**918**	**52.2**	**18:24**	**7**	**1**	**1**	**2**	**4**	**1**	**0**	**1**	**26:1**
2007-08	**Dallas**	**NHL**	**82**	**21**	**36**	**57**	**48**	**5**	**1**	**4**	**200**	**10.5**	**–11**	**1145**	**49.2**	**19:14**	**18**	**5**	**7**	**12**	**22**	**5**	**0**	**3**	**19:4**
2008-09	**Dallas**	**NHL**	**80**	**15**	**31**	**46**	**46**	**4**	**0**	**4**	**197**	**7.6**	**–13**	**1176**	**52.5**	**18:18**	....	....	....	....	....	....	....	....	....
2009-10	**Dallas**	**NHL**	**59**	**14**	**16**	**30**	**22**	**3**	**0**	**2**	**115**	**12.2**	**–6**	**847**	**50.4**	**14:18**	....	....	....	....	....	....	....	....	....
	NHL Totals		**1459**	**557**	**802**	**1359**	**922**	**156**	**29**	**92**	**4194**	**13.3**		**15674**	**51.7**	**20:08**	**174**	**58**	**87**	**145**	**128**	**24**	**2**	**15**	**23:5**

WHL East First All-Star Team (1989) • NHL All-Rookie Team (1990) • NHL Second All-Star Team (2000)
Played in NHL All-Star Game (1993, 1998, 1999, 2000, 2003, 2004, 2009)
• Transferred to **Dallas** after **Minnesota** franchise relocated, June 9, 1993. Signed as a free agent by **Detroit**, August 5, 2010.

MODIN, Fredrik

(moh-DEEN, FREHD-rihk)

Left wing. Shoots left. 6'4", 218 lbs. Born, Sundsvall, Sweden, October 8, 1974. Toronto's 3rd choice, 64th overall, in 1994 Entry Draft.

Season	Club	League	GP	G	A	Pts	PIM	PP	SH	GW	S	%	+/-	TF	F%	Min	GP	G	A	Pts	PIM	PP	SH	GW	M
1991-92	Sundsvall/Timra	Sweden-2	11	1	0	1	0	....	....	....	....	....	....	....	....	....	....	....	....	....	....	....	....	....	....
1992-93	Sundsvall/Timra	Sweden-2	30	5	7	12	12	....	....	....	....	....	....	....	....	....	5	1	0	1	0	....	....	....	....
1993-94	Sundsvall/Timra	Sweden-2	30	16	15	31	36	....	....	....	....	....	....	....	....	....	2	0	1	1	6	....	....	....	....
1994-95	Brynas IF Gavle	Sweden	38	9	10	19	33	....	....	....	....	....	....	....	....	....	14	4	4	8	6	....	....	....	....
1995-96	Brynas IF Gavle	Sweden	22	4	8	12	22	....	....	....	....	....	....	....	....	....	....	....	....	....	....	....	....	....	....
1996-97	**Toronto**	**NHL**	**76**	**6**	**7**	**13**	**24**	**0**	**0**	**0**	**85**	**7.1**	**–14**	....	....	....	....	....	....	....	....	....	....	....	....
1997-98	**Toronto**	**NHL**	**74**	**16**	**16**	**32**	**32**	**1**	**0**	**4**	**137**	**11.7**	**–5**	....	....	....	....	....	....	....	....	....	....	....	....
1998-99	**Toronto**	**NHL**	**67**	**16**	**15**	**31**	**35**	**1**	**0**	**3**	**108**	**14.8**	**14**	**2**	**50.0**	**13:34**	**8**	**0**	**0**	**0**	**6**	**0**	**0**	**0**	**9:5**
99-2000	**Tampa Bay**	**NHL**	**80**	**22**	**26**	**48**	**18**	**3**	**0**	**5**	**167**	**13.2**	**–26**	**6**	**50.0**	**15:32**	....	....	....	....	....	....	....	....	....
2000-01	**Tampa Bay**	**NHL**	**76**	**32**	**24**	**56**	**48**	**8**	**0**	**4**	**217**	**14.7**	**–1**	**21**	**42.9**	**17:15**	....	....	....	....	....	....	....	....	....
2001-02	**Tampa Bay**	**NHL**	**54**	**14**	**17**	**31**	**27**	**2**	**0**	**4**	**141**	**9.9**	**0**	**25**	**40.0**	**19:05**	....	....	....	....	....	....	....	....	....
2002-03	**Tampa Bay**	**NHL**	**76**	**17**	**23**	**40**	**43**	**2**	**1**	**4**	**179**	**9.5**	**7**	**35**	**28.6**	**17:35**	**11**	**2**	**0**	**2**	**18**	**0**	**0**	**0**	**19:18**
2003-04♦	**Tampa Bay**	**NHL**	**82**	**29**	**28**	**57**	**32**	**5**	**1**	**2**	**206**	**14.1**	**31**	**138**	**38.4**	**18:12**	**23**	**8**	**11**	**19**	**10**	**3**	**0**	**2**	**20:47**
2004-05	Timra IK	Sweden	43	12	24	36	58	....	....	....	....	....	....	....	....	....	7	1	1	2	8	....	....	....	....
2005-06	**Tampa Bay**	**NHL**	**77**	**31**	**23**	**54**	**56**	**12**	**1**	**4**	**221**	**14.0**	**5**	**171**	**51.5**	**19:35**	**5**	**0**	**0**	**0**	**6**	**0**	**0**	**0**	**18:46**
	Sweden	Olympics	8	2	1	3	6	....	....	....	....	....	....	....	....	....	....	....	....	....	....	....	....	....	....
2006-07	**Columbus**	**NHL**	**79**	**22**	**20**	**42**	**50**	**6**	**0**	**4**	**220**	**10.0**	**–3**	**508**	**46.5**	**19:07**	....	....	....	....	....	....	....	....	....
2007-08	**Columbus**	**NHL**	**23**	**6**	**6**	**12**	**20**	**2**	**0**	**1**	**41**	**14.6**	**1**	**103**	**44.7**	**16:51**	....	....	....	....	....	....	....	....	....
2008-09	**Columbus**	**NHL**	**50**	**9**	**16**	**25**	**28**	**2**	**0**	**0**	**113**	**8.0**	**2**	**122**	**40.2**	**16:53**	**4**	**1**	**0**	**1**	**0**	**0**	**0**	**0**	**13:07**
2009-10	**Columbus**	**NHL**	**24**	**2**	**4**	**6**	**12**	**0**	**0**	**2**	**35**	**5.7**	**–6**	**12**	**58.3**	**14:41**	....	....	....	....	....	....	....	....	....
	Sweden	Olympics	3	0	1	1	0	....	....	....	....	....	....	....	....	....	....	....	....	....	....	....	....	....	....
	Los Angeles	**NHL**	**20**	**3**	**2**	**5**	**14**	**2**	**0**	**0**	**32**	**9.4**	**–2**	**16**	**68.8**	**14:55**	**6**	**3**	**1**	**4**	**2**	**2**	**0**	**0**	**17:22**
	NHL Totals		**858**	**225**	**227**	**452**	**439**	**46**	**3**	**37**	**1902**	**11.8**		**1159**	**45.1**	**17:16**	**57**	**14**	**12**	**26**	**42**	**5**	**0**	**2**	**17:53**

Played in NHL All-Star Game (2001)
Traded to **Tampa Bay** by **Toronto** for Cory Cross and Tampa Bay's 7th round choice (Ivan Kolozvary) in 2001 Entry Draft, October 1, 1999. Signed as a free agent by **Timra** (Sweden), October 5, 2004. Traded to **Columbus** by **Tampa Bay** with Fredrik Norrena for Marc Denis, June 30, 2006. • Missed majority of 2007-08 season recovering from shoulder injury suffered in game at Anaheim, November 1, 2007. Traded to **Los Angeles** by **Columbus** for future considerations, March 3, 2010.

MOEN, Travis

(MOH-ehn, TRA-vihs) **MTL.**

Left wing. Shoots left. 6'2", 215 lbs. Born, Stewart Valley, Sask., April 6, 1982. Calgary's 6th choice, 155th overall, in 2000 Entry Draft.

Season	Club	League	GP	G	A	Pts	PIM	PP	SH	GW	S	%	+/-	TF	F%	Min	GP	G	A	Pts	PIM	PP	SH	GW	M
1998-99	Swift Current	SMHL	STATISTICS NOT AVAILABLE																						
	Kelowna Rockets	WHL	4	0	0	0	0	....	....	....	....	....	....	....	....	....	....	....	....	....	....	....	....	....	....
99-2000	Kelowna Rockets	WHL	66	9	6	15	96	....	....	....	....	....	....	....	....	....	5	1	1	2	2	....	....	....	....
2000-01	Kelowna Rockets	WHL	40	8	8	16	106	....	....	....	....	....	....	....	....	....	....	....	....	....	....	....	....	....	....
2001-02	Kelowna Rockets	WHL	71	10	17	27	197	....	....	....	....	....	....	....	....	....	13	1	0	1	28	....	....	....	....
2002-03	Norfolk Admirals	AHL	42	1	2	3	62	....	....	....	....	....	....	....	....	....	9	0	0	0	20	....	....	....	....
2003-04	**Chicago**	**NHL**	**82**	**4**	**2**	**6**	**142**	**0**	**0**	**2**	**51**	**7.8**	**–17**	**19**	**15.8**	**10:57**	....	....	....	....	....	....	....	....	....
2004-05	Norfolk Admirals	AHL	79	8	12	20	187	....	....	....	....	....	....	....	....	....	6	0	1	1	6	....	....	....	....
2005-06	**Anaheim**	**NHL**	**39**	**4**	**1**	**5**	**72**	**0**	**0**	**0**	**28**	**14.3**	**–3**	**8**	**12.5**	**11:03**	**9**	**1**	**0**	**1**	**10**	**0**	**0**	**0**	**8:25**
2006-07♦	**Anaheim**	**NHL**	**82**	**11**	**10**	**21**	**101**	**0**	**0**	**0**	**124**	**8.9**	**–4**	**10**	**30.0**	**14:48**	**21**	**7**	**5**	**12**	**22**	**0**	**0**	**3**	**17:19**
2007-08	**Anaheim**	**NHL**	**77**	**3**	**5**	**8**	**81**	**0**	**1**	**1**	**98**	**3.1**	**–10**	**25**	**32.0**	**15:50**	**6**	**1**	**1**	**2**	**2**	**0**	**0**	**0**	**14:09**
2008-09	**Anaheim**	**NHL**	**63**	**4**	**7**	**11**	**77**	**0**	**2**	**1**	**77**	**5.2**	**–17**	**7**	**28.6**	**14:53**	....	....	....	....	....	....	....	....	....
	San Jose	**NHL**	**19**	**3**	**2**	**5**	**14**	**0**	**1**	**1**	**24**	**12.5**	**–1**	**11**	**18.2**	**15:21**	**6**	**0**	**0**	**0**	**2**	**0**	**0**	**0**	**12:54**
2009-10	**Montreal**	**NHL**	**81**	**8**	**11**	**19**	**57**	**1**	**2**	**0**	**107**	**7.5**	**–2**	**12**	**25.0**	**15:00**	**19**	**2**	**1**	**3**	**4**	**0**	**1**	**1**	**13:15**
	NHL Totals		**443**	**37**	**38**	**75**	**544**	**1**	**6**	**5**	**509**	**7.3**		**92**	**23.9**	**14:00**	**61**	**11**	**7**	**18**	**40**	**0**	**1**	**4**	**13:59**

Signed as a free agent by **Chicago**, October 21, 2002. Traded to **Anaheim** by **Chicago** for Michael Holmqvist, July 30, 2005. • Missed majority of 2005-06 season recovering from recurring knee and shoulder injuries and as a healthy reserve. Traded to **San Jose** by **Anaheim** with Kent Huskins for Timo Pielmeier, Nick Bonino and future considerations, March 4, 2009. Signed as a free agent by **Montreal**, July 10, 2009.

MOJZIS, Tomas

(moi-ZHEESH, TAW-mash)

Defense. Shoots left. 6'1", 192 lbs. Born, Kolin, Czech., May 2, 1982. Toronto's 11th choice, 246th overall, in 2001 Entry Draft.

Season	Club	League	GP	G	A	Pts	PIM	PP	SH	GW	S	%	+/-	TF	F%	Min	GP	G	A	Pts	PIM	PP	SH	GW	M
99-2000	HC Pardubice Jr.	CzRep-Jr.	40	7	1	8	....	....	....	....	....	....	....	....	....	....	....	....	....	....	....	....	....	....	....
2000-01	Moose Jaw	WHL	72	11	25	36	115	....	....	....	....	....	....	....	....	....	4	0	1	1	8	....	....	....	....
2001-02	Moose Jaw	WHL	28	2	11	13	43	....	....	....	....	....	....	....	....	....	....	....	....	....	....	....	....	....	....
	Seattle	WHL	36	8	15	23	66	....	....	....	....	....	....	....	....	....	11	1	3	4	20	....	....	....	....
2002-03	Seattle	WHL	62	21	49	70	126	....	....	....	....	....	....	....	....	....	15	1	6	7	36	....	....	....	....
2003-04	Manitoba Moose	AHL	63	5	13	18	50	....	....	....	....	....	....	....	....	....	....	....	....	....	....	....	....	....	....
2004-05	Manitoba Moose	AHL	80	7	23	30	62	....	....	....	....	....	....	....	....	....	14	0	2	2	28	....	....	....	....
2005-06	**Vancouver**	**NHL**	**7**	**0**	**1**	**1**	**12**	**0**	**0**	**0**	**7**	**0.0**	**2**	**0**	**0.0**	**13:57**	....	....	....	....	....	....	....	....	....
	Manitoba Moose	AHL	37	5	13	18	52	....	....	....	....	....	....	....	....	....	....	....	....	....	....	....	....	....	....
	Peoria Rivermen	AHL	12	3	4	7	14	....	....	....	....	....	....	....	....	....	1	0	0	0	0	....	....	....	....
2006-07	**St. Louis**	**NHL**	**6**	**1**	**0**	**1**	**0**	**0**	**0**	**0**	**7**	**14.3**	**0**	**0**	**0.0**	**10:03**	....	....	....	....	....	....	....	....	....
	Peoria Rivermen	AHL	69	2	24	26	112	....	....	....	....	....	....	....	....	....	....	....	....	....	....	....	....	....	....
2007-08	Sibir Novosibirsk	Russia	28	2	2	4	38	....	....	....	....	....	....	....	....	....	....	....	....	....	....	....	....	....	....
2008-09	**Minnesota**	**NHL**	**4**	**0**	**1**	**1**	**2**	**0**	**0**	**0**	**2**	**0.0**	**–1**	**0**	**0.0**	**7:15**	....	....	....	....	....	....	....	....	....
	Houston Aeros	AHL	46	7	15	22	51	....	....	....	....	....	....	....	....	....	15	2	0	2	8	....	....	....	....
2009-10	MODO	Sweden	52	5	5	10	44	....	....	....	....	....	....	....	....	....	....	....	....	....	....	....	....	....	....
	NHL Totals		**17**	**1**	**2**	**3**	**14**	**0**	**0**	**0**	**16**	**6.3**		**0**	**0.0**	**11:00**	....	....	....	....	....	....	....	....	....

WHL West First All-Star Team (2003) • Canadian Major Junior First All-Star Team (2003)
Traded to **Vancouver** by **Toronto** for Brad Leeb, September 4, 2002. Traded to **St. Louis** by **Vancouver** with Vancouver's 3rd round choice (later traded to New Jersey - New Jersey selected Vladimir Zharkov) in 2006 Entry Draft for Eric Weinrich, March 9, 2006. Signed as a free agent by **Novosibirsk** (Russia), May 21, 2007. Signed as a free agent by **Minesota**, July 7, 2008. Signed as a free agent by **MODO** (Sweden), September 15, 2009.

MOLLER, Oscar

(MOH-luhr, AH-skuhr) **L.A.**

Center. Shoots right. 5'10", 186 lbs. Born, Stockholm, Sweden, January 22, 1989. Los Angeles' 2nd choice, 52nd overall, in 2007 Entry Draft.

Season	Club	League	GP	G	A	Pts	PIM	PP	SH	GW	S	%	+/-	TF	F%	Min	GP	G	A	Pts	PIM	PP	SH	GW	M
2003-04	Spanga U18	Swe-U18	32	28	12	40	68	....	....	....	....	....	....	....	....	....	....	....	....	....	....	....	....	....	....
2004-05	Spanga U18	Swe-U18	24	28	16	44	52	....	....	....	....	....	....	....	....	....	....	....	....	....	....	....	....	....	....
	Spanga Jr.	Swe-Jr.	4	6	1	7	6	....	....	....	....	....	....	....	....	....	....	....	....	....	....	....	....	....	....
	Spanga	Sweden-4	6	6	4	10	0	....	....	....	....	....	....	....	....	....	....	....	....	....	....	....	....	....	....
2005-06	Djurgarden U18	Swe-U18	8	8	5	13	6	....	....	....	....	....	....	....	....	....	2	1	0	1	0	....	....	....	....
	Djurgarden Jr.	Swe-Jr.	25	8	5	13	41	....	....	....	....	....	....	....	....	....	4	2	0	2	0	....	....	....	....
2006-07	Chilliwack Bruins	WHL	68	32	37	69	50	....	....	....	....	....	....	....	....	....	5	0	3	3	6	....	....	....	....
2007-08	Chilliwack Bruins	WHL	63	39	43	82	42	....	....	....	....	....	....	....	....	....	4	2	1	3	4	....	....	....	....
	Manchester	AHL	....	....	....	....	....	....	....	....	....	....	....	....	....	....	2	0	1	1	0	....	....	....	....
2008-09	**Los Angeles**	**NHL**	**40**	**7**	**8**	**15**	**16**	**5**	**0**	**0**	**81**	**8.6**	**–3**	**86**	**43.0**	**13:22**	....	....	....	....	....	....	....	....	....
	Manchester	AHL	8	2	3	5	6	....	....	....	....	....	....	....	....	....	....	....	....	....	....	....	....	....	....

			Regular Season														Playoffs								
Season	Club	League	GP	G	A	Pts	PIM	PP	SH	GW	S	%	+/-	TF	F%	Min	GP	G	A	Pts	PIM	PP	SH	GW	Min
2009-10	Los Angeles	NHL	34	4	3	7	4	1	0	0	42	9.5	-6	104	30.8	8:35	....	....	....	....	....	....	....	....	....
	Manchester	AHL	43	15	18	33	20	....	....	....	....	....	....	....	....	....	16	2	5	7	0	....	....	....	....
	NHL Totals		74	11	11	22	20	6	0	0	123	8.9		190	36.3	11:10	....	....	....	....	....	....	....	....	....

VHL West First All-Star Team (2008)

MONTADOR, Steve

(MAWN-tuh-dohr, STEEV) **BUF.**

Defense. Shoots right. 6', 207 lbs. Born, Vancouver, B.C., December 21, 1979.

Season	Club	League	GP	G	A	Pts	PIM	PP	SH	GW	S	%	+/-	TF	F%	Min	GP	G	A	Pts	PIM	PP	SH	GW	Min
1995-96	St. Mike's B's	OPJHL	46	3	16	19	145	....	....	....	....	....	....	....	....	....	7	1	2	3	10	....	....	....	....
1996-97	North Bay	OHL	63	7	28	35	129	....	....	....	....	....	....	....	....	....	....	....	....	....	....	....	....	....	....
1997-98	North Bay	OHL	37	5	16	21	54	....	....	....	....	....	....	....	....	....	....	....	....	....	....	....	....	....	....
	Erie Otters	OHL	26	3	17	20	35	....	....	....	....	....	....	....	....	....	7	1	1	2	9	....	....	....	....
1998-99	Erie Otters	OHL	61	9	33	42	114	....	....	....	....	....	....	....	....	....	5	0	2	2	4	....	....	....	....
99-2000	Peterborough	OHL	64	14	42	56	97	....	....	....	....	....	....	....	....	....	5	0	2	2	4	....	....	....	....
	Saint John Flames	AHL	....	....	....	....	....	....	....	....	....	....	....	....	....	....	2	0	0	0	0	....	....	....	....
2000-01	Saint John Flames	AHL	58	1	6	7	95	....	....	....	....	....	....	....	....	....	19	0	8	8	13	....	....	....	....
2001-02	**Calgary**	**NHL**	**11**	**1**	**2**	**3**	**26**	**0**	**0**	**0**	**10**	**10.0**	**-2**	**0**	**0.0**	**12:12**	....	....	....	....	....	....	....	....	....
	Saint John Flames	AHL	67	9	16	25	107	....	....	....	....	....	....	....	....	....	....	....	....	....	....	....	....	....	....
2002-03	**Calgary**	**NHL**	**50**	**1**	**1**	**2**	**114**	**0**	**0**	**0**	**64**	**1.6**	**-9**	**0**	**0.0**	**15:11**	....	....	....	....	....	....	....	....	....
	Saint John Flames	AHL	11	1	7	8	20	....	....	....	....	....	....	....	....	....	....	....	....	....	....	....	....	....	....
2003-04	**Calgary**	**NHL**	**26**	**1**	**2**	**3**	**50**	**0**	**0**	**1**	**31**	**3.2**	**-1**	**1**	**0.0**	**11:46**	**20**	**1**	**2**	**3**	**6**	**0**	**0**	**1**	**17:43**
2004-05	HC Mulhouse	France	15	1	7	8	69	....	....	....	....	....	....	....	....	....	....	....	....	....	....	....	....	....	....
2005-06	**Calgary**	**NHL**	**7**	**1**	**0**	**1**	**11**	**0**	**0**	**0**	**13**	**7.7**	**0**	**0**	**0.0**	**11:49**	....	....	....	....	....	....	....	....	....
	Florida	**NHL**	**51**	**1**	**5**	**6**	**68**	**0**	**0**	**0**	**42**	**2.4**	**4**	**0**	**0.0**	**14:04**	....	....	....	....	....	....	....	....	....
2006-07	**Florida**	**NHL**	**72**	**1**	**8**	**9**	**119**	**0**	**0**	**0**	**88**	**1.1**	**1**	**0**	**0.0**	**13:08**	....	....	....	....	....	....	....	....	....
2007-08	**Florida**	**NHL**	**73**	**8**	**15**	**23**	**73**	**2**	**0**	**0**	**96**	**8.3**	**1**	**0**	**0.0**	**11:39**	....	....	....	....	....	....	....	....	....
2008-09	**Anaheim**	**NHL**	**65**	**4**	**16**	**20**	**125**	**0**	**0**	**0**	**100**	**4.0**	**14**	**0**	**0.0**	**16:12**	....	....	....	....	....	....	....	....	....
	Boston	**NHL**	**13**	**0**	**1**	**1**	**18**	**0**	**0**	**0**	**17**	**0.0**	**3**	**1**	**0.0**	**15:55**	**11**	**1**	**2**	**3**	**18**	**0**	**0**	**0**	**19:33**
2009-10	**Buffalo**	**NHL**	**78**	**5**	**18**	**23**	**75**	**0**	**0**	**2**	**134**	**3.7**	**0**	**1**	**0.0**	**17:06**	**6**	**1**	**0**	**1**	**4**	**0**	**0**	**0**	**23:54**
	NHL Totals		**446**	**23**	**68**	**91**	**679**	**2**	**0**	**3**	**595**	**3.9**		**3**	**0.0**	**14:20**	**37**	**3**	**4**	**7**	**28**	**0**	**0**	**1**	**19:16**

igned as a free agent by **Calgary**, April 10, 2000. • Missed majority of 2003-04 season as a healthy reserve. Signed as a free agent by **Mulhouse** (France), September 17, 2004. Traded to **Florida** by **algary** with Dustin Johner for Kristian Huselius, December 2, 2005. Signed as a free agent by **Anaheim**, July 11, 2008. Traded to **Boston** by **Anaheim** for Petteri Nokelainen, March 4, 2009. Signed as a ee agent by **Buffalo**, July 1, 2009.

MOORE, Dominic

(MOOR, DOHM-ihn-ihk) **T.B.**

Center. Shoots left. 6', 196 lbs. Born, Sarnia, Ont., August 3, 1980. NY Rangers' 2nd choice, 95th overall, in 2000 Entry Draft.

Season	Club	League	GP	G	A	Pts	PIM	PP	SH	GW	S	%	+/-	TF	F%	Min	GP	G	A	Pts	PIM	PP	SH	GW	Min
1996-97	Thornhill Islanders	MTJHL	29	4	6	10	48	....	....	....	....	....	....	....	....	....	1	0	1	1	0	....	....	....	....
1997-98	Aurora Tigers	OPJHL	51	10	15	25	16	....	....	....	....	....	....	....	....	....	....	....	....	....	....	....	....	....	....
1998-99	Aurora Tigers	OPJHL	51	34	53	87	70	....	....	....	....	....	....	....	....	....	....	....	....	....	....	....	....	....	....
99-2000	Harvard Crimson	ECAC	30	12	24	28	16	....	....	....	....	....	....	....	....	....	....	....	....	....	....	....	....	....	....
2000-01	Harvard Crimson	ECAC	32	15	28	43	40	....	....	....	....	....	....	....	....	....	....	....	....	....	....	....	....	....	....
2001-02	Harvard Crimson	ECAC	32	13	16	29	37	....	....	....	....	....	....	....	....	....	....	....	....	....	....	....	....	....	....
2002-03	Harvard Crimson	ECAC	34	*24	27	*51	30	....	....	....	....	....	....	....	....	....	....	....	....	....	....	....	....	....	....
2003-04	**NY Rangers**	**NHL**	**5**	**0**	**3**	**3**	**0**	**0**	**0**	**0**	**3**	**0.0**	**0**	**36**	**30.6**	**9:18**	....	....	....	....	....	....	....	....	....
	Hartford	AHL	70	14	25	39	60	....	....	....	....	....	....	....	....	....	16	3	3	6	8	....	....	....	....
2004-05	Hartford	AHL	78	19	31	50	78	....	....	....	....	....	....	....	....	....	6	1	1	2	4	....	....	....	....
2005-06	**NY Rangers**	**NHL**	**82**	**9**	**9**	**18**	**28**	**2**	**0**	**1**	**139**	**6.5**	**4**	**814**	**46.3**	**12:28**	**4**	**0**	**0**	**0**	**2**	**0**	**0**	**0**	**11:21**
2006-07	**Pittsburgh**	**NHL**	**59**	**6**	**9**	**15**	**46**	**0**	**0**	**0**	**100**	**6.0**	**1**	**678**	**51.6**	**13:04**	....	....	....	....	....	....	....	....	....
	Minnesota	**NHL**	**10**	**2**	**0**	**2**	**10**	**0**	**0**	**1**	**11**	**18.2**	**3**	**66**	**62.1**	**10:12**	....	....	....	....	....	....	....	....	....
2007-08	**Minnesota**	**NHL**	**30**	**1**	**2**	**3**	**10**	**0**	**0**	**0**	**28**	**3.6**	**-11**	**311**	**52.4**	**11:57**	....	....	....	....	....	....	....	....	....
	Toronto	**NHL**	**38**	**4**	**10**	**14**	**14**	**1**	**0**	**0**	**72**	**5.6**	**7**	**393**	**50.6**	**14:21**	....	....	....	....	....	....	....	....	....
2008-09	**Toronto**	**NHL**	**63**	**12**	**29**	**41**	**69**	**4**	**1**	**1**	**132**	**9.1**	**-1**	**1007**	**54.8**	**17:18**	....	....	....	....	....	....	....	....	....
	Buffalo	**NHL**	**18**	**1**	**3**	**4**	**23**	**0**	**0**	**0**	**33**	**3.0**	**-1**	**237**	**51.1**	**15:12**	....	....	....	....	....	....	....	....	....
2009-10	**Florida**	**NHL**	**48**	**8**	**9**	**17**	**35**	**2**	**1**	**0**	**81**	**9.9**	**-7**	**462**	**55.8**	**14:55**	....	....	....	....	....	....	....	....	....
	Montreal	**NHL**	**21**	**2**	**9**	**11**	**8**	**0**	**1**	**0**	**38**	**5.3**	**4**	**201**	**53.2**	**14:40**	**19**	**4**	**1**	**5**	**6**	**0**	**0**	**1**	**14:34**
	NHL Totals		**374**	**45**	**83**	**128**	**243**	**9**	**3**	**3**	**637**	**7.1**		**4205**	**51.8**	**14:00**	**23**	**4**	**1**	**5**	**8**	**0**	**0**	**1**	**14:00**

CAC All-Rookie Team (2000) • ECAC Second All-Star Team (2001) • ECAC First All-Star Team (2003) • NCAA East First All-American Team (2003)

raded to **Nashville** by **NY Rangers** for Adam Hall, July 19, 2006. Traded to **Pittsburgh** by **Nashville** with Libor Pivko for Pittsburgh's 3rd round choice (Ryan Thang) in 2007 Entry Draft, July 19, 2006. raded to **Minnesota** by **Pittsburgh** for Minnesota's 3rd round choice (Casey Pierro-Zabotel) in 2007 Entry Draft, February 27, 2007. Claimed on waivers by **Toronto** from **Minnesota**, January 11, 2008. raded to **Buffalo** by **Toronto** for Carolina's 2nd round choice (previously acquired, Toronto selected Jesse Blacker) in 2009 Entry Draft, March 4, 2009. Signed as a free agent by **Florida**, October 5, 2009. raded to **Montreal** by **Florida** for Montreal's 2nd round choice in 2011 Entry Draft, February 11, 2010. Signed as a free agent by **Tampa Bay**, July 30, 2010.

MOORE, Greg

(MOOR, GREHG) **PHI.**

Right wing. Shoots right. 6'1", 214 lbs. Born, Lisbon, ME, March 26, 1984. Calgary's 5th choice, 143rd overall, in 2003 Entry Draft.

Season	Club	League	GP	G	A	Pts	PIM	PP	SH	GW	S	%	+/-	TF	F%	Min	GP	G	A	Pts	PIM	PP	SH	GW	Min
99-2000	St. Dominic	High-ME	31	32	40	72		....	....	....	....	....	....	....	....	....	....	....	....	....	....	....	....	....	....
2000-01	USNTDP	U-17	13	4	6	10	1	....	....	....	....	....	....	....	....	....	....	....	....	....	....	....	....	....	....
	USNTDP	NAHL	56	8	12	20	22	....	....	....	....	....	....	....	....	....	....	....	....	....	....	....	....	....	....
2001-02	USNTDP	U-18	35	8	20	28	14	....	....	....	....	....	....	....	....	....	....	....	....	....	....	....	....	....	....
	USNTDP	USHL	12	2	2	4	4	....	....	....	....	....	....	....	....	....	....	....	....	....	....	....	....	....	....
	USNTDP	NAHL	6	3	2	5	2	....	....	....	....	....	....	....	....	....	....	....	....	....	....	....	....	....	....
2002-03	U. of Maine	H-East	33	9	7	16	10	....	....	....	....	....	....	....	....	....	....	....	....	....	....	....	....	....	....
2003-04	U. of Maine	H-East	39	15	8	23	44	....	....	....	....	....	....	....	....	....	....	....	....	....	....	....	....	....	....
2004-05	U. of Maine	H-East	40	14	9	23	16	....	....	....	....	....	....	....	....	....	....	....	....	....	....	....	....	....	....
2005-06	U. of Maine	H-East	42	28	17	45	47	....	....	....	....	....	....	....	....	....	....	....	....	....	....	....	....	....	....
	Hartford	AHL	2	1	1	2	2	....	....	....	....	....	....	....	....	....	13	2	5	7	6	....	....	....	....
2006-07	Hartford	AHL	79	8	17	25	41	....	....	....	....	....	....	....	....	....	7	0	1	1	4	....	....	....	....
2007-08	**NY Rangers**	**NHL**	**6**	**0**	**0**	**0**	**0**	**0**	**0**	**0**	**13**	**0.0**	**-2**	**8**	**37.5**	**11:49**	....	....	....	....	....	....	....	....	....
	Hartford	AHL	72	26	40	66	31	....	....	....	....	....	....	....	....	....	5	1	2	3	2	....	....	....	....
2008-09	Hartford	AHL	71	23	16	39	28	....	....	....	....	....	....	....	....	....	6	0	2	2	0	....	....	....	....
2009-10	Bridgeport	AHL	62	14	17	31	28	....	....	....	....	....	....	....	....	....	....	....	....	....	....	....	....	....	....
	Columbus	**NHL**	**4**	**0**	**0**	**0**	**0**	**0**	**0**	**0**	**2**	**0.0**	**0**	**8**	**50.0**	**5:54**	....	....	....	....	....	....	....	....	....
	Syracuse Crunch	AHL	16	5	5	10	10	....	....	....	....	....	....	....	....	....	....	....	....	....	....	....	....	....	....
	NHL Totals		**10**	**0**	**0**	**0**	**0**	**0**	**0**	**0**	**15**	**0.0**		**16**	**43.8**	**9:27**	....	....	....	....	....	....	....	....	....

ockey East First All-Star Team (2006) • NCAA East First All-American Team (2006)

raded to **NY Rangers** by **Calgary** with Jamie McLennan and Blair Betts for Chris Simon and NY Rangers' 7th round choice (Matt Schneider) in 2004 Entry Draft, March 6, 2004. Signed as a free agent by **Y Islanders**, July 6, 2009. Traded to **Columbus** by **NY Islanders** for Dylan Reese, March 1, 2010.

MORAN, Brad

(moh-RAN, BRAD) **EDM.**

Center. Shoots left. 5'11", 187 lbs. Born, Abbotsford, B.C., March 20, 1979. Buffalo's 8th choice, 191st overall, in 1998 Entry Draft.

Season	Club	League	GP	G	A	Pts	PIM	PP	SH	GW	S	%	+/-	TF	F%	Min	GP	G	A	Pts	PIM	PP	SH	GW	Min
1994-95	Abbotsford	Minor-BC	56	66	93	159	40	....	....	....	....	....	....	....	....	....	....	....	....	....	....	....	....	....	....
1995-96	Calgary Hitmen	WHL	70	13	31	44	28	....	....	....	....	....	....	....	....	....	....	....	....	....	....	....	....	....	....
1996-97	Calgary Hitmen	WHL	72	30	36	66	61	....	....	....	....	....	....	....	....	....	....	....	....	....	....	....	....	....	....
1997-98	Calgary Hitmen	WHL	72	53	49	102	64	....	....	....	....	....	....	....	....	....	18	10	8	18	20	....	....	....	....
1998-99	Calgary Hitmen	WHL	71	60	58	118	96	....	....	....	....	....	....	....	....	....	21	17	*25	42	26	....	....	....	....
99-2000	Calgary Hitmen	WHL	72	48	*72	*120	84	....	....	....	....	....	....	....	....	....	13	7	15	22	18	....	....	....	....
2000-01	Syracuse Crunch	AHL	71	11	19	30	30	....	....	....	....	....	....	....	....	....	5	3	4	7	2	....	....	....	....
2001-02	**Columbus**	**NHL**	**3**	**0**	**0**	**0**	**0**	**0**	**0**	**0**	**2**	**0.0**	**0**	**22**	**40.9**	**7:39**	....	....	....	....	....	....	....	....	....
	Syracuse Crunch	AHL	64	25	24	49	51	....	....	....	....	....	....	....	....	....	10	5	8	13	2	....	....	....	....
2002-03	Syracuse Crunch	AHL	47	12	19	31	22	....	....	....	....	....	....	....	....	....	....	....	....	....	....	....	....	....	....
2003-04	**Columbus**	**NHL**	**2**	**1**	**1**	**2**	**2**	**0**	**0**	**0**	**4**	**25.0**	**-1**	**25**	**64.0**	**10:03**	....	....	....	....	....	....	....	....	....
	Syracuse Crunch	AHL	72	24	35	59	44	....	....	....	....	....	....	....	....	....	7	5	3	8	2	....	....	....	....
2004-05	Syracuse Crunch	AHL	80	26	46	72	70	....	....	....	....	....	....	....	....	....	....	....	....	....	....	....	....	....	....
2005-06	Langnau	Swiss	18	4	4	8	18	....	....	....	....	....	....	....	....	....	6	4	6	10	10	....	....	....	....
2006-07	**Vancouver**	**NHL**	**3**	**0**	**1**	**1**	**2**	**0**	**0**	**0**	**3**	**0.0**	**0**	**24**	**58.3**	**12:38**	....	....	....	....	....	....	....	....	....
	Manitoba Moose	AHL	69	25	47	72	52	....	....	....	....	....	....	....	....	....	13	5	6	11	12	....	....	....	....
2007-08	Manitoba Moose	AHL	74	22	55	77	44	....	....	....	....	....	....	....	....	....	6	1	4	5	4	....	....	....	....

Season	Club	League	GP	G	A	Pts	PIM	PP	SH	GW	S	%	+/-	TF	F%	Min	GP	G	A	Pts	PIM	PP	SH	GW	M
			Regular Season														Playoffs								
2008-09	Skelleftea AIK	Sweden	55	11	31	42	28	....	....	....	....	....	....	....	....	....	9	2	2	4	6	....	....	....	
2009-10	Skelleftea AIK	Sweden	55	14	26	40	32	....	....	....	....	....	....	....	....	....	12	0	5	5	6	....	....	....	
	NHL Totals		**8**	**1**	**2**	**3**	**4**	**0**	**0**	**0**	**9**	**11.1**		**71**	**54.9**	**10:07**	....	....	....	....	....	....	....	....	

WHL East First All-Star Team (1999, 2000) • WHL Player of the Year (2000)

Signed as a free agent by **Columbus**, June 5, 2000. Signed as a free agent by **Vancouver**, June 19, 2006. Signed as a free agent by **Skelleftea** (Sweden), June 15, 2008. Signed as a free agent by **Edmonton**, July 7, 2010.

MOREAU, Ethan

(moh-ROH, EE-thuhn) **CB**

Left wing. Shoots left. 6'2", 220 lbs. Born, Huntsville, Ont., September 22, 1975. Chicago's 1st choice, 14th overall, in 1994 Entry Draft.

Season	Club	League	GP	G	A	Pts	PIM	PP	SH	GW	S	%	+/-	TF	F%	Min	GP	G	A	Pts	PIM	PP	SH	GW	Min
1990-91	Orillia Terriers	OHA-B	42	17	22	39	26	....	....	....	....	....	....	....	....	....	12	6	6	12	18	....	....	....	....
1991-92	Niagara Falls	OHL	62	20	35	55	39	....	....	....	....	....	....	....	....	....	17	4	6	10	4	....	....	....	....
1992-93	Niagara Falls	OHL	65	32	41	73	69	....	....	....	....	....	....	....	....	....	4	0	3	3	4	....	....	....	....
1993-94	Niagara Falls	OHL	59	44	54	98	100	....	....	....	....	....	....	....	....	....	....	....	....	....	....	....	....	....	....
1994-95	Niagara Falls	OHL	39	25	41	66	69	....	....	....	....	....	....	....	....	....	....	....	....	....	....	....	....	....	....
	Sudbury Wolves	OHL	23	13	17	30	22	....	....	....	....	....	....	....	....	....	18	6	12	18	26	....	....	....	....
1995-96	**Chicago**	**NHL**	**8**	**0**	**1**	**1**	**4**	**0**	**0**	**0**	**1**	**0.0**	**1**	....	....	....	....	....	....	....	....	....	....	....	....
	Indianapolis Ice	IHL	71	21	20	41	126	....	....	....	....	....	....	....	....	....	5	4	0	4	8	....	....	....	....
1996-97	**Chicago**	**NHL**	**82**	**15**	**16**	**31**	**123**	**0**	**0**	**1**	**114**	**13.2**	**13**	....	....	....	**6**	**1**	**0**	**1**	**9**	**0**	**0**	**0**	....
1997-98	**Chicago**	**NHL**	**54**	**9**	**9**	**18**	**73**	**2**	**0**	**0**	**87**	**10.3**	**0**	....	....	....	....	....	....	....	....	....	....	....	....
1998-99	**Chicago**	**NHL**	**66**	**9**	**6**	**15**	**84**	**0**	**0**	**1**	**80**	**11.3**	**−5**	**3**	**33.3**	**12:30**	....	....	....	....	....	....	....	....	....
	Edmonton	**NHL**	**14**	**1**	**5**	**6**	**8**	**0**	**0**	**1**	**16**	**6.3**	**2**	**1**	**0.0**	**11:47**	**4**	**0**	**3**	**3**	**6**	**0**	**0**	**0**	**17:26**
99-2000	**Edmonton**	**NHL**	**73**	**17**	**10**	**27**	**62**	**1**	**0**	**3**	**106**	**16.0**	**8**	**8**	**62.5**	**15:07**	**5**	**0**	**1**	**1**	**0**	**0**	**0**	**0**	**15:46**
2000-01	**Edmonton**	**NHL**	**68**	**9**	**10**	**19**	**90**	**0**	**1**	**3**	**97**	**9.3**	**−6**	**2**	**0.0**	**14:11**	**4**	**0**	**0**	**0**	**2**	**0**	**0**	**0**	**10:35**
2001-02	**Edmonton**	**NHL**	**80**	**11**	**5**	**16**	**81**	**0**	**2**	**1**	**129**	**8.5**	**4**	**11**	**54.6**	**12:43**	....	....	....	....	....	....	....	....	....
2002-03	**Edmonton**	**NHL**	**78**	**14**	**17**	**31**	**112**	**2**	**3**	**2**	**137**	**10.2**	**−7**	**25**	**12.0**	**13:30**	**6**	**0**	**1**	**1**	**16**	**0**	**0**	**0**	**12:23**
2003-04	**Edmonton**	**NHL**	**81**	**20**	**12**	**32**	**96**	**0**	**3**	**5**	**180**	**11.1**	**7**	**59**	**44.1**	**15:04**	....	....	....	....	....	....	....	....	....
2004-05	EC Villacher SV	Austria	16	10	6	16	73	....	....	....	....	....	....	....	....	....	3	4	0	4	0	....	....	....	....
2005-06	**Edmonton**	**NHL**	**74**	**11**	**16**	**27**	**87**	**2**	**4**	**4**	**151**	**7.3**	**6**	**29**	**48.3**	**15:59**	**21**	**2**	**1**	**3**	**19**	**0**	**0**	**0**	**14:35**
2006-07	**Edmonton**	**NHL**	**7**	**1**	**0**	**1**	**12**	**0**	**0**	**0**	**18**	**5.6**	**−4**	**20**	**50.0**	**15:08**	....	....	....	....	....	....	....	....	....
2007-08	**Edmonton**	**NHL**	**25**	**5**	**4**	**9**	**39**	**1**	**0**	**0**	**54**	**9.3**	**−4**	**23**	**43.5**	**15:55**	....	....	....	....	....	....	....	....	....
2008-09	**Edmonton**	**NHL**	**77**	**14**	**12**	**26**	**133**	**0**	**1**	**2**	**159**	**8.8**	**0**	**36**	**30.6**	**15:22**	....	....	....	....	....	....	....	....	....
2009-10	**Edmonton**	**NHL**	**76**	**9**	**9**	**18**	**62**	**0**	**3**	**2**	**143**	**6.3**	**−18**	**17**	**41.2**	**14:24**	....	....	....	....	....	....	....	....	....
	NHL Totals		**863**	**145**	**132**	**277**	**1066**	**8**	**17**	**25**	**1472**	**9.9**		**234**	**39.7**	**14:21**	**46**	**3**	**6**	**9**	**52**	**0**	**0**	**0**	**14:17**

OHL All-Rookie Team (1992) • King Clancy Memorial Trophy (2009)

Traded to **Edmonton** by **Chicago** with Daniel Cleary, Chad Kilger and Christian Laflamme for Boris Mironov, Dean McAmmond and Jonas Elofsson, March 20, 1999. Signed as a free agent by **Villacher** (Austria), December 20, 2004. • Missed majority of 2006-07 season recovering from shoulder injury suffered in game vs. Detroit, October 21, 2006. • Missed majority of 2007-08 season recovering from foot injury suffered in training camp. Claimed on waivers by **Columbus** from **Edmonton**, June 30, 2010.

MORMINA, Joey

(mohr-MEE-nah, JOH-ee)

Defense. Shoots left. 6'6", 220 lbs. Born, Montreal, Que., June 29, 1982. Philadelphia's 6th choice, 193rd overall, in 2002 Entry Draft.

Season	Club	League	GP	G	A	Pts	PIM	PP	SH	GW	S	%	+/-	TF	F%	Min	GP	G	A	Pts	PIM	PP	SH	GW	Min
2000-01	Holderness	High-NH	29	15	15	30	....	....	....	....	....	....	....	....	....	....	....	....	....	....	....	....	....	....	....
2001-02	Colgate	ECAC	34	2	13	15	28	....	....	....	....	....	....	....	....	....	....	....	....	....	....	....	....	....	....
2002-03	Colgate	ECAC	40	4	9	13	52	....	....	....	....	....	....	....	....	....	....	....	....	....	....	....	....	....	....
2003-04	Colgate	ECAC	28	2	10	12	26	....	....	....	....	....	....	....	....	....	....	....	....	....	....	....	....	....	....
2004-05	Colgate	ECAC	39	8	8	16	50	....	....	....	....	....	....	....	....	....	....	....	....	....	....	....	....	....	....
2005-06	Manchester	AHL	61	0	13	13	70	....	....	....	....	....	....	....	....	....	7	0	0	0	4	....	....	....	....
2006-07	Manchester	AHL	62	2	9	11	108	....	....	....	....	....	....	....	....	....	1	0	0	0	2	....	....	....	....
2007-08	**Carolina**	**NHL**	**1**	**0**	**0**	**0**	**0**	**0**	**0**	**0**	**1**	**0.0**	**0**	**0**	**0.0**	**7:45**	....	....	....	....	....	....	....	....	....
	Albany River Rats	AHL	77	4	9	13	96	....	....	....	....	....	....	....	....	....	7	0	0	0	4	....	....	....	....
2008-09	Wilkes-Barre	AHL	70	2	9	11	71	....	....	....	....	....	....	....	....	....	12	0	0	0	12	....	....	....	....
2009-10	Adirondack	AHL	77	5	18	23	102	....	....	....	....	....	....	....	....	....	....	....	....	....	....	....	....	....	....
	NHL Totals		**1**	**0**	**0**	**0**	**0**	**0**	**0**	**0**	**1**	**0.0**		**0**	**0.0**	**7:45**	....	....	....	....	....	....	....	....	....

Signed as a free agent by **Los Angeles**, August 24, 2005. Signed as a free agent by **Carolina**, July 2, 2007. Signed as a free agent by **Pittsburgh**, July 10, 2008. Signed as a free agent by **Philadelphia**, July 23, 2009. Signed as a free agent by **Kassel** (Germany), August 5, 2010.

MORRIS, Derek

(MOH-rihs, DAIR-ihk) **PHX.**

Defense. Shoots right. 6', 221 lbs. Born, Edmonton, Alta., August 24, 1978. Calgary's 1st choice, 13th overall, in 1996 Entry Draft.

Season	Club	League	GP	G	A	Pts	PIM	PP	SH	GW	S	%	+/-	TF	F%	Min	GP	G	A	Pts	PIM	PP	SH	GW	Min
1994-95	Red Deer Vipers	AMHL	31	6	35	41	74	....	....	....	....	....	....	....	....	....	....	....	....	....	....	....	....	....	....
1995-96	Regina Pats	WHL	67	8	44	52	70	....	....	....	....	....	....	....	....	....	11	1	7	8	26	....	....	....	....
1996-97	Regina Pats	WHL	67	18	57	75	180	....	....	....	....	....	....	....	....	....	5	0	3	3	9	....	....	....	....
	Saint John Flames	AHL	7	0	3	3	7	....	....	....	....	....	....	....	....	....	5	0	3	3	7	....	....	....	....
1997-98	**Calgary**	**NHL**	**82**	**9**	**20**	**29**	**88**	**5**	**1**	**1**	**120**	**7.5**	**1**	....	....	....	....	....	....	....	....	....	....	....	....
1998-99	**Calgary**	**NHL**	**71**	**7**	**27**	**34**	**73**	**3**	**0**	**2**	**150**	**4.7**	**4**	**0**	**0.0**	**20:44**	....	....	....	....	....	....	....	....	....
99-2000	**Calgary**	**NHL**	**78**	**9**	**29**	**38**	**80**	**3**	**0**	**2**	**193**	**4.7**	**2**	**0**	**0.0**	**24:51**	....	....	....	....	....	....	....	....	....
2000-01	**Calgary**	**NHL**	**51**	**5**	**23**	**28**	**56**	**3**	**1**	**4**	**142**	**3.5**	**−15**	**0**	**0.0**	**25:51**	....	....	....	....	....	....	....	....	....
	Saint John Flames	AHL	3	1	2	3	2	....	....	....	....	....	....	....	....	....	....	....	....	....	....	....	....	....	....
2001-02	**Calgary**	**NHL**	**61**	**4**	**30**	**34**	**88**	**2**	**0**	**1**	**166**	**2.4**	**−4**	**1**	**100.0**	**24:40**	....	....	....	....	....	....	....	....	....
2002-03	**Colorado**	**NHL**	**75**	**11**	**37**	**48**	**68**	**9**	**0**	**7**	**191**	**5.8**	**16**	**0**	**0.0**	**23:49**	**7**	**0**	**3**	**3**	**6**	**0**	**0**	**0**	**22:44**
2003-04	**Colorado**	**NHL**	**69**	**6**	**22**	**28**	**47**	**2**	**0**	**1**	**139**	**4.3**	**4**	**0**	**0.0**	**20:53**	....	....	....	....	....	....	....	....	....
	Phoenix	**NHL**	**14**	**0**	**4**	**4**	**2**	**0**	**0**	**0**	**28**	**0.0**	**−5**	**0**	**0.0**	**25:02**	....	....	....	....	....	....	....	....	....
2004-05			DID NOT PLAY														....	....	....	....	....	....	....	....	....
2005-06	**Phoenix**	**NHL**	**53**	**6**	**21**	**27**	**54**	**4**	**1**	**2**	**91**	**6.6**	**−7**	**1**	**0.0**	**20:52**	....	....	....	....	....	....	....	....	....
2006-07	**Phoenix**	**NHL**	**82**	**6**	**19**	**25**	**115**	**2**	**0**	**1**	**129**	**4.7**	**−18**	**1**	**100.0**	**20:29**	....	....	....	....	....	....	....	....	....
2007-08	**Phoenix**	**NHL**	**82**	**8**	**17**	**25**	**83**	**2**	**0**	**0**	**135**	**5.9**	**8**	**1**	**0.0**	**21:43**	....	....	....	....	....	....	....	....	....
2008-09	**Phoenix**	**NHL**	**57**	**5**	**7**	**12**	**24**	**0**	**1**	**0**	**89**	**5.6**	**−13**	**0**	**0.0**	**21:16**	....	....	....	....	....	....	....	....	....
	NY Rangers	**NHL**	**18**	**0**	**8**	**8**	**16**	**0**	**0**	**0**	**31**	**0.0**	**3**	**0**	**0.0**	**19:41**	**7**	**0**	**2**	**2**	**0**	**0**	**0**	**0**	**16:24**
2009-10	**Boston**	**NHL**	**58**	**3**	**22**	**25**	**26**	**2**	**0**	**0**	**95**	**3.2**	**−2**	**1**	**0.0**	**22:00**	....	....	....	....	....	....	....	....	....
	Phoenix	**NHL**	**18**	**1**	**3**	**4**	**11**	**0**	**0**	**0**	**25**	**4.0**	**4**	**0**	**0.0**	**19:39**	**7**	**1**	**3**	**4**	**11**	**1**	**0**	**1**	**19:35**
	NHL Totals		**869**	**80**	**289**	**369**	**831**	**37**	**4**	**21**	**1724**	**4.6**		**5**	**40.0**	**22:20**	**21**	**1**	**8**	**9**	**17**	**1**	**0**	**1**	**19:34**

WHL East First All-Star Team (1997) • NHL All-Rookie Team (1998)

Traded to **Colorado** by **Calgary** with Jeff Shantz and Dean McAmmond for Chris Drury and Stephane Yelle, October 1, 2002. Traded to **Phoenix** by **Colorado** with Keith Ballard for Ossi Vaananen, Chris Gratton and Phoenix's 2nd round choice (Paul Stastny) in 2005 Entry Draft, March 9, 2004. Traded to **NY Rangers** by **Phoenix** for Dmitri Kalinin, Nigel Dawes and Petr Prucha, March 4, 2009. Signed as a free agent by **Boston**, July 25, 2009. Traded to **Phoenix** by **Boston** for future considerations, March 3, 2010.

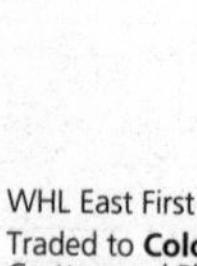

MORRISON, Brendan

(MOHR-ih-suhn, BREHN-duhn)

Center. Shoots left. 5'11", 185 lbs. Born, Pitt Meadows, B.C., August 15, 1975. New Jersey's 3rd choice, 39th overall, in 1993 Entry Draft.

Season	Club	League	GP	G	A	Pts	PIM	PP	SH	GW	S	%	+/-	TF	F%	Min	GP	G	A	Pts	PIM	PP	SH	GW	Min
1990-91	Ridge Meadows	Minor-BC	77	126	127	253	88	....	....	....	....	....	....	....	....	....	....	....	....	....	....	....	....	....	....
1991-92	Ridge Meadows	Minor-BC	55	56	111	167	56	....	....	....	....	....	....	....	....	....	....	....	....	....	....	....	....	....	....
1992-93	Penticton	BCJHL	56	35	59	94	45	....	....	....	....	....	....	....	....	....	....	....	....	....	....	....	....	....	....
1993-94	U. of Michigan	CCHA	38	20	28	48	24	....	....	....	....	....	....	....	....	....	....	....	....	....	....	....	....	....	....
1994-95	U. of Michigan	CCHA	39	23	*53	*76	42	....	....	....	....	....	....	....	....	....	....	....	....	....	....	....	....	....	....
1995-96	U. of Michigan	CCHA	35	28	44	*72	41	....	....	....	....	....	....	....	....	....	....	....	....	....	....	....	....	....	....
1996-97	U. of Michigan	CCHA	43	31	*57	*88	52	....	....	....	....	....	....	....	....	....	....	....	....	....	....	....	....	....	....
1997-98	**New Jersey**	**NHL**	**11**	**5**	**4**	**9**	**0**	**0**	**0**	**1**	**19**	**26.3**	**3**	....	....	....	**3**	**0**	**1**	**1**	**0**	**0**	**0**	**0**	....
	Albany River Rats	AHL	72	35	49	84	44	....	....	....	....	....	....	....	....	....	8	3	4	7	19	....	....	....	....
1998-99	**New Jersey**	**NHL**	**76**	**13**	**33**	**46**	**18**	**5**	**0**	**2**	**111**	**11.7**	**−4**	**920**	**51.1**	**13:55**	**7**	**0**	**2**	**2**	**0**	**0**	**0**	**0**	**13:04**
99-2000	Trebic	CzRep-2	2	0	0	0	0	....	....	....	....	....	....	....	....	....	....	....	....	....	....	....	....	....	....
	Pardubice	CzRep	6	5	2	7	2	....	....	....	....	....	....	....	....	....	....	....	....	....	....	....	....	....	....
	New Jersey	**NHL**	**44**	**5**	**21**	**26**	**8**	**2**	**0**	**1**	**79**	**6.3**	**8**	**572**	**51.1**	**16:09**	....	....	....	....	....	....	....	....	....
	Vancouver	**NHL**	**12**	**2**	**7**	**9**	**10**	**0**	**0**	**0**	**17**	**11.8**	**4**	**48**	**54.2**	**14:41**	....	....	....	....	....	....	....	....	....
2000-01	**Vancouver**	**NHL**	**82**	**16**	**38**	**54**	**42**	**3**	**2**	**3**	**179**	**8.9**	**2**	**1685**	**50.1**	**18:22**	**4**	**1**	**2**	**3**	**0**	**1**	**0**	**0**	**20:50**
2001-02	**Vancouver**	**NHL**	**82**	**23**	**44**	**67**	**26**	**6**	**0**	**4**	**183**	**12.6**	**18**	**1307**	**49.9**	**19:21**	**6**	**0**	**2**	**2**	**6**	**0**	**0**	**0**	**19:44**
2002-03	**Vancouver**	**NHL**	**82**	**25**	**46**	**71**	**36**	**6**	**2**	**8**	**167**	**15.0**	**18**	**1585**	**48.3**	**21:13**	**14**	**4**	**7**	**11**	**18**	**1**	**0**	**1**	**20:18**
2003-04	**Vancouver**	**NHL**	**82**	**22**	**38**	**60**	**50**	**5**	**1**	**4**	**161**	**13.7**	**16**	**1486**	**51.0**	**20:08**	**7**	**2**	**3**	**5**	**8**	**1**	**0**	**1**	**22:00**
2004-05	Linkopings HC	Sweden	45	16	28	44	50	....	....	....	....	....	....	....	....	....	6	0	2	2	10	....	....	....	....
2005-06	**Vancouver**	**NHL**	**82**	**19**	**37**	**56**	**84**	**8**	**0**	**5**	**156**	**12.2**	**−1**	**1328**	**50.5**	**19:31**	....	....	....	....	....	....	....	....	....

			Regular Season														Playoffs								
Season	Club	League	GP	G	A	Pts	PIM	PP	SH	GW	S	%	+/-	TF	F%	Min	GP	G	A	Pts	PIM	PP	SH	GW	Min
2006-07	Vancouver	NHL	82	20	31	51	60	6	2	3	139	14.4	-9	1230	50.8	17:57	12	1	3	4	6	0	0	0	23:09
2007-08	Vancouver	NHL	39	9	16	25	18	3	0	3	54	16.7	-3	370	45.1	15:23	....	....	....	....	....	....	....	....	....
2008-09	Anaheim	NHL	62	10	12	22	16	1	0	2	82	12.2	0	350	46.0	13:51	....	....	....	....	....	....	....	....	....
	Dallas	NHL	19	6	3	9	16	2	0	2	29	20.7	3	100	43.0	15:23	....	....	....	....	....	....	....	....	....
2009-10	Washington	NHL	74	12	30	42	40	3	0	3	105	11.4	23	978	51.2	15:44	5	0	1	1	2	0	0	0	12:00
	NHL Totals		**829**	**187**	**360**	**547**	**424**	**50**	**7**	**41**	**1481**	**12.6**		**11959**	**50.0**	**17:37**	**58**	**8**	**21**	**29**	**40**	**3**	**0**	**2**	**19:26**

CHA Rookie of the Year (1994) • CCHA First All-Star Team (1995, 1996, 1997) • NCAA West First All-American Team (1995, 1996, 1997) • CCHA Player of the Year (1996, 1997) • NCAA Championship l-Tournament Team (1996) • NCAA Championship Tournament MVP (1996) • Hobey Baker Memorial Award (Top U.S. Collegiate Player) (1997) • AHL All-Rookie Team (1998)

aded to **Vancouver** by **New Jersey** with Denis Pederson for Alexander Mogilny, March 14, 2000. Signed as a free agent by **Linkopings** (Sweden), September, 2004. Signed as a free agent by **Anaheim**, ly 8, 2008. Claimed on waivers by **Dallas** from **Anaheim**, March 4, 2009. Signed as a free agent by **Washington**, July 10, 2009.

MORRISONN, Shaone

(MOHR-ih-suhn, SHAWN) **BUF.**

Defense. Shoots left. 6'4", 217 lbs. Born, Vancouver, B.C., December 23, 1982. Boston's 1st choice, 19th overall, in 2001 Entry Draft.

Season	Club	League	GP	G	A	Pts	PIM	PP	SH	GW	S	%	+/-	TF	F%	Min	GP	G	A	Pts	PIM	PP	SH	GW	Min
1997-98	Vancouver T-Birds	Minor-BC	45	16	44	60	75	....	....	....	....	....	....	....	....	....	....	....	....	....	....	....	....	....	....
1998-99	South Surrey	BCHL	19	0	2	2	13	....	....	....	....	....	....	....	....	....	....	....	....	....	....	....	....	....	....
99-2000	Kamloops Blazers	WHL	57	1	6	7	80	....	....	....	....	....	....	....	....	....	4	0	0	0	6	....	....	....	....
2000-01	Kamloops Blazers	WHL	61	13	25	38	132	....	....	....	....	....	....	....	....	....	4	0	0	0	6	....	....	....	....
2001-02	Kamloops Blazers	WHL	61	11	26	37	106	....	....	....	....	....	....	....	....	....	4	0	2	2	2	....	....	....	....
2002-03	**Boston**	**NHL**	**11**	**0**	**0**	**0**	**8**	**0**	**0**	**0**	**4**	**0.0**	**0**	**0**	**0.0**	**8:57**	....	....	....	....	....	....	....	....	....
	Providence Bruins	AHL	60	5	16	21	103	....	....	....	....	....	....	....	....	....	4	0	0	0	6	....	....	....	....
2003-04	**Boston**	**NHL**	**30**	**1**	**7**	**8**	**10**	**0**	**0**	**0**	**13**	**7.7**	**10**	**0**	**0.0**	**18:11**	....	....	....	....	....	....	....	....	....
	Providence Bruins	AHL	18	0	2	2	16	....	....	....	....	....	....	....	....	....	....	....	....	....	....	....	....	....	....
	Washington	**NHL**	**3**	**0**	**0**	**0**	**0**	**0**	**0**	**0**	**1**	**0.0**	**0**	**0**	**0.0**	**18:52**	....	....	....	....	....	....	....	....	....
	Portland Pirates	AHL	13	1	4	5	10	....	....	....	....	....	....	....	....	....	7	0	1	1	4	....	....	....	....
2004-05	Portland Pirates	AHL	71	4	14	18	63	....	....	....	....	....	....	....	....	....	....	....	....	....	....	....	....	....	....
2005-06	**Washington**	**NHL**	**80**	**1**	**13**	**14**	**91**	**0**	**0**	**0**	**56**	**1.8**	**7**	**4**	**0.0**	**20:44**	....	....	....	....	....	....	....	....	....
2006-07	**Washington**	**NHL**	**78**	**3**	**10**	**13**	**106**	**0**	**0**	**0**	**46**	**6.5**	**3**	**2**	**0.0**	**20:57**	....	....	....	....	....	....	....	....	....
2007-08	**Washington**	**NHL**	**76**	**1**	**9**	**10**	**63**	**0**	**0**	**1**	**47**	**2.1**	**4**	**1**	**100.0**	**20:16**	**7**	**0**	**1**	**1**	**6**	**0**	**0**	**0**	**21:18**
2008-09	**Washington**	**NHL**	**72**	**3**	**10**	**13**	**77**	**0**	**0**	**1**	**50**	**6.0**	**4**	**0**	**0.0**	**17:59**	**14**	**0**	**1**	**1**	**8**	**0**	**0**	**0**	**18:03**
2009-10	**Washington**	**NHL**	**68**	**1**	**11**	**12**	**68**	**0**	**0**	**1**	**32**	**3.1**	**8**	**0**	**0.0**	**17:34**	**5**	**0**	**0**	**0**	**2**	**0**	**0**	**0**	**15:54**
	NHL Totals		**418**	**10**	**60**	**70**	**423**	**0**	**0**	**3**	**249**	**4.0**		**7**	**14.3**	**19:12**	**26**	**0**	**2**	**2**	**16**	**0**	**0**	**0**	**18:31**

aded to **Washington** by **Boston** with Boston's 1st (Jeff Schultz) and 2nd (Michail Yunkov) round choices in 2004 Entry Draft for Sergei Gonchar, March 3, 2004. Signed as a free agent by **Buffalo**, ugust 2, 2010.

MORROW, Brenden

(MOHR-roh, BREHN-duhn) **DAL.**

Left wing. Shoots left. 6', 205 lbs. Born, Carlyle, Sask., January 16, 1979. Dallas' 1st choice, 25th overall, in 1997 Entry Draft.

Season	Club	League	GP	G	A	Pts	PIM	PP	SH	GW	S	%	+/-	TF	F%	Min	GP	G	A	Pts	PIM	PP	SH	GW	Min
1994-95	Estevan	SMBHL	60	117	72	189	45	....	....	....	....	....	....	....	....	....	....	....	....	....	....	....	....	....	....
1995-96	Portland	WHL	65	13	12	25	61	....	....	....	....	....	....	....	....	....	7	0	0	0	8	....	....	....	....
1996-97	Portland	WHL	71	39	49	88	178	....	....	....	....	....	....	....	....	....	6	2	1	3	4	....	....	....	....
1997-98	Portland	WHL	68	34	52	86	184	....	....	....	....	....	....	....	....	....	16	10	8	18	65	....	....	....	....
1998-99	Portland	WHL	61	41	44	85	248	....	....	....	....	....	....	....	....	....	4	0	4	4	18	....	....	....	....
99-2000	**Dallas**	**NHL**	**64**	**14**	**19**	**33**	**81**	**3**	**0**	**3**	**113**	**12.4**	**8**	**25**	**48.0**	**15:51**	**21**	**2**	**4**	**6**	**22**	**1**	**0**	**0**	**15:04**
	Michigan	IHL	9	2	0	2	18	....	....	....	....	....	....	....	....	....	....	....	....	....	....	....	....	....	....
2000-01	**Dallas**	**NHL**	**82**	**20**	**24**	**44**	**128**	**7**	**0**	**6**	**121**	**16.5**	**18**	**22**	**45.5**	**15:29**	**10**	**0**	**3**	**3**	**12**	**0**	**0**	**0**	**17:00**
2001-02	**Dallas**	**NHL**	**72**	**17**	**18**	**35**	**109**	**4**	**0**	**3**	**102**	**16.7**	**12**	**39**	**41.0**	**16:52**	....	....	....	....	....	....	....	....	....
2002-03	**Dallas**	**NHL**	**71**	**21**	**22**	**43**	**134**	**2**	**3**	**4**	**105**	**20.0**	**20**	**29**	**27.6**	**15:43**	**12**	**3**	**5**	**8**	**16**	**2**	**0**	**0**	**21:03**
2003-04	**Dallas**	**NHL**	**81**	**25**	**24**	**49**	**121**	**9**	**0**	**3**	**132**	**18.9**	**10**	**38**	**47.4**	**19:24**	**5**	**0**	**1**	**1**	**4**	**0**	**0**	**0**	**21:29**
2004-05	Oklahoma City	CHL	19	8	14	22	31	....	....	....	....	....	....	....	....	....	....	....	....	....	....	....	....	....	....
2005-06	**Dallas**	**NHL**	**81**	**23**	**42**	**65**	**183**	**8**	**1**	**4**	**146**	**15.8**	**30**	**32**	**37.5**	**19:15**	**5**	**1**	**5**	**6**	**6**	**0**	**0**	**0**	**21:57**
2006-07	**Dallas**	**NHL**	**40**	**16**	**15**	**31**	**33**	**8**	**0**	**3**	**101**	**15.8**	**-2**	**51**	**39.2**	**18:16**	**7**	**2**	**1**	**3**	**18**	**2**	**0**	**1**	**21:54**
2007-08	**Dallas**	**NHL**	**82**	**32**	**42**	**74**	**105**	**12**	**2**	**7**	**207**	**15.5**	**23**	**41**	**39.0**	**20:00**	**18**	**9**	**6**	**15**	**22**	**4**	**0**	**2**	**23:17**
2008-09	**Dallas**	**NHL**	**18**	**5**	**10**	**15**	**49**	**2**	**0**	**0**	**52**	**9.6**	**-4**	**9**	**33.3**	**21:21**	....	....	....	....	....	....	....	....	....
2009-10	**Dallas**	**NHL**	**76**	**20**	**26**	**46**	**69**	**9**	**1**	**2**	**155**	**12.9**	**-3**	**31**	**29.0**	**19:10**	....	....	....	....	....	....	....	....	....
	Canada	Olympics	7	2	1	3	2	....	....	....	....	....	....	....	....	....	....	....	....	....	....	....	....	....	....
	NHL Totals		**667**	**193**	**242**	**435**	**1012**	**64**	**7**	**35**	**1234**	**15.6**		**317**	**39.1**	**17:56**	**78**	**17**	**25**	**42**	**100**	**9**	**0**	**3**	**19:36**

VHL West First All-Star Team (1999)

igned as a free agent by **Oklahoma City** (CHL), October 19, 2004. • Missed majority of 2006-07 season recovering from groin (November 22, 2006 vs. Nashville) and wrist (December 26, 2006 at hicago) injuries. • Missed majority of 2008-09 recovering from knee injury suffered in game vs. Chicago, November 20, 2008.

MOSS, Dave

(MAWS, DAYV) **CGY.**

Left wing. Shoots left. 6'3", 200 lbs. Born, Livonia, MI, December 28, 1981. Calgary's 9th choice, 220th overall, in 2001 Entry Draft.

Season	Club	League	GP	G	A	Pts	PIM	PP	SH	GW	S	%	+/-	TF	F%	Min	GP	G	A	Pts	PIM	PP	SH	GW	Min
99-2000	Catholic Central	High-MI	28	18	20	28	20	....	....	....	....	....	....	....	....	....	....	....	....	....	....	....	....	....	....
2000-01	St. Louis Jr. Blues	CSJHL	9	2	2	4	2	....	....	....	....	....	....	....	....	....	....	....	....	....	....	....	....	....	....
	Cedar Rapids	USHL	51	20	18	38	14	....	....	....	....	....	....	....	....	....	4	0	1	1	2	....	....	....	....
2001-02	U. of Michigan	CCHA	43	4	9	13	10	....	....	....	....	....	....	....	....	....	....	....	....	....	....	....	....	....	....
2002-03	U. of Michigan	CCHA	43	14	17	31	37	....	....	....	....	....	....	....	....	....	....	....	....	....	....	....	....	....	....
2003-04	U. of Michigan	CCHA	38	8	12	20	18	....	....	....	....	....	....	....	....	....	....	....	....	....	....	....	....	....	....
2004-05	U. of Michigan	CCHA	38	10	20	30	26	....	....	....	....	....	....	....	....	....	....	....	....	....	....	....	....	....	....
2005-06	Omaha	AHL	63	21	27	48	28	....	....	....	....	....	....	....	....	....	....	....	....	....	....	....	....	....	....
2006-07	**Calgary**	**NHL**	**41**	**10**	**8**	**18**	**12**	**3**	**0**	**1**	**70**	**14.3**	**5**	**11**	**36.4**	**11:13**	**6**	**0**	**1**	**1**	**0**	**0**	**0**	**0**	**10:30**
	Omaha	AHL	28	9	12	21	22	....	....	....	....	....	....	....	....	....	....	....	....	....	....	....	....	....	....
2007-08	**Calgary**	**NHL**	**41**	**4**	**7**	**11**	**10**	**0**	**0**	**0**	**60**	**6.7**	**-4**	**17**	**41.2**	**12:24**	**5**	**1**	**1**	**2**	**4**	**0**	**0**	**0**	**10:20**
2008-09	**Calgary**	**NHL**	**81**	**20**	**19**	**39**	**22**	**8**	**0**	**4**	**194**	**10.3**	**-5**	**46**	**50.0**	**13:36**	**6**	**3**	**0**	**3**	**0**	**0**	**0**	**1**	**12:50**
2009-10	**Calgary**	**NHL**	**64**	**8**	**9**	**17**	**20**	**3**	**0**	**2**	**133**	**6.0**	**-9**	**43**	**34.9**	**13:43**	....	....	....	....	....	....	....	....	....
	NHL Totals		**227**	**42**	**43**	**85**	**64**	**14**	**0**	**7**	**457**	**9.2**		**117**	**41.9**	**12:59**	**17**	**4**	**2**	**6**	**4**	**0**	**0**	**1**	**11:16**

MOTIN, Johan

(MOH-tihn, YOH-han) **EDM.**

Defense. Shoots right. 6'1", 202 lbs. Born, Karlskoga, Sweden, October 10, 1989. Edmonton's 2nd choice, 103rd overall, in 2008 Entry Draft.

Season	Club	League	GP	G	A	Pts	PIM	PP	SH	GW	S	%	+/-	TF	F%	Min	GP	G	A	Pts	PIM	PP	SH	GW	Min
2005-06	Farjestad U18	Swe-U18	14	0	7	7	6	....	....	....	....	....	....	....	....	....	8	0	2	2	8	....	....	....	....
2006-07	Farjestad U18	Swe-U18	1	0	0	0	0	....	....	....	....	....	....	....	....	....	1	1	1	2	0	....	....	....	....
	Skare BK Karlstad	Sweden-3	18	0	4	4	30	....	....	....	....	....	....	....	....	....	....	....	....	....	....	....	....	....	....
	Farjestad	Sweden	22	0	4	4	8	....	....	....	....	....	....	....	....	....	9	0	0	0	2	....	....	....	....
2007-08	Farjestad	Sweden	28	0	2	2	10	....	....	....	....	....	....	....	....	....	....	....	....	....	....	....	....	....	....
	Bofors	Sweden-2	15	2	3	5	18	....	....	....	....	....	....	....	....	....	....	....	....	....	....	....	....	....	....
	Skare BK	Sweden-3	3	0	2	2	2	....	....	....	....	....	....	....	....	....	....	....	....	....	....	....	....	....	....
2008-09	Skare BK Karlstad	Sweden-3	8	0	3	3	8	....	....	....	....	....	....	....	....	....	....	....	....	....	....	....	....	....	....
	Farjestad	Sweden	52	0	3	3	28	....	....	....	....	....	....	....	....	....	13	0	1	1	6	....	....	....	....
2009-10	**Edmonton**	**NHL**	**1**	**0**	**0**	**0**	**0**	**0**	**0**	**0**	**0**	**0.0**	**-1**	**0**	**0.0**	**14:08**	....	....	....	....	....	....	....	....	....
	Springfield	AHL	55	1	5	6	33	....	....	....	....	....	....	....	....	....	....	....	....	....	....	....	....	....	....
	NHL Totals		**1**	**0**	**0**	**0**	**0**	**0**	**0**	**0**	**0**	**0.0**		**0**	**0.0**	**14:08**	....	....	....	....	....	....	....	....	....

MOTTAU, Mike

(MAW-tuh, MIGHK)

Defense. Shoots left. 6', 190 lbs. Born, Quincy, MA, March 19, 1978. NY Rangers' 10th choice, 182nd overall, in 1997 Entry Draft.

Season	Club	League	GP	G	A	Pts	PIM	PP	SH	GW	S	%	+/-	TF	F%	Min	GP	G	A	Pts	PIM	PP	SH	GW	Min
1994-95	Thayer Academy	High-MA	29	7	19	26	....	....	....	....	....	....	....	....	....	....	....	....	....	....	....	....	....	....	....
1995-96	Thayer Academy	High-MA	31	6	20	26	14	....	....	....	....	....	....	....	....	....	....	....	....	....	....	....	....	....	....
1996-97	Boston College	H-East	38	5	18	23	77	....	....	....	....	....	....	....	....	....	....	....	....	....	....	....	....	....	....
1997-98	Boston College	H-East	40	13	36	49	50	....	....	....	....	....	....	....	....	....	....	....	....	....	....	....	....	....	....
1998-99	Boston College	H-East	43	3	39	42	44	....	....	....	....	....	....	....	....	....	....	....	....	....	....	....	....	....	....
99-2000	Boston College	H-East	42	6	37	43	61	....	....	....	....	....	....	....	....	....	....	....	....	....	....	....	....	....	....
2000-01	**NY Rangers**	**NHL**	**18**	**0**	**3**	**3**	**13**	**0**	**0**	**0**	**17**	**0.0**	**-6**	**0**	**0.0**	**15:18**	....	....	....	....	....	....	....	....	....
	Hartford	AHL	61	10	33	43	45	....	....	....	....	....	....	....	....	....	5	0	1	1	19	....	....	....	....
2001-02	**NY Rangers**	**NHL**	**1**	**0**	**0**	**0**	**0**	**0**	**0**	**0**	**0**	**0.0**	**0**	**0**	**0.0**	**6:20**	....	....	....	....	....	....	....	....	....
	Hartford	AHL	80	9	42	51	56	....	....	....	....	....	....	....	....	....	10	0	5	5	4	....	....	....	....

			Regular Season														Playoffs								
Season	Club	League	GP	G	A	Pts	PIM	PP	SH	GW	S	%	+/-	TF	F%	Min	GP	G	A	Pts	PIM	PP	SH	GW	Mi
2002-03	Hartford	AHL	29	1	18	19	24																		
	Calgary	**NHL**	4	0	0	0	0	0	0	0	0	0.0	−1	0	0.0	9:50									
	Saint John Flames	AHL	32	5	12	17	14																		
2003-04	Cincinnati	AHL	69	9	22	31	79										9	1	2	3	8				
2004-05	Worcester IceCats	AHL	73	4	31	35	23																		
2005-06	Peoria Rivermen	AHL	76	8	48	56	81										4	0	1	1	6				
2006-07	Lowell Devils	AHL	43	1	26	27	33																		
2007-08	**New Jersey**	**NHL**	76	4	13	17	48	1	0	1	68	5.9	−11	0	0.0	20:39	5	1	0	1	0	0	0	0	21:2
2008-09	**New Jersey**	**NHL**	80	1	14	15	35	0	0	0	71	1.4	24	0	0.0	17:47	7	1	1	2	0	0	0	0	17:5
2009-10	**New Jersey**	**NHL**	79	2	16	18	41	0	0	0	74	2.7	4	0	0.0	22:16	5	0	1	1	0	0	0	0	17:5
	NHL Totals		258	7	46	53	137	1	0	1	230	3.0		0	0.0	19:40	17	2	2	4	0	0	0	0	18:5

Hockey East First All-Star Team (1998, 2000) • NCAA East Second All-American Team (1998) • NCAA Championship All-Tournament Team (1998, 2000) • Hockey East Second All-Star Team (1999) • NCAA East First All-American Team (1999, 2000) • Hockey East Player of the Year (2000) (co-winner - Ty Conklin) • Hobey Baker Memorial Award (Top U.S. Collegiate Player) (2000) • AHL All-Rookie Team (2001)

Traded to **Calgary** by **NY Rangers** for Calgary's 6th round choice (Ivan Dornic) in 2003 Entry Draft and future considerations, January 22, 2003. Signed as a free agent by **Anaheim**, July 25, 2003. Signed as a free agent by **Worcester** (AHL), September 30, 2004. Signed as a free agent by **New Jersey**, July 17, 2006.

MOTZKO, Joe

(MAWTS-koh, JOH)

Right wing. Shoots right. 6', 184 lbs. Born, Bemidji, MN, March 14, 1980.

Season	Club	League	GP	G	A	Pts	PIM	PP	SH	GW	S	%	+/-	TF	F%	Min	GP	G	A	Pts	PIM	PP	SH	GW	Mi
1997-98	Bemidji Jacks	High-MN	25	24	28	52																			
1998-99	Omaha Lancers	USHL	51	15	21	36	60										12	7	3	10	12				
99-2000	St. Cloud State	WCHA	36	9	15	24	52																		
2000-01	St. Cloud State	WCHA	41	17	20	37	54																		
2001-02	St. Cloud State	WCHA	39	9	30	39	34																		
2002-03	St. Cloud State	WCHA	38	17	25	42	59																		
	Syracuse Crunch	AHL	2	0	0	0	0																		
2003-04	**Columbus**	**NHL**	2	0	0	0	0	0	0	0	1	0.0	0	0	0.0	7:16									
	Syracuse Crunch	AHL	70	17	24	41	38										7	2	2	4	6				
2004-05	Syracuse Crunch	AHL	79	28	38	66	72																		
2005-06	**Columbus**	**NHL**	2	0	0	0	0	0	0	0	3	0.0	−2	1	0.0	10:35									
	Syracuse Crunch	AHL	61	27	34	61	54										3	0	0	0	0				
2006-07	**Columbus**	**NHL**	7	1	0	1	0	0	0	0	10	10.0	0	1	0.0	6:27									
	Syracuse Crunch	AHL	33	13	23	36	29																		
	Portland Pirates	AHL	34	15	14	29	20																		
	♦ **Anaheim**	**NHL**															3	0	0	0	2	0	0	0	3:5
2007-08	**Washington**	**NHL**	8	2	2	4	0	0	0	0	10	20.0	1	3	0.0	12:27									
	Hershey Bears	AHL	48	21	27	48	44																		
	Chicago Wolves	AHL	24	6	16	22	16										16	2	9	11	12				
2008-09	**Atlanta**	**NHL**	6	1	0	1	0	0	0	0	8	12.5	1	3	33.3	11:39									
	Chicago Wolves	AHL	73	29	27	56	82																		
2009-10	ERC Ingolstadt	Germany	48	18	16	34	74										10	3	5	8	10				
	NHL Totals		25	4	2	6	0	0	0	0	32	12.5		8	12.5	10:01	3	0	0	0	2	0	0	0	3:5

Signed as a free agent by **Columbus**, May 15, 2003. Traded to **Anaheim** by **Columbus** with Mark Hartigan and Columbus' 4th round choice (Sebastian Stefaniszin) in 2007 Entry Draft for Zenon Konopka, Curtis Glencross and Anaheim's 7th round choice (Trent Vogelhuber) in 2007 Entry Draft, January 26, 2007. Signed as a free agent by **Washington**, July 9, 2007. Traded to **Atlanta** by **Washington** for Alexandre Giroux, February 26, 2008. Signed as a free agent by **Ingolstadt** (Germany), September 16, 2009.

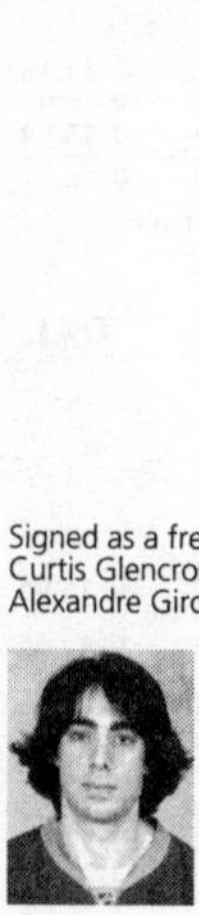

MOULSON, Matt

(MOHL-suhn, MAT) **NY**

Left wing. Shoots left. 6'1", 206 lbs. Born, North York, Ont., November 1, 1983. Pittsburgh's 11th choice, 263rd overall, in 2003 Entry Draft.

Season	Club	League	GP	G	A	Pts	PIM	PP	SH	GW	S	%	+/-	TF	F%	Min	GP	G	A	Pts	PIM	PP	SH	GW	Mi
2001-02	Guelph	OHA-B	42	56	46	102	80																		
2002-03	Cornell Big Red	ECAC	33	13	10	23	22																		
2003-04	Cornell Big Red	ECAC	32	18	17	35	37																		
2004-05	Cornell Big Red	ECAC	34	22	20	42	33																		
2005-06	Cornell Big Red	ECAC	35	18	20	38	14																		
2006-07	Manchester	AHL	77	25	32	57	23										16	2	3	5	8				
2007-08	**Los Angeles**	**NHL**	22	5	4	9	4	0	0	0	35	14.3	2	4	25.0	12:05									
	Manchester	AHL	57	28	28	56	29										4	2	0	2	4				
2008-09	**Los Angeles**	**NHL**	7	1	0	1	2	0	0	1	6	16.7	−4	0	0.0	14:30									
	Manchester	AHL	54	21	26	47	35																		
2009-10	**NY Islanders**	**NHL**	82	30	18	48	16	8	0	5	208	14.4	−1	4	75.0	16:38									
	NHL Totals		111	36	22	58	22	8	0	6	249	14.5		8	50.0	15:36									

ECAC First All-Star Team (2005) • NCAA East Second All-American Team (2005) • ECAC Second All-Star Team (2006)

Signed as a free agent by **Los Angeles**, September 1, 2006. Signed as a free agent by **NY Islanders**, July 6, 2009.

MUELLER, Peter

(MEW-luhr, PEE-tuhr) **COL.**

Center. Shoots right. 6'2", 205 lbs. Born, Bloomington, MN, April 14, 1988. Phoenix's 1st choice, 8th overall, in 2006 Entry Draft.

Season	Club	League	GP	G	A	Pts	PIM	PP	SH	GW	S	%	+/-	TF	F%	Min	GP	G	A	Pts	PIM	PP	SH	GW	Mi
2003-04	USNTDP	U-17	17	4	9	13	25																		
	USNTDP	NAHL	43	10	16	26	26										7	3	2	5	4				
2004-05	USNTDP	U-18	43	27	27	64	75																		
	USNTDP	NAHL	14	11	13	24	16																		
2005-06	Everett Silvertips	WHL	52	26	32	58	44										15	7	6	13	10				
2006-07	Everett Silvertips	WHL	51	21	57	78	45										12	7	9	16	12				
2007-08	**Phoenix**	**NHL**	81	22	32	54	32	7	0	3	201	10.9	−13	251	41.8	17:16									
2008-09	**Phoenix**	**NHL**	72	13	23	36	24	5	0	4	138	9.4	−7	92	44.6	16:05									
2009-10	**Phoenix**	**NHL**	54	4	13	17	8	1	0	1	89	4.5	−5	42	42.9	12:55									
	Colorado	**NHL**	15	9	11	20	8	3	0	1	35	25.7	4	2	0.0	17:50									
	NHL Totals		222	48	79	127	72	16	0	9	463	10.4		387	42.4	15:52									

WHL Rookie ot the Year (2006) • WHL West First All-Star Team (2007) • Canadian Major Junior Second All-Star Team (2007)

Traded to **Colorado** by **Phoenix** with Kevin Porter for Wojtek Wolski, March 3, 2010.

MURPHY, Cory

(MUHR-fee, KOH-ree)

Defense. Shoots left. 5'9", 175 lbs. Born, Kanata, Ont., February 13, 1978.

Season	Club	League	GP	G	A	Pts	PIM	PP	SH	GW	S	%	+/-	TF	F%	Min	GP	G	A	Pts	PIM	PP	SH	GW	Mi
1997-98	Colgate	ECAC	35	8	19	27	38																		
1998-99	Colgate	ECAC	34	3	23	26	26																		
99-2000	Colgate	ECAC	35	10	19	29	26																		
2000-01	Colgate	ECAC	34	7	22	29	34																		
2001-02	Blues Espoo	Finland	46	9	15	24	38										3	0	1	1	0				
2002-03	Blues Espoo	Finland	45	11	4	15	49										7	1	0	1	2				
2003-04	Ilves Tampere	Finland	56	18	26	44	22										7	1	2	3	2				
2004-05	Ilves Tampere	Finland	56	12	23	35	36										7	1	3	4	18				
2005-06	Fribourg	Swiss	44	13	22	35	52																		
2006-07	HIFK Helsinki	Finland	45	13	37	50	46										5	0	1	1	4				
2007-08	**Florida**	**NHL**	47	2	15	17	22	1	0	0	65	3.1	0	0	0.0	15:23									
2008-09	**Florida**	**NHL**	7	0	1	1	2	0	0	0	8	0.0	−1	0	0.0	10:10									
	Rochester	AHL	5	2	4	6	2																		
	Tampa Bay	**NHL**	25	5	10	15	12	4	0	0	47	10.6	−3	0	0.0	20:08									
2009-10	**New Jersey**	**NHL**	12	2	1	3	2	0	0	0	9	22.2	−2	0	0.0	12:26									
	Lowell Devils	AHL	64	6	38	44	30										5	0	0	0	2				
	NHL Totals		91	9	27	36	38	5	0	0	129	7.0		0	0.0	15:54									

ECAC First All-Star Team (2000) • ECAC Second All-Star Team (2001)

Signed as a free agent by **Florida**, March 26, 2007. Claimed on wiavers by **Tampa Bay** from **Florida**, January 19, 2009. Signed as a free agent by **New Jersey**, July 17, 2009. Signed as a free agent by **ZSC Lions** (Swiss), June 4, 2010.

MURRAY, Andrew

(MUHR-ree, AN-droo) **CBJ**

Center. Shoots left. 6'2", 210 lbs. Born, Selkirk, Man., November 6, 1981. Columbus' 11th choice, 242nd overall, in 2001 Entry Draft.

Season	Club	League	GP	G	A	Pts	PIM	PP	SH	GW	S	%	+/-	TF	F%	Min	GP	G	A	Pts	PIM	PP	SH	GW	Min
			Regular Season														Playoffs								
99-2000	Selkirk Steelers	MJHL	63	29	48	77	....	....	....	....	....	....	....	....	....	....	....	....	....	....	....	....	....	....	....
2000-01	Selkirk Steelers	MJHL	64	46	56	102	72	....	....	....	....	....	....	....	....	....	5	3	0	3	6	....	....	....	....
2001-02	Bemidji State	CHA	35	15	15	30	22	....	....	....	....	....	....	....	....	....	....	....	....	....	....	....	....	....	....
2002-03	Bemidji State	CHA	36	9	18	27	38	....	....	....	....	....	....	....	....	....	....	....	....	....	....	....	....	....	....
2003-04	Bemidji State	CHA	25	6	14	20	41	....	....	....	....	....	....	....	....	....	....	....	....	....	....	....	....	....	....
2004-05	Bemidji State	CHA	32	16	22	38	30	....	....	....	....	....	....	....	....	....	....	....	....	....	....	....	....	....	....
2005-06	Syracuse Crunch	AHL	77	13	16	29	73	....	....	....	....	....	....	....	....	....	6	0	1	1	17	....	....	....	....
2006-07	Syracuse Crunch	AHL	72	10	12	22	62	....	....	....	....	....	....	....	....	....	....	....	....	....	....	....	....	....	....
2007-08	**Columbus**	**NHL**	**39**	**6**	**4**	**10**	**12**	**0**	**0**	**0**	**45**	**13.3**	**0**	**32**	**46.9**	**11:42**	....	....	....	....	....	....	....	....	....
	Syracuse Crunch	AHL	34	13	2	15	15	....	....	....	....	....	....	....	....	....	....	....	....	....	....	....	....	....	....
2008-09	**Columbus**	**NHL**	**67**	**8**	**3**	**11**	**10**	**1**	**0**	**3**	**89**	**9.0**	**–6**	**85**	**45.9**	**11:16**	....	....	....	....	....	....	....	....	....
2009-10	**Columbus**	**NHL**	**46**	**5**	**2**	**7**	**6**	**0**	**0**	**0**	**73**	**6.8**	**–6**	**118**	**41.5**	**10:22**	....	....	....	....	....	....	....	....	....
	NHL Totals		**152**	**19**	**9**	**28**	**28**	**1**	**0**	**3**	**207**	**9.2**		**235**	**43.8**	**11:06**	....	....	....	....	....	....	....	....	....

HA All-Rookie Team (2002)

MURRAY, Brady

(MUHR-ree, BRAY-dee) **L.A.**

Center. Shoots left. 5'9", 185 lbs. Born, Brandon, Man., August 17, 1984. Los Angeles' 6th choice, 152nd overall, in 2003 Entry Draft.

Season	Club	League	GP	G	A	Pts	PIM	PP	SH	GW	S	%	+/-	TF	F%	Min	GP	G	A	Pts	PIM	PP	SH	GW	Min
2001-02	Shat.-St. Mary's	High-MN	60	58	92	150	50	....	....	....	....	....	....	....	....	....	....	....	....	....	....	....	....	....	....
2002-03	Salmon Arm	BCHL	59	42	59	101	30	....	....	....	....	....	....	....	....	....	....	....	....	....	....	....	....	....	....
2003-04	North Dakota	WCHA	37	19	27	46	32	....	....	....	....	....	....	....	....	....	....	....	....	....	....	....	....	....	....
2004-05	North Dakota	WCHA	25	8	12	20	22	....	....	....	....	....	....	....	....	....	....	....	....	....	....	....	....	....	....
2005-06	Rapperswil	Swiss	36	3	9	12	28	....	....	....	....	....	....	....	....	....	10	3	2	5	10	....	....	....	....
2006-07	Rapperswil	Swiss	38	12	20	32	38	....	....	....	....	....	....	....	....	....	7	4	2	6	6	....	....	....	....
2007-08	**Los Angeles**	**NHL**	**4**	**1**	**0**	**1**	**6**	**0**	**0**	**0**	**2**	**50.0**	**–2**	**31**	**51.6**	**11:18**	....	....	....	....	....	....	....	....	....
	Manchester	AHL	58	14	13	27	50	....	....	....	....	....	....	....	....	....	4	1	0	1	2	....	....	....	....
2008-09	HC Lugano	Swiss	36	*26	14	40	26	....	....	....	....	....	....	....	....	....	7	1	4	5	0	....	....	....	....
2009-10	HC Lugano	Swiss	47	6	13	19	12	....	....	....	....	....	....	....	....	....	4	1	0	1	2	....	....	....	....
	NHL Totals		**4**	**1**	**0**	**1**	**6**	**0**	**0**	**0**	**2**	**50.0**		**31**	**51.6**	**11:18**	....	....	....	....	....	....	....	....	....

CHA All-Rookie Team (2004) • WCHA Rookie of the Year (2004)
Assigned to **Lugano** (Swiss) by **Los Angeles**, October 9, 2008.

MURRAY, Douglas

(MUHR-ree, DUHG-luhs) **S.J.**

Defense. Shoots left. 6'3", 240 lbs. Born, Bromma, Sweden, March 12, 1980. San Jose's 6th choice, 241st overall, in 1999 Entry Draft.

Season	Club	League	GP	G	A	Pts	PIM	PP	SH	GW	S	%	+/-	TF	F%	Min	GP	G	A	Pts	PIM	PP	SH	GW	Min
1998-99	NY Apple Core	EJHL	60	17	47	64	62	....	....	....	....	....	....	....	....	....	....	....	....	....	....	....	....	....	....
99-2000	Cornell Big Red	ECAC	32	3	6	9	38	....	....	....	....	....	....	....	....	....	....	....	....	....	....	....	....	....	....
2000-01	Cornell Big Red	ECAC	25	5	13	18	39	....	....	....	....	....	....	....	....	....	....	....	....	....	....	....	....	....	....
2001-02	Cornell Big Red	ECAC	35	11	21	32	67	....	....	....	....	....	....	....	....	....	....	....	....	....	....	....	....	....	....
2002-03	Cornell Big Red	ECAC	35	5	20	25	30	....	....	....	....	....	....	....	....	....	....	....	....	....	....	....	....	....	....
2003-04	Cleveland Barons	AHL	72	10	12	22	75	....	....	....	....	....	....	....	....	....	9	3	0	3	37	....	....	....	....
2004-05	Cleveland Barons	AHL	54	6	17	23	56	....	....	....	....	....	....	....	....	....	....	....	....	....	....	....	....	....	....
2005-06	**San Jose**	**NHL**	**34**	**0**	**1**	**1**	**27**	**0**	**0**	**0**	**21**	**0.0**	**3**	**0**	**0.0**	**13:53**	....	....	....	....	....	....	....	....	....
	Cleveland Barons	AHL	20	1	7	8	37	....	....	....	....	....	....	....	....	....	....	....	....	....	....	....	....	....	....
2006-07	**San Jose**	**NHL**	**35**	**0**	**3**	**3**	**31**	**0**	**0**	**0**	**18**	**0.0**	**0**	**0**	**0.0**	**10:46**	....	....	....	....	....	....	....	....	....
	Worcester Sharks	AHL	5	2	1	3	8	....	....	....	....	....	....	....	....	....	....	....	....	....	....	....	....	....	....
2007-08	**San Jose**	**NHL**	**66**	**1**	**9**	**10**	**98**	**0**	**0**	**0**	**48**	**2.1**	**20**	**2**	**50.0**	**17:28**	**13**	**1**	**1**	**2**	**2**	**0**	**0**	**0**	**18:09**
2008-09	**San Jose**	**NHL**	**75**	**0**	**7**	**7**	**38**	**0**	**0**	**0**	**56**	**0.0**	**6**	**0**	**0.0**	**16:39**	**6**	**0**	**0**	**0**	**9**	**0**	**0**	**0**	**16:51**
2009-10	**San Jose**	**NHL**	**79**	**4**	**13**	**17**	**66**	**1**	**0**	**1**	**85**	**4.7**	**3**	**0**	**0.0**	**20:20**	**15**	**1**	**6**	**7**	**8**	**0**	**0**	**0**	**20:21**
	Sweden	Olympics	4	0	0	0	0	....	....	....	....	....	....	....	....	....	....	....	....	....	....	....	....	....	....
	NHL Totals		**289**	**5**	**33**	**38**	**260**	**1**	**0**	**1**	**228**	**2.2**		**2**	**50.0**	**16:48**	**34**	**2**	**7**	**9**	**19**	**0**	**0**	**0**	**18:53**

CAC First All-Star Team (2002, 2003) • NCAA East First All-American Team (2003)
Missed majority of 2006-07 season recovering from respiratory infection.

MURRAY, Garth

(MUHR-ree, GARTH)

Center. Shoots left. 6'2", 210 lbs. Born, Regina, Sask., September 17, 1982. NY Rangers' 3rd choice, 79th overall, in 2001 Entry Draft.

Season	Club	League	GP	G	A	Pts	PIM	PP	SH	GW	S	%	+/-	TF	F%	Min	GP	G	A	Pts	PIM	PP	SH	GW	Min
1997-98	Calgary Buffaloes	AMHL	56	26	34	60	110	....	....	....	....	....	....	....	....	....	....	....	....	....	....	....	....	....	....
	Regina Pats	WHL	4	0	0	0	2	....	....	....	....	....	....	....	....	....	2	0	0	0	0	....	....	....	....
1998-99	Regina Pats	WHL	60	3	5	8	101	....	....	....	....	....	....	....	....	....	....	....	....	....	....	....	....	....	....
99-2000	Regina Pats	WHL	68	14	26	40	155	....	....	....	....	....	....	....	....	....	7	1	1	2	7	....	....	....	....
2000-01	Regina Pats	WHL	72	28	16	44	183	....	....	....	....	....	....	....	....	....	6	1	1	2	10	....	....	....	....
2001-02	Regina Pats	WHL	62	33	30	63	154	....	....	....	....	....	....	....	....	....	6	2	3	5	9	....	....	....	....
	Hartford	AHL	4	0	0	0	0	....	....	....	....	....	....	....	....	....	9	1	3	4	6	....	....	....	....
2002-03	Hartford	AHL	64	10	14	24	121	....	....	....	....	....	....	....	....	....	2	0	0	0	6	....	....	....	....
2003-04	**NY Rangers**	**NHL**	**20**	**1**	**0**	**1**	**24**	**0**	**0**	**0**	**18**	**5.6**	**–5**	**5**	**20.0**	**9:16**	....	....	....	....	....	....	....	....	....
	Hartford	AHL	63	11	11	22	159	....	....	....	....	....	....	....	....	....	16	0	4	4	29	....	....	....	....
2004-05	Hartford	AHL	55	4	5	9	182	....	....	....	....	....	....	....	....	....	5	1	0	1	8	....	....	....	....
2005-06	**Montreal**	**NHL**	**36**	**5**	**1**	**6**	**44**	**0**	**0**	**1**	**25**	**20.0**	**–2**	**99**	**46.5**	**9:15**	**6**	**0**	**0**	**0**	**0**	**0**	**0**	**0**	**12:39**
	Hamilton	AHL	26	1	1	2	46	....	....	....	....	....	....	....	....	....	....	....	....	....	....	....	....	....	....
2006-07	**Montreal**	**NHL**	**43**	**2**	**1**	**3**	**32**	**0**	**0**	**0**	**28**	**7.1**	**–10**	**107**	**42.1**	**8:23**	....	....	....	....	....	....	....	....	....
2007-08	**Montreal**	**NHL**	**1**	**0**	**0**	**0**	**0**	**0**	**0**	**0**	**0**	**0.0**	**0**	**1**	**0.0**	**12:46**	....	....	....	....	....	....	....	....	....
	Florida	**NHL**	**6**	**0**	**0**	**0**	**19**	**0**	**0**	**0**	**3**	**0.0**	**0**	**2**	**0.0**	**5:09**	....	....	....	....	....	....	....	....	....
2008-09	**Phoenix**	**NHL**	**10**	**0**	**0**	**0**	**12**	**0**	**0**	**0**	**12**	**0.0**	**–2**	**80**	**45.0**	**9:20**	....	....	....	....	....	....	....	....	....
	San Antonio	AHL	64	11	10	21	146	....	....	....	....	....	....	....	....	....	....	....	....	....	....	....	....	....	....
2009-10	Abbotsford Heat	AHL	80	9	22	31	169	....	....	....	....	....	....	....	....	....	13	1	2	3	34	....	....	....	....
	NHL Totals		**116**	**8**	**2**	**10**	**131**	**0**	**0**	**1**	**86**	**9.3**		**294**	**43.5**	**8:45**	**6**	**0**	**0**	**0**	**0**	**0**	**0**	**0**	**12:39**

raded to **Montreal** by **NY Rangers** for Marcel Hossa, September 30, 2005. Claimed on waivers by **Florida** from **Montreal**, November 13, 2007. Signed as a free agent by **Phoenix**, July 18, 2008. Signed s a free agent by **Calgary**, July 2, 2009.

MURRAY, Marty

(MUHR-ree, MAHR-tee)

Center. Shoots left. 5'9", 180 lbs. Born, Deloraine, Man., February 16, 1975. Calgary's 5th choice, 96th overall, in 1993 Entry Draft.

Season	Club	League	GP	G	A	Pts	PIM	PP	SH	GW	S	%	+/-	TF	F%	Min	GP	G	A	Pts	PIM	PP	SH	GW	Min
1990-91	S-W Cougars	MMMHL	36	46	47	93	50	....	....	....	....	....	....	....	....	....	....	....	....	....	....	....	....	....	....
1991-92	Brandon	WHL	68	20	36	56	22	....	....	....	....	....	....	....	....	....	....	....	....	....	....	....	....	....	....
1992-93	Brandon	WHL	67	29	65	94	50	....	....	....	....	....	....	....	....	....	4	1	3	4	0	....	....	....	....
1993-94	Brandon	WHL	64	43	71	114	33	....	....	....	....	....	....	....	....	....	14	6	14	20	14	....	....	....	....
1994-95	Brandon	WHL	65	40	*88	128	53	....	....	....	....	....	....	....	....	....	18	9	*20	29	16	....	....	....	....
1995-96	**Calgary**	**NHL**	**15**	**3**	**3**	**6**	**0**	**2**	**0**	**0**	**22**	**13.6**	**–4**				....	....	....	....	....	....	....	....	....
	Saint John Flames	AHL	58	25	31	56	20	....	....	....	....	....	....	....	....	....	14	2	4	6	4	....	....	....	....
1996-97	**Calgary**	**NHL**	**2**	**0**	**0**	**0**	**4**	**0**	**0**	**0**	**2**	**0.0**	**0**				....	....	....	....	....	....	....	....	....
	Saint John Flames	AHL	67	19	39	58	40	....	....	....	....	....	....	....	....	....	5	2	3	5	4	....	....	....	....
1997-98	**Calgary**	**NHL**	**2**	**0**	**0**	**0**	**2**	**0**	**0**	**0**	**2**	**0.0**	**1**				....	....	....	....	....	....	....	....	....
	Saint John Flames	AHL	41	10	30	40	16	....	....	....	....	....	....	....	....	....	21	10	10	20	12	....	....	....	....
1998-99	EC Villacher SV	Alpenliga	33	26	41	67	12	....	....	....	....	....	....	....	....	....	....	....	....	....	....	....	....	....	....
	EC Villacher SV	Austria	17	13	17	30	6	....	....	....	....	....	....	....	....	....	6	1	4	5	0	....	....	....	....
99-2000	Kolner Haie	Germany	56	12	47	59	28	....	....	....	....	....	....	....	....	....	10	4	3	7	2	....	....	....	....
2000-01	**Calgary**	**NHL**	**7**	**0**	**0**	**0**	**0**	**0**	**0**	**0**	**6**	**0.0**	**–2**	**88**	**55.7**	**14:28**	....	....	....	....	....	....	....	....	....
	Saint John Flames	AHL	56	24	52	76	36	....	....	....	....	....	....	....	....	....	19	4	16	20	18	....	....	....	....
2001-02	**Philadelphia**	**NHL**	**74**	**12**	**15**	**27**	**10**	**1**	**1**	**2**	**109**	**11.0**	**10**	**913**	**50.7**	**13:56**	**5**	**0**	**1**	**1**	**0**	**0**	**0**	**0**	**13:14**
	Philadelphia	AHL	3	0	3	3	2	....	....	....	....	....	....	....	....	....	....	....	....	....	....	....	....	....	....
2002-03	**Philadelphia**	**NHL**	**76**	**11**	**15**	**26**	**13**	**1**	**1**	**0**	**105**	**10.5**	**–1**	**472**	**55.1**	**12:22**	**4**	**0**	**0**	**0**	**4**	**0**	**0**	**0**	**11:01**
2003-04	**Carolina**	**NHL**	**66**	**5**	**7**	**12**	**8**	**0**	**0**	**0**	**56**	**8.9**	**6**	**229**	**52.8**	**11:49**	....	....	....	....	....	....	....	....	....
2004-05			DID NOT PLAY																						
2005-06	Hannover	Germany	24	7	15	22	16	....	....	....	....	....	....	....	....	....	9	4	3	7	35	....	....	....	....

			Regular Season														Playoffs								
Season	Club	League	GP	G	A	Pts	PIM	PP	SH	GW	S	%	+/-	TF	F%	Min	GP	G	A	Pts	PIM	PP	SH	GW	M
2006-07	Philadelphia	AHL	11	2	13	15	4	....	....	....	....	....	....	....	....	....	....	....	....	....	....	....	....	....	....
	Los Angeles	**NHL**	19	0	2	2	4	0	0	0	4	0.0	–5	139	46.8	9:32	....	....	....	....	....	....	....	....	....
	Manchester	AHL	34	12	28	40	24	....	....	....	....	....	....	....	....	....	16	6	8	14	11	....	....	....	....
2007-08	HC Lugano	Swiss	49	7	25	32	22	....	....	....	....	....	....	....	....	....	5	2	3	5	0	....	....	....	....
2008-09	Manchester	AHL	76	15	39	54	37	....	....	....	....	....	....	....	....	....	....	....	....	....	....	....	....	....	....
2009-10	Manitoba Moose	AHL	59	10	20	30	26	....	....	....	....	....	....	....	....	....	....	....	....	....	....	....	....	....	....
	Milwaukee	AHL	15	5	5	10	10	....	....	....	....	....	....	....	....	....	7	2	3	5	2	....	....	....	....
	NHL Totals		261	31	42	73	41	4	2	2	306	10.1		1841	52.0	12:32	9	0	1	1	4	0	0	0	12:1

WHL East First All-Star Team (1994, 1995) • Canadian Major Junior Second All-Star Team (1994) • WHL Player of the Year (1995)

Signed as a free agent by **Philadelphia**, July 9, 2001. Traded to **Carolina** by **Philadelphia** for Carolina's 6th round choice (Frederik Cabana) in 2004 Entry Draft, June 22, 2003. Signed as a free agent by **Hannover** (Germany), August 16, 2005. Signed as a free agent by **Philadelphia**, June 15, 2006. Claimed on waivers by **Los Angeles** from **Philadelphia**, November 11, 2006. Signed as a free agent by **Lugano** (Swiss), May 27, 2007. Signed as a free agent by **Manitoba** (AHL). August 18, 2009. • Loaned to **Milwaukee** (AHL) by **Manitoba** (AHL) in return for the loan of Peter Olvecky, March 10, 2010.

MYERS, Tyler

(MIGH-uhrz, TIGH-luhr) **BUF**

Defense. Shoots right. 6'8", 219 lbs. Born, Houston, TX, February 1, 1990. Buffalo's 1st choice, 12th overall, in 2008 Entry Draft.

2005-06	Notre Dame	SMHL	34	4	6	10	78	....	....	....	....	....	....	....	....	....	....	....	....	....	....	....	....	....	....
	Kelowna Rockets	WHL	9	0	1	1	2	....	....	....	....	....	....	....	....	....	8	1	0	1	2	....	....	....	....
2006-07	Kelowna Rockets	WHL	59	2	13	15	78	....	....	....	....	....	....	....	....	....	....	....	....	....	....	....	....	....	....
2007-08	Kelowna Rockets	WHL	65	6	13	19	97	....	....	....	....	....	....	....	....	....	7	1	2	3	12	....	....	....	....
2008-09	Kelowna Rockets	WHL	58	9	33	42	105	....	....	....	....	....	....	....	....	....	22	5	15	20	29	....	....	....	....
2009-10	**Buffalo**	**NHL**	82	11	37	48	32	3	0	1	104	10.6	13	0	0.0	23:44	6	1	0	1	4	0	0	0	25:54
	NHL Totals		82	11	37	48	32	3	0	1	104	10.6		0	0.0	23:44	6	1	0	1	4	0	0	0	25:54

WHL West Second All-Star Team (2009) • NHL All-Rookie Team (2010) • Calder Memorial Trophy (2010)

NASH, Rick

(NASH, RIHK) **CBJ**

Left wing. Shoots left. 6'4", 218 lbs. Born, Brampton, Ont., June 16, 1984. Columbus' 1st choice, 1st overall, in 2002 Entry Draft.

99-2000	Tor. Marlboros	GTHL	34	61	54	115	34	....	....	....	....	....	....	....	....	....	....	....	....	....	....	....	....	....	....
2000-01	London Knights	OHL	58	31	35	66	56	....	....	....	....	....	....	....	....	....	4	3	3	6	8	....	....	....	....
2001-02	London Knights	OHL	54	32	40	72	88	....	....	....	....	....	....	....	....	....	12	10	9	19	21	....	....	....	....
2002-03	**Columbus**	**NHL**	74	17	22	39	78	6	0	2	154	11.0	–27	14	35.7	13:57	....	....	....	....	....	....	....	....	....
2003-04	**Columbus**	**NHL**	80	*41	16	57	87	*19	0	7	269	15.2	–35	21	28.6	17:38	....	....	....	....	....	....	....	....	....
2004-05	HC Davos	Swiss	44	26	20	46	83	....	....	....	....	....	....	....	....	....	15	9	2	11	26	....	....	....	....
2005-06	**Columbus**	**NHL**	54	31	23	54	51	11	0	4	170	18.2	5	38	50.0	18:16	....	....	....	....	....	....	....	....	....
	Canada	Olympics	6	0	1	1	10	....	....	....	....	....	....	....	....	....	....	....	....	....	....	....	....	....	....
2006-07	**Columbus**	**NHL**	75	27	30	57	73	9	1	5	228	11.8	–8	143	42.7	19:12	....	....	....	....	....	....	....	....	....
2007-08	**Columbus**	**NHL**	80	38	31	69	95	10	4	6	329	11.6	2	44	31.8	20:29	....	....	....	....	....	....	....	....	....
2008-09	**Columbus**	**NHL**	78	40	39	79	52	6	5	5	263	15.2	11	18	27.8	21:10	4	1	2	3	2	0	0	0	20:52
2009-10	**Columbus**	**NHL**	76	33	34	67	58	10	2	6	254	13.0	–2	22	50.0	20:56	....	....	....	....	....	....	....	....	....
	Canada	Olympics	7	2	3	5	0	....	....	....	....	....	....	....	....	....	....	....	....	....	....	....	....	....	....
	NHL Totals		517	227	195	422	494	71	12	35	1667	13.6		300	40.3	18:51	4	1	2	3	2	0	0	0	20:52

OHL All-Rookie Team (2001) • OHL Rookie of the Year (2001) • CHL All-Rookie Team (2001) • NHL All-Rookie Team (2003) • Maurice "Rocket" Richard Trophy (2004) (tied with Jarome Iginla and Ilya Kovalchuk)

Played in NHL All-Star Game (2004, 2007, 2008, 2009)

Signed as a free agent by **Davos** (Swiss), August 3, 2004.

NEAL, James

(NEEL, JAYMS) **DAL.**

Left wing. Shoots left. 6'2", 208 lbs. Born, Whitby, Ont., September 3, 1987. Dallas' 2nd choice, 33rd overall, in 2005 Entry Draft.

2003-04	Bowmanville	OPJHL	43	28	27	55	....	....	....	....	....	....	....	....	....	....	....	....	....	....	....	....	....	....	....
	Plymouth Whalers	OHL	9	2	4	6	0	....	....	....	....	....	....	....	....	....	....	....	....	....	....	....	....	....	....
2004-05	Plymouth Whalers	OHL	67	18	26	44	32	....	....	....	....	....	....	....	....	....	4	1	1	2	6	....	....	....	....
2005-06	Plymouth Whalers	OHL	66	21	37	58	109	....	....	....	....	....	....	....	....	....	13	9	7	16	33	....	....	....	....
2006-07	Plymouth Whalers	OHL	45	27	38	65	94	....	....	....	....	....	....	....	....	....	20	13	12	25	54	....	....	....	....
2007-08	Iowa Stars	AHL	62	18	19	37	63	....	....	....	....	....	....	....	....	....	....	....	....	....	....	....	....	....	....
2008-09	**Dallas**	**NHL**	77	24	13	37	51	9	0	2	171	14.0	–11	31	35.5	15:52	....	....	....	....	....	....	....	....	....
	Manitoba Moose	AHL	5	4	1	5	2	....	....	....	....	....	....	....	....	....	....	....	....	....	....	....	....	....	....
2009-10	**Dallas**	**NHL**	78	27	28	55	64	2	1	4	200	13.5	–5	60	31.7	18:12	....	....	....	....	....	....	....	....	....
	NHL Totals		155	51	41	92	115	11	1	6	371	13.7		91	33.0	17:02	....	....	....	....	....	....	....	....	....

OHL First All-Star Team (2007) • Canadian Major Junior Second All-Star Team (2007)

NEGRIN, John

(NEH-grihn, JAWN) **CGY.**

Defense. Shoots left. 6'3", 200 lbs. Born, West Vancouver, B.C., March 25, 1989. Calgary's 2nd choice, 70th overall, in 2007 Entry Draft.

2004-05	North Delta Flyers	PIJHL	45	3	12	15	53	....	....	....	....	....	....	....	....	....	....	....	....	....	....	....	....	....	....
	Kootenay Ice	WHL	2	0	0	0	0	....	....	....	....	....	....	....	....	....	....	....	....	....	....	....	....	....	....
2005-06	Kootenay Ice	WHL	55	3	7	10	48	....	....	....	....	....	....	....	....	....	6	0	0	0	6	....	....	....	....
2006-07	Kootenay Ice	WHL	44	1	15	16	57	....	....	....	....	....	....	....	....	....	7	0	2	2	8	....	....	....	....
2007-08	Kootenay Ice	WHL	71	1	41	42	68	....	....	....	....	....	....	....	....	....	10	1	1	2	8	....	....	....	....
2008-09	Kootenay Ice	WHL	38	5	26	31	27	....	....	....	....	....	....	....	....	....	....	....	....	....	....	....	....	....	....
	Swift Current	WHL	25	3	15	18	22	....	....	....	....	....	....	....	....	....	7	2	4	6	8	....	....	....	....
	Calgary	**NHL**	3	0	1	1	2	0	0	0	3	0.0	–2	0	0.0	9:59	....	....	....	....	....	....	....	....	....
2009-10	Abbotsford Heat	AHL	45	5	10	15	28	....	....	....	....	....	....	....	....	....	....	....	....	....	....	....	....	....	....
	NHL Totals		3	0	1	1	2	0	0	0	3	0.0		0	0.0	9:59	....	....	....	....	....	....	....	....	....

WHL East Second All-Star Team (2009)

NEIL, Chris

(NEEL, KRIHS) **OTT.**

Right wing. Shoots right. 6'1", 212 lbs. Born, Markdale, Ont., June 18, 1979. Ottawa's 7th choice, 161st overall, in 1998 Entry Draft.

1995-96	Orangeville	OHA-B	43	15	15	30	50	....	....	....	....	....	....	....	....	....	....	....	....	....	....	....	....	....	....
1996-97	North Bay	OHL	65	13	16	29	150	....	....	....	....	....	....	....	....	....	....	....	....	....	....	....	....	....	....
1997-98	North Bay	OHL	59	26	29	55	231	....	....	....	....	....	....	....	....	....	....	....	....	....	....	....	....	....	....
1998-99	North Bay	OHL	66	26	46	72	215	....	....	....	....	....	....	....	....	....	4	1	0	1	15	....	....	....	....
99-2000	Mobile Mysticks	ECHL	4	0	2	2	39	....	....	....	....	....	....	....	....	....	....	....	....	....	....	....	....	....	....
	Grand Rapids	IHL	51	9	10	19	301	....	....	....	....	....	....	....	....	....	8	0	2	2	24	....	....	....	....
2000-01	Grand Rapids	IHL	78	15	21	36	354	....	....	....	....	....	....	....	....	....	10	2	2	4	22	....	....	....	....
2001-02	**Ottawa**	**NHL**	72	10	7	17	231	1	0	0	56	17.9	5	0	0.0	8:22	12	0	0	0	12	0	0	0	7:12
2002-03	**Ottawa**	**NHL**	68	6	4	10	147	0	0	0	62	9.7	8	5	60.0	7:40	15	1	0	1	24	0	0	0	7:57
2003-04	**Ottawa**	**NHL**	82	8	8	16	194	0	0	1	76	10.5	13	14	42.9	8:51	7	0	1	1	19	0	0	0	6:45
2004-05	Binghamton	AHL	22	4	6	10	132	....	....	....	....	....	....	....	....	....	6	1	1	2	26	....	....	....	....
2005-06	**Ottawa**	**NHL**	79	16	17	33	204	8	0	0	126	12.7	9	9	22.2	12:18	10	1	0	1	14	0	0	0	6:58
2006-07	**Ottawa**	**NHL**	82	12	16	28	177	3	0	3	139	8.6	6	13	38.5	13:08	20	2	2	4	20	0	0	0	10:40
2007-08	**Ottawa**	**NHL**	68	6	14	20	199	0	0	1	78	7.7	–3	0	0.0	12:46	4	0	1	1	22	0	0	0	11:17
2008-09	**Ottawa**	**NHL**	60	3	7	10	146	0	0	0	59	5.1	–13	6	16.7	10:58	....	....	....	....	....	....	....	....	....
2009-10	**Ottawa**	**NHL**	68	10	12	22	175	1	0	2	100	10.0	–1	4	50.0	11:59	6	3	1	4	20	0	0	0	14:11
	NHL Totals		579	71	85	156	1473	13	0	7	696	10.2		51	37.3	10:46	74	7	5	12	131	0	0	0	9:00

Signed as a free agent by **Binghamton** (AHL), March 2, 2005.

NEWBURY, Kris

(new-BUHR-ee, KRIHS) **NYR**

Center. Shoots left. 5'10", 205 lbs. Born, Brampton, Ont., February 19, 1982. San Jose's 4th choice, 139th overall, in 2002 Entry Draft.

			Regular Season														Playoffs								
Season	Club	League	GP	G	A	Pts	PIM	PP	SH	GW	S	%	+/-	TF	F%	Min	GP	G	A	Pts	PIM	PP	SH	GW	Min
1996-97	Brampton	OPJHL	28	9	4	13	36																		
1997-98	Brampton	OPJHL	46	11	21	32	161																		
1998-99	Belleville Bulls	OHL	51	6	8	14	89																		
99-2000	Belleville Bulls	OHL	34	6	18	24	72																		
	Sarnia Sting	OHL	27	6	8	14	44										7	0	3	3	16				
2000-01	Sarnia Sting	OHL	64	28	30	58	126										4	1	3	4	20				
2001-02	Sarnia Sting	OHL	66	42	62	104	141										5	1	3	4	15				
2002-03	Sarnia Sting	OHL	64	34	58	92	149										6	4	4	8	16				
2003-04	St. John's	AHL	72	5	15	20	153																		
2004-05	St. John's	AHL	55	4	9	13	103										5	0	0	0	36				
	Pensacola	ECHL	6	2	4	6	20																		
2005-06	Toronto Marlies	AHL	74	22	37	59	215										5	0	1	1	12				
2006-07	**Toronto**	**NHL**	**15**	**2**	**2**	**4**	**26**	**0**	**0**	**0**	**30**	**6.7**	**4**	**20**	**45.0**	**7:42**									
	Toronto Marlies	AHL	37	12	24	36	87																		
2007-08	**Toronto**	**NHL**	**28**	**1**	**1**	**2**	**32**	**0**	**0**	**0**	**14**	**7.1**	**-7**	**55**	**40.0**	**4:22**									
	Toronto Marlies	AHL	54	16	27	43	101										19	4	9	13	*73				
2008-09	**Toronto**	**NHL**	**1**	**0**	**0**	**0**	**2**	**0**	**0**	**0**	**0**	**0.0**	**0**	**3**	**33.3**	**4:55**									
	Toronto Marlies	AHL	33	6	23	29	72																		
2009-10	**Detroit**	**NHL**	**4**	**1**	**0**	**1**	**4**	**0**	**0**	**0**	**3**	**33.3**	**1**	**18**	**38.9**	**8:41**									
	Grand Rapids	AHL	52	11	22	33	144																		
	Hartford	AHL	18	4	14	18	61																		
	NHL Totals		**48**	**4**	**3**	**7**	**64**	**0**	**0**	**0**	**47**	**8.5**		**96**	**40.6**	**5:47**									

HL Second All-Star Team (2002)

gned as a free agent by **St. John's** (AHL), October 2, 2003. Signed as a free agent by **Toronto**, July 17, 2006. Signed as a free agent by **Detroit**, July 7, 2009. Traded to **NY Rangers** by **Detroit** for rdan Owens, March 3, 2010.

NICHOL, Scott

(NIH-KOHL, SKAWT) **S.J.**

Center. Shoots right. 5'9", 180 lbs. Born, Edmonton, Alta., December 31, 1974. Buffalo's 9th choice, 272nd overall, in 1993 Entry Draft.

Season	Club	League	GP	G	A	Pts	PIM	PP	SH	GW	S	%	+/-	TF	F%	Min	GP	G	A	Pts	PIM	PP	SH	GW	Min
1991-92	Cgy. AAA Flames	AMHL	23	26	16	42	132																		
1992-93	Portland	WHL	67	31	33	64	146										16	8	8	16	41				
1993-94	Portland	WHL	65	40	53	93	144										10	3	8	11	16				
1994-95	Rochester	AHL	71	11	16	27	136										5	0	3	3	14				
1995-96	**Buffalo**	**NHL**	**2**	**0**	**0**	**0**	**10**	**0**	**0**	**0**	**4**	**0.0**	**0**												
	Rochester	AHL	62	14	18	32	170										19	7	6	13	36				
1996-97	Rochester	AHL	68	22	21	43	133										10	2	1	3	26				
1997-98	**Buffalo**	**NHL**	**3**	**0**	**0**	**0**	**4**	**0**	**0**	**0**	**5**	**0.0**	**0**												
	Rochester	AHL	35	13	7	20	113										17	0	6	6	18				
1998-99	Rochester	AHL	52	13	20	33	120																		
99-2000	Rochester	AHL	37	7	11	18	141										12	0	3	3	10				
2000-01	Detroit Vipers	IHL	67	7	24	31	198										11	1	1	2	12				
2001-02	**Calgary**	**NHL**	**60**	**8**	**9**	**17**	**107**	**2**	**1**	**0**	**49**	**16.3**	**-9**	**458**	**53.1**	**12:41**									
2002-03	**Calgary**	**NHL**	**68**	**5**	**5**	**10**	**149**	**0**	**1**	**0**	**66**	**7.6**	**-7**	**357**	**58.3**	**10:47**									
2003-04	**Chicago**	**NHL**	**75**	**7**	**11**	**18**	**145**	**0**	**0**	**1**	**112**	**6.3**	**-16**	**1178**	**57.4**	**15:46**									
2004-05	London Racers	Britain	16	7	12	19	86																		
2005-06	**Nashville**	**NHL**	**34**	**3**	**3**	**6**	**79**	**0**	**1**	**0**	**32**	**9.4**	**3**	**242**	**58.3**	**10:30**	**3**	**0**	**0**	**0**	**2**	**0**	**0**	**0**	**7:45**
	Milwaukee	AHL	6	3	5	8	18																		
2006-07	**Nashville**	**NHL**	**59**	**7**	**6**	**13**	**79**	**1**	**1**	**2**	**58**	**12.1**	**7**	**623**	**58.0**	**12:32**	**5**	**0**	**0**	**0**	**17**	**0**	**0**	**0**	**10:22**
2007-08	**Nashville**	**NHL**	**73**	**10**	**8**	**18**	**72**	**0**	**2**	**1**	**101**	**9.9**	**12**	**738**	**59.8**	**13:16**	**2**	**0**	**0**	**0**	**0**	**0**	**0**	**0**	**7:31**
2008-09	**Nashville**	**NHL**	**43**	**4**	**6**	**10**	**41**	**0**	**0**	**0**	**42**	**9.5**	**0**	**359**	**54.6**	**11:04**									
2009-10	**San Jose**	**NHL**	**79**	**4**	**15**	**19**	**72**	**0**	**1**	**0**	**93**	**4.3**	**0**	**832**	**60.6**	**13:04**	**15**	**1**	**1**	**2**	**17**	**0**	**0**	**0**	**8:54**
	NHL Totals		**496**	**48**	**63**	**111**	**758**	**3**	**7**	**4**	**562**	**8.5**		**4787**	**57.9**	**12:44**	**25**	**1**	**1**	**2**	**36**	**0**	**0**	**0**	**8:57**

Missed majority of 1999-2000 season recovering from knee injury suffered in game vs. Saint John (AHL), February 16, 2000. Signed as a free agent by **Calgary**, July 1, 2001. Signed as a free agent by **Chicago**, July 1, 2003. Signed as a free agent by **London** (Britain), October 26, 2004. Signed as a free agent by **Nashville**, August 6, 2005. Signed as a free agent by **San Jose**, July 15, 2009.

NIEDERMAYER, Rob

(NEE-duhr-MIGH-uhr, RAWB) **BUF.**

Center. Shoots left. 6'2", 200 lbs. Born, Cassiar, B.C., December 28, 1974. Florida's 1st choice, 5th overall, in 1993 Entry Draft.

Season	Club	League	GP	G	A	Pts	PIM	PP	SH	GW	S	%	+/-	TF	F%	Min	GP	G	A	Pts	PIM	PP	SH	GW	Min
1989-90	Cranbrook Blazers	Minor-BC	35	42	40	82	30																		
1990-91	Medicine Hat	WHL	71	24	26	50	8										12	3	7	10	2				
1991-92	Medicine Hat	WHL	71	32	46	78	77										4	2	3	5	2				
1992-93	Medicine Hat	WHL	52	43	34	77	67																		
1993-94	**Florida**	**NHL**	**65**	**9**	**17**	**26**	**51**	**3**	**0**	**2**	**67**	**13.4**	**-11**												
1994-95	Medicine Hat	WHL	13	9	15	24	14																		
	Florida	**NHL**	**48**	**4**	**6**	**10**	**36**	**1**	**0**	**0**	**58**	**6.9**	**-13**												
1995-96	**Florida**	**NHL**	**82**	**26**	**35**	**61**	**107**	**11**	**0**	**6**	**155**	**16.8**	**1**				**22**	**5**	**3**	**8**	**12**	**2**	**0**	**2**	
1996-97	**Florida**	**NHL**	**60**	**14**	**24**	**38**	**54**	**3**	**0**	**2**	**136**	**10.3**	**4**				**5**	**2**	**1**	**3**	**6**	**1**	**0**	**0**	
1997-98	**Florida**	**NHL**	**33**	**8**	**7**	**15**	**41**	**5**	**0**	**2**	**64**	**12.5**	**-9**												
1998-99	**Florida**	**NHL**	**82**	**18**	**33**	**51**	**50**	**6**	**1**	**3**	**142**	**12.7**	**-13**	**1895**	**47.1**	**21:17**									
99-2000	**Florida**	**NHL**	**81**	**10**	**23**	**33**	**46**	**1**	**0**	**4**	**135**	**7.4**	**-5**	**1632**	**47.9**	**19:04**	**4**	**1**	**0**	**1**	**6**	**0**	**0**	**0**	**15:55**
2000-01	**Florida**	**NHL**	**67**	**12**	**20**	**32**	**50**	**3**	**1**	**0**	**115**	**10.4**	**-12**	**997**	**45.0**	**20:30**									
2001-02	**Calgary**	**NHL**	**57**	**6**	**14**	**20**	**49**	**1**	**2**	**1**	**87**	**6.9**	**-15**	**777**	**48.4**	**18:01**									
2002-03	**Calgary**	**NHL**	**54**	**8**	**10**	**18**	**42**	**2**	**0**	**1**	**104**	**7.7**	**-13**	**139**	**48.9**	**17:29**									
	Anaheim	**NHL**	**12**	**2**	**2**	**4**	**15**	**1**	**0**	**0**	**21**	**9.5**	**3**	**14**	**42.9**	**15:21**	**21**	**3**	**7**	**10**	**18**	**0**	***2**	**0**	**23:35**
2003-04	**Anaheim**	**NHL**	**55**	**12**	**16**	**28**	**34**	**6**	**0**	**2**	**111**	**10.8**	**-6**	**45**	**64.4**	**19:28**									
2004-05	Ferencvaros	Hungary	5	2	1	3	14																		
2005-06	**Anaheim**	**NHL**	**76**	**15**	**24**	**39**	**89**	**4**	**1**	**2**	**140**	**10.7**	**-5**	**447**	**45.6**	**17:52**	**16**	**1**	**3**	**4**	**10**	**1**	**0**	**0**	**19:36**
2006-07 ♦	**Anaheim**	**NHL**	**82**	**5**	**11**	**16**	**77**	**0**	**0**	**0**	**106**	**4.7**	**-8**	**76**	**40.8**	**16:39**	**21**	**5**	**5**	**10**	**39**	**0**	**1**	**1**	**18:35**
2007-08	**Anaheim**	**NHL**	**78**	**8**	**8**	**16**	**54**	**0**	**1**	**1**	**111**	**7.2**	**1**	**69**	**33.3**	**17:43**	**2**	**0**	**0**	**0**	**0**	**0**	**0**	**0**	**13:47**
2008-09	**Anaheim**	**NHL**	**79**	**14**	**7**	**21**	**42**	**1**	**1**	**2**	**88**	**15.9**	**-17**	**68**	**38.2**	**15:34**	**13**	**0**	**3**	**3**	**12**	**0**	**0**	**0**	**16:13**
2009-10	**New Jersey**	**NHL**	**71**	**10**	**12**	**22**	**45**	**0**	**1**	**0**	**93**	**10.8**	**3**	**945**	**50.6**	**16:49**	**5**	**0**	**0**	**0**	**6**	**0**	**0**	**0**	**12:39**
	NHL Totals		**1082**	**181**	**269**	**450**	**882**	**48**	**8**	**28**	**1733**	**10.4**		**7104**	**47.4**	**18:10**	**109**	**17**	**22**	**39**	**109**	**4**	**3**	**3**	**19:05**

VHL East First All-Star Team (1993)

• Missed majority of 1997-98 season recovering from thumb (November 26, 1997 vs. Boston) and head (March 19, 1998 vs. Buffalo) injuries. Traded to **Calgary** by **Florida** with Philadelphia's 2nd round choice (previously acquired, Calgary selected Andrei Medvedev) in 2001 Entry Draft for Valeri Bure and Jason Wiemer, June 23, 2001. Traded to **Anaheim** by **Calgary** for Mike Commodore and Jean-Francois Damphousse, March 11, 2003. Signed as a free agent by **Ferencvaros** (Hungary), January 17, 2005. Signed as a free agent by **New Jersey**, September 25, 2009. Signed as a free agent by **Buffalo**, July 7, 2010.

NIEDERMAYER, Scott

(NEE-duhr-MIGH-uhr, SKAWT)

Defense. Shoots left. 6'1", 194 lbs. Born, Edmonton, Alta., August 31, 1973. New Jersey's 1st choice, 3rd overall, in 1991 Entry Draft.

Season	Club	League	GP	G	A	Pts	PIM	PP	SH	GW	S	%	+/-	TF	F%	Min	GP	G	A	Pts	PIM	PP	SH	GW	Min
1988-89	Cranbrook Blazers	Minor-BC	62	55	37	92	100																		
1989-90	Kamloops Blazers	WHL	64	14	55	69	64										17	2	14	16	35				
1990-91	Kamloops Blazers	WHL	57	26	56	82	52																		
1991-92	Kamloops Blazers	WHL	35	7	32	39	61										17	9	14	23	28				
	New Jersey	**NHL**	**4**	**0**	**1**	**1**	**2**	**0**	**0**	**0**	**4**	**0.0**	**1**												
1992-93	**New Jersey**	**NHL**	**80**	**11**	**29**	**40**	**47**	**5**	**0**	**0**	**131**	**8.4**	**8**				**5**	**0**	**3**	**3**	**2**	**0**	**0**	**0**	
1993-94	**New Jersey**	**NHL**	**81**	**10**	**36**	**46**	**42**	**5**	**0**	**2**	**135**	**7.4**	**34**				**20**	**2**	**2**	**4**	**8**	**1**	**0**	**0**	
1994-95 ♦	**New Jersey**	**NHL**	**48**	**4**	**15**	**19**	**18**	**4**	**0**	**0**	**52**	**7.7**	**19**				**20**	**4**	**7**	**11**	**10**	**2**	**0**	**1**	
1995-96	**New Jersey**	**NHL**	**79**	**8**	**25**	**33**	**46**	**6**	**0**	**0**	**179**	**4.5**	**5**												
1996-97	**New Jersey**	**NHL**	**81**	**5**	**30**	**35**	**64**	**3**	**0**	**3**	**159**	**3.1**	**-4**				**10**	**2**	**4**	**6**	**6**	**2**	**0**	**1**	
1997-98	**New Jersey**	**NHL**	**81**	**14**	**43**	**57**	**27**	**11**	**0**	**1**	**175**	**8.0**	**5**				**6**	**0**	**2**	**2**	**4**	**0**	**0**	**0**	
1998-99	Utah Grizzlies	IHL	5	0	2	2	0																		
	New Jersey	**NHL**	**72**	**11**	**35**	**46**	**26**	**1**	**1**	**3**	**161**	**6.8**	**16**	**13**	**15.4**	**24:40**	**7**	**1**	**3**	**4**	**18**	**1**	**0**	**0**	**25:30**
99-2000 ♦	**New Jersey**	**NHL**	**71**	**7**	**31**	**38**	**48**	**1**	**0**	**0**	**109**	**6.4**	**19**	**8**	**37.5**	**24:21**	**22**	**5**	**2**	**7**	**10**	**0**	***2**	**1**	**25:28**
2000-01	**New Jersey**	**NHL**	**57**	**6**	**29**	**35**	**22**	**1**	**0**	**5**	**87**	**6.9**	**14**	**5**	**0.0**	**23:19**	**21**	**0**	**6**	**6**	**14**	**0**	**0**	**0**	**23:53**
2001-02	**New Jersey**	**NHL**	**76**	**11**	**22**	**33**	**30**	**2**	**0**	**6**	**129**	**8.5**	**12**	**1**	**100.0**	**24:17**	**6**	**0**	**2**	**2**	**6**	**0**	**0**	**0**	**26:37**
	Canada	Olympics	6	1	1	2	4																		

Season	Club	League	GP	G	A	Pts	PIM	PP	SH	GW	S	%	+/-	TF	F%	Min	GP	G	A	Pts	PIM	PP	SH	GW	Mi
																					Playoffs				
2002-03 ◆	New Jersey	NHL	81	11	28	39	62	3	0	3	164	6.7	23	1	0.0	24:30	24	2	*16	*18	16	1	0	0	26:0
2003-04	New Jersey	NHL	81	14	40	54	44	9	0	3	165	8.5	20	1	0.0	25:56	5	1	0	1	6	0	0	0	27:2
2004-05			DID NOT PLAY																						
2005-06	Anaheim	NHL	82	13	50	63	96	9	0	3	181	7.2	8	7	28.6	25:30	16	2	9	11	14	1	1	1	28:5
	Canada	Olympics	DID NOT PLAY – INJURED																						
2006-07 ◆	Anaheim	NHL	79	15	54	69	86	9	0	3	172	8.7	6	1	100.0	27:31	21	3	8	11	26	1	0	2	29:5
2007-08	Anaheim	NHL	48	8	17	25	16	7	0	3	87	9.2	-2	0	0.0	23:54	6	0	2	2	4	0	0	0	24:2
2008-09	Anaheim	NHL	82	14	45	59	70	9	0	2	178	7.9	-8	1	0.0	26:55	13	3	7	10	11	3	0	2	26:1
2009-10	Anaheim	NHL	80	10	38	48	38	5	0	2	168	6.0	-9	1	0.0	26:30									
	Canada	Olympics	7	1	2	3	4																		
	NHL Totals		1263	172	568	740	784	90	1	39	2436	7.1		39	23.1	25:21	202	25	73	98	126	12	3	8	26:32

WHL West First All-Star Team (1991, 1992) • Canadian Major Junior Scholastic Player of the Year (1991) • Memorial Cup Tournament All-Star Team (1992) • Stafford Smythe Memorial Trophy (Memorial Cup Tournament - MVP) (1992) • NHL All-Rookie Team (1993) • NHL Second All-Star Team (1998) • NHL First All-Star Team (2004, 2006, 2007) • James Norris Memorial Trophy (2004) • Conn Smythe Trophy (2007)
Played in NHL All-Star Game (1998, 2001, 2004, 2008, 2009)
Signed to PTO (professional tryout) contract by **Utah** (IHL) with **New Jersey** retaining NHL rights, October 19, 1998. Signed as a free agent by **Anaheim**, August 4, 2005. • Officially announced his retirement, June 22, 2010.

NIELSEN, Frans

Center. Shoots left. 5'11", 172 lbs.   Born, Herning, Denmark, April 24, 1984. NY Islanders' 2nd choice, 87th overall, in 2002 Entry Draft.   (NEEL-sehn, FRAHNZ)   NYI

Season	Club	League	GP	G	A	Pts	PIM	PP	SH	GW	S	%	+/-	TF	F%	Min	GP	G	A	Pts	PIM
99-2000	Herning IK Jr.	Den-Jr.	36	18	16	34	6														
	Denmark	WJ18-B	5	3	4	7	0														
2000-01	Herning IK	Denmark	38	18	19	37	6														
	Denmark	WJ18-B	3	2	1	3	0														
2001-02	Malmo	Sweden	20	0	1	1	0														
	Malmo Jr.	Swe-Jr.	29	15	27	42	8										7	3	7	10	2
2002-03	Malmo	Sweden	47	3	6	9	10														
	Malmo Jr.	Swe-Jr.	2	1	3	4	0														
2003-04	Malmo	Sweden	50	9	7	16	28														
	Malmo	Sweden-Q	10	3	5	8	2														
2004-05	Malmo	Sweden	49	8	7	15	6														
	Malmo	Sweden-Q	10	7	2	9	0														
2005-06	Timra IK	Sweden	50	5	13	18	22														
2006-07	NY Islanders	NHL	15	1	1	2	0	0	0	1	16	6.3	-2	53	45.3	5:13					
	Bridgeport	AHL	54	20	24	44	10														
2007-08	NY Islanders	NHL	16	2	1	3	0	0	0	0	17	11.8	1	111	48.7	8:42					
	Bridgeport	AHL	48	10	28	38	18														
2008-09	NY Islanders	NHL	59	9	24	33	18	3	1	2	101	8.9	-4	758	47.2	16:32					
2009-10	NY Islanders	NHL	76	12	26	38	6	0	1	1	136	8.8	4	1165	50.0	17:13					
	NHL Totals		166	24	52	76	24	3	2	4	270	8.9		2087	48.8	15:04					

NIKULIN, Alexander

Center. Shoots left. 6'1", 205 lbs.   Born, Moscow, USSR, August 25, 1985. Ottawa's 6th choice, 122nd overall, in 2004 Entry Draft.   (nih-KOO-lihn, al-EHX-AN-duhr)   PHX.

Season	Club	League	GP	G	A	Pts	PIM	PP	SH	GW	S	%	+/-	TF	F%	Min	GP	G	A	Pts	PIM
2002-03	CSKA Moscow 2	Russia-3	46	22	14	36															
2003-04	CSKA Moscow 2	Russia-3	47	21	20	41	46														
2004-05	CSKA Moscow	Russia	16	3	3	6	0														
2005-06	CSKA Moscow	Russia	51	10	12	22	22										7	1	0	1	2
2006-07	CSKA Moscow	Russia	33	5	11	16	8										12	4	2	6	4
2007-08	Ottawa	NHL	2	0	0	0	0	0	0	0	0	0.0	-2	1	100.0	4:56					
	Binghamton	AHL	71	14	36	50	34														
2008-09	Binghamton	AHL	5	2	0	2	0														
	Phoenix	NHL	1	0	0	0	0	0	0	0	1	0.0	-1	3	0.0	5:35					
	San Antonio	AHL	64	7	16	23	20										3	0	0	0	0
2009-10	CSKA Moscow	Rus-KHL	42	5	17	22	2														
	NHL Totals		3	0	0	0	0	0	0	0	1	0.0		4	25.0	5:09					

Traded to **Phoenix** by **Ottawa** for Drew Fata, November 3, 2008. Signed as a free agent by **CSKA Moscow** (Russia-KHL), June 24, 2009.

NILSSON, Robert

Center. Shoots left. 5'11", 185 lbs.   Born, Calgary, Alta., January 10, 1985. NY Islanders' 1st choice, 15th overall, in 2003 Entry Draft.   (NIHL-suhn, RAW-buhrt)

Season	Club	League	GP	G	A	Pts	PIM	PP	SH	GW	S	%	+/-	TF	F%	Min	GP	G	A	Pts	PIM
2000-01	Leksands IF Jr.	Swe-Jr.	23	14	28	42	26										2	0	0	0	2
	Leksands IF U18	Swe-U18	4	6	3	9	6										2	0	2	2	2
2001-02	Leksands IF Jr.	Swe-Jr.	21	13	18	31	24										5	0	5	5	8
	Leksands IF	Sweden-2	14	1	4	5	8														
2002-03	Leksands IF	Sweden	41	8	13	21	10										5	0	1	1	2
	Leksands IF Jr.	Swe-Jr.															2	1	1	2	2
2003-04	Leksands IF Jr.	Swe-Jr.	4	2	8	10	4														
	Leksands IF	Sweden	34	2	4	6	6														
	Fribourg	Swiss	7	1	3	4	2														
2004-05	Almtuna	Sweden-2	3	0	1	1	2										4	1	0	1	2
	Hammarby	Sweden-2	7	0	4	4	4														
	Djurgarden Jr.	Swe-Jr.	8	8	4	12	12														
	Djurgarden	Sweden	23	2	4	6	6														
2005-06	NY Islanders	NHL	53	6	14	20	26	1	0	1	70	8.6	-6	31	29.0	11:52	3	0	0	0	0
	Bridgeport	AHL	29	8	20	28	12														
2006-07	Bridgeport	AHL	50	12	34	46	34										7	1	4	5	0
	Edmonton	NHL	4	1	0	1	4	0	0	0	8	12.5	-1	2	50.0	17:21					
	Wilkes-Barre	AHL	19	6	14	20	14										11	3	12	15	8
2007-08	Edmonton	NHL	71	10	31	41	22	3	0	0	102	9.8	8	15	46.7	13:56					
	Springfield	AHL	5	2	2	4	4														
2008-09	Edmonton	NHL	64	9	20	29	26	4	0	1	77	11.7	1	10	40.0	15:11					
2009-10	Edmonton	NHL	60	11	16	27	12	3	0	1	104	10.6	-17	3	33.3	14:45					
	NHL Totals		252	37	81	118	90	11	0	3	361	10.2		61	36.1	14:04					

Traded to **Edmonton** by **NY Islanders** with Ryan O'Marra and NY Islanders' 1st round choice (Alex Plante) in 2007 Entry Draft for Ryan Smyth, February 27, 2007. Signed as a free agent by **Ufa** (Sweden), July 25, 2010.

NISKANEN, Matt

Defense. Shoots right. 6', 204 lbs.   Born, Virginia, MN, December 6, 1986. Dallas' 1st choice, 28th overall, in 2005 Entry Draft.   (NIHS-kah-nehn, MAT)   DAL.

Season	Club	League	GP	G	A	Pts	PIM	PP	SH	GW	S	%	+/-	TF	F%	Min	GP	G	A	Pts	PIM	PP	SH	GW	Mi
2003-04	Virginia	High-MN		24	37	61																			
2004-05	Virginia	High-MN	29	27	38	65	34																		
2005-06	U. Minn-Duluth	WCHA	38	1	13	14	40																		
2006-07	U. Minn-Duluth	WCHA	39	9	22	31	42																		
	Iowa Stars	AHL	13	0	3	3	6										12	2	5	7	10				
2007-08	Dallas	NHL	78	7	19	26	36	2	0	0	99	7.1	22	0	0.0	20:30									
2008-09	Dallas	NHL	80	6	29	35	52	2	0	0	111	5.4	-11	0	0.0	19:58	16	0	3	3	10	0	0	0	16:23
2009-10	Dallas	NHL	74	3	12	15	18	0	0	2	110	2.7	-15	0	0.0	18:16									
	NHL Totals		232	16	60	76	106	4	0	2	320	5.0		0	0.0	19:36	16	0	3	3	10	0	0	0	16:23

WCHA First All-Star Team (2007)

NODL, Andreas

(NOHD'L, awn-DRAY-uhs) **PHI.**

Right wing. Shoots left. 6'1", 196 lbs. Born, Vienna, Austria, February 28, 1987. Philadelphia's 2nd choice, 39th overall, in 2006 Entry Draft.

			Regular Season														Playoffs								
Season	Club	League	GP	G	A	Pts	PIM	PP	SH	GW	S	%	+/-	TF	F%	Min	GP	G	A	Pts	PIM	PP	SH	GW	Min
2001-02	Wien Jr.	Austria-Jr.	1	0	0	0	0																		
2002-03	Wien Jr.	Austria-Jr.	STATISTICS NOT AVAILABLE																						
	Austria	WJ18-B	5	2	2	4	4																		
2003-04	Vienna Capitals	Austria	25	15	22	37	26																		
	Wien Jr.	Austria-Jr.	15	11	10	21	47																		
	Austria	WJ18-B	5	2	3	5	26																		
2004-05	Sioux Falls	USHL	44	7	9	16	24																		
	Sioux Falls	USHL	44	7	9	16	24																		
2005-06	Sioux Falls	USHL	58	29	30	59	16										14	6	9	15	6				
2006-07	St. Cloud State	WCHA	40	18	28	46	32																		
2007-08	St. Cloud State	WCHA	40	18	26	44	22																		
	Philadelphia	AHL	3	1	0	1	0										10	1	0	1	2				
2008-09	**Philadelphia**	**NHL**	**38**	**1**	**3**	**4**	**2**	0	0	0	33	3.0	-15	0	0.0	11:09									
	Philadelphia	AHL	39	6	14	20	20										4	0	1	1	2				
2009-10	**Philadelphia**	**NHL**	**10**	**0**	**1**	**1**	**0**	0	0	0	2	0.0	-2	0	0.0	8:55	10	0	0	0	0	0	0	0	8:28
	Adirondack	AHL	65	14	20	34	24																		
	NHL Totals		**48**	**1**	**4**	**5**	**2**	**0**	**0**	**0**	**35**	**2.9**		**0**	**0.0**	**10:41**	**10**	**0**	**0**	**0**	**0**	**0**	**0**	**0**	**8:28**

USHL First All-Star Team (2006) • WCHA All-Rookie Team (2007) • WCHA Rookie of the Year (2007) • NCAA Rookie of the Year (2007) • WCHA Second All-Star Team (2008)

NOKELAINEN, Petteri

(noh-kuh-LAY-nehn, PEH-tuh-ree)

Center. Shoots right. 6'1", 191 lbs. Born, Imatra, Finland, January 16, 1986. NY Islanders' 1st choice, 16th overall, in 2004 Entry Draft.

Season	Club	League	GP	G	A	Pts	PIM	PP	SH	GW	S	%	+/-	TF	F%	Min	GP	G	A	Pts	PIM	PP	SH	GW	Min
2001-02	SaiPa U18	Fin-U18	6	2	1	3	14																		
2002-03	SaiPa U18	Fin-U18	10	3	8	11	18																		
	SaiPa Jr.	Fin-Jr.	28	7	4	11	28										3	1	0	1	4				
	SaiPa	Finland	2	1	0	1	2																		
2003-04	Suomi U20	Finland-2	3	0	1	1	0																		
	SaiPa Jr.	Fin-Jr.	10	5	3	8	4										4	0	1	1	0				
	SaiPa	Finland	40	4	4	8	16																		
2004-05	SaiPa	Finland	52	15	5	20	34																		
2005-06	**NY Islanders**	**NHL**	**15**	**1**	**1**	**2**	**4**	0	0	1	13	7.7	-1	82	48.8	7:47									
2006-07	Bridgeport	AHL	60	6	10	16	51																		
2007-08	**Boston**	**NHL**	**57**	**7**	**3**	**10**	**19**	0	0	1	40	17.5	0	288	52.8	8:16	7	0	2	2	4	0	0	0	12:38
	Providence Bruins	AHL	8	3	5	8	4										6	4	1	5	0				
2008-09	**Boston**	**NHL**	**33**	**0**	**3**	**3**	**10**	0	0	0	30	0.0	-1	87	62.1	9:40									
	Anaheim	**NHL**	**17**	**4**	**2**	**6**	**6**	0	1	0	26	15.4	3	205	49.8	14:20	9	0	0	0	2	0	0	0	8:42
2009-10	**Anaheim**	**NHL**	**50**	**4**	**7**	**11**	**21**	0	0	0	70	5.7	-7	354	43.5	12:56									
	Phoenix	**NHL**	**17**	**1**	**1**	**2**	**6**	0	0	0	18	5.6	-2	90	51.1	10:24	5	0	0	0	2	0	0	0	8:22
	NHL Totals		**189**	**17**	**17**	**34**	**66**	**0**	**1**	**2**	**197**	**8.6**		**1106**	**49.5**	**10:27**	**21**	**0**	**2**	**2**	**8**	**0**	**0**	**0**	**9:56**

Missed majority of 2005-06 season recovering from knee injury suffered in game vs. Pittsburgh, November 3, 2005. Traded to **Boston** by **NY Islanders** for Ben Walter and Boston's 2nd round choice (later traded to Columbus – Columbus selected Kevin Lynch) in 2009 Entry Draft, September 11, 2007. Traded to **Anaheim** by **Boston** for Steve Montador, March 4, 2009. Traded to **Phoenix** by **Anaheim** for Phoenix's 6th round choice in 2011 Entry Draft, March 3, 2010.

NOLAN, Owen

(NOH-lan, OH-wehn)

Right wing. Shoots right. 6'1", 214 lbs. Born, Belfast, N.Ireland, February 12, 1972. Quebec's 1st choice, 1st overall, in 1990 Entry Draft.

Season	Club	League	GP	G	A	Pts	PIM	PP	SH	GW	S	%	+/-	TF	F%	Min	GP	G	A	Pts	PIM	PP	SH	GW	Min
1987-88	Thorold	Minor-ON	28	53	32	85	24																		
	Thorold	OHA-B	3	1	0	1	2																		
1988-89	Cornwall Royals	OHL	62	34	25	59	213										18	5	11	16	41				
1989-90	Cornwall Royals	OHL	58	51	59	110	240										6	7	5	12	26				
1990-91	**Quebec**	**NHL**	**59**	**3**	**10**	**13**	**109**	0	0	0	54	5.6	-19												
	Halifax Citadels	AHL	6	4	4	8	11																		
1991-92	**Quebec**	**NHL**	**75**	**42**	**31**	**73**	**183**	17	0	0	190	22.1	-9												
1992-93	**Quebec**	**NHL**	**73**	**36**	**41**	**77**	**185**	15	0	4	241	14.9	-1				5	1	0	1	2	0	0	0	
1993-94	**Quebec**	**NHL**	**6**	**2**	**2**	**4**	**8**	0	0	0	15	13.3	2												
1994-95	**Quebec**	**NHL**	**46**	**30**	**19**	**49**	**46**	13	2	*8	137	21.9	21				6	2	3	5	6	0	0	0	
1995-96	**Colorado**	**NHL**	**9**	**4**	**4**	**8**	**9**	4	0	0	23	17.4	-3												
	San Jose	**NHL**	**72**	**29**	**32**	**61**	**137**	12	1	2	184	15.8	-30												
1996-97	**San Jose**	**NHL**	**72**	**31**	**32**	**63**	**155**	10	0	3	225	13.8	-19												
1997-98	**San Jose**	**NHL**	**75**	**14**	**27**	**41**	**144**	3	1	1	192	7.3	-2				6	2	2	4	26	2	0	1	
1998-99	**San Jose**	**NHL**	**78**	**19**	**26**	**45**	**129**	6	2	3	207	9.2	16	657	49.3	19:09	6	1	1	2	6	0	0	0	20:15
99-2000	**San Jose**	**NHL**	**78**	**44**	**40**	**84**	**110**	*18	4	6	261	16.9	-1	357	50.7	21:07	10	8	2	10	6	2	*2	3	22:14
2000-01	**San Jose**	**NHL**	**57**	**24**	**25**	**49**	**75**	10	1	4	191	12.6	0	407	46.9	21:49	6	1	1	2	8	0	0	1	22:45
2001-02	**San Jose**	**NHL**	**75**	**23**	**43**	**66**	**93**	8	2	2	217	10.6	7	545	47.0	19:23	12	3	6	9	8	0	0	0	19:46
	Canada	Olympics	6	0	3	3	2																		
2002-03	**San Jose**	**NHL**	**61**	**22**	**20**	**42**	**91**	8	3	4	192	11.5	-5	226	50.4	18:08									
	Toronto	**NHL**	**14**	**7**	**5**	**12**	**16**	5	0	1	29	24.1	2	56	48.2	17:00	7	0	2	2	2	0	0	0	23:19
2003-04	**Toronto**	**NHL**	**65**	**19**	**29**	**48**	**110**	7	2	3	154	12.3	4	242	53.3	17:57									
2004-05			DID NOT PLAY																						
2005-06			DID NOT PLAY – INJURED																						
2006-07	**Phoenix**	**NHL**	**76**	**16**	**24**	**40**	**56**	2	3	1	154	10.4	-2	238	52.5	15:25									
2007-08	**Calgary**	**NHL**	**77**	**16**	**16**	**32**	**71**	1	1	3	163	9.8	6	346	52.3	16:33	7	3	2	5	2	0	0	2	19:11
2008-09	**Minnesota**	**NHL**	**59**	**25**	**20**	**45**	**26**	12	0	5	148	16.9	5	161	46.6	16:24									
2009-10	**Minnesota**	**NHL**	**73**	**16**	**17**	**33**	**40**	4	1	3	151	10.6	-12	390	47.2	16:36									
	NHL Totals		**1200**	**422**	**463**	**885**	**1793**	**155**	**23**	**53**	**3128**	**13.5**		**3625**	**49.3**	**18:12**	**65**	**21**	**19**	**40**	**66**	**4**	**2**	**7**	**21:09**

OHL Rookie of the Year (1989) • OHL First All-Star Team (1990)

Played in NHL All-Star Game (1992, 1996, 1997, 2000, 2002)

• Missed majority of 1993-94 season recovering from shoulder injury suffered in game vs. Tampa Bay, November 13, 1993. • Transferred to **Colorado** after **Quebec** franchise relocated, June 21, 1995. Traded to **San Jose** by **Colorado** for Sandis Ozolinsh, October 26, 1995. Traded to **Toronto** by **San Jose** for Alyn McCauley, Brad Boyes and Toronto's 1st round choice (later traded to Boston – Boston selected Mark Stuart) in 2003 Entry Draft, March 5, 2003. • Missed entire 2005-06 season recovering from knee surgery, July, 2005. Signed as a free agent by **Phoenix**, August 16, 2006. Signed as a free agent by **Calgary**, July 3, 2007. Signed as a free agent by **Minnesota**, July 6, 2008.

NOREAU, Maxim

(NOHR-oh, max-EEM) **MIN.**

Defense. Shoots right. 5'11", 192 lbs. Born, Montreal, Que., May 14, 1987.

Season	Club	League	GP	G	A	Pts	PIM	PP	SH	GW	S	%	+/-	TF	F%	Min	GP	G	A	Pts	PIM	PP	SH	GW	Min
2004-05	Victoriaville Tigres	QMJHL	65	5	8	13	47										7	0	0	0	8				
2005-06	Victoriaville Tigres	QMJHL	69	22	43	65	116										5	2	4	6	7				
2006-07	Victoriaville Tigres	QMJHL	69	17	53	70	106										6	2	1	3	8				
2007-08	Houston Aeros	AHL	50	8	8	16	48										5	0	0	0	4				
	Texas Wildcatters	ECHL	2	0	3	3	0																		
2008-09	Houston Aeros	AHL	77	14	25	39	49										20	4	7	11	2				
2009-10	**Minnesota**	**NHL**	**1**	**0**	**0**	**0**	**0**	0	0	0	0	0.0	0	0	0.0	7:01									
	Houston Aeros	AHL	76	18	34	52	60																		
	NHL Totals		**1**	**0**	**0**	**0**	**0**	**0**	**0**	**0**	**0**	**0.0**		**0**	**0.0**	**7:01**									

Signed as a free agent by **Minnesota**, May 22, 2008.

NOVOTNY, Jiri

(nuh-VAWT-nee, YIH-ree)

Center. Shoots right. 6'3", 204 lbs. Born, Pelhrimov, Czech., August 12, 1983. Buffalo's 1st choice, 22nd overall, in 2001 Entry Draft.

Season	Club	League	GP	G	A	Pts	PIM	PP	SH	GW	S	%	+/-	TF	F%	Min	GP	G	A	Pts	PIM	PP	SH	GW	Min
99-2000	C. Budejovice Jr.	CzRep-Jr.	36	11	10	21	6																		
	C. Budejovice U17	CzR-U17	11	5	7	12	4																		
	HC Slezan Opava	CzRep-2	17	2	2	4	6																		
2000-01	C. Budejovice Jr.	CzRep-Jr.	33	10	10	20	....																		
	Havl. Brod	CzRep-3	1	0	0	0	0																		
2001-02	C. Budejovice Jr.	CzRep-Jr.	7	4	4	8	4																		
	Jind. Hradec	CzRep-3	3	1	3	4	0																		
	C. Budejovice	CzRep	41	8	6	14	6																		

			Regular Season														Playoffs								
Season	Club	League	GP	G	A	Pts	PIM	PP	SH	GW	S	%	+/-	TF	F%	Min	GP	G	A	Pts	PIM	PP	SH	GW	Min
2002-03	Rochester	AHL	43	2	9	11	14	....	....	....	....	....	....	....	....	....	3	0	1	1	10	....	....	....	....
2003-04	Rochester	AHL	48	1	14	15	16	....	....	....	....	....	....	....	....	....	13	0	1	1	10	....	....	....	....
2004-05	Rochester	AHL	61	5	20	25	36	....	....	....	....	....	....	....	....	....	9	2	2	4	4	....	....	....	....
2005-06	**Buffalo**	**NHL**	**14**	**2**	**1**	**3**	**0**	**0**	**1**	**0**	**15**	**13.3**	**-5**	**139**	**45.3**	**12:15**	**4**	**0**	**0**	**0**	**0**	**0**	**0**	**0**	**10:2**
	Rochester	AHL	66	17	37	54	40	....	....	....	....	....	....	....	....	....	....	....	....	....	....	....	....	....	....
2006-07	**Buffalo**	**NHL**	**50**	**6**	**7**	**13**	**26**	**0**	**0**	**0**	**60**	**10.0**	**-2**	**324**	**44.1**	**12:19**	....	....	....	....	....	....	....	....	....
	Washington	**NHL**	**18**	**0**	**6**	**6**	**2**	**0**	**0**	**0**	**19**	**0.0**	**-2**	**202**	**51.5**	**14:36**	....	....	....	....	....	....	....	....	....
2007-08	**Columbus**	**NHL**	**65**	**8**	**14**	**22**	**24**	**1**	**0**	**0**	**91**	**8.8**	**-10**	**791**	**47.4**	**17:43**	....	....	....	....	....	....	....	....	....
2008-09	**Columbus**	**NHL**	**42**	**4**	**3**	**7**	**14**	**0**	**1**	**0**	**56**	**7.1**	**4**	**293**	**52.9**	**13:21**	....	....	....	....	....	....	....	....	....
2009-10	Mytischi	Rus-KHL	45	12	21	33	8	....	....	....	....	....	....	....	....	....	4	0	1	1	0	....	....	....	....
	NHL Totals		**189**	**20**	**31**	**51**	**66**	**1**	**2**	**0**	**241**	**8.3**		**1749**	**48.0**	**14:37**	**4**	**0**	**0**	**0**	**0**	**0**	**0**	**0**	**10:2**

Traded to **Washington** by **Buffalo** with Buffalo's 1st round choice (later traded to San Jose - San Jose selected Nicholas Petrecki) in 2007 Entry Draft for Dainius Zubrus and Timo Helbling, February 27, 2007. Signed as a free agent by **Columbus**, July 3, 2007. Signed as a free agent by **Mytischi** (Russia-KHL), September 7, 2009.

NYCHOLAT, Lawrence

(NIH-koh-lat, LAW-rehnts)

Defense. Shoots left. 6', 200 lbs. Born, Calgary, Alta., May 7, 1979.

1995-96	Notre Dame	SMHL	42	10	36	46	66	....	....	....	....	....	....	....	....	....	....	....	....	....	....	....	....	....	....
1996-97	Swift Current	WHL	67	8	13	21	82	....	....	....	....	....	....	....	....	....	10	0	0	0	24	....	....	....	....
1997-98	Swift Current	WHL	71	13	35	48	108	....	....	....	....	....	....	....	....	....	1	0	0	0	0	....	....	....	....
1998-99	Swift Current	WHL	72	16	44	60	125	....	....	....	....	....	....	....	....	....	6	2	2	4	12	....	....	....	....
99-2000	Swift Current	WHL	70	22	58	80	92	....	....	....	....	....	....	....	....	....	2	0	0	0	0	....	....	....	....
2000-01	Jackson Bandits	ECHL	5	1	2	3	5	....	....	....	....	....	....	....	....	....	....	....	....	....	....	....	....	....	....
	Cleveland	IHL	42	3	7	10	69	....	....	....	....	....	....	....	....	....	4	0	0	0	2	....	....	....	....
2001-02	Houston Aeros	AHL	72	3	11	14	92	....	....	....	....	....	....	....	....	....	14	1	0	1	23	....	....	....	....
2002-03	Houston Aeros	AHL	66	11	28	39	155	....	....	....	....	....	....	....	....	....	....	....	....	....	....	....	....	....	....
	Hartford	AHL	15	2	9	11	6	....	....	....	....	....	....	....	....	....	2	2	0	2	0	....	....	....	....
2003-04	**NY Rangers**	**NHL**	**9**	**0**	**0**	**0**	**6**	**0**	**0**	**0**	**6**	**0.0**	**-2**	**0**	**0.0**	**17:09**	....	....	....	....	....	....	....	....	....
	Hartford	AHL	72	6	26	32	130	....	....	....	....	....	....	....	....	....	16	0	5	5	28	....	....	....	....
2004-05	Hartford	AHL	79	5	38	43	132	....	....	....	....	....	....	....	....	....	6	0	3	3	11	....	....	....	....
2005-06	Hershey Bears	AHL	73	13	44	57	94	....	....	....	....	....	....	....	....	....	16	2	12	14	12	....	....	....	....
2006-07	**Washington**	**NHL**	**18**	**2**	**6**	**8**	**12**	**0**	**0**	**0**	**22**	**9.1**	**-3**	**0**	**0.0**	**20:32**	....	....	....	....	....	....	....	....	....
	Hershey Bears	AHL	29	3	25	28	39	....	....	....	....	....	....	....	....	....	....	....	....	....	....	....	....	....	....
	Ottawa	**NHL**	**1**	**0**	**0**	**0**	**0**	**0**	**0**	**0**	**3**	**0.0**	**0**	**0**	**0.0**	**12:48**	....	....	....	....	....	....	....	....	....
2007-08	**Ottawa**	**NHL**	**3**	**0**	**0**	**0**	**0**	**0**	**0**	**0**	**4**	**0.0**	**1**	**0**	**0.0**	**11:57**	....	....	....	....	....	....	....	....	....
	Binghamton	AHL	77	12	37	49	74	....	....	....	....	....	....	....	....	....	....	....	....	....	....	....	....	....	....
2008-09	**Vancouver**	**NHL**	**14**	**0**	**1**	**1**	**6**	**0**	**0**	**0**	**8**	**0.0**	**3**	**0**	**0.0**	**9:41**	....	....	....	....	....	....	....	....	....
	Manitoba Moose	AHL	3	0	3	3	4	....	....	....	....	....	....	....	....	....	....	....	....	....	....	....	....	....	....
	Colorado	**NHL**	**5**	**0**	**0**	**0**	**0**	**0**	**0**	**0**	**1**	**0.0**	**-2**	**0**	**0.0**	**10:33**	....	....	....	....	....	....	....	....	....
2009-10	Manitoba Moose	AHL	37	5	17	22	49	....	....	....	....	....	....	....	....	....	4	0	1	1	4	....	....	....	....
	NHL Totals		**50**	**2**	**7**	**9**	**24**	**0**	**0**	**0**	**44**	**4.5**		**0**	**0.0**	**15:13**	....	....	....	....	....	....	....	....	....

AHL First All-Star Team (2008)

Signed as a free agent by **Minnesota**, August 31, 2000. Traded to **NY Rangers** by **Minnesota** for Johan Holmqvist, March 11, 2003. Signed as a free agent by **Washington**, August 9, 2005. Traded to **Ottawa** by **Washington** for Andy Hedlund and Ottawa's 6th round choice (Justin Taylor) in 2007 Entry Draft, February 26, 2007. Traded to **Vancouver** by **Ottawa** for Ryan Shannon, September 2, 2008. Claimed on waivers by **Calgary** from **Vancouver**, March 3, 2009. Traded to **Colorado** by **Calgary** with Ryan Wilson and and Montreal's 2nd round choice (previously acquired, Colorado selected Stefan Elliott) in 2009 Entry Draft for Jordan Leopold, March 4, 2009. Signed as a free agent by **Vancouver**, July 2, 2009.

NYSTROM, Eric

(NIGH-stuhm, AIR-ihk) **MIN.**

Left wing. Shoots left. 6'1", 193 lbs. Born, Syosset, NY, February 14, 1983. Calgary's 1st choice, 10th overall, in 2002 Entry Draft.

99-2000	USNTDP	NAHL	55	7	16	23	57	....	....	....	....	....	....	....	....	....	3	0	0	0	0	....	....	....	....
2000-01	USNTDP	U-18	43	10	12	22	52	....	....	....	....	....	....	....	....	....	....	....	....	....	....	....	....	....	....
	USNTDP	USHL	23	5	5	10	50	....	....	....	....	....	....	....	....	....	....	....	....	....	....	....	....	....	....
2001-02	U. of Michigan	CCHA	40	18	13	31	42	....	....	....	....	....	....	....	....	....	....	....	....	....	....	....	....	....	....
2002-03	U. of Michigan	CCHA	39	15	11	26	24	....	....	....	....	....	....	....	....	....	....	....	....	....	....	....	....	....	....
2003-04	U. of Michigan	CCHA	43	10	12	22	50	....	....	....	....	....	....	....	....	....	....	....	....	....	....	....	....	....	....
2004-05	U. of Michigan	CCHA	38	13	19	32	33	....	....	....	....	....	....	....	....	....	....	....	....	....	....	....	....	....	....
2005-06	**Calgary**	**NHL**	**2**	**0**	**0**	**0**	**0**	**0**	**0**	**0**	**0**	**0.0**	**-1**	**5**	**60.0**	**12:01**	....	....	....	....	....	....	....	....	....
	Omaha	AHL	78	15	18	33	37	....	....	....	....	....	....	....	....	....	....	....	....	....	....	....	....	....	....
2006-07	Omaha	AHL	12	2	0	2	0	....	....	....	....	....	....	....	....	....	5	0	0	0	2	....	....	....	....
2007-08	**Calgary**	**NHL**	**44**	**3**	**7**	**10**	**48**	**0**	**0**	**0**	**42**	**7.1**	**-5**	**14**	**50.0**	**11:30**	**7**	**0**	**0**	**0**	**2**	**0**	**0**	**0**	**7:39**
	Quad City Flames	AHL	18	4	3	7	15	....	....	....	....	....	....	....	....	....	....	....	....	....	....	....	....	....	....
2008-09	**Calgary**	**NHL**	**76**	**5**	**5**	**10**	**89**	**0**	**1**	**3**	**83**	**6.0**	**-7**	**29**	**37.9**	**9:16**	**6**	**2**	**2**	**4**	**0**	**0**	**0**	**1**	**10:57**
2009-10	**Calgary**	**NHL**	**82**	**11**	**8**	**19**	**54**	**0**	**0**	**2**	**91**	**12.1**	**0**	**279**	**45.5**	**13:11**	....	....	....	....	....	....	....	....	....
	NHL Totals		**204**	**19**	**20**	**39**	**191**	**0**	**1**	**5**	**216**	**8.8**		**327**	**45.3**	**11:21**	**13**	**2**	**2**	**4**	**2**	**0**	**0**	**1**	**9:10**

CCHA All-Rookie Team (2002)

• Missed majority of 2006-07 season recovering from shoulder injury suffered during pre-season game. Signed as a free agent by **Minnesota**, July 1, 2010.

OBERG, Evan

(OH-buhrg, EH-vuhn) **VAN.**

Defense. Shoots left. 6', 178 lbs. Born, Forestburg, Alta., February 16, 1988.

2005-06	Camrose Kodiaks	AJHL	44	4	9	13	56	....	....	....	....	....	....	....	....	....	14	1	1	2	14	....	....	....	....
2006-07	Camrose Kodiaks	AJHL	52	9	14	23	86	....	....	....	....	....	....	....	....	....	16	3	11	14	24	....	....	....	....
2007-08	U. Minn-Duluth	WCHA	24	1	2	3	10	....	....	....	....	....	....	....	....	....	....	....	....	....	....	....	....	....	....
2008-09	U. Minn-Duluth	WCHA	43	7	20	27	50	....	....	....	....	....	....	....	....	....	....	....	....	....	....	....	....	....	....
2009-10	**Vancouver**	**NHL**	**2**	**0**	**0**	**0**	**0**	**0**	**0**	**0**	**0**	**0.0**	**0**	**0**	**0.0**	**6:17**	....	....	....	....	....	....	....	....	....
	Manitoba Moose	AHL	70	3	23	26	64	....	....	....	....	....	....	....	....	....	5	1	1	2	4	....	....	....	....
	NHL Totals		**2**	**0**	**0**	**0**	**0**	**0**	**0**	**0**	**0**	**0.0**		**0**	**0.0**	**6:17**	....	....	....	....	....	....	....	....	....

Signed as a free agent by **Vancouver**, April 10, 2009.

O'BRIEN, Shane

(oh-BRIGH-uhn, SHAYN) **VAN.**

Defense. Shoots left. 6'3", 230 lbs. Born, Port Hope, Ont., August 9, 1983. Anaheim's 8th choice, 250th overall, in 2003 Entry Draft.

99-2000	Port Hope	OPJHL	47	6	27	33	110	....	....	....	....	....	....	....	....	....	....	....	....	....	....	....	....	....	....
2000-01	Kingston	OHL	61	2	12	14	89	....	....	....	....	....	....	....	....	....	4	0	1	1	6	....	....	....	....
2001-02	Kingston	OHL	67	10	23	33	132	....	....	....	....	....	....	....	....	....	1	0	0	0	2	....	....	....	....
2002-03	Kingston	OHL	28	8	15	23	100	....	....	....	....	....	....	....	....	....	....	....	....	....	....	....	....	....	....
	St. Michael's	OHL	34	8	11	19	108	....	....	....	....	....	....	....	....	....	19	4	10	14	*79	....	....	....	....
2003-04	Cincinnati	AHL	60	2	8	10	163	....	....	....	....	....	....	....	....	....	9	0	2	2	20	....	....	....	....
2004-05	Cincinnati	AHL	77	5	20	25	319	....	....	....	....	....	....	....	....	....	12	1	3	4	57	....	....	....	....
2005-06	Portland Pirates	AHL	77	8	33	41	287	....	....	....	....	....	....	....	....	....	19	6	16	22	*81	....	....	....	....
2006-07	**Anaheim**	**NHL**	**62**	**2**	**12**	**14**	**140**	**1**	**0**	**2**	**55**	**3.6**	**5**	**0**	**0.0**	**14:04**	....	....	....	....	....	....	....	....	....
	Tampa Bay	**NHL**	**18**	**0**	**2**	**2**	**36**	**0**	**0**	**0**	**17**	**0.0**	**-8**	**0**	**0.0**	**18:08**	**6**	**0**	**0**	**0**	**12**	**0**	**0**	**0**	**17:12**
2007-08	**Tampa Bay**	**NHL**	**77**	**4**	**17**	**21**	**154**	**0**	**0**	**1**	**69**	**5.8**	**-2**	**0**	**0.0**	**21:13**	....	....	....	....	....	....	....	....	....
2008-09	**Tampa Bay**	**NHL**	**1**	**0**	**0**	**0**	**0**	**0**	**0**	**0**	**0**	**0.0**	**-1**	**0**	**0.0**	**14:04**	....	....	....	....	....	....	....	....	....
	Vancouver	**NHL**	**76**	**0**	**10**	**10**	**196**	**0**	**0**	**0**	**39**	**0.0**	**6**	**0**	**0.0**	**14:56**	**10**	**1**	**1**	**2**	**24**	**0**	**0**	**0**	**12:06**
2009-10	**Vancouver**	**NHL**	**65**	**2**	**6**	**8**	**79**	**0**	**0**	**0**	**37**	**5.4**	**15**	**0**	**0.0**	**17:01**	**12**	**1**	**2**	**3**	**25**	**0**	**0**	**0**	**17:44**
	NHL Totals		**299**	**8**	**47**	**55**	**605**	**1**	**0**	**3**	**217**	**3.7**		**0**	**0.0**	**17:01**	**28**	**2**	**3**	**5**	**61**	**0**	**0**	**0**	**15:36**

Traded to **Tampa Bay** by **Anaheim** with Colorado's 3rd round choice (previously acquired, Tampa Bay selected Luca Cunti) in 2007 Entry Draft for Gerald Coleman and Tampa Bay's 1st round choice (later traded to Minnesota - Minnesota selected Colton Gillies) in 2007 Entry Draft, February 24, 2007. Traded to **Vancouver** by **Tampa Bay** with Michel Ouellet for Lukas Krajicek and Juraj Simek, October 6, 2008.

Season	Club	League	Regular Season GP	G	A	Pts	PIM	PP	SH	GW	S	%	+/-	TF	F%	Min	Playoffs GP	G	A	Pts	PIM	PP	SH	GW	Min

O'BYRNE, Ryan

(oh-BUHRN, RIGH-uhn) **MTL.**

Defense. Shoots right. 6'5", 234 lbs. Born, Victoria, B.C., July 19, 1984. Montreal's 4th choice, 79th overall, in 2003 Entry Draft.

Season	Club	League	GP	G	A	Pts	PIM	PP	SH	GW	S	%	+/-	TF	F%	Min	GP	G	A	Pts	PIM	PP	SH	GW	Min
2001-02	Victoria Salsa	BCHL	52	2	9	11	91	....	....	....	....	....	....	....	....	....	....	....	....	....	....	....	....	....	....
2002-03	Victoria Salsa	BCHL	32	3	6	9	94	....	....	....	....	....	....	....	....	....	....	....	....	....	....	....	....	....	....
	Nanaimo Clippers	BCHL	9	2	4	6	24	....	....	....	....	....	....	....	....	....	....	....	....	....	....	....	....	....	....
2003-04	Cornell Big Red	ECAC	31	0	2	2	71	....	....	....	....	....	....	....	....	....	....	....	....	....	....	....	....	....	....
2004-05	Cornell Big Red	ECAC	33	3	7	10	68	....	....	....	....	....	....	....	....	....	....	....	....	....	....	....	....	....	....
2005-06	Cornell Big Red	ECAC	28	7	6	13	69	....	....	....	....	....	....	....	....	....	....	....	....	....	....	....	....	....	....
2006-07	Hamilton	AHL	80	0	12	12	129	....	....	....	....	....	....	....	....	....	22	2	5	7	32	....	....	....	....
2007-08	**Montreal**	**NHL**	**33**	**1**	**6**	**7**	**45**	**0**	**0**	**0**	**10**	**10.0**	**7**	**0**	**0.0**	**13:24**	**4**	**0**	**0**	**0**	**0**	**0**	**0**	**0**	**10:46**
	Hamilton	AHL	20	2	6	8	49	....	....	....	....	....	....	....	....	....	....	....	....	....	....	....	....	....	....
2008-09	**Montreal**	**NHL**	**37**	**0**	**5**	**5**	**58**	**0**	**0**	**0**	**14**	**0.0**	**–7**	**0**	**0.0**	**15:06**	**2**	**0**	**0**	**0**	**2**	**0**	**0**	**0**	**13:04**
	Hamilton	AHL	18	1	5	6	35	....	....	....	....	....	....	....	....	....	....	....	....	....	....	....	....	....	....
2009-10	**Montreal**	**NHL**	**55**	**1**	**3**	**4**	**74**	**0**	**0**	**1**	**27**	**3.7**	**–3**	**0**	**0.0**	**15:16**	**13**	**0**	**0**	**0**	**10**	**0**	**0**	**0**	**12:43**
	NHL Totals		**125**	**2**	**14**	**16**	**177**	**0**	**0**	**1**	**51**	**3.9**		**0**	**0.0**	**14:43**	**19**	**0**	**0**	**0**	**12**	**0**	**0**	**0**	**12:20**

O'DONNELL, Sean

(oh-DAHN-uhl, SHAWN) **PHI.**

Defense. Shoots left. 6'2", 237 lbs. Born, Ottawa, Ont., October 13, 1971. Buffalo's 6th choice, 123rd overall, in 1991 Entry Draft.

Season	Club	League	GP	G	A	Pts	PIM	PP	SH	GW	S	%	+/-	TF	F%	Min	GP	G	A	Pts	PIM	PP	SH	GW	Min
1987-88	Kanata Valley	CJHL	54	4	25	29	96	....	....	....	....	....	....	....	....	....	....	....	....	....	....	....	....	....	....
1988-89	Sudbury Wolves	OHL	56	1	9	10	49	....	....	....	....	....	....	....	....	....	....	....	....	....	....	....	....	....	....
1989-90	Sudbury Wolves	OHL	64	7	19	26	84	....	....	....	....	....	....	....	....	....	7	1	2	3	8	....	....	....	....
1990-91	Sudbury Wolves	OHL	66	8	23	31	114	....	....	....	....	....	....	....	....	....	5	1	4	5	10	....	....	....	....
1991-92	Rochester	AHL	73	4	9	13	193	....	....	....	....	....	....	....	....	....	16	1	2	3	21	....	....	....	....
1992-93	Rochester	AHL	74	3	18	21	203	....	....	....	....	....	....	....	....	....	17	1	6	7	38	....	....	....	....
1993-94	Rochester	AHL	64	2	10	12	242	....	....	....	....	....	....	....	....	....	4	0	1	1	21	....	....	....	....
1994-95	Phoenix	IHL	61	2	18	20	132	....	....	....	....	....	....	....	....	....	9	0	1	1	21	....	....	....	....
	Los Angeles	**NHL**	**15**	**0**	**2**	**2**	**49**	**0**	**0**	**0**	**12**	**0.0**	**–2**	....	....	....	....	....	....	....	....	....	....	....	....
1995-96	**Los Angeles**	**NHL**	**71**	**2**	**5**	**7**	**127**	**0**	**0**	**0**	**65**	**3.1**	**3**	....	....	....	....	....	....	....	....	....	....	....	....
1996-97	**Los Angeles**	**NHL**	**55**	**5**	**12**	**17**	**144**	**2**	**0**	**0**	**68**	**7.4**	**–13**	....	....	....	....	....	....	....	....	....	....	....	....
1997-98	**Los Angeles**	**NHL**	**80**	**2**	**15**	**17**	**179**	**0**	**0**	**1**	**71**	**2.8**	**7**	....	....	....	**4**	**1**	**0**	**1**	**36**	**0**	**0**	**0**	....
1998-99	**Los Angeles**	**NHL**	**80**	**1**	**13**	**14**	**186**	**0**	**0**	**0**	**64**	**1.6**	**1**	**0**	**0.0**	**19:10**	....	....	....	....	....	....	....	....	....
99-2000	**Los Angeles**	**NHL**	**80**	**2**	**12**	**14**	**114**	**0**	**0**	**1**	**51**	**3.9**	**4**	**0**	**0.0**	**17:41**	**4**	**1**	**0**	**1**	**4**	**0**	**0**	**0**	**16:26**
2000-01	**Minnesota**	**NHL**	**63**	**4**	**12**	**16**	**128**	**1**	**0**	**2**	**58**	**6.9**	**–2**	**12**	**50.0**	**23:00**	....	....	....	....	....	....	....	....	....
	New Jersey	**NHL**	**17**	**0**	**1**	**1**	**33**	**0**	**0**	**0**	**9**	**0.0**	**2**	**0**	**0.0**	**16:27**	**23**	**1**	**2**	**3**	**41**	**0**	**0**	**0**	**16:21**
2001-02	**Boston**	**NHL**	**80**	**3**	**22**	**25**	**89**	**1**	**0**	**2**	**112**	**2.7**	**27**	**0**	**0.0**	**24:50**	**6**	**0**	**2**	**2**	**4**	**0**	**0**	**0**	**24:58**
2002-03	**Boston**	**NHL**	**70**	**1**	**15**	**16**	**76**	**0**	**0**	**1**	**61**	**1.6**	**8**	**1**	**0.0**	**22:05**	....	....	....	....	....	....	....	....	....
2003-04	**Boston**	**NHL**	**82**	**1**	**10**	**11**	**110**	**0**	**0**	**0**	**72**	**1.4**	**10**	**3**	**33.3**	**20:36**	**7**	**0**	**0**	**0**	**0**	**0**	**0**	**0**	**19:53**
2004-05			DID NOT PLAY																						
2005-06	**Phoenix**	**NHL**	**57**	**1**	**7**	**8**	**121**	**0**	**0**	**0**	**23**	**4.3**	**3**	**0**	**0.0**	**16:18**	....	....	....	....	....	....	....	....	....
	Anaheim	**NHL**	**21**	**1**	**2**	**3**	**26**	**0**	**0**	**0**	**10**	**10.0**	**3**	**0**	**0.0**	**17:13**	**16**	**2**	**3**	**5**	**23**	**0**	**0**	**1**	**16:44**
2006-07 ♦	**Anaheim**	**NHL**	**79**	**2**	**15**	**17**	**92**	**0**	**0**	**1**	**47**	**4.3**	**9**	**1**	**0.0**	**19:55**	**21**	**0**	**2**	**2**	**10**	**0**	**0**	**0**	**20:20**
2007-08	**Anaheim**	**NHL**	**82**	**2**	**7**	**9**	**84**	**0**	**1**	**0**	**25**	**8.0**	**9**	**2**	**100.0**	**17:14**	**6**	**1**	**1**	**2**	**2**	**0**	**0**	**0**	**15:32**
2008-09	**Los Angeles**	**NHL**	**82**	**0**	**12**	**12**	**71**	**0**	**0**	**0**	**32**	**0.0**	**2**	**1**	**0.0**	**20:29**	....	....	....	....	....	....	....	....	....
2009-10	**Los Angeles**	**NHL**	**78**	**3**	**12**	**15**	**70**	**0**	**0**	**1**	**44**	**6.8**	**14**	**1**	**0.0**	**18:44**	**6**	**0**	**1**	**1**	**4**	**0**	**0**	**0**	**18:27**
	NHL Totals		**1092**	**30**	**174**	**204**	**1699**	**4**	**1**	**9**	**824**	**3.6**		**21**	**42.9**	**19:53**	**93**	**6**	**11**	**17**	**124**	**0**	**0**	**1**	**18:18**

Traded to **Los Angeles** by **Buffalo** for Doug Houda, July 26, 1994. Claimed by **Minnesota** from **Los Angeles** in Expansion Draft, June 23, 2000. Traded to **New Jersey** by **Minnesota** for Willie Mitchell, March 4, 2001. Signed as a free agent by **Boston**, July 2, 2001. Signed as a free agent by **Phoenix**, July 6, 2004. Traded to **Anaheim** by **Phoenix** for Joel Perreault, March 9, 2006. Traded to **Los Angeles** by **Anaheim** for future considerations, September 30, 2008. Signed as a free agent by **Philadelphia**, July 1, 2010.

ODUYA, Johnny

(oh-DOO-yuh, JAW-nee) **ATL.**

Defense. Shoots left. 6', 200 lbs. Born, Stockholm, Sweden, October 1, 1981. Washington's 6th choice, 221st overall, in 2001 Entry Draft.

Season	Club	League	GP	G	A	Pts	PIM	PP	SH	GW	S	%	+/-	TF	F%	Min	GP	G	A	Pts	PIM	PP	SH	GW	Min
1996-97	Hammarby Jr.	Swe-Jr.	13	0	0	0	....	....	....	....	....	....	....	....	....	....	....	....	....	....	....	....	....	....	....
1997-98	Hammarby Jr.	Swe-Jr.	26	3	11	14	70	....	....	....	....	....	....	....	....	....	....	....	....	....	....	....	....	....	....
1998-99	Hammarby Jr.	Swe-Jr.	38	14	31	45	45	....	....	....	....	....	....	....	....	....	....	....	....	....	....	....	....	....	....
99-2000	Hammarby Jr.	Swe-Jr.	32	3	18	21	48	....	....	....	....	....	....	....	....	....	6	1	2	3	4	....	....	....	....
	Hammarby	Sweden-2	1	0	0	0	0	....	....	....	....	....	....	....	....	....	1	0	0	0	0	....	....	....	....
2000-01	Moncton Wildcats	QMJHL	44	11	38	49	147	....	....	....	....	....	....	....	....	....	....	....	....	....	....	....	....	....	....
	Victoriaville Tigres	QMJHL	24	3	16	19	112	....	....	....	....	....	....	....	....	....	13	4	9	13	10	....	....	....	....
2001-02	Hammarby	Sweden-2	46	11	14	25	66	....	....	....	....	....	....	....	....	....	2	1	0	1	4	....	....	....	....
2002-03	Hammarby	Sweden-2	48	15	25	40	200	....	....	....	....	....	....	....	....	....	....	....	....	....	....	....	....	....	....
2003-04	Djurgarden	Sweden	42	4	4	8	*173	....	....	....	....	....	....	....	....	....	4	0	0	0	6	....	....	....	....
2004-05	Djurgarden	Sweden	49	2	4	6	139	....	....	....	....	....	....	....	....	....	12	0	2	2	39	....	....	....	....
2005-06	Frolunda	Sweden	47	8	11	19	95	....	....	....	....	....	....	....	....	....	17	1	2	3	16	....	....	....	....
2006-07	**New Jersey**	**NHL**	**76**	**2**	**9**	**11**	**61**	**0**	**0**	**0**	**55**	**3.6**	**–5**	**0**	**0.0**	**18:31**	**6**	**0**	**1**	**1**	**6**	**0**	**0**	**0**	**12:59**
2007-08	**New Jersey**	**NHL**	**75**	**6**	**20**	**26**	**46**	**2**	**0**	**0**	**63**	**9.5**	**27**	**0**	**0.0**	**19:02**	**5**	**0**	**1**	**1**	**6**	**0**	**0**	**0**	**20:40**
2008-09	**New Jersey**	**NHL**	**82**	**7**	**22**	**29**	**30**	**1**	**1**	**4**	**108**	**6.5**	**21**	**0**	**0.0**	**20:52**	**7**	**0**	**0**	**0**	**2**	**0**	**0**	**0**	**20:19**
2009-10	**New Jersey**	**NHL**	**40**	**2**	**2**	**4**	**18**	**0**	**0**	**0**	**44**	**4.5**	**2**	**0**	**0.0**	**21:11**	....	....	....	....	....	....	....	....	....
	Atlanta	**NHL**	**27**	**1**	**8**	**9**	**12**	**0**	**0**	**0**	**24**	**4.2**	**6**	**0**	**0.0**	**21:22**	....	....	....	....	....	....	....	....	....
	Sweden	Olympics	4	0	0	0	12	....	....	....	....	....	....	....	....	....	....	....	....	....	....	....	....	....	....
	NHL Totals		**300**	**18**	**61**	**79**	**167**	**3**	**1**	**4**	**294**	**6.1**		**0**	**0.0**	**19:54**	**18**	**0**	**2**	**2**	**14**	**0**	**0**	**0**	**17:58**

Signed as a free agent by **New Jersey**, July 24, 2006. Traded to **Atlanta** by **New Jersey** with Niclas Bergfors, Patrice Cormier and New Jersey's 1st (later traded to Chicago - Chicago selected Kevin Hayes) and 2nd (later traded to Chicago - Chicago selected Justin Holl) round choices in 2010 Entry Draft for Ilya Kovalchuk, Anssi Salmela and Atlanta's 2nd round choice (Jonathon Merrill) in 2010 Entry Draft, February 4, 2010.

OHLUND, Mattias

(OH-luhnd, mat-TEE-uhs) **T.B.**

Defense. Shoots left. 6'4", 225 lbs. Born, Pitea, Sweden, September 9, 1976. Vancouver's 1st choice, 13th overall, in 1994 Entry Draft.

Season	Club	League	GP	G	A	Pts	PIM	PP	SH	GW	S	%	+/-	TF	F%	Min	GP	G	A	Pts	PIM	PP	SH	GW	Min
1992-93	Pitea HC	Sweden-2	22	0	6	6	16	....	....	....	....	....	....	....	....	....	....	....	....	....	....	....	....	....	....
1993-94	Pitea HC	Sweden-2	28	7	10	17	66	....	....	....	....	....	....	....	....	....	....	....	....	....	....	....	....	....	....
1994-95	Lulea HF	Sweden	34	6	10	16	34	....	....	....	....	....	....	....	....	....	9	4	0	4	16	....	....	....	....
1995-96	Lulea HF	Sweden	38	4	10	14	26	....	....	....	....	....	....	....	....	....	13	1	3	4	47	....	....	....	....
1996-97	Lulea HF	Sweden	47	7	9	16	38	....	....	....	....	....	....	....	....	....	10	1	2	3	8	....	....	....	....
	Lulea HF	EuroHL	6	0	3	3	0	....	....	....	....	....	....	....	....	....	....	....	....	....	....	....	....	....	....
1997-98	**Vancouver**	**NHL**	**77**	**7**	**23**	**30**	**76**	**1**	**0**	**0**	**172**	**4.1**	**3**	....	....	....	....	....	....	....	....	....	....	....	....
	Sweden	Olympics	4	0	1	1	4	....	....	....	....	....	....	....	....	....	....	....	....	....	....	....	....	....	....
1998-99	**Vancouver**	**NHL**	**74**	**9**	**26**	**35**	**83**	**2**	**1**	**1**	**129**	**7.0**	**–19**	**0**	**0.0**	**26:04**	....	....	....	....	....	....	....	....	....
99-2000	**Vancouver**	**NHL**	**42**	**4**	**16**	**20**	**24**	**2**	**1**	**1**	**63**	**6.3**	**6**	**0**	**0.0**	**27:41**	....	....	....	....	....	....	....	....	....
2000-01	**Vancouver**	**NHL**	**65**	**8**	**20**	**28**	**46**	**1**	**1**	**4**	**136**	**5.9**	**–16**	**0**	**0.0**	**25:00**	**4**	**1**	**3**	**4**	**6**	**1**	**0**	**0**	**26:32**
2001-02	**Vancouver**	**NHL**	**81**	**10**	**26**	**36**	**56**	**4**	**1**	**3**	**193**	**5.2**	**16**	**0**	**0.0**	**25:17**	**6**	**1**	**1**	**2**	**6**	**0**	**0**	**0**	**28:48**
	Sweden	Olympics	4	0	2	2	2	....	....	....	....	....	....	....	....	....	....	....	....	....	....	....	....	....	....
2002-03	**Vancouver**	**NHL**	**59**	**2**	**27**	**29**	**42**	**0**	**0**	**0**	**100**	**2.0**	**1**	**0**	**0.0**	**25:23**	**13**	**3**	**4**	**7**	**12**	**0**	**0**	**0**	**24:01**
2003-04	**Vancouver**	**NHL**	**82**	**14**	**20**	**34**	**73**	**5**	**0**	**3**	**129**	**10.9**	**14**	**0**	**0.0**	**25:47**	**7**	**1**	**4**	**5**	**13**	**0**	**0**	**1**	**27:25**
2004-05	Lulea HF	Sweden	2	1	0	1	4	....	....	....	....	....	....	....	....	....	....	....	....	....	....	....	....	....	....
2005-06	**Vancouver**	**NHL**	**78**	**13**	**20**	**33**	**92**	**8**	**1**	**2**	**183**	**7.1**	**–6**	**1**	**0.0**	**25:40**	....	....	....	....	....	....	....	....	....
	Sweden	Olympics	6	0	2	2	2	....	....	....	....	....	....	....	....	....	....	....	....	....	....	....	....	....	....
2006-07	**Vancouver**	**NHL**	**77**	**11**	**20**	**31**	**80**	**6**	**0**	**2**	**170**	**6.5**	**–3**	**1**	**0.0**	**24:47**	**12**	**2**	**5**	**7**	**12**	**1**	**0**	**0**	**28:18**
2007-08	**Vancouver**	**NHL**	**53**	**9**	**15**	**24**	**79**	**4**	**0**	**2**	**128**	**7.0**	**–1**	**0**	**0.0**	**23:46**	....	....	....	....	....	....	....	....	....
2008-09	**Vancouver**	**NHL**	**82**	**6**	**19**	**25**	**105**	**3**	**0**	**1**	**131**	**4.6**	**14**	**0**	**0.0**	**21:34**	**10**	**1**	**2**	**3**	**6**	**1**	**0**	**0**	**23:54**
2009-10	**Tampa Bay**	**NHL**	**67**	**0**	**13**	**13**	**59**	**0**	**0**	**0**	**71**	**0.0**	**–8**	**0**	**0.0**	**22:49**	....	....	....	....	....	....	....	....	....
	Sweden	Olympics	4	1	0	1	2	....	....	....	....	....	....	....	....	....	....	....	....	....	....	....	....	....	....
	NHL Totals		**837**	**93**	**245**	**338**	**815**	**36**	**5**	**19**	**1605**	**5.8**		**2**	**0.0**	**24:48**	**52**	**9**	**19**	**28**	**55**	**3**	**0**	**1**	**26:11**

NHL All-Rookie Team (1998)

Played in NHL All-Star Game (1999)

Signed as a free agent by **Lulea** (Sweden), December 21, 2004. Signed as a free agent by **Tampa Bay**, July 1, 2009.

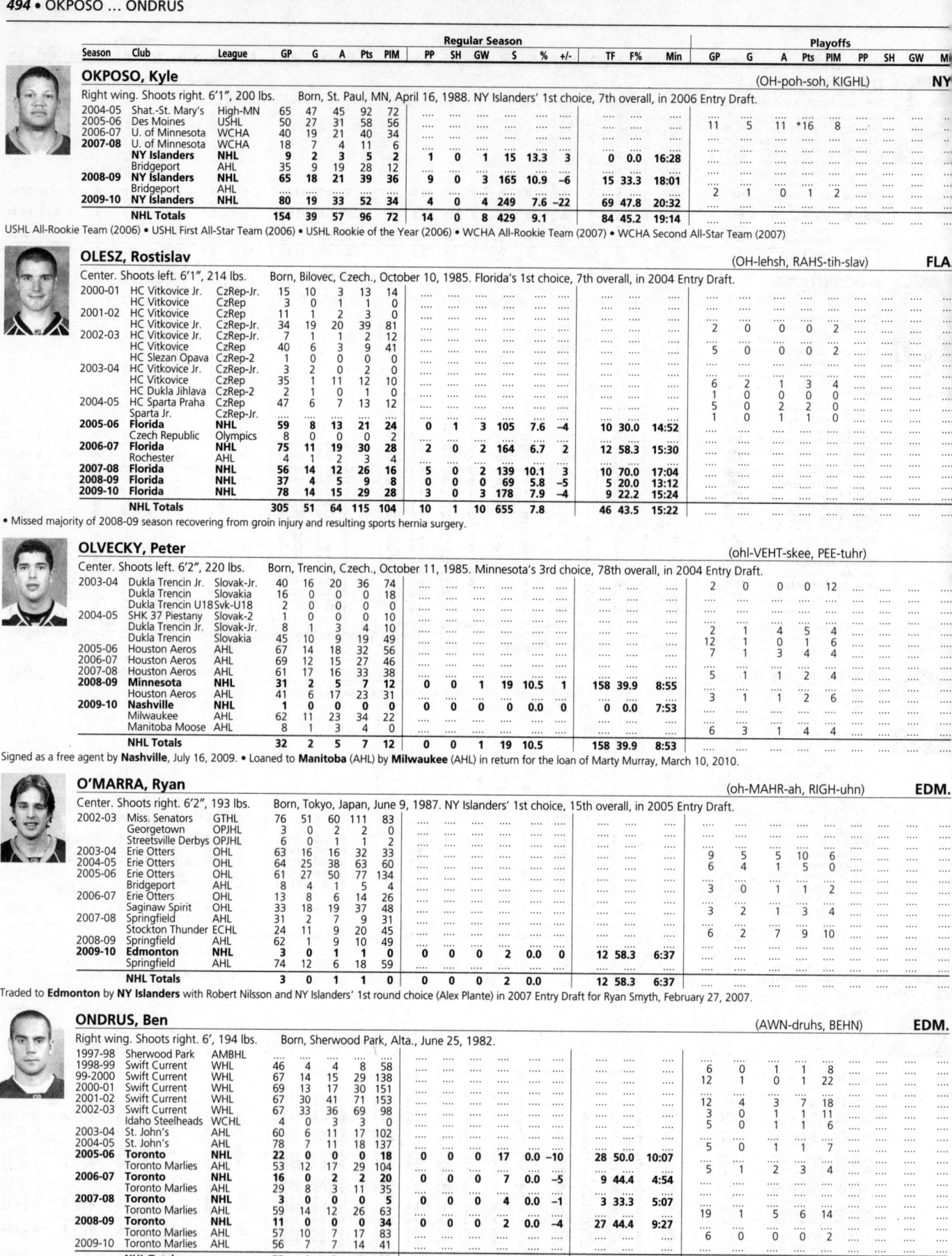

OKPOSO, Kyle
(OH-poh-soh, KIGHL)   NY

Right wing. Shoots right. 6'1", 200 lbs.   Born, St. Paul, MN, April 16, 1988. NY Islanders' 1st choice, 7th overall, in 2006 Entry Draft.

					Regular Season															**Playoffs**					
Season	Club	League	GP	G	A	Pts	PIM	PP	SH	GW	S	%	+/-	TF	F%	Min	GP	G	A	Pts	PIM	PP	SH	Mi
2004-05	Shat.-St. Mary's	High-MN	65	47	45	92	72	....	....	....	....	....	....	....	....	....	....	....	....	....	....	....	....	
2005-06	Des Moines	USHL	50	27	31	58	56	....	....	....	....	....	....	....	....	....	11	5	11	*16	8	....	....	
2006-07	U. of Minnesota	WCHA	40	19	21	40	34	....	....	....	....	....	....	....	....	....	....	....	....	....	....	....	....	
2007-08	U. of Minnesota	WCHA	18	7	4	11	6	....	....	....	....	....	....	....	....	....	....	....	....	....	....	....	....	
	NY Islanders	**NHL**	9	2	3	5	2	1	0	1	15	13.3	3	0	0.0	16:28	....	....	....	....	....	....	....	
	Bridgeport	AHL	35	9	19	28	12	....	....	....	....	....	....	....	....	....	....	....	....	....	....	....	....	
2008-09	**NY Islanders**	**NHL**	65	18	21	39	36	9	0	3	165	10.9	–6	15	33.3	18:01	....	....	....	....	....	....	....	
	Bridgeport	AHL	....	....	....	....	....	....	....	....	....	....	....	....	....	....	2	1	0	1	2	....	....	
2009-10	**NY Islanders**	**NHL**	80	19	33	52	34	4	0	4	249	7.6	–22	69	47.8	20:32	....	....	....	....	....	....	....	
	NHL Totals		154	39	57	96	72	14	0	8	429	9.1		84	45.2	19:14	....	....	....	....	....	....	....	

USHL All-Rookie Team (2006) • USHL First All-Star Team (2006) • USHL Rookie of the Year (2006) • WCHA All-Rookie Team (2007) • WCHA Second All-Star Team (2007)

OLESZ, Rostislav
(OH-lehsh, RAHS-tih-slav)   FLA

Center. Shoots left. 6'1", 214 lbs.   Born, Bilovec, Czech., October 10, 1985. Florida's 1st choice, 7th overall, in 2004 Entry Draft.

Season	Club	League	GP	G	A	Pts	PIM	PP	SH	GW	S	%	+/-	TF	F%	Min	GP	G	A	Pts	PIM
2000-01	HC Vitkovice Jr.	CzRep-Jr.	15	10	3	13	14														
	HC Vitkovice	CzRep	3	0	1	1	0														
2001-02	HC Vitkovice	CzRep	11	1	2	3	0														
	HC Vitkovice Jr.	CzRep-Jr.	34	19	20	39	81										2	0	0	0	2
2002-03	HC Vitkovice Jr.	CzRep-Jr.	7	1	1	2	12														
	HC Vitkovice	CzRep	40	6	3	9	41										5	0	0	0	2
	HC Slezan Opava	CzRep-2	1	0	0	0	0														
2003-04	HC Vitkovice Jr.	CzRep-Jr.	3	2	0	2	0														
	HC Vitkovice	CzRep	35	1	11	12	10										6	2	1	3	4
	HC Dukla Jihlava	CzRep-2	2	1	0	1	0										1	0	0	0	0
2004-05	HC Sparta Praha	CzRep	47	6	7	13	12										5	0	2	2	0
	Sparta Jr.	CzRep-Jr.															1	0	1	1	0
2005-06	**Florida**	**NHL**	59	8	13	21	24	0	1	3	105	7.6	–4	10	30.0	14:52					
	Czech Republic	Olympics	8	0	0	0	2														
2006-07	**Florida**	**NHL**	75	11	19	30	28	2	0	2	164	6.7	2	12	58.3	15:30					
	Rochester	AHL	4	1	2	3	4														
2007-08	**Florida**	**NHL**	56	14	12	26	16	5	0	2	139	10.1	3	10	70.0	17:04					
2008-09	**Florida**	**NHL**	37	4	5	9	8	0	0	0	69	5.8	–5	5	20.0	13:12					
2009-10	**Florida**	**NHL**	78	14	15	29	28	3	0	3	178	7.9	–4	9	22.2	15:24					
	NHL Totals		305	51	64	115	104	10	1	10	655	7.8		46	43.5	15:22					

• Missed majority of 2008-09 season recovering from groin injury and resulting sports hernia surgery.

OLVECKY, Peter
(ohl-VEHT-skee, PEE-tuhr)

Center. Shoots left. 6'2", 220 lbs.   Born, Trencin, Czech., October 11, 1985. Minnesota's 3rd choice, 78th overall, in 2004 Entry Draft.

Season	Club	League	GP	G	A	Pts	PIM	PP	SH	GW	S	%	+/-	TF	F%	Min	GP	G	A	Pts	PIM
2003-04	Dukla Trencin Jr.	Slovak-Jr.	40	16	20	36	74										2	0	0	0	12
	Dukla Trencin	Slovakia	16	0	0	0	18														
	Dukla Trencin U18	Svk-U18	2	0	0	0	0														
2004-05	SHK 37 Piestany	Slovak-2	1	0	0	0	10														
	Dukla Trencin Jr.	Slovak-Jr.	8	1	3	4	10										2	1	4	5	4
	Dukla Trencin	Slovakia	45	10	9	19	49										12	1	0	1	6
2005-06	Houston Aeros	AHL	67	14	18	32	56										7	1	3	4	4
2006-07	Houston Aeros	AHL	69	12	15	27	46														
2007-08	Houston Aeros	AHL	61	17	16	33	38										5	1	1	2	4
2008-09	**Minnesota**	**NHL**	31	2	5	7	12	0	0	1	19	10.5	1	158	39.9	8:55					
	Houston Aeros	AHL	41	6	17	23	31										3	1	1	2	6
2009-10	**Nashville**	**NHL**	1	0	0	0	0	0	0	0	0	0.0	0	0	0.0	7:53					
	Milwaukee	AHL	62	11	23	34	22														
	Manitoba Moose	AHL	8	1	3	4	0										6	3	1	4	4
	NHL Totals		32	2	5	7	12	0	0	1	19	10.5		158	39.9	8:53					

Signed as a free agent by **Nashville**, July 16, 2009. • Loaned to **Manitoba** (AHL) by **Milwaukee** (AHL) in return for the loan of Marty Murray, March 10, 2010.

O'MARRA, Ryan
(oh-MAHR-ah, RIGH-uhn)   EDM.

Center. Shoots right. 6'2", 193 lbs.   Born, Tokyo, Japan, June 9, 1987. NY Islanders' 1st choice, 15th overall, in 2005 Entry Draft.

Season	Club	League	GP	G	A	Pts	PIM	PP	SH	GW	S	%	+/-	TF	F%	Min	GP	G	A	Pts	PIM
2002-03	Miss. Senators	GTHL	76	51	60	111	83														
	Georgetown	OPJHL	3	0	2	2	0														
	Streetsville Derbys	OPJHL	0	1	1	2															
2003-04	Erie Otters	OHL	63	16	16	32	33										9	5	5	10	6
2004-05	Erie Otters	OHL	64	25	38	63	60										6	4	1	5	0
2005-06	Erie Otters	OHL	61	27	50	77	134														
	Bridgeport	AHL	8	4	1	5	4										3	0	1	1	2
2006-07	Erie Otters	OHL	13	8	6	14	26														
	Saginaw Spirit	OHL	33	18	19	37	48										3	2	1	3	4
2007-08	Springfield	AHL	31	2	7	9	31														
	Stockton Thunder	ECHL	24	11	9	20	45										6	2	7	9	10
2008-09	Springfield	AHL	62	1	9	10	49														
2009-10	**Edmonton**	**NHL**	3	0	1	1	0	0	0	0	2	0.0	0	12	58.3	6:37					
	Springfield	AHL	74	12	6	18	59														
	NHL Totals		3	0	1	1	0	0	0	0	2	0.0		12	58.3	6:37					

Traded to **Edmonton** by **NY Islanders** with Robert Nilsson and NY Islanders' 1st round choice (Alex Plante) in 2007 Entry Draft for Ryan Smyth, February 27, 2007.

ONDRUS, Ben
(AWN-druhs, BEHN)   EDM.

Right wing. Shoots right. 6', 194 lbs.   Born, Sherwood Park, Alta., June 25, 1982.

Season	Club	League	GP	G	A	Pts	PIM	PP	SH	GW	S	%	+/-	TF	F%	Min	GP	G	A	Pts	PIM
1997-98	Sherwood Park	AMBHL																			
1998-99	Swift Current	WHL	46	4	4	8	58										6	0	1	1	8
99-2000	Swift Current	WHL	67	14	15	29	138										12	1	0	1	22
2000-01	Swift Current	WHL	69	13	17	30	151														
2001-02	Swift Current	WHL	67	30	41	71	153										12	4	3	7	18
2002-03	Swift Current	WHL	67	33	36	69	98										3	0	1	1	11
	Idaho Steelheads	WCHL	4	0	3	3	0										5	0	1	1	6
2003-04	St. John's	AHL	60	6	11	17	102														
2004-05	St. John's	AHL	78	7	11	18	137										5	0	1	1	7
2005-06	**Toronto**	**NHL**	22	0	0	0	18	0	0	0	17	0.0	–10	28	50.0	10:07					
	Toronto Marlies	AHL	53	12	17	29	104										5	1	2	3	4
2006-07	**Toronto**	**NHL**	16	0	2	2	20	0	0	0	7	0.0	–5	9	44.4	4:54					
	Toronto Marlies	AHL	29	8	3	11	35														
2007-08	**Toronto**	**NHL**	3	0	0	0	5	0	0	0	4	0.0	–1	3	33.3	5:07					
	Toronto Marlies	AHL	59	14	12	26	63										19	1	5	6	14
2008-09	**Toronto**	**NHL**	11	0	0	0	34	0	0	0	2	0.0	–4	27	44.4	9:27					
	Toronto Marlies	AHL	57	10	7	17	83										6	0	0	0	2
2009-10	Toronto Marlies	AHL	56	7	7	14	41														
	NHL Totals		52	0	2	2	77	0	0	0	30	0.0		67	46.3	8:05					

Signed as a free agent by **Idaho** (WCHL), March 23, 2003. Signed as a free agent by **St. John's** (AHL), September 1, 2003. Signed as a free agent by **Toronto**, May 27, 2004. Signed as a free agent by **Edmonton**, July 9, 2010.

			Regular Season														Playoffs							
Season	Club	League	GP	G	A	Pts	PIM	PP	SH	GW	S	%	+/-	TF	F%	Min	GP	G	A	Pts	PIM	PP	SH	GW	Min

O'NEILL, Wes
(oh-NEEL, WEHS)

Defense. Shoots left. 6'4", 215 lbs.　　Born, Windsor, Ont., March 3, 1986. NY Islanders' 4th choice, 115th overall, in 2004 Entry Draft.

Season	Club	League	GP	G	A	Pts	PIM	PP	SH	GW	S	%	+/-	TF	F%	Min	GP	G	A	Pts	PIM
2000-01	Chatham	OHA-B	51	6	9	15	50	....	....	....	....	....	....	....	....	....					
2001-02	Chatham	OHA-B	51	9	36	45	....	....	....	....	....	....	....	....	....	....					
2002-03	Green Bay	USHL	50	2	15	17	79	....	....	....	....	....	....	....	....	....					
2003-04	U. of Notre Dame	CCHA	39	2	10	12	28	....	....	....	....	....	....	....	....	....					
2004-05	U. of Notre Dame	CCHA	38	6	14	20	52	....	....	....	....	....	....	....	....	....					
2005-06	U. of Notre Dame	CCHA	35	6	19	25	40	....	....	....	....	....	....	....	....	....					
2006-07	U. of Notre Dame	CCHA	42	3	18	21	40	....	....	....	....	....	....	....	....	....					
2007-08	Lake Erie	AHL	51	2	4	6	50	....	....	....	....	....	....	....	....	....	6	0	0	0	8
	Johnstown Chiefs	ECHL	6	0	1	1	2	....	....	....	....	....	....	....	....	....					
2008-09	**Colorado**	**NHL**	**3**	**0**	**0**	**0**	**4**	0	0	0	1	0.0	-2	0	0.0	10:52					
	Lake Erie	AHL	54	1	5	6	34	....	....	....	....	....	....	....	....	....					
	Johnstown Chiefs	ECHL	6	0	1	1	0	....	....	....	....	....	....	....	....	....					
2009-10	**Colorado**	**NHL**	**2**	**0**	**0**	**0**	**2**	0	0	0	1	0.0	1	0	0.0	9:43					
	Lake Erie	AHL	54	1	14	15	41	....	....	....	....	....	....	....	....	....					
	NHL Totals		**5**	**0**	**0**	**0**	**6**	**0**	**0**	**0**	**2**	**0.0**		**0**	**0.0**	**10:24**					

Signed as a free agent by **Colorado**, August 20, 2007.

O'REILLY, Cal
(oh-RIGH-lee, KAL)　　**NSH.**

Center. Shoots left. 6', 187 lbs.　　Born, Toronto, Ont., September 30, 1986. Nashville's 4th choice, 150th overall, in 2005 Entry Draft.

Season	Club	League	GP	G	A	Pts	PIM	PP	SH	GW	S	%	+/-	TF	F%	Min	GP	G	A	Pts	PIM
2002-03	St. Mary's Lincolns	OJHL-B	46	11	19	30	2	....	....	....	....	....	....	....	....	....	3	0	1	1	0
2003-04	Windsor Spitfires	OHL	61	3	18	21	2	....	....	....	....	....	....	....	....	....	11	4	5	9	4
2004-05	Windsor Spitfires	OHL	68	24	50	74	16	....	....	....	....	....	....	....	....	....	7	3	8	11	0
2005-06	Windsor Spitfires	OHL	68	18	81	99	8	....	....	....	....	....	....	....	....	....	10	0	1	1	0
	Milwaukee	AHL	2	0	0	0	0	....	....	....	....	....	....	....	....	....	4	1	2	3	0
2006-07	Milwaukee	AHL	78	18	47	65	20	....	....	....	....	....	....	....	....	....	6	1	2	3	0
2007-08	Milwaukee	AHL	80	16	63	79	22	....	....	....	....	....	....	....	....	....					
2008-09	**Nashville**	**NHL**	**11**	**3**	**2**	**5**	**2**	0	0	0	6	50.0	2	88	39.8	12:36	11	2	6	8	0
	Milwaukee	AHL	67	13	56	69	20	....	....	....	....	....	....	....	....	....					
2009-10	**Nashville**	**NHL**	**31**	**2**	**9**	**11**	**4**	1	0	0	23	8.7	1	281	47.3	13:38					
	Milwaukee	AHL	35	9	31	40	8	....	....	....	....	....	....	....	....	....					
	NHL Totals		**42**	**5**	**11**	**16**	**6**	**1**	**0**	**0**	**29**	**17.2**		**369**	**45.5**	**13:22**					

O'REILLY, Ryan
(oh-RIGH-lee, RIGH-uhn)　　**COL.**

Center. Shoots left. 6', 200 lbs.　　Born, Clinton, Ont., February 7, 1991. Colorado's 2nd choice, 33rd overall, in 2009 Entry Draft.

Season	Club	League	GP	G	A	Pts	PIM	PP	SH	GW	S	%	+/-	TF	F%	Min	GP	G	A	Pts	PIM	PP	SH	GW	Min
2006-07	Tor. Jr. Canadiens	GTHL	50	31	43	74	....	....	....	....	....	....	....	....	....	....									
	Tor. Canadiens	OPJHL	1	1	0	1	0	....	....	....	....	....	....	....	....	....									
2007-08	Erie Otters	OHL	61	19	33	52	14	....	....	....	....	....	....	....	....	....	5	0	5	5	2				
2008-09	Erie Otters	OHL	68	16	50	66	26	....	....	....	....	....	....	....	....	....	6	3	4	7	4				
2009-10	**Colorado**	**NHL**	**81**	**8**	**18**	**26**	**18**	0	2	2	135	5.9	4	1014	47.8	16:46	6	1	0	1	2	0	0	1	17:05
	NHL Totals		**81**	**8**	**18**	**26**	**18**	**0**	**2**	**2**	**135**	**5.9**		**1014**	**47.8**	**16:46**	**6**	**1**	**0**	**1**	**2**	**0**	**0**	**1**	**17:05**

ORESKOVIC, Phil
(oh-rehs-KOH-vihch, FIHL)

Defense. Shoots right. 6'4", 217 lbs.　　Born, North York, Ont., January 26, 1987. Toronto's 2nd choice, 82nd overall, in 2005 Entry Draft.

Season	Club	League	GP	G	A	Pts	PIM	PP	SH	GW	S	%	+/-	TF	F%	Min	GP	G	A	Pts	PIM
2003-04	Brampton	OHL	66	0	7	7	64	....	....	....	....	....	....	....	....	....	12	0	2	2	16
2004-05	Brampton	OHL	61	1	6	7	147	....	....	....	....	....	....	....	....	....	6	0	0	0	4
2005-06	Brampton	OHL	65	3	9	12	202	....	....	....	....	....	....	....	....	....	11	0	0	0	34
2006-07	Brampton	OHL	36	2	12	14	113	....	....	....	....	....	....	....	....	....					
	Owen Sound	OHL	26	1	7	8	66	....	....	....	....	....	....	....	....	....	4	0	0	0	2
	Toronto Marlies	AHL	3	0	1	1	2	....	....	....	....	....	....	....	....	....					
2007-08	Toronto Marlies	AHL	54	1	9	10	68	....	....	....	....	....	....	....	....	....	7	0	1	1	11
	Columbia Inferno	ECHL	13	0	4	4	19	....	....	....	....	....	....	....	....	....					
2008-09	**Toronto**	**NHL**	**10**	**1**	**1**	**2**	**21**	0	0	0	12	8.3	-2	0	0.0	16:14					
	Toronto Marlies	AHL	65	1	10	11	103	....	....	....	....	....	....	....	....	....	6	0	0	0	12
2009-10	Toronto Marlies	AHL	74	2	7	9	142	....	....	....	....	....	....	....	....	....					
	NHL Totals		**10**	**1**	**1**	**2**	**21**	**0**	**0**	**0**	**12**	**8.3**		**0**	**0.0**	**16:14**					

ORESKOVICH, Victor
(oh-rehs-KOH-vihch, VIHK-tohr)　　**VAN.**

Right wing. Shoots right. 6'3", 215 lbs.　　Born, Whitby, Ont., August 15, 1986. Colorado's 2nd choice, 55th overall, in 2004 Entry Draft.

Season	Club	League	GP	G	A	Pts	PIM	PP	SH	GW	S	%	+/-	TF	F%	Min	GP	G	A	Pts	PIM
2002-03	Milton IceHawks	OPJHL	49	28	46	74	51	....	....	....	....	....	....	....	....	....					
2003-04	Green Bay	USHL	58	11	26	37	33	....	....	....	....	....	....	....	....	....					
2004-05	U. of Notre Dame	CCHA	37	1	2	3	69	....	....	....	....	....	....	....	....	....					
2005-06	U. of Notre Dame	CCHA	10	2	1	3	8	....	....	....	....	....	....	....	....	....	5	0	2	2	4
	Kitchener Rangers	OHL	19	6	10	16	16	....	....	....	....	....	....	....	....	....	5	2	0	2	4
2006-07	Kitchener Rangers	OHL	62	28	32	60	48	....	....	....	....	....	....	....	....	....					
2007-08				OUT OF HOCKEY – RETIRED																	
2008-09				OUT OF HOCKEY – RETIRED																	
2009-10	**Florida**	**NHL**	**50**	**2**	**4**	**6**	**26**	0	0	0	55	3.6	-8	3	33.3	8:53	6	0	0	0	10
	Rochester	AHL	34	6	9	15	18	....	....	....	....	....	....	....	....	....					
	NHL Totals		**50**	**2**	**4**	**6**	**26**	**0**	**0**	**0**	**55**	**3.6**		**3**	**33.3**	**8:53**					

Signed as a free agent by **Florida**, October 9, 2009. Traded to **Vancouver** by **Florida** with Keith Ballard for Steve Bernier, Michael Grabner and Vancouver's 1st round choice (Quinton Howden) in 2010 Entry Draft, June 25, 2010.

ORPIK, Brooks
(OHR-pihk, BRUKS)　　**PIT.**

Defense. Shoots left. 6'2", 219 lbs.　　Born, San Francisco, CA, September 26, 1980. Pittsburgh's 1st choice, 18th overall, in 2000 Entry Draft.

Season	Club	League	GP	G	A	Pts	PIM	PP	SH	GW	S	%	+/-	TF	F%	Min	GP	G	A	Pts	PIM	PP	SH	GW	Min
1996-97	Thayer Academy	High-MA	20	4	1	5	....	....	....	....	....	....	....	....	....	....									
1997-98	Thayer Academy	High-MA	22	0	7	7	....	....	....	....	....	....	....	....	....	....									
1998-99	Boston College	H-East	41	1	10	11	*96	....	....	....	....	....	....	....	....	....									
99-2000	Boston College	H-East	38	1	9	10	102	....	....	....	....	....	....	....	....	....									
2000-01	Boston College	H-East	40	0	20	20	*124	....	....	....	....	....	....	....	....	....									
2001-02	Wilkes-Barre	AHL	78	2	18	20	99	....	....	....	....	....	....	....	....	....									
2002-03	**Pittsburgh**	**NHL**	**6**	**0**	**0**	**0**	**2**	0	0	0	2	0.0	-5	0	0.0	18:19	6	0	0	0	14				
	Wilkes-Barre	AHL	71	4	14	18	105	....	....	....	....	....	....	....	....	....									
2003-04	**Pittsburgh**	**NHL**	**79**	**1**	**9**	**10**	**127**	0	0	0	56	1.8	-36	0	0.0	18:25	24	0	4	4	53				
	Wilkes-Barre	AHL	3	0	0	0	2	....	....	....	....	....	....	....	....	....									
2005-06	**Pittsburgh**	**NHL**	**64**	**2**	**7**	**9**	**124**	0	0	0	32	6.3	-3	0	0.0	18:50	5	0	0	0	8	0	0	0	15:43
2006-07	**Pittsburgh**	**NHL**	**70**	**0**	**6**	**6**	**82**	0	0	0	59	0.0	4	0	0.0	16:37	20	0	2	2	18	0	0	0	20:47
2007-08	**Pittsburgh**	**NHL**	**78**	**1**	**10**	**11**	**57**	0	0	0	50	2.0	11	0	0.0	16:58	20	0	4	4	22	0	0	0	20:04
2008-09 ◆	**Pittsburgh**	**NHL**	**79**	**2**	**17**	**19**	**73**	1	0	0	39	5.1	10	0	0.0	20:20	24	0	4	4	22	0	0	0	21:40
2009-10	**Pittsburgh**	**NHL**	**73**	**2**	**23**	**25**	**64**	0	0	0	61	3.3	6	0	0.0	20:06	13	0	2	2	12	0	0	0	21:40
	United States	Olympics	6	0	0	0	0	....	....	....	....	....	....	....	....	....									
	NHL Totals		**449**	**8**	**72**	**80**	**529**	**1**	**0**	**0**	**299**	**2.7**		**0**	**0.0**	**18:33**	**62**	**0**	**8**	**8**	**60**	**0**	**0**	**0**	**20:17**

ORR, Colton
(OHR, KOHL-tuhn)　　**TOR.**

Right wing. Shoots right. 6'3", 222 lbs.　　Born, Winnipeg, Man., March 3, 1982.

Season	Club	League	GP	G	A	Pts	PIM	PP	SH	GW	S	%	+/-	TF	F%	Min	GP	G	A	Pts	PIM
1998-99	St. Boniface	MJHL			STATISTICS NOT AVAILABLE																
	Swift Current	WHL	2	0	0	0	0	....	....	....	....	....	....	....	....	....	12	1	0	1	25
99-2000	Swift Current	WHL	61	3	2	5	130	....	....	....	....	....	....	....	....	....					
2000-01	Swift Current	WHL	19	0	4	4	67	....	....	....	....	....	....	....	....	....	3	0	0	0	20
	Kamloops Blazers	WHL	41	8	1	9	179	....	....	....	....	....	....	....	....	....	2	0	0	0	2
2001-02	Kamloops Blazers	WHL	1	0	0	0	7	....	....	....	....	....	....	....	....	....					

			Regular Season														Playoffs								
Season	Club	League	GP	G	A	Pts	PIM	PP	SH	GW	S	%	+/-	TF	F%	Min	GP	G	A	Pts	PIM	PP	SH	GW	M
2002-03	Kamloops Blazers	WHL	3	2	0	2	17	....	....	....	....	....	....	....	....	....	....	....	....	....	....	....	....	....	....
	Regina Pats	WHL	37	6	2	8	170	....	....	....	....	....	....	....	....	....	3	0	0	0	19	....	....	....	....
	Providence Bruins	AHL	1	0	0	0	7	....	....	....	....	....	....	....	....	....	....	....	....	....	....	....	....	....	....
2003-04	**Boston**	**NHL**	**1**	**0**	**0**	**0**	**0**	**0**	**0**	**0**	**0**	**0.0**	**–1**	**0**	**0.0**	**2:13**	....	....	....	....	....	....	....	....	....
	Providence Bruins	AHL	64	1	4	5	257	....	....	....	....	....	....	....	....	....	2	0	0	0	9	....	....	....	....
2004-05	Providence Bruins	AHL	61	1	6	7	279	....	....	....	....	....	....	....	....	....	17	1	0	1	44	....	....	....	....
2005-06	**Boston**	**NHL**	**20**	**0**	**0**	**0**	**27**	**0**	**0**	**0**	**1**	**0.0**	**0**	**0**	**0.0**	**1:49**	....	....	....	....	....	....	....	....	....
	NY Rangers	**NHL**	**15**	**0**	**1**	**1**	**44**	**0**	**0**	**0**	**0**	**0.0**	**1**	**0**	**0.0**	**4:19**	**1**	**0**	**0**	**0**	**2**	**0**	**0**	**0**	**4:1**
2006-07	**NY Rangers**	**NHL**	**53**	**2**	**1**	**3**	**126**	**0**	**0**	**1**	**23**	**8.7**	**–2**	**0**	**0.0**	**5:20**	**4**	**0**	**0**	**0**	**12**	**0**	**0**	**0**	**4:5**
2007-08	**NY Rangers**	**NHL**	**74**	**1**	**1**	**2**	**159**	**0**	**0**	**1**	**24**	**4.2**	**–13**	**2**	**50.0**	**7:49**	**2**	**0**	**0**	**0**	**0**	**0**	**0**	**0**	**4:2**
2008-09	**NY Rangers**	**NHL**	**82**	**1**	**4**	**5**	**193**	**0**	**0**	**0**	**40**	**2.5**	**–15**	**16**	**25.0**	**6:29**	**5**	**0**	**0**	**0**	**16**	**0**	**0**	**0**	**3:5**
2009-10	**Toronto**	**NHL**	**82**	**4**	**2**	**6**	**239**	**0**	**0**	**1**	**43**	**9.3**	**–4**	**2**	**50.0**	**6:52**	....	....	....	....	....	....	....	....	....
	NHL Totals		**327**	**8**	**9**	**17**	**788**	**0**	**0**	**3**	**131**	**6.1**		**20**	**30.0**	**6:18**	**12**	**0**	**0**	**0**	**30**	**0**	**0**	**0**	**4:2**

Signed as a free agent by **Boston**, September 19, 2001. • Missed majority of 2001-02 season recovering from wrist injury suffered in game vs. Red Deer (WHL), October 20, 2001. Claimed on waivers by **NY Rangers** from **Boston**, November 29, 2005. Signed as a free agent by **Toronto**, July 1, 2009.

ORTMEYER, Jed

(OHRT-migh-uhr, JEHD)

Center. Shoots right. 6', 200 lbs. Born, Omaha, NE, September 3, 1978.

Season	Club	League	GP	G	A	Pts	PIM	PP	SH	GW	S	%	+/-	TF	F%	Min	GP	G	A	Pts	PIM	PP	SH	GW	Min
1997-98	Omaha Lancers	USHL	54	23	25	48	52	....	....	....	....	....	....	....	....	....	14	3	4	7	31	....	....	....	....
1998-99	Omaha Lancers	USHL	52	23	36	59	81	....	....	....	....	....	....	....	....	....	12	5	6	11	16	....	....	....	....
99-2000	U. of Michigan	CCHA	41	8	16	24	40	....	....	....	....	....	....	....	....	....	....	....	....	....	....	....	....	....	....
2000-01	U. of Michigan	CCHA	27	10	11	21	52	....	....	....	....	....	....	....	....	....	....	....	....	....	....	....	....	....	....
2001-02	U. of Michigan	CCHA	41	15	23	38	40	....	....	....	....	....	....	....	....	....	....	....	....	....	....	....	....	....	....
2002-03	U. of Michigan	CCHA	36	18	16	34	48	....	....	....	....	....	....	....	....	....	....	....	....	....	....	....	....	....	....
2003-04	**NY Rangers**	**NHL**	**58**	**2**	**4**	**6**	**16**	**0**	**0**	**0**	**48**	**4.2**	**–10**	**16**	**31.3**	**9:52**	....	....	....	....	....	....	....	....	....
	Hartford	AHL	13	2	8	10	4	....	....	....	....	....	....	....	....	....	16	5	2	7	6	....	....	....	....
2004-05	Hartford	AHL	61	7	20	27	63	....	....	....	....	....	....	....	....	....	6	0	1	1	4	....	....	....	....
2005-06	**NY Rangers**	**NHL**	**78**	**5**	**2**	**7**	**38**	**0**	**0**	**1**	**90**	**5.6**	**2**	**21**	**23.8**	**11:06**	**4**	**1**	**0**	**1**	**4**	**0**	**0**	**0**	**11:4**
2006-07	**NY Rangers**	**NHL**	**41**	**2**	**9**	**11**	**22**	**0**	**1**	**0**	**67**	**3.0**	**7**	**8**	**12.5**	**12:35**	**9**	**0**	**0**	**0**	**2**	**0**	**0**	**0**	**9:3**
	Hartford	AHL	8	1	3	4	6	....	....	....	....	....	....	....	....	....	....	....	....	....	....	....	....	....	....
2007-08	**Nashville**	**NHL**	**51**	**4**	**4**	**8**	**32**	**0**	**1**	**0**	**68**	**5.9**	**–8**	**12**	**50.0**	**12:27**	....	....	....	....	....	....	....	....	....
2008-09	**Nashville**	**NHL**	**2**	**0**	**0**	**0**	**0**	**0**	**0**	**0**	**4**	**0.0**	**0**	**0**	**0.0**	**11:01**	....	....	....	....	....	....	....	....	....
	Milwaukee	AHL	55	10	13	23	51	....	....	....	....	....	....	....	....	....	11	1	6	7	8	....	....	....	....
2009-10	**San Jose**	**NHL**	**76**	**8**	**11**	**19**	**37**	**0**	**0**	**1**	**131**	**6.1**	**4**	**18**	**27.8**	**11:31**	**4**	**0**	**1**	**1**	**0**	**0**	**0**	**0**	**6:5**
	NHL Totals		**306**	**21**	**30**	**51**	**145**	**0**	**2**	**2**	**408**	**5.1**		**75**	**29.3**	**11:24**	**17**	**1**	**1**	**2**	**6**	**0**	**0**	**0**	**9:2**

Signed as a free agent by **NY Rangers**, May 10, 2003. Signed as a free agent by **Nashville**, July 2, 2007. Signed as a free agent by **San Jose**, July 16, 2009.

OSALA, Oskar

(OH-sa-la, AWZ-kuhr) **CAR**

Left wing. Shoots left. 6'4", 219 lbs. Born, Vaasa, Finland, December 26, 1987. Washington's 6th choice, 97th overall, in 2006 Entry Draft.

Season	Club	League	GP	G	A	Pts	PIM	PP	SH	GW	S	%	+/-	TF	F%	Min	GP	G	A	Pts	PIM	PP	SH	GW	Min
2003-04	Sport Vaasa U18	Fin-U18	25	19	18	37	32	....	....	....	....	....	....	....	....	....	....	....	....	....	....	....	....	....	....
	Sport Vaasa Jr.	Fin-Jr.	2	0	0	0	4	....	....	....	....	....	....	....	....	....	....	....	....	....	....	....	....	....	....
	Sport Vaasa	Finland-2	5	0	0	0	0	....	....	....	....	....	....	....	....	....	....	....	....	....	....	....	....	....	....
2004-05	Sport Vaasa U18	Fin-U18	4	4	2	6	16	....	....	....	....	....	....	....	....	....	....	....	....	....	....	....	....	....	....
	Sport Vaasa Jr.	Fin-Jr.	19	13	14	27	28	....	....	....	....	....	....	....	....	....	2	0	0	0	2	....	....	....	....
	Sport Vaasa	Finland-2	21	1	4	5	6	....	....	....	....	....	....	....	....	....	7	0	0	0	6	....	....	....	....
2005-06	Mississauga	OHL	68	17	26	43	86	....	....	....	....	....	....	....	....	....	....	....	....	....	....	....	....	....	....
2006-07	Mississauga	OHL	54	22	22	44	81	....	....	....	....	....	....	....	....	....	5	2	2	4	0	....	....	....	....
	Suomi U20	Finland-2	2	1	0	1	0	....	....	....	....	....	....	....	....	....	....	....	....	....	....	....	....	....	....
2007-08	Blues Espoo	Finland	53	18	17	35	62	....	....	....	....	....	....	....	....	....	17	7	3	10	8	....	....	....	....
2008-09	**Washington**	**NHL**	**2**	**0**	**0**	**0**	**0**	**0**	**0**	**0**	**1**	**0.0**	**–1**	**0**	**0.0**	**8:44**	....	....	....	....	....	....	....	....	....
	Hershey Bears	AHL	75	23	14	37	47	....	....	....	....	....	....	....	....	....	22	6	4	10	17	....	....	....	....
2009-10	**Carolina**	**NHL**	**1**	**0**	**0**	**0**	**0**	**0**	**0**	**0**	**1**	**0.0**	**0**	**0**	**0.0**	**6:46**	....	....	....	....	....	....	....	....	....
	Hershey Bears	AHL	53	15	14	29	57	....	....	....	....	....	....	....	....	....	....	....	....	....	....	....	....	....	....
	Albany River Rats	AHL	16	9	3	12	11	....	....	....	....	....	....	....	....	....	8	2	1	3	2	....	....	....	....
	NHL Totals		**3**	**0**	**0**	**0**	**0**	**0**	**0**	**0**	**2**	**0.0**		**0**	**0.0**	**8:04**	....	....	....	....	....	....	....	....	....

Signed as a free agent by **Espoo** (Finland), July 23, 2007. Traded to **Carolina** by **Washington** with Brian Pothier and Washington's 2nd round choice (later traded to NY Rangers) in 2011 Entry Draft for Joe Corvo, March 3, 2010.

OSHIE, T.J.

(OH-shee, TEE-JAY) **ST.L.**

Center. Shoots right. 5'11", 194 lbs. Born, Mt. Vernon, WA, December 23, 1986. St. Louis' 1st choice, 24th overall, in 2005 Entry Draft.

Season	Club	League	GP	G	A	Pts	PIM	PP	SH	GW	S	%	+/-	TF	F%	Min	GP	G	A	Pts	PIM	PP	SH	GW	Min
2004-05	Warroad Warriors	High-MN	31	37	62	99	22	....	....	....	....	....	....	....	....	....	....	....	....	....	....	....	....	....	....
	Sioux Falls	USHL	11	3	2	5	6	....	....	....	....	....	....	....	....	....	....	....	....	....	....	....	....	....	....
2005-06	North Dakota	WCHA	44	24	21	45	33	....	....	....	....	....	....	....	....	....	....	....	....	....	....	....	....	....	....
2006-07	North Dakota	WCHA	43	17	*35	52	30	....	....	....	....	....	....	....	....	....	....	....	....	....	....	....	....	....	....
2007-08	North Dakota	WCHA	42	18	27	45	57	....	....	....	....	....	....	....	....	....	....	....	....	....	....	....	....	....	....
2008-09	**St. Louis**	**NHL**	**57**	**14**	**25**	**39**	**30**	**6**	**1**	**1**	**101**	**13.9**	**16**	**109**	**43.1**	**16:35**	**4**	**0**	**0**	**0**	**2**	**0**	**0**	**0**	**19:01**
2009-10	**St. Louis**	**NHL**	**76**	**18**	**30**	**48**	**36**	**1**	**1**	**3**	**158**	**11.4**	**–1**	**153**	**41.8**	**18:19**	....	....	....	....	....	....	....	....	....
	NHL Totals		**133**	**32**	**55**	**87**	**66**	**7**	**2**	**4**	**259**	**12.4**		**262**	**42.4**	**17:34**	**4**	**0**	**0**	**0**	**2**	**0**	**0**	**0**	**19:01**

WCHA All-Rookie Team (2006) • WCHA First All-Star Team (2008) • NCAA West First All-American Team (2008)

O'SULLIVAN, Patrick

(Oh-SUHL-ih-vihn, PAT-rihk)

Center. Shoots left. 5'11", 190 lbs. Born, Toronto, Ont., February 1, 1985. Minnesota's 2nd choice, 56th overall, in 2003 Entry Draft.

Season	Club	League	GP	G	A	Pts	PIM	PP	SH	GW	S	%	+/-	TF	F%	Min	GP	G	A	Pts	PIM	PP	SH	GW	Min
99-2000	Strathroy Rockets	OHA-B	45	6	13	19	53	....	....	....	....	....	....	....	....	....	....	....	....	....	....	....	....	....	....
2000-01	USNTDP	U-17	8	8	10	18	12	....	....	....	....	....	....	....	....	....	....	....	....	....	....	....	....	....	....
	USNTDP	NAHL	56	22	35	57	57	....	....	....	....	....	....	....	....	....	....	....	....	....	....	....	....	....	....
2001-02	Mississauga	OHL	68	34	58	92	61	....	....	....	....	....	....	....	....	....	....	....	....	....	....	....	....	....	....
	USNTDP	USHL	1	1	0	1	2	....	....	....	....	....	....	....	....	....	....	....	....	....	....	....	....	....	....
2002-03	Mississauga	OHL	56	40	41	81	57	....	....	....	....	....	....	....	....	....	5	2	9	11	18	....	....	....	....
2003-04	Mississauga	OHL	53	43	39	82	32	....	....	....	....	....	....	....	....	....	24	12	11	23	16	....	....	....	....
2004-05	Mississauga	OHL	57	31	59	90	63	....	....	....	....	....	....	....	....	....	5	0	4	4	6	....	....	....	....
2005-06	Houston Aeros	AHL	78	47	46	93	64	....	....	....	....	....	....	....	....	....	8	5	5	10	4	....	....	....	....
2006-07	**Los Angeles**	**NHL**	**44**	**5**	**14**	**19**	**14**	**2**	**0**	**1**	**92**	**5.4**	**–6**	**127**	**46.5**	**14:04**	....	....	....	....	....	....	....	....	....
	Manchester	AHL	41	18	21	39	12	....	....	....	....	....	....	....	....	....	16	8	9	17	10	....	....	....	....
2007-08	**Los Angeles**	**NHL**	**82**	**22**	**31**	**53**	**36**	**3**	**3**	**2**	**220**	**10.0**	**–8**	**461**	**44.0**	**18:42**	....	....	....	....	....	....	....	....	....
2008-09	**Los Angeles**	**NHL**	**62**	**14**	**23**	**37**	**16**	**2**	**1**	**1**	**200**	**7.0**	**1**	**39**	**46.2**	**19:26**	....	....	....	....	....	....	....	....	....
	Edmonton	**NHL**	**19**	**2**	**4**	**6**	**12**	**0**	**0**	**0**	**59**	**3.4**	**–7**	**60**	**38.3**	**18:14**	....	....	....	....	....	....	....	....	....
2009-10	**Edmonton**	**NHL**	**73**	**11**	**23**	**34**	**32**	**3**	**1**	**3**	**191**	**5.8**	**–35**	**195**	**36.4**	**17:31**	....	....	....	....	....	....	....	....	....
	NHL Totals		**280**	**54**	**95**	**149**	**110**	**10**	**5**	**7**	**762**	**7.1**		**882**	**42.4**	**17:48**	....	....	....	....	....	....	....	....	....

Canadian Major Junior Rookie of the Year (2002) • AHL All-Rookie Team (2006) • Dudley "Red" Garrett Memorial Trophy (AHL - Top Rookie) (2006)

Traded to **Los Angeles** by **Minnesota** with Edmonton's 1st round choice (previously acquired, Los Angeles selected Trevor Lewis) in 2006 Entry Draft for Pavol Demitra, June 24, 2006. Traded to **Carolina** by **Los Angeles** with Calgary's 2nd round choice (previously acquired, Carolina selected Brian Dumoulin) in 2009 Entry Draft for Justin Williams, March 4, 2009. Traded to **Edmonton** by **Carolina** with Carolina's 2nd round choice (later traded to Buffalo, later traded to Toronto – Toronto selected Jesse Blacker) in 2009 Entry Draft for Erik Cole and Edmonton's 5th round choice (Matt Kennedy) in 2009 Entry Draft, March 4, 2009. Traded to **Phoenix** by **Edmonton** for Jim Vandermeer, June 30, 2010.

OTT, Steve

(AWT, STEEV) **DAL.**

Center. Shoots left. 6', 194 lbs. Born, Summerside, P.E.I., August 19, 1982. Dallas' 1st choice, 25th overall, in 2000 Entry Draft.

Season	Club	League	GP	G	A	Pts	PIM	PP	SH	GW	S	%	+/-	TF	F%	Min	GP	G	A	Pts	PIM	PP	SH	GW	Min
1998-99	Leamington Flyers	OHA-B	48	14	30	44	110	....	....	....	....	....	....	....	....	....	....	....	....	....	....	....	....	....	....
99-2000	Windsor Spitfires	OHL	66	23	39	62	131	....	....	....	....	....	....	....	....	....	12	3	5	8	21	....	....	....	....
2000-01	Windsor Spitfires	OHL	55	50	37	87	164	....	....	....	....	....	....	....	....	....	9	3	8	11	27	....	....	....	....
2001-02	Windsor Spitfires	OHL	53	43	45	88	178	....	....	....	....	....	....	....	....	....	14	6	10	16	49	....	....	....	....
2002-03	**Dallas**	**NHL**	**26**	**3**	**4**	**7**	**31**	**0**	**0**	**0**	**25**	**12.0**	**6**	**4**	**50.0**	**8:46**	**1**	**0**	**0**	**0**	**0**	**0**	**0**	**0**	**6:57**
	Utah Grizzlies	AHL	40	9	11	20	98	....	....	....	....	....	....	....	....	....	....	....	....	....	....	....	....	....	....
2003-04	**Dallas**	**NHL**	**73**	**2**	**10**	**12**	**152**	**0**	**0**	**1**	**74**	**2.7**	**–2**	**59**	**49.2**	**10:14**	**4**	**1**	**0**	**1**	**0**	**0**	**0**	**1**	**6:55**
2004-05	Hamilton	AHL	67	18	21	39	279	....	....	....	....	....	....	....	....	....	4	0	0	0	20	....	....	....	....

			Regular Season														Playoffs								
Season	Club	League	GP	G	A	Pts	PIM	PP	SH	GW	S	%	+/-	TF	F%	Min	GP	G	A	Pts	PIM	PP	SH	GW	Min
2005-06	**Dallas**	**NHL**	**82**	**5**	**17**	**22**	**178**	**0**	**0**	**1**	**89**	**5.6**	**1**	**535**	**49.2**	**11:54**	**5**	**0**	**1**	**1**	**2**	**0**	**0**	**0**	**7:41**
2006-07	**Dallas**	**NHL**	**19**	**0**	**4**	**4**	**35**	**0**	**0**	**0**	**17**	**0.0**	**–4**	**39**	**59.0**	**9:11**	**6**	**0**	**0**	**0**	**8**	**0**	**0**	**0**	**6:43**
	Iowa Stars	AHL	3	0	0	0	8	....	....	....	....	....	....	....	....	....	....	....	....	....	....	....	....	....	....
2007-08	**Dallas**	**NHL**	**73**	**11**	**11**	**22**	**147**	**0**	**1**	**2**	**89**	**12.4**	**2**	**311**	**58.8**	**14:28**	**18**	**2**	**1**	**3**	**22**	**1**	**0**	**1**	**13:46**
2008-09	**Dallas**	**NHL**	**64**	**19**	**27**	**46**	**135**	**5**	**0**	**0**	**132**	**14.4**	**3**	**172**	**46.5**	**17:35**	....	....	....	....	....	....	....	....	....
2009-10	**Dallas**	**NHL**	**73**	**22**	**14**	**36**	**153**	**8**	**1**	**2**	**146**	**15.1**	**–14**	**352**	**56.8**	**16:28**	....	....	....	....	....	....	....	....	....
	NHL Totals		**410**	**62**	**87**	**149**	**831**	**13**	**2**	**6**	**572**	**10.8**		**1472**	**53.0**	**13:26**	**34**	**3**	**2**	**5**	**32**	**1**	**0**	**2**	**10:37**

:anadian Major Junior Second All-Star Team (2001) • OHL Second All-Star Team (2002)

Missed majority of 2006-07 season recovering from ankle injury suffered in game vs. Los Angeles, October 28, 2006.

OUELLET, Michel

(oo-LEHT, mee-SHEHL)

Right wing. Shoots right. 6'1", 193 lbs. Born, Rimouski, Que., March 5, 1982. Pittsburgh's 4th choice, 124th overall, in 2000 Entry Draft.

Season	Club	League	GP	G	A	Pts	PIM	PP	SH	GW	S	%	+/-	TF	F%	Min	GP	G	A	Pts	PIM	PP	SH	GW	Min
1997-98	Jonquiere Elites	QAAA	33	20	32	52	52	....	....	....	....	....	....	....	....	....	....	....	....	....	....	....	....	....	....
1998-99	Rimouski Oceanic	QMJHL	28	7	13	20	10	....	....	....	....	....	....	....	....	....	11	0	1	1	6	....	....	....	....
99-2000	Rimouski Oceanic	QMJHL	72	36	53	89	38	....	....	....	....	....	....	....	....	....	14	4	5	9	14	....	....	....	....
2000-01	Rimouski Oceanic	QMJHL	63	42	50	92	50	....	....	....	....	....	....	....	....	....	11	6	7	13	8	....	....	....	....
2001-02	Rimouski Oceanic	QMJHL	61	40	58	98	66	....	....	....	....	....	....	....	....	....	7	3	6	9	4	....	....	....	....
2002-03	Wilkes-Barre	AHL	4	0	2	2	0	....	....	....	....	....	....	....	....	....	....	....	....	....	....	....	....	....	....
	Wheeling Nailers	ECHL	55	20	26	46	40	....	....	....	....	....	....	....	....	....	....	....	....	....	....	....	....	....	....
2003-04	Wilkes-Barre	AHL	79	30	19	49	34	....	....	....	....	....	....	....	....	....	22	2	10	12	6	....	....	....	....
2004-05	Wilkes-Barre	AHL	80	31	32	63	56	....	....	....	....	....	....	....	....	....	11	2	3	5	6	....	....	....	....
2005-06	**Pittsburgh**	**NHL**	**50**	**16**	**16**	**32**	**16**	**11**	**0**	**0**	**87**	**18.4**	**–13**	**16**	**37.5**	**14:02**	....	....	....	....	....	....	....	....	....
	Wilkes-Barre	AHL	19	10	20	30	12	....	....	....	....	....	....	....	....	....	....	....	....	....	....	....	....	....	....
2006-07	**Pittsburgh**	**NHL**	**73**	**19**	**29**	**48**	**30**	**11**	**0**	**2**	**148**	**12.8**	**–3**	**8**	**37.5**	**13:20**	**5**	**0**	**2**	**2**	**6**	**0**	**0**	**0**	**12:54**
2007-08	**Tampa Bay**	**NHL**	**64**	**17**	**19**	**36**	**12**	**5**	**0**	**0**	**132**	**12.9**	**11**	**42**	**45.2**	**13:38**	....	....	....	....	....	....	....	....	....
2008-09	**Vancouver**	**NHL**	**3**	**0**	**0**	**0**	**0**	**0**	**0**	**0**	**3**	**0.0**	**1**	**1**	**0.0**	**9:39**	....	....	....	....	....	....	....	....	....
	Manitoba Moose	AHL	46	13	27	40	30	....	....	....	....	....	....	....	....	....	....	....	....	....	....	....	....	....	....
2009-10	Fribourg	Swiss	11	1	4	5	4	....	....	....	....	....	....	....	....	....	5	1	1	2	4	....	....	....	....
	NHL Totals		**190**	**52**	**64**	**116**	**58**	**27**	**0**	**2**	**370**	**14.1**		**67**	**41.8**	**13:33**	**5**	**0**	**2**	**2**	**6**	**0**	**0**	**0**	**12:54**

\HL All-Rookie Team (2004)

igned as a free agent by **Tampa Bay**, July 1, 2007. Traded to **Vancouver** by **Tampa Bay** with Shane O'Brien for Lukas Krajicek and Juraj Simek, October 6, 2008. Signed as a free agent by **Fribourg** ;wiss), October 5, 2009.

OVECHKIN, Alex

(oh-VEHCH-kihn, AL-ehx) **WSH.**

Left wing. Shoots right. 6'2", 223 lbs. Born, Moscow, USSR, September 17, 1985. Washington's 1st choice, 1st overall, in 2004 Entry Draft.

Season	Club	League	GP	G	A	Pts	PIM	PP	SH	GW	S	%	+/-	TF	F%	Min	GP	G	A	Pts	PIM	PP	SH	GW	Min
2001-02	Dyn'o Moscow 2	Russia-3	19	18	8	26	20	....	....	....	....	....	....	....	....	....	....	....	....	....	....	....	....	....	....
	Dynamo Moscow	Russia	22	2	2	4	4	....	....	....	....	....	....	....	....	....	3	0	0	0	0	....	....	....	....
2002-03	Dynamo Moscow	Russia	40	8	7	15	28	....	....	....	....	....	....	....	....	....	5	0	0	0	2	....	....	....	....
2003-04	Dynamo Moscow	Russia	53	13	11	24	40	....	....	....	....	....	....	....	....	....	3	0	0	0	2	....	....	....	....
2004-05	Dynamo Moscow	Russia	37	13	13	26	32	....	....	....	....	....	....	....	....	....	10	2	4	6	31	....	....	....	....
2005-06	**Washington**	**NHL**	**81**	**52**	**54**	**106**	**52**	**21**	**3**	**5**	**425**	**12.2**	**2**	**16**	**12.5**	**21:37**	....	....	....	....	....	....	....	....	....
	Russia	Olympics	8	5	0	5	8	....	....	....	....	....	....	....	....	....	....	....	....	....	....	....	....	....	....
2006-07	**Washington**	**NHL**	**82**	**46**	**46**	**92**	**52**	**16**	**0**	**8**	**392**	**11.7**	**–19**	**17**	**47.1**	**21:23**	....	....	....	....	....	....	....	....	....
2007-08	**Washington**	**NHL**	**82**	***65**	**47**	***112**	**40**	***22**	**0**	***11**	**446**	**14.6**	**28**	**18**	**38.9**	**23:06**	**7**	**4**	**5**	**9**	**0**	**1**	**0**	**2**	**24:03**
2008-09	**Washington**	**NHL**	**79**	***56**	**54**	**110**	**72**	**19**	**1**	**10**	**528**	**10.6**	**8**	**32**	**25.0**	**23:00**	**14**	**11**	**10**	**21**	**8**	**3**	**0**	**1**	**23:21**
2009-10	**Washington**	**NHL**	**72**	**50**	**59**	**109**	**89**	**13**	**0**	**7**	**368**	**13.6**	**45**	**22**	**45.5**	**21:48**	**7**	**5**	**5**	**10**	**0**	**1**	**0**	**0**	**23:06**
	Russia	Olympics	4	2	2	4	2	....	....	....	....	....	....	....	....	....	....	....	....	....	....	....	....	....	....
	NHL Totals		**396**	**269**	**260**	**529**	**305**	**91**	**4**	**41**	**2159**	**12.5**		**105**	**33.3**	**22:11**	**28**	**20**	**20**	**40**	**8**	**5**	**0**	**3**	**23:28**

)lympic Tournament All-Star Team (2006) • NHL All-Rookie Team (2006) • NHL First All-Star Team (2006, 2007, 2008, 2009, 2010) • Calder Memorial Trophy (2006) • Maurice "Rocket" Richard Trophy 2008, 2009) • Art Ross Trophy (2008) • Lester B. Pearson Award (2008, 2009) • Hart Memorial Trophy (2008, 2009) • Ted Lindsay Award (2010)

layed in NHL All-Star Game (2007, 2008, 2009)

OYSTRICK, Nathan

(OI-strihk, NAY-thuhn) **ST.L.**

Defense. Shoots left. 6', 210 lbs. Born, Regina, Sask., December 17, 1982. Atlanta's 7th choice, 198th overall, in 2002 Entry Draft.

Season	Club	League	GP	G	A	Pts	PIM	PP	SH	GW	S	%	+/-	TF	F%	Min	GP	G	A	Pts	PIM	PP	SH	GW	Min
99-2000	Reg. Pat Cdns.	SMHL	43	6	22	28	214	....	....	....	....	....	....	....	....	....	....	....	....	....	....	....	....	....	....
2000-01	South Surrey	BCHL	STATISTICS NOT AVAILABLE																						
2001-02	South Surrey	BCHL	50	15	42	57	142	....	....	....	....	....	....	....	....	....	....	....	....	....	....	....	....	....	....
2002-03	Northern Mich.	CCHA	34	2	10	12	26	....	....	....	....	....	....	....	....	....	....	....	....	....	....	....	....	....	....
2003-04	Northern Mich.	CCHA	39	8	20	28	98	....	....	....	....	....	....	....	....	....	....	....	....	....	....	....	....	....	....
2004-05	Northern Mich.	CCHA	40	7	13	20	87	....	....	....	....	....	....	....	....	....	....	....	....	....	....	....	....	....	....
2005-06	Northern Mich.	CCHA	38	9	20	29	58	....	....	....	....	....	....	....	....	....	....	....	....	....	....	....	....	....	....
	Chicago Wolves	AHL	2	0	1	1	4	....	....	....	....	....	....	....	....	....	....	....	....	....	....	....	....	....	....
2006-07	Chicago Wolves	AHL	80	15	32	47	105	....	....	....	....	....	....	....	....	....	15	0	6	6	16	....	....	....	....
2007-08	Chicago Wolves	AHL	80	15	28	43	112	....	....	....	....	....	....	....	....	....	24	3	8	11	35	....	....	....	....
2008-09	**Atlanta**	**NHL**	**53**	**4**	**8**	**12**	**50**	**0**	**0**	**0**	**43**	**9.3**	**–2**	**0**	**0.0**	**15:45**	....	....	....	....	....	....	....	....	....
2009-10	Chicago Wolves	AHL	43	7	16	23	96	....	....	....	....	....	....	....	....	....	14	2	8	10	8	....	....	....	....
	Anaheim	**NHL**	**3**	**0**	**0**	**0**	**2**	**0**	**0**	**0**	**1**	**0.0**	**–1**	**0**	**0.0**	**10:35**	....	....	....	....	....	....	....	....	....
	NHL Totals		**56**	**4**	**8**	**12**	**52**	**0**	**0**	**0**	**44**	**9.1**		**0**	**0.0**	**15:28**	....	....	....	....	....	....	....	....	....

CHA Second All-Star Team (2004) • CCHA First All-Star Team (2005, 2006) • NCAA West Second All-American Team (2006) • AHL All-Rookie Team (2007) • AHL Second All-Star Team (2007)

raded to **Anaheim** by **Atlanta** with future considerations for Evgeny Artyukhin, March 1, 2010.

PACIORETTY, Max

(pahk-OHR-eht-tee, MAX) **MTL.**

Left wing. Shoots left. 6'2", 196 lbs. Born, New Canaan, CT, November 20, 1988. Montreal's 2nd choice, 22nd overall, in 2007 Entry Draft.

Season	Club	League	GP	G	A	Pts	PIM	PP	SH	GW	S	%	+/-	TF	F%	Min	GP	G	A	Pts	PIM	PP	SH	GW	Min
2004-05	Taft Rhinos	High-CT	23	5	14	19	....	....	....	....	....	....	....	....	....	....	....	....	....	....	....	....	....	....	....
2005-06	Taft Rhinos	High-CT	26	7	26	33	....	....	....	....	....	....	....	....	....	....	....	....	....	....	....	....	....	....	....
2006-07	Sioux City	USHL	60	21	42	63	119	....	....	....	....	....	....	....	....	....	7	4	6	10	10	....	....	....	....
2007-08	U. of Michigan	CCHA	37	15	24	39	59	....	....	....	....	....	....	....	....	....	....	....	....	....	....	....	....	....	....
2008-09	**Montreal**	**NHL**	**34**	**3**	**8**	**11**	**27**	**1**	**0**	**0**	**57**	**5.3**	**–3**	**2**	**50.0**	**12:37**	....	....	....	....	....	....	....	....	....
	Hamilton	AHL	37	6	23	29	43	....	....	....	....	....	....	....	....	....	....	....	....	....	....	....	....	....	....
2009-10	**Montreal**	**NHL**	**52**	**3**	**11**	**14**	**20**	**0**	**0**	**0**	**74**	**4.1**	**–5**	**7**	**14.3**	**12:43**	....	....	....	....	....	....	....	....	....
	Hamilton	AHL	18	2	9	11	10	....	....	....	....	....	....	....	....	....	5	1	0	1	2	....	....	....	....
	NHL Totals		**86**	**6**	**19**	**25**	**47**	**1**	**0**	**0**	**131**	**4.6**		**9**	**22.2**	**12:40**	....	....	....	....	....	....	....	....	....

SHL All-Rookie Team (2007) • USHL Rookie of the Year (2007) • CCHA All-Rookie Team (2008) • CCHA Rookie of the Year (2008)

PADDOCK, Cam

(PA-dawk, KAM)

Center. Shoots right. 6', 178 lbs. Born, Vancouver, B.C., March 22, 1983. Pittsburgh's 6th choice, 137th overall, in 2002 Entry Draft.

Season	Club	League	GP	G	A	Pts	PIM	PP	SH	GW	S	%	+/-	TF	F%	Min	GP	G	A	Pts	PIM	PP	SH	GW	Min
99-2000	Kelowna Rockets	WHL	46	5	5	10	42	....	....	....	....	....	....	....	....	....	5	0	0	0	0	....	....	....	....
2000-01	Kelowna Rockets	WHL	72	14	10	24	110	....	....	....	....	....	....	....	....	....	6	0	0	0	4	....	....	....	....
2001-02	Kelowna Rockets	WHL	72	38	35	73	122	....	....	....	....	....	....	....	....	....	15	8	6	14	35	....	....	....	....
2002-03	Kelowna Rockets	WHL	71	33	26	59	107	....	....	....	....	....	....	....	....	....	19	11	8	19	18	....	....	....	....
2003-04	Wilkes-Barre	AHL	1	0	0	0	2	....	....	....	....	....	....	....	....	....	....	....	....	....	....	....	....	....	....
	Kelowna Rockets	WHL	62	17	22	39	86	....	....	....	....	....	....	....	....	....	16	3	4	7	22	....	....	....	....
2004-05	Wilkes-Barre	AHL	16	0	0	0	13	....	....	....	....	....	....	....	....	....	....	....	....	....	....	....	....	....	....
	Wheeling Nailers	ECHL	53	11	18	29	70	....	....	....	....	....	....	....	....	....	....	....	....	....	....	....	....	....	....
2005-06	Wilkes-Barre	AHL	4	0	0	0	2	....	....	....	....	....	....	....	....	....	....	....	....	....	....	....	....	....	....
	Wheeling Nailers	ECHL	61	14	24	38	90	....	....	....	....	....	....	....	....	....	9	0	0	0	12	....	....	....	....
2006-07	San Antonio	AHL	22	0	2	2	13	....	....	....	....	....	....	....	....	....	....	....	....	....	....	....	....	....	....
	Phoenix	ECHL	46	11	20	31	117	....	....	....	....	....	....	....	....	....	3	2	0	2	9	....	....	....	....
2007-08	San Antonio	AHL	78	12	13	25	107	....	....	....	....	....	....	....	....	....	7	0	2	2	18	....	....	....	....

			Regular Season														Playoffs								
Season	Club	League	GP	G	A	Pts	PIM	PP	SH	GW	S	%	+/-	TF	F%	Min	GP	G	A	Pts	PIM	PP	SH	GW	Min
2008-09	St. Louis	NHL	16	2	1	3	0	0	0	0	17	11.8	–4	87	46.0	10:41									
	Peoria Rivermen	AHL	60	8	7	15	96										7	2	2	4	0				
2009-10	Peoria Rivermen	AHL	80	15	12	27	95																		
	NHL Totals		16	2	1	3	0	0	0	0	17	11.8		87	46.0	10:41									

Signed as a free agent by **San Antonio** (AHL), December 26, 2006. Signed as a free agent by **St. Louis**, July 15, 2008.

PAETSCH, Nathan

(PASH, NAY-thuhn) **FLA.**

Defense. Shoots left. 6'1", 195 lbs. Born, Humboldt, Sask., March 30, 1983. Buffalo's 8th choice, 202nd overall, in 2003 Entry Draft.

1998-99	Tisdale Trojans	SMHL	74	20	55	75	120																		
	Moose Jaw	WHL	2	0	0	0	0																		
99-2000	Moose Jaw	WHL	68	9	35	44	49										4	0	1	1	0				
2000-01	Moose Jaw	WHL	70	8	54	62	118										4	1	2	3	6				
2001-02	Moose Jaw	WHL	59	16	36	52	86										12	0	4	4	16				
2002-03	Moose Jaw	WHL	59	15	39	54	81										13	3	10	13	6				
2003-04	Rochester	AHL	54	5	5	10	49										16	1	1	2	28				
2004-05	Rochester	AHL	80	4	19	23	150										9	1	1	2	16				
2005-06	Buffalo	NHL	1	0	1	1	0	0	0	0	0	0.0	–1	0	0.0	15:38	1	0	0	0	0	0	0	0	12:06
	Rochester	AHL	72	11	39	50	90																		
2006-07	Buffalo	NHL	63	2	22	24	50	0	0	0	62	3.2	10	0	0.0	15:15									
2007-08	Buffalo	NHL	59	2	7	9	27	0	0	0	49	4.1	3	0	0.0	13:38									
2008-09	Buffalo	NHL	23	2	4	6	25	0	0	0	21	9.5	3	0	0.0	12:11									
2009-10	Buffalo	NHL	11	1	1	2	6	0	0	0	9	11.1	2	0	0.0	9:39									
	Columbus	NHL	10	0	0	0	6	0	0	0	8	0.0	–5	0	0.0	11:14									
	NHL Totals		167	7	35	42	114	0	0	0	149	4.7		0	0.0	13:39	1	0	0	0	0	0	0	0	12:06

• Re-entered NHL Entry Draft. Originally Washington's 1st choice, 58th overall, in 2001 Entry Draft.
WHL East Second All-Star Team (2003)
• Missed majority of 2008-09 season as a healthy reserve. Traded to **Columbus** by **Buffalo** with Vancouver's 2nd round choice (previously acquired, Columbus selected Petr Straka) in 2010 Entry Draft for Raffi Torres, March 3, 2010. • Missed majority of 2009-10 season as a healthy reserve. Signed as a free agent by **Florida**, July 7, 2010.

PAHLSSON, Samuel

(PAWL-suhn, SAM-yoo-ehl) **CBJ**

Center. Shoots left. 6', 203 lbs. Born, Ange, Sweden, December 17, 1977. Colorado's 10th choice, 176th overall, in 1996 Entry Draft.

1992-93	Ange IK	Sweden-4	9	0	0	0	0																		
1993-94	Ange IK	Sweden-4	STATISTICS NOT AVAILABLE																						
1994-95	MoDo	Sweden	1	0	0	0	0																		
1995-96	MoDo Jr.	Swe-Jr.	30	10	11	21	26																		
	MoDo	Sweden	36	1	3	4	8										4	0	0	0	0				
1996-97	MoDo	Sweden	49	8	9	17	83																		
	MoDo Jr.	Swe-Jr.	5	2	6	8	2																		
1997-98	MoDo	Sweden	23	6	11	17	24										9	3	0	3	6				
1998-99	MoDo	Sweden	50	17	17	34	44										13	3	3	6	10				
99-2000	MoDo	Sweden	47	16	11	27	67										13	3	3	6	8				
	MoDo	EuroHL	4	1	0	1	0										3	1	1	2	2				
2000-01	Boston	NHL	17	1	1	2	6	0	0	0	13	7.7	–5	239	40.2	14:19									
	Anaheim	NHL	59	3	4	7	14	1	1	1	46	6.5	–9	867	45.1	14:14									
2001-02	Anaheim	NHL	80	6	14	20	26	1	1	0	99	6.1	–16	1201	49.8	16:24									
2002-03	Anaheim	NHL	34	4	11	15	18	0	1	2	28	14.3	10	118	52.5	13:20	21	2	4	6	12	0	0	0	16:41
	Cincinnati	AHL	13	1	7	8	24																		
2003-04	Anaheim	NHL	82	8	14	22	52	1	0	2	134	6.0	–2	908	55.3	16:51									
2004-05	Frolunda	Sweden	48	6	18	24	56										14	4	7	11	24				
2005-06	Anaheim	NHL	82	11	10	21	34	0	3	1	116	9.5	–1	1517	52.8	16:30	16	2	3	5	18	0	0	2	17:06
	Sweden	Olympics	8	2	2	4	8																		
2006-07 ♦	Anaheim	NHL	82	8	18	26	42	0	0	1	111	7.2	–4	1523	52.7	17:22	21	3	9	12	20	0	0	2	19:25
2007-08	Anaheim	NHL	56	6	9	15	34	0	3	3	94	6.4	–2	1066	55.0	18:46	6	0	0	0	0	0	0	0	18:18
2008-09	Anaheim	NHL	52	5	10	15	32	1	0	1	74	6.8	–16	1064	53.5	18:31									
	Chicago	NHL	13	2	1	3	2	0	0	1	14	14.3	–1	173	53.8	17:25	17	2	3	5	4	1	0	0	16:38
2009-10	Columbus	NHL	79	3	13	16	32	0	0	0	93	3.2	–9	1273	52.9	16:17									
	Sweden	Olympics	3	0	1	1	2																		
	NHL Totals		636	57	105	162	292	4	9	12	822	6.9		9949	52.0	16:34	81	9	19	28	54	1	0	4	17:35

Traded to **Boston** by **Colorado** with Brian Rolston, Martin Grenier and New Jersey's 1st round choice (previously acquired, Boston selected Martin Samuelsson) in 2000 Entry Draft for Raymond Bourque and Dave Andreychuk, March 6, 2000. Traded to **Anaheim** by **Boston** for Patrick Traverse and Andrei Nazarov, November 18, 2000. Signed as a free agent by **Frolunda** (Sweden), September, 2004. Traded to **Chicago** by **Anaheim** with Logan Stephenson and future considerations for James Wisniewski and Petri Kontiola, March 4, 2009. Signed as a free agent by **Columbus**, July 1, 2009.

PAILLE, Daniel

(PIGH-yay, DAN-yehl) **BOS.**

Left wing. Shoots left. 6'1", 200 lbs. Born, Welland, Ont., April 15, 1984. Buffalo's 2nd choice, 20th overall, in 2002 Entry Draft.

99-2000	Welland Cougars	OHA-B	42	14	17	31	19										16	16	16	32					
2000-01	Guelph Storm	OHL	64	22	31	53	57										4	2	0	2	2				
2001-02	Guelph Storm	OHL	62	27	30	57	54										9	5	2	7	9				
2002-03	Guelph Storm	OHL	54	30	27	57	28										11	8	6	14	6				
2003-04	Guelph Storm	OHL	59	37	43	80	63										22	9	9	18	14				
2004-05	Rochester	AHL	79	14	15	29	54										9	2	2	4	6				
2005-06	Buffalo	NHL	14	1	2	3	2	0	0	0	15	6.7	5	4	25.0	10:24									
	Rochester	AHL	45	14	13	27	29																		
2006-07	Buffalo	NHL	29	3	8	11	18	0	0	0	45	6.7	5	6	33.3	12:47	1	0	0	0	0	0	0	0	4:52
	Rochester	AHL	29	7	14	21	12																		
2007-08	Buffalo	NHL	77	19	16	35	14	0	3	2	110	17.3	9	41	36.6	13:16									
2008-09	Buffalo	NHL	73	12	15	27	20	0	0	2	80	15.0	0	17	17.7	11:54									
2009-10	Buffalo	NHL	2	0	1	1	0	0	0	0	2	0.0	1	0	0.0	10:22									
	Boston	NHL	74	10	9	19	12	0	1	0	118	8.5	–4	13	30.8	13:49	13	0	2	2	2	0	0	0	16:01
	NHL Totals		269	45	51	96	66	0	4	4	370	12.2		81	30.9	12:49	14	0	2	2	2	0	0	0	15:13

Traded to **Boston** by **Buffalo** for Boston's 3rd round choice (Kevin Sundher) in 2010 Entry Draft, October 20, 2009.

PALMIERI, Nick

(pawl-mee-AIR-ee, NIHK) **N.J.**

Right wing. Shoots right. 6'3", 220 lbs. Born, Utica, NY, July 12, 1989. New Jersey's 2nd choice, 79th overall, in 2007 Entry Draft.

2004-05	Northwood	High-NY	STATISTICS NOT AVAILABLE																						
2005-06	Erie Otters	OHL	68	13	10	23	79																		
2006-07	Erie Otters	OHL	56	24	21	45	99																		
2007-08	Erie Otters	OHL	50	28	18	46	122																		
	Lowell Devils	AHL	9	1	0	1	4																		
2008-09	Erie Otters	OHL	18	7	5	12	41																		
	Belleville Bulls	OHL	43	20	9	29	75										17	14	3	17	27				
2009-10	New Jersey	NHL	6	0	1	1	0	0	0	0	10	0.0	0	2	50.0	11:45									
	Lowell Devils	AHL	69	21	15	36	36										5	1	3	4	2				
	NHL Totals		6	0	1	1	0	0	0	0	10	0.0		2	50.0	11:45									

PANDOLFO, Jay

(pan-DAWL-foh, JAY)

Left wing. Shoots left. 6'1", 190 lbs. Born, Winchester, MA, December 27, 1974. New Jersey's 2nd choice, 32nd overall, in 1993 Entry Draft.

1989-90	Burlington	High-MA	23	33	30	63	18																		
1990-91	Burlington	High-MA	20	19	27	46	10																		
1991-92	Burlington	High-MA	20	35	34	69	14																		
1992-93	Boston University	H-East	37	16	22	38	16																		
1993-94	Boston University	H-East	37	17	25	42	27																		
1994-95	Boston University	H-East	20	7	13	20	6																		
1995-96	Boston University	H-East	39	*38	29	67	6																		
	Albany River Rats	AHL	5	3	1	4	0										3	0	0	0	0				

			Regular Season														Playoffs								
Season	Club	League	GP	G	A	Pts	PIM	PP	SH	GW	S	%	+/-	TF	F%	Min	GP	G	A	Pts	PIM	PP	SH	GW	Min
1996-97	**New Jersey**	**NHL**	**46**	**6**	**8**	**14**	**6**	**0**	**0**	**1**	**61**	**9.8**	**–1**	....	....	....	**6**	**0**	**1**	**1**	**0**	**0**	**0**	**0**	....
	Albany River Rats	AHL	12	3	9	12	0	....	....	....	....	....	....	....	....	....	....	....	....	....	....	....	....	....	....
1997-98	**New Jersey**	**NHL**	**23**	**1**	**3**	**4**	**4**	**0**	**0**	**0**	**23**	**4.3**	**–4**	....	....	....	**3**	**0**	**2**	**2**	**0**	**0**	**0**	**0**	....
	Albany River Rats	AHL	51	18	19	37	24	....	....	....	....	....	....	....	....	....	....	....	....	....	....	....	....	....	....
1998-99	**New Jersey**	**NHL**	**70**	**14**	**13**	**27**	**10**	**1**	**1**	**4**	**100**	**14.0**	**3**	**10**	**40.0**	**15:13**	**7**	**1**	**0**	**1**	**0**	**0**	**0**	**0**	**13:19**
99-2000♦	**New Jersey**	**NHL**	**71**	**7**	**8**	**15**	**4**	**0**	**0**	**0**	**86**	**8.1**	**0**	**19**	**47.4**	**13:25**	**23**	**0**	**5**	**5**	**0**	**0**	**0**	**0**	**15:35**
2000-01	**New Jersey**	**NHL**	**63**	**4**	**12**	**16**	**16**	**0**	**0**	**0**	**57**	**7.0**	**3**	**15**	**53.3**	**14:05**	**25**	**1**	**4**	**5**	**4**	**0**	**0**	**0**	**12:38**
2001-02	**New Jersey**	**NHL**	**65**	**4**	**10**	**14**	**15**	**0**	**1**	**0**	**72**	**5.6**	**12**	**12**	**41.7**	**13:59**	**6**	**0**	**0**	**0**	**0**	**0**	**0**	**0**	**16:11**
2002-03♦	**New Jersey**	**NHL**	**68**	**6**	**11**	**17**	**23**	**0**	**1**	**4**	**92**	**6.5**	**12**	**13**	**23.1**	**16:08**	**24**	**6**	**6**	**12**	**2**	**0**	**0**	**1**	**16:34**
2003-04	**New Jersey**	**NHL**	**82**	**13**	**13**	**26**	**14**	**1**	**2**	**4**	**140**	**9.3**	**5**	**25**	**44.0**	**16:00**	**5**	**0**	**0**	**0**	**0**	**0**	**0**	**0**	**13:41**
2004-05	Salzburg	Austria	19	5	7	12	0	....	....	....	....	....	....	....	....	....	....	....	....	....	....	....	....	....	....
2005-06	**New Jersey**	**NHL**	**82**	**10**	**10**	**20**	**16**	**0**	**0**	**0**	**116**	**8.6**	**2**	**13**	**30.8**	**18:03**	**9**	**1**	**4**	**5**	**0**	**0**	**1**	**1**	**18:37**
2006-07	**New Jersey**	**NHL**	**82**	**13**	**14**	**27**	**8**	**0**	**1**	**1**	**109**	**11.9**	**–5**	**16**	**6.3**	**18:37**	**11**	**1**	**0**	**1**	**4**	**0**	**0**	**0**	**19:39**
2007-08	**New Jersey**	**NHL**	**54**	**12**	**12**	**24**	**22**	**0**	**0**	**1**	**78**	**15.4**	**10**	**7**	**42.9**	**17:17**	**5**	**0**	**0**	**0**	**2**	**0**	**0**	**0**	**16:15**
2008-09	**New Jersey**	**NHL**	**61**	**5**	**5**	**10**	**10**	**0**	**1**	**1**	**63**	**7.9**	**–12**	**18**	**22.2**	**14:50**	**7**	**1**	**0**	**1**	**0**	**0**	**0**	**0**	**16:35**
2009-10	**New Jersey**	**NHL**	**52**	**4**	**5**	**9**	**6**	**0**	**0**	**3**	**71**	**5.6**	**–10**	**12**	**41.7**	**13:55**	....	....	....	....	....	....	....	....	....
	NHL Totals		**819**	**99**	**124**	**223**	**154**	**2**	**7**	**19**	**1068**	**9.3**		**160**	**35.6**	**15:43**	**131**	**11**	**22**	**33**	**12**	**0**	**1**	**2**	**15:40**

ockey East First All-Star Team (1996) • Hockey East Player of the Year (1996) • NCAA East First All-American Team (1996)
igned as a free agent by **Salzburg** (Austria), December 27, 2004.

PARDY, Adam (PAHR-dee, A-duhm) CGY.

Defense. Shoots left. 6'2", 206 lbs. Born, Bonavista, Nfld., March 29, 1984. Calgary's 6th choice, 173rd overall, in 2004 Entry Draft.

Season	Club	League	GP	G	A	Pts	PIM	PP	SH	GW	S	%	+/-	TF	F%	Min	GP	G	A	Pts	PIM	PP	SH	GW	Min
2002-03	Yarmouth	MJrHL	1	0	0	0	2	....	....	....	....	....	....	....	....	....	....	....	....	....	....	....	....	....	....
	Antigonish	MJrHL	31	5	16	21	42	....	....	....	....	....	....	....	....	....	....	....	....	....	....	....	....	....	....
	Cape Breton	QMJHL	7	0	1	1	2	....	....	....	....	....	....	....	....	....	2	0	0	0	0	....	....	....	....
2003-04	Cape Breton	QMJHL	68	4	12	16	137	....	....	....	....	....	....	....	....	....	5	0	1	1	8	....	....	....	....
2004-05	Cape Breton	QMJHL	69	12	27	39	163	....	....	....	....	....	....	....	....	....	5	2	2	4	8	....	....	....	....
2005-06	Omaha	AHL	24	0	0	0	18	....	....	....	....	....	....	....	....	....	....	....	....	....	....	....	....	....	....
	Las Vegas	ECHL	41	1	11	12	55	....	....	....	....	....	....	....	....	....	10	2	1	3	12	....	....	....	....
2006-07	Omaha	AHL	70	2	6	8	60	....	....	....	....	....	....	....	....	....	6	1	1	2	0	....	....	....	....
2007-08	Quad City Flames	AHL	65	5	13	18	67	....	....	....	....	....	....	....	....	....	....	....	....	....	....	....	....	....	....
2008-09	**Calgary**	**NHL**	**60**	**1**	**9**	**10**	**69**	**0**	**0**	**0**	**38**	**2.6**	**3**	**0**	**0.0**	**15:00**	**6**	**0**	**2**	**2**	**5**	**0**	**0**	**0**	**14:51**
2009-10	**Calgary**	**NHL**	**57**	**2**	**7**	**9**	**48**	**0**	**0**	**0**	**40**	**5.0**	**–3**	**0**	**0.0**	**15:51**	....	....	....	....	....	....	....	....	....
	NHL Totals		**117**	**3**	**16**	**19**	**117**	**0**	**0**	**0**	**78**	**3.8**		**0**	**0.0**	**15:25**	**6**	**0**	**2**	**2**	**5**	**0**	**0**	**0**	**14:51**

PARENT, Ryan (PAIR-ehnt, RIGH-uhn) NSH.

Defense. Shoots left. 6'3", 198 lbs. Born, Prince Albert, Sask., March 17, 1987. Nashville's 1st choice, 18th overall, in 2005 Entry Draft.

Season	Club	League	GP	G	A	Pts	PIM	PP	SH	GW	S	%	+/-	TF	F%	Min	GP	G	A	Pts	PIM	PP	SH	GW	Min
2002-03	Waterloo Siskins	OHA-B	41	2	8	10	35	....	....	....	....	....	....	....	....	....	....	....	....	....	....	....	....	....	....
2003-04	Guelph Storm	OHL	58	1	5	6	18	....	....	....	....	....	....	....	....	....	22	0	0	0	2	....	....	....	....
2004-05	Guelph Storm	OHL	66	2	17	19	36	....	....	....	....	....	....	....	....	....	4	0	1	1	4	....	....	....	....
2005-06	Guelph Storm	OHL	60	4	17	21	122	....	....	....	....	....	....	....	....	....	15	1	4	5	24	....	....	....	....
	Milwaukee	AHL	....	....	....	....	....	....	....	....	....	....	....	....	....	....	10	0	0	0	4	....	....	....	....
2006-07	**Philadelphia**	**NHL**	**1**	**0**	**0**	**0**	**0**	**0**	**0**	**0**	**1**	**0.0**	**0**	**0**	**0.0**	**14:10**	....	....	....	....	....	....	....	....	....
	Philadelphia	AHL	6	1	0	1	4	....	....	....	....	....	....	....	....	....	....	....	....	....	....	....	....	....	....
	Guelph Storm	OHL	43	3	7	10	86	....	....	....	....	....	....	....	....	....	4	0	1	1	14	....	....	....	....
2007-08	**Philadelphia**	**NHL**	**22**	**0**	**0**	**0**	**6**	**0**	**0**	**0**	**9**	**0.0**	**–4**	**0**	**0.0**	**14:59**	**4**	**0**	**1**	**1**	**0**	**0**	**0**	**0**	**16:36**
	Philadelphia	AHL	53	1	7	8	42	....	....	....	....	....	....	....	....	....	....	....	....	....	....	....	....	....	....
2008-09	**Philadelphia**	**NHL**	**31**	**0**	**4**	**4**	**10**	**0**	**0**	**0**	**9**	**0.0**	**3**	**0**	**0.0**	**18:12**	**6**	**0**	**0**	**0**	**6**	**0**	**0**	**0**	**18:52**
	Philadelphia	AHL	15	0	1	1	18	....	....	....	....	....	....	....	....	....	....	....	....	....	....	....	....	....	....
2009-10	**Philadelphia**	**NHL**	**48**	**1**	**2**	**3**	**20**	**0**	**0**	**0**	**27**	**3.7**	**–14**	**0**	**0.0**	**14:46**	**17**	**1**	**0**	**1**	**2**	**0**	**0**	**0**	**7:28**
	NHL Totals		**102**	**1**	**6**	**7**	**36**	**0**	**0**	**0**	**46**	**2.2**		**0**	**0.0**	**15:51**	**27**	**1**	**1**	**2**	**8**	**0**	**0**	**0**	**11:21**

HL Second All-Star Team (2006, 2007)
raded to **Philadelphia** by **Nashville** with Scottie Upshall and Nashville's 1st (later traded back to Nashville - Nashville selected Jonathon Blum) and 3rd (later traded to Washington - Washington selected nil Desimone) round choices in 2007 Entry Draft for Peter Forsberg, February 15, 2007. Traded to **Nashville** by **Philadelphia** with future considerations for Dan Hamhuis, June 19, 2010.

PARENTEAU, P.A. (pair-ehn-TOH, PEE-AY) NYI

Left wing. Shoots right. 6', 198 lbs. Born, Hull, Que., March 24, 1983. Anaheim's 11th choice, 264th overall, in 2001 Entry Draft.

Season	Club	League	GP	G	A	Pts	PIM	PP	SH	GW	S	%	+/-	TF	F%	Min	GP	G	A	Pts	PIM	PP	SH	GW	Min
99-2000	Charles-Lemoyne	QAAA	40	25	40	65	18	....	....	....	....	....	....	....	....	....	16	4	9	13	8	....	....	....	....
2000-01	Moncton Wildcats	QMJHL	45	10	19	29	38	....	....	....	....	....	....	....	....	....	....	....	....	....	....	....	....	....	....
	Chicoutimi	QMJHL	28	10	13	23	14	....	....	....	....	....	....	....	....	....	7	4	7	11	2	....	....	....	....
2001-02	Chicoutimi	QMJHL	68	51	67	118	120	....	....	....	....	....	....	....	....	....	4	3	1	4	10	....	....	....	....
2002-03	Chicoutimi	QMJHL	31	20	35	55	56	....	....	....	....	....	....	....	....	....	....	....	....	....	....	....	....	....	....
	Sherbrooke	QMJHL	28	13	35	48	84	....	....	....	....	....	....	....	....	....	12	8	11	19	6	....	....	....	....
2003-04	Cincinnati	AHL	66	14	16	30	20	....	....	....	....	....	....	....	....	....	7	1	2	3	6	....	....	....	....
2004-05	Cincinnati	AHL	76	17	24	41	58	....	....	....	....	....	....	....	....	....	9	2	0	2	8	....	....	....	....
2005-06	Portland Pirates	AHL	56	22	27	49	42	....	....	....	....	....	....	....	....	....	19	5	17	22	24	....	....	....	....
	Augusta Lynx	ECHL	2	0	1	1	0	....	....	....	....	....	....	....	....	....	....	....	....	....	....	....	....	....	....
2006-07	Portland Pirates	AHL	28	15	13	28	35	....	....	....	....	....	....	....	....	....	....	....	....	....	....	....	....	....	....
	Chicago	**NHL**	**5**	**0**	**1**	**1**	**2**	**0**	**0**	**0**	**7**	**0.0**	**–1**	**2**	**50.0**	**11:05**	....	....	....	....	....	....	....	....	....
	Norfolk Admirals	AHL	40	15	36	51	12	....	....	....	....	....	....	....	....	....	6	2	1	3	2	....	....	....	....
2007-08	Hartford	AHL	75	34	47	81	81	....	....	....	....	....	....	....	....	....	5	3	2	5	13	....	....	....	....
2008-09	Hartford	AHL	74	29	49	78	142	....	....	....	....	....	....	....	....	....	....	....	....	....	....	....	....	....	....
2009-10	**NY Rangers**	**NHL**	**22**	**3**	**5**	**8**	**4**	**1**	**0**	**0**	**38**	**7.9**	**–2**	**12**	**33.3**	**13:42**	....	....	....	....	....	....	....	....	....
	Hartford	AHL	35	20	25	45	63	....	....	....	....	....	....	....	....	....	....	....	....	....	....	....	....	....	....
	NHL Totals		**27**	**3**	**6**	**9**	**6**	**1**	**0**	**0**	**45**	**6.7**		**14**	**35.7**	**13:13**	....	....	....	....	....	....	....	....	....

HL Second All-Star Team (2008) • AHL First All-Star Team (2009)
raded to **Chicago** by **Anaheim** with Bruno St. Jacques for Sebastien Caron, Matt Keith and Chris Durno, December 28, 2006. Traded to **NY Rangers** by **Chicago** for future considerations, October 11, 007. Signed as a free agent by **NY Islanders**, July 2, 2010.

PARISE, Zach (pah-REE-say, ZAK) N.J.

Left wing. Shoots left. 5'11", 190 lbs. Born, Minneapolis, MN, July 28, 1984. New Jersey's 1st choice, 17th overall, in 2003 Entry Draft.

Season	Club	League	GP	G	A	Pts	PIM	PP	SH	GW	S	%	+/-	TF	F%	Min	GP	G	A	Pts	PIM	PP	SH	GW	Min
2000-01	Shat.-St. Mary's	High-MN	58	69	93	162	....	....	....	....	....	....	....	....	....	....	....	....	....	....	....	....	....	....	....
2001-02	Shat.-St. Mary's	High-MN	67	77	101	178	58	....	....	....	....	....	....	....	....	....	....	....	....	....	....	....	....	....	....
	USNTDP	U-18	12	7	7	14	6	....	....	....	....	....	....	....	....	....	....	....	....	....	....	....	....	....	....
2002-03	North Dakota	WCHA	39	26	35	61	34	....	....	....	....	....	....	....	....	....	....	....	....	....	....	....	....	....	....
2003-04	North Dakota	WCHA	37	23	32	55	24	....	....	....	....	....	....	....	....	....	....	....	....	....	....	....	....	....	....
2004-05	Albany River Rats	AHL	73	18	40	58	56	....	....	....	....	....	....	....	....	....	....	....	....	....	....	....	....	....	....
2005-06	**New Jersey**	**NHL**	**81**	**14**	**18**	**32**	**28**	**2**	**0**	**5**	**133**	**10.5**	**–1**	**162**	**42.6**	**13:08**	**9**	**1**	**2**	**3**	**2**	**0**	**0**	**0**	**15:03**
2006-07	**New Jersey**	**NHL**	**82**	**31**	**31**	**62**	**30**	**9**	**0**	**7**	**247**	**12.6**	**–3**	**52**	**44.2**	**17:32**	**11**	**7**	**3**	**10**	**8**	**2**	**0**	**1**	**19:08**
2007-08	**New Jersey**	**NHL**	**81**	**32**	**33**	**65**	**25**	**10**	**1**	**8**	**266**	**12.0**	**13**	**104**	**48.1**	**18:04**	**5**	**1**	**4**	**5**	**2**	**1**	**0**	**0**	**18:29**
2008-09	**New Jersey**	**NHL**	**82**	**45**	**49**	**94**	**24**	**14**	**0**	**8**	**364**	**12.4**	**30**	**121**	**44.6**	**18:45**	**7**	**3**	**3**	**6**	**2**	**1**	**0**	**1**	**19:02**
2009-10	**New Jersey**	**NHL**	**81**	**38**	**44**	**82**	**32**	**9**	**1**	**5**	**347**	**11.0**	**24**	**48**	**37.5**	**19:46**	**5**	**1**	**3**	**4**	**0**	**0**	**1**	**0**	**20:44**
	United States	Olympics	6	4	4	8	0	....	....	....	....	....	....	....	....	....	....	....	....	....	....	....	....	....	....
	NHL Totals		**407**	**160**	**175**	**335**	**139**	**44**	**2**	**33**	**1357**	**11.8**		**487**	**43.9**	**17:27**	**37**	**13**	**15**	**28**	**14**	**4**	**1**	**2**	**18:15**

/CHA All-Rookie Team (2003) • WCHA First All-Star Team (2004) • NCAA West First All-American Team (2004) • NHL Second All-Star Team (2009) • Olympic Tournament All-Star Team (2010)
ayed in NHL All-Star Game (2009)

			Regular Season														Playoffs								
Season	Club	League	GP	G	A	Pts	PIM	PP	SH	GW	S	%	+/-	TF	F%	Min	GP	G	A	Pts	PIM	PP	SH	GW	Min

PARK, Richard

(PAHRK, RIH-chuhrd)

Right wing. Shoots right. 5'11", 190 lbs. Born, Seoul, South Korea, May 27, 1976. Pittsburgh's 2nd choice, 50th overall, in 1994 Entry Draft.

Season	Club	League	GP	G	A	Pts	PIM	PP	SH	GW	S	%	+/-	TF	F%	Min	GP	G	A	Pts	PIM	PP	SH	GW	Min
1991-92	Tor. Young Nats	MTHL	76	49	58	107	91																		
1992-93	Belleville Bulls	OHL	66	23	38	61	38										5	0	0	0	14				
1993-94	Belleville Bulls	OHL	59	27	49	76	70										12	3	5	8	18				
1994-95	Belleville Bulls	OHL	45	28	51	79	35										16	9	18	27	12				
	Pittsburgh	**NHL**	**1**	**0**	**1**	**1**	**2**	**0**	**0**	**0**	**4**	**0.0**	**1**				**3**	**0**	**0**	**0**	**2**	**0**	**0**	**0**	
1995-96	Belleville Bulls	OHL	6	7	6	13	2										14	18	12	30	10				
	Pittsburgh	**NHL**	**56**	**4**	**6**	**10**	**36**	**0**	**1**	**1**	**62**	**6.5**	**3**				**1**	**0**	**0**	**0**	**0**	**0**	**0**	**0**	
1996-97	**Pittsburgh**	**NHL**	**1**	**0**	**0**	**0**	**0**	**0**	**0**	**0**	**1**	**0.0**	**–1**												
	Cleveland	IHL	50	12	15	27	30																		
	Anaheim	**NHL**	**11**	**1**	**1**	**2**	**10**	**0**	**0**	**0**	**9**	**11.1**	**0**				**11**	**0**	**1**	**1**	**2**	**0**	**0**	**0**	
1997-98	**Anaheim**	**NHL**	**15**	**0**	**2**	**2**	**8**	**0**	**0**	**0**	**14**	**0.0**	**–3**												
	Cincinnati	AHL	56	17	26	43	36																		
1998-99	**Philadelphia**	**NHL**	**7**	**0**	**0**	**0**	**0**	**0**	**0**	**0**	**5**	**0.0**	**–1**	**15**	**53.3**	**9:21**									
	Philadelphia	AHL	75	41	42	83	33										16	9	6	15	4				
99-2000	Utah Grizzlies	IHL	82	28	32	60	36										5	1	0	1	0				
2000-01	Cleveland	IHL	75	27	21	48	29										4	0	2	2	4				
2001-02	**Minnesota**	**NHL**	**63**	**10**	**15**	**25**	**10**	**2**	**1**	**2**	**115**	**8.7**	**–1**	**79**	**41.8**	**16:28**									
	Houston Aeros	AHL	13	4	10	14	6																		
2002-03	**Minnesota**	**NHL**	**81**	**14**	**10**	**24**	**16**	**2**	**2**	**3**	**149**	**9.4**	**–3**	**178**	**48.9**	**16:36**	**18**	**3**	**3**	**6**	**4**	**0**	**0**	**1**	**17:03**
2003-04	**Minnesota**	**NHL**	**73**	**13**	**12**	**25**	**28**	**4**	**0**	**1**	**142**	**9.2**	**0**	**379**	**40.1**	**16:30**									
2004-05	Malmo	Sweden	9	1	3	4	4																		
	Langnau	Swiss	10	3	0	3	8										6	4	1	5	6				
2005-06	**Vancouver**	**NHL**	**60**	**8**	**10**	**18**	**29**	**0**	**1**	**2**	**97**	**8.2**	**–2**	**26**	**26.9**	**11:00**									
2006-07	**NY Islanders**	**NHL**	**82**	**10**	**16**	**26**	**33**	**0**	**2**	**2**	**93**	**10.8**	**4**	**218**	**39.0**	**11:39**	**5**	**0**	**1**	**1**	**2**	**0**	**0**	**0**	**9:16**
2007-08	**NY Islanders**	**NHL**	**82**	**12**	**20**	**32**	**20**	**1**	**4**	**2**	**132**	**9.1**	**–4**	**626**	**50.2**	**15:14**									
2008-09	**NY Islanders**	**NHL**	**71**	**14**	**17**	**31**	**34**	**4**	**2**	**1**	**138**	**10.1**	**–13**	**809**	**49.0**	**17:10**									
2009-10	**NY Islanders**	**NHL**	**81**	**9**	**22**	**31**	**28**	**0**	**1**	**4**	**146**	**6.2**	**–9**	**1040**	**51.5**	**15:45**									
	NHL Totals		**684**	**95**	**132**	**227**	**254**	**13**	**14**	**18**	**1107**	**8.6**		**3370**	**48.0**	**15:01**	**38**	**3**	**5**	**8**	**10**	**0**	**0**	**1**	**15:22**

OHL All-Rookie Team (1993) • AHL Second All-Star Team (1999)

Traded to **Anaheim** by **Pittsburgh** for Roman Oksiuta, March 18, 1997. Signed as a free agent by **Philadelphia**, August 24, 1998. Signed as a free agent by **Utah** (IHL), September 22, 1999. Signed as a free agent by **Minnesota**, June 6, 2000. Signed as a free agent by **Malmo** (Sweden), November 8, 2004. Signed as a free agent by **Langnau** (Swiss), January 4, 2005. Signed as a free agent by **Vancouver**, August 8, 2005. Signed as a free agent by **NY Islanders**, October 2, 2006.

PARRISH, Mark

(PAIR-ihsh, MAHRK)

Right wing. Shoots right. 5'11", 199 lbs. Born, Bloomington, MN, February 2, 1977. Colorado's 3rd choice, 79th overall, in 1996 Entry Draft.

Season	Club	League	GP	G	A	Pts	PIM	PP	SH	GW	S	%	+/-	TF	F%	Min	GP	G	A	Pts	PIM	PP	SH	GW	Min
1994-95	Jefferson Jaguars	High-MN	27	40	20	60	42																		
1995-96	St. Cloud State	WCHA	39	15	13	28	30																		
1996-97	St. Cloud State	WCHA	35	*27	15	42	60																		
1997-98	Seattle	WHL	54	54	38	92	29										5	2	3	5	2				
	New Haven	AHL	1	1	0	1	2																		
1998-99	**Florida**	**NHL**	**73**	**24**	**13**	**37**	**25**	**5**	**0**	**5**	**129**	**18.6**	**–6**	**1**	**0.0**	**13:59**									
	New Haven	AHL	2	1	0	1	0																		
99-2000	**Florida**	**NHL**	**81**	**26**	**18**	**44**	**39**	**6**	**0**	**3**	**152**	**17.1**	**1**	**8**	**75.0**	**14:04**	**4**	**0**	**1**	**1**	**0**	**0**	**0**	**0**	**12:37**
2000-01	**NY Islanders**	**NHL**	**70**	**17**	**13**	**30**	**28**	**6**	**0**	**3**	**123**	**13.8**	**–27**	**3**	**33.3**	**15:27**									
2001-02	**NY Islanders**	**NHL**	**78**	**30**	**30**	**60**	**32**	**9**	**1**	**6**	**162**	**18.5**	**10**	**10**	**40.0**	**16:48**	**7**	**2**	**1**	**3**	**6**	**2**	**0**	**0**	**17:2**
2002-03	**NY Islanders**	**NHL**	**81**	**23**	**25**	**48**	**28**	**9**	**0**	**5**	**147**	**15.6**	**–11**	**9**	**44.4**	**16:12**	**5**	**1**	**0**	**1**	**4**	**1**	**0**	**0**	**16:0**
2003-04	**NY Islanders**	**NHL**	**59**	**24**	**11**	**35**	**18**	**6**	**0**	**6**	**105**	**22.9**	**8**	**5**	**20.0**	**17:20**	**5**	**1**	**2**	**3**	**0**	**0**	**0**	**0**	**20:3**
2004-05			DID NOT PLAY																						
2005-06	**NY Islanders**	**NHL**	**57**	**24**	**17**	**41**	**16**	**13**	**0**	**5**	**102**	**23.5**	**–14**	**12**	**16.7**	**19:34**									
	Los Angeles	**NHL**	**19**	**5**	**3**	**8**	**4**	**3**	**0**	**0**	**35**	**14.3**	**–9**	**0**	**0.0**	**15:29**									
	United States	Olympics	6	0	0	0	4																		
2006-07	**Minnesota**	**NHL**	**76**	**19**	**20**	**39**	**18**	**5**	**0**	**4**	**141**	**13.5**	**9**	**13**	**30.8**	**14:20**	**5**	**1**	**0**	**1**	**0**	**0**	**0**	**0**	**15:4**
2007-08	**Minnesota**	**NHL**	**66**	**16**	**14**	**30**	**16**	**7**	**0**	**0**	**95**	**16.8**	**2**	**10**	**40.0**	**14:56**	**1**	**0**	**0**	**0**	**0**	**0**	**0**	**0**	**5:0**
2008-09	**Dallas**	**NHL**	**44**	**8**	**5**	**13**	**18**	**4**	**0**	**3**	**46**	**17.4**	**–3**	**5**	**20.0**	**11:16**									
	Bridgeport	AHL	3	1	1	2	2																		
2009-10	Norfolk Admirals	AHL	56	17	21	38	32																		
	Tampa Bay	**NHL**	**16**	**0**	**2**	**2**	**4**	**0**	**0**	**0**	**10**	**0.0**	**–5**	**10**	**40.0**	**15:10**									
	NHL Totals		**720**	**216**	**171**	**387**	**246**	**73**	**1**	**40**	**1247**	**17.3**		**86**	**36.0**	**15:26**	**27**	**5**	**4**	**9**	**10**	**3**	**0**	**0**	**16:1**

NCAA West Second All-American Team (1997) • WHL West First All-Star Team (1998)

Played in NHL All-Star Game (2002)

• Rights traded to **Florida** by **Colorado** with Anaheim's 3rd round choice (previously acquired, Florida selected Lance Ward) in 1998 Entry Draft for Tom Fitzgerald, March 24, 1998. Traded to **NY Islanders** by **Florida** with Oleg Kvasha for Roberto Luongo and Olli Jokinen, June 24, 2000. Traded to **Los Angeles** by **NY Islanders** with Brent Sopel for Denis Grebeshkov and Jeff Tambellini, March 8, 2006. Signed as a free agent by **Minnesota**, July 1, 2006. Signed as a free agent by **Dallas**, November 5, 2008. Signed as a free agent by **Norfolk** (AHL), October 8, 2009. Signed as a free agent by **Tampa Bay**, February 9, 2010.

PARROS, George

(PAIR-ohs, JOHRJ) **ANA**

Right wing. Shoots right. 6'5", 222 lbs. Born, Washington, PA, December 29, 1979. Los Angeles' 9th choice, 222nd overall, in 1999 Entry Draft.

Season	Club	League	GP	G	A	Pts	PIM	PP	SH	GW	S	%	+/-	TF	F%	Min	GP	G	A	Pts	PIM	PP	SH	GW	Min
1996-97	Delbarton	High-NJ	14	15	8	23																			
1997-98	Delbarton	High-NJ	15	22	17	39																			
1998-99	Chicago Freeze	NAHL	54	30	20	50	126																		
99-2000	Princeton	ECAC	27	4	2	6	14																		
2000-01	Princeton	ECAC	31	7	10	17	38																		
2001-02	Princeton	ECAC	31	9	13	22	36																		
2002-03	Princeton	ECAC	22	0	7	7	29																		
	Manchester	AHL	9	0	1	1	7																		
2003-04	Manchester	AHL	57	3	6	9	126										5	0	0	0	4				
2004-05	Manchester	AHL	67	14	8	22	247										6	1	1	2	27				
	Reading Royals	ECHL	3	0	0	0	9																		
2005-06	**Los Angeles**	**NHL**	**55**	**2**	**3**	**5**	**138**	**0**	**0**	**0**	**23**	**8.7**	**1**	**1**	**0.0**	**4:56**									
2006-07	**Colorado**	**NHL**	**2**	**0**	**0**	**0**	**0**	**0**	**0**	**0**	**1**	**0.0**	**–1**	**0**	**0.0**	**3:33**									
	♦ **Anaheim**	**NHL**	**32**	**1**	**0**	**1**	**102**	**0**	**0**	**0**	**18**	**5.6**	**–2**	**0**	**0.0**	**5:09**	**5**	**0**	**0**	**0**	**10**	**0**	**0**	**0**	**3:4**
2007-08	**Anaheim**	**NHL**	**69**	**1**	**4**	**5**	**183**	**0**	**0**	**0**	**30**	**3.3**	**3**	**10**	**30.0**	**5:57**	**1**	**0**	**0**	**0**	**0**	**0**	**0**	**0**	**2:4**
2008-09	**Anaheim**	**NHL**	**74**	**5**	**5**	**10**	**135**	**0**	**0**	**0**	**47**	**10.6**	**8**	**3**	**0.0**	**6:16**	**7**	**0**	**0**	**0**	**9**	**0**	**0**	**0**	**5:3**
2009-10	**Anaheim**	**NHL**	**57**	**4**	**0**	**4**	**136**	**0**	**0**	**0**	**25**	**16.0**	**4**	**7**	**14.3**	**6:00**									
	NHL Totals		**289**	**13**	**12**	**25**	**694**	**0**	**0**	**0**	**144**	**9.0**		**21**	**19.0**	**5:44**	**13**	**0**	**0**	**0**	**19**	**0**	**0**	**0**	**4:4**

Claimed on waivers by **Colorado** from **Los Angeles**, October 3, 2006. Traded to **Anaheim** by **Colorado** with Colorado's 3rd round choice (later traded to Tampa Bay - Tampa Bay selected Luca Cunti) in 2007 Entry Draft for Atlanta's 2nd round choice (previously acquired, Colorado selected T.J. Galiardi) in 2007 Entry Draft and Anaheim's 3rd round choice (later traded to San Jose - San Jose selected Tyson Sexsmith) in 2007 Entry Draft, November 13, 2006.

PARSE, Scott

(PARS, SKAWT) **L.A**

Center. Shoots right. 5'11", 197 lbs. Born, Portage, MI, September 5, 1984. Los Angeles' 5th choice, 174th overall, in 2004 Entry Draft.

Season	Club	League	GP	G	A	Pts	PIM	PP	SH	GW	S	%	+/-	TF	F%	Min	GP	G	A	Pts	PIM	PP	SH	GW	Min
2002-03	Tri-City Storm	USHL	48	21	23	44	32										3	2	1	3	8				
2003-04	Nebraska-Omaha	CCHA	39	16	19	35	52																		
2004-05	Nebraska-Omaha	CCHA	39	19	30	49	32																		
2005-06	Nebraska-Omaha	CCHA	41	20	*41	*61	40																		
2006-07	Nebraska-Omaha	CCHA	40	24	28	52	36																		
	Grand Rapids	AHL	10	2	5	7	6										7	1	0	1	8				
2007-08	Manchester	AHL	14	0	3	3	4																		
	Reading Royals	ECHL	18	5	11	16	14																		
2008-09	Manchester	AHL	74	15	24	39	38																		
2009-10	**Los Angeles**	**NHL**	**59**	**11**	**13**	**24**	**22**	**0**	**0**	**1**	**78**	**14.1**	**13**	**11**	**54.6**	**10:32**	**4**	**0**	**0**	**0**	**0**	**0**	**0**	**0**	**6:3**
	Manchester	AHL	14	4	11	15	21																		
	NHL Totals		**59**	**11**	**13**	**24**	**22**	**0**	**0**	**1**	**78**	**14.1**		**11**	**54.5**	**10:32**	**4**	**0**	**0**	**0**	**0**	**0**	**0**	**0**	**6:3**

USHL All-Rookie Team (2003) • CCHA First All-Star Team (2005, 2007) • CCHA Player of the Year (2006) • NCAA West First All-American Team (2006) • NCAA West Second All-American Team (2007)

			Regular Season														Playoffs								
Season	Club	League	GP	G	A	Pts	PIM	PP	SH	GW	S	%	+/-	TF	F%	Min	GP	G	A	Pts	PIM	PP	SH	GW	Min

PAVELSKI, Joe

(pah-VEHL-skee, JOH) **S.J.**

Center. Shoots right. 5'11", 195 lbs. Born, Plover, WI, July 11, 1984. San Jose's 7th choice, 205th overall, in 2003 Entry Draft.

Season	Club	League	GP	G	A	Pts	PIM	PP	SH	GW	S	%	+/-	TF	F%	Min	GP	G	A	Pts	PIM	PP	SH	GW	Min
2002-03	Waterloo	USHL	60	36	33	69	32	....	....	....	....	....	....	....	....	....	7	5	7	12	8	....	....	....	....
2003-04	Waterloo	USHL	54	21	31	52	58	....	....	....	....	....	....	....	....	....	12	6	6	12	10	....	....	....	....
2004-05	U. of Wisconsin	WCHA	41	16	29	45	26	....	....	....	....	....	....	....	....	....	....	....	....	....	....	....	....	....	....
2005-06	U. of Wisconsin	WCHA	43	23	33	56	34	....	....	....	....	....	....	....	....	....	....	....	....	....	....	....	....	....	....
2006-07	**San Jose**	**NHL**	**46**	**14**	**14**	**28**	**18**	**5**	**0**	**3**	**111**	**12.6**	**4**	**389**	**48.6**	**15:02**	**6**	**1**	**0**	**1**	**0**	**0**	**0**	**0**	**10:27**
	Worcester Sharks	AHL	16	8	18	26	8	....	....	....	....	....	....	....	....	....	....	....	....	....	....	....	....	....	....
2007-08	**San Jose**	**NHL**	**82**	**19**	**21**	**40**	**28**	**8**	**1**	**4**	**207**	**9.2**	**1**	**501**	**53.5**	**14:07**	**13**	**5**	**4**	**9**	**0**	**2**	**0**	**3**	**22:03**
2008-09	**San Jose**	**NHL**	**80**	**25**	**34**	**59**	**46**	**8**	**3**	**3**	**266**	**9.4**	**5**	**1274**	**56.3**	**18:58**	**6**	**0**	**1**	**1**	**9**	**0**	**0**	**0**	**19:21**
2009-10	**San Jose**	**NHL**	**67**	**25**	**26**	**51**	**26**	**3**	**1**	**5**	**228**	**11.0**	**1**	**821**	**58.1**	**19:29**	**15**	**9**	**8**	**17**	**6**	**5**	**0**	**3**	**21:32**
	United States	Olympics	6	0	3	3	4	....	....	....	....	....	....	....	....	....	....	....	....	....	....	....	....	....	....
	NHL Totals		**275**	**83**	**95**	**178**	**118**	**24**	**5**	**15**	**812**	**10.2**		**2985**	**55.3**	**16:59**	**40**	**15**	**13**	**28**	**15**	**7**	**0**	**6**	**19:43**

SHL All-Rookie Team (2003) • USHL First All-Star Team (2003) • USHL Rookie of the Year (2003) • WCHA All-Rookie Team (2005) • WCHA Second All-Star Team (2006) • NCAA West Second All-American eam (2006)

PECKHAM, Theo

(PEHK-uhm, THEE-oh) **EDM.**

Defense. Shoots left. 6'2", 223 lbs. Born, Richmond Hill, Ont., November 10, 1987. Edmonton's 2nd choice, 75th overall, in 2006 Entry Draft.

Season	Club	League	GP	G	A	Pts	PIM	PP	SH	GW	S	%	+/-	TF	F%	Min	GP	G	A	Pts	PIM	PP	SH	GW	Min
2003-04	North York	OPJHL	29	1	4	5	46	....	....	....	....	....	....	....	....	....	....	....	....	....	....	....	....	....	....
2004-05	Owen Sound	OHL	61	1	9	10	209	....	....	....	....	....	....	....	....	....	8	0	0	0	8	....	....	....	....
2005-06	Owen Sound	OHL	67	6	9	15	236	....	....	....	....	....	....	....	....	....	11	1	6	7	32	....	....	....	....
2006-07	Owen Sound	OHL	53	10	25	35	173	....	....	....	....	....	....	....	....	....	4	0	1	1	0	....	....	....	....
2007-08	**Edmonton**	**NHL**	**1**	**0**	**0**	**0**	**2**	**0**	**0**	**0**	**0**	**0.0**	**0**	**0**	**0.0**	**13:22**	....	....	....	....	....	....	....	....	....
	Springfield	AHL	59	6	7	13	174	....	....	....	....	....	....	....	....	....	....	....	....	....	....	....	....	....	....
2008-09	**Edmonton**	**NHL**	**15**	**0**	**0**	**0**	**59**	**0**	**0**	**0**	**8**	**0.0**	**–1**	**0**	**0.0**	**11:38**	....	....	....	....	....	....	....	....	....
	Springfield	AHL	47	6	13	19	107	....	....	....	....	....	....	....	....	....	....	....	....	....	....	....	....	....	....
2009-10	**Edmonton**	**NHL**	**15**	**0**	**1**	**1**	**43**	**0**	**0**	**0**	**9**	**0.0**	**–8**	**0**	**0.0**	**16:04**	....	....	....	....	....	....	....	....	....
	Springfield	AHL	37	0	6	6	106	....	....	....	....	....	....	....	....	....	....	....	....	....	....	....	....	....	....
	NHL Totals		**31**	**0**	**1**	**1**	**104**	**0**	**0**	**0**	**17**	**0.0**		**0**	**0.0**	**13:50**	....	....	....	....	....	....	....	....	....

PELECH, Matt

(PEH-lihk, MAT) **CGY.**

Defense. Shoots right. 6'5", 216 lbs. Born, Toronto, Ont., September 4, 1987. Calgary's 1st choice, 26th overall, in 2005 Entry Draft.

Season	Club	League	GP	G	A	Pts	PIM	PP	SH	GW	S	%	+/-	TF	F%	Min	GP	G	A	Pts	PIM	PP	SH	GW	Min
2002-03	Vaughan	GTHL	44	3	13	16	113	....	....	....	....	....	....	....	....	....	....	....	....	....	....	....	....	....	....
2003-04	Sarnia Sting	OHL	62	4	6	10	39	....	....	....	....	....	....	....	....	....	5	0	1	1	12	....	....	....	....
2004-05	Sarnia Sting	OHL	31	1	5	6	74	....	....	....	....	....	....	....	....	....	....	....	....	....	....	....	....	....	....
2005-06	Sarnia Sting	OHL	18	0	2	2	59	....	....	....	....	....	....	....	....	....	....	....	....	....	....	....	....	....	....
	London Knights	OHL	34	1	7	8	80	....	....	....	....	....	....	....	....	....	19	0	0	0	48	....	....	....	....
2006-07	Belleville Bulls	OHL	58	5	30	35	171	....	....	....	....	....	....	....	....	....	12	0	3	3	22	....	....	....	....
2007-08	Quad City Flames	AHL	77	3	6	9	141	....	....	....	....	....	....	....	....	....	....	....	....	....	....	....	....	....	....
2008-09	**Calgary**	**NHL**	**5**	**0**	**3**	**3**	**9**	**0**	**0**	**0**	**4**	**0.0**	**1**	**0**	**0.0**	**13:16**	....	....	....	....	....	....	....	....	....
	Quad City Flames	AHL	59	3	6	9	130	....	....	....	....	....	....	....	....	....	....	....	....	....	....	....	....	....	....
2009-10	Abbotsford Heat	AHL	42	2	8	10	125	....	....	....	....	....	....	....	....	....	13	0	4	4	31	....	....	....	....
	NHL Totals		**5**	**0**	**3**	**3**	**9**	**0**	**0**	**0**	**4**	**0.0**		**0**	**0.0**	**13:16**	....	....	....	....	....	....	....	....	....

PELLETIER, Pascal

(PEHL-tyay, pas-KAL)

Left wing. Shoots right. 5'11", 191 lbs. Born, Labrador City, Nfld., June 16, 1983.

Season	Club	League	GP	G	A	Pts	PIM	PP	SH	GW	S	%	+/-	TF	F%	Min	GP	G	A	Pts	PIM	PP	SH	GW	Min
2000-01	Baie-Comeau	QMJHL	70	15	44	59	176	....	....	....	....	....	....	....	....	....	11	2	11	13	6	....	....	....	....
2001-02	Baie-Comeau	QMJHL	56	12	25	37	115	....	....	....	....	....	....	....	....	....	5	3	4	7	0	....	....	....	....
2002-03	Baie-Comeau	QMJHL	67	46	55	101	113	....	....	....	....	....	....	....	....	....	12	5	7	12	14	....	....	....	....
2003-04	Shawinigan	QMJHL	64	39	52	91	85	....	....	....	....	....	....	....	....	....	11	3	9	12	20	....	....	....	....
2004-05	Louisiana	ECHL	61	10	28	38	75	....	....	....	....	....	....	....	....	....	....	....	....	....	....	....	....	....	....
	Gwinnett	ECHL	6	0	1	1	2	....	....	....	....	....	....	....	....	....	5	0	2	2	2	....	....	....	....
2005-06	Providence Bruins	AHL	53	20	26	46	42	....	....	....	....	....	....	....	....	....	6	2	4	6	23	....	....	....	....
	Gwinnett	ECHL	21	18	12	30	18	....	....	....	....	....	....	....	....	....	....	....	....	....	....	....	....	....	....
2006-07	Providence Bruins	AHL	80	14	35	49	60	....	....	....	....	....	....	....	....	....	13	5	4	9	16	....	....	....	....
2007-08	**Boston**	**NHL**	**6**	**0**	**0**	**0**	**0**	**0**	**0**	**0**	**8**	**0.0**	**–2**	**1**	**100.0**	**11:04**	....	....	....	....	....	....	....	....	....
	Providence Bruins	AHL	73	37	38	75	66	....	....	....	....	....	....	....	....	....	10	6	6	12	4	....	....	....	....
2008-09	**Chicago**	**NHL**	**7**	**0**	**0**	**0**	**0**	**0**	**0**	**0**	**7**	**0.0**	**–4**	**33**	**39.4**	**9:08**	....	....	....	....	....	....	....	....	....
	Rockford IceHogs	AHL	71	29	26	55	45	....	....	....	....	....	....	....	....	....	4	1	0	1	6	....	....	....	....
2009-10	Syracuse Crunch	AHL	25	3	13	16	23	....	....	....	....	....	....	....	....	....	....	....	....	....	....	....	....	....	....
	Peoria Rivermen	AHL	55	14	28	42	41	....	....	....	....	....	....	....	....	....	....	....	....	....	....	....	....	....	....
	NHL Totals		**13**	**0**	**0**	**0**	**0**	**0**	**0**	**0**	**15**	**0.0**		**34**	**41.2**	**10:01**	....								

HL First All-Star Team (2008)

gned as a free agent by **Boston**, August 7, 2006. Traded to **Chicago** by **Boston** for Martin St. Pierre, July 24, 2008. Signed as a free agent by **Columbus**, July 6, 2009. Traded to **St. Louis** by **Columbus** r Tomas Kana and Brendan Bell, December 8, 2009. Signed as a free agent by **Langnau** (Swiss), May 20, 2010.

PELLEY, Rod

(PEHL-lee, RAWD) **N.J.**

Center. Shoots left. 5'11", 195 lbs. Born, Kitimat, B.C., September 1, 1984.

Season	Club	League	GP	G	A	Pts	PIM	PP	SH	GW	S	%	+/-	TF	F%	Min	GP	G	A	Pts	PIM	PP	SH	GW	Min
2002-03	Ohio State	CCHA	43	8	3	11	26	....	....	....	....	....	....	....	....	....	....	....	....	....	....	....	....	....	....
2003-04	Ohio State	CCHA	42	10	12	22	38	....	....	....	....	....	....	....	....	....	....	....	....	....	....	....	....	....	....
2004-05	Ohio State	CCHA	41	22	19	41	54	....	....	....	....	....	....	....	....	....	....	....	....	....	....	....	....	....	....
2005-06	Ohio State	CCHA	39	7	7	14	42	....	....	....	....	....	....	....	....	....	....	....	....	....	....	....	....	....	....
2006-07	**New Jersey**	**NHL**	**9**	**0**	**0**	**0**	**0**	**0**	**0**	**0**	**8**	**0.0**	**–3**	**98**	**40.8**	**11:00**	....	....	....	....	....	....	....	....	....
	Lowell Devils	AHL	65	17	12	29	35	....	....	....	....	....	....	....	....	....	....	....	....	....	....	....	....	....	....
2007-08	**New Jersey**	**NHL**	**58**	**2**	**4**	**6**	**19**	**0**	**0**	**1**	**59**	**3.4**	**–3**	**321**	**46.7**	**9:19**	....	....	....	....	....	....	....	....	....
	Lowell Devils	AHL	11	2	1	3	18	....	....	....	....	....	....	....	....	....	....	....	....	....	....	....	....	....	....
2008-09	Lowell Devils	AHL	75	15	23	38	78	....	....	....	....	....	....	....	....	....	....	....	....	....	....	....	....	....	....
2009-10	**New Jersey**	**NHL**	**63**	**2**	**8**	**10**	**40**	**0**	**0**	**0**	**74**	**2.7**	**–4**	**198**	**49.5**	**7:52**	**3**	**0**	**0**	**0**	**2**	**0**	**0**	**0**	**9:12**
	NHL Totals		**130**	**4**	**12**	**16**	**59**	**0**	**0**	**1**	**141**	**2.8**		**617**	**46.7**	**8:44**	**3**	**0**	**0**	**0**	**2**	**0**	**0**	**0**	**9:12**

CHA Second All-Star Team (2005)

gned as a free agent by **New Jersey**, July 24, 2006.

PELTIER, Derek

(PEHL-tyay, DAIR-ihk)

Defense. Shoots left. 5'11", 190 lbs. Born, Plymouth, MN, March 14, 1985. Colorado's 5th choice, 184th overall, in 2004 Entry Draft.

Season	Club	League	GP	G	A	Pts	PIM	PP	SH	GW	S	%	+/-	TF	F%	Min	GP	G	A	Pts	PIM	PP	SH	GW	Min
2003-04	Cedar Rapids	USHL	55	7	26	33	34	....	....	....	....	....	....	....	....	....	4	0	0	0	4	....	....	....	....
2004-05	U. of Minnesota	WCHA	43	6	13	19	22	....	....	....	....	....	....	....	....	....	....	....	....	....	....	....	....	....	....
2005-06	U. of Minnesota	WCHA	41	1	17	18	30	....	....	....	....	....	....	....	....	....	....	....	....	....	....	....	....	....	....
2006-07	U. of Minnesota	WCHA	44	4	11	15	28	....	....	....	....	....	....	....	....	....	....	....	....	....	....	....	....	....	....
2007-08	U. of Minnesota	WCHA	45	4	17	21	38	....	....	....	....	....	....	....	....	....	....	....	....	....	....	....	....	....	....
	Lake Erie	AHL	6	0	1	1	4	....	....	....	....	....	....	....	....	....	....	....	....	....	....	....	....	....	....
2008-09	**Colorado**	**NHL**	**11**	**0**	**0**	**0**	**2**	**0**	**0**	**0**	**7**	**0.0**	**–4**	**0**	**0.0**	**13:15**	....	....	....	....	....	....	....	....	....
	Lake Erie	AHL	63	2	17	19	32	....	....	....	....	....	....	....	....	....	....	....	....	....	....	....	....	....	....
2009-10	**Colorado**	**NHL**	**3**	**0**	**0**	**0**	**0**	**0**	**0**	**0**	**1**	**0.0**	**0**	**0**	**0.0**	**9:00**	....	....	....	....	....	....	....	....	....
	Lake Erie	AHL	44	1	12	13	26	....	....	....	....	....	....	....	....	....	....	....	....	....	....	....	....	....	....
	NHL Totals		**14**	**0**	**0**	**0**	**2**	**0**	**0**	**0**	**8**	**0.0**		**0**	**0.0**	**12:21**	....	....	....	....	....	....	....	....	....

PELTONEN, Ville

(PEHL-TOH-nen, VIHL-ee)

Left wing. Shoots left. 5'11", 182 lbs. Born, Vantaa, Finland, May 24, 1973. San Jose's 4th choice, 58th overall, in 1993 Entry Draft.

			Regular Season															Playoffs								
Season	Club	League	GP	G	A	Pts	PIM	PP	SH	GW	S	%	+/-	TF	F%	Min	GP	G	A	Pts	PIM	PP	SH	GW	Min
1989-90	HIFK Helsinki U18	Fin-U18	24	21	24	45	14	....	....	....	....	....	....	....	....	....	....	....	....	....	....	....	....	....	....
1990-91	HIFK Helsinki Jr.	Fin-Jr.	36	21	16	37	16	....	....	....	....	....	....	....	....	....	7	2	3	5	10	....	....	....	....
1991-92	HIFK Helsinki Jr.	Fin-Jr.	37	28	23	51	28	....	....	....	....	....	....	....	....	....	4	0	2	2	0	....	....	....	....
	HIFK Helsinki	Finland	6	0	0	0	0	....	....	....	....	....	....	....	....	....	....	....	....	....	....	....	....	....	....
1992-93	HIFK Helsinki Jr.	Fin-Jr.	2	4	2	6	4	....	....	....	....	....	....	....	....	....	....	....	....	....	....	....	....	....	....
	HIFK Helsinki	Finland	46	13	24	37	16	....	....	....	....	....	....	....	....	....	4	0	2	2	2	....	....	....	....
1993-94	HIFK Helsinki	Finland	43	16	22	38	14	....	....	....	....	....	....	....	....	....	3	0	0	0	2	....	....	....	....
	Finland	Olympics	8	4	3	7	0	....	....	....	....	....	....	....	....	....	....	....	....	....	....	....	....	....	....
1994-95	HIFK Helsinki	Finland	45	20	16	36	16	....	....	....	....	....	....	....	....	....	3	0	0	0	0	....	....	....	....
1995-96	**San Jose**	**NHL**	**31**	**2**	**11**	**13**	**14**	**0**	**0**	**0**	**58**	**3.4**	**–7**	....	....	....	....	....	....	....	....	....	....	....	....
	Kansas City	IHL	29	5	13	18	8	....	....	....	....	....	....	....	....	....	....	....	....	....	....	....	....	....	....
1996-97	**San Jose**	**NHL**	**28**	**2**	**3**	**5**	**0**	**1**	**0**	**0**	**35**	**5.7**	**–8**	....	....	....	....	....	....	....	....	....	....	....	....
	Kentucky	AHL	40	22	30	52	21	....	....	....	....	....	....	....	....	....	....	....	....	....	....	....	....	....	....
1997-98	V.Frolunda	Sweden	45	22	29	51	44	....	....	....	....	....	....	....	....	....	7	4	2	6	0	....	....	....	....
	Finland	Olympics	6	2	1	3	6	....	....	....	....	....	....	....	....	....	....	....	....	....	....	....	....	....	....
1998-99	**Nashville**	**NHL**	**14**	**5**	**5**	**10**	**2**	**1**	**0**	**0**	**31**	**16.1**	**1**	**0**	**0.0**	**15:54**	....	....	....	....	....	....	....	....	....
99-2000	**Nashville**	**NHL**	**79**	**6**	**22**	**28**	**22**	**2**	**0**	**2**	**125**	**4.8**	**–1**	**1**	**100.0**	**14:41**	....	....	....	....	....	....	....	....	....
2000-01	**Nashville**	**NHL**	**23**	**3**	**1**	**4**	**2**	**0**	**0**	**0**	**38**	**7.9**	**–7**	**2**	**0.0**	**11:40**	....	....	....	....	....	....	....	....	....
	Milwaukee	IHL	53	27	33	60	26	....	....	....	....	....	....	....	....	....	5	2	1	3	6	....	....	....	....
2001-02	Jokerit Helsinki	Finland	30	11	18	29	8	....	....	....	....	....	....	....	....	....	....	....	....	....	....	....	....	....	....
2002-03	Jokerit Helsinki	Finland	49	23	19	42	14	....	....	....	....	....	....	....	....	....	10	4	6	10	0	....	....	....	....
2003-04	HC Lugano	Swiss	48	28	44	72	14	....	....	....	....	....	....	....	....	....	16	4	7	11	8	....	....	....	....
2004-05	HC Lugano	Swiss	44	24	33	57	16	....	....	....	....	....	....	....	....	....	5	0	3	3	2	....	....	....	....
2005-06	HC Lugano	Swiss	39	22	25	47	22	....	....	....	....	....	....	....	....	....	17	*12	12	24	8	....	....	....	....
	Finland	Olympics	8	4	5	9	6	....	....	....	....	....	....	....	....	....	....	....	....	....	....	....	....	....	....
2006-07	**Florida**	**NHL**	**72**	**17**	**20**	**37**	**28**	**4**	**0**	**0**	**145**	**11.7**	**7**	**35**	**31.4**	**16:25**	....	....	....	....	....	....	....	....	....
2007-08	**Florida**	**NHL**	**56**	**5**	**15**	**20**	**20**	**1**	**0**	**0**	**108**	**4.6**	**–2**	**16**	**18.8**	**15:49**	....	....	....	....	....	....	....	....	....
2008-09	**Florida**	**NHL**	**79**	**12**	**19**	**31**	**31**	**0**	**0**	**1**	**121**	**9.9**	**6**	**64**	**28.1**	**15:15**	....	....	....	....	....	....	....	....	....
2009-10	Dynamo Minsk	Rus-KHL	51	6	20	26	54	....	....	....	....	....	....	....	....	....	....	....	....	....	....	....	....	....	....
	Finland	Olympics	6	0	1	1	2	....	....	....	....	....	....	....	....	....	....	....	....	....	....	....	....	....	....
	NHL Totals		**382**	**52**	**96**	**148**	**119**	**9**	**0**	**3**	**661**	**7.9**		**118**	**28.0**	**15:15**	....	....	....	....	....	....	....	....	....

IHL Second All-Star Team (2001)

Traded to **Nashville** by **San Jose** for Nashville's 5th round choice (later traded to Phoenix – Phoenix selected Josh Blackburn) in 1998 Entry Draft, June 26, 1998. • Missed majority of 1998-99 season recovering from shoulder surgery, December 10, 1998. Signed as a free agent by **Jokerit Helsinki** (Finland), April 26, 2001. Signed as a free agent by **Lugano** (Swiss), April 9, 2003. Signed as a free agent by **Florida**, June 15, 2006. Signed as a free agent by **Minsk** (Russia-KHL), July 31, 2009.

PENNER, Dustin

(PEH-nuhr, DUHS-tihn) **EDM**

Left wing. Shoots left. 6'4", 245 lbs. Born, Winkler, Man., September 28, 1982.

2001-02	MSU - Bottineau	NJCAA	23	20	12	32	30	....	....	....	....	....	....	....	....	....	....	....	....	....	....	....	....	....	....
2002-03	U. of Maine	H-East	DID NOT PLAY – FRESHMAN																						
2003-04	U. of Maine	H-East	43	11	12	23	52	....	....	....	....	....	....	....	....	....	....	....	....	....	....	....	....	....	....
2004-05	Cincinnati	AHL	77	10	18	28	82	....	....	....	....	....	....	....	....	....	9	2	3	5	13	....	....	....	....
2005-06	**Anaheim**	**NHL**	**19**	**4**	**3**	**7**	**14**	**2**	**0**	**1**	**46**	**8.7**	**3**	**1**	**0.0**	**11:58**	**13**	**3**	**6**	**9**	**12**	**0**	**0**	**0**	**13:16**
	Portland Pirates	AHL	57	39	45	84	68	....	....	....	....	....	....	....	....	....	5	4	3	7	0	....	....	....	....
2006-07♦	**Anaheim**	**NHL**	**82**	**29**	**16**	**45**	**58**	**9**	**0**	**5**	**204**	**14.2**	**–2**	**58**	**46.6**	**13:59**	**21**	**3**	**5**	**8**	**2**	**0**	**0**	**2**	**14:05**
2007-08	**Edmonton**	**NHL**	**82**	**23**	**24**	**47**	**45**	**13**	**0**	**4**	**201**	**11.4**	**–12**	**189**	**55.0**	**17:12**	....	....	....	....	....	....	....	....	....
2008-09	**Edmonton**	**NHL**	**78**	**17**	**20**	**37**	**61**	**5**	**0**	**5**	**137**	**12.4**	**7**	**114**	**47.4**	**15:23**	....	....	....	....	....	....	....	....	....
2009-10	**Edmonton**	**NHL**	**82**	**32**	**31**	**63**	**38**	**9**	**0**	**1**	**203**	**15.8**	**6**	**421**	**47.7**	**18:23**	....	....	....	....	....	....	....	....	....
	NHL Totals		**343**	**105**	**94**	**199**	**216**	**38**	**0**	**16**	**791**	**13.3**		**783**	**49.3**	**16:01**	**34**	**6**	**11**	**17**	**14**	**0**	**0**	**2**	**13:4**

NCAA Championship All-Tournament Team (2004) • AHL Second All-Star Team (2006)

Signed as a free agent by **Anaheim**, May 12, 2004. Signed as a free agent by **Edmonton**, August 2, 2007.

PENNER, Jeff

(PEH-nuhr, JEHF) **BOS**

Defense. Shoots left. 5'10", 191 lbs. Born, Winnipeg, Man., April 13, 1987.

2005-06	Dauphin Kings	MJHL	44	8	27	35	46	....	....	....	....	....	....	....	....	....	....	....	....	....	....	....	....	....	....
2006-07	Dauphin Kings	MJHL	45	9	44	53	....	....	....	....	....	....	....	....	....	....	....	....	....	....	....	....	....	....	....
2007-08	Alaska	CCHA	35	5	7	12	49	....	....	....	....	....	....	....	....	....	....	....	....	....	....	....	....	....	....
	Providence Bruins	AHL	2	0	0	0	0	....	....	....	....	....	....	....	....	....	....	....	....	....	....	....	....	....	....
2008-09	Providence Bruins	AHL	80	10	18	28	50	....	....	....	....	....	....	....	....	....	16	6	5	11	8	....	....	....	....
2009-10	**Boston**	**NHL**	**2**	**0**	**0**	**0**	**0**	**0**	**0**	**0**	**1**	**0.0**	**0**	**0**	**0.0**	**14:01**	....	....	....	....	....	....	....	....	....
	Providence Bruins	AHL	68	7	28	35	28	....	....	....	....	....	....	....	....	....	....	....	....	....	....	....	....	....	....
	NHL Totals		**2**	**0**	**0**	**0**	**0**	**0**	**0**	**0**	**1**	**0.0**		**0**	**0.0**	**14:01**	....	....	....	....	....	....	....	....	....

MJHL Rookie All-Star Team (2006) • MJHL First All-Star Team (2007)

Signed as a free agent by **Boston**, March 29, 2008.

PEREZHOGIN, Alexander

(pehr-eh-ZHOI-gihn, al-EHX-AN-duhr) **MTL**

Left wing. Shoots left. 6', 211 lbs. Born, Ust-Kamenogorsk, USSR, August 10, 1983. Montreal's 2nd choice, 25th overall, in 2001 Entry Draft.

1998-99	Omsk 2	Russia-4	10	3	4	7	0	....	....	....	....	....	....	....	....	....	....	....	....	....	....	....	....	....	....
99-2000	Omsk 2	Russia-3	22	12	11	23	12	....	....	....	....	....	....	....	....	....	....	....	....	....	....	....	....	....	....
	Avangard Omsk	Russia	1	0	0	0	0	....	....	....	....	....	....	....	....	....	....	....	....	....	....	....	....	....	....
2000-01	Omsk 2	Russia-3	41	47	24	71	40	....	....	....	....	....	....	....	....	....	....	....	....	....	....	....	....	....	....
	Avangard Omsk	Russia	....	....	....	....	....	....	....	....	....	....	....	....	....	....	1	0	0	0	0	....	....	....	....
2001-02	Avangard Omsk	Russia	4	1	0	1	4	....	....	....	....	....	....	....	....	....	....	....	....	....	....	....	....	....	....
	Mostovik Kurgan	Russia-2	19	14	10	24	10	....	....	....	....	....	....	....	....	....	....	....	....	....	....	....	....	....	....
2002-03	Avangard Omsk	Russia	48	15	6	21	28	....	....	....	....	....	....	....	....	....	8	0	2	2	4	....	....	....	....
2003-04	Hamilton	AHL	77	23	27	50	52	....	....	....	....	....	....	....	....	....	5	3	3	6	16	....	....	....	....
2004-05	Avangard Omsk	Russia	43	15	18	33	18	....	....	....	....	....	....	....	....	....	11	3	2	5	8	....	....	....	....
2005-06	**Montreal**	**NHL**	**67**	**9**	**10**	**19**	**38**	**3**	**0**	**2**	**109**	**8.3**	**5**	**6**	**33.3**	**10:08**	**6**	**1**	**1**	**2**	**4**	**0**	**0**	**0**	**13:4**
	Hamilton	AHL	11	0	2	2	8	....	....	....	....	....	....	....	....	....	....	....	....	....	....	....	....	....	....
2006-07	**Montreal**	**NHL**	**61**	**6**	**9**	**15**	**48**	**1**	**0**	**1**	**103**	**5.8**	**11**	**7**	**0.0**	**11:51**	....	....	....	....	....	....	....	....	....
2007-08	Ufa	Russia	50	21	20	41	42	....	....	....	....	....	....	....	....	....	16	3	2	5	14	....	....	....	....
2008-09	Ufa	Rus-KHL	55	29	24	53	32	....	....	....	....	....	....	....	....	....	4	0	0	0	2	....	....	....	....
2009-10	Ufa	Rus-KHL	56	13	19	32	36	....	....	....	....	....	....	....	....	....	16	4	1	5	22	....	....	....	....
	NHL Totals		**128**	**15**	**19**	**34**	**86**	**4**	**0**	**3**	**212**	**7.1**		**13**	**15.4**	**10:57**	**6**	**1**	**1**	**2**	**4**	**0**	**0**	**0**	**13:4**

Signed as a free agent by **Ufa** ((Russia), May 5, 2007.

PERRAULT, Joel

(pair-OH, JOHL) **VAN**

Center. Shoots right. 6'2", 205 lbs. Born, Montreal, Que., April 6, 1983. Anaheim's 7th choice, 137th overall, in 2001 Entry Draft.

99-2000	Antoine-Girouard	QAAA	19	4	7	11	6	....	....	....	....	....	....	....	....	....	....	....	....	....	....	....	....	....	....
2000-01	Baie-Comeau	QMJHL	68	10	14	24	46	....	....	....	....	....	....	....	....	....	11	1	1	2	10	....	....	....	....
2001-02	Baie-Comeau	QMJHL	57	18	44	62	96	....	....	....	....	....	....	....	....	....	5	2	0	2	6	....	....	....	....
2002-03	Baie-Comeau	QMJHL	70	51	65	*116	93	....	....	....	....	....	....	....	....	....	12	3	7	10	14	....	....	....	....
2003-04	Cincinnati	AHL	65	14	14	28	38	....	....	....	....	....	....	....	....	....	9	1	1	2	2	....	....	....	....
2004-05	Cincinnati	AHL	51	9	19	28	40	....	....	....	....	....	....	....	....	....	....	....	....	....	....	....	....	....	....
2005-06	Portland Pirates	AHL	25	12	12	24	20	....	....	....	....	....	....	....	....	....	....	....	....	....	....	....	....	....	....
	Phoenix	**NHL**	**5**	**1**	**1**	**2**	**2**	**0**	**0**	**0**	**7**	**14.3**	**0**	**47**	**34.0**	**11:29**	....	....	....	....	....	....	....	....	....
	San Antonio	AHL	12	1	6	7	4	....	....	....	....	....	....	....	....	....	....	....	....	....	....	....	....	....	....
2006-07	**Phoenix**	**NHL**	**15**	**1**	**2**	**3**	**14**	**0**	**0**	**0**	**18**	**9.1**	**–3**	**109**	**82.6**	**11:29**	....	....	....	....	....	....	....	....	....
	St. Louis	**NHL**	**11**	**0**	**0**	**0**	**0**	**0**	**0**	**0**	**13**	**0.0**	**–4**	**20**	**25.0**	**8:19**	....	....	....	....	....	....	....	....	....
	Peoria Rivermen	AHL	2	0	2	2	7	....	....	....	....	....	....	....	....	....	....	....	....	....	....	....	....	....	....
	San Antonio	AHL	21	10	4	14	8	....	....	....	....	....	....	....	....	....	....	....	....	....	....	....	....	....	....

			Regular Season														Playoffs								
Season	Club	League	GP	G	A	Pts	PIM	PP	SH	GW	S	%	+/-	TF	F%	Min	GP	G	A	Pts	PIM	PP	SH	GW	Min
2007-08	**Phoenix**	**NHL**	**49**	**7**	**10**	**17**	**48**	**3**	**0**	**2**	**87**	**8.0**	**-11**	**599**	**49.1**	**14:26**	....	....	....	....	....	....	....	....	....
	San Antonio	AHL	28	14	13	27	36	....	....	....	....	....	....	....	....	....	....	....	....	....	....	....	....	....	....
2008-09	**Phoenix**	**NHL**	**7**	**2**	**1**	**3**	**4**	**0**	**0**	**0**	**15**	**13.3**	**2**	**76**	**44.7**	**12:52**	....	....	....	....	....	....	....	....	....
	San Antonio	AHL	46	18	31	49	46	....	....	....	....	....	....	....	....	....	....	....	....	....	....	....	....	....	....
2009-10	**Phoenix**	**NHL**	**2**	**1**	**0**	**1**	**0**	**0**	**0**	**0**	**7**	**14.3**	**-1**	**25**	**40.0**	**9:55**	....	....	....	....	....	....	....	....	....
	San Antonio	AHL	47	17	19	36	38	....	....	....	....	....	....	....	....	....	....	....	....	....	....	....	....	....	....
	NHL Totals		**89**	**12**	**14**	**26**	**68**	**3**	**0**	**2**	**147**	**8.2**		**876**	**51.3**	**12:47**	....	....	....	....	....	....	....	....	....

MJHL First All-Star Team (2003) • Canadian Major Junior First All-Star Team (2003)

raded to **Phoenix** by **Anaheim** for Sean O'Donnell, March 9, 2006. Claimed on waivers by **St. Louis** from **Phoenix**, October 31, 2006. Claimed on waivers by **Phoenix** from **St. Louis**, December 19, 006. Signed as a free agent by **Vancouver**, July 1, 2010.

PERREAULT, Mathieu

(pair-OH, MA-tyew) **WSH.**

Center. Shoots left. 5'8", 166 lbs. Born, Drummondville, Que., January 5, 1988. Washington's 10th choice, 177th overall, in 2006 Entry Draft.

Season	Club	League	GP	G	A	Pts	PIM	PP	SH	GW	S	%	+/-	TF	F%	Min	GP	G	A	Pts	PIM	PP	SH	GW	Min
2004-05	Magog	QAAA	41	25	47	72	68	....	....	....	....	....	....	....	....	....	9	5	10	15	12	....	....	....	....
2005-06	Acadie-Bathurst	QMJHL	62	18	34	52	42	....	....	....	....	....	....	....	....	....	17	10	11	21	8	....	....	....	....
2006-07	Acadie-Bathurst	QMJHL	67	41	78	119	66	....	....	....	....	....	....	....	....	....	12	6	8	14	8	....	....	....	....
2007-08	Acadie-Bathurst	QMJHL	65	34	*80	*114	61	....	....	....	....	....	....	....	....	....	12	3	19	22	6	....	....	....	....
	Hershey Bears	AHL	....	....	....	....	....	....	....	....	....	....	....	....	....	....	3	0	0	0	0	....	....	....	....
2008-09	Hershey Bears	AHL	77	11	39	50	36	....	....	....	....	....	....	....	....	....	21	2	6	8	8	....	....	....	....
2009-10	**Washington**	**NHL**	**21**	**4**	**5**	**9**	**6**	**1**	**0**	**0**	**27**	**14.8**	**4**	**210**	**45.2**	**11:21**	....	....	....	....	....	....	....	....	....
	Hershey Bears	AHL	56	16	34	50	34	....	....	....	....	....	....	....	....	....	21	7	12	19	18	....	....	....	....
	NHL Totals		**21**	**4**	**5**	**9**	**6**	**1**	**0**	**0**	**27**	**14.8**		**210**	**45.2**	**11:21**	....	....	....	....	....	....	....	....	....

MJHL First All-Star Team (2007) • QMJHL Player of the Year (2007) • QMJHL Second All-Star Team (2008) • Canadian Major Junior Second All-Star Team (2007, 2008)

PERRIN, Eric

(peh-REHN, AIR-ihk)

Center. Shoots left. 5'9", 180 lbs. Born, Laval, Que., November 1, 1975.

Season	Club	League	GP	G	A	Pts	PIM	PP	SH	GW	S	%	+/-	TF	F%	Min	GP	G	A	Pts	PIM	PP	SH	GW	Min
1991-92	Laval-Laurentides	QAAA	42	41	50	91	....	....	....	....	....	....	....	....	....	....	12	7	16	23	....	....	....	....	....
1992-93	Laval College	CEGEP	STATISTICS NOT AVAILABLE																						
1993-94	U. of Vermont	ECAC	32	24	21	45	34	....	....	....	....	....	....	....	....	....	....	....	....	....	....	....	....	....	....
1994-95	U. of Vermont	ECAC	35	28	39	67	38	....	....	....	....	....	....	....	....	....	....	....	....	....	....	....	....	....	....
1995-96	U. of Vermont	ECAC	38	29	56	85	38	....	....	....	....	....	....	....	....	....	....	....	....	....	....	....	....	....	....
1996-97	U. of Vermont	ECAC	36	26	33	59	40	....	....	....	....	....	....	....	....	....	....	....	....	....	....	....	....	....	....
1997-98	Cleveland	IHL	69	12	31	43	34	....	....	....	....	....	....	....	....	....	....	....	....	....	....	....	....	....	....
	Quebec Rafales	IHL	13	2	12	14	4	....	....	....	....	....	....	....	....	....	....	....	....	....	....	....	....	....	....
1998-99	Kansas City	IHL	82	24	37	61	71	....	....	....	....	....	....	....	....	....	3	0	0	0	0	....	....	....	....
99-2000	Kansas City	IHL	21	3	15	18	16	....	....	....	....	....	....	....	....	....	....	....	....	....	....	....	....	....	....
2000-01	Jokerit Helsinki	Finland	6	1	1	2	4	....	....	....	....	....	....	....	....	....	....	....	....	....	....	....	....	....	....
	Assat Pori	Finland	43	15	23	38	70	....	....	....	....	....	....	....	....	....	....	....	....	....	....	....	....	....	....
2001-02	Assat Pori	Finland	45	13	13	26	16	....	....	....	....	....	....	....	....	....	....	....	....	....	....	....	....	....	....
	HPK Hameenlinna	Finland	12	5	10	15	4	....	....	....	....	....	....	....	....	....	8	2	4	6	6	....	....	....	....
2002-03	JYP Jyvaskyla	Finland	56	18	28	46	36	....	....	....	....	....	....	....	....	....	7	4	6	10	8	....	....	....	....
2003-04♦	**Tampa Bay**	**NHL**	**4**	**0**	**0**	**0**	**0**	**0**	**0**	**0**	**3**	**0.0**	**-1**	**30**	**60.0**	**8:32**	**12**	**0**	**1**	**1**	**6**	**0**	**0**	**0**	**5:20**
	Hershey Bears	AHL	71	21	54	75	49	....	....	....	....	....	....	....	....	....	....	....	....	....	....	....	....	....	....
2004-05	Hershey Bears	AHL	80	24	49	73	46	....	....	....	....	....	....	....	....	....	....	....	....	....	....	....	....	....	....
2005-06	SC Bern	Swiss	44	13	25	38	28	....	....	....	....	....	....	....	....	....	6	2	4	6	8	....	....	....	....
2006-07	**Tampa Bay**	**NHL**	**82**	**13**	**23**	**36**	**30**	**2**	**1**	**0**	**151**	**8.6**	**-7**	**407**	**50.9**	**17:00**	**6**	**1**	**1**	**2**	**2**	**0**	**0**	**0**	**12:32**
2007-08	**Atlanta**	**NHL**	**81**	**12**	**33**	**45**	**26**	**2**	**2**	**0**	**121**	**9.9**	**-5**	**717**	**53.0**	**17:50**	....	....	....	....	....	....	....	....	....
2008-09	**Atlanta**	**NHL**	**78**	**7**	**16**	**23**	**36**	**1**	**1**	**0**	**109**	**6.4**	**-2**	**213**	**52.1**	**14:11**	....	....	....	....	....	....	....	....	....
2009-10	Omsk	Rus-KHL	55	7	12	19	36	....	....	....	....	....	....	....	....	....	3	1	0	1	16	....	....	....	....
	NHL Totals		**245**	**32**	**72**	**104**	**92**	**5**	**4**	**0**	**384**	**8.3**		**1367**	**52.4**	**16:14**	**18**	**1**	**2**	**3**	**8**	**0**	**0**	**0**	**7:44**

CAC All-Rookie Team (1994) • ECAC Rookie of the Year (1994) • ECAC First All-Star Team (1995, 1996) • ECAC Player of the Year (1996) • NCAA East First All-American Team (1996) • AHL First All-Star eam (2004)

gned as a free agent by **Tampa Bay**, June 19, 2003. Signed as a free agent by **Bern** (Swiss), August 22, 2005. Signed as a free agent by **Atlanta**, July 1, 2007. Signed as a free agent by **Omsk** ussia-KHL), September 2, 2009.

PERRON, David

(peh-RAWN, DAY-vihd) **ST.L.**

Left wing. Shoots right. 6', 200 lbs. Born, Sherbrooke, Que., May 28, 1988. St. Louis' 3rd choice, 26th overall, in 2007 Entry Draft.

Season	Club	League	GP	G	A	Pts	PIM	PP	SH	GW	S	%	+/-	TF	F%	Min	GP	G	A	Pts	PIM	PP	SH	GW	Min
2005-06	St-Jerome	QJHL	51	24	45	69	92	....	....	....	....	....	....	....	....	....	8	4	5	9	8	....	....	....	....
2006-07	Lewiston	QMJHL	70	39	44	83	75	....	....	....	....	....	....	....	....	....	17	12	16	28	22	....	....	....	....
2007-08	**St. Louis**	**NHL**	**62**	**13**	**14**	**27**	**38**	**3**	**0**	**1**	**68**	**19.1**	**16**	**14**	**35.7**	**12:33**	....	....	....	....	....	....	....	....	....
2008-09	**St. Louis**	**NHL**	**81**	**15**	**35**	**50**	**50**	**4**	**0**	**3**	**161**	**9.3**	**13**	**6**	**16.7**	**14:32**	**4**	**1**	**1**	**2**	**4**	**0**	**0**	**0**	**17:12**
2009-10	**St. Louis**	**NHL**	**82**	**20**	**27**	**47**	**60**	**5**	**1**	**2**	**166**	**12.0**	**-10**	**21**	**38.1**	**16:09**	....	....	....	....	....	....	....	....	....
	NHL Totals		**225**	**48**	**76**	**124**	**148**	**12**	**1**	**6**	**395**	**12.2**		**41**	**34.1**	**14:35**	**4**	**1**	**1**	**2**	**4**	**0**	**0**	**0**	**17:12**

PERRY, Corey

(PAIR-ee, KOH-ree) **ANA.**

Right wing. Shoots right. 6'3", 206 lbs. Born, Peterborough, Ont., May 16, 1985. Anaheim's 2nd choice, 28th overall, in 2003 Entry Draft.

Season	Club	League	GP	G	A	Pts	PIM	PP	SH	GW	S	%	+/-	TF	F%	Min	GP	G	A	Pts	PIM	PP	SH	GW	Min
2000-01	Peterborough	Minor-ON	64	69	46	115	20	....	....	....	....	....	....	....	....	....	3	3	0	3	0	....	....	....	....
2001-02	London Knights	OHL	67	28	31	59	56	....	....	....	....	....	....	....	....	....	12	2	3	5	30	....	....	....	....
2002-03	London Knights	OHL	67	25	53	78	145	....	....	....	....	....	....	....	....	....	14	7	16	23	27	....	....	....	....
2003-04	London Knights	OHL	66	40	*73	113	98	....	....	....	....	....	....	....	....	....	15	7	15	22	20	....	....	....	....
	Cincinnati	AHL	....	....	....	....	....	....	....	....	....	....	....	....	....	....	3	1	1	2	4	....	....	....	....
2004-05	London Knights	OHL	60	*47	*83	*130	117	....	....	....	....	....	....	....	....	....	18	11	*27	*38	46	....	....	....	....
2005-06	**Anaheim**	**NHL**	**56**	**13**	**12**	**25**	**50**	**4**	**0**	**2**	**98**	**13.3**	**1**	**11**	**27.3**	**11:34**	**11**	**0**	**3**	**3**	**16**	**0**	**0**	**0**	**9:33**
	Portland Pirates	AHL	19	16	18	34	32	....	....	....	....	....	....	....	....	....	1	1	0	1	0	....	....	....	....
2006-07♦	**Anaheim**	**NHL**	**82**	**17**	**27**	**44**	**55**	**4**	**0**	**3**	**194**	**8.8**	**12**	**21**	**42.9**	**12:28**	**21**	**6**	**9**	**15**	**37**	**1**	**0**	**1**	**16:30**
2007-08	**Anaheim**	**NHL**	**70**	**29**	**25**	**54**	**108**	**11**	**0**	**4**	**200**	**14.5**	**12**	**16**	**18.8**	**17:57**	**3**	**2**	**1**	**3**	**8**	**0**	**0**	**0**	**14:55**
2008-09	**Anaheim**	**NHL**	**78**	**32**	**40**	**72**	**109**	**10**	**0**	**8**	**283**	**11.3**	**10**	**31**	**29.0**	**18:36**	**13**	**8**	**6**	**14**	**36**	**2**	**0**	**1**	**22:00**
2009-10	**Anaheim**	**NHL**	**82**	**27**	**49**	**76**	**111**	**6**	**1**	**2**	**270**	**10.0**	**0**	**28**	**21.4**	**21:04**	....	....	....	....	....	....	....	....	....
	Canada	Olympics	7	4	1	5	2	....	....	....	....	....	....	....	....	....	....	....	....	....	....	....	....	....	....
	NHL Totals		**368**	**118**	**153**	**271**	**433**	**35**	**1**	**19**	**1045**	**11.3**		**107**	**28.0**	**16:35**	**48**	**16**	**19**	**35**	**97**	**3**	**0**	**2**	**16:18**

HL First All-Star Team (2004, 2005) • Canadian Major Junior Second All-Star Team (2004) • Canadian Major Junior First All-Star Team (2005) • Memorial Cup Tournament All-Star Team (2005) • Stafford nythe Memorial Trophy (Memorial Cup Tournament - MVP) (2005)

ayed in NHL All-Star Game (2008)

PESONEN, Janne

(PEHS-oh-nihn, YAH-nee)

Left wing. Shoots left. 5'11", 180 lbs. Born, Suomussalmi, Finland, May 11, 1982. Anaheim's 8th choice, 269th overall, in 2004 Entry Draft.

Season	Club	League	GP	G	A	Pts	PIM	PP	SH	GW	S	%	+/-	TF	F%	Min	GP	G	A	Pts	PIM	PP	SH	GW	Min
1998-99	Hokki Kajaani	Finland-3	2	0	0	0	0	....	....	....	....	....	....	....	....	....	....	....	....	....	....	....	....	....	....
99-2000	Karpat Oulu U18	Fin-U18	33	6	12	18	30	....	....	....	....	....	....	....	....	....	3	0	1	1	0	....	....	....	....
2000-01	Karpat Oulu Jr.	Fin-Jr.	41	9	22	31	18	....	....	....	....	....	....	....	....	....	6	1	1	2	0	....	....	....	....
2001-02	Karpat Oulu Jr.	Fin-Jr.	42	12	19	31	18	....	....	....	....	....	....	....	....	....	3	2	0	2	2	....	....	....	....
	Karpat Oulu	Finland	9	2	0	2	0	....	....	....	....	....	....	....	....	....	1	0	0	0	0	....	....	....	....
2002-03	Hokki Kajaani	Finland-2	40	15	21	36	62	....	....	....	....	....	....	....	....	....	3	2	0	2	4	....	....	....	....
2003-04	Karpat Oulu	Finland	56	17	13	30	28	....	....	....	....	....	....	....	....	....	15	1	1	2	4	....	....	....	....
2004-05	Karpat Oulu	Finland	55	11	18	29	42	....	....	....	....	....	....	....	....	....	12	2	0	2	0	....	....	....	....
2005-06	Karpat Oulu	Finland	53	8	14	22	34	....	....	....	....	....	....	....	....	....	11	4	0	4	8	....	....	....	....
2006-07	Karpat Oulu	Finland	56	22	33	55	38	....	....	....	....	....	....	....	....	....	9	4	3	7	10	....	....	....	....
2007-08	Karpat Oulu	Finland	56	*34	44	*78	58	....	....	....	....	....	....	....	....	....	14	7	9	16	10	....	....	....	....
2008-09	**Pittsburgh**	**NHL**	**7**	**0**	**0**	**0**	**0**	**0**	**0**	**0**	**3**	**0.0**	**-3**	**3**	**0.0**	**7:27**	....	....	....	....	....	....	....	....	....
	Wilkes-Barre	AHL	70	32	50	82	33	....	....	....	....	....	....	....	....	....	5	1	5	6	0	....	....	....	....
2009-10	Ak Bars Kazan	Rus-KHL	42	14	11	25	12	....	....	....	....	....	....	....	....	....	8	1	0	1	4	....	....	....	....
	NHL Totals		**7**	**0**	**0**	**0**	**0**	**0**	**0**	**0**	**3**	**0.0**		**3**	**0.0**	**7:27**	....	....	....	....	....	....	....	....	....

HL Second All-Star Team (2009)

gned as a free agent by **Pittsburgh**, July 7, 2008. Signed as a free agent by **Kazan** (Russia-KHL), August 4, 2009.

PETERS, Andrew

Left wing. Shoots left. 6'4", 240 lbs. Born, St. Catharines, Ont., May 5, 1980. Buffalo's 2nd choice, 34th overall, in 1998 Entry Draft.   (PEE-tuhrz, AN-droo)

Season	Club	League	GP	G	A	Pts	PIM	PP	SH	GW	S	%	+/-	TF	F%	Min	GP	G	A	Pts	PIM	PP	SH	GW	Min
1996-97	Georgetown	OPJHL	46	11	16	27	65																		
1997-98	Oshawa Generals	OHL	60	11	7	18	220																		
1998-99	Oshawa Generals	OHL	54	14	10	24	137										7	2	0	2	19				
99-2000	Kitchener Rangers	OHL	42	6	13	19	95										15	2	7	9	36				
2000-01	Rochester	AHL	49	0	4	4	118										4	0	1	1	14				
2001-02	Rochester	AHL	67	4	1	5	*388																		
2002-03	Rochester	AHL	57	3	0	3	223										3	0	0	0	24				
2003-04	**Buffalo**	**NHL**	42	2	0	2	151	0	0	0	19	10.5	-3	2	0.0	4:10									
2004-05	Bodens IK	Sweden-2	22	2	4	6	195																		
2005-06	**Buffalo**	**NHL**	28	0	0	0	100	0	0	0	6	0.0	-2	2	100.0	3:16									
2006-07	**Buffalo**	**NHL**	58	1	1	2	125	0	0	0	19	5.3	-1	1	0.0	3:46									
2007-08	**Buffalo**	**NHL**	44	1	1	2	100	0	0	0	18	5.6	-4	1	0.0	3:09									
2008-09	**Buffalo**	**NHL**	28	0	1	1	81	0	0	0	10	0.0	-2	1	0.0	4:01									
2009-10	**New Jersey**	**NHL**	29	0	0	0	93	0	0	0	15	0.0	-5	4	50.0	5:12									
	NHL Totals		229	4	3	7	650	0	0	0	87	4.6		10	40.0	3:52									

Signed as a free agent by **Bodens** (Sweden-2), August 20, 2004. • Missed majority of 2008-09 season as a healthy reserve. Signed as a free agent by **New Jersey**, September 25, 2009. • Missed majority of 2009-10 season as a healthy reserve.

PETERS, Warren

Center. Shoots left. 6', 195 lbs. Born, Saskatoon, Sask., July 10, 1982.   (PEE-tuhrz, WAHR-ihn)   **MIN.**

Season	Club	League	GP	G	A	Pts	PIM	PP	SH	GW	S	%	+/-	TF	F%	Min	GP	G	A	Pts	PIM	PP	SH	GW	Min
1998-99	Saskatoon Blades	WHL	53	8	6	14	111																		
99-2000	Saskatoon Blades	WHL	70	11	17	28	97										10	1	2	3	13				
2000-01	Saskatoon Blades	WHL	63	27	14	41	111																		
2001-02	Saskatoon Blades	WHL	72	34	26	60	115										7	1	4	5	13				
2002-03	Saskatoon Blades	WHL	71	31	44	75	108										6	1	6	7	6				
	Portland Pirates	AHL	1	0	0	0	0																		
2003-04	Utah Grizzlies	AHL	55	4	4	8	63																		
	Idaho Steelheads	ECHL	21	6	7	13	33																		
2004-05	Idaho Steelheads	ECHL	69	23	23	46	131										4	0	1	1	12				
2005-06	Omaha	AHL	77	15	10	25	133																		
2006-07	Omaha	AHL	79	17	16	33	95										6	2	1	3	4				
2007-08	Quad City Flames	AHL	75	11	13	24	74																		
2008-09	**Calgary**	**NHL**	16	1	0	1	12	0	0	0	13	7.7	-2	69	58.0	7:05	4	0	0	0	0	0	0	0	7:03
	Quad City Flames	AHL	62	11	6	17	51																		
2009-10	**Dallas**	**NHL**	11	1	0	1	2	0	0	0	8	12.5	1	80	48.8	7:13									
	Texas Stars	AHL	61	20	14	34	52										23	4	4	8	*56				
	NHL Totals		27	2	0	2	14	0	0	0	21	9.5		149	53.0	7:08	4	0	0	0	0	0	0	0	7:03

Signed as a free agent by **Calgary**, August 5, 2005. Signed as a free agent by **Dallas**, July 6, 2009. Signed as a free agent by **Minnesota**, July 2, 2010.

PETERSEN, Toby

Center. Shoots left. 5'10", 198 lbs. Born, Minneapolis, MN, October 27, 1978. Pittsburgh's 9th choice, 244th overall, in 1998 Entry Draft.   (PEE-tuhr-suhn, TOH-bee)   **DAL.**

Season	Club	League	GP	G	A	Pts	PIM	PP	SH	GW	S	%	+/-	TF	F%	Min	GP	G	A	Pts	PIM	PP	SH	GW	Min
1995-96	Jefferson Jaguars	High-MN	25	29	30	59																			
1996-97	Colorado College	WCHA	40	17	21	38	18																		
1997-98	Colorado College	WCHA	40	16	17	33	34																		
1998-99	Colorado College	WCHA	21	12	12	24	2																		
99-2000	Colorado College	WCHA	37	14	19	33	8																		
2000-01	**Pittsburgh**	**NHL**	12	2	6	8	4	0	0	1	25	8.0	3	39	35.9	13:22									
	Wilkes-Barre	AHL	73	26	41	67	22										21	7	6	13	4				
2001-02	**Pittsburgh**	**NHL**	79	8	10	18	4	1	1	0	116	6.9	-15	338	45.6	12:16									
2002-03	Wilkes-Barre	AHL	80	31	35	66	24										6	1	3	4	4				
2003-04	Wilkes-Barre	AHL	62	15	29	44	4										21	2	10	12	12				
2004-05	Edmonton	AHL	78	14	15	29	21																		
2005-06	**Edmonton**	**NHL**															2	1	0	1	0	0	0	0	6:23
	Iowa Stars	AHL	79	26	47	73	48										7	2	4	6	2				
2006-07	**Edmonton**	**NHL**	64	6	9	15	4	0	2	1	92	6.5	-18	214	48.1	13:40									
	Iowa Stars	AHL	7	2	6	8	0																		
2007-08	**Dallas**	**NHL**	8	0	3	3	4	0	0	0	6	0.0		44	50.0	7:50	16	0	0	0	2	0	0	0	9:45
	Iowa Stars	AHL	63	21	30	51	24																		
2008-09	**Dallas**	**NHL**	57	4	7	11	14	0	0	0	80	5.0	1	283	45.2	11:25									
2009-10	**Dallas**	**NHL**	78	9	6	15	6	0	1	0	110	8.2	3	171	44.4	10:55									
	NHL Totals		298	29	41	70	36	1	4	2	429	6.8		1089	45.6	11:59	18	1	0	1	2	0	0	0	9:23

WCHA All-Rookie Team (1997) • AHL All-Rookie Team (2001)
Signed as a free agent by **Edmonton**, July 30, 2004. Signed as a free agent by **Dallas**, July 6, 2007.

PETIOT, Richard

Defense. Shoots left. 6'4", 215 lbs. Born, Daysland, Alta., August 20, 1982. Los Angeles' 6th choice, 116th overall, in 2001 Entry Draft.   (PEH-tee-awt, RIH-chuhrd)   **EDM.**

Season	Club	League	GP	G	A	Pts	PIM	PP	SH	GW	S	%	+/-	TF	F%	Min	GP	G	A	Pts	PIM	PP	SH	GW	Min
2000-01	Camrose Kodiaks	AJHL	55	8	16	24	81										8	2	1	3	8				
2001-02	Colorado College	WCHA	39	4	6	10	35																		
2002-03	Colorado College	WCHA	38	1	6	7	86																		
2003-04	Colorado College	WCHA	39	3	5	8	61																		
2004-05	Colorado College	WCHA	26	3	5	8	42																		
2005-06	**Los Angeles**	**NHL**	2	0	0	0	0	0	0	0	1	0.0	-2	0	0.0	4:47									
	Manchester	AHL	63	4	10	14	52										7	1	0	1	6				
2006-07	Manchester	AHL	13	1	1	2	25										2	0	0	0	2				
2007-08	Manchester	AHL	40	2	5	7	56																		
2008-09	Toronto Marlies	AHL	45	3	11	14	59																		
	Tampa Bay	**NHL**	11	0	3	3	21	0	0	0	10	0.0	5	0	0.0	20:37									
2009-10	Norfolk Admirals	AHL	1	0	0	0	0																		
	Rockford IceHogs	AHL	80	8	29	37	88										4	0	0	0	4				
	NHL Totals		13	0	3	3	23	0	0	0	11	0.0		0	0.0	18:11									

AJHL All-Rookie Team (2001) • AJHL South Second All-Star Team (2001)
• Missed majority of 2006-07 season recovering from knee injury suffered in rookie training camp and resulting surgery, October 6, 2006. Signed as a free agent by **Toronto**, July 15, 2008. Traded to **Tampa Bay** by **Toronto** for Olaf Kolzig, Jamie Heward, Andy Rogers and Carolina's 4th round choice (previously acquired – later forfeited) in 2009 Entry Draft, March 4, 2009. Signed as a free agent by **Chicago**, July 9, 2009.

PETRUZALEK, Jakub

Center/Right wing. Shoots right. 5'10", 176 lbs. Born, Most, Czech., April 24, 1985. NY Rangers' 13th choice, 266th overall, in 2004 Entry Draft.   (peh-troo-ZAL-ehk, YA-kuhb)

Season	Club	League	GP	G	A	Pts	PIM	PP	SH	GW	S	%	+/-	TF	F%	Min	GP	G	A	Pts	PIM	PP	SH	GW	Min
2002-03	Litvinov Jr.	CzRep-Jr.	21	17	13	30	10																		
	Litvinov	CzRep	5	0	0	0	0																		
2003-04	Litvinov Jr.	CzRep-Jr.	53	38	51	89	110										2	0	0	0	0				
	Litvinov	CzRep	7	0	0	0	2																		
	Most	CzRep-3	0	0	0	0	0																		
2004-05	Ottawa 67's	OHL	59	23	40	63	64										21	8	10	18	30				
2005-06	Litvinov Jr.	CzRep-Jr.	3	4	2	6	4																		
	Litvinov	CzRep	19	1	1	2	6																		
	Barrie Colts	OHL	24	11	20	31	28										14	8	11	19	14				
2006-07	Hartford	AHL	6	0	2	2	0																		
	Charlotte	ECHL	7	1	9	10	4																		
	Albany River Rats	AHL	54	10	18	28	16										5	2	2	4	10				
2007-08	Albany River Rats	AHL	78	14	31	45	52										7	2	1	3	8				

			Regular Season														Playoffs								
Season	Club	League	GP	G	A	Pts	PIM	PP	SH	GW	S	%	+/-	TF	F%	Min	GP	G	A	Pts	PIM	PP	SH	GW	Min
2008-09	Carolina	NHL	2	0	1	1	0	0	0	0	0	0.0	1	7	57.1	8:05	....	....	....	....	....	....	....	....	....
	Albany River Rats	AHL	77	19	35	54	35	....	....	....	....	....	....	....	....	....	....	....	....	....	....	....	....	....	....
2009-10	Lukko Rauma	Finland	55	17	24	41	78	....	....	....	....	....	....	....	....	....	4	0	1	1	4	....	....	....	....
	NHL Totals		2	0	1	1	0	0	0	0	0	0.0		7	57.1	8:04	....	....	....	....	....	....	....	....	....

raded to **Carolina** by **NY Rangers** with future considerations for Brad Isbister, November 21, 2006. Signed as a free agent by **Rauma** (Finland), May 15, 2009.

PETTINGER, Matt

(PEH-tihn-juhr, MAT)

Left wing. Shoots left. 6'1", 205 lbs. Born, Edmonton, Alta., October 22, 1980. Washington's 2nd choice, 43rd overall, in 2000 Entry Draft.

1994-95	Victoria Racquet	Minor-BC	55	52	48	100	41	....	....	....	....	....	....	....	....	....	....	....	....	....	....	....	....	....	....
1995-96	Victoria Racquet	Minor-BC	60	80	65	145	45	....	....	....	....	....	....	....	....	....	....	....	....	....	....	....	....	....	....
1996-97	Victoria Salsa	BCHL	49	22	14	36	31	....	....	....	....	....	....	....	....	....	....	....	....	....	....	....	....	....	....
1997-98	Victoria Salsa	BCHL	55	22	20	42	56	....	....	....	....	....	....	....	....	....	7	5	1	6	8	....	....	....	....
1998-99	U. of Denver	WCHA	33	6	14	20	44	....	....	....	....	....	....	....	....	....	....	....	....	....	....	....	....	....	....
99-2000	U. of Denver	WCHA	19	2	6	8	49	....	....	....	....	....	....	....	....	....	....	....	....	....	....	....	....	....	....
	Calgary Hitmen	WHL	27	14	6	20	41	....	....	....	....	....	....	....	....	....	11	2	6	8	30	....	....	....	....
2000-01	Washington	NHL	10	0	0	0	2	0	0	0	6	0.0	–1	2	50.0	7:47	....	....	....	....	....	....	....	....	....
	Portland Pirates	AHL	64	19	17	36	92	....	....	....	....	....	....	....	....	....	2	0	0	0	4	....	....	....	....
2001-02	Washington	NHL	61	7	3	10	44	1	0	1	73	9.6	–8	5	20.0	9:39	....	....	....	....	....	....	....	....	....
	Portland Pirates	AHL	9	3	3	6	24	....	....	....	....	....	....	....	....	....	....	....	....	....	....	....	....	....	....
2002-03	Washington	NHL	1	0	0	0	0	0	0	0	0	0.0	0	1	0.0	3:30	....	....	....	....	....	....	....	....	....
	Portland Pirates	AHL	69	14	13	27	72	....	....	....	....	....	....	....	....	....	3	0	2	2	2	....	....	....	....
2003-04	Washington	NHL	71	7	5	12	37	1	0	1	92	7.6	–9	18	44.4	11:25	....	....	....	....	....	....	....	....	....
2004-05	Ljubljana	Slovenia	1	0	1	1	0	....	....	....	....	....	....	....	....	....	....	....	....	....	....	....	....	....	....
	Ljubljana	Interliga	7	2	4	6	41	....	....	....	....	....	....	....	....	....	....	....	....	....	....	....	....	....	....
2005-06	Washington	NHL	71	20	18	38	39	4	5	2	134	14.9	–2	39	12.8	15:29	....	....	....	....	....	....	....	....	....
2006-07	Washington	NHL	64	16	16	32	22	4	3	2	111	14.4	–13	23	30.4	16:53	....	....	....	....	....	....	....	....	....
2007-08	Washington	NHL	56	2	5	7	25	1	0	1	98	2.0	–11	12	58.3	14:43	....	....	....	....	....	....	....	....	....
	Vancouver	NHL	20	4	2	6	11	0	0	2	29	13.8	0	7	57.1	13:10	....	....	....	....	....	....	....	....	....
2008-09	Manitoba Moose	AHL	2	3	0	3	0	....	....	....	....	....	....	....	....	....	....	....	....	....	....	....	....	....	....
	Tampa Bay	NHL	59	8	7	15	24	2	0	1	82	9.8	–14	18	16.7	12:19	....	....	....	....	....	....	....	....	....
2009-10	Vancouver	NHL	9	1	2	3	6	0	0	0	8	12.5	3	13	23.1	10:45	1	0	0	0	0	0	0	0	4:12
	Manitoba Moose	AHL	54	14	16	30	31	....	....	....	....	....	....	....	....	....	....	....	....	....	....	....	....	....	....
	NHL Totals		422	65	58	123	210	13	8	10	633	10.3		138	28.3	13:12	1	0	0	0	0	0	0	0	4:12

• Left **University of Denver** (WCHA) and signed as a free agent with **Calgary** (WHL), January 10, 2000. Signed as a free agent by **Ljubljana** (Slovenia), December 6, 2004. Traded to **Vancouver** by **Vashington** for Matt Cooke, February 26, 2008. Claimed on waivers by **Tampa Bay** from **Vancouver**, October 21, 2008. Signed as a free agent by **Vancouver**, November 2, 2009. Signed as a free agent y **Koln** (Germany). August 6, 2010.

PEVERLEY, Rich

(PEH-vuhr-lee, RIHTCH) **ATL.**

Center. Shoots right. 6', 200 lbs. Born, Guelph, Ont., July 8, 1982.

2000-01	St. Lawrence	ECAC	29	2	4	6	4	....	....	....	....	....	....	....	....	....	....	....	....	....	....	....	....	....	....
2001-02	St. Lawrence	ECAC	34	10	21	31	18	....	....	....	....	....	....	....	....	....	....	....	....	....	....	....	....	....	....
2002-03	St. Lawrence	ECAC	34	15	23	38	12	....	....	....	....	....	....	....	....	....	....	....	....	....	....	....	....	....	....
2003-04	St. Lawrence	ECAC	41	17	25	42	34	....	....	....	....	....	....	....	....	....	....	....	....	....	....	....	....	....	....
2004-05	Portland Pirates	AHL	1	0	0	0	0	....	....	....	....	....	....	....	....	....	....	....	....	....	....	....	....	....	....
	South Carolina	ECHL	69	30	28	58	72	....	....	....	....	....	....	....	....	....	4	2	2	4	6	....	....	....	....
2005-06	Milwaukee	AHL	65	12	34	46	44	....	....	....	....	....	....	....	....	....	21	2	9	11	18	....	....	....	....
	Reading Royals	ECHL	11	4	11	15	4	....	....	....	....	....	....	....	....	....	....	....	....	....	....	....	....	....	....
2006-07	Milwaukee	AHL	66	30	38	68	62	....	....	....	....	....	....	....	....	....	4	1	2	3	8	....	....	....	....
	Nashville	NHL	13	0	1	1	0	0	0	0	9	0.0	–1	45	48.9	7:31	....	....	....	....	....	....	....	....	....
2007-08	Nashville	NHL	33	5	5	10	8	0	0	2	43	11.6	4	132	46.2	10:20	6	0	2	2	0	0	0	0	8:52
	Milwaukee	AHL	45	14	40	54	50	....	....	....	....	....	....	....	....	....	3	1	0	1	0	....	....	....	....
2008-09	Nashville	NHL	27	2	7	9	15	0	0	0	42	4.8	–3	130	49.2	12:08	....	....	....	....	....	....	....	....	....
	Atlanta	NHL	39	13	22	35	18	2	1	5	75	17.3	16	554	52.4	18:49	....	....	....	....	....	....	....	....	....
2009-10	Atlanta	NHL	82	22	33	55	36	7	2	7	166	13.3	–14	1193	54.2	18:40	....	....	....	....	....	....	....	....	....
	NHL Totals		194	42	68	110	77	9	3	14	335	12.5		2054	52.8	15:37	6	0	2	2	0	0	0	0	8:52

igned as a free agent by **Nashville**, January 18, 2007. Claimed on waivers by **Atlanta** from **Nashville**, January 10, 2009.

PHANEUF, Dion

(fah-NUF, DEE-awn) **TOR.**

Defense. Shoots left. 6'3", 214 lbs. Born, Edmonton, Alta., April 10, 1985. Calgary's 1st choice, 9th overall, in 2003 Entry Draft.

2000-01	Southgate Lions	AMBHL	35	15	50	65	208	....	....	....	....	....	....	....	....	....	4	3	4	7	15	....	....	....	....
2001-02	Red Deer Rebels	WHL	67	5	12	17	170	....	....	....	....	....	....	....	....	....	21	0	2	2	14	....	....	....	....
2002-03	Red Deer Rebels	WHL	71	16	14	30	185	....	....	....	....	....	....	....	....	....	23	7	7	14	34	....	....	....	....
2003-04	Red Deer Rebels	WHL	62	19	24	43	126	....	....	....	....	....	....	....	....	....	19	2	9	11	30	....	....	....	....
2004-05	Red Deer Rebels	WHL	55	24	32	56	73	....	....	....	....	....	....	....	....	....	7	1	4	5	12	....	....	....	....
2005-06	Calgary	NHL	82	20	29	49	93	16	0	7	242	8.3	5	0	0.0	21:44	7	1	0	1	7	1	0	0	18:37
2006-07	Calgary	NHL	79	17	33	50	98	13	0	4	230	7.4	10	0	0.0	25:40	6	1	0	1	7	1	0	0	26:24
2007-08	Calgary	NHL	82	17	43	60	182	10	1	4	263	6.5	12	0	0.0	26:25	7	3	4	7	4	1	0	0	27:07
2008-09	Calgary	NHL	80	11	36	47	100	4	0	4	277	4.0	–11	0	0.0	26:32	5	0	3	3	4	0	0	0	24:48
2009-10	Calgary	NHL	55	10	12	22	49	5	0	2	138	7.2	3	0	0.0	23:14	....	....	....	....	....	....	....	....	....
	Toronto	NHL	26	2	8	10	34	0	0	1	87	2.3	–2	0	0.0	26:22	....	....	....	....	....	....	....	....	....
	NHL Totals		404	77	161	238	556	48	1	22	1237	6.2		0	0.0	24:54	25	5	7	12	22	3	0	0	24:06

VHL East First All-Star Team (2004, 2005) • WHL Defenseman of the Year (2004, 2005) • Canadian Major Junior First All-Star Team (2004, 2005) • NHL All-Rookie Team (2006) • NHL First All-Star Team 2008)

layed in NHL All-Star Game (2007, 2008)

raded to **Toronto** by **Calgary** with Fredrik Sjostrom and Keith Aulie for Matt Stajan, Niklas Hagman, Jamal Mayers and Ian White, January 31, 2010.

PHILLIPS, Chris

(FIHL-ihps, KRIHS) **OTT.**

Defense. Shoots left. 6'3", 216 lbs. Born, Calgary, Alta., March 9, 1978. Ottawa's 1st choice, 1st overall, in 1996 Entry Draft.

1993-94	Fort McMurray	AJHL	56	6	16	22	72	....	....	....	....	....	....	....	....	....	10	0	3	3	16	....	....	....	....
1994-95	Fort McMurray	AJHL	48	16	32	48	127	....	....	....	....	....	....	....	....	....	11	4	2	6	10	....	....	....	....
1995-96	Prince Albert	WHL	61	10	30	40	97	....	....	....	....	....	....	....	....	....	18	2	12	14	30	....	....	....	....
1996-97	Prince Albert	WHL	32	3	23	26	58	....	....	....	....	....	....	....	....	....	....	....	....	....	....	....	....	....	....
	Lethbridge	WHL	26	4	18	22	28	....	....	....	....	....	....	....	....	....	19	4	*21	25	20	....	....	....	....
1997-98	Ottawa	NHL	72	5	11	16	38	2	0	2	107	4.7	2	....	....	....	11	0	2	2	2	0	0	0	....
1998-99	Ottawa	NHL	34	3	3	6	32	2	0	0	51	5.9	–5	0	0.0	18:06	3	0	0	0	0	0	0	0	13:50
99-2000	Ottawa	NHL	65	5	14	19	39	0	0	1	96	5.2	12	0	0.0	16:50	6	0	1	1	4	0	0	0	18:17
2000-01	Ottawa	NHL	73	2	12	14	31	2	0	0	77	2.6	8	1	0.0	21:28	1	1	0	1	0	0	0	0	20:52
2001-02	Ottawa	NHL	63	6	16	22	29	1	0	1	103	5.8	5	0	0.0	19:31	12	0	0	0	12	0	0	0	21:44
2002-03	Ottawa	NHL	78	3	16	19	71	2	0	1	97	3.1	7	0	0.0	20:13	18	2	4	6	12	0	0	1	21:36
2003-04	Ottawa	NHL	82	7	16	23	46	0	0	1	93	7.5	15	1	100.0	20:50	7	1	0	1	12	1	0	0	20:26
2004-05	Brynas IF Gavle	Sweden	27	5	3	8	45	....	....	....	....	....	....	....	....	....	....	....	....	....	....	....	....	....	....
	Brynas IF Gavle	Sweden-Q	9	1	2	3	2	....	....	....	....	....	....	....	....	....	....	....	....	....	....	....	....	....	....
2005-06	Ottawa	NHL	69	1	18	19	90	0	0	0	79	1.3	19	0	0.0	20:52	9	2	0	2	6	0	0	0	21:41
2006-07	Ottawa	NHL	82	8	18	26	80	0	1	3	94	8.5	36	2	0.0	22:22	20	0	0	0	24	0	0	0	23:11
2007-08	Ottawa	NHL	81	5	13	18	56	1	0	1	80	6.3	15	1	0.0	22:29	4	0	0	0	4	0	0	0	22:00
2008-09	Ottawa	NHL	82	6	16	22	66	0	1	0	88	6.8	–14	0	0.0	21:52	....	....	....	....	....	....	....	....	....
2009-10	Ottawa	NHL	82	8	16	24	45	1	1	2	82	9.8	8	0	0.0	22:21	6	0	0	0	4	0	0	0	24:57
	NHL Totals		863	59	169	228	623	11	3	12	1047	5.6		5	20.0	20:52	97	6	7	13	80	1	0	1	21:39

VHL Rookie of the Year (1996) • WHL East First All-Star Team (1997) • Canadian Major Junior First All-Star Team (1997) • Memorial Cup Tournament All-Star Team (1997)

Missed majority of 1998-99 season recovering from ankle injury suffered in game vs. Buffalo, December 30, 1998. Signed as a free agent by **Gavle** (Sweden), November 2, 2004.

PICARD, Alexandre
(pee-KARD, al-ehx-AHN-druh) **MTL.**

Defense. Shoots left. 6'3", 215 lbs. Born, Gatineau, Que., July 5, 1985. Philadelphia's 5th choice, 85th overall, in 2003 Entry Draft.

			Regular Season														Playoffs								
Season	Club	League	GP	G	A	Pts	PIM	PP	SH	GW	S	%	+/-	TF	F%	Min	GP	G	A	Pts	PIM	PP	SH	GW	Min
2000-01	Gatineau	QAAA	42	6	15	21	38										11	0	1	1	8				
2001-02	Halifax	QMJHL	59	2	12	14	28										13	2	3	5	6				
2002-03	Halifax	QMJHL	71	4	30	34	64										25	1	5	6	14				
2003-04	Cape Breton	QMJHL	57	10	26	36	44										5	0	0	0	0				
2004-05	Halifax	QMJHL	68	15	23	38	46										13	1	5	6	14				
	Philadelphia	AHL															2	0	0	0	0				
2005-06	**Philadelphia**	**NHL**	**6**	**0**	**0**	**0**	**4**	**0**	**0**	**0**	**9**	**0.0**	**–2**	**0**	**0.0**	**9:33**									
	Philadelphia	AHL	75	7	26	33	82																		
2006-07	**Philadelphia**	**NHL**	**62**	**3**	**19**	**22**	**17**	**1**	**0**	**0**	**56**	**5.4**	**–19**	**0**	**0.0**	**18:29**									
	Philadelphia	AHL	6	1	2	3	2																		
2007-08	**Philadelphia**	**NHL**	**4**	**0**	**0**	**0**	**2**	**0**	**0**	**0**	**3**	**0.0**	**–3**	**0**	**0.0**	**13:02**									
	Philadelphia	AHL	53	8	30	38	31																		
	Tampa Bay	**NHL**	**20**	**3**	**3**	**6**	**8**	**1**	**0**	**1**	**21**	**14.3**	**–9**	**0**	**0.0**	**21:54**									
	Norfolk Admirals	AHL	1	0	0	0	0																		
2008-09	**Ottawa**	**NHL**	**47**	**6**	**8**	**14**	**8**	**6**	**0**	**1**	**72**	**8.3**	**–2**	**0**	**0.0**	**18:52**									
2009-10	**Ottawa**	**NHL**	**45**	**4**	**11**	**15**	**20**	**1**	**0**	**1**	**64**	**6.3**	**–2**	**0**	**0.0**	**19:03**									
	Carolina	**NHL**	**9**	**0**	**0**	**0**	**6**	**0**	**0**	**0**	**7**	**0.0**	**2**	**0**	**0.0**	**15:04**									
	NHL Totals		**193**	**16**	**41**	**57**	**65**	**9**	**0**	**3**	**232**	**6.9**		**0**	**0.0**	**18:31**									

QMJHL Second All-Star Team (2005)

Traded to **Tampa Bay** by **Philadelphia** with Philadelphia's 2nd round choice (Richard Panik) in 2009 Entry Draft for Vaclav Prospal, February 25, 2008. Traded to **Ottawa** by **Tampa Bay** with Filip Kuba and San Jose's 1st round choice (previously acquired, later traded to Columbus, later traded to NY Islanders, later traded to Anaheim - Anaheim selected Kyle Palmieri) in 2009 Entry Draft for Andrej Meszaros, August 29, 2008. Traded to **Carolina** by **Ottawa** with Ottawa's 2nd round choice (later traded to Edmonton - Edmonton selected Martin Marincin) in 2010 Entry Draft for Matt Cullen, February 12, 2010. Signed as a free agent by **Montreal**, July 31, 2010.

PICARD, Alexandre
(pee-KARD, al-ehx-AHN-druh) **PHX.**

Left wing. Shoots left. 6'2", 206 lbs. Born, Les Saules, Que., October 9, 1985. Columbus' 1st choice, 8th overall, in 2004 Entry Draft.

			Regular Season														Playoffs								
Season	Club	League	GP	G	A	Pts	PIM	PP	SH	GW	S	%	+/-	TF	F%	Min	GP	G	A	Pts	PIM	PP	SH	GW	Min
2000-01	St-Francois	QAAA	5	1	1	2	0																		
2001-02	St-Francois	QAAA	41	21	30	51	48										8	2	7	9	8				
	Sherbrooke	QMJHL	6	0	3	3	0																		
2002-03	Sherbrooke	QMJHL	66	14	15	29	41										12	4	0	4	10				
2003-04	Lewiston	QMJHL	69	39	41	80	88										7	7	4	11	6				
2004-05	Lewiston	QMJHL	65	40	45	85	160										8	5	2	7	18				
2005-06	**Columbus**	**NHL**	**17**	**0**	**0**	**0**	**14**	**0**	**0**	**0**	**10**	**0.0**	**–2**	**3**	**33.3**	**9:09**									
	Syracuse Crunch	AHL	45	15	15	30	54										6	1	0	1	19				
2006-07	**Columbus**	**NHL**	**23**	**0**	**1**	**1**	**6**	**0**	**0**	**0**	**20**	**0.0**	**–3**	**0**	**0.0**	**7:49**									
	Syracuse Crunch	AHL	48	11	18	29	73																		
2007-08	**Columbus**	**NHL**	**3**	**0**	**0**	**0**	**2**	**0**	**0**	**0**	**1**	**0.0**	**0**	**0**	**0.0**	**6:46**									
	Syracuse Crunch	AHL	50	7	13	20	116										13	2	1	3	14				
2008-09	**Columbus**	**NHL**	**15**	**0**	**1**	**1**	**26**	**0**	**0**	**0**	**10**	**0.0**	**–1**	**0**	**0.0**	**6:53**									
	Syracuse Crunch	AHL	49	22	10	32	107																		
2009-10	**Columbus**	**NHL**	**9**	**0**	**0**	**0**	**10**	**0**	**0**	**0**	**12**	**0.0**	**–3**	**0**	**0.0**	**7:13**									
	Syracuse Crunch	AHL	42	17	18	35	111																		
	San Antonio	AHL	16	9	6	15	14																		
	NHL Totals		**67**	**0**	**2**	**2**	**58**	**0**	**0**	**0**	**53**	**0.0**		**3**	**33.3**	**7:49**									

QMJHL Second All-Star Team (2004)

Traded to **Phoenix** by **Columbus** for Chad Kolarik, March 3, 2010.

PIETRANGELO, Alex
(puh-TRAN-geh-loh, AL-ehx) **ST.L.**

Defense. Shoots right. 6'3", 206 lbs. Born, King City, Ont., January 18, 1990. St. Louis' 1st choice, 4th overall, in 2008 Entry Draft.

			Regular Season														Playoffs								
Season	Club	League	GP	G	A	Pts	PIM	PP	SH	GW	S	%	+/-	TF	F%	Min	GP	G	A	Pts	PIM	PP	SH	GW	Min
2005-06	Tor. Jr. Canadiens	GTHL	44	13	31	44	33																		
2006-07	Mississauga	OHL	59	7	45	52	45										4	0	0	0	8				
2007-08	Niagara Ice Dogs	OHL	60	13	40	53	94										6	5	4	9	4				
2008-09	Niagara Ice Dogs	OHL	36	8	21	29	32										12	1	5	6	20				
	St. Louis	**NHL**	**8**	**0**	**1**	**1**	**2**	**0**	**0**	**0**	**7**	**0.0**	**0**	**0**	**0.0**	**16:31**									
	Peoria Rivermen	AHL	1	0	0	0	4										7	0	3	3	2				
2009-10	**St. Louis**	**NHL**	**9**	**1**	**1**	**2**	**6**	**0**	**0**	**0**	**7**	**14.3**	**–9**	**0**	**0.0**	**16:34**									
	Barrie Colts	OHL	25	9	20	29	27										17	2	12	14	8				
	NHL Totals		**17**	**1**	**2**	**3**	**8**	**0**	**0**	**0**	**14**	**7.1**		**0**	**0.0**	**16:33**									

• Missed majority of 2009-10 season as a healthy reserve.

PIHLSTROM, Antti
(PIHL-stuhm, AN-tee) **NSH.**

Left wing. Shoots left. 5'11", 190 lbs. Born, Vanntaa, Finland, October 22, 1984.

			Regular Season														Playoffs								
Season	Club	League	GP	G	A	Pts	PIM	PP	SH	GW	S	%	+/-	TF	F%	Min	GP	G	A	Pts	PIM	PP	SH	GW	Min
2001-02	Jokerit U18	Fin-U18	26	15	14	29	41										8	0	5	5	18				
	Jokerit Helsinki Jr.	Fin-Jr.	1	0	0	0	0																		
2002-03	Blues Espoo Jr.	Fin-Jr.	36	10	16	26	38										10	1	1	2	8				
2003-04	Blues Espoo Jr.	Fin-Jr.	23	9	19	28	42										1	0	2	2	0				
	Suomi U20	Finland-2	4	0	1	1	2																		
	Blues Espoo	Finland	49	1	3	4	18										9	0	0	0	0				
2004-05	Blues Espoo	Finland	53	4	3	7	30																		
	Blues Espoo Jr.	Fin-Jr.	11	7	3	10	36										7	0	2	2	26				
2005-06	SaiPa	Finland	54	10	11	21	60										8	1	0	1	2				
2006-07	HPK Hameenlinna	Finland	56	16	23	39	63										9	3	5	8	4				
2007-08	**Nashville**	**NHL**	**1**	**0**	**0**	**0**	**0**	**0**	**0**	**0**	**1**	**0.0**	**–1**	**0**	**0.0**	**9:08**									
	Milwaukee	AHL	78	27	18	45	62										6	1	0	1	8				
2008-09	**Nashville**	**NHL**	**53**	**2**	**5**	**7**	**10**	**1**	**0**	**0**	**88**	**2.3**	**–1**	**1**	**0.0**	**11:27**									
	Milwaukee	AHL	15	8	4	12	10																		
2009-10	Farjestad	Sweden	43	4	6	10	44																		
	JYP Jyvaskyla	Finland	19	7	14	21	14										14	4	4	8	18				
	NHL Totals		**54**	**2**	**5**	**7**	**10**	**1**	**0**	**0**	**89**	**2.2**		**1**	**0.0**	**11:24**									

Signed as a free agent by **Nashville**, June 1, 2007. Signed as a free agent by **Farjestad** (Sweden), August 6, 2009. • Loaned to **Jyvaskyla** (Finland) by **Farjestad** (Sweden), January 29, 2010.

PIKKARAINEN, Ilkka
(pih-kar-AY-nihn, IHL-kah)

Right wing. Shoots right. 6'2", 215 lbs. Born, Sonkajarvi, Finland, April 19, 1981. New Jersey's 9th choice, 218th overall, in 2002 Entry Draft.

			Regular Season														Playoffs								
Season	Club	League	GP	G	A	Pts	PIM	PP	SH	GW	S	%	+/-	TF	F%	Min	GP	G	A	Pts	PIM	PP	SH	GW	Min
1998-99	HIFK Helsinki U18	Fin-U18	24	6	12	18	26										2	1	0	1	27				
	HIFK Helsinki Jr.	Fin-Jr.	13	6	1	7	12																		
99-2000	HIFK Helsinki Jr.	Fin-Jr.	28	3	2	5	14										3	1	1	2	2				
2000-01	HIFK Helsinki Jr.	Fin-Jr.	38	27	31	58	186										9	2	5	7	26				
	HIFK Helsinki	Finland	4	0	0	0	8										2	0	0	0	0				
2001-02	HIFK Helsinki	Finland	54	9	9	18	111																		
2002-03	HIFK Helsinki	Finland	47	11	12	23	40																		
2003-04	Albany River Rats	AHL	63	8	10	18	118																		
2004-05	Albany River Rats	AHL	71	12	12	24	102																		
2005-06	Albany River Rats	AHL	62	9	11	20	85																		
2006-07	HIFK Helsinki	Finland	53	17	20	37	140										5	0	1	1	2				
2007-08	HIFK Helsinki	Finland	37	8	10	18	100										7	1	2	3	6				
2008-09	HIFK Helsinki	Finland	54	24	13	37	149										2	0	0	0	0				
2009-10	**New Jersey**	**NHL**	**31**	**1**	**3**	**4**	**10**	**0**	**0**	**0**	**26**	**3.8**	**–3**	**6**	**16.7**	**8:09**									
	Lowell Devils	AHL	1	0	0	0	0																		
	CSKA Moscow	Rus-KHL	6	0	2	2	0										3	0	0	0	6				
	NHL Totals		**31**	**1**	**3**	**4**	**10**	**0**	**0**	**0**	**26**	**3.8**		**6**	**16.7**	**8:09**									

• Assigned to **CSKA Moscow** (Russia-KHL) by **New Jersey**, January 28, 2010. Signed as a free agent by **Timra** (Sweden), May 27, 2010.

PINEAULT, Adam

(PEE-noh, A-duhm)

Right wing. Shoots right. 6'1", 211 lbs. Born, Holyoke, MA, May 23, 1986. Columbus' 2nd choice, 46th overall, in 2004 Entry Draft.

			Regular Season														Playoffs								
Season	Club	League	GP	G	A	Pts	PIM	PP	SH	GW	S	%	+/-	TF	F%	Min	GP	G	A	Pts	PIM	PP	SH	GW	Min
2000-01	Bos. Jr. Bruins	EJHL	57	30	35	65	56	....	....	....	....	....	....	....	....	....	....	....	....	....	....	....	....	....	....
2001-02	USNTDP	U-17	20	5	4	9	14	....	....	....	....	....	....	....	....	....	....	....	....	....	....	....	....	....	....
	USNTDP	NAHL	38	11	4	15	11	....	....	....	....	....	....	....	....	....	....	....	....	....	....	....	....	....	....
2002-03	USNTDP	U-17	43	13	15	28	76	....	....	....	....	....	....	....	....	....	....	....	....	....	....	....	....	....	....
	USNTDP	U-18	4	4	3	7	6	....	....	....	....	....	....	....	....	....	....	....	....	....	....	....	....	....	....
	USNTDP	NAHL	9	5	4	9	13	....	....	....	....	....	....	....	....	....	....	....	....	....	....	....	....	....	....
2003-04	Boston College	H-East	30	4	4	8	32	....	....	....	....	....	....	....	....	....	....	....	....	....	....	....	....	....	....
2004-05	Moncton Wildcats	QMJHL	61	26	20	46	64	....	....	....	....	....	....	....	....	....	12	2	6	8	18	....	....	....	....
2005-06	Moncton Wildcats	QMJHL	55	29	30	59	94	....	....	....	....	....	....	....	....	....	21	14	8	22	25	....	....	....	....
2006-07	Syracuse Crunch	AHL	57	12	16	28	66	....	....	....	....	....	....	....	....	....	....	....	....	....	....	....	....	....	....
2007-08	**Columbus**	**NHL**	**3**	**0**	**0**	**0**	**0**	**0**	**0**	**0**	**5**	**0.0**	**-2**	**1**	**0.0**	**11:03**	....	....	....	....	....	....	....	....	....
	Syracuse Crunch	AHL	74	21	27	48	64	....	....	....	....	....	....	....	....	....	8	0	2	2	2	....	....	....	....
2008-09	Syracuse Crunch	AHL	29	5	7	12	36	....	....	....	....	....	....	....	....	....	....	....	....	....	....	....	....	....	....
	Rockford IceHogs	AHL	41	5	9	14	16	....	....	....	....	....	....	....	....	....	4	0	0	0	2	....	....	....	....
2009-10	Pardubice	CzRep	31	10	10	20	67	....	....	....	....	....	....	....	....	....	13	0	5	5	12	....	....	....	....
	NHL Totals		**3**	**0**	**0**	**0**	**0**	**0**	**0**	**0**	**5**	**0.0**		**1**	**0.0**	**11:03**	....	....	....	....	....	....	....	....	....

lemorial Cup Tournament All-Star Team (2006)

raded to **Chicago** by **Columbus** for Michael Blunden, January 10, 2009. Signed as a free agent by **Pardubice** (CzRep), November 2, 2009.

PISANI, Fernando

(pih-ZAN-ee, FUHR-nan-DOH)

Right wing. Shoots left. 6'1", 205 lbs. Born, Edmonton, Alta., December 27, 1976. Edmonton's 9th choice, 195th overall, in 1996 Entry Draft.

			Regular Season														Playoffs								
Season	Club	League	GP	G	A	Pts	PIM	PP	SH	GW	S	%	+/-	TF	F%	Min	GP	G	A	Pts	PIM	PP	SH	GW	Min
1993-94	St. Albert Saints	AJHL	50	6	21	27	24	....	....	....	....	....	....	....	....	....	....	....	....	....	....	....	....	....	....
1994-95	Bonnyville	AJHL	16	4	34	37	97	....	....	....	....	....	....	....	....	....	....	....	....	....	....	....	....	....	....
	St. Albert Saints	AJHL	40	26	21	47	16	....	....	....	....	....	....	....	....	....	....	....	....	....	....	....	....	....	....
1995-96	St. Albert Saints	AJHL	58	40	63	103	134	....	....	....	....	....	....	....	....	....	18	7	22	29	28	....	....	....	....
1996-97	Providence	H-East	35	12	18	30	36	....	....	....	....	....	....	....	....	....	....	....	....	....	....	....	....	....	....
1997-98	Providence	H-East	36	16	18	34	20	....	....	....	....	....	....	....	....	....	....	....	....	....	....	....	....	....	....
1998-99	Providence	H-East	38	14	37	51	42	....	....	....	....	....	....	....	....	....	....	....	....	....	....	....	....	....	....
99-2000	Providence	H-East	38	14	24	38	56	....	....	....	....	....	....	....	....	....	....	....	....	....	....	....	....	....	....
2000-01	Hamilton	AHL	52	12	13	25	28	....	....	....	....	....	....	....	....	....	....	....	....	....	....	....	....	....	....
2001-02	Hamilton	AHL	79	26	34	60	60	....	....	....	....	....	....	....	....	....	15	4	6	10	4	....	....	....	....
2002-03	**Edmonton**	**NHL**	**35**	**8**	**5**	**13**	**10**	**0**	**1**	**0**	**32**	**25.0**	**9**	**1**	**100.0**	**10:43**	**6**	**1**	**0**	**1**	**2**	**0**	**0**	**0**	**13:48**
	Hamilton	AHL	41	17	15	32	24	....	....	....	....	....	....	....	....	....	....	....	....	....	....	....	....	....	....
2003-04	**Edmonton**	**NHL**	**76**	**16**	**14**	**30**	**46**	**4**	**1**	**1**	**99**	**16.2**	**14**	**10**	**20.0**	**12:46**	....	....	....	....	....	....	....	....	....
2004-05	Langnau	Swiss	7	1	3	4	0	....	....	....	....	....	....	....	....	....	....	....	....	....	....	....	....	....	....
	Asiago	Italy	12	1	5	6	6	....	....	....	....	....	....	....	....	....	9	4	6	10	0	....	....	....	....
2005-06	**Edmonton**	**NHL**	**80**	**18**	**19**	**37**	**42**	**4**	**1**	**2**	**131**	**13.7**	**5**	**35**	**22.9**	**13:51**	**24**	***14**	**4**	**18**	**10**	**3**	**1**	***5**	**17:12**
2006-07	**Edmonton**	**NHL**	**77**	**14**	**14**	**28**	**40**	**2**	**1**	**0**	**142**	**9.9**	**-1**	**20**	**40.0**	**16:54**	....	....	....	....	....	....	....	....	....
2007-08	**Edmonton**	**NHL**	**56**	**13**	**9**	**22**	**28**	**4**	**0**	**3**	**96**	**13.5**	**-5**	**7**	**28.6**	**16:32**	....	....	....	....	....	....	....	....	....
2008-09	**Edmonton**	**NHL**	**38**	**7**	**8**	**15**	**14**	**0**	**0**	**0**	**72**	**9.7**	**-1**	**123**	**40.7**	**15:19**	....	....	....	....	....	....	....	....	....
2009-10	**Edmonton**	**NHL**	**40**	**4**	**4**	**8**	**10**	**0**	**0**	**0**	**54**	**7.4**	**-16**	**16**	**18.8**	**14:35**	....	....	....	....	....	....	....	....	....
	NHL Totals		**402**	**80**	**73**	**153**	**190**	**14**	**4**	**6**	**626**	**12.8**		**212**	**34.9**	**14:32**	**30**	**15**	**4**	**19**	**12**	**3**	**1**	**5**	**16:31**

gned as a free agent by **Langnau** (Swiss), October 24, 2004. Signed as a free agent by **Asiago** (Italy), December 23, 2004. • Missed majority of 2008-09 season recovering from ankle injury suffered in ame at Detroit, November 17, 2008.

PISKULA, Joe

(pihs-KOO-luh, JOH)

Defense. Shoots left. 6'3", 208 lbs. Born, Antigo, WI, July 5, 1984.

			Regular Season														Playoffs								
Season	Club	League	GP	G	A	Pts	PIM	PP	SH	GW	S	%	+/-	TF	F%	Min	GP	G	A	Pts	PIM	PP	SH	GW	Min
2002-03	Chicago Steel	USHL	13	0	0	0	18	....	....	....	....	....	....	....	....	....	....	....	....	....	....	....	....	....	....
	Des Moines	USHL	32	2	6	8	18	....	....	....	....	....	....	....	....	....	4	0	1	1	4	....	....	....	....
2003-04	Des Moines	USHL	58	2	4	6	68	....	....	....	....	....	....	....	....	....	3	0	1	1	0	....	....	....	....
2004-05	U. of Wisconsin	WCHA	40	0	6	6	24	....	....	....	....	....	....	....	....	....	....	....	....	....	....	....	....	....	....
2005-06	U. of Wisconsin	WCHA	34	2	9	11	22	....	....	....	....	....	....	....	....	....	....	....	....	....	....	....	....	....	....
2006-07	U. of Wisconsin	WCHA	38	1	4	5	34	....	....	....	....	....	....	....	....	....	....	....	....	....	....	....	....	....	....
	Los Angeles	**NHL**	**5**	**0**	**0**	**0**	**6**	**0**	**0**	**0**	**4**	**0.0**	**-3**	**0**	**0.0**	**9:59**	....	....	....	....	....	....	....	....	....
2007-08	Manchester	AHL	55	0	7	7	57	....	....	....	....	....	....	....	....	....	4	0	0	0	4	....	....	....	....
2008-09	Manchester	AHL	67	0	12	12	40	....	....	....	....	....	....	....	....	....	....	....	....	....	....	....	....	....	....
2009-10	Manchester	AHL	72	2	10	12	51	....	....	....	....	....	....	....	....	....	16	2	2	4	12	....	....	....	....
	NHL Totals		**5**	**0**	**0**	**0**	**6**	**0**	**0**	**0**	**4**	**0.0**		**0**	**0.0**	**9:59**	....	....	....	....	....	....	....	....	....

gned as a free agent by **Los Angeles**, March 21, 2007.

PITKANEN, Joni

(PIHT-ka-nuhn, YOH-nee) **CAR.**

Defense. Shoots left. 6'3", 210 lbs. Born, Oulu, Finland, September 19, 1983. Philadelphia's 1st choice, 4th overall, in 2002 Entry Draft.

			Regular Season														Playoffs								
Season	Club	League	GP	G	A	Pts	PIM	PP	SH	GW	S	%	+/-	TF	F%	Min	GP	G	A	Pts	PIM	PP	SH	GW	Min
1998-99	Karpat Oulu U18	Fin-U18	30	1	5	6	12	....	....	....	....	....	....	....	....	....	....	....	....	....	....	....	....	....	....
99-2000	Karpat Oulu U18	Fin-U18	36	12	14	26	26	....	....	....	....	....	....	....	....	....	6	1	4	5	2	....	....	....	....
	Karpat Oulu Jr.	Fin-Jr.	2	0	0	0	0	....	....	....	....	....	....	....	....	....	....	....	....	....	....	....	....	....	....
2000-01	Karpat Oulu Jr.	Fin-Jr.	24	6	11	17	77	....	....	....	....	....	....	....	....	....	....	....	....	....	....	....	....	....	....
	Karpat Oulu	Finland	21	0	0	0	10	....	....	....	....	....	....	....	....	....	2	0	0	0	2	....	....	....	....
2001-02	Karpat Oulu Jr.	Fin-Jr.	....	....	....	....	....	....	....	....	....	....	....	....	....	....	1	0	0	0	0	....	....	....	....
	Karpat Oulu	Finland	49	4	15	19	65	....	....	....	....	....	....	....	....	....	4	0	0	0	12	....	....	....	....
2002-03	Karpat Oulu	Finland	35	5	15	20	38	....	....	....	....	....	....	....	....	....	....	....	....	....	....	....	....	....	....
2003-04	**Philadelphia**	**NHL**	**71**	**8**	**19**	**27**	**44**	**5**	**0**	**2**	**133**	**6.0**	**15**	**0**	**0.0**	**16:35**	**15**	**0**	**3**	**3**	**6**	**0**	**0**	**0**	**12:13**
2004-05	Philadelphia	AHL	76	6	35	41	105	....	....	....	....	....	....	....	....	....	21	3	4	7	16	....	....	....	....
2005-06	**Philadelphia**	**NHL**	**58**	**13**	**33**	**46**	**78**	**5**	**0**	**3**	**118**	**11.0**	**22**	**0**	**0.0**	**23:43**	**6**	**0**	**2**	**2**	**2**	**0**	**0**	**0**	**24:12**
	Finland	Olympics	DID NOT PLAY – INJURED																						
2006-07	**Philadelphia**	**NHL**	**77**	**4**	**39**	**43**	**88**	**1**	**0**	**0**	**137**	**2.9**	**-25**	**0**	**0.0**	**24:33**	....	....	....	....	....	....	....	....	....
2007-08	**Edmonton**	**NHL**	**63**	**8**	**18**	**26**	**56**	**1**	**1**	**1**	**101**	**7.9**	**-5**	**0**	**0.0**	**24:07**	....	....	....	....	....	....	....	....	....
2008-09	**Carolina**	**NHL**	**71**	**7**	**26**	**33**	**58**	**2**	**0**	**3**	**147**	**4.8**	**11**	**0**	**0.0**	**24:48**	**18**	**0**	**8**	**8**	**16**	**0**	**0**	**0**	**26:29**
2009-10	**Carolina**	**NHL**	**71**	**6**	**40**	**46**	**72**	**1**	**0**	**1**	**161**	**3.7**	**-11**	**0**	**0.0**	**27:23**	....	....	....	....	....	....	....	....	....
	Finland	Olympics	5	1	2	3	*29	....	....	....	....	....	....	....	....	....	....	....	....	....	....	....	....	....	....
	NHL Totals		**411**	**46**	**175**	**221**	**396**	**15**	**1**	**10**	**797**	**5.8**		**0**	**0.0**	**23:31**	**39**	**0**	**13**	**13**	**24**	**0**	**0**	**0**	**20:39**

HL All-Rookie Team (2004)

aded to **Edmonton** by **Philadelphia** with Geoff Sanderson and Philadelphia's 3rd round choice (Cameron Abney) in 2009 Entry Draft for Joffrey Lupul and Jason Smith, July 1, 2007. Traded to **Carolina** **Edmonton** for Erik Cole, July 1, 2008.

PLANTE, Alex

(PLAWNT, AL-ehx) **EDM.**

Defense. Shoots right. 6'4", 225 lbs. Born, Brandon, Man., May 9, 1989. Edmonton's 2nd choice, 15th overall, in 2007 Entry Draft.

			Regular Season														Playoffs								
Season	Club	League	GP	G	A	Pts	PIM	PP	SH	GW	S	%	+/-	TF	F%	Min	GP	G	A	Pts	PIM	PP	SH	GW	Min
2004-05	Brandon	MMHL	37	5	21	26	120	....	....	....	....	....	....	....	....	....	....	....	....	....	....	....	....	....	....
	Calgary Hitmen	WHL	8	0	0	0	6	....	....	....	....	....	....	....	....	....	11	0	0	0	17	....	....	....	....
2005-06	Calgary Hitmen	WHL	54	1	3	4	72	....	....	....	....	....	....	....	....	....	13	0	0	0	6	....	....	....	....
2006-07	Calgary Hitmen	WHL	58	8	30	38	81	....	....	....	....	....	....	....	....	....	13	5	6	11	14	....	....	....	....
2007-08	Calgary Hitmen	WHL	36	1	1	2	28	....	....	....	....	....	....	....	....	....	15	0	4	4	10	....	....	....	....
2008-09	Calgary Hitmen	WHL	68	8	37	45	157	....	....	....	....	....	....	....	....	....	18	6	9	15	41	....	....	....	....
2009-10	**Edmonton**	**NHL**	**4**	**0**	**1**	**1**	**2**	**0**	**0**	**0**	**4**	**0.0**	**1**	**0**	**0.0**	**13:36**	....	....	....	....	....	....	....	....	....
	Springfield	AHL	49	2	7	9	122	....	....	....	....	....	....	....	....	....	....	....	....	....	....	....	....	....	....
	NHL Totals		**4**	**0**	**1**	**1**	**2**	**0**	**0**	**0**	**4**	**0.0**		**0**	**0.0**	**13:36**	....	....	....	....	....	....	....	....	....

PLATT, Geoff
(PLAT, JEHF) **ANA.**

Center. Shoots left. 5'9", 175 lbs. Born, Toronto, Ont., July 10, 1985.

			Regular Season														Playoffs								
Season	Club	League	GP	G	A	Pts	PIM	PP	SH	GW	S	%	+/-	TF	F%	Min	GP	G	A	Pts	PIM	PP	SH	GW	Min
2000-01	St. Mike's B's	OPJHL	6	2	0	2	4	....	....	....	....	....	....	....	....	....	....	....	....	....	....	....	....	....	....
2001-02	North Bay	OHL	63	4	6	10	34	....	....	....	....	....	....	....	....	....	5	0	0	0	6	....	....	....	....
2002-03	Saginaw Spirit	OHL	62	32	22	54	81	....	....	....	....	....	....	....	....	....	....	....	....	....	....	....	....	....	....
2003-04	Saginaw Spirit	OHL	27	7	13	20	49	....	....	....	....	....	....	....	....	....	....	....	....	....	....	....	....	....	....
	Erie Otters	OHL	28	18	11	29	22	....	....	....	....	....	....	....	....	....	9	9	1	10	22	....	....	....	....
2004-05	Erie Otters	OHL	68	45	34	79	84	....	....	....	....	....	....	....	....	....	6	2	3	5	16	....	....	....	....
	Atlantic City	ECHL	2	0	2	2	0	....	....	....	....	....	....	....	....	....	3	0	0	0	0	....	....	....	....
2005-06	Syracuse Crunch	AHL	66	31	34	65	58	....	....	....	....	....	....	....	....	....	6	3	0	3	6	....	....	....	....
	Columbus	**NHL**	**15**	**0**	**5**	**5**	**16**	**0**	**0**	**0**	**29**	**0.0**	**-4**	**53**	**45.3**	**11:12**	....	....	....	....	....	....	....	....	....
2006-07	**Columbus**	**NHL**	**26**	**4**	**5**	**9**	**10**	**0**	**0**	**0**	**40**	**10.0**	**1**	**168**	**56.6**	**10:04**	....	....	....	....	....	....	....	....	....
	Syracuse Crunch	AHL	53	28	21	49	59	....	....	....	....	....	....	....	....	....	....	....	....	....	....	....	....	....	....
2007-08	Syracuse Crunch	AHL	15	4	3	7	6	....	....	....	....	....	....	....	....	....	....	....	....	....	....	....	....	....	....
	Anaheim	**NHL**	**5**	**0**	**0**	**0**	**2**	**0**	**0**	**0**	**4**	**0.0**	**2**	**7**	**28.6**	**11:17**	....	....	....	....	....	....	....	....	....
	Portland Pirates	AHL	60	28	30	58	49	....	....	....	....	....	....	....	....	....	18	8	9	17	24	....	....	....	....
2008-09	Dynamo Minsk	Rus-KHL	13	2	3	5	8	....	....	....	....	....	....	....	....	....	....	....	....	....	....	....	....	....	....
	Ilves Tampere	Finland	45	19	18	37	54	....	....	....	....	....	....	....	....	....	3	1	0	1	4	....	....	....	....
2009-10	Dynamo Minsk	Rus-KHL	56	26	18	44	77	....	....	....	....	....	....	....	....	....	....	....	....	....	....	....	....	....	....
	NHL Totals		**46**	**4**	**10**	**14**	**28**	**0**	**0**	**0**	**73**	**5.5**		**228**	**53.1**	**10:34**	....	....	....	....	....	....	....	....	....

Signed as a free agent by **Syracuse** (AHL), September 23, 2005. Signed as a free agent by **Columbus**, November 25, 2005. Traded to **Anaheim** by **Columbus** for Aaron Rome and Clay Wilson, November 15, 2007. Signed as a free agent by **Minsk** (Russia-KHL), May 15, 2009.

PLEKANEC, Tomas
(pleh-KA-nyehts, TAW-mahsh) **MTL.**

Left wing. Shoots left. 5'11", 198 lbs. Born, Kladno, Czech., October 31, 1982. Montreal's 4th choice, 71st overall, in 2001 Entry Draft.

1996-97	Kladno U17	CzR-U17	13	1	3	4	....	....	....	....	....	....	....	....	....	....	....	....	....	....	....	....	....	....	....
1997-98	HC Kladno U17	CzR-U17	45	38	26	64	....	....	....	....	....	....	....	....	....	....	....	....	....	....	....	....	....	....	....
1998-99	HC Kladno Jr.	CzRep-Jr.	53	22	20	42	....	....	....	....	....	....	....	....	....	....	....	....	....	....	....	....	....	....	....
99-2000	HC Kladno Jr.	CzRep-Jr.	43	14	16	30	....	....	....	....	....	....	....	....	....	....	....	....	....	....	....	....	....	....	....
	Kralupy	CzRep-3	6	2	2	4	2	....	....	....	....	....	....	....	....	....	....	....	....	....	....	....	....	....	....
	HC CKD Slany	CzRep-3	3	0	1	1	6	....	....	....	....	....	....	....	....	....	....	....	....	....	....	....	....	....	....
2000-01	Kladno	CzRep	47	9	9	18	24	....	....	....	....	....	....	....	....	....	....	....	....	....	....	....	....	....	....
	HC Kladno Jr.	CzRep-Jr.	9	6	4	10	4	....	....	....	....	....	....	....	....	....	....	....	....	....	....	....	....	....	....
2001-02	Kladno	CzRep	48	7	16	23	28	....	....	....	....	....	....	....	....	....	....	....	....	....	....	....	....	....	....
	BK Mlada Boleslav	CzRep-3	6	6	3	9	14	....	....	....	....	....	....	....	....	....	....	....	....	....	....	....	....	....	....
	Kladno	CzRep-Q	5	0	1	1	0	....	....	....	....	....	....	....	....	....	....	....	....	....	....	....	....	....	....
2002-03	Hamilton	AHL	77	19	27	46	74	....	....	....	....	....	....	....	....	....	13	3	2	5	8	....	....	....	....
2003-04	**Montreal**	**NHL**	**2**	**0**	**0**	**0**	**0**	**0**	**0**	**0**	**0**	**0.0**	**0**	**11**	**45.5**	**9:02**	....	....	....	....	....	....	....	....	....
	Hamilton	AHL	74	23	43	66	90	....	....	....	....	....	....	....	....	....	10	2	5	7	6	....	....	....	....
2004-05	Hamilton	AHL	80	29	35	64	68	....	....	....	....	....	....	....	....	....	4	2	4	6	6	....	....	....	....
2005-06	**Montreal**	**NHL**	**67**	**9**	**20**	**29**	**32**	**1**	**0**	**0**	**99**	**9.1**	**4**	**708**	**50.3**	**13:15**	**6**	**0**	**4**	**4**	**6**	**0**	**0**	**0**	**18:00**
	Hamilton	AHL	2	0	0	0	2	....	....	....	....	....	....	....	....	....	....	....	....	....	....	....	....	....	....
2006-07	**Montreal**	**NHL**	**81**	**20**	**27**	**47**	**36**	**5**	**2**	**1**	**150**	**13.3**	**10**	**1159**	**48.3**	**15:59**	....	....	....	....	....	....	....	....	....
2007-08	**Montreal**	**NHL**	**81**	**29**	**40**	**69**	**42**	**12**	**2**	**6**	**186**	**15.6**	**15**	**1381**	**49.5**	**18:05**	**12**	**4**	**5**	**9**	**2**	**2**	**0**	**0**	**18:02**
2008-09	**Montreal**	**NHL**	**80**	**20**	**19**	**39**	**54**	**6**	**3**	**2**	**202**	**9.9**	**-9**	**1351**	**50.6**	**17:15**	**3**	**0**	**0**	**0**	**4**	**0**	**0**	**0**	**13:36**
2009-10	**Montreal**	**NHL**	**82**	**25**	**45**	**70**	**50**	**3**	**1**	**4**	**216**	**11.6**	**5**	**1615**	**49.0**	**19:58**	**19**	**4**	**7**	**11**	**20**	**1**	**0**	**1**	**19:57**
	Czech Republic	Olympics	5	2	1	3	2	....	....	....	....	....	....	....	....	....	....	....	....	....	....	....	....	....	....
	NHL Totals		**393**	**103**	**151**	**254**	**214**	**27**	**8**	**13**	**853**	**12.1**		**6225**	**49.5**	**17:00**	**40**	**8**	**16**	**24**	**32**	**3**	**0**	**1**	**18:36**

PLIHAL, Tomas
(PLEE-hahl, TOH-mahs)

Center. Shoots left. 6'1", 210 lbs. Born, Frydlant, Czech., March 28, 1983. San Jose's 4th choice, 140th overall, in 2001 Entry Draft.

99-2000	Liberec U17	CzR-U17	38	22	14	36	....	....	....	....	....	....	....	....	....	....	....	....	....	....	....	....	....	....	....
	Liberec Jr.	CzRep-Jr.	2	0	0	0	0	....	....	....	....	....	....	....	....	....	....	....	....	....	....	....	....	....	....
2000-01	HC Liberec U17	CzR-U17	18	3	5	8	....	....	....	....	....	....	....	....	....	....	....	....	....	....	....	....	....	....	....
	HC Liberec Jr.	CzRep-Jr.	33	16	12	28	....	....	....	....	....	....	....	....	....	....	....	....	....	....	....	....	....	....	....
2001-02	Kootenay Ice	WHL	72	32	54	86	28	....	....	....	....	....	....	....	....	....	22	4	10	14	14	....	....	....	....
2002-03	Kootenay Ice	WHL	67	35	42	77	113	....	....	....	....	....	....	....	....	....	11	2	4	6	18	....	....	....	....
2003-04	Cleveland Barons	AHL	51	4	12	16	16	....	....	....	....	....	....	....	....	....	6	0	3	3	2	....	....	....	....
2004-05	Cleveland Barons	AHL	62	17	11	28	26	....	....	....	....	....	....	....	....	....	....	....	....	....	....	....	....	....	....
2005-06	Cleveland Barons	AHL	74	11	19	30	53	....	....	....	....	....	....	....	....	....	....	....	....	....	....	....	....	....	....
2006-07	**San Jose**	**NHL**	**3**	**0**	**0**	**0**	**0**	**0**	**0**	**0**	**10**	**0.0**	**0**	**8**	**75.0**	**9:44**	....	....	....	....	....	....	....	....	....
	Worcester Sharks	AHL	47	6	9	15	28	....	....	....	....	....	....	....	....	....	....	....	....	....	....	....	....	....	....
2007-08	**San Jose**	**NHL**	**22**	**2**	**1**	**3**	**4**	**0**	**0**	**0**	**34**	**5.9**	**4**	**19**	**26.3**	**10:50**	**4**	**0**	**0**	**0**	**0**	**0**	**0**	**0**	**13:16**
	Worcester Sharks	AHL	22	5	7	12	12	....	....	....	....	....	....	....	....	....	....	....	....	....	....	....	....	....	....
2008-09	**San Jose**	**NHL**	**64**	**5**	**8**	**13**	**22**	**0**	**1**	**1**	**79**	**6.3**	**-4**	**248**	**52.8**	**10:08**	....	....	....	....	....	....	....	....	....
2009-10	TPS Turku	Finland	52	19	18	37	73	....	....	....	....	....	....	....	....	....	15	4	4	8	28	....	....	....	....
	NHL Totals		**89**	**7**	**9**	**16**	**26**	**0**	**1**	**1**	**123**	**5.7**		**275**	**51.6**	**10:17**	**4**	**0**	**0**	**0**	**0**	**0**	**0**	**0**	**13:16**

George Parsons Trophy (Memorial Cup Tournament - Most Sportsmanlike Player) (2002)

Signed as a free agent by **Turku** (Finland), September 7, 2009.

POCK, Thomas
(POHK, TAW-muhs)

Defense. Shoots left. 6'1", 210 lbs. Born, Klagenfurt, Austria, December 2, 1981.

1998-99	Klagenfurt Jr.	Austria-Jr.	31	0	0	0	2	....	....	....	....	....	....	....	....	....	....	....	....	....	....	....	....	....	....
99-2000	Klagenfurter AC	Austria	15	3	8	11	14	....	....	....	....	....	....	....	....	....	....	....	....	....	....	....	....	....	....
	Klagenfurt	Alpenliga	33	4	11	15	48	....	....	....	....	....	....	....	....	....	....	....	....	....	....	....	....	....	....
2000-01	Massachusetts	H-East	33	6	6	12	59	....	....	....	....	....	....	....	....	....	....	....	....	....	....	....	....	....	....
2001-02	Massachusetts	H-East	23	5	7	12	26	....	....	....	....	....	....	....	....	....	....	....	....	....	....	....	....	....	....
	Austria	Nat-Tm	10	1	2	3	4	....	....	....	....	....	....	....	....	....	....	....	....	....	....	....	....	....	....
	Austria	Olympics	4	0	0	0	2	....	....	....	....	....	....	....	....	....	....	....	....	....	....	....	....	....	....
2002-03	Massachusetts	H-East	37	17	20	37	46	....	....	....	....	....	....	....	....	....	....	....	....	....	....	....	....	....	....
	Austria	WC-A	6	1	0	1	4	....	....	....	....	....	....	....	....	....	....	....	....	....	....	....	....	....	....
2003-04	Massachusetts	H-East	37	16	25	41	48	....	....	....	....	....	....	....	....	....	....	....	....	....	....	....	....	....	....
	NY Rangers	**NHL**	**6**	**2**	**2**	**4**	**0**	**0**	**0**	**0**	**8**	**25.0**	**-4**	**0**	**0.0**	**18:38**	....	....	....	....	....	....	....	....	....
2004-05	Hartford	AHL	50	1	5	6	55	....	....	....	....	....	....	....	....	....	6	0	1	1	8	....	....	....	....
	Charlotte	ECHL	3	0	2	2	2	....	....	....	....	....	....	....	....	....	....	....	....	....	....	....	....	....	....
2005-06	**NY Rangers**	**NHL**	**8**	**1**	**1**	**2**	**4**	**0**	**0**	**0**	**15**	**6.7**	**-3**	**0**	**0.0**	**15:10**	....	....	....	....	....	....	....	....	....
	Hartford	AHL	67	15	46	61	99	....	....	....	....	....	....	....	....	....	6	0	3	3	15	....	....	....	....
2006-07	**NY Rangers**	**NHL**	**44**	**4**	**4**	**8**	**16**	**0**	**0**	**0**	**76**	**5.3**	**-4**	**0**	**0.0**	**16:14**	**4**	**0**	**3**	**3**	**4**	**0**	**0**	**0**	**13:29**
	Hartford	AHL	4	0	1	1	2	....	....	....	....	....	....	....	....	....	....	....	....	....	....	....	....	....	....
2007-08	**NY Rangers**	**NHL**	**1**	**0**	**0**	**0**	**0**	**0**	**0**	**0**	**2**	**0.0**	**-2**	**0**	**0.0**	**18:53**	....	....	....	....	....	....	....	....	....
	Hartford	AHL	74	7	37	44	63	....	....	....	....	....	....	....	....	....	5	0	0	0	8	....	....	....	....
2008-09	**NY Islanders**	**NHL**	**59**	**1**	**2**	**3**	**35**	**0**	**0**	**0**	**51**	**2.0**	**-17**	**0**	**0.0**	**12:42**	....	....	....	....	....	....	....	....	....
2009-10	Rapperswil	Swiss	49	11	22	33	58	....	....	....	....	....	....	....	....	....	7	2	7	9	8	....	....	....	....
	NHL Totals		**118**	**8**	**9**	**17**	**55**	**0**	**0**	**0**	**152**	**5.3**		**0**	**0.0**	**14:32**	**4**	**0**	**3**	**3**	**4**	**0**	**0**	**0**	**13:2**

Hockey East Second All-Star Team (2003) • Hockey East First All-Star Team (2004) • NCAA East First All-American Team (2004) • AHL Second All-Star Team (2006)

Signed as a free agent by **NY Rangers**, March 23, 2004. Claimed on waivers by **NY Islanders** from **NY Rangers**, September 29, 2008. Signed as a free agent by **Rapperswil** (Swiss), May 28, 2009.

POHL, John
(PAWL, JAWN)

Center. Shoots right. 6'1", 196 lbs. Born, Rochester, MN, June 29, 1979. St. Louis' 8th choice, 255th overall, in 1998 Entry Draft.

1997-98	Red Wing High	High-MN	28	30	77	107	18	....	....	....	....	....	....	....	....	....	....	....	....	....	....	....	....	....	....
	Twin Cities	USHL	10	5	3	8	10	....	....	....	....	....	....	....	....	....	....	....	....	....	....	....	....	....	....
1998-99	U. of Minnesota	WCHA	42	7	10	17	18	....	....	....	....	....	....	....	....	....	....	....	....	....	....	....	....	....	....
99-2000	U. of Minnesota	WCHA	41	18	41	59	26	....	....	....	....	....	....	....	....	....	....	....	....	....	....	....	....	....	....
2000-01	U. of Minnesota	WCHA	38	19	26	45	24	....	....	....	....	....	....	....	....	....	....	....	....	....	....	....	....	....	....
2001-02	U. of Minnesota	WCHA	44	27	*52	*79	26	....	....	....	....	....	....	....	....	....	....	....	....	....	....	....	....	....	....

			Regular Season														Playoffs								
Season	Club	League	GP	G	A	Pts	PIM	PP	SH	GW	S	%	+/-	TF	F%	Min	GP	G	A	Pts	PIM	PP	SH	GW	Min
2002-03	Worcester IceCats	AHL	58	26	32	58	34										3	0	1	1	6				
2003-04	**St. Louis**	**NHL**	**1**	**0**	**0**	**0**	**0**	**0**	**0**	**0**	**1**	**0.0**	**–2**	**9**	**55.6**	**8:18**									
	Worcester IceCats	AHL	65	16	25	41	65										3	0	1	1	2				
2004-05	Worcester IceCats	AHL	13	3	6	9	2																		
2005-06	**Toronto**	**NHL**	**7**	**3**	**1**	**4**	**4**	**1**	**0**	**0**	**17**	**17.6**	**2**	**41**	**53.7**	**12:47**									
	Toronto Marlies	AHL	60	36	39	75	42										5	1	5	6	10				
2006-07	**Toronto**	**NHL**	**74**	**13**	**16**	**29**	**10**	**3**	**0**	**1**	**105**	**12.4**	**–4**	**553**	**53.4**	**11:21**									
2007-08	**Toronto**	**NHL**	**33**	**1**	**4**	**5**	**10**	**0**	**0**	**1**	**23**	**4.3**	**–4**	**94**	**43.6**	**7:06**									
2008-09	HC Lugano	Swiss	22	3	22	25	26																		
	Frolunda	Sweden	12	5	7	12	6										11	2	7	9	8				
2009-10	Chicago Wolves	AHL	66	20	33	53	12										14	3	3	6	2				
	NHL Totals		**115**	**17**	**21**	**38**	**24**	**4**	**0**	**2**	**146**	**11.6**		**697**	**52.1**	**10:11**									

WCHA Second All-Star Team (2000) • WCHA First All-Star Team (2002) • NCAA Championship All-Tournament Team (2002)

Traded to **Toronto** by **St. Louis** for future considerations, August 24, 2005. Signed as a free agent by **Lugano** (Swiss), May 27, 2008. Signed as a free agent by **Frolunda** (Sweden), January 22, 2009. Signed as a free agent by **Chicago** (AHL), July 29, 2009

POLAK, Roman

(POH-lahk, ROH-muhn) **ST.L.**

Defense. Shoots right. 6'1", 225 lbs. Born, Ostrava, Czech., April 28, 1986. St. Louis' 6th choice, 180th overall, in 2004 Entry Draft.

Season	Club	League	GP	G	A	Pts	PIM	PP	SH	GW	S	%	+/-	TF	F%	Min	GP	G	A	Pts	PIM	PP	SH	GW	Min
2001-02	HC Ostrava Jr.	CzRep-Jr.	46	4	9	13	84																		
2002-03	HC Ostrava Jr.	CzRep-Jr.	32	3	12	15	34																		
2003-04	HC Vitkovice Jr.	CzRep-Jr.	52	4	8	12	48																		
2004-05	Kootenay Ice	WHL	65	5	18	23	85										9	0	0	0	6				
2005-06	HC Vitkovice Jr.	CzRep-Jr.	1	0	0	0	4																		
	Vitkovice	CzRep	37	0	1	1	16										6	0	0	0	6				
2006-07	**St. Louis**	**NHL**	**19**	**0**	**0**	**0**	**6**	**0**	**0**	**0**	**13**	**0.0**	**–3**	**0**	**0.0**	**13:38**									
	Peoria Rivermen	AHL	53	4	8	12	66																		
2007-08	**St. Louis**	**NHL**	**6**	**0**	**1**	**1**	**0**	**0**	**0**	**0**	**2**	**0.0**	**1**	**0**	**0.0**	**11:32**									
	Peoria Rivermen	AHL	34	0	7	7	33																		
2008-09	**St. Louis**	**NHL**	**69**	**1**	**14**	**15**	**45**	**0**	**0**	**1**	**73**	**1.4**	**–15**	**1**	**0.0**	**21:32**	**4**	**0**	**0**	**0**	**0**	**0**	**0**	**0**	**21:49**
2009-10	**St. Louis**	**NHL**	**78**	**4**	**17**	**21**	**59**	**0**	**0**	**1**	**73**	**5.5**	**7**	**0**	**0.0**	**19:59**									
	Czech Republic	Olympics	5	0	0	0	4																		
	NHL Totals		**172**	**5**	**32**	**37**	**110**	**0**	**0**	**2**	**161**	**3.1**		**1**	**0.0**	**19:36**	**4**	**0**	**0**	**0**	**0**	**0**	**0**	**0**	**21:49**

POLAK, Vojtech

(POH-lahk, VOI-tehk) **DAL.**

Left wing. Shoots left. 5'10", 180 lbs. Born, Ostrov nad Ohri, Czech., June 27, 1985. Dallas' 2nd choice, 36th overall, in 2003 Entry Draft.

Season	Club	League	GP	G	A	Pts	PIM	PP	SH	GW	S	%	+/-	TF	F%	Min	GP	G	A	Pts	PIM	PP	SH	GW	Min
99-2000	Karlovy Vary Jr.	CzRep-Jr.	49	17	23	40	48																		
2000-01	Karlovy Vary Jr.	CzRep-Jr.	47	36	33	69	38																		
	Karlovy Vary	CzRep	2	0	0	0	0																		
2001-02	Karlovy Vary Jr.	CzRep-Jr.	37	11	14	25	26																		
	Karlovy Vary	CzRep	9	1	1	2	2																		
2002-03	Karlovy Vary	CzRep	41	7	9	16	51																		
	Karlovy Vary Jr.	CzRep-Jr.	6	3	7	10	18																		
2003-04	HC Sparta Praha	CzRep	1	1	0	1	0																		
	Karlovy Vary	CzRep	44	0	8	8	42																		
	Karlovy Vary Jr.	CzRep-Jr.	5	8	4	12	2																		
2004-05	Jihlava Jr.	CzRep-Jr.	5	4	1	5	6																		
	HC Dukla Jihlava	CzRep	16	1	2	3	12																		
	Karlovy Vary Jr.	CzRep-Jr.	3	5	5	10	6																		
	SK Kadan	CzRep-2	7	1	2	3	39																		
	Karlovy Vary	CzRep	26	1	5	6	4																		
2005-06	**Dallas**	**NHL**	**3**	**0**	**0**	**0**	**0**	**0**	**0**	**0**	**3**	**0.0**	**–1**	**2**	**50.0**	**6:31**									
	Iowa Stars	AHL	60	12	22	34	41										3	0	1	1	0				
2006-07	**Dallas**	**NHL**	**2**	**0**	**0**	**0**	**0**	**0**	**0**	**0**	**2**	**0.0**	**–1**	**0**	**0.0**	**7:43**									
	Iowa Stars	AHL	67	17	28	45	48										7	1	0	1	8				
2007-08	Iowa Stars	AHL	35	6	10	16	18																		
	Karlovy Vary	CzRep	5	1	0	1	4										19	1	3	4	8				
2008-09	HC Ocelari Trinec	CzRep	45	21	13	34	42										5	0	1	1	6				
2009-10	HC Ocelari Trinec	CzRep	49	10	9	19	48										5	0	1	1	0				
	NHL Totals		**5**	**0**	**0**	**0**	**0**	**0**	**0**	**0**	**5**	**0.0**		**2**	**50.0**	**7:00**									

Signed as a free agent by **Trinec** (CzRep), May 19, 2008.

POMINVILLE, Jason

(paw-MIHN-vihl, JAY-suhn) **BUF.**

Right wing. Shoots right. 6', 189 lbs. Born, Repentigny, Que., November 30, 1982. Buffalo's 4th choice, 55th overall, in 2001 Entry Draft.

Season	Club	League	GP	G	A	Pts	PIM	PP	SH	GW	S	%	+/-	TF	F%	Min	GP	G	A	Pts	PIM	PP	SH	GW	Min
1997-98	Cap-d-Madeleine	QAAA	13	3	7	10																			
1998-99	Cap-d-Madeleine	QAAA	41	18	38	56	16										7	2	7	9	0				
	Shawinigan	QMJHL	2	0	0	0	0																		
99-2000	Shawinigan	QMJHL	60	4	17	21	12										13	2	3	5	0				
2000-01	Shawinigan	QMJHL	71	46	67	113	24										10	6	6	12	0				
2001-02	Shawinigan	QMJHL	66	57	64	121	32										2	0	0	0	0				
2002-03	Rochester	AHL	73	13	21	34	16										3	1	1	2	0				
2003-04	**Buffalo**	**NHL**	**1**	**0**	**0**	**0**	**0**	**0**	**0**	**0**	**3**	**0.0**	**0**	**0**	**0.0**	**14:22**									
	Rochester	AHL	66	34	30	64	30										16	9	10	19	6				
2004-05	Rochester	AHL	78	30	38	68	43																		
2005-06	**Buffalo**	**NHL**	**57**	**18**	**12**	**30**	**22**	**10**	**2**	**2**	**124**	**14.5**	**–4**	**5**	**20.0**	**14:07**	**18**	**5**	**5**	**10**	**8**	**0**	**1**	**1**	**12:11**
	Rochester	AHL	18	19	7	26	11																		
2006-07	**Buffalo**	**NHL**	**82**	**34**	**34**	**68**	**30**	**2**	**2**	**5**	**212**	**16.0**	**25**	**14**	**42.9**	**17:25**	**16**	**4**	**6**	**10**	**0**	**0**	**0**	**0**	**17:54**
2007-08	**Buffalo**	**NHL**	**82**	**27**	**53**	**80**	**20**	**2**	**1**	**1**	**232**	**11.6**	**16**	**67**	**37.3**	**19:58**									
2008-09	**Buffalo**	**NHL**	**82**	**20**	**46**	**66**	**18**	**6**	**1**	**2**	**239**	**8.4**	**–4**	**67**	**37.3**	**19:46**									
2009-10	**Buffalo**	**NHL**	**82**	**24**	**38**	**62**	**22**	**8**	**0**	**2**	**252**	**9.5**	**13**	**120**	**35.0**	**18:45**	**6**	**2**	**2**	**4**	**2**	**0**	**0**	**1**	**20:17**
	NHL Totals		**386**	**123**	**183**	**306**	**112**	**28**	**6**	**12**	**1062**	**11.6**		**273**	**36.3**	**18:15**	**40**	**11**	**13**	**24**	**10**	**0**	**1**	**2**	**15:41**

QMJHL First All-Star Team (2002)

PONIKAROVSKY, Alexei

(poh-nih-kahr-OHV-skee, al-EHX-ay) **L.A.**

Left wing. Shoots left. 6'4", 229 lbs. Born, Kiev, USSR, April 9, 1980. Toronto's 4th choice, 87th overall, in 1998 Entry Draft.

Season	Club	League	GP	G	A	Pts	PIM	PP	SH	GW	S	%	+/-	TF	F%	Min	GP	G	A	Pts	PIM	PP	SH	GW	Min
1996-97	Dyn'o Moscow 2	Russia-3	60	12	15	27	30																		
	Dyn'o Moscow 2	Russia-3	2	0	0	0	2																		
1997-98	Dynamo Moscow	Russia	24	1	2	3	30																		
1998-99	Krylja Sovetov	Russia	13	2	1	3	2																		
	Dynamo Moscow	Russia															3	0	0	0	2				
99-2000	THK Tver	Russia-2	29	8	14	22	26																		
	Dynamo Moscow	Russia	19	1	0	1	8										1	0	0	0	0				
	Dynamo Moscow	EuroHL	2	0	2	2	0																		
2000-01	**Toronto**	**NHL**	**22**	**1**	**3**	**4**	**14**	**0**	**0**	**0**	**21**	**4.8**	**–1**	**7**	**28.6**	**8:32**									
	St. John's	AHL	49	12	24	36	44										4	0	0	0	4				
2001-02	**Toronto**	**NHL**	**8**	**2**	**0**	**2**	**0**	**0**	**0**	**1**	**8**	**25.0**	**2**	**2**	**50.0**	**8:03**	**10**	**0**	**0**	**0**	**4**	**0**	**0**	**0**	**8:15**
	St. John's	AHL	72	21	27	48	74										5	2	1	3	8				
	Ukraine	Olympics	4	1	1	2	6																		
2002-03	**Toronto**	**NHL**	**13**	**0**	**3**	**3**	**11**	**0**	**0**	**0**	**13**	**0.0**	**4**	**4**	**25.0**	**10:43**									
	St. John's	AHL	63	24	22	46	68																		
2003-04	**Toronto**	**NHL**	**73**	**9**	**19**	**28**	**44**	**1**	**0**	**2**	**110**	**8.2**	**14**	**20**	**30.0**	**11:36**	**13**	**1**	**3**	**4**	**8**	**0**	**0**	**1**	**14:20**
2004-05	Voskresensk	Russia	19	1	5	6	16																		
2005-06	**Toronto**	**NHL**	**81**	**21**	**17**	**38**	**68**	**2**	**4**	**3**	**157**	**13.4**	**15**	**13**	**30.8**	**14:06**									
2006-07	**Toronto**	**NHL**	**71**	**21**	**24**	**45**	**63**	**6**	**0**	**1**	**198**	**10.6**	**8**	**4**	**25.0**	**17:06**									
2007-08	**Toronto**	**NHL**	**66**	**18**	**17**	**35**	**36**	**1**	**0**	**1**	**150**	**12.0**	**3**	**4**	**25.0**	**15:58**									
2008-09	**Toronto**	**NHL**	**82**	**23**	**38**	**61**	**38**	**5**	**0**	**3**	**185**	**12.4**	**6**	**11**	**54.6**	**15:47**									

			Regular Season														Playoffs								
Season	Club	League	GP	G	A	Pts	PIM	PP	SH	GW	S	%	+/-	TF	F%	Min	GP	G	A	Pts	PIM	PP	SH	GW	Min
2009-10	**Toronto**	**NHL**	**61**	**19**	**22**	**41**	**44**	**4**	**0**	**1**	**147**	**12.9**	**5**	**37**	**32.4**	**16:50**									
	Pittsburgh	**NHL**	**16**	**2**	**7**	**9**	**17**	**1**	**0**	**0**	**37**	**5.4**	**–6**	**1**	**0.0**	**15:05**	**11**	**1**	**4**	**5**	**4**	**0**	**0**	**0**	**13:1**
	NHL Totals		**493**	**116**	**150**	**266**	**335**	**20**	**4**	**12**	**1026**	**11.3**		**103**	**33.0**	**14:38**	**34**	**2**	**7**	**9**	**16**	**0**	**0**	**1**	**12:1**

Signed as a free agent by **Voskresensk** (Russia), November 13, 2004. Traded to **Pittsburgh** by **Toronto** for Martin Skoula and Luca Caputi, March 2, 2010. Signed as a free agent by **Los Angeles**, July 27, 2010.

POPOVIC, Mark

(poh-PUH-vihk, MAHRK)

Defense. Shoots left. 6'1", 205 lbs. Born, Stoney Creek, Ont., October 11, 1982. Anaheim's 2nd choice, 35th overall, in 2001 Entry Draft.

Season	Club	League	GP	G	A	Pts	PIM	PP	SH	GW	S	%	+/-	TF	F%	Min	GP	G	A	Pts	PIM	PP	SH	GW	Min
1997-98	Mississauga	OPJHL	51	10	16	26	32																		
1998-99	St. Michael's	OHL	60	6	26	32	46																		
99-2000	St. Michael's	OHL	68	11	29	40	68																		
2000-01	St. Michael's	OHL	61	7	35	42	54										18	3	5	8	22				
2001-02	St. Michael's	OHL	58	12	29	41	42										15	1	11	12	10				
2002-03	Cincinnati	AHL	73	3	21	24	46																		
2003-04	**Anaheim**	**NHL**	**1**	**0**	**0**	**0**	**0**	**0**	**0**	**0**	**1**	**0.0**	**0**	**0**	**0.0**	**13:48**									
	Cincinnati	AHL	74	4	10	14	63										9	1	2	3	4				
2004-05	Cincinnati	AHL	74	1	17	18	47										11	2	3	5	6				
2005-06	**Atlanta**	**NHL**	**7**	**0**	**0**	**0**	**0**	**0**	**0**	**0**	**6**	**0.0**	**–5**	**0**	**0.0**	**11:04**									
	Chicago Wolves	AHL	73	12	26	38	51																		
2006-07	**Atlanta**	**NHL**	**3**	**0**	**1**	**1**	**0**	**0**	**0**	**0**	**1**	**0.0**	**1**	**0**	**0.0**	**10:15**									
	Chicago Wolves	AHL	65	16	24	40	51										15	3	6	9	4				
2007-08	**Atlanta**	**NHL**	**33**	**0**	**2**	**2**	**10**	**0**	**0**	**0**	**25**	**0.0**	**–4**	**0**	**0.0**	**14:28**									
2008-09	St. Petersburg	Rus-KHL	52	8	15	23	40										3	0	0	0	2				
2009-10	**Atlanta**	**NHL**	**37**	**2**	**2**	**4**	**10**	**0**	**0**	**0**	**24**	**8.3**	**0**	**0**	**0.0**	**14:48**									
	NHL Totals		**81**	**2**	**5**	**7**	**20**	**0**	**0**	**0**	**57**	**3.5**		**0**	**0.0**	**14:10**									

OHL First All-Star Team (2002)

Traded to **Atlanta** by **Anaheim** for Kip Brennan, August 23, 2005. Signed as a free agent by **St. Petersburg** (Russia-KHL), August 29, 2008. • Missed majority of 2009-10 season recovering from foot and upper body injuries.

PORTER, Chris

(POHR-tuhr, KRIHS) **ST.L**

Center. Shoots left. 6'1", 210 lbs. Born, Toronto, Ont., May 29, 1984. Chicago's 10th choice, 282nd overall, in 2003 Entry Draft.

Season	Club	League	GP	G	A	Pts	PIM	PP	SH	GW	S	%	+/-	TF	F%	Min	GP	G	A	Pts	PIM	PP	SH	GW	Min
2001-02	Shat.-St. Mary's	High-MN	75	10	25	35	32																		
2002-03	Lincoln Stars	USHL	59	13	22	35	74										10	4	3	7	10				
2003-04	North Dakota	WCHA	41	10	15	25	46																		
2004-05	North Dakota	WCHA	45	12	3	15	36																		
2005-06	North Dakota	WCHA	46	7	16	23	40																		
2006-07	North Dakota	WCHA	43	13	17	30	38																		
2007-08	Peoria Rivermen	AHL	80	12	25	37	72																		
2008-09	**St. Louis**	**NHL**	**6**	**1**	**1**	**2**	**0**	**0**	**0**	**0**	**7**	**14.3**	**–1**	**3**	**33.3**	**10:32**									
	Peoria Rivermen	AHL	74	7	16	23	72										7	1	1	2	0				
2009-10	Peoria Rivermen	AHL	80	13	18	31	53																		
	NHL Totals		**6**	**1**	**1**	**2**	**0**	**0**	**0**	**0**	**7**	**14.3**		**3**	**33.3**	**10:32**									

Signed as a free agent by **St. Louis**, August 21, 2007.

PORTER, Kevin

(POHR-tuhr, KEH-vihn) **CO**

Center. Shoots left. 6', 190 lbs. Born, Detroit, MI, March 12, 1986. Phoenix's 5th choice, 119th overall, in 2004 Entry Draft.

Season	Club	League	GP	G	A	Pts	PIM	PP	SH	GW	S	%	+/-	TF	F%	Min	GP	G	A	Pts	PIM	PP	SH	GW	Min
2002-03	USNTDP	U-17	19	9	11	20	8																		
	USNTDP	U-18	13	1	2	3	2																		
	USNTDP	NAHL	40	19	9	28	17																		
2003-04	USNTDP	U-18	44	5	21	26	26																		
	USNTDP	NAHL	11	3	8	11	4																		
2004-05	U. of Michigan	CCHA	39	11	13	24	51																		
2005-06	U. of Michigan	CCHA	39	17	21	38	30																		
2006-07	U. of Michigan	CCHA	41	24	34	58	16																		
2007-08	U. of Michigan	CCHA	43	*33	30	*63	18																		
	San Antonio	AHL															7	0	4	4	0				
2008-09	**Phoenix**	**NHL**	**34**	**5**	**5**	**10**	**4**	**1**	**0**	**2**	**39**	**12.8**	**–2**	**95**	**29.5**	**13:38**									
	San Antonio	AHL	42	13	22	35	14																		
2009-10	**Phoenix**	**NHL**	**4**	**0**	**0**	**0**	**0**	**0**	**0**	**0**	**3**	**0.0**	**1**	**15**	**33.3**	**7:22**									
	San Antonio	AHL	52	15	25	40	31																		
	Colorado	**NHL**	**16**	**2**	**1**	**3**	**0**	**0**	**1**	**0**	**18**	**11.1**	**–4**	**27**	**48.2**	**13:13**	**4**	**0**	**0**	**0**	**0**	**0**	**0**	**0**	**10:3**
	Lake Erie	AHL	4	1	0	1	2																		
	NHL Totals		**54**	**7**	**6**	**13**	**4**	**1**	**1**	**2**	**60**	**11.7**		**137**	**33.6**	**13:03**	**4**	**0**	**0**	**0**	**0**	**0**	**0**	**0**	**10:3**

CCHA Second All-Star Team (2007) • CCHA First All-Star Team (2008) • CCHA Player of the Year (2008) • NCAA West First All-American Team (2008)

Traded to **Colorado** by **Phoenix** with Peter Mueller for Wojtek Wolski, March 3, 2010.

POTHIER, Brian

(POH-thee-uhr, BRIGH-uhn)

Defense. Shoots right. 6', 204 lbs. Born, New Bedford, MA, April 15, 1977.

Season	Club	League	GP	G	A	Pts	PIM	PP	SH	GW	S	%	+/-	TF	F%	Min	GP	G	A	Pts	PIM	PP	SH	GW	Min
1995-96	NMH School	High-MA	27	11	22	33	36																		
1996-97	RPI Engineers	ECAC	34	1	11	12	42																		
1997-98	RPI Engineers	ECAC	35	2	9	11	28																		
1998-99	RPI Engineers	ECAC	37	5	13	18	36																		
99-2000	RPI Engineers	ECAC	36	9	24	33	44																		
2000-01	**Atlanta**	**NHL**	**3**	**0**	**0**	**0**	**2**	**0**	**0**	**0**	**0**	**0.0**	**4**	**0**	**0.0**	**20:38**									
	Orlando	IHL	76	12	29	41	69										16	3	5	8	11				
2001-02	**Atlanta**	**NHL**	**33**	**3**	**6**	**9**	**22**	**1**	**0**	**1**	**65**	**4.6**	**–19**	**0**	**0.0**	**21:41**									
	Chicago Wolves	AHL	39	6	13	19	30																		
2002-03	**Ottawa**	**NHL**	**14**	**2**	**4**	**6**	**6**	**0**	**0**	**1**	**23**	**8.7**	**11**	**0**	**0.0**	**15:23**	**1**	**0**	**0**	**0**	**2**	**0**	**0**	**0**	**13:1**
	Binghamton	AHL	68	7	40	47	58										8	2	8	10	4				
2003-04	**Ottawa**	**NHL**	**55**	**2**	**6**	**8**	**24**	**1**	**0**	**1**	**78**	**2.6**	**6**	**0**	**0.0**	**16:43**	**7**	**0**	**0**	**0**	**6**	**0**	**0**	**0**	**17:1**
2004-05	Binghamton	AHL	77	12	36	48	64										6	0	1	1	6				
2005-06	**Ottawa**	**NHL**	**77**	**5**	**30**	**35**	**59**	**3**	**0**	**0**	**133**	**3.8**	**29**	**0**	**0.0**	**16:46**	**8**	**2**	**1**	**3**	**2**	**0**	**0**	**0**	**15:**
2006-07	**Washington**	**NHL**	**72**	**3**	**25**	**28**	**44**	**2**	**0**	**0**	**118**	**2.5**	**–11**	**0**	**0.0**	**23:59**									
2007-08	**Washington**	**NHL**	**38**	**5**	**9**	**14**	**20**	**1**	**0**	**1**	**65**	**7.7**	**5**	**0**	**0.0**	**18:42**									
2008-09	**Washington**	**NHL**	**9**	**1**	**2**	**3**	**4**	**0**	**0**	**1**	**8**	**12.5**	**0**	**0**	**0.0**	**16:35**	**13**	**0**	**2**	**2**	**8**	**0**	**0**	**0**	**16:4**
	Hershey Bears	AHL	4	0	0	0	2																		
2009-10	**Washington**	**NHL**	**41**	**4**	**7**	**11**	**10**	**1**	**0**	**1**	**57**	**7.0**	**12**	**0**	**0.0**	**18:03**									
	Carolina	**NHL**	**20**	**1**	**3**	**4**	**11**	**0**	**0**	**1**	**24**	**4.2**	**–8**	**0**	**0.0**	**21:01**									
	NHL Totals		**362**	**26**	**92**	**118**	**202**	**9**	**0**	**7**	**571**	**4.6**		**0**	**0.0**	**19:12**	**29**	**2**	**3**	**5**	**18**	**0**	**0**	**0**	**16:**

ECAC Second All-Star Team (2000) • ECAC All-Tournament Team (2000) • NCAA East Second All-American Team (2000) • Ken McKenzie Trophy (IHL – U.S. - Born Rookie of the Year) (2001) • Garry F. Longman Memorial Trophy (IHL – Rookie of the Year) (2001) • AHL Second All-Star Team (2003, 2005)

Signed as a free agent by **Atlanta**, March 27, 2000. Traded to **Ottawa** by **Atlanta** for Shawn McEachern and Ottawa's 6th round choice (Dan Turple) in 2004 Entry Draft, June 29, 2002. Signed as a free agent by **Washington**, July 1, 2006. • Missed remainder of 2007-08 season and majority of 2008-09 season recovering from head injury suffered in game at Boston, January 3, 2008. Traded to **Carolina** by **Washington** with Oskar Osala and Washington's 2nd round choice (later traded to NY Rangers) in 2011 Entry Draft for Joe Corvo, March 3, 2010.

POTI, Tom

(POH-tee, TAWM) **WS**

Defense. Shoots left. 6'3", 197 lbs. Born, Worcester, MA, March 22, 1977. Edmonton's 4th choice, 59th overall, in 1996 Entry Draft.

Season	Club	League	GP	G	A	Pts	PIM	PP	SH	GW	S	%	+/-	TF	F%	Min	GP	G	A	Pts	PIM	PP	SH	GW	Min
1992-93	St. Peter's Marian	High-MA	55	25	46	71																			
1993-94	Cushing	High-MA	30	10	35	45																			
1994-95	Cushing	High-MA	36	17	54	71	35																		
	Central-Mass	MBAHL	8	8	10	18																			
1995-96	Cushing	High-MA	29	14	59	73	18																		
1996-97	Boston University	H-East	38	4	17	21	54																		
1997-98	Boston University	H-East	38	13	29	42	60																		

			Regular Season														Playoffs								
Season	Club	League	GP	G	A	Pts	PIM	PP	SH	GW	S	%	+/-	TF	F%	Min	GP	G	A	Pts	PIM	PP	SH	GW	Min
1998-99	**Edmonton**	**NHL**	**73**	**5**	**16**	**21**	**42**	**2**	**0**	**3**	**94**	**5.3**	**10**	**0**	**0.0**	**19:33**	**4**	**0**	**1**	**1**	**2**	**0**	**0**	**0**	**28:02**
99-2000	**Edmonton**	**NHL**	**76**	**9**	**26**	**35**	**65**	**2**	**1**	**1**	**125**	**7.2**	**8**	**0**	**0.0**	**24:10**	**5**	**0**	**1**	**1**	**0**	**0**	**0**	**0**	**23:53**
2000-01	**Edmonton**	**NHL**	**81**	**12**	**20**	**32**	**60**	**6**	**0**	**3**	**161**	**7.5**	**–4**	**0**	**0.0**	**22:44**	**6**	**0**	**2**	**2**	**2**	**0**	**0**	**0**	**20:25**
2001-02	**Edmonton**	**NHL**	**55**	**1**	**16**	**17**	**42**	**1**	**0**	**0**	**100**	**1.0**	**–6**	**0**	**0.0**	**24:32**	....	....	....	....	....	....	....	....	....
	United States	Olympics	6	0	1	1	4	....	....	....	....	....	....	....	....	....	....	....	....	....	....	....	....	....	....
	NY Rangers	**NHL**	**11**	**1**	**7**	**8**	**2**	**1**	**0**	**1**	**9**	**11.1**	**–4**	**0**	**0.0**	**21:45**	....	....	....	....	....	....	....	....	....
2002-03	**NY Rangers**	**NHL**	**80**	**11**	**37**	**48**	**58**	**3**	**0**	**2**	**148**	**7.4**	**–6**	**0**	**0.0**	**24:43**	....	....	....	....	....	....	....	....	....
2003-04	**NY Rangers**	**NHL**	**67**	**10**	**14**	**24**	**47**	**4**	**0**	**5**	**124**	**8.1**	**–1**	**0**	**0.0**	**22:28**	....	....	....	....	....	....	....	....	....
2004-05		DID NOT PLAY																							
2005-06	**NY Rangers**	**NHL**	**73**	**3**	**20**	**23**	**70**	**2**	**0**	**2**	**122**	**2.5**	**16**	**4**	**25.0**	**20:46**	**4**	**0**	**0**	**0**	**2**	**0**	**0**	**0**	**19:39**
2006-07	**NY Islanders**	**NHL**	**78**	**6**	**38**	**44**	**74**	**6**	**0**	**1**	**134**	**4.5**	**–1**	**0**	**0.0**	**25:43**	**5**	**0**	**3**	**3**	**6**	**0**	**0**	**0**	**27:34**
2007-08	**Washington**	**NHL**	**71**	**2**	**27**	**29**	**46**	**0**	**0**	**0**	**99**	**2.0**	**9**	**0**	**0.0**	**23:29**	**7**	**0**	**1**	**1**	**8**	**0**	**0**	**0**	**24:01**
2008-09	**Washington**	**NHL**	**52**	**3**	**10**	**13**	**28**	**0**	**0**	**1**	**48**	**6.3**	**3**	**0**	**0.0**	**21:09**	**14**	**2**	**5**	**7**	**4**	**1**	**0**	**0**	**21:37**
2009-10	**Washington**	**NHL**	**70**	**4**	**20**	**24**	**42**	**2**	**0**	**0**	**69**	**5.8**	**26**	**0**	**0.0**	**21:24**	**6**	**0**	**4**	**4**	**5**	**0**	**0**	**0**	**21:23**
	NHL Totals		**787**	**67**	**251**	**318**	**576**	**29**	**1**	**19**	**1233**	**5.4**		**4**	**25.0**	**22:50**	**51**	**2**	**17**	**19**	**29**	**1**	**0**	**0**	**22:56**

NCAA Championship All-Tournament Team (1997) • Hockey East First All-Star Team (1998) • NCAA East First All-American Team (1998) • NHL All-Rookie Team (1999)

Played in NHL All-Star Game (2003)

Traded to **NY Rangers** by **Edmonton** with Rem Murray for Mike York and NY Rangers' 4th round choice (Ivan Koltsov) in 2002 Entry Draft, March 19, 2002. Signed as a free agent by **NY Islanders**, July 8, 2006. Signed as a free agent by **Washington**, July 1, 2007.

POTTER, Corey (PAW-tuhr, KOHR-ee) PIT.

Defense. Shoots right. 6'3", 205 lbs. Born, Lansing, MI, January 5, 1984. NY Rangers' 4th choice, 122nd overall, in 2003 Entry Draft.

Season	Club	League	GP	G	A	Pts	PIM	PP	SH	GW	S	%	+/-	TF	F%	Min	GP	G	A	Pts	PIM	PP	SH	GW	Min
99-2000	Det. Honeybaked	MWEHL	58	10	38	48	....	....	....	....	....	....	....	....	....	....	....	....	....	....	....	....	....	....	....
2000-01	USNTDP	U-17	13	0	0	0	6	....	....	....	....	....	....	....	....	....	....	....	....	....	....	....	....	....	....
	USNTDP	NAHL	53	4	4	8	20	....	....	....	....	....	....	....	....	....	....	....	....	....	....	....	....	....	....
2001-02	USNTDP	U-18	38	4	6	10	49	....	....	....	....	....	....	....	....	....	....	....	....	....	....	....	....	....	....
	USNTDP	USHL	13	2	2	4	12	....	....	....	....	....	....	....	....	....	....	....	....	....	....	....	....	....	....
	USNTDP	NAHL	10	0	3	3	4	....	....	....	....	....	....	....	....	....	....	....	....	....	....	....	....	....	....
2002-03	Michigan State	CCHA	35	4	4	8	30	....	....	....	....	....	....	....	....	....	....	....	....	....	....	....	....	....	....
2003-04	Michigan State	CCHA	38	0	8	8	63	....	....	....	....	....	....	....	....	....	....	....	....	....	....	....	....	....	....
2004-05	Michigan State	CCHA	32	0	6	6	73	....	....	....	....	....	....	....	....	....	....	....	....	....	....	....	....	....	....
2005-06	Michigan State	CCHA	45	4	18	22	117	....	....	....	....	....	....	....	....	....	....	....	....	....	....	....	....	....	....
2006-07	Hartford	AHL	30	2	8	10	21	....	....	....	....	....	....	....	....	....	7	1	4	5	12	....	....	....	....
	Charlotte	ECHL	43	6	13	19	56	....	....	....	....	....	....	....	....	....	....	....	....	....	....	....	....	....	....
2007-08	Hartford	AHL	80	5	27	32	102	....	....	....	....	....	....	....	....	....	5	0	1	1	14	....	....	....	....
2008-09	**NY Rangers**	**NHL**	**5**	**1**	**1**	**2**	**0**	**0**	**0**	**0**	**4**	**25.0**	**–1**	**0**	**0.0**	**13:15**	....	....	....	....	....	....	....	....	....
	Hartford	AHL	67	10	22	32	82	....	....	....	....	....	....	....	....	....	6	1	3	4	23	....	....	....	....
2009-10	**NY Rangers**	**NHL**	**3**	**0**	**0**	**0**	**2**	**0**	**0**	**0**	**2**	**0.0**	**0**	**0**	**0.0**	**12:07**	....	....	....	....	....	....	....	....	....
	Hartford	AHL	69	4	24	28	54	....	....	....	....	....	....	....	....	....	....	....	....	....	....	....	....	....	....
	NHL Totals		**8**	**1**	**1**	**2**	**2**	**0**	**0**	**0**	**6**	**16.7**		**0**	**0.0**	**12:50**	....	....	....	....	....	....	....	....	....

Signed as a free agent by **Pittsburgh**, July 16, 2010.

POTULNY, Ryan (poh-TUHL-nee, RIGH-uhn)

Center. Shoots left. 6', 190 lbs. Born, Grand Forks, ND, September 5, 1984. Philadelphia's 6th choice, 87th overall, in 2003 Entry Draft.

Season	Club	League	GP	G	A	Pts	PIM	PP	SH	GW	S	%	+/-	TF	F%	Min	GP	G	A	Pts	PIM	PP	SH	GW	Min
2001-02	Lincoln Stars	USHL	60	23	34	57	65	....	....	....	....	....	....	....	....	....	4	0	1	1	2	....	....	....	....
2002-03	Lincoln Stars	USHL	54	35	*43	*78	18	....	....	....	....	....	....	....	....	....	10	6	*11	*17	8	....	....	....	....
2003-04	U. of Minnesota	WCHA	15	6	8	14	10	....	....	....	....	....	....	....	....	....	....	....	....	....	....	....	....	....	....
2004-05	U. of Minnesota	WCHA	44	24	17	41	20	....	....	....	....	....	....	....	....	....	....	....	....	....	....	....	....	....	....
2005-06	U. of Minnesota	WCHA	41	*38	25	*63	31	....	....	....	....	....	....	....	....	....	....	....	....	....	....	....	....	....	....
	Philadelphia	**NHL**	**2**	**0**	**1**	**1**	**0**	**0**	**0**	**0**	**0**	**0.0**	**1**	**9**	**44.4**	**6:09**	....	....	....	....	....	....	....	....	....
2006-07	**Philadelphia**	**NHL**	**35**	**7**	**5**	**12**	**22**	**0**	**0**	**2**	**56**	**12.5**	**1**	**278**	**43.5**	**11:00**	....	....	....	....	....	....	....	....	....
	Philadelphia	AHL	30	12	14	26	34	....	....	....	....	....	....	....	....	....	....	....	....	....	....	....	....	....	....
2007-08	**Philadelphia**	**NHL**	**7**	**0**	**1**	**1**	**4**	**0**	**0**	**0**	**5**	**0.0**	**0**	**32**	**43.8**	**6:30**	....	....	....	....	....	....	....	....	....
	Philadelphia	AHL	58	21	26	47	51	....	....	....	....	....	....	....	....	....	12	3	5	8	10	....	....	....	....
2008-09	**Edmonton**	**NHL**	**8**	**0**	**3**	**3**	**0**	**0**	**0**	**0**	**9**	**0.0**	**2**	**10**	**10.0**	**10:29**	....	....	....	....	....	....	....	....	....
	Springfield	AHL	70	38	24	62	48	....	....	....	....	....	....	....	....	....	....	....	....	....	....	....	....	....	....
2009-10	**Edmonton**	**NHL**	**64**	**15**	**17**	**32**	**28**	**7**	**1**	**2**	**152**	**9.9**	**–21**	**820**	**47.4**	**16:17**	....	....	....	....	....	....	....	....	....
	Springfield	AHL	14	3	5	8	8	....	....	....	....	....	....	....	....	....	....	....	....	....	....	....	....	....	....
	NHL Totals		**116**	**22**	**27**	**49**	**54**	**7**	**1**	**4**	**222**	**9.9**		**1149**	**46.0**	**13:31**	....	....	....	....	....	....	....	....	....

USHL First All-Star Team (2003) • USHL Player of the Year (2003) • WCHA First All-Star Team (2006) • NCAA West First All-American Team (2006)

• Missed majority of 2003-04 season recovering from knee injury suffered in game vs. North Dakota (WCHA), November 7, 2003. Traded to **Edmonton** by **Philadelphia** for Danny Syvret, June 6, 2008.

POULIOT, Benoit (POO-lee-oh, BEHN-wah) MTL.

Left wing. Shoots Left. 6'3", 199 lbs. Born, Alfred, Ont., September 29, 1986. Minnesota's 1st choice, 4th overall, in 2005 Entry Draft.

Season	Club	League	GP	G	A	Pts	PIM	PP	SH	GW	S	%	+/-	TF	F%	Min	GP	G	A	Pts	PIM	PP	SH	GW	Min
2002-03	Clarence Beavers	OHA-B	38	13	17	30	86	....	....	....	....	....	....	....	....	....	5	0	2	2	8	....	....	....	....
	Hawkesbury	CJHL	1	1	0	1	0	....	....	....	....	....	....	....	....	....	....	....	....	....	....	....	....	....	....
2003-04	Hawkesbury	CJHL	45	21	21	42	85	....	....	....	....	....	....	....	....	....	6	3	7	10	10	....	....	....	....
	Sudbury Wolves	OHL	4	2	2	4	0	....	....	....	....	....	....	....	....	....	4	2	1	3	0	....	....	....	....
2004-05	Sudbury Wolves	OHL	67	29	38	67	102	....	....	....	....	....	....	....	....	....	12	6	8	14	20	....	....	....	....
2005-06	Sudbury Wolves	OHL	51	35	30	65	141	....	....	....	....	....	....	....	....	....	8	8	3	11	16	....	....	....	....
	Houston Aeros	AHL	....	....	....	....	....	....	....	....	....	....	....	....	....	....	2	0	0	0	2	....	....	....	....
2006-07	**Minnesota**	**NHL**	**3**	**0**	**0**	**0**	**0**	**0**	**0**	**0**	**1**	**0.0**	**–1**	**2**	**0.0**	**6:58**	....	....	....	....	....	....	....	....	....
	Houston Aeros	AHL	67	19	17	36	109	....	....	....	....	....	....	....	....	....	....	....	....	....	....	....	....	....	....
2007-08	**Minnesota**	**NHL**	**11**	**2**	**1**	**3**	**0**	**0**	**0**	**0**	**10**	**20.0**	**–1**	**65**	**40.0**	**8:49**	**1**	**0**	**0**	**0**	**0**	**0**	**0**	**0**	**10:16**
	Houston Aeros	AHL	46	10	14	24	67	....	....	....	....	....	....	....	....	....	3	0	0	0	2	....	....	....	....
2008-09	**Minnesota**	**NHL**	**37**	**5**	**6**	**11**	**18**	**2**	**0**	**1**	**34**	**14.7**	**1**	**217**	**42.9**	**11:51**	....	....	....	....	....	....	....	....	....
	Houston Aeros	AHL	30	9	15	24	20	....	....	....	....	....	....	....	....	....	20	1	7	8	28	....	....	....	....
2009-10	**Minnesota**	**NHL**	**14**	**2**	**2**	**4**	**12**	**0**	**0**	**0**	**19**	**10.5**	**0**	**8**	**50.0**	**11:56**	....	....	....	....	....	....	....	....	....
	Montreal	**NHL**	**39**	**15**	**9**	**24**	**31**	**4**	**0**	**3**	**92**	**16.3**	**8**	**3**	**33.3**	**16:44**	**18**	**0**	**2**	**2**	**6**	**0**	**0**	**0**	**11:45**
	Hamilton	AHL	3	1	2	3	4	....	....	....	....	....	....	....	....	....	....	....	....	....	....	....	....	....	....
	NHL Totals		**104**	**24**	**18**	**42**	**61**	**6**	**0**	**4**	**156**	**15.4**		**295**	**42.0**	**13:14**	**19**	**0**	**2**	**2**	**6**	**0**	**0**	**0**	**11:41**

OHL All-Rookie Team (2005) • OHL First All-Star Team (2005) • OHL Rookie of the Year (2005) • Canadian Major Junior All-Rookie Team (2005) • Canadian Major Junior Rookie of the Year (2005)

Traded to **Montreal** by **Minnesota** for Guillaume Latendresse, November 23, 2009.

POULIOT, Marc (POO-lee-oh, MAHRK) T.B.

Center. Shoots right. 6'1", 195 lbs. Born, Quebec City, Que., May 22, 1985. Edmonton's 1st choice, 22nd overall, in 2003 Entry Draft.

Season	Club	League	GP	G	A	Pts	PIM	PP	SH	GW	S	%	+/-	TF	F%	Min	GP	G	A	Pts	PIM	PP	SH	GW	Min
2000-01	Ste-Foy	QAAA	38	16	39	55	52	....	....	....	....	....	....	....	....	....	16	8	12	20	16	....	....	....	....
2001-02	Rimouski Oceanic	QMJHL	28	9	14	23	32	....	....	....	....	....	....	....	....	....	5	0	0	0	4	....	....	....	....
2002-03	Rimouski Oceanic	QMJHL	65	32	41	73	100	....	....	....	....	....	....	....	....	....	....	....	....	....	....	....	....	....	....
2003-04	Rimouski Oceanic	QMJHL	42	25	33	58	62	....	....	....	....	....	....	....	....	....	9	5	7	12	12	....	....	....	....
2004-05	Rimouski Oceanic	QMJHL	70	45	69	114	83	....	....	....	....	....	....	....	....	....	13	4	15	19	8	....	....	....	....
2005-06	**Edmonton**	**NHL**	**8**	**1**	**0**	**1**	**0**	**0**	**0**	**0**	**5**	**20.0**	**1**	**56**	**55.4**	**8:30**	....	....	....	....	....	....	....	....	....
	Hamilton	AHL	65	15	31	46	63	....	....	....	....	....	....	....	....	....	....	....	....	....	....	....	....	....	....
2006-07	**Edmonton**	**NHL**	**46**	**4**	**7**	**11**	**18**	**0**	**0**	**0**	**73**	**5.5**	**–2**	**353**	**48.7**	**13:03**	....	....	....	....	....	....	....	....	....
	Wilkes-Barre	AHL	33	14	17	31	20	....	....	....	....	....	....	....	....	....	11	5	5	10	4	....	....	....	....
2007-08	**Edmonton**	**NHL**	**24**	**1**	**6**	**7**	**12**	**0**	**0**	**0**	**32**	**3.1**	**–1**	**44**	**47.7**	**10:20**	....	....	....	....	....	....	....	....	....
	Springfield	AHL	55	21	26	47	47	....	....	....	....	....	....	....	....	....	....	....	....	....	....	....	....	....	....
2008-09	**Edmonton**	**NHL**	**63**	**8**	**12**	**20**	**23**	**0**	**0**	**2**	**94**	**8.5**	**1**	**211**	**48.3**	**11:30**	....	....	....	....	....	....	....	....	....
2009-10	**Edmonton**	**NHL**	**35**	**7**	**7**	**14**	**21**	**1**	**0**	**1**	**60**	**11.7**	**–4**	**235**	**44.3**	**12:48**	....	....	....	....	....	....	....	....	....
	Springfield	AHL	4	1	5	6	12	....	....	....	....	....	....	....	....	....	....	....	....	....	....	....	....	....	....
	NHL Totals		**176**	**21**	**32**	**53**	**74**	**1**	**0**	**3**	**264**	**8.0**		**899**	**47.8**	**11:52**	....	....	....	....	....	....	....	....	....

QMJHL First All-Star Team (2005) • George Parsons Trophy (Memorial Cup Tournament - Most Sportsmanlike Player) (2005)

• Missed majority of 2009-10 season recovering from lower body injury. Signed as a free agent by **Tampa Bay**, July 23, 2010.

POWE, Darroll

(POW, DAIR-ohl) **PHI.**

Left wing. Shoots left. 5'11", 212 lbs. Born, Saskatoon, Sask., June 22, 1985.

			Regular Season														Playoffs								
Season	Club	League	GP	G	A	Pts	PIM	PP	SH	GW	S	%	+/-	TF	F%	Min	GP	G	A	Pts	PIM	PP	SH	GW	Min
2003-04	Princeton	ECAC	29	4	5	9	28																		
2004-05	Princeton	ECAC	30	5	2	7	41																		
2005-06	Princeton	ECAC	27	6	10	16	48																		
2006-07	Princeton	ECAC	34	13	15	28	63																		
	Philadelphia	AHL	11	2	2	4	20																		
2007-08	Philadelphia	AHL	76	9	14	23	133										10	1	0	1	6				
2008-09	**Philadelphia**	**NHL**	60	6	5	11	35	0	0	0	72	8.3	–8	263	48.7	10:32	6	1	2	3	7	0	0	0	14:02
	Philadelphia	AHL	8	4	3	7	20																		
2009-10	**Philadelphia**	**NHL**	63	9	6	15	54	0	0	0	103	8.7	0	210	45.2	12:05	23	0	1	1	6	0	0	0	12:33
	NHL Totals		123	15	11	26	89	0	0	0	175	8.6		473	47.1	11:20	29	1	3	4	13	0	0	0	12:52

Signed as a free agent by **Philadelphia**, April 17, 2008.

PREISSING, Tom

(PRIGH-sihng, TAHM)

Defense. Shoots right. 6', 197 lbs. Born, Arlington Heights, IL, December 3, 1978.

			Regular Season														Playoffs								
Season	Club	League	GP	G	A	Pts	PIM	PP	SH	GW	S	%	+/-	TF	F%	Min	GP	G	A	Pts	PIM	PP	SH	GW	Min
1997-98	Green Bay	USHL	56	8	13	21	30										4	0	2	2	2				
1998-99	Green Bay	USHL	53	18	37	55	40										6	3	6	9	2				
99-2000	Colorado College	WCHA	36	4	14	18	20																		
2000-01	Colorado College	WCHA	33	6	18	24	26																		
2001-02	Colorado College	WCHA	43	6	26	32	42																		
2002-03	Colorado College	WCHA	42	23	29	52	16																		
2003-04	**San Jose**	**NHL**	69	2	17	19	12	2	0	1	89	2.2	8	0	0.0	18:12	11	0	1	1	0	0	0	0	12:49
2004-05	Krefeld Pinguine	Germany	33	1	6	7	32																		
2005-06	**San Jose**	**NHL**	74	11	32	43	26	2	0	2	131	8.4	17	1	0.0	20:30	11	1	6	7	4	0	0	0	23:50
2006-07	**Ottawa**	**NHL**	80	7	31	38	18	3	0	0	94	7.4	40	0	0.0	15:15	20	2	5	7	10	1	0	1	15:02
2007-08	**Los Angeles**	**NHL**	77	8	16	24	16	6	0	1	93	8.6	–6	9	22.2	17:53									
2008-09	**Los Angeles**	**NHL**	22	3	4	7	6	2	0	0	40	7.5	–7	0	0.0	16:45									
	Manchester	AHL	14	2	4	6	6																		
2009-10	**Colorado**	**NHL**	4	0	1	1	0	0	0	0	6	0.0	–6	0	0.0	13:05									
	Lake Erie	AHL	49	9	22	31	38																		
	NHL Totals		326	31	101	132	78	15	0	4	453	6.8		10	20.0	17:46	42	3	12	15	14	1	0	1	16:45

USHL First All-Star Team (1999) • USHL Defenseman of the Year (1999) • WCHA First All-Star Team (2003) • NCAA West First All-American Team (2003)

Signed as a free agent by **San Jose**, April 4, 2003. Signed as a free agent by **Krefeld** (Germany), November 15, 2004. Traded to **Chicago** by **San Jose** with Josh Hennessy for Mark Bell, July 9, 2006. Traded to **Ottawa** by **Chicago** with Josh Hennessy, Michal Barinka and Chicago's 2nd round choice (Patrick Wiercioch) in 2008 Entry Draft for Martin Havlat and Bryan Smolinski, July 10, 2006. Signed as a free agent by **Los Angeles**, July 2, 2007. Traded to **Colorado** by **Los Angeles** with Kyle Quincey and Los Angeles' 5th round choice (Luke Walker) in 2010 Entry Draft for Ryan Smyth, July 3, 2009.

PRIMEAU, Wayne

(PREE-moh, WAYN)

Center. Shoots left. 6'4", 225 lbs. Born, Scarborough, Ont., June 4, 1976. Buffalo's 1st choice, 17th overall, in 1994 Entry Draft.

			Regular Season														Playoffs								
Season	Club	League	GP	G	A	Pts	PIM	PP	SH	GW	S	%	+/-	TF	F%	Min	GP	G	A	Pts	PIM	PP	SH	GW	Min
1991-92	Whitby Flyers	Minor-ON	63	36	50	86	96																		
1992-93	Owen Sound	OHL	66	10	27	37	108										8	1	4	5	0				
1993-94	Owen Sound	OHL	65	25	50	75	75										9	1	6	7	8				
1994-95	Owen Sound	OHL	66	34	62	96	84										10	4	9	13	15				
	Buffalo	**NHL**	1	1	0	1	0	0	0	1	2	50.0	–2												
1995-96	Owen Sound	OHL	28	15	29	44	52																		
	Oshawa Generals	OHL	24	12	13	25	33										3	2	3	5	2				
	Buffalo	**NHL**	2	0	0	0	0	0	0	0	0	0.0	0												
	Rochester	AHL	8	2	3	5	6										17	3	1	4	11				
1996-97	**Buffalo**	**NHL**	45	2	4	6	64	1	0	0	25	8.0	–2				9	0	0	0	6	0	0	0	
	Rochester	AHL	24	9	5	14	27										1	0	0	0	0				
1997-98	**Buffalo**	**NHL**	69	6	6	12	87	2	0	1	51	11.8	9				14	1	3	4	6	0	0	0	
1998-99	**Buffalo**	**NHL**	67	5	8	13	38	0	0	0	55	9.1	–6	529	48.6	10:19	19	3	4	7	6	1	0	0	13:29
99-2000	**Buffalo**	**NHL**	41	5	7	12	38	2	0	1	40	12.5	–8	430	45.6	11:03									
	Tampa Bay	**NHL**	17	2	3	5	25	0	0	0	35	5.7	–4	290	45.5	14:21									
2000-01	**Tampa Bay**	**NHL**	47	2	13	15	77	0	0	0	47	4.3	–17	630	52.2	14:11									
	Pittsburgh	**NHL**	28	1	6	7	54	0	0	0	30	3.3	0	318	51.3	12:45	18	1	3	4	2	0	0	0	15:06
2001-02	**Pittsburgh**	**NHL**	33	3	7	10	18	0	1	0	28	10.7	–1	519	53.2	12:38									
2002-03	**Pittsburgh**	**NHL**	70	5	11	16	55	1	0	0	101	5.0	–30	1240	50.4	16:17									
	San Jose	**NHL**	7	1	1	2	0	0	0	0	13	7.7	2	98	45.9	15:59									
2003-04	**San Jose**	**NHL**	72	9	20	29	90	0	1	1	142	6.3	4	867	46.6	15:28	17	1	2	3	4	0	0	0	15:41
2004-05				DID NOT PLAY																					
2005-06	**San Jose**	**NHL**	21	5	3	8	17	1	1	1	35	14.3	–6	194	41.8	13:55									
	Boston	**NHL**	50	6	8	14	40	0	0	0	66	9.1	–10	749	49.8	17:16									
2006-07	**Boston**	**NHL**	51	7	8	15	75	2	1	1	72	9.7	–15	652	50.5	15:05									
	Calgary	**NHL**	27	3	4	7	36	0	1	2	35	8.6	–2	199	46.2	10:38	6	0	2	2	14	0	0	0	13:29
2007-08	**Calgary**	**NHL**	43	3	7	10	26	0	0	0	39	7.7	–3	94	54.3	11:03	7	1	0	1	4	0	0	0	10:35
2008-09	**Calgary**	**NHL**	24	0	4	4	14	0	0	0	22	0.0	–3	217	53.0	10:23									
2009-10	**Toronto**	**NHL**	59	3	5	8	35	0	0	0	47	6.4	–1	512	55.3	11:03									
	NHL Totals		774	69	125	194	789	9	5	8	885	7.8		7538	49.8	13:22	90	7	14	21	42	1	0	0	14:11

Traded to **Tampa Bay** by **Buffalo** with Cory Sarich, Brian Holzinger and Buffalo's 3rd round choice (Alexander Kharitonov) in 2000 Entry Draft for Chris Gratton and Tampa Bay's 2nd round choice (Derek Roy) in 2001 Entry Draft, March 9, 2000. Traded to **Pittsburgh** by **Tampa Bay** for Matthew Barnaby, February 1, 2001. • Missed majority of 2001-02 season recovering from knee injury suffered in game vs. Buffalo, January 8, 2002. Traded to **San Jose** by **Pittsburgh** for Matt Bradley, March 11, 2003. Traded to **Boston** by **San Jose** with Brad Stuart and Marco Sturm for Joe Thornton, November 30, 2005. Traded to **Calgary** by **Boston** with Brad Stuart and Washington's 4th round choice (previously acquired, Calgary selected T.J. Brodie) in 2008 Entry Draft for Andrew Ference and Chuck Kobasew, February 10, 2007. • Missed remainder of 2008-09 season recovering from ankle injury suffered in game at St, Louis. December 5, 2008. Traded to **Toronto** by **Calgary** with Calgary's 2nd round choice in 2011 Entry Draft for Anton Stralman, Colin Stuart and Toronto's 7th round choice in 2012 Entry Draft, July 27, 2009.

PRONGER, Chris

(PRAWN-guhr, KRIHS) **PHI.**

Defense. Shoots left. 6'6", 220 lbs. Born, Dryden, Ont., October 10, 1974. Hartford's 1st choice, 2nd overall, in 1993 Entry Draft.

			Regular Season														Playoffs								
Season	Club	League	GP	G	A	Pts	PIM	PP	SH	GW	S	%	+/-	TF	F%	Min	GP	G	A	Pts	PIM	PP	SH	GW	Min
1990-91	Stratford Cullitons	OHA-B	48	15	37	52	132																		
1991-92	Peterborough	OHL	63	17	45	62	90										10	1	8	9	28				
1992-93	Peterborough	OHL	61	15	62	77	108										21	15	25	40	51				
1993-94	**Hartford**	**NHL**	81	5	25	30	113	2	0	0	174	2.9	–3												
1994-95	**Hartford**	**NHL**	43	5	9	14	54	3	0	1	94	5.3	–12												
1995-96	**St. Louis**	**NHL**	78	7	18	25	110	3	1	1	138	5.1	–18				13	1	5	6	16	0	0	0	
1996-97	**St. Louis**	**NHL**	79	11	24	35	143	4	0	0	147	7.5	15				6	1	1	2	22	0	0	0	
1997-98	**St. Louis**	**NHL**	81	9	27	36	180	1	0	2	145	6.2	*47				10	1	9	10	26	0	0	0	
	Canada	Olympics	6	0	0	0	4																		
1998-99	**St. Louis**	**NHL**	67	13	33	46	113	8	0	0	172	7.6	3	0	0.0	30:36	13	1	4	5	28	1	0	0	35:53
99-2000	**St. Louis**	**NHL**	79	14	48	62	92	8	0	3	192	7.3	*52	1	0.0	30:14	7	3	4	7	32	2	0	2	30:14
2000-01	**St. Louis**	**NHL**	51	8	39	47	75	4	0	0	121	6.6	21	0	0.0	27:45	15	1	7	8	32	0	0	0	33:50
2001-02	**St. Louis**	**NHL**	78	7	40	47	120	4	1	3	204	3.4	23	0	0.0	29:28	9	1	7	8	24	0	0	0	27:51
	Canada	Olympics	6	0	1	1	2																		
2002-03	**St. Louis**	**NHL**	5	1	3	4	10	0	0	0	11	9.1	–2	1	0.0	21:39	7	1	3	4	14	0	0	0	24:36
2003-04	**St. Louis**	**NHL**	80	14	40	54	88	7	0	3	203	6.9	–1	2	0.0	27:28	5	0	1	1	16	0	0	0	27:54
2004-05				DID NOT PLAY																					
2005-06	**Edmonton**	**NHL**	80	12	44	56	74	10	0	3	155	7.7	2	1	0.0	27:59	24	5	16	21	26	3	0	0	30:57
	Canada	Olympics	6	1	2	3	16																		
2006-07 ♦	**Anaheim**	**NHL**	66	13	46	59	69	8	0	2	166	7.8	27	4	25.0	27:06	19	3	12	15	26	1	0	0	30:11
2007-08	**Anaheim**	**NHL**	72	12	31	43	128	8	0	4	182	6.6	–1	7	57.1	26:00	6	2	3	5	12	2	0	1	24:14
2008-09	**Anaheim**	**NHL**	82	11	37	48	88	4	0	2	196	5.6	0	7	28.6	26:56	13	2	8	10	12	1	0	0	27:13

			Regular Season														Playoffs								
Season	Club	League	GP	G	A	Pts	PIM	PP	SH	GW	S	%	+/-	TF	F%	Min	GP	G	A	Pts	PIM	PP	SH	GW	Min
2009-10	**Philadelphia**	**NHL**	**82**	**10**	**45**	**55**	**79**	**5**	**0**	**2**	**175**	**5.7**	**22**	**0**	**0.0**	**25:56**	**23**	**4**	**14**	**18**	***36**	**3**	**0**	**0**	**29:03**
	Canada	Olympics	7	0	5	5	2	....	....	....	....	....	....	....	....	....	....	....	....	....	....	....	....	....	....
	NHL Totals		**1104**	**152**	**509**	**661**	**1536**	**79**	**2**	**26**	**2475**	**6.1**		**23**	**30.4**	**27:53**	**170**	**26**	**94**	**120**	**322**	**13**	**0**	**3**	**30:01**

OHL All-Rookie Team (1992) • OHL First All-Star Team (1993) • Canadian Major Junior First All-Star Team (1993) • Canadian Major Junior Defenseman of the Year (1993) • NHL All-Rookie Team (1994) • NHL Second All-Star Team (1998, 2004, 2007) • Bud Ice Plus/Minus Award (1998) • NHL First All-Star Team (2000) • Bud Light Plus/Minus Award (2000) • James Norris Memorial Trophy (2000) • Hart Memorial Trophy (2000)

Played in NHL All-Star Game (1999, 2000, 2002, 2004, 2008)

Traded to **St. Louis** by **Hartford** for Brendan Shanahan, July 27, 1995. • Missed majority of 2002-03 season recovering from wrist and knee surgery, September 10, 2002. Traded to **Edmonton** by **St. Louis** for Eric Brewer, Doug Lynch and Jeff Woywitka, August 2, 2005. Traded to **Anaheim** by **Edmonton** for Joffrey Lupul, Ladislav Smid, Anaheim's 1st round choice (later traded to Phoenix - Phoenix selected Nick Ross) in 2007 Entry Draft and Anaheim's 1st (Jordan Eberle) and 2nd (later traded to NY Islanders - NY Islanders selected Travis Hamonic) round choices in 2008 Entry Draft, July 3, 2006. Traded to **Philadelphia** by **Anaheim** with Ryan Dingle for Joffrey Lupul, Luca Sbisa, Philadelphia's 1st round choices in 2009 (later traded to Columbus - Columbus selected John Moore) and 2010 (Emerson Etem) Entry Drafts and future considerations, June 26, 2009.

PROSPAL, Vinny

(PRAWS-puhl, vih-NEE) **NYR**

Center. Shoots left. 6'2", 198 lbs. Born, Ceske Budejovice, Czech., February 17, 1975. Philadelphia's 2nd choice, 71st overall, in 1993 Entry Draft.

Season	Club	League	GP	G	A	Pts	PIM	PP	SH	GW	S	%	+/-	TF	F%	Min	GP	G	A	Pts	PIM	PP	SH	GW	Min
1991-92	C. Budejovice Jr.	Czech-Jr.	36	16	16	32	12	....	....	....	....	....	....	....	....	....	....	....	....	....	....	....	....	....	....
1992-93	C. Budejovice Jr.	Czech-Jr.	32	26	31	57	24	....	....	....	....	....	....	....	....	....	....	....	....	....	....	....	....	....	....
1993-94	Hershey Bears	AHL	55	14	21	35	38	....	....	....	....	....	....	....	....	....	2	0	0	0	2	....	....	....	....
1994-95	Hershey Bears	AHL	69	13	32	45	36	....	....	....	....	....	....	....	....	....	2	1	0	1	4	....	....	....	....
1995-96	Hershey Bears	AHL	68	15	36	51	59	....	....	....	....	....	....	....	....	....	5	2	4	6	2	....	....	....	....
1996-97	**Philadelphia**	**NHL**	**18**	**5**	**10**	**15**	**4**	**0**	**0**	**0**	**35**	**14.3**	**3**	....	....	....	**5**	**1**	**3**	**4**	**4**	**0**	**0**	**0**	....
	Philadelphia	AHL	63	32	63	95	70	....	....	....	....	....	....	....	....	....	....	....	....	....	....	....	....	....	....
1997-98	**Philadelphia**	**NHL**	**41**	**5**	**13**	**18**	**17**	**4**	**0**	**0**	**60**	**8.3**	**-10**	....	....	....	....	....	....	....	....	....	....	....	....
	Ottawa	**NHL**	**15**	**1**	**6**	**7**	**4**	**0**	**0**	**0**	**28**	**3.6**	**-1**	....	....	....	**6**	**0**	**0**	**0**	**0**	**0**	**0**	**0**	....
1998-99	**Ottawa**	**NHL**	**79**	**10**	**26**	**36**	**58**	**2**	**0**	**3**	**114**	**8.8**	**8**	**997**	**56.2**	**13:03**	**4**	**0**	**0**	**0**	**0**	**0**	**0**	**0**	**12:37**
99-2000	**Ottawa**	**NHL**	**79**	**22**	**33**	**55**	**40**	**5**	**0**	**4**	**204**	**10.8**	**-2**	**1331**	**49.6**	**16:26**	**6**	**0**	**4**	**4**	**4**	**0**	**0**	**0**	**17:40**
2000-01	**Ottawa**	**NHL**	**40**	**1**	**12**	**13**	**12**	**0**	**0**	**0**	**68**	**1.5**	**1**	**501**	**50.1**	**12:57**	....	....	....	....	....	....	....	....	....
	Florida	**NHL**	**34**	**4**	**12**	**16**	**10**	**1**	**0**	**0**	**68**	**5.9**	**-2**	**487**	**54.6**	**16:36**	....	....	....	....	....	....	....	....	....
2001-02	**Tampa Bay**	**NHL**	**81**	**18**	**37**	**55**	**38**	**7**	**0**	**2**	**166**	**10.8**	**-11**	**555**	**52.8**	**17:31**	....	....	....	....	....	....	....	....	....
2002-03	**Tampa Bay**	**NHL**	**80**	**22**	**57**	**79**	**53**	**9**	**0**	**4**	**134**	**16.4**	**9**	**161**	**51.6**	**18:39**	**11**	**4**	**2**	**6**	**8**	**2**	**0**	**0**	**21:15**
2003-04	**Anaheim**	**NHL**	**82**	**19**	**35**	**54**	**54**	**7**	**0**	**4**	**185**	**10.3**	**-9**	**45**	**46.7**	**18:37**	....	....	....	....	....	....	....	....	....
2004-05	C. Budejovice	CzRep-2	39	28	60	88	82	....	....	....	....	....	....	....	....	....	16	15	15	30	32	....	....	....	....
2005-06	**Tampa Bay**	**NHL**	**81**	**25**	**55**	**80**	**50**	**10**	**0**	**3**	**236**	**10.6**	**-3**	**267**	**45.3**	**19:10**	**5**	**0**	**2**	**2**	**0**	**0**	**0**	**0**	**15:56**
	Czech Republic	Olympics	8	4	2	6	2	....	....	....	....	....	....	....	....	....	....	....	....	....	....	....	....	....	....
2006-07	**Tampa Bay**	**NHL**	**82**	**14**	**41**	**55**	**36**	**2**	**0**	**1**	**219**	**6.4**	**-24**	**124**	**52.4**	**19:04**	**6**	**1**	**4**	**5**	**4**	**0**	**0**	**1**	**22:19**
2007-08	**Tampa Bay**	**NHL**	**62**	**29**	**28**	**57**	**39**	**9**	**0**	**4**	**175**	**16.6**	**-7**	**176**	**54.6**	**20:00**	....	....	....	....	....	....	....	....	....
	Philadelphia	**NHL**	**18**	**4**	**10**	**14**	**6**	**1**	**0**	**1**	**40**	**10.0**	**7**	**86**	**58.1**	**17:15**	**17**	**3**	**10**	**13**	**6**	**1**	**0**	**0**	**16:49**
2008-09	**Tampa Bay**	**NHL**	**82**	**19**	**26**	**45**	**52**	**7**	**0**	**2**	**194**	**9.8**	**-20**	**202**	**53.0**	**17:41**	....	....	....	....	....	....	....	....	....
2009-10	**NY Rangers**	**NHL**	**75**	**20**	**38**	**58**	**32**	**6**	**1**	**4**	**180**	**11.1**	**8**	**639**	**51.2**	**20:06**	....	....	....	....	....	....	....	....	....
	NHL Totals		**949**	**218**	**439**	**657**	**505**	**70**	**1**	**32**	**2106**	**10.4**		**5571**	**52.1**	**17:41**	**60**	**9**	**25**	**34**	**26**	**3**	**0**	**1**	**18:09**

AHL First All-Star Team (1997)

Traded to **Ottawa** by **Philadelphia** with Pat Falloon and Dallas' 2nd round choice (previously acquired, Ottawa selected Chris Bala) in 1998 Entry Draft for Alexandre Daigle, January 17, 1998. Traded to **Florida** by **Ottawa** for future considerations, January 20, 2001. Traded to **Tampa Bay** by **Florida** for Ryan Johnson and Tampa Bay's 6th round choice (later traded back to Tampa Bay – Tampa Bay selected Doug O'Brien) in 2003 Entry Draft, July 10, 2001. Signed as a free agent by **Anaheim**, July 17, 2003. Traded to **Tampa Bay** by **Anaheim** for Tampa Bay's 2nd round choice (Brendan Mikkelson) in 2005 Entry Draft, August 16, 2004. Signed as a free agent by **Ceske Budejovice** (CzRep-2), September 17, 2004. Traded to **Philadelphia** by **Tampa Bay** for Alexandre Picard and Philadelphia's 2nd round choice (Richard Panik) in 2009 Entry Draft, February 25, 2008. Traded to **Tampa Bay** by **Philadelphia** for Nashville's 7th round choice (previously acquired, Philadelphia selected Joacim Eriksson) in 2008 Entry Draft and future considerations, June 18, 2008. Signed as a free agent by **NY Rangers**, August 17, 2009.

PROSSER, Nate

(PRAW-suhr, NAYT) **MIN.**

Defense. Shoots right. 6'2", 215 lbs. Born, Elk River, MN, May 7, 1986.

Season	Club	League	GP	G	A	Pts	PIM	PP	SH	GW	S	%	+/-	TF	F%	Min	GP	G	A	Pts	PIM	PP	SH	GW	Min
2006-07	Colorado College	WCHA	21	0	3	3	8	....	....	....	....	....	....	....	....	....	....	....	....	....	....	....	....	....	....
2007-08	Colorado College	WCHA	39	3	17	20	51	....	....	....	....	....	....	....	....	....	....	....	....	....	....	....	....	....	....
2008-09	Colorado College	WCHA	38	5	8	13	61	....	....	....	....	....	....	....	....	....	....	....	....	....	....	....	....	....	....
2009-10	Colorado College	WCHA	39	4	24	28	58	....	....	....	....	....	....	....	....	....	....	....	....	....	....	....	....	....	....
	Minnesota	**NHL**	**3**	**0**	**1**	**1**	**8**	**0**	**0**	**0**	**4**	**0.0**	**2**	**0**	**0.0**	**19:37**	....	....	....	....	....	....	....	....	....
	NHL Totals		**3**	**0**	**1**	**1**	**8**	**0**	**0**	**0**	**4**	**0.0**		**0**	**0.0**	**19:37**	....	....	....	....	....	....	....	....	....

WCHA Second All-Star Team (2010)

Signed as a free agent by **Minnesota**, March 18, 2010.

PRUCHA, Petr

(PROO-khah, PEE-tuhr) **PHX.**

Right wing. Shoots right. 6', 175 lbs. Born, Chrudim, Czech., September 14, 1982. NY Rangers' 8th choice, 240th overall, in 2002 Entry Draft.

Season	Club	League	GP	G	A	Pts	PIM	PP	SH	GW	S	%	+/-	TF	F%	Min	GP	G	A	Pts	PIM	PP	SH	GW	Min
99-2000	HC Chrudim Jr.	CzRep-Jr.	43	35	27	62	62	....	....	....	....	....	....	....	....	....	....	....	....	....	....	....	....	....	....
2000-01	HC Pardubice Jr.	CzRep-Jr.	54	39	22	61	18	....	....	....	....	....	....	....	....	....	....	....	....	....	....	....	....	....	....
2001-02	HC Pardubice Jr.	CzRep-Jr.	28	38	28	66	18	....	....	....	....	....	....	....	....	....	3	2	6	8	0	....	....	....	....
	Sumperk	CzRep-2	8	6	4	10	0	....	....	....	....	....	....	....	....	....	....	....	....	....	....	....	....	....	....
	Sumperk	CzRep-Q	5	5	3	8	0	....	....	....	....	....	....	....	....	....	....	....	....	....	....	....	....	....	....
	Pardubice	CzRep	20	1	1	2	2	....	....	....	....	....	....	....	....	....	5	0	0	0	0	....	....	....	....
2002-03	Pardubice	CzRep	49	7	9	16	12	....	....	....	....	....	....	....	....	....	17	2	6	8	8	....	....	....	....
	HC Pardubice Jr.	CzRep-Jr.	4	5	4	9	25	....	....	....	....	....	....	....	....	....	....	....	....	....	....	....	....	....	....
	Hr. Kralove	CzRep-2	11	3	5	8	35	....	....	....	....	....	....	....	....	....	....	....	....	....	....	....	....	....	....
2003-04	Pardubice	CzRep	48	11	13	24	24	....	....	....	....	....	....	....	....	....	7	4	3	7	2	....	....	....	....
	Hr. Kralove	CzRep-2	3	1	0	1	25	....	....	....	....	....	....	....	....	....	....	....	....	....	....	....	....	....	....
2004-05	Pardubice	CzRep	47	7	10	17	24	....	....	....	....	....	....	....	....	....	16	6	7	13	2	....	....	....	....
2005-06	**NY Rangers**	**NHL**	**68**	**30**	**17**	**47**	**32**	**16**	**0**	**2**	**130**	**23.1**	**3**	**150**	**52.0**	**13:42**	**4**	**1**	**0**	**1**	**0**	**1**	**0**	**0**	**14:13**
	Hartford	AHL	2	2	1	3	0	....	....	....	....	....	....	....	....	....	....	....	....	....	....	....	....	....	....
2006-07	**NY Rangers**	**NHL**	**79**	**22**	**18**	**40**	**30**	**8**	**0**	**2**	**136**	**16.2**	**-7**	**70**	**50.0**	**13:00**	**10**	**0**	**1**	**1**	**4**	**0**	**0**	**0**	**13:35**
2007-08	**NY Rangers**	**NHL**	**62**	**7**	**10**	**17**	**22**	**2**	**0**	**1**	**89**	**7.9**	**3**	**3**	**66.7**	**11:38**	**3**	**0**	**0**	**0**	**0**	**0**	**0**	**0**	**8:13**
2008-09	**NY Rangers**	**NHL**	**28**	**4**	**5**	**9**	**16**	**0**	**0**	**0**	**44**	**9.1**	**-2**	**0**	**0.0**	**12:09**	....	....	....	....	....	....	....	....	....
	Phoenix	**NHL**	**19**	**2**	**8**	**10**	**6**	**1**	**0**	**1**	**23**	**8.7**	**1**	**8**	**12.5**	**18:26**	....	....	....	....	....	....	....	....	....
2009-10	**Phoenix**	**NHL**	**79**	**13**	**9**	**22**	**23**	**4**	**0**	**2**	**128**	**10.2**	**-2**	**151**	**45.0**	**14:02**	**7**	**1**	**2**	**3**	**4**	**0**	**0**	**1**	**13:31**
	NHL Totals		**335**	**78**	**67**	**145**	**129**	**31**	**0**	**8**	**550**	**14.2**		**382**	**48.2**	**13:22**	**24**	**2**	**3**	**5**	**8**	**1**	**0**	**1**	**13:00**

Traded to **Phoenix** by **NY Rangers** with Dmitri Kalinin and Nigel Dawes for Derek Morris, March 4, 2009.

PRUST, Brandon

(PROOST, BRAN-duhn) **NYR**

Left wing. Shoots left. 5'11", 195 lbs. Born, London, Ont., March 16, 1984. Calgary's 2nd choice, 70th overall, in 2004 Entry Draft.

Season	Club	League	GP	G	A	Pts	PIM	PP	SH	GW	S	%	+/-	TF	F%	Min	GP	G	A	Pts	PIM	PP	SH	GW	Min
2001-02	London Nationals	OHA-B	52	17	35	52	38	....	....	....	....	....	....	....	....	....	....	....	....	....	....	....	....	....	....
2002-03	London Knights	OHL	65	12	17	29	94	....	....	....	....	....	....	....	....	....	14	2	1	3	21	....	....	....	....
2003-04	London Knights	OHL	64	19	33	52	269	....	....	....	....	....	....	....	....	....	15	7	13	20	33	....	....	....	....
2004-05	London Knights	OHL	48	10	20	30	174	....	....	....	....	....	....	....	....	....	15	3	5	8	*71	....	....	....	....
2005-06	Omaha	AHL	79	12	14	26	294	....	....	....	....	....	....	....	....	....	....	....	....	....	....	....	....	....	....
2006-07	**Calgary**	**NHL**	**10**	**0**	**0**	**0**	**25**	**0**	**0**	**0**	**1**	**0.0**	**1**	**0**	**0.0**	**6:03**	....	....	....	....	....	....	....	....	....
	Omaha	AHL	63	17	10	27	211	....	....	....	....	....	....	....	....	....	6	0	3	3	20	....	....	....	....
2007-08	Quad City Flames	AHL	79	10	27	37	248	....	....	....	....	....	....	....	....	....	....	....	....	....	....	....	....	....	....
2008-09	**Calgary**	**NHL**	**25**	**1**	**1**	**2**	**79**	**0**	**0**	**1**	**15**	**6.7**	**-4**	**15**	**53.3**	**6:21**	....	....	....	....	....	....	....	....	....
	Phoenix	**NHL**	**11**	**0**	**1**	**1**	**29**	**0**	**0**	**0**	**8**	**0.0**	**-4**	**16**	**56.3**	**9:59**	....	....	....	....	....	....	....	....	....
2009-10	**Calgary**	**NHL**	**43**	**1**	**4**	**5**	**98**	**0**	**0**	**1**	**23**	**4.3**	**6**	**29**	**37.9**	**6:33**	....	....	....	....	....	....	....	....	....
	NY Rangers	**NHL**	**26**	**4**	**5**	**9**	**65**	**0**	**0**	**2**	**21**	**19.0**	**3**	**2**	**100.0**	**9:20**	....	....	....	....	....	....	....	....	....
	NHL Totals		**115**	**6**	**11**	**17**	**296**	**0**	**0**	**4**	**68**	**8.8**		**62**	**48.4**	**7:25**	....	....	....	....	....	....	....	....	....

Traded to **Phoenix** by **Calgary** with Matthew Lombardi and Calgary's 1st round choice (Brandon Gormley) in 2010 Entry Draft for Olli Jokinen and Phoenix's 3rd round choice (later traded to Florida – Florida selected Josh Birkholz) in 2009 Entry Draft, March 4, 2009. Traded to **Calgary** by **Phoenix** for Jim Vandermeer, June 27, 2009. Traded to **NY Rangers** by **Calgary** with Olli Jokinen for Christopher Higgins and Ales Kotalik, February 2, 2010.

PURCELL, Teddy

(PUHR-sihl, TEH-dee) **T.B.**

Right wing. Shoots right. 6'2", 198 lbs. Born, St. Johns, Nfld., September 8, 1985.

			Regular Season														Playoffs								
Season	Club	League	GP	G	A	Pts	PIM	PP	SH	GW	S	%	+/-	TF	F%	Min	GP	G	A	Pts	PIM	PP	SH	GW	Mi
2003-04	Notre Dame	SJHL	51	21	25	46	8	....	....	....	....	....	....	....	....	....	....	....	....	....	....	....	....	....	....
2004-05	Cedar Rapids	USHL	58	20	47	67	22	....	....	....	....	....	....	....	....	....	11	5	9	14	4	....	....	....	....
2005-06	Cedar Rapids	USHL	55	19	*52	71	14	....	....	....	....	....	....	....	....	....	8	3	8	11	4	....	....	....	....
2006-07	U. of Maine	H-East	40	16	27	43	34	....	....	....	....	....	....	....	....	....	....	....	....	....	....	....	....	....	....
2007-08	**Los Angeles**	**NHL**	**10**	**1**	**2**	**3**	**0**	**0**	**0**	**0**	**10**	**10.0**	**2**	**0**	**0.0**	**11:59**	....	....	....	....	....	....	....	....	....
	Manchester	AHL	67	25	58	83	34	....	....	....	....	....	....	....	....	....	4	0	3	3	0	....	....	....	....
2008-09	**Los Angeles**	**NHL**	**40**	**4**	**12**	**16**	**4**	**2**	**0**	**1**	**68**	**5.9**	**–4**	**29**	**17.2**	**13:31**	....	....	....	....	....	....	....	....	....
	Manchester	AHL	38	16	22	38	12	....	....	....	....	....	....	....	....	....	....	....	....	....	....	....	....	....	....
2009-10	**Los Angeles**	**NHL**	**41**	**3**	**3**	**6**	**4**	**1**	**0**	**1**	**55**	**5.5**	**–1**	**3**	**33.3**	**11:22**	....	....	....	....	....	....	....	....	....
	Tampa Bay	**NHL**	**19**	**3**	**6**	**9**	**6**	**1**	**0**	**0**	**46**	**6.5**	**–8**	**1**	**100.0**	**16:05**	....	....	....	....	....	....	....	....	....
	NHL Totals		**110**	**11**	**23**	**34**	**14**	**4**	**0**	**2**	**179**	**6.1**		**33**	**21.2**	**13:01**	....	....	....	....	....	....	....	....	....

AHL First All-Star Team (2008)

Signed as a free agent by **Los Angeles**, April 27, 2007. Traded to **Tampa Bay** by **Los Angeles** with Florida's 3rd round choice (previously acquired, Tampa Bay selected Brock Beukeboom) in 2010 Entry Draft for Jeff Halpern, March 3, 2010.

PUSHKAREV, Konstantin

(puhsh-KAR-ehv, KAWN-stan-tihn)

Right wing. Shoots left. 6', 180 lbs. Born, Ust-Kamenogorsk, USSR, February 12, 1985. Los Angeles' 4th choice, 44th overall, in 2003 Entry Draft.

Season	Club	League	GP	G	A	Pts	PIM	PP	SH	GW	S	%	+/-	TF	F%	Min	GP	G	A	Pts	PIM	PP	SH	GW	Mi
2002-03	Ust-Kam'gorsk 2	Russia-3	STATISTICS NOT AVAILABLE																						
	Ust-Kamenogorsk	Russia-2	4	0	0	0	4	....	....	....	....	....	....	....	....	....	....	....	....	....	....	....	....	....	....
2003-04	Omsk 2	Russia-3	34	17	11	28	64	....	....	....	....	....	....	....	....	....	....	....	....	....	....	....	....	....	....
	Avangard Omsk	Russia	5	1	0	1	0	....	....	....	....	....	....	....	....	....	....	....	....	....	....	....	....	....	....
2004-05	Avangard Omsk	Russia	1	0	0	0	0	....	....	....	....	....	....	....	....	....	....	....	....	....	....	....	....	....	....
	Calgary Hitmen	WHL	69	22	30	52	50	....	....	....	....	....	....	....	....	....	12	2	5	7	4	....	....	....	....
2005-06	**Los Angeles**	**NHL**	**1**	**0**	**1**	**1**	**0**	**0**	**0**	**0**	**0**	**0.0**	**0**	**0**	**0.0**	**9:33**	....	....	....	....	....	....	....	....	....
	Manchester	AHL	77	19	19	38	95	....	....	....	....	....	....	....	....	....	7	1	1	2	4	....	....	....	....
2006-07	**Los Angeles**	**NHL**	**16**	**2**	**2**	**4**	**8**	**0**	**0**	**0**	**10**	**20.0**	**–2**	**1**	**0.0**	**9:10**	....	....	....	....	....	....	....	....	....
	Manchester	AHL	35	4	11	15	29	....	....	....	....	....	....	....	....	....	....	....	....	....	....	....	....	....	....
	Iowa Stars	AHL	15	2	5	7	25	....	....	....	....	....	....	....	....	....	12	1	4	5	18	....	....	....	....
2007-08	Iowa Stars	AHL	49	13	27	40	52	....	....	....	....	....	....	....	....	....	....	....	....	....	....	....	....	....	....
	CSKA Moscow	Russia	5	0	1	1	2	....	....	....	....	....	....	....	....	....	....	....	....	....	....	....	....	....	....
2008-09	Magnitogorsk	Rus-KHL	30	5	1	6	14	....	....	....	....	....	....	....	....	....	4	0	0	0	0	....	....	....	....
2009-10	Wilkes-Barre	AHL	58	9	10	19	47	....	....	....	....	....	....	....	....	....	4	1	1	2	2	....	....	....	....
	NHL Totals		**17**	**2**	**3**	**5**	**8**	**0**	**0**	**0**	**10**	**20.0**		**1**	**0.0**	**9:12**	....	....	....	....	....	....	....	....	....

Traded to **Dallas** by **Los Angeles** with Mattias Norstrom and Los Angeles' 3rd (Sergei Korostin) and 4th (later traded to Columbus - Columbus selected Maxim Mayorov) round choices in 2007 Entry Draft for Jaroslav Modry, the rights to Johan Fransson, Dallas' 2nd (Oscar Moller) and 3rd (Bryan Cameron) round choices in 2007 Entry Draft and Dallas' 1st round choice (later traded to Phoenix - Phoenix selected Viktor Tikhonov) in 2008 Entry Draft , February 27, 2007. Signed as a free agent by **CSKA Moscow** (Russia), November 5, 2007. Signed as a fre agent by **Magnitogorsk** (Russia-KHL), November 2, 2008.

PYATT, Taylor

(PIGH-at, TAY-luhr) **PHX**

Left wing. Shoots left. 6'4", 230 lbs. Born, Thunder Bay, Ont., August 19, 1981. NY Islanders' 2nd choice, 8th overall, in 1999 Entry Draft.

Season	Club	League	GP	G	A	Pts	PIM	PP	SH	GW	S	%	+/-	TF	F%	Min	GP	G	A	Pts	PIM	PP	SH	GW	Mi
1996-97	Thunder Bay	TBAHA	60	52	61	113	72	....	....	....	....	....	....	....	....	....	....	....	....	....	....	....	....	....	....
1997-98	Sudbury Wolves	OHL	58	14	17	31	104	....	....	....	....	....	....	....	....	....	10	3	1	4	8	....	....	....	....
1998-99	Sudbury Wolves	OHL	68	37	38	75	95	....	....	....	....	....	....	....	....	....	4	0	4	4	6	....	....	....	....
99-2000	Sudbury Wolves	OHL	68	40	49	89	98	....	....	....	....	....	....	....	....	....	12	8	7	15	25	....	....	....	....
2000-01	**NY Islanders**	**NHL**	**78**	**4**	**14**	**18**	**39**	**1**	**0**	**2**	**86**	**4.7**	**–17**	**1**	**0.0**	**12:14**	....	....	....	....	....	....	....	....	....
2001-02	**Buffalo**	**NHL**	**48**	**10**	**10**	**20**	**35**	**0**	**0**	**0**	**61**	**16.4**	**4**	**0**	**0.0**	**13:30**	....	....	....	....	....	....	....	....	....
	Rochester	AHL	27	6	4	10	36	....	....	....	....	....	....	....	....	....	....	....	....	....	....	....	....	....	....
2002-03	**Buffalo**	**NHL**	**78**	**14**	**14**	**28**	**38**	**2**	**0**	**0**	**110**	**12.7**	**–8**	**8**	**25.0**	**14:06**	....	....	....	....	....	....	....	....	....
2003-04	**Buffalo**	**NHL**	**63**	**8**	**12**	**20**	**25**	**1**	**2**	**4**	**98**	**8.2**	**–7**	**19**	**26.3**	**15:36**	....	....	....	....	....	....	....	....	....
2004-05	Hammarby	Sweden-2	24	11	9	20	20	....	....	....	....	....	....	....	....	....	....	....	....	....	....	....	....	....	....
2005-06	**Buffalo**	**NHL**	**41**	**6**	**6**	**12**	**33**	**0**	**0**	**1**	**62**	**9.7**	**–1**	**11**	**18.2**	**11:14**	**14**	**0**	**5**	**5**	**10**	**0**	**0**	**0**	**11:0**
2006-07	**Vancouver**	**NHL**	**76**	**23**	**14**	**37**	**42**	**9**	**0**	**4**	**150**	**15.3**	**5**	**4**	**0.0**	**13:58**	**12**	**2**	**4**	**6**	**6**	**0**	**0**	**1**	**18:0**
2007-08	**Vancouver**	**NHL**	**79**	**16**	**21**	**37**	**60**	**7**	**0**	**2**	**167**	**9.6**	**9**	**36**	**33.3**	**15:47**	....	....	....	....	....	....	....	....	....
2008-09	**Vancouver**	**NHL**	**69**	**10**	**9**	**19**	**43**	**0**	**0**	**1**	**99**	**10.1**	**0**	**33**	**48.5**	**14:43**	**4**	**0**	**0**	**0**	**2**	**0**	**0**	**0**	**14:1**
2009-10	**Phoenix**	**NHL**	**74**	**12**	**11**	**23**	**39**	**1**	**0**	**3**	**121**	**9.9**	**13**	**1**	**0.0**	**13:27**	**7**	**1**	**1**	**2**	**2**	**1**	**0**	**0**	**14:2**
	NHL Totals		**606**	**103**	**111**	**214**	**354**	**21**	**2**	**17**	**954**	**10.8**		**113**	**32.7**	**13:58**	**37**	**3**	**10**	**13**	**20**	**1**	**0**	**1**	**14:1**

OHL First All-Star Team (2000)

Traded to **Buffalo** by **NY Islanders** with Tim Connolly for Michael Peca, June 24, 2001. Signed as a free agent by **Hammarby** (Sweden-2), November 16, 2004. • Rights traded to **Vancouver** by **Buffalo** for Vancouver's 4th round choice (later traded to Calgary - Calgary selected Keith Aulie) in 2007 Entry Draft, July 14, 2006. Signed as a free agent by **Phoenix**, September 2, 2009.

PYATT, Tom

(PIGH-at, TAWM) **MTL**

Center. Shoots left. 5'11", 183 lbs. Born, Thunder Bay, Ont., February 14, 1987. NY Rangers' 6th choice, 107th overall, in 2005 Entry Draft.

Season	Club	League	GP	G	A	Pts	PIM	PP	SH	GW	S	%	+/-	TF	F%	Min	GP	G	A	Pts	PIM	PP	SH	GW	Mi
2003-04	Saginaw Spirit	OHL	67	9	9	18	21	....	....	....	....	....	....	....	....	....	....	....	....	....	....	....	....	....	....
2004-05	Saginaw Spirit	OHL	57	18	30	48	14	....	....	....	....	....	....	....	....	....	....	....	....	....	....	....	....	....	....
2005-06	Saginaw Spirit	OHL	58	24	29	53	29	....	....	....	....	....	....	....	....	....	4	1	2	3	4	....	....	....	....
2006-07	Saginaw Spirit	OHL	58	43	38	81	18	....	....	....	....	....	....	....	....	....	6	3	5	8	0	....	....	....	....
	Hartford	AHL	1	0	0	0	0	....	....	....	....	....	....	....	....	....	....	....	....	....	....	....	....	....	....
2007-08	Hartford	AHL	41	4	7	11	6	....	....	....	....	....	....	....	....	....	3	0	0	0	0	....	....	....	....
	Charlotte	ECHL	16	6	9	15	8	....	....	....	....	....	....	....	....	....	3	0	0	0	0	....	....	....	....
2008-09	Hartford	AHL	73	15	22	37	22	....	....	....	....	....	....	....	....	....	4	0	0	0	2	....	....	....	....
2009-10	**Montreal**	**NHL**	**40**	**2**	**3**	**5**	**10**	**0**	**0**	**0**	**48**	**4.2**	**–5**	**50**	**42.0**	**11:04**	**18**	**2**	**2**	**4**	**2**	**0**	**0**	**1**	**13:0**
	Hamilton	AHL	41	13	22	35	8	....	....	....	....	....	....	....	....	....	....	....	....	....	....	....	....	....	....
	NHL Totals		**40**	**2**	**3**	**5**	**10**	**0**	**0**	**0**	**48**	**4.2**		**50**	**42.0**	**11:04**	**18**	**2**	**2**	**4**	**2**	**0**	**0**	**1**	**13:0**

Traded to **Montreal** by **NY Rangers** with Scott Gomez and Michael Busto for Christopher Higgins, Ryan McDonagh and Pavel Valentenko, June 30, 2009.

PYORALA, Mika

(P'YOHR-ah-lah, MEE-kah)

Center. Shoots left. 6', 190 lbs. Born, Oulu, Finland, July 13, 1981.

Season	Club	League	GP	G	A	Pts	PIM	PP	SH	GW	S	%	+/-	TF	F%	Min	GP	G	A	Pts	PIM	PP	SH	GW	Mi
2001-02	Karpat Oulu	Finland	51	4	2	6	35	....	....	....	....	....	....	....	....	....	4	0	1	1	2	....	....	....	....
2002-03	Karpat Oulu	Finland	56	17	11	28	22	....	....	....	....	....	....	....	....	....	15	2	3	5	6	....	....	....	....
2003-04	Karpat Oulu	Finland	53	12	19	31	8	....	....	....	....	....	....	....	....	....	13	0	1	1	0	....	....	....	....
2004-05	Karpat Oulu	Finland	56	9	13	22	18	....	....	....	....	....	....	....	....	....	11	3	1	4	4	....	....	....	....
2005-06	Karpat Oulu	Finland	41	13	8	21	10	....	....	....	....	....	....	....	....	....	11	5	6	11	0	....	....	....	....
2006-07	Karpat Oulu	Finland	56	28	17	45	30	....	....	....	....	....	....	....	....	....	10	4	2	6	2	....	....	....	....
2007-08	Timra IK	Sweden	46	17	16	33	18	....	....	....	....	....	....	....	....	....	11	6	4	10	0	....	....	....	....
2008-09	Timra IK	Sweden	55	21	22	43	10	....	....	....	....	....	....	....	....	....	7	2	1	3	6	....	....	....	....
2009-10	**Philadelphia**	**NHL**	**36**	**2**	**2**	**4**	**10**	**0**	**0**	**0**	**41**	**4.9**	**–3**	**207**	**45.9**	**13:36**	....	....	....	....	....	....	....	....	....
	Adirondack	AHL	35	8	10	18	10	....	....	....	....	....	....	....	....	....	....	....	....	....	....	....	....	....	....
	NHL Totals		**36**	**2**	**2**	**4**	**10**	**0**	**0**	**0**	**41**	**4.9**		**207**	**45.9**	**13:36**	....	....	....	....	....	....	....	....	....

Signed as a free agent by **Philadelphia**, July 23, 2009. Signed as a free agent by **Frolunda** (Sweden), July 29, 2010.

QUICK, Kevin

(KWIHK, KEH-vihn) **T.B.**

Defense. Shoots left. 6', 195 lbs. Born, Buffalo, NY, March 29, 1988. Tampa Bay's 2nd choice, 78th overall, in 2006 Entry Draft.

Season	Club	League	GP	G	A	Pts	PIM	PP	SH	GW	S	%	+/-	TF	F%	Min	GP	G	A	Pts	PIM	PP	SH	GW	Mi
2004-05	Salisbury School	High-CT	27	3	9	12	3	....	....	....	....	....	....	....	....	....	....	....	....	....	....	....	....	....	....
2005-06	Salisbury School	High-CT	28	3	20	23	6	....	....	....	....	....	....	....	....	....	....	....	....	....	....	....	....	....	....
2006-07	Salisbury School	High-CT	25	1	10	11	10	....	....	....	....	....	....	....	....	....	....	....	....	....	....	....	....	....	....
2007-08	U. of Michigan	CCHA	21	2	2	4	12	....	....	....	....	....	....	....	....	....	....	....	....	....	....	....	....	....	....
	Norfolk Admirals	AHL	18	0	4	4	6	....	....	....	....	....	....	....	....	....	....	....	....	....	....	....	....	....	....

			Regular Season														Playoffs								
Season	Club	League	GP	G	A	Pts	PIM	PP	SH	GW	S	%	+/-	TF	F%	Min	GP	G	A	Pts	PIM	PP	SH	GW	Min
2008-09	Tampa Bay	NHL	6	0	1	1	0	0	0	0	7	0.0	0	0	0.0	13:23									
	Norfolk Admirals	AHL	49	1	8	9	8																		
	Elmira Jackals	ECHL															9	0	1	1	0				
2009-10	Norfolk Admirals	AHL	47	0	4	4	10																		
	NHL Totals		6	0	1	1	0	0	0	0	7	0.0		0	0.0	13:23									

QUINCEY, Kyle

(KWIHN-see, KIGHL) **COL.**

Defense. Shoots left. 6'2", 207 lbs. Born, Kitchener, Ont., August 12, 1985. Detroit's 2nd choice, 132nd overall, in 2003 Entry Draft.

Season	Club	League	GP	G	A	Pts	PIM	PP	SH	GW	S	%	+/-	TF	F%	Min	GP	G	A	Pts	PIM	PP	SH	GW	Min
2001-02	Mississauga	OPJHL	27	5	14	19	31																		
2002-03	London Knights	OHL	66	6	12	18	77										14	3	4	7	11				
2003-04	London Knights	OHL	3	0	2	2	4																		
	Mississauga	OHL	61	14	23	37	135										24	3	13	16	32				
2004-05	Mississauga	OHL	59	15	31	46	111										5	0	3	3	4				
2005-06	**Detroit**	**NHL**	**1**	**0**	**0**	**0**	**0**	**0**	**0**	**0**	**1**	**0.0**	**0**	**0**	**0.0**	**11:37**									
	Grand Rapids	AHL	70	7	26	33	107										16	0	1	1	27				
2006-07	**Detroit**	**NHL**	**6**	**1**	**0**	**1**	**0**	**0**	**0**	**0**	**7**	**14.3**	**0**	**0**	**0.0**	**11:26**	**13**	**0**	**0**	**0**	**2**	**0**	**0**	**0**	**8:11**
	Grand Rapids	AHL	65	4	18	22	126										2	0	0	0	0				
2007-08	**Detroit**	**NHL**	**6**	**0**	**0**	**0**	**4**	**0**	**0**	**0**	**5**	**0.0**	**–3**	**0**	**0.0**	**13:58**									
	Grand Rapids	AHL	66	5	15	20	149																		
2008-09	**Los Angeles**	**NHL**	**72**	**4**	**34**	**38**	**63**	**2**	**0**	**2**	**150**	**2.7**	**–5**	**0**	**0.0**	**20:59**									
2009-10	**Colorado**	**NHL**	**79**	**6**	**23**	**29**	**76**	**1**	**0**	**0**	**139**	**4.3**	**9**	**1**	**0.0**	**23:37**	**6**	**0**	**0**	**0**	**8**	**0**	**0**	**0**	**22:06**
	NHL Totals		**164**	**11**	**57**	**68**	**143**	**3**	**0**	**2**	**302**	**3.6**		**1**	**0.0**	**21:35**	**19**	**0**	**0**	**0**	**10**	**0**	**0**	**0**	**12:35**

OHL Second All-Star Team (2005)

Claimed on waivers by **Los Angeles** from **Detroit**, October 13, 2008. Traded to **Colorado** by **Los Angeles** with Tom Preissing and Los Angeles' 5th round choice (Luke Walker) in 2010 Entry Draft for Ryan Smyth, July 3, 2009.

RADIVOJEVIC, Branko

(ra-dih-VOI-uh-vihch, BRAN-koh)

Right wing. Shoots right. 6', 208 lbs. Born, Piestany, Czech., November 24, 1980. Colorado's 3rd choice, 93rd overall, in 1999 Entry Draft.

Season	Club	League	GP	G	A	Pts	PIM	PP	SH	GW	S	%	+/-	TF	F%	Min	GP	G	A	Pts	PIM	PP	SH	GW	Min
1997-98	Dukla Trencin Jr.	Slovak-Jr.	52	30	31	61	50																		
	Dukla Trencin	Slovakia	1	0	0	0	2																		
1998-99	Belleville Bulls	OHL	68	20	38	58	61										21	7	17	24	18				
99-2000	Belleville Bulls	OHL	59	23	49	72	86										16	5	8	13	32				
2000-01	Belleville Bulls	OHL	61	34	70	104	77										10	6	10	16	18				
2001-02	**Phoenix**	**NHL**	**18**	**4**	**2**	**6**	**4**	**0**	**0**	**1**	**19**	**21.1**	**1**	**0**	**0.0**	**9:22**	**1**	**0**	**0**	**0**	**2**	**0**	**0**	**0**	**8:07**
	Springfield	AHL	62	18	21	39	64																		
2002-03	**Phoenix**	**NHL**	**79**	**12**	**15**	**27**	**63**	**1**	**0**	**3**	**109**	**11.0**	**–2**	**20**	**40.0**	**13:18**									
2003-04	**Phoenix**	**NHL**	**53**	**9**	**14**	**23**	**36**	**2**	**1**	**2**	**83**	**10.8**	**–5**	**30**	**30.0**	**16:27**									
	Philadelphia	**NHL**	**24**	**1**	**8**	**9**	**36**	**0**	**0**	**0**	**24**	**4.2**	**0**	**11**	**54.6**	**10:28**	**18**	**1**	**1**	**2**	**32**	**0**	**0**	**0**	**9:56**
2004-05	HC Vsetin	CzRep	31	7	11	18	114																		
	Lulea HF	Sweden	10	6	5	11	8										4	0	0	0	44				
2005-06	**Philadelphia**	**NHL**	**64**	**8**	**6**	**14**	**44**	**1**	**0**	**1**	**84**	**9.5**	**–6**	**14**	**42.9**	**12:46**	**5**	**1**	**0**	**1**	**0**	**0**	**0**	**0**	**10:34**
2006-07	**Minnesota**	**NHL**	**82**	**11**	**13**	**24**	**21**	**4**	**0**	**3**	**116**	**9.5**	**–9**	**18**	**50.0**	**12:59**	**5**	**0**	**0**	**0**	**2**	**0**	**0**	**0**	**14:14**
2007-08	**Minnesota**	**NHL**	**73**	**7**	**10**	**17**	**48**	**1**	**0**	**3**	**91**	**7.7**	**–14**	**39**	**38.5**	**14:55**	**2**	**0**	**0**	**0**	**0**	**0**	**0**	**0**	**14:35**
2008-09	Spartak Moscow	Rus-KHL	49	17	26	43	86										6	2	1	3	6				
2009-10	Spartak Moscow	Rus-KHL	56	18	37	55	115										9	0	5	5	33				
	Slovakia	Olympics	7	0	0	0	6																		
	NHL Totals		**393**	**52**	**68**	**120**	**252**	**9**	**1**	**13**	**526**	**9.9**		**132**	**40.2**	**13:31**	**31**	**2**	**1**	**3**	**36**	**0**	**0**	**0**	**10:58**

OHL First All-Star Team (2001)

Signed as a free agent by **Phoenix**, June 19, 2001. Traded to **Philadelphia** by **Phoenix** with Sean Burke and Ben Eager for Mike Comrie, February 9, 2004. Signed as a free agent by **Vsetin** (CzRep), September 17, 2004. Signed as a free agent by **Lulea** (Sweden), January 27, 2005. Signed as a free agent by **Minnesota**, July 6, 2006. Signed as a free agent by **Spartak Moscow** (Russia-KHL), June 8, 2008.

RADULOV, Alexander

(ra-DEW-lahf, al-EHX-AN-duhr) **NSH.**

Right wing. Shoots left. 6'1", 188 lbs. Born, Nizhny Tagil, USSR, July 5, 1986. Nashville's 1st choice, 15th overall, in 2004 Entry Draft.

Season	Club	League	GP	G	A	Pts	PIM	PP	SH	GW	S	%	+/-	TF	F%	Min	GP	G	A	Pts	PIM	PP	SH	GW	Min
2002-03	Dyn'o Moscow 2	Russia-3	STATISTICS NOT AVAILABLE																						
2003-04	Dyn'o Moscow 2	Russia-3	STATISTICS NOT AVAILABLE																						
	THK Tver	Russia-2	42	15	16	31	102																		
	Dynamo Moscow	Russia	1	0	0	0	2																		
2004-05	Quebec Remparts	QMJHL	65	32	43	75	64										13	6	5	11	15				
2005-06	Quebec Remparts	QMJHL	62	61	*91	*152	101										23	21	*34	*55	30				
2006-07	**Nashville**	**NHL**	**64**	**18**	**19**	**37**	**26**	**5**	**0**	**4**	**96**	**18.8**	**19**	**0**	**0.0**	**11:38**	**4**	**3**	**1**	**4**	**19**	**0**	**0**	**0**	**13:10**
	Milwaukee	AHL	11	6	12	18	26																		
2007-08	**Nashville**	**NHL**	**81**	**26**	**32**	**58**	**44**	**4**	**0**	**2**	**183**	**14.2**	**7**	**1**	**0.0**	**16:24**	**6**	**2**	**2**	**4**	**6**	**1**	**0**	**0**	**15:59**
2008-09	Ufa	Rus-KHL	52	22	26	48	92										4	0	2	2	4				
2009-10	Ufa	Rus-KHL	54	24	39	63	62										16	8	*11	*19	10				
	Russia	Olympics	4	1	1	2	4																		
	NHL Totals		**145**	**44**	**51**	**95**	**70**	**9**	**0**	**6**	**279**	**15.8**		**1**	**0.0**	**14:18**	**10**	**5**	**3**	**8**	**25**	**1**	**0**	**0**	**14:51**

QMJHL All-Rookie Team (2005) • QMJHL First All-Star Team (2006) • QMJHL Player of the Year (2006) • Canadian Major Junior First All-Star Team (2006) • Canadian Major Junior Player of the Year (2006) • Memorial Cup Tournament All-Star Team (2006) • Stafford Smythe Memorial Trophy (Memorial Cup Tournament - MVP) (2006)

Signed as a free agent by **Ufa** (Russia-KHL), July 11, 2008.

RADUNS, Nate

(RAH-duhnz, NAYT)

Right wing. Shoots right. 6'3", 205 lbs. Born, Sauk Rapids, MN, May 17, 1984.

Season	Club	League	GP	G	A	Pts	PIM	PP	SH	GW	S	%	+/-	TF	F%	Min	GP	G	A	Pts	PIM	PP	SH	GW	Min
2001-02	USNTDP	USHL	13	3	3	6	14																		
	USNTDP	NAHL	10	0	4	4	7																		
2002-03	River City Lancers	USHL	48	5	17	22	50										11	1	3	4	8				
2003-04	St. Cloud State	WCHA	34	4	7	11	40																		
2004-05	St. Cloud State	WCHA	28	4	8	12	32																		
2005-06	St. Cloud State	WCHA	41	5	10	15	50																		
2006-07	St. Cloud State	WCHA	40	6	6	12	53																		
2007-08	Worcester Sharks	AHL	56	12	15	27	42																		
2008-09	**Philadelphia**	**NHL**	**1**	**0**	**0**	**0**	**0**	**0**	**0**	**0**	**0**	**0.0**	**0**	**1**	**0.0**	**6:02**									
	Philadelphia	AHL	70	5	9	14	71										3	0	0	0	2				
2009-10	SG Pontebba	Italy	40	13	25	38	44																		
	NHL Totals		**1**	**0**	**0**	**0**	**0**	**0**	**0**	**0**	**0**	**0.0**		**1**	**0.0**	**6:02**									

Signed as a free agent by **Philadelphia**, July 1, 2008. Signed as a free agent by **Pontebba** (Italy), July 7, 2009.

RAFALSKI, Brian

(ra-FAWL-skee, BRIGH-uhn) **DET.**

Defense. Shoots right. 5'10", 194 lbs. Born, Dearborn, MI, September 28, 1973.

Season	Club	League	GP	G	A	Pts	PIM	PP	SH	GW	S	%	+/-	TF	F%	Min	GP	G	A	Pts	PIM	PP	SH	GW	Min
1990-91	Madison Capitols	USHL	47	12	11	23	28																		
1991-92	U. of Wisconsin	WCHA	34	3	14	17	34																		
1992-93	U. of Wisconsin	WCHA	32	0	13	13	10																		
1993-94	U. of Wisconsin	WCHA	37	6	17	23	26																		
1994-95	U. of Wisconsin	WCHA	43	11	34	45	48																		
1995-96	Brynas IF Gavle	Sweden	40	4	14	18	26										9	0	1	1	2				
1996-97	HPK Hameenlinna	Finland	49	11	24	35	26										10	6	5	11	4				
1997-98	HIFK Helsinki	Finland	40	13	10	23	20										9	5	6	11	0				
1998-99	HIFK Helsinki	Finland	53	19	34	53	18										11	5	*9	*14	4				
	HIFK Helsinki	EuroHL	6	4	6	10	10										4	1	0	1	2				
99-2000♦	**New Jersey**	**NHL**	**75**	**5**	**27**	**32**	**28**	**1**	**0**	**1**	**128**	**3.9**	**21**	**1**	**0.0**	**18:51**	**23**	**2**	**6**	**8**	**8**	**0**	**0**	**1**	**21:25**
2000-01	**New Jersey**	**NHL**	**78**	**9**	**43**	**52**	**26**	**6**	**0**	**1**	**142**	**6.3**	**36**	**2**	**100.0**	**21:41**	**25**	**7**	**11**	**18**	**7**	**1**	**0**	***3**	**22:08**
2001-02	**New Jersey**	**NHL**	**76**	**7**	**40**	**47**	**18**	**2**	**0**	**4**	**125**	**5.6**	**15**	**0**	**0.0**	**22:08**	**6**	**3**	**2**	**5**	**4**	**3**	**0**	**0**	**21:45**
	United States	Olympics	6	1	2	3	2																		
2002-03♦	**New Jersey**	**NHL**	**79**	**3**	**37**	**40**	**14**	**2**	**0**	**0**	**178**	**1.7**	**18**	**1**	**0.0**	**23:09**	**23**	**2**	**9**	**11**	**8**	**2**	**0**	**0**	**25:46**

			Regular Season														Playoffs								
Season	Club	League	GP	G	A	Pts	PIM	PP	SH	GW	S	%	+/-	TF	F%	Min	GP	G	A	Pts	PIM	PP	SH	GW	Min
2003-04	New Jersey	NHL	69	6	30	36	24	2	0	1	130	4.6	6	0	0.0	22:48	5	0	1	1	0	0	0	0	22:22
2004-05			DID NOT PLAY																						
2005-06	New Jersey	NHL	82	6	43	49	36	3	0	2	126	4.8	0	1	0.0	25:32	9	1	8	9	2	1	0	0	27:26
	United States	Olympics	5	0	2	2	0	....	....	....	....	....	....	....	....	....	....	....	....	....	....	....	....	....	....
2006-07	New Jersey	NHL	82	8	47	55	34	3	1	4	148	5.4	4	0	0.0	25:29	11	2	6	8	8	2	0	0	22:54
2007-08 ♦	Detroit	NHL	73	13	42	55	34	10	0	1	175	7.4	27	0	0.0	24:04	22	4	10	14	12	2	0	0	24:53
2008-09	Detroit	NHL	78	10	49	59	20	5	0	1	141	7.1	17	0	0.0	23:10	18	3	9	12	11	3	0	1	22:27
2009-10	Detroit	NHL	78	8	34	42	26	5	0	1	134	6.0	23	0	0.0	24:14	12	3	8	11	2	1	0	0	23:58
	United States	Olympics	6	4	4	8	2	....	....	....	....	....	....	....	....	....	....	....	....	....	....	....	....	....	....
	NHL Totals		770	75	392	467	260	39	1	16	1427	5.3		5	40.0	23:09	154	27	70	97	62	15	0	5	23:30

WCHA First All-Star Team (1995) • NCAA West First All-American Team (1995) • NHL All-Rookie Team (2000) • Olympic Tournament All-Star Team (2010) • Olympic Tournament Best Defenseman (2010)
Played in NHL All-Star Game (2004, 2007)
Signed as a free agent by **New Jersey**, June 18, 1999. Signed as a free agent by **Detroit**, July 1, 2007.

RANGER, Paul

(RAIN-juhr, PAWL) **T.B.**

Defense. Shoots left. 6'3", 208 lbs. Born, Whitby, Ont., September 12, 1984. Tampa Bay's 7th choice, 183rd overall, in 2002 Entry Draft.

Season	Club	League	GP	G	A	Pts	PIM	PP	SH	GW	S	%	+/-	TF	F%	Min	GP	G	A	Pts	PIM	PP	SH	GW	Min
2000-01	Oshawa Generals	OHL	32	0	1	1	2	....	....	....	....	....	....	....	....	....	....	....	....	....	....	....	....	....	....
2001-02	Oshawa Generals	OHL	62	0	9	9	49	....	....	....	....	....	....	....	....	....	5	0	0	0	4	....	....	....	....
2002-03	Oshawa Generals	OHL	68	10	28	38	70	....	....	....	....	....	....	....	....	....	13	0	3	3	10	....	....	....	....
2003-04	Oshawa Generals	OHL	62	12	31	43	72	....	....	....	....	....	....	....	....	....	7	0	1	1	10	....	....	....	....
2004-05	Springfield	AHL	69	3	8	11	46	....	....	....	....	....	....	....	....	....	....	....	....	....	....	....	....	....	....
2005-06	Tampa Bay	NHL	76	1	17	18	58	0	0	1	73	1.4	5	0	0.0	17:07	5	2	4	6	0	1	0	0	21:43
	Springfield	AHL	1	1	2	3	0	....	....	....	....	....	....	....	....	....	....	....	....	....	....	....	....	....	....
2006-07	Tampa Bay	NHL	72	4	24	28	42	0	0	2	90	4.4	5	0	0.0	20:19	6	0	1	1	4	0	0	0	21:22
2007-08	Tampa Bay	NHL	72	10	21	31	56	0	1	0	105	9.5	−13	0	0.0	25:13	....	....	....	....	....	....	....	....	....
2008-09	Tampa Bay	NHL	42	2	11	13	56	0	0	0	69	2.9	−5	0	0.0	24:30	....	....	....	....	....	....	....	....	....
2009-10	Tampa Bay	NHL	8	1	1	2	6	0	0	0	11	9.1	−2	0	0.0	20:19	....	....	....	....	....	....	....	....	....
	NHL Totals		270	18	74	92	218	0	1	3	348	5.2		0	0.0	21:23	11	2	5	7	4	1	0	0	21:3

• Missed majority of 2009-10 season for personal reasons.

RAYMOND, Mason

(RAY-muhnd, MAY-sohn) **VAN**

Left wing. Shoots left. 6', 185 lbs. Born, Cochrane, Alta., September 17, 1985. Vancouver's 2nd choice, 51st overall, in 2005 Entry Draft.

Season	Club	League	GP	G	A	Pts	PIM	PP	SH	GW	S	%	+/-	TF	F%	Min	GP	G	A	Pts	PIM	PP	SH	GW	Min
2003-04	Camrose Kodiaks	AJHL	....	27	35	62	....	....	....	....	....	....	....	....	....	....	....	....	....	....	....	....	....	....	....
2004-05	Camrose Kodiaks	AJHL	55	*41	41	82	80	....	....	....	....	....	....	....	....	....	15	8	*12	20	....	....	....	....	....
2005-06	U. Minn-Duluth	WCHA	40	11	17	28	30	....	....	....	....	....	....	....	....	....	....	....	....	....	....	....	....	....	....
2006-07	U. Minn-Duluth	WCHA	39	14	32	46	45	....	....	....	....	....	....	....	....	....	....	....	....	....	....	....	....	....	....
	Manitoba Moose	AHL	11	2	2	4	6	....	....	....	....	....	....	....	....	....	13	0	1	1	0	....	....	....	....
2007-08	Vancouver	NHL	49	9	12	21	2	1	0	0	80	11.3	1	63	38.1	12:31	....	....	....	....	....	....	....	....	....
	Manitoba Moose	AHL	20	7	10	17	6	....	....	....	....	....	....	....	....	....	....	....	....	....	....	....	....	....	....
2008-09	Vancouver	NHL	72	11	12	23	24	4	0	0	145	7.6	2	50	34.0	13:43	10	2	1	3	2	0	0	0	15:1
2009-10	Vancouver	NHL	82	25	28	53	48	8	0	4	217	11.5	0	23	34.8	17:20	12	3	1	4	6	0	0	1	17:3
	NHL Totals		203	45	52	97	74	13	0	4	442	10.2		136	36.0	14:53	22	5	2	7	8	0	0	1	16:3

AJHL MVP (2005) • WCHA All-Rookie Team (2006) • WCHA First All-Star Team (2007)

REASONER, Marty

(REE-suh-nuhr, MAHR-tee) **FLA**

Center. Shoots left. 6'1", 205 lbs. Born, Honeoye Falls, NY, February 26, 1977. St. Louis' 1st choice, 14th overall, in 1996 Entry Draft.

Season	Club	League	GP	G	A	Pts	PIM	PP	SH	GW	S	%	+/-	TF	F%	Min	GP	G	A	Pts	PIM	PP	SH	GW	Min
1993-94	Deerfield	High-MA	22	27	25	52	....	....	....	....	....	....	....	....	....	....	....	....	....	....	....	....	....	....	....
1994-95	Deerfield	High-MA	26	25	32	57	14	....	....	....	....	....	....	....	....	....	....	....	....	....	....	....	....	....	....
1995-96	Boston College	H-East	34	16	29	45	32	....	....	....	....	....	....	....	....	....	....	....	....	....	....	....	....	....	....
1996-97	Boston College	H-East	35	20	24	44	31	....	....	....	....	....	....	....	....	....	....	....	....	....	....	....	....	....	....
1997-98	Boston College	H-East	42	*33	40	*73	56	....	....	....	....	....	....	....	....	....	....	....	....	....	....	....	....	....	....
1998-99	St. Louis	NHL	22	3	7	10	8	1	0	0	33	9.1	2	224	53.6	13:55	....	....	....	....	....	....	....	....	....
	Worcester IceCats	AHL	44	17	22	39	24	....	....	....	....	....	....	....	....	....	4	2	1	3	6	....	....	....	....
99-2000	St. Louis	NHL	32	10	14	24	20	3	0	0	51	19.6	9	379	49.6	15:20	7	2	1	3	4	1	0	0	13:1
	Worcester IceCats	AHL	44	23	28	51	39	....	....	....	....	....	....	....	....	....	....	....	....	....	....	....	....	....	....
2000-01	St. Louis	NHL	41	4	9	13	14	0	0	0	65	6.2	−5	454	53.1	14:00	10	3	1	4	0	0	0	1	12:2
	Worcester IceCats	AHL	34	17	18	35	25	....	....	....	....	....	....	....	....	....	....	....	....	....	....	....	....	....	....
2001-02	Edmonton	NHL	52	6	5	11	41	3	0	2	66	9.1	0	470	55.5	11:44	....	....	....	....	....	....	....	....	....
2002-03	Edmonton	NHL	70	11	20	31	28	2	2	0	102	10.8	19	968	53.5	14:50	6	1	0	1	2	1	0	0	14:2
	Hamilton	AHL	2	0	2	2	2	....	....	....	....	....	....	....	....	....	....	....	....	....	....	....	....	....	....
2003-04	Edmonton	NHL	17	2	6	8	10	0	1	0	28	7.1	5	321	52.7	16:30	....	....	....	....	....	....	....	....	....
2004-05	Salzburg	Austria	11	5	4	9	12	....	....	....	....	....	....	....	....	....	....	....	....	....	....	....	....	....	....
2005-06	Edmonton	NHL	58	9	17	26	20	5	0	1	63	14.3	−12	524	52.5	12:45	....	....	....	....	....	....	....	....	....
	Boston	NHL	19	2	6	8	8	1	0	0	39	5.1	−2	227	46.7	15:09	....	....	....	....	....	....	....	....	....
2006-07	Edmonton	NHL	72	6	14	20	60	0	0	1	84	7.1	−15	765	54.6	13:52	....	....	....	....	....	....	....	....	....
2007-08	Edmonton	NHL	82	11	14	25	50	0	0	0	113	9.7	−17	906	52.8	14:58	....	....	....	....	....	....	....	....	....
2008-09	Atlanta	NHL	79	14	16	30	36	0	1	2	131	10.7	11	1141	52.9	15:19	....	....	....	....	....	....	....	....	....
2009-10	Atlanta	NHL	80	4	13	17	24	0	0	0	86	4.7	−3	1006	50.9	12:30	....	....	....	....	....	....	....	....	....
	NHL Totals		624	82	141	223	319	15	4	6	861	9.5		7385	52.7	14:03	23	6	2	8	6	2	0	1	13:0

Hockey East Rookie of the Year (1996) • Hockey East First All-Star Team (1997, 1998) • NCAA East First All-American Team (1998) • NCAA Championship All-Tournament Team (1998)

Traded to **Edmonton** by **St. Louis** with Jochen Hecht and Jan Horacek for Doug Weight and Michel Riesen, July 1, 2001. • Missed majority of 2003-04 season recovering from ankle (November 8, 2003 vs. Toronto) and knee (January 13, 2004 vs. Florida) injuries. Signed as a free agent by **Salzburg** (Austria), January 30, 2005. Traded to **Boston** by **Edmonton** with Yan Stastny and Edmonton's 2nd round choice (Milan Lucic) in 2006 Entry Draft for Sergei Samsonov, March 9, 2006. Signed as a free agent by **Edmonton**, July 4, 2006. Signed as a free agent by **Atlanta**, July 17, 2008. Traded to **Chicago** by **Atlanta** with Joey Crabb, Jeremy Morin and New Jersey's 1st (prevously acquired, Chicago selected Kevin Hayes) and 2nd (previously acquired, Chicago selected Justin Holl) round choices in 2010 Entry Draft for Brent Sopel, Dustin Byfuglien, Ben Eager and Akim Aliu, June 24, 2010. Traded to **Florida** by **Chicago** for Jeff Taffe, July 22, 2010.

RECCHI, Mark

(REH-kee, MAHRK) **BOS**

Right wing. Shoots left. 5'10", 195 lbs. Born, Kamloops, B.C., February 1, 1968. Pittsburgh's 4th choice, 67th overall, in 1988 Entry Draft.

Season	Club	League	GP	G	A	Pts	PIM	PP	SH	GW	S	%	+/-	TF	F%	Min	GP	G	A	Pts	PIM	PP	SH	GW	Min
1984-85	Langley Eagles	BCJHL	51	26	39	65	39	....	....	....	....	....	....	....	....	....	....	....	....	....	....	....	....	....	....
	New Westminster	WHL	4	1	0	1	0	....	....	....	....	....	....	....	....	....	....	....	....	....	....	....	....	....	....
1985-86	New Westminster	WHL	72	21	40	61	55	....	....	....	....	....	....	....	....	....	....	....	....	....	....	....	....	....	....
1986-87	Kamloops Blazers	WHL	40	26	50	76	63	....	....	....	....	....	....	....	....	....	13	3	16	19	17	....	....	....	....
1987-88	Kamloops Blazers	WHL	62	61	*93	154	75	....	....	....	....	....	....	....	....	....	17	10	*21	*31	18	....	....	....	....
1988-89	Pittsburgh	NHL	15	1	1	2	0	0	0	0	11	9.1	−2	....	....	....	....	....	....	....	....	....	....	....	....
	Muskegon	IHL	63	50	49	99	86	....	....	....	....	....	....	....	....	....	14	7	*14	*21	28	....	....	....	....
1989-90	Pittsburgh	NHL	74	30	37	67	44	6	2	4	143	21.0	6	....	....	....	....	....	....	....	....	....	....	....	....
	Muskegon	IHL	4	7	4	11	2	....	....	....	....	....	....	....	....	....	....	....	....	....	....	....	....	....	....
1990-91 ♦	Pittsburgh	NHL	78	40	73	113	48	12	0	9	184	21.7	0	....	....	....	24	10	24	34	33	5	0	2	
1991-92	Pittsburgh	NHL	58	33	37	70	78	16	1	4	156	21.2	−16	....	....	....	....	....	....	....	....	....	....	....	
	Philadelphia	NHL	22	10	17	27	18	4	0	1	54	18.5	−5	....	....	....	....	....	....	....	....	....	....	....	
1992-93	Philadelphia	NHL	84	53	70	123	95	15	4	6	274	19.3	1	....	....	....	....	....	....	....	....	....	....	....	
1993-94	Philadelphia	NHL	84	40	67	107	46	11	0	5	217	18.4	−2	....	....	....	....	....	....	....	....	....	....	....	
1994-95	Philadelphia	NHL	10	2	3	5	12	1	0	2	17	11.8	−6	....	....	....	....	....	....	....	....	....	....	....	
	Montreal	NHL	39	14	29	43	16	8	0	1	104	13.5	−3	....	....	....	....	....	....	....	....	....	....	....	
1995-96	Montreal	NHL	82	28	50	78	69	11	2	6	191	14.7	20	....	....	....	6	3	3	6	0	3	0	0	
1996-97	Montreal	NHL	82	34	46	80	58	7	2	3	202	16.8	−1	....	....	....	5	4	2	6	2	0	0	0	
1997-98	Montreal	NHL	82	32	42	74	51	9	1	6	216	14.8	11	....	....	....	10	4	8	12	6	0	0	2	
	Canada	Olympics	5	0	2	2	0	....	....	....	....	....	....	....	....	....	....	....	....	....	....	....	....	....	
1998-99	Montreal	NHL	61	12	35	47	28	3	0	2	152	7.9	−4	239	44.8	20:37	....	....	....	....	....	....	....	....	
	Philadelphia	NHL	10	4	2	6	6	0	0	0	19	21.1	−3	4	25.0	19:30	6	0	1	1	2	0	0	0	19:
99-2000	Philadelphia	NHL	82	28	*63	91	50	7	1	5	223	12.6	20	353	49.6	21:43	18	6	12	18	6	2	0	1	23:
2000-01	Philadelphia	NHL	69	27	50	77	33	7	1	8	191	14.1	15	138	42.8	21:40	6	2	2	4	2	1	0	1	23:
2001-02	Philadelphia	NHL	80	22	42	64	46	7	2	4	205	10.7	5	82	53.7	20:40	4	0	0	0	2	0	0	0	21:
2002-03	Philadelphia	NHL	79	20	32	52	35	8	1	3	171	11.7	0	168	52.4	18:50	13	7	3	10	2	1	0	1	18:
2003-04	Philadelphia	NHL	82	26	49	75	47	14	1	5	167	15.6	18	298	52.4	17:12	18	4	2	6	4	2	0	0	16:

Season	Club	League	GP	G	A	Pts	PIM	PP	SH	GW	S	%	+/-	TF	F%	Min	GP	G	A	Pts	PIM	PP	SH	GW	Min
								Regular Season												Playoffs					
2004-05				DID NOT PLAY																					
2005-06	Pittsburgh	NHL	63	24	33	57	56	11	0	2	164	14.6	-28	387	48.3	21:17	....	....	....	....	....	....	....		
	◆ Carolina	NHL	20	4	3	7	12	2	0	1	35	11.4	-8	6	33.3	17:37	25	7	9	16	18	2	0	2	16:34
2006-07	Pittsburgh	NHL	82	24	44	68	62	14	0	3	190	12.6	1	26	46.2	19:42	5	0	4	4	0	0	0	0	19:09
2007-08	Pittsburgh	NHL	19	2	6	8	12	2	0	0	36	5.6	-2	9	44.4	16:25	....	....	....	....	....	....	....		
	Atlanta	NHL	53	12	28	40	20	5	0	1	85	14.1	-16	49	46.9	18:23									
2008-09	Tampa Bay	NHL	62	13	32	45	20	2	0	1	97	13.4	-15	54	40.7	16:53	....	....	....	....	....	....	....		
	Boston	NHL	18	10	6	16	2	4	0	2	32	31.3	-3		2100.0	16:22	11	3	3	6	2	1	0	1	16:57
2009-10	Boston	NHL	81	18	25	43	34	8	0	2	152	11.8	4	146	37.0	17:03	13	6	4	10	6	3	0	0	19:29
	NHL Totals		1571	563	922	1485	998	194	18	85	3688	15.3		1961	47.7	19:17	164	56	77	133	85	20	0	10	18:51

WHL West First All-Star Team (1988) • IHL Second All-Star Team (1989) • NHL Second All-Star Team (1992)
Played in NHL All-Star Game (1991, 1993, 1994, 1997, 1998, 1999, 2000)

Traded to **Philadelphia** by **Pittsburgh** with Brian Benning and Los Angeles' 1st round choice (previously acquired, Philadelphia selected Jason Bowen) in 1992 Entry Draft for Rick Tocchet, Kjell Samuelsson, Ken Wregget and Philadelphia's 3rd round choice (Dave Roche) in 1993 Entry Draft, February 19, 1992. Traded to **Montreal** by **Philadelphia** with Philadelphia's 3rd round choice (Martin Hohenberger) in 1995 Entry Draft for Eric Desjardins, Gilbert Dionne and John LeClair, February 9, 1995. Traded to **Philadelphia** by **Montreal** for Danius Zubrus, Philadelphia's 2nd round choice (Matt Carkner) in 1999 Entry Draft and NY Islanders' 6th round choice (previously acquired, Montreal selected Scott Selig) in 2000 Entry Draft, March 10, 1999. Signed as a free agent by **Pittsburgh**, July 9, 2004. Traded to **Carolina** by **Pittsburgh** for Niklas Nordgren, Krys Kolanos and Carolina's 2nd round choice (later traded to San Jose, later traded to Philadelphia - Philadelphia selected Kevin Marshall) in 2007 Entry Draft, March 9, 2006. Signed as a free agent by **Pittsburgh**, July 25, 2006. Claimed on waivers by **Atlanta** from **Pittsburgh**, December 8, 2007. Signed as a free agent by **Tampa Bay**, July 8, 2008. Traded to **Boston** by **Tampa Bay** with Tampa Bay's 2nd round choice (later traded to Florida - Florida selected Alexander Petrovic) in 2010 Entry Draft for Matt Lashoff and Martins Karsums, March 4, 2009.

RECHLICZ, Joel

Right wing. Shoots right. 6'4", 220 lbs.   Born, Brookfield, WI, June 14, 1987.   (REHK-lihj, JOHL)

Season	Club	League	GP	G	A	Pts	PIM	PP	SH	GW	S	%	+/-	TF	F%	Min	GP	G	A	Pts	PIM	PP	SH	GW	Min
2004-05	Santa Fe	NAHL	3	0	1	1	29	....			....			....			....								
2005-06	Des Moines	USHL	2	0	0	0	4	....			....			....			....								
	Indiana Ice	USHL	2	0	0	0	16	....			....			....			....								
	Gatineau	QMJHL	3	0	0	0	17	....			....			....			....								
2006-07	Chicoutimi	QMJHL	55	0	1	1	159	....			....			....			1	0	0	0	2				
	Chicago Hounds	UHL	2	0	0	0	9	....			....			....			....								
2007-08	Albany River Rats	AHL	25	0	1	1	106	....			....			....			....								
	Kalamazoo Wings	IHL	25	1	0	1	100	....			....			....			....								
2008-09	**NY Islanders**	**NHL**	17	0	1	1	68	0	0	0	7	0.0	-1	0	0.0	4:52	....								
	Bridgeport	AHL	4	0	0	0	12	....			....			....			....								
	Utah Grizzlies	ECHL	45	0	1	1	110	....			....			....			....								
2009-10	**NY Islanders**	**NHL**	6	0	0	0	27	0	0	0	1	0.0	-2	0	0.0	2:41	....								
	Bridgeport	AHL	21	0	0	0	128	....			....			....			....								
	NHL Totals		23	0	1	1	95	0	0	0	8	0.0		0	0.0	4:18	....								

Signed as a free agent by **NY Islanders**, May 6, 2008. • Missed majority of 2009-10 season as a healthy reserve. Signed as a free agent by **Hershey** (AHL), July 29, 2010.

REDDEN, Wade

Defense. Shoots left. 6'2", 210 lbs.   Born, Lloydminster, Sask., June 12, 1977. NY Islanders' 1st choice, 2nd overall, in 1995 Entry Draft.   (REH-duhn, WAYD)   **NYR**

Season	Club	League	GP	G	A	Pts	PIM	PP	SH	GW	S	%	+/-	TF	F%	Min	GP	G	A	Pts	PIM	PP	SH	GW	Min
1992-93	Lloydminster	AJHL	34	4	11	15	64	....			....			....			....								
1993-94	Brandon	WHL	63	4	35	39	98	....			....			....			14	2	4	6	10				
1994-95	Brandon	WHL	64	14	46	60	83	....			....			....			18	5	10	15	8				
1995-96	Brandon	WHL	51	9	45	54	55	....			....			....			19	5	10	15	19				
1996-97	**Ottawa**	**NHL**	82	6	24	30	41	2	0	1	102	5.9	1				7	1	3	4	2	0	0	0	
1997-98	**Ottawa**	**NHL**	80	8	14	22	27	3	0	2	103	7.8	17				9	0	2	2	2	0	0	0	
1998-99	**Ottawa**	**NHL**	72	8	21	29	54	3	0	1	127	6.3	7	0	0.0	23:27	4	1	2	3	2	1	0	0	26:39
99-2000	**Ottawa**	**NHL**	81	10	26	36	49	3	0	2	163	6.1	-1	0	0.0	23:43	....								
2000-01	**Ottawa**	**NHL**	78	10	37	47	49	4	0	0	159	6.3	22	0	0.0	25:17	4	0	0	0	0	0	0	0	27:29
2001-02	**Ottawa**	**NHL**	79	9	25	34	48	4	1	1	156	5.8	22	1	0.0	25:06	12	3	2	5	6	1	0	1	27:56
2002-03	**Ottawa**	**NHL**	76	10	35	45	70	4	0	3	154	6.5	23	0	0.0	25:24	18	1	8	9	10	0	0	1	25:28
2003-04	**Ottawa**	**NHL**	81	17	26	43	65	12	0	3	175	9.7	21	0	0.0	24:54	7	1	0	1	2	1	0	0	26:47
2004-05				DID NOT PLAY																					
2005-06	**Ottawa**	**NHL**	65	10	40	50	63	8	0	4	153	6.5	*35		1100.0	23:28	9	2	8	10	10	2	0	1	25:06
	Canada	Olympics	6	1	0	1	0	....			....			....			....								
2006-07	**Ottawa**	**NHL**	64	7	29	36	50	4	0	3	122	5.7	1	0	0.0	22:54	20	3	7	10	10	3	0	1	23:37
2007-08	**Ottawa**	**NHL**	80	6	32	38	60	4	0	1	136	4.4	11	0	0.0	22:13	4	0	1	1	11	0	0	0	23:31
2008-09	**NY Rangers**	**NHL**	81	3	23	26	51	2	0	0	161	1.9	-5	0	0.0	22:20	7	0	2	2	0	0	0	0	23:24
2009-10	**NY Rangers**	**NHL**	75	2	12	14	27	0	0	0	66	3.0	8		1100.0	17:31	....								
	NHL Totals		994	106	344	450	654	53	1	21	1777	6.0		3	66.7	23:19	101	12	35	47	55	8	0	4	25:08

WHL Rookie of the Year (1994) • WHL East Second All-Star Team (1995) • WHL East First All-Star Team (1996) • Memorial Cup Tournament All-Star Team (1996)
Played in NHL All-Star Game (2002)

Traded to **Ottawa** by **NY Islanders** with Damian Rhodes for Don Beaupre, Martin Straka and Bryan Berard, January 23, 1996. Signed as a free agent by **NY Rangers**, July 1, 2008.

REDDOX, Liam

Left wing. Shoots left. 5'10", 180 lbs.   Born, East York, Ont., January 27, 1986. Edmonton's 5th choice, 112th overall, in 2004 Entry Draft.   (REH-dawks, LEE-uhm)   **EDM.**

Season	Club	League	GP	G	A	Pts	PIM	PP	SH	GW	S	%	+/-	TF	F%	Min	GP	G	A	Pts	PIM	PP	SH	GW	Min
2002-03	Wellington Dukes	OPJHL	45	32	32	64	29	....			....			....			....								
	Peterborough	OHL	4	0	0	0	0	....			....			....			....								
2003-04	Peterborough	OHL	68	31	33	64	24	....			....			....			14	3	10	13	10				
2004-05	Peterborough	OHL	68	36	46	82	38	....			....			....			19	5	9	14	20				
2005-06	Peterborough	OHL	68	19	45	64	74	....			....			....			6	2	1	3	4				
2006-07	Stockton Thunder	ECHL	70	8	18	26	49	....			....			....			....								
2007-08	**Edmonton**	**NHL**	1	0	0	0	0	0	0	0	1	0.0	-1	0	0.0	5:55	....								
	Springfield	AHL	65	16	28	44	48	....			....			....			....								
2008-09	**Edmonton**	**NHL**	46	5	7	12	10	1	0	0	39	12.8	-6	25	44.0	10:28	....								
	Springfield	AHL	14	5	4	9	2	....			....			....			....								
2009-10	**Edmonton**	**NHL**	9	0	2	2	4	0	0	0	11	0.0	-2	0	0.0	12:32	....								
	Springfield	AHL	70	18	17	35	24	....			....			....			....								
	NHL Totals		56	5	9	14	14	1	0	0	51	9.8		25	44.0	10:43	....								

AHL All-Rookie Team (2004)

REESE, Dylan

Defense. Shoots right. 6', 195 lbs.   Born, Pittsburgh, PA, August 29, 1984. NY Rangers' 9th choice, 209th overall, in 2003 Entry Draft.   (REES, DIH-luhn)   **NYI**

Season	Club	League	GP	G	A	Pts	PIM	PP	SH	GW	S	%	+/-	TF	F%	Min	GP	G	A	Pts	PIM	PP	SH	GW	Min
2000-01	Pittsburgh	MWEHL	66	14	42	66		....			....			....			....								
2001-02	Pittsburgh Forge	NAHL	48	7	16	23	70	....			....			....			7	0	2	2	4				
2002-03	Pittsburgh Forge	NAHL	56	11	30	41	98	....			....			....			5	2	3	5	6				
2003-04	Harvard Crimson	ECAC	21	1	4	5	18	....			....			....			....								
2004-05	Harvard Crimson	ECAC	34	7	12	19	44	....			....			....			....								
2005-06	Harvard Crimson	ECAC	33	4	15	19	36	....			....			....			....								
2006-07	Harvard Crimson	ECAC	33	9	9	18	26	....			....			....			....								
	Hartford	AHL	10	0	4	4	12	....			....			....			2	0	0	0	2				
2007-08	San Antonio	AHL	59	1	6	7	49	....			....			....			3	1	1	2	4				
2008-09	San Antonio	AHL	75	1	27	28	64	....			....			....			....								
2009-10	Syracuse Crunch	AHL	51	4	18	22	31	....			....			....			....								
	NY Islanders	**NHL**	19	2	2	4	14	0	0	1	16	12.5	4	0	0.0	15:02	....								
	Bridgeport	AHL	1	1	1	2	0	....			....			....			5	1	3	4	0				
	NHL Totals		19	2	2	4	14	0	0	1	16	12.5		0	0.0	15:02	....								

ECAC Second All-Star Team (2006, 2007)
Signed as a free agent by **San Antonio** (AHL), September 5, 2007. Signed as a free agent by **Columbus**, September 29, 2009. Traded to **NY Islanders** by **Columbus** for Greg Moore, March 1, 2010.

REGEHR, Robyn

(reh-GEER, RAW-bihn) **CGY.**

Defense. Shoots left. 6'3", 225 lbs. Born, Recife, Brazil, April 19, 1980. Colorado's 3rd choice, 19th overall, in 1998 Entry Draft.

			Regular Season														Playoffs								
Season	Club	League	GP	G	A	Pts	PIM	PP	SH	GW	S	%	+/-	TF	F%	Min	GP	G	A	Pts	PIM	PP	SH	GW	Min
1995-96	Prince Albert	SMHL	59	8	24	32	157	....	....	....	....	....	....	....	....	....	....	....	....	....	....	....	....	....	....
1996-97	Kamloops Blazers	WHL	64	4	19	23	96	....	....	....	....	....	....	....	....	....	5	0	1	1	18	....	....	....	....
1997-98	Kamloops Blazers	WHL	65	4	10	14	120	....	....	....	....	....	....	....	....	....	5	0	3	3	8	....	....	....	....
1998-99	Kamloops Blazers	WHL	54	12	20	32	130	....	....	....	....	....	....	....	....	....	12	1	4	5	21	....	....	....	....
99-2000	**Calgary**	**NHL**	**57**	**5**	**7**	**12**	**46**	**2**	**0**	**0**	**64**	**7.8**	**-2**	**0**	**0.0**	**18:24**	....	....	....	....	....	....	....	....	....
	Saint John Flames	AHL	5	0	0	0	0	....	....	....	....	....	....	....	....	....	....	....	....	....	....	....	....	....	....
2000-01	**Calgary**	**NHL**	**71**	**1**	**3**	**4**	**70**	**0**	**0**	**0**	**62**	**1.6**	**-7**	**1**	**0.0**	**19:43**	....	....	....	....	....	....	....	....	....
2001-02	**Calgary**	**NHL**	**77**	**2**	**6**	**8**	**93**	**0**	**0**	**0**	**82**	**2.4**	**-24**	**0**	**0.0**	**20:54**	....	....	....	....	....	....	....	....	....
2002-03	**Calgary**	**NHL**	**76**	**0**	**12**	**12**	**87**	**0**	**0**	**0**	**109**	**0.0**	**-9**	**1**	**100.0**	**22:45**	....	....	....	....	....	....	....	....	....
2003-04	**Calgary**	**NHL**	**82**	**4**	**14**	**18**	**74**	**2**	**0**	**1**	**106**	**3.8**	**14**	**2**	**50.0**	**22:21**	**26**	**2**	**7**	**9**	**20**	**0**	**0**	**0**	**26:27**
2004-05			DID NOT PLAY																						
2005-06	**Calgary**	**NHL**	**68**	**6**	**20**	**26**	**67**	**5**	**0**	**2**	**89**	**6.7**	**6**	**1**	**100.0**	**23:08**	**7**	**1**	**3**	**4**	**6**	**1**	**0**	**0**	**22:22**
	Canada	Olympics	6	0	1	1	2	....	....	....	....	....	....	....	....	....	....	....	....	....	....	....	....	....	....
2006-07	**Calgary**	**NHL**	**78**	**2**	**19**	**21**	**75**	**0**	**0**	**0**	**66**	**3.0**	**27**	**1**	**0.0**	**21:55**	**1**	**0**	**0**	**0**	**0**	**0**	**0**	**0**	**11:15**
2007-08	**Calgary**	**NHL**	**82**	**5**	**15**	**20**	**79**	**1**	**1**	**0**	**93**	**5.4**	**11**	**0**	**0.0**	**21:20**	**7**	**0**	**2**	**2**	**2**	**0**	**0**	**0**	**21:50**
2008-09	**Calgary**	**NHL**	**75**	**0**	**8**	**8**	**73**	**0**	**0**	**0**	**79**	**0.0**	**10**	**0**	**0.0**	**21:09**	....	....	....	....	....	....	....	....	....
2009-10	**Calgary**	**NHL**	**81**	**2**	**15**	**17**	**80**	**0**	**0**	**0**	**78**	**2.6**	**2**	**1**	**0.0**	**21:38**	....	....	....	....	....	....	....	....	....
	NHL Totals		**747**	**27**	**119**	**146**	**744**	**10**	**1**	**3**	**828**	**3.3**		**7**	**42.9**	**21:24**	**41**	**3**	**12**	**15**	**28**	**1**	**0**	**0**	**24:36**

WHL West First All-Star Team (1999)

Traded to **Calgary** by **Colorado** with Rene Corbet, Wade Belak and Colorado's 2nd round compensatory choice (Jarret Stoll) in 2000 Entry Draft for Theoren Fleury and Chris Dingman, February 28, 1999.

REGIER, Steve

(reh-GEER, STEEV)

Left wing. Shoots left. 6'4", 194 lbs. Born, Edmonton, Alta., August 31, 1984. NY Islanders' 5th choice, 148th overall, in 2004 Entry Draft.

			Regular Season														Playoffs								
Season	Club	League	GP	G	A	Pts	PIM	PP	SH	GW	S	%	+/-	TF	F%	Min	GP	G	A	Pts	PIM	PP	SH	GW	Min
2000-01	Leduc Oil Kings	AMHL	35	22	39	61	135	....	....	....	....	....	....	....	....	....	....	....	....	....	....	....	....	....	....
2001-02	Medicine Hat	WHL	59	1	4	5	31	....	....	....	....	....	....	....	....	....	....	....	....	....	....	....	....	....	....
2002-03	Medicine Hat	WHL	61	11	10	21	114	....	....	....	....	....	....	....	....	....	11	2	2	4	20	....	....	....	....
2003-04	Medicine Hat	WHL	72	25	35	60	111	....	....	....	....	....	....	....	....	....	18	5	11	16	20	....	....	....	....
2004-05	Bridgeport	AHL	75	7	15	22	43	....	....	....	....	....	....	....	....	....	....	....	....	....	....	....	....	....	....
2005-06	**NY Islanders**	**NHL**	**9**	**0**	**0**	**0**	**0**	**0**	**0**	**0**	**4**	**0.0**	**-1**	**0**	**0.0**	**6:02**	....	....	....	....	....	....	....	....	....
	Bridgeport	AHL	73	16	21	37	54	....	....	....	....	....	....	....	....	....	7	0	2	2	6	....	....	....	....
2006-07	**NY Islanders**	**NHL**	**1**	**0**	**0**	**0**	**0**	**0**	**0**	**0**	**0**	**0.0**	**0**	**0**	**0.0**	**4:41**	....	....	....	....	....	....	....	....	....
	Bridgeport	AHL	77	19	27	46	77	....	....	....	....	....	....	....	....	....	....	....	....	....	....	....	....	....	....
2007-08	**NY Islanders**	**NHL**	**8**	**0**	**0**	**0**	**4**	**0**	**0**	**0**	**7**	**0.0**	**-1**	**1**	**0.0**	**7:59**	....	....	....	....	....	....	....	....	....
	Bridgeport	AHL	65	19	25	44	60	....	....	....	....	....	....	....	....	....	....	....	....	....	....	....	....	....	....
2008-09	**St. Louis**	**NHL**	**8**	**3**	**1**	**4**	**4**	**2**	**0**	**0**	**11**	**27.3**	**-1**	**7**	**42.9**	**10:59**	....	....	....	....	....	....	....	....	....
	Peoria Rivermen	AHL	73	22	28	50	61	....	....	....	....	....	....	....	....	....	7	2	2	4	4	....	....	....	....
2009-10	Salzburg	Austria	56	10	27	37	85	....	....	....	....	....	....	....	....	....	....	....	....	....	....	....	....	....	....
	NHL Totals		**26**	**3**	**1**	**4**	**8**	**2**	**0**	**0**	**22**	**13.6**		**8**	**37.5**	**8:06**	....	....	....	....	....	....	....	....	....

Signed as a free agent by **St. Louis**, July 15, 2008. Signed as a free agent by **Salzburg** (Austria), July 22, 2009.

REGIN, Peter

(REE-gihn, PEE-tuhr) **OTT.**

Center. Shoots left. 6'2", 197 lbs. Born, Herning, Denmark, April 16, 1986. Ottawa's 4th choice, 87th overall, in 2004 Entry Draft.

			Regular Season														Playoffs								
Season	Club	League	GP	G	A	Pts	PIM	PP	SH	GW	S	%	+/-	TF	F%	Min	GP	G	A	Pts	PIM	PP	SH	GW	Min
2002-03	Herning IK	Denmark	24	0	1	1	4	....	....	....	....	....	....	....	....	....	10	1	3	4	4	....	....	....	....
2003-04	Herning IK	Denmark	33	9	11	20	14	....	....	....	....	....	....	....	....	....	....	....	....	....	....	....	....	....	....
2004-05	Herning Blue Fox	Denmark	36	19	27	46	43	....	....	....	....	....	....	....	....	....	16	5	8	13	2	....	....	....	....
2005-06	Timra IK	Sweden	44	4	7	11	14	....	....	....	....	....	....	....	....	....	....	....	....	....	....	....	....	....	....
2006-07	Timra IK	Sweden	51	9	7	16	16	....	....	....	....	....	....	....	....	....	7	2	2	4	2	....	....	....	....
2007-08	Timra IK	Sweden	55	12	19	31	36	....	....	....	....	....	....	....	....	....	11	2	7	9	2	....	....	....	....
2008-09	**Ottawa**	**NHL**	**11**	**1**	**1**	**2**	**2**	**0**	**0**	**1**	**7**	**14.3**	**0**	**77**	**53.3**	**10:32**	....	....	....	....	....	....	....	....	....
	Binghamton	AHL	56	18	29	47	36	....	....	....	....	....	....	....	....	....	....	....	....	....	....	....	....	....	....
2009-10	**Ottawa**	**NHL**	**75**	**13**	**16**	**29**	**20**	**1**	**0**	**1**	**135**	**9.6**	**10**	**538**	**44.6**	**12:54**	**6**	**3**	**1**	**4**	**6**	**0**	**0**	**0**	**18:06**
	NHL Totals		**86**	**14**	**17**	**31**	**22**	**1**	**0**	**2**	**142**	**9.9**		**615**	**45.7**	**12:36**	**6**	**3**	**1**	**4**	**6**	**0**	**0**	**0**	**18:06**

REICH, Jeremy

(REECH, JAIR-eh-mee) **BOS.**

Left wing. Shoots left. 6'1", 203 lbs. Born, Craik, Sask., February 11, 1979. Chicago's 3rd choice, 39th overall, in 1997 Entry Draft.

			Regular Season														Playoffs								
Season	Club	League	GP	G	A	Pts	PIM	PP	SH	GW	S	%	+/-	TF	F%	Min	GP	G	A	Pts	PIM	PP	SH	GW	Min
1993-94	Pilote Butte	SAHA	80	70	65	135	120	....	....	....	....	....	....	....	....	....	....	....	....	....	....	....	....	....	....
1994-95	Sask. Contacts	SMHL	35	13	20	33	81	....	....	....	....	....	....	....	....	....	....	....	....	....	....	....	....	....	....
1995-96	Seattle	WHL	65	11	11	22	88	....	....	....	....	....	....	....	....	....	5	0	1	1	10	....	....	....	....
1996-97	Seattle	WHL	62	19	31	50	134	....	....	....	....	....	....	....	....	....	15	2	5	7	36	....	....	....	....
1997-98	Seattle	WHL	43	24	23	47	121	....	....	....	....	....	....	....	....	....	....	....	....	....	....	....	....	....	....
	Swift Current	WHL	22	8	8	16	47	....	....	....	....	....	....	....	....	....	12	5	6	11	37	....	....	....	....
1998-99	Swift Current	WHL	67	21	28	49	220	....	....	....	....	....	....	....	....	....	6	0	3	3	26	....	....	....	....
99-2000	Swift Current	WHL	72	33	58	91	167	....	....	....	....	....	....	....	....	....	12	2	10	12	19	....	....	....	....
2000-01	Syracuse Crunch	AHL	56	6	9	15	108	....	....	....	....	....	....	....	....	....	5	0	0	0	6	....	....	....	....
2001-02	Syracuse Crunch	AHL	59	9	7	16	178	....	....	....	....	....	....	....	....	....	10	4	0	4	16	....	....	....	....
2002-03	Syracuse Crunch	AHL	78	14	13	27	195	....	....	....	....	....	....	....	....	....	....	....	....	....	....	....	....	....	....
2003-04	**Columbus**	**NHL**	**9**	**0**	**1**	**1**	**20**	**0**	**0**	**0**	**3**	**0.0**	**-3**	**0**	**0.0**	**7:38**	....	....	....	....	....	....	....	....	....
	Syracuse Crunch	AHL	72	14	37	51	150	....	....	....	....	....	....	....	....	....	6	1	1	2	13	....	....	....	....
2004-05	Syracuse Crunch	AHL	50	4	5	9	189	....	....	....	....	....	....	....	....	....	....	....	....	....	....	....	....	....	....
	Houston Aeros	AHL	18	3	4	7	34	....	....	....	....	....	....	....	....	....	5	0	1	1	28	....	....	....	....
2005-06	Providence Bruins	AHL	77	8	15	23	235	....	....	....	....	....	....	....	....	....	6	0	0	0	27	....	....	....	....
2006-07	**Boston**	**NHL**	**32**	**0**	**1**	**1**	**63**	**0**	**0**	**0**	**27**	**0.0**	**-10**	**4**	**25.0**	**8:14**	....	....	....	....	....	....	....	....	....
	Providence Bruins	AHL	46	4	7	11	105	....	....	....	....	....	....	....	....	....	....	....	....	....	....	....	....	....	....
2007-08	**Boston**	**NHL**	**58**	**2**	**2**	**4**	**78**	**0**	**0**	**1**	**39**	**5.1**	**-5**	**31**	**48.4**	**8:15**	**4**	**0**	**0**	**0**	**8**	**0**	**0**	**0**	**10:27**
2008-09	Providence Bruins	AHL	76	21	13	34	139	....	....	....	....	....	....	....	....	....	16	3	5	8	21	....	....	....	....
2009-10	Bridgeport	AHL	33	12	8	20	24	....	....	....	....	....	....	....	....	....	5	1	2	3	4	....	....	....	....
	NHL Totals		**99**	**2**	**4**	**6**	**161**	**0**	**0**	**1**	**69**	**2.9**		**35**	**45.7**	**8:12**	**4**	**0**	**0**	**0**	**8**	**0**	**0**	**0**	**10:27**

Signed as a free agent by **Columbus**, May 17, 2000. • Loaned to **Houston** (AHL) by **Syracuse** (AHL) for the loan of Jason Beckett, March 10, 2005. Signed as a free agent by **Boston**, September 7, 2005. Signed as a free agent by **NY Islanders**, July 2, 2009. Signed as a free agent by **Boston**, July 1, 2010.

REINPRECHT, Steve

(RIGHN-prehkt, STEEV) **FLA.**

Center. Shoots left. 6', 195 lbs. Born, Edmonton, Alta., May 7, 1976.

			Regular Season														Playoffs								
Season	Club	League	GP	G	A	Pts	PIM	PP	SH	GW	S	%	+/-	TF	F%	Min	GP	G	A	Pts	PIM	PP	SH	GW	Min
1993-94	Edmonton SSAC	AMHL	71	48	77	125	....	....	....	....	....	....	....	....	....	....	....	....	....	....	....	....	....	....	....
1994-95	St. Albert Saints	AJHL	56	35	44	79	14	....	....	....	....	....	....	....	....	....	....	....	....	....	....	....	....	....	....
1995-96	St. Albert Saints	AJHL	39	24	33	57	16	....	....	....	....	....	....	....	....	....	....	....	....	....	....	....	....	....	....
1996-97	U. of Wisconsin	WCHA	38	11	9	20	12	....	....	....	....	....	....	....	....	....	....	....	....	....	....	....	....	....	....
1997-98	U. of Wisconsin	WCHA	41	19	24	43	18	....	....	....	....	....	....	....	....	....	....	....	....	....	....	....	....	....	....
1998-99	U. of Wisconsin	WCHA	38	16	17	33	14	....	....	....	....	....	....	....	....	....	....	....	....	....	....	....	....	....	....
99-2000	U. of Wisconsin	WCHA	37	26	40	*66	14	....	....	....	....	....	....	....	....	....	....	....	....	....	....	....	....	....	....
	Los Angeles	**NHL**	**1**	**0**	**0**	**0**	**2**	**0**	**0**	**0**	**0**	**0.0**	**0**	**6**	**50.0**	**6:01**	....	....	....	....	....	....	....	....	....
2000-01	**Los Angeles**	**NHL**	**59**	**12**	**17**	**29**	**12**	**3**	**2**	**3**	**72**	**16.7**	**11**	**676**	**41.4**	**12:39**	....	....	....	....	....	....	....	....	....
	♦ Colorado	**NHL**	**21**	**3**	**4**	**7**	**2**	**0**	**0**	**0**	**28**	**10.7**	**-1**	**209**	**51.2**	**15:38**	**22**	**2**	**3**	**5**	**2**	**0**	**0**	**0**	**12:09**
2001-02	**Colorado**	**NHL**	**67**	**19**	**27**	**46**	**18**	**4**	**0**	**3**	**111**	**17.1**	**14**	**413**	**52.1**	**16:32**	**21**	**7**	**5**	**12**	**8**	**0**	**0**	**2**	**16:23**
2002-03	**Colorado**	**NHL**	**77**	**18**	**33**	**51**	**18**	**2**	**1**	**1**	**146**	**12.3**	**-6**	**928**	**46.4**	**17:22**	**7**	**1**	**2**	**3**	**0**	**0**	**0**	**0**	**15:32**
2003-04	**Calgary**	**NHL**	**44**	**7**	**22**	**29**	**4**	**3**	**0**	**1**	**68**	**10.3**	**1**	**120**	**40.0**	**17:05**	....	....	....	....	....	....	....	....	....
2004-05	HC Mulhouse	France	22	20	27	47	6	....	....	....	....	....	....	....	....	....	10	7	6	13	2	....	....	....	....
2005-06	**Calgary**	**NHL**	**52**	**10**	**19**	**29**	**24**	**5**	**0**	**1**	**72**	**13.9**	**10**	**340**	**49.4**	**14:49**	....	....	....	....	....	....	....	....	....
	Phoenix	**NHL**	**28**	**12**	**11**	**23**	**8**	**4**	**1**	**2**	**58**	**20.7**	**1**	**526**	**47.3**	**19:06**	....	....	....	....	....	....	....	....	....
2006-07	**Phoenix**	**NHL**	**49**	**9**	**24**	**33**	**28**	**2**	**0**	**1**	**71**	**12.7**	**-3**	**537**	**52.3**	**15:40**	....	....	....	....	....	....	....	....	....
2007-08	**Phoenix**	**NHL**	**81**	**16**	**30**	**46**	**26**	**5**	**1**	**0**	**105**	**15.2**	**-3**	**1020**	**50.6**	**15:42**	....	....	....	....	....	....	....	....	....

			Regular Season														Playoffs								
Season	Club	League	GP	G	A	Pts	PIM	PP	SH	GW	S	%	+/-	TF	F%	Min	GP	G	A	Pts	PIM	PP	SH	GW	Min
2008-09	**Phoenix**	**NHL**	**73**	**14**	**27**	**41**	**20**	**3**	**0**	**3**	**95**	**14.7**	**0**	**886**	**46.3**	**15:54**	....	....	....	....	....	....	....	....	....
2009-10	**Florida**	**NHL**	**82**	**16**	**22**	**38**	**18**	**3**	**0**	**1**	**124**	**12.9**	**–1**	**989**	**47.7**	**16:05**	....	....	....	....	....	....	....	....	....
	NHL Totals		**634**	**136**	**236**	**372**	**180**	**34**	**5**	**16**	**950**	**14.3**		**6650**	**47.8**	**15:56**	**50**	**10**	**10**	**20**	**10**	**0**	**0**	**2**	**14:24**

WCHA Second All-Star Team (1998) • WCHA First All-Star Team (2000) • WCHA Player of the Year (2000) • NCAA West First All-American Team (2000)

Signed as a free agent by **Los Angeles**, March 31, 2000. Traded to **Colorado** by **Los Angeles** with Rob Blake for Adam Deadmarsh, Aaron Miller, a player to be named later (Jared Aulin, March 22, 2001) and Colorado's 1st round choices in 2001 (Dave Steckel) and 2003 (Brian Boyle) Entry Drafts, February 21, 2001. Traded to **Buffalo** by **Colorado** for Keith Ballard, July 3, 2003. Traded to **Calgary** by **Buffalo** with Rhett Warrener for Chris Drury and Steve Begin, July 3, 2003. Signed as a free agent by **Mulhouse** (France), September 28, 2004. Traded to **Phoenix** by **Calgary** with Philippe Sauve for Brian Boucher and Mike Leclerc, February 2, 2006. Traded to **Florida** by **Phoenix** for Stefan Meyer, June 19, 2009.

REITZ, Erik

(REETZ, AIR-ihk)

Defense. Shoots right. 6'1", 222 lbs. Born, Detroit, MI, July 29, 1982. Minnesota's 5th choice, 170th overall, in 2000 Entry Draft.

Season	Club	League	GP	G	A	Pts	PIM	PP	SH	GW	S	%	+/-	TF	F%	Min	GP	G	A	Pts	PIM	PP	SH	GW	Min
1998-99	Leamington Flyers	OHA-B	50	5	10	15	80	....	....	....	....	....	....	....	....	....	....	....	....	....	....	....	....	....	....
99-2000	Barrie Colts	OHL	63	2	10	12	85	....	....	....	....	....	....	....	....	....	25	0	5	5	44	....	....	....	....
2000-01	Barrie Colts	OHL	68	5	21	26	178	....	....	....	....	....	....	....	....	....	5	1	0	1	21	....	....	....	....
2001-02	Barrie Colts	OHL	61	13	27	40	153	....	....	....	....	....	....	....	....	....	20	4	16	20	40	....	....	....	....
2002-03	Houston Aeros	AHL	62	6	13	19	112	....	....	....	....	....	....	....	....	....	11	0	3	3	31	....	....	....	....
2003-04	Houston Aeros	AHL	69	5	19	24	148	....	....	....	....	....	....	....	....	....	2	0	0	0	0	....	....	....	....
2004-05	Houston Aeros	AHL	38	2	12	14	91	....	....	....	....	....	....	....	....	....	....	....	....	....	....	....	....	....	....
2005-06	**Minnesota**	**NHL**	**5**	**0**	**0**	**0**	**4**	**0**	**0**	**0**	**0**	**0.0**	**–2**	**0**	**0.0**	**13:09**	....	....	....	....	....	....	....	....	....
	Houston Aeros	AHL	72	5	23	28	139	....	....	....	....	....	....	....	....	....	8	0	5	5	20	....	....	....	....
2006-07	**Minnesota**	**NHL**	**1**	**0**	**0**	**0**	**0**	**0**	**0**	**0**	**0**	**0.0**	**1**	**0**	**0.0**	**10:36**	....	....	....	....	....	....	....	....	....
	Houston Aeros	AHL	73	9	25	34	132	....	....	....	....	....	....	....	....	....	....	....	....	....	....	....	....	....	....
2007-08	Houston Aeros	AHL	49	8	26	34	99	....	....	....	....	....	....	....	....	....	3	0	0	0	2	....	....	....	....
	Minnesota	**NHL**	....	....	....	....	....	....	....	....	....	....	....	....	....	....	**2**	**0**	**0**	**0**	**0**	**0**	**0**	**0**	**6:18**
2008-09	**Minnesota**	**NHL**	**31**	**1**	**1**	**2**	**41**	**0**	**0**	**0**	**15**	**6.7**	**–2**	**0**	**0.0**	**9:52**	....	....	....	....	....	....	....	....	....
	NY Rangers	**NHL**	**11**	**0**	**0**	**0**	**24**	**0**	**0**	**0**	**7**	**0.0**	**–4**	**0**	**0.0**	**10:16**	....	....	....	....	....	....	....	....	....
2009-10	Sibir Novosibirsk	Rus-KHL	38	1	5	6	146	....	....	....	....	....	....	....	....	....	....	....	....	....	....	....	....	....	....
	NHL Totals		**48**	**1**	**1**	**2**	**69**	**0**	**0**	**0**	**22**	**4.5**		**0**	**0.0**	**10:19**	**2**	**0**	**0**	**0**	**0**	**0**	**0**	**0**	**6:18**

Memorial Cup Tournament All-Star Team (2000) • OHL First All-Star Team (2002)

• Missed majority of 2004-05 season recovering from elbow injury suffered in game vs. Milwaukee (AHL), February 5, 2005. Traded to **NY Rangers** by **Minnesota** for Dan Fritsche, January 29, 2009. Claimed on waivers by **Toronto** from **NY Rangers**, March 4, 2009. Signed as a free agent by **Novosibirsk** (Russia-KHL), August 22, 2009.

REPIK, Michal

(REH-pihk, MEE-khahl) **FLA.**

Right wing. Shoots right. 5'10", 180 lbs. Born, Vlasim, Czech., December 31, 1988. Florida's 2nd choice, 40th overall, in 2007 Entry Draft.

Season	Club	League	GP	G	A	Pts	PIM	PP	SH	GW	S	%	+/-	TF	F%	Min	GP	G	A	Pts	PIM	PP	SH	GW	Min
2002-03	Sparta U17	CzR-U17	18	7	10	17	6	....	....	....	....	....	....	....	....	....	2	0	0	0	0	....	....	....	....
2003-04	Sparta U17	CzR-U17	33	25	17	42	42	....	....	....	....	....	....	....	....	....	3	0	0	0	0	....	....	....	....
	Sparta Jr.	CzRep-Jr.	23	12	5	17	10	....	....	....	....	....	....	....	....	....	....	....	....	....	....	....	....	....	....
2004-05	Sparta U17	CzR-U17	2	2	3	5	6	....	....	....	....	....	....	....	....	....	....	....	....	....	....	....	....	....	....
	Sparta Jr.	CzRep-Jr.	45	26	31	57	24	....	....	....	....	....	....	....	....	....	8	2	4	6	10	....	....	....	....
2005-06	Vancouver Giants	WHL	69	24	28	52	55	....	....	....	....	....	....	....	....	....	14	3	3	6	19	....	....	....	....
2006-07	Vancouver Giants	WHL	56	24	31	55	56	....	....	....	....	....	....	....	....	....	22	10	*16	*26	24	....	....	....	....
2007-08	Vancouver Giants	WHL	51	27	34	61	62	....	....	....	....	....	....	....	....	....	10	5	6	11	18	....	....	....	....
2008-09	**Florida**	**NHL**	**5**	**2**	**0**	**2**	**2**	**0**	**0**	**0**	**7**	**28.6**	**1**	**1**	**100.0**	**7:32**	....	....	....	....	....	....	....	....	....
	Rochester	AHL	75	19	30	49	58	....	....	....	....	....	....	....	....	....	....	....	....	....	....	....	....	....	....
2009-10	**Florida**	**NHL**	**19**	**3**	**2**	**5**	**6**	**0**	**0**	**0**	**23**	**13.0**	**1**	**1**	**100.0**	**8:35**	....	....	....	....	....	....	....	....	....
	Rochester	AHL	60	22	31	53	57	....	....	....	....	....	....	....	....	....	7	1	1	2	4	....	....	....	....
	NHL Totals		**24**	**5**	**2**	**7**	**8**	**0**	**0**	**0**	**30**	**16.7**		**2**	**100.0**	**8:22**	....	....	....	....	....	....	....	....	....

Memorial Cup Tournament All-Star Team (2007) • Ed Chynoweth Trophy (Memorial Cup Tournament - Leading Scorer) (2007)

RIBEIRO, Mike

(rih-BAIR-roh, MIGHK) **DAL.**

Center. Shoots left. 6', 173 lbs. Born, Montreal, Que., February 10, 1980. Montreal's 2nd choice, 45th overall, in 1998 Entry Draft.

Season	Club	League	GP	G	A	Pts	PIM	PP	SH	GW	S	%	+/-	TF	F%	Min	GP	G	A	Pts	PIM	PP	SH	GW	Min
1996-97	Mtl-Bourassa	QAAA	43	32	57	89	48	....	....	....	....	....	....	....	....	....	16	15	23	38	14	....	....	....	....
1997-98	Rouyn-Noranda	QMJHL	67	40	*85	125	55	....	....	....	....	....	....	....	....	....	6	3	1	4	0	....	....	....	....
1998-99	Rouyn-Noranda	QMJHL	69	*67	*100	*167	137	....	....	....	....	....	....	....	....	....	11	5	11	16	12	....	....	....	....
	Fredericton	AHL	....	....	....	....	....	....	....	....	....	....	....	....	....	....	5	0	1	1	2	....	....	....	....
99-2000	**Montreal**	**NHL**	**19**	**1**	**1**	**2**	**2**	**1**	**0**	**0**	**18**	**5.6**	**–6**	**95**	**34.7**	**10:40**	....	....	....	....	....	....	....	....	....
	Quebec Citadelles	AHL	3	0	0	0	2	....	....	....	....	....	....	....	....	....	....	....	....	....	....	....	....	....	....
	Rouyn-Noranda	QMJHL	2	1	3	4	0	....	....	....	....	....	....	....	....	....	....	....	....	....	....	....	....	....	....
	Quebec Remparts	QMJHL	21	17	28	45	30	....	....	....	....	....	....	....	....	....	11	3	20	23	38	....	....	....	....
2000-01	**Montreal**	**NHL**	**2**	**0**	**0**	**0**	**2**	**0**	**0**	**0**	**3**	**0.0**	**0**	**11**	**18.2**	**10:38**	....	....	....	....	....	....	....	....	....
	Quebec Citadelles	AHL	74	26	40	66	44	....	....	....	....	....	....	....	....	....	9	1	5	6	23	....	....	....	....
2001-02	**Montreal**	**NHL**	**43**	**8**	**10**	**18**	**12**	**3**	**0**	**0**	**48**	**16.7**	**–11**	**141**	**44.0**	**13:55**	....	....	....	....	....	....	....	....	....
	Quebec Citadelles	AHL	23	9	14	23	36	....	....	....	....	....	....	....	....	....	3	0	3	3	0	....	....	....	....
2002-03	**Montreal**	**NHL**	**52**	**5**	**12**	**17**	**6**	**2**	**0**	**0**	**57**	**8.8**	**–3**	**358**	**50.3**	**11:07**	....	....	....	....	....	....	....	....	....
	Hamilton	AHL	3	0	1	1	0	....	....	....	....	....	....	....	....	....	....	....	....	....	....	....	....	....	....
2003-04	**Montreal**	**NHL**	**81**	**20**	**45**	**65**	**34**	**7**	**0**	**5**	**103**	**19.4**	**15**	**913**	**44.8**	**17:05**	**11**	**2**	**1**	**3**	**18**	**0**	**0**	**0**	**16:31**
2004-05	Blues Espoo	Finland	17	8	9	17	4	....	....	....	....	....	....	....	....	....	....	....	....	....	....	....	....	....	....
2005-06	**Montreal**	**NHL**	**79**	**16**	**35**	**51**	**36**	**8**	**0**	**2**	**130**	**12.3**	**–6**	**843**	**44.7**	**16:35**	**6**	**0**	**2**	**2**	**0**	**0**	**0**	**0**	**18:22**
2006-07	**Dallas**	**NHL**	**81**	**18**	**41**	**59**	**22**	**6**	**0**	**3**	**111**	**16.2**	**3**	**678**	**46.6**	**14:56**	**7**	**0**	**3**	**3**	**4**	**0**	**0**	**0**	**18:28**
2007-08	**Dallas**	**NHL**	**76**	**27**	**56**	**83**	**46**	**7**	**0**	**5**	**107**	**25.2**	**21**	**883**	**45.0**	**18:26**	**18**	**3**	**14**	**17**	**16**	**0**	**0**	**0**	**21:45**
2008-09	**Dallas**	**NHL**	**82**	**22**	**56**	**78**	**52**	**7**	**0**	**1**	**163**	**13.5**	**–4**	**1240**	**45.5**	**20:57**	....	....	....	....	....	....	....	....	....
2009-10	**Dallas**	**NHL**	**66**	**19**	**34**	**53**	**38**	**8**	**2**	**0**	**155**	**12.3**	**–5**	**1102**	**44.8**	**19:32**	....	....	....	....	....	....	....	....	....
	NHL Totals		**581**	**136**	**290**	**426**	**250**	**49**	**2**	**16**	**895**	**15.2**		**6264**	**45.2**	**16:43**	**42**	**5**	**20**	**25**	**38**	**0**	**0**	**0**	**19:21**

QMJHL Second All-Star Team (1998) • QMJHL First All-Star Team (1999) • Canadian Major Junior First All-Star Team (1999)

Played in NHL All-Star Game (2008)

Signed as a free agent by **Espoo** (Finland), January 17, 2005. Traded to **Dallas** by **Montreal** with Montreal's 6th round choice (Matthew Tassone) in 2008 Entry Draft for Janne Niinimaa and Dallas' 5th round choice (Andrew Conboy) in 2007 Entry Draft, September 30, 2006.

RICHARDS, Brad

(RIH-chuhrds, BRAD) **DAL.**

Center. Shoots left. 6', 196 lbs. Born, Murray Harbour, P.E.I., May 2, 1980. Tampa Bay's 2nd choice, 64th overall, in 1998 Entry Draft.

Season	Club	League	GP	G	A	Pts	PIM	PP	SH	GW	S	%	+/-	TF	F%	Min	GP	G	A	Pts	PIM	PP	SH	GW	Min
1996-97	Notre Dame	SJHL	63	39	48	87	73	....	....	....	....	....	....	....	....	....	....	....	....	....	....	....	....	....	....
1997-98	Rimouski Oceanic	QMJHL	68	33	82	115	44	....	....	....	....	....	....	....	....	....	19	8	24	32	2	....	....	....	....
1998-99	Rimouski Oceanic	QMJHL	59	39	92	131	55	....	....	....	....	....	....	....	....	....	11	9	12	21	6	....	....	....	....
99-2000	Rimouski Oceanic	QMJHL	63	*71	*115	*186	69	....	....	....	....	....	....	....	....	....	12	13	*24	*37	16	....	....	....	....
2000-01	**Tampa Bay**	**NHL**	**82**	**21**	**41**	**62**	**14**	**7**	**0**	**3**	**179**	**11.7**	**–10**	**955**	**41.4**	**16:54**	....	....	....	....	....	....	....	....	....
2001-02	**Tampa Bay**	**NHL**	**82**	**20**	**42**	**62**	**13**	**5**	**0**	**0**	**251**	**8.0**	**–18**	**911**	**41.2**	**19:48**	....	....	....	....	....	....	....	....	....
2002-03	**Tampa Bay**	**NHL**	**80**	**17**	**57**	**74**	**24**	**4**	**0**	**2**	**277**	**6.1**	**3**	**1007**	**47.5**	**19:56**	**11**	**0**	**5**	**5**	**12**	**0**	**0**	**0**	**22:21**
2003-04 ♦	**Tampa Bay**	**NHL**	**82**	**26**	**53**	**79**	**12**	**5**	**1**	**6**	**244**	**10.7**	**13**	**1167**	**46.7**	**20:26**	**23**	**12**	**14**	***26**	**4**	***7**	**0**	***7**	**23:28**
2004-05	Ak Bars Kazan	Russia	6	2	5	7	16	....	....	....	....	....	....	....	....	....	....	....	....	....	....	....	....	....	....
2005-06	**Tampa Bay**	**NHL**	**82**	**23**	**68**	**91**	**32**	**7**	**4**	**0**	**282**	**8.2**	**0**	**1288**	**50.2**	**22:45**	**5**	**3**	**5**	**8**	**6**	**0**	**0**	**0**	**24:11**
	Canada	Olympics	6	2	2	4	6	....	....	....	....	....	....	....	....	....	....	....	....	....	....	....	....	....	....
2006-07	**Tampa Bay**	**NHL**	**82**	**25**	**45**	**70**	**23**	**12**	**1**	**3**	**272**	**9.2**	**–19**	**1580**	**51.4**	**24:07**	**6**	**3**	**5**	**8**	**6**	**2**	**0**	**0**	**25:39**
2007-08	**Tampa Bay**	**NHL**	**62**	**18**	**33**	**51**	**15**	**9**	**1**	**4**	**228**	**7.9**	**–25**	**944**	**48.1**	**24:17**	....	....	....	....	....	....	....	....	....
	Dallas	**NHL**	**12**	**2**	**9**	**11**	**0**	**0**	**1**	**0**	**21**	**9.5**	**–2**	**130**	**56.2**	**19:15**	**18**	**3**	**12**	**15**	**8**	**0**	**0**	**0**	**21:06**
2008-09	**Dallas**	**NHL**	**56**	**16**	**32**	**48**	**6**	**5**	**0**	**2**	**180**	**8.9**	**–4**	**911**	**50.6**	**20:29**	....	....	....	....	....	....	....	....	....
2009-10	**Dallas**	**NHL**	**80**	**24**	**67**	**91**	**14**	**13**	**0**	**2**	**284**	**8.5**	**–12**	**1140**	**51.5**	**20:52**	....	....	....	....	....	....	....	....	....
	NHL Totals		**700**	**192**	**447**	**639**	**153**	**67**	**8**	**22**	**2218**	**8.7**		**10033**	**48.1**	**20:58**	**63**	**21**	**41**	**62**	**36**	**9**	**0**	**7**	**22:52**

QMJHL First All-Star Team (2000) • Canadian Major Junior First All-Star Team (2000) • Canadian Major Junior Player of the Year (2000) • Memorial Cup Tournament All-Star Team (2000) • Stafford Smythe Memorial Trophy (Memorial Cup Tournament - MVP) (2000) • NHL All-Rookie Team (2001) • Lady Byng Memorial Trophy (2004) • Conn Smythe Trophy (2004)

Signed as a free agent by **Kazan** (Russia), November 8, 2004. Traded to **Dallas** by **Tampa Bay** with Johan Holmqvist for Jussi Jokinen, Jeff Halpern, Mike Smith and Dallas' 4th round choice (later traded to Minnesota, later traded to Edmonton – Edmonton selected Kyle Bigos) in 2009 Entry Draft, February 26, 2008.

RICHARDS, Mike
(RIH-chuhrds, MIGHK) **PHI.**

Center. Shoots left. 5'11", 195 lbs. Born, Kenora, Ont., February 11, 1985. Philadelphia's 2nd choice, 24th overall, in 2003 Entry Draft.

			Regular Season														Playoffs								
Season	Club	League	GP	G	A	Pts	PIM	PP	SH	GW	S	%	+/-	TF	F%	Min	GP	G	A	Pts	PIM	PP	SH	GW	Min
2000-01	Kenora Stars	NOHA	85	76	73	149	20	....	....	....	....	....	....	....	....	....	....	....	....	....	....	....	....	....	....
2001-02	Kitchener Rangers	OHL	65	20	38	58	52	....	....	....	....	....	....	....	....	....	4	0	1	1	6	....	....	....	....
2002-03	Kitchener Rangers	OHL	67	37	50	87	99	....	....	....	....	....	....	....	....	....	21	9	18	27	24	....	....	....	....
2003-04	Kitchener Rangers	OHL	58	36	53	89	82	....	....	....	....	....	....	....	....	....	1	0	0	0	0	....	....	....	....
2004-05	Kitchener Rangers	OHL	43	22	36	58	75	....	....	....	....	....	....	....	....	....	15	11	17	28	36	....	....	....	....
	Philadelphia	AHL	....	....	....	....	....	....	....	....	....	....	....	....	....	....	14	7	8	15	28	....	....	....	....
2005-06	**Philadelphia**	**NHL**	**79**	**11**	**23**	**34**	**65**	**1**	**3**	**1**	**168**	**6.5**	**6**	**914**	**45.7**	**15:23**	**6**	**0**	**1**	**1**	**0**	**0**	**0**	**0**	**15:41**
2006-07	**Philadelphia**	**NHL**	**59**	**10**	**22**	**32**	**52**	**1**	**4**	**3**	**130**	**7.7**	**-12**	**978**	**47.8**	**17:50**	....	....	....	....	....	....	....	....	....
2007-08	**Philadelphia**	**NHL**	**73**	**28**	**47**	**75**	**76**	**8**	**5**	**6**	**212**	**13.2**	**14**	**1381**	**50.5**	**21:31**	**17**	**7**	**7**	**14**	**10**	**1**	***2**	**0**	**20:55**
2008-09	**Philadelphia**	**NHL**	**79**	**30**	**50**	**80**	**63**	**8**	***7**	**4**	**238**	**12.6**	**22**	**1660**	**49.0**	**21:44**	**6**	**1**	**4**	**5**	**6**	**1**	**0**	**0**	**22:58**
2009-10	**Philadelphia**	**NHL**	**82**	**31**	**31**	**62**	**79**	**13**	**1**	**3**	**237**	**13.1**	**-2**	**1373**	**50.7**	**20:24**	**23**	**7**	**16**	**23**	**18**	**2**	**1**	**1**	**21:45**
	Canada	Olympics	7	2	3	5	0	....	....	....	....	....	....	....	....	....	....	....	....	....	....	....	....	....	....
	NHL Totals		**372**	**110**	**173**	**283**	**335**	**31**	**20**	**17**	**985**	**11.2**		**6306**	**49.0**	**19:26**	**52**	**15**	**28**	**43**	**34**	**4**	**3**	**1**	**20:55**

Memorial Cup Tournament All-Star Team (2003) • OHL Second All-Star Team (2005) • Canadian Major Junior Second All-Star Team (2005)
Played in NHL All-Star Game (2008)

RICHARDSON, Brad
(RIH-chuhrd-suhn, BRAD) **L.A.**

Center. Shoots left. 5'11", 195 lbs. Born, Belleville, Ont., February 4, 1985. Colorado's 4th choice, 163rd overall, in 2003 Entry Draft.

			Regular Season														Playoffs								
Season	Club	League	GP	G	A	Pts	PIM	PP	SH	GW	S	%	+/-	TF	F%	Min	GP	G	A	Pts	PIM	PP	SH	GW	Min
2001-02	Owen Sound	OHL	58	12	21	33	20	....	....	....	....	....	....	....	....	....	....	....	....	....	....	....	....	....	....
2002-03	Owen Sound	OHL	67	27	40	67	54	....	....	....	....	....	....	....	....	....	4	1	1	2	10	....	....	....	....
2003-04	Owen Sound	OHL	15	7	9	16	4	....	....	....	....	....	....	....	....	....	....	....	....	....	....	....	....	....	....
2004-05	Owen Sound	OHL	68	41	56	97	60	....	....	....	....	....	....	....	....	....	8	6	4	10	8	....	....	....	....
2005-06	**Colorado**	**NHL**	**41**	**3**	**10**	**13**	**12**	**1**	**0**	**0**	**51**	**5.9**	**0**	**305**	**41.0**	**10:44**	**9**	**1**	**0**	**1**	**6**	**0**	**0**	**0**	**11:4**
	Lowell	AHL	29	4	13	17	20	....	....	....	....	....	....	....	....	....	....	....	....	....	....	....	....	....	....
2006-07	**Colorado**	**NHL**	**73**	**14**	**8**	**22**	**28**	**0**	**3**	**3**	**129**	**10.9**	**4**	**358**	**40.8**	**13:10**	....	....	....	....	....	....	....	....	....
	Albany River Rats	AHL	3	0	1	1	2	....	....	....	....	....	....	....	....	....	....	....	....	....	....	....	....	....	....
2007-08	**Colorado**	**NHL**	**22**	**2**	**3**	**5**	**8**	**0**	**0**	**0**	**32**	**6.3**	**-3**	**60**	**43.3**	**13:29**	....	....	....	....	....	....	....	....	....
	Lake Erie	AHL	38	14	26	40	18	....	....	....	....	....	....	....	....	....	....	....	....	....	....	....	....	....	....
2008-09	**Los Angeles**	**NHL**	**31**	**0**	**5**	**5**	**11**	**0**	**0**	**0**	**37**	**0.0**	**-6**	**95**	**54.7**	**10:48**	....	....	....	....	....	....	....	....	....
	Manchester	AHL	3	1	2	3	0	....	....	....	....	....	....	....	....	....	....	....	....	....	....	....	....	....	....
2009-10	**Los Angeles**	**NHL**	**81**	**11**	**16**	**27**	**37**	**0**	**1**	**4**	**148**	**7.4**	**1**	**391**	**48.1**	**12:51**	**6**	**1**	**1**	**2**	**2**	**0**	**0**	**1**	**14:4**
	NHL Totals		**248**	**30**	**42**	**72**	**96**	**1**	**4**	**7**	**397**	**7.6**		**1209**	**44.4**	**12:24**	**15**	**2**	**1**	**3**	**8**	**0**	**0**	**1**	**12:5**

Traded to **Los Angeles** by **Colorado** for Detroit's 2nd round choice (previously acquired, Colorado selected Peter Delmas) in 2008 Entry Draft, June 21, 2008.

RICHMOND, Danny
(RIHCH-muhnd, DA-nee) **TOR.**

Defense. Shoots left. 6', 192 lbs. Born, Chicago, IL, August 1, 1984. Carolina's 2nd choice, 31st overall, in 2003 Entry Draft.

			Regular Season														Playoffs								
Season	Club	League	GP	G	A	Pts	PIM	PP	SH	GW	S	%	+/-	TF	F%	Min	GP	G	A	Pts	PIM	PP	SH	GW	Min
2000-01	Team Illinois	MWEHL	79	25	40	65	....	....	....	....	....	....	....	....	....	....	....	....	....	....	....	....	....	....	....
2001-02	Chicago Steel	USHL	56	8	45	53	129	....	....	....	....	....	....	....	....	....	4	0	4	4	20	....	....	....	....
2002-03	U. of Michigan	CCHA	43	3	19	22	48	....	....	....	....	....	....	....	....	....	....	....	....	....	....	....	....	....	....
2003-04	London Knights	OHL	59	13	22	35	92	....	....	....	....	....	....	....	....	....	15	5	6	11	10	....	....	....	....
2004-05	Lowell	AHL	63	4	9	13	139	....	....	....	....	....	....	....	....	....	6	0	2	2	8	....	....	....	....
2005-06	**Carolina**	**NHL**	**10**	**0**	**1**	**1**	**7**	**0**	**0**	**0**	**7**	**0.0**	**-3**	**0**	**0.0**	**9:00**	....	....	....	....	....	....	....	....	....
	Lowell	AHL	32	4	11	15	60	....	....	....	....	....	....	....	....	....	....	....	....	....	....	....	....	....	....
	Chicago	**NHL**	**10**	**0**	**0**	**0**	**18**	**0**	**0**	**0**	**6**	**0.0**	**-3**	**0**	**0.0**	**13:36**	....	....	....	....	....	....	....	....	....
	Norfolk Admirals	AHL	31	4	8	12	42	....	....	....	....	....	....	....	....	....	3	0	1	1	2	....	....	....	....
2006-07	**Chicago**	**NHL**	**22**	**0**	**2**	**2**	**48**	**0**	**0**	**0**	**13**	**0.0**	**-1**	**0**	**0.0**	**12:20**	....	....	....	....	....	....	....	....	....
	Norfolk Admirals	AHL	57	10	24	34	144	....	....	....	....	....	....	....	....	....	6	0	0	0	8	....	....	....	....
2007-08	**Chicago**	**NHL**	**7**	**0**	**0**	**0**	**2**	**0**	**0**	**0**	**2**	**0.0**	**-5**	**0**	**0.0**	**9:24**	....	....	....	....	....	....	....	....	....
	Rockford IceHogs	AHL	40	2	12	14	156	....	....	....	....	....	....	....	....	....	....	....	....	....	....	....	....	....	....
2008-09	Wilkes-Barre	AHL	55	3	14	17	108	....	....	....	....	....	....	....	....	....	....	....	....	....	....	....	....	....	....
	Peoria Rivermen	AHL	18	1	4	5	21	....	....	....	....	....	....	....	....	....	7	0	4	4	2	....	....	....	....
2009-10	Peoria Rivermen	AHL	54	1	15	16	135	....	....	....	....	....	....	....	....	....	....	....	....	....	....	....	....	....	....
	Rockford IceHogs	AHL	15	0	6	6	31	....	....	....	....	....	....	....	....	....	4	0	1	1	5	....	....	....	....
	NHL Totals		**49**	**0**	**3**	**3**	**75**	**0**	**0**	**0**	**28**	**0.0**		**0**	**0.0**	**11:29**	....	....	....	....	....	....	....	....	....

USHL All-Rookie Team (2002) • USHL First All-Star Team (2002) • USHL Rookie of the Year (2002) • CCHA All-Rookie Team (2003)

• Left **University of Michigan** (CCHA) and signed with **London** (OHL), June 6, 2003. Traded to **Chicago** by **Carolina** with Columbus' 4th round choice (previously acquired, later traded to Toronto - Toronto selected James Reimer) in 2006 Entry Draft for Anton Babchuk and Chicago's 4th round choice (later traded to St. Louis - St. Louis selected Cade Fairchild) in 2007 Entry Draft, January 20, 2006. Traded to **Pittsburgh** by **Chicago** for Tim Brent, July 17, 2008. Traded to **St. Louis** by **Pittsburgh** for Andy Wozniewski, March 4, 2009. Traded to **Chicago** by **St. Louis** with Hannu Toivonen for Joe Fallon, March 1, 2010. Signed as a free agent by **Toronto**, July 15, 2010.

RISSMILLER, Patrick
(RIGHZ-mih-luhr, PAT-rihk) **ATL.**

Left wing. Shoots left. 6'4", 215 lbs. Born, Belmont, MA, October 26, 1978.

			Regular Season														Playoffs								
Season	Club	League	GP	G	A	Pts	PIM	PP	SH	GW	S	%	+/-	TF	F%	Min	GP	G	A	Pts	PIM	PP	SH	GW	Min
1997-98	The Hill School	High-PA	STATISTICS NOT AVAILABLE																						
1998-99	Holy Cross	MAAC	34	13	28	41	23	....	....	....	....	....	....	....	....	....	....	....	....	....	....	....	....	....	....
99-2000	Holy Cross	MAAC	35	10	17	27	22	....	....	....	....	....	....	....	....	....	....	....	....	....	....	....	....	....	....
2000-01	Holy Cross	MAAC	29	14	15	29	40	....	....	....	....	....	....	....	....	....	....	....	....	....	....	....	....	....	....
2001-02	Holy Cross	MAAC	33	16	*30	*46	31	....	....	....	....	....	....	....	....	....	....	....	....	....	....	....	....	....	....
2002-03	Cleveland Barons	AHL	72	14	26	40	24	....	....	....	....	....	....	....	....	....	....	....	....	....	....	....	....	....	....
	Cincinnati	ECHL	2	2	2	4	0	....	....	....	....	....	....	....	....	....	....	....	....	....	....	....	....	....	....
2003-04	**San Jose**	**NHL**	**4**	**0**	**0**	**0**	**0**	**0**	**0**	**0**	**2**	**0.0**	**0**	**26**	**53.9**	**7:07**	....	....	....	....	....	....	....	....	....
	Cleveland Barons	AHL	75	14	31	45	66	....	....	....	....	....	....	....	....	....	9	0	1	1	8	....	....	....	....
2004-05	Cleveland Barons	AHL	69	21	23	44	50	....	....	....	....	....	....	....	....	....	....	....	....	....	....	....	....	....	....
2005-06	**San Jose**	**NHL**	**18**	**3**	**3**	**6**	**8**	**1**	**0**	**1**	**26**	**11.5**	**1**	**3**	**0.0**	**9:22**	**11**	**2**	**1**	**3**	**6**	**0**	**0**	**0**	**8:**
	Cleveland Barons	AHL	68	15	37	52	30	....	....	....	....	....	....	....	....	....	....	....	....	....	....	....	....	....	....
2006-07	**San Jose**	**NHL**	**79**	**7**	**15**	**22**	**22**	**1**	**0**	**0**	**100**	**7.0**	**1**	**25**	**36.0**	**12:10**	**11**	**1**	**3**	**4**	**0**	**0**	**0**	**1**	**12:**
2007-08	**San Jose**	**NHL**	**79**	**8**	**9**	**17**	**30**	**0**	**0**	**2**	**119**	**6.7**	**-8**	**214**	**50.9**	**13:10**	**8**	**0**	**0**	**0**	**4**	**0**	**0**	**0**	**11:**
2008-09	**NY Rangers**	**NHL**	**2**	**0**	**0**	**0**	**0**	**0**	**0**	**0**	**2**	**0.0**	**-2**	**0**	**0.0**	**9:13**	....	....	....	....	....	....	....	....	....
	Hartford	AHL	64	14	40	54	24	....	....	....	....	....	....	....	....	....	6	0	1	1	6	....	....	....	....
2009-10	Hartford	AHL	6	0	2	2	8	....	....	....	....	....	....	....	....	....	....	....	....	....	....	....	....	....	....
	Grand Rapids	AHL	63	20	25	45	18	....	....	....	....	....	....	....	....	....	....	....	....	....	....	....	....	....	....
	NHL Totals		**182**	**18**	**27**	**45**	**60**	**2**	**0**	**3**	**249**	**7.2**		**268**	**49.3**	**12:11**	**30**	**3**	**4**	**7**	**10**	**0**	**0**	**1**	**10:**

MAAC All-Rookie Team (1999) • MAAC First All-Star Team (2002) • MAAC Offensive Player of the Year (2002)

Signed as a free agent by **Cleveland** (AHL), September 23, 2002. Signed as a free agent by **San Jose**, June 30, 2003. Signed as a free agent by **NY Rangers**, July 1, 2008. Traded to **Atlanta** by **NY Rangers** with Donald Brashear for Todd White, August 2, 2010.

RITOLA, Mattias
(RIH-toh-lah, mat-TEE-uhs) **DET.**

Right wing. Shoots left. 5'11", 205 lbs. Born, Borlange, Sweden, March 14, 1987. Detroit's 4th choice, 103rd overall, in 2005 Entry Draft.

			Regular Season														Playoffs								
Season	Club	League	GP	G	A	Pts	PIM	PP	SH	GW	S	%	+/-	TF	F%	Min	GP	G	A	Pts	PIM	PP	SH	GW	Min
2003-04	V.Frolunda U18	Swe-U18	11	4	11	15	35	....	....	....	....	....	....	....	....	....	7	2	7	9	12	....	....	....	....
	V.Frolunda Jr.	Swe-Jr.	24	7	4	11	8	....	....	....	....	....	....	....	....	....	5	0	1	1	0	....	....	....	....
2004-05	Frolunda Jr.	Swe-Jr.	9	2	6	8	6	....	....	....	....	....	....	....	....	....	....	....	....	....	....	....	....	....	....
	Leksands IF U18	Swe-U18	STATISTICS NOT AVAILABLE																						
	Leksands IF Jr.	Swe-Jr.	18	8	10	18	14	....	....	....	....	....	....	....	....	....	5	1	1	2	2	....	....	....	....
2005-06	Leksands IF Jr.	Swe-Jr.	14	4	2	6	16	....	....	....	....	....	....	....	....	....	....	....	....	....	....	....	....	....	....
	Leksands IF	Sweden	30	0	3	3	10	....	....	....	....	....	....	....	....	....	....	....	....	....	....	....	....	....	....
	Leksands IF	Sweden-Q	8	0	0	0	4	....	....	....	....	....	....	....	....	....	....	....	....	....	....	....	....	....	....
2006-07	Leksands IF Jr.	Swe-Jr.	12	5	7	12	16	....	....	....	....	....	....	....	....	....	....	....	....	....	....	....	....	....	....
	Leksands IF	Sweden-2	23	1	4	5	4	....	....	....	....	....	....	....	....	....	....	....	....	....	....	....	....	....	....
	IFK Arboga IK	Sweden-2	3	1	0	1	2	....	....	....	....	....	....	....	....	....	....	....	....	....	....	....	....	....	....
	Borlange HF	Sweden-3	11	4	6	10	14	....	....	....	....	....	....	....	....	....	....	....	....	....	....	....	....	....	....
2007-08	**Detroit**	**NHL**	**2**	**0**	**1**	**1**	**0**	**0**	**0**	**0**	**2**	**0.0**	**0**	**0**	**0.0**	**5:47**	....	....	....	....	....	....	....	....	....
	Grand Rapids	AHL	72	7	15	22	62	....	....	....	....	....	....	....	....	....	....	....	....	....	....	....	....	....	....
2008-09	Grand Rapids	AHL	66	15	27	42	32	....	....	....	....	....	....	....	....	....	8	0	2	2	0	....	....	....	....

			Regular Season													Playoffs								
Season	Club	League	GP	G	A	Pts	PIM	PP	SH	GW	S	%	+/-	TF	F%	Min	GP	G	A	Pts	PIM	PP	SH	GW	Min
2009-10	Detroit	NHL	5	0	0	0	0	0	0	0	9	0.0	0	3	0.0	11:42	1	0	0	0	0	0	0	0	7:45
	Grand Rapids	AHL	73	19	23	42	50	....	....	....	....	....	....	....	....	....	....	....	....	....	....	....	....	....	....
	NHL Totals		7	0	1	1	0	0	0	0	11	0.0		3	0.0	10:00	1	0	0	0	0	0	0	0	7:45

RIVERS, Jamie

(RIH-vuhrs, JAY-mee)

Defense. Shoots left. 6'1", 206 lbs. Born, Ottawa, Ont., March 16, 1975. St. Louis' 2nd choice, 63rd overall, in 1993 Entry Draft.

Season	Club	League	GP	G	A	Pts	PIM	PP	SH	GW	S	%	+/-	TF	F%	Min	GP	G	A	Pts	PIM	PP	SH	GW	Min
1989-90	Ottawa South	ODMHA	50	26	46	72	46	....	....	....	....	....	....	....	....	....	....	....	....	....	....	....	....	....	....
1990-91	Ott. Jr. Senators	CJHL	55	4	30	34	74	....	....	....	....	....	....	....	....	....	....	....	....	....	....	....	....	....	....
1991-92	Sudbury Wolves	OHL	55	3	13	16	20	....	....	....	....	....	....	....	....	....	8	0	0	0	0	....	....	....	....
1992-93	Sudbury Wolves	OHL	62	12	43	55	20	....	....	....	....	....	....	....	....	....	14	7	19	26	4	....	....	....	....
1993-94	Sudbury Wolves	OHL	65	32	*89	121	58	....	....	....	....	....	....	....	....	....	10	1	9	10	14	....	....	....	....
1994-95	Sudbury Wolves	OHL	46	9	56	65	30	....	....	....	....	....	....	....	....	....	18	7	26	33	22	....	....	....	....
1995-96	St. Louis	NHL	3	0	0	0	2	0	0	0	5	0.0	-1	....	....	....	....	....	....	....	....	....	....	....	....
	Worcester IceCats	AHL	75	7	45	52	130	....	....	....	....	....	....	....	....	....	4	0	1	1	4	....	....	....	....
1996-97	St. Louis	NHL	15	2	5	7	6	1	0	0	9	22.2	-4	....	....	....	....	....	....	....	....	....	....	....	....
	Worcester IceCats	AHL	63	8	35	43	83	....	....	....	....	....	....	....	....	....	5	1	2	3	14	....	....	....	....
1997-98	St. Louis	NHL	59	2	4	6	36	1	0	1	53	3.8	5	....	....	....	....	....	....	....	....	....	....	....	....
1998-99	St. Louis	NHL	76	2	5	7	47	1	0	0	78	2.6	-3	0	0.0	14:10	9	1	1	2	2	1	0	1	6:29
99-2000	NY Islanders	NHL	75	1	16	17	84	1	0	0	95	1.1	-4	0	0.0	19:39	....	....	....	....	....	....	....	....	....
2000-01	Ottawa	NHL	45	2	4	6	44	0	0	0	41	4.9	6	0	0.0	14:01	1	0	0	0	4	0	0	0	12:45
	Grand Rapids	IHL	2	0	0	0	2	....	....	....	....	....	....	....	....	....	....	....	....	....	....	....	....	....	....
2001-02	Ottawa	NHL	2	0	0	0	4	0	0	0	3	0.0	-3	0	0.0	11:37	....	....	....	....	....	....	....	....	....
	Boston	NHL	64	4	2	6	45	1	0	1	48	8.3	6	39	33.3	8:27	3	0	0	0	0	0	0	0	4:57
2002-03	Florida	NHL	1	0	0	0	2	0	0	0	2	0.0	-2	0	0.0	18:27	....	....	....	....	....	....	....	....	....
	San Antonio	AHL	50	6	19	25	68	....	....	....	....	....	....	....	....	....	3	0	1	1	10	....	....	....	....
2003-04	Detroit	NHL	50	3	4	7	41	0	0	0	31	9.7	9	1	0.0	10:14	2	0	0	0	2	0	0	0	5:40
	Grand Rapids	AHL	2	0	0	0	4	....	....	....	....	....	....	....	....	....	....	....	....	....	....	....	....	....	....
2004-05	Hershey Bears	AHL	50	7	13	20	46	....	....	....	....	....	....	....	....	....	....	....	....	....	....	....	....	....	....
2005-06	Detroit	NHL	15	0	1	1	12	0	0	0	4	0.0	0	0	0.0	8:51	....	....	....	....	....	....	....	....	....
	Phoenix	NHL	18	0	5	5	26	0	0	0	32	0.0	2	0	0.0	20:06	....	....	....	....	....	....	....	....	....
2006-07	St. Louis	NHL	31	1	3	4	36	1	0	0	17	5.9	-7	0	0.0	14:11	....	....	....	....	....	....	....	....	....
	Peoria Rivermen	AHL	30	4	19	23	24	....	....	....	....	....	....	....	....	....	....	....	....	....	....	....	....	....	....
2007-08	Spartak Moscow	Russia	19	0	3	3	42	....	....	....	....	....	....	....	....	....	4	0	0	0	8	....	....	....	....
2008-09	Chicago Wolves	AHL	69	4	24	28	72	....	....	....	....	....	....	....	....	....	....	....	....	....	....	....	....	....	....
2009-10	HC Ambri-Piotta	Swiss	24	0	8	8	34	....	....	....	....	....	....	....	....	....	6	1	4	5	2	....	....	....	....
	NHL Totals		454	17	49	66	385	6	0	2	418	4.1		40	32.5	13:49	15	1	1	2	8	1	0	1	6:29

OHL First All-Star Team (1994) • Canadian Major Junior Second All-Star Team (1994) • OHL Second All-Star Team (1995) • AHL Second All-Star Team (1997)

Claimed by **NY Islanders** from **St. Louis** in Waiver Draft, September 27, 1999. Signed as a free agent by **Ottawa**, November 30, 2000. Claimed on waivers by **Boston** from **Ottawa**, October 13, 2001. Signed as a free agent by **San Antonio** (AHL), November 2, 2002. Signed as a free agent by **Florida**, December 16, 2002. Signed as a free agent by **Detroit**, July 29, 2003. Signed as a free agent by **Hershey** (AHL), November 3, 2004. Traded to **Phoenix** by **Detroit** for Phoenix's 7th round choice (Nick Oslund) in 2006 Entry Draft, March 9, 2006. • Missed majority of 2005-06 season as a healthy reserve. Signed as a free agent by **St. Louis**, August 18, 2006. Signed as a free agent by **Montreal**, July 5, 2007. Signed as a free agent by **Spartak Moscow** (Russia), October 12, 2007. Signed as a free agent by **Ambri-Piotta** (Swiss), December 16, 2009.

RIVET, Craig

(rih-VAY, KRAYG) **BUF.**

Defense. Shoots right. 6'2", 210 lbs. Born, North Bay, Ont., September 13, 1974. Montreal's 4th choice, 68th overall, in 1992 Entry Draft.

Season	Club	League	GP	G	A	Pts	PIM	PP	SH	GW	S	%	+/-	TF	F%	Min	GP	G	A	Pts	PIM	PP	SH	GW	Min
1990-91	Barrie Colts	OHA-B	42	9	17	26	55	....	....	....	....	....	....	....	....	....	....	....	....	....	....	....	....	....	....
1991-92	Kingston	OHL	66	5	21	26	97	....	....	....	....	....	....	....	....	....	....	....	....	....	....	....	....	....	....
1992-93	Kingston	OHL	64	19	55	74	117	....	....	....	....	....	....	....	....	....	16	5	7	12	39	....	....	....	....
1993-94	Kingston	OHL	61	12	52	64	100	....	....	....	....	....	....	....	....	....	6	0	3	3	6	....	....	....	....
	Fredericton	AHL	4	0	2	2	2	....	....	....	....	....	....	....	....	....	....	....	....	....	....	....	....	....	....
1994-95	Fredericton	AHL	78	5	27	32	126	....	....	....	....	....	....	....	....	....	12	0	4	4	17	....	....	....	....
	Montreal	NHL	5	0	1	1	5	0	0	0	2	0.0	2	....	....	....	....	....	....	....	....	....	....	....	....
1995-96	Montreal	NHL	19	1	4	5	54	0	0	0	9	11.1	4	....	....	....	....	....	....	....	....	....	....	....	....
	Fredericton	AHL	49	5	18	23	189	....	....	....	....	....	....	....	....	....	6	0	0	0	12	....	....	....	....
1996-97	Montreal	NHL	35	0	4	4	54	0	0	0	24	0.0	7	....	....	....	5	0	1	1	14	0	0	0	....
	Fredericton	AHL	23	3	12	15	99	....	....	....	....	....	....	....	....	....	....	....	....	....	....	....	....	....	....
1997-98	Montreal	NHL	61	0	2	2	93	0	0	0	26	0.0	-3	....	....	....	5	0	0	0	2	0	0	0	....
1998-99	Montreal	NHL	66	2	8	10	66	0	0	0	39	5.1	-3	0	0.0	14:20	....	....	....	....	....	....	....	....	....
99-2000	Montreal	NHL	61	3	14	17	76	0	0	1	71	4.2	11	0	0.0	19:03	....	....	....	....	....	....	....	....	....
2000-01	Montreal	NHL	26	1	2	3	36	0	0	0	22	4.5	-8	0	0.0	19:04	....	....	....	....	....	....	....	....	....
2001-02	Montreal	NHL	82	8	17	25	76	0	0	0	90	8.9	1	1	0.0	19:00	12	0	3	3	4	0	0	0	21:26
2002-03	Montreal	NHL	82	7	15	22	71	3	0	2	118	5.9	1	0	0.0	22:00	....	....	....	....	....	....	....	....	....
2003-04	Montreal	NHL	80	4	8	12	98	2	0	1	96	4.2	-1	0	0.0	19:28	11	1	4	5	2	1	0	0	24:07
2004-05	TPS Turku	Finland	18	3	1	4	28	....	....	....	....	....	....	....	....	....	6	0	0	0	39	....	....	....	....
2005-06	Montreal	NHL	82	7	27	34	109	5	0	1	122	5.7	-5	2	0.0	22:27	6	0	2	2	2	0	0	0	24:09
2006-07	Montreal	NHL	54	6	10	16	57	2	0	0	58	10.3	-7	0	0.0	21:04	....	....	....	....	....	....	....	....	....
	San Jose	NHL	17	1	7	8	12	0	0	0	31	3.2	8	0	0.0	23:31	11	2	3	5	18	1	0	0	25:18
2007-08	San Jose	NHL	74	5	30	35	104	2	0	0	105	4.8	3	0	0.0	21:12	13	0	6	6	16	0	0	0	23:01
2008-09	Buffalo	NHL	64	2	22	24	125	1	0	0	80	2.5	4	0	0.0	20:14	....	....	....	....	....	....	....	....	....
2009-10	Buffalo	NHL	78	1	14	15	100	0	0	0	63	1.6	-6	0	0.0	18:13	6	1	0	1	11	0	0	1	14:35
	NHL Totals		886	48	185	233	1136	15	0	5	956	5.0		3	0.0	19:49	69	4	19	23	69	2	0	1	22:35

• Missed majority of 2000-01 season recovering from shoulder injury suffered in game vs. Vancouver, October 30, 2000. Signed as a free agent by **Turku** (Finland), January 11, 2005. Traded to **San Jose** by **Montreal** with Montreal's 5th round choice (Julien Demers) in 2008 Entry Draft for Josh Gorges and San Jose's 1st round choice (Max Pacioretty) in 2007 Entry Draft, February 25, 2007. Traded to **Buffalo** by **San Jose** with San Jose's 7th round choice (Riley Boychuk) in 2010 Entry Draft for Buffalo's 2nd round choices in 2009 (William Wrenn) and 2010 (later traded to Carolina - Carolina selected Mark Alt) Entry Drafts, July 4, 2008.

ROBIDAS, Stephane

(ROH-bih-dah, STEH-fan) **DAL.**

Defense. Shoots right. 5'11", 193 lbs. Born, Sherbrooke, Que., March 3, 1977. Montreal's 7th choice, 164th overall, in 1995 Entry Draft.

Season	Club	League	GP	G	A	Pts	PIM	PP	SH	GW	S	%	+/-	TF	F%	Min	GP	G	A	Pts	PIM	PP	SH	GW	Min
1992-93	Magog	QAAA	41	3	12	15	16	....	....	....	....	....	....	....	....	....	5	1	1	2	2	....	....	....	....
1993-94	Shawinigan	QMJHL	67	3	18	21	33	....	....	....	....	....	....	....	....	....	1	0	0	0	0	....	....	....	....
1994-95	Shawinigan	QMJHL	71	13	56	69	44	....	....	....	....	....	....	....	....	....	15	7	12	19	4	....	....	....	....
1995-96	Shawinigan	QMJHL	67	23	56	79	53	....	....	....	....	....	....	....	....	....	6	1	5	6	10	....	....	....	....
1996-97	Shawinigan	QMJHL	67	24	51	75	59	....	....	....	....	....	....	....	....	....	7	4	6	10	14	....	....	....	....
1997-98	Fredericton	AHL	79	10	21	31	50	....	....	....	....	....	....	....	....	....	4	0	2	2	0	....	....	....	....
1998-99	Fredericton	AHL	79	8	33	41	59	....	....	....	....	....	....	....	....	....	15	1	5	6	10	....	....	....	....
99-2000	Montreal	NHL	1	0	0	0	0	0	0	0	0	0.0	0	0	0.0	15:54	....	....	....	....	....	....	....	....	....
	Quebec Citadelles	AHL	76	14	31	45	36	....	....	....	....	....	....	....	....	....	3	0	1	1	0	....	....	....	....
2000-01	Montreal	NHL	65	6	6	12	14	1	0	0	77	7.8	0	1	100.0	20:44	....	....	....	....	....	....	....	....	....
2001-02	Montreal	NHL	56	1	10	11	14	1	0	0	68	1.5	-25	3	33.3	18:58	2	0	0	0	4	0	0	0	13:07
2002-03	Dallas	NHL	76	3	7	10	35	0	0	1	47	6.4	15	1	100.0	12:54	12	0	1	1	20	0	0	0	13:54
2003-04	Dallas	NHL	14	1	0	1	8	1	0	0	8	12.5	-2	1	100.0	12:57	....	....	....	....	....	....	....	....	....
	Chicago	NHL	45	2	10	12	33	0	1	1	55	3.6	6	0	0.0	20:56	....	....	....	....	....	....	....	....	....
2004-05	Frankfurt Lions	Germany	51	15	32	47	64	....	....	....	....	....	....	....	....	....	6	1	2	3	6	....	....	....	....
2005-06	Dallas	NHL	75	5	15	20	67	1	1	0	95	5.3	15	0	0.0	16:59	5	0	2	2	4	0	0	0	16:42
2006-07	Dallas	NHL	75	0	17	17	86	0	0	0	106	0.0	-1	0	0.0	18:04	7	0	1	1	2	0	0	0	19:02
2007-08	Dallas	NHL	82	9	17	26	85	7	0	2	153	5.9	0	0	0.0	20:39	18	3	8	11	12	3	0	0	25:31
2008-09	Dallas	NHL	72	3	23	26	76	1	0	0	158	1.9	10	1	100.0	24:32	....	....	....	....	....	....	....	....	....
2009-10	Dallas	NHL	82	10	31	41	70	7	0	1	199	5.0	-10	0	0.0	24:29	....	....	....	....	....	....	....	....	....
	NHL Totals		643	40	136	176	488	19	2	5	966	4.1		7	71.4	19:38	44	3	12	15	42	3	0	0	19:45

QMJHL First All-Star Team (1996, 1997)

Played in NHL All-Star Game (2009)

Claimed by **Atlanta** from **Montreal** in Waiver Draft, October 4, 2002. Traded to **Dallas** by **Atlanta** for future considerations, October 4, 2002. Traded to **Chicago** by **Dallas** with Dallas' 2nd round choice (Jakub Sindel) in 2004 Entry Draft for Jon Klemm and NY Rangers' 4th round choice (previously acquired, Dallas selected Fredrik Naslund) in 2004 Entry Draft, November 17, 2003. Signed as a free agent by **Frankfurt** (Germany), September 17, 2004. Signed as a free agent by **Dallas**, August 6, 2005.

RODNEY, Bryan

(ROHD-nee, BRIGH-uhn) **CAR.**

Defense. Shoots right. 6', 195 lbs. Born, London, Ont., April 22, 1984.

Season	Club	League	Regular Season GP	G	A	Pts	PIM	PP	SH	GW	S	%	+/-	TF	F%	Min	Playoffs GP	G	A	Pts	PIM	PP	SH	GW	M
2000-01	Ottawa 67's	OHL	65	0	15	15	26										20	1	4	5	20				
2001-02	Ottawa 67's	OHL	30	3	8	11	14																		
	Kingston	OHL	18	2	8	10	8										1	0	0	0	0				
2002-03	Kingston	OHL	67	8	52	60	60																		
2003-04	Kingston	OHL	67	11	65	76	68										5	1	4	5	8				
2004-05	London Knights	OHL	64	23	39	62	48										12	5	10	15	20				
2005-06	Hartford	AHL	8	1	2	3	0																		
	Charlotte	ECHL	59	4	21	25	47										3	0	1	1	0				
2006-07	Charlotte	ECHL	31	2	19	21	14																		
	Columbia Inferno	ECHL	14	2	9	11	12																		
2007-08	Albany River Rats	AHL	42	4	11	15	22										7	3	3	6	2				
	Columbia Inferno	ECHL	17	2	9	11	10																		
	Elmira Jackals	ECHL	6	5	5	10	2																		
2008-09	**Carolina**	**NHL**	**8**	**0**	**2**	**2**	**2**	**0**	**0**	**0**	**3**	**0.0**	**–3**	**0**	**0.0**	**12:38**									
	Albany River Rats	AHL	58	3	33	36	28																		
2009-10	**Carolina**	**NHL**	**22**	**1**	**10**	**11**	**8**	**0**	**0**	**0**	**24**	**4.2**	**–4**	**0**	**0.0**	**16:44**									
	Albany River Rats	AHL	54	7	28	35	42										8	0	4	4	8				
	NHL Totals		**30**	**1**	**12**	**13**	**10**	**0**	**0**	**0**	**27**	**3.7**		**0**	**0.0**	**15:38**									

Signed as a free agent by **Charlotte** (ECHL), October 21, 2005. Signed as a free agent by **Albany** (AHL), December 16, 2007. Signed as a free agent by **Carolina**, May 12, 2008.

ROLSTON, Brian

(ROHL-stuhn, BRIGH-uhn) **N.J.**

Center. Shoots left. 6'2", 210 lbs. Born, Flint, MI, February 21, 1973. New Jersey's 2nd choice, 11th overall, in 1991 Entry Draft.

Season	Club	League	Regular Season GP	G	A	Pts	PIM	PP	SH	GW	S	%	+/-	TF	F%	Min	Playoffs GP	G	A	Pts	PIM	PP	SH	GW	M
1989-90	Det. Compuware	NAHL	40	36	37	73	57																		
1990-91	Det. Compuware	NAHL	36	49	46	95	14																		
1991-92	Lake Superior	CCHA	37	14	23	37	14																		
1992-93	Lake Superior	CCHA	39	33	31	64	20																		
1993-94	United States	Nat-Tm	41	20	28	48	36																		
	United States	Olympics	8	7	0	7	8																		
	Albany River Rats	AHL	17	5	5	10	8										5	1	2	3	0				
1994-95	Albany River Rats	AHL	18	9	11	20	10																		
	♦ New Jersey	**NHL**	**40**	**7**	**11**	**18**	**17**	**2**	**0**	**3**	**92**	**7.6**	**5**				**6**	**2**	**1**	**3**	**4**	**1**	**0**	**0**	
1995-96	**New Jersey**	**NHL**	**58**	**13**	**11**	**24**	**8**	**3**	**1**	**4**	**139**	**9.4**	**9**												
1996-97	**New Jersey**	**NHL**	**81**	**18**	**27**	**45**	**20**	**2**	**2**	**3**	**237**	**7.6**	**6**				**10**	**4**	**1**	**5**	**6**	**1**	**2**	**0**	
1997-98	**New Jersey**	**NHL**	**76**	**16**	**14**	**30**	**16**	**0**	**2**	**1**	**185**	**8.6**	**7**				**6**	**1**	**0**	**1**	**2**	**0**	**1**	**0**	
1998-99	**New Jersey**	**NHL**	**82**	**24**	**33**	**57**	**14**	**5**	***5**	**3**	**210**	**11.4**	**11**	**51**	**45.1**	**18:49**	**7**	**1**	**0**	**1**	**2**	**0**	**1**	**0**	**17:36**
99-2000	**New Jersey**	**NHL**	**11**	**3**	**1**	**4**	**0**	**1**	**0**	**2**	**33**	**9.1**	**–2**	**37**	**37.8**	**19:09**									
	Colorado	**NHL**	**50**	**8**	**10**	**18**	**12**	**1**	**0**	**3**	**107**	**7.5**	**–6**	**65**	**41.5**	**16:18**									
	Boston	**NHL**	**16**	**5**	**4**	**9**	**6**	**3**	**0**	**1**	**66**	**7.6**	**–4**	**265**	**41.1**	**22:13**									
2000-01	**Boston**	**NHL**	**77**	**19**	**39**	**58**	**28**	**5**	**0**	**4**	**286**	**6.6**	**6**	**666**	**45.7**	**19:19**									
2001-02	**Boston**	**NHL**	**82**	**31**	**31**	**62**	**30**	**6**	***9**	**7**	**331**	**9.4**	**11**	**1289**	**46.6**	**20:24**	**6**	**4**	**1**	**5**	**0**	**1**	**1**	**0**	**20:37**
	United States	Olympics	6	0	3	3	0																		
2002-03	**Boston**	**NHL**	**81**	**27**	**32**	**59**	**32**	**6**	**5**	**5**	**281**	**9.6**	**1**	**1148**	**47.6**	**20:28**	**5**	**0**	**2**	**2**	**0**	**0**	**0**	**0**	**18:39**
2003-04	**Boston**	**NHL**	**82**	**19**	**29**	**48**	**40**	**3**	**2**	**3**	**257**	**7.4**	**9**	**1205**	**50.7**	**19:38**	**7**	**1**	**0**	**1**	**8**	**0**	**0**	**0**	**16:33**
2004-05			DID NOT PLAY																						
2005-06	**Minnesota**	**NHL**	**82**	**34**	**45**	**79**	**50**	**15**	**5**	**7**	**293**	**11.6**	**14**	**403**	**46.4**	**20:21**									
	United States	Olympics	6	3	1	4	4																		
2006-07	**Minnesota**	**NHL**	**78**	**31**	**33**	**64**	**46**	**13**	**1**	**6**	**305**	**10.2**	**6**	**295**	**45.4**	**21:16**	**5**	**1**	**1**	**2**	**4**	**0**	**0**	**0**	**20:25**
2007-08	**Minnesota**	**NHL**	**81**	**31**	**28**	**59**	**53**	**11**	**1**	**8**	**289**	**10.7**	**–1**	**165**	**40.6**	**20:04**	**6**	**2**	**4**	**6**	**8**	**0**	**1**	**0**	**22:27**
2008-09	**New Jersey**	**NHL**	**64**	**15**	**17**	**32**	**30**	**8**	**0**	**3**	**174**	**8.6**	**2**	**180**	**46.1**	**15:06**	**7**	**1**	**1**	**2**	**4**	**1**	**0**	**0**	**14:09**
2009-10	**New Jersey**	**NHL**	**80**	**20**	**17**	**37**	**22**	**7**	**0**	**3**	**232**	**8.6**	**2**	**63**	**50.8**	**16:56**	**5**	**2**	**1**	**3**	**0**	**2**	**0**	**0**	**14:48**
	NHL Totals		**1121**	**321**	**382**	**703**	**424**	**91**	**33**	**66**	**3517**	**9.1**		**5832**	**46.9**	**19:12**	**70**	**19**	**12**	**31**	**38**	**6**	**6**	**0**	**18:03**

NCAA Championship All-Tournament Team (1992, 1993) • CCHA First All-Star Team (1993) • NCAA West Second All-American Team (1993)

Played in NHL All-Star Game (2007)

Traded to **Colorado** by **New Jersey** with New Jersey's 1st round choice (later traded to Boston – Boston selected Martin Samuelsson) in 2000 Entry Draft for Claude Lemieux and Colorado's 1st (David Hale) and 2nd (Matt DeMarchi) round choices in 2000 Entry Draft, November 3, 1999. Traded to **Boston** by **Colorado** with Martin Grenier, Samuel Pahlsson and New Jersey's 1st round choice (previously acquired, Boston selected Martin Samuelsson) in 2000 Entry Draft for Raymond Bourque and Dave Andreychuk, March 6, 2000. Signed as a free agent by **Minnesota**, July 8, 2004. Traded to **Tampa Bay** by **Minnesota** for Dallas' 4th round choice (previously acquired, later traded to Edmonton – Edmonton selected Kyle Bigos) in 2009 Entry Draft, June 29, 2008. Signed as a free agent by **New Jersey**, July 1, 2008.

ROME, Aaron

(ROHM, AIR-uhn) **VAN.**

Defense. Shoots left. 6'1", 218 lbs. Born, Nesbitt, Man., September 27, 1983. Los Angeles' 4th choice, 104th overall, in 2002 Entry Draft.

Season	Club	League	Regular Season GP	G	A	Pts	PIM	PP	SH	GW	S	%	+/-	TF	F%	Min	Playoffs GP	G	A	Pts	PIM	PP	SH	GW	M
1998-99	Sask. Contacts	SMHL	STATISTICS NOT AVAILABLE																						
	Saskatoon Blades	WHL	1	0	0	0	0																		
99-2000	Saskatoon Blades	WHL	47	0	6	6	22										1	0	0	0	0				
2000-01	Saskatoon Blades	WHL	3	0	0	0	2																		
	Kootenay Ice	WHL	53	2	8	10	43										11	1	3	4	6				
2001-02	Kootenay Ice	WHL	33	4	13	17	55																		
	Swift Current	WHL	37	3	11	14	113										10	1	4	5	23				
2002-03	Swift Current	WHL	61	12	44	56	201										4	1	0	1	20				
2003-04	Swift Current	WHL	41	7	26	33	122																		
	Moose Jaw	WHL	28	3	16	19	88										8	0	6	6	17				
2004-05	Cincinnati	AHL	75	2	14	16	130										12	3	3	6	33				
2005-06	Portland Pirates	AHL	64	5	19	24	87										18	1	4	5	33				
2006-07	**♦ Anaheim**	**NHL**	**1**	**0**	**0**	**0**	**0**	**0**	**0**	**0**	**1**	**0.0**	**–1**	**0**	**0.0**	**14:31**	**1**	**0**	**0**	**0**	**0**	**0**	**0**	**0**	**11:01**
	Portland Pirates	AHL	76	8	17	25	139																		
2007-08	**Columbus**	**NHL**	**17**	**1**	**1**	**2**	**33**	**0**	**0**	**0**	**15**	**6.7**	**–4**	**0**	**0.0**	**18:11**									
	Portland Pirates	AHL	14	2	3	5	31																		
	Syracuse Crunch	AHL	41	3	21	24	126																		
2008-09	**Columbus**	**NHL**	**8**	**0**	**1**	**1**	**0**	**0**	**0**	**0**	**7**	**0.0**	**1**	**0**	**0.0**	**15:28**	**1**	**0**	**1**	**1**	**0**	**0**	**0**	**0**	**15:24**
	Syracuse Crunch	AHL	48	7	21	28	153																		
2009-10	**Vancouver**	**NHL**	**49**	**0**	**4**	**4**	**24**	**0**	**0**	**0**	**49**	**0.0**	**–2**	**0**	**0.0**	**15:11**	**1**	**0**	**0**	**0**	**0**	**0**	**0**	**0**	**9:32**
	Manitoba Moose	AHL	7	6	1	7	15																		
	NHL Totals		**75**	**1**	**6**	**7**	**57**	**0**	**0**	**0**	**72**	**1.4**		**0**	**0.0**	**15:53**	**3**	**0**	**1**	**1**	**0**	**0**	**0**	**0**	**11:59**

WHL East Second All-Star Team (2004)

Signed as a free agent by **Anaheim**, June 7, 2004. Traded to **Columbus** by **Anaheim** with Clay Wilson for Geoff Platt, November 15, 2007. Signed as a free agent by **Vancouver**, July 1, 2009.

ROSEHILL, Jay

(ROHZ-hihl, JAY) **TOR.**

Left wing. Shoots left. 6'3", 215 lbs. Born, Olds, Alta., July 16, 1985. Tampa Bay's 6th choice, 227th overall, in 2003 Entry Draft.

Season	Club	League	Regular Season GP	G	A	Pts	PIM	PP	SH	GW	S	%	+/-	TF	F%	Min	Playoffs GP	G	A	Pts	PIM	PP	SH	GW	M
2002-03	Olds Grizzlys	AJHL	59	1	4	5	219																		
2003-04	Olds Grizzlys	AJHL	42	4	12	16	172										14	2	2	4					
2004-05	U. Minn-Duluth	WCHA	34	0	5	5	103																		
2005-06	Springfield	AHL	45	1	2	3	68																		
	Johnstown Chiefs	ECHL	5	0	0	0	13										5	0	0	0	4				
2006-07	Springfield	AHL	64	0	6	6	85																		
	Johnstown Chiefs	ECHL	1	0	0	0	2																		
2007-08	Norfolk Admirals	AHL	66	3	4	7	194																		
	Mississippi	ECHL	2	0	0	0	6																		
2008-09	Norfolk Admirals	AHL	57	5	7	12	221																		
	Toronto Marlies	AHL	13	2	1	3	54										6	0	0	0	4				
2009-10	**Toronto**	**NHL**	**15**	**1**	**1**	**2**	**67**	**0**	**0**	**0**	**6**	**16.7**	**–2**	**3**	**33.3**	**6:14**									
	Toronto Marlies	AHL	46	1	2	3	172																		
	NHL Totals		**15**	**1**	**1**	**2**	**67**	**0**	**0**	**0**	**6**	**16.7**		**3**	**33.3**	**6:14**									

Signed as a free agent by **Toronto**, July 6 2009.

Season	Club	League	GP	G	A	Pts	PIM	PP	SH	GW	S	%	+/-	TF	F%	Min	Playoffs GP	G	A	Pts	PIM	PP	SH	GW	Min
			Regular Season														Playoffs								

ROSS, Jared

(RAWS, JAIR-uhd) **ATL.**

Center. Shoots left. 5'9", 165 lbs. Born, Huntsville, AL, September 18, 1982.

Season	Club	League	GP	G	A	Pts	PIM	PP	SH	GW	S	%	+/-	TF	F%	Min	GP	G	A	Pts	PIM	PP	SH	GW	Min
2001-02	AL-Huntsville	CHA	37	11	17	28	8																		
2002-03	AL-Huntsville	CHA	35	20	20	40	30																		
2003-04	AL-Huntsville	CHA	31	19	31	50	46																		
2004-05	AL-Huntsville	CHA	30	22	18	40	53																		
	Motor City	UHL	12	3	5	8	2																		
2005-06	Chicago Wolves	AHL	62	10	27	37	37																		
	Gwinnett	ECHL	1	0	0	0	0																		
2006-07	Chicago Wolves	AHL	41	7	8	15	14																		
	Philadelphia	AHL	21	4	10	14	6																		
2007-08	Philadelphia	AHL	67	23	39	62	56											12	5	4	9	4				
2008-09	**Philadelphia**	**NHL**	**10**	**0**	**0**	**0**	**2**	**0**	**0**	**0**	**12**	**0.0**	**–4**	**48**	**56.3**	**7:44**	**6**	**1**	**0**	**1**	**0**	**0**	**0**	**0**	**4:10**
	Philadelphia	AHL	64	29	40	69	26																		
2009-10	**Philadelphia**	**NHL**	**3**	**0**	**0**	**0**	**0**	**0**	**0**	**0**	**4**	**0.0**	**–1**	**11**	**54.6**	**7:39**	**3**	**0**	**0**	**0**	**0**	**0**	**0**	**0**	**5:37**
	Adirondack	AHL	73	12	34	46	40																		
	NHL Totals		**13**	**0**	**0**	**0**	**2**	**0**	**0**	**0**	**16**	**0.0**		**59**	**55.9**	**7:43**	**9**	**1**	**0**	**1**	**0**	**0**	**0**	**0**	**4:39**

Traded to **Philadelphia** (AHL) by **Chicago** (AHL) for the loan of Niko Dimitrakos, March 1, 2007. Signed as a free agent by **Philadelphia**, April 8, 2008. Signed as a free agent by **Atlanta**, July 7, 2010.

ROY, Derek

(ROI, DAIR-ihk) **BUF.**

Center. Shoots left. 5'9", 188 lbs. Born, Ottawa, Ont., May 4, 1983. Buffalo's 2nd choice, 32nd overall, in 2001 Entry Draft.

Season	Club	League	GP	G	A	Pts	PIM	PP	SH	GW	S	%	+/-	TF	F%	Min	GP	G	A	Pts	PIM	PP	SH	GW	Min
1998-99	Ontario East	Minor-ON	34	61	31	92	42																		
99-2000	Kitchener Rangers	OHL	66	34	53	87	44										5	4	1	5	6				
2000-01	Kitchener Rangers	OHL	65	42	39	81	114																		
2001-02	Kitchener Rangers	OHL	62	43	46	89	92										4	1	2	3	2				
2002-03	Kitchener Rangers	OHL	49	28	50	78	73										21	9	*23	32	14				
2003-04	**Buffalo**	**NHL**	**49**	**9**	**10**	**19**	**12**	**1**	**0**	**4**	**71**	**12.7**	**–8**	**715**	**47.4**	**15:19**									
	Rochester	AHL	26	10	16	26	20										16	6	8	14	18				
2004-05	Rochester	AHL	67	16	45	61	60										9	6	5	11	6				
2005-06	**Buffalo**	**NHL**	**70**	**18**	**28**	**46**	**57**	**5**	**1**	**1**	**151**	**11.9**	**1**	**807**	**48.0**	**17:02**	**18**	**5**	**10**	**15**	**16**	**1**	**1**	**0**	**17:03**
	Rochester	AHL	8	7	13	20	10																		
2006-07	**Buffalo**	**NHL**	**75**	**21**	**42**	**63**	**60**	**6**	**1**	**3**	**130**	**16.2**	**37**	**1129**	**48.5**	**18:28**	**16**	**2**	**5**	**7**	**14**	**0**	**0**	**0**	**18:03**
2007-08	**Buffalo**	**NHL**	**78**	**32**	**49**	**81**	**46**	**6**	**3**	**4**	**218**	**14.7**	**13**	**1393**	**51.2**	**20:58**									
2008-09	**Buffalo**	**NHL**	**82**	**28**	**42**	**70**	**38**	**9**	**1**	**9**	**221**	**12.7**	**–5**	**1469**	**50.7**	**21:12**									
2009-10	**Buffalo**	**NHL**	**80**	**26**	**43**	**69**	**48**	**10**	**1**	**6**	**215**	**12.1**	**9**	**1225**	**50.4**	**19:23**	**6**	**0**	**2**	**2**	**4**	**0**	**0**	**0**	**22:59**
	NHL Totals		**434**	**134**	**214**	**348**	**261**	**37**	**7**	**27**	**1006**	**13.3**		**6738**	**49.7**	**19:01**	**40**	**7**	**17**	**24**	**34**	**1**	**1**	**0**	**18:21**

OHL All-Rookie Team (2000) • OHL Rookie of the Year (2000) • CHL All-Rookie Team (2000) • CHL Plus/Minus Award (2000) • CHL Most Sportsmanlike Player (2000) • Memorial Cup Tournament All-Star Team (2003) • Stafford Smythe Memorial Trophy (Memorial Cup Tournament - MVP) (2003)

ROY, Mathieu

(WAH, MA-tyew) **T.B.**

Defense. Shoots right. 6'2", 210 lbs. Born, St-Georges, Que., August 10, 1983. Edmonton's 10th choice, 215th overall, in 2003 Entry Draft.

Season	Club	League	GP	G	A	Pts	PIM	PP	SH	GW	S	%	+/-	TF	F%	Min	GP	G	A	Pts	PIM	PP	SH	GW	Min
1998-99	Levis	QAAA	11	4	1	5	16																		
99-2000	Levis	QAAA	24	3	4	7	88										6	1	1	2	22				
	Val-d'Or Foreurs	QMJHL	48	1	4	5	66																		
2000-01	Val-d'Or Foreurs	QMJHL	30	0	7	7	60										17	0	0	0	4				
2001-02	Val-d'Or Foreurs	QMJHL	53	7	26	33	103										7	0	2	2	19				
2002-03	Val-d'Or Foreurs	QMJHL	52	11	21	32	164										7	1	0	1	8				
2003-04	Toronto	AHL	30	0	2	2	46																		
	Columbus	ECHL	10	1	2	3	13																		
2004-05	Edmonton	AHL	51	3	22	25	68																		
2005-06	**Edmonton**	**NHL**	**1**	**0**	**0**	**0**	**0**	**0**	**0**	**0**	**0**	**0.0**	**–1**	**0**	**0.0**	**13:00**									
	Hamilton	AHL	50	3	16	19	82																		
2006-07	**Edmonton**	**NHL**	**16**	**2**	**0**	**2**	**30**	**0**	**0**	**0**	**18**	**11.1**	**–7**	**0**	**0.0**	**14:06**									
	Hamilton	AHL	31	6	12	18	40																		
2007-08	**Edmonton**	**NHL**	**13**	**0**	**1**	**1**	**27**	**0**	**0**	**0**	**8**	**0.0**	**0**	**0**	**0.0**	**10:23**									
	Springfield	AHL	20	2	8	10	34																		
2008-09	Springfield	AHL	59	2	15	17	120																		
2009-10	**Columbus**	**NHL**	**31**	**0**	**10**	**10**	**17**	**0**	**0**	**0**	**32**	**0.0**	**–2**	**1**	**100.0**	**18:19**									
	Syracuse Crunch	AHL	14	0	4	4	32																		
	Rochester	AHL	1	0	0	0	0										6	0	0	0	11				
	NHL Totals		**61**	**2**	**11**	**13**	**74**	**0**	**0**	**0**	**58**	**3.4**		**1**	**100.0**	**15:26**									

• Missed majority of 2007-08 season recovering from recurring shoulder injury and as a healthy reserve. Signed as a free agent by **Columbus**, July 14, 2009. Traded to **Florida** by **Columbus** for Matt Rust, March 3, 2010. Signed as a free agent by **Tampa Bay**, July 29, 2010.

ROZSIVAL, Michal

(roh-ZIH-vahl, MEE-khahl) **NYR**

Defense. Shoots right. 6'2", 205 lbs. Born, Vlasim, Czech., September 3, 1978. Pittsburgh's 5th choice, 105th overall, in 1996 Entry Draft.

Season	Club	League	GP	G	A	Pts	PIM	PP	SH	GW	S	%	+/-	TF	F%	Min	GP	G	A	Pts	PIM	PP	SH	GW	Min
1994-95	Jihlava Jr.	CzRep-Jr.	31	8	13	21																			
1995-96	HC Dukla Jihlava	CzRep	36	3	4	7																			
1996-97	Swift Current	WHL	63	8	31	39	80										10	0	6	6	15				
1997-98	Swift Current	WHL	71	14	55	69	122										12	0	5	5	33				
1998-99	Syracuse Crunch	AHL	49	3	22	25	72																		
99-2000	**Pittsburgh**	**NHL**	**75**	**4**	**17**	**21**	**48**	**1**	**0**	**1**	**73**	**5.5**	**11**	**1**	**0.0**	**19:01**	**2**	**0**	**0**	**0**	**4**	**0**	**0**	**0**	**30:56**
2000-01	**Pittsburgh**	**NHL**	**30**	**1**	**4**	**5**	**26**	**0**	**0**	**0**	**17**	**5.9**	**3**	**1**	**100.0**	**17:06**									
	Wilkes-Barre	AHL	29	8	8	16	32										21	3	*19	22	23				
2001-02	**Pittsburgh**	**NHL**	**79**	**9**	**20**	**29**	**47**	**4**	**0**	**4**	**89**	**10.1**	**–6**	**0**	**0.0**	**20:01**									
2002-03	**Pittsburgh**	**NHL**	**53**	**4**	**6**	**10**	**40**	**1**	**0**	**0**	**61**	**6.6**	**–5**	**0**	**0.0**	**20:25**									
2003-04	Wilkes-Barre	AHL	1	0	0	0	2																		
2004-05	HC Ocelari Trinec	CzRep	35	1	10	11	40																		
	Pardubice	CzRep	16	1	3	4	30										16	1	2	3	34				
2005-06	**NY Rangers**	**NHL**	**82**	**5**	**25**	**30**	**90**	**3**	**0**	**3**	**115**	**4.3**	***35**	**1**	**0.0**	**22:27**	**4**	**0**	**1**	**1**	**8**	**0**	**0**	**0**	**24:31**
2006-07	**NY Rangers**	**NHL**	**80**	**10**	**30**	**40**	**52**	**7**	**0**	**3**	**104**	**9.6**	**10**	**3**	**0.0**	**23:46**	**10**	**3**	**4**	**7**	**10**	**2**	**0**	**1**	**24:45**
2007-08	**NY Rangers**	**NHL**	**80**	**13**	**25**	**38**	**80**	**6**	**2**	**0**	**127**	**10.2**	**0**	**0**	**0.0**	**24:33**	**10**	**1**	**5**	**6**	**10**	**0**	**0**	**0**	**25:05**
2008-09	**NY Rangers**	**NHL**	**76**	**8**	**22**	**30**	**52**	**3**	**0**	**2**	**120**	**6.7**	**–7**	**0**	**0.0**	**22:31**	**7**	**0**	**0**	**0**	**4**	**0**	**0**	**0**	**22:41**
2009-10	**NY Rangers**	**NHL**	**82**	**3**	**20**	**23**	**78**	**1**	**0**	**1**	**80**	**3.8**	**3**	**1**	**100.0**	**21:26**									
	NHL Totals		**637**	**57**	**169**	**226**	**513**	**26**	**2**	**14**	**786**	**7.3**		**7**	**28.6**	**21:38**	**33**	**4**	**10**	**14**	**36**	**2**	**0**	**1**	**24:46**

WHL East First All-Star Team (1998)

• Missed majority of 2003-04 season recovering from knee injury suffered in training camp, September 18, 2003. Signed as a free agent by **Trinec** (CzRep), September 17, 2004. Signed as a free agent by **Pardubice** (CzRep), January, 2005. Signed as a free agent by **NY Rangers**, August 29, 2005.

RUPP, Mike

(RUHP, MIGHK) **PIT.**

Center. Shoots left. 6'5", 230 lbs. Born, Cleveland, OH, January 13, 1980. New Jersey's 7th choice, 76th overall, in 2000 Entry Draft.

Season	Club	League	GP	G	A	Pts	PIM	PP	SH	GW	S	%	+/-	TF	F%	Min	GP	G	A	Pts	PIM	PP	SH	GW	Min
1996-97	St. Edward's	High-OH	20	26	24	50																			
1997-98	Windsor Spitfires	OHL	38	9	8	17	60																		
	Erie Otters	OHL	26	7	3	10	57										7	3	1	4	6				
1998-99	Erie Otters	OHL	63	22	25	47	102										5	0	2	2	25				
99-2000	Erie Otters	OHL	58	32	21	53	134										13	5	5	10	22				
2000-01	Albany River Rats	AHL	71	10	10	20	63																		
2001-02	Albany River Rats	AHL	78	13	17	30	90																		
2002-03 ♦	**New Jersey**	**NHL**	**26**	**5**	**3**	**8**	**21**	**2**	**0**	**3**	**34**	**14.7**	**0**	**150**	**44.7**	**11:39**	**4**	**1**	**3**	**4**	**0**	**0**	**0**	**1**	**11:28**
	Albany River Rats	AHL	47	8	11	19	74																		
2003-04	**New Jersey**	**NHL**	**51**	**6**	**5**	**11**	**41**	**1**	**0**	**1**	**64**	**9.4**	**–1**	**386**	**47.9**	**10:38**									
	Phoenix	**NHL**	**6**	**0**	**1**	**1**	**6**	**0**	**0**	**0**	**12**	**0.0**	**–3**	**94**	**57.5**	**16:59**									
2004-05	Danbury Trashers	UHL	14	5	5	10	30										11	3	4	7	38				

			Regular Season														Playoffs								
Season	Club	League	GP	G	A	Pts	PIM	PP	SH	GW	S	%	+/-	TF	F%	Min	GP	G	A	Pts	PIM	PP	SH	GW	Mi
2005-06	**Phoenix**	**NHL**	**1**	**0**	**0**	**0**	**0**	**0**	**0**	**0**	**1**	**0.0**	**0**	**1**	**0.0**	**6:30**	....	....	....	....	....	....	....	....	....
	Columbus	**NHL**	**39**	**4**	**2**	**6**	**58**	**0**	**0**	**0**	**38**	**10.5**	**–3**	**264**	**48.1**	**9:04**	....	....	....	....	....	....	....	....	....
	Syracuse Crunch	AHL	3	1	2	3	12	....	....	....	....	....	....	....	....	....	....	....	....	....	....	....	....	....	....
2006-07	**New Jersey**	**NHL**	**76**	**6**	**3**	**9**	**92**	**0**	**0**	**1**	**60**	**10.0**	**–10**	**33**	**45.5**	**6:27**	**9**	**0**	**1**	**1**	**7**	**0**	**0**	**0**	**2:4**
2007-08	**New Jersey**	**NHL**	**64**	**3**	**6**	**9**	**58**	**1**	**0**	**0**	**69**	**4.3**	**–8**	**155**	**48.4**	**8:04**	**5**	**0**	**1**	**1**	**2**	**0**	**0**	**0**	**7:4**
2008-09	**New Jersey**	**NHL**	**72**	**3**	**6**	**9**	**136**	**0**	**0**	**0**	**76**	**3.9**	**–2**	**90**	**51.1**	**8:44**	**7**	**0**	**0**	**0**	**14**	**0**	**0**	**0**	**6:5**
2009-10	**Pittsburgh**	**NHL**	**81**	**13**	**6**	**19**	**120**	**0**	**0**	**1**	**87**	**14.9**	**5**	**143**	**44.1**	**9:03**	**11**	**0**	**0**	**0**	**8**	**0**	**0**	**0**	**7:2**
	NHL Totals		**416**	**40**	**32**	**72**	**532**	**4**	**0**	**6**	**441**	**9.1**		**1316**	**48.0**	**8:50**	**36**	**1**	**5**	**6**	**31**	**0**	**0**	**1**	**6:4**

• Re-entered NHL Entry Draft. Originally NY Islanders' 1st choice, 9th overall, in 1998 Entry Draft.

Traded to **Phoenix** by **New Jersey** with New Jersey's 2nd round choice (later traded to Edmonton – Edmonton selected Geoff Paukovich) in 2004 Entry Draft for Jan Hrdina, March 5, 2004. Signed as a fre agent by **Danbury** (UHL), February 10, 2005. Traded to **Columbus** by **Phoenix** with Cale Hulse and Jason Chimera for Geoff Sanderson and Tim Jackman, October 8, 2005. Signed as a free agent by **New Jersey**, July 10, 2006. Signed as a free agent by **Pittsburgh**, July 1, 2009.

RUSSELL, Kris

(RUH-sehl, KRIHS) **CB**

Defense. Shoots left. 5'10", 185 lbs. Born, Red Deer, Alta., May 2, 1987. Columbus' 3rd choice, 67th overall, in 2005 Entry Draft.

Season	Club	League	GP	G	A	Pts	PIM	PP	SH	GW	S	%	+/-	TF	F%	Min	GP	G	A	Pts	PIM	PP	SH	GW	Mi
2003-04	Medicine Hat	WHL	55	4	15	19	30	....	....	....	....	....	....	....	....	....	20	3	2	5	4	....	....	....	....
2004-05	Medicine Hat	WHL	72	26	35	61	37	....	....	....	....	....	....	....	....	....	10	2	1	3	4	....	....	....	....
2005-06	Medicine Hat	WHL	55	14	33	47	18	....	....	....	....	....	....	....	....	....	13	4	8	12	11	....	....	....	....
2006-07	Medicine Hat	WHL	59	32	37	69	56	....	....	....	....	....	....	....	....	....	23	4	15	19	24	....	....	....	....
2007-08	**Columbus**	**NHL**	**67**	**2**	**8**	**10**	**14**	**1**	**0**	**1**	**90**	**2.2**	**–12**	**0**	**0.0**	**14:47**	....	....	....	....	....	....	....	....	....
2008-09	**Columbus**	**NHL**	**66**	**2**	**19**	**21**	**28**	**1**	**0**	**1**	**86**	**2.3**	**–10**	**0**	**0.0**	**16:07**	**4**	**1**	**1**	**2**	**2**	**0**	**0**	**0**	**16:4**
	Syracuse Crunch	AHL	14	3	5	8	0	....	....	....	....	....	....	....	....	....	....	....	....	....	....	....	....	....	....
2009-10	**Columbus**	**NHL**	**70**	**7**	**15**	**22**	**32**	**0**	**0**	**1**	**108**	**6.5**	**3**	**0**	**0.0**	**18:35**	....	....	....	....	....	....	....	....	....
	NHL Totals		**203**	**11**	**42**	**53**	**74**	**2**	**0**	**3**	**284**	**3.9**		**0**	**0.0**	**16:32**	**4**	**1**	**1**	**2**	**2**	**0**	**0**	**0**	**16:4**

WHL East Second All-Star Team (2005) • WHL East First All-Star Team (2006, 2007) • WHL Defenseman of the Year (2006, 2007) • Canadian Major Junior Second All-Star Team (2006) • Canadian Major Junior Sportsman of the Year (2006) • WHL Player of the Year (2007) • Canadian Major Junior First All-Star Team (2007) • Canadian Major Junior Defenseman of the Year (2007)

RUUTU, Jarkko

(ROO-too, YAHR-koh) **OT**

Right wing. Shoots left. 6'1", 204 lbs. Born, Vantaa, Finland, August 23, 1975. Vancouver's 3rd choice, 68th overall, in 1998 Entry Draft.

Season	Club	League	GP	G	A	Pts	PIM	PP	SH	GW	S	%	+/-	TF	F%	Min	GP	G	A	Pts	PIM	PP	SH	GW	Mi
1991-92	HIFK Helsinki Jr.	Fin-Jr.	1	0	0	0	0	....	....	....	....	....	....	....	....	....	....	....	....	....	....	....	....	....	....
1992-93	HIFK Helsinki U18	Fin-U18	33	26	21	47	53	....	....	....	....	....	....	....	....	....	....	....	....	....	....	....	....	....	....
	HIFK Helsinki Jr.	Fin-Jr.	1	0	0	0	0	....	....	....	....	....	....	....	....	....	....	....	....	....	....	....	....	....	....
1993-94	HIFK Helsinki Jr.	Fin-Jr.	19	9	12	21	44	....	....	....	....	....	....	....	....	....	....	....	....	....	....	....	....	....	....
1994-95	HIFK Helsinki Jr.	Fin-Jr.	35	26	22	48	117	....	....	....	....	....	....	....	....	....	....	....	....	....	....	....	....	....	....
1995-96	Michigan Tech	WCHA	39	12	10	22	96	....	....	....	....	....	....	....	....	....	....	....	....	....	....	....	....	....	....
1996-97	HIFK Helsinki	Finland	48	11	10	21	155	....	....	....	....	....	....	....	....	....	....	....	....	....	....	....	....	....	....
1997-98	HIFK Helsinki	Finland	37	10	10	20	166	....	....	....	....	....	....	....	....	....	9	7	4	11	10	....	....	....	....
1998-99	HIFK Helsinki	Finland	25	10	4	14	136	....	....	....	....	....	....	....	....	....	9	0	2	2	43	....	....	....	....
	HIFK Helsinki	EuroHL	5	1	2	3	8	....	....	....	....	....	....	....	....	....	....	....	....	....	....	....	....	....	....
99-2000	**Vancouver**	**NHL**	**8**	**0**	**1**	**1**	**6**	**0**	**0**	**0**	**4**	**0.0**	**–1**	**0**	**0.0**	**8:47**	....	....	....	....	....	....	....	....	....
	Syracuse Crunch	AHL	65	26	32	58	164	....	....	....	....	....	....	....	....	....	4	3	1	4	8	....	....	....	....
2000-01	**Vancouver**	**NHL**	**21**	**3**	**3**	**6**	**32**	**0**	**1**	**0**	**23**	**13.0**	**1**	**0**	**0.0**	**10:39**	**4**	**0**	**1**	**1**	**8**	**0**	**0**	**0**	**10:1**
	Kansas City	IHL	46	11	18	29	111	....	....	....	....	....	....	....	....	....	....	....	....	....	....	....	....	....	....
2001-02	**Vancouver**	**NHL**	**49**	**2**	**7**	**9**	**74**	**0**	**0**	**0**	**37**	**5.4**	**–1**	**5**	**0.0**	**10:11**	**1**	**0**	**0**	**0**	**0**	**0**	**0**	**0**	**8:5**
	Finland	Olympics	4	0	0	0	4	....	....	....	....	....	....	....	....	....	....	....	....	....	....	....	....	....	....
2002-03	**Vancouver**	**NHL**	**36**	**2**	**2**	**4**	**66**	**0**	**0**	**1**	**36**	**5.6**	**–7**	**6**	**16.7**	**8:58**	**13**	**0**	**2**	**2**	**14**	**0**	**0**	**0**	**11:5**
2003-04	**Vancouver**	**NHL**	**71**	**6**	**8**	**14**	**133**	**1**	**0**	**0**	**70**	**8.6**	**–13**	**20**	**30.0**	**11:29**	**6**	**1**	**0**	**1**	**10**	**0**	**0**	**0**	**9:1**
2004-05	HIFK Helsinki	Finland	50	10	18	28	215	....	....	....	....	....	....	....	....	....	3	0	0	0	41	....	....	....	....
2005-06	**Vancouver**	**NHL**	**82**	**10**	**7**	**17**	**142**	**2**	**0**	**2**	**85**	**11.8**	**1**	**11**	**0.0**	**11:42**	....	....	....	....	....	....	....	....	....
	Finland	Olympics	8	0	0	0	31	....	....	....	....	....	....	....	....	....	....	....	....	....	....	....	....	....	....
2006-07	**Pittsburgh**	**NHL**	**81**	**7**	**9**	**16**	**125**	**0**	**0**	**2**	**63**	**11.1**	**0**	**3**	**100.0**	**9:20**	**5**	**0**	**0**	**0**	**10**	**0**	**0**	**0**	**6:3**
2007-08	**Pittsburgh**	**NHL**	**71**	**6**	**10**	**16**	**138**	**0**	**1**	**1**	**55**	**10.9**	**3**	**10**	**40.0**	**10:12**	**20**	**2**	**1**	**3**	**26**	**0**	**0**	**1**	**10:3**
2008-09	**Ottawa**	**NHL**	**78**	**7**	**14**	**21**	**144**	**0**	**1**	**0**	**89**	**7.9**	**0**	**8**	**25.0**	**11:43**	....	....	....	....	....	....	....	....	....
2009-10	**Ottawa**	**NHL**	**82**	**12**	**14**	**26**	**121**	**0**	**0**	**1**	**106**	**11.3**	**–2**	**24**	**20.8**	**13:21**	**6**	**2**	**1**	**3**	**34**	**0**	**0**	**1**	**18:2**
	Finland	Olympics	6	2	1	3	14	....	....	....	....	....	....	....	....	....	....	....	....	....	....	....	....	....	....
	NHL Totals		**579**	**55**	**75**	**130**	**981**	**3**	**3**	**7**	**568**	**9.7**		**87**	**24.1**	**11:01**	**55**	**5**	**5**	**10**	**102**	**0**	**0**	**2**	**11:1**

• Missed majority of 2002-03 season as a healthy reserve. Signed as a free agent by **HIFK Helsinki** (Finland), September 23, 2004. Signed as a free agent by **Pittsburgh**, July 4, 2006. Signed as a free ager by **Ottawa**, July 2, 2008.

RUUTU, Tuomo

(ROO-too, TOO-oh-moh) **CA**

Center/Left wing. Shoots left. 6', 205 lbs. Born, Vantaa, Finland, February 16, 1983. Chicago's 1st choice, 9th overall, in 2001 Entry Draft.

Season	Club	League	GP	G	A	Pts	PIM	PP	SH	GW	S	%	+/-	TF	F%	Min	GP	G	A	Pts	PIM	PP	SH	GW	Mi
1998-99	HIFK Helsinki U18	Fin-U18	25	9	11	20	88	....	....	....	....	....	....	....	....	....	2	1	1	2	2	....	....	....	....
99-2000	HIFK Helsinki U18	Fin-U18	5	0	3	3	12	....	....	....	....	....	....	....	....	....	3	1	2	3	2	....	....	....	....
	HIFK Helsinki Jr.	Fin-Jr.	35	11	16	27	32	....	....	....	....	....	....	....	....	....	3	0	1	1	4	....	....	....	....
	HIFK Helsinki	Finland	1	0	0	0	2	....	....	....	....	....	....	....	....	....	....	....	....	....	....	....	....	....	....
2000-01	Jokerit Helsinki Jr.	Fin-Jr.	2	1	0	1	0	....	....	....	....	....	....	....	....	....	....	....	....	....	....	....	....	....	....
	Jokerit Helsinki	Finland	47	11	11	22	94	....	....	....	....	....	....	....	....	....	5	0	0	0	4	....	....	....	....
2001-02	Jokerit Helsinki	Finland	51	7	16	23	69	....	....	....	....	....	....	....	....	....	10	0	6	6	29	....	....	....	....
2002-03	HIFK Helsinki	Finland	30	12	15	27	24	....	....	....	....	....	....	....	....	....	....	....	....	....	....	....	....	....	....
2003-04	**Chicago**	**NHL**	**82**	**23**	**21**	**44**	**58**	**10**	**0**	**3**	**174**	**13.2**	**–31**	**317**	**46.4**	**16:24**	....	....	....	....	....	....	....	....	....
2004-05			DID NOT PLAY																						
2005-06	**Chicago**	**NHL**	**15**	**2**	**3**	**5**	**31**	**1**	**0**	**0**	**30**	**6.7**	**–7**	**90**	**46.7**	**14:43**	....	....	....	....	....	....	....	....	....
2006-07	**Chicago**	**NHL**	**71**	**17**	**21**	**38**	**95**	**1**	**0**	**1**	**115**	**14.8**	**4**	**347**	**42.7**	**17:21**	....	....	....	....	....	....	....	....	....
2007-08	**Chicago**	**NHL**	**60**	**6**	**15**	**21**	**75**	**1**	**0**	**1**	**71**	**8.5**	**3**	**49**	**53.1**	**15:35**	....	....	....	....	....	....	....	....	....
	Carolina	**NHL**	**17**	**4**	**7**	**11**	**16**	**3**	**0**	**0**	**29**	**13.8**	**1**	**17**	**11.8**	**17:01**	....	....	....	....	....	....	....	....	....
2008-09	**Carolina**	**NHL**	**79**	**26**	**28**	**54**	**79**	**10**	**0**	**4**	**190**	**13.7**	**0**	**37**	**51.4**	**18:19**	**16**	**1**	**3**	**4**	**8**	**0**	**0**	**0**	**14:**
2009-10	**Carolina**	**NHL**	**54**	**14**	**21**	**35**	**50**	**5**	**0**	**1**	**122**	**11.5**	**–4**	**47**	**40.4**	**16:23**	....	....	....	....	....	....	....	....	....
	Finland	Olympics	6	1	0	1	2	....	....	....	....	....	....	....	....	....	....	....	....	....	....	....	....	....	....
	NHL Totals		**378**	**92**	**116**	**208**	**404**	**31**	**0**	**10**	**731**	**12.6**		**904**	**44.6**	**16:48**	**16**	**1**	**3**	**4**	**8**	**0**	**0**	**0**	**14:**

• Missed majority of 2005-06 season recovering from back (October 15, 2005 at San Jose) and ankle (January 8, 2006 vs. Nashville) injuries. Traded to **Carolina** by **Chicago** for Andrew Ladd, February 26, 2008.

RUZICKA, Stefan

(roo-ZHEECH-kuh, STEH-fan) **PH**

Right wing. Shoots right. 6', 205 lbs. Born, Nitra, Czech., February 17, 1985. Philadelphia's 4th choice, 81st overall, in 2003 Entry Draft.

Season	Club	League	GP	G	A	Pts	PIM	PP	SH	GW	S	%	+/-	TF	F%	Min	GP	G	A	Pts	PIM	PP	SH	GW	Mi
2000-01	Nitra Jr.	Slovak-Jr.	38	30	15	45	....	....	....	....	....	....	....	....	....	....	....	....	....	....	....	....	....	....	....
2001-02	HKM Nitra Jr.	Slovak-Jr.	29	27	25	52	....	....	....	....	....	....	....	....	....	....	....	....	....	....	....	....	....	....	....
	HKM Nitra	Slovakia	19	0	5	5	29	....	....	....	....	....	....	....	....	....	....	....	....	....	....	....	....	....	....
2002-03	HKM Nitra Jr.	Slovak-Jr.	30	18	22	40	64	....	....	....	....	....	....	....	....	....	....	....	....	....	....	....	....	....	....
	HKM Nitra	Slovak-2	17	5	7	12	4	....	....	....	....	....	....	....	....	....	....	....	....	....	....	....	....	....	....
2003-04	Owen Sound	OHL	62	34	38	72	63	....	....	....	....	....	....	....	....	....	7	1	6	7	8	....	....	....	....
	Philadelphia	AHL	2	0	0	0	0	....	....	....	....	....	....	....	....	....	3	1	0	1	2	....	....	....	....
2004-05	Owen Sound	OHL	62	37	33	70	61	....	....	....	....	....	....	....	....	....	8	3	3	6	14	....	....	....	....
2005-06	**Philadelphia**	**NHL**	**1**	**0**	**0**	**0**	**2**	**0**	**0**	**0**	**1**	**0.0**	**0**	**1**	**0.0**	**4:48**	....	....	....	....	....	....	....	....	....
	Philadelphia	AHL	73	16	32	48	88	....	....	....	....	....	....	....	....	....	....	....	....	....	....	....	....	....	....
2006-07	**Philadelphia**	**NHL**	**40**	**3**	**10**	**13**	**18**	**1**	**0**	**0**	**75**	**4.0**	**–6**	**3**	**0.0**	**12:44**	....	....	....	....	....	....	....	....	....
	Philadelphia	AHL	32	16	11	27	29	....	....	....	....	....	....	....	....	....	....	....	....	....	....	....	....	....	....
2007-08	**Philadelphia**	**NHL**	**14**	**1**	**3**	**4**	**27**	**0**	**0**	**0**	**10**	**10.0**	**5**	**5**	**0.0**	**8:40**	....	....	....	....	....	....	....	....	....
	Philadelphia	AHL	59	19	31	50	105	....	....	....	....	....	....	....	....	....	12	4	9	13	30	....	....	....	....
2008-09	Spartak Moscow	Rus-KHL	55	18	19	37	81	....	....	....	....	....	....	....	....	....	6	3	4	7	6	....	....	....	....
2009-10	Spartak Moscow	Rus-KHL	56	16	20	36	72	....	....	....	....	....	....	....	....	....	10	3	1	4	24	....	....	....	....
	NHL Totals		**55**	**4**	**13**	**17**	**47**	**1**	**0**	**0**	**86**	**4.7**		**9**	**0.0**	**11:33**	....	....	....	....	....	....	....	....	....

OHL All-Rookie Team (2004) • OHL Second All-Star Team (2004)

Signed as a free agent by **Spartak Moscow** (Russia-KHL), July 3, 2008.

RYAN, Bobby

(RIGH-uhn, BAW-bee) **ANA.**

Right wing. Shoots right. 6'2", 208 lbs. Born, Cherry Hill, NJ, March 17, 1987. Anaheim's 1st choice, 2nd overall, in 2005 Entry Draft.

Season	Club	League	Regular Season GP	G	A	Pts	PIM	PP	SH	GW	S	%	+/-	TF	F%	Min	Playoffs GP	G	A	Pts	PIM	PP	SH	GW	Min
2003-04	Owen Sound	OHL	65	22	17	39	52	....	....	....	....	....	....	....	....	....	7	1	2	3	2	....	....	....	....
2004-05	Owen Sound	OHL	62	37	52	89	51	....	....	....	....	....	....	....	....	....	8	2	7	9	8	....	....	....	....
2005-06	Owen Sound	OHL	59	31	64	95	44	....	....	....	....	....	....	....	....	....	11	5	7	12	14	....	....	....	....
	Portland Pirates	AHL	....	....	....	....	....	....	....	....	....	....	....	....	....	....	19	1	7	8	22	....	....	....	....
2006-07	Owen Sound	OHL	63	43	59	102	63	....	....	....	....	....	....	....	....	....	4	1	1	2	2	....	....	....	....
	Portland Pirates	AHL	8	3	6	9	6	....	....	....	....	....	....	....	....	....	....	....	....	....	....	....	....	....	....
2007-08	**Anaheim**	**NHL**	**23**	**5**	**5**	**10**	**6**	**3**	**0**	**0**	**37**	**13.5**	**–1**	**1**	**100.0**	**11:16**	**2**	**0**	**0**	**0**	**2**	**0**	**0**	**0**	**11:09**
	Portland Pirates	AHL	48	21	28	49	38	....	....	....	....	....	....	....	....	....	16	8	12	20	18	....	....	....	....
2008-09	**Anaheim**	**NHL**	**64**	**31**	**26**	**57**	**33**	**12**	**0**	**3**	**174**	**17.8**	**13**	**13**	**46.2**	**15:26**	**13**	**5**	**2**	**7**	**0**	**2**	**0**	**1**	**19:41**
	Iowa Chops	AHL	14	9	10	19	19	....	....	....	....	....	....	....	....	....	....	....	....	....	....	....	....	....	....
2009-10	**Anaheim**	**NHL**	**81**	**35**	**29**	**64**	**81**	**11**	**0**	**3**	**258**	**13.6**	**9**	**93**	**44.1**	**18:29**	....	....	....	....	....	....	....	....	....
	United States	Olympics	6	1	1	2	2	....	....	....	....	....	....	....	....	....	....	....	....	....	....	....	....	....	....
	NHL Totals		**168**	**71**	**60**	**131**	**120**	**26**	**0**	**6**	**469**	**15.1**		**107**	**44.9**	**16:20**	**15**	**5**	**2**	**7**	**2**	**2**	**0**	**1**	**18:32**

L First All-Star Team (2005) • NHL All-Rookie Team (2009)

RYAN, Michael

(RIGH-uhn, MIGH-kuhl)

Center. Shoots left. 6'1", 188 lbs. Born, Boston, MA, May 16, 1980. Dallas' 1st choice, 32nd overall, in 1999 Entry Draft.

Season	Club	League	GP	G	A	Pts	PIM	PP	SH	GW	S	%	+/-	TF	F%	Min	GP	G	A	Pts	PIM	PP	SH	GW	Min
1997-98	Bos. College High	High-MA	23	22	14	36	28	....	....	....	....	....	....	....	....	....	....	....	....	....	....	....	....	....	....
1998-99	Bos. College High	High-MA	21	20	24	44	22	....	....	....	....	....	....	....	....	....	....	....	....	....	....	....	....	....	....
99-2000	Northeastern	H-East	32	4	9	13	47	....	....	....	....	....	....	....	....	....	....	....	....	....	....	....	....	....	....
2000-01	Northeastern	H-East	33	17	12	29	52	....	....	....	....	....	....	....	....	....	....	....	....	....	....	....	....	....	....
2001-02	Northeastern	H-East	36	24	15	39	54	....	....	....	....	....	....	....	....	....	....	....	....	....	....	....	....	....	....
2002-03	Northeastern	H-East	34	18	14	32	30	....	....	....	....	....	....	....	....	....	....	....	....	....	....	....	....	....	....
2003-04	Rochester	AHL	45	3	9	12	31	....	....	....	....	....	....	....	....	....	....	....	....	....	....	....	....	....	....
2004-05	Rochester	AHL	59	11	11	22	20	....	....	....	....	....	....	....	....	....	5	0	1	1	4	....	....	....	....
2005-06	Rochester	AHL	56	15	22	37	70	....	....	....	....	....	....	....	....	....	....	....	....	....	....	....	....	....	....
2006-07	**Buffalo**	**NHL**	**19**	**3**	**2**	**5**	**2**	**0**	**1**	**0**	**34**	**8.8**	**–8**	**2**	**0.0**	**13:40**	....	....	....	....	....	....	....	....	....
	Rochester	AHL	50	28	23	51	68	....	....	....	....	....	....	....	....	....	6	4	0	4	4	....	....	....	....
2007-08	**Buffalo**	**NHL**	**46**	**4**	**4**	**8**	**30**	**0**	**0**	**0**	**60**	**6.7**	**–4**	**2**	**0.0**	**9:53**	....	....	....	....	....	....	....	....	....
2008-09	**Carolina**	**NHL**	**18**	**0**	**2**	**2**	**2**	**0**	**0**	**0**	**24**	**0.0**	**–3**	**6**	**16.7**	**8:12**	....	....	....	....	....	....	....	....	....
	Albany River Rats	AHL	40	25	17	42	34	....	....	....	....	....	....	....	....	....	....	....	....	....	....	....	....	....	....
2009-10	Albany River Rats	AHL	3	0	0	0	2	....	....	....	....	....	....	....	....	....	....	....	....	....	....	....	....	....	....
	NHL Totals		**83**	**7**	**8**	**15**	**34**	**0**	**1**	**0**	**118**	**5.9**		**10**	**10.0**	**10:23**									

ded to **Buffalo** by **Dallas** with Dallas's 2nd round choice (Branislav Fabry) in 2003 Entry Draft for Stu Barnes, March 10, 2003. Signed as a free agent by **Carolina**, October 31, 2008.

RYDER, Michael

(RIGH-duhr, MIGH-kuhl) **BOS.**

Right wing. Shoots right. 6', 192 lbs. Born, St. John's, Nfld., March 31, 1980. Montreal's 9th choice, 216th overall, in 1998 Entry Draft.

Season	Club	League	GP	G	A	Pts	PIM	PP	SH	GW	S	%	+/-	TF	F%	Min	GP	G	A	Pts	PIM	PP	SH	GW	Min
1996-97	Bonavista Saints	NFAHA	23	31	17	48	....	....	....	....	....	....	....	....	....	....	....	....	....	....	....	....	....	....	....
1997-98	Hull Olympiques	QMJHL	69	34	28	62	41	....	....	....	....	....	....	....	....	....	10	4	2	6	4	....	....	....	....
1998-99	Hull Olympiques	QMJHL	69	44	43	87	65	....	....	....	....	....	....	....	....	....	23	*20	16	36	39	....	....	....	....
99-2000	Hull Olympiques	QMJHL	63	50	58	108	50	....	....	....	....	....	....	....	....	....	15	11	17	28	28	....	....	....	....
2000-01	Tallahassee	ECHL	5	4	5	9	6	....	....	....	....	....	....	....	....	....	....	....	....	....	....	....	....	....	....
	Quebec Citadelles	AHL	61	6	9	15	14	....	....	....	....	....	....	....	....	....	....	....	....	....	....	....	....	....	....
2001-02	Mississippi	ECHL	20	14	13	27	2	....	....	....	....	....	....	....	....	....	....	....	....	....	....	....	....	....	....
	Quebec Citadelles	AHL	50	11	17	28	9	....	....	....	....	....	....	....	....	....	3	0	1	1	2	....	....	....	....
2002-03	Hamilton	AHL	69	34	33	67	43	....	....	....	....	....	....	....	....	....	23	11	6	17	8	....	....	....	....
2003-04	**Montreal**	**NHL**	**81**	**25**	**38**	**63**	**26**	**10**	**0**	**4**	**215**	**11.6**	**10**	**25**	**24.0**	**16:00**	**11**	**1**	**2**	**3**	**4**	**0**	**0**	**0**	**16:52**
2004-05	Leksands IF	Sweden-2	42	34	27	61	32	....	....	....	....	....	....	....	....	....	....	....	....	....	....	....	....	....	....
2005-06	**Montreal**	**NHL**	**81**	**30**	**25**	**55**	**40**	**18**	**0**	**6**	**243**	**12.3**	**–5**	**17**	**52.9**	**16:10**	**6**	**2**	**3**	**5**	**0**	**1**	**0**	**1**	**16:09**
2006-07	**Montreal**	**NHL**	**82**	**30**	**28**	**58**	**60**	**17**	**2**	**3**	**221**	**13.6**	**–25**	**28**	**42.9**	**16:17**	....	....	....	....	....	....	....	....	....
2007-08	**Montreal**	**NHL**	**70**	**14**	**17**	**31**	**30**	**1**	**0**	**2**	**134**	**10.4**	**–4**	**19**	**26.3**	**13:15**	**4**	**0**	**0**	**0**	**2**	**0**	**0**	**0**	**10:46**
2008-09	**Boston**	**NHL**	**74**	**27**	**26**	**53**	**26**	**10**	**0**	**7**	**185**	**14.6**	**28**	**15**	**46.7**	**14:55**	**11**	**5**	**8**	**13**	**8**	**1**	**0**	**1**	**15:45**
2009-10	**Boston**	**NHL**	**82**	**18**	**15**	**33**	**35**	**7**	**0**	**1**	**191**	**9.4**	**3**	**15**	**13.3**	**15:18**	**13**	**4**	**1**	**5**	**2**	**1**	**0**	**0**	**15:47**
	NHL Totals		**470**	**144**	**149**	**293**	**217**	**63**	**2**	**23**	**1189**	**12.1**		**119**	**34.5**	**15:23**	**45**	**12**	**14**	**26**	**16**	**3**	**0**	**2**	**15:39**

L All-Rookie Team (2004)

ned as a free agent by **Leksands** (Sweden-2), September 19, 2004. Signed as a free agent by **Boston**, July 1, 2008.

RYPIEN, Rick

(RIH-pihn, RIHK) **VAN.**

Center. Shoots right. 5'11", 190 lbs. Born, Coleman, Alta., May 16, 1984.

Season	Club	League	GP	G	A	Pts	PIM	PP	SH	GW	S	%	+/-	TF	F%	Min	GP	G	A	Pts	PIM	PP	SH	GW	Min
2001-02	Crowsnest Pass	AJHL	57	12	10	22	143	....	....	....	....	....	....	....	....	....	....	....	....	....	....	....	....	....	....
	Regina Pats	WHL	1	0	0	0	0	....	....	....	....	....	....	....	....	....	....	....	....	....	....	....	....	....	....
2002-03	Regina Pats	WHL	50	6	12	18	159	....	....	....	....	....	....	....	....	....	5	1	1	2	21	....	....	....	....
2003-04	Regina Pats	WHL	65	19	26	45	186	....	....	....	....	....	....	....	....	....	4	0	1	1	18	....	....	....	....
2004-05	Regina Pats	WHL	63	22	29	51	148	....	....	....	....	....	....	....	....	....	....	....	....	....	....	....	....	....	....
	Manitoba Moose	AHL	8	1	1	2	5	....	....	....	....	....	....	....	....	....	14	0	0	0	35	....	....	....	....
2005-06	Manitoba Moose	AHL	49	9	6	15	122	....	....	....	....	....	....	....	....	....	13	1	1	2	22	....	....	....	....
	Vancouver	**NHL**	**5**	**1**	**0**	**1**	**4**	**0**	**0**	**0**	**6**	**16.7**	**1**	**22**	**36.4**	**6:19**	....	....	....	....	....	....	....	....	....
2006-07	**Vancouver**	**NHL**	**2**	**0**	**0**	**0**	**5**	**0**	**0**	**0**	**0**	**0.0**	**0**	**6**	**66.7**	**4:46**	....	....	....	....	....	....	....	....	....
	Manitoba Moose	AHL	14	3	3	6	35	....	....	....	....	....	....	....	....	....	....	....	....	....	....	....	....	....	....
2007-08	**Vancouver**	**NHL**	**22**	**1**	**2**	**3**	**41**	**0**	**0**	**0**	**8**	**12.5**	**–5**	**106**	**41.5**	**8:07**	....	....	....	....	....	....	....	....	....
	Manitoba Moose	AHL	34	3	11	14	81	....	....	....	....	....	....	....	....	....	6	0	0	0	10	....	....	....	....
2008-09	**Vancouver**	**NHL**	**12**	**3**	**0**	**3**	**19**	**0**	**1**	**0**	**16**	**18.8**	**–3**	**18**	**50.0**	**9:20**	**10**	**0**	**2**	**2**	**40**	**0**	**0**	**0**	**7:30**
2009-10	**Vancouver**	**NHL**	**69**	**4**	**4**	**8**	**126**	**0**	**0**	**1**	**61**	**6.6**	**–3**	**153**	**43.1**	**7:14**	**7**	**0**	**1**	**1**	**7**	**0**	**0**	**0**	**4:40**
	NHL Totals		**110**	**9**	**6**	**15**	**195**	**0**	**1**	**1**	**91**	**9.9**		**305**	**43.0**	**7:33**	**17**	**0**	**3**	**3**	**47**	**0**	**0**	**0**	**6:20**

ned to an ATO (amateur tryout) contract by **Manitoba** (AHL), March 22, 2005. Signed as a free agent by **Vancouver**, November 9, 2005. • Missed majority of 2006-07 season recovering from recurring n injury. • Missed majority of 2008-09 season recovering from viral infection.

ST. LOUIS, Martin

(SAINT loo-EE, mahr-TEHN) **T.B.**

Right wing. Shoots left. 5'9", 177 lbs. Born, Laval, Que., June 18, 1975.

Season	Club	League	GP	G	A	Pts	PIM	PP	SH	GW	S	%	+/-	TF	F%	Min	GP	G	A	Pts	PIM	PP	SH	GW	Min
1991-92	Laval-Laurentides	QAAA	42	29	*74	*103	38	....	....	....	....	....	....	....	....	....	12	7	15	22	16	....	....	....	....
1992-93	Hawkesbury	CJHL	31	37	50	87	70	....	....	....	....	....	....	....	....	....	....	....	....	....	....	....	....	....	....
1993-94	U. of Vermont	ECAC	33	15	36	51	24	....	....	....	....	....	....	....	....	....	....	....	....	....	....	....	....	....	....
1994-95	U. of Vermont	ECAC	35	23	48	71	36	....	....	....	....	....	....	....	....	....	....	....	....	....	....	....	....	....	....
1995-96	U. of Vermont	ECAC	35	29	56	85	38	....	....	....	....	....	....	....	....	....	....	....	....	....	....	....	....	....	....
1996-97	U. of Vermont	ECAC	36	24	*36	60	65	....	....	....	....	....	....	....	....	....	....	....	....	....	....	....	....	....	....
1997-98	Cleveland	IHL	56	16	34	50	24	....	....	....	....	....	....	....	....	....	....	....	....	....	....	....	....	....	....
	Saint John Flames	AHL	25	15	11	26	20	....	....	....	....	....	....	....	....	....	20	5	15	20	16	....	....	....	....
1998-99	**Calgary**	**NHL**	**13**	**1**	**1**	**2**	**10**	**0**	**0**	**0**	**14**	**7.1**	**–2**	**0**	**0.0**	**8:15**	....	....	....	....	....	....	....	....	....
	Saint John Flames	AHL	53	28	34	62	30	....	....	....	....	....	....	....	....	....	7	4	4	8	2	....	....	....	....
99-2000	**Calgary**	**NHL**	**56**	**3**	**15**	**18**	**22**	**0**	**0**	**1**	**73**	**4.1**	**–5**	**3**	**0.0**	**14:41**	....	....	....	....	....	....	....	....	....
	Saint John Flames	AHL	17	15	11	26	14	....	....	....	....	....	....	....	....	....	....	....	....	....	....	....	....	....	....
2000-01	**Tampa Bay**	**NHL**	**78**	**18**	**22**	**40**	**12**	**3**	**3**	**4**	**141**	**12.8**	**–4**	**48**	**41.7**	**15:14**	....	....	....	....	....	....	....	....	....
2001-02	**Tampa Bay**	**NHL**	**53**	**16**	**19**	**35**	**20**	**6**	**1**	**2**	**105**	**15.2**	**4**	**33**	**39.4**	**18:41**	....	....	....	....	....	....	....	....	....
2002-03	**Tampa Bay**	**NHL**	**82**	**33**	**37**	**70**	**32**	**12**	**3**	**5**	**201**	**16.4**	**10**	**37**	**37.8**	**19:43**	**11**	**7**	**5**	**12**	**0**	**1**	***2**	**3**	**22:21**
2003-04 ♦	**Tampa Bay**	**NHL**	**82**	**38**	***56**	***94**	**24**	**8**	***8**	**7**	**212**	**17.9**	***35**	**24**	**33.3**	**20:35**	**23**	**9**	***15**	**24**	**14**	**3**	**1**	**3**	**22:52**
2004-05	Lausanne HC	Swiss	23	9	16	25	16	....	....	....	....	....	....	....	....	....	....	....	....	....	....	....	....	....	....
2005-06	**Tampa Bay**	**NHL**	**80**	**31**	**30**	**61**	**38**	**9**	**3**	**7**	**221**	**14.0**	**–3**	**13**	**23.1**	**20:59**	**5**	**4**	**0**	**4**	**2**	**1**	**0**	**1**	**22:53**
	Canada	Olympics	6	2	1	3	0	....	....	....	....	....	....	....	....	....	....	....	....	....	....	....	....	....	....
2006-07	**Tampa Bay**	**NHL**	**82**	**43**	**59**	**102**	**28**	**14**	**5**	**7**	**273**	**15.8**	**7**	**20**	**35.0**	**24:09**	**6**	**3**	**5**	**8**	**8**	**1**	**0**	**0**	**28:07**
2007-08	**Tampa Bay**	**NHL**	**82**	**25**	**58**	**83**	**26**	**10**	**2**	**5**	**241**	**10.4**	**–23**	**12**	**25.0**	**24:17**	....	....	....	....	....	....	....	....	....

			Regular Season														Playoffs								
Season	Club	League	GP	G	A	Pts	PIM	PP	SH	GW	S	%	+/-	TF	F%	Min	GP	G	A	Pts	PIM	PP	SH	GW	M
2008-09	**Tampa Bay**	**NHL**	82	30	50	80	14	7	2	3	262	11.5	4	30	46.7	21:17	....	....	....	....	....	....	....	....	
2009-10	**Tampa Bay**	**NHL**	82	29	65	94	12	7	1	7	242	12.0	–8	157	45.2	21:49	....	....	....	....	....	....	....	....	
	NHL Totals		772	267	412	679	238	76	28	48	1985	13.5		377	40.6	20:12	45	23	25	48	24	6	3	7	23:

ECAC First All-Star Team (1995, 1996, 1997) • ECAC Player of the Year (1995) • NCAA East First All-American Team (1995, 1996, 1997) • NCAA Championship All-Tournament Team (1996) • NHL First All-Star Team (2004) • Art Ross Trophy (2004) • Lester B. Pearson Award (2004) • Hart Memorial Trophy (2004) • NHL Second All-Star Team (2007, 2010) • Lady Byng Memorial Trophy (2010)

Played in NHL All-Star Game (2003, 2004, 2007, 2008, 2009)

Signed as a free agent by **Calgary**, February 19, 1998. Signed as a free agent by **Tampa Bay**, July 31, 2000. Signed as a free agent by **Lausanne** (Swiss), November 4, 2004.

ST. PIERRE, Martin

(SAINT PEE-aihr, mahr-TEHN)

Center. Shoots left. 5'9", 185 lbs. Born, Ottawa, Ont., August 11, 1983.

Season	Club	League	GP	G	A	Pts	PIM	PP	SH	GW	S	%	+/-	TF	F%	Min	GP	G	A	Pts	PIM	PP	SH	GW	M
2000-01	Guelph Storm	OHL	68	20	49	69	40	....	....	....	....	....	....	....	....	....	4	0	0	0	4	....	....	....	
2001-02	Guelph Storm	OHL	66	32	53	85	68	....	....	....	....	....	....	....	....	....	9	3	9	12	12	....	....	....	
2002-03	Guelph Storm	OHL	55	11	45	56	74	....	....	....	....	....	....	....	....	....	11	5	11	16	4	....	....	....	
2003-04	Guelph Storm	OHL	68	45	65	110	95	....	....	....	....	....	....	....	....	....	22	8	*27	*35	20	....	....	....	
2004-05	Greenville	ECHL	45	14	39	53	55	....	....	....	....	....	....	....	....	....	7	2	5	7	6	....	....	....	
	Edmonton	AHL	18	4	3	7	8	....	....	....	....	....	....	....	....	....	....	....	....	....	....	....	....	....	
2005-06	**Chicago**	**NHL**	2	0	0	0	0	0	0	0	1	0.0	–1	15	33.3	12:02	....	....	....	....	....	....	....	....	
	Norfolk Admirals	AHL	77	23	50	73	98	....	....	....	....	....	....	....	....	....	4	0	3	3	2	....	....	....	
2006-07	**Chicago**	**NHL**	14	1	3	4	8	1	0	0	13	7.7	–3	129	48.1	12:29	....	....	....	....	....	....	....	....	
	Norfolk Admirals	AHL	65	27	72	99	100	....	....	....	....	....	....	....	....	....	6	0	1	1	6	....	....	....	
2007-08	Mytischi	Russia	14	1	6	7	16	....	....	....	....	....	....	....	....	....	....	....	....	....	....	....	....	....	
	Chicago	**NHL**	5	0	0	0	0	0	0	0	2	0.0	–3	59	55.9	15:17	....	....	....	....	....	....	....	....	
	Rockford IceHogs	AHL	69	21	67	88	80	....	....	....	....	....	....	....	....	....	12	2	12	14	12	....	....	....	
2008-09	**Boston**	**NHL**	14	2	2	4	4	0	1	1	15	13.3	–1	101	42.6	11:24	....	....	....	....	....	....	....	....	
	Providence Bruins	AHL	61	15	51	66	58	....	....	....	....	....	....	....	....	....	16	5	11	16	26	....	....	....	
2009-10	**Ottawa**	**NHL**	3	0	0	0	0	0	0	0	0	0.0	–2	20	45.0	9:37	....	....	....	....	....	....	....	....	
	Binghamton	AHL	77	24	48	72	50	....	....	....	....	....	....	....	....	....	....	....	....	....	....	....	....	....	
	NHL Totals		38	3	5	8	12	1	1	1	31	9.7		324	46.9	12:12	....	....	....	....	....	....	....	....	

AHL All-Rookie Team (2006) • AHL First All-Star Team (2007) • AHL Second All-Star Team (2008)

Signed as a free agent by **Chicago**, November 3, 2005. Signed as a free agent by **Mytischi** (Russia), June 22, 2007. Traded to **Boston** by **Chicago** for Pascal Pelletier, July 24, 2008. Signed as a free agent by **Ottawa**, July 1, 2009. Signed as a free agent by **Nizhnekamsk** (Russia-KHL), June 7, 2010.

SALCIDO, Brian

(sal-SEE-doh, BRIGH-uhn)

Defense. Shoots left. 6'2", 188 lbs. Born, Los Angeles, CA, April 14, 1985. Anaheim's 5th choice, 141st overall, in 2005 Entry Draft.

Season	Club	League	GP	G	A	Pts	PIM	PP	SH	GW	S	%	+/-	TF	F%	Min	GP	G	A	Pts	PIM	PP	SH	GW	M
2002-03	Shat.-St. Mary's	High-MN	53	8	35	43	....	....	....	....	....	....	....	....	....	....	....	....	....	....	....	....	....	....	
2003-04	Colorado College	WCHA	12	1	0	1	48	....	....	....	....	....	....	....	....	....	....	....	....	....	....	....	....	....	
2004-05	Colorado College	WCHA	38	7	23	30	52	....	....	....	....	....	....	....	....	....	....	....	....	....	....	....	....	....	
2005-06	Colorado College	WCHA	42	8	32	40	69	....	....	....	....	....	....	....	....	....	....	....	....	....	....	....	....	....	
2006-07	Portland Pirates	AHL	76	7	20	27	80	....	....	....	....	....	....	....	....	....	....	....	....	....	....	....	....	....	
2007-08	Portland Pirates	AHL	71	11	42	53	58	....	....	....	....	....	....	....	....	....	18	0	6	6	18	....	....	....	
2008-09	**Anaheim**	**NHL**	2	0	1	1	0	0	0	0	1	0.0	2	0	0.0	12:18	....	....	....	....	....	....	....	....	
	Iowa Chops	AHL	76	10	33	43	108	....	....	....	....	....	....	....	....	....	....	....	....	....	....	....	....	....	
2009-10	Manitoba Moose	AHL	68	8	10	18	50	....	....	....	....	....	....	....	....	....	5	0	1	1	6	....	....	....	
	NHL Totals		2	0	1	1	0	0	0	0	1	0.0		0	0.0	12:18	....	....	....	....	....	....	....	....	

WCHA Second All-Star Team (2006) • AHL Second All-Star Team (2008)

SALEI, Ruslan

(sah-LAY, roos-LAHN) **DE**

Defense. Shoots left. 6'1", 212 lbs. Born, Minsk, USSR, November 2, 1974. Anaheim's 1st choice, 9th overall, in 1996 Entry Draft.

Season	Club	League	GP	G	A	Pts	PIM	PP	SH	GW	S	%	+/-	TF	F%	Min	GP	G	A	Pts	PIM	PP	SH	GW	M
1992-93	Dynamo Moscow	CIS	9	1	0	1	10	....	....	....	....	....	....	....	....	....	....	....	....	....	....	....	....	....	
1993-94	Tivali Minsk	CIS	39	2	3	5	50	....	....	....	....	....	....	....	....	....	....	....	....	....	....	....	....	....	
1994-95	Tivali Minsk	CIS	51	4	2	6	44	....	....	....	....	....	....	....	....	....	....	....	....	....	....	....	....	....	
1995-96	Las Vegas	IHL	76	7	23	30	123	....	....	....	....	....	....	....	....	....	15	3	7	10	18	....	....	....	
1996-97	**Anaheim**	**NHL**	30	0	1	1	37	0	0	0	14	0.0	–8	....	....	....	....	....	....	....	....	....	....	....	
	Baltimore Bandits	AHL	12	1	4	5	12	....	....	....	....	....	....	....	....	....	....	....	....	....	....	....	....	....	
	Las Vegas	IHL	8	0	2	2	24	....	....	....	....	....	....	....	....	....	3	2	1	3	6	....	....	....	
1997-98	**Anaheim**	**NHL**	66	5	10	15	70	1	0	0	104	4.8	7	....	....	....	....	....	....	....	....	....	....	....	
	Cincinnati	AHL	6	3	6	9	14	....	....	....	....	....	....	....	....	....	....	....	....	....	....	....	....	....	
	Belarus	Olympics	7	1	0	1	4	....	....	....	....	....	....	....	....	....	....	....	....	....	....	....	....	....	
1998-99	**Anaheim**	**NHL**	74	2	14	16	65	1	0	0	123	1.6	1	0	0.0	22:03	3	0	0	0	4	0	0	0	15:
99-2000	**Anaheim**	**NHL**	71	5	5	10	94	1	0	0	116	4.3	3	0	0.0	20:21	....	....	....	....	....	....	....	....	
2000-01	**Anaheim**	**NHL**	50	1	5	6	70	0	0	0	73	1.4	–14	0	0.0	20:40	....	....	....	....	....	....	....	....	
2001-02	**Anaheim**	**NHL**	82	4	7	11	97	0	0	1	96	4.2	–10	0	0.0	21:25	....	....	....	....	....	....	....	....	
	Belarus	Olympics	6	2	1	3	4	....	....	....	....	....	....	....	....	....	....	....	....	....	....	....	....	....	
2002-03	**Anaheim**	**NHL**	61	4	8	12	78	0	0	0	93	4.3	2	0	0.0	21:53	21	2	3	5	26	0	0	1	26:
2003-04	**Anaheim**	**NHL**	82	4	11	15	110	0	1	2	145	2.8	–1	0	0.0	23:42	....	....	....	....	....	....	....	....	
2004-05	Ak Bars Kazan	Russia	35	8	12	20	36	....	....	....	....	....	....	....	....	....	4	0	0	0	2	....	....	....	
2005-06	**Anaheim**	**NHL**	78	1	18	19	114	0	0	0	108	0.9	17	2	100.0	22:31	16	3	2	5	18	0	0	1	22:
2006-07	**Florida**	**NHL**	82	6	26	32	102	2	0	0	148	4.1	–13	0	0.0	23:20	....	....	....	....	....	....	....	....	
2007-08	**Florida**	**NHL**	65	3	20	23	75	1	0	0	81	3.7	–5	1	0.0	23:17	....	....	....	....	....	....	....	....	
	Colorado	**NHL**	17	3	4	7	23	0	0	1	30	10.0	1	0	0.0	19:17	10	1	4	5	4	1	0	0	20:
2008-09	**Colorado**	**NHL**	70	4	17	21	72	1	0	0	93	4.3	–4	0	0.0	21:06	....	....	....	....	....	....	....	....	
2009-10	**Colorado**	**NHL**	14	1	5	6	10	0	0	0	22	4.5	–1	0	0.0	18:46	1	0	0	0	0	0	0	0	21:
	Belarus	Olympics	4	1	0	1	0	....	....	....	....	....	....	....	....	....	....	....	....	....	....	....	....	....	
	NHL Totals		842	43	151	194	1017	7	1	4	1246	3.5		3	66.7	21:59	51	6	9	15	52	1	0	2	23:

Signed as a free agent by **Kazan** (Russia), October 20, 2004. Signed as a free agent by **Florida**, July 2, 2006. Traded to **Colorado** by **Florida** for Karlis Skrastins and Colorado's 3rd round choice (Adam Comrie) in 2008 Entry Draft, February 26, 2008. • Missed majority of 2009-10 season recovering from back injury suffered in game at Nashville, October 8, 2009. Signed as a free agent by **Detroit**, August 9, 2010.

SALMELA, Anssi

(sahl-MEHL-ah, AN-see) **N**

Defense. Shoots left. 6'1", 200 lbs. Born, Nokia, Finland, August 13, 1984.

Season	Club	League	GP	G	A	Pts	PIM	PP	SH	GW	S	%	+/-	TF	F%	Min	GP	G	A	Pts	PIM	PP	SH	GW	M
2000-01	Tappara U18	Fin-U18	32	7	3	10	24	....	....	....	....	....	....	....	....	....	2	0	1	1	4	....	....	....	
2001-02	Tappara U18	Fin-U18	11	6	4	10	12	....	....	....	....	....	....	....	....	....	....	....	....	....	....	....	....	....	
	Tappara Jr.	Fin-Jr.	26	3	4	7	22	....	....	....	....	....	....	....	....	....	2	2	1	3	0	....	....	....	
2002-03	Tappara Jr.	Fin-Jr.	23	5	9	14	22	....	....	....	....	....	....	....	....	....	....	....	....	....	....	....	....	....	
2003-04	Suomi U20	Finland-2	5	2	2	4	0	....	....	....	....	....	....	....	....	....	....	....	....	....	....	....	....	....	
	Tappara Jr.	Fin-Jr.	27	10	9	19	22	....	....	....	....	....	....	....	....	....	12	5	3	8	4	....	....	....	
	Tappara Tampere	Finland	10	0	0	0	2	....	....	....	....	....	....	....	....	....	3	0	0	0	2	....	....	....	
2004-05	Tappara Jr.	Fin-Jr.	10	2	4	6	6	....	....	....	....	....	....	....	....	....	1	0	0	0	0	....	....	....	
	Tappara Tampere	Finland	48	1	5	6	49	....	....	....	....	....	....	....	....	....	8	0	0	0	0	....	....	....	
2005-06	Tappara Tampere	Finland	8	0	1	1	0	....	....	....	....	....	....	....	....	....	....	....	....	....	....	....	....	....	
	Pelicans Lahti	Finland	40	8	7	15	59	....	....	....	....	....	....	....	....	....	....	....	....	....	....	....	....	....	
2006-07	Pelicans Lahti	Finland	56	11	12	23	58	....	....	....	....	....	....	....	....	....	6	1	1	2	4	....	....	....	
2007-08	Tappara Tampere	Finland	56	16	16	32	40	....	....	....	....	....	....	....	....	....	11	0	6	6	14	....	....	....	
2008-09	**New Jersey**	**NHL**	17	0	3	3	6	0	0	0	33	0.0	1	0	0.0	15:10	....	....	....	....	....	....	....	....	
	Lowell Devils	AHL	38	8	16	24	41	....	....	....	....	....	....	....	....	....	....	....	....	....	....	....	....	....	
	Atlanta	**NHL**	9	1	2	3	2	1	0	0	8	12.5	0	0	0.0	17:31	....	....	....	....	....	....	....	....	
	Chicago Wolves	AHL	2	0	0	0	0	....	....	....	....	....	....	....	....	....	....	....	....	....	....	....	....	....	
2009-10	**Atlanta**	**NHL**	29	1	4	5	22	0	0	0	27	3.7	4	0	0.0	13:10	....	....	....	....	....	....	....	....	
	New Jersey	**NHL**	9	1	2	3	0	0	1	0	14	7.1	–5	0	0.0	14:27	....	....	....	....	....	....	....	....	
	NHL Totals		64	3	11	14	30	1	1	0	82	3.7		0	0.0	14:30	....	....	....	....	....	....	....	....	

Signed as a free agent by **New Jersey**, May 30, 2008. Traded to **Atlanta** by **New Jersey** for Niclas Havelid and Myles Stoesz, March 2, 2009. Traded to **New Jersey** by **Atlanta** with Ilya Kovalchuk and Atlanta's 2nd round choice (Jonathon Merrill) in 2010 Entry Draft for Johnny Oduya, Niclas Bergfors, Patrice Cormier and New Jersey's 1st (later traded to Chicago - Chicago selected Kevin Hayes) and 2nd (later traded to Chicago - Chicago selected Justin Holl) round choices in 2010 Entry Draft, February 4, 2010. • Missed majority of 2009-10 season as a healthy reserve.

SALO, Sami

(SA-loh, SA-mee) **VAN.**

Defense. Shoots right. 6'3", 212 lbs. Born, Turku, Finland, September 2, 1974. Ottawa's 7th choice, 239th overall, in 1996 Entry Draft.

Season	Club	League	GP	G	A	Pts	PIM	PP	SH	GW	S	%	+/-	TF	F%	Min	Playoffs GP	G	A	Pts	PIM	PP	SH	GW	Min
1991-92	Kiekko-67 Jr.	Fin-Jr.	23	4	5	9	26																		
1992-93	Kiekko-67 Jr.	Fin-Jr.	21	9	4	13	4																		
1993-94	TPS Turku Jr.	Fin-Jr.	36	7	13	20	16										7	0	1	1	10				
1994-95	TPS Turku Jr.	Fin-Jr.	14	1	3	4	6																		
	Kiekko-67 Turku	Finland-2	19	4	2	6	4																		
	TPS Turku	Finland	7	1	2	3	6										1	0	0	0	0				
1995-96	TPS Turku	Finland	47	7	14	21	32										11	1	3	4	8				
1996-97	TPS Turku	Finland	48	9	6	15	10										10	2	3	5	4				
	TPS Turku	EuroHL	6	0	2	2	6										2	0	0	0	2				
1997-98	Jokerit Helsinki	Finland	35	3	5	8	24										8	0	1	1	2				
	Jokerit Helsinki	EuroHL	6	1	1	2	2																		
1998-99	**Ottawa**	**NHL**	61	7	12	19	24	2	0	1	106	6.6	20	0	0.0	19:42	4	0	0	0	0	0	0	0	21:32
	Detroit Vipers	IHL	5	0	2	2	0																		
99-2000	**Ottawa**	**NHL**	37	6	8	14	2	3	0	1	85	7.1	6	0	0.0	20:18	6	1	1	2	0	1	0	0	24:11
2000-01	**Ottawa**	**NHL**	31	2	16	18	10	1	0	0	61	3.3	9	0	0.0	19:44	4	0	0	0	0	0	0	0	22:30
2001-02	**Ottawa**	**NHL**	66	4	14	18	14	1	1	2	122	3.3	1	0	0.0	19:52	12	2	1	3	4	0	0	0	20:23
	Finland	Olympics	4	0	0	0	0																		
2002-03	**Vancouver**	**NHL**	79	9	21	30	10	4	0	1	126	7.1	9	0	0.0	20:08	12	1	3	4	0	0	0	0	20:52
2003-04	**Vancouver**	**NHL**	74	7	19	26	22	5	0	2	143	4.9	8	1	100.0	22:14	7	1	2	3	2	1	0	0	22:59
2004-05	Frolunda	Sweden	41	6	8	14	18										14	1	6	7	2				
2005-06	**Vancouver**	**NHL**	59	10	23	33	38	9	0	2	140	7.1	9	0	0.0	24:30									
	Finland	Olympics	6	1	3	4	0																		
2006-07	**Vancouver**	**NHL**	67	14	23	37	26	5	0	6	143	9.8	21	0	0.0	21:27	10	0	1	1	4	0	0	0	25:53
2007-08	**Vancouver**	**NHL**	63	8	17	25	38	6	0	1	122	6.6	8	0	0.0	23:39									
2008-09	**Vancouver**	**NHL**	60	5	20	25	26	5	0	2	110	4.5	5	0	0.0	20:11	7	3	4	7	2	2	0	2	18:36
2009-10	**Vancouver**	**NHL**	68	9	19	28	18	6	0	3	119	7.6	14	0	0.0	20:41	12	1	5	6	2	1	0	0	20:40
	Finland	Olympics	6	1	1	2	4																		
	NHL Totals		665	81	192	273	228	47	1	21	1277	6.3		1	100.0	21:12	74	9	17	26	14	5	0	2	21:49

NHL All-Rookie Team (1999)

• Missed majority of 1999-2000 season recovering from wrist injury suffered in game vs. Philadelphia, November 28, 1999. • Missed majority of 2000-01 season recovering from shoulder injury suffered in game vs. Atlanta, December 14, 2000. Traded to **Vancouver** by **Ottawa** for Peter Schaefer, September 21, 2002. Signed as a free agent by **Frolunda** (Sweden), September 24, 2004.

SALVADOR, Bryce

(SAL-vuh-dohr, BRIGHS) **N.J.**

Defense. Shoots left. 6'3", 215 lbs. Born, Brandon, Man., February 11, 1976. Tampa Bay's 6th choice, 138th overall, in 1994 Entry Draft.

Season	Club	League	GP	G	A	Pts	PIM	PP	SH	GW	S	%	+/-	TF	F%	Min	Playoffs GP	G	A	Pts	PIM	PP	SH	GW	Min
1991-92	Brandon	MAHA	52	6	23	29	38																		
1992-93	Lethbridge	WHL	64	1	4	5	29										4	0	0	0	0				
1993-94	Lethbridge	WHL	61	4	14	18	36										9	0	1	1	2				
1994-95	Lethbridge	WHL	67	1	9	10	88																		
1995-96	Lethbridge	WHL	56	4	12	16	75										3	0	1	1	2				
1996-97	Lethbridge	WHL	63	8	32	40	81										19	0	7	7	14				
1997-98	Worcester IceCats	AHL	46	2	8	10	74										11	0	1	1	45				
1998-99	Worcester IceCats	AHL	69	5	13	18	129										4	0	1	1	2				
99-2000	Worcester IceCats	AHL	55	0	13	13	53										9	0	1	1	2				
2000-01	**St. Louis**	**NHL**	75	2	8	10	69	0	0	1	60	3.3	–4	1	0.0	16:38	14	2	0	2	18	0	0	1	14:41
2001-02	**St. Louis**	**NHL**	66	5	7	12	78	1	0	2	37	13.5	3	0	0.0	16:55	10	0	1	1	4	0	0	0	12:34
2002-03	**St. Louis**	**NHL**	71	2	8	10	95	1	0	0	73	2.7	7	0	0.0	18:57	7	0	0	0	2	0	0	0	17:17
2003-04	**St. Louis**	**NHL**	69	3	5	8	47	0	0	1	60	5.0	–4	0	0.0	17:29	5	0	0	0	2	0	0	0	14:31
	Worcester IceCats	AHL	2	0	1	1	0																		
2004-05	Missouri	UHL	7	0	0	0	16										3	0	0	0	0				
2005-06	**St. Louis**	**NHL**	46	1	4	5	26	0	0	0	23	4.3	–24	1	0.0	19:48									
2006-07	**St. Louis**	**NHL**	64	2	5	7	55	0	0	0	40	5.0	–5	0	0.0	19:44									
2007-08	**St. Louis**	**NHL**	56	1	10	11	43	0	0	1	29	3.4	12	1	0.0	19:38									
	New Jersey	**NHL**	8	0	0	0	11	0	0	0	0	0.0	0	0	0.0	20:54	5	1	0	1	2	0	0	0	17:55
2008-09	**New Jersey**	**NHL**	76	3	13	16	78	0	0	2	68	4.4	–1	1	100.0	19:29	4	0	0	0	4	0	0	0	15:29
2009-10	**New Jersey**	**NHL**	79	4	10	14	57	0	0	2	47	8.5	8	0	0.0	18:52	5	0	0	0	6	0	0	0	16:04
	NHL Totals		610	23	70	93	559	2	0	9	437	5.3		4	25.0	18:34	50	3	1	4	38	0	0	1	15:08

Signed as a free agent by **St. Louis**, December 16, 1996. Signed as a free agent by **Missouri** (UHL), March 11, 2005. Traded to **New Jersey** by **St. Louis** for Cam Janssen, February 26, 2008.

SAMSON, Jerome

(SAM-sohn, jeh-ROHM) **CAR.**

Right wing. Shoots right. 6', 195 lbs. Born, Greenfield Park, Que., September 4, 1987.

Season	Club	League	GP	G	A	Pts	PIM	PP	SH	GW	S	%	+/-	TF	F%	Min	Playoffs GP	G	A	Pts	PIM	PP	SH	GW	Min
2004-05	Moncton Wildcats	QMJHL	63	6	11	17	22										12	1	4	5	8				
2005-06	Moncton Wildcats	QMJHL	62	20	32	52	46										21	6	12	18	15				
2006-07	Moncton Wildcats	QMJHL	38	19	33	52	20																		
	Val-d'Or Foreurs	QMJHL	33	25	22	47	16										20	14	12	26	10				
2007-08	Albany River Rats	AHL	65	21	18	39	38										7	1	1	2	2				
2008-09	Albany River Rats	AHL	70	22	32	54	56																		
2009-10	**Carolina**	**NHL**	7	0	2	2	10	0	0	0	17	0.0	–1	1	0.0	8:27									
	Albany River Rats	AHL	74	37	41	78	66										8	6	3	9	8				
	NHL Totals		7	0	2	2	10	0	0	0	17	0.0		1	0.0	8:27									

Signed as a free agent by **Carolina**, July 2, 2007.

SAMSONOV, Sergei

(sam-SAW-nahf, SAIR-gay) **CAR.**

Left wing. Shoots right. 5'8", 188 lbs. Born, Moscow, USSR, October 27, 1978. Boston's 2nd choice, 8th overall, in 1997 Entry Draft.

Season	Club	League	GP	G	A	Pts	PIM	PP	SH	GW	S	%	+/-	TF	F%	Min	Playoffs GP	G	A	Pts	PIM	PP	SH	GW	Min
1994-95	CSKA Moscow 2	CIS-2	50	110	72	182																			
	CSKA Moscow	CIS	13	2	2	4	14										2	0	0	0	0				
1995-96	CSKA Moscow	CIS	51	21	17	38	12										3	1	1	2	4				
1996-97	Detroit Vipers	IHL	73	29	35	64	18										19	8	4	12	12				
1997-98	**Boston**	**NHL**	81	22	25	47	8	7	0	3	159	13.8	9				6	2	5	7	0	0	0	1	
1998-99	**Boston**	**NHL**	79	25	26	51	18	6	0	8	160	15.6	–6	0	0.0	16:23	11	3	1	4	0	0	0	0	16:11
99-2000	**Boston**	**NHL**	77	19	26	45	4	6	0	3	145	13.1	–6	3	0.0	16:32									
2000-01	**Boston**	**NHL**	82	29	46	75	18	3	0	3	215	13.5	6	14	42.9	19:23									
2001-02	**Boston**	**NHL**	74	29	41	70	27	3	0	4	192	15.1	21	1	0.0	18:47	6	2	2	4	0	0	0	0	17:41
	Russia	Olympics	6	1	2	3	4																		
2002-03	**Boston**	**NHL**	8	5	6	11	2	1	0	3	23	21.7	8	0	0.0	20:20	5	0	2	2	0	0	0	0	17:07
2003-04	**Boston**	**NHL**	58	17	23	40	4	3	0	5	132	12.9	12	4	25.0	17:27	7	2	5	7	0	0	0	0	17:18
2004-05	Dynamo Moscow	Russia	3	1	0	1	0										3	1	2	3	0				
2005-06	**Boston**	**NHL**	55	18	19	37	22	6	0	1	107	16.8	–3	1	100.0	16:53									
	Edmonton	**NHL**	19	5	11	16	6	4	0	0	36	13.9	0	2	0.0	15:26	24	4	11	15	14	1	0	0	14:30
2006-07	**Montreal**	**NHL**	63	9	17	26	10	0	0	0	114	7.9	–4	14	14.3	13:59									
2007-08	**Chicago**	**NHL**	23	0	4	4	6	0	0	0	38	0.0	–7	1	0.0	12:21									
	Rockford IceHogs	AHL	2	1	0	1	0																		
	Carolina	**NHL**	38	14	18	32	10	3	0	2	71	19.7	6	2	0.0	18:02									
2008-09	**Carolina**	**NHL**	81	16	32	48	28	3	0	3	155	10.3	–8	7	57.1	17:19	17	5	3	8	6	0	0	0	15:48
2009-10	**Carolina**	**NHL**	72	14	15	29	32	2	0	2	104	13.5	–15	4	0.0	13:23									
	NHL Totals		810	222	309	531	195	47	0	37	1651	13.4		53	26.4	16:41	76	18	29	47	20	1	0	1	15:49

Garry F. Longman Memorial Trophy (IHL – Rookie of the Year) (1997) • NHL All-Rookie Team (1998) • Calder Memorial Trophy (1998)

Played in NHL All-Star Game (2001)

• Missed majority of 2002-03 season recovering from wrist injury suffered in game vs. Columbus, October 18, 2002. Signed as a free agent by **Dynamo Moscow** (Russia), February 2, 2005. Traded to **Edmonton** by **Boston** for Marty Reasoner, Yan Stastny and Edmonton's 2nd round choice (Milan Lucic) in 2006 Entry Draft, March 9, 2006. Signed as a free agent by **Montreal**, July 12, 2006. Traded to **Chicago** by **Montreal** for Jassen Cullimore and Tony Salmelainen, June 16, 2007. Claimed on waivers by **Carolina** from **Chicago**, January 8, 2008.

			Regular Season														Playoffs								
Season	Club	League	GP	G	A	Pts	PIM	PP	SH	GW	S	%	+/-	TF	F%	Min	GP	G	A	Pts	PIM	PP	SH	GW	Min

SAMUELSSON, Mikael

(SAM-yuhl-suhn, MIH-kigh-ehl) **VAN.**

Right wing. Shoots right. 6'2", 218 lbs. Born, Mariefred, Sweden, December 23, 1976. San Jose's 7th choice, 145th overall, in 1998 Entry Draft.

1994-95	Sodertalje SK Jr.	Swe-Jr.	30	8	6	14	12	....	....	....	....	....	....	....	....	....	....	....	....	....	....	....	....	....	....
1995-96	Sodertalje SK Jr.	Swe-Jr.	22	13	12	25	20	....	....	....	....	....	....	....	....	....	....	....	....	....	....	....	....	....	....
	Sodertalje SK	Sweden-2	18	5	1	6	0	....	....	....	....	....	....	....	....	....	4	0	0	0	0	....	....	....	....
1996-97	Sodertalje SK Jr.	Swe-Jr.	2	2	1	3	....	....	....	....	....	....	....	....	....	....	....	....	....	....	....	....	....	....	....
	Sodertalje SK	Sweden	29	3	2	5	10	....	....	....	....	....	....	....	....	....	10	0	0	0	4	....	....	....	....
1997-98	Nykoping	Sweden-2	10	5	1	6	14	....	....	....	....	....	....	....	....	....	....	....	....	....	....	....	....	....	....
	Sodertalje SK	Sweden	41	11	9	20	66	....	....	....	....	....	....	....	....	....	....	....	....	....	....	....	....	....	....
1998-99	Sodertalje SK	Sweden-2	18	13	10	23	26	....	....	....	....	....	....	....	....	....	10	2	2	4	12	....	....	....	....
	V.Frolunda	Sweden	27	0	5	5	10	....	....	....	....	....	....	....	....	....	....	....	....	....	....	....	....	....	....
99-2000	Brynas IF Gavle	Sweden	40	4	3	7	76	....	....	....	....	....	....	....	....	....	11	7	2	9	6	....	....	....	....
	Brynas IF Gavle	EuroHL	4	0	2	2	4	....	....	....	....	....	....	....	....	....	....	....	....	....	....	....	....	....	....
2000-01	**San Jose**	**NHL**	4	0	0	0	0	0	0	0	3	0.0	0	0	0.0	4:41	....	....	....	....	....	....	....	....	....
	Kentucky	AHL	66	32	46	78	58	....	....	....	....	....	....	....	....	....	3	1	0	1	0	....	....	....	....
2001-02	**NY Rangers**	**NHL**	67	6	10	16	23	1	2	1	94	6.4	10	5	40.0	11:52	....	....	....	....	....	....	....	....	....
	Hartford	AHL	8	3	6	9	12	....	....	....	....	....	....	....	....	....	....	....	....	....	....	....	....	....	....
2002-03	**NY Rangers**	**NHL**	58	8	14	22	32	1	1	2	118	6.8	0	35	42.9	15:32	....	....	....	....	....	....	....	....	....
	Pittsburgh	**NHL**	22	2	0	2	8	1	0	0	36	5.6	–21	8	75.0	14:04	....	....	....	....	....	....	....	....	....
2003-04	**Florida**	**NHL**	37	3	6	9	35	0	0	1	50	6.0	0	28	28.6	12:15	....	....	....	....	....	....	....	....	....
2004-05	Geneve	Swiss	12	2	4	6	14	....	....	....	....	....	....	....	....	....	....	....	....	....	....	....	....	....	....
	Sodertalje SK	Sweden	29	7	13	20	45	....	....	....	....	....	....	....	....	....	10	3	3	6	24	....	....	....	....
2005-06	Rapperswil	Swiss	1	0	0	0	0	....	....	....	....	....	....	....	....	....	....	....	....	....	....	....	....	....	....
	Detroit	**NHL**	71	23	22	45	42	7	0	3	187	12.3	27	11	27.3	13:31	6	0	1	1	6	0	0	0	15:33
	Sweden	Olympics	8	1	3	4	2	....	....	....	....	....	....	....	....	....	....	....	....	....	....	....	....	....	....
2006-07	**Detroit**	**NHL**	53	14	20	34	28	6	0	2	189	7.4	1	3	66.7	15:09	18	3	8	11	14	1	0	1	15:27
2007-08♦	**Detroit**	**NHL**	73	11	29	40	26	3	0	1	249	4.4	21	14	42.9	16:16	22	5	8	13	8	0	0	1	15:56
2008-09	**Detroit**	**NHL**	81	19	21	40	50	7	0	1	257	7.4	0	8	25.0	15:22	23	5	5	10	6	0	0	2	15:08
2009-10	**Vancouver**	**NHL**	74	30	23	53	64	7	0	4	219	13.7	10	31	35.5	17:10	12	8	7	15	16	3	0	1	17:58
	NHL Totals		**540**	**116**	**145**	**261**	**308**	**33**	**3**	**15**	**1402**	**8.3**		**143**	**38.5**	**14:43**	**81**	**21**	**29**	**50**	**50**	**4**	**0**	**5**	**15:52**

Traded to **NY Rangers** by **San Jose** with Christian Gosselin for Adam Graves and future considerations, June 24, 2001. Traded to **Pittsburgh** by **NY Rangers** with Joel Bouchard, Richard Lintner and Rico Fata for Mike Wilson, Alex Kovalev, Janne Laukkanen and Dan LaCouture, February 10, 2003. Traded to **Florida** by **Pittsburgh** with Pittsburgh's 1st round choice (Nathan Horton) and 2nd round compensatory choice (Stefan Meyer) in 2003 Entry Draft for Florida's 1st (Marc-Andre Fleury) and 3rd (Daniel Carcillo) round choices in 2003 Entry Draft, June 21, 2003. • Missed majority of 2003-04 season recovering from jaw (November 21, 2003 vs. Washington) and hand (January 21, 2004 vs. Columbus) injuries. Signed as a free agent by **Geneve** (Swiss), September 8, 2004. Signed as a free agent by **Sodertalje** (Sweden), October 26, 2004. Signed as a free agent by **Detroit**, September 17, 2005. Signed as a free agent by **Vancouver**, July 3, 2009.

SANGUINETTI, Bobby

(san-GIH-neh-tee, BAW-bee) **CAR.**

Defense. Shoots right. 6'3", 190 lbs. Born, Trenton, NJ, February 29, 1988. NY Rangers' 1st choice, 21st overall, in 2006 Entry Draft.

2003-04	Lawrenceville	High-NJ	26	4	17	21	....	....	....	....	....	....	....	....	....	....	....	....	....	....	....	....	....	....	....
2004-05	Owen Sound	OHL	67	4	20	24	12	....	....	....	....	....	....	....	....	....	5	0	2	2	0	....	....	....	....
2005-06	Owen Sound	OHL	68	14	51	65	44	....	....	....	....	....	....	....	....	....	11	5	10	15	4	....	....	....	....
2006-07	Owen Sound	OHL	67	23	30	53	48	....	....	....	....	....	....	....	....	....	4	3	3	6	2	....	....	....	....
	Hartford	AHL	5	0	3	3	2	....	....	....	....	....	....	....	....	....	7	0	1	1	2	....	....	....	....
2007-08	Brampton	OHL	61	29	41	70	38	....	....	....	....	....	....	....	....	....	5	1	3	4	10	....	....	....	....
	Hartford	AHL	6	0	1	1	2	....	....	....	....	....	....	....	....	....	5	0	0	0	2	....	....	....	....
2008-09	Hartford	AHL	78	6	36	42	42	....	....	....	....	....	....	....	....	....	6	1	4	5	6	....	....	....	....
2009-10	**NY Rangers**	**NHL**	5	0	0	0	4	0	0	0	5	0.0	0	0	0.0	11:32	....	....	....	....	....	....	....	....	....
	Hartford	AHL	61	9	29	38	22	....	....	....	....	....	....	....	....	....	....	....	....	....	....	....	....	....	....
	NHL Totals		**5**	**0**	**0**	**0**	**4**	**0**	**0**	**0**	**5**	**0.0**		**0**	**0.0**	**11:32**	....	....	....	....	....	....	....	....	....

OHL Second All-Star Team (2008)

Traded to **Carolina** by **NY Rangers** for Carolina's 6th round choice (Jesper Fasth) in 2010 Entry Draft and Washington's 2nd round choice (previously acquired) in 2011 Entry Draft, June 25, 2010.

SANTORELLI, Mike

(san-toh-REHL-ee, MIGHK) **FLA.**

Center. Shoots right. 6', 189 lbs. Born, Vancouver, B.C., December 14, 1985. Nashville's 6th choice, 178th overall, in 2004 Entry Draft.

2003-04	Vernon Vipers	BCHL	60	43	53	96	26	....	....	....	....	....	....	....	....	....	5	0	2	2	0	....	....	....	....
2004-05	Northern Mich.	CCHA	40	16	14	30	22	....	....	....	....	....	....	....	....	....	....	....	....	....	....	....	....	....	....
2005-06	Northern Mich.	CCHA	40	15	18	33	24	....	....	....	....	....	....	....	....	....	....	....	....	....	....	....	....	....	....
2006-07	Northern Mich.	CCHA	41	*30	17	47	28	....	....	....	....	....	....	....	....	....	....	....	....	....	....	....	....	....	....
2007-08	Milwaukee	AHL	80	21	21	42	60	....	....	....	....	....	....	....	....	....	6	0	0	0	2	....	....	....	....
2008-09	**Nashville**	**NHL**	7	0	0	0	2	0	0	0	11	0.0	–5	47	44.7	12:15	....	....	....	....	....	....	....	....	....
	Milwaukee	AHL	70	27	43	70	36	....	....	....	....	....	....	....	....	....	11	6	5	11	6	....	....	....	....
2009-10	**Nashville**	**NHL**	25	2	1	3	8	0	0	0	36	5.6	–8	105	45.7	10:57	....	....	....	....	....	....	....	....	....
	Milwaukee	AHL	57	26	33	59	20	....	....	....	....	....	....	....	....	....	7	3	4	7	2	....	....	....	....
	NHL Totals		**32**	**2**	**1**	**3**	**10**	**0**	**0**	**0**	**47**	**4.3**		**152**	**45.4**	**11:14**	....	....	....	....	....	....	....	....	....

CCHA All-Rookie Team (2005) • CCHA First All-Star Team (2007) • NCAA West Second All-American Team (2007)

Traded to **Florida** by **Nashville** for a conditional choice in 2011 Entry Draft, August 5, 2010.

SARICH, Cory

(SAHR-ihch, KOH-ree) **CGY.**

Defense. Shoots right. 6'4", 207 lbs. Born, Saskatoon, Sask., August 16, 1978. Buffalo's 2nd choice, 27th overall, in 1996 Entry Draft.

1994-95	Sask. Contacts	SMHL	31	5	22	27	99	....	....	....	....	....	....	....	....	....	....	....	....	....	....	....	....	....	....
	Saskatoon Blades	WHL	6	0	0	0	4	....	....	....	....	....	....	....	....	....	3	0	1	1	0	....	....	....	....
1995-96	Saskatoon Blades	WHL	59	5	18	23	54	....	....	....	....	....	....	....	....	....	3	0	0	0	4	....	....	....	....
1996-97	Saskatoon Blades	WHL	58	6	27	33	158	....	....	....	....	....	....	....	....	....	....	....	....	....	....	....	....	....	....
1997-98	Saskatoon Blades	WHL	33	5	24	29	90	....	....	....	....	....	....	....	....	....	....	....	....	....	....	....	....	....	....
	Seattle	WHL	13	3	16	19	47	....	....	....	....	....	....	....	....	....	....	....	....	....	....	....	....	....	....
1998-99	**Buffalo**	**NHL**	4	0	0	0	0	0	0	0	2	0.0	3	0	0.0	13:11	....	....	....	....	....	....	....	....	....
	Rochester	AHL	77	3	26	29	82	....	....	....	....	....	....	....	....	....	20	2	4	6	14	....	....	....	....
99-2000	**Buffalo**	**NHL**	42	0	4	4	35	0	0	0	49	0.0	2	0	0.0	17:42	....	....	....	....	....	....	....	....	....
	Rochester	AHL	15	0	6	6	44	....	....	....	....	....	....	....	....	....	....	....	....	....	....	....	....	....	....
	Tampa Bay	**NHL**	17	0	2	2	42	0	0	0	20	0.0	–8	0	0.0	20:42	....	....	....	....	....	....	....	....	....
2000-01	**Tampa Bay**	**NHL**	73	1	8	9	106	0	0	1	66	1.5	–25	3	0.0	18:44	....	....	....	....	....	....	....	....	....
	Detroit Vipers	IHL	3	0	2	2	2	....	....	....	....	....	....	....	....	....	....	....	....	....	....	....	....	....	....
2001-02	**Tampa Bay**	**NHL**	72	0	11	11	105	0	0	0	55	0.0	–4	2	50.0	16:06	....	....	....	....	....	....	....	....	....
	Springfield	AHL	2	0	0	0	0	....	....	....	....	....	....	....	....	....	....	....	....	....	....	....	....	....	....
2002-03	**Tampa Bay**	**NHL**	82	5	9	14	63	0	0	2	79	6.3	–3	3	0.0	19:36	11	0	2	2	6	0	0	0	21:18
2003-04♦	**Tampa Bay**	**NHL**	82	3	16	19	89	0	1	1	93	3.2	5	1	0.0	18:31	23	0	2	2	25	0	0	0	19:11
2004-05			DID NOT PLAY																						
2005-06	**Tampa Bay**	**NHL**	82	1	14	15	79	0	0	0	88	1.1	–2	0	0.0	18:34	5	0	1	1	4	0	0	0	15:46
2006-07	**Tampa Bay**	**NHL**	82	0	15	15	70	0	0	0	64	0.0	–6	1	0.0	18:07	6	0	0	0	2	0	0	0	16:37
2007-08	**Calgary**	**NHL**	80	2	5	7	135	0	0	0	57	3.5	2	0	0.0	18:49	7	0	1	1	4	0	0	0	19:35
2008-09	**Calgary**	**NHL**	76	2	18	20	112	0	0	0	57	3.5	12	0	0.0	17:53	5	0	1	1	4	0	0	0	18:44
2009-10	**Calgary**	**NHL**	57	1	5	6	58	0	0	1	46	2.2	4	0	0.0	15:57	....	....	....	....	....	....	....	....	....
	NHL Totals		**749**	**15**	**107**	**122**	**894**	**0**	**1**	**5**	**676**	**2.2**		**10**	**10.0**	**18:08**	**57**	**0**	**7**	**7**	**45**	**0**	**0**	**0**	**19:02**

WHL West Second All-Star Team (1998) • AHL All-Rookie Team (1999)

Traded to **Tampa Bay** by **Buffalo** with Wayne Primeau, Brian Holzinger and Buffalo's 3rd round choice (Alexander Kharitonov) in 2000 Entry Draft for Chris Gratton and Tampa Bay's 2nd round choice (Derek Roy) in 2001 Entry Draft, March 9, 2000. Signed as a free agent by **Calgary**, July 1, 2007.

SATAN, Miroslav
(shuh-TAN, MEER-oh-slav)

Left wing. Shoots left. 6'3", 191 lbs. Born, Topolcany, Czech., October 22, 1974. Edmonton's 6th choice, 111th overall, in 1993 Entry Draft.

Season	Club	League	GP	G	A	Pts	PIM	PP	SH	GW	S	%	+/-	TF	F%	Min	GP	G	A	Pts	PIM	PP	SH	GW	Min
			Regular Season														Playoffs								
1991-92	Topolcany Jr.	Czech-Jr.	31	30	22	52	....	....	....	....	....	....	....	....	....	....	....	....	....	....	....	....	....	....	....
	VTJ Topolcany	Czech-2	9	2	1	3	6	....	....	....	....	....	....	....	....	....	....	....	....	....	....	....	....	....	....
1992-93	Dukla Trencin	Czech	38	11	6	17	....	....	....	....	....	....	....	....	....	....	....	....	....	....	....	....	....	....	....
1993-94	Dukla Trencin	Slovakia	30	32	16	48	16	....	....	....	....	....	....	....	....	....	....	....	....	....	....	....	....	....	....
	Slovakia	Olympics	8	*9	0	9	0	....	....	....	....	....	....	....	....	....	....	....	....	....	....	....	....	....	....
1994-95	Cape Breton	AHL	25	24	16	40	15	....	....	....	....	....	....	....	....	....	....	....	....	....	....	....	....	....	....
	Detroit Vipers	IHL	8	1	3	4	4	....	....	....	....	....	....	....	....	....	....	....	....	....	....	....	....	....	....
	San Diego Gulls	IHL	6	0	2	2	6	....	....	....	....	....	....	....	....	....	....	....	....	....	....	....	....	....	....
1995-96	**Edmonton**	**NHL**	**62**	**18**	**17**	**35**	**22**	**6**	**0**	**4**	**113**	**15.9**	**0**	....	....	....	....	....	....	....	....	....	....	....	....
1996-97	**Edmonton**	**NHL**	**64**	**17**	**11**	**28**	**22**	**5**	**0**	**2**	**90**	**18.9**	**-4**	....	....	....	....	....	....	....	....	....	....	....	....
	Buffalo	**NHL**	**12**	**8**	**2**	**10**	**4**	**2**	**0**	**1**	**29**	**27.6**	**1**	....	....	....	**7**	**0**	**0**	**0**	**0**	**0**	**0**	**0**	....
1997-98	**Buffalo**	**NHL**	**79**	**22**	**24**	**46**	**34**	**9**	**0**	**4**	**139**	**15.8**	**2**	....	....	....	**14**	**5**	**4**	**9**	**4**	***4**	**0**	**1**	....
1998-99	**Buffalo**	**NHL**	**81**	**40**	**26**	**66**	**44**	**13**	**3**	**6**	**208**	**19.2**	**24**	**9**	**55.6**	**20:49**	**12**	**3**	**5**	**8**	**2**	**1**	**0**	**1**	**21:18**
99-2000	Dukla Trencin	Slovakia	3	2	8	10	2	....	....	....	....	....	....	....	....	....	....	....	....	....	....	....	....	....	....
	Buffalo	**NHL**	**81**	**33**	**34**	**67**	**32**	**5**	**3**	**5**	**265**	**12.5**	**16**	**7**	**14.3**	**20:35**	**5**	**3**	**2**	**5**	**0**	**0**	**0**	**0**	**19:52**
2000-01	**Buffalo**	**NHL**	**82**	**29**	**33**	**62**	**36**	**8**	**2**	**4**	**206**	**14.1**	**5**	**11**	**36.4**	**19:56**	**13**	**3**	**10**	**13**	**8**	**1**	**0**	**0**	**21:18**
2001-02	**Buffalo**	**NHL**	**82**	**37**	**36**	**73**	**33**	**15**	**5**	**5**	**267**	**13.9**	**14**	**4**	**50.0**	**21:10**	....	....	....	....	....	....	....	....	....
	Slovakia	Olympics	2	0	1	1	0	....	....	....	....	....	....	....	....	....	....	....	....	....	....	....	....	....	....
2002-03	**Buffalo**	**NHL**	**79**	**26**	**49**	**75**	**20**	**11**	**1**	**3**	**240**	**10.8**	**-3**	**10**	**20.0**	**21:23**	....	....	....	....	....	....	....	....	....
2003-04	Bratislava	Slovakia	7	6	4	10	41	....	....	....	....	....	....	....	....	....	....	....	....	....	....	....	....	....	....
	Buffalo	**NHL**	**82**	**29**	**28**	**57**	**30**	**11**	**1**	**5**	**206**	**14.1**	**-15**	**9**	**22.2**	**20:02**	....	....	....	....	....	....	....	....	....
2004-05	Bratislava	Slovakia	18	11	9	20	14	....	....	....	....	....	....	....	....	....	18	*15	7	*22	16	....	....	....	....
2005-06	**NY Islanders**	**NHL**	**82**	**35**	**31**	**66**	**54**	**17**	**0**	**2**	**253**	**13.8**	**-8**	**342**	**53.2**	**19:10**	....	....	....	....	....	....	....	....	....
	Slovakia	Olympics	6	0	2	2	2	....	....	....	....	....	....	....	....	....	....	....	....	....	....	....	....	....	....
2006-07	**NY Islanders**	**NHL**	**81**	**27**	**32**	**59**	**46**	**7**	**1**	**2**	**216**	**12.5**	**-12**	**164**	**55.5**	**18:35**	**5**	**1**	**2**	**3**	**0**	**0**	**0**	**0**	**15:15**
2007-08	**NY Islanders**	**NHL**	**80**	**16**	**25**	**41**	**39**	**5**	**0**	**4**	**171**	**9.4**	**-11**	**38**	**50.0**	**18:19**	....	....	....	....	....	....	....	....	....
2008-09 ♦	**Pittsburgh**	**NHL**	**65**	**17**	**19**	**36**	**36**	**6**	**0**	**2**	**120**	**14.2**	**3**	**12**	**41.7**	**15:45**	**17**	**1**	**5**	**6**	**11**	**0**	**0**	**0**	**9:55**
	Wilkes-Barre	AHL	10	3	6	9	4	....	....	....	....	....	....	....	....	....	....	....	....	....	....	....	....	....	....
2009-10	**Boston**	**NHL**	**38**	**9**	**5**	**14**	**12**	**0**	**0**	**1**	**59**	**15.3**	**8**	**26**	**57.7**	**15:46**	**13**	**5**	**5**	**10**	**16**	**2**	**0**	**3**	**18:31**
	Slovakia	Olympics	6	1	1	2	0	....	....	....	....	....	....	....	....	....	....	....	....	....	....	....	....	....	....
	NHL Totals		**1050**	**363**	**372**	**735**	**464**	**120**	**16**	**50**	**2582**	**14.1**		**632**	**51.9**	**19:28**	**86**	**21**	**33**	**54**	**41**	**8**	**0**	**5**	**17:11**

ayed in NHL All-Star Game (2000, 2003)

aded to **Buffalo** by **Edmonton** for Barrie Moore and Craig Millar, March 18, 1997. Signed as a free agent by **Bratislava** (Slovakia), December 29, 2004. Signed as a free agent by **NY Islanders**, August 2005. Signed as a free agent by **Pittsburgh**, July 3, 2008. Signed as a free agent by **Boston**, January 3, 2010.

SAUER, Kurt
(SAW-uhr, KUHRT) **PHX.**

Defense. Shoots left. 6'4", 222 lbs. Born, St. Cloud, MN, January 16, 1981. Colorado's 5th choice, 88th overall, in 2000 Entry Draft.

Season	Club	League	GP	G	A	Pts	PIM	PP	SH	GW	S	%	+/-	TF	F%	Min	GP	G	A	Pts	PIM	PP	SH	GW	Min
1998-99	North Iowa	USHL	52	1	4	5	67	....	....	....	....	....	....	....	....	....	....	....	....	....	....	....	....	....	....
99-2000	Spokane Chiefs	WHL	71	3	12	15	48	....	....	....	....	....	....	....	....	....	15	2	1	3	8	....	....	....	....
2000-01	Spokane Chiefs	WHL	48	5	10	15	85	....	....	....	....	....	....	....	....	....	3	1	0	1	2	....	....	....	....
2001-02	Spokane Chiefs	WHL	61	4	20	24	73	....	....	....	....	....	....	....	....	....	11	0	3	3	12	....	....	....	....
2002-03	**Anaheim**	**NHL**	**80**	**1**	**2**	**3**	**74**	**0**	**0**	**0**	**50**	**2.0**	**-23**	**0**	**0.0**	**18:33**	**21**	**1**	**1**	**2**	**6**	**0**	**1**	**1**	**20:45**
2003-04	**Anaheim**	**NHL**	**55**	**1**	**4**	**5**	**32**	**0**	**0**	**0**	**32**	**3.1**	**-8**	**0**	**0.0**	**16:54**	....	....	....	....	....	....	....	....	....
	Colorado	**NHL**	**14**	**0**	**1**	**1**	**19**	**0**	**0**	**0**	**12**	**0.0**	**-3**	**0**	**0.0**	**15:04**	**3**	**0**	**0**	**0**	**0**	**0**	**0**	**0**	**11:56**
2004-05			DID NOT PLAY																						
2005-06	**Colorado**	**NHL**	**37**	**1**	**4**	**5**	**24**	**0**	**0**	**0**	**19**	**5.3**	**5**	**0**	**0.0**	**12:48**	**9**	**0**	**0**	**0**	**4**	**0**	**0**	**0**	**8:39**
	Lowell	AHL	4	0	0	0	0	....	....	....	....	....	....	....	....	....	....	....	....	....	....	....	....	....	....
2006-07	**Colorado**	**NHL**	**48**	**0**	**6**	**6**	**24**	**0**	**0**	**0**	**29**	**0.0**	**-3**	**0**	**0.0**	**18:20**	....	....	....	....	....	....	....	....	....
2007-08	**Colorado**	**NHL**	**54**	**1**	**5**	**6**	**41**	**0**	**0**	**0**	**28**	**3.6**	**17**	**0**	**0.0**	**18:41**	**10**	**1**	**0**	**1**	**8**	**0**	**0**	**0**	**19:23**
2008-09	**Phoenix**	**NHL**	**68**	**1**	**6**	**7**	**36**	**0**	**0**	**0**	**33**	**3.0**	**-1**	**1**	**0.0**	**20:37**	....	....	....	....	....	....	....	....	....
2009-10	**Phoenix**	**NHL**	**1**	**0**	**0**	**0**	**0**	**0**	**0**	**0**	**2**	**0.0**	**1**	**0**	**0.0**	**16:32**	....	....	....	....	....	....	....	....	....
	NHL Totals		**357**	**5**	**28**	**33**	**250**	**0**	**0**	**0**	**205**	**2.4**		**1**	**0.0**	**17:56**	**43**	**2**	**1**	**3**	**18**	**0**	**1**	**1**	**17:17**

HL West First All-Star Team (2002)

gned as a free agent by **Anaheim**, July 6, 2002. Traded to **Colorado** by **Anaheim** with Anaheim's 4th round choice (Raymond Macias) in 2005 Entry Draft for Martin Skoula, February 21, 2004. Signed as ree agent by **Phoenix**, July 1, 2008. • Missed majority of 2009-10 season recovering from upper body injury.

SAUER, Michael
(SAW-uhr, MIGH-kuhl) **NYR**

Defense. Shoots right. 6'3", 220 lbs. Born, St. Cloud, MN, August 7, 1987. NY Rangers' 2nd choice, 40th overall, in 2005 Entry Draft.

Season	Club	League	GP	G	A	Pts	PIM	PP	SH	GW	S	%	+/-	TF	F%	Min	GP	G	A	Pts	PIM	PP	SH	GW	Min
2003-04	St. Cloud Tech	High-MN	18	12	16	28	34	....	....	....	....	....	....	....	....	....	....	....	....	....	....	....	....	....	....
2004-05	Portland	WHL	32	2	11	13	10	....	....	....	....	....	....	....	....	....	....	....	....	....	....	....	....	....	....
2005-06	Portland	WHL	59	8	23	31	68	....	....	....	....	....	....	....	....	....	12	4	2	6	8	....	....	....	....
2006-07	Portland	WHL	33	4	8	12	46	....	....	....	....	....	....	....	....	....	....	....	....	....	....	....	....	....	....
	Medicine Hat	WHL	32	1	10	11	29	....	....	....	....	....	....	....	....	....	23	1	5	6	34	....	....	....	....
2007-08	Hartford	AHL	71	4	7	11	80	....	....	....	....	....	....	....	....	....	2	0	0	0	0	....	....	....	....
2008-09	**NY Rangers**	**NHL**	**3**	**0**	**0**	**0**	**0**	**0**	**0**	**0**	**2**	**0.0**	**-1**	**0**	**0.0**	**9:21**	....	....	....	....	....	....	....	....	....
	Hartford	AHL	64	6	17	23	35	....	....	....	....	....	....	....	....	....	6	0	0	0	10	....	....	....	....
2009-10	Hartford	AHL	42	3	9	12	45	....	....	....	....	....	....	....	....	....	....	....	....	....	....	....	....	....	....
	NHL Totals		**3**	**0**	**0**	**0**	**0**	**0**	**0**	**0**	**2**	**0.0**		**0**	**0.0**	**9:21**	....	....	....	....	....	....	....	....	....

Missed majority of 2004-05 season recovering from recurring hip injury and resulting surgery.

SAVARD, Marc
(suh-VAHRD, MAHRK) **BOS.**

Center. Shoots left. 5'10", 191 lbs. Born, Ottawa, Ont., July 17, 1977. NY Rangers' 3rd choice, 91st overall, in 1995 Entry Draft.

Season	Club	League	GP	G	A	Pts	PIM	PP	SH	GW	S	%	+/-	TF	F%	Min	GP	G	A	Pts	PIM	PP	SH	GW	Min
1992-93	Metcalfe Jets	OHA-B	36	*44	55	*99	38	....	....	....	....	....	....	....	....	....	....	....	....	....	....	....	....	....	....
1993-94	Oshawa Generals	OHL	61	18	39	57	20	....	....	....	....	....	....	....	....	....	5	4	3	7	8	....	....	....	....
1994-95	Oshawa Generals	OHL	66	43	96	*139	78	....	....	....	....	....	....	....	....	....	7	5	6	11	8	....	....	....	....
1995-96	Oshawa Generals	OHL	48	28	59	87	77	....	....	....	....	....	....	....	....	....	5	4	5	9	6	....	....	....	....
1996-97	Oshawa Generals	OHL	64	43	*87	*130	94	....	....	....	....	....	....	....	....	....	18	13	*24	*37	20	....	....	....	....
1997-98	**NY Rangers**	**NHL**	**28**	**1**	**5**	**6**	**4**	**0**	**0**	**0**	**32**	**3.1**	**-4**	....	....	....	....	....	....	....	....	....	....	....	....
	Hartford	AHL	58	21	53	74	66	....	....	....	....	....	....	....	....	....	15	8	19	27	24	....	....	....	....
1998-99	**NY Rangers**	**NHL**	**70**	**9**	**36**	**45**	**38**	**4**	**0**	**1**	**116**	**7.8**	**-7**	**956**	**48.4**	**14:35**	....	....	....	....	....	....	....	....	....
	Hartford	AHL	9	3	10	13	16	....	....	....	....	....	....	....	....	....	7	1	12	13	16	....	....	....	....
99-2000	**Calgary**	**NHL**	**78**	**22**	**31**	**53**	**56**	**4**	**0**	**3**	**184**	**12.0**	**-2**	**1021**	**49.6**	**16:36**	....	....	....	....	....	....	....	....	....
2000-01	**Calgary**	**NHL**	**77**	**23**	**42**	**65**	**46**	**10**	**1**	**5**	**197**	**11.7**	**-12**	**1050**	**53.1**	**19:13**	....	....	....	....	....	....	....	....	....
2001-02	**Calgary**	**NHL**	**56**	**14**	**19**	**33**	**48**	**7**	**0**	**3**	**140**	**10.0**	**-18**	**577**	**54.8**	**17:20**	....	....	....	....	....	....	....	....	....
2002-03	**Calgary**	**NHL**	**10**	**1**	**2**	**3**	**8**	**0**	**0**	**0**	**21**	**4.8**	**-3**	**89**	**52.8**	**14:41**	....	....	....	....	....	....	....	....	....
	Atlanta	**NHL**	**57**	**16**	**31**	**47**	**77**	**6**	**0**	**4**	**127**	**12.6**	**-11**	**1247**	**50.9**	**19:50**	....	....	....	....	....	....	....	....	....
2003-04	**Atlanta**	**NHL**	**45**	**19**	**33**	**52**	**85**	**6**	**1**	**3**	**133**	**14.3**	**-8**	**1083**	**49.9**	**22:19**	....	....	....	....	....	....	....	....	....
2004-05	HC Thurgau	Swiss-2	13	9	19	28	10	....	....	....	....	....	....	....	....	....	....	....	....	....	....	....	....	....	....
	SC Bern	Swiss	5	1	2	3	0	....	....	....	....	....	....	....	....	....	....	....	....	....	....	....	....	....	....
2005-06	**Atlanta**	**NHL**	**82**	**28**	**69**	**97**	**100**	**14**	**1**	**4**	**212**	**13.2**	**7**	**1529**	**51.6**	**20:30**	....	....	....	....	....	....	....	....	....
2006-07	**Boston**	**NHL**	**82**	**22**	**74**	**96**	**96**	**10**	**1**	**3**	**221**	**10.0**	**-19**	**1420**	**50.1**	**20:13**	....	....	....	....	....	....	....	....	....
2007-08	**Boston**	**NHL**	**74**	**15**	**63**	**78**	**66**	**4**	**0**	**2**	**196**	**7.7**	**3**	**1555**	**51.6**	**20:31**	**7**	**1**	**5**	**6**	**6**	**0**	**0**	**1**	**17:06**
2008-09	**Boston**	**NHL**	**82**	**25**	**63**	**88**	**70**	**9**	**0**	**5**	**213**	**11.7**	**25**	**1289**	**49.9**	**19:32**	**11**	**6**	**7**	**13**	**4**	**3**	**0**	**2**	**19:36**
2009-10	**Boston**	**NHL**	**41**	**10**	**23**	**33**	**14**	**6**	**0**	**2**	**90**	**11.1**	**2**	**648**	**48.8**	**18:35**	**7**	**1**	**2**	**3**	**12**	**0**	**0**	**1**	**17:22**
	NHL Totals		**782**	**205**	**491**	**696**	**708**	**80**	**4**	**35**	**1882**	**10.9**		**12464**	**50.8**	**18:55**	**25**	**8**	**14**	**22**	**22**	**3**	**0**	**4**	**18:16**

HL Second All-Star Team (1995)
ayed in NHL All-Star Game (2008, 2009)

aded to **Calgary** by **NY Rangers** with NY Rangers 1st round choice (Oleg Saprykin) in 1999 Entry Draft for the rights to Jan Hlavac and Calgary's 1st (Jamie Lundmark) and 3rd (later traded back to algary – Calgary selected Craig Andersson) round choices in 1999 Entry Draft, June 26, 1999. Traded to **Atlanta** by **Calgary** for Ruslan Zainullin, November 15, 2002. Signed as a free agent by **Thurgau** viss-2), October 11, 2004. Signed as a free agent by **Bern** (Swiss), November 23, 2004. Signed as a free agent by **Boston**, July 1, 2006.

SAWADA, Raymond
(suh-WAW-duh, RAY-muhnd) **DAL**

Right wing. Shoots right. 6'2", 207 lbs. Born, Richmond, B.C., February 19, 1985. Dallas' 3rd choice, 52nd overall, in 2004 Entry Draft.

Season	Club	League	GP	G	A	Pts	PIM	PP	SH	GW	S	%	+/-	TF	F%	Min	Playoffs GP	G	A	Pts	PIM	PP	SH	GW	Min
2002-03	Richmond	PIJHL	36	7	17	24	155																		
2003-04	Nanaimo Clippers	BCHL	54	20	32	52	93										25	6	16	22	22				
2004-05	Cornell Big Red	ECAC	35	4	5	9	48																		
2005-06	Cornell Big Red	ECAC	35	7	13	20	20																		
2006-07	Cornell Big Red	ECAC	31	10	11	21	29																		
2007-08	Cornell Big Red	ECAC	36	10	16	26	34																		
	Iowa Stars	AHL	10	2	7	9	14																		
2008-09	**Dallas**	**NHL**	**5**	**1**	**0**	**1**	**0**	**0**	**0**	**0**	**2**	**50.0**	**–1**	**0**	**0.0**	**8:42**									
	Manitoba Moose	AHL	52	6	15	21	31										22	4	4	8	4				
2009-10	**Dallas**	**NHL**	**5**	**0**	**0**	**0**	**0**	**0**	**0**	**0**	**2**	**0.0**	**1**	**0**	**0.0**	**8:09**									
	Texas Stars	AHL	60	8	11	19	92										24	3	5	8	20				
	NHL Totals		**10**	**1**	**0**	**1**	**0**	**0**	**0**	**0**	**4**	**25.0**		**0**	**0.0**	**8:25**									

SBISA, Luca
(S'BEE-za, LOO-ka) **ANA.**

Defense. Shoots left. 6'2", 204 lbs. Born, Ozieri, Italy, January 30, 1990. Philadelphia's 1st choice, 19th overall, in 2008 Entry Draft.

Season	Club	League	GP	G	A	Pts	PIM	PP	SH	GW	S	%	+/-	TF	F%	Min	Playoffs GP	G	A	Pts	PIM	PP	SH	GW	Min
2005-06	EV Zug Jr.	Swiss-Jr.	18	0	3	3	18																		
2006-07	EV Zug Jr.	Swiss-Jr.	STATISTICS NOT AVAILABLE																						
	EHC Seewen	Swiss-3	6	1	2	3	4																		
	EV Zug	Swiss	7	0	0	0	0										1	0	0	0	0				
2007-08	Lethbridge	WHL	62	6	27	33	63										19	3	12	15	17				
2008-09	**Philadelphia**	**NHL**	**39**	**0**	**7**	**7**	**36**	**0**	**0**	**0**	**38**	**0.0**	**–6**	**0**	**0.0**	**17:29**	**1**	**0**	**0**	**0**	**2**	**0**	**0**	**0**	**5:37**
	Lethbridge	WHL	18	4	11	15	19										11	2	1	3	12				
	Philadelphia	AHL	2	1	1	2	2																		
2009-10	**Anaheim**	**NHL**	**8**	**0**	**0**	**0**	**6**	**0**	**0**	**0**	**3**	**0.0**	**–1**	**0**	**0.0**	**12:38**									
	Lethbridge	WHL	17	1	12	13	18																		
	Portland	WHL	12	3	2	5	11										13	2	2	4	26				
	Switzerland	Olympics	5	0	0	0	0																		
	NHL Totals		**47**	**0**	**7**	**7**	**42**	**0**	**0**	**0**	**41**	**0.0**		**0**	**0.0**	**16:39**	**1**	**0**	**0**	**0**	**2**	**0**	**0**	**0**	**5:37**

Traded to **Anaheim** by **Philadelphia** with Joffrey Lupul, Philadelphia's 1st round choices in 2009 (later traded to Columbus - Columbus selected John Moore) and 2010 (Emerson Etem) Entry Drafts and future considerations for Chris Pronger and Ryan Dingle, June 26, 2009.

SCATCHARD, Dave
(SKAT-chuhrd, DAYV) **ST.L.**

Center. Shoots right. 6'3", 210 lbs. Born, Hinton, Alta., February 20, 1976. Vancouver's 3rd choice, 42nd overall, in 1994 Entry Draft.

Season	Club	League	GP	G	A	Pts	PIM	PP	SH	GW	S	%	+/-	TF	F%	Min	Playoffs GP	G	A	Pts	PIM	PP	SH	GW	Min
1991-92	Salmon Arm	Minor-BC	65	98	100	198	167																		
1992-93	Kimberley	RMJHL	51	20	23	43	61																		
1993-94	Portland	WHL	47	9	11	20	46										10	2	1	3	4				
1994-95	Portland	WHL	71	20	30	50	148										8	0	3	3	21				
1995-96	Portland	WHL	59	19	28	47	146										7	1	8	9	14				
	Syracuse Crunch	AHL	1	0	0	0	0										15	2	5	7	29				
1996-97	Syracuse Crunch	AHL	26	8	7	15	65																		
1997-98	**Vancouver**	**NHL**	**76**	**13**	**11**	**24**	**165**	**0**	**0**	**1**	**85**	**15.3**	**–4**												
1998-99	**Vancouver**	**NHL**	**82**	**13**	**13**	**26**	**140**	**0**	**2**	**2**	**130**	**10.0**	**–12**	**1007**	**56.3**	**13:46**									
99-2000	**Vancouver**	**NHL**	**21**	**0**	**4**	**4**	**24**	**0**	**0**	**0**	**25**	**0.0**	**–3**	**190**	**59.5**	**10:12**									
	NY Islanders	**NHL**	**44**	**12**	**14**	**26**	**93**	**0**	**1**	**1**	**103**	**11.7**	**0**	**710**	**55.8**	**13:42**									
2000-01	**NY Islanders**	**NHL**	**81**	**21**	**24**	**45**	**114**	**4**	**0**	**5**	**176**	**11.9**	**–9**	**1322**	**55.1**	**16:50**									
2001-02	**NY Islanders**	**NHL**	**80**	**12**	**15**	**27**	**111**	**3**	**1**	**4**	**117**	**10.3**	**–4**	**788**	**53.8**	**12:31**	**7**	**1**	**1**	**2**	**22**	**0**	**0**	**0**	**12:38**
2002-03	**NY Islanders**	**NHL**	**81**	**27**	**18**	**45**	**108**	**5**	**0**	**2**	**165**	**16.4**	**9**	**1147**	**52.7**	**14:30**	**5**	**1**	**0**	**1**	**6**	**0**	**0**	**1**	**15:58**
2003-04	**NY Islanders**	**NHL**	**61**	**9**	**16**	**25**	**78**	**1**	**1**	**1**	**111**	**8.1**	**12**	**1052**	**52.7**	**16:13**	**5**	**0**	**1**	**1**	**6**	**0**	**0**	**0**	**16:18**
2004-05			DID NOT PLAY																						
2005-06	**Boston**	**NHL**	**16**	**4**	**6**	**10**	**28**	**1**	**0**	**0**	**40**	**10.0**	**–2**	**272**	**54.8**	**16:56**									
	Phoenix	**NHL**	**47**	**11**	**12**	**23**	**84**	**4**	**0**	**3**	**81**	**13.6**	**–11**	**594**	**53.2**	**14:44**									
2006-07	**Phoenix**	**NHL**	**46**	**3**	**5**	**8**	**72**	**0**	**0**	**1**	**77**	**3.9**	**–18**	**385**	**52.5**	**13:31**									
2007-08	Hartford	AHL	3	0	1	1	0																		
	Milwaukee	AHL	8	1	2	3	14																		
2008-09			DID NOT PLAY – INJURED																						
2009-10	**Nashville**	**NHL**	**16**	**3**	**2**	**5**	**17**	**0**	**0**	**0**	**25**	**12.0**	**3**	**81**	**51.9**	**10:42**									
	Milwaukee	AHL	36	20	10	30	59										3	0	0	0	2				
	NHL Totals		**651**	**128**	**140**	**268**	**1034**	**18**	**5**	**20**	**1135**	**11.3**		**7548**	**54.3**	**14:19**	**17**	**2**	**2**	**4**	**34**	**0**	**0**	**1**	**14:41**

Traded to **NY Islanders** by **Vancouver** with Kevin Weekes and Bill Muckalt for Felix Potvin, NY Islanders' 2nd round compensatory choice (later traded to New Jersey – New Jersey selected Teemu Laine) in 2000 Entry Draft and NY Islanders' 3rd round choice (Thatcher Bell) in 2000 Entry Draft, December 19, 1999. Signed as a free agent by **Boston**, August 2, 2005. Traded to **Phoenix** by **Boston** for David Tanabe, November 18, 2005. Signed to a PTO (professional tryout) contract by **Hartford** (AHL), October 17, 2007. Signed to a PTO (professional tryout) contract by **Milwaukee** (AHL), November 15, 2007. • Missed entire 2008-09 season recovering from head injury. Signed as a free agent by **Nashville**, October 7, 2009. Signed as a free agent by **St. Louis**, August 4, 2010.

SCHENN, Brayden
(SHEHN, BRAY-duhn) **L.A.**

Center. Shoots left. 6'1", 192 lbs. Born, Saskatoon, Sask., August 22, 1991. Los Angeles' 1st choice, 5th overall, in 2009 Entry Draft.

Season	Club	League	GP	G	A	Pts	PIM	PP	SH	GW	S	%	+/-	TF	F%	Min	Playoffs GP	G	A	Pts	PIM	PP	SH	GW	Min
2006-07	Sask. Contacts	SMHL	41	27	43	70	63																		
2007-08	Brandon	WHL	66	28	43	71	48										6	2	1	3	14				
2008-09	Brandon	WHL	70	32	56	88	82										12	8	10	18	12				
2009-10	**Los Angeles**	**NHL**	**1**	**0**	**0**	**0**	**0**	**0**	**0**	**0**	**0**	**0.0**	**–1**	**14**	**28.6**	**12:31**									
	Brandon	WHL	59	34	65	99	55										15	8	11	19	2				
	NHL Totals		**1**	**0**	**0**	**0**	**0**	**0**	**0**	**0**	**0**	**0.0**		**14**	**28.6**	**12:31**									

WHL Rookie of the Year (2008) • Canadian Major Junior All-Rookie Team (2008) • WHL East Second All-Star Team (2009) • WHL East First All-Star Team (2010)

SCHENN, Luke
(SHEHN, LEWK) **TOR.**

Defense. Shoots right. 6'2", 215 lbs. Born, Saskatoon, Sask., November 2, 1989. Toronto's 1st choice, 5th overall, in 2008 Entry Draft.

Season	Club	League	GP	G	A	Pts	PIM	PP	SH	GW	S	%	+/-	TF	F%	Min	Playoffs GP	G	A	Pts	PIM	PP	SH	GW	Min
2004-05	Sask. Contacts	SMHL	41	5	22	27	69																		
2005-06	Kelowna Rockets	WHL	60	3	8	11	86										12	0	0	0	14				
2006-07	Kelowna Rockets	WHL	72	2	27	29	139																		
2007-08	Kelowna Rockets	WHL	57	7	21	28	100										7	2	2	4	6				
2008-09	**Toronto**	**NHL**	**70**	**2**	**12**	**14**	**71**	**1**	**0**	**0**	**102**	**2.0**	**–12**	**0**	**0.0**	**21:32**									
2009-10	**Toronto**	**NHL**	**79**	**5**	**12**	**17**	**50**	**0**	**0**	**1**	**101**	**5.0**	**2**	**0**	**0.0**	**16:53**									
	NHL Totals		**149**	**7**	**24**	**31**	**121**	**1**	**0**	**1**	**203**	**3.4**		**0**	**0.0**	**19:04**									

WHL West Second All-Star Team (2008) • NHL All-Rookie Team (2009)

SCHLEMKO, David
(SHLEHM-koh, DAY-vihd) **PHX.**

Defense. Shoots left. 6'2", 196 lbs. Born, Edmonton, Alta., May 7, 1987.

Season	Club	League	GP	G	A	Pts	PIM	PP	SH	GW	S	%	+/-	TF	F%	Min	Playoffs GP	G	A	Pts	PIM	PP	SH	GW	Min
2004-05	Medicine Hat	WHL	65	5	24	29	23										13	0	3	3	10				
2005-06	Medicine Hat	WHL	69	9	35	44	44										13	2	5	7	15				
2006-07	Medicine Hat	WHL	64	8	50	58	78										23	3	13	16	12				
2007-08	San Antonio	AHL	1	0	0	0	4																		
	Arizona Sundogs	CHL	58	10	29	39	24										14	3	5	8	6				
2008-09	**Phoenix**	**NHL**	**3**	**0**	**1**	**1**	**0**	**0**	**0**	**0**	**3**	**0.0**	**–2**	**0**	**0.0**	**19:16**									
	San Antonio	AHL	68	7	22	29	20																		
2009-10	**Phoenix**	**NHL**	**17**	**1**	**4**	**5**	**8**	**0**	**0**	**0**	**19**	**5.3**	**1**	**0**	**0.0**	**17:49**									
	San Antonio	AHL	55	5	26	31	30																		
	NHL Totals		**20**	**1**	**5**	**6**	**8**	**0**	**0**	**0**	**22**	**4.5**		**0**	**0.0**	**18:02**									

WHL East Second All-Star Team (2007)
Signed as a free agent by **Phoenix**, July 19, 2007.

SCHNEIDER, Mathieu

(SHNIGH-duhr, MA-thew)

Defense. Shoots left. 5'11", 192 lbs. Born, New York, NY, June 12, 1969. Montreal's 4th choice, 44th overall, in 1987 Entry Draft.

			Regular Season														Playoffs								
Season	**Club**	**League**	**GP**	**G**	**A**	**Pts**	**PIM**	**PP**	**SH**	**GW**	**S**	**%**	**+/-**	**TF**	**F%**	**Min**	**GP**	**G**	**A**	**Pts**	**PIM**	**PP**	**SH**	**GW**	**Min**
1985-86	Mount St. Charles	High-RI	19	3	27	30	....	....	....	....	....	....	....	....	....	....	....	....	....	....	....	....	....	....	....
1986-87	Cornwall Royals	OHL	63	7	29	36	75	....	....	....	....	....	....	....	....	....	5	0	0	0	22	....	....	....	....
1987-88	Cornwall Royals	OHL	48	21	40	61	83	....	....	....	....	....	....	....	....	....	11	2	6	8	14	....	....	....	....
	Montreal	**NHL**	**4**	**0**	**0**	**0**	**2**	**0**	**0**	**0**	**2**	**0.0**	**-1**	....	....	....	....	....	....	....	....	....	....	....	....
	Sherbrooke	AHL	....	....	....	....	....	....	....	....	....	....	....	....	....	....	3	0	3	3	12	....	....	....	....
1988-89	Cornwall Royals	OHL	59	16	57	73	96	....	....	....	....	....	....	....	....	....	18	7	20	27	30	....	....	....	....
1989-90	**Montreal**	**NHL**	**44**	**7**	**14**	**21**	**25**	**5**	**0**	**1**	**84**	**8.3**	**2**	....	....	....	**9**	**1**	**3**	**4**	**31**	**1**	**0**	**0**	....
	Sherbrooke	AHL	28	6	13	19	20	....	....	....	....	....	....	....	....	....	....	....	....	....	....	....	....	....	....
1990-91	**Montreal**	**NHL**	**69**	**10**	**20**	**30**	**63**	**5**	**0**	**3**	**164**	**6.1**	**7**	....	....	....	**13**	**2**	**7**	**9**	**18**	**1**	**0**	**0**	....
1991-92	**Montreal**	**NHL**	**78**	**8**	**24**	**32**	**72**	**2**	**0**	**1**	**194**	**4.1**	**10**	....	....	....	**10**	**1**	**4**	**5**	**6**	**1**	**0**	**0**	....
1992-93 ♦	**Montreal**	**NHL**	**60**	**13**	**31**	**44**	**91**	**3**	**0**	**2**	**169**	**7.7**	**8**	....	....	....	**11**	**1**	**2**	**3**	**16**	**0**	**0**	**0**	....
1993-94	**Montreal**	**NHL**	**75**	**20**	**32**	**52**	**62**	**11**	**0**	**4**	**193**	**10.4**	**15**	....	....	....	**1**	**0**	**0**	**0**	**0**	**0**	**0**	**0**	....
1994-95	**Montreal**	**NHL**	**30**	**5**	**15**	**20**	**49**	**2**	**0**	**0**	**82**	**6.1**	**-3**	....	....	....	....	....	....	....	....	....	....	....	....
	NY Islanders	**NHL**	**13**	**3**	**6**	**9**	**30**	**1**	**0**	**2**	**36**	**8.3**	**-5**	....	....	....	....	....	....	....	....	....	....	....	....
1995-96	**NY Islanders**	**NHL**	**65**	**11**	**36**	**47**	**93**	**7**	**0**	**1**	**155**	**7.1**	**-18**	....	....	....	....	....	....	....	....	....	....	....	....
	Toronto	**NHL**	**13**	**2**	**5**	**7**	**10**	**0**	**0**	**0**	**36**	**5.6**	**-2**	....	....	....	**6**	**0**	**4**	**4**	**8**	**0**	**0**	**0**	....
1996-97	**Toronto**	**NHL**	**26**	**5**	**7**	**12**	**20**	**1**	**0**	**1**	**63**	**7.9**	**3**	....	....	....	....	....	....	....	....	....	....	....	....
1997-98	**Toronto**	**NHL**	**76**	**11**	**26**	**37**	**44**	**4**	**1**	**1**	**181**	**6.1**	**-12**	....	....	....	....	....	....	....	....	....	....	....	....
	United States	Olympics	4	0	0	0	6	....	....	....	....	....	....	....	....	....	....	....	....	....	....	....	....	....	....
1998-99	**NY Rangers**	**NHL**	**75**	**10**	**24**	**34**	**71**	**5**	**0**	**2**	**159**	**6.3**	**-19**	**0**	**0.0**	**24:35**	....	....	....	....	....	....	....	....	....
99-2000	**NY Rangers**	**NHL**	**80**	**10**	**20**	**30**	**78**	**3**	**0**	**1**	**228**	**4.4**	**-6**	**0**	**0.0**	**22:31**	....	....	....	....	....	....	....	....	....
2000-01	**Los Angeles**	**NHL**	**73**	**16**	**35**	**51**	**56**	**7**	**1**	**2**	**183**	**8.7**	**0**	**0**	**0.0**	**23:04**	**13**	**0**	**9**	**9**	**10**	**0**	**0**	**0**	**25:51**
2001-02	**Los Angeles**	**NHL**	**55**	**7**	**23**	**30**	**68**	**4**	**0**	**0**	**123**	**5.7**	**3**	**0**	**0.0**	**22:25**	**7**	**0**	**1**	**1**	**18**	**0**	**0**	**0**	**22:52**
2002-03	**Los Angeles**	**NHL**	**65**	**14**	**29**	**43**	**57**	**10**	**0**	**1**	**162**	**8.6**	**0**	**0**	**0.0**	**22:20**	....	....	....	....	....	....	....	....	....
	Detroit	**NHL**	**13**	**2**	**5**	**7**	**16**	**1**	**0**	**0**	**37**	**5.4**	**2**	**0**	**0.0**	**22:42**	**4**	**0**	**0**	**0**	**6**	**0**	**0**	**0**	**28:16**
2003-04	**Detroit**	**NHL**	**78**	**14**	**32**	**46**	**56**	**4**	**1**	**4**	**165**	**8.5**	**22**	**4**	**0.0**	**24:29**	**12**	**1**	**2**	**3**	**8**	**1**	**0**	**1**	**26:30**
2004-05			DID NOT PLAY																						
2005-06	**Detroit**	**NHL**	**72**	**21**	**38**	**59**	**86**	**11**	**0**	**4**	**188**	**11.2**	**33**	**4**	**25.0**	**24:31**	**6**	**1**	**7**	**8**	**6**	**0**	**0**	**0**	**26:44**
	United States	Olympics	6	1	2	3	16	....	....	....	....	....	....	....	....	....	....	....	....	....	....	....	....	....	....
2006-07	**Detroit**	**NHL**	**68**	**11**	**41**	**52**	**66**	**2**	**1**	**2**	**184**	**6.0**	**12**	**0**	**0.0**	**23:35**	**11**	**2**	**4**	**6**	**16**	**1**	**0**	**1**	**23:35**
2007-08	**Anaheim**	**NHL**	**65**	**12**	**27**	**39**	**50**	**5**	**0**	**2**	**139**	**8.6**	**22**	**0**	**0.0**	**22:18**	**6**	**1**	**0**	**1**	**8**	**0**	**0**	**0**	**20:29**
2008-09	**Atlanta**	**NHL**	**44**	**4**	**11**	**15**	**50**	**1**	**0**	**0**	**82**	**4.9**	**-10**	**0**	**0.0**	**21:02**	....	....	....	....	....	....	....	....	....
	Montreal	**NHL**	**23**	**5**	**12**	**17**	**14**	**5**	**0**	**2**	**46**	**10.9**	**-2**	**0**	**0.0**	**20:57**	**2**	**0**	**0**	**0**	**4**	**0**	**0**	**0**	**18:58**
2009-10	**Vancouver**	**NHL**	**17**	**2**	**3**	**5**	**12**	**1**	**0**	**0**	**14**	**14.3**	**0**	**0**	**0.0**	**15:15**	....	....	....	....	....	....	....	....	....
	Manitoba Moose	AHL	8	3	2	5	8	....	....	....	....	....	....	....	....	....	....	....	....	....	....	....	....	....	....
	Phoenix	**NHL**	**8**	**0**	**4**	**4**	**4**	**0**	**0**	**0**	**23**	**0.0**	**5**	**0**	**0.0**	**20:50**	**3**	**1**	**0**	**1**	**0**	**1**	**0**	**0**	**13:38**
	NHL Totals		**1289**	**223**	**520**	**743**	**1245**	**100**	**4**	**36**	**3092**	**7.2**		**8**	**12.5**	**22:55**	**114**	**11**	**43**	**54**	**155**	**6**	**0**	**2**	**24:12**

OHL First All-Star Team (1988, 1989)

Played in NHL All-Star Game (1996, 2003)

Traded to **NY Islanders** by **Montreal** with Kirk Muller and Craig Darby for Pierre Turgeon and Vladimir Malakhov, April 5, 1995. Traded to **Toronto** by **NY Islanders** with Wendel Clark and D.J. Smith for Darby Hendrickson, Sean Haggerty, Kenny Jonsson and Toronto's 1st round choice (Roberto Luongo) in 1997 Entry Draft, March 13, 1996. • Missed majority of 1996-97 season recovering from groin injury suffered in game vs. St. Louis, December 27, 1996. • Rights traded to **NY Rangers** by **Toronto** for Alexander Karpovtsev and NY Rangers' 4th round choice (Mirko Murovic) in 1999 Entry Draft, October 14, 1998. Claimed by **Columbus** from **NY Rangers** in Expansion Draft, June 23, 2000. Signed as a free agent by **Los Angeles**, August 14, 2000. Traded to **Detroit** by **Los Angeles** for Sean Avery, Maxim Kuznetsov, Detroit's 1st round choice (Jeff Tambellini) in 2003 Entry Draft and Detroit's 2nd round choice (later traded to Boston – Boston selected Martins Karsums) in 2004 Entry Draft, March 11, 2003. Signed as a free agent by **Anaheim**, July 1, 2007. Traded to **Atlanta** by **Anaheim** for Ken Klee, Brad Larsen and Chad Painchaud, September 26, 2008. Traded to **Montreal** by **Atlanta** with Atlanta's 3rd round choice (Joonas Nattinen) in 2009 Entry Draft for Anaheim's 2nd round choice (previously acquired, Atlanta selected Jeremy Morin) in 2009 Entry Draft and Montreal's 3rd round choice (Julian Melchiori) in 2010 Entry Draft, February 16, 2009. Signed as a free agent by **Vancouver**, August 28, 2009. Traded to **Phoenix** by **Vancouver** for Sean Zimmerman and Phoenix's 6th round choice (Alex Friesen) in 2010 Entry Draft, March 3, 2010.

SCHREMP, Rob

(SHREHMP, RAWB) **NYI**

Center. Shoots left. 5'11", 200 lbs. Born, Syracuse, NY, July 1, 1986. Edmonton's 2nd choice, 25th overall, in 2004 Entry Draft.

2000-01	Syracuse	OPJHL	49	32	46	78	....	....	....	....	....	....	....	....	....	....	....	....	....	....	....	....	....	....	....
2001-02	Syracuse	OPJHL	47	41	47	88	93	....	....	....	....	....	....	....	....	....	1	1	2	3	0	....	....	....	....
2002-03	Mississauga	OHL	65	26	48	74	25	....	....	....	....	....	....	....	....	....	2	1	0	1	0	....	....	....	....
2003-04	USNTDP	U-18	2	0	0	0	8	....	....	....	....	....	....	....	....	....	....	....	....	....	....	....	....	....	....
	Mississauga	OHL	3	2	4	6	0	....	....	....	....	....	....	....	....	....	....	....	....	....	....	....	....	....	....
	London Knights	OHL	60	28	41	69	18	....	....	....	....	....	....	....	....	....	15	7	6	13	2	....	....	....	....
2004-05	London Knights	OHL	62	41	49	90	54	....	....	....	....	....	....	....	....	....	18	13	16	29	16	....	....	....	....
2005-06	London Knights	OHL	57	*57	*88	*145	74	....	....	....	....	....	....	....	....	....	19	10	*37	*47	35	....	....	....	....
2006-07	**Edmonton**	**NHL**	**1**	**0**	**0**	**0**	**0**	**0**	**0**	**0**	**2**	**0.0**	**0**	**12**	**50.0**	**13:50**	....	....	....	....	....	....	....	....	....
	Wilkes-Barre	AHL	69	17	36	53	36	....	....	....	....	....	....	....	....	....	....	....	....	....	....	....	....	....	....
2007-08	**Edmonton**	**NHL**	**2**	**0**	**0**	**0**	**0**	**0**	**0**	**0**	**3**	**0.0**	**-1**	**1**	**0.0**	**6:57**	....	....	....	....	....	....	....	....	....
	Springfield	AHL	78	23	53	76	64	....	....	....	....	....	....	....	....	....	....	....	....	....	....	....	....	....	....
2008-09	**Edmonton**	**NHL**	**4**	**0**	**3**	**3**	**2**	**0**	**0**	**0**	**3**	**0.0**	**2**	**2**	**50.0**	**13:35**	....	....	....	....	....	....	....	....	....
	Springfield	AHL	69	7	35	42	50	....	....	....	....	....	....	....	....	....	....	....	....	....	....	....	....	....	....
2009-10	**NY Islanders**	**NHL**	**44**	**7**	**18**	**25**	**8**	**5**	**0**	**0**	**74**	**9.5**	**-4**	**395**	**47.3**	**13:54**	....	....	....	....	....	....	....	....	....
	NHL Totals		**51**	**7**	**21**	**28**	**10**	**5**	**0**	**0**	**82**	**8.5**		**410**	**47.3**	**13:36**	....	....	....	....	....	....	....	....	....

OPJHL Rookie of the Year (2001) • OHL All-Rookie Team (2003) • OHL Rookie of the Year (2003) • OHL First All-Star Team (2006) • Canadian Major Junior First All-Star Team (2006)

Claimed on waivers by **NY Islanders** from **Edmonton**, September 29, 2009.

SCHUBERT, Christoph

(SHOO-buhrt, KRIHS-tawf)

Defense. Shoots left. 6'3", 230 lbs. Born, Munich, West Germany, February 5, 1982. Ottawa's 5th choice, 127th overall, in 2001 Entry Draft.

1998-99	EV Landshut Jr.	Ger-Jr.	28	15	20	35	77	....	....	....	....	....	....	....	....	....	....	....	....	....	....	....	....	....	....
99-2000	EV Landshut Jr.	Ger-Jr.	11	14	11	25	51	....	....	....	....	....	....	....	....	....	....	....	....	....	....	....	....	....	....
	EV Landshut	German-3	55	7	5	12	68	....	....	....	....	....	....	....	....	....	....	....	....	....	....	....	....	....	....
2000-01	Munchen Barons	Germany	55	6	3	9	80	....	....	....	....	....	....	....	....	....	10	0	2	2	27	....	....	....	....
2001-02	Munchen Barons	Germany	50	5	11	16	125	....	....	....	....	....	....	....	....	....	9	3	4	7	32	....	....	....	....
2002-03	Binghamton	AHL	70	2	8	10	102	....	....	....	....	....	....	....	....	....	8	0	1	1	2	....	....	....	....
2003-04	Binghamton	AHL	70	2	10	12	69	....	....	....	....	....	....	....	....	....	1	0	0	0	0	....	....	....	....
2004-05	Binghamton	AHL	76	10	22	32	110	....	....	....	....	....	....	....	....	....	6	2	2	4	20	....	....	....	....
2005-06	**Ottawa**	**NHL**	**56**	**4**	**6**	**10**	**48**	**0**	**1**	**0**	**72**	**5.6**	**4**	**5**	**0.0**	**11:06**	**7**	**0**	**1**	**1**	**4**	**0**	**0**	**0**	**7:53**
	Germany	Olympics	5	0	1	1	2	....	....	....	....	....	....	....	....	....	....	....	....	....	....	....	....	....	....
2006-07	**Ottawa**	**NHL**	**80**	**8**	**17**	**25**	**56**	**1**	**0**	**1**	**97**	**8.2**	**30**	**1**	**0.0**	**11:13**	**20**	**0**	**1**	**1**	**22**	**0**	**0**	**0**	**9:10**
2007-08	**Ottawa**	**NHL**	**82**	**8**	**16**	**24**	**64**	**1**	**0**	**0**	**137**	**5.8**	**7**	**4**	**25.0**	**13:34**	**4**	**0**	**0**	**0**	**8**	**0**	**0**	**0**	**11:58**
2008-09	**Ottawa**	**NHL**	**50**	**3**	**3**	**6**	**26**	**1**	**0**	**0**	**57**	**5.3**	**-8**	**0**	**0.0**	**13:36**	....	....	....	....	....	....	....	....	....
2009-10	**Atlanta**	**NHL**	**47**	**2**	**5**	**7**	**69**	**0**	**0**	**0**	**73**	**2.7**	**-6**	**0**	**0.0**	**15:47**	....	....	....	....	....	....	....	....	....
	NHL Totals		**315**	**25**	**47**	**72**	**263**	**3**	**1**	**1**	**436**	**5.7**		**10**	**10.0**	**12:52**	**31**	**0**	**2**	**2**	**34**	**0**	**0**	**0**	**9:14**

Claimed on waivers by **Atlanta** from **Ottawa**, October 2, 2009.

SCHULTZ, Jeff

(SHUHLTZ, JEHF) **WSH.**

Defense. Shoots left. 6'6", 230 lbs. Born, Calgary, Alta., February 25, 1986. Washington's 2nd choice, 27th overall, in 2004 Entry Draft.

2000-01	Calgary Hawks	CBHL	27	7	8	15	20	....	....	....	....	....	....	....	....	....	....	....	....	....	....	....	....	....	....
2001-02	Calgary Rangers	CBHL	27	5	18	23	42	....	....	....	....	....	....	....	....	....	....	....	....	....	....	....	....	....	....
2002-03	Calgary Hitmen	WHL	50	2	1	3	4	....	....	....	....	....	....	....	....	....	4	0	0	0	0	....	....	....	....
2003-04	Calgary Hitmen	WHL	72	11	24	35	33	....	....	....	....	....	....	....	....	....	7	1	1	2	0	....	....	....	....
2004-05	Calgary Hitmen	WHL	72	2	27	29	31	....	....	....	....	....	....	....	....	....	12	2	1	3	6	....	....	....	....
2005-06	Calgary Hitmen	WHL	68	7	33	40	36	....	....	....	....	....	....	....	....	....	13	4	6	10	6	....	....	....	....
	Hershey Bears	AHL	....	....	....	....	....	....	....	....	....	....	....	....	....	....	7	1	3	4	4	....	....	....	....
2006-07	**Washington**	**NHL**	**38**	**0**	**3**	**3**	**16**	**0**	**0**	**0**	**22**	**0.0**	**5**	**0**	**0.0**	**18:13**	....	....	....	....	....	....	....	....	....
	Hershey Bears	AHL	44	2	10	12	39	....	....	....	....	....	....	....	....	....	19	0	1	1	18	....	....	....	....
2007-08	**Washington**	**NHL**	**72**	**5**	**13**	**18**	**28**	**0**	**0**	**0**	**36**	**13.9**	**12**	**1**	**100.0**	**18:05**	**2**	**0**	**0**	**0**	**2**	**0**	**0**	**0**	**10:25**
	Hershey Bears	AHL	1	0	0	0	0	....	....	....	....	....	....	....	....	....	....	....	....	....	....	....	....	....	....

			Regular Season														Playoffs								
Season	Club	League	GP	G	A	Pts	PIM	PP	SH	GW	S	%	+/-	TF	F%	Min	GP	G	A	Pts	PIM	PP	SH	GW	M
2008-09	Washington	NHL	64	1	11	12	21	0	1	0	40	2.5	13	0	0.0	19:46	1	0	0	0	0	0	0	0	12:2
2009-10	Washington	NHL	73	3	20	23	32	0	0	0	43	7.0	50	0	0.0	19:52	7	0	1	1	4	0	0	0	19:4
	NHL Totals		247	9	47	56	97	0	1	0	141	6.4		1	100.0	19:04	10	0	1	1	6	0	0	0	17:0

WHL East Second All-Star Team (2006)

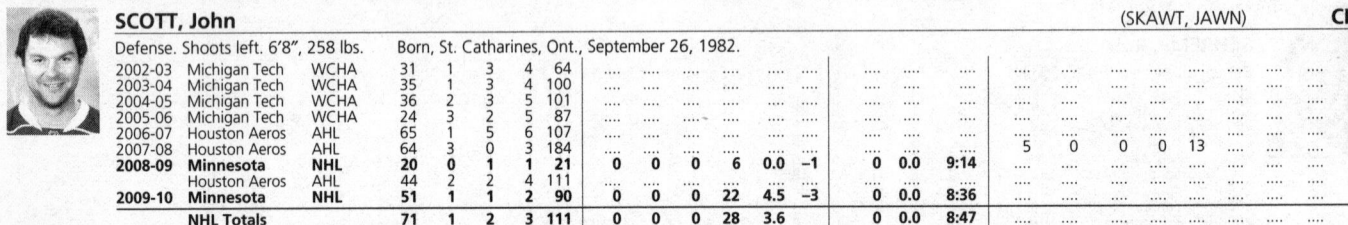

SCHULTZ, Jesse

(SHUHLTZ, JEH-see)

Right wing. Shoots right. 6'1", 195 lbs. Born, Strasbourg, Sask., September 28, 1982.

Season	Club	League	GP	G	A	Pts	PIM	PP	SH	GW	S	%	+/-	TF	F%	Min	GP	G	A	Pts	PIM	PP	SH	GW	M
99-2000	Tri-City	WHL	62	10	6	16	34	....	....	....	....	....	....	....	....	....	4	1	1	2	2	....	....	....	.
2000-01	Tri-City	WHL	30	5	8	13	16	....	....	....	....	....	....	....	....	....	....	....	....	....	....	....	....	....	.
	Prince Albert	WHL	35	14	18	32	14	....	....	....	....	....	....	....	....	....	....	....	....	....	....	....	....	....	.
2001-02	Prince Albert	WHL	45	18	24	42	16	....	....	....	....	....	....	....	....	....	....	....	....	....	....	....	....	....	.
	Kelowna Rockets	WHL	28	10	12	22	14	....	....	....	....	....	....	....	....	....	....	....	....	....	....	....	....	....	.
2002-03	Kelowna Rockets	WHL	72	53	51	104	47	....	....	....	....	....	....	....	....	....	19	*12	16	*28	21	....	....	....	.
2003-04	Manitoba Moose	AHL	2	0	1	1	0	....	....	....	....	....	....	....	....	....	....	....	....	....	....	....	....	....	.
	Columbia Inferno	ECHL	52	27	21	48	72	....	....	....	....	....	....	....	....	....	4	1	2	3	2	....	....	....	.
2004-05	Manitoba Moose	AHL	70	9	15	24	33	....	....	....	....	....	....	....	....	....	14	3	2	5	2	....	....	....	.
2005-06	Manitoba Moose	AHL	80	37	30	67	63	....	....	....	....	....	....	....	....	....	13	5	7	12	10	....	....	....	.
2006-07	Vancouver	NHL	2	0	0	0	0	0	0	0	6	0.0	0	0	0.0	10:09	....	....	....	....	....	....	....	....	.
	Manitoba Moose	AHL	67	18	21	39	35	....	....	....	....	....	....	....	....	....	7	0	0	0	2	....	....	....	.
2007-08	Chicago Wolves	AHL	80	26	40	66	43	....	....	....	....	....	....	....	....	....	24	8	6	14	18	....	....	....	.
2008-09	Houston Aeros	AHL	76	22	33	55	51	....	....	....	....	....	....	....	....	....	8	1	1	2	2	....	....	....	.
2009-10	Nurnberg	Germany	21	4	8	12	16	....	....	....	....	....	....	....	....	....	4	0	2	2	27	....	....	....	.
	NHL Totals		2	0	0	0	0	0	0	0	6	0.0		0	0.0	10:09	....	....	....	....	....	....	....	....	.

WHL West First All-Star Team (2003)

Signed as a free agent by **Vancouver**, July 31, 2003. Traded to **Atlanta** by **Vancouver** for Jim Sharrow, June 23, 2007. Signed as a free agent by **Minnesota**, July 6, 2008. Signed as a free agent by **Nurnberg** (Germany), January 6, 2010.

SCHULTZ, Nick

(SHUHLTZ, NIHK) **MI**

Defense. Shoots left. 6'1", 200 lbs. Born, Strasbourg, Sask., August 25, 1982. Minnesota's 2nd choice, 33rd overall, in 2000 Entry Draft.

Season	Club	League	GP	G	A	Pts	PIM	PP	SH	GW	S	%	+/-	TF	F%	Min	GP	G	A	Pts	PIM	PP	SH	GW	M
1997-98	Yorkton Mallers	SMHL	59	10	30	40	74	....	....	....	....	....	....	....	....	....	....	....	....	....	....	....	....	....	.
1998-99	Prince Albert	WHL	58	5	18	23	37	....	....	....	....	....	....	....	....	....	14	0	7	7	0	....	....	....	.
99-2000	Prince Albert	WHL	72	11	33	44	38	....	....	....	....	....	....	....	....	....	6	0	3	3	2	....	....	....	.
2000-01	Prince Albert	WHL	59	17	30	47	120	....	....	....	....	....	....	....	....	....	....	....	....	....	....	....	....	....	.
	Cleveland	IHL	4	1	1	2	2	....	....	....	....	....	....	....	....	....	3	0	1	1	0	....	....	....	.
2001-02	Minnesota	NHL	52	4	6	10	14	1	0	1	47	8.5	0	0	0.0	16:08	....	....	....	....	....	....	....	....	.
	Houston Aeros	AHL	....	....	....	....	....	....	....	....	....	....	....	....	....	....	14	1	5	6	2	....	....	....	.
2002-03	Minnesota	NHL	75	3	7	10	23	0	0	1	70	4.3	11	0	0.0	18:28	18	0	1	1	10	0	0	0	19:
2003-04	Minnesota	NHL	79	6	10	16	16	1	0	0	72	8.3	12	0	0.0	20:19	....	....	....	....	....	....	....	....	.
2004-05	Kassel Huskies	Germany	46	7	15	22	26	....	....	....	....	....	....	....	....	....	7	0	4	4	6	....	....	....	.
2005-06	Minnesota	NHL	79	2	12	14	43	0	0	0	45	4.4	2	0	0.0	17:58	....	....	....	....	....	....	....	....	.
2006-07	Minnesota	NHL	82	2	10	12	42	0	0	1	69	2.9	0	0	0.0	20:13	5	0	1	1	0	0	0	0	18:
2007-08	Minnesota	NHL	81	2	13	15	42	0	0	0	52	3.8	9	0	0.0	20:10	1	0	0	0	0	0	0	0	16:
2008-09	Minnesota	NHL	79	2	9	11	31	0	0	0	48	4.2	–4	1	0.0	20:33	....	....	....	....	....	....	....	....	.
2009-10	Minnesota	NHL	80	1	19	20	43	1	0	0	83	1.2	–8	0	0.0	20:58	....	....	....	....	....	....	....	....	.
	NHL Totals		607	22	86	108	254	3	0	3	486	4.5		1	0.0	19:30	24	0	2	2	10	0	0	0	19:

Signed as a free agent by **Kassel** (Germany), September 24, 2004.

SCOTT, John

(SKAWT, JAWN) **CH**

Defense. Shoots left. 6'8", 258 lbs. Born, St. Catharines, Ont., September 26, 1982.

Season	Club	League	GP	G	A	Pts	PIM	PP	SH	GW	S	%	+/-	TF	F%	Min	GP	G	A	Pts	PIM	PP	SH	GW	M
2002-03	Michigan Tech	WCHA	31	1	3	4	64	....	....	....	....	....	....	....	....	....	....	....	....	....	....	....	....	....	
2003-04	Michigan Tech	WCHA	35	1	3	4	100	....	....	....	....	....	....	....	....	....	....	....	....	....	....	....	....	....	
2004-05	Michigan Tech	WCHA	36	2	3	5	101	....	....	....	....	....	....	....	....	....	....	....	....	....	....	....	....	....	
2005-06	Michigan Tech	WCHA	24	3	2	5	87	....	....	....	....	....	....	....	....	....	....	....	....	....	....	....	....	....	
2006-07	Houston Aeros	AHL	65	1	5	6	107	....	....	....	....	....	....	....	....	....	....	....	....	....	....	....	....	....	
2007-08	Houston Aeros	AHL	64	3	0	3	184	....	....	....	....	....	....	....	....	....	5	0	0	0	13	....	....	....	
2008-09	Minnesota	NHL	20	0	1	1	21	0	0	0	6	0.0	–1	0	0.0	9:14	....	....	....	....	....	....	....	....	
	Houston Aeros	AHL	44	2	2	4	111	....	....	....	....	....	....	....	....	....	....	....	....	....	....	....	....	....	
2009-10	Minnesota	NHL	51	1	1	2	90	0	0	0	22	4.5	–3	0	0.0	8:36	....	....	....	....	....	....	....	....	
	NHL Totals		71	1	2	3	111	0	0	0	28	3.6		0	0.0	8:47	....	....	....	....	....	....	....	....	

Signed as a free agent by **Houston** (AHL), September 26, 2006. Signed as a free agent by **Minnesota**, December 31, 2006. Signed as a free agent by **Chicago**, July 2, 2010.

SCUDERI, Rob

(SKUD-uh-ree, RAWB) **L.**

Defense. Shoots left. 6'1", 211 lbs. Born, Syosset, NY, December 30, 1978. Pittsburgh's 5th choice, 134th overall, in 1998 Entry Draft.

Season	Club	League	GP	G	A	Pts	PIM	PP	SH	GW	S	%	+/-	TF	F%	Min	GP	G	A	Pts	PIM	PP	SH	GW	M
1995-96	NY Apple Core	MtJHL	76	18	60	78	....	....	....	....	....	....	....	....	....	....	....	....	....	....	....	....	....	....	.
1996-97	NY Apple Core	MtJHL	82	42	70	112	64	....	....	....	....	....	....	....	....	....	....	....	....	....	....	....	....	....	.
1997-98	Boston College	H-East	42	0	24	24	12	....	....	....	....	....	....	....	....	....	....	....	....	....	....	....	....	....	.
1998-99	Boston College	H-East	41	2	8	10	20	....	....	....	....	....	....	....	....	....	....	....	....	....	....	....	....	....	.
99-2000	Boston College	H-East	42	1	12	13	22	....	....	....	....	....	....	....	....	....	....	....	....	....	....	....	....	....	.
2000-01	Boston College	H-East	43	4	19	23	42	....	....	....	....	....	....	....	....	....	....	....	....	....	....	....	....	....	.
2001-02	Wilkes-Barre	AHL	75	1	22	23	66	....	....	....	....	....	....	....	....	....	....	....	....	....	....	....	....	....	.
2002-03	Wilkes-Barre	AHL	74	4	17	21	44	....	....	....	....	....	....	....	....	....	6	0	1	1	4	....	....	....	.
2003-04	Pittsburgh	NHL	13	1	2	3	4	0	0	0	4	25.0	2	0	0.0	20:06	....	....	....	....	....	....	....	....	.
	Wilkes-Barre	AHL	64	1	15	16	54	....	....	....	....	....	....	....	....	....	24	0	3	3	14	....	....	....	.
2004-05	Wilkes-Barre	AHL	79	2	18	20	34	....	....	....	....	....	....	....	....	....	11	2	1	3	2	....	....	....	.
2005-06	Pittsburgh	NHL	57	0	4	4	36	0	0	0	28	0.0	–18	0	0.0	20:15	....	....	....	....	....	....	....	....	.
	Wilkes-Barre	AHL	13	0	8	8	8	....	....	....	....	....	....	....	....	....	....	....	....	....	....	....	....	....	.
2006-07	Pittsburgh	NHL	78	1	10	11	28	0	0	0	31	3.2	3	0	0.0	18:49	5	0	0	0	2	0	0	0	17:
2007-08	Pittsburgh	NHL	71	0	5	5	26	0	0	0	28	0.0	3	0	0.0	18:45	20	0	3	3	2	0	0	0	19:
2008-09♦	Pittsburgh	NHL	81	1	15	16	18	0	0	0	51	2.0	23	0	0.0	19:10	24	1	4	5	6	0	0	0	20:
2009-10	Los Angeles	NHL	73	0	11	11	21	0	0	0	38	0.0	16	0	0.0	19:16	6	0	0	0	6	0	0	0	20:
	NHL Totals		373	3	47	50	133	0	0	0	180	1.7		0	0.0	19:14	55	1	7	8	16	0	0	0	19:

NCAA Championship All-Tournament Team (2001)

Signed as a free agent by **Los Angeles** July 2, 2009.

SEABROOK, Brent

(SEE-bruk, BREHNT) **CH**

Defense. Shoots right. 6'3", 218 lbs. Born, Richmond, B.C., April 20, 1985. Chicago's 1st choice, 14th overall, in 2003 Entry Draft.

Season	Club	League	GP	G	A	Pts	PIM	PP	SH	GW	S	%	+/-	TF	F%	Min	GP	G	A	Pts	PIM	PP	SH	GW	M
2000-01	Delta Ice Hawks	PIJHL	54	16	26	42	55	....	....	....	....	....	....	....	....	....	....	....	....	....	....	....	....	....	
	Lethbridge	WHL	4	0	0	0	0	....	....	....	....	....	....	....	....	....	....	....	....	....	....	....	....	....	
2001-02	Lethbridge	WHL	67	6	33	39	70	....	....	....	....	....	....	....	....	....	4	1	1	2	2	....	....	....	
2002-03	Lethbridge	WHL	69	9	33	42	113	....	....	....	....	....	....	....	....	....	....	....	....	....	....	....	....	....	
2003-04	Lethbridge	WHL	61	12	29	41	107	....	....	....	....	....	....	....	....	....	....	....	....	....	....	....	....	....	
2004-05	Lethbridge	WHL	63	12	42	54	107	....	....	....	....	....	....	....	....	....	5	1	2	3	10	....	....	....	
	Norfolk Admirals	AHL	3	0	0	0	2	....	....	....	....	....	....	....	....	....	6	0	1	1	6	....	....	....	
2005-06	Chicago	NHL	69	5	27	32	60	1	0	2	114	4.4	5	0	0.0	20:02	....	....	....	....	....	....	....	....	
2006-07	Chicago	NHL	81	4	20	24	104	0	0	0	144	2.8	–6	2	50.0	20:46	....	....	....	....	....	....	....	....	
2007-08	Chicago	NHL	82	9	23	32	90	4	0	2	152	5.9	13	1	0.0	21:30	....	....	....	....	....	....	....	....	
2008-09	Chicago	NHL	82	8	18	26	62	3	1	1	132	6.1	23	0	0.0	23:19	17	1	11	12	14	1	0	0	26:
2009-10♦	Chicago	NHL	78	4	26	30	59	0	0	2	129	3.1	20	0	0.0	23:13	22	4	7	11	14	1	0	0	24:
	Canada	Olympics	7	0	1	1	2	....	....	....	....	....	....	....	....	....	....	....	....	....	....	....	....	....	
	NHL Totals		392	30	114	144	375	8	1	7	671	4.5		3	33.3	21:49	39	5	18	23	28	2	0	0	24:

WHL East Second All-Star Team (2005)

SEDIN, Daniel

(suh-DEEN, DAN-yehl) **VAN.**

Left wing. Shoots left. 6'1", 187 lbs. Born, Ornskoldsvik, Sweden, September 26, 1980. Vancouver's 1st choice, 2nd overall, in 1999 Entry Draft.

			Regular Season														Playoffs								
Season	Club	League	GP	G	A	Pts	PIM	PP	SH	GW	S	%	+/-	TF	F%	Min	GP	G	A	Pts	PIM	PP	SH	GW	Min
1997-98	Malmo Jr.	Swe-Jr.	4	3	3	6	4	....	....	....	....	....	....	....	....	....	....	....	....	....	....	....	....	....	....
	MoDo Jr.	Swe-Jr.	26	26	14	40	....	....	....	....	....	....	....	....	....	....	....	....	....	....	....	....	....	....	....
	MoDo	Sweden	45	4	8	12	26	....	....	....	....	....	....	....	....	....	9	0	0	0	2	....	....	....	....
1998-99	MoDo	Sweden	50	21	21	42	20	....	....	....	....	....	....	....	....	....	13	4	8	12	14	....	....	....	....
99-2000	MoDo	Sweden	50	19	26	45	28	....	....	....	....	....	....	....	....	....	13	*8	6	14	18	....	....	....	....
	MoDo	EuroHL	4	3	3	6	0	....	....	....	....	....	....	....	....	....	2	0	0	0	0	....	....	....	....
2000-01	**Vancouver**	**NHL**	**75**	**20**	**14**	**34**	**24**	**10**	**0**	**3**	**127**	**15.7**	**–3**	**10**	**60.0**	**13:00**	**4**	**1**	**2**	**3**	**0**	**0**	**0**	**0**	**16:15**
2001-02	**Vancouver**	**NHL**	**79**	**9**	**23**	**32**	**32**	**4**	**0**	**2**	**117**	**7.7**	**1**	**18**	**33.3**	**12:22**	**6**	**0**	**1**	**1**	**0**	**0**	**0**	**0**	**10:44**
2002-03	**Vancouver**	**NHL**	**79**	**14**	**17**	**31**	**34**	**4**	**0**	**2**	**134**	**10.4**	**8**	**24**	**45.8**	**12:26**	**14**	**1**	**5**	**6**	**8**	**1**	**0**	**1**	**12:23**
2003-04	**Vancouver**	**NHL**	**82**	**18**	**36**	**54**	**18**	**1**	**0**	**3**	**153**	**11.8**	**18**	**71**	**47.9**	**13:33**	**7**	**1**	**2**	**3**	**0**	**1**	**0**	**0**	**16:03**
2004-05	MODO	Sweden	49	13	20	33	40	....	....	....	....	....	....	....	....	....	6	0	3	3	6	....	....	....	....
2005-06	**Vancouver**	**NHL**	**82**	**22**	**49**	**71**	**34**	**11**	**0**	**4**	**204**	**10.8**	**7**	**49**	**42.9**	**16:40**	....	....	....	....	....	....	....	....	....
	Sweden	Olympics	8	1	3	4	2	....	....	....	....	....	....	....	....	....	....	....	....	....	....	....	....	....	....
2006-07	**Vancouver**	**NHL**	**81**	**36**	**48**	**84**	**36**	**16**	**0**	**8**	**236**	**15.3**	**19**	**44**	**22.7**	**18:04**	**12**	**2**	**3**	**5**	**4**	**0**	**0**	**0**	**21:31**
2007-08	**Vancouver**	**NHL**	**82**	**29**	**45**	**74**	**50**	**12**	**0**	**7**	**247**	**11.7**	**6**	**38**	**44.7**	**19:03**	....	....	....	....	....	....	....	....	....
2008-09	**Vancouver**	**NHL**	**82**	**31**	**51**	**82**	**36**	**9**	**0**	**7**	**285**	**10.9**	**24**	**35**	**40.0**	**18:48**	**10**	**4**	**6**	**10**	**8**	**2**	**0**	**0**	**18:37**
2009-10	**Vancouver**	**NHL**	**63**	**29**	**56**	**85**	**28**	**8**	**0**	**8**	**225**	**12.9**	**36**	**33**	**33.3**	**19:08**	**12**	**5**	**9**	**14**	**12**	**1**	**0**	**2**	**19:46**
	Sweden	Olympics	4	1	2	3	0	....	....	....	....	....	....	....	....	....	....	....	....	....	....	....	....	....	....
	NHL Totals		**705**	**208**	**339**	**547**	**292**	**75**	**0**	**44**	**1728**	**12.0**		**322**	**40.4**	**15:52**	**65**	**14**	**28**	**42**	**32**	**5**	**0**	**3**	**16:52**

HL Second All-Star Team (2010)

gned as a free agent by **MODO** (Sweden), September 18, 2004.

SEDIN, Henrik

(suh-DEEN, HEHN-rihk) **VAN.**

Center. Shoots left. 6'2", 188 lbs. Born, Ornskoldsvik, Sweden, September 26, 1980. Vancouver's 2nd choice, 3rd overall, in 1999 Entry Draft.

			Regular Season														Playoffs								
Season	Club	League	GP	G	A	Pts	PIM	PP	SH	GW	S	%	+/-	TF	F%	Min	GP	G	A	Pts	PIM	PP	SH	GW	Min
1997-98	Malmo Jr.	Swe-Jr.	8	4	7	11	6	....	....	....	....	....	....	....	....	....	....	....	....	....	....	....	....	....	....
	MoDo Jr.	Swe-Jr.	26	14	22	36	....	....	....	....	....	....	....	....	....	....	....	....	....	....	....	....	....	....	....
	MoDo	Sweden	39	1	4	5	8	....	....	....	....	....	....	....	....	....	7	0	0	0	0	....	....	....	....
1998-99	MoDo	Sweden	49	12	22	34	32	....	....	....	....	....	....	....	....	....	13	2	8	10	6	....	....	....	....
99-2000	MoDo	Sweden	50	9	38	47	22	....	....	....	....	....	....	....	....	....	13	5	9	14	2	....	....	....	....
2000-01	**Vancouver**	**NHL**	**82**	**9**	**20**	**29**	**38**	**2**	**0**	**1**	**98**	**9.2**	**–2**	**1020**	**44.1**	**13:31**	**4**	**0**	**4**	**4**	**0**	**0**	**0**	**0**	**16:31**
2001-02	**Vancouver**	**NHL**	**82**	**16**	**20**	**36**	**36**	**3**	**0**	**1**	**78**	**20.5**	**9**	**785**	**47.4**	**12:48**	**6**	**3**	**0**	**3**	**0**	**0**	**0**	**1**	**11:55**
2002-03	**Vancouver**	**NHL**	**78**	**8**	**31**	**39**	**38**	**4**	**1**	**1**	**81**	**9.9**	**9**	**995**	**48.2**	**13:58**	**14**	**3**	**2**	**5**	**8**	**1**	**0**	**0**	**13:01**
2003-04	**Vancouver**	**NHL**	**76**	**11**	**31**	**42**	**32**	**2**	**0**	**2**	**99**	**11.1**	**23**	**961**	**50.0**	**14:02**	**7**	**2**	**2**	**4**	**2**	**2**	**0**	**0**	**16:02**
2004-05	MODO	Sweden	44	14	22	36	50	....	....	....	....	....	....	....	....	....	6	1	3	4	6	....	....	....	....
2005-06	**Vancouver**	**NHL**	**82**	**18**	**57**	**75**	**56**	**5**	**1**	**0**	**113**	**15.9**	**11**	**1238**	**50.7**	**16:54**	....	....	....	....	....	....	....	....	....
	Sweden	Olympics	8	3	1	4	2	....	....	....	....	....	....	....	....	....	....	....	....	....	....	....	....	....	....
2006-07	**Vancouver**	**NHL**	**82**	**10**	**71**	**81**	**66**	**1**	**0**	**2**	**134**	**7.5**	**19**	**1220**	**52.5**	**18:26**	**12**	**2**	**2**	**4**	**14**	**1**	**0**	**1**	**22:12**
2007-08	**Vancouver**	**NHL**	**82**	**15**	**61**	**76**	**56**	**4**	**1**	**2**	**141**	**10.6**	**6**	**1369**	**47.0**	**19:31**	....	....	....	....	....	....	....	....	....
2008-09	**Vancouver**	**NHL**	**82**	**22**	**60**	**82**	**48**	**4**	**0**	**8**	**143**	**15.4**	**22**	**1364**	**49.6**	**19:31**	**10**	**4**	**6**	**10**	**2**	**1**	**0**	**0**	**20:07**
2009-10	**Vancouver**	**NHL**	**82**	**29**	***83**	***112**	**48**	**4**	**2**	**5**	**166**	**17.5**	**35**	**1527**	**49.5**	**19:41**	**12**	**3**	**11**	**14**	**6**	**0**	**0**	**1**	**20:38**
	Sweden	Olympics	4	0	2	2	2	....	....	....	....	....	....	....	....	....	....	....	....	....	....	....	....	....	....
	NHL Totals		**728**	**138**	**434**	**572**	**418**	**29**	**5**	**22**	**1053**	**13.1**		**10479**	**48.9**	**16:31**	**65**	**17**	**27**	**44**	**32**	**5**	**0**	**3**	**17:39**

HL First All-Star Team (2010) • Art Ross Trophy (2010) • Hart Memorial Trophy (2010)

ayed in NHL All-Star Game (2008)

gned as a free agent by **MODO** (Sweden), September 18, 2004.

SEGAL, Brandon

(SEE-guhl, BRAN-duhn) **DAL.**

Right wing. Shoots right. 6'2", 209 lbs. Born, Richmond, B.C., July 12, 1983. Nashville's 2nd choice, 102nd overall, in 2002 Entry Draft.

			Regular Season														Playoffs								
Season	Club	League	GP	G	A	Pts	PIM	PP	SH	GW	S	%	+/-	TF	F%	Min	GP	G	A	Pts	PIM	PP	SH	GW	Min
99-2000	Calgary Hitmen	WHL	44	2	6	8	76	....	....	....	....	....	....	....	....	....	13	1	1	2	13	....	....	....	....
	Delta Ice Hawks	PIJHL	....	....	....	....	....	....	....	....	....	....	....	....	....	....	3	0	1	1	2	....	....	....	....
2000-01	Calgary Hitmen	WHL	72	16	11	27	103	....	....	....	....	....	....	....	....	....	12	1	1	2	17	....	....	....	....
2001-02	Calgary Hitmen	WHL	71	43	40	83	122	....	....	....	....	....	....	....	....	....	7	1	4	5	16	....	....	....	....
2002-03	Calgary Hitmen	WHL	71	31	27	58	104	....	....	....	....	....	....	....	....	....	5	2	2	4	4	....	....	....	....
2003-04	Calgary Hitmen	WHL	28	18	12	30	29	....	....	....	....	....	....	....	....	....	....	....	....	....	....	....	....	....	....
	Milwaukee	AHL	44	11	10	21	54	....	....	....	....	....	....	....	....	....	13	2	1	3	21	....	....	....	....
2004-05	Milwaukee	AHL	59	7	8	15	45	....	....	....	....	....	....	....	....	....	3	1	0	1	11	....	....	....	....
	Rockford IceHogs	UHL	10	5	4	9	27	....	....	....	....	....	....	....	....	....	11	11	5	16	10	....	....	....	....
2005-06	Milwaukee	AHL	79	18	15	33	126	....	....	....	....	....	....	....	....	....	21	1	2	3	16	....	....	....	....
2006-07	Milwaukee	AHL	77	20	9	29	84	....	....	....	....	....	....	....	....	....	4	1	0	1	2	....	....	....	....
2007-08	Portland Pirates	AHL	54	5	9	14	46	....	....	....	....	....	....	....	....	....	....	....	....	....	....	....	....	....	....
	Norfolk Admirals	AHL	22	7	6	13	25	....	....	....	....	....	....	....	....	....	....	....	....	....	....	....	....	....	....
2008-09	**Tampa Bay**	**NHL**	**2**	**0**	**0**	**0**	**0**	**0**	**0**	**0**	**2**	**0.0**	**0**	**0**	**0.0**	**13:48**	....	....	....	....	....	....	....	....	....
	Norfolk Admirals	AHL	69	26	26	52	95	....	....	....	....	....	....	....	....	....	....	....	....	....	....	....	....	....	....
2009-10	**Los Angeles**	**NHL**	**25**	**1**	**1**	**2**	**20**	**0**	**0**	**0**	**24**	**4.2**	**0**	**3**	**0.0**	**6:47**	....	....	....	....	....	....	....	....	....
	Manchester	AHL	21	6	8	14	34	....	....	....	....	....	....	....	....	....	....	....	....	....	....	....	....	....	....
	Dallas	**NHL**	**19**	**5**	**5**	**10**	**18**	**0**	**0**	**2**	**31**	**16.1**	**3**	**0**	**0.0**	**11:20**	....	....	....	....	....	....	....	....	....
	NHL Totals		**46**	**6**	**6**	**12**	**38**	**0**	**0**	**2**	**57**	**10.5**		**3**	**0.0**	**8:58**	....	....	....	....	....	....	....	....	....

aded to **Anaheim** by **Nashville** for future considerations, June 25, 2007. Traded to **Tampa Bay** by **Anaheim** with Anaheim's 7th round choice (David Carle) in 2008 Entry Draft for Jay Leach, February ;, 2008. Signed as a free agent by **Los Angeles**, July 13, 2009. Claimed on waivers by **Dallas** from **Los Angeles**, February 11, 2010.

SEIDENBERG, Dennis

(SIGH-dehn-buhrg, DEH-nihs) **BOS.**

Defense. Shoots left. 6'1", 210 lbs. Born, Schwenningen, West Germany, July 18, 1981. Philadelphia's 6th choice, 172nd overall, in 2001 Entry Draft.

			Regular Season														Playoffs								
Season	Club	League	GP	G	A	Pts	PIM	PP	SH	GW	S	%	+/-	TF	F%	Min	GP	G	A	Pts	PIM	PP	SH	GW	Min
99-2000	Mannheim Jr.	Ger-Jr.	52	12	28	40	28	....	....	....	....	....	....	....	....	....	....	....	....	....	....	....	....	....	....
	Adler Mannheim	Germany	3	0	0	0	0	....	....	....	....	....	....	....	....	....	....	....	....	....	....	....	....	....	....
2000-01	Mannheim Jr.	Ger-Jr.	9	3	8	11	20	....	....	....	....	....	....	....	....	....	....	....	....	....	....	....	....	....	....
	Adler Mannheim	Germany	55	2	5	7	6	....	....	....	....	....	....	....	....	....	12	0	1	1	10	....	....	....	....
2001-02	Adler Mannheim	Germany	55	7	13	20	56	....	....	....	....	....	....	....	....	....	8	0	0	0	2	....	....	....	....
2002-03	**Philadelphia**	**NHL**	**58**	**4**	**9**	**13**	**20**	**1**	**0**	**0**	**123**	**3.3**	**8**	**1**	**0.0**	**16:50**	....	....	....	....	....	....	....	....	....
	Philadelphia	AHL	19	5	6	11	17	....	....	....	....	....	....	....	....	....	....	....	....	....	....	....	....	....	....
2003-04	**Philadelphia**	**NHL**	**5**	**0**	**0**	**0**	**2**	**0**	**0**	**0**	**14**	**0.0**	**–4**	**0**	**0.0**	**17:20**	**3**	**0**	**0**	**0**	**0**	**0**	**0**	**0**	**7:36**
	Philadelphia	AHL	33	7	12	19	31	....	....	....	....	....	....	....	....	....	9	2	2	4	4	....	....	....	....
2004-05	Philadelphia	AHL	79	13	28	41	47	....	....	....	....	....	....	....	....	....	18	2	8	10	19	....	....	....	....
2005-06	**Philadelphia**	**NHL**	**29**	**2**	**5**	**7**	**4**	**1**	**0**	**0**	**34**	**5.9**	**–4**	**1**	**0.0**	**14:22**	....	....	....	....	....	....	....	....	....
	Phoenix	**NHL**	**34**	**1**	**10**	**11**	**14**	**1**	**0**	**0**	**49**	**2.0**	**–9**	**0**	**0.0**	**19:13**	....	....	....	....	....	....	....	....	....
	Germany	Olympics	5	0	0	0	6	....	....	....	....	....	....	....	....	....	....	....	....	....	....	....	....	....	....
2006-07	**Phoenix**	**NHL**	**32**	**1**	**1**	**2**	**16**	**0**	**0**	**0**	**36**	**2.8**	**–4**	**0**	**0.0**	**14:43**	....	....	....	....	....	....	....	....	....
	Carolina	**NHL**	**20**	**1**	**5**	**6**	**2**	**0**	**0**	**0**	**47**	**2.1**	**–12**	**0**	**0.0**	**18:29**	....	....	....	....	....	....	....	....	....
2007-08	**Carolina**	**NHL**	**47**	**0**	**15**	**15**	**18**	**0**	**0**	**0**	**80**	**0.0**	**6**	**1**	**100.0**	**18:50**	....	....	....	....	....	....	....	....	....
2008-09	**Carolina**	**NHL**	**70**	**5**	**25**	**30**	**37**	**2**	**0**	**1**	**129**	**3.9**	**–9**	**0**	**0.0**	**22:20**	**16**	**1**	**5**	**6**	**16**	**0**	**0**	**0**	**22:25**
2009-10	**Florida**	**NHL**	**62**	**2**	**21**	**23**	**33**	**1**	**0**	**0**	**116**	**1.7**	**–3**	**1**	**0.0**	**22:55**	....	....	....	....	....	....	....	....	....
	Boston	**NHL**	**17**	**2**	**7**	**9**	**6**	**1**	**0**	**1**	**37**	**5.4**	**9**	**0**	**0.0**	**22:57**	....	....	....	....	....	....	....	....	....
	Germany	Olympics	4	1	0	1	2	....	....	....	....	....	....	....	....	....	....	....	....	....	....	....	....	....	....
	NHL Totals		**374**	**18**	**98**	**116**	**152**	**7**	**0**	**2**	**665**	**2.7**		**4**	**25.0**	**19:20**	**19**	**1**	**5**	**6**	**16**	**0**	**0**	**0**	**20:05**

Missed majority of 2003-04 season recovering from leg injury suffered in game vs. Edmonton, January 10, 2004. Traded to **Phoenix** by **Philadelphia** with Philadelphia's 4th round choice (later traded to Y Islanders - NY Islanders selected Tomas Marcinko) in 2006 Entry Draft for Petr Nedved and Phoenix's 4th round choice (Joonas Lehtivuori) in 2006 Entry Draft, January 20, 2006. Traded to **Carolina** by **hoenix** for Kevyn Adams, January 8, 2007. Signed as a free agent by **Florida**, September 14, 2009. Traded to **Boston** by **Florida** with Matt Bartkowski for Byron Bitz, Craig Weller and Tampa Bay's 2nd und choice (previously acquired, Florida selected Alexander Petrovic) in 2010 Entry Draft, March 3, 2010.

SEKERA, Andrej

(seh-KAIR-ah, AWN-dray) **BUF**

Defense. Shoots left. 6', 202 lbs. Born, Bojnice, Czech., June 8, 1986. Buffalo's 3rd choice, 71st overall, in 2004 Entry Draft.

			Regular Season														Playoffs								
Season	Club	League	GP	G	A	Pts	PIM	PP	SH	GW	S	%	+/-	TF	F%	Min	GP	G	A	Pts	PIM	PP	SH	GW	Min
2001-02	Dukla Trencin Jr.	Slovak-Jr.	52	5	10	15	10	....	....	....	....	....	....	....	....	....	....	....	....	....	....	....	....	....	....
2002-03	Dukla Trencin Jr.	Slovak-Jr.	48	9	15	24	20	....	....	....	....	....	....	....	....	....	....	....	....	....	....	....	....	....	....
2003-04	Dukla Trencin Jr.	Slovak-Jr.	42	5	12	17	40	....	....	....	....	....	....	....	....	....	2	0	1	1	4	....	....	....	....
	Dukla Trencin	Slovakia	3	0	0	0	2	....	....	....	....	....	....	....	....	....	....	....	....	....	....	....	....	....	....
	Dukla Trencin U18	Svk-U18	5	0	0	0	0	....	....	....	....	....	....	....	....	....	....	....	....	....	....	....	....	....	....
2004-05	Owen Sound	OHL	51	7	21	28	18	....	....	....	....	....	....	....	....	....	6	0	4	4	4	....	....	....	....
2005-06	Owen Sound	OHL	51	21	34	55	54	....	....	....	....	....	....	....	....	....	11	5	8	13	9	....	....	....	....
2006-07	**Buffalo**	**NHL**	**2**	**0**	**0**	**0**	**2**	**0**	**0**	**0**	**0**	**0.0**	**1**	**0**	**0.0**	**7:31**	....	....	....	....	....	....	....	....	....
	Rochester	AHL	54	3	16	19	28	....	....	....	....	....	....	....	....	....	....	....	....	....	....	....	....	....	....
2007-08	**Buffalo**	**NHL**	**37**	**2**	**6**	**8**	**16**	**0**	**0**	**1**	**28**	**7.1**	**5**	**0**	**0.0**	**19:37**	....	....	....	....	....	....	....	....	....
	Rochester	AHL	40	2	15	17	22	....	....	....	....	....	....	....	....	....	....	....	....	....	....	....	....	....	....
2008-09	**Buffalo**	**NHL**	**69**	**3**	**16**	**19**	**22**	**1**	**0**	**1**	**84**	**3.6**	**–11**	**1**	**0.0**	**20:42**	....	....	....	....	....	....	....	....	....
2009-10	**Buffalo**	**NHL**	**49**	**4**	**7**	**11**	**6**	**0**	**0**	**0**	**59**	**6.8**	**–1**	**1**	**0.0**	**17:27**	**6**	**0**	**0**	**0**	**7**	**0**	**0**	**0**	**13:55**
	Slovakia	Olympics	7	1	0	1	0	....	....	....	....	....	....	....	....	....	....	....	....	....	....	....	....	....	....
	NHL Totals		**157**	**9**	**29**	**38**	**46**	**1**	**0**	**2**	**171**	**5.3**		**2**	**0.0**	**19:16**	**6**	**0**	**0**	**0**	**7**	**0**	**0**	**0**	**13:55**

OHL All-Rookie Team (2005) • OHL First All-Star Team (2006)

SELANNE, Teemu

(seh-LAH-nee, TEE-moo) **ANA**

Right wing. Shoots right. 6', 196 lbs. Born, Helsinki, Finland, July 3, 1970. Winnipeg's 1st choice, 10th overall, in 1988 Entry Draft.

Season	Club	League	GP	G	A	Pts	PIM	PP	SH	GW	S	%	+/-	TF	F%	Min	GP	G	A	Pts	PIM	PP	SH	GW	Min
1986-87	Jokerit U18	Fin-U18	....	....	....	....	....	....	....	....	....	....	....	....	....	....	7	10	3	13	2	....	....	....	....
	Jokerit Helsinki Jr.	Fin-Jr.	33	10	12	22	8	....	....	....	....	....	....	....	....	....	....	....	....	....	....	....	....	....	....
1987-88	Jokerit Helsinki Jr.	Fin-Jr.	33	43	23	66	18	....	....	....	....	....	....	....	....	....	5	4	3	7	2	....	....	....	....
	Jokerit Helsinki	Finland-2	5	1	1	2	0	....	....	....	....	....	....	....	....	....	....	....	....	....	....	....	....	....	....
1988-89	PvUK Lahti Jr.	Fin-Jr.	3	3	1	4	2	....	....	....	....	....	....	....	....	....	....	....	....	....	....	....	....	....	....
	Jokerit Helsinki Jr.	Fin-Jr.	3	8	8	16	4	....	....	....	....	....	....	....	....	....	....	....	....	....	....	....	....	....	....
	Jokerit Helsinki	Finland-2	35	36	33	69	14	....	....	....	....	....	....	....	....	....	5	7	3	10	4	....	....	....	....
1989-90	Jokerit Helsinki	Finland	11	4	8	12	0	....	....	....	....	....	....	....	....	....	....	....	....	....	....	....	....	....	....
1990-91	Jokerit Helsinki Jr.	Fin-Jr.	4	3	2	5	10	....	....	....	....	....	....	....	....	....	....	....	....	....	....	....	....	....	....
	Jokerit Helsinki	Finland	42	33	25	58	12	....	....	....	....	....	....	....	....	....	....	....	....	....	....	....	....	....	....
1991-92	Jokerit Helsinki	Finland	44	39	23	62	20	....	....	....	....	....	....	....	....	....	10	10	7	17	18	....	....	....	....
	Finland	Olympics	8	7	4	11	6	....	....	....	....	....	....	....	....	....	....	....	....	....	....	....	....	....	....
1992-93	**Winnipeg**	**NHL**	**84**	***76**	**56**	**132**	**45**	**24**	**0**	**7**	**387**	**19.6**	**8**	....	....	....	**6**	**4**	**2**	**6**	**2**	**2**	**0**	**2**	....
1993-94	**Winnipeg**	**NHL**	**51**	**25**	**29**	**54**	**22**	**11**	**0**	**2**	**191**	**13.1**	**–23**	....	....	....	....	....	....	....	....	....	....	....	....
1994-95	Jokerit Helsinki	Finland	20	7	12	19	6	....	....	....	....	....	....	....	....	....	....	....	....	....	....	....	....	....	....
	Winnipeg	**NHL**	**45**	**22**	**26**	**48**	**2**	**8**	**2**	**1**	**167**	**13.2**	**1**	....	....	....	....	....	....	....	....	....	....	....	....
1995-96	**Winnipeg**	**NHL**	**51**	**24**	**48**	**72**	**18**	**6**	**1**	**4**	**163**	**14.7**	**3**	....	....	....	....	....	....	....	....	....	....	....	....
	Anaheim	**NHL**	**28**	**16**	**20**	**36**	**4**	**3**	**0**	**1**	**104**	**15.4**	**2**	....	....	....	....	....	....	....	....	....	....	....	....
1996-97	**Anaheim**	**NHL**	**78**	**51**	**58**	**109**	**34**	**11**	**1**	**8**	**273**	**18.7**	**28**	....	....	....	**11**	**7**	**3**	**10**	**4**	**3**	**0**	**1**	....
1997-98	**Anaheim**	**NHL**	**73**	***52**	**34**	**86**	**30**	**10**	**1**	**10**	**268**	**19.4**	**12**	....	....	....	....	....	....	....	....	....	....	....	....
	Finland	Olympics	5	4	6	10	8	....	....	....	....	....	....	....	....	....	....	....	....	....	....	....	....	....	....
1998-99	**Anaheim**	**NHL**	**75**	***47**	**60**	**107**	**30**	***25**	**0**	**7**	**281**	**16.7**	**18**	**5**	**20.0**	**22:47**	**4**	**2**	**2**	**4**	**2**	**1**	**0**	**0**	**22:23**
99-2000	**Anaheim**	**NHL**	**79**	**33**	**52**	**85**	**12**	**8**	**0**	**6**	**236**	**14.0**	**6**	**13**	**23.1**	**22:44**	....	....	....	....	....	....	....	....	....
2000-01	**Anaheim**	**NHL**	**61**	**26**	**33**	**59**	**36**	**10**	**0**	**5**	**202**	**12.9**	**–8**	**4**	**50.0**	**21:51**	....	....	....	....	....	....	....	....	....
	San Jose	**NHL**	**12**	**7**	**6**	**13**	**0**	**2**	**0**	**2**	**31**	**22.6**	**1**	**4**	**75.0**	**18:14**	**6**	**0**	**2**	**2**	**2**	**0**	**0**	**0**	**17:13**
2001-02	**San Jose**	**NHL**	**82**	**29**	**25**	**54**	**40**	**9**	**1**	**8**	**202**	**14.4**	**–11**	**12**	**25.0**	**16:58**	**12**	**5**	**3**	**8**	**2**	**2**	**0**	**1**	**16:51**
	Finland	Olympics	4	3	0	3	2	....	....	....	....	....	....	....	....	....	....	....	....	....	....	....	....	....	....
2002-03	**San Jose**	**NHL**	**82**	**28**	**36**	**64**	**30**	**7**	**0**	**5**	**253**	**11.1**	**–6**	**107**	**42.1**	**19:14**	....	....	....	....	....	....	....	....	....
2003-04	**Colorado**	**NHL**	**78**	**16**	**16**	**32**	**32**	**6**	**1**	**4**	**182**	**8.8**	**2**	**80**	**43.8**	**16:10**	**10**	**0**	**3**	**3**	**2**	**0**	**0**	**0**	**12:53**
2004-05			DID NOT PLAY																						
2005-06	**Anaheim**	**NHL**	**80**	**40**	**50**	**90**	**44**	**18**	**0**	**5**	**267**	**15.0**	**28**	**209**	**41.6**	**17:48**	**16**	**6**	**8**	**14**	**6**	**1**	**0**	**2**	**17:56**
	Finland	Olympics	8	*6	5	*11	4	....	....	....	....	....	....	....	....	....	....	....	....	....	....	....	....	....	....
2006-07 ♦	**Anaheim**	**NHL**	**82**	**48**	**46**	**94**	**82**	***25**	**0**	***10**	**257**	**18.7**	**26**	**351**	**50.7**	**17:42**	**21**	**5**	**10**	**15**	**10**	**0**	**0**	**2**	**19:08**
2007-08	**Anaheim**	**NHL**	**26**	**12**	**11**	**23**	**8**	**7**	**0**	**2**	**87**	**13.8**	**5**	**67**	**50.8**	**18:07**	**6**	**2**	**2**	**4**	**6**	**2**	**0**	**1**	**19:35**
2008-09	**Anaheim**	**NHL**	**65**	**27**	**27**	**54**	**36**	**16**	**0**	**5**	**186**	**14.5**	**–3**	**224**	**49.1**	**16:29**	**13**	**4**	**2**	**6**	**4**	**2**	**0**	**1**	**15:08**
2009-10	**Anaheim**	**NHL**	**54**	**27**	**21**	**48**	**16**	**14**	**0**	**5**	**173**	**15.6**	**3**	**131**	**47.3**	**17:19**	....	....	....	....	....	....	....	....	....
	Finland	Olympics	6	0	2	2	0	....	....	....	....	....	....	....	....	....	....	....	....	....	....	....	....	....	....
	NHL Totals		**1186**	**606**	**654**	**1260**	**521**	**220**	**7**	**97**	**3910**	**15.5**		**1207**	**46.6**	**18:52**	**105**	**35**	**37**	**72**	**40**	**13**	**0**	**10**	**17:21**

NHL All-Rookie Team (1993) • NHL First All-Star Team (1993, 1997) • Calder Memorial Trophy (1993) • NHL Second All-Star Team (1998, 1999) • Maurice "Rocket" Richard Trophy (1999) • Olympic Tournament All-Star Team (2006) • Best Forward - Olympic Tournament (2006) • Bill Masterton Memorial Trophy (2006)

Played in NHL All-Star Game (1993, 1994, 1996, 1997, 1998, 1999, 2000, 2002, 2003, 2007)

• Missed majority of 1989-90 season recovering from leg injury suffered in game vs. HIFK Helsinki (Finland), October 19, 1989. Traded to **Anaheim** by **Winnipeg** with Marc Chouinard and Winnipeg's 4th round choice (later traded to Toronto, later traded to Montreal – Montreal selected Kim Staal) in 1996 Entry Draft for Chad Kilger, Oleg Tverdovsky and Anaheim's 3rd round choice (Per-Anton Lundstrom) in 1996 Entry Draft, February 7, 1996. Traded to **San Jose** by **Anaheim** for Jeff Friesen, Steve Shields and San Jose's 2nd round choice (later traded to Dallas – Dallas selected Vojtech Polak) in 2003 Entry Draft, March 5, 2001. Signed as a free agent by **Colorado**, July 3, 2003. Signed as a free agent by **Anaheim**, August 22, 2005. • Missed majority of 2007-08 season contemplating retirement.

SEMENOV, Alexei

(seh-MEH-nahv, al-EHX-ay)

Defense. Shoots left. 6'6", 245 lbs. Born, Murmansk, USSR, April 10, 1981. Edmonton's 2nd choice, 36th overall, in 1999 Entry Draft.

Season	Club	League	GP	G	A	Pts	PIM	PP	SH	GW	S	%	+/-	TF	F%	Min	GP	G	A	Pts	PIM	PP	SH	GW	Min
1997-98	Krylja Sovetov 2	Russia-3	52	1	2	3	48	....	....	....	....	....	....	....	....	....	....	....	....	....	....	....	....	....	....
1998-99	St. Petersburg 2	Russia-4	19	0	1	1	20	....	....	....	....	....	....	....	....	....	....	....	....	....	....	....	....	....	....
	Sudbury Wolves	OHL	28	0	3	3	28	....	....	....	....	....	....	....	....	....	2	0	0	0	4	....	....	....	....
99-2000	Sudbury Wolves	OHL	65	9	35	44	135	....	....	....	....	....	....	....	....	....	12	1	3	4	23	....	....	....	....
	Hamilton	AHL	....	....	....	....	....	....	....	....	....	....	....	....	....	....	3	0	0	0	0	....	....	....	....
2000-01	Sudbury Wolves	OHL	65	21	42	63	106	....	....	....	....	....	....	....	....	....	12	4	13	17	17	....	....	....	....
2001-02	Hamilton	AHL	78	5	11	16	67	....	....	....	....	....	....	....	....	....	....	....	....	....	....	....	....	....	....
2002-03	**Edmonton**	**NHL**	**46**	**1**	**6**	**7**	**58**	**0**	**0**	**0**	**33**	**3.0**	**–7**	**0**	**0.0**	**19:41**	**6**	**0**	**0**	**0**	**0**	**0**	**0**	**0**	**13:05**
	Hamilton	AHL	37	4	3	7	45	....	....	....	....	....	....	....	....	....	....	....	....	....	....	....	....	....	....
2003-04	**Edmonton**	**NHL**	**46**	**2**	**3**	**5**	**32**	**1**	**0**	**0**	**36**	**5.6**	**8**	**0**	**0.0**	**17:16**	....	....	....	....	....	....	....	....	....
2004-05	St. Petersburg	Russia	50	0	8	8	26	....	....	....	....	....	....	....	....	....	....	....	....	....	....	....	....	....	....
2005-06	Yaroslavl	Russia	2	0	1	1	2	....	....	....	....	....	....	....	....	....	....	....	....	....	....	....	....	....	....
	Edmonton	**NHL**	**11**	**1**	**1**	**2**	**17**	**0**	**0**	**0**	**3**	**33.3**	**–3**	**0**	**0.0**	**10:49**	....	....	....	....	....	....	....	....	....
	Florida	**NHL**	**16**	**1**	**1**	**2**	**21**	**1**	**0**	**0**	**13**	**7.7**	**–1**	**0**	**0.0**	**12:33**	....	....	....	....	....	....	....	....	....
	Rochester	AHL	3	0	0	0	7	....	....	....	....	....	....	....	....	....	....	....	....	....	....	....	....	....	....
2006-07	**Florida**	**NHL**	**23**	**0**	**5**	**5**	**28**	**0**	**0**	**0**	**23**	**0.0**	**9**	**1**	**0.0**	**12:22**	....	....	....	....	....	....	....	....	....
	Rochester	AHL	4	0	0	0	6	....	....	....	....	....	....	....	....	....	....	....	....	....	....	....	....	....	....
	Ufa	Russia	20	1	2	3	32	....	....	....	....	....	....	....	....	....	....	....	....	....	....	....	....	....	....
2007-08	**San Jose**	**NHL**	**22**	**1**	**3**	**4**	**36**	**1**	**0**	**0**	**23**	**4.3**	**–8**	**0**	**0.0**	**15:15**	**2**	**0**	**0**	**0**	**2**	**0**	**0**	**0**	**11:15**
2008-09	**San Jose**	**NHL**	**47**	**1**	**7**	**8**	**57**	**0**	**0**	**0**	**28**	**3.6**	**3**	**1**	**0.0**	**13:03**	....	....	....	....	....	....	....	....	....
2009-10	Dynamo Moscow	Rus-KHL	34	1	3	4	30	....	....	....	....	....	....	....	....	....	4	0	1	1	4	....	....	....	....
	NHL Totals		**211**	**7**	**26**	**33**	**249**	**3**	**0**	**0**	**159**	**4.4**		**2**	**0.0**	**15:25**	**8**	**0**	**0**	**0**	**2**	**0**	**0**	**0**	**12:37**

OHL First All-Star Team (2001)

Signed as a free agent by **St. Petersburg** (Russia), July 30, 2004. Traded to **Florida** by **Edmonton** for Florida's 5th round choice (Bryan Pitton) in 2006 Entry Draft, November 19, 2005. Signed as a free agent by **San Jose**, July 27, 2007. Signed as a free agent by **Dynamo Moscow** (Russia-KHL), October 9, 2009.

SEMIN, Alexander

(SEH-min, al-EHX-AN-duhr) **WSH.**

Left wing. Shoots left. 6'2", 208 lbs. Born, Krasnoyarsk, USSR, March 3, 1984. Washington's 2nd choice, 13th overall, in 2002 Entry Draft.

Season	Club	League	GP	G	A	Pts	PIM	PP	SH	GW	S	%	+/-	TF	F%	Min	GP	G	A	Pts	PIM	PP	SH	GW	Min
2001-02	Chelyabinsk	Russia-2	46	13	8	21	52	....	....	....	....	....	....	....	....	....	2	2	0	2	0	....	....	....	....
2002-03	Lada Togliatti	Russia	47	10	7	17	36	....	....	....	....	....	....	....	....	....	10	*5	3	8	10	....	....	....	....
2003-04	**Washington**	**NHL**	**52**	**10**	**12**	**22**	**36**	**4**	**0**	**2**	**92**	**10.9**	**–2**	**6**	**50.0**	**12:37**	....	....	....	....	....	....	....	....	....
	Portland Pirates	AHL	4	3	1	4	6	....	....	....	....	....	....	....	....	....	7	4	7	11	19	....	....	....	....
2004-05	Lada Togliatti	Russia	50	19	11	30	56	....	....	....	....	....	....	....	....	....	10	1	1	2	0	....	....	....	....
2005-06	Lada Togliatti	Russia	16	5	4	9	52	....	....	....	....	....	....	....	....	....	....	....	....	....	....	....	....	....	....
	Mytischi	Russia	26	3	7	10	24	....	....	....	....	....	....	....	....	....	8	3	2	5	6	....	....	....	....
2006-07	**Washington**	**NHL**	**77**	**38**	**35**	**73**	**90**	**17**	**0**	**6**	**243**	**15.6**	**–7**	**44**	**27.3**	**18:24**	....	....	....	....	....	....	....	....	....
2007-08	**Washington**	**NHL**	**63**	**26**	**16**	**42**	**54**	**10**	**0**	**2**	**185**	**14.1**	**–18**	**11**	**36.4**	**16:55**	**7**	**3**	**5**	**8**	**8**	**2**	**0**	**1**	**19:45**
2008-09	**Washington**	**NHL**	**62**	**34**	**45**	**79**	**77**	**8**	**0**	**8**	**223**	**15.2**	**25**	**24**	**50.0**	**19:14**	**14**	**5**	**9**	**14**	**16**	**1**	**0**	**1**	**19:58**

Season	Club	League	GP	G	A	Pts	PIM	PP	SH	GW	S	%	+/-	TF	F%	Min	GP	G	A	Pts	PIM	PP	SH	GW	Min
2009-10	Washington	NHL	73	40	44	84	66	8	2	5	278	14.4	36	16	37.5	19:07	7	0	2	2	4	0	0	0	19:21
	Russia	Olympics	4	0	2	2	4	....	....	....	....	....	....												
	NHL Totals		327	148	152	300	323	47	2	23	1021	14.5		101	36.6	17:31	28	8	16	24	28	3	0	2	19:46

gned as a free agent by **Togliatti** (Russia), September 25, 2004. • Suspended by **Washington** for failing to report to **Portland** (AHL), September 28, 2004. Signed as a free agent by **Mytischi** (Russia), ovember 22, 2005.

SESTITO, Tim
(sehs-TEE-toh, TIHM)   N.J.

Center. Shoots left. 6′, 200 lbs.   Born, Rome, NY, August 28, 1984.

Season	Club	League	GP	G	A	Pts	PIM	PP	SH	GW	S	%	+/-	TF	F%	Min	GP	G	A	Pts	PIM	PP	SH	GW	Min
2001-02	Plymouth Whalers	OHL	51	10	11	21	40										6	0	0	0	0				
2002-03	Plymouth Whalers	OHL	61	11	7	18	49										18	2	3	5	4				
2003-04	Plymouth Whalers	OHL	57	10	20	30	68										9	4	1	5	14				
2004-05	Plymouth Whalers	OHL	67	14	18	32	93										4	0	0	0	14				
	Bridgeport	AHL	9	2	1	3	12																		
2005-06	Greenville	ECHL	72	21	23	44	127										6	2	2	4	24				
2006-07	Wilkes-Barre	AHL	4	0	0	0	6																		
	Stockton Thunder	ECHL	66	13	13	26	132										6	2	1	3	6				
2007-08	Springfield	AHL	77	7	10	17	175																		
2008-09	**Edmonton**	**NHL**	1	0	0	0	0	0	0	0	1	0.0	0	2	50.0	5:53									
	Springfield	AHL	51	5	3	8	77																		
2009-10	**New Jersey**	**NHL**	9	0	1	1	2	0	0	0	7	0.0	-2	64	53.1	12:16									
	Lowell Devils	AHL	66	18	17	35	38										5	0	0	0	8				
	NHL Totals		10	0	1	1	2	0	0	0	8	0.0		66	53.0	11:38									

gned as a free agent by **Edmonton**, August 28, 2006. Traded to **New Jersey** by **Edmonton** for future considerations, July 9, 2009.

SESTITO, Tom
(sehs-TEE-toh, TAWM)   CBJ

Left wing. Shoots left. 6′5″, 228 lbs.   Born, Rome, NY, September 28, 1987. Columbus' 3rd choice, 85th overall, in 2006 Entry Draft.

Season	Club	League	GP	G	A	Pts	PIM	PP	SH	GW	S	%	+/-	TF	F%	Min	GP	G	A	Pts	PIM	PP	SH	GW	Min
2003-04	Syracuse Jr. Stars	EmJHL	31	13	16	29	137										6	5	6	11	32				
2004-05	Plymouth Whalers	OHL	35	1	3	4	88																		
2005-06	Plymouth Whalers	OHL	57	10	10	20	176										13	5	2	7	29				
2006-07	Plymouth Whalers	OHL	60	42	22	64	135										19	11	6	17	57				
2007-08	**Columbus**	**NHL**	1	0	0	0	17	0	0	0	0	0.0	0	0	0.0	4:36									
	Syracuse Crunch	AHL	66	7	16	23	202										9	3	0	3	57				
2008-09	Syracuse Crunch	AHL	52	8	12	20	168																		
2009-10	**Columbus**	**NHL**	3	0	0	0	7	0	0	0	0	0.0	0	0	0.0	5:34									
	Syracuse Crunch	AHL	36	10	7	17	138																		
	NHL Totals		4	0	0	0	24	0	0	0	0	0.0		0	0.0	5:19									

SETOGUCHI, Devin
(SEHT-oh-GOO-chee, DEH-vihn)   S.J.

Right wing. Shoots right. 6′, 200 lbs.   Born, Taber, Alta., January 1, 1987. San Jose's 1st choice, 8th overall, in 2005 Entry Draft.

Season	Club	League	GP	G	A	Pts	PIM	PP	SH	GW	S	%	+/-	TF	F%	Min	GP	G	A	Pts	PIM	PP	SH	GW	Min
2003-04	Saskatoon Blades	WHL	66	13	18	31	53										4	0	1	1	0				
2004-05	Saskatoon Blades	WHL	69	33	31	64	34										10	8	4	12	8				
2005-06	Saskatoon Blades	WHL	65	36	47	83	69										15	*11	10	21	24				
2006-07	Prince George	WHL	55	36	29	65	55																		
2007-08	**San Jose**	**NHL**	44	11	6	17	8	3	0	2	105	10.5	6	17	64.7	14:15	9	1	1	2	2	0	0	0	10:25
	Worcester Sharks	AHL	23	8	11	19	25																		
2008-09	**San Jose**	**NHL**	81	31	34	65	25	11	0	3	246	12.6	16	21	28.6	16:13	6	1	2	3	2	0	0	0	16:21
2009-10	**San Jose**	**NHL**	70	20	16	36	19	8	0	4	165	12.1	0	10	30.0	15:18	15	5	4	9	6	1	0	1	18:25
	NHL Totals		195	62	56	118	52	22	0	9	516	12.0		48	41.7	15:26	30	7	7	14	10	1	0	1	15:36

VHL East Second All-Star Team (2006)

SEXTON, Dan
(SEHKS-tuhn, DAN)   ANA.

Right wing. Shoots right. 5′10″, 170 lbs.   Born, Apple Valley, MN, April 29, 1987.

Season	Club	League	GP	G	A	Pts	PIM	PP	SH	GW	S	%	+/-	TF	F%	Min	GP	G	A	Pts	PIM	PP	SH	GW	Min
2005-06	Wichita Falls	NAHL	58	22	37	59	16										5	2	1	3	0				
2006-07	Sioux Falls	USHL	58	14	10	24	20										8	*8	1	9	0				
2007-08	Bowling Green	CCHA	38	7	14	21	42																		
2008-09	Bowling Green	CCHA	38	17	22	39	20																		
2009-10	**Anaheim**	**NHL**	41	9	10	19	16	2	0	0	93	9.7	-3	1	0.0	13:30									
	Manitoba Moose	AHL	13	5	7	12	2										6	2	3	5	2				
	Bakersfield	ECHL	18	13	13	26	14																		
	NHL Totals		41	9	10	19	16	2	0	0	93	9.7		1	0.0	13:30									

igned as a free agent by **Anaheim**, April 7, 2009.

SHANNON, Ryan
(SHA-nuhn, RIGH-uhn)   OTT.

Center. Shoots right. 5′9″, 171 lbs.   Born, Darien, CT, March 2, 1983.

Season	Club	League	GP	G	A	Pts	PIM	PP	SH	GW	S	%	+/-	TF	F%	Min	GP	G	A	Pts	PIM	PP	SH	GW	Min
2001-02	Boston College	H-East	38	8	17	25	12																		
2002-03	Boston College	H-East	36	14	24	38	4																		
2003-04	Boston College	H-East	42	15	27	42	22																		
2004-05	Boston College	H-East	38	14	31	45	22																		
	Cincinnati	AHL	4	1	0	1	2																		
2005-06	Portland Pirates	AHL	71	27	59	86	44										19	11	11	22	8				
2006-07 ♦	**Anaheim**	**NHL**	53	2	9	11	10	0	0	0	77	2.6	-2	25	52.0	10:39	11	0	0	0	6	0	0	0	4:04
	Portland Pirates	AHL	14	2	7	9	12																		
2007-08	**Vancouver**	**NHL**	27	5	8	13	24	4	0	0	34	14.7	-1	82	39.0	12:53									
	Manitoba Moose	AHL	13	1	7	8	10																		
2008-09	**Ottawa**	**NHL**	35	8	12	20	2	3	0	1	61	13.1	-1	6	33.3	15:04									
	Binghamton	AHL	36	10	25	35	16																		
2009-10	**Ottawa**	**NHL**	66	5	11	16	20	1	0	1	109	4.6	-12	51	37.3	12:40	2	0	0	0	0	0	0	0	6:13
	NHL Totals		181	20	40	60	56	8	0	2	281	7.1		164	40.2	12:35	13	0	0	0	6	0	0	0	4:24

Hockey East First All-Star Team (2004) • NCAA East Second All-American Team (2004) • AHL All-Rookie Team (2006)

igned as a free agent by **Anaheim**, November 28, 2005. Traded to **Vancouver** by **Anaheim** for Jason King and future considerations, June 23, 2007. Traded to **Ottawa** by **Vancouver** for Lawrence Nycholat, September 2, 2008.

SHARP, MacGregor
(SHAHRP, muh-GREHG-uhr)   ANA.

Center. Shoots left. 6′1″, 186 lbs.   Born, Vancouver, B.C., October 1, 1985.

Season	Club	League	GP	G	A	Pts	PIM	PP	SH	GW	S	%	+/-	TF	F%	Min	GP	G	A	Pts	PIM	PP	SH	GW	Min
2002-03	Camrose Kodiaks	AJHL	60	23	25	48	96																		
2003-04	Camrose Kodiaks	AJHL	44	20	26	46	45																		
2004-05	Camrose Kodiaks	AJHL	57	19	30	49	32																		
2005-06	U. Minn-Duluth	WCHA	40	6	8	14	31																		
2006-07	U. Minn-Duluth	WCHA	38	11	16	27	35																		
2007-08	U. Minn-Duluth	WCHA	36	7	10	17	14																		
2008-09	U. Minn-Duluth	WCHA	43	*26	24	*50	20																		
	Iowa Chops	AHL	6	1	1	2	4																		
2009-10	**Anaheim**	**NHL**	8	0	0	0	0	0	0	0	6	0.0	0	28	53.6	4:10									
	San Antonio	AHL	40	9	9	18	16										10	3	5	8	10				
	Bakersfield	ECHL	17	4	12	16	10																		
	NHL Totals		8	0	0	0	0	0	0	0	6	0.0		28	53.6	4:10									

igned as a free agent by **Anaheim**, April 1, 2009.

SHARP, Patrick
(SHAHRP, PAT-rihk) CH

Center. Shoots right. 6'1", 199 lbs. Born, Winnipeg, Man., December 27, 1981. Philadelphia's 2nd choice, 95th overall, in 2001 Entry Draft.

Season	Club	League	GP	G	A	Pts	PIM	PP	SH	GW	S	%	+/-	TF	F%	Min	GP	G	A	Pts	PIM	PP	SH	GW	M
			Regular Season														Playoffs								
1998-99	Thunder Bay	USHL	55	19	24	43	48										3	1	1	2	0				
99-2000	Thunder Bay	USHL	56	20	35	55	41																		
2000-01	U. of Vermont	ECAC	34	12	15	27	36																		
2001-02	U. of Vermont	ECAC	31	13	13	26	50																		
2002-03	**Philadelphia**	**NHL**	3	0	0	0	2	0	0	0	3	0.0	0	7	42.9	5:59									
	Philadelphia	AHL	53	14	19	33	39																		
2003-04	**Philadelphia**	**NHL**	41	5	2	7	55	0	0	1	44	11.4	–3	272	46.7	9:56	12	1	0	1	2	0	0	0	6:1
	Philadelphia	AHL	35	15	14	29	45										1	2	0	2	0				
2004-05	Philadelphia	AHL	75	23	29	52	80										21	8	13	*21	20				
2005-06	**Philadelphia**	**NHL**	22	5	3	8	10	1	0	3	33	15.2	4	38	52.6	7:43									
	Chicago	**NHL**	50	9	14	23	36	0	1	2	111	8.1	1	664	48.0	16:19									
2006-07	**Chicago**	**NHL**	80	20	15	35	74	5	3	1	160	12.5	–15	1008	46.5	17:04									
2007-08	**Chicago**	**NHL**	80	36	26	62	55	9	*7	7	209	17.2	23	594	51.4	18:47									
2008-09	**Chicago**	**NHL**	61	26	18	44	41	9	0	4	184	14.1	6	566	45.8	17:57	17	7	4	11	6	3	0	2	16:1
2009-10♦	**Chicago**	**NHL**	82	25	41	66	28	4	2	4	266	9.4	24	466	51.7	18:07	22	11	11	22	16	3	1	1	17:5
	NHL Totals		**419**	**126**	**119**	**245**	**301**	**28**	**13**	**22**	**1010**	**12.5**		**3615**	**48.2**	**16:22**	**51**	**19**	**15**	**34**	**24**	**6**	**1**	**3**	**14:3**

Traded to **Chicago** by **Philadelphia** with Eric Meloche for Matt Ellison and Chicago's 3rd round choice (later traded to Montreal - Montreal selected Ryan White) in 2006 Entry Draft, December 5, 2005.

SHELLEY, Jody
(SHEH-lee, JOH-dee) PH

Left wing. Shoots left. 6'3", 230 lbs. Born, Thompson, Man., February 7, 1976.

Season	Club	League	GP	G	A	Pts	PIM	PP	SH	GW	S	%	+/-	TF	F%	Min	GP	G	A	Pts	PIM	PP	SH	GW	M
1994-95	Halifax	QMJHL	72	10	12	22	194										7	0	1	1	12				
1995-96	Halifax	QMJHL	50	13	19	32	319										6	0	2	2	36				
1996-97	Halifax	QMJHL	58	25	19	44	*448										17	6	6	12	*123				
1997-98	Dalhousie	AUAA	19	6	11	17	145																		
	Saint John Flames	AHL	18	1	1	2	50																		
1998-99	Saint John Flames	AHL	8	0	0	0	46																		
	Johnstown Chiefs	ECHL	52	12	17	29	325																		
99-2000	Johnstown Chiefs	ECHL	36	9	17	26	256																		
	Saint John Flames	AHL	22	1	4	5	93										3	0	0	0	2				
2000-01	Syracuse Crunch	AHL	69	1	7	8	*357										5	0	0	0	21				
	Columbus	**NHL**	1	0	0	0	10	0	0	0	0	0.0	0	0	0.0	1:33									
2001-02	**Columbus**	**NHL**	52	3	3	6	206	0	0	0	35	8.6	1	0	0.0	6:32									
	Syracuse Crunch	AHL	22	3	5	8	165																		
2002-03	**Columbus**	**NHL**	68	1	4	5	*249	0	0	0	39	2.6	–5	1	0.0	6:08									
2003-04	**Columbus**	**NHL**	76	3	3	6	228	1	0	0	62	4.8	–10	3	0.0	7:14									
2004-05	JYP Jyvaskyla	Finland	11	0	1	1	20										3	0	0	0	25				
2005-06	**Columbus**	**NHL**	80	3	7	10	163	0	0	1	39	7.7	–4	7	14.3	5:58									
2006-07	**Columbus**	**NHL**	72	1	1	2	125	0	0	0	32	3.1	–6	2	0.0	4:52									
2007-08	**Columbus**	**NHL**	31	0	0	0	44	0	0	0	10	0.0	–2	1	0.0	4:20									
	San Jose	**NHL**	31	1	6	7	91	0	0	0	31	3.2	–2	1	0.0	7:24	6	0	0	0	2	0	0	0	3:1
2008-09	**San Jose**	**NHL**	70	2	2	4	116	0	0	1	44	4.5	–6	7	42.9	6:11	1	0	0	0	0	0	0	0	2:0
2009-10	**San Jose**	**NHL**	36	0	3	3	78	0	0	0	20	0.0	1	5	40.0	6:34									
	NY Rangers	**NHL**	21	2	4	6	37	0	0	0	29	6.9	4	1	0.0	7:07									
	NHL Totals		**538**	**16**	**33**	**49**	**1347**	**1**	**0**	**2**	**341**	**4.7**		**28**	**21.4**	**6:10**	**7**	**0**	**0**	**0**	**2**	**0**	**0**	**0**	**3:0**

Signed as a free agent by **Calgary**, September 1, 1998. Signed as a free agent by **Syracuse** (AHL), September 15, 2000. Signed as a free agent by **Columbus**, January 31, 2001. Signed as a free agent by **Jyvaskyla** (Finland), January 17, 2005. Traded to **San Jose** by **Columbus** for San Jose's 6th round choice (later traded to Atlanta, later traded to Chicago – Chicago selected David Pacan) in 2009 Entry Draft, January 29, 2008. Traded to **NY Rangers** by **San Jose** for NY Rangers' 6th round choice in 2011 Entry Draft, February 12, 2010. Signed as a free agent by **Philadelphia**, July 1, 2010.

SHEPPARD, James
(sheh-PUHRD, JAYMZ) MIN

Center. Shoots left. 6'2", 210 lbs. Born, Halifax, N.S., April 25, 1988. Minnesota's 1st choice, 9th overall, in 2006 Entry Draft.

Season	Club	League	GP	G	A	Pts	PIM	PP	SH	GW	S	%	+/-	TF	F%	Min	GP	G	A	Pts	PIM	PP	SH	GW	M
2003-04	Dartmouth	NSMHL	61	38	54	92	46																		
2004-05	Cape Breton	QMJHL	65	14	31	45	40										5	1	3	4	2				
2005-06	Cape Breton	QMJHL	66	30	54	84	78										9	2	5	7	12				
2006-07	Cape Breton	QMJHL	56	33	63	96	62										16	8	12	20	14				
2007-08	**Minnesota**	**NHL**	78	4	15	19	29	0	0	1	57	7.0	0	655	41.5	10:37	6	0	1	1	4	0	0	0	10:3
2008-09	**Minnesota**	**NHL**	82	5	19	24	41	0	0	1	88	5.7	–14	870	41.5	15:11									
2009-10	**Minnesota**	**NHL**	64	2	4	6	38	0	0	0	64	3.1	–14	343	45.2	11:59									
	NHL Totals		**224**	**11**	**38**	**49**	**108**	**0**	**0**	**2**	**209**	**5.3**		**1868**	**42.2**	**12:41**	**6**	**0**	**1**	**1**	**4**	**0**	**0**	**0**	**10:3**

QMJHL Second All-Star Team (2007)

SHIROKOV, Sergei
(sheer-OH-kawv, SAIR-gay) VAN

Left wing. Shoots right. 5'10", 195 lbs. Born, Ozery, USSR, March 10, 1986. Vancouver's 3rd choice, 163rd overall, in 2006 Entry Draft.

Season	Club	League	GP	G	A	Pts	PIM	PP	SH	GW	S	%	+/-	TF	F%	Min	GP	G	A	Pts	PIM	PP	SH	GW	M
2001-02	HK CSKA 2	Russia-3	18	2	3	5	0																		
2002-03	CSKA Moscow 2	Russia-3	2	0	0	0	0																		
2003-04	CSKA Moscow 2	Russia-3	66	39	41	80	66																		
2004-05	CSKA Moscow 2	Russia-3	25	16	13	29	47																		
	CSKA Moscow	Russia	8	0	0	0	0																		
	CSKA Moscow	Russia	8	0	0	0	0																		
2005-06	CSKA Moscow	Russia	39	7	7	14	26										4	0	0	0	0				
2006-07	CSKA Moscow	Russia	52	16	19	35	36										12	4	6	10	4				
2007-08	CSKA Moscow	Russia	57	12	21	33	28										6	0	3	3	4				
2008-09	CSKA Moscow	Rus-KHL	56	17	23	40	36										8	1	3	4	4				
2009-10	**Vancouver**	**NHL**	6	0	0	0	2	0	0	0	4	0.0	–4	2	50.0	12:50									
	Manitoba Moose	AHL	76	22	23	45	32										6	0	2	2	4				
	NHL Totals		**6**	**0**	**0**	**0**	**2**	**0**	**0**	**0**	**4**	**0.0**		**2**	**50.0**	**12:50**									

SIFERS, Jaime
(SIH-fuhrs, JAY-mee) ATL

Defense. Shoots right. 5'11", 210 lbs. Born, Stratford, CT, January 18, 1983.

Season	Club	League	GP	G	A	Pts	PIM	PP	SH	GW	S	%	+/-	TF	F%	Min	GP	G	A	Pts	PIM	PP	SH	GW	M
2002-03	U. of Vermont	ECAC	34	4	14	18	66																		
2003-04	U. of Vermont	ECAC	35	4	14	18	93																		
2004-05	U. of Vermont	ECAC	36	4	12	16	57																		
2005-06	U. of Vermont	H-East	38	3	15	18	60																		
	Toronto Marlies	AHL	2	0	0	0	2																		
2006-07	Toronto Marlies	AHL	80	7	18	25	75																		
2007-08	Toronto Marlies	AHL	80	3	10	13	57										19	2	3	5	6				
2008-09	**Toronto**	**NHL**	23	0	2	2	18	0	0	0	25	0.0	–4	0	0.0	12:50									
	Toronto Marlies	AHL	43	4	16	20	47										4	0	1	1	4				
2009-10	**Minnesota**	**NHL**	14	0	0	0	6	0	0	0	9	0.0	1	0	0.0	12:59									
	Houston Aeros	AHL	54	3	5	8	58																		
	NHL Totals		**37**	**0**	**2**	**2**	**24**	**0**	**0**	**0**	**34**	**0.0**		**0**	**0.0**	**12:53**									

ECAC Second All-Star Team (2005)

Signed as a free agent by **Toronto**, July 20, 2006. Signed as a free agent by **Minnesota**, July 8, 2009. Signed as a free agent by **Atlanta**, July 7, 2010.

SIGALET, Jonathan
(SIH-ga-leht, JAWN-ah-thuhn) CB

Defense. Shoots left. 6'1", 199 lbs. Born, Vancouver, B.C., February 12, 1986. Boston's 4th choice, 100th overall, in 2005 Entry Draft.

Season	Club	League	GP	G	A	Pts	PIM	PP	SH	GW	S	%	+/-	TF	F%	Min	GP	G	A	Pts	PIM	PP	SH	GW	M
2002-03	Salmon Arm	BCHL	52	13	39	52	34																		
2003-04	Bowling Green	CCHA	37	3	12	15	26																		
2004-05	Bowling Green	CCHA	35	3	13	16	36																		
2005-06	Providence Bruins	AHL	75	9	27	36	59										6	2	1	3	9				
2006-07	**Boston**	**NHL**	1	0	0	0	4	0	0	0	1	0.0	–2	0	0.0	14:41									
	Providence Bruins	AHL	50	9	13	22	37																		

						Regular Season													Playoffs							
Season	Club	League	GP	G	A	Pts	PIM	PP	SH	GW	S	%	+/-	TF	F%	Min	GP	G	A	Pts	PIM	PP	SH	GW	Min
2007-08	Providence Bruins	AHL	74	3	20	23	58	....	....	....	....	....	....	....	....	....	10	0	3	3	12	....	....	....	....
2008-09	Syracuse Crunch	AHL	19	5	6	11	16	....	....	....	....	....	....	....	....	....	....	....	....	....	....	....	....	....	....
2009-10	Syracuse Crunch	AHL	69	8	11	19	66	....	....	....	....	....	....	....	....	....	....	....	....	....	....	....	....	....	....
	NHL Totals		**1**	**0**	**0**	**0**	**4**	0	0	0	1	0.0		0	0.0	14:41									

Traded to **Columbus** by **Boston** for Matt Marquardt, May 27, 2008.

SIM, Jon

(SIHM, JAWN)   **NYI**

Left wing. Shoots left. 5'10", 195 lbs.   Born, New Glasgow, N.S., September 29, 1977. Dallas' 2nd choice, 70th overall, in 1996 Entry Draft.

Season	Club	League	GP	G	A	Pts	PIM	PP	SH	GW	S	%	+/-	TF	F%	Min	GP	G	A	Pts	PIM	PP	SH	GW	Min
1994-95	Laval Titan	QMJHL	9	0	1	1	6	....	....	....	....	....	....	....	....	....	4	3	2	5	2	....	....	....	....
	Sarnia Sting	OHL	25	9	12	21	19	....	....	....	....	....	....	....	....	....	10	8	7	15	26	....	....	....	....
1995-96	Sarnia Sting	OHL	63	56	46	102	130	....	....	....	....	....	....	....	....	....	12	9	5	14	32	....	....	....	....
1996-97	Sarnia Sting	OHL	64	*56	39	95	109	....	....	....	....	....	....	....	....	....	5	1	4	5	14	....	....	....	....
1997-98	Sarnia Sting	OHL	59	44	50	94	95	....	....	....	....	....	....	....	....	....	4	0	0	0	0	0	0	0	6:27
1998-99 ♦	**Dallas**	NHL	7	1	0	1	12	0	0	0	8	12.5	1	6	50.0	11:26	5	3	1	4	18	....	....	....	....
	Michigan	IHL	68	24	27	51	91	....	....	....	....	....	....	....	....	....	7	1	0	1	6	0	0	0	11:11
99-2000	**Dallas**	NHL	25	5	3	8	10	2	0	1	44	11.4	4	4	75.0	10:51	....	....	....	....	....	....	....	....	....
	Michigan	IHL	35	14	16	30	65	....	....	....	....	....	....	....	....	....	....	....	....	....	....	....	....	....	....
2000-01	**Dallas**	NHL	15	0	3	3	6	0	0	0	18	0.0	-2	1000.0		8:47	....	....	....	....	....	....	....	....	....
	Utah Grizzlies	IHL	39	16	13	29	44	....	....	....	....	....	....	3	0.0	9:30	....	....	....	....	....	....	....	....	....
2001-02	**Dallas**	NHL	26	3	0	3	10	1	0	0	43	7.0	-3	2	50.0	9:10	....	....	....	....	....	....	....	....	....
	Utah Grizzlies	AHL	31	21	6	27	63	....	....	....	....	....	....	....	....	....	....	....	....	....	....	....	....	....	....
2002-03	**Dallas**	NHL	4	0	0	0	0	0	0	0	7	0.0	-1	....	....	....	....	....	....	....	....	....	....	....	....
	Utah Grizzlies	AHL	42	16	31	47	85	....	....	....	....	....	....	14	35.7	9:18	....	....	....	....	....	....	....	....	....
	Nashville	NHL	4	1	0	1	0	0	0	0	3	33.3	0	3	33.3	12:05	....	....	....	....	....	....	....	....	....
	Los Angeles	NHL	14	0	2	2	19	0	0	0	29	0.0	-3	19	31.6	10:01	....	....	....	....	....	....	....	....	....
2003-04	**Los Angeles**	NHL	48	6	7	13	27	0	0	1	73	8.2	0	0	0.0	13:39	....	....	....	....	....	....	....	....	....
	Pittsburgh	NHL	15	2	3	5	6	0	0	0	27	7.4	-4	....	....	....	....	....	....	....	....	....	....	....	....
2004-05	Utah Grizzlies	AHL	10	2	2	4	12	....	....	....	....	....	....	....	....	....	21	*10	7	17	44	....	....	....	....
	Philadelphia	AHL	63	35	26	61	66	....	....	....	....	....	....	1	0.0	10:59	....	....	....	....	....	....	....	....	....
2005-06	**Philadelphia**	NHL	39	7	7	14	28	4	0	2	80	8.8	-6	0	0.0	12:28	....	....	....	....	....	....	....	....	....
	Florida	NHL	33	10	8	18	26	4	0	3	92	10.9	-1	9	22.2	11:45	4	0	0	0	0	0	0	0	5:29
2006-07	**Atlanta**	NHL	77	17	12	29	60	2	0	1	141	12.1	-1	0	0.0	14:19	....	....	....	....	....	....	....	....	....
2007-08	**NY Islanders**	NHL	2	0	1	1	2	0	0	0	8	0.0	-1	0	0.0	14:19	....	....	....	....	....	....	....	....	....
2008-09	**NY Islanders**	NHL	49	9	6	15	42	3	0	0	90	10.0	-12	6	16.7	12:10	5	2	3	5	2	....	....	....	....
	Bridgeport	AHL	18	13	10	23	12	....	....	....	....	....	....	....	....	....	....	....	....	....	....	....	....	....	....
2009-10	**NY Islanders**	NHL	77	13	9	22	44	1	0	0	128	10.2	-4	18	50.0	11:39	....	....	....	....	....	....	....	....	....
	NHL Totals		**435**	**74**	**61**	**135**	**292**	17	0	9	791	9.4		86	37.2	11:19	15	1	0	1	6	0	0	0	8:24

OHL Second All-Star Team (1998)
Traded to **Nashville** by **Dallas** for Bubba Berenzweig and future considerations, February 17, 2003. Claimed on waivers by **Los Angeles** from **Nashville**, March 8, 2003. Claimed on waivers by **Pittsburgh** from **Los Angeles**, March 4, 2004. Signed as a free agent by **Phoenix**, September 2, 2004. • Loaned to Philadelphia (AHL) by **Phoenix** (Utah - AHL) for the loan of Peter White, November 14, 2004. Signed as a free agent by **Philadelphia**, August 2, 2005. Traded to **Florida** by Philadelphia for Florida's 6th round choice (Patrick Maroon) in 2007 Entry Draft, January 23, 2006. Signed as a free agent by **Atlanta**, July 14, 2006. Signed as a free agent by **NY Islanders**, July 1, 2007.

SIMMONDS, Wayne

(SIH-muhnds, WAYN)   **L.A.**

Right wing. Shoots right. 6'2", 183 lbs.   Born, Scarborough, Ont., August 26, 1988. Los Angeles' 3rd choice, 61st overall, in 2007 Entry Draft.

Season	Club	League	GP	G	A	Pts	PIM	PP	SH	GW	S	%	+/-	TF	F%	Min	GP	G	A	Pts	PIM	PP	SH	GW	Min
2004-05	Tor. Jr. Canadiens	GTHL	67	32	40	72	97	....	....	....	....	....	....	....	....	....	7	4	2	6	12	....	....	....	....
2005-06	Brockville Braves	CJHL	49	24	19	43	127	....	....	....	....	....	....	....	....	....	4	1	1	2	4	....	....	....	....
2006-07	Owen Sound	OHL	66	23	26	49	112	....	....	....	....	....	....	....	....	....	....	....	....	....	....	....	....	....	....
2007-08	Owen Sound	OHL	29	17	22	39	43	....	....	....	....	....	....	....	....	....	14	5	9	14	22	....	....	....	....
	Sault Ste. Marie	OHL	31	16	20	36	68	....	....	....	....	....	....	....	....	....	....	....	....	....	....	....	....	....	....
2008-09	**Los Angeles**	NHL	82	9	14	23	73	2	0	2	127	7.1	-8	25	36.0	13:50	6	2	1	3	9	0	0	0	14:21
2009-10	**Los Angeles**	NHL	78	16	24	40	116	0	0	2	127	12.6	22	10	30.0	14:29	6	2	1	3	9	0	0	0	14:21
	NHL Totals		**160**	**25**	**38**	**63**	**189**	2	0	4	254	9.8		35	34.3	14:09									

SIMON, Ben

(SIGH-muhn, BEHN)

Left wing. Shoots left. 6', 195 lbs.   Born, Shaker Heights, OH, June 14, 1978. Chicago's 5th choice, 110th overall, in 1997 Entry Draft.

Season	Club	League	GP	G	A	Pts	PIM	PP	SH	GW	S	%	+/-	TF	F%	Min	GP	G	A	Pts	PIM	PP	SH	GW	Min
1992-93	Shaker Heights	High-OH	25	15	21	36	....	....	....	....	....	....	....	....	....	....	....	....	....	....	....	....	....	....	....
1993-94	Shaker Heights	High-OH	24	45	41	86	....	....	....	....	....	....	....	....	....	....	....	....	....	....	....	....	....	....	....
1994-95	Shaker Heights	High-OH	25	61	68	129	....	....	....	....	....	....	....	....	....	....	5	7	13	20	....	....	....	....	....
1995-96	Cleveland Barons	NAHL	45	38	33	71	....	....	....	....	....	....	....	....	....	....	....	....	....	....	....	....	....	....	....
1996-97	U. of Notre Dame	CCHA	30	4	15	19	79	....	....	....	....	....	....	....	....	....	....	....	....	....	....	....	....	....	....
1997-98	U. of Notre Dame	CCHA	37	9	28	37	91	....	....	....	....	....	....	....	....	....	....	....	....	....	....	....	....	....	....
1998-99	U. of Notre Dame	CCHA	37	18	24	42	65	....	....	....	....	....	....	....	....	....	....	....	....	....	....	....	....	....	....
99-2000	U. of Notre Dame	CCHA	40	13	19	32	53	....	....	....	....	....	....	....	....	....	16	6	5	11	20	....	....	....	....
2000-01	Orlando	IHL	77	8	12	20	47	....	....	....	....	....	....	....	....	....	....	....	....	....	....	....	....	....	....
2001-02	**Atlanta**	NHL	6	0	0	0	6	0	0	0	7	0.0	1	32	40.6	9:20	25	2	3	5	24	....	....	....	....
	Chicago Wolves	AHL	74	11	23	34	56	....	....	....	....	....	....	54	31.5	9:25	....	....	....	....	....	....	....	....	....
2002-03	**Atlanta**	NHL	10	0	1	1	9	0	0	0	7	0.0	0	....	....	....	9	0	0	0	6	....	....	....	....
	Chicago Wolves	AHL	69	15	17	32	78	....	....	....	....	....	....	....	....	....	....	....	....	....	....	....	....	....	....
2003-04	Milwaukee	AHL	18	1	3	4	6	....	....	....	....	....	....	203	33.0	6:05	....	....	....	....	....	....	....	....	....
	Atlanta	NHL	52	3	0	3	28	0	0	0	30	10.0	-10	....	....	....	18	1	5	6	44	....	....	....	....
2004-05	Chicago Wolves	AHL	53	11	10	21	58	....	....	....	....	....	....	53	24.5	5:38	....	....	....	....	....	....	....	....	....
2005-06	**Columbus**	NHL	13	0	0	0	4	0	0	0	7	0.0	-4	....	....	....	3	0	1	1	2	....	....	....	....
	Syracuse Crunch	AHL	66	13	24	37	88	....	....	....	....	....	....	....	....	....	....	....	....	....	....	....	....	....	....
2006-07	Syracuse Crunch	AHL	56	9	12	21	77	....	....	....	....	....	....	....	....	....	7	0	0	0	9	....	....	....	....
	Grand Rapids	AHL	21	4	5	9	28	....	....	....	....	....	....	....	....	....	....	....	....	....	....	....	....	....	....
2007-08	Springfield	AHL	80	12	10	22	88	....	....	....	....	....	....	....	....	....	....	....	....	....	....	....	....	....	....
2008-09	Iserlohn Roosters	Germany	51	5	10	15	64	....	....	....	....	....	....	....	....	....	3	3	0	3	14	....	....	....	....
2009-10	Kalamazoo Wings	ECHL	18	4	9	13	16	....	....	....	....	....	....	....	....	....	....	....	....	....	....	....	....	....	....
	Toronto Marlies	AHL	44	2	6	8	51	....	....	....	....	....	....	....	....	....	....	....	....	....	....	....	....	....	....
	NHL Totals		**81**	**3**	**1**	**4**	**47**	0	0	0	51	5.9		342	32.2	6:40									

CCHA Second All-Star Team (1999)
• Rights traded to **Atlanta** by **Chicago** for Atlanta's 9th round choice (Peter Flache) in 2000 Entry Draft, June 25, 2000. Signed as a free agent by **Nashville**, July 14, 2003. Traded to **Atlanta** by **Nashville** with Tomas Kloucek for Simon Gamache and Kirill Safronov, December 2, 2003. Signed as a free agent by **Columbus**, August 11, 2005. Signed as a free agent by **Iserlohn** (Germany), August 5, 2008. Signed as a free agent by **Kalamazoo** (ECHL), November 11, 2009. Signed to a PTO (professional tryout) contract by **Toronto** (AHL), January 2, 2010.

SJOSTROM, Fredrik

(SHAW-strahm, FREHD-rihk)   **TOR.**

Right wing. Shoots left. 6'1", 218 lbs.   Born, Fargelanda, Sweden, May 6, 1983. Phoenix's 1st choice, 11th overall, in 2001 Entry Draft.

Season	Club	League	GP	G	A	Pts	PIM	PP	SH	GW	S	%	+/-	TF	F%	Min	GP	G	A	Pts	PIM	PP	SH	GW	Min
99-2000	MoDo U18	Swe-U18	4	0	2	2	6	....	....	....	....	....	....	....	....	....	....	....	....	....	....	....	....	....	....
	Malmo Jr.	Swe-Jr.	18	4	6	10	8	....	....	....	....	....	....	....	....	....	4	1	2	3	6	....	....	....	....
2000-01	V.Frolunda Jr.	Swe-Jr.	11	3	7	10	12	....	....	....	....	....	....	....	....	....	5	0	0	0	2	....	....	....	....
	V.Frolunda	Sweden	31	3	2	5	6	....	....	....	....	....	....	....	....	....	4	1	1	2	8	....	....	....	....
2001-02	Calgary Hitmen	WHL	58	19	31	50	51	....	....	....	....	....	....	....	....	....	5	1	3	4	4	....	....	....	....
2002-03	Calgary Hitmen	WHL	63	34	43	77	95	....	....	....	....	....	....	....	....	....	6	2	0	2	12	....	....	....	....
	Springfield	AHL	2	1	0	1	0	....	....	....	....	....	....	....	....	....	....	....	....	....	....	....	....	....	....
2003-04	**Phoenix**	NHL	57	7	6	13	22	0	0	1	73	9.6	-7	7	28.6	11:35	....	....	....	....	....	....	....	....	....
	Springfield	AHL	17	0	7	7	8	....	....	....	....	....	....	....	....	....	....	....	....	....	....	....	....	....	....
2004-05	Utah Grizzlies	AHL	80	14	24	38	57	....	....	....	....	....	....	8	12.5	13:20	....	....	....	....	....	....	....	....	....
2005-06	**Phoenix**	NHL	75	6	17	23	42	1	0	1	109	5.5	1	15	13.3	14:07	....	....	....	....	....	....	....	....	....
2006-07	**Phoenix**	NHL	78	9	9	18	48	2	0	1	125	7.2	-11	33	18.2	13:33	....	....	....	....	....	....	....	....	....
2007-08	**Phoenix**	NHL	51	10	9	19	14	2	1	0	84	11.9	-2	3	0.0	8:05	10	0	1	1	2	0	0	0	6:28
	NY Rangers	NHL	18	2	0	2	8	0	0	0	26	7.7	0	....	....	....	7	0	1	1	0	0	0	0	11:46
2008-09	**NY Rangers**	NHL	79	7	6	13	30	0	2	0	95	7.4	-11	5	60.0	12:10	....	....	....	....	....	....	....	....	....

Season	Club	League	GP	G	A	Pts	PIM	PP	SH	GW	S	%	+/-	TF	F%	Min	GP	G	A	Pts	PIM	PP	SH	GW	Min
							Regular Season										Playoffs								
2009-10	Calgary	NHL	46	1	5	6	8	0	0	0	33	3.0	2	2	0.0	9:31	....	....	....	....	....	....	....	....	....
	Toronto	NHL	19	2	3	5	4	0	0	0	31	6.5	−4	5	0.0	13:52	....	....	....	....	....	....	....	....	....
	NHL Totals		**423**	**44**	**55**	**99**	**176**	**5**	**4**	**5**	**576**	**7.6**		**78**	**17.9**	**12:26**	**17**	**0**	**2**	**2**	**2**	**0**	**0**	**0**	**8:39**

Traded to **NY Rangers** by **Phoenix** with Josh Gratton, David LeNeveu and Phoenix's 5th round choice (Roman Horak) in 2009 Entry Draft for Marcel Hossa and Al Montoya, February 26, 2008. Signed as a free agent by **Calgary**, July 1, 2009. Traded to **Toronto** by **Calgary** with Dion Phaneuf and Keith Aulie for Matt Stajan, Niklas Hagman, Jamal Mayers and Ian White, January 31, 2010.

SKILLE, Jack

(SKIH-lee, JAK) **CHI.**

Right wing. Shoots right. 6'1", 215 lbs. Born, Madison, WI, May 19, 1987. Chicago's 1st choice, 7th overall, in 2005 Entry Draft.

Season	Club	League	GP	G	A	Pts	PIM	PP	SH	GW	S	%	+/-	TF	F%	Min	GP	G	A	Pts	PIM	PP	SH	GW	Min
2003-04	USNTDP	U-17	33	14	10	24	30	....	....	....	....	....	....	....	....	....	....	....	....	....	....	....	....	....	....
	USNTDP	NAHL	28	11	9	20	31	....	....	....	....	....	....	....	....	....	....	....	....	....	....	....	....	....	....
2004-05	USNTDP	U-18	26	9	11	20	36	....	....	....	....	....	....	....	....	....	....	....	....	....	....	....	....	....	....
	USNTDP	NAHL	16	6	11	17	20	....	....	....	....	....	....	....	....	....	....	....	....	....	....	....	....	....	....
2005-06	U. of Wisconsin	WCHA	41	13	8	21	37	....	....	....	....	....	....	....	....	....	....	....	....	....	....	....	....	....	....
2006-07	U. of Wisconsin	WCHA	26	8	10	18	12	....	....	....	....	....	....	....	....	....	....	....	....	....	....	....	....	....	....
	Norfolk Admirals	AHL	9	4	4	8	0	....	....	....	....	....	....	....	....	....	3	0	0	0	2	....	....	....	....
2007-08	**Chicago**	**NHL**	**16**	**3**	**2**	**5**	**0**	**0**	**0**	**0**	**23**	**13.0**	**1**	**4**	**50.0**	**11:59**	....	....	....	....	....	....	....	....	....
	Rockford IceHogs	AHL	59	16	18	34	44	....	....	....	....	....	....	....	....	....	12	2	1	3	6	....	....	....	....
2008-09	**Chicago**	**NHL**	**8**	**1**	**0**	**1**	**5**	**0**	**0**	**0**	**14**	**7.1**	**−3**	**0**	**0.0**	**9:26**	....	....	....	....	....	....	....	....	....
	Rockford IceHogs	AHL	58	20	25	45	56	....	....	....	....	....	....	....	....	....	....	....	....	....	....	....	....	....	....
2009-10	**Chicago**	**NHL**	**6**	**1**	**1**	**2**	**0**	**0**	**0**	**0**	**9**	**11.1**	**−3**	**0**	**0.0**	**7:40**	....	....	....	....	....	....	....	....	....
	Rockford IceHogs	AHL	63	23	26	49	50	....	....	....	....	....	....	....	....	....	4	0	0	0	0	....	....	....	....
	NHL Totals		**30**	**5**	**3**	**8**	**5**	**0**	**0**	**0**	**46**	**10.9**		**4**	**50.0**	**10:26**	....	....	....	....	....	....	....	....	....

SKINNER, Brett

(SKIH-nuhr, BREHT)

Defense. Shoots left. 6'1", 183 lbs. Born, Brandon, Man., June 28, 1983. Vancouver's 3rd choice, 68th overall, in 2002 Entry Draft.

Season	Club	League	GP	G	A	Pts	PIM	PP	SH	GW	S	%	+/-	TF	F%	Min	GP	G	A	Pts	PIM	PP	SH	GW	Min
1998-99	Brandon Kings	MMBHL	29	3	18	21	20	....	....	....	....	....	....	....	....	....	....	....	....	....	....	....	....	....	....
99-2000	Brandon Kings	MMMHL	40	8	27	35	48	....	....	....	....	....	....	....	....	....	....	....	....	....	....	....	....	....	....
2000-01	Trail	BCHL	59	11	24	35	43	....	....	....	....	....	....	....	....	....	....	....	....	....	....	....	....	....	....
2001-02	Des Moines	USHL	44	9	38	47	25	....	....	....	....	....	....	....	....	....	3	0	1	1	0	....	....	....	....
2002-03	U. of Denver	WCHA	37	4	13	17	27	....	....	....	....	....	....	....	....	....	....	....	....	....	....	....	....	....	....
2003-04	U. of Denver	WCHA	44	7	23	30	32	....	....	....	....	....	....	....	....	....	....	....	....	....	....	....	....	....	....
2004-05	U. of Denver	WCHA	43	4	36	40	30	....	....	....	....	....	....	....	....	....	....	....	....	....	....	....	....	....	....
2005-06	Manitoba Moose	AHL	65	4	21	25	33	....	....	....	....	....	....	....	....	....	13	0	4	4	19	....	....	....	....
2006-07	Portland Pirates	AHL	41	6	12	18	24	....	....	....	....	....	....	....	....	....	....	....	....	....	....	....	....	....	....
	Augusta Lynx	ECHL	5	1	3	4	8	....	....	....	....	....	....	....	....	....	....	....	....	....	....	....	....	....	....
	Omaha	AHL	21	0	6	6	2	....	....	....	....	....	....	....	....	....	5	0	3	3	2	....	....	....	....
2007-08	Providence Bruins	AHL	68	7	40	47	47	....	....	....	....	....	....	....	....	....	10	0	1	1	0	....	....	....	....
2008-09	**NY Islanders**	**NHL**	**11**	**0**	**0**	**0**	**4**	**0**	**0**	**0**	**5**	**0.0**	**3**	**0**	**0.0**	**11:43**	....	....	....	....	....	....	....	....	....
	Bridgeport	AHL	24	1	11	12	10	....	....	....	....	....	....	....	....	....	....	....	....	....	....	....	....	....	....
	Chicago Wolves	AHL	37	3	20	23	4	....	....	....	....	....	....	....	....	....	....	....	....	....	....	....	....	....	....
2009-10	Lake Erie	AHL	73	3	25	28	43	....	....	....	....	....	....	....	....	....	....	....	....	....	....	....	....	....	....
	NHL Totals		**11**	**0**	**0**	**0**	**4**	**0**	**0**	**0**	**5**	**0.0**		**0**	**0.0**	**11:43**	....	....	....	....	....	....	....	....	....

USHL First All-Star Team (2002) • USHL Defenseman of the Year (2002) • WCHA First All-Star Team (2005) • NCAA West Second All-American Team (2005) • NCAA Championship All-Tournament Team (2005)

Traded to **Anaheim** by **Vancouver** with NY Islanders' 2nd round choice (previously acquired, Anaheim selected Bryce Swan) in 2006 Entry Draft for Keith Carney and Juha Alen, March 9, 2006. Traded to **Boston** by **Anaheim** with Nathan Saunders for Mark Mowers, September 24, 2007. Signed as a free agent by **NY Islanders**, July 3, 2008. Traded to **Atlanta** by **NY Islanders** for Junior Lessard, January 13, 2009. Signed as a free agent by **Colorado**, July 8, 2009.

SKOULA, Martin

(SKOO-la, MAHR-tihn)

Defense. Shoots left. 6'3", 226 lbs. Born, Litomerice, Czech., October 28, 1979. Colorado's 2nd choice, 17th overall, in 1998 Entry Draft.

Season	Club	League	GP	G	A	Pts	PIM	PP	SH	GW	S	%	+/-	TF	F%	Min	GP	G	A	Pts	PIM	PP	SH	GW	Min
1995-96	Litvinov Jr.	CzRep-Jr.	38	0	4	4	....	....	....	....	....	....	....	....	....	....	....	....	....	....	....	....	....	....	....
	Litvinov	CzRep	....	....	....	....	....	....	....	....	....	....	....	....	....	....	1	0	0	0	0	....	....	....	....
1996-97	Litvinov Jr.	CzRep-Jr.	38	2	9	11	....	....	....	....	....	....	....	....	....	....	....	....	....	....	....	....	....	....	....
	Litvinov	CzRep	1	0	0	0	0	....	....	....	....	....	....	....	....	....	....	....	....	....	....	....	....	....	....
1997-98	Barrie Colts	OHL	66	8	36	44	36	....	....	....	....	....	....	....	....	....	6	1	3	4	4	....	....	....	....
1998-99	Barrie Colts	OHL	67	13	46	59	46	....	....	....	....	....	....	....	....	....	12	3	10	13	13	....	....	....	....
	Hershey Bears	AHL	....	....	....	....	....	....	....	....	....	....	....	....	....	....	1	0	0	0	0	....	....	....	....
99-2000	**Colorado**	**NHL**	**80**	**3**	**13**	**16**	**20**	**2**	**0**	**0**	**66**	**4.5**	**5**	**0**	**0.0**	**18:15**	**17**	**0**	**2**	**2**	**4**	**0**	**0**	**0**	**18:45**
2000-01♦	**Colorado**	**NHL**	**82**	**8**	**17**	**25**	**38**	**3**	**0**	**2**	**108**	**7.4**	**8**	**1**	**100.0**	**20:41**	**23**	**1**	**4**	**5**	**8**	**0**	**0**	**0**	**11:59**
2001-02	**Colorado**	**NHL**	**82**	**10**	**21**	**31**	**42**	**5**	**0**	**1**	**100**	**10.0**	**−3**	**0**	**0.0**	**22:18**	**21**	**0**	**6**	**6**	**2**	**0**	**0**	**0**	**14:37**
	Czech Republic	Olympics	4	0	0	0	0	....	....	....	....	....	....	....	....	....	....	....	....	....	....	....	....	....	....
2002-03	**Colorado**	**NHL**	**81**	**4**	**21**	**25**	**68**	**2**	**0**	**0**	**93**	**4.3**	**11**	**1**	**100.0**	**18:27**	**7**	**0**	**1**	**1**	**4**	**0**	**0**	**0**	**11:05**
2003-04	**Colorado**	**NHL**	**58**	**2**	**14**	**16**	**30**	**0**	**0**	**0**	**54**	**3.7**	**2**	**0**	**0.0**	**17:21**	....	....	....	....	....	....	....	....	....
	Anaheim	**NHL**	**21**	**2**	**7**	**9**	**2**	**1**	**0**	**0**	**30**	**6.7**	**3**	**1**	**0.0**	**21:14**	....	....	....	....	....	....	....	....	....
2004-05	Litvinov	CzRep	47	4	15	19	101	....	....	....	....	....	....	....	....	....	6	0	0	0	6	....	....	....	....
2005-06	**Dallas**	**NHL**	**61**	**4**	**11**	**15**	**36**	**3**	**0**	**1**	**78**	**5.1**	**6**	**0**	**0.0**	**18:41**	....	....	....	....	....	....	....	....	....
	Minnesota	**NHL**	**17**	**1**	**5**	**6**	**10**	**0**	**0**	**0**	**14**	**7.1**	**0**	**0**	**0.0**	**20:49**	....	....	....	....	....	....	....	....	....
2006-07	**Minnesota**	**NHL**	**81**	**0**	**15**	**15**	**36**	**0**	**0**	**0**	**91**	**0.0**	**9**	**0**	**0.0**	**20:14**	**5**	**0**	**0**	**0**	**4**	**0**	**0**	**0**	**19:02**
2007-08	**Minnesota**	**NHL**	**80**	**3**	**8**	**11**	**26**	**0**	**0**	**1**	**63**	**4.8**	**−16**	**0**	**0.0**	**20:29**	**6**	**0**	**0**	**0**	**0**	**0**	**0**	**0**	**26:41**
2008-09	**Minnesota**	**NHL**	**81**	**4**	**12**	**16**	**10**	**0**	**0**	**0**	**55**	**7.3**	**−12**	**0**	**0.0**	**19:58**	....	....	....	....	....	....	....	....	....
2009-10	**Pittsburgh**	**NHL**	**33**	**3**	**5**	**8**	**6**	**1**	**0**	**0**	**23**	**13.0**	**−4**	**0**	**0.0**	**16:43**	....	....	....	....	....	....	....	....	....
	New Jersey	**NHL**	**19**	**0**	**3**	**3**	**4**	**0**	**0**	**0**	**11**	**0.0**	**7**	**0**	**0.0**	**18:37**	**4**	**0**	**0**	**0**	**0**	**0**	**0**	**0**	**16:39**
	NHL Totals		**776**	**44**	**152**	**196**	**328**	**17**	**0**	**5**	**786**	**5.6**		**3**	**66.7**	**19:37**	**83**	**1**	**13**	**14**	**22**	**0**	**0**	**0**	**15:40**

OHL All-Rookie Team (1998) • OHL Second All-Star Team (1999)

Traded to **Anaheim** by **Colorado** for Kurt Sauer and Anaheim's 4th round choice (Raymond Macias) in 2005 Entry Draft, February 21, 2004. Signed as a free agent by **Litvinov** (CzRep), September 17, 2004. Signed as a free agent by **Dallas**, August 3, 2005. Traded to **Minnesota** by **Dallas** with Shawn Belle for Willie Mitchell and Minnesota's 2nd round choice (Nico Sacchetti) in 2007 Entry Draft, March 8, 2006. Signed as a free agent by **Pittsburgh**, September 29, 2009. Traded to **Toronto** by **Pittsburgh** with Luca Caputi for Alexei Ponikarovsky, March 2, 2010. Traded to **New Jersey** by **Toronto** for New Jersey's 5th round choice (Sam Carrick) in 2010 Entry Draft, March 3, 2010. Signed as a free agent by **Omsk** (Russia-KHL), June 23, 2010.

SKRASTINS, Karlis

(SKRAS-tihnz, KAR-lihs) **DAL.**

Defense. Shoots left. 6'1", 208 lbs. Born, Riga, Latvia, July 9, 1974. Nashville's 8th choice, 230th overall, in 1998 Entry Draft.

Season	Club	League	GP	G	A	Pts	PIM	PP	SH	GW	S	%	+/-	TF	F%	Min	GP	G	A	Pts	PIM	PP	SH	GW	Min
1992-93	Pardaugava Riga	CIS	40	3	5	8	16	....	....	....	....	....	....	....	....	....	2	0	0	0	0	....	....	....	....
1993-94	Pardaugava Riga	CIS	42	7	5	12	18	....	....	....	....	....	....	....	....	....	2	1	0	1	4	....	....	....	....
1994-95	Pardaugava Riga	CIS	52	4	14	18	69	....	....	....	....	....	....	....	....	....	....	....	....	....	....	....	....	....	....
1995-96	TPS Turku	Finland	50	4	11	15	32	....	....	....	....	....	....	....	....	....	11	2	2	4	10	....	....	....	....
1996-97	TPS Turku	Finland	50	2	8	10	20	....	....	....	....	....	....	....	....	....	12	0	4	4	2	....	....	....	....
	TPS Turku	EuroHL	6	0	1	1	4	....	....	....	....	....	....	....	....	....	4	0	0	0	14	....	....	....	....
1997-98	TPS Turku	Finland	48	4	15	19	67	....	....	....	....	....	....	....	....	....	4	0	0	0	0	....	....	....	....
	TPS Turku	EuroHL	6	0	1	1	6	....	....	....	....	....	....	....	....	....	....	....	....	....	....	....	....	....	....
1998-99	**Nashville**	**NHL**	**2**	**0**	**1**	**1**	**0**	**0**	**0**	**0**	**0**	**0.0**	**0**	**0**	**0.0**	**11:47**	....	....	....	....	....	....	....	....	....
	Milwaukee	IHL	75	8	36	44	47	....	....	....	....	....	....	....	....	....	2	0	1	1	2	....	....	....	....
99-2000	**Nashville**	**NHL**	**59**	**5**	**6**	**11**	**20**	**1**	**0**	**2**	**51**	**9.8**	**−7**	**0**	**0.0**	**20:51**	....	....	....	....	....	....	....	....	....
	Milwaukee	IHL	19	3	8	11	10	....	....	....	....	....	....	....	....	....	....	....	....	....	....	....	....	....	....
2000-01	**Nashville**	**NHL**	**82**	**1**	**11**	**12**	**30**	**0**	**0**	**1**	**66**	**1.5**	**−12**	**0**	**0.0**	**19:12**	....	....	....	....	....	....	....	....	....
2001-02	**Nashville**	**NHL**	**82**	**4**	**13**	**17**	**36**	**0**	**0**	**1**	**84**	**4.8**	**−12**	**0**	**0.0**	**20:29**	....	....	....	....	....	....	....	....	....
	Latvia	Olympics	1	0	0	0	0	....	....	....	....	....	....	....	....	....	....	....	....	....	....	....	....	....	....
2002-03	**Nashville**	**NHL**	**82**	**3**	**10**	**13**	**44**	**0**	**1**	**0**	**86**	**3.5**	**−18**	**0**	**0.0**	**20:17**	....	....	....	....	....	....	....	....	....
2003-04	**Colorado**	**NHL**	**82**	**5**	**8**	**13**	**26**	**0**	**1**	**1**	**102**	**4.9**	**18**	**0**	**0.0**	**21:49**	**11**	**0**	**2**	**2**	**2**	**0**	**0**	**0**	**23:07**
2004-05	HK Riga 2000	Latvia	4	0	4	4	0	....	....	....	....	....	....	....	....	....	9	3	10	13	33	....	....	....	....
	HK Riga 2000	BelOpen	34	8	17	25	30	....	....	....	....	....	....	....	....	....	3	0	0	0	25	....	....	....	....
2005-06	**Colorado**	**NHL**	**82**	**3**	**11**	**14**	**65**	**0**	**2**	**0**	**58**	**5.2**	**−7**	**0**	**0.0**	**21:49**	**9**	**0**	**1**	**1**	**10**	**0**	**0**	**0**	**23:24**
	Latvia	Olympics	5	0	1	1	0	....	....	....	....	....	....	....	....	....	....	....	....	....	....	....	....	....	....
2006-07	**Colorado**	**NHL**	**68**	**0**	**11**	**11**	**30**	**0**	**0**	**0**	**65**	**0.0**	**0**	**0**	**0.0**	**21:14**	....	....	....	....	....	....	....	....	....
2007-08	**Colorado**	**NHL**	**43**	**1**	**3**	**4**	**20**	**0**	**0**	**0**	**34**	**2.9**	**−2**	**0**	**0.0**	**18:02**	....	....	....	....	....	....	....	....	....
	Florida	**NHL**	**17**	**1**	**0**	**1**	**12**	**0**	**0**	**1**	**11**	**9.1**	**−9**	**0**	**0.0**	**20:03**	....	....	....	....	....	....	....	....	....
2008-09	**Florida**	**NHL**	**80**	**4**	**14**	**18**	**30**	**0**	**0**	**0**	**55**	**7.3**	**9**	**0**	**0.0**	**20:34**	....	....	....	....	....	....	....	....	....

			Regular Season														Playoffs								
Season	Club	League	GP	G	A	Pts	PIM	PP	SH	GW	S	%	+/-	TF	F%	Min	GP	G	A	Pts	PIM	PP	SH	GW	Min
2009-10	**Dallas**	**NHL**	**79**	**2**	**11**	**13**	**24**	**0**	**0**	**1**	**53**	**3.8**	**–4**	**0**	**0.0**	**19:34**	....	....	....	....	....	....	....	....	....
	Latvia	Olympics	4	0	0	0	0	....	....	....	....	....	....	....	....	....	....	....	....	....	....	....	....	....	....
	NHL Totals		**758**	**29**	**99**	**128**	**337**	**1**	**4**	**7**	**665**	**4.4**		**0**	**0.0**	**20:27**	**20**	**0**	**3**	**3**	**12**	**0**	**0**	**0**	**23:15**

aded to **Colorado** by **Nashville** for Colorado's 3rd round choice (later traded to Ottawa – Ottawa selected Peter Regin Jensen) in 2004 Entry Draft, June 30, 2003. Signed as a free agent by **Riga** (Latvia), ptember 25, 2004. Traded to **Florida** by **Colorado** with Colorado's 3rd round choice (Adam Comrie) in 2008 Entry Draft for Ruslan Salei, February 26, 2008. Signed as a free agent by **Dallas**, July 2, 09.

SLATER, Jim
(SLAY-tuhr, JIHM) **ATL.**

Center. Shoots left. 6', 200 lbs. Born, Lapeer, MI, December 9, 1982. Atlanta's 2nd choice, 30th overall, in 2002 Entry Draft.

1998-99	USNTDP	U-18	3	0	1	1	0	....	....	....	....	....	....	....	....	....	....	....	....	....	....	....	....	....	....
	Cleveland Barons	NAHL	50	13	20	33	58	....	....	....	....	....	....	....	....	....	2	0	0	0	2	....	....	....	....
99-2000	Cleveland Barons	NAHL	56	35	50	85	129	....	....	....	....	....	....	....	....	....	3	1	3	4	4	....	....	....	....
2000-01	Cleveland Barons	NAHL	48	27	37	64	122	....	....	....	....	....	....	....	....	....	6	6	6	12	6	....	....	....	....
2001-02	Michigan State	CCHA	37	11	21	32	50	....	....	....	....	....	....	....	....	....	....	....	....	....	....	....	....	....	....
2002-03	Michigan State	CCHA	37	18	26	44	26	....	....	....	....	....	....	....	....	....	....	....	....	....	....	....	....	....	....
2003-04	Michigan State	CCHA	42	19	29	*48	38	....	....	....	....	....	....	....	....	....	....	....	....	....	....	....	....	....	....
2004-05	Michigan State	CCHA	41	16	32	48	30	....	....	....	....	....	....	....	....	....	....	....	....	....	....	....	....	....	....
2005-06	**Atlanta**	**NHL**	**71**	**10**	**10**	**20**	**46**	**1**	**0**	**0**	**108**	**9.3**	**1**	**287**	**56.5**	**10:06**	....	....	....	....	....	....	....	....	....
	Chicago Wolves	AHL	4	0	2	2	2	....	....	....	....	....	....	....	....	....	....	....	....	....	....	....	....	....	....
2006-07	**Atlanta**	**NHL**	**74**	**5**	**14**	**19**	**62**	**0**	**0**	**2**	**90**	**5.6**	**8**	**373**	**54.4**	**10:14**	**4**	**0**	**0**	**0**	**2**	**0**	**0**	**0**	**5:10**
2007-08	**Atlanta**	**NHL**	**69**	**8**	**5**	**13**	**41**	**0**	**2**	**0**	**95**	**8.4**	**–10**	**367**	**52.0**	**10:24**	....	....	....	....	....	....	....	....	....
	Chicago Wolves	AHL	3	0	0	0	0	....	....	....	....	....	....	....	....	....	....	....	....	....	....	....	....	....	....
2008-09	**Atlanta**	**NHL**	**60**	**8**	**10**	**18**	**52**	**0**	**2**	**0**	**94**	**8.5**	**0**	**462**	**53.0**	**11:15**	....	....	....	....	....	....	....	....	....
2009-10	**Atlanta**	**NHL**	**61**	**11**	**7**	**18**	**60**	**1**	**0**	**2**	**107**	**10.3**	**1**	**431**	**58.9**	**12:12**	....	....	....	....	....	....	....	....	....
	NHL Totals		**335**	**42**	**46**	**88**	**261**	**2**	**4**	**4**	**494**	**8.5**		**1920**	**54.9**	**10:47**	**4**	**0**	**0**	**0**	**2**	**0**	**0**	**0**	**5:10**

HA All-Rookie Team (2002) • CCHA First All-Star Team (2003, 2004) • NCAA West Second All-American Team (2004)

SLOAN, Tyler
(SLOHN, TIGH-luhr) **WSH.**

Defense. Shoots left. 6'4", 204 lbs. Born, Calgary, Alta., March 15, 1981.

1997-98	Calgary Buffaloes	AMHL	36	2	11	13	24	....	....	....	....	....	....	....	....	....	10	0	4	4	2	....	....	....	....
1998-99	Calgary Royals	AJHL	STATISTICS NOT AVAILABLE																						
99-2000	Calgary Royals	AJHL	45	5	26	31	80	....	....	....	....	....	....	....	....	....	....	....	....	....	....	....	....	....	....
2000-01	Kamloops Blazers	WHL	70	5	28	33	146	....	....	....	....	....	....	....	....	....	4	0	0	0	4	....	....	....	....
2001-02	Kamloops Blazers	WHL	70	3	29	32	89	....	....	....	....	....	....	....	....	....	4	0	0	0	15	....	....	....	....
	Syracuse Crunch	AHL	2	0	0	0	5	....	....	....	....	....	....	....	....	....	....	....	....	....	....	....	....	....	....
2002-03	Syracuse Crunch	AHL	39	2	1	3	46	....	....	....	....	....	....	....	....	....	....	....	....	....	....	....	....	....	....
	Dayton Bombers	ECHL	14	1	2	3	22	....	....	....	....	....	....	....	....	....	....	....	....	....	....	....	....	....	....
2003-04	Syracuse Crunch	AHL	69	2	4	6	50	....	....	....	....	....	....	....	....	....	7	0	0	0	8	....	....	....	....
2004-05	Syracuse Crunch	AHL	14	0	2	2	18	....	....	....	....	....	....	....	....	....	....	....	....	....	....	....	....	....	....
	Dayton Bombers	ECHL	43	6	11	17	84	....	....	....	....	....	....	....	....	....	....	....	....	....	....	....	....	....	....
2005-06	Las Vegas	ECHL	48	4	16	20	71	....	....	....	....	....	....	....	....	....	13	0	4	4	27	....	....	....	....
	Manitoba Moose	AHL	4	0	0	0	0	....	....	....	....	....	....	....	....	....	....	....	....	....	....	....	....	....	....
	Hershey Bears	AHL	....	....	....	....	....	....	....	....	....	....	....	....	....	....	2	0	1	1	2	....	....	....	....
2006-07	Hershey Bears	AHL	68	2	9	11	104	....	....	....	....	....	....	....	....	....	17	0	7	7	30	....	....	....	....
2007-08	Hershey Bears	AHL	56	1	7	8	90	....	....	....	....	....	....	....	....	....	5	0	0	0	8	....	....	....	....
2008-09	**Washington**	**NHL**	**26**	**1**	**4**	**5**	**14**	**0**	**0**	**0**	**8**	**12.5**	**4**	**0**	**0.0**	**16:39**	**2**	**0**	**1**	**1**	**0**	**0**	**0**	**0**	**18:24**
	Hershey Bears	AHL	46	2	10	12	61	....	....	....	....	....	....	....	....	....	16	0	5	5	14	....	....	....	....
2009-10	**Washington**	**NHL**	**40**	**2**	**4**	**6**	**22**	**0**	**0**	**0**	**34**	**5.9**	**–1**	**3**	**66.7**	**14:15**	**2**	**0**	**0**	**0**	**0**	**0**	**0**	**0**	**13:06**
	Hershey Bears	AHL	2	0	1	1	0	....	....	....	....	....	....	....	....	....	....	....	....	....	....	....	....	....	....
	NHL Totals		**66**	**3**	**8**	**11**	**36**	**0**	**0**	**0**	**42**	**7.1**		**3**	**66.7**	**15:11**	**4**	**0**	**1**	**1**	**0**	**0**	**0**	**0**	**15:45**

gned as a free agent by **Columbus**, September 24, 2000. Signed as a free agent by **Hershey** (AHL), August 15, 2007. Signed as a free agent by **Washington**, July 2, 2008.

SLOANE, David
(SLOHN, DAY-vihd)

Right wing. Shoots right. 6'4", 220 lbs. Born, Philadelphia, PA, April 6, 1985.

2004-05	Chicago Steel	USHL	17	0	1	1	12	....	....	....	....	....	....	....	....	....	....	....	....	....	....	....	....	....	....
2005-06	Colgate	ECAC	27	4	1	5	16	....	....	....	....	....	....	....	....	....	....	....	....	....	....	....	....	....	....
2006-07	Colgate	ECAC	35	4	5	9	27	....	....	....	....	....	....	....	....	....	....	....	....	....	....	....	....	....	....
2007-08	Colgate	ECAC	32	2	3	5	20	....	....	....	....	....	....	....	....	....	....	....	....	....	....	....	....	....	....
2008-09	Colgate	ECAC	35	0	4	4	37	....	....	....	....	....	....	....	....	....	....	....	....	....	....	....	....	....	....
	Philadelphia	**NHL**	**1**	**0**	**0**	**0**	**0**	**0**	**0**	**0**	**0**	**0.0**	**0**	**0**	**0.0**	**6:44**	....	....	....	....	....	....	....	....	....
	Philadelphia	AHL	1	0	0	0	2	....	....	....	....	....	....	....	....	....	....	....	....	....	....	....	....	....	....
2009-10	Adirondack	AHL	20	0	1	1	23	....	....	....	....	....	....	....	....	....	....	....	....	....	....	....	....	....	....
	Kalamazoo Wings	ECHL	5	0	2	2	4	....	....	....	....	....	....	....	....	....	....	....	....	....	....	....	....	....	....
	NHL Totals		**1**	**0**	**0**	**0**	**0**	**0**	**0**	**0**	**0**	**0.0**		**0**	**0.0**	**6:44**									

gned to an ATO (amateur tryout) contract by **Philadelphia**, April 9, 2009. Signed as a free agent by **Philadelphia** (AHL), August 11, 2009. • Missed majority of 2009-10 season as a healthy reserve.

SMABY, Matt
(SMA-bee, MAT) **T.B.**

Defense. Shoots left. 6'4", 240 lbs. Born, Minneapolis, MN, October 14, 1984. Tampa Bay's 2nd choice, 41st overall, in 2003 Entry Draft.

2001-02	Shat.-St. Mary's	High-MN	65	7	18	25	134	....	....	....	....	....	....	....	....	....	....	....	....	....	....	....	....	....	....
2002-03	Shat.-St. Mary's	High-MN	57	3	20	23	114	....	....	....	....	....	....	....	....	....	....	....	....	....	....	....	....	....	....
2003-04	North Dakota	WCHA	39	1	6	7	81	....	....	....	....	....	....	....	....	....	....	....	....	....	....	....	....	....	....
2004-05	North Dakota	WCHA	44	1	2	3	86	....	....	....	....	....	....	....	....	....	....	....	....	....	....	....	....	....	....
2005-06	North Dakota	WCHA	46	4	15	19	*113	....	....	....	....	....	....	....	....	....	....	....	....	....	....	....	....	....	....
2006-07	Springfield	AHL	66	2	14	16	43	....	....	....	....	....	....	....	....	....	....	....	....	....	....	....	....	....	....
2007-08	**Tampa Bay**	**NHL**	**14**	**0**	**0**	**0**	**12**	**0**	**0**	**0**	**7**	**0.0**	**–6**	**0**	**0.0**	**12:08**	....	....	....	....	....	....	....	....	....
	Norfolk Admirals	AHL	58	1	5	6	66	....	....	....	....	....	....	....	....	....	....	....	....	....	....	....	....	....	....
2008-09	**Tampa Bay**	**NHL**	**43**	**0**	**4**	**4**	**50**	**0**	**0**	**0**	**28**	**0.0**	**–11**	**1**	**100.0**	**19:05**	....	....	....	....	....	....	....	....	....
	Norfolk Admirals	AHL	25	2	4	6	30	....	....	....	....	....	....	....	....	....	....	....	....	....	....	....	....	....	....
2009-10	**Tampa Bay**	**NHL**	**33**	**0**	**2**	**2**	**27**	**0**	**0**	**0**	**17**	**0.0**	**–4**	**0**	**0.0**	**13:29**	....	....	....	....	....	....	....	....	....
	Norfolk Admirals	AHL	7	0	2	2	9	....	....	....	....	....	....	....	....	....	....	....	....	....	....	....	....	....	....
	NHL Totals		**90**	**0**	**6**	**6**	**89**	**0**	**0**	**0**	**52**	**0.0**		**1**	**100.0**	**15:57**	....	....	....	....	....	....	....	....	....

Missed majority of 2009-10 season recovering from various injuries and as a healthy reserve.

SMID, Ladislav
(SHMIHD, LA-dih-slahv) **EDM.**

Defense. Shoots left. 6'3", 226 lbs. Born, Frydlant V Cechach, Czech., February 1, 1986. Anaheim's 1st choice, 9th overall, in 2004 Entry Draft.

2001-02	HC Liberec Jr.	CzRep-Jr.	43	6	10	16	87	....	....	....	....	....	....	....	....	....	....	....	....	....	....	....	....	....	....
2002-03	HC Liberec Jr.	CzRep-Jr.	32	1	14	15	12	....	....	....	....	....	....	....	....	....	8	2	1	3	31	....	....	....	....
	Liberec	CzRep	4	0	0	0	0	....	....	....	....	....	....	....	....	....	....	....	....	....	....	....	....	....	....
2003-04	HC Liberec Jr.	CzRep-Jr.	14	4	10	14	38	....	....	....	....	....	....	....	....	....	2	1	0	1	6	....	....	....	....
	Liberec	CzRep	45	1	1	2	51	....	....	....	....	....	....	....	....	....	....	....	....	....	....	....	....	....	....
	Beroun	CzRep-2	....	....	....	....	....	....	....	....	....	....	....	....	....	....	3	1	1	2	4	....	....	....	....
2004-05	HC Liberec Jr.	CzRep-Jr.	3	0	1	1	4	....	....	....	....	....	....	....	....	....	....	....	....	....	....	....	....	....	....
	Liberec	CzRep	39	1	3	4	14	....	....	....	....	....	....	....	....	....	12	0	0	0	6	....	....	....	....
2005-06	Portland Pirates	AHL	71	3	25	28	48	....	....	....	....	....	....	....	....	....	16	0	1	1	16	....	....	....	....
2006-07	**Edmonton**	**NHL**	**77**	**3**	**7**	**10**	**37**	**0**	**0**	**0**	**53**	**5.7**	**–16**	**0**	**0.0**	**19:14**	....	....	....	....	....	....	....	....	....
2007-08	**Edmonton**	**NHL**	**65**	**0**	**4**	**4**	**58**	**0**	**0**	**0**	**45**	**0.0**	**–15**	**0**	**0.0**	**17:52**	....	....	....	....	....	....	....	....	....
	Springfield	AHL	8	1	4	5	15	....	....	....	....	....	....	....	....	....	....	....	....	....	....	....	....	....	....
2008-09	**Edmonton**	**NHL**	**60**	**0**	**11**	**11**	**57**	**0**	**0**	**0**	**33**	**0.0**	**–6**	**0**	**0.0**	**14:57**	....	....	....	....	....	....	....	....	....
2009-10	**Edmonton**	**NHL**	**51**	**1**	**8**	**9**	**39**	**0**	**0**	**0**	**36**	**2.8**	**5**	**0**	**0.0**	**19:11**	....	....	....	....	....	....	....	....	....
	NHL Totals		**253**	**4**	**30**	**34**	**191**	**0**	**0**	**0**	**167**	**2.4**		**0**	**0.0**	**17:51**	....	....	....	....	....	....	....	....	....

raded to **Edmonton** by **Anaheim** with Joffrey Lupul, Anaheim's 1st round choice (later traded to Phoenix - Phoenix selected Nick Ross) in 2007 Entry Draft and Anaheim's 1st (Jordan Eberle) and 2nd (later raded to NY Islanders - NY Islanders selected Travis Hamonic) round choices in 2008 Entry Draft for Chris Pronger, July 3, 2006.

SMITH, Derek (SMIHTH, DAIR-ihk) OT

Defense. Shoots left. 6'2", 200 lbs. Born, Belleville, Ont., October 13, 1984.

			Regular Season														Playoffs								
Season	Club	League	GP	G	A	Pts	PIM	PP	SH	GW	S	%	+/-	TF	F%	Min	GP	G	A	Pts	PIM	PP	SH	GW	
2002-03	Wellington Dukes	OPJHL	21	6	10	16	26																		
2003-04	Wellington Dukes	OPJHL	44	8	26	34	34																		
2004-05	Lake Superior	CCHA	38	1	4	5	28																		
2005-06	Lake Superior	CCHA	36	2	8	10	18																		
2006-07	Lake Superior	CCHA	43	10	20	30	10																		
2007-08	Binghamton	AHL	52	2	11	13	18																		
	Elmira Jackals	ECHL	1	0	1	1	0																		
2008-09	Binghamton	AHL	75	7	17	24	49																		
2009-10	**Ottawa**	**NHL**	**2**	**0**	**0**	**0**	**0**	**0**	**0**	**0**	**4**	**0.0**	**-4**	**0**	**0.0**	**12:20**									
	Binghamton	AHL	74	14	37	51	24																		
	NHL Totals		**2**	**0**	**0**	**0**	**0**	**0**	**0**	**0**	**4**	**0.0**		**0**	**0.0**	**12:20**									

Signed as a free agent by **Ottawa**, April 12, 2007.

SMITH, Nathan (SMIHTH, NAY-thun)

Center. Shoots left. 6'2", 190 lbs. Born, Edmonton, Alta., February 9, 1982. Vancouver's 1st choice, 23rd overall, in 2000 Entry Draft.

			Regular Season														Playoffs								
Season	Club	League	GP	G	A	Pts	PIM	PP	SH	GW	S	%	+/-	TF	F%	Min	GP	G	A	Pts	PIM	PP	SH	GW	
1997-98	Sherwood Park	AMHL	35	15	13	28	24																		
1998-99	Swift Current	WHL	47	5	8	13	26																		
99-2000	Swift Current	WHL	70	21	28	49	72										12	1	6	7	4				
2000-01	Swift Current	WHL	67	28	62	90	78										19	4	3	7	20				
2001-02	Swift Current	WHL	47	22	38	60	52										12	3	6	9	18				
2002-03	Manitoba Moose	AHL	53	9	8	17	30										14	1	3	4	25				
2003-04	**Vancouver**	**NHL**	**2**	**0**	**0**	**0**	**0**	**0**	**0**	**0**	**1**	**0.0**	**-1**	**12**	**33.3**	**5:16**									
	Manitoba Moose	AHL	76	4	16	20	71																		
2004-05	Manitoba Moose	AHL	72	7	9	16	67										14	2	4	6	20				
2005-06	**Vancouver**	**NHL**	**1**	**0**	**0**	**0**	**0**	**0**	**0**	**0**	**2**	**0.0**	**0**	**9**	**33.3**	**10:52**									
	Manitoba Moose	AHL	20	5	4	9	57																		
2006-07	**Vancouver**	**NHL**	**1**	**0**	**0**	**0**	**0**	**0**	**0**	**0**	**0**	**0.0**	**0**	**9**	**66.7**	**8:45**	**4**	**0**	**0**	**0**	**0**	**0**	**0**	**0**	**6**
	Manitoba Moose	AHL	72	19	21	40	76										6	0	1	1	12				
2007-08	**Pittsburgh**	**NHL**	**13**	**0**	**0**	**0**	**2**	**0**	**0**	**0**	**3**	**0.0**	**0**	**75**	**53.3**	**7:41**									
	Wilkes-Barre	AHL	68	22	28	50	61										22	7	11	18	40				
2008-09	Lake Erie	AHL	44	6	10	16	42																		
2009-10	**Minnesota**	**NHL**	**9**	**0**	**0**	**0**	**12**	**0**	**0**	**0**	**4**	**0.0**	**-4**	**49**	**53.1**	**7:51**									
	Houston Aeros	AHL	67	14	23	37	83																		
	NHL Totals		**26**	**0**	**0**	**0**	**14**	**0**	**0**	**0**	**10**	**0.0**		**154**	**51.3**	**7:43**	**4**	**0**	**0**	**0**	**0**	**0**	**0**	**0**	**6**

• Missed remainder of 2005-06 season recovering from knee injury suffered in game vs. Cleveland (AHL), November 27, 2005. Signed as a free agent by **Pittsburgh**, July 12, 2007. Signed as a free agent **Colorado**, July 14, 2008. Signed as a free agent by **Minnesota**, July 22, 2009. Signed as a free agent by **Augsburg** (Germany), August 6, 2010.

SMITH, Trevor (SMIHTH, TREH-vuhr) AN

Left wing. Shoots left. 6'1", 195 lbs. Born, North Vancouver, B.C., February 8, 1985.

			Regular Season														Playoffs								
Season	Club	League	GP	G	A	Pts	PIM	PP	SH	GW	S	%	+/-	TF	F%	Min	GP	G	A	Pts	PIM	PP	SH	GW	
2003-04	Quesnel	BCHL	44	28	19	47	50																		
2004-05	Omaha Lancers	USHL	60	29	39	68	78										5	3	1	4	2				
2005-06	New Hampshire	H-East	39	10	10	20	34																		
2006-07	New Hampshire	H-East	39	21	22	43	39																		
	Bridgeport	AHL	8	1	2	3	2																		
2007-08	Bridgeport	AHL	53	20	17	37	16																		
	Utah Grizzlies	ECHL	22	11	14	25	28																		
2008-09	**NY Islanders**	**NHL**	**7**	**1**	**0**	**1**	**0**	**0**	**0**	**0**	**7**	**14.3**	**-3**	**9**	**66.7**	**11:48**									
	Bridgeport	AHL	76	30	32	62	40										5	1	3	4	0				
2009-10	Bridgeport	AHL	77	21	26	47	73										5	1	2	3	2				
	NHL Totals		**7**	**1**	**0**	**1**	**0**	**0**	**0**	**0**	**7**	**14.3**		**9**	**66.7**	**11:48**									

NCAA East Second All-American Team (2007)

Signed as a free agent by **NY Islanders**, April 2, 2007. Signed as a free agent by **Anaheim**, July 2, 2010.

SMITH, Wyatt (SMIHTH, WIGH-uht)

Center. Shoots left. 5'11", 205 lbs. Born, Thief River Falls, MN, February 13, 1977. Phoenix's 6th choice, 233rd overall, in 1997 Entry Draft.

			Regular Season														Playoffs								
Season	Club	League	GP	G	A	Pts	PIM	PP	SH	GW	S	%	+/-	TF	F%	Min	GP	G	A	Pts	PIM	PP	SH	GW	
1994-95	Warroad Warriors	High-MN	28	29	31	60	28																		
1995-96	U. of Minnesota	WCHA	32	4	5	9	32																		
1996-97	U. of Minnesota	WCHA	38	16	14	30	44																		
1997-98	U. of Minnesota	WCHA	39	24	23	47	62																		
1998-99	U. of Minnesota	WCHA	43	23	20	43	37																		
99-2000	**Phoenix**	**NHL**	**2**	**0**	**0**	**0**	**0**	**0**	**0**	**0**	**0**	**0.0**	**-2**	**20**	**30.0**	**11:39**									
	Springfield	AHL	60	14	26	40	26										5	2	3	5	13				
2000-01	**Phoenix**	**NHL**	**42**	**3**	**7**	**10**	**13**	**0**	**1**	**0**	**40**	**7.5**	**7**	**335**	**40.9**	**12:20**									
	Springfield	AHL	18	5	7	12	11																		
2001-02	**Phoenix**	**NHL**	**10**	**0**	**0**	**0**	**0**	**0**	**0**	**0**	**4**	**0.0**	**-5**	**81**	**48.2**	**10:36**									
	Springfield	AHL	69	23	32	55	69																		
2002-03	**Nashville**	**NHL**	**11**	**1**	**0**	**1**	**0**	**0**	**0**	**0**	**8**	**12.5**	**-1**	**123**	**49.6**	**11:56**									
	Milwaukee	AHL	56	24	27	51	89										4	1	0	1	2				
2003-04	**Nashville**	**NHL**	**18**	**3**	**1**	**4**	**2**	**0**	**1**	**0**	**21**	**14.3**	**2**	**193**	**57.0**	**10:22**									
	Milwaukee	AHL	40	9	7	16	40										22	5	7	12	25				
2004-05	Milwaukee	AHL	69	19	28	47	89										7	1	4	5	10				
2005-06	**NY Islanders**	**NHL**	**42**	**0**	**8**	**8**	**26**	**0**	**0**	**0**	**37**	**0.0**	**-7**	**384**	**48.4**	**11:14**									
	Bridgeport	AHL	39	13	16	29	40																		
2006-07	**Minnesota**	**NHL**	**61**	**3**	**3**	**6**	**16**	**1**	**0**	**0**	**44**	**6.8**	**-8**	**508**	**43.5**	**9:31**	**4**	**0**	**0**	**0**	**0**	**0**	**0**	**0**	**11:**
	Houston Aeros	AHL	12	4	3	7	12																		
2007-08	**Colorado**	**NHL**	**25**	**0**	**3**	**3**	**8**	**0**	**0**	**0**	**25**	**0.0**	**-4**	**108**	**50.9**	**11:38**	**1**	**0**	**0**	**0**	**0**	**0**	**0**	**0**	**10:**
	Lake Erie	AHL	40	17	18	35	34																		
2008-09	Norfolk Admirals	AHL	18	3	4	7	12																		
	San Antonio	AHL	53	16	24	40	59																		
2009-10	Wilkes-Barre	AHL	76	13	35	48	70										4	1	0	1	4				
	NHL Totals		**211**	**10**	**22**	**32**	**65**	**1**	**2**	**0**	**179**	**5.6**		**1752**	**46.5**	**10:56**	**5**	**0**	**0**	**0**	**0**	**0**	**0**	**0**	**10:**

Signed as a free agent by **Nashville**, July 15, 2002. Signed as a free agent by **NY Islanders**, August 10, 2005. Signed as a free agent by **Minnesota**, July 19, 2006. Signed as a free agent by **Colorado**, August 20, 2007. Signed as a free agent by **Tampa Bay**, July 3, 2008. Traded to **Phoenix** by **Tampa Bay** for future consideratons, November 25, 2008. Signed as a free agent by **Pittsburgh**, July 31, 2009.

SMITH, Zack (SMIHTH, ZAK) OT

Center. Shoots left. 6'2", 210 lbs. Born, Medicine Hat, Alta., April 5, 1988. Ottawa's 3rd choice, 79th overall, in 2008 Entry Draft.

			Regular Season														Playoffs								
Season	Club	League	GP	G	A	Pts	PIM	PP	SH	GW	S	%	+/-	TF	F%	Min	GP	G	A	Pts	PIM	PP	SH	GW	
2004-05	Swift Current	SMHL	43	15	27	42	83																		
	Swift Current	WHL	14	1	1	2	0																		
2005-06	Swift Current	WHL	64	2	5	7	78										3	0	0	0	9				
2006-07	Swift Current	WHL	71	16	15	31	130										6	0	2	2	11				
2007-08	Swift Current	WHL	72	22	47	69	136										12	5	5	10	29				
	Manitoba Moose	AHL															6	0	1	1	0				
2008-09	**Ottawa**	**NHL**	**1**	**0**	**0**	**0**	**0**	**0**	**0**	**0**	**0**	**0.0**	**0**	**1**	**0.0**	**7:01**									
	Binghamton	AHL	79	24	24	48	132																		
2009-10	**Ottawa**	**NHL**	**15**	**2**	**1**	**3**	**14**	**0**	**1**	**0**	**11**	**18.2**	**1**	**61**	**47.5**	**9:03**	**6**	**0**	**0**	**0**	**5**	**0**	**0**	**0**	**7:**
	Binghamton	AHL	68	14	27	41	100																		
	NHL Totals		**16**	**2**	**1**	**3**	**14**	**0**	**1**	**0**	**11**	**18.2**		**62**	**46.8**	**8:55**	**6**	**0**	**0**	**0**	**5**	**0**	**0**	**0**	**7:**

SMITHSON, Jerred
(SMIHTH-suhn, JEHR-rehd) **NSH.**

Center. Shoots right. 6'3", 206 lbs. Born, Vernon, B.C., February 4, 1979.

			Regular Season														Playoffs								
Season	Club	League	GP	G	A	Pts	PIM	PP	SH	GW	S	%	+/-	TF	F%	Min	GP	G	A	Pts	PIM	PP	SH	GW	Min
1994-95	Vernon	Minor-BC	64	39	46	85	120	....	....	....	....	....	....	....	....	....	....	....	....	....	....	....	....	....	....
1995-96	Calgary Hitmen	WHL	60	4	2	6	16	....	....	....	....	....	....	....	....	....	....	....	....	....	....	....	....	....	....
1996-97	Calgary Hitmen	WHL	65	3	6	9	49	....	....	....	....	....	....	....	....	....	....	....	....	....	....	....	....	....	....
1997-98	Calgary Hitmen	WHL	65	12	9	21	65	....	....	....	....	....	....	....	....	....	18	0	2	2	25	....	....	....	....
1998-99	Calgary Hitmen	WHL	63	14	22	36	108	....	....	....	....	....	....	....	....	....	21	3	7	10	17	....	....	....	....
99-2000	Calgary Hitmen	WHL	66	14	25	39	111	....	....	....	....	....	....	....	....	....	10	1	1	2	16	....	....	....	....
2000-01	Lowell	AHL	24	1	1	2	10	....	....	....	....	....	....	....	....	....	4	0	0	0	2	....	....	....	....
	Trenton Titans	ECHL	3	0	1	1	2	....	....	....	....	....	....	....	....	....	....	....	....	....	....	....	....	....	....
2001-02	Manchester	AHL	78	5	13	18	45	....	....	....	....	....	....	....	....	....	5	0	1	1	4	....	....	....	....
2002-03	**Los Angeles**	**NHL**	**22**	**0**	**2**	**2**	**21**	**0**	**0**	**0**	**9**	**0.0**	**–5**	**175**	**48.0**	**8:50**	....	....	....	....	....	....	....	....	....
	Manchester	AHL	38	4	21	25	60	....	....	....	....	....	....	....	....	....	3	0	0	0	4	....	....	....	....
2003-04	**Los Angeles**	**NHL**	**8**	**0**	**1**	**1**	**4**	**0**	**0**	**0**	**2**	**0.0**	**0**	**86**	**64.0**	**10:39**	....	....	....	....	....	....	....	....	....
	Manchester	AHL	66	7	13	20	51	....	....	....	....	....	....	....	....	....	6	0	1	1	10	....	....	....	....
2004-05	Milwaukee	AHL	80	11	11	22	92	....	....	....	....	....	....	....	....	....	5	0	0	0	4	....	....	....	....
2005-06	**Nashville**	**NHL**	**66**	**5**	**9**	**14**	**54**	**0**	**0**	**1**	**50**	**10.0**	**9**	**613**	**54.3**	**11:50**	**3**	**0**	**0**	**0**	**4**	**0**	**0**	**0**	**9:26**
	Milwaukee	AHL	8	0	0	0	12	....	....	....	....	....	....	....	....	....	....	....	....	....	....	....	....	....	....
2006-07	**Nashville**	**NHL**	**64**	**5**	**7**	**12**	**42**	**1**	**1**	**2**	**47**	**10.6**	**–8**	**420**	**56.4**	**11:03**	**5**	**0**	**0**	**0**	**17**	**0**	**0**	**0**	**11:30**
2007-08	**Nashville**	**NHL**	**81**	**7**	**9**	**16**	**50**	**0**	**2**	**2**	**61**	**11.5**	**–9**	**572**	**52.1**	**12:05**	**6**	**0**	**0**	**0**	**2**	**0**	**0**	**0**	**11:52**
2008-09	**Nashville**	**NHL**	**82**	**4**	**9**	**13**	**49**	**0**	**0**	**0**	**74**	**5.4**	**–6**	**722**	**52.6**	**13:51**	....	....	....	....	....	....	....	....	....
2009-10	**Nashville**	**NHL**	**69**	**9**	**4**	**13**	**54**	**0**	**2**	**1**	**54**	**16.7**	**–4**	**548**	**54.9**	**13:58**	**6**	**1**	**0**	**1**	**6**	**0**	**0**	**0**	**15:36**
	NHL Totals		**392**	**30**	**41**	**71**	**274**	**1**	**5**	**6**	**297**	**10.1**		**3136**	**53.8**	**12:22**	**20**	**1**	**0**	**1**	**29**	**0**	**0**	**0**	**12:32**

gned as a free agent by **Los Angeles**, February 18, 2000. Signed as a free agent by **Nashville**, July 22, 2004.

SMOLENAK, Radek
(SMOH-lehn-ahk, RA-dehk)

Left wing. Shoots left. 6'3", 180 lbs. Born, Prague, Czech., December 3, 1986. Tampa Bay's 2nd choice, 73rd overall, in 2005 Entry Draft.

			Regular Season														Playoffs								
Season	Club	League	GP	G	A	Pts	PIM	PP	SH	GW	S	%	+/-	TF	F%	Min	GP	G	A	Pts	PIM	PP	SH	GW	Min
2001-02	HC Kladno U17	CzR-U17	47	29	20	49	42	....	....	....	....	....	....	....	....	....	....	....	....	....	....	....	....	....	....
2002-03	HC Kladno U17	CzR-U17	41	39	27	66	52	....	....	....	....	....	....	....	....	....	9	7	3	10	18	....	....	....	....
	HC Kladno Jr.	CzRep-Jr.	4	2	0	2	6	....	....	....	....	....	....	....	....	....	....	....	....	....	....	....	....	....	....
2003-04	HC Kladno Jr.	CzRep-Jr.	54	27	25	52	51	....	....	....	....	....	....	....	....	....	7	3	4	7	0	....	....	....	....
2004-05	Kingston	OHL	67	32	28	60	58	....	....	....	....	....	....	....	....	....	....	....	....	....	....	....	....	....	....
2005-06	Kingston	OHL	65	42	42	84	109	....	....	....	....	....	....	....	....	....	6	1	3	4	20	....	....	....	....
2006-07	Springfield	AHL	20	0	1	1	8	....	....	....	....	....	....	....	....	....	....	....	....	....	....	....	....	....	....
	Johnstown Chiefs	ECHL	43	15	20	35	35	....	....	....	....	....	....	....	....	....	1	0	0	0	0	....	....	....	....
2007-08	Norfolk Admirals	AHL	56	15	11	26	108	....	....	....	....	....	....	....	....	....	....	....	....	....	....	....	....	....	....
	Mississippi	ECHL	19	7	8	15	14	....	....	....	....	....	....	....	....	....	....	....	....	....	....	....	....	....	....
2008-09	**Tampa Bay**	**NHL**	**6**	**0**	**1**	**1**	**10**	**0**	**0**	**0**	**14**	**0.0**	**1**	**0**	**0.0**	**8:21**	....	....	....	....	....	....	....	....	....
	Norfolk Admirals	AHL	71	24	25	49	165	....	....	....	....	....	....	....	....	....	....	....	....	....	....	....	....	....	....
2009-10	**Chicago**	**NHL**	**1**	**0**	**0**	**0**	**5**	**0**	**0**	**0**	**1**	**0.0**	**0**	**0**	**0.0**	**4:41**	....	....	....	....	....	....	....	....	....
	Norfolk Admirals	AHL	39	7	14	21	49	....	....	....	....	....	....	....	....	....	....	....	....	....	....	....	....	....	....
	Abbotsford Heat	AHL	21	2	4	6	26	....	....	....	....	....	....	....	....	....	....	....	....	....	....	....	....	....	....
	NHL Totals		**7**	**0**	**1**	**1**	**15**	**0**	**0**	**0**	**15**	**0.0**		**0**	**0.0**	**7:49**	....	....	....	....	....	....	....	....	....

aimed on waivers by **Chicago** from **Tampa Bay**, September 25, 2009. Claimed on waivers by **Tampa Bay** from **Chicago**, October 10, 2009. • Reassigned to **Abbotsford** (AHL) by **Tampa Bay**, February 2, 2010.

SMYTH, Ryan
(SMIHTH, RIGH-uhn) **L.A.**

Left wing. Shoots left. 6'2", 189 lbs. Born, Banff, Alta., February 21, 1976. Edmonton's 2nd choice, 6th overall, in 1994 Entry Draft.

			Regular Season														Playoffs								
Season	Club	League	GP	G	A	Pts	PIM	PP	SH	GW	S	%	+/-	TF	F%	Min	GP	G	A	Pts	PIM	PP	SH	GW	Min
1990-91	Banff Blazers	Minor-AB	25	100	50	150	....	....	....	....	....	....	....	....	....	....	....	....	....	....	....	....	....	....	....
	Lethbridge	AMHL	34	8	21	29	....	....	....	....	....	....	....	....	....	....	....	....	....	....	....	....	....	....	....
1991-92	Caronport	SMHL	35	55	61	116	98	....	....	....	....	....	....	....	....	....	....	....	....	....	....	....	....	....	....
	Moose Jaw	WHL	2	0	0	0	0	....	....	....	....	....	....	....	....	....	....	....	....	....	....	....	....	....	....
1992-93	Moose Jaw	WHL	64	19	14	33	59	....	....	....	....	....	....	....	....	....	....	....	....	....	....	....	....	....	....
1993-94	Moose Jaw	WHL	72	50	55	105	88	....	....	....	....	....	....	....	....	....	....	....	....	....	....	....	....	....	....
1994-95	Moose Jaw	WHL	50	41	45	86	66	....	....	....	....	....	....	....	....	....	10	6	9	15	22	....	....	....	....
	Edmonton	**NHL**	**3**	**0**	**0**	**0**	**0**	**0**	**0**	**0**	**2**	**0.0**	**–1**	....	....	....	....	....	....	....	....	....	....	....	....
1995-96	**Edmonton**	**NHL**	**48**	**2**	**9**	**11**	**28**	**1**	**0**	**0**	**65**	**3.1**	**–10**	....	....	....	....	....	....	....	....	....	....	....	....
	Cape Breton	AHL	9	6	5	11	4	....	....	....	....	....	....	....	....	....	....	....	....	....	....	....	....	....	....
1996-97	**Edmonton**	**NHL**	**82**	**39**	**22**	**61**	**76**	***20**	**0**	**4**	**265**	**14.7**	**–7**	....	....	....	**12**	**5**	**5**	**10**	**12**	**1**	**0**	**2**	....
1997-98	**Edmonton**	**NHL**	**65**	**20**	**13**	**33**	**44**	**10**	**0**	**2**	**205**	**9.8**	**–24**	....	....	....	**12**	**1**	**3**	**4**	**16**	**1**	**0**	**0**	....
1998-99	**Edmonton**	**NHL**	**71**	**13**	**18**	**31**	**62**	**6**	**0**	**2**	**161**	**8.1**	**0**	**5**	**20.0**	**14:26**	**3**	**3**	**0**	**3**	**0**	**2**	**0**	**0**	**24:35**
99-2000	**Edmonton**	**NHL**	**82**	**28**	**26**	**54**	**58**	**11**	**0**	**4**	**238**	**11.8**	**–2**	**24**	**54.2**	**19:12**	**5**	**1**	**0**	**1**	**6**	**0**	**1**	**0**	**19:18**
2000-01	**Edmonton**	**NHL**	**82**	**31**	**39**	**70**	**58**	**11**	**0**	**6**	**245**	**12.7**	**10**	**17**	**35.3**	**19:58**	**6**	**3**	**4**	**7**	**4**	**0**	**0**	**0**	**24:46**
2001-02	**Edmonton**	**NHL**	**61**	**15**	**35**	**50**	**48**	**7**	**1**	**5**	**150**	**10.0**	**7**	**12**	**41.7**	**19:27**	....	....	....	....	....	....	....	....	....
	Canada	Olympics	6	0	1	1	0	....	....	....	....	....	....	....	....	....	....	....	....	....	....	....	....	....	....
2002-03	**Edmonton**	**NHL**	**66**	**27**	**34**	**61**	**67**	**10**	**0**	**3**	**199**	**13.6**	**5**	**42**	**42.9**	**19:21**	**6**	**2**	**0**	**2**	**16**	**0**	**1**	**0**	**17:39**
2003-04	**Edmonton**	**NHL**	**82**	**23**	**36**	**59**	**70**	**8**	**2**	**6**	**245**	**9.4**	**11**	**484**	**47.1**	**19:39**	....	....	....	....	....	....	....	....	....
2004-05			DID NOT PLAY																						
2005-06	**Edmonton**	**NHL**	**75**	**36**	**30**	**66**	**58**	**19**	**2**	**3**	**230**	**15.7**	**–5**	**159**	**47.8**	**20:13**	**24**	**7**	**9**	**16**	**22**	**4**	**0**	**1**	**21:27**
	Canada	Olympics	6	0	1	1	4	....	....	....	....	....	....	....	....	....	....	....	....	....	....	....	....	....	....
2006-07	**Edmonton**	**NHL**	**53**	**31**	**22**	**53**	**38**	**14**	**1**	**5**	**161**	**19.3**	**2**	**63**	**47.6**	**20:09**	....	....	....	....	....	....	....	....	....
	NY Islanders	**NHL**	**18**	**5**	**10**	**15**	**14**	**1**	**0**	**0**	**49**	**10.2**	**0**	**9**	**22.2**	**22:26**	**5**	**1**	**3**	**4**	**4**	**0**	**0**	**0**	**22:42**
2007-08	**Colorado**	**NHL**	**55**	**14**	**23**	**37**	**50**	**2**	**0**	**3**	**168**	**8.3**	**–4**	**33**	**39.4**	**19:37**	**8**	**2**	**3**	**5**	**2**	**1**	**0**	**1**	**17:29**
2008-09	**Colorado**	**NHL**	**77**	**26**	**33**	**59**	**62**	**10**	**1**	**3**	**257**	**10.1**	**–15**	**174**	**51.2**	**20:17**	....	....	....	....	....	....	....	....	....
2009-10	**Los Angeles**	**NHL**	**67**	**22**	**31**	**53**	**42**	**11**	**0**	**3**	**206**	**10.7**	**8**	**62**	**50.0**	**19:41**	**6**	**1**	**1**	**2**	**6**	**0**	**0**	**0**	**18:39**
	NHL Totals		**987**	**332**	**381**	**713**	**775**	**141**	**7**	**49**	**2846**	**11.7**		**1084**	**47.2**	**19:20**	**87**	**26**	**28**	**54**	**88**	**9**	**2**	**4**	**20:43**

/HL East Second All-Star Team (1995)
ayed in NHL All-Star Game (2007)

raded to **NY Islanders** by **Edmonton** for Ryan O'Marra, Robert Nilsson and NY Islanders' 1st round choice (Alex Plante) in 2007 Entry Draft, February 27, 2007. Signed as a free agent by **Colorado**, July 1, 007. Traded to **Los Angeles** by **Colorado** for Kyle Quincey, Tom Preissing and Los Angeles' 5th round choice (Luke Walker) in 2010 Entry Draft, July 3, 2009.

SOBOTKA, Vladimir
(suh-BOHT-kah, vla-DIH-meer) **ST.L.**

Center. Shoots left. 5'10", 183 lbs. Born, Trebic, Czech., July 2, 1987. Boston's 5th choice, 106th overall, in 2005 Entry Draft.

			Regular Season														Playoffs								
Season	Club	League	GP	G	A	Pts	PIM	PP	SH	GW	S	%	+/-	TF	F%	Min	GP	G	A	Pts	PIM	PP	SH	GW	Min
2002-03	Slavia U17	CzR-U17	46	16	24	40	48	....	....	....	....	....	....	....	....	....	8	1	1	2	29	....	....	....	....
2003-04	Slavia U17	CzR-U17	35	24	41	65	109	....	....	....	....	....	....	....	....	....	7	7	12	19	8	....	....	....	....
	Slavia Jr.	CzRep-Jr.	18	6	6	12	16	....	....	....	....	....	....	....	....	....	....	....	....	....	....	....	....	....	....
	HC Slavia Praha	CzRep	1	0	0	0	0	....	....	....	....	....	....	....	....	....	....	....	....	....	....	....	....	....	....
2004-05	Slavia Jr.	CzRep-Jr.	27	12	21	33	93	....	....	....	....	....	....	....	....	....	....	....	....	....	....	....	....	....	....
	HC Slavia Praha	CzRep	18	0	1	1	8	....	....	....	....	....	....	....	....	....	....	....	....	....	....	....	....	....	....
	Havl. Brod	CzRep-3	7	3	0	3	31	....	....	....	....	....	....	....	....	....	7	1	5	6	0	....	....	....	....
2005-06	Slavia Jr.	CzRep-Jr.	8	10	4	14	42	....	....	....	....	....	....	....	....	....	....	....	....	....	....	....	....	....	....
	HC Slavia Praha	CzRep	33	1	9	10	28	....	....	....	....	....	....	....	....	....	11	2	3	5	10	....	....	....	....
2006-07	HC Slavia Praha	CzRep	33	7	6	13	38	....	....	....	....	....	....	....	....	....	....	....	....	....	....	....	....	....	....
2007-08	**Boston**	**NHL**	**48**	**1**	**6**	**7**	**24**	**0**	**0**	**1**	**40**	**2.5**	**1**	**247**	**48.6**	**8:50**	**6**	**2**	**0**	**2**	**0**	**0**	**0**	**0**	**8:37**
	Providence Bruins	AHL	18	10	10	20	37	....	....	....	....	....	....	....	....	....	6	0	4	4	0	....	....	....	....
2008-09	**Boston**	**NHL**	**25**	**1**	**4**	**5**	**10**	**0**	**0**	**0**	**19**	**5.3**	**–10**	**52**	**57.7**	**10:33**	....	....	....	....	....	....	....	....	....
	Providence Bruins	AHL	44	20	24	44	83	....	....	....	....	....	....	....	....	....	14	2	11	13	43	....	....	....	....
2009-10	**Boston**	**NHL**	**61**	**4**	**6**	**10**	**30**	**0**	**0**	**0**	**67**	**6.0**	**–7**	**361**	**54.3**	**11:06**	**13**	**0**	**2**	**2**	**15**	**0**	**0**	**0**	**13:20**
	Providence Bruins	AHL	6	4	6	10	4	....	....	....	....	....	....	....	....	....	....	....	....	....	....	....	....	....	....
	NHL Totals		**134**	**6**	**16**	**22**	**64**	**0**	**0**	**1**	**126**	**4.8**		**660**	**52.4**	**10:11**	**19**	**2**	**2**	**4**	**15**	**0**	**0**	**0**	**11:51**

raded to **St. Louis** by **Boston** for David Warsofsky, June 26, 2010.

SOPEL, Brent

(SOH-puhl, BREHNT) **AT**

Defense. Shoots right. 6'1", 200 lbs. Born, Calgary, Alta., January 7, 1977. Vancouver's 6th choice, 144th overall, in 1995 Entry Draft.

			Regular Season														Playoffs								
Season	Club	League	GP	G	A	Pts	PIM	PP	SH	GW	S	%	+/-	TF	F%	Min	GP	G	A	Pts	PIM	PP	SH	GW	M
1992-93	Sask. Legion	SMHL	36	7	17	24	95	....	....	....	....	....	....	....	....	....	....	....	....	....	....	....	....	....	
1993-94	Saskatoon Blazers	SMHL	34	9	30	39	180	....	....	....	....	....	....	....	....	....	....	....	....	....	....	....	....	....	
	Saskatoon Blades	WHL	11	2	2	4	2	....	....	....	....	....	....	....	....	....	....	....	....	....	....	....	....	....	
1994-95	Saskatoon Blades	WHL	22	1	10	11	31	....	....	....	....	....	....	....	....	....	....	....	....	....	....	....	....	....	
	Swift Current	WHL	41	4	19	23	50	....	....	....	....	....	....	....	....	....	3	0	3	3	0	....	....	....	
1995-96	Swift Current	WHL	71	13	48	61	87	....	....	....	....	....	....	....	....	....	6	1	2	3	4	....	....	....	
	Syracuse Crunch	AHL	1	0	0	0	0	....	....	....	....	....	....	....	....	....	....	....	....	....	....	....	....	....	
1996-97	Swift Current	WHL	62	15	41	56	109	....	....	....	....	....	....	....	....	....	10	5	11	16	32	....	....	....	
	Syracuse Crunch	AHL	2	0	0	0	0	....	....	....	....	....	....	....	....	....	3	0	0	0	0	....	....	....	
1997-98	Syracuse Crunch	AHL	76	10	33	43	70	....	....	....	....	....	....	....	....	....	5	0	7	7	12	....	....	....	
1998-99	**Vancouver**	**NHL**	**5**	**1**	**0**	**1**	**4**	**1**	**0**	**0**	**5**	**20.0**	**-1**	**0**	**0.0**	**11:58**	....	....	....	....	....	....	....	....	
	Syracuse Crunch	AHL	53	10	21	31	59	....	....	....	....	....	....	....	....	....	....	....	....	....	....	....	....	....	
99-2000	**Vancouver**	**NHL**	**18**	**2**	**4**	**6**	**12**	**0**	**0**	**1**	**11**	**18.2**	**9**	**0**	**0.0**	**10:31**	....	....	....	....	....	....	....	....	
	Syracuse Crunch	AHL	50	6	25	31	67	....	....	....	....	....	....	....	....	....	4	0	2	2	8	....	....	....	
2000-01	**Vancouver**	**NHL**	**52**	**4**	**10**	**14**	**10**	**0**	**0**	**1**	**57**	**7.0**	**4**	**0**	**0.0**	**16:01**	**4**	**0**	**0**	**0**	**2**	**0**	**0**	**0**	**19:**
	Kansas City	IHL	4	0	1	1	0	....	....	....	....	....	....	....	....	....	....	....	....	....	....	....	....	....	
2001-02	**Vancouver**	**NHL**	**66**	**8**	**17**	**25**	**44**	**1**	**0**	**3**	**116**	**6.9**	**21**	**0**	**0.0**	**19:01**	**6**	**0**	**2**	**2**	**2**	**0**	**0**	**0**	**24:**
2002-03	**Vancouver**	**NHL**	**81**	**7**	**30**	**37**	**23**	**6**	**0**	**1**	**167**	**4.2**	**-15**	**0**	**0.0**	**21:42**	**14**	**2**	**6**	**8**	**4**	**1**	**0**	**1**	**22:**
2003-04	**Vancouver**	**NHL**	**80**	**10**	**32**	**42**	**36**	**6**	**0**	**2**	**173**	**5.8**	**11**	**0**	**0.0**	**21:56**	**7**	**0**	**1**	**1**	**0**	**0**	**0**	**0**	**23:**
2004-05			DID NOT PLAY																						
2005-06	**NY Islanders**	**NHL**	**57**	**2**	**25**	**27**	**64**	**2**	**0**	**0**	**121**	**1.7**	**-9**	**0**	**0.0**	**23:35**	....	....	....	....	....	....	....	....	
	Los Angeles	**NHL**	**11**	**0**	**1**	**1**	**6**	**0**	**0**	**0**	**12**	**0.0**	**-4**	**0**	**0.0**	**22:02**	....	....	....	....	....	....	....	....	
2006-07	**Los Angeles**	**NHL**	**44**	**4**	**19**	**23**	**14**	**2**	**0**	**2**	**104**	**3.8**	**2**	**3**	**33.3**	**21:06**	....	....	....	....	....	....	....	....	
	Vancouver	**NHL**	**20**	**1**	**4**	**5**	**10**	**0**	**0**	**0**	**27**	**3.7**	**0**	**0**	**0.0**	**18:25**	**11**	**0**	**0**	**0**	**2**	**0**	**0**	**0**	**19:**
2007-08	**Chicago**	**NHL**	**58**	**1**	**19**	**20**	**28**	**0**	**0**	**0**	**56**	**1.8**	**9**	**0**	**0.0**	**20:18**	....	....	....	....	....	....	....	....	
2008-09	**Chicago**	**NHL**	**23**	**1**	**1**	**2**	**8**	**0**	**0**	**1**	**15**	**6.7**	**-4**	**0**	**0.0**	**13:49**	....	....	....	....	....	....	....	....	
2009-10♦	**Chicago**	**NHL**	**73**	**1**	**7**	**8**	**34**	**0**	**0**	**0**	**48**	**2.1**	**3**	**0**	**0.0**	**14:52**	**22**	**1**	**5**	**6**	**8**	**0**	**0**	**0**	**18:**
	NHL Totals		**588**	**42**	**169**	**211**	**293**	**18**	**0**	**11**	**912**	**4.6**		**3**	**33.3**	**19:14**	**64**	**3**	**14**	**17**	**18**	**1**	**0**	**1**	**20:**

Traded to **NY Islanders** by **Vancouver** for NY Islanders' 2nd round choice (later traded to Anaheim - Anaheim selected Bryce Swan) in 2006 Entry Draft, August 3, 2005. Traded to **Los Angeles** by **NY Islanders** with Mark Parrish for Denis Grebeshkov and Jeff Tambellini, March 8, 2006. Traded to **Vancouver** by **Los Angeles** for Anaheim's 2nd round choice (previously acquired, Los Angeles selected Wayne Simmonds) in 2007 Entry Draft and and Vancouver's 4th round choice (later traded to Buffalo - Buffalo selected Justin Jokinen) in 2008 Entry Draft, February 26, 2006. Signed as a free agent by **Chicago**, October 3, 2007. • Missed majority of 2008-09 season recovering from recurring elbow injury. Traded to **Atlanta** by **Chicago** with Dustin Byfuglien, Ben Eager and Akim Aliu for Marty Reasoner Joey Crabb, Jeremy Morin and New Jersey's 1st (previously acquired, Chicago selected Kevin Hayes) and 2nd (previously acquired, Chicago selected Justin Holl) round choices in 2010 Entry Draft, June 24, 2010.

SOURAY, Sheldon

(SOO-ray, SHEHL-duhn) **ED**

Defense. Shoots left. 6'4", 233 lbs. Born, Elk Point, Alta., July 13, 1976. New Jersey's 3rd choice, 71st overall, in 1994 Entry Draft.

			Regular Season														Playoffs								
Season	Club	League	GP	G	A	Pts	PIM	PP	SH	GW	S	%	+/-	TF	F%	Min	GP	G	A	Pts	PIM	PP	SH	GW	M
1990-91	Bonnyville Sabres	AAHA	30	15	20	35	100	....	....	....	....	....	....	....	....	....	....	....	....	....	....	....	....	....	
1991-92	Quesnel	Minor-BC	20	5	15	20	200	....	....	....	....	....	....	....	....	....	....	....	....	....	....	....	....	....	
	Alberta Cycle	AMHL	11	0	5	5	67	....	....	....	....	....	....	....	....	....	....	....	....	....	....	....	....	....	
1992-93	Ft. Saskatchewan	AJHL	35	0	12	12	125	....	....	....	....	....	....	....	....	....	....	....	....	....	....	....	....	....	
	Tri-City	WHL	2	0	0	0	0	....	....	....	....	....	....	....	....	....	....	....	....	....	....	....	....	....	
1993-94	Tri-City	WHL	42	3	6	9	122	....	....	....	....	....	....	....	....	....	....	....	....	....	....	....	....	....	
1994-95	Tri-City	WHL	40	2	24	26	140	....	....	....	....	....	....	....	....	....	....	....	....	....	....	....	....	....	
	Prince George	WHL	11	2	3	5	23	....	....	....	....	....	....	....	....	....	....	....	....	....	....	....	....	....	
	Albany River Rats	AHL	7	0	2	2	8	....	....	....	....	....	....	....	....	....	....	....	....	....	....	....	....	....	
1995-96	Prince George	WHL	32	9	18	27	91	....	....	....	....	....	....	....	....	....	....	....	....	....	....	....	....	....	
	Kelowna Rockets	WHL	27	7	20	27	94	....	....	....	....	....	....	....	....	....	6	0	5	5	2	....	....	....	
	Albany River Rats	AHL	6	0	2	2	12	....	....	....	....	....	....	....	....	....	4	0	1	1	4	....	....	....	
1996-97	Albany River Rats	AHL	70	2	11	13	160	....	....	....	....	....	....	....	....	....	16	2	3	5	47	....	....	....	
1997-98	**New Jersey**	**NHL**	**60**	**3**	**7**	**10**	**85**	**0**	**0**	**1**	**74**	**4.1**	**18**	....	....	....	**3**	**0**	**1**	**1**	**2**	**0**	**0**	**0**	
	Albany River Rats	AHL	6	0	0	0	8	....	....	....	....	....	....	....	....	....	....	....	....	....	....	....	....	....	
1998-99	**New Jersey**	**NHL**	**70**	**1**	**7**	**8**	**110**	**0**	**0**	**0**	**101**	**1.0**	**5**	**0**	**0.0**	**14:56**	**2**	**0**	**1**	**1**	**0**	**0**	**0**	**0**	**12:**
99-2000	**New Jersey**	**NHL**	**52**	**0**	**8**	**8**	**70**	**0**	**0**	**0**	**74**	**0.0**	**-6**	**0**	**0.0**	**17:12**	....	....	....	....	....	....	....	....	
	Montreal	**NHL**	**19**	**3**	**0**	**3**	**44**	**0**	**0**	**0**	**39**	**7.7**	**7**	**0**	**0.0**	**19:18**	....	....	....	....	....	....	....	....	
2000-01	**Montreal**	**NHL**	**52**	**3**	**8**	**11**	**95**	**0**	**0**	**2**	**103**	**2.9**	**-11**	**0**	**0.0**	**20:36**	....	....	....	....	....	....	....	....	
2001-02	**Montreal**	**NHL**	**34**	**3**	**5**	**8**	**62**	**1**	**0**	**0**	**56**	**5.4**	**-5**	**1**	**100.0**	**18:11**	**12**	**0**	**1**	**1**	**16**	**0**	**0**	**0**	**19:**
2002-03	**Montreal**	**NHL**	DID NOT PLAY – INJURED																						
2003-04	**Montreal**	**NHL**	**63**	**15**	**20**	**35**	**104**	**6**	**1**	**3**	**186**	**8.1**	**4**	**0**	**0.0**	**23:26**	**11**	**0**	**2**	**2**	**39**	**0**	**0**	**0**	**23:**
2004-05	Farjestad	Sweden	39	9	8	17	117	....	....	....	....	....	....	....	....	....	15	1	6	7	77	....	....	....	
2005-06	**Montreal**	**NHL**	**75**	**12**	**27**	**39**	**116**	**7**	**1**	**0**	**202**	**5.9**	**-11**	**0**	**0.0**	**22:15**	**6**	**3**	**2**	**5**	**8**	**2**	**0**	**0**	**18:**
2006-07	**Montreal**	**NHL**	**81**	**26**	**38**	**64**	**135**	**19**	**1**	**6**	**224**	**11.6**	**-28**	**2**	**100.0**	**23:11**	....	....	....	....	....	....	....	....	
2007-08	**Edmonton**	**NHL**	**26**	**3**	**7**	**10**	**36**	**2**	**0**	**1**	**71**	**4.2**	**-7**	**0**	**0.0**	**24:21**	....	....	....	....	....	....	....	....	
2008-09	**Edmonton**	**NHL**	**81**	**23**	**30**	**53**	**98**	**12**	**1**	**5**	**268**	**8.6**	**1**	**0**	**0.0**	**24:51**	....	....	....	....	....	....	....	....	
2009-10	**Edmonton**	**NHL**	**37**	**4**	**9**	**13**	**65**	**0**	**0**	**0**	**113**	**3.5**	**-19**	**0**	**0.0**	**22:37**	....	....	....	....	....	....	....	....	
	NHL Totals		**650**	**96**	**166**	**262**	**1020**	**47**	**4**	**18**	**1511**	**6.4**		**3**	**100.0**	**21:11**	**34**	**3**	**7**	**10**	**65**	**2**	**0**	**0**	**20:**

WHL West Second All-Star Team (1996)

Played in NHL All-Star Game (2004, 2007, 2009)

Traded to **Montreal** by **New Jersey** with Josh DeWolf and New Jersey's 2nd round choice (later traded to Washington, later traded to Tampa Bay – Tampa Bay selected Andreas Holmqvist) in 2001 Entry Draft for Vladimir Malakhov, March 1, 2000. • Missed remainder of 2001-02 season and entire 2002-03 season recovering from wrist injury suffered in game vs. Tampa Bay, November 17, 2001. Signed as a free agent by **Farjestad** (Sweden), September 22, 2004. Signed as a free agent by **Edmonton**, July 12, 2007. • Missed majority of 2007-08 season recovering from shoulder injury suffered in game at Vancouver, October 13, 2007 and resulting surgery, February 8, 2008. • Missed majority of 2009-10 season recovering from head injury suffered in game vs. Calgary (October 8, 2009) and hand injury suffered in game at Calgary (January 30, 2010).

SPACEK, Jaroslav

(SPAH-chehk, YAHR-roh-slav) **MT**

Defense. Shoots left. 6', 210 lbs. Born, Rokycany, Czech., February 11, 1974. Florida's 5th choice, 117th overall, in 1998 Entry Draft.

			Regular Season														Playoffs								
Season	Club	League	GP	G	A	Pts	PIM	PP	SH	GW	S	%	+/-	TF	F%	Min	GP	G	A	Pts	PIM	PP	SH	GW	M
1992-93	HC Skoda Plzen	Czech	16	1	3	4	....	....	....	....	....	....	....	....	....	....	....	....	....	....	....	....	....	....	
1993-94	HC Skoda Plzen	CzRep	34	2	6	8	....	....	....	....	....	....	....	....	....	....	....	....	....	....	....	....	....	....	
1994-95	Plzen	CzRep	38	4	8	12	14	....	....	....	....	....	....	....	....	....	3	1	0	1	2	....	....	....	
1995-96	HC ZKZ Plzen	CzRep	40	3	10	13	42	....	....	....	....	....	....	....	....	....	3	0	1	1	4	....	....	....	
1996-97	HC ZKZ Plzen	CzRep	52	9	29	38	44	....	....	....	....	....	....	....	....	....	....	....	....	....	....	....	....	....	
1997-98	Farjestad	Sweden	45	10	16	26	63	....	....	....	....	....	....	....	....	....	12	2	5	7	14	....	....	....	
	Farjestad	EuroHL	6	2	3	5	2	....	....	....	....	....	....	....	....	....	....	....	....	....	....	....	....	....	
1998-99	**Florida**	**NHL**	**63**	**3**	**12**	**15**	**28**	**2**	**1**	**0**	**92**	**3.3**	**15**	**1**	**100.0**	**19:27**	....	....	....	....	....	....	....	....	
	New Haven	AHL	14	4	8	12	15	....	....	....	....	....	....	....	....	....	....	....	....	....	....	....	....	....	
99-2000	**Florida**	**NHL**	**82**	**10**	**26**	**36**	**53**	**4**	**0**	**1**	**111**	**9.0**	**7**	**1**	**0.0**	**22:40**	**4**	**0**	**0**	**0**	**0**	**0**	**0**	**0**	**20:**
2000-01	**Florida**	**NHL**	**12**	**2**	**1**	**3**	**8**	**1**	**0**	**0**	**21**	**9.5**	**-4**	**0**	**0.0**	**19:12**	....	....	....	....	....	....	....	....	
	Chicago	**NHL**	**50**	**5**	**18**	**23**	**20**	**2**	**0**	**1**	**85**	**5.9**	**7**	**0**	**0.0**	**21:31**	....	....	....	....	....	....	....	....	
2001-02	**Chicago**	**NHL**	**60**	**3**	**10**	**13**	**29**	**0**	**0**	**1**	**64**	**4.7**	**5**	**0**	**0.0**	**16:25**	....	....	....	....	....	....	....	....	
	Czech Republic	Olympics	4	0	0	0	0	....	....	....	....	....	....	....	....	....	....	....	....	....	....	....	....	....	
	Columbus	**NHL**	**14**	**2**	**3**	**5**	**24**	**1**	**1**	**1**	**29**	**6.9**	**-9**	**0**	**0.0**	**23:35**	....	....	....	....	....	....	....	....	
2002-03	**Columbus**	**NHL**	**81**	**9**	**36**	**45**	**70**	**5**	**0**	**1**	**166**	**5.4**	**-23**	**0**	**0.0**	**24:47**	....	....	....	....	....	....	....	....	
2003-04	**Columbus**	**NHL**	**58**	**5**	**17**	**22**	**45**	**2**	**1**	**2**	**108**	**4.6**	**-13**	**0**	**0.0**	**23:26**	....	....	....	....	....	....	....	....	
2004-05	Plzen	CzRep	30	3	8	11	26	....	....	....	....	....	....	....	....	....	....	....	....	....	....	....	....	....	
	HC Slavia Praha	CzRep	17	4	9	13	29	....	....	....	....	....	....	....	....	....	7	0	2	2	8	....	....	....	
2005-06	**Chicago**	**NHL**	**45**	**7**	**17**	**24**	**72**	**1**	**0**	**0**	**80**	**8.8**	**8**	**0**	**0.0**	**23:00**	....	....	....	....	....	....	....	....	
	Edmonton	**NHL**	**31**	**5**	**14**	**19**	**24**	**3**	**0**	**0**	**70**	**7.1**	**3**	**0**	**0.0**	**24:37**	**24**	**3**	**11**	**14**	**24**	**2**	**0**	**0**	**25:**
2006-07	**Buffalo**	**NHL**	**65**	**5**	**16**	**21**	**62**	**1**	**0**	**2**	**78**	**6.4**	**20**	**0**	**0.0**	**19:09**	**16**	**0**	**0**	**0**	**10**	**0**	**0**	**0**	**14:**
2007-08	**Buffalo**	**NHL**	**60**	**9**	**23**	**32**	**42**	**7**	**0**	**1**	**95**	**9.5**	**7**	**0**	**0.0**	**22:59**	....	....	....	....	....	....	....	....	
2008-09	**Buffalo**	**NHL**	**80**	**8**	**37**	**45**	**38**	**4**	**0**	**0**	**130**	**6.2**	**2**	**0**	**0.0**	**22:17**	....	....	....	....	....	....	....	....	
2009-10	**Montreal**	**NHL**	**74**	**3**	**18**	**21**	**50**	**1**	**0**	**0**	**99**	**3.0**	**9**	**0**	**0.0**	**21:48**	**10**	**1**	**3**	**4**	**6**	**0**	**0**	**0**	**18:**
	NHL Totals		**775**	**76**	**248**	**324**	**565**	**34**	**3**	**10**	**1228**	**6.2**		**2**	**50.0**	**21:48**	**54**	**4**	**14**	**18**	**40**	**2**	**0**	**0**	**20:**

Traded to **Chicago** by **Florida** for Anders Eriksson, November 6, 2000. Traded to **Columbus** by **Chicago** with Chicago's 2nd round choice (Dan Fritsche) in 2003 Entry Draft for Lyle Odelein, March 19, 2002. Signed as a free agent by **Plzen** (CzRep), September 17, 2004. Signed as a free agent by **Slavia Praha** (CzRep), January 4, 2005. Signed as a free agent by **Chicago**, August 3, 2005. Traded to **Edmonton** by **Chicago** for Tony Salmelainen, January 26, 2006. Signed as a free agent by **Buffalo**, July 5, 2006. Signed as a free agent by **Montreal**, July 1, 2009.

SPALING, Nick

(SPAHL-ihng, NIHK) **NSH.**

Center. Shoots left. 6'1", 195 lbs. Born, Palmerston, Ont., September 19, 1988. Nashville's 3rd choice, 58th overall, in 2007 Entry Draft.

			Regular Season														Playoffs								
Season	Club	League	GP	G	A	Pts	PIM	PP	SH	GW	S	%	+/-	TF	F%	Min	GP	G	A	Pts	PIM	PP	SH	GW	Min
2004-05	Listowel Cyclones	OJHL-B	61	25	27	52	58																		
2005-06	Kitchener Rangers	OHL	62	10	15	25	22										5	0	3	3	0				
2006-07	Kitchener Rangers	OHL	61	23	36	59	41										9	2	3	5	4				
2007-08	Kitchener Rangers	OHL	56	38	34	72	18										20	14	16	30	9				
2008-09	Milwaukee	AHL	79	12	23	35	28										11	0	3	3	8				
2009-10	**Nashville**	**NHL**	**28**	**0**	**3**	**3**	**0**	**0**	**0**	**0**	**26**	**0.0**	**3**	**95**	**41.1**	**11:03**	**6**	**0**	**0**	**0**	**0**	**0**	**0**	**0**	**8:24**
	Milwaukee	AHL	48	7	10	17	21																		
	NHL Totals		**28**	**0**	**3**	**3**	**0**	**0**	**0**	**0**	**26**	**0.0**		**95**	**41.1**	**11:03**	**6**	**0**	**0**	**0**	**0**	**0**	**0**	**0**	**8:24**

SPEZZA, Jason

(SPEHT-zuh, JAY-suhn) **OTT.**

Center. Shoots right. 6'3", 215 lbs. Born, Mississauga, Ont., June 13, 1983. Ottawa's 1st choice, 2nd overall, in 2001 Entry Draft.

Season	Club	League	GP	G	A	Pts	PIM	PP	SH	GW	S	%	+/-	TF	F%	Min	GP	G	A	Pts	PIM	PP	SH	GW	Min
1997-98	Toronto Marlies	MTHL	54	53	61	114	42																		
1998-99	Brampton	OHL	67	22	49	71	18																		
99-2000	Mississauga	OHL	52	24	37	61	33																		
2000-01	Mississauga	OHL	15	7	23	30	11																		
	Windsor Spitfires	OHL	41	36	50	86	32										9	4	5	9	10				
2001-02	Windsor Spitfires	OHL	27	19	26	45	16																		
	Belleville Bulls	OHL	26	23	37	60	26										11	5	6	11	18				
	Grand Rapids	AHL															3	1	0	1	2				
2002-03	**Ottawa**	**NHL**	**33**	**7**	**14**	**21**	**8**	**3**	**0**	**0**	**65**	**10.8**	**–3**	**330**	**45.8**	**12:40**	**3**	**1**	**1**	**2**	**0**	**1**	**0**	**0**	**11:34**
	Binghamton	AHL	43	22	32	54	71										2	1	2	3	4				
2003-04	**Ottawa**	**NHL**	**78**	**22**	**33**	**55**	**71**	**5**	**0**	**3**	**142**	**15.5**	**22**	**956**	**47.7**	**14:38**	**3**	**0**	**0**	**0**	**2**	**0**	**0**	**0**	**9:44**
2004-05	Binghamton	AHL	80	32	*85	*117	50										6	1	3	4	6				
2005-06	**Ottawa**	**NHL**	**68**	**19**	**71**	**90**	**33**	**7**	**0**	**5**	**156**	**12.2**	**23**	**1220**	**52.6**	**19:00**	**10**	**5**	**9**	**14**	**2**	**3**	**0**	**1**	**17:59**
2006-07	**Ottawa**	**NHL**	**67**	**34**	**53**	**87**	**45**	**13**	**1**	**5**	**162**	**21.0**	**19**	**1261**	**53.0**	**19:17**	**20**	**7**	***15**	***22**	**10**	**3**	**0**	**0**	**20:58**
2007-08	**Ottawa**	**NHL**	**76**	**34**	**58**	**92**	**66**	**11**	**0**	**6**	**210**	**16.2**	**26**	**1445**	**50.5**	**20:40**	**4**	**0**	**1**	**1**	**0**	**0**	**0**	**0**	**19:45**
2008-09	**Ottawa**	**NHL**	**82**	**32**	**41**	**73**	**79**	**13**	**1**	**3**	**246**	**13.0**	**–14**	**1477**	**53.3**	**19:41**									
2009-10	**Ottawa**	**NHL**	**60**	**23**	**34**	**57**	**20**	**11**	**0**	**5**	**165**	**13.9**	**0**	**1018**	**50.5**	**19:04**	**6**	**1**	**6**	**7**	**4**	**1**	**0**	**0**	**22:46**
	NHL Totals		**464**	**171**	**304**	**475**	**322**	**63**	**2**	**27**	**1146**	**14.9**		**7707**	**51.2**	**18:16**	**46**	**14**	**32**	**46**	**18**	**8**	**0**	**1**	**19:06**

HL All-Rookie Team (1999) • AHL All-Rookie Team (2003) • AHL First All-Star Team (2005) • John P. Sollenberger Trophy (AHL - Top Scorer) (2005) • Les Cunningham Award (AHL – MVP) (2005)
yed in NHL All-Star Game (2008)

SPILLER, Matthew

(SPIHL-uhr, MA-thew)

Defense. Shoots left. 6'5", 235 lbs. Born, Daysland, Alta., February 7, 1983. Phoenix's 2nd choice, 31st overall, in 2001 Entry Draft.

Season	Club	League	GP	G	A	Pts	PIM	PP	SH	GW	S	%	+/-	TF	F%	Min	GP	G	A	Pts	PIM	PP	SH	GW	Min
1998-99	East Central Chill	AMBHL	36	8	19	27	140																		
99-2000	Seattle	WHL	60	1	10	11	108										7	0	0	0	25				
2000-01	Seattle	WHL	71	4	7	11	174																		
2001-02	Seattle	WHL	72	8	23	31	168										1	0	0	0	4				
2002-03	Seattle	WHL	68	11	24	35	198										15	2	7	9	36				
2003-04	**Phoenix**	**NHL**	**51**	**0**	**0**	**0**	**54**	**0**	**0**	**0**	**22**	**0.0**	**–11**	**0**	**0.0**	**10:42**									
	Springfield	AHL	21	1	2	3	32																		
2004-05	Utah Grizzlies	AHL	79	4	7	11	160																		
2005-06	**Phoenix**	**NHL**	**8**	**0**	**1**	**1**	**13**	**0**	**0**	**0**	**3**	**0.0**	**–1**	**0**	**0.0**	**10:30**									
	San Antonio	AHL	69	2	7	9	167																		
2006-07	San Antonio	AHL	80	1	7	8	187																		
2007-08	**NY Islanders**	**NHL**	**9**	**0**	**1**	**1**	**7**	**0**	**0**	**0**	**6**	**0.0**	**–2**	**0**	**0.0**	**19:47**									
	Bridgeport	AHL	75	1	6	7	177																		
2008-09	Lowell Devils	AHL	71	2	11	13	90																		
2009-10	Liberec	CzRep	8	0	0	0	8																		
	Bloomington	IHL	43	8	13	21	124																		
	NHL Totals		**68**	**0**	**2**	**2**	**74**	**0**	**0**	**0**	**31**	**0.0**		**0**	**0.0**	**11:53**									

gned as a free agent by **NY Islanders**, July 3, 2007. Signed as a free agent by **New Jersey**, September 6, 2008. Signed as a free agent by **Liberec** (CzRep), October 17, 2009. Signed as a free agent by
berec (CzRep), October 17, 2009. Signed as a free agent by **Bloomington** (IHL), December 8, 2009.

SPRUKTS, Janis

(SPRUKTS, YAN-ish)

Center. Shoots left. 6'3", 235 lbs. Born, Riga, Latvia, January 31, 1982. Florida's 7th choice, 234th overall, in 2000 Entry Draft.

Season	Club	League	GP	G	A	Pts	PIM	PP	SH	GW	S	%	+/-	TF	F%	Min	GP	G	A	Pts	PIM	PP	SH	GW	Min
99-2000	Lukko Rauma Jr.	Fin-Jr.	26	2	5	7	6										3	0	0	0	0				
	HC Essamika Jr.	EEHL-2	2	4	4	8	0																		
2000-01	Lukko Rauma Jr.	Fin-Jr.	36	15	22	37	24										3	0	0	0	0				
	Lukko Rauma	Finland	9	0	0	0	2																		
2001-02	Acadie-Bathurst	QMJHL	63	35	44	79	46										16	14	8	22	12				
2002-03	Sport Vaasa	Finland-2	21	5	6	11	8																		
	Acadie-Bathurst	QMJHL	30	9	29	38	12										11	3	5	8	0				
2003-04	ASK Ogre	Latvia	5	2	4	6	0																		
	Odense IK	Denmark	2	0	1	1	2																		
2004-05	HK Riga 2000	BelOpen	21	7	9	16	10										3	0	0	0	2				
	HK Riga 2000	Latvia	3	2	3	5	0										9	3	4	7	2				
2005-06	HPK Hameenlinna	Finland	35	18	10	28	14										13	3	4	7	14				
2006-07	**Florida**	**NHL**	**13**	**1**	**2**	**3**	**2**	**0**	**0**	**0**	**10**	**10.0**	**1**	**61**	**44.3**	**6:19**									
	Rochester	AHL	58	18	41	59	60										6	1	3	4	4				
2007-08	Lukko Rauma	Finland	53	12	17	29	20										3	0	1	1	0				
2008-09	**Florida**	**NHL**	**1**	**0**	**0**	**0**	**0**	**0**	**0**	**0**	**1**	**0.0**	**0**	**0**	**0.0**	**12:19**									
	Rochester	AHL	59	16	31	47	20																		
2009-10	Dynamo Riga	Rus-KHL	53	11	25	36	34										9	1	4	5	10				
	Latvia	Olympics	4	0	1	1	0																		
	NHL Totals		**14**	**1**	**2**	**3**	**2**	**0**	**0**	**0**	**11**	**9.1**		**61**	**44.3**	**6:45**									

Released by **Vaasa** (Finland-2) and returned to **Acadie-Bathurst** (QMJHL), January 3, 2003. Signed as a free agent by **Riga**, (Russia-KHL), July 17, 2009.

STAAL, Eric

(STAHL, AIR-ihk) **CAR.**

Center. Shoots left. 6'4", 205 lbs. Born, Thunder Bay, Ont., October 29, 1984. Carolina's 1st choice, 2nd overall, in 2003 Entry Draft.

Season	Club	League	GP	G	A	Pts	PIM	PP	SH	GW	S	%	+/-	TF	F%	Min	GP	G	A	Pts	PIM	PP	SH	GW	Min
99-2000	Thunder Bay	Exhib.	7	4	8	12	0																		
2000-01	Peterborough	OHL	63	19	30	49	23										7	2	5	7	4				
2001-02	Peterborough	OHL	56	23	39	62	40										6	3	6	9	10				
2002-03	Peterborough	OHL	66	39	59	98	36										7	9	5	14	6				
2003-04	**Carolina**	**NHL**	**81**	**11**	**20**	**31**	**40**	**2**	**1**	**3**	**164**	**6.7**	**–6**	**669**	**43.1**	**16:40**									
2004-05	Lowell	AHL	77	26	51	77	88										11	2	8	10	12				
2005-06 ♦	**Carolina**	**NHL**	**82**	**45**	**55**	**100**	**81**	**19**	**4**	**4**	**279**	**16.1**	**–8**	**1309**	**42.6**	**19:39**	**25**	**9**	***19**	***28**	**8**	***7**	**0**	**1**	**19:48**
2006-07	**Carolina**	**NHL**	**82**	**30**	**40**	**70**	**68**	**12**	**1**	**1**	**288**	**10.4**	**–6**	**1238**	**45.2**	**20:08**									
2007-08	**Carolina**	**NHL**	**82**	**38**	**44**	**82**	**50**	**14**	**0**	**7**	**310**	**12.3**	**–2**	**1708**	**44.9**	**21:38**									
2008-09	**Carolina**	**NHL**	**82**	**40**	**35**	**75**	**50**	**14**	**1**	**8**	**372**	**10.8**	**15**	**1586**	**45.3**	**21:03**	**18**	**10**	**5**	**15**	**4**	**3**	**0**	**1**	**21:31**
2009-10	**Carolina**	**NHL**	**70**	**29**	**41**	**70**	**68**	**13**	**0**	**5**	**277**	**10.5**	**4**	**1162**	**41.8**	**20:43**									
	Canada	Olympics	7	1	5	6	6																		
	NHL Totals		**479**	**193**	**235**	**428**	**357**	**74**	**7**	**28**	**1690**	**11.4**		**7672**	**44.0**	**19:58**	**43**	**19**	**24**	**43**	**12**	**10**	**0**	**2**	**20:31**

HL Second All-Star Team (2003) • Canadian Major Junior First All-Star Team (2003) • NHL Second All-Star Team (2006)
ayed in NHL All-Star Game (2007, 2008, 2009)

STAAL, Jordan
(STAHL, JOHR-dahn) **PIT**

Center. Shoots left. 6'4", 220 lbs. Born, Thunder Bay, Ont., September 10, 1988. Pittsburgh's 1st choice, 2nd overall, in 2006 Entry Draft.

			Regular Season														Playoffs								
Season	Club	League	GP	G	A	Pts	PIM	PP	SH	GW	S	%	+/-	TF	F%	Min	GP	G	A	Pts	PIM	PP	SH	GW	Mi
2004-05	Peterborough	OHL	66	9	19	28	29	....	....	....	....	....	....	....	....	....	14	5	5	10	16	....	....	....	..
2005-06	Peterborough	OHL	68	28	40	68	69	....	....	....	....	....	....	....	....	....	19	10	6	16	16	....	....	....	..
2006-07	**Pittsburgh**	**NHL**	**81**	**29**	**13**	**42**	**24**	**4**	***7**	**4**	**131**	**22.1**	**16**	**383**	**37.1**	**14:56**	**5**	**3**	**0**	**3**	**2**	**0**	**0**	**0**	**16:0**
2007-08	**Pittsburgh**	**NHL**	**82**	**12**	**16**	**28**	**55**	**3**	**0**	**4**	**183**	**6.6**	**–5**	**1202**	**42.2**	**18:16**	**20**	**6**	**1**	**7**	**14**	**1**	**0**	**1**	**18:1**
2008-09 ♦	**Pittsburgh**	**NHL**	**82**	**22**	**27**	**49**	**37**	**2**	**1**	**3**	**166**	**13.3**	**5**	**1206**	**47.0**	**19:51**	**24**	**4**	**5**	**9**	**8**	**0**	**1**	**0**	**19:1**
2009-10	**Pittsburgh**	**NHL**	**82**	**21**	**28**	**49**	**57**	**1**	**2**	**1**	**195**	**10.8**	**19**	**1324**	**48.3**	**19:24**	**11**	**3**	**2**	**5**	**6**	**2**	**0**	**0**	**18:1**
	NHL Totals		**327**	**84**	**84**	**168**	**173**	**10**	**10**	**12**	**675**	**12.4**		**4115**	**45.1**	**18:07**	**60**	**16**	**8**	**24**	**30**	**3**	**1**	**1**	**18:2**

NHL All-Rookie Team (2007)

STAAL, Marc
(STAHL, MAHRK) **NY**

Defense. Shoots left. 6'4", 209 lbs. Born, Thunder Bay, Ont., January 13, 1987. NY Rangers' 1st choice, 12th overall, in 2005 Entry Draft.

Season	Club	League	GP	G	A	Pts	PIM	PP	SH	GW	S	%	+/-	TF	F%	Min	GP	G	A	Pts	PIM	PP	SH	GW	Mi
2003-04	Sudbury Wolves	OHL	61	1	13	14	34	....	....	....	....	....	....	....	....	....	7	1	2	3	2	....	....	....	..
2004-05	Sudbury Wolves	OHL	65	6	20	26	53	....	....	....	....	....	....	....	....	....	12	0	4	4	15	....	....	....	..
2005-06	Sudbury Wolves	OHL	57	11	38	49	60	....	....	....	....	....	....	....	....	....	10	0	8	8	8	....	....	....	..
	Hartford	AHL	....	....	....	....	....	....	....	....	....	....	....	....	....	....	12	0	2	2	8	....	....	....	..
2006-07	Sudbury Wolves	OHL	53	5	29	34	68	....	....	....	....	....	....	....	....	....	21	5	15	20	22	....	....	....	..
2007-08	**NY Rangers**	**NHL**	**80**	**2**	**8**	**10**	**42**	**0**	**0**	**0**	**78**	**2.6**	**2**	**0**	**0.0**	**18:48**	**10**	**1**	**2**	**3**	**8**	**0**	**0**	**1**	**22:2**
2008-09	**NY Rangers**	**NHL**	**82**	**3**	**12**	**15**	**64**	**0**	**0**	**1**	**96**	**3.1**	**–7**	**0**	**0.0**	**21:08**	**7**	**1**	**0**	**1**	**0**	**0**	**0**	**0**	**21:3**
2009-10	**NY Rangers**	**NHL**	**82**	**8**	**19**	**27**	**44**	**0**	**0**	**2**	**78**	**10.3**	**11**	**0**	**0.0**	**23:08**	....	....	....	....	....	....	....	....	..
	NHL Totals		**244**	**13**	**39**	**52**	**150**	**0**	**0**	**3**	**252**	**5.2**		**0**	**0.0**	**21:02**	**17**	**2**	**2**	**4**	**8**	**0**	**0**	**1**	**22:0**

OHL First All-Star Team (2006, 2007) • Canadian Major Junior First All-Star Team (2006, 2007)

STAFFORD, Drew
(STA-fuhrd, DROO) **BUF**

Right wing. Shoots right. 6'1", 216 lbs. Born, Milwaukee, WI, October 30, 1985. Buffalo's 1st choice, 13th overall, in 2004 Entry Draft.

Season	Club	League	GP	G	A	Pts	PIM	PP	SH	GW	S	%	+/-	TF	F%	Min	GP	G	A	Pts	PIM	PP	SH	GW	Mi
2001-02	Shat.-St. Mary's	High-MN	45	35	53	88	30	....	....	....	....	....	....	....	....	....	....	....	....	....	....	....	....	....	..
2002-03	Shat.-St. Mary's	High-MN	65	49	67	116	....	....	....	....	....	....	....	....	....	....	....	....	....	....	....	....	....	....	..
2003-04	North Dakota	WCHA	36	11	21	32	30	....	....	....	....	....	....	....	....	....	....	....	....	....	....	....	....	....	..
2004-05	North Dakota	WCHA	42	13	25	38	34	....	....	....	....	....	....	....	....	....	....	....	....	....	....	....	....	....	..
2005-06	North Dakota	WCHA	42	24	24	48	63	....	....	....	....	....	....	....	....	....	....	....	....	....	....	....	....	....	..
2006-07	**Buffalo**	**NHL**	**41**	**13**	**14**	**27**	**33**	**3**	**0**	**3**	**67**	**19.4**	**5**	**13**	**46.2**	**13:08**	**10**	**2**	**2**	**4**	**4**	**0**	**0**	**0**	**11:5**
	Rochester	AHL	34	22	22	44	30	....	....	....	....	....	....	....	....	....	....	....	....	....	....	....	....	....	..
2007-08	**Buffalo**	**NHL**	**64**	**16**	**22**	**38**	**51**	**1**	**0**	**5**	**103**	**15.5**	**3**	**21**	**38.1**	**13:32**	....	....	....	....	....	....	....	....	..
2008-09	**Buffalo**	**NHL**	**79**	**20**	**25**	**45**	**29**	**9**	**0**	**0**	**183**	**10.9**	**3**	**20**	**20.0**	**15:38**	....	....	....	....	....	....	....	....	..
2009-10	**Buffalo**	**NHL**	**71**	**14**	**20**	**34**	**35**	**5**	**0**	**1**	**181**	**7.7**	**4**	**86**	**47.7**	**14:28**	**3**	**0**	**0**	**0**	**0**	**0**	**0**	**0**	**14:0**
	NHL Totals		**255**	**63**	**81**	**144**	**148**	**18**	**0**	**9**	**534**	**11.8**		**140**	**42.1**	**14:23**	**13**	**2**	**2**	**4**	**4**	**0**	**0**	**0**	**12:2**

STAFFORD, Garrett
(STA-fuhrd, GAIR-reht) **PHX**

Defense. Shoots right. 6'1", 207 lbs. Born, Los Angeles, CA, January 28, 1980.

Season	Club	League	GP	G	A	Pts	PIM	PP	SH	GW	S	%	+/-	TF	F%	Min	GP	G	A	Pts	PIM	PP	SH	GW	Mi
1996-97	Des Moines	USHL	37	1	10	11	40	....	....	....	....	....	....	....	....	....	5	0	0	0	0	....	....	....	..
1997-98	Des Moines	USHL	53	6	17	23	89	....	....	....	....	....	....	....	....	....	12	1	3	4	42	....	....	....	..
1998-99	Des Moines	USHL	56	8	33	41	54	....	....	....	....	....	....	....	....	....	13	2	2	4	18	....	....	....	..
99-2000	New Hampshire	H-East	38	3	9	12	28	....	....	....	....	....	....	....	....	....	....	....	....	....	....	....	....	....	..
2000-01	New Hampshire	H-East	37	5	21	26	44	....	....	....	....	....	....	....	....	....	....	....	....	....	....	....	....	....	..
2001-02	New Hampshire	H-East	36	5	22	27	42	....	....	....	....	....	....	....	....	....	....	....	....	....	....	....	....	....	..
2002-03	New Hampshire	H-East	23	1	15	16	24	....	....	....	....	....	....	....	....	....	....	....	....	....	....	....	....	....	..
2003-04	Cleveland Barons	AHL	73	12	34	46	71	....	....	....	....	....	....	....	....	....	6	0	0	0	6	....	....	....	..
2004-05	Cleveland Barons	AHL	68	6	18	24	55	....	....	....	....	....	....	....	....	....	....	....	....	....	....	....	....	....	..
2005-06	Cleveland Barons	AHL	80	11	28	39	86	....	....	....	....	....	....	....	....	....	....	....	....	....	....	....	....	....	..
2006-07	Worcester Sharks	AHL	77	11	30	41	58	....	....	....	....	....	....	....	....	....	6	0	3	3	2	....	....	....	..
2007-08	**Detroit**	**NHL**	**2**	**0**	**0**	**0**	**0**	**0**	**0**	**0**	**1**	**0.0**	**0**	**0**	**0.0**	**6:45**	....	....	....	....	....	....	....	....	..
	Grand Rapids	AHL	69	11	33	44	36	....	....	....	....	....	....	....	....	....	....	....	....	....	....	....	....	....	..
2008-09	**Dallas**	**NHL**	**3**	**0**	**2**	**2**	**0**	**0**	**0**	**0**	**5**	**0.0**	**0**	**0**	**0.0**	**18:00**	....	....	....	....	....	....	....	....	..
	Grand Rapids	AHL	70	11	34	45	50	....	....	....	....	....	....	....	....	....	10	0	5	5	4	....	....	....	..
2009-10	Texas Stars	AHL	60	7	25	32	22	....	....	....	....	....	....	....	....	....	21	4	6	10	10	....	....	....	..
	NHL Totals		**5**	**0**	**2**	**2**	**0**	**0**	**0**	**0**	**6**	**0.0**		**0**	**0.0**	**13:30**	....	....	....	....	....	....	....	....	..

Hockey East Second All-Star Team (2002) • AHL All-Rookie Team (2004) • AHL Second All-Star Team (2004)

Signed as a free agent by **Cleveland** (AHL), October 10, 2003. Signed as a free agent by **San Jose**, December 9, 2003. Signed as a free agent by **Detroit**, July 16, 2007. Signed as a free agent by **Dallas**, July 3, 2008. Signed as a free agent by **Phoenix**, July 3, 2010.

STAIOS, Steve
(STAY-ohs, STEEV) **CGY**

Defense. Shoots right. 6'1", 200 lbs. Born, Hamilton, Ont., July 28, 1973. St. Louis' 1st choice, 27th overall, in 1991 Entry Draft.

Season	Club	League	GP	G	A	Pts	PIM	PP	SH	GW	S	%	+/-	TF	F%	Min	GP	G	A	Pts	PIM	PP	SH	GW	Mi
1988-89	Hamilton Huskies	Minor-ON	58	13	39	52	78	....	....	....	....	....	....	....	....	....	....	....	....	....	....	....	....	....	..
1989-90	Hamilton Kilty B's	OHA-B	40	9	27	36	66	....	....	....	....	....	....	....	....	....	....	....	....	....	....	....	....	....	..
1990-91	Niagara Falls	OHL	66	17	29	46	115	....	....	....	....	....	....	....	....	....	12	2	3	5	10	....	....	....	..
1991-92	Niagara Falls	OHL	65	11	42	53	122	....	....	....	....	....	....	....	....	....	17	7	8	15	27	....	....	....	..
1992-93	Niagara Falls	OHL	12	4	14	18	30	....	....	....	....	....	....	....	....	....	....	....	....	....	....	....	....	....	..
	Sudbury Wolves	OHL	53	13	44	57	67	....	....	....	....	....	....	....	....	....	11	5	6	11	22	....	....	....	..
1993-94	Peoria Rivermen	IHL	38	3	9	12	42	....	....	....	....	....	....	....	....	....	....	....	....	....	....	....	....	....	..
1994-95	Peoria Rivermen	IHL	60	3	13	16	64	....	....	....	....	....	....	....	....	....	6	0	0	0	10	....	....	....	..
1995-96	Peoria Rivermen	IHL	6	0	1	1	14	....	....	....	....	....	....	....	....	....	....	....	....	....	....	....	....	....	..
	Worcester IceCats	AHL	57	1	11	12	114	....	....	....	....	....	....	....	....	....	....	....	....	....	....	....	....	....	..
	Boston	**NHL**	**12**	**0**	**0**	**0**	**4**	**0**	**0**	**0**	**4**	**0.0**	**–5**	....	....	....	**3**	**0**	**0**	**0**	**0**	**0**	**0**	**0**	..
	Providence Bruins	AHL	7	1	4	5	8	....	....	....	....	....	....	....	....	....	....	....	....	....	....	....	....	....	..
1996-97	**Boston**	**NHL**	**54**	**3**	**8**	**11**	**71**	**0**	**0**	**0**	**56**	**5.4**	**–26**	....	....	....	....	....	....	....	....	....	....	....	..
	Vancouver	**NHL**	**9**	**0**	**6**	**6**	**20**	**0**	**0**	**0**	**10**	**0.0**	**2**	....	....	....	....	....	....	....	....	....	....	....	..
1997-98	**Vancouver**	**NHL**	**77**	**3**	**4**	**7**	**134**	**0**	**0**	**1**	**45**	**6.7**	**–3**	....	....	....	....	....	....	....	....	....	....	....	..
1998-99	**Vancouver**	**NHL**	**57**	**0**	**2**	**2**	**54**	**0**	**0**	**0**	**33**	**0.0**	**–12**	**4**	**25.0**	**6:53**	....	....	....	....	....	....	....	....	..
99-2000	**Atlanta**	**NHL**	**27**	**2**	**3**	**5**	**66**	**0**	**0**	**0**	**38**	**5.3**	**–5**	**2**	**50.0**	**13:01**	....	....	....	....	....	....	....	....	..
2000-01	**Atlanta**	**NHL**	**70**	**9**	**13**	**22**	**137**	**4**	**0**	**0**	**156**	**5.8**	**–23**	**1**	**0.0**	**21:45**	....	....	....	....	....	....	....	....	..
2001-02	**Edmonton**	**NHL**	**73**	**5**	**5**	**10**	**108**	**0**	**0**	**1**	**101**	**5.0**	**10**	**0**	**0.0**	**18:05**	....	....	....	....	....	....	....	....	..
2002-03	**Edmonton**	**NHL**	**76**	**5**	**21**	**26**	**96**	**1**	**3**	**0**	**126**	**4.0**	**13**	**1**	**0.0**	**22:17**	**6**	**0**	**0**	**0**	**4**	**0**	**0**	**0**	**23:27**
2003-04	**Edmonton**	**NHL**	**82**	**6**	**22**	**28**	**86**	**1**	**0**	**1**	**153**	**3.9**	**17**	**0**	**0.0**	**23:03**	....	....	....	....	....	....	....	....	..
2004-05	Lulea HF	Sweden	7	2	1	3	12	....	....	....	....	....	....	....	....	....	....	....	....	....	....	....	....	....	..
2005-06	**Edmonton**	**NHL**	**82**	**8**	**20**	**28**	**84**	**1**	**0**	**1**	**140**	**5.7**	**10**	**0**	**0.0**	**20:53**	**24**	**1**	**5**	**6**	**28**	**1**	**0**	**0**	**21:31**
2006-07	**Edmonton**	**NHL**	**58**	**2**	**15**	**17**	**97**	**0**	**0**	**0**	**71**	**2.8**	**–5**	**0**	**0.0**	**21:23**	....	....	....	....	....	....	....	....	..
2007-08	**Edmonton**	**NHL**	**82**	**7**	**9**	**16**	**121**	**1**	**0**	**0**	**73**	**9.6**	**–14**	**1**	**100.0**	**22:01**	....	....	....	....	....	....	....	....	..
2008-09	**Edmonton**	**NHL**	**80**	**2**	**12**	**14**	**92**	**0**	**0**	**0**	**78**	**2.6**	**–5**	**0**	**0.0**	**19:48**	....	....	....	....	....	....	....	....	..
2009-10	**Edmonton**	**NHL**	**40**	**0**	**7**	**7**	**59**	**0**	**0**	**0**	**45**	**0.0**	**–19**	**0**	**0.0**	**18:51**	....	....	....	....	....	....	....	....	..
	Calgary	**NHL**	**18**	**1**	**2**	**3**	**16**	**1**	**0**	**0**	**16**	**6.3**	**–8**	**0**	**0.0**	**18:23**	....	....	....	....	....	....	....	....	..
	NHL Totals		**897**	**53**	**149**	**202**	**1245**	**9**	**3**	**4**	**1145**	**4.6**		**9**	**33.3**	**19:36**	**33**	**1**	**5**	**6**	**32**	**1**	**0**	**0**	**21:54**

Traded to **Boston** by **St. Louis** with Kevin Sawyer for Steve Leach, March 8, 1996. Claimed on waivers by **Vancouver** from **Boston**, March 18, 1997. Claimed by **Atlanta** from **Vancouver** in Expansion Draft, June 25, 1999. • Missed majority of 1999-2000 season recovering from knee injury suffered in game vs. Colorado, October 23, 1999. Traded to **New Jersey** by **Atlanta** for New Jersey's 9th round choice (Simon Gamache) in 2000 Entry Draft, June 12, 2000. Traded to **Atlanta** by **New Jersey** for future considerations, July 10, 2000. Signed as a free agent by **Edmonton**, July 12, 2001. Signed as a free agent by **Lulea** (Sweden), January 28, 2005. Traded to **Calgary** by **Edmonton** for Aaron Johnson and Calgary's 3rd round choice in 2011 Entry Draft, March 3, 2010.

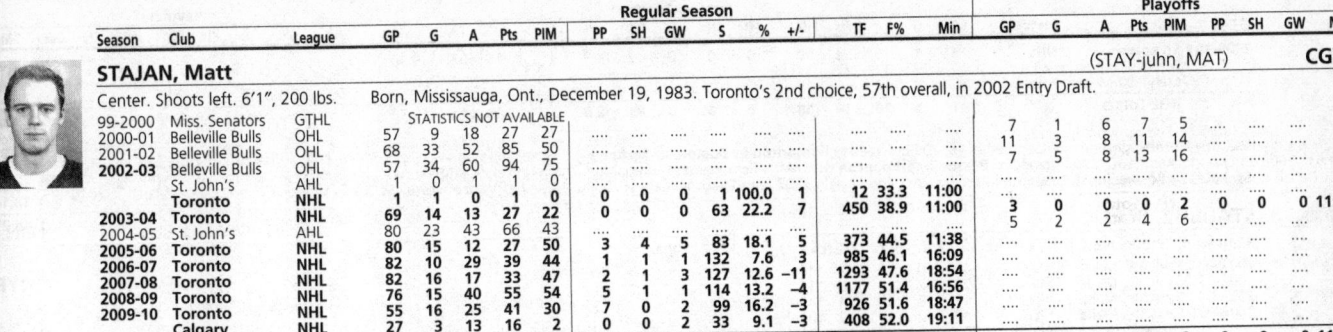

Season	Club	League	Regular Season GP	G	A	Pts	PIM	PP	SH	GW	S	%	+/-	TF	F%	Min	Playoffs GP	G	A	Pts	PIM	PP	SH	GW	Min

STAJAN, Matt

(STAY-juhn, MAT) **CGY.**

Center. Shoots left. 6'1", 200 lbs. Born, Mississauga, Ont., December 19, 1983. Toronto's 2nd choice, 57th overall, in 2002 Entry Draft.

Season	Club	League	GP	G	A	Pts	PIM	PP	SH	GW	S	%	+/-	TF	F%	Min	GP	G	A	Pts	PIM	PP	SH	GW	Min
99-2000	Miss. Senators	GTHL	STATISTICS NOT AVAILABLE																						
2000-01	Belleville Bulls	OHL	57	9	18	27	27	....	....	....	....	....	....	....	....	....	7	1	6	7	5	....	....	....	....
2001-02	Belleville Bulls	OHL	68	33	52	85	50	....	....	....	....	....	....	....	....	....	11	3	8	11	14	....	....	....	....
2002-03	Belleville Bulls	OHL	57	34	60	94	75	....	....	....	....	....	....	....	....	....	7	5	8	13	16	....	....	....	....
	St. John's	AHL	1	0	1	1	0	....	....	....	....	....	....	....	....	....	....	....	....	....	....	....	....	....	....
	Toronto	**NHL**	1	1	0	1	0	0	0	0	1	100.0	1	12	33.3	11:00	....	....	....	....	....	....	....	....	....
2003-04	**Toronto**	**NHL**	69	14	13	27	22	0	0	0	63	22.2	7	450	38.9	11:00	3	0	0	0	2	0	0	0	11:13
2004-05	St. John's	AHL	80	23	43	66	43	....	....	....	....	....	....	....	....	....	5	2	2	4	6	....	....	....	....
2005-06	**Toronto**	**NHL**	80	15	12	27	50	3	4	5	83	18.1	5	373	44.5	11:38	....	....	....	....	....	....	....	....	....
2006-07	**Toronto**	**NHL**	82	10	29	39	44	1	1	1	132	7.6	3	985	46.1	16:09	....	....	....	....	....	....	....	....	....
2007-08	**Toronto**	**NHL**	82	16	17	33	47	2	1	3	127	12.6	–11	1293	47.6	18:54	....	....	....	....	....	....	....	....	....
2008-09	**Toronto**	**NHL**	76	15	40	55	54	5	1	1	114	13.2	–4	1177	51.4	16:56	....	....	....	....	....	....	....	....	....
2009-10	**Toronto**	**NHL**	55	16	25	41	30	7	0	2	99	16.2	–3	926	51.6	18:47	....	....	....	....	....	....	....	....	....
	Calgary	**NHL**	27	3	13	16	2	0	0	2	33	9.1	–3	408	52.0	19:11	....	....	....	....	....	....	....	....	....
	NHL Totals		**472**	**90**	**149**	**239**	**249**	**18**	**7**	**14**	**652**	**13.8**		**5624**	**48.2**	**15:42**	**3**	**0**	**0**	**0**	**2**	**0**	**0**	**0**	**11:13**

Scored a goal in his first NHL game (April 5, 2003 vs. Ottawa).

raded to **Calgary** by **Toronto** with Niklas Hagman, Jamal Mayers and Ian White for Dion Phaneuf, Fredrik Sjostrom and Keith Aulie, January 31, 2010.

STALBERG, Viktor

(STAHL-buhrg, VIHK-tohr) **CHI.**

Left wing. Shoots left. 6'3", 210 lbs. Born, Stockholm, Sweden, January 17, 1986. Toronto's 5th choice, 161st overall, in 2006 Entry Draft.

Season	Club	League	GP	G	A	Pts	PIM	PP	SH	GW	S	%	+/-	TF	F%	Min	GP	G	A	Pts	PIM	PP	SH	GW	Min
2003-04	Molndal U18	Swe-U18	13	14	13	27	....	....	....	....	....	....	....	....	....	....	....	....	....	....	....	....	....	....	....
	Molndal Jr.	Swe-Jr.	18	25	10	35	....	....	....	....	....	....	....	....	....	....	....	....	....	....	....	....	....	....	....
	Molndal	Sweden-4	....	11	9	20	....	....	....	....	....	....	....	....	....	....	....	....	....	....	....	....	....	....	....
2004-05	Molndal Jr.	Swe-Jr.	11	16	7	23	....	....	....	....	....	....	....	....	....	....	....	....	....	....	....	....	....	....	....
	Molndal	Sweden-3	29	6	9	15	54	....	....	....	....	....	....	....	....	....	....	....	....	....	....	....	....	....	....
2005-06	Frolunda Jr.	Swe-Jr.	41	27	26	53	89	....	....	....	....	....	....	....	....	....	7	6	5	11	6	....	....	....	....
2006-07	U. of Vermont	H-East	39	7	8	15	53	....	....	....	....	....	....	....	....	....	....	....	....	....	....	....	....	....	....
2007-08	U. of Vermont	H-East	39	10	13	23	34	....	....	....	....	....	....	....	....	....	....	....	....	....	....	....	....	....	....
2008-09	U. of Vermont	H-East	39	24	22	46	32	....	....	....	....	....	....	....	....	....	....	....	....	....	....	....	....	....	....
	Toronto Marlies	AHL	....	....	....	....	....	....	....	....	....	....	....	....	....	....	2	0	1	1	0	....	....	....	....
2009-10	**Toronto**	**NHL**	40	9	5	14	30	0	0	0	117	7.7	–13	9	33.3	14:37	....	....	....	....	....	....	....	....	....
	Toronto Marlies	AHL	39	12	21	33	36	....	....	....	....	....	....	....	....	....	....	....	....	....	....	....	....	....	....
	NHL Totals		**40**	**9**	**5**	**14**	**30**	**0**	**0**	**0**	**117**	**7.7**		**9**	**33.3**	**14:37**	....	....	....	....	....	....	....	....	....

Hockey East First All-Star Team (2009) • NCAA East First All-American Team (2009)

Traded to **Chicago** by **Toronto** with Christopher Didomenico and Phillipe Paradis for Kris Versteeg and Bill Sweatt, June 30, 2010.

STAMKOS, Steven

(STAM-kohs, STEE-vehn) **T.B.**

Center. Shoots right. 6'1", 196 lbs. Born, Markham, Ont., February 7, 1990. Tampa Bay's 1st choice, 1st overall, in 2008 Entry Draft.

Season	Club	League	GP	G	A	Pts	PIM	PP	SH	GW	S	%	+/-	TF	F%	Min	GP	G	A	Pts	PIM	PP	SH	GW	Min
2005-06	Markham Waxers	Minor-ON	66	105	92	197	87	....	....	....	....	....	....	....	....	....	....	....	....	....	....	....	....	....	....
2006-07	Sarnia Sting	OHL	63	42	50	92	56	....	....	....	....	....	....	....	....	....	4	3	3	6	0	....	....	....	....
2007-08	Sarnia Sting	OHL	61	58	47	105	88	....	....	....	....	....	....	....	....	....	9	11	0	11	20	....	....	....	....
2008-09	**Tampa Bay**	**NHL**	79	23	23	46	39	9	0	1	181	12.7	–13	557	45.4	14:56	....	....	....	....	....	....	....	....	....
2009-10	**Tampa Bay**	**NHL**	82	*51	44	95	38	24	1	5	297	17.2	–2	1004	47.9	20:33	....	....	....	....	....	....	....	....	....
	NHL Totals		**161**	**74**	**67**	**141**	**77**	**33**	**1**	**6**	**478**	**15.5**		**1561**	**47.0**	**17:48**	....	....	....	....	....	....	....	....	....

OHL Second All-Star Team (2008) • Canadian Major Junior First All-Star Team (2008) • Maurice "Rocket" Richard Trophy (2010) (tied with Sidney Crosby)

STAPLETON, Tim

(STAY-puhl-TOHN, TIHM)

Center. Shoots right. 5'9", 160 lbs. Born, La Grange, IL, July 9, 1982.

Season	Club	League	GP	G	A	Pts	PIM	PP	SH	GW	S	%	+/-	TF	F%	Min	GP	G	A	Pts	PIM	PP	SH	GW	Min
2000-01	Green Bay	USHL	52	7	15	22	8	....	....	....	....	....	....	....	....	....	4	1	2	3	4	....	....	....	....
2001-02	Green Bay	USHL	61	24	36	60	10	....	....	....	....	....	....	....	....	....	7	4	7	11	0	....	....	....	....
2002-03	U. Minn-Duluth	WCHA	42	14	28	42	6	....	....	....	....	....	....	....	....	....	....	....	....	....	....	....	....	....	....
2003-04	U. Minn-Duluth	WCHA	43	16	25	41	18	....	....	....	....	....	....	....	....	....	....	....	....	....	....	....	....	....	....
2004-05	U. Minn-Duluth	WCHA	38	19	20	39	6	....	....	....	....	....	....	....	....	....	....	....	....	....	....	....	....	....	....
2005-06	U. Minn-Duluth	WCHA	39	14	16	30	4	....	....	....	....	....	....	....	....	....	....	....	....	....	....	....	....	....	....
	Portland Pirates	AHL	9	0	5	5	4	....	....	....	....	....	....	....	....	....	4	0	0	0	2	....	....	....	....
2006-07	Jokerit Helsinki	Finland	56	19	29	48	24	....	....	....	....	....	....	....	....	....	10	6	4	10	8	....	....	....	....
2007-08	Jokerit Helsinki	Finland	55	29	33	62	36	....	....	....	....	....	....	....	....	....	14	*9	8	17	8	....	....	....	....
2008-09	**Toronto**	**NHL**	4	1	0	1	0	0	0	0	9	11.1	–3	5	20.0	15:06	....	....	....	....	....	....	....	....	....
	Toronto Marlies	AHL	70	28	51	79	26	....	....	....	....	....	....	....	....	....	6	2	0	2	2	....	....	....	....
2009-10	**Atlanta**	**NHL**	6	2	0	2	2	1	0	0	6	33.3	1	36	61.1	11:53	....	....	....	....	....	....	....	....	....
	Chicago Wolves	AHL	73	30	29	59	18	....	....	....	....	....	....	....	....	....	14	4	9	13	12	....	....	....	....
	NHL Totals		**10**	**3**	**0**	**3**	**2**	**1**	**0**	**0**	**15**	**20.0**		**41**	**56.1**	**13:10**	....	....	....	....	....	....	....	....	....

Signed as a free agent by **Toronto**, June 6, 2008. Traded to **Atlanta** by **Toronto** with Pavel Kubina for Garnet Exelby and Colin Stuart, July 1, 2009.

STASTNY, Paul

(STAS-nee, PAWL) **COL.**

Center. Shoots left. 6', 205 lbs. Born, Quebec City, Que., December 27, 1985. Colorado's 2nd choice, 44th overall, in 2005 Entry Draft.

Season	Club	League	GP	G	A	Pts	PIM	PP	SH	GW	S	%	+/-	TF	F%	Min	GP	G	A	Pts	PIM	PP	SH	GW	Min
2003-04	River City Lancers	USHL	56	30	*47	77	46	....	....	....	....	....	....	....	....	....	3	1	2	3	0	....	....	....	....
2004-05	U. of Denver	WCHA	42	17	28	45	30	....	....	....	....	....	....	....	....	....	....	....	....	....	....	....	....	....	....
2005-06	U. of Denver	WCHA	39	19	34	53	79	....	....	....	....	....	....	....	....	....	....	....	....	....	....	....	....	....	....
2006-07	**Colorado**	**NHL**	82	28	50	78	42	11	0	6	185	15.1	4	1226	48.5	18:10	....	....	....	....	....	....	....	....	....
2007-08	**Colorado**	**NHL**	66	24	47	71	24	3	0	4	138	17.4	22	1101	51.0	21:05	9	2	1	3	6	0	0	1	19:56
2008-09	**Colorado**	**NHL**	45	11	25	36	22	7	0	2	118	9.3	–9	850	51.8	21:14	....	....	....	....	....	....	....	....	....
2009-10	**Colorado**	**NHL**	81	20	59	79	50	9	0	2	199	10.1	2	1703	50.0	21:24	6	1	4	5	4	1	0	0	20:23
	United States	Olympics	6	1	2	3	0	....	....	....	....	....	....	....	....	....	....	....	....	....	....	....	....	....	....
	NHL Totals		**274**	**83**	**181**	**264**	**138**	**30**	**0**	**14**	**640**	**13.0**		**4880**	**50.1**	**20:20**	**15**	**3**	**5**	**8**	**10**	**1**	**0**	**1**	**20:06**

WCHA All-Rookie Team (2005) • WCHA Rookie of the Year (2005) • NCAA Championship All-Tournament Team (2005) • WCHA First All-Star Team (2006) • NCAA West Second All-American Team (2006) • NHL All-Rookie Team (2007)

STASTNY, Yan

(STAS-nee, YAHN)

Center. Shoots left. 5'10", 191 lbs. Born, Quebec City, Que., September 30, 1982. Boston's 6th choice, 259th overall, in 2002 Entry Draft.

Season	Club	League	GP	G	A	Pts	PIM	PP	SH	GW	S	%	+/-	TF	F%	Min	GP	G	A	Pts	PIM	PP	SH	GW	Min
99-2000	St. Louis Sting	NAHL	45	12	23	35	77	....	....	....	....	....	....	....	....	....	....	....	....	....	....	....	....	....	....
2000-01	St. Louis Jr. Blues	CSJHL	6	0	2	2	23	....	....	....	....	....	....	....	....	....	....	....	....	....	....	....	....	....	....
	Omaha Lancers	USHL	44	17	14	31	101	....	....	....	....	....	....	....	....	....	11	6	6	12	12	....	....	....	....
2001-02	U. of Notre Dame	CCHA	33	6	11	17	38	....	....	....	....	....	....	....	....	....	....	....	....	....	....	....	....	....	....
2002-03	U. of Notre Dame	CCHA	39	14	9	23	44	....	....	....	....	....	....	....	....	....	....	....	....	....	....	....	....	....	....
2003-04	Nurnberg	Germany	44	9	20	29	83	....	....	....	....	....	....	....	....	....	6	0	1	1	6	....	....	....	....
2004-05	Nurnberg	Germany	51	24	30	54	60	....	....	....	....	....	....	....	....	....	6	2	1	3	8	....	....	....	....
2005-06	**Edmonton**	**NHL**	3	0	0	0	0	0	0	0	1	0.0	–2	17	41.2	6:53	....	....	....	....	....	....	....	....	....
	Iowa Stars	AHL	51	14	17	31	42	....	....	....	....	....	....	....	....	....	....	....	....	....	....	....	....	....	....
	Boston	**NHL**	17	1	3	4	10	0	0	0	13	7.7	–2	122	42.6	10:16	....	....	....	....	....	....	....	....	....
	Providence Bruins	AHL	....	....	....	....	....	....	....	....	....	....	....	....	....	....	6	0	5	5	12	....	....	....	....
2006-07	**Boston**	**NHL**	21	0	2	2	19	0	0	0	7	0.0	–3	51	45.1	7:28	....	....	....	....	....	....	....	....	....
	Providence Bruins	AHL	11	3	9	12	12	....	....	....	....	....	....	....	....	....	....	....	....	....	....	....	....	....	....
	Peoria Rivermen	AHL	39	11	17	28	35	....	....	....	....	....	....	....	....	....	....	....	....	....	....	....	....	....	....
2007-08	**St. Louis**	**NHL**	12	1	1	2	9	0	0	0	10	10.0	0	61	44.3	10:59	....	....	....	....	....	....	....	....	....
	Peoria Rivermen	AHL	43	13	11	24	69	....	....	....	....	....	....	....	....	....	....	....	....	....	....	....	....	....	....
2008-09	**St. Louis**	**NHL**	34	3	4	7	20	0	0	0	30	10.0	–14	102	45.1	12:45	....	....	....	....	....	....	....	....	....
	Peoria Rivermen	AHL	30	12	7	19	21	....	....	....	....	....	....	....	....	....	6	2	2	4	2	....	....	....	....

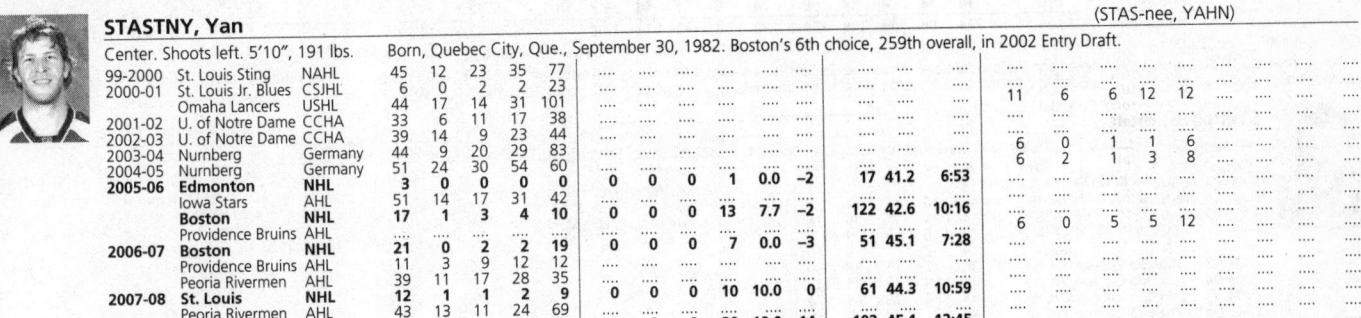

Season	Club	League	Regular Season GP	G	A	Pts	PIM	PP	SH	GW	S	%	+/-	TF	F%	Min	Playoffs GP	G	A	Pts	PIM	PP	SH	GW	Min
2009-10	St. Louis	NHL	4	1	0	1	0	0	0	0	7	14.3	1	15	60.0	9:30	....	....	....	....	....	....	....	....	....
	Peoria Rivermen	AHL	49	10	17	27	51	....	....	....	....	....	....	....	....	....	....	....	....	....	....	....	....	....	....
	Manitoba Moose	AHL	16	2	4	6	18	....	....	....	....	....	....	....	....	....	6	2	2	4	8	....	....	....	....
	NHL Totals		91	6	10	16	58	0	0	0	68	8.8		368	44.6	10:30	....	....	....	....	....	....	....	....	....

Signed as a free agent by **Nurnberg** (Germany), September 18, 2003. Traded to **Edmonton** by **Boston** for Boston's 4th round choice (previously acquired, later traded to San Jose - San Jose selected James Delory) in 2006 Entry Draft, August 30, 2005. Traded to **Boston** by **Edmonton** with Marty Reasoner and Edmonton's 2nd round choice (Milan Lucic) in 2006 Entry Draft for Sergei Samsonov, March 9, 2006. Traded to **St. Louis** by **Boston** for St. Louis' 5th round choice (Denis Reul) in 2007 Entry Draft, January 16, 2006. Traded to **Vancouver** by **St. Louis** for Pierre-Cedric Labrie, March 3, 2010.

STAUBITZ, Brad

(STAW-bihtz, BRAD) **MIN.**

Right wing. Shoots right. 6'1", 210 lbs. Born, Bright's Grove, Ont., July 28, 1984.

Season	Club	League	GP	G	A	Pts	PIM	PP	SH	GW	S	%	+/-	TF	F%	Min	GP	G	A	Pts	PIM	PP	SH	GW	Min
2001-02	Sault Ste. Marie	OHL	45	0	3	3	46	....	....	....	....	....	....	....	....	....	3	0	0	0	2	....	....	....	....
2002-03	Sault Ste. Marie	OHL	55	2	6	8	116	....	....	....	....	....	....	....	....	....	4	0	0	0	7	....	....	....	....
2003-04	Sault Ste. Marie	OHL	66	6	18	24	140	....	....	....	....	....	....	....	....	....	....	....	....	....	....	....	....	....	....
2004-05	Sault Ste. Marie	OHL	40	2	11	13	101	....	....	....	....	....	....	....	....	....	....	....	....	....	....	....	....	....	....
	Ottawa 67's	OHL	30	5	8	13	80	....	....	....	....	....	....	....	....	....	....	....	....	....	....	....	....	....	....
2005-06	Cleveland Barons	AHL	71	0	6	6	245	....	....	....	....	....	....	....	....	....	21	4	16	20	70	....	....	....	....
2006-07	Worcester Sharks	AHL	51	1	4	5	137	....	....	....	....	....	....	....	....	....	....	....	....	....	....	....	....	....	....
2007-08	Worcester Sharks	AHL	73	6	14	20	195	....	....	....	....	....	....	....	....	....	5	0	0	0	13	....	....	....	....
2008-09	**San Jose**	**NHL**	**35**	**1**	**2**	**3**	**76**	**0**	**0**	**1**	**22**	**4.5**	**0**	**2**	**0.0**	**6:13**	....	....	....	....	....	....	....	....	....
	Worcester Sharks	AHL	38	0	5	5	130	....	....	....	....	....	....	....	....	....	10	0	2	2	15	....	....	....	....
2009-10	**San Jose**	**NHL**	**47**	**3**	**3**	**6**	**110**	**0**	**0**	**1**	**24**	**12.5**	**0**	**4**	**0.0**	**6:13**	....	....	....	....	....	....	....	....	....
	NHL Totals		**82**	**4**	**5**	**9**	**186**	**0**	**0**	**2**	**46**	**8.7**		**6**	**0.0**	**6:13**	....	....	....	....	....	....	....	....	....

Signed as a free agent by **San Jose**, September 19, 2005. Traded to **Minnesota** by **San Jose** for Minnesota's 5th round choice (Freddie Hamiton) in 2010 Entry Draft, June 21, 2010.

STECKEL, David

(STEH-kuhl, DAY-vihd) **WSH.**

Center. Shoots left. 6'5", 217 lbs. Born, Westbend, WI, March 15, 1982. Los Angeles' 2nd choice, 30th overall, in 2001 Entry Draft.

Season	Club	League	GP	G	A	Pts	PIM	PP	SH	GW	S	%	+/-	TF	F%	Min	GP	G	A	Pts	PIM	PP	SH	GW	Min
1998-99	USNTDP	USHL	2	0	0	0	2	....	....	....	....	....	....	....	....	....	....	....	....	....	....	....	....	....	....
	USNTDP	NAHL	51	3	14	17	18	....	....	....	....	....	....	....	....	....	....	....	....	....	....	....	....	....	....
99-2000	USNTDP	U-18	6	2	5	7	14	....	....	....	....	....	....	....	....	....	....	....	....	....	....	....	....	....	....
	USNTDP	USHL	52	13	13	26	94	....	....	....	....	....	....	....	....	....	....	....	....	....	....	....	....	....	....
2000-01	Ohio State	CCHA	33	17	18	35	80	....	....	....	....	....	....	....	....	....	....	....	....	....	....	....	....	....	....
2001-02	Ohio State	CCHA	36	6	16	22	75	....	....	....	....	....	....	....	....	....	....	....	....	....	....	....	....	....	....
2002-03	Ohio State	CCHA	36	10	8	18	50	....	....	....	....	....	....	....	....	....	....	....	....	....	....	....	....	....	....
2003-04	Ohio State	CCHA	41	17	13	30	44	....	....	....	....	....	....	....	....	....	....	....	....	....	....	....	....	....	....
2004-05	Manchester	AHL	63	10	7	17	26	....	....	....	....	....	....	....	....	....	6	1	1	2	4	....	....	....	....
2005-06	**Washington**	**NHL**	**7**	**0**	**0**	**0**	**0**	**0**	**0**	**0**	**6**	**0.0**	**1**	**48**	**35.4**	**7:39**	....	....	....	....	....	....	....	....	....
	Hershey Bears	AHL	74	14	20	34	58	....	....	....	....	....	....	....	....	....	21	10	5	15	20	....	....	....	....
2006-07	**Washington**	**NHL**	**5**	**0**	**0**	**0**	**2**	**0**	**0**	**0**	**4**	**0.0**	**–2**	**43**	**65.1**	**12:26**	....	....	....	....	....	....	....	....	....
	Hershey Bears	AHL	71	30	31	61	46	....	....	....	....	....	....	....	....	....	19	6	9	15	16	....	....	....	....
2007-08	**Washington**	**NHL**	**67**	**5**	**7**	**12**	**34**	**0**	**0**	**1**	**66**	**7.6**	**1**	**900**	**56.3**	**13:34**	**7**	**1**	**1**	**2**	**4**	**0**	**0**	**0**	**14:23**
2008-09	**Washington**	**NHL**	**76**	**8**	**11**	**19**	**34**	**0**	**2**	**1**	**103**	**7.8**	**2**	**886**	**57.9**	**13:49**	**14**	**3**	**2**	**5**	**4**	**0**	**0**	**1**	**16:03**
2009-10	**Washington**	**NHL**	**79**	**5**	**11**	**16**	**19**	**1**	**0**	**1**	**90**	**5.6**	**4**	**1076**	**59.2**	**12:24**	**3**	**0**	**0**	**0**	**0**	**0**	**0**	**0**	**10:28**
	NHL Totals		**234**	**18**	**29**	**47**	**89**	**1**	**2**	**3**	**269**	**6.7**		**2953**	**57.6**	**13:03**	**24**	**4**	**3**	**7**	**8**	**0**	**0**	**1**	**14:52**

CCHA All-Rookie Team (2001)

Signed as a free agent by **Washington**, August 25, 2005.

STEEN, Alex

(STEEN, AL-ehx) **ST.L.**

Center. Shoots left. 6'1", 206 lbs. Born, Winnipeg, Man., March 1, 1984. Toronto's 1st choice, 24th overall, in 2002 Entry Draft.

Season	Club	League	GP	G	A	Pts	PIM	PP	SH	GW	S	%	+/-	TF	F%	Min	GP	G	A	Pts	PIM	PP	SH	GW	Min
99-2000	V.Frolunda Jr.	Swe-Jr.	8	5	7	12	0	....	....	....	....	....	....	....	....	....	....	....	....	....	....	....	....	....	....
	V.Frolunda U18	Swe-U18	14	3	5	8	16	....	....	....	....	....	....	....	....	....	....	....	....	....	....	....	....	....	....
2000-01	V.Frolunda Jr.	Swe-Jr.	23	11	12	23	15	....	....	....	....	....	....	....	....	....	3	1	0	1	2	....	....	....	....
	V.Frolunda U18	Swe-U18	6	3	3	6	9	....	....	....	....	....	....	....	....	....	....	....	....	....	....	....	....	....	....
2001-02	V.Frolunda Jr.	Swe-Jr.	23	21	17	38	47	....	....	....	....	....	....	....	....	....	2	1	1	2	2	....	....	....	....
	V.Frolunda	Sweden	26	0	3	3	14	....	....	....	....	....	....	....	....	....	10	1	2	3	0	....	....	....	....
2002-03	V.Frolunda	Sweden	45	5	10	15	18	....	....	....	....	....	....	....	....	....	16	2	3	5	4	....	....	....	....
	V.Frolunda Jr.	Swe-Jr.	2	0	2	2	0	....	....	....	....	....	....	....	....	....	....	....	....	....	....	....	....	....	....
2003-04	V.Frolunda	Sweden	48	10	14	24	50	....	....	....	....	....	....	....	....	....	10	4	6	10	14	....	....	....	....
2004-05	MODO	Sweden	50	9	8	17	26	....	....	....	....	....	....	....	....	....	6	1	0	1	4	....	....	....	....
2005-06	**Toronto**	**NHL**	**75**	**18**	**27**	**45**	**42**	**9**	**1**	**3**	**176**	**10.2**	**–9**	**29**	**24.1**	**17:37**	....	....	....	....	....	....	....	....	....
2006-07	**Toronto**	**NHL**	**82**	**15**	**20**	**35**	**26**	**4**	**0**	**5**	**192**	**7.8**	**5**	**44**	**34.1**	**15:42**	....	....	....	....	....	....	....	....	....
2007-08	**Toronto**	**NHL**	**76**	**15**	**27**	**42**	**32**	**2**	**1**	**2**	**169**	**8.9**	**0**	**179**	**33.0**	**18:05**	....	....	....	....	....	....	....	....	....
2008-09	**Toronto**	**NHL**	**20**	**2**	**2**	**4**	**6**	**1**	**0**	**0**	**31**	**6.5**	**–4**	**82**	**52.4**	**15:38**	....	....	....	....	....	....	....	....	....
	St. Louis	**NHL**	**61**	**6**	**18**	**24**	**24**	**2**	**1**	**0**	**117**	**5.1**	**–6**	**154**	**41.6**	**16:34**	**4**	**0**	**1**	**1**	**0**	**0**	**0**	**0**	**17:47**
2009-10	**St. Louis**	**NHL**	**68**	**24**	**23**	**47**	**30**	**7**	**2**	**4**	**189**	**12.7**	**6**	**73**	**41.1**	**16:17**	....	....	....	....	....	....	....	....	....
	NHL Totals		**382**	**80**	**117**	**197**	**160**	**25**	**5**	**14**	**874**	**9.2**		**561**	**38.9**	**16:47**	**4**	**0**	**1**	**1**	**0**	**0**	**0**	**0**	**17:47**

Traded to **St. Louis** by **Toronto** with Carlo Colaiacovo for Lee Stempniak, November 24, 2008.

STEMPNIAK, Lee

(STEHMP-nee-ak, LEE)

Right wing. Shoots right. 6', 195 lbs. Born, Buffalo, NY, February 4, 1983. St. Louis' 7th choice, 148th overall, in 2003 Entry Draft.

Season	Club	League	GP	G	A	Pts	PIM	PP	SH	GW	S	%	+/-	TF	F%	Min	GP	G	A	Pts	PIM	PP	SH	GW	Min
2000-01	Buffalo Lightning	OPJHL	48	34	51	86	36	....	....	....	....	....	....	....	....	....	....	....	....	....	....	....	....	....	....
2001-02	Dartmouth	ECAC	32	12	9	21	8	....	....	....	....	....	....	....	....	....	....	....	....	....	....	....	....	....	....
2002-03	Dartmouth	ECAC	34	21	28	49	32	....	....	....	....	....	....	....	....	....	....	....	....	....	....	....	....	....	....
2003-04	Dartmouth	ECAC	34	16	22	38	42	....	....	....	....	....	....	....	....	....	....	....	....	....	....	....	....	....	....
2004-05	Dartmouth	ECAC	35	14	*29	43	34	....	....	....	....	....	....	....	....	....	....	....	....	....	....	....	....	....	....
2005-06	**St. Louis**	**NHL**	**57**	**14**	**13**	**27**	**22**	**5**	**0**	**2**	**100**	**14.0**	**–10**	**7**	**42.9**	**14:22**	....	....	....	....	....	....	....	....	....
	Peoria Rivermen	AHL	26	8	7	15	32	....	....	....	....	....	....	....	....	....	3	0	3	3	2	....	....	....	....
2006-07	**St. Louis**	**NHL**	**82**	**27**	**25**	**52**	**33**	**8**	**0**	**4**	**166**	**16.3**	**–2**	**7**	**14.3**	**14:43**	....	....	....	....	....	....	....	....	....
2007-08	**St. Louis**	**NHL**	**80**	**13**	**25**	**38**	**40**	**3**	**0**	**2**	**162**	**8.0**	**0**	**11**	**36.4**	**15:53**	....	....	....	....	....	....	....	....	....
2008-09	**St. Louis**	**NHL**	**14**	**3**	**10**	**13**	**2**	**0**	**0**	**1**	**43**	**7.0**	**–3**	**1**	**0.0**	**19:28**	....	....	....	....	....	....	....	....	....
	Toronto	**NHL**	**61**	**11**	**20**	**31**	**31**	**3**	**0**	**0**	**128**	**8.6**	**–9**	**12**	**33.3**	**15:52**	....	....	....	....	....	....	....	....	....
2009-10	**Toronto**	**NHL**	**62**	**14**	**16**	**30**	**18**	**5**	**1**	**1**	**164**	**8.5**	**–10**	**25**	**36.0**	**17:53**	....	....	....	....	....	....	....	....	....
	Phoenix	**NHL**	**18**	**14**	**4**	**18**	**8**	**4**	**0**	**1**	**48**	**29.2**	**10**	**14**	**57.1**	**15:22**	**7**	**0**	**2**	**2**	**0**	**0**	**0**	**0**	**14:28**
	NHL Totals		**374**	**96**	**113**	**209**	**154**	**28**	**1**	**11**	**811**	**11.8**		**77**	**37.7**	**15:50**	**7**	**0**	**2**	**2**	**0**	**0**	**0**	**0**	**14:28**

ECAC All-Rookie Team (2002) • ECAC First All-Star Team (2004, 2005) • NCAA East First All-American Team (2004) • NCAA East Second All-American Team (2005)

Traded to **Toronto** by **St. Louis** for Alex Steen and Carlo Colaiacovo, November 24, 2008. Traded to **Phoenix** by **Toronto** for Matt Jones and Phoenix's 4th (later traded to Washington – Washington selected Philipp Grubauer) and 7th (later traded to Edmonton – Edmonton selected Kellen Jones) round choices in 2010 Entry Draft, March 3, 2010.

STERLING, Brett

(STUHR-lihng, BREHT) **PIT.**

Left wing. Shoots left. 5'7", 175 lbs. Born, Los Angeles, CA, April 24, 1984. Atlanta's 5th choice, 145th overall, in 2003 Entry Draft.

Season	Club	League	GP	G	A	Pts	PIM	PP	SH	GW	S	%	+/-	TF	F%	Min	GP	G	A	Pts	PIM	PP	SH	GW	Min
99-2000	L.A. Jr. Kings	SCAHA	35	45	25	70	....	....	....	....	....	....	....	....	....	....	....	....	....	....	....	....	....	....	....
2000-01	USNTDP	U-17	13	....	....	....	....	....	....	....	....	....	....	....	....	....	....	....	....	....	....	....	....	....	....
	USNTDP	NAHL	47	29	15	44	72	....	....	....	....	....	....	....	....	....	....	....	....	....	....	....	....	....	....
2001-02	USNTDP	U-18	31	21	15	36	18	....	....	....	....	....	....	....	....	....	....	....	....	....	....	....	....	....	....
	USNTDP	USHL	10	6	3	9	8	....	....	....	....	....	....	....	....	....	....	....	....	....	....	....	....	....	....
	USNTDP	NAHL	9	2	1	3	10	....	....	....	....	....	....	....	....	....	....	....	....	....	....	....	....	....	....
2002-03	Colorado College	WCHA	36	27	11	38	30	....	....	....	....	....	....	....	....	....	....	....	....	....	....	....	....	....	....
2003-04	Colorado College	WCHA	30	16	12	28	40	....	....	....	....	....	....	....	....	....	....	....	....	....	....	....	....	....	....
2004-05	Colorado College	WCHA	43	*34	29	63	74	....	....	....	....	....	....	....	....	....	....	....	....	....	....	....	....	....	....
2005-06	Colorado College	WCHA	42	31	24	55	66	....	....	....	....	....	....	....	....	....	....	....	....	....	....	....	....	....	....
2006-07	Chicago Wolves	AHL	77	*55	42	97	96	....	....	....	....	....	....	....	....	....	15	7	5	12	24	....	....	....	....
2007-08	**Atlanta**	**NHL**	**13**	**1**	**2**	**3**	**14**	**0**	**0**	**0**	**14**	**7.1**	**–2**	**3**	**66.7**	**12:24**	....	....	....	....	....	....	....	....	....
	Chicago Wolves	AHL	70	38	33	71	116	....	....	....	....	....	....	....	....	....	16	4	5	9	18	....	....	....	....

			Regular Season														Playoffs								
Season	Club	League	GP	G	A	Pts	PIM	PP	SH	GW	S	%	+/-	TF	F%	Min	GP	G	A	Pts	PIM	PP	SH	GW	Min
2008-09	**Atlanta**	**NHL**	**6**	**1**	**0**	**1**	**2**	**0**	**0**	**0**	**11**	**9.1**	**–3**	**0**	**0.0**	**13:53**	....	....	....	....	....	....	....	....	....
	Chicago Wolves	AHL	52	16	23	39	84	....	....	....	....	....	....	....	....	....	....	....	....	....	....	....	....	....	....
2009-10	Chicago Wolves	AHL	55	34	22	56	38	....	....	....	....	....	....	....	....	....	9	4	6	10	4	....	....	....	....
	NHL Totals		**19**	**2**	**2**	**4**	**16**	**0**	**0**	**0**	**25**	**8.0**		**3**	**66.7**	**12:52**	....	....	....	....	....	....	....	....	....

WCHA All-Rookie Team (2003) • WCHA First All-Star Team (2005, 2006) • NCAA West First All-American Team (2005, 2006) • AHL All-Rookie Team (2007) • AHL First All-Star Team (2007) • Dudley "Red" Garrett Memorial Award (AHL - Rookie of the Year) (2007) • Willie Marshall Award (AHL - Top Goal-scorer) (2007) • AHL Second All-Star Team (2008)

Traded to **San Jose** by **Atlanta** with Michael Vernace and Atlanta's 7th round choice (Lee Moffie) in 2010 Entry Draft for future considerations, June 23, 2010. Signed as a free agent by **Pittsburgh**, July 3, 2010.

STEVENSON, Grant

(STEE-vehn-suhn, GRANT)

Center. Shoots right. 5'11", 170 lbs. Born, Spruce Grove, Alta., October 15, 1981.

Season	Club	League	GP	G	A	Pts	PIM	PP	SH	GW	S	%	+/-	TF	F%	Min	GP	G	A	Pts	PIM	PP	SH	GW	Min
1998-99	Spruce Grove	RAMHL	26	15	32	47	90	....	....	....	....	....	....	....	....	....	8	10	10	20	30	....	....	....	....
99-2000	Bonnyville	AJHL	63	20	38	58	....	....	....	....	....	....	....	....	....	....	....	....	....	....	....	....	....	....	....
2000-01	Grande Prairie	AJHL	53	24	49	73	62	....	....	....	....	....	....	....	....	....	15	7	2	9	38	....	....	....	....
2001-02	Minnesota State	WCHA	38	8	8	16	36	....	....	....	....	....	....	....	....	....	....	....	....	....	....	....	....	....	....
2002-03	Minnesota State	WCHA	38	27	36	63	38	....	....	....	....	....	....	....	....	....	....	....	....	....	....	....	....	....	....
2003-04	Cleveland Barons	AHL	71	13	26	39	45	....	....	....	....	....	....	....	....	....	9	0	7	7	6	....	....	....	....
2004-05	Cleveland Barons	AHL	77	14	25	39	70	....	....	....	....	....	....	....	....	....	....	....	....	....	....	....	....	....	....
	Johnstown Chiefs	ECHL	2	1	0	1	2	....	....	....	....	....	....	....	....	....	....	....	....	....	....	....	....	....	....
2005-06	**San Jose**	**NHL**	**47**	**10**	**12**	**22**	**14**	**5**	**0**	**2**	**67**	**14.9**	**–7**	**6**	**33.3**	**11:57**	**5**	**0**	**0**	**0**	**4**	**0**	**0**	**0**	**6:59**
	Cleveland Barons	AHL	17	8	8	16	8	....	....	....	....	....	....	....	....	....	....	....	....	....	....	....	....	....	....
2006-07	Worcester Sharks	AHL	59	14	25	39	30	....	....	....	....	....	....	....	....	....	6	2	0	2	2	....	....	....	....
2007-08	Quad City Flames	AHL	80	30	43	73	58	....	....	....	....	....	....	....	....	....	....	....	....	....	....	....	....	....	....
2008-09	Chicago Wolves	AHL	59	10	11	21	31	....	....	....	....	....	....	....	....	....	....	....	....	....	....	....	....	....	....
2009-10	Kloten Flyers	Swiss	3	0	0	0	0	....	....	....	....	....	....	....	....	....	....	....	....	....	....	....	....	....	....
	Hamilton	AHL	53	8	9	17	22	....	....	....	....	....	....	....	....	....	19	1	9	10	8	....	....	....	....
	NHL Totals		**47**	**10**	**12**	**22**	**14**	**5**	**0**	**2**	**67**	**14.9**		**6**	**33.3**	**11:57**	**5**	**0**	**0**	**0**	**4**	**0**	**0**	**0**	**6:59**

WCHA First All-Star Team (2003) • NCAA West Second All-American Team (2003)

Signed as a free agent by **San Jose**, April 18, 2003. Signed as a free agent by **Calgary**, July 4, 2007. Signed as a free agent by **Atlanta**, July 9, 2008. Signed as a free agent by **Kloten** (Swiss), June 25, 2009. Signed as a free agent by **Hamilton** (AHL), November 26, 2009. Signed as a free agent by **Augsburg** (Germany), July 29, 2010.

STEWART, Anthony

(STEW-ahrt, AN-thu-nee) **ATL.**

Right wing. Shoots right. 6'2", 235 lbs. Born, LaSalle, Que., January 5, 1985. Florida's 2nd choice, 25th overall, in 2003 Entry Draft.

Season	Club	League	GP	G	A	Pts	PIM	PP	SH	GW	S	%	+/-	TF	F%	Min	GP	G	A	Pts	PIM	PP	SH	GW	Min
2000-01	North York	MTHL	34	30	70	100	....	....	....	....	....	....	....	....	....	....	....	....	....	....	....	....	....	....	....
	St. Mike's B's	OPJHL	5	0	2	2	0	....	....	....	....	....	....	....	....	....	....	....	....	....	....	....	....	....	....
2001-02	Kingston	OHL	65	19	24	43	12	....	....	....	....	....	....	....	....	....	1	0	0	0	0	....	....	....	....
2002-03	Kingston	OHL	68	32	38	70	47	....	....	....	....	....	....	....	....	....	....	....	....	....	....	....	....	....	....
2003-04	Kingston	OHL	53	35	23	58	76	....	....	....	....	....	....	....	....	....	5	3	4	7	7	....	....	....	....
2004-05	Kingston	OHL	62	32	35	67	70	....	....	....	....	....	....	....	....	....	....	....	....	....	....	....	....	....	....
	San Antonio	AHL	10	1	2	3	14	....	....	....	....	....	....	....	....	....	....	....	....	....	....	....	....	....	....
2005-06	**Florida**	**NHL**	**10**	**2**	**1**	**3**	**2**	**1**	**0**	**0**	**16**	**12.5**	**2**	**1**	**0.0**	**7:13**	....	....	....	....	....	....	....	....	....
	Rochester	AHL	4	2	3	5	0	....	....	....	....	....	....	....	....	....	....	....	....	....	....	....	....	....	....
2006-07	**Florida**	**NHL**	**10**	**0**	**1**	**1**	**2**	**0**	**0**	**0**	**8**	**0.0**	**1**	**0**	**0.0**	**6:51**	....	....	....	....	....	....	....	....	....
	Rochester	AHL	62	13	14	27	64	....	....	....	....	....	....	....	....	....	6	2	0	2	2	....	....	....	....
2007-08	**Florida**	**NHL**	**26**	**0**	**1**	**1**	**0**	**0**	**0**	**0**	**21**	**0.0**	**–1**	**0**	**0.0**	**6:08**	....	....	....	....	....	....	....	....	....
	Rochester	AHL	54	13	18	31	61	....	....	....	....	....	....	....	....	....	....	....	....	....	....	....	....	....	....
2008-09	**Florida**	**NHL**	**59**	**2**	**5**	**7**	**34**	**0**	**0**	**0**	**56**	**3.6**	**–6**	**3**	**33.3**	**7:39**	....	....	....	....	....	....	....	....	....
2009-10	Chicago Wolves	AHL	77	12	19	31	67	....	....	....	....	....	....	....	....	....	13	9	3	12	6	....	....	....	....
	NHL Totals		**105**	**4**	**8**	**12**	**38**	**1**	**0**	**0**	**101**	**4.0**		**4**	**25.0**	**7:09**	....	....	....	....	....	....	....	....	....

• Missed remainder of 2005-06 season recovering from wrist injury suffered in game vs. Carolina, November 11, 2005. Signed as a free agent by **Atlanta**, July 13, 2009.

STEWART, Chris

(STEW-ahrt, KRIHS) **COL.**

Right wing. Shoots right. 6'2", 228 lbs. Born, Toronto, Ont., October 30, 1987. Colorado's 1st choice, 18th overall, in 2006 Entry Draft.

Season	Club	League	GP	G	A	Pts	PIM	PP	SH	GW	S	%	+/-	TF	F%	Min	GP	G	A	Pts	PIM	PP	SH	GW	Min
2004-05	Kingston	OHL	64	18	12	30	45	....	....	....	....	....	....	....	....	....	....	....	....	....	....	....	....	....	....
2005-06	Kingston	OHL	62	37	50	87	118	....	....	....	....	....	....	....	....	....	6	2	0	2	13	....	....	....	....
2006-07	Kingston	OHL	61	36	46	82	108	....	....	....	....	....	....	....	....	....	5	4	2	6	6	....	....	....	....
	Albany River Rats	AHL	5	1	2	3	2	....	....	....	....	....	....	....	....	....	1	0	0	0	0	....	....	....	....
2007-08	Lake Erie	AHL	77	25	19	44	93	....	....	....	....	....	....	....	....	....	....	....	....	....	....	....	....	....	....
2008-09	**Colorado**	**NHL**	**53**	**11**	**8**	**19**	**54**	**1**	**1**	**1**	**98**	**11.2**	**–18**	**21**	**33.3**	**12:20**	....	....	....	....	....	....	....	....	....
	Lake Erie	AHL	19	5	6	11	23	....	....	....	....	....	....	....	....	....	....	....	....	....	....	....	....	....	....
2009-10	**Colorado**	**NHL**	**77**	**28**	**36**	**64**	**73**	**3**	**0**	**5**	**221**	**12.7**	**4**	**8**	**37.5**	**16:42**	**6**	**3**	**0**	**3**	**4**	**0**	**0**	**1**	**18:00**
	Lake Erie	AHL	2	0	0	0	2	....	....	....	....	....	....	....	....	....	....	....	....	....	....	....	....	....	....
	NHL Totals		**130**	**39**	**44**	**83**	**127**	**4**	**1**	**6**	**319**	**12.2**		**29**	**34.5**	**14:55**	**6**	**3**	**0**	**3**	**4**	**0**	**0**	**1**	**18:00**

STEWART, Greg

(STEW-ahrt, GREHG) **EDM.**

Left wing. Shoots left. 6'2", 197 lbs. Born, Kitchener, Ont., May 21, 1986. Montreal's 7th choice, 246th overall, in 2004 Entry Draft.

Season	Club	League	GP	G	A	Pts	PIM	PP	SH	GW	S	%	+/-	TF	F%	Min	GP	G	A	Pts	PIM	PP	SH	GW	Min
2003-04	Peterborough	OHL	58	4	6	10	76	....	....	....	....	....	....	....	....	....	....	....	....	....	....	....	....	....	....
2004-05	Peterborough	OHL	68	16	18	34	111	....	....	....	....	....	....	....	....	....	14	3	3	6	20	....	....	....	....
2005-06	Peterborough	OHL	60	24	15	39	83	....	....	....	....	....	....	....	....	....	19	1	6	7	30	....	....	....	....
2006-07	Cincinnati	ECHL	62	8	15	23	126	....	....	....	....	....	....	....	....	....	10	5	2	7	36	....	....	....	....
2007-08	**Montreal**	**NHL**	**1**	**0**	**0**	**0**	**5**	**0**	**0**	**0**	**2**	**0.0**	**0**	**0**	**0.0**	**11:26**	....	....	....	....	....	....	....	....	....
	Hamilton	AHL	69	10	7	17	137	....	....	....	....	....	....	....	....	....	....	....	....	....	....	....	....	....	....
2008-09	**Montreal**	**NHL**	**20**	**0**	**1**	**1**	**32**	**0**	**0**	**0**	**16**	**0.0**	**–4**	**1**	**100.0**	**8:37**	**2**	**0**	**0**	**0**	**2**	**0**	**0**	**0**	**8:31**
	Hamilton	AHL	51	7	10	17	170	....	....	....	....	....	....	....	....	....	2	1	0	1	9	....	....	....	....
2009-10	**Montreal**	**NHL**	**5**	**0**	**0**	**0**	**11**	**0**	**0**	**0**	**4**	**0.0**	**–3**	**1**	**0.0**	**4:12**	....	....	....	....	....	....	....	....	....
	Hamilton	AHL	45	5	5	10	90	....	....	....	....	....	....	....	....	....	....	....	....	....	....	....	....	....	....
	Chicago Wolves	AHL	9	1	0	1	39	....	....	....	....	....	....	....	....	....	10	0	1	1	20	....	....	....	....
	NHL Totals		**26**	**0**	**1**	**1**	**48**	**0**	**0**	**0**	**22**	**0.0**		**2**	**50.0**	**7:52**	**2**	**0**	**0**	**0**	**2**	**0**	**0**	**0**	**8:31**

Signed as a free agent by **Edmonton**, July 16, 2010. • Reassigned to **Chicago** (AHL) by **Edmonton**, March 10, 2010.

STEWART, Karl

(STEW-ahrt, KAHRL)

Left wing. Shoots left. 5'11", 185 lbs. Born, Aurora, Ont., June 30, 1983.

Season	Club	League	GP	G	A	Pts	PIM	PP	SH	GW	S	%	+/-	TF	F%	Min	GP	G	A	Pts	PIM	PP	SH	GW	Min
99-2000	Thornhill Rattlers	OPJHL	49	15	19	34	61	....	....	....	....	....	....	....	....	....	....	....	....	....	....	....	....	....	....
2000-01	Plymouth Whalers	OHL	68	9	14	23	87	....	....	....	....	....	....	....	....	....	19	3	4	7	14	....	....	....	....
2001-02	Plymouth Whalers	OHL	65	20	23	43	104	....	....	....	....	....	....	....	....	....	6	0	2	2	21	....	....	....	....
2002-03	Plymouth Whalers	OHL	68	35	50	85	120	....	....	....	....	....	....	....	....	....	17	7	10	17	31	....	....	....	....
2003-04	**Atlanta**	**NHL**	**5**	**0**	**1**	**1**	**4**	**0**	**0**	**0**	**2**	**0.0**	**0**	**10**	**10.0**	**4:27**	....	....	....	....	....	....	....	....	....
	Chicago Wolves	AHL	72	10	32	42	186	....	....	....	....	....	....	....	....	....	10	2	3	5	29	....	....	....	....
2004-05	Chicago Wolves	AHL	77	16	8	24	226	....	....	....	....	....	....	....	....	....	12	4	2	6	32	....	....	....	....
2005-06	**Atlanta**	**NHL**	**8**	**0**	**0**	**0**	**15**	**0**	**0**	**0**	**6**	**0.0**	**–3**	**3**	**100.0**	**5:40**	....	....	....	....	....	....	....	....	....
	Chicago Wolves	AHL	71	22	18	40	184	....	....	....	....	....	....	....	....	....	....	....	....	....	....	....	....	....	....
2006-07	**Pittsburgh**	**NHL**	**3**	**0**	**0**	**0**	**2**	**0**	**0**	**0**	**0**	**0.0**	**–1**	**1**	**100.0**	**3:23**	....	....	....	....	....	....	....	....	....
	Chicago	**NHL**	**37**	**2**	**3**	**5**	**43**	**0**	**1**	**0**	**19**	**10.5**	**–2**	**2**	**50.0**	**9:22**	....	....	....	....	....	....	....	....	....
	Tampa Bay	**NHL**	**7**	**0**	**0**	**0**	**2**	**0**	**0**	**0**	**2**	**0.0**	**–2**	**0**	**0.0**	**7:10**	....	....	....	....	....	....	....	....	....
2007-08	**Tampa Bay**	**NHL**	**9**	**0**	**0**	**0**	**2**	**0**	**0**	**0**	**2**	**0.0**	**–2**	**0**	**0.0**	**4:06**	....	....	....	....	....	....	....	....	....
	Norfolk Admirals	AHL	62	14	13	27	96	....	....	....	....	....	....	....	....	....	....	....	....	....	....	....	....	....	....
2008-09	Rochester	AHL	72	20	8	28	70	....	....	....	....	....	....	....	....	....	....	....	....	....	....	....	....	....	....
2009-10	Straubing Tigers	Germany	40	12	14	26	30	....	....	....	....	....	....	....	....	....	....	....	....	....	....	....	....	....	....
	NHL Totals		**69**	**2**	**4**	**6**	**68**	**0**	**1**	**0**	**31**	**6.5**		**16**	**37.5**	**7:25**	....	....	....	....	....	....	....	....	....

Signed as a free agent by **Atlanta**, September 28, 2001. Traded to **Anaheim** by **Atlanta** with Atlanta's 2nd round choice (later traded to Colorado - Colorado selected T.J. Galiardi) in 2007 Entry Draft and future considerations for Vitaly Vishnevski, August 17, 2006. Claimed on waivers by **Pittsburgh** from **Anaheim**, September 27, 2006. Claimed on waivers by **Chicago** from **Pittsburgh**, October 26, 2006. Traded to **Tampa Bay** by **Chicago** with Florida's 6th round choice (previously acquired, Tampa Bay selected Luke Witkowski) in 2008 Entry Draft for Nikita Alexeev, February 27, 2007. Signed as a free agent by **Straubing** (Germany), April 6, 2009.

STILLMAN, Cory

(STIHL-mahn, KOHR-ee) **FLA.**

Left wing. Shoots left. 6', 200 lbs. Born, Peterborough, Ont., December 20, 1973. Calgary's 1st choice, 6th overall, in 1992 Entry Draft.

Season	Club	League	Regular Season GP	G	A	Pts	PIM	PP	SH	GW	S	%	+/-	TF	F%	Min	Playoffs GP	G	A	Pts	PIM	PP	SH	GW	Min
1989-90	Peterborough	OHA-B	41	30	*54	84	76	....	....	....	....	....	....	....	....	....	....	....	....	....	....	....	....	....	....
1990-91	Windsor Spitfires	OHL	64	31	70	101	31	....	....	....	....	....	....	....	....	....	11	3	6	9	8	....	....	....	....
1991-92	Windsor Spitfires	OHL	53	29	61	90	59	....	....	....	....	....	....	....	....	....	7	2	4	6	8	....	....	....	....
1992-93	Peterborough	OHL	61	25	55	80	55	....	....	....	....	....	....	....	....	....	18	3	8	11	18	....	....	....	....
1993-94	Saint John Flames	AHL	79	35	48	83	52	....	....	....	....	....	....	....	....	....	7	2	4	6	16	....	....	....	....
1994-95	Saint John Flames	AHL	63	28	53	81	70	....	....	....	....	....	....	....	....	....	5	0	2	2	2	....	....	....	....
	Calgary	NHL	10	0	2	2	2	0	0	0	7	0.0	1	....	....	....	....	....	....	....	....	....	....	....	....
1995-96	Calgary	NHL	74	16	19	35	41	4	1	3	132	12.1	–5	....	....	....	2	1	1	2	0	0	0	0	....
1996-97	Calgary	NHL	58	6	20	26	14	2	0	0	112	5.4	–6	....	....	....	....	....	....	....	....	....	....	....	....
1997-98	Calgary	NHL	72	27	22	49	40	9	4	1	178	15.2	–9	....	....	....	....	....	....	....	....	....	....	....	....
1998-99	Calgary	NHL	76	27	30	57	38	9	3	5	175	15.4	7	535	46.5	16:19	....	....	....	....	....	....	....	....	....
99-2000	Calgary	NHL	37	12	9	21	12	6	0	3	59	20.3	–9	283	54.4	17:45	....	....	....	....	....	....	....	....	....
2000-01	Calgary	NHL	66	21	24	45	45	7	0	4	148	14.2	–6	346	43.9	18:50	....	....	....	....	....	....	....	....	....
	St. Louis	NHL	12	3	4	7	6	3	0	0	26	11.5	–2	36	61.1	18:37	15	3	5	8	8	1	0	1	14:58
2001-02	St. Louis	NHL	80	23	22	45	36	6	0	4	140	16.4	8	196	46.4	15:03	9	0	2	2	2	0	0	0	12:46
2002-03	St. Louis	NHL	79	24	43	67	56	6	0	4	157	15.3	12	266	41.7	18:20	6	2	2	4	2	2	0	1	18:05
2003-04♦	Tampa Bay	NHL	81	25	55	80	36	11	1	6	178	14.0	18	38	31.6	19:32	21	2	5	7	15	0	1	0	17:22
2004-05			DID NOT PLAY																						
2005-06♦	Carolina	NHL	72	21	55	76	32	10	0	3	177	11.9	–9	11	27.3	18:40	25	9	17	26	14	4	0	3	18:42
2006-07	Carolina	NHL	43	5	22	27	24	1	0	0	85	5.9	–8	7	28.6	17:25	....	....	....	....	....	....	....	....	....
2007-08	Carolina	NHL	55	21	25	46	14	10	0	6	124	16.9	–7	11	54.6	19:53	....	....	....	....	....	....	....	....	....
	Ottawa	NHL	24	3	16	19	10	1	0	0	42	7.1	–8	6	16.7	16:54	4	2	0	2	2	1	0	0	18:26
2008-09	Florida	NHL	63	17	32	49	37	8	0	2	115	14.8	1	30	36.7	16:35	....	....	....	....	....	....	....	....	....
2009-10	Florida	NHL	58	15	22	37	22	3	0	4	126	11.9	–3	29	62.1	17:34	....	....	....	....	....	....	....	....	....
	NHL Totals		960	266	422	688	465	96	9	45	1981	13.4		1794	46.4	17:46	82	19	32	51	43	8	1	5	16:55

OHL Rookie of the Year (1991)

• Missed majority of 1999-2000 season recovering from shoulder injury suffered in game vs. Philadelphia, December 27, 1999. Traded to **St. Louis by Calgary** for Craig Conroy and St. Louis' 7th round choice (David Moss) in 2001 Entry Draft, March 13, 2001. Traded to **Tampa Bay** by **St. Louis** for Tampa Bay's 2nd round choice (David Backes) in 2003 Entry Draft, June 21, 2003. Signed as a free agent by **Carolina**, August 2, 2005. Traded to **Ottawa** by **Carolina** with Mike Commodore for Joe Corvo and Patrick Eaves, February 11, 2008. Signed as a free agent by **Florida**, July 1, 2008.

STOA, Ryan

(STOH-ah, RIGH-uhn) **COL.**

Center. Shoots left. 6'3", 200 lbs. Born, Bloomington, MN, April 13, 1987. Colorado's 1st choice, 34th overall, in 2005 Entry Draft.

Season	Club	League	Regular Season GP	G	A	Pts	PIM	PP	SH	GW	S	%	+/-	TF	F%	Min	Playoffs GP	G	A	Pts	PIM	PP	SH	GW	Min
2003-04	USNTDP	U-17	18	9	8	17	....	....	....	....	....	....	....	....	....	....	....	....	....	....	....	....	....	....	....
	USNTDP	NAHL	42	10	12	22	26	....	....	....	....	....	....	....	....	....	7	7	1	8	2	....	....	....	....
2004-05	USNTDP	U-18	23	4	11	15	16	....	....	....	....	....	....	....	....	....	....	....	....	....	....	....	....	....	....
	USNTDP	NAHL	15	10	13	23	20	....	....	....	....	....	....	....	....	....	....	....	....	....	....	....	....	....	....
2005-06	U. of Minnesota	WCHA	41	10	15	25	43	....	....	....	....	....	....	....	....	....	....	....	....	....	....	....	....	....	....
2006-07	U. of Minnesota	WCHA	41	12	12	24	44	....	....	....	....	....	....	....	....	....	....	....	....	....	....	....	....	....	....
2007-08	U. of Minnesota	WCHA	2	1	1	2	2	....	....	....	....	....	....	....	....	....	....	....	....	....	....	....	....	....	....
2008-09	U. of Minnesota	WCHA	36	24	22	46	76	....	....	....	....	....	....	....	....	....	....	....	....	....	....	....	....	....	....
2009-10	Colorado	NHL	12	2	1	3	0	0	0	0	26	7.7	–3	0	0.0	11:04	1	0	0	0	2	0	0	0	8:45
	Lake Erie	AHL	54	23	17	40	42	....	....	....	....	....	....	....	....	....	....	....	....	....	....	....	....	....	....
	NHL Totals		12	2	1	3	0	0	0	0	26	7.7		0	0.0	11:04	1	0	0	0	2	0	0	0	8:45

WCHA First All-Star Team (2009) • NCAA West First All-American Team (2009)

• Missed remainder of 2007-08 season recovering from knee injury suffered in game vs. University of Michigan, October 13, 2007.

STOLL, Jarret

(STOHL, JAIR-iht) **L.A.**

Center. Shoots right. 6'1", 215 lbs. Born, Melville, Sask., June 25, 1982. Edmonton's 3rd choice, 36th overall, in 2002 Entry Draft.

Season	Club	League	Regular Season GP	G	A	Pts	PIM	PP	SH	GW	S	%	+/-	TF	F%	Min	Playoffs GP	G	A	Pts	PIM	PP	SH	GW	Min
1997-98	Saskatoon Blazers	SMHL	44	45	44	*89	78	....	....	....	....	....	....	....	....	....	....	....	....	....	....	....	....	....	....
	Edmonton Ice	WHL	8	2	3	5	4	....	....	....	....	....	....	....	....	....	....	....	....	....	....	....	....	....	....
1998-99	Kootenay Ice	WHL	57	13	21	34	38	....	....	....	....	....	....	....	....	....	4	0	0	0	2	....	....	....	....
99-2000	Kootenay Ice	WHL	71	37	38	75	64	....	....	....	....	....	....	....	....	....	20	7	9	16	24	....	....	....	....
2000-01	Kootenay Ice	WHL	62	40	66	106	105	....	....	....	....	....	....	....	....	....	11	5	9	14	22	....	....	....	....
2001-02	Kootenay Ice	WHL	47	32	34	66	64	....	....	....	....	....	....	....	....	....	22	6	14	20	35	....	....	....	....
2002-03	Edmonton	NHL	4	0	1	1	0	0	0	0	5	0.0	–3	30	63.3	7:44	....	....	....	....	....	....	....	....	....
	Hamilton	AHL	76	21	33	54	86	....	....	....	....	....	....	....	....	....	23	5	8	13	25	....	....	....	....
2003-04	Edmonton	NHL	68	10	11	21	42	1	1	2	107	9.3	8	1019	54.1	13:54	....	....	....	....	....	....	....	....	....
2004-05	Edmonton	AHL	66	21	17	38	92	....	....	....	....	....	....	....	....	....	....	....	....	....	....	....	....	....	....
2005-06	Edmonton	NHL	82	22	46	68	74	11	1	4	243	9.1	4	1348	56.8	18:23	24	4	6	10	24	2	0	1	17:06
2006-07	Edmonton	NHL	51	13	26	39	48	6	1	2	115	11.3	2	901	55.6	18:12	....	....	....	....	....	....	....	....	....
2007-08	Edmonton	NHL	81	14	22	36	74	8	3	1	187	7.5	–23	1229	55.1	17:56	....	....	....	....	....	....	....	....	....
2008-09	Los Angeles	NHL	74	18	23	41	68	10	0	1	155	11.6	–7	1047	57.2	17:05	....	....	....	....	....	....	....	....	....
2009-10	Los Angeles	NHL	73	16	31	47	40	4	0	4	164	9.8	13	1105	56.0	17:25	6	1	0	1	4	1	0	0	15:51
	NHL Totals		433	93	160	253	346	40	6	14	976	9.5		6679	55.9	17:05	30	5	6	11	28	3	0	1	16:51

• Re-entered NHL Entry Draft. Originally Calgary's 3rd choice, 46th overall, in 2000 Entry Draft.

WHL East First All-Star Team (2001) • Canadian Major Junior First All-Star Team (2001) • WHL West First All-Star Team (2002)

Traded to **Los Angeles** by **Edmonton** with Matt Greene for Lubomir Visnovsky, June 29, 2008.

STONE, Ryan

(STOHN, RIGH-uhn) **CGY.**

Center. Shoots left. 6'2", 200 lbs. Born, Calgary, Alta., March 20, 1985. Pittsburgh's 2nd choice, 32nd overall, in 2003 Entry Draft.

Season	Club	League	Regular Season GP	G	A	Pts	PIM	PP	SH	GW	S	%	+/-	TF	F%	Min	Playoffs GP	G	A	Pts	PIM	PP	SH	GW	Min
2000-01	Cgy. North Stars	AMHL	34	37	28	55	90	....	....	....	....	....	....	....	....	....	....	....	....	....	....	....	....	....	....
2001-02	Brandon	WHL	65	11	27	38	128	....	....	....	....	....	....	....	....	....	19	0	3	3	39	....	....	....	....
2002-03	Brandon	WHL	54	14	31	45	158	....	....	....	....	....	....	....	....	....	12	4	2	6	20	....	....	....	....
2003-04	Brandon	WHL	50	20	38	58	125	....	....	....	....	....	....	....	....	....	11	1	3	4	24	....	....	....	....
2004-05	Brandon	WHL	70	33	*66	99	127	....	....	....	....	....	....	....	....	....	24	4	*23	27	48	....	....	....	....
2005-06	Wilkes-Barre	AHL	75	14	22	36	109	....	....	....	....	....	....	....	....	....	11	4	7	11	12	....	....	....	....
2006-07	Wilkes-Barre	AHL	41	7	26	33	86	....	....	....	....	....	....	....	....	....	10	2	3	5	21	....	....	....	....
2007-08	Pittsburgh	NHL	6	0	1	1	5	0	0	0	3	0.0	–1	5	60.0	6:25	....	....	....	....	....	....	....	....	....
	Wilkes-Barre	AHL	65	11	28	39	129	....	....	....	....	....	....	....	....	....	23	5	12	17	33	....	....	....	....
2008-09	Pittsburgh	NHL	2	0	0	0	2	0	0	0	5	0.0	1	0	0.0	10:20	....	....	....	....	....	....	....	....	....
	Wilkes-Barre	AHL	38	9	19	28	53	....	....	....	....	....	....	....	....	....	....	....	....	....	....	....	....	....	....
	Springfield	AHL	39	8	21	29	64	....	....	....	....	....	....	....	....	....	....	....	....	....	....	....	....	....	....
2009-10	Edmonton	NHL	27	0	6	6	48	0	0	0	25	0.0	2	21	33.3	10:52	....	....	....	....	....	....	....	....	....
	NHL Totals		35	0	7	7	55	0	0	0	33	0.0		26	38.5	10:04	....	....	....	....	....	....	....	....	....

WHL East First All-Star Team (2005)

Traded to **Edmonton** by **Pittsburgh** with Dany Sabourin and Pittsburgh's 4th round choice in 2011 Entry Draft for Mathieu Garon, January 17, 2009. • Missed majority of 2009-10 season recovering from knee inury suffered in game vs. Vancouver (October 19, 2009) and re-injured in game vs. Pittsburgh (January 14, 2010). Signed as a free agent by **Calgary**, July 7, 2010.

STONER, Clayton

(STOH-nuhr, KLAY-tuhn) **MIN.**

Defense. Shoots left. 6'3", 225 lbs. Born, Port McNeill, B.C., February 19, 1985. Minnesota's 4th choice, 79th overall, in 2004 Entry Draft.

Season	Club	League	Regular Season GP	G	A	Pts	PIM	PP	SH	GW	S	%	+/-	TF	F%	Min	Playoffs GP	G	A	Pts	PIM	PP	SH	GW	Min
2000-01	Campbell River	VIJHL	47	4	16	20	57	....	....	....	....	....	....	....	....	....	....	....	....	....	....	....	....	....	....
2001-02	Campbell River	VIJHL	42	12	35	47	199	....	....	....	....	....	....	....	....	....	....	....	....	....	....	....	....	....	....
2002-03	Tri-City	WHL	58	4	12	16	85	....	....	....	....	....	....	....	....	....	....	....	....	....	....	....	....	....	....
2003-04	Tri-City	WHL	71	7	24	31	109	....	....	....	....	....	....	....	....	....	11	1	1	2	8	....	....	....	....
2004-05	Tri-City	WHL	60	12	34	46	81	....	....	....	....	....	....	....	....	....	4	0	3	3	2	....	....	....	....
2005-06	Houston Aeros	AHL	73	6	18	24	92	....	....	....	....	....	....	....	....	....	3	1	1	2	7	....	....	....	....
2006-07	Houston Aeros	AHL	65	1	6	7	104	....	....	....	....	....	....	....	....	....	....	....	....	....	....	....	....	....	....
2007-08	Houston Aeros	AHL	56	3	12	15	78	....	....	....	....	....	....	....	....	....	....	....	....	....	....	....	....	....	....
2008-09	Houston Aeros	AHL	63	2	22	24	81	....	....	....	....	....	....	....	....	....	20	1	4	5	27	....	....	....	....

Season	Club	League	Regular Season														Playoffs								
			GP	G	A	Pts	PIM	PP	SH	GW	S	%	+/-	TF	F%	Min	GP	G	A	Pts	PIM	PP	SH	GW	Min
2009-10	**Minnesota**	**NHL**	**8**	**0**	**2**	**2**	**12**	**0**	**0**	**0**	**5**	**0.0**	**1**	**0**	**0.0**	**13:19**	....	....	....	....	....	....	....	....	....
	Houston Aeros	AHL	26	3	7	10	52	....	....	....	....	....	....	....	....	....	....	....	....	....	....	....	....	....	....
	NHL Totals		**8**	**0**	**2**	**2**	**12**	**0**	**0**	**0**	**5**	**0.0**		**0**	**0.0**	**13:19**	....	....	....	....	....	....	....	....	....

WHL West Second All-Star Team (2005)
• Missed majority of 2009-10 season recovering from recurring groin injury.

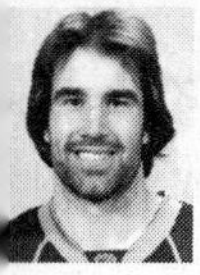

STORTINI, Zack (stohr-TEE-nee, ZAK) EDM.

Right wing. Shoots right. 6'3", 228 lbs. Born, Elliot Lake, Ont., September 11, 1985. Edmonton's 5th choice, 94th overall, in 2003 Entry Draft.

Season	Club	League	GP	G	A	Pts	PIM	PP	SH	GW	S	%	+/-	TF	F%	Min	GP	G	A	Pts	PIM	PP	SH	GW	Min
2000-01	Newmarket	OPJHL	34	3	10	13	68	....	....	....	....	....	....	....	....	....	....	....	....	....	....	....	....	....	....
2001-02	Sudbury Wolves	OHL	65	8	6	14	187	....	....	....	....	....	....	....	....	....	5	1	0	1	24	....	....	....	....
2002-03	Sudbury Wolves	OHL	62	13	16	29	222	....	....	....	....	....	....	....	....	....	....	....	....	....	....	....	....	....	....
2003-04	Sudbury Wolves	OHL	62	21	16	37	151	....	....	....	....	....	....	....	....	....	7	1	1	2	14	....	....	....	....
	Toronto	AHL	2	0	0	0	7	....	....	....	....	....	....	....	....	....	3	0	0	0	4	....	....	....	....
2004-05	Sudbury Wolves	OHL	58	13	27	40	186	....	....	....	....	....	....	....	....	....	12	2	5	7	27	....	....	....	....
2005-06	Iowa Stars	AHL	27	2	1	3	108	....	....	....	....	....	....	....	....	....	....	....	....	....	....	....	....	....	....
	Milwaukee	AHL	37	0	7	7	153	....	....	....	....	....	....	....	....	....	....	....	....	....	....	....	....	....	....
2006-07	**Edmonton**	**NHL**	**29**	**1**	**0**	**1**	**105**	**0**	**0**	**0**	**17**	**5.9**	**-7**	**3**	**100.0**	**7:09**	....	....	....	....	....	....	....	....	....
	Hamilton	AHL	47	9	6	15	195	....	....	....	....	....	....	....	....	....	22	3	0	3	*56	....	....	....	....
2007-08	**Edmonton**	**NHL**	**66**	**3**	**9**	**12**	**201**	**0**	**0**	**0**	**38**	**7.9**	**3**	**7**	**42.9**	**8:10**	....	....	....	....	....	....	....	....	....
	Springfield	AHL	4	3	2	5	21	....	....	....	....	....	....	....	....	....	....	....	....	....	....	....	....	....	....
2008-09	**Edmonton**	**NHL**	**52**	**6**	**5**	**11**	**181**	**0**	**0**	**0**	**23**	**26.1**	**-3**	**11**	**63.6**	**7:17**	....	....	....	....	....	....	....	....	....
2009-10	**Edmonton**	**NHL**	**77**	**4**	**9**	**13**	**155**	**1**	**0**	**1**	**46**	**8.7**	**3**	**183**	**47.5**	**9:17**	....	....	....	....	....	....	....	....	....
	NHL Totals		**224**	**14**	**23**	**37**	**642**	**1**	**0**	**1**	**124**	**11.3**		**204**	**49.0**	**8:13**	....	....	....	....	....	....	....	....	....

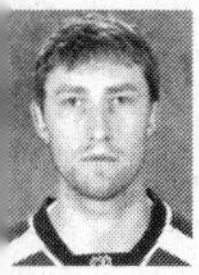

STRACHAN, Tyson (STRAWN, TIGH-suhn) ST.L.

Defense. Shoots right. 6'2", 215 lbs. Born, Melfort, Sask., October 30, 1984. Carolina's 6th choice, 137th overall, in 2003 Entry Draft.

Season	Club	League	GP	G	A	Pts	PIM	PP	SH	GW	S	%	+/-	TF	F%	Min	GP	G	A	Pts	PIM	PP	SH	GW	Min
2001-02	Tisdale Trojans	SMHL	42	5	18	23	70	....	....	....	....	....	....	....	....	....	....	....	....	....	....	....	....	....	....
	Melville	SJHL	2	0	0	0	0	....	....	....	....	....	....	....	....	....	....	....	....	....	....	....	....	....	....
2002-03	Vernon Vipers	BCHL	56	6	22	28	99	....	....	....	....	....	....	....	....	....	....	....	....	....	....	....	....	....	....
2003-04	Ohio State	CCHA	30	2	5	7	8	....	....	....	....	....	....	....	....	....	....	....	....	....	....	....	....	....	....
2004-05	Ohio State	CCHA	31	1	4	5	32	....	....	....	....	....	....	....	....	....	....	....	....	....	....	....	....	....	....
2005-06	Ohio State	CCHA	23	3	2	5	37	....	....	....	....	....	....	....	....	....	....	....	....	....	....	....	....	....	....
2006-07	Ohio State	CCHA	35	7	11	18	55	....	....	....	....	....	....	....	....	....	....	....	....	....	....	....	....	....	....
	Albany River Rats	AHL	1	0	0	0	0	....	....	....	....	....	....	....	....	....	....	....	....	....	....	....	....	....	....
2007-08	Peoria Rivermen	AHL	34	1	2	3	61	....	....	....	....	....	....	....	....	....	....	....	....	....	....	....	....	....	....
	Las Vegas	ECHL	25	2	7	9	68	....	....	....	....	....	....	....	....	....	16	0	4	4	12	....	....	....	....
2008-09	**St. Louis**	**NHL**	**30**	**0**	**3**	**3**	**39**	**0**	**0**	**0**	**21**	**0.0**	**8**	**0**	**0.0**	**13:26**	....	....	....	....	....	....	....	....	....
	Peoria Rivermen	AHL	29	2	3	5	67	....	....	....	....	....	....	....	....	....	3	0	0	0	11	....	....	....	....
2009-10	**St. Louis**	**NHL**	**8**	**0**	**2**	**2**	**4**	**0**	**0**	**0**	**7**	**0.0**	**3**	**0**	**0.0**	**14:02**	....	....	....	....	....	....	....	....	....
	Peoria Rivermen	AHL	65	5	21	26	75	....	....	....	....	....	....	....	....	....	....	....	....	....	....	....	....	....	....
	NHL Totals		**38**	**0**	**5**	**5**	**43**	**0**	**0**	**0**	**28**	**0.0**		**0**	**0.0**	**13:34**	....	....	....	....	....	....	....	....	....

Signed as a free agent by **St. Louis**, October 9, 2008.

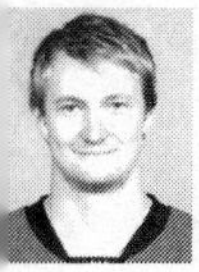

STRALMAN, Anton (STROHL-muhn, AN-tawn) CBJ

Defense. Shoots right. 6'1", 193 lbs. Born, Tibro, Sweden, August 1, 1986. Toronto's 5th choice, 216th overall, in 2005 Entry Draft.

Season	Club	League	GP	G	A	Pts	PIM	PP	SH	GW	S	%	+/-	TF	F%	Min	GP	G	A	Pts	PIM	PP	SH	GW	Min
2002-03	Skovde IK Jr.	Swe-Jr.	46	20	9	29	38	....	....	....	....	....	....	....	....	....	....	....	....	....	....	....	....	....	....
2003-04	Skovde IK	Sweden-3	27	4	8	12	18	....	....	....	....	....	....	....	....	....	....	....	....	....	....	....	....	....	....
2004-05	Skovde IK	Sweden-2	50	10	11	21	40	....	....	....	....	....	....	....	....	....	....	....	....	....	....	....	....	....	....
2005-06	Timra IK	Sweden	45	1	4	5	28	....	....	....	....	....	....	....	....	....	....	....	....	....	....	....	....	....	....
	Timra IK Jr.	Swe-Jr.	....	....	....	....	....	....	....	....	....	....	....	....	....	....	3	0	0	0	4	....	....	....	....
2006-07	Timra IK	Sweden	53	10	11	21	34	....	....	....	....	....	....	....	....	....	7	1	3	4	10	....	....	....	....
2007-08	**Toronto**	**NHL**	**50**	**3**	**6**	**9**	**18**	**0**	**0**	**0**	**40**	**7.5**	**-10**	**0**	**0.0**	**12:49**	....	....	....	....	....	....	....	....	....
	Toronto Marlies	AHL	21	0	11	11	22	....	....	....	....	....	....	....	....	....	....	....	....	....	....	....	....	....	....
2008-09	**Toronto**	**NHL**	**38**	**1**	**12**	**13**	**20**	**0**	**0**	**1**	**43**	**2.3**	**-2**	**1**	**100.0**	**15:34**	....	....	....	....	....	....	....	....	....
	Toronto Marlies	AHL	36	7	9	16	24	....	....	....	....	....	....	....	....	....	6	1	2	3	0	....	....	....	....
2009-10	**Columbus**	**NHL**	**73**	**6**	**28**	**34**	**37**	**4**	**0**	**0**	**121**	**5.0**	**-17**	**0**	**0.0**	**20:29**	....	....	....	....	....	....	....	....	....
	NHL Totals		**161**	**10**	**46**	**56**	**75**	**4**	**0**	**1**	**204**	**4.9**		**1**	**100.0**	**16:57**	....	....	....	....	....	....	....	....	....

Traded to **Calgary** by **Toronto** with Colin Stuart and Toronto's 7th round choice in 2012 Entry Draft for Wayne Primeau and Calgary's 2nd round choice in 2011 Entry Draft, July 27, 2009. Traded to **Columbus** by **Calgary** for Columbus' 3rd round choice (Max Reinhart) in 2010 Entry Draft, September 29, 2009.

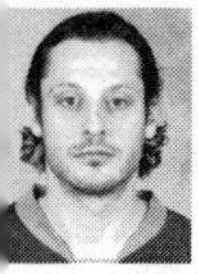

STREIT, Mark (STRIGHT, MAHRK) NYI

Defense. Shoots left. 6', 197 lbs. Born, Bern, Switz., December 11, 1977. Montreal's 8th choice, 262nd overall, in 2004 Entry Draft.

Season	Club	League	GP	G	A	Pts	PIM	PP	SH	GW	S	%	+/-	TF	F%	Min	GP	G	A	Pts	PIM	PP	SH	GW	Min
1995-96	Fribourg	Swiss	34	2	2	4	6	....	....	....	....	....	....	....	....	....	4	0	0	0	2	....	....	....	....
1996-97	HC Davos	Swiss	46	2	9	11	18	....	....	....	....	....	....	....	....	....	6	0	0	0	0	....	....	....	....
1997-98	HC Ambri-Piotta	Swiss	2	0	0	0	0	....	....	....	....	....	....	....	....	....	....	....	....	....	....	....	....	....	....
	HC Davos	Swiss	38	4	10	14	14	....	....	....	....	....	....	....	....	....	18	1	5	6	20	....	....	....	....
1998-99	HC Davos	Swiss	44	7	18	25	42	....	....	....	....	....	....	....	....	....	6	3	3	6	8	....	....	....	....
99-2000	Springfield	AHL	43	3	12	15	18	....	....	....	....	....	....	....	....	....	5	0	0	0	2	....	....	....	....
	Utah Grizzlies	IHL	1	0	1	1	2	....	....	....	....	....	....	....	....	....	....	....	....	....	....	....	....	....	....
	Tallahassee	ECHL	14	0	5	5	16	....	....	....	....	....	....	....	....	....	....	....	....	....	....	....	....	....	....
2000-01	ZSC Lions Zurich	Swiss	44	5	11	16	48	....	....	....	....	....	....	....	....	....	16	2	5	7	37	....	....	....	....
2001-02	ZSC Lions Zurich	Swiss	28	6	17	23	36	....	....	....	....	....	....	....	....	....	16	0	6	6	14	....	....	....	....
	Switzerland	Olympics	4	1	1	2	0	....	....	....	....	....	....	....	....	....	....	....	....	....	....	....	....	....	....
2002-03	ZSC Lions Zurich	Swiss	37	4	19	23	62	....	....	....	....	....	....	....	....	....	12	1	7	8	2	....	....	....	....
2003-04	ZSC Lions Zurich	Swiss	48	12	24	36	78	....	....	....	....	....	....	....	....	....	13	5	2	7	14	....	....	....	....
2004-05	ZSC Lions Zurich	Swiss	44	14	29	43	46	....	....	....	....	....	....	....	....	....	15	4	11	15	20	....	....	....	....
2005-06	**Montreal**	**NHL**	**48**	**2**	**9**	**11**	**28**	**2**	**0**	**0**	**52**	**3.8**	**-6**	**1**	**0.0**	**14:36**	**1**	**0**	**0**	**0**	**0**	**0**	**0**	**0**	**3:29**
	Switzerland	Olympics	6	2	1	3	6	....	....	....	....	....	....	....	....	....	....	....	....	....	....	....	....	....	....
2006-07	**Montreal**	**NHL**	**76**	**10**	**26**	**36**	**14**	**2**	**1**	**1**	**102**	**9.8**	**-5**	**12**	**33.3**	**14:01**	....	....	....	....	....	....	....	....	....
2007-08	**Montreal**	**NHL**	**81**	**13**	**49**	**62**	**28**	**7**	**0**	**3**	**165**	**7.9**	**-6**	**1**	**0.0**	**17:31**	**11**	**1**	**3**	**4**	**8**	**0**	**0**	**0**	**14:48**
2008-09	**NY Islanders**	**NHL**	**74**	**16**	**40**	**56**	**62**	**10**	**1**	**1**	**150**	**10.7**	**5**	**0**	**0.0**	**25:13**	....	....	....	....	....	....	....	....	....
2009-10	**NY Islanders**	**NHL**	**82**	**11**	**38**	**49**	**48**	**9**	**0**	**2**	**187**	**5.9**	**0**	**1**	**0.0**	**25:42**	....	....	....	....	....	....	....	....	....
	Switzerland	Olympics	5	0	3	3	0	....	....	....	....	....	....	....	....	....	....	....	....	....	....	....	....	....	....
	NHL Totals		**361**	**52**	**162**	**214**	**180**	**30**	**2**	**7**	**656**	**7.9**		**15**	**26.7**	**19:50**	**12**	**1**	**3**	**4**	**8**	**0**	**0**	**0**	**13:51**

Played in NHL All-Star Game (2009)
Signed as a free agent by **NY Islanders**, July 1, 2008.

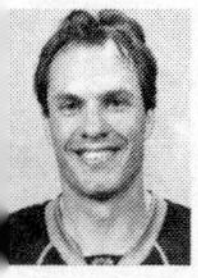

STRUDWICK, Jason (STRUHD-wihk, JAY-suhn) EDM.

Defense. Shoots left. 6'4", 225 lbs. Born, Edmonton, Alta., July 17, 1975. NY Islanders' 3rd choice, 63rd overall, in 1994 Entry Draft.

Season	Club	League	GP	G	A	Pts	PIM	PP	SH	GW	S	%	+/-	TF	F%	Min	GP	G	A	Pts	PIM	PP	SH	GW	Min
1991-92	Edmonton Legion	AMHL	35	3	8	11	67	....	....	....	....	....	....	....	....	....	....	....	....	....	....	....	....	....	....
1992-93	Edmonton Pats	AMHL	33	8	20	28	135	....	....	....	....	....	....	....	....	....	....	....	....	....	....	....	....	....	....
1993-94	Kamloops Blazers	WHL	61	6	8	14	118	....	....	....	....	....	....	....	....	....	19	0	4	4	24	....	....	....	....
1994-95	Kamloops Blazers	WHL	72	3	11	14	183	....	....	....	....	....	....	....	....	....	21	1	1	2	39	....	....	....	....
1995-96	**NY Islanders**	**NHL**	**1**	**0**	**0**	**0**	**7**	**0**	**0**	**0**	**0**	**0.0**	**0**	....	....	....	....	....	....	....	....	....	....	....	....
	Worcester IceCats	AHL	60	2	7	9	119	....	....	....	....	....	....	....	....	....	4	0	1	1	0	....	....	....	....
1996-97	Kentucky	AHL	80	1	9	10	198	....	....	....	....	....	....	....	....	....	4	0	0	0	0	....	....	....	....
1997-98	**NY Islanders**	**NHL**	**17**	**0**	**1**	**1**	**36**	**0**	**0**	**0**	**3**	**0.0**	**1**	....	....	....	....	....	....	....	....	....	....	....	....
	Kentucky	AHL	39	3	1	4	87	....	....	....	....	....	....	....	....	....	....	....	....	....	....	....	....	....	....
	Vancouver	**NHL**	**11**	**0**	**1**	**1**	**29**	**0**	**0**	**0**	**5**	**0.0**	**-3**	....	....	....	....	....	....	....	....	....	....	....	....
	Syracuse Crunch	AHL	....	....	....	....	....	....	....	....	....	....	....	....	....	....	3	0	0	0	6	....	....	....	....
1998-99	**Vancouver**	**NHL**	**65**	**0**	**3**	**3**	**114**	**0**	**0**	**0**	**25**	**0.0**	**-19**	**0**	**0.0**	**12:49**	....	....	....	....	....	....	....	....	....
99-2000	**Vancouver**	**NHL**	**63**	**1**	**3**	**4**	**64**	**0**	**0**	**0**	**18**	**5.6**	**-13**	**0**	**0.0**	**15:12**	....	....	....	....	....	....	....	....	....
2000-01	**Vancouver**	**NHL**	**60**	**1**	**4**	**5**	**64**	**0**	**0**	**1**	**21**	**4.8**	**16**	**0**	**0.0**	**9:59**	**2**	**0**	**0**	**0**	**0**	**0**	**0**	**0**	**2:15**
2001-02	**Vancouver**	**NHL**	**44**	**2**	**4**	**6**	**96**	**0**	**0**	**0**	**13**	**15.4**	**4**	**0**	**0.0**	**9:45**	....	....	....	....	....	....	....	....	....

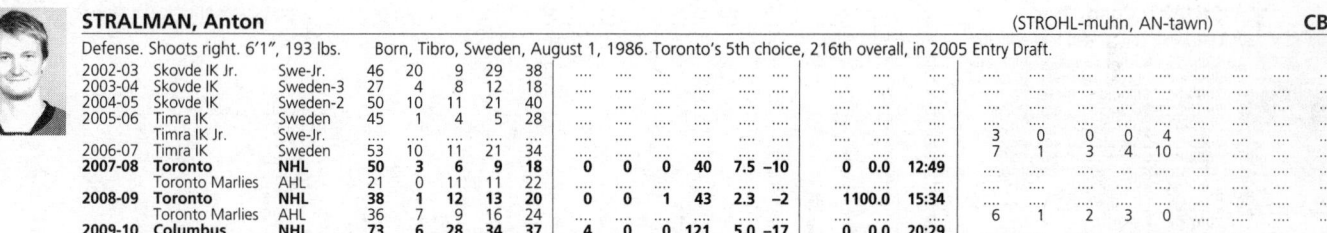

Season	Club	League	Regular Season GP	G	A	Pts	PIM	PP	SH	GW	S	%	+/-	TF	F%	Min	Playoffs GP	G	A	Pts	PIM	PP	SH	GW	Min
2002-03	Chicago	NHL	48	2	3	5	87	0	0	0	19	10.5	-4	3	0.0	8:32	....	....	....	....	....	....	....	....	....
2003-04	Chicago	NHL	54	1	3	4	73	0	0	0	32	3.1	-16	1	0.0	14:55	....	....	....	....	....	....	....	....	....
2004-05	Ferencvaros	Hungary	6	1	2	3	8	....	....	....	....	....	....	....	....	....	....	....	....	....	....	....	....	....	....
2005-06	NY Rangers	NHL	65	3	4	7	66	0	0	0	31	9.7	-10	3	33.3	15:31	3	0	0	0	0	0	0	0	13:35
2006-07	HC Lugano	Swiss	34	2	3	5	28	....	....	....	....	....	....	....	....	....	6	0	0	0	4	....	....	....	....
	NY Rangers	NHL	8	0	0	0	2	0	0	0	3	0.0	0	0	0.0	13:40	....	....	....	....	....	....	....	....	....
2007-08	NY Rangers	NHL	52	1	1	2	40	0	0	1	21	4.8	0	0	0.0	12:57	2	0	0	0	0	0	0	0	9:41
2008-09	Edmonton	NHL	71	2	7	9	60	0	0	0	32	6.3	-4	0	0.0	12:38	....	....	....	....	....	....	....	....	....
2009-10	Edmonton	NHL	72	0	6	6	50	0	0	0	19	0.0	-18	0	0.0	16:56	....	....	....	....	....	....	....	....	....
	NHL Totals		631	13	40	53	788	0	0	2	242	5.4		7	14.3	13:11	7	0	0	0	0	0	0	0	9:14

Traded to **Vancouver** by **NY Islanders** for Gino Odjick, March 23, 1998. Signed as a free agent by **Chicago**, July 15, 2002. Signed as a free agent by **NY Rangers**, July 20, 2004. Signed as a free agent by **Ferencvaros** (Hungary), January 17, 2005. Signed as a free agent by **Lugano**, September 12, 2006. Signed as a free agent by **NY Rangers**, March 19, 2007. Signed as a free agent by **Edmonton**, July 10, 2008.

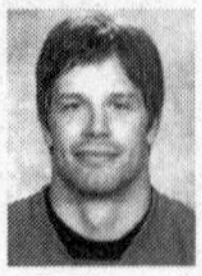

STUART, Brad

(STEW-ahrt, BRAD) **DET.**

Defense. Shoots left. 6'2", 210 lbs. Born, Rocky Mountain House, Alta., November 6, 1979. San Jose's 1st choice, 3rd overall, in 1998 Entry Draft.

1995-96	Red Deer	AMHL	35	12	25	37	83	....	....	....	....	....	....	....	....	....	....	....	....	....	....	....	....	....	....
	Regina Pats	WHL	3	0	0	0	0	....	....	....	....	....	....	....	....	....	....	....	....	....	....	....	....	....	....
1996-97	Regina Pats	WHL	57	7	36	43	58	....	....	....	....	....	....	....	....	....	5	0	4	4	14	....	....	....	....
1997-98	Regina Pats	WHL	72	20	45	65	82	....	....	....	....	....	....	....	....	....	9	3	4	7	10	....	....	....	....
1998-99	Regina Pats	WHL	29	10	19	29	43	....	....	....	....	....	....	....	....	....	....	....	....	....	....	....	....	....	....
	Calgary Hitmen	WHL	30	11	22	33	26	....	....	....	....	....	....	....	....	....	21	8	15	23	59	....	....	....	....
99-2000	San Jose	NHL	82	10	26	36	32	5	1	3	133	7.5	3	0	0.0	20:24	12	1	0	1	6	1	0	0	16:30
2000-01	San Jose	NHL	77	5	18	23	56	1	0	2	119	4.2	10	0	0.0	20:06	5	1	0	1	0	0	0	0	20:19
2001-02	San Jose	NHL	82	6	23	29	39	2	0	2	96	6.3	13	0	0.0	21:41	12	0	3	3	8	0	0	0	19:42
2002-03	San Jose	NHL	36	4	10	14	46	2	0	1	63	6.3	-6	0	0.0	20:53	....	....	....	....	....	....	....	....	....
2003-04	San Jose	NHL	77	9	30	39	34	5	0	0	129	7.0	9	0	0.0	22:09	17	1	5	6	13	0	0	0	23:23
2004-05			DID NOT PLAY																						
2005-06	San Jose	NHL	23	2	10	12	14	1	0	0	41	4.9	-2	0	0.0	23:15	....	....	....	....	....	....	....	....	....
	Boston	NHL	55	10	21	31	38	6	0	2	122	8.2	-6	0	0.0	25:40	....	....	....	....	....	....	....	....	....
2006-07	Boston	NHL	48	7	10	17	26	1	0	2	74	9.5	-22	0	0.0	22:55	....	....	....	....	....	....	....	....	....
	Calgary	NHL	27	0	5	5	18	0	0	0	35	0.0	12	0	0.0	22:48	6	0	1	1	6	0	0	0	25:16
2007-08	Los Angeles	NHL	63	5	16	21	67	2	0	1	111	4.5	-16	4	0.0	21:13	....	....	....	....	....	....	....	....	....
	♦ Detroit	NHL	9	1	1	2	2	0	0	0	21	4.8	6	0	0.0	20:46	21	1	6	7	14	0	0	1	21:40
2008-09	Detroit	NHL	67	2	13	15	26	1	0	0	105	1.9	-3	0	0.0	20:13	23	3	6	9	12	1	0	0	24:09
2009-10	Detroit	NHL	82	4	16	20	22	1	0	2	153	2.6	-12	2	50.0	23:10	12	2	4	6	8	0	0	0	22:04
	NHL Totals		728	65	199	264	420	27	1	15	1202	5.4		6	16.7	21:50	108	9	25	34	67	2	0	1	21:51

WHL East Second All-Star Team (1998) • WHL East First All-Star Team (1999) • Canadian Major Junior First All-Star Team (1999) • Canadian Major Junior Defenseman of the Year (1999) • NHL All-Rookie Team (2000)

• Missed majority of 2002-03 season recovering from ankle (January 4, 2003 vs. Los Angeles) and head (February 21, 2003 vs. Columbus) injuries. Traded to **Boston** by **San Jose** with Marco Sturm and Wayne Primeau for Joe Thornton, November 30, 2005. Traded to **Calgary** by **Boston** with Wayne Primeau and Washington's 4th round choice (previously acquired, Calgary selected T.J. Brodie) in 2008 Entry Draft for Andrew Ference and Chuck Kobasew, February 10, 2007. Signed as a free agent by **Los Angeles**, July 3, 2007. Traded to **Detroit** by **Los Angeles** for Detroit's 2nd round choice (later traded to Colorado – Colorado selected Peter Delmas) in 2008 Entry Draft and Detroit's 4th round choice (later traded to Atlanta – Atlanta selected Ben Chiarot) in 2009 Entry Draft, February 26, 2008.

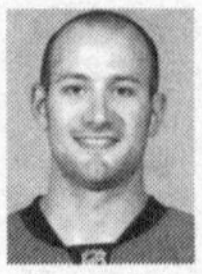

STUART, Colin

(STEW-ahrt, KAW-lihn)

Left wing. Shoots left. 6'2", 205 lbs. Born, Rochester, MN, July 8, 1982. Atlanta's 5th choice, 135th overall, in 2001 Entry Draft.

1998-99	Roch. Lourdes	High-MN	23	22	32	54	....	....	....	....	....	....	....	....	....	....	....	....	....	....	....	....	....	....	....
99-2000	Lincoln Stars	USHL	53	18	19	37	38	....	....	....	....	....	....	....	....	....	9	1	3	4	2	....	....	....	....
2000-01	Colorado College	WCHA	41	2	7	9	26	....	....	....	....	....	....	....	....	....	....	....	....	....	....	....	....	....	....
2001-02	Colorado College	WCHA	43	13	9	22	34	....	....	....	....	....	....	....	....	....	....	....	....	....	....	....	....	....	....
2002-03	Colorado College	WCHA	42	13	11	24	56	....	....	....	....	....	....	....	....	....	....	....	....	....	....	....	....	....	....
2003-04	Colorado College	WCHA	30	10	12	22	38	....	....	....	....	....	....	....	....	....	....	....	....	....	....	....	....	....	....
2004-05	Chicago Wolves	AHL	39	3	2	5	12	....	....	....	....	....	....	....	....	....	....	....	....	....	....	....	....	....	....
	Gwinnett	ECHL	5	1	3	4	4	....	....	....	....	....	....	....	....	....	....	....	....	....	....	....	....	....	....
2005-06	Chicago Wolves	AHL	78	13	14	27	65	....	....	....	....	....	....	....	....	....	....	....	....	....	....	....	....	....	....
2006-07	Chicago Wolves	AHL	67	18	11	29	75	....	....	....	....	....	....	....	....	....	15	2	5	7	10	....	....	....	....
2007-08	Atlanta	NHL	18	3	2	5	6	0	1	1	19	15.8	2	7	57.1	12:20	....	....	....	....	....	....	....	....	....
	Chicago Wolves	AHL	58	8	8	16	45	....	....	....	....	....	....	....	....	....	24	3	3	6	18	....	....	....	....
2008-09	Atlanta	NHL	33	5	3	8	18	0	3	0	54	9.3	3	12	41.7	12:29	....	....	....	....	....	....	....	....	....
	Chicago Wolves	AHL	42	9	6	15	38	....	....	....	....	....	....	....	....	....	....	....	....	....	....	....	....	....	....
2009-10	Abbotsford Heat	AHL	67	17	19	36	36	....	....	....	....	....	....	....	....	....	3	0	0	0	6	....	....	....	....
	NHL Totals		51	8	5	13	24	0	4	1	73	11.0		19	47.4	12:26	....	....	....	....	....	....	....	....	....

Traded to **Toronto** by **Atlanta** with Garnet Exelby for Pavel Kubina and Tim Stapleton, July 1, 2009. Traded to **Calgary** by **Toronto** with Anton Stralman and Toronto's 7th round choice in 2012 Entry Draft for Wayne Primeau and Calgary's 2nd round choice in 2011 Entry Draft, July 27, 2009.

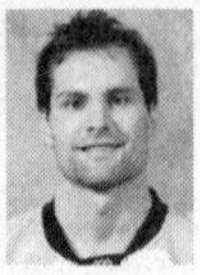

STUART, Mark

(STEW-uhrt, MAHRK) **BOS.**

Defense. Shoots left. 6'2", 213 lbs. Born, Rochester, MN, April 27, 1984. Boston's 1st choice, 21st overall, in 2003 Entry Draft.

99-2000	Roch. Lourdes	High-MN	28	19	22	41	....	....	....	....	....	....	....	....	....	....	....	....	....	....	....	....	....	....	....
2000-01	USNTDP	U-17	12	1	5	6	6	....	....	....	....	....	....	....	....	....	....	....	....	....	....	....	....	....	....
	USNTDP	NAHL	52	2	11	13	114	....	....	....	....	....	....	....	....	....	....	....	....	....	....	....	....	....	....
2001-02	USNTDP	U-18	40	9	9	18	....	....	....	....	....	....	....	....	....	....	....	....	....	....	....	....	....	....	....
	USNTDP	USHL	12	0	1	1	25	....	....	....	....	....	....	....	....	....	....	....	....	....	....	....	....	....	....
	USNTDP	NAHL	9	0	1	1	18	....	....	....	....	....	....	....	....	....	....	....	....	....	....	....	....	....	....
2002-03	Colorado College	WCHA	38	3	17	20	81	....	....	....	....	....	....	....	....	....	....	....	....	....	....	....	....	....	....
2003-04	Colorado College	WCHA	37	4	11	15	100	....	....	....	....	....	....	....	....	....	....	....	....	....	....	....	....	....	....
2004-05	Colorado College	WCHA	43	5	14	19	94	....	....	....	....	....	....	....	....	....	....	....	....	....	....	....	....	....	....
2005-06	Boston	NHL	17	1	1	2	10	0	0	0	9	11.1	-1	0	0.0	17:46	....	....	....	....	....	....	....	....	....
	Providence Bruins	AHL	60	4	3	7	76	....	....	....	....	....	....	....	....	....	6	0	0	0	25	....	....	....	....
2006-07	Boston	NHL	15	0	1	1	14	0	0	0	4	0.0	7	0	0.0	10:23	....	....	....	....	....	....	....	....	....
	Providence Bruins	AHL	49	4	16	20	62	....	....	....	....	....	....	....	....	....	3	0	1	1	9	....	....	....	....
2007-08	Boston	NHL	82	4	4	8	81	0	0	1	60	6.7	2	0	0.0	15:22	7	0	1	1	8	0	0	0	16:00
2008-09	Boston	NHL	82	5	12	17	76	0	0	1	61	8.2	20	0	0.0	15:25	11	0	1	1	7	0	0	0	17:57
2009-10	Boston	NHL	56	2	5	7	80	0	0	0	53	3.8	1	0	0.0	17:01	4	0	0	0	6	0	0	0	14:39
	NHL Totals		252	12	23	35	261	0	0	2	187	6.4		0	0.0	15:37	22	0	2	2	21	0	0	0	16:44

WCHA All-Rookie Team (2003) • WCHA Second All-Star Team (2005) • NCAA West First All-American Team (2005)

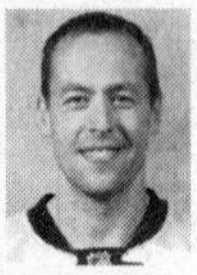

STURM, Marco

(STUHRM, MAHR-koh) **BOS**

Left wing. Shoots left. 6', 194 lbs. Born, Dingolfing, West Germany, September 8, 1978. San Jose's 2nd choice, 21st overall, in 1996 Entry Draft.

1995-96	EV Landshut	Germany	47	12	20	32	50	....	....	....	....	....	....	....	....	....	11	1	3	4	18	....	....	....	....
1996-97	EV Landshut	Germany	46	16	27	43	40	....	....	....	....	....	....	....	....	....	7	1	4	5	6	....	....	....	....
1997-98	San Jose	NHL	74	10	20	30	40	2	0	3	118	8.5	-2	....	....	....	2	0	0	0	0	0	0	0	....
	Germany	Olympics	2	0	0	0	0	....	....	....	....	....	....	....	....	....	....	....	....	....	....	....	....	....	....
1998-99	San Jose	NHL	78	16	22	38	52	3	2	3	140	11.4	7	576	45.0	15:23	6	2	2	4	4	0	0	1	14:16
99-2000	San Jose	NHL	74	12	15	27	22	2	4	3	120	10.0	4	183	45.4	14:07	12	1	3	4	6	0	0	0	13:00
2000-01	San Jose	NHL	81	14	18	32	28	2	3	5	153	9.2	9	517	40.2	16:06	6	0	2	2	0	0	0	0	18:18
2001-02	San Jose	NHL	77	21	20	41	32	4	3	5	174	12.1	23	105	47.6	15:39	12	3	2	5	2	0	0	0	15:33
	Germany	Olympics	5	0	1	1	0	....	....	....	....	....	....	....	....	....	....	....	....	....	....	....	....	....	....
2002-03	San Jose	NHL	82	28	20	48	16	6	0	2	208	13.5	9	83	48.2	16:31	....	....	....	....	....	....	....	....	....
2003-04	San Jose	NHL	64	21	20	41	36	10	2	6	158	13.3	0	7	42.9	16:25	....	....	....	....	....	....	....	....	....
2004-05	ERC Ingolstadt	Germany	45	22	16	38	56	....	....	....	....	....	....	....	....	....	11	3	4	7	12	....	....	....	....
2005-06	San Jose	NHL	23	6	10	16	16	3	0	0	48	12.5	-8	9	44.4	17:28	....	....	....	....	....	....	....	....	....
	Boston	NHL	51	23	20	43	32	5	0	6	132	17.4	14	3	33.3	18:44	....	....	....	....	....	....	....	....	....
2006-07	Boston	NHL	76	27	17	44	46	10	2	1	224	12.1	-24	13	61.5	18:36	....	....	....	....	....	....	....	....	....
2007-08	Boston	NHL	80	27	29	56	40	10	1	5	229	11.8	11	34	29.4	18:00	7	2	2	4	6	0	1	1	18:20
2008-09	Boston	NHL	19	7	6	13	8	4	0	0	45	15.6	9	4	75.0	16:01	....	....	....	....	....	....	....	....	....

			Regular Season														Playoffs								
Season	Club	League	GP	G	A	Pts	PIM	PP	SH	GW	S	%	+/-	TF	F%	Min	GP	G	A	Pts	PIM	PP	SH	GW	Min
2009-10	**Boston**	**NHL**	**76**	**22**	**15**	**37**	**30**	**4**	**1**	**2**	**203**	**10.8**	**14**	**11**	**18.2**	**16:46**	**7**	**0**	**0**	**0**	**4**	**0**	**0**	**0**	**14:15**
	Germany	Olympics	4	0	1	1	0	....	....	....	....	....	....	....	....	....	....	....	....	....	....	....	....	....	....
	NHL Totals		**855**	**234**	**232**	**466**	**398**	**65**	**18**	**41**	**1952**	**12.0**		**1545**	**43.4**	**16:35**	**52**	**8**	**11**	**19**	**22**	**0**	**1**	**2**	**15:19**

ayed in NHL All-Star Game (1999)

gned as a free agent by **Ingolstadt** (Germany), August 8, 2004. Traded to **Boston** by **San Jose** with Brad Stuart and Wayne Primeau for Joe Thornton, November 30, 2005. • Missed majority of 2008-09 eason recovering from knee injury suffered in game vs. Toronto, December 18, 2008.

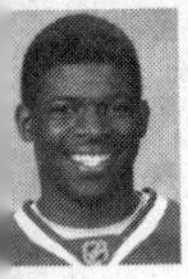

SUBBAN, P.K.

(soo-BAHN, PEE-KAY) **MTL.**

Defense. Shoots right. 6', 206 lbs. Born, Toronto, Ont., May 13, 1989. Montreal's 3rd choice, 43rd overall, in 2007 Entry Draft.

2004-05	Markham	GTHL	67	15	28	43	179	....	....	....	....	....	....	....	....	....	....	....	....	....	....	....	....	....	....
2005-06	Belleville Bulls	OHL	52	5	7	12	70	....	....	....	....	....	....	....	....	....	3	0	0	0	2	....	....	....	....
2006-07	Belleville Bulls	OHL	68	15	41	56	89	....	....	....	....	....	....	....	....	....	15	5	8	13	26	....	....	....	....
2007-08	Belleville Bulls	OHL	58	8	38	46	100	....	....	....	....	....	....	....	....	....	21	8	15	23	28	....	....	....	....
2008-09	Belleville Bulls	OHL	56	14	62	76	94	....	....	....	....	....	....	....	....	....	17	3	12	15	22	....	....	....	....
2009-10	**Montreal**	**NHL**	**2**	**0**	**2**	**2**	**2**	**0**	**0**	**0**	**4**	**0.0**	**1**	**0**	**0.0**	**20:06**	**14**	**1**	**7**	**8**	**6**	**0**	**0**	**0**	**20:44**
	Hamilton	AHL	77	18	35	53	82	....	....	....	....	....	....	....	....	....	7	3	7	10	6	....	....	....	....
	NHL Totals		**2**	**0**	**2**	**2**	**2**	**0**	**0**	**0**	**4**	**0.0**		**0**	**0.0**	**20:06**	**14**	**1**	**7**	**8**	**6**	**0**	**0**	**0**	**20:44**

)HL First All-Star Team (2009)

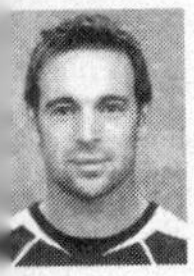

SULLIVAN, Steve

(SUHL-ih-vuhn, STEEV) **NSH.**

Right wing. Shoots right. 5'8", 161 lbs. Born, Timmins, Ont., July 6, 1974. New Jersey's 10th choice, 233rd overall, in 1994 Entry Draft.

1991-92	Timmins	NOJHA	47	66	55	121	141	....	....	....	....	....	....	....	....	....	....	....	....	....	....	....	....	....	....
1992-93	Sault Ste. Marie	OHL	62	36	27	63	44	....	....	....	....	....	....	....	....	....	16	3	8	11	18	....	....	....	....
1993-94	Sault Ste. Marie	OHL	63	51	62	113	82	....	....	....	....	....	....	....	....	....	14	9	16	25	22	....	....	....	....
1994-95	Albany River Rats	AHL	75	31	50	81	124	....	....	....	....	....	....	....	....	....	14	4	7	11	10	....	....	....	....
1995-96	**New Jersey**	**NHL**	**16**	**5**	**4**	**9**	**8**	**2**	**0**	**1**	**23**	**21.7**	**3**	....	....	....	....	....	....	....	....	....	....	....	....
	Albany River Rats	AHL	53	33	42	75	127	....	....	....	....	....	....	....	....	....	4	3	0	3	6	....	....	....	....
1996-97	**New Jersey**	**NHL**	**33**	**8**	**14**	**22**	**14**	**2**	**0**	**2**	**63**	**12.7**	**9**	....	....	....	....	....	....	....	....	....	....	....	....
	Albany River Rats	AHL	15	8	7	15	16	....	....	....	....	....	....	....	....	....	....	....	....	....	....	....	....	....	....
	Toronto	**NHL**	**21**	**5**	**11**	**16**	**23**	**1**	**0**	**1**	**45**	**11.1**	**5**	....	....	....	....	....	....	....	....	....	....	....	....
1997-98	**Toronto**	**NHL**	**63**	**10**	**18**	**28**	**40**	**1**	**0**	**1**	**112**	**8.9**	**–8**	....	....	....	....	....	....	....	....	....	....	....	....
1998-99	**Toronto**	**NHL**	**63**	**20**	**20**	**40**	**28**	**4**	**0**	**5**	**110**	**18.2**	**12**	**685**	**44.4**	**14:12**	**13**	**3**	**3**	**6**	**14**	**2**	**0**	**0**	**16:20**
99-2000	**Toronto**	**NHL**	**7**	**0**	**1**	**1**	**4**	**0**	**0**	**0**	**11**	**0.0**	**–1**	**47**	**48.9**	**11:52**	....	....	....	....	....	....	....	....	....
	Chicago	**NHL**	**73**	**22**	**42**	**64**	**52**	**2**	**1**	**6**	**169**	**13.0**	**20**	**692**	**48.0**	**18:05**	....	....	....	....	....	....	....	....	....
2000-01	**Chicago**	**NHL**	**81**	**34**	**41**	**75**	**54**	**6**	***8**	**3**	**204**	**16.7**	**3**	**649**	**42.4**	**20:32**	....	....	....	....	....	....	....	....	....
2001-02	**Chicago**	**NHL**	**78**	**21**	**39**	**60**	**67**	**3**	**0**	**8**	**155**	**13.5**	**23**	**758**	**48.9**	**19:10**	**5**	**1**	**0**	**1**	**2**	**0**	**0**	**0**	**18:04**
2002-03	**Chicago**	**NHL**	**82**	**26**	**35**	**61**	**42**	**4**	**2**	**3**	**190**	**13.7**	**15**	**382**	**46.1**	**19:15**	....	....	....	....	....	....	....	....	....
2003-04	**Chicago**	**NHL**	**56**	**15**	**28**	**43**	**36**	**4**	**2**	**4**	**140**	**10.7**	**–7**	**103**	**44.7**	**21:19**	....	....	....	....	....	....	....	....	....
	Nashville	**NHL**	**24**	**9**	**21**	**30**	**12**	**7**	**0**	**0**	**78**	**11.5**	**8**	**124**	**43.6**	**20:02**	**6**	**1**	**1**	**2**	**6**	**0**	**0**	**1**	**18:58**
2004-05			DID NOT PLAY																						
2005-06	**Nashville**	**NHL**	**69**	**31**	**37**	**68**	**50**	**13**	**4**	**5**	**192**	**16.1**	**2**	**42**	**52.4**	**19:06**	**5**	**0**	**2**	**2**	**0**	**0**	**0**	**0**	**17:02**
2006-07	**Nashville**	**NHL**	**57**	**22**	**38**	**60**	**20**	**6**	**3**	**4**	**122**	**18.0**	**16**	**39**	**38.5**	**19:25**	....	....	....	....	....	....	....	....	....
2007-08	**Nashville**	**NHL**	DID NOT PLAY – INJURED																						
2008-09	**Nashville**	**NHL**	**41**	**11**	**21**	**32**	**30**	**3**	**0**	**2**	**83**	**13.3**	**2**	**4**	**0.0**	**18:29**	....	....	....	....	....	....	....	....	....
2009-10	**Nashville**	**NHL**	**82**	**17**	**34**	**51**	**35**	**5**	**0**	**4**	**152**	**11.2**	**2**	**10**	**10.0**	**17:55**	**6**	**0**	**3**	**3**	**2**	**0**	**0**	**0**	**17:59**
	NHL Totals		**846**	**256**	**404**	**660**	**515**	**63**	**20**	**49**	**1849**	**13.8**		**3535**	**45.8**	**18:44**	**35**	**5**	**9**	**14**	**24**	**2**	**0**	**1**	**17:25**

AHL First All-Star Team (1996) • Bill Masterton Memorial Trophy (2009)

Traded to **Toronto** by **New Jersey** with Jason Smith and the rights to Alyn McCauley for Doug Gilmour, Dave Ellett and New Jersey's 3rd round choice (previously acquired, New Jersey selected Andre Lakos) in 1999 Entry Draft, February 25, 1997. Claimed on waivers by **Chicago** from **Toronto**, October 23, 1999. Traded to **Nashville** by **Chicago** for Nashville's 2nd round choices in 2004 (Ryan Garlock) and 2005 (Michael Blunden) Entry Drafts, February 16, 2004. • Missed remainder of 2006-07 season, entire 2007-08 season and start of 2008-09 season recovering from back injury suffered in game vs. Montreal, February 22, 2006.

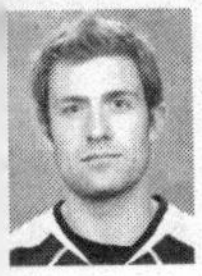

SULZER, Alexander

(ZUHLT-suhr, al-EHX-AN-duhr) **NSH.**

Defense. Shoots left. 6'1", 204 lbs. Born, Kaufbeuren, West Germany, May 30, 1984. Nashville's 7th choice, 92nd overall, in 2003 Entry Draft.

2000-01	ESV Kaufbeuren	German-3	38	3	6	9	20	....	....	....	....	....	....	....	....	....	....	....	....	....	....	....	....	....	....
	Kaufbeuren Jr.	Ger-Jr.	1	0	2	2	2	....	....	....	....	....	....	....	....	....	....	....	....	....	....	....	....	....	....
2001-02	ESV Kaufbeuren	German-3	19	1	9	10	14	....	....	....	....	....	....	....	....	....	....	....	....	....	....	....	....	....	....
	Kaufbeuren Jr.	Ger-Jr.	1	0	0	0	4	....	....	....	....	....	....	....	....	....	....	....	....	....	....	....	....	....	....
2002-03	ESV Kaufbeuren	German-2	26	5	3	8	38	....	....	....	....	....	....	....	....	....	1	0	1	1	4	....	....	....	....
	Hamburg Freezers	Germany	18	0	1	1	18	....	....	....	....	....	....	....	....	....	5	0	0	0	12	....	....	....	....
2003-04	Dusseldorf	Germany	46	4	1	5	56	....	....	....	....	....	....	....	....	....	4	0	0	0	8	....	....	....	....
2004-05	Dusseldorf	Germany	42	5	6	11	68	....	....	....	....	....	....	....	....	....	....	....	....	....	....	....	....	....	....
	EV Duisburg	German-2	....	....	....	....	....	....	....	....	....	....	....	....	....	....	7	0	3	3	6	....	....	....	....
2005-06	Dusseldorf	Germany	48	3	15	18	82	....	....	....	....	....	....	....	....	....	13	3	6	9	22	....	....	....	....
	Germany	Olympics	5	0	1	1	2	....	....	....	....	....	....	....	....	....	....	....	....	....	....	....	....	....	....
2006-07	Dusseldorf	Germany	44	4	11	15	82	....	....	....	....	....	....	....	....	....	9	2	1	3	20	....	....	....	....
2007-08	Milwaukee	AHL	61	7	25	32	47	....	....	....	....	....	....	....	....	....	....	....	....	....	....	....	....	....	....
2008-09	**Nashville**	**NHL**	**2**	**0**	**0**	**0**	**0**	**0**	**0**	**0**	**0**	**0.0**	**0**	**0**	**0.0**	**6:34**	....	....	....	....	....	....	....	....	....
	Milwaukee	AHL	48	8	26	34	36	....	....	....	....	....	....	....	....	....	....	....	....	....	....	....	....	....	....
2009-10	**Nashville**	**NHL**	**20**	**0**	**2**	**2**	**4**	**0**	**0**	**0**	**15**	**0.0**	**4**	**0**	**0.0**	**13:23**	....	....	....	....	....	....	....	....	....
	Milwaukee	AHL	36	7	23	30	8	....	....	....	....	....	....	....	....	....	7	1	5	6	2	....	....	....	....
	Germany	Olympics	4	0	0	0	4	....	....	....	....	....	....	....	....	....	....	....	....	....	....	....	....	....	....
	NHL Totals		**22**	**0**	**2**	**2**	**4**	**0**	**0**	**0**	**15**	**0.0**		**0**	**0.0**	**12:46**	....	....	....	....	....	....	....	....	....

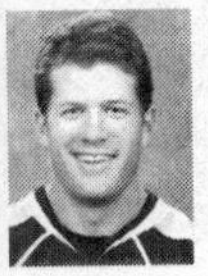

SUTER, Ryan

(SOO-tuhr, RIGH-uhn) **NSH.**

Defense. Shoots left. 6'1", 198 lbs. Born, Madison, WI, January 21, 1985. Nashville's 1st choice, 7th overall, in 2003 Entry Draft.

2000-01	Culver Academy	High-IN	26	13	32	45	....	....	....	....	....	....	....	....	....	....	....	....	....	....	....	....	....	....	....
2001-02	USNTDP	U-17	8	2	11	13	21	....	....	....	....	....	....	....	....	....	....	....	....	....	....	....	....	....	....
	USNTDP	U-18	27	4	10	14	6	....	....	....	....	....	....	....	....	....	....	....	....	....	....	....	....	....	....
	USNTDP	NAHL	35	2	10	12	75	....	....	....	....	....	....	....	....	....	....	....	....	....	....	....	....	....	....
2002-03	USNTDP	NAHL	9	2	5	7	12	....	....	....	....	....	....	....	....	....	....	....	....	....	....	....	....	....	....
	USNTDP	U-18	42	7	17	24	124	....	....	....	....	....	....	....	....	....	....	....	....	....	....	....	....	....	....
2003-04	U. of Wisconsin	WCHA	39	3	16	19	93	....	....	....	....	....	....	....	....	....	....	....	....	....	....	....	....	....	....
2004-05	Milwaukee	AHL	63	7	16	23	70	....	....	....	....	....	....	....	....	....	7	1	5	6	16	....	....	....	....
2005-06	**Nashville**	**NHL**	**71**	**1**	**15**	**16**	**66**	**0**	**0**	**0**	**84**	**1.2**	**7**	**0**	**0.0**	**17:21**	....	....	....	....	....	....	....	....	....
2006-07	**Nashville**	**NHL**	**82**	**8**	**16**	**24**	**54**	**1**	**0**	**0**	**87**	**9.2**	**10**	**0**	**0.0**	**20:09**	**5**	**1**	**0**	**1**	**8**	**0**	**0**	**0**	**23:19**
2007-08	**Nashville**	**NHL**	**76**	**7**	**24**	**31**	**71**	**1**	**0**	**1**	**138**	**5.1**	**3**	**0**	**0.0**	**20:35**	**6**	**1**	**1**	**2**	**4**	**0**	**0**	**0**	**21:12**
2008-09	**Nashville**	**NHL**	**82**	**7**	**38**	**45**	**73**	**3**	**0**	**3**	**143**	**4.9**	**–16**	**0**	**0.0**	**24:16**	....	....	....	....	....	....	....	....	....
2009-10	**Nashville**	**NHL**	**82**	**4**	**33**	**37**	**48**	**2**	**0**	**1**	**125**	**3.2**	**4**	**1**	**0.0**	**23:59**	**6**	**0**	**0**	**0**	**0**	**0**	**0**	**0**	**24:09**
	United States	Olympics	6	0	4	4	2	....	....	....	....	....	....	....	....	....	....	....	....	....	....	....	....	....	....
	NHL Totals		**393**	**27**	**126**	**153**	**312**	**7**	**0**	**5**	**577**	**4.7**		**1**	**0.0**	**21:23**	**17**	**2**	**1**	**3**	**12**	**0**	**0**	**0**	**22:52**

WCHA All-Rookie Team (2004)

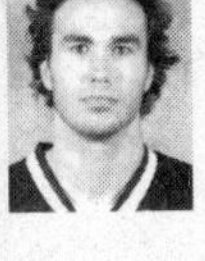

SUTHERBY, Brian

(SUH-thur-bee, BRIGH-uhn) **DAL.**

Center. Shoots left. 6'2", 204 lbs. Born, Edmonton, Alta., March 1, 1982. Washington's 1st choice, 26th overall, in 2000 Entry Draft.

1997-98	CAC Cement	AMHL	36	36	23	59	60	....	....	....	....	....	....	....	....	....	....	....	....	....	....	....	....	....	....
1998-99	Moose Jaw	WHL	66	9	12	21	47	....	....	....	....	....	....	....	....	....	11	0	1	1	0	....	....	....	....
99-2000	Moose Jaw	WHL	47	18	17	35	102	....	....	....	....	....	....	....	....	....	4	1	1	2	12	....	....	....	....
2000-01	Moose Jaw	WHL	59	34	43	77	138	....	....	....	....	....	....	....	....	....	4	2	1	3	10	....	....	....	....
2001-02	**Washington**	**NHL**	**7**	**0**	**0**	**0**	**2**	**0**	**0**	**0**	**3**	**0.0**	**–3**	**39**	**35.9**	**7:17**	....	....	....	....	....	....	....	....	....
	Moose Jaw	WHL	36	18	27	45	75	....	....	....	....	....	....	....	....	....	12	7	5	12	33	....	....	....	....
2002-03	**Washington**	**NHL**	**72**	**2**	**9**	**11**	**93**	**0**	**0**	**0**	**38**	**5.3**	**7**	**288**	**43.8**	**9:44**	**5**	**0**	**0**	**0**	**10**	**0**	**0**	**0**	**4:10**
	Portland Pirates	AHL	5	0	5	5	11	....	....	....	....	....	....	....	....	....	....	....	....	....	....	....	....	....	....

			Regular Season														Playoffs								
Season	Club	League	GP	G	A	Pts	PIM	PP	SH	GW	S	%	+/-	TF	F%	Min	GP	G	A	Pts	PIM	PP	SH	GW	M
2003-04	**Washington**	**NHL**	**30**	**2**	**0**	**2**	**28**	**0**	**0**	**0**	**24**	**8.3**	**–5**	**116**	**41.4**	**10:15**	....	....	....	....	....	....	....	....	
	Portland Pirates	AHL	6	2	4	6	16	....	....	....	....	....	....	....	....	....	....	....	....	....	....	....	....	....	
2004-05	Portland Pirates	AHL	53	10	19	29	115	....	....	....	....	....	....	....	....	....	....	....	....	....	....	....	....	....	
2005-06	**Washington**	**NHL**	**76**	**14**	**16**	**30**	**73**	**0**	**2**	**0**	**85**	**16.5**	**–17**	**904**	**48.7**	**13:44**	....	....	....	....	....	....	....	....	
2006-07	**Washington**	**NHL**	**69**	**7**	**10**	**17**	**78**	**1**	**0**	**0**	**87**	**8.0**	**–9**	**762**	**50.1**	**13:41**	....	....	....	....	....	....	....	....	
2007-08	**Washington**	**NHL**	**5**	**1**	**0**	**1**	**7**	**0**	**0**	**0**	**3**	**33.3**	**–2**	**23**	**52.2**	**6:49**	....	....	....	....	....	....	....	....	
	Anaheim	**NHL**	**45**	**0**	**1**	**1**	**57**	**0**	**0**	**0**	**46**	**0.0**	**–2**	**255**	**45.5**	**8:47**	**5**	**0**	**0**	**0**	**2**	**0**	**0**	**0**	**5:**
2008-09	**Anaheim**	**NHL**	**17**	**3**	**3**	**6**	**19**	**0**	**0**	**0**	**17**	**17.6**	**6**	**45**	**48.9**	**7:12**	....	....	....	....	....	....	....	....	
	Dallas	**NHL**	**42**	**5**	**4**	**9**	**52**	**0**	**1**	**0**	**50**	**10.0**	**–5**	**219**	**41.1**	**12:25**	....	....	....	....	....	....	....	....	
2009-10	**Dallas**	**NHL**	**46**	**5**	**4**	**9**	**66**	**0**	**0**	**0**	**49**	**10.2**	**8**	**41**	**43.9**	**8:37**	....	....	....	....	....	....	....	....	
	NHL Totals		**409**	**39**	**47**	**86**	**475**	**1**	**3**	**0**	**402**	**9.7**		**2692**	**47.1**	**11:03**	**10**	**0**	**0**	**0**	**12**	**0**	**0**	**0**	**4:**

• Missed majority of 2003-04 season recovering from groin injury suffered in game vs. St. Louis, October 18, 2003. Traded to **Anaheim** by **Washington** for Anaheim's 2nd round choice (later traded to Montreal, later traded to Atlanta – Atlanta selected Jeremy Morin) in 2009 Entry Draft, November 19, 2007. Traded to **Dallas** by **Anaheim** for David McIntyre and Dallas' 6th round choice (Andreas Dahlstrom) in 2010 Entry Draft, December 14, 2008.

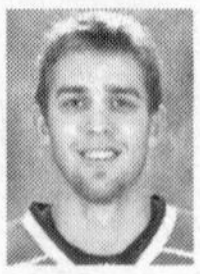

SUTTER, Brandon
(SUH-tuhr, BRAN-duhn) **CA**

Center/Right wing. Shoots right. 6'3", 183 lbs. Born, Huntington, NY, February 14, 1989. Carolina's 1st choice, 11th overall, in 2007 Entry Draft.

Season	Club	League	GP	G	A	Pts	PIM	PP	SH	GW	S	%	+/-	TF	F%	Min	GP	G	A	Pts	PIM	PP	SH	GW	M
2003-04	Red Deer Chiefs	AMBHL	35	25	34	59	28	....	....	....	....	....	....	....	....	....	11	5	4	9	....	....	....	....	
2004-05	Red Deer	AMHL	34	4	16	20	28	....	....	....	....	....	....	....	....	....	....	....	....	....	....	....	....	....	
	Red Deer Rebels	WHL	7	0	2	2	8	....	....	....	....	....	....	....	....	....	7	1	4	5	2	....	....	....	
2005-06	Red Deer Rebels	WHL	68	22	24	46	36	....	....	....	....	....	....	....	....	....	....	....	....	....	....	....	....	....	
2006-07	Red Deer Rebels	WHL	71	20	37	57	54	....	....	....	....	....	....	....	....	....	7	0	3	3	14	....	....	....	
2007-08	Red Deer Rebels	WHL	59	26	23	49	38	....	....	....	....	....	....	....	....	....	....	....	....	....	....	....	....	....	
	Albany River Rats	AHL	7	1	1	2	2	....	....	....	....	....	....	....	....	....	7	0	2	2	4	....	....	....	
2008-09	**Carolina**	**NHL**	**50**	**1**	**5**	**6**	**16**	**0**	**0**	**0**	**57**	**1.8**	**–1**	**332**	**38.6**	**8:50**	....	....	....	....	....	....	....	....	
	Albany River Rats	AHL	22	4	8	12	6	....	....	....	....	....	....	....	....	....	....	....	....	....	....	....	....	....	
2009-10	**Carolina**	**NHL**	**72**	**21**	**19**	**40**	**2**	**5**	**0**	**3**	**168**	**12.5**	**–1**	**997**	**49.1**	**16:33**	....	....	....	....	....	....	....	....	
	Albany River Rats	AHL	7	1	3	4	2	....	....	....	....	....	....	....	....	....	....	....	....	....	....	....	....	....	
	NHL Totals		**122**	**22**	**24**	**46**	**18**	**5**	**0**	**3**	**225**	**9.8**		**1329**	**46.4**	**13:23**	....	....	....	....	....	....	....	....	

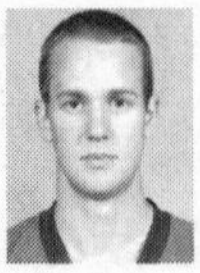

SUTTER, Brett
(SUH-tuhr, BREHT) **CG**

Center/Left wing. Shoots left. 6', 192 lbs. Born, Viking, Alta., June 2, 1987. Calgary's 7th choice, 179th overall, in 2005 Entry Draft.

Season	Club	League	GP	G	A	Pts	PIM	PP	SH	GW	S	%	+/-	TF	F%	Min	GP	G	A	Pts	PIM	PP	SH	GW	M
2003-04	Kootenay Ice	WHL	44	5	7	12	26	....	....	....	....	....	....	....	....	....	4	0	0	0	4	....	....	....	
2004-05	Kootenay Ice	WHL	70	8	11	19	70	....	....	....	....	....	....	....	....	....	16	1	2	3	16	....	....	....	
2005-06	Kootenay Ice	WHL	16	8	7	15	21	....	....	....	....	....	....	....	....	....	....	....	....	....	....	....	....	....	
	Red Deer Rebels	WHL	57	9	26	35	80	....	....	....	....	....	....	....	....	....	....	....	....	....	....	....	....	....	
2006-07	Red Deer Rebels	WHL	67	28	29	57	77	....	....	....	....	....	....	....	....	....	7	3	4	7	11	....	....	....	
2007-08	Quad City Flames	AHL	75	4	6	10	63	....	....	....	....	....	....	....	....	....	....	....	....	....	....	....	....	....	
2008-09	**Calgary**	**NHL**	**4**	**1**	**0**	**1**	**2**	**0**	**0**	**0**	**6**	**16.7**	**–2**	**1**	**0.0**	**8:04**	....	....	....	....	....	....	....	....	
	Quad City Flames	AHL	71	10	15	25	50	....	....	....	....	....	....	....	....	....	....	....	....	....	....	....	....	....	
2009-10	**Calgary**	**NHL**	**10**	**0**	**0**	**0**	**5**	**0**	**0**	**0**	**9**	**0.0**	**–1**	**5**	**20.0**	**9:40**	....	....	....	....	....	....	....	....	
	Abbotsford Heat	AHL	66	9	15	24	69	....	....	....	....	....	....	....	....	....	13	4	7	11	20	....	....	....	
	NHL Totals		**14**	**1**	**0**	**1**	**7**	**0**	**0**	**0**	**15**	**6.7**		**6**	**16.7**	**9:12**	....	....	....	....	....	....	....	....	

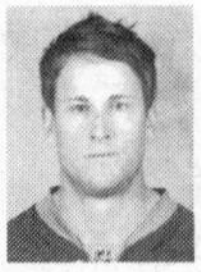

SUTTON, Andy
(SUH-tuhn, AN-dee) **AN**

Defense. Shoots left. 6'6", 245 lbs. Born, Kingston, Ont., March 10, 1975.

Season	Club	League	GP	G	A	Pts	PIM	PP	SH	GW	S	%	+/-	TF	F%	Min	GP	G	A	Pts	PIM	PP	SH	GW	M
1991-92	Gananoque	OHA-B	36	11	9	20	....	....	....	....	....	....	....	....	....	....	14	9	21	30	....	....	....	....	
1992-93	Gananoque	OHA-B	38	14	9	23	....	....	....	....	....	....	....	....	....	....	12	16	13	29	....	....	....	....	
1993-94	St. Mike's B's	MTJHL	48	17	23	40	161	....	....	....	....	....	....	....	....	....	3	0	0	0	20	....	....	....	
1994-95	Michigan Tech	WCHA	19	2	1	3	42	....	....	....	....	....	....	....	....	....	....	....	....	....	....	....	....	....	
1995-96	Michigan Tech	WCHA	33	2	2	4	58	....	....	....	....	....	....	....	....	....	....	....	....	....	....	....	....	....	
1996-97	Michigan Tech	WCHA	32	2	7	9	73	....	....	....	....	....	....	....	....	....	....	....	....	....	....	....	....	....	
1997-98	Michigan Tech	WCHA	38	16	24	40	97	....	....	....	....	....	....	....	....	....	....	....	....	....	....	....	....	....	
	Kentucky	AHL	7	0	0	0	33	....	....	....	....	....	....	....	....	....	....	....	....	....	....	....	....	....	
1998-99	**San Jose**	**NHL**	**31**	**0**	**3**	**3**	**65**	**0**	**0**	**0**	**24**	**0.0**	**–4**	**0**	**0.0**	**12:58**	....	....	....	....	....	....	....	....	
	Kentucky	AHL	21	5	10	15	53	....	....	....	....	....	....	....	....	....	5	0	0	0	23	....	....	....	
99-2000	**San Jose**	**NHL**	**40**	**1**	**1**	**2**	**80**	**0**	**0**	**0**	**29**	**3.4**	**–5**	**0**	**0.0**	**12:57**	....	....	....	....	....	....	....	....	
	Kentucky	AHL	3	0	1	1	0	....	....	....	....	....	....	....	....	....	....	....	....	....	....	....	....	....	
2000-01	**Minnesota**	**NHL**	**69**	**3**	**4**	**7**	**131**	**2**	**0**	**0**	**64**	**4.7**	**–11**	**3**	**33.3**	**12:55**	....	....	....	....	....	....	....	....	
2001-02	**Minnesota**	**NHL**	**19**	**2**	**4**	**6**	**35**	**1**	**0**	**0**	**21**	**9.5**	**–4**	**2**	**0.0**	**10:57**	....	....	....	....	....	....	....	....	
	Atlanta	**NHL**	**24**	**0**	**4**	**4**	**46**	**0**	**0**	**0**	**20**	**0.0**	**0**	**0**	**0.0**	**15:25**	....	....	....	....	....	....	....	....	
2002-03	**Atlanta**	**NHL**	**53**	**3**	**18**	**21**	**114**	**1**	**1**	**0**	**65**	**4.6**	**–8**	**3**	**33.3**	**18:00**	....	....	....	....	....	....	....	....	
2003-04	**Atlanta**	**NHL**	**65**	**8**	**13**	**21**	**94**	**7**	**1**	**1**	**102**	**7.8**	**0**	**1**	**0.0**	**23:21**	....	....	....	....	....	....	....	....	
2004-05	GCK Lions Zurich	Swiss-2	18	8	18	26	58	....	....	....	....	....	....	....	....	....	6	2	4	6	16	....	....	....	
	ZSC Lions Zurich	Swiss	8	2	2	4	32	....	....	....	....	....	....	....	....	....	1	0	1	1	2	....	....	....	
2005-06	**Atlanta**	**NHL**	**76**	**8**	**17**	**25**	**144**	**2**	**1**	**3**	**86**	**9.3**	**13**	**1**	**0.0**	**21:05**	....	....	....	....	....	....	....	....	
2006-07	**Atlanta**	**NHL**	**55**	**2**	**14**	**16**	**76**	**0**	**1**	**0**	**51**	**3.9**	**6**	**0**	**0.0**	**19:28**	**4**	**0**	**0**	**0**	**10**	**0**	**0**	**0**	**17:**
2007-08	**NY Islanders**	**NHL**	**58**	**1**	**7**	**8**	**86**	**0**	**0**	**1**	**57**	**1.8**	**–6**	**0**	**0.0**	**18:10**	....	....	....	....	....	....	....	....	
2008-09	**NY Islanders**	**NHL**	**23**	**2**	**8**	**10**	**40**	**0**	**0**	**0**	**19**	**10.5**	**3**	**0**	**0.0**	**20:14**	....	....	....	....	....	....	....	....	
2009-10	**NY Islanders**	**NHL**	**54**	**4**	**8**	**12**	**73**	**0**	**0**	**0**	**58**	**6.9**	**–3**	**0**	**0.0**	**20:49**	....	....	....	....	....	....	....	....	
	Ottawa	**NHL**	**18**	**1**	**0**	**1**	**34**	**0**	**0**	**0**	**19**	**5.3**	**–7**	**0**	**0.0**	**19:13**	**6**	**0**	**0**	**0**	**8**	**0**	**0**	**0**	**23:**
	NHL Totals		**585**	**35**	**101**	**136**	**1018**	**13**	**4**	**5**	**615**	**5.7**		**10**	**20.0**	**17:59**	**10**	**0**	**0**	**0**	**18**	**0**	**0**	**0**	**20.**

WCHA Second All-Star Team (1998)

Signed as a free agent by **San Jose**, March 20, 1998. Traded to **Minnesota** by **San Jose** with San Jose's 7th round choice (Peter Bartos) in 2000 Entry Draft and San Jose's 3rd round choice (later traded to Atlanta, later traded to Pittsburgh, later traded to Columbus – Columbus selected Aaron Johnson) in 2001 Entry Draft for Minnesota's 8th round choice (later traded to Calgary – Calgary selected Joe Campbell) in 2001 Entry Draft and future considerations, June 12, 2000. Traded to **Atlanta** by **Minnesota** for Hnat Domenichelli, January 22, 2002. Signed as a free agent by **GCK Zurich** (Swiss-2), September 24, 2004. • Loaned to **ZSC Zurich** (Swiss) by **GCK Zurich** (Swiss-2), February 22, 2005. Signed as a free agent by **NY Islanders**, August 10, 2007. • Missed majority of 2008-09 season recovering from broken foot suffered in game at Minnesota, December 19, 2008. Traded to **Ottawa** by **NY Islanders** for San Jose's 2nd round choice (previously acquired, later traded to Chicago – Chicago selected Kent Simpson) in 2010 Entry Draft, March 2, 2010. Signed as a free agent by **Anaheim**, August 2, 2010.

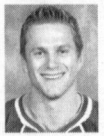

SVATOS, Marek
(SVA-tohs, MAIR-ehk)

Right wing. Shoots right. 5'10", 185 lbs. Born, Kosice, Czech., June 17, 1982. Colorado's 10th choice, 227th overall, in 2001 Entry Draft.

Season	Club	League	GP	G	A	Pts	PIM	PP	SH	GW	S	%	+/-	TF	F%	Min	GP	G	A	Pts	PIM	PP	SH	GW	M
99-2000	HC VSZ Kosice Jr.	Slovak-Jr.	39	43	30	73	28	....	....	....	....	....	....	....	....	....	....	....	....	....	....	....	....	....	
	HC VSZ Kosice	Slovakia	19	2	2	4	0	....	....	....	....	....	....	....	....	....	....	....	....	....	....	....	....	....	
2000-01	Kootenay Ice	WHL	39	23	18	41	47	....	....	....	....	....	....	....	....	....	11	7	2	9	26	....	....	....	
2001-02	Kootenay Ice	WHL	53	38	39	77	58	....	....	....	....	....	....	....	....	....	21	12	6	18	40	....	....	....	
2002-03	Hershey Bears	AHL	30	9	4	13	10	....	....	....	....	....	....	....	....	....	....	....	....	....	....	....	....	....	
2003-04	**Colorado**	**NHL**	**4**	**2**	**0**	**2**	**0**	**1**	**0**	**1**	**6**	**33.3**	**1**	**0**	**0.0**	**10:18**	**11**	**1**	**5**	**6**	**2**	**0**	**0**	**1**	**12:**
2004-05	Hershey Bears	AHL	72	18	28	46	69	....	....	....	....	....	....	....	....	....	....	....	....	....	....	....	....	....	
2005-06	**Colorado**	**NHL**	**61**	**32**	**18**	**50**	**60**	**12**	**0**	**9**	**165**	**19.4**	**0**	**5**	**20.0**	**13:45**	....	....	....	....	....	....	....	....	
	Slovakia	Olympics	6	0	0	0	0	....	....	....	....	....	....	....	....	....	....	....	....	....	....	....	....	....	
2006-07	**Colorado**	**NHL**	**66**	**15**	**15**	**30**	**46**	**8**	**0**	**2**	**179**	**8.4**	**1**	**1**	**100.0**	**12:30**	....	....	....	....	....	....	....	....	
2007-08	**Colorado**	**NHL**	**62**	**26**	**11**	**37**	**32**	**3**	**0**	**6**	**140**	**18.6**	**13**	**3**	**33.3**	**13:39**	....	....	....	....	....	....	....	....	
2008-09	**Colorado**	**NHL**	**69**	**14**	**20**	**34**	**34**	**6**	**0**	**1**	**140**	**10.0**	**–6**	**3**	**0.0**	**13:06**	....	....	....	....	....	....	....	....	
2009-10	**Colorado**	**NHL**	**54**	**7**	**4**	**11**	**35**	**3**	**0**	**1**	**84**	**8.3**	**–13**	**0**	**0.0**	**11:25**	**3**	**1**	**0**	**1**	**2**	**0**	**0**	**0**	**13:**
	NHL Totals		**316**	**96**	**68**	**164**	**207**	**33**	**0**	**20**	**714**	**13.4**		**12**	**25.0**	**12:53**	**14**	**2**	**5**	**7**	**4**	**0**	**0**	**1**	**12:**

WHL West Second All-Star Team (2002)

• Missed majority of 2002-03 season recovering from recurring shoulder injury and resulting surgery, January 28, 2003. • Missed majority of 2003-04 season recovering from shoulder injury suffered in game vs. St. Louis, October 12, 2003.

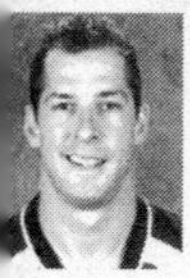

SYDOR, Darryl

(sih-DOHR, DAIR-uhl)

Defense. Shoots left. 6'1", 211 lbs. Born, Edmonton, Alta., May 13, 1972. Los Angeles' 1st choice, 7th overall, in 1990 Entry Draft.

			Regular Season														Playoffs								
Season	Club	League	GP	G	A	Pts	PIM	PP	SH	GW	S	%	+/-	TF	F%	Min	GP	G	A	Pts	PIM	PP	SH	GW	Min
1985-86	Genstar Cement	AAHA	34	20	17	37	60																		
1986-87	Genstar Cement	AAHA	36	15	20	35	60																		
1987-88	Edmonton Mets	AJHL	38	10	11	21	54																		
1988-89	Kamloops Blazers	WHL	65	12	14	26	86										15	1	4	5	19				
1989-90	Kamloops Blazers	WHL	67	29	66	95	129										17	2	9	11	28				
1990-91	Kamloops Blazers	WHL	66	27	78	105	88										12	3	*22	25	10				
1991-92	Kamloops Blazers	WHL	29	9	39	48	33										17	3	15	18	18				
	Los Angeles	**NHL**	**18**	**1**	**5**	**6**	**22**	**0**	**0**	**0**	**18**	**5.6**	**-3**												
1992-93	**Los Angeles**	**NHL**	**80**	**6**	**23**	**29**	**63**	**0**	**0**	**1**	**112**	**5.4**	**-2**				**24**	**3**	**8**	**11**	**16**	**2**	**0**	**0**	
1993-94	**Los Angeles**	**NHL**	**84**	**8**	**27**	**35**	**94**	**1**	**0**	**0**	**146**	**5.5**	**-9**												
1994-95	**Los Angeles**	**NHL**	**48**	**4**	**19**	**23**	**36**	**3**	**0**	**0**	**96**	**4.2**	**-2**												
1995-96	**Los Angeles**	**NHL**	**58**	**1**	**11**	**12**	**34**	**1**	**0**	**0**	**84**	**1.2**	**-11**												
	Dallas	**NHL**	**26**	**2**	**6**	**8**	**41**	**1**	**0**	**0**	**33**	**6.1**	**-1**												
1996-97	**Dallas**	**NHL**	**82**	**8**	**40**	**48**	**51**	**2**	**0**	**2**	**142**	**5.6**	**37**				**7**	**0**	**2**	**2**	**0**	**0**	**0**	**0**	
1997-98	**Dallas**	**NHL**	**79**	**11**	**35**	**46**	**51**	**4**	**1**	**1**	**166**	**6.6**	**17**				**17**	**0**	**5**	**5**	**14**	**0**	**0**	**0**	
1998-99♦	**Dallas**	**NHL**	**74**	**14**	**34**	**48**	**50**	**9**	**0**	**2**	**163**	**8.6**	**-1**	**1**	**100.0**	**21:16**	**23**	**3**	**9**	**12**	**16**	**1**	**0**	**1**	**22:20**
99-2000	**Dallas**	**NHL**	**74**	**8**	**26**	**34**	**32**	**5**	**0**	**1**	**132**	**6.1**	**6**	**1**	**0.0**	**23:09**	**23**	**1**	**6**	**7**	**6**	**0**	**0**	**0**	**20:48**
2000-01	**Dallas**	**NHL**	**81**	**10**	**37**	**47**	**34**	**8**	**0**	**1**	**140**	**7.1**	**5**	**1**	**0.0**	**21:25**	**10**	**1**	**3**	**4**	**0**	**1**	**0**	**0**	**22:42**
2001-02	**Dallas**	**NHL**	**78**	**4**	**29**	**33**	**50**	**2**	**0**	**0**	**183**	**2.2**	**3**	**0**	**0.0**	**21:07**									
2002-03	**Dallas**	**NHL**	**81**	**5**	**31**	**36**	**40**	**2**	**0**	**1**	**132**	**3.8**	**22**	**0**	**0.0**	**18:19**	**12**	**0**	**6**	**6**	**6**	**0**	**0**	**0**	**19:14**
2003-04	**Columbus**	**NHL**	**49**	**2**	**13**	**15**	**26**	**1**	**0**	**0**	**80**	**2.5**	**-19**	**1**	**0.0**	**21:54**									
	♦ Tampa Bay	**NHL**	**31**	**1**	**6**	**7**	**6**	**0**	**0**	**0**	**42**	**2.4**	**3**	**0**	**0.0**	**19:06**	**23**	**0**	**6**	**6**	**9**	**0**	**0**	**0**	**21:50**
2004-05			DID NOT PLAY																						
2005-06	**Tampa Bay**	**NHL**	**80**	**4**	**19**	**23**	**30**	**1**	**0**	**0**	**64**	**6.3**	**-18**	**1**	**0.0**	**19:06**	**5**	**0**	**1**	**1**	**0**	**0**	**0**	**0**	**17:54**
2006-07	**Dallas**	**NHL**	**74**	**5**	**16**	**21**	**36**	**2**	**0**	**1**	**75**	**6.7**	**-4**	**0**	**0.0**	**20:09**	**7**	**1**	**1**	**2**	**4**	**0**	**0**	**0**	**23:19**
2007-08	**Pittsburgh**	**NHL**	**74**	**1**	**12**	**13**	**26**	**1**	**0**	**0**	**59**	**1.7**	**1**	**0**	**0.0**	**17:33**	**4**	**0**	**0**	**0**	**2**	**0**	**0**	**0**	**16:20**
2008-09	**Pittsburgh**	**NHL**	**8**	**1**	**1**	**2**	**2**	**0**	**0**	**0**	**7**	**14.3**	**5**	**0**	**0.0**	**14:23**									
	Dallas	**NHL**	**65**	**2**	**11**	**13**	**16**	**0**	**0**	**0**	**66**	**3.0**	**-2**	**0**	**0.0**	**18:42**									
2009-10	**St. Louis**	**NHL**	**47**	**0**	**8**	**8**	**15**	**0**	**0**	**0**	**26**	**0.0**	**-6**	**1**	**0.0**	**16:42**									
	NHL Totals		**1291**	**98**	**409**	**507**	**755**	**43**	**1**	**10**	**1966**	**5.0**		**6**	**16.7**	**19:55**	**155**	**9**	**47**	**56**	**73**	**4**	**0**	**1**	**21:13**

VHL West First All-Star Team (1990, 1991, 1992)
layed in NHL All-Star Game (1998, 1999)

raded to **Dallas** by **Los Angeles** with Los Angeles' 5th round choice (Ryan Christie) in 1996 Entry Draft for Shane Churla and Doug Zmolek, February 17, 1996. Traded to **Columbus** by **Dallas** for Mike illinger and Columbus' 2nd round choice (Johan Fransson) in 2004 Entry Draft, July 22, 2003. Traded to **Tampa Bay** by **Columbus** with Columbus' 4th round choice (Mike Lundin) in 2004 Entry Draft for lexander Svitov and Tampa Bay's 3rd round choice (later traded to Calgary – Calgary selected Dustin Boyd) in 2004 Entry Draft, January 27, 2004. Traded to **Dallas** by **Tampa Bay** for Dallas' 4th round hoice (later traded to Ottawa - Ottawa selected Derek Grant) in 2008 Entry Draft, July 2, 2006. Signed as a free agent by **Pittsburgh**, July 2, 2007. Traded to **Dallas** by **Pittsburgh** for Philippe Boucher, lovember 16, 2008. Signed as a free agent by **St. Louis**, September 25, 2009. • Officially announced his retirement, July 13, 2010.

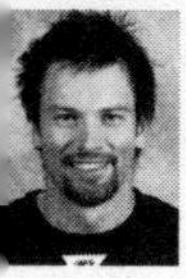

SYKORA, Petr

(sih-KOH-ra, PEE-tuhr)

Right wing. Shoots left. 6', 190 lbs. Born, Plzen, Czech., November 19, 1976. New Jersey's 1st choice, 18th overall, in 1995 Entry Draft.

			Regular Season														Playoffs								
Season	Club	League	GP	G	A	Pts	PIM	PP	SH	GW	S	%	+/-	TF	F%	Min	GP	G	A	Pts	PIM	PP	SH	GW	Min
1991-92	Plzen Jr.	Czech-Jr.	30	50	50	100	....																		
1992-93	HC Skoda Plzen	Czech	19	12	5	17	....																		
1993-94	HC Skoda Plzen	CzRep	37	10	16	26	....										4	0	1	1	....				
	Cleveland	IHL	13	4	5	9	8																		
1994-95	Detroit Vipers	IHL	29	12	17	29	16																		
1995-96	**New Jersey**	**NHL**	**63**	**18**	**24**	**42**	**32**	**8**	**0**	**3**	**128**	**14.1**	**7**												
	Albany River Rats	AHL	5	4	1	5	0																		
1996-97	**New Jersey**	**NHL**	**19**	**1**	**2**	**3**	**4**	**0**	**0**	**0**	**26**	**3.8**	**-8**				**2**	**0**	**0**	**0**	**2**	**0**	**0**	**0**	
	Albany River Rats	AHL	43	20	25	45	48										4	1	4	5	2				
1997-98	**New Jersey**	**NHL**	**58**	**16**	**20**	**36**	**22**	**3**	**1**	**4**	**130**	**12.3**	**0**				**2**	**0**	**0**	**0**	**0**	**0**	**0**	**0**	
	Albany River Rats	AHL	2	4	1	5	0																		
1998-99	**New Jersey**	**NHL**	**80**	**29**	**43**	**72**	**22**	**15**	**0**	**7**	**222**	**13.1**	**16**	**33**	**33.3**	**16:14**	**7**	**3**	**3**	**6**	**4**	**0**	**0**	**1**	**18:11**
99-2000♦	**New Jersey**	**NHL**	**79**	**25**	**43**	**68**	**26**	**5**	**1**	**4**	**222**	**11.3**	**24**	**47**	**61.7**	**17:06**	**23**	**9**	**8**	**17**	**10**	**1**	**0**	**3**	**15:20**
2000-01	**New Jersey**	**NHL**	**73**	**35**	**46**	**81**	**32**	**9**	**2**	**3**	**249**	**14.1**	**36**	**15**	**33.3**	**17:44**	**25**	**10**	**12**	**22**	**12**	**2**	***2**	**2**	**18:40**
2001-02	**New Jersey**	**NHL**	**73**	**21**	**27**	**48**	**44**	**4**	**0**	**4**	**194**	**10.8**	**12**	**1**	**0.0**	**17:51**	**4**	**0**	**1**	**1**	**0**	**0**	**0**	**0**	**17:57**
	Czech Republic	Olympics	4	1	0	1	0																		
2002-03	**Anaheim**	**NHL**	**82**	**34**	**25**	**59**	**24**	**15**	**1**	**5**	**299**	**11.4**	**-7**	**23**	**39.1**	**18:29**	**21**	**4**	**9**	**13**	**12**	**1**	**0**	**2**	**18:39**
2003-04	**Anaheim**	**NHL**	**81**	**23**	**29**	**52**	**34**	**6**	**0**	**2**	**277**	**8.3**	**-9**	**9**	**22.2**	**17:57**									
2004-05	Magnitogorsk	Russia	45	18	13	31	46										5	2	3	5	8				
2005-06	**Anaheim**	**NHL**	**34**	**7**	**13**	**20**	**28**	**1**	**0**	**0**	**118**	**5.9**	**1**	**5**	**40.0**	**17:11**									
	NY Rangers	**NHL**	**40**	**16**	**15**	**31**	**22**	**7**	**0**	**0**	**112**	**14.3**	**5**	**69**	**37.7**	**15:11**	**4**	**0**	**0**	**0**	**0**	**0**	**0**	**0**	**17:45**
2006-07	**Edmonton**	**NHL**	**82**	**22**	**31**	**53**	**40**	**6**	**0**	**6**	**206**	**10.7**	**-20**	**462**	**48.1**	**16:40**									
2007-08	**Pittsburgh**	**NHL**	**81**	**28**	**35**	**63**	**41**	**15**	**0**	**4**	**201**	**13.9**	**1**	**15**	**60.0**	**16:51**	**20**	**6**	**3**	**9**	**16**	**2**	**0**	**1**	**14:57**
2008-09♦	**Pittsburgh**	**NHL**	**76**	**25**	**21**	**46**	**36**	**13**	**0**	**10**	**180**	**13.9**	**3**	**12**	**41.7**	**16:17**	**7**	**0**	**1**	**1**	**0**	**0**	**0**	**0**	**11:55**
2009-10	**Minnesota**	**NHL**	**14**	**2**	**1**	**3**	**8**	**0**	**0**	**0**	**13**	**15.4**	**-7**	**4**	**50.0**	**11:59**									
	NHL Totals		**935**	**302**	**375**	**677**	**415**	**107**	**5**	**52**	**2577**	**11.7**		**695**	**46.0**	**17:02**	**115**	**32**	**37**	**69**	**56**	**6**	**2**	**9**	**16:47**

HL All-Rookie Team (1996)

raded to **Anaheim** by **New Jersey** with Mike Commodore, Jean-Francois Damphousse and Igor Pohanka for Jeff Friesen, Oleg Tverdovsky and Maxim Balmochnykh, July 6, 2002. Signed as a free agent by **lagnitogorsk** (Russia), August 12, 2004. Traded to **NY Rangers** by **Anaheim** with NY Rangers' 4th round choice (previously acquired, later traded to Washington - Washington selected Brett Bruneteau) 2007 Entry Draft for Maxim Kondratiev, January 8, 2006. Signed as a free agent by **Edmonton**, August 11, 2006. Signed as a free agent by **Pittsburgh**, July 2, 2007. Signed as a free agent by **linnesota**, September 17, 2009. • Missed majority of 2009-10 season recovering from concussion suffered in game vs. Dallas, November 7, 2009.

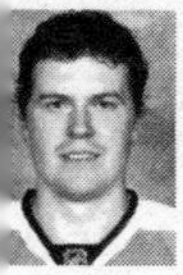

SYVRET, Danny

(SIHV-reht, DA-nee) **ANA.**

Defense. Shoots left. 5'11", 203 lbs. Born, Millgrove, Ont., June 13, 1985. Edmonton's 3rd choice, 81st overall, in 2005 Entry Draft.

			Regular Season														Playoffs								
Season	Club	League	GP	G	A	Pts	PIM	PP	SH	GW	S	%	+/-	TF	F%	Min	GP	G	A	Pts	PIM	PP	SH	GW	Min
2001-02	Cambridge	OHA-B	43	6	41	47	23																		
	London Knights	OHL	1	0	0	0	0																		
2002-03	London Knights	OHL	68	8	14	22	31										14	1	6	7	11				
2003-04	London Knights	OHL	68	3	28	31	32										15	1	6	7	4				
2004-05	London Knights	OHL	62	23	46	69	33										18	5	15	20	4				
2005-06	**Edmonton**	**NHL**	**10**	**0**	**0**	**0**	**6**	**0**	**0**	**0**	**8**	**0.0**	**-1**	**0**	**0.0**	**12:19**									
	Hamilton	AHL	62	0	21	21	38																		
2006-07	**Edmonton**	**NHL**	**16**	**0**	**1**	**1**	**6**	**0**	**0**	**0**	**15**	**0.0**	**-10**	**0**	**0.0**	**18:28**									
	Grand Rapids	AHL	57	4	16	20	16																		
2007-08	Springfield	AHL	36	1	7	8	14																		
	Hershey Bears	AHL	27	1	11	12	29										5	0	0	0	0				
2008-09	**Philadelphia**	**NHL**	**2**	**0**	**0**	**0**	**0**	**0**	**0**	**0**	**0**	**0.0**	**-1**	**0**	**0.0**	**9:26**									
	Philadelphia	AHL	76	12	45	57	44										4	0	1	1	0				
2009-10	**Philadelphia**	**NHL**	**21**	**2**	**2**	**4**	**12**	**0**	**0**	**0**	**14**	**14.3**	**1**	**0**	**0.0**	**12:29**									
	Adirondack	AHL	15	5	8	13	6																		
	NHL Totals		**49**	**2**	**3**	**5**	**24**	**0**	**0**	**0**	**37**	**5.4**		**0**	**0.0**	**14:17**									

HL First All-Star Team (2005) • Canadian Major Junior Defenseman of the Year (2005) • Canadian Major Junior First All-Star Team (2005) • Memorial Cup Tournament All-Star Team (2005) • AHL First ll-Star Team (2009)

raded to **Philadelphia** by **Edmonton** for Ryan Potulny, June 6, 2008. • Missed majority of 2009-10 season recovering from upper body injury and as a healthy reserve. Signed as a free agent by **Anaheim**, ıly 21, 2010.

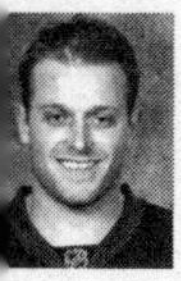

SZCZECHURA, Paul

(sha-HUR-uh, PAWL) **T.B.**

Right wing. Shoots right. 5'11", 190 lbs. Born, Brantford, Ont., November 30, 1985.

			Regular Season														Playoffs								
Season	Club	League	GP	G	A	Pts	PIM	PP	SH	GW	S	%	+/-	TF	F%	Min	GP	G	A	Pts	PIM	PP	SH	GW	Min
2003-04	Western Mich.	CCHA	39	9	11	20	12																		
2004-05	Western Mich.	CCHA	37	6	23	29	22																		
2005-06	Western Mich.	CCHA	40	10	26	36	47																		
2006-07	Western Mich.	CCHA	37	19	26	45	26																		
	Iowa Stars	AHL	14	3	4	7	19										10	3	1	4	8				
2007-08	Iowa Stars	AHL	29	2	3	5	15																		
	Norfolk Admirals	AHL	24	14	12	26	16																		

Season	Club	League	GP	G	A	Pts	PIM	PP	SH	GW	S	%	+/-	TF	F%	Min	GP	G	A	Pts	PIM	PP	SH	GW	M
			Regular Season														Playoffs								
2008-09	**Tampa Bay**	**NHL**	**31**	**4**	**5**	**9**	**12**	**1**	**0**	**0**	**51**	**7.8**	**–1**	**232**	**40.5**	**13:33**	....	....	....	....	....	....	....	....	....
	Norfolk Admirals	AHL	33	13	16	29	26	....	....	....	....	....	....	....	....	....	....	....	....	....	....	....	....	....	....
2009-10	**Tampa Bay**	**NHL**	**52**	**5**	**2**	**7**	**18**	**1**	**0**	**1**	**83**	**6.0**	**–15**	**403**	**46.2**	**13:05**	....	....	....	....	....	....	....	....	....
	Norfolk Admirals	AHL	35	8	21	29	24	....	....	....	....	....	....	....	....	....	....	....	....	....	....	....	....	....	....
	NHL Totals		**83**	**9**	**7**	**16**	**30**	**2**	**0**	**1**	**134**	**6.7**		**635**	**44.1**	**13:16**	....	....	....	....	....	....	....	....	....

Signed as a free agent by **Tampa Bay**, April 24, 2008.

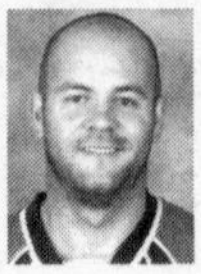

TAFFE, Jeff

(TAYF, JEHF) **CH**

Center. Shoots left. 6'3", 207 lbs. Born, Hastings, MN, February 19, 1981. St. Louis' 1st choice, 30th overall, in 2000 Entry Draft.

Season	Club	League	GP	G	A	Pts	PIM	PP	SH	GW	S	%	+/-	TF	F%	Min	GP	G	A	Pts	PIM	PP	SH	GW	M
1996-97	Hastings Huskies	High-MN	25	21	37	58	....	....	....	....	....	....	....	....	....	....	....	....	....	....	....	....	....	....	....
1997-98	Hastings Huskies	High-MN	28	37	29	66	....	....	....	....	....	....	....	....	....	....	....	....	....	....	....	....	....	....	....
1998-99	Hastings Huskies	High-MN	28	39	51	90	....	....	....	....	....	....	....	....	....	....	....	....	....	....	....	....	....	....	....
	Rochester	USHL	17	12	9	21	26	....	....	....	....	....	....	....	....	....	....	....	....	....	....	....	....	....	....
99-2000	U. of Minnesota	WCHA	39	10	10	20	22	....	....	....	....	....	....	....	....	....	....	....	....	....	....	....	....	....	....
2000-01	U. of Minnesota	WCHA	38	12	23	35	56	....	....	....	....	....	....	....	....	....	....	....	....	....	....	....	....	....	....
2001-02	U. of Minnesota	WCHA	43	34	24	58	86	....	....	....	....	....	....	....	....	....	....	....	....	....	....	....	....	....	....
2002-03	**Phoenix**	**NHL**	**20**	**3**	**1**	**4**	**4**	**1**	**0**	**1**	**18**	**16.7**	**–4**	**113**	**29.2**	**11:34**	....	....	....	....	....	....	....	....	....
	Springfield	AHL	57	23	26	49	44	....	....	....	....	....	....	....	....	....	5	0	3	3	8	....	....	....	....
2003-04	**Phoenix**	**NHL**	**59**	**8**	**10**	**18**	**20**	**5**	**0**	**0**	**67**	**11.9**	**–8**	**219**	**43.4**	**11:02**	....	....	....	....	....	....	....	....	....
	Springfield	AHL	15	10	6	16	19	....	....	....	....	....	....	....	....	....	....	....	....	....	....	....	....	....	....
2004-05	Utah Grizzlies	AHL	27	9	10	19	35	....	....	....	....	....	....	....	....	....	....	....	....	....	....	....	....	....	....
2005-06	**NY Rangers**	**NHL**	**2**	**0**	**0**	**0**	**0**	**0**	**0**	**0**	**1**	**0.0**	**0**	**0**	**0.0**	**3:49**	....	....	....	....	....	....	....	....	....
	Hartford	AHL	36	6	16	22	34	....	....	....	....	....	....	....	....	....	....	....	....	....	....	....	....	....	....
	Phoenix	**NHL**	**2**	**0**	**0**	**0**	**0**	**0**	**0**	**0**	**2**	**0.0**	**0**	**1**	**100.0**	**9:06**	....	....	....	....	....	....	....	....	....
	San Antonio	AHL	33	5	6	11	29	....	....	....	....	....	....	....	....	....	....	....	....	....	....	....	....	....	....
2006-07	**Phoenix**	**NHL**	**17**	**4**	**2**	**6**	**2**	**1**	**0**	**0**	**34**	**11.8**	**–7**	**64**	**39.1**	**14:12**	....	....	....	....	....	....	....	....	....
	San Antonio	AHL	59	20	20	40	22	....	....	....	....	....	....	....	....	....	....	....	....	....	....	....	....	....	....
2007-08	**Pittsburgh**	**NHL**	**45**	**5**	**7**	**12**	**8**	**1**	**0**	**1**	**56**	**8.9**	**2**	**152**	**48.7**	**9:35**	....	....	....	....	....	....	....	....	....
	Wilkes-Barre	AHL	27	11	10	21	22	....	....	....	....	....	....	....	....	....	....	....	....	....	....	....	....	....	....
2008-09	**Pittsburgh**	**NHL**	**8**	**0**	**2**	**2**	**2**	**0**	**0**	**0**	**5**	**0.0**	**–4**	**40**	**52.5**	**8:30**	....	....	....	....	....	....	....	....	....
	Wilkes-Barre	AHL	74	25	50	75	65	....	....	....	....	....	....	....	....	....	12	5	6	11	22	....	....	....	....
2009-10	**Florida**	**NHL**	**21**	**1**	**1**	**2**	**4**	**0**	**0**	**0**	**18**	**5.6**	**–1**	**74**	**44.6**	**8:25**	....	....	....	....	....	....	....	....	....
	Rochester	AHL	61	28	28	56	47	....	....	....	....	....	....	....	....	....	7	1	6	7	9	....	....	....	....
	NHL Totals		**174**	**21**	**23**	**44**	**40**	**8**	**0**	**2**	**201**	**10.4**		**663**	**42.5**	**10:29**	....	....	....	....	....	....	....	....	....

• Rights traded to **Phoenix** by **St. Louis** with Michal Handzus, Ladislav Nagy and St. Louis' 1st round choice (Ben Eager) in 2002 Entry Draft for Keith Tkachuk, March 13, 2001. Traded to **NY Rangers** by **Phoenix** for Jamie Lundmark, October 18, 2005. Traded to **Phoenix** by **NY Rangers** for Martin Sonnenberg, January 24, 2006. Signed as a free agent by **Pittsburgh**, July 13, 2007. Signed as a free agent by **Florida**, July 6, 2009. Traded to **Chicago** by **Florida** for Marty Reasoner, July 22, 2010.

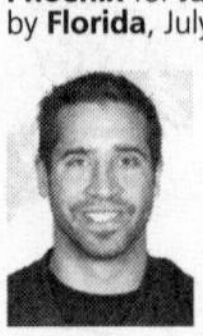

TALBOT, Maxime

(TAL-buht, max-EEM) **PI**

Center. Shoots left. 5'11", 190 lbs. Born, Lemoyne, Que., February 11, 1984. Pittsburgh's 9th choice, 234th overall, in 2002 Entry Draft.

Season	Club	League	GP	G	A	Pts	PIM	PP	SH	GW	S	%	+/-	TF	F%	Min	GP	G	A	Pts	PIM	PP	SH	GW	M
99-2000	Antoine-Girouard	QAAA	42	19	21	40	32	....	....	....	....	....	....	....	....	....	7	3	6	9	0	....	....	....	....
2000-01	Rouyn-Noranda	QMJHL	40	9	15	24	78	....	....	....	....	....	....	....	....	....	....	....	....	....	....	....	....	....	....
	Hull Olympiques	QMJHL	24	6	7	13	60	....	....	....	....	....	....	....	....	....	5	1	0	1	2	....	....	....	....
2001-02	Hull Olympiques	QMJHL	65	24	36	60	174	....	....	....	....	....	....	....	....	....	12	4	6	10	51	....	....	....	....
2002-03	Hull Olympiques	QMJHL	69	46	58	104	130	....	....	....	....	....	....	....	....	....	20	14	*30	*44	33	....	....	....	....
2003-04	Gatineau	QMJHL	51	25	73	98	41	....	....	....	....	....	....	....	....	....	15	*11	*16	*27	0	....	....	....	....
2004-05	Wilkes-Barre	AHL	75	7	12	19	62	....	....	....	....	....	....	....	....	....	11	0	1	1	22	....	....	....	....
2005-06	**Pittsburgh**	**NHL**	**48**	**5**	**3**	**8**	**59**	**0**	**2**	**1**	**45**	**11.1**	**–12**	**473**	**42.9**	**10:58**	....	....	....	....	....	....	....	....	....
	Wilkes-Barre	AHL	42	12	20	32	80	....	....	....	....	....	....	....	....	....	11	3	6	9	16	....	....	....	....
2006-07	**Pittsburgh**	**NHL**	**75**	**13**	**11**	**24**	**53**	**0**	**4**	**4**	**88**	**14.8**	**–2**	**903**	**44.4**	**13:54**	**5**	**0**	**1**	**1**	**7**	**0**	**0**	**0**	**15:5**
	Wilkes-Barre	AHL	5	4	0	4	2	....	....	....	....	....	....	....	....	....	....	....	....	....	....	....	....	....	....
2007-08	**Pittsburgh**	**NHL**	**63**	**12**	**14**	**26**	**53**	**0**	**2**	**1**	**80**	**15.0**	**8**	**513**	**45.0**	**15:28**	**17**	**3**	**6**	**9**	**36**	**0**	**0**	**1**	**14:2**
2008-09♦	**Pittsburgh**	**NHL**	**75**	**12**	**10**	**22**	**63**	**0**	**2**	**1**	**102**	**11.8**	**–9**	**542**	**51.1**	**14:08**	**24**	**8**	**5**	**13**	**19**	**0**	**0**	**2**	**15:1**
2009-10	**Pittsburgh**	**NHL**	**45**	**2**	**5**	**7**	**30**	**0**	**0**	**0**	**49**	**4.1**	**–9**	**165**	**41.2**	**12:13**	**13**	**2**	**4**	**6**	**11**	**0**	**1**	**1**	**14:1**
	NHL Totals		**306**	**44**	**43**	**87**	**258**	**0**	**10**	**7**	**364**	**12.1**		**2596**	**45.5**	**13:34**	**59**	**13**	**16**	**29**	**73**	**0**	**1**	**4**	**14:5**

QMJHL Second All-Star Team (2003, 2004)

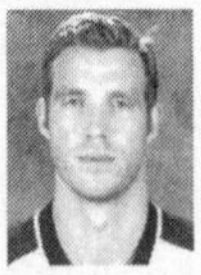

TALLACKSON, Barry

(TAL-ak-suhn, BAIR-ee)

Right wing. Shoots right. 6'5", 215 lbs. Born, Grafton, ND, April 14, 1983. New Jersey's 2nd choice, 53rd overall, in 2002 Entry Draft.

Season	Club	League	GP	G	A	Pts	PIM	PP	SH	GW	S	%	+/-	TF	F%	Min	GP	G	A	Pts	PIM	PP	SH	GW	M
99-2000	USNTDP	NAHL	53	14	6	20	90	....	....	....	....	....	....	....	....	....	3	1	0	1	8	....	....	....	....
2000-01	USNTDP	U-18	40	16	17	33	45	....	....	....	....	....	....	....	....	....	....	....	....	....	....	....	....	....	....
	USNTDP	USHL	23	7	7	14	32	....	....	....	....	....	....	....	....	....	....	....	....	....	....	....	....	....	....
2001-02	U. of Minnesota	WCHA	44	13	10	23	44	....	....	....	....	....	....	....	....	....	....	....	....	....	....	....	....	....	....
2002-03	U. of Minnesota	WCHA	32	9	14	23	18	....	....	....	....	....	....	....	....	....	....	....	....	....	....	....	....	....	....
2003-04	U. of Minnesota	WCHA	44	10	15	25	46	....	....	....	....	....	....	....	....	....	....	....	....	....	....	....	....	....	....
2004-05	U. of Minnesota	WCHA	36	11	8	19	54	....	....	....	....	....	....	....	....	....	....	....	....	....	....	....	....	....	....
	Albany River Rats	AHL	4	1	1	2	0	....	....	....	....	....	....	....	....	....	....	....	....	....	....	....	....	....	....
2005-06	**New Jersey**	**NHL**	**10**	**1**	**1**	**2**	**2**	**0**	**0**	**0**	**11**	**9.1**	**–2**	**2**	**0.0**	**8:04**	....	....	....	....	....	....	....	....	....
	Albany River Rats	AHL	60	14	23	37	62	....	....	....	....	....	....	....	....	....	....	....	....	....	....	....	....	....	....
2006-07	**New Jersey**	**NHL**	**3**	**0**	**0**	**0**	**0**	**0**	**0**	**0**	**3**	**0.0**	**–1**	**0**	**0.0**	**12:06**	....	....	....	....	....	....	....	....	....
	Lowell Devils	AHL	58	10	24	34	33	....	....	....	....	....	....	....	....	....	....	....	....	....	....	....	....	....	....
2007-08	**New Jersey**	**NHL**	**3**	**0**	**0**	**0**	**0**	**0**	**0**	**0**	**0**	**0.0**	**0**	**0**	**0.0**	**7:03**	....	....	....	....	....	....	....	....	....
	Lowell Devils	AHL	63	22	23	45	54	....	....	....	....	....	....	....	....	....	....	....	....	....	....	....	....	....	....
2008-09	**New Jersey**	**NHL**	**4**	**0**	**0**	**0**	**0**	**0**	**0**	**0**	**2**	**0.0**	**–1**	**1**	**0.0**	**4:29**	....	....	....	....	....	....	....	....	....
	Lowell Devils	AHL	56	11	10	21	29	....	....	....	....	....	....	....	....	....	....	....	....	....	....	....	....	....	....
2009-10	Peoria Rivermen	AHL	74	19	8	27	34	....	....	....	....	....	....	....	....	....	....	....	....	....	....	....	....	....	....
	NHL Totals		**20**	**1**	**1**	**2**	**2**	**0**	**0**	**0**	**16**	**6.3**		**3**	**0.0**	**7:48**									

Signed as a free agent by **St. Louis**, July 23, 2009. Signed as a free agent by **Augsburg** (Germany), July 17, 2010.

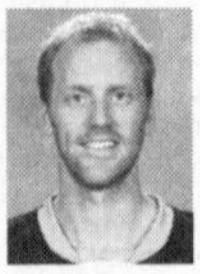

TALLINDER, Henrik

(tah-LIHN-duhr, HEHN-rihk) **N.**

Defense. Shoots left. 6'3", 215 lbs. Born, Stockholm, Sweden, January 10, 1979. Buffalo's 2nd choice, 48th overall, in 1997 Entry Draft.

Season	Club	League	GP	G	A	Pts	PIM	PP	SH	GW	S	%	+/-	TF	F%	Min	GP	G	A	Pts	PIM	PP	SH	GW	M
1996-97	AIK Solna Jr.	Swe-Jr.	40	4	13	17	55	....	....	....	....	....	....	....	....	....	....	....	....	....	....	....	....	....	....
	AIK Solna	Sweden	1	0	0	0	0	....	....	....	....	....	....	....	....	....	....	....	....	....	....	....	....	....	....
1997-98	AIK Solna	Sweden	34	0	0	0	26	....	....	....	....	....	....	....	....	....	....	....	....	....	....	....	....	....	....
1998-99	AIK Solna	Sweden	36	0	0	0	30	....	....	....	....	....	....	....	....	....	....	....	....	....	....	....	....	....	....
99-2000	AIK Solna	Sweden	50	0	2	2	59	....	....	....	....	....	....	....	....	....	....	....	....	....	....	....	....	....	....
2000-01	TPS Turku	Finland	56	5	9	14	62	....	....	....	....	....	....	....	....	....	10	2	1	3	8	....	....	....	....
2001-02	**Buffalo**	**NHL**	**2**	**0**	**0**	**0**	**0**	**0**	**0**	**0**	**4**	**0.0**	**–1**	**0**	**0.0**	**18:10**	....	....	....	....	....	....	....	....	....
	Rochester	AHL	73	6	14	20	26	....	....	....	....	....	....	....	....	....	2	0	0	0	0	....	....	....	....
2002-03	**Buffalo**	**NHL**	**46**	**3**	**10**	**13**	**28**	**1**	**0**	**0**	**37**	**8.1**	**–3**	**0**	**0.0**	**19:53**	....	....	....	....	....	....	....	....	....
2003-04	**Buffalo**	**NHL**	**72**	**1**	**9**	**10**	**26**	**0**	**0**	**0**	**63**	**1.6**	**5**	**1**	**0.0**	**18:23**	....	....	....	....	....	....	....	....	....
2004-05	Linkopings HC	Sweden	44	6	10	16	63	....	....	....	....	....	....	....	....	....	....	....	....	....	....	....	....	....	....
	SC Bern	Swiss															10	1	1	2	4	....	....	....	....
2005-06	**Buffalo**	**NHL**	**82**	**6**	**15**	**21**	**74**	**0**	**1**	**1**	**79**	**7.6**	**10**	**0**	**0.0**	**20:21**	**14**	**2**	**6**	**8**	**16**	**0**	**0**	**0**	**22:**
2006-07	**Buffalo**	**NHL**	**47**	**4**	**10**	**14**	**34**	**0**	**0**	**0**	**34**	**11.8**	**19**	**1**	**0.0**	**21:07**	**16**	**0**	**2**	**2**	**10**	**0**	**0**	**0**	**23:**
2007-08	**Buffalo**	**NHL**	**71**	**1**	**17**	**18**	**48**	**0**	**0**	**0**	**70**	**1.4**	**5**	**0**	**0.0**	**21:02**	....	....	....	....	....	....	....	....	....
2008-09	**Buffalo**	**NHL**	**66**	**1**	**11**	**12**	**36**	**0**	**0**	**1**	**35**	**2.9**	**–2**	**0**	**0.0**	**18:26**	....	....	....	....	....	....	....	....	....
2009-10	**Buffalo**	**NHL**	**82**	**4**	**16**	**20**	**32**	**0**	**0**	**0**	**53**	**7.5**	**13**	**0**	**0.0**	**20:37**	**6**	**0**	**2**	**2**	**2**	**0**	**0**	**0**	**22:**
	Sweden	Olympics	4	0	0	0	4	....	....	....	....	....	....	....	....	....	....	....	....	....	....	....	....	....	....
	NHL Totals		**468**	**20**	**88**	**108**	**278**	**1**	**1**	**2**	**375**	**5.3**		**2**	**0.0**	**19:57**	**36**	**2**	**10**	**12**	**28**	**0**	**0**	**0**	**22:5**

Signed as a free agent by **Linkopings** (Sweden), September 9, 2004. Signed as a free agent by **Bern** (Swiss), February 22, 2005. Signed as a free agent by **New Jersey**, July 1, 2010.

			Regular Season														Playoffs								
Season	Club	League	GP	G	A	Pts	PIM	PP	SH	GW	S	%	+/-	TF	F%	Min	GP	G	A	Pts	PIM	PP	SH	GW	Min

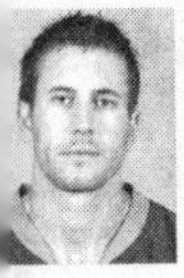

TAMBELLINI, Jeff (tam-buh-LEE-nee, JEHF) **VAN.**

Left wing. Shoots left. 5'11", 186 lbs. Born, Calgary, Alta., April 13, 1984. Los Angeles' 3rd choice, 27th overall, in 2003 Entry Draft.

Season	Club	League	GP	G	A	Pts	PIM	PP	SH	GW	S	%	+/-	TF	F%	Min	GP	G	A	Pts	PIM	PP	SH	GW	Min
99-2000	Port Coquitlam	PIJHL	41	30	34	64	....	....	....	....	....	....	....	....	....	....	....	....	....	....	....	....	....	....	....
2000-01	Chilliwack Chiefs	BCHL	54	21	30	51	13	....	....	....	....	....	....	....	....	....	....	....	....	....	....	....	....	....	....
2001-02	Chilliwack Chiefs	BCHL	34	46	71	117	23	....	....	....	....	....	....	....	....	....	29	27	27	54	....	....	....	....	....
2002-03	U. of Michigan	CCHA	43	26	19	45	24	....	....	....	....	....	....	....	....	....	....	....	....	....	....	....	....	....	....
2003-04	U. of Michigan	CCHA	39	15	12	27	18	....	....	....	....	....	....	....	....	....	....	....	....	....	....	....	....	....	....
2004-05	U. of Michigan	CCHA	42	*24	33	*57	32	....	....	....	....	....	....	....	....	....	....	....	....	....	....	....	....	....	....
2005-06	**Los Angeles**	**NHL**	**4**	**0**	**0**	**0**	**2**	**0**	**0**	**0**	**6**	**0.0**	**-1**	**1**	**0.0**	**9:23**	....	....	....	....	....	....	....	....	....
	Manchester	AHL	56	25	31	56	26	....	....	....	....	....	....	....	....	....	....	....	....	....	....	....	....	....	....
	NY Islanders	**NHL**	**21**	**1**	**3**	**4**	**8**	**0**	**0**	**0**	**11**	**9.1**	**2**	**3**	**33.3**	**9:54**	....	....	....	....	....	....	....	....	....
	Bridgeport	AHL	....	....	....	....	....	....	....	....	....	....	....	....	....	....	7	1	2	3	2	....	....	....	....
2006-07	**NY Islanders**	**NHL**	**23**	**2**	**7**	**9**	**6**	**0**	**0**	**0**	**20**	**10.0**	**6**	**1**	**0.0**	**7:14**	....	....	....	....	....	....	....	....	....
	Bridgeport	AHL	50	30	29	59	46	....	....	....	....	....	....	....	....	....	....	....	....	....	....	....	....	....	....
2007-08	**NY Islanders**	**NHL**	**31**	**1**	**3**	**4**	**8**	**0**	**0**	**0**	**43**	**2.3**	**-9**	**0**	**0.0**	**10:25**	....	....	....	....	....	....	....	....	....
	Bridgeport	AHL	57	38	38	76	38	....	....	....	....	....	....	....	....	....	....	....	....	....	....	....	....	....	....
2008-09	**NY Islanders**	**NHL**	**65**	**7**	**8**	**15**	**32**	**0**	**0**	**0**	**98**	**7.1**	**-20**	**5**	**60.0**	**13:07**	....	....	....	....	....	....	....	....	....
	Bridgeport	AHL	6	3	0	3	2	....	....	....	....	....	....	....	....	....	....	....	....	....	....	....	....	....	....
2009-10	**NY Islanders**	**NHL**	**36**	**7**	**7**	**14**	**14**	**3**	**0**	**0**	**55**	**12.7**	**-8**	**4**	**0.0**	**11:28**	....	....	....	....	....	....	....	....	....
	NHL Totals		**180**	**18**	**28**	**46**	**70**	**3**	**0**	**0**	**233**	**7.7**		**14**	**28.6**	**11:07**	....	....	....	....	....	....	....	....	....

CCHA All-Rookie Team (2003) • CCHA Second All-Star Team (2003) • CCHA Rookie of the Year (2003) • CCHA First All-Star Team (2005) • NCAA West Second All-American Team (2005)

Traded to **NY Islanders** by **Los Angeles** with Denis Grebeshkov for Mark Parrish and Brent Sopel, March 8, 2006. • Missed majority of 2009-10 season as a healthy reserve. Signed as a free agent by **Vancouver**, July 1, 2010.

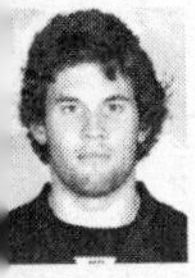

TANGRADI, Eric (tan-GRAY-dee, AIR-ihk) **PIT.**

Center. Shoots left. 6'4", 221 lbs. Born, Philadelphia, PA, February 10, 1989. Anaheim's 2nd choice, 42nd overall, in 2007 Entry Draft.

Season	Club	League	GP	G	A	Pts	PIM	PP	SH	GW	S	%	+/-	TF	F%	Min	GP	G	A	Pts	PIM	PP	SH	GW	Min
2005-06	Wyoming Prep	High-PA	38	21	23	44	120	....	....	....	....	....	....	....	....	....	....	....	....	....	....	....	....	....	....
2006-07	Belleville Bulls	OHL	65	5	15	20	32	....	....	....	....	....	....	....	....	....	15	8	9	17	14	....	....	....	....
2007-08	Belleville Bulls	OHL	56	24	36	60	41	....	....	....	....	....	....	....	....	....	21	7	11	18	20	....	....	....	....
2008-09	Belleville Bulls	OHL	55	38	50	88	61	....	....	....	....	....	....	....	....	....	16	8	13	21	12	....	....	....	....
2009-10	**Pittsburgh**	**NHL**	**1**	**0**	**0**	**0**	**0**	**0**	**0**	**0**	**3**	**0.0**	**0**	**0**	**0.0**	**13:49**	....	....	....	....	....	....	....	....	....
	Wilkes-Barre	AHL	65	17	22	39	31	....	....	....	....	....	....	....	....	....	4	1	1	2	6	....	....	....	....
	NHL Totals		**1**	**0**	**0**	**0**	**0**	**0**	**0**	**0**	**3**	**0.0**		**0**	**0.0**	**13:49**	....	....	....	....	....	....	....	....	....

Traded to **Pittsburgh** by **Anaheim** with Chris Kunitz for Ryan Whitney, February 26, 2009.

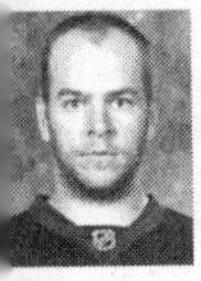

TANGUAY, Alex (TAHNG-ay, AL-ehx) **CGY.**

Left wing. Shoots left. 6'1", 192 lbs. Born, Ste-Justine, Que., November 21, 1979. Colorado's 1st choice, 12th overall, in 1998 Entry Draft.

Season	Club	League	GP	G	A	Pts	PIM	PP	SH	GW	S	%	+/-	TF	F%	Min	GP	G	A	Pts	PIM	PP	SH	GW	Min
1994-95	Cap-d-Madeleine	QAAA	1	0	1	1	0	....	....	....	....	....	....	....	....	....	....	....	....	....	....	....	....	....	....
1995-96	Cap-d-Madeleine	QAAA	44	29	34	63	64	....	....	....	....	....	....	....	....	....	5	2	4	6	14	....	....	....	....
1996-97	Halifax	QMJHL	70	27	41	68	60	....	....	....	....	....	....	....	....	....	12	5	8	13	8	....	....	....	....
1997-98	Halifax	QMJHL	51	47	38	85	32	....	....	....	....	....	....	....	....	....	5	7	6	13	4	....	....	....	....
1998-99	Halifax	QMJHL	31	27	34	61	30	....	....	....	....	....	....	....	....	....	5	1	2	3	2	....	....	....	....
	Hershey Bears	AHL	5	1	2	3	2	....	....	....	....	....	....	....	....	....	5	0	2	2	0	....	....	....	....
99-2000	**Colorado**	**NHL**	**76**	**17**	**34**	**51**	**22**	**5**	**0**	**3**	**74**	**23.0**	**6**	**11**	**45.5**	**15:38**	**17**	**2**	**1**	**3**	**2**	**1**	**0**	**1**	**10:49**
2000-01 ♦	**Colorado**	**NHL**	**82**	**27**	**50**	**77**	**37**	**7**	**1**	**3**	**135**	**20.0**	**35**	**30**	**43.3**	**17:51**	**23**	**6**	**15**	**21**	**8**	**1**	**0**	**2**	**19:18**
2001-02	**Colorado**	**NHL**	**70**	**13**	**35**	**48**	**36**	**7**	**0**	**2**	**90**	**14.4**	**8**	**37**	**40.5**	**18:20**	**19**	**5**	**8**	**13**	**0**	**3**	**0**	**0**	**17:25**
2002-03	**Colorado**	**NHL**	**82**	**26**	**41**	**67**	**36**	**3**	**0**	**5**	**142**	**18.3**	**34**	**123**	**39.0**	**17:48**	**7**	**1**	**2**	**3**	**4**	**0**	**0**	**1**	**19:06**
2003-04	**Colorado**	**NHL**	**69**	**25**	**54**	**79**	**42**	**7**	**0**	**5**	**117**	**21.4**	**30**	**71**	**40.9**	**18:21**	**8**	**2**	**2**	**4**	**2**	**1**	**0**	**1**	**15:46**
2004-05	HC Lugano	Swiss	6	3	3	6	4	....	....	....	....	....	....	....	....	....	....	....	....	....	....	....	....	....	....
2005-06	**Colorado**	**NHL**	**71**	**29**	**49**	**78**	**46**	**8**	**0**	**4**	**125**	**23.2**	**8**	**20**	**30.0**	**18:22**	**9**	**2**	**4**	**6**	**12**	**0**	**0**	**1**	**18:20**
2006-07	**Calgary**	**NHL**	**81**	**22**	**59**	**81**	**44**	**5**	**0**	**0**	**107**	**20.6**	**12**	**24**	**25.0**	**17:40**	**6**	**1**	**3**	**4**	**8**	**1**	**0**	**0**	**17:56**
2007-08	**Calgary**	**NHL**	**78**	**18**	**40**	**58**	**48**	**3**	**2**	**3**	**121**	**14.9**	**11**	**20**	**35.0**	**18:46**	**7**	**0**	**4**	**4**	**4**	**0**	**0**	**0**	**18:15**
2008-09	**Montreal**	**NHL**	**50**	**16**	**25**	**41**	**34**	**5**	**0**	**3**	**76**	**21.1**	**13**	**9**	**33.3**	**16:05**	**2**	**0**	**1**	**1**	**2**	**0**	**0**	**0**	**15:29**
2009-10	**Tampa Bay**	**NHL**	**80**	**10**	**27**	**37**	**32**	**3**	**0**	**2**	**91**	**11.0**	**-2**	**25**	**44.0**	**15:47**	....	....	....	....	....	....	....	....	....
	NHL Totals		**739**	**203**	**414**	**617**	**377**	**53**	**3**	**30**	**1078**	**18.8**		**370**	**38.6**	**17:30**	**98**	**19**	**40**	**59**	**42**	**7**	**0**	**6**	**16:50**

QMJHL All-Rookie Team (1997)

Played in NHL All-Star Game (2004)

Signed as a free agent by **Lugano** (Swiss), October 7, 2004. Traded to **Calgary** by **Colorado** for Jordan Leopold, Calgary's 2nd round choice (Codey Burki) in 2006 Entry Draft and Calgary's 2nd round choice (Trevor Cann) in 2007 Entry Draft, June 24, 2006. Traded to **Montreal** by **Calgary** with Calgary's 5th round choice (Maxim Trunev) in 2008 Entry Draft for Montreal's 1st round choice (Greg Nemisz) in 2008 Entry Draft and Montreal's 2nd round choice (later traded to Colorado – Colorado selected Stefan Elliott) in 2009 Entry Draft, June 20, 2008. Signed as a free agent by **Tampa Bay**, September 1, 2009. Signed as a free agent by **Calgary**, July 1, 2010.

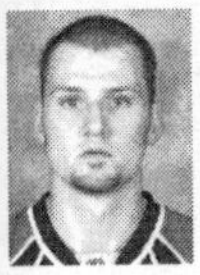

TARNASKY, Nick (tahr-NAS-kee, NIHK)

Center. Shoots left. 6'2", 224 lbs. Born, Rocky Mtn. House, Alta., November 25, 1984. Tampa Bay's 11th choice, 287th overall, in 2003 Entry Draft.

Season	Club	League	GP	G	A	Pts	PIM	PP	SH	GW	S	%	+/-	TF	F%	Min	GP	G	A	Pts	PIM	PP	SH	GW	Min
99-2000	Leduc Oil Kings	AMBHL	36	21	11	32	59	....	....	....	....	....	....	....	....	....	....	....	....	....	....	....	....	....	....
2000-01	Leduc Oil Kings	AMHL	35	39	29	68	95	....	....	....	....	....	....	....	....	....	....	....	....	....	....	....	....	....	....
2001-02	Drayton Valley	AJHL	20	7	4	11	10	....	....	....	....	....	....	....	....	....	....	....	....	....	....	....	....	....	....
	Vancouver Giants	WHL	10	1	0	1	5	....	....	....	....	....	....	....	....	....	....	....	....	....	....	....	....	....	....
2002-03	Kelowna Rockets	WHL	39	4	12	16	39	....	....	....	....	....	....	....	....	....	....	....	....	....	....	....	....	....	....
	Lethbridge	WHL	30	5	8	13	45	....	....	....	....	....	....	....	....	....	....	....	....	....	....	....	....	....	....
2003-04	Lethbridge	WHL	71	26	23	49	108	....	....	....	....	....	....	....	....	....	....	....	....	....	....	....	....	....	....
2004-05	Springfield	AHL	80	7	10	17	176	....	....	....	....	....	....	....	....	....	....	....	....	....	....	....	....	....	....
2005-06	**Tampa Bay**	**NHL**	**12**	**0**	**1**	**1**	**4**	**0**	**0**	**0**	**9**	**0.0**	**-3**	**15**	**40.0**	**4:40**	....	....	....	....	....	....	....	....	....
	Springfield	AHL	68	14	9	23	100	....	....	....	....	....	....	....	....	....	....	....	....	....	....	....	....	....	....
2006-07	**Tampa Bay**	**NHL**	**77**	**5**	**4**	**9**	**80**	**0**	**0**	**1**	**41**	**12.2**	**-6**	**13**	**30.8**	**6:30**	**6**	**0**	**0**	**0**	**10**	**0**	**0**	**0**	**6:13**
2007-08	**Tampa Bay**	**NHL**	**80**	**6**	**4**	**10**	**78**	**1**	**0**	**1**	**91**	**6.6**	**-15**	**9**	**44.4**	**8:15**	....	....	....	....	....	....	....	....	....
2008-09	**Nashville**	**NHL**	**11**	**0**	**1**	**1**	**17**	**0**	**0**	**0**	**6**	**0.0**	**1**	**0**	**0.0**	**5:38**	....	....	....	....	....	....	....	....	....
	Florida	**NHL**	**34**	**1**	**5**	**6**	**33**	**0**	**0**	**0**	**32**	**3.1**	**-2**	**1**	**0.0**	**7:52**	....	....	....	....	....	....	....	....	....
2009-10	**Florida**	**NHL**	**31**	**1**	**2**	**3**	**85**	**0**	**0**	**0**	**19**	**5.3**	**-5**	**0**	**0.0**	**6:49**	....	....	....	....	....	....	....	....	....
	Rochester	AHL	5	3	0	3	7	....	....	....	....	....	....	....	....	....	....	....	....	....	....	....	....	....	....
	NHL Totals		**245**	**13**	**17**	**30**	**297**	**1**	**0**	**2**	**198**	**6.6**		**38**	**36.8**	**7:10**	**6**	**0**	**0**	**0**	**10**	**0**	**0**	**0**	**6:13**

Traded to **Nashville** by **Tampa Bay** for Nashville's 6th round choice (Jaroslav Janus) in 2009 Entry Draft, September 29, 2008. Traded to **Florida** by **Nashville** for Wade Belak, November 27, 2008. • Missed majority of 2009-10 season recovering from eye injury suffered in pre-season game at Ottawa, September 16, 2009.

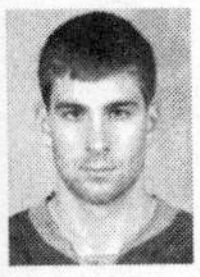

TAVARES, John (tah-VAHR-ehs, JAWN) **NYI**

Left wing. Shoots left. 6', 195 lbs. Born, Mississauga, Ont., September 20, 1990. NY Islanders' 1st choice, 1st overall, in 2009 Entry Draft.

Season	Club	League	GP	G	A	Pts	PIM	PP	SH	GW	S	%	+/-	TF	F%	Min	GP	G	A	Pts	PIM	PP	SH	GW	Min
2004-05	Tor. Marlboros	GTHL	72	91	67	158	....	....	....	....	....	....	....	....	....	....	....	....	....	....	....	....	....	....	....
	Milton Icehawks	OPJHL	20	13	15	28	10	....	....	....	....	....	....	....	....	....	....	....	....	....	....	....	....	....	....
2005-06	Oshawa Generals	OHL	65	45	32	77	72	....	....	....	....	....	....	....	....	....	9	7	12	19	6	....	....	....	....
2006-07	Oshawa Generals	OHL	67	*72	62	134	60	....	....	....	....	....	....	....	....	....	15	3	13	16	20	....	....	....	....
2007-08	Oshawa Generals	OHL	59	40	78	118	69	....	....	....	....	....	....	....	....	....	....	....	....	....	....	....	....	....	....
2008-09	Oshawa Generals	OHL	32	*26	28	*54	32	....	....	....	....	....	....	....	....	....	....	....	....	....	....	....	....	....	....
	London Knights	OHL	24	*32	18	*50	22	....	....	....	....	....	....	....	....	....	14	10	11	21	8	....	....	....	....
2009-10	**NY Islanders**	**NHL**	**82**	**24**	**30**	**54**	**22**	**11**	**0**	**2**	**186**	**12.9**	**-15**	**1129**	**47.5**	**18:00**	....	....	....	....	....	....	....	....	....
	NHL Totals		**82**	**24**	**30**	**54**	**22**	**11**	**0**	**2**	**186**	**12.9**		**1129**	**47.5**	**18:00**	....	....	....	....	....	....	....	....	....

OHL All-Rookie Team (2006) • Canadian Major Junior Rookie of the Year (2006) • OHL First All-Star Team (2007) • Canadian Major Junior First All-Star Team (2007, 2009) • Canadian Major Junior Player of the Year (2007) • OHL Second All-Star Team (2009) • NHL All-Rookie Team (2010)

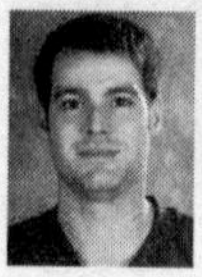

THOMAS, Bill

(TAW-mas, BIHL) **FLA.**

Right wing. Shoots right. 6'1", 191 lbs. Born, Pittsburgh, PA, June 20, 1983.

			Regular Season													Playoffs								
Season	Club	League	GP	G	A	Pts	PIM	PP	SH	GW	S	%	+/-	TF	F%	Min	GP	G	A	Pts	PIM	PP	SH	GW	Min
2002-03	Tri-City Storm	USHL	60	29	21	50	20	....	....	....	....	....	....	....	....	....	3	0	3	3	4	....	....	....	....
2003-04	Tri-City Storm	USHL	60	31	38	69	30	....	....	....	....	....	....	....	....	....	11	*9	7	*16	4	....	....	....	....
2004-05	Nebraska-Omaha	CCHA	39	19	26	45	12	....	....	....	....	....	....	....	....	....	....	....	....	....	....	....	....	....	....
2005-06	Nebraska-Omaha	CCHA	41	*27	23	50	43	....	....	....	....	....	....	....	....	....	....	....	....	....	....	....	....	....	....
	Phoenix	**NHL**	**9**	**1**	**2**	**3**	**8**	**1**	**0**	**0**	**15**	**6.7**	**–2**	**2**	**50.0**	**13:30**	....	....	....	....	....	....	....	....	....
2006-07	**Phoenix**	**NHL**	**24**	**8**	**6**	**14**	**2**	**4**	**0**	**1**	**60**	**13.3**	**–6**	**0**	**0.0**	**13:29**	....	....	....	....	....	....	....	....	....
	San Antonio	AHL	47	13	20	33	20	....	....	....	....	....	....	....	....	....	....	....	....	....	....	....	....	....	....
2007-08	**Phoenix**	**NHL**	**7**	**0**	**0**	**0**	**0**	**0**	**0**	**0**	**9**	**0.0**	**–2**	**0**	**0.0**	**13:08**	....	....	....	....	....	....	....	....	....
	San Antonio	AHL	75	24	28	52	40	....	....	....	....	....	....	....	....	....	7	1	2	3	0	....	....	....	....
2008-09	**Pittsburgh**	**NHL**	**16**	**2**	**1**	**3**	**2**	**0**	**1**	**0**	**17**	**11.8**	**–4**	**101**	**51.5**	**9:31**	....	....	....	....	....	....	....	....	....
	Wilkes-Barre	AHL	39	8	10	18	24	....	....	....	....	....	....	....	....	....	12	1	4	5	12	....	....	....	....
2009-10	Springfield	AHL	33	5	12	17	14	....	....	....	....	....	....	....	....	....	....	....	....	....	....	....	....	....	....
	HC Lugano	Swiss	6	2	1	3	2	....	....	....	....	....	....	....	....	....	2	0	0	0	0	....	....	....	....
	NHL Totals		**56**	**11**	**9**	**20**	**12**	**5**	**1**	**1**	**101**	**10.9**		**103**	**51.5**	**12:19**	....	....	....	....	....	....	....	....	....

CCHA All-Rookie Team (2005) • CCHA Rookie of the Year (2005) • CCHA Second All-Star Team (2005) • CCHA First All-Star Team (2006)

Signed as a free agent by **Phoenix**. March 27, 2006. Signed as a free agent by **Pittsburgh**. July 15, 2008. Signed to a PTO (professional tryout) contract by **Springfield** (AHL), November 3, 2009. Signed as a free agent by **Lugano** (Swiss), January 12, 2010. Signed as a free agent by **Florida**, July 2, 2010.

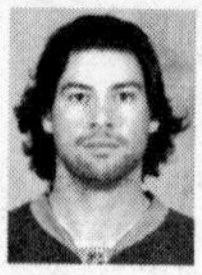

THOMPSON, Nate

(TAWM-suhn, NAYT) **T.B.**

Center. Shoots left. 6', 207 lbs. Born, Anchorage, AK, October 5, 1984. Boston's 8th choice, 183rd overall, in 2003 Entry Draft.

Season	Club	League	GP	G	A	Pts	PIM	PP	SH	GW	S	%	+/-	TF	F%	Min	GP	G	A	Pts	PIM	PP	SH	GW	Min
2001-02	Seattle	WHL	69	13	26	39	42	....	....	....	....	....	....	....	....	....	11	1	3	4	13	....	....	....	....
2002-03	Seattle	WHL	61	10	24	34	48	....	....	....	....	....	....	....	....	....	15	5	4	9	6	....	....	....	....
2003-04	Seattle	WHL	65	13	23	36	24	....	....	....	....	....	....	....	....	....	....	....	....	....	....	....	....	....	....
2004-05	Seattle	WHL	58	19	15	34	39	....	....	....	....	....	....	....	....	....	12	1	2	3	2	....	....	....	....
	Providence Bruins	AHL	....	....	....	....	....	....	....	....	....	....	....	....	....	....	11	0	1	1	6	....	....	....	....
2005-06	Providence Bruins	AHL	74	8	10	18	58	....	....	....	....	....	....	....	....	....	3	0	0	0	10	....	....	....	....
2006-07	**Boston**	**NHL**	**4**	**0**	**0**	**0**	**0**	**0**	**0**	**0**	**5**	**0.0**	**0**	**10**	**40.0**	**4:46**	....	....	....	....	....	....	....	....	....
	Providence Bruins	AHL	67	8	15	23	74	....	....	....	....	....	....	....	....	....	13	0	2	2	9	....	....	....	....
2007-08	Providence Bruins	AHL	75	19	20	39	83	....	....	....	....	....	....	....	....	....	10	2	3	5	4	....	....	....	....
2008-09	**NY Islanders**	**NHL**	**43**	**2**	**2**	**4**	**49**	**0**	**1**	**0**	**56**	**3.6**	**–11**	**429**	**50.4**	**12:05**	....	....	....	....	....	....	....	....	....
2009-10	**NY Islanders**	**NHL**	**39**	**1**	**5**	**6**	**39**	**0**	**0**	**0**	**48**	**2.1**	**–14**	**210**	**49.5**	**12:56**	....	....	....	....	....	....	....	....	....
	Tampa Bay	**NHL**	**32**	**1**	**3**	**4**	**17**	**0**	**0**	**0**	**44**	**2.3**	**–3**	**385**	**56.9**	**13:58**	....	....	....	....	....	....	....	....	....
	NHL Totals		**118**	**4**	**10**	**14**	**105**	**0**	**1**	**0**	**153**	**2.6**		**1034**	**52.5**	**12:38**	....	....	....	....	....	....	....	....	....

Claimed on waivers by **NY Islanders** from **Boston**, October 8, 2008. Claimed on waivers by **Tampa Bay** from **NY Islanders**, January 21, 2010.

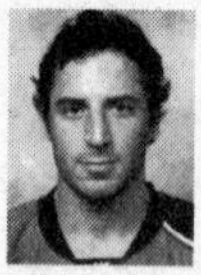

THORBURN, Chris

(THOHR-buhrn, KRIHS) **ATL.**

Right wing. Shoots right. 6'3", 230 lbs. Born, Sault Ste. Marie, Ont., June 3, 1983. Buffalo's 3rd choice, 50th overall, in 2001 Entry Draft.

Season	Club	League	GP	G	A	Pts	PIM	PP	SH	GW	S	%	+/-	TF	F%	Min	GP	G	A	Pts	PIM	PP	SH	GW	Min
1998-99	Elliot Lake Vikings	NOJHA	40	21	12	33	28	....	....	....	....	....	....	....	....	....	....	....	....	....	....	....	....	....	....
99-2000	North Bay	OHL	56	12	8	20	33	....	....	....	....	....	....	....	....	....	6	0	2	2	0	....	....	....	....
2000-01	North Bay	OHL	66	22	32	54	64	....	....	....	....	....	....	....	....	....	4	0	1	1	9	....	....	....	....
2001-02	North Bay	OHL	67	15	43	58	112	....	....	....	....	....	....	....	....	....	5	1	2	3	8	....	....	....	....
2002-03	Saginaw Spirit	OHL	37	19	19	38	68	....	....	....	....	....	....	....	....	....	....	....	....	....	....	....	....	....	....
	Plymouth Whalers	OHL	27	11	22	33	56	....	....	....	....	....	....	....	....	....	18	11	9	20	10	....	....	....	....
2003-04	Rochester	AHL	58	6	16	22	77	....	....	....	....	....	....	....	....	....	16	3	2	5	18	....	....	....	....
2004-05	Rochester	AHL	73	12	17	29	185	....	....	....	....	....	....	....	....	....	4	0	1	1	2	....	....	....	....
2005-06	**Buffalo**	**NHL**	**2**	**0**	**1**	**1**	**7**	**0**	**0**	**0**	**1**	**0.0**	**–1**	**1**	**0.0**	**6:52**	....	....	....	....	....	....	....	....	....
	Rochester	AHL	77	23	27	50	134	....	....	....	....	....	....	....	....	....	....	....	....	....	....	....	....	....	....
2006-07	**Pittsburgh**	**NHL**	**39**	**3**	**2**	**5**	**69**	**0**	**0**	**1**	**40**	**7.5**	**1**	**8**	**25.0**	**7:54**	....	....	....	....	....	....	....	....	....
	Wilkes-Barre	AHL	3	0	1	1	2	....	....	....	....	....	....	....	....	....	....	....	....	....	....	....	....	....	....
2007-08	**Atlanta**	**NHL**	**73**	**5**	**13**	**18**	**92**	**0**	**0**	**1**	**72**	**6.9**	**–4**	**20**	**60.0**	**8:56**	....	....	....	....	....	....	....	....	....
2008-09	**Atlanta**	**NHL**	**82**	**7**	**8**	**15**	**104**	**0**	**0**	**1**	**85**	**8.2**	**–10**	**37**	**40.5**	**9:35**	....	....	....	....	....	....	....	....	....
2009-10	**Atlanta**	**NHL**	**76**	**4**	**9**	**13**	**89**	**0**	**3**	**0**	**63**	**6.3**	**6**	**29**	**55.2**	**9:59**	....	....	....	....	....	....	....	....	....
	NHL Totals		**272**	**19**	**33**	**52**	**361**	**0**	**3**	**3**	**261**	**7.3**		**95**	**47.4**	**9:16**	....	....	....	....	....	....	....	....	....

Claimed on waivers by **Pittsburgh** from **Buffalo**, October 3, 2006. Traded to **Atlanta** by **Pittsburgh** for NY Rangers' 3rd round choice (previously acquired, Pittsburgh selected Robert Bortuzzo) in 2007 Entry Draft, June 22, 2007.

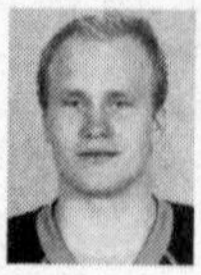

THORESEN, Patrick

(THOR-eh-sehn, PAT-rihk) **PHI.**

Center. Shoots left. 5'11", 188 lbs. Born, Oslo, Norway, November 7, 1983.

Season	Club	League	GP	G	A	Pts	PIM	PP	SH	GW	S	%	+/-	TF	F%	Min	GP	G	A	Pts	PIM	PP	SH	GW	Min
99-2000	Storhamar	Norway	25	1	8	9	4	....	....	....	....	....	....	....	....	....	....	....	....	....	....	....	....	....	....
	Norway	WJ18-B	5	3	2	5	6	....	....	....	....	....	....	....	....	....	....	....	....	....	....	....	....	....	....
2000-01	Storhamar	Norway	40	18	27	45	24	....	....	....	....	....	....	....	....	....	....	....	....	....	....	....	....	....	....
2001-02	Moncton Wildcats	QMJHL	60	30	43	73	50	....	....	....	....	....	....	....	....	....	....	....	....	....	....	....	....	....	....
2002-03	Baie-Comeau	QMJHL	71	33	*75	108	57	....	....	....	....	....	....	....	....	....	12	2	8	10	8	....	....	....	....
2003-04	Morrums GoIS IK	Sweden-2	38	19	22	41	40	....	....	....	....	....	....	....	....	....	....	....	....	....	....	....	....	....	....
	Djurgarden	Sweden	3	0	0	0	2	....	....	....	....	....	....	....	....	....	....	....	....	....	....	....	....	....	....
2004-05	Djurgarden	Sweden	30	10	7	17	33	....	....	....	....	....	....	....	....	....	12	2	2	4	29	....	....	....	....
2005-06	Djurgarden	Sweden	50	17	19	36	44	....	....	....	....	....	....	....	....	....	....	....	....	....	....	....	....	....	....
	Salzburg	Austria	....	....	....	....	....	....	....	....	....	....	....	....	....	....	9	4	7	11	12	....	....	....	....
2006-07	**Edmonton**	**NHL**	**68**	**4**	**12**	**16**	**52**	**0**	**1**	**2**	**73**	**5.5**	**–1**	**82**	**51.2**	**11:25**	....	....	....	....	....	....	....	....	....
	Wilkes-Barre	AHL	5	1	5	6	4	....	....	....	....	....	....	....	....	....	....	....	....	....	....	....	....	....	....
2007-08	**Edmonton**	**NHL**	**17**	**2**	**1**	**3**	**6**	**0**	**0**	**0**	**18**	**11.1**	**–4**	**19**	**52.6**	**10:43**	....	....	....	....	....	....	....	....	....
	Springfield	AHL	29	13	13	26	13	....	....	....	....	....	....	....	....	....	....	....	....	....	....	....	....	....	....
	Philadelphia	**NHL**	**21**	**0**	**5**	**5**	**8**	**0**	**0**	**0**	**21**	**0.0**	**–6**	**81**	**38.3**	**12:36**	**14**	**0**	**2**	**2**	**4**	**0**	**0**	**0**	**9:22**
2008-09	HC Lugano	Swiss	48	22	41	63	83	....	....	....	....	....	....	....	....	....	7	1	7	8	2	....	....	....	....
2009-10	Ufa	Rus-KHL	56	24	33	57	71	....	....	....	....	....	....	....	....	....	15	5	9	14	37	....	....	....	....
	Norway	Olympics	4	0	5	5	0	....	....	....	....	....	....	....	....	....	....	....	....	....	....	....	....	....	....
	NHL Totals		**106**	**6**	**18**	**24**	**66**	**0**	**1**	**2**	**112**	**5.4**		**182**	**45.6**	**11:32**	**14**	**0**	**2**	**2**	**4**	**0**	**0**	**0**	**9:22**

Signed as a free agent by **Edmonton**, June 12, 2006. Claimed on waivers by **Philadelphia** from **Edmonton**, February 22, 2008. Signed as a free agent by **Lugano** (Swiss), July 14, 2008. Signed as a free agent by **Ufa** (Russia-KHL), May 21, 2009.

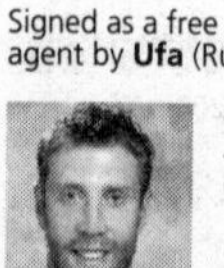

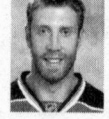

THORNTON, Joe

(THOHRN-tuhn, JOH) **S.J.**

Center. Shoots left. 6'4", 235 lbs. Born, London, Ont., July 2, 1979. Boston's 1st choice, 1st overall, in 1997 Entry Draft.

Season	Club	League	GP	G	A	Pts	PIM	PP	SH	GW	S	%	+/-	TF	F%	Min	GP	G	A	Pts	PIM	PP	SH	GW	Min
1993-94	Elgin-Mid. Chiefs	Minor-ON	67	*83	*85	*168	45	....	....	....	....	....	....	....	....	....	....	....	....	....	....	....	....	....	....
	St. Thomas Stars	OHA-B	6	2	6	8	2	....	....	....	....	....	....	....	....	....	....	....	....	....	....	....	....	....	....
1994-95	St. Thomas Stars	OHA-B	50	40	64	104	53	....	....	....	....	....	....	....	....	....	....	....	....	....	....	....	....	....	....
1995-96	Sault Ste. Marie	OHL	66	30	46	76	53	....	....	....	....	....	....	....	....	....	4	1	1	2	11	....	....	....	....
1996-97	Sault Ste. Marie	OHL	59	41	81	122	123	....	....	....	....	....	....	....	....	....	11	11	8	19	24	....	....	....	....
1997-98	**Boston**	**NHL**	**55**	**3**	**4**	**7**	**19**	**0**	**0**	**1**	**33**	**9.1**	**–6**	....	....	....	**6**	**0**	**0**	**0**	**9**	**0**	**0**	**0**	....
1998-99	**Boston**	**NHL**	**81**	**16**	**25**	**41**	**69**	**7**	**0**	**1**	**128**	**12.5**	**3**	**1073**	**48.7**	**15:21**	**11**	**3**	**6**	**9**	**4**	**2**	**0**	**2**	**19:52**
99-2000	**Boston**	**NHL**	**81**	**23**	**37**	**60**	**82**	**5**	**0**	**3**	**171**	**13.5**	**–5**	**1861**	**49.5**	**21:18**	....	....	....	....	....	....	....	....	....
2000-01	**Boston**	**NHL**	**72**	**37**	**34**	**71**	**107**	**19**	**1**	**5**	**181**	**20.4**	**–4**	**1651**	**52.1**	**21:45**	....	....	....	....	....	....	....	....	....
2001-02	**Boston**	**NHL**	**66**	**22**	**46**	**68**	**127**	**6**	**0**	**5**	**152**	**14.5**	**7**	**1341**	**49.1**	**19:59**	**6**	**2**	**4**	**6**	**10**	**0**	**0**	**0**	**21:09**
2002-03	**Boston**	**NHL**	**77**	**36**	**65**	**101**	**109**	**12**	**2**	**4**	**196**	**18.4**	**12**	**1766**	**49.5**	**22:33**	**5**	**1**	**2**	**3**	**4**	**1**	**0**	**0**	**20:13**
2003-04	**Boston**	**NHL**	**77**	**23**	**50**	**73**	**98**	**4**	**0**	**6**	**187**	**12.3**	**18**	**1671**	**56.3**	**21:38**	**7**	**0**	**0**	**0**	**14**	**0**	**0**	**0**	**21:30**
2004-05	HC Davos	Swiss	40	10	44	54	80	....	....	....	....	....	....	....	....	....	14	4	*20	*24	29	....	....	....	....
2005-06	**Boston**	**NHL**	**23**	**9**	***24**	***33**	**6**	**3**	**0**	**2**	**60**	**15.0**	**0**	**511**	**52.3**	**21:33**	....	....	....	....	....	....	....	....	....
	San Jose	**NHL**	**58**	**20**	***72**	***92**	**55**	**8**	**0**	**4**	**135**	**14.8**	**31**	**1287**	**50.9**	**21:15**	**11**	**2**	**7**	**9**	**12**	**1**	**0**	**1**	**25:09**
	Canada	Olympics	6	1	2	3	0	....	....	....	....	....	....	....	....	....	....	....	....	....	....	....	....	....	....
2006-07	**San Jose**	**NHL**	**82**	**22**	***92**	**114**	**44**	**10**	**0**	**5**	**213**	**10.3**	**24**	**1522**	**51.1**	**20:19**	**11**	**1**	**10**	**11**	**10**	**0**	**0**	**0**	**22:00**
2007-08	**San Jose**	**NHL**	**82**	**29**	***67**	**96**	**59**	**11**	**0**	**5**	**178**	**16.3**	**18**	**1485**	**52.9**	**21:24**	**13**	**2**	**8**	**10**	**2**	**1**	**0**	**1**	**24:42**
2008-09	**San Jose**	**NHL**	**82**	**25**	**61**	**86**	**56**	**11**	**0**	**3**	**139**	**18.0**	**16**	**1295**	**55.4**	**19:28**	**6**	**1**	**4**	**5**	**5**	**1**	**0**	**0**	**19:14**

Season	Club	League	GP	G	A	Pts	PIM	PP	SH	GW	S	%	+/-	TF	F%	Min	GP	G	A	Pts	PIM	PP	SH	GW	Min
			Regular Season														Playoffs								
2009-10	**San Jose**	**NHL**	**79**	**20**	**69**	**89**	**54**	**4**	**1**	**2**	**141**	**14.2**	**17**	**1228**	**53.9**	**19:51**	**15**	**3**	**9**	**12**	**18**	**1**	**0**	**1**	**21:20**
	Canada	Olympics	7	1	1	2	0	....	....	....	....	....	....	....	....	....	....	....	....	....	....	....	....	....	....
	NHL Totals		**915**	**285**	**646**	**931**	**885**	**100**	**4**	**46**	**1914**	**14.9**		**16691**	**51.8**	**20:26**	**91**	**15**	**50**	**65**	**88**	**7**	**0**	**5**	**22:01**

HL All-Rookie Team (1996) • OHL Rookie of the Year (1996) • Canadian Major Junior Rookie of the Year (1996) • OHL Second All-Star Team (1997) • NHL Second All-Star Team (2003, 2008) • NHL First ll-Star Team (2006) • Art Ross Trophy (2006) • Hart Memorial Trophy (2006)

layed in NHL All-Star Game (2002, 2003, 2004, 2007, 2008, 2009

igned as a free agent by **Davos** (Swiss), July 8, 2004. Traded to **San Jose** by **Boston** for Brad Stuart, Marco Sturm and Wayne Primeau, November 30, 2005.

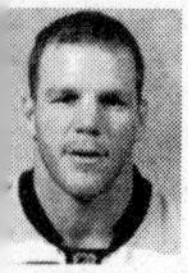

THORNTON, Shawn (THOHRN-tuhn, SHAWN) BOS.

Right wing. Shoots right. 6'2", 217 lbs. Born, Oshawa, Ont., July 23, 1977. Toronto's 6th choice, 190th overall, in 1997 Entry Draft.

Season	Club	League	GP	G	A	Pts	PIM	PP	SH	GW	S	%	+/-	TF	F%	Min	GP	G	A	Pts	PIM	PP	SH	GW	Min
1995-96	Peterborough	OHL	63	4	10	14	192	....	....	....	....	....	....	....	....	....	24	3	0	3	25	....	....	....	....
1996-97	Peterborough	OHL	61	19	10	29	204	....	....	....	....	....	....	....	....	....	11	2	4	6	20	....	....	....	....
1997-98	St. John's	AHL	59	0	3	3	225	....	....	....	....	....	....	....	....	....	....	....	....	....	....	....	....	....	....
1998-99	St. John's	AHL	78	8	11	19	354	....	....	....	....	....	....	....	....	....	5	0	0	0	9	....	....	....	....
99-2000	St. John's	AHL	60	4	12	16	316	....	....	....	....	....	....	....	....	....	....	....	....	....	....	....	....	....	....
2000-01	St. John's	AHL	79	5	12	17	320	....	....	....	....	....	....	....	....	....	3	1	2	3	2	....	....	....	....
2001-02	Norfolk Admirals	AHL	70	8	14	22	281	....	....	....	....	....	....	....	....	....	4	0	0	0	4	....	....	....	....
2002-03	**Chicago**	**NHL**	**13**	**1**	**1**	**2**	**31**	**0**	**0**	**0**	**15**	**6.7**	**-4**	**3**	**66.7**	**8:30**	....	....	....	....	....	....	....	....	....
	Norfolk Admirals	AHL	50	11	2	13	213	....	....	....	....	....	....	....	....	....	9	0	2	2	28	....	....	....	....
2003-04	**Chicago**	**NHL**	**8**	**1**	**0**	**1**	**23**	**0**	**0**	**0**	**14**	**7.1**	**2**	**19**	**42.1**	**11:14**	....	....	....	....	....	....	....	....	....
	Norfolk Admirals	AHL	64	6	11	17	259	....	....	....	....	....	....	....	....	....	8	1	1	2	6	....	....	....	....
2004-05	Norfolk Admirals	AHL	71	5	9	14	253	....	....	....	....	....	....	....	....	....	6	0	0	0	8	....	....	....	....
2005-06	**Chicago**	**NHL**	**10**	**0**	**0**	**0**	**16**	**0**	**0**	**0**	**16**	**0.0**	**-5**	**17**	**58.8**	**7:18**	....	....	....	....	....	....	....	....	....
	Norfolk Admirals	AHL	59	10	22	32	192	....	....	....	....	....	....	....	....	....	4	0	0	0	35	....	....	....	....
2006-07♦	**Anaheim**	**NHL**	**48**	**2**	**7**	**9**	**88**	**0**	**0**	**0**	**60**	**3.3**	**3**	**8**	**25.0**	**8:26**	**15**	**0**	**0**	**0**	**19**	**0**	**0**	**0**	**3:58**
	Portland Pirates	AHL	15	4	4	8	55	....	....	....	....	....	....	....	....	....	....	....	....	....	....	....	....	....	....
2007-08	**Boston**	**NHL**	**58**	**4**	**3**	**7**	**74**	**0**	**0**	**1**	**65**	**6.2**	**-1**	**7**	**28.6**	**7:24**	**7**	**0**	**0**	**0**	**6**	**0**	**0**	**0**	**8:04**
2008-09	**Boston**	**NHL**	**79**	**6**	**5**	**11**	**123**	**0**	**0**	**2**	**136**	**4.4**	**-2**	**5**	**20.0**	**10:02**	**10**	**1**	**0**	**1**	**6**	**0**	**0**	**0**	**9:07**
2009-10	**Boston**	**NHL**	**74**	**1**	**9**	**10**	**141**	**0**	**0**	**0**	**119**	**0.8**	**-9**	**23**	**47.8**	**9:03**	**12**	**0**	**0**	**0**	**4**	**0**	**0**	**0**	**7:08**
	NHL Totals		**290**	**15**	**25**	**40**	**496**	**0**	**0**	**3**	**425**	**3.5**		**82**	**43.9**	**8:52**	**44**	**1**	**0**	**1**	**35**	**0**	**0**	**0**	**6:39**

raded to **Chicago** by **Toronto** for Marty Wilford, September 30, 2001. Signed as a free agent by **Anaheim**, July 14, 2006. Signed as a free agent by **Boston**, July 1, 2007.

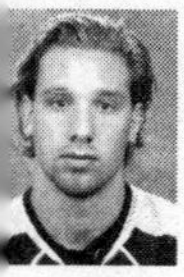

THURESSON, Andreas (THUR-eh-suhn, an-DRAY-uhs) NSH.

Center. Shoots right. 6'1", 212 lbs. Born, Kristianstad, Sweden, November 18, 1987. Nashville's 7th choice, 144th overall, in 2007 Entry Draft.

Season	Club	League	GP	G	A	Pts	PIM	PP	SH	GW	S	%	+/-	TF	F%	Min	GP	G	A	Pts	PIM	PP	SH	GW	Min
2003-04	Malmo U18	Swe-U18	3	0	0	0	4	....	....	....	....	....	....	....	....	....	....	....	....	....	....	....	....	....	....
	Tyringe SoSS	Sweden-3	12	0	1	1	0	....	....	....	....	....	....	....	....	....	....	....	....	....	....	....	....	....	....
	Malmo Jr.	Swe-Jr.	19	2	2	4	16	....	....	....	....	....	....	....	....	....	8	0	0	0	6	....	....	....	....
2004-05	Malmo U18	Swe-U18	3	1	1	2	4	....	....	....	....	....	....	....	....	....	....	....	....	....	....	....	....	....	....
	Malmo Jr.	Swe-Jr.	30	4	4	8	28	....	....	....	....	....	....	....	....	....	3	2	1	3	2	....	....	....	....
2005-06	Malmo U18	Swe-U18	2	1	0	1	4	....	....	....	....	....	....	....	....	....	....	....	....	....	....	....	....	....	....
	Malmo Jr.	Swe-Jr.	38	15	18	33	71	....	....	....	....	....	....	....	....	....	....	....	....	....	....	....	....	....	....
	Malmo	Sweden-2	20	0	2	2	10	....	....	....	....	....	....	....	....	....	....	....	....	....	....	....	....	....	....
2006-07	Malmo	Sweden	48	10	5	15	26	....	....	....	....	....	....	....	....	....	....	....	....	....	....	....	....	....	....
	Malmo	Sweden-Q	10	2	2	4	2	....	....	....	....	....	....	....	....	....	....	....	....	....	....	....	....	....	....
2007-08	Milwaukee	AHL	77	11	7	18	37	....	....	....	....	....	....	....	....	....	6	0	0	0	4	....	....	....	....
2008-09	Milwaukee	AHL	74	14	15	29	32	....	....	....	....	....	....	....	....	....	11	3	1	4	4	....	....	....	....
2009-10	**Nashville**	**NHL**	**22**	**1**	**2**	**3**	**4**	**0**	**0**	**0**	**30**	**3.3**	**-5**	**10**	**30.0**	**9:59**	....	....	....	....	....	....	....	....	....
	Milwaukee	AHL	50	14	19	33	24	....	....	....	....	....	....	....	....	....	7	2	7	9	16	....	....	....	....
	NHL Totals		**22**	**1**	**2**	**3**	**4**	**0**	**0**	**0**	**30**	**3.3**		**10**	**30.0**	**9:59**	....	....	....	....	....	....	....	....	....

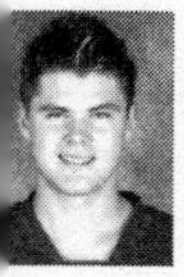

TIKHONOV, Viktor (TIHK-uh-nawf, VIHK-tohr) PHX.

Center. Shoots right. 6'2", 187 lbs. Born, Riga, Latvia, May 12, 1988. Phoenix's 2nd choice, 28th overall, in 2008 Entry Draft.

Season	Club	League	GP	G	A	Pts	PIM	PP	SH	GW	S	%	+/-	TF	F%	Min	GP	G	A	Pts	PIM	PP	SH	GW	Min
2004-05	CSKA Moscow 2	Russia-3	STATISTICS NOT AVAILABLE																						
2005-06	CSKA Moscow 2	Russia-3	STATISTICS NOT AVAILABLE																						
	HK Dmitrov	Russia-2	36	6	8	14	10	....	....	....	....	....	....	....	....	....	....	....	....	....	....	....	....	....	....
2006-07	Cherepovets 2	Russia-3	STATISTICS NOT AVAILABLE																						
	Cherepovets	Russia	4	0	0	0	0	....	....	....	....	....	....	....	....	....	....	....	....	....	....	....	....	....	....
2007-08	Cherepovets	Russia	43	7	5	12	43	....	....	....	....	....	....	....	....	....	8	0	1	1	4	....	....	....	....
2008-09	**Phoenix**	**NHL**	**61**	**8**	**8**	**16**	**20**	**1**	**0**	**1**	**71**	**11.3**	**-3**	**60**	**38.3**	**12:08**	....	....	....	....	....	....	....	....	....
	San Antonio	AHL	4	2	1	3	0	....	....	....	....	....	....	....	....	....	....	....	....	....	....	....	....	....	....
2009-10	San Antonio	AHL	18	2	6	8	12	....	....	....	....	....	....	....	....	....	....	....	....	....	....	....	....	....	....
	Cherepovets	Rus-KHL	25	14	1	15	12	....	....	....	....	....	....	....	....	....	....	....	....	....	....	....	....	....	....
	NHL Totals		**61**	**8**	**8**	**16**	**20**	**1**	**0**	**1**	**71**	**11.3**		**60**	**38.3**	**12:08**	....	....	....	....	....	....	....	....	....

Loaned to **Cherepovets** (Russia-KHL) by **Phoenix**, November 28, 2009.

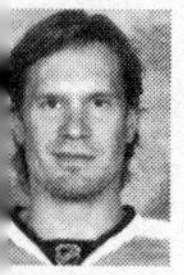

TIMONEN, Kimmo (TEEM-oh-nehn, KEE-moh) PHI.

Defense. Shoots left. 5'10", 194 lbs. Born, Kuopio, Finland, March 18, 1975. Los Angeles' 11th choice, 250th overall, in 1993 Entry Draft.

Season	Club	League	GP	G	A	Pts	PIM	PP	SH	GW	S	%	+/-	TF	F%	Min	GP	G	A	Pts	PIM	PP	SH	GW	Min
1990-91	KalPa Kuopio Jr.	Fin-Jr.	4	0	1	1	2	....	....	....	....	....	....	....	....	....	....	....	....	....	....	....	....	....	....
1991-92	KalPa Kuopio Jr.	Fin-Jr.	32	7	10	17	4	....	....	....	....	....	....	....	....	....	....	....	....	....	....	....	....	....	....
	KalPa Kuopio	Finland	5	0	0	0	0	....	....	....	....	....	....	....	....	....	....	....	....	....	....	....	....	....	....
1992-93	KalPa Kuopio U18	Fin-U18	3	0	5	5	0	....	....	....	....	....	....	....	....	....	....	....	....	....	....	....	....	....	....
	KalPa Kuopio Jr.	Fin-Jr.	16	9	15	24	10	....	....	....	....	....	....	....	....	....	....	....	....	....	....	....	....	....	....
	KalPa Kuopio	Finland	33	0	2	2	4	....	....	....	....	....	....	....	....	....	....	....	....	....	....	....	....	....	....
1993-94	KalPa Kuopio Jr.	Fin-Jr.	5	4	7	11	0	....	....	....	....	....	....	....	....	....	....	....	....	....	....	....	....	....	....
	KalPa Kuopio	Finland	46	6	7	13	55	....	....	....	....	....	....	....	....	....	....	....	....	....	....	....	....	....	....
1994-95	TPS Turku Jr.	Fin-Jr.	1	0	0	0	0	....	....	....	....	....	....	....	....	....	....	....	....	....	....	....	....	....	....
	TPS Turku	Finland	45	3	4	7	10	....	....	....	....	....	....	....	....	....	13	0	1	1	6	....	....	....	....
1995-96	TPS Turku	Finland	48	3	21	24	22	....	....	....	....	....	....	....	....	....	9	1	2	3	12	....	....	....	....
1996-97	TPS Turku	Finland	50	10	14	24	18	....	....	....	....	....	....	....	....	....	12	2	7	9	6	....	....	....	....
	TPS Turku	EuroHL	6	1	0	1	27	....	....	....	....	....	....	....	....	....	4	0	1	1	0	....	....	....	....
1997-98	HIFK Helsinki	Finland	45	10	15	25	24	....	....	....	....	....	....	....	....	....	9	3	4	7	8	....	....	....	....
	Finland	Olympics	6	0	1	1	2	....	....	....	....	....	....	....	....	....	....	....	....	....	....	....	....	....	....
1998-99	**Nashville**	**NHL**	**50**	**4**	**8**	**12**	**30**	**1**	**0**	**0**	**75**	**5.3**	**-4**	**0**	**0.0**	**19:04**	....	....	....	....	....	....	....	....	....
	Milwaukee	IHL	29	2	13	15	22	....	....	....	....	....	....	....	....	....	....	....	....	....	....	....	....	....	....
99-2000	**Nashville**	**NHL**	**51**	**8**	**25**	**33**	**26**	**2**	**1**	**2**	**97**	**8.2**	**-5**	**0**	**0.0**	**21:06**	....	....	....	....	....	....	....	....	....
2000-01	**Nashville**	**NHL**	**82**	**12**	**13**	**25**	**50**	**6**	**0**	**3**	**151**	**7.9**	**-6**	**2**	**50.0**	**23:11**	....	....	....	....	....	....	....	....	....
2001-02	**Nashville**	**NHL**	**82**	**13**	**29**	**42**	**28**	**9**	**0**	**1**	**154**	**8.4**	**2**	**0**	**0.0**	**24:12**	....	....	....	....	....	....	....	....	....
	Finland	Olympics	4	0	1	1	2	....	....	....	....	....	....	....	....	....	....	....	....	....	....	....	....	....	....
2002-03	**Nashville**	**NHL**	**72**	**6**	**34**	**40**	**46**	**4**	**0**	**0**	**144**	**4.2**	**-3**	**0**	**0.0**	**22:25**	....	....	....	....	....	....	....	....	....
2003-04	**Nashville**	**NHL**	**77**	**12**	**32**	**44**	**52**	**8**	**0**	**1**	**180**	**6.7**	**-7**	**1**	**0.0**	**23:52**	**6**	**0**	**0**	**0**	**10**	**0**	**0**	**0**	**24:16**
2004-05	HC Lugano	Swiss	3	0	1	1	0	....	....	....	....	....	....	....	....	....	....	....	....	....	....	....	....	....	....
	Brynas IF Gavle	Sweden	10	5	3	8	8	....	....	....	....	....	....	....	....	....	....	....	....	....	....	....	....	....	....
	KalPa Kuopio	Finland-2	12	4	13	17	6	....	....	....	....	....	....	....	....	....	8	3	7	10	4	....	....	....	....
2005-06	**Nashville**	**NHL**	**79**	**11**	**39**	**50**	**74**	**8**	**0**	**1**	**156**	**7.1**	**-3**	**5**	**80.0**	**22:26**	**5**	**1**	**3**	**4**	**4**	**0**	**1**	**0**	**24:42**
	Finland	Olympics	8	1	4	5	2	....	....	....	....	....	....	....	....	....	....	....	....	....	....	....	....	....	....
2006-07	**Nashville**	**NHL**	**80**	**13**	**42**	**55**	**42**	**8**	**0**	**2**	**121**	**10.7**	**20**	**1**	**0.0**	**21:51**	**5**	**0**	**2**	**2**	**4**	**0**	**0**	**0**	**24:33**
2007-08	**Philadelphia**	**NHL**	**80**	**8**	**36**	**44**	**50**	**3**	**1**	**1**	**125**	**6.4**	**0**	**0**	**0.0**	**23:35**	**13**	**0**	**6**	**6**	**8**	**0**	**0**	**0**	**24:41**
2008-09	**Philadelphia**	**NHL**	**77**	**3**	**40**	**43**	**54**	**2**	**0**	**0**	**104**	**2.9**	**19**	**2**	**0.0**	**24:31**	**6**	**0**	**1**	**1**	**12**	**0**	**0**	**0**	**26:21**

			Regular Season														Playoffs								
Season	Club	League	GP	G	A	Pts	PIM	PP	SH	GW	S	%	+/-	TF	F%	Min	GP	G	A	Pts	PIM	PP	SH	GW	Min
2009-10	Philadelphia	NHL	82	6	33	39	50	1	2	1	121	5.0	–2	0	0.0	22:53	23	1	10	11	20	0	0	0	26:3
	Finland	Olympics	6	2	2	4	2																		
	NHL Totals		812	96	331	427	502	52	4	12	1428	6.7		11	45.5	22:50	58	2	22	24	58	0	1	0	25:3

Olympic Tournament All-Star Team (2006)

Played in NHL All-Star Game (2004, 2007, 2008)

Traded to **Nashville** by **Los Angeles** with Jan Vopat for future considerations, June 26, 1998. Signed as a free agent by **Lugano** (Swiss), October 31, 2004. Signed as a free agent by **Gavle** (Sweden), November 8, 2004. Signed as a free agent by **Kuopio** (Finland-2), January 3, 2005. Traded to **Philadelphia** by **Nashville** with Scott Hartnell for Nashville's 1st round choice (previously acquired, Nashville selected Jonathon Blum) in 2007 Entry Draft, June 18, 2007.

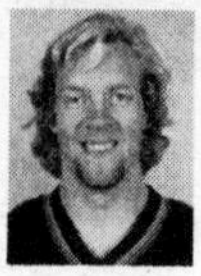

TJARNQVIST, Daniel

(T'YAHRN-kvihst, DAN-yehl)

Defense. Shoots left. 6'1", 207 lbs. Born, Umea, Sweden, October 14, 1976. Florida's 5th choice, 88th overall, in 1995 Entry Draft.

Season	Club	League	GP	G	A	Pts	PIM	PP	SH	GW	S	%	+/-	TF	F%	Min	GP	G	A	Pts	PIM	PP	SH	GW	Min
1992-93	Rogle Jr.	Swe-Jr.	7	1	0	1	0																		
1993-94	Rogle U18	Swe-U18	Statistics Not Available																						
1994-95	Rogle	Sweden	18	0	1	1	2																		
	Rogle	Sweden-Q	15	2	3	5	0																		
1995-96	Rogle	Sweden	22	1	7	8	6																		
1996-97	Jokerit Helsinki	Finland	44	3	8	11	4										9	0	3	3	4				
	Jokerit Helsinki	EuroHL	6	1	1	2	2																		
1997-98	Djurgarden	Sweden	40	5	9	14	12										15	1	1	2	2				
1998-99	Djurgarden	Sweden	40	4	3	7	16										4	0	0	0	2				
99-2000	Djurgarden	Sweden	42	3	16	19	8										5	0	0	0	2				
2000-01	Djurgarden	Sweden	45	9	17	26	26										16	6	5	11	2				
2001-02	Atlanta	NHL	75	2	16	18	14	1	0	0	68	2.9	–22	4	25.0	21:32									
2002-03	Atlanta	NHL	75	3	12	15	26	1	0	0	65	4.6	–20	3	66.7	21:53									
2003-04	Atlanta	NHL	68	5	15	20	20	0	2	1	65	7.7	–4	4	25.0	22:17									
2004-05	Djurgarden	Sweden	49	12	12	24	30										12	2	5	7	10				
2005-06	Minnesota	NHL	60	3	15	18	32	3	0	1	54	5.6	–11	0	0.0	19:46									
	Sweden	Olympics	8	2	1	3	4																		
2006-07	Edmonton	NHL	37	3	12	15	30	2	0	0	33	9.1	3	0	0.0	22:42									
2007-08	Yaroslavl	Russia	18	1	2	3	14										8	0	4	4	4				
2008-09	Colorado	NHL	37	2	2	4	8	0	0	0	19	10.5	1	0	0.0	14:40									
2009-10	Yaroslavl	Rus-KHL	54	3	7	10	26										17	0	3	3	8				
	NHL Totals		352	18	72	90	130	7	2	2	304	5.9		11	36.4	20:51									

Traded to **Atlanta** by **Florida** with Gord Murphy, Herbert Vasiljevs and Ottawa's 6th round choice (previously acquired, later traded to Dallas – Dallas selected Justin Cox) in 1999 Entry Draft for Trevor Kidd, June 25, 1999. Signed as a free agent by **Djurgarden** (Sweden), September 16, 2004. Signed as a free agent by **Minnesota**, August 15, 2005. Signed as a free agent by **Edmonton**, July 6, 2006. • Missed majority of 2006-07 season recovering from recurring groin injury. Signed as a free agent by **Yaroslavl** (Russia), August 23, 2007. Signed as a free agent by **Colorado**, July 3, 2008. Signed as a free agent by **Yaroslavl** (Russia-KHL), July 23, 2009.

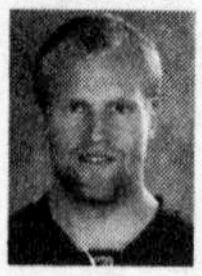

TJARNQVIST, Mathias

(T'YAHRN-kvihst, MAT-ee-uhs)

Right wing. Shoots left. 6'2", 196 lbs. Born, Umea, Sweden, April 15, 1979. Dallas' 3rd choice, 96th overall, in 1999 Entry Draft.

Season	Club	League	GP	G	A	Pts	PIM	PP	SH	GW	S	%	+/-	TF	F%	Min	GP	G	A	Pts	PIM	PP	SH	GW	Min
1995-96	Rogle Jr.	Swe-Jr.	4	2	0	2	0																		
1996-97	Rogle Jr.	Swe-Jr.	18	5	8	13																			
	Rogle	Sweden-2	15	1	4	5	4																		
1997-98	Rogle	Sweden-2	31	12	11	23	30										4	2	0	2	6				
1998-99	Rogle	Sweden-2	34	18	16	34	44										5	4	1	5	4				
99-2000	Djurgarden	Sweden	50	12	12	24	20										13	3	2	5	16				
2000-01	Djurgarden	Sweden	47	11	8	19	53										16	1	2	3	6				
2001-02	Djurgarden	Sweden	6	0	1	1	4										2	0	0	0	2				
2002-03	Djurgarden	Sweden	38	11	13	24	30										9	4	1	5	12				
2003-04	Dallas	NHL	18	1	1	2	2	0	0	1	11	9.1	–6	4	25.0	9:43									
	Utah Grizzlies	AHL	60	15	13	28	51																		
2004-05	HV 71 Jonkoping	Sweden	46	8	9	17	18																		
2005-06	Dallas	NHL	33	2	4	6	18	0	0	0	36	5.6	4	4	75.0	8:10									
	Iowa Stars	AHL	34	17	12	29	28										1	0	0	0	0				
2006-07	Dallas	NHL	18	1	3	4	4	0	0	0	13	7.7	–3	7	42.9	9:15									
	Iowa Stars	AHL	2	1	1	2	0																		
	Phoenix	NHL	26	5	4	9	2	0	1	0	31	16.1	–2	11	54.6	14:50									
2007-08	Phoenix	NHL	78	4	7	11	34	0	0	0	90	4.4	–1	46	32.6	13:39									
2008-09	Rogle	Sweden	40	11	10	21	16																		
	Rogle	Sweden-Q	8	0	2	2	4																		
2009-10	Djurgarden	Sweden	18	2	2	4	8										16	1	2	3	8				
	NHL Totals		173	13	19	32	60	0	1	1	181	7.2		72	38.9	11:55									

Signed as a free agent by **Jonkoping** (Sweden), August 30, 2004. Traded to **Phoenix** by **Dallas** with Dallas' 1st round choice (later traded to Edmonton - Edmonton selected Riley Nash) in 2007 Entry Draft for Ladislav Nagy, February 12, 2007. Signed as a free agent by **Rogle** (Sweden), August 3, 2008. Signed as a free agent by **Djurgarden** (Sweden), August 12, 2009.

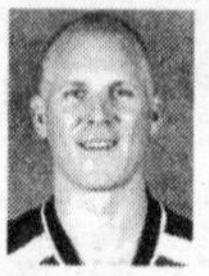

TKACHUK, Keith

(kuh-CHUK, KEETH)

Left wing. Shoots left. 6'2", 235 lbs. Born, Melrose, MA, March 28, 1972. Winnipeg's 1st choice, 19th overall, in 1990 Entry Draft.

Season	Club	League	GP	G	A	Pts	PIM	PP	SH	GW	S	%	+/-	TF	F%	Min	GP	G	A	Pts	PIM	PP	SH	GW	Min
1988-89	Malden Cath.	High-MA	21	30	16	46																			
1989-90	Malden Cath.	High-MA	6	12	14	26																			
1990-91	Boston University	H-East	36	17	23	40	70																		
1991-92	United States	Nat-Tm	45	10	10	20	141																		
	United States	Olympics	8	1	1	2	12																		
	Winnipeg	NHL	17	3	5	8	28	2	0	0	22	13.6	0				7	3	0	3	30	0	0	0	
1992-93	Winnipeg	NHL	83	28	23	51	201	12	0	2	199	14.1	–13				6	4	0	4	14	1	0	0	
1993-94	Winnipeg	NHL	84	41	40	81	255	22	3	3	218	18.8	–12												
1994-95	Winnipeg	NHL	48	22	29	51	152	7	2	2	129	17.1	–4												
1995-96	Winnipeg	NHL	76	50	48	98	156	20	2	6	249	20.1	11				6	1	2	3	22	0	0	0	
1996-97	Phoenix	NHL	81	*52	34	86	228	9	2	7	296	17.6	–1				7	6	0	6	7	2	0	0	
1997-98	Phoenix	NHL	69	40	26	66	147	11	0	8	232	17.2	9				6	3	3	6	10	0	0	0	
	United States	Olympics	4	0	2	2	6																		
1998-99	Phoenix	NHL	68	36	32	68	151	11	2	7	258	14.0	22	770	47.7	20:59	7	1	3	4	13	1	0	0	25:09
99-2000	Phoenix	NHL	50	22	21	43	82	5	1	1	183	12.0	7	500	50.4	19:21	5	1	1	2	4	1	0	0	18:46
2000-01	Phoenix	NHL	64	29	42	71	108	15	0	4	230	12.6	6	646	51.9	20:11									
	St. Louis	NHL	12	6	2	8	14	2	0	1	41	14.6	–3	87	54.0	19:39	15	2	7	9	20	2	0	1	19:17
2001-02	St. Louis	NHL	73	38	37	75	117	13	0	7	244	15.6	21	88	43.2	19:38	10	5	5	10	18	1	0	0	19:24
	United States	Olympics	5	2	0	2	2																		
2002-03	St. Louis	NHL	56	31	24	55	139	14	0	5	185	16.8	1	346	55.8	19:16	7	1	3	4	14	0	0	0	19:22
2003-04	St. Louis	NHL	75	33	38	71	83	18	0	8	233	14.2	8	410	49.5	19:39	5	0	2	2	10	0	0	0	19:18
2004-05			Did Not Play																						
2005-06	St. Louis	NHL	41	15	21	36	46	10	0	1	133	11.3	–15	250	50.4	19:27									
	United States	Olympics	6	0	0	0	8																		
2006-07	St. Louis	NHL	61	20	23	43	92	8	0	1	160	12.5	3	678	49.4	17:26									
	Atlanta	NHL	18	7	8	15	34	2	0	3	36	19.4	8	348	52.9	17:41	4	1	2	3	12	0	0	0	16:33
2007-08	St. Louis	NHL	79	27	31	58	69	12	1	1	177	15.3	–2	1118	49.4	16:51									
2008-09	St. Louis	NHL	79	25	24	49	61	14	0	4	185	13.5	–11	918	51.4	16:57	4	0	0	0	2	0	0	0	18:28
2009-10	St. Louis	NHL	67	13	19	32	56	5	0	1	120	10.8	–2	695	56.0	13:30									
	NHL Totals		1201	538	527	1065	2219	212	13	72	3530	15.2		6854	51.0	18:23	89	28	28	56	176	8	0	1	19:44

NHL Second All-Star Team (1995, 1998)

Played in NHL All-Star Game (1997, 1998, 1999, 2004, 2009)

• Transferred to **Phoenix** after **Winnipeg** franchise relocated, July 1, 1996. Traded to **St. Louis** by **Phoenix** for Michal Handzus, Ladislav Nagy, the rights to Jeff Taffe and St. Louis' 1st round choice (Ben Eager) in 2002 Entry Draft, March 13, 2001. Traded to **Atlanta** by **St. Louis** for Glen Metropolit, Atlanta's 1st (later traded to Calgary - Calgary selected Mikael Backlund) and 3rd (Brett Sonne) round choices in 2007 Entry Draft, and Atlanta's 1st (later traded back to Atlanta - Atlanta selected Zach Bogosian) and 2nd (Philip McRae) round choices in 2008 Entry Draft, February 25, 2007. Traded to **St. Louis** by **Atlanta** with future considerations for Atlanta's 1st round choice (previously acquired, Atlanta selected Zach Bogosian) in 2008 Entry Draft, June 26, 2007. • Officially announced his retirement, April 13, 2010.

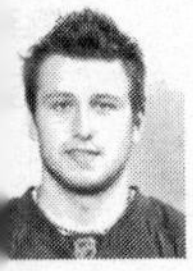

TLUSTY, Jiri

(T'LOO-stee, YIH-ree) **CAR.**

Center. Shoots left. 6', 209 lbs. Born, Slany, Czech., March 16, 1988. Toronto's 1st choice, 13th overall, in 2006 Entry Draft.

			Regular Season														Playoffs								
Season	Club	League	GP	G	A	Pts	PIM	PP	SH	GW	S	%	+/-	TF	F%	Min	GP	G	A	Pts	PIM	PP	SH	GW	Min
2001-02	HC Kladno U17	CzR-U17	1	0	0	0	0	....	....	....	....	....	....	....	....	....	....	....	....	....	....	....	....	....	....
2002-03	HC Kladno U17	CzR-U17	48	28	17	45	22	....	....	....	....	....	....	....	....	....	10	5	4	9	12	....	....	....	....
2003-04	HC Kladno U17	CzR-U17	1	0	0	0	2	....	....	....	....	....	....	....	....	....	1	0	0	0	2	....	....	....	....
	HC Kladno Jr.	CzRep-Jr.	51	10	3	13	12	....	....	....	....	....	....	....	....	....	1	0	0	0	0	....	....	....	....
2004-05	HC Kladno Jr.	CzRep-Jr.	42	15	12	27	54	....	....	....	....	....	....	....	....	....	10	2	2	4	8	....	....	....	....
2005-06	HC Kladno Jr.	CzRep-Jr.	6	4	2	6	2	....	....	....	....	....	....	....	....	....	6	7	6	13	6	....	....	....	....
	HC Rabat Kladno	CzRep	44	7	3	10	51	....	....	....	....	....	....	....	....	....	....	....	....	....	....	....	....	....	....
2006-07	Sault Ste. Marie	OHL	37	13	21	34	28	....	....	....	....	....	....	....	....	....	13	9	8	17	14	....	....	....	....
	Toronto Marlies	AHL	6	3	1	4	4	....	....	....	....	....	....	....	....	....	....	....	....	....	....	....	....	....	....
2007-08	**Toronto**	**NHL**	**58**	**10**	**6**	**16**	**14**	**2**	**0**	**2**	**69**	**14.5**	**-12**	**2**	**50.0**	**10:55**	....	....	....	....	....	....	....	....	....
	Toronto Marlies	AHL	14	7	11	18	8	....	....	....	....	....	....	....	....	....	19	2	8	10	8	....	....	....	....
2008-09	**Toronto**	**NHL**	**14**	**0**	**4**	**4**	**0**	**0**	**0**	**0**	**22**	**0.0**	**0**	**3**	**33.3**	**12:42**	....	....	....	....	....	....	....	....	....
	Toronto Marlies	AHL	66	25	41	66	26	....	....	....	....	....	....	....	....	....	6	1	2	3	2	....	....	....	....
2009-10	**Toronto**	**NHL**	**2**	**0**	**0**	**0**	**0**	**0**	**0**	**0**	**2**	**0.0**	**-2**	**0**	**0.0**	**12:13**	....	....	....	....	....	....	....	....	....
	Toronto Marlies	AHL	19	8	7	15	4	....	....	....	....	....	....	....	....	....	....	....	....	....	....	....	....	....	....
	Carolina	**NHL**	**18**	**1**	**5**	**6**	**6**	**0**	**0**	**0**	**15**	**6.7**	**2**	**2**	**100.0**	**12:36**	....	....	....	....	....	....	....	....	....
	Albany River Rats	AHL	20	6	9	15	10	....	....	....	....	....	....	....	....	....	5	0	1	1	0	....	....	....	....
	NHL Totals		**92**	**11**	**15**	**26**	**20**	**2**	**0**	**2**	**108**	**10.2**		**7**	**57.1**	**11:33**	....	....	....	....	....	....	....	....	....

Traded to **Carolina** by **Toronto** for Philippe Paradis, December 3, 2009.

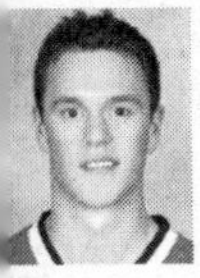

TOEWS, Jonathan

(TAYVZ, JAWN-ah-thuhn) **CHI.**

Center. Shoots left. 6'2", 210 lbs. Born, Winnipeg, Man., April 29, 1988. Chicago's 1st choice, 3rd overall, in 2006 Entry Draft.

			Regular Season														Playoffs								
Season	Club	League	GP	G	A	Pts	PIM	PP	SH	GW	S	%	+/-	TF	F%	Min	GP	G	A	Pts	PIM	PP	SH	GW	Min
2004-05	Shat.-St. Mary's	High-MN	64	48	62	110	38	....	....	....	....	....	....	....	....	....	....	....	....	....	....	....	....	....	....
2005-06	North Dakota	WCHA	42	22	17	39	22	....	....	....	....	....	....	....	....	....	....	....	....	....	....	....	....	....	....
2006-07	North Dakota	WCHA	34	18	28	46	10	....	....	....	....	....	....	....	....	....	....	....	....	....	....	....	....	....	....
2007-08	**Chicago**	**NHL**	**64**	**24**	**30**	**54**	**44**	**7**	**0**	**4**	**144**	**16.7**	**11**	**956**	**53.2**	**18:40**	....	....	....	....	....	....	....	....	....
2008-09	**Chicago**	**NHL**	**82**	**34**	**35**	**69**	**51**	**12**	**0**	**7**	**195**	**17.4**	**12**	**1287**	**54.7**	**18:38**	**17**	**7**	**6**	**13**	**26**	**5**	**0**	**2**	**16:14**
2009-10 ♦	**Chicago**	**NHL**	**76**	**25**	**43**	**68**	**47**	**9**	**1**	**3**	**202**	**12.4**	**22**	**1397**	**57.3**	**20:00**	**22**	**7**	***22**	**29**	**4**	**5**	**0**	**3**	**20:58**
	Canada	Olympics	7	1	*7	8	2	....	....	....	....	....	....	....	....	....	....	....	....	....	....	....	....	....	....
	NHL Totals		**222**	**83**	**108**	**191**	**142**	**28**	**1**	**14**	**541**	**15.3**		**3640**	**55.3**	**19:07**	**39**	**14**	**28**	**42**	**30**	**10**	**0**	**5**	**18:54**

WCHA Second All-Star Team (2007) • NCAA West First All-American Team (2007) • NHL All-Rookie Team (2008) • Olympic Tournament All-Star Team (2010) • Olympic Tournament – Best Forward (2010) • Conn Smythe Trophy (2010)

Played in NHL All-Star Game (2009)

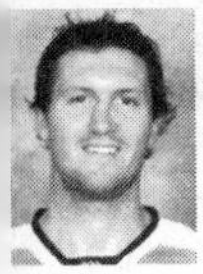

TOLLEFSEN, Ole-Kristian

(TOHL-uhf-suhn, OH-lay-KRIHS-tyahn) **DET.**

Defense. Shoots left. 6'2", 211 lbs. Born, Oslo, Norway, March 29, 1984. Columbus' 3rd choice, 65th overall, in 2002 Entry Draft.

			Regular Season														Playoffs								
Season	Club	League	GP	G	A	Pts	PIM	PP	SH	GW	S	%	+/-	TF	F%	Min	GP	G	A	Pts	PIM	PP	SH	GW	Min
2000-01	Lillehammer IK	Norway	4	0	0	0	2	....	....	....	....	....	....	....	....	....	....	....	....	....	....	....	....	....	....
2001-02	Lillehammer IK	Norway	37	1	5	6	63	....	....	....	....	....	....	....	....	....	6	1	1	2	10	....	....	....	....
	Lillehammer IK	Nor-Jr.	....	....	....	....	....	....	....	....	....	....	....	....	....	....	1	0	2	2	4	....	....	....	....
2002-03	Brandon	WHL	43	6	14	20	73	....	....	....	....	....	....	....	....	....	17	0	2	2	38	....	....	....	....
2003-04	Brandon	WHL	53	3	27	30	94	....	....	....	....	....	....	....	....	....	11	0	4	4	15	....	....	....	....
2004-05	Syracuse Crunch	AHL	64	0	3	3	115	....	....	....	....	....	....	....	....	....	....	....	....	....	....	....	....	....	....
	Dayton Bombers	ECHL	2	0	0	0	0	....	....	....	....	....	....	....	....	....	....	....	....	....	....	....	....	....	....
2005-06	**Columbus**	**NHL**	**5**	**0**	**0**	**0**	**2**	**0**	**0**	**0**	**3**	**0.0**	**-2**	**0**	**0.0**	**16:18**	....	....	....	....	....	....	....	....	....
	Syracuse Crunch	AHL	58	2	16	18	155	....	....	....	....	....	....	....	....	....	1	0	0	0	6	....	....	....	....
2006-07	**Columbus**	**NHL**	**70**	**2**	**3**	**5**	**123**	**1**	**0**	**0**	**39**	**5.1**	**2**	**0**	**0.0**	**14:14**	....	....	....	....	....	....	....	....	....
2007-08	**Columbus**	**NHL**	**51**	**2**	**2**	**4**	**111**	**0**	**1**	**0**	**21**	**9.5**	**-3**	**0**	**0.0**	**12:18**	....	....	....	....	....	....	....	....	....
2008-09	**Columbus**	**NHL**	**19**	**0**	**1**	**1**	**37**	**0**	**0**	**0**	**12**	**0.0**	**-4**	**0**	**0.0**	**10:20**	....	....	....	....	....	....	....	....	....
2009-10	**Philadelphia**	**NHL**	**18**	**0**	**2**	**2**	**23**	**0**	**0**	**0**	**12**	**0.0**	**1**	**0**	**0.0**	**9:52**	....	....	....	....	....	....	....	....	....
	Grand Rapids	AHL	16	1	0	1	44	....	....	....	....	....	....	....	....	....	....	....	....	....	....	....	....	....	....
	Norway	Olympics	3	0	0	0	25	....	....	....	....	....	....	....	....	....	....	....	....	....	....	....	....	....	....
	NHL Totals		**163**	**4**	**8**	**12**	**296**	**1**	**1**	**0**	**87**	**4.6**		**0**	**0.0**	**12:45**	....	....	....	....	....	....	....	....	....

• Missed majority of 2008-09 season recovering from knee surgery, December 17, 2008. Signed as a free agent by **Philadelphia**, July 30, 2009. Traded to **Detroit** by **Philadelphia** with Philadelphia's 5th round choice in 2011 Entry Draft for Ville Leino, February 6, 2010. • Missed majority of 2009-10 season recovering from concussion and knee injuries. Signed as a free agent by **MODO** (Sweden), May 13. 2010.

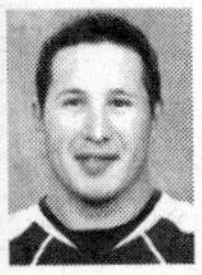

TOOTOO, Jordin

(TOO-TOO, JOHR-dahn) **NSH.**

Right wing. Shoots right. 5'9", 197 lbs. Born, Churchill, Man., February 2, 1983. Nashville's 6th choice, 98th overall, in 2001 Entry Draft.

			Regular Season														Playoffs								
Season	Club	League	GP	G	A	Pts	PIM	PP	SH	GW	S	%	+/-	TF	F%	Min	GP	G	A	Pts	PIM	PP	SH	GW	Min
1997-98	Spruce Grove	AMBHL	STATISTICS NOT AVAILABLE																						
1998-99	OCN Blizzard	MJHL	47	16	21	37	251	....	....	....	....	....	....	....	....	....	....	....	....	....	....	....	....	....	....
99-2000	Brandon	WHL	45	6	10	16	214	....	....	....	....	....	....	....	....	....	....	....	....	....	....	....	....	....	....
2000-01	Brandon	WHL	60	20	28	48	172	....	....	....	....	....	....	....	....	....	6	2	4	6	18	....	....	....	....
2001-02	Brandon	WHL	64	32	39	71	272	....	....	....	....	....	....	....	....	....	16	4	3	7	*58	....	....	....	....
2002-03	Brandon	WHL	51	35	39	74	216	....	....	....	....	....	....	....	....	....	17	6	3	9	49	....	....	....	....
2003-04	**Nashville**	**NHL**	**70**	**4**	**4**	**8**	**137**	**2**	**0**	**0**	**92**	**4.3**	**-6**	**18**	**55.6**	**8:29**	**5**	**0**	**0**	**0**	**4**	**0**	**0**	**0**	**5:09**
2004-05	Milwaukee	AHL	59	10	12	22	266	....	....	....	....	....	....	....	....	....	6	0	0	0	41	....	....	....	....
2005-06	**Nashville**	**NHL**	**34**	**4**	**6**	**10**	**55**	**0**	**0**	**0**	**61**	**6.6**	**9**	**17**	**70.6**	**9:15**	**3**	**0**	**0**	**0**	**0**	**0**	**0**	**0**	**4:04**
	Milwaukee	AHL	41	13	14	27	133	....	....	....	....	....	....	....	....	....	15	9	2	11	35	....	....	....	....
2006-07	**Nashville**	**NHL**	**65**	**3**	**6**	**9**	**116**	**0**	**0**	**0**	**77**	**3.9**	**-11**	**12**	**33.3**	**8:24**	**4**	**0**	**1**	**1**	**21**	**0**	**0**	**0**	**9:32**
2007-08	**Nashville**	**NHL**	**63**	**11**	**7**	**18**	**100**	**0**	**0**	**1**	**98**	**11.2**	**-8**	**4**	**50.0**	**9:54**	**6**	**2**	**0**	**2**	**4**	**0**	**0**	**0**	**12:31**
2008-09	**Nashville**	**NHL**	**72**	**4**	**12**	**16**	**124**	**0**	**0**	**1**	**138**	**2.9**	**-15**	**16**	**56.3**	**12:05**	....	....	....	....	....	....	....	....	....
2009-10	**Nashville**	**NHL**	**51**	**6**	**10**	**16**	**40**	**0**	**0**	**1**	**101**	**5.9**	**2**	**8**	**25.0**	**10:50**	**6**	**0**	**1**	**1**	**2**	**0**	**0**	**0**	**7:58**
	NHL Totals		**355**	**32**	**45**	**77**	**572**	**2**	**0**	**3**	**567**	**5.6**		**75**	**52.0**	**9:52**	**24**	**2**	**2**	**4**	**31**	**0**	**0**	**0**	**8:17**

WHL East First All-Star Team (2003)

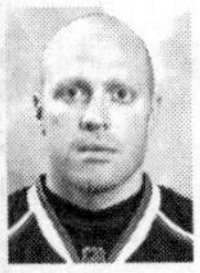

TORRES, Raffi

(TOHR-ehz, RA-fee)

Left wing. Shoots left. 6', 216 lbs. Born, Toronto, Ont., October 8, 1981. NY Islanders' 2nd choice, 5th overall, in 2000 Entry Draft.

			Regular Season														Playoffs								
Season	Club	League	GP	G	A	Pts	PIM	PP	SH	GW	S	%	+/-	TF	F%	Min	GP	G	A	Pts	PIM	PP	SH	GW	Min
1997-98	Thornhill Rattlers	MTJHL	46	17	16	33	90	....	....	....	....	....	....	....	....	....	....	....	....	....	....	....	....	....	....
1998-99	Brampton	OHL	62	35	27	62	32	....	....	....	....	....	....	....	....	....	....	....	....	....	....	....	....	....	....
99-2000	Brampton	OHL	68	43	48	91	40	....	....	....	....	....	....	....	....	....	6	5	2	7	23	....	....	....	....
2000-01	Brampton	OHL	55	33	37	70	76	....	....	....	....	....	....	....	....	....	8	7	4	11	19	....	....	....	....
2001-02	**NY Islanders**	**NHL**	**14**	**0**	**1**	**1**	**6**	**0**	**0**	**0**	**9**	**0.0**	**2**	**0**	**0.0**	**7:35**	....	....	....	....	....	....	....	....	....
	Bridgeport	AHL	59	20	10	30	45	....	....	....	....	....	....	....	....	....	20	8	9	17	26	....	....	....	....
2002-03	**NY Islanders**	**NHL**	**17**	**0**	**5**	**5**	**10**	**0**	**0**	**0**	**12**	**0.0**	**0**	**4**	**25.0**	**7:40**	....	....	....	....	....	....	....	....	....
	Bridgeport	AHL	49	17	15	32	54	....	....	....	....	....	....	....	....	....	....	....	....	....	....	....	....	....	....
	Hamilton	AHL	11	1	7	8	14	....	....	....	....	....	....	....	....	....	23	6	1	7	29	....	....	....	....
2003-04	**Edmonton**	**NHL**	**80**	**20**	**14**	**34**	**65**	**5**	**0**	**3**	**136**	**14.7**	**12**	**21**	**28.6**	**12:38**	....	....	....	....	....	....	....	....	....
2004-05	Edmonton	AHL	67	21	25	46	165	....	....	....	....	....	....	....	....	....	....	....	....	....	....	....	....	....	....
2005-06	**Edmonton**	**NHL**	**82**	**27**	**14**	**41**	**50**	**6**	**0**	**3**	**164**	**16.5**	**4**	**60**	**41.7**	**13:24**	**22**	**4**	**7**	**11**	**16**	**1**	**0**	**1**	**13:15**
2006-07	**Edmonton**	**NHL**	**82**	**15**	**19**	**34**	**88**	**1**	**0**	**0**	**154**	**9.7**	**-7**	**50**	**44.0**	**14:19**	....	....	....	....	....	....	....	....	....
2007-08	**Edmonton**	**NHL**	**32**	**5**	**6**	**11**	**36**	**1**	**0**	**2**	**87**	**5.7**	**-4**	**20**	**65.0**	**17:01**	....	....	....	....	....	....	....	....	....
2008-09	**Columbus**	**NHL**	**51**	**12**	**8**	**20**	**23**	**2**	**0**	**6**	**74**	**16.2**	**-4**	**19**	**57.9**	**12:06**	**4**	**0**	**2**	**2**	**2**	**0**	**0**	**0**	**12:04**
2009-10	**Columbus**	**NHL**	**60**	**19**	**12**	**31**	**32**	**7**	**0**	**3**	**99**	**19.2**	**-8**	**47**	**36.2**	**13:34**	....	....	....	....	....	....	....	....	....
	Buffalo	**NHL**	**14**	**0**	**5**	**5**	**2**	**0**	**0**	**0**	**21**	**0.0**	**-3**	**3**	**33.3**	**13:21**	**4**	**0**	**2**	**2**	**12**	**0**	**0**	**0**	**12:55**
	NHL Totals		**432**	**98**	**84**	**182**	**312**	**22**	**0**	**17**	**756**	**13.0**		**224**	**42.9**	**13:09**	**30**	**4**	**11**	**15**	**30**	**1**	**0**	**1**	**13:03**

OHL All-Rookie Team (1999) • OHL Second All-Star Team (2000, 2001)

Traded to **Edmonton** by **NY Islanders** with Brad Isbister for Janne Niinimaa and Washington's 2nd round choice (previously acquired, NY Islanders selected Evgeni Tunik) in 2003 Entry Draft, March 11, 2003. • Missed majority of 2007-08 season recovering from knee injury suffered in game vs. Detroit, December 15, 2007. Traded to **Columbus** by **Edmonton** for Gilbert Brule, July 1, 2008. Traded to **Buffalo** by **Columbus** for Nathan Paetsch and Vancouver's 2nd round choice (previously acquired, Columbus selected Petr Straka) in 2010 Entry Draft, March 3, 2010.

			Regular Season														Playoffs								
Season	Club	League	GP	G	A	Pts	PIM	PP	SH	GW	S	%	+/-	TF	F%	Min	GP	G	A	Pts	PIM	PP	SH	GW	Min

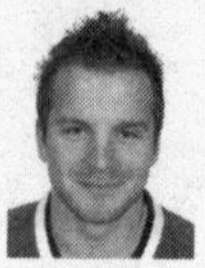

TROTTER, Brock

(TRAW-tuhr, BRAWK) **MTL.**

Center. Shoots right. 5'10", 180 lbs. Born, Brandon, Man., September 18, 1987.

Season	Club	League	GP	G	A	Pts	PIM	PP	SH	GW	S	%	+/-	TF	F%	Min	GP	G	A	Pts	PIM	PP	SH	GW	Min
2003-04	Dauphin Kings	MJHL	63	32	33	65	108	....	....	....	....	....	....	....	....	....	....	....	....	....	....	....	....	....	....
2004-05	Lincoln Stars	USHL	60	20	38	58	84	....	....	....	....	....	....	....	....	....	4	2	3	5	0	....	....	....	....
2005-06	U. of Denver	WCHA	5	3	2	5	2	....	....	....	....	....	....	....	....	....	....	....	....	....	....	....	....	....	....
2006-07	U. of Denver	WCHA	40	16	24	40	22	....	....	....	....	....	....	....	....	....	....	....	....	....	....	....	....	....	....
2007-08	U. of Denver	WCHA	24	13	18	31	18	....	....	....	....	....	....	....	....	....	....	....	....	....	....	....	....	....	....
	Hamilton	AHL	21	3	6	9	4	....	....	....	....	....	....	....	....	....	....	....	....	....	....	....	....	....	....
2008-09	Hamilton	AHL	76	18	31	49	32	....	....	....	....	....	....	....	....	....	6	0	1	1	13	....	....	....	....
2009-10	**Montreal**	**NHL**	**2**	**0**	**0**	**0**	**0**	**0**	**0**	**0**	**6**	**0.0**	**–1**	**0**	**0.0**	**9:03**	....	....	....	....	....	....	....	....	....
	Hamilton	AHL	75	36	41	77	56	....	....	....	....	....	....	....	....	....	19	8	11	19	14	....	....	....	....
	NHL Totals		**2**	**0**	**0**	**0**	**0**	**0**	**0**	**0**	**6**	**0.0**		**0**	**0.0**	**9:02**	....	....	....	....	....	....	....	....	....

• Missed majority of 2005-06 season recovering from achilles tendon injury suffered in game vs. North Dakota (WCHA), October 29, 2005. Signed as a free agent by **Montreal**, February 7, 2008.

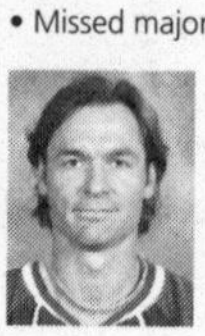

TUCKER, Darcy

(TUH-kuhr, DAHR-see)

Right wing. Shoots left. 5'10", 178 lbs. Born, Castor, Alta., March 15, 1975. Montreal's 8th choice, 151st overall, in 1993 Entry Draft.

Season	Club	League	GP	G	A	Pts	PIM	PP	SH	GW	S	%	+/-	TF	F%	Min	GP	G	A	Pts	PIM	PP	SH	GW	Min
1990-91	Red Deer	AMHL	47	70	90	160	48	....	....	....	....	....	....	....	....	....	....	....	....	....	....	....	....	....	....
1991-92	Kamloops Blazers	WHL	26	3	10	13	32	....	....	....	....	....	....	....	....	....	9	0	1	1	16	....	....	....	....
1992-93	Kamloops Blazers	WHL	67	31	58	89	155	....	....	....	....	....	....	....	....	....	13	7	6	13	34	....	....	....	....
1993-94	Kamloops Blazers	WHL	66	52	88	140	143	....	....	....	....	....	....	....	....	....	19	9	*18	*27	43	....	....	....	....
1994-95	Kamloops Blazers	WHL	64	64	73	137	94	....	....	....	....	....	....	....	....	....	21	*16	15	*31	19	....	....	....	....
1995-96	**Montreal**	**NHL**	**3**	**0**	**0**	**0**	**0**	**0**	**0**	**0**	**1**	**0.0**	**–1**	....	....	....	....	....	....	....	....	....	....	....	....
	Fredericton	AHL	74	29	64	93	174	....	....	....	....	....	....	....	....	....	7	7	3	10	14	....	....	....	....
1996-97	**Montreal**	**NHL**	**73**	**7**	**13**	**20**	**110**	**1**	**0**	**3**	**62**	**11.3**	**–5**	....	....	....	**4**	**0**	**0**	**0**	**0**	**0**	**0**	**0**	....
1997-98	**Montreal**	**NHL**	**39**	**1**	**5**	**6**	**57**	**0**	**0**	**0**	**19**	**5.3**	**–6**	....	....	....	....	....	....	....	....	....	....	....	....
	Tampa Bay	**NHL**	**35**	**6**	**8**	**14**	**89**	**1**	**1**	**0**	**44**	**13.6**	**–8**	....	....	....	....	....	....	....	....	....	....	....	....
1998-99	**Tampa Bay**	**NHL**	**82**	**21**	**22**	**43**	**176**	**8**	**2**	**3**	**178**	**11.8**	**–34**	**1470**	**45.6**	**19:24**	....	....	....	....	....	....	....	....	....
99-2000	**Tampa Bay**	**NHL**	**50**	**14**	**20**	**34**	**108**	**1**	**0**	**2**	**98**	**14.3**	**–15**	**152**	**48.7**	**19:58**	....	....	....	....	....	....	....	....	....
	Toronto	**NHL**	**27**	**7**	**10**	**17**	**55**	**0**	**2**	**3**	**40**	**17.5**	**3**	**11**	**54.6**	**16:41**	**12**	**4**	**2**	**6**	**15**	**1**	**0**	**2**	**17:23**
2000-01	**Toronto**	**NHL**	**82**	**16**	**21**	**37**	**141**	**2**	**0**	**4**	**122**	**13.1**	**6**	**413**	**47.0**	**16:09**	**11**	**0**	**2**	**2**	**6**	**0**	**0**	**0**	**13:59**
2001-02	**Toronto**	**NHL**	**77**	**24**	**35**	**59**	**92**	**7**	**0**	**5**	**124**	**19.4**	**24**	**138**	**43.5**	**16:59**	**17**	**4**	**4**	**8**	**38**	**1**	**0**	**1**	**16:50**
2002-03	**Toronto**	**NHL**	**77**	**10**	**26**	**36**	**119**	**4**	**1**	**2**	**108**	**9.3**	**–7**	**68**	**45.6**	**15:21**	**6**	**0**	**3**	**3**	**6**	**0**	**0**	**0**	**21:07**
2003-04	**Toronto**	**NHL**	**64**	**21**	**11**	**32**	**68**	**8**	**1**	**2**	**146**	**14.4**	**4**	**136**	**50.7**	**17:50**	**12**	**2**	**0**	**2**	**14**	**1**	**0**	**0**	**13:54**
2004-05			DID NOT PLAY																						
2005-06	**Toronto**	**NHL**	**74**	**28**	**33**	**61**	**100**	**18**	**0**	**4**	**189**	**14.8**	**–12**	**29**	**58.6**	**17:38**	....	....	....	....	....	....	....	....	....
2006-07	**Toronto**	**NHL**	**56**	**24**	**19**	**43**	**81**	**15**	**0**	**6**	**143**	**16.8**	**–11**	**15**	**40.0**	**17:47**	....	....	....	....	....	....	....	....	....
2007-08	**Toronto**	**NHL**	**74**	**18**	**16**	**34**	**100**	**7**	**0**	**3**	**152**	**11.8**	**–8**	**25**	**52.0**	**16:26**	....	....	....	....	....	....	....	....	....
2008-09	**Colorado**	**NHL**	**63**	**8**	**8**	**16**	**67**	**2**	**0**	**1**	**94**	**8.5**	**–13**	**35**	**42.9**	**14:07**	....	....	....	....	....	....	....	....	....
2009-10	**Colorado**	**NHL**	**71**	**10**	**14**	**24**	**47**	**3**	**0**	**1**	**73**	**13.7**	**–3**	**45**	**64.4**	**12:07**	**6**	**0**	**0**	**0**	**2**	**0**	**0**	**0**	**11:59**
	NHL Totals		**947**	**215**	**261**	**476**	**1410**	**77**	**7**	**39**	**1593**	**13.5**		**2537**	**46.7**	**16:38**	**68**	**10**	**11**	**21**	**81**	**3**	**0**	**3**	**15:51**

WHL West First All-Star Team (1994, 1995) • Canadian Major Junior First All-Star Team (1994) • Memorial Cup Tournament All-Star Team (1994, 1995) • Stafford Smythe Memorial Trophy (Memorial Cup Tournament - MVP) (1994) • Dudley "Red" Garrett Memorial Award (AHL – Rookie of the Year) (1996)

Traded to **Tampa Bay** by **Montreal** with Stephane Richer and David Wilkie for Patrick Poulin, Mick Vukota and Igor Ulanov, January 15, 1998. Traded to **Toronto** by **Tampa Bay** with Tampa Bay's 4th round choice (Miguel Delisle) in 2000 Entry Draft for Mike Johnson, Marek Posmyk and Toronto's 5th (Pavel Sedov) and 6th (Aaron Gionet) round choices in 2000 Entry Draft, February 9, 2000. Signed as a free agent by **Colorado**, July 1, 2008.

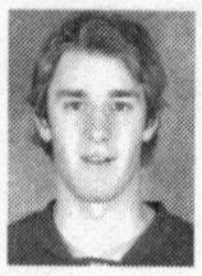

TURRIS, Kyle

(TUH-rihs, KIGHL) **PHX.**

Center. Shoots right. 6'1", 188 lbs. Born, New Westminster, B.C., August 14, 1989. Phoenix's 1st choice, 3rd overall, in 2007 Entry Draft.

Season	Club	League	GP	G	A	Pts	PIM	PP	SH	GW	S	%	+/-	TF	F%	Min	GP	G	A	Pts	PIM	PP	SH	GW	Min
2004-05	Grandview	Minor-BC	30	13	20	33	....	....	....	....	....	....	....	....	....	....	12	3	6	9	....	....	....	....	....
2005-06	Burnaby Express	BCHL	57	36	36	72	32	....	....	....	....	....	....	....	....	....	20	10	13	23	6	....	....	....	....
2006-07	Burnaby Express	BCHL	53	66	55	121	83	....	....	....	....	....	....	....	....	....	14	12	14	26	16	....	....	....	....
2007-08	U. of Wisconsin	WCHA	36	11	24	35	38	....	....	....	....	....	....	....	....	....	....	....	....	....	....	....	....	....	....
	Phoenix	**NHL**	**3**	**0**	**1**	**1**	**2**	**0**	**0**	**0**	**11**	**0.0**	**–5**	**42**	**40.5**	**19:45**	....	....	....	....	....	....	....	....	....
2008-09	**Phoenix**	**NHL**	**63**	**8**	**12**	**20**	**21**	**3**	**0**	**3**	**91**	**8.8**	**–15**	**567**	**42.9**	**12:55**	....	....	....	....	....	....	....	....	....
	San Antonio	AHL	8	4	3	7	6	....	....	....	....	....	....	....	....	....	....	....	....	....	....	....	....	....	....
2009-10	San Antonio	AHL	76	24	39	63	60	....	....	....	....	....	....	....	....	....	....	....	....	....	....	....	....	....	....
	NHL Totals		**66**	**8**	**13**	**21**	**23**	**3**	**0**	**3**	**102**	**7.8**		**609**	**42.7**	**13:14**	....	....	....	....	....	....	....	....	....

WCHA All-Rookie Team (2008)

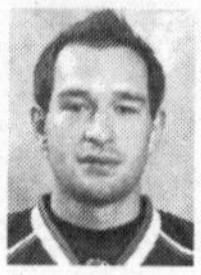

TYUTIN, Fedor

(T'YOO-tihn, FEH-duhr) **CBJ**

Defense. Shoots left. 6'3", 218 lbs. Born, Izhevsk, USSR, July 19, 1983. NY Rangers' 2nd choice, 40th overall, in 2001 Entry Draft.

Season	Club	League	GP	G	A	Pts	PIM	PP	SH	GW	S	%	+/-	TF	F%	Min	GP	G	A	Pts	PIM	PP	SH	GW	Min
1998-99	Magnitogorsk 2	Russia-4	7	0	1	1	2	....	....	....	....	....	....	....	....	....	....	....	....	....	....	....	....	....	....
99-2000	Izhstal Izhevsk 2	Russia-3	38	11	8	19	68	....	....	....	....	....	....	....	....	....	....	....	....	....	....	....	....	....	....
	Izhstal Izhevsk	Russia-2	10	0	1	1	12	....	....	....	....	....	....	....	....	....	....	....	....	....	....	....	....	....	....
2000-01	St. Petersburg	Russia	34	2	4	6	20	....	....	....	....	....	....	....	....	....	....	....	....	....	....	....	....	....	....
2001-02	Guelph Storm	OHL	53	19	40	59	54	....	....	....	....	....	....	....	....	....	9	2	8	10	8	....	....	....	....
2002-03	St. Petersburg	Russia	10	1	1	2	16	....	....	....	....	....	....	....	....	....	....	....	....	....	....	....	....	....	....
	Ak Bars Kazan	Russia	10	0	0	0	8	....	....	....	....	....	....	....	....	....	5	0	0	0	4	....	....	....	....
2003-04	**NY Rangers**	**NHL**	**25**	**2**	**5**	**7**	**14**	**0**	**1**	**0**	**33**	**6.1**	**–4**	**1**	**0.0**	**20:08**	....	....	....	....	....	....	....	....	....
	Hartford	AHL	43	5	9	14	50	....	....	....	....	....	....	....	....	....	16	0	5	5	18	....	....	....	....
2004-05	Hartford	AHL	13	2	1	3	10	....	....	....	....	....	....	....	....	....	....	....	....	....	....	....	....	....	....
	St. Petersburg	Russia	35	5	3	8	24	....	....	....	....	....	....	....	....	....	....	....	....	....	....	....	....	....	....
2005-06	**NY Rangers**	**NHL**	**77**	**6**	**19**	**25**	**58**	**4**	**0**	**2**	**102**	**5.9**	**1**	**1**	**0.0**	**20:33**	**4**	**0**	**1**	**1**	**0**	**0**	**0**	**0**	**17:50**
	Russia	Olympics	8	0	1	1	4	....	....	....	....	....	....	....	....	....	....	....	....	....	....	....	....	....	....
2006-07	**NY Rangers**	**NHL**	**66**	**2**	**12**	**14**	**44**	**1**	**1**	**0**	**75**	**2.7**	**–8**	**1**	**0.0**	**20:02**	**10**	**0**	**5**	**5**	**8**	**0**	**0**	**0**	**19:30**
2007-08	**NY Rangers**	**NHL**	**82**	**5**	**15**	**20**	**43**	**1**	**0**	**0**	**131**	**3.8**	**5**	**0**	**0.0**	**20:27**	**10**	**0**	**3**	**3**	**4**	**0**	**0**	**0**	**19:52**
2008-09	**Columbus**	**NHL**	**82**	**9**	**25**	**34**	**81**	**5**	**1**	**0**	**167**	**5.4**	**1**	**1**	**100.0**	**23:31**	**4**	**0**	**0**	**0**	**0**	**0**	**0**	**0**	**23:16**
2009-10	**Columbus**	**NHL**	**80**	**6**	**26**	**32**	**49**	**3**	**0**	**2**	**149**	**4.0**	**–7**	**3**	**33.3**	**23:31**	....	....	....	....	....	....	....	....	....
	Russia	Olympics	4	0	2	2	2	....	....	....	....	....	....	....	....	....	....	....	....	....	....	....	....	....	....
	NHL Totals		**412**	**30**	**102**	**132**	**289**	**14**	**3**	**4**	**657**	**4.6**		**7**	**28.6**	**21:35**	**28**	**0**	**9**	**9**	**12**	**0**	**0**	**0**	**19:56**

Signed as a free agent by **St. Petersburg** (Russia), November 11, 2004. Traded to **Columbus** by **NY Rangers** with Christian Backman for Nikolai Zherdev and Dan Fritsche, July 2, 2008.

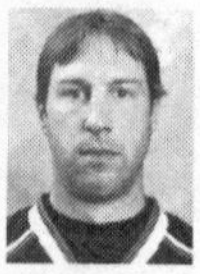

UMBERGER, R.J.

(UHM-buhr-guhr, AHR-JAY) **CBJ**

Center. Shoots left. 6'2", 219 lbs. Born, Pittsburgh, PA, May 3, 1982. Vancouver's 1st choice, 16th overall, in 2001 Entry Draft.

Season	Club	League	GP	G	A	Pts	PIM	PP	SH	GW	S	%	+/-	TF	F%	Min	GP	G	A	Pts	PIM	PP	SH	GW	Min
1997-98	Plum Mustangs	High-PA	26	*60	*56	*116	....	....	....	....	....	....	....	....	....	....	....	....	....	....	....	....	....	....	....
1998-99	USNTDP	USHL	5	2	2	4	0	....	....	....	....	....	....	....	....	....	....	....	....	....	....	....	....	....	....
	USNTDP	NAHL	50	21	21	42	32	....	....	....	....	....	....	....	....	....	....	....	....	....	....	....	....	....	....
99-2000	USNTDP	U-18	6	1	0	1	2	....	....	....	....	....	....	....	....	....	....	....	....	....	....	....	....	....	....
	USNTDP	USHL	57	33	35	68	20	....	....	....	....	....	....	....	....	....	....	....	....	....	....	....	....	....	....
2000-01	Ohio State	CCHA	32	14	23	37	18	....	....	....	....	....	....	....	....	....	....	....	....	....	....	....	....	....	....
2001-02	Ohio State	CCHA	37	18	21	39	31	....	....	....	....	....	....	....	....	....	....	....	....	....	....	....	....	....	....
2002-03	Ohio State	CCHA	43	26	27	53	16	....	....	....	....	....	....	....	....	....	....	....	....	....	....	....	....	....	....
2003-04			DID NOT PLAY																						
2004-05	Philadelphia	AHL	80	21	44	65	36	....	....	....	....	....	....	....	....	....	21	3	7	10	12	....	....	....	....
2005-06	**Philadelphia**	**NHL**	**73**	**20**	**18**	**38**	**18**	**5**	**0**	**2**	**138**	**14.5**	**9**	**163**	**50.3**	**13:14**	**5**	**1**	**0**	**1**	**2**	**0**	**0**	**0**	**11:15**
	Philadelphia	AHL	8	3	7	10	8	....	....	....	....	....	....	....	....	....	....	....	....	....	....	....	....	....	....
2006-07	**Philadelphia**	**NHL**	**81**	**16**	**12**	**28**	**41**	**2**	**2**	**1**	**134**	**11.9**	**–32**	**535**	**44.5**	**14:32**	....	....	....	....	....	....	....	....	....
2007-08	**Philadelphia**	**NHL**	**74**	**13**	**37**	**50**	**19**	**4**	**0**	**3**	**173**	**7.5**	**0**	**117**	**38.5**	**17:52**	**17**	**10**	**5**	**15**	**10**	**1**	**0**	**2**	**16:51**

			Regular Season														Playoffs								
Season	Club	League	GP	G	A	Pts	PIM	PP	SH	GW	S	%	+/-	TF	F%	Min	GP	G	A	Pts	PIM	PP	SH	GW	Min
2008-09	**Columbus**	**NHL**	**82**	**26**	**20**	**46**	**53**	**9**	**0**	**2**	**234**	**11.1**	**–10**	**841**	**48.0**	**18:46**	**4**	**3**	**0**	**3**	**0**	**2**	**0**	**0**	**16:22**
2009-10	**Columbus**	**NHL**	**82**	**23**	**32**	**55**	**40**	**8**	**1**	**4**	**221**	**10.4**	**–16**	**704**	**52.8**	**19:10**	....	....	....	....	....	....	....	....	....
	NHL Totals		**392**	**98**	**119**	**217**	**171**	**28**	**3**	**12**	**900**	**10.9**		**2360**	**48.3**	**16:47**	**26**	**14**	**5**	**19**	**12**	**3**	**0**	**2**	**15:42**

CHA All-Rookie Team (2001) • CCHA Rookie of the Year (2001) • CCHA First All-Star Team (2003) • NCAA West Second All-American Team (2003)

Missed entire 2003-04 season due to contract dispute. Traded to **NY Rangers** by **Vancouver** with Martin Grenier for Martin Rucinsky, March 9, 2004. Signed as a free agent by **Philadelphia**, June 16, 04. Traded to **Columbus** by **Philadelphia** with Philadelphia's 4th round choice (Drew Olson) in 2008 Entry Draft for Colorado's 1st round choice (previously acquired, Philadelphia selected Luca Sbisa) in 08 Entry Draft and Columbus's 3rd round choice (Marc-Andre Bourdon) in 2008 Entry Draft, June 20, 2008.

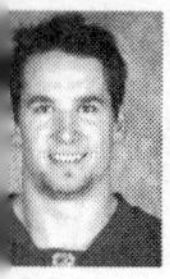

UPSHALL, Scottie

(UHP-shuhl, SKAW-tee) **PHX.**

Left wing. Shoots left. 6', 197 lbs. Born, Fort McMurray, Alta., October 7, 1983. Nashville's 1st choice, 6th overall, in 2002 Entry Draft.

Season	Club	League	GP	G	A	Pts	PIM	PP	SH	GW	S	%	+/-	TF	F%	Min	GP	G	A	Pts	PIM	PP	SH	GW	Min
1998-99	Fort McMurray	AMHL	28	62	40	102	100	....	....	....	....	....	....	....	....	....	....	....	....	....	....	....	....	....	....
99-2000	Fort McMurray	AJHL	52	26	26	52	65	....	....	....	....	....	....	....	....	....	....	....	....	....	....	....	....	....	....
2000-01	Kamloops Blazers	WHL	70	42	45	87	111	....	....	....	....	....	....	....	....	....	4	0	2	2	10	....	....	....	....
2001-02	Kamloops Blazers	WHL	61	32	51	83	139	....	....	....	....	....	....	....	....	....	4	1	2	3	21	....	....	....	....
2002-03	**Nashville**	**NHL**	**8**	**1**	**0**	**1**	**0**	**0**	**0**	**0**	**6**	**16.7**	**2**	**2**	**0.0**	**8:42**	....	....	....	....	....	....	....	....	....
	Kamloops Blazers	WHL	42	25	31	56	111	....	....	....	....	....	....	....	....	....	6	0	2	2	34	....	....	....	....
	Milwaukee	AHL	2	1	0	1	2	....	....	....	....	....	....	....	....	....	6	0	0	0	2	....	....	....	....
2003-04	**Nashville**	**NHL**	**7**	**0**	**1**	**1**	**0**	**0**	**0**	**0**	**6**	**0.0**	**–2**	**8**	**37.5**	**9:11**	....	....	....	....	....	....	....	....	....
	Milwaukee	AHL	31	13	11	24	42	....	....	....	....	....	....	....	....	....	8	3	0	3	4	....	....	....	....
2004-05	Milwaukee	AHL	62	19	27	46	108	....	....	....	....	....	....	....	....	....	5	2	2	4	8	....	....	....	....
2005-06	**Nashville**	**NHL**	**48**	**8**	**16**	**24**	**34**	**1**	**0**	**2**	**72**	**11.1**	**14**	**11**	**45.5**	**10:26**	**2**	**0**	**0**	**0**	**0**	**0**	**0**	**0**	**11:57**
	Milwaukee	AHL	23	17	16	33	44	....	....	....	....	....	....	....	....	....	14	6	10	16	20	....	....	....	....
2006-07	**Nashville**	**NHL**	**14**	**2**	**1**	**3**	**18**	**0**	**0**	**2**	**27**	**7.4**	**–1**	**0**	**0.0**	**10:28**	....	....	....	....	....	....	....	....	....
	Milwaukee	AHL	5	0	1	1	6	....	....	....	....	....	....	....	....	....	....	....	....	....	....	....	....	....	....
	Philadelphia	**NHL**	**18**	**6**	**7**	**13**	**8**	**1**	**1**	**2**	**60**	**10.0**	**4**	**18**	**44.4**	**18:05**	....	....	....	....	....	....	....	....	....
2007-08	**Philadelphia**	**NHL**	**61**	**14**	**16**	**30**	**74**	**3**	**0**	**1**	**128**	**10.9**	**2**	**7**	**28.6**	**13:20**	**17**	**3**	**4**	**7**	***44**	**1**	**0**	**1**	**13:57**
2008-09	**Philadelphia**	**NHL**	**55**	**7**	**14**	**21**	**63**	**2**	**0**	**0**	**126**	**5.6**	**5**	**10**	**10.0**	**13:13**	....	....	....	....	....	....	....	....	....
	Phoenix	**NHL**	**19**	**8**	**5**	**13**	**26**	**3**	**0**	**1**	**66**	**12.1**	**2**	**9**	**44.4**	**18:35**	....	....	....	....	....	....	....	....	....
2009-10	**Phoenix**	**NHL**	**49**	**18**	**14**	**32**	**50**	**2**	**0**	**4**	**119**	**15.1**	**5**	**17**	**41.2**	**15:03**	....	....	....	....	....	....	....	....	....
	NHL Totals		**279**	**64**	**74**	**138**	**273**	**12**	**1**	**12**	**610**	**10.5**		**82**	**36.6**	**13:24**	**19**	**3**	**4**	**7**	**44**	**1**	**0**	**1**	**13:44**

HL All-Rookie Team (2001) • WHL Rookie of the Year (2001) • CHL All-Rookie Team (2001) • Canadian Major Junior Rookie of the Year (2001) • WHL West Second All-Star Team (2002)

Missed majority of 2003-04 season recovering from knee injury suffered in game vs. Phoenix, December 22, 2003. Traded to **Philadelphia** by **Nashville** with Ryan Parent and Nashville's 1st (later traded ck to Nashville - Nashville selected Jonathon Blum) and 3rd (later traded to Washington - Washington selected Phil Desimone) round choices in 2007 Entry Draft for Peter Forsberg, February 15, 2007. ded to **Phoenix** by **Philadelphia** with Philadelphia's 2nd round choice in 2011 Entry Draft for Daniel Carcillo, March 4, 2009.

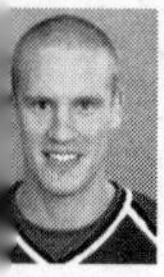

VAANANEN, Ossi

(VAN-ih-nehn, AW-see)

Defense. Shoots left. 6'4", 215 lbs. Born, Vantaa, Finland, August 18, 1980. Phoenix's 2nd choice, 43rd overall, in 1998 Entry Draft.

Season	Club	League	GP	G	A	Pts	PIM	PP	SH	GW	S	%	+/-	TF	F%	Min	GP	G	A	Pts	PIM	PP	SH	GW	Min
1995-96	Jokerit U18	Fin-U18	8	0	0	0	2	....	....	....	....	....	....	....	....	....	2	0	0	0	0	....	....	....	....
1996-97	Jokerit U18	Fin-U18	18	1	2	3	43	....	....	....	....	....	....	....	....	....	....	....	....	....	....	....	....	....	....
	Jokerit Helsinki Jr.	Fin-Jr.	1	0	0	0	0	....	....	....	....	....	....	....	....	....	....	....	....	....	....	....	....	....	....
1997-98	Jokerit U18	Fin-U18	7	3	3	6	8	....	....	....	....	....	....	....	....	....	....	....	....	....	....	....	....	....	....
	Jokerit Helsinki Jr.	Fin-Jr.	31	0	6	6	24	....	....	....	....	....	....	....	....	....	7	0	2	2	16	....	....	....	....
1998-99	Jokerit Helsinki Jr.	Fin-Jr.	12	1	6	7	16	....	....	....	....	....	....	....	....	....	6	1	0	1	12	....	....	....	....
	Jokerit Helsinki	Finland	48	0	1	1	42	....	....	....	....	....	....	....	....	....	3	0	1	1	2	....	....	....	....
	Jokerit Helsinki	EuroHL	5	0	0	0	2	....	....	....	....	....	....	....	....	....	1	0	1	1	2	....	....	....	....
99-2000	Jokerit Helsinki	Finland	49	1	6	7	46	....	....	....	....	....	....	....	....	....	11	1	1	2	2	....	....	....	....
2000-01	**Phoenix**	**NHL**	**81**	**4**	**12**	**16**	**90**	**0**	**0**	**2**	**69**	**5.8**	**9**	**0**	**0.0**	**19:09**	....	....	....	....	....	....	....	....	....
2001-02	**Phoenix**	**NHL**	**76**	**2**	**12**	**14**	**74**	**0**	**1**	**0**	**41**	**4.9**	**6**	**0**	**0.0**	**20:13**	**5**	**0**	**0**	**0**	**6**	**0**	**0**	**0**	**20:33**
	Finland	Olympics	2	0	1	1	0	....	....	....	....	....	....	....	....	....	....	....	....	....	....	....	....	....	....
2002-03	**Phoenix**	**NHL**	**67**	**2**	**7**	**9**	**82**	**0**	**0**	**0**	**49**	**4.1**	**1**	**0**	**0.0**	**19:15**	....	....	....	....	....	....	....	....	....
2003-04	**Phoenix**	**NHL**	**67**	**2**	**4**	**6**	**87**	**0**	**0**	**1**	**39**	**5.1**	**–10**	**0**	**0.0**	**19:21**	....	....	....	....	....	....	....	....	....
	Colorado	**NHL**	**12**	**0**	**0**	**0**	**2**	**0**	**0**	**0**	**6**	**0.0**	**–4**	**0**	**0.0**	**18:36**	**11**	**0**	**1**	**1**	**18**	**0**	**0**	**0**	**22:06**
2004-05	Jokerit Helsinki	Finland	28	2	2	4	30	....	....	....	....	....	....	....	....	....	12	0	0	0	26	....	....	....	....
2005-06	**Colorado**	**NHL**	**53**	**0**	**4**	**4**	**56**	**0**	**0**	**0**	**34**	**0.0**	**10**	**1**	**0.0**	**13:34**	**1**	**0**	**0**	**0**	**0**	**0**	**0**	**0**	**13:58**
2006-07	**Colorado**	**NHL**	**74**	**2**	**6**	**8**	**69**	**0**	**0**	**1**	**32**	**6.3**	**6**	**0**	**0.0**	**14:20**	....	....	....	....	....	....	....	....	....
2007-08	Djurgarden	Sweden	45	7	8	15	102	....	....	....	....	....	....	....	....	....	5	0	0	0	2	....	....	....	....
2008-09	**Philadelphia**	**NHL**	**46**	**1**	**9**	**10**	**22**	**0**	**0**	**0**	**18**	**5.6**	**7**	**0**	**0.0**	**18:28**	....	....	....	....	....	....	....	....	....
	Vancouver	**NHL**	**3**	**0**	**1**	**1**	**0**	**0**	**0**	**0**	**2**	**0.0**	**1**	**0**	**0.0**	**9:28**	**3**	**0**	**0**	**0**	**2**	**0**	**0**	**0**	**9:14**
2009-10	Dynamo Minsk	Rus-KHL	52	0	6	6	76	....	....	....	....	....	....	....	....	....	....	....	....	....	....	....	....	....	....
	NHL Totals		**479**	**13**	**55**	**68**	**482**	**0**	**1**	**4**	**290**	**4.5**		**1**	**0.0**	**17:52**	**20**	**0**	**1**	**1**	**26**	**0**	**0**	**0**	**19:23**

ded to **Colorado** by **Phoenix** with Chris Gratton and Phoenix's 2nd round choice (Paul Stastny) in 2005 Entry Draft for Derek Morris and Keith Ballard, March 9, 2004. Signed as a free agent by **Jokerit sinki** (Finland), December 1, 2004. Signed as a free agent by **Djurgarden** (Sweden), September 26, 2007. Signed as a free agent by **Philadelphia**, July 1, 2008. Claimed on waivers by **Vancouver** from **ladelphia**, February 27, 2009. Signed as a free agent by **Minsk** (Russia-KHL), August 2, 2009.

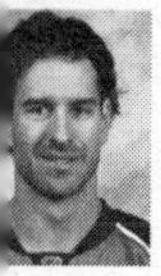

VALABIK, Boris

(vuh-LA-bihk, BOHR-ihs) **ATL.**

Defense. Shoots left. 6'7", 245 lbs. Born, Nitra, Czech., February 14, 1986. Atlanta's 1st choice, 10th overall, in 2004 Entry Draft.

Season	Club	League	GP	G	A	Pts	PIM	PP	SH	GW	S	%	+/-	TF	F%	Min	GP	G	A	Pts	PIM	PP	SH	GW	Min
2002-03	HKM Nitra Jr.	Slovak-Jr.	46	2	12	14	145	....	....	....	....	....	....	....	....	....	....	....	....	....	....	....	....	....	....
2003-04	Kitchener Rangers	OHL	68	3	13	16	278	....	....	....	....	....	....	....	....	....	5	0	0	0	8	....	....	....	....
2004-05	Kitchener Rangers	OHL	43	0	4	4	231	....	....	....	....	....	....	....	....	....	15	0	0	0	56	....	....	....	....
2005-06	Kitchener Rangers	OHL	52	1	9	10	216	....	....	....	....	....	....	....	....	....	5	0	2	2	14	....	....	....	....
2006-07	Chicago Wolves	AHL	50	2	7	9	184	....	....	....	....	....	....	....	....	....	8	0	1	1	37	....	....	....	....
2007-08	**Atlanta**	**NHL**	**7**	**0**	**0**	**0**	**42**	**0**	**0**	**0**	**5**	**0.0**	**–2**	**0**	**0.0**	**16:42**	....	....	....	....	....	....	....	....	....
	Chicago Wolves	AHL	58	1	7	8	229	....	....	....	....	....	....	....	....	....	24	3	1	4	71	....	....	....	....
2008-09	**Atlanta**	**NHL**	**50**	**0**	**5**	**5**	**132**	**0**	**0**	**0**	**16**	**0.0**	**–14**	**0**	**0.0**	**15:15**	....	....	....	....	....	....	....	....	....
	Chicago Wolves	AHL	11	1	2	3	21	....	....	....	....	....	....	....	....	....	....	....	....	....	....	....	....	....	....
2009-10	**Atlanta**	**NHL**	**23**	**0**	**2**	**2**	**36**	**0**	**0**	**0**	**22**	**0.0**	**2**	**0**	**0.0**	**13:14**	....	....	....	....	....	....	....	....	....
	Chicago Wolves	AHL	6	0	0	0	10	....	....	....	....	....	....	....	....	....	....	....	....	....	....	....	....	....	....
	NHL Totals		**80**	**0**	**7**	**7**	**210**	**0**	**0**	**0**	**43**	**0.0**		**0**	**0.0**	**14:47**	....	....	....	....	....	....	....	....	....

All-Rookie Team (2004) • Canadian Major Junior All-Rookie Team (2004)

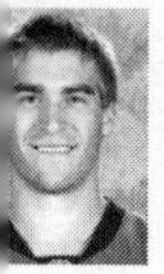

VAN DER GULIK, David

(VAN DUHR-GOO-lihk, DAY-vihd) **COL.**

Right wing. Shoots left. 5'10", 173 lbs. Born, Abbotsford, B.C., April 20, 1983. Calgary's 10th choice, 206th overall, in 2002 Entry Draft.

Season	Club	League	GP	G	A	Pts	PIM	PP	SH	GW	S	%	+/-	TF	F%	Min	GP	G	A	Pts	PIM	PP	SH	GW	Min
99-2000	Chilliwack Chiefs	BCHL	41	35	46	81	....	....	....	....	....	....	....	....	....	....	....	....	....	....	....	....	....	....	....
2000-01	Chilliwack Chiefs	BCHL	60	42	38	80	....	....	....	....	....	....	....	....	....	....	....	....	....	....	....	....	....	....	....
2001-02	Chilliwack Chiefs	BCHL	56	38	62	100	90	....	....	....	....	....	....	....	....	....	13	8	11	19	....	....	....	....	....
2002-03	Boston University	H-East	40	10	10	20	56	....	....	....	....	....	....	....	....	....	....	....	....	....	....	....	....	....	....
2003-04	Boston University	H-East	35	13	7	20	74	....	....	....	....	....	....	....	....	....	....	....	....	....	....	....	....	....	....
2004-05	Boston University	H-East	41	18	13	31	48	....	....	....	....	....	....	....	....	....	....	....	....	....	....	....	....	....	....
2005-06	Boston University	H-East	25	11	11	22	26	....	....	....	....	....	....	....	....	....	....	....	....	....	....	....	....	....	....
2006-07	Omaha	AHL	80	16	27	43	69	....	....	....	....	....	....	....	....	....	6	0	2	2	4	....	....	....	....
2007-08	Quad City Flames	AHL	80	19	23	42	62	....	....	....	....	....	....	....	....	....	....	....	....	....	....	....	....	....	....
2008-09	**Calgary**	**NHL**	**6**	**0**	**2**	**2**	**0**	**0**	**0**	**0**	**11**	**0.0**	**–1**	**1**	**0.0**	**8:29**	....	....	....	....	....	....	....	....	....
	Quad City Flames	AHL	73	17	19	36	58	....	....	....	....	....	....	....	....	....	....	....	....	....	....	....	....	....	....
2009-10	Abbotsford Heat	AHL	64	16	24	40	58	....	....	....	....	....	....	....	....	....	13	4	2	6	10	....	....	....	....
	NHL Totals		**6**	**0**	**2**	**2**	**0**	**0**	**0**	**0**	**11**	**0.0**		**1**	**0.0**	**8:29**	....	....	....	....	....	....	....	....	....

key East All-Rookie Team (2003)

ed as a free agent by **Colorado**, July 2, 2010.

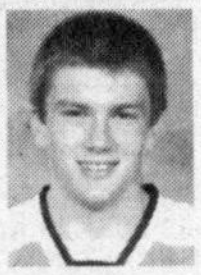

van RIEMSDYK, James

(VAN REEMZ-dighk, JAYMZ) **PH**

Left wing. Shoots left. 6'3", 200 lbs. Born, Middletown, NJ, May 4, 1989. Philadelphia's 1st choice, 2nd overall, in 2007 Entry Draft.

			Regular Season														Playoffs								
Season	Club	League	GP	G	A	Pts	PIM	PP	SH	GW	S	%	+/-	TF	F%	Min	GP	G	A	Pts	PIM	PP	SH	GW	Mi
2004-05	Christian Bros.	High-NJ	30	36	24	60	....	....	....	....	....	....	....	....	....	....	....	....	....	....	....	....	....	....	....
2005-06	USNTDP	U-17	11	7	5	12	18	....	....	....	....	....	....	....	....	....	....	....	....	....	....	....	....	....	....
	USNTDP	U-18	14	1	3	4	6	....	....	....	....	....	....	....	....	....	....	....	....	....	....	....	....	....	....
	USNTDP	NAHL	37	18	11	29	36	....	....	....	....	....	....	....	....	....	7	1	0	1	8	....	....	....	....
2006-07	USNTDP	U-18	39	25	28	53	48	....	....	....	....	....	....	....	....	....	....	....	....	....	....	....	....	....	....
	USNTDP	NAHL	12	13	12	25	37	....	....	....	....	....	....	....	....	....	....	....	....	....	....	....	....	....	....
2007-08	New Hampshire	H-East	31	11	23	34	36	....	....	....	....	....	....	....	....	....	....	....	....	....	....	....	....	....	....
2008-09	New Hampshire	H-East	36	17	23	40	47	....	....	....	....	....	....	....	....	....	....	....	....	....	....	....	....	....	....
	Philadelphia	AHL	7	1	1	2	2	....	....	....	....	....	....	....	....	....	4	0	0	0	2	....	....	....	....
2009-10	**Philadelphia**	**NHL**	**78**	**15**	**20**	**35**	**30**	**4**	**0**	**6**	**173**	**8.7**	**–1**	**2**	**0.0**	**12:58**	**21**	**3**	**3**	**6**	**4**	**0**	**0**	**0**	**11:5**
	NHL Totals		**78**	**15**	**20**	**35**	**30**	**4**	**0**	**6**	**173**	**8.7**		**2**	**0.0**	**12:58**	**21**	**3**	**3**	**6**	**4**	**0**	**0**	**0**	**11:5**

Hockey East All-Rookie Team (2008) • Hockey East Second All-Star Team (2009)

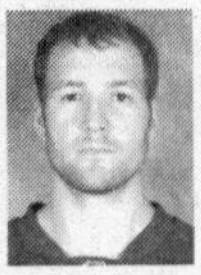

VANDERMEER, Jim

(VAN-duhr-meer, JIHM) **EDM**

Defense. Shoots left. 6'1", 210 lbs. Born, Caroline, Alta., February 21, 1980.

Season	Club	League	GP	G	A	Pts	PIM	PP	SH	GW	S	%	+/-	TF	F%	Min	GP	G	A	Pts	PIM	PP	SH	GW	Mi
1997-98	Red Deer	AMHL	26	4	8	12	51	....	....	....	....	....	....	....	....	....	....	....	....	....	....	....	....	....	....
	Red Deer Rebels	WHL	35	0	3	3	55	....	....	....	....	....	....	....	....	....	2	0	0	0	0	....	....	....	....
1998-99	Red Deer Rebels	WHL	70	5	23	28	258	....	....	....	....	....	....	....	....	....	9	0	1	1	24	....	....	....	....
99-2000	Red Deer Rebels	WHL	71	8	30	38	221	....	....	....	....	....	....	....	....	....	4	0	1	1	16	....	....	....	....
2000-01	Red Deer Rebels	WHL	72	21	44	65	180	....	....	....	....	....	....	....	....	....	22	3	13	16	43	....	....	....	....
2001-02	Philadelphia	AHL	74	1	13	14	88	....	....	....	....	....	....	....	....	....	5	0	2	2	14	....	....	....	....
2002-03	**Philadelphia**	**NHL**	**24**	**2**	**1**	**3**	**27**	**0**	**0**	**0**	**22**	**9.1**	**9**	**0**	**0.0**	**13:42**	**8**	**0**	**1**	**1**	**9**	**0**	**0**	**0**	**12:4**
	Philadelphia	AHL	48	4	8	12	122	....	....	....	....	....	....	....	....	....	....	....	....	....	....	....	....	....	....
2003-04	**Philadelphia**	**NHL**	**23**	**3**	**2**	**5**	**25**	**0**	**0**	**1**	**24**	**12.5**	**–5**	**0**	**0.0**	**15:47**	....	....	....	....	....	....	....	....	....
	Philadelphia	AHL	26	1	6	7	120	....	....	....	....	....	....	....	....	....	....	....	....	....	....	....	....	....	....
	Chicago	**NHL**	**23**	**2**	**10**	**12**	**58**	**1**	**1**	**0**	**37**	**5.4**	**–6**	**1**	**100.0**	**22:03**	....	....	....	....	....	....	....	....	....
2004-05	Norfolk Admirals	AHL	52	3	10	13	164	....	....	....	....	....	....	....	....	....	....	....	....	....	....	....	....	....	....
2005-06	**Chicago**	**NHL**	**76**	**6**	**18**	**24**	**116**	**2**	**0**	**1**	**93**	**6.5**	**–2**	**1**	**100.0**	**21:47**	....	....	....	....	....	....	....	....	....
2006-07	**Chicago**	**NHL**	**46**	**1**	**6**	**7**	**53**	**0**	**0**	**0**	**50**	**2.0**	**–3**	**0**	**0.0**	**17:50**	....	....	....	....	....	....	....	....	....
2007-08	**Chicago**	**NHL**	**26**	**2**	**7**	**9**	**44**	**1**	**0**	**0**	**23**	**8.7**	**3**	**0**	**0.0**	**19:37**	....	....	....	....	....	....	....	....	....
	Philadelphia	**NHL**	**28**	**1**	**5**	**6**	**27**	**1**	**0**	**0**	**26**	**3.8**	**–1**	**0**	**0.0**	**19:34**	....	....	....	....	....	....	....	....	....
	Calgary	**NHL**	**21**	**0**	**2**	**2**	**39**	**0**	**0**	**0**	**23**	**0.0**	**4**	**0**	**0.0**	**19:44**	**7**	**0**	**0**	**0**	**4**	**0**	**0**	**0**	**16:1**
2008-09	**Calgary**	**NHL**	**45**	**1**	**6**	**7**	**108**	**0**	**0**	**0**	**31**	**3.2**	**1**	**0**	**0.0**	**16:01**	**6**	**0**	**1**	**1**	**4**	**0**	**0**	**0**	**16:3**
2009-10	**Phoenix**	**NHL**	**62**	**4**	**8**	**12**	**60**	**0**	**0**	**1**	**64**	**6.3**	**3**	**0**	**0.0**	**17:41**	....	....	....	....	....	....	....	....	....
	NHL Totals		**374**	**22**	**65**	**87**	**557**	**5**	**1**	**3**	**393**	**5.6**		**2**	**100.0**	**18:37**	**21**	**0**	**2**	**2**	**17**	**0**	**0**	**0**	**15:**

WHL East First All-Star Team (2001) • Canadian Major Junior Humanitarian Player of the Year (2001)

Signed as a free agent by **Philadelphia**, December 21, 2000. Traded to **Chicago** by **Philadelphia** with the rights to Colin Fraser and Los Angeles' 2nd round choice (previously acquired, Chicago selected Bryan Bickell) in 2004 Entry Draft for Alex Zhamnov and Washington's 4th round choice (previously acquired, Philadelphia selected R.J. Anderson) in 2004 Entry Draft, February 19, 2004. Traded to **Philadelphia** by **Chicago** for Ben Eager, December 18, 2007. Traded to **Calgary** by **Philadelphia** for Calgary's 3rd round choice (Adam Morrison) in 2009 Entry Draft, February 20, 2008. Traded to **Phoenix** by **Calgary** for Brandon Prust, June 27, 2009. Traded to **Edmonton** by **Phoenix** for Patrick O'Sullivan, June 30, 2010.

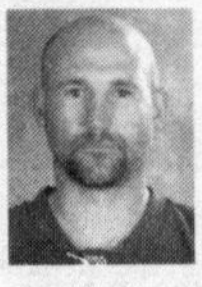

VANDERMEER, Peter

(VAN-duhr-meer, PEE-tuhr)

Left wing. Shoots left. 6', 209 lbs. Born, Caroline, Alta., October 14, 1975.

Season	Club	League	GP	G	A	Pts	PIM	PP	SH	GW	S	%	+/-	TF	F%	Min	GP	G	A	Pts	PIM	PP	SH	GW	Mi
1992-93	Red Deer	AMHL	34	26	30	56	172	....	....	....	....	....	....	....	....	....	....	....	....	....	....	....	....	....	....
	Red Deer Rebels	WHL	2	0	0	0	2	....	....	....	....	....	....	....	....	....	....	....	....	....	....	....	....	....	....
1993-94	Red Deer Rebels	WHL	54	4	9	13	170	....	....	....	....	....	....	....	....	....	....	....	....	....	....	....	....	....	....
1994-95	Red Deer Rebels	WHL	61	16	16	32	218	....	....	....	....	....	....	....	....	....	....	....	....	....	....	....	....	....	....
1995-96	Red Deer Rebels	WHL	63	21	40	61	207	....	....	....	....	....	....	....	....	....	....	....	....	....	....	....	....	....	....
1996-97	Columbus Chill	ECHL	30	6	11	17	195	....	....	....	....	....	....	....	....	....	7	2	1	3	26	....	....	....	....
1997-98	Columbus Chill	ECHL	20	4	7	11	78	....	....	....	....	....	....	....	....	....	....	....	....	....	....	....	....	....	....
	Richmond	ECHL	18	2	5	7	165	....	....	....	....	....	....	....	....	....	....	....	....	....	....	....	....	....	....
	Rochester	AHL	30	4	2	6	140	....	....	....	....	....	....	....	....	....	4	1	0	1	13	....	....	....	....
1998-99	Rochester	AHL	2	1	0	1	16	....	....	....	....	....	....	....	....	....	16	1	0	1	38	....	....	....	....
	Binghamton	UHL	62	15	21	36	*390	....	....	....	....	....	....	....	....	....	5	2	2	4	0	....	....	....	....
99-2000	Wilkes-Barre	AHL	4	0	0	0	7	....	....	....	....	....	....	....	....	....	....	....	....	....	....	....	....	....	....
	Richmond	ECHL	58	31	25	56	*457	....	....	....	....	....	....	....	....	....	3	0	1	1	20	....	....	....	....
	Providence Bruins	AHL	....	....	....	....	....	....	....	....	....	....	....	....	....	....	9	0	3	3	2	....	....	....	....
2000-01	Providence Bruins	AHL	62	19	18	37	240	....	....	....	....	....	....	....	....	....	4	0	0	0	16	....	....	....	....
2001-02	Philadelphia	AHL	61	5	1	6	313	....	....	....	....	....	....	....	....	....	5	0	0	0	8	....	....	....	....
	Trenton Titans	ECHL	2	0	1	1	2	....	....	....	....	....	....	....	....	....	....	....	....	....	....	....	....	....	....
2002-03	Philadelphia	AHL	77	5	8	13	335	....	....	....	....	....	....	....	....	....	....	....	....	....	....	....	....	....	....
2003-04	Philadelphia	AHL	71	5	8	13	*398	....	....	....	....	....	....	....	....	....	12	1	0	1	29	....	....	....	....
2004-05	Grand Rapids	AHL	73	4	13	17	310	....	....	....	....	....	....	....	....	....	....	....	....	....	....	....	....	....	....
2005-06	Hamilton	AHL	67	6	6	12	276	....	....	....	....	....	....	....	....	....	....	....	....	....	....	....	....	....	....
2006-07	Hershey Bears	AHL	26	2	5	7	129	....	....	....	....	....	....	....	....	....	2	0	0	0	0	....	....	....	....
2007-08	San Antonio	AHL	38	2	6	8	332	....	....	....	....	....	....	....	....	....	....	....	....	....	....	....	....	....	....
	Phoenix	**NHL**	**2**	**0**	**0**	**0**	**0**	**0**	**0**	**0**	**0**	**0.0**	**0**	**0**	**0.0**	**7:33**	....	....	....	....	....	....	....	....	....
2008-09	Quad City Flames	AHL	80	5	1	6	185	....	....	....	....	....	....	....	....	....	....	....	....	....	....	....	....	....	....
2009-10	Utah Grizzlies	ECHL	11	0	6	6	19	....	....	....	....	....	....	....	....	....	9	1	0	1	49	....	....	....	....
	Abbotsford Heat	AHL	20	2	2	4	91	....	....	....	....	....	....	....	....	....	....	....	....	....	....	....	....	....	....
	NHL Totals		**2**	**0**	**0**	**0**	**0**	**0**	**0**	**0**	**0**	**0.0**		**0**	**0.0**	**7:33**	....	....	....	....	....	....	....	....	....

Signed as a free agent by **Philadelphia**, July 6, 2001. Signed as a free agent by **Detroit**, August 16, 2004. Signed as a free agent by **Montreal**, August 2, 2005. Signed as a free agent by **Washington**, July 21, 2006. Signed as a free agent by **San Antonio** (AHL), August 16, 2007. Signed as a free agent by **Phoenix**, February 8, 2008. Signed as a free agent by **Calgary**, July 2, 2008.

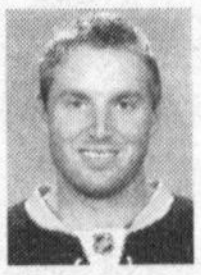

VANEK, Thomas

(VAN-ehk, TAW-muhs) **BU**

Left wing. Shoots right. 6'2", 212 lbs. Born, Vienna, Austria, January 19, 1984. Buffalo's 1st choice, 5th overall, in 2003 Entry Draft.

Season	Club	League	GP	G	A	Pts	PIM	PP	SH	GW	S	%	+/-	TF	F%	Min	GP	G	A	Pts	PIM	PP	SH	GW	Mi
99-2000	Sioux Falls	USHL	35	15	18	33	12	....	....	....	....	....	....	....	....	....	3	0	1	1	0	....	....	....	....
2000-01	Sioux Falls	USHL	20	19	10	29	15	....	....	....	....	....	....	....	....	....	8	5	4	9	2	....	....	....	....
2001-02	Sioux Falls	USHL	53	46	45	91	54	....	....	....	....	....	....	....	....	....	3	0	0	0	9	....	....	....	....
2002-03	U. of Minnesota	WCHA	45	31	31	62	60	....	....	....	....	....	....	....	....	....	....	....	....	....	....	....	....	....	....
2003-04	U. of Minnesota	WCHA	38	26	25	51	72	....	....	....	....	....	....	....	....	....	....	....	....	....	....	....	....	....	....
2004-05	Rochester	AHL	74	42	26	68	62	....	....	....	....	....	....	....	....	....	5	2	3	5	10	....	....	....	....
2005-06	**Buffalo**	**NHL**	**81**	**25**	**23**	**48**	**72**	**11**	**0**	**4**	**204**	**12.3**	**–11**	**23**	**21.7**	**14:44**	**10**	**2**	**0**	**2**	**6**	**2**	**0**	**0**	**10**
2006-07	**Buffalo**	**NHL**	**82**	**43**	**41**	**84**	**40**	**15**	**0**	**5**	**237**	**18.1**	***47**	**39**	**28.2**	**16:47**	**16**	**6**	**4**	**10**	**10**	**1**	**0**	**2**	**16:**
2007-08	**Buffalo**	**NHL**	**82**	**36**	**28**	**64**	**64**	**19**	**0**	**9**	**240**	**15.0**	**–5**	**13**	**46.2**	**16:51**	....	....	....	....	....	....	....	....	....
2008-09	**Buffalo**	**NHL**	**73**	**40**	**24**	**64**	**44**	***20**	**2**	**5**	**211**	**19.0**	**–1**	**6**	**16.7**	**17:12**	....	....	....	....	....	....	....	....	....
2009-10	**Buffalo**	**NHL**	**71**	**28**	**25**	**53**	**42**	**10**	**0**	**6**	**182**	**15.4**	**9**	**9**	**22.2**	**16:46**	**3**	**2**	**1**	**3**	**2**	**0**	**0**	**0**	**13**
	NHL Totals		**389**	**172**	**141**	**313**	**262**	**75**	**2**	**29**	**1074**	**16.0**		**90**	**27.8**	**16:27**	**29**	**10**	**5**	**15**	**18**	**3**	**0**	**2**	**14**

USHL First All-Star Team (2002) • USHL MVP (2002) • WCHA All-Rookie Team (2003) • WCHA Second All-Star Team (2003, 2004) • WCHA Rookie of the Year (2003) • NCAA Championship All-Tournament Team (2003) • NCAA Championship Tournament MVP (2003) • NCAA West Second All-American Team (2004) • AHL All-Rookie Team (2005) • NHL Second All-Star Team (2007)

Played in NHL All-Star Game (2009)

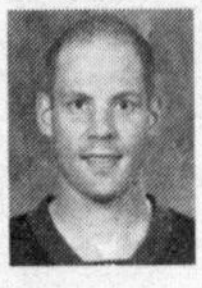

VEILLEUX, Stephane

(VAY-oo, STEH-fan)

Left wing. Shoots left. 6'1", 190 lbs. Born, Beauceville, Que., November 16, 1981. Minnesota's 4th choice, 93rd overall, in 2001 Entry Draft.

Season	Club	League	GP	G	A	Pts	PIM	PP	SH	GW	S	%	+/-	TF	F%	Min	GP	G	A	Pts	PIM	PP	SH	GW	Mi
1997-98	Beauce-Amiante	QAAA	21	20	17	37	....	....	....	....	....	....	....	....	....	....	....	....	....	....	....	....	....	....	....
	Levis-Lauzon	QAAA	14	3	5	8	....	....	....	....	....	....	....	....	....	....	1	0	0	0	0	....	....	....	....
1998-99	Victoriaville Tigres	QMJHL	65	6	13	19	35	....	....	....	....	....	....	....	....	....	6	1	3	4	2	....	....	....	....
99-2000	Victoriaville Tigres	QMJHL	22	1	4	5	17	....	....	....	....	....	....	....	....	....	....	....	....	....	....	....	....	....	....
	Val-d'Or Foreurs	QMJHL	50	14	28	42	100	....	....	....	....	....	....	....	....	....	....	....	....	....	....	....	....	....	....
2000-01	Val-d'Or Foreurs	QMJHL	68	48	67	115	90	....	....	....	....	....	....	....	....	....	21	15	18	33	42	....	....	....	....
2001-02	Houston Aeros	AHL	77	13	22	35	113	....	....	....	....	....	....	....	....	....	14	2	4	6	20	....	....	....	....

Season	Club	League	GP	G	A	Pts	PIM	PP	SH	GW	S	%	+/-	TF	F%	Min	GP	G	A	Pts	PIM	PP	SH	GW	Min
2002-03	Minnesota	NHL	38	3	2	5	23	1	0	0	52	5.8	-6	13	7.7	12:08	....	....	....	....	....				
	Houston Aeros	AHL	29	8	4	12	43										23	7	11	18	12				
2003-04	Minnesota	NHL	19	2	8	10	20	1	1	1	37	5.4	0	10	40.0	14:20	....	....	....	....	....				
	Houston Aeros	AHL	64	13	25	38	66										2	1	1	2	2				
2004-05	Houston Aeros	AHL	59	15	24	39	35										....	....	....	....	....				
2005-06	Minnesota	NHL	71	7	9	16	63	0	0	1	87	8.0	-13	33	33.3	12:58	....	....	....	....	....				
2006-07	Minnesota	NHL	75	7	11	18	47	0	0	1	84	8.3	3	32	21.9	12:17	5	0	0	0	4	0	0	0	12:40
2007-08	Minnesota	NHL	77	11	7	18	61	0	0	0	136	8.1	-13	45	37.8	14:32	6	0	0	0	27	0	0	0	15:43
2008-09	Minnesota	NHL	81	13	10	23	40	0	1	1	146	8.9	-17	22	27.3	15:48	....	....	....	....	....				
2009-10	Tampa Bay	NHL	77	3	6	9	48	0	0	0	94	3.2	-14	25	40.0	12:17	....	....	....	....	....				
	NHL Totals		438	46	53	99	302	2	2	4	636	7.2		180	31.1	13:31	11	0	0	0	31	0	0	0	14:20

Signed as a free agent by **Tampa Bay**, July 7, 2009.

VERMETTE, Antoine

(vuhr-MEHT, AN-twuhn) **CBJ**

Center. Shoots left. 6'1", 200 lbs. Born, St-Agapit, Que., July 20, 1982. Ottawa's 3rd choice, 55th overall, in 2000 Entry Draft.

Season	Club	League	GP	G	A	Pts	PIM	PP	SH	GW	S	%	+/-	TF	F%	Min	GP	G	A	Pts	PIM	PP	SH	GW	Min
1997-98	Quebec Select	QAHA	19	11	20	31	36										1	0	0	0	0				
	Levis-Lauzon	QAAA	8	1	1	2	4										13	0	0	0	2				
1998-99	Quebec Remparts	QMJHL	57	9	17	26	32										6	0	1	1	6				
99-2000	Victoriaville Tigres	QMJHL	71	30	41	71	87										9	4	6	10	14				
2000-01	Victoriaville Tigres	QMJHL	71	57	62	119	102										22	10	16	26	10				
2001-02	Victoriaville Tigres	QMJHL	4	0	2	2	6										14	2	9	11	10				
2002-03	Binghamton	AHL	80	34	28	62	57										4	0	1	1	4	0	0	0	11:35
2003-04	Ottawa	NHL	57	7	7	14	16	0	1	0	63	11.1	5	100	44.0	11:59									
	Binghamton	AHL	3	0	0	0	6										6	1	4	5	10				
2004-05	Binghamton	AHL	78	28	45	73	36																		
2005-06	Ottawa	NHL	82	21	12	33	44	1	6	4	123	17.1	17	537	57.9	12:35	10	2	0	2	4	0	0	1	15:00
2006-07	Ottawa	NHL	77	19	20	39	52	2	3	2	151	12.6	-2	834	53.0	15:42	20	2	3	5	6	0	0	0	16:20
2007-08	Ottawa	NHL	81	24	29	53	51	4	3	3	175	13.7	3	1217	56.7	17:35	4	0	0	0	0	0	0	0	20:33
2008-09	Ottawa	NHL	62	9	19	28	42	2	0	0	141	6.4	-12	771	58.4	18:03									
	Columbus	NHL	17	7	6	13	8	1	1	1	33	21.2	5	341	56.3	19:29	4	0	0	0	10	0	0	0	16:47
2009-10	Columbus	NHL	82	27	38	65	32	6	2	1	156	17.3	2	1573	54.2	20:09									
	NHL Totals		458	114	131	245	245	16	16	11	842	13.5		5373	55.5	16:16	42	4	4	8	28	0	0	1	16:00

AHL All-Rookie Team (2003)

• Missed majority of 2001-02 season recovering from neck injury suffered at Team Canada Jr. Selection Camp, June 3, 2001. Traded to **Columbus** by **Ottawa** for Pascal Leclaire and Columbus' 2nd round choice (Robin Lehner) in 2009 Entry Draft, March 4, 2009.

VERNACE, Michael

(vuhr-NAYS, MIGH-kuhl) **T.B.**

Defense. Shoots left. 6'2", 200 lbs. Born, Toronto, Ont., May 26, 1986. San Jose's 6th choice, 201st overall, in 2004 Entry Draft.

Season	Club	League	GP	G	A	Pts	PIM	PP	SH	GW	S	%	+/-	TF	F%	Min	GP	G	A	Pts	PIM	PP	SH	GW	Min
2003-04	Bramalea Blues	OPJHL	33	3	12	15	16										11	2	3	5	8				
	Brampton	OHL	2	1	1	2	0										6	2	2	4	0				
2004-05	Brampton	OHL	68	12	38	50	42										11	1	5	6	6				
2005-06	Brampton	OHL	68	10	62	72	54																		
2006-07	Albany River Rats	AHL	30	1	11	12	35																		
	Arizona Sundogs	CHL	24	3	11	14	20																		
2007-08	Lake Erie	AHL	79	3	26	29	59																		
2008-09	Colorado	NHL	12	0	0	0	8	0	0	0	9	0.0	-5	0	0.0	19:39									
	Lake Erie	AHL	65	3	14	17	52																		
2009-10	Chicago Wolves	AHL	47	2	10	12	29										18	0	4	4	8				
	Hamilton	AHL	15	0	1	1	23																		
	NHL Totals		12	0	0	0	8	0	0	0	9	0.0		0	0.0	19:39									

OHL All-Rookie Team (2005)

• Rights traded to **San Jose** by **Colorado** for Colorado's 6th round choice (Patrick Zackrisson) in 2007 Entry Draft, June 1, 2006. Signed as a free agent by **Atlanta**, July 30, 2009. Traded to **San Jose** by **Atlanta** with Brett Sterling and Atlanta's 7th round choice (Lee Moffie) in 2010 Entry Draft for future considerations, June 23, 2010. Signed as a free agent by **Tampa Bay**, July 29, 2010.

VERSTEEG, Kris

(vuhr-STEEG, KRIHS) **TOR.**

Right wing. Shoots right. 5'10", 182 lbs. Born, Lethbridge, Alta., May 13, 1986. Boston's 4th choice, 134th overall, in 2004 Entry Draft.

Season	Club	League	GP	G	A	Pts	PIM	PP	SH	GW	S	%	+/-	TF	F%	Min	GP	G	A	Pts	PIM	PP	SH	GW	Min
2002-03	Lethbridge	WHL	57	8	10	18	32																		
2003-04	Lethbridge	WHL	68	16	33	49	85																		
2004-05	Lethbridge	WHL	68	22	30	52	68										5	0	1	1	4				
2005-06	Kamloops Blazers	WHL	14	6	6	12	24																		
	Red Deer Rebels	WHL	57	10	26	36	103										3	0	0	0	6				
	Providence Bruins	AHL	13	2	4	6	13																		
2006-07	Providence Bruins	AHL	43	22	27	49	19										2	0	0	0	2				
	Norfolk Admirals	AHL	27	4	19	23	20																		
2007-08	Chicago	NHL	13	2	2	4	6	0	0	0	21	9.5	-1	3	66.7	15:52									
	Rockford IceHogs	AHL	56	18	31	49	174										12	6	5	11	6				
2008-09	Chicago	NHL	78	22	31	53	55	6	4	3	139	15.8	15	266	46.6	17:02	17	4	8	12	22	3	0	0	16:14
2009-10 ♦	Chicago	NHL	79	20	24	44	35	4	3	4	184	10.9	8	183	42.1	15:44	22	6	8	14	14	0	0	2	17:13
	NHL Totals		170	44	57	101	96	10	7	7	344	12.8		452	44.9	16:20	39	10	16	26	36	3	0	2	16:47

NHL All-Rookie Team (2009)

Traded to **Chicago** by **Boston** with future considerations for Brandon Bochenski, February 3, 2007. Traded to **Toronto** by **Chicago** with Bill Sweatt for Viktor Stalberg, Christopher Didomenico and Phillipe Paradis, June 30, 2010.

VESCE, Ryan

(veks-KEE, RIGH-uhn)

Center. Shoots right. 5'8", 175 lbs. Born, Lloyd Harbor, NY, April 7, 1982.

Season	Club	League	GP	G	A	Pts	PIM	PP	SH	GW	S	%	+/-	TF	F%	Min	GP	G	A	Pts	PIM	PP	SH	GW	Min
2000-01	Cornell Big Red	ECAC	33	7	20	27	10																		
2001-02	Cornell Big Red	ECAC	35	10	20	30	10																		
2002-03	Cornell Big Red	ECAC	36	19	26	45	16																		
2003-04	Cornell Big Red	ECAC	27	10	16	26	14																		
2004-05	Rogle	Sweden-2	43	20	25	45	51																		
2005-06	Springfield	AHL	80	18	49	67	50																		
2006-07	Binghamton	AHL	80	16	35	51	51																		
2007-08	HIFK Helsinki	Finland	56	26	18	44	42										7	1	2	3	2				
2008-09	San Jose	NHL	10	0	0	0	4	0	0	0	11	0.0	-2	64	46.9	9:45									
	Worcester Sharks	AHL	67	24	47	71	28										12	3	7	10	22				
2009-10	San Jose	NHL	9	3	2	5	0	0	0	1	20	15.0	-1	50	50.0	10:57									
	Worcester Sharks	AHL	35	14	16	30	20										6	3	1	4	0				
	NHL Totals		19	3	2	5	4	0	0	1	31	9.7		114	48.2	10:19									

Signed as a free agent by **Rogle** (Sweden), August, 2004. Signed as a free agent by **Ottawa**, July 17, 2006. Signed as a free agent by **HIFK Helsinki** (Finland), July 17, 2007. Signed as a free agent by **San Jose**, August 13, 2008. Signed as a free agent by **Nizhny Novgorod** (Russia-KHL), June 28, 2010.

VISHNEVSKIY, Ivan

(vihsh-NEHV-skee, ee-VAHN) **CHI.**

Defense. Shoots left. 6', 193 lbs. Born, Barnaul, USSR, February 18, 1988. Dallas' 1st choice, 27th overall, in 2006 Entry Draft.

Season	Club	League	GP	G	A	Pts	PIM	PP	SH	GW	S	%	+/-	TF	F%	Min	GP	G	A	Pts	PIM	PP	SH	GW	Min
2003-04	Lada Togliatti 2	Russia-3	16	0	0	0	10																		
2004-05	Lada Togliatti 2	Russia-3			STATISTICS NOT AVAILABLE																				
2005-06	Rouyn-Noranda	QMJHL	54	13	35	48	57										5	2	1	3	2				
2006-07	Rouyn-Noranda	QMJHL	60	14	37	51	90										16	5	8	13	8				
2007-08	Rouyn-Noranda	QMJHL	45	17	28	45	50										17	0	6	6	16				
2008-09	Dallas	NHL	3	0	2	2	2	0	0	0	9	0.0	1	0	0.0	19:33									
	Peoria Rivermen	AHL	67	6	13	19	28										5	0	2	2	4				

			Regular Season														Playoffs								
Season	Club	League	GP	G	A	Pts	PIM	PP	SH	GW	S	%	+/-	TF	F%	Min	GP	G	A	Pts	PIM	PP	SH	GW	Min
2009-10	**Dallas**	**NHL**	**2**	**0**	**0**	**0**	**0**	**0**	**0**	**0**	**4**	**0.0**	**–2**	**0**	**0.0**	**16:39**	....	....	....	....	....	....	....	....	....
	Texas Stars	AHL	51	8	16	24	18	....	....	....	....	....	....	....	....	....	....	....	....	....	....	....	....	....	....
	Chicago Wolves	AHL	28	2	10	12	10	....	....	....	....	....	....	....	....	....	14	0	6	6	4	....	....	....	....
	NHL Totals		**5**	**0**	**2**	**2**	**2**	**0**	**0**	**0**	**13**	**0.0**		**0**	**0.0**	**18:23**	....	....	....	....	....	....	....	....	....

QMJHL All-Rookie Team (2006) • QMJHL Second All-Star Team (2008)

Traded to **Atlanta** by **Dallas** with Dallas' 4th round choice (Ivan Telegin) in 2010 Entry Draft for Kari Lehtonen, February 9, 2010. Traded to **Chicago** by **Atlanta** with a 2nd round choice in the 2011 Entry Draft for Andrew Ladd, July 1, 2010.

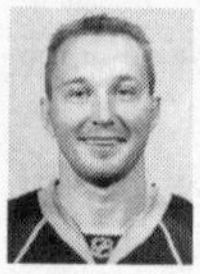

VISNOVSKY, Lubomir

(vihsh-NAWV-skee, LOO-boh-mihr) **ANA.**

Defense. Shoots left. 5'10", 188 lbs. Born, Topolcany, Czech., August 11, 1976. Los Angeles' 4th choice, 118th overall, in 2000 Entry Draft.

1994-95	Bratislava	Slovakia	36	11	12	23	10	....	....	....	....	....	....	....	....	....	9	1	3	4	2	....	....	....	....
1995-96	Bratislava	Slovakia	35	8	6	14	22	....	....	....	....	....	....	....	....	....	13	1	5	6	2	....	....	....	....
1996-97	Bratislava	Slovakia	44	11	12	23	....	....	....	....	....	....	....	....	....	....	2	0	1	1	....	....	....	....	....
	Bratislava	EuroHL	6	3	1	4	2	....	....	....	....	....	....	....	....	....	2	0	0	0	6	....	....	....	....
1997-98	Bratislava	Slovakia	36	7	9	16	16	....	....	....	....	....	....	....	....	....	11	2	4	6	8	....	....	....	....
	Bratislava	EuroHL	6	1	0	1	4	....	....	....	....	....	....	....	....	....	....	....	....	....	....	....	....	....	....
	Slovakia	Olympics	3	0	0	0	2	....	....	....	....	....	....	....	....	....	....	....	....	....	....	....	....	....	....
1998-99	Bratislava	Slovakia	40	9	10	19	31	....	....	....	....	....	....	....	....	....	10	5	5	10	0	....	....	....	....
	Bratislava	EuroHL	6	0	3	3	4	....	....	....	....	....	....	....	....	....	....	....	....	....	....	....	....	....	....
99-2000	Bratislava	Slovakia	52	21	24	45	38	....	....	....	....	....	....	....	....	....	8	5	3	8	16	....	....	....	....
2000-01	**Los Angeles**	**NHL**	**81**	**7**	**32**	**39**	**36**	**3**	**0**	**3**	**105**	**6.7**	**16**	**0**	**0.0**	**16:58**	**8**	**0**	**0**	**0**	**0**	**0**	**0**	**0**	**13:57**
2001-02	**Los Angeles**	**NHL**	**72**	**4**	**17**	**21**	**14**	**1**	**0**	**2**	**95**	**4.2**	**–5**	**0**	**0.0**	**16:15**	**4**	**0**	**1**	**1**	**0**	**0**	**0**	**0**	**8:22**
	Slovakia	Olympics	3	1	2	3	0	....	....	....	....	....	....	....	....	....	....	....	....	....	....	....	....	....	....
2002-03	**Los Angeles**	**NHL**	**57**	**8**	**16**	**24**	**28**	**1**	**0**	**1**	**85**	**9.4**	**2**	**0**	**0.0**	**19:20**	....	....	....	....	....	....	....	....	....
2003-04	**Los Angeles**	**NHL**	**58**	**8**	**21**	**29**	**26**	**5**	**0**	**0**	**114**	**7.0**	**8**	**0**	**0.0**	**24:02**	....	....	....	....	....	....	....	....	....
2004-05	Bratislava	Slovakia	43	13	25	38	40	....	....	....	....	....	....	....	....	....	14	2	10	12	10	....	....	....	....
2005-06	**Los Angeles**	**NHL**	**80**	**17**	**50**	**67**	**50**	**10**	**0**	**3**	**152**	**11.2**	**7**	**1**	**100.0**	**23:16**	....	....	....	....	....	....	....	....	....
	Slovakia	Olympics	6	1	1	2	0	....	....	....	....	....	....	....	....	....	....	....	....	....	....	....	....	....	....
2006-07	**Los Angeles**	**NHL**	**69**	**18**	**40**	**58**	**26**	**8**	**0**	**0**	**159**	**11.3**	**1**	**6**	**33.3**	**24:27**	....	....	....	....	....	....	....	....	....
2007-08	**Los Angeles**	**NHL**	**82**	**8**	**33**	**41**	**34**	**3**	**0**	**1**	**153**	**5.2**	**–18**	**8**	**12.5**	**23:00**	....	....	....	....	....	....	....	....	....
2008-09	**Edmonton**	**NHL**	**50**	**8**	**23**	**31**	**30**	**5**	**0**	**1**	**86**	**9.3**	**6**	**0**	**0.0**	**23:01**	....	....	....	....	....	....	....	....	....
2009-10	**Edmonton**	**NHL**	**57**	**10**	**22**	**32**	**16**	**4**	**0**	**1**	**78**	**12.8**	**–4**	**0**	**0.0**	**20:45**	....	....	....	....	....	....	....	....	....
	Slovakia	Olympics	7	2	1	3	0	....	....	....	....	....	....	....	....	....	....	....	....	....	....	....	....	....	....
	Anaheim	**NHL**	**16**	**5**	**8**	**13**	**4**	**1**	**0**	**1**	**53**	**9.4**	**–6**	**0**	**0.0**	**26:00**	....	....	....	....	....	....	....	....	....
	NHL Totals		**622**	**93**	**262**	**355**	**264**	**41**	**0**	**13**	**1080**	**8.6**		**15**	**26.7**	**21:16**	**12**	**0**	**1**	**1**	**0**	**0**	**0**	**0**	**12:05**

NHL All-Rookie Team (2001)

Played in NHL All-Star Game (2007)

Signed as a free agent by **Bratislava** (Slovakia), September 27, 2004. Traded to **Edmonton** by **Los Angeles** for Jarret Stoll and Matt Greene, June 29, 2008. Traded to **Anaheim** by **Edmonton** for Ryan Whitney and Anaheim's 6th round choice (Brandon Davidson) in 2010 Entry Draft, March 3, 2010.

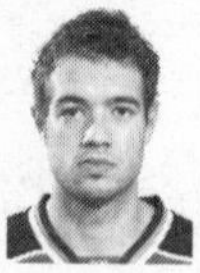

VLASIC, Marc-Edouard

(vih-LASH-ihc, MAHRK-EHD-wahrd) **S.J.**

Defense. Shoots left. 6'1", 200 lbs. Born, Montreal, Que., March 30, 1987. San Jose's 2nd choice, 35th overall, in 2005 Entry Draft.

2003-04	Quebec Remparts	QMJHL	41	1	9	10	4	....	....	....	....	....	....	....	....	....	5	0	1	1	0	....	....	....	....
2004-05	Quebec Remparts	QMJHL	70	5	25	30	33	....	....	....	....	....	....	....	....	....	13	2	7	9	2	....	....	....	....
2005-06	Quebec Remparts	QMJHL	66	16	57	73	57	....	....	....	....	....	....	....	....	....	23	5	24	29	10	....	....	....	....
2006-07	**San Jose**	**NHL**	**81**	**3**	**23**	**26**	**18**	**2**	**0**	**0**	**66**	**4.5**	**13**	**0**	**0.0**	**22:12**	**11**	**0**	**1**	**1**	**2**	**0**	**0**	**0**	**22:52**
2007-08	**San Jose**	**NHL**	**82**	**2**	**12**	**14**	**24**	**1**	**0**	**0**	**72**	**2.8**	**–12**	**0**	**0.0**	**21:37**	**13**	**0**	**1**	**1**	**0**	**0**	**0**	**0**	**24:39**
	Worcester Sharks	AHL	1	0	2	2	0	....	....	....	....	....	....	....	....	....	....	....	....	....	....	....	....	....	....
2008-09	**San Jose**	**NHL**	**82**	**6**	**30**	**36**	**42**	**3**	**0**	**1**	**104**	**5.8**	**15**	**0**	**0.0**	**23:54**	**6**	**0**	**1**	**1**	**0**	**0**	**0**	**0**	**20:39**
2009-10	**San Jose**	**NHL**	**64**	**3**	**13**	**16**	**33**	**1**	**0**	**0**	**74**	**4.1**	**21**	**0**	**0.0**	**22:05**	**15**	**0**	**3**	**3**	**4**	**0**	**0**	**0**	**21:53**
	NHL Totals		**309**	**14**	**78**	**92**	**117**	**7**	**0**	**1**	**316**	**4.4**		**0**	**0.0**	**22:28**	**45**	**0**	**6**	**6**	**6**	**0**	**0**	**0**	**22:46**

NHL All-Rookie Team (2007)

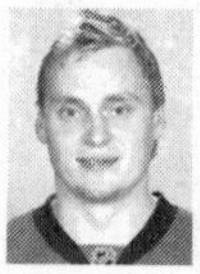

VOLCHENKOV, Anton

(vohl-chen-KAHF, AN-tawn) **N.J.**

Defense. Shoots left. 6'1", 225 lbs. Born, Moscow, USSR, February 25, 1982. Ottawa's 1st choice, 21st overall, in 2000 Entry Draft.

99-2000	HK Moscow 2	Russia-3	6	0	1	1	10	....	....	....	....	....	....	....	....	....	....	....	....	....	....	....	....	....	....
	HK Moscow	Russia-2	30	2	9	11	36	....	....	....	....	....	....	....	....	....	....	....	....	....	....	....	....	....	....
2000-01	Krylja Sovetov	Russia-2	34	3	4	7	56	....	....	....	....	....	....	....	....	....	....	....	....	....	....	....	....	....	....
2001-02	Krylja Sovetov 2	Russia-3	1	0	0	0	0	....	....	....	....	....	....	....	....	....	....	....	....	....	....	....	....	....	....
	Krylja Sovetov	Russia	47	4	16	20	50	....	....	....	....	....	....	....	....	....	3	0	0	0	29	....	....	....	....
2002-03	**Ottawa**	**NHL**	**57**	**3**	**13**	**16**	**40**	**0**	**0**	**0**	**75**	**4.0**	**–4**	**0**	**0.0**	**15:30**	**17**	**1**	**1**	**2**	**4**	**0**	**0**	**1**	**13:31**
2003-04	**Ottawa**	**NHL**	**19**	**1**	**2**	**3**	**8**	**0**	**0**	**0**	**15**	**6.7**	**1**	**0**	**0.0**	**13:04**	**5**	**0**	**0**	**0**	**6**	**0**	**0**	**0**	**11:52**
2004-05	Binghamton	AHL	69	10	35	45	62	....	....	....	....	....	....	....	....	....	6	0	3	3	0	....	....	....	....
2005-06	**Ottawa**	**NHL**	**75**	**4**	**13**	**17**	**53**	**0**	**0**	**0**	**82**	**4.9**	**21**	**0**	**0.0**	**18:03**	**9**	**0**	**4**	**4**	**8**	**0**	**0**	**0**	**13:53**
	Russia	Olympics	8	0	0	0	2	....	....	....	....	....	....	....	....	....	....	....	....	....	....	....	....	....	....
2006-07	**Ottawa**	**NHL**	**78**	**1**	**18**	**19**	**67**	**0**	**0**	**0**	**85**	**1.2**	**37**	**0**	**0.0**	**21:17**	**20**	**2**	**4**	**6**	**24**	**0**	**0**	**1**	**23:19**
2007-08	**Ottawa**	**NHL**	**67**	**1**	**14**	**15**	**55**	**0**	**0**	**1**	**71**	**1.4**	**14**	**0**	**0.0**	**20:31**	**4**	**0**	**1**	**1**	**2**	**0**	**0**	**0**	**17:11**
2008-09	**Ottawa**	**NHL**	**68**	**2**	**8**	**10**	**36**	**0**	**0**	**1**	**79**	**2.5**	**–10**	**0**	**0.0**	**20:08**	....	....	....	....	....	....	....	....	....
2009-10	**Ottawa**	**NHL**	**64**	**4**	**10**	**14**	**38**	**0**	**0**	**0**	**69**	**5.8**	**2**	**0**	**0.0**	**20:41**	**6**	**0**	**2**	**2**	**4**	**0**	**0**	**0**	**22:30**
	Russia	Olympics	4	0	1	1	2	....	....	....	....	....	....	....	....	....	....	....	....	....	....	....	....	....	....
	NHL Totals		**428**	**16**	**78**	**94**	**297**	**0**	**0**	**2**	**476**	**3.4**		**0**	**0.0**	**19:11**	**61**	**3**	**12**	**15**	**48**	**0**	**0**	**2**	**17:47**

• Missed majority of 2003-04 season recovering from shoulder injury suffered in game vs. Boston, December 8, 2003. Signed as a free agent by **New Jersey**, July 1, 2010.

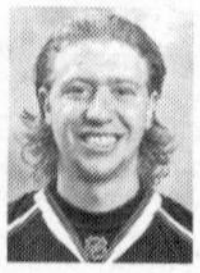

VORACEK, Jakub

(VOHR-rah-chehk, YA-kuhb) **CBJ**

Right wing. Shoots left. 6'2", 213 lbs. Born, Kladno, Czech., August 15, 1989. Columbus' 1st choice, 7th overall, in 2007 Entry Draft.

2002-03	HC Kladno U17	CzR-U17	2	1	1	2	2	....	....	....	....	....	....	....	....	....	2	1	1	2	0	....	....	....	....
2003-04	HC Kladno U17	CzR-U17	52	30	24	54	26	....	....	....	....	....	....	....	....	....	2	0	0	0	2	....	....	....	....
2004-05	HC Kladno U17	CzR-U17	30	23	39	62	44	....	....	....	....	....	....	....	....	....	7	5	4	9	14	....	....	....	....
	HC Kladno Jr.	CzRep-Jr.	16	5	7	12	6	....	....	....	....	....	....	....	....	....	1	1	0	1	2	....	....	....	....
2005-06	HC Kladno U17	CzR-U17	....	....	....	....	....	....	....	....	....	....	....	....	....	....	2	1	3	4	31	....	....	....	....
	HC Kladno Jr.	CzRep-Jr.	46	21	38	59	54	....	....	....	....	....	....	....	....	....	6	7	4	11	2	....	....	....	....
	HC Rabat Kladno	CzRep	1	0	0	0	0	....	....	....	....	....	....	....	....	....	....	....	....	....	....	....	....	....	....
2006-07	Halifax	QMJHL	59	23	63	86	26	....	....	....	....	....	....	....	....	....	12	7	17	24	6	....	....	....	....
2007-08	Halifax	QMJHL	53	33	68	101	42	....	....	....	....	....	....	....	....	....	15	5	13	18	14	....	....	....	....
2008-09	**Columbus**	**NHL**	**80**	**9**	**29**	**38**	**44**	**0**	**0**	**1**	**101**	**8.9**	**11**	**3**	**0.0**	**12:40**	**4**	**0**	**1**	**1**	**8**	**0**	**0**	**0**	**12:06**
2009-10	**Columbus**	**NHL**	**81**	**16**	**34**	**50**	**26**	**4**	**0**	**1**	**154**	**10.4**	**–7**	**6**	**33.3**	**15:37**	....	....	....	....	....	....	....	....	....
	NHL Totals		**161**	**25**	**63**	**88**	**70**	**4**	**0**	**2**	**255**	**9.8**		**9**	**22.2**	**14:09**	**4**	**0**	**1**	**1**	**8**	**0**	**0**	**0**	**12:06**

QMJHL All-Rookie Team (2007) • QMJHL Rookie of the Year (2007) • QMJHL Second All-Star Team (2008)

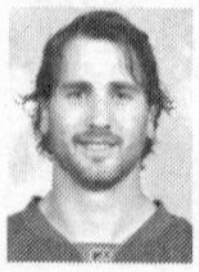

VOROS, Aaron

(VOH-ruhs, AIR-ruhn) **ANA.**

Center. Shoots left. 6'4", 215 lbs. Born, Vancouver, B.C., July 2, 1981. New Jersey's 10th choice, 229th overall, in 2001 Entry Draft.

99-2000	Victoria Salsa	BCHL	58	14	21	35	285	....	....	....	....	....	....	....	....	....	....	....	....	....	....	....	....	....	....
2000-01	Victoria Salsa	BCHL	57	34	34	68	196	....	....	....	....	....	....	....	....	....	30	16	15	31	....	....	....	....	....
2001-02	Alaska	CCHA	37	18	12	30	*101	....	....	....	....	....	....	....	....	....	....	....	....	....	....	....	....	....	....
2002-03	Alaska	CCHA	16	2	5	7	42	....	....	....	....	....	....	....	....	....	....	....	....	....	....	....	....	....	....
2003-04	Alaska	CCHA	36	16	8	24	*132	....	....	....	....	....	....	....	....	....	....	....	....	....	....	....	....	....	....
	Albany River Rats	AHL	9	2	1	3	14	....	....	....	....	....	....	....	....	....	....	....	....	....	....	....	....	....	....
2004-05	Albany River Rats	AHL	71	11	17	28	220	....	....	....	....	....	....	....	....	....	....	....	....	....	....	....	....	....	....
2005-06	Albany River Rats	AHL	73	16	14	30	180	....	....	....	....	....	....	....	....	....	....	....	....	....	....	....	....	....	....
2006-07	Lowell Devils	AHL	39	9	8	17	111	....	....	....	....	....	....	....	....	....	....	....	....	....	....	....	....	....	....
	Houston Aeros	AHL	19	2	3	5	58	....	....	....	....	....	....	....	....	....	....	....	....	....	....	....	....	....	....
2007-08	**Minnesota**	**NHL**	**55**	**7**	**7**	**14**	**141**	**0**	**0**	**1**	**52**	**13.5**	**–7**	**15**	**20.0**	**9:11**	**5**	**1**	**0**	**1**	**16**	**0**	**0**	**0**	**10:39**
	Houston Aeros	AHL	12	4	4	8	46	....	....	....	....	....	....	....	....	....	....	....	....	....	....	....	....	....	....

Season	Club	League	GP	G	A	Pts	PIM	PP	SH	GW	S	%	+/-	TF	F%	Min	GP	G	A	Pts	PIM	PP	SH	GW	Min
2008-09	NY Rangers	NHL	54	8	8	16	122	3	0	1	66	12.1	-9	10	40.0	11:11	4	0	0	0	14	0	0	0	6:51
2009-10	NY Rangers	NHL	41	3	4	7	89	1	0	0	22	13.6	-2	6	50.0	6:09	....	....	....	....	....	....	....	....	....
	NHL Totals		150	18	19	37	352	4	0	2	140	12.9		31	32.3	9:04	9	1	0	1	30	0	0	0	8:58

CCHA All-Rookie Team (2002)
• Missed majority of 2002-03 season recovering from leg surgery, January 30, 2003. Traded to **Minnesota** by New Jersey for Minnesota's 7th round choice (Jean-Sebastien Berube) in 2008 Entry Draft, February 28, 2007. Signed as a free agent by **NY Rangers**, July 1, 2008. Traded to **Anaheim** by NY Rangers with Ryan Hillier for Steve Eminger, July 9, 2010.

VRANA, Petr
(vuh-RA-nuh, PEE-tuhr)   **N.J.**

Center. Shoots left. 5'10", 190 lbs.   Born, Sternberk, Czech., March 29, 1985. New Jersey's 2nd choice, 42nd overall, in 2003 Entry Draft.

Season	Club	League	GP	G	A	Pts	PIM	PP	SH	GW	S	%	+/-	TF	F%	Min	GP	G	A	Pts	PIM	PP	SH	GW	Min
2001-02	HC Havirov Jr.	CzRep-Jr.	38	11	12	23	....																		
	HC Femax Havirov	CzRep	6	0	0	0	4																		
2002-03	Halifax	QMJHL	72	37	46	83	32										24	5	15	20	12				
2003-04	Halifax	QMJHL	48	13	25	38	56																		
2004-05	Halifax	QMJHL	60	16	35	51	77										12	10	4	14	12				
2005-06	Albany River Rats	AHL	74	12	23	35	91																		
2006-07	Lowell Devils	AHL	61	13	19	32	44																		
2007-08	Lowell Devils	AHL	80	20	41	61	64																		
2008-09	**New Jersey**	**NHL**	16	1	0	1	2	0	0	0	6	16.7	-4	36	41.7	6:54									
	Lowell Devils	AHL	14	5	4	9	6																		
2009-10	Vitkovice	CzRep	39	7	6	13	10										16	3	3	6	8				
	NHL Totals		16	1	0	1	2	0	0	0	6	16.7		36	41.7	6:54									

QMJHL All-Rookie Team (2003) • QMJHL Rookie of the Year (2003)
Signed as a free agent by **Vitkovice** (CzRep), June 1, 2009.

VRBATA, Radim
(vuhr-BA-tuh, RA-dihm)   **PHX.**

Right wing. Shoots right. 6'1", 190 lbs.   Born, Mlada Boleslav, Czech., June 13, 1981. Colorado's 10th choice, 212th overall, in 1999 Entry Draft.

Season	Club	League	GP	G	A	Pts	PIM	PP	SH	GW	S	%	+/-	TF	F%	Min	GP	G	A	Pts	PIM	PP	SH	GW	Min
1997-98	Ml. Boleslav Jr.	CzRep-Jr.	35	42	31	73	4																		
1998-99	Hull Olympiques	QMJHL	54	22	38	60	16										23	6	13	19	6				
99-2000	Hull Olympiques	QMJHL	58	29	45	74	26										15	3	9	12	8				
2000-01	Shawinigan	QMJHL	55	56	64	120	67										10	4	7	11	4				
	Hershey Bears	AHL															1	0	1	1	2				
2001-02	**Colorado**	**NHL**	52	18	12	30	14	6	0	3	112	16.1	7	8	37.5	14:32	9	0	0	0	0	0	0	0	13:05
	Hershey Bears	AHL	20	8	14	22	8																		
2002-03	**Colorado**	**NHL**	66	11	19	30	16	3	0	4	171	6.4	0	14	50.0	13:55									
	Carolina	**NHL**	10	5	0	5	2	3	0	0	44	11.4	-7	15	46.7	19:00									
2003-04	**Carolina**	**NHL**	80	12	13	25	24	4	0	2	195	6.2	-10	21	38.1	13:42									
2004-05	Liberec	CzRep	45	18	21	39	91										12	3	2	5	0				
2005-06	**Carolina**	**NHL**	16	2	3	5	4	1	0	0	38	5.3	0	3	33.3	12:37									
	Chicago	**NHL**	45	13	21	34	16	5	0	0	147	8.8	4	6	50.0	15:43									
2006-07	**Chicago**	**NHL**	77	14	27	41	26	5	0	2	215	6.5	-4	12	33.3	16:53									
2007-08	**Phoenix**	**NHL**	76	27	29	56	14	7	3	5	246	11.0	6	19	36.8	18:12									
2008-09	**Tampa Bay**	**NHL**	18	3	3	6	8	1	0	0	41	7.3	-1	3	33.3	14:13									
	BK Mlada Boleslav	CzRep	11	5	3	8	18										3	0	1	1	2				
	Liberec	CzRep	7	7	2	9	2																		
2009-10	**Phoenix**	**NHL**	82	24	19	43	24	7	0	4	266	9.0	6	8	25.0	16:13	7	2	2	4	4	1	0	1	15:42
	NHL Totals		522	129	146	275	150	42	3	20	1475	8.7		109	39.4	15:35	16	2	2	4	4	1	0	1	14:13

QMJHL First All-Star Team (2001)
Traded to **Carolina** by **Colorado** for Bates Battaglia, March 11, 2003. Signed as a free agent by **Liberec** (CzRep), September 4, 2004. Traded to **Chicago** by Carolina for Chicago's 4th round choice (later traded to St. Louis - St. Louis selected Cade Fairchild) in 2007 Entry Draft, December 29, 2005. Traded to **Phoenix** by **Chicago** for Kevyn Adams, August 11, 2007. Signed as a free agent by **Tampa Bay**, July 1, 2008. • Assigned to **Mlada Boleslav** (CzRep) by **Tampa Bay**, December 9, 2008. • Loaned to **Liberec** (CzRep) by **Mlada Boleslav** (CzRep), January 29, 2009. Traded to **Phoenix** by **Tampa Bay** for Todd Fedoruk and David Hale, July 21, 2009.

WAGNER, Steve
(WAG-nuhr, STEEV)   **PIT.**

Defense. Shoots left. 6'2", 200 lbs.   Born, Grand Rapids, MN, March 6, 1984.

Season	Club	League	GP	G	A	Pts	PIM	PP	SH	GW	S	%	+/-	TF	F%	Min	GP	G	A	Pts	PIM	PP	SH	GW	Min
2002-03	Des Moines	USHL	14	0	1	1	17																		
	Tri-City Storm	USHL	27	0	5	5	52										3	1	0	1	0				
2003-04	Tri-City Storm	USHL	43	3	19	22	52										9	0	4	4	13				
2004-05	Minnesota State	WCHA	37	1	9	10	40																		
2005-06	Minnesota State	WCHA	38	5	11	16	53																		
2006-07	Minnesota State	WCHA	38	6	23	29	63																		
	Peoria Rivermen	AHL	14	1	2	3	8																		
2007-08	**St. Louis**	**NHL**	24	2	6	8	8	1	0	0	25	8.0	-4	0	0.0	18:29									
	Peoria Rivermen	AHL	23	5	7	12	16																		
2008-09	**St. Louis**	**NHL**	22	2	2	4	18	0	0	0	16	12.5	-5	0	0.0	15:38									
	Peoria Rivermen	AHL	47	6	16	22	38										7	1	3	4	4				
2009-10	Peoria Rivermen	AHL	46	3	12	15	20																		
	Wilkes-Barre	AHL	20	1	6	7	10										4	0	1	1	2				
	NHL Totals		46	4	8	12	26	1	0	0	41	9.8		0	0.0	17:07									

Signed as a free agent by **St. Louis**, March 20, 2007. Traded to **Pittsburgh** by **St. Louis** for Nate Guenin, February 11, 2010.

WALKER, Matt
(WAH-kuhr, MAT)   **PHI.**

Defense. Shoots right. 6'4", 214 lbs.   Born, Beaverlodge, Alta., April 7, 1980. St. Louis' 3rd choice, 83rd overall, in 1998 Entry Draft.

Season	Club	League	GP	G	A	Pts	PIM	PP	SH	GW	S	%	+/-	TF	F%	Min	GP	G	A	Pts	PIM	PP	SH	GW	Min
1996-97	Grand Prairie	AAHA	68	22	62	74	186																		
1997-98	Portland	WHL	64	2	13	15	124										16	0	0	0	21				
1998-99	Portland	WHL	64	1	10	11	151										4	0	1	1	6				
99-2000	Portland	WHL	38	2	7	9	97																		
	Kootenay Ice	WHL	31	4	19	23	53										21	5	13	18	24				
2000-01	Worcester IceCats	AHL	61	4	8	12	131										11	0	0	0	6				
	Peoria Rivermen	ECHL	8	1	0	1	70																		
2001-02	Worcester IceCats	AHL	49	2	11	13	164										3	0	0	0	8				
2002-03	**St. Louis**	**NHL**	16	0	1	1	38	0	0	0	13	0.0	0	1100.0	11:09									
	Worcester IceCats	AHL	40	1	8	9	58																		
2003-04	**St. Louis**	**NHL**	14	0	1	1	25	0	0	0	8	0.0	0	0	0.0	11:23	4	0	0	0	0	0	0	0	9:43
	Worcester IceCats	AHL	4	0	1	1	7																		
2004-05	Worcester IceCats	AHL	20	2	4	6	44																		
2005-06	**St. Louis**	**NHL**	54	0	2	2	79	0	0	0	59	0.0	-7	0	0.0	14:15									
2006-07	**St. Louis**	**NHL**	48	0	5	5	72	0	0	0	34	0.0	7	0	0.0	15:15									
	Peoria Rivermen	AHL	2	0	1	1	0																		
2007-08	**St. Louis**	**NHL**	43	1	1	2	61	0	0	0	47	2.1	-3	0	0.0	15:54									
2008-09	**Chicago**	**NHL**	65	1	13	14	79	0	0	0	83	1.2	7	0	0.0	16:38	17	0	2	2	14	0	0	0	15:21
2009-10	**Tampa Bay**	**NHL**	66	2	3	5	90	0	0	0	54	3.7	-11	0	0.0	16:09									
	NHL Totals		306	4	26	30	444	0	0	0	298	1.3		1100.0	15:16	21	0	2	2	14	0	0	0	14:17

• Missed majority of 2003-04 season recovering from groin injury suffered in training camp, September 23, 2003. Signed as a free agent by **Chicago**, July 7, 2008. Signed as a free agent by **Tampa Bay**, July 1, 2009. Traded to **Philadelphia** by **Tampa Bay** with Tampa Bay's 4th round choice in 2011 Entry Draft for Simon Gagne, July 19. 2010.

			Regular Season														Playoffs								
Season	Club	League	GP	G	A	Pts	PIM	PP	SH	GW	S	%	+/-	TF	F%	Min	GP	G	A	Pts	PIM	PP	SH	GW	Min

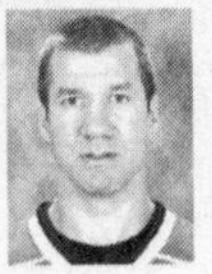

WALKER, Scott

(WAH-kuhr, SKAWT)

Right wing. Shoots right. 5'10", 196 lbs. Born, Cambridge, Ont., July 19, 1973. Vancouver's 4th choice, 124th overall, in 1993 Entry Draft.

1989-90	Kitchener	OHA-B	6	0	5	5	4	....	....	....	....	....	....	....	....	....	....	....	....	....	....	....	....	....	....
	Cambridge	OHA-B	27	7	22	29	87	....	....	....	....	....	....	....	....	....	....	....	....	....	....	....	....	....	....
1990-91	Cambridge	OHA-B	45	10	27	37	241	....	....	....	....	....	....	....	....	....	....	....	....	....	....	....	....	....	....
1991-92	Owen Sound	OHL	53	7	31	38	128	....	....	....	....	....	....	....	....	....	5	0	7	7	8	....	....	....	....
1992-93	Owen Sound	OHL	57	23	68	91	110	....	....	....	....	....	....	....	....	....	8	1	5	6	16	....	....	....	....
1993-94	Hamilton	AHL	77	10	29	39	272	....	....	....	....	....	....	....	....	....	4	0	1	1	25	....	....	....	....
1994-95	Syracuse Crunch	AHL	74	14	38	52	334	....	....	....	....	....	....	....	....	....	....	....	....	....	....	....	....	....	....
	Vancouver	NHL	11	0	1	1	33	0	0	0	8	0.0	0	....	....	....	....	....	....	....	....	....	....	....	....
1995-96	Vancouver	NHL	63	4	8	12	137	0	1	1	45	8.9	–7	....	....	....	....	....	....	....	....	....	....	....	....
	Syracuse Crunch	AHL	15	3	12	15	52	....	....	....	....	....	....	....	....	....	16	9	8	17	39	....	....	....	....
1996-97	Vancouver	NHL	64	3	15	18	132	0	0	0	55	5.5	2	....	....	....	....	....	....	....	....	....	....	....	....
1997-98	Vancouver	NHL	59	3	10	13	164	0	1	1	40	7.5	–8	....	....	....	....	....	....	....	....	....	....	....	....
1998-99	Nashville	NHL	71	15	25	40	103	0	1	2	96	15.6	0	265	48.3	16:21	....	....	....	....	....	....	....	....	....
99-2000	Nashville	NHL	69	7	21	28	90	0	1	0	98	7.1	–16	30	36.7	15:49	....	....	....	....	....	....	....	....	....
2000-01	Nashville	NHL	74	25	29	54	66	9	3	1	159	15.7	–2	541	51.4	19:17	....	....	....	....	....	....	....	....	....
2001-02	Nashville	NHL	28	4	5	9	18	1	0	0	46	8.7	–13	149	38.9	18:38	....	....	....	....	....	....	....	....	....
2002-03	Nashville	NHL	60	15	18	33	58	7	0	5	124	12.1	2	336	49.1	19:50	....	....	....	....	....	....	....	....	....
2003-04	Nashville	NHL	75	25	42	67	94	9	3	3	157	15.9	4	367	41.4	20:03	6	0	1	1	6	0	0	0	20:10
2004-05	Cambridge	OHA-Sr.	5	2	6	8	4	....	....	....	....	....	....	....	....	....	....	....	....	....	....	....	....	....	....
	Dundas	OHA-Sr.	3	3	2	5	8	....	....	....	....	....	....	....	....	....	....	....	....	....	....	....	....	....	....
2005-06	Nashville	NHL	33	5	11	16	36	1	0	0	57	8.8	2	87	44.8	17:23	5	0	0	0	6	0	0	0	16:01
2006-07	Carolina	NHL	81	21	30	51	45	6	0	6	183	11.5	–10	95	42.1	16:10	....	....	....	....	....	....	....	....	....
2007-08	Carolina	NHL	58	14	18	32	115	4	2	4	122	11.5	–3	48	43.8	16:37	....	....	....	....	....	....	....	....	....
2008-09	Carolina	NHL	41	5	10	15	39	1	0	0	71	7.0	–4	4	50.0	13:20	18	1	6	7	19	0	0	1	11:31
2009-10	Carolina	NHL	33	3	2	5	23	1	0	0	50	6.0	–4	3	0.0	9:50	....	....	....	....	....	....	....	....	....
	Washington	NHL	9	2	1	3	9	0	0	1	13	15.4	1	1	0.0	9:11	1	0	0	0	0	0	0	0	6:47
	NHL Totals		829	151	246	397	1162	39	12	24	1324	11.4		1926	46.4	16:55	30	1	7	8	31	0	0	1	13:50

OHL Second All-Star Team (1993)

Claimed by **Nashville** from **Vancouver** in Expansion Draft, June 26, 1998. Signed as a free agent by **Cambridge** (OHA-Sr.), October 21, 2004. Signed as a free agent by **Dundas** (OHA-Sr.), February 10, 2005. • Missed majority of 2005-06 season recovering from sports hernia (October 25, 2005 vs. Chicago) and wrist (February 6, 2006 at Dallas) injuries. Traded to **Carolina** by **Nashville** for Josef Vasicek, July 18, 2006. Traded to **Washington** by **Carolina** for Washington's 7th round choice (later traded to Philadelphia – Philadelphia selected Ricard Blidstrand) in 2010 Entry Draft, March 3, 2010.

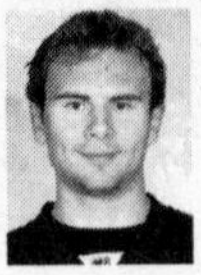

WALLACE, Tim

(WAHL-uhs, TIHM) **PIT.**

Right wing. Shoots right. 6'1", 207 lbs. Born, Anchorage, AK, August 6, 1984.

2002-03	U. of Notre Dame	CCHA	40	6	5	11	28	....	....	....	....	....	....	....	....	....	....	....	....	....	....	....	....	....	....
2003-04	U. of Notre Dame	CCHA	39	3	8	11	10	....	....	....	....	....	....	....	....	....	....	....	....	....	....	....	....	....	....
2004-05	U. of Notre Dame	CCHA	38	5	9	14	20	....	....	....	....	....	....	....	....	....	....	....	....	....	....	....	....	....	....
2005-06	U. of Notre Dame	CCHA	36	11	12	23	28	....	....	....	....	....	....	....	....	....	....	....	....	....	....	....	....	....	....
2006-07	Wilkes-Barre	AHL	32	5	9	14	39	....	....	....	....	....	....	....	....	....	11	1	1	2	2	....	....	....	....
	Wheeling Nailers	ECHL	19	6	11	17	23	....	....	....	....	....	....	....	....	....	....	....	....	....	....	....	....	....	....
2007-08	Wilkes-Barre	AHL	74	12	14	26	82	....	....	....	....	....	....	....	....	....	23	2	6	8	21	....	....	....	....
2008-09	Pittsburgh	NHL	16	0	2	2	7	0	0	0	17	0.0	2	3	66.7	8:07	....	....	....	....	....	....	....	....	....
	Wilkes-Barre	AHL	58	11	8	19	51	....	....	....	....	....	....	....	....	....	7	0	2	2	2	....	....	....	....
2009-10	Pittsburgh	NHL	1	0	0	0	0	0	0	0	0	0.0	0	0	0.0	5:50	....	....	....	....	....	....	....	....	....
	Wilkes-Barre	AHL	78	27	14	41	61	....	....	....	....	....	....	....	....	....	4	0	0	0	2	....	....	....	....
	NHL Totals		17	0	2	2	7	0	0	0	17	0.0		3	66.7	7:59	....	....	....	....	....	....	....	....	....

Signed as a free agent by **Pittsburgh**, May 29, 2007.

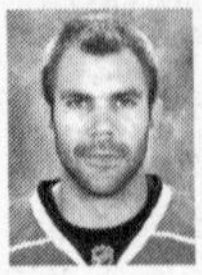

WALLIN, Niclas

(WAHL-ihn, NIHK-luhs) **S.J**

Defense. Shoots left. 6'3", 220 lbs. Born, Boden, Sweden, February 20, 1975. Carolina's 3rd choice, 97th overall, in 2000 Entry Draft.

1994-95	Bodens IK	Swe-Jr.	30	2	13	15	125	....	....	....	....	....	....	....	....	....	....	....	....	....	....	....	....	....	....
	Bodens IK	Sweden-2	13	0	0	0	0	....	....	....	....	....	....	....	....	....	2	0	0	0	0	....	....	....	....
1995-96	Bodens IK	Swe-Jr.	2	2	2	4	0	....	....	....	....	....	....	....	....	....	....	....	....	....	....	....	....	....	....
	Bodens IK	Sweden-2	30	2	7	9	26	....	....	....	....	....	....	....	....	....	2	0	1	1	2	....	....	....	....
1996-97	Brynas IF Gavle	Sweden	47	1	1	2	14	....	....	....	....	....	....	....	....	....	....	....	....	....	....	....	....	....	....
1997-98	Brynas IF Gavle	Sweden	44	2	3	5	57	....	....	....	....	....	....	....	....	....	3	0	1	1	4	....	....	....	....
1998-99	Brynas IF Gavle	Sweden	46	2	4	6	52	....	....	....	....	....	....	....	....	....	14	0	1	1	8	....	....	....	....
99-2000	Brynas IF Gavle	Sweden	48	7	9	16	73	....	....	....	....	....	....	....	....	....	11	2	1	3	14	....	....	....	....
	Brynas IF Gavle	EuroHL	5	1	1	2	10	....	....	....	....	....	....	....	....	....	....	....	....	....	....	....	....	....	....
2000-01	Carolina	NHL	37	2	3	5	21	0	0	0	19	10.5	–11	0	0.0	14:57	3	0	0	0	2	0	0	0	19:1
	Cincinnati	IHL	8	1	2	3	4	....	....	....	....	....	....	....	....	....	3	0	0	0	2	....	....	....	....
2001-02	Carolina	NHL	52	1	2	3	36	0	0	0	33	3.0	1	0	0.0	12:12	23	2	1	3	12	0	0	2	15:2
2002-03	Carolina	NHL	77	2	8	10	71	0	0	2	69	2.9	–19	0	0.0	16:12	....	....	....	....	....	....	....	....	....
2003-04	Carolina	NHL	57	3	7	10	51	0	0	0	74	4.1	–8	0	0.0	18:40	....	....	....	....	....	....	....	....	....
2004-05	Lulea HF	Sweden	39	6	7	13	89	....	....	....	....	....	....	....	....	....	3	0	1	1	6	....	....	....	....
2005-06 ♦	Carolina	NHL	50	4	4	8	42	0	0	0	44	9.1	2	0	0.0	16:50	25	1	4	5	14	0	0	1	16:3
2006-07	Carolina	NHL	67	2	8	10	48	0	0	0	76	2.6	–2	0	0.0	18:33	....	....	....	....	....	....	....	....	....
2007-08	Carolina	NHL	66	2	6	8	54	0	0	0	60	3.3	–18	1	0.0	18:08	....	....	....	....	....	....	....	....	....
2008-09	Carolina	NHL	64	2	8	10	42	0	0	1	53	3.8	–1	1	0.0	16:16	18	0	0	0	4	0	0	0	13:4
2009-10	Carolina	NHL	47	0	5	5	26	0	0	0	50	0.0	–5	1	0.0	17:47	....	....	....	....	....	....	....	....	....
	San Jose	NHL	23	0	2	2	23	0	0	0	22	0.0	0	0	0.0	16:23	6	0	0	0	2	0	0	0	11:1
	NHL Totals		540	18	53	71	414	0	0	3	500	3.6		3	0.0	16:44	75	3	5	8	34	0	0	3	15:1

Signed as a free agent by **Lulea** (Sweden), September 19, 2004. Traded to **San Jose** by **Carolina** with Carolina's 5th round choice (Cody Ferriero) in 2010 Entry Draft for Buffalo's 2nd round choice (previously acquired, Carolina selected Mark Alt) in 2010 Entry Draft, February 7, 2010.

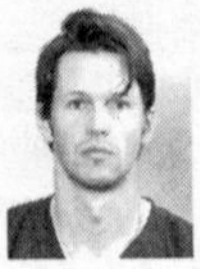

WALLIN, Rickard

(WAHL-ihn, RIH-kahrd)

Center. Shoots left. 6'2", 195 lbs. Born, Stockholm, Sweden, April 19, 1980. Phoenix's 8th choice, 160th overall, in 1998 Entry Draft.

1996-97	Vasteras IK Jr.	Swe-Jr.	26	3	3	6	....	....	....	....	....	....	....	....	....	....	....	....	....	....	....	....	....	....	....
1997-98	Farjestad Jr.	Swe-Jr.	29	20	30	50	32	....	....	....	....	....	....	....	....	....	2	1	1	2	2	....	....	....	....
1998-99	Farjestad Jr.	Swe-Jr.	21	11	15	26	30	....	....	....	....	....	....	....	....	....	....	....	....	....	....	....	....	....	....
	Farjestad	Sweden	5	0	0	0	0	....	....	....	....	....	....	....	....	....	....	....	....	....	....	....	....	....	....
99-2000	IF Troja-Ljungby	Sweden-2	46	15	22	37	54	....	....	....	....	....	....	....	....	....	....	....	....	....	....	....	....	....	....
2000-01	Farjestad	Sweden	47	9	22	31	24	....	....	....	....	....	....	....	....	....	16	11	3	14	4	....	....	....	....
2001-02	Farjestad	Sweden	50	12	31	43	56	....	....	....	....	....	....	....	....	....	10	4	9	13	8	....	....	....	....
2002-03	Minnesota	NHL	4	1	0	1	0	0	0	1	1	100.0	1	28	53.6	7:44	....	....	....	....	....	....	....	....	....
	Houston Aeros	AHL	52	13	22	35	70	....	....	....	....	....	....	....	....	....	23	4	11	15	22	....	....	....	....
2003-04	Minnesota	NHL	15	5	4	9	14	3	0	1	16	31.3	1	189	45.5	14:20	....	....	....	....	....	....	....	....	....
	Houston Aeros	AHL	47	14	18	32	36	....	....	....	....	....	....	....	....	....	2	0	0	0	2	....	....	....	....
2004-05	Houston Aeros	AHL	79	12	31	43	61	....	....	....	....	....	....	....	....	....	5	1	0	1	29	....	....	....	....
2005-06	Farjestad	Sweden	50	11	19	30	82	....	....	....	....	....	....	....	....	....	18	6	3	9	28	....	....	....	....
2006-07	HC Lugano	Swiss	44	14	35	49	87	....	....	....	....	....	....	....	....	....	6	3	3	6	16	....	....	....	....
2007-08	Farjestad	Sweden	55	17	23	40	54	....	....	....	....	....	....	....	....	....	12	1	5	6	18	....	....	....	....
2008-09	Farjestad	Sweden	55	18	27	45	56	....	....	....	....	....	....	....	....	....	13	1	4	5	8	....	....	....	....
2009-10	Toronto	NHL	60	2	7	9	20	0	0	0	72	2.8	–7	506	44.5	12:39	....	....	....	....	....	....	....	....	....
	NHL Totals		79	8	11	19	34	3	0	2	89	9.0		723	45.1	12:43	....	....	....	....	....	....	....	....	....

• Rights traded to **Minnesota** by **Phoenix** for Joe Juneau, June 23, 2000. • Assigned to **Farjestad** (Sweden) by **Minnesota**, September 22, 2005. Signed as a free agent by **Lugano** (Swiss), July 23, 2006 Signed as a free agent by **Toronto**, July 10, 2009. Signed as a free agent by **Farjestad** (Sweden), May 26, 2010.

			Regular Season														Playoffs								
Season	Club	League	GP	G	A	Pts	PIM	PP	SH	GW	S	%	+/-	TF	F%	Min	GP	G	A	Pts	PIM	PP	SH	GW	Min

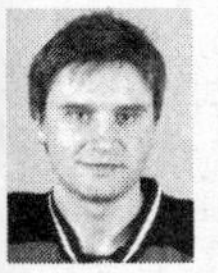

WALTER, Ben

(WAHL-tuhr, BEHN) **COL.**

Center. Shoots left. 6'1", 195 lbs. Born, Beaconsfield, Que., May 11, 1984. Boston's 5th choice, 160th overall, in 2004 Entry Draft.

Season	Club	League	GP	G	A	Pts	PIM	PP	SH	GW	S	%	+/-	TF	F%	Min	GP	G	A	Pts	PIM	PP	SH	GW	Min
2000-01	Langley Hornets	BCHL	50	8	22	30	19	....	....	....	....	....	....	....	....	....	....	....	....	....	....	....	....	....	....
2001-02	Langley Hornets	BCHL	50	29	47	76	29	....	....	....	....	....	....	....	....	....	....	....	....	....	....	....	....	....	....
2002-03	U. Mass-Lowell	H-East	35	5	12	17	12	....	....	....	....	....	....	....	....	....	....	....	....	....	....	....	....	....	....
2003-04	U. Mass-Lowell	H-East	36	18	16	34	18	....	....	....	....	....	....	....	....	....	....	....	....	....	....	....	....	....	....
2004-05	U. Mass-Lowell	H-East	36	*26	13	39	28	....	....	....	....	....	....	....	....	....	....	....	....	....	....	....	....	....	....
2005-06	**Boston**	**NHL**	**6**	**0**	**0**	**0**	**4**	**0**	**0**	**0**	**6**	**0.0**	**2**	**32**	**53.1**	**11:49**	....	....	....	....	....	....	....	....	....
	Providence Bruins	AHL	62	16	25	41	33	....	....	....	....	....	....	....	....	....	3	2	0	2	2	....	....	....	....
2006-07	**Boston**	**NHL**	**4**	**0**	**0**	**0**	**0**	**0**	**0**	**0**	**0**	**0.0**	**0**	**24**	**41.7**	**6:11**	....	....	....	....	....	....	....	....	....
	Providence Bruins	AHL	73	24	43	67	58	....	....	....	....	....	....	....	....	....	13	4	4	8	6	....	....	....	....
2007-08	**NY Islanders**	**NHL**	**8**	**1**	**0**	**1**	**0**	**1**	**0**	**0**	**6**	**16.7**	**–1**	**33**	**30.3**	**6:05**	....	....	....	....	....	....	....	....	....
	Bridgeport	AHL	68	20	46	66	31	....	....	....	....	....	....	....	....	....	....	....	....	....	....	....	....	....	....
2008-09	**NY Islanders**	**NHL**	**4**	**0**	**0**	**0**	**0**	**0**	**0**	**0**	**2**	**0.0**	**–2**	**43**	**41.9**	**10:58**	....	....	....	....	....	....	....	....	....
	Bridgeport	AHL	65	20	30	50	10	....	....	....	....	....	....	....	....	....	5	1	4	5	2	....	....	....	....
2009-10	**New Jersey**	**NHL**	**2**	**0**	**0**	**0**	**2**	**0**	**0**	**0**	**0**	**0.0**	**0**	**6**	**33.3**	**5:48**	....	....	....	....	....	....	....	....	....
	Lowell Devils	AHL	78	22	36	58	26	....	....	....	....	....	....	....	....	....	5	1	1	2	2	....	....	....	....
	NHL Totals		**24**	**1**	**0**	**1**	**6**	**1**	**0**	**0**	**14**	**7.1**		**138**	**41.3**	**8:19**	....	....	....	....	....	....	....	....	....

Hockey East Second All-Star Team (2005)

Traded to **NY Islanders** by **Boston** with Boston's 2nd round choice (later traded to Columbus – Columbus selected Kevin Lynch) in 2009 Entry Draft for Petteri Nokelainen, September 11, 2007. Traded to **New Jersey** by **NY Islanders** with future considerations for Tony Romano, June 30, 2009. Signed as a free agent by **Colorado**, July 7, 2010.

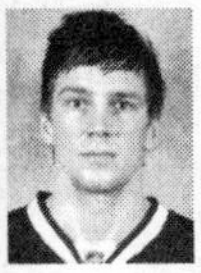

WANDELL, Tom

(VAHN-dehl, TAWM) **DAL.**

Center. Shoots left. 6'1", 195 lbs. Born, Sodertalje, Sweden, January 29, 1987. Dallas' 5th choice, 146th overall, in 2005 Entry Draft.

Season	Club	League	GP	G	A	Pts	PIM	PP	SH	GW	S	%	+/-	TF	F%	Min	GP	G	A	Pts	PIM	PP	SH	GW	Min
2002-03	Sodertalje SK U18	Swe-U18	13	8	7	15	6	....	....	....	....	....	....	....	....	....	....	....	....	....	....	....	....	....	....
2003-04	Sodertalje SK U18	Swe-U18	6	5	7	12	6	....	....	....	....	....	....	....	....	....	2	0	0	0	0	....	....	....	....
	Sodertalje SK Jr.	Swe-Jr.	33	7	15	22	14	....	....	....	....	....	....	....	....	....	2	0	0	0	0	....	....	....	....
2004-05	Sodertalje SK Jr.	Swe-Jr.	5	1	2	3	4	....	....	....	....	....	....	....	....	....	....	....	....	....	....	....	....	....	....
2005-06	Sodertalje SK Jr.	Swe-Jr.	41	19	20	39	45	....	....	....	....	....	....	....	....	....	4	1	0	1	2	....	....	....	....
	Sodertalje SK	Sweden	6	0	0	0	0	....	....	....	....	....	....	....	....	....	....	....	....	....	....	....	....	....	....
	Sodertalje SK	Sweden-Q	1	1	0	1	0	....	....	....	....	....	....	....	....	....	....	....	....	....	....	....	....	....	....
2006-07	Assat Pori Jr.	Fin-Jr.	4	1	1	2	0	....	....	....	....	....	....	....	....	....	....	....	....	....	....	....	....	....	....
	Assat Pori	Finland	50	6	6	12	20	....	....	....	....	....	....	....	....	....	....	....	....	....	....	....	....	....	....
2007-08	Iowa Stars	AHL	53	10	9	19	16	....	....	....	....	....	....	....	....	....	....	....	....	....	....	....	....	....	....
	Idaho Steelheads	ECHL	3	3	0	3	2	....	....	....	....	....	....	....	....	....	....	....	....	....	....	....	....	....	....
2008-09	Timra IK	Sweden	51	15	26	41	26	....	....	....	....	....	....	....	....	....	7	0	4	4	0	....	....	....	....
	Dallas	**NHL**	**14**	**1**	**2**	**3**	**4**	**0**	**0**	**0**	**23**	**4.3**	**–1**	**113**	**51.3**	**11:09**	....	....	....	....	....	....	....	....	....
2009-10	**Dallas**	**NHL**	**50**	**5**	**10**	**15**	**14**	**0**	**0**	**3**	**85**	**5.9**	**2**	**486**	**44.0**	**13:52**	....	....	....	....	....	....	....	....	....
	NHL Totals		**64**	**6**	**12**	**18**	**18**	**0**	**0**	**3**	**108**	**5.6**		**599**	**45.4**	**13:17**	....	....	....	....	....	....	....	....	....

• Assigned to **Timra** (Sweden) by **Dallas**, July 24, 2008 .

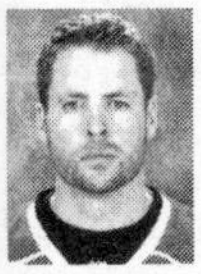

WARD, Aaron

(WOHRD, AIR-ruhn)

Defense. Shoots right. 6'2", 209 lbs. Born, Windsor, Ont., January 17, 1973. Winnipeg's 1st choice, 5th overall, in 1991 Entry Draft.

Season	Club	League	GP	G	A	Pts	PIM	PP	SH	GW	S	%	+/-	TF	F%	Min	GP	G	A	Pts	PIM	PP	SH	GW	Min
1988-89	Nepean Raiders	CJHL	54	1	14	15	40	....	....	....	....	....	....	....	....	....	....	....	....	....	....	....	....	....	....
1989-90	Nepean Raiders	CJHL	52	6	33	39	85	....	....	....	....	....	....	....	....	....	....	....	....	....	....	....	....	....	....
1990-91	U. of Michigan	CCHA	46	8	11	19	126	....	....	....	....	....	....	....	....	....	....	....	....	....	....	....	....	....	....
1991-92	U. of Michigan	CCHA	42	7	12	19	64	....	....	....	....	....	....	....	....	....	....	....	....	....	....	....	....	....	....
1992-93	U. of Michigan	CCHA	30	5	8	13	73	....	....	....	....	....	....	....	....	....	....	....	....	....	....	....	....	....	....
1993-94	**Detroit**	**NHL**	**5**	**1**	**0**	**1**	**4**	**0**	**0**	**0**	**3**	**33.3**	**2**	....	....	....	....	....	....	....	....	....	....	....	....
	Adirondack	AHL	58	4	12	16	87	....	....	....	....	....	....	....	....	....	9	2	6	8	6	....	....	....	....
1994-95	Adirondack	AHL	76	11	24	35	87	....	....	....	....	....	....	....	....	....	4	0	1	1	0	....	....	....	....
	Detroit	**NHL**	**1**	**0**	**1**	**1**	**2**	**0**	**0**	**0**	**0**	**0.0**	**1**	....	....	....	....	....	....	....	....	....	....	....	....
1995-96	Adirondack	AHL	74	5	10	15	133	....	....	....	....	....	....	....	....	....	3	0	0	0	6	....	....	....	....
1996-97♦	**Detroit**	**NHL**	**49**	**2**	**5**	**7**	**52**	**0**	**0**	**0**	**40**	**5.0**	**–9**	....	....	....	**19**	**0**	**0**	**0**	**17**	**0**	**0**	**0**	....
1997-98♦	**Detroit**	**NHL**	**52**	**5**	**5**	**10**	**47**	**0**	**0**	**1**	**47**	**10.6**	**–1**	....	....	....	....	....	....	....	....	....	....	....	....
1998-99	**Detroit**	**NHL**	**60**	**3**	**8**	**11**	**52**	**0**	**0**	**0**	**46**	**6.5**	**–5**	**0**	**0.0**	**13:55**	**8**	**0**	**1**	**1**	**8**	**0**	**0**	**0**	**10:15**
99-2000	**Detroit**	**NHL**	**36**	**1**	**3**	**4**	**24**	**0**	**0**	**0**	**25**	**4.0**	**–4**	**0**	**0.0**	**12:36**	**3**	**0**	**0**	**0**	**0**	**0**	**0**	**0**	**7:36**
2000-01	**Detroit**	**NHL**	**73**	**4**	**5**	**9**	**57**	**0**	**0**	**1**	**48**	**8.3**	**–4**	**0**	**0.0**	**17:00**	....	....	....	....	....	....	....	....	....
2001-02	**Carolina**	**NHL**	**79**	**3**	**11**	**14**	**74**	**0**	**0**	**2**	**69**	**4.3**	**0**	**1**	**100.0**	**19:40**	**23**	**1**	**1**	**2**	**22**	**0**	**0**	**0**	**21:12**
2002-03	**Carolina**	**NHL**	**77**	**3**	**6**	**9**	**90**	**0**	**0**	**1**	**66**	**4.5**	**–23**	**0**	**0.0**	**18:43**	....	....	....	....	....	....	....	....	....
2003-04	**Carolina**	**NHL**	**49**	**3**	**5**	**8**	**37**	**2**	**0**	**0**	**51**	**5.9**	**1**	**0**	**0.0**	**17:52**	....	....	....	....	....	....	....	....	....
2004-05	ERC Ingolstadt	Germany	8	0	3	3	16	....	....	....	....	....	....	....	....	....	11	1	1	2	16	....	....	....	....
2005-06♦	**Carolina**	**NHL**	**71**	**6**	**19**	**25**	**62**	**0**	**0**	**1**	**60**	**10.0**	**2**	**1**	**0.0**	**19:07**	**25**	**2**	**3**	**5**	**18**	**0**	**0**	**0**	**21:42**
2006-07	**NY Rangers**	**NHL**	**60**	**3**	**10**	**13**	**57**	**0**	**0**	**0**	**45**	**6.7**	**–3**	**0**	**0.0**	**19:42**	....	....	....	....	....	....	....	....	....
	Boston	**NHL**	**20**	**1**	**2**	**3**	**18**	**0**	**0**	**0**	**17**	**5.9**	**–8**	**0**	**0.0**	**21:36**	....	....	....	....	....	....	....	....	....
2007-08	**Boston**	**NHL**	**65**	**5**	**8**	**13**	**54**	**0**	**0**	**3**	**68**	**7.4**	**9**	**0**	**0.0**	**20:45**	**6**	**0**	**1**	**1**	**6**	**0**	**0**	**0**	**22:20**
2008-09	**Boston**	**NHL**	**65**	**3**	**7**	**10**	**44**	**0**	**1**	**0**	**53**	**5.7**	**16**	**0**	**0.0**	**19:01**	**11**	**1**	**0**	**1**	**2**	**0**	**0**	**0**	**19:41**
2009-10	**Carolina**	**NHL**	**60**	**1**	**10**	**11**	**54**	**0**	**0**	**0**	**32**	**3.1**	**–17**	**0**	**0.0**	**18:07**	....	....	....	....	....	....	....	....	....
	Anaheim	**NHL**	**17**	**0**	**2**	**2**	**8**	**0**	**0**	**0**	**9**	**0.0**	**2**	**0**	**0.0**	**14:26**	....	....	....	....	....	....	....	....	....
	NHL Totals		**839**	**44**	**107**	**151**	**736**	**2**	**1**	**9**	**679**	**6.5**		**2**	**50.0**	**18:09**	**95**	**4**	**6**	**10**	**73**	**0**	**0**	**0**	**19:33**

Traded to **Detroit** by **Winnipeg** with Toronto's 4th round choice (previously acquired, Detroit selected John Jakopin) in 1993 Entry Draft for Paul Ysebaert and future considerations (Alan Kerr, June 18, 1993), June 11, 1993. • Missed majority of 1999-2000 season recovering from shoulder injury suffered in game vs. Vancouver, January 19, 2000. Traded to **Carolina** by **Detroit** for Carolina's 2nd round choice (Jiri Hudler) in 2002 Entry Draft, July 9, 2001. Signed as a free agent by **Ingolstadt** (Germany), February 15, 2005. Signed as a free agent by **NY Rangers**, July 3, 2006. Traded to **Boston** by **NY Rangers** for Paul Mara, February 27, 2007. Traded to **Carolina** by **Boston** for Patrick Eaves and Carolina's 4th round choice (Craig Cunningham) in 2010 Entry Draft, July 24, 2009. Traded to **Anaheim** by **Carolina** for Justin Pogge and Boston's 4th round choice (previously acquired, Carolina selected Justin Shugg) in 2010 Entry Draft), March 3, 2010.

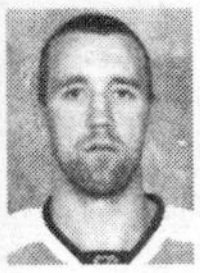

WARD, Jason

(WOHRD, JAY-suhn)

Right wing. Shoots right. 6'2", 208 lbs. Born, Chapleau, Ont., January 16, 1979. Montreal's 1st choice, 11th overall, in 1997 Entry Draft.

Season	Club	League	GP	G	A	Pts	PIM	PP	SH	GW	S	%	+/-	TF	F%	Min	GP	G	A	Pts	PIM	PP	SH	GW	Min
1994-95	Oshawa	OHA-B	47	30	31	61	75	....	....	....	....	....	....	....	....	....	....	....	....	....	....	....	....	....	....
1995-96	Niagara Falls	OHL	64	15	35	50	139	....	....	....	....	....	....	....	....	....	10	6	4	10	23	....	....	....	....
1996-97	Erie Otters	OHL	58	25	39	64	137	....	....	....	....	....	....	....	....	....	5	1	2	3	2	....	....	....	....
1997-98	Erie Otters	OHL	21	7	9	16	42	....	....	....	....	....	....	....	....	....	....	....	....	....	....	....	....	....	....
	Windsor Spitfires	OHL	26	19	27	46	34	....	....	....	....	....	....	....	....	....	....	....	....	....	....	....	....	....	....
	Fredericton	AHL	7	1	0	1	2	....	....	....	....	....	....	....	....	....	1	0	0	0	2	....	....	....	....
1998-99	Windsor Spitfires	OHL	12	8	11	19	25	....	....	....	....	....	....	....	....	....	....	....	....	....	....	....	....	....	....
	Plymouth Whalers	OHL	23	14	13	27	28	....	....	....	....	....	....	....	....	....	11	6	8	14	12	....	....	....	....
	Fredericton	AHL	....	....	....	....	....	....	....	....	....	....	....	....	....	....	10	4	2	6	22	....	....	....	....
99-2000	**Montreal**	**NHL**	**32**	**2**	**1**	**3**	**10**	**1**	**0**	**0**	**24**	**8.3**	**–1**	**86**	**44.2**	**9:10**	....	....	....	....	....	....	....	....	....
	Quebec Citadelles	AHL	40	14	12	26	30	....	....	....	....	....	....	....	....	....	3	2	1	3	4	....	....	....	....
2000-01	**Montreal**	**NHL**	**12**	**0**	**0**	**0**	**12**	**0**	**0**	**0**	**4**	**0.0**	**3**	**2**	**50.0**	**8:16**	....	....	....	....	....	....	....	....	....
	Quebec Citadelles	AHL	23	7	12	19	69	....	....	....	....	....	....	....	....	....	....	....	....	....	....	....	....	....	....
2001-02	Quebec Citadelles	AHL	78	24	33	57	128	....	....	....	....	....	....	....	....	....	3	0	0	0	2	....	....	....	....
2002-03	**Montreal**	**NHL**	**8**	**3**	**2**	**5**	**0**	**0**	**0**	**0**	**10**	**30.0**	**3**	**6**	**50.0**	**11:17**	....	....	....	....	....	....	....	....	....
	Hamilton	AHL	69	31	41	72	78	....	....	....	....	....	....	....	....	....	23	*12	9	*21	20	....	....	....	....
2003-04	**Montreal**	**NHL**	**53**	**5**	**7**	**12**	**21**	**2**	**0**	**1**	**56**	**8.9**	**3**	**98**	**41.8**	**12:39**	**5**	**0**	**2**	**2**	**2**	**0**	**0**	**0**	**15:39**
	Hamilton	AHL	2	0	3	3	17	....	....	....	....	....	....	....	....	....	....	....	....	....	....	....	....	....	....
2004-05	Hamilton	AHL	77	20	34	54	66	....	....	....	....	....	....	....	....	....	4	2	1	3	2	....	....	....	....
2005-06	**NY Rangers**	**NHL**	**81**	**10**	**18**	**28**	**44**	**0**	**2**	**1**	**125**	**8.0**	**–4**	**153**	**47.7**	**13:12**	**1**	**0**	**0**	**0**	**2**	**0**	**0**	**0**	**2:39**
2006-07	**NY Rangers**	**NHL**	**46**	**4**	**6**	**10**	**26**	**0**	**1**	**1**	**68**	**5.9**	**–3**	**191**	**41.9**	**12:19**	....	....	....	....	....	....	....	....	....
	Los Angeles	**NHL**	**7**	**0**	**1**	**1**	**4**	**0**	**0**	**0**	**2**	**0.0**	**–1**	**7**	**14.3**	**4:51**	....	....	....	....	....	....	....	....	....
	Tampa Bay	**NHL**	**17**	**4**	**4**	**8**	**10**	**0**	**0**	**0**	**38**	**10.5**	**–11**	**16**	**37.5**	**16:38**	**6**	**0**	**1**	**1**	**6**	**0**	**0**	**0**	**20:03**
2007-08	**Tampa Bay**	**NHL**	**79**	**8**	**6**	**14**	**42**	**1**	**1**	**0**	**85**	**9.4**	**–18**	**45**	**40.0**	**12:33**	....	....	....	....	....	....	....	....	....

			Regular Season														Playoffs								
Season	Club	League	GP	G	A	Pts	PIM	PP	SH	GW	S	%	+/-	TF	F%	Min	GP	G	A	Pts	PIM	PP	SH	GW	Mi
2008-09	**Tampa Bay**	**NHL**	**1**	**0**	**0**	**0**	**2**	**0**	**0**	**0**	**1**	**0.0**	**0**	**0**	**0.0**	**9:31**	....	....	....	....	....	....	....	....	....
	Norfolk Admirals	AHL	21	2	7	9	16	....	....	....	....	....	....	....	....	....	....	....	....	....	....	....	....	....	....
2009-10	Adirondack	AHL	56	12	17	29	30	....	....	....	....	....	....	....	....	....	....	....	....	....	....	....	....	....	....
	NHL Totals		**336**	**36**	**45**	**81**	**171**	**4**	**4**	**3**	**413**	**8.7**		**604**	**43.2**	**12:13**	**12**	**0**	**3**	**3**	**10**	**0**	**0**	**0**	**16:4**

AHL First All-Star Team (2003) • Les Cunningham Award (AHL – MVP) (2003)

• Missed majority of 2000-01 season recovering from knee injury suffered in game vs. Carolina, January 16, 2001. Signed as a free agent by **Hamilton** (AHL), October 19, 2004. Signed as a free agent by **NY Rangers**, August 4, 2005. Traded to **Los Angeles** by **NY Rangers** with Jan Marek, Marc-Andre Cliche and NY Rangers' 3rd round choice (later traded to Buffalo - Buffalo selected Corey Fienhage) in 2008 Entry Draft for Sean Avery and John Seymour, February 5, 2007. Traded to **Tampa Bay** by **Los Angeles** for Tampa Bay's 5th round choice (Joshua Turnbull) in 2007 Entry Draft, February 27, 2007. • Missed majority of 2008-09 season recovering from lower body injury suffered in game at Portland (AHL), December 31, 2008. Signed as a free agent by **Philadelphia**, July 23, 2009.

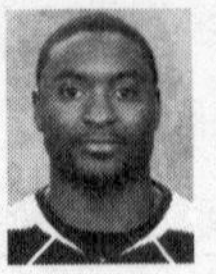

WARD, Joel

(WOHRD, JOHL) **NSH**

Right wing. Shoots right. 6'1", 218 lbs. Born, Toronto, Ont., December 2, 1980.

Season	Club	League	GP	G	A	Pts	PIM	PP	SH	GW	S	%	+/-	TF	F%	Min	GP	G	A	Pts	PIM	PP	SH	GW	Mi
1997-98	Owen Sound	OHL	47	8	4	12	14	....	....	....	....	....	....	....	....	....	11	1	1	2	5	....	....	....	....
1998-99	Owen Sound	OHL	58	19	16	35	23	....	....	....	....	....	....	....	....	....	16	2	4	6	0	....	....	....	....
99-2000	Owen Sound	OHL	63	23	20	43	51	....	....	....	....	....	....	....	....	....	....	....	....	....	....	....	....	....	....
2000-01	Owen Sound	OHL	67	26	36	62	45	....	....	....	....	....	....	....	....	....	5	2	4	6	4	....	....	....	....
	Long Beach	WCHL	....	....	....	....	....	....	....	....	....	....	....	....	....	....	8	0	0	0	0	....	....	....	....
2001-02	U. of P.E.I.	CIS	22	13	14	27	16	....	....	....	....	....	....	....	....	....	....	....	....	....	....	....	....	....	....
2002-03	U. of P.E.I.	CIS	19	11	15	26	24	....	....	....	....	....	....	....	....	....	....	....	....	....	....	....	....	....	....
2003-04	U. of P.E.I.	CIS	27	14	24	38	42	....	....	....	....	....	....	....	....	....	....	....	....	....	....	....	....	....	....
2004-05	U. of P.E.I.	CIS	28	16	28	44	42	....	....	....	....	....	....	....	....	....	....	....	....	....	....	....	....	....	....
2005-06	Houston Aeros	AHL	66	8	14	22	34	....	....	....	....	....	....	....	....	....	8	4	2	6	4	....	....	....	....
2006-07	**Minnesota**	**NHL**	**11**	**0**	**1**	**1**	**0**	**0**	**0**	**0**	**12**	**0.0**	**0**	**1**	**0.0**	**7:42**	....	....	....	....	....	....	....	....	....
	Houston Aeros	AHL	64	9	14	23	45	....	....	....	....	....	....	....	....	....	....	....	....	....	....	....	....	....	....
2007-08	Houston Aeros	AHL	79	21	20	41	47	....	....	....	....	....	....	....	....	....	4	0	2	2	0	....	....	....	....
2008-09	**Nashville**	**NHL**	**79**	**17**	**18**	**35**	**29**	**3**	**2**	**2**	**133**	**12.8**	**1**	**46**	**43.5**	**16:01**	....	....	....	....	....	....	....	....	....
2009-10	**Nashville**	**NHL**	**71**	**13**	**21**	**34**	**18**	**3**	**1**	**1**	**134**	**9.7**	**–5**	**81**	**38.3**	**17:33**	**6**	**2**	**2**	**4**	**2**	**0**	**1**	**0**	**19:5**
	NHL Totals		**161**	**30**	**40**	**70**	**47**	**6**	**3**	**3**	**279**	**10.8**		**128**	**39.8**	**16:07**	**6**	**2**	**2**	**4**	**2**	**0**	**1**	**0**	**19:5**

Signed as a free agent by **Houston** (AHL), December 4, 2005. Signed as a free agent by **Minnesota**, September 27, 2006. Signed as a free agent by **Nashville**, July 14, 2008.

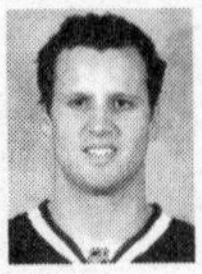

WATHIER, Francis

(waw-TEE-ay, FRAN-sihs) **DA**

Left wing. Shoots left. 6'4", 208 lbs. Born, St Isidore, Ont., December 7, 1984. Dallas' 8th choice, 185th overall, in 2003 Entry Draft.

Season	Club	League	GP	G	A	Pts	PIM	PP	SH	GW	S	%	+/-	TF	F%	Min	GP	G	A	Pts	PIM	PP	SH	GW	Mi
2001-02	Hull Olympiques	QMJHL	63	1	3	4	68	....	....	....	....	....	....	....	....	....	12	1	2	3	30	....	....	....	....
2002-03	Hull Olympiques	QMJHL	72	9	18	27	143	....	....	....	....	....	....	....	....	....	20	1	6	7	20	....	....	....	....
2003-04	Gatineau	QMJHL	51	9	16	25	127	....	....	....	....	....	....	....	....	....	15	0	2	2	23	....	....	....	....
2004-05	Gatineau	QMJHL	67	15	20	35	96	....	....	....	....	....	....	....	....	....	10	0	2	2	8	....	....	....	....
2005-06	Iowa Stars	AHL	11	0	1	1	26	....	....	....	....	....	....	....	....	....	....	....	....	....	....	....	....	....	....
2006-07	Iowa Stars	AHL	57	14	3	17	78	....	....	....	....	....	....	....	....	....	12	0	4	4	25	....	....	....	....
	Idaho Steelheads	ECHL	17	4	9	13	31	....	....	....	....	....	....	....	....	....	7	1	1	2	4	....	....	....	....
2007-08	Iowa Stars	AHL	19	2	3	5	17	....	....	....	....	....	....	....	....	....	....	....	....	....	....	....	....	....	....
2008-09	Iowa Chops	AHL	77	6	10	16	127	....	....	....	....	....	....	....	....	....	....	....	....	....	....	....	....	....	....
2009-10	**Dallas**	**NHL**	**5**	**0**	**0**	**0**	**5**	**0**	**0**	**0**	**4**	**0.0**	**0**	**1**	**100.0**	**5:18**	....	....	....	....	....	....	....	....	....
	Texas Stars	AHL	76	19	21	40	101	....	....	....	....	....	....	....	....	....	24	2	6	8	18	....	....	....	....
	NHL Totals		**5**	**0**	**0**	**0**	**5**	**0**	**0**	**0**	**4**	**0.0**		**1**	**100.0**	**5:18**	....	....	....	....	....	....	....	....	....

• Missed majority of 2005-06 and 2007-08 seasons recovering from shoulder injuries.

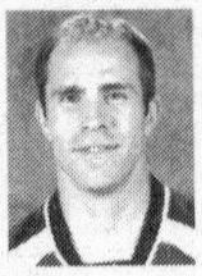

WEAVER, Mike

(WEE-vuhr, MIGHK) **FL**

Defense. Shoots right. 5'9", 186 lbs. Born, Bramalea, Ont., May 2, 1978.

Season	Club	League	GP	G	A	Pts	PIM	PP	SH	GW	S	%	+/-	TF	F%	Min	GP	G	A	Pts	PIM	PP	SH	GW	Mi
1995-96	Bramalea Blues	OPJHL	48	10	39	49	103	....	....	....	....	....	....	....	....	....	....	....	....	....	....	....	....	....	....
1996-97	Michigan State	CCHA	39	0	7	7	46	....	....	....	....	....	....	....	....	....	....	....	....	....	....	....	....	....	....
1997-98	Michigan State	CCHA	44	4	22	26	68	....	....	....	....	....	....	....	....	....	....	....	....	....	....	....	....	....	....
1998-99	Michigan State	CCHA	42	1	6	7	54	....	....	....	....	....	....	....	....	....	....	....	....	....	....	....	....	....	....
99-2000	Michigan State	CCHA	26	0	7	7	20	....	....	....	....	....	....	....	....	....	....	....	....	....	....	....	....	....	....
2000-01	Orlando	IHL	68	0	8	8	34	....	....	....	....	....	....	....	....	....	16	0	2	2	8	....	....	....	....
2001-02	**Atlanta**	**NHL**	**16**	**0**	**1**	**1**	**10**	**0**	**0**	**0**	**9**	**0.0**	**0**	**0**	**0.0**	**13:54**	....	....	....	....	....	....	....	....	....
	Chicago Wolves	AHL	58	2	8	10	67	....	....	....	....	....	....	....	....	....	25	1	3	4	21	....	....	....	....
2002-03	**Atlanta**	**NHL**	**40**	**0**	**5**	**5**	**20**	**0**	**0**	**0**	**21**	**0.0**	**–5**	**0**	**0.0**	**18:38**	....	....	....	....	....	....	....	....	....
	Chicago Wolves	AHL	33	2	2	4	32	....	....	....	....	....	....	....	....	....	9	0	3	3	4	....	....	....	....
2003-04	**Atlanta**	**NHL**	**1**	**0**	**0**	**0**	**0**	**0**	**0**	**0**	**0**	**0.0**	**–1**	**0**	**0.0**	**8:28**	....	....	....	....	....	....	....	....	....
	Chicago Wolves	AHL	78	3	14	17	89	....	....	....	....	....	....	....	....	....	9	2	2	4	20	....	....	....	....
2004-05	Manchester	AHL	79	1	22	23	61	....	....	....	....	....	....	....	....	....	6	0	1	1	0	....	....	....	....
2005-06	**Los Angeles**	**NHL**	**53**	**0**	**9**	**9**	**14**	**0**	**0**	**0**	**21**	**0.0**	**–3**	**0**	**0.0**	**15:03**	....	....	....	....	....	....	....	....	....
2006-07	**Los Angeles**	**NHL**	**39**	**3**	**6**	**9**	**16**	**1**	**0**	**1**	**22**	**13.6**	**–4**	**3**	**66.7**	**15:20**	....	....	....	....	....	....	....	....	....
	Manchester	AHL	7	1	3	4	2	....	....	....	....	....	....	....	....	....	....	....	....	....	....	....	....	....	....
2007-08	**Vancouver**	**NHL**	**55**	**0**	**1**	**1**	**33**	**0**	**0**	**0**	**33**	**0.0**	**1**	**1**	**0.0**	**14:02**	....	....	....	....	....	....	....	....	....
2008-09	**St. Louis**	**NHL**	**58**	**0**	**7**	**7**	**12**	**0**	**0**	**0**	**36**	**0.0**	**–3**	**0**	**0.0**	**17:16**	**4**	**0**	**0**	**0**	**0**	**0**	**0**	**0**	**17:**
2009-10	**St. Louis**	**NHL**	**77**	**1**	**9**	**10**	**29**	**0**	**0**	**0**	**33**	**3.0**	**10**	**2**	**50.0**	**16:58**	....	....	....	....	....	....	....	....	....
	NHL Totals		**339**	**4**	**38**	**42**	**134**	**1**	**0**	**1**	**175**	**2.3**		**6**	**50.0**	**16:05**	**4**	**0**	**0**	**0**	**0**	**0**	**0**	**0**	**17:**

OPJHL Defenseman of the Year (1996) • CCHA All-Tournament Team (1997) • CCHA First All-Star Team (1999, 2000) • CCHA Best Defensive Defenseman Award (1999, 2000) • NCAA West Second All-American Team (1999, 2000)

Signed as a free agent by **Atlanta**, June 15, 2000. Signed as a free agent by **Los Angeles**, July 16, 2004. Signed as a free agent by **Pittsburgh**, August 8, 2007. Claimed on waivers by **Vancouver** from **Pittsburgh**, October 2, 2007. Signed as a free agent by **St. Louis**, July 10, 2008. Signed as a free agent by **Florida**, August 3, 2010.

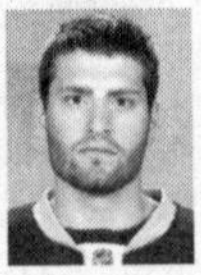

WEBER, Mike

(WEH-buhr, MIGHK) **BU**

Defense. Shoots left. 6'2", 211 lbs. Born, Pittsburgh, PA, December 16, 1987. Buffalo's 3rd choice, 57th overall, in 2006 Entry Draft.

Season	Club	League	GP	G	A	Pts	PIM	PP	SH	GW	S	%	+/-	TF	F%	Min	GP	G	A	Pts	PIM	PP	SH	GW	Mi
2002-03	Jr. Penguins	EmJHL	28	4	11	15	109	....	....	....	....	....	....	....	....	....	3	0	0	0	20	....	....	....	....
2003-04	Windsor Spitfires	OHL	65	0	2	2	49	....	....	....	....	....	....	....	....	....	....	....	....	....	....	....	....	....	....
2004-05	Windsor Spitfires	OHL	68	2	6	8	132	....	....	....	....	....	....	....	....	....	11	0	1	1	18	....	....	....	....
2005-06	Windsor Spitfires	OHL	68	5	21	26	181	....	....	....	....	....	....	....	....	....	7	0	0	0	12	....	....	....	....
2006-07	Windsor Spitfires	OHL	30	3	16	19	86	....	....	....	....	....	....	....	....	....	....	....	....	....	....	....	....	....	....
	Barrie Colts	OHL	30	3	12	15	86	....	....	....	....	....	....	....	....	....	7	0	6	6	10	....	....	....	....
2007-08	**Buffalo**	**NHL**	**16**	**0**	**3**	**3**	**14**	**0**	**0**	**0**	**12**	**0.0**	**12**	**0**	**0.0**	**16:41**	....	....	....	....	....	....	....	....	....
	Rochester	AHL	59	1	13	14	178	....	....	....	....	....	....	....	....	....	....	....	....	....	....	....	....	....	....
2008-09	**Buffalo**	**NHL**	**7**	**0**	**0**	**0**	**19**	**0**	**0**	**0**	**2**	**0.0**	**–3**	**0**	**0.0**	**14:10**	....	....	....	....	....	....	....	....	....
	Portland Pirates	AHL	42	1	7	8	94	....	....	....	....	....	....	....	....	....	....	....	....	....	....	....	....	....	....
2009-10	Portland Pirates	AHL	80	5	16	21	153	....	....	....	....	....	....	....	....	....	4	1	0	1	14	....	....	....	....
	NHL Totals		**23**	**0**	**3**	**3**	**33**	**0**	**0**	**0**	**14**	**0.0**		**0**	**0.0**	**15:55**	....	....	....	....	....	....	....	....	....

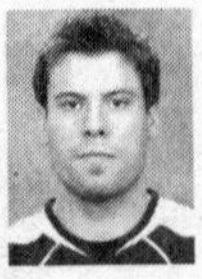

WEBER, Shea

(WEH-buhr, SHAY) **NS**

Defense. Shoots right. 6'4", 234 lbs. Born, Sicamous, B.C., August 14, 1985. Nashville's 4th choice, 49th overall, in 2003 Entry Draft.

Season	Club	League	GP	G	A	Pts	PIM	PP	SH	GW	S	%	+/-	TF	F%	Min	GP	G	A	Pts	PIM	PP	SH	GW	Mi
2001-02	Sicamous Eagles	KIJHL	47	9	33	42	87	....	....	....	....	....	....	....	....	....	....	....	....	....	....	....	....	....	....
	Kelowna Rockets	WHL	5	0	0	0	0	....	....	....	....	....	....	....	....	....	....	....	....	....	....	....	....	....	....
2002-03	Kelowna Rockets	WHL	70	2	16	18	167	....	....	....	....	....	....	....	....	....	19	1	4	5	26	....	....	....	....
2003-04	Kelowna Rockets	WHL	60	12	20	32	126	....	....	....	....	....	....	....	....	....	17	3	14	17	16	....	....	....	....
2004-05	Kelowna Rockets	WHL	55	12	29	41	95	....	....	....	....	....	....	....	....	....	18	9	8	17	25	....	....	....	....
2005-06	**Nashville**	**NHL**	**28**	**2**	**8**	**10**	**42**	**2**	**0**	**1**	**46**	**4.3**	**8**	**0**	**0.0**	**17:00**	**4**	**2**	**0**	**2**	**8**	**1**	**0**	**0**	**14**
	Milwaukee	AHL	46	12	15	27	49	....	....	....	....	....	....	....	....	....	14	6	5	11	16	....	....	....	....
2006-07	**Nashville**	**NHL**	**79**	**17**	**23**	**40**	**60**	**6**	**0**	**2**	**152**	**11.2**	**13**	**0**	**0.0**	**19:23**	**5**	**0**	**3**	**3**	**2**	**0**	**0**	**0**	**21**
2007-08	**Nashville**	**NHL**	**54**	**6**	**14**	**20**	**49**	**5**	**0**	**2**	**152**	**3.9**	**–6**	**0**	**0.0**	**19:30**	**6**	**1**	**3**	**4**	**6**	**0**	**0**	**0**	**19**
2008-09	**Nashville**	**NHL**	**81**	**23**	**30**	**53**	**80**	**10**	**1**	**4**	**251**	**9.2**	**1**	**0**	**0.0**	**23:58**	....	....	....	....	....	....	....	....	....

Season	Club	League	Regular Season GP	G	A	Pts	PIM	PP	SH	GW	S	%	+/-	TF	F%	Min	Playoffs GP	G	A	Pts	PIM	PP	SH	GW	Min
2009-10	**Nashville**	**NHL**	**78**	**16**	**27**	**43**	**36**	**7**	**0**	**3**	**222**	**7.2**	**0**	**0**	**0.0**	**23:10**	**6**	**2**	**1**	**3**	**4**	**0**	**0**	**0**	**24:27**
	Canada	Olympics	7	2	4	6	2	....	....	....	....	....	....	....	....	....	....	....	....	....	....	....	....	....	....
	NHL Totals		**320**	**64**	**102**	**166**	**267**	**30**	**1**	**12**	**823**	**7.8**		**0**	**0.0**	**21:17**	**21**	**5**	**7**	**12**	**20**	**1**	**0**	**0**	**20:25**

/HL West Second All-Star Team (2004) • Memorial Cup Tournament All-Star Team (2004) • WHL West First All-Star Team (2005) • Canadian Major Junior Second All-Star Team (2005) • Olympic
ournament All-Star Team (2010)
ayed in NHL All-Star Game (2009)

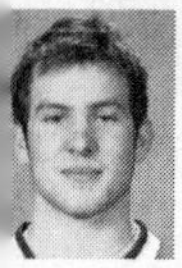

WEBER, Yannick

(WEH-buhr, YAH-nihk) **MTL.**

Defense. Shoots right. 5'11", 193 lbs. Born, Morges, Switz., September 23, 1988. Montreal's 5th choice, 73rd overall, in 2007 Entry Draft.

Season	Club	League	GP	G	A	Pts	PIM	PP	SH	GW	S	%	+/-	TF	F%	Min	GP	G	A	Pts	PIM	PP	SH	GW	Min
2003-04	SC Bern Jr.	Swiss-Jr.	32	2	3	5	39	....	....	....	....	....	....	....	....	....	8	2	0	2	8	....	....	....	....
2004-05	SC Bern Jr.	Swiss-Jr.	37	5	4	9	62	....	....	....	....	....	....	....	....	....	5	0	0	0	22	....	....	....	....
2005-06	SC Bern Future Jr.	Swiss-Jr.	17	1	6	7	46	....	....	....	....	....	....	....	....	....	....	....	....	....	....	....	....	....	....
	SC Langenthal	Swiss-2	28	3	0	3	8	....	....	....	....	....	....	....	....	....	....	....	....	....	....	....	....	....	....
2006-07	SC Bern Future Jr.	Swiss-Jr.	1	0	0	0	2	....	....	....	....	....	....	....	....	....	....	....	....	....	....	....	....	....	....
	Kitchener Rangers	OHL	51	13	28	41	42	....	....	....	....	....	....	....	....	....	9	3	6	9	8	....	....	....	....
2007-08	Kitchener Rangers	OHL	59	20	35	55	79	....	....	....	....	....	....	....	....	....	17	4	13	17	24	....	....	....	....
2008-09	**Montreal**	**NHL**	**3**	**0**	**1**	**1**	**2**	**0**	**0**	**0**	**6**	**0.0**	**–1**	**0**	**0.0**	**15:06**	**3**	**1**	**1**	**2**	**0**	**0**	**0**	**0**	**13:36**
	Hamilton	AHL	68	16	28	44	42	....	....	....	....	....	....	....	....	....	2	0	1	1	10	....	....	....	....
2009-10	**Montreal**	**NHL**	**5**	**0**	**0**	**0**	**4**	**0**	**0**	**0**	**2**	**0.0**	**–5**	**0**	**0.0**	**13:53**	....	....	....	....	....	....	....	....	....
	Hamilton	AHL	65	7	25	32	58	....	....	....	....	....	....	....	....	....	3	0	0	0	2	....	....	....	....
	Switzerland	Olympics	5	0	0	0	6	....	....	....	....	....	....	....	....	....	....	....	....	....	....	....	....	....	....
	NHL Totals		**8**	**0**	**1**	**1**	**6**	**0**	**0**	**0**	**8**	**0.0**		**0**	**0.0**	**14:20**	**3**	**1**	**1**	**2**	**0**	**0**	**0**	**0**	**13:36**

HL Second All-Star Team (2008) • AHL All-Rookie Team (2009)

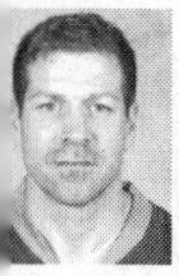

WEIGHT, Doug

(WAYT, DUHG)

Center. Shoots left. 5'11", 196 lbs. Born, Warren, MI, January 21, 1971. NY Rangers' 2nd choice, 34th overall, in 1990 Entry Draft.

Season	Club	League	GP	G	A	Pts	PIM	PP	SH	GW	S	%	+/-	TF	F%	Min	GP	G	A	Pts	PIM	PP	SH	GW	Min
1988-89	Bloomfield Jets	NAHL	34	26	53	79	105	....	....	....	....	....	....	....	....	....	....	....	....	....	....	....	....	....	....
1989-90	Lake Superior	CCHA	46	21	48	69	44	....	....	....	....	....	....	....	....	....	....	....	....	....	....	....	....	....	....
1990-91	Lake Superior	CCHA	42	29	46	75	86	....	....	....	....	....	....	....	....	....	....	....	....	....	....	....	....	....	....
	NY Rangers	**NHL**	....	....	....	....	....	....	....	....	....	....	....	....	....	....	**1**	**0**	**0**	**0**	**0**	**0**	**0**	**0**	....
1991-92	**NY Rangers**	**NHL**	**53**	**8**	**22**	**30**	**23**	**0**	**0**	**2**	**72**	**11.1**	**–3**	....	....	....	**7**	**2**	**2**	**4**	**0**	**1**	**0**	**0**	....
	Binghamton	AHL	9	3	14	17	2	....	....	....	....	....	....	....	....	....	4	1	4	5	6	....	....	....	....
1992-93	**NY Rangers**	**NHL**	**65**	**15**	**25**	**40**	**55**	**3**	**0**	**1**	**90**	**16.7**	**4**	....	....	....	....	....	....	....	....	....	....	....	....
	Edmonton	**NHL**	**13**	**2**	**6**	**8**	**10**	**0**	**0**	**0**	**35**	**5.7**	**–2**	....	....	....	....	....	....	....	....	....	....	....	....
1993-94	**Edmonton**	**NHL**	**84**	**24**	**50**	**74**	**47**	**4**	**1**	**1**	**188**	**12.8**	**–22**	....	....	....	....	....	....	....	....	....	....	....	....
1994-95	Rosenheim	Germany	8	2	3	5	18	....	....	....	....	....	....	....	....	....	....	....	....	....	....	....	....	....	....
	Edmonton	**NHL**	**48**	**7**	**33**	**40**	**69**	**1**	**0**	**1**	**104**	**6.7**	**–17**	....	....	....	....	....	....	....	....	....	....	....	....
1995-96	**Edmonton**	**NHL**	**82**	**25**	**79**	**104**	**95**	**9**	**0**	**2**	**204**	**12.3**	**–19**	....	....	....	....	....	....	....	....	....	....	....	....
1996-97	**Edmonton**	**NHL**	**80**	**21**	**61**	**82**	**80**	**4**	**0**	**2**	**235**	**8.9**	**1**	....	....	....	**12**	**3**	**8**	**11**	**8**	**0**	**0**	**0**	....
1997-98	**Edmonton**	**NHL**	**79**	**26**	**44**	**70**	**69**	**9**	**0**	**4**	**205**	**12.7**	**1**	....	....	....	**12**	**2**	**7**	**9**	**14**	**2**	**0**	**1**	....
	United States	Olympics	4	0	2	2	2	....	....	....	....	....	....	....	....	....	....	....	....	....	....	....	....	....	....
1998-99	**Edmonton**	**NHL**	**43**	**6**	**31**	**37**	**12**	**1**	**0**	**0**	**79**	**7.6**	**–8**	**853**	**49.5**	**19:51**	**4**	**1**	**1**	**2**	**15**	**0**	**0**	**0**	**14:43**
99-2000	**Edmonton**	**NHL**	**77**	**21**	**51**	**72**	**54**	**3**	**1**	**4**	**167**	**12.6**	**6**	**1588**	**50.4**	**20:35**	**5**	**3**	**2**	**5**	**4**	**2**	**0**	**1**	**21:05**
2000-01	**Edmonton**	**NHL**	**82**	**25**	**65**	**90**	**91**	**8**	**0**	**3**	**188**	**13.3**	**12**	**1514**	**51.3**	**22:08**	**6**	**1**	**5**	**6**	**17**	**0**	**0**	**0**	**22:45**
2001-02	**St. Louis**	**NHL**	**61**	**15**	**34**	**49**	**40**	**3**	**0**	**1**	**131**	**11.5**	**20**	**1123**	**49.2**	**19:48**	**10**	**1**	**1**	**2**	**4**	**1**	**0**	**1**	**16:26**
	United States	Olympics	6	0	3	3	4	....	....	....	....	....	....	....	....	....	....	....	....	....	....	....	....	....	....
2002-03	**St. Louis**	**NHL**	**70**	**15**	**52**	**67**	**52**	**7**	**0**	**3**	**182**	**8.2**	**–6**	**1048**	**50.4**	**20:23**	**7**	**5**	**8**	**13**	**2**	***5**	**0**	**1**	**22:26**
2003-04	**St. Louis**	**NHL**	**75**	**14**	**51**	**65**	**37**	**6**	**0**	**5**	**198**	**7.1**	**–3**	**1115**	**50.4**	**20:25**	**5**	**2**	**1**	**3**	**6**	**1**	**1**	**0**	**19:24**
2004-05	Frankfurt Lions	Germany	7	6	9	15	26	....	....	....	....	....	....	....	....	....	11	2	10	12	8	....	....	....	....
2005-06	**St. Louis**	**NHL**	**47**	**11**	**33**	**44**	**50**	**7**	**0**	**1**	**123**	**8.9**	**–11**	**638**	**49.8**	**22:17**	....	....	....	....	....	....	....	....	....
	♦ **Carolina**	**NHL**	**23**	**4**	**9**	**13**	**25**	**2**	**0**	**0**	**52**	**7.7**	**–6**	**256**	**46.1**	**17:35**	**23**	**3**	**13**	**16**	**20**	**2**	**0**	**0**	**15:27**
	United States	Olympics	6	0	3	3	4	....	....	....	....	....	....	....	....	....	....	....	....	....	....	....	....	....	....
2006-07	**St. Louis**	**NHL**	**82**	**16**	**43**	**59**	**56**	**5**	**0**	**3**	**123**	**13.0**	**10**	**1025**	**47.7**	**18:17**	....	....	....	....	....	....	....	....	....
2007-08	**St. Louis**	**NHL**	**29**	**4**	**7**	**11**	**12**	**0**	**0**	**0**	**47**	**8.5**	**4**	**289**	**49.5**	**16:11**	....	....	....	....	....	....	....	....	....
	Anaheim	**NHL**	**38**	**6**	**8**	**14**	**20**	**2**	**0**	**1**	**49**	**12.2**	**0**	**325**	**45.2**	**13:25**	**5**	**0**	**1**	**1**	**4**	**0**	**0**	**0**	**7:39**
2008-09	**NY Islanders**	**NHL**	**53**	**10**	**28**	**38**	**55**	**5**	**0**	**0**	**96**	**10.4**	**–15**	**679**	**45.1**	**18:17**	....	....	....	....	....	....	....	....	....
2009-10	**NY Islanders**	**NHL**	**36**	**1**	**16**	**17**	**8**	**0**	**0**	**0**	**61**	**1.6**	**–1**	**152**	**45.4**	**15:51**	....	....	....	....	....	....	....	....	....
	NHL Totals		**1220**	**276**	**748**	**1024**	**960**	**79**	**2**	**34**	**2629**	**10.5**		**10605**	**49.3**	**19:24**	**97**	**23**	**49**	**72**	**94**	**14**	**1**	**4**	**17:07**

CHA First All-Star Team (1991) • NCAA West Second All-American Team (1991)
ayed in NHL All-Star Game (1996, 1998, 2001, 2003)

aded to **Edmonton** by **NY Rangers** for Esa Tikkanen, March 17, 1993. Traded to **St. Louis** by **Edmonton** with Michel Riesen for Marty Reasoner, Jochen Hecht and Jan Horacek, July 1, 2001. Signed as a ee agent by **Frankfurt** (Germany), February 11, 2005. Traded to **Carolina** by **St. Louis** with Erkki Rajamaki for Jesse Boulerice, Mike Zigomanis, the rights to Magnus Kahnberg, Carolina's 1st round oice (later traded to New Jersey - New Jersey selected Matthew Corrente) in 2006 Entry Draft, Toronto's 4th round choice (previously acquired, St. Louis selected Reto Berra) in 2006 Entry Draft and iicago's 4th round choice (previously acquired, St. Louis selected Cade Fairchild) in 2007 Entry Draft, January 30, 2006. Signed as a free agent by **St. Louis**, July 2, 2006. Traded to **Anaheim** by **St. Louis** th Michal Birner and St. Louis' 7th round choice (later traded to Los Angeles, later traded back to St. Louis - St. Louis selected Paul Karpowich) in 2008 Entry Draft for Andy McDonald, December 14, 07. Signed as a free agent by **NY Islanders**, July 2, 2008. • Missed majority of 2009-10 season recovering from various injuries.

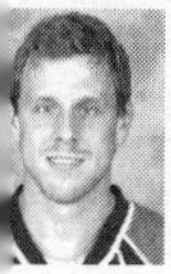

WEISS, Stephen

(WIGHS, STEE-vehn) **FLA.**

Center. Shoots left. 5'11", 185 lbs. Born, Toronto, Ont., April 3, 1983. Florida's 1st choice, 4th overall, in 2001 Entry Draft.

Season	Club	League	GP	G	A	Pts	PIM	PP	SH	GW	S	%	+/-	TF	F%	Min	GP	G	A	Pts	PIM	PP	SH	GW	Min
1997-98	Tor. Young Nats	MTHL	48	51	58	109	....	....	....	....	....	....	....	....	....	....	....	....	....	....	....	....	....	....	....
1998-99	North York	OPJHL	35	15	22	37	10	....	....	....	....	....	....	....	....	....	....	....	....	....	....	....	....	....	....
99-2000	Plymouth Whalers	OHL	64	24	42	66	35	....	....	....	....	....	....	....	....	....	23	8	18	26	18	....	....	....	....
2000-01	Plymouth Whalers	OHL	62	40	47	87	45	....	....	....	....	....	....	....	....	....	18	7	16	23	10	....	....	....	....
2001-02	**Florida**	**NHL**	**7**	**1**	**1**	**2**	**0**	**1**	**0**	**0**	**15**	**6.7**	**0**	**107**	**52.3**	**16:14**	....	....	....	....	....	....	....	....	....
	Plymouth Whalers	OHL	46	25	45	70	69	....	....	....	....	....	....	....	....	....	6	2	7	9	13	....	....	....	....
2002-03	**Florida**	**NHL**	**77**	**6**	**15**	**21**	**17**	**0**	**0**	**2**	**87**	**6.9**	**–13**	**1065**	**46.3**	**14:17**	....	....	....	....	....	....	....	....	....
2003-04	**Florida**	**NHL**	**50**	**12**	**17**	**29**	**10**	**3**	**0**	**2**	**82**	**14.6**	**–10**	**799**	**44.9**	**17:42**	....	....	....	....	....	....	....	....	....
	San Antonio	AHL	10	6	3	9	14	....	....	....	....	....	....	....	....	....	....	....	....	....	....	....	....	....	....
2004-05	San Antonio	AHL	62	15	23	38	38	....	....	....	....	....	....	....	....	....	....	....	....	....	....	....	....	....	....
	Chicago Wolves	AHL	18	7	9	16	12	....	....	....	....	....	....	....	....	....	18	2	7	9	17	....	....	....	....
2005-06	**Florida**	**NHL**	**41**	**9**	**12**	**21**	**22**	**5**	**0**	**1**	**74**	**12.2**	**–2**	**514**	**49.6**	**15:15**	....	....	....	....	....	....	....	....	....
2006-07	**Florida**	**NHL**	**74**	**20**	**28**	**48**	**28**	**10**	**0**	**1**	**176**	**11.4**	**–1**	**1182**	**45.9**	**17:07**	....	....	....	....	....	....	....	....	....
2007-08	**Florida**	**NHL**	**74**	**13**	**29**	**42**	**40**	**4**	**0**	**4**	**132**	**9.8**	**14**	**1198**	**51.2**	**17:35**	....	....	....	....	....	....	....	....	....
2008-09	**Florida**	**NHL**	**78**	**14**	**47**	**61**	**22**	**4**	**1**	**4**	**154**	**9.1**	**19**	**1277**	**50.9**	**17:48**	....	....	....	....	....	....	....	....	....
2009-10	**Florida**	**NHL**	**80**	**28**	**32**	**60**	**40**	**12**	**0**	**2**	**180**	**15.6**	**–7**	**1551**	**52.4**	**20:00**	....	....	....	....	....	....	....	....	....
	NHL Totals		**481**	**103**	**181**	**284**	**179**	**39**	**1**	**16**	**900**	**11.4**		**7693**	**49.2**	**17:13**	....	....	....	....	....	....	....	....	....

HL All-Rookie Team (2000)
.oaned to **Chicago** (AHL) by **San Antonio** (AHL) for cash, March 8, 2005.

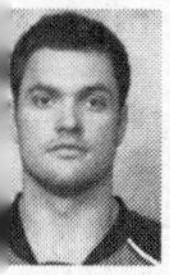

WELCH, Noah

(WEHLCH, NOH-uh) **ATL.**

Defense. Shoots left. 6'4", 220 lbs. Born, Brighton, MA, August 26, 1982. Pittsburgh's 2nd choice, 54th overall, in 2001 Entry Draft.

Season	Club	League	GP	G	A	Pts	PIM	PP	SH	GW	S	%	+/-	TF	F%	Min	GP	G	A	Pts	PIM	PP	SH	GW	Min
99-2000	St. Sebastian's	High-MA	26	4	11	15	35	....	....	....	....	....	....	....	....	....	....	....	....	....	....	....	....	....	....
	Eastern-Mass	MBAHL	4	0	3	3	6	....	....	....	....	....	....	....	....	....	....	....	....	....	....	....	....	....	....
2000-01	St. Sebastian's	High-MA	30	11	20	31	37	....	....	....	....	....	....	....	....	....	....	....	....	....	....	....	....	....	....
2001-02	Harvard Crimson	ECAC	27	5	6	11	56	....	....	....	....	....	....	....	....	....	....	....	....	....	....	....	....	....	....
2002-03	Harvard Crimson	ECAC	34	6	22	28	70	....	....	....	....	....	....	....	....	....	....	....	....	....	....	....	....	....	....
2003-04	Harvard Crimson	ECAC	34	6	13	19	58	....	....	....	....	....	....	....	....	....	....	....	....	....	....	....	....	....	....
2004-05	Harvard Crimson	ECAC	34	6	12	18	*86	....	....	....	....	....	....	....	....	....	....	....	....	....	....	....	....	....	....
2005-06	**Pittsburgh**	**NHL**	**5**	**1**	**3**	**4**	**2**	**0**	**0**	**0**	**5**	**20.0**	**0**	**0**	**0.0**	**17:24**	....	....	....	....	....	....	....	....	....
	Wilkes-Barre	AHL	77	9	20	29	99	....	....	....	....	....	....	....	....	....	11	1	0	1	18	....	....	....	....
2006-07	**Pittsburgh**	**NHL**	**22**	**1**	**1**	**2**	**22**	**0**	**0**	**0**	**14**	**7.1**	**1**	**0**	**0.0**	**13:34**	....	....	....	....	....	....	....	....	....
	Wilkes-Barre	AHL	27	5	16	21	24	....	....	....	....	....	....	....	....	....	....	....	....	....	....	....	....	....	....
	Florida	**NHL**	**2**	**1**	**0**	**1**	**2**	**0**	**0**	**0**	**4**	**25.0**	**3**	**0**	**0.0**	**18:08**	....	....	....	....	....	....	....	....	....
	Rochester	AHL	11	2	4	6	21	....	....	....	....	....	....	....	....	....	6	0	2	2	12	....	....	....	....
2007-08	**Florida**	**NHL**	**4**	**0**	**0**	**0**	**7**	**0**	**0**	**0**	**0**	**0.0**	**1**	**0**	**0.0**	**8:04**	....	....	....	....	....	....	....	....	....

			Regular Season														Playoffs							
Season	Club	League	GP	G	A	Pts	PIM	PP	SH	GW	S	%	+/-	TF	F%	Min	GP	G	A	Pts	PIM	PP	SH	GW	M
2008-09	Florida	NHL	23	1	1	2	11	0	0	0	11	9.1	–5	0	0.0	6:38	....	....	....	....	....				
	Rochester	AHL	7	0	3	3	10										....	....	....	....	....				
	Tampa Bay	NHL	17	0	0	0	14	0	0	0	11	0.0	–4	0	0.0	16:45	....	....	....	....	....				
2009-10	Chicago Wolves	AHL	37	1	4	5	33										14	0	2	2	10				
	NHL Totals		73	4	5	9	58	0	0	0	45	8.9		0	0.0	12:13									

ECAC All-Rookie Team (2002) • ECAC Second All-Star Team (2002, 2003) • NCAA East Second All-American Team (2003) • ECAC First All-Star Team (2005) • NCAA East First All-American Team (2005)
Traded to **Florida** by **Pittsburgh** for Gary Roberts, February 27, 2007. • Missed remainder of 2007-08 season recovering from shoulder injury suffered in game at Montreal, October 16, 2007. Traded to **Tampa Bay** by **Florida** with Florida's 3rd round choice (later traded to Detroit – Detroit selected Andrej Nestrasil) in 2009 Entry Draft for Steve Eminger, March 4, 2009. Signed as a free agent by **Atlanta**, July 13, 2009. • Missed majority of 2009-10 season recovering from knee injury.

WELLER, Craig

Right wing. Shoots right. 6'4", 220 lbs.   Born, Calgary, Alta., January 17, 1981. St. Louis' 6th choice, 167th overall, in 2000 Entry Draft.   (WEHL-uhr, KRAIG)

Season	Club	League	GP	G	A	Pts	PIM	PP	SH	GW	S	%	+/-	TF	F%	Min	GP	G	A	Pts	PIM	PP	SH	GW	M
1997-98	Cgy. AAA Flames	AMHL	33	2	10	12	65										3	0	1	1	2				
1998-99	Calgary Canucks	AJHL	49	4	14	18	80										13	0	1	1	10				
99-2000	Calgary Canucks	AJHL	53	3	14	17	100										4	0	0	0	4				
2000-01	U. Minn-Duluth	WCHA	6	0	1	1	0																		
	Kootenay Ice	WHL	30	1	5	6	40										11	0	2	2	26				
2001-02	Kootenay Ice	WHL	69	5	13	18	127										22	3	7	10	27				
2002-03	Hartford	AHL	11	0	0	0	8										2	0	0	0	0				
	Charlotte	ECHL	48	3	11	14	84																		
2003-04	Hartford	AHL	68	5	9	14	86										16	2	2	4	30				
2004-05	Hartford	AHL	76	10	9	19	182										6	0	1	1	6				
2005-06	Hartford	AHL	80	12	21	33	152										13	2	3	5	44				
2006-07	Hartford	AHL	56	11	6	17	96										4	0	0	0	4				
2007-08	**Phoenix**	NHL	59	3	8	11	80	0	0	1	72	4.2	–7	2	0.0	10:23									
2008-09	**Minnesota**	NHL	36	1	2	3	47	1	0	0	27	3.7	–3	5	0.0	6:57									
2009-10	Houston Aeros	AHL	5	0	1	1	7																		
	Providence Bruins	AHL	55	4	10	14	62																		
	Chicago Wolves	AHL	14	0	3	3	21										4	0	0	0	4				
	NHL Totals		95	4	10	14	127	1	0	1	99	4.0		7	0.0	9:05									

WHL West Second All-Star Team (2002)
• Left **University of Minnesota-Duluth** (WCHA) and signed as a free agent by **Kootenay** (WHL), January 7, 2001. Signed as a free agent by **NY Rangers**, July 11, 2002. Signed as a free agent by **Phoenix**, July 19, 2007. Signed as a free agent by **Minnesota**, July 1, 2008. • Missed majority of 2008-09 season recovering from various injuries and as a healthy reserve. Traded to **Boston** by **Minnesota** with Alexander Fallstrom and Minnesota's 2nd round choice in 2011 Entry Draft for Chuck Kobasew, October 18, 2009. Traded to **Florida** by **Boston** with Byron Bitz and Tampa Bay's 2nd round choice (previously acquired, Florida selected Alexander Petrovic) in 2010 Entry Draft for Dennis Seidenberg and Matt Bartkowski, March 3, 2010.

WELLMAN, Casey

Right wing. Shoots right. 6', 184 lbs.   Born, Brentwood, CA, October 18, 1987.   (WEHL-man, KAY-see)   MIN

Season	Club	League	GP	G	A	Pts	PIM	PP	SH	GW	S	%	+/-	TF	F%	Min	GP	G	A	Pts	PIM	PP	SH	GW	M
2006-07	Cedar Rapids	USHL	50	6	13	19	30										6	1	2	3	0				
2007-08	Cedar Rapids	USHL	59	22	23	45	30										3	1	1	2	4				
2008-09	Massachusetts	H-East	39	111	22	33	32																		
2009-10	Massachusetts	H-East	36	23	22	45	38																		
	Minnesota	NHL	12	1	3	4	0	0	0	0	18	5.6	–2	32	53.1	12:03									
	NHL Totals		12	1	3	4	0	0	0	0	18	5.6		32	53.1	12:03									

Hockey East All-Rookie Team (2009)
Signed as a free agent by **Minnesota**, March 16, 2010.

WELLWOOD, Kyle

Center. Shoots right. 5'10", 181 lbs.   Born, Windsor, Ont., May 16, 1983. Toronto's 6th choice, 134th overall, in 2001 Entry Draft.   (WEHL-wud, KIGHL)

Season	Club	League	GP	G	A	Pts	PIM	PP	SH	GW	S	%	+/-	TF	F%	Min	GP	G	A	Pts	PIM	PP	SH	GW	M
1998-99	Tecumseh	OHA-B	51	22	41	63	12										16	3	7	10	6				
99-2000	Belleville Bulls	OHL	65	14	37	51	14										10	3	16	19	4				
2000-01	Belleville Bulls	OHL	68	35	*83	*118	24																		
2001-02	Belleville Bulls	OHL	28	16	24	40	4										16	12	12	24	0				
	Windsor Spitfires	OHL	26	14	21	35	0										7	5	9	14	0				
2002-03	Windsor Spitfires	OHL	57	41	59	100	0																		
2003-04	**Toronto**	NHL	1	0	0	0	0	0	0	0	1	0.0	–1	13	30.8	7:56									
	St. John's	AHL	76	20	35	55	6										5	2	2	4	2				
2004-05	St. John's	AHL	80	38	49	87	20																		
2005-06	**Toronto**	NHL	81	11	34	45	14	3	0	0	117	9.4	0	593	56.3	12:47									
2006-07	**Toronto**	NHL	48	12	30	42	0	7	0	2	99	12.1	3	291	56.4	16:38									
2007-08	**Toronto**	NHL	59	8	13	21	0	5	0	1	57	14.0	–12	325	54.8	12:39									
2008-09	**Vancouver**	NHL	74	18	9	27	4	10	0	3	94	19.1	2	621	57.5	13:48	10	1	5	6	0	0	0	0	15:
2009-10	**Vancouver**	NHL	75	14	11	25	12	3	0	2	98	14.3	6	725	53.8	13:52	12	2	5	7	0	1	0	0	15:
	NHL Totals		338	63	97	160	30	28	0	8	466	13.5		2568	55.6	13:45	22	3	10	13	0	1	0	0	15:

OHL First All-Star Team (2001) • Canadian Major Junior Sportsman of the Year (2003)
Claimed on waivers by **Vancouver** from **Toronto**, June 25, 2008.

WESTGARTH, Kevin

Right wing. Shoots right. 6'4", 243 lbs.   Born, Amherstburg, Ont., February 7, 1984.   (WEHST-garth, KEH-vihn)   L.

Season	Club	League	GP	G	A	Pts	PIM	PP	SH	GW	S	%	+/-	TF	F%	Min	GP	G	A	Pts	PIM	PP	SH	GW	M
2003-04	Princeton	ECAC	25	3	3	6	48																		
2004-05	Princeton	ECAC	29	4	3	7	36																		
2005-06	Princeton	ECAC	29	10	13	23	36																		
2006-07	Princeton	ECAC	33	8	16	24	40																		
	Manchester	AHL	14	1	2	3	44										4	0	0	0	6				
2007-08	Manchester	AHL	69	6	6	12	191																		
2008-09	**Los Angeles**	NHL	9	0	0	0	9	0	0	0	1	0.0	1	1	0.0	5:02									
	Manchester	AHL	65	4	6	10	165										6	1	0	1	10				
2009-10	Manchester	AHL	76	11	14	25	180																		
	NHL Totals		9	0	0	0	9	0	0	0	1	0.0		1	0.0	5:02									

Signed as a free agent by **Los Angeles**, March 16, 2007.

WHEELER, Blake

Right wing. Shoots right. 6'5", 208 lbs.   Born, Robbinsdale, MN, August 31, 1986. Phoenix's 1st choice, 5th overall, in 2004 Entry Draft.   (WEE-luhr, BLAYK)   BO

Season	Club	League	GP	G	A	Pts	PIM	PP	SH	GW	S	%	+/-	TF	F%	Min	GP	G	A	Pts	PIM	PP	SH	GW	M
2002-03	Breck Mustangs	High-MN	26	15	27	42	....																		
2003-04	Team Northwest	UMEHL	24	5	6	11	....										3	6	5	11	0				
	Breck Mustangs	High-MN	27	39	50	89	34																		
2004-05	Green Bay	USHL	58	19	28	47	43																		
2005-06	U. of Minnesota	WCHA	39	9	14	23	41																		
2006-07	U. of Minnesota	WCHA	44	18	20	38	42																		
2007-08	U. of Minnesota	WCHA	44	15	20	35	72																		
2008-09	**Boston**	NHL	81	21	24	45	46	3	2	3	150	14.0	36	34	38.2	13:41	8	0	0	0	0	0	0	0	12
2009-10	**Boston**	NHL	82	18	20	38	53	3	1	2	159	11.3	–4	27	48.2	15:47	13	1	5	6	6	0	0	0	14
	NHL Totals		163	39	44	83	99	6	3	5	309	12.6		61	42.6	14:45	21	1	5	6	6	0	0	0	13

USHL All-Rookie Team (2005)
Signed as a free agent by **Boston**, July 1, 2008.

			Regular Season														Playoffs								
Season	Club	League	GP	G	A	Pts	PIM	PP	SH	GW	S	%	+/-	TF	F%	Min	GP	G	A	Pts	PIM	PP	SH	GW	Min

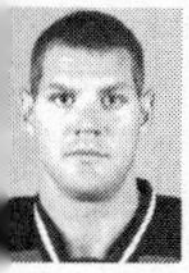

WHITE, Colin
(WIGHT, KAW-lihn) **N.J.**

Defense. Shoots left. 6'4", 215 lbs. Born, New Glasgow, N.S., December 12, 1977. New Jersey's 5th choice, 49th overall, in 1996 Entry Draft.

Season	Club	League	GP	G	A	Pts	PIM	PP	SH	GW	S	%	+/-	TF	F%	Min	GP	G	A	Pts	PIM	PP	SH	GW	Min
1994-95	Laval Titan	QMJHL	7	0	1	1	32	....	....	....	....	....	....	....	....	....	....	....	....	....	....	....	....	....	....
	Hull Olympiques	QMJHL	5	0	1	1	4	....	....	....	....	....	....	....	....	....	12	0	0	0	23	....	....	....	....
1995-96	Hull Olympiques	QMJHL	62	2	8	10	303	....	....	....	....	....	....	....	....	....	18	0	4	4	42	....	....	....	....
1996-97	Hull Olympiques	QMJHL	63	3	12	15	297	....	....	....	....	....	....	....	....	....	14	3	12	15	65	....	....	....	....
1997-98	Albany River Rats	AHL	76	3	13	16	235	....	....	....	....	....	....	....	....	....	13	0	0	0	55	....	....	....	....
1998-99	Albany River Rats	AHL	77	2	12	14	265	....	....	....	....	....	....	....	....	....	5	0	1	1	8	....	....	....	....
99-2000♦	**New Jersey**	**NHL**	**21**	**2**	**1**	**3**	**40**	**0**	**0**	**1**	**29**	**6.9**	**3**	**0**	**0.0**	**14:45**	**23**	**1**	**5**	**6**	**18**	**0**	**0**	**1**	**14:25**
	Albany River Rats	AHL	52	5	21	26	176	....	....	....	....	....	....	....	....	....	....	....	....	....	....	....	....	....	....
2000-01	**New Jersey**	**NHL**	**82**	**1**	**19**	**20**	**155**	**0**	**0**	**1**	**114**	**0.9**	**32**	**0**	**0.0**	**19:06**	**25**	**0**	**3**	**3**	**42**	**0**	**0**	**0**	**16:45**
2001-02	**New Jersey**	**NHL**	**73**	**2**	**3**	**5**	**133**	**0**	**0**	**0**	**81**	**2.5**	**6**	**0**	**0.0**	**20:06**	**6**	**0**	**0**	**0**	**2**	**0**	**0**	**0**	**21:50**
2002-03♦	**New Jersey**	**NHL**	**72**	**5**	**8**	**13**	**98**	**0**	**0**	**1**	**81**	**6.2**	**19**	**0**	**0.0**	**19:41**	**24**	**0**	**5**	**5**	**29**	**0**	**0**	**0**	**22:02**
2003-04	**New Jersey**	**NHL**	**75**	**2**	**11**	**13**	**96**	**0**	**0**	**0**	**61**	**3.3**	**10**	**0**	**0.0**	**21:02**	**5**	**0**	**0**	**0**	**4**	**0**	**0**	**0**	**19:40**
2004-05		DID NOT PLAY																							
2005-06	**New Jersey**	**NHL**	**73**	**3**	**14**	**17**	**91**	**1**	**0**	**1**	**60**	**5.0**	**–2**	**0**	**0.0**	**21:48**	**4**	**0**	**0**	**0**	**4**	**0**	**0**	**0**	**17:39**
2006-07	**New Jersey**	**NHL**	**69**	**0**	**8**	**8**	**69**	**0**	**0**	**0**	**47**	**0.0**	**–8**	**0**	**0.0**	**22:28**	**7**	**0**	**0**	**0**	**6**	**0**	**0**	**0**	**21:16**
2007-08	**New Jersey**	**NHL**	**57**	**2**	**8**	**10**	**26**	**0**	**0**	**1**	**27**	**7.4**	**–5**	**0**	**0.0**	**19:40**	**5**	**0**	**0**	**0**	**6**	**0**	**0**	**0**	**20:27**
2008-09	**New Jersey**	**NHL**	**71**	**1**	**17**	**18**	**46**	**0**	**0**	**0**	**68**	**1.5**	**18**	**1**	**0.0**	**19:01**	**7**	**0**	**1**	**1**	**6**	**0**	**0**	**0**	**19:46**
2009-10	**New Jersey**	**NHL**	**81**	**2**	**10**	**12**	**46**	**0**	**0**	**0**	**47**	**4.3**	**8**	**0**	**0.0**	**20:04**	**5**	**1**	**0**	**1**	**8**	**0**	**0**	**0**	**18:56**
	NHL Totals		**674**	**20**	**99**	**119**	**800**	**1**	**0**	**5**	**615**	**3.3**		**1**	**0.0**	**20:09**	**111**	**2**	**14**	**16**	**125**	**0**	**0**	**1**	**18:35**

QMJHL All-Rookie Team (1996) • NHL All-Rookie Team (2001)

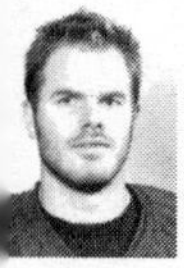

WHITE, Ian
(WIGHT, EE-an) **CGY.**

Defense. Shoots right. 5'10", 191 lbs. Born, Steinbach, Man., June 4, 1984. Toronto's 6th choice, 191st overall, in 2002 Entry Draft.

Season	Club	League	GP	G	A	Pts	PIM	PP	SH	GW	S	%	+/-	TF	F%	Min	GP	G	A	Pts	PIM	PP	SH	GW	Min
99-2000	Eastman Selects	MAHA	32	29	33	62	36	....	....	....	....	....	....	....	....	....	....	....	....	....	....	....	....	....	....
2000-01	Swift Current	WHL	69	12	31	43	24	....	....	....	....	....	....	....	....	....	....	....	....	....	....	....	....	....	....
2001-02	Swift Current	WHL	70	32	47	79	40	....	....	....	....	....	....	....	....	....	12	4	5	9	12	....	....	....	....
2002-03	Swift Current	WHL	64	24	44	68	44	....	....	....	....	....	....	....	....	....	4	0	4	4	0	....	....	....	....
2003-04	Swift Current	WHL	43	9	23	32	32	....	....	....	....	....	....	....	....	....	5	1	3	4	8	....	....	....	....
	St. John's	AHL	8	0	4	4	2	....	....	....	....	....	....	....	....	....	....	....	....	....	....	....	....	....	....
2004-05	St. John's	AHL	78	4	22	26	54	....	....	....	....	....	....	....	....	....	5	0	2	2	2	....	....	....	....
2005-06	**Toronto**	**NHL**	**12**	**1**	**5**	**6**	**10**	**0**	**0**	**0**	**21**	**4.8**	**2**	**0**	**0.0**	**19:07**	....	....	....	....	....	....	....	....	....
	Toronto Marlies	AHL	59	7	30	37	42	....	....	....	....	....	....	....	....	....	5	1	4	5	4	....	....	....	....
2006-07	**Toronto**	**NHL**	**76**	**3**	**23**	**26**	**40**	**1**	**0**	**1**	**138**	**2.2**	**8**	**0**	**0.0**	**18:32**	....	....	....	....	....	....	....	....	....
2007-08	**Toronto**	**NHL**	**81**	**5**	**16**	**21**	**44**	**0**	**0**	**2**	**116**	**4.3**	**–9**	**0**	**0.0**	**18:48**	....	....	....	....	....	....	....	....	....
2008-09	**Toronto**	**NHL**	**71**	**10**	**16**	**26**	**57**	**2**	**0**	**2**	**158**	**6.3**	**6**	**0**	**0.0**	**22:51**	....	....	....	....	....	....	....	....	....
2009-10	**Toronto**	**NHL**	**56**	**9**	**17**	**26**	**39**	**2**	**0**	**1**	**130**	**6.9**	**1**	**0**	**0.0**	**23:47**	....	....	....	....	....	....	....	....	....
	Calgary	**NHL**	**27**	**4**	**8**	**12**	**12**	**1**	**0**	**0**	**43**	**9.3**	**7**	**0**	**0.0**	**20:43**	....	....	....	....	....	....	....	....	....
	NHL Totals		**323**	**32**	**85**	**117**	**202**	**6**	**0**	**6**	**606**	**5.3**		**0**	**0.0**	**20:40**	....	....	....	....	....	....	....	....	....

WHL East Second All-Star Team (2002) • WHL East First All-Star Team (2003) • Canadian Major Junior Second All-Star Team (2003)

raded to **Calgary** by **Toronto** with Matt Stajan, Niklas Hagman and Jamal Mayers for Dion Phaneuf, Fredrik Sjostrom and Keith Aulie, January 31, 2010.

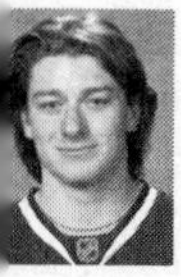

WHITE, Ryan
(WIGHT, RIGH-uhn) **MTL.**

Center. Shoots right. 6', 193 lbs. Born, Brandon, Man., March 17, 1988. Montreal's 4th choice, 66th overall, in 2006 Entry Draft.

Season	Club	League	GP	G	A	Pts	PIM	PP	SH	GW	S	%	+/-	TF	F%	Min	GP	G	A	Pts	PIM	PP	SH	GW	Min
2003-04	Brandon	MMHL	39	21	41	62	90	....	....	....	....	....	....	....	....	....	11	7	7	14	22	....	....	....	....
2004-05	Calgary Hitmen	WHL	63	9	14	23	95	....	....	....	....	....	....	....	....	....	12	2	1	3	26	....	....	....	....
2005-06	Calgary Hitmen	WHL	72	20	33	53	121	....	....	....	....	....	....	....	....	....	13	3	4	7	18	....	....	....	....
2006-07	Calgary Hitmen	WHL	72	34	55	89	97	....	....	....	....	....	....	....	....	....	18	6	8	14	36	....	....	....	....
2007-08	Calgary Hitmen	WHL	68	28	44	72	98	....	....	....	....	....	....	....	....	....	16	6	11	17	8	....	....	....	....
2008-09	Hamilton	AHL	80	11	18	29	68	....	....	....	....	....	....	....	....	....	6	3	1	4	9	....	....	....	....
2009-10	**Montreal**	**NHL**	**16**	**0**	**2**	**2**	**16**	**0**	**0**	**0**	**5**	**0.0**	**–6**	**10**	**70.0**	**11:09**	....	....	....	....	....	....	....	....	....
	Hamilton	AHL	62	17	17	34	173	....	....	....	....	....	....	....	....	....	19	4	5	9	47	....	....	....	....
	NHL Totals		**16**	**0**	**2**	**2**	**16**	**0**	**0**	**0**	**5**	**0.0**		**10**	**70.0**	**11:09**	....	....	....	....	....	....	....	....	....

WHL East First All-Star Team (2007) • WHL East Second All-Star Team (2008)

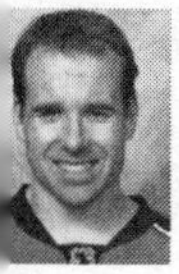

WHITE, Todd
(WIGHT, TAWD) **NYR**

Center. Shoots left. 5'10", 195 lbs. Born, Kanata, Ont., May 21, 1975.

Season	Club	League	GP	G	A	Pts	PIM	PP	SH	GW	S	%	+/-	TF	F%	Min	GP	G	A	Pts	PIM	PP	SH	GW	Min
1990-91	Powassan	NOJHA	38	34	38	72	118	....	....	....	....	....	....	....	....	....	....	....	....	....	....	....	....	....	....
1991-92	Kanata Valley	CJHL	55	39	49	88	30	....	....	....	....	....	....	....	....	....	....	....	....	....	....	....	....	....	....
1992-93	Kanata Valley	CJHL	49	51	87	138	46	....	....	....	....	....	....	....	....	....	....	....	....	....	....	....	....	....	....
1993-94	Clarkson Knights	ECAC	33	10	12	22	28	....	....	....	....	....	....	....	....	....	....	....	....	....	....	....	....	....	....
1994-95	Clarkson Knights	ECAC	34	13	16	29	44	....	....	....	....	....	....	....	....	....	....	....	....	....	....	....	....	....	....
1995-96	Clarkson Knights	ECAC	38	29	43	72	36	....	....	....	....	....	....	....	....	....	....	....	....	....	....	....	....	....	....
1996-97	Clarkson Knights	ECAC	37	*38	*36	*74	22	....	....	....	....	....	....	....	....	....	....	....	....	....	....	....	....	....	....
1997-98	**Chicago**	**NHL**	**7**	**1**	**0**	**1**	**2**	**0**	**0**	**0**	**3**	**33.3**	**0**	....	....	....	....	....	....	....	....	....	....	....	....
	Indianapolis Ice	IHL	65	46	36	82	28	....	....	....	....	....	....	....	....	....	5	2	3	5	4	....	....	....	....
1998-99	**Chicago**	**NHL**	**35**	**5**	**8**	**13**	**20**	**2**	**0**	**0**	**43**	**11.6**	**–1**	**452**	**46.0**	**13:39**	....	....	....	....	....	....	....	....	....
	Chicago Wolves	IHL	25	11	13	24	8	....	....	....	....	....	....	....	....	....	10	1	4	5	8	....	....	....	....
99-2000	**Chicago**	**NHL**	**1**	**0**	**0**	**0**	**0**	**0**	**0**	**0**	**0**	**0.0**	**0**	**9**	**55.6**	**13:02**	....	....	....	....	....	....	....	....	....
	Cleveland	IHL	42	21	30	51	32	....	....	....	....	....	....	....	....	....	....	....	....	....	....	....	....	....	....
	Philadelphia	**NHL**	**3**	**1**	**0**	**1**	**0**	**0**	**0**	**0**	**4**	**25.0**	**–1**	**25**	**40.0**	**10:29**	....	....	....	....	....	....	....	....	....
	Philadelphia	AHL	32	19	24	43	12	....	....	....	....	....	....	....	....	....	5	2	1	3	8	....	....	....	....
2000-01	**Ottawa**	**NHL**	**16**	**4**	**1**	**5**	**4**	**0**	**0**	**0**	**12**	**33.3**	**5**	**133**	**57.1**	**8:33**	**2**	**0**	**0**	**0**	**0**	**0**	**0**	**0**	**7:29**
	Grand Rapids	IHL	64	22	32	54	20	....	....	....	....	....	....	....	....	....	10	4	4	8	10	....	....	....	....
2001-02	**Ottawa**	**NHL**	**81**	**20**	**30**	**50**	**24**	**4**	**0**	**1**	**147**	**13.6**	**12**	**1508**	**50.5**	**18:22**	**12**	**2**	**2**	**4**	**6**	**0**	**0**	**0**	**18:57**
2002-03	**Ottawa**	**NHL**	**80**	**25**	**35**	**60**	**28**	**8**	**1**	**5**	**144**	**17.4**	**19**	**1396**	**50.5**	**17:58**	**18**	**5**	**1**	**6**	**6**	**1**	**1**	**2**	**16:59**
2003-04	**Ottawa**	**NHL**	**53**	**9**	**20**	**29**	**22**	**1**	**1**	**2**	**98**	**9.2**	**12**	**879**	**52.0**	**17:32**	**7**	**1**	**0**	**1**	**4**	**0**	**0**	**0**	**18:04**
2004-05	Sodertalje SK	Sweden	1	0	1	1	4	....	....	....	....	....	....	....	....	....	....	....	....	....	....	....	....	....	....
2005-06	**Minnesota**	**NHL**	**61**	**19**	**21**	**40**	**18**	**5**	**0**	**0**	**109**	**17.4**	**–1**	**886**	**49.1**	**17:12**	....	....	....	....	....	....	....	....	....
2006-07	**Minnesota**	**NHL**	**77**	**13**	**31**	**44**	**24**	**6**	**1**	**1**	**162**	**8.0**	**8**	**1051**	**49.2**	**17:13**	**4**	**0**	**0**	**0**	**0**	**0**	**0**	**0**	**14:18**
2007-08	**Atlanta**	**NHL**	**74**	**14**	**23**	**37**	**36**	**6**	**1**	**4**	**111**	**12.6**	**–12**	**1166**	**46.6**	**18:26**	....	....	....	....	....	....	....	....	....
2008-09	**Atlanta**	**NHL**	**82**	**22**	**51**	**73**	**24**	**12**	**1**	**0**	**150**	**14.7**	**–9**	**1329**	**50.6**	**18:04**	....	....	....	....	....	....	....	....	....
2009-10	**Atlanta**	**NHL**	**65**	**7**	**19**	**26**	**24**	**2**	**0**	**3**	**92**	**7.6**	**–11**	**745**	**53.8**	**15:15**	....	....	....	....	....	....	....	....	....
	NHL Totals		**635**	**140**	**239**	**379**	**226**	**46**	**5**	**16**	**1075**	**13.0**		**9579**	**50.0**	**17:04**	**43**	**8**	**3**	**11**	**16**	**1**	**1**	**2**	**17:01**

ECAC Second All-Star Team (1996) • NCAA East Second All-American Team (1996) • ECAC First All-Star Team (1997) • ECAC Player of the Year (1997) • NCAA East First All-American Team (1997) • Garry Longman Memorial Trophy (IHL – Rookie of the Year) (1998)

gned as a free agent by **Chicago**, August 27, 1997. Traded to **Philadelphia** by **Chicago** for future considerations, January 26, 2000. Signed as a free agent by **Ottawa**, July 12, 2000. Signed as a free ent by **Sodertalje** (Sweden), December 21, 2004. Traded to **Minnesota** by **Ottawa** for Colorado's 4th round choice (previously acquired, Ottawa selected Cody Bass) in 2005 Entry Draft, July 30, 2005. gned as a free agent by **Atlanta**, July 1, 2007. Traded to **NY Rangers** by **Atlanta** for Donald Brashear and Patrick Rissmiller, August 2, 2010.

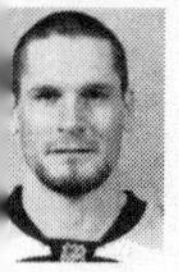

WHITFIELD, Trent
(WHIHT-feeld, TREHNT) **BOS.**

Center. Shoots left. 5'11", 209 lbs. Born, Estevan, Sask., June 17, 1977. Boston's 5th choice, 100th overall, in 1996 Entry Draft.

Season	Club	League	GP	G	A	Pts	PIM	PP	SH	GW	S	%	+/-	TF	F%	Min	GP	G	A	Pts	PIM	PP	SH	GW	Min
1993-94	Saskatoon Blazers	SMHL	36	26	22	48	42	....	....	....	....	....	....	....	....	....	....	....	....	....	....	....	....	....	....
	Spokane Chiefs	WHL	5	1	1	2	0	....	....	....	....	....	....	....	....	....	....	....	....	....	....	....	....	....	....
1994-95	Spokane Chiefs	WHL	48	8	17	25	26	....	....	....	....	....	....	....	....	....	11	7	6	13	5	....	....	....	....
1995-96	Spokane Chiefs	WHL	72	33	51	84	75	....	....	....	....	....	....	....	....	....	18	8	10	18	10	....	....	....	....
1996-97	Spokane Chiefs	WHL	58	34	42	76	74	....	....	....	....	....	....	....	....	....	9	5	7	12	10	....	....	....	....
1997-98	Spokane Chiefs	WHL	65	38	44	82	97	....	....	....	....	....	....	....	....	....	18	9	10	19	15	....	....	....	....
1998-99	Portland Pirates	AHL	50	10	8	18	20	....	....	....	....	....	....	....	....	....	....	....	....	....	....	....	....	....	....
	Hampton Roads	ECHL	19	13	12	25	12	....	....	....	....	....	....	....	....	....	4	2	0	2	14	....	....	....	....
99-2000	Portland Pirates	AHL	79	18	35	53	52	....	....	....	....	....	....	....	....	....	3	1	1	2	2	....	....	....	....
	Washington	**NHL**	....	....	....	....	....	....	....	....	....	....	....	....	....	....	**3**	**0**	**0**	**0**	**0**	**0**	**0**	**0**	**5:47**
2000-01	**Washington**	**NHL**	**61**	**2**	**4**	**6**	**35**	**0**	**0**	**0**	**47**	**4.3**	**3**	**520**	**51.9**	**9:39**	**5**	**0**	**0**	**0**	**2**	**0**	**0**	**0**	**7:07**
	Portland Pirates	AHL	19	9	11	20	27	....	....	....	....	....	....	....	....	....	....	....	....	....	....	....	....	....	....

			Regular Season														Playoffs								
Season	Club	League	GP	G	A	Pts	PIM	PP	SH	GW	S	%	+/-	TF	F%	Min	GP	G	A	Pts	PIM	PP	SH	GW	Mi
2001-02	Washington	NHL	24	0	1	1	28	0	0	0	15	0.0	–3	189	54.0	7:06	....	....	....	....	....	....	....	....	..
	Portland Pirates	AHL	10	4	4	8	8	....	....	....	....	....	....	....	....	....	....	....	....	....	....	....	....	....	..
	NY Rangers	NHL	1	0	0	0	0	0	0	0	0	0.0	1	18	50.0	12:44	....	....	....	....	....	....	....	....	..
	Portland Pirates	AHL	24	10	16	26	16	....	....	....	....	....	....	....	....	....	....	....	....	....	....	....	....	....	..
2002-03	Washington	NHL	14	1	1	2	6	0	0	1	4	25.0	1	124	57.3	8:30	6	0	0	0	10	0	0	0	11:0
	Portland Pirates	AHL	64	27	34	61	42	....	....	....	....	....	....	....	....	....	....	....	....	....	....	....	....	....	..
2003-04	Washington	NHL	44	6	5	11	14	0	1	2	38	15.8	–2	598	55.4	12:48	....	....	....	....	....	....	....	....	..
	Portland Pirates	AHL	24	8	7	15	22	....	....	....	....	....	....	....	....	....	....	....	....	....	....	....	....	....	..
2004-05	Portland Pirates	AHL	67	17	38	55	75	....	....	....	....	....	....	....	....	....	....	....	....	....	....	....	....	....	..
2005-06	St. Louis	NHL	30	2	5	7	14	1	0	0	41	4.9	–3	330	54.6	11:56	....	....	....	....	....	....	....	....	..
	Peoria Rivermen	AHL	41	19	34	53	18	....	....	....	....	....	....	....	....	....	....	....	....	....	....	....	....	....	..
2006-07	Peoria Rivermen	AHL	79	33	45	78	70	....	....	....	....	....	....	....	....	....	....	....	....	....	....	....	....	....	..
2007-08	Peoria Rivermen	AHL	80	22	30	52	51	....	....	....	....	....	....	....	....	....	....	....	....	....	....	....	....	....	..
2008-09	St. Louis	NHL	3	0	1	1	0	0	0	0	4	0.0	2	26	73.1	11:03	....	....	....	....	....	....	....	....	..
	Peoria Rivermen	AHL	69	20	30	50	37	....	....	....	....	....	....	....	....	....	7	2	1	3	0	....	....	....	..
2009-10	Boston	NHL	16	0	1	1	7	0	0	0	15	0.0	–2	178	57.9	11:03	4	0	0	0	0	0	0	0	8:3
	Providence Bruins	AHL	52	17	26	43	22	....	....	....	....	....	....	....	....	....	....	....	....	....	....	....	....	....	..
	NHL Totals		**193**	**11**	**18**	**29**	**104**	**1**	**1**	**3**	**164**	**6.7**		**1983**	**54.7**	**10:28**	**18**	**0**	**0**	**0**	**12**	**0**	**0**	**0**	**8:3**

WHL West First All-Star Team (1997) • WHL West Second All-Star Team (1998)

Signed as a free agent by **Washington**, September 1, 1998. Claimed on waivers by **NY Rangers** from **Washington**, January 16, 2002. Claimed on waivers by **Washington** from **NY Rangers**, February 1, 2002. Signed as a free agent by **St. Louis**, August 2, 2005. Signed as a free agent by **Boston**, July 13, 2009.

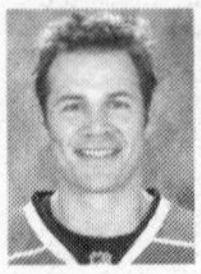

WHITNEY, Ray

(WHIHT-nee, RAY) **PHX**

Left wing. Shoots right. 5'10", 180 lbs. Born, Fort Saskatchewan, Alta., May 8, 1972. San Jose's 2nd choice, 23rd overall, in 1991 Entry Draft.

Season	Club	League	GP	G	A	Pts	PIM	PP	SH	GW	S	%	+/-	TF	F%	Min	GP	G	A	Pts	PIM	PP	SH	GW	Mi
1987-88	Ft. Saskatchewan	AMHL	71	80	155	235	119	....	....	....	....	....	....	....	....	....	....	....	....	....	....	....	....	....	..
1988-89	Spokane Chiefs	WHL	71	17	33	50	16	....	....	....	....	....	....	....	....	....	....	....	....	....	....	....	....	....	..
1989-90	Spokane Chiefs	WHL	71	57	56	113	50	....	....	....	....	....	....	....	....	....	6	3	4	7	6	....	....	....	..
1990-91	Spokane Chiefs	WHL	72	67	118	*185	36	....	....	....	....	....	....	....	....	....	15	13	18	*31	12	....	....	....	..
1991-92	Kolner EC	Germany	10	3	6	9	4	....	....	....	....	....	....	....	....	....	....	....	....	....	....	....	....	....	..
	Canada	Nat-Tm	5	1	0	1	6	....	....	....	....	....	....	....	....	....	....	....	....	....	....	....	....	....	..
	San Jose	NHL	2	0	3	3	0	0	0	0	4	0.0	–1	....	....	....	....	....	....	....	....	....	....	....	..
	San Diego Gulls	IHL	63	36	54	90	12	....	....	....	....	....	....	....	....	....	4	0	0	0	0	....	....	....	..
1992-93	San Jose	NHL	26	4	6	10	4	1	0	0	24	16.7	–14	....	....	....	....	....	....	....	....	....	....	....	..
	Kansas City	IHL	46	20	33	53	14	....	....	....	....	....	....	....	....	....	12	5	7	12	2	....	....	....	..
1993-94	San Jose	NHL	61	14	26	40	14	1	0	0	82	17.1	2	....	....	....	14	0	4	4	8	0	0	0	..
1994-95	San Jose	NHL	39	13	12	25	14	4	0	1	67	19.4	–7	....	....	....	11	4	4	8	2	0	0	1	..
1995-96	San Jose	NHL	60	17	24	41	16	4	2	2	106	16.0	–23	....	....	....	....	....	....	....	....	....	....	....	..
1996-97	San Jose	NHL	12	0	2	2	4	0	0	0	24	0.0	–6	....	....	....	....	....	....	....	....	....	....	....	..
	Kentucky	AHL	9	1	7	8	2	....	....	....	....	....	....	....	....	....	....	....	....	....	....	....	....	....	..
	Utah Grizzlies	IHL	43	13	35	48	34	....	....	....	....	....	....	....	....	....	7	3	1	4	6	....	....	....	..
1997-98	Edmonton	NHL	9	1	3	4	0	0	0	0	19	5.3	–1	....	....	....	....	....	....	....	....	....	....	....	..
	Florida	NHL	68	32	29	61	28	12	0	2	156	20.5	10	....	....	....	....	....	....	....	....	....	....	....	..
1998-99	Florida	NHL	81	26	38	64	18	7	0	6	193	13.5	–3	144	43.8	18:20	....	....	....	....	....	....	....	....	..
99-2000	Florida	NHL	81	29	42	71	35	5	0	3	198	14.6	16	198	49.0	18:41	4	1	0	1	4	0	0	0	18:1
2000-01	Florida	NHL	43	10	21	31	28	5	0	0	117	8.5	–16	38	39.5	17:41	....	....	....	....	....	....	....	....	..
	Columbus	NHL	3	0	3	3	2	0	0	0	3	0.0	–1	19	36.8	20:17	....	....	....	....	....	....	....	....	..
2001-02	Columbus	NHL	67	21	40	61	12	6	0	3	210	10.0	–22	21	47.6	20:13	....	....	....	....	....	....	....	....	..
2002-03	Columbus	NHL	81	24	52	76	22	8	2	2	235	10.2	–26	29	44.8	21:00	....	....	....	....	....	....	....	....	..
2003-04	Detroit	NHL	67	14	29	43	22	3	1	4	119	11.8	7	18	38.9	16:24	12	1	3	4	4	0	0	1	11:5
2004-05			DID NOT PLAY																						
2005-06 ♦	Carolina	NHL	63	17	38	55	42	12	0	2	147	11.6	0	13	38.5	17:11	24	9	6	15	14	5	0	1	14:0
2006-07	Carolina	NHL	81	32	51	83	46	6	0	6	215	14.9	–5	7	28.6	18:42	....	....	....	....	....	....	....	....	..
2007-08	Carolina	NHL	66	25	36	61	30	6	0	4	204	12.3	–6	5	60.0	18:56	....	....	....	....	....	....	....	....	..
2008-09	Carolina	NHL	82	24	53	77	32	7	0	2	219	11.0	2	4	50.0	18:25	18	3	8	11	4	0	0	1	18:3
2009-10	Carolina	NHL	80	21	37	58	26	7	0	5	171	12.3	–6	9	33.3	19:09	....	....	....	....	....	....	....	....	..
	NHL Totals		**1072**	**324**	**545**	**869**	**395**	**94**	**5**	**42**	**2513**	**12.9**		**505**	**45.0**	**18:42**	**83**	**18**	**25**	**43**	**36**	**5**	**0**	**4**	**15:2**

WHL West First All-Star Team (1991) • WHL Player of the Year (1991) • Memorial Cup Tournament All-Star Team (1991) • George Parsons Trophy (Memorial Cup Tournament - Most Sportsmanlike Player) (1991)

Played in NHL All-Star Game (2000, 2003)

Signed as a free agent by **Edmonton**, October 1, 1997. Claimed on waivers by **Florida** from **Edmonton**, November 6, 1997. Traded to **Columbus** by **Florida** with future considerations for Kevyn Adams and Columbus's 4th round choice (Michael Woodford) in 2001 Entry Draft, March 13, 2001. Signed as a free agent by **Detroit**, July 30, 2003. Signed as a free agent by **Carolina**, August 7, 2005. Signed as a free agent by **Phoenix**, July 1, 2010.

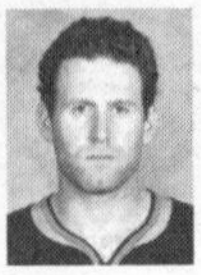

WHITNEY, Ryan

(WHIHT-nee, RIGH-uhn) **EDM**

Defense. Shoots left. 6'4", 219 lbs. Born, Boston, MA, February 19, 1983. Pittsburgh's 1st choice, 5th overall, in 2002 Entry Draft.

Season	Club	League	GP	G	A	Pts	PIM	PP	SH	GW	S	%	+/-	TF	F%	Min	GP	G	A	Pts	PIM	PP	SH	GW	Mi
99-2000	Thayer Academy	High-MA	22	5	33	38	....	....	....	....	....	....	....	....	....	....	....	....	....	....	....	....	....	....	..
2000-01	USNTDP	U-18	40	7	23	30	64	....	....	....	....	....	....	....	....	....	....	....	....	....	....	....	....	....	..
	USNTDP	USHL	20	2	8	10	22	....	....	....	....	....	....	....	....	....	....	....	....	....	....	....	....	....	..
2001-02	Boston University	H-East	35	4	17	21	46	....	....	....	....	....	....	....	....	....	....	....	....	....	....	....	....	....	..
2002-03	Boston University	H-East	34	3	10	13	48	....	....	....	....	....	....	....	....	....	....	....	....	....	....	....	....	....	..
2003-04	Boston University	H-East	38	9	16	25	56	....	....	....	....	....	....	....	....	....	....	....	....	....	....	....	....	....	..
	Wilkes-Barre	AHL	....	....	....	....	....	....	....	....	....	....	....	....	....	....	20	1	9	10	6	....	....	....	..
2004-05	Wilkes-Barre	AHL	80	6	35	41	101	....	....	....	....	....	....	....	....	....	11	2	7	9	12	....	....	....	..
2005-06	Pittsburgh	NHL	68	6	32	38	85	2	0	1	113	5.3	–7	1	0.0	23:50	....	....	....	....	....	....	....	....	..
	Wilkes-Barre	AHL	9	5	9	14	6	....	....	....	....	....	....	....	....	....	11	1	4	5	8	....	....	....	..
2006-07	Pittsburgh	NHL	81	14	45	59	77	9	0	2	129	10.9	9	5	20.0	23:56	5	1	1	2	6	1	0	0	22:5
2007-08	Pittsburgh	NHL	76	12	28	40	45	7	1	1	119	10.1	–2	0	0.0	22:27	20	1	5	6	25	1	0	0	20:4
2008-09	Pittsburgh	NHL	28	2	11	13	16	1	0	0	42	4.8	–15	0	0.0	24:34	....	....	....	....	....	....	....	....	..
	Wilkes-Barre	AHL	1	0	1	1	2	....	....	....	....	....	....	....	....	....	....	....	....	....	....	....	....	....	..
	Anaheim	NHL	20	0	10	10	12	0	0	0	29	0.0	1	0	0.0	22:53	13	1	5	6	9	1	0	0	21:3
2009-10	Anaheim	NHL	62	4	24	28	48	3	0	0	107	3.7	–6	1	0.0	24:34	....	....	....	....	....	....	....	....	..
	United States	Olympics	6	0	0	0	0	....	....	....	....	....	....	....	....	....	....	....	....	....	....	....	....	....	..
	Edmonton	NHL	19	3	8	11	22	0	0	1	44	6.8	7	0	0.0	25:23	....	....	....	....	....	....	....	....	..
	NHL Totals		**354**	**41**	**158**	**199**	**305**	**22**	**1**	**5**	**583**	**7.0**		**7**	**14.3**	**23:46**	**38**	**3**	**11**	**14**	**40**	**3**	**0**	**0**	**21:**

Hockey East All-Rookie Team (2002)

Traded to **Anaheim** by **Pittsburgh** for Chris Kunitz and Eric Tangradi, February 26, 2009. Traded to **Edmonton** by **Anaheim** with Anaheim's 6th round choice (Brandon Davidson) in 2010 Entry Draft for Lubomir Visnovsky, March 3, 2010.

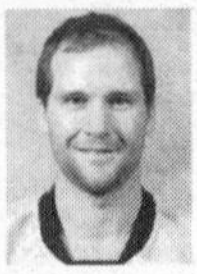

WIDEMAN, Dennis

(WIGHD-muhn, DEH-nihs) **FLA**

Defense. Shoots right. 6', 196 lbs. Born, Kitchener, Ont., March 20, 1983. Buffalo's 9th choice, 241st overall, in 2002 Entry Draft.

Season	Club	League	GP	G	A	Pts	PIM	PP	SH	GW	S	%	+/-	TF	F%	Min	GP	G	A	Pts	PIM	PP	SH	GW	Mi
1998-99	Elmira	OHA-B	47	18	30	48	142	....	....	....	....	....	....	....	....	....	....	....	....	....	....	....	....	....	..
99-2000	Sudbury Wolves	OHL	63	10	26	36	64	....	....	....	....	....	....	....	....	....	12	1	2	3	22	....	....	....	..
2000-01	Sudbury Wolves	OHL	25	7	11	18	37	....	....	....	....	....	....	....	....	....	....	....	....	....	....	....	....	....	..
	London Knights	OHL	24	8	8	16	38	....	....	....	....	....	....	....	....	....	5	0	4	4	6	....	....	....	..
2001-02	London Knights	OHL	65	27	42	69	141	....	....	....	....	....	....	....	....	....	12	4	9	13	26	....	....	....	..
2002-03	London Knights	OHL	55	20	27	47	83	....	....	....	....	....	....	....	....	....	14	6	6	12	10	....	....	....	..
2003-04	London Knights	OHL	60	24	41	65	85	....	....	....	....	....	....	....	....	....	15	7	10	17	17	....	....	....	..
2004-05	Worcester IceCats	AHL	79	13	30	43	65	....	....	....	....	....	....	....	....	....	....	....	....	....	....	....	....	....	..
2005-06	St. Louis	NHL	67	8	16	24	83	5	1	1	150	5.3	–31	1	0.0	21:41	....	....	....	....	....	....	....	....	..
	Peoria Rivermen	AHL	12	2	4	6	31	....	....	....	....	....	....	....	....	....	....	....	....	....	....	....	....	....	..
2006-07	St. Louis	NHL	55	5	17	22	44	4	0	1	94	5.3	–7	0	0.0	20:12	....	....	....	....	....	....	....	....	..
	Boston	NHL	20	1	2	3	27	0	0	0	28	3.6	–3	1	0.0	17:20	....	....	....	....	....	....	....	....	..
2007-08	Boston	NHL	81	13	23	36	70	9	0	1	171	7.6	11	0	0.0	25:09	6	0	3	3	0	0	0	0	24:

			Regular Season														Playoffs								
Season	Club	League	GP	G	A	Pts	PIM	PP	SH	GW	S	%	+/-	TF	F%	Min	GP	G	A	Pts	PIM	PP	SH	GW	Min
2008-09	Boston	NHL	79	13	37	50	34	6	1	2	169	7.7	32	0	0.0	24:39	11	0	7	7	4	0	0	0	24:42
2009-10	Boston	NHL	76	6	24	30	34	2	0	2	146	4.1	-14	0	0.0	23:33	13	1	11	12	4	0	0	0	26:02
	NHL Totals		378	46	119	165	292	26	2	7	758	6.1		2	0.0	22:59	30	1	21	22	8	0	0	0	25:13

OHL First All-Star Team (2004) • Canadian Major Junior Second All-Star Team (2004)

Signed as a free agent by **St. Louis**, June 30, 2004. Traded to **Boston** by **St. Louis** for Brad Boyes, February 27, 2007. Traded to **Florida** by **Boston** with Boston's 1st round choice (later traded to Los Angeles – Los Angeles selected Derek Forbert) in 2010 Entry Draft and Boston's 3rd round choice in 2011 Entry Draft for Nathan Horton and Gregory Campbell, June 22, 2010.

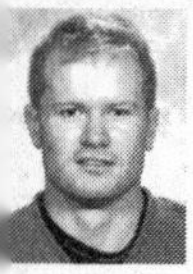

WILLIAMS, Jason

(WIHL-yuhms, JAY-suhn)

Center. Shoots right. 5'11", 192 lbs. Born, London, Ont., August 11, 1980.

Season	Club	League	GP	G	A	Pts	PIM	PP	SH	GW	S	%	+/-	TF	F%	Min	GP	G	A	Pts	PIM	PP	SH	GW	Min
1995-96	Mount Brydges	OHA-D	36	31	28	59	18																		
1996-97	Peterborough	OHL	60	4	8	12	8										10	1	0	1	2				
1997-98	Peterborough	OHL	55	8	27	35	31										4	0	1	1	2				
1998-99	Peterborough	OHL	68	26	48	74	42										5	1	2	3	2				
99-2000	Peterborough	OHL	66	36	37	75	64										5	2	1	3	2				
2000-01	**Detroit**	**NHL**	**5**	**0**	**3**	**3**	**2**	**0**	**0**	**0**	**7**	**0.0**	**1**	**56**	**39.3**	**12:24**	**2**	**0**	**0**	**0**	**0**	**0**	**0**	**0**	**11:45**
	Cincinnati	AHL	76	24	45	69	48										1	0	0	0	2				
2001-02♦	**Detroit**	**NHL**	**25**	**8**	**2**	**10**	**4**	**4**	**0**	**0**	**32**	**25.0**	**2**	**208**	**47.6**	**10:50**	**9**	**0**	**0**	**0**	**2**	**0**	**0**	**0**	**6:12**
	Cincinnati	AHL	52	23	27	50	27										3	0	1	1	6				
2002-03	**Detroit**	**NHL**	**16**	**3**	**3**	**6**	**2**	**1**	**0**	**0**	**20**	**15.0**	**3**	**78**	**51.3**	**10:43**									
	Grand Rapids	AHL	45	23	22	45	18										15	1	7	8	16				
2003-04	**Detroit**	**NHL**	**49**	**6**	**7**	**13**	**15**	**0**	**0**	**0**	**44**	**13.6**	**1**	**315**	**49.2**	**9:27**	**3**	**0**	**0**	**0**	**2**	**0**	**0**	**0**	**6:11**
2004-05	Assat Pori	Finland	43	26	17	43	52										2	1	1	2	4				
2005-06	**Detroit**	**NHL**	**80**	**21**	**37**	**58**	**26**	**6**	**0**	**4**	**177**	**11.9**	**4**	**29**	**55.2**	**14:55**	**6**	**1**	**1**	**2**	**6**	**0**	**0**	**0**	**18:10**
2006-07	**Detroit**	**NHL**	**58**	**11**	**15**	**26**	**24**	**3**	**0**	**2**	**111**	**9.9**	**7**	**11**	**45.5**	**14:26**									
	Chicago	**NHL**	**20**	**4**	**2**	**6**	**20**	**2**	**1**	**0**	**38**	**10.5**	**-6**	**193**	**42.5**	**18:17**									
2007-08	**Chicago**	**NHL**	**43**	**13**	**23**	**36**	**22**	**6**	**0**	**4**	**101**	**12.9**	**-2**	**15**	**60.0**	**16:35**									
2008-09	**Atlanta**	**NHL**	**41**	**7**	**11**	**18**	**8**	**4**	**0**	**2**	**79**	**8.9**	**-9**	**381**	**49.1**	**16:05**									
	Columbus	**NHL**	**39**	**12**	**17**	**29**	**16**	**3**	**0**	**2**	**74**	**16.2**	**5**	**237**	**40.9**	**15:38**	**4**	**0**	**1**	**1**	**2**	**0**	**0**	**0**	**14:12**
2009-10	**Detroit**	**NHL**	**44**	**6**	**9**	**15**	**8**	**3**	**0**	**1**	**96**	**6.3**	**-7**	**60**	**50.0**	**13:32**	**3**	**0**	**0**	**0**	**0**	**0**	**0**	**0**	**8:12**
	NHL Totals		**420**	**91**	**129**	**220**	**147**	**32**	**1**	**15**	**779**	**11.7**		**1583**	**46.9**	**14:09**	**27**	**1**	**2**	**3**	**12**	**0**	**0**	**0**	**10:40**

Signed as a free agent by **Detroit**, September 18, 2000. Signed as a free agent by **Pori** (Finland), October 18, 2004. Traded to **Chicago** by **Detroit** for Kyle Calder, February 26, 2007. Signed as a free agent by **Atlanta**, July 14, 2008. Traded to **Columbus** by **Atlanta** for Clay Wilson and San Jose's 6th round choice (previously acquired, later traded to Chicago – Chicago selected David Pacan) in 2009 Entry Draft, January 14, 2009. Signed as a free agent by **Detroit**, August 4, 2009.

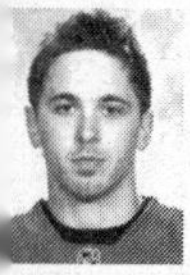

WILLIAMS, Jeremy

(WIHL-yuhms, JAIR-eh-mee) **NYR**

Right wing. Shoots right. 6', 195 lbs. Born, Regina, Sask., January 26, 1984. Toronto's 5th choice, 220th overall, in 2003 Entry Draft.

Season	Club	League	GP	G	A	Pts	PIM	PP	SH	GW	S	%	+/-	TF	F%	Min	GP	G	A	Pts	PIM	PP	SH	GW	Min
2001-02	Swift Current	SMMHL	24	18	23	41	64																		
	Swift Current	WHL	32	6	7	13	30										12	1	0	1	4				
2002-03	Swift Current	WHL	72	41	52	93	117										4	1	0	1	6				
2003-04	Swift Current	WHL	68	*52	49	101	82										5	2	1	3	12				
	St. John's	AHL	4	0	2	2	0																		
2004-05	St. John's	AHL	75	16	20	36	24										5	0	0	0	0				
2005-06	**Toronto**	**NHL**	**1**	**1**	**0**	**1**	**0**	**0**	**0**	**0**	**1**	**100.0**	**0**	**0**	**0.0**	**9:31**									
	Toronto Marlies	AHL	55	23	33	56	62										5	1	0	1	6				
2006-07	**Toronto**	**NHL**	**1**	**1**	**0**	**1**	**0**	**0**	**0**	**0**	**3**	**33.3**	**1**	**1**	**0.0**	**7:18**									
	Toronto Marlies	AHL	23	6	9	15	27																		
2007-08	**Toronto**	**NHL**	**18**	**2**	**0**	**2**	**4**	**0**	**0**	**0**	**16**	**12.5**	**-3**	**4**	**0.0**	**7:20**									
	Toronto Marlies	AHL	49	18	15	33	36																		
2008-09	**Toronto**	**NHL**	**11**	**5**	**2**	**7**	**2**	**0**	**0**	**0**	**21**	**23.8**	**2**	**1**	**0.0**	**13:26**									
	Toronto Marlies	AHL	46	27	13	40	29										6	0	1	1	6				
2009-10	Grand Rapids	AHL	77	32	31	63	55																		
	NHL Totals		**31**	**9**	**2**	**11**	**6**	**0**	**0**	**0**	**41**	**22.0**		**6**	**0.0**	**9:34**									

WHL East First All-Star Team (2004) • Canadian Major Junior First All-Star Team (2004)

Signed as a free agent by **Detroit**, July 7, 2009. Signed as a free agent by **NY Rangers**, July 12, 2010.

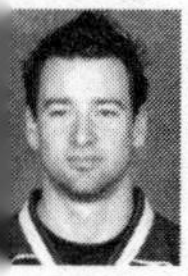

WILLIAMS, Justin

(WIHL-yuhms, JUHS-tihn) **L.A.**

Right wing. Shoots right. 6'1", 193 lbs. Born, Cobourg, Ont., October 4, 1981. Philadelphia's 1st choice, 28th overall, in 2000 Entry Draft.

Season	Club	League	GP	G	A	Pts	PIM	PP	SH	GW	S	%	+/-	TF	F%	Min	GP	G	A	Pts	PIM	PP	SH	GW	Min
1997-98	Colborne Colts	OHA-C	36	32	35	67	26																		
	Cobourg Cougars	OPJHL	17	0	3	3	5																		
1998-99	Plymouth Whalers	OHL	47	4	8	12	28										7	1	2	3	0				
99-2000	Plymouth Whalers	OHL	68	37	46	83	46										23	*14	16	*30	10				
2000-01	**Philadelphia**	**NHL**	**63**	**12**	**13**	**25**	**22**	**0**	**0**	**0**	**99**	**12.1**	**6**	**13**	**53.9**	**12:31**									
2001-02	**Philadelphia**	**NHL**	**75**	**17**	**23**	**40**	**32**	**0**	**0**	**1**	**162**	**10.5**	**11**	**16**	**25.0**	**14:27**	**5**	**0**	**0**	**0**	**4**	**0**	**0**	**0**	**16:42**
2002-03	**Philadelphia**	**NHL**	**41**	**8**	**16**	**24**	**22**	**0**	**0**	**2**	**105**	**7.6**	**15**	**16**	**50.0**	**15:57**	**12**	**1**	**5**	**6**	**8**	**0**	**0**	**1**	**14:11**
2003-04	**Philadelphia**	**NHL**	**47**	**6**	**20**	**26**	**32**	**3**	**0**	**1**	**107**	**5.6**	**10**	**38**	**31.6**	**15:30**									
	Carolina	**NHL**	**32**	**5**	**13**	**18**	**32**	**1**	**0**	**0**	**96**	**5.2**	**2**	**25**	**36.0**	**18:52**									
2004-05	Lulea HF	Sweden	49	14	18	32	61										4	0	1	1	29				
2005-06♦	**Carolina**	**NHL**	**82**	**31**	**45**	**76**	**60**	**8**	**4**	**4**	**255**	**12.2**	**1**	**17**	**29.4**	**21:08**	**25**	**7**	**11**	**18**	**34**	**0**	**1**	**1**	**21:36**
2006-07	**Carolina**	**NHL**	**82**	**33**	**34**	**67**	**73**	**12**	**2**	**8**	**258**	**12.8**	**-11**	**24**	**37.5**	**20:51**									
2007-08	**Carolina**	**NHL**	**37**	**9**	**21**	**30**	**43**	**2**	**0**	**0**	**106**	**8.5**	**2**	**13**	**38.5**	**19:18**									
2008-09	**Carolina**	**NHL**	**32**	**3**	**7**	**10**	**9**	**2**	**0**	**0**	**80**	**3.8**	**-9**	**20**	**30.0**	**15:08**									
	Los Angeles	**NHL**	**12**	**1**	**3**	**4**	**8**	**1**	**0**	**0**	**28**	**3.6**	**1**	**2**	**50.0**	**17:51**									
2009-10	**Los Angeles**	**NHL**	**49**	**10**	**19**	**29**	**39**	**1**	**0**	**1**	**140**	**7.1**	**3**	**11**	**36.4**	**16:23**	**3**	**0**	**1**	**1**	**2**	**0**	**0**	**0**	**11:24**
	NHL Totals		**552**	**135**	**214**	**349**	**372**	**30**	**6**	**17**	**1436**	**9.4**		**195**	**35.9**	**17:14**	**45**	**8**	**17**	**25**	**48**	**0**	**1**	**2**	**18:24**

Played in NHL All-Star Game (2007)

Missed majority of 2002-03 season recovering from shoulder (November 15, 2002 vs. Carolina) and knee (January 18, 2003 vs. Tampa Bay) injuries. Traded to **Carolina** by **Philadelphia** for Danny Markov, January 20, 2004. Signed as a free agent by **Lulea** (Sweden), September 21, 2004. • Missed majority of 2007-08 season recovering from knee injury suffered in game at Florida, December 20, 2007. Traded to **Los Angeles** by **Carolina** for Patrick O'Sullivan and Calgary's 2nd round choice (previously acquired, Carolina selected Brian Dumoulin) in 2009 Entry Draft, March 4. 2009.

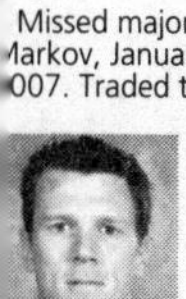

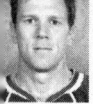

WILLSIE, Brian

(WIHL-see, BRIGH-uhn) **WSH.**

Right wing. Shoots right. 6'1", 202 lbs. Born, Belmont, Ont., March 16, 1978. Colorado's 7th choice, 146th overall, in 1996 Entry Draft.

Season	Club	League	GP	G	A	Pts	PIM	PP	SH	GW	S	%	+/-	TF	F%	Min	GP	G	A	Pts	PIM	PP	SH	GW	Min
1993-94	Belmont Bombers	OHA-D	13	9	5	14	14																		
1994-95	St. Thomas Stars	OHA-B	45	35	47	82	47																		
1995-96	Guelph Storm	OHL	65	13	21	34	18										16	4	2	6	6				
1996-97	Guelph Storm	OHL	64	37	31	68	37										18	15	4	19	10				
1997-98	Guelph Storm	OHL	57	45	31	76	41										12	9	5	14	18				
1998-99	Hershey Bears	AHL	72	19	10	29	28										3	1	0	1	0				
99-2000	**Colorado**	**NHL**	**1**	**0**	**0**	**0**	**0**	**0**	**0**	**0**	**1**	**0.0**	**0**	**0**	**0.0**	**8:16**									
	Hershey Bears	AHL	78	20	39	59	44										12	2	6	8	8				
2000-01	Hershey Bears	AHL	48	18	23	41	20										12	7	2	9	14				
2001-02	**Colorado**	**NHL**	**56**	**7**	**7**	**14**	**14**	**2**	**0**	**1**	**66**	**10.6**	**4**	**8**	**12.5**	**11:24**	**4**	**0**	**1**	**1**	**2**	**0**	**0**	**0**	**11:54**
2002-03	**Colorado**	**NHL**	**12**	**0**	**1**	**1**	**15**	**0**	**0**	**0**	**12**	**0.0**	**0**	**7**	**14.3**	**9:36**	**6**	**1**	**0**	**1**	**2**	**0**	**0**	**1**	**10:48**
	Hershey Bears	AHL	59	29	28	57	49																		
2003-04	**Washington**	**NHL**	**49**	**10**	**5**	**15**	**18**	**1**	**1**	**1**	**85**	**11.8**	**-7**	**46**	**34.8**	**12:42**									
2004-05	Ljubljana	Slovenia	2	0	3	3	4																		
	Ljubljana	Interliga	12	7	6	13	34																		
	Portland Pirates	AHL	53	23	17	40	47																		
2005-06	**Washington**	**NHL**	**82**	**19**	**22**	**41**	**77**	**8**	**1**	**2**	**185**	**10.3**	**-19**	**52**	**51.9**	**16:40**									
2006-07	**Los Angeles**	**NHL**	**81**	**11**	**10**	**21**	**49**	**2**	**0**	**1**	**131**	**8.4**	**-20**	**201**	**45.3**	**13:23**									
2007-08	**Los Angeles**	**NHL**	**53**	**4**	**8**	**12**	**30**	**0**	**0**	**0**	**62**	**6.5**	**-8**	**24**	**58.3**	**10:38**									
2008-09	**Colorado**	**NHL**	**42**	**1**	**3**	**4**	**14**	**0**	**0**	**0**	**59**	**1.7**	**-6**	**89**	**33.7**	**11:47**									
	Lake Erie	AHL	12	8	6	14	8																		

Season	Club	League	GP	G	A	Pts	PIM	PP	SH	GW	S	%	+/-	TF	F%	Min	Playoffs GP	G	A	Pts	PIM	PP	SH	GW	Min
2009-10	**Colorado**	**NHL**	**4**	**0**	**0**	**0**	**0**	**0**	**0**	**0**	**2**	**0.0**	**–1**	**18**	**55.6**	**11:05**									
	Lake Erie	AHL	75	26	31	57	44																		
	NHL Totals		**380**	**52**	**56**	**108**	**217**	**13**	**2**	**5**	**603**	**8.6**		**445**	**42.7**	**13:00**	**10**	**1**	**1**	**2**	**4**	**0**	**0**	**1**	**11:14**

OHL First All-Star Team (1998)

Claimed by **Washington** from **Colorado** in Waiver Draft, October 3, 2003. Signed as a free agent by **Ljubljana** (Slovenia), October 8, 2004. Signed as a free agent by **Portland** (AHL), December 15, 2004. Signed as a free agent by **Los Angeles**, July 4, 2006. Signed as a free agent by **Colorado**, July 15, 2008. Signed as a free agent by **Washington**, July 14, 2010.

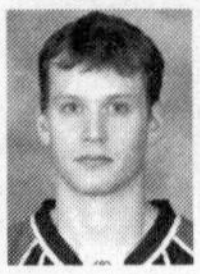

WILSON, Clay

(WIHL-suhn, KLAY) **FLA**

Defense. Shoots left. 6', 195 lbs. Born, Sturgeon Lake, MN, April 5, 1983.

Season	Club	League	GP	G	A	Pts	PIM	PP	SH	GW	S	%	+/-	TF	F%	Min	Playoffs GP	G	A	Pts	PIM	PP	SH	GW	Min
2001-02	Michigan Tech	WCHA	38	4	8	12	18																		
2002-03	Michigan Tech	WCHA	38	8	17	25	37																		
2003-04	Michigan Tech	WCHA	37	2	11	13	22																		
2004-05	Michigan Tech	WCHA	35	3	4	7	42																		
	Muskegon Fury	UHL	14	3	3	6	2										17	0	2	2	8				
2005-06	Muskegon Fury	UHL	13	3	9	12	9																		
	Grand Rapids	AHL	60	10	27	37	40										16	0	3	3	8				
2006-07	Portland Pirates	AHL	79	9	34	43	52																		
2007-08	Portland Pirates	AHL	14	3	5	8	6																		
	Columbus	**NHL**	**7**	**1**	**1**	**2**	**2**	**0**	**0**	**0**	**12**	**8.3**	**3**	**0**	**0.0**	**16:55**									
	Syracuse Crunch	AHL	57	11	28	39	29										13	2	5	7	4				
2008-09	**Columbus**	**NHL**	**5**	**0**	**1**	**1**	**0**	**0**	**0**	**0**	**9**	**0.0**	**–2**	**0**	**0.0**	**9:26**									
	Syracuse Crunch	AHL	33	8	12	20	6																		
	Atlanta	**NHL**	**2**	**0**	**0**	**0**	**0**	**0**	**0**	**0**	**4**	**0.0**	**–1**	**0**	**0.0**	**15:55**									
	Chicago Wolves	AHL	37	6	18	24	10																		
2009-10	**Florida**	**NHL**	**2**	**0**	**0**	**0**	**0**	**0**	**0**	**0**	**0**	**0.0**	**–5**	**0**	**0.0**	**11:07**									
	Rochester	AHL	75	14	46	60	58										7	2	0	2	22				
	NHL Totals		**16**	**1**	**2**	**3**	**2**	**0**	**0**	**0**	**25**	**4.0**		**0**	**0.0**	**13:44**									

Signed as a free agent by **Anaheim**, July 11, 2006. Traded to **Columbus** by **Anaheim** with Aaron Rome for Geoff Platt, November 15, 2007. Traded to **Atlanta** by **Columbus** with San Jose's 6th round choice (previously acquired, later traded to Chicago – Chicago selected David Pacan) in 2009 Entry Draft for Jason Williams, January 14, 2009. Signed as a free agent by **Florida**, July 2, 2009.

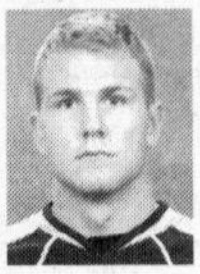

WILSON, Colin

(WIHL-suhn, KAW-lihn) **NSH**

Center. Shoots left. 6'1", 219 lbs. Born, Greenwich, CT, October 20, 1989. Nashville's 1st choice, 7th overall, in 2008 Entry Draft.

Season	Club	League	GP	G	A	Pts	PIM	PP	SH	GW	S	%	+/-	TF	F%	Min	Playoffs GP	G	A	Pts	PIM	PP	SH	GW	Min
2005-06	USNTDP	U-17	15	9	7	16	2																		
	USNTDP	U-18	16	2	4	6	8																		
	USNTDP	NAHL	34	10	11	21	10										2	0	0	0	2				
2006-07	USNTDP	U-18	41	19	31	50	32																		
	USNTDP	NAHL	15	11	13	24	21																		
2007-08	Boston University	H-East	37	12	23	35	22																		
2008-09	Boston University	H-East	43	17	*38	*55	52																		
2009-10	**Nashville**	**NHL**	**35**	**8**	**7**	**15**	**7**	**1**	**0**	**3**	**58**	**13.8**	**–2**	**124**	**50.0**	**15:10**	**6**	**0**	**1**	**1**	**0**	**0**	**0**	**0**	**13:4**
	Milwaukee	AHL	40	13	21	34	19																		
	NHL Totals		**35**	**8**	**7**	**15**	**7**	**1**	**0**	**3**	**58**	**13.8**		**124**	**50.0**	**15:10**	**6**	**0**	**1**	**1**	**0**	**0**	**0**	**0**	**13:4**

Hockey East All-Rookie Team (2008) • Hockey East Rookie of the Year (2008) • Hockey East First All-Star Team (2009) • NCAA East First All-American Team (2009) • NCAA Championship All-Tournament Team (2009)

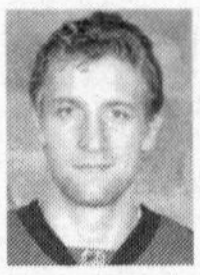

WILSON, Kyle

(WIHL-suhn, KIGHL) **CB**

Center. Shoots right. 6'1", 201 lbs. Born, Oakville, Ont., December 15, 1984. Minnesota's 12th choice, 272nd overall, in 2004 Entry Draft.

Season	Club	League	GP	G	A	Pts	PIM	PP	SH	GW	S	%	+/-	TF	F%	Min	Playoffs GP	G	A	Pts	PIM	PP	SH	GW	Min
2000-01	Strathroy Rockets	OHA-B	33	12	17	29	15										5	2	2	4	2				
2001-02	Strathroy Rockets	OHA-B	53	42	25	67	16																		
2002-03	Colgate	ECAC	33	4	2	6	15																		
2003-04	Colgate	ECAC	37	14	17	31	23																		
2004-05	Colgate	ECAC	30	5	18	23	12																		
2005-06	Colgate	ECAC	39	*23	18	41	22																		
2006-07	San Antonio	AHL	7	1	0	1	2																		
	South Carolina	ECHL	5	3	2	5	4																		
	Hershey Bears	AHL	54	24	30	54	26										19	7	9	16	8				
2007-08	Hershey Bears	AHL	80	30	31	61	26										5	0	3	3	2				
2008-09	Hershey Bears	AHL	80	28	30	58	31										22	3	7	10	2				
2009-10	**Washington**	**NHL**	**2**	**0**	**2**	**2**	**0**	**0**	**0**	**0**	**1**	**0.0**	**1**	**13**	**30.8**	**9:42**									
	Hershey Bears	AHL	77	24	29	53	23										21	6	6	12	4				
	NHL Totals		**2**	**0**	**2**	**2**	**0**	**0**	**0**	**0**	**1**	**0.0**		**13**	**30.8**	**9:42**									

ECAC Second All-Star Team (2006)

Signed as a free agent by **San Antonio** (AHL), October 6, 2006. Signed as a free agent by **Washington**, July 5, 2007. Signed as a free agent by **Columbus**, July 2, 2010.

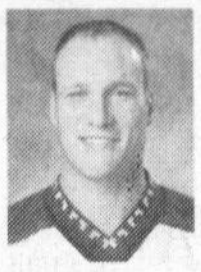

WILSON, Landon

(WIHL-suhn, LAN-duhn)

Right wing. Shoots right. 6'3", 224 lbs. Born, St. Louis, MO, March 13, 1975. Toronto's 2nd choice, 19th overall, in 1993 Entry Draft.

Season	Club	League	GP	G	A	Pts	PIM	PP	SH	GW	S	%	+/-	TF	F%	Min	Playoffs GP	G	A	Pts	PIM	PP	SH	GW	Min
1991-92	California	WSJHL	38	50	42	92	135																		
1992-93	Dubuque	USHL	43	29	36	65	284																		
1993-94	North Dakota	WCHA	35	18	15	33	*147																		
1994-95	North Dakota	WCHA	31	7	16	23	141																		
	Cornwall Aces	AHL	8	4	4	8	25										13	3	4	7	68				
1995-96	**Colorado**	**NHL**	**7**	**1**	**0**	**1**	**6**	**0**	**0**	**0**	**6**	**16.7**	**3**												
	Cornwall Aces	AHL	53	21	13	34	154										8	1	3	4	22				
1996-97	**Colorado**	**NHL**	**9**	**1**	**2**	**3**	**23**	**0**	**0**	**0**	**7**	**14.3**	**1**												
	Boston	**NHL**	**40**	**7**	**10**	**17**	**49**	**0**	**0**	**0**	**76**	**9.2**	**–6**												
	Providence Bruins	AHL	2	2	1	3	2										10	3	4	7	16				
1997-98	**Boston**	**NHL**	**28**	**1**	**5**	**6**	**7**	**0**	**0**	**0**	**26**	**3.8**	**3**				**1**	**0**	**0**	**0**	**0**	**0**	**0**	**0**	
	Providence Bruins	AHL	42	18	10	28	146																		
1998-99	**Boston**	**NHL**	**22**	**3**	**3**	**6**	**17**	**0**	**0**	**0**	**32**	**9.4**	**0**	**3**	**0.0**	**10:04**	**8**	**1**	**1**	**2**	**8**	**1**	**0**	**1**	**13:4**
	Providence Bruins	AHL	48	31	22	53	89										11	7	1	8	19				
99-2000	**Boston**	**NHL**	**40**	**1**	**3**	**4**	**18**	**0**	**0**	**0**	**67**	**1.5**	**–6**	**14**	**42.9**	**10:09**									
	Providence Bruins	AHL	17	5	5	10	45										9	2	3	5	38				
2000-01	**Phoenix**	**NHL**	**70**	**18**	**13**	**31**	**92**	**2**	**0**	**3**	**123**	**14.6**	**3**	**13**	**46.2**	**11:26**									
2001-02	**Phoenix**	**NHL**	**47**	**7**	**12**	**19**	**46**	**1**	**0**	**0**	**100**	**7.0**	**4**	**15**	**53.3**	**12:51**	**4**	**0**	**0**	**0**	**12**	**0**	**0**	**0**	**12:0**
	Springfield	AHL	2	2	1	3	2																		
2002-03	**Phoenix**	**NHL**	**31**	**6**	**8**	**14**	**26**	**0**	**0**	**3**	**92**	**6.5**	**1**	**35**	**54.3**	**12:11**									
2003-04	**Phoenix**	**NHL**	**35**	**1**	**3**	**4**	**16**	**0**	**0**	**0**	**41**	**2.4**	**–3**	**44**	**31.8**	**9:51**									
	Pittsburgh	**NHL**	**19**	**5**	**1**	**6**	**31**	**2**	**0**	**0**	**35**	**14.3**	**0**	**2**	**0.0**	**11:21**									
2004-05	Blues Espoo	Finland	37	8	11	19	80																		
2005-06	HC Davos	Swiss	36	27	14	41	142										11	5	3	8	40				
2006-07	HC Lugano	Swiss	35	20	11	31	67										6	3	2	5	12				
2007-08	HC Lugano	Swiss	30	13	7	20	67										3	4	0	4	2				
2008-09	**Dallas**	**NHL**	**27**	**2**	**6**	**8**	**21**	**0**	**0**	**0**	**34**	**5.9**	**5**	**3**	**0.0**	**9:14**									
	Grand Rapids	AHL	15	8	7	15	37																		
2009-10	Texas Stars	AHL	11	4	1	5	11										19	1	6	7	20				
	NHL Totals		**375**	**53**	**66**	**119**	**352**	**5**	**0**	**6**	**639**	**8.3**		**129**	**41.1**	**11:04**	**13**	**1**	**1**	**2**	**20**	**1**	**0**	**1**	**13:0**

WCHA Rookie of the Year (1994) • AHL First All-Star Team (1999)

Traded to **Quebec** by **Toronto** with Wendel Clark, Sylvain Lefebvre and Toronto's 1st round choice (Jeffrey Kealty) in 1994 Entry Draft for Mats Sundin, Garth Butcher, Todd Warriner and Philadelphia's 1st round choice (previously acquired, later traded to Washington – Washington selected Nolan Baumgartner) in 1994 Entry Draft, June 28, 1994. Transferred to **Colorado** after **Quebec** franchise relocated, June 21, 1995. Traded to **Boston** by **Colorado** with Anders Myrvold for Boston's 1st round choice (Robyn Regehr) in 1998 Entry Draft, November 22, 1996. Signed as a free agent by **Phoenix**, July 7, 2000. • Missed majority of 2002-03 season recovering from eye injury suffered in game vs. Washington, December 13, 2002. Traded to **Pittsburgh** by **Phoenix** for future considerations, February 22, 2004. Signed as a free agent by **Espoo** (Finland), June 23, 2004. Signed as a free agent by **Davos** (Swiss), August 31, 2005. Signed as a free agent by **Lugano** (Swiss), July 17, 2006. Signed as a free agent by **Dallas**, July 3, 2008. • Missed majority of 2009-10 season recovering from various injuries.

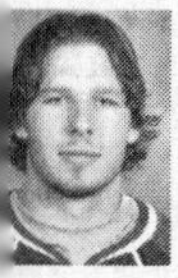

WILSON, Ryan
(WIHL-suhn, RIGH-uhn) **COL.**

Defense. Shoots left. 6'1", 207 lbs. Born, Windsor, Ont., February 3, 1987.

Season	Club	League	GP	G	A	Pts	PIM	PP	SH	GW	S	%	+/-	TF	F%	Min	GP	G	A	Pts	PIM	PP	SH	GW	Min
			Regular Season														Playoffs								
2003-04	St. Michael's	OHL	58	3	22	25	88										18	3	7	10	16				
2004-05	St. Michael's	OHL	68	13	24	37	149										10	4	5	9	12				
2005-06	St. Michael's	OHL	64	12	49	61	145										4	1	3	4	12				
2006-07	Sarnia Sting	OHL	68	17	58	75	136										4	1	3	4	14				
2007-08	Sarnia Sting	OHL	58	7	64	71	84										9	0	7	7	19				
2008-09	Quad City Flames	AHL	60	4	16	20	56																		
	Lake Erie	AHL	8	0	2	2	25																		
2009-10	**Colorado**	**NHL**	**61**	**3**	**18**	**21**	**36**	**0**	**0**	**0**	**46**	**6.5**	**13**	**0**	**0.0**	**16:16**	**4**	**0**	**1**	**1**	**0**	**0**	**0**	**0**	**14:39**
	Lake Erie	AHL	3	0	0	0	17																		
	NHL Totals		**61**	**3**	**18**	**21**	**36**	**0**	**0**	**0**	**46**	**6.5**		**0**	**0.0**	**16:16**	**4**	**0**	**1**	**1**	**0**	**0**	**0**	**0**	**14:39**

gned as a free agent by **Calgary**, July 1, 2008. Traded to **Colorado** by **Calgary** with Lawrence Nycholat and Montreal's 2nd round choice (previously acquired, Colorado selected Stefan Elliott) in 2009 ntry Draft for Jordan Leopold, March 4, 2009.

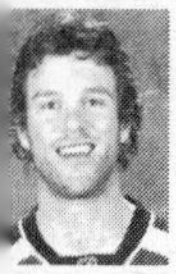

WINCHESTER, Brad
(WIHN-chehs-tuhr, BRAD) **ST.L.**

Center/left wing. Shoots left. 6'5", 231 lbs. Born, Madison, WI, March 1, 1981. Edmonton's 2nd choice, 35th overall, in 2000 Entry Draft.

Season	Club	League	GP	G	A	Pts	PIM	PP	SH	GW	S	%	+/-	TF	F%	Min	GP	G	A	Pts	PIM	PP	SH	GW	Min
1997-98	USNTDP	U-17	24	8	5	13	64																		
	USNTDP	USHL	5	2	1	3	6																		
	USNTDP	NAHL	40	11	17	28	84										5	1	0	1	8				
1998-99	USNTDP	U-18	6	0	3	3	6																		
	USNTDP	USHL	48	14	23	37	103																		
99-2000	U. of Wisconsin	WCHA	33	9	9	18	48																		
2000-01	U. of Wisconsin	WCHA	41	7	9	16	71																		
2001-02	U. of Wisconsin	WCHA	38	14	20	34	38																		
2002-03	U. of Wisconsin	WCHA	38	10	6	16	58																		
2003-04	Toronto	AHL	65	13	6	19	85										3	0	0	0	2				
2004-05	Edmonton	AHL	76	22	18	40	143																		
2005-06	**Edmonton**	**NHL**	**19**	**0**	**1**	**1**	**21**	**0**	**0**	**0**	**19**	**0.0**	**–2**	**2**	**100.0**	**6:05**	**10**	**1**	**2**	**3**	**4**	**0**	**0**	**1**	**9:14**
	Hamilton	AHL	40	26	14	40	118																		
2006-07	**Edmonton**	**NHL**	**59**	**4**	**5**	**9**	**86**	**0**	**0**	**0**	**66**	**6.1**	**–10**	**3**	**33.3**	**8:04**									
2007-08	**Dallas**	**NHL**	**41**	**1**	**2**	**3**	**46**	**0**	**0**	**0**	**36**	**2.8**	**–9**	**2**	**0.0**	**7:34**	**6**	**0**	**0**	**0**	**8**	**0**	**0**	**0**	**6:50**
	Iowa Stars	AHL	1	0	0	0	2																		
2008-09	**St. Louis**	**NHL**	**64**	**13**	**8**	**21**	**89**	**5**	**0**	**3**	**82**	**15.9**	**–1**	**20**	**45.0**	**12:10**	**4**	**0**	**0**	**0**	**10**	**0**	**0**	**0**	**11:42**
	Peoria Rivermen	AHL	13	4	2	6	46																		
2009-10	**St. Louis**	**NHL**	**64**	**3**	**5**	**8**	**108**	**1**	**0**	**0**	**69**	**4.3**	**3**	**12**	**25.0**	**9:04**									
	NHL Totals		**247**	**21**	**21**	**42**	**350**	**6**	**0**	**3**	**272**	**7.7**		**39**	**38.5**	**9:09**	**20**	**1**	**2**	**3**	**22**	**0**	**0**	**1**	**9:00**

gned as a free agent by **Dallas**, July 6, 2007. Signed as a free agent by **St. Louis**, July 16, 2008. Signed as a free agent by **Ottawa**, July 1, 2010.

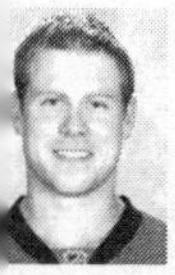

WINCHESTER, Jesse
(WIHN-chehs-tuhr, JEH-see) **OTT.**

Center. Shoots right. 6'1", 203 lbs. Born, Long Sault, Ont., October 4, 1983.

Season	Club	League	GP	G	A	Pts	PIM	PP	SH	GW	S	%	+/-	TF	F%	Min	GP	G	A	Pts	PIM	PP	SH	GW	Min
2004-05	Colgate	ECAC	28	2	2	4	22																		
2005-06	Colgate	ECAC	37	14	22	36	31																		
2006-07	Colgate	ECAC	37	16	21	37	52																		
2007-08	Colgate	ECAC	40	8	*29	37	51																		
	Ottawa	**NHL**	**1**	**0**	**0**	**0**	**2**	**0**	**0**	**0**	**1**	**0.0**	**0**	**0**	**0.0**	**14:00**									
2008-09	**Ottawa**	**NHL**	**76**	**3**	**15**	**18**	**33**	**0**	**0**	**1**	**115**	**2.6**	**0**	**199**	**56.8**	**10:35**									
2009-10	**Ottawa**	**NHL**	**52**	**2**	**11**	**13**	**22**	**0**	**1**	**0**	**77**	**2.6**	**–1**	**377**	**55.4**	**10:01**	**6**	**0**	**0**	**0**	**0**	**0**	**0**	**0**	**9:38**
	Binghamton	AHL	4	2	2	4	0																		
	NHL Totals		**129**	**5**	**26**	**31**	**57**	**0**	**1**	**1**	**193**	**2.6**		**576**	**55.9**	**10:23**	**6**	**0**	**0**	**0**	**0**	**0**	**0**	**0**	**9:38**

gned as a free agent by **Ottawa**, March 24, 2008.

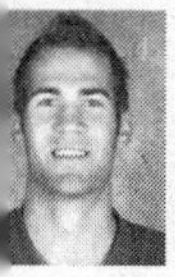

WINNIK, Daniel
(WIHN-ihk, DAN-yehl) **COL.**

Center/Left wing. Shoots right. 6'2", 210 lbs. Born, Toronto, Ont., March 6, 1985. Phoenix's 10th choice, 265th overall, in 2004 Entry Draft.

Season	Club	League	GP	G	A	Pts	PIM	PP	SH	GW	S	%	+/-	TF	F%	Min	GP	G	A	Pts	PIM	PP	SH	GW	Min
2002-03	Wexford	OPJHL	47	20	33	53	70										18	11	11	22	24				
2003-04	New Hampshire	H-East	38	4	10	14	12																		
2004-05	New Hampshire	H-East	42	18	22	40	26																		
2005-06	New Hampshire	H-East	39	15	26	41	44																		
	San Antonio	AHL	7	1	1	2	8																		
2006-07	San Antonio	AHL	66	9	12	21	34																		
	Phoenix	ECHL	5	0	6	6	9																		
2007-08	**Phoenix**	**NHL**	**79**	**11**	**15**	**26**	**25**	**0**	**0**	**1**	**122**	**9.0**	**–3**	**154**	**42.2**	**14:06**									
2008-09	**Phoenix**	**NHL**	**49**	**3**	**4**	**7**	**63**	**0**	**0**	**0**	**66**	**4.5**	**1**	**138**	**37.0**	**13:04**									
	San Antonio	AHL	5	0	0	0	4																		
2009-10	**Phoenix**	**NHL**	**74**	**4**	**15**	**19**	**12**	**0**	**0**	**1**	**83**	**4.8**	**1**	**110**	**45.5**	**13:09**	**7**	**0**	**0**	**0**	**0**	**0**	**0**	**0**	**12:45**
	NHL Totals		**202**	**18**	**34**	**52**	**100**	**0**	**0**	**2**	**271**	**6.6**		**402**	**41.3**	**13:30**	**7**	**0**	**0**	**0**	**0**	**0**	**0**	**0**	**12:45**

ockey East Second All-Star Team (2006)

aded to **Colorado** by **Phoenix** for Colorado's 4th round choice in 2012 Entry Draft, June 28, 2010.

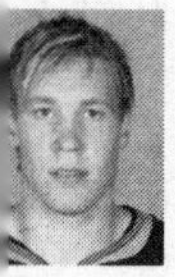

WIRTANEN, Petteri
(WEER-tah-nehn, PEH-tuh-ree) **ANA.**

Center. Shoots left. 6'1", 203 lbs. Born, Hyvinkaa, Finland, May 28, 1986. Anaheim's 5th choice, 172nd overall, in 2006 Entry Draft.

Season	Club	League	GP	G	A	Pts	PIM	PP	SH	GW	S	%	+/-	TF	F%	Min	GP	G	A	Pts	PIM	PP	SH	GW	Min
2001-02	Ahmat Jr.	Fin-Jr.	1	1	0	1	2																		
2002-03	HPK U18	Fin-U18	27	17	12	29	36										2	0	0	0	2				
	HPK Jr.	Fin-Jr.	2	1	0	1	0																		
2003-04	HPK U18	Fin-U18	7	2	3	5	10										2	0	0	0	0				
	HPK Jr.	Fin-Jr.	40	7	11	18	26																		
2004-05	HPK Jr.	Fin-Jr.	43	14	25	39	42										2	0	0	0	10				
	HPK Hameenlinna	Finland	8	0	0	0	0																		
2005-06	Suomi U20	Finland-2	2	2	0	2	2																		
	HPK Jr.	Fin-Jr.	3	4	2	6	4																		
	HPK Hameenlinna	Finland	50	8	3	11	24										13	1	0	1	12				
2006-07	Portland Pirates	AHL	67	7	11	18	40																		
2007-08	**Anaheim**	**NHL**	**3**	**1**	**0**	**1**	**2**	**0**	**0**	**1**	**1**	**100.0**	**1**	**11**	**45.5**	**4:11**									
	Portland Pirates	AHL	78	10	27	37	58										18	0	0	0	14				
2008-09	Iowa Chops	AHL	78	15	26	41	50																		
2009-10	HIFK Helsinki	Finland	56	10	17	27	32										6	4	1	5	4				
	NHL Totals		**3**	**1**	**0**	**1**	**2**	**0**	**0**	**1**	**1**	**100.0**		**11**	**45.5**	**4:11**									

gned as a free agent by **HIFK Helsinki** (Finland), July 29, 2009,

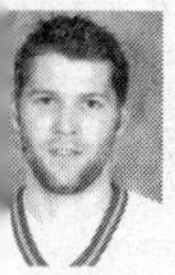

WISEMAN, Chad
(WIGHZ-man, CHAD) **N.J.**

Left wing. Shoots left. 6'1", 210 lbs. Born, Burlington, Ont., March 25, 1981. San Jose's 8th choice, 246th overall, in 2000 Entry Draft.

Season	Club	League	GP	G	A	Pts	PIM	PP	SH	GW	S	%	+/-	TF	F%	Min	GP	G	A	Pts	PIM	PP	SH	GW	Min
1997-98	Burlington	OPJHL	50	28	36	64	31																		
1998-99	Mississauga	OHL	64	11	25	36	29																		
99-2000	Mississauga	OHL	68	23	45	68	53																		
2000-01	Mississauga	OHL	30	15	29	44	22																		
	Plymouth Whalers	OHL	32	11	16	27	12										19	12	8	20	22				
2001-02	Cleveland Barons	AHL	76	21	29	50	61																		
2002-03	**San Jose**	**NHL**	**4**	**0**	**0**	**0**	**4**	**0**	**0**	**0**	**1**	**0.0**	**–2**	**0**	**0.0**	**9:19**									
	Cleveland Barons	AHL	77	17	35	52	44																		
2003-04	**NY Rangers**	**NHL**	**4**	**1**	**0**	**1**	**0**	**0**	**0**	**0**	**3**	**33.3**	**–1**	**0**	**0.0**	**8:49**									
	Hartford	AHL	62	25	27	52	45										15	5	6	11	12				
2004-05	Hartford	AHL	60	17	16	33	74										6	1	1	2	6				

			Regular Season														Playoffs								
Season	Club	League	GP	G	A	Pts	PIM	PP	SH	GW	S	%	+/-	TF	F%	Min	GP	G	A	Pts	PIM	PP	SH	GW	M
2005-06	**NY Rangers**	**NHL**	**1**	**0**	**1**	**1**	**4**	**0**	**0**	**0**	**1**	**0.0**	**2**	**0**	**0.0**	**8:47**	**1**	**0**	**0**	**0**	**2**	**0**	**0**	**0**	**6:0**
	Hartford	AHL	69	19	35	54	65	....	....	....	....	....	....	....	....	....	11	3	6	9	22	....	....	....	
2006-07	Hershey Bears	AHL	48	15	20	35	80	....	....	....	....	....	....	....	....	....	16	2	6	8	16	....	....	....	
2007-08	Wolfsburg	Germany	28	10	13	23	41	....	....	....	....	....	....	....	....	....	....	....	....	....	....	....	....	....	
2008-09	Lowell Devils	AHL	23	9	10	19	23	....	....	....	....	....	....	....	....	....	....	....	....	....	....	....	....	....	
2009-10	Springfield	AHL	67	24	35	59	83	....	....	....	....	....	....	....	....	....	....	....	....	....	....	....	....	....	
	NHL Totals		**9**	**1**	**1**	**2**	**8**	**0**	**0**	**0**	**5**	**20.0**		**0**	**0.0**	**9:02**	**1**	**0**	**0**	**0**	**2**	**0**	**0**	**0**	**6:0**

Traded to **NY Rangers** by **San Jose** for Nils Ekman, August 12, 2003. Signed as a free agent by **Washington**, July 14, 2006. Signed as a free agent by **Wolfsburg** (Germany), July 9, 2007. Signed as a fre agent by **New Jersey**, July 17, 2008. • Missed majority of 2007-08 and 2008-09 seasons recovering from three sports hernia surgeries. Signed as a free agent by **Springfield** (AHL), December 17, 2009. Signed as a free agent by **New Jersey** July 29, 2010.

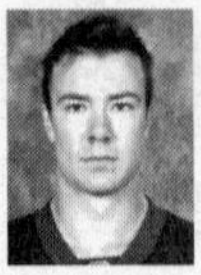

WISHART, Ty

(wih-SHAHRT, TIGH) **T.B**

Defense. Shoots left. 6'4", 215 lbs. Born, Belleville, Ont., May 19, 1988. San Jose's 1st choice, 16th overall, in 2006 Entry Draft.

Season	Club	League	GP	G	A	Pts	PIM	PP	SH	GW	S	%	+/-	TF	F%	Min	GP	G	A	Pts	PIM	PP	SH	GW	M
2003-04	Comox Valley	Minor-BC	47	26	27	53	48	....	....	....	....	....	....	....	....	....	....	....	....	....	....	....	....	....	
2004-05	Prince George	WHL	58	1	7	8	41	....	....	....	....	....	....	....	....	....	....	....	....	....	....	....	....	....	
2005-06	Prince George	WHL	70	5	32	37	68	....	....	....	....	....	....	....	....	....	5	0	0	0	4	....	....	....	
2006-07	Prince George	WHL	62	11	38	49	59	....	....	....	....	....	....	....	....	....	15	3	8	11	6	....	....	....	
2007-08	Prince George	WHL	40	12	28	40	34	....	....	....	....	....	....	....	....	....	....	....	....	....	....	....	....	....	
	Moose Jaw	WHL	32	4	23	27	18	....	....	....	....	....	....	....	....	....	6	1	3	4	2	....	....	....	
	Worcester Sharks	AHL	5	0	0	0	0	....	....	....	....	....	....	....	....	....	....	....	....	....	....	....	....	....	
2008-09	**Tampa Bay**	**NHL**	**5**	**0**	**1**	**1**	**0**	**0**	**0**	**0**	**2**	**0.0**	**0**	**0**	**0.0**	**10:07**	....	....	....	....	....	....	....	....	
	Norfolk Admirals	AHL	61	1	6	7	25	....	....	....	....	....	....	....	....	....	....	....	....	....	....	....	....	....	
2009-10	Norfolk Admirals	AHL	76	9	23	32	44	....	....	....	....	....	....	....	....	....	....	....	....	....	....	....	....	....	
	NHL Totals		**5**	**0**	**1**	**1**	**0**	**0**	**0**	**0**	**2**	**0.0**		**0**	**0.0**	**10:07**	....	....	....	....	....	....	....	....	

WHL West Second All-Star Team (2007) • WHL East Second All-Star Team (2008)

Traded to **Tampa Bay** by **San Jose** with Matt Carle, San Jose's 1st round choice (later traded to Ottawa, later traded to NY Islanders, later traded to Columbus, later traded to Anaheim - Anaheim selected Kyle Palmieri) in 2009 Entry Draft and San Jose's 4th round choice (James Mullin) in 2010 Entry Draft for Dan Boyle and Brad Lukowich, July 4, 2008.

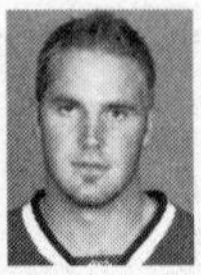

WISNIEWSKI, James

(wihz-NOO-skee, JAYMZ) **NY**

Defense. Shoots right. 5'11", 205 lbs. Born, Canton, MI, February 21, 1984. Chicago's 5th choice, 156th overall, in 2002 Entry Draft.

Season	Club	League	GP	G	A	Pts	PIM	PP	SH	GW	S	%	+/-	TF	F%	Min	GP	G	A	Pts	PIM	PP	SH	GW	M
99-2000	Det. Compuware	NAHL	50	5	11	16	67	....	....	....	....	....	....	....	....	....	5	0	3	3	4	....	....	....	
2000-01	Plymouth Whalers	OHL	53	6	23	29	72	....	....	....	....	....	....	....	....	....	19	3	10	13	34	....	....	....	
2001-02	Plymouth Whalers	OHL	62	11	25	36	100	....	....	....	....	....	....	....	....	....	6	1	2	3	6	....	....	....	
2002-03	Plymouth Whalers	OHL	52	18	34	52	60	....	....	....	....	....	....	....	....	....	18	2	10	12	14	....	....	....	
2003-04	Plymouth Whalers	OHL	50	17	53	70	63	....	....	....	....	....	....	....	....	....	9	3	7	10	8	....	....	....	
2004-05	Norfolk Admirals	AHL	66	7	18	25	110	....	....	....	....	....	....	....	....	....	5	1	3	4	2	....	....	....	
2005-06	**Chicago**	**NHL**	**19**	**2**	**5**	**7**	**36**	**0**	**0**	**0**	**25**	**8.0**	**0**	**1**	**0.0**	**15:52**	....	....	....	....	....	....	....	....	
	Norfolk Admirals	AHL	61	7	28	35	67	....	....	....	....	....	....	....	....	....	4	1	2	3	6	....	....	....	
2006-07	**Chicago**	**NHL**	**50**	**2**	**8**	**10**	**39**	**0**	**0**	**0**	**55**	**3.6**	**3**	**1**	**0.0**	**19:00**	....	....	....	....	....	....	....	....	
	Norfolk Admirals	AHL	10	0	6	6	8	....	....	....	....	....	....	....	....	....	....	....	....	....	....	....	....	....	
2007-08	**Chicago**	**NHL**	**68**	**7**	**19**	**26**	**103**	**1**	**1**	**0**	**82**	**8.5**	**12**	**0**	**0.0**	**17:00**	....	....	....	....	....	....	....	....	
2008-09	**Chicago**	**NHL**	**31**	**2**	**11**	**13**	**14**	**1**	**0**	**0**	**70**	**2.9**	**6**	**0**	**0.0**	**19:15**	....	....	....	....	....	....	....	....	
	Rockford IceHogs	AHL	2	3	1	4	0	....	....	....	....	....	....	....	....	....	....	....	....	....	....	....	....	....	
	Anaheim	**NHL**	**17**	**1**	**10**	**11**	**16**	**0**	**0**	**0**	**19**	**5.3**	**3**	**0**	**0.0**	**20:57**	**12**	**1**	**2**	**3**	**10**	**0**	**0**	**0**	**20:**
2009-10	**Anaheim**	**NHL**	**69**	**3**	**27**	**30**	**56**	**2**	**0**	**0**	**146**	**2.1**	**–5**	**0**	**0.0**	**24:21**	....	....	....	....	....	....	....	....	
	NHL Totals		**254**	**17**	**80**	**97**	**264**	**4**	**1**	**0**	**397**	**4.3**		**2**	**0.0**	**19:51**	**12**	**1**	**2**	**3**	**10**	**0**	**0**	**0**	**20:**

OHL First All-Star Team (2004) • OHL Defenseman of the Year (2004) • Canadian Major Junior First All-Star Team (2004) • Canadian Major Junior Defenseman of the Year (2004)

Traded to **Anaheim** by **Chicago** with Petri Kontiola for Samuel Pahlsson, Logan Stephenson and future considerations, March 4, 2009. Traded to **NY Islanders** by **Anaheim** for an optional 3rd round choice in 2011 Entry Draft, July 30, 2010.

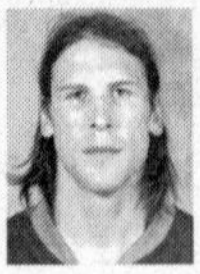

WITT, Brendan

(WIHT, BREHN-duhn)

Defense. Shoots left. 6'2", 223 lbs. Born, Humboldt, Sask., February 20, 1975. Washington's 1st choice, 11th overall, in 1993 Entry Draft.

Season	Club	League	GP	G	A	Pts	PIM	PP	SH	GW	S	%	+/-	TF	F%	Min	GP	G	A	Pts	PIM	PP	SH	GW	M
1990-91	Saskatoon Blazers	SMHL	31	5	13	18	42	....	....	....	....	....	....	....	....	....	....	....	....	....	....	....	....	....	
	Seattle	WHL	....	....	....	....	....	....	....	....	....	....	....	....	....	....	1	0	0	0	0	....	....	....	
1991-92	Seattle	WHL	67	3	9	12	212	....	....	....	....	....	....	....	....	....	15	1	1	2	84	....	....	....	
1992-93	Seattle	WHL	70	2	26	28	239	....	....	....	....	....	....	....	....	....	5	1	2	3	30	....	....	....	
1993-94	Seattle	WHL	56	8	31	39	235	....	....	....	....	....	....	....	....	....	9	3	8	11	23	....	....	....	
1994-95			DID NOT PLAY																						
1995-96	**Washington**	**NHL**	**48**	**2**	**3**	**5**	**85**	**0**	**0**	**1**	**44**	**4.5**	**–4**	....	....	....	....	....	....	....	....	....	....	....	
1996-97	**Washington**	**NHL**	**44**	**3**	**2**	**5**	**88**	**0**	**0**	**0**	**41**	**7.3**	**–20**	....	....	....	....	....	....	....	....	....	....	....	
	Portland Pirates	AHL	30	2	4	6	56	....	....	....	....	....	....	....	....	....	5	1	0	1	30	....	....	....	
1997-98	**Washington**	**NHL**	**64**	**1**	**7**	**8**	**112**	**0**	**0**	**0**	**68**	**1.5**	**–11**	....	....	....	**16**	**1**	**0**	**1**	**14**	**0**	**0**	**0**	
1998-99	**Washington**	**NHL**	**54**	**2**	**5**	**7**	**87**	**0**	**0**	**0**	**51**	**3.9**	**–6**	**0**	**0.0**	**15:50**	....	....	....	....	....	....	....	....	
99-2000	**Washington**	**NHL**	**77**	**1**	**7**	**8**	**114**	**0**	**0**	**0**	**64**	**1.6**	**5**	**2**	**50.0**	**20:56**	**3**	**0**	**0**	**0**	**0**	**0**	**0**	**0**	**20:**
2000-01	**Washington**	**NHL**	**72**	**3**	**3**	**6**	**101**	**0**	**0**	**0**	**87**	**3.4**	**2**	**1**	**100.0**	**20:41**	**6**	**2**	**0**	**2**	**12**	**1**	**0**	**0**	**20:**
2001-02	**Washington**	**NHL**	**68**	**3**	**7**	**10**	**78**	**0**	**0**	**0**	**81**	**3.7**	**–1**	**1**	**100.0**	**20:03**	....	....	....	....	....	....	....	....	
2002-03	**Washington**	**NHL**	**69**	**2**	**9**	**11**	**106**	**0**	**0**	**0**	**80**	**2.5**	**12**	**0**	**0.0**	**20:55**	**6**	**1**	**0**	**1**	**0**	**0**	**0**	**0**	**23:**
2003-04	**Washington**	**NHL**	**72**	**2**	**10**	**12**	**123**	**0**	**0**	**0**	**91**	**2.2**	**–22**	**3**	**66.7**	**22:48**	....	....	....	....	....	....	....	....	
2004-05	Bracknell Bees	Britain-2	3	1	4	5	0	....	....	....	....	....	....	....	....	....	....	....	....	....	....	....	....	....	
2005-06	**Washington**	**NHL**	**58**	**1**	**10**	**11**	**141**	**0**	**0**	**0**	**62**	**1.6**	**–5**	**0**	**0.0**	**21:41**	....	....	....	....	....	....	....	....	
	Nashville	**NHL**	**17**	**0**	**3**	**3**	**68**	**0**	**0**	**0**	**13**	**0.0**	**5**	**0**	**0.0**	**17:29**	**5**	**0**	**0**	**0**	**12**	**0**	**0**	**0**	**17:**
2006-07	**NY Islanders**	**NHL**	**81**	**1**	**13**	**14**	**131**	**0**	**0**	**0**	**75**	**1.3**	**14**	**0**	**0.0**	**21:39**	**5**	**0**	**1**	**1**	**6**	**0**	**0**	**0**	**20:**
2007-08	**NY Islanders**	**NHL**	**59**	**2**	**5**	**7**	**51**	**0**	**0**	**0**	**58**	**3.4**	**–8**	**0**	**0.0**	**21:46**	....	....	....	....	....	....	....	....	
2008-09	**NY Islanders**	**NHL**	**65**	**0**	**9**	**9**	**94**	**0**	**0**	**0**	**52**	**0.0**	**–34**	**2**	**50.0**	**20:18**	....	....	....	....	....	....	....	....	
2009-10	**NY Islanders**	**NHL**	**42**	**2**	**3**	**5**	**45**	**0**	**0**	**1**	**25**	**8.0**	**–18**	**1**	**0.0**	**15:15**	....	....	....	....	....	....	....	....	
	Bridgeport	AHL	27	2	4	6	49	....	....	....	....	....	....	....	....	....	....	....	....	....	....	....	....	....	
	NHL Totals		**890**	**25**	**96**	**121**	**1424**	**0**	**0**	**2**	**892**	**2.8**		**10**	**60.0**	**20:23**	**41**	**4**	**1**	**5**	**44**	**1**	**0**	**0**	**20:**

WHL West First All-Star Team (1993, 1994) • Canadian Major Junior First All-Star Team (1994)

• Missed entire 1994-95 season after failing to come to contract terms with **Washington**. Signed as a free agent by **Bracknell** (Britain-2), December 21, 2004. Traded to **Nashville** by **Washington** for K Beech and Nashville's 1st round choice (Semyon Varlamov) in 2006 Entry Draft, March 9, 2006. Signed as a free agent by **NY Islanders**, July 3, 2006.

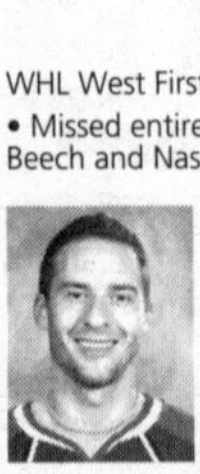

WOLSKI, Wojtek

(VOHL-skee, VOI-tehk) **PH**

Left wing. Shoots left. 6'3", 210 lbs. Born, Zabrze, Poland, February 24, 1986. Colorado's 1st choice, 21st overall, in 2004 Entry Draft.

Season	Club	League	GP	G	A	Pts	PIM	PP	SH	GW	S	%	+/-	TF	F%	Min	GP	G	A	Pts	PIM	PP	SH	GW	M
2001-02	St. Mike's B's	OPJHL	33	16	33	49	40	....	....	....	....	....	....	....	....	....	....	....	....	....	....	....	....	....	
2002-03	Brampton	OHL	64	25	32	57	26	....	....	....	....	....	....	....	....	....	11	5	0	5	6	....	....	....	
2003-04	Brampton	OHL	66	29	41	70	30	....	....	....	....	....	....	....	....	....	12	5	3	8	8	....	....	....	
2004-05	Brampton	OHL	67	29	44	73	41	....	....	....	....	....	....	....	....	....	6	2	5	7	6	....	....	....	
2005-06	**Colorado**	**NHL**	**9**	**2**	**4**	**6**	**4**	**2**	**0**	**0**	**9**	**22.2**	**–5**	**4**	**0.0**	**9:44**	**8**	**1**	**3**	**4**	**2**	**0**	**0**	**0**	**12.**
	Brampton	OHL	56	47	81	128	46	....	....	....	....	....	....	....	....	....	11	7	11	18	4	....	....	....	
2006-07	**Colorado**	**NHL**	**76**	**22**	**28**	**50**	**14**	**7**	**0**	**2**	**165**	**13.3**	**2**	**3**	**100.0**	**15:31**	....	....	....	....	....	....	....	....	
2007-08	**Colorado**	**NHL**	**77**	**18**	**30**	**48**	**14**	**4**	**0**	**6**	**158**	**11.4**	**10**	**48**	**50.0**	**15:56**	**7**	**2**	**3**	**5**	**2**	**1**	**0**	**1**	**13:**
2008-09	**Colorado**	**NHL**	**78**	**14**	**28**	**42**	**28**	**2**	**1**	**3**	**169**	**8.3**	**–13**	**515**	**48.2**	**18:23**	....	....	....	....	....	....	....	....	
2009-10	**Colorado**	**NHL**	**62**	**17**	**30**	**47**	**21**	**2**	**0**	**4**	**156**	**10.9**	**15**	**23**	**47.8**	**18:57**	....	....	....	....	....	....	....	....	
	Phoenix	**NHL**	**18**	**6**	**12**	**18**	**6**	**0**	**0**	**1**	**39**	**15.4**	**6**	**13**	**38.5**	**18:01**	**7**	**4**	**1**	**5**	**0**	**1**	**0**	**0**	**17:**
	NHL Totals		**320**	**79**	**132**	**211**	**87**	**17**	**1**	**16**	**696**	**11.4**		**606**	**48.0**	**16:58**	**22**	**7**	**7**	**14**	**4**	**2**	**0**	**1**	**14.**

OHL First All-Star Team (2004) • OHL Second All-Star Team (2006)

Traded to **Phoenix** by **Colorado** for Peter Mueller and Kevin Porter, March 3, 2010.

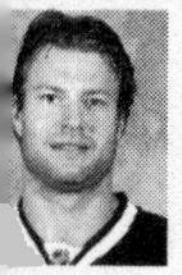

WOYWITKA, Jeff

(WOI-wiht-ka, JEHF) **DAL.**

Defense. Shoots left. 6'2", 224 lbs. Born, Vermilion, Alta., September 1, 1983. Philadelphia's 1st choice, 27th overall, in 2001 Entry Draft.

			Regular Season														Playoffs								
Season	Club	League	GP	G	A	Pts	PIM	PP	SH	GW	S	%	+/-	TF	F%	Min	GP	G	A	Pts	PIM	PP	SH	GW	Min
1998-99	Wainwright	AAHA	26	7	15	22	60																		
99-2000	Red Deer Rebels	WHL	67	4	12	16	40										4	0	3	3	2				
2000-01	Red Deer Rebels	WHL	72	7	28	35	113										22	2	8	10	25				
2001-02	Red Deer Rebels	WHL	72	14	23	37	109										23	2	10	12	22				
2002-03	Red Deer Rebels	WHL	57	16	36	52	65										23	1	9	10	25				
2003-04	Philadelphia	AHL	29	0	6	6	51																		
	Toronto	AHL	53	4	18	22	41										3	0	0	0	2				
2004-05	Edmonton	AHL	80	6	20	26	84																		
2005-06	**St. Louis**	**NHL**	**26**	**0**	**2**	**2**	**25**	**0**	**0**	**0**	**23**	**0.0**	**–12**	**0**	**0.0**	**10:38**									
	Peoria Rivermen	AHL	53	1	14	15	58										4	0	0	0	4				
2006-07	**St. Louis**	**NHL**	**34**	**1**	**6**	**7**	**12**	**0**	**0**	**0**	**28**	**3.6**	**4**	**0**	**0.0**	**14:45**									
	Peoria Rivermen	AHL	41	0	18	18	20																		
2007-08	**St. Louis**	**NHL**	**27**	**2**	**6**	**8**	**12**	**0**	**0**	**0**	**25**	**8.0**	**2**	**0**	**0.0**	**16:04**									
	Peoria Rivermen	AHL	52	10	20	30	35																		
2008-09	**St. Louis**	**NHL**	**65**	**3**	**15**	**18**	**57**	**2**	**0**	**1**	**71**	**4.2**	**8**	**0**	**0.0**	**18:29**	**4**	**0**	**0**	**0**	**0**	**0**	**0**	**0**	**18:48**
	Peoria Rivermen	AHL	7	0	7	7	2																		
2009-10	**Dallas**	**NHL**	**36**	**0**	**3**	**3**	**11**	**0**	**0**	**0**	**44**	**0.0**	**–6**	**0**	**0.0**	**14:06**									
	NHL Totals		**188**	**6**	**32**	**38**	**117**	**2**	**0**	**1**	**191**	**3.1**		**0**	**0.0**	**15:32**	**4**	**0**	**0**	**0**	**0**	**0**	**0**	**0**	**18:48**

HL East Second All-Star Team (2002) • WHL East First All-Star Team (2003)

aded to **Edmonton** by **Philadelphia** with Philadelphia's 1st round choice (Rob Schremp) in 2004 Entry Draft and Philadelphia's 3rd round choice (Danny Syvret) in 2005 Entry Draft for Mike Comrie, cember 16, 2003. Traded to **St. Louis** by **Edmonton** with Eric Brewer and Doug Lynch for Chris Pronger, August 2, 2005. Signed as a free agent by **Dallas**, July 7, 2009. • Missed majority of 2009-10 ason as a healthy reserve.

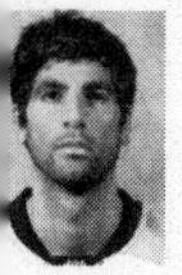

WOZNIEWSKI, Andy

(wuhz-NYOO-skee, AN-dee)

Defense. Shoots left. 6'5", 225 lbs. Born, Buffalo Grove, IL, May 25, 1980.

			Regular Season														Playoffs								
Season	Club	League	GP	G	A	Pts	PIM	PP	SH	GW	S	%	+/-	TF	F%	Min	GP	G	A	Pts	PIM	PP	SH	GW	Min
99-2000	U. Mass-Lowell	H-East	17	1	1	2	8																		
2000-01	Texas Tornado	NAHL	54	10	34	44	98										8	2	7	9	12				
2001-02	U. of Wisconsin	WCHA	39	3	13	16	54																		
2002-03	U. of Wisconsin	WCHA	33	1	7	8	47																		
2003-04	U. of Wisconsin	WCHA	43	6	8	14	*104																		
	St. John's	AHL	3	0	1	1	0																		
2004-05	St. John's	AHL	28	1	4	5	20																		
2005-06	**Toronto**	**NHL**	**13**	**0**	**1**	**1**	**13**	**0**	**0**	**0**	**6**	**0.0**	**–8**	**0**	**0.0**	**17:55**									
	Toronto Marlies	AHL	31	4	11	15	42																		
2006-07	**Toronto**	**NHL**	**15**	**0**	**2**	**2**	**14**	**0**	**0**	**0**	**10**	**0.0**	**–1**	**0**	**0.0**	**13:55**									
	Toronto Marlies	AHL	5	0	3	3	8																		
2007-08	**Toronto**	**NHL**	**48**	**2**	**7**	**9**	**54**	**0**	**0**	**0**	**34**	**5.9**	**5**	**0**	**0.0**	**14:10**									
	Toronto Marlies	AHL	33	7	10	17	26										19	4	5	9	14				
2008-09	**St. Louis**	**NHL**	**1**	**0**	**0**	**0**	**0**	**0**	**0**	**0**	**0**	**0.0**	**0**	**0**	**0.0**	**6:44**									
	Peoria Rivermen	AHL	56	1	16	17	56																		
	Wilkes-Barre	AHL	18	2	2	4	26										6	1	1	2	2				
2009-10	**Boston**	**NHL**	**2**	**0**	**0**	**0**	**0**	**0**	**0**	**0**	**1**	**0.0**	**0**	**0**	**0.0**	**9:17**									
	Providence Bruins	AHL	68	10	33	43	69																		
	NHL Totals		**79**	**2**	**10**	**12**	**81**	**0**	**0**	**0**	**51**	**3.9**		**0**	**0.0**	**14:31**									

gned as a free agent by **Toronto**, May 27, 2004. • Missed majority of 2006-07 season recovering from shoulder surgery, October 10, 2006. Signed as a free agent by **St. Louis**, July 17, 2008. Traded to **ttsburgh** by **St. Louis** for Danny Richmond, March 4, 2009. Signed as a free agent by **Boston**, September 9, 2009. Signed as a free agent by **Zug** (Swiss), May 20, 2010.

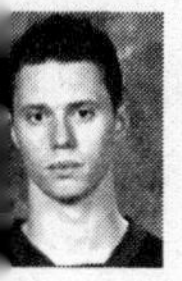

WRIGHT, James

(RIGHT, JAYMZ) **T.B.**

Center. Shoots left. 6'3", 175 lbs. Born, Saskatoon, Sask., March 24, 1990. Tampa Bay's 2nd choice, 117th overall, in 2008 Entry Draft.

			Regular Season														Playoffs								
Season	Club	League	GP	G	A	Pts	PIM	PP	SH	GW	S	%	+/-	TF	F%	Min	GP	G	A	Pts	PIM	PP	SH	GW	Min
2005-06	Sask. Contacts	SMHL	41	13	19	32	43																		
	Vancouver Giants	WHL	2	0	0	0	2																		
2006-07	Vancouver Giants	WHL	48	5	7	12	31										14	3	1	4	0				
2007-08	Vancouver Giants	WHL	60	13	23	36	21										6	1	0	1	2				
2008-09	Vancouver Giants	WHL	71	21	26	47	54										17	3	7	10	13				
2009-10	**Tampa Bay**	**NHL**	**48**	**2**	**3**	**5**	**18**	**0**	**0**	**0**	**25**	**8.0**	**–9**	**169**	**45.6**	**11:39**									
	Vancouver Giants	WHL	21	6	13	19	17										16	7	9	16	4				
	NHL Totals		**48**	**2**	**3**	**5**	**18**	**0**	**0**	**0**	**25**	**8.0**		**169**	**45.6**	**11:39**									

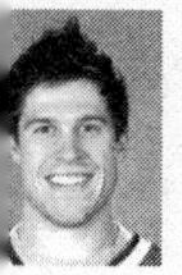

WYMAN, James

(WIGH-muhn, JAYMZ) **MTL.**

Right wing. Shoots right. 6'2", 199 lbs. Born, Edina, MN, February 27, 1986. Montreal's 3rd choice, 100th overall, in 2004 Entry Draft.

			Regular Season														Playoffs								
Season	Club	League	GP	G	A	Pts	PIM	PP	SH	GW	S	%	+/-	TF	F%	Min	GP	G	A	Pts	PIM	PP	SH	GW	Min
2001-02	Blake Bears	High-MN	26	7	5	12																			
2002-03	Blake Bears	High-MN	28	17	23	40	12																		
2003-04	Blake Bears	High-MN	27	31	24	55	4																		
	Team Southwest	UMEHL	24	8	8	16																			
2004-05	Dartmouth	ECAC	33	5	6	11	4																		
2005-06	Dartmouth	ECAC	28	8	12	20	6																		
2006-07	Dartmouth	ECAC	33	13	11	24	20																		
2007-08	Dartmouth	ECAC	29	15	15	30	18																		
	Hamilton	AHL	8	0	1	1	5																		
2008-09	Hamilton	AHL	52	6	5	11	8										6	0	1	1	2				
	Cincinnati	ECHL	15	0	8	8	4																		
2009-10	**Montreal**	**NHL**	**3**	**0**	**0**	**0**	**0**	**0**	**0**	**0**	**0**	**0.0**	**–2**	**1**	**0.0**	**4:23**									
	Hamilton	AHL	76	17	20	37	12										19	1	3	4	2				
	NHL Totals		**3**	**0**	**0**	**0**	**0**	**0**	**0**	**0**	**0**	**0.0**		**1**	**0.0**	**4:23**									

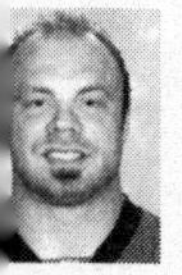

YABLONSKI, Jeremy

(ya-BLAWN-skee, JAIR-eh-mee) **NYI**

Left wing. Shoots right. 6', 240 lbs. Born, Meadow Lake, Sask., March 21, 1980.

			Regular Season														Playoffs								
Season	Club	League	GP	G	A	Pts	PIM	PP	SH	GW	S	%	+/-	TF	F%	Min	GP	G	A	Pts	PIM	PP	SH	GW	Min
1996-97	Beardy's	SMHL	38	7	3	10	284																		
1997-98	Edmonton Ice	WHL	47	3	0	3	143																		
1998-99	Kootenay Ice	WHL	27	1	1	2	77																		
99-2000	Kootenay Ice	WHL	DID NOT PLAY – INJURED																						
2000-01	Phoenix	WCHL	44	2	1	3	169																		
2001-02	Idaho Steelheads	WCHL	69	2	1	3	303																		
2002-03	Peoria Rivermen	ECHL	24	1	2	3	154																		
	Cincinnati	AHL	9	0	0	0	42																		
	Worcester IceCats	AHL	20	1	0	1	50																		
2003-04	Worcester IceCats	AHL	6	0	0	0	19																		
	St. Louis	**NHL**	**1**	**0**	**0**	**0**	**5**	**0**	**0**	**0**	**1**	**0.0**	**–1**	**0**	**0.0**	**7:53**									
	Peoria Rivermen	ECHL	13	0	2	2	62																		
	Milwaukee	AHL	2	0	0	0	11																		
2004-05	Milwaukee	AHL	32	3	2	5	116																		
2005-06	Milwaukee	AHL	30	0	1	1	82																		
	Idaho Steelheads	ECHL	3	0	1	1	25																		
2006-07	Idaho Steelheads	ECHL	41	3	3	6	163																		
2007-08	Binghamton	AHL	76	3	10	13	228																		
2008-09	Binghamton	AHL	64	1	2	3	215																		
2009-10	Binghamton	AHL	27	1	0	1	128																		
	NHL Totals		**1**	**0**	**0**	**0**	**5**	**0**	**0**	**0**	**1**	**0.0**		**0**	**0.0**	**7:53**									

Aissed majority of 1998-99 season and entire 1999-2000 season recovering from head injury suffered in practice, January 3, 1999. Signed as a free agent by **Worcester** (AHL), July 17, 2003. Signed as a e agent by **St. Louis**, December 30, 2003. Claimed on waivers by **Nashville** from **St. Louis**, January 30, 2004. Signed as a free agent by **Binghamton** (AHL), August 9, 2007. Signed as a free agent by **tawa**, June 30, 2008. • Missed majority of 2009-10 season recovering from various injuries. Signed as a free agent by **NY Islanders**, July 21, 2010.

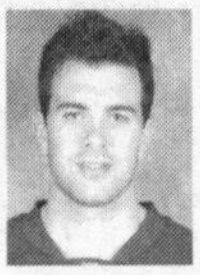

YANDLE, Keith

(Yan-duhl, KEETH) **PHX**

Defense. Shoots left. 6'1", 195 lbs. Born, Boston, MA, September 9, 1986. Phoenix's 3rd choice, 105th overall, in 2005 Entry Draft.

			Regular Season														Playoffs								
Season	Club	League	GP	G	A	Pts	PIM	PP	SH	GW	S	%	+/-	TF	F%	Min	GP	G	A	Pts	PIM	PP	SH	GW	Min
2004-05	Cushing	High-MA	34	14	40	54	52																		
2005-06	Moncton Wildcats	QMJHL	66	25	59	84	109										21	6	14	20	36				
2006-07	**Phoenix**	**NHL**	**7**	**0**	**2**	**2**	**8**	**0**	**0**	**0**	**10**	**0.0**	**0**	**0**	**0.0**	**20:10**									
	San Antonio	AHL	69	6	27	33	97																		
2007-08	**Phoenix**	**NHL**	**43**	**5**	**7**	**12**	**14**	**4**	**0**	**0**	**72**	**6.9**	**–12**	**0**	**0.0**	**14:04**									
	San Antonio	AHL	30	1	14	15	80										5	0	0	0	8				
2008-09	**Phoenix**	**NHL**	**69**	**4**	**26**	**30**	**37**	**1**	**0**	**0**	**118**	**3.4**	**–4**	**0**	**0.0**	**16:37**									
2009-10	**Phoenix**	**NHL**	**82**	**12**	**29**	**41**	**45**	**5**	**0**	**2**	**145**	**8.3**	**16**	**0**	**0.0**	**20:14**	**7**	**2**	**3**	**5**	**4**	**1**	**0**	**0**	**17:1**
	NHL Totals		**201**	**21**	**64**	**85**	**104**	**10**	**0**	**2**	**345**	**6.1**		**0**	**0.0**	**17:40**	**7**	**2**	**3**	**5**	**4**	**1**	**0**	**0**	**17:1**

QMJHL First All-Star Team (2006) • Canadian Major Junior First All-Star Team (2006) • Canadian Major Junior Defenseman of the Year (2006)

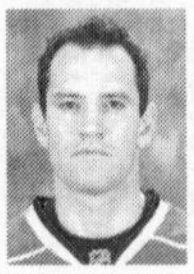

YELLE, Stephane

(YEHL, STEH-fan)

Center. Shoots left. 6'2", 182 lbs. Born, Ottawa, Ont., May 9, 1974. New Jersey's 9th choice, 186th overall, in 1992 Entry Draft.

			Regular Season														Playoffs								
Season	Club	League	GP	G	A	Pts	PIM	PP	SH	GW	S	%	+/-	TF	F%	Min	GP	G	A	Pts	PIM	PP	SH	GW	Min
1990-91	Cumberland	OHA-B	33	20	30	50	16																		
1991-92	Oshawa Generals	OHL	55	12	14	26	20										7	2	0	2	2				
1992-93	Oshawa Generals	OHL	66	24	50	74	20										10	2	4	6	4				
1993-94	Oshawa Generals	OHL	66	35	69	104	22										5	1	7	8	2				
1994-95	Cornwall Aces	AHL	40	18	15	33	22										13	7	7	14	8				
1995-96♦	**Colorado**	**NHL**	**71**	**13**	**14**	**27**	**30**	**0**	**2**	**1**	**93**	**14.0**	**15**				**22**	**1**	**4**	**5**	**8**	**0**	**1**	**0**	
1996-97	**Colorado**	**NHL**	**79**	**9**	**17**	**26**	**38**	**0**	**1**	**1**	**89**	**10.1**	**1**				**12**	**1**	**6**	**7**	**2**	**0**	**0**	**0**	
1997-98	**Colorado**	**NHL**	**81**	**7**	**15**	**22**	**48**	**0**	**1**	**0**	**93**	**7.5**	**–10**				**7**	**1**	**0**	**1**	**12**	**0**	**0**	**0**	
1998-99	**Colorado**	**NHL**	**72**	**8**	**7**	**15**	**40**	**1**	**0**	**0**	**99**	**8.1**	**–8**	**1201**	**51.2**	**15:15**	**10**	**0**	**1**	**1**	**6**	**0**	**0**	**0**	**15:1**
99-2000	**Colorado**	**NHL**	**79**	**8**	**14**	**22**	**28**	**0**	**1**	**1**	**90**	**8.9**	**9**	**1294**	**52.2**	**15:51**	**17**	**1**	**2**	**3**	**4**	**0**	**0**	**0**	**15:3**
2000-01♦	**Colorado**	**NHL**	**50**	**4**	**10**	**14**	**20**	**0**	**1**	**0**	**54**	**7.4**	**–3**	**736**	**56.4**	**14:28**	**23**	**1**	**2**	**3**	**8**	**0**	**0**	**1**	**13:5**
2001-02	**Colorado**	**NHL**	**73**	**5**	**12**	**17**	**48**	**0**	**1**	**1**	**71**	**7.0**	**1**	**1036**	**51.8**	**14:02**	**20**	**0**	**2**	**2**	**14**	**0**	**0**	**0**	**13:2**
2002-03	**Calgary**	**NHL**	**82**	**10**	**15**	**25**	**50**	**3**	**0**	**3**	**121**	**8.3**	**–10**	**1494**	**53.4**	**18:06**									
2003-04	**Calgary**	**NHL**	**53**	**4**	**13**	**17**	**24**	**1**	**0**	**0**	**76**	**5.3**	**1**	**996**	**56.6**	**15:48**	**23**	**3**	**3**	**6**	**16**	**0**	**1**	**1**	**17:0**
2004-05			DID NOT PLAY																						
2005-06	**Calgary**	**NHL**	**74**	**4**	**14**	**18**	**48**	**1**	**1**	**1**	**93**	**4.3**	**10**	**1072**	**55.4**	**14:27**	**7**	**1**	**0**	**1**	**8**	**0**	**0**	**0**	**15:2**
2006-07	**Calgary**	**NHL**	**56**	**10**	**14**	**24**	**32**	**1**	**1**	**1**	**55**	**18.2**	**5**	**808**	**50.4**	**14:37**	**6**	**0**	**0**	**0**	**2**	**0**	**0**	**0**	**15:1**
2007-08	**Calgary**	**NHL**	**74**	**3**	**9**	**12**	**20**	**0**	**1**	**0**	**62**	**4.8**	**–4**	**381**	**49.9**	**11:57**	**7**	**2**	**0**	**2**	**6**	**0**	**0**	**1**	**14:3**
2008-09	**Boston**	**NHL**	**77**	**7**	**11**	**18**	**32**	**1**	**0**	**2**	**72**	**9.7**	**6**	**792**	**52.0**	**13:16**	**11**	**0**	**1**	**1**	**2**	**0**	**0**	**0**	**12:3**
2009-10	**Carolina**	**NHL**	**59**	**4**	**3**	**7**	**28**	**0**	**1**	**0**	**34**	**11.8**	**–6**	**296**	**48.7**	**9:22**									
	Colorado	**NHL**	**11**	**0**	**1**	**1**	**4**	**0**	**0**	**0**	**5**	**0.0**	**0**	**84**	**44.1**	**10:00**	**6**	**0**	**0**	**0**	**2**	**0**	**0**	**0**	**11:1**
	NHL Totals		**991**	**96**	**169**	**265**	**490**	**8**	**11**	**11**	**1107**	**8.7**		**10190**	**52.9**	**14:19**	**171**	**11**	**21**	**32**	**90**	**0**	**2**	**3**	**14:3**

Traded to **Quebec** by **New Jersey** with New Jersey's 11th round choice (Steven Low) in 1994 Entry Draft for Quebec's 11th round choice (Mike Hanson) in 1994 Entry Draft, June 1, 1994. • Transferred to **Colorado** after **Quebec** franchise relocated, June 21, 1995. Traded to **Calgary** by **Colorado** with Chris Drury for Derek Morris, Jeff Shantz and Dean McAmmond, October 1, 2002. Signed as a free agent by **Boston**, September 3, 2008. Signed as a free agent by **Carolina**, August 19, 2009. Traded to **Colorado** by **Carolina** with Harrison Reed for Cedric Lalonde-McNicoll and Colorado's 6th round choice (Tyler Stahl) in 2010 Entry Draft, March 3, 2010.

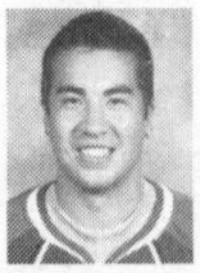

YIP, Brandon

(YIHP, BRAN-duhn) **CO**

Right wing. Shoots right. 6'1", 195 lbs. Born, Vancouver, B.C., April 25, 1985. Colorado's 7th choice, 239th overall, in 2004 Entry Draft.

			Regular Season														Playoffs								
Season	Club	League	GP	G	A	Pts	PIM	PP	SH	GW	S	%	+/-	TF	F%	Min	GP	G	A	Pts	PIM	PP	SH	GW	Min
2003-04	Coquitlam	BCHL	56	31	38	69	87										4	1	2	3	14				
2004-05	Coquitlam	BCHL	43	20	42	62	92										7	6	1	7	12				
2005-06	Boston University	H-East	39	9	22	31	59																		
2006-07	Boston University	H-East	18	5	6	11	29																		
2007-08	Boston University	H-East	37	11	12	23	28																		
2008-09	Boston University	H-East	45	20	23	43	118																		
2009-10	**Colorado**	**NHL**	**32**	**11**	**8**	**19**	**22**	**4**	**0**	**2**	**65**	**16.9**	**5**	**1**	**0.0**	**14:41**	**6**	**2**	**2**	**4**	**6**	**0**	**0**	**0**	**17:5**
	Lake Erie	AHL	6	2	0	2	4																		
	NHL Totals		**32**	**11**	**8**	**19**	**22**	**4**	**0**	**2**	**65**	**16.9**		**1**	**0.0**	**14:41**	**6**	**2**	**2**	**4**	**6**	**0**	**0**	**0**	**17:5**

Hockey East All-Rookie Team (2006) • Hockey East Rookie of the Year (2006)

• Missed majority of 2009-10 season recovering from hand injury suffered in pre-season game at St. Louis, September 18, 2009.

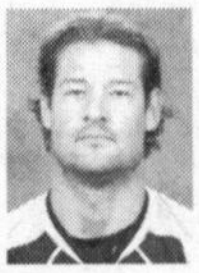

YONKMAN, Nolan

(YAWNK-man, NOH-luhn) **PHX**

Defense. Shoots right. 6'6", 253 lbs. Born, Punnichy, Sask., April 1, 1981. Washington's 5th choice, 37th overall, in 1999 Entry Draft.

			Regular Season														Playoffs								
Season	Club	League	GP	G	A	Pts	PIM	PP	SH	GW	S	%	+/-	TF	F%	Min	GP	G	A	Pts	PIM	PP	SH	GW	Min
1996-97	Naicam Vikings	SAHA	64	15	23	38	36																		
	Kelowna Rockets	WHL	4	0	0	0	0																		
1997-98	Kelowna Rockets	WHL	65	0	2	2	36										7	0	0	0	2				
1998-99	Kelowna Rockets	WHL	61	1	6	7	129										6	0	0	0	6				
99-2000	Kelowna Rockets	WHL	71	5	7	12	153										5	0	0	0	8				
2000-01	Kelowna Rockets	WHL	7	0	1	1	19																		
	Brandon	WHL	51	6	10	16	94										6	0	1	1	12				
2001-02	**Washington**	**NHL**	**11**	**1**	**0**	**1**	**4**	**0**	**0**	**0**	**7**	**14.3**	**3**	**0**	**0.0**	**12:44**									
	Portland Pirates	AHL	59	4	3	7	116																		
2002-03	Portland Pirates	AHL	24	1	4	5	40										3	0	1	1	2				
2003-04	**Washington**	**NHL**	**1**	**0**	**0**	**0**	**0**	**0**	**0**	**0**	**0**	**0.0**	**0**	**0**	**0.0**	**5:00**									
	Portland Pirates	AHL	4	0	0	0	11																		
2004-05	Portland Pirates	AHL	32	0	3	3	68																		
2005-06	**Washington**	**NHL**	**38**	**0**	**7**	**7**	**86**	**0**	**0**	**0**	**14**	**0.0**	**1**	**0**	**0.0**	**8:13**									
	Hershey Bears	AHL	6	0	0	0	15																		
2006-07	Milwaukee	AHL	77	3	10	13	113										4	0	0	0	2				
2007-08	Milwaukee	AHL	69	0	7	7	103										6	0	1	1	18				
2008-09	Milwaukee	AHL	61	3	7	10	80										11	0	0	0	15				
2009-10	Milwaukee	AHL	76	2	7	9	170										7	0	1	1	2				
	NHL Totals		**50**	**1**	**7**	**8**	**90**	**0**	**0**	**0**	**21**	**4.8**		**0**	**0.0**	**9:09**									

• Missed majority of 2002-03 season recovering from abdominal injury suffered in training camp, September 25, 2002. • Missed majority of 2003-04 and 2004-05 seasons recovering from knee injury suffered in game vs. Worcester (AHL), October 23, 2003. Signed as a free agent by **Nashville**, July 17, 2006. Signed as a free agent by **Phoenix**, July 3, 2010.

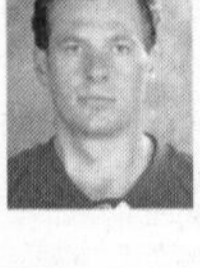

YORK, Mike

(YOHRK, MIGHK)

Left wing. Shoots right. 5'10", 185 lbs. Born, Waterford, MI, January 3, 1978. NY Rangers' 7th choice, 136th overall, in 1997 Entry Draft.

			Regular Season														Playoffs								
Season	Club	League	GP	G	A	Pts	PIM	PP	SH	GW	S	%	+/-	TF	F%	Min	GP	G	A	Pts	PIM	PP	SH	GW	Min
1992-93	Michigan	MNHL	50	45	50	95																			
1993-94	Det. Compuware	MNHL	85	136	140	276																			
1994-95	Thornhill Islanders	MTJHL	49	39	54	*93	44										11	7	6	13	0				
1995-96	Michigan State	CCHA	39	12	27	39	20																		
1996-97	Michigan State	CCHA	37	18	29	47	42																		
1997-98	Michigan State	CCHA	40	27	34	61	38																		
1998-99	Michigan State	CCHA	42	22	32	*54	41																		
	Hartford	AHL	3	2	2	4	0										6	3	1	4	0				
99-2000	**NY Rangers**	**NHL**	**82**	**26**	**24**	**50**	**18**	**8**	**0**	**4**	**177**	**14.7**	**–17**	**1131**	**48.1**	**1:35**									
2000-01	**NY Rangers**	**NHL**	**79**	**14**	**17**	**31**	**20**	**3**	**2**	**4**	**171**	**8.2**	**1**	**1098**	**46.9**	**17:45**									
2001-02	**NY Rangers**	**NHL**	**69**	**18**	**39**	**57**	**16**	**2**	**0**	**5**	**188**	**9.6**	**8**	**267**	**43.1**	**20:24**									
	United States	Olympics	6	0	1	1	0																		
	Edmonton	**NHL**	**12**	**2**	**2**	**4**	**0**	**1**	**0**	**1**	**30**	**6.7**	**–1**	**100**	**56.0**	**16:35**									
2002-03	**Edmonton**	**NHL**	**71**	**22**	**29**	**51**	**10**	**7**	**2**	**4**	**177**	**12.4**	**–8**	**390**	**43.9**	**19:04**	**6**	**0**	**2**	**2**	**2**	**0**	**0**	**0**	**14:**
2003-04	**Edmonton**	**NHL**	**61**	**16**	**26**	**42**	**15**	**1**	**2**	**0**	**144**	**11.1**	**18**	**656**	**45.9**	**19:17**									
2004-05	Iserlohn Roosters	Germany	52	16	46	62	77																		
2005-06	**NY Islanders**	**NHL**	**75**	**13**	**39**	**52**	**30**	**4**	**1**	**2**	**146**	**8.9**	**–9**	**1289**	**46.1**	**19:55**									
2006-07	**NY Islanders**	**NHL**	**32**	**6**	**7**	**13**	**14**	**2**	**0**	**1**	**46**	**13.0**	**–9**	**432**	**45.6**	**14:47**									
	Philadelphia	**NHL**	**34**	**4**	**4**	**8**	**8**	**0**	**0**	**1**	**41**	**9.8**	**–9**	**272**	**47.8**	**10:22**									
2007-08	**Phoenix**	**NHL**	**63**	**6**	**8**	**14**	**4**	**4**	**0**	**1**	**85**	**7.1**	**–8**	**205**	**50.7**	**11:59**									

			Regular Season														Playoffs								
Season	Club	League	GP	G	A	Pts	PIM	PP	SH	GW	S	%	+/-	TF	F%	Min	GP	G	A	Pts	PIM	PP	SH	GW	Min
2008-09	**Columbus**	**NHL**	**1**	**0**	**0**	**0**	**0**	**0**	**0**	**0**	**1**	**0.0**	**0**	**0**	**0.0**	**13:15**									
	Syracuse Crunch	AHL	75	11	47	58	30																		
2009-10	Rochester	AHL	45	14	27	41	8										7	2	10	12	2				
	NHL Totals		**579**	**127**	**195**	**322**	**135**	**32**	**7**	**23**	**1206**	**10.5**		**5840**	**46.7**	**15:07**	**6**	**0**	**2**	**2**	**2**	**0**	**0**	**0**	**14:20**

CHA Second All-Star Team (1998) • NCAA West First All-American Team (1998, 1999) • CCHA First All-Star Team (1999) • CCHA Player of the Year (1999) • NHL All-Rookie Team (2000)

ayed in NHL All-Star Game (2002)

raded to **Edmonton** by **NY Rangers** with NY Rangers' 4th round choice (Ivan Koltsov) in 2002 Entry Draft for Tom Poti and Rem Murray, March 19, 2002. Signed as a free agent by **Iserlohn** (Germany), ebruary 25, 2005. Traded to **NY Islanders** by **Edmonton** with Edmonton's 4th round choice (later traded to Colorado - Colorado selected Kevin Montgomery) in 2006 Entry Draft for Michael Peca, August , 2005. Traded to **Philadelphia** by **NY Islanders** for Randy Robitaille and Philadelphia's 5th round choice (Matthew Martin) in 2008 Entry Draft, December 20, 2006. Signed as a free agent by **Phoenix**, ly 9, 2007. Signed as a free agent by **Columbus**, July 25, 2008. Signed as a free agent by **Rochester** (AHL), August 20, 2009.

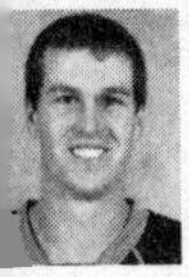

YOUNG, Bryan

(YUHNG, BRIGH-uhn)

Defense. Shoots left. 6'1", 191 lbs. Born, Kitchener, Ont., August 6, 1986. Edmonton's 6th choice, 146th overall, in 2004 Entry Draft.

Season	Club	League	GP	G	A	Pts	PIM	PP	SH	GW	S	%	+/-	TF	F%	Min	GP	G	A	Pts	PIM	PP	SH	GW	Min
2002-03	Lindsay Muskies	OPJHL	47	1	9	10	56																		
	Peterborough	OHL	2	0	0	0	0																		
2003-04	Peterborough	OHL	60	0	8	8	63																		
2004-05	Peterborough	OHL	60	1	11	12	44										14	0	1	1	10				
2005-06	Peterborough	OHL	64	0	10	10	113										19	0	0	0	37				
2006-07	**Edmonton**	**NHL**	**15**	**0**	**0**	**0**	**10**	**0**	**0**	**0**	**2**	**0.0**	**-8**	**0**	**0.0**	**10:06**									
	Milwaukee	AHL	22	0	0	0	6																		
	Stockton Thunder	ECHL	17	0	4	4	24																		
	Wilkes-Barre	AHL	10	0	1	1	2										4	0	1	1	2				
2007-08	**Edmonton**	**NHL**	**2**	**0**	**0**	**0**	**0**	**0**	**0**	**0**	**0**	**0.0**	**-1**	**0**	**0.0**	**2:08**									
	Springfield	AHL	74	0	7	7	62																		
2008-09	Springfield	AHL	63	3	7	10	64																		
2009-10	Springfield	AHL	7	0	0	0	11																		
	Stockton Thunder	ECHL	45	4	7	11	49										15	2	1	3	16				
	NHL Totals		**17**	**0**	**0**	**0**	**10**	**0**	**0**	**0**	**2**	**0.0**		**0**	**0.0**	**9:10**									

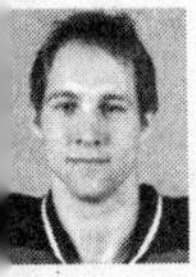

ZAJAC, Travis

(ZAY-jak, TRA-vihs) **N.J.**

Center. Shoots right. 6'3", 200 lbs. Born, Winnipeg, Man., May 13, 1985. New Jersey's 1st choice, 20th overall, in 2004 Entry Draft.

Season	Club	League	GP	G	A	Pts	PIM	PP	SH	GW	S	%	+/-	TF	F%	Min	GP	G	A	Pts	PIM	PP	SH	GW	Min
2002-03	Salmon Arm	BCHL	59	16	36	52	27										11	2	4	6	6				
2003-04	Salmon Arm	BCHL	59	43	69	112	110										14	10	13	23	10				
2004-05	North Dakota	WCHA	45	20	19	39	16																		
2005-06	North Dakota	WCHA	46	18	29	47	20																		
	Albany River Rats	AHL	2	0	1	1	2																		
2006-07	**New Jersey**	**NHL**	**80**	**17**	**25**	**42**	**16**	**6**	**0**	**2**	**134**	**12.7**	**1**	**904**	**46.9**	**16:03**	**11**	**1**	**4**	**5**	**4**	**0**	**0**	**0**	**16:22**
2007-08	**New Jersey**	**NHL**	**82**	**14**	**20**	**34**	**31**	**5**	**0**	**1**	**155**	**9.0**	**-11**	**1032**	**51.2**	**16:44**	**5**	**0**	**1**	**1**	**4**	**0**	**0**	**0**	**13:35**
2008-09	**New Jersey**	**NHL**	**82**	**20**	**42**	**62**	**29**	**5**	**1**	**2**	**185**	**10.8**	**33**	**1287**	**53.1**	**18:39**	**7**	**1**	**3**	**4**	**6**	**0**	**0**	**1**	**17:51**
2009-10	**New Jersey**	**NHL**	**82**	**25**	**42**	**67**	**24**	**6**	**0**	**4**	**210**	**11.9**	**22**	**1373**	**52.9**	**20:13**	**5**	**1**	**1**	**2**	**2**	**0**	**0**	**0**	**21:46**
	NHL Totals		**326**	**76**	**129**	**205**	**100**	**22**	**1**	**9**	**684**	**11.1**		**4596**	**51.4**	**17:55**	**28**	**3**	**9**	**12**	**16**	**0**	**0**	**1**	**17:12**

WCHA All-Rookie Team (2005) • NCAA Championship All-Tournament Team (2005)

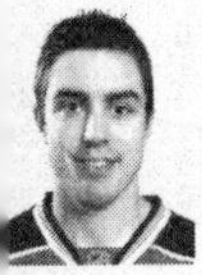

ZALEWSKI, Steven

(zuh-LEH-skee, STEE-vehn) **S.J.**

Center. Shoots left. 6', 195 lbs. Born, Utica, NY, August 20, 1986. San Jose's 5th choice, 153rd overall, in 2004 Entry Draft.

Season	Club	League	GP	G	A	Pts	PIM	PP	SH	GW	S	%	+/-	TF	F%	Min	GP	G	A	Pts	PIM	PP	SH	GW	Min
2003-04	Northwood	High-NY	40	32	34	66	22																		
2004-05	Clarkson Knights	ECAC	39	12	7	19	60																		
2005-06	Clarkson Knights	ECAC	35	9	13	22	50																		
2006-07	Clarkson Knights	ECAC	39	16	18	34	44																		
2007-08	Clarkson Knights	ECAC	38	21	12	33	34																		
	Worcester Sharks	AHL	7	2	4	6	0																		
2008-09	Worcester Sharks	AHL	75	13	26	39	26										12	0	1	1	6				
2009-10	**San Jose**	**NHL**	**3**	**0**	**0**	**0**	**0**	**0**	**0**	**0**	**3**	**0.0**	**-2**	**5**	**40.0**	**8:19**									
	Worcester Sharks	AHL	78	22	40	62	20										11	1	5	6	4				
	NHL Totals		**3**	**0**	**0**	**0**	**0**	**0**	**0**	**0**	**3**	**0.0**		**5**	**40.0**	**8:19**									

ECAC First All-Star Team (2008)

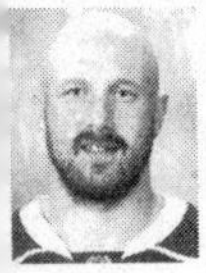

ZANON, Greg

(ZA-nuhn, GREHG) **MIN.**

Defense. Shoots left. 5'11", 201 lbs. Born, Burnaby, B.C., June 5, 1980. Ottawa's 6th choice, 156th overall, in 2000 Entry Draft.

Season	Club	League	GP	G	A	Pts	PIM	PP	SH	GW	S	%	+/-	TF	F%	Min	GP	G	A	Pts	PIM	PP	SH	GW	Min
1995-96	Burnaby Beavers	Minor-BC	49	16	27	43	142																		
1996-97	Victoria Salsa	BCHL	53	4	13	17	124																		
1997-98	Victoria Salsa	BCHL	59	11	21	32	108										7	0	2	2	10				
1998-99	South Surrey	BCHL	59	17	54	71	154																		
99-2000	Nebraska-Omaha	CCHA	42	3	26	29	56																		
2000-01	Nebraska-Omaha	CCHA	39	12	16	28	64																		
2001-02	Nebraska-Omaha	CCHA	41	9	16	25	54																		
2002-03	Nebraska-Omaha	CCHA	32	6	19	25	44																		
2003-04	Milwaukee	AHL	62	4	12	16	59										22	2	6	8	31				
2004-05	Milwaukee	AHL	80	2	17	19	59										7	0	1	1	10				
2005-06	**Nashville**	**NHL**	**4**	**0**	**2**	**2**	**6**	**0**	**0**	**0**	**3**	**0.0**	**0**	**0**	**0.0**	**17:19**									
	Milwaukee	AHL	71	8	27	35	55										21	1	7	8	24				
2006-07	**Nashville**	**NHL**	**66**	**3**	**5**	**8**	**32**	**0**	**0**	**0**	**43**	**7.0**	**16**	**0**	**0.0**	**17:20**	**5**	**0**	**2**	**2**	**2**	**0**	**0**	**0**	**20:44**
	Milwaukee	AHL	2	0	2	2	0																		
2007-08	**Nashville**	**NHL**	**78**	**0**	**5**	**5**	**24**	**0**	**0**	**0**	**38**	**0.0**	**-5**	**0**	**0.0**	**18:28**	**6**	**0**	**2**	**2**	**4**	**0**	**0**	**0**	**18:45**
2008-09	**Nashville**	**NHL**	**82**	**4**	**7**	**11**	**38**	**0**	**0**	**1**	**54**	**7.4**	**8**	**0**	**0.0**	**20:51**									
2009-10	**Minnesota**	**NHL**	**81**	**2**	**13**	**15**	**36**	**0**	**0**	**0**	**59**	**3.4**	**-10**	**1**	**0.0**	**22:22**									
	NHL Totals		**311**	**9**	**32**	**41**	**136**	**0**	**0**	**1**	**197**	**4.6**		**1**	**0.0**	**19:51**	**11**	**0**	**4**	**4**	**6**	**0**	**0**	**0**	**19:39**

CCHA First All-Star Team (2001) • NCAA West Second All-American Team (2001, 2002) • CCHA Second All-Star Team (2002)

Signed as a free agent by **Nashville**, July 9, 2004. Signed as a free agent by **Minnesota**, July 1, 2009.

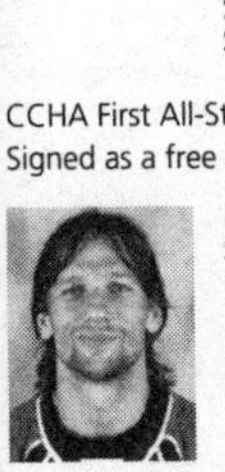

ZEDNIK, Richard

(ZEHD-nihk, RIH-chuhrd)

Right wing. Shoots left. 6', 200 lbs. Born, Banska Bystrica, Czech., January 6, 1976. Washington's 10th choice, 249th overall, in 1994 Entry Draft.

Season	Club	League	GP	G	A	Pts	PIM	PP	SH	GW	S	%	+/-	TF	F%	Min	GP	G	A	Pts	PIM	PP	SH	GW	Min
1993-94	B. Bystrica	Slovak-2	25	3	6	9																			
1994-95	Portland	WHL	65	35	51	86	89										9	5	5	10	20				
1995-96	Portland	WHL	61	44	37	81	154										7	8	4	12	23				
	Washington	**NHL**	**1**	**0**	**0**	**0**	**0**	**0**	**0**	**0**	**0**	**0.0**	**0**												
	Portland Pirates	AHL	1	1	1	2	0										21	4	5	9	26				
1996-97	**Washington**	**NHL**	**11**	**2**	**1**	**3**	**4**	**1**	**0**	**0**	**21**	**9.5**	**-5**												
	Portland Pirates	AHL	56	15	20	35	70										5	1	0	1	6				
1997-98	**Washington**	**NHL**	**65**	**17**	**9**	**26**	**28**	**2**	**0**	**2**	**148**	**11.5**	**-2**				**17**	**7**	**3**	**10**	**16**	**2**	**0**	**0**	
1998-99	**Washington**	**NHL**	**49**	**9**	**8**	**17**	**50**	**1**	**0**	**2**	**115**	**7.8**	**-6**	**2**	**0.0**	**15:08**									
99-2000	**Washington**	**NHL**	**69**	**19**	**16**	**35**	**54**	**1**	**0**	**2**	**179**	**10.6**	**6**	**1**	**100.0**	**15:34**	**5**	**0**	**0**	**0**	**5**	**0**	**0**	**0**	**16:57**
2000-01	**Washington**	**NHL**	**62**	**16**	**19**	**35**	**61**	**4**	**0**	**3**	**155**	**10.3**	**-2**	**1**	**0.0**	**15:32**									
	Montreal	**NHL**	**12**	**3**	**6**	**9**	**10**	**1**	**0**	**0**	**23**	**13.0**	**-2**	**0**	**0.0**	**18:29**									
2001-02	**Montreal**	**NHL**	**82**	**22**	**22**	**44**	**59**	**4**	**0**	**3**	**249**	**8.8**	**-3**	**10**	**30.0**	**17:39**	**4**	**4**	**4**	**8**	**6**	**2**	**0**	**0**	**21:19**
2002-03	**Montreal**	**NHL**	**80**	**31**	**19**	**50**	**79**	**9**	**0**	**2**	**250**	**12.4**	**4**	**10**	**30.0**	**18:25**									
2003-04	**Montreal**	**NHL**	**81**	**26**	**24**	**50**	**63**	**7**	**0**	**9**	**218**	**11.9**	**5**	**6**	**50.0**	**17:30**	**11**	**3**	**3**	**6**	**2**	**0**	**0**	**1**	**18:52**
2004-05	HKm Zvolen	Slovakia	36	15	19	34	56										17	9	10	19	12				
2005-06	**Montreal**	**NHL**	**67**	**16**	**14**	**30**	**48**	**6**	**0**	**4**	**161**	**9.9**	**-2**	**6**	**16.7**	**15:46**	**6**	**2**	**0**	**2**	**4**	**1**	**0**	**0**	**15:13**
	Slovakia	Olympics	6	1	0	1	12																		
2006-07	**Washington**	**NHL**	**32**	**6**	**12**	**18**	**16**	**1**	**0**	**1**	**68**	**8.8**	**-4**	**3**	**33.3**	**15:42**									
	NY Islanders	**NHL**	**10**	**1**	**2**	**3**	**2**	**0**	**0**	**0**	**15**	**6.7**	**-2**	**1**	**0.0**	**12:51**	**5**	**0**	**0**	**0**	**8**	**0**	**0**	**0**	**10:45**
2007-08	**Florida**	**NHL**	**54**	**15**	**11**	**26**	**43**	**6**	**0**	**5**	**140**	**10.7**	**-5**	**2**	**0.0**	**17:35**									
2008-09	**Florida**	**NHL**	**70**	**17**	**16**	**33**	**46**	**3**	**0**	**4**	**153**	**11.1**	**2**	**1**	**0.0**	**15:35**									

			Regular Season														Playoffs								
Season	Club	League	GP	G	A	Pts	PIM	PP	SH	GW	S	%	+/-	TF	F%	Min	GP	G	A	Pts	PIM	PP	SH	GW	M
2009-10	Yaroslavl	Rus-KHL	37	6	12	18	56	....	....	....	....	....	....	....	....	....	17	3	5	8	22	....	....	....	.
	Slovakia	Olympics	7	2	4	6	6	....	....	....	....	....	....	....	....	....	....	....	....	....	....	....	....	....	.
	NHL Totals		**745**	**200**	**179**	**379**	**563**	**46**	**0**	**37**	**1895**	**10.6**		**43**	**27.9**	**16:34**	**48**	**16**	**10**	**26**	**41**	**5**	**0**	**1**	**16:5**

WHL West Second All-Star Team (1996)

Traded to **Montreal** by **Washington** with Jan Bulis and Washington's 1st round choice (Alexander Perezhogin) in 2001 Entry Draft for Trevor Linden, Dainius Zubrus and New Jersey's 2nd round choice (previously acquired, later traded to Tampa Bay – Tampa Bay selected Andreas Holmqvist) in 2001 Entry Draft, March 13, 2001. Signed as a free agent by **Zvolen** (Slovakia), October 7, 2004. Traded to **Washington** by **Montreal** for Washington's 3rd round choice (Olivier Fortier) in 2007 Entry Draft, July 12, 2006. Traded to **NY Islanders** by **Washington** for NY Islanders' 2nd round choice (Theo Ruth) ir 2007 Entry Draft, February 26, 2007. Signed as a free agent by **Florida**, July 1, 2007. Signed as a free agent by **Yaroslavl** (Russia-KHL), April 30, 2009.

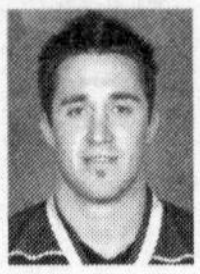

ZEILER, John

(ZIGH-luhr, JAWN) **L.A**

Right wing. Shoots right. 6', 203 lbs. Born, Jefferson Hills, PA, November 21, 1982. Phoenix's 7th choice, 132nd overall, in 2002 Entry Draft.

99-2000	Pittsburgh	PAHA	27	17	15	32	94	....	....	....	....	....	....	....	....	....	....	....	....	....	....	....	....	....	.
2000-01	Sioux City	USHL	56	8	20	28	45	....	....	....	....	....	....	....	....	....	2	0	0	0	26	....	....	....	.
2001-02	Sioux City	USHL	60	23	27	50	116	....	....	....	....	....	....	....	....	....	12	2	3	5	25	....	....	....	.
2002-03	St. Lawrence	ECAC	37	10	17	27	28	....	....	....	....	....	....	....	....	....	....	....	....	....	....	....	....	....	.
2003-04	St. Lawrence	ECAC	41	8	*28	36	42	....	....	....	....	....	....	....	....	....	....	....	....	....	....	....	....	....	.
2004-05	St. Lawrence	ECAC	38	9	23	32	42	....	....	....	....	....	....	....	....	....	....	....	....	....	....	....	....	....	.
2005-06	St. Lawrence	ECAC	28	13	15	28	28	....	....	....	....	....	....	....	....	....	....	....	....	....	....	....	....	....	.
	San Antonio	AHL	8	0	1	1	10	....	....	....	....	....	....	....	....	....	....	....	....	....	....	....	....	....	.
	Lubbock	CHL	4	2	0	2	16	....	....	....	....	....	....	....	....	....	....	....	....	....	....	....	....	....	.
2006-07	Manchester	AHL	56	12	16	28	70	....	....	....	....	....	....	....	....	....	16	3	2	5	14	....	....	....	.
	Los Angeles	**NHL**	**23**	**1**	**2**	**3**	**22**	**0**	**0**	**0**	**12**	**8.3**	**–2**	**22**	**40.9**	**8:36**	....	....	....	....	....	....	....	....	.
2007-08	**Los Angeles**	**NHL**	**36**	**0**	**1**	**1**	**23**	**0**	**0**	**0**	**18**	**0.0**	**–6**	**31**	**38.7**	**8:29**	....	....	....	....	....	....	....	....	.
	Manchester	AHL	45	6	5	11	40	....	....	....	....	....	....	....	....	....	4	0	2	2	8	....	....	....	.
2008-09	**Los Angeles**	**NHL**	**27**	**0**	**1**	**1**	**42**	**0**	**0**	**0**	**3**	**0.0**	**–2**	**5**	**60.0**	**6:33**	....	....	....	....	....	....	....	....	.
	Manchester	AHL	2	0	1	1	4	....	....	....	....	....	....	....	....	....	....	....	....	....	....	....	....	....	.
2009-10	Manchester	AHL	65	11	9	20	31	....	....	....	....	....	....	....	....	....	16	4	3	7	4	....	....	....	.
	NHL Totals		**86**	**1**	**4**	**5**	**87**	**0**	**0**	**0**	**33**	**3.0**		**58**	**41.4**	**7:54**	....	....	....	....	....	....	....	....	.

ECAC All-Rookie Team (2003)

Signed as a free agent by **San Antonio** (AHL), March 18, 2006. Signed as a free agent by **Los Angeles**, February 17, 2007. • Missed majority of 2008-09 season recovering from pre-season groin injury ar as a healthy reserve.

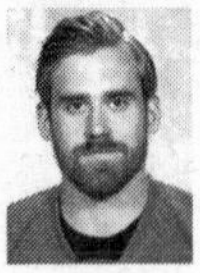

ZETTERBERG, Henrik

(ZEH-tuhr-buhrg, HEHN-rihk) **DE**

Left wing. Shoots left. 5'11", 195 lbs. Born, Njurunda, Sweden, October 9, 1980. Detroit's 4th choice, 210th overall, in 1999 Entry Draft.

1997-98	Timra IK Jr.	Swe-Jr.	18	9	5	14	4	....	....	....	....	....	....	....	....	....	....	....	....	....	....	....	....	....	.
	Timra IK	Sweden-2	16	1	2	3	4	....	....	....	....	....	....	....	....	....	4	0	1	1	0	....	....	....	.
1998-99	Timra IK	Sweden-2	37	15	13	28	2	....	....	....	....	....	....	....	....	....	4	2	1	3	2	....	....	....	.
99-2000	Timra IK	Sweden-2	32	20	14	34	20	....	....	....	....	....	....	....	....	....	10	10	4	14	4	....	....	....	.
2000-01	Timra IK	Sweden	47	15	31	46	24	....	....	....	....	....	....	....	....	....	....	....	....	....	....	....	....	....	.
2001-02	Timra IK	Sweden	48	10	22	32	20	....	....	....	....	....	....	....	....	....	....	....	....	....	....	....	....	....	.
	Sweden	Olympics	4	0	1	1	0	....	....	....	....	....	....	....	....	....	....	....	....	....	....	....	....	....	.
2002-03	**Detroit**	**NHL**	**79**	**22**	**22**	**44**	**8**	**5**	**1**	**4**	**135**	**16.3**	**6**	**401**	**46.1**	**16:19**	**4**	**1**	**0**	**1**	**0**	**0**	**0**	**0**	**18:**
2003-04	**Detroit**	**NHL**	**61**	**15**	**28**	**43**	**14**	**7**	**1**	**2**	**137**	**10.9**	**15**	**627**	**45.6**	**18:15**	**12**	**2**	**2**	**4**	**4**	**0**	**0**	**0**	**17:**
2004-05	Timra IK	Sweden	50	19	31	*50	24	....	....	....	....	....	....	....	....	....	7	6	2	8	2	....	....	....	.
2005-06	**Detroit**	**NHL**	**77**	**39**	**46**	**85**	**30**	**17**	**1**	**9**	**270**	**14.4**	**29**	**583**	**50.3**	**18:57**	**6**	**6**	**0**	**6**	**2**	**4**	**0**	**0**	**21:**
	Sweden	Olympics	8	3	3	6	0	....	....	....	....	....	....	....	....	....	....	....	....	....	....	....	....	....	.
2006-07	**Detroit**	**NHL**	**63**	**33**	**35**	**68**	**36**	**11**	**1**	***10**	**224**	**14.7**	**26**	**888**	**52.5**	**20:50**	**18**	**6**	**8**	**14**	**12**	**3**	**0**	**1**	**22:**
2007-08 ♦	**Detroit**	**NHL**	**75**	**43**	**49**	**92**	**34**	**16**	**1**	**7**	**358**	**12.0**	**30**	**1210**	**55.0**	**22:04**	**22**	***13**	**14**	***27**	**16**	**4**	***2**	**4**	**22:**
2008-09	**Detroit**	**NHL**	**77**	**31**	**42**	**73**	**36**	**12**	**2**	**5**	**309**	**10.0**	**13**	**1189**	**53.3**	**19:53**	**23**	**11**	**13**	**24**	**13**	**4**	**0**	**0**	**22:**
2009-10	**Detroit**	**NHL**	**74**	**23**	**47**	**70**	**26**	**3**	**0**	**6**	**309**	**7.4**	**12**	**1098**	**49.5**	**20:04**	**12**	**7**	**8**	**15**	**6**	**2**	**0**	**2**	**20:**
	Sweden	Olympics	4	1	0	1	2	....	....	....	....	....	....	....	....	....	....	....	....	....	....	....	....	....	.
	NHL Totals		**506**	**206**	**269**	**475**	**184**	**71**	**7**	**43**	**1742**	**11.8**		**5996**	**51.3**	**19:27**	**97**	**46**	**45**	**91**	**53**	**17**	**2**	**7**	**21:**

Swedish Elite League Rookie of the Year (2001) • NHL All-Rookie Team (2003) • NHL Second All-Star Team (2008) • Conn Smythe Trophy (2008)

Signed as a free agent by **Timra** (Sweden), September 20, 2004.

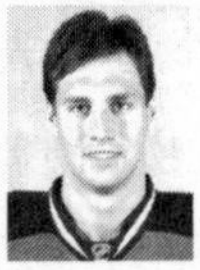

ZHARKOV, Vladimir

(zhar-KAWV, vla-DIH-meer) **N.**

Right wing. Shoots left. 6'1", 200 lbs. Born, Elektrostal, USSR, January 10, 1988. New Jersey's 4th choice, 77th overall, in 2006 Entry Draft.

2004-05	CSKA Moscow 2	Russia-3	STATISTICS NOT AVAILABLE																						
2005-06	CSKA Moscow	Russia	4	0	1	1	4	....	....	....	....	....	....	....	....	....	1	0	0	0	0	....	....	....	.
	CSKA Moscow 2	Russia-3	48	17	22	39	86	....	....	....	....	....	....	....	....	....	....	....	....	....	....	....	....	....	.
2006-07	CSKA Moscow	Russia	47	4	1	5	18	....	....	....	....	....	....	....	....	....	12	0	1	1	2	....	....	....	.
2007-08	CSKA Moscow	Russia	30	5	2	7	6	....	....	....	....	....	....	....	....	....	....	....	....	....	....	....	....	....	.
	CSKA Moscow 2	Russia-3	4	3	4	7	4	....	....	....	....	....	....	....	....	....	12	8	7	15	8	....	....	....	.
2008-09	Lowell Devils	AHL	69	11	23	34	26	....	....	....	....	....	....	....	....	....	....	....	....	....	....	....	....	....	.
2009-10	**New Jersey**	**NHL**	**40**	**0**	**10**	**10**	**8**	**0**	**0**	**0**	**54**	**0.0**	**2**	**4**	**25.0**	**11:26**	....	....	....	....	....	....	....	....	.
	Lowell Devils	AHL	23	6	15	21	6	....	....	....	....	....	....	....	....	....	....	....	....	....	....	....	....	....	.
	NHL Totals		**40**	**0**	**10**	**10**	**8**	**0**	**0**	**0**	**54**	**0.0**		**4**	**25.0**	**11:26**	....	....	....	....	....	....	....	....	.

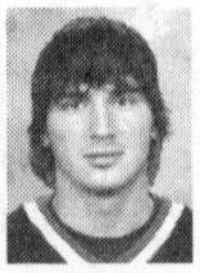

ZHERDEV, Nikolai

(ZHAIR-dehv, NIH-koh-ligh) **PH**

Wing. Shoots right. 6'2", 203 lbs. Born, Kiev, USSR, November 5, 1984. Columbus' 1st choice, 4th overall, in 2003 Entry Draft.

99-2000	Elektrostal 2	Russia-3	21	10	7	17	26	....	....	....	....	....	....	....	....	....	7	0	0	0	0	....	....	....	.
2000-01	Elektrostal	Russia-2	18	5	8	13	12	....	....	....	....	....	....	....	....	....	....	....	....	....	....	....	....	....	.
	Russia	Exhib.	17	10	11	21	17	....	....	....	....	....	....	....	....	....	....	....	....	....	....	....	....	....	.
2001-02	Elektrostal	Russia-2	53	13	15	28	62	....	....	....	....	....	....	....	....	....	....	....	....	....	....	....	....	....	.
	Elektrostal 2	Russia-3	1	1	0	1	4	....	....	....	....	....	....	....	....	....	....	....	....	....	....	....	....	....	.
2002-03	CSKA Moscow	Russia	44	12	12	24	34	....	....	....	....	....	....	....	....	....	....	....	....	....	....	....	....	....	.
2003-04	CSKA Moscow	Russia	20	2	2	4	14	....	....	....	....	....	....	....	....	....	....	....	....	....	....	....	....	....	.
	Columbus	**NHL**	**57**	**13**	**21**	**34**	**54**	**5**	**0**	**1**	**137**	**9.5**	**–11**	**9**	**11.1**	**16:11**	....	....	....	....	....	....	....	....	.
2004-05	CSKA Moscow	Russia	51	19	21	40	62	....	....	....	....	....	....	....	....	....	....	....	....	....	....	....	....	....	.
2005-06	**Columbus**	**NHL**	**73**	**27**	**27**	**54**	**50**	**10**	**0**	**0**	**194**	**13.9**	**–13**	**20**	**10.0**	**17:36**	....	....	....	....	....	....	....	....	.
	Syracuse Crunch	AHL	2	1	0	1	0	....	....	....	....	....	....	....	....	....	....	....	....	....	....	....	....	....	.
2006-07	Mytischi	Russia	8	2	4	6	10	....	....	....	....	....	....	....	....	....	....	....	....	....	....	....	....	....	.
	Columbus	**NHL**	**71**	**10**	**22**	**32**	**26**	**3**	**0**	**2**	**164**	**6.1**	**–19**	**17**	**23.5**	**16:13**	....	....	....	....	....	....	....	....	.
2007-08	**Columbus**	**NHL**	**82**	**26**	**35**	**61**	**34**	**7**	**0**	**3**	**254**	**10.2**	**–9**	**29**	**41.4**	**19:22**	....	....	....	....	....	....	....	....	.
2008-09	**NY Rangers**	**NHL**	**82**	**23**	**35**	**58**	**39**	**4**	**1**	**3**	**219**	**10.5**	**6**	**11**	**9.1**	**16:50**	**7**	**0**	**0**	**0**	**2**	**0**	**0**	**0**	**12:**
2009-10	Mytischi	Rus-KHL	52	13	26	39	79	....	....	....	....	....	....	....	....	....	4	0	1	1	4	....	....	....	.
	NHL Totals		**365**	**99**	**140**	**239**	**203**	**29**	**1**	**9**	**968**	**10.2**		**86**	**23.3**	**17:20**	**7**	**0**	**0**	**0**	**2**	**0**	**0**	**0**	**12:**

Signed as a free agent by **CSKA Moscow** (Russia), July 27, 2004. Signed as a free agent by **Mystichi** (Russia), July 20, 2006. Traded to **NY Rangers** by **Columbus** with Dan Fritsche for Fedor Tyutin and Christian Backman, July 2, 2008. Signed as a free agent by **Mytischi** (Russia-KHL), September 16, 2009. Signed as a free agent by **Philadelphia**, July 9, 2010.

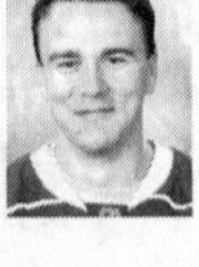

ZIDLICKY, Marek

(zihd-LIH-kee, MAIR-ehk) **MI**

Defense. Shoots right. 5'11", 190 lbs. Born, Most, Czech., February 3, 1977. NY Rangers' 6th choice, 176th overall, in 2001 Entry Draft.

1994-95	HC Kladno	CzRep	30	2	2	4	38	....	....	....	....	....	....	....	....	....	11	1	1	2	10	....	....	....	.
1995-96	HC Poldi Kladno	CzRep	37	4	5	9	74	....	....	....	....	....	....	....	....	....	7	1	1	2	8	....	....	....	.
1996-97	HC Poldi Kladno	CzRep	49	5	16	21	60	....	....	....	....	....	....	....	....	....	2	0	0	0	0	....	....	....	.
1997-98	Kladno	CzRep	51	2	13	15	121	....	....	....	....	....	....	....	....	....	....	....	....	....	....	....	....	....	.
1998-99	Kladno	CzRep	50	10	12	22	94	....	....	....	....	....	....	....	....	....	....	....	....	....	....	....	....	....	.
99-2000	HIFK Helsinki	Finland	47	4	16	20	66	....	....	....	....	....	....	....	....	....	9	3	2	5	24	....	....	....	.
	HIFK Helsinki	EuroHL	4	2	2	4	10	....	....	....	....	....	....	....	....	....	1	0	0	0	0	....	....	....	.
2000-01	HIFK Helsinki	Finland	51	12	25	37	146	....	....	....	....	....	....	....	....	....	5	0	1	1	6	....	....	....	.
2001-02	HIFK Helsinki	Finland	56	11	29	40	107	....	....	....	....	....	....	....	....	....	....	....	....	....	....	....	....	....	.
2002-03	HIFK Helsinki	Finland	54	10	37	47	79	....	....	....	....	....	....	....	....	....	4	0	0	0	4	....	....	....	.
2003-04	**Nashville**	**NHL**	**82**	**14**	**39**	**53**	**82**	**9**	**0**	**4**	**143**	**9.8**	**–16**	**0**	**0.0**	**20:02**	**1**	**0**	**0**	**0**	**0**	**0**	**0**	**0**	**2:**
2004-05	HIFK Helsinki	Finland	49	11	20	31	91	....	....	....	....	....	....	....	....	....	5	0	3	3	14	....	....	....	.

			Regular Season														Playoffs								
Season	Club	League	GP	G	A	Pts	PIM	PP	SH	GW	S	%	+/-	TF	F%	Min	GP	G	A	Pts	PIM	PP	SH	GW	Min
2005-06	**Nashville**	**NHL**	**67**	**12**	**37**	**49**	**82**	**10**	**0**	**1**	**113**	**10.6**	**8**	**0**	**0.0**	**20:04**	**2**	**0**	**1**	**1**	**2**	**0**	**0**	**0**	**15:19**
	Czech Republic	Olympics	7	4	1	5	16	....	....	....	....	....	....	....	....	....	....	....	....	....	....	....	....	....	....
2006-07	**Nashville**	**NHL**	**79**	**4**	**26**	**30**	**72**	**2**	**0**	**1**	**114**	**3.5**	**8**	**0**	**0.0**	**19:43**	**5**	**0**	**2**	**2**	**4**	**0**	**0**	**0**	**19:19**
2007-08	**Nashville**	**NHL**	**79**	**5**	**38**	**43**	**63**	**4**	**0**	**0**	**122**	**4.1**	**–5**	**0**	**0.0**	**20:50**	**6**	**0**	**3**	**3**	**8**	**0**	**0**	**0**	**19:04**
2008-09	**Minnesota**	**NHL**	**76**	**12**	**30**	**42**	**76**	**10**	**0**	**3**	**147**	**8.2**	**–12**	**0**	**0.0**	**22:07**	....	....	....	....	....	....	....	....	....
2009-10	**Minnesota**	**NHL**	**78**	**6**	**37**	**43**	**67**	**4**	**0**	**3**	**116**	**5.2**	**–16**	**0**	**0.0**	**24:10**	....	....	....	....	....	....	....	....	....
	Czech Republic	Olympics	5	0	5	5	2	....	....	....	....	....	....	....	....	....	....	....	....	....	....	....	....	....	....
	NHL Totals		**461**	**53**	**207**	**260**	**442**	**39**	**0**	**12**	**755**	**7.0**		**0**	**0.0**	**21:10**	**14**	**0**	**6**	**6**	**14**	**0**	**0**	**0**	**17:25**

Traded to **Nashville** by **NY Rangers** with Rem Murray and Tomas Kloucek for Mike Dunham, December 12, 2002. Signed as a free agent by **HIFK Helsinki** (Finland), September 17, 2004. Traded to **Minnesota** by **Nashville** for Ryan Jones and Minnesota's 2nd round choice (Charles-Olivier Roussel) in 2009 Entry Draft, July 1, 2008.

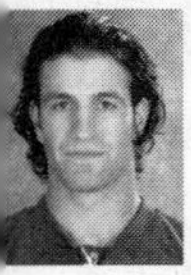

ZIGOMANIS, Mike

(zih-goh-MAN-ihs, MIGHK) **TOR.**

Center. Shoots right. 6', 200 lbs. Born, Toronto, Ont., January 17, 1981. Carolina's 2nd choice, 46th overall, in 2001 Entry Draft.

1996-97	Wexford Raiders	MTHL	40	37	48	85	23	....	....	....	....	....	....	....	....	....	....	....	....	....	....	....	....	....	....
	Wexford Raiders	MTJHL	8	2	5	7	2	....	....	....	....	....	....	....	....	....	....	....	....	....	....	....	....	....	....
1997-98	Kingston	OHL	62	23	51	74	30	....	....	....	....	....	....	....	....	....	12	1	6	7	2	....	....	....	....
1998-99	Kingston	OHL	67	29	56	85	36	....	....	....	....	....	....	....	....	....	5	1	7	8	2	....	....	....	....
99-2000	Kingston	OHL	59	40	54	94	49	....	....	....	....	....	....	....	....	....	5	0	4	4	0	....	....	....	....
2000-01	Kingston	OHL	52	40	37	77	44	....	....	....	....	....	....	....	....	....	....	....	....	....	....	....	....	....	....
2001-02	Lowell	AHL	79	18	30	48	24	....	....	....	....	....	....	....	....	....	5	1	1	2	2	....	....	....	....
2002-03	**Carolina**	**NHL**	**19**	**2**	**1**	**3**	**0**	**1**	**1**	**0**	**19**	**10.5**	**–4**	**147**	**59.2**	**9:43**	....	....	....	....	....	....	....	....	....
	Lowell	AHL	38	13	18	31	19	....	....	....	....	....	....	....	....	....	....	....	....	....	....	....	....	....	....
2003-04	**Carolina**	**NHL**	**17**	**0**	**3**	**3**	**2**	**0**	**0**	**0**	**13**	**0.0**	**–1**	**108**	**53.7**	**8:37**	....	....	....	....	....	....	....	....	....
	Lowell	AHL	61	17	35	52	56	....	....	....	....	....	....	....	....	....	....	....	....	....	....	....	....	....	....
2004-05	Lowell	AHL	76	29	31	60	71	....	....	....	....	....	....	....	....	....	11	4	7	11	8	....	....	....	....
2005-06	**Carolina**	**NHL**	**21**	**1**	**0**	**1**	**4**	**0**	**0**	**0**	**16**	**6.3**	**1**	**72**	**50.0**	**9:25**	....	....	....	....	....	....	....	....	....
	Lowell	AHL	11	6	7	13	19	....	....	....	....	....	....	....	....	....	....	....	....	....	....	....	....	....	....
	St. Louis	**NHL**	**2**	**0**	**0**	**0**	**0**	**0**	**0**	**0**	**1**	**0.0**	**0**	**1**	**100.0**	**7:39**	....	....	....	....	....	....	....	....	....
	Peoria Rivermen	AHL	28	10	18	28	16	....	....	....	....	....	....	....	....	....	4	2	4	6	6	....	....	....	....
2006-07	**Phoenix**	**NHL**	**75**	**14**	**9**	**23**	**46**	**2**	**1**	**0**	**142**	**9.9**	**–8**	**1010**	**56.2**	**14:53**	....	....	....	....	....	....	....	....	....
2007-08	**Phoenix**	**NHL**	**33**	**2**	**1**	**3**	**6**	**0**	**0**	**0**	**35**	**5.7**	**–7**	**328**	**59.8**	**12:24**	....	....	....	....	....	....	....	....	....
	San Antonio	AHL	27	10	15	25	14	....	....	....	....	....	....	....	....	....	7	0	5	5	10	....	....	....	....
2008-09 •	**Pittsburgh**	**NHL**	**22**	**2**	**4**	**6**	**27**	**0**	**0**	**0**	**23**	**8.7**	**–2**	**251**	**63.0**	**11:26**	....	....	....	....	....	....	....	....	....
2009-10	Toronto Marlies	AHL	7	0	13	13	0	....	....	....	....	....	....	....	....	....	....	....	....	....	....	....	....	....	....
	Djurgarden	Sweden	27	4	7	11	12	....	....	....	....	....	....	....	....	....	5	0	0	0	8	....	....	....	....
	NHL Totals		**189**	**21**	**18**	**39**	**85**	**3**	**2**	**0**	**249**	**8.4**		**1917**	**57.6**	**12:17**	....	....	....	....	....	....	....	....	....

• Re-entered NHL Entry Draft. Originally Buffalo's 4th choice, 64th overall, in 1999 Entry Draft.

Traded to **St. Louis** by **Carolina** with Jesse Boulerice, the rights to Magnus Kahnberg, Carolina's 1st round choice (later traded to New Jersey - New Jersey selected Matthew Corrente) in 2006 Entry Draft, Toronto's 4th round choice (previously acquired, St. Louis selected Reto Berra) in 2006 Entry Draft and Chicago's 4th round choice (previously acquired, St. Louis selected Cade Fairchild) in 2007 Entry Draft for Doug Weight and Erkki Rajamaki, January 30, 2006. Signed as a free agent by **Phoenix**, July 21, 2006. Traded to **Pittsburgh** by **Phoenix** for future considerations, October 9, 2008. • Missed majority of 2008-09 season recovering from shoulder surgery. Signed to a PTO (professional tryout) contract by **Toronto** (AHL), October 19, 2009. Signed as a free agent by **Djurgarden** (Sweden), November 10, 2009. Signed as a free agent by **Toronto**, July 15, 2010.

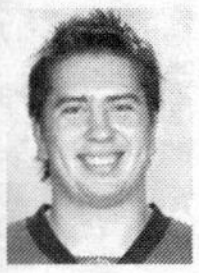

ZUBOV, Ilya

(ZOO-bahf, IHL-yah) **OTT.**

Center. Shoots left. 6', 211 lbs. Born, Chelyabinsk, USSR, February 14, 1987. Ottawa's 4th choice, 98th overall, in 2005 Entry Draft.

2003-04	Chelyabinsk	Russia-2	33	7	7	14	16	....	....	....	....	....	....	....	....	....	8	2	1	3	2	....	....	....	....
2004-05	Chelyabinsk	Russia-2	40	9	8	17	36	....	....	....	....	....	....	....	....	....	....	....	....	....	....	....	....	....	....
	Chelyabinsk 2	Russia-3	1	0	0	0	0	....	....	....	....	....	....	....	....	....	....	....	....	....	....	....	....	....	....
2005-06	Spartak 2	Russia-3	1	0	1	1	4	....	....	....	....	....	....	....	....	....	....	....	....	....	....	....	....	....	....
	Spartak Moscow	Russia	43	4	8	12	12	....	....	....	....	....	....	....	....	....	3	2	2	4	0	....	....	....	....
2006-07	Mytischi	Russia	16	1	1	2	4	....	....	....	....	....	....	....	....	....	....	....	....	....	....	....	....	....	....
	Ufa	Russia	26	3	7	10	4	....	....	....	....	....	....	....	....	....	8	2	3	5	2	....	....	....	....
2007-08	**Ottawa**	**NHL**	**1**	**0**	**0**	**0**	**0**	**0**	**0**	**0**	**0**	**0.0**	**0**	**5**	**40.0**	**14:38**	....	....	....	....	....	....	....	....	....
	Binghamton	AHL	74	15	23	38	18	....	....	....	....	....	....	....	....	....	....	....	....	....	....	....	....	....	....
2008-09	**Ottawa**	**NHL**	**10**	**0**	**2**	**2**	**0**	**0**	**0**	**0**	**11**	**0.0**	**–1**	**1**	**0.0**	**10:17**	....	....	....	....	....	....	....	....	....
	Binghamton	AHL	63	14	38	52	26	....	....	....	....	....	....	....	....	....	....	....	....	....	....	....	....	....	....
2009-10	Binghamton	AHL	1	0	0	0	2	....	....	....	....	....	....	....	....	....	....	....	....	....	....	....	....	....	....
	Ufa	Rus-KHL	25	3	3	6	6	....	....	....	....	....	....	....	....	....	....	....	....	....	....	....	....	....	....
	CSKA Moscow	Rus-KHL	6	1	0	1	2	....	....	....	....	....	....	....	....	....	3	1	1	2	2	....	....	....	....
	NHL Totals		**11**	**0**	**2**	**2**	**0**	**0**	**0**	**0**	**11**	**0.0**		**6**	**33.3**	**10:40**	....	....	....	....	....	....	....	....	....

• Loaned to **Ufa** (Russia-KHL) by **Ottawa** for remainder of 2009-10 season, October 20, 2009. Traded to **CSKA Moscow** (Russia-KHL) by **Ufa** (Russia-KHL) with future considerations for Peter Schastlivy, April 3, 2010.

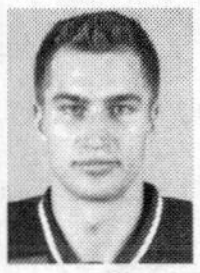

ZUBRUS, Dainius

(ZOO-bruhs, DAYN-ihs) **N.J.**

Center/Right wing. Shoots left. 6'5", 225 lbs. Born, Elektrenai, USSR, June 16, 1978. Philadelphia's 1st choice, 15th overall, in 1996 Entry Draft.

1995-96	Pembroke	CJHL	28	19	13	32	73	....	....	....	....	....	....	....	....	....	....	....	....	....	....	....	....	....	....
	Caledon	MTJHL	7	3	7	10	2	....	....	....	....	....	....	....	....	....	17	11	12	23	4	....	....	....	....
1996-97	**Philadelphia**	**NHL**	**68**	**8**	**13**	**21**	**22**	**1**	**0**	**2**	**71**	**11.3**	**3**	....	....	....	**19**	**5**	**4**	**9**	**12**	**1**	**0**	**1**	....
1997-98	**Philadelphia**	**NHL**	**69**	**8**	**25**	**33**	**42**	**1**	**0**	**5**	**101**	**7.9**	**29**	....	....	....	**5**	**0**	**1**	**1**	**2**	**0**	**0**	**0**	....
1998-99	**Philadelphia**	**NHL**	**63**	**3**	**5**	**8**	**25**	**0**	**1**	**0**	**49**	**6.1**	**–5**	**29**	**51.7**	**11:00**	....	....	....	....	....	....	....	....	....
	Montreal	**NHL**	**17**	**3**	**5**	**8**	**4**	**0**	**0**	**1**	**31**	**9.7**	**–3**	**2**	**50.0**	**16:53**	....	....	....	....	....	....	....	....	....
99-2000	**Montreal**	**NHL**	**73**	**14**	**28**	**42**	**54**	**3**	**0**	**1**	**139**	**10.1**	**–1**	**212**	**39.2**	**17:37**	....	....	....	....	....	....	....	....	....
2000-01	**Montreal**	**NHL**	**49**	**12**	**12**	**24**	**30**	**3**	**0**	**0**	**70**	**17.1**	**–7**	**190**	**41.1**	**18:30**	....	....	....	....	....	....	....	....	....
	Washington	**NHL**	**12**	**1**	**1**	**2**	**7**	**1**	**0**	**0**	**13**	**7.7**	**–4**	**0**	**0.0**	**13:05**	**6**	**0**	**0**	**0**	**2**	**0**	**0**	**0**	**17:24**
2001-02	**Washington**	**NHL**	**71**	**17**	**26**	**43**	**38**	**4**	**0**	**3**	**138**	**12.3**	**5**	**131**	**37.4**	**18:52**	....	....	....	....	....	....	....	....	....
2002-03	**Washington**	**NHL**	**63**	**13**	**22**	**35**	**43**	**2**	**0**	**0**	**104**	**12.5**	**15**	**565**	**50.3**	**16:26**	**6**	**2**	**2**	**4**	**4**	**1**	**0**	**0**	**21:30**
2003-04	**Washington**	**NHL**	**54**	**12**	**15**	**27**	**38**	**6**	**1**	**2**	**115**	**10.4**	**–16**	**916**	**48.0**	**19:32**	....	....	....	....	....	....	....	....	....
2004-05	Lada Togliatti	Russia	42	8	11	19	85	....	....	....	....	....	....	....	....	....	10	3	1	4	22	....	....	....	....
2005-06	**Washington**	**NHL**	**71**	**23**	**34**	**57**	**84**	**13**	**0**	**5**	**181**	**12.7**	**3**	**1118**	**50.3**	**20:22**	....	....	....	....	....	....	....	....	....
2006-07	**Washington**	**NHL**	**60**	**20**	**32**	**52**	**50**	**9**	**0**	**4**	**127**	**15.7**	**–16**	**1096**	**49.7**	**19:51**	....	....	....	....	....	....	....	....	....
	Buffalo	**NHL**	**19**	**4**	**4**	**8**	**12**	**1**	**0**	**0**	**31**	**12.9**	**–3**	**69**	**39.1**	**18:22**	**15**	**0**	**8**	**8**	**8**	**0**	**0**	**0**	**18:38**
2007-08	**New Jersey**	**NHL**	**82**	**13**	**25**	**38**	**38**	**4**	**0**	**2**	**128**	**10.2**	**2**	**144**	**55.6**	**15:42**	**5**	**0**	**1**	**1**	**8**	**0**	**0**	**0**	**16:18**
2008-09	**New Jersey**	**NHL**	**82**	**15**	**25**	**40**	**69**	**1**	**0**	**3**	**130**	**11.5**	**6**	**923**	**51.3**	**15:16**	**7**	**0**	**1**	**1**	**10**	**0**	**0**	**0**	**13:57**
2009-10	**New Jersey**	**NHL**	**51**	**10**	**17**	**27**	**28**	**1**	**0**	**4**	**86**	**11.6**	**4**	**400**	**48.5**	**16:29**	**5**	**1**	**0**	**1**	**8**	**0**	**0**	**1**	**16:25**
	NHL Totals		**904**	**176**	**289**	**465**	**584**	**50**	**2**	**32**	**1514**	**11.6**		**5795**	**48.9**	**17:07**	**68**	**8**	**17**	**25**	**54**	**2**	**0**	**2**	**17:36**

Traded to **Montreal** by **Philadelphia** with Philadelphia's 2nd round choice (Matt Carkner) in 1999 Entry Draft and NY Islanders' 6th round choice (previously acquired, Montreal selected Scott Selig) in 2000 Entry Draft for Mark Recchi, March 10, 1999. Traded to **Washington** by **Montreal** with Trevor Linden and New Jersey's 2nd round choice (previously acquired, later traded to Tampa Bay – Tampa Bay selected Andreas Holmqvist) in 2001 Entry Draft for Richard Zednik, Jan Bulis and Washington's 1st round choice (Alexander Perezhogin) in 2001 Entry Draft, March 13, 2001. Signed as a free agent by **Togliatti** (Russia), July 1, 2004. Traded to **Buffalo** by **Washington** with Timo Helbling for Jiri Novotny and Buffalo's 1st round choice (later traded to San Jose - San Jose selected Nicholas Petrecki) in 2007 Entry Draft, February 27, 2007. Signed as a free agent by **New Jersey**, July 3, 2007.

NHL Goaltenders

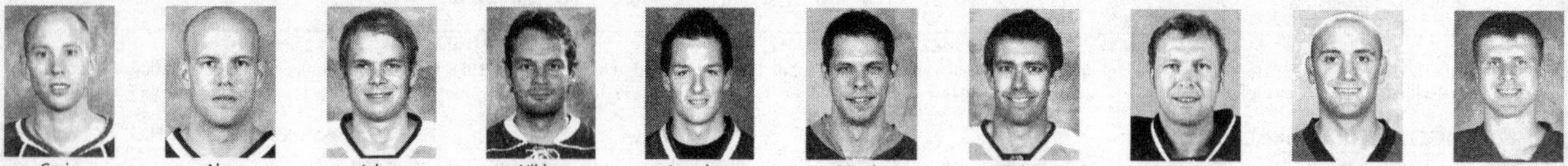

Craig Anderson · Alex Auld · Johan Backlund · Niklas Backstrom · Jonathan Bernier · Martin Biron · Brian Boucher · Martin Brodeur · Mike Brodeur · Ilya Bryzgalov

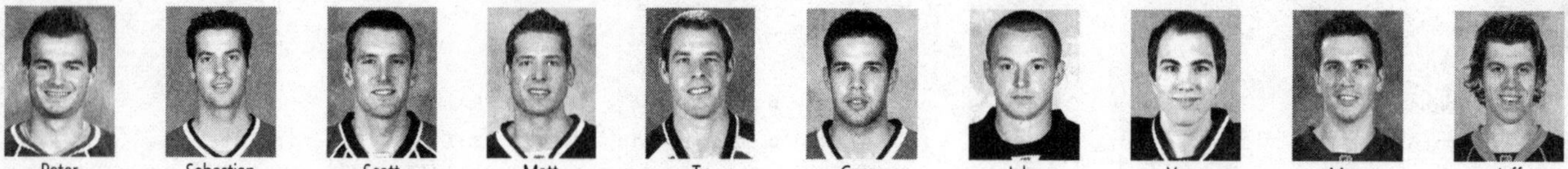

Peter Budaj · Sebastian Caron · Scott Clemmensen · Matt Climie · Ty Conklin · Corey Crawford · John Curry · Yann Danis · Marc Denis · Jeff Deslauriers

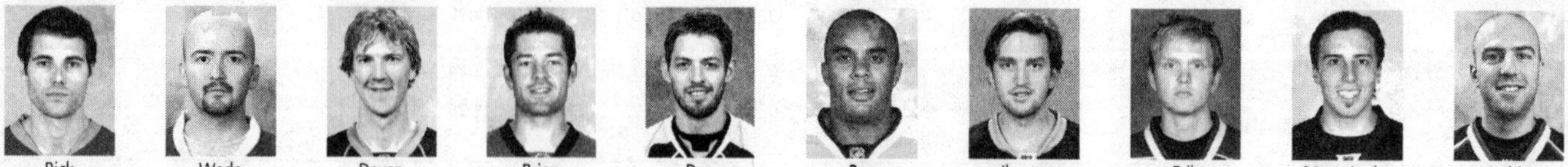

Rick DiPietro · Wade Dubielewicz · Devan Dubnyk · Brian Elliott · Dan Ellis · Ray Emery · Jhonas Enroth · Erik Ersberg · Marc-Andre Fleury · Mathieu Garon

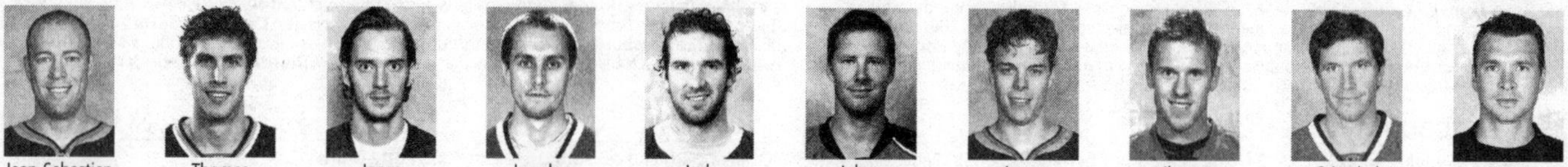

Jean-Sebastien Giguere · Thomas Greiss · Jonas Gustavsson · Jaroslav Halak · Josh Harding · Johan Hedberg · Jonas Hiller · Jimmy Howard · Cristobal Huet · Brent Johnson

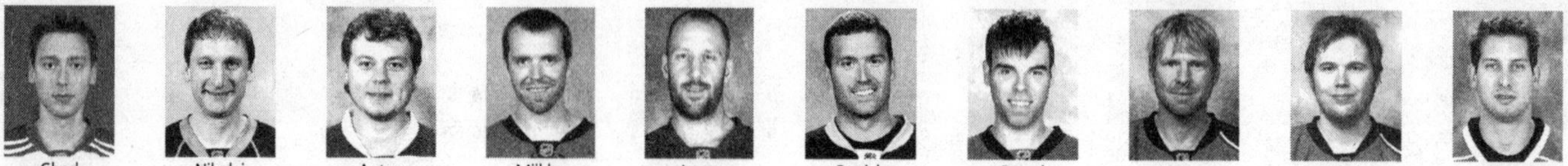

Chad Johnson · Nikolai Khabibulin · Anton Khudobin · Miikka Kiprusoff · Jason LaBarbera · Patrick Lalime · Pascal Leclaire · Manny Legace · Kari Lehtonen · Michael Leighton

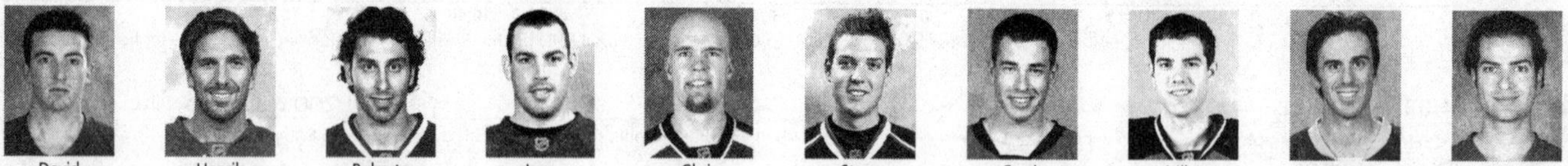

David LeNeveu · Henrik Lundqvist · Roberto Luongo · Joey MacDonald · Chris Mason · Steve Mason · Curtis McElhinney · Mike McKenna · Ryan Miller · Al Montoya

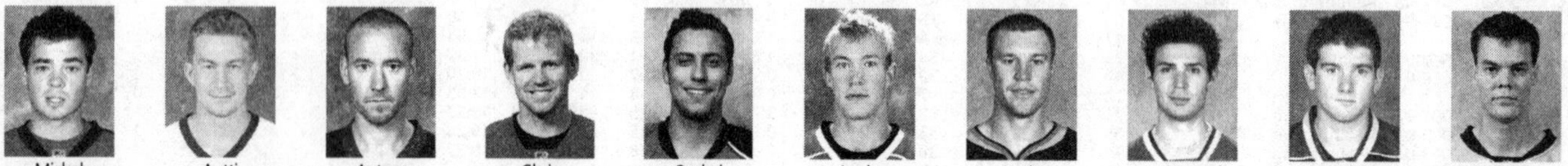

Michal Neuvirth · Antti Niemi · Antero Niittymaki · Chris Osgood · Ondrej Pavelec · Justin Peters · Justin Pogge · Carey Price · Jonathan Quick · Tuukka Rask

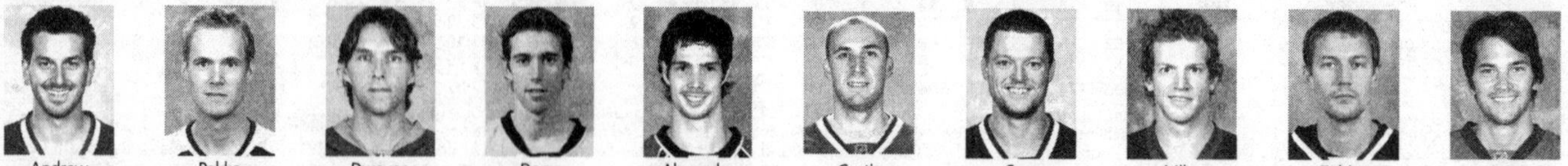

Andrew Raycroft · Pekka Rinne · Dwayne Roloson · Dany Sabourin · Alexander Salak · Curtis Sanford · Cory Schneider · Mike Smith · Tobias Stephan · Jose Theodore

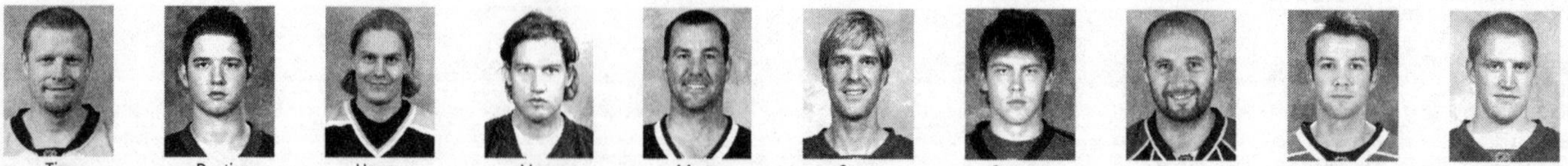

Tim Thomas · Dustin Tokarski · Hannu Toivonen · Vesa Toskala · Marty Turco · Steve Valiquette · Semyon Varlamov · Tomas Vokoun · Cam Ward · Matt Zaba

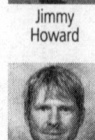

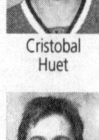

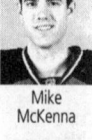

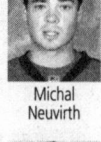

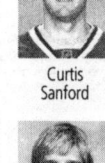

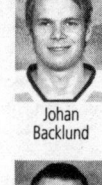

2010-11 Goaltender Register

ote: The 2010-11 Goaltender Register lists all active NHL goaltenders, every goaltender afted in the 2010 Entry Draft, goaltenders on NHL Reserve Lists and other goaltenders. ades and roster changes are current as of August 15, 2010.

› calculate a goaltender's goals-against per game average **(Avg)**, divide goals jainst **(GA)** by minutes played **(Mins)** and multiply this result by **60**.

bbreviations: GP – games played; **W** – wins; **L** – losses; **O/T** – overtime losses/ties; **lins** – minutes played; **GA** – goals against; **SO** – shutouts; **vg** – goals-against-per-game average; ***** – league-leading total
– member of Stanley Cup-winning team.

HL Player Register begins on page 345.
rospect Register begins on page 275.
eague Abbreviations are listed on page 662.

EBISCHER, David (A-bih-shuhr, DAY-vihd)

oaltender. Catches left. 6'1", 185 lbs. Born, Fribourg, Switz., February 7, 1978.
Colorado's 7th choice, 161st overall, in 1997 Entry Draft).

			Regular Season								Playoffs						
eason	Club	League	GP	W	L	O/T	Mins	GA	SO	Avg	GP	W	L	Mins	GA	SO	Avg
996-97	Fribourg	Swiss	10	....	....	....	577	34	0	3.54	3	1	2	184	13	0	4.24
997-98	Chesapeake	ECHL	17	5	7	2	930	52	0	3.35	....	....	....	....	....	....	....
	Wheeling Nailers	ECHL	10	5	3	1	564	30	1	3.19	....	....	....	....	....	....	....
	Hershey Bears	AHL	2	0	0	1	79	5	0	3.76	....	....	....	....	....	....	....
	Fribourg	Swiss	1	1	0	0	60	1	0	1.00	4	....	....	240	17	....	4.25
998-99	Hershey Bears	AHL	38	17	10	5	1932	79	2	2.45	3	1	2	152	6	0	2.37
-2000	Hershey Bears	AHL	58	29	23	2	3259	180	1	3.31	14	7	6	788	40	2	3.05
000-01 ♦	**Colorado**	**NHL**	**26**	**12**	**7**	**3**	**1393**	**52**	**3**	**2.24**	**1**	**0**	**0**	**1**	**0**	**0**	**0.00**
001-02	**Colorado**	**NHL**	**21**	**13**	**6**	**0**	**1184**	**37**	**2**	**1.88**	**1**	**0**	**0**	**34**	**1**	**0**	**1.76**
	Switzerland	Olympics	2	1	0	0	81	6	0	4.43	....	....	....	....	....	....	....
002-03	**Colorado**	**NHL**	**22**	**7**	**12**	**0**	**1235**	**50**	**1**	**2.43**	....	....	....	....	....	....	....
003-04	**Colorado**	**NHL**	**62**	**32**	**19**	**9**	**3703**	**129**	**4**	**2.09**	**11**	**6**	**5**	**662**	**23**	**1**	**2.08**
004-05	HC Lugano	Swiss	18	12	2	3	1019	41	0	2.41	4	1	3	240	10	0	2.50
	EHC Chur	Swiss-2	....	....	....	....	....	....	....	....	2	....	....	130	4	0	1.84
005-06	**Colorado**	**NHL**	**43**	**25**	**14**	**2**	**2477**	**123**	**3**	**2.98**	....	....	....	....	....	....	....
	Switzerland	Olympics	4	1	0	2	200	7	0	2.10	....	....	....	....	....	....	....
	Montreal	**NHL**	**7**	**4**	**3**	**0**	**418**	**26**	**0**	**3.73**	....	....	....	....	....	....	....
006-07	**Montreal**	**NHL**	**32**	**13**	**12**	**3**	**1760**	**93**	**0**	**3.17**	....	....	....	....	....	....	....
007-08	**Phoenix**	**NHL**	**1**	**0**	**1**	**0**	**60**	**3**	**0**	**3.00**	....	....	....	....	....	....	....
	San Antonio	AHL	5	2	3	0	302	13	0	2.58	....	....	....	....	....	....	....
	HC Lugano	Swiss	26	12	14	0	1576	69	2	2.63	5	4	1	301	14	0	2.79
008-09	HC Lugano	Swiss	49	27	22	0	2953	140	2	2.84	7	3	4	452	26	0	3.45
009-10	HC Lugano	Swiss	48	23	24	0	2897	156	2	3.23	4	0	4	240	22	0	5.50
	NHL Totals		**214**	**106**	**74**	**17**	**12230**	**513**	**13**	**2.52**	**13**	**6**	**5**	**697**	**24**	**1**	**2.07**

igned as a free agent by **Lugano** (Swiss), September 17, 2004. Traded to **Montreal** by **Colorado** or Jose Theodore, March 8, 2006. Signed as a free agent by **Phoenix**, July 19, 2007. • Loaned to **ugano** (Swiss) by **Phoenix**, November 23, 2007.

ITTOKALLIO, Sami (ay-toh-KAHL-ee-oh, SAHM-ee) COL.

oaltender. Catches left. 6'1", 174 lbs. Born, Tampere, Finland, August 6, 1992.
Colorado's 5th choice, 107th overall, in 2010 Entry Draft).

			Regular Season								Playoffs						
eason	Club	League	GP	W	L	O/T	Mins	GA	SO	Avg	GP	W	L	Mins	GA	SO	Avg
008-09	Ilves Tampere U18	Fin-U18	5	5	0	0	305	9	1	1.77	....	....	....	....	....	....	....
	Ilves Tampere Jr.	Fin-Jr.	13	7	6	0	731	33	1	2.71	....	....	....	....	....	....	....
009-10	Ilves Tampere	Finland	1	0	0	0	2	0	0	0.00	....	....	....	....	....	....	....
	LeKi Lempaala	Finland-2	2	1	1	0	124	7	0	3.38	....	....	....	....	....	....	....
	Suomi U20	Finland-2	2	1	1	0	120	8	0	4.00	....	....	....	....	....	....	....
	Ilves Tampere U18	Fin-U18	9	6	3	0	542	19	1	2.10	....	....	....	....	....	....	....
	Ilves Tampere Jr.	Fin-Jr.	23	13	9	0	1257	67	2	3.20	9	6	3	504	19	0	2.26

LLEN, Jake (A-lehn, JAYK) ST.L.

oaltender. Catches left. 6'1", 190 lbs. Born, Fredericton, N.B., August 7, 1990.
St. Louis' 3rd choice, 34th overall, in 2008 Entry Draft).

			Regular Season								Playoffs						
eason	Club	League	GP	W	L	O/T	Mins	GA	SO	Avg	GP	W	L	Mins	GA	SO	Avg
006-07	Fredericton	NBPEI					STATISTICS NOT AVAILABLE										
007-08	St. John's	QMJHL	30	9	12	....	1507	79	2	3.14	4	2	1	128	8	0	3.74
008-09	Montreal	QMJHL	53	28	25	....	3023	144	3	2.86	10	4	6	585	35	1	3.59
009-10	Montreal	QMJHL	23	11	11	....	1241	55	1	2.66	....	....	....	....	....	....	....
	Drummondville	QMJHL	22	18	3	....	1271	37	3	1.75	14	9	5	840	34	1	2.43

MJHL First All-Star Team (2010) • Canadian Major Junior First All-Star Team (2010) • Canadian Major Junior Goaltender of the Year (2010)

NDERSEN, Frederik (AHN-duhr-suhn, FREH-duhr-ihk) CAR.

oaltender. Catches left. 6'4", 220 lbs. Born, Herning, Denmark, October 2, 1989.
Carolina's 8th choice, 187th overall, in 2010 Entry Draft).

			Regular Season								Playoffs						
eason	Club	League	GP	W	L	O/T	Mins	GA	SO	Avg	GP	W	L	Mins	GA	SO	Avg
007-08	Herning IK Jr.	Den-Jr.	17	....	....	....	....	....	....	....	....	....	....	....	....	....	....
	Herning IK	Denmark-2	9	....	....	....	....	....	....	....	....	....	....	....	....	....	....
008-09	Herning IK	Denmark-2	1	....	....	....	....	....	....	....	....	....	....	....	....	....	....
	Herning Blue Fox	Denmark	22	....	....	....	1249	51	1	2.45	....	....	....	....	....	....	....
009-10	Frederikshavn	Denmark	30	....	....	....	1754	64	6	2.19	10	....	....	607	29	0	2.86

ANDERSON, Craig (AN-duhr-suhn, KRAYG) COL.

Goaltender. Catches left. 6'2", 180 lbs. Born, Park Ridge, IL, May 21, 1981.
(Chicago's 4th choice, 73rd overall, in 2001 Entry Draft).

			Regular Season								Playoffs						
Season	Club	League	GP	W	L	O/T	Mins	GA	SO	Avg	GP	W	L	Mins	GA	SO	Avg
1997-98	Chicago Jets	MEHL	50	....	....	....	2991	143	2	2.86	....	....	....	....	....	....	....
1998-99	Chicago Freeze	NAHL	14	11	3	0	840	40	0	2.56	....	....	....	....	....	....	....
	Guelph Storm	OHL	21	12	5	1	1006	52	1	3.10	3	0	2	114	9	0	4.74
99-2000	Guelph Storm	OHL	38	12	17	2	1955	117	0	3.59	3	0	1	110	5	0	2.73
2000-01	Guelph Storm	OHL	59	30	19	9	3555	156	3	2.63	4	0	4	240	17	0	4.25
2001-02	Norfolk Admirals	AHL	28	9	13	4	1568	77	2	2.95	1	0	1	21	1	0	2.83
2002-03	**Chicago**	**NHL**	**6**	**0**	**3**	**2**	**270**	**18**	**0**	**4.00**	....	....	....	....	....	....	....
	Norfolk Admirals	AHL	32	15	11	5	1795	58	4	1.94	5	2	3	345	15	0	2.61
2003-04	**Chicago**	**NHL**	**21**	**6**	**14**	**0**	**1205**	**57**	**1**	**2.84**	....	....	....	....	....	....	....
	Norfolk Admirals	AHL	37	17	20	0	2108	74	3	2.11	5	2	3	327	10	0	1.84
2004-05	Norfolk Admirals	AHL	15	9	4	1	886	27	2	1.83	6	2	4	356	14	0	2.36
2005-06	**Chicago**	**NHL**	**29**	**6**	**12**	**4**	**1554**	**86**	**1**	**3.32**	....	....	....	....	....	....	....
2006-07	**Florida**	**NHL**	**5**	**1**	**1**	**1**	**217**	**8**	**0**	**2.21**	....	....	....	....	....	....	....
	Rochester	AHL	34	23	10	1	2060	88	1	2.56	6	2	4	376	18	0	2.87
2007-08	**Florida**	**NHL**	**17**	**8**	**6**	**1**	**935**	**35**	**2**	**2.25**	....	....	....	....	....	....	....
2008-09	**Florida**	**NHL**	**31**	**15**	**7**	**5**	**1636**	**74**	**3**	**2.71**	....	....	....	....	....	....	....
2009-10	**Colorado**	**NHL**	**71**	**38**	**25**	**7**	**4235**	**186**	**7**	**2.64**	**6**	**2**	**4**	**366**	**16**	**1**	**2.62**
	NHL Totals		**180**	**74**	**68**	**20**	**10052**	**464**	**14**	**2.77**	**6**	**2**	**4**	**366**	**16**	**1**	**2.62**

• Re-entered NHL Entry Draft. Originally Calgary's 3rd choice, 77th overall, in 1999 Entry Draft.

OHL First All-Star Team (2001)

Claimed on waivers by **Boston** from **Chicago**, January 19, 2006. Claimed on waivers by **St. Louis** from **Boston**, January 31, 2006. Claimed on waivers by **Chicago** from **St. Louis**, February 3, 2006. Traded to **Florida** by **Chicago** for Florida's 6th round choice (later traded to Tampa Bay - Tampa Bay selected Luke Witkowski) in 2008 Entry Draft, June 24, 2006. Signed as a free agent by **Colorado**, July 1, 2009.

AUBIN, Jean-Sebastien (oh-BEHN, ZHAWN-suh-BAS-tee-yeh)

Goaltender. Catches right. 5'11", 180 lbs. Born, Montreal, Que., July 19, 1977.
(Pittsburgh's 2nd choice, 76th overall, in 1995 Entry Draft).

			Regular Season								Playoffs						
Season	Club	League	GP	W	L	O/T	Mins	GA	SO	Avg	GP	W	L	Mins	GA	SO	Avg
1993-94	Montreal-Bourassa	QAAA	27	14	13	0	1524	96	1	3.74	4	1	3	222	19	0	5.14
1994-95	Sherbrooke	QMJHL	27	13	10	1	1287	73	1	3.40	3	1	2	185	11	0	3.57
1995-96	Sherbrooke	QMJHL	40	18	14	2	2140	127	0	3.57	4	1	3	238	23	0	5.55
1996-97	Sherbrooke	QMJHL	4	3	1	0	249	8	0	1.93	1	0	1	60	4	0	4.00
	Moncton Wildcats	QMJHL	22	9	12	0	1252	67	1	3.21	....	....	....	....	....	....	....
	Laval Titan	QMJHL	11	2	6	1	532	41	0	4.62	....	....	....	....	....	....	....
1997-98	Syracuse Crunch	AHL	8	2	4	1	380	26	0	4.10	....	....	....	....	....	....	....
	Dayton Bombers	ECHL	21	15	2	2	1177	59	1	3.01	3	1	1	142	4	0	1.69
1998-99	**Pittsburgh**	**NHL**	**17**	**4**	**3**	**6**	**756**	**28**	**2**	**2.22**	....	....	....	....	....	....	....
	Kansas City Blades	IHL	13	5	7	1	751	41	0	3.28	....	....	....	....	....	....	....
99-2000	**Pittsburgh**	**NHL**	**51**	**23**	**21**	**3**	**2789**	**120**	**2**	**2.58**	....	....	....	....	....	....	....
	Wilkes-Barre	AHL	11	2	8	0	538	39	0	4.35	....	....	....	....	....	....	....
2000-01	**Pittsburgh**	**NHL**	**36**	**20**	**14**	**1**	**2050**	**107**	**0**	**3.13**	**1**	**0**	**0**	**1**	**0**	**0**	**0.00**
2001-02	**Pittsburgh**	**NHL**	**21**	**3**	**12**	**1**	**1094**	**65**	**0**	**3.56**	....	....	....	....	....	....	....
2002-03	**Pittsburgh**	**NHL**	**21**	**6**	**13**	**0**	**1132**	**59**	**1**	**3.13**	....	....	....	....	....	....	....
	Wilkes-Barre	AHL	16	8	6	1	919	29	3	1.89	6	3	3	356	12	0	2.02
2003-04	**Pittsburgh**	**NHL**	**22**	**7**	**9**	**0**	**1067**	**53**	**1**	**2.98**	....	....	....	....	....	....	....
	Wilkes-Barre	AHL	13	4	5	2	670	31	0	2.78	....	....	....	....	....	....	....
2004-05	St. John's	AHL	23	12	9	0	1336	64	3	2.87	1	0	0	47	1	0	1.27
2005-06	**Toronto**	**NHL**	**11**	**9**	**0**	**2**	**677**	**25**	**1**	**2.22**	....	....	....	....	....	....	....
	Toronto Marlies	AHL	46	19	18	2	2491	126	2	3.03	5	1	4	359	17	0	2.84
2006-07	**Toronto**	**NHL**	**20**	**3**	**5**	**2**	**804**	**46**	**0**	**3.43**	....	....	....	....	....	....	....
2007-08	**Los Angeles**	**NHL**	**19**	**5**	**6**	**1**	**828**	**44**	**0**	**3.19**	....	....	....	....	....	....	....
	Manchester	AHL	1	0	0	0	9	4	0	27.69	....	....	....	....	....	....	....
	Portland Pirates	AHL	11	6	4	0	645	18	3	1.67	12	9	3	757	29	0	2.30
2008-09	Philadelphia	AHL	23	10	10	1	1252	70	0	3.36	1	0	1	58	1	0	1.03
2009-10	Dusseldorf	Germany	*54	27	25	....	3179	130	2	2.45	3	0	3	174	11	0	3.78
	NHL Totals		**218**	**80**	**83**	**16**	**11197**	**547**	**7**	**2.93**	**1**	**0**	**0**	**1**	**0**	**0**	**0.00**

Signed to a PTO (professional tryout) contract by **St. John's** (AHL), November 13, 2004. Signed as a free agent by **Toronto**, August 18, 2005. Signed as a free agent by **Los Angeles**, August 28, 2007. Traded to **Anaheim** by **Los Angeles** for St. Louis' 7th round choice (previously acquired, later traded back to St. Louis - St. Louis selected Paul Karpowich) in 2008 Entry Draft, February 26, 2008. Signed as a free agent by **Philadelphia**, September 18, 2008. Signed as a free agent by **Dusseldorf** (Germany), July 23, 2009.

AULD, Alex (AWLD, AL-ehx) MTL.

Goaltender. Catches left. 6'4", 223 lbs. Born, Cold Lake, Alta., January 7, 1981.
(Florida's 2nd choice, 40th overall, in 1999 Entry Draft).

			Regular Season								Playoffs						
Season	Club	League	GP	W	L	O/T	Mins	GA	SO	Avg	GP	W	L	Mins	GA	SO	Avg
1996-97	Thunder Bay Kings	TBMHL	35	....	....	....	2100	46	10	1.35	....	....	....	....	....	....	....
1997-98	Sturgeon Falls Lynx	NOJHA	11	4	6	0	611	46	0	4.52	....	....	....	....	....	....	....
	North Bay	OHL	6	0	4	0	206	17	0	4.95	....	....	....	....	....	....	....
1998-99	North Bay	OHL	37	9	20	1	1894	106	1	3.36	3	0	3	170	10	0	3.53
99-2000	North Bay	OHL	55	21	26	6	3047	167	2	3.29	6	2	4	374	12	0	*1.93
2000-01	North Bay	OHL	40	22	11	5	2319	98	1	2.54	4	0	4	240	15	0	3.75
2001-02	Vancouver	NHL	1	1	0	0	60	2	0	2.00	....	....	....	....	....	....	....
	Columbia Inferno	ECHL	6	3	1	2	375	12	0	1.92	....	....	....	....	....	....	....
	Manitoba Moose	AHL	21	11	9	0	1104	65	1	3.53	1	0	0	20	0	0	0.00
2002-03	Vancouver	NHL	7	3	3	0	382	10	1	1.57	1	0	0	20	1	0	3.00
	Manitoba Moose	AHL	37	15	19	3	2209	97	3	2.64	....	....	....	....	....	....	....
2003-04	Vancouver	NHL	6	2	2	2	349	12	0	2.06	3	1	2	222	9	0	2.43
	Manitoba Moose	AHL	40	18	16	4	2329	99	4	2.55	....	....	....	....	....	....	....
2004-05	Manitoba Moose	AHL	50	25	18	4	2764	118	2	2.56	3	0	2	128	7	0	3.29
2005-06	Vancouver	NHL	67	33	26	6	3859	189	0	2.94	....	....	....	....	....	....	....
2006-07	Florida	NHL	27	7	13	5	1471	82	1	3.34	....	....	....	....	....	....	....
2007-08	Phoenix	NHL	9	3	6	0	509	30	1	3.54	....	....	....	....	....	....	....
	San Antonio	AHL	2	1	1	0	119	5	1	2.53	....	....	....	....	....	....	....
	Boston	NHL	23	9	7	5	1213	47	2	2.32	....	....	....	....	....	....	....
2008-09	Ottawa	NHL	43	16	18	7	2449	101	1	2.47	....	....	....	....	....	....	....
2009-10	Dallas	NHL	21	9	6	3	1181	59	0	3.00	....	....	....	....	....	....	....
	NY Rangers	NHL	3	0	1	0	119	5	0	2.52	....	....	....	....	....	....	....
	NHL Totals		207	83	82	28	11592	537	6	2.78	4	1	2	242	10	0	2.48

• Rights traded to **Vancouver** by **Florida** for Vancouver's 2nd round compensatory choice (later traded to New Jersey – New Jersey selected Tuomas Pihlman) in 2001 Entry Draft and Vancouver's 3rd round choice (later traded to Atlanta, later traded to Buffalo – Buffalo selected John Adams) in 2002 Entry Draft, May 31, 2001. Traded to **Florida** by **Vancouver** with Todd Bertuzzi and Bryan Allen for Roberto Luongo, Lukas Krajicek and Florida's 6th round choice (Sergei Shirokov) in 2006 Entry Draft, June 23, 2006. Signed as a free agent by **Phoenix**, August 13, 2007. Traded to **Boston** by **Phoenix** for Nate DiCasmirro and Boston's 5th round choice (later traded to Ottawa – Ottawa selected Jeff Costello) in 2009 Entry Draft, December 6, 2007. Signed as a free agent by **Ottawa**, July 1, 2008. Traded to **Dallas** by **Ottawa** for San Jose's 6th round choice (previously acquired, Ottawa selected Mark Stone) in 2010 Entry Draft, July 8, 2009. Claimed on waivers by **NY Rangers** from **Dallas**, February 27, 2010. Signed as a free agent by **Montreal**, July 1, 2010.

BACASHIHUA, Jason (buh-KAH-shoo-wuh, JAY-suhn) COL.

Goaltender. Catches left. 5'11", 175 lbs. Born, Dearborn Heights, MI, September 20, 1982.
(Dallas' 1st choice, 26th overall, in 2001 Entry Draft).

			Regular Season								Playoffs						
Season	Club	League	GP	W	L	O/T	Mins	GA	SO	Avg	GP	W	L	Mins	GA	SO	Avg
99-2000	Chicago Freeze	NAHL	41	20	19	2	2432	118	2	2.91	2	0	2	103	12	0	6.97
2000-01	Chicago Freeze	NAHL	39	24	14	0	2246	121	1	3.23	3	1	2	190	12	0	3.79
2001-02	Plymouth Whalers	OHL	46	26	12	7	2688	105	*5	2.34	6	2	4	360	15	0	2.50
	Utah Grizzlies	AHL	1	0	1	0	61	3	0	2.97	....	....	....	....	....	....	....
2002-03	Utah Grizzlies	AHL	39	18	18	2	2245	118	3	3.15	1	0	1	59	2	0	2.05
2003-04	Utah Grizzlies	AHL	39	13	19	5	2234	99	3	2.66	....	....	....	....	....	....	....
2004-05	Worcester IceCats	AHL	35	18	13	1	1909	80	2	2.51	....	....	....	....	....	....	....
2005-06	St. Louis	NHL	19	4	10	1	966	52	0	3.23	....	....	....	....	....	....	....
	Peoria Rivermen	AHL	15	9	4	0	820	36	2	2.63	....	....	....	....	....	....	....
2006-07	St. Louis	NHL	19	3	7	3	894	47	0	3.15	....	....	....	....	....	....	....
	Peoria Rivermen	AHL	20	5	10	4	1139	55	1	2.90	....	....	....	....	....	....	....
2007-08	Peoria Rivermen	AHL	4	1	3	0	208	11	0	3.17	....	....	....	....	....	....	....
	Johnstown Chiefs	ECHL	1	1	0	0	65	4	0	3.70	....	....	....	....	....	....	....
	Lake Erie Monsters	AHL	19	5	11	2	1074	60	1	3.35	....	....	....	....	....	....	....
2008-09	Lake Erie Monsters	AHL	39	13	21	3	2255	104	2	2.77	....	....	....	....	....	....	....
2009-10	Hershey Bears	AHL	22	17	3	1	1258	52	1	2.48	....	....	....	....	....	....	....
	NHL Totals		38	7	17	4	1860	99	0	3.19	....	....	....	....	....	....	....

Traded to **St. Louis** by **Dallas** for the rights to Shawn Belle, June 25, 2004. Traded to **Colorado** by **St. Louis** for future considerations, November 8, 2007. Signed as a free agent by **Hershey** (AHL), July 31, 2009. Signed as a free agent by **Colorado**, July 2, 2010.

BACHMAN, Richard (BAWK-mahn, RIH-chuhrd) DAL.

Goaltender. Catches left. 5'10", 170 lbs. Born, Salt Lake City, UT, July 25, 1987.
(Dallas' 3rd choice, 120th overall, in 2006 Entry Draft).

			Regular Season								Playoffs						
Season	Club	League	GP	W	L	O/T	Mins	GA	SO	Avg	GP	W	L	Mins	GA	SO	Avg
2004-05	Cushing	High-MA	28	....	....	....	1498	53	3	1.89	....	....	....	....	....	....	....
	Boston Jr. Bruins	EmJHL	25	....	....	....	....	....	....	....	....	....	....	....	....	....	....
2005-06	Cushing	High-MA	30	....	....	....	1598	60	4	2.25	....	....	....	....	....	....	....
	Boston Jr. Bruins	EmJHL	....	31	1	2	....	....	....	1.69	....	....	....	....	....	....	....
2006-07	Chicago Steel	USHL	7	2	5	0	359	29	0	4.85	....	....	....	....	....	....	....
	Cedar Rapids	USHL	26	14	10	2	1565	78	4	2.99	6	4	1	329	7	*2	*1.28
2007-08	Colorado College	WCHA	35	25	9	1	2103	65	4	1.85	....	....	....	....	....	....	....
2008-09	Colorado College	WCHA	35	14	11	10	2073	91	3	2.63	....	....	....	....	....	....	....
2009-10	Texas Stars	AHL	8	4	4	0	446	16	1	2.15	....	....	....	....	....	....	....
	Idaho Steelheads	ECHL	35	22	7	4	2028	77	*4	*2.28	8	6	1	492	13	1	1.59

WCHA All-Rookie Team (2008) • WCHA First All-Star Team (2008) • WCHA Rookie of the Year (2008) • WCHA Player of the Year (2008) • NCAA West First All-American Team (2008) • NCAA Rookie of the Year (2008)

BACKLUND, Johan (BAHK-luhnd, YOH-han) PHI.

Goaltender. Catches left. 6'2", 198 lbs. Born, Skelleftea, Sweden, July 24, 1981.

			Regular Season								Playoffs						
Season	Club	League	GP	W	L	O/T	Mins	GA	SO	Avg	GP	W	L	Mins	GA	SO	Avg
2005-06	Leksands IF	Sweden	32	....	....	....	1843	81	1	2.64	....	....	....	....	....	....	....
2006-07	Timra IK	Sweden	*49	....	....	....	2835	106	*6	2.24	7	....	....	444	16	0	2.16
2007-08	Timra IK	Sweden	47	....	....	....	2794	107	6	2.30	11	....	....	662	27	1	2.45
2008-09	Timra IK	Sweden	*49	....	....	....	*2840	121	*4	2.56	5	....	....	317	18	0	3.41
2009-10	Philadelphia	NHL	1	0	1	0	40	2	0	3.00	1	0	0	1	0	0	0.00
	Adirondack	AHL	41	21	17	2	2451	114	2	2.79	....	....	....	....	....	....	....
	NHL Totals		1	0	1	0	40	2	0	3.00	1	0	0	1	0	0	0.00

Signed as a free agent by **Philadelphia**, March 26, 2009.

BACKSTROM, Niklas (BAK-struhm, NIHK-luhs) MI

Goaltender. Catches left. 6'1", 189 lbs. Born, Helsinki, Finland, February 13, 1978.

			Regular Season								Playoffs						
Season	Club	League	GP	W	L	O/T	Mins	GA	SO	Avg	GP	W	L	Mins	GA	SO	Av
1994-95	HIFK Helsinki U18	Fin-U18	STATISTICS NOT AVAILABLE														
1995-96	HIFK Helsinki U18	Fin-U18	12	....	....	....	699	44	....	3.77	4	....	....	203	9	....	2.6
1996-97	HIFK Helsinki Jr.	Fin-Jr.	21	....	....	....	1243	57	....	2.75	....	....	....	....	....	....	....
	PiTa Helsinki	Finland-2	8	....	....	....	390	24	....	3.69	....	....	....	....	....	....	....
	HIFK Helsinki	Finland	2	0	0	0	30	3	0	5.85	....	....	....	....	....	....	....
1997-98	HIFK Helsinki Jr.	Fin-Jr.	14	7	7	0	847	42	....	2.98	....	....	....	....	....	....	....
	Hermes Kokkola	Finland-2	9	4	3	1	468	23	1	2.95	....	....	....	....	....	....	....
1998-99	HIFK Helsinki	Finland	16	9	5	1	923	26	1	*1.69	....	....	....	....	....	....	....
	HIFK Helsinki Jr.	Fin-Jr.	15	7	7	1	898	45	1	3.01	....	....	....	....	....	....	....
99-2000	HIFK Helsinki	Finland	4	0	4	0	155	17	0	6.58	....	....	....	....	....	....	....
	FPS Forssa	Finland-2	22	13	8	1	1320	50	1	2.27	3	1	2	178	8	0	2.6
2000-01	SaiPa	Finland	49	22	24	3	2826	120	2	2.55	....	....	....	....	....	....	....
2001-02	AIK Solna	Sweden	40	....	....	....	2186	111	1	3.05	....	....	....	....	....	....	....
	AIK Solna	Sweden-Q	9	....	....	....	543	20	0	2.21	....	....	....	....	....	....	....
2002-03	Karpat Oulu	Finland	36	16	8	9	2136	77	4	2.16	*15	7	8	*990	33	1	2.0
2003-04	Karpat Oulu	Finland	43	24	8	0	2572	87	7	2.03	*15	*9	6	*927	36	1	2.3
2004-05	Karpat Oulu	Finland	47	27	10	10	2819	102	7	2.17	*12	*10	2	720	15	*3	*1.2
2005-06	Karpat Oulu	Finland	51	*32	9	10	3077	86	*10	*1.68	4	3	1	195	6	0	1.8
	Finland	Olympics	DID NOT PLAY – SPARE GOALTENDER														
2006-07	Minnesota	NHL	41	23	8	6	2227	73	5	*1.97	5	1	4	297	11	0	2.2
2007-08	Minnesota	NHL	58	33	13	8	3409	131	4	2.31	6	2	4	361	17	0	2.8
2008-09	Minnesota	NHL	71	37	24	8	4088	159	8	2.33	....	....	....	....	....	....	....
2009-10	Minnesota	NHL	60	26	23	8	3489	158	2	2.72	....	....	....	....	....	....	....
	Finland	Olympics	2	1	0	0	110	2	1	*1.09	....	....	....	....	....	....	....
	NHL Totals		230	119	68	30	13213	521	19	2.37	11	3	8	658	28	0	2.5

MBNA Roger Crozier Saving Grace Award (2007) • William M. Jennings Trophy (2007) (shared with Manny Fernandez)

Played in NHL All-Star Game (2009)

Signed as a free agent by **Minnesota**, June 1, 2006.

BARULIN, Konstantin (bah-ROO-lihn, KAWN-stan-tihn) ST.L

Goaltender. Catches left. 6'2", 200 lbs. Born, Karaganda, USSR, September 4, 1984.
(St. Louis' 3rd choice, 84th overall, in 2003 Entry Draft).

			Regular Season								Playoffs						
Season	Club	League	GP	W	L	O/T	Mins	GA	SO	Avg	GP	W	L	Mins	GA	SO	Av
2001-02	Gazovik Tyumen	Russia-2	4	....	....	....	190	15	0	4.73	....	....	....	....	....	....	....
2002-03	Gazovik Tyumen	Russia-2	41	....	....	....	2361	67	5	1.70	....	....	....	....	....	....	....
2003-04	Gazovik Tyumen	Russia-2	11	....	....	....	663	24	....	2.17	....	....	....	....	....	....	....
	SKA St. Petersburg	Russia	1	....	....	....	1	0	0	0.00	....	....	....	....	....	....	....
	St. Petersburg 2	Russia-3	11	....	....	....	668	24	1	2.15	....	....	....	....	....	....	....
2004-05	Gazovik Tyumen	Russia-2	30	....	....	....	1773	59	6	2.00	3	....	....	136	9	0	3.9
2005-06	Spartak Moscow	Russia	36	....	....	....	2102	75	2	2.14	2	....	....	104	4	0	2.3
2006-07	Mytischi	Russia	26	....	....	....	1249	45	1	2.16	1	....	....	48	3	0	3.7
2007-08	Mytischi	Russia	11	....	....	....	434	20	0	2.77	....	....	....	....	....	....	....
2008-09	CSKA Moscow	Rus-KHL	41	....	....	....	2443	100	2	2.46	2	....	....	100	9	0	5.4
2009-10	CSKA Moscow	Rus-KHL	45	....	....	....	2277	80	3	2.11	3	....	....	136	10	0	4.4

BECKFORD-TSEU, Chris (BEHK-fuhrd-TSEW, KRIHS)

Goaltender. Catches left. 6'2", 201 lbs. Born, Toronto, Ont., June 22, 1984.
(St. Louis' 8th choice, 159th overall, in 2003 Entry Draft).

			Regular Season								Playoffs						
Season	Club	League	GP	W	L	O/T	Mins	GA	SO	Avg	GP	W	L	Mins	GA	SO	Av
2000-01	St. Mike's B's	OPJHL	25	9	15	1	1506	119	1	4.75	4	1	3	240	10	0	2.5
2001-02	Oshawa	OPJHL	STATISTICS NOT AVAILABLE														
	Guelph Storm	OHL	5	2	0	0	207	16	0	4.64	....	....	....	....	....	....	....
	Oshawa Generals	OHL	7	2	3	0	341	19	0	3.34	5	1	4	310	16	0	3.1
2002-03	Oshawa Generals	OHL	54	25	26	2	2978	157	4	3.16	13	6	7	727	48	1	3.9
2003-04	Oshawa Generals	OHL	9	1	5	2	495	28	0	3.39	....	....	....	....	....	....	....
	Kingston	OHL	40	16	19	2	2226	121	3	3.26	5	1	4	303	18	0	3.5
2004-05	Worcester IceCats	AHL	1	0	0	0	29	0	0	0.00	....	....	....	....	....	....	....
	Peoria Rivermen	ECHL	29	11	12	3	1594	72	1	2.71	....	....	....	....	....	....	....
2005-06	Peoria Rivermen	AHL	16	7	5	1	737	38	0	3.10	4	0	4	238	15	0	3.7
	Alaska Aces	ECHL	19	16	1	2	1152	36	2	1.87	12	8	4	795	27	*3	*2.0
2006-07	Peoria Rivermen	AHL	29	12	11	4	1654	75	1	2.72	....	....	....	....	....	....	....
	Alaska Aces	ECHL	7	7	0	0	426	9	2	1.27	....	....	....	....	....	....	....
2007-08	St. Louis	NHL	1	0	0	0	27	1	0	2.22	....	....	....	....	....	....	....
	Peoria Rivermen	AHL	34	15	14	2	1871	82	1	2.63	....	....	....	....	....	....	....
	Alaska Aces	ECHL	16	12	4	0	921	36	1	2.34	2	0	2	98	7	0	4.2
2008-09	Rochester	AHL	22	3	14	1	1112	73	0	3.94	....	....	....	....	....	....	....
	Florida Everblades	ECHL	1	0	0	1	65	5	0	4.62	....	....	....	....	....	....	....
	Phoenix	ECHL	11	2	7	1	577	49	0	5.09	....	....	....	....	....	....	....
2009-10	Rochester	AHL	6	0	4	0	296	23	0	4.66	....	....	....	....	....	....	....
	Florida Everblades	ECHL	38	19	11	4	2145	114	2	3.19	9	3	5	467	30	0	3.8
	NHL Totals		1	0	0	0	27	1	0	2.22	....	....	....	....	....	....	....

Signed as a free agent by **Florida**, July 3, 2008.

BENNETT, Brett (BEHN-eht, BREHT) PHX

Goaltender. Catches left. 6'1", 185 lbs. Born, Buffalo, NY, March 8, 1988.
(Phoenix's 4th choice, 130th overall, in 2006 Entry Draft).

			Regular Season								Playoffs						
Season	Club	League	GP	W	L	O/T	Mins	GA	SO	Avg	GP	W	L	Mins	GA	SO	Av
2003-04	Det. Honeybaked	MWEHL	31	....	....	....	....	....	....	....	....	....	....	....	....	....	....
2004-05	USNTDP	U-17	14	10	6	1	930	41	0	2.65	....	....	....	....	....	....	....
	USNTDP	NAHL	23	10	7	1	1217	56	1	2.76	10	7	3	598	20	3	2.0
2005-06	USNTDP	U-18	12	7	2	0	593	24	0	2.43	....	....	....	....	....	....	....
	USNTDP	NAHL	5	3	0	0	238	5	0	1.26	....	....	....	....	....	....	....
2006-07	Boston University	H-East	1	1	0	0	60	1	0	1.00	....	....	....	....	....	....	....
2007-08	Boston University	H-East	31	16	10	3	1780	78	*3	2.63	....	....	....	....	....	....	....
2008-09	Indiana Ice	USHL	*54	*35	17	2	*3110	134	*4	2.59	*13	*9	4	*789	31	*1	*2.3
2009-10	U. of Wisconsin	WCHA	14	8	6	0	765	36	1	2.82	....	....	....	....	....	....	....

ERKHOEL, Adam (BUHRK-uhl, A-duhm)

oaltender. Catches left. 5'11", 185 lbs. Born, St. Paul, MN, May 16, 1981.
hicago's 12th choice, 240th overall, in 2000 Entry Draft).

Season	Club	League	GP	W	L	O/T	Mins	GA	SO	Avg	GP	W	L	Mins	GA	SO	Avg
			Regular Season								Playoffs						
-2000	Twin Cities	USHL	49	25	15	7	2848	129	0	2.72	13	7	6	797	43	0	3.24
00-01	U. of Denver	WCHA	15	7	6	1	745	38	1	3.06							
01-02	U. of Denver	WCHA	18	12	4	1	1026	40	1	2.34							
02-03	U. of Denver	WCHA	26	12	6	4	1436	55	3	*2.30							
03-04	U. of Denver	WCHA	39	24	11	4	2225	91	*7	2.45							
04-05	Chicago Wolves	AHL	1	0	1	0	59	4	0	4.04							
	Gwinnett	ECHL	24	9	10	5	1458	59	2	2.43	7	4	1	353	9	0	*1.53
05-06	Atlanta	NHL	9	2	4	1	473	30	0	3.81							
	Chicago Wolves	AHL	11	3	6	0	526	32	0	3.65							
	Gwinnett	ECHL	15	10	4	1	902	41	1	2.73	9	6	3	551	30	0	3.27
06-07	Rochester	AHL	6	2	3	0	316	17	0	3.22							
	Dayton Bombers	ECHL	43	23	17	3	2584	105	5	2.44	*22	12	10	1385	59	*3	2.56
07-08	Grand Rapids	AHL	31	10	14	4	1697	83	1	2.93							
08-09	Wilkes-Barre	AHL	28	15	11	2	1635	69	4	2.53	6	3	2	340	12	0	2.12
09-10	Wheeling Nailers	ECHL	28	12	11	3	1590	83	0	3.03							
	Wilkes-Barre	AHL	7	4	3	0	403	20	1	2.98							
	NHL Totals		9	2	4	1	473	30	0	3.81							

SHL All-Rookie Team (2000) • USHL Second All-Star Team (2000) • NCAA Championship
-Tournament Team (2004) • NCAA Championship Tournament MVP (2004) • ECHL First All-Star
eam (2007) • ECHL Goaltender of the Year (2007)

aded to **Atlanta** by **Chicago** for Atlanta's 7th round choice (Adam Hobson) in 2005 Entry Draft,
ne 27, 2004. Signed as a free agent by **Detroit**, July 3, 2007.

ERNIER, Jonathan (BAIRN-yay, JAWN-ah-thuhn) L.A.

oaltender. Catches left. 5'11", 184 lbs. Born, Laval, Que., August 7, 1988.
os Angeles' 1st choice, 11th overall, in 2006 Entry Draft).

Season	Club	League	GP	W	L	O/T	Mins	GA	SO	Avg	GP	W	L	Mins	GA	SO	Avg
			Regular Season								Playoffs						
03-04	Laval Regents	QAAA	27	16	4	0	1329	62	2	2.80	3	1	2	180	5	0	1.70
04-05	Lewiston	QMJHL	23	7	12	3	1353	67	0	2.97	1	0	0	20	0	0	0.00
05-06	Lewiston	QMJHL	54	27	26	0	3241	146	2	2.70	6	2	4	359	17	1	2.84
06-07	Lewiston	QMJHL	37	26	10	....	2186	94	2	2.58	17	*16	1	1025	40	1	2.34
07-08	Los Angeles	NHL	4	1	3	0	238	16	0	4.03							
	Lewiston	QMJHL	34	18	15	....	2024	92	0	2.73	6	2	4	348	17	0	2.93
	Manchester	AHL	3	1	1	1	184	5	0	1.63	3	0	3	195	9	0	2.76
08-09	Manchester	AHL	54	23	24	4	3101	124	5	2.40							
09-10	Los Angeles	NHL	3	3	0	0	185	4	1	1.30							
	Manchester	AHL	58	30	21	6	3424	116	*9	2.03	16	10	6	996	30	*3	*1.81
	NHL Totals		7	4	3	0	423	20	1	2.84							

MJHL Second All-Star Team (2007) • Canadian Major Junior Second All-Star Team (2007) • Aldege
Baz" Bastien Award (AHL – Outstanding Goaltender) (2010)

ERRA, Reto (BAIR-uh, REH-toh) ST.L.

oaltender. Catches left. 6'4", 209 lbs. Born, Bulach, Switz., January 3, 1987.
t. Louis' 6th choice, 106th overall, in 2006 Entry Draft).

Season	Club	League	GP	W	L	O/T	Mins	GA	SO	Avg	GP	W	L	Mins	GA	SO	Avg
			Regular Season								Playoffs						
04-05	GCK Zurich Jr.	Swiss-Jr.	22														
	GCK Lions Zurich	Swiss-2	3				180	12	0	4.00							
	EHC Dubendorf	Swiss-3	STATISTICS NOT AVAILABLE														
05-06	GCK Zurich Jr.	Swiss-Jr.	23														
	GCK Lions Zurich	Swiss-2	15				835	51	1	3.56							
	ZSC Lions Zurich	Swiss	2	0	1	0	90	6	0	3.99							
06-07	Switzerland U20	Swiss-2	3	0	3	0	179	13	0	4.69							
	GCK Lions Zurich	Swiss-2	6	4	2	0	359	18	0	3.01							
	ZSC Lions Zurich	Swiss	2	1	0	0	78	4	0	3.08	4	0	3	188	9	0	2.87
07-08	HC Davos	Swiss	16	9	7	0	966	44	0	2.73							
08-09	EV Zug	Swiss	6	1	5	0	368	17	0	2.77							
	SCL Tigers Langnau	Swiss	2	1	1	0	120	9	0	4.50							
	HC Davos	Swiss	8	3	4	0	445	20	0	2.70	4	3	1	216	5	0	1.39
09-10	EHC Biel-Bienne	Swiss	40	16	20	0	2319	130	3	3.36	10	3	7	582	33	0	3.40
	EHC Biel-Bienne	Swiss-Q									7	4	3	419	20	0	2.86

ERUBE, Jean-Francois (beh-ROO-bay, ZHAWN-fran-SWUH) L.A.

oaltender. Catches left. 6'1", 155 lbs. Born, Repentigny, Que., July 13, 1991.
os Angeles' 4th choice, 95th overall, in 2009 Entry Draft).

Season	Club	League	GP	W	L	O/T	Mins	GA	SO	Avg	GP	W	L	Mins	GA	SO	Avg
			Regular Season								Playoffs						
07-08	Laurentides	QAAA	10	0	6	1	511	35	0	4.11							
	Lachute Stars	QueAA	STATISTICS NOT AVAILABLE														
08-09	Montreal	QMJHL	20	6	9	....	1059	51	1	2.89	1	0	0	20	1	0	3.00
09-10	Montreal	QMJHL	45	17	23	....	2394	121	1	3.03	7	3	4	449	18	0	2.40
	Manchester	AHL	3	2	1	0	180	11	0	3.67							

ESKOROWANY, Tyler (behs-koor-WAH-nee, TIGH-luhr) DAL.

oaltender. Catches left. 6'4", 208 lbs. Born, Sudbury, Ont., April 28, 1990.
Dallas' 1st choice, 59th overall, in 2008 Entry Draft).

Season	Club	League	GP	W	L	O/T	Mins	GA	SO	Avg	GP	W	L	Mins	GA	SO	Avg
			Regular Season								Playoffs						
06-07	Valley East Cobras	GNML	32				1443	80	1	3.33	7			410	22	2	3.22
07-08	Owen Sound	OHL	35	12	19	3	2021	136	0	4.04							
08-09	Owen Sound	OHL	37	11	12	10	2160	131	1	3.64	1	0	1	27	5	0	11.16
09-10	Kingston	OHL	62	29	25	4	3461	203	1	3.52	7	3	3	424	23	0	3.26

IRON, Martin (BEE-rawn, MAHR-tihn) NYR

oaltender. Catches left. 6'3", 180 lbs. Born, Lac-St-Charles, Que., August 15, 1977.
Buffalo's 2nd choice, 16th overall, in 1995 Entry Draft).

Season	Club	League	GP	W	L	O/T	Mins	GA	SO	Avg	GP	W	L	Mins	GA	SO	Avg
			Regular Season								Playoffs						
993-94	Trois-Rivieres	QAAA	23	14	8	1	1412	80	1	3.40	2	1	1	112	7	0	3.73
994-95	Beauport Harfangs	QMJHL	56	29	16	9	3193	132	3	*2.48	16	8	7	900	37	*4	2.47
995-96	Beauport Harfangs	QMJHL	55	29	17	7	3201	152	1	2.85	*19	*12	7	1134	64	0	3.39
	Buffalo	NHL	3	0	2	0	119	10	0	5.04							
1996-97	Beauport Harfangs	QMJHL	18	6	9	1	928	61	1	3.94							
	Hull Olympiques	QMJHL	16	11	4	1	974	43	2	2.65	6	3	1	325	19	0	3.51
1997-98	South Carolina	ECHL	2	0	1	1	86	3	0	2.09							
	Rochester	AHL	41	14	18	6	2312	113	*5	2.93	4	1	3	239	16	0	4.01
1998-99	Buffalo	NHL	6	1	2	1	281	10	0	2.14							
	Rochester	AHL	52	36	13	3	3129	108	*6	*2.07	*20	12	8	1167	42	1	*2.16
99-2000	Buffalo	NHL	41	19	18	2	2229	90	5	2.42							
	Rochester	AHL	6	6	0	0	344	12	1	2.09							
2000-01	Buffalo	NHL	18	7	7	1	918	39	2	2.55							
	Rochester	AHL	4	3	1	0	239	4	1	1.00							
2001-02	Buffalo	NHL	72	31	28	10	4085	151	4	2.22							
2002-03	Buffalo	NHL	54	17	28	6	3170	135	4	2.56							
2003-04	Buffalo	NHL	52	26	18	5	2972	125	2	2.52							
2004-05			DID NOT PLAY														
2005-06	Buffalo	NHL	35	21	8	3	1934	93	1	2.89							
2006-07	Buffalo	NHL	19	12	4	1	1066	54	0	3.04							
	Philadelphia	NHL	16	6	8	2	935	47	0	3.02							
2007-08	Philadelphia	NHL	62	30	20	9	3539	153	5	2.59	17	9	8	1049	52	1	2.97
2008-09	Philadelphia	NHL	55	29	19	5	3177	146	2	2.76	6	2	4	375	16	1	2.56
2009-10	NY Islanders	NHL	29	9	14	4	1634	89	1	3.27							
	Bridgeport	AHL	2	1	1	0	124	7	0	3.40							
	NHL Totals		462	208	176	49	26059	1142	26	2.63	23	11	12	1424	68	2	2.87

QMJHL All-Rookie Team (1995) • Canadian Major Junior First All-Star Team (1995) • Canadian Major Junior Goaltender of the Year (1995) • AHL First All-Star Team (1999) • Harry "Hap" Holmes Memorial Award (AHL – fewest goals against) (1999) (shared with Tom Draper) • Aldege "Baz" Bastien Memorial Award (AHL – Outstanding Goaltender) (1999)

Traded to **Philadelphia** by **Buffalo** for Philadelphia's 2nd round choice (T.J. Brennan) in 2007 Entry Draft, February 27, 2007. Signed as a free agent by **NY Islanders**, July 22, 2009. Signed as a free agent by **NY Rangers**, July 1, 2010.

BISHOP, Ben (BIH-shuhp, BEHN) ST.L.

Goaltender. Catches left. 6'7", 215 lbs. Born, Denver, CO, November 21, 1986.
(St. Louis' 3rd choice, 85th overall, in 2005 Entry Draft).

Season	Club	League	GP	W	L	O/T	Mins	GA	SO	Avg	GP	W	L	Mins	GA	SO	Avg
			Regular Season								Playoffs						
2003-04	St.L. AAA Blues	MAHL	11	8	1	2	660	19	1	1.73							
	St.L. AAA Blues	Exhib.	26	15	7	4	1480	62	3	2.51							
2004-05	Texas Tornado	NAHL	45	*35	8	0	2577	83	5	1.93	*11	*9	2	*660	30	0	2.73
2005-06	University of Maine	H-East	31	21	8	2	1788	68	0	2.28							
2006-07	University of Maine	H-East	34	21	9	2	1907	68	3	2.14							
2007-08	University of Maine	H-East	34	13	18	3	1972	80	2	2.43							
	Peoria Rivermen	AHL	5	2	2	1	302	12	0	2.38							
2008-09	St. Louis	NHL	6	1	1	1	245	12	0	2.94							
	Peoria Rivermen	AHL	33	15	16	1	1898	89	1	2.81							
2009-10	Peoria Rivermen	AHL	48	23	18	4	2793	129	0	2.77							
	NHL Totals		6	1	1	1	245	12	0	2.94							

Hockey East All-Rookie Team (2006) • Hockey East Second All-Star Team (2008)

BOBKOV, Igor (bawb-KAWF, EE-gohr) ANA.

Goaltender. Catches left. 6'4", 192 lbs. Born, Surgut, USSR, January 2, 1991.
(Anaheim's 4th choice, 76th overall, in 2009 Entry Draft).

Season	Club	League	GP	W	L	O/T	Mins	GA	SO	Avg	GP	W	L	Mins	GA	SO	Avg
			Regular Season								Playoffs						
2008-09	Magnitogorsk 2	Russia-3	9					24									
2009-10	Magnitogorsk Jr.	Russia-Jr.	14				665	30	2	2.71	2			59	3	0	3.05

BOBROVSKY, Sergei (bawb-RAWF-skee, SAIR-gay) PHI.

Goaltender. Catches left. 6'1", 174 lbs. Born, Novokuznetsk, USSR, September 20, 1988.

Season	Club	League	GP	W	L	O/T	Mins	GA	SO	Avg	GP	W	L	Mins	GA	SO	Avg
			Regular Season								Playoffs						
2006-07	Novokuznetsk	Russia	8				280	13	0	2.78							
2007-08	Novokuznetsk	Russia	24				1153	57	1	2.97							
2008-09	Novokuznetsk	Rus-KHL	32				1636	69	1	2.53							
2009-10	Novokuznetsk	Rus-KHL	35				1964	89	1	2.72							

Signed as a free agent by **Philadelphia**, May 6, 2010.

BOUCHER, Brian (BOO-shay, BRIGH-uhn) PHI.

Goaltender. Catches left. 6'2", 200 lbs. Born, Woonsocket, RI, January 2, 1977.
(Philadelphia's 1st choice, 22nd overall, in 1995 Entry Draft).

Season	Club	League	GP	W	L	O/T	Mins	GA	SO	Avg	GP	W	L	Mins	GA	SO	Avg
			Regular Season								Playoffs						
1993-94	Mount St. Charles	High-RI	15	*14	0	1	*504	*8	*9	*0.57	4	*4	0	*180	*6	*1	*1.20
1994-95	Wexford Raiders	MTJHL	8				425	23	0	3.25							
	Tri-City Americans	WHL	35	17	11	2	1969	108	1	3.29	13	6	5	795	50	0	3.77
1995-96	Tri-City Americans	WHL	55	33	19	2	3183	181	1	3.41	11	6	5	653	37	*2	3.40
1996-97	Tri-City Americans	WHL	41	10	24	6	2458	149	1	3.64							
1997-98	Philadelphia	AHL	34	16	12	3	1901	101	0	3.19	2	0	0	30	1	0	1.95
1998-99	Philadelphia	AHL	36	20	8	5	2061	89	2	2.59	16	9	7	947	45	0	2.85
99-2000	Philadelphia	NHL	35	20	10	3	2038	65	4	*1.91	18	11	7	1183	40	1	2.03
	Philadelphia	AHL	1	0	0	1	65	3	0	2.77							
2000-01	Philadelphia	NHL	27	8	12	5	1470	80	1	3.27	1	0	0	37	3	0	4.86
2001-02	Philadelphia	NHL	41	18	16	4	2295	92	2	2.41	2	0	1	88	2	0	1.36
2002-03	Phoenix	NHL	45	15	20	8	2544	128	0	3.02							
2003-04	Phoenix	NHL	40	10	19	10	2364	108	5	2.74							
2004-05	HV 71 Jonkoping	Sweden	4				235	13	0	3.32							
2005-06	Phoenix	NHL	11	3	6	0	512	33	0	3.87							
	San Antonio	AHL	6	2	3	0	345	8	0	1.39							
	Calgary	NHL	3	1	2	0	182	15	0	4.95							
2006-07	Chicago	NHL	15	1	10	3	827	45	1	3.26							
	Columbus	NHL	3	1	1	0	142	9	0	3.80							
2007-08	Philadelphia	AHL	42	23	16	1	2288	94	4	2.47							
	San Jose	NHL	5	3	1	1	238	7	1	1.76	1	0	0	2	0	0	0.00
2008-09	San Jose	NHL	22	12	6	3	1291	47	2	2.18							
2009-10	Philadelphia	NHL	33	9	18	3	1742	80	1	2.76	12	6	6	656	27	1	2.47
	Adirondack	AHL	1	1	0	0	60	2	0	2.00							
	NHL Totals		280	101	121	40	15645	709	17	2.72	34	17	14	1966	72	2	2.20

WHL West Second All-Star Team (1996) • WHL West First All-Star Team (1997) • WHL Goaltender of the Year (1997) • NHL All-Rookie Team (2000)

Traded to **Phoenix** by **Philadelphia** with Nashville's 3rd round choice (previously acquired, Phoenix selected Joe Callahan) in 2002 Entry Draft for Michal Handzus and Robert Esche, June 12, 2002. Signed as a free agent by **Jonkoping** (Sweden), October 20, 2004. Traded to **Calgary** by **Phoenix** with Mike Leclerc for Steve Reinprecht and Philippe Sauve, February 2, 2006. Signed as a free agent by **Chicago**, September 24, 2006. Claimed on waivers by **Columbus** from **Chicago**, February 27, 2007. Signed as a free agent by **Philadelphia** (AHL), July 23, 2007. Signed as a free agent by **San Jose**, February 26, 2008. Signed as a free agent by **Philadelphia**, July 1, 2009.

BRITTAIN, Sam (brih-TAYN, SAM) FLA.

Goaltender. Catches left. 6'3", 215 lbs. Born, Calgary, Alta., May 10, 1992.
(Florida's 8th choice, 92nd overall, in 2010 Entry Draft).

			Regular Season								Playoffs						
Season	Club	League	GP	W	L	O/T	Mins	GA	SO	Avg	GP	W	L	Mins	GA	SO	Avg
2008-09	Calgary Buffaloes	AMHL	26	14	9	3	1542	67	....	2.61	15	11	4	901	45	....	3.00
	Canmore Eagles	AJHL	3	1	2	0	179	9	0	3.02	....	....	....	....	....	....	....
2009-10	Canmore Eagles	AJHL	52	23	19	8	3065	167	2	3.27	9	5	4	559	28	0	3.01

• Signed Letter of Intent to attend **University of Denver** (WCHA) in fall of 2010.

BRODEUR, Martin (broh-DUHR, MAHR-tihn) N.J.

Goaltender. Catches left. 6'2", 215 lbs. Born, Montreal, Que., May 6, 1972.
(New Jersey's 1st choice, 20th overall, in 1990 Entry Draft).

			Regular Season								Playoffs						
Season	Club	League	GP	W	L	O/T	Mins	GA	SO	Avg	GP	W	L	Mins	GA	SO	Avg
1988-89	Montreal-Bourassa	QAAA	27	13	12	1	1580	98	0	3.72	3	0	3	210	14	0	3.99
1989-90	St-Hyacinthe Laser	QMJHL	42	23	13	2	2333	156	0	4.01	12	5	7	678	46	0	4.07
1990-91	St-Hyacinthe Laser	QMJHL	52	22	24	4	2946	162	2	3.30	4	0	4	232	16	0	4.14
1991-92	St-Hyacinthe Laser	QMJHL	48	27	16	4	2846	161	2	3.39	5	2	3	317	14	0	2.65
	New Jersey	**NHL**	**4**	**2**	**1**	**0**	**179**	**10**	**0**	**3.35**	**1**	**0**	**1**	**32**	**3**	**0**	**5.63**
1992-93	Utica Devils	AHL	32	14	13	5	1952	131	0	4.03	4	1	3	258	18	0	4.19
1993-94	**New Jersey**	**NHL**	**47**	**27**	**11**	**8**	**2625**	**105**	**3**	**2.40**	**17**	**8**	**9**	**1171**	**38**	**1**	**1.95**
1994-95 ♦	**New Jersey**	**NHL**	**40**	**19**	**11**	**6**	**2184**	**89**	**3**	**2.45**	***20**	***16**	**4**	***1222**	**34**	***3**	***1.67**
1995-96	**New Jersey**	**NHL**	**77**	**34**	**30**	**12**	***4433**	**173**	**6**	**2.34**	....	....	....	....	....	....	....
1996-97	**New Jersey**	**NHL**	**67**	**37**	**14**	**13**	**3838**	**120**	***10**	***1.88**	**10**	**5**	**5**	**659**	**19**	**2**	***1.73**
1997-98	**New Jersey**	**NHL**	**70**	***43**	**17**	**8**	**4128**	**130**	**10**	**1.89**	**6**	**2**	**4**	**366**	**12**	**0**	**1.97**
1998-99	**New Jersey**	**NHL**	***70**	***39**	**21**	**10**	***4239**	**162**	**4**	**2.29**	**7**	**3**	**4**	**425**	**20**	**0**	**2.82**
99-2000 ♦	**New Jersey**	**NHL**	**72**	***43**	**20**	**8**	**4312**	**161**	**6**	**2.24**	***23**	***16**	**7**	***1450**	**39**	**2**	***1.61**
2000-01	**New Jersey**	**NHL**	**72**	***42**	**17**	**11**	**4297**	**166**	**9**	**2.32**	***25**	**15**	**10**	***1505**	**52**	***4**	**2.07**
2001-02	**New Jersey**	**NHL**	***73**	**38**	**26**	**9**	***4347**	**156**	**4**	**2.15**	**6**	**2**	**4**	**381**	**9**	**1**	**1.42**
	Canada	Olympics	5	*4	0	1	300	9	0	*1.80	....	....	....	....	....	....	....
2002-03 ♦	**New Jersey**	**NHL**	**73**	***41**	**23**	**9**	**4374**	**147**	***9**	**2.02**	***24**	***16**	**8**	***1491**	**41**	***7**	**1.65**
2003-04	**New Jersey**	**NHL**	***75**	***38**	**26**	**11**	***4555**	**154**	***11**	**2.03**	**5**	**1**	**4**	**298**	**13**	**0**	**2.62**
2004-05			DID NOT PLAY														
2005-06	**New Jersey**	**NHL**	**73**	***43**	**23**	**7**	**4365**	**187**	**5**	**2.57**	**9**	**5**	**4**	**533**	**20**	**1**	**2.25**
	Canada	Olympics	4	2	2	0	239	8	0	2.01	....	....	....	....	....	....	....
2006-07	**New Jersey**	**NHL**	***78**	***48**	**23**	**7**	***4697**	**171**	***12**	**2.18**	**11**	**5**	**6**	**688**	**28**	**1**	**2.44**
2007-08	**New Jersey**	**NHL**	***77**	**44**	**27**	**6**	***4635**	**168**	**4**	**2.17**	**5**	**1**	**4**	**301**	**16**	**0**	**3.19**
2008-09	**New Jersey**	**NHL**	**31**	**19**	**9**	**3**	**1814**	**73**	**5**	**2.41**	**7**	**3**	**4**	**427**	**17**	**1**	**2.39**
2009-10	**New Jersey**	**NHL**	***77**	***45**	**25**	**6**	***4499**	**168**	***9**	**2.24**	**5**	**1**	**4**	**299**	**15**	**0**	**3.01**
	Canada	Olympics	2	1	1	0	124	6	0	2.90	....	....	....	....	....	....	....
	NHL Totals		**1076**	**602**	**324**	**134**	**63521**	**2340**	**110**	**2.21**	**181**	**99**	**82**	**11248**	**376**	**23**	**2.01**

QMJHL All-Rookie Team (1990) • QMJHL Second All-Star Team (1992) • NHL All-Rookie Team (1994) • Calder Memorial Trophy (1994) • NHL Second All-Star Team (1997, 1998, 2006, 2008) • William M. Jennings Trophy (1997) (shared with Mike Dunham) • William M. Jennings Trophy (1998, 2004, 2010) • NHL First All-Star Team (2003, 2004, 2007) • William M. Jennings Trophy (2003) (tied with Roman Cechmanek/Robert Esche) • Vezina Trophy (2003, 2004, 2007, 2008)

Played in NHL All-Star Game (1996, 1997, 1998, 1999, 2000, 2001, 2003, 2004, 2007)

• Scored a goal in playoffs vs. Montreal, April 17, 1997. • Missed majority of 2008-09 season recovering from elbow injury suffered in game vs. Atlanta, November 1, 2008 and resulting surgery, November 6, 2008.

BRODEUR, Mike (broh-DUHR, MIGHK) OTT.

Goaltender. Catches left. 6'2", 186 lbs. Born, Calgary, Alta., March 30, 1983.
(Chicago's 7th choice, 211th overall, in 2003 Entry Draft).

			Regular Season								Playoffs						
Season	Club	League	GP	W	L	O/T	Mins	GA	SO	Avg	GP	W	L	Mins	GA	SO	Avg
2000-01	Cgy. AAA Flames	AMHL	21	11	8	3	1231	54	1	2.63	10	6	4	620	31	0	3.00
2001-02	Camrose Kodiaks	AJHL	24	13	9	1	1299	65	1	2.91	....	....	....	....	....	....	....
2002-03	Camrose Kodiaks	AJHL	48	28	16	2	2570	113	2	2.64	21	16	5	1378	48	4	2.09
2003-04	Moose Jaw	WHL	41	23	12	5	2385	84	5	2.11	10	6	4	624	18	1	*1.73
2004-05	Norfolk Admirals	AHL	1	0	1	0	39	4	0	6.17	....	....	....	....	....	....	....
	Greenville Grrrowl	ECHL	35	19	15	1	2081	93	2	2.68	5	2	3	302	10	1	1.98
2005-06	Greenville Grrrowl	ECHL	24	14	8	2	1466	63	1	2.58	....	....	....	....	....	....	....
2006-07	Norfolk Admirals	AHL	10	4	3	0	495	28	0	3.39	1	0	0	8	2	0	14.17
	Augusta Lynx	ECHL	2	2	0	0	120	4	1	2.00	....	....	....	....	....	....	....
	Toledo Storm	ECHL	5	3	2	0	300	10	2	2.00	....	....	....	....	....	....	....
2007-08	Rockford IceHogs	AHL	8	2	3	0	341	16	0	2.81	....	....	....	....	....	....	....
	Pensacola Ice Pilots	ECHL	26	10	9	5	1504	71	1	2.83	....	....	....	....	....	....	....
2008-09	Rochester	AHL	38	18	13	4	2127	87	2	2.45	....	....	....	....	....	....	....
	Augusta Lynx	ECHL	8	2	4	1	457	23	1	3.02	....	....	....	....	....	....	....
2009-10	**Ottawa**	**NHL**	**3**	**3**	**0**	**0**	**180**	**3**	**1**	**1.00**	....	....	....	....	....	....	....
	Binghamton	AHL	36	13	13	2	1881	96	2	3.06	....	....	....	....	....	....	....
	NHL Totals		**3**	**3**	**0**	**0**	**180**	**3**	**1**	**1.00**	....	....	....	....	....	....	....

Signed as a free agent by **Ottawa**, July 1, 2009.

BRUST, Barry (BRUHST, BAIR-ree)

Goaltender. Catches left. 6'2", 235 lbs. Born, Swan River, Man., August 8, 1983.
(Minnesota's 4th choice, 73rd overall, in 2002 Entry Draft).

			Regular Season								Playoffs						
Season	Club	League	GP	W	L	O/T	Mins	GA	SO	Avg	GP	W	L	Mins	GA	SO	Avg
99-2000	Swan Valley	MJHL	19	10	9	0	1140	67	0	3.50	....	....	....	....	....	....	....
2000-01	Spokane Chiefs	WHL	16	4	6	1	777	42	0	3.24	....	....	....	....	....	....	....
2001-02	Spokane Chiefs	WHL	60	28	21	10	3540	152	1	2.58	11	6	5	677	23	0	2.04
2002-03	Spokane Chiefs	WHL	*59	22	31	4	*3385	194	0	3.44	11	4	7	722	37	0	3.07
2003-04	Spokane Chiefs	WHL	27	10	13	2	1505	75	0	2.99	....	....	....	....	....	....	....
	Calgary Hitmen	WHL	25	12	8	3	1448	54	2	2.24	7	3	4	457	15	2	1.97
2004-05	Reading Royals	ECHL	42	27	9	4	2413	79	4	1.96	8	4	4	481	14	2	1.74
2005-06	Manchester	AHL	35	19	14	1	1971	89	2	2.71	5	2	2	279	17	1	3.66
	Reading Royals	ECHL	6	3	3	0	361	18	0	3.00	....	....	....	....	....	....	....
2006-07	**Los Angeles**	**NHL**	**11**	**2**	**4**	**1**	**486**	**30**	**0**	**3.70**	....	....	....	....	....	....	....
	Manchester	AHL	18	9	7	0	951	38	2	2.40	5	2	1	199	6	0	1.81
2007-08	Houston Aeros	AHL	43	24	16	3	2380	90	4	2.27	3	1	2	202	6	1	1.78
2008-09	Houston Aeros	AHL	28	9	9	3	1548	65	0	2.52	....	....	....	....	....	....	....
2009-10	Houston Aeros	AHL	15	6	6	0	756	31	1	2.46	....	....	....	....	....	....	....
	Florida Everblades	ECHL	16	9	3	2	882	33	0	2.24	....	....	....	....	....	....	....
	NHL Totals		**11**	**2**	**4**	**1**	**486**	**30**	**0**	**3.70**	....	....	....	....	....	....	....

WHL West First All-Star Team (2002) • Harry "Hap" Holmes Memorial Award (AHL – fewest goals against) (2008) (shared with Nolan Schaefer)

Signed as a free agent by **Los Angeles**, June 10, 2004. Signed as a free agent by **Minnesota**, July 6, 2008.

BRYZGALOV, Ilya (breez-GAH-lahf, IHL-yah) PH

Goaltender. Catches left. 6'3", 210 lbs. Born, Togliatti, USSR, June 22, 1980.
(Anaheim's 2nd choice, 44th overall, in 2000 Entry Draft).

			Regular Season								Playoffs						
Season	Club	League	GP	W	L	O/T	Mins	GA	SO	Avg	GP	W	L	Mins	GA	SO	Av
1996-97	Lada Togliatti 2	Russia-3	5	....	....	....	....	....	....	....	....	....	....	....	....	....	....
1997-98	Lada Togliatti 2	Russia-3	8	....	....	....	....	28	....	....	....	....	....	....	....	....	....
1998-99	Lada Togliatti 2	Russia-4	20	....	....	....	....	43	....	....	....	....	....	....	....	....	....
99-2000	Spartak Moscow	Russia-2	10	....	....	....	500	21	....	2.52	....	....	....	....	....	....	....
	Lada Togliatti 2	Russia-3	2	....	....	....	....	5	....	....	....	....	....	....	....	....	....
	Lada Togliatti	Russia	14	....	....	....	796	18	3	1.36	7	....	....	407	10	1	1.4
2000-01	Lada Togliatti	Russia	34	....	....	....	1992	61	8	1.84	5	....	....	249	8	0	1.9
2001-02	**Anaheim**	**NHL**	**1**	**0**	**0**	**0**	**32**	**1**	**0**	**1.88**	....	....	....	....	....	....	....
	Cincinnati	AHL	45	20	16	4	2399	99	4	2.48	....	....	....	....	....	....	....
	Russia	Olympics	DID NOT PLAY – SPARE GOALTENDER														
2002-03	Cincinnati	AHL	54	12	26	9	3020	142	1	2.82	....	....	....	....	....	....	....
2003-04	**Anaheim**	**NHL**	**1**	**1**	**0**	**0**	**60**	**2**	**0**	**2.00**	....	....	....	....	....	....	....
	Cincinnati	AHL	*64	27	25	10	*3748	145	6	2.32	9	5	4	536	27	1	3.0
2004-05	Cincinnati	AHL	36	17	13	1	2007	87	4	2.60	7	3	3	314	13	0	2.4
2005-06	**Anaheim**	**NHL**	**31**	**13**	**12**	**1**	**1575**	**66**	**1**	**2.51**	**11**	**6**	**4**	**659**	**16**	***3**	***1.4**
	Russia	Olympics	1	0	1	0	60	5	0	5.00	....	....	....	....	....	....	....
2006-07 ♦	**Anaheim**	**NHL**	**27**	**10**	**8**	**6**	**1509**	**62**	**1**	**2.47**	**5**	**3**	**1**	**267**	**10**	**0**	**2.2**
2007-08	**Anaheim**	**NHL**	**9**	**2**	**3**	**1**	**447**	**19**	**0**	**2.55**	....	....	....	....	....	....	....
	Phoenix	**NHL**	**55**	**26**	**22**	**5**	**3167**	**128**	**3**	**2.43**	....	....	....	....	....	....	....
2008-09	**Phoenix**	**NHL**	**65**	**26**	**31**	**6**	**3760**	**187**	**3**	**2.98**	....	....	....	....	....	....	....
2009-10	**Phoenix**	**NHL**	**69**	**42**	**20**	**6**	**4084**	**156**	**8**	**2.29**	**7**	**3**	**4**	**419**	**24**	**0**	**3.4**
	Russia	Olympics	2	0	1	0	101	3	0	1.78	....	....	....	....	....	....	....
	NHL Totals		**258**	**120**	**96**	**25**	**14634**	**621**	**16**	**2.55**	**23**	**12**	**9**	**1345**	**50**	**3**	**2.2**

NHL Second All-Star Team (2010)

Claimed on waivers by **Phoenix** from **Anaheim**, November 17, 2007.

BUDAJ, Peter (BOO-digh, PEE-tuhr) CO

Goaltender. Catches left. 6'1", 200 lbs. Born, Banska Bystrica, Czech., September 18, 1982.
(Colorado's 1st choice, 63rd overall, in 2001 Entry Draft).

			Regular Season								Playoffs						
Season	Club	League	GP	W	L	O/T	Mins	GA	SO	Avg	GP	W	L	Mins	GA	SO	Av
99-2000	St. Michael's	OHL	34	6	18	1	1676	112	1	4.01	....	....	....	....	....	....	....
2000-01	St. Michael's	OHL	37	17	12	3	1996	95	3	2.86	11	6	4	621	26	1	2.5
2001-02	St. Michael's	OHL	42	26	9	5	2329	89	2	*2.29	12	5	6	620	34	*1	3.2
2002-03	Hershey Bears	AHL	28	10	10	2	1467	65	2	2.66	1	0	0	6	2	0	20.8
2003-04	Hershey Bears	AHL	46	17	20	6	2574	120	3	2.80	....	....	....	....	....	....	....
2004-05	Hershey Bears	AHL	59	29	25	2	3356	148	5	2.65	....	....	....	....	....	....	....
2005-06	**Colorado**	**NHL**	**34**	**14**	**10**	**6**	**1803**	**86**	**2**	**2.86**	....	....	....	....	....	....	....
	Slovakia	Olympics	3	2	1	0	179	6	0	2.01	....	....	....	....	....	....	....
2006-07	**Colorado**	**NHL**	**57**	**31**	**16**	**6**	**3199**	**143**	**3**	**2.68**	....	....	....	....	....	....	....
2007-08	**Colorado**	**NHL**	**35**	**16**	**10**	**4**	**1912**	**82**	**0**	**2.57**	**3**	**0**	**0**	**108**	**6**	**0**	**3.3**
2008-09	**Colorado**	**NHL**	**56**	**20**	**29**	**5**	**3232**	**154**	**2**	**2.86**	....	....	....	....	....	....	....
2009-10	**Colorado**	**NHL**	**15**	**5**	**5**	**2**	**728**	**32**	**1**	**2.64**	**1**	**0**	**0**	**9**	**1**	**0**	**6.6**
	Slovakia	Olympics	DID NOT PLAY – SPARE GOALTENDER														
	NHL Totals		**197**	**86**	**70**	**23**	**10874**	**497**	**8**	**2.74**	**4**	**0**	**0**	**117**	**7**	**0**	**3.5**

OHL Second All-Star Team (2002)

BUNZ, Tyler (BUHNZ, TIGH-luhr) EDM

Goaltender. Catches left. 6'1", 196 lbs. Born, Regina, Sask., February 11, 1992.
(Edmonton's 7th choice, 121st overall, in 2010 Entry Draft).

			Regular Season								Playoffs						
Season	Club	League	GP	W	L	O/T	Mins	GA	SO	Avg	GP	W	L	Mins	GA	SO	Av
2007-08	St. Albert	AMHL	24	11	9	4	1503	80	....	3.19	4	2	2	240	16	....	4.0
	Medicine Hat	WHL	1	1	0	0	60	3	0	3.00	....	....	....	....	....	....	....
2008-09	Medicine Hat	WHL	22	9	6	1	1007	58	0	3.46	2	0	1	....	6	0	4.9
2009-10	Medicine Hat	WHL	57	31	19	5	3214	156	2	2.91	12	6	5	720	35	0	2.9

CAMPBELL, Jack (KAM-behl, JAK) DAL

Goaltender. Catches left. 6'3", 175 lbs. Born, Port Huron, MI, January 9, 1992.
(Dallas' 1st choice, 11th overall, in 2010 Entry Draft).

			Regular Season								Playoffs						
Season	Club	League	GP	W	L	O/T	Mins	GA	SO	Avg	GP	W	L	Mins	GA	SO	Av
2007-08	Det. Honeybaked	MWEHL	12	8	2	2	630	24	2	2.06	....	....	....	....	....	....	....
	Det. Honeybaked	Minor-MI	25	20	4	1	....	....	....	....	....	....	....	....	....	....	....
2008-09	USNTDP	NAHL	21	14	6	1	1262	53	1	2.52	....	....	....	....	....	....	....
	USNTDP	U-17	7	6	0	1	394	7	3	1.07	....	....	....	....	....	....	....
	USNTDP	U-18	7	7	0	0	421	12	2	1.71	....	....	....	....	....	....	....
2009-10	USNTDP	USHL	11	6	3	1	569	21	1	2.21	....	....	....	....	....	....	....
	USNTDP	U-18	25	16	9	0	1469	54	3	2.21	....	....	....	....	....	....	....

CANN, Trevor (KAN, TREH-vuhr) COL

Goaltender. Catches left. 5'11", 199 lbs. Born, Oakville, Ont., March 30, 1989.
(Colorado's 3rd choice, 49th overall, in 2007 Entry Draft).

			Regular Season								Playoffs						
Season	Club	League	GP	W	L	O/T	Mins	GA	SO	Avg	GP	W	L	Mins	GA	SO	Av
2005-06	Peterborough	OHL	20	16	2	0	1176	52	1	2.65	1	0	0	35	3	0	5.1
2006-07	Peterborough	OHL	*62	23	32	5	3565	219	0	3.69	....	....	....	....	....	....	....
2007-08	Peterborough	OHL	51	20	28	3	2976	178	2	3.59	5	1	4	317	21	0	3.9
2008-09	Peterborough	OHL	10	5	5	0	545	28	1	3.08	....	....	....	....	....	....	....
	London Knights	OHL	42	30	10	1	2482	104	5	2.51	13	9	4	805	38	0	2.8
2009-10	Lake Erie Monsters	AHL	13	3	6	1	671	40	1	3.58	....	....	....	....	....	....	....
	Tulsa Oilers	CHL	18	11	6	1	1088	51	0	2.81	....	....	....	....	....	....	....

CANNATA, Joe (ka-NA-tuh, JOH) VAN

Goaltender. Catches left. 6'1", 202 lbs. Born, Wakefield, MA, January 2, 1990.
(Vancouver's 6th choice, 173rd overall, in 2009 Entry Draft).

			Regular Season								Playoffs						
Season	Club	League	GP	W	L	O/T	Mins	GA	SO	Avg	GP	W	L	Mins	GA	SO	Av
2007-08	USNTDP	NAHL	5	3	1	1	307	12	0	2.35	....	....	....	....	....	....	....
	USNTDP	U-18	28	13	13	2	1474	64	1	2.61	....	....	....	....	....	....	....
2008-09	Merrimack College	H-East	23	7	11	4	1353	53	2	2.35	....	....	....	....	....	....	....
2009-10	Merrimack College	H-East	24	10	13	1	1362	69	2	3.04	....	....	....	....	....	....	....

CARON, Sebastien

(KAIR-aw, suh-BAS-tee-yeh)

Goaltender. Catches left. 6'1", 170 lbs. Born, Amqui, Que., June 25, 1980.
(Pittsburgh's 4th choice, 86th overall, in 1999 Entry Draft).

			Regular Season								Playoffs						
Season	Club	League	GP	W	L	O/T	Mins	GA	SO	Avg	GP	W	L	Mins	GA	SO	Avg
1997-98	TGV Pentagone	QAHA	17	....	....	....	762	48	1	2.84	....	....	....	....	....	....	....
1998-99	Rimouski Oceanic	QMJHL	30	13	10	3	1570	85	0	3.25	2	1	0	68	0	0	0.00
99-2000	Rimouski Oceanic	QMJHL	54	*38	11	3	3040	179	1	3.53	14	*12	2	828	50	0	3.62
2000-01	Wilkes-Barre	AHL	30	12	14	3	1746	103	4	3.54	....	....	....	....	....	....	....
2001-02	Wilkes-Barre	AHL	46	14	22	8	2671	139	1	3.12	....	....	....	....	....	....	....
2002-03	**Pittsburgh**	**NHL**	**24**	**7**	**14**	**2**	**1408**	**62**	**2**	**2.64**	....	....	....	....	....	....	....
	Wilkes-Barre	AHL	27	12	14	1	1561	81	1	3.11	....	....	....	....	....	....	....
2003-04	**Pittsburgh**	**NHL**	**40**	**9**	**24**	**5**	**2213**	**138**	**1**	**3.74**	....	....	....	....	....	....	....
	Wilkes-Barre	AHL	14	7	3	4	811	26	2	1.92	7	3	4	395	23	0	3.50
2004-05	Saguenay Fjord	QNAHL	STATISTICS NOT AVAILABLE														
2005-06	**Pittsburgh**	**NHL**	**26**	**8**	**9**	**5**	**1312**	**87**	**1**	**3.98**	....	....	....	....	....	....	....
	Wilkes-Barre	AHL	6	3	3	0	357	7	2	1.18	....	....	....	....	....	....	....
2006-07	**Chicago**	**NHL**	**1**	**1**	**0**	**0**	**60**	**1**	**0**	**1.00**	....	....	....	....	....	....	....
	Norfolk Admirals	AHL	9	4	4	0	506	34	0	4.03	....	....	....	....	....	....	....
	Anaheim	**NHL**	**1**	**0**	**0**	**0**	**28**	**1**	**0**	**2.14**	....	....	....	....	....	....	....
	Portland Pirates	AHL	17	7	6	4	1025	40	0	2.34	....	....	....	....	....	....	....
2007-08	Fribourg	Swiss	48	24	24	0	2851	144	5	3.03	7	4	3	437	21	0	2.88
2008-09	Fribourg	Swiss	39	21	17	0	2265	101	4	2.68	11	7	3	668	19	2	1.71
2009-10	Fribourg	Swiss	46	20	26	0	2739	142	1	3.11	7	3	4	429	23	0	3.22
	NHL Totals		**92**	**25**	**47**	**12**	**5021**	**289**	**4**	**3.45**	....	....	....	....	....	....	....

Memorial Cup Tournament All-Star Team (2000) • Hap Emms Memorial Trophy (Memorial Cup Tournament - Top Goaltender) (2000) • NHL All-Rookie Team (2003)

Signed as a free agent by **Saguenay** (QNAHL), September 21, 2004. Signed as a free agent by **Chicago**, August 8, 2006. Traded to **Anaheim** by **Chicago** with Matt Keith and Chris Durno for P. A. Parenteau and Bruno St. Jacques, December 28, 2006. Signed as a free agent by **Fribourg** (Swiss), June 21, 2007. Signed as a free agent by **Philadelphia**, April 2, 2010.

CARROZZI, Chris

(ka-ROH-zee, KRIHS) **ATL.**

Goaltender. Catches left. 6'3", 200 lbs. Born, Ottawa, Ont., March 2, 1990.
(Atlanta's 6th choice, 154th overall, in 2008 Entry Draft).

			Regular Season								Playoffs						
Season	Club	League	GP	W	L	O/T	Mins	GA	SO	Avg	GP	W	L	Mins	GA	SO	Avg
2005-06	Nepean Raiders	Minor-ON	23	....	....	....	....	42	4	1.82	....	....	....	....	....	....	....
2006-07	St. Michael's	OHL	25	6	7	2	1130	81	0	4.30	....	....	....	....	....	....	....
2007-08	St. Michael's	OHL	47	25	18	2	2505	115	*4	2.75	4	0	4	240	18	0	4.50
2008-09	St. Michael's	OHL	47	27	14	3	2715	133	2	2.94	2	0	0	33	3	0	5.52
2009-10	St. Michael's	OHL	37	19	10	5	2089	82	*5	2.36	8	5	1	448	16	1	*2.14

OHL First All-Star Team (2010)

CARRUTH, Mac

(kair-UHTH, MAK) **CHI.**

Goaltender. Catches left. 6'2", 169 lbs. Born, Salt Lake City, UT, March 25, 1992.
(Chicago's 10th choice, 191st overall, in 2010 Entry Draft).

			Regular Season								Playoffs						
Season	Club	League	GP	W	L	O/T	Mins	GA	SO	Avg	GP	W	L	Mins	GA	SO	Avg
2008-09	Wenatchee Wild	NAHL	26	18	7	1	1462	74	1	3.04	5	2	2	232	15	0	3.88
2009-10	Wenatchee Wild	NAHL	16	11	4	0	866	35	1	2.42	....	....	....	....	....	....	....
	Portland	WHL	26	14	9	1	1427	81	1	3.41	11	5	4	614	39	0	3.81

CHEVERIE, Marc

(sheh-VEH-ree, MAHRK) **FLA.**

Goaltender. Catches left. 6'3", 183 lbs. Born, Cole Harbour, N.S., February 22, 1987.
(Florida's 6th choice, 193rd overall, in 2006 Entry Draft).

			Regular Season								Playoffs						
Season	Club	League	GP	W	L	O/T	Mins	GA	SO	Avg	GP	W	L	Mins	GA	SO	Avg
2003-04	Dartmouth	NSMHL	....	19	4	2	1521	76	1	2.99	....	....	....	....	....	....	....
2004-05	Notre Dame	SMHL	25	....	....	....	....	....	....	2.25	....	....	....	....	....	....	....
2005-06	Nanaimo Clippers	BCHL	46	23	9	0	2032	86	4	2.54	....	....	....	....	....	....	....
2006-07	Nanaimo Clippers	BCHL	34	21	9	2	2015	104	3	3.10	....	....	....	....	....	....	....
2007-08	U. of Denver	WCHA	5	1	0	0	141	4	0	1.70	....	....	....	....	....	....	....
2008-09	U. of Denver	WCHA	40	23	12	5	2383	93	4	2.34	....	....	....	....	....	....	....
2009-10	U. of Denver	WCHA	35	*24	6	3	2044	71	*6	*2.08	....	....	....	....	....	....	....

WCHA Second All-Star Team (2009) • WCHA First All-Star Team (2010) • WCHA Player of the Year (2010) • NCAA West First All-American Team (2010)

CLEMMENSEN, Scott

(KLEH-mehn-sehn, SKAWT) **FLA.**

Goaltender. Catches left. 6'3", 205 lbs. Born, Des Moines, IA, July 23, 1977.
(New Jersey's 7th choice, 215th overall, in 1997 Entry Draft).

			Regular Season								Playoffs						
Season	Club	League	GP	W	L	O/T	Mins	GA	SO	Avg	GP	W	L	Mins	GA	SO	Avg
1995-96	Dubuque	USHL	20	10	7	1	1082	62	0	3.44	....	....	....	....	....	....	....
1996-97	Des Moines	USHL	36	22	9	2	2042	111	1	3.26	4	1	2	200	9	1	2.70
1997-98	Boston College	H-East	37	24	9	4	2205	102	*4	2.78	....	....	....	....	....	....	....
1998-99	Boston College	H-East	*42	26	12	4	*2507	120	1	2.87	....	....	....	....	....	....	....
99-2000	Boston College	H-East	29	19	7	0	1610	59	*5	2.20	....	....	....	....	....	....	....
2000-01	Boston College	H-East	*39	*30	7	2	*2312	82	3	2.13	....	....	....	....	....	....	....
2001-02	**New Jersey**	**NHL**	**2**	**0**	**0**	**0**	**20**	**1**	**0**	**3.00**	....	....	....	....	....	....	....
	Albany River Rats	AHL	29	5	19	4	1677	92	0	3.29	....	....	....	....	....	....	....
2002-03	Albany River Rats	AHL	47	12	24	8	2694	119	1	2.65	....	....	....	....	....	....	....
2003-04	**New Jersey**	**NHL**	**4**	**3**	**1**	**0**	**238**	**4**	**2**	**1.01**	....	....	....	....	....	....	....
	Albany River Rats	AHL	22	5	12	4	1309	67	0	3.07	....	....	....	....	....	....	....
2004-05	Albany River Rats	AHL	46	13	25	5	2645	124	2	2.81	....	....	....	....	....	....	....
2005-06	**New Jersey**	**NHL**	**13**	**3**	**4**	**2**	**627**	**35**	**0**	**3.35**	**1**	**0**	**0**	**7**	**0**	**0**	**0.00**
	Albany River Rats	AHL	1	0	1	0	59	5	0	5.05	....	....	....	....	....	....	....
2006-07	**New Jersey**	**NHL**	**6**	**1**	**1**	**2**	**305**	**16**	**0**	**3.15**	....	....	....	....	....	....	....
	Lowell Devils	AHL	1	1	0	0	60	0	1	0.00	....	....	....	....	....	....	....
2007-08	**Toronto**	**NHL**	**3**	**1**	**1**	**0**	**154**	**10**	**0**	**3.90**	....	....	....	....	....	....	....
	Toronto Marlies	AHL	40	23	14	2	2363	96	1	2.44	17	8	9	992	50	0	3.02
2008-09	**New Jersey**	**NHL**	**40**	**25**	**13**	**1**	**2356**	**94**	**2**	**2.39**	....	....	....	....	....	....	....
	Lowell Devils	AHL	12	6	5	1	707	40	0	3.39	....	....	....	....	....	....	....
2009-10	**Florida**	**NHL**	**23**	**9**	**8**	**2**	**1215**	**59**	**1**	**2.91**	....	....	....	....	....	....	....
	NHL Totals		**91**	**42**	**28**	**7**	**4915**	**219**	**5**	**2.67**	**1**	**0**	**0**	**7**	**0**	**0**	**0.00**

NCAA Championship All-Tournament Team (2001)

Signed as a free agent by **Toronto**, July 6, 2007. Signed as a free agent by **New Jersey**, July 10, 2008. Signed as a free agent by **Florida**, July 1, 2009.

CLERMONT, Maxime

(KLAIR-mawnt, max-EEM) **N.J.**

Goaltender. Catches left. 6'1", 195 lbs. Born, Montreal, Que., December 31, 1991.
(New Jersey's 4th choice, 174th overall, in 2010 Entry Draft).

			Regular Season								Playoffs						
Season	Club	League	GP	W	L	O/T	Mins	GA	SO	Avg	GP	W	L	Mins	GA	SO	Avg
2006-07	Crabtree Draveurs	QAAA	26	10	11	2	1436	74	1	3.09	3	0	2	95	10	0	6.31
2007-08	Gatineau	QMJHL	29	13	7	....	1285	62	1	2.89	3	0	1	56	3	0	3.20
2008-09	Gatineau	QMJHL	49	25	20	....	2665	143	1	3.22	2	0	0	10	1	0	5.99
2009-10	Gatineau	QMJHL	59	24	31	....	3354	157	4	2.81	11	4	6	635	38	0	3.59

CLIMIE, Matt

(KLIGH-mee, MAT) **PHX.**

Goaltender. Catches left. 6'3", 194 lbs. Born, Leduc, Alta., February 11, 1983.

			Regular Season								Playoffs						
Season	Club	League	GP	W	L	O/T	Mins	GA	SO	Avg	GP	W	L	Mins	GA	SO	Avg
2002-03	Truro Bearcats	MJrHL	STATISTICS NOT AVAILABLE														
2003-04	Truro Bearcats	MJrHL	45	30	10	0	2731	119	0	2.61	....	....	....	....	....	....	....
2004-05	Bemidji State	CHA	21	12	5	1	1167	35	4	*1.80	....	....	....	....	....	....	....
2005-06	Bemidji State	CHA	18	8	7	2	1065	48	1	2.70	....	....	....	....	....	....	....
2006-07	Bemidji State	CHA	29	11	10	5	*1666	84	*2	*3.03	....	....	....	....	....	....	....
2007-08	Bemidji State	CHA	27	14	8	3	1529	55	*5	*2.16	....	....	....	....	....	....	....
	Iowa Stars	AHL	6	1	4	1	346	23	0	....	....	....	....	....	....	....	....
2008-09	**Dallas**	**NHL**	**3**	**2**	**1**	**0**	**185**	**9**	**0**	**2.92**	....	....	....	....	....	....	....
	Idaho Steelheads	ECHL	42	27	12	1	2404	92	4	2.30	4	0	3	199	8	0	2.41
	Houston Aeros	AHL	....	....	....	....	....	....	....	....	5	1	1	191	6	0	1.88
2009-10	**Dallas**	**NHL**	**1**	**0**	**1**	**0**	**60**	**5**	**0**	**5.00**	....	....	....	....	....	....	....
	Texas Stars	AHL	43	21	17	3	2539	104	3	2.46	15	7	6	885	40	0	2.71
	NHL Totals		**4**	**2**	**2**	**0**	**245**	**14**	**0**	**3.43**	....	....	....	....	....	....	....

CHA Second All-Star Team (2008)

Signed as a free agent by **Dallas**, March 20, 2008. Signed as a free agent by **Phoenix**, July 3, 2010.

COLEMAN, Gerald

(KOHL-man, JAIR-uhld)

Goaltender. Catches left. 6'4", 214 lbs. Born, Romeoville, IL, April 3, 1985.
(Tampa Bay's 5th choice, 224th overall, in 2003 Entry Draft).

			Regular Season								Playoffs						
Season	Club	League	GP	W	L	O/T	Mins	GA	SO	Avg	GP	W	L	Mins	GA	SO	Avg
99-2000	Chicago	MEHL	26	....	....	....	1560	65	0	2.50	....	....	....	....	....	....	....
2000-01	USNTDP	U-17	9	3	0	4	527	26	0	2.96	....	....	....	....	....	....	....
	USNTDP	NAHL	36	8	23	1	1859	132	0	4.26	....	....	....	....	....	....	....
2001-02	USNTDP	U-18	13	8	1	3	667	38	1	3.42	....	....	....	....	....	....	....
	USNTDP	USHL	2	1	1	0	76	4	0	3.15	....	....	....	....	....	....	....
	USNTDP	NAHL	22	5	14	2	1263	75	0	3.56	....	....	....	....	....	....	....
2002-03	London Knights	OHL	26	6	9	3	1074	59	1	3.30	....	....	....	....	....	....	....
2003-04	London Knights	OHL	33	24	8	0	1852	68	*5	2.20	8	5	2	442	19	1	2.58
2004-05	London Knights	OHL	38	*32	2	2	2224	63	*8	*1.70	8	7	1	455	13	0	*1.71
2005-06	**Tampa Bay**	**NHL**	**2**	**0**	**0**	**1**	**43**	**2**	**0**	**2.79**	....	....	....	....	....	....	....
	Springfield Falcons	AHL	43	14	21	3	2413	156	2	3.88	....	....	....	....	....	....	....
2006-07	Springfield Falcons	AHL	3	2	1	0	179	6	0	2.01	....	....	....	....	....	....	....
	Johnstown Chiefs	ECHL	17	7	9	0	914	52	0	3.41	....	....	....	....	....	....	....
	Portland Pirates	AHL	11	4	5	0	603	29	0	2.89	....	....	....	....	....	....	....
2007-08	Portland Pirates	AHL	18	8	7	1	968	47	2	2.91	1	0	0	39	4	0	6.09
	Augusta Lynx	ECHL	9	2	5	0	500	22	0	2.64	....	....	....	....	....	....	....
2008-09	Worcester Sharks	AHL	3	0	2	0	112	6	0	3.23	....	....	....	....	....	....	....
	Phoenix	ECHL	4	2	1	1	244	6	1	1.48	....	....	....	....	....	....	....
	Trenton Devils	ECHL	40	27	8	2	2322	92	3	2.38	3	1	1	246	15	0	3.66
2009-10	Lowell Devils	AHL	3	1	2	0	182	13	0	4.28	....	....	....	....	....	....	....
	Trenton Devils	ECHL	28	11	9	7	1563	94	0	3.61	....	....	....	....	....	....	....
	NHL Totals		**2**	**0**	**0**	**1**	**43**	**2**	**0**	**2.79**	....	....	....	....	....	....	....

ECHL Second All-Star Team (2009)

Traded to **Anaheim** by **Tampa Bay** with Tampa Bay's 1st round choice (later traded to Minnesota - Minnesota selected Colton Gillies) in 2007 Entry Draft for Shane O'Brien and Colorado's 3rd round choice (previously acquired, Tampa Bay selected Luca Cunti) in 2007 Entry Draft, February 24, 2007. Signed as a free agent by **New Jersey**, July 31, 2009.

CONKLIN, Ty

(KAWN-klihn, TIGH) **ST.L.**

Goaltender. Catches left. 6'1", 190 lbs. Born, Anchorage, AK, March 30, 1976.

			Regular Season								Playoffs						
Season	Club	League	GP	W	L	O/T	Mins	GA	SO	Avg	GP	W	L	Mins	GA	SO	Avg
1995-96	Green Bay	USHL	30	....	....	....	1727	82	1	2.85	....	....	....	....	....	....	....
1996-97	Alaska Anchorage	WCHA	DID NOT PLAY – FRESHMAN														
	Green Bay	USHL	30	19	7	1	1609	86	1	3.21	17	8	9	980	56	1	3.43
1997-98	New Hampshire	H-East	DID NOT PLAY – TRANSFERRED COLLEGES														
1998-99	New Hampshire	H-East	22	18	3	1	1338	41	0	*1.84	....	....	....	....	....	....	....
99-2000	New Hampshire	H-East	*37	*22	8	6	*2194	91	2	2.49	....	....	....	....	....	....	....
2000-01	New Hampshire	H-East	34	17	12	5	2048	70	*5	*2.05	....	....	....	....	....	....	....
2001-02	**Edmonton**	**NHL**	**4**	**2**	**0**	**0**	**148**	**4**	**0**	**1.62**	....	....	....	....	....	....	....
	Hamilton Bulldogs	AHL	37	13	12	8	2043	89	1	2.61	7	4	2	416	18	0	2.60
2002-03	Hamilton Bulldogs	AHL	38	19	13	3	2140	91	4	2.55	17	9	6	1024	38	1	2.23
2003-04	**Edmonton**	**NHL**	**38**	**17**	**14**	**4**	**2086**	**84**	**1**	**2.42**	....	....	....	....	....	....	....
2004-05	Wolfsburg	Germany	11	....	....	....	623	31	0	2.99	7	....	....	414	11	2	1.59
2005-06	**Edmonton**	**NHL**	**18**	**8**	**5**	**1**	**922**	**43**	**1**	**2.80**	**1**	**0**	**1**	**6**	**1**	**0**	**10.00**
	Hamilton Bulldogs	AHL	3	1	2	0	152	8	0	3.17	....	....	....	....	....	....	....
	Hartford Wolf Pack	AHL	2	1	0	1	130	5	0	2.31	....	....	....	....	....	....	....
2006-07	**Columbus**	**NHL**	**11**	**2**	**3**	**2**	**491**	**27**	**0**	**3.30**	....	....	....	....	....	....	....
	Syracuse Crunch	AHL	19	3	12	3	1085	60	0	3.32	....	....	....	....	....	....	....
	Buffalo	**NHL**	**5**	**1**	**2**	**0**	**227**	**13**	**0**	**3.44**	....	....	....	....	....	....	....
2007-08	**Pittsburgh**	**NHL**	**33**	**18**	**8**	**5**	**1866**	**78**	**2**	**2.51**	....	....	....	....	....	....	....
	Wilkes-Barre	AHL	18	11	7	0	1058	39	2	2.21	....	....	....	....	....	....	....
2008-09	**Detroit**	**NHL**	**40**	**25**	**11**	**2**	**2246**	**94**	**6**	**2.51**	**1**	**0**	**0**	**20**	**0**	**0**	**0.00**
2009-10	**St. Louis**	**NHL**	**26**	**10**	**10**	**2**	**1451**	**60**	**4**	**2.48**	....	....	....	....	....	....	....
	NHL Totals		**175**	**83**	**53**	**16**	**9437**	**403**	**14**	**2.56**	**2**	**0**	**1**	**26**	**1**	**0**	**2.31**

USHL Second All-Star Team (1996) • Hockey East All-Rookie Team (1999) • Hockey East Second All-Star Team (1999) • Hockey East First All-Star Team (2000, 2001) • Hockey East Player of the Year (2000) (co-winner - Mike Mottau) • NCAA East Second All-American Team (2000) • NCAA East First All-American Team (2001)

• Left **Alaska-Anchorage** (WCHA) and returned to **Green Bay** (USHL), November 14, 1996. Signed as a free agent by **Edmonton**, April 18, 2001. Signed as a free agent by **Wolfsburg** (Germany), January 25, 2005. • Loaned to **Hartford** (AHL) by **Edmonton**, March 8, 2006. Signed as a free agent by **Columbus**, July 6, 2006. Traded to **Buffalo** by **Columbus** for Buffalo's 5th round choice (later traded to Dallas - Dallas selected Michael Neal) in 2007 Entry Draft, February 27, 2007. Signed as a free agent by **Pittsburgh**, July 19, 2007. Signed as a free agent by **Detroit**, July 1, 2008. Signed as a free agent by **St. Louis**, July 1, 2009.

CORBEIL, Mathieu

(kawr-BAY, MA-tyew) **CBJ**

Goaltender. Catches left. 6'6", 186 lbs. Born, Montreal, Que., September 27, 1991.
(Columbus' 5th choice, 102nd overall, in 2010 Entry Draft).

			Regular Season								Playoffs						
Season	Club	League	GP	W	L	O/T	Mins	GA	SO	Avg	GP	W	L	Mins	GA	SO	Avg
2007-08	Mtl. Predateurs	QAAA	27	3	21	0	1296	109	1	5.04	2	0	1	95	9	0	5.70
2008-09	Halifax	QMJHL	24	3	14	....	1094	81	0	4.44	....	....	....	....	....	....	....
2009-10	Halifax	QMJHL	50	8	39	....	2692	172	0	3.83	....	....	....	....	....	....	....

COURCHAINE, Adam (KOOR-shayn, A-duhm) BOS.

Goaltender. Catches left. 6'2", 191 lbs. Born, Calgary, Alta., February 20, 1989.

			Regular Season								Playoffs						
Season	Club	League	GP	W	L	O/T	Mins	GA	SO	Avg	GP	W	L	Mins	GA	SO	Avg
2006-07	Orleans Blues	CJHL	39	19	11	5	2285	119	1	3.12	6	2	2	372	16	0	2.58
2007-08	Ottawa 67's	OHL	48	17	25	4	2813	152	2	3.24	4	0	4	158	12	0	4.56
	Providence Bruins	AHL	3	2	0	0	144	4	0	1.67	....	....	....	....	....	....	....
2008-09	Ottawa 67's	OHL	30	13	11	2	1520	83	2	3.28	5	2	3	280	14	*1	3.00
	Providence Bruins	AHL	1	0	1	0	60	3	0	3.00	....	....	....	....	....	....	....
2009-10	Sarnia Sting	OHL	27	8	16	2	1520	89	1	3.51	....	....	....	....	....	....	....
	Erie Otters	OHL	21	12	8	0	1200	58	2	2.90	2	0	2	120	9	0	4.50

Signed as a free agent by **Boston**, September 30, 2007.

COUSINEAU, Marco (KOO-zih-noh, MAHR-koh) ANA.

Goaltender. Catches left. 6', 200 lbs. Born, St.Lazare, Que., November 9, 1989.
(Anaheim's 6th choice, 83rd overall, in 2008 Entry Draft).

			Regular Season								Playoffs						
Season	Club	League	GP	W	L	O/T	Mins	GA	SO	Avg	GP	W	L	Mins	GA	SO	Avg
2006-07	Baie-Comeau	QMJHL	23	4	12	....	1015	71	0	4.20	1	0	0	10	2	0	11.88
2007-08	Baie-Comeau	QMJHL	58	34	19	....	3227	151	4	2.81	5	1	4	305	11	0	*2.17
2008-09	Baie-Comeau	QMJHL	34	9	25	....	1878	115	1	3.67	....	....	....	....	....	....	....
	Drummondville	QMJHL	16	12	4	....	919	36	0	2.35	17	*13	3	1009	41	0	2.44
2009-10	P.E.I. Rocket	QMJHL	25	10	14	....	1441	77	1	3.20	....	....	....	....	....	....	....
	Saint John	QMJHL	20	15	5	....	1218	48	3	2.36	21	14	7	1222	57	2	2.80

QMJHL Second All-Star Team (2008)

CRAWFORD, Corey (KRAW-fohrd, KOH-ree) CHI.

Goaltender. Catches left. 6'2", 200 lbs. Born, Montreal, Que., December 31, 1984.
(Chicago's 2nd choice, 52nd overall, in 2003 Entry Draft).

			Regular Season								Playoffs						
Season	Club	League	GP	W	L	O/T	Mins	GA	SO	Avg	GP	W	L	Mins	GA	SO	Avg
2000-01	Gatineau Intrepide	QAAA	21	17	3	1	1260	40	2	1.92	....	....	....	....	....	....	....
2001-02	Moncton Wildcats	QMJHL	38	9	20	3	1863	116	1	3.74	....	....	....	....	....	....	....
2002-03	Moncton Wildcats	QMJHL	50	24	17	6	2855	130	2	2.73	6	2	3	303	20	0	3.97
2003-04	Moncton Wildcats	QMJHL	54	*35	15	3	3019	132	2	2.62	*20	*13	6	*1170	42	0	2.15
2004-05	Moncton Wildcats	QMJHL	51	28	16	6	2942	121	*6	2.47	12	6	6	725	33	*1	2.73
2005-06	**Chicago**	**NHL**	**2**	**0**	**0**	**1**	**86**	**5**	**0**	**3.49**	....	....	....	....	....	....	....
	Norfolk Admirals	AHL	48	22	23	1	2734	134	1	2.94	1	0	0	17	1	0	3.49
2006-07	Norfolk Admirals	AHL	60	38	20	2	3467	164	1	2.84	6	2	4	363	20	0	3.31
2007-08	**Chicago**	**NHL**	**5**	**1**	**2**	**0**	**224**	**8**	**1**	**2.14**	....	....	....	....	....	....	....
	Rockford IceHogs	AHL	55	29	19	5	3028	143	3	2.83	12	7	5	741	27	0	2.19
2008-09	Rockford IceHogs	AHL	47	22	20	3	2686	116	2	2.59	2	0	2	117	5	0	2.57
	Chicago	**NHL**	....	....	....	....	....	....	....	....	**1**	**0**	**0**	**16**	**1**	**0**	**3.75**
2009-10	**Chicago**	**NHL**	**1**	**0**	**1**	**0**	**59**	**3**	**0**	**3.05**	....	....	....	....	....	....	....
	Rockford IceHogs	AHL	45	24	16	2	2521	112	1	2.67	4	0	4	216	13	0	3.61
	NHL Totals		**8**	**1**	**3**	**1**	**369**	**16**	**1**	**2.60**	**1**	**0**	**0**	**16**	**1**	**0**	**3.75**

QMJHL Second All-Star Team (2004, 2005)

CURRY, John (KUH-ree, JAWN) PIT.

Goaltender. Catches left. 5'11", 185 lbs. Born, Shorewood, MN, February 27, 1984.

			Regular Season								Playoffs						
Season	Club	League	GP	W	L	O/T	Mins	GA	SO	Avg	GP	W	L	Mins	GA	SO	Avg
2003-04	Boston University	H-East	1	0	0	0	5	0	0	0.00	....	....	....	....	....	....	....
2004-05	Boston University	H-East	33	18	11	3	1950	64	3	1.97	....	....	....	....	....	....	....
2005-06	Boston University	H-East	37	24	8	4	2166	81	3	2.24	....	....	....	....	....	....	....
2006-07	Boston University	H-East	36	17	10	8	2154	72	7	2.01	....	....	....	....	....	....	....
2007-08	Wilkes-Barre	AHL	40	24	12	3	2343	87	3	2.23	23	14	9	1358	64	1	2.83
	Las Vegas	ECHL	6	4	1	0	342	16	0	2.81	....	....	....	....	....	....	....
	Wheeling Nailers	ECHL	1	0	1	0	60	4	0	4.00	....	....	....	....	....	....	....
2008-09	**Pittsburgh**	**NHL**	**3**	**2**	**1**	**0**	**150**	**6**	**0**	**2.40**	....	....	....	....	....	....	....
	Wilkes-Barre	AHL	50	33	15	1	2996	119	4	2.38	7	4	3	393	22	0	3.36
2009-10	**Pittsburgh**	**NHL**	**1**	**0**	**1**	**0**	**24**	**5**	**0**	**12.50**	....	....	....	....	....	....	....
	Wilkes-Barre	AHL	46	23	19	2	2657	127	1	2.87	3	0	3	176	9	0	3.07
	NHL Totals		**4**	**2**	**2**	**0**	**174**	**11**	**0**	**3.79**	....	....	....	....	....	....	....

NCAA East Second All-American Team (2006) • NCAA East First All-American Team (2007)

Signed as a free agent by **Pittsburgh**, July 13, 2007.

DALTON, Matt (DAWL-tuhn, MAT) BOS.

Goaltender. Catches left. 6'1", 181 lbs. Born, Clinton, Ont., July 4, 1986.

			Regular Season								Playoffs						
Season	Club	League	GP	W	L	O/T	Mins	GA	SO	Avg	GP	W	L	Mins	GA	SO	Avg
2005-06	Bozeman Icedogs	NAHL	39	33	5	1	2315	63	*9	*1.63	11	9	2	658	17	2	1.55
2006-07	Des Moines	USHL	*53	*27	15	9	*3030	143	*5	2.83	*8	6	2	*540	14	1	1.56
2007-08	Bemidji State	CHA	5	1	3	0	233	12	1	3.09	....	....	....	....	....	....	....
2008-09	Bemidji State	CHA	31	*19	11	1	1861	68	2	2.19	....	....	....	....	....	....	....
2009-10	Providence Bruins	AHL	6	0	4	1	331	18	0	3.26	....	....	....	....	....	....	....
	Reading Royals	ECHL	46	22	20	4	2735	158	1	3.47	16	*10	4	955	48	0	3.02

CHA Second All-Star Team (2009)

Signed as a free agent by **Boston**, April 22, 2009.

DANIS, Yann (DA-nihs, YAN)

Goaltender. Catches left. 6', 185 lbs. Born, Lafontaine, Que., June 21, 1981.

			Regular Season								Playoffs						
Season	Club	League	GP	W	L	O/T	Mins	GA	SO	Avg	GP	W	L	Mins	GA	SO	Avg
99-2000	St-Jerome	QJHL					STATISTICS NOT AVAILABLE										
	Cornwall Colts	CJHL	26	....	....	....	1367	71	0	3.12	....	....	....	....	....	....	....
2000-01	Brown U.	ECAC	12	2	8	1	667	40	0	3.60	....	....	....	....	....	....	....
2001-02	Brown U.	ECAC	24	11	10	2	1451	45	3	1.86	....	....	....	....	....	....	....
2002-03	Brown U.	ECAC	*34	15	14	5	*2074	80	5	2.31	....	....	....	....	....	....	....
2003-04	Brown U.	ECAC	30	15	11	4	1821	55	*5	*1.81	....	....	....	....	....	....	....
	Hamilton Bulldogs	AHL	2	2	0	0	120	3	1	1.50	1	0	0	12	0	0	0.00
2004-05	Hamilton Bulldogs	AHL	53	28	17	6	3075	120	5	2.34	4	0	4	237	13	0	3.29
2005-06	**Montreal**	**NHL**	**6**	**3**	**2**	**0**	**312**	**14**	**1**	**2.69**	....	....	....	....	....	....	....
	Hamilton Bulldogs	AHL	39	17	17	3	2242	111	0	2.97	....	....	....	....	....	....	....
2006-07	Hamilton Bulldogs	AHL	44	23	14	5	2540	119	1	2.81	1	1	0	54	1	0	1.12
2007-08	Hamilton Bulldogs	AHL	38	11	19	4	2064	113	0	3.28	....	....	....	....	....	....	....
2008-09	**NY Islanders**	**NHL**	**31**	**10**	**17**	**3**	**1760**	**84**	**2**	**2.86**	....	....	....	....	....	....	....
	Bridgeport	AHL	10	7	3	0	611	23	0	2.26	....	....	....	....	....	....	....
2009-10	**New Jersey**	**NHL**	**12**	**3**	**2**	**1**	**467**	**16**	**0**	**2.06**	....	....	....	....	....	....	....
	NHL Totals		**49**	**16**	**21**	**4**	**2539**	**114**	**3**	**2.69**	....	....	....	....	....	....	....

ECAC Second All-Star Team (2002, 2003) • ECAC First All-Star Team (2004) • ECAC Goaltender of the Year (2004) • ECAC Player of the Year (2004) • NCAA East First All-American Team (2004)

Signed as a free agent by **Montreal**, March 19, 2004. Signed as a free agent by **NY Islanders**, July 2, 2008. Signed as a free agent by **New Jersey**, July 10, 2009.

DARLING, Scott (DAHR-lihng, SKAWT) PHX

Goaltender. Catches left. 6'6", 190 lbs. Born, Lemont, IL, December 22, 1988.
(Phoenix's 7th choice, 153rd overall, in 2007 Entry Draft).

			Regular Season								Playoffs						
Season	Club	League	GP	W	L	O/T	Mins	GA	SO	Avg	GP	W	L	Mins	GA	SO	Avg
2005-06	Chicago	MWEHL	2	0	2	0	120	10	0	5.00	....	....	....	....	....	....	....
	North Iowa	NAHL	8	2	4	0	405	28	0	4.15	....	....	....	....	....	....	....
2006-07	Capital District	EJHL	22	9	9	3	1243	70	1	3.38	....	....	....	....	....	....	....
	North Iowa	NAHL	1	0	0	0	15	3	0	12.00	....	....	....	....	....	....	....
2007-08	Indiana Ice	USHL	42	27	10	2	2391	121	1	3.04	3	1	2	179	11	0	3.6
2008-09	University of Maine	H-East	27	10	14	3	1566	72	*3	2.76	....	....	....	....	....	....	....
2009-10	University of Maine	H-East	27	15	6	3	1511	78	0	3.10	....	....	....	....	....	....	....

DEKANICH, Mark (deh-KAN-ihch, MAHRK) NSH

Goaltender. Catches left. 6'2", 190 lbs. Born, N. Vancouver, B.C., May 10, 1986.
(Nashville's 3rd choice, 146th overall, in 2006 Entry Draft).

			Regular Season								Playoffs						
Season	Club	League	GP	W	L	O/T	Mins	GA	SO	Avg	GP	W	L	Mins	GA	SO	Avg
2003-04	Coquitlam Express	BCHL	30	13	15	1	1647	89	2	3.24	....	....	....	....	....	....	....
2004-05	Colgate	ECAC	5	1	1	0	162	5	0	1.85	....	....	....	....	....	....	....
2005-06	Colgate	ECAC	36	18	11	6	2126	81	4	2.29	....	....	....	....	....	....	....
2006-07	Colgate	ECAC	36	15	17	4	2136	83	1	2.33	....	....	....	....	....	....	....
2007-08	Colgate	ECAC	*41	18	16	6	*2389	86	*6	2.16	....	....	....	....	....	....	....
2008-09	Milwaukee	AHL	30	15	10	2	1663	58	1	2.09	....	....	....	....	....	....	....
2009-10	Milwaukee	AHL	49	27	16	4	2804	109	4	2.33	7	3	4	408	19	1	2.79
	Cincinnati	ECHL	2	2	0	0	125	1	1	0.48	....	....	....	....	....	....	....

ECAC First All-Star Team (2006) • ECAC Second All-Star Team (2007)

DESJARDINS, Cedrick (deh-ZHAHR-dai, SEH-DRIHK) MTL.

Goaltender. Catches left. 6', 194 lbs. Born, Edmunston, N.B., September 30, 1985.

			Regular Season								Playoffs						
Season	Club	League	GP	W	L	O/T	Mins	GA	SO	Avg	GP	W	L	Mins	GA	SO	Avg
2002-03	Coaticook	QJHL					STATISTICS NOT AVAILABLE										
	Rimouski Oceanic	QMJHL	23	1	19	0	1239	109	0	5.28	....	....	....	....	....	....	....
2003-04	Rimouski Oceanic	QMJHL	20	8	11	0	1119	72	0	3.86	1	0	0	14	0	0	0.00
2004-05	Rimouski Oceanic	QMJHL	44	*30	7	4	2439	120	2	2.95	13	*12	1	*767	34	*1	2.66
2005-06	Quebec Remparts	QMJHL	41	28	10	0	2254	111	*5	2.95	*23	14	9	*1413	60	1	2.55
2006-07	Hamilton Bulldogs	AHL	3	0	2	0	142	7	0	2.96	....	....	....	....	....	....	....
	Cincinnati	ECHL	45	24	19	1	2648	112	4	2.54	....	....	....	....	....	....	....
2007-08	Hamilton Bulldogs	AHL	12	4	3	2	572	29	0	3.04	....	....	....	....	....	....	....
	Cincinnati	ECHL	22	16	4	2	1285	41	*5	1.91	16	11	4	947	29	1	*1.83
2008-09	Hamilton Bulldogs	AHL	30	16	12	0	1718	73	4	2.55	....	....	....	....	....	....	....
2009-10	Hamilton Bulldogs	AHL	47	29	9	4	2576	86	6	*2.00	10	6	4	596	26	1	2.62

Memorial Cup Tournament All-Star Team (2006) • Hap Emms Memorial Trophy (Memorial Cup Tournament - Top Goaltender) (2006) • ECHL All-Rookie-Team (2007) • ECHL Playoff MVP (2009) • Harry "Hap" Holmes Memorial Award (AHL – fewest goals against) (2010) (shared with Curtis Sanford)

Signed as a free agent by **Hamilton** (AHL), July 26, 2006. Signed as a free agent by **Montreal**, July 3, 2008.

DESLAURIERS, Jeff (duh-LAW-ree-yay, JEHF) EDM.

Goaltender. Catches right. 6'4", 200 lbs. Born, St-Jean-Richelieu, Que., May 15, 1984.
(Edmonton's 2nd choice, 31st overall, in 2002 Entry Draft).

			Regular Season								Playoffs						
Season	Club	League	GP	W	L	O/T	Mins	GA	SO	Avg	GP	W	L	Mins	GA	SO	Avg
2000-01	Gatineau Intrepide	QAAA	22	10	9	2	1194	61	2	3.07	2	1	0	125	6	0	2.89
2001-02	Chicoutimi	QMJHL	51	28	20	1	2909	170	1	3.51	4	0	3	197	20	0	6.11
2002-03	Chicoutimi	QMJHL	54	18	24	1	2582	164	0	3.81	4	0	4	240	15	0	9.00
2003-04	Chicoutimi	QMJHL	50	21	20	6	2701	129	1	2.87	18	10	8	956	50	1	3.14
2004-05	Greenville Grrrowl	ECHL	11	7	3	1	673	26	1	2.32	....	....	....	....	....	....	....
	Edmonton	AHL	22	6	13	2	1258	62	0	2.96	....	....	....	....	....	....	....
2005-06	Hamilton Bulldogs	AHL	13	4	7	0	666	35	0	3.15	....	....	....	....	....	....	....
	Greenville Grrrowl	ECHL	6	2	4	0	335	17	0	3.05	....	....	....	....	....	....	....
2006-07	Wilkes-Barre	AHL	40	22	12	3	2231	92	4	2.47	....	....	....	....	....	....	....
2007-08	Springfield Falcons	AHL	57	26	23	5	3045	147	0	2.90	....	....	....	....	....	....	....
2008-09	**Edmonton**	**NHL**	**10**	**4**	**3**	**0**	**540**	**30**	**0**	**3.33**	....	....	....	....	....	....	....
	Springfield Falcons	AHL	5	1	4	0	286	13	0	2.73	....	....	....	....	....	....	....
2009-10	**Edmonton**	**NHL**	**48**	**16**	**28**	**4**	**2798**	**152**	**3**	**3.26**	....	....	....	....	....	....	....
	NHL Totals		**58**	**20**	**31**	**4**	**3338**	**182**	**3**	**3.27**	....	....	....	....	....	....	....

QMJHL All-Rookie Team (2002)

DiPIETRO, Rick (dee-pee-EHT-roh, RIHK) NYI

Goaltender. Catches right. 6'1", 210 lbs. Born, Winthrop, MA, September 19, 1981.
(NY Islanders' 1st choice, 1st overall, in 2000 Entry Draft).

			Regular Season								Playoffs						
Season	Club	League	GP	W	L	O/T	Mins	GA	SO	Avg	GP	W	L	Mins	GA	SO	Avg
1997-98	USNTDP	U-17	10	6	4	0	800	31	0	2.33	....	....	....	....	....	....	....
	USNTDP	USHL	3	0	2	0	117	8	0	4.09	....	....	....	....	....	....	....
	USNTDP	NAHL	30	13	12	0	1602	85	1	3.18	3	2	1	179	7	1	2.35
1998-99	USNTDP	U-18	16	9	5	1	1027	46	....	2.69	....	....	....	....	....	....	....
	USNTDP	USHL	30	22	6	1	1733	67	3	2.32	....	....	....	....	....	....	....
99-2000	Boston University	H-East	29	18	5	5	1790	73	2	2.45	....	....	....	....	....	....	....
2000-01	**NY Islanders**	**NHL**	**20**	**3**	**15**	**1**	**1083**	**63**	**0**	**3.49**	....	....	....	....	....	....	....
	Chicago Wolves	IHL	14	4	5	2	778	44	0	3.39	....	....	....	....	....	....	....
2001-02	Bridgeport	AHL	59	*30	22	7	3472	134	4	2.32	20	12	8	*1270	45	*3	2.13
2002-03	**NY Islanders**	**NHL**	**10**	**2**	**5**	**2**	**585**	**29**	**0**	**2.97**	**1**	**0**	**0**	**15**	**0**	**0**	**0.00**
	Bridgeport	AHL	34	16	10	8	2044	73	3	2.14	5	2	3	299	10	1	2.01
2003-04	**NY Islanders**	**NHL**	**50**	**23**	**18**	**5**	**2844**	**112**	**5**	**2.36**	**5**	**1**	**4**	**303**	**11**	**1**	**2.18**
	Bridgeport	AHL	2	0	2	0	119	3	0	1.51	....	....	....	....	....	....	....
2004-05							DID NOT PLAY										
2005-06	**NY Islanders**	**NHL**	**63**	**30**	**24**	**5**	**3572**	**180**	**1**	**3.02**	....	....	....	....	....	....	....
	United States	Olympics	4	1	3	0	237	9	0	2.28	....	....	....	....	....	....	....
2006-07	**NY Islanders**	**NHL**	**62**	**32**	**19**	**9**	**3627**	**156**	**5**	**2.58**	**4**	**1**	**3**	**236**	**13**	**0**	**3.31**
2007-08	**NY Islanders**	**NHL**	**63**	**26**	**28**	**7**	**3707**	**174**	**3**	**2.82**	....	....	....	....	....	....	....
2008-09	**NY Islanders**	**NHL**	**5**	**1**	**3**	**0**	**256**	**15**	**0**	**3.52**	....	....	....	....	....	....	....
2009-10	**NY Islanders**	**NHL**	**8**	**2**	**5**	**0**	**462**	**20**	**1**	**2.60**	....	....	....	....	....	....	....
	Bridgeport	AHL	4	1	2	0	199	11	0	3.31	....	....	....	....	....	....	....
	NHL Totals		**281**	**119**	**117**	**29**	**16136**	**749**	**15**	**2.79**	**10**	**2**	**7**	**554**	**24**	**1**	**2.60**

Hockey East Second All-Star Team (2000) • Hockey East Rookie of the Year (2000)

Played in NHL All-Star Game (2008)

• Missed majority of 2008-09 and 2009-10 seasons recovering from arthroscopic knee surgery, October 31, 2008.

DOMINGUE, Louis
(doh-MIHN-gay, LOO-ee) **PHX.**

Goaltender. Catches right. 6'3", 180 lbs. Born, St-Hyacinthe, Que., March 6, 1992.
(Phoenix's 5th choice, 138th overall, in 2010 Entry Draft).

			Regular Season								Playoffs						
Season	Club	League	GP	W	L	O/T	Mins	GA	SO	Avg	GP	W	L	Mins	GA	SO	Avg
2007-08	Lac St-Louis Lions	QAAA	35	22	9	0	1732	90	2	3.12	13	8	2	761	33	1	2.60
2008-09	Moncton Wildcats	QMJHL	12	5	5	....	621	26	0	2.51	....	....	....	....	....	....	....
2009-10	Moncton Wildcats	QMJHL	22	11	9	....	1195	56	1	2.81	....	....	....	....	....	....	....
	Quebec Remparts	QMJHL	19	9	8	....	1016	43	2	2.54	9	3	5	455	33	0	4.35

DUBIELEWICZ, Wade
(DOO-bih-wihtz, WAYD)

Goaltender. Catches left. 5'10", 180 lbs. Born, Invermere, B.C., January 30, 1979.

			Regular Season								Playoffs						
Season	Club	League	GP	W	L	O/T	Mins	GA	SO	Avg	GP	W	L	Mins	GA	SO	Avg
1997-98	Trail Smoke Eaters	BCHL	41	....	....	....	2225	118	0	3.18	....	....	....	....	....	....	....
1998-99	Trail Smoke Eaters	BCHL	STATISTICS NOT AVAILABLE														
	Chilliwack Chiefs	BCHL	14	10	4	0	834	....	0	....	....	....	....	....	....	....	....
99-2000	U. of Denver	WCHA	13	3	5	1	596	27	1	2.72	....	....	....	....	....	....	....
2000-01	U. of Denver	WCHA	29	12	9	3	1542	59	2	2.30	....	....	....	....	....	....	....
2001-02	U. of Denver	WCHA	24	20	4	0	1431	41	2	*1.72	....	....	....	....	....	....	....
2002-03	U. of Denver	WCHA	19	9	8	2	1060	43	3	2.43	....	....	....	....	....	....	....
2003-04	**NY Islanders**	**NHL**	**2**	**1**	**0**	**1**	**105**	**3**	**0**	**1.71**	....	....	....	....	....	....	....
	Bridgeport	AHL	33	20	8	5	1959	45	9	*1.38	3	2	1	181	11	0	3.64
2004-05	Bridgeport	AHL	43	18	23	1	2539	113	1	2.67	....	....	....	....	....	....	....
2005-06	**NY Islanders**	**NHL**	**7**	**2**	**3**	**0**	**310**	**15**	**0**	**2.90**	....	....	....	....	....	....	....
	Bridgeport	AHL	46	20	21	2	2575	134	3	3.12	7	3	4	435	16	0	2.21
2006-07	**NY Islanders**	**NHL**	**8**	**4**	**1**	**0**	**379**	**13**	**0**	**2.06**	**1**	**0**	**1**	**59**	**4**	**0**	**4.07**
	Bridgeport	AHL	40	22	12	5	2405	108	2	2.69	....	....	....	....	....	....	....
2007-08	**NY Islanders**	**NHL**	**20**	**9**	**9**	**1**	**1132**	**51**	**0**	**2.70**	....	....	....	....	....	....	....
	Bridgeport	AHL	2	1	1	0	124	5	0	2.42	....	....	....	....	....	....	....
2008-09	**Columbus**	**NHL**	**3**	**1**	**2**	**0**	**169**	**10**	**0**	**3.55**	....	....	....	....	....	....	....
	Ak Bars Kazan	Rus-KHL	21	....	....	....	1236	58	0	2.82	....	....	....	....	....	....	....
2009-10	**Minnesota**	**NHL**	**3**	**1**	**1**	**0**	**101**	**5**	**0**	**2.97**	....	....	....	....	....	....	....
	Houston Aeros	AHL	32	12	14	1	1564	71	0	2.72	....	....	....	....	....	....	....
	NHL Totals		**43**	**18**	**16**	**2**	**2196**	**97**	**0**	**2.65**	**1**	**0**	**1**	**59**	**4**	**0**	**4.07**

WCHA Second All-Star Team (2001, 2003) • WCHA First All-Star Team (2002) • AHL All-Rookie Team (2004) • AHL Second All-Star Team (2004) • Dudley "Red" Garrett Memorial Award (AHL - Rookie of the Year) (2004) • Harry "Hap" Holmes Memorial Award (AHL - fewest goals against) (2004) (shared with Dieter Kochan)

Signed as a free agent by **NY Islanders**, May 25, 2003. Signed as a free agent by **Kazan** (Russia-KHL), June 25, 2008. Signed as a free agent by **NY Islanders**, January 15, 2009. Claimed on waivers by **Columbus** from **NY Islanders**, January 17, 2009. Signed as a free agent by **Minnesota**, July 17, 2009.

DUBNYK, Devan
(DOOB-nihk, DEH-vuhn) **EDM.**

Goaltender. Catches left. 6'6", 194 lbs. Born, Regina, Sask., May 4, 1986.
(Edmonton's 1st choice, 14th overall, in 2004 Entry Draft).

			Regular Season								Playoffs						
Season	Club	League	GP	W	L	O/T	Mins	GA	SO	Avg	GP	W	L	Mins	GA	SO	Avg
2000-01	Calgary Bruins	CBHL	14	....	....	....	815	39	2	3.10	....	....	....	....	....	....	....
2001-02	Calgary Bruins	CBHL	18	7	9	2	1105	68	1	3.69	....	....	....	....	....	....	....
	Titaanit Kotka Jr.	Fin-Jr.	5	5	0	0	300	7	....	1.40	....	....	....	....	....	....	....
	Kamloops Blazers	WHL	3	1	1	0	143	13	0	5.45	....	....	....	....	....	....	....
2002-03	Kamloops Blazers	WHL	26	12	8	1	1279	68	2	3.19	....	....	....	....	....	....	....
2003-04	Kamloops Blazers	WHL	44	20	18	5	2533	106	6	2.51	4	1	3	245	12	0	2.94
2004-05	Kamloops Blazers	WHL	*65	23	34	7	3699	166	6	2.69	6	2	4	363	22	0	3.64
2005-06	Kamloops Blazers	WHL	54	27	26	1	3207	136	1	2.54	....	....	....	....	....	....	....
2006-07	Wilkes-Barre	AHL	4	2	1	0	204	10	0	2.94	....	....	....	....	....	....	....
	Stockton Thunder	ECHL	43	24	11	7	2529	108	2	2.56	6	2	4	395	18	0	2.73
2007-08	Springfield Falcons	AHL	33	9	17	0	1772	92	0	3.12	....	....	....	....	....	....	....
2008-09	Springfield Falcons	AHL	*62	18	41	2	*3635	180	3	2.97	....	....	....	....	....	....	....
2009-10	**Edmonton**	**NHL**	**19**	**4**	**10**	**2**	**1075**	**64**	**0**	**3.57**	....	....	....	....	....	....	....
	Springfield Falcons	AHL	33	13	17	2	1985	100	0	3.02	....	....	....	....	....	....	....
	NHL Totals		**19**	**4**	**10**	**2**	**1075**	**64**	**0**	**3.57**	....	....	....	....	....	....	....

Canadian Major Junior Scholastic Player of the Year (2004)

DUCHESNE, Jeremy
(DOO-shayn, JAIR-eh-mee)

Goaltender. Catches left. 6', 201 lbs. Born, Silver Spring, MD, October 17, 1986.
(Philadelphia's 3rd choice, 119th overall, in 2005 Entry Draft).

			Regular Season								Playoffs						
Season	Club	League	GP	W	L	O/T	Mins	GA	SO	Avg	GP	W	L	Mins	GA	SO	Avg
2002-03	St-Francois Blizzard	QAAA	26	7	11	5	1341	75	0	3.35	....	....	....	....	....	....	....
2003-04	Victoriaville Tigres	QMJHL	17	3	8	1	870	60	0	4.14	....	....	....	....	....	....	....
2004-05	Victoriaville Tigres	QMJHL	15	2	9	0	711	41	2	*3.46	....	....	....	....	....	....	....
	Halifax	QMJHL	18	12	0	2	921	23	3	*1.50	12	8	4	723	33	*1	2.74
2005-06	Halifax	QMJHL	55	25	29	0	3175	185	4	3.50	11	5	6	626	34	1	3.26
2006-07	Halifax	QMJHL	28	12	15	....	1580	97	1	3.68	....	....	....	....	....	....	....
	Val-d'Or Foreurs	QMJHL	24	13	10	....	1356	66	1	2.92	*18	11	7	*1157	56	0	2.90
2007-08	Philadelphia	AHL	2	1	0	0	80	6	0	4.50	....	....	....	....	....	....	....
	Dayton Bombers	ECHL	31	13	13	5	1838	91	1	2.97	....	....	....	....	....	....	....
2008-09	Mississippi	ECHL	13	3	7	2	718	57	1	4.77	....	....	....	....	....	....	....
	South Carolina	ECHL	5	2	2	0	206	17	0	4.94	....	....	....	....	....	....	....
2009-10	**Philadelphia**	**NHL**	**1**	**0**	**0**	**0**	**17**	**1**	**0**	**3.53**	....	....	....	....	....	....	....
	Adirondack	AHL	5	1	4	0	263	13	1	2.97	....	....	....	....	....	....	....
	Kalamazoo Wings	ECHL	19	9	4	5	1162	62	1	3.20	....	....	....	....	....	....	....
	NHL Totals		**1**	**0**	**0**	**0**	**17**	**1**	**0**	**3.53**	....	....	....	....	....	....	....

DUNN, Dan
(DUHN, DAN) **WSH.**

Goaltender. Catches left. 6'5", 204 lbs. Born, Oshawa, Ont., June 20, 1988.
(Washington's 7th choice, 154th overall, in 2007 Entry Draft).

			Regular Season								Playoffs						
Season	Club	League	GP	W	L	O/T	Mins	GA	SO	Avg	GP	W	L	Mins	GA	SO	Avg
2005-06	Oshawa	OPJHL	10	2	4	2	494	29	1	3.52	....	....	....	....	....	....	....
	Cobourg Cougars	OPJHL	6	0	5	0	277	33	0	7.14	....	....	....	....	....	....	....
2006-07	Wellington Dukes	OPJHL	27	19	4	2	1546	50	2	1.94	....	....	....	....	....	....	....
2007-08	St. Cloud State	WCHA	9	3	2	2	433	19	0	2.63	....	....	....	....	....	....	....
2008-09	St. Cloud State	WCHA	9	2	4	1	393	17	0	2.60	....	....	....	....	....	....	....
2009-10	St. Cloud State	WCHA	21	12	5	2	1140	49	0	2.58	....	....	....	....	....	....	....

EHELECHNER, Patrick
(eh-heh-LEHCH-nuhr, PAT-rihk) **PIT.**

Goaltender. Catches left. 6'2", 176 lbs. Born, Rosenheim, West Germany, September 23, 1984.
(San Jose's 5th choice, 139th overall, in 2003 Entry Draft).

			Regular Season								Playoffs						
Season	Club	League	GP	W	L	O/T	Mins	GA	SO	Avg	GP	W	L	Mins	GA	SO	Avg
2000-01	Jung. Mannheim	German-4	40	....	....	....	2423	171	2	4.23	....	....	....	....	....	....	....
2001-02	EV Landshut	German-3	2	....	....	....	130	6	0	2.77	....	....	....	....	....	....	....
	Hannover	Germany	8	....	....	....	475	24	0	3.03	....	....	....	....	....	....	....
2002-03	ESC Wedemark	German-4	STATISTICS NOT AVAILABLE														
	Hannover	Germany	4	....	....	....	162	16	0	5.90	....	....	....	....	....	....	....
2003-04	Sudbury Wolves	OHL	56	22	26	6	3089	148	3	2.87	7	2	4	390	14	2	2.15
2004-05	Sudbury Wolves	OHL	51	23	21	4	2997	128	3	2.56	10	4	5	497	29	0	3.50
2005-06	Adler Mannheim	Germany	1	....	....	....	59	5	0	5.02	....	....	....	....	....	....	....
	Fuchse Duisburg	Germany	26	....	....	....	1243	75	2	3.62	....	....	....	....	....	....	....
2006-07	Fuchse Duisburg	Germany	6	....	....	....	244	28	0	6.89	....	....	....	....	....	....	....
2007-08	Nurnberg	Germany	15	10	4	0	820	37	0	2.71	2	0	0	17	1	0	3.57
2008-09	Nurnberg	Germany	7	4	3	....	428	15	0	2.10	....	....	....	....	....	....	....
2009-10	Nurnberg	Germany	49	25	22	....	2848	123	1	2.59	4	1	3	286	12	0	2.52

OHL Second All-Star Team (2004)

Signed as a free agent by **Mannheim** (Germany), April 25, 2005. Traded to **Pittsburgh** by **San Jose** with Nils Ekman for Carolina's 2nd round choice (previously acquired, later traded to Philadelphia - Philadelphia selected Kevin Marshall) in 2007 Entry Draft, July 20, 2006. Signed as a free agent by **Nurnberg** (Germany), April 25, 2007.

EIDSNESS, Brad
(IGHD-nehz, BRAD) **BUF.**

Goaltender. Catches left. 6', 175 lbs. Born, Chestermere, Alta., June 2, 1989.
(Buffalo's 4th choice, 139th overall, in 2007 Entry Draft).

			Regular Season								Playoffs						
Season	Club	League	GP	W	L	O/T	Mins	GA	SO	Avg	GP	W	L	Mins	GA	SO	Avg
2005-06	Okotoks Oilers	AJHL	4	3	1	0	238	4	2	1.01	....	....	....	....	....	....	....
	UFA Bisons	AMHL	18	12	4	2	1046	45	....	2.58	8	5	3	512	14	....	1.64
2006-07	Okotoks Oilers	AJHL	48	24	18	2	2658	127	4	2.87	....	....	....	....	....	....	....
2007-08	Okotoks Oilers	AJHL	....	29	4	4	2264	80	3	2.12	9	4	5	547	25	0	2.74
2008-09	North Dakota	WCHA	41	*24	12	0	2441	104	1	2.56	....	....	....	....	....	....	....
2009-10	North Dakota	WCHA	*41	*24	10	4	*2388	84	3	2.11	....	....	....	....	....	....	....

WCHA All-Rookie Team (2009) • WCHA Second All-Star Team (2010)

ELLIOTT, Brian
(EHL-lee-awt, BRIGH-uhn) **OTT.**

Goaltender. Catches left. 6'2", 201 lbs. Born, Newmarket, Ont., April 9, 1985.
(Ottawa's 9th choice, 291st overall, in 2003 Entry Draft).

			Regular Season								Playoffs						
Season	Club	League	GP	W	L	O/T	Mins	GA	SO	Avg	GP	W	L	Mins	GA	SO	Avg
2002-03	Ajax Axemen	OPJHL	39	....	....	....	2097	135	0	3.86	....	....	....	....	....	....	....
2003-04	U. of Wisconsin	WCHA	6	3	3	0	336	12	0	2.14	....	....	....	....	....	....	....
2004-05	U. of Wisconsin	WCHA	9	6	2	1	467	9	3	1.16	....	....	....	....	....	....	....
2005-06	U. of Wisconsin	WCHA	35	*27	5	3	2128	55	*8	*1.55	....	....	....	....	....	....	....
2006-07	U. of Wisconsin	WCHA	36	15	17	2	2053	72	*5	2.10	....	....	....	....	....	....	....
	Binghamton	AHL	8	3	4	0	425	30	0	4.24	....	....	....	....	....	....	....
2007-08	**Ottawa**	**NHL**	**1**	**1**	**0**	**0**	**60**	**1**	**0**	**1.00**	....	....	....	....	....	....	....
	Binghamton	AHL	44	18	19	1	2394	112	2	2.81	....	....	....	....	....	....	....
2008-09	**Ottawa**	**NHL**	**31**	**16**	**8**	**3**	**1667**	**77**	**1**	**2.77**	....	....	....	....	....	....	....
	Binghamton	AHL	30	18	8	1	1691	65	2	2.31	....	....	....	....	....	....	....
2009-10	**Ottawa**	**NHL**	**55**	**29**	**18**	**4**	**3038**	**130**	**5**	**2.57**	**4**	**1**	**2**	**203**	**14**	**0**	**4.14**
	NHL Totals		**87**	**46**	**26**	**7**	**4765**	**208**	**6**	**2.62**	**4**	**1**	**2**	**203**	**14**	**0**	**4.14**

WCHA Second All-Star Team (2006, 2007) • NCAA West First All-American Team (2006) • NCAA Championship All-Tournament Team (2006)

ELLIS, Dan
(EHL-ihs, DAN) **T.B.**

Goaltender. Catches left. 6', 193 lbs. Born, Orangeville, Ont., June 19, 1980.
(Dallas' 2nd choice, 60th overall, in 2000 Entry Draft).

			Regular Season								Playoffs						
Season	Club	League	GP	W	L	O/T	Mins	GA	SO	Avg	GP	W	L	Mins	GA	SO	Avg
1998-99	Newmarket	OPJHL	28	24	3	1	1670	63	3	2.25	....	....	....	....	....	....	....
99-2000	Omaha Lancers	USHL	55	*34	16	4	*3274	123	*11	*2.25	4	1	3	238	10	0	2.52
2000-01	Nebraska-Omaha	CCHA	40	21	14	3	2285	95	2	2.49	....	....	....	....	....	....	....
2001-02	Nebraska-Omaha	CCHA	40	20	15	4	2405	97	3	2.42	....	....	....	....	....	....	....
2002-03	Nebraska-Omaha	CCHA	39	11	21	5	2211	117	3	3.18	....	....	....	....	....	....	....
2003-04	**Dallas**	**NHL**	**1**	**1**	**0**	**0**	**60**	**3**	**0**	**3.00**	....	....	....	....	....	....	....
	Utah Grizzlies	AHL	20	5	14	0	1130	55	2	2.92	....	....	....	....	....	....	....
	Idaho Steelheads	ECHL	23	13	8	1	1334	57	2	2.56	*16	*13	3	*966	30	*3	*1.86
2004-05	Hamilton Bulldogs	AHL	31	10	19	0	1774	82	1	2.77	....	....	....	....	....	....	....
2005-06	Iowa Stars	AHL	34	16	13	1	1857	86	2	2.78	....	....	....	....	....	....	....
2006-07	Iowa Stars	AHL	55	30	21	1	3194	148	4	2.78	12	6	6	679	35	0	3.09
2007-08	**Nashville**	**NHL**	**44**	**23**	**10**	**3**	**2229**	**87**	**6**	**2.34**	**6**	**2**	**4**	**357**	**15**	**0**	**2.52**
2008-09	**Nashville**	**NHL**	**35**	**11**	**19**	**4**	**1965**	**96**	**3**	**2.93**	....	....	....	....	....	....	....
2009-10	**Nashville**	**NHL**	**31**	**15**	**13**	**1**	**1715**	**77**	**1**	**2.69**	....	....	....	....	....	....	....
	NHL Totals		**111**	**50**	**42**	**8**	**5969**	**263**	**10**	**2.64**	**6**	**2**	**4**	**357**	**15**	**0**	**2.52**

USHL First All-Star Team (2000) • USHL Goaltender of the Year (2000) • USHL Player of the Year (2000) • CCHA Second All-Star Team (2002) • ECHL Playoff MVP (2004)

Signed as a free agent by **Nashville**, July 5, 2007. Traded to **Montreal** by **Nashville** with Dustin Boyd and future considerations for Sergei Kostitsyn and future considerations, June 29, 2010. Signed as a free agent by **Tampa Bay**, July 1, 2010.

EMERY, Ray
(EH-muhr-ee, RAY)

Goaltender. Catches left. 6'2", 196 lbs. Born, Cayuga, Ont., September 28, 1982.
(Ottawa's 4th choice, 99th overall, in 2001 Entry Draft).

			Regular Season								Playoffs						
Season	Club	League	GP	W	L	O/T	Mins	GA	SO	Avg	GP	W	L	Mins	GA	SO	Avg
1998-99	Dunnville Terriers	OJHL-C	22	3	19	0	1320	140	0	6.37	....	....	....	....	....	....	....
99-2000	Welland Cougars	OHA-B	23	13	10	1	1323	62	1	2.68	....	....	....	....	....	....	....
	Sault Ste. Marie	OHL	16	9	3	0	716	36	1	3.02	15	8	7	883	33	*3	2.24
2000-01	Sault Ste. Marie	OHL	52	18	29	2	2938	174	1	3.55	....	....	....	....	....	....	....
2001-02	Sault Ste. Marie	OHL	*59	*33	17	9	*3477	158	4	2.73	6	2	4	360	19	*1	3.17
2002-03	**Ottawa**	**NHL**	**3**	**1**	**0**	**0**	**85**	**2**	**0**	**1.41**	....	....	....	....	....	....	....
	Binghamton	AHL	50	27	17	6	2924	118	*7	2.42	14	8	6	848	40	*2	2.83
2003-04	**Ottawa**	**NHL**	**3**	**2**	**0**	**0**	**126**	**5**	**0**	**2.38**	....	....	....	....	....	....	....
	Binghamton	AHL	53	21	23	7	3109	128	3	2.47	2	0	2	120	6	0	3.01
2004-05	Binghamton	AHL	51	28	18	5	2993	132	0	2.65	6	2	4	409	14	0	2.05
2005-06	**Ottawa**	**NHL**	**39**	**23**	**11**	**4**	**2168**	**102**	**3**	**2.82**	**10**	**5**	**5**	**604**	**29**	**0**	**2.88**
2006-07	**Ottawa**	**NHL**	**58**	**33**	**16**	**6**	**3351**	**138**	**5**	**2.47**	***20**	***13**	**7**	***1249**	**47**	***3**	**2.26**
2007-08	**Ottawa**	**NHL**	**31**	**12**	**13**	**4**	**1689**	**88**	**0**	**3.13**	....	....	....	....	....	....	....
	Binghamton	AHL	2	1	1	0	120	6	0	3.00	....	....	....	....	....	....	....
2008-09	Mytischi	Rus-KHL	36	....	....	....	2070	73	2	2.12	7	....	....	419	13	1	1.86
2009-10	**Philadelphia**	**NHL**	**29**	**16**	**11**	**1**	**1684**	**74**	**3**	**2.64**	....	....	....	....	....	....	....
	Adirondack	AHL	1	0	1	0	59	2	0	2.03	....	....	....	....	....	....	....
	NHL Totals		**163**	**87**	**51**	**15**	**9103**	**409**	**11**	**2.70**	**30**	**18**	**12**	**1853**	**76**	**3**	**2.46**

OHL First All-Star Team (2002) • Canadian Major Junior First All-Star Team (2002) • Canadian Major Junior Goaltender of the Year (2002) • AHL All-Rookie Team (2003)

Signed as a free agent by **Mytischi** (Rus-KHL), July 9, 2008. Signed as a free agent by **Philadelphia** June 10, 2009.

ENDRAS, Dennis (EHN-dras, DEHN-his) MIN.

Goaltender. Catches left. 6', 166 lbs. Born, Immenstadt, West Germany, July 14, 1985.

			Regular Season								Playoffs						
Season	Club	League	GP	W	L	O/T	Mins	GA	SO	Avg	GP	W	L	Mins	GA	SO	Avg
2003-04	Bayreuth Tigers	German-3	26	....	....	....	1395	76	1	3.27	....	....	....	....	....	....	....
2004-05	Augsburg	Germany	2	....	....	....	120	3	1	1.50	....	....	....	....	....	....	....
	Bayreuth Tigers	German-3	17	....	....	....	996	70	0	4.22	....	....	....	....	....	....	....
2005-06	Augsburg	Germany	5	....	....	....	145	14	0	5.79	....	....	....	....	....	....	....
	EV Landsberg 2000	German-3	20	....	....	....	1185	39	1	1.97	8	....	....	498	10	2	1.21
2006-07	Frankfurt Lions	Germany	2	....	....	....	122	6	0	2.96	....	....	....	....	....	....	....
	EV Landsberg 2000	German-2	42	....	....	....	2483	124	1	3.00	....	....	....	....	....	....	....
2007-08	EV Landsberg 2000	German-2	29	....	....	....	1728	83	0	2.88	....	....	....	....	....	....	....
	Ravensburg	German-2	20	....	....	....	1146	58	0	3.04	4	....	....	242	13	0	3.23
2008-09	Augsburg	Germany	50	26	24	....	2933	149	6	3.05	4	1	3	240	10	0	2.50
2009-10	Augsburg	Germany	52	28	24	....	3036	166	2	3.28	*14	8	6	*838	33	*1	2.36

Signed as a free agent by **Minnesota**, July 7, 2010.

ENGREN, Atte (EHN-grehn, AH-tay) NSH.

Goaltender. Catches left. 6'1", 184 lbs. Born, Rauma, Finland, February 19, 1988.
(Nashville's 9th choice, 204th overall, in 2007 Entry Draft).

			Regular Season								Playoffs						
Season	Club	League	GP	W	L	O/T	Mins	GA	SO	Avg	GP	W	L	Mins	GA	SO	Avg
2004-05	Lukko Rauma U18	Fin-U18	10	....	....	....	603	22	0	2.19	....	....	....	....	....	....	....
2005-06	Lukko Rauma U18	Fin-U18	16	....	....	....	966	44	0	2.73	....	....	....	....	....	....	....
	Lukko Rauma Jr.	Fin-Jr.	11	....	....	....	637	30	0	2.83	9	....	....	509	27	0	3.18
2006-07	Lukko Rauma Jr.	Fin-Jr.	38	....	....	....	2277	115	1	3.03	....	....	....	....	....	....	....
	Suomi U20	Finland-2	2	....	....	....	100	7	0	4.20	....	....	....	....	....	....	....
2007-08	Hokki Kajaani	Finland-2	1	0	0	0	15	4	0	15.70	....	....	....	....	....	....	....
	Lukko Rauma	Finland	1	0	1	0	59	3	0	3.04	....	....	....	....	....	....	....
	Lukko Rauma Jr.	Fin-Jr.	31	14	13	0	1791	89	1	2.98	2	2	0	120	3	0	1.50
2008-09	TPS Turku Jr.	Fin-Jr.	4	3	1	0	240	11	0	2.75	....	....	....	....	....	....	....
	Kiekko-Vantaa	Finland-2	5	3	2	0	264	9	0	2.05	....	....	....	....	....	....	....
	TPS Turku	Finland	6	1	4	1	317	17	1	3.22	....	....	....	....	....	....	....
2009-10	TuTo Turku	Finland-2	1	1	0	0	60	1	1	1.00	2	....	....	59	3	0	3.05
	TPS Turku	Finland	35	15	13	1	1778	78	2	2.63	8	7	1	494	15	1	1.82

ENO, Nick (EE-noh, NIHK) BUF.

Goaltender. Catches left. 6'3", 193 lbs. Born, Howell, MI, February 12, 1989.
(Buffalo's 7th choice, 187th overall, in 2007 Entry Draft).

			Regular Season								Playoffs						
Season	Club	League	GP	W	L	O/T	Mins	GA	SO	Avg	GP	W	L	Mins	GA	SO	Avg
2005-06	Howell	High-MI	25	....	....	....	1020	52	5	2.29	....	....	....	....	....	....	....
2006-07	Green Mountain	EJHL	25	9	14	2	1398	84	1	3.60	....	....	....	....	....	....	....
2007-08	Bowling Green	CCHA	22	12	10	0	1269	59	0	2.79	....	....	....	....	....	....	....
2008-09	Bowling Green	CCHA	7	0	5	0	328	25	0	4.58	....	....	....	....	....	....	....
2009-10	Bowling Green	CCHA	27	5	13	4	1343	74	0	3.30	....	....	....	....	....	....	....

CCHA All-Rookie Team (2008)

ENROTH, Jhonas (EHN-rawth, YOH-nuhs) BUF.

Goaltender. Catches left. 5'10", 170 lbs. Born, Stockholm, Sweden, June 25, 1988.
(Buffalo's 2nd choice, 46th overall, in 2006 Entry Draft).

			Regular Season								Playoffs						
Season	Club	League	GP	W	L	O/T	Mins	GA	SO	Avg	GP	W	L	Mins	GA	SO	Avg
2003-04	Huddinge IK U18	Swe-U18	6	....	....	....	324	15	0	2.77	....	....	....	....	....	....	....
2004-05	Huddinge IK Jr.	Swe-Jr.	19	....	....	....	1144	49	3	2.57	3	....	....	186	6	1	1.93
	Huddinge IK U18	Swe-U18	2	....	....	....	125	5	0	2.40	....	....	....	....	....	....	....
	Huddinge IK	Sweden-2	2	....	....	....	51	6	0	6.95	....	....	....	....	....	....	....
2005-06	Sodertalje SK Jr.	Swe-Jr.	39	....	....	....	2378	86	1	2.17	4	....	....	243	9	0	2.22
	Sodertalje SK U18	Swe-U18	2	....	....	....	120	5	0	2.50	....	....	....	....	....	....	....
2006-07	Sodertalje SK Jr.	Swe-Jr.	3	....	....	....	180	4	0	1.33	....	....	....	....	....	....	....
	Sodertalje SK	Sweden-2	33	....	....	....	1938	57	3	1.76	....	....	....	....	....	....	....
2007-08	Sodertalje SK Jr.	Swe-Jr.	1	....	....	....	59	4	0	4.05	....	....	....	....	....	....	....
	Sodertalje SK	Sweden	27	....	....	....	1578	56	2	*2.13	....	....	....	....	....	....	....
2008-09	Portland Pirates	AHL	58	26	23	6	3424	157	3	2.75	5	1	4	264	10	1	2.27
2009-10	**Buffalo**	**NHL**	**1**	**0**	**1**	**0**	**58**	**4**	**0**	**4.14**	....	....	....	....	....	....	....
	Portland Pirates	AHL	48	28	18	1	2781	110	5	2.37	....	....	....	....	....	....	....
	NHL Totals		**1**	**0**	**1**	**0**	**58**	**4**	**0**	**4.14**	....	....	....	....	....	....	....

ERIKSSON, Joacim (AIR-ihk-suhn, YOH-a-kihm) PHI.

Goaltender. Catches right. 6'1", 189 lbs. Born, Gavle, Sweden, April 9, 1990.
(Philadelphia's 5th choice, 196th overall, in 2008 Entry Draft).

			Regular Season								Playoffs						
Season	Club	League	GP	W	L	O/T	Mins	GA	SO	Avg	GP	W	L	Mins	GA	SO	Avg
2006-07	Valbo AIF Jr.	Swe-Jr.	18	....	....	....	1072	55	....	3.08	....	....	....	....	....	....	....
	Valbo AIF	Sweden-3	1	....	....	....	34	2	0	3.51	....	....	....	....	....	....	....
2007-08	Brynas U18	Swe-U18	9	....	....	....	545	21	2	2.31	5	....	....	296	7	2	1.42
	Brynas IF Gavle Jr.	Swe-Jr.	16	....	....	....	960	53	0	3.31	7	....	....	426	13	1	1.83
	Valbo HC	Sweden-3	2	....	....	....	123	8	0	3.91	....	....	....	....	....	....	....
2008-09	Brynas IF Gavle Jr.	Swe-Jr.	33	....	....	....	1962	65	6	1.99	7	....	....	468	19	0	2.43
2009-10	Leksands IF Jr.	Swe-Jr.	1	....	....	....	60	0	1	0.00	....	....	....	....	....	....	....
	Leksands IF	Sweden-2	48	....	....	....	2877	115	5	2.40	....	....	....	....	....	....	....

ERSBERG, Erik (AIRZH-buhrg, AIR-ihk) L.A.

Goaltender. Catches left. 6', 165 lbs. Born, Sala, Sweden, March 8, 1982.

			Regular Season								Playoffs						
Season	Club	League	GP	W	L	O/T	Mins	GA	SO	Avg	GP	W	L	Mins	GA	SO	Avg
99-2000	Vasteras IK U18	Swe-U18	1	....	....	....	60	2	0	2.00	2	....	....	119	10	0	5.02
	Vasteras IK Jr.	Swe-Jr.	16	....	....	....	885	36	0	2.44	....	....	....	....	....	....	....
2000-01	Vasteras	Sweden-4	33	....	....	....	....	....	....	1.48	....	....	....	....	....	....	....
2001-02	Vasteras Jr.	Swe-Jr.	....	....	....	....	....	....	....	....	2	....	....	118	11	0	5.61
	Vasteras	Sweden-3	37	....	....	....	....	....	....	....	....	....	....	....	....	....	....
2002-03	Vasteras	Sweden-2	32	....	....	....	1920	91	1	2.84	....	....	....	....	....	....	....
2003-04	Vasteras	Sweden-2	32	....	....	....	1850	79	3	2.56	....	....	....	....	....	....	....
2004-05	Vasteras	Sweden-2	37	....	....	....	2189	76	3	2.08	5	....	....	308	8	2	1.56
2005-06	VIK Vasteras HK	Sweden-2	2	....	....	....	118	4	0	2.02	....	....	....	....	....	....	....
	HV 71 Jonkoping	Sweden	10	....	....	....	602	18	2	1.79	2	....	....	79	4	0	3.05
	HV 71 Jr.	Swe-Jr.	1	....	....	....	60	1	0	1.00	....	....	....	....	....	....	....
2006-07	HV 71 Jonkoping	Sweden	41	....	....	....	2455	98	4	2.39	14	....	....	834	39	0	2.81
2007-08	**Los Angeles**	**NHL**	**14**	**6**	**5**	**3**	**799**	**33**	**2**	**2.48**	....	....	....	....	....	....	....
	Manchester	AHL	30	10	13	2	1540	75	1	2.92	....	....	....	....	....	....	....
2008-09	**Los Angeles**	**NHL**	**28**	**8**	**11**	**5**	**1477**	**65**	**0**	**2.64**	....	....	....	....	....	....	....
2009-10	**Los Angeles**	**NHL**	**11**	**4**	**3**	**2**	**551**	**22**	**0**	**2.40**	**1**	**0**	**0**	**13**	**2**	**0**	**9.23**
	NHL Totals		**53**	**18**	**19**	**10**	**2827**	**120**	**2**	**2.55**	**1**	**0**	**0**	**13**	**2**	**0**	**9.23**

Signed as a free agent by **Los Angeles**, May 31, 2007.

FALLON, Joe (FA-luhn, JOH)

Goaltender. Catches left. 6'4", 200 lbs. Born, Bemidji, MN, February 1, 1985.
(Chicago's 9th choice, 167th overall, in 2005 Entry Draft).

			Regular Season								Playoffs						
Season	Club	League	GP	W	L	O/T	Mins	GA	SO	Avg	GP	W	L	Mins	GA	SO	Av
2001-02	Rochester	USHL	27	7	16	1	1484	93	0	3.76	....	....	....	....	....	....	.
2002-03	Cedar Rapids	USHL	42	20	15	6	2495	108	2	2.60	7	3	4	426	21	0	2.9
2003-04	Cedar Rapids	USHL	42	25	13	2	2370	108	4	2.73	4	1	3	237	9	0	2.2
2004-05	U. of Vermont	ECAC	32	17	10	4	1932	63	5	1.96	....	....	....	....	....	....	.
2005-06	U. of Vermont	H-East	33	14	14	5	1931	65	6	2.02	....	....	....	....	....	....	..
2006-07	U. of Vermont	H-East	34	17	14	3	1997	62	6	*1.86	....	....	....	....	....	....	.
2007-08	U. of Vermont	H-East	33	15	13	5	1942	77	*3	2.38	....	....	....	....	....	....	.
2008-09	Rockford IceHogs	AHL	2	0	0	0	63	1	0	0.95	....	....	....	....	....	....	.
	Fresno Falcons	ECHL	13	8	4	1	747	32	1	2.57	....	....	....	....	....	....	.
	Gwinnett	ECHL	22	10	10	1	1246	67	1	3.23	....	....	....	....	....	....	.
2009-10	Rockford IceHogs	AHL	29	15	10	1	1545	68	1	2.64	....	....	....	....	....	....	..
	Peoria Rivermen	AHL	10	4	6	0	532	31	0	3.50	....	....	....	....	....	....	..

ECAC All-Rookie Team (2005) • ECAC Rookie of the Year (2005)

Traded to **St. Louis** by **Chicago** for Hannu Toivonen and Danny Richmond, March 1, 2010.

FLEURY, Marc-Andre (fluh-REE, MAHRK-AWN-dray) PIT

Goaltender. Catches left. 6'2", 180 lbs. Born, Sorel, Que., November 28, 1984.
(Pittsburgh's 1st choice, 1st overall, in 2003 Entry Draft).

			Regular Season								Playoffs						
Season	Club	League	GP	W	L	O/T	Mins	GA	SO	Avg	GP	W	L	Mins	GA	SO	Av
99-2000	Charles-Lemoyne	QAAA	15	4	9	0	780	36	1	2.77	....	....	....	....	....	....	..
2000-01	Cape Breton	QMJHL	35	12	13	2	1705	115	0	4.05	2	0	1	32	4	0	7.5
2001-02	Cape Breton	QMJHL	55	26	14	8	3043	141	2	2.78	16	9	7	1003	55	0	3.2
2002-03	Cape Breton	QMJHL	51	17	24	6	2889	162	2	3.36	4	0	4	228	17	0	4.4
2003-04	**Pittsburgh**	**NHL**	**21**	**4**	**14**	**2**	**1154**	**70**	**1**	**3.64**	....	....	....	....	....	....	..
	Cape Breton	QMJHL	10	8	1	1	606	20	0	1.98	4	1	3	251	13	0	3.1
	Wilkes-Barre	AHL	....	....	....	....	....	....	....	....	2	0	1	92	6	0	3.9
2004-05	Wilkes-Barre	AHL	54	26	19	4	3029	127	5	2.52	4	0	2	151	11	0	4.3
2005-06	**Pittsburgh**	**NHL**	**50**	**13**	**27**	**6**	**2809**	**152**	**1**	**3.25**	....	....	....	....	....	....	..
	Wilkes-Barre	AHL	12	10	2	0	727	19	0	1.57	5	2	3	311	18	0	3.4
2006-07	**Pittsburgh**	**NHL**	**67**	**40**	**16**	**9**	**3905**	**184**	**5**	**2.83**	**5**	**1**	**4**	**287**	**18**	**0**	**3.7**
2007-08	**Pittsburgh**	**NHL**	**35**	**19**	**10**	**2**	**1857**	**72**	**4**	**2.33**	***20**	***14**	**6**	***1251**	**41**	***3**	**1.9**
	Wilkes-Barre	AHL	5	3	2	0	297	7	0	1.42	....	....	....	....	....	....	..
2008-09 ♦	**Pittsburgh**	**NHL**	**62**	**35**	**18**	**7**	**3641**	**162**	**4**	**2.67**	***24**	***16**	**8**	***1447**	**63**	**0**	**2.6**
2009-10	**Pittsburgh**	**NHL**	**67**	**37**	**21**	**6**	**3798**	**168**	**1**	**2.65**	**13**	**7**	**6**	**798**	**37**	**1**	**2.7**
	Canada	Olympics					DID NOT PLAY – SPARE GOALTENDER										
	NHL Totals		**302**	**148**	**106**	**32**	**17164**	**808**	**16**	**2.82**	**62**	**38**	**24**	**3783**	**159**	**4**	**2.5**

QMJHL Second All-Star Team (2003)

FOSTER, Brian (FAW-stuhr, BRIGH-uhn) FLA

Goaltender. Catches left. 6'1", 155 lbs. Born, Pembroke, NH, February 4, 1987.
(Florida's 6th choice, 161st overall, in 2005 Entry Draft).

			Regular Season								Playoffs						
Season	Club	League	GP	W	L	O/T	Mins	GA	SO	Avg	GP	W	L	Mins	GA	SO	Av
2003-04	N.H. Jr. Monarchs	EJHL					STATISTICS NOT AVAILABLE										
2004-05	N.H. Jr. Monarchs	EJHL	41	30	6	4	2339	....	3	2.51	....	....	....	....	....	....	..
2005-06	Des Moines	USHL	26	12	9	3	1516	71	0	2.81	1	0	0	12	0	0	0.00
2006-07	New Hampshire	H-East	7	2	2	0	298	11	2	2.21	....	....	....	....	....	....	..
2007-08	New Hampshire	H-East	6	2	2	2	372	19	0	3.06	....	....	....	....	....	....	..
2008-09	New Hampshire	H-East	35	19	11	4	2080	93	*3	2.68	....	....	....	....	....	....	..
2009-10	New Hampshire	H-East	*38	17	14	7	*2297	114	0	2.98	....	....	....	....	....	....	..

Hockey East First All-Star Team (2010) • NCAA East Second All-American Team (2010)

FRAZEE, Jeff (FRAY-zee, JEHF) N.J

Goaltender. Catches left. 6', 200 lbs. Born, Edina, MN, May 13, 1987.
(New Jersey's 2nd choice, 38th overall, in 2005 Entry Draft).

			Regular Season								Playoffs						
Season	Club	League	GP	W	L	O/T	Mins	GA	SO	Avg	GP	W	L	Mins	GA	SO	Avg
2001-02	Holy Angels	High-MN	6	6	0	0	....	....	....	....	....	....	....	....	....	....	..
2002-03	Holy Angels	High-MN	16	14	1	1	....	....	....	....	....	....	....	....	....	....	..
2003-04	USNTDP	U-17	16	9	3	0	781	31	....	2.38	....	....	....	....	....	....	..
	USNTDP	NAHL	25	14	8	3	1463	71	3	2.91	....	....	....	....	....	....	..
2004-05	USNTDP	U-18	24	....	....	....	1309	59	3	2.71	....	....	....	....	....	....	..
	USNTDP	NAHL	9	8	1	0	500	18	1	2.16	....	....	....	....	....	....	..
2005-06	U. of Minnesota	WCHA	12	6	3	2	660	26	2	2.36	....	....	....	....	....	....	..
2006-07	U. of Minnesota	WCHA	20	14	3	1	1148	45	1	2.35	....	....	....	....	....	....	..
2007-08	U. of Minnesota	WCHA	14	6	7	0	798	39	1	2.93	....	....	....	....	....	....	..
	Lowell Devils	AHL	1	0	1	0	40	3	0	4.50	....	....	....	....	....	....	..
2008-09	Lowell Devils	AHL	58	28	22	6	3407	149	4	2.62	....	....	....	....	....	....	..
	Trenton Devils	ECHL	5	2	2	0	272	12	0	2.65	4	2	2	271	10	0	2.22
2009-10	Lowell Devils	AHL	31	14	16	0	1778	83	1	2.80	....	....	....	....	....	....	..

GARON, Mathieu (gah-ROHN, MA-tyew) CBJ

Goaltender. Catches right. 6'2", 202 lbs. Born, Chandler, Que., January 9, 1978.
(Montreal's 2nd choice, 44th overall, in 1996 Entry Draft).

			Regular Season								Playoffs						
Season	Club	League	GP	W	L	O/T	Mins	GA	SO	Avg	GP	W	L	Mins	GA	SO	Avg
1993-94	Jonquiere Elites	QAAA	17	0	13	0	834	88	0	6.33	....	....	....	....	....	....	....
1994-95	Jonquiere Elites	QAAA	27	13	13	1	1554	94	0	3.63	9	6	2	467	26	0	3.34
1995-96	Victoriaville Tigres	QMJHL	51	18	27	0	2709	189	1	4.19	12	7	4	676	38	1	3.39
1996-97	Victoriaville Tigres	QMJHL	53	29	18	3	3032	150	*6	2.97	6	2	4	330	23	0	4.18
1997-98	Victoriaville Tigres	QMJHL	47	27	18	2	2802	125	5	2.68	6	2	4	345	22	0	3.82
1998-99	Fredericton	AHL	40	14	22	2	2222	114	3	3.08	6	1	1	208	12	0	3.47
99-2000	Quebec Citadelles	AHL	53	17	28	3	2884	149	2	3.10	1	0	0	20	3	0	8.82
2000-01	**Montreal**	**NHL**	**11**	**4**	**5**	**1**	**589**	**24**	**2**	**2.44**	....	....	....	....	....	....	....
	Quebec Citadelles	AHL	31	16	13	1	1768	86	1	2.92	8	4	4	459	22	1	2.88
2001-02	**Montreal**	**NHL**	**5**	**1**	**4**	**0**	**261**	**19**	**0**	**4.37**	....	....	....	....	....	....	....
	Quebec Citadelles	AHL	50	21	15	12	2988	136	2	2.73	3	0	3	198	12	0	3.63
2002-03	**Montreal**	**NHL**	**8**	**3**	**5**	**0**	**482**	**16**	**2**	**1.99**	....	....	....	....	....	....	....
	Hamilton Bulldogs	AHL	20	15	2	2	1150	34	4	1.77	....	....	....	....	....	....	....
2003-04	**Montreal**	**NHL**	**19**	**8**	**6**	**2**	**1003**	**38**	**0**	**2.27**	**1**	**0**	**0**	**12**	**0**	**0**	**0.00**
2004-05	Manchester	AHL	52	32	14	4	2969	105	8	2.12	6	2	4	285	17	0	3.58
2005-06	**Los Angeles**	**NHL**	**63**	**31**	**26**	**3**	**3446**	**185**	**4**	**3.22**	....	....	....	....	....	....	....
2006-07	**Los Angeles**	**NHL**	**32**	**13**	**10**	**6**	**1779**	**79**	**2**	**2.66**	....	....	....	....	....	....	....
2007-08	**Edmonton**	**NHL**	**47**	**26**	**18**	**1**	**2658**	**118**	**4**	**2.66**	....	....	....	....	....	....	....
2008-09	**Edmonton**	**NHL**	**15**	**6**	**8**	**0**	**815**	**43**	**0**	**3.17**	....	....	....	....	....	....	....
	♦ **Pittsburgh**	**NHL**	**4**	**2**	**1**	**0**	**206**	**10**	**0**	**2.91**	**1**	**0**	**0**	**24**	**0**	**0**	**0.00**

9-10	Columbus	NHL	35	12	9	6	1771	83	2	2.81	....	....	....	....	....	....	....
	NHL Totals		239	106	92	19	13010	615	16	2.84	2	0	0	36	0	0	0.00

IJHL All-Rookie Team (1996) • QMJHL Defensive Rookie of the Year (1996) • QMJHL First All-Star am (1998) • Canadian Major Junior First All-Star Team (1998) • Canadian Major Junior altender of the Year (1998)

ded to **Los Angeles** by **Montreal** with San Jose's 3rd round choice (previously acquired, Los geles selected Paul Baier) in 2004 Entry Draft for Radek Bonk and Cristobal Huet, June 26, 2004. ned as a free agent by **Edmonton**, July 3, 2007. Traded to **Pittsburgh** by **Edmonton** for Dany ourin, Ryan Stone and Pittsburgh's 4th round choice in 2011 Entry Draft, January 17, 2009. ned as a free agent by **Columbus**, July 1, 2009.

AYDUCHENKO, Sergei (gay-doo-CHEHN-koh, SAIR-gay) FLA.

altender. Catches left. 6'5", 222 lbs. Born, Kiev, USSR, June 6, 1989.
rida's 8th choice, 202nd overall, in 2007 Entry Draft).

			Regular Season								Playoffs						
ason	Club	League	GP	W	L	O/T	Mins	GA	SO	Avg	GP	W	L	Mins	GA	SO	Avg
6-07	Yaroslavl 2	Russia-3	23	....	....	....	1180	57	3	2.90	....	....	....	....	....	....	....
7-08	Novokuznetsk 2	Russia-3	2	....	....	....	....	5	....	....	....	....	....	....	....	....	....
	Novokuznetsk	Russia	11	....	....	....	533	27	0	3.04	....	....	....	....	....	....	....
8-09	Yaroslavl 2	Russia-3					STATISTICS NOT AVAILABLE										
	Yaroslavl	Rus-KHL	3	....	....	....	185	6	0	1.95	....	....	....	....	....	....	....
9-10	Yaroslavl	Rus-KHL	20	....	....	....	1091	44	0	2.42	....	....	....	....	....	....	....

ERBER, Martin (GUHR-buhr, MAHR-tihn) EDM.

altender. Catches left. 5'11", 199 lbs. Born, Burgdorf, Switz., September 3, 1974.
naheim's 10th choice, 232nd overall, in 2001 Entry Draft).

			Regular Season								Playoffs						
ason	Club	League	GP	W	L	O/T	Mins	GA	SO	Avg	GP	W	L	Mins	GA	SO	Avg
6-97	SC Langnau	Swiss-2	38	....	....	....	2286	121	0	3.18	8	....	....	488	29	0	3.57
7-98	SC Langnau	Swiss-2	40	....	....	....	2430	141	2	3.48	16	....	....	961	42	0	2.62
8-99	SC Langnau	Swiss	42	....	....	....	2521	203	1	4.83	11	....	....	664	50	0	4.52
2000	SC Langnau	Swiss	44	....	....	....	2652	161	3	3.64	6	....	....	360	13	*2	*2.17
0-01	SCL Tigers Langnau	Swiss	*44	....	....	....	2671	114	3	2.56	5	....	....	319	7	1	1.32
1-02	Farjestad	Sweden	44	....	....	....	2664	87	*4	*1.96	*10	....	....	*657	18	*2	*1.64
	Switzerland	Olympics	3	1	1	1	158	4	0	1.52	....	....	....	....	....	....	....
2-03	**Anaheim**	**NHL**	**22**	**6**	**11**	**3**	**1203**	**39**	**1**	**1.95**	**2**	**0**	**0**	**20**	**1**	**0**	**3.00**
	Cincinnati	AHL	1	1	0	0	60	2	0	2.00	....	....	....	....	....	....	....
3-04	**Anaheim**	**NHL**	**32**	**11**	**12**	**4**	**1698**	**64**	**2**	**2.26**	....	....	....	....	....	....	....
4-05	SCL Tigers Langnau	Swiss	20	6	10	4	1220	59	0	2.90	....	....	....	....	....	....	....
	Farjestad	Sweden	30	20	6	4	1827	58	4	1.90	*15	9	6	*900	36	1	2.40
5-06 ◆	**Carolina**	**NHL**	**60**	**38**	**14**	**6**	**3493**	**162**	**3**	**2.78**	**6**	**1**	**1**	**221**	**13**	**1**	**3.53**
	Switzerland	Olympics	3	1	2	0	160	11	1	4.13	....	....	....	....	....	....	....
6-07	**Ottawa**	**NHL**	**29**	**15**	**9**	**3**	**1599**	**74**	**1**	**2.78**	....	....	....	....	....	....	....
7-08	**Ottawa**	**NHL**	**57**	**30**	**18**	**4**	**3197**	**145**	**2**	**2.72**	**4**	**0**	**4**	**238**	**14**	**0**	**3.53**
8-09	**Ottawa**	**NHL**	**14**	**4**	**9**	**1**	**839**	**40**	**1**	**2.86**	....	....	....	....	....	....	....
	Binghamton	AHL	14	6	7	0	783	38	1	2.91	....	....	....	....	....	....	....
	Toronto	**NHL**	**12**	**6**	**5**	**0**	**706**	**38**	**0**	**3.23**	....	....	....	....	....	....	....
9-10	Mytischi	Rus-KHL	30	....	....	....	1750	64	2	2.19	....	....	....	....	....	....	....
	NHL Totals		**226**	**110**	**78**	**21**	**12735**	**562**	**10**	**2.65**	**12**	**1**	**5**	**479**	**28**	**1**	**3.51**

Scored a goal in playoffs vs. Martigny (Swiss-2), February 27, 1997. Traded to **Carolina** by **naheim** for Tomas Malec and Carolina's 3rd round choice (Kyle Klubertanz) in 2004 Entry Draft, ne 18, 2004. Signed as a free agent by **Langnau** (Swiss), September 17, 2004. Signed as a free ent by **Farjestad** (Sweden), November 7, 2004. Signed as a free agent by **Ottawa**, July 1, 2006. aimed on waivers by **Toronto** from **Ottawa**, March 4, 2009. Signed as a free agent by **Mytischi** ussia-KHL), July 21, 2009. Signed as a free agent by **Edmonton**, August 7, 2010.

IGUERE, Jean-Sebastien (zhih-GAIR, ZHAWN-suh-BAS-t'yehn) TOR.

altender. Catches left. 6'1", 202 lbs. Born, Montreal, Que., May 16, 1977.
artford's 1st choice, 13th overall, in 1995 Entry Draft).

			Regular Season								Playoffs						
ason	Club	League	GP	W	L	O/T	Mins	GA	SO	Avg	GP	W	L	Mins	GA	SO	Avg
92-93	Laval-Laurentides	QAAA	25	12	11	2	1498	76	0	3.02	11	6	5	654	38	0	3.49
93-94	Verdun	QMJHL	25	13	5	2	1234	66	1	3.21	....	....	....	....	....	....	....
94-95	Halifax	QMJHL	47	14	27	5	2755	181	2	3.94	7	3	4	417	17	1	*2.45
95-96	Halifax	QMJHL	55	26	23	2	3230	185	1	3.44	6	1	5	354	24	0	4.07
96-97	**Hartford**	**NHL**	**8**	**1**	**4**	**0**	**394**	**24**	**0**	**3.65**	....	....	....	....	....	....	....
	Halifax	QMJHL	50	28	19	3	3014	170	2	3.38	16	9	7	954	58	0	3.65
97-98	Saint John Flames	AHL	31	16	10	3	1758	72	2	2.46	10	5	3	536	27	0	3.02
98-99	**Calgary**	**NHL**	**15**	**6**	**7**	**1**	**860**	**46**	**0**	**3.21**	....	....	....	....	....	....	....
	Saint John Flames	AHL	39	18	16	3	2145	123	3	3.44	7	3	2	304	21	0	4.14
-2000	**Calgary**	**NHL**	**7**	**1**	**3**	**1**	**330**	**15**	**0**	**2.73**	....	....	....	....	....	....	....
	Saint John Flames	AHL	41	17	17	3	2243	114	0	3.05	3	0	3	178	9	0	3.03
00-01	**Anaheim**	**NHL**	**34**	**11**	**17**	**5**	**2031**	**87**	**4**	**2.57**	....	....	....	....	....	....	....
	Cincinnati	AHL	23	12	7	2	1306	53	0	2.43	....	....	....	....	....	....	....
01-02	**Anaheim**	**NHL**	**53**	**20**	**25**	**6**	**3127**	**111**	**4**	**2.13**	....	....	....	....	....	....	....
02-03	**Anaheim**	**NHL**	**65**	**34**	**22**	**6**	**3775**	**145**	**8**	**2.30**	**21**	**15**	**6**	**1407**	**38**	**5**	***1.62**
03-04	**Anaheim**	**NHL**	**55**	**17**	**31**	**6**	**3210**	**140**	**3**	**2.62**	....	....	....	....	....	....	....
04-05	Hamburg Freezers	Germany	6	....	....	....	301	12	0	2.39	2	....	....	100	7	0	4.20
05-06	**Anaheim**	**NHL**	**60**	**30**	**15**	**11**	**3381**	**150**	**2**	**2.66**	**6**	**3**	**3**	**318**	**18**	**0**	**3.40**
06-07 ◆	**Anaheim**	**NHL**	**56**	**36**	**10**	**8**	**3245**	**122**	**4**	**2.26**	**18**	***13**	**4**	**1067**	**35**	**1**	**1.97**
07-08	**Anaheim**	**NHL**	**58**	**35**	**17**	**6**	**3310**	**117**	**4**	**2.12**	**6**	**2**	**4**	**358**	**19**	**0**	**3.18**
08-09	**Anaheim**	**NHL**	**46**	**19**	**18**	**6**	**2458**	**127**	**2**	**3.10**	**1**	**0**	**0**	**17**	**0**	**0**	**0.00**
09-10	**Anaheim**	**NHL**	**20**	**4**	**8**	**5**	**1108**	**58**	**1**	**3.14**	....	....	....	....	....	....	....
	Toronto	**NHL**	**15**	**6**	**7**	**2**	**915**	**38**	**2**	**2.49**	....	....	....	....	....	....	....
	NHL Totals		**492**	**220**	**184**	**63**	**28144**	**1180**	**34**	**2.52**	**52**	**33**	**17**	**3167**	**110**	**6**	**2.08**

MJHL Second All-Star Team (1997) • AHL All-Rookie Team (1998) • Harry "Hap" Holmes Memorial ward (AHL – fewest goals against) (1998) (shared with Tyler Moss) • Conn Smythe Trophy (2003)

ayed in NHL All-Star Game (2009)

Transferred to **Carolina** after **Hartford** franchise relocated, June 25, 1997. Traded to **Calgary** by **arolina** with Andrew Cassels for Gary Roberts and Trevor Kidd, August 25, 1997. Traded to **naheim** by **Calgary** for Anaheim's 2nd round choice (later traded to Washington – Washington lected Matt Pettinger) in 2000 Entry Draft, June 10, 2000. Signed as a free agent by **Hamburg** ermany), January 31, 2005. Traded to **Toronto** by **Anaheim** for Vesa Toskala and Jason Blake, nuary 31, 2010.

GISTEDT, Joel (JIHZ-tehd, JOHL) PHX.

Goaltender. Catches left. 5'11", 176 lbs. Born, Uddevalla, Sweden, December 7, 1987.
(Phoenix's 4th choice, 36th overall, in 2007 Entry Draft).

			Regular Season								Playoffs						
Season	Club	League	GP	W	L	O/T	Mins	GA	SO	Avg	GP	W	L	Mins	GA	SO	Avg
2003-04	V.Frolunda U18	Swe-U18	21	....	....	....	1258	49	1	2.34	7	....	....	422	11	2	1.57
2004-05	Frolunda U18	Swe-U18	2	....	....	....	120	6	0	3.00	6	....	....	366	14	1	2.30
	Frolunda Jr.	Swe-Jr.	8	....	....	....	485	14	0	1.73	....	....	....	....	....	....	....
2005-06	Frolunda Jr.	Swe-Jr.	32	....	....	....	1926	76	5	2.37	7	....	....	434	18	0	2.49
	Frolunda	Sweden	3	....	....	....	181	5	1	1.66	....	....	....	....	....	....	....
2006-07	Frolunda Jr.	Swe-Jr.	2	....	....	....	120	3	1	1.50	8	....	....	484	15	0	1.86
	Frolunda	Sweden	35	....	....	....	2050	88	2	2.58	....	....	....	....	....	....	....
2007-08	Frolunda Jr.	Swe-Jr.	5	....	....	....	303	7	0	1.38	....	....	....	....	....	....	....
	Frolunda	Sweden	11	....	....	....	578	37	0	3.84	....	....	....	....	....	....	....
2008-09	San Antonio	AHL	1	0	0	0	20	2	0	6.00	....	....	....	....	....	....	....
	Arizona Sundogs	CHL	29	10	15	1	1533	106	0	4.15	....	....	....	....	....	....	....
2009-10	Las Vegas	ECHL	20	7	8	2	991	67	0	4.06	....	....	....	....	....	....	....

Signed as a free agent by **Rogle** (Sweden-2), April 21, 2010.

GOTHBERG, Zane (GAWTH-buhrg, ZAYN) BOS.

Goaltender. Catches left. 6'2", 188 lbs. Born, Grand Forks, ND, August 20, 1992.
(Boston's 6th choice, 165th overall, in 2010 Entry Draft).

			Regular Season								Playoffs						
Season	Club	League	GP	W	L	O/T	Mins	GA	SO	Avg	GP	W	L	Mins	GA	SO	Avg
2007-08	Thief River Falls	High-MN	....	14	12	0	....	....	....	2.15	....	....	....	....	....	....	....
2008-09	Thief River Falls	High-MN	27	20	5	2	1354	....	4	1.49	....	....	....	....	....	....	....
2009-10	Team Great Plains	UMHSEL	5	0	4	0	250	32	0	7.68	....	....	....	....	....	....	....
	Thief River Falls	High-MN	28	18	8	1	1434	51	3	1.84	....	....	....	....	....	....	....

• Signed Letter of Intent to attend **University of North Dakota** (WCHA) in fall of 2011.

GRAHAME, John (GRAY-uhm, JAWN) COL.

Goaltender. Catches left. 6'3", 220 lbs. Born, Denver, CO, August 31, 1975.
(Boston's 7th choice, 229th overall, in 1994 Entry Draft).

			Regular Season								Playoffs						
Season	Club	League	GP	W	L	O/T	Mins	GA	SO	Avg	GP	W	L	Mins	GA	SO	Avg
1993-94	Sioux City	USHL	20	....	....	....	1200	73	0	3.70	....	....	....	....	....	....	....
1994-95	Lake Superior State	CCHA	28	16	7	3	1616	75	2	2.79	....	....	....	....	....	....	....
1995-96	Lake Superior State	CCHA	29	21	4	2	1558	66	2	2.54	....	....	....	....	....	....	....
1996-97	Lake Superior State	CCHA	37	19	13	4	2197	134	3	3.66	....	....	....	....	....	....	....
1997-98	Providence Bruins	AHL	55	15	31	4	3053	164	3	3.22	....	....	....	....	....	....	....
1998-99	Providence Bruins	AHL	48	*37	9	1	2771	134	3	2.90	19	*15	4	*1209	48	1	2.38
99-2000	**Boston**	**NHL**	**24**	**7**	**10**	**5**	**1344**	**55**	**2**	**2.46**	....	....	....	....	....	....	....
	Providence Bruins	AHL	27	11	13	2	1528	86	1	3.38	13	10	3	839	35	0	2.50
2000-01	**Boston**	**NHL**	**10**	**3**	**4**	**0**	**471**	**28**	**0**	**3.57**	....	....	....	....	....	....	....
	Providence Bruins	AHL	16	4	7	3	893	47	0	3.16	17	8	9	1043	46	2	2.65
2001-02	**Boston**	**NHL**	**19**	**8**	**7**	**2**	**1079**	**52**	**1**	**2.89**	....	....	....	....	....	....	....
2002-03	**Boston**	**NHL**	**23**	**11**	**9**	**2**	**1352**	**61**	**1**	**2.71**	....	....	....	....	....	....	....
	Tampa Bay	**NHL**	**17**	**6**	**5**	**4**	**914**	**34**	**2**	**2.23**	**1**	**0**	**1**	**111**	**2**	**0**	**1.08**
2003-04 ◆	**Tampa Bay**	**NHL**	**29**	**18**	**9**	**1**	**1688**	**58**	**1**	**2.06**	**1**	**0**	**0**	**34**	**2**	**0**	**3.53**
2004-05							DID NOT PLAY										
2005-06	**Tampa Bay**	**NHL**	**57**	**29**	**22**	**1**	**3152**	**161**	**5**	**3.06**	**4**	**1**	**3**	**188**	**15**	**0**	**4.79**
	United States	Olympics	1	0	0	1	60	3	0	3.00	....	....	....	....	....	....	....
2006-07	**Carolina**	**NHL**	**28**	**10**	**13**	**2**	**1515**	**72**	**0**	**2.85**	....	....	....	....	....	....	....
2007-08	**Carolina**	**NHL**	**17**	**5**	**7**	**1**	**848**	**53**	**0**	**3.75**	....	....	....	....	....	....	....
	Albany River Rats	AHL	7	4	3	0	415	21	0	3.04	....	....	....	....	....	....	....
2008-09	Omsk	Rus-KHL	20	9	10	0	1195	57	3	2.86	....	....	....	....	....	....	....
2009-10	Adirondack	AHL	12	2	10	0	717	34	0	2.84	....	....	....	....	....	....	....
	Lake Erie Monsters	AHL	14	4	7	3	837	48	0	3.44	....	....	....	....	....	....	....
	NHL Totals		**224**	**97**	**86**	**18**	**12363**	**574**	**12**	**2.79**	**6**	**1**	**4**	**333**	**19**	**0**	**3.42**

Traded to **Tampa Bay** by **Boston** for Tampa Bay's 4th round choice (later traded to San Jose – San Jose selected Jason Churchill) in 2004 Entry Draft, January 13, 2003. Signed as a free agent by **Carolina**, July 1, 2006. Signed as a free agent by **Omsk** (Russia-KHL), May 17, 2008. Signed to a PTO (professional tryout) contract by **Adirondack** (AHL), December 13, 2009. Signed as a free agent by **Colorado**, March 3, 2010.

GREISS, Thomas (GRIGHS, TAW-muhs) S.J.

Goaltender. Catches left. 6'1", 210 lbs. Born, Straubing, West Germany, January 29, 1986.
(San Jose's 2nd choice, 94th overall, in 2004 Entry Draft).

			Regular Season								Playoffs						
Season	Club	League	GP	W	L	O/T	Mins	GA	SO	Avg	GP	W	L	Mins	GA	SO	Avg
2001-02	EV Fussen Jr.	Ger-Jr.					STATISTICS NOT AVAILABLE										
2002-03	Koln Jr.	Ger-Jr.	25	....	....	....	1613	58	0	2.16	3	1	2	180	8	1	2.67
2003-04	Koln Jr.	Ger-Jr.	24	....	....	....	1286	56	....	2.61	....	....	....	....	....	....	....
	Kolner Haie	Germany	1	....	....	....	20	4	0	12.00	....	....	....	....	....	....	....
2004-05	Kolner Haie	Germany	8	....	....	....	459	16	0	2.09	....	....	....	....	....	....	....
	Regensburg	German-2	1	....	....	....	60	2	0	2.00	2	....	....	56	2	0	2.14
2005-06	Kolner Haie	Germany	27	....	....	....	1560	64	1	2.46	9	....	....	533	27	*1	3.04
	Germany	Olympics	1	0	1	0	60	5	0	5.00	....	....	....	....	....	....	....
2006-07	Worcester Sharks	AHL	43	26	15	2	2555	111	0	2.61	3	0	3	172	12	0	4.18
	Fresno Falcons	ECHL	3	1	2	0	180	7	0	2.34	....	....	....	....	....	....	....
2007-08	**San Jose**	**NHL**	**3**	**0**	**1**	**1**	**129**	**7**	**0**	**3.26**	....	....	....	....	....	....	....
	Worcester Sharks	AHL	41	18	21	2	2424	125	0	3.09	....	....	....	....	....	....	....
2008-09	Worcester Sharks	AHL	57	30	24	2	3346	138	1	2.47	12	6	6	742	30	2	2.43
2009-10	**San Jose**	**NHL**	**16**	**7**	**4**	**1**	**782**	**35**	**0**	**2.69**	**1**	**0**	**0**	**40**	**2**	**0**	**3.00**
	Germany	Olympics	3	0	3	0	179	15	0	5.03	....	....	....	....	....	....	....
	NHL Totals		**19**	**7**	**5**	**2**	**911**	**42**	**0**	**2.77**	**1**	**0**	**0**	**40**	**2**	**0**	**3.00**

GRUBAUER, Philipp (groo-BAHW-uhr, FIHL-ihp) WSH.

Goaltender. Catches left. 6', 180 lbs. Born, Rosenheim, Germany, November 25, 1991.
(Washington's 3rd choice, 112th overall, in 2010 Entry Draft).

			Regular Season								Playoffs						
Season	Club	League	GP	W	L	O/T	Mins	GA	SO	Avg	GP	W	L	Mins	GA	SO	Avg
2006-07	Rosenheim Jr.	Ger-Jr.	6	....	....	....	354	49	....	8.32	3	....	....	180	12	....	4.00
2007-08	Rosenheim Jr.	Ger-Jr.	23	....	....	....	1288	71	....	3.31	3	....	....	181	8	....	2.65
	Rosenheim	German-3	5	....	....	....	307	14	1	2.74	7	....	....	420	12	....	1.71
2008-09	Belleville Bulls	OHL	17	7	8	0	947	62	0	3.93	1	0	0	....	4	0	4.29
2009-10	Belleville Bulls	OHL	31	10	14	5	1717	90	0	3.15	....	....	....	....	....	....	....
	Windsor Spitfires	OHL	19	13	1	2	1011	40	2	2.37	18	*16	1	1094	49	*2	2.69

GUSTAFSSON, Johan (GUHS-tahf-suhn, YOH-han) MIN.

Goaltender. Catches left. 6'2", 213 lbs. Born, Koping, Sweden, February 28, 1992.
(Minnesota's 5th choice, 159th overall, in 2010 Entry Draft).

			Regular Season								Playoffs						
Season	Club	League	GP	W	L	O/T	Mins	GA	SO	Avg	GP	W	L	Mins	GA	SO	Avg
2006-07	IFK Arboga IK	Sweden-2	4	....	....	....	201	22	0	6.55	....	....	....	....	....	....	....
2007-08	Kopings HC	Sweden-4					STATISTICS NOT AVAILABLE										
2008-09	Farjestad U18	Swe-U18	27	....	....	....	1581	47	5	1.78	4	....	....	228	14	0	3.68
2009-10	Farjestad U18	Swe-U18	10	....	....	....	600	34	1	3.40	7	....	....	417	22	0	3.16
	Farjestad	Sweden	3	....	....	....	136	9	0	3.96	....	....	....	....	....	....	....
	Skare BK	Sweden-3	26	....	....	....	1553	74	2	2.86	....	....	....	....	....	....	....

GUSTAVSSON, Jonas (GUHS-tahv-suhn, YOH-nuhs) TOR.

Goaltender. Catches left. 6'3", 192 lbs. Born, Danderyd, Sweden, October 24, 1984.

			Regular Season								Playoffs						
Season	Club	League	GP	W	L	O/T	Mins	GA	SO	Avg	GP	W	L	Mins	GA	SO	Avg
2000-01	AIK Solna U18	Swe-U18	12	....	....	....	667	42	1	3.78	....	....	....	....	....	....	....
2001-02	AIK Solna U18	Swe-U18	8	....	....	....	439	13	2	1.78	4	....	....	239	12	0	3.01
2002-03	AIK Solna Jr.	Swe-Jr.	21	....	....	....	1261	69	0	3.28	4	....	....	198	9	0	2.72
2003-04	AIK Solna Jr.	Swe-Jr.	9	....	....	....	505	24	0	2.85	....	....	....	....	....	....	....
	AIK Solna	Sweden-2	1	....	....	....	20	1	0	2.95	....	....	....	....	....	....	....
2004-05	AIK Solna Jr.	Swe-Jr.	10	....	....	....	557	32	0	3.45	....	....	....	....	....	....	....
	AIK Solna	Sweden-3	22	....	....	....	1270	32	4	1.51	....	....	....	....	....	....	....
2005-06	AIK Solna Jr.	Swe-Jr.	5	....	....	....	258	14	0	3.26	....	....	....	....	....	....	....
	AIK Solna	Sweden-2	6	....	....	....	351	14	0	2.39	....	....	....	....	....	....	....
2006-07	AIK IF Solna	Sweden-2	23	....	....	....	1269	59	2	2.79	....	....	....	....	....	....	....
2007-08	Skare BK	Sweden-3	6	....	....	....	368	16	0	2.61	....	....	....	....	....	....	....
	Farjestad	Sweden	20	....	....	....	1102	44	2	2.40	10	....	....	517	31	0	3.60
2008-09	Farjestad	Sweden	42	....	....	....	2475	81	3	*1.96	13	....	....	819	14	*5	*1.03
2009-10	**Toronto**	**NHL**	**42**	**16**	**15**	**9**	**2340**	**112**	**1**	**2.87**	....	....	....	....	....	....	....
	Sweden	Olympics	1	1	0	0	60	2	0	2.00	....	....	....	....	....	....	....
	NHL Totals		**42**	**16**	**15**	**9**	**2340**	**112**	**1**	**2.87**	....	....	....	....	....	....	....

Signed as a free agent by **Toronto**, July 7, 2009.

HACKETT, Matt (HA-keht, MA-thew) MIN.

Goaltender. Catches left. 6'2", 179 lbs. Born, London, Ont., March 7, 1990.
(Minnesota's 2nd choice, 77th overall, in 2009 Entry Draft).

			Regular Season								Playoffs						
Season	Club	League	GP	W	L	O/T	Mins	GA	SO	Avg	GP	W	L	Mins	GA	SO	Avg
2006-07	London Jr. Knights	Minor-ON	38	28	7	3	....	52	20	1.39	6	5	1	....	12	2	2.00
	St. Catharines	OJHL-B	16	7	7	0	902	63	0	4.19	....	....	....	....	....	....	....
	Windsor Spitfires	OHL	7	0	7	0	429	36	0	5.04	....	....	....	....	....	....	....
2007-08	Windsor Spitfires	OHL	4	1	1	0	130	10	0	4.61	....	....	....	....	....	....	....
	Plymouth Whalers	OHL	18	6	9	1	978	56	0	3.44	1	0	0	16	0	0	0.00
2008-09	Plymouth Whalers	OHL	55	34	15	3	3036	154	2	3.04	11	6	5	638	32	*1	3.01
2009-10	Plymouth Whalers	OHL	56	33	18	3	3165	138	4	2.62	8	3	4	429	24	0	3.36

OHL Second All-Star Team (2010)

HALAK, Jaroslav (HA-lak, YAHR-roh-slav) ST.L.

Goaltender. Catches left. 5'11", 179 lbs. Born, Bratislava, Czech., May 13, 1985.
(Montreal's 11th choice, 271st overall, in 2003 Entry Draft).

			Regular Season								Playoffs						
Season	Club	League	GP	W	L	O/T	Mins	GA	SO	Avg	GP	W	L	Mins	GA	SO	Avg
2001-02	Bratislava Jr.	Slovak-Jr.	22	....	....	....	1257	41	0	1.96	6	6	0	353	7	2	1.19
2002-03	Bratislava Jr.	Slovak-Jr.	20	13	3	3	1200	41	1	2.02	....	....	....	....	....	....	....
2003-04	Bratislava Jr.	Slovak-Jr.	29	....	....	....	1694	51	....	1.81	....	....	....	....	....	....	....
	HK 91 Senica	Slovak-2	21	....	....	....	1240	54	....	2.61	....	....	....	....	....	....	....
	Bratislava	Slovakia	12	....	....	....	650	18	0	1.66	1	....	....	45	6	0	8.00
2004-05	Lewiston	QMJHL	47	24	17	4	2697	125	4	2.78	8	4	4	460	27	0	3.52
2005-06	Hamilton Bulldogs	AHL	13	7	6	0	786	30	3	2.29	....	....	....	....	....	....	....
	Long Beach	ECHL	20	11	4	2	1026	35	2	2.05	4	2	2	252	13	0	3.10
2006-07	**Montreal**	**NHL**	**16**	**10**	**6**	**0**	**912**	**44**	**2**	**2.89**	....	....	....	....	....	....	....
	Hamilton Bulldogs	AHL	28	16	11	0	1618	54	6	*2.00	....	....	....	....	....	....	....
2007-08	**Montreal**	**NHL**	**6**	**2**	**1**	**1**	**285**	**10**	**1**	**2.11**	**2**	**0**	**1**	**77**	**3**	**0**	**2.34**
	Hamilton Bulldogs	AHL	28	15	10	2	1630	57	2	2.10	....	....	....	....	....	....	....
2008-09	**Montreal**	**NHL**	**34**	**18**	**14**	**1**	**1931**	**92**	**1**	**2.86**	**1**	**0**	**0**	**20**	**0**	**0**	**0.00**
2009-10	**Montreal**	**NHL**	**45**	**26**	**13**	**5**	**2630**	**105**	**5**	**2.40**	**18**	**9**	**9**	**1013**	**43**	**0**	**2.55**
	Slovakia	Olympics	7	3	4	0	423	17	1	2.41	....	....	....	....	....	....	....
	NHL Totals		**101**	**56**	**34**	**7**	**5758**	**251**	**9**	**2.62**	**21**	**9**	**10**	**1110**	**46**	**0**	**2.49**

AHL All-Rookie Team (2007)

Traded to **St. Louis** by **Montreal** for Lars Eller and Ian Schultz, June 17, 2010.

HARDING, Josh (HAHR-dihng, JAWSH) MIN.

Goaltender. Catches right. 6'1", 197 lbs. Born, Regina, Sask., June 18, 1984.
(Minnesota's 2nd choice, 38th overall, in 2002 Entry Draft).

			Regular Season								Playoffs						
Season	Club	League	GP	W	L	O/T	Mins	GA	SO	Avg	GP	W	L	Mins	GA	SO	Avg
2000-01	Reg. Pat Cdns.	SMHL	36	17	13	0	2106	96	2	2.75	3	1	2	170	11	0	3.88
2001-02	Regina Pats	WHL	42	27	13	1	2389	95	*4	2.39	6	2	4	325	16	0	2.95
2002-03	Regina Pats	WHL	57	18	24	13	*3385	155	3	2.75	5	1	4	321	13	0	2.43
2003-04	Regina Pats	WHL	28	12	14	2	1665	67	2	2.41	....	....	....	....	....	....	....
	Brandon	WHL	27	13	11	3	1612	65	5	2.42	11	5	6	660	36	0	3.27
2004-05	Houston Aeros	AHL	42	21	16	3	2388	80	4	2.01	2	0	2	119	8	0	4.03
2005-06	**Minnesota**	**NHL**	**3**	**2**	**1**	**0**	**185**	**8**	**1**	**2.59**	....	....	....	....	....	....	....
	Houston Aeros	AHL	38	29	8	0	2215	99	2	2.68	8	4	4	476	30	0	3.79
2006-07	**Minnesota**	**NHL**	**7**	**3**	**2**	**1**	**361**	**7**	**1**	**1.16**	....	....	....	....	....	....	....
	Houston Aeros	AHL	38	17	16	4	2270	94	1	2.48	....	....	....	....	....	....	....
2007-08	**Minnesota**	**NHL**	**29**	**11**	**15**	**2**	**1571**	**77**	**1**	**2.94**	**1**	**0**	**0**	**20**	**0**	**0**	**0.00**
2008-09	**Minnesota**	**NHL**	**19**	**3**	**9**	**1**	**870**	**32**	**0**	**2.21**	....	....	....	....	....	....	....
2009-10	**Minnesota**	**NHL**	**25**	**9**	**12**	**0**	**1300**	**66**	**1**	**3.05**	....	....	....	....	....	....	....
	NHL Totals		**83**	**28**	**39**	**4**	**4287**	**190**	**4**	**2.66**	**1**	**0**	**0**	**20**	**0**	**0**	**0.00**

WHL East Second All-Star Team (2002) • WHL East First All-Star Team (2003) • WHL Goaltender of the Year (2003) • WHL Player of the Year (2003) • Canadian Major Junior Second All-Star Team (2003)

HEDBERG, Johan (HEHD-buhrg, YOH-han) N.J.

Goaltender. Catches left. 6', 190 lbs. Born, Leksand, Sweden, May 5, 1973.
(Philadelphia's 8th choice, 218th overall, in 1994 Entry Draft).

			Regular Season								Playoffs						
Season	Club	League	GP	W	L	O/T	Mins	GA	SO	Avg	GP	W	L	Mins	GA	SO	Avg
1992-93	Leksands IF	Sweden	10	....	....	....	600	24	....	2.40	....	....	....	....	....	....	....
1993-94	Leksands IF	Sweden	17	....	....	....	1020	48	....	2.82	....	....	....	....	....	....	....
1994-95	Leksands IF	Sweden	17	....	....	....	986	58	....	3.53	....	....	....	....	....	....	....
1995-96	Leksands IF	Sweden	34	....	....	....	2013	95	....	2.83	4	....	....	240	13	....	3.25
1996-97	Leksands IF	Sweden	38	....	....	....	2260	95	3	2.52	8	....	....	581	18	1	1.86
1997-98	Detroit Vipers	IHL	16	7	2	2	726	32	1	2.64	....	....	....	....	....	....	....
	Baton Rouge	ECHL	2	1	1	0	100	7	0	4.20	....	....	....	....	....	....	....
	Manitoba Moose	IHL	14	8	4	1	745	32	1	2.58	2	0	2	105	6	0	3.40
	Sweden	Olympics					DID NOT PLAY – SPARE GOALTENDER										
1998-99	Leksands IF	Sweden	*48	....	....	....	*2940	140	0	2.86	4	....	....	255	15	0	3.53
99-2000	Kentucky	AHL	33	18	9	5	1973	88	3	2.68	5	3	2	311	10	1	1.93
2000-01	Manitoba Moose	IHL	46	23	13	7	2697	115	1	2.56	....	....	....	....	....	....	....
	Pittsburgh	**NHL**	**9**	**7**	**1**	**1**	**545**	**24**	**0**	**2.64**	**18**	**9**	**9**	**1123**	**43**	**2**	**2.30**
2001-02	**Pittsburgh**	**NHL**	**66**	**25**	**34**	**7**	**3877**	**178**	**6**	**2.75**	....	....	....	....	....	....	....
	Sweden	Olympics	1	1	0	0	60	1	0	1.00	....	....	....	....	....	....	....
2002-03	**Pittsburgh**	**NHL**	**41**	**14**	**22**	**4**	**2410**	**126**	**1**	**3.14**	....	....	....	....	....	....	....
2003-04	**Vancouver**	**NHL**	**21**	**8**	**6**	**2**	**1098**	**46**	**3**	**2.51**	**2**	**1**	**1**	**98**	**4**	**0**	**2.**
	Manitoba Moose	AHL	2	0	2	0	125	9	0	4.32	....	....	....	....	....	....	....
2004-05	Leksands IF	Sweden-2	21	....	....	....	1274	45	1	2.12	....	....	....	....	....	....	....
2005-06	**Dallas**	**NHL**	**19**	**12**	**4**	**1**	**1079**	**48**	**0**	**2.67**	....	....	....	....	....	....	....
2006-07	**Atlanta**	**NHL**	**21**	**9**	**4**	**2**	**1057**	**51**	**0**	**2.89**	**2**	**0**	**2**	**117**	**5**	**0**	**2.**
2007-08	**Atlanta**	**NHL**	**36**	**14**	**15**	**3**	**1927**	**111**	**1**	**3.46**	....	....	....	....	....	....	....
2008-09	**Atlanta**	**NHL**	**33**	**13**	**12**	**3**	**1717**	**100**	**0**	**3.49**	....	....	....	....	....	....	....
2009-10	**Atlanta**	**NHL**	**47**	**21**	**16**	**6**	**2632**	**115**	**3**	**2.62**	....	....	....	....	....	....	....
	NHL Totals		**293**	**123**	**114**	**29**	**16342**	**799**	**14**	**2.93**	**22**	**10**	**12**	**1338**	**52**	**2**	**2.**

• Rights traded to **San Jose** by **Philadelphia** for San Jose's 7th round choice (Pavel Kasparik) in 1999 Entry Draft, August 6, 1998. Traded to **Pittsburgh** by **San Jose** with Bobby Dollas for Jeff Norton, March 12, 2001. Traded to **Vancouver** by **Pittsburgh** for Vancouver's 2nd round choice (Alex Goligoski) in 2004 Entry Draft, August 25, 2003. Signed as a free agent by **Leksands** (Sweden-2), August 1, 2004. Signed as a free agent by **Dallas**, August 5, 2005. Signed as a free agent by **Atlanta**, July 1, 2006. Signed as a free agent by **New Jersey**, July 1, 2010.

HEEMSKERK, Thomas (HEEMZ-kuhrk, TAW-muhs) S.

Goaltender. Catches left. 6', 185 lbs. Born, Chilliwack, B.C., April 11, 1990.

			Regular Season								Playoffs						
Season	Club	League	GP	W	L	O/T	Mins	GA	SO	Avg	GP	W	L	Mins	GA	SO	Av
2006-07	Fraser Valley Bruins	BCMML	20	....	....	....	1125	68	1	3.31	....	....	....	....	....	....	
2007-08	Kootenay Ice	WHL	27	15	4	3	1379	61	1	2.65	....	....	....	....	....	....	
2008-09	Kootenay Ice	WHL	18	7	6	4	978	47	0	2.88	....	....	....	....	....	....	
	Everett Silvertips	WHL	27	9	15	2	1481	82	2	3.32	5	1	4	306	22	0	4.3
2009-10	Everett Silvertips	WHL	42	24	12	4	2415	94	4	2.34	2	1	0	146	9	0	3.

Signed as a free agent by **San Jose**, September 29, 2009.

HELENIUS, Riku (heh-lehn-NEE-uhs, REE-koo) T.B

Goaltender. Catches left. 6'3", 202 lbs. Born, Palkane, Finland, March 1, 1988.
(Tampa Bay's 1st choice, 15th overall, in 2006 Entry Draft).

			Regular Season								Playoffs						
Season	Club	League	GP	W	L	O/T	Mins	GA	SO	Avg	GP	W	L	Mins	GA	SO	Av
2004-05	Ilves Tampere U18	Fin-U18	16	....	....	....	903	30	3	1.99	5	....	....	295	15	0	3.0
	Ilves Tampere Jr.	Fin-Jr.	2	....	....	....	86	4	0	2.77	....	....	....	....	....	....	
2005-06	Suomi U20	Finland-2	1	....	....	....	60	3	0	3.00	....	....	....	....	....	....	
	Ilves Tampere U18	Fin-U18	2	....	....	....	120	2	0	1.00	5	....	....	300	13	0	2.6
	Ilves Tampere Jr.	Fin-Jr.	26	....	....	....	1565	70	4	2.68	2	....	....	135	7	0	3.
2006-07	Ilves Tampere Jr.	Fin-Jr.	2	2	0	0	120	4	0	2.00	....	....	....	....	....	....	
2007-08	Seattle	WHL	41	22	12	6	2358	95	3	2.42	9	4	5	534	24	0	2.7
2008-09	**Tampa Bay**	**NHL**	**1**	**0**	**0**	**0**	**7**	**0**	**0**	**0.00**	....	....	....	....	....	....	
	Norfolk Admirals	AHL	25	9	15	0	1388	63	1	2.72	....	....	....	....	....	....	
	Augusta Lynx	ECHL	8	3	4	1	463	34	0	4.41	....	....	....	....	....	....	
	Mississippi	ECHL	3	1	1	1	184	7	0	2.28	....	....	....	....	....	....	
	Elmira Jackals	ECHL	....	....	....	....	....	....	....	....	2	0	1	87	10	0	6.9
2009-10	Norfolk Admirals	AHL	12	5	7	0	719	33	0	2.75	....	....	....	....	....	....	
	Sodertalje SK	Sweden	9	....	....	....	545	22	0	2.42	....	....	....	....	....	....	
	Sodertalje SK	Sweden-Q	9	....	....	....	548	25	1	2.74	....	....	....	....	....	....	
	NHL Totals		**1**	**0**	**0**	**0**	**7**	**0**	**0**	**0.00**	....	....	....	....	....	....	

• Assigned to **Sodertalje** (Sweden) by **Tampa Bay**, January 24, 2010.

HILLER, Jonas (HIHL-uhr, YOH-nuhs) ANA

Goaltender. Catches right. 6'2", 190 lbs. Born, Felben Wellhausen, Switz., February 12, 1982.

			Regular Season								Playoffs						
Season	Club	League	GP	W	L	O/T	Mins	GA	SO	Avg	GP	W	L	Mins	GA	SO	Av
2000-01	HC Davos	Swiss	1	0	0	0	9	0	0	0.00	....	....	....	....	....	....	
2001-02	HC Davos	Swiss					DID NOT PLAY										
2002-03	HC Davos	Swiss					DID NOT PLAY										
2003-04	Lausanne HC	Swiss	21	....	....	....	1161	64	1	3.31	....	....	....	....	....	....	
	Chaux-de-Fonds	Swiss-2	1	0	1	0	60	4	0	4.00	....	....	....	....	....	....	
	Lausanne HC	Swiss-Q	....	....	....	....	....	....	....	....	4	4	0	251	7	0	1.6
2004-05	HC Davos	Swiss	43	26	12	4	2519	95	*8	2.26	*15	12	3	*932	34	0	*2.1
2005-06	HC Davos	Swiss	*44	23	16	5	*2676	110	3	2.47	15	9	6	900	45	1	3.0
2006-07	HC Davos	Swiss	*44	*28	16	0	*2656	115	3	2.60	*19	*12	7	*1138	39	3	2.0
2007-08	**Anaheim**	**NHL**	**23**	**10**	**7**	**1**	**1223**	**42**	**0**	**2.06**	....	....	....	....	....	....	
	Portland Pirates	AHL	6	3	2	1	370	13	0	2.11	....	....	....	....	....	....	
2008-09	**Anaheim**	**NHL**	**46**	**23**	**15**	**1**	**2486**	**99**	**4**	**2.39**	**13**	**7**	**6**	**807**	**30**	***2**	**2.2**
2009-10	**Anaheim**	**NHL**	**59**	**30**	**23**	**4**	**3338**	**152**	**2**	**2.73**	....	....	....	....	....	....	
	Switzerland	Olympics	5	2	3	0	316	13	0	2.47	....	....	....	....	....	....	
	NHL Totals		**128**	**63**	**45**	**6**	**7047**	**293**	**6**	**2.49**	**13**	**7**	**6**	**807**	**30**	**2**	**2.2**

Signed as a free agent by **Anaheim**, May 25, 2007.

HOLMQVIST, Johan (HOHLM-kvihst, YOH-han)

Goaltender. Catches left. 6'3", 198 lbs. Born, Tolfta, Sweden, May 24, 1978.
(NY Rangers' 9th choice, 175th overall, in 1997 Entry Draft).

			Regular Season								Playoffs						
Season	Club	League	GP	W	L	O/T	Mins	GA	SO	Avg	GP	W	L	Mins	GA	SO	Av
1996-97	Brynas IF Gavle	Sweden	2	0	0	0	80	4	0	3.00	....	....	....	....	....	....	
1997-98	Brynas IF Gavle	Sweden	33	....	....	....	1897	82	....	2.59	3	0	3	180	14	....	4.6
1998-99	Brynas IF Gavle	Sweden	41	....	....	....	2383	111	4	2.79	*14	9	5	*855	34	0	2.3
99-2000	Brynas IF Gavle	Sweden	41	....	....	....	2402	104	4	2.60	11	....	....	671	30	1	2.6
2000-01	**NY Rangers**	**NHL**	**2**	**0**	**2**	**0**	**119**	**10**	**0**	**5.04**	....	....	....	....	....	....	
	Hartford Wolf Pack	AHL	43	19	14	4	2305	111	2	2.89	5	2	3	314	13	0	2.4
2001-02	**NY Rangers**	**NHL**	**1**	**0**	**0**	**0**	**9**	**0**	**0**	**0.00**	....	....	....	....	....	....	
	Hartford Wolf Pack	AHL	48	26	12	6	2734	140	1	3.07	4	1	2	163	12	0	4.4
2002-03	**NY Rangers**	**NHL**	**1**	**0**	**1**	**0**	**39**	**2**	**0**	**3.08**	....	....	....	....	....	....	
	Hartford Wolf Pack	AHL	35	14	13	5	1904	84	2	2.65	....	....	....	....	....	....	
	Charlotte Checkers	ECHL	1	1	0	0	60	2	0	2.00	....	....	....	....	....	....	
	Houston Aeros	AHL	8	5	3	0	479	23	1	2.88	*23	*15	8	*1499	50	1	2.0
2003-04	Houston Aeros	AHL	59	23	27	7	3467	148	4	2.56	....	....	....	....	....	....	
2004-05	Brynas IF Gavle	Sweden	42	....	....	....	2445	138	1	3.39	....	....	....	....	....	....	
2005-06	Brynas IF Gavle	Sweden	26	....	....	....	1539	50	3	*1.95	4	....	....	194	13	0	4.0
2006-07	**Tampa Bay**	**NHL**	**48**	**27**	**15**	**3**	**2548**	**121**	**1**	**2.85**	**6**	**2**	**4**	**370**	**18**	**0**	**2.9**
2007-08	**Tampa Bay**	**NHL**	**45**	**20**	**16**	**6**	**2469**	**124**	**2**	**3.01**	....	....	....	....	....	....	
	Dallas	**NHL**	**2**	**1**	**0**	**0**	**80**	**5**	**0**	**3.75**	....	....	....	....	....	....	
2008-09	Frolunda	Sweden	*49	....	....	....	2799	101	2	2.17	11	....	....	623	25	1	2.4
2009-10	Frolunda	Sweden	*53	....	....	....	*3181	142	0	2.68	7	....	....	429	22	0	3.0
	NHL Totals		**99**	**48**	**34**	**9**	**5264**	**262**	**3**	**2.99**	**6**	**2**	**4**	**370**	**18**	**0**	**2.9**

Jack A. Butterfield Trophy (AHL –Playoff MVP) (2003)

Traded to **Minnesota** by **NY Rangers** for Lawrence Nycholat, March 11, 2003. Signed as a free agent by **Gavle** (Sweden), July 29, 2004. Signed as a free agent by **Tampa Bay**, June 1, 2006. Traded to **Dallas** by **Tampa Bay** with Brad Richards for Jussi Jokinen, Jeff Halpern, Mike Smith and Dallas' 4th round choice (later traded to Minnesota, later traded to Edmonton – Edmonton selected Kyle Bigos) in 2009 Entry Draft, February 26, 2008. Signed as a free agent by **Frolunda** (Sweden), July 23, 2008.

HOLT, Chris (HOHLT, KRIHS)

oaltender. Catches left. 6'3", 221 lbs. Born, Vancouver, B.C., June 5, 1985.
Y Rangers' 8th choice, 180th overall, in 2003 Entry Draft).

			Regular Season								Playoffs						
Season	Club	League	GP	W	L	O/T	Mins	GA	SO	Avg	GP	W	L	Mins	GA	SO	Avg
001-02	Billings Bulls	AWHL	24	13	7	1	1184	59	2	2.99	....	....	....	....	....	....	....
002-03	USNTDP	U-18	27	7	12	2	1519	81	1	3.20	....	....	....	....	....	....	....
	USNTDP	NAHL	5	2	3	0	255	14	0	3.30	....	....	....	....	....	....	....
003-04	Nebraska-Omaha	CCHA	27	5	17	2	1499	81	0	3.24	....	....	....	....	....	....	....
004-05	Nebraska-Omaha	CCHA	37	19	14	4	2190	106	1	2.90	....	....	....	....	....	....	....
005-06	**NY Rangers**	**NHL**	**1**	**0**	**0**	**0**	**10**	**0**	**0**	**0.00**	....	....	....	....	....	....	....
	Hartford Wolf Pack	AHL	9	3	2	1	459	31	0	4.06	8	4	4	487	24	0	2.96
	Charlotte Checkers	ECHL	23	7	11	1	1229	84	0	4.10	....	....	....	....	....	....	....
006-07	Hartford Wolf Pack	AHL	6	2	1	0	240	8	0	2.00	1	0	0	26	1	0	2.28
	Charlotte Checkers	ECHL	45	24	18	2	2650	139	1	3.15	4	2	2	223	11	0	2.97
007-08	Hartford Wolf Pack	AHL	9	5	3	0	447	18	0	2.42	....	....	....	....	....	....	....
	Charlotte Checkers	ECHL	32	15	13	2	1808	82	3	2.72	3	0	3	179	10	0	3.35
008-09	**St. Louis**	**NHL**	**1**	**0**	**0**	**0**	**19**	**0**	**0**	**0.00**	....	....	....	....	....	....	....
	Peoria Rivermen	AHL	20	10	6	2	1111	32	1	1.73	....	....	....	....	....	....	....
	Alaska Aces	ECHL	5	3	2	0	300	9	1	1.80	....	....	....	....	....	....	....
009-10	Binghamton	AHL	33	16	15	1	1872	92	4	2.95	....	....	....	....	....	....	....
	Elmira Jackals	ECHL	15	9	5	1	896	45	0	3.01	5	2	3	297	16	0	3.23
	NHL Totals		**2**	**0**	**0**	**0**	**29**	**0**	**0**	**0.00**	....	....	....	....	....	....	....

gned as a free agent by **St. Louis**, October 30, 2008. Signed as a free agent by **Binghamton** AHL), August 25, 2009. Signed as a free agent by **Riga** (Russia-KHL), June 18, 2010.

HOLTBY, Braden (HOHLT-bee, BRAY-duhn) WSH.

oaltender. Catches left. 6'1", 202 lbs. Born, Lloydminster, Sask., September 16, 1989.
Vashington's 5th choice, 93rd overall, in 2008 Entry Draft).

			Regular Season								Playoffs						
Season	Club	League	GP	W	L	O/T	Mins	GA	SO	Avg	GP	W	L	Mins	GA	SO	Avg
005-06	Saskatoon Blazers	SMHL	STATISTICS NOT AVAILABLE														
	Saskatoon Blades	WHL	1	0	1	0	59	4	0	4.07	....	....	....	....	....	....	....
006-07	Saskatoon Blades	WHL	51	17	29	3	2725	146	0	3.21	....	....	....	....	....	....	....
007-08	Saskatoon Blades	WHL	*64	25	29	0	3632	172	1	2.84	....	....	....	....	....	....	....
008-09	Saskatoon Blades	WHL	*61	40	16	4	*3571	156	6	2.62	7	3	4	414	16	0	2.32
009-10	Hershey Bears	AHL	37	25	8	2	2146	83	2	2.32	3	2	1	200	12	0	3.60
	South Carolina	ECHL	12	7	2	3	712	35	0	2.95	....	....	....	....	....	....	....

VHL East First All-Star Team (2009)

HOWARD, Jimmy (HOW-uhrd, JIHM-ee) DET.

oaltender. Catches left. 6', 210 lbs. Born, Syracuse, NY, March 26, 1984.
etroit's 1st choice, 64th overall, in 2003 Entry Draft).

			Regular Season								Playoffs						
Season	Club	League	GP	W	L	O/T	Mins	GA	SO	Avg	GP	W	L	Mins	GA	SO	Avg
001-02	USNTDP	U-18	19	15	4	1	1170	37	4	1.90	....	....	....	....	....	....	....
	USNTDP	USHL	8	4	3	0	425	14	0	1.98	....	....	....	....	....	....	....
	USNTDP	NAHL	8	3	4	0	381	25	0	3.93	....	....	....	....	....	....	....
002-03	University of Maine	H-East	21	14	6	0	1151	47	3	2.45	....	....	....	....	....	....	....
003-04	University of Maine	H-East	23	14	4	3	1364	27	*6	*1.19	....	....	....	....	....	....	....
004-05	University of Maine	H-East	*39	*19	13	7	*2310	74	*6	1.92	....	....	....	....	....	....	....
005-06	**Detroit**	**NHL**	**4**	**1**	**2**	**0**	**201**	**10**	**0**	**2.99**	....	....	....	....	....	....	....
	Grand Rapids	AHL	38	27	6	2	2140	92	2	2.58	13	5	7	763	44	0	3.46
006-07	Grand Rapids	AHL	49	21	21	3	2776	125	6	2.70	7	3	4	434	14	0	*1.93
007-08	**Detroit**	**NHL**	**4**	**0**	**2**	**0**	**197**	**7**	**0**	**2.13**	....	....	....	....	....	....	....
	Grand Rapids	AHL	54	21	28	2	3097	146	2	2.83	....	....	....	....	....	....	....
008-09	**Detroit**	**NHL**	**1**	**0**	**1**	**0**	**59**	**4**	**0**	**4.07**	....	....	....	....	....	....	....
	Grand Rapids	AHL	45	21	18	4	2644	112	4	2.54	10	4	6	598	24	0	2.41
009-10	**Detroit**	**NHL**	**63**	**37**	**15**	**10**	**3740**	**141**	**3**	**2.26**	**12**	**5**	**7**	**720**	**33**	**1**	**2.75**
	NHL Totals		**72**	**38**	**20**	**10**	**4197**	**162**	**3**	**2.32**	**12**	**5**	**7**	**720**	**33**	**1**	**2.75**

ockey East All-Rookie Team (2003) • Hockey East Rookie of the Year (2003) • Hockey East First ll-Star Team (2004) • NCAA East Second All-American Team (2004) • AHL All-Rookie Team (2006) NHL All-Rookie Team (2010)

HUET, Cristobal (hew-AY, KRIHS-toh-bahl) CHI.

oaltender. Catches left. 6'1", 206 lbs. Born, St. Martin d'Heres, France, September 3, 1975.
os Angeles' 9th choice, 214th overall, in 2001 Entry Draft).

			Regular Season								Playoffs						
Season	Club	League	GP	W	L	O/T	Mins	GA	SO	Avg	GP	W	L	Mins	GA	SO	Avg
997-98	CSG Grenoble	France	STATISTICS NOT AVAILABLE														
	France	Olympics	2	1	1	0	120	5	0	2.50	....	....	....	....	....	....	....
998-99	HC Lugano	Swiss	21	....	....	....	1275	58	1	2.73	10	....	....	628	18	1	*1.72
9-2000	HC Lugano	Swiss	31	....	....	....	1886	50	*8	*1.59	13	....	....	783	29	0	2.22
000-01	HC Lugano	Swiss	39	....	....	....	2365	77	*6	*1.95	*18	....	....	*1141	39	2	2.05
001-02	HC Lugano	Swiss	39	....	....	....	2313	107	*4	2.78	1	0	1	60	3	0	3.00
	France	Olympics	3	0	2	1	179	10	0	3.36	....	....	....	....	....	....	....
	France	WC-B	5	4	1	0	299	5	2	1.00	....	....	....	....	....	....	....
002-03	**Los Angeles**	**NHL**	**12**	**4**	**4**	**1**	**541**	**21**	**1**	**2.33**	....	....	....	....	....	....	....
	Manchester	AHL	30	16	8	5	1784	68	1	2.29	1	0	1	30	4	0	8.08
003-04	**Los Angeles**	**NHL**	**41**	**10**	**16**	**10**	**2199**	**89**	**3**	**2.43**	....	....	....	....	....	....	....
004-05	Adler Mannheim	Germany	36	....	....	....	2001	93	1	2.79	*14	....	....	*850	40	2	2.82
005-06	**Montreal**	**NHL**	**36**	**18**	**11**	**4**	**2103**	**77**	**7**	**2.20**	**6**	**2**	**4**	**386**	**15**	**0**	**2.33**
	Hamilton Bulldogs	AHL	4	0	4	0	237	15	0	3.79	....	....	....	....	....	....	....
006-07	**Montreal**	**NHL**	**42**	**19**	**16**	**3**	**2286**	**107**	**2**	**2.81**	....	....	....	....	....	....	....
007-08	**Montreal**	**NHL**	**39**	**21**	**12**	**6**	**2278**	**97**	**2**	**2.55**	....	....	....	....	....	....	....
	Washington	**NHL**	**13**	**11**	**2**	**0**	**771**	**21**	**2**	**1.63**	**7**	**3**	**4**	**451**	**22**	**0**	**2.93**
008-09	**Chicago**	**NHL**	**41**	**20**	**15**	**4**	**2351**	**99**	**3**	**2.53**	**3**	**1**	**2**	**130**	**7**	**0**	**3.23**
009-10 ♦	**Chicago**	**NHL**	**48**	**26**	**14**	**4**	**2731**	**114**	**4**	**2.50**	**1**	**0**	**0**	**20**	**0**	**0**	**0.00**
	NHL Totals		**272**	**129**	**90**	**32**	**15260**	**625**	**24**	**2.46**	**17**	**6**	**10**	**987**	**44**	**0**	**2.67**

ayed in NHL All-Star Game (2007)

raded to **Montreal** by **Los Angeles** with Radek Bonk for Mathieu Garon and San Jose's 3rd round hoice (previously acquired, Los Angeles selected Piaul Baier) in 2004 Entry Draft, June 26, 2004. gned as a free agent by **Mannheim** (Germany), September 14, 2004. Traded to **Washington** by **Montreal** for Anaheim's 2nd round choice (previously acquired, later traded to Atlanta – Atlanta elected Jeremy Morin) in 2009 Entry Draft, February 26, 2008. Signed as a free agent by **Chicago**, ly 1, 2008.

HUTCHINSON, Michael (HUH-chihn-suhn, MIGH-kuhl) BOS.

oaltender. Catches right. 6'3", 192 lbs. Born, Barrie, Ont., March 2, 1990.
oston's 3rd choice, 77th overall, in 2008 Entry Draft).

			Regular Season								Playoffs						
Season	Club	League	GP	W	L	O/T	Mins	GA	SO	Avg	GP	W	L	Mins	GA	SO	Avg
006-07	Orangeville	OPJHL	8	1	4	0	289	24	0	4.99	....	....	....	....	....	....	....
	Barrie Colts	OHL	14	8	3	0	768	27	0	2.11	1	1	0	45	1	0	1.33
007-08	Barrie Colts	OHL	32	12	15	4	1826	92	1	3.02	8	4	4	500	22	1	2.64
008-09	Barrie Colts	OHL	38	15	20	1	2146	108	5	3.02	3	0	2	112	10	0	5.37
009-10	London Knights	OHL	46	32	12	2	2667	127	3	2.86	12	7	4	686	47	0	4.11

HUTTON, Carter (HUH-tuhn, KAR-tuhr) S.J.

Goaltender. Catches left. 6'1", 195 lbs. Born, Thunder Bay, Ont., December 19, 1985.

			Regular Season								Playoffs						
Season	Club	League	GP	W	L	O/T	Mins	GA	SO	Avg	GP	W	L	Mins	GA	SO	Avg
2005-06	F-Wm. North Stars	SIJHL	36	33	1	0	2053	63	10	1.84	15	12	3	928	36	2	2.33
2006-07	U. Mass-Lowell	H-East	19	3	10	5	1097	52	1	2.84	....	....	....	....	....	....	....
2007-08	U. Mass-Lowell	H-East	20	7	11	2	1187	49	2	2.48	....	....	....	....	....	....	....
2008-09	U. Mass-Lowell	H-East	19	9	8	1	1106	38	*3	2.06	....	....	....	....	....	....	....
2009-10	U. Mass-Lowell	H-East	27	13	12	2	1614	55	*4	*2.04	....	....	....	....	....	....	....
	Adirondack	AHL	4	1	2	1	244	11	0	2.71	....	....	....	....	....	....	....

Hockey East Second All-Star Team (2010)

Signed to an ATO (amateur tryout) contract by **Adirondack** (AHL), March 20, 2010. Signed as a free agent by **San Jose**, June 1, 2010.

IILAHTI, Jonathan (ee-eh-LAH-tee, JAWN-ah-thuhn) VAN.

Goaltender. Catches left. 6'1", 175 lbs. Born, Vaasa, Finland, April 27, 1992.
(Vancouver's 4th choice, 175th overall, in 2010 Entry Draft).

			Regular Season								Playoffs						
Season	Club	League	GP	W	L	O/T	Mins	GA	SO	Avg	GP	W	L	Mins	GA	SO	Avg
2007-08	Sport Vaasa U18	Fin-U18	2	0	2	0	119	8	0	4.03	....	....	....	....	....	....	....
2008-09	Blues Espoo U18	Fin-U18	19	9	10	0	1096	63	0	3.45	2	0	2	98	9	0	5.51
2009-10	Blues Espoo U18	Fin-U18	21	15	5	0	1176	47	1	2.40	11	5	6	667	31	1	2.79
	Blues Espoo Jr.	Fin-Jr.	14	8	6	0	832	37	1	2.67	....	....	....	....	....	....	....

IRVING, Leland (UHR-vihng, LEE-land) CGY.

Goaltender. Catches left. 6', 175 lbs. Born, Barrhead, Alta., April 11, 1988.
(Calgary's 1st choice, 26th overall, in 2006 Entry Draft).

			Regular Season								Playoffs						
Season	Club	League	GP	W	L	O/T	Mins	GA	SO	Avg	GP	W	L	Mins	GA	SO	Avg
2002-03	Spruce Grove	AMBHL	....	11	11	4	1559	94	....	3.62	....	....	....	....	....	....	....
2003-04	Spruce Grove	RAMHL	19	....	....	....	1017	44	1	2.60	....	....	....	....	....	....	....
	Everett Silvertips	WHL	1	0	0	0	8	0	0	0.00	....	....	....	....	....	....	....
2004-05	Everett Silvertips	WHL	23	9	8	1	1132	34	2	1.80	....	....	....	....	....	....	....
2005-06	Everett Silvertips	WHL	*67	37	22	4	*3791	121	4	1.92	12	8	4	747	21	3	1.69
2006-07	Everett Silvertips	WHL	48	34	9	3	2802	87	*11	1.86	12	6	5	639	30	0	2.82
2007-08	Everett Silvertips	WHL	56	27	24	0	3258	133	4	2.45	3	0	3	139	10	0	4.32
2008-09	Quad City Flames	AHL	47	24	18	2	2658	99	1	2.23	....	....	....	....	....	....	....
2009-10	Abbotsford Heat	AHL	35	14	17	2	1850	85	1	2.76	1	0	1	14	3	0	12.97
	Victoria	ECHL	8	2	4	2	490	25	0	3.06	....	....	....	....	....	....	....

WHL West Second All-Star Team (2006, 2007)

JANUS, Jaroslav (YA-nuhs, YAHR-roh-slav) T.B.

Goaltender. Catches left. 5'11", 190 lbs. Born, Presov, Czechoslovakia, September 21, 1989.
(Tampa Bay's 6th choice, 162nd overall, in 2009 Entry Draft).

			Regular Season								Playoffs						
Season	Club	League	GP	W	L	O/T	Mins	GA	SO	Avg	GP	W	L	Mins	GA	SO	Avg
2003-04	Presov U18	Svk-U18	14	....	....	....	....	....	....	....	....	....	....	....	....	....	....
2004-05	PHK Presov U18	Svk-U18	34	....	....	....	1743	53	3	1.82	....	....	....	....	....	....	....
	PHK Presov Jr.	Slovak-Jr.	1	....	....	....	60	7	0	7.00	1	....	....	23	1	0	2.61
2005-06	Bratislava U18	Svk-U18	37	....	....	....	1913	92	2	2.89	8	....	....	486	19	0	2.34
	Bratislava Jr.	Slovak-Jr.	13	....	....	....	609	25	0	2.46	....	....	....	....	....	....	....
2006-07	Bratislava U18	Svk-U18	35	....	....	....	2010	84	1	2.51	....	....	....	....	....	....	....
	Bratislava Jr.	Slovak-Jr.	24	....	....	....	1355	49	4	2.17	1	....	....	33	4	0	7.28
2007-08	Erie Otters	OHL	48	13	29	3	2740	201	0	4.40	....	....	....	....	....	....	....
2008-09	Erie Otters	OHL	49	25	20	4	2818	152	3	3.24	5	1	4	285	20	*1	4.21
2009-10	Erie Otters	OHL	13	7	4	2	770	36	0	2.81	....	....	....	....	....	....	....
	Norfolk Admirals	AHL	13	7	6	0	783	27	1	2.07	....	....	....	....	....	....	....

JOHNSON, Brent (JAWN-suhn, BREHNT) PIT.

Goaltender. Catches left. 6'3", 199 lbs. Born, Farmington, MI, March 12, 1977.
(Colorado's 5th choice, 129th overall, in 1995 Entry Draft).

			Regular Season								Playoffs						
Season	Club	League	GP	W	L	O/T	Mins	GA	SO	Avg	GP	W	L	Mins	GA	SO	Avg
1993-94	Det. Compuware	NAHL	18	....	....	....	1024	49	1	3.52	....	....	....	....	....	....	....
1994-95	Owen Sound	OHL	18	3	9	1	904	75	0	4.98	....	....	....	....	....	....	....
1995-96	Owen Sound	OHL	58	24	28	1	3211	243	1	4.54	6	2	4	371	29	0	4.69
1996-97	Owen Sound	OHL	50	20	28	1	2798	201	1	4.31	4	0	4	253	24	0	5.69
1997-98	Worcester IceCats	AHL	42	14	15	7	2240	119	0	3.19	6	3	2	332	19	0	3.43
1998-99	**St. Louis**	**NHL**	**6**	**3**	**2**	**0**	**286**	**10**	**0**	**2.10**	....	....	....	....	....	....	....
	Worcester IceCats	AHL	49	22	22	4	2925	146	2	2.99	4	1	3	238	12	0	3.02
99-2000	Worcester IceCats	AHL	58	24	27	5	3319	161	3	2.91	9	4	5	561	23	1	2.46
2000-01	**St. Louis**	**NHL**	**31**	**19**	**9**	**2**	**1744**	**63**	**4**	**2.17**	**2**	**0**	**1**	**62**	**2**	**0**	**1.94**
2001-02	**St. Louis**	**NHL**	**58**	**34**	**20**	**4**	**3491**	**127**	**5**	**2.18**	**10**	**5**	**5**	**590**	**18**	**3**	**1.83**
2002-03	**St. Louis**	**NHL**	**38**	**16**	**13**	**5**	**2042**	**84**	**2**	**2.47**	....	....	....	....	....	....	....
	Worcester IceCats	AHL	2	0	1	1	125	8	0	3.84	....	....	....	....	....	....	....
2003-04	**St. Louis**	**NHL**	**10**	**4**	**3**	**1**	**493**	**20**	**1**	**2.43**	....	....	....	....	....	....	....
	Worcester IceCats	AHL	8	2	2	2	365	14	0	2.30	....	....	....	....	....	....	....
	Phoenix	**NHL**	**8**	**1**	**6**	**1**	**486**	**21**	**0**	**2.59**	....	....	....	....	....	....	....
2004-05			DID NOT PLAY														
2005-06	**Washington**	**NHL**	**26**	**9**	**12**	**1**	**1413**	**81**	**1**	**3.44**	....	....	....	....	....	....	....
2006-07	**Washington**	**NHL**	**30**	**6**	**15**	**7**	**1644**	**99**	**0**	**3.61**	....	....	....	....	....	....	....
2007-08	**Washington**	**NHL**	**19**	**7**	**8**	**2**	**1032**	**46**	**0**	**2.67**	....	....	....	....	....	....	....
	Hershey Bears	AHL	1	0	1	0	59	3	0	3.04	....	....	....	....	....	....	....
2008-09	**Washington**	**NHL**	**21**	**12**	**6**	**2**	**1131**	**53**	**0**	**2.81**	....	....	....	....	....	....	....
2009-10	**Pittsburgh**	**NHL**	**23**	**10**	**6**	**1**	**1108**	**51**	**0**	**2.76**	**1**	**0**	**0**	**31**	**1**	**0**	**1.94**
	NHL Totals		**270**	**121**	**100**	**26**	**14870**	**655**	**13**	**2.64**	**13**	**5**	**6**	**683**	**21**	**3**	**1.84**

Traded to **St. Louis** by **Colorado** for San Jose's 3rd round choice (previously acquired, Colorado selected Rick Berry) in 1997 Entry Draft, May 30, 1997. Traded to **Phoenix** by **St. Louis** for Mike Sillinger, March 4, 2004. Signed as a free agent by **Vancouver**, September 1, 2005. Claimed on waivers by **Washington** from **Vancouver**, October 4, 2005. Signed as a free agent by **Pittsburgh**, July 21, 2009.

JOHNSON, Chad (JAWN-suhn, CHAD) NYR

Goaltender. Catches left. 6'3", 200 lbs. Born, Calgary, Alta., June 10, 1986.
(Pittsburgh's 4th choice, 125th overall, in 2006 Entry Draft).

			Regular Season								Playoffs						
Season	Club	League	GP	W	L	O/T	Mins	GA	SO	Avg	GP	W	L	Mins	GA	SO	Avg
2002-03	Calgary Buffaloes	AMHL	....	8	8	2	1145	62	....	3.25	1	0	1	60	3	0	3.00
2003-04	Brooks Bandits	AJHL	31	6	20	3	1782	117	0	3.94	....	....	....	....	....	....	....
2004-05	Brooks Bandits	AJHL	43	25	16	2	2505	109	2	2.61	119	4	5	493	....	....	....
2005-06	Alaska	CCHA	18	6	7	4	985	42	0	2.56	....	....	....	....	....	....	....
2006-07	Alaska	CCHA	19	5	6	2	1002	52	1	3.11	....	....	....	....	....	....	....
2007-08	Alaska	CCHA	7	0	6	0	357	20	0	3.36	....	....	....	....	....	....	....
2008-09	Alaska	CCHA	35	14	16	5	2062	57	6	*1.66	....	....	....	....	....	....	....
2009-10	**NY Rangers**	**NHL**	**5**	**1**	**2**	**1**	**281**	**11**	**0**	**2.35**	....	....	....	....	....	....	....
	Hartford Wolf Pack	AHL	47	24	18	2	2649	112	3	2.54	....	....	....	....	....	....	....
	NHL Totals		**5**	**1**	**2**	**1**	**281**	**11**	**0**	**2.35**	....	....	....	....	....	....	....

AJHL South Division First All-Star Team (2005) • CCHA First All-Star Team (2009) • CCHA Rookie of the Year (2009) • NCAA West Second All-American Team (2009)

Traded to **NY Rangers** by **Pittsburgh** for Pittsburgh's 5th round choice (previously acquired, Pittsburgh selected Andy Bathgate) in 2009 Entry Draft, June 27, 2009.

JONES, Martin (JOHNZ, MAR-tihn) L.A.

Goaltender. Catches left. 6'4", 185 lbs. Born, North Vancouver, B.C., January 10, 1990.

			Regular Season								Playoffs						
Season	Club	League	GP	W	L	O/T	Mins	GA	SO	Avg	GP	W	L	Mins	GA	SO	Avg
2006-07	Calgary Hitmen	WHL	18	9	4	3	1029	52	0	3.03	....	....	....	....	....	....	....
2007-08	Calgary Hitmen	WHL	27	18	8	1	1529	54	1	2.12	5	2	1	250	12	0	2.88
2008-09	Calgary Hitmen	WHL	55	*45	5	4	3295	114	*7	2.08	18	14	4	1095	34	2	1.86
2009-10	Calgary Hitmen	WHL	48	36	11	1	2851	105	*8	*2.21	*23	*16	6	*1401	55	*2	*2.36

WHL East Second All-Star Team (2009) • WHL East First All-Star Team (2010) • WHL Goaltender of the Year (2010) • Canadian Major Junior Second All-Star Team (2010) • Memorial Cup All-Star Team (2010) • Hap Emms Memorial Trophy (Memorial Cup Tournament – Top Goaltender) (2010)

Signed as a free agent by **Los Angeles**, October 2, 2008.

KANGAS, Alex (KANG-uhs, AL-ehx) ATL.

Goaltender. Catches left. 6'3", 200 lbs. Born, Rochester, NY, May 28, 1987.
(Atlanta's 4th choice, 135th overall, in 2006 Entry Draft).

			Regular Season								Playoffs						
Season	Club	League	GP	W	L	O/T	Mins	GA	SO	Avg	GP	W	L	Mins	GA	SO	Avg
2001-02	Rochester Century	High-MN	3	3	0	0	....	3	2	1.00	....	....	....	....	....	....	....
2002-03	Rochester Century	High-MN	27	17	9	0	....	50	6	1.76	....	....	....	....	....	....	....
2003-04	Rochester Century	High-MN	28	15	12	1	....	59	3	2.08	....	....	....	....	....	....	....
2004-05	Rochester Century	High-MN	30	23	4	3	....	55	7	1.86	....	....	....	....	....	....	....
2005-06	Sioux Falls	USHL	29	20	6	3	1733	62	3	2.15	6	4	2	359	17	0	2.84
2006-07	Indiana Ice	USHL	46	19	19	5	2467	136	1	3.31	7	6	1	434	18	0	2.49
2007-08	U. of Minnesota	WCHA	31	12	10	9	1967	65	0	1.98	....	....	....	....	....	....	....
2008-09	U. of Minnesota	WCHA	36	17	11	6	2019	94	3	2.79	....	....	....	....	....	....	....
2009-10	U. of Minnesota	WCHA	33	16	15	1	1934	84	1	2.61	....	....	....	....	....	....	....

USHL All-Rookie Team (2006)

KARLSSON, Henrik (KARL-suhn, HEHN-rihk) CGY.

Goaltender. Catches left. 6'6", 215 lbs. Born, Stockholm, Sweden, November 27, 1983.

			Regular Season								Playoffs						
Season	Club	League	GP	W	L	O/T	Mins	GA	SO	Avg	GP	W	L	Mins	GA	SO	Avg
2000-01	Hammarby U18	Swe-U18	2	....	....	....	120	7	0	3.50	....	....	....	....	....	....	....
	Hammarby Jr.	Swe-Jr.	13	....	....	....	706	56	0	4.76	....	....	....	....	....	....	....
2001-02	Hammarby Jr.	Swe-Jr.	23	....	....	....	1356	97	1	4.29	....	....	....	....	....	....	....
2002-03	Botkyrka	Sweden-3	....	....	....	....	....	....	....	2.58	....	....	....	....	....	....	....
2003-04	Botkyrka	Sweden-3	21	....	....	....	....	....	....	2.49	6	....	....	236	15	0	3.82
2004-05	Olofstroms IK	Sweden-3	1	....	....	....	60	0	1	0.00	....	....	....	....	....	....	....
	IK Oskarshamn	Sweden-2	11	....	....	....	613	25	1	2.45	2	....	....	109	7	0	3.87
2005-06	IK Oskarshamn	Sweden-2	1	....	....	....	40	3	0	4.54	....	....	....	....	....	....	....
2006-07	Hammarby Jr.	Swe-Jr.	1	....	....	....	59	2	0	2.04	....	....	....	....	....	....	....
	Hammarby	Sweden-2	35	....	....	....	1893	111	1	3.52	....	....	....	....	....	....	....
2007-08	Hammarby	Sweden-2	29	....	....	....	1692	109	1	3.86	....	....	....	....	....	....	....
	Malmo	Sweden-2	3	....	....	....	180	8	0	2.67	....	....	....	....	....	....	....
2008-09	Malmo	Sweden-2	32	....	....	....	1888	77	4	2.45	....	....	....	....	....	....	....
	Sodertalje SK	Sweden	7	....	....	....	410	17	0	2.49	....	....	....	....	....	....	....
	Sodertalje SK	Sweden-Q	8	....	....	....	483	16	0	1.99	....	....	....	....	....	....	....
2009-10	Farjestad	Sweden	34	....	....	....	1934	79	3	2.45	....	....	....	....	....	....	....

Signed as a free agent by **San Jose**, August 12, 2009. Signed as a free agent by **Riga** (Russia-KHL), June 14, 2010. • Rights traded to **Calgary** by **San Jose** for Calgary's 6th round choice (Konrad Abeltshauser) in 2010 Entry Draft, June 25, 2010.

KARPOWICH, Paul (KAHR-puh-wihch, PAWL) ST.L.

Goaltender. Catches left. 6'2", 190 lbs. Born, Thunder Bay, Ont., October 25, 1988.
(St. Louis' 10th choice, 185th overall, in 2008 Entry Draft).

			Regular Season								Playoffs						
Season	Club	League	GP	W	L	O/T	Mins	GA	SO	Avg	GP	W	L	Mins	GA	SO	Avg
2004-05	Thunder Bay Kings	Minor-ON	38	25	7	3	2057	103	2	3.00	....	....	....	....	....	....	....
2005-06	Thunder Bay Kings	Minor-ON	42	29	8	3	2280	91	6	2.39	....	....	....	....	....	....	....
2006-07	Brooks Bandits	AJHL	18	6	6	2	1010	59	0	3.51	2	1	0	92	8	0	5.21
2007-08	Wellington Dukes	OPJHL	22	15	3	2	1202	43	3	2.15	13	9	4	771	35	1	2.72
2008-09	Clarkson Knights	ECAC	27	7	14	4	1516	72	1	2.85	....	....	....	....	....	....	....
2009-10	Clarkson Knights	ECAC	31	8	19	4	1744	101	0	3.48	....	....	....	....	....	....	....

KEETLEY, Matt (KEET-lee, MAT) CGY.

Goaltender. Catches right. 6'1", 187 lbs. Born, Medicine Hat, Alta., April 27, 1986.
(Calgary's 6th choice, 158th overall, in 2005 Entry Draft).

			Regular Season								Playoffs						
Season	Club	League	GP	W	L	O/T	Mins	GA	SO	Avg	GP	W	L	Mins	GA	SO	Avg
2003-04	Medicine Hat	AMHL	....	7	4	2	813	48	....	3.54	....	....	....	....	....	....	....
	Medicine Hat	WHL	3	0	1	0	72	5	0	4.17	2	0	0	15	1	0	4.00
2004-05	Medicine Hat	WHL	32	21	5	3	1846	51	6	*1.66	3	1	0	103	8	0	4.66
2005-06	Medicine Hat	WHL	62	*42	13	6	3741	130	6	2.09	13	9	4	864	30	0	2.08
2006-07	Medicine Hat	WHL	55	*42	11	1	3258	119	6	2.19	*23	*16	7	*1407	51	*4	2.18
2007-08	**Calgary**	**NHL**	**1**	**0**	**0**	**0**	**9**	**0**	**0**	**0.00**	....	....	....	....	....	....	....
	Quad City Flames	AHL	26	10	8	3	1393	54	1	2.33	....	....	....	....	....	....	....
2008-09	Quad City Flames	AHL	33	8	18	4	1853	88	2	2.85	....	....	....	....	....	....	....
	Las Vegas	ECHL	7	1	3	3	429	19	0	2.66	....	....	....	....	....	....	....
2009-10	Abbotsford Heat	AHL	23	10	7	1	1205	52	2	2.59	....	....	....	....	....	....	....
	Victoria	ECHL	9	2	7	0	484	31	2	3.84	5	2	3	298	13	0	2.62
	NHL Totals		**1**	**0**	**0**	**0**	**9**	**0**	**0**	**0.00**	....	....	....	....	....	....	....

WHL East Second All-Star Team (2006) • WHL East First All-Star Team (2007) • Memorial Cup Tournament All-Star Team (2007) • Hap Emms Memorial Trophy (Memorial Cup Tournament - Top Goaltender) (2007)

KHABIBULIN, Nikolai (khah-bee-BOO-lihn, NIH-koh-ligh) EDM

Goaltender. Catches left. 6'1", 209 lbs. Born, Sverdlovsk, USSR, January 13, 1973.
(Winnipeg's 8th choice, 204th overall, in 1992 Entry Draft).

			Regular Season								Playoffs						
Season	Club	League	GP	W	L	O/T	Mins	GA	SO	Avg	GP	W	L	Mins	GA	SO	Avg
1988-89	Sverdlovsk	USSR	1	....	....	....	3	0	0	0.00	....	....	....	....	....	....	..
1989-90	Luch Sverdlovsk	USSR-2					STATISTICS NOT AVAILABLE										
1990-91	Nizhny Tagil	USSR-3	10	....	....	....	....	....	....	....	....	....	....	....	....	....	..
	Sverdlovsk	USSR-Q	2	....	....	....	....	7	....	....	....	....	....	....	....	....	..
1991-92	CSKA Moscow 2	CIS-3	11	....	....	....	....	....	....	....	....	....	....	....	....	....	..
	CSKA Moscow	CIS	2	....	....	....	34	2	0	3.53	....	....	....	....	....	....	..
	Russia	Olympics					DID NOT PLAY – SPARE GOALTENDER										
1992-93	CSKA Moscow	CIS	13	....	....	....	491	27	....	3.29	....	....	....	....	....	....	..
	Serov	CIS-2	18	....	....	....	....	....	....	....	....	....	....	....	....	....	..
1993-94	CSKA Moscow	CIS	46	....	....	....	2625	116	....	2.65	....	....	....	....	....	....	..
	Russian Penguins	IHL	12	2	7	2	639	47	0	4.41	....	....	....	....	....	....	..
1994-95	Springfield Indians	AHL	23	9	9	3	1240	80	0	3.87	....	....	....	....	....	....	..
	Winnipeg	**NHL**	**26**	**8**	**9**	**4**	**1339**	**76**	**0**	**3.41**	....	....	....	....	....	....	..
1995-96	**Winnipeg**	**NHL**	**53**	**26**	**20**	**3**	**2914**	**152**	**2**	**3.13**	**6**	**2**	**4**	**359**	**19**	**0**	**3.1**
1996-97	**Phoenix**	**NHL**	**72**	**30**	**33**	**6**	**4091**	**193**	**7**	**2.83**	**7**	**3**	**4**	**426**	**15**	**1**	**2.1**
1997-98	**Phoenix**	**NHL**	**70**	**30**	**28**	**10**	**4026**	**184**	**4**	**2.74**	**4**	**2**	**1**	**185**	**13**	**0**	**4.2**
1998-99	**Phoenix**	**NHL**	**63**	**32**	**23**	**7**	**3657**	**130**	**8**	**2.13**	**7**	**3**	**4**	**449**	**18**	**0**	**2.4**
99-2000	Long Beach	IHL	33	21	11	1	1936	59	5	*1.83	5	2	3	321	15	0	2.8
2000-01	**Tampa Bay**	**NHL**	**2**	**1**	**1**	**0**	**123**	**6**	**0**	**2.93**	....	....	....	....	....	....	..
2001-02	**Tampa Bay**	**NHL**	**70**	**24**	**32**	**10**	**3896**	**153**	**7**	**2.36**	....	....	....	....	....	....	..
	Russia	Olympics	6	3	2	1	*359	14	*1	2.34	....	....	....	....	....	....	..
2002-03	**Tampa Bay**	**NHL**	**65**	**30**	**22**	**11**	**3787**	**156**	**4**	**2.47**	**10**	**5**	**5**	**644**	**26**	**0**	**2.4**
2003-04 ♦	**Tampa Bay**	**NHL**	**55**	**28**	**19**	**7**	**3274**	**127**	**3**	**2.33**	**23**	***16**	**7**	**1401**	**40**	***5**	**1.7**
2004-05	Ak Bars Kazan	Russia	24	....	....	....	1457	40	5	1.65	2	....	....	118	6	0	3.0
2005-06	**Chicago**	**NHL**	**50**	**17**	**26**	**6**	**2815**	**157**	**0**	**3.35**	....	....	....	....	....	....	..
	Russia	Olympics					DID NOT PLAY – INJURED										
2006-07	**Chicago**	**NHL**	**60**	**25**	**26**	**5**	**3425**	**163**	**1**	**2.86**	....	....	....	....	....	....	..
2007-08	**Chicago**	**NHL**	**50**	**23**	**20**	**6**	**2892**	**127**	**2**	**2.63**	....	....	....	....	....	....	..
2008-09	**Chicago**	**NHL**	**42**	**25**	**8**	**7**	**2467**	**96**	**3**	**2.33**	**15**	**8**	**6**	**881**	**43**	**0**	**2.9**
2009-10	**Edmonton**	**NHL**	**18**	**7**	**9**	**2**	**1089**	**55**	**0**	**3.03**	....	....	....	....	....	....	..
	NHL Totals		**696**	**306**	**276**	**84**	**39795**	**1775**	**41**	**2.68**	**72**	**39**	**31**	**4345**	**174**	**6**	**2.4**

James Gatschene Memorial Trophy (IHL – MVP) (2000) (co-winner - Frederic Chabot)

Played in NHL All-Star Game (1998, 1999, 2002, 2003)

• Transferred to **Phoenix** after **Winnipeg** franchise relocated, July 1, 1996. • Missed entire 1999-2000 NHL season and majority of 2000-01 season after failing to come to contract terms with **Phoenix**. Signed as a free agent by **Long Beach** (IHL) with **Phoenix** retaining NHL rights, January 14, 2000. Traded to **Tampa Bay** by **Phoenix** with Stan Neckar for Mike Johnson, Paul Mara, Ruslan Zainullin and NY Islanders' 2nd round choice (previously acquired, Phoenix selected Matthew Spiller) in 2001 Entry Draft, March 5, 2001. Signed as a free agent by **Kazan** (Russia), November 8, 2004. Signed as a free agent by **Chicago**, August 5, 2005. Signed as a free agent by **Edmonton**, July 1, 2009.

KHUDOBIN, Anton (khuh-DAW-bihn, AN-tawn) MIN

Goaltender. Catches left. 5'11", 203 lbs. Born, Ust-Kamenogorsk, USSR, May 7, 1986.
(Minnesota's 11th choice, 206th overall, in 2004 Entry Draft).

			Regular Season								Playoffs						
Season	Club	League	GP	W	L	O/T	Mins	GA	SO	Avg	GP	W	L	Mins	GA	SO	Avg
2003-04	Magnitogorsk 2	Russia-3	38	....	....	....	....	80	....	....	....	....	....	....	....	....	..
2004-05	Magnitogorsk	Russia	4	....	....	....	133	0	1	0.00	....	....	....	....	....	....	..
	Magnitogorsk 2	Russia-3	27	....	....	....	....	52	....	....	....	....	....	....	....	....	..
2005-06	Saskatoon Blades	WHL	44	23	13	3	2362	114	4	2.90	10	4	6	685	32	0	2.8
2006-07	Magnitogorsk	Russia	16	....	....	....	618	28	0	2.72	3	....	....	26	1	0	2.3
2007-08	Houston Aeros	AHL	12	2	2	1	482	16	1	1.99	....	....	....	....	....	....	..
	Texas Wildcatters	ECHL	27	20	1	4	1549	51	3	*1.98	9	5	2	547	20	1	2.1
2008-09	Houston Aeros	AHL	10	3	6	1	512	26	0	3.04	17	8	8	890	40	2	2.7
	Florida Everblades	ECHL	33	18	10	1	1706	77	4	2.71	....	....	....	....	....	....	..
2009-10	**Minnesota**	**NHL**	**2**	**2**	**0**	**0**	**69**	**1**	**0**	**0.87**	....	....	....	....	....	....	..
	Houston Aeros	AHL	40	14	19	4	2247	91	4	2.43	....	....	....	....	....	....	..
	NHL Totals		**2**	**2**	**0**	**0**	**69**	**1**	**0**	**0.87**	....	....	....	....	....	....	..

ECHL First All-Star Team (2008) • ECHL Goaltender of the Year (2008)

KILLEEN, Patrick (kih-LEEN, PAT-rihk) PIT

Goaltender. Catches left. 6'4", 194 lbs. Born, Almonte, Ont., April 15, 1990.
(Pittsburgh's 3rd choice, 180th overall, in 2008 Entry Draft).

			Regular Season								Playoffs						
Season	Club	League	GP	W	L	O/T	Mins	GA	SO	Avg	GP	W	L	Mins	GA	SO	Avg
2006-07	Ottawa Jr. Sens	CJHL	7	5	1	0	376	20	0	3.19	....	....	....	....	....	....	..
	Brampton Battalion	OHL	8	1	3	0	304	29	0	5.72	....	....	....	....	....	....	..
2007-08	Brampton Battalion	OHL	34	20	9	2	1959	90	1	2.76	....	....	....	....	....	....	..
2008-09	Brampton Battalion	OHL	34	19	11	2	1916	91	2	2.85	2	0	0	26	4	0	9.2
2009-10	Brampton Battalion	OHL	*63	23	25	13	*3693	149	*5	2.42	11	4	6	664	38	0	3.4

KIPRUSOFF, Miikka (KIHP-roo-sawf, MEE-kah) CGY.

Goaltender. Catches left. 6'1", 184 lbs. Born, Turku, Finland, October 26, 1976.
(San Jose's 5th choice, 116th overall, in 1995 Entry Draft).

			Regular Season								Playoffs						
Season	**Club**	**League**	**GP**	**W**	**L**	**O/T**	**Mins**	**GA**	**SO**	**Avg**	**GP**	**W**	**L**	**Mins**	**GA**	**SO**	**Avg**
1993-94	TPS Turku Jr.	Fin-Jr.	35	20	9	5	2101	100	0	2.85	6	3	3	369	26	0	4.23
1994-95	TPS Turku Jr.	Fin-Jr.	31	13	14	4	1896	92	2	2.91	....	....	....	....	....	....	....
	Kiekko-67 Turku	Finland-2	1	0	1	0	60	6	0	6.00	....	....	....	....	....	....	....
	TPS Turku	Finland	4	3	1	0	240	12	0	3.00	2	2	0	120	7	0	3.50
1995-96	TPS Turku Jr.	Fin-Jr.	3	1	2	0	180	9	0	3.00	....	....	....	....	....	....	....
	Kiekko-67 Turku	Finland-2	5	5	0	0	300	7	1	1.40	....	....	....	....	....	....	....
	TPS Turku	Finland	12	5	3	1	550	38	0	4.14	3	0	1	113	4	0	2.12
1996-97	AIK Solna	Sweden	42	....	....	....	2440	93	3	2.29	7	....	....	420	22	0	3.14
1997-98	AIK Solna	Sweden	43	....	....	....	2517	111	1	2.65	....	....	....	....	....	....	....
	AIK Solna	Sweden-Q	9	....	....	....	540	15	2	1.67	....	....	....	....	....	....	....
1998-99	TPS Turku	Finland	39	26	6	6	2259	70	4	1.86	10	9	1	580	15	3	1.55
99-2000	Kentucky	AHL	47	23	19	4	2759	114	3	2.48	5	1	3	239	13	0	3.27
2000-01	**San Jose**	**NHL**	**5**	**2**	**1**	**0**	**154**	**5**	**0**	**1.95**	**3**	**1**	**1**	**149**	**5**	**0**	**2.01**
	Kentucky	AHL	36	19	9	6	2038	76	2	2.24	....	....	....	....	....	....	....
2001-02	**San Jose**	**NHL**	**20**	**7**	**6**	**3**	**1037**	**43**	**2**	**2.49**	**1**	**0**	**0**	**8**	**0**	**0**	**0.00**
	Cleveland Barons	AHL	4	4	0	0	242	7	0	1.73	....	....	....	....	....	....	....
2002-03	**San Jose**	**NHL**	**22**	**5**	**14**	**0**	**1199**	**65**	**1**	**3.25**	....	....	....	....	....	....	....
2003-04	**Calgary**	**NHL**	**38**	**24**	**10**	**4**	**2301**	**65**	**4**	***1.69**	***26**	**15**	**11**	***1655**	**51**	***5**	**1.85**
2004-05	Timra IK	Sweden	46	....	....	....	2719	97	5	2.14	6	....	....	356	13	0	2.19
2005-06	**Calgary**	**NHL**	**74**	**42**	**20**	**11**	***4380**	**151**	***10**	***2.07**	**7**	**3**	**4**	**428**	**16**	**0**	**2.24**
	Finland	Olympics					DID NOT PLAY – INJURED										
2006-07	**Calgary**	**NHL**	**74**	**40**	**24**	**9**	**4419**	**181**	**7**	**2.46**	**6**	**2**	**4**	**384**	**18**	**0**	**2.81**
2007-08	**Calgary**	**NHL**	**76**	**39**	**26**	**10**	**4398**	**197**	**2**	**2.69**	**7**	**2**	**4**	**336**	**18**	**1**	**3.21**
2008-09	**Calgary**	**NHL**	***76**	***45**	**24**	**5**	***4418**	**209**	**4**	**2.84**	**6**	**2**	**4**	**324**	**19**	**0**	**3.52**
2009-10	**Calgary**	**NHL**	**73**	**35**	**28**	**10**	**4235**	**163**	**4**	**2.31**	....	....	....	....	....	....	....
	Finland	Olympics	5	3	2	0	250	11	1	2.64	....	....	....	....	....	....	....
	NHL Totals		**458**	**239**	**153**	**52**	**26541**	**1079**	**34**	**2.44**	**56**	**25**	**28**	**3284**	**127**	**6**	**2.32**

NHL First All-Star Team (2006) • Vezina Trophy (2006)

Played in NHL All-Star Game (2007)

Traded to **Calgary** by **San Jose** for Calgary's 2nd round choice (Marc-Edouard Vlasic) in 2005 Entry Draft, November 16, 2003. Signed as a free agent by **Timra** (Sweden), September 20, 2004.

KNAPP, Connor (NAP, KAW-nuhr) BUF.

Goaltender. Catches left. 6'6", 224 lbs. Born, New York, NY, May 1, 1990.
(Buffalo's 5th choice, 164th overall, in 2009 Entry Draft).

			Regular Season								Playoffs						
Season	**Club**	**League**	**GP**	**W**	**L**	**O/T**	**Mins**	**GA**	**SO**	**Avg**	**GP**	**W**	**L**	**Mins**	**GA**	**SO**	**Avg**
2006-07	Bos. Jr. Bruins	EmJHL	23	*22	1	0	1340	37	3	*1.66	5	5	0	290	6	*2	*1.24
2007-08	Bos. Jr. Bruins	EJHL	....	14	7	2	1307	....	....	1.92	....	....	....	....	....	....	....
2008-09	Miami U.	CCHA	23	13	5	3	1350	47	2	2.09	....	....	....	....	....	....	....
2009-10	Miami U.	CCHA	20	10	4	4	1127	37	4	1.97	....	....	....	....	....	....	....

CCHA All-Rookie Team (2009)

KOSHECHKIN, Vasily (KOH-shech-kihn, va-SEE-lee) T.B.

Goaltender. Catches left. 6'6", 210 lbs. Born, Togliatti, USSR, March 27, 1983.
(Tampa Bay's 9th choice, 233rd overall, in 2002 Entry Draft).

			Regular Season								Playoffs						
Season	**Club**	**League**	**GP**	**W**	**L**	**O/T**	**Mins**	**GA**	**SO**	**Avg**	**GP**	**W**	**L**	**Mins**	**GA**	**SO**	**Avg**
1998-99	Lada Togliatti 2	Russia-4	8	....	....	....	....	8	....	....	....	....	....	....	....	....	....
99-2000	Lada Togliatti 2	Russia-3	18	....	....	....	....	20	....	....	....	....	....	....	....	....	....
2000-01	Lada Togliatti 2	Russia-3					STATISTICS NOT AVAILABLE										
2001-02	Lada Togliatti 2	Russia-3					STATISTICS NOT AVAILABLE										
2002-03	Lada Togliatti 2	Russia-3					STATISTICS NOT AVAILABLE										
	Kirovo-Chepetsk	Russia-2	10	....	....	....	613	14	3	1.37	....	....	....	....	....	....	....
	Almetjevsk	Russia-2	14	....	....	....	675	29	1	2.58	....	....	....	....	....	....	....
2003-04	Lada Togliatti 2	Russia-3	13	....	....	....	....	19	1	....	3	....	....	....	....	....	....
	Lada Togliatti	Russia	8	....	....	....	247	10	0	2.43	1	....	....	40	3	0	4.50
2004-05	Lada Togliatti	Russia	4	....	....	....	121	5	0	2.47	....	....	....	....	....	....	....
	Lada Togliatti	Russia	4	....	....	....	121	5	0	2.47	....	....	....	....	....	....	....
2005-06	Lada Togliatti	Russia	41	....	....	....	2375	63	9	1.59	8	....	....	474	20	1	2.53
2006-07	Lada Togliatti	Russia	42	....	....	....	2430	82	5	2.02	3	....	....	179	13	0	4.35
2007-08	Ak Bars Kazan	Russia	19	....	....	....	990	45	0	2.73	....	....	....	....	....	....	....
2008-09	Lada Togliatti	Rus-KHL	43	....	....	....	2404	67	8	1.67	5	....	....	280	9	1	1.93
2009-10	Lada Togliatti	Rus-KHL	*23	....	....	....	1304	46	*2	2.12	....	....	....	....	....	....	....
	Magnitogorsk	Rus-KHL	*26	....	....	....	1536	47	*6	1.84	9	....	....	535	18	1	2.02

KOSKINEN, Mikko (KAWS-kih-nehn, MEE-koh) NYI

Goaltender. Catches left. 6'5", 187 lbs. Born, Vantaa, Finland, July 18, 1988.
(NY Islanders' 3rd choice, 31st overall, in 2009 Entry Draft).

			Regular Season								Playoffs						
Season	**Club**	**League**	**GP**	**W**	**L**	**O/T**	**Mins**	**GA**	**SO**	**Avg**	**GP**	**W**	**L**	**Mins**	**GA**	**SO**	**Avg**
2004-05	Blues-T U18	Fin-U18	21	....	....	....	1138	67	0	3.53	....	....	....	....	....	....	....
2005-06	Blues Espoo U18	Fin-U18	3	....	....	....	142	12	0	5.07	....	....	....	....	....	....	....
2006-07	Kiekko-Vantaa Jr.	Fin-Jr.	27	16	8	0	1567	62	3	2.37	....	....	....	....	....	....	....
2007-08	Blues Espoo Jr.	Fin-Jr.	20	12	4	0	1176	45	2	2.30	2	0	2	81	7	0	5.18
	Blues Espoo	Finland	1	1	0	0	60	0	1	0.00	....	....	....	....	....	....	....
2008-09	Blues Espoo Jr.	Fin-Jr.	9	9	0	0	545	15	2	1.65	....	....	....	....	....	....	....
	Blues Espoo	Finland	33	17	9	7	1921	61	1	1.91	14	6	8	856	37	0	2.59
2009-10	Bridgeport	AHL	2	1	1	0	123	5	0	2.45	3	1	1	147	7	0	2.85
	Utah Grizzlies	ECHL	6	6	0	0	360	15	0	2.50	4	2	1	172	10	0	3.49

KOVAR, Jakub (KOH-vahr, YA-kuhb) PHI.

Goaltender. Catches left. 6', 176 lbs. Born, Pisek, Czech., July 19, 1988.
(Philadelphia's 7th choice, 109th overall, in 2006 Entry Draft).

			Regular Season								Playoffs						
Season	**Club**	**League**	**GP**	**W**	**L**	**O/T**	**Mins**	**GA**	**SO**	**Avg**	**GP**	**W**	**L**	**Mins**	**GA**	**SO**	**Avg**
2004-05	IHC Pisek U17	CzR-U17	40	....	....	....	2298	137	4	3.58	....	....	....	....	....	....	....
2005-06	C. Budejovice Jr.	CzRep-Jr.	19	....	....	....	1048	39	2	2.23	5	....	....	304	8	0	1.58
2006-07	C. Budejovice Jr.	CzRep-Jr.	38	....	....	....	2231	77	3	2.07	3	....	....	160	16	0	6.00
2007-08	Oshawa Generals	OHL	16	12	3	0	917	48	0	3.14	....	....	....	....	....	....	....
	Windsor Spitfires	OHL	20	14	3	3	1194	68	1	3.42	4	1	2	188	13	0	4.15
2008-09	C. Budejovice	CzRep	25	....	....	....	1355	63	0	2.79	....	....	....	....	....	....	....
2009-10	C. Budejovice	CzRep	17	....	....	....	879	36	1	2.46	....	....	....	....	....	....	....
	HC Tabor	CzRep-2	13	....	....	....	758	32	1	2.53	5	....	....	300	18	0	3.60

KRAHN, Brent (KRAWN, BREHNT) DAL.

Goaltender. Catches left. 6'4", 232 lbs. Born, Winnipeg, Man., April 2, 1982.
(Calgary's 1st choice, 9th overall, in 2000 Entry Draft).

			Regular Season								Playoffs						
Season	**Club**	**League**	**GP**	**W**	**L**	**O/T**	**Mins**	**GA**	**SO**	**Avg**	**GP**	**W**	**L**	**Mins**	**GA**	**SO**	**Avg**
1997-98	Pembina Valley	MMMHL	22	20	0	1	1265	40	3	1.90	2	2	0	120	2	1	1.00
1998-99	Pembina Valley	MMMHL	13	10	3	0	770	30	2	2.34	....	....	....	....	....	....	....
99-2000	Calgary Hitmen	WHL	39	33	6	0	2315	92	4	2.38	5	2	2	266	13	0	2.93
2000-01	Calgary Hitmen	WHL	37	22	10	3	2087	104	1	2.99	....	....	....	....	....	....	....
2001-02	Calgary Hitmen	WHL	18	8	6	2	1033	61	0	3.54	2	1	1	119	6	0	3.03
2002-03	Calgary Hitmen	WHL	23	11	10	2	1343	72	2	3.22	....	....	....	....	....	....	....
	Seattle	WHL	5	5	0	0	302	9	2	1.79	15	9	6	960	38	2	2.38
2003-04	San Antonio	AHL	14	3	7	1	715	41	0	3.44	....	....	....	....	....	....	....
	Lowell	AHL	7	2	3	0	344	15	0	2.62	....	....	....	....	....	....	....
	Las Vegas	ECHL	14	7	5	2	828	36	0	2.61	....	....	....	....	....	....	....
2004-05	Lowell	AHL	35	20	11	2	1998	83	6	2.49	1	0	0	1	0	0	0.00
2005-06	Omaha	AHL	57	26	20	9	3241	135	3	2.50	....	....	....	....	....	....	....
2006-07	Omaha	AHL	28	14	12	0	1564	63	2	2.42	1	0	1	59	3	0	3.06
2007-08	Quad City Flames	AHL	14	6	6	2	795	33	0	2.49	....	....	....	....	....	....	....
2008-09	**Dallas**	**NHL**	**1**	**0**	**0**	**0**	**20**	**3**	**0**	**9.00**	....	....	....	....	....	....	....
	Chicago Wolves	AHL	13	6	6	0	738	26	2	2.11	....	....	....	....	....	....	....
	Las Vegas	ECHL	6	1	4	1	342	23	0	4.04	....	....	....	....	....	....	....
2009-10	Texas Stars	AHL	22	17	4	0	1246	38	5	1.83	11	7	4	628	26	0	2.48
	NHL Totals		**1**	**0**	**0**	**0**	**20**	**3**	**0**	**9.00**	....	....	....	....	....	....	....

Signed as a free agent by **Dallas**, September 24, 2008.

KUEMPER, Darcy (KEHM-puhr, DAHR-see) MIN.

Goaltender. Catches left. 6'4", 200 lbs. Born, Saskatoon, Sask., May 5, 1990.
(Minnesota's 5th choice, 161st overall, in 2009 Entry Draft).

			Regular Season								Playoffs						
Season	**Club**	**League**	**GP**	**W**	**L**	**O/T**	**Mins**	**GA**	**SO**	**Avg**	**GP**	**W**	**L**	**Mins**	**GA**	**SO**	**Avg**
2006-07	Sask. Contacts	SMHL	25	8	14	3	1489	87	1	3.51	4	1	3	200	19	0	5.70
	Spokane Chiefs	WHL	....	....	....	....	....	....	....	....	1	0	0	0	0	0	0.00
2007-08	Saskatoon Blazers	SMHL	26	15	7	4	1578	62	1	2.36	13	7	6	781	34	1	2.61
2008-09	Red Deer Rebels	WHL	55	21	25	8	3167	156	3	2.96	....	....	....	....	....	....	....
2009-10	Red Deer Rebels	WHL	61	28	23	4	3234	147	3	2.73	2	0	2	61	6	0	5.90
	Houston Aeros	AHL	4	2	1	0	199	8	0	2.41	....	....	....	....	....	....	....

WHL East Second All-Star Team (2010)

LaBARBERA, Jason (luh-BAHR-buhr-ah, JAY-suhn) PHX.

Goaltender. Catches left. 6'3", 234 lbs. Born, Burnaby, B.C., January 18, 1980.
(NY Rangers' 3rd choice, 66th overall, in 1998 Entry Draft).

			Regular Season								Playoffs						
Season	**Club**	**League**	**GP**	**W**	**L**	**O/T**	**Mins**	**GA**	**SO**	**Avg**	**GP**	**W**	**L**	**Mins**	**GA**	**SO**	**Avg**
1995-96	Prince George	Minor-BC	31	....	....	....	1860	83	0	2.68	....	....	....	....	....	....	....
1996-97	Tri-City Americans	WHL	2	1	0	0	63	4	0	3.81	....	....	....	....	....	....	....
	Portland	WHL	9	5	1	1	443	18	0	2.44	....	....	....	....	....	....	....
1997-98	Portland	WHL	23	18	4	0	1305	72	1	3.31	....	....	....	....	....	....	....
1998-99	Portland	WHL	51	18	23	9	2991	170	4	3.41	4	0	4	252	19	0	4.52
99-2000	Portland	WHL	34	8	24	2	2005	123	1	3.68	....	....	....	....	....	....	....
	Spokane Chiefs	WHL	21	12	6	2	1146	50	0	2.62	9	6	1	435	18	1	2.48
2000-01	**NY Rangers**	**NHL**	**1**	**0**	**0**	**0**	**10**	**0**	**0**	**0.00**	....	....	....	....	....	....	....
	Hartford Wolf Pack	AHL	4	1	1	0	156	12	0	4.61	....	....	....	....	....	....	....
	Charlotte Checkers	ECHL	35	18	10	7	2100	112	1	3.20	2	1	1	143	5	0	2.09
2001-02	Hartford Wolf Pack	AHL	20	7	11	1	1058	55	0	3.12	....	....	....	....	....	....	....
	Charlotte Checkers	ECHL	13	9	3	1	744	29	0	2.34	4	2	2	212	12	0	3.39
2002-03	Hartford Wolf Pack	AHL	46	18	17	6	2452	105	2	2.57	2	0	2	117	6	0	3.07
2003-04	**NY Rangers**	**NHL**	**4**	**1**	**2**	**0**	**198**	**16**	**0**	**4.85**	....	....	....	....	....	....	....
	Hartford Wolf Pack	AHL	59	34	9	9	3393	90	*13	1.59	16	11	5	1043	30	*3	*1.73
2004-05	Hartford Wolf Pack	AHL	53	31	16	2	2937	90	6	1.84	4	1	3	238	9	0	2.27
2005-06	**Los Angeles**	**NHL**	**29**	**11**	**9**	**2**	**1433**	**69**	**1**	**2.89**	....	....	....	....	....	....	....
	Manchester	AHL	3	1	1	1	185	10	0	3.25	....	....	....	....	....	....	....
2006-07	Manchester	AHL	*62	*39	20	1	*3619	133	*7	2.21	13	6	7	824	38	1	2.77
2007-08	**Los Angeles**	**NHL**	**45**	**17**	**23**	**2**	**2421**	**121**	**1**	**3.00**	....	....	....	....	....	....	....
2008-09	**Los Angeles**	**NHL**	**19**	**5**	**8**	**4**	**995**	**47**	**2**	**2.83**	....	....	....	....	....	....	....
	Vancouver	**NHL**	**9**	**3**	**2**	**2**	**451**	**20**	**0**	**2.66**	....	....	....	....	....	....	....
2009-10	**Phoenix**	**NHL**	**17**	**8**	**5**	**1**	**928**	**33**	**0**	**2.13**	....	....	....	....	....	....	....
	NHL Totals		**124**	**45**	**49**	**11**	**6436**	**306**	**4**	**2.85**	....	....	....	....	....	....	....

AHL First All-Star Team (2004, 2007) • Aldege "Baz" Bastien Memorial Award (AHL - Outstanding Goaltender) (2004, 2007) • Les Cunningham Award (AHL - MVP) (2004) • Harry "Hap" Holmes Memorial Trophy (AHL - fewest goals against) (2005) (shared with Steve Valiquette) • Harry "Hap" Holmes Memorial Trophy (AHL - fewest goals against) (2007)

Signed as a free agent by **Los Angeles**, August 2, 2005. Traded to **Vancouver** by **Los Angeles** for Vancouver's 7th round choice (later traded to Atlanta – Atlanta selected Jordan Samuels-Thomas) in 2009 Entry Draft, December 30, 2008. Signed as a free agent by **Phoenix**, July 1, 2009.

LACK, Eddie (LAK, EH-dee) VAN.

Goaltender. Catches left. 6'5", 194 lbs. Born, Norrtalje, Sweden, January 5, 1988.

			Regular Season								Playoffs						
Season	**Club**	**League**	**GP**	**W**	**L**	**O/T**	**Mins**	**GA**	**SO**	**Avg**	**GP**	**W**	**L**	**Mins**	**GA**	**SO**	**Avg**
2004-05	Djurgarden U18	Swe-U18	9	....	....	....	527	21	1	2.39	3	....	....	140	6	0	2.57
	Djurgarden Jr.	Swe-Jr.	1	....	....	....	60	6	0	6.00	....	....	....	....	....	....	....
2005-06	Djurgarden Jr.	Swe-Jr.	23	....	....	....	1400	49	3	2.10	....	....	....	....	....	....	....
2006-07	Leksands IF Jr.	Swe-Jr.	30	....	....	....	1782	85	0	2.86	....	....	....	....	....	....	....
	Leksands IF	Sweden-2	3	....	....	....	137	7	0	3.06	....	....	....	....	....	....	....
2007-08	Leksands IF Jr.	Swe-Jr.	18	....	....	....	1077	47	4	2.62	3	....	....	179	8	0	2.68
	Leksands IF	Sweden-2	26	....	....	....	1530	50	4	1.96	....	....	....	....	....	....	....
2008-09	Leksands IF Jr.	Swe-Jr.	2	....	....	....	120	4	1	2.00	....	....	....	....	....	....	....
	Leksands IF	Sweden-2	38	....	....	....	2260	78	4	2.07	....	....	....	....	....	....	....
2009-10	Brynas IF Gavle Jr.	Swe-Jr.	6	....	....	....	359	21	0	....	....	....	....	....	....	....	....
	Brynas IF Gavle	Sweden	14	....	....	....	809	36	0	2.67	2	....	....	79	2	0	1.53

Signed as a free agent by **Vancouver**, April 6, 2010.

LaCOSTA, Dan (luh-KAWS-tah, DAN)

Goaltender. Catches left. 6'1", 186 lbs. Born, Labrador City, Nfld., March 28, 1986.
(Columbus' 4th choice, 93rd overall, in 2004 Entry Draft).

			Regular Season								Playoffs						
Season	Club	League	GP	W	L	O/T	Mins	GA	SO	Avg	GP	W	L	Mins	GA	SO	Avg
2001-02	Wellington Dukes	OPJHL	24	19	2	3	1377	44	2	*1.92	....	....	....	....	....	....	....
2002-03	Owen Sound	OHL	28	8	10	3	1321	82	0	3.72	....	....	....	....	....	....	....
2003-04	Owen Sound	OHL	37	17	10	1	1810	82	4	2.72	....	....	....	....	....	....	....
2004-05	Owen Sound	OHL	25	15	7	2	1423	70	0	2.95	....	....	....	....	....	....	....
	Barrie Colts	OHL	21	10	5	2	1054	48	1	2.73	5	1	2	215	11	0	3.07
2005-06	Barrie Colts	OHL	*59	36	17	4	3340	142	6	2.55	11	5	5	654	34	0	3.12
2006-07	Syracuse Crunch	AHL	19	5	7	1	852	40	3	2.82	....	....	....	....	....	....	....
	Dayton Bombers	ECHL	10	3	5	1	556	32	0	3.45	....	....	....	....	....	....	....
2007-08	**Columbus**	**NHL**	**1**	**0**	**0**	**0**	**13**	**0**	**0**	**0.00**	....	....	....	....	....	....	....
	Syracuse Crunch	AHL	15	9	2	3	848	30	1	2.12	....	....	....	....	....	....	....
	Elmira Jackals	ECHL	14	7	4	1	754	27	0	2.15	....	....	....	....	....	....	....
2008-09	**Columbus**	**NHL**	**3**	**2**	**0**	**0**	**156**	**4**	**1**	**1.54**	....	....	....	....	....	....	....
	Syracuse Crunch	AHL	45	19	18	2	2469	115	2	2.79	....	....	....	....	....	....	....
2009-10	Syracuse Crunch	AHL	26	7	15	1	1362	90	1	3.96	....	....	....	....	....	....	....
	NHL Totals		**4**	**2**	**0**	**0**	**169**	**4**	**1**	**1.42**	....	....	....	....	....	....	....

LALANDE, Kevin (lah-LAWND, KEH-vihn)

Goaltender. Catches left. 6', 175 lbs. Born, Kingston, Ont., February 19, 1987.
(Calgary's 5th choice, 128th overall, in 2005 Entry Draft).

			Regular Season								Playoffs						
Season	Club	League	GP	W	L	O/T	Mins	GA	SO	Avg	GP	W	L	Mins	GA	SO	Avg
2003-04	Hawkesbury	CJHL	35	....	....	....	2010	105	3	3.13	6	....	....	286	19	0	3.99
	Belleville Bulls	OHL	3	1	2	0	133	15	0	6.77	....	....	....	....	....	....	....
2004-05	Belleville Bulls	OHL	30	15	11	3	1797	79	1	2.64	2	0	2	120	8	0	4.00
2005-06	Belleville Bulls	OHL	50	24	17	5	2789	143	3	3.08	....	....	....	....	....	....	....
2006-07	Belleville Bulls	OHL	48	27	17	3	2772	139	3	3.01	15	10	5	989	42	*1	2.55
2007-08	Quad City Flames	AHL	7	2	3	0	360	20	0	3.34	....	....	....	....	....	....	....
	Las Vegas	ECHL	27	17	5	4	1607	55	3	2.05	*20	*13	6	1142	48	3	2.52
2008-09	Quad City Flames	AHL	6	4	1	1	340	11	1	1.94	....	....	....	....	....	....	....
	Las Vegas	ECHL	21	9	8	2	1181	47	3	2.39	....	....	....	....	....	....	....
	Syracuse Crunch	AHL	15	9	5	1	848	32	0	2.26	....	....	....	....	....	....	....
2009-10	Syracuse Crunch	AHL	56	25	24	2	3067	146	3	2.86	....	....	....	....	....	....	....

Traded to **Columbus** by **Calgary** for Columbus' 4th round choice (later traded to Los Angeles, later traded to Florida – Florida selected Garrett Wilson) in 2009 Entry Draft, March 4, 2009.

LALIME, Patrick (lah-LEEM, PAT-rihk) BUF.

Goaltender. Catches left. 6'3", 198 lbs. Born, St-Bonaventure, Que., July 7, 1974.
(Pittsburgh's 6th choice, 156th overall, in 1993 Entry Draft).

			Regular Season								Playoffs						
Season	Club	League	GP	W	L	O/T	Mins	GA	SO	Avg	GP	W	L	Mins	GA	SO	Avg
1990-91	Abitibi Forestiers	QAAA	26	9	17	0	1595	151	0	5.81	....	....	....	....	....	....	....
1991-92	Shawinigan	QMJHL	6	....	....	....	272	25	0	5.50	....	....	....	....	....	....	....
1992-93	Shawinigan	QMJHL	44	10	24	4	2467	192	0	4.67	....	....	....	....	....	....	....
1993-94	Shawinigan	QMJHL	48	22	20	0	2733	192	1	4.22	5	1	3	223	25	0	6.73
1994-95	Hampton Roads	ECHL	26	15	7	3	1470	82	2	3.35	....	....	....	....	....	....	....
	Cleveland	IHL	23	7	10	4	1230	91	0	4.44	....	....	....	....	....	....	....
1995-96	Cleveland	IHL	41	20	12	7	2314	149	0	3.86	....	....	....	....	....	....	....
1996-97	**Pittsburgh**	**NHL**	**39**	**21**	**12**	**2**	**2058**	**101**	**3**	**2.94**	....	....	....	....	....	....	....
	Cleveland	IHL	14	6	6	2	834	45	1	3.24	....	....	....	....	....	....	....
1997-98	Grand Rapids	IHL	31	10	10	9	1749	76	2	2.61	1	0	1	77	4	0	3.11
1998-99	Kansas City Blades	IHL	*66	*39	20	4	*3789	190	2	3.01	3	1	2	179	6	1	2.01
99-2000	**Ottawa**	**NHL**	**38**	**19**	**14**	**3**	**2038**	**79**	**3**	**2.33**	....	....	....	....	....	....	....
2000-01	**Ottawa**	**NHL**	**60**	**36**	**19**	**5**	**3607**	**141**	**7**	**2.35**	**4**	**0**	**4**	**251**	**10**	**0**	**2.39**
2001-02	**Ottawa**	**NHL**	**61**	**27**	**24**	**8**	**3583**	**148**	**7**	**2.48**	**12**	**7**	**5**	**778**	**18**	**4**	***1.39**
2002-03	**Ottawa**	**NHL**	**67**	**39**	**20**	**7**	**3943**	**142**	**8**	**2.16**	**18**	**11**	**7**	**1122**	**34**	**1**	**1.82**
2003-04	**Ottawa**	**NHL**	**57**	**25**	**23**	**7**	**3324**	**127**	**5**	**2.29**	**7**	**3**	**4**	**398**	**13**	**0**	**1.96**
2004-05							DID NOT PLAY										
2005-06	**St. Louis**	**NHL**	**31**	**4**	**18**	**8**	**1699**	**103**	**0**	**3.64**	....	....	....	....	....	....	....
	Peoria Rivermen	AHL	14	6	6	1	798	38	1	2.86	....	....	....	....	....	....	....
2006-07	**Chicago**	**NHL**	**12**	**4**	**6**	**1**	**645**	**33**	**1**	**3.07**	....	....	....	....	....	....	....
	Norfolk Admirals	AHL	4	3	1	0	241	10	0	2.49	....	....	....	....	....	....	....
2007-08	**Chicago**	**NHL**	**32**	**16**	**12**	**2**	**1828**	**86**	**1**	**2.82**	....	....	....	....	....	....	....
2008-09	**Buffalo**	**NHL**	**24**	**5**	**13**	**3**	**1297**	**67**	**0**	**3.10**	....	....	....	....	....	....	....
2009-10	**Buffalo**	**NHL**	**16**	**4**	**8**	**2**	**854**	**40**	**0**	**2.81**	....	....	....	....	....	....	....
	Portland Pirates	AHL	2	0	1	1	124	6	0	2.91	....	....	....	....	....	....	....
	NHL Totals		**437**	**200**	**169**	**48**	**24876**	**1067**	**35**	**2.57**	**41**	**21**	**20**	**2549**	**75**	**5**	**1.77**

NHL All-Rookie Team (1997) • IHL First All-Star Team (1999)

Played in NHL All-Star Game (2003)

• Rights traded to **Anaheim** by **Pittsburgh** for Sean Pronger, March 24, 1998. Traded to **Ottawa** by **Anaheim** for Ted Donato and the rights to Antti-Jussi Niemi, June 18, 1999. Traded to **St. Louis** by **Ottawa** for St. Louis' 4th round choice (Ilya Zubov) in 2005 Entry Draft, June 27, 2004. Signed as a free agent by **Chicago**, July 1, 2006. Signed as a free agent by **Buffalo**, July 1, 2008.

LAMOUREUX, Jean-Philippe (LA-muh-roo, ZHAWN-fihl-EEP) CGY.

Goaltender. Catches left. 5'10", 165 lbs. Born, Grand Forks, ND, August 20, 1984.

			Regular Season								Playoffs						
Season	Club	League	GP	W	L	O/T	Mins	GA	SO	Avg	GP	W	L	Mins	GA	SO	Avg
2001-02	Lincoln Stars	USHL	31	20	8	1	1758	66	6	2.25	....	....	....	....	....	....	....
2002-03	Lincoln Stars	USHL	34	22	7	4	1968	71	4	2.16	4	4	0	228	6	0	1.58
2003-04	Lincoln Stars	USHL	50	22	23	3	2874	134	3	2.80	....	....	....	....	....	....	....
2004-05	North Dakota	WCHA	18	7	8	2	1043	38	0	2.19	....	....	....	....	....	....	....
2005-06	North Dakota	WCHA	14	5	7	0	734	32	1	2.61	....	....	....	....	....	....	....
2006-07	North Dakota	WCHA	*37	*21	12	4	*2184	88	3	2.42	....	....	....	....	....	....	....
2007-08	North Dakota	WCHA	*42	*27	11	4	*2508	73	*6	*1.75	....	....	....	....	....	....	....
2008-09	Alaska Aces	ECHL	51	*33	16	2	3071	117	*8	2.29	*21	*15	5	*1263	41	*4	*1.95
2009-10	Portland Pirates	AHL	31	14	12	2	1750	87	2	2.98	4	0	3	207	10	0	2.90

ECHL Goaltender of the Year (2009)

Signed as a free agent by **Buffalo**, July 30, 2009. Signed as a free agent by **Abbotsford** (AHL), July 22, 2010.

LARSSON, Daniel (LAR-suhn, DAN-yehl) DET.

Goaltender. Catches left. 6', 180 lbs. Born, Boden, Sweden, February 7, 1986.
(Detroit's 4th choice, 92nd overall, in 2006 Entry Draft).

			Regular Season								Playoffs						
Season	Club	League	GP	W	L	O/T	Mins	GA	SO	Avg	GP	W	L	Mins	GA	SO	Avg
2002-03	Lulea HF U18	Swe-U18	12	....	....	....	731	50	0	4.10	....	....	....	....	....	....	....
2003-04	Lulea HF Jr.	Swe-Jr.	4	....	....	....	239	12	0	3.01	....	....	....	....	....	....	....
	Bodens IK	Sweden-2	1	....	....	....	20	1	0	3.00	....	....	....	....	....	....	....
2004-05	Bodens IK	Sweden-2	28	....	....	....	1514	97	1	3.84	....	....	....	....	....	....	....
2005-06	Hammarby Jr.	Swe-Jr.	9	....	....	....	548	24	1	2.63	....	....	....	....	....	....	....
	Hammarby	Sweden-2	36	....	....	....	2001	90	0	2.70	....	....	....	....	....	....	....
2006-07	Djurgarden	Sweden	24	....	....	....	1259	53	3	2.53	....	....	....	....	....	....	....
2007-08	Djurgarden	Sweden	46	....	....	....	2721	104	6	2.29	5	....	....	295	13	0	2.64
2008-09	Grand Rapids	AHL	40	22	12	2	2152	99	5	2.76	....	....	....	....	....	....	....
2009-10	Grand Rapids	AHL	53	23	24	2	2840	135	1	2.85	....	....	....	....	....	....	....

LAWSON, Nathan (LAW-suhn, NAY-thuhn) NY

Goaltender. Catches left. 6'2", 200 lbs. Born, Calgary, Alta., September 29, 1983.

			Regular Season								Playoffs						
Season	Club	League	GP	W	L	O/T	Mins	GA	SO	Avg	GP	W	L	Mins	GA	SO	A
2004-05	Alaska Anchorage	WCHA	27	7	15	3	1482	82	1	3.32	....	....	....	....	....	....	
2005-06	Alaska Anchorage	WCHA	21	4	11	3	1063	61	1	3.44	....	....	....	....	....	....	
2006-07	Alaska Anchorage	WCHA	27	10	15	2	1523	77	0	3.03	....	....	....	....	....	....	
2007-08	Phoenix	ECHL	5	3	2	0	279	14	1	3.01	....	....	....	....	....	....	
	Utah Grizzlies	ECHL	24	14	7	1	1390	67	1	2.89	10	5	4	543	26	2	2.
2008-09	Bridgeport	AHL	31	19	9	2	1723	62	2	2.16	2	0	2	123	8	0	3.
	Utah Grizzlies	ECHL	3	2	0	0	158	6	0	2.28	....	....	....	....	....	....	
2009-10	Bridgeport	AHL	36	16	16	3	2121	89	1	2.52	1	0	0	46	2	0	2.

Signed as a free agent by **NY Islanders**, March 2, 2008.

LECLAIRE, Pascal (luh-KLAIR, pas-KAL) OT

Goaltender. Catches left. 6'2", 202 lbs. Born, Repentigny, Que., November 7, 1982.
(Columbus' 1st choice, 8th overall, in 2001 Entry Draft).

			Regular Season								Playoffs						
Season	Club	League	GP	W	L	O/T	Mins	GA	SO	Avg	GP	W	L	Mins	GA	SO	A
1997-98	Cap-d-Madeleine	QAAA	26	6	17	3	1580	127	0	4.90	....	....	....	....	....	....	
1998-99	Halifax	QMJHL	33	19	11	1	1828	96	2	3.15	1	0	0	17	2	0	7.
99-2000	Halifax	QMJHL	31	16	8	4	1729	103	1	3.57	5	1	2	198	12	0	3.
2000-01	Halifax	QMJHL	35	14	16	5	2111	126	1	3.58	2	0	2	109	10	0	5.
2001-02	Montreal Rocket	QMJHL	45	15	23	4	2513	138	1	3.29	7	3	4	441	15	0	*2.
2002-03	Syracuse Crunch	AHL	36	8	21	3	1886	112	0	3.56	....	....	....	....	....	....	
2003-04	**Columbus**	**NHL**	**2**	**0**	**2**	**0**	**119**	**7**	**0**	**3.53**	....	....	....	....	....	....	
	Syracuse Crunch	AHL	44	21	16	3	2447	125	2	3.06	3	1	2	142	12	0	5.
2004-05	Syracuse Crunch	AHL	14	5	6	3	845	33	2	2.34	....	....	....	....	....	....	
2005-06	**Columbus**	**NHL**	**33**	**11**	**15**	**3**	**1804**	**97**	**0**	**3.23**	....	....	....	....	....	....	
	Syracuse Crunch	AHL	7	3	3	0	340	16	1	2.82	5	2	3	288	11	1	2.
2006-07	**Columbus**	**NHL**	**24**	**6**	**15**	**2**	**1315**	**65**	**1**	**2.97**	....	....	....	....	....	....	
2007-08	**Columbus**	**NHL**	**54**	**24**	**17**	**6**	**2986**	**112**	**9**	**2.25**	....	....	....	....	....	....	
2008-09	**Columbus**	**NHL**	**12**	**4**	**6**	**1**	**674**	**43**	**0**	**3.83**	....	....	....	....	....	....	
2009-10	**Ottawa**	**NHL**	**34**	**12**	**14**	**2**	**1745**	**93**	**0**	**3.20**	**3**	**1**	**2**	**211**	**10**	**0**	**2.**
	NHL Totals		**159**	**57**	**69**	**14**	**8643**	**417**	**10**	**2.89**	**3**	**1**	**2**	**211**	**10**	**0**	**2.**

• Missed majority of 2008-09 season recovering from ankle injury suffered in game vs. Minnesota, October 25, 2008. Traded to **Ottawa** by **Columbus** with Columbus' 2nd round choice (Robin Lehner) in 2009 Entry Draft for Antoine Vermette, March 4, 2009.

LEE, Michael (LEE, MIGH-kuhl) PH

Goaltender. Catches left. 6'1", 185 lbs. Born, Fargo, ND, October 5, 1990.
(Phoenix's 3rd choice, 91st overall, in 2009 Entry Draft).

			Regular Season								Playoffs						
Season	Club	League	GP	W	L	O/T	Mins	GA	SO	Avg	GP	W	L	Mins	GA	SO	A
2006-07	Roseau Rams	High-MN	12	12	0	0	612	9	6	0.75	....	....	....	....	....	....	
2007-08	Roseau Rams	High-MN	29	27	2	0	1482	32	12	1.10	1	0	0	16	0	0	0.
2008-09	Fargo Force	USHL	48	26	15	4	2745	110	3	2.40	10	7	3	546	24	*1	2.
2009-10	St. Cloud State	WCHA	26	12	9	3	1477	69	2	2.80	....	....	....	....	....	....	

USHL All-Rookie Team (2009) • USHL Goaltender of the Year (2009)

LEGACE, Manny (LEH-gah-see, MAN-ee)

Goaltender. Catches left. 5'10", 200 lbs. Born, Toronto, Ont., February 4, 1973.
(Hartford's 5th choice, 188th overall, in 1993 Entry Draft).

			Regular Season								Playoffs						
Season	Club	League	GP	W	L	O/T	Mins	GA	SO	Avg	GP	W	L	Mins	GA	SO	A
1987-88	Alliston Hornets	OJHL-C	16	7	9	0	960	83	0	5.17	....	....	....	....	....	....	
1988-89	Vaughan Raiders	MTJHL	23	....	....	....	1303	92	1	4.24	....	....	....	....	....	....	
1989-90	Vaughan Raiders	MTJHL	21	8	11	1	1180	89	1	4.53	....	....	....	....	....	....	
	Thornhill	OHA-B	8	3	3	2	480	30	0	3.75	....	....	....	....	....	....	
1990-91	Niagara Falls	OHL	30	13	11	2	1515	107	0	4.24	4	1	1	119	10	0	5.
1991-92	Niagara Falls	OHL	43	21	16	3	2384	143	0	3.60	14	8	5	791	56	0	4.
1992-93	Niagara Falls	OHL	48	22	19	3	2630	171	0	3.90	4	0	4	240	18	0	4.
1993-94	Canada	Nat-Tm	16	8	6	0	859	36	2	2.51	....	....	....	....	....	....	
1994-95	Springfield Indians	AHL	39	12	17	6	2169	128	2	3.54	....	....	....	....	....	....	
1995-96	Springfield Falcons	AHL	37	20	12	4	2196	83	*5	*2.27	4	1	3	220	18	0	4.
1996-97	Springfield Falcons	AHL	36	17	14	5	2119	107	1	3.03	12	9	3	745	25	*2	2.
	Richmond	ECHL	3	2	1	0	157	8	0	3.05	....	....	....	....	....	....	
1997-98	Springfield Falcons	AHL	6	4	2	0	345	16	0	2.78	....	....	....	....	....	....	
	Las Vegas Thunder	IHL	41	18	16	4	2106	111	1	3.16	4	1	3	237	16	0	4.
1998-99	**Los Angeles**	**NHL**	**17**	**2**	**9**	**2**	**899**	**39**	**0**	**2.60**	....	....	....	....	....	....	
	Long Beach	IHL	33	22	8	1	1796	67	2	2.24	6	4	2	338	9	0	*1
99-2000	**Detroit**	**NHL**	**4**	**4**	**0**	**0**	**240**	**11**	**0**	**2.75**	....	....	....	....	....	....	
	Manitoba Moose	IHL	42	17	18	5	2409	104	2	2.59	2	0	2	141	7	0	2.
2000-01	**Detroit**	**NHL**	**39**	**24**	**5**	**5**	**2136**	**73**	**2**	**2.05**	....	....	....	....	....	....	
2001-02 ♦	**Detroit**	**NHL**	**20**	**10**	**6**	**2**	**1117**	**45**	**1**	**2.42**	**1**	**0**	**0**	**11**	**1**	**0**	**5.**
2002-03	**Detroit**	**NHL**	**25**	**14**	**5**	**4**	**1406**	**51**	**0**	**2.18**	....	....	....	....	....	....	
2003-04	**Detroit**	**NHL**	**41**	**23**	**10**	**5**	**2325**	**82**	**3**	**2.12**	**4**	**2**	**2**	**220**	**8**	**0**	**2**
2004-05	Voskresensk	Russia	2	....	....	....	89	10	0	6.73	....	....	....	....	....	....	
2005-06	**Detroit**	**NHL**	**51**	**37**	**8**	**3**	**2905**	**106**	**7**	**2.19**	**6**	**2**	**4**	**408**	**18**	**0**	**2**
	Grand Rapids	AHL	1	1	0	0	60	2	0	2.00	....	....	....	....	....	....	
2006-07	**St. Louis**	**NHL**	**45**	**23**	**15**	**5**	**2522**	**109**	**5**	**2.59**	....	....	....	....	....	....	
2007-08	**St. Louis**	**NHL**	**66**	**27**	**25**	**8**	**3666**	**147**	**5**	**2.41**	....	....	....	....	....	....	
2008-09	**St. Louis**	**NHL**	**29**	**13**	**9**	**2**	**1452**	**77**	**0**	**3.18**	....	....	....	....	....	....	
	Peoria Rivermen	AHL	23	14	7	1	1290	43	3	2.00	7	3	4	429	18	0	2
2009-10	Chicago Wolves	AHL	6	2	2	1	317	17	1	3.21	....	....	....	....	....	....	
	Carolina	**NHL**	**28**	**10**	**7**	**5**	**1472**	**69**	**1**	**2.81**	....	....	....	....	....	....	
	NHL Totals		**365**	**187**	**99**	**41**	**20140**	**809**	**24**	**2.41**	**11**	**4**	**6**	**639**	**27**	**0**	**2.**

OHL First All-Star Team (1993) • AHL First All-Star Team (1996) • Harry "Hap" Holmes Memorial Award (AHL – fewest goals against) (1996) (shared with Scott Langkow) • Aldege "Baz" Bastien Memorial Award (AHL – Outstanding Goaltender) (1996)

Played in NHL All-Star Game (2008)

• Rights transferred to **Carolina** after **Hartford** franchise relocated, June 25, 1997. Traded to **Los Angeles** by **Carolina** for future considerations, July 31, 1998. Signed as a free agent by **Detroit**, August 9, 1999. Claimed on waivers by **Vancouver** from **Detroit**, September 30, 1999. Claimed on waivers by **Detroit** from **Vancouver**, October 13, 1999. Signed as a free agent by **Voskresensk** (Russia), December 20, 2004. Signed as a free agent by **St. Louis**, August 8, 2006. Signed to a PTO (professional tryout) contract by **Chicago** (AHL), October 12, 2009. Signed as a fr agent by **Carolina**, November 9, 2009.

LEHNER, Robin (LEH-nuhr, RAW-bihn) OT

Goaltender. Catches left. 6'4", 225 lbs. Born, Goteborg, Sweden, July 24, 1991.
(Ottawa's 3rd choice, 46th overall, in 2009 Entry Draft).

			Regular Season								Playoffs						
Season	Club	League	GP	W	L	O/T	Mins	GA	SO	Avg	GP	W	L	Mins	GA	SO	A
2007-08	Frolunda U18	Swe-U18	19	....	....	....	1147	34	6	1.78	4	....	....	243	15	0	3
2008-09	Frolunda U18	Swe-U18	2	....	....	....	117	5	0	2.56	7	....	....	438	19	0	2
	Frolunda Jr.	Swe-Jr.	22	....	....	....	1318	67	1	3.05	1	....	....	58	3	0	3
2009-10	Sault Ste. Marie	OHL	47	27	13	3	2574	120	*5	2.80	5	1	4	279	20	0	4
	Binghamton	AHL	2	2	0	0	120	6	0	3.00	....	....	....	....	....	....	

EHTONEN, Kari (LEH-tuh-nehn, KAH-ree) DAL.

oaltender. Catches left. 6'4", 215 lbs. Born, Helsinki, Finland, November 16, 1983.
tlanta's 1st choice, 2nd overall, in 2002 Entry Draft).

			Regular Season								Playoffs						
ason	Club	League	GP	W	L	O/T	Mins	GA	SO	Avg	GP	W	L	Mins	GA	SO	Avg
98-99	Jokerit U18	Fin-U18	2	....	....	....	....	....	....	....	4	2	2	240	7	0	1.75
-2000	Jokerit Helsinki Jr.	Fin-Jr.	33	21	9	3	1974	86	2	2.61	12	9	3	758	14	4	1.11
00-01	Jokerit U18	Fin-U18	....	....	....	....	....	....	....	....	6	....	....	....	....	....	....
	Jokerit Helsinki Jr.	Fin-Jr.	31	20	9	1	1799	71	3	2.37	1	0	1	54	4	0	4.44
	Jokerit Helsinki	Finland	4	3	1	0	189	6	0	1.90	....	....	....	....	....	....	....
01-02	Jokerit Helsinki Jr.	Fin-Jr.	6	5	1	0	360	11	1	1.83	....	....	....	....	....	....	....
	Jokerit Helsinki	Finland	23	13	5	2	1242	37	4	1.79	11	8	2	623	18	3	1.73
02-03	Jokerit Helsinki	Finland	45	23	14	6	2634	87	5	1.98	10	6	4	626	17	2	1.63
03-04	**Atlanta**	**NHL**	**4**	**4**	**0**	**0**	**240**	**5**	**1**	**1.25**	....	....	....	....	....	....	....
	Chicago Wolves	AHL	39	20	14	2	2192	88	3	2.41	10	6	4	663	23	1	2.08
04-05	Chicago Wolves	AHL	57	38	17	2	3378	128	5	2.27	16	10	6	983	28	2	*1.71
05-06	**Atlanta**	**NHL**	**38**	**20**	**15**	**0**	**2166**	**106**	**2**	**2.94**	....	....	....	....	....	....	....
06-07	**Atlanta**	**NHL**	**68**	**34**	**24**	**9**	**3934**	**183**	**4**	**2.79**	**2**	**0**	**2**	**118**	**11**	**0**	**5.59**
07-08	**Atlanta**	**NHL**	**48**	**17**	**22**	**5**	**2707**	**131**	**4**	**2.90**	....	....	....	....	....	....	....
	Chicago Wolves	AHL	2	2	0	0	124	4	0	1.93	....	....	....	....	....	....	....
08-09	**Atlanta**	**NHL**	**46**	**19**	**22**	**3**	**2624**	**134**	**3**	**3.06**	....	....	....	....	....	....	....
09-10	Chicago Wolves	AHL	4	1	1	2	247	11	0	2.67	....	....	....	....	....	....	....
	Dallas	**NHL**	**12**	**6**	**4**	**0**	**663**	**31**	**0**	**2.81**	....	....	....	....	....	....	....
	NHL Totals		**216**	**100**	**87**	**17**	**12334**	**590**	**14**	**2.87**	**2**	**0**	**2**	**118**	**11**	**0**	**5.59**

HL Second All-Star Team (2005)

Missed majority of 2009-10 season recovering from off-season back surgery. Traded to **Dallas** by **tlanta** for Ivan Vishnevskiy and Dallas' 4th round choice (Ivan Telegin) in 2010 Entry Draft, ebruary 9, 2010.

EIGHTON, Michael (LAY-tohn, MIGH-kuhl) PHI.

oaltender. Catches left. 6'3", 186 lbs. Born, Petrolia, Ont., May 19, 1981.
Chicago's 5th choice, 165th overall, in 1999 Entry Draft).

			Regular Season								Playoffs						
eason	Club	League	GP	W	L	O/T	Mins	GA	SO	Avg	GP	W	L	Mins	GA	SO	Avg
997-98	Petrolia Jets	OHA-B	30	....	....	....	1583	87	2	3.30	....	....	....	....	....	....	....
998-99	Windsor Spitfires	OHL	28	4	17	2	1389	112	0	4.84	3	0	1	80	10	0	7.50
9-2000	Windsor Spitfires	OHL	42	17	17	2	2272	118	1	3.12	12	5	6	616	32	0	3.12
000-01	Windsor Spitfires	OHL	54	32	13	5	3035	138	2	2.73	9	4	5	519	27	1	3.12
001-02	Norfolk Admirals	AHL	52	27	16	8	3114	111	6	2.14	4	1	2	238	8	0	2.02
002-03	**Chicago**	**NHL**	**8**	**2**	**3**	**2**	**447**	**21**	**1**	**2.82**	....	....	....	....	....	....	....
	Norfolk Admirals	AHL	36	18	13	5	2184	91	4	2.50	4	3	1	240	7	1	1.75
003-04	**Chicago**	**NHL**	**34**	**6**	**18**	**8**	**1988**	**99**	**2**	**2.99**	....	....	....	....	....	....	....
	Norfolk Admirals	AHL	18	10	7	1	1081	33	1	1.83	4	2	1	212	2	2	0.57
004-05	Norfolk Admirals	AHL	41	20	16	3	2319	78	7	2.02	....	....	....	....	....	....	....
005-06	Rochester	AHL	40	15	22	1	2318	124	2	3.21	....	....	....	....	....	....	....
006-07	Portland Pirates	AHL	16	8	6	1	962	37	2	2.31	....	....	....	....	....	....	....
	Nashville	**NHL**	**1**	**0**	**0**	**0**	**20**	**2**	**0**	**6.00**	....	....	....	....	....	....	....
	Philadelphia	**NHL**	**4**	**2**	**2**	**0**	**195**	**12**	**0**	**3.69**	....	....	....	....	....	....	....
	Philadelphia	AHL	5	2	0	2	270	7	0	1.56	....	....	....	....	....	....	....
007-08	**Carolina**	**NHL**	**3**	**1**	**1**	**0**	**158**	**7**	**0**	**2.66**	....	....	....	....	....	....	....
	Albany River Rats	AHL	58	28	25	4	3451	121	*7	2.10	7	3	4	510	10	*2	*1.18
008-09	**Carolina**	**NHL**	**19**	**6**	**7**	**2**	**1029**	**50**	**0**	**2.92**	....	....	....	....	....	....	....
009-10	**Carolina**	**NHL**	**7**	**1**	**4**	**0**	**350**	**25**	**0**	**4.29**	....	....	....	....	....	....	....
	Philadelphia	**NHL**	**27**	**16**	**5**	**2**	**1449**	**60**	**1**	**2.48**	**14**	**8**	**3**	**757**	**31**	***3**	***2.46**
	NHL Totals		**103**	**34**	**40**	**14**	**5636**	**276**	**4**	**2.94**	**14**	**8**	**3**	**757**	**31**	**3**	**2.46**

AHL All-Rookie Team (2002) • AHL First All-Star Team (2008) • Aldege "Baz" Bastien Memorial Award (AHL – Outstanding Goaltender) (2008)

Traded to **Buffalo** by **Chicago** for Milan Bartovic, October 4, 2005. Signed as a free agent by **Anaheim**, July 13, 2006. Claimed on waivers by **Nashville** from **Anaheim**, November 27, 2006. Claimed on waivers by **Philadelphia** from **Nashville**, January 11, 2007. Claimed on waivers by **Montreal** from **Philadelphia**, February 27, 2007. Traded to **Carolina** by **Montreal** for Carolina's 7th round choice (Scott Kishel) in 2007 Entry Draft, June 23, 2007. Claimed on waivers by **Philadelphia** from **Carolina**, December 15, 2009.

LeNEVEU, David (LEH-neh-voo, DAY-vihd) CBJ

Goaltender. Catches left. 6'1", 187 lbs. Born, Fernie, B.C., May 23, 1983.
(Phoenix's 3rd choice, 46th overall, in 2002 Entry Draft).

			Regular Season								Playoffs						
Season	Club	League	GP	W	L	O/T	Mins	GA	SO	Avg	GP	W	L	Mins	GA	SO	Avg
99-2000	Fernie Ghostriders	AWHL	22	15	2	0	1140	48	0	2.49	....	....	....	....	....	....	....
2000-01	Nanaimo Clippers	BCHL	41	....	....	....	2330	127	6	3.29	....	....	....	....	....	....	....
2001-02	Cornell Big Red	ECAC	14	11	2	1	842	21	2	*1.50	....	....	....	....	....	....	....
2002-03	Cornell Big Red	ECAC	32	*28	3	1	1946	39	*9	*1.20	....	....	....	....	....	....	....
2003-04	Springfield Falcons	AHL	38	16	19	3	2217	102	1	2.76	....	....	....	....	....	....	....
2004-05	Utah Grizzlies	AHL	48	11	32	3	2702	132	0	2.93	....	....	....	....	....	....	....
2005-06	**Phoenix**	**NHL**	**15**	**3**	**8**	**2**	**814**	**44**	**0**	**3.24**	....	....	....	....	....	....	....
	San Antonio	AHL	28	10	16	2	1646	80	2	2.92	....	....	....	....	....	....	....
2006-07	**Phoenix**	**NHL**	**6**	**2**	**1**	**0**	**233**	**15**	**0**	**3.86**	....	....	....	....	....	....	....
	San Antonio	AHL	37	13	20	2	2101	104	2	2.97	....	....	....	....	....	....	....
2007-08	San Antonio	AHL	21	9	7	3	1172	52	1	2.66	....	....	....	....	....	....	....
	Hartford Wolf Pack	AHL	13	8	3	2	786	24	1	1.83	4	1	3	266	11	0	2.48
2008-09	Iowa Chops	AHL	46	20	19	6	2627	129	0	2.95	....	....	....	....	....	....	....
2009-10	Salzburg	Austria	43	....	....	....	2467	106	2	2.58	9	6	2	....	....	....	2.17
	NHL Totals		**21**	**5**	**9**	**2**	**1047**	**59**	**0**	**3.38**	....	....	....	....	....	....	....

ECAC All-Rookie Team (2002) • ECAC First All-Star Team (2003) • ECAC Goaltender of the Year (2003) • ECAC Player of the Year (2003) (co-winner - Christopher Higgins) • NCAA East First All-American Team (2003)

Traded to **NY Rangers** by **Phoenix** with Josh Gratton, Fredrik Sjostrom and Phoenix's 5th round choice (Roman Horak) in 2009 Entry Draft for Marcel Hossa and Al Montoya, February 26, 2008. Signed as a free agent by **Anaheim**, July 7, 2008. Signed as a free agent by **Salzburg** (Austria), August 7, 2009. Signed as a free agent by **Columbus**, July 7, 2010.

LEVASSEUR, Jean-Philippe (leh-VAH-soor, ZHAWN-fihl-EEP) ANA.

Goaltender. Catches right. 6'1", 199 lbs. Born, Victoriaville, Que., January 15, 1987.
(Anaheim's 6th choice, 197th overall, in 2005 Entry Draft).

			Regular Season								Playoffs						
Season	Club	League	GP	W	L	O/T	Mins	GA	SO	Avg	GP	W	L	Mins	GA	SO	Avg
2002-03	Magog	QAAA	28	15	10	1	1563	71	3	2.73	....	....	....	....	....	....	....
2003-04	Magog	QAAA	24	12	11	2	1424	86	0	3.62	13	7	5	762	35	0	2.80
	Rouyn-Noranda	QMJHL	3	0	2	1	184	14	0	4.57	....	....	....	....	....	....	....
2004-05	Rouyn-Noranda	QMJHL	29	8	14	3	1393	89	0	3.83	3	0	0	48	3	0	3.76
2005-06	Rouyn-Noranda	QMJHL	58	*35	19	0	3125	178	2	3.42	5	1	4	297	16	0	3.23
2006-07	Rouyn-Noranda	QMJHL	58	*31	21	....	3118	182	1	3.50	15	8	6	852	51	0	3.59
2007-08	Portland Pirates	AHL	10	4	5	1	600	25	1	2.50	....	....	....	....	....	....	....
	Augusta Lynx	ECHL	29	10	11	2	1527	76	1	2.99	1	0	1	59	2	0	2.02
2008-09	Iowa Chops	AHL	41	13	18	4	2217	115	0	3.11	....	....	....	....	....	....	....
2009-10	Springfield Falcons	AHL	25	8	16	1	1438	86	1	3.59	....	....	....	....	....	....	....
	Laredo Bucks	CHL	16	10	3	3	986	38	0	2.31	....	....	....	....	....	....	....
	Bakersfield	ECHL	5	2	3	0	298	18	0	3.63	6	3	2	368	16	1	2.61

LINDBACK, Anders (LIHND-bak, AN-duhrs) NSH.

Goaltender. Catches left. 6'6", 212 lbs. Born, Gavle, Sweden, May 3, 1988.
(Nashville's 7th choice, 207th overall, in 2008 Entry Draft).

			Regular Season								Playoffs						
Season	Club	League	GP	W	L	O/T	Mins	GA	SO	Avg	GP	W	L	Mins	GA	SO	Avg
2003-04	Brynas U18	Swe-U18	3	....	....	....	178	13	0	4.38	....	....	....	....	....	....	....
2004-05	Brynas U18	Swe-U18	49	....	....	....	2940	108	7	2.20	....	....	....	....	....	....	....
2005-06	Brynas U18	Swe-U18	11	....	....	....	666	36	2	3.24	....	....	....	....	....	....	....
	Brynas IF Gavle Jr.	Swe-Jr.	5	....	....	....	257	7	2	1.64	....	....	....	....	....	....	....
2006-07	Brynas IF Gavle Jr.	Swe-Jr.	36	....	....	....	2143	81	5	2.27	3	....	....	180	6	0	2.00
2007-08	Almtuna	Sweden-2	18	....	....	....	1034	53	0	3.07	....	....	....	....	....	....	....
2008-09	Brynas IF Gavle Jr.	Swe-Jr.	3	....	....	....	179	7	0	2.35	....	....	....	....	....	....	....
	Brynas IF Gavle	Sweden	24	....	....	....	1332	57	1	2.57	3	....	....	177	7	0	2.37
2009-10	Timra IK	Sweden	42	....	....	....	2537	104	3	2.46	5	....	....	306	15	0	2.94

LUNDQVIST, Henrik (LUHND-kvihst, HEHN-rihk) NYR

Goaltender. Catches left. 6'1", 198 lbs. Born, Are, Sweden, March 2, 1982.
(NY Rangers' 7th choice, 205th overall, in 2000 Entry Draft).

			Regular Season								Playoffs						
Season	Club	League	GP	W	L	O/T	Mins	GA	SO	Avg	GP	W	L	Mins	GA	SO	Avg
1998-99	V.Frolunda Jr.	Swe-Jr.	35	....	....	....	2100	95	0	2.73	....	....	....	....	....	....	....
99-2000	V.Frolunda Jr.	Swe-Jr.	30	....	....	....	1726	73	0	2.54	5	4	1	300	7	2	1.40
2000-01	V.Frolunda U18	Swe-U18	2	....	....	....	120	5	0	2.50	3	2	1	182	5	0	1.62
	V.Frolunda Jr.	Swe-Jr.	19	....	....	....	1140	50	2	2.64	....	....	....	....	....	....	....
	IF Molndal Hockey	Sweden-2	7	....	....	....	420	29	0	4.22	....	....	....	....	....	....	....
	V.Frolunda	Sweden	4	....	....	....	190	11	0	3.47	....	....	....	....	....	....	....
2001-02	V.Frolunda	Sweden	20	....	....	....	1152	52	2	2.71	8	8	0	489	18	*2	2.21
	V.Frolunda Jr.	Swe-Jr.	1	1	0	0	60	4	0	4.00	....	....	....	....	....	....	....
2002-03	V.Frolunda	Sweden	28	....	....	....	1650	40	*6	*1.45	12	....	....	739	26	*2	2.11
	V.Frolunda Jr.	Swe-Jr.	1	1	0	0	60	4	0	4.00	....	....	....	....	....	....	....
2003-04	V.Frolunda	Sweden	*48	....	....	....	*2897	105	7	2.17	10	....	....	610	20	0	1.97
2004-05	Frolunda	Sweden	44	*33	8	3	2642	79	*6	*1.79	*14	*12	2	854	15	*6	*1.05
2005-06	**NY Rangers**	**NHL**	**53**	**30**	**12**	**9**	**3112**	**116**	**2**	**2.24**	**3**	**0**	**3**	**177**	**13**	**0**	**4.41**
	Sweden	Olympics	6	5	1	0	360	14	0	2.33	....	....	....	....	....	....	....
2006-07	**NY Rangers**	**NHL**	**70**	**37**	**22**	**8**	**4109**	**160**	**5**	**2.34**	**10**	**6**	**4**	**637**	**22**	**1**	**2.07**
2007-08	**NY Rangers**	**NHL**	**72**	**37**	**24**	**10**	**4305**	**160**	***10**	**2.23**	**10**	**5**	**5**	**608**	**26**	**1**	**2.57**
2008-09	**NY Rangers**	**NHL**	**70**	**38**	**25**	**7**	**4153**	**168**	**3**	**2.43**	**7**	**3**	**4**	**380**	**19**	**1**	**3.00**
2009-10	**NY Rangers**	**NHL**	**73**	**35**	**27**	**10**	**4204**	**167**	**4**	**2.38**	....	....	....	....	....	....	....
	Sweden	Olympics	3	2	1	0	179	4	*2	1.34	....	....	....	....	....	....	....
	NHL Totals		**338**	**177**	**110**	**44**	**19883**	**771**	**24**	**2.33**	**30**	**14**	**16**	**1802**	**80**	**3**	**2.66**

NHL All-Rookie Team (2006)

Played in NHL All-Star Game (2009)

LUONGO, Roberto (loo-WAHN-goh, roh-BUHR-toh) VAN.

Goaltender. Catches left. 6'3", 217 lbs. Born, Montreal, Que., April 4, 1979.
(NY Islanders' 1st choice, 4th overall, in 1997 Entry Draft).

			Regular Season								Playoffs						
Season	Club	League	GP	W	L	O/T	Mins	GA	SO	Avg	GP	W	L	Mins	GA	SO	Avg
1994-95	Montreal-Bourassa	QAAA	25	10	14	0	1465	94	0	3.85	....	....	....	....	....	....	....
1995-96	Val-d'Or Foreurs	QMJHL	23	6	11	4	1201	74	0	3.70	3	0	1	68	5	0	4.41
1996-97	Val-d'Or Foreurs	QMJHL	60	32	22	2	3305	171	2	3.10	13	8	5	777	44	0	3.40
1997-98	Val-d'Or Foreurs	QMJHL	54	27	20	5	3046	157	*7	3.09	*17	*14	3	*1019	37	*2	*2.18
1998-99	Val-d'Or Foreurs	QMJHL	21	6	10	2	1176	77	1	3.93	....	....	....	....	....	....	....
	Acadie-Bathurst	QMJHL	22	14	7	1	1340	74	0	3.31	*23	*16	6	*1400	64	0	2.74
99-2000	**NY Islanders**	**NHL**	**24**	**7**	**14**	**1**	**1292**	**70**	**1**	**3.25**	....	....	....	....	....	....	....
	Lowell	AHL	26	10	12	4	1517	74	1	2.93	6	3	3	359	18	0	3.01
2000-01	**Florida**	**NHL**	**47**	**12**	**24**	**7**	**2628**	**107**	**5**	**2.44**	....	....	....	....	....	....	....
	Louisville Panthers	AHL	3	1	2	0	178	10	0	3.38	....	....	....	....	....	....	....
2001-02	**Florida**	**NHL**	**58**	**16**	**33**	**4**	**3030**	**140**	**4**	**2.77**	....	....	....	....	....	....	....
2002-03	**Florida**	**NHL**	**65**	**20**	**34**	**7**	**3627**	**164**	**6**	**2.71**	....	....	....	....	....	....	....
2003-04	**Florida**	**NHL**	**72**	**25**	**33**	**14**	**4252**	**172**	**7**	**2.43**	....	....	....	....	....	....	....
2004-05							DID NOT PLAY										
2005-06	**Florida**	**NHL**	***75**	**35**	**30**	**9**	**4305**	**213**	**4**	**2.97**	....	....	....	....	....	....	....
	Canada	Olympics	2	1	1	0	119	3	0	1.51	....	....	....	....	....	....	....
2006-07	**Vancouver**	**NHL**	**76**	**47**	**22**	**6**	**4490**	**171**	**5**	**2.29**	**12**	**5**	**7**	**847**	**25**	**0**	**1.77**
2007-08	**Vancouver**	**NHL**	**73**	**35**	**29**	**9**	**4233**	**168**	**6**	**2.38**	....	....	....	....	....	....	....
2008-09	**Vancouver**	**NHL**	**54**	**33**	**13**	**7**	**3181**	**124**	**9**	**2.34**	**10**	**6**	**4**	**618**	**26**	**1**	**2.52**
2009-10	**Vancouver**	**NHL**	**68**	**40**	**22**	**4**	**3899**	**167**	**4**	**2.57**	**12**	**6**	**6**	**707**	**38**	**0**	**3.22**
	Canada	Olympics	5	5	0	0	308	9	1	1.76	....	....	....	....	....	....	....
	NHL Totals		**612**	**270**	**254**	**68**	**34937**	**1496**	**51**	**2.57**	**34**	**17**	**17**	**2172**	**89**	**1**	**2.46**

NHL Second All-Star Team (2004, 2007)

Played in NHL All-Star Game (2004, 2007, 2009)

Traded to **Florida** by **NY Islanders** with Olli Jokinen for Mark Parrish and Oleg Kvasha, June 24, 2000. Traded to **Vancouver** by **Florida** with Lukas Krajicek and Florida's 6th round choice (Sergei Shirokov) in 2006 Entry Draft for Todd Bertuzzi, Bryan Allen and Alex Auld, June 23, 2006.

MacDONALD, Joey (MAK-DAWN-uhld, JOH-ee) DET.

Goaltender. Catches left. 6', 197 lbs. Born, Pictou, N.S., February 7, 1980.

			Regular Season								Playoffs						
Season	Club	League	GP	W	L	O/T	Mins	GA	SO	Avg	GP	W	L	Mins	GA	SO	Avg
1997-98	Halifax	QMJHL	17	3	12	0	815	54	0	3.97	3	1	2	140	15	0	6.43
1998-99	Peterborough	OHL	47	22	15	2	2483	123	3	2.97	3	0	2	145	13	0	5.38
99-2000	Peterborough	OHL	48	20	15	6	2641	125	2	2.84	5	1	4	280	16	1	3.43
2000-01	Peterborough	OHL	57	25	21	7	3284	161	1	2.94	7	3	4	425	18	0	2.54
2001-02	Toledo Storm	ECHL	38	12	15	7	2084	100	1	2.88	....	....	....	....	....	....	....
2002-03	Grand Rapids	AHL	25	14	6	0	1337	49	3	2.20	1	0	0	8	1	0	7.95
2003-04	Grand Rapids	AHL	39	22	12	3	2249	74	6	1.97	1	0	1	40	4	0	6.04
2004-05	Grand Rapids	AHL	*66	34	29	2	*3755	143	5	2.29	....	....	....	....	....	....	....
2005-06	Grand Rapids	AHL	32	17	9	2	1745	91	2	3.13	....	....	....	....	....	....	....
	Toledo Storm	ECHL	1	1	0	0	60	1	0	1.00	....	....	....	....	....	....	....
2006-07	**Detroit**	**NHL**	**8**	**1**	**5**	**1**	**468**	**27**	**0**	**3.46**	....	....	....	....	....	....	....
	Grand Rapids	AHL	2	1	1	0	123	6	0	2.93	....	....	....	....	....	....	....
	Boston	**NHL**	**7**	**2**	**2**	**1**	**358**	**16**	**0**	**2.68**	....	....	....	....	....	....	....
2007-08	**NY Islanders**	**NHL**	**2**	**0**	**1**	**1**	**120**	**6**	**0**	**3.00**	....	....	....	....	....	....	....
	Bridgeport	AHL	38	16	19	2	2266	109	2	2.89	....	....	....	....	....	....	....
2008-09	**NY Islanders**	**NHL**	**49**	**14**	**26**	**6**	**2792**	**157**	**1**	**3.37**	....	....	....	....	....	....	....
2009-10	**Toronto**	**NHL**	**6**	**1**	**4**	**0**	**319**	**17**	**0**	**3.20**	....	....	....	....	....	....	....
	Toronto Marlies	AHL	36	14	19	3	2112	112	2	3.18	....	....	....	....	....	....	....
	NHL Totals		**72**	**18**	**38**	**9**	**4057**	**223**	**1**	**3.30**	....	....	....	....	....	....	....

Harry "Hap" Holmes Memorial Award (AHL – fewest goals against) (2003) (shared with Marc Lamothe)

Signed as a free agent by **Detroit**, December 21, 2001. Claimed on waivers by **Boston** from **Detroit**, February 24, 2007. Signed as a free agent by **NY Islanders**, July 7, 2007. Signed as a free agent by **Toronto**, August 10, 2009. Traded to **Anaheim** by **Toronto** for Anaheim's 7th round choice in 2011 Entry Draft, March 3, 2010. Signed as a free agent by **Detroit**, July 6, 2010.

MACHESNEY, Daren (muh-KEHS-nee, DAIR-ehn)

Goaltender. Catches left. 6', 182 lbs. Born, Hamilton, Ont., December 13, 1986.
(Washington's 5th choice, 143rd overall, in 2005 Entry Draft).

			Regular Season								Playoffs						
Season	Club	League	GP	W	L	O/T	Mins	GA	SO	Avg	GP	W	L	Mins	GA	SO	Avg
2003-04	Newmarket	OPJHL	32	....	....	....	1868	82	1	2.63	....	....	....	....	....	....	....
	Brampton Battalion	OHL	5	3	2	0	300	15	0	3.00	....	....	....	....	....	....	....
2004-05	Brampton Battalion	OHL	38	16	13	6	2166	99	1	2.74	5	2	3	331	15	0	2.72
2005-06	Brampton Battalion	OHL	49	28	17	3	2830	143	3	3.03	11	5	6	633	32	0	3.03
2006-07	Hershey Bears	AHL	10	3	3	1	377	20	0	3.18	....	....	....	....	....	....	....
	South Carolina	ECHL	15	5	8	2	836	46	1	3.30	....	....	....	....	....	....	....
2007-08	Hershey Bears	AHL	38	22	10	2	2139	91	1	2.55	2	0	1	21	3	0	8.54
2008-09	Hershey Bears	AHL	36	19	12	1	1981	107	3	3.24	....	....	....	....	....	....	....
2009-10	Manitoba Moose	AHL	21	5	14	0	1186	66	0	3.34	1	0	0	27	3	0	6.59

OHL All-Rookie Team (2005)

Signed as a free agent by **Manitoba** (AHL), July 20, 2009.

MacINTYRE, Drew (MAK-ihn-tighr, DROO) ATL.

Goaltender. Catches left. 6', 190 lbs. Born, Charlottetown, P.E.I., June 24, 1983.
(Detroit's 2nd choice, 121st overall, in 2001 Entry Draft).

			Regular Season								Playoffs						
Season	Club	League	GP	W	L	O/T	Mins	GA	SO	Avg	GP	W	L	Mins	GA	SO	Avg
1998-99	Trenton Sting	OPJHL	20	....	....	....	1173	71	2	3.63	....	....	....	....	....	....	....
99-2000	Sherbrooke	QMJHL	24	10	7	2	1253	67	0	3.21	....	....	....	....	....	....	....
2000-01	Sherbrooke	QMJHL	48	17	22	3	2552	139	4	3.27	4	0	4	238	19	0	4.78
2001-02	Sherbrooke	QMJHL	55	15	34	3	3028	201	1	3.98	....	....	....	....	....	....	....
2002-03	Sherbrooke	QMJHL	*61	31	24	5	*3515	161	2	2.75	12	5	7	767	52	0	4.07
2003-04	Toledo Storm	ECHL	11	6	4	0	574	25	0	2.61	....	....	....	....	....	....	....
2004-05	Grand Rapids	AHL	24	7	8	0	1049	47	1	2.69	....	....	....	....	....	....	....
	Toledo Storm	ECHL	2	0	1	0	87	6	0	4.12	....	....	....	....	....	....	....
2005-06	Grand Rapids	AHL	13	8	4	0	681	33	0	2.91	5	3	1	260	7	0	1.62
	Toledo Storm	ECHL	33	24	7	2	1981	68	2	*2.06	6	5	1	360	12	0	2.00
2006-07	Manitoba Moose	AHL	41	24	12	2	2290	83	3	2.17	11	4	6	633	21	1	1.99
2007-08	**Vancouver**	**NHL**	**2**	**0**	**1**	**0**	**61**	**3**	**0**	**2.95**	....	....	....	....	....	....	....
	Manitoba Moose	AHL	46	25	18	2	2736	106	2	2.32	1	1	0	31	2	0	3.93
2008-09	Milwaukee	AHL	55	*34	15	4	3180	122	4	2.30	11	7	4	655	18	1	*1.65
2009-10	Chicago Wolves	AHL	41	20	17	2	2246	95	3	2.54	5	1	2	228	11	1	2.90
	NHL Totals		**2**	**0**	**1**	**0**	**61**	**3**	**0**	**2.95**	....	....	....	....	....	....	....

AHL Second All-Star Team (2008, 2009)

• Missed majority of 2003-04 season recovering from thigh injury suffered in practice, December 27, 2003. Traded to **Vancouver** by **Detroit** for future considerations, September 12, 2006. Signed as a free agent by **Nashville**, July 1, 2008. Signed as a free agent by **Atlanta**, July 6, 2009.

MANNINO, Peter (ma-NEE-noh, PE-tuhr) ATL.

Goaltender. Catches right. 6', 190 lbs. Born, Farmington Hills, MI, February 17, 1984.

			Regular Season								Playoffs						
Season	Club	League	GP	W	L	O/T	Mins	GA	SO	Avg	GP	W	L	Mins	GA	SO	Avg
2001-02	Pittsburgh Forge	NAHL	11	....	....	....	....	....	....	....	....	....	....	....	....	....	....
2002-03	Pittsburgh Forge	NAHL	45	....	....	....	....	....	....	....	....	....	....	....	....	....	....
2003-04	Tri-City Storm	USHL	38	26	7	0	1988	70	5	*2.11	7	4	1	334	12	*1	2.15
2004-05	U. of Denver	WCHA	21	16	4	1	1224	46	*5	2.25	....	....	....	....	....	....	....
2005-06	U. of Denver	WCHA	22	12	8	1	1241	56	1	2.71	....	....	....	....	....	....	....
2006-07	U. of Denver	WCHA	18	8	6	2	1021	39	3	2.29	....	....	....	....	....	....	....
2007-08	U. of Denver	WCHA	40	25	14	1	2302	87	*6	2.27	....	....	....	....	....	....	....
2008-09	**NY Islanders**	**NHL**	**3**	**1**	**1**	**0**	**133**	**10**	**0**	**4.51**	....	....	....	....	....	....	....
	Bridgeport	AHL	34	17	12	2	1959	96	1	2.94	3	1	2	189	10	0	3.18
	Utah Grizzlies	ECHL	9	4	3	2	549	25	0	2.73	....	....	....	....	....	....	....
2009-10	Chicago Wolves	AHL	38	26	5	1	2026	79	2	2.34	12	6	5	653	34	2	3.12
	NHL Totals		**3**	**1**	**1**	**0**	**133**	**10**	**0**	**4.51**	....	....	....	....	....	....	....

Signed as a free agent by **NY Islanders**, July 3, 2008. Signed as a free agent by **Atlanta**, July 6, 2009.

MARKSTROM, Jacob (MAHRK-struhm, JAY-kawb) FLA.

Goaltender. Catches left. 6'3", 178 lbs. Born, Gavle, Sweden, January 31, 1990.
(Florida's 1st choice, 31st overall, in 2008 Entry Draft).

			Regular Season								Playoffs						
Season	Club	League	GP	W	L	O/T	Mins	GA	SO	Avg	GP	W	L	Mins	GA	SO	Avg
2006-07	Brynas U18	Swe-U18	13	....	....	....	789	27	0	2.05	3	....	....	193	6	1	1.86
	Brynas IF Gavle Jr.	Swe-Jr.	1	....	....	....	65	3	0	2.77	1	....	....	25	4	0	9.76
2007-08	Brynas U18	Swe-U18	1	....	....	....	60	3	0	3.00	....	....	....	....	....	....	....
	Brynas IF Gavle Jr.	Swe-Jr.	22	....	....	....	1320	44	2	2.00	....	....	....	....	....	....	....
	Brynas IF Gavle	Sweden	7	....	....	....	423	22	0	3.12	....	....	....	....	....	....	....
	Brynas IF Gavle	Sweden-Q	9	....	....	....	505	15	2	1.78	....	....	....	....	....	....	....
2008-09	Brynas IF Gavle	Sweden	35	....	....	....	1992	79	3	2.38	1	....	....	59	2	0	2.02
2009-10	Brynas IF Gavle	Sweden	43	....	....	....	2542	85	*5	*2.01	4	....	....	224	12	0	3.21
	Brynas IF Gavle Jr.	Swe-Jr.	....	....	....	....	....	....	....	....	2	....	....	119	6	0	3.03

MASON, Chris (MAY-sohn, KRIHS) ATL.

Goaltender. Catches left. 6', 200 lbs. Born, Red Deer, Alta., April 20, 1976.
(New Jersey's 7th choice, 122nd overall, in 1995 Entry Draft).

			Regular Season								Playoffs						
Season	Club	League	GP	W	L	O/T	Mins	GA	SO	Avg	GP	W	L	Mins	GA	SO	Avg
1992-93	Red Deer	AMHL	20	....	....	....	1280	76	0	3.35	....	....	....	....	....	....	....
1993-94	Victoria Cougars	WHL	5	1	4	0	237	27	0	6.84	....	....	....	....	....	....	....
1994-95	Prince George	WHL	44	8	30	1	2288	192	1	5.03	....	....	....	....	....	....	....
1995-96	Prince George	WHL	59	16	37	1	3289	236	1	4.31	....	....	....	....	....	....	....
1996-97	Prince George	WHL	50	19	24	4	2851	172	2	3.62	15	9	6	938	44	*1	2.81
1997-98	Cincinnati	AHL	47	13	19	7	2368	136	0	3.45	....	....	....	....	....	....	....
1998-99	**Nashville**	**NHL**	**3**	**0**	**0**	**0**	**69**	**6**	**0**	**5.22**	....	....	....	....	....	....	....
	Milwaukee	IHL	34	15	12	6	1901	92	1	2.90	....	....	....	....	....	....	....
99-2000	Milwaukee	IHL	53	20	21	8	2952	137	2	2.78	3	1	2	252	11	0	2.62
2000-01	**Nashville**	**NHL**	**1**	**0**	**1**	**0**	**59**	**2**	**0**	**2.03**	....	....	....	....	....	....	....
	Milwaukee	IHL	37	17	14	5	2226	87	5	2.35	4	1	3	239	12	0	3.02
2001-02	Milwaukee	AHL	48	17	21	7	2755	116	2	2.53	....	....	....	....	....	....	....
2002-03	San Antonio	AHL	50	25	18	6	2914	122	1	2.51	3	0	3	195	9	0	2.77
2003-04	**Nashville**	**NHL**	**17**	**4**	**4**	**1**	**744**	**27**	**1**	**2.18**	....	....	....	....	....	....	....
	Milwaukee	AHL	1	1	0	0	60	2	0	2.00	....	....	....	....	....	....	....
2004-05	Valerengen IF Oslo	Norway	20	....	....	....	1204	36	1	1.79	11	....	....	657	22	1	2.01
2005-06	**Nashville**	**NHL**	**23**	**12**	**5**	**1**	**1227**	**52**	**2**	**2.54**	**5**	**1**	**4**	**296**	**17**	**0**	**3.45**
2006-07	**Nashville**	**NHL**	**40**	**24**	**11**	**4**	**2342**	**93**	**5**	**2.38**	....	....	....	....	....	....	....
2007-08	**Nashville**	**NHL**	**51**	**18**	**22**	**6**	**2692**	**130**	**4**	**2.90**	....	....	....	....	....	....	....
2008-09	**St. Louis**	**NHL**	**57**	**27**	**21**	**7**	**3215**	**129**	**6**	**2.41**	**4**	**0**	**4**	**256**	**10**	**0**	**2.34**
2009-10	**St. Louis**	**NHL**	**61**	**30**	**22**	**8**	**3512**	**148**	**2**	**2.53**	....	....	....	....	....	....	....
	NHL Totals		**253**	**115**	**86**	**27**	**13860**	**587**	**20**	**2.54**	**9**	**1**	**8**	**552**	**27**	**0**	**2.93**

Signed as a free agent by **Anaheim**, June 27, 1997. Traded to **Nashville** by **Anaheim** with Marc Moro for Dominic Roussel, October 5, 1998. Signed as a free agent by **Florida**, August 20, 2002. Claimed by **Nashville** from **Florida** in Waiver Draft, October 3, 2003. Signed as a free agent by **Oslo** (Norway), November 30, 2004. Traded to **St. Louis** by **Nashville** for NY Rangers' 4th round choice (previously acquired, later traded back to NY Rangers - NY Rangers selected Dale Weise) in 2008 Entry Draft, June 20, 2008. Signed as a free agent by **Atlanta**, July 1, 2010.

MASON, Steve (MAY-sohn, STEEV) C

Goaltender. Catches right. 6'4", 220 lbs. Born, Oakville, Ont., May 29, 1988.
(Columbus' 2nd choice, 69th overall, in 2006 Entry Draft).

			Regular Season								Playoffs						
Season	Club	League	GP	W	L	O/T	Mins	GA	SO	Avg	GP	W	L	Mins	GA	SO	Av
2004-05	Grimsby	OJHL-C	45	....	....	....	2800	....	6	1.75	....	....	....	....	....	....	
2005-06	Petrolia Jets	OJHL-B	9	6	3	0	521	....	1	2.53	....	....	....	....	....	....	
	London Knights	OHL	12	5	3	0	497	22	0	2.66	4	0	1	150	7	0	2.
2006-07	London Knights	OHL	*62	*45	13	4	*3733	199	2	3.20	16	9	7	931	54	0	3.
2007-08	London Knights	OHL	26	19	4	3	1569	73	2	2.79	....	....	....	....	....	....	
	Kitchener Rangers	OHL	16	13	3	0	961	33	1	2.06	5	5	0	313	10	1	1.
2008-09	**Columbus**	**NHL**	**61**	**33**	**20**	**7**	**3664**	**140**	***10**	**2.29**	**4**	**0**	**4**	**239**	**17**	**0**	**4.2**
	Syracuse Crunch	AHL	3	2	1	0	184	5	0	1.63	....	....	....	....	....	....	
2009-10	**Columbus**	**NHL**	**58**	**20**	**26**	**9**	**3201**	**163**	**5**	**3.06**	....	....	....	....	....	....	
	NHL Totals		**119**	**53**	**46**	**16**	**6865**	**303**	**15**	**2.65**	**4**	**0**	**4**	**239**	**17**	**0**	**4.2**

OHL First All-Star Team (2007) • OHL Second All-Star Team (2008) • NHL All-Rookie Team (2009) • NHL Second All-Star Team (2009) • Calder Memorial Trophy (2009)

MAXWELL, Brandon (MAX-wehl, BRAN-duhn) CO

Goaltender. Catches left. 6', 195 lbs. Born, Winter Park, FL, March 22, 1991.
(Colorado's 6th choice, 154th overall, in 2009 Entry Draft).

			Regular Season								Playoffs						
Season	Club	League	GP	W	L	O/T	Mins	GA	SO	Avg	GP	W	L	Mins	GA	SO	Av
2007-08	USNTDP	NAHL	21	8	10	1	1201	68	1	3.40	....	....	....	....	....	....	
	USNTDP	U-17	5	3	2	0	....	....	0	....	....	....	....	....	....	....	
	USNTDP	U-18	13	9	3	1	....	....	1	1.91	....	....	....	....	....	....	
2008-09	USNTDP	NAHL	11	7	3	1	666	35	0	3.15	9	5	4	535	23	0	2.5
	USNTDP	U-17	15	8	6	1	900	43	0	2.87	....	....	....	....	....	....	
	USNTDP	U-18	3	3	0	0	185	8	0	2.59	....	....	....	....	....	....	
2009-10	Kitchener Rangers	OHL	41	22	14	4	2362	147	1	3.73	*20	11	9	*1181	76	0	3.8

MAYER, Robert (MAY-uhr, RAW-buhrt) MTL

Goaltender. Catches left. 6'1", 188 lbs. Born, Havirov, Czech., October 9, 1989.

			Regular Season								Playoffs						
Season	Club	League	GP	W	L	O/T	Mins	GA	SO	Avg	GP	W	L	Mins	GA	SO	Av
2005-06	ESV Kaufbeuren	German-2	3	....	....	....	....	....	....	....	....	....	....	....	....	....	
2006-07	ESV Kaufbeuren	German-2	7	....	....	....	....	....	....	....	....	....	....	....	....	....	
	Kloten Flyers	Swiss	1	0	0	0	10	1	0	6.00	....	....	....	....	....	....	
2007-08	Saint John	QMJHL	32	16	10	1	1669	105	2	3.77	....	....	....	....	....	....	
2008-09	Saint John	QMJHL	57	26	28	....	3155	169	2	3.21	4	0	3	204	16	0	4.7
2009-10	Hamilton Bulldogs	AHL	1	0	0	1	65	2	0	1.85	1	0	0	37	3	0	4.8
	Cincinnati	ECHL	31	19	10	1	1750	82	2	2.81	9	6	0	508	13	*3	*1.5

Signed as a free agent by **Montreal**, September 25, 2008.

McCOLLUM, Thomas (muh-KAW-luhm, TAW-muhs) DET

Goaltender. Catches left. 6'2", 210 lbs. Born, Amherst, NY, December 7, 1989.
(Detroit's 1st choice, 30th overall, in 2008 Entry Draft).

			Regular Season								Playoffs						
Season	Club	League	GP	W	L	O/T	Mins	GA	SO	Avg	GP	W	L	Mins	GA	SO	Avg
2005-06	Wheatfield Blades	EmJHL	24	2	19	3	1448	109	1	4.52	....	....	....	....	....	....	....
2006-07	Guelph Storm	OHL	55	26	18	10	3158	126	*5	2.39	4	0	4	233	17	0	4.3
2007-08	Guelph Storm	OHL	51	25	17	6	2978	124	*4	2.50	10	5	5	596	19	1	1.9
2008-09	Guelph Storm	OHL	31	17	10	4	1859	69	*3	2.23	....	....	....	....	....	....	....
	Brampton Battalion	OHL	23	17	6	0	1333	43	*4	1.94	*21	13	8	*1284	62	*1	2.9
2009-10	Grand Rapids	AHL	32	10	16	2	1741	101	0	3.48	....	....	....	....	....	....	....
	Toledo Walleye	ECHL	4	2	1	0	188	14	0	4.48	....	....	....	....	....	....	....

OHL Second All-Star Team (2009)

McELHINNEY, Curtis (MAK-IHL-ehn-ee, KUHR-this) ANA.

Goaltender. Catches left. 6'2", 196 lbs. Born, London, Ont., May 23, 1983.
(Calgary's 9th choice, 176th overall, in 2002 Entry Draft).

			Regular Season								Playoffs						
Season	Club	League	GP	W	L	O/T	Mins	GA	SO	Avg	GP	W	L	Mins	GA	SO	Avg
2000-01	Notre Dame	SJHL					Statistics not available										
2001-02	Colorado College	WCHA	9	6	0	1	441	15	1	2.04	....	....	....	....	....	....	....
2002-03	Colorado College	WCHA	*37	*25	6	5	*2147	85	*4	2.37	....	....	....	....	....	....	....
2003-04	Colorado College	WCHA	19	10	6	1	1015	41	2	2.42	....	....	....	....	....	....	....
2004-05	Colorado College	WCHA	26	*21	4	1	1550	58	2	2.24	....	....	....	....	....	....	....
2005-06	Omaha	AHL	33	9	14	2	1621	68	3	2.52	....	....	....	....	....	....	....
2006-07	Omaha	AHL	57	35	17	1	3181	113	*7	2.13	5	2	3	311	11	0	2.12
2007-08	**Calgary**	**NHL**	**5**	**0**	**2**	**0**	**150**	**5**	**0**	**2.00**	....	....	....	....	....	....	....
	Quad City Flames	AHL	41	20	18	2	2320	88	3	2.28	....	....	....	....	....	....	....
2008-09	**Calgary**	**NHL**	**14**	**1**	**6**	**1**	**518**	**31**	**0**	**3.59**	**1**	**0**	**0**	**34**	**1**	**0**	**1.76**
2009-10	**Calgary**	**NHL**	**10**	**3**	**4**	**0**	**502**	**27**	**0**	**3.23**	....	....	....	....	....	....	....
	Anaheim	**NHL**	**10**	**5**	**1**	**2**	**521**	**24**	**0**	**2.76**	....	....	....	....	....	....	....
	NHL Totals		**39**	**9**	**13**	**3**	**1691**	**87**	**0**	**3.09**	**1**	**0**	**0**	**34**	**1**	**0**	**1.76**

WCHA First All-Star Team (2003, 2005) • NCAA West Second All-American Team (2003) • NCAA West First All-American Team (2005) • AHL Second All-Star Team (2007)

Traded to **Anaheim** by **Calgary** for Vesa Toskala, March 3, 2010.

McGANN, Pat (muh-GAN, PAT) DAL.

Goaltender. Catches right. 5'11", 160 lbs. Born, Evergreen Park, IL, January 27, 1987.
(Dallas' 7th choice, 223rd overall, in 2005 Entry Draft).

			Regular Season								Playoffs						
Season	Club	League	GP	W	L	O/T	Mins	GA	SO	Avg	GP	W	L	Mins	GA	SO	Avg
2003-04	Chicago Chill	MAHL	31	14	16	1	....	....	....	3.40	....	....	....	....	....	....	....
2004-05	Team Illinois	MWEHL	50	31	18	1	....	91	5	2.21	....	....	....	....	....	....	....
2005-06	Cedar Rapids	USHL	17	5	8	3	998	49	1	2.95	....	....	....	....	....	....	....
2006-07	Cedar Rapids	USHL	6	3	3	0	357	22	0	3.70	....	....	....	....	....	....	....
	Chicago Steel	USHL	17	2	14	1	935	67	0	4.30	....	....	....	....	....	....	....
2007-08	Quinnipiac	ECAC	8	2	1	0	242	19	0	4.72	....	....	....	....	....	....	....
2008-09	Quinnipiac	ECAC					Did not play – Spare Goaltender										
2009-10	Quinnipiac	ECAC	1	0	0	0	3	0	0	0.00	....	....	....	....	....	....	....

ıcKENNA, Mike (mih-KEHN-ah, MIGHK) N.J.

oaltender. Catches right. 6'3", 195 lbs. Born, St. Louis, MO, April 11, 1983.
ıashville's 4th choice, 172nd overall, in 2002 Entry Draft).

			Regular Season								Playoffs						
eason	Club	League	GP	W	L	O/T	Mins	GA	SO	Avg	GP	W	L	Mins	GA	SO	Avg
)01-02	St. Lawrence	ECAC	20	7	10	1	1121	59	0	3.16	....	....	....	....	....	....	....
)02-03	St. Lawrence	ECAC	15	1	7	2	618	38	0	3.69	....	....	....	....	....	....	....
)03-04	St. Lawrence	ECAC	27	9	10	3	1475	60	3	2.44	....	....	....	....	....	....	....
)04-05	St. Lawrence	ECAC	35	15	17	2	2022	92	3	2.73	....	....	....	....	....	....	....
)05-06	Las Vegas	ECHL	25	19	2	1	1383	49	1	2.13	4	1	1	173	9	0	3.12
	Norfolk Admirals	AHL	7	4	2	1	388	25	0	3.86	....	....	....	....	....	....	....
)06-07	Milwaukee	AHL	1	0	0	0	11	3	0	15.72	....	....	....	....	....	....	....
	Las Vegas	ECHL	38	27	4	7	2258	83	5	*2.21	6	3	3	358	15	0	2.51
	Omaha	AHL	2	0	1	0	96	6	0	3.74	....	....	....	....	....	....	....
)07-08	Portland Pirates	AHL	41	24	13	1	2269	103	3	2.72	6	2	4	320	18	0	3.38
)08-09	**Tampa Bay**	**NHL**	**15**	**4**	**8**	**1**	**776**	**46**	**1**	**3.56**	....	....	....	....	....	....	....
	Norfolk Admirals	AHL	24	11	10	1	1315	65	1	2.97	....	....	....	....	....	....	....
)09-10	Lowell Devils	AHL	50	24	17	6	2891	119	3	2.47	5	1	4	317	17	0	3.22
	NHL Totals		**15**	**4**	**8**	**1**	**776**	**46**	**1**	**3.56**	....	....	....	....	....	....	....

CHL Second All-Star Team (2007)

gned as a free agent by **Tampa Bay**, February 3, 2009.

ıILLAN, Kieran (MIH-luhn, KEER-uhn) COL.

oaltender. Catches left. 6', 190 lbs. Born, Edmonton, Alta., August 31, 1989.
Colorado's 5th choice, 124th overall, in 2009 Entry Draft).

			Regular Season								Playoffs						
eason	Club	League	GP	W	L	O/T	Mins	GA	SO	Avg	GP	W	L	Mins	GA	SO	Avg
)06-07	Spruce Grove	AJHL	32	20	7	4	1883	82	3	2.61	4	2	2	200	10	1	3.00
)07-08	Spruce Grove	AJHL	43	21	12	8	2391	121	1	3.04	15	8	7	931	34	1	2.19
)08-09	Boston University	H-East	35	29	2	3	2073	67	3	1.94	....	....	....	....	....	....	....
)09-10	Boston University	H-East	32	16	16	0	1869	98	1	3.15	....	....	....	....	....	....	....

ockey East Second All-Star Team (2009) • Hockey East All-Rookie Team (2009) • Hockey East ookie of the Year (2009) • NCAA Rookie of the Year (2009) • NCAA Championship ll-Tournament Team (2009)

ıILLER, Ryan (MIH-luhr, RIGH-uhn) BUF.

oaltender. Catches left. 6'2", 175 lbs. Born, East Lansing, MI, July 17, 1980.
uffalo's 7th choice, 138th overall, in 1999 Entry Draft).

			Regular Season								Playoffs						
eason	Club	League	GP	W	L	O/T	Mins	GA	SO	Avg	GP	W	L	Mins	GA	SO	Avg
)97-98	Soo Indians	NAHL	37	21	14	0	2113	82	3	2.33	2	0	2	158	7	0	2.66
)98-99	Soo Indians	NAHL	47	31	14	1	2711	104	8	2.30	4	2	2	218	10	1	2.76
-2000	Michigan State	CCHA	26	16	5	3	1525	39	*8	*1.53	....	....	....	....	....	....	....
)00-01	Michigan State	CCHA	40	*31	5	4	2447	54	*10	*1.32	....	....	....	....	....	....	....
)01-02	Michigan State	CCHA	40	26	9	5	2411	71	*8	*1.77	....	....	....	....	....	....	....
02-03	**Buffalo**	**NHL**	**15**	**6**	**8**	**1**	**912**	**40**	**1**	**2.63**	....	....	....	....	....	....	....
	Rochester	AHL	47	23	18	5	2817	110	2	2.34	3	1	2	190	13	0	4.11
03-04	**Buffalo**	**NHL**	**3**	**0**	**3**	**0**	**178**	**15**	**0**	**5.06**	....	....	....	....	....	....	....
	Rochester	AHL	60	27	25	7	3579	132	5	2.21	14	7	7	857	26	2	1.82
04-05	Rochester	AHL	63	*41	17	4	3741	153	8	2.45	9	5	4	547	24	0	2.63
05-06	**Buffalo**	**NHL**	**48**	**30**	**14**	**3**	**2862**	**124**	**1**	**2.60**	**18**	**11**	**7**	**1123**	**48**	**1**	**2.56**
	Rochester	AHL	2	1	1	0	120	5	0	2.50	....	....	....	....	....	....	....
06-07	**Buffalo**	**NHL**	**63**	**40**	**16**	**6**	**3692**	**168**	**2**	**2.73**	**16**	**9**	**7**	**1029**	**38**	**0**	**2.22**
07-08	**Buffalo**	**NHL**	**76**	**36**	**27**	**10**	**4474**	**197**	**3**	**2.64**	....	....	....	....	....	....	....
08-09	**Buffalo**	**NHL**	**59**	**34**	**18**	**6**	**3443**	**145**	**5**	**2.53**	....	....	....	....	....	....	....
09-10	**Buffalo**	**NHL**	**69**	**41**	**18**	**8**	**4047**	**150**	**5**	**2.22**	**6**	**2**	**4**	**384**	**15**	**0**	**2.34**
	United States	Olympics	6	5	1	0	355	8	1	1.35	....	....	....	....	....	....	....
	NHL Totals		**333**	**187**	**104**	**34**	**19608**	**839**	**17**	**2.57**	**40**	**22**	**18**	**2536**	**101**	**1**	**2.39**

CHA Second All-Star Team (2000) • CCHA First All-Star Team (2001, 2002) • CCHA Player of the ear (2001, 2002) • NCAA West First All-American Team (2001, 2002) • Hobey Baker Memorial ward (Top U.S. Collegiate Player) (2001) • AHL First All-Star Team (2005) • Aldege "Baz" Bastien emorial Award (AHL – Outstanding Goaltender) (2005) • NHL First All-Star Team (2010) • Vezina ophy (2010) • Olympic Tournament All-Star Team (2010) • Olympic Tournament – Best oaltender (2010) • Olympic Tournament – MVP (2010)

ayed in NHL All-Star Game (2007)

ıODIG, Mattias (moh-DIHG, mat-TEE-uhs) PIT.

oaltender. Catches left. 6', 163 lbs. Born, Lulea, Sweden, April 1, 1987.
naheim's 7th choice, 121st overall, in 2007 Entry Draft).

			Regular Season								Playoffs						
ason	Club	League	GP	W	L	O/T	Mins	GA	SO	Avg	GP	W	L	Mins	GA	SO	Avg
02-03	Lulea HF U18	Swe-U18	2	....	....	....	120	4	0	2.00	....	....	....	....	....	....	....
03-04	Lulea HF U18	Swe-U18	14	....	....	....	854	30	2	2.11	7	....	....	449	14	0	1.87
	Lulea HF Jr.	Swe-Jr.	2	....	....	....	66	2	0	1.81	....	....	....	....	....	....	....
04-05	Lulea HF U18	Swe-U18	2	....	....	....	120	4	0	2.00	....	....	....	....	....	....	....
	Lulea HF Jr.	Swe-Jr.	14	....	....	....	819	42	2	3.08	5	....	....	306	16	0	3.14
05-06	Lulea HF Jr.	Swe-Jr.	19	....	....	....	1154	42	1	2.18	3	....	....	175	10	0	3.43
	Lulea HF	Sweden	2	....	....	....	66	3	0	2.74	....	....	....	....	....	....	....
06-07	Lulea HF Jr.	Swe-Jr.	2	....	....	....	120	7	0	3.50	....	....	....	....	....	....	....
	Lulea HF	Sweden	32	....	....	....	1636	69	1	2.53	1	....	....	20	1	0	3.00
07-08	Lulea HF Jr.	Swe-Jr.	5	....	....	....	297	14	0	2.83	....	....	....	....	....	....	....
	Lulea HF	Sweden	13	....	....	....	696	41	1	3.53	....	....	....	....	....	....	....
08-09	Lulea HF	Sweden	40	....	....	....	2268	85	*4	2.25	4	....	....	238	13	0	3.28
09-10	Lulea HF	Sweden	34	....	....	....	1925	80	2	2.49	....	....	....	....	....	....	....

aded to **Pittsburgh** by **Anaheim** for Montreal's 6th round choice (previously acquired, Anaheim lected Kevin Lind) in 2010 Entry Draft, May 28, 2010.

MONTOYA, Al (mawn-TOI-uh, AL) PHX.

Goaltender. Catches left. 6'2", 195 lbs. Born, Chicago, IL, February 13, 1985.
(NY Rangers' 1st choice, 6th overall, in 2004 Entry Draft).

			Regular Season								Playoffs						
Season	Club	League	GP	W	L	O/T	Mins	GA	SO	Avg	GP	W	L	Mins	GA	SO	Avg
99-2000	Loyola Academy	High-MN	28	12	13	3	1685	56	1	2.01	....	....	....	....	....	....	....
2000-01	Texas Tornado	NAHL	15	10	3	0	780	38	0	2.92	1	1	0	60	2	0	2.00
	United States	Nat-Tm	2	2	0	0	120	4	0	2.00	....	....	....	....	....	....	....
2001-02	USNTDP	U-17	10	5	5	0	570	24	0	2.53	....	....	....	....	....	....	....
	USNTDP	NAHL	24	6	11	4	1344	79	0	3.53	....	....	....	....	....	....	....
2002-03	U. of Michigan	CCHA	*43	*30	10	3	*2547	99	4	2.33	....	....	....	....	....	....	....
2003-04	U. of Michigan	CCHA	*40	*26	12	2	*2340	87	6	2.23	....	....	....	....	....	....	....
2004-05	U. of Michigan	CCHA	*40	*30	7	3	*2359	99	3	2.52	....	....	....	....	....	....	....
2005-06	Hartford Wolf Pack	AHL	40	23	9	1	2094	91	2	2.61	5	2	1	257	8	1	1.87
	Charlotte Checkers	ECHL	2	1	1	0	123	8	0	3.92	....	....	....	....	....	....	....
2006-07	Hartford Wolf Pack	AHL	48	27	17	0	2556	98	6	2.30	7	3	4	391	20	1	3.07
2007-08	Hartford Wolf Pack	AHL	31	16	8	3	1704	72	0	2.54	....	....	....	....	....	....	....
	San Antonio	AHL	14	8	6	0	789	34	1	2.59	1	0	1	59	4	0	4.04
2008-09	**Phoenix**	**NHL**	**5**	**3**	**1**	**0**	**259**	**9**	**1**	**2.08**	....	....	....	....	....	....	....
	San Antonio	AHL	29	7	17	2	1562	84	0	3.23	....	....	....	....	....	....	....
2009-10	San Antonio	AHL	14	4	7	1	771	34	0	2.65	....	....	....	....	....	....	....
	NHL Totals		**5**	**3**	**1**	**0**	**259**	**9**	**1**	**2.08**	....	....	....	....	....	....	....

CCHA All-Rookie Team (2003) • NCAA West Second All-American Team (2004)

Traded to **Phoenix** by **NY Rangers** with Marcel Hossa for Josh Gratton, David LeNeveu, Fredrik Sjostrom and Phoenix's 5th round choice (Roman Horak) in 2009 Entry Draft, February 26, 2008.

MORRISON, Adam (MOHR-ih-suhn, A-duhm) PHI.

Goaltender. Catches left. 6'3", 166 lbs. Born, Edmonton, Alta., February 9, 1991.
(Philadelphia's 1st choice, 81st overall, in 2009 Entry Draft).

			Regular Season								Playoffs						
Season	Club	League	GP	W	L	O/T	Mins	GA	SO	Avg	GP	W	L	Mins	GA	SO	Avg
2007-08	Valley West Hawks	BCMML	....	12	6	2	....	....	....	2.92	....	....	....	....	....	....	....
2008-09	Saskatoon Blades	WHL	13	9	1	1	746	31	1	2.49	....	....	....	....	....	....	....
2009-10	Saskatoon Blades	WHL	36	18	13	3	2040	112	1	3.29	....	....	....	....	....	....	....

MRAZEK, Petr (M'RAZ-ihk, PEH-tuhr) DET.

Goaltender. Catches left. 6', 162 lbs. Born, Ostrava, Czechoslovakia, February 14, 1992.
(Detroit's 5th choice, 141st overall, in 2010 Entry Draft).

			Regular Season								Playoffs						
Season	Club	League	GP	W	L	O/T	Mins	GA	SO	Avg	GP	W	L	Mins	GA	SO	Avg
2006-07	HC Vitkovice U17	CzR-U17	23	....	....	....	1273	51	2	2.40	9	....	....	486	15	1	1.85
2007-08	HC Vitkovice U17	CzR-U17	34	....	....	....	1974	81	4	2.46	3	....	....	179	8	0	2.68
	HC Vitkovice Steel	CzRep	1	....	....	....	24	4	0	10.00	....	....	....	....	....	....	....
2008-09	HC Vitkovice U17	CzR-U17	28	....	....	....	1601	53	5	1.99	4	....	....	193	3	2	0.93
	HC Vitkovice Jr.	CzRep-Jr.	13	....	....	....	795	33	0	2.49	1	....	....	60	1	0	1.00
2009-10	Ottawa 67's	OHL	30	12	9	1	1562	78	3	3.00	8	4	4	451	18	0	2.40

MUNRO, Adam (muhn-ROH, A-duhm)

Goaltender. Catches left. 6'2", 219 lbs. Born, St. George, Ont., November 12, 1982.
(Chicago's 1st choice, 29th overall, in 2001 Entry Draft).

			Regular Season								Playoffs						
Season	Club	League	GP	W	L	O/T	Mins	GA	SO	Avg	GP	W	L	Mins	GA	SO	Avg
1997-98	Brantford Classics	Minor-ON	15	13	2	0	660	20	*4	*1.36	....	....	....	....	....	....	....
1998-99	Brant County	OJHL-B	10	....	....	....	348	30	0	5.17	....	....	....	....	....	....	....
	Bowmanville	OPJHL	14	....	....	....	816	50	0	3.68	....	....	....	....	....	....	....
	Erie Otters	OHL	1	0	0	0	1	0	0	0.00	....	....	....	....	....	....	....
99-2000	Bowmanville	OPJHL	2	2	0	0	125	5	0	2.40	....	....	....	....	....	....	....
	Erie Otters	OHL	22	8	7	1	948	48	1	3.04	1	0	0	5	1	0	12.00
2000-01	Erie Otters	OHL	41	26	6	6	2283	88	*4	2.31	10	6	2	509	27	1	3.18
2001-02	Erie Otters	OHL	43	24	13	1	2277	128	3	3.37	6	4	2	361	17	0	2.83
2002-03	Erie Otters	OHL	8	2	6	0	426	24	1	3.38	....	....	....	....	....	....	....
	Sault Ste. Marie	OHL	42	20	20	2	2494	160	1	3.85	4	0	4	240	12	0	3.00
2003-04	**Chicago**	**NHL**	**7**	**1**	**5**	**1**	**426**	**26**	**0**	**3.66**	....	....	....	....	....	....	....
	Norfolk Admirals	AHL	12	5	4	1	695	26	0	2.24	....	....	....	....	....	....	....
	Gwinnett	ECHL	6	4	1	1	370	17	0	2.76	1	0	1	60	2	0	2.01
2004-05	Norfolk Admirals	AHL	30	14	10	2	1595	66	4	2.48	....	....	....	....	....	....	....
	Atlantic City	ECHL	5	2	2	1	272	9	0	1.99	....	....	....	....	....	....	....
2005-06	**Chicago**	**NHL**	**10**	**3**	**5**	**2**	**501**	**25**	**1**	**2.99**	....	....	....	....	....	....	....
	Norfolk Admirals	AHL	28	17	8	1	1612	73	1	2.72	4	0	4	239	15	0	3.77
2006-07	Fribourg	Swiss	41	12	28	0	2488	149	0	3.59	....	....	....	....	....	....	....
2007-08	Syracuse Crunch	AHL	25	13	9	1	1414	57	2	2.42	1	0	0	20	4	0	12.04
2008-09	Toronto Marlies	AHL	26	12	11	2	1511	61	2	2.42	1	0	1	58	4	0	4.11
2009-10	Toronto Marlies	AHL	14	3	8	1	727	38	0	3.14	....	....	....	....	....	....	....
	Sibir Novosibirsk	Rus-KHL	4	....	....	....	120	7	0	3.50	....	....	....	....	....	....	....
	NHL Totals		**17**	**4**	**10**	**3**	**927**	**51**	**1**	**3.30**	....	....	....	....	....	....	....

Signed as a free agent by **Fribourg** (Swiss), July 7, 2006. Signed as a free agent by **Syracuse** (AHL), July 23, 2007. Signed to a PTO (professional tryout) contract by **Toronto** (AHL), October 15, 2009. Signed as a free agent by **Novosibirsk** (Russia-KHL), January 15, 2010.

MUNROE, Scott (muhn-ROH, SKAWT)

Goaltender. Catches left. 6'2", 195 lbs. Born, Moose Jaw, Sask., January 20, 1982.

			Regular Season								Playoffs						
Season	Club	League	GP	W	L	O/T	Mins	GA	SO	Avg	GP	W	L	Mins	GA	SO	Avg
2002-03	AL-Huntsville	CHA	20	11	6	1	1049	49	1	2.80	....	....	....	....	....	....	....
2003-04	AL-Huntsville	CHA	17	5	9	1	891	47	0	3.16	....	....	....	....	....	....	....
2004-05	AL-Huntsville	CHA	31	16	10	4	1805	69	3	2.29	....	....	....	....	....	....	....
2005-06	AL-Huntsville	CHA	31	17	11	2	1813	91	0	3.01	....	....	....	....	....	....	....
	Philadelphia	AHL	2	0	2	0	119	7	0	3.54	....	....	....	....	....	....	....
2006-07	Philadelphia	AHL	40	15	19	2	2298	117	2	3.05	....	....	....	....	....	....	....
2007-08	Philadelphia	AHL	36	18	8	2	1779	68	4	2.29	12	5	7	784	29	*2	2.22
2008-09	Philadelphia	AHL	56	31	19	4	3271	134	4	2.46	3	0	3	180	12	0	4.01
2009-10	Bridgeport	AHL	40	19	16	3	2310	97	3	2.52	3	0	3	110	10	0	5.46

CHA All-Rookie Team (2003) • CHA Rookie of the Year (2003)

Signed as a free agent by **Philadelphia** (AHL), March 18, 2006. Signed as a free agent by **NY Islanders**, July 2, 2009.

MURPHY, Mike (MUHR-fee, MIGHK) CAR.

Goaltender. Catches left. 5'11", 165 lbs. Born, Kingston, Ont., January 15, 1989.
(Carolina's 4th choice, 165th overall, in 2008 Entry Draft).

			Regular Season								Playoffs						
Season	Club	League	GP	W	L	O/T	Mins	GA	SO	Avg	GP	W	L	Mins	GA	SO	Avg
2005-06	Kingston	OPJHL	33	16	13	2	....	102	3	3.30	4	0	3	174	19	0	6.55
	Belleville Bulls	OHL	3	1	1	0	93	9	0	5.81	....	....	....	....	....	....	....
2006-07	Belleville Bulls	OHL	18	8	6	2	995	61	0	3.68	....	....	....	....	....	....	....
2007-08	Belleville Bulls	OHL	49	36	7	4	2942	110	3	*2.24	*19	*14	4	*1085	42	1	2.32
2008-09	Belleville Bulls	OHL	54	40	9	4	3169	110	5	*2.08	17	10	7	1007	43	0	2.56
2009-10	Albany River Rats	AHL	20	10	9	0	1109	52	2	2.81	....	....	....	....	....	....	....

OHL First All-Star Team (2008, 2009) • Canadian Major Junior Second All-Star Team (2008) • Canadian Major Junior First All-Star Team (2009) • Canadian Major Junior Goaltender of the Year (2009)

NABOKOV, Evgeni (na-BAW-kahv, ehv-GEH-nee)

Goaltender. Catches left. 6', 200 lbs. Born, Ust-Kamenogorsk, USSR, July 25, 1975.
(San Jose's 9th choice, 219th overall, in 1994 Entry Draft).

			Regular Season								Playoffs						
Season	Club	League	GP	W	L	O/T	Mins	GA	SO	Avg	GP	W	L	Mins	GA	SO	Avg
1991-92	Ust-Kamenogorsk	CIS	1	....	....	....	20	1	0	3.00	....	....	....	....	....	....	....
1992-93	Ust-Kam'gorsk 2	CIS-2	19	....	....	....	....	....	....	....	....	....	....	....	....	....	....
	Ust-Kamenogorsk	CIS	4	....	....	....	109	5	0	2.75	....	....	....	....	....	....	....
1993-94	Ust-Kamenogorsk	CIS	11	....	....	....	539	29	....	3.23	....	....	....	....	....	....	....
1994-95	Dynamo Moscow	CIS	24	....	....	....	1326	40	3	1.81	13	....	....	806	30	2	2.23
1995-96	Dynamo Moscow	CIS	39	....	....	....	2008	67	5	2.00	....	....	....	....	....	....	....
1996-97	Dynamo Moscow	Russia	27	....	....	....	1588	56	2	2.11	4	....	....	255	12	0	2.82
	Dynamo Moscow 2	Russia-3	1	....	....	....	....	2	....	....	....	....	....	....	....	....	....
1997-98	Kentucky	AHL	33	10	21	2	1866	122	0	3.92	1	0	0	23	1	0	2.59
1998-99	Kentucky	AHL	43	26	14	1	2429	106	5	2.62	11	6	5	599	30	*2	3.00
99-2000	**San Jose**	**NHL**	**11**	**2**	**2**	**1**	**414**	**15**	**1**	**2.17**	**1**	**0**	**0**	**20**	**0**	**0**	**0.00**
	Kentucky	AHL	2	1	1	0	120	3	1	1.50	....	....	....	....	....	....	....
	Cleveland	IHL	20	12	4	3	1164	52	0	2.68	....	....	....	....	....	....	....
2000-01	**San Jose**	**NHL**	**66**	**32**	**21**	**7**	**3700**	**135**	**6**	**2.19**	**4**	**1**	**3**	**218**	**10**	**1**	**2.75**
2001-02	**San Jose**	**NHL**	**67**	**37**	**24**	**5**	**3901**	**149**	**7**	**2.29**	**12**	**7**	**5**	**712**	**31**	**0**	**2.61**
2002-03	**San Jose**	**NHL**	**55**	**19**	**28**	**8**	**3227**	**146**	**3**	**2.71**	....	....	....	....	....	....	....
2003-04	**San Jose**	**NHL**	**59**	**31**	**19**	**8**	**3456**	**127**	**9**	**2.20**	**17**	**10**	**7**	**1052**	**30**	**3**	**1.71**
2004-05	Magnitogorsk	Russia	14	....	....	....	808	27	3	2.00	5	....	....	307	13	0	2.53
2005-06	**San Jose**	**NHL**	**45**	**16**	**19**	**7**	**2575**	**133**	**1**	**3.10**	**1**	**0**	**0**	**12**	**1**	**0**	**5.00**
	Russia	Olympics	7	4	2	0	359	8	3	1.34	....	....	....	....	....	....	....
2006-07	**San Jose**	**NHL**	**50**	**25**	**16**	**4**	**2778**	**106**	**7**	**2.29**	**11**	**6**	**5**	**701**	**26**	**1**	**2.23**
2007-08	**San Jose**	**NHL**	***77**	***46**	**21**	**8**	**4561**	**163**	**6**	**2.14**	**13**	**6**	**7**	**853**	**31**	**1**	**2.18**
2008-09	**San Jose**	**NHL**	**62**	**41**	**12**	**8**	**3686**	**150**	**7**	**2.44**	**6**	**2**	**4**	**362**	**17**	**0**	**2.82**
2009-10	**San Jose**	**NHL**	**71**	**44**	**16**	**10**	**4194**	**170**	**3**	**2.43**	**15**	**8**	**7**	**890**	**38**	**1**	**2.56**
	Russia	Olympics	3	2	1	0	144	10	0	4.16	....	....	....	....	....	....	....
	NHL Totals		**563**	**293**	**178**	**66**	**32492**	**1294**	**50**	**2.39**	**80**	**40**	**38**	**4820**	**184**	**7**	**2.29**

NHL All-Rookie Team (2001) • Calder Memorial Trophy (2001) • NHL First All-Star Team (2008)

Played in NHL All-Star Game (2001, 2008)

• Scored a goal vs. Vancouver, March 10, 2002. Signed as a free agent by **Magnitogorsk** (Russia), December 2, 2004. Signed as a free agent by **St. Petersburg** (Russia-KHL), July 7, 2010.

NEUVIRTH, Michal (NOI-vihrt, MIGHK-ahl) WSH.

Goaltender. Catches left. 6'1", 200 lbs. Born, Usti nad Labem, Czech., March 23, 1988.
(Washington's 3rd choice, 34th overall, in 2006 Entry Draft).

			Regular Season								Playoffs						
Season	Club	League	GP	W	L	O/T	Mins	GA	SO	Avg	GP	W	L	Mins	GA	SO	Avg
2003-04	Sparta U17	CzR-U17	55	....	....	....	3137	96	5	1.84	3	....	....	180	13	0	4.33
2004-05	Sparta U17	CzR-U17	20	....	....	....	1178	49	3	2.50	8	....	....	482	17	0	2.12
	Sparta Jr.	CzRep-Jr.	10	....	....	....	501	20	1	2.40	....	....	....	....	....	....	....
2005-06	Sparta Jr.	CzRep-Jr.	42	....	....	....	2516	82	5	1.96	3	....	....	179	9	0	3.02
2006-07	Plymouth Whalers	OHL	41	26	8	4	2223	86	4	*2.32	*18	*14	4	*1080	44	0	*2.44
2007-08	Plymouth Whalers	OHL	10	5	4	1	600	26	0	2.60	....	....	....	....	....	....	....
	Windsor Spitfires	OHL	8	6	1	1	482	17	0	2.12	....	....	....	....	....	....	....
	Oshawa Generals	OHL	15	6	2	6	844	57	0	4.05	9	7	2	507	21	0	2.49
2008-09	**Washington**	**NHL**	**5**	**2**	**1**	**0**	**220**	**11**	**0**	**3.00**	....	....	....	....	....	....	....
	Hershey Bears	AHL	17	9	5	2	1001	45	1	2.70	*22	*16	6	*1346	43	*4	1.92
	South Carolina	ECHL	13	6	7	0	762	29	2	2.28	....	....	....	....	....	....	....
2009-10	**Washington**	**NHL**	**17**	**9**	**4**	**0**	**872**	**40**	**0**	**2.75**	....	....	....	....	....	....	....
	Hershey Bears	AHL	22	15	6	0	1231	46	1	2.24	*18	*14	4	*1133	39	1	2.07
	NHL Totals		**22**	**11**	**5**	**0**	**1092**	**51**	**0**	**2.80**	....	....	....	....	....	....	....

OHL Second All-Star Team (2007)

NIEMI, Antti (nee-YEH-mee, AN-tee)

Goaltender. Catches left. 6'2", 210 lbs. Born, Vantaa, Finland, August 29, 1983.

			Regular Season								Playoffs						
Season	Club	League	GP	W	L	O/T	Mins	GA	SO	Avg	GP	W	L	Mins	GA	SO	Avg
2000-01	Kiekko-Vantaa Jr.	Fin-Jr.	4	....	....	....	....	....	....	6.86	....	....	....	....	....	....	....
2001-02	Kiekko-Vantaa	Finland-2	24	....	....	....	....	....	....	....	3	....	....	....	....	....	....
2002-03	Kiekko-Vantaa	Finland-2	....	....	....	....	364	16	0	2.63	....	....	....	....	....	....	....
2003-04	Kiekko-Vantaa Jr.	Fin-Jr.	19	....	....	....	1095	58	2	3.18	....	....	....	....	....	....	....
	Kiekko-Vantaa	Finland-2	19	....	....	....	1048	47	1	2.52	3	....	....	187	13	0	4.17
2004-05	Kiekko-Vantaa	Finland-2	38	....	....	....	2261	95	1	2.52	3	....	....	187	13	0	4.17
2005-06	Pelicans Lahti	Finland	40	12	17	8	2263	103	3	2.73	....	....	....	....	....	....	....
2006-07	Pelicans Lahti	Finland	48	18	21	7	2780	119	3	2.57	6	2	4	371	9	1	1.46
2007-08	Pelicans Lahti	Finland	49	26	14	6	2778	109	4	2.35	6	2	3	327	21	0	3.85
2008-09	**Chicago**	**NHL**	**3**	**1**	**1**	**1**	**141**	**8**	**0**	**3.40**	....	....	....	....	....	....	....
	Rockford IceHogs	AHL	38	18	14	3	2095	85	2	2.43	2	0	2	115	7	0	3.65
2009-10 ♦	**Chicago**	**NHL**	**39**	**26**	**7**	**4**	**2190**	**82**	**7**	**2.25**	***22**	***16**	**6**	***1322**	**58**	**2**	**2.63**
	NHL Totals		**42**	**27**	**8**	**5**	**2331**	**90**	**7**	**2.32**	**22**	**16**	**6**	**1322**	**58**	**2**	**2.63**

Signed as a free agent by **Chicago**, May 5, 2008.

NIITTYMAKI, Antero (nih-tih-MA-kee, AN-tehr-oh) S.J.

Goaltender. Catches left. 6'1", 190 lbs. Born, Turku, Finland, June 18, 1980.
(Philadelphia's 7th choice, 168th overall, in 1998 Entry Draft).

			Regular Season								Playoffs						
Season	Club	League	GP	W	L	O/T	Mins	GA	SO	Avg	GP	W	L	Mins	GA	SO	Avg
1997-98	TPS Turku U18	Fin-U18	12	....	....	....	....	....	....	....	1	1	0	60	1	0	1.00
	TPS Turku Jr.	Fin-Jr.	19	10	8	1	1131	34	....	1.80	4	3	1	220	7	0	1.91
1998-99	TPS Turku Jr.	Fin-Jr.	35	27	8	0	2095	60	3	1.72	6	3	3	362	14	0	2.32
99-2000	TPS Turku Jr.	Fin-Jr.	1	1	0	0	60	1	0	1.00	1	0	1	60	5	0	5.00
	TPS Turku	Finland	32	23	6	3	1899	68	3	2.15	8	6	2	453	13	0	1.72
2000-01	TPS Turku Jr.	Fin-Jr.	....	....	....	....	....	....	....	....	2	1	1	120	4	1	2.00
	TPS Turku	Finland	21	10	5	1	1112	46	2	2.48	....	....	....	....	....	....	....
2001-02	TPS Turku	Finland	27	16	8	1	1498	46	3	1.84	4	2	2	295	11	0	2.24
2002-03	Philadelphia	AHL	40	14	21	2	2283	98	0	2.58	....	....	....	....	....	....	....
2003-04	**Philadelphia**	**NHL**	**3**	**3**	**0**	**0**	**180**	**3**	**0**	**1.00**	....	....	....	....	....	....	....
	Philadelphia	AHL	49	24	13	6	2728	92	7	2.02	12	6	6	796	24	0	1.81
2004-05	Philadelphia	AHL	58	33	21	4	3453	119	6	2.07	*21	*15	5	*1269	37	*3	1.75
2005-06	**Philadelphia**	**NHL**	**46**	**23**	**15**	**6**	**2690**	**133**	**2**	**2.97**	**2**	**0**	**0**	**73**	**5**	**0**	**4.11**
	Finland	Olympics	6	5	1	0	359	8	3	1.34	....	....	....	....	....	....	....
2006-07	**Philadelphia**	**NHL**	**52**	**9**	**29**	**9**	**2943**	**166**	**0**	**3.38**	....	....	....	....	....	....	....
2007-08	**Philadelphia**	**NHL**	**28**	**12**	**9**	**2**	**1424**	**69**	**1**	**2.91**	....	....	....	....	....	....	....
2008-09	**Philadelphia**	**NHL**	**32**	**15**	**8**	**6**	**1805**	**83**	**1**	**2.76**	....	....	....	....	....	....	....
2009-10	**Tampa Bay**	**NHL**	**49**	**21**	**18**	**5**	**2657**	**127**	**1**	**2.87**	....	....	....	....	....	....	....
	Finland	Olympics	DID NOT PLAY – SPARE GOALTENDER														
	NHL Totals		**210**	**83**	**79**	**28**	**11699**	**581**	**5**	**2.98**	**2**	**0**	**0**	**73**	**5**	**0**	**4.11**

Jack A. Butterfield Trophy (AHL – Playoff MVP) (2005) • Olympic Tournament All-Star Team (2006) • Olympic Tournament – Best Goaltender (2006) • Olympic Tournament – MVP (2006)

Signed as a free agent by **Tampa Bay**, July 10, 2009. Signed as a free agent by **San Jose**, July 1, 2010.

NILSSON, Anders (NIHL-suhn, AN-duhrz) NY

Goaltender. Catches left. 6'5", 220 lbs. Born, Lulea, Sweden, March 19, 1990.
(NY Islanders' 4th choice, 62nd overall, in 2009 Entry Draft).

			Regular Season								Playoffs						
Season	Club	League	GP	W	L	O/T	Mins	GA	SO	Avg	GP	W	L	Mins	GA	SO	Av
2004-05	Lulea HF Jr.	Swe-Jr.	1	....	....	....	24	4	0	9.90	....	....	....	....	....	....	..
2007-08	Lulea HF U18	Swe-U18	11	....	....	....	625	31	0	2.97	....	....	....	....	....	....	..
	Lulea HF Jr.	Swe-Jr.	16	....	....	....	898	31	2	2.07	1	....	....	60	6	0	6.0
2008-09	Lulea HF Jr.	Swe-Jr.	37	....	....	....	2199	75	4	2.05	6	....	....	357	14	1	2.3
	Lulea HF	Sweden	1	....	....	....	28	0	0	0.00	....	....	....	....	....	....	..
	Kalix Ungdoms HC	Sweden-3	1	....	....	....	59	3	0	3.05	....	....	....	....	....	....	..
2009-10	Lulea HF Jr.	Swe-Jr.	4	....	....	....	244	12	0	2.95	....	....	....	....	....	....	..
	Lulea HF	Sweden	27	....	....	....	1383	61	2	2.65	....	....	....	....	....	....	..

ORTIO, Joni (OHR-tee-oh, YOH-nee) CGY

Goaltender. Catches left. 6'1", 185 lbs. Born, Turku, Finland, April 16, 1991.
(Calgary's 5th choice, 171st overall, in 2009 Entry Draft).

			Regular Season								Playoffs						
Season	Club	League	GP	W	L	O/T	Mins	GA	SO	Avg	GP	W	L	Mins	GA	SO	Av
2007-08	TuTo Turku U18	Fin-U18	7	1	6	0	392	34	0	5.20	....	....	....	....	....	....	..
	TuTo Turku Jr.	Fin-Jr.	5	1	3	0	302	16	0	3.18	....	....	....	....	....	....	..
2008-09	TPS Turku U18	Fin-U18	1	1	0	0	60	4	0	4.00	....	....	....	....	....	....	..
	TPS Turku Jr.	Fin-Jr.	26	18	8	0	1573	69	1	2.63	12	6	6	716	23	0	1.9
2009-10	Suomi U20	Finland-2	5	3	2	0	312	11	0	2.12	....	....	....	....	....	....	..
	TuTo Turku	Finland-2	9	5	4	0	546	27	0	2.96	....	....	....	....	....	....	..
	TPS Turku Jr.	Fin-Jr.	16	8	6	0	935	45	1	2.89	....	....	....	....	....	....	..
	TPS Turku	Finland	3	1	0	0	108	8	0	4.45	....	....	....	....	....	....	..

OSGOOD, Chris (AWS-gud, KRIHS) DET

Goaltender. Catches left. 5'10", 180 lbs. Born, Peace River, Alta., November 26, 1972.
(Detroit's 3rd choice, 54th overall, in 1991 Entry Draft).

			Regular Season								Playoffs						
Season	Club	League	GP	W	L	O/T	Mins	GA	SO	Avg	GP	W	L	Mins	GA	SO	Av
1988-89	Medicine Hat	AMHL	26	....	....	....	1441	88	0	3.66	....	....	....	....	....	....	.
1989-90	Medicine Hat	WHL	57	24	28	2	3094	228	0	4.42	3	0	3	173	17	0	5.9
1990-91	Medicine Hat	WHL	46	23	18	3	2630	173	2	3.95	12	7	5	712	42	0	3.5
1991-92	Medicine Hat	WHL	15	10	3	0	819	44	0	3.22	....	....	....	....	....	....	.
	Brandon	WHL	16	3	10	1	890	60	1	4.04	....	....	....	....	....	....	.
	Seattle	WHL	21	12	7	1	1217	65	1	3.20	15	9	6	904	51	0	3.3
1992-93	Adirondack	AHL	45	19	19	4	2438	159	0	3.91	1	0	1	59	2	0	2.0
1993-94	**Detroit**	**NHL**	**41**	**23**	**8**	**5**	**2206**	**105**	**2**	**2.86**	**6**	**3**	**2**	**307**	**12**	**1**	**2.3**
	Adirondack	AHL	4	3	1	0	239	13	0	3.26	....	....	....	....	....	....	.
1994-95	**Detroit**	**NHL**	**19**	**14**	**5**	**0**	**1087**	**41**	**1**	**2.26**	**2**	**0**	**0**	**68**	**2**	**0**	**1.7**
	Adirondack	AHL	2	1	1	0	120	6	0	3.00	....	....	....	....	....	....	.
1995-96	**Detroit**	**NHL**	**50**	***39**	**6**	**5**	**2933**	**106**	**5**	**2.17**	**15**	**8**	**7**	**936**	**33**	**2**	**2.1**
1996-97 ♦	**Detroit**	**NHL**	**47**	**23**	**13**	**9**	**2769**	**106**	**6**	**2.30**	**2**	**0**	**0**	**47**	**2**	**0**	**2.5**
1997-98 ♦	**Detroit**	**NHL**	**64**	**33**	**20**	**11**	**3807**	**140**	**6**	**2.21**	***22**	***16**	**6**	***1361**	**48**	**2**	**2.1**
1998-99	**Detroit**	**NHL**	**63**	**34**	**25**	**4**	**3691**	**149**	**3**	**2.42**	**6**	**4**	**2**	**358**	**14**	**1**	**2.3**
99-2000	**Detroit**	**NHL**	**53**	**30**	**14**	**8**	**3148**	**126**	**6**	**2.40**	**9**	**5**	**4**	**547**	**18**	**2**	**1.9**
2000-01	**Detroit**	**NHL**	**52**	**25**	**19**	**4**	**2834**	**127**	**1**	**2.69**	**6**	**2**	**4**	**365**	**15**	**1**	**2.4**
2001-02	**NY Islanders**	**NHL**	**66**	**32**	**25**	**6**	**3743**	**156**	**4**	**2.50**	**7**	**3**	**4**	**392**	**17**	**0**	**2.6**
2002-03	**NY Islanders**	**NHL**	**37**	**17**	**14**	**4**	**1993**	**97**	**2**	**2.92**	....	....	....	....	....	....	.
	St. Louis	**NHL**	**9**	**4**	**3**	**2**	**532**	**27**	**2**	**3.05**	**7**	**3**	**4**	**417**	**17**	**1**	**2.4**
2003-04	**St. Louis**	**NHL**	**67**	**31**	**25**	**8**	**3861**	**144**	**3**	**2.24**	**5**	**1**	**4**	**287**	**12**	**0**	**2.5**
2004-05			DID NOT PLAY														
2005-06	**Detroit**	**NHL**	**32**	**20**	**6**	**5**	**1846**	**85**	**2**	**2.76**	....	....	....	....	....	....	.
	Grand Rapids	AHL	3	2	1	0	180	10	0	3.34	....	....	....	....	....	....	.
2006-07	**Detroit**	**NHL**	**21**	**11**	**3**	**6**	**1161**	**46**	**0**	**2.38**	....	....	....	....	....	....	.
2007-08 ♦	**Detroit**	**NHL**	**43**	**27**	**9**	**4**	**2409**	**84**	**4**	***2.09**	**19**	***14**	**4**	**1160**	**30**	***3**	***1.5**
2008-09	**Detroit**	**NHL**	**46**	**26**	**9**	**8**	**2663**	**137**	**2**	**3.09**	**23**	**15**	**8**	**1406**	**47**	***2**	**2.0**
2009-10	**Detroit**	**NHL**	**23**	**7**	**9**	**4**	**1252**	**63**	**1**	**3.02**	....	....	....	....	....	....	.
	NHL Totals		**733**	**396**	**213**	**93**	**41935**	**1739**	**50**	**2.49**	**129**	**74**	**49**	**7651**	**267**	**15**	**2.0**

WHL East Second All-Star Team (1991) • NHL Second All-Star Team (1996) • William M. Jennings Trophy (1996) (shared with Mike Vernon) • William M. Jennings Trophy (2008) (shared with Dominik Hasek)

Played in NHL All-Star Game (1996, 2008)

• Scored a goal while with Medicine Hat (WHL), January 3, 1991. • Scored a goal vs. Hartford, March 6, 1996. Claimed by **NY Islanders** from **Detroit** in Waiver Draft, September 28, 2001. Traded to **St. Louis** by **NY Islanders** with NY Islanders' 3rd round choice (Konstantin Barulin) in 2003 Entry Draft for Justin Papineau and St. Louis' 2nd round choice (Jeremy Colliton) in 2003 Entr Draft, March 11, 2003. Signed as a free agent by **Detroit**, August 8, 2005.

OUELLETTE, Martin (OO-leht, MAHR-tihn) CE

Goaltender. Catches left. 6'2", 168 lbs. Born, Saint-Jerome, Que., December 30, 1991.
(Columbus' 8th choice, 184th overall, in 2010 Entry Draft).

			Regular Season								Playoffs						
Season	Club	League	GP	W	L	O/T	Mins	GA	SO	Avg	GP	W	L	Mins	GA	SO	A
2008-09	Kimball Union	High-NH	16	....	....	....	....	....	....	2.93	....	....	....	....	....	....	
2009-10	Kimball Union	High-NH	29	21	6	2	1461	45	....	1.61	....	....	....	....	....	....	

• Signed Letter of Intent to attend **University of Maine** (Hockey East) in fall of 2010.

PALMER, Joe (PAHL-muhr, JOH) CH

Goaltender. Catches left. 6'2", 190 lbs. Born, Yorkville, NY, February 19, 1988.
(Chicago's 6th choice, 96th overall, in 2006 Entry Draft).

			Regular Season								Playoffs						
Season	Club	League	GP	W	L	O/T	Mins	GA	SO	Avg	GP	W	L	Mins	GA	SO	A
2003-04	Syracuse Jr. Stars	EmJHL	31	....	....	....	1147	69	1	3.61	6	....	....	368	19	0	3.
	USNTDP	U-17	1	0	0	0	11	2	0	10.91	....	....	....	....	....	....	
2004-05	USNTDP	U-17	8	6	1	1	495	22	0	2.67	....	....	....	....	....	....	
	USNTDP	NAHL	19	10	8	1	1020	56	0	3.29	....	....	....	....	....	....	
2005-06	USNTDP	U-18	33	16	14	3	1900	99	0	3.13	....	....	....	....	....	....	
	USNTDP	NAHL	14	13	1	0	776	22	1	1.70	....	....	....	....	....	....	
2006-07	Ohio State	CCHA	34	15	15	4	1968	97	1	2.96	....	....	....	....	....	....	
2007-08	Ohio State	CCHA	34	10	19	4	1980	103	1	3.12	....	....	....	....	....	....	
2008-09	Ohio State	CCHA	3	0	2	1	122	11	0	5.40	....	....	....	....	....	....	
2009-10	Texas Brahmas	CHL	32	13	10	4	1786	82	*3	2.75	3	0	1	117	4	0	2.

PASQUALE, Edward (pas-KWAHL-ee, EHD-wuhrd) AT

Goaltender. Catches left. 6'2", 220 lbs. Born, Toronto, Ont., November 20, 1990.
(Atlanta's 4th choice, 117th overall, in 2009 Entry Draft).

			Regular Season								Playoffs						
Season	Club	League	GP	W	L	O/T	Mins	GA	SO	Avg	GP	W	L	Mins	GA	SO	A
2006-07	Wellington Dukes	OPJHL	18	13	3	2	1091	35	1	1.92	....	....	....	....	....	....	
	Belleville Bulls	OHL	7	4	1	0	367	19	0	3.11	....	....	....	....	....	....	
2007-08	Belleville Bulls	OHL	10	4	4	2	558	27	1	2.90	....	....	....	....	....	....	
	Saginaw Spirit	OHL	13	8	5	0	661	39	0	3.54	2	0	1	97	5	0	3.
2008-09	Saginaw Spirit	OHL	*61	32	21	6	*3536	178	0	3.02	8	4	4	530	34	0	3.
2009-10	Saginaw Spirit	OHL	51	27	17	5	2898	153	1	3.17	6	2	3	361	14	0	2.

ATTERSON, Kent (PA-tuhr-suhn, KEHNT) COL.

oaltender. Catches left. 6', 184 lbs. Born, St. Louis Park, MN, September 15, 1989.
Colorado's 6th choice, 113th overall, in 2007 Entry Draft).

			Regular Season								Playoffs						
eason	Club	League	GP	W	L	O/T	Mins	GA	SO	Avg	GP	W	L	Mins	GA	SO	Avg
04-05	Blake Bears	High-MN	14	9	4	1	673	27	....	2.05	....	....	....	....	....	....	....
05-06	Blake Bears	High-MN	25	14	8	2	1249	66	....	2.70	....	....	....	....	....	....	....
06-07	Cedar Rapids	USHL	29	20	5	3	1710	83	2	2.91	1	0	1	41	6	0	8.78
07-08	Cedar Rapids	USHL	20	10	6	1	1110	46	1	2.49	....	....	....	....	....	....	....
08-09	U. of Minnesota	WCHA	7	0	2	1	231	9	0	2.34	....	....	....	....	....	....	....
09-10	U. of Minnesota	WCHA	8	2	4	1	406	21	0	3.10	....	....	....	....	....	....	....

SHL All-Rookie Team (2007)

AVELEC, Ondrej (pah-vah-LEK, AWN-dray) ATL.

oaltender. Catches left. 6'3", 220 lbs. Born, Kladno, Czech., August 31, 1987.
tlanta's 2nd choice, 41st overall, in 2005 Entry Draft).

			Regular Season								Playoffs						
eason	Club	League	GP	W	L	O/T	Mins	GA	SO	Avg	GP	W	L	Mins	GA	SO	Avg
03-04	HC Kladno U17	CzR-U17	38	....	....	....	2079	77	3	2.22	2	....	....	67	7	0	6.27
04-05	HC Kladno Jr.	CzRep-Jr.	39	....	....	....	2218	85	7	2.30	10	....	....	587	24	1	2.45
	HK LEV Slany	CzRep-3	1	....	....	....	60	4	0	4.00	....	....	....	....	....	....	....
05-06	Cape Breton	QMJHL	47	27	18	0	2578	108	3	2.51	9	4	5	507	19	0	*2.25
06-07	Cape Breton	QMJHL	43	28	11	....	2335	98	1	*2.52	16	11	5	970	37	*2	*2.29
07-08	**Atlanta**	**NHL**	**7**	**3**	**3**	**0**	**347**	**18**	**0**	**3.11**	....	....	....	....	....	....	....
	Chicago Wolves	AHL	52	33	16	3	3033	140	2	2.77	*24	*16	8	*1438	56	*2	2.34
08-09	**Atlanta**	**NHL**	**12**	**3**	**7**	**0**	**599**	**36**	**0**	**3.61**	....	....	....	....	....	....	....
	Chicago Wolves	AHL	40	18	20	2	2417	104	3	2.58	....	....	....	....	....	....	....
09-10	**Atlanta**	**NHL**	**42**	**14**	**18**	**7**	**2317**	**127**	**2**	**3.29**	....	....	....	....	....	....	....
	Czech Republic	Olympics	DID NOT PLAY – SPARE GOALTENDER														
	NHL Totals		**61**	**20**	**28**	**7**	**3263**	**181**	**2**	**3.33**	....	....	....	....	....	....	....

MJHL All-Rookie Team (2006) • QMJHL First All-Star Team (2006, 2007) • QMJHL Defensive
ookie of the Year (2006)

EARCE, Jordan (PEERS-JOHR-dahn) DET.

oaltender. Catches left. 6'1", 201 lbs. Born, Anchorage, AK, October 10, 1986.

			Regular Season								Playoffs						
ason	Club	League	GP	W	L	O/T	Mins	GA	SO	Avg	GP	W	L	Mins	GA	SO	Avg
04-05	Lincoln Stars	USHL	38	22	10	4	2227	114	0	3.07	2	0	1	69	7	0	6.06
05-06	U. of Notre Dame	CCHA	9	4	4	0	442	24	1	3.25	....	....	....	....	....	....	....
06-07	U. of Notre Dame	CCHA	3	2	1	0	180	6	1	2.01	....	....	....	....	....	....	....
07-08	U. of Notre Dame	CCHA	*43	23	15	4	*2558	87	2	2.04	....	....	....	....	....	....	....
08-09	U. of Notre Dame	CCHA	*39	*30	6	3	*2326	65	8	1.68	....	....	....	....	....	....	....
	Grand Rapids	AHL	1	0	1	0	59	5	0	5.11	....	....	....	....	....	....	....
09-10	Grand Rapids	AHL	5	1	2	0	236	15	0	3.82	....	....	....	....	....	....	....
	Toledo Walleye	ECHL	37	15	16	2	2047	124	2	3.63	4	1	2	247	16	0	3.88

gned as a free agent by **Detroit**, April 10, 2009.

ECHURSKI, Alexander (puh-CHUHR-skee, al-ehx-AN-duhr) PIT.

oaltender. Catches left. 6', 187 lbs. Born, Magnitogorsk, USSR, June 4, 1990.
ttsburgh's 2nd choice, 150th overall, in 2008 Entry Draft).

			Regular Season								Playoffs						
ason	Club	League	GP	W	L	O/T	Mins	GA	SO	Avg	GP	W	L	Mins	GA	SO	Avg
07-08	Magnitogorsk 2	Russia-3	27	....	....	....	....	62	....	....	....	....	....	....	....	....	....
	Magnitogorsk	Russia	1	....	....	....	1	0	0	0.00	....	....	....	....	....	....	....
08-09	Magnitogorsk 2	Russia-3	20	....	....	....	....	54	....	....	....	....	....	....	....	....	....
09-10	Magnitogorsk	Rus-KHL	1	....	....	....	30	3	0	6.00	....	....	....	....	....	....	....
	Magnitogorsk Jr.	Russia-Jr.	5	....	....	....	299	14	0	2.81	....	....	....	....	....	....	....
	Pittsburgh	**NHL**	**1**	**0**	**0**	**0**	**36**	**1**	**0**	**1.67**	....	....	....	....	....	....	....
	Tri-City Americans	WHL	27	13	10	1	1403	61	4	2.61	7	1	2	305	15	0	2.95
	NHL Totals		**1**	**0**	**0**	**0**	**36**	**1**	**0**	**1.67**	....	....	....	....	....	....	....

ETERS, Justin (PEE-tuhrz, JUHS-tihn) CAR.

oaltender. Catches left. 6'1", 205 lbs. Born, Blyth, Ont., August 30, 1986.
arolina's 2nd choice, 38th overall, in 2004 Entry Draft).

			Regular Season								Playoffs						
ason	Club	League	GP	W	L	O/T	Mins	GA	SO	Avg	GP	W	L	Mins	GA	SO	Avg
01-02	Huron-Perth	Minor-ON	17	11	2	4	810	32	1	1.89	13	9	4	285	30	1	2.31
02-03	St. Michael's	OHL	23	6	10	1	1052	54	0	3.08	7	1	0	126	4	0	1.90
03-04	St. Michael's	OHL	53	30	16	6	3149	139	4	2.65	18	10	8	1109	37	4	2.00
4-05	St. Michael's	OHL	58	23	23	5	3150	146	3	2.78	10	4	4	524	25	0	2.86
5-06	St. Michael's	OHL	20	10	6	3	1174	75	0	3.83	....	....	....	....	....	....	....
	Plymouth Whalers	OHL	35	19	15	1	2073	95	1	2.75	13	6	7	789	42	0	3.19
06-07	Albany River Rats	AHL	34	10	18	0	1765	96	1	3.26	....	....	....	....	....	....	....
	Florida Everblades	ECHL	1	0	0	1	65	6	0	5.54	....	....	....	....	....	....	....
07-08	Albany River Rats	AHL	11	7	3	0	645	29	0	2.70	....	....	....	....	....	....	....
	Florida Everblades	ECHL	31	18	10	2	1846	79	1	2.57	....	....	....	....	....	....	....
08-09	Albany River Rats	AHL	56	19	30	4	3178	153	4	2.89	....	....	....	....	....	....	....
09-10	**Carolina**	**NHL**	**9**	**6**	**3**	**0**	**488**	**23**	**0**	**2.83**	....	....	....	....	....	....	....
	Albany River Rats	AHL	47	26	18	2	2763	117	1	2.54	8	4	4	509	29	0	3.42
	NHL Totals		**9**	**6**	**3**	**0**	**488**	**23**	**0**	**2.83**	....	....	....	....	....	....	....

TTERSSON-WENTZEL, Fredrik PEH-tuhr-suhn-WEHNT-zuhl, FREH-drik ATL.

altender. Catches left. 6'1", 180 lbs. Born, Uppsala, Sweden, July 23, 1991.
lanta's 4th choice, 128th overall, in 2010 Entry Draft).

			Regular Season								Playoffs						
ason	Club	League	GP	W	L	O/T	Mins	GA	SO	Avg	GP	W	L	Mins	GA	SO	Avg
08-09	Almtuna U18	Swe-U18	25	....	....	....	1457	59	3	2.43	....	....	....	....	....	....	....
	Almtuna Jr.	Swe-Jr.	1	....	....	....	29	0	0	0.00	....	....	....	....	....	....	....
09-10	Almtuna Jr.	Swe-Jr.	5	....	....	....	299	10	2	2.01	....	....	....	....	....	....	....
	Nykopings HK	Sweden-3	1	....	....	....	60	3	0	3.00	....	....	....	....	....	....	....
	Almtuna	Sweden-2	47	....	....	....	2746	88	7	1.92	5	....	....	311	11	0	2.12

ILLIPS, Brad (FIHL-ihps , BRAD) PHI.

altender. Catches left. 6'2", 163 lbs. Born, Allen Park, MI, April 22, 1989.
iladelphia's 7th choice, 182nd overall, in 2007 Entry Draft).

			Regular Season								Playoffs						
ason	Club	League	GP	W	L	O/T	Mins	GA	SO	Avg	GP	W	L	Mins	GA	SO	Avg
4-05	Det. Honeybaked	MWEHL	38	32	3	3	....	50	10	1.32	....	....	....	....	....	....	....
5-06	USNTDP	U-17	13	8	5	0	610	28	....	2.75	....	....	....	....	....	....	....
	USNTDP	NAHL	21	12	6	3	1261	51	0	2.43	4	1	3	254	12	0	2.83
6-07	USNTDP	U-18	12	7	1	2	706	29	0	2.46	....	....	....	....	....	....	....
	USNTDP	NAHL	11	8	3	0	660	24	2	2.18	1	0	1	60	3	0	3.00
7-08	U. of Notre Dame	CCHA	5	4	1	0	275	7	1	1.53	....	....	....	....	....	....	....
8-09	U. of Notre Dame	CCHA	DID NOT PLAY – INJURED														
9-10	U. of Notre Dame	CCHA	10	2	3	3	559	23	1	2.47	....	....	....	....	....	....	....

lissed entire 2008-09 season recovering from pre-season knee injury.

PICKARD, Calvin (pih-KARD, KAL-vihn) COL.

Goaltender. Catches left. 6'1", 195 lbs. Born, Moncton, N.B., April 15, 1992.
(Colorado's 2nd choice, 49th overall, in 2010 Entry Draft).

			Regular Season								Playoffs						
Season	Club	League	GP	W	L	O/T	Mins	GA	SO	Avg	GP	W	L	Mins	GA	SO	Avg
2007-08	Winnipeg Wild	MMHL	40	....	....	....	....	....	....	1.91	....	....	....	....	....	....	....
2008-09	Seattle	WHL	47	23	16	5	2694	137	3	3.05	5	1	4	....	15	0	3.03
2009-10	Seattle	WHL	*62	16	34	12	*3688	190	3	3.09	....	....	....	....	....	....	....

WHL West First All-Star Team (2010)

PICKARD, Chet (PIH-kuhrd, CHEHT) NSH.

Goaltender. Catches left. 6'2", 210 lbs. Born, Moncton, N.B., November 29, 1989.
(Nashville's 2nd choice, 18th overall, in 2008 Entry Draft).

			Regular Season								Playoffs						
Season	Club	League	GP	W	L	O/T	Mins	GA	SO	Avg	GP	W	L	Mins	GA	SO	Avg
2004-05	Wpg. Monarchs	MMHL	22	....	....	....	1264	55	2	2.61	....	....	....	....	....	....	....
2005-06	Tri-City Americans	WHL	26	9	9	1	1270	62	3	2.93	....	....	....	....	....	....	....
2006-07	Tri-City Americans	WHL	29	17	10	1	1577	75	1	2.85	1	0	0	20	1	0	3.00
2007-08	Tri-City Americans	WHL	*64	*46	12	4	*3779	146	2	2.32	16	11	5	1010	30	*3	1.78
2008-09	Tri-City Americans	WHL	50	35	12	3	2947	112	6	2.28	11	6	5	650	37	0	3.41
2009-10	Milwaukee	AHL	36	14	16	3	2024	96	1	2.85	1	0	0	12	1	0	5.08

WHL West First All-Star Team (2008, 2009) • WHL Goaltender of the Year (2008, 2009) • Canadian Major Junior First All-Star Team (2008) • Canadian Major Junior Goaltender of the Year (2008)

PIELMEIER, Timo (PEEL-migh-uhr, TEE-moh) ANA.

Goaltender. Catches left. 6', 167 lbs. Born, Deggendorf, West Germany, July 7, 1989.
(San Jose's 3rd choice, 83rd overall, in 2007 Entry Draft).

			Regular Season								Playoffs						
Season	Club	League	GP	W	L	O/T	Mins	GA	SO	Avg	GP	W	L	Mins	GA	SO	Avg
2004-05	Mannheimer ERC	German-5	1	....	....	....	....	....	....	8.15	....	....	....	....	....	....	....
	Mannheim Jr.	Ger-Jr.	10	....	....	....	568	33	....	3.49	....	....	....	....	....	....	....
2005-06	Koln Jr.	Ger-Jr.	8	....	....	....	459	52	....	6.79	2	....	....	100	17	....	10.20
2006-07	Koln Jr.	Ger-Jr.	20	....	....	....	1159	77	....	3.99	6	....	....	370	17	....	2.76
2007-08	St. John's	QMJHL	50	23	26	....	2719	133	1	2.94	5	0	3	231	22	0	5.71
2008-09	Shawinigan	QMJHL	43	29	11	....	2407	106	2	2.64	*18	12	5	1021	47	0	2.76
2009-10	Bakersfield	ECHL	57	27	22	5	3251	178	0	3.29	4	1	2	247	14	0	3.39

Traded to **Anaheim** by **San Jose** with Nick Bonino and future considerations for Travis Moen and Kent Huskins, March 4, 2009.

PITTON, Bryan (PIH-tuhn, BRIGH-uhn) EDM.

Goaltender. Catches left. 6'2", 168 lbs. Born, Mississauga, Ont., January 26, 1988.
(Edmonton's 3rd choice, 133rd overall, in 2006 Entry Draft).

			Regular Season								Playoffs						
Season	Club	League	GP	W	L	O/T	Mins	GA	SO	Avg	GP	W	L	Mins	GA	SO	Avg
2004-05	Wellington Dukes	OPJHL	....	24	7	3	....	....	2	2.93	....	....	....	....	....	....	....
2005-06	Brampton Battalion	OHL	24	16	4	0	1293	74	0	3.43	2	0	0	45	5	0	6.67
2006-07	Brampton Battalion	OHL	61	26	29	4	3494	208	0	3.57	4	0	4	270	15	0	3.33
2007-08	Brampton Battalion	OHL	39	22	13	2	2153	91	*4	2.54	5	1	4	333	10	0	*1.80
	Springfield Falcons	AHL	1	0	0	0	12	1	0	4.88	....	....	....	....	....	....	....
2008-09	Stockton Thunder	ECHL	34	9	19	3	1949	110	0	3.39	3	1	2	144	12	0	5.01
2009-10	Springfield Falcons	AHL	8	2	6	0	458	36	0	4.71	....	....	....	....	....	....	....
	Stockton Thunder	ECHL	22	9	9	3	1242	59	1	2.85	4	2	1	247	7	1	1.70

PLANTE, Tyler (PLAWNT, TIGH-luhr) FLA.

Goaltender. Catches left. 6'3", 191 lbs. Born, Milwaukee, WI, April 16, 1987.
(Florida's 2nd choice, 32nd overall, in 2005 Entry Draft).

			Regular Season								Playoffs						
Season	Club	League	GP	W	L	O/T	Mins	GA	SO	Avg	GP	W	L	Mins	GA	SO	Avg
2003-04	Brandon	WHL	2	0	0	1	58	2	0	2.07	....	....	....	....	....	....	....
2004-05	Brandon	WHL	48	34	11	2	2833	122	6	2.58	*24	*13	11	*1408	69	0	2.94
2005-06	Brandon	WHL	60	25	24	9	3414	189	2	3.32	6	2	4	360	18	0	3.00
2006-07	Brandon	WHL	54	30	14	9	3215	145	4	2.71	11	6	5	659	37	0	3.37
2007-08	Rochester	AHL	25	6	16	1	1451	86	0	3.56	....	....	....	....	....	....	....
	Florida Everblades	ECHL	10	4	5	1	598	28	1	2.81	....	....	....	....	....	....	....
2008-09	Rochester	AHL	19	5	10	1	904	49	0	3.25	....	....	....	....	....	....	....
	Dayton Bombers	ECHL	19	6	11	1	1076	60	0	3.35	....	....	....	....	....	....	....
2009-10	Rochester	AHL	27	12	12	1	1487	66	3	2.66	7	3	3	346	14	0	2.43

WHL Rookie of the Year (2005) • Canadian Major Junior All-Rookie Team (2005)

POGGE, Justin (POH-gee, JUHS-tihn) CAR.

Goaltender. Catches left. 6'3", 204 lbs. Born, Ft. McMurray, Alta., April 22, 1986.
(Toronto's 1st choice, 90th overall, in 2004 Entry Draft).

			Regular Season								Playoffs						
Season	Club	League	GP	W	L	O/T	Mins	GA	SO	Avg	GP	W	L	Mins	GA	SO	Avg
2002-03	Summerland Sting	KIJHL	30	....	....	....	1761	91	0	3.13	....	....	....	....	....	....	....
2003-04	Prince George	WHL	44	17	18	2	2271	107	3	2.83	....	....	....	....	....	....	....
2004-05	Prince George	WHL	24	10	9	2	1198	56	4	2.80	....	....	....	....	....	....	....
	Calgary Hitmen	WHL	29	14	12	3	1727	66	2	2.29	12	7	5	742	24	1	1.94
2005-06	Calgary Hitmen	WHL	54	38	10	6	3237	93	*11	*1.72	13	7	6	802	34	2	2.54
2006-07	Toronto Marlies	AHL	48	19	25	2	2812	142	3	3.03	....	....	....	....	....	....	....
2007-08	Toronto Marlies	AHL	41	26	10	4	2415	94	4	2.34	4	1	1	172	6	0	2.09
2008-09	**Toronto**	**NHL**	**7**	**1**	**4**	**1**	**372**	**27**	**0**	**4.35**	....	....	....	....	....	....	....
	Toronto Marlies	AHL	53	26	21	5	3155	142	0	2.70	5	2	3	304	16	0	3.15
2009-10	San Antonio	AHL	23	12	7	3	1332	57	1	2.57	....	....	....	....	....	....	....
	Bakersfield	ECHL	9	6	2	0	491	22	1	2.69	....	....	....	....	....	....	....
	Albany River Rats	AHL	4	1	0	2	199	8	0	2.41	....	....	....	....	....	....	....
	NHL Totals		**7**	**1**	**4**	**1**	**372**	**27**	**0**	**4.35**	....	....	....	....	....	....	....

WHL East First All-Star Team (2006) • WHL Goaltender of the Year (2006) • WHL Player of the Year (2006) • Canadian Major Junior First All-Star Team (2006) • Canadian Major Junior Goaltender of the Year (2006)

Traded to **Anaheim** by **Toronto** for future considerations, August 10, 2009. Traded to **Carolina** by **Anaheim** with Boston's 4th round choice (previously acquired, Carolina selected Justin Shugg) in 2010 Entry Draft for Aaron Ward, March 3, 2010.

POULIN, Kevin (POO-lihn, KEH-vihn) NYI

Goaltender. Catches left. 6'2", 210 lbs. Born, Montreal, Que., April 12, 1990.
(NY Islanders' 10th choice, 126th overall, in 2008 Entry Draft).

			Regular Season								Playoffs						
Season	Club	League	GP	W	L	O/T	Mins	GA	SO	Avg	GP	W	L	Mins	GA	SO	Avg
2005-06	C.C. Lemoyne	QAAA	27	13	8	2	1440	71	1	2.96	7	4	3	373	16	1	2.57
2006-07	Victoriaville Tigres	QMJHL	24	10	6	....	1220	68	0	3.34	2	0	0	42	5	0	7.20
2007-08	Victoriaville Tigres	QMJHL	52	18	24	....	2734	168	0	3.69	6	2	4	279	27	0	5.80
2008-09	Victoriaville Tigres	QMJHL	39	18	19	....	2273	120	1	3.17	4	0	4	249	18	0	4.34
2009-10	Victoriaville Tigres	QMJHL	54	35	16	....	3105	136	7	2.63	16	10	6	971	46	0	2.84

QMJHL Second All-Star Team (2010)

PRICE, Carey (PRIGHS, KAIR-ee) MTL.

Goaltender. Catches left. 6'3", 219 lbs. Born, Vancouver, B.C., August 16, 1987.
(Montreal's 1st choice, 5th overall, in 2005 Entry Draft).

			Regular Season								Playoffs						
Season	Club	League	GP	W	L	O/T	Mins	GA	SO	Avg	GP	W	L	Mins	GA	SO	Avg
2002-03	Williams Lake	Minor-BC	18	....	....	....	1050	48	1	2.70	....	....	....	....	....	....	....
	Tri-City Americans	WHL	1	0	0	0	20	2	0	6.00	....	....	....	....	....	....	....
2003-04	Tri-City Americans	WHL	28	8	9	3	1363	54	1	2.38	8	5	3	470	19	0	2.43
2004-05	Tri-City Americans	WHL	63	24	31	8	3712	145	8	2.34	5	1	4	325	12	0	2.22
2005-06	Tri-City Americans	WHL	55	21	25	6	3072	147	3	2.87	5	1	4	302	12	0	2.38
2006-07	Tri-City Americans	WHL	46	30	13	1	2722	111	3	2.45	6	2	4	348	17	0	2.93
	Hamilton Bulldogs	AHL	2	1	1	0	117	3	0	1.53	*22	*15	6	*1314	45	*2	2.06
2007-08	**Montreal**	**NHL**	**41**	**24**	**12**	**3**	**2413**	**103**	**3**	**2.56**	**11**	**5**	**6**	**648**	**30**	**2**	**2.78**
	Hamilton Bulldogs	AHL	10	6	4	0	581	26	1	2.69	....	....	....	....	....	....	....
2008-09	**Montreal**	**NHL**	**52**	**23**	**16**	**10**	**3036**	**143**	**1**	**2.83**	**4**	**0**	**4**	**219**	**15**	**0**	**4.11**
2009-10	**Montreal**	**NHL**	**41**	**13**	**20**	**5**	**2358**	**109**	**0**	**2.77**	**4**	**0**	**1**	**135**	**8**	**0**	**3.56**
	NHL Totals		**134**	**60**	**48**	**18**	**7807**	**355**	**4**	**2.73**	**19**	**5**	**11**	**1002**	**53**	**2**	**3.17**

WHL West First All-Star Team (2007) • WHL Goaltender of the Year (2007) • Canadian Major Junior First All-Star Team (2007) • Canadian Major Junior Goaltender of the Year (2007) • Jack A. Butterfield Trophy (AHL - Playoff MVP) (2007) • NHL All-Rookie Team (2008)

Played in NHL All-Star Game (2009)

QUICK, Jonathan (KWIHK, JAWN-ah-thuhn) L.A.

Goaltender. Catches left. 6'1", 223 lbs. Born, Milford, CT, January 21, 1986.
(Los Angeles' 4th choice, 72nd overall, in 2005 Entry Draft).

			Regular Season								Playoffs						
Season	Club	League	GP	W	L	O/T	Mins	GA	SO	Avg	GP	W	L	Mins	GA	SO	Avg
2002-03	Avon Old Farms	High-CT	13	8	5	0	780	38	0	2.92	....	....	....	....	....	....	....
2003-04	Avon Old Farms	High-CT	21	20	1	0	1260	26	2	1.71	....	....	....	....	....	....	....
2004-05	Avon Old Farms	High-CT	27	25	2	0	1413	27	9	1.14	....	....	....	....	....	....	....
2005-06	Massachusetts	H-East	17	4	10	1	905	45	0	2.98	....	....	....	....	....	....	....
2006-07	Massachusetts	H-East	37	19	12	5	2224	80	3	2.16	....	....	....	....	....	....	....
2007-08	**Los Angeles**	**NHL**	**3**	**1**	**2**	**0**	**141**	**9**	**0**	**3.83**	....	....	....	....	....	....	....
	Manchester	AHL	19	11	8	0	1085	42	3	2.32	1	0	1	59	1	0	1.02
	Reading Royals	ECHL	38	23	11	3	2257	105	1	2.79	....	....	....	....	....	....	....
2008-09	**Los Angeles**	**NHL**	**44**	**21**	**18**	**2**	**2495**	**103**	**4**	**2.48**	....	....	....	....	....	....	....
	Manchester	AHL	14	6	5	2	827	37	0	2.68	....	....	....	....	....	....	....
2009-10	**Los Angeles**	**NHL**	**72**	**39**	**24**	**7**	**4258**	**180**	**4**	**2.54**	**6**	**2**	**4**	**360**	**21**	**0**	**3.50**
	United States	Olympics	DID NOT PLAY – SPARE GOALTENDER														
	NHL Totals		**119**	**61**	**44**	**9**	**6894**	**292**	**8**	**2.54**	**6**	**2**	**4**	**360**	**21**	**0**	**3.50**

Hockey East Second All-Star Team (2007) • NCAA East Second All-American Team (2007)

RAMO, Karri (RAH-moh, KAH-ree) T.B.

Goaltender. Catches left. 6'2", 201 lbs. Born, Asikkala, Finland, July 1, 1986.
(Tampa Bay's 7th choice, 191st overall, in 2004 Entry Draft).

			Regular Season								Playoffs						
Season	Club	League	GP	W	L	O/T	Mins	GA	SO	Avg	GP	W	L	Mins	GA	SO	Avg
2002-03	K-Reipas U18	Fin-U18	19	12	3	2	1013	47	0	2.78	4	2	2	182	11	0	3.62
2003-04	Pelicans Lahti U18	Fin-U18	3	3	0	0	180	7	0	2.33	5	2	2	268	10	0	2.24
	Pelicans Lahti Jr.	Fin-Jr.	18	5	9	2	960	53	0	3.31	2	2	0	120	1	1	0.50
	Pelicans Lahti	Finland	3	0	2	0	138	10	0	4.34	....	....	....	....	....	....	....
2004-05	Pelicans Lahti Jr.	Fin-Jr.	21	10	5	6	1269	36	6	1.70	4	1	3	206	16	0	4.66
	Pelicans Lahti	Finland	26	4	12	4	1267	84	1	3.98	....	....	....	....	....	....	....
2005-06	Haukat Jarvenpaa	Finland-2	1	....	....	....	60	5	0	5.00	....	....	....	....	....	....	....
	Suomi U20	Finland-2	3	....	....	....	183	12	0	3.93	....	....	....	....	....	....	....
	HPK Hameenlinna	Finland	24	7	8	7	1359	49	2	2.16	3	2	1	204	5	1	1.46
2006-07	**Tampa Bay**	**NHL**	**2**	**0**	**0**	**0**	**70**	**4**	**0**	**3.43**	....	....	....	....	....	....	....
	Springfield Falcons	AHL	45	15	24	1	2432	127	1	3.13	....	....	....	....	....	....	....
2007-08	**Tampa Bay**	**NHL**	**22**	**7**	**11**	**3**	**1269**	**64**	**0**	**3.03**	....	....	....	....	....	....	....
	Norfolk Admirals	AHL	6	2	4	0	342	19	0	3.33	....	....	....	....	....	....	....
2008-09	**Tampa Bay**	**NHL**	**24**	**4**	**10**	**7**	**1312**	**80**	**0**	**3.66**	....	....	....	....	....	....	....
	Norfolk Admirals	AHL	26	7	14	4	1507	95	0	3.78	....	....	....	....	....	....	....
2009-10	Omsk	Rus-KHL	44	....	....	....	2582	91	4	2.11	3	....	....	158	8	0	3.04
	NHL Totals		**48**	**11**	**21**	**10**	**2651**	**148**	**0**	**3.35**	....	....	....	....	....	....	....

Signed as a free agent by **Omsk** (Russia-KHL), June 23, 2009.

RASK, Tuukka (RASK, TU-kah) BOS.

Goaltender. Catches left. 6'2", 171 lbs. Born, Savonlinna, Finland, March 10, 1987.
(Toronto's 1st choice, 21st overall, in 2005 Entry Draft).

			Regular Season								Playoffs						
Season	Club	League	GP	W	L	O/T	Mins	GA	SO	Avg	GP	W	L	Mins	GA	SO	Avg
2003-04	Ilves Tampere U18	Fin-U18	9	4	3	2	533	25	0	2.81	....	....	....	....	....	....	....
	Ilves Tampere Jr.	Fin-Jr.	30	12	10	7	1767	65	2	2.21	3	1	2	178	6	0	2.02
2004-05	Ilves Tampere Jr.	Fin-Jr.	26	17	3	4	1517	47	2	1.86	10	9	1	619	9	6	0.87
	Ilves Tampere	Finland	4	0	1	1	201	15	0	4.46	....	....	....	....	....	....	....
2005-06	Ilves Tampere Jr.	Fin-Jr.	1	....	....	....	60	2	0	2.00	....	....	....	....	....	....	....
	Suomi U20	Finland-2	3	....	....	....	179	6	0	2.01	....	....	....	....	....	....	....
	Ilves Tampere	Finland	30	12	8	7	1724	60	2	2.09	3	0	3	180	7	0	2.33
2006-07	Suomi U20	Finland-2	1	0	1	0	58	4	0	4.14	....	....	....	....	....	....	....
	Ilves Tampere	Finland	49	18	18	10	2872	114	3	2.38	7	2	5	397	20	0	3.02
2007-08	**Boston**	**NHL**	**4**	**2**	**1**	**1**	**184**	**10**	**0**	**3.26**	....	....	....	....	....	....	....
	Providence Bruins	AHL	45	27	13	2	2570	100	1	2.33	10	6	4	605	22	*2	2.18
2008-09	**Boston**	**NHL**	**1**	**1**	**0**	**0**	**60**	**0**	**1**	**0.00**	....	....	....	....	....	....	....
	Providence Bruins	AHL	57	33	20	4	3340	139	4	2.50	16	9	7	977	36	0	2.21
2009-10	**Boston**	**NHL**	**45**	**22**	**12**	**5**	**2562**	**84**	**5**	***1.97**	**13**	**7**	**6**	**829**	**36**	**0**	**2.61**
	NHL Totals		**50**	**25**	**13**	**6**	**2806**	**94**	**6**	**2.01**	**13**	**7**	**6**	**829**	**36**	**0**	**2.61**

Traded to **Boston** by **Toronto** for Andrew Raycroft, June 24, 2006.

RAYCROFT, Andrew (RAY-krawft, AN-droo) DAL

Goaltender. Catches left. 6', 173 lbs. Born, Belleville, Ont., May 4, 1980.
(Boston's 4th choice, 135th overall, in 1998 Entry Draft).

			Regular Season								Playoffs						
Season	Club	League	GP	W	L	O/T	Mins	GA	SO	Avg	GP	W	L	Mins	GA	SO	Av
1996-97	Wellington Dukes	MTJHL	27	....	....	....	1402	92	0	3.94	....	....	....	....	....	....	..
1997-98	Sudbury Wolves	OHL	33	8	16	5	1802	125	0	4.16	2	0	1	89	8	0	5.3
1998-99	Sudbury Wolves	OHL	45	17	22	5	2528	173	1	4.11	3	0	2	96	13	0	8.1
99-2000	Kingston	OHL	*61	33	20	5	3340	191	0	3.43	5	1	4	300	21	0	4.2
2000-01	**Boston**	**NHL**	**15**	**4**	**6**	**0**	**649**	**32**	**0**	**2.96**	....	....	....	....	....	....	..
	Providence Bruins	AHL	26	8	14	4	1459	82	1	3.37	....	....	....	....	....	....	..
2001-02	**Boston**	**NHL**	**1**	**0**	**0**	**1**	**65**	**3**	**0**	**2.77**	....	....	....	....	....	....	..
	Providence Bruins	AHL	56	25	24	6	3317	142	4	2.57	2	0	2	119	5	0	2.5
2002-03	**Boston**	**NHL**	**5**	**2**	**3**	**0**	**300**	**12**	**0**	**2.40**	....	....	....	....	....	....	..
	Providence Bruins	AHL	39	23	10	3	2255	94	1	2.50	4	1	3	264	6	1	*1.3
2003-04	**Boston**	**NHL**	**57**	**29**	**18**	**9**	**3420**	**117**	**3**	**2.05**	**7**	**3**	**4**	**447**	**16**	**1**	**2.1**
2004-05	Tappara Tampere	Finland	11	4	5	2	657	32	1	2.92	3	0	2	104	11	0	6.3
2005-06	**Boston**	**NHL**	**30**	**8**	**19**	**2**	**1619**	**100**	**0**	**3.71**	....	....	....	....	....	....	..
	Providence Bruins	AHL	1	1	0	0	64	3	0	2.80	....	....	....	....	....	....	..
2006-07	**Toronto**	**NHL**	**72**	**37**	**25**	**9**	**4108**	**205**	**2**	**2.99**	....	....	....	....	....	....	..
2007-08	**Toronto**	**NHL**	**19**	**2**	**9**	**5**	**965**	**63**	**1**	**3.92**	....	....	....	....	....	....	..
2008-09	**Colorado**	**NHL**	**31**	**12**	**16**	**0**	**1722**	**90**	**0**	**3.14**	....	....	....	....	....	....	..
2009-10	**Vancouver**	**NHL**	**21**	**9**	**5**	**1**	**967**	**39**	**1**	**2.42**	**1**	**0**	**0**	**25**	**1**	**0**	**2.4**
	NHL Totals		**251**	**103**	**101**	**27**	**13815**	**661**	**7**	**2.87**	**8**	**3**	**4**	**472**	**17**	**1**	**2.1**

OHL First All-Star Team (2000) • Canadian Major Junior First All-Star Team (2000) • Canadian Major Junior Goaltender of the Year (2000) • NHL All-Rookie Team (2004) • Calder Memorial Trophy (2004)

Signed as a free agent by **Tappara Tampere** (Finland), January 17, 2005. Traded to **Toronto** by **Boston** for Tuukka Rask, June 24, 2006. Signed as a free agent by **Colorado**, July 1, 2008. Signed as a free agent by **Vancouver**, July 6, 2009. Signed as a free agent by **Dallas**, July 1, 2010.

REGAN, Kevin (REE-guhn, KEH-vihn)

Goaltender. Catches left. 6', 195 lbs. Born, Boston, MA, July 25, 1984.
(Boston's 10th choice, 277th overall, in 2003 Entry Draft).

			Regular Season								Playoffs						
Season	Club	League	GP	W	L	O/T	Mins	GA	SO	Avg	GP	W	L	Mins	GA	SO	Av
2001-02	St. Sebastian's	High-MA	31	27	4	0	1860	56	0	1.91	....	....	....	....	....	....	.
	USNTDP	U-18	1	0	0	0	12	0	0	0.00	....	....	....	....	....	....	.
	South Boston	USHA	3	3	0	0	158	8	0	2.58	....	....	....	....	....	....	.
2002-03	St. Sebastian's	High-MA	28	....	....	....	1215	47	4	1.81	....	....	....	....	....	....	.
2003-04	Waterloo	USHL	50	*28	19	1	0	111	*6	2.37	*12	*9	3	*735	19	*1	*1.5
2004-05	New Hampshire	H-East	23	15	4	2	1276	50	0	2.35	....	....	....	....	....	....	.
2005-06	New Hampshire	H-East	23	8	8	5	1299	57	3	2.63	....	....	....	....	....	....	.
2006-07	New Hampshire	H-East	35	24	9	2	2066	71	3	2.06	....	....	....	....	....	....	.
2007-08	New Hampshire	H-East	32	23	8	1	1958	72	*3	2.21	....	....	....	....	....	....	.
	Providence Bruins	AHL	1	1	0	0	60	0	1	0.00	....	....	....	....	....	....	.
2008-09	Providence Bruins	AHL	21	9	7	2	1124	56	0	2.99	....	....	....	....	....	....	.
	Gwinnett	ECHL	2	1	1	0	120	5	0	2.50	....	....	....	....	....	....	.
	Alaska Aces	ECHL	4	2	2	0	243	10	0	2.47	....	....	....	....	....	....	.
2009-10	Providence Bruins	AHL	21	8	11	0	1159	49	0	2.54	....	....	....	....	....	....	.
	Reading Royals	ECHL	6	2	2	2	367	23	0	3.76	....	....	....	....	....	....	.

Hockey East All-Rookie Team (2005) (co-winners - Cory Schneider and Peter Vetri) • Hockey East First All-Star Team (2008) • Hockey East Player of the Year (2008) • NCAA East First All-American Team (2008)

REIMER, James (RIGH-muhr, JAYMZ) TOR

Goaltender. Catches left. 6'2", 208 lbs. Born, Winnipeg, Man., March 15, 1988.
(Toronto's 3rd choice, 99th overall, in 2006 Entry Draft).

			Regular Season								Playoffs						
Season	Club	League	GP	W	L	O/T	Mins	GA	SO	Avg	GP	W	L	Mins	GA	SO	Av
2003-04	Interlake Lightning	MMHL	27	6	5	2	863	41	1	2.85	....	....	....	....	....	....	.
2004-05	Interlake Lightning	MMHL	37	19	6	2	1646	58	4	2.11	435	26	0	3.59	....	....	.
2005-06	Red Deer Rebels	WHL	34	7	18	3	1709	80	0	2.81	....	....	....	....	....	....	.
2006-07	Red Deer Rebels	WHL	60	26	23	7	3339	148	3	2.66	7	3	4	417	27	0	3.8
2007-08	Red Deer Rebels	WHL	30	8	15	0	1668	76	1	2.73	....	....	....	....	....	....	.
2008-09	Toronto Marlies	AHL	3	1	2	0	183	10	0	3.28	....	....	....	....	....	....	.
	Reading Royals	ECHL	22	10	7	3	1236	68	0	3.30	....	....	....	....	....	....	.
	South Carolina	ECHL	6	6	0	0	363	8	2	1.32	8	4	1	497	18	1	2.
2009-10	Toronto Marlies	AHL	26	14	8	2	1520	57	1	2.25	....	....	....	....	....	....	.

ECHL Playoff MVP (2009)

RICHARDS, Alec (RIH-chuhrds, ALEHK) CH

Goaltender. Catches left. 6'4", 190 lbs. Born, Robbinsdale, MN, June 29, 1987.

			Regular Season								Playoffs						
Season	Club	League	GP	W	L	O/T	Mins	GA	SO	Avg	GP	W	L	Mins	GA	SO	Av
2003-04	Breck Mustangs	High-MN	....	19	1	1	....	....	....	1.70	....	....	....	....	....	....	
2004-05	Breck Mustangs	High-MN	....	15	2	2	....	....	....	1.90	....	....	....	....	....	....	
	Indiana Ice	USHL	4	1	2	1	241	14	0	3.47	....	....	....	....	....	....	
2005-06	Yale	ECAC	29	8	15	3	1686	85	1	3.02	....	....	....	....	....	....	
2006-07	Yale	ECAC	26	9	15	2	1518	79	0	3.12	....	....	....	....	....	....	
2007-08	Yale	ECAC	11	3	4	0	563	19	1	2.02	....	....	....	....	....	....	
2008-09	Yale	ECAC	25	19	5	1	1458	50	4	2.06	....	....	....	....	....	....	
2009-10	Rockford IceHogs	AHL	6	3	2	0	307	16	0	3.12	....	....	....	....	....	....	
	Toledo Walleye	ECHL	34	17	12	5	2004	112	1	3.35	....	....	....	....	....	....	

Signed as a free agent by **Chicago**, June 8, 2009.

RINNE, Pekka (RIH-neh, PEH-kuh) NSH

Goaltender. Catches left. 6'5", 207 lbs. Born, Kempele, Finland, November 3, 1982.
(Nashville's 10th choice, 258th overall, in 2004 Entry Draft).

			Regular Season								Playoffs						
Season	Club	League	GP	W	L	O/T	Mins	GA	SO	Avg	GP	W	L	Mins	GA	SO	A
2000-01	Karpat Oulu Jr.	Fin-Jr.	20	9	4	5	1148	63	0	3.29	....	....	....	....	....	....	
2001-02	Karpat Oulu Jr.	Fin-Jr.	30	19	7	3	1724	61	3	2.12	3	1	2	184	10	1	3.
2002-03	Karpat Oulu Jr.	Fin-Jr.	25	14	8	3	1479	48	5	1.95	4	1	3	238	7	0	1.
	Karpat Oulu	Finland	1	0	1	0	60	7	0	7.00	....	....	....	....	....	....	
2003-04	Karpat Oulu	Finland	14	5	4	4	824	41	0	2.99	2	1	0	22	0	0	0.
	Hokki Kajaani	Finland-2	8	5	2	1	463	16	2	2.07	....	....	....	....	....	....	
2004-05	Karpat Oulu	Finland	10	8	0	1	571	16	0	1.68	....	....	....	....	....	....	
2005-06	**Nashville**	**NHL**	**2**	**1**	**1**	**0**	**63**	**4**	**0**	**3.81**	....	....	....	....	....	....	
	Milwaukee	AHL	51	30	18	2	2960	139	2	2.82	14	10	4	734	35	3	2.
2006-07	Milwaukee	AHL	29	15	7	6	1670	65	3	2.34	4	0	4	247	12	0	2.
2007-08	**Nashville**	**NHL**	**1**	**0**	**0**	**0**	**29**	**0**	**0**	**0.00**	....	....	....	....	....	....	
	Milwaukee	AHL	*65	*36	24	3	*3840	158	5	2.47	6	2	4	358	15	1	2.
2008-09	**Nashville**	**NHL**	**52**	**29**	**15**	**4**	**2999**	**119**	**7**	**2.38**	....	....	....	....	....	....	
2009-10	**Nashville**	**NHL**	**58**	**32**	**16**	**5**	**3246**	**137**	**7**	**2.53**	**6**	**2**	**4**	**358**	**16**	**0**	**2**
	NHL Totals		**113**	**62**	**32**	**9**	**6337**	**260**	**14**	**2.46**	**6**	**2**	**4**	**358**	**16**	**0**	**2.**

IOPEL, Nic — (ree-OH-pehl, NIHK) PHI.

oaltender. Catches left. 6', 172 lbs. Born, St-Pie de Bagot, Que., February 20, 1989.
hiladelphia's 3rd choice, 142nd overall, in 2009 Entry Draft).

			Regular Season								Playoffs						
eason	Club	League	GP	W	L	O/T	Mins	GA	SO	Avg	GP	W	L	Mins	GA	SO	Avg
)06-07	Moncton Wildcats	QMJHL	37	17	12	....	1914	107	1	3.35	4	1	3	185	16	0	5.19
)07-08	Moncton Wildcats	QMJHL	47	15	29	....	2662	135	1	3.04	....	....	....	....	....	....	....
)08-09	Moncton Wildcats	QMJHL	*59	*43	15	....	*3487	117	5	*2.01	10	5	5	620	21	*2	*2.03
09-10	Moncton Wildcats	QMJHL	25	19	5	....	1455	50	3	*2.06	*21	*16	4	*1291	46	*3	*2.14
	Adirondack	AHL	10	4	6	0	573	32	0	3.35	....	....	....	....	....	....	....

MJHL All-Rookie Team (2009) • QMJHL First All-Star Team (2009) • Canadian Major Junior Second l-Star Team (2009)

OLLHEISER, Grant — (rohl-HIGH-zuhr, GRANT) TOR.

oaltender. Catches left. 6'4", 195 lbs. Born, Chilliwak, B.C., July 24, 1989.
oronto's 7th choice, 158th overall, in 2008 Entry Draft).

			Regular Season								Playoffs						
eason	Club	League	GP	W	L	O/T	Mins	GA	SO	Avg	GP	W	L	Mins	GA	SO	Avg
06-07	Nelson Leafs	KIJHL	35	25	8	0	1990	110	2	3.32	15	9	6	907	35	2	2.31
07-08	Trail Smoke Eaters	BCHL	46	19	26	0	2557	136	2	3.19	3	0	3	159	13	0	4.90
08-09	Boston University	H-East	12	6	4	1	648	23	1	2.13	....	....	....	....	....	....	....
09-10	Boston University	H-East	7	2	1	3	389	22	0	3.39	....	....	....	....	....	....	....

OLOSON, Dwayne — (ROH-loh-suhn, DWAYN) NYI

oaltender. Catches left. 6'1", 180 lbs. Born, Simcoe, Ont., October 12, 1969.

			Regular Season								Playoffs						
eason	Club	League	GP	W	L	O/T	Mins	GA	SO	Avg	GP	W	L	Mins	GA	SO	Avg
84-85	Simcoe Penguins	OJHL-C	3	....	....	....	100	21	0	12.60	....	....	....	....	....	....	....
85-86	Simcoe Rams	OJHL-C	1	....	....	....	60	6	0	6.00	....	....	....	....	....	....	....
86-87	Norwich	OJHL-C	19	....	....	....	1091	55	0	*3.03	....	....	....	....	....	....	....
87-88	Belleville Bobcats	OJHL-B	21	9	6	1	1070	60	*2	3.36	....	....	....	....	....	....	....
88-89	Thorold	OJHL-B	27	15	6	4	1490	82	0	3.30	....	....	....	....	....	....	....
89-90	Thorold	OHA-B	30	18	8	1	1683	108	0	3.85	....	....	....	....	....	....	....
90-91	U. Mass-Lowell	H-East	15	5	9	0	823	63	0	4.59	....	....	....	....	....	....	....
91-92	U. Mass-Lowell	H-East	12	3	8	0	660	52	0	4.73	....	....	....	....	....	....	....
92-93	U. Mass-Lowell	H-East	*39	20	17	2	*2342	150	0	3.84	....	....	....	....	....	....	....
93-94	U. Mass-Lowell	H-East	*40	*23	10	7	*2305	106	0	2.76	....	....	....	....	....	....	....
94-95	Saint John Flames	AHL	46	16	21	8	2734	156	1	3.42	5	1	4	298	13	0	2.61
95-96	Saint John Flames	AHL	67	*33	22	11	4026	190	1	2.83	16	10	6	1027	49	1	2.86
96-97	**Calgary**	**NHL**	**31**	**9**	**14**	**3**	**1618**	**78**	**1**	**2.89**	....	....	....	....	....	....	....
	Saint John Flames	AHL	8	6	2	0	481	22	1	2.75	....	....	....	....	....	....	....
97-98	**Calgary**	**NHL**	**39**	**11**	**16**	**8**	**2205**	**110**	**0**	**2.99**	....	....	....	....	....	....	....
	Saint John Flames	AHL	4	3	0	1	245	8	0	1.96	....	....	....	....	....	....	....
98-99	**Buffalo**	**NHL**	**18**	**6**	**8**	**2**	**911**	**42**	**1**	**2.77**	**4**	**1**	**1**	**139**	**10**	**0**	**4.32**
	Rochester	AHL	2	2	0	0	120	4	0	2.00	....	....	....	....	....	....	....
-2000	**Buffalo**	**NHL**	**14**	**1**	**7**	**3**	**677**	**32**	**0**	**2.84**	....	....	....	....	....	....	....
00-01	Worcester IceCats	AHL	52	*32	15	5	*3127	113	*6	*2.17	11	6	5	697	23	1	1.98
01-02	**Minnesota**	**NHL**	**45**	**14**	**20**	**7**	**2506**	**112**	**5**	**2.68**	....	....	....	....	....	....	....
02-03	**Minnesota**	**NHL**	**50**	**23**	**16**	**8**	**2945**	**98**	**4**	**2.00**	**11**	**5**	**6**	**579**	**25**	**0**	**2.59**
03-04	**Minnesota**	**NHL**	**48**	**19**	**18**	**11**	**2847**	**89**	**5**	**1.88**	....	....	....	....	....	....	....
04-05	Lukko Rauma	Finland	34	20	10	4	2048	70	4	2.05	9	4	5	512	18	2	2.11
05-06	**Minnesota**	**NHL**	**24**	**6**	**17**	**1**	**1361**	**68**	**1**	**3.00**	....	....	....	....	....	....	....
	Edmonton	**NHL**	**19**	**8**	**7**	**4**	**1163**	**47**	**1**	**2.42**	**18**	**12**	**5**	**1160**	**45**	**1**	**2.33**
06-07	**Edmonton**	**NHL**	**68**	**27**	**34**	**6**	**3932**	**180**	**4**	**2.75**	....	....	....	....	....	....	....
07-08	**Edmonton**	**NHL**	**43**	**15**	**17**	**5**	**2340**	**119**	**0**	**3.05**	....	....	....	....	....	....	....
08-09	**Edmonton**	**NHL**	**63**	**28**	**24**	**9**	**3597**	**166**	**1**	**2.77**	....	....	....	....	....	....	....
09-10	**NY Islanders**	**NHL**	**50**	**23**	**18**	**7**	**2897**	**145**	**1**	**3.00**	....	....	....	....	....	....	....
	NHL Totals		**512**	**190**	**216**	**74**	**28999**	**1286**	**24**	**2.66**	**33**	**18**	**12**	**1878**	**80**	**1**	**2.56**

ockey East First All-Star Team (1994) • Hockey East Player of the Year (1994) • NCAA East First -American Team (1994) • AHL First All-Star Team (2001) • Aldege "Baz" Bastien Memorial Award HL – Outstanding Goaltender) (2001) • MBNA/Mastercard Roger Crozier Saving Grace Award 004)

ayed in NHL All-Star Game (2004)

gned as a free agent by **Calgary**, July 4, 1994. Signed as a free agent by **Buffalo**, July 15, 1998. aimed by **Columbus** from **Buffalo** in Expansion Draft, June 23, 2000. Signed as a free agent by **Louis**, July 14, 2000. Signed as a free agent by **Minnesota**, July 2, 2001. Signed as a free agent **Rauma** (Finland), October 18, 2004. Traded to **Edmonton** by **Minnesota** for Edmonton's 1st und choice (later traded to Los Angeles - Los Angeles selected Trevor Lewis) in 2006 Entry Draft d Edmonton's 3rd round chocie (later traded to Atlanta - Atlanta selected Spencer Machacek) in 07 Entry Draft, March 8, 2006. Signed as a free agent by **NY Islanders**, July 1, 2009.

SEN, Cody — (ROH-zehn, KOH-dee) NYI

altender. Catches left. 5'11", 180 lbs. Born, Kingston, Ont., September 27, 1990.
Y Islanders' 6th choice, 185th overall, in 2010 Entry Draft).

			Regular Season								Playoffs						
ason	Club	League	GP	W	L	O/T	Mins	GA	SO	Avg	GP	W	L	Mins	GA	SO	Avg
)8-09	Kingston	OJHL	18	14	3	1	1055	51	3	2.90	....	....	....	....	....	....	....
)9-10	Clarkson Knights	ECAC	1	0	0	0	20	3	0	9.00	....	....	....	....	....	....	....

)Y, Olivier — (WAH, oh-LIHV-ee-ay) EDM.

altender. Catches left. 6', 165 lbs. Born, Amqui, Que., July 12, 1991.
dmonton's 7th choice, 133rd overall, in 2009 Entry Draft).

			Regular Season								Playoffs						
ason	Club	League	GP	W	L	O/T	Mins	GA	SO	Avg	GP	W	L	Mins	GA	SO	Avg
)6-07	Ecole Notre Dame	QAAA	27	15	8	0	1459	65	2	2.67	4	2	1	206	13	0	3.79
)7-08	Cape Breton	QMJHL	47	27	15	....	2428	116	4	2.87	11	5	6	707	30	1	2.55
)8-09	Cape Breton	QMJHL	54	35	13	....	2935	137	3	2.80	11	7	4	740	30	0	2.43
)9-10	Cape Breton	QMJHL	54	32	21	....	3156	138	5	2.62	5	1	4	311	19	0	3.66
	Springfield Falcons	AHL	3	1	1	0	140	6	0	2.57	....	....	....	....	....	....	....

MJHL All-Rookie Team (2008)

YNNAS, Jussi — (RIH-nuhs, YEW-see) TOR.

altender. Catches left. 6'5", 205 lbs. Born, Pori, Finland, May 22, 1987.

			Regular Season								Playoffs						
ason	Club	League	GP	W	L	O/T	Mins	GA	SO	Avg	GP	W	L	Mins	GA	SO	Avg
)6-07	Assat Pori Jr.	Fin-Jr.	23	....	....	....	....	....	....	4.20	....	....	....	....	....	....	....
)7-08	Assat Pori Jr.	Fin-Jr.	27	....	....	....	....	....	....	2.90	....	....	....	....	....	....	....
)8-09	Assat Pori	Finland	DID NOT PLAY – SPARE GOALTENDER														
	Sport Vaasa	Finland-2	1	....	....	....	....	....	....	6.00	....	....	....	....	....	....	....
	Kiekko-Vantaa	Finland-2	7	....	....	....	....	....	....	3.99	....	....	....	....	....	....	....
9-10	Assat Pori	Finland	31	14	13	1	1717	71	2	2.48	....	....	....	....	....	....	....

ned as a free agent by **Toronto**, April 23, 2010.

SABOURIN, Dany — (SA-boo-rihn, DA-nee) WSH.

Goaltender. Catches left. 6'4", 200 lbs. Born, Val-d'Or, Que., September 2, 1980.
(Calgary's 5th choice, 108th overall, in 1998 Entry Draft).

			Regular Season								Playoffs						
Season	Club	League	GP	W	L	O/T	Mins	GA	SO	Avg	GP	W	L	Mins	GA	SO	Avg
1996-97	Amos Forestiers	QAAA	24	6	16	0	1440	107	0	4.48	....	....	....	....	....	....	....
1997-98	Sherbrooke	QMJHL	37	15	15	2	1906	128	1	4.03	....	....	....	....	....	....	....
1998-99	Sherbrooke	QMJHL	30	8	13	2	1477	102	1	4.14	1	0	1	49	2	0	2.45
	Saint John Flames	AHL	....	....	....	....	....	....	....	....	1	0	1	57	4	0	4.19
99-2000	Sherbrooke	QMJHL	55	25	22	5	3067	181	1	3.54	5	1	4	324	18	0	3.33
2000-01	Saint John Flames	AHL	1	1	0	0	40	0	0	0.00	....	....	....	....	....	....	....
	Johnstown Chiefs	ECHL	19	4	9	1	903	56	0	3.72	1	0	0	40	2	0	3.00
2001-02	Johnstown Chiefs	ECHL	27	14	10	1	1539	84	0	3.28	3	0	2	137	5	0	2.18
2002-03	Saint John Flames	AHL	41	15	17	4	2220	100	4	2.70	....	....	....	....	....	....	....
2003-04	**Calgary**	**NHL**	**4**	**0**	**3**	**0**	**169**	**10**	**0**	**3.55**	....	....	....	....	....	....	....
	Lowell	AHL	14	5	7	2	821	39	0	2.85	....	....	....	....	....	....	....
	Las Vegas	ECHL	10	6	3	1	613	24	0	2.35	1	0	1	58	2	0	2.07
2004-05	Wilkes-Barre	AHL	20	8	8	2	1029	38	1	2.22	....	....	....	....	....	....	....
	Wheeling Nailers	ECHL	27	19	6	1	1579	44	5	*1.67	....	....	....	....	....	....	....
2005-06	**Pittsburgh**	**NHL**	**1**	**0**	**1**	**0**	**21**	**4**	**0**	**11.43**	....	....	....	....	....	....	....
	Wilkes-Barre	AHL	49	30	14	4	2943	111	4	*2.26	6	2	4	362	13	1	2.15
2006-07	**Vancouver**	**NHL**	**9**	**2**	**4**	**1**	**480**	**21**	**0**	**2.63**	**2**	**0**	**0**	**14**	**1**	**0**	**4.29**
	Manitoba Moose	AHL	2	1	1	0	119	4	1	2.01	....	....	....	....	....	....	....
2007-08	**Pittsburgh**	**NHL**	**24**	**10**	**9**	**1**	**1242**	**57**	**2**	**2.75**	....	....	....	....	....	....	....
2008-09	**Pittsburgh**	**NHL**	**19**	**6**	**8**	**2**	**989**	**47**	**0**	**2.85**	....	....	....	....	....	....	....
	Springfield Falcons	AHL	13	5	6	2	795	42	0	3.17	....	....	....	....	....	....	....
2009-10	Providence Bruins	AHL	56	28	27	0	3278	146	3	2.67	....	....	....	....	....	....	....
	NHL Totals		**57**	**18**	**25**	**4**	**2901**	**139**	**2**	**2.87**	**2**	**0**	**0**	**14**	**1**	**0**	**4.29**

AHL First All-Star Team (2006) • Aldege "Baz" Bastien Memorial Award (AHL – Outstanding Goaltender) (2006)

Signed as a free agent by **Pittsburgh**, August 10, 2005. Claimed on waivers by **Vancouver** from **Pittsburgh**, October 4, 2006. Signed as a free agent by **Pittsburgh**, July 1, 2007. Traded to **Edmonton** by **Pittsburgh** with Ryan Stone and Pittsburgh's 4th round choice in 2011 Entry Draft for Mathieu Garon, January 17, 2009. Signed as a free agent by **Boston**, July 7, 2009. Signed as a free agent by **Washington**, July 1, 2010.

SALAK, Alexander — (SAL-ak, al-EHX-AN-duhr) FLA.

Goaltender. Catches left. 6'1", 189 lbs. Born, Strakonice, Czech., January 5, 1987.

			Regular Season								Playoffs						
Season	Club	League	GP	W	L	O/T	Mins	GA	SO	Avg	GP	W	L	Mins	GA	SO	Avg
2006-07	Jokipojat Joensuu	Finland-2	35	....	....	....	....	....	....	2.81	....	....	....	....	....	....	....
2007-08	TPS Turku	Finland	31	....	....	....	1757	76	1	2.59	....	....	....	....	....	....	....
2008-09	TPS Turku	Finland	52	20	20	9	2981	119	4	2.40	8	4	4	489	16	0	1.96
2009-10	**Florida**	**NHL**	**2**	**0**	**1**	**0**	**67**	**6**	**0**	**5.37**	....	....	....	....	....	....	....
	Rochester	AHL	48	29	14	0	2557	123	1	2.89	2	0	1	69	5	0	4.37
	NHL Totals		**2**	**0**	**1**	**0**	**67**	**6**	**0**	**5.37**	....	....	....	....	....	....	....

Signed as a free agent by **Florida**, May 29, 2009.

SANFORD, Curtis — (SAN-fohrd, KUHR-this) MTL.

Goaltender. Catches left. 5'11", 185 lbs. Born, Owen Sound, Ont., October 5, 1979.

			Regular Season								Playoffs						
Season	Club	League	GP	W	L	O/T	Mins	GA	SO	Avg	GP	W	L	Mins	GA	SO	Avg
1994-95	Wiarton Wolves	OJHL-C	18	....	....	....	949	98	0	6.20	....	....	....	....	....	....	....
1995-96	Collingwood	OJHL	21	....	....	....	2128	74	0	3.54	....	....	....	....	....	....	....
1996-97	Owen Sound	OHL	19	4	8	1	847	77	0	5.45	....	....	....	....	....	....	....
	Owen Sound	OJHL-B	6	....	....	....	360	28	0	4.68	....	....	....	....	....	....	....
1997-98	Owen Sound	OHL	30	13	10	2	1542	114	1	4.44	9	4	4	456	30	1	3.95
1998-99	Owen Sound	OHL	56	30	16	5	2998	191	2	3.82	16	9	7	960	58	0	3.63
99-2000	Owen Sound	OHL	53	18	26	6	3124	198	1	3.80	....	....	....	....	....	....	....
	Missouri	UHL	6	3	1	0	237	6	0	1.52	....	....	....	....	....	....	....
2000-01	Worcester IceCats	AHL	5	3	0	1	237	16	0	4.06	....	....	....	....	....	....	....
	Peoria Rivermen	ECHL	27	15	7	4	1511	48	3	*1.91	14	9	4	813	28	*2	2.07
2001-02	Worcester IceCats	AHL	9	5	4	0	537	22	0	2.46	....	....	....	....	....	....	....
	Peoria Rivermen	ECHL	24	13	8	2	1418	58	1	2.45	....	....	....	....	....	....	....
2002-03	**St. Louis**	**NHL**	**8**	**5**	**1**	**0**	**397**	**13**	**1**	**1.96**	....	....	....	....	....	....	....
	Worcester IceCats	AHL	41	18	14	8	2317	93	3	2.41	3	0	3	179	8	0	2.68
2003-04	Worcester IceCats	AHL	43	20	16	3	2367	84	5	2.13	9	4	5	569	24	0	2.53
2004-05	Worcester IceCats	AHL	50	19	25	2	2743	123	2	2.69	....	....	....	....	....	....	....
2005-06	**St. Louis**	**NHL**	**34**	**13**	**13**	**5**	**1830**	**81**	**3**	**2.66**	....	....	....	....	....	....	....
	Peoria Rivermen	AHL	6	4	2	0	358	11	2	1.84	....	....	....	....	....	....	....
2006-07	**St. Louis**	**NHL**	**31**	**8**	**12**	**5**	**1492**	**79**	**0**	**3.18**	....	....	....	....	....	....	....
	Peoria Rivermen	AHL	2	1	1	0	119	5	0	2.52	....	....	....	....	....	....	....
2007-08	**Vancouver**	**NHL**	**16**	**4**	**3**	**1**	**679**	**32**	**0**	**2.83**	....	....	....	....	....	....	....
2008-09	**Vancouver**	**NHL**	**19**	**7**	**8**	**0**	**973**	**42**	**1**	**2.59**	....	....	....	....	....	....	....
	Manitoba Moose	AHL	16	7	3	3	865	25	2	1.73	1	0	1	43	1	0	1.40
2009-10	Hamilton Bulldogs	AHL	41	23	11	3	2230	79	4	2.13	9	5	4	565	19	2	2.02
	NHL Totals		**108**	**37**	**37**	**11**	**5371**	**247**	**5**	**2.76**	....	....	....	....	....	....	....

ECHL Second All-Star Team (2001) • Harry "Hap" Holmes Memorial Award (AHL – fewest goals against) (2010) (shared with Cedrick Desjardins)

Signed as a free agent by **St. Louis**, October 1, 2000. Signed as a free agent by **Vancouver**, July 2, 2007. Signed as a free agent by **Montreal**, July 20, 2009.

SATERI, Harri — (SA-teh-ree, HAR-ree) S.J.

Goaltender. Catches left. 6'1", 210 lbs. Born, Toijala, Finland, December 29, 1989.
(San Jose's 3rd choice, 106th overall, in 2008 Entry Draft).

			Regular Season								Playoffs						
Season	Club	League	GP	W	L	O/T	Mins	GA	SO	Avg	GP	W	L	Mins	GA	SO	Avg
2005-06	HPK U18	Fin-U18	27	....	....	....	1515	66	5	2.61	2	....	....	118	10	0	5.08
	HPK Jr.	Fin-Jr.	1	....	....	....	50	3	0	3.60	....	....	....	....	....	....	....
2006-07	Tappara U18	Fin-U18	2	....	....	....	119	4	0	2.02	....	....	....	....	....	....	....
	Tappara Jr.	Fin-Jr.	23	....	....	....	1346	59	2	2.63	10	....	....	614	31	0	3.03
2007-08	Tappara Jr.	Fin-Jr.	34	13	17	0	2048	102	1	2.99	3	0	3	178	8	0	2.70
2008-09	Suomi U20	Finland-2	4	2	2	0	247	12	0	2.91	....	....	....	....	....	....	....
2009-10	Tappara Tampere	Finland	49	21	22	4	2836	129	2	2.73	9	4	5	572	27	0	2.83

SCHAEFER, Nolan (SHAY-fuhr, NOH-luhn) BOS.

Goaltender. Catches right. 6'2", 195 lbs. Born, Regina, Sask., January 15, 1980.
(San Jose's 4th choice, 166th overall, in 2000 Entry Draft).

			Regular Season								Playoffs						
Season	Club	League	GP	W	L	O/T	Mins	GA	SO	Avg	GP	W	L	Mins	GA	SO	Avg
1996-97	Yorkton Mallers	SMHL	36	....	....	....	1854	132	0	4.27	....	....	....	....	....	....	....
1997-98	Yorkton Mallers	SMHL	5	....	....	....	239	17	0	4.25	....	....	....	....	....	....	....
	Nipawin Hawks	SJHL	21	12	4	3	1080	42	*3	*2.33	....	....	....	....	....	....	....
1998-99	Nipawin Hawks	SJHL	46	....	....	....	2478	165	0	3.60	....	....	....	....	....	....	....
99-2000	Providence College	H-East	14	6	5	1	778	42	0	3.24	....	....	....	....	....	....	....
2000-01	Providence College	H-East	25	15	8	2	1529	63	3	2.47	....	....	....	....	....	....	....
2001-02	Providence College	H-East	*35	11	18	5	*2062	113	0	3.29	....	....	....	....	....	....	....
2002-03	Providence College	H-East	25	13	8	2	1440	71	0	2.96	....	....	....	....	....	....	....
2003-04	Cleveland Barons	AHL	27	14	9	3	1592	62	2	2.34	9	4	5	573	24	0	2.51
	Fresno Falcons	ECHL	12	5	5	0	654	34	1	3.12	....	....	....	....	....	....	....
2004-05	Cleveland Barons	AHL	43	17	23	1	2418	110	3	2.73	....	....	....	....	....	....	....
2005-06	**San Jose**	**NHL**	**7**	**5**	**1**	**0**	**352**	**11**	**1**	**1.88**	....	....	....	....	....	....	....
	Cleveland Barons	AHL	36	12	21	2	2058	118	2	3.44	....	....	....	....	....	....	....
2006-07	Worcester Sharks	AHL	16	5	8	3	921	43	0	2.80	....	....	....	....	....	....	....
	Hershey Bears	AHL	3	0	3	0	162	10	0	3.70	....	....	....	....	....	....	....
	Wilkes-Barre	AHL	15	9	5	0	804	30	1	2.24	11	5	6	699	32	0	2.75
2007-08	Houston Aeros	AHL	34	19	13	0	1980	68	6	*2.06	2	0	2	117	4	0	2.05
2008-09	Houston Aeros	AHL	51	26	17	5	2711	114	1	2.52	4	1	1	148	11	0	4.46
2009-10	CSKA Moscow	Rus-KHL	22	....	....	....	1107	49	1	2.66	1	....	....	44	2	0	2.73
	NHL Totals		**7**	**5**	**1**	**0**	**352**	**11**	**1**	**1.88**	....	....	....	....	....	....	....

Hockey East Second All-Star Team (2001) • NCAA East Second All-American Team (2001) • Harry "Hap" Holmes Memorial Award (AHL – fewest goals against) (2008) (shared with Barry Brust)

Traded to **Pittsburgh** by **San Jose** for Pittsburgh's 7th round choice (Justin Braun) in 2007 Entry Draft, February 27, 2007. Signed as a free agent by **Minnesota**, July 3, 2007. Signed as a free agent by **CSKA Moscow** (Russia-KHL), August 4, 2009. Signed as a free agent by **Boston**, July 5, 2010.

SCHNEIDER, Cory (SHNIGH-duhr, KOHR-ee) VAN.

Goaltender. Catches left. 6'2", 195 lbs. Born, Marblehead, MA, March 18, 1986.
(Vancouver's 1st choice, 26th overall, in 2004 Entry Draft).

			Regular Season								Playoffs						
Season	Club	League	GP	W	L	O/T	Mins	GA	SO	Avg	GP	W	L	Mins	GA	SO	Avg
2002-03	Andover	High-MA	23	13	7	2	1385	39	3	1.69	....	....	....	....	....	....	....
2003-04	Andover	High-MA	24	17	5	2	1336	32	6	1.42	....	....	....	....	....	....	....
	USNTDP	U-18	10	9	1	0	559	15	1	1.61	....	....	....	....	....	....	....
	USNTDP	NAHL	2	2	0	0	120	6	0	3.00	....	....	....	....	....	....	....
2004-05	Boston College	H-East	18	13	1	4	1102	35	1	1.90	....	....	....	....	....	....	....
2005-06	Boston College	H-East	*39	*24	13	2	*2362	83	*8	2.11	....	....	....	....	....	....	....
2006-07	Boston College	H-East	*42	*29	12	1	*2517	90	6	2.15	....	....	....	....	....	....	....
2007-08	Manitoba Moose	AHL	36	21	12	2	2054	78	3	2.28	6	1	4	375	12	0	1.92
2008-09	**Vancouver**	**NHL**	**8**	**2**	**4**	**1**	**355**	**20**	**0**	**3.38**	....	....	....	....	....	....	....
	Manitoba Moose	AHL	40	28	10	1	2324	79	5	*2.04	*22	14	7	1315	47	0	2.15
2009-10	**Vancouver**	**NHL**	**2**	**0**	**1**	**0**	**79**	**5**	**0**	**3.80**	....	....	....	....	....	....	....
	Manitoba Moose	AHL	60	35	23	2	*3557	149	4	2.51	6	2	4	366	19	0	3.12
	NHL Totals		**10**	**2**	**5**	**1**	**434**	**25**	**0**	**3.46**	....	....	....	....	....	....	....

Hockey East All-Rookie Team (2005) (co-winners - Kevin Regan and Peter Vetri) • Hockey East Second All-Star Team (2006) • NCAA East First All-American Team (2006) • AHL First All-Star Team (2009) • Harry "Hap" Holmes Memorial Award (AHL – fewest goals against) (2009) (shared with Karl Goehring) • Aldege "Baz" Bastien Memorial Award (AHL – Outstanding Goaltender) (2009)

SCHWARZ, Marek (SHWAHRTS, MAIR-ehk)

Goaltender. Catches right. 6', 180 lbs. Born, Mlada Boleslav, Czech., April 1, 1986.
(St. Louis' 1st choice, 17th overall, in 2004 Entry Draft).

			Regular Season								Playoffs						
Season	Club	League	GP	W	L	O/T	Mins	GA	SO	Avg	GP	W	L	Mins	GA	SO	Avg
2000-01	Ml. Boleslav Jr.	CzRep-Jr.	45	....	....	....	1969	154	0	4.69	....	....	....	....	....	....	....
2001-02	Sparta Jr.	CzRep-Jr.	46	....	....	....	2692	86	9	1.92	6	....	....	368	16	0	2.61
2002-03	Sparta Jr.	CzRep-Jr.	34	....	....	....	1778	57	3	1.92	2	....	....	120	5	0	2.50
	HC Sparta Praha	CzRep	1	....	....	....	1	0	0	0.00	....	....	....	....	....	....	....
2003-04	Sparta Jr.	CzRep-Jr.	7	....	....	....	352	14	2	2.39	....	....	....	....	....	....	....
	Plzen	CzRep	10	....	....	....	603	33	0	3.28	....	....	....	....	....	....	....
	HC Sparta Praha	CzRep	8	....	....	....	335	20	0	3.58	....	....	....	....	....	....	....
	HC Ocelari Trinec	CzRep	5	....	....	....	280	12	0	2.57	....	....	....	....	....	....	....
	BK Mlada Boleslav	CzRep-2	1	....	....	....	63	6	0	5.71	....	....	....	....	....	....	....
2004-05	Vancouver Giants	WHL	56	26	24	4	3304	147	2	2.67	6	2	4	378	18	0	2.86
2005-06	Sparta Jr.	CzRep-Jr.	3	....	....	....	178	5	0	1.69	....	....	....	....	....	....	....
	HC Sparta Praha	CzRep	15	....	....	....	746	32	1	2.57	1	....	....	1	0	0	0.00
	Beroun	CzRep-2	4	....	....	....	229	17	0	4.45	....	....	....	....	....	....	....
2006-07	**St. Louis**	**NHL**	**2**	**0**	**1**	**0**	**60**	**3**	**0**	**3.00**	....	....	....	....	....	....	....
	Peoria Rivermen	AHL	34	19	13	0	1912	88	1	2.76	....	....	....	....	....	....	....
2007-08	**St. Louis**	**NHL**	**2**	**0**	**1**	**0**	**50**	**6**	**0**	**7.20**	....	....	....	....	....	....	....
	Peoria Rivermen	AHL	33	14	14	2	1808	84	0	2.79	....	....	....	....	....	....	....
	Alaska Aces	ECHL	6	6	0	0	375	13	0	2.08	8	5	2	468	25	0	3.21
2008-09	**St. Louis**	**NHL**	**2**	**0**	**0**	**0**	**15**	**0**	**0**	**0.00**	....	....	....	....	....	....	....
	Peoria Rivermen	AHL	10	4	4	0	523	31	0	3.56	....	....	....	....	....	....	....
	Alaska Aces	ECHL	5	2	2	1	304	16	0	3.15	....	....	....	....	....	....	....
	BK Mlada Boleslav	CzRep	19	....	....	....	1132	49	3	2.60	....	....	....	....	....	....	....
	BK Mlada Boleslav	CzRep-Q	4	....	....	....	249	2	2	0.48	....	....	....	....	....	....	....
2009-10	BK Mlada Boleslav	CzRep	*54	....	....	....	*2899	134	2	2.77	....	....	....	....	....	....	....
	BK Mlada Boleslav	CzRep-Q	....	....	....	....	....	....	....	....	5	....	....	299	11	0	2.21
	NHL Totals		**6**	**0**	**2**	**0**	**125**	**9**	**0**	**4.32**	....	....	....	....	....	....	....

SCRIVENS, Ben (SKRIH-vehnz, BEHN) TOR.

Goaltender. Catches left. 6'2", 192 lbs. Born, Spruce Grove, Alta., September 11, 1986.

			Regular Season								Playoffs						
Season	Club	League	GP	W	L	O/T	Mins	GA	SO	Avg	GP	W	L	Mins	GA	SO	Avg
2004-05	Drayton Valley	AJHL	1	0	1	0	59	3	0	3.03	....	....	....	....	....	....	....
	Calgary Canucks	AJHL	16	7	3	3	857	43	1	3.01	....	....	....	....	....	....	....
2005-06	Spruce Grove	AJHL	45	27	12	2	2469	100	3	2.43	....	....	....	....	....	....	....
2006-07	Cornell Big Red	ECAC	12	3	6	2	574	22	1	2.30	....	....	....	....	....	....	....
2007-08	Cornell Big Red	ECAC	35	*19	12	3	1965	66	4	*2.02	....	....	....	....	....	....	....
2008-09	Cornell Big Red	ECAC	36	*22	10	4	2153	65	*7	*1.81	....	....	....	....	....	....	....
2009-10	Cornell Big Red	ECAC	34	*21	9	4	*2018	63	*7	*1.87	....	....	....	....	....	....	....

ECAC Second All-Star Team (2009) • ECAC First All-Star Team (2010) • NCAA East First All-American Team (2010)

Signed as a free agent by **Toronto**, April 28, 2010.

SEXSMITH, Tyson (SEHX-smihth, TIGH-suhn) S.J

Goaltender. Catches left. 5'11", 210 lbs. Born, Calgary, Alta., March 19, 1989.
(San Jose's 4th choice, 91st overall, in 2007 Entry Draft).

			Regular Season								Playoffs						
Season	Club	League	GP	W	L	O/T	Mins	GA	SO	Avg	GP	W	L	Mins	GA	SO	Avg
2004-05	Olds Grizzlys	AJHL	STATISTICS NOT AVAILABLE														
	Medicine Hat	WHL	1	0	0	0	5	0	0	0.00	....	....	....	....	....	....	....
	Vancouver Giants	WHL	2	1	0	0	80	4	0	3.00	....	....	....	....	....	....	....
2005-06	Vancouver Giants	WHL	11	6	3	1	547	21	1	2.30	....	....	....	....	....	....	....
2006-07	Vancouver Giants	WHL	51	31	12	8	3047	91	10	*1.79	22	14	7	1339	40	*4	*1.79
2007-08	Vancouver Giants	WHL	62	43	11	0	3678	116	*9	*1.89	10	6	4	658	20	0	1.82
2008-09	Vancouver Giants	WHL	52	39	9	4	3109	117	6	2.26	17	10	5	....	36	1	1.88
2009-10	Worcester Sharks	AHL	13	4	6	1	716	47	1	3.94	....	....	....	....	....	....	....
	Kalamazoo Wings	ECHL	2	2	0	0	120	5	0	2.50	....	....	....	....	....	....	....

WHL West Second All-Star Team (2008)

SHANTZ, David (SHAWNTS, DAY-vihd)

Goaltender. Catches left. 6'1", 202 lbs. Born, Burlington, Ont., May 5, 1986.
(Florida's 2nd choice, 37th overall, in 2004 Entry Draft).

			Regular Season								Playoffs						
Season	Club	League	GP	W	L	O/T	Mins	GA	SO	Avg	GP	W	L	Mins	GA	SO	Avg
2002-03	Thorold	OJHL-B	36	30	3	3	2107	63	8	1.79	....	....	....	....	....	....	....
2003-04	Mississauga	OHL	43	21	18	3	2483	120	1	2.90	*24	12	12	*1449	49	*5	2.03
2004-05	Mississauga	OHL	27	10	11	3	1524	72	0	2.83	2	0	1	80	2	0	1.50
2005-06	Peterborough	OHL	49	31	14	3	2946	141	2	2.87	*19	*16	3	*1239	54	1	2.62
2006-07	Rochester	AHL	2	1	1	0	120	9	0	4.51	....	....	....	....	....	....	....
	Florida Everblades	ECHL	23	13	7	1	1338	66	0	2.96	1	0	0	20	1	0	3.00
2007-08	Rochester	AHL	14	1	10	1	780	53	0	4.07	....	....	....	....	....	....	....
	Florida Everblades	ECHL	20	11	5	3	1101	47	0	2.56	2	0	1	77	3	0	2.33
2008-09	Rochester	AHL	12	3	6	2	690	30	1	2.61	....	....	....	....	....	....	....
	Elmira Jackals	ECHL	11	5	4	1	645	31	1	2.88	....	....	....	....	....	....	....
	Dayton Bombers	ECHL	23	10	9	3	1326	69	1	3.12	....	....	....	....	....	....	....
2009-10	Abbotsford Heat	AHL	32	15	10	4	1813	83	1	2.75	13	6	6	762	34	1	2.68
	Victoria	ECHL	28	18	5	4	1585	76	2	2.88	....	....	....	....	....	....	....

OHL All-Rookie Team (2004) • Canadian Major Junior All-Rookie Team (2004)

Signed as a free agent by **Abbotsford** (AHL), September 14, 2009.

SIMILA, Petteri (sih-MIH-la, PEH-tuhr-ree) MTL.

Goaltender. Catches left. 6'6", 189 lbs. Born, Oulu, Finland, April 9, 1990.
(Montreal's 8th choice, 211th overall, in 2009 Entry Draft).

			Regular Season								Playoffs						
Season	Club	League	GP	W	L	O/T	Mins	GA	SO	Avg	GP	W	L	Mins	GA	SO	Avg
2006-07	Karpat Oulu U18	Fin-U18	15	7	5	0	826	46	0	3.34	....	....	....	....	....	....	....
2007-08	Karpat Oulu U18	Fin-U18	12	4	3	0	738	35	0	2.84	3	0	2	162	9	0	3.33
2008-09	Karpat Oulu Jr.	Fin-Jr.	18	7	9	0	980	58	0	3.55	....	....	....	....	....	....	....
2009-10	Niagara Ice Dogs	OHL	11	1	4	3	550	38	0	4.15	....	....	....	....	....	....	....

SIMPSON, Kent (SIHMP-suhn, KEHNT) CHI.

Goaltender. Catches left. 6'3", 182 lbs. Born, Edmonton, Alta., March 26, 1992.
(Chicago's 4th choice, 58th overall, in 2010 Entry Draft).

			Regular Season								Playoffs						
Season	Club	League	GP	W	L	O/T	Mins	GA	SO	Avg	GP	W	L	Mins	GA	SO	Avg
2007-08	AMC Bulldogs	Minor-AB	....	4	10	6	1126	93	....	4.96	....	....	....	....	....	....	....
	Everett Silvertips	WHL	1	0	0	0	29	1	0	2.07	....	....	....	....	....	....	....
2008-09	Everett Silvertips	WHL	27	8	11	4	1451	93	1	3.85	....	....	....	....	....	....	....
2009-10	Everett Silvertips	WHL	34	22	9	1	1938	73	1	2.26	5	2	3	298	13	1	2.62

SMITH, Jeremy (SMIHTH, JAIR-eh-mee) NSH.

Goaltender. Catches left. 6', 171 lbs. Born, Dearborn, MI, April 13, 1989.
(Nashville's 2nd choice, 54th overall, in 2007 Entry Draft).

			Regular Season								Playoffs						
Season	Club	League	GP	W	L	O/T	Mins	GA	SO	Avg	GP	W	L	Mins	GA	SO	Avg
2005-06	Det. Compuware	MWEHL	13	5	6	0	696	31	0	2.67	....	....	....	....	....	....	....
	Det. Compuware	Exhib.	3	2	1	0	178	8	0	2.70	....	....	....	....	....	....	....
	Plymouth Whalers	OHL	5	0	2	0	111	11	0	5.95	....	....	....	....	....	....	....
2006-07	Plymouth Whalers	OHL	34	23	6	1	1901	82	4	2.59	3	2	0	149	8	0	3.22
2007-08	Plymouth Whalers	OHL	40	23	13	4	2431	116	3	2.86	4	0	4	224	29	0	7.77
2008-09	Plymouth Whalers	OHL	17	3	9	2	901	72	0	4.80	....	....	....	....	....	....	....
	Niagara Ice Dogs	OHL	26	12	9	3	1488	79	1	3.19	12	5	7	724	45	*1	3.73
2009-10	Milwaukee	AHL	1	0	0	0	5	0	0	0.00	....	....	....	....	....	....	....
	Cincinnati	ECHL	42	23	15	2	2468	108	2	2.63	*17	9	7	*988	44	1	2.67

ECHL Playoff MVP (Co-Winner)

SMITH, Mike (SMIHTH, MIGHK) T.B.

Goaltender. Catches left. 6'4", 219 lbs. Born, Kingston, Ont., March 22, 1982.
(Dallas' 5th choice, 161st overall, in 2001 Entry Draft).

			Regular Season								Playoffs						
Season	Club	League	GP	W	L	O/T	Mins	GA	SO	Avg	GP	W	L	Mins	GA	SO	Avg
1998-99	Kingston	OPJHL	16	....	....	....	906	53	0	3.51	....	....	....	....	....	....	....
99-2000	Kingston	OHL	15	4	5	0	666	42	0	3.78	....	....	....	....	....	....	....
2000-01	Kingston	OHL	3	0	0	2	136	8	0	3.53	....	....	....	....	....	....	....
	Sudbury Wolves	OHL	43	22	13	7	2571	108	3	2.52	12	7	5	735	26	2	*2.12
2001-02	Sudbury Wolves	OHL	53	19	28	5	3082	157	3	3.06	5	1	4	302	15	0	2.98
2002-03	Utah Grizzlies	AHL	11	5	5	0	614	33	0	3.23	....	....	....	....	....	....	....
	Lexington	ECHL	27	11	10	4	1553	66	1	2.55	2	0	1	93	8	0	5.14
2003-04	Utah Grizzlies	AHL	21	8	11	0	1186	56	2	2.83	....	....	....	....	....	....	....
2004-05	Houston Aeros	AHL	45	19	17	3	2408	97	5	2.42	3	1	2	181	4	0	1.33
2005-06	Iowa Stars	AHL	50	25	19	6	2998	125	3	2.50	7	3	4	417	19	0	2.74
2006-07	**Dallas**	**NHL**	**23**	**12**	**5**	**2**	**1213**	**45**	**3**	**2.23**	....	....	....	....	....	....	....
2007-08	**Dallas**	**NHL**	**21**	**12**	**9**	**0**	**1172**	**48**	**2**	**2.46**	....	....	....	....	....	....	....
	Tampa Bay	**NHL**	**13**	**3**	**10**	**0**	**774**	**36**	**1**	**2.79**	....	....	....	....	....	....	....
2008-09	**Tampa Bay**	**NHL**	**41**	**14**	**18**	**9**	**2471**	**108**	**2**	**2.62**	....	....	....	....	....	....	....
2009-10	**Tampa Bay**	**NHL**	**42**	**13**	**18**	**7**	**2273**	**117**	**2**	**3.09**	....	....	....	....	....	....	....
	NHL Totals		**140**	**54**	**60**	**18**	**7903**	**354**	**10**	**2.69**	....	....	....	....	....	....	....

NHL All-Rookie Team (2007)

Traded to **Tampa Bay** by **Dallas** with Jussi Jokinen, Jeff Halpern and Dallas' 4th round choice (later traded to Minnesota, later traded to Edmonton – Edmonton selected Kyle Bigos) in 2009 Entry Draft for Brad Richards and Johan Holmqvist, February 26, 2008.

STAJCER, Scott (STA-chuhr, SKAWT) NYR

Goaltender. Catches left. 6'3", 200 lbs. Born, Cambridge, Ont., June 14, 1991.
(NY Rangers' 5th choice, 140th overall, in 2009 Entry Draft).

			Regular Season								Playoffs						
Season	Club	League	GP	W	L	O/T	Mins	GA	SO	Avg	GP	W	L	Mins	GA	SO	Avg
2007-08	Owen Sound	OJHL-B	32	8	21	2	1862	130	0	3.90	....	....	....	....	....	....	....
	Owen Sound	OHL	6	1	3	1	306	22	0	4.31	....	....	....	....	....	....	....
2008-09	Owen Sound	OHL	35	15	15	5	1969	117	0	3.57	4	0	3	211	20	0	5.70
2009-10	Owen Sound	OHL	55	21	23	6	3042	186	1	3.67	....	....	....	....	....	....	....

STALOCK, Alex

(STAY-lahk, AL-ehx) **S.J.**

ioaltender. Catches left. 6', 180 lbs. Born, St. Paul, MN, July 28, 1987.
San Jose's 3rd choice, 112th overall, in 2005 Entry Draft).

			Regular Season								Playoffs						
eason	Club	League	GP	W	L	O/T	Mins	GA	SO	Avg	GP	W	L	Mins	GA	SO	Avg
003-04	South St. Paul	High-MN	31	23	7	1	....	....	....	2.20	....	....	....	....	....	....	....
004-05	Cedar Rapids	USHL	32	19	9	3	1801	82	1	2.73	9	7	2	582	14	*1	*1.44
005-06	Cedar Rapids	USHL	44	*28	13	3	2641	112	4	2.54	8	3	5	472	25	0	3.18
006-07	U. Minn-Duluth	WCHA	23	5	14	3	1364	76	1	3.34	....	....	....	....	....	....	....
007-08	U. Minn-Duluth	WCHA	36	13	17	6	2170	85	3	2.35	....	....	....	....	....	....	....
008-09	U. Minn-Duluth	WCHA	*42	21	13	8	*2534	90	*5	*2.13	....	....	....	....	....	....	....
009-10	Worcester Sharks	AHL	*61	*39	19	2	3534	155	4	2.63	11	6	5	683	26	0	2.28

SHL Playoff MVP (2005) • USHL First All-Star Team (2006) • USHL Goaltender of the Year (2006) • VCHA All-Rookie Team (2007) • WCHA First All-Star Team (2009) • NCAA West First All-American eam (2009)

STEFANISZIN, Sebastian

steh-fan-IHSH-ihn,suh-BAS-tee-yehn **ANA.**

ioaltender. Catches left. 6', 194 lbs. Born, Berlin, East Germany, July 22, 1987.
Anaheim's 6th choice, 98th overall, in 2007 Entry Draft).

			Regular Season								Playoffs						
eason	Club	League	GP	W	L	O/T	Mins	GA	SO	Avg	GP	W	L	Mins	GA	SO	Avg
002-03	Eisb. Jrs. Berl. Jr.	Ger-Jr.	12	....	....	....	....	....	....	....	....	....	....	....	....	....	....
003-04	Eisb. Jrs. Berl. Jr.	Ger-Jr.	23	....	....	....	....	....	....	2.87	3	....	....	....	....	....	5.45
004-05	Eisb. Jrs. Berlin	German-3	4	....	....	....	183	10	1	3.28	....	....	....	....	....	....	....
	Eisb. Jrs. Berl. Jr.	Ger-Jr.	20	....	....	....	1048	55	1	3.15	4	....	....	240	21	0	5.25
005-06	Eisbaren Berlin	Germany	3	....	....	....	175	11	0	3.77	....	....	....	....	....	....	....
	Eisb. Jrs. Berlin	German-3	16	....	....	....	818	57	0	4.18	....	....	....	....	....	....	....
	Hamburg Freezers	Germany	4	....	....	....	240	8	0	2.00	....	....	....	....	....	....	....
006-07	Eisbaren Berlin	Germany	2	....	....	....	39	3	0	4.59	....	....	....	....	....	....	....
	Eisb. Jrs. Berlin	German-3	36	....	....	....	2005	130	1	3.89	2	....	....	120	11	0	5.50
007-08	Essen	German-2	10	0	5	0	492	37	0	4.51	....	....	....	....	....	....	....
	Iserlohn Roosters	Germany	9	1	6	0	467	35	0	4.50	....	....	....	....	....	....	....
008-09	Iserlohn Roosters	Germany	23	8	12	0	1275	71	0	3.34	....	....	....	....	....	....	....
009-10	Landshut Cann.	German-2	5	3	2	0	304	10	0	1.97	....	....	....	....	....	....	....
	Iserlohn Roosters	Germany	14	3	9	0	636	43	0	4.06	....	....	....	....	....	....	....

TEPHAN, Tobias

(STEH-fan, toh-BUY-uhs)

oaltender. Catches left. 6'2", 180 lbs. Born, Zurich, Switz., January 21, 1984.
Dallas' 3rd choice, 34th overall, in 2002 Entry Draft).

			Regular Season								Playoffs						
eason	Club	League	GP	W	L	O/T	Mins	GA	SO	Avg	GP	W	L	Mins	GA	SO	Avg
000-01	Kloten Flyers Jr.	Swiss-Jr.					STATISTICS NOT AVAILABLE										
001-02	EHC Chur	Swiss	23	....	....	....	1396	80	0	3.44	10	....	....	604	39	0	3.87
002-03	Kloten Flyers	Swiss	*44	....	....	....	2670	125	2	2.81	5	....	....	292	20	0	4.11
003-04	Kloten Flyers	Swiss	26	....	....	....	1547	61	5	2.37	....	....	....	....	....	....	....
004-05	Kloten Flyers	Swiss	*44	....	....	....	2580	123	4	2.86	5	....	....	301	11	0	2.19
005-06	Kloten Flyers	Swiss	*44	16	19	8	2663	125	*5	2.82	11	5	6	683	34	0	2.98
006-07	Iowa Stars	AHL	27	10	15	0	1396	67	1	2.88	2	0	0	52	3	0	3.46
007-08	**Dallas**	**NHL**	**1**	**0**	**0**	**1**	**61**	**2**	**0**	**1.97**	....	....	....	....	....	....	....
	Iowa Stars	AHL	60	27	25	2	3329	147	6	2.65	....	....	....	....	....	....	....
008-09	**Dallas**	**NHL**	**10**	**1**	**3**	**1**	**438**	**27**	**0**	**3.70**	....	....	....	....	....	....	....
	Bridgeport	AHL	5	4	0	1	313	10	0	1.91	....	....	....	....	....	....	....
009-10	Geneve	Swiss	*50	*34	16	0	*3024	113	3	*2.24	*20	11	9	*1195	62	0	3.11
	Switzerland	Olympics					DID NOT PLAY – SPARE GOALTENDER										
	NHL Totals		**11**	**1**	**3**	**2**	**499**	**29**	**0**	**3.49**	....	....	....	....	....	....	....

TEWART, Brian

(STEW-ahrt, BRIGH-uhn) **PHI.**

oaltender. Catches left. 6'4", 200 lbs. Born, Burnaby, B.C., February 19, 1985.

			Regular Season								Playoffs						
eason	Club	League	GP	W	L	O/T	Mins	GA	SO	Avg	GP	W	L	Mins	GA	SO	Avg
06-07	Northern Mich.	CCHA	13	3	3	0	557	31	0	3.34	....	....	....	....	....	....	....
07-08	Northern Mich.	CCHA	35	15	15	4	1993	87	3	2.62	....	....	....	....	....	....	....
08-09	Northern Mich.	CCHA	32	14	13	3	1812	70	3	2.32	....	....	....	....	....	....	....
09-10	Northern Mich.	CCHA	37	18	11	7	2153	87	4	2.43	....	....	....	....	....	....	....
	Adirondack	AHL	3	1	2	0	182	11	0	3.63	....	....	....	....	....	....	....

gned as a free agent by **Philadelphia**, May 6, 2010.

ALBOT, Cameron

(TAL-buht, KAM-ruhn) **NYR**

oaltender. Catches left. 6'4", 205 lbs. Born, Caledonia, Ont., June 5, 1987.

			Regular Season								Playoffs						
eason	Club	League	GP	W	L	O/T	Mins	GA	SO	Avg	GP	W	L	Mins	GA	SO	Avg
07-08	AL-Huntsville	CHA	13	1	10	0	583	45	0	4.63	....	....	....	....	....	....	....
08-09	AL-Huntsville	CHA	24	2	16	3	1320	65	1	2.95	....	....	....	....	....	....	....
09-10	AL-Huntsville	CHA	*33	12	18	3	*1958	85	1	2.61	....	....	....	....	....	....	....
	Hartford Wolf Pack	AHL	1	0	0	0	19	3	0	9.70	....	....	....	....	....	....	....

gned as a free agent by **NY Rangers**, March 30, 2010.

AYLOR, Daniel

(TAY-luhr, DAN-yehl)

oaltender. Catches left. 5'11", 179 lbs. Born, Plymouth, England, April 28, 1986.
os Angeles' 8th choice, 221st overall, in 2004 Entry Draft).

			Regular Season								Playoffs						
eason	Club	League	GP	W	L	O/T	Mins	GA	SO	Avg	GP	W	L	Mins	GA	SO	Avg
02-03	Cumberland Grads	CJHL	23	13	3	1	1009	41	1	2.44	6	3	3	432	17	0	2.36
03-04	Guelph Storm	OHL	26	16	4	3	1462	66	0	2.71	3	1	1	159	9	0	3.40
04-05	Guelph Storm	OHL	31	13	14	3	1821	80	2	2.64	1	0	1	59	4	0	4.07
05-06	Kingston	OHL	57	32	15	6	3319	172	3	3.11	....	....	....	....	....	....	....
06-07	Bakersfield	ECHL	17	7	7	2	969	70	0	4.33	....	....	....	....	....	....	....
	Wheeling Nailers	ECHL	1	0	0	1	62	4	0	3.86	....	....	....	....	....	....	....
	Texas Wildcatters	ECHL	2	0	1	0	74	2	0	1.61	....	....	....	....	....	....	....
07-08	**Los Angeles**	**NHL**	**1**	**0**	**0**	**0**	**20**	**2**	**0**	**6.00**	....	....	....	....	....	....	....
	Manchester	AHL	23	13	5	2	1275	51	4	2.40	....	....	....	....	....	....	....
	Reading Royals	ECHL	5	3	0	0	182	8	0	2.63	13	7	6	815	38	1	2.80
08-09	Manchester	AHL	15	7	4	2	744	33	0	2.66	....	....	....	....	....	....	....
09-10	Syracuse Crunch	AHL	9	2	4	0	397	24	0	3.63	....	....	....	....	....	....	....
	Gwinnett	ECHL	37	18	13	5	2181	126	1	3.47	....	....	....	....	....	....	....
	NHL Totals		**1**	**0**	**0**	**0**	**20**	**2**	**0**	**6.00**	....	....	....	....	....	....	....

TELLQVIST, Mikael

(TEHL-kvihst, MIGH-kuhl)

Goaltender. Catches left. 5'11", 185 lbs. Born, Sundbyberg, Sweden, September 19, 1979.
(Toronto's 3rd choice, 70th overall, in 2000 Entry Draft).

			Regular Season								Playoffs						
Season	Club	League	GP	W	L	O/T	Mins	GA	SO	Avg	GP	W	L	Mins	GA	SO	Avg
1997-98	Djurgarden Jr.	Swe-Jr.	23	....	....	....	1380	55	....	2.39	2	0	2	120	8	0	4.00
1998-99	Djurgarden	Sweden	3	1	2	0	124	8	0	3.87	4	....	....	240	11	0	2.75
	Djurgarden	EuroHL	3	2	1	0	180	8	....	2.33	....	....	....	....	....	....	....
99-2000	Huddinge IK	Sweden-2	11	4	7	0	660	33	....	3.30	....	....	....	....	....	....	....
	Djurgarden	Sweden	30	....	....	....	1909	66	2	*2.07	*13	....	....	*814	21	*3	*1.55
2000-01	Djurgarden	Sweden	43	....	....	....	2622	91	*5	*2.08	*16	....	....	*1006	45	*1	2.68
2001-02	St. John's	AHL	28	8	11	6	1521	79	0	3.12	1	1	0	15	0	0	0.00
	Sweden	Olympics					DID NOT PLAY – SPARE GOALTENDER										
2002-03	**Toronto**	**NHL**	**3**	**1**	**1**	**0**	**86**	**4**	**0**	**2.79**	....	....	....	....	....	....	....
	St. John's	AHL	47	17	25	3	2651	148	1	3.35	....	....	....	....	....	....	....
2003-04	**Toronto**	**NHL**	**11**	**5**	**3**	**2**	**647**	**31**	**0**	**2.87**	....	....	....	....	....	....	....
	St. John's	AHL	23	10	11	1	1343	59	1	2.64	....	....	....	....	....	....	....
2004-05	St. John's	AHL	45	24	16	4	2600	115	0	2.65	5	1	4	253	15	0	3.56
2005-06	**Toronto**	**NHL**	**25**	**10**	**11**	**2**	**1399**	**73**	**2**	**3.13**	....	....	....	....	....	....	....
	Sweden	Olympics	1	0	1	0	60	3	0	3.00	....	....	....	....	....	....	....
2006-07	**Toronto**	**NHL**	**1**	**0**	**1**	**0**	**59**	**2**	**0**	**2.03**	....	....	....	....	....	....	....
	Toronto Marlies	AHL	3	2	1	0	182	12	0	3.95	....	....	....	....	....	....	....
	Phoenix	**NHL**	**30**	**11**	**11**	**3**	**1591**	**90**	**2**	**3.39**	....	....	....	....	....	....	....
2007-08	**Phoenix**	**NHL**	**22**	**9**	**8**	**2**	**1224**	**56**	**2**	**2.75**	....	....	....	....	....	....	....
2008-09	**Phoenix**	**NHL**	**15**	**7**	**5**	**1**	**798**	**38**	**0**	**2.86**	....	....	....	....	....	....	....
	Buffalo	**NHL**	**6**	**2**	**1**	**0**	**230**	**9**	**0**	**2.35**	....	....	....	....	....	....	....
2009-10	Ak Bars Kazan	Rus-KHL	11	....	....	....	588	24	0	2.45	....	....	....	....	....	....	....
	Lukko Rauma	Finland	26	11	10	5	1588	62	0	2.34	4	0	4	236	12	0	3.05
	NHL Totals		**113**	**45**	**41**	**10**	**6034**	**303**	**6**	**3.01**	....	....	....	....	....	....	....

Traded to **Phoenix** by **Toronto** for Tyson Nash and Boston's 4th round choice (previously acquired, Toronto selected Matt Frattin) in 2007 Entry Draft, November 28, 2006. Traded to **Buffalo** by **Phoenix** for Buffalo's 4th round choice (later traded to Montreal - Montreal selected Mark MacMillan) in 2010 Entry Draft, March 4, 2009. Signed as a free agent by **Kazan** (Russia - KHL), May 1, 2009. Signed as a free agent by **Rauma** (Finland), November 19, 2009.

THEODORE, Jose

(THEE-uh-dohr, joh-SAY)

Goaltender. Catches right. 5'11", 185 lbs. Born, Laval, Que., September 13, 1976.
(Montreal's 2nd choice, 44th overall, in 1994 Entry Draft).

			Regular Season								Playoffs						
Season	Club	League	GP	W	L	O/T	Mins	GA	SO	Avg	GP	W	L	Mins	GA	SO	Avg
1990-91	Richelieu	QAHA	42	....	....	....	2520	80	0	1.90	....	....	....	....	....	....	....
1991-92	Richelieu Riverains	QAAA	24	9	13	2	1440	96	0	3.99	5	2	3	295	26	0	5.28
1992-93	St-Jean Lynx	QMJHL	34	12	16	2	1776	112	0	3.78	3	0	2	175	11	0	3.77
1993-94	St-Jean Lynx	QMJHL	57	20	29	6	3225	194	0	3.61	5	1	4	296	18	0	3.65
1994-95	Hull Olympiques	QMJHL	*58	*32	22	2	*3348	193	5	3.46	*21	*15	6	*1263	59	*1	2.80
	Fredericton	AHL	....	....	....	....	....	....	....	....	1	0	1	60	3	0	3.00
1995-96	**Montreal**	**NHL**	**1**	**0**	**0**	**0**	**9**	**1**	**0**	**6.67**	....	....	....	....	....	....	....
	Hull Olympiques	QMJHL	48	33	11	2	2807	158	0	3.38	5	2	3	299	20	0	4.01
1996-97	**Montreal**	**NHL**	**16**	**5**	**6**	**2**	**821**	**53**	**0**	**3.87**	**2**	**1**	**1**	**168**	**7**	**0**	**2.50**
	Fredericton	AHL	26	12	12	0	1469	87	0	3.55	....	....	....	....	....	....	....
1997-98	Fredericton	AHL	53	20	23	8	3053	145	2	2.85	4	1	3	237	13	0	3.28
	Montreal	**NHL**	....	....	....	....	....	....	....	....	**3**	**0**	**1**	**120**	**1**	**0**	**0.50**
1998-99	**Montreal**	**NHL**	**18**	**4**	**12**	**0**	**913**	**50**	**1**	**3.29**	....	....	....	....	....	....	....
	Fredericton	AHL	27	12	13	2	1609	77	2	2.87	13	8	5	694	35	1	3.03
99-2000	**Montreal**	**NHL**	**30**	**12**	**13**	**2**	**1655**	**58**	**5**	**2.10**	....	....	....	....	....	....	....
2000-01	**Montreal**	**NHL**	**59**	**20**	**29**	**5**	**3298**	**141**	**2**	**2.57**	....	....	....	....	....	....	....
	Quebec Citadelles	AHL	3	3	0	0	180	9	0	3.00	....	....	....	....	....	....	....
2001-02	**Montreal**	**NHL**	**67**	**30**	**24**	**10**	**3864**	**136**	**7**	**2.11**	**12**	**6**	**6**	**686**	**35**	**0**	**3.06**
2002-03	**Montreal**	**NHL**	**57**	**20**	**31**	**6**	**3419**	**165**	**2**	**2.90**	....	....	....	....	....	....	....
2003-04	**Montreal**	**NHL**	**67**	**33**	**28**	**5**	**3961**	**150**	**6**	**2.27**	**11**	**4**	**7**	**678**	**27**	**1**	**2.39**
2004-05	Djurgarden	Sweden	17	....	....	....	1024	42	0	2.46	12	....	....	728	27	0	2.23
2005-06	**Montreal**	**NHL**	**38**	**17**	**15**	**5**	**2114**	**122**	**0**	**3.46**	....	....	....	....	....	....	....
	Colorado	**NHL**	**5**	**1**	**3**	**1**	**296**	**15**	**0**	**3.04**	**9**	**4**	**5**	**573**	**29**	**0**	**3.04**
2006-07	**Colorado**	**NHL**	**33**	**13**	**15**	**1**	**1748**	**95**	**0**	**3.26**	....	....	....	....	....	....	....
2007-08	**Colorado**	**NHL**	**53**	**28**	**21**	**3**	**3028**	**123**	**3**	**2.44**	**10**	**4**	**6**	**514**	**27**	**0**	**3.15**
	Lake Erie Monsters	AHL	1	0	1	0	60	3	0	3.02	....	....	....	....	....	....	....
2008-09	**Washington**	**NHL**	**57**	**32**	**17**	**5**	**3287**	**157**	**2**	**2.87**	**2**	**0**	**1**	**97**	**6**	**0**	**3.71**
2009-10	**Washington**	**NHL**	**47**	**30**	**7**	**7**	**2586**	**121**	**1**	**2.81**	**2**	**0**	**1**	**81**	**5**	**0**	**3.70**
	NHL Totals		**548**	**245**	**221**	**52**	**30999**	**1387**	**29**	**2.68**	**51**	**19**	**28**	**2917**	**137**	**1**	**2.82**

QMJHL Second All-Star Team (1995, 1996) • NHL Second All-Star Team (2002) • MBNA Roger Crozier Saving Grace Award (2002) • Vezina Trophy (2002) • Hart Trophy (2002) • Bill Masterton Memorial Trophy (2010)

Played in NHL All-Star Game (2002, 2004)

• Scored a goal vs. NY Islanders, January 2, 2001. Signed as a free agent by **Djurgarden** (Sweden), December 20, 2004. Traded to **Colorado** by **Montreal** for David Aebischer, March 8, 2006. Signed as a free agent by **Washington**, July 1, 2008.

THIESSEN, Brad

(THEE-suhn, BRAD) **PIT.**

Goaltender. Catches left. 6', 180 lbs. Born, Aldergrove, B.C., March 19, 1986.

			Regular Season								Playoffs						
Season	Club	League	GP	W	L	O/T	Mins	GA	SO	Avg	GP	W	L	Mins	GA	SO	Avg
2003-04	Penticton Panthers	BCHL	42	13	17	1	2131	122	2	3.44	....	....	....	....	....	....	....
2004-05	Penticton Vees	BCHL	26	7	18	1	1492	86	1	3.46	....	....	....	....	....	....	....
	Prince George	BCHL	10	5	4	0	561	31	0	3.31	....	....	....	....	....	....	....
2005-06	Prince George	BCHL	36	14	17	4	2058	99	5	2.89	....	....	....	....	....	....	....
	Merritt	BCHL	13	8	4	0	754	2	36	2.87	....	....	....	....	....	....	....
2006-07	Northeastern	H-East	33	11	17	5	1985	82	4	2.48	....	....	....	....	....	....	....
2007-08	Northeastern	H-East	37	16	17	3	2180	96	2	2.64	....	....	....	....	....	....	....
2008-09	Northeastern	H-East	41	25	12	4	2496	88	3	2.12	....	....	....	....	....	....	....
2009-10	Wilkes-Barre	AHL	30	14	14	1	1763	72	4	2.45	....	....	....	....	....	....	....
	Wheeling Nailers	ECHL	12	8	3	0	674	30	1	2.67	....	....	....	....	....	....	....

Signed as a free agent by **Pittsburgh**, April 8, 2009.

THOMAS, Tim (TAW-mas, TIHM) BOS.

Goaltender. Catches left. 5'11", 208 lbs. Born, Flint, MI, April 15, 1974.
(Quebec's 11th choice, 217th overall, in 1994 Entry Draft).

			Regular Season								Playoffs						
Season	**Club**	**League**	**GP**	**W**	**L**	**O/T**	**Mins**	**GA**	**SO**	**Avg**	**GP**	**W**	**L**	**Mins**	**GA**	**SO**	**Avg**
1992-93	Davison High	High-MI	27	....	....	....	1580	87	....	3.30	....	....	....	....	....	....	....
1993-94	U. of Vermont	ECAC	*33	15	12	6	1864	94	0	3.03	....	....	....	....	....	....	....
1994-95	U. of Vermont	ECAC	34	18	13	2	2010	90	*4	*2.69	....	....	....	....	....	....	....
1995-96	U. of Vermont	ECAC	37	*26	7	4	*2254	88	*3	*2.34	....	....	....	....	....	....	....
1996-97	U. of Vermont	ECAC	36	22	11	3	2158	101	2	2.81	....	....	....	....	....	....	....
1997-98	Birmingham Bulls	ECHL	6	4	1	1	360	13	1	2.17	....	....	....	....	....	....	....
	Houston Aeros	IHL	1	0	1	0	59	4	0	4.01	....	....	....	....	....	....	....
	HIFK Helsinki	Finland	18	13	4	1	1034	28	2	1.62	9	9	0	551	14	3	1.52
1998-99	Hamilton Bulldogs	AHL	15	6	8	0	837	45	0	3.23	....	....	....	....	....	....	....
	HIFK Helsinki	Finland	14	8	3	3	833	31	2	2.23	11	7	4	658	25	0	2.28
99-2000	Detroit Vipers	IHL	36	10	21	3	2020	120	1	3.56	....	....	....	....	....	....	....
2000-01	AIK Solna	Sweden	43	....	....	....	2542	105	3	2.48	5	....	....	299	20	0	4.01
2001-02	Karpat Oulu	Finland	32	15	12	5	1937	79	4	2.44	3	1	2	180	12	0	4.00
2002-03	**Boston**	**NHL**	**4**	**3**	**1**	**0**	**220**	**11**	**0**	**3.00**	....	....	....	....	....	....	....
	Providence Bruins	AHL	35	18	12	5	2049	98	1	2.87	....	....	....	....	....	....	....
2003-04	Providence Bruins	AHL	43	20	16	6	2544	78	9	1.84	2	0	2	84	10	0	7.13
2004-05	Jokerit Helsinki	Finland	54	34	13	7	3266	86	15	1.58	12	8	4	720	22	0	1.83
2005-06	**Boston**	**NHL**	**38**	**12**	**13**	**10**	**2187**	**101**	**1**	**2.77**	....	....	....	....	....	....	....
	Providence Bruins	AHL	26	15	11	0	1515	57	1	2.26	....	....	....	....	....	....	....
2006-07	**Boston**	**NHL**	**66**	**30**	**29**	**4**	**3619**	**189**	**3**	**3.13**	....	....	....	....	....	....	....
2007-08	**Boston**	**NHL**	**57**	**28**	**19**	**6**	**3342**	**136**	**3**	**2.44**	**7**	**3**	**4**	**430**	**19**	**0**	**2.65**
2008-09	**Boston**	**NHL**	**54**	**36**	**11**	**7**	**3259**	**114**	**5**	***2.10**	**11**	**7**	**4**	**680**	**21**	**1**	***1.85**
2009-10	**Boston**	**NHL**	**43**	**17**	**18**	**8**	**2442**	**104**	**5**	**2.56**	....	....	....	....	....	....	....
	United States	Olympics	1	0	0	0	12	1	0	5.21	....	....	....	....	....	....	....
	NHL Totals		**262**	**126**	**91**	**35**	**15069**	**655**	**17**	**2.61**	**18**	**10**	**8**	**1110**	**40**	**1**	**2.16**

ECAC First All-Star Team (1995, 1996) • ECAC Goaltender of the Year (1996) • NCAA East Second All-American Team (1995) • NCAA East First All-American Team (1996) • NHL First All-Star Team (2009) • William M. Jennings Trophy (2009) (shared with Manny Fernandez) • Vezina Trophy (2009)

Played in NHL All-Star Game (2008, 2009)

• Rights transferred to **Colorado** after **Quebec** franchise relocated, June 21, 1995. Signed as a free agent by **Edmonton**, June 4, 1998. Signed as free agent by **Solna** (Sweden), July 26. 2000. Signed as a free agent by **Boston**, August 8, 2002. Signed as a free agent by **Jokerit Helsinki** (Finland), May 17, 2004. Signed as a free agent by **Boston**, September 14, 2005.

TOIVONEN, Hannu (TOI-voh-nuhn, HA-noo) CHI.

Goaltender. Catches left. 6'2", 200 lbs. Born, Kalvola, Finland, May 18, 1984.
(Boston's 1st choice, 29th overall, in 2002 Entry Draft).

			Regular Season								Playoffs						
Season	**Club**	**League**	**GP**	**W**	**L**	**O/T**	**Mins**	**GA**	**SO**	**Avg**	**GP**	**W**	**L**	**Mins**	**GA**	**SO**	**Avg**
2000-01	HPK U18	Fin-U18	....	....	....	....	....	....	....	....	....	....	....	....	....	....	....
2001-02	HPK U18	Fin-U18	5	4	1	0	277	14	0	3.03	....	....	....	....	....	....	....
	HPK Jr.	Fin-Jr.	31	15	12	4	1877	103	2	3.29	7	3	4	440	31	0	4.23
2002-03	HPK Jr.	Fin-Jr.	6	3	3	0	359	20	0	3.34	....	....	....	....	....	....	....
	HPK Hameenlinna	Finland	24	16	2	4	1432	54	2	2.26	2	1	1	117	3	1	1.53
2003-04	Providence Bruins	AHL	36	15	16	4	2162	83	2	2.30	0	0	0	0	0	0	0.00
2004-05	Providence Bruins	AHL	54	29	18	3	3017	103	7	2.05	17	10	7	1038	42	0	2.43
2005-06	**Boston**	**NHL**	**20**	**9**	**5**	**4**	**1163**	**51**	**1**	**2.63**	....	....	....	....	....	....	....
2006-07	**Boston**	**NHL**	**18**	**3**	**9**	**1**	**894**	**63**	**0**	**4.23**	....	....	....	....	....	....	....
	Providence Bruins	AHL	27	13	13	1	1618	64	2	2.37	13	6	7	742	36	0	2.91
2007-08	**St. Louis**	**NHL**	**23**	**6**	**10**	**5**	**1202**	**69**	**0**	**3.44**	....	....	....	....	....	....	....
	Peoria Rivermen	AHL	11	6	4	0	627	33	0	3.16	....	....	....	....	....	....	....
2008-09	Ilves Tampere	Finland	52	19	23	9	2913	130	3	2.68	3	1	2	198	6	1	1.82
2009-10	Peoria Rivermen	AHL	26	11	11	3	1516	69	0	2.73	....	....	....	....	....	....	....
	Rockford IceHogs	AHL	6	1	4	0	296	17	0	3.44	1	0	0	20	1	0	3.00
	NHL Totals		**61**	**18**	**24**	**10**	**3259**	**183**	**1**	**3.37**	....	....	....	....	....	....	....

Traded to **St. Louis** by **Boston** for Carl Soderberg, July 23, 2007. Signed as a free agent by **Ilves Tampere** (Finland), July 15, 2008. Signed as a free agent by **St. Louis**, July 9, 2009. Traded to **Chicago** by **St. Louis** with Danny Richmond for Joe Fallon, March 1, 2010.

TOKARSKI, Dustin (toh-KAHR-skee, DUHS-tihn) T.B.

Goaltender. Catches left. 5'11", 190 lbs. Born, Humboldt, Sask., September 16, 1989.
(Tampa Bay's 3rd choice, 122nd overall, in 2008 Entry Draft).

			Regular Season								Playoffs						
Season	**Club**	**League**	**GP**	**W**	**L**	**O/T**	**Mins**	**GA**	**SO**	**Avg**	**GP**	**W**	**L**	**Mins**	**GA**	**SO**	**Avg**
2006-07	Spokane Chiefs	WHL	30	13	11	2	1674	78	2	2.80	6	2	4	364	17	0	2.80
2007-08	Spokane Chiefs	WHL	45	30	10	0	2543	87	6	2.05	*21	*16	5	*1352	31	*3	*1.38
2008-09	Spokane Chiefs	WHL	54	34	18	2	3264	107	*7	*1.97	12	7	5	812	23	1	*1.70
2009-10	**Tampa Bay**	**NHL**	**2**	**0**	**0**	**0**	**44**	**3**	**0**	**4.09**	....	....	....	....	....	....	....
	Norfolk Admirals	AHL	55	27	25	3	3319	139	4	2.51	....	....	....	....	....	....	....
	NHL Totals		**2**	**0**	**0**	**0**	**44**	**3**	**0**	**4.09**	....	....	....	....	....	....	....

Memorial Cup All-Star Team (2008) • Hap Emms Memorial Trophy (Memorial Cup Tournament - Top Goaltender) (2008) • Stafford Smythe Memorial Trophy (Memorial Cup Tournament - MVP) (2008) • WHL West Second All-Star Team (2009)

TORDJMAN, Josh (TOHRJ-man, JAWSH)

Goaltender. Catches left. 6'1", 156 lbs. Born, Montreal, Que., January 11, 1985.

			Regular Season								Playoffs						
Season	**Club**	**League**	**GP**	**W**	**L**	**O/T**	**Mins**	**GA**	**SO**	**Avg**	**GP**	**W**	**L**	**Mins**	**GA**	**SO**	**Avg**
2002-03	Valleyfield Braves	QJHL					STATISTICS NOT AVAILABLE										
	Victoriaville Tigres	QMJHL	10	4	3	0	432	24	1	3.33	2	0	1	112	12	0	6.46
2003-04	Victoriaville Tigres	QMJHL	42	10	24	4	2177	143	2	3.94	....	....	....	....	....	....	....
2004-05	Victoriaville Tigres	QMJHL	56	22	28	4	3185	171	5	3.22	7	3	4	435	24	0	3.31
2005-06	Victoriaville Tigres	QMJHL	31	13	17	0	1792	106	2	3.55	....	....	....	....	....	....	....
	Moncton Wildcats	QMJHL	25	18	6	0	1427	55	2	*2.31	21	*15	5	1238	48	*2	2.33
2006-07	San Antonio	AHL	37	15	18	2	2114	91	1	2.58	....	....	....	....	....	....	....
	Phoenix	ECHL	9	4	4	0	480	25	0	3.12	....	....	....	....	....	....	....
2007-08	San Antonio	AHL	43	22	14	4	2466	109	1	2.65	6	3	3	357	11	1	1.85
2008-09	**Phoenix**	**NHL**	**2**	**0**	**2**	**0**	**118**	**8**	**0**	**4.07**	....	....	....	....	....	....	....
	San Antonio	AHL	51	25	22	2	2921	127	6	2.61	....	....	....	....	....	....	....
2009-10	San Antonio	AHL	45	20	22	2	2537	125	1	2.96	....	....	....	....	....	....	....
	NHL Totals		**2**	**0**	**2**	**0**	**118**	**8**	**0**	**4.07**	....	....	....	....	....	....	....

QMJHL Second All-Star Team (2006) • Yanick Dupre Memorial Award (AHL – Outstanding Humanitarian Contribution) (2010)

Signed as a free agent by **Phoenix**, July 2, 2006.

TOSKALA, Vesa (TAWS-kah-lah, VEH-sa)

Goaltender. Catches left. 5'10", 195 lbs. Born, Tampere, Finland, May 20, 1977.
(San Jose's 4th choice, 90th overall, in 1995 Entry Draft).

			Regular Season								Playoffs						
Season	**Club**	**League**	**GP**	**W**	**L**	**O/T**	**Mins**	**GA**	**SO**	**Avg**	**GP**	**W**	**L**	**Mins**	**GA**	**SO**	**Av**
1994-95	Ilves Tampere Jr.	Fin-Jr.	17	10	5	1	956	36	2	2.26	7	....	....	393	22	....	3.3
1995-96	Ilves Tampere Jr.	Fin-Jr.	3	3	0	0	180	3	0	1.00	....	....	....	....	....	....	....
	KooVee Tampere	Finland-2	2	1	1	0	119	5	1	2.51	....	....	....	....	....	....	....
	Ilves Tampere	Finland	37	14	14	7	2072	109	1	3.16	2	0	2	78	11	0	8.4
1996-97	Ilves Tampere Jr.	Fin-Jr.	3	....	....	....	184	....	....	2.93	....	....	....	....	....	....	....
	Ilves Tampere	Finland	40	22	12	5	2270	108	0	2.85	8	3	5	479	29	0	3.6
1997-98	Ilves Tampere Jr.	Fin-Jr.	2	2	0	0	120	4	0	2.00	....	....	....	....	....	....	....
	Ilves Tampere	Finland	43	26	13	3	2554	118	1	2.77	9	6	3	519	18	1	2.
1998-99	Ilves Tampere	Finland	33	21	12	0	1966	70	5	2.14	4	1	3	248	14	0	3.
99-2000	Farjestad	Sweden	44	....	....	....	2652	118	3	2.67	7	....	....	439	19	0	2.
2000-01	Kentucky	AHL	44	22	13	5	2466	114	2	2.77	3	0	3	197	8	0	2.
2001-02	**San Jose**	**NHL**	**1**	**0**	**0**	**0**	**10**	**0**	**0**	**0.00**	....	....	....	....	....	....	....
	Cleveland Barons	AHL	*62	19	33	7	*3574	178	3	2.99	....	....	....	....	....	....	....
2002-03	**San Jose**	**NHL**	**11**	**4**	**3**	**1**	**537**	**21**	**1**	**2.35**	....	....	....	....	....	....	....
	Cleveland Barons	AHL	49	15	30	2	2824	151	1	3.21	....	....	....	....	....	....	....
2003-04	**San Jose**	**NHL**	**28**	**12**	**8**	**4**	**1541**	**53**	**1**	**2.06**	....	....	....	....	....	....	....
2004-05	Ilves Tampere	Finland	3	0	1	2	186	8	0	2.58	6	3	3	357	19	0	3.
2005-06	**San Jose**	**NHL**	**37**	**23**	**7**	**4**	**2039**	**87**	**2**	**2.56**	**11**	**6**	**5**	**686**	**28**	**1**	**2.**
	Cleveland Barons	AHL	1	0	0	1	65	0	1	0.00	....	....	....	....	....	....	....
2006-07	**San Jose**	**NHL**	**38**	**26**	**10**	**1**	**2142**	**84**	**4**	**2.35**	....	....	....	....	....	....	....
2007-08	**Toronto**	**NHL**	**66**	**33**	**25**	**6**	**3837**	**175**	**3**	**2.74**	....	....	....	....	....	....	....
2008-09	**Toronto**	**NHL**	**53**	**22**	**17**	**11**	**3056**	**166**	**1**	**3.26**	....	....	....	....	....	....	....
2009-10	**Toronto**	**NHL**	**26**	**7**	**12**	**3**	**1393**	**85**	**1**	**3.66**	....	....	....	....	....	....	....
	Calgary	**NHL**	**6**	**2**	**0**	**0**	**212**	**8**	**0**	**2.26**	....	....	....	....	....	....	....
	NHL Totals		**266**	**129**	**82**	**30**	**14767**	**679**	**13**	**2.76**	**11**	**6**	**5**	**686**	**28**	**1**	**2.**

Signed as a free agent by **Ilves Tampere** (Finland), January 31, 2005. Traded to **Toronto** by **San Jose** with Mark Bell for Toronto's 1st (later traded to St. Louis – St. Louis selected Lars Eller) and 2n (later traded to St. Louis – St. Louis selected Aaron Palushaj) round choices in 2007 Entry Draft and Toronto's 4th round choice (later traded to Nashville – Nashville selected Craig Smith) in 2009 Entry Draft, June 22, 2007. Traded to **Anaheim** by **Toronto** with Jason Blake for Jean-Sebastien Giguer January 31, 2010. Traded to **Calgary** by **Anaheim** for Curtis McElhinney, March 3, 2010.

TURCO, Marty (TUHR-koh, MAHR-tee) CH

Goaltender. Catches left. 5'11", 184 lbs. Born, Sault Ste. Marie, Ont., August 13, 1975.
(Dallas' 4th choice, 124th overall, in 1994 Entry Draft).

			Regular Season								Playoffs						
Season	**Club**	**League**	**GP**	**W**	**L**	**O/T**	**Mins**	**GA**	**SO**	**Avg**	**GP**	**W**	**L**	**Mins**	**GA**	**SO**	**A**
1993-94	Cambridge	OJHL-B	34	19	10	3	1973	114	0	3.47	....	....	....	....	....	....	
1994-95	U. of Michigan	CCHA	37	*27	7	1	2063	95	1	2.76	....	....	....	....	....	....	
1995-96	U. of Michigan	CCHA	*42	*34	7	1	*2335	84	*5	*2.16	....	....	....	....	....	....	
1996-97	U. of Michigan	CCHA	*41	*33	4	4	*2296	87	*4	*2.27	....	....	....	....	....	....	
1997-98	U. of Michigan	CCHA	*45	*33	10	1	*2640	95	4	2.16	....	....	....	....	....	....	
1998-99	Michigan K-Wings	IHL	54	24	17	10	3127	136	1	2.61	5	2	3	300	14	0	2.
99-2000	Michigan K-Wings	IHL	60	23	27	*7	3399	139	*7	2.45	....	....	....	....	....	....	
2000-01	**Dallas**	**NHL**	**26**	**13**	**6**	**1**	**1266**	**40**	**3**	***1.90**	....	....	....	....	....	....	
2001-02	**Dallas**	**NHL**	**31**	**15**	**6**	**2**	**1519**	**53**	**2**	**2.09**	....	....	....	....	....	....	
2002-03	**Dallas**	**NHL**	**55**	**31**	**10**	**10**	**3203**	**92**	**7**	***1.72**	**12**	**6**	**6**	**798**	**25**	**0**	**1**
2003-04	**Dallas**	**NHL**	**73**	**37**	**21**	**13**	**4359**	**144**	**9**	**1.98**	**5**	**1**	**4**	**325**	**18**	**0**	**3.**
2004-05	Djurgarden	Sweden	6	....	....	....	356	12	1	2.02	....	....	....	....	....	....	
2005-06	**Dallas**	**NHL**	**68**	**41**	**19**	**5**	**3910**	**166**	**3**	**2.55**	**5**	**1**	**4**	**319**	**18**	**0**	**3.**
	Canada	Olympics					DID NOT PLAY – SPARE GOALTENDER										
2006-07	**Dallas**	**NHL**	**67**	**38**	**20**	**5**	**3764**	**140**	**6**	**2.23**	**7**	**3**	**4**	**509**	**11**	**3**	***1.**
2007-08	**Dallas**	**NHL**	**62**	**32**	**21**	**6**	**3629**	**140**	**3**	**2.31**	**18**	**10**	**8**	**1152**	**40**	**1**	**2**
2008-09	**Dallas**	**NHL**	**74**	**33**	**31**	**10**	**4327**	**203**	**3**	**2.81**	....	....	....	....	....	....	
2009-10	**Dallas**	**NHL**	**53**	**22**	**20**	**11**	**3088**	**140**	**4**	**2.72**	....	....	....	....	....	....	
	NHL Totals		**509**	**262**	**154**	**63**	**29065**	**1118**	**40**	**2.31**	**47**	**21**	**26**	**3103**	**112**	**4**	**2.**

CCHA Rookie of the Year (1995) • NCAA Championship All-Tournament Team (1996, 1998) • CCHA First All-Star Team (1997) • NCAA West First All-American Team (1997) • CCHA Second All-Star Team (1998) • NCAA Championship Tournament MVP (1998) • Garry F. Longman Memori Trophy (IHL – Rookie of the Year) (1999) • MBNA Roger Crozier Saving Grace Award (2001, 2003) • NHL Second All-Star Team (2003)

Played in NHL All-Star Game (2003, 2004, 2007)

Signed as a free agent by **Djurgarden** (Sweden), November 13, 2004. Signed as a free agent by **Chicago**, August 2, 2010.

VALIQUETTE, Steve (val-ih-KEHT, STEEV)

Goaltender. Catches left. 6'6", 210 lbs. Born, Etobicoke, Ont., August 20, 1977.
(Los Angeles' 8th choice, 190th overall, in 1996 Entry Draft).

			Regular Season								Playoffs						
Season	**Club**	**League**	**GP**	**W**	**L**	**O/T**	**Mins**	**GA**	**SO**	**Avg**	**GP**	**W**	**L**	**Mins**	**GA**	**SO**	**Avg**
1993-94	Burlington	OPJHL	30	....	....	....	1663	112	1	4.04	....	....	....	....	....	....	....
1994-95	Rayside-Balfour	NOJHA	2	0	2	0	89	12	0	8.09	....	....	....	....	....	....	....
	Smiths Falls Bears	CJHL	21	10	8	3	1275	75	0	3.53	....	....	....	....	....	....	....
	Sudbury Wolves	OHL	4	2	0	0	138	6	0	2.61	....	....	....	....	....	....	....
1995-96	Sudbury Wolves	OHL	39	13	16	2	1887	123	0	3.91	....	....	....	....	....	....	....
1996-97	Sudbury Wolves	OHL	*61	21	29	7	3311	232	1	4.20	....	....	....	....	....	....	....
	Dayton Bombers	ECHL	3	1	0	0	89	6	0	4.03	2	1	1	118	5	0	2.54
1997-98	Sudbury Wolves	OHL	14	5	7	1	807	50	0	3.72	....	....	....	....	....	....	....
	Erie Otters	OHL	28	16	7	3	1525	65	3	2.56	7	3	4	467	15	1	1.93
1998-99	Lowell	AHL	1	0	1	0	59	3	0	3.05	....	....	....	....	....	....	....
	Hampton Roads	ECHL	31	18	7	3	1713	84	1	2.94	2	0	1	60	7	0	7.00
99-2000	**NY Islanders**	**NHL**	**6**	**2**	**0**	**0**	**193**	**6**	**0**	**1.87**	....	....	....	....	....	....	....
	Lowell	AHL	14	8	5	0	727	36	0	2.97	....	....	....	....	....	....	....
	Providence Bruins	AHL	1	1	0	0	60	3	0	3.00	....	....	....	....	....	....	....
	Trenton Titans	ECHL	12	5	6	1	692	36	1	3.12	....	....	....	....	....	....	....
2000-01	Springfield Falcons	AHL	20	7	10	1	1066	54	0	3.04	....	....	....	....	....	....	....
2001-02	Bridgeport	AHL	20	10	5	1	1071	45	2	2.52	1	0	0	18	1	0	3.30
2002-03	Bridgeport	AHL	34	15	14	3	1962	86	2	2.63	4	3	1	253	9	0	2.13
2003-04	**Edmonton**	**NHL**	**1**	**0**	**0**	**0**	**14**	**2**	**0**	**8.57**	....	....	....	....	....	....	....
	Toronto	AHL	35	14	14	5	2064	89	2	2.59	....	....	....	....	....	....	....
	NY Rangers	**NHL**	**2**	**1**	**1**	**0**	**120**	**6**	**0**	**3.00**	....	....	....	....	....	....	....
	Hartford Wolf Pack	AHL	7	2	4	1	400	15	1	2.25	1	0	0	11	0	0	0.00
2004-05	Hartford Wolf Pack	AHL	35	19	11	1	1900	56	7	*1.77	2	1	1	118	4	0	2.03
2005-06	Yaroslavl	Russia	45	....	....	....	2734	89	4	1.95	8	....	....	458	23	0	3.01
2006-07	**NY Rangers**	**NHL**	**3**	**1**	**2**	**0**	**115**	**6**	**0**	**3.13**	....	....	....	....	....	....	....
	Hartford Wolf Pack	AHL	30	17	12	0	1694	66	2	2.34	....	....	....	....	....	....	....
2007-08	**NY Rangers**	**NHL**	**13**	**5**	**3**	**3**	**686**	**25**	**2**	**2.19**	....	....	....	....	....	....	....
2008-09	**NY Rangers**	**NHL**	**15**	**5**	**5**	**2**	**823**	**39**	**1**	**2.84**	**2**	**0**	**0**	**40**	**0**	**0**	**0.00**
2009-10	**NY Rangers**	**NHL**	**6**	**2**	**3**	**0**	**305**	**19**	**1**	**3.74**	....	....	....	....	....	....	....
	Hartford Wolf Pack	AHL	11	4	5	1	547	34	0	3.73	....	....	....	....	....	....	....
	NHL Totals		**46**	**16**	**14**	**5**	**2256**	**103**	**4**	**2.74**	**2**	**0**	**0**	**40**	**0**	**0**	**0.00**

Harry "Hap" Holmes Memorial Trophy (AHL - fewest goals against) (2005) (shared with Jason LaBarbera)

Signed as a free agent by **NY Islanders**, August 18, 1998. Signed as a free agent by **Edmonton**, July 20, 2003. Claimed by **Florida** from **Edmonton** in Waiver Draft, October 3, 2003. Claimed on waivers by **Edmonton** from **Florida**, October 9, 2003. Traded to **NY Rangers** by **Edmonton** with Dwight Helminen and Edmonton's 2nd round compensatory choice (Dane Byers) in 2004 Entry Draft for Petr Nedved and Jussi Markkanen, March 3, 2004. Signed as a free agent by **Yaroslavl** (Russia), April 26, 2005. Signed as a free agent by **NY Rangers**, July 1, 2006.

VARLAMOV, Semyon (vahr-LA-mawv, sehm-YAWN) WSH.

Goaltender. Catches left. 6'2", 209 lbs. Born, Kuybyshev, USSR, April 27, 1988.
(Washington's 2nd choice, 23rd overall, in 2006 Entry Draft).

			Regular Season								Playoffs						
Season	**Club**	**League**	**GP**	**W**	**L**	**O/T**	**Mins**	**GA**	**SO**	**Avg**	**GP**	**W**	**L**	**Mins**	**GA**	**SO**	**Avg**
2004-05	Yaroslavl 2	Russia-3	8	....	....	....	369	15	1	2.43	....	....	....	....	....	....	....
2005-06	Yaroslavl 2	Russia-3	33	....	....	....	1782	60	8	2.02	....	....	....	....	....	....	....
2006-07	Yaroslavl 2	Russia-3	2	....	....	....	120	3	0	1.50	....	....	....	....	....	....	....
	Yaroslavl	Russia	33	....	....	....	1936	70	3	2.17	6	....	....	368	18	0	2.94
2007-08	Yaroslavl	Russia	44	....	....	....	2592	106	3	2.45	*16	....	....	*924	25	*5	1.62
2008-09	**Washington**	**NHL**	**6**	**4**	**0**	**1**	**329**	**13**	**0**	**2.37**	**13**	**7**	**6**	**759**	**32**	***2**	**2.53**
	Hershey Bears	AHL	27	19	7	1	1551	62	2	2.40	....	....	....	....	....	....	....
2009-10	**Washington**	**NHL**	**26**	**15**	**4**	**6**	**1527**	**65**	**2**	**2.55**	**6**	**3**	**3**	**349**	**14**	**0**	**2.41**
	Hershey Bears	AHL	3	3	0	0	185	6	0	1.95	....	....	....	....	....	....	....
	Russia	Olympics					DID NOT PLAY – SPARE GOALTENDER										
	NHL Totals		**32**	**19**	**4**	**7**	**1856**	**78**	**2**	**2.52**	**19**	**10**	**9**	**1108**	**46**	**2**	**2.49**

VISENTIN, Mark (vih-SEHN-tihn, MAHRK) PHX.

Goaltender. Catches left. 6'2", 187 lbs. Born, Hamilton, Ont., August 7, 1992.
(Phoenix's 2nd choice, 27th overall, in 2010 Entry Draft).

			Regular Season								Playoffs						
Season	**Club**	**League**	**GP**	**W**	**L**	**O/T**	**Mins**	**GA**	**SO**	**Avg**	**GP**	**W**	**L**	**Mins**	**GA**	**SO**	**Avg**
2007-08	Halton Hurricanes	Minor-ON	44	....	....	....	1980	98	3	2.22	....	....	....	....	....	....	....
2008-09	Niagara Ice Dogs	OHL	23	5	11	3	1099	78	0	4.26	....	....	....	....	....	....	....
2009-10	Niagara Ice Dogs	OHL	55	24	26	5	3209	160	0	2.99	5	1	3	305	18	0	3.54

VOKOUN, Tomas (voh-KOON, TAW-mas) FLA.

Goaltender. Catches right. 6', 195 lbs. Born, Karlovy Vary, Czech., July 2, 1976.
(Montreal's 11th choice, 226th overall, in 1994 Entry Draft).

			Regular Season								Playoffs						
Season	**Club**	**League**	**GP**	**W**	**L**	**O/T**	**Mins**	**GA**	**SO**	**Avg**	**GP**	**W**	**L**	**Mins**	**GA**	**SO**	**Avg**
1993-94	HC Kladno	CzRep	1	0	0	0	20	2	0	6.01	....	....	....	....	....	....	....
1994-95	HC Kladno	CzRep	26	....	....	....	1368	70	....	3.07	5	....	....	240	19	....	4.75
1995-96	Wheeling	ECHL	35	20	10	2	1912	117	0	3.67	7	4	3	436	19	0	2.61
	Fredericton	AHL	....	....	....	....	....	....	....	....	1	0	1	59	4	0	4.09
1996-97	**Montreal**	**NHL**	**1**	**0**	**0**	**0**	**20**	**4**	**0**	**12.00**	....	....	....	....	....	....	....
	Fredericton	AHL	47	12	26	7	2645	154	2	3.49	....	....	....	....	....	....	....
1997-98	Fredericton	AHL	31	13	13	2	1735	90	0	3.11	....	....	....	....	....	....	....
1998-99	**Nashville**	**NHL**	**37**	**12**	**18**	**4**	**1954**	**96**	**1**	**2.95**	....	....	....	....	....	....	....
	Milwaukee	IHL	9	3	2	4	539	22	1	2.45	2	0	2	149	8	0	3.22
99-2000	**Nashville**	**NHL**	**33**	**9**	**20**	**1**	**1879**	**87**	**1**	**2.78**	....	....	....	....	....	....	....
	Milwaukee	IHL	7	5	2	0	364	17	0	2.80	....	....	....	....	....	....	....
2000-01	**Nashville**	**NHL**	**37**	**13**	**17**	**5**	**2088**	**85**	**2**	**2.44**	....	....	....	....	....	....	....
2001-02	**Nashville**	**NHL**	**29**	**5**	**14**	**4**	**1471**	**66**	**2**	**2.69**	....	....	....	....	....	....	....
2002-03	**Nashville**	**NHL**	**69**	**25**	**31**	**11**	**3974**	**146**	**3**	**2.20**	....	....	....	....	....	....	....
2003-04	**Nashville**	**NHL**	**73**	**34**	**29**	**10**	**4221**	**178**	**3**	**2.53**	**6**	**2**	**4**	**356**	**12**	**1**	**2.02**
2004-05	Znojmo	CzRep	27	....	....	....	1599	69	3	2.59	....	....	....	....	....	....	....
	HIFK Helsinki	Finland	19	11	4	4	1149	35	2	1.83	4	0	3	205	12	0	3.51
2005-06	**Nashville**	**NHL**	**61**	**36**	**18**	**7**	**3601**	**160**	**4**	**2.67**	....	....	....	....	....	....	....
	Czech Republic	Olympics	7	3	4	0	342	14	1	2.46	....	....	....	....	....	....	....
2006-07	**Nashville**	**NHL**	**44**	**27**	**12**	**4**	**2601**	**104**	**5**	**2.40**	**5**	**1**	**4**	**324**	**16**	**0**	**2.96**
2007-08	**Florida**	**NHL**	**69**	**30**	**29**	**8**	**4031**	**180**	**4**	**2.68**	....	....	....	....	....	....	....
2008-09	**Florida**	**NHL**	**59**	**26**	**23**	**6**	**3324**	**138**	**6**	**2.49**	....	....	....	....	....	....	....
2009-10	**Florida**	**NHL**	**63**	**23**	**28**	**11**	**3695**	**157**	**7**	**2.55**	....	....	....	....	....	....	....
	Czech Republic	Olympics	5	3	2	0	304	9	0	1.78	....	....	....	....	....	....	....
	NHL Totals		**575**	**240**	**239**	**71**	**32859**	**1401**	**38**	**2.56**	**11**	**3**	**8**	**680**	**28**	**1**	**2.47**

Played in NHL All-Star Game (2004, 2008)

Claimed by **Nashville** from **Montreal** in Expansion Draft, June 26, 1998. Signed as a free agent by **Znojmo** (CzRep), September 6, 2004. Signed as a free agent by **HIFK Helsinki** (Finland), December 20, 2004. Traded to **Florida** by **Nashville** for Detroit's 2nd round choice (previously acquired, Nashville selected Nick Spaling) in 2007 Entry Draft and Florida's 1st (later traded to NY Islanders - NY Islanders selected Joshua Bailey) and 2nd (later traded to NY Islanders - NY Islanders selected Aaron Ness) round choices in 2008 Entry Draft, June 22, 2007.

WARD, Cam (WOHRD, KAM) CAR.

Goaltender. Catches left. 6'1", 185 lbs. Born, Saskatoon, Sask., February 29, 1984.
(Carolina's 1st choice, 25th overall, in 2002 Entry Draft).

			Regular Season								Playoffs						
Season	**Club**	**League**	**GP**	**W**	**L**	**O/T**	**Mins**	**GA**	**SO**	**Avg**	**GP**	**W**	**L**	**Mins**	**GA**	**SO**	**Avg**
1998-99	Sherwood Park	Minor-AB	24	13	7	4	1403	85	0	3.64	....	....	....	....	....	....	....
99-2000	Sherwood Park	AMHL	20	9	5	1	1194	71	0	3.57	7	4	3	262	22	0	3.57
2000-01	Sherwood Park	AMHL	25	14	6	3	1449	70	0	2.90	....	....	....	....	....	....	....
	Red Deer Rebels	WHL	1	1	0	0	60	0	1	0.00	....	....	....	....	....	....	....
2001-02	Red Deer Rebels	WHL	46	30	11	4	2694	102	1	*2.27	*23	14	9	*1502	53	*2	2.12
2002-03	Red Deer Rebels	WHL	57	*40	13	3	3368	118	5	2.10	*23	14	9	*1407	49	3	2.09
2003-04	Red Deer Rebels	WHL	56	31	16	8	3338	114	4	2.05	19	10	9	1200	37	3	1.85
2004-05	Lowell	AHL	50	27	17	3	2829	94	6	1.99	11	5	6	664	28	2	2.53
2005-06 ♦	**Carolina**	**NHL**	**28**	**14**	**8**	**2**	**1484**	**91**	**0**	**3.68**	***23**	***15**	**8**	***1320**	**47**	**2**	**2.14**
	Lowell	AHL	2	0	2	0	118	5	0	2.54	....	....	....	....	....	....	....
2006-07	**Carolina**	**NHL**	**60**	**30**	**21**	**6**	**3422**	**167**	**2**	**2.93**	....	....	....	....	....	....	....
2007-08	**Carolina**	**NHL**	**69**	**37**	**25**	**5**	**3930**	**180**	**4**	**2.75**	....	....	....	....	....	....	....
2008-09	**Carolina**	**NHL**	**68**	**39**	**23**	**5**	**3928**	**160**	**6**	**2.44**	**18**	**8**	**10**	**1101**	**49**	***2**	**2.67**
2009-10	**Carolina**	**NHL**	**47**	**18**	**23**	**5**	**2651**	**119**	**0**	**2.69**	....	....	....	....	....	....	....
	NHL Totals		**272**	**138**	**100**	**23**	**15415**	**717**	**12**	**2.79**	**41**	**23**	**18**	**2421**	**96**	**4**	**2.38**

WHL East First All-Star Team (2002, 2004) • Canadian Major Junior Second All-Star Team (2002) • WHL East Second All-Star Team (2003) • WHL Goaltender of the Year (2002, 2004) • WHL Player of the Year (2004) • Canadian Major Junior First All-Star Team (2004) • Canadian Major Junior Goaltender of the Year (2004) • AHL All-Rookie Team (2005) • Conn Smythe Trophy (2006)

WEDGEWOOD, Scott (WEHJ-wud, SKAWT) N.J.

Goaltender. Catches left. 6'1", 190 lbs. Born, Etobicoke, Ont., August 14, 1992.
(New Jersey's 2nd choice, 84th overall, in 2010 Entry Draft).

			Regular Season								Playoffs						
Season	**Club**	**League**	**GP**	**W**	**L**	**O/T**	**Mins**	**GA**	**SO**	**Avg**	**GP**	**W**	**L**	**Mins**	**GA**	**SO**	**Avg**
2007-08	Miss. Senators	GTHL	29	....	....	....	1305	63	2	2.17	....	....	....	....	....	....	....
2008-09	Plymouth Whalers	OHL	6	0	2	0	158	12	0	4.56	3	0	0	26	2	0	4.62
2009-10	Plymouth Whalers	OHL	18	5	9	0	938	51	1	3.26	4	1	0	116	4	0	2.07

WEIMAN, Tyler (WIGH-muhn, TIGH-luhr) VAN.

Goaltender. Catches left. 5'11", 180 lbs. Born, Saskatoon, Sask., June 5, 1984.
(Colorado's 6th choice, 164th overall, in 2002 Entry Draft).

			Regular Season								Playoffs						
Season	**Club**	**League**	**GP**	**W**	**L**	**O/T**	**Mins**	**GA**	**SO**	**Avg**	**GP**	**W**	**L**	**Mins**	**GA**	**SO**	**Avg**
99-2000	Ft. Saskatchewan	AMBHL	21	15	4	2	1239	60	0	2.91	....	....	....	....	....	....	....
2000-01	Tri-City Americans	WHL	44	10	25	4	2464	155	0	3.77	....	....	....	....	....	....	....
2001-02	Tri-City Americans	WHL	47	18	17	5	2492	149	2	3.59	5	1	4	300	14	0	2.80
2002-03	Tri-City Americans	WHL	55	16	34	2	3129	207	1	3.97	....	....	....	....	....	....	....
2003-04	Tri-City Americans	WHL	54	23	21	7	3023	134	1	2.66	5	1	2	234	11	0	2.82
2004-05	Colorado Eagles	CHL	44	*33	6	5	2630	79	*8	*1.80	*13	*8	4	*744	32	1	2.58
2005-06	Lowell	AHL	14	6	6	1	844	36	0	2.56	....	....	....	....	....	....	....
	San Diego Gulls	ECHL	32	14	12	3	1797	84	1	2.81	4	0	4	251	15	0	3.59
2006-07	Albany River Rats	AHL	54	27	22	3	3047	152	2	2.99	5	1	4	294	17	0	3.47
2007-08	**Colorado**	**NHL**	**1**	**0**	**0**	**0**	**16**	**0**	**0**	**0.00**	....	....	....	....	....	....	....
	Lake Erie Monsters	AHL	31	9	19	1	1769	98	2	3.32	....	....	....	....	....	....	....
2008-09	Lake Erie Monsters	AHL	44	21	20	2	2559	105	*8	2.46	....	....	....	....	....	....	....
2009-10	Lake Erie Monsters	AHL	43	21	18	3	2538	105	3	2.48	....	....	....	....	....	....	....
	NHL Totals		**1**	**0**	**0**	**0**	**16**	**0**	**0**	**0.00**	....	....	....	....	....	....	....

Signed as a free agent by **Vancouver**, July 12, 2010.

WESLOSKY, Jase (wehs-LAWZ-kee, JAYS) NYI

Goaltender. Catches left. 6'2", 170 lbs. Born, St. Albert, Alta., August 14, 1988.
(NY Islanders' 5th choice, 108th overall, in 2006 Entry Draft).

			Regular Season								Playoffs						
Season	**Club**	**League**	**GP**	**W**	**L**	**O/T**	**Mins**	**GA**	**SO**	**Avg**	**GP**	**W**	**L**	**Mins**	**GA**	**SO**	**Avg**
2004-05	St. Albert Blues	EMHA	....	13	3	2	1043	38	....	2.19	....	....	....	....	....	....	....
2005-06	Sherwood Park	AJHL	58	....	....	....	2123	110	2	3.11	....	....	....	....	....	....	....
2006-07	St. Cloud State	WCHA	6	5	1	0	359	16	1	2.67	....	....	....	....	....	....	....
2007-08	St. Cloud State	WCHA	33	16	13	2	1901	67	3	2.11	....	....	....	....	....	....	....
2008-09	St. Cloud State	WCHA	33	16	13	2	1889	85	2	2.70	....	....	....	....	....	....	....
2009-10	Bemidji State	CHA					DID NOT PLAY – TRANSFERRED COLLEGES										

• Ruled academically ineligible by **St. Cloud State**, August 25, 2009.

WESSLAU, Gustaf (VEHS-low, GUHS-tahf) CBJ

Goaltender. Catches left. 6'4", 199 lbs. Born, Upplands Vasby, Sweden, February 5, 1985.

			Regular Season								Playoffs						
Season	**Club**	**League**	**GP**	**W**	**L**	**O/T**	**Mins**	**GA**	**SO**	**Avg**	**GP**	**W**	**L**	**Mins**	**GA**	**SO**	**Avg**
2005-06	Malmo Jr.	Swe-Jr.	2	....	....	....	126	7	0	3.32	....	....	....	....	....	....	....
	Malmo	Sweden-2	5	....	....	....	300	7	0	1.40	....	....	....	....	....	....	....
	AIK Solna	Sweden-2	30	....	....	....	1777	84	1	2.84	....	....	....	....	....	....	....
2006-07	Malmo Jr.	Swe-Jr.	7	....	....	....	420	13	1	1.86	....	....	....	....	....	....	....
	Malmo	Sweden	12	....	....	....	614	37	0	3.61	....	....	....	....	....	....	....
	Almtuna	Sweden-2	2	....	....	....	120	6	0	3.00	....	....	....	....	....	....	....
2007-08	Boras HC	Sweden-2	37	....	....	....	2247	126	2	3.36	....	....	....	....	....	....	....
2008-09	Djurgarden	Sweden	33	....	....	....	1857	77	1	2.49	....	....	....	....	....	....	....
2009-10	Djurgarden	Sweden	32	....	....	....	1836	70	2	2.29	15	....	....	965	29	1	*1.80

Signed as a free agent by **Columbus**, May 5, 2010.

WIIKMAN, Miika (VEEK-man, MEE-kah)

Goaltender. Catches left. 5'11", 187 lbs. Born, Toreboda, Sweden, October 17, 1984.

			Regular Season								Playoffs						
Season	**Club**	**League**	**GP**	**W**	**L**	**O/T**	**Mins**	**GA**	**SO**	**Avg**	**GP**	**W**	**L**	**Mins**	**GA**	**SO**	**Avg**
99-2000	HV 71 U18	Swe-U18	4	....	....	....	240	23	0	5.75	....	....	....	....	....	....	....
	HV 71 Jr.	Swe-Jr.	1	....	....	....	20	0	0	0.00	....	....	....	....	....	....	....
2000-01	HV 71 U18	Swe-U18	13	....	....	....	740	45	1	3.65	2	....	....	120	12	0	6.00
	HV 71 Jr.	Swe-Jr.	3	....	....	....	100	6	0	3.60	....	....	....	....	....	....	....
2001-02	HV 71 U18	Swe-U18	7	....	....	....	416	33	0	4.76	....	....	....	....	....	....	....
	HV 71 Jr.	Swe-Jr.	9	....	....	....	501	28	0	3.36	....	....	....	....	....	....	....
2002-03	HV 71 Jr.	Swe-Jr.	27	....	....	....	1569	72	1	2.75	7	....	....	423	28	0	3.97
2003-04	Suomi U20	Finland-2	4	....	....	....	240	9	1	2.25	....	....	....	....	....	....	....
	Hermes Kokkola	Finland-2	31	....	....	....	1845	67	3	2.18	6	....	....	375	15	0	2.40
2004-05	HPK Hameenlinna	Finland	23	9	5	9	1361	54	2	2.38	2	1	1	118	4	0	2.03
2005-06	HPK Hameenlinna	Finland	34	21	5	7	1949	68	3	2.09	11	*8	2	607	20	*3	*1.98
2006-07	HPK Hameenlinna	Finland	18	8	6	4	1066	46	0	2.59	....	....	....	....	....	....	....
2007-08	Hartford Wolf Pack	AHL	34	21	8	3	1907	73	2	2.30	1	0	1	59	3	0	3.07
	Charlotte Checkers	ECHL	4	1	1	2	254	10	0	2.36	....	....	....	....	....	....	....
2008-09	Hartford Wolf Pack	AHL	43	21	18	4	2463	111	2	2.70	....	....	....	....	....	....	....
2009-10	Hartford Wolf Pack	AHL	7	2	4	0	343	24	0	4.20	....	....	....	....	....	....	....
	Charlotte Checkers	ECHL	17	9	3	3	971	46	1	2.84	....	....	....	....	....	....	....
	San Antonio	AHL	5	0	1	1	198	8	0	2.42	....	....	....	....	....	....	....

Signed as a free agent by **NY Rangers**, April 24, 2008. Traded to **Phoenix** by **NY Rangers** with NY Rangers' 7th round choice in 2011 Entry Draft for Anders Eriksson, March 3, 2010.

YORK, Allen
(YOHRK, AL-ihn) **CBJ**

Goaltender. Catches left. 6'3", 190 lbs. Born, Wetaskiwin, Alta., June 17, 1989.
(Columbus' 6th choice, 158th overall, in 2007 Entry Draft).

						Regular Season							Playoffs				
Season	Club	League	GP	W	L	O/T	Mins	GA	SO	Avg	GP	W	L	Mins	GA	SO	Avg
2006-07	Camrose Kodiaks	AJHL	32	23	4	0	1661	60	2	2.17	22	16	6	1391	46	4	1.98
2007-08	Camrose Kodiaks	AJHL	....	24	5	3	2005	75	3	2.24	....	....	....	....	....	....	....
2008-09	RPI Engineers	ECAC	16	5	10	0	913	46	1	3.02	....	....	....	....	....	....	....
2009-10	RPI Engineers	ECAC	33	14	12	4	1935	82	1	2.54	....	....	....	....	....	....	....

ECAC Second All-Star Team (2010)

ZABA, Matt
(ZA-buh, MAT)

Goaltender. Catches left. 6'1", 185 lbs. Born, Yorkton, Sask., July 14, 1983.
(Los Angeles' 8th choice, 231st overall, in 2003 Entry Draft).

						Regular Season							Playoffs				
Season	Club	League	GP	W	L	O/T	Mins	GA	SO	Avg	GP	W	L	Mins	GA	SO	Avg
2000-01	Yorkton Mallers	SMHL	26	13	10	3	1480	79	0	3.20	....	....	....	....	....	....	....
2001-02	Penticton Panthers	BCHL	33	....	....	....	1980	128	0	3.69	....	....	....	....	....	....	....
2002-03	Vernon Vipers	BCHL	44	34	9	0	2012	96	2	2.21	17	14	3	1006	25	3	1.49
2003-04	Colorado College	WCHA	23	10	10	2	1323	50	1	2.27	....	....	....	....	....	....	....
2004-05	Colorado College	WCHA	18	10	5	2	1050	43	2	2.46	....	....	....	....	....	....	....
2005-06	Colorado College	WCHA	36	20	14	2	2068	87	4	2.52	....	....	....	....	....	....	....
2006-07	Colorado College	WCHA	33	15	13	4	1908	76	3	2.39	....	....	....	....	....	....	....
2007-08	Charlotte Checkers	ECHL	9	3	4	1	496	30	0	3.63	....	....	....	....	....	....	....
	Idaho Steelheads	ECHL	19	12	4	1	1070	39	3	2.19	2	0	1	129	6	0	2.78
2008-09	Hartford Wolf Pack	AHL	41	25	10	0	2262	88	2	2.33	6	2	4	378	20	1	3.17
2009-10	**NY Rangers**	**NHL**	**1**	**0**	**0**	**0**	**34**	**2**	**0**	**3.53**	....	....	....	....	....	....	....
	Hartford Wolf Pack	AHL	25	6	12	2	1296	68	0	3.15	....	....	....	....	....	....	....
	Charlotte Checkers	ECHL	3	2	1	0	185	11	0	3.58	....	....	....	....	....	....	....
	NHL Totals		**1**	**0**	**0**	**0**	**34**	**2**	**0**	**3.53**	....	....	....	....	....	....	....

WCHA All-Rookie Team (2004)
Signed as a free agent by **NY Rangers**, August 20, 2007.

ZADOR, Michael
(ZAY-dohr, MIGH-kuhl) **T.B**

Goaltender. Catches left. 6'2", 172 lbs. Born, Toronto, Ont., May 8, 1991.
(Tampa Bay's 5th choice, 148th overall, in 2009 Entry Draft).

						Regular Season							Playoffs				
Season	Club	League	GP	W	L	O/T	Mins	GA	SO	Avg	GP	W	L	Mins	GA	SO	Avg
2007-08	Petrolia Jets	OJHL-B	17	0	16	0	917	122	0	7.98	....	....	....	....	....	....	....
	London Knights	OHL	1	0	1	0	20	3	0	9.00	....	....	....	....	....	....	....
2008-09	St. Mary's Lincolns	OJHL-B	5	4	1	0	300	14	0	2.80	....	....	....	....	....	....	....
	London Knights	OHL	10	6	1	0	462	28	0	3.64	....	....	....	....	....	....	....
2009-10	Oshawa Generals	OHL	18	5	12	1	1002	61	0	3.65	....	....	....	....	....	....	....
	Oshawa Generals	OHL	49	14	28	3	2574	178	2	4.15	....	....	....	....	....	....	....

ZATKOFF, Jeff
(ZAT-kawf, JEHF) **L.A.**

Goaltender. Catches left. 6'2", 169 lbs. Born, Detroit, MI, June 9, 1987.
(Los Angeles' 4th choice, 74th overall, in 2006 Entry Draft).

						Regular Season							Playoffs				
Season	Club	League	GP	W	L	O/T	Mins	GA	SO	Avg	GP	W	L	Mins	GA	SO	Avg
2004-05	Sioux City	USHL	24	13	6	3	1271	54	1	2.55	2	0	0	68	10	0	8.88
2005-06	Miami U.	CCHA	20	14	5	1	1217	41	3	2.02	....	....	....	....	....	....	....
2006-07	Miami U.	CCHA	26	14	8	3	1542	58	1	2.26	....	....	....	....	....	....	....
2007-08	Miami U.	CCHA	36	27	8	1	2161	62	3	*1.72	....	....	....	....	....	....	....
2008-09	Manchester	AHL	3	1	2	0	182	7	0	2.31	....	....	....	....	....	....	....
	Ontario Reign	ECHL	37	17	15	3	2164	107	1	2.97	7	3	3	418	26	0	3.73
2009-10	Manchester	AHL	22	10	9	0	1170	57	2	2.92	....	....	....	....	....	....	....

CCHA Second All-Star Team (2008)

Late Additions to Player Register

FREE AGENT SIGNINGS

BERGENHEIM, Sean   *(see page 356 for data panel)*   **T.B.**
Left wing.   Signed as a free agent by **Tampa Bay**, August 17, 2010.

GUITE, Ben   *(see page 417 for data panel)*   **CBJ**
Right wing.   Signed as a free agent by **Columbus**, August 18, 2010.

HILBERT, Andy   *(see page 426 for data panel)*   **NYI**
Center.   Signed as a free agent by **NY Islanders**, August 18, 2010.

HISEY, Rob   (HIGH-zee, RAWB)   **NYI**
Center. Shoots left. 5'9", 180 lbs.   Born, Oakville, Ont., September 24, 1984.

			Regular Season					Playoffs				
Season	Club	League	GP	G	A	Pts	PIM	GP	G	A	Pts	PIM
2000-01	Aurora Tigers	OPJHL	49	27	41	68	44	...	...	...	...	...
2001-02	Sault Ste. Marie	OHL	68	20	33	53	33	6	0	0	0	6
2002-03	Sault Ste. Marie	OHL	23	9	16	25	10	...	...	...	...	...
2002-03	Erie Otters	OHL	50	19	30	49	46	...	...	...	...	...
2003-04	Erie Otters	OHL	63	38	58	96	63	8	2	3	5	8
2003-04	Port Huron	UHL	...	...	...	...	...	6	3	6	9	4
2004-05	Erie Otters	OHL	25	8	26	34	41	...	...	...	...	...
	Barrie Colts	OHL	41	21	31	52	40	6	2	8	10	6
	Reading	ECHL	...	...	...	...	...	7	2	2	4	2
2005-06	Assat Pori	Finland	46	12	13	25	101	14	4	2	6	40
2006-07	Hannover Scorpions	Germany	51	12	17	29	54	6	0	1	1	8
2007-08	Graz EC	Austria	22	3	13	16	36	...	...	...	...	...
	Assat Pori	Finland	14	2	4	6	16	...	...	...	...	...
	Mora IK	Sweden	12	6	4	10	10	...	...	...	...	...
2008-09	Hannover Indians	German-2	34	19	39	58	137	7	10	8	18	8
2009-10	Tulsa Oilers	CHL	24	19	22	41	27	...	...	...	...	...
	Springfield	AHL	37	11	14	25	29	...	...	...	...	...

Signed as a free agent by **NY Islanders**, August 18, 2010.

MEYER, Freddy   *(see page 478 for data panel)*   **ATL**
Defense.   Signed as a free agent by **Atlanta**, August 19, 2010.

PETERS, Andrew   *(see page 504 for data panel)*   **FLA**
Left wing.   Signed as a free agent by **Florida**, August 19, 2010.

PISANI, Fernando   *(see page 507 for data panel)*   **CHI**
Right wing.   Signed as a free agent by **Chicago**, August 18, 2010.

TRADES

DESJARDINS, Cedrick   *(see page 588 for data panel)*   **T.B.**
Goaltender.
Traded to **Tampa Bay** by **Montreal** for Karri Ramo, August 16, 2010.

RAMO, Karri   *(see page 602 for data panel)*   **MTL.**
Goaltender.
Traded to **Montreal** by **Tampa Bay** for Cedrick Desjardins, August 16, 2010.

CLUB FRONT OFFICE ADDITIONS

GOULET, Michel   *(see page 622 for career totals)*   **CGY**
Hired by **Calgary** as Western Professional Scout, August 18, 2010.

Retired NHL Player Index

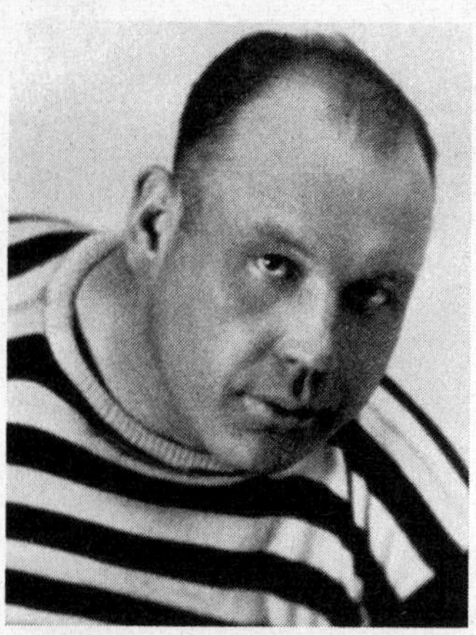

Clarence "Taffy" Abel

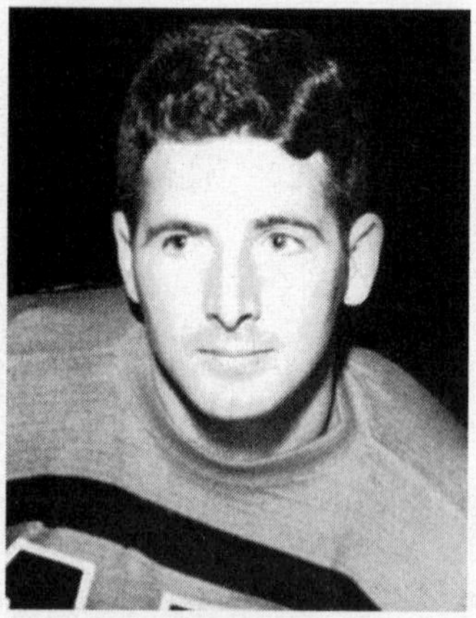

Douglas Adam

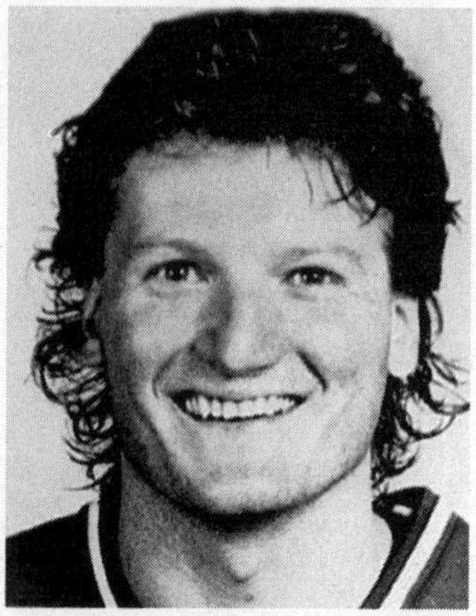

Dave Allison

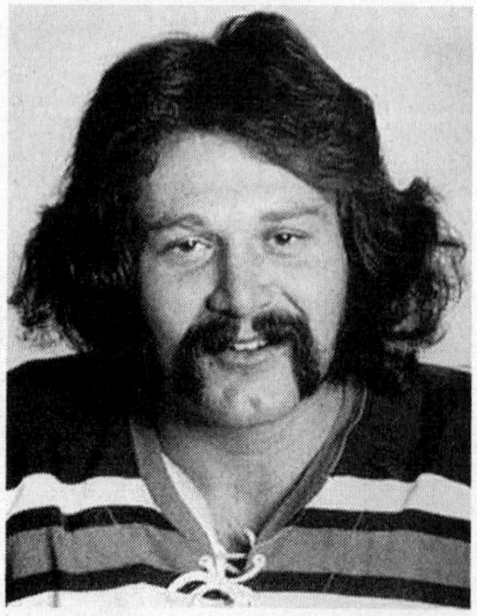

Mike Amodeo

Abbreviations: Teams/Cities: – **Ana.** – Anaheim; **Atl.** – Atlanta; **Bos.** – Boston; **Bro.** – Brooklyn; **Buf.** – Buffalo; **Cgy.** – Calgary; **Cal.** – California; **Car.** – Carolina; **Chi.** – Chicago; **Cle.** – Cleveland; **Col.** – Colorado; **CBJ** – Columbus; **Dal.** – Dallas; **Det.** – Detroit; **Edm.** – Edmonton; **Fla.** – Florida; **Ham.** – Hamilton; **Hfd.** – Hartford; **K.C.** – Kansas City; **L.A.** – Los Angeles; **Min.** – Minnesota; **Mtl.** – Montreal; **Mtl.M.** – Montreal Maroons; **Mtl.W.** – Montreal Wanderers; **Nsh.** – Nashville; **N.J.** – New Jersey; **NYA** – NY Americans; **NYI** – NY Islanders; **NYR** – New York Rangers; **Oak.** – Oakland; **Ott.** – Ottawa; **Phi.** – Philadelphia; **Phx.** – Phoenix; **Pit.** – Pittsburgh; **Que.** – Quebec; **St.L.** – St. Louis; **S.J.** – San Jose; **T.B.** – Tampa Bay; **Tor.** – Toronto; **Van.** – Vancouver; **Wsh.** – Washington; **Wpg.** – Winnipeg

A – assists; **G** – goals; **GP** – games played; **PIM** – penalties in minutes; **TP** – total points.
• – deceased. Assists not recorded during 1917-18 season ‡ – Remains active in other leagues.

NHL Seasons – A player or goaltender who does not play in a regular season but who does appear in that year's playoffs is credited with an NHL Season in this Index. Total seasons are rounded off to the nearest full season.

			Regular Schedule					Playoffs							
Name	NHL Teams	NHL Seasons	GP	G	A	TP	PIM	GP	G	A	TP	PIM	NHL Cup Wins	First NHL Season	Last NHL Season
A															
Aalto, Antti	Ana.	4	151	11	17	28	52	4	0	0	0	2	....	1997-98	2000-01
Abbott, Reg	Mtl.	1	3	0	0	0	0	....	....	....	....	....	....	1952-53	1952-53
• Abel, Clarence	NYR, Chi.	8	333	19	18	37	359	38	1	1	2	58	2	1926-27	1933-34
Abel, Gerry	Det.	1	1	0	0	0	0	....	....	....	....	....	....	1966-67	1966-67
• Abel, Sid	Det., Chi.	14	612	189	283	472	376	97	28	30	58	79	3	1938-39	1953-54
Abgrall, Dennis	L.A.	1	13	0	2	2	4	....	....	....	....	....	....	1975-76	1975-76
‡ Abid, Ramzi	Phx., Pit., Atl., Nsh.	4	68	14	16	30	78	2	0	0	0	0	....	2002-03	2006-07
Abrahamsson, Thommy	Hfd.	1	32	6	11	17	16	....	....	....	....	....	....	1980-81	1980-81
Achtymichuk, Gene	Mtl., Det.	4	32	3	5	8	2	....	....	....	....	....	....	1951-52	1958-59
Acomb, Doug	Tor.	1	2	0	1	1	0	....	....	....	....	....	....	1969-70	1969-70
Acton, Keith	Mtl., Min., Edm., Phi., Wsh., NYI	15	1023	226	358	584	1172	66	12	21	33	88	1	1979-80	1993-94
• Adam, Douglas	NYR	1	4	0	1	1	0	....	....	....	....	....	....	1949-50	1949-50
Adam, Russ	Tor.	1	8	1	2	3	11	....	....	....	....	....	....	1982-83	1982-83
‡ Adams, Bryan	Atl.	2	11	0	1	1	2	....	....	....	....	....	....	1999-00	2000-01
Adams, Greg	Phi., Hfd., Wsh., Edm., Van., Que., Det.	10	545	84	143	227	1173	43	2	11	13	153	....	1980-81	1989-90
Adams, Greg	N.J., Van., Dal., Phx., Fla.	17	1056	355	388	743	326	81	20	22	42	16	....	1984-85	2000-01
• Adams, Jack	Tor., Ott.	7	173	83	32	115	366	10	2	0	2	13	2	1917-18	1926-27
Adams, John	Mtl.	1	42	6	12	18	11	3	0	0	0	0	....	1940-41	1940-41
Adams, Kevyn	Tor., CBJ, Fla., Car., Phx., Chi.	10	540	59	77	136	317	67	2	2	4	39	1	1997-98	2007-08
• Adams, Stew	Chi., Tor.	4	95	9	26	35	60	11	3	3	6	14	....	1929-30	1932-33
Adduono, Rick	Bos., Atl.	2	4	0	0	0	2	....	....	....	....	....	....	1975-76	1979-80
‡ Afanasenkov, Dmitry	T.B., Phi.	5	227	27	27	54	52	28	1	3	4	8	1	2000-01	2006-07
Affleck, Bruce	St.L., Van., NYI	7	280	14	66	80	86	8	0	0	0	0	....	1974-75	1983-84
Agnew, Jim	Van., Hfd.	6	81	0	1	1	257	4	0	0	0	6	....	1986-87	1992-93
Ahern, Fred	Cal., Cle., Col.	4	146	31	30	61	130	2	0	1	1	2	....	1974-75	1977-78
• Ahlin, Rudy	Chi.	1	1	0	0	0	0	....	....	....	....	....	....	1937-38	1937-38
Ahola, Peter	L.A., Pit., S.J., Cgy.	3	123	10	17	27	137	6	0	0	0	2	....	1991-92	1993-94
Ahrens, Chris	Min.	6	52	0	3	3	84	1	0	0	0	0	....	1972-73	1977-78
• Ailsby, Lloyd	NYR	1	3	0	0	0	2	....	....	....	....	....	....	1951-52	1951-52
Aitken, Brad	Pit., Edm.	2	14	1	3	4	25	....	....	....	....	....	....	1987-88	1990-91
Aitken, Johnathan	Bos., Chi.	2	44	0	1	1	70	....	....	....	....	....	....	1999-00	2003-04
Aivazoff, Micah	Det., Edm., NYI	3	92	4	6	10	46	....	....	....	....	....	....	1993-94	1995-96
Alatalo, Mika	Phx.	2	152	17	29	46	58	5	0	0	0	2	....	1999-00	2000-01
Albelin, Tommy	Que., N.J., Cgy.	18	952	44	211	255	417	81	7	15	22	22	2	1987-88	2005-06
• Albright, Clint	NYR	1	59	14	5	19	19	....	....	....	....	....	....	1948-49	1948-49
Aldcorn, Gary	Tor., Det., Bos.	5	226	41	56	97	78	6	1	2	3	4	....	1956-57	1960-61
Aldridge, Keith	Dal.	1	4	0	0	0	0	....	....	....	....	....	....	1999-00	1999-00
Alexander, Claire	Tor., Van.	4	155	18	47	65	36	16	2	4	6	4	....	1974-75	1977-78
• Alexandre, Art	Mtl.	2	11	0	2	2	8	4	0	0	0	0	....	1931-32	1932-33
‡ Alexeev, Nikita	T.B., Chi.	3	159	20	17	37	28	11	1	0	1	0	....	2001-02	2006-07
Allan, Jeff	Cle.	1	4	0	0	0	2	....	....	....	....	....	....	1977-78	1977-78
Allen, Bobby	Edm., Bos.	3	51	0	3	3	12	....	....	....	....	....	....	2002-03	2007-08
Allen, Chris	Fla.	2	2	0	0	0	2	....	....	....	....	....	....	1997-98	1998-99
• Allen, George	NYR, Chi., Mtl.	8	339	82	115	197	179	41	9	10	19	32	....	1938-39	1946-47
Allen, Keith	Det.	2	28	0	4	4	8	5	0	0	0	0	1	1953-54	1954-55
Allen, Peter	Pit.	1	8	0	0	0	8	....	....	....	....	....	....	1995-96	1995-96
• Allen, Viv	NYA	1	6	0	1	1	0	....	....	....	....	....	....	1940-41	1940-41
Alley, Steve	Hfd.	2	15	3	3	6	11	3	0	1	1	0	....	1979-80	1980-81
Allison, Dave	Mtl.	1	3	0	0	0	12	....	....	....	....	....	....	1983-84	1983-84
Allison, Jamie	Cgy., Chi., CBJ, Nsh., Fla.	10	372	7	23	30	639	....	....	....	....	....	....	1994-95	2005-06
Allison, Jason	Wsh., Bos., L.A., Tor.	12	552	154	331	485	441	25	7	18	25	14	....	1993-94	2005-06
Allison, Mike	NYR, Tor., L.A.	10	499	102	166	268	630	82	9	17	26	135	....	1980-81	1989-90
Allison, Ray	Hfd., Phi.	7	238	64	93	157	223	12	2	3	5	20	....	1979-80	1986-87
• Allum, Bill	NYR	1	1	0	1	1	0	....	....	....	....	....	....	1940-41	1940-41
• Amadio, Dave	Det., L.A.	3	125	5	11	16	163	16	1	2	3	18	....	1957-58	1968-69
Ambroziak, Peter	Buf.	1	12	0	1	1	0	....	....	....	....	....	....	1994-95	1994-95
Amodeo, Mike	Wpg.	1	19	0	0	0	2	....	....	....	....	....	....	1979-80	1979-80
Amonte, Tony	NYR, Chi., Phx., Phi., Cgy.	16	1174	416	484	900	752	99	22	33	55	56	....	1990-91	2006-07
• Anderson, Bill	Bos.	1	....	....	....	....	....	1	0	0	0	0	....	1942-43	1942-43
Anderson, Dale	Det.	1	13	0	0	0	6	2	0	0	0	0	....	1956-57	1956-57
Anderson, Doug	Mtl.	1	....	....	....	....	....	2	0	0	0	0	....	1952-53	1952-53
Anderson, Earl	Det., Bos.	3	109	19	19	38	22	5	0	1	1	0	....	1974-75	1976-77
Anderson, Glenn	Edm., Tor., NYR, St.L.	16	1129	498	601	1099	1120	225	93	121	214	442	6	1980-81	1995-96
Anderson, Jim	L.A.	1	7	1	2	3	2	....	....	....	....	....	....	1967-68	1967-68
Anderson, John	Tor., Que., Hfd.	12	814	282	349	631	263	37	9	18	27	2	....	1977-78	1988-89
Anderson, Murray	Wsh.	1	40	0	1	1	68	....	....	....	....	....	....	1974-75	1974-75
Anderson, Perry	St.L., N.J., S.J.	10	400	50	59	109	1051	36	2	1	3	161	....	1981-82	1991-92
Anderson, Ron	Det., L.A., St.L., Buf.	5	251	28	30	58	146	5	0	0	0	4	....	1967-68	1971-72
Anderson, Ron	Wsh.	1	28	9	7	16	8	....	....	....	....	....	....	1974-75	1974-75
Anderson, Russ	Pit., Hfd., L.A.	9	519	22	99	121	1086	10	0	3	3	28	....	1976-77	1984-85
Anderson, Shawn	Buf., Que., Wsh., Phi.	8	255	11	51	62	117	19	1	1	2	16	....	1986-87	1994-95
• Anderson, Tom	Det., NYA, Bro.	8	319	62	127	189	180	16	2	7	9	8	....	1934-35	1941-42
Andersson, Erik	Cgy.	1	12	2	1	3	8	....	....	....	....	....	....	1997-98	1997-98
Andersson, Kent-Erik	Min., NYR	7	456	72	103	175	78	50	4	11	15	4	....	1977-78	1983-84
Andersson, Mikael	Buf., Hfd., T.B., Phi., NYI	15	761	95	169	264	134	25	2	7	9	10	....	1985-86	1999-00
‡ Andersson, Niklas	Que., NYI, S.J., Nsh., Cgy.	6	164	29	53	82	85	....	....	....	....	....	....	1992-93	2000-01
Andersson, Peter	Wsh., Que.	3	172	10	41	51	81	7	0	2	2	2	....	1983-84	1985-86
Andersson, Peter	NYR, Fla.	2	47	6	13	19	20	....	....	....	....	....	....	1992-93	1993-94
Andrascik, Steve	NYR	1	....	....	....	....	....	1	0	0	0	0	....	1971-72	1971-72
Andrea, Paul	NYR, Pit., Cal., Buf.	4	150	31	49	80	10	....	....	....	....	....	....	1965-66	1970-71
• Andrews, Lloyd	Tor.	4	53	8	5	13	10	2	0	0	0	0	1	1921-22	1924-25
Andreychuk, Dave	Buf., Tor., N.J., Bos., Col., T.B.	23	1639	640	698	1338	1125	162	43	54	97	162	1	1982-83	2005-06
Andrievski, Alexander	Chi.	1	1	0	0	0	0	....	....	....	....	....	....	1992-93	1992-93
Andruff, Ron	Mtl., Col.	5	153	19	36	55	54	2	0	0	0	0	....	1974-75	1978-79
Andrusak, Greg	Pit., Tor.	5	28	0	6	6	16	15	1	0	1	8	....	1993-94	1999-00
Angelstad, Mel	Wsh.	1	2	0	0	0	2	....	....	....	....	....	....	2003-04	2003-04
Angotti, Lou	NYR, Chi., Phi., Pit., St.L.	10	653	103	186	289	228	65	8	8	16	17	....	1964-65	1973-74
Anholt, Darrel	Chi.	1	1	0	0	0	0	....	....	....	....	....	....	1983-84	1983-84
• Anslow, Hub	NYR	1	2	0	0	0	0	....	....	....	....	....	....	1947-48	1947-48
Antonovich, Mike	Min., Hfd., N.J.	5	87	10	15	25	37	....	....	....	....	....	....	1975-76	1983-84
Antoski, Shawn	Van., Phi., Pit., Ana.	8	183	3	5	8	599	36	1	3	4	74	....	1990-91	1997-98
• Apps, Syl	Tor.	10	423	201	231	432	56	69	25	29	54	8	3	1936-37	1947-48
Apps, Syl	NYR, Pit., L.A.	10	727	183	423	606	311	23	5	5	10	23	....	1970-71	1979-80
Arbour, Al	Det., Chi., Tor., St.L.	16	626	12	58	70	617	86	1	8	9	92	4	1953-54	1970-71
• Arbour, Amos	Mtl., Ham., Tor.	6	113	52	20	72	77	....	....	....	....	....	....	1918-19	1923-24
• Arbour, Jack	Det., Tor.	2	47	5	1	6	56	....	....	....	....	....	....	1926-27	1928-29
Arbour, John	Bos., Pit., Van., St.L.	5	106	1	9	10	149	5	0	0	0	0	....	1965-66	1971-72
• Arbour, Ty	Pit., Chi.	5	207	28	28	56	112	11	2	0	2	6	....	1926-27	1930-31
Archambault, Michel	Chi.	1	3	0	0	0	0	....	....	....	....	....	....	1976-77	1976-77
Archibald, Dave	Min., NYR, Ott., NYI	8	323	57	67	124	139	5	0	1	1	0	....	1987-88	1996-97
Archibald, Jim	Min.	3	16	1	2	3	45	....	....	....	....	....	....	1984-85	1986-87

			Regular Schedule					Playoffs							
ame	NHL Teams	NHL Seasons	GP	G	A	TP	PIM	GP	G	A	TP	PIM	NHL Cup Wins	First NHL Season	Last NHL Season
'eshenkoff, Ron	Edm.	1	4	0	0	0	0	....	....	....	....	....	....	1979-80	1979-80
'khipov, Denis	Nsh., Chi.	5	352	56	82	138	128	....	....	....	....	....	....	2000-01	2006-07
'mstrong, Bill	Phi.	1	1	0	1	1	0	....	....	....	....	....	....	1990-91	1990-91
'mstrong, Bob	Bos.	12	542	13	86	99	671	42	1	7	8	28	....	1950-51	1961-62
'mstrong, Chris	Min., Ana.	2	7	0	1	1	0	....	....	....	....	....	....	2000-01	2003-04
'mstrong, George	Tor.	21	1187	296	417	713	721	110	26	34	60	52	4	1949-50	1970-71
'mstrong, Murray	Tor., NYA, Bro., Det.	8	270	67	121	188	72	30	4	6	10	2	....	1937-38	1945-46
'mstrong, Norm	Tor.	1	7	1	1	2	2	....	....	....	....	....	....	1962-63	1962-63
'mstrong, Tim	Tor.	1	11	1	0	1	6	....	....	....	....	....	....	1988-89	1988-89
'nason, Chuck	Mtl., Atl., Pit., K.C., Col., Cle., Min., Wsh.	8	401	109	90	199	122	9	2	4	6	4	....	1971-72	1978-79
'niel, Scott	Wpg., Buf., Bos.	12	730	149	189	338	599	34	3	3	6	39	....	1981-82	1991-92
'sene, Dean	Edm.	1	13	0	0	0	41	....	....	....	....	....	....	2009-10	2009-10
'thur, Fred	Hfd., Phi.	3	80	1	8	9	49	4	0	0	0	2	....	1980-81	1982-83
undel, John	Tor.	1	3	0	0	0	9	....	....	....	....	....	....	1949-50	1949-50
vedson, Magnus	Ott., Van.	7	434	100	125	225	241	52	3	8	11	34	....	1997-98	2003-04
hbee, Barry	Bos., Phi.	5	284	15	70	85	291	17	0	4	4	22	1	1965-66	1973-74
hby, Don	Tor., Col., Edm.	6	188	40	56	96	40	12	1	0	1	4	....	1975-76	1980-81
shton, Brent	Van., Col., N.J., Min., Que., Det., Wpg., Bos., Cgy.	14	998	284	345	629	635	85	24	25	49	70	....	1979-80	1992-93
shworth, Frank	Chi.	1	18	5	4	9	2	....	....	....	....	....	....	1946-47	1946-47
smundson, Oscar	NYR, Det., St.L., NYA, Mtl.	5	111	11	23	34	30	9	0	2	2	4	1	1932-33	1937-38
stashenko, Kaspars	T.B.	2	23	1	2	3	8	....	....	....	....	....	....	1999-00	2000-01
stley, Mark	Buf.	3	75	4	19	23	92	2	0	0	0	0	....	1993-94	1995-96
anas, Walt	NYR	1	49	13	8	21	40	....	....	....	....	....	....	1944-45	1944-45
cheynum, Blair	Ott., St.L., Nsh., Chi.	5	196	27	33	60	36	23	1	3	4	8	....	1992-93	2000-01
kinson, Steve	Bos., Buf., Wsh.	6	302	60	51	111	104	1	0	0	0	0	....	1968-69	1974-75
twell, Bob	Col.	2	22	1	5	6	0	....	....	....	....	....	....	1979-80	1980-81
twell, Ron	St.L., NYR	1	22	1	7	8	8	....	....	....	....	....	....	1967-68	1967-68
ibin, Norm	Tor.	2	69	18	13	31	30	1	0	0	0	0	....	1981-82	1982-83
ibin, Serge	Col., CBJ, Atl.	7	374	44	64	108	361	22	0	1	1	10	....	1998-99	2005-06
ibry, Pierre	Que., Det.	5	202	24	26	50	133	20	1	1	2	32	....	1980-81	1984-85
ibuchon, Ossie	Bos., NYR	2	50	20	12	32	4	6	1	0	1	0	....	1942-43	1943-44
idet, Philippe	Det.	1	4	0	0	0	0	....	....	....	....	....	....	1998-99	1998-99
idette, Donald	Buf., L.A., Atl., Dal., Mtl., Fla.	15	735	260	249	509	584	73	21	27	48	46	....	1989-90	2003-04
ge, Les	Col.	1	6	0	3	3	4	....	....	....	....	....	....	1980-81	1980-81
gusta, Patrik	Tor., Wsh.	2	4	0	0	0	0	....	....	....	....	....	....	1993-94	1998-99
lin, Jared	L.A.	1	17	2	2	4	0	....	....	....	....	....	....	2002-03	2002-03
rie, Larry	Det.	12	489	147	129	276	279	24	6	9	15	10	2	1927-28	1938-39
vrey, Don	Bos., St.L., Mtl., Pit., NYR, Col.	16	979	31	158	189	1065	71	0	18	18	150	2	1963-64	1978-79
'es, Vern	NYA, Mtl.M., St.L., NYR	6	211	6	11	17	350	....	....	....	....	....	....	1930-31	1935-36

oando, Pete	Bos., Det., Chi., NYR	6	351	86	73	159	194	17	3	3	6	6	1	1947-48	1952-53
ocock, Bobby	Wsh.	2	2	0	0	0	2	....	....	....	....	....	....	1990-91	1992-93
oe, Warren	Min.	3	21	2	5	7	23	2	0	0	0	0	....	1987-88	1990-91
oenko, Yuri	Col.	1	3	0	0	0	0	....	....	....	....	....	....	2000-01	2000-01
oin, Mitch	St.L.	1	8	0	0	0	0	....	....	....	....	....	....	1975-76	1975-76
oy, John	Cle., Min.	2	26	2	8	10	26	....	....	....	....	....	....	1977-78	1978-79
oych, Dave	Wpg., Hfd., Van., Phi., L.A.	19	1195	142	581	723	970	114	21	41	62	113	....	1980-81	1998-99
oych, Wayne	St.L., Pit., Que., Hfd.	9	519	192	246	438	498	41	7	9	16	24	....	1978-79	1986-87
ca, Jergus	Hfd.	2	10	0	2	2	14	....	....	....	....	....	....	1990-91	1991-92
ckman, Mike	NYR	3	18	1	6	7	18	10	2	2	4	2	....	1981-82	1983-84
ckor, Pete	Tor.	1	36	4	5	9	6	....	....	....	....	....	1	1944-45	1944-45
ckstrom, Ralph	Mtl., L.A., Chi.	17	1032	278	361	639	386	116	27	32	59	68	6	1956-57	1972-73
ley, Ace	Tor.	8	313	111	82	193	472	21	3	4	7	12	1	1926-27	1933-34
ley, Bob	Tor., Det., Chi.	5	150	15	21	36	207	15	0	4	4	22	....	1953-54	1957-58
ley, Garnet	Bos., Det., St.L., Wsh.	10	568	107	171	278	633	15	2	4	6	28	2	1968-69	1977-78
ley, Reid	Phi., Tor., Hfd.	4	40	1	3	4	105	16	0	2	2	25	....	1980-81	1983-84
llargeon, Joel	Wpg., Que.	3	20	0	2	2	31	....	....	....	....	....	....	1986-87	1988-89
rd, Ken	Cal.	1	10	0	2	2	15	....	....	....	....	....	....	1971-72	1971-72
ker, Bill	Mtl., Col., St.L., NYR	3	143	7	25	32	175	6	0	0	0	0	....	1980-81	1982-83
ker, Jamie	Que., Ott., S.J., Tor.	10	404	71	79	150	271	25	5	4	9	42	....	1989-90	1998-99
kovic, Peter	Van.	1	10	2	0	2	48	....	....	....	....	....	....	1987-88	1987-88
a, Chris	Ott.	1	6	0	1	1	0	....	....	....	....	....	....	2001-02	2001-02
astik, Jaroslav	CBJ	2	74	13	11	24	30	....	....	....	....	....	....	2005-06	2006-07
deris, Helmut	Min.	1	26	3	6	9	2	....	....	....	....	....	....	1989-90	1989-90
dwin, Doug	Tor., Det., Chi.	3	24	0	1	1	8	....	....	....	....	....	....	1945-46	1947-48
ej, Jozef	Mtl., NYR, Van.	2	18	1	5	6	4	....	....	....	....	....	....	2003-04	2005-06
'our, Earl	Tor., Chi.	7	288	30	22	52	78	26	0	3	3	4	1	1951-52	1960-61
'our, Murray	Mtl., Chi., Bos.	8	306	67	90	157	393	40	9	10	19	45	1	1956-57	1964-65
, Terry	Phi., Buf.	4	74	7	19	26	26	....	....	....	....	....	....	1967-68	1971-72
nochnykh, Maxim	Ana.	1	6	0	1	1	2	....	....	....	....	....	....	1999-00	1999-00
on, Dave	NYR, Mtl., Min., Van.	14	776	192	222	414	607	78	14	21	35	109	2	1959-60	1972-73
timore, Bryon	Edm.	1	2	0	0	0	4	....	....	....	....	....	....	1979-80	1979-80
uik, Stan	Bos.	1	7	0	0	0	2	....	....	....	....	....	....	1959-60	1959-60
croft, Steve	Chi., S.J.	2	6	0	1	1	2	....	....	....	....	....	....	1992-93	2001-02
dura, Jeff	NYR	1	2	0	1	1	0	....	....	....	....	....	....	1980-81	1980-81
ham, Frank	Ana., Phx.	4	32	9	2	11	16	....	....	....	....	....	....	1996-97	2002-03
ks, Darren	Bos.	2	20	2	2	4	73	....	....	....	....	....	....	1992-93	1993-94
ahona, Ralph	Bos.	2	6	2	2	4	0	....	....	....	....	....	....	1990-91	1991-92
be, Andy	Tor.	1	1	0	0	0	2	....	....	....	....	....	....	1950-51	1950-51
ber, Bill	Phi.	14	903	420	463	883	623	129	53	55	108	109	2	1972-73	1983-84
ber, Don	Min., Wpg., Que., S.J.	4	115	25	32	57	64	11	4	4	8	10	....	1988-89	1991-92
lko, Bill	Tor.	5	252	26	36	62	456	47	5	7	12	104	4	1946-47	1950-51
nka, Michal	Chi.	2	34	0	2	2	26	....	....	....	....	....	....	2003-04	2005-06
kley, Doug	Chi., Det.	6	253	24	80	104	382	30	0	9	9	63	....	1957-58	1965-66
ow, Bob	Min.	2	77	16	17	33	10	6	2	2	4	6	....	1969-70	1970-71
naby, Matthew	Buf., Pit., T.B., NYR, Col., Chi., Dal.	14	834	113	187	300	2562	62	7	15	22	170	....	1992-93	2006-07
nes, Blair	L.A.	1	1	0	0	0	0	....	....	....	....	....	....	1982-83	1982-83
nes, Norm	Phi., Hfd.	5	156	6	38	44	178	12	0	0	0	8	....	1976-77	1981-82
nes, Ryan	Det.	1	2	0	0	0	0	....	....	....	....	....	....	2003-04	2003-04
nes, Stu	Wpg., Fla., Pit., Buf., Dal.	16	1136	261	336	597	438	116	30	32	62	24	....	1991-92	2007-08
ney, Scott	L.A., Atl.	3	27	5	6	11	4	....	....	....	....	....	....	2002-03	2005-06
on, Murray	Phi., St.L., Mtl., Phx., Van.	15	988	35	94	129	1309	73	2	8	10	78	....	1989-90	2003-04
on, Normand	Mtl., St.L.	2	27	2	0	2	51	3	0	0	0	22	....	1983-84	1985-86
, Dave	Bos., NYR, St.L., Hfd., Det., N.J., Dal.	13	614	128	204	332	520	71	12	10	22	70	....	1981-82	1993-94
'ault, Doug	Min., Fla.	2	4	0	0	0	2	....	....	....	....	....	....	1992-93	1993-94
'ett, Fred	Min., L.A.	13	745	25	123	148	671	44	0	2	2	60	....	1970-71	1983-84
'ett, John	Det., Wsh., Min.	8	488	20	77	97	604	16	2	2	4	50	....	1980-81	1987-88
'ie, Doug	Pit., Buf., L.A.	3	158	10	42	52	268	....	....	....	....	....	....	1968-69	1971-72
'ie, Len	Phi., Fla., Pit., L.A.	7	184	19	45	64	290	8	1	0	1	8	....	1989-90	2000-01
y, Ed	Bos.	1	19	1	3	4	2	....	....	....	....	....	....	1946-47	1946-47
y, Marty	NYA, Bos., Det., Mtl.	12	509	195	192	387	231	43	15	18	33	34	2	1927-28	1939-40
y, Ray	Bos.	1	18	1	2	3	6	....	....	....	....	....	....	1951-52	1951-52
ecko, Lubos	St.L., Atl.	5	257	46	65	111	107	12	1	1	2	2	....	1998-99	2002-03
el, Robin	Cgy., Van.	2	41	0	1	1	14	6	0	0	0	16	....	1985-86	1986-87
lett, Jim	Mtl., NYR, Bos.	5	191	34	23	57	273	2	0	0	0	0	....	1954-55	1960-61
on, Cliff	Pit., Phi., NYR	3	85	10	9	19	22	....	....	....	....	....	....	1929-30	1939-40
os, Peter	Min.	1	13	4	2	6	6	....	....	....	....	....	....	2000-01	2000-01
ovic, Milan	Buf., Chi.	3	50	3	14	17	26	....	....	....	....	....	....	2002-03	2005-06
kirov, Andrei	Mtl.	3	30	0	3	3	0	....	....	....	....	....	....	1998-99	2000-01
en, Bob	NYI, Chi., St.L., Que., Dal., Cgy.	15	765	88	144	232	1004	93	9	15	24	134	....	1985-86	1999-00
, Ryan	Phi.	1	2	0	1	1	0	....	....	....	....	....	....	1998-99	1998-99
s, Shawn	Bos., NYI	10	465	72	126	198	266	29	3	4	7	19	....	1997-98	2007-08
e, Frank	Det., Phi.	9	224	3	28	31	542	27	1	3	4	42	....	1974-75	1983-84
gate, Andy	NYR, Tor., Det., Pit.	17	1069	349	624	973	624	54	21	14	35	76	1	1952-53	1970-71
gate, Frank	NYR	1	2	0	0	0	2	....	....	....	....	....	....	1952-53	1952-53
ers, Jeff	St.L.	2	16	0	0	0	28	....	....	....	....	....	....	1993-94	1994-95
rshin, Ruslan	L.A.	1	2	0	0	0	6	....	....	....	....	....	....	1995-96	1995-96
er, Bobby	Bos.	9	327	123	137	260	36	48	11	8	19	6	2	1936-37	1951-52
ngartner, Ken	L.A., NYI, Tor., Ana., Bos.	12	696	13	41	54	2244	51	1	2	3	106	....	1987-88	1998-99
ngartner, Mike	K.C.	1	17	0	0	0	0	....	....	....	....	....	....	1974-75	1974-75
, Bob	Tor., Oak., Det.	17	964	37	187	224	1493	96	3	12	15	171	4	1956-57	1972-73
in, Sergei	Wpg., Det., S.J.	3	132	5	25	30	176	6	0	0	0	2	....	1992-93	1995-96

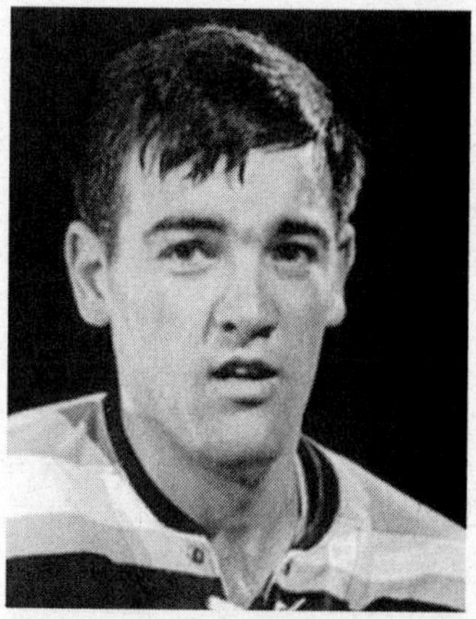
John Arbour

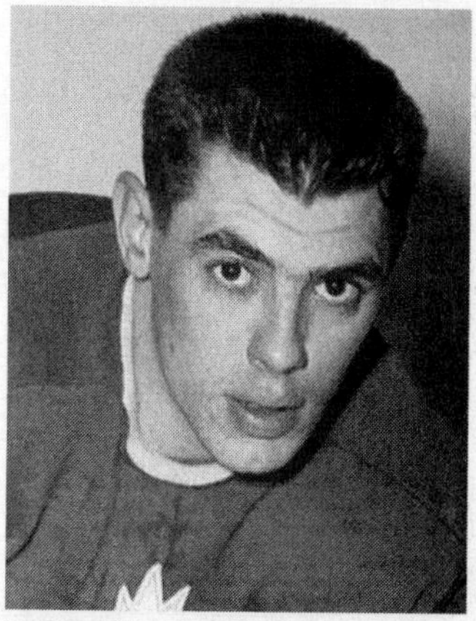
Earl Balfour

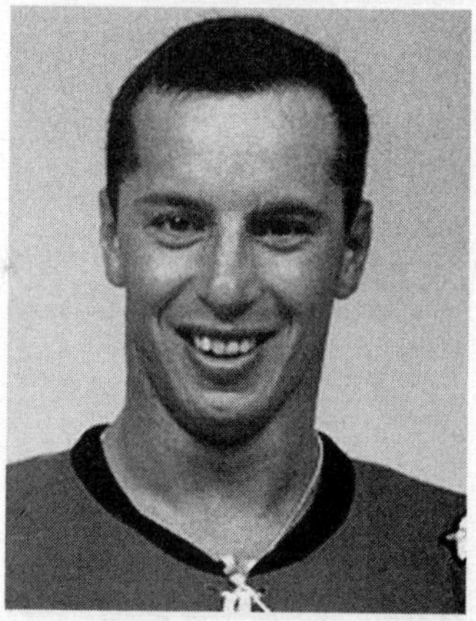
Murray Balfour

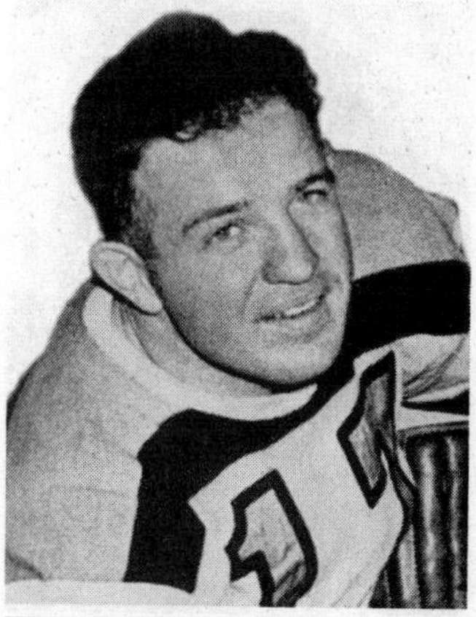
Bobby Bauer

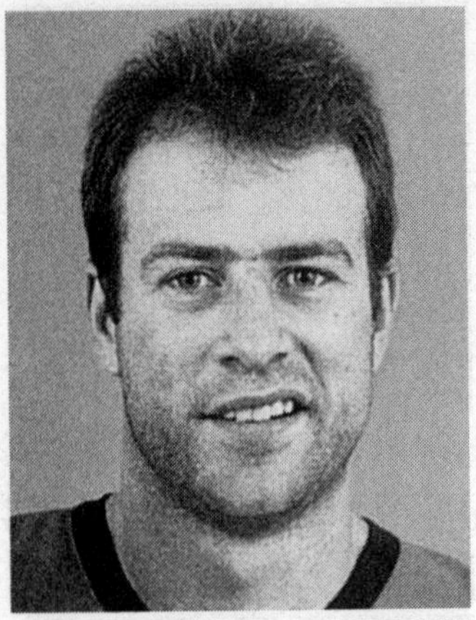

Brian Benning

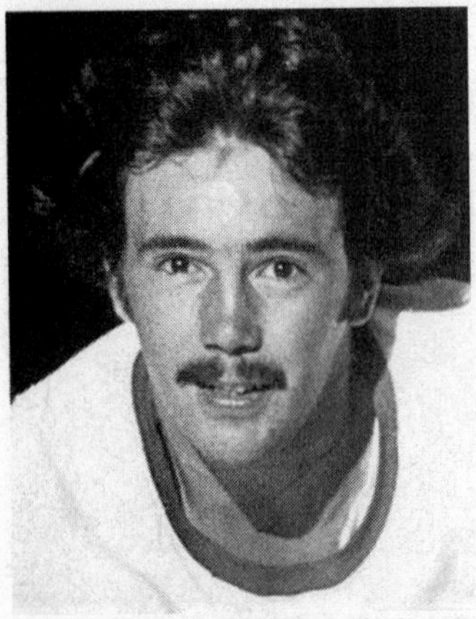

Michel Bergeron

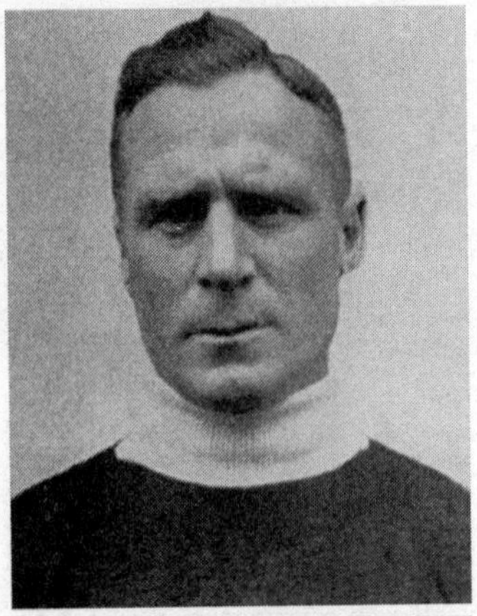

Louis Berlinguette

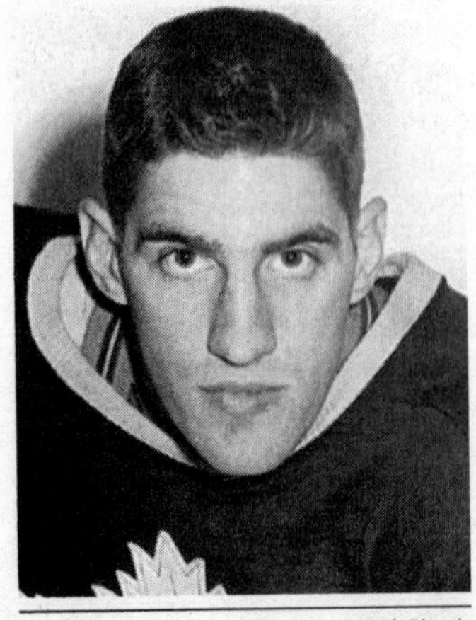

Jack Bionda

			Regular Schedule					Playoffs							
Name	NHL Teams	NHL Seasons	GP	G	A	TP	PIM	GP	G	A	TP	PIM	NHL Cup Wins	First NHL Season	Last NHL Seaso
Bawa, Robin	Wsh., Van., S.J., Ana.	4	61	6	1	7	60	1	0	0	0	0	....	1989-90	1993-9
Baxter, Paul	Que., Pit., Cgy.	8	472	48	121	169	1564	40	0	5	5	162	....	1979-80	1986-8
Beadle, Sandy	Wpg.	1	6	1	0	1	2	....	....	....	....	....	....	1980-81	1980-8
Beaton, Frank	NYR	2	25	1	1	2	43	....	....	....	....	....	....	1978-79	1979-8
• Beattie, Red	Bos., Det., NYA	9	334	62	85	147	137	24	4	2	6	8	....	1930-31	1938-3
Beaudin, Norm	St.L., Min.	2	25	1	2	3	4	....	....	....	....	....	....	1967-68	1970-7
‡ Beaudoin, Eric	Fla.	3	53	3	8	11	41	....	....	....	....	....	....	2001-02	2003-0
Beaudoin, Serge	Atl.	1	3	0	0	0	0	....	....	....	....	....	....	1979-80	1979-8
Beaudoin, Yves	Wsh.	3	11	0	0	0	5	....	....	....	....	....	....	1985-86	1987-8
‡ Beaufait, Mark	S.J.	1	5	1	0	1	0	....	....	....	....	....	....	1992-93	1992-9
Beck, Barry	Col., NYR, L.A.	10	615	104	251	355	1016	51	10	23	33	77	....	1977-78	1989-9
Beckett, Bob	Bos.	4	68	7	6	13	18	....	....	....	....	....	....	1956-57	1963-6
Bedard, James	Chi.	2	22	1	1	2	8	....	....	....	....	....	....	1949-50	1950-5
Beddoes, Clayton	Bos.	2	60	2	8	10	57	....	....	....	....	....	....	1995-96	1996-9
‡ Bednar, Jaroslav	L.A., Fla.	3	102	10	25	35	30	3	0	0	0	0	....	2001-02	2003-0
Bednarski, John	NYR, Edm.	4	100	2	18	20	114	1	0	0	0	17	....	1974-75	1979-8
‡ Beech, Kris	Wsh., Pit., Nsh., CBJ, Van.	7	198	25	42	67	113	....	....	....	....	....	....	2000-01	2007-0
Beers, Bob	Bos., T.B., Edm., NYI	8	258	28	79	107	225	21	1	1	2	22	....	1989-90	1996-9
Beers, Eddy	Cgy., St.L.	5	250	94	116	210	256	41	7	10	17	47	....	1981-82	1985-8
• Behling, Dick	Det.	2	5	1	0	1	2	....	....	....	....	....	....	1940-41	1942-4
• Beisler, Frank	NYA	2	2	0	0	0	0	....	....	....	....	....	....	1936-37	1939-4
Bekar, Derek	St.L., L.A., NYI	3	11	0	0	0	6	....	....	....	....	....	....	1999-00	2003-0
Belanger, Alain	Tor.	1	9	0	1	1	6	....	....	....	....	....	....	1977-78	1977-7
Belanger, Francis	Mtl.	1	10	0	0	0	29	....	....	....	....	....	....	2000-01	2000-0
Belanger, Jesse	Mtl., Fla., Van., Edm., NYI	8	246	59	76	135	56	12	0	3	3	2	1	1991-92	2000-0
Belanger, Ken	Tor., NYI, Bos., L.A.	11	248	11	12	23	695	12	1	0	1	16	....	1994-95	2005-
Belanger, Roger	Pit.	1	44	3	5	8	32	....	....	....	....	....	....	1984-85	1984-
Belisle, Danny	NYR	1	4	2	0	2	0	....	....	....	....	....	....	1960-61	1960-6
Beliveau, Jean	Mtl.	20	1125	507	712	1219	1029	162	79	97	176	211	10	1950-51	1970-
• Bell, Billy	Mtl.W., Mtl., Ott.	6	66	3	2	5	14	5	0	0	0	0	1	1917-18	1923-
Bell, Bruce	Que., St.L., NYR, Edm.	5	209	12	64	76	113	34	3	5	8	41	....	1984-85	1989-
• Bell, Huddy	NYR	1	1	0	1	1	0	....	....	....	....	....	....	1946-47	1946-
Bell, Joe	NYR	2	62	8	9	17	18	....	....	....	....	....	....	1942-43	1946-
‡ Bell, Mark	Chi., S.J., Tor.	7	445	87	95	182	597	9	0	0	0	10	....	2000-01	2007-
Belland, Neil	Van., Pit.	6	109	13	32	45	54	21	2	9	11	23	....	1981-82	1986-
‡ Bellefeuille, Blake	CBJ	2	5	0	1	1	0	....	....	....	....	....	....	2001-02	2002-
• Bellefeuille, Pete	Tor., Det.	4	92	26	4	30	58	....	....	....	....	....	....	1925-26	1929-
• Bellemer, Andy	Mtl.M.	1	15	0	0	0	0	....	....	....	....	....	....	1932-33	1932-
Bellows, Brian	Min., Mtl., T.B., Ana., Wsh.	17	1188	485	537	1022	718	143	51	71	122	143	1	1982-83	1998-
• Bend, Lin	NYR	1	8	3	1	4	2	....	....	....	....	....	....	1942-43	1942-
‡ Benda, Jan	Wsh.	1	9	0	3	3	6	....	....	....	....	....	....	1997-98	1997-
Bennett, Adam	Chi., Edm.	3	69	3	8	11	69	....	....	....	....	....	....	1991-92	1993-
Bennett, Bill	Bos., Hfd.	2	31	4	7	11	65	....	....	....	....	....	....	1978-79	1979-
Bennett, Curt	St.L., NYR, Atl.	10	580	152	182	334	347	21	1	1	2	57	....	1970-71	1979-
Bennett, Frank	Det.	1	7	0	1	1	2	....	....	....	....	....	....	1943-44	1943-
Bennett, Harvey	Pit., Wsh., Phi., Min., St.L.	5	268	44	46	90	347	4	0	0	0	2	....	1974-75	1978-
• Bennett, Max	Mtl.	1	1	0	0	0	0	....	....	....	....	....	....	1935-36	1935-
Bennett, Rick	NYR	3	15	1	1	2	13	....	....	....	....	....	....	1989-90	1991-
Benning, Brian	St.L., L.A., Phi., Edm., Fla.	11	568	63	233	296	963	48	3	20	23	74	....	1984-85	1994-
Benning, Jim	Tor., Van.	9	605	52	191	243	461	7	1	1	2	2	....	1981-82	1989-
• Benoit, Joe	Mtl.	5	185	75	69	144	94	11	6	3	9	11	1	1940-41	1946-
Benson, Bill	NYA, Bro.	2	67	11	25	36	35	....	....	....	....	....	....	1940-41	1941-
• Benson, Bobby	Bos.	1	8	0	1	1	4	....	....	....	....	....	....	1924-25	1924-
• Bentley, Doug	Chi., NYR	13	566	219	324	543	217	23	9	8	17	12	....	1939-40	1953-
• Bentley, Max	Chi., Tor., NYR	12	646	245	299	544	179	51	18	27	45	14	3	1940-41	1953-
• Bentley, Reg	Chi.	1	11	1	2	3	2	....	....	....	....	....	....	1942-43	1942-
‡ Benysek, Ladislav	Edm., Min.	4	161	3	12	15	74	....	....	....	....	....	....	1997-98	2002-
Beraldo, Paul	Bos.	2	10	0	0	0	4	....	....	....	....	....	....	1987-88	1988-
‡ Beranek, Josef	Edm., Phi., Van., Pit.	9	531	118	144	262	398	57	5	8	13	24	....	1991-92	2000-
Berard, Bryan	NYI, Tor., NYR, Bos., Chi., CBJ	10	619	76	247	323	500	20	2	8	10	10	....	1996-97	2007-
Berehowsky, Drake	Tor., Pit., Edm., Nsh., Van., Phx.	13	549	37	112	149	848	22	1	3	4	30	....	1990-91	2003
Berenson, Red	Mtl., NYR, St.L., Det.	17	987	261	397	658	305	85	23	14	37	49	1	1961-62	1977
Berenzweig, Bubba	Nsh.	4	37	3	7	10	14	....	....	....	....	....	....	1999-00	2002
Berezan, Perry	Cgy., Min., S.J.	9	378	61	75	136	279	31	4	7	11	34	....	1984-85	1992
Berezin, Sergei	Tor., Phx., Mtl., Chi., Wsh.	7	502	160	126	286	54	52	13	17	30	6	....	1996-97	2002
‡ Berg, Aki	L.A., Tor.	9	606	15	70	85	374	54	1	7	8	47	....	1995-96	2005
Berg, Bill	NYI, Tor., NYR, Ott.	10	546	55	67	122	488	61	3	4	7	34	....	1988-89	1998
• Bergdinon, Fred	Bos.	1	2	0	0	0	0	....	....	....	....	....	....	1925-26	1925
Bergen, Todd	Phi.	1	14	11	5	16	4	17	4	9	13	8	....	1984-85	1984
Berger, Mike	Min.	2	30	3	1	4	67	....	....	....	....	....	....	1987-88	1988
Bergeron, Michel	Det., NYI, Wsh.	5	229	80	58	138	165	....	....	....	....	....	....	1974-75	1978
Bergeron, Yves	Pit.	2	3	0	0	0	0	....	....	....	....	....	....	1974-75	1976
Bergevin, Marc	Chi., NYI, Hfd., T.B., Det., St.L., Pit., Van.	20	1191	36	145	181	1090	80	3	6	9	52	....	1984-85	2003
Bergkvist, Stefan	Pit.	2	7	0	0	0	9	4	0	0	0	2	....	1995-96	1996
Bergland, Tim	Wsh., T.B.	5	182	17	26	43	75	26	2	2	4	22	....	1989-90	1993
Bergloff, Bob	Min.	1	2	0	0	0	5	....	....	....	....	....	....	1982-83	1982
Berglund, Bo	Que., Min., Phi.	3	130	28	39	67	40	9	2	0	2	6	....	1983-84	1985
‡ Berglund, Christian	N.J., Fla.	3	86	11	16	27	42	3	0	0	0	2	....	2001-02	2003
• Bergman, Gary	Det., Min., K.C.	12	838	68	299	367	1249	21	0	5	5	20	....	1964-65	1975
Bergman, Thommie	Det.	6	246	21	44	65	243	7	0	2	2	2	....	1972-73	1979
Bergqvist, Jonas	Cgy.	1	22	2	5	7	10	....	....	....	....	....	....	1989-90	1989
• Berlinguette, Louis	Mtl., Mtl.M., Pit.	8	193	45	33	78	129	11	0	5	5	9	....	1917-18	1925
Bernier, Serge	Phi., L.A., Que.	7	302	78	119	197	234	5	1	1	2	0	....	1968-69	1980
Berry, Bob	Mtl., L.A.	8	541	159	191	350	344	26	2	6	8	6	....	1968-69	1976
Berry, Brad	Wpg., Min., Dal.	8	241	4	28	32	323	13	0	1	1	16	....	1985-86	1993
Berry, Doug	Col.	2	121	10	33	43	25	....	....	....	....	....	....	1979-80	1980
Berry, Fred	Det.	1	3	0	0	0	0	....	....	....	....	....	....	1976-77	1976
Berry, Ken	Edm., Van.	4	55	8	10	18	30	....	....	....	....	....	....	1981-82	1988
‡ Berry, Rick	Col., Pit., Wsh.	4	197	2	13	15	314	....	....	....	....	....	....	2000-01	2003
‡ Berti, Adam	Chi.	1	2	0	0	0	0	....	....	....	....	....	....	2007-08	2007
‡ Bertrand, Eric	N.J., Atl., Mtl.	2	15	0	0	0	4	....	....	....	....	....	....	1999-00	2000
Berube, Craig	Phi., Tor., Cgy., Wsh., NYI	17	1054	61	98	159	3149	89	3	1	4	211	....	1986-87	2002
• Besler, Phil	Bos., Chi., Det.	2	30	1	4	5	18	....	....	....	....	....	....	1935-36	1938
• Bessone, Pete	Det.	1	6	0	1	1	6	....	....	....	....	....	....	1937-38	1937
Bethel, John	Wpg.	1	17	0	2	2	4	....	....	....	....	....	....	1979-80	1979
Betik, Karel	T.B.	1	3	0	2	2	2	....	....	....	....	....	....	1998-99	1998
Bets, Maxim	Ana.	1	3	0	0	0	0	....	....	....	....	....	....	1993-94	1993
• Bettio, Sam	Bos.	1	44	9	12	21	32	....	....	....	....	....	....	1949-50	1949
Beukeboom, Jeff	Edm., NYR	14	804	30	129	159	1890	99	3	16	19	197	4	1985-86	1998
Beverley, Nick	Bos., Pit., NYR, Min., L.A., Col.	11	502	18	94	112	156	7	0	1	1	0	....	1966-67	1979
‡ Bezina, Goran	Phx.	1	3	0	0	0	2	....	....	....	....	....	....	2003-04	2003
Bialowas, Dwight	Atl., Min.	4	164	11	46	57	46	....	....	....	....	....	....	1973-74	197
Bialowas, Frank	Tor.	1	3	0	0	0	12	....	....	....	....	....	....	1993-94	199
Bianchin, Wayne	Pit., Edm.	7	276	68	41	109	137	3	0	1	1	6	....	1973-74	197
Bicanek, Radim	Ott., Chi., CBJ	7	122	1	11	12	62	7	0	0	0	8	....	1994-95	200
‡ Bicek, Jiri	N.J.	4	62	6	7	13	29	7	0	0	0	0	1	2000-01	200
Bidner, Todd	Wsh.	1	12	2	1	3	7	....	....	....	....	....	....	1981-82	198
Biggs, Don	Min., Phi.	2	12	2	0	2	8	....	....	....	....	....	....	1984-85	198
Bignell, Larry	Pit.	2	20	0	3	3	2	3	0	0	0	2	....	1973-74	197
• Bilodeau, Gilles	Que.	1	9	0	1	1	25	....	....	....	....	....	....	1979-80	197
• Bionda, Jack	Tor., Bos.	4	93	3	9	12	113	11	0	1	1	14	....	1955-56	195
‡ Biron, Mathieu	NYI, T.B., Fla., Wsh.	6	253	12	32	44	177	....	....	....	....	....	....	1999-00	200
‡ Bisaillon, Sebastien	Edm.	1	2	0	0	0	0	....	....	....	....	....	....	2006-07	200
‡ Bishai, Mike	Edm.	1	14	0	2	2	19	....	....	....	....	....	....	2003-04	200
Bissett, Tom	Det.	1	5	0	0	0	0	....	....	....	....	....	....	1990-91	199
Bjugstad, Scott	Min., Pit., L.A.	9	317	76	68	144	144	9	0	1	1	2	....	1983-84	199
Black, James	Hfd., Min., Dal., Buf., Chi., Wsh.	11	352	58	57	115	84	13	2	1	3	4	....	1989-90	200
• Black, Steve	Det., Chi.	2	113	11	20	31	77	13	0	0	0	13	1	1949-50	195
Blackburn, Bob	NYR, Pit.	3	135	8	12	20	105	6	0	0	0	4	....	1968-69	197
Blackburn, Don	Bos., Phi., NYR, NYI, Min.	6	185	23	44	67	87	12	3	0	3	10	....	1962-63	197
• Blade, Hank	Chi.	2	24	2	3	5	2	....	....	....	....	....	....	1946-47	194
Bladon, Tom	Phi., Pit., Edm., Wpg., Det.	9	610	73	197	270	392	86	8	29	37	70	2	1972-73	198
• Blaine, Garry	Mtl.	1	1	0	0	0	0	....	....	....	....	....	....	1954-55	195
• Blair, Andy	Tor., Chi.	9	402	74	86	160	323	38	6	6	12	32	1	1928-29	193
• Blair, Chuck	Tor.	1	1	0	0	0	0	....	....	....	....	....	....	1948-49	194

Name	NHL Teams	NHL Seasons	Regular Schedule					Playoffs					NHL Cup Wins	First NHL Season	Last NHL Season
			GP	G	A	TP	PIM	GP	G	A	TP	PIM			
lair, Dusty	Tor.	1	2	0	0	0	0	....	....	....	....	....	....	1950-51	1950-51
laisdell, Mike	Det., NYR, Pit., Tor.	9	343	70	84	154	166	6	1	2	3	10	....	1980-81	1988-89
lake, Bob	Bos.	1	12	0	0	0	0	....	....	....	....	....	....	1935-36	1935-36
lake, Mickey	Mtl.M., St.L., Tor.	3	10	1	1	2	4	....	....	....	....	....	....	1932-33	1935-36
lake, Toe	Mtl.M., Mtl.	14	577	235	292	527	272	58	25	37	62	23	3	1934-35	1947-48
latny, Zdenek	Atl., Bos.	3	25	3	0	3	8	....	....	....	....	....	....	2002-03	2005-06
light, Rick	Van., L.A.	7	326	96	125	221	170	5	0	5	5	2	....	1975-76	1982-83
linco, Russ	Mtl.M., Chi.	6	268	59	66	125	24	19	3	3	6	4	1	1933-34	1938-39
lock, Ken	Van.	1	1	0	0	0	0	....	....	....	....	....	....	1970-71	1970-71
loemberg, Jeff	NYR	4	43	3	6	9	25	7	0	3	3	5	....	1988-89	1991-92
lomqvist, Timo	Wsh., N.J.	5	243	4	53	57	293	13	0	0	0	24	....	1981-82	1986-87
lomsten, Arto	Wpg., L.A.	3	25	0	4	4	8	....	....	....	....	....	....	1993-94	1995-96
loom, Mike	Wsh., Det.	3	201	30	47	77	215	....	....	....	....	....	....	1974-75	1976-77
louin, Sylvain	NYR, Mtl., Min.	6	115	3	4	7	336	....	....	....	....	....	....	1996-97	2002-03
lum, John	Edm., Bos., Wsh., Det.	8	250	7	34	41	610	20	0	2	2	27	....	1982-83	1989-90
odak, Bob	Cgy., Hfd.	2	4	0	0	0	29	....	....	....	....	....	....	1987-88	1989-90
oddy, Gregg	Van.	5	273	23	44	67	263	3	0	0	0	0	....	1971-72	1975-76
odger, Doug	Pit., Buf., S.J., N.J., L.A., Van.	16	1071	106	422	528	1007	47	6	18	24	25	....	1984-85	1999-00
odnar, Gus	Tor., Chi., Bos.	12	667	142	254	396	207	32	4	3	7	10	2	1943-44	1954-55
oehm, Ron	Oak.	1	16	2	1	3	10	....	....	....	....	....	....	1967-68	1967-68
oesch, Garth	Tor.	4	197	9	28	37	205	34	2	5	7	18	3	1946-47	1949-50
oguniecki, Eric	Fla., St.L., Pit., NYI	7	178	34	42	76	105	9	1	3	4	2	....	1999-00	2006-07
oh, Rick	Min.	1	8	2	1	3	4	....	....	....	....	....	....	1987-88	1987-88
ohonos, Lonny	Van., Tor.	4	83	19	16	35	22	9	3	6	9	2	....	1995-96	1998-99
oikov, Alexandre	Nsh.	2	10	0	0	0	15	....	....	....	....	....	....	1999-00	2000-01
oileau, Marc	Det.	1	54	5	6	11	8	....	....	....	....	....	....	1961-62	1961-62
oileau, Patrick	Wsh., Det., Pit.	5	48	5	11	16	26	....	....	....	....	....	....	1996-97	2003-04
oileau, Rene	NYA	1	7	0	0	0	0	....	....	....	....	....	....	1925-26	1925-26
oimistruck, Fred	Tor.	2	83	4	14	18	45	....	....	....	....	....	....	1981-82	1982-83
oisvert, Serge	Tor., Mtl.	5	46	5	7	12	8	23	3	7	10	4	1	1982-83	1987-88
oivin, Claude	Phi., Ott.	4	132	12	19	31	364	....	....	....	....	....	....	1991-92	1994-95
oivin, Leo	Tor., Bos., Det., Pit., Min.	19	1150	72	250	322	1192	54	3	10	13	59	....	1951-52	1969-70
Boland, Mike	Phi.	1	2	0	0	0	0	....	....	....	....	....	....	1974-75	1974-75
Boland, Mike	K.C., Buf.	2	23	1	2	3	29	3	1	0	1	2	....	1974-75	1978-79
Boldirev, Ivan	Bos., Cal., Chi., Atl., Van., Det.	16	1052	361	505	866	507	48	13	20	33	14	1	1969-70	1984-85
Bolduc, Danny	Det., Cgy.	3	102	22	19	41	33	1	0	0	0	0	....	1978-79	1983-84
Bolduc, Michel	Que.	2	10	0	0	0	6	....	....	....	....	....	....	1981-82	1982-83
Boll, Buzz	Tor., NYA, Bro., Bos.	12	437	133	130	263	148	31	7	3	10	13	....	1932-33	1943-44
Bolonchuk, Larry	Van., Wsh.	4	74	3	9	12	97	....	....	....	....	....	....	1972-73	1977-78
Bolton, Hugh	Tor.	8	235	10	51	61	221	17	0	5	5	14	1	1949-50	1956-57
Bombardir, Brad	N.J., Min., Nsh.	7	356	8	46	54	127	16	0	1	1	2	1	1997-98	2003-04
Bonar, Dan	L.A.	3	170	25	39	64	208	14	3	4	7	22	....	1980-81	1982-83
Bondra, Peter	Wsh., Ott., Atl., Chi.	16	1081	503	389	892	761	80	30	26	56	60	....	1990-91	2006-07
Bonin, Brian	Pit., Min.	2	12	0	0	0	0	3	0	0	0	0	....	1998-99	2000-01
Bonin, Marcel	Det., Bos., Mtl.	9	454	97	175	272	336	50	11	14	25	51	4	1952-53	1961-62
Bonk, Radek	Ott., Mtl., Nsh.	14	969	194	303	497	581	73	12	15	27	42	....	1994-95	2008-09
Bonni, Ryan	Van.	1	3	0	0	0	0	....	....	....	....	....	....	1999-00	1999-00
Bonsignore, Jason	Edm., T.B.	4	79	3	13	16	34	....	....	....	....	....	....	1994-95	1998-99
Bonvie, Dennis	Edm., Chi., Pit., Bos., Ott., Col.	9	92	1	2	3	311	1	0	0	0	0	....	1994-95	2003-04
Boo, Jim	Min.	1	6	0	0	0	22	....	....	....	....	....	....	1977-78	1977-78
Boone, Buddy	Bos.	2	34	5	3	8	28	22	2	1	3	25	....	1956-57	1957-58
Boothman, George	Tor.	2	58	17	19	36	18	5	2	1	3	2	....	1942-43	1943-44
Bordeleau, Christian	Mtl., St.L., Chi.	4	205	38	65	103	82	19	4	7	11	17	1	1968-69	1971-72
Bordeleau, J.P.	Chi.	10	519	97	126	223	143	48	3	6	9	12	....	1969-70	1979-80
Bordeleau, Paulin	Van.	3	183	33	56	89	47	5	2	1	3	0	....	1973-74	1975-76
Bordeleau, Sebastien	Mtl., Nsh., Min., Phx.	7	251	37	61	98	118	5	0	0	0	2	....	1995-96	2001-02
Borotsik, Jack	St.L.	1	1	0	0	0	0	....	....	....	....	....	....	1974-75	1974-75
Borsato, Luciano	Wpg.	5	203	35	55	90	113	7	1	0	1	4	....	1990-91	1994-95
Borschevsky, Nikolai	Tor., Cgy., Dal.	4	162	49	73	122	44	31	4	9	13	4	....	1992-93	1995-96
Boschman, Laurie	Tor., Edm., Wpg., N.J., Ott.	14	1009	229	348	577	2265	57	8	13	21	140	....	1979-80	1992-93
Bossy, Mike	NYI	10	752	573	553	1126	210	129	85	75	160	38	4	1977-78	1986-87
Bostrom, Helge	Chi.	4	96	3	3	6	58	13	0	0	0	16	....	1929-30	1932-33
Botell, Mark	Phi.	1	32	4	10	14	31	....	....	....	....	....	....	1981-82	1981-82
Bothwell, Tim	NYR, St.L., Hfd.	12	502	28	93	121	382	49	0	3	3	56	....	1978-79	1988-89
Botterill, Jason	Dal., Atl., Cgy., Buf.	6	88	5	9	14	89	....	....	....	....	....	....	1997-98	2003-04
Botting, Cam	Atl.	1	2	0	1	1	0	....	....	....	....	....	....	1975-76	1975-76
Boucha, Henry	Det., Min., K.C., Col.	6	247	53	49	102	157	....	....	....	....	....	....	1971-72	1976-77
Bouchard, Butch	Mtl.	15	785	49	144	193	863	113	11	21	32	121	4	1941-42	1955-56
Bouchard, Dick	NYR	1	1	0	0	0	0	....	....	....	....	....	....	1954-55	1954-55
Bouchard, Edmond	Mtl., Ham., NYA, Pit.	8	211	19	21	40	117	....	....	....	....	....	....	1921-22	1928-29
Bouchard, Joel	Cgy., Nsh., Dal., Phx., N.J., NYR, Pit., NYI	11	364	22	53	75	264	....	....	....	....	....	....	1994-95	2005-06
Bouchard, Pierre	Mtl., Wsh.	12	595	24	82	106	433	76	3	10	13	56	5	1970-71	1981-82
Boucher, Billy	Mtl., Bos., NYA	7	213	93	38	131	409	14	3	0	3	17	1	1921-22	1927-28
Boucher, Bobby	Mtl.	1	11	1	0	1	0	2	0	0	0	0	1	1923-24	1923-24
Boucher, Clarence	NYA	2	47	2	2	4	133	....	....	....	....	....	....	1926-27	1927-28
Boucher, Frank	Ott., NYR	14	557	160	263	423	119	55	16	20	36	12	2	1921-22	1943-44
Boucher, Georges	Ott., Mtl.M., Chi.	15	449	117	87	204	838	28	5	3	8	88	4	1917-18	1931-32
Boucher, Philippe	Buf., L.A., Dal., Pit.	16	748	94	206	300	702	65	4	10	14	39	1	1992-93	2008-09
Bouck, Tyler	Dal., Phx., Van.	5	91	4	8	12	93	2	0	0	0	0	....	2000-01	2006-07
Boudreau, Bruce	Tor., Chi.	8	141	28	42	70	46	9	2	0	2	0	....	1976-77	1985-86
Boudrias, Andre	Mtl., Min., Chi., St.L., Van.	12	662	151	340	491	216	34	6	10	16	12	....	1963-64	1975-76
Boughner, Barry	Oak., Cal.	2	20	0	0	0	11	....	....	....	....	....	....	1969-70	1970-71
Boughner, Bob	Buf., Nsh., Pit., Cgy., Car., Col.	10	630	15	57	72	1382	65	0	12	12	67	....	1995-96	2005-06
Boumedienne, Josef	N.J., T.B., Wsh.	3	47	4	12	16	36	....	....	....	....	....	....	2001-02	2003-04
Bourbonnais, Dan	Hfd.	2	59	3	25	28	11	....	....	....	....	....	....	1981-82	1983-84
Bourbonnais, Rick	St.L.	3	71	9	15	24	29	4	0	1	1	0	....	1975-76	1977-78
Bourcier, Conrad	Mtl.	1	6	0	0	0	0	....	....	....	....	....	....	1935-36	1935-36
Bourcier, Jean	Mtl.	1	9	0	1	1	0	....	....	....	....	....	....	1935-36	1935-36
Bourdon, Luc	Van.	2	36	2	0	2	24	....	....	....	....	....	....	2006-07	2007-08
Bourgeault, Leo	Tor., NYR, Ott., Mtl.	8	307	24	20	44	334	24	1	1	2	18	1	1926-27	1934-35
Bourgeois, Charlie	Cgy., St.L., Hfd.	7	290	16	54	70	788	40	2	3	5	194	....	1981-82	1987-88
Bourne, Bob	NYI, L.A.	14	964	258	324	582	605	139	40	56	96	108	4	1974-75	1987-88
Bourque, Phil	Pit., NYR, Ott.	12	477	88	111	199	516	56	13	12	25	107	2	1983-84	1995-96
Bourque, Raymond	Bos., Col.	22	1612	410	1169	1579	1141	214	41	139	180	171	1	1979-80	2000-01
Boutette, Pat	Tor., Hfd., Pit.	10	756	171	282	453	1354	46	10	14	24	109	....	1975-76	1984-85
Boutilier, Paul	NYI, Bos., Min., NYR, Wpg.	8	288	27	83	110	358	41	1	9	10	45	1	1981-82	1988-89
Bowen, Jason	Phi., Edm.	6	77	2	6	8	109	....	....	....	....	....	....	1992-93	1997-98
Bowler, Bill	CBJ	1	9	0	2	2	8	....	....	....	....	....	....	2000-01	2000-01
Bowman, Kirk	Chi.	3	88	11	17	28	19	7	1	0	1	0	....	1976-77	1978-79
Bowman, Ralph	Ott., St.L., Det.	7	274	8	17	25	260	22	2	2	4	6	2	1933-34	1939-40
Bownass, Jack	Mtl., NYR	4	80	3	8	11	58	....	....	....	....	....	....	1957-58	1961-62
Bowness, Rick	Atl., Det., St.L., Wpg.	7	173	18	37	55	191	5	0	0	0	2	....	1975-76	1981-82
Boyd, Bill	NYR, NYA	4	138	15	7	22	72	10	0	0	0	4	1	1926-27	1929-30
Boyd, Irwin	Bos., Det.	4	96	10	10	20	30	5	0	1	1	4	....	1931-32	1943-44
Boyd, Randy	Pit., Chi., NYI, Van.	8	257	20	67	87	328	13	0	2	2	26	....	1981-82	1988-89
Boyer, Wally	Tor., Chi., Oak., Pit.	7	365	54	105	159	163	15	1	3	4	0	....	1965-66	1971-72
Boyer, Zac	Dal.	2	3	0	0	0	0	2	0	0	0	0	....	1994-95	1995-96
Boyko, Darren	Wpg.	1	1	0	0	0	0	....	....	....	....	....	....	1988-89	1988-89
Bozek, Steve	L.A., Cgy., St.L., Van., S.J.	11	641	164	167	331	309	58	12	11	23	69	....	1981-82	1991-92
Bozon, Philippe	St.L.	4	144	16	25	41	101	19	2	0	2	31	....	1991-92	1994-95
Brackenborough, John	Bos.	1	7	0	0	0	0	....	....	....	....	....	....	1925-26	1925-26
Brackenbury, Curt	Que., Edm., St.L.	4	141	9	17	26	226	2	0	0	0	0	....	1979-80	1982-83
Bradley, Bart	Bos.	1	1	0	0	0	0	....	....	....	....	....	....	1949-50	1949-50
Bradley, Brian	Cgy., Van., Tor., T.B.	13	651	182	321	503	528	13	3	7	10	16	....	1985-86	1997-98
Bradley, Lyle	Cal., Cle.	2	6	1	0	1	2	....	....	....	....	....	....	1973-74	1976-77
Brady, Neil	N.J., Ott., Dal.	5	89	9	22	31	95	....	....	....	....	....	....	1989-90	1993-94
Bragnalo, Rick	Wsh.	4	145	15	35	50	46	....	....	....	....	....	....	1975-76	1978-79
Brandner, Christoph	Min.	1	35	4	5	9	8	....	....	....	....	....	....	2003-04	2003-04
Branigan, Andy	NYA, Bro.	2	27	1	2	3	31	....	....	....	....	....	....	1940-41	1941-42
Brasar, Per-Olov	Min., Van.	5	348	64	142	206	33	13	1	2	3	0	....	1977-78	1981-82
Brayshaw, Russ	Chi.	1	43	5	9	14	24	....	....	....	....	....	....	1944-45	1944-45
Breault, Francois	L.A.	3	27	2	4	6	42	....	....	....	....	....	....	1990-91	1992-93
Breitenbach, Ken	Buf.	3	68	1	13	14	49	8	0	1	1	4	....	1975-76	1978-79
Bremberg, Fredrik	Edm.	1	8	0	0	0	2	....	....	....	....	....	....	1998-99	1998-99
Brendl, Pavel	Phi., Car., Phx.	4	78	11	11	22	16	2	0	0	0	0	....	2001-02	2005-06

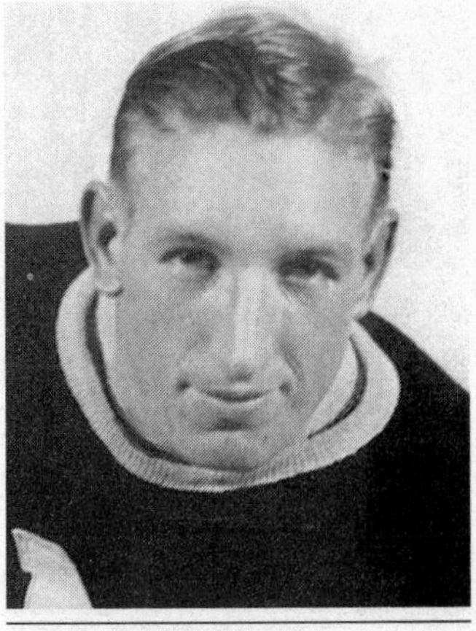

Russ Blinco

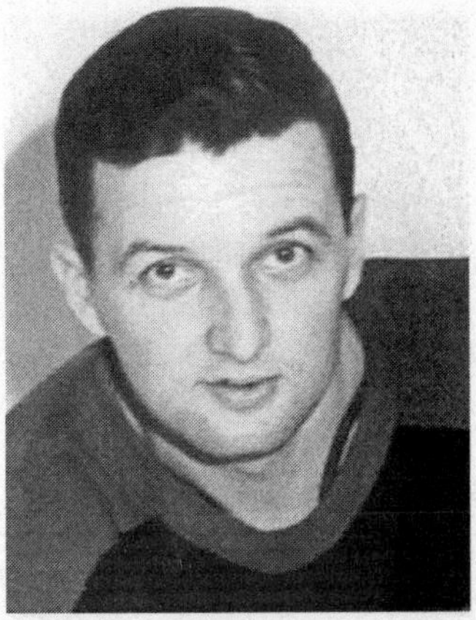

Gus Bodnar

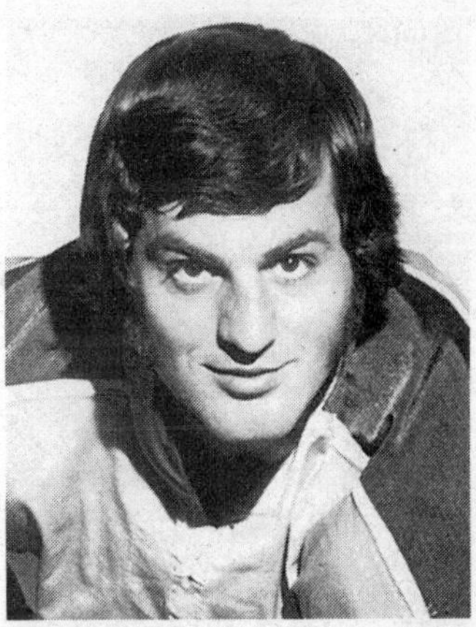

Ivan Boldirev

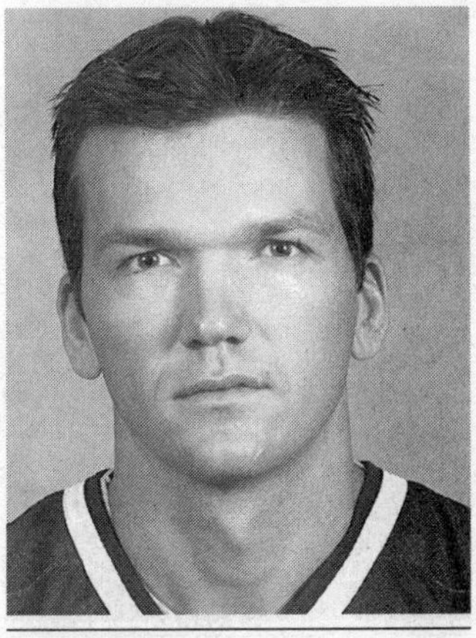

Philippe Boucher

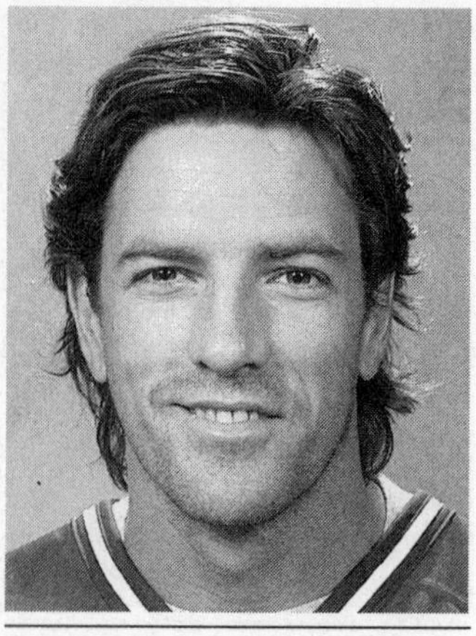
Patrice Brisebois

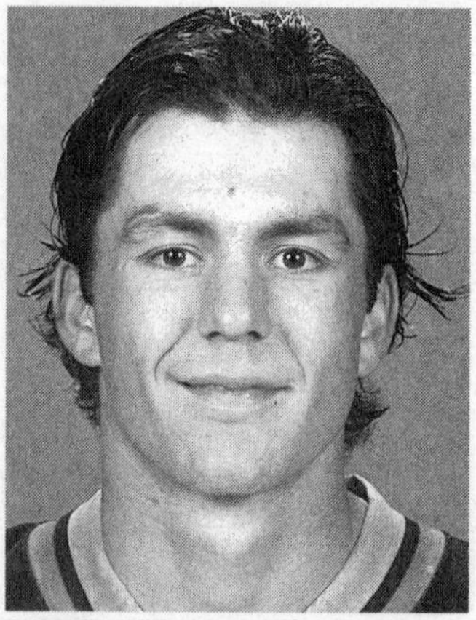
Curtis Brown

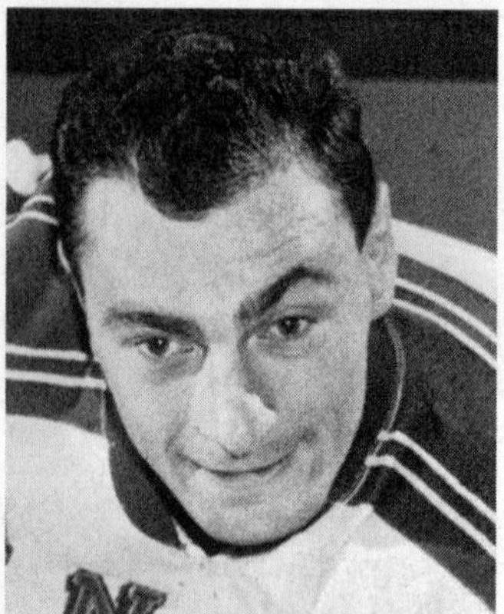
Hy Buller

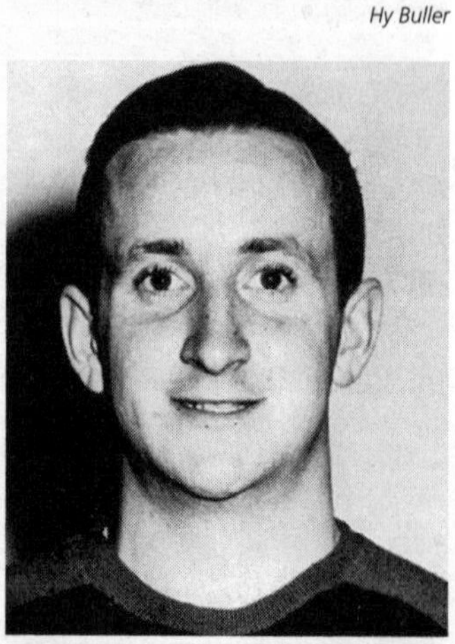
Dick Butler

Name	NHL Teams	NHL Seasons	Regular Schedule GP	G	A	TP	PIM	Playoffs GP	G	A	TP	PIM	NHL Cup Wins	First NHL Season	Last NHL Season
Brennan, Dan	L.A.	2	8	0	1	1	9	....	....	....	....	....	....	1983-84	1985-86
● Brennan, Doug	NYR	3	123	9	7	16	152	16	1	0	1	21	1	1931-32	1933-34
Brennan, Rich	Col., S.J., NYR, L.A., Nsh., Bos.	6	50	2	6	8	33	....	....	....	....	....	....	1996-97	2002-03
● Brennan, Tom	Bos.	2	12	2	2	4	2	....	....	....	....	....	....	1943-44	1944-45
Brenneman, John	Chi., NYR, Tor., Det., Oak.	5	152	21	19	40	46	....	....	....	....	....	1	1964-65	1968-69
● Bretto, Joe	Chi.	1	3	0	0	0	4	....	....	....	....	....	....	1944-45	1944-45
● Brewer, Carl	Tor., Det., St.L.	12	604	25	198	223	1037	72	3	17	20	146	3	1957-58	1979-80
Brickley, Andy	Phi., Pit., N.J., Bos., Wpg.	11	385	82	140	222	81	17	1	4	5	4	....	1982-83	1993-94
● Briden, Archie	Bos., Det., Pit.	2	71	9	5	14	56	....	....	....	....	....	....	1926-27	1929-30
Bridgman, Mel	Phi., Cgy., N.J., Det., Van.	14	977	252	449	701	1625	125	28	39	67	298	....	1975-76	1988-89
● Briere, Michel	Pit.	1	76	12	32	44	20	10	5	3	8	17	....	1969-70	1969-70
‡ Brigley, Travis	Cgy., Col.	3	55	3	6	9	16	....	....	....	....	....	....	1997-98	2003-04
‡ Brimanis, Aris	Phi., NYI, Ana., St.L.	7	113	2	12	14	57	....	....	....	....	....	....	1993-94	2003-04
Brindley, Doug	Tor.	1	3	0	0	0	0	....	....	....	....	....	....	1970-71	1970-71
● Brink, Milt	Chi.	1	5	0	0	0	0	....	....	....	....	....	....	1936-37	1936-37
Brisebois, Patrice	Mtl., Col.	18	1009	98	322	420	623	98	9	23	32	76	1	1990-91	2008-09
Brisson, Gerry	Mtl.	1	4	0	2	2	4	....	....	....	....	....	....	1962-63	1962-63
Britz, Greg	Tor., Hfd.	3	8	0	0	0	4	....	....	....	....	....	....	1983-84	1986-87
● Broadbent, Punch	Ott., Mtl.M., NYA	11	303	121	51	172	564	23	4	6	10	60	4	1918-19	1928-29
Brochu, Stephane	NYR	1	1	0	0	0	0	....	....	....	....	....	....	1988-89	1988-89
Broden, Connie	Mtl.	3	6	2	1	3	2	7	0	1	1	0	2	1955-56	1957-58
Brooke, Bob	NYR, Min., N.J.	7	447	69	97	166	520	34	9	9	18	59	....	1983-84	1989-90
‡ Brooks, Alex	N.J.	1	19	0	1	1	4	....	....	....	....	....	....	2006-07	2006-07
Brooks, Gord	St.L., Wsh.	3	70	7	18	25	37	....	....	....	....	....	....	1971-72	1974-75
● Brophy, Bernie	Mtl.M., Det.	3	62	4	4	8	25	2	0	0	0	2	1	1925-26	1929-30
Brossart, Willie	Phi., Tor., Wsh.	6	129	1	14	15	88	1	0	0	0	0	....	1970-71	1975-76
Broten, Aaron	Col., N.J., Min., Que., Tor., Wpg.	12	748	186	329	515	441	34	7	18	25	40	....	1980-81	1991-92
Broten, Neal	Min., Dal., N.J., L.A.	17	1099	289	634	923	569	135	35	63	98	77	1	1980-81	1996-97
Broten, Paul	NYR, Dal., St.L.	7	322	46	55	101	264	38	4	6	10	18	....	1989-90	1995-96
Brousseau, Paul	Col., T.B., Fla.	4	26	1	3	4	29	....	....	....	....	....	....	1995-96	2000-01
● Brown, Adam	Det., Chi., Bos.	10	391	104	113	217	378	26	2	4	6	14	1	1941-42	1951-52
Brown, Arnie	Tor., NYR, Det., NYI, Atl.	12	681	44	141	185	738	22	0	6	6	23	....	1961-62	1973-74
‡ Brown, Brad	Mtl., Chi., NYR, Min., Buf.	7	330	2	27	29	747	11	0	0	0	16	....	1996-97	2003-04
Brown, Cam	Van.	1	1	0	0	0	7	....	....	....	....	....	....	1990-91	1990-91
● Brown, Connie	Det.	5	73	15	24	39	12	14	2	3	5	0	1	1938-39	1942-43
‡ Brown, Curtis	Buf., S.J., Chi.	13	736	129	171	300	398	87	14	15	29	58	....	1994-95	2007-08
Brown, Dave	Phi., Edm., S.J.	14	729	45	52	97	1789	80	2	3	5	209	1	1982-83	1995-96
Brown, Doug	N.J., Pit., Det.	15	854	160	214	374	210	109	23	23	46	26	2	1986-87	2000-01
● Brown, Fred	Mtl.M.	1	19	1	0	1	0	9	0	0	0	0	....	1927-28	1927-28
Brown, George	Mtl.	3	79	6	22	28	34	7	0	0	0	2	....	1936-37	1938-39
● Brown, Gerry	Det.	2	23	4	5	9	2	12	2	1	3	4	....	1941-42	1945-46
Brown, Greg	Buf., Pit., Wpg.	4	94	4	14	18	86	6	0	1	1	4	....	1990-91	1994-95
Brown, Harold	NYR	1	13	2	1	3	2	....	....	....	....	....	....	1945-46	1945-46
Brown, Jeff	Que., St.L., Van., Hfd., Car., Tor., Wsh.	13	747	154	430	584	498	87	20	45	65	59	....	1985-86	1997-98
Brown, Jim	L.A.	1	3	0	1	1	5	....	....	....	....	....	....	1982-83	1982-83
Brown, Keith	Chi., Fla.	16	876	68	274	342	916	103	4	32	36	184	....	1979-80	1994-95
Brown, Kevin	L.A., Hfd., Car., Edm.	6	64	7	9	16	28	1	0	0	0	0	....	1994-95	1999-00
Brown, Larry	NYR, Det., Phi., L.A.	9	455	7	53	60	180	35	0	4	4	10	....	1969-70	1977-78
Brown, Mike	Van., Ana., Chi.	4	34	1	2	3	130	....	....	....	....	....	....	2000-01	2005-06
Brown, Rob	Pit., Hfd., Chi., Dal., L.A.	11	543	190	248	438	599	54	12	14	26	45	....	1987-88	1999-00
‡ Brown, Sean	Edm., Bos., N.J., Van.	9	436	14	43	57	907	9	0	0	0	37	....	1996-97	2005-06
● Brown, Stan	NYR, Det.	2	48	8	2	10	18	2	0	0	0	0	....	1926-27	1927-28
Brown, Wayne	Bos.	1	....	....	....	....	....	4	0	0	0	2	....	1953-54	1953-54
● Browne, Cecil	Chi.	1	13	2	0	2	4	....	....	....	....	....	....	1927-28	1927-28
Brownschidle, Jack	St.L., Hfd.	9	494	39	162	201	151	26	0	5	5	18	....	1977-78	1985-86
● Brownschidle, Jeff	Hfd.	2	7	0	1	1	2	....	....	....	....	....	....	1981-82	1982-83
Brubaker, Jeff	Hfd., Mtl., Cgy., Tor., Edm., NYR, Det.	8	178	16	9	25	512	2	0	0	0	27	....	1979-80	1988-89
Bruce, David	Van., St.L., S.J.	8	234	48	39	87	338	3	0	0	0	2	....	1985-86	1993-94
● Bruce, Gordie	Bos.	3	28	4	9	13	13	7	2	3	5	4	....	1940-41	1945-46
● Bruce, Morley	Ott.	4	71	8	3	11	27	3	0	0	0	2	2	1917-18	1921-22
Brule, Steve	N.J., Col.	2	2	0	0	0	0	1	0	0	0	0	1	1999-00	2002-03
Brumwell, Murray	Min., N.J.	7	128	12	31	43	70	2	0	0	0	2	....	1980-81	1987-88
Brunet, Benoit	Mtl., Dal., Ott.	13	539	101	161	262	229	54	5	20	25	32	1	1988-89	2001-02
● Bruneteau, Eddie	Det.	7	180	40	42	82	35	31	7	6	13	0	....	1940-41	1948-49
● Bruneteau, Mud	Det.	11	411	139	138	277	80	77	23	14	37	22	3	1935-36	1945-46
● Brydge, Bill	Tor., Det., NYA	9	368	26	52	78	506	2	0	0	0	4	....	1926-27	1935-36
Brydges, Paul	Buf.	1	15	2	2	4	6	....	....	....	....	....	....	1986-87	1986-87
● Brydson, Glenn	Mtl.M., St.L., NYR, Chi.	8	299	56	79	135	203	11	0	0	0	8	....	1930-31	1937-38
● Brydson, Gord	Tor.	1	8	2	0	2	8	....	....	....	....	....	....	1929-30	1929-30
‡ Brylin, Sergei	N.J.	13	765	129	179	308	273	109	15	19	34	32	3	1994-95	2007-08
Bubla, Jiri	Van.	5	256	17	101	118	202	6	0	0	0	7	....	1981-82	1985-86
● Buchanan, Al	Tor.	2	4	0	1	1	2	....	....	....	....	....	....	1948-49	1949-50
● Buchanan, Bucky	NYR	1	2	0	0	0	0	....	....	....	....	....	....	1948-49	1948-49
Buchanan, Jeff	Col.	1	6	0	0	0	6	....	....	....	....	....	....	1998-99	1998-99
Buchanan, Mike	Chi.	1	1	0	0	0	0	....	....	....	....	....	....	1951-52	1951-52
Buchanan, Ron	Bos., St.L.	2	5	0	0	0	0	....	....	....	....	....	....	1966-67	1969-70
Buchberger, Kelly	Edm., Atl., L.A., Phx., Pit.	18	1182	105	204	309	2297	97	10	15	25	129	2	1986-87	2003-04
Bucyk, John	Det., Bos.	23	1540	556	813	1369	497	124	41	62	103	42	2	1955-56	1977-78
Bucyk, Randy	Mtl., Cgy.	2	19	4	2	6	8	2	0	0	0	0	....	1985-86	1987-88
● Buhr, Doug	K.C.	1	6	0	2	2	4	....	....	....	....	....	....	1974-75	1974-75
Bukovich, Tony	Det.	2	17	7	3	10	6	6	0	1	1	0	....	1943-44	1944-45
‡ Bulis, Jan	Wsh., Mtl., Van.	9	552	96	149	245	268	35	3	3	6	14	....	1997-98	2006-07
Bullard, Mike	Pit., Cgy., St.L., Phi., Tor.	11	727	329	345	674	703	40	11	18	29	44	....	1980-81	1991-92
● Buller, Hy	Det., NYR	5	188	22	58	80	215	....	....	....	....	....	....	1943-44	1953-54
Bulley, Ted	Chi., Wsh., Pit.	8	414	101	113	214	704	29	5	5	10	24	....	1976-77	1983-84
Burakovsky, Robert	Ott.	1	23	2	3	5	6	....	....	....	....	....	....	1993-94	1993-94
● Burch, Billy	Ham., NYA, Bos., Chi.	11	390	137	61	198	255	2	0	0	0	0	....	1922-23	1932-33
● Burchell, Fred	Mtl.	2	4	0	0	0	2	....	....	....	....	....	....	1950-51	1953-54
Burdon, Glen	K.C.	1	11	0	2	2	0	....	....	....	....	....	....	1974-75	1974-75
Bure, Pavel	Van., Fla., NYR	12	702	437	342	779	484	64	35	35	70	74	....	1991-92	2002-03
Bure, Valeri	Mtl., Cgy., Fla., St.L., Dal.	10	621	174	226	400	221	22	0	7	7	16	....	1994-95	2003-04
Bureau, Marc	Cgy., Min., T.B., Mtl., Phi.	11	567	55	83	138	327	50	5	7	12	46	....	1989-90	1999-00
Burega, Bill	Tor.	1	4	0	1	1	4	....	....	....	....	....	....	1955-56	1955-56
● Burke, Eddie	Bos., NYA	4	106	29	20	49	55	....	....	....	....	....	....	1931-32	1934-35
● Burke, Marty	Mtl., Pit., Ott., Chi.	11	494	19	47	66	560	31	2	4	6	44	2	1927-28	1937-38
● Burmister, Roy	NYA	3	67	4	3	7	2	....	....	....	....	....	....	1929-30	1931-32
Burnett, Garrett	Ana.	1	39	1	2	3	184	....	....	....	....	....	....	2003-04	2003-04
Burnett, Kelly	NYR	1	3	1	0	1	0	....	....	....	....	....	....	1952-53	1952-53
● Burns, Bobby	Chi.	3	20	1	0	1	8	....	....	....	....	....	....	1927-28	1929-30
Burns, Charlie	Det., Bos., Oak., Pit., Min.	11	749	106	198	304	252	31	5	4	9	6	....	1958-59	1972-73
Burns, Gary	NYR	2	11	2	2	4	18	5	0	0	0	2	....	1980-81	1981-82
● Burns, Norm	NYR	1	11	0	4	4	2	....	....	....	....	....	....	1941-42	1941-42
Burns, Robin	Pit., K.C.	5	190	31	38	69	139	....	....	....	....	....	....	1970-71	1975-76
Burr, Shawn	Det., T.B., S.J.	16	878	181	259	440	1069	91	16	19	35	95	....	1984-85	1999-00
Burridge, Randy	Bos., Wsh., L.A., Buf.	13	706	199	251	450	458	107	18	34	52	103	....	1985-86	1997-98
Burrows, Dave	Pit., Tor.	10	724	29	135	164	373	29	1	5	6	25	....	1971-72	1980-81
● Burry, Bert	Ott.	1	4	0	0	0	0	....	....	....	....	....	....	1932-33	1932-33
Burt, Adam	Hfd., Car., Phi., Atl.	13	737	37	115	152	961	21	0	1	1	8	....	1988-89	2000-01
Burton, Cummy	Det.	3	43	0	2	2	21	3	0	0	0	0	....	1955-56	1958-59
Burton, Nelson	Wsh.	2	8	1	0	1	21	....	....	....	....	....	....	1977-78	1978-79
● Bush, Eddie	Det.	2	26	4	6	10	40	11	1	6	7	23	....	1938-39	1941-42
Buskas, Rod	Pit., Van., L.A., Chi.	11	556	19	63	82	1294	18	0	3	3	45	....	1982-83	1992-93
Busniuk, Mike	Phi.	2	143	3	23	26	297	25	2	5	7	34	....	1979-80	1980-81
Busniuk, Ron	Buf.	2	6	0	3	3	13	....	....	....	....	....	....	1972-73	1973-74
● Buswell, Walt	Det., Mtl.	8	368	10	40	50	164	24	2	1	3	10	....	1932-33	1939-40
Butcher, Garth	Van., St.L., Que., Tor.	14	897	48	158	206	2302	50	6	5	11	122	....	1981-82	1994-95
‡ Butenschon, Sven	Pit., Edm., NYI, Van.	8	140	2	12	14	86	4	0	0	0	0	....	1997-98	2005-06
● Butler, Dick	Chi.	1	7	2	0	2	0	....	....	....	....	....	....	1947-48	1947-48
Butler, Jerry	NYR, St.L., Tor., Van., Wpg.	11	641	99	120	219	515	48	3	3	6	79	....	1972-73	1982-83
Butsayev, Viacheslav	Phi., S.J., Ana., Fla., Ott., T.B.	6	132	17	26	43	133	....	....	....	....	....	....	1992-93	1999-00
‡ Butsayev, Yuri	Det., Atl.	4	99	10	4	14	28	....	....	....	....	....	....	1999-00	2002-03
Butters, Bill	Min.	2	72	1	4	5	77	....	....	....	....	....	....	1977-78	1978-79
Buttrey, Gord	Chi.	1	10	0	0	0	0	....	....	....	....	....	....	1943-44	1943-44
Buynak, Gord	St.L.	1	4	0	0	0	2	....	....	....	....	....	....	1974-75	1974-75
Buzek, Petr	Dal., Atl., Cgy.	6	157	9	22	31	94	....	....	....	....	....	....	1997-98	2002-03
Byakin, Ilja	Edm., S.J.	2	57	8	25	33	44	....	....	....	....	....	....	1993-94	1994-95

Name	NHL Teams	NHL Seasons	Regular Schedule GP	G	A	TP	PIM	Playoffs GP	G	A	TP	PIM	NHL Cup Wins	First NHL Season	Last NHL Season
Byce, John	Bos.	3	21	2	3	5	6	8	2	0	2	2	....	1989-90	1991-92
Byers, Gord	Bos.	1	1	0	1	1	0	....	....	....	....	....	....	1949-50	1949-50
Byers, Jerry	Min., Atl., NYR	4	43	3	4	7	15	....	....	....	....	....	....	1972-73	1977-78
Byers, Lyndon	Bos., S.J.	10	279	28	43	71	1081	37	2	2	4	96	....	1983-84	1992-93
Byers, Mike	Tor., Phi., L.A., Buf.	4	166	42	34	76	39	4	0	1	1	0	....	1967-68	1971-72
Bykov, Dmitri	Det.	1	71	2	10	12	43	4	0	0	0	0	....	2002-03	2002-03
Bylsma, Dan	L.A., Ana.	9	429	19	43	62	184	16	0	1	1	2	....	1995-96	2003-04
Byram, Shawn	NYI, Chi.	2	5	0	0	0	14	....	....	....	....	....	....	1990-91	1991-92

C

Name	NHL Teams	NHL Seasons	Regular Schedule GP	G	A	TP	PIM	Playoffs GP	G	A	TP	PIM	NHL Cup Wins	First NHL Season	Last NHL Season
Caffery, Jack	Tor., Bos.	3	57	3	2	5	22	10	1	0	1	4	....	1954-55	1957-58
Caffery, Terry	Chi., Min.	2	14	0	0	0	0	1	0	0	0	0	....	1969-70	1970-71
Cahan, Larry	Tor., NYR, Oak., L.A.	13	666	38	92	130	700	29	1	1	2	38	....	1954-55	1970-71
Cahill, Charles	Bos.	2	32	0	1	1	4	....	....	....	....	....	....	1925-26	1926-27
Cain, Francis	Mtl.M., Tor.	2	61	4	0	4	35	....	....	....	....	....	....	1924-25	1925-26
Cain, Herb	Mtl.M., Mtl., Bos.	13	570	206	194	400	178	67	16	13	29	13	2	1933-34	1945-46
Cairns, Don	K.C., Col.	2	9	0	1	1	2	....	....	....	....	....	....	1975-76	1976-77
Cairns, Eric	NYR, NYI, Fla., Pit.	10	457	10	32	42	1182	16	0	0	0	28	....	1996-97	2006-07
Cajanek, Petr	St.L.	4	269	46	107	153	144	7	0	2	2	4	....	2002-03	2006-07
Calder, Eric	Wsh.	2	2	0	0	0	0	....	....	....	....	....	....	1981-82	1982-83
Calladine, Norm	Bos.	3	63	19	29	48	8	....	....	....	....	....	....	1942-43	1944-45
Callander, Drew	Phi., Van.	4	39	6	2	8	7	....	....	....	....	....	....	1976-77	1979-80
Callander, Jock	Pit., T.B.	5	109	22	29	51	116	22	3	8	11	12	1	1987-88	1992-93
Callighen, Brett	Edm.	3	160	56	89	145	132	14	4	6	10	8	....	1979-80	1981-82
Callighen, Patsy	NYR	1	36	0	0	0	32	9	0	0	0	0	1	1927-28	1927-28
Caloun, Jan	S.J., CBJ	3	24	8	6	14	2	....	....	....	....	....	....	1995-96	2000-01
Camazzola, James	Chi.	2	3	0	0	0	0	....	....	....	....	....	....	1983-84	1986-87
Camazzola, Tony	Wsh.	1	3	0	0	0	4	....	....	....	....	....	....	1981-82	1981-82
Cameron, Al	Det., Wpg.	6	282	11	44	55	356	7	0	1	1	2	....	1975-76	1980-81
Cameron, Billy	Mtl., NYA	2	39	0	0	0	2	2	0	0	0	0	1	1923-24	1925-26
Cameron, Craig	Det., St.L., Min., NYI	9	552	87	65	152	196	27	3	1	4	17	....	1966-67	1975-76
Cameron, Dave	Col., N.J.	3	168	25	28	53	238	....	....	....	....	....	....	1981-82	1983-84
Cameron, Harry	Tor., Ott., Mtl.	6	128	88	51	139	189	11	5	4	9	16	2	1917-18	1922-23
Cameron, Scotty	NYR	1	35	8	11	19	0	....	....	....	....	....	....	1942-43	1942-43
Campbell, Bryan	L.A., Chi.	5	260	35	71	106	74	22	3	4	7	2	....	1967-68	1971-72
Campbell, Colin	Pit., Col., Edm., Van., Det.	11	636	25	103	128	1292	45	4	10	14	181	....	1974-75	1984-85
Campbell, Dave	Mtl.	1	2	0	0	0	0	....	....	....	....	....	....	1920-21	1920-21
Campbell, Don	Chi.	1	17	1	3	4	8	....	....	....	....	....	....	1943-44	1943-44
Campbell, Earl	Ott., NYA	3	76	6	3	9	14	1	0	0	0	6	....	1923-24	1925-26
Campbell, Jim	Ana., St.L., Mtl., Chi., Fla., T.B.	9	285	61	75	136	268	14	8	3	11	18	....	1995-96	2005-06
Campbell, Scott	Wpg., St.L.	3	80	4	21	25	243	....	....	....	....	....	....	1979-80	1981-82
Campbell, Wade	Wpg., Bos.	6	213	9	27	36	305	10	0	0	0	20	....	1982-83	1987-88
ampeau, Tod	Mtl.	3	42	5	9	14	16	1	0	0	0	0	....	1943-44	1948-49
ampedelli, Dom	Mtl.	1	2	0	0	0	0	....	....	....	....	....	....	1985-86	1985-86
apuano, Dave	Pit., Van., T.B., S.J.	4	104	17	38	55	56	6	1	1	2	5	....	1989-90	1993-94
apuano, Jack	Tor., Van., Bos.	3	6	0	0	0	0	....	....	....	....	....	....	1989-90	1991-92
arbol, Leo	Chi.	1	6	0	1	1	4	....	....	....	....	....	....	1942-43	1942-43
arbonneau, Guy	Mtl., St.L., Dal.	19	1318	260	403	663	820	231	38	55	93	161	3	1980-81	1999-00
ard, Mike	Buf.	1	4	0	0	0	0	....	....	....	....	....	....	2006-07	2006-07
ardin, Claude	St.L.	1	1	0	0	0	0	....	....	....	....	....	....	1967-68	1967-68
ardwell, Steve	Pit.	3	53	9	11	20	35	4	0	0	0	2	....	1970-71	1972-73
arey, George	Que., Ham., Tor.	5	72	21	12	33	20	....	....	....	....	....	....	1919-20	1923-24
arkner, Terry	NYR, Que., Phi., Det., Fla.	13	858	42	188	230	1588	54	1	9	10	48	....	1986-87	1998-99
arleton, Wayne	Tor., Bos., Cal.	7	278	55	73	128	172	18	2	4	6	14	1	1965-66	1971-72
arlin, Brian	L.A.	1	5	1	0	1	0	....	....	....	....	....	....	1971-72	1971-72
arlson, Jack	Min., St.L.	6	236	30	15	45	417	25	1	2	3	72	....	1978-79	1986-87
arlson, Kent	Mtl., St.L., Wsh.	5	113	7	11	18	148	8	0	0	0	13	....	1983-84	1988-89
arlson, Steve	L.A.	1	52	9	12	21	23	4	1	1	2	7	....	1979-80	1979-80
arlsson, Anders	N.J.	3	104	7	26	33	34	3	1	0	1	2	....	1986-87	1988-89
arlyle, Randy	Tor., Pit., Wpg.	18	1055	148	499	647	1400	69	9	24	33	120	....	1976-77	1992-93
arnback, Patrik	Mtl., Ana.	4	154	24	38	62	122	....	....	....	....	....	....	1992-93	1995-96
arney, Keith	Buf., Chi., Phx., Ana., Van., Min.	16	1018	45	183	228	904	91	3	19	22	67	....	1991-92	2007-08
aron, Alain	Oak., Mtl.	2	60	9	13	22	18	....	....	....	....	....	....	1967-68	1968-69
arpenter, Bob	Wsh., NYR, L.A., Bos., N.J.	18	1178	320	408	728	919	140	21	38	59	136	1	1981-82	1998-99
arpenter, Ed	Que., Ham.	2	45	10	5	15	41	....	....	....	....	....	....	1919-20	1920-21
arr, Gene	St.L., NYR, L.A., Pit., Atl.	8	465	79	136	215	365	35	5	8	13	66	....	1971-72	1978-79
arr, Lorne	NYR, NYA, Tor.	13	580	204	222	426	132	53	10	9	19	13	2	1933-34	1945-46
arr, Red	Tor.	1	5	0	1	1	2	....	....	....	....	....	....	1943-44	1943-44
arriere, Larry	Buf., Atl., Van., L.A., Tor.	7	367	16	74	90	462	27	0	3	3	42	....	1972-73	1979-80
arrigan, Gene	NYR, Det., St.L.	3	37	2	1	3	13	4	0	0	0	0	....	1930-31	1934-35
arroll, Billy	NYI, Edm., Det.	7	322	30	54	84	113	71	6	12	18	18	4	1980-81	1986-87
arroll, George	Mtl.M., Bos.	1	16	0	0	0	11	....	....	....	....	....	....	1924-25	1924-25
arroll, Greg	Wsh., Det., Hfd.	2	131	20	34	54	44	....	....	....	....	....	....	1978-79	1979-80
arruthers, Dwight	Det., Phi.	2	2	0	0	0	0	....	....	....	....	....	....	1965-66	1967-68
arse, Bill	NYR, Chi.	4	124	28	43	71	38	13	3	2	5	0	....	1938-39	1941-42
arse, Bob	Chi., Mtl.	5	167	32	55	87	52	10	0	2	2	2	....	1939-40	1947-48
arson, Bill	Tor., Bos.	4	159	54	24	78	156	11	3	0	3	14	1	1926-27	1929-30
arson, Frank	Mtl.M., NYA, Det.	7	248	42	48	90	166	27	0	2	2	9	1	1925-26	1933-34
arson, Gerry	Mtl., NYR, Mtl.M.	6	261	12	11	23	205	22	0	0	0	12	1	1928-29	1936-37
arson, Jimmy	L.A., Edm., Det., Van., Hfd.	10	626	275	286	561	254	55	17	15	32	22	....	1986-87	1995-96
arson, Lindsay	Phi., Hfd.	7	373	66	80	146	524	49	4	10	14	56	....	1981-82	1987-88
arter, Anson	Wsh., Bos., Edm., NYR, L.A., Van., CBJ, Car.	10	674	202	219	421	229	24	8	5	13	4	....	1996-97	2006-07
arter, Billy	Mtl., Bos.	3	16	0	0	0	6	....	....	....	....	....	....	1957-58	1961-62
arter, John	Bos., S.J.	8	244	40	50	90	201	31	7	5	12	51	....	1985-86	1992-93
arter, Ron	Edm.	1	2	0	0	0	0	....	....	....	....	....	....	1979-80	1979-80
arveth, Joe	Det., Bos., Mtl.	11	504	150	189	339	81	69	21	16	37	28	2	1940-41	1950-51
ashman, Wayne	Bos.	17	1027	277	516	793	1041	145	31	57	88	250	2	1964-65	1982-83
asselman, Mike	Fla.	1	3	0	0	0	0	....	....	....	....	....	....	1995-96	1995-96
assels, Andrew	Mtl., Hfd., Cgy., Van., CBJ, Wsh.	16	1015	204	528	732	410	21	4	7	11	8	....	1989-90	2005-06
ssidy, Bruce	Chi.	6	36	4	13	17	10	1	0	0	0	0	....	1983-84	1989-90
ssidy, Tom	Pit.	1	26	3	4	7	15	....	....	....	....	....	....	1977-78	1977-78
ssolato, Tony	Wsh.	3	23	1	6	7	4	....	....	....	....	....	....	1979-80	1981-82
ufield, Jay	NYR, Min., Pit.	7	208	5	8	13	759	17	0	0	0	42	2	1986-87	1992-93
vallini, Gino	Cgy., St.L., Que.	9	593	114	159	273	507	74	14	19	33	66	....	1984-85	1992-93
vallini, Paul	Wsh., St.L., Dal.	10	564	56	177	233	750	69	8	27	35	114	....	1986-87	1995-96
resino, Ray	Tor.	1	12	1	1	2	2	....	....	....	....	....	....	1948-49	1948-49
rnik, Frantisek	Det.	1	49	5	4	9	13	....	....	....	....	....	....	1984-85	1984-85
abot, John	Mtl., Pit., Det.	8	508	84	228	312	85	33	6	20	26	2	....	1983-84	1990-91
ad, John	Chi.	3	80	15	22	37	29	10	0	1	1	2	....	1939-40	1945-46
almers, Chick	NYR	1	1	0	0	0	0	....	....	....	....	....	....	1953-54	1953-54
alupa, Milan	Det.	1	14	0	5	5	6	....	....	....	....	....	....	1984-85	1984-85
amberlain, Murph	Tor., Mtl., Bro., Bos.	12	510	100	175	275	769	66	14	17	31	96	2	1937-38	1948-49
ambers, Shawn	Min., Wsh., T.B., N.J., Dal.	13	625	50	185	235	364	94	7	26	33	72	2	1987-88	1999-00
ampagne, Andre	Tor.	1	2	0	0	0	0	....	....	....	....	....	....	1962-63	1962-63
apdelaine, Rene	L.A.	3	32	0	2	2	32	....	....	....	....	....	....	1990-91	1992-93
apman, Art	Bos., NYA	10	438	62	176	238	140	26	1	5	6	9	....	1930-31	1939-40
apman, Blair	Pit., St.L.	7	402	106	125	231	158	25	4	6	10	15	....	1976-77	1982-83
apman, Brian	Hfd.	1	3	0	0	0	29	....	....	....	....	....	....	1990-91	1990-91
arbonneau, Jose	Mtl., Van.	4	71	9	13	22	67	11	1	0	1	8	....	1987-88	1994-95
arbonneau, Stephane	Que.	1	2	0	0	0	0	....	....	....	....	....	....	1991-92	1991-92
arlebois, Bob	Min.	1	7	1	0	1	0	....	....	....	....	....	....	1967-68	1967-68
arlesworth, Todd	Pit., NYR	6	93	3	9	12	47	....	....	....	....	....	....	1983-84	1989-90
arron, Eric	Mtl., T.B., Wsh., Cgy.	8	130	2	7	9	127	6	0	0	0	8	....	1992-93	1999-00
arron, Guy	Mtl., Det., K.C., Wsh.	12	734	221	309	530	146	....	....	....	....	....	....	1969-70	1980-81
artier, Dave	Wpg.	1	1	0	0	0	0	....	....	....	....	....	....	1980-81	1980-81
artrand, Brad	L.A.	5	215	25	25	50	122	11	1	1	2	8	....	1999-00	2003-04
artraw, Rick	Mtl., L.A., NYR, Edm.	10	420	28	64	92	399	75	7	9	16	80	4	1974-75	1983-84
ase, Kelly	St.L., Hfd., Tor.	11	458	17	36	53	2017	27	1	1	2	100	....	1989-90	1999-00
asse, Denis	St.L., Wsh., Wpg., Ott.	4	132	11	14	25	292	7	1	7	8	23	....	1993-94	1996-97
ebaturkin, Vladimir	NYI, St.L., Chi.	5	62	2	7	9	52	3	0	0	0	2	....	1997-98	2001-02
eck, Lude	Det., Chi.	2	27	6	2	8	4	....	....	....	....	....	....	1943-44	1944-45
ernoff, Mike	Min.	1	1	0	0	0	0	....	....	....	....	....	....	1968-69	1968-69
ernomaz, Rich	Col., N.J., Cgy.	7	51	9	7	16	18	....	....	....	....	....	....	1981-82	1991-92
erry, Dick	Bos., Phi.	3	145	12	10	22	45	4	1	0	1	4	....	1956-57	1969-70

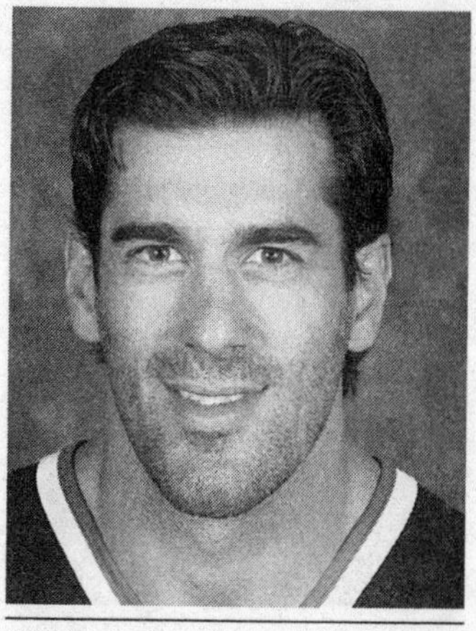
Keith Carney

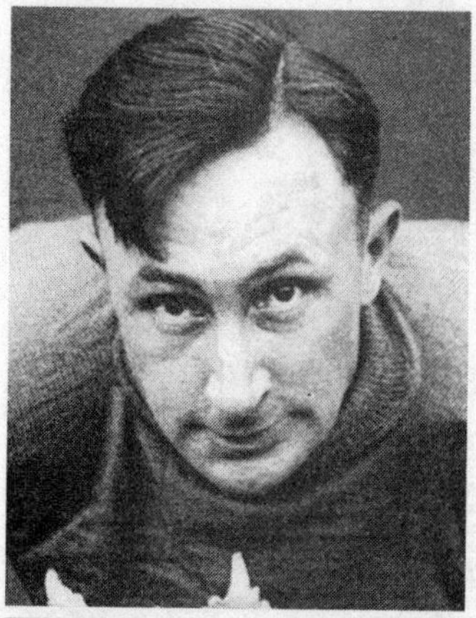
Bill Carson

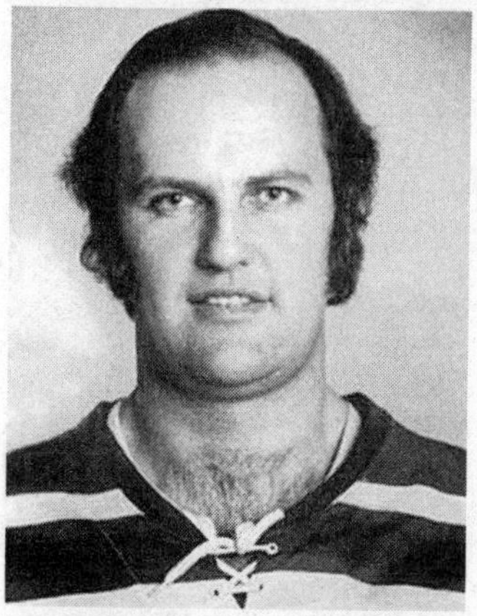
Bob Charlebois

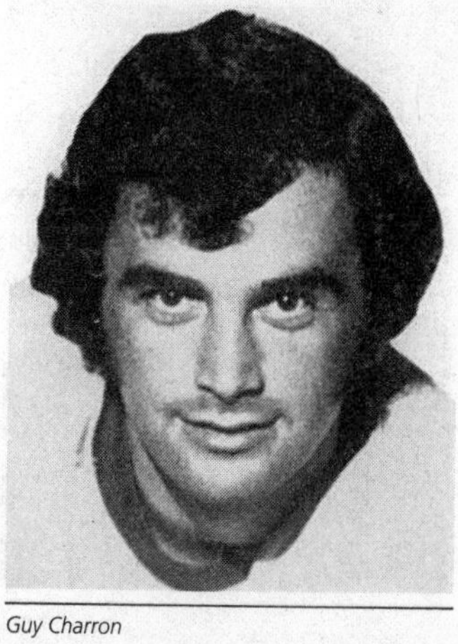
Guy Charron

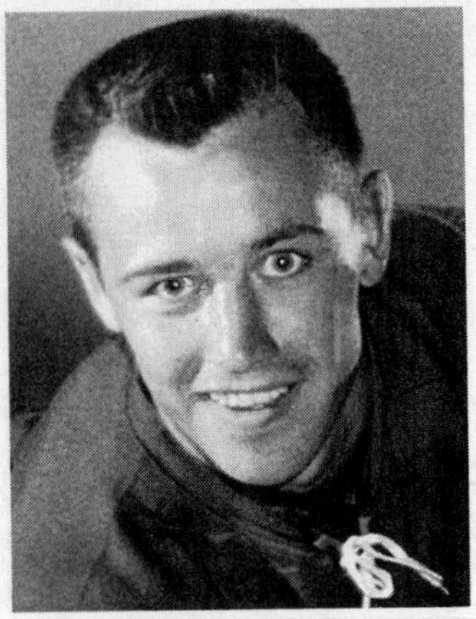
Bruce Cline

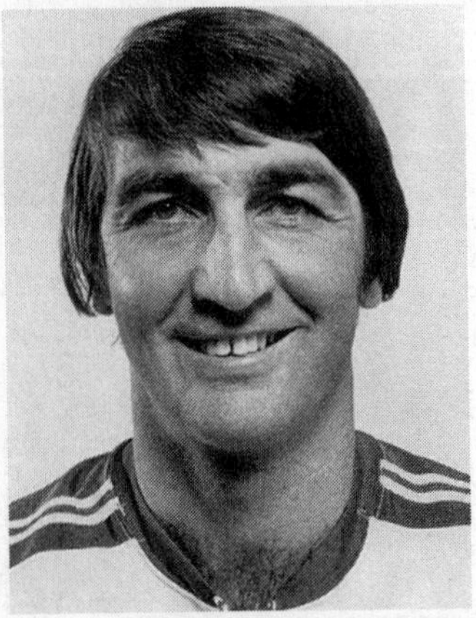
Bill Collins

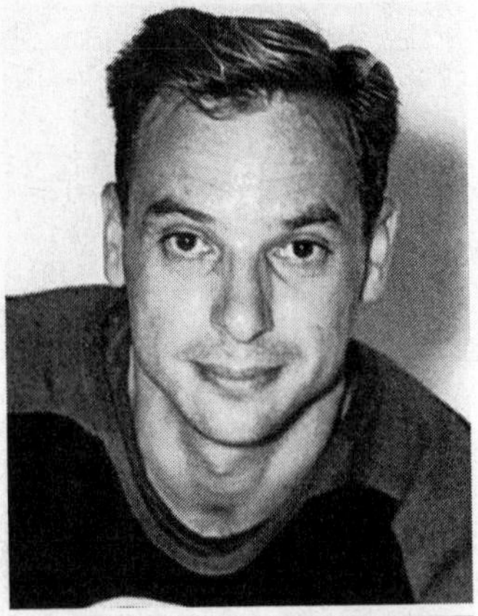
Roy Conacher

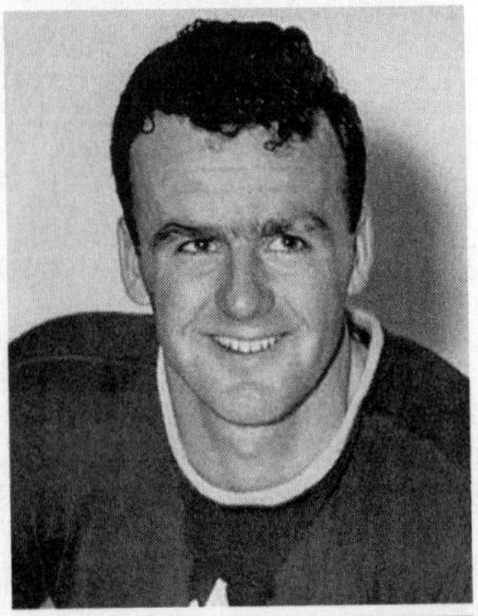
Les Costello

Name	NHL Teams	NHL Seasons	Regular Schedule GP	G	A	TP	PIM	Playoffs GP	G	A	TP	PIM	NHL Cup Wins	First NHL Season	Last NHL Season
Cherry, Don	Bos.	1	....	....	....	....	....	1	0	0	0	0	....	1954-55	1954-55
Chervyakov, Denis	Bos.	1	2	0	0	0	2	....	....	....	....	....	....	1992-93	1992-93
● Chevrefils, Real	Bos., Det.	8	387	104	97	201	185	30	5	4	9	20	....	1951-52	1958-59
● Chiasson, Steve	Det., Cgy., Hfd., Car.	13	751	93	305	398	1107	63	16	19	35	119	....	1986-87	1998-99
Chibirev, Igor	Hfd.	2	45	7	12	19	2	....	....	....	....	....	....	1993-94	1994-95
Chicoine, Dan	Cle., Min.	3	31	1	2	3	12	1	0	0	0	0	....	1977-78	1979-80
Chinnick, Rick	Min.	2	4	0	2	2	0	....	....	....	....	....	....	1973-74	1974-75
Chipperfield, Ron	Edm., Que.	2	83	22	24	46	34	....	....	....	....	....	....	1979-80	1980-81
Chisholm, Art	Bos.	1	3	0	0	0	0	....	....	....	....	....	....	1960-61	1960-61
Chisholm, Colin	Min.	1	1	0	0	0	0	....	....	....	....	....	....	1986-87	1986-87
● Chisholm, Lex	Tor.	2	54	10	8	18	19	3	1	0	1	0	....	1939-40	1940-41
‡ Chistov, Stanislav	Ana., Bos.	3	196	19	42	61	116	21	4	2	6	8	....	2002-03	2006-07
Chorney, Marc	Pit., L.A.	4	210	8	27	35	209	7	0	1	1	2	....	1980-81	1983-84
Chorske, Tom	Mtl., N.J., Ott., NYI, Wsh., Cgy., Pit.	11	596	115	122	237	225	50	5	12	17	10	1	1989-90	1999-00
‡ Chouinard, Eric	Mtl., Phi., Min.	4	90	11	11	22	16	....	....	....	....	....	....	2000-01	2005-06
● Chouinard, Gene	Ott.	1	8	0	0	0	0	....	....	....	....	....	....	1927-28	1927-28
Chouinard, Guy	Atl., Cgy., St.L.	10	578	205	370	575	120	46	9	28	37	12	....	1974-75	1983-84
‡ Chouinard, Marc	Ana., Min., Van.	6	320	37	41	78	123	15	1	0	1	0	....	2000-01	2006-07
Christian, Dave	Wpg., Wsh., Bos., St.L., Chi.	15	1009	340	433	773	284	102	32	25	57	27	....	1979-80	1993-94
Christian, Jeff	N.J., Pit., Phx.	5	18	2	2	4	17	....	....	....	....	....	....	1991-92	1997-98
Christie, Mike	Cal., Cle., Col., Van.	7	412	15	101	116	550	2	0	0	0	0	....	1974-75	1980-81
‡ Christie, Ryan	Dal., Cgy.	2	7	0	0	0	0	....	....	....	....	....	....	1999-00	2001-02
Christoff, Steve	Min., Cgy., L.A.	5	248	77	64	141	108	35	16	12	28	25	....	1979-80	1983-84
Chrystal, Bob	NYR	2	132	11	14	25	112	....	....	....	....	....	....	1953-54	1954-55
‡ Chubarov, Artem	Van.	5	228	25	33	58	40	27	0	4	4	4	....	1999-00	2003-04
Church, Brad	Wsh.	1	2	0	0	0	0	....	....	....	....	....	....	1997-98	1997-98
● Church, Jack	Tor., Bro., Bos.	5	130	4	19	23	154	25	1	1	2	18	....	1938-39	1945-46
Churla, Shane	Hfd., Cgy., Min., Dal., L.A., NYR	11	488	26	45	71	2301	78	5	7	12	282	....	1986-87	1996-97
Chychrun, Jeff	Phi., L.A., Pit., Edm.	8	262	3	22	25	744	19	0	2	2	65	1	1986-87	1993-94
Chynoweth, Dean	NYI, Bos.	9	241	4	18	22	667	6	0	0	0	26	....	1988-89	1997-98
Chyzowski, Dave	NYI, Chi.	6	126	15	16	31	144	2	0	0	0	0	....	1989-90	1996-97
Ciavaglia, Peter	Buf.	2	5	0	0	0	0	....	....	....	....	....	....	1991-92	1992-93
‡ Cibak, Martin	T.B.	3	154	5	18	23	60	11	0	1	1	0	1	2001-02	2005-06
Ciccarelli, Dino	Min., Wsh., Det., T.B., Fla.	19	1232	608	592	1200	1425	141	73	45	118	211	....	1980-81	1998-99
Ciccone, Enrico	Min., Wsh., T.B., Chi., Car., Van., Mtl.	9	374	10	18	28	1469	13	1	0	1	48	....	1991-92	2000-01
Cichocki, Chris	Det., N.J.	4	68	11	12	23	27	....	....	....	....	....	....	1985-86	1988-89
‡ Ciernik, Ivan	Ott., Wsh.	5	89	12	14	26	32	2	0	1	1	6	....	1997-98	2003-04
‡ Cierny, Jozef	Edm.	1	1	0	0	0	0	....	....	....	....	....	....	1993-94	1993-94
● Ciesla, Hank	Chi., NYR	4	269	26	51	77	87	6	0	2	2	0	....	1955-56	1958-59
Ciger, Zdeno	N.J., Edm., NYR, T.B.	7	352	94	134	228	101	13	2	6	8	4	....	1990-91	2001-02
Cimellaro, Tony	Ott.	1	2	0	0	0	0	....	....	....	....	....	....	1992-93	1992-93
Cimetta, Rob	Bos., Tor.	4	103	16	16	32	66	1	0	0	0	15	....	1988-89	1991-92
Cirella, Joe	Col., N.J., Que., NYR, Fla., Ott.	15	828	64	211	275	1446	38	0	13	13	98	....	1981-82	1995-96
Cirone, Jason	Wpg.	1	3	0	0	0	2	....	....	....	....	....	....	1991-92	1991-92
Cisar, Marian	Nsh.	3	73	13	17	30	57	....	....	....	....	....	....	1999-00	2001-02
Clackson, Kim	Pit., Que.	2	106	0	8	8	370	8	0	0	0	70	....	1979-80	1980-81
● Clancy, King	Ott., Tor.	16	592	136	147	283	914	55	8	8	16	88	3	1921-22	1936-37
Clancy, Terry	Oak., Tor.	4	93	6	6	12	39	....	....	....	....	....	....	1967-68	1972-73
● Clapper, Dit	Bos.	20	833	228	246	474	462	82	13	17	30	50	3	1927-28	1946-47
Clark, Dan	NYR	1	4	0	1	1	6	....	....	....	....	....	....	1978-79	1978-79
Clark, Dean	Edm.	1	1	0	0	0	0	....	....	....	....	....	....	1983-84	1983-84
Clark, Gordie	Bos.	2	8	0	1	1	0	1	0	0	0	0	....	1974-75	1975-76
● Clark, Nobby	Bos.	1	5	0	0	0	0	....	....	....	....	....	....	1927-28	1927-28
Clark, Wendel	Tor., Que., NYI, T.B., Det., Chi.	15	793	330	234	564	1690	95	37	32	69	201	....	1985-86	1999-00
Clarke, Bobby	Phi.	15	1144	358	852	1210	1453	136	42	77	119	152	2	1969-70	1983-84
‡ Clarke, Dale	St.L.	1	3	0	0	0	0	....	....	....	....	....	....	2000-01	2000-01
‡ Clarke, Noah	L.A., N.J.	4	21	3	1	4	4	....	....	....	....	....	....	2003-04	2007-08
‡ Classen, Greg	Nsh.	3	90	7	10	17	48	....	....	....	....	....	....	2000-01	2002-03
● Cleghorn, Odie	Mtl., Pit.	10	181	95	34	129	142	12	7	2	9	5	1	1918-19	1927-28
● Cleghorn, Sprague	Ott., Tor., Mtl., Bos.	10	259	83	55	138	538	21	4	3	7	26	2	1918-19	1927-28
Clement, Bill	Phi., Wsh., Atl., Cgy.	11	719	148	208	356	383	50	5	3	8	26	2	1971-72	1981-82
Cline, Bruce	NYR	1	30	2	3	5	10	....	....	....	....	....	....	1956-57	1956-57
Clippingdale, Steve	L.A., Wsh.	2	19	1	2	3	9	1	0	0	0	0	....	1976-77	1979-80
Cloutier, Real	Que., Buf.	6	317	146	198	344	119	25	7	5	12	20	....	1979-80	1984-85
Cloutier, Rejean	Det.	2	5	0	2	2	2	....	....	....	....	....	....	1979-80	1981-82
Cloutier, Roland	Det., Que.	3	34	8	9	17	2	....	....	....	....	....	....	1977-78	1979-80
Cloutier, Sylvain	Chi.	1	7	0	0	0	0	....	....	....	....	....	....	1998-99	1998-99
● Clune, Wally	Mtl.	1	5	0	0	0	6	....	....	....	....	....	....	1955-56	1955-56
‡ Clymer, Ben	T.B., Wsh.	7	438	52	77	129	367	16	0	2	2	6	1	1999-00	2006-
Coalter, Gary	Cal., K.C.	2	34	2	4	6	2	....	....	....	....	....	....	1973-74	1974-
Coates, Steve	Det.	1	5	1	0	1	24	....	....	....	....	....	....	1976-77	1976-
Cochrane, Glen	Phi., Van., Chi., Edm.	10	411	17	72	89	1556	18	1	1	2	31	....	1978-79	1988-
Coffey, Paul	Edm., Pit., L.A., Det., Hfd., Phi., Chi., Car., Bos.	21	1409	396	1135	1531	1802	194	59	137	196	264	4	1980-81	2000-
Coflin, Hugh	Chi.	1	31	0	3	3	33	....	....	....	....	....	....	1950-51	1950-
Cole, Danton	Wpg., T.B., N.J., NYI, Chi.	7	318	58	60	118	125	1	0	0	0	0	1	1989-90	1995-
Colley, Kevin	NYI	1	16	0	0	0	52	....	....	....	....	....	....	2005-06	2005-
Colley, Tom	Min.	1	1	0	0	0	2	....	....	....	....	....	....	1974-75	1974-
Collings, Norm	Mtl.	1	1	0	1	1	0	....	....	....	....	....	....	1934-35	1934-
Collins, Bill	Min., Mtl., Det., St.L., NYR, Phi., Wsh.	11	768	157	154	311	415	18	3	5	8	12	....	1967-68	1977-
Collins, Gary	Tor.	1	....	....	....	....	....	2	0	0	0	0	....	1958-59	1958-
‡ Collins, Rob	NYI	1	8	1	1	2	0	....	....	....	....	....	....	2005-06	2005-
Collyard, Bob	St.L.	1	10	1	3	4	4	....	....	....	....	....	....	1973-74	1973-
● Colman, Michael	S.J.	1	15	0	1	1	32	....	....	....	....	....	....	1991-92	1991-
● Colville, Mac	NYR	9	353	71	104	175	130	40	9	10	19	14	1	1935-36	1946-
● Colville, Neil	NYR	12	464	99	166	265	213	46	7	19	26	32	1	1935-36	1948-
Colwill, Les	NYR	1	69	7	6	13	16	....	....	....	....	....	....	1958-59	1958-
Comeau, Rey	Mtl., Atl., Col.	9	564	98	141	239	175	9	2	1	3	8	....	1971-72	1979-
Comrie, Paul	Edm.	1	15	1	2	3	4	....	....	....	....	....	....	1999-00	1999-
Conacher, Brian	Tor., Det.	5	155	28	28	56	84	12	3	2	5	21	1	1961-62	1971-
● Conacher, Charlie	Tor., Det., NYA	12	459	225	173	398	523	49	17	18	35	49	1	1929-30	1940-
Conacher, Jim	Det., Chi., NYR	8	328	85	117	202	91	19	5	2	7	4	....	1945-46	1952-
● Conacher, Lionel	Pit., NYA, Mtl.M., Chi.	12	498	80	105	185	882	35	2	2	4	34	2	1925-26	1936-
Conacher, Pat	NYR, Edm., N.J., L.A., Cgy., NYI	13	521	63	76	139	235	67	11	10	21	40	1	1979-80	1995
Conacher, Pete	Chi., NYR, Tor.	6	229	47	39	86	57	7	0	0	0	0	....	1951-52	1957
● Conacher, Roy	Bos., Det., Chi.	11	490	226	200	426	90	42	15	15	30	14	2	1938-39	1951
● Conn, Red	NYA	2	96	9	28	37	22	....	....	....	....	....	....	1933-34	1934
Conn, Rob	Chi., Buf.	2	30	2	5	7	20	....	....	....	....	....	....	1991-92	1995
● Connelly, Bert	NYR, Chi.	3	87	13	15	28	37	14	1	0	1	0	1	1934-35	1937
Connelly, Wayne	Mtl., Bos., Min., Det., St.L., Van.	10	543	133	174	307	156	24	11	7	18	4	....	1960-61	1971
Connor, Cam	Mtl., Edm., NYR	5	89	9	22	31	256	20	5	0	5	6	1	1978-79	1982
● Connor, Harry	Bos., NYA, Ott.	4	134	16	5	21	149	10	0	0	0	2	....	1927-28	1930
● Connors, Bob	NYA, Det.	3	78	17	10	27	110	2	0	0	0	10	....	1926-27	1929
Conroy, Al	Phi.	3	114	9	14	23	156	....	....	....	....	....	....	1991-92	1993
Contini, Joe	Col., Min.	3	68	17	21	38	34	2	0	0	0	0	....	1977-78	1980
Convery, Brandon	Tor., Van., L.A.	4	72	9	19	28	36	5	0	0	0	2	....	1995-96	1998
● Convey, Eddie	NYA	3	36	1	1	2	33	....	....	....	....	....	....	1930-31	1932
● Cook, Bill	NYR	11	474	229	138	367	386	46	13	11	24	68	2	1926-27	1936
● Cook, Bob	Van., Det., NYI, Min.	4	72	13	9	22	22	....	....	....	....	....	....	1970-71	1974
● Cook, Bud	Bos., Ott., St.L.	3	50	5	4	9	22	....	....	....	....	....	....	1931-32	1934
● Cook, Bun	NYR, Bos.	11	473	158	144	302	444	46	15	3	18	50	2	1926-27	1936
● Cook, Lloyd	Bos.	1	4	1	0	1	0	....	....	....	....	....	....	1924-25	1924
● Cook, Tom	Chi., Mtl.M.	9	349	77	98	175	184	24	2	4	6	19	1	1929-30	1937
● Cooper, Carson	Bos., Mtl., Det.	8	294	110	57	167	111	7	0	0	0	2	....	1924-25	1931
Cooper, David	Tor.	3	30	3	7	10	24	....	....	....	....	....	....	1996-97	2000
Cooper, Ed	Col.	2	49	8	7	15	46	....	....	....	....	....	....	1980-81	1981
● Cooper, Hal	NYR	1	8	0	0	0	2	....	....	....	....	....	....	1944-45	1944
● Cooper, Joe	NYR, Chi.	11	420	30	66	96	442	35	3	5	8	58	....	1935-36	1946
● Copp, Bobby	Tor.	2	40	3	9	12	26	....	....	....	....	....	....	1942-43	1950
‡ Corazzini, Carl	Bos., Chi.	2	19	2	1	3	2	....	....	....	....	....	....	2003-04	2006
● Corbeau, Bert	Mtl., Ham., Tor.	10	258	63	49	112	629	9	2	2	4	38	....	1917-18	1926
Corbet, Rene	Que., Col., Cgy., Pit.	8	362	58	74	132	420	53	7	6	13	52	1	1993-94	2000
● Corbett, Mike	L.A.	1	....	....	....	....	....	2	0	1	1	2	....	1967-68	1967
Corcoran, Norm	Bos., Det., Chi.	4	29	1	3	4	21	4	0	0	0	6	....	1949-50	1955
Corkum, Bob	Buf., Ana., Phi., Phx., L.A., N.J., Atl.	12	720	97	103	200	281	62	7	7	14	24	....	1989-90	2001
● Cormier, Roger	Mtl.	1	1	0	0	0	0	....	....	....	....	....	....	1925-26	1925

Name	NHL Teams	NHL Seasons	Regular Schedule GP	G	A	TP	PIM	Playoffs GP	G	A	TP	PIM	NHL Cup Wins	First NHL Season	Last NHL Season
ornforth, Mark	Bos.	1	6	0	0	0	4	....	....	....	....	....	....	1995-96	1995-96
orrigan, Chuck	Tor., NYA	2	19	2	2	4	2	....	....	....	....	....	....	1937-38	1940-41
orrigan, Mike	L.A., Van., Pit.	10	594	152	195	347	698	17	2	3	5	20	....	1967-68	1977-78
orrinet, Chris	Wsh.	1	8	0	1	1	6	....	....	....	....	....	....	2001-02	2001-02
orriveau, Andre	Mtl.	1	3	0	1	1	0	....	....	....	....	....	....	1953-54	1953-54
orriveau, Yvon	Wsh., Hfd., S.J.	9	280	48	40	88	310	29	5	7	12	50	....	1985-86	1993-94
orso, Daniel	St.L., Atl.	4	77	14	11	25	20	14	0	1	1	0	....	2000-01	2003-04
orson, Shayne	Mtl., Edm., St.L., Tor., Dal.	19	1156	273	420	693	2357	140	38	49	87	291	....	1985-86	2003-04
ory, Ross	Wpg.	2	51	2	10	12	41	....	....	....	....	....	....	1979-80	1980-81
ossette, Jacques	Pit.	3	64	8	6	14	29	3	0	1	1	4	....	1975-76	1978-79
ostello, Les	Tor.	3	15	2	3	5	11	6	2	2	4	2	1	1947-48	1949-50
ostello, Murray	Chi., Bos., Det.	4	162	13	19	32	54	5	0	0	0	2	....	1953-54	1956-57
ostello, Rich	Tor.	2	12	2	2	4	2	....	....	....	....	....	....	1983-84	1985-86
otch, Charlie	Ham., Tor.	1	12	1	0	1	0	....	....	....	....	....	....	1924-25	1924-25
ote, Alain	Que.	10	696	103	190	293	383	67	9	15	24	44	....	1979-80	1988-89
ote, Alain	Bos., Wsh., Mtl., T.B., Que.	9	119	2	18	20	124	11	0	2	2	26	....	1985-86	1993-94
ote, Jean-Philippe	Mtl.	1	8	0	0	0	4	....	....	....	....	....	....	2005-06	2005-06
ote, Patrick	Dal., Nsh., Edm.	6	105	1	2	3	377	....	....	....	....	....	....	1995-96	2000-01
ote, Ray	Edm.	3	15	0	0	0	4	14	3	2	5	0	....	1982-83	1984-85
ote, Sylvain	Hfd., Wsh., Tor., Chi., Dal.	19	1171	122	313	435	545	102	11	22	33	62	....	1984-85	2002-03
otton, Baldy	Pit., Tor., NYA	12	503	101	103	204	419	43	4	9	13	46	1	1925-26	1936-37
oughlin, Jack	Tor., Que., Mtl., Ham.	3	19	2	0	2	3	....	....	....	....	....	1	1917-18	1920-21
oulis, Tim	Wsh., Min.	4	47	4	5	9	138	3	1	0	1	2	....	1979-80	1985-86
oulombe, Patrick	Van.	1	7	0	1	1	4	....	....	....	....	....	....	2006-07	2006-07
oulson, D'arcy	Phi.	1	28	0	0	0	103	....	....	....	....	....	....	1930-31	1930-31
oulter, Art	Chi., NYR	11	465	30	82	112	543	49	4	5	9	61	2	1931-32	1941-42
oulter, Neal	NYI	3	26	5	5	10	11	....	....	....	....	....	....	1985-86	1987-88
oulter, Thomas	Chi.	1	2	0	0	0	0	....	....	....	....	....	....	1933-34	1933-34
ournoyer, Yvan	Mtl.	16	968	428	435	863	255	147	64	63	127	47	10	1963-64	1978-79
ourteau, Yves	Cgy., Hfd.	3	22	2	5	7	4	1	0	0	0	0	....	1984-85	1986-87
ourtenay, Ed	S.J.	2	44	7	13	20	10	....	....	....	....	....	....	1991-92	1992-93
ourtnall, Geoff	Bos., Edm., Wsh., St.L., Van.	17	1048	367	432	799	1465	156	39	70	109	262	1	1983-84	1999-00
ourtnall, Russ	Tor., Mtl., Min., Dal., Van., NYR, L.A.	16	1029	297	447	744	557	129	39	44	83	83	....	1983-84	1998-99
ourville, Larry	Van.	3	33	1	2	3	16	....	....	....	....	....	....	1995-96	1997-98
outu, Billy	Mtl., Ham., Bos.	10	244	33	21	54	478	19	1	1	2	39	1	1917-18	1926-27
outure, Gerry	Det., Mtl., Chi.	10	385	86	70	156	89	45	9	7	16	4	1	1944-45	1953-54
outure, Rosie	Chi., Mtl.	8	309	48	56	104	184	23	1	5	6	15	1	1928-29	1935-36
outurier, Sylvain	L.A.	3	33	4	5	9	4	....	....	....	....	....	....	1988-89	1991-92
owick, Bruce	Phi., Wsh., St.L.	3	70	5	6	11	43	8	0	0	0	9	1	1973-74	1975-76
owie, Rob	L.A.	2	78	7	12	19	52	....	....	....	....	....	....	1994-95	1995-96
owley, Bill	St.L., Bos.	13	549	195	353	548	143	64	12	34	46	22	2	1934-35	1946-47
ox, Danny	Tor., Ott., Det., NYR	8	319	47	49	96	128	10	0	1	1	6	....	1926-27	1933-34
oxe, Craig	Van., Cgy., St.L., S.J.	8	235	14	31	45	713	5	1	0	1	18	....	1984-85	1991-92
raig, Mike	Min., Dal., Tor., S.J.	9	423	71	97	168	550	26	2	2	4	49	....	1990-91	2001-02
raighead, John	Tor.	1	5	0	0	0	10	....	....	....	....	....	....	1996-97	1996-97
raigwell, Dale	S.J.	3	98	11	18	29	28	....	....	....	....	....	....	1991-92	1993-94
rashley, Bart	Det., K.C., L.A.	6	140	7	36	43	50	....	....	....	....	....	....	1965-66	1975-76
raven, Murray	Det., Phi., Hfd., Van., Chi., S.J.	18	1071	266	493	759	524	118	27	43	70	64	....	1982-83	1999-00
rawford, Bob	St.L., Hfd., NYR, Wsh.	7	246	71	71	142	72	11	0	1	1	8	....	1979-80	1986-87
rawford, Bobby	Col., Det.	2	16	1	3	4	6	....	....	....	....	....	....	1980-81	1982-83
rawford, Jack	Bos.	13	548	38	140	178	202	66	3	13	16	36	2	1937-38	1949-50
rawford, Lou	Bos.	2	26	2	1	3	29	1	0	0	0	0	....	1989-90	1991-92
rawford, Marc	Van.	6	176	19	31	50	229	20	1	2	3	44	....	1981-82	1986-87
rawford, Rusty	Ott., Tor.	2	38	10	8	18	117	2	2	1	3	9	1	1917-18	1918-19
reighton, Adam	Buf., Chi., NYI, T.B., St.L.	14	708	187	216	403	1077	61	11	14	25	137	....	1983-84	1996-97
reighton, Dave	Bos., Tor., Chi., NYR	12	616	140	174	314	223	51	11	13	24	20	....	1948-49	1959-60
reighton, Jimmy	Det.	1	11	1	0	1	2	....	....	....	....	....	....	1930-31	1930-31
ressman, Dave	Min.	2	85	6	8	14	37	....	....	....	....	....	....	1974-75	1975-76
ressman, Glen	Mtl.	1	4	0	0	0	2	....	....	....	....	....	....	1956-57	1956-57
risp, Terry	Bos., St.L., NYI, Phi.	11	536	67	134	201	135	110	15	28	43	40	2	1965-66	1976-77
ristofoli, Ed	Mtl.	1	9	0	1	1	4	....	....	....	....	....	....	1989-90	1989-90
roghan, Maurice	Mtl.M.	1	16	0	0	0	4	....	....	....	....	....	....	1937-38	1937-38
rombeen, Mike	Cle., St.L., Hfd.	8	475	55	68	123	218	27	6	2	8	32	....	1977-78	1984-85
ronin, Shawn	Wsh., Wpg., Phi., S.J.	7	292	3	18	21	877	32	1	0	1	38	....	1988-89	1994-95
ross, Cory	T.B., Tor., NYR, Edm., Pit., Det.	12	659	34	97	131	684	47	2	4	6	62	....	1993-94	2005-06
rossett, Stan	Phi.	1	21	0	0	0	10	....	....	....	....	....	....	1930-31	1930-31
rossman, Doug	Chi., Phi., L.A., NYI, Hfd., Det., T.B., St.L.	14	914	105	359	464	534	97	12	39	51	105	....	1980-81	1993-94
roteau, Gary	L.A., Det., Cal., K.C., Col.	12	684	144	175	319	143	11	3	2	5	8	....	1968-69	1979-80
rowder, Bruce	Bos., Pit.	4	243	47	51	98	156	31	8	4	12	41	....	1981-82	1984-85
rowder, Keith	Bos., L.A.	10	662	223	271	494	1354	85	14	22	36	218	....	1980-81	1989-90
rowder, Troy	N.J., Det., L.A., Van.	7	150	9	7	16	433	4	0	0	0	22	....	1987-88	1996-97
rowe, Phil	L.A., Phi., Ott., Nsh.	6	94	4	5	9	173	3	0	0	0	16	....	1993-94	1999-00
rowley, Mike	Ana.	3	67	5	15	20	44	....	....	....	....	....	....	1997-98	2000-01
rowley, Ted	Hfd., Col., NYI	2	34	2	4	6	12	....	....	....	....	....	....	1993-94	1998-99
rozier, Greg	Pit.	1	1	0	0	0	0	....	....	....	....	....	....	2000-01	2000-01
rozier, Joe	Tor.	1	5	0	3	3	2	....	....	....	....	....	....	1959-60	1959-60
rutchfield, Nels	Mtl.	1	41	5	5	10	20	2	0	1	1	22	....	1934-35	1934-35
ulhane, Jim	Hfd.	1	6	0	1	1	4	....	....	....	....	....	....	1989-90	1989-90
ullen, Barry	Tor., Det.	5	219	32	52	84	111	6	0	0	0	2	....	1955-56	1959-60
ullen, Brian	Tor., NYR	7	326	56	100	156	92	19	3	0	3	2	....	1954-55	1960-61
ullen, David	Phx., Min.	2	19	0	0	0	6	....	....	....	....	....	....	2000-01	2001-02
ullen, John	Pit., Hfd., Tor., T.B.	11	621	187	363	550	898	53	12	22	34	58	....	1988-89	1998-99
ullen, Ray	NYR, Det., Min., Van.	6	313	92	123	215	120	20	3	10	13	2	....	1965-66	1970-71
ummins, Barry	Cal.	1	36	1	2	3	39	....	....	....	....	....	....	1973-74	1973-74
ummins, Jim	Det., Phi., T.B., Chi., Phx., Mtl., Ana., NYI, Col.	12	511	24	36	60	1538	37	1	2	3	43	....	1991-92	2003-04
unneyworth, Randy	Buf., Pit., Wpg., Hfd., Chi., Ott.	16	866	189	225	414	1280	45	7	7	14	61	....	1980-81	1998-99
unningham, Bob	NYR	2	4	0	1	1	0	....	....	....	....	....	....	1960-61	1961-62
unningham, Jim	Phi.	1	1	0	0	0	4	....	....	....	....	....	....	1977-78	1977-78
unningham, Les	NYA, Chi.	2	60	7	19	26	21	1	0	0	0	0	....	1936-37	1939-40
upolo, Bill	Bos.	1	47	11	13	24	10	7	1	2	3	0	....	1944-45	1944-45
urran, Brian	Bos., NYI, Tor., Buf., Wsh.	10	381	7	33	40	1461	24	0	1	1	122	....	1983-84	1993-94
urrie, Dan	Edm., L.A.	4	22	2	1	3	4	....	....	....	....	....	....	1990-91	1993-94
urrie, Glen	Wsh., L.A.	8	326	39	79	118	100	12	1	3	4	4	....	1979-80	1987-88
urrie, Hugh	Mtl.	1	1	0	0	0	0	....	....	....	....	....	....	1950-51	1950-51
urrie, Tony	St.L., Van., Hfd.	8	290	92	119	211	83	16	4	12	16	14	....	1977-78	1984-85
urry, Floyd	Mtl.	11	601	105	99	204	147	91	23	17	40	38	4	1947-48	1957-58
urtale, Tony	Cgy.	1	2	0	0	0	0	....	....	....	....	....	....	1980-81	1980-81
urtis, Paul	Mtl., L.A., St.L.	4	185	3	34	37	161	5	0	0	0	2	....	1969-70	1972-73
ushenan, Ian	Chi., Mtl., NYR, Det.	5	129	3	11	14	134	....	....	....	....	....	1	1956-57	1963-64
usson, Jean	Oak.	1	2	0	0	0	0	....	....	....	....	....	....	1967-68	1967-68
utta, Jakub	Wsh.	3	8	0	0	0	0	....	....	....	....	....	....	2000-01	2003-04
r, Denis	Cgy., Chi., St.L.	6	193	41	43	84	36	4	0	0	0	0	....	1980-81	1985-86
r, Paul	Buf., NYR, Hfd.	9	470	101	140	241	623	24	4	6	10	31	....	1982-83	1991-92
erkawski, Mariusz	Bos., Edm., NYI, Mtl., Tor.	12	745	215	220	435	274	42	8	7	15	18	....	1993-94	2005-06

D

Name	NHL Teams	NHL Seasons	Regular Schedule GP	G	A	TP	PIM	Playoffs GP	G	A	TP	PIM	NHL Cup Wins	First NHL Season	Last NHL Season
ckell, Andreas	Ott., Mtl.	8	613	91	159	250	162	44	5	5	10	10	....	1996-97	2003-04
genais, Pierre	N.J., Fla., Mtl.	5	142	35	23	58	58	8	0	1	1	6	....	2000-01	2005-06
hl, Kevin	Cgy., Phx., Tor., CBJ	8	188	7	22	29	153	16	0	2	2	12	....	1992-93	2000-01
hlen, Ulf	NYR, Min., Dal., S.J., Chi., Wsh.	14	966	301	354	655	230	85	15	25	40	12	....	1987-88	2002-03
hlin, Kjell	Mtl.	3	166	57	59	116	10	35	6	11	17	6	1	1985-86	1987-88
hlman, Toni	Ott.	2	22	1	1	2	0	....	....	....	....	....	....	2001-02	2002-03
hlquist, Chris	Pit., Min., Cgy., Ott.	11	532	19	71	90	488	39	4	7	11	30	....	1985-86	1995-96
hlstrom, Cully	Chi.	8	342	88	118	206	58	29	6	8	14	4	1	1937-38	1944-45
igle, Alain	Chi.	6	389	56	50	106	122	17	0	1	1	0	....	1974-75	1979-80
igle, Alexandre	Ott., Phi., T.B., NYR, Pit., Min.	10	616	129	198	327	186	12	0	2	2	2	....	1993-94	2005-06
igneault, J.J.	Van., Phi., Mtl., St.L., Pit., Ana., NYI, Nsh., Phx., Min.	16	899	53	197	250	687	99	5	26	31	100	1	1984-85	2000-01
ley, Bob	Van., Phi.	9	561	94	231	325	814	63	12	34	46	105	....	1973-74	1981-82
ley, Frank	Det.	1	5	0	0	0	0	2	0	0	0	0	....	1928-29	1928-29
ley, Pat	Wpg.	2	12	1	0	1	13	....	....	....	....	....	....	1979-80	1980-81
garno, Brad	NYI	10	321	49	71	120	332	27	2	4	6	37	....	1985-86	1995-96
lman, Kevin	Bos., St.L., L.A.	3	154	8	23	31	45	....	....	....	....	....	....	2005-06	2007-08

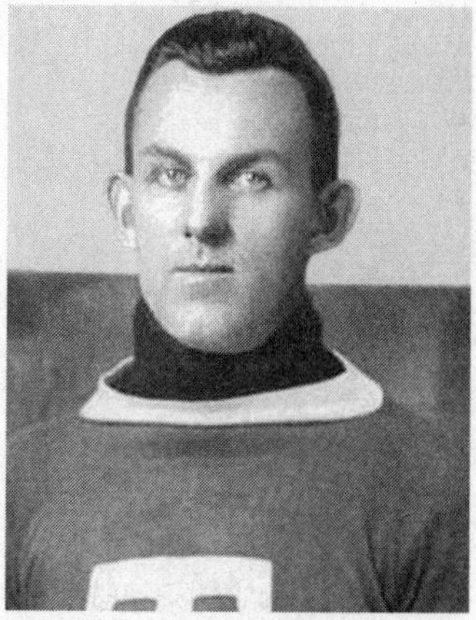
Jack Coughlin

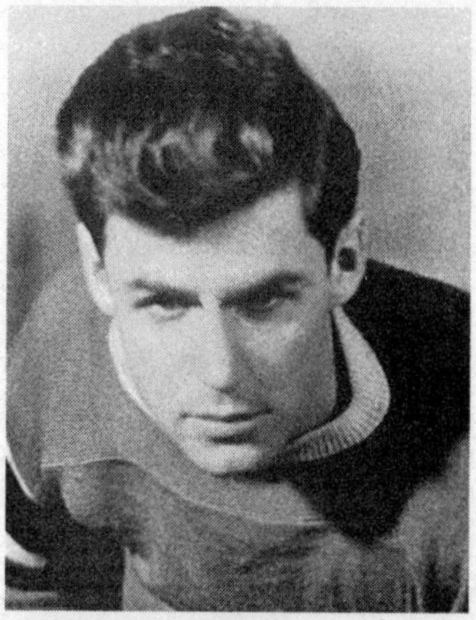
Nels Crutchfield

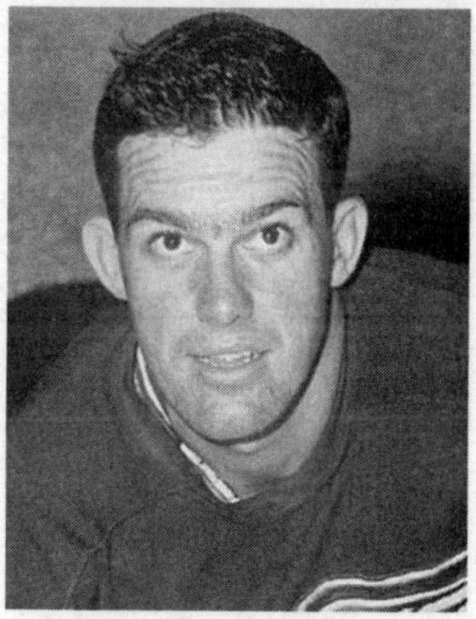
Barry Cullen

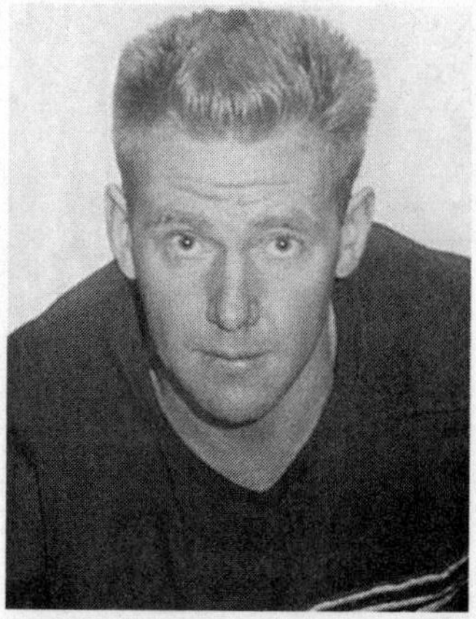
Lorne Davis

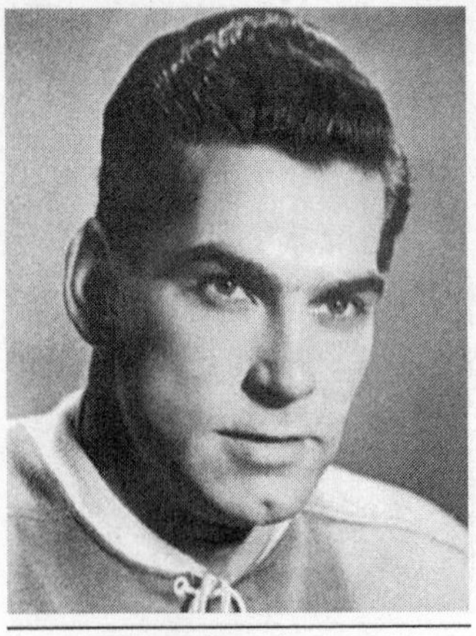

Bob Dawes

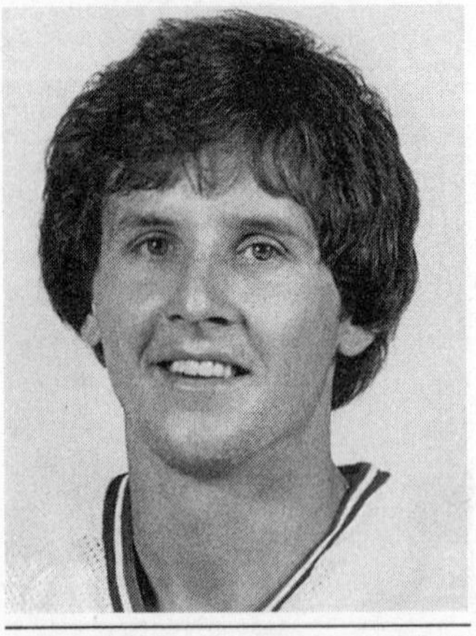

Dave Debol

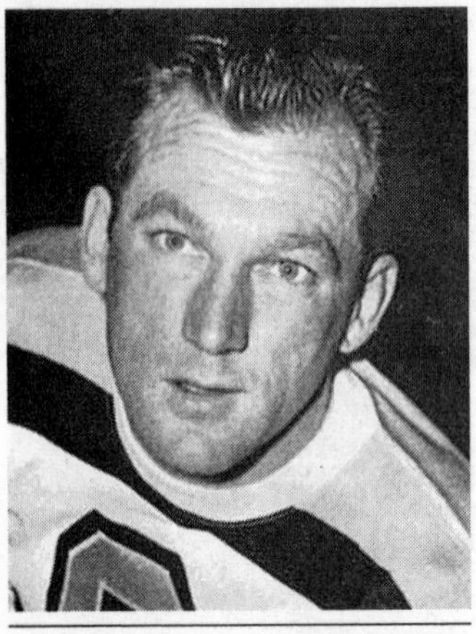

Marcel Dheere

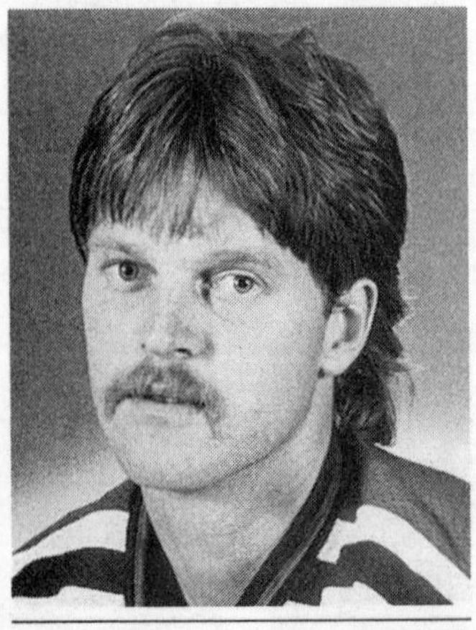

Don Dietrich

Name	NHL Teams	NHL Seasons	Regular Schedule GP	G	A	TP	PIM	Playoffs GP	G	A	TP	PIM	NHL Cup Wins	First NHL Season	Last NHL Season
Dallman, Marty	Tor.	2	6	0	1	1	0	....	....	....	....	....	....	1987-88	1988-8
Dallman, Rod	NYI, Phi.	4	6	1	0	1	26	1	0	1	1	0	....	1987-88	1991-9
● Dame, Bunny	Mtl.	1	34	2	5	7	4	....	....	....	....	....	....	1941-42	1941-4
● Damore, Hank	NYR	1	4	1	0	1	2	....	....	....	....	....	....	1943-44	1943-4
Damphousse, Vincent	Tor., Edm., Mtl., S.J.	18	1378	432	773	1205	1190	140	41	63	104	144	1	1986-87	2003-0
‡ Dandenault, Mathieu	Det., Mtl.	13	868	68	135	203	516	83	3	8	11	24	3	1995-96	2008-0
Daneyko, Ken	N.J.	20	1283	36	142	178	2519	175	5	17	22	296	3	1983-84	2002-0
Daniels, Jeff	Pit., Fla., Hfd., Car., Nsh.	12	425	17	26	43	83	41	3	5	8	2	1	1990-91	2002-0
‡ Daniels, Kimbi	Phi.	2	27	1	2	3	4	....	....	....	....	....	....	1990-91	1991-9
Daniels, Scott	Hfd., Phi., N.J.	6	149	8	12	20	667	1	0	0	0	0	....	1992-93	1998-9
‡ Danton, Mike	N.J., St.L.	3	87	9	5	14	182	5	1	0	1	2	....	2000-01	2003-0
Daoust, Dan	Mtl., Tor.	8	522	87	167	254	544	32	7	5	12	83	....	1982-83	1989-9
‡ Darby, Craig	Mtl., NYI, Phi., N.J.	9	196	21	35	56	32	....	....	....	....	....	....	1994-95	2003-0
Dark, Michael	St.L.	2	43	5	6	11	14	....	....	....	....	....	....	1986-87	1987-8
● Darragh, Harold	Pit., Phi., Bos., Tor.	8	308	68	49	117	50	16	1	3	4	4	1	1925-26	1932-3
● Darragh, Jack	Ott.	6	121	66	46	112	113	11	3	0	3	9	3	1917-18	1923-2
David, Richard	Que.	3	31	4	4	8	10	1	0	0	0	0	....	1979-80	1982-8
● Davidson, Bob	Tor.	12	491	94	160	254	398	79	5	17	22	76	2	1934-35	1945-4
● Davidson, Gord	NYR	2	51	3	6	9	8	....	....	....	....	....	....	1942-43	1943-4
Davidson, Matt	CBJ	3	56	5	7	12	28	....	....	....	....	....	....	2000-01	2002-0
‡ Davidsson, Johan	Ana., NYI	2	83	6	9	15	16	1	0	0	0	0	....	1998-99	1999-0
● Davie, Bob	Bos.	3	41	0	1	1	25	....	....	....	....	....	....	1933-34	1935-3
● Davies, Buck	NYR	1	....	....	....	....	....	1	0	0	0	0	....	1947-48	1947-4
● Davis, Bob	Det.	1	3	0	0	0	0	....	....	....	....	....	....	1932-33	1932-3
Davis, Kim	Pit., Tor.	4	36	5	7	12	51	4	0	0	0	0	....	1977-78	1980-8
● Davis, Lorne	Mtl., Chi., Det., Bos.	6	95	8	12	20	20	18	3	1	4	10	1	1951-52	1959-6
Davis, Mal	Det., Buf.	6	100	31	22	53	34	7	1	0	1	0	....	1978-79	1985-8
● Davison, Murray	Bos.	1	1	0	0	0	0	....	....	....	....	....	....	1965-66	1965-6
Davydov, Evgeny	Wpg., Fla., Ott.	4	155	40	39	79	120	11	2	2	4	2	....	1991-92	1994-9
Daw, Jeff	Col.	1	1	0	1	1	0	....	....	....	....	....	....	2001-02	2001-0
Dawe, Jason	Buf., NYI, Mtl., NYR	8	366	86	90	176	162	22	4	3	7	18	....	1993-94	2001-0
● Dawes, Bob	Tor., Mtl.	4	32	2	7	9	6	10	0	0	0	2	1	1946-47	1950-5
● Day, Hap	Tor., NYA	14	581	86	116	202	601	53	4	7	11	56	1	1924-25	1937-3
Day, Joe	Hfd., NYI	3	72	1	10	11	87	....	....	....	....	....	....	1991-92	1993-9
Daze, Eric	Chi.	11	601	226	172	398	176	37	5	7	12	8	....	1994-95	2005-0
de Vries, Greg	Edm., Nsh., Col., NYR, Ott., Atl.	13	878	48	146	194	780	111	8	14	22	91	1	1995-96	2008-0
Dea, Billy	NYR, Det., Chi., Pit.	8	397	67	54	121	44	11	2	1	3	6	....	1953-54	1970-7
● Deacon, Don	Det.	3	30	6	4	10	6	2	2	1	3	0	....	1936-37	1939-4
Deadmarsh, Adam	Que., Col., L.A.	10	567	184	189	373	819	105	26	40	66	100	1	1994-95	2003-0
Deadmarsh, Butch	Buf., Atl., K.C.	5	137	12	5	17	155	4	0	0	0	17	....	1970-71	1974-7
Dean, Barry	Col., Phi.	3	165	25	56	81	146	....	....	....	....	....	....	1976-77	1978-7
Dean, Kevin	N.J., Atl., Dal., Chi.	7	331	7	48	55	138	16	2	2	4	2	1	1994-95	2000-0
Debenedet, Nelson	Det., Pit.	2	46	10	4	14	13	....	....	....	....	....	....	1973-74	1974-7
DeBlois, Lucien	NYR, Col., Wpg., Mtl., Que., Tor.	15	993	249	276	525	814	52	7	6	13	38	1	1977-78	1991-9
Debol, Dave	Hfd.	2	92	26	26	52	4	3	0	0	0	0	....	1979-80	1980-8
DeBrusk, Louie	Edm., T.B., Phx., Chi.	11	401	24	17	41	1161	15	2	0	2	10	....	1991-92	2002-0
DeFauw, Brad	Car.	1	9	3	0	3	2	....	....	....	....	....	....	2002-03	2002-0
Defazio, Dean	Pit.	1	22	0	2	2	28	....	....	....	....	....	....	1983-84	1983-8
Degray, Dale	Cgy., Tor., L.A., Buf.	5	153	18	47	65	195	13	1	3	4	28	....	1985-86	1989-9
● Delisle, Jonathan	Mtl.	1	1	0	0	0	0	....	....	....	....	....	....	1998-99	1998-9
Delisle, Xavier	T.B., Mtl.	2	16	3	2	5	6	....	....	....	....	....	....	1998-99	2000-0
● Delmonte, Armand	Bos.	1	1	0	0	0	0	....	....	....	....	....	....	1945-46	1945-4
Delorme, Gilbert	Mtl., St.L., Que., Det., Pit.	9	541	31	92	123	520	56	1	9	10	56	....	1981-82	1989-9
Delorme, Ron	Col., Van.	9	524	83	83	166	667	25	1	2	3	59	....	1976-77	1984-8
Delory, Val	NYR	1	1	0	0	0	0	....	....	....	....	....	....	1948-49	1948-4
Delparte, Guy	Col.	1	48	1	8	9	18	....	....	....	....	....	....	1976-77	1976-7
Delvecchio, Alex	Det.	24	1549	456	825	1281	383	121	35	69	104	29	3	1950-51	1973-7
● DeMarco, Ab	Chi., Tor., Bos., NYR	7	209	72	93	165	53	11	3	0	3	2	....	1938-39	1946-4
DeMarco, Ab	NYR, St.L., Pit., Van., L.A., Bos.	9	344	44	80	124	75	25	1	2	3	17	....	1969-70	1978-7
● Demers, Tony	Mtl., NYR	6	83	20	22	42	23	2	0	0	0	0	....	1937-38	1943-4
‡ Dempsey, Nathan	Tor., Chi., L.A., Bos.	8	260	21	67	88	120	6	0	2	2	0	....	1996-97	2006-0
Denis, Jean-Paul	NYR	2	10	0	2	2	2	....	....	....	....	....	....	1946-47	1949-5
Denis, Lulu	Mtl.	2	3	0	1	1	0	....	....	....	....	....	....	1949-50	1950-5
● Denneny, Corb	Tor., Ham., Chi.	9	176	103	42	145	148	6	1	0	1	7	2	1917-18	1927-2
● Denneny, Cy	Ott., Bos.	12	328	248	85	333	301	25	16	2	18	23	5	1917-18	1928-2
Dennis, Norm	St.L.	4	12	3	0	3	11	5	0	0	0	2	....	1968-69	1971-7
● Denoird, Gerry	Tor.	1	17	0	1	1	0	....	....	....	....	....	....	1922-23	1922-2
DePalma, Larry	Min., S.J., Pit.	7	148	21	20	41	408	3	0	0	0	6	....	1985-86	1993-9
Derlago, Bill	Van., Tor., Bos., Wpg., Que.	9	555	189	227	416	247	13	5	0	5	8	....	1978-79	1986-8
● Desaulniers, Gerard	Mtl.	3	8	0	2	2	4	....	....	....	....	....	....	1950-51	1953-5
Descoteaux, Matthieu	Mtl.	1	5	1	1	2	4	....	....	....	....	....	....	2000-01	2000-
● Desilets, Joffre	Mtl., Chi.	5	192	37	45	82	57	7	1	0	1	7	....	1935-36	1939-
Desjardins, Eric	Mtl., Phi.	17	1143	136	439	575	757	168	23	57	80	93	1	1988-89	2005-
Desjardins, Martin	Mtl.	1	8	0	2	2	2	....	....	....	....	....	....	1989-90	1989-
● Desjardins, Vic	Chi., NYR	2	87	6	15	21	27	16	0	0	0	0	....	1930-31	1931-
Deslauriers, Jacques	Mtl.	1	2	0	0	0	0	....	....	....	....	....	....	1955-56	1955-
Deuling, Jarrett	NYI	2	15	0	1	1	11	....	....	....	....	....	....	1995-96	1996-
Devine, Kevin	NYI	1	2	0	1	1	8	....	....	....	....	....	....	1982-83	1982-
● Dewar, Tom	NYR	1	9	0	2	2	4	....	....	....	....	....	....	1943-44	1943-
● Dewsbury, Al	Det., Chi.	9	347	30	78	108	365	14	1	5	6	16	1	1946-47	1955-
Deziel, Michel	Buf.	1	....	....	....	....	....	1	0	0	0	0	....	1974-75	1974-
● Dheere, Marcel	Mtl.	1	11	1	2	3	2	5	0	0	0	6	....	1942-43	1942-
Diachuk, Edward	Det.	1	12	0	0	0	19	....	....	....	....	....	....	1960-61	1960-
● Dick, Harry	Chi.	1	12	0	1	1	12	....	....	....	....	....	....	1946-47	1946-
● Dickens, Ernie	Tor., Chi.	6	278	12	44	56	98	13	0	0	0	4	1	1941-42	1950-
Dickenson, Herb	NYR	2	48	18	17	35	10	....	....	....	....	....	....	1951-52	1952-
Diduck, Gerald	NYI, Mtl., Van., Chi., Hfd., Phx., Tor., Dal.	17	932	56	156	212	1612	114	8	16	24	212	....	1984-85	2000-
Dietrich, Don	Chi., N.J.	2	28	0	7	7	10	....	....	....	....	....	....	1983-84	1985-
● Dill, Bob	NYR	2	76	15	15	30	135	....	....	....	....	....	....	1943-44	1944-
● Dillabough, Bob	Det., Bos., Pit., Oak.	9	283	32	54	86	76	17	3	0	3	0	....	1961-62	1969-
● Dillon, Cecil	NYR, Det.	10	453	167	131	298	105	43	14	9	23	14	1	1930-31	1939-
Dillon, Gary	Col.	1	13	1	1	2	29	....	....	....	....	....	....	1980-81	1980-
Dillon, Wayne	NYR, Wpg.	4	229	43	66	109	60	3	0	1	1	0	....	1975-76	1979-
DiMaio, Rob	NYI, T.B., Phi., Bos., NYR, Car., Dal.	17	894	106	171	277	840	62	7	9	16	40	....	1988-89	2005-
‡ Dimitrakos, Niko	S.J., Phi.	4	158	24	38	62	95	20	1	8	9	10	....	2002-03	2006-
Dineen, Bill	Det., Chi.	5	323	51	44	95	122	37	1	1	2	18	2	1953-54	1957-
● Dineen, Gary	Min.	1	4	0	1	1	0	....	....	....	....	....	....	1968-69	1968-
Dineen, Gord	NYI, Min., Pit., Ott.	13	528	16	90	106	695	40	1	7	8	68	....	1982-83	1994-
Dineen, Kevin	Hfd., Phi., Car., Ott., CBJ	19	1188	355	405	760	2229	59	23	18	41	127	....	1984-85	2002-
Dineen, Peter	L.A., Det.	2	13	0	2	2	13	....	....	....	....	....	....	1986-87	1989-
Dingman, Chris	Cgy., Col., Car., T.B.	8	385	15	19	34	769	52	2	5	7	100	2	1997-98	2005-
● Dinsmore, Chuck	Mtl.M.	4	100	6	2	8	50	8	1	0	1	2	1	1924-25	1929-
Dionne, Gilbert	Mtl., Phi., Fla.	6	223	61	79	140	108	39	10	12	22	34	1	1990-91	1995-
Dionne, Marcel	Det., L.A., NYR	18	1348	731	1040	1771	600	49	21	24	45	17	....	1971-72	1988-
‡ DiPietro, Paul	Mtl., Tor., L.A.	6	192	31	49	80	96	31	11	10	21	10	1	1991-92	1996-
Dirk, Robert	St.L., Van., Chi., Ana., Mtl.	9	402	13	29	42	786	39	0	1	1	56	....	1987-88	1995-
‡ Divisek, Tomas	Phi.	2	5	1	0	1	0	....	....	....	....	....	....	2000-01	2001-
Djoos, Per	Det., NYR	3	82	2	31	33	58	....	....	....	....	....	....	1990-91	1992-
Doak, Gary	Det., Bos., Van., NYR	16	789	23	107	130	908	78	2	4	6	121	1	1965-66	1980-
Dobbin, Brian	Phi., Bos.	5	63	7	8	15	61	2	0	0	0	17	....	1986-87	1991-
Dobson, Jim	Min., Col., Que.	4	12	0	0	0	6	....	....	....	....	....	....	1979-80	1983-
● Doherty, Fred	Mtl.	1	1	0	0	0	0	....	....	....	....	....	....	1918-19	1918-
‡ Doig, Jason	Wpg., Phx., NYR, Wsh.	7	158	6	18	24	285	6	0	1	1	6	....	1995-96	2003-
Dollas, Bobby	Wpg., Que., Det., Ana., Edm., Pit., Ott., Cgy., S.J.	16	646	42	96	138	467	47	2	1	3	41	....	1983-84	2000-
‡ Dome, Robert	Pit., Cgy.	3	53	7	7	14	12	....	....	....	....	....	....	1997-98	2002-
‡ Domenichelli, Hnat	Hfd., Cgy., Atl., Min.	7	267	52	61	113	104	....	....	....	....	....	....	1996-97	2002-
Domi, Tie	Tor., NYR, Wpg.	16	1020	104	141	245	3515	98	7	12	19	238	....	1989-90	2005-
Donaldson, Gary	Chi.	1	1	0	0	0	0	....	....	....	....	....	....	1973-74	1973-
Donatelli, Clark	Min., Bos.	2	35	3	4	7	39	2	0	0	0	0	....	1989-90	1991-
Donato, Ted	Bos., NYI, Ott., Ana., Dal., St.L., L.A., NYR	13	796	150	197	347	396	58	8	10	18	22	....	1991-92	2003-
● Donnelly, Babe	Mtl.M.	1	34	0	1	1	14	2	0	0	0	0	....	1926-27	1926-
Donnelly, Dave	Bos., Chi., Edm.	5	137	15	24	39	150	5	0	0	0	0	....	1983-84	1987-
Donnelly, Gord	Que., Wpg., Buf., Dal.	12	554	28	41	69	2069	26	0	2	2	61	....	1983-84	1994-

ame	NHL Teams	NHL Seasons	Regular Schedule GP	G	A	TP	PIM	Playoffs GP	G	A	TP	PIM	NHL Cup Wins	First NHL Season	Last NHL Season
onnelly, Mike	NYR, Buf., L.A., Dal., NYI	11	465	114	121	235	255	47	12	12	24	30	....	1986-87	1996-97
opita, Jiri	Phi., Edm.	2	73	12	21	33	19	....	....	....	....	....	....	2001-02	2002-03
oran, John	NYA, Det., Mtl.	5	98	5	10	15	110	3	0	0	0	0	....	1933-34	1939-40
oran, Lloyd	Det.	1	24	3	2	5	10	....	....	....	....	....	....	1946-47	1946-47
oraty, Ken	Chi., Tor., Det.	5	103	15	26	41	24	15	7	2	9	2	....	1926-27	1937-38
ore, Andre	NYR, St.L., Que.	7	257	14	81	95	261	23	1	2	3	32	....	1978-79	1984-85
ore, Daniel	Que.	2	17	2	3	5	59	....	....	....	....	....	....	1989-90	1990-91
orey, Jim	Tor., NYR	4	232	25	74	99	553	11	0	2	2	40	....	1968-69	1971-72
orion, Dan	N.J.	2	4	1	1	2	2	....	....	....	....	....	....	1985-86	1987-88
ornhoefer, Gary	Bos., Phi.	14	787	214	328	542	1291	80	17	19	36	203	2	1963-64	1977-78
orohoy, Eddie	Mtl.	1	16	0	0	0	6	....	....	....	....	....	....	1948-49	1948-49
ouglas, Jordy	Hfd., Min., Wpg.	6	268	76	62	138	160	6	0	0	0	4	....	1979-80	1984-85
ouglas, Kent	Tor., Oak., Det.	7	428	33	115	148	631	19	1	3	4	33	3	1962-63	1968-69
ouglas, Les	Det.	4	52	6	12	18	8	10	3	2	5	2	1	1940-41	1946-47
oull, Doug	Bos., Wsh.	2	37	0	1	1	151	....	....	....	....	....	....	2003-04	2005-06
ouris, Peter	Wpg., Bos., Ana., Dal.	11	321	54	67	121	80	27	3	5	8	14	....	1985-86	1997-98
owd, Jim	N.J., Van., NYI, Cgy., Edm., Min., Mtl., Chi., Col., Phi.	16	728	71	168	239	390	99	9	17	26	50	1	1991-92	2007-08
owney, Aaron	Bos., Chi., Dal., St.L., Mtl., Det.	9	243	8	10	18	494	5	0	0	0	8	1	1999-00	2008-09
ownie, Dave	Tor.	1	11	0	1	1	2	....	....	....	....	....	....	1932-33	1932-33
oyon, Mario	Chi., Que.	3	28	3	4	7	16	....	....	....	....	....	....	1988-89	1990-91
rake, Dallas	Det., Wpg., Phx., St.L.	15	1009	177	300	477	885	90	14	19	33	79	1	1992-93	2007-08
raper, Bruce	Tor.	1	1	0	0	0	0	....	....	....	....	....	....	1962-63	1962-63
rillon, Gordie	Tor., Mtl.	7	311	155	139	294	56	50	26	15	41	10	1	1936-37	1942-43
riscoll, Peter	Edm.	2	60	3	8	11	97	3	0	0	0	0	....	1979-80	1980-81
river, Bruce	N.J., NYR	15	922	96	390	486	670	108	10	40	50	64	1	1983-84	1997-98
rolet, Rene	Phi., Det.	2	2	0	0	0	0	....	....	....	....	....	....	1971-72	1974-75
roppa, Ivan	Chi.	2	19	0	1	1	14	....	....	....	....	....	....	1993-94	1995-96
rouillard, Clarence	Det.	1	10	0	1	1	0	....	....	....	....	....	....	1937-38	1937-38
rouin, Jude	Mtl., Min., NYI, Wpg.	12	666	151	305	456	346	72	27	41	68	33	....	1968-69	1980-81
rouin, P.C.	Bos.	1	3	0	0	0	0	....	....	....	....	....	....	1996-97	1996-97
rouin, Polly	Mtl.	7	160	23	50	73	80	5	0	1	1	5	....	1934-35	1940-41
ruce, John	Wsh., Wpg., L.A., Phi.	10	531	113	126	239	347	53	17	6	23	38	....	1988-89	1997-98
ruken, Harold	Van., Car., Tor.	5	146	27	36	63	36	4	0	1	1	0	....	1999-00	2003-04
rulia, Stan	T.B.	3	126	15	27	42	52	....	....	....	....	....	....	1992-93	2000-01
rummond, Jim	NYR	1	2	0	0	0	0	....	....	....	....	....	....	1944-45	1944-45
rury, Herb	Pit., Phi.	6	213	24	13	37	203	4	1	1	2	0	....	1925-26	1930-31
rury, Ted	Cgy., Hfd., Ott., Ana., NYI, CBJ	8	414	41	52	93	367	14	1	0	1	4	....	1993-94	2000-01
ube, Christian	NYR	2	33	1	1	2	4	3	0	0	0	0	....	1996-97	1998-99
ube, Gilles	Mtl., Det.	2	12	1	2	3	2	2	0	0	0	0	1	1949-50	1953-54
ube, Norm	K.C.	2	57	8	10	18	54	....	....	....	....	....	....	1974-75	1975-76
uberman, Justin	Pit.	1	4	0	0	0	0	....	....	....	....	....	....	1993-94	1993-94
ubinsky, Steve	Chi., Cgy., Nsh., St.L.	10	375	25	45	70	164	10	1	0	1	14	....	1993-94	2002-03
uchesne, Gaetan	Wsh., Que., Min., S.J., Fla.	14	1028	179	254	433	617	84	14	13	27	97	....	1981-82	1994-95
uchesne, Steve	L.A., Phi., Que., St.L., Ott., Det.	16	1113	227	525	752	824	121	16	61	77	96	1	1986-87	2001-02
Dudley, Rick	Buf., Wpg.	6	309	75	99	174	292	25	7	2	9	69	....	1972-73	1980-81
Duerden, Dave	Fla.	1	2	0	0	0	0	....	....	....	....	....	....	1999-00	1999-00
Duff, Dick	Tor., NYR, Mtl., L.A., Buf.	18	1030	283	289	572	743	114	30	49	79	78	6	1954-55	1971-72
Dufour, Luc	Bos., Que., St.L.	3	167	23	21	44	199	18	1	0	1	32	....	1982-83	1984-85
Dufour, Marc	NYR, L.A.	3	14	1	0	1	2	....	....	....	....	....	....	1963-64	1968-69
Dufresne, Donald	Mtl., T.B., L.A., St.L., Edm.	9	268	6	36	42	258	34	1	3	4	47	1	1988-89	1996-97
Duggan, John	Ott.	1	27	0	0	0	0	2	0	0	0	0	....	1925-26	1925-26
Duggan, Ken	Min.	1	1	0	0	0	0	....	....	....	....	....	....	1987-88	1987-88
Duguay, Ron	NYR, Det., Pit., L.A.	12	864	274	346	620	582	89	31	22	53	118	....	1977-78	1988-89
Duguid, Lorne	Mtl.M., Det., Bos.	6	135	9	15	24	57	4	1	0	1	6	....	1931-32	1936-37
Dukowski, Duke	Chi., NYA, NYR	5	200	16	30	46	172	6	0	0	0	6	....	1926-27	1933-34
Dumart, Woody	Bos.	16	772	211	218	429	99	88	12	15	27	23	2	1935-36	1953-54
Dunbar, Dale	Van., Bos.	2	2	0	0	0	2	....	....	....	....	....	....	1985-86	1988-89
Duncan, Art	Det., Tor.	5	156	18	16	34	225	5	0	0	0	4	....	1926-27	1930-31
Duncan, Iain	Wpg.	4	127	34	55	89	149	11	0	3	3	6	....	1986-87	1990-91
Duncanson, Craig	L.A., Wpg., NYR	7	38	5	4	9	61	....	....	....	....	....	....	1985-86	1992-93
Dundas, Rocky	Tor.	1	5	0	0	0	14	....	....	....	....	....	....	1989-90	1989-90
Dunlap, Frank	Tor.	1	15	0	1	1	2	....	....	....	....	....	....	1943-44	1943-44
Dunlop, Blake	Min., Phi., St.L., Det.	11	550	130	274	404	172	40	4	10	14	18	....	1973-74	1983-84
Dunn, Dave	Van., Tor.	3	184	14	41	55	313	10	1	1	2	41	....	1973-74	1975-76
Dunn, Richie	Buf., Cgy., Hfd.	12	483	36	140	176	314	36	3	15	18	24	....	1977-78	1988-89
Dupere, Denis	Tor., Wsh., St.L., K.C., Col.	8	421	80	99	179	66	16	1	0	1	0	....	1970-71	1977-78
Dupont, Andre	NYR, St.L., Phi., Que.	13	800	59	185	244	1986	140	14	18	32	352	2	1970-71	1982-83
Dupont, Jerome	Chi., Tor.	6	214	7	29	36	468	20	0	2	2	56	....	1981-82	1986-87
DuPont, Micki	Cgy., Pit., St.L.	4	23	1	3	4	12	....	....	....	....	....	....	2001-02	2007-08
Dupont, Norm	Mtl., Wpg., Hfd.	5	256	55	85	140	52	13	4	2	6	0	....	1979-80	1983-84
Dupre, Yanick	Phi.	3	35	2	0	2	16	....	....	....	....	....	....	1991-92	1995-96
Durbano, Steve	St.L., Pit., K.C., Col.	6	220	13	60	73	1127	5	0	2	2	8	....	1972-73	1978-79
Duris, Vitezslav	Tor.	2	89	3	20	23	62	3	0	1	1	2	....	1980-81	1982-83
Dusablon, Benoit	NYR	1	3	0	0	0	2	....	....	....	....	....	....	2003-04	2003-04
Dussault, Norm	Mtl.	4	206	31	62	93	47	7	3	1	4	0	....	1947-48	1950-51
Dutton, Red	Mtl.M., NYA	10	449	29	67	96	871	18	1	0	1	33	....	1926-27	1935-36
Dvorak, Miroslav	Phi.	3	193	11	74	85	51	18	0	2	2	6	....	1982-83	1984-85
Dwyer, Gordie	T.B., NYR, Mtl.	5	108	0	5	5	394	....	....	....	....	....	....	1999-00	2003-04
Dwyer, Mike	Col., Cgy.	4	31	2	6	8	25	1	1	0	1	0	....	1978-79	1981-82
Dyck, Henry	NYR	1	1	0	0	0	0	....	....	....	....	....	....	1943-44	1943-44
Dye, Babe	Tor., Ham., Chi., NYA	11	271	201	47	248	221	10	2	0	2	11	1	1919-20	1930-31
Dykhuis, Karl	Chi., Phi., T.B., Mtl.	12	644	42	91	133	495	62	8	10	18	50	....	1991-92	2003-04
Dykstra, Steve	Buf., Edm., Pit., Hfd.	5	217	8	32	40	545	1	0	0	0	2	....	1985-86	1989-90
Dyte, Jack	Chi.	1	27	1	0	1	31	....	....	....	....	....	....	1943-44	1943-44
Dziedzic, Joe	Pit., Phx.	3	130	14	14	28	131	21	1	3	4	23	....	1995-96	1998-99

E

Name	NHL Teams	NHL Seasons	Regular Schedule GP	G	A	TP	PIM	Playoffs GP	G	A	TP	PIM	NHL Cup Wins	First NHL Season	Last NHL Season
Eagles, Mike	Que., Chi., Wpg., Wsh.	16	853	74	122	196	928	44	2	6	8	34	....	1982-83	1999-00
Eakin, Bruce	Cgy., Det.	4	13	2	2	4	4	....	....	....	....	....	....	1981-82	1985-86
Eakins, Dallas	Wpg., Fla., St.L., Phx., NYR, Tor., NYI, Cgy.	10	120	0	9	9	208	5	0	0	0	4	....	1992-93	2001-02
Eastwood, Mike	Tor., Wpg., Phx., NYR, St.L., Chi., Pit.	13	783	87	149	236	354	97	8	11	19	64	....	1991-92	2003-04
Eatough, Jeff	Buf.	1	1	0	0	0	0	....	....	....	....	....	....	1981-82	1981-82
Eaves, Mike	Min., Cgy.	8	324	83	143	226	80	43	7	10	17	14	....	1978-79	1985-86
Eaves, Murray	Wpg., Det.	8	57	4	13	17	9	4	0	1	1	2	....	1980-81	1989-90
Ecclestone, Tim	St.L., Det., Tor., Atl.	11	692	126	233	359	344	48	6	11	17	76	....	1967-68	1977-78
Edberg, Rolf	Wsh.	3	184	45	58	103	24	....	....	....	....	....	....	1978-79	1980-81
Eddolls, Frank	Mtl., NYR	8	317	23	43	66	114	31	0	2	2	10	1	1944-45	1951-52
Edestrand, Darryl	St.L., Phi., Pit., Bos., L.A.	10	455	34	90	124	404	42	3	9	12	57	....	1967-68	1978-79
Edmundson, Garry	Mtl., Tor.	3	43	4	6	10	49	11	0	1	1	8	....	1951-52	1960-61
Edur, Tom	Col., Pit.	2	158	17	70	87	67	....	....	....	....	....	....	1976-77	1977-78
• Egan, Pat	NYA, Bro., Det., Bos., NYR	11	554	77	153	230	776	46	9	4	13	48	....	1939-40	1950-51
Egeland, Allan	T.B.	3	17	0	0	0	16	....	....	....	....	....	....	1995-96	1997-98
Egers, Jack	NYR, St.L., Wsh.	7	284	64	69	133	154	32	5	6	11	32	....	1969-70	1975-76
• Ehman, Gerry	Bos., Det., Tor., Oak., Cal.	9	429	96	118	214	100	41	10	10	20	12	1	1957-58	1970-71
Eisenhut, Neil	Van., Cgy.	2	16	1	3	4	21	....	....	....	....	....	....	1993-94	1994-95
Eklund, Pelle	Phi., Dal.	9	594	120	335	455	109	66	10	36	46	8	....	1985-86	1993-94
Ekman, Nils	T.B., S.J., Pit.	5	264	60	91	151	188	28	2	5	7	16	....	1999-00	2006-07
Eldebrink, Anders	Van., Que.	2	55	3	11	14	29	14	0	0	0	10	....	1981-82	1982-83
Elich, Matt	T.B.	2	16	1	1	2	0	....	....	....	....	....	....	1999-00	2000-01
Elik, Bo	Det.	1	3	0	0	0	0	....	....	....	....	....	....	1962-63	1962-63
Elik, Todd	L.A., Min., Edm., S.J., St.L., Bos.	8	448	110	219	329	453	52	15	27	42	48	....	1989-90	1996-97
Ellett, Dave	Wpg., Tor., N.J., Bos., St.L.	16	1129	153	415	568	985	116	11	46	57	87	....	1984-85	1999-00
• Elliott, Fred	Ott.	1	43	2	0	2	6	....	....	....	....	....	....	1928-29	1928-29
Ellis, Ron	Tor.	16	1034	332	308	640	207	70	18	8	26	20	1	1963-64	1980-81
Elomo, Miika	Wsh.	1	2	0	1	1	2	....	....	....	....	....	....	1999-00	1999-00
Eloranta, Kari	Cgy., St.L.	5	267	13	103	116	155	26	1	7	8	19	....	1981-82	1986-87
Eloranta, Mikko	Bos., L.A.	4	264	32	44	76	186	7	1	1	2	2	....	1999-00	2002-03
Elynuik, Pat	Wpg., Wsh., T.B., Ott.	9	506	154	188	342	459	20	6	9	15	25	....	1987-88	1995-96
• Emberg, Eddie	Mtl.	1	....	....	....	....	....	2	1	0	1	0	....	1944-45	1944-45
Emerson, Nelson	St.L., Wpg., Hfd., Car., Chi., Ott., Atl., L.A.	12	771	195	293	488	575	40	7	15	22	33	....	1990-91	2001-02
Emma, David	N.J., Bos., Fla.	5	34	5	6	11	2	....	....	....	....	....	....	1992-93	2000-01
Emmons, Gary	S.J.	1	3	1	0	1	0	....	....	....	....	....	....	1993-94	1993-94

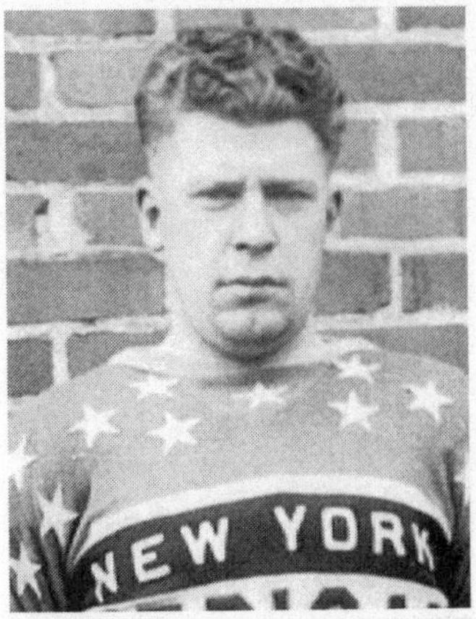

John Doran

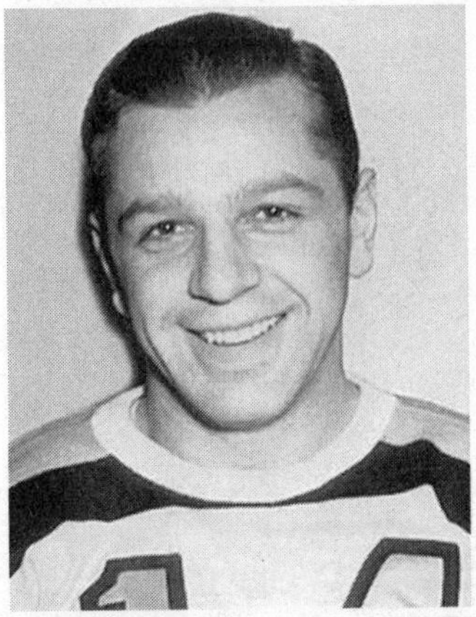
Woody Dumart

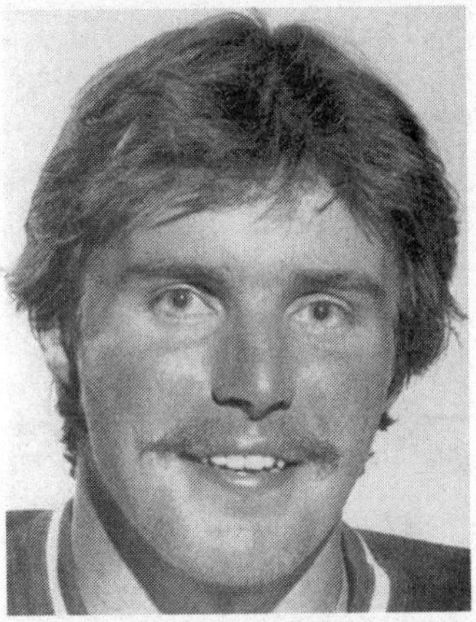
Kari Eloranta

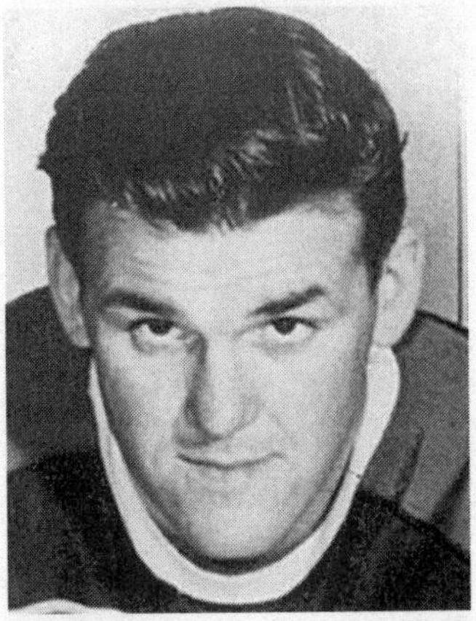
Jack Evans

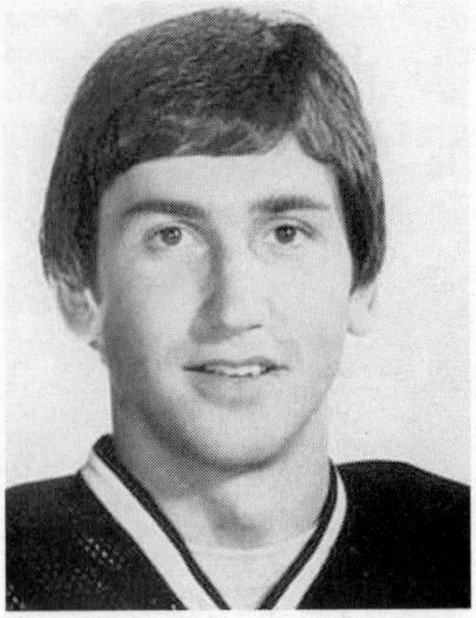

Mario Faubert

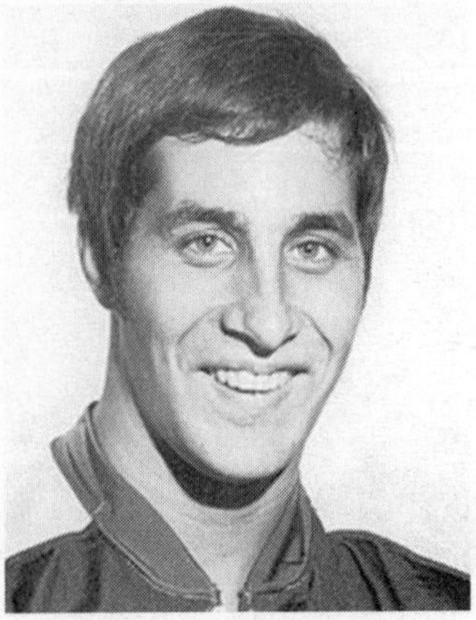

Tony Featherstone

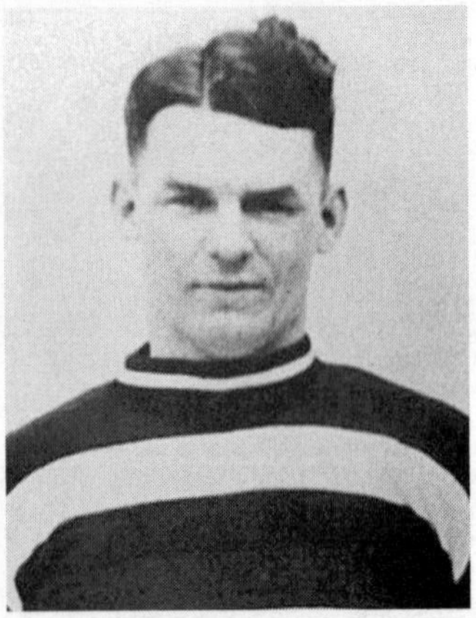

Frank Finnigan

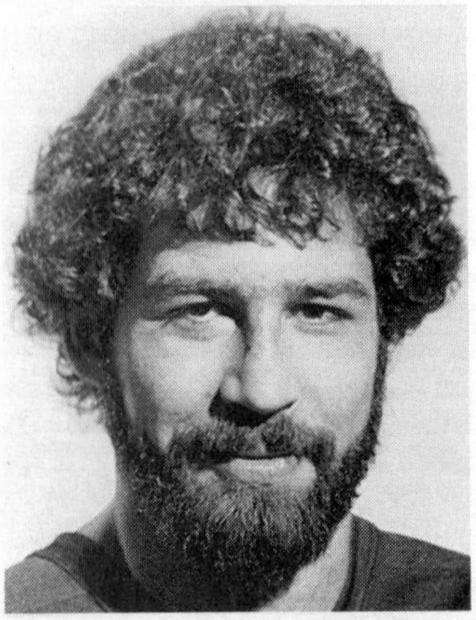

Dwight Foster

Name	NHL Teams	NHL Seasons	Regular Schedule GP	G	A	TP	PIM	Playoffs GP	G	A	TP	PIM	NHL Cup Wins	First NHL Season	Last NHL Seaso
Emmons, John	Ott., T.B., Bos.	3	85	2	4	6	64	....	....	....	....	....	....	1999-00	2001-0
• Emms, Hap	Mtl.M., NYA, Det., Bos.	10	320	36	53	89	311	14	0	0	0	12	....	1926-27	1937-3
Endean, Craig	Wpg.	1	2	0	1	1	0	....	....	....	....	....	....	1986-87	1986-8
‡ Endicott, Shane	Pit.	2	45	1	2	3	47	....	....	....	....	....	....	2001-02	2005-0
Engblom, Brian	Mtl., Wsh., L.A., Buf., Cgy.	11	659	29	177	206	599	48	3	9	12	43	2	1976-77	1986-8
Engele, Jerry	Min.	3	100	2	13	15	162	2	0	1	1	0	....	1975-76	1977-7
English, John	L.A.	1	3	1	3	4	4	1	0	0	0	0	....	1987-88	1987-8
Ennis, Jim	Edm.	1	5	1	0	1	10	....	....	....	....	....	....	1987-88	1987-8
Erickson, Aut	Bos., Chi., Tor., Oak.	7	226	7	24	31	182	7	0	0	0	2	1	1959-60	1969-7
Erickson, Bryan	Wsh., L.A., Pit., Wpg.	9	351	80	125	205	141	14	3	4	7	7	....	1983-84	1993-9
Erickson, Grant	Bos., Min.	2	6	1	0	1	0	....	....	....	....	....	....	1968-69	1969-7
Eriksson, Peter	Edm.	1	20	3	3	6	24	....	....	....	....	....	....	1989-90	1989-9
Eriksson, Roland	Min., Van.	3	193	48	95	143	26	2	1	0	1	0	....	1976-77	1978-7
Eriksson, Thomas	Phi.	5	208	22	76	98	107	19	0	3	3	12	....	1980-81	1985-8
Erixon, Jan	NYR	10	556	57	159	216	167	58	7	7	14	16	....	1983-84	1992-9
Errey, Bob	Pit., Buf., S.J., Det., Dal., NYR	15	895	170	212	382	1005	99	13	16	29	109	2	1983-84	1997-9
Esau, Len	Tor., Que., Cgy., Edm.	4	27	0	10	10	24	....	....	....	....	....	....	1991-92	1994-9
Esposito, Phil	Chi., Bos., NYR	18	1282	717	873	1590	910	130	61	76	137	138	2	1963-64	1980-8
• Evans, Chris	Tor., Buf., St.L., Det., K.C.	5	241	19	42	61	143	12	1	1	2	8	....	1969-70	1974-7
Evans, Daryl	L.A., Wsh., Tor.	6	113	22	30	52	25	11	5	8	13	12	....	1981-82	1986-8
Evans, Doug	St.L., Wpg., Phi.	8	355	48	87	135	502	22	3	4	7	38	....	1985-86	1992-9
• Evans, Jack	NYR, Chi.	14	752	19	80	99	989	56	2	2	4	97	1	1948-49	1962-6
Evans, Kevin	Min., S.J.	2	9	0	1	1	44	....	....	....	....	....	....	1990-91	1991-9
Evans, Paul	Tor.	2	11	1	1	2	21	2	0	0	0	0	....	1976-77	1977-7
Evans, Paul	Phi.	3	103	14	25	39	34	1	0	0	0	0	....	1978-79	1982-8
Evans, Shawn	St.L., NYI	2	9	1	0	1	2	....	....	....	....	....	....	1985-86	1989-9
• Evans, Stewart	Det., Mtl.M., Mtl.	8	367	28	49	77	425	26	0	0	0	20	1	1930-31	1938-3
Evason, Dean	Wsh., Hfd., S.J., Dal., Cgy.	13	803	139	233	372	1002	55	9	20	29	132	....	1983-84	1995-9
Ewen, Todd	St.L., Mtl., Ana., S.J.	11	518	36	40	76	1911	26	0	0	0	87	1	1986-87	1996-9
Ezinicki, Bill	Tor., Bos., NYR	9	368	79	105	184	713	40	5	8	13	87	3	1944-45	1954-5

F

Name	NHL Teams	NHL Seasons	Regular Schedule GP	G	A	TP	PIM	Playoffs GP	G	A	TP	PIM	NHL Cup Wins	First NHL Season	Last NHL Seaso
‡ Fahey, Jim	S.J., N.J.	4	92	1	24	25	67	2	0	0	0	0	....	2002-03	2006-0
Fahey, Trevor	NYR	1	1	0	0	0	0	....	....	....	....	....	....	1964-65	1964-6
Fairbairn, Bill	NYR, Min., St.L.	11	658	162	261	423	173	54	13	22	35	42	....	1968-69	1978-7
Fairchild, Kelly	Tor., Dal., Col.	4	34	2	3	5	6	....	....	....	....	....	....	1995-96	2001-0
Falkenberg, Bob	Det.	5	54	1	5	6	26	....	....	....	....	....	....	1966-67	1971-7
Falloon, Pat	S.J., Phi., Ott., Edm., Pit.	9	575	143	179	322	141	66	11	7	18	16	....	1991-92	1999-0
Farkas, Jeff	Tor., Atl.	4	11	0	2	2	6	5	1	0	1	0	....	1999-00	2002-0
• Farrant, Walt	Chi.	1	1	0	0	0	0	....	....	....	....	....	....	1943-44	1943-4
Farrell, Mike	Wsh., Nsh.	3	13	0	0	0	2	....	....	....	....	....	....	2001-02	2003-0
Farrish, Dave	NYR, Que., Tor.	7	430	17	110	127	440	14	0	2	2	24	....	1976-77	1983-8
Fashoway, Gordie	Chi.	1	13	3	2	5	14	....	....	....	....	....	....	1950-51	1950-5
‡ Fast, Brad	Car.	1	1	1	0	1	0	....	....	....	....	....	....	2003-04	2003-0
‡ Fata, Rico	Cgy., NYR, Pit., Atl., Wsh.	8	230	27	36	63	104	....	....	....	....	....	....	1998-99	2006-0
Faubert, Mario	Pit.	7	231	21	90	111	292	10	2	2	4	6	....	1974-75	1981-8
Faulkner, Alex	Tor., Det.	3	101	15	17	32	15	12	5	0	5	2	....	1961-62	1963-6
Fauss, Ted	Tor.	2	28	0	2	2	15	....	....	....	....	....	....	1986-87	1987-8
Faust, Andre	Phi.	2	47	10	7	17	14	....	....	....	....	....	....	1992-93	1993-9
Feamster, Dave	Chi.	4	169	13	24	37	154	33	3	5	8	61	....	1981-82	1984-8
Featherstone, Glen	St.L., Bos., NYR, Hfd., Cgy.	9	384	19	61	80	939	28	0	2	2	103	....	1988-89	1996-9
Featherstone, Tony	Oak., Cal., Min.	3	130	17	21	38	65	2	0	0	0	0	....	1969-70	1973-7
Federko, Bernie	St.L., Det.	14	1000	369	761	1130	487	91	35	66	101	83	....	1976-77	1989-9
‡ Fedorov, Fedor	Van., NYR	3	18	0	2	2	14	....	....	....	....	....	....	2002-03	2005-0
‡ Fedorov, Sergei	Det., Ana., CBJ, Wsh.	18	1248	483	696	1179	839	183	52	124	176	133	3	1990-91	2008-0
Fedotov, Anatoli	Wpg., Ana.	2	4	0	2	2	0	....	....	....	....	....	....	1992-93	1993-9
Fedyk, Brent	Det., Phi., Dal., NYR	10	470	97	112	209	308	16	3	2	5	12	....	1987-88	1998-9
Felix, Chris	Wsh.	4	35	1	12	13	10	2	0	1	1	0	....	1987-88	1990-9
Felsner, Brian	Chi.	1	12	1	3	4	12	....	....	....	....	....	....	1997-98	1997-9
Felsner, Denny	St.L.	4	18	1	4	5	6	10	2	3	5	2	....	1991-92	1994-9
Feltrin, Tony	Pit., NYR	4	48	3	3	6	65	....	....	....	....	....	....	1980-81	1985-8
Fenton, Paul	Hfd., NYR, L.A., Wpg., Tor., Cgy., S.J.	8	411	100	83	183	198	17	4	1	5	27	....	1984-85	1991-9
Fenyves, David	Buf., Phi.	9	206	3	32	35	119	11	0	0	0	9	....	1982-83	1990-9
Ference, Brad	Fla., Phx., Cgy.	6	250	4	30	34	565	....	....	....	....	....	....	1999-00	2006-0
Fergus, Tom	Bos., Tor., Van.	12	726	235	346	581	499	65	21	17	38	48	....	1981-82	1992-9
Ferguson, Craig	Mtl., Cgy., Fla.	5	27	1	1	2	6	....	....	....	....	....	....	1993-94	1999-0
Ferguson, George	Tor., Pit., Min.	12	797	160	238	398	431	86	14	23	37	44	....	1972-73	1983-8
• Ferguson, John	Mtl.	8	500	145	158	303	1214	85	20	18	38	260	5	1963-64	1970-
• Ferguson, Lorne	Bos., Det., Chi.	8	422	82	80	162	193	31	6	3	9	24	....	1949-50	1958-
Ferguson, Norm	Oak., Cal.	4	279	73	66	139	72	10	1	4	5	7	....	1968-69	1971-
Ferguson, Scott	Edm., Ana., Min.	7	218	7	14	21	310	11	0	0	0	8	....	1997-98	2005-
‡ Ferland, Jonathan	Mtl.	1	7	1	0	1	2	....	....	....	....	....	....	2005-06	2005-
Ferner, Mark	Buf., Wsh., Ana., Det.	6	91	3	10	13	51	....	....	....	....	....	....	1986-87	1994-
‡ Ferraro, Chris	NYR, Pit., Edm., NYI, Wsh.	6	74	7	9	16	57	....	....	....	....	....	....	1995-96	2001-
‡ Ferraro, Peter	NYR, Pit., Bos., Wsh.	6	92	9	15	24	58	2	0	0	0	0	....	1995-96	2001-
Ferraro, Ray	Hfd., NYI, NYR, L.A., Atl., St.L.	18	1258	408	490	898	1288	68	21	22	43	54	....	1984-85	2001-
Fetisov, Viacheslav	N.J., Det.	9	546	36	192	228	656	116	2	26	28	147	2	1989-90	1997-
‡ Fibiger, Jesse	S.J.	1	16	0	0	0	2	....	....	....	....	....	....	2002-03	2002-
Fidler, Mike	Cle., Min., Hfd., Chi.	7	271	84	97	181	124	....	....	....	....	....	....	1976-77	1982-
• Field, Wilf	NYA, Bro., Mtl., Chi.	6	219	17	25	42	151	2	0	0	0	2	....	1936-37	1944-
Fielder, Guyle	Chi., Det., Bos.	4	9	0	0	0	2	6	0	0	0	2	....	1950-51	1957-
Filimonov, Dmitri	Ott.	1	30	1	4	5	18	....	....	....	....	....	....	1993-94	1993-
Fillion, Bob	Mtl.	7	327	42	61	103	84	33	7	4	11	10	2	1943-44	1949-
• Fillion, Marcel	Bos.	1	1	0	0	0	0	....	....	....	....	....	....	1944-45	1944-
• Filmore, Tommy	Det., NYA, Bos.	4	117	15	12	27	33	....	....	....	....	....	....	1930-31	1933-
• Finkbeiner, Lloyd	NYA	1	2	0	0	0	0	....	....	....	....	....	....	1940-41	1940-
Finley, Jeff	NYI, Phi., Wpg., Phx., NYR, St.L.	15	708	13	70	83	457	52	1	6	7	38	....	1987-88	2003-
Finn, Steven	Que., T.B., L.A.	12	725	34	78	112	1724	23	0	4	4	39	....	1985-86	1996-
• Finney, Sid	Chi.	3	59	10	7	17	4	7	0	2	2	0	....	1951-52	1953-
• Finnigan, Ed	St.L., Bos.	2	15	1	1	2	2	....	....	....	....	....	....	1934-35	1935-
• Finnigan, Frank	Ott., Tor., St.L.	14	553	115	88	203	407	38	6	9	15	22	2	1923-24	1936-
Fiorentino, Peter	NYR	1	1	0	0	0	0	....	....	....	....	....	....	1991-92	1991-
Fischer, Jiri	Det.	6	305	11	49	60	295	38	4	3	7	55	1	1999-00	2005-
‡ Fischer, Patrick	Phx.	1	27	4	6	10	24	....	....	....	....	....	....	2006-07	2006-
Fischer, Ron	Buf.	2	18	0	7	7	6	....	....	....	....	....	....	1981-82	1982-
• Fisher, Alvin	Tor.	1	9	1	0	1	4	....	....	....	....	....	....	1924-25	1924-
Fisher, Craig	Phi., Wpg., Fla.	4	12	0	0	0	2	....	....	....	....	....	....	1989-90	1996-
Fisher, Dunc	NYR, Bos., Det.	7	275	45	70	115	104	21	4	4	8	14	....	1947-48	1958-
• Fisher, Joe	Det.	4	65	8	12	20	13	12	2	1	3	6	1	1939-40	1942-
Fitchner, Bob	Que.	2	78	12	20	32	59	3	0	0	0	10	....	1979-80	1980-
Fitzgerald, Rusty	Pit.	2	25	2	2	4	12	5	0	0	0	4	....	1994-95	1995-
Fitzgerald, Tom	NYI, Fla., Col., Nsh., Chi., Tor., Bos.	17	1097	139	190	329	776	78	7	12	19	90	....	1988-89	2005-
Fitzpatrick, Ross	Phi.	4	20	5	2	7	0	....	....	....	....	....	....	1982-83	1985-
Fitzpatrick, Sandy	NYR, Min.	2	22	3	6	9	8	12	0	0	0	0	....	1964-65	1967-
Flaman, Fern	Bos., Tor.	17	910	34	174	208	1370	63	4	8	12	93	1	1944-45	1960-
Flatley, Pat	NYI, NYR	14	780	170	340	510	686	70	18	15	33	75	....	1983-84	1996-
Fleming, Gerry	Mtl.	2	11	0	0	0	42	....	....	....	....	....	....	1993-94	1994-
• Fleming, Reggie	Mtl., Chi., Bos., NYR, Phi., Buf.	12	749	108	132	240	1468	50	3	6	9	106	1	1959-60	1970-
Flesch, John	Min., Pit., Col.	4	124	18	23	41	117	....	....	....	....	....	....	1974-75	1979-
Fletcher, Steven	Mtl., Wpg.	2	3	0	0	0	5	1	0	0	0	5	....	1987-88	1988-
• Flett, Bill	L.A., Phi., Tor., Atl., Edm.	11	689	202	215	417	501	52	7	16	23	42	1	1967-68	1979-
Fleury, Theoren	Cgy., Col., NYR, Chi.	15	1084	455	633	1088	1840	77	34	45	79	116	1	1988-89	2002-
Flichel, Todd	Wpg.	3	6	0	1	1	4	....	....	....	....	....	....	1987-88	1989-
Flockhart, Rob	Van., Min.	5	55	2	5	7	14	1	1	0	1	2	....	1976-77	1980-
Flockhart, Ron	Phi., Pit., Mtl., St.L., Bos.	9	453	145	183	328	208	19	4	6	10	14	....	1980-81	1988-
Floyd, Larry	N.J.	2	12	2	3	5	9	....	....	....	....	....	....	1982-83	1983-
Focht, Dan	Phx., Pit.	3	82	2	6	8	145	1	0	1	1	0	....	2001-02	2003-
• Fogarty, Bryan	Que., Pit., Mtl.	6	156	22	52	74	119	....	....	....	....	....	....	1989-90	1994-
• Fogolin, Lee	Det., Chi.	9	427	10	48	58	575	28	0	2	2	30	1	1947-48	1955-
Fogolin, Lee	Buf., Edm.	13	924	44	195	239	1318	108	5	19	24	173	2	1974-75	1986-
Folco, Peter	Van.	1	2	0	0	0	0	....	....	....	....	....	....	1973-74	1973-
Foley, Gerry	Tor., NYR, L.A.	4	142	9	14	23	99	9	0	1	1	2	....	1954-55	1968-
Foley, Rick	Chi., Phi., Det.	3	67	11	26	37	180	4	0	1	1	4	....	1970-71	1973-
Foligno, Mike	Det., Buf., Tor., Fla.	15	1018	355	372	727	2049	57	15	17	32	185	....	1979-80	1993-
Folk, Bill	Det.	2	12	0	0	0	4	....	....	....	....	....	....	1951-52	1952-

Name	NHL Teams	NHL Seasons	Regular Schedule GP	G	A	TP	PIM	Playoffs GP	G	A	TP	PIM	NHL Cup Wins	First NHL Season	Last NHL Season
ontaine, Len	Det.	2	46	8	11	19	10	....	....	....	....	....	....	1972-73	1973-74
ontas, Jon	Min.	2	2	0	0	0	0	....	....	....	....	....	....	1979-80	1980-81
onteyne, Val	Det., NYR, Pit.	13	820	75	154	229	26	59	3	10	13	8	....	1959-60	1971-72
ontinato, Lou	NYR, Mtl.	9	535	26	78	104	1247	21	0	2	2	42	....	1954-55	1962-63
orbes, Colin	Phi., T.B., Ott., NYR, Wsh.	9	311	33	28	61	213	13	1	0	1	16	....	1996-97	2005-06
orbes, Dave	Bos., Wsh.	6	363	64	64	128	341	45	1	4	5	13	....	1973-74	1978-79
orbes, Mike	Bos., Edm.	3	50	1	11	12	41	....	....	....	....	....	....	1977-78	1981-82
orey, Connie	St.L.	1	4	0	0	0	2	....	....	....	....	....	....	1973-74	1973-74
orsberg, Peter	Que., Col., Phi., Nsh.	13	706	249	636	885	686	151	64	107	171	163	2	1994-95	2007-08
orsey, Jack	Tor.	1	19	7	9	16	10	3	0	1	1	0	....	1942-43	1942-43
orslund, Gus	Ott.	1	48	4	9	13	2	....	....	....	....	....	....	1932-33	1932-33
orslund, Tomas	Cgy.	2	44	5	11	16	12	....	....	....	....	....	....	1991-92	1992-93
orsyth, Alex	Wsh.	1	1	0	0	0	0	....	....	....	....	....	....	1976-77	1976-77
ortier, Dave	Tor., NYI, Van.	4	205	8	21	29	335	20	0	2	2	33	....	1972-73	1976-77
ortier, Marc	Que., Ott., L.A.	6	212	42	60	102	135	....	....	....	....	....	....	1987-88	1992-93
ortin, Jean-Francois	Wsh.	3	71	1	4	5	42	....	....	....	....	....	....	2001-02	2003-04
ortin, Ray	St.L.	3	92	2	6	8	33	6	0	0	0	8	....	1967-68	1969-70
oster, Corey	N.J., Phi., Pit., NYI	4	45	5	6	11	24	3	0	0	0	4	....	1988-89	1996-97
oster, Dwight	Bos., Col., N.J., Det.	10	541	111	163	274	420	35	5	12	17	4	....	1977-78	1986-87
oster, Herb	NYR	2	6	1	0	1	5	....	....	....	....	....	....	1940-41	1947-48
oster, Yip	NYR, Bos., Det.	4	83	3	2	5	32	....	....	....	....	....	....	1929-30	1934-35
otiu, Nick	NYR, Hfd., Cgy., Phi., Edm.	13	646	60	77	137	1362	38	0	4	4	67	....	1976-77	1988-89
owler, Jimmy	Tor.	3	135	18	29	47	39	18	0	3	3	2	....	1936-37	1938-39
owler, Tom	Chi.	1	24	0	1	1	18	....	....	....	....	....	....	1946-47	1946-47
ox, Greg	Atl., Chi., Pit.	8	494	14	92	106	637	44	1	9	10	67	....	1977-78	1984-85
ox, Jim	L.A.	9	578	186	293	479	143	22	4	8	12	0	....	1980-81	1989-90
oy, Matt	Min.	3	56	6	7	13	48	1	0	0	0	0	....	2005-06	2007-08
oyston, Frank	Det.	2	64	17	7	24	32	....	....	....	....	....	....	1926-27	1927-28
rampton, Bob	Mtl.	1	2	0	0	0	0	3	0	0	0	0	....	1949-50	1949-50
ranceschetti, Lou	Wsh., Tor., Buf.	10	459	59	81	140	747	44	3	2	5	111	....	1981-82	1991-92
rancis, Bobby	Det.	1	14	2	0	2	0	....	....	....	....	....	....	1982-83	1982-83
rancis, Ron	Hfd., Pit., Car., Tor.	23	1731	549	1249	1798	979	171	46	97	143	95	2	1981-82	2003-04
raser, Archie	NYR	1	3	0	1	1	0	....	....	....	....	....	....	1943-44	1943-44
raser, Charles	Ham.	1	1	0	0	0	0	....	....	....	....	....	....	1923-24	1923-24
raser, Curt	Van., Chi., Min.	12	704	193	240	433	1306	65	15	18	33	198	....	1978-79	1989-90
raser, Gord	Chi., Det., Mtl., Pit., Phi.	5	144	24	12	36	224	2	1	0	1	6	....	1926-27	1930-31
raser, Harvey	Chi.	1	21	5	4	9	0	....	....	....	....	....	....	1944-45	1944-45
raser, Iain	NYI, Que., Dal., Edm., Wpg., S.J.	5	94	23	23	46	31	4	0	0	0	0	....	1992-93	1996-97
raser, Scott	Mtl., Edm., NYR	3	72	16	15	31	24	11	1	1	2	0	....	1995-96	1998-99
rawley, Dan	Chi., Pit.	6	273	37	40	77	674	1	0	0	0	0	....	1983-84	1988-89
readrich, Kyle	T.B.	2	23	0	1	1	75	....	....	....	....	....	....	1999-00	2000-01
redrickson, Frank	Det., Bos., Pit.	5	161	39	34	73	206	10	2	3	5	24	....	1926-27	1930-31
reer, Mark	Phi., Ott., Cgy.	7	124	16	23	39	61	....	....	....	....	....	....	1986-87	1993-94
rew, Irv	Mtl.M., St.L., Mtl.	3	96	2	5	7	146	4	0	0	0	6	....	1933-34	1935-36
riday, Tim	Det.	1	23	0	3	3	6	....	....	....	....	....	....	1985-86	1985-86
ridgen, Dan	Hfd.	2	13	2	3	5	2	....	....	....	....	....	....	1981-82	1982-83
riedman, Doug	Edm., Nsh.	2	18	0	1	1	34	....	....	....	....	....	....	1997-98	1998-99
riesen, Jeff	S.J., Ana., N.J., Wsh., Cgy.	12	893	218	298	516	488	84	18	15	33	48	1	1994-95	2006-07
riest, Ron	Min.	3	64	7	7	14	191	6	1	0	1	7	....	1980-81	1982-83
rig, Len	Chi., Cal., Cle., St.L.	7	311	13	51	64	479	14	2	1	3	0	....	1972-73	1979-80
ritsch, Jamie	Phi.	1	1	0	0	0	0	....	....	....	....	....	....	2008-09	2008-09
rost, Harry	Bos.	1	4	0	0	0	0	1	0	0	0	0	1	1938-39	1938-39
rycer, Miroslav	Que., Tor., Det., Edm.	8	415	147	183	330	486	17	3	8	11	16	....	1981-82	1988-89
ryday, Bob	Mtl.	2	5	1	0	1	0	....	....	....	....	....	....	1949-50	1951-52
torek, Robbie	Det., Que., NYR	8	334	77	150	227	262	19	9	6	15	28	....	1972-73	1984-85
ullan, Larry	Wsh.	1	4	1	0	1	0	....	....	....	....	....	....	1974-75	1974-75
usco, Mark	Hfd.	2	80	3	12	15	42	....	....	....	....	....	....	1983-84	1984-85
ussey, Owen	Wsh.	1	4	0	1	1	0	....	....	....	....	....	....	2003-04	2003-04
G															
adsby, Bill	Chi., NYR, Det.	20	1248	130	438	568	1539	67	4	23	27	92	....	1946-47	1965-66
aetz, Link	Min., S.J.	3	65	6	8	14	412	....	....	....	....	....	....	1988-89	1991-92
age, Jody	Det., Buf.	6	68	14	15	29	26	....	....	....	....	....	....	1980-81	1991-92
agne, Art	Mtl., Bos., Ott., Det.	6	228	67	33	100	257	11	2	1	3	20	....	1926-27	1931-32
agne, Paul	Col., N.J., Tor., NYI	8	390	110	101	211	127	....	....	....	....	....	....	1980-81	1989-90
agne, Pierre	Bos.	1	2	0	0	0	0	....	....	....	....	....	....	1959-60	1959-60
agner, Dave	NYR, Min., Dal., Tor., Cgy., Fla., Van.	15	946	318	401	719	1018	57	22	26	48	64	....	1984-85	1998-99
agnon, Germain	Mtl., NYI, Chi., K.C.	5	259	40	101	141	72	19	2	3	5	2	....	1971-72	1975-76
agnon, Johnny	Mtl., Bos., NYA	10	454	120	141	261	295	32	12	12	24	37	1	1930-31	1939-40
agnon, Sean	Phx., Ott.	3	12	0	1	1	34	....	....	....	....	....	....	1997-98	2000-01
ainey, Bob	Mtl.	16	1160	239	262	501	585	182	25	48	73	151	5	1973-74	1988-89
ainey, Steve	Dal., Phx.	4	33	0	2	2	34	....	....	....	....	....	....	2000-01	2005-06
ainor, Dutch	Bos., NYR, Ott., Mtl.M.	7	246	51	56	107	129	22	2	1	3	14	2	1927-28	1934-35
alanov, Maxim	NYR, Pit., Atl., T.B.	4	122	8	12	20	44	1	0	0	0	0	....	1997-98	2000-01
alarneau, Michel	Hfd.	3	78	7	10	17	34	....	....	....	....	....	....	1980-81	1982-83
albraith, Percy	Bos., Ott.	8	347	29	31	60	224	31	4	7	11	24	1	1926-27	1933-34
allagher, John	Mtl.M., Det., NYA	7	205	14	19	33	153	24	2	3	5	27	1	1930-31	1938-39
allant, Gerard	Det., T.B.	11	615	211	269	480	1674	58	18	21	39	178	....	1984-85	1994-95
alley, Garry	L.A., Wsh., Bos., Phi., Buf., NYI	17	1149	125	475	600	1218	89	7	23	30	119	....	1984-85	2000-01
allimore, Jamie	Min.	1	2	0	0	0	0	....	....	....	....	....	....	1977-78	1977-78
allinger, Don	Bos.	5	222	65	88	153	89	23	5	5	10	19	....	1942-43	1947-48
amache, Simon	Atl., Nsh., St.L., Tor.	4	48	6	7	13	18	....	....	....	....	....	....	2002-03	2007-08
amble, Dick	Mtl., Chi., Tor.	8	195	41	41	82	66	14	1	2	3	4	1	1950-51	1966-67
ambucci, Gary	Min.	2	51	2	7	9	9	....	....	....	....	....	....	1971-72	1973-74
anchar, Perry	St.L., Mtl., Pit.	4	42	3	7	10	36	7	3	1	4	0	....	1983-84	1988-89
ans, Dave	L.A.	2	6	0	0	0	2	....	....	....	....	....	....	1982-83	1985-86
ardiner, Bruce	Ott., T.B., CBJ, N.J.	6	312	34	54	88	263	21	1	4	5	8	....	1996-97	2001-02
ardiner, Herb	Mtl., Chi.	3	108	10	9	19	52	9	0	1	1	16	....	1926-27	1928-29
ardner, Bill	Chi., Hfd.	9	380	73	115	188	68	45	3	8	11	17	....	1980-81	1988-89
ardner, Cal	NYR, Tor., Chi., Bos.	12	696	154	238	392	517	61	7	10	17	20	2	1945-46	1956-57
ardner, Dave	Mtl., St.L., Cal., Cle., Phi.	7	350	75	115	190	41	....	....	....	....	....	....	1972-73	1979-80
ardner, Paul	Col., Tor., Pit., Wsh., Buf.	10	447	201	201	402	207	16	2	6	8	14	....	1976-77	1985-86
are, Danny	Buf., Det., Edm.	13	827	354	331	685	1285	64	25	21	46	195	....	1974-75	1986-87
ariepy, Ray	Bos., Tor.	2	36	1	6	7	43	....	....	....	....	....	....	1953-54	1955-56
arland, Scott	Tor., L.A.	3	91	13	24	37	115	7	1	2	3	35	....	1975-76	1978-79
arner, Rob	Pit.	1	1	0	0	0	0	....	....	....	....	....	....	1982-83	1982-83
arpenlov, Johan	Det., S.J., Fla., Atl.	10	609	114	197	311	276	44	10	9	19	22	....	1990-91	1999-00
arrett, Red	NYR	1	23	1	1	2	18	....	....	....	....	....	....	1942-43	1942-43
artner, Mike	Wsh., Min., NYR, Tor., Phx.	19	1432	708	627	1335	1159	122	43	50	93	125	....	1979-80	1997-98
assoff, Bob	St.L.	4	245	11	47	58	866	9	0	1	1	16	....	1973-74	1976-77
assoff, Brad	Van.	4	122	19	17	36	163	3	0	0	0	0	....	1975-76	1978-79
atzos, Steve	Pit.	4	89	15	20	35	83	1	0	0	0	0	....	1981-82	1984-85
audreau, Rob	S.J., Ott.	4	231	51	54	105	69	14	2	0	2	0	....	1992-93	1995-96
audreault, Armand	Bos.	1	44	15	9	24	27	7	0	2	2	8	....	1944-45	1944-45
audreault, Leo	Mtl.	3	67	8	4	12	30	....	....	....	....	....	....	1927-28	1932-33
aul, Mike	Col., CBJ	2	3	0	0	0	4	....	....	....	....	....	....	1998-99	2000-01
aulin, Jean-Marc	Que.	4	26	4	3	7	8	1	0	0	0	0	....	1982-83	1985-86
aume, Dallas	Hfd.	1	4	1	1	2	0	....	....	....	....	....	....	1988-89	1988-89
authier, Art	Mtl.	1	13	0	0	0	0	1	0	0	0	0	....	1926-27	1926-27
authier, Daniel	Chi.	1	5	0	0	0	0	....	....	....	....	....	....	1994-95	1994-95
authier, Denis	Cgy., Phx., Phi., L.A.	10	554	17	60	77	748	12	0	2	2	23	....	1997-98	2008-09
authier, Fern	NYR, Mtl., Det.	6	229	46	50	96	35	22	5	1	6	7	....	1943-44	1948-49
authier, Jean	Mtl., Phi., Bos.	10	166	6	29	35	150	14	1	3	4	22	1	1960-61	1969-70
authier, Luc	Mtl.	1	3	0	0	0	2	....	....	....	....	....	....	1990-91	1990-91
auvreau, Jocelyn	Mtl.	1	2	0	0	0	0	....	....	....	....	....	....	1983-84	1983-84
avey, Aaron	T.B., Cgy., Dal., Min., Tor., Ana.	9	360	41	50	91	272	19	1	2	3	14	....	1995-96	2005-06
avin, Stew	Tor., Hfd., Min.	13	768	130	155	285	584	66	14	20	34	75	....	1980-81	1992-93
eale, Bob	Pit.	1	1	0	0	0	2	....	....	....	....	....	....	1984-85	1984-85
ee, George	Chi., Det.	9	551	135	183	318	345	41	6	13	19	32	1	1945-46	1953-54
eldart, Gary	Min.	1	4	0	0	0	5	....	....	....	....	....	....	1970-71	1970-71
elinas, Martin	Edm., Que., Van., Car., Cgy., Fla., Nsh.	19	1273	309	351	660	820	147	23	33	56	120	1	1988-89	2007-08
endron, Jean-Guy	NYR, Bos., Mtl., Phi.	14	863	182	201	383	701	42	7	4	11	47	....	1955-56	1971-72
endron, Martin	Wsh., Chi.	3	30	4	2	6	10	....	....	....	....	....	....	1994-95	1997-98
eoffrion, Bernie	Mtl., NYR	16	883	393	429	822	689	132	58	60	118	88	6	1950-51	1967-68
eoffrion, Danny	Mtl., Wpg.	3	111	20	32	52	99	2	0	0	0	7	....	1979-80	1981-82

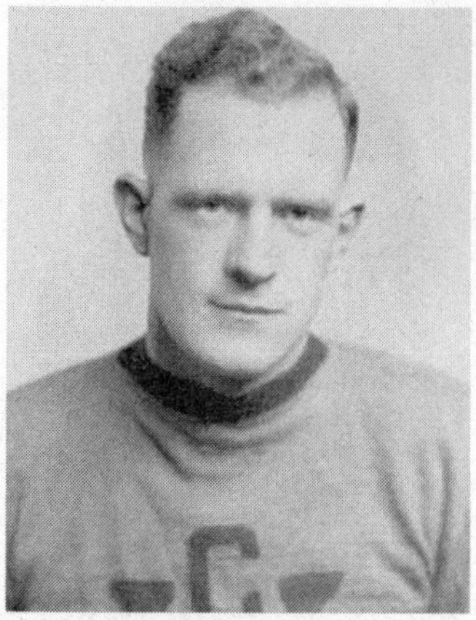

Gord Fraser

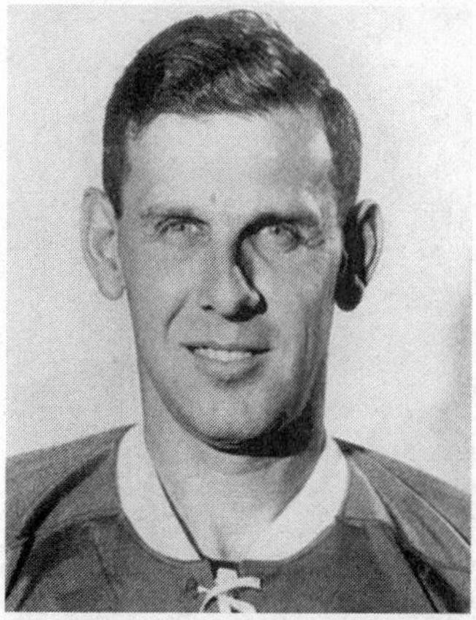

Dick Gamble

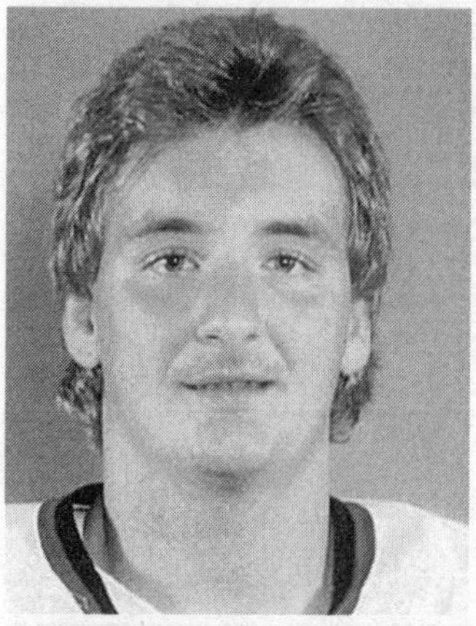

Bill Gardner

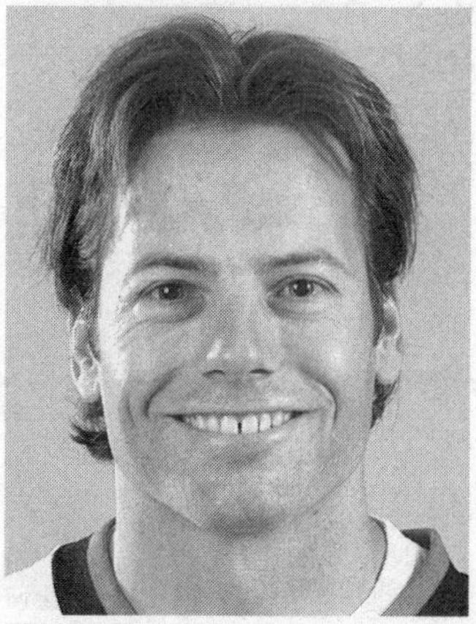

Martin Gelinas

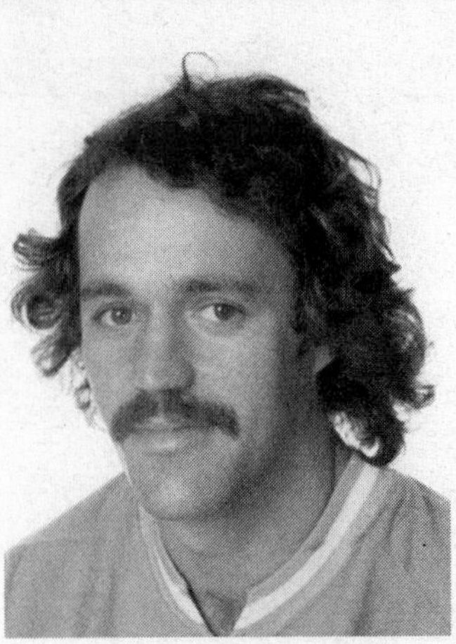

Bob Girard

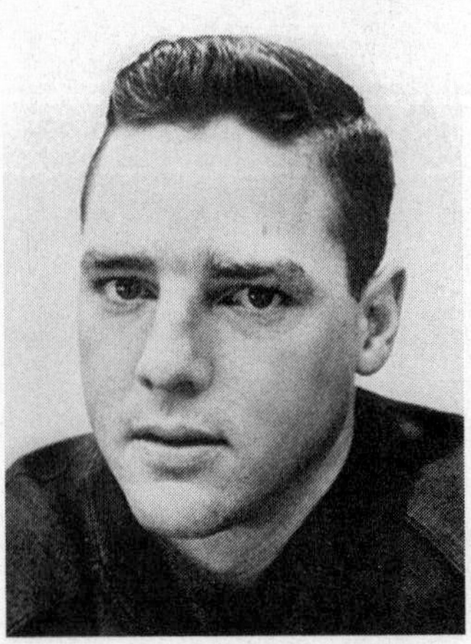

Howie Glover

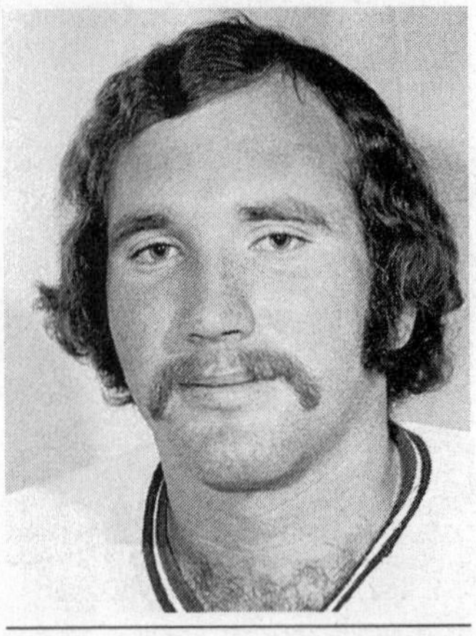

Larry Gould

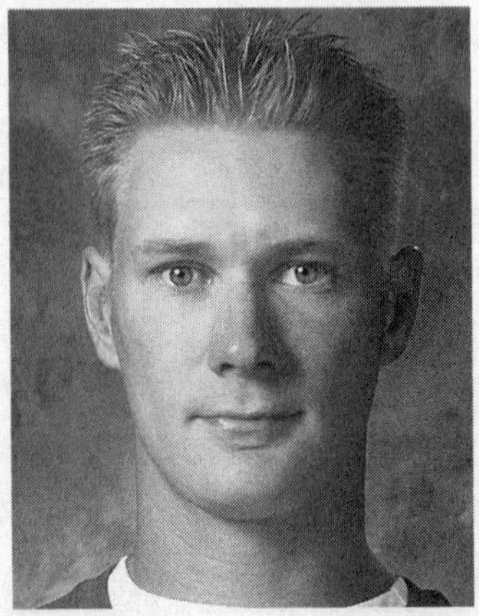

Chris Gratton

Name	NHL Teams	NHL Seasons	Regular Schedule GP	G	A	TP	PIM	Playoffs GP	G	A	TP	PIM	NHL Cup Wins	First NHL Season	Last NHL Season
• Geran, Gerry	Mtl.W., Bos.	2	37	5	1	6	6	....	....	....	....	....	....	1917-18	1925-26
• Gerard, Eddie	Ott.	6	128	50	48	98	108	11	4	0	4	17	3	1917-18	1922-23
Germain, Eric	L.A.	1	4	0	1	1	13	1	0	0	0	4	....	1987-88	1987-88
Gernander, Ken	NYR	3	12	2	3	5	6	15	0	0	0	0	....	1995-96	2003-04
• Getliffe, Ray	Bos., Mtl.	10	393	136	137	273	250	45	9	10	19	30	2	1935-36	1944-45
Giallonardo, Mario	Col.	2	23	0	3	3	6	....	....	....	....	....	....	1979-80	1980-81
Gibbs, Barry	Bos., Min., Atl:, St.L., L.A.	13	797	58	224	282	945	36	4	2	6	67	....	1967-68	1979-80
Gibson, Don	Van.	1	14	0	3	3	20	....	....	....	....	....	....	1990-91	1990-91
Gibson, Doug	Bos., Wsh.	3	63	9	19	28	0	1	0	0	0	0	....	1973-74	1977-78
Gibson, John	L.A., Tor., Wpg.	3	48	0	2	2	120	....	....	....	....	....	....	1980-81	1983-84
• Giesebrecht, Gus	Det.	4	135	27	51	78	13	17	2	3	5	0	....	1938-39	1941-42
Giffin, Lee	Pit.	2	27	1	3	4	9	....	....	....	....	....	....	1986-87	1987-88
Gilbert, Ed	K.C., Pit.	3	166	21	31	52	22	....	....	....	....	....	....	1974-75	1976-77
Gilbert, Greg	NYI, Chi., NYR, St.L.	15	837	150	228	378	576	133	17	33	50	162	3	1981-82	1995-96
Gilbert, Jeannot	Bos.	2	9	0	1	1	4	....	....	....	....	....	....	1962-63	1964-65
Gilbert, Rod	NYR	18	1065	406	615	1021	508	79	34	33	67	43	....	1960-61	1977-78
Gilbertson, Stan	Cal., St.L., Wsh., Pit.	6	428	85	89	174	148	3	1	1	2	2	....	1971-72	1976-77
Gilchrist, Brent	Mtl., Edm., Min., Dal., Det., Nsh.	15	792	135	170	305	400	90	17	14	31	48	1	1988-89	2002-03
Giles, Curt	Min., NYR, St.L.	14	895	43	199	242	733	103	6	16	22	118	....	1979-80	1992-93
Gilhen, Randy	Hfd., Wpg., Pit., L.A., NYR, T.B., Fla.	11	457	55	60	115	314	33	3	2	5	26	1	1982-83	1995-96
Gill, Todd	Tor., S.J., St.L., Det., Phx., Col., Chi.	19	1007	82	272	354	1214	103	7	30	37	193	....	1984-85	2002-03
Gillen, Don	Phi., Hfd.	2	35	2	4	6	22	....	....	....	....	....	....	1979-80	1981-82
• Gillie, Farrand	Det.	1	1	0	0	0	0	....	....	....	....	....	....	1928-29	1928-29
Gillies, Clark	NYI, Buf.	14	958	319	378	697	1023	164	47	47	94	287	4	1974-75	1987-88
Gillis, Jere	Van., NYR, Que., Buf., Phi.	9	386	78	95	173	230	19	4	7	11	9	....	1977-78	1986-87
Gillis, Mike	Col., Bos.	6	246	33	43	76	186	27	2	5	7	10	....	1978-79	1983-84
Gillis, Paul	Que., Chi., Hfd.	11	624	88	154	242	1498	42	3	14	17	156	....	1982-83	1992-93
Gilmour, Doug	St.L., Cgy., Tor., N.J., Chi., Buf., Mtl.	20	1474	450	964	1414	1301	182	60	128	188	235	1	1983-84	2002-03
Gingras, Gaston	Mtl., Tor., St.L.	10	476	61	174	235	161	52	6	18	24	20	1	1979-80	1988-89
Girard, Bob	Cal., Cle., Wsh.	5	305	45	69	114	140	....	....	....	....	....	....	1975-76	1979-80
Girard, Jonathan	Bos.	5	150	10	34	44	46	3	0	1	1	2	....	1998-99	2002-03
Girard, Kenny	Tor.	3	7	0	1	1	2	....	....	....	....	....	....	1956-57	1959-60
• Giroux, Art	Mtl., Bos., Det.	3	54	6	4	10	14	2	0	0	0	0	....	1932-33	1935-36
Giroux, Larry	St.L., K.C., Det., Hfd.	7	274	15	74	89	333	5	0	0	0	4	....	1973-74	1979-80
Giroux, Pierre	L.A.	1	6	1	0	1	17	....	....	....	....	....	....	1982-83	1982-83
‡ Giroux, Raymond	NYI, N.J.	4	38	0	13	13	22	4	0	0	0	0	....	1999-00	2003-04
‡ Giuliano, Jeff	L.A.	2	101	3	10	13	40	....	....	....	....	....	....	2005-06	2007-08
Gladney, Bob	L.A., Pit.	2	14	1	5	6	4	....	....	....	....	....	....	1982-83	1983-84
Gladu, Jean-Paul	Bos.	1	40	6	14	20	2	7	2	2	4	0	....	1944-45	1944-45
Glennie, Brian	Tor., L.A.	10	572	14	100	114	621	32	0	1	1	66	....	1969-70	1978-79
Glennon, Matt	Bos.	1	3	0	0	0	2	....	....	....	....	....	....	1991-92	1991-92
‡ Globke, Rob	Fla.	3	46	1	1	2	8	....	....	....	....	....	....	2005-06	2007-08
Gloeckner, Lorry	Det.	1	13	0	2	2	6	....	....	....	....	....	....	1978-79	1978-79
Gloor, Dan	Van.	1	2	0	0	0	0	....	....	....	....	....	....	1973-74	1973-74
• Glover, Fred	Det., Chi.	5	92	13	11	24	62	8	0	0	0	0	1	1948-49	1952-5
Glover, Howie	Chi., Det., NYR, Mtl.	5	144	29	17	46	101	11	1	2	3	2	....	1958-59	1968-69
Glynn, Brian	Cgy., Min., Edm., Ott., Van., Hfd.	10	431	25	79	104	410	57	6	10	16	40	....	1987-88	1996-9
‡ Goc, Sascha	N.J., T.B.	2	22	0	0	0	4	....	....	....	....	....	....	2000-01	2001-02
Godden, Ernie	Tor.	1	5	1	1	2	6	....	....	....	....	....	....	1981-82	1981-82
• Godfrey, Warren	Bos., Det.	16	786	32	125	157	752	52	1	4	5	42	....	1952-53	1967-68
Godin, Eddy	Wsh.	2	27	3	6	9	12	....	....	....	....	....	....	1977-78	1978-79
• Godin, Sam	Ott., Mtl.	3	83	4	3	7	36	....	....	....	....	....	....	1927-28	1933-3
Godynyuk, Alexander	Tor., Cgy., Fla., Hfd.	7	223	10	39	49	224	....	....	....	....	....	....	1990-91	1996-9
• Goegan, Pete	Det., NYR, Min.	11	383	19	67	86	365	33	1	3	4	61	....	1957-58	1967-68
Goertz, Dave	Pit.	1	2	0	0	0	2	....	....	....	....	....	....	1987-88	1987-88
• Goldham, Bob	Tor., Chi., Det.	12	650	28	143	171	400	66	3	14	17	53	5	1941-42	1955-5
Goldmann, Erich	Ott.	1	1	0	0	0	0	....	....	....	....	....	....	1999-00	1999-0
• Goldsworthy, Bill	Bos., Min., NYR	14	771	283	258	541	793	40	18	19	37	30	....	1964-65	1977-7
• Goldsworthy, Leroy	NYR, Det., Chi., Mtl., Bos., NYA	10	336	66	57	123	79	24	1	0	1	4	1	1928-29	1938-3
Goldup, Glenn	Mtl., L.A.	9	291	52	67	119	303	16	4	3	7	22	....	1973-74	1981-8
• Goldup, Hank	Tor., NYR	6	202	63	80	143	97	26	5	1	6	6	1	1939-40	1945-4
Golubovsky, Yan	Det., Fla.	4	56	1	7	8	32	....	....	....	....	....	....	1997-98	2000-0
Goneau, Daniel	NYR	3	53	12	3	15	14	....	....	....	....	....	....	1996-97	1999-0
• Gooden, Bill	NYR	2	53	9	11	20	15	....	....	....	....	....	....	1942-43	1943-4
Goodenough, Larry	Phi., Van.	6	242	22	77	99	179	22	3	15	18	10	1	1974-75	1979-8
• Goodfellow, Ebbie	Det.	14	557	134	190	324	511	45	8	8	16	65	3	1929-30	1942-4
Gordiouk, Viktor	Buf.	2	26	3	8	11	0	....	....	....	....	....	....	1992-93	1994-9
• Gordon, Fred	Det., Bos.	2	81	8	7	15	68	2	0	0	0	0	....	1926-27	1927-2
Gordon, Jack	NYR	3	36	3	10	13	0	9	1	1	2	7	....	1948-49	1950-5
Gordon, Robb	Van.	1	4	0	0	0	2	....	....	....	....	....	....	1998-99	1998-9
‡ Goren, Lee	Bos., Fla., Van.	5	67	5	4	9	44	5	0	0	0	5	....	2000-01	2006-0
Gorence, Tom	Phi., Edm.	6	303	58	53	111	89	37	9	6	15	47	....	1978-79	1983-8
Goring, Butch	L.A., NYI, Bos.	16	1107	375	513	888	102	134	38	50	88	32	4	1969-70	1984-8
Gorman, Dave	Atl.	1	3	0	0	0	0	....	....	....	....	....	....	1979-80	1979-8
• Gorman, Ed	Ott., Tor.	4	111	14	6	20	108	8	0	0	0	2	1	1924-25	1927-2
Gosselin, Benoit	NYR	1	7	0	0	0	33	....	....	....	....	....	....	1977-78	1977-7
Gosselin, David	Nsh.	2	13	2	1	3	11	....	....	....	....	....	....	1999-00	2001-0
Gosselin, Guy	Wpg.	1	5	0	0	0	6	....	....	....	....	....	....	1987-88	1987-8
Gotaas, Steve	Pit., Min.	3	49	6	9	15	53	3	0	1	1	5	....	1987-88	1990-9
• Gottselig, Johnny	Chi.	16	589	176	195	371	203	43	13	13	26	18	2	1928-29	1944-4
Gould, Bobby	Atl., Cgy., Wsh., Bos.	11	697	145	159	304	572	78	15	13	28	58	....	1979-80	1989-9
Gould, John	Buf., Van., Atl.	9	504	131	138	269	113	14	3	2	5	4	....	1971-72	1979-8
Gould, Larry	Van.	1	2	0	0	0	0	....	....	....	....	....	....	1973-74	1973-7
Goulet, Michel	Que., Chi.	15	1089	548	604	1152	825	92	39	39	78	110	....	1979-80	1993-9
• Goupille, Red	Mtl.	8	222	12	28	40	256	8	2	0	2	6	....	1935-36	1942-4
Gove, David	Car.	2	2	0	1	1	0	....	....	....	....	....	....	2005-06	2006-0
Govedaris, Chris	Hfd., Tor.	4	45	4	6	10	24	4	0	0	0	2	....	1989-90	1993-9
Goyer, Gerry	Chi.	1	40	1	2	3	4	3	0	0	0	2	....	1967-68	1967-6
Goyette, Phil	Mtl., NYR, St.L., Buf.	16	941	207	467	674	131	94	17	29	46	26	4	1956-57	1971-7
• Graboski, Tony	Mtl.	3	66	6	10	16	24	3	0	0	0	6	....	1940-41	1942-4
• Gracie, Bob	Tor., Bos., NYA, Mtl.M., Mtl., Chi.	9	379	82	109	191	205	33	4	7	11	4	2	1930-31	1938-3
Gradin, Thomas	Van., Bos.	9	677	209	384	593	298	42	17	25	42	20	....	1978-79	1986-8
Graham, Dirk	Min., Chi.	12	772	219	270	489	917	90	17	27	44	92	....	1983-84	1994-9
• Graham, Leth	Ott., Ham.	6	27	3	0	3	0	1	0	0	0	0	1	1920-21	1925-2
Graham, Pat	Pit., Tor.	3	103	11	17	28	136	4	0	0	0	2	....	1981-82	1983-8
Graham, Rod	Bos.	1	14	2	1	3	7	....	....	....	....	....	....	1974-75	1974-7
• Graham, Ted	Chi., Mtl.M., Det., St.L., Bos., NYA	9	346	14	25	39	300	24	3	1	4	30	....	1927-28	1936-3
Granato, Tony	NYR, L.A., S.J.	13	773	248	244	492	1425	79	16	27	43	141	....	1988-89	2000-0
‡ Grand-Pierre, Jean-Luc	Buf., CBJ, Atl., Wsh.	6	269	7	13	20	311	4	0	0	0	4	....	1998-99	2003-0
Grant, Danny	Mtl., Min., Det., L.A.	13	736	263	273	536	239	43	10	14	24	19	1	1965-66	1978-7
‡ Gratton, Benoit	Wsh., Cgy., Mtl.	6	58	6	10	16	58	....	....	....	....	....	....	1997-98	2003-0
Gratton, Chris	T.B., Phi., Buf., Phx., Col., Fla., CBJ	15	1092	214	354	568	1638	40	8	7	15	82	....	1993-94	2008-0
Gratton, Dan	L.A.	1	7	1	0	1	5	....	....	....	....	....	....	1987-88	1987-8
Gratton, Norm	NYR, Atl., Buf., Min.	5	201	39	44	83	64	6	0	1	1	2	....	1971-72	1975-7
Gravelle, Leo	Mtl., Det.	5	223	44	34	78	42	17	4	1	5	2	....	1946-47	1950-5
Graves, Adam	Det., Edm., NYR, S.J.	16	1152	329	287	616	1224	125	38	27	65	119	2	1987-88	2002-0
Graves, Hilliard	Cal., Atl., Van., Wpg.	9	556	118	163	281	209	2	0	0	0	0	....	1970-71	1979-8
Graves, Steve	Edm.	3	35	5	4	9	10	....	....	....	....	....	....	1983-84	1987-8
• Gray, Alex	NYR, Tor.	2	50	7	0	7	32	13	1	0	1	0	1	1927-28	1928-2
Gray, Terry	Bos., Mtl., L.A., St.L.	6	147	26	28	54	64	35	5	5	10	22	....	1961-62	1970-7
‡ Green, Mike	Fla., NYR	1	24	1	3	4	4	....	....	....	....	....	....	2003-04	2003-0
• Green, Red	Ham., NYA, Bos., Det.	6	195	59	26	85	290	1	0	0	0	0	1	1923-24	1928-2
Green, Rick	Wsh., Mtl., Det., NYI	15	845	43	220	263	588	100	3	16	19	73	1	1976-77	1991-9
• Green, Shorty	Ham., NYA	4	103	33	20	53	151	....	....	....	....	....	....	1923-24	1926-2
Green, Ted	Bos.	11	620	48	206	254	1029	31	4	8	12	54	1	1960-61	1971-7
Green, Travis	NYI, Ana., Phx., Tor., Bos.	14	970	193	262	455	764	56	10	11	21	60	....	1992-93	2006-0
Greenlaw, Jeff	Wsh., Fla.	6	57	3	6	9	108	2	0	0	0	21	....	1986-87	1993-9
Gregg, Randy	Edm., Van.	10	474	41	152	193	333	137	13	38	51	127	5	1981-82	1991-9
• Greig, Bruce	Cal.	2	9	0	1	1	46	....	....	....	....	....	....	1973-74	1974-7
Greig, Mark	Hfd., Tor., Cgy., Phi.	9	125	13	27	40	90	5	0	1	1	0	....	1990-91	2002-0
Grenier, Lucien	Mtl., L.A.	4	151	14	14	28	18	2	0	0	0	0	....	1968-69	1971-7
‡ Grenier, Martin	Phx., Van., Phi.	4	18	1	0	1	14	....	....	....	....	....	....	2001-02	2006-0
Grenier, Richard	NYI	1	10	1	1	2	2	....	....	....	....	....	....	1972-73	1972-7
Greschner, Ron	NYR	16	982	179	431	610	1226	84	17	32	49	106	....	1974-75	1989-9
Gretzky, Brent	T.B.	2	13	1	3	4	2	....	....	....	....	....	....	1993-94	1994-9
Gretzky, Wayne	Edm., L.A., St.L., NYR	20	1487	894	1963	2857	577	208	122	260	382	66	4	1979-80	1998-9

Name	NHL Teams	NHL Seasons	Regular Schedule GP	G	A	TP	PIM	Playoffs GP	G	A	TP	PIM	NHL Cup Wins	First NHL Season	Last NHL Season
ieve, Brent	NYI, Edm., Chi., L.A.	4	97	20	16	36	87	....	....	....	....	....	....	1993-94	1996-97
igor, George	Chi.	1	2	1	0	1	0	1	0	0	0	0	....	1943-44	1943-44
imson, Stu	Cgy., Chi., Ana., Det., Hfd., Car., L.A., Nsh.	14	729	17	22	39	2113	42	1	1	2	120	....	1988-89	2001-02
sdale, John	Tor., Van.	6	250	4	39	43	346	10	0	1	1	15	....	1972-73	1978-79
oleau, Francois	Mtl.	3	8	0	1	1	6	....	....	....	....	....	....	1995-96	1997-98
on, Stanislav	N.J.	1	1	0	0	0	0	....	....	....	....	....	....	2000-01	2000-01
onman, Tuomas	Chi., Pit.	2	38	1	3	4	38	1	0	0	0	0	....	1996-97	1997-98
onsdahl, Lloyd	Bos.	1	10	1	2	3	0	....	....	....	....	....	....	1941-42	1941-42
onstrand, Jari	Min., NYR, Que., NYI	5	185	8	26	34	135	3	0	0	0	4	....	1986-87	1990-91
osek, Michal	Wpg., Buf., Chi., NYR, Bos.	11	526	84	137	221	509	45	9	11	20	77	....	1993-94	2003-04
oss, Lloyd	Tor., NYA, Bos., Det.	3	52	11	5	16	20	1	0	0	0	0	....	1926-27	1934-35
osso, Don	Det., Chi., Bos.	9	336	87	117	204	90	48	15	14	29	63	1	1938-39	1946-47
osvenor, Len	Ott., NYA, Mtl.	6	149	9	11	20	78	4	0	0	0	2	....	1927-28	1932-33
oulx, Wayne	Que.	1	1	0	0	0	0	....	....	....	....	....	....	1984-85	1984-85
uden, John	Bos., Ott., Wsh.	6	92	1	8	9	46	3	0	1	1	0	....	1993-94	2003-04
uen, Danny	Det., Col.	3	49	9	13	22	19	....	....	....	....	....	....	1972-73	1976-77
uhl, Scott	L.A., Pit.	3	20	3	3	6	6	....	....	....	....	....	....	1981-82	1987-88
yp, Bob	Bos., Wsh.	3	74	11	13	24	33	....	....	....	....	....	....	1973-74	1975-76
ay, Francois	Buf.	1	1	0	0	0	0	....	....	....	....	....	....	1989-90	1989-90
ay, Paul	Phi., L.A., Bos., NYI	7	117	11	23	34	92	9	0	1	1	12	....	1983-84	1990-91
erard, Daniel	Ott.	1	2	0	0	0	0	....	....	....	....	....	....	1994-95	1994-95
erard, Stephane	Que.	2	34	0	0	0	40	....	....	....	....	....	....	1987-88	1989-90
evremont, Jocelyn	Van., Buf., NYR	9	571	84	223	307	319	40	4	17	21	18	....	1971-72	1979-80
idolin, Aldo	NYR	4	182	9	15	24	117	....	....	....	....	....	....	1952-53	1955-56
idolin, Bep	Bos., Det., Chi.	9	519	107	171	278	606	24	5	7	12	35	....	1942-43	1951-52
indon, Bobby	Wpg.	1	6	0	1	1	0	....	....	....	....	....	....	1979-80	1979-80
olla, Steve	S.J., T.B., Atl., N.J.	6	205	40	46	86	60	....	....	....	....	....	....	1996-97	2002-03
ren, Miloslav	Mtl.	2	36	1	3	4	16	....	....	....	....	....	....	1998-99	1999-00
sarov, Alexei	Que., Col., NYR, St.L.	11	607	39	128	167	313	68	0	14	14	38	1	1990-91	2000-01
sev, Sergey	Dal., T.B.	4	89	4	10	14	34	....	....	....	....	....	....	1997-98	2000-01
smanov, Ravil	Wpg.	1	4	0	0	0	0	....	....	....	....	....	....	1995-96	1995-96
stafsson, Bengt-Ake	Wsh.	9	629	196	359	555	196	32	9	19	28	16	....	1979-80	1988-89
stafsson, Per	Fla., Tor., Ott.	2	89	8	27	35	38	1	0	0	0	0	....	1996-97	1997-98
stavsson, Peter	Col.	1	2	0	0	0	0	....	....	....	....	....	....	1981-82	1981-82
y, Kevan	Cgy., Van.	6	156	5	20	25	138	5	0	1	1	23	....	1986-87	1991-92
akana, Kari	Edm.	1	13	0	0	0	4	....	....	....	....	....	....	2002-03	2002-03
anpaa, Ari	NYI	3	60	6	11	17	37	6	0	0	0	10	....	1985-86	1987-88
as, David	Edm., Cgy.	2	7	2	1	3	7	....	....	....	....	....	....	1990-91	1993-94
bscheid, Marc	Edm., Min., Det., Cgy.	11	345	72	91	163	171	12	1	3	4	13	....	1981-82	1991-92
chborn, Len	Phi., L.A.	3	102	20	39	59	29	7	0	3	3	7	....	1983-84	1985-86
ddon, Lloyd	Det.	1	8	0	0	0	2	1	0	0	0	0	....	1959-60	1959-60
dfield, Vic	NYR, Pit.	16	1002	323	389	712	1154	73	27	21	48	117	....	1961-62	1976-77
ggarty, Jim	Mtl.	1	5	1	1	2	0	3	2	1	3	0	....	1941-42	1941-42
ggerty, Sean	Tor., NYI, Nsh.	4	14	1	2	3	4	....	....	....	....	....	....	1995-96	2000-01
gglund, Roger	Que.	1	3	0	0	0	0	....	....	....	....	....	....	1984-85	1984-85
gman, Matti	Bos., Edm.	4	237	56	89	145	36	20	5	2	7	6	....	1976-77	1981-82
nl, Riku	Col.	3	92	5	8	13	38	34	2	4	6	4	....	2001-02	2003-04
dy, Gord	Det.	1	....	....	....	....	....	1	0	0	0	0	....	1949-50	1949-50
du, Richard	Buf.	2	5	0	0	0	4	....	....	....	....	....	....	1985-86	1986-87
t, Bill	Buf.	14	854	42	202	244	433	80	2	16	18	70	....	1973-74	1986-87
t, Chris	Edm., Wsh.	2	6	0	0	0	2	....	....	....	....	....	....	2000-01	2003-04
kansson, Anders	Min., Pit., L.A.	5	330	52	46	98	141	6	0	0	0	2	....	1981-82	1985-86
derson, Harold	Det., Tor.	1	44	3	2	5	65	....	....	....	....	....	....	1926-27	1926-27
e, Larry	Phi.	4	196	5	37	42	90	8	0	0	0	12	....	1968-69	1971-72
ey, Len	Det.	2	30	2	2	4	14	6	1	3	4	6	....	1959-60	1960-61
kidis, Bob	Buf., L.A., Tor., Det., T.B., NYI	11	256	8	32	40	825	20	0	1	1	51	....	1984-85	1995-96
ko, Steven	Car.	6	155	0	15	15	71	4	0	0	0	2	....	1997-98	2002-03
l, Bob	NYA	1	8	0	0	0	0	....	....	....	....	....	....	1925-26	1925-26
l, Del	Cal.	3	9	2	0	2	2	....	....	....	....	....	....	1971-72	1973-74
l, Joe	Mtl.	2	37	15	9	24	235	7	0	1	1	38	....	1917-18	1918-19
l, Murray	Chi., Det., Min., Van.	9	164	35	48	83	46	6	0	0	0	0	....	1961-62	1971-72
l, Taylor	Van., Bos.	5	41	7	9	16	29	....	....	....	....	....	....	1983-84	1987-88
l, Wayne	NYR	1	4	0	0	0	0	....	....	....	....	....	....	1960-61	1960-61
ler, Kevin	Buf., Mtl., Phi., Hfd., Car., Ana., NYI	13	642	41	97	138	907	64	7	16	23	71	1	1989-90	2001-02
liday, Milt	Ott.	3	67	1	0	1	4	6	0	0	0	0	1	1926-27	1928-29
lin, Mats	NYI, Min.	5	152	17	14	31	193	15	1	0	1	13	1	1982-83	1986-87
lverson, Trevor	Wsh.	1	17	0	4	4	28	....	....	....	....	....	....	1998-99	1998-99
ward, Doug	Bos., L.A., Van., Det., Edm.	14	653	69	224	293	774	47	7	10	17	113	....	1975-76	1988-89
nel, Gilles	Buf., Wpg., L.A.	9	519	127	147	274	276	27	4	5	9	10	....	1980-81	1988-89
nel, Herb	Tor.	1	2	0	0	0	4	....	....	....	....	....	....	1930-31	1930-31
nel, Jean	St.L., Det., Que., Mtl.	12	699	26	95	121	766	33	0	2	2	44	....	1972-73	1983-84
nill, Red	Bos., Chi.	12	419	128	94	222	160	24	1	2	3	20	1	1937-38	1950-51
nilton, Al	NYR, Buf., Edm.	7	257	10	78	88	258	7	0	0	0	2	....	1965-66	1979-80
nilton, Chuck	Mtl., St.L.	2	4	0	2	2	2	....	....	....	....	....	....	1961-62	1972-73
nilton, Jack	Tor.	3	102	28	32	60	20	11	2	1	3	0	....	1942-43	1945-46
nilton, Jim	Pit.	8	95	14	18	32	28	6	3	0	3	0	....	1977-78	1984-85
nilton, Reg	Tor., Chi.	12	424	21	87	108	412	64	3	8	11	46	2	1935-36	1946-47
nmarstrom, Inge	Tor., St.L.	6	427	116	123	239	86	13	2	3	5	4	....	1973-74	1978-79
nmond, Ken	L.A., Edm., NYR, Tor., Bos., S.J., Van., Ott.	8	193	18	29	47	290	15	0	0	0	24	....	1984-85	1992-93
npson, Gord	Cgy.	1	4	0	0	0	5	....	....	....	....	....	....	1982-83	1982-83
npson, Ted	Tor., NYR, Det., Oak., Cal., Min.	12	676	108	245	353	94	35	7	10	17	2	....	1959-60	1971-72
npton, Rick	Cal., Cle., L.A.	6	337	59	113	172	147	2	0	0	0	0	....	1974-75	1979-80
nr, Radek	Ott.	2	11	0	0	0	0	....	....	....	....	....	....	1992-93	1993-94
nway, Mark	NYI	3	53	5	13	18	9	1	0	0	0	0	....	1984-85	1986-87
ndy, Ron	NYI, St.L.	2	14	0	3	3	0	....	....	....	....	....	....	1984-85	1987-88
ngsleben, Al	Hfd., Wsh., L.A.	3	185	21	48	69	396	....	....	....	....	....	....	1979-80	1981-82
nkinson, Ben	N.J., T.B.	3	43	3	3	6	45	2	1	0	1	4	....	1992-93	1994-95
nkinson, Casey	Chi., Ana.	3	18	0	1	1	13	....	....	....	....	....	....	2000-01	2003-04
nna, John	NYR, Mtl., Phi.	5	198	6	26	32	206	....	....	....	....	....	....	1958-59	1967-68
nnan, Dave	Pit., Edm., Tor., Buf., Col., Ott.	16	841	114	191	305	942	63	6	7	13	46	2	1981-82	1996-97
nnigan, Gord	Tor.	4	161	29	31	60	117	9	2	0	2	8	....	1952-53	1955-56
nnigan, Pat	Tor., NYR, Phi.	5	182	30	39	69	116	11	1	2	3	11	....	1959-60	1968-69
nnigan, Ray	Tor.	1	3	0	0	0	2	....	....	....	....	....	....	1948-49	1948-49
nsen, Richie	NYI, St.L.	4	20	2	8	10	4	....	....	....	....	....	....	1976-77	1981-82
nsen, Tavis	Wpg., Phx.	5	34	2	1	3	16	2	0	0	0	0	....	1994-95	2000-01
nson, Dave	Det., Min.	2	33	1	1	2	65	....	....	....	....	....	....	1978-79	1979-80
nson, Emil	Det.	1	7	0	0	0	6	....	....	....	....	....	....	1932-33	1932-33
nson, Keith	Cgy.	1	25	0	2	2	77	....	....	....	....	....	....	1983-84	1983-84
nson, Oscar	Chi.	1	8	0	0	0	0	....	....	....	....	....	....	1937-38	1937-38
baruk, Nick	Pit., St.L.	5	364	45	75	120	273	14	3	1	4	20	....	1969-70	1973-74
ding, Jeff	Phi.	2	15	0	0	0	47	....	....	....	....	....	....	1988-89	1989-90
dy, Joe	Oak., Cal.	2	63	9	14	23	51	4	0	0	0	0	....	1969-70	1970-71
dy, Mark	L.A., NYR, Min.	15	915	62	306	368	1293	67	5	16	21	158	....	1979-80	1993-94
greaves, Jim	Van.	2	66	1	7	8	105	....	....	....	....	....	....	1970-71	1972-73
kins, Brett	Bos., Fla., CBJ	4	78	6	30	36	22	....	....	....	....	....	....	1994-95	2001-02
kins, Todd	Cgy., Hfd.	3	48	3	3	6	78	....	....	....	....	....	....	1991-92	1993-94
lock, David	Tor., Wsh., NYI, Atl.	8	212	2	14	16	188	....	....	....	....	....	....	1993-94	2001-02
low, Scott	St.L.	1	1	0	1	1	0	....	....	....	....	....	....	1987-88	1987-88
mon, Glen	Mtl.	9	452	50	96	146	334	53	5	10	15	37	2	1942-43	1950-51
ms, John	Chi.	2	44	5	5	10	21	4	3	0	3	2	....	1943-44	1944-45
nott, Walter	Bos.	1	6	0	0	0	2	....	....	....	....	....	....	1933-34	1933-34
per, Terry	Mtl., L.A., Det., St.L., Col.	19	1066	35	221	256	1362	112	4	13	17	140	5	1962-63	1980-81
rer, Tim	Cgy.	1	3	0	0	0	2	....	....	....	....	....	....	1982-83	1982-83
rington, Hago	Bos., Mtl.	3	72	9	3	12	15	4	1	0	1	2	....	1925-26	1932-33
ris, Billy	Tor., Det., Oak., Pit.	13	769	126	219	345	205	62	8	10	18	30	3	1955-56	1968-69
ris, Billy	NYI, L.A., Tor.	12	897	231	327	558	394	71	19	19	38	48	....	1972-73	1983-84
ris, Duke	Min., Tor.	1	26	1	4	5	4	....	....	....	....	....	....	1967-68	1967-68
ris, Henry	Bos.	1	32	2	4	6	20	....	....	....	....	....	....	1930-31	1930-31
ris, Hugh	Buf.	1	60	12	26	38	17	3	0	0	0	0	....	1972-73	1972-73
ris, Ron	Det., Oak., Atl., NYR	11	476	20	91	111	474	28	4	3	7	33	....	1962-63	1975-76
ris, Smokey	Bos.	1	6	3	1	4	8	....	....	....	....	....	....	1924-25	1924-25

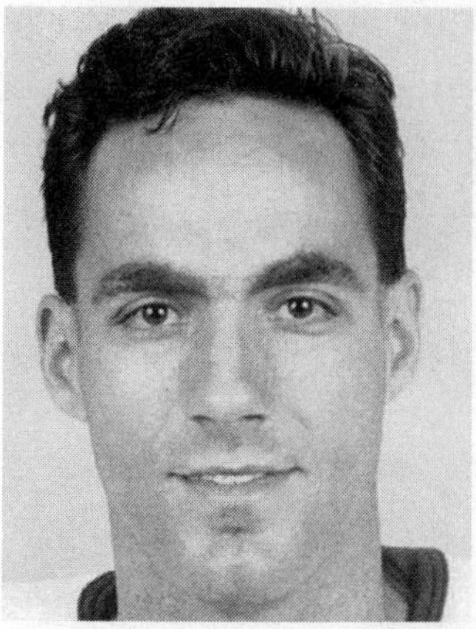

Paul Guay

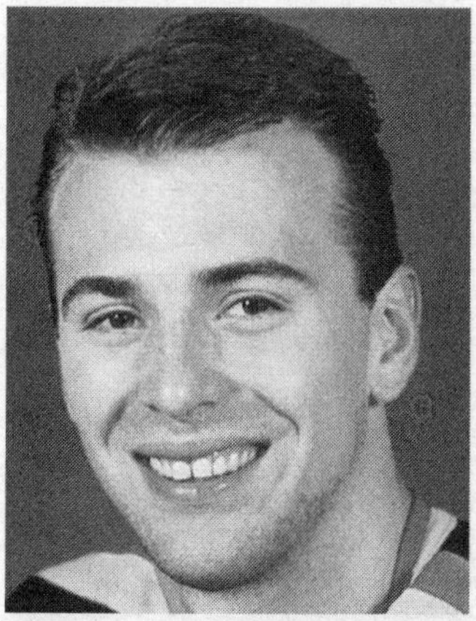

Taylor Hall

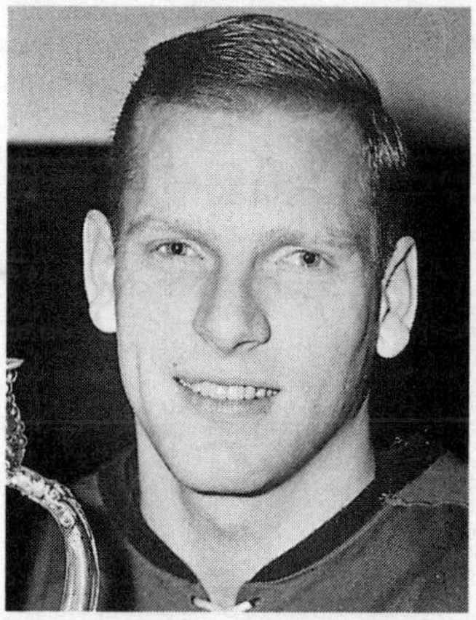

Bill Hay

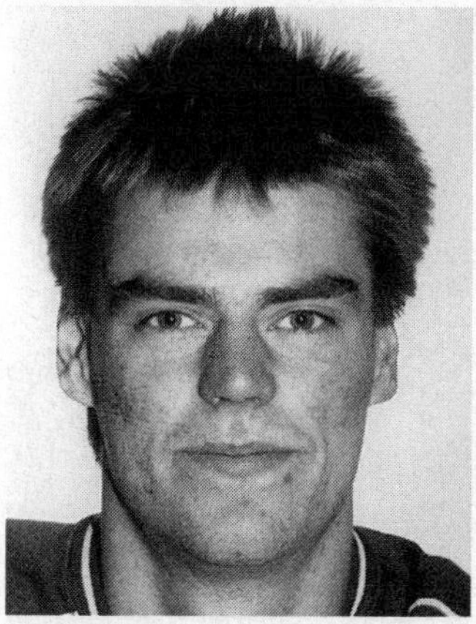

Raimo Helminen

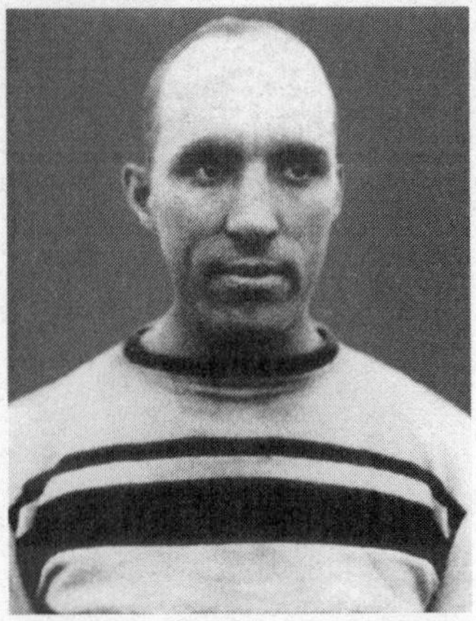

Henry Hicks

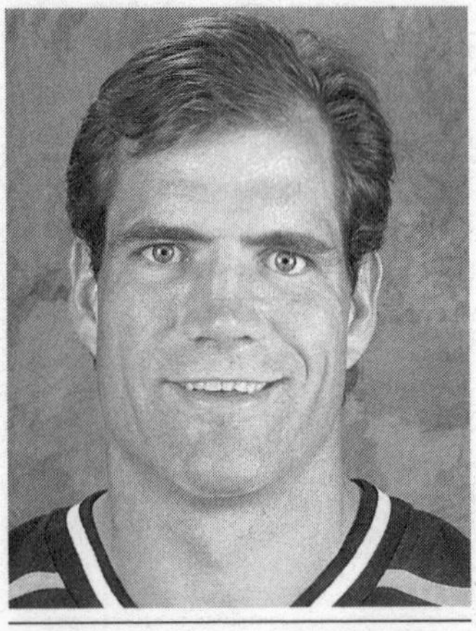

Sean Hill

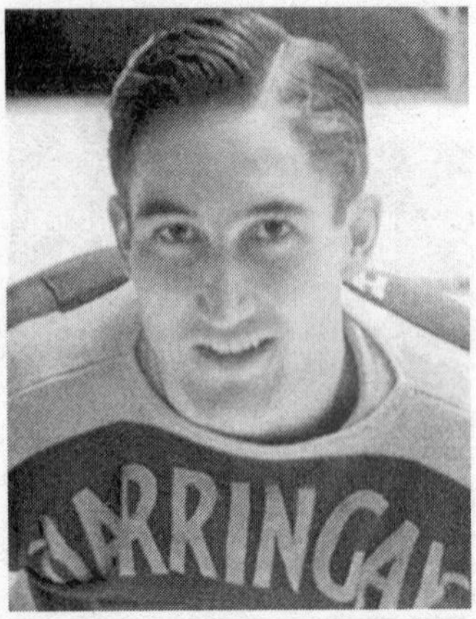

Dutch Hiller

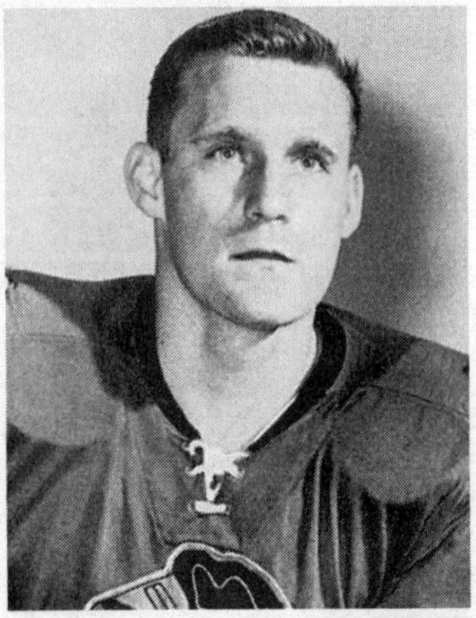

Wayne Hillman

			Regular Schedule					Playoffs					NHL	First	Last
Name	NHL Teams	NHL Seasons	GP	G	A	TP	PIM	GP	G	A	TP	PIM	Cup Wins	NHL Season	NHL Seaso
Harris, Ted	Mtl., Min., Det., St.L., Phi.	12	788	30	168	198	1000	100	1	22	23	230	5	1963-64	1974-7
Harrison, Ed	Bos., NYR	4	194	27	24	51	53	9	1	0	1	2	....	1947-48	1950-5
Harrison, Jim	Bos., Tor., Chi., Edm.	8	324	67	86	153	435	13	1	1	2	43	....	1968-69	1979-8
Hart, Gerry	Det., NYI, Que., St.L.	15	730	29	150	179	1240	78	3	12	15	175	....	1968-69	1982-8
• Hart, Gizzy	Det., Mtl.	3	104	6	8	14	12	8	0	1	1	0	....	1926-27	1932-3
‡ Hartigan, Mark	Atl., CBJ, Ana., Det.	6	102	19	11	30	58	5	0	1	1	4	1	2001-02	2007-0
Hartman, Mike	Buf., Wpg., T.B., NYR	9	397	43	35	78	1388	21	0	0	0	106	1	1986-87	1994-9
Hartsburg, Craig	Min.	10	570	98	315	413	818	61	15	27	42	70	....	1979-80	1988-8
• Harvey, Buster	Min., Atl., K.C., Det.	7	407	90	118	208	131	14	0	2	2	8	....	1970-71	1976-7
• Harvey, Doug	Mtl., NYR, Det., St.L.	20	1113	88	452	540	1216	137	8	64	72	152	6	1947-48	1968-6
Harvey, Hugh	K.C.	2	18	1	1	2	4	....	....	....	....	....	....	1974-75	1975-7
Harvey, Todd	Dal., NYR, S.J., Edm.	11	671	91	132	223	950	68	3	6	9	52	....	1994-95	2005-0
Hassard, Bob	Tor., Chi.	5	126	9	28	37	22	....	....	....	....	....	1	1949-50	1954-5
Hatcher, Derian	Min., Dal., Det., Phi.	16	1045	80	251	331	1581	133	7	26	33	248	1	1991-92	2007-0
Hatcher, Kevin	Wsh., Dal., Pit., NYR, Car.	17	1157	227	450	677	1392	118	22	37	59	252	....	1984-85	2000-0
Hatoum, Ed	Det., Van.	3	47	3	6	9	25	....	....	....	....	....	....	1968-69	1970-7
‡ Hauer, Brett	Edm., Nsh.	3	37	4	4	8	38	....	....	....	....	....	....	1995-96	2001-0
Hawerchuk, Dale	Wpg., Buf., St.L., Phi.	16	1188	518	891	1409	730	97	30	69	99	67	....	1981-82	1996-9
Hawgood, Greg	Bos., Edm., Phi., Fla., Pit., S.J., Van., Dal.	12	474	60	164	224	426	42	2	8	10	37	....	1987-88	2001-0
Hawkins, Todd	Van., Tor.	3	10	0	0	0	15	....	....	....	....	....	....	1988-89	1991-9
Haworth, Alan	Buf., Wsh., Que.	8	524	189	211	400	425	42	12	16	28	28	....	1980-81	1987-8
Haworth, Gord	NYR	1	2	0	1	1	0	....	....	....	....	....	....	1952-53	1952-5
Hawryliw, Neil	NYI	1	1	0	0	0	0	....	....	....	....	....	....	1981-82	1981-8
Hay, Bill	Chi.	8	506	113	273	386	244	67	15	21	36	62	1	1959-60	1966-6
Hay, Dwayne	Wsh., Fla., T.B., Cgy.	4	79	2	4	6	22	....	....	....	....	....	....	1997-98	2000-0
• Hay, George	Chi., Det.	7	239	74	60	134	84	8	2	3	5	2	....	1926-27	1933-3
Hay, Jim	Det.	3	75	1	5	6	22	9	1	0	1	2	1	1952-53	1954-5
Hayek, Peter	Min.	1	1	0	0	0	0	....	....	....	....	....	....	1981-82	1981-8
Hayes, Chris	Bos.	1	....	....	....	....	....	1	0	0	0	0	....	1971-72	1971-7
• Haynes, Paul	Mtl.M., Bos., Mtl.	11	391	61	134	195	164	24	2	8	10	13	....	1930-31	1940-4
Hayward, Rick	L.A.	1	4	0	0	0	5	....	....	....	....	....	....	1990-91	1990-9
Hazlett, Steve	Van.	1	1	0	0	0	0	....	....	....	....	....	....	1979-80	1979-8
Head, Galen	Det.	1	1	0	0	0	0	....	....	....	....	....	....	1967-68	1967-6
• Headley, Fern	Bos., Mtl.	1	30	1	3	4	10	1	0	0	0	0	....	1924-25	1924-2
‡ Healey, Eric	Bos.	1	2	0	0	0	2	....	....	....	....	....	....	2005-06	2005-0
‡ Healey, Paul	Phi., Tor., NYR, Col.	6	77	6	14	20	44	22	0	2	2	4	....	1996-97	2005-0
Healey, Rich	Det.	1	1	0	0	0	2	....	....	....	....	....	....	1960-61	1960-6
Heaphy, Shawn	Cgy.	1	1	0	0	0	0	....	....	....	....	....	....	1992-93	1992-9
Heaslip, Mark	NYR, L.A.	3	117	10	19	29	110	5	0	0	0	2	....	1976-77	1978-7
Heath, Randy	NYR	2	13	2	4	6	15	....	....	....	....	....	....	1984-85	1985-8
Hebenton, Andy	NYR, Bos.	9	630	189	202	391	83	22	6	5	11	8	....	1955-56	1963-6
Hecl, Radoslav	Buf.	1	14	0	0	0	2	....	....	....	....	....	....	2002-03	2002-0
Hedberg, Anders	NYR	7	465	172	225	397	144	58	22	24	46	31	....	1978-79	1984-8
Hedican, Bret	St.L., Van., Fla., Car., Ana.	17	1039	55	239	294	893	108	4	22	26	108	1	1991-92	2008-0
‡ Hedin, Pierre	Tor.	1	3	0	1	1	0	....	....	....	....	....	....	2003-04	2003-0
‡ Hedstrom, Jonathan	Ana.	2	83	13	14	27	48	3	0	1	1	2	....	2002-03	2005-0
‡ Heerema, Jeff	Car., St.L.	2	32	4	2	6	6	....	....	....	....	....	....	2002-03	2003-0
• Heffernan, Frank	Tor.	1	19	0	1	1	10	....	....	....	....	....	....	1919-20	1919-2
• Heffernan, Gerry	Mtl.	3	83	33	35	68	27	11	3	3	6	8	1	1941-42	1943-4
Heidt, Mike	L.A.	1	6	0	1	1	7	....	....	....	....	....	....	1983-84	1983-8
• Heindl, Bill	Min., NYR	3	18	2	1	3	0	....	....	....	....	....	....	1970-71	1972-
Heinrich, Lionel	Bos.	1	35	1	1	2	33	....	....	....	....	....	....	1955-56	1955-
‡ Heins, Shawn	S.J., Pit., Atl.	6	125	4	12	16	154	2	0	0	0	0	....	1998-99	2003-0
Heinze, Steve	Bos., CBJ, Buf., L.A.	12	694	178	158	336	379	69	11	15	26	48	....	1991-92	2002-0
Heiskala, Earl	Phi.	3	127	13	11	24	294	....	....	....	....	....	....	1968-69	1970-
‡ Heisten, Barrett	NYR	1	10	0	0	0	2	....	....	....	....	....	....	2001-02	2001-0
Helander, Peter	L.A.	1	7	0	1	1	0	....	....	....	....	....	....	1982-83	1982-
‡ Helbling, Timo	T.B., Wsh.	2	11	0	1	1	8	....	....	....	....	....	....	2005-06	2006-
‡ Helenius, Sami	Cgy., T.B., Col., Dal., Chi.	6	155	2	4	6	260	1	0	0	0	0	....	1996-97	2002-0
• Heller, Ott	NYR	15	647	55	176	231	465	61	6	8	14	61	2	1931-32	1945-
• Helman, Harry	Ott.	3	44	1	0	1	7	2	0	0	0	0	1	1922-23	1924-
‡ Helminen, Raimo	NYR, Min., NYI	3	117	13	46	59	16	2	0	0	0	0	....	1985-86	1988-8
‡ Hemingway, Colin	St.L.	1	3	0	0	0	0	....	....	....	....	....	....	2005-06	2005-0
• Hemmerling, Tony	NYA	2	22	3	3	6	4	....	....	....	....	....	....	1935-36	1936-
Henderson, Archie	Wsh., Min., Hfd.	3	23	3	1	4	92	....	....	....	....	....	....	1980-81	1982-
‡ Henderson, Jay	Bos.	4	33	1	3	4	37	....	....	....	....	....	....	1998-99	2001-0
Henderson, Matt	Nsh., Chi.	2	6	0	1	1	2	....	....	....	....	....	....	1998-99	2001-0
Henderson, Murray	Bos.	8	405	24	62	86	305	41	2	3	5	23	....	1944-45	1951-
Henderson, Paul	Det., Tor., Atl.	13	707	236	241	477	304	56	11	14	25	28	....	1962-63	1979-
Hendrickson, Darby	Tor., NYI, Van., Min., Col.	11	518	65	64	129	370	25	3	3	6	6	....	1993-94	2003-
Hendrickson, John	Det.	3	5	0	0	0	4	....	....	....	....	....	....	1957-58	1961-
Henning, Lorne	NYI	9	543	73	111	184	102	81	7	7	14	8	2	1972-73	1980-
Henry, Burke	Chi.	2	39	2	6	8	33	....	....	....	....	....	....	2002-03	2003-
• Henry, Camille	NYR, Chi., St.L.	14	727	279	249	528	88	47	6	12	18	7	....	1953-54	1969-
Henry, Dale	NYI	6	132	13	26	39	263	14	1	0	1	19	....	1984-85	1989-
‡ Hentunen, Jukka	Cgy., Nsh.	1	38	4	5	9	4	....	....	....	....	....	....	2001-02	2001-
Hepple, Alan	N.J.	3	3	0	0	0	7	....	....	....	....	....	....	1983-84	1985-
Herbers, Ian	Edm., T.B., NYI	2	65	0	5	5	79	....	....	....	....	....	....	1993-94	1999-
• Herberts, Jimmy	Bos., Tor., Det.	6	206	83	31	114	253	9	3	0	3	10	....	1924-25	1929-
• Herchenratter, Art	Det.	1	10	1	2	3	2	....	....	....	....	....	....	1940-41	1940-
• Hergerts, Fred	NYA	2	20	2	4	6	2	....	....	....	....	....	....	1934-35	1935-
• Hergesheimer, Phil	Chi., Bos.	4	125	21	41	62	19	6	0	0	0	2	....	1939-40	1942-
Hergesheimer, Wally	NYR, Chi.	7	351	114	85	199	106	5	1	0	1	0	....	1951-52	1958-
• Heron, Red	Tor., Bro., Mtl.	4	106	21	19	40	38	21	2	2	4	6	....	1938-39	1941-
Heroux, Yves	Que.	1	1	0	0	0	0	....	....	....	....	....	....	1986-87	1986-
‡ Herperger, Chris	Chi., Ott., Atl.	4	169	18	25	43	75	....	....	....	....	....	....	1999-00	2002-
Herr, Matt	Wsh., Fla., Bos.	4	58	4	5	9	25	....	....	....	....	....	....	1998-99	2002-
Herter, Jason	NYI	1	1	0	1	1	0	....	....	....	....	....	....	1995-96	1995-
Hervey, Matt	Wpg., Bos., T.B.	3	35	0	5	5	97	5	0	0	0	6	....	1988-89	1992-
Hess, Bob	St.L., Buf., Hfd.	8	329	27	95	122	178	4	1	1	2	2	....	1974-75	1983-
Heward, Jamie	Tor., Nsh., NYI, CBJ, Wsh., L.A., T.B.	9	394	38	86	124	221	....	....	....	....	....	....	1995-96	2008-
• Heximer, Obs	NYR, Bos., NYA	3	84	13	7	20	16	5	0	0	0	2	....	1929-30	1934-
• Hextall, Bryan	NYR	11	449	187	175	362	227	37	8	9	17	19	1	1936-37	1947-
Hextall, Bryan	NYR, Pit., Atl., Det., Min.	8	549	99	161	260	738	18	0	4	4	59	....	1962-63	1975-
Hextall, Dennis	NYR, L.A., Cal., Min., Det., Wsh.	13	681	153	350	503	1398	22	3	3	6	45	....	1967-68	1979-
• Heyliger, Vic	Chi.	2	33	2	3	5	2	....	....	....	....	....	....	1937-38	1943-
• Hicke, Bill	Mtl., NYR, Oak., Cal., Pit.	14	729	168	234	402	395	42	3	10	13	41	2	1958-59	1971-
Hicke, Ernie	Cal., Atl., NYI, Min., L.A.	8	520	132	140	272	407	2	1	0	1	0	....	1970-71	1977-
Hickey, Greg	NYR	1	1	0	0	0	0	....	....	....	....	....	....	1977-78	1977-
Hickey, Pat	NYR, Col., Tor., Que., St.L.	10	646	192	212	404	351	55	5	11	16	37	....	1975-76	1984-
Hicks, Alex	Ana., Pit., S.J., Fla.	5	258	25	54	79	247	15	0	2	2	8	....	1995-96	1999-
Hicks, Doug	Min., Chi., Edm., Wsh.	9	561	37	131	168	442	18	2	1	3	15	....	1974-75	1982-
Hicks, Glenn	Det.	2	108	6	12	18	127	....	....	....	....	....	....	1979-80	1980-
• Hicks, Henry	Mtl.M., Det.	3	96	7	2	9	72	....	....	....	....	....	....	1928-29	1930-
Hicks, Wayne	Chi., Bos., Mtl., Phi., Pit.	5	115	13	23	36	22	2	0	1	1	2	1	1959-60	1967-
Hidi, Andre	Wsh.	2	7	2	1	3	9	2	0	0	0	0	....	1983-84	1984-
Hiemer, Uli	N.J.	3	143	19	54	73	176	....	....	....	....	....	....	1984-85	1986-
‡ Higgins, Matt	Mtl.	4	57	1	2	3	6	....	....	....	....	....	....	1997-98	2000-
Higgins, Paul	Tor.	2	25	0	0	0	152	1	0	0	0	0	....	1981-82	1982-
Higgins, Tim	Chi., N.J., Det.	11	706	154	198	352	719	65	5	8	13	77	....	1978-79	1988-
• Hildebrand, Ike	NYR, Chi.	2	41	7	11	18	16	....	....	....	....	....	....	1953-54	1954-
Hill, Al	Phi.	8	221	40	55	95	227	51	8	11	19	43	....	1976-77	1987-
Hill, Brian	Hfd.	1	19	1	1	2	4	....	....	....	....	....	....	1979-80	1979-
• Hill, Mel	Bos., Bro., Tor.	9	324	89	109	198	128	43	12	7	19	18	3	1937-38	1945-
‡ Hill, Sean	Mtl., Ana., Ott., Car., St.L., Fla., NYI, Min.	17	876	62	236	298	1008	55	5	5	10	42	1	1990-91	2007-
• Hiller, Dutch	NYR, Det., Bos., Mtl.	9	383	91	113	204	163	48	9	8	17	21	2	1937-38	1945-
Hiller, Jim	L.A., Det., NYR	2	63	8	12	20	116	2	0	0	0	4	....	1992-93	1993-
Hillier, Randy	Bos., Pit., NYI, Buf.	11	543	16	110	126	906	28	0	2	2	93	1	1981-82	1991-
Hillman, Floyd	Bos.	1	6	0	0	0	10	....	....	....	....	....	....	1956-57	1956
Hillman, Larry	Det., Bos., Tor., Min., Mtl., Phi., L.A., Buf.	19	790	36	196	232	579	74	2	9	11	30	6	1954-55	1972
• Hillman, Wayne	Chi., NYR, Min., Phi.	13	691	18	86	104	534	28	0	3	3	19	1	1960-61	1972
Hilworth, John	Det.	3	57	1	1	2	89	....	....	....	....	....	....	1977-78	1979
• Himes, Normie	NYA	9	402	106	113	219	127	2	0	0	0	0	....	1926-27	1934

			Regular Schedule					Playoffs					NHL	First	Last
lame	NHL Teams	NHL Seasons	GP	G	A	TP	PIM	GP	G	A	TP	PIM	Cup Wins	NHL Season	NHL Season
indmarch, Dave	Cgy.	4	99	21	17	38	25	10	0	0	0	6	....	1980-81	1983-84
inse, Andre	Tor.	1	4	0	0	0	0	....	....	....	....	....	....	1967-68	1967-68
inton, Dan	Chi.	1	14	0	0	0	16	....	....	....	....	....	....	1976-77	1976-77
irsch, Tom	Min.	3	31	1	7	8	30	12	0	0	0	6	....	1983-84	1987-88
irschfeld, Bert	Mtl.	2	33	1	4	5	2	5	1	0	1	0	....	1949-50	1950-51
islop, Jamie	Que., Cgy.	5	345	75	103	178	86	28	3	2	5	11	....	1979-80	1983-84
itchman, Lionel	Ott., Bos.	12	417	28	34	62	523	35	2	2	4	73	2	1922-23	1933-34
lavac, Jan	NYR, Phi., Van., Car., T.B., Nsh.	6	436	90	134	224	138	11	0	3	3	2	....	1999-00	2007-08
linka, Ivan	Van.	2	137	42	81	123	28	16	3	10	13	8	....	1981-82	1982-83
linka, Jaroslav	Col.	1	63	8	20	28	16	1	0	0	0	0	....	2007-08	2007-08
lushko, Todd	Phi., Cgy., Pit.	6	79	8	13	21	84	3	0	0	0	2	....	1993-94	1998-99
ocking, Justin	L.A.	1	1	0	0	0	0	....	....	....	....	....	....	1993-94	1993-94
odge, Ken	Chi., Bos., NYR	14	881	328	472	800	779	97	34	47	81	120	2	1964-65	1977-78
odge, Ken	Min., Bos., T.B.	4	142	39	48	87	32	15	4	6	10	6	....	1988-89	1992-93
odgson, Dan	Tor., Van.	4	114	29	45	74	64	....	....	....	....	....	....	1985-86	1988-89
odgson, Rick	Hfd.	1	6	0	0	0	6	1	0	0	0	0	....	1979-80	1979-80
odgson, Ted	Bos.	1	4	0	0	0	0	....	....	....	....	....	....	1966-67	1966-67
oekstra, Cec	Mtl.	1	4	0	0	0	0	....	....	....	....	....	....	1959-60	1959-60
oekstra, Ed	Phi.	1	70	15	21	36	6	7	0	1	1	0	....	1967-68	1967-68
oene, Phil	L.A.	3	37	2	4	6	22	....	....	....	....	....	....	1972-73	1974-75
offinger, Val	Chi.	2	28	0	1	1	30	....	....	....	....	....	....	1927-28	1928-29
offman, Mike	Hfd.	3	9	1	3	4	2	....	....	....	....	....	....	1982-83	1985-86
offmeyer, Bob	Chi., Phi., N.J.	6	198	14	52	66	325	3	0	1	1	25	....	1977-78	1984-85
offord, Jim	Buf., L.A.	3	18	0	0	0	47	....	....	....	....	....	....	1985-86	1988-89
ogaboam, Bill	Atl., Det., Min.	8	332	80	109	189	100	2	0	0	0	0	....	1972-73	1979-80
oganson, Dale	L.A., Mtl., Que.	7	343	13	77	90	186	11	0	3	3	12	....	1969-70	1981-82
oglund, Jonas	Cgy., Mtl., Tor.	7	545	117	145	262	112	59	8	11	19	8	....	1996-97	2002-03
ogue, Benoit	Buf., NYI, Tor., Dal., T.B., Phx., Bos., Wsh.	15	863	222	321	543	877	92	17	16	33	124	1	1987-88	2001-02
olan, Milos	Phi., Ana.	3	49	5	11	16	42	....	....	....	....	....	....	1993-94	1995-96
olbrook, Terry	Min.	2	43	3	6	9	4	6	0	0	0	0	....	1972-73	1973-74
olden, Josh	Van., Car., Tor.	6	60	5	9	14	16	....	....	....	....	....	....	1998-99	2003-04
olik, Bobby	Hfd., N.J., NYR, Atl.	18	1314	326	421	747	1423	141	20	39	59	120	2	1990-91	2008-09
olland, Jason	NYI, Buf., L.A.	7	81	4	5	9	36	1	0	0	0	0	....	1996-97	2003-04
olland, Jerry	NYR	2	37	8	4	12	6	....	....	....	....	....	....	1974-75	1975-76
ollett, Flash	Tor., Ott., Bos., Det.	13	562	132	181	313	358	79	8	26	34	38	2	1933-34	1945-46
ollinger, Terry	St.L.	2	7	0	0	0	2	....	....	....	....	....	....	1993-94	1994-95
ollingworth, Gord	Chi., Det.	4	163	4	14	18	201	3	0	0	0	2	....	1954-55	1957-58
olloway, Bruce	Van.	1	2	0	0	0	0	....	....	....	....	....	....	1984-85	1984-85
olmes, Bill	Mtl., NYA	3	52	6	4	10	35	....	....	....	....	....	....	1925-26	1929-30
olmes, Chuck	Det.	2	23	1	3	4	10	....	....	....	....	....	....	1958-59	1961-62
olmes, Lou	Chi.	2	59	1	4	5	6	2	0	0	0	2	....	1931-32	1932-33
olmes, Warren	L.A.	3	45	8	18	26	7	....	....	....	....	....	....	1981-82	1983-84
olmgren, Paul	Phi., Min.	10	527	144	179	323	1684	82	19	32	51	195	....	1975-76	1984-85
olmqvist, Michael	Ana., Chi.	3	156	18	17	35	72	....	....	....	....	....	....	2003-04	2006-07
olota, John	Det.	2	15	2	0	2	0	....	....	....	....	....	....	1942-43	1945-46
olst, Greg	NYR	3	11	0	0	0	0	....	....	....	....	....	....	1975-76	1977-78
olt, Gary	Cal., Cle., St.L.	5	101	13	11	24	133	....	....	....	....	....	....	1973-74	1977-78
olt, Randy	Chi., Cle., Van., L.A., Cgy., Wsh., Phi.	10	395	4	37	41	1438	21	2	3	5	83	....	1974-75	1983-84
olway, Albert	Tor., Mtl.M., Pit.	5	112	7	2	9	48	6	0	0	0	0	1	1923-24	1928-29
olzinger, Brian	Buf., T.B., Pit., CBJ	10	547	93	145	238	339	52	11	18	29	61	....	1994-95	2003-04
omenuke, Ron	Van.	1	1	0	0	0	0	....	....	....	....	....	....	1972-73	1972-73
oover, Ron	Bos., St.L.	3	18	4	0	4	31	8	0	0	0	18	....	1989-90	1991-92
opkins, Dean	L.A., Edm., Que.	6	223	23	51	74	306	18	1	5	6	29	....	1979-80	1988-89
opkins, Larry	Tor., Wpg.	4	60	13	16	29	26	6	0	0	0	2	....	1977-78	1982-83
oracek, Tony	Phi., Chi.	5	154	10	19	29	316	2	1	0	1	2	....	1989-90	1994-95
orava, Miloslav	NYR	3	80	5	17	22	38	2	0	1	1	0	....	1988-89	1990-91
orbul, Doug	K.C.	1	4	1	0	1	2	....	....	....	....	....	....	1974-75	1974-75
ordy, Mike	NYI	2	11	0	0	0	7	....	....	....	....	....	....	1978-79	1979-80
oreck, Pete	Chi., Det., Bos.	8	426	106	118	224	340	34	6	8	14	43	....	1944-45	1951-52
orne, George	Mtl.M., Tor.	3	54	9	3	12	34	4	0	0	0	4	1	1925-26	1928-29
orner, Red	Tor.	12	490	42	110	152	1254	71	7	10	17	170	1	1928-29	1939-40
ornung, Larry	St.L.	2	48	2	9	11	10	11	0	2	2	2	....	1970-71	1971-72
orton, Tim	Tor., NYR, Pit., Buf.	24	1446	115	403	518	1611	126	11	39	50	183	4	1949-50	1973-74
orvath, Bronco	NYR, Mtl., Bos., Chi., Tor., Min.	9	434	141	185	326	319	36	12	9	21	18	....	1955-56	1967-68
ospodar, Ed	NYR, Hfd., Phi., Min., Buf.	9	450	17	51	68	1314	44	4	1	5	208	....	1979-80	1987-88
ostak, Martin	Phi.	2	55	3	11	14	24	....	....	....	....	....	....	1990-91	1991-92
otham, Greg	Tor., Pit.	6	230	15	74	89	139	5	0	3	3	6	....	1979-80	1984-85
ouck, Paul	Min.	3	16	1	2	3	2	....	....	....	....	....	....	1985-86	1987-88
ouda, Doug	Det., Hfd., L.A., Buf., NYI, Ana.	15	561	19	63	82	1104	18	0	3	3	21	....	1985-86	2002-03
oude, Claude	K.C.	2	59	3	6	9	40	....	....	....	....	....	....	1974-75	1975-76
oude, Eric	Mtl.	3	30	2	3	5	4	....	....	....	....	....	....	1996-97	1998-99
ough, Mike	Que., Fla., NYI	14	707	100	156	256	675	44	5	5	10	38	....	1984-85	1998-99
oulder, Bill	Wsh., Buf., Ana., St.L., T.B., S.J., Nsh.	16	846	59	191	250	412	30	5	6	11	14	....	1987-88	2002-03
oule, Rejean	Mtl.	11	635	161	247	408	395	90	14	34	48	66	5	1969-70	1982-83
ousley, Phil	Buf., Wpg., St.L., Cgy., N.J., Wsh., Chi., Tor.	21	1495	338	894	1232	822	85	13	43	56	36	....	1982-83	2002-03
ouston, Ken	Atl., Cgy., Wsh., L.A.	9	570	161	167	328	624	35	10	9	19	66	....	1975-76	1983-84
oward, Jack	Tor.	1	2	0	0	0	0	....	....	....	....	....	....	1936-37	1936-37
owatt, Garry	NYI, Hfd., N.J.	12	720	112	156	268	1836	87	12	14	26	289	2	1972-73	1983-84
owe, Gordie	Det., Hfd.	26	1767	801	1049	1850	1685	157	68	92	160	220	4	1946-47	1979-80
owe, Mark	Hfd., Phi., Det.	16	929	197	545	742	455	101	10	51	61	34	....	1979-80	1994-95
owe, Marty	Hfd., Bos.	6	197	2	29	31	99	15	1	2	3	9	....	1979-80	1984-85
owe, Syd	Ott., Phi., Tor., St.L., Det.	17	698	237	291	528	212	70	17	27	44	10	3	1929-30	1945-46
owe, Vic	NYR	3	33	3	4	7	10	....	....	....	....	....	....	1950-51	1954-55
owell, Harry	NYR, Oak., Cal., L.A.	21	1411	94	324	418	1298	38	3	3	6	32	....	1952-53	1972-73
owell, Ron	NYR	2	4	0	0	0	0	....	....	....	....	....	....	1954-55	1955-56
owse, Don	L.A.	1	33	2	5	7	6	2	0	0	0	0	....	1979-80	1979-80
owson, Scott	NYI	2	18	5	3	8	4	....	....	....	....	....	....	1984-85	1985-86
oyda, Dave	Phi., Wpg.	4	132	6	17	23	299	12	0	0	0	17	....	1977-78	1980-81
dina, Jan	Pit., Phx., N.J., CBJ	7	513	101	196	297	341	45	12	14	26	24	....	1998-99	2005-06
dina, Jiri	Cgy., Pit.	5	250	45	85	130	92	46	2	5	7	24	3	1987-88	1991-92
echkosy, Dave	Cal., St.L.	4	140	42	24	66	41	3	1	0	1	2	....	1973-74	1976-77
kac, Tony	St.L., Que., S.J., Chi., Dal., Edm., NYI, Ana., Atl.	13	758	132	239	371	173	41	7	7	14	12	1	1986-87	2002-03
ycuik, Jim	Wsh.	1	21	5	5	10	12	....	....	....	....	....	....	1974-75	1974-75
ymnak, Steve	Chi., Det.	2	18	2	1	3	4	2	0	0	0	0	....	1951-52	1952-53
ynewich, Tim	Pit.	2	55	6	8	14	82	....	....	....	....	....	....	1982-83	1983-84
uard, Bill	Bos., Ott., Que., Dal., Edm., L.A.	8	223	16	18	34	594	5	0	0	0	2	....	1992-93	1999-00
uard, Rolly	Tor.	1	1	1	0	1	0	....	....	....	....	....	....	1930-31	1930-31
ubacek, Petr	Phi.	1	6	1	0	1	2	....	....	....	....	....	....	2000-01	2000-01
uber, Willie	Det., NYR, Van., Phi.	10	655	104	217	321	950	33	5	5	10	35	....	1978-79	1987-88
ubick, Greg	Tor., Van.	2	77	6	9	15	10	....	....	....	....	....	....	1975-76	1979-80
uck, Fran	Mtl., St.L.	3	94	24	30	54	38	11	3	4	7	2	....	1969-70	1972-73
ucul, Fred	Chi., St.L.	5	164	11	30	41	113	6	1	0	1	10	....	1950-51	1967-68
uddy, Charlie	Edm., L.A., Buf., St.L.	17	1017	99	354	453	785	183	19	66	85	135	5	1980-81	1996-97
udson, Dave	NYI, K.C., Col.	6	409	59	124	183	89	2	1	1	2	0	....	1972-73	1977-78
udson, Lex	Pit.	1	2	0	0	0	0	2	0	0	0	0	....	1978-79	1978-79
udson, Mike	Chi., Edm., NYR, Pit., Tor., St.L., Phx.	9	416	49	87	136	414	49	4	10	14	64	1	1988-89	1996-97
udson, Ron	Det.	2	33	5	2	7	2	....	....	....	....	....	....	1937-38	1939-40
uffman, Kerry	Phi., Que., Ott.	10	401	37	108	145	361	11	0	0	0	2	....	1986-87	1995-96
uggins, Al	Mtl.M.	1	20	1	1	2	2	....	....	....	....	....	....	1930-31	1930-31
ughes, Albert	NYA	2	60	6	8	14	22	....	....	....	....	....	....	1930-31	1931-32
ughes, Brent	L.A., Phi., St.L., Det., K.C.	8	435	15	117	132	440	22	1	3	4	53	....	1967-68	1974-75
ughes, Brent	Wpg., Bos., Buf., NYI	8	357	41	39	80	831	29	4	1	5	53	....	1988-89	1996-97
ughes, Frank	Cal.	1	5	0	0	0	0	....	....	....	....	....	....	1971-72	1971-72
ughes, Howie	L.A.	3	168	25	32	57	30	14	2	0	2	2	....	1967-68	1969-70
ughes, Jack	Col.	2	46	2	5	7	104	....	....	....	....	....	....	1980-81	1981-82
ughes, James	Det.	1	40	0	1	1	48	....	....	....	....	....	....	1929-30	1929-30
ughes, John	Van., Edm., NYR	2	70	2	14	16	211	7	0	1	1	16	....	1979-80	1980-81
ughes, Pat	Mtl., Pit., Edm., Buf., St.L., Hfd.	10	573	130	128	258	646	71	8	25	33	77	3	1977-78	1986-87
ughes, Ryan	Bos.	1	3	0	0	0	0	....	....	....	....	....	....	1995-96	1995-96
ulbig, Joe	Edm., Bos.	5	55	4	4	8	16	6	0	1	1	2	....	1996-97	2000-01
ull, Bobby	Chi., Wpg., Hfd.	16	1063	610	560	1170	640	119	62	67	129	102	1	1957-58	1979-80
ull, Brett	Cgy., St.L., Dal., Det., Phx.	20	1269	741	650	1391	458	202	103	87	190	73	2	1985-86	2005-06
ull, Dennis	Chi., Det.	14	959	303	351	654	261	104	33	34	67	30	....	1964-65	1977-78

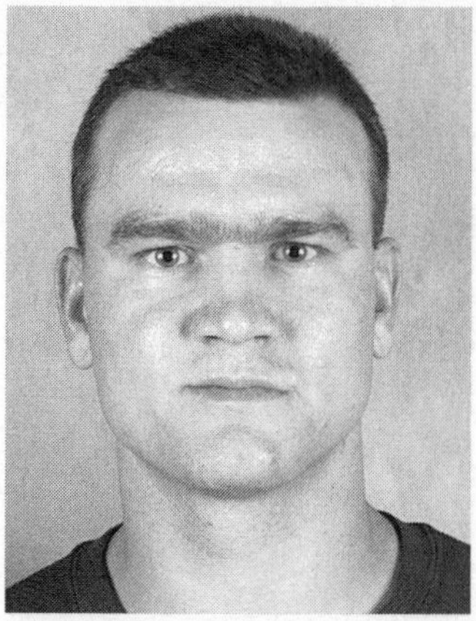

Bobby Holik

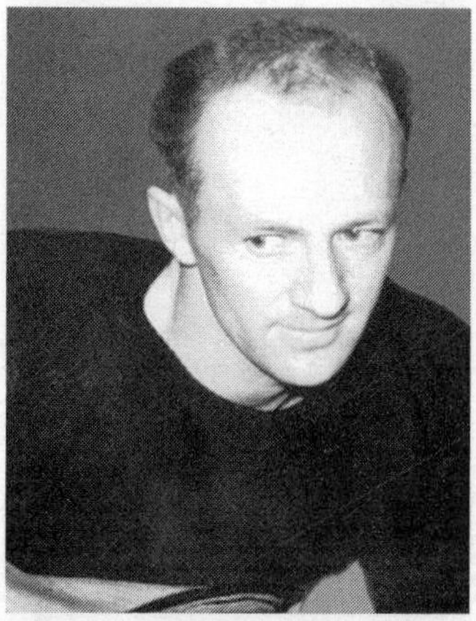

Lou Holmes

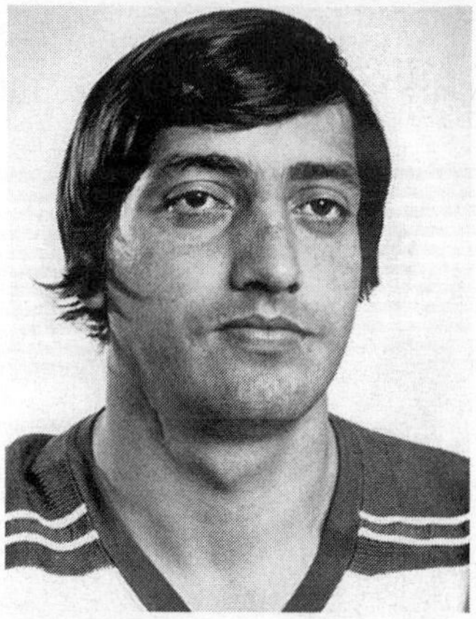

Claude Houde

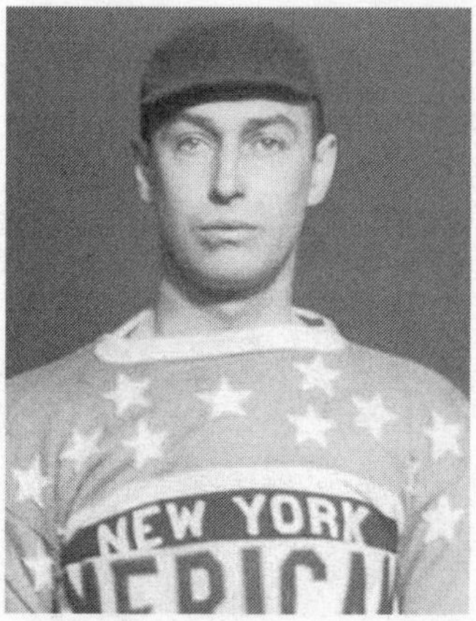

Albert Hughes

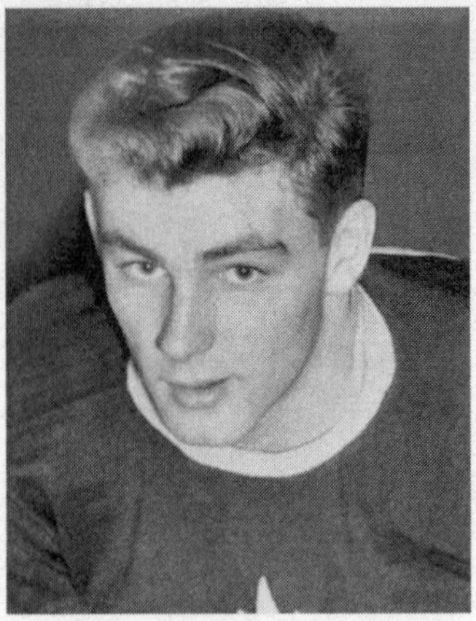

Jack Ingoldsby

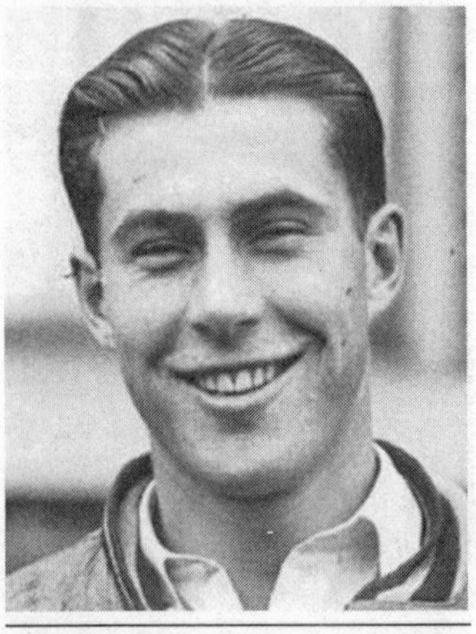

Busher Jackson

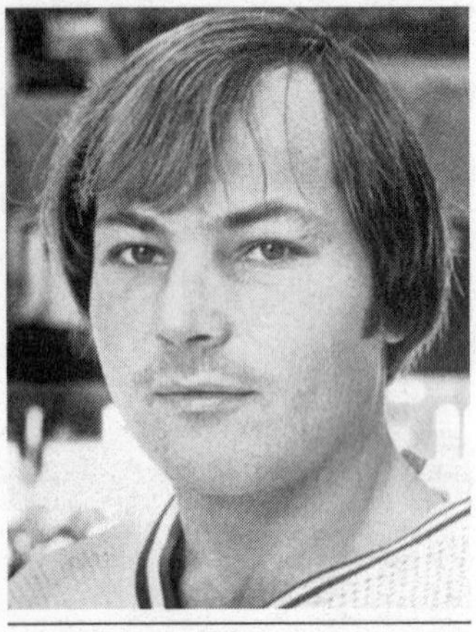

Tim Jacobs

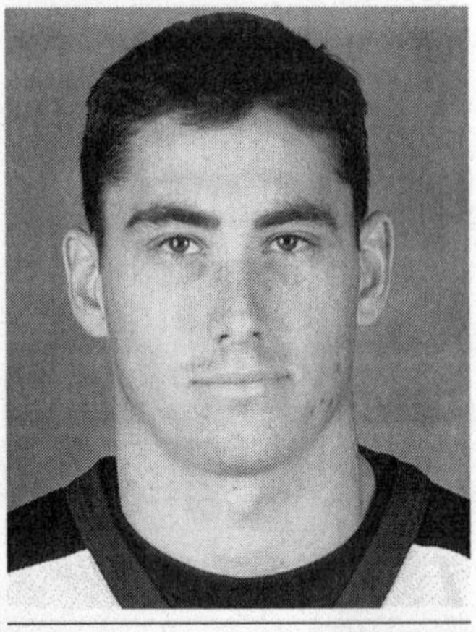

Mike Johnson

Name	NHL Teams	NHL Seasons	Regular Schedule GP	G	A	TP	PIM	Playoffs GP	G	A	TP	PIM	NHL Cup Wins	First NHL Season	Last NHL Season
Hull, Jody	Hfd., NYR, Ott., Fla., T.B., Phi.	16	831	124	137	261	156	69	4	5	9	14	....	1988-89	2003-0
Hulse, Cale	N.J., Cgy., Nsh., Phx., CBJ	10	619	16	79	95	1000	1	0	0	0	0	....	1995-96	2005-0
‡ Huml, Ivan	Bos.	3	49	6	12	18	36	....	....	....	....	....	....	2001-02	2003-0
• Hunt, Fred	NYA, NYR	2	59	15	14	29	6	....	....	....	....	....	....	1940-41	1944-4
Hunter, Dale	Que., Wsh., Col.	19	1407	323	697	1020	3565	186	42	76	118	729	....	1980-81	1998-9
Hunter, Dave	Edm., Pit., Wpg.	10	746	133	190	323	918	105	16	24	40	211	3	1979-80	1988-8
Hunter, Mark	Mtl., St.L., Cgy., Hfd., Wsh.	12	628	213	171	384	1426	79	18	20	38	230	1	1981-82	1992-9
Hunter, Tim	Cgy., Que., Van., S.J.	16	815	62	76	138	3146	132	5	7	12	426	1	1981-82	1996-9
Huras, Larry	NYR	1	2	0	0	0	0	....	....	....	....	....	....	1976-77	1976-7
Hurlburt, Bob	Van.	1	1	0	0	0	2	....	....	....	....	....	....	1974-75	1974-7
Hurlbut, Mike	NYR, Que., Buf.	5	29	1	8	9	20	....	....	....	....	....	....	1992-93	1999-0
Hurley, Paul	Bos.	1	1	0	1	1	0	....	....	....	....	....	....	1968-69	1968-6
Hurst, Ron	Tor.	2	64	9	7	16	70	3	0	2	2	4	....	1955-56	1956-5
Huscroft, Jamie	N.J., Bos., Cgy., T.B., Van., Phx., Wsh.	10	352	5	33	38	1065	21	0	1	1	46	....	1988-89	1999-0
Huska, Ryan	Chi.	1	1	0	0	0	0	....	....	....	....	....	....	1997-98	1997-9
‡ Hussey, Matt	Pit., Det.	3	21	2	2	4	2	....	....	....	....	....	....	2003-04	2006-0
Huston, Ron	Cal.	2	79	15	31	46	8	....	....	....	....	....	....	1973-74	1974-7
Hutchinson, Ron	NYR	1	9	0	0	0	0	....	....	....	....	....	....	1960-61	1960-6
Hutchison, Dave	L.A., Tor., Chi., N.J.	10	584	19	97	116	1550	48	2	12	14	149	....	1974-75	1983-8
• Hutton, Bill	Bos., Ott., Phi.	2	64	3	2	5	8	2	0	0	0	0	....	1929-30	1930-3
• Hyland, Harry	Mtl.W., Ott.	1	17	14	2	16	65	....	....	....	....	....	....	1917-18	1917-1
Hynes, Dave	Bos.	2	22	4	0	4	2	....	....	....	....	....	....	1973-74	1974-7
Hynes, Gord	Bos., Phi.	2	52	3	9	12	22	12	1	2	3	6	....	1991-92	1992-9
‡ Hyvonen, Hannes	S.J., CBJ	2	42	4	5	9	22	....	....	....	....	....	....	2001-02	2002-0

I

Name	NHL Teams	NHL Seasons	Regular Schedule GP	G	A	TP	PIM	Playoffs GP	G	A	TP	PIM	NHL Cup Wins	First NHL Season	Last NHL Season
Iafrate, Al	Tor., Wsh., Bos., S.J.	12	799	152	311	463	1301	71	19	16	35	77	....	1984-85	1997-9
Ignatjev, Victor	Pit.	1	11	0	1	1	6	1	0	0	0	2	....	1998-99	1998-9
Ihnacak, Miroslav	Tor., Det.	3	56	8	9	17	39	1	0	0	0	0	....	1985-86	1988-8
Ihnacak, Peter	Tor.	8	417	102	165	267	175	28	4	10	14	25	....	1982-83	1989-9
Imlach, Brent	Tor.	2	3	0	0	0	0	....	....	....	....	....	....	1965-66	1966-6
‡ Immonen, Jarkko	NYR	2	20	3	5	8	4	....	....	....	....	....	....	2005-06	2006-0
Ingarfield, Earl	NYR, Pit., Oak., Cal.	13	746	179	226	405	239	21	9	8	17	10	....	1958-59	1970-7
Ingarfield, Earl	Atl., Cgy., Det.	2	39	4	4	8	22	2	0	1	1	0	....	1979-80	1980-8
Inglis, Billy	L.A., Buf.	3	36	1	3	4	4	11	1	2	3	4	....	1967-68	1970-7
• Ingoldsby, Jack	Tor.	2	29	5	1	6	15	....	....	....	....	....	....	1942-43	1943-4
• Ingram, Frank	Chi.	3	101	24	16	40	69	11	0	1	1	2	....	1929-30	1931-3
• Ingram, John	Bos.	1	1	0	0	0	0	....	....	....	....	....	....	1924-25	1924-2
• Ingram, Ron	Chi., Det., NYR	4	114	5	15	20	81	2	0	0	0	0	....	1956-57	1964-6
Intranuovo, Ralph	Edm., Tor.	3	22	2	4	6	4	....	....	....	....	....	....	1994-95	1996-9
• Irvin, Dick	Chi.	3	94	29	23	52	78	2	2	0	2	4	....	1926-27	1928-2
Irvine, Ted	Bos., L.A., NYR, St.L.	11	724	154	177	331	657	83	16	24	40	115	....	1963-64	1976-7
Irwin, Ivan	Mtl., NYR	5	155	2	27	29	214	5	0	0	0	8	....	1952-53	1957-5
• Isaksson, Ulf	L.A.	1	50	7	15	22	10	....	....	....	....	....	....	1982-83	1982-8
Isbister, Brad	Phx., NYI, Edm., Bos., NYR, Van.	10	541	106	116	222	615	18	1	2	3	33	....	1997-98	2007-0
Issel, Kim	Edm.	1	4	0	0	0	0	....	....	....	....	....	....	1988-89	1988-8

J

Name	NHL Teams	NHL Seasons	Regular Schedule GP	G	A	TP	PIM	Playoffs GP	G	A	TP	PIM	NHL Cup Wins	First NHL Season	Last NHL Season
‡ Jacina, Greg	Fla.	2	14	0	1	1	6	....	....	....	....	....	....	2005-06	2006-0
‡ Jackman, Ric	Dal., Bos., Tor., Pit., Fla., Ana.	7	231	19	58	77	166	7	1	1	2	2	1	1999-00	2006-0
• Jackson, Art	Tor., Bos., NYA	11	468	123	178	301	144	52	8	12	20	29	2	1934-35	1944-4
• Jackson, Busher	Tor., NYA, Bos.	15	633	241	234	475	437	71	18	12	30	53	1	1929-30	1943-4
Jackson, Dane	Van., Buf., NYI	4	45	12	6	18	58	6	0	0	0	10	....	1993-94	1997-9
Jackson, Don	Min., Edm., NYR	10	311	16	52	68	640	53	4	5	9	147	2	1977-78	1986-8
• Jackson, Harold	Chi., Det.	8	219	17	34	51	208	31	1	2	3	33	2	1936-37	1946-4
Jackson, Jack	Chi.	1	48	2	5	7	38	....	....	....	....	....	....	1946-47	1946-4
Jackson, Jeff	Tor., NYR, Que., Chi.	8	263	38	48	86	313	6	1	1	2	16	....	1984-85	1991-9
Jackson, Jim	Cgy., Buf.	4	112	17	30	47	20	14	3	2	5	6	....	1982-83	1987-8
• Jackson, Lloyd	NYA	1	14	1	1	2	0	....	....	....	....	....	....	1936-37	1936-3
• Jackson, Stan	Tor., Bos., Ott.	5	86	9	6	15	75	....	....	....	....	....	1	1921-22	1926-2
Jackson, Walter	NYA, Bos.	4	84	16	11	27	18	....	....	....	....	....	....	1932-33	1935-3
• Jacobs, Paul	Tor.	1	1	0	0	0	0	....	....	....	....	....	....	1918-19	1918-1
Jacobs, Tim	Cal.	1	46	0	10	10	35	....	....	....	....	....	....	1975-76	1975-7
‡ Jagr, Jaromir	Pit., Wsh., NYR	17	1273	646	953	1599	907	169	77	104	181	149	2	1990-91	2007-0
Jakopin, John	Fla., Pit., S.J.	6	113	1	6	7	145	....	....	....	....	....	....	1997-98	2002-0
Jalo, Risto	Edm.	1	3	0	3	3	0	....	....	....	....	....	....	1985-86	1985-8
Jalonen, Kari	Cgy., Edm.	2	37	9	6	15	4	5	1	0	1	0	....	1982-83	1983-8
James, Gerry	Tor.	5	149	14	26	40	257	15	1	0	1	8	....	1954-55	1959-6
James, Val	Buf., Tor.	2	11	0	0	0	30	3	0	0	0	0	....	1981-82	1986-8
Jamieson, Jim	NYR	1	1	0	1	1	0	....	....	....	....	....	....	1943-44	1943-4
• Jankowski, Lou	Det., Chi.	4	127	19	18	37	15	1	0	0	0	0	....	1950-51	1954-5
Janney, Craig	Bos., St.L., S.J., Wpg., Phx., T.B., NYI	12	760	188	563	751	170	120	24	86	110	53	....	1987-88	1998-9
Janssens, Mark	NYR, Min., Hfd., Ana., NYI, Phx., Chi.	14	711	40	73	113	1422	27	5	1	6	33	....	1987-88	2000-0
‡ Jantunen, Marko	Cgy.	1	3	0	0	0	0	....	....	....	....	....	....	1996-97	1996-9
Jardine, Ryan	Fla.	1	8	0	2	2	2	....	....	....	....	....	....	2001-02	2001-0
‡ Jarrett, Cole	NYI	1	1	0	0	0	0	....	....	....	....	....	....	2005-06	2005-0
Jarrett, Doug	Chi., NYR	13	775	38	182	220	631	99	7	16	23	82	....	1964-65	1976-7
Jarrett, Gary	Tor., Det., Oak., Cal.	7	341	72	92	164	131	11	3	1	4	9	....	1960-61	1971-7
Jarry, Pierre	NYR, Tor., Det., Min.	7	344	88	117	205	142	5	0	1	1	0	....	1971-72	1977-7
Jarvenpaa, Hannu	Wpg.	3	114	11	26	37	83	....	....	....	....	....	....	1986-87	1988-8
‡ Jarventie, Martti	Mtl.	1	1	0	0	0	0	....	....	....	....	....	....	2001-02	2001-0
Jarvi, Iiro	Que.	2	116	18	43	61	58	....	....	....	....	....	....	1988-89	1989-9
Jarvis, Doug	Mtl., Wsh., Hfd.	13	964	139	264	403	263	105	14	27	41	42	4	1975-76	1987-8
• Jarvis, James	Pit., Phi., Tor.	3	112	17	15	32	62	....	....	....	....	....	....	1929-30	1936-3
Jarvis, Wes	Wsh., Min., L.A., Tor.	9	237	31	55	86	98	2	0	0	0	2	....	1979-80	1987-8
‡ Jaspers, Jason	Phx.	3	9	0	1	1	6	....	....	....	....	....	....	2001-02	2003-0
Javanainen, Arto	Pit.	1	14	4	1	5	2	....	....	....	....	....	....	1984-85	1984-8
Jay, Bob	L.A.	1	3	0	1	1	0	....	....	....	....	....	....	1993-94	1993-9
Jeffrey, Larry	Det., Tor., NYR	8	368	39	62	101	293	38	4	10	14	42	1	1961-62	1968-6
Jelinek, Tomas	Ott.	1	49	7	6	13	52	....	....	....	....	....	....	1992-93	1992-9
Jenkins, Dean	L.A.	1	5	0	0	0	2	....	....	....	....	....	....	1983-84	1983-8
• Jenkins, Roger	Chi., Tor., Mtl., Bos., Mtl.M., NYA	8	325	15	39	54	253	27	1	7	8	12	2	1930-31	1938-3
Jennings, Bill	Det., Bos.	5	108	32	33	65	45	20	4	4	8	6	....	1940-41	1944-4
Jennings, Grant	Wsh., Hfd., Pit., Tor., Buf.	9	389	14	43	57	804	54	2	1	3	68	2	1987-88	1995-9
Jensen, Chris	NYR, Phi.	6	74	9	12	21	27	....	....	....	....	....	....	1985-86	1991-9
Jensen, David	Min.	3	18	0	2	2	11	....	....	....	....	....	....	1983-84	1985-8
Jensen, David	Hfd., Wsh.	4	69	9	13	22	22	11	0	0	0	2	....	1984-85	1987-8
Jensen, Joe	Car.	1	6	1	0	1	2	....	....	....	....	....	....	2007-08	2007-0
Jensen, Steve	Min., L.A.	7	438	113	107	220	318	12	0	3	3	9	....	1975-76	1981-8
• Jeremiah, Ed	NYA, Bos.	1	15	0	1	1	0	....	....	....	....	....	....	1931-32	1931-3
Jerrard, Paul	Min.	1	5	0	0	0	4	....	....	....	....	....	....	1988-89	1988-8
• Jerwa, Frank	Bos., St.L.	4	81	11	16	27	53	....	....	....	....	....	....	1931-32	1934-3
• Jerwa, Joe	NYR, Bos., NYA	7	234	29	58	87	309	17	2	3	5	16	....	1930-31	1938-3
‡ Jillson, Jeff	S.J., Bos., Buf.	4	140	9	32	41	96	8	0	0	0	0	....	2001-02	2005-0
Jirik, Jaroslav	St.L.	1	3	0	0	0	0	....	....	....	....	....	....	1969-70	1969-7
• Joanette, Rosario	Mtl.	1	2	0	1	1	4	....	....	....	....	....	....	1944-45	1944-4
Jodzio, Rick	Col., Cle.	1	70	2	8	10	71	....	....	....	....	....	....	1977-78	1977-7
Johannesen, Glenn	NYI	1	2	0	0	0	0	....	....	....	....	....	....	1985-86	1985-8
Johannson, John	N.J.	1	5	0	0	0	0	....	....	....	....	....	....	1983-84	1983-8
• Johansen, Bill	Tor.	1	1	0	0	0	0	....	....	....	....	....	....	1949-50	1949-5
Johansen, Trevor	Tor., Col., L.A.	5	286	11	46	57	282	13	0	3	3	21	....	1977-78	1981-8
‡ Johansson, Andreas	NYI, Pit., Ott., T.B., Cgy., NYR, Nsh.	8	377	81	88	169	190	9	0	0	0	0	....	1995-96	2003-0
Johansson, Bjorn	Cle.	2	15	1	1	2	10	....	....	....	....	....	....	1976-77	1977-7
Johansson, Calle	Buf., Wsh., Tor.	17	1109	119	416	535	519	105	12	43	55	44	....	1987-88	2003-0
‡ Johansson, Jonas	Wsh.	1	1	0	0	0	2	....	....	....	....	....	....	2005-06	2005-0
‡ Johansson, Magnus	Chi., Fla.	1	45	0	14	14	18	....	....	....	....	....	....	2007-08	2007-0
‡ Johansson, Mathias	Cgy., Pit.	1	58	5	10	15	16	....	....	....	....	....	....	2002-03	2002-0
Johansson, Roger	Cgy., Chi.	4	161	9	34	43	163	5	0	1	1	2	....	1989-90	1994-9
Johns, Don	NYR, Mtl., Min.	6	153	2	21	23	76	....	....	....	....	....	....	1960-61	1967-6
Johnson, Allan	Mtl., Det.	4	105	21	28	49	30	11	2	2	4	6	....	1956-57	1962-6
Johnson, Brian	Det.	1	3	0	0	0	5	....	....	....	....	....	....	1983-84	1983-8
• Johnson, Ching	NYR, NYA	12	436	38	48	86	808	61	5	2	7	161	2	1926-27	1937-3
Johnson, Craig	St.L., L.A., Ana., Tor., Wsh.	10	557	75	98	173	260	16	3	2	5	10	....	1994-95	2003-0
• Johnson, Danny	Tor., Van., Det.	3	121	18	19	37	24	....	....	....	....	....	....	1969-70	1971-7

Name	NHL Teams	NHL Seasons	Regular Schedule GP	G	A	TP	PIM	Playoffs GP	G	A	TP	PIM	NHL Cup Wins	First NHL Season	Last NHL Season
ohnson, Earl	Det.	1	1	0	0	0	0	....	....	....	....	....	1	1953-54	1953-54
ohnson, Greg	Det., Pit., Chi., Nsh.	12	785	145	224	369	345	37	7	6	13	14	....	1993-94	2005-06
ohnson, Jim	NYR, Phi., L.A.	8	302	75	111	186	73	7	0	2	2	2	....	1964-65	1971-72
ohnson, Jim	Pit., Min., Dal., Wsh., Phx.	13	829	29	166	195	1197	51	1	11	12	132	....	1985-86	1997-98
ohnson, Mark	Pit., Min., Hfd., St.L., N.J.	11	669	203	305	508	260	37	16	12	28	10	....	1979-80	1989-90
ohnson, Matt	L.A., Atl., Min.	10	473	23	20	43	1523	16	0	0	0	31	....	1994-95	2003-04
ohnson, Mike	Tor., T.B., Phx., Mtl., St.L.	11	661	129	246	375	315	22	4	3	7	10	....	1996-97	2007-08
ohnson, Norm	Bos., Chi.	3	61	5	20	25	41	14	4	0	4	6	....	1957-58	1959-60
ohnson, Terry	Que., St.L., Cgy., Tor.	9	285	3	24	27	580	38	0	4	4	118	....	1979-80	1987-88
ohnson, Tom	Mtl., Bos.	17	978	51	213	264	960	111	8	15	23	109	6	1947-48	1964-65
ohnson, Virgil	Chi.	3	75	1	11	12	27	19	0	3	3	4	1	1937-38	1944-45
ohnston, Bernie	Hfd.	2	57	12	24	36	16	3	0	1	1	0	....	1979-80	1980-81
ohnston, George	Chi.	4	58	20	12	32	2	....	....	....	....	....	....	1941-42	1946-47
ohnston, Greg	Bos., Tor.	9	187	26	29	55	124	22	2	1	3	12	....	1983-84	1991-92
ohnston, Jay	Wsh.	2	8	0	0	0	13	....	....	....	....	....	....	1980-81	1981-82
ohnston, Joey	Min., Cal., Chi.	6	331	85	106	191	320	....	....	....	....	....	....	1968-69	1975-76
ohnston, Larry	L.A., Det., K.C., Col.	7	320	9	64	73	580	....	....	....	....	....	....	1967-68	1976-77
ohnston, Marshall	Min., Cal.	7	251	14	52	66	58	6	0	0	0	2	....	1967-68	1973-74
ohnston, Randy	NYI	1	4	0	0	0	4	....	....	....	....	....	....	1979-80	1979-80
ohnstone, Eddie	NYR, Det.	10	426	122	136	258	375	55	13	10	23	83	....	1975-76	1986-87
ohnstone, Ross	Tor.	2	42	5	4	9	14	3	0	0	0	0	1	1943-44	1944-45
okela, Mikko	Van.	1	1	0	0	0	0	....	....	....	....	....	....	2002-03	2002-03
oliat, Aurele	Mtl.	16	655	270	190	460	771	45	9	13	22	66	3	1922-23	1937-38
oliat, Rene	Mtl.	1	1	0	0	0	0	....	....	....	....	....	....	1924-25	1924-25
oly, Greg	Wsh., Det.	9	365	21	76	97	250	5	0	0	0	8	....	1974-75	1982-83
oly, Yvan	Mtl.	3	2	0	0	0	0	1	0	0	0	0	....	1979-80	1982-83
omphe, Jean-Francois	Ana., Phx., Mtl.	4	111	10	29	39	102	....	....	....	....	....	....	1995-96	1998-99
onathan, Stan	Bos., Pit.	8	411	91	110	201	751	63	8	4	12	137	....	1975-76	1982-83
ones, Bob	NYR	1	2	0	0	0	0	....	....	....	....	....	....	1968-69	1968-69
ones, Brad	Wpg., L.A., Phi.	6	148	25	31	56	122	9	1	1	2	2	....	1986-87	1991-92
ones, Buck	Det., Tor.	4	50	2	2	4	36	12	0	1	1	18	....	1938-39	1942-43
ones, Jim	Cal.	1	2	0	0	0	0	....	....	....	....	....	....	1971-72	1971-72
ones, Jimmy	Tor.	3	148	13	18	31	68	19	1	5	6	11	....	1977-78	1979-80
ones, Keith	Wsh., Col., Phi.	9	491	117	141	258	765	63	12	12	24	120	....	1992-93	2000-01
ones, Matt	Phx.	3	106	1	10	11	63	....	....	....	....	....	....	2005-06	2007-08
ones, Ron	Bos., Pit., Wsh.	5	54	1	4	5	31	....	....	....	....	....	....	1971-72	1975-76
ones, Ty	Chi., Fla.	2	14	0	0	0	19	....	....	....	....	....	....	1998-99	2003-04
onsson, Hans	Pit.	4	242	10	38	48	92	27	0	1	1	14	....	1999-00	2002-03
onsson, Jorgen	NYI, Ana.	1	81	12	19	31	16	....	....	....	....	....	....	1999-00	1999-00
onsson, Kenny	Tor., NYI	10	686	63	204	267	298	19	1	3	4	6	....	1994-95	2003-04
onsson, Lars	Phi.	1	8	0	2	2	6	....	....	....	....	....	....	2006-07	2006-07
onsson, Tomas	NYI, Edm.	8	552	85	259	344	482	80	11	26	37	97	2	1981-82	1988-89
oseph, Chris	Pit., Edm., T.B., Van., Phi., Phx., Atl.	14	510	39	112	151	567	31	3	4	7	24	....	1987-88	2000-01
oseph, Tony	Wpg.	1	2	1	0	1	0	....	....	....	....	....	....	1988-89	1988-89
oyal, Eddie	Det., Tor., L.A., Phi.	9	466	128	134	262	103	50	11	8	19	18	....	1962-63	1971-72
oyce, Bob	Bos., Wsh., Wpg.	6	158	34	49	83	90	46	15	9	24	29	....	1987-88	1992-93
oyce, Duane	Dal.	1	3	0	0	0	0	....	....	....	....	....	....	1993-94	1993-94
uckes, Bing	NYR	2	16	2	1	3	6	....	....	....	....	....	....	1947-48	1949-50
uhlin, Patrik	Phi.	2	56	7	6	13	23	13	1	0	1	2	....	1994-95	1995-96
ulien, Claude	Que.	2	14	0	1	1	25	....	....	....	....	....	....	1984-85	1985-86
uneau, Joe	Bos., Wsh., Buf., Ott., Phx., Mtl.	13	828	156	416	572	272	112	25	54	79	69	....	1991-92	2003-04
unker, Steve	NYI	2	5	0	0	0	0	3	0	1	1	0	....	1992-93	1993-94
utila, Timo	Buf.	1	10	1	5	6	13	....	....	....	....	....	....	1984-85	1984-85
uzda, Bill	NYR, Tor.	9	398	14	54	68	398	42	0	3	3	46	2	1940-41	1951-52

K

abel, Bob	NYR	2	48	5	13	18	34	....	....	....	....	....	....	1959-60	1960-61
achowski, Mark	Pit.	3	64	6	5	11	209	....	....	....	....	....	....	1987-88	1989-90
achur, Ed	Chi.	2	96	10	14	24	35	....	....	....	....	....	....	1956-57	1957-58
aese, Trent	Buf.	1	1	0	0	0	0	....	....	....	....	....	....	1988-89	1988-89
aiser, Vern	Mtl.	1	50	7	5	12	33	2	0	0	0	0	....	1950-51	1950-51
albfleisch, Walter	Ott., St.L., NYA, Bos.	4	36	0	4	4	32	5	0	0	0	2	....	1933-34	1936-37
aleta, Alex	Chi., NYR	7	387	92	121	213	190	17	1	6	7	2	....	1941-42	1950-51
allio, Tomi	Atl., CBJ, Phi.	3	140	24	31	55	48	....	....	....	....	....	....	2000-01	2002-03
allur, Anders	NYI	6	383	101	110	211	149	78	12	23	35	32	4	1979-80	1984-85
amensky, Valeri	Que., Col., NYR, Dal., N.J.	11	637	200	301	501	383	66	25	35	60	72	1	1991-92	2001-02
aminski, Kevin	Min., Que., Wsh.	7	139	3	10	13	528	8	0	0	0	52	....	1988-89	1996-97
aminsky, Max	Ott., St.L., Bos., Mtl.M.	4	130	22	34	56	38	4	0	0	0	0	....	1933-34	1936-37
aminsky, Yan	Wpg., NYI	2	26	3	2	5	4	2	0	0	0	4	....	1993-94	1994-95
ampman, Bingo	Tor.	5	189	14	30	44	287	47	1	4	5	38	1	1937-38	1941-42
ane, Francis	Det.	1	2	0	0	0	0	....	....	....	....	....	....	1943-44	1943-44
anko, Petr	L.A.	1	10	1	0	1	0	....	....	....	....	....	....	2005-06	2005-06
annegiesser, Gord	St.L.	2	23	0	1	1	15	....	....	....	....	....	....	1967-68	1971-72
annegiesser, Sheldon	Pit., NYR, L.A., Van.	8	366	14	67	81	292	18	0	2	2	10	....	1970-71	1977-78
apanen, Niko	Dal., Atl., Phx.	6	397	36	90	126	160	18	5	4	9	22	....	2001-02	2007-08
apanen, Sami	Hfd., Car., Phi.	12	831	189	269	458	175	87	13	22	35	22	....	1995-96	2007-08
arabin, Ladislav	Pit.	1	9	0	0	0	2	....	....	....	....	....	....	1993-94	1993-94
aralahti, Jere	L.A., Nsh.	3	149	8	19	27	97	17	0	1	1	20	....	1999-00	2001-02
aramnov, Vitali	St.L.	3	92	12	20	32	65	2	0	0	0	2	....	1992-93	1994-95
ariya, Steve	Van.	3	65	9	18	27	32	....	....	....	....	....	....	1999-00	2001-02
arjalainen, Kyosti	L.A.	1	28	1	8	9	12	3	0	1	1	2	....	1991-92	1991-92
arlander, Al	Det.	4	212	36	56	92	70	4	0	1	1	0	....	1969-70	1972-73
arlsson, Andreas	Atl., T.B.	5	264	16	35	51	72	6	0	0	0	0	....	1999-00	2007-08
arpa, Dave	Que., Ana., Car., NYR	12	557	18	80	98	1374	19	1	1	2	39	....	1991-92	2002-03
arpov, Valeri	Ana.	3	76	14	15	29	32	....	....	....	....	....	....	1994-95	1996-97
arpovtsev, Alexander	NYR, Tor., Chi., NYI, Fla.	12	596	34	154	188	430	74	4	14	18	52	1	1993-94	2005-06
asatonov, Alexei	N.J., Ana., St.L., Bos.	7	383	38	122	160	326	33	4	7	11	40	....	1989-90	1995-96
asparaitis, Darius	NYI, Pit., Col., NYR	14	863	27	136	163	1379	83	2	10	12	107	....	1992-93	2006-07
asper, Steve	Bos., L.A., Phi., T.B.	13	821	177	291	468	554	94	20	28	48	82	....	1980-81	1992-93
astelic, Ed	Wsh., Hfd.	7	220	11	10	21	719	8	1	0	1	32	....	1985-86	1991-92
aszycki, Mike	NYI, Wsh., Tor.	5	226	42	80	122	108	19	2	6	8	10	....	1977-78	1982-83
avanagh, Pat	Van., Phi.	4	14	2	0	2	4	3	0	0	0	2	....	2000-01	2005-06
ea, Ed	Atl., St.L.	10	583	30	145	175	508	32	2	4	6	39	....	1973-74	1982-83
eane, Mike	Mtl., Col., NYR, Dal., St.L., Van.	16	1161	168	302	470	881	220	34	40	74	135	3	1988-89	2003-04
earns, Dennis	Van.	10	677	31	290	321	386	11	1	2	3	8	....	1971-72	1980-81
eating, Jack	Det.	2	11	3	0	3	4	....	....	....	....	....	....	1938-39	1939-40
eating, John	NYA	2	35	5	5	10	17	....	....	....	....	....	....	1931-32	1932-33
eating, Mike	NYR	1	1	0	0	0	0	....	....	....	....	....	....	1977-78	1977-78
eats, Duke	Bos., Det., Chi.	3	82	30	19	49	113	....	....	....	....	....	....	1926-27	1928-29
eczmer, Dan	Min., Hfd., Cgy., Dal., Nsh.	10	235	8	38	46	212	12	0	1	1	8	....	1990-91	1999-00
eefe, Sheldon	T.B.	3	125	12	12	24	78	....	....	....	....	....	....	2000-01	2002-03
eeling, Butch	Tor., NYR	12	525	157	63	220	331	47	11	11	22	34	1	1926-27	1937-38
eenan, Larry	Tor., St.L., Buf., Phi.	6	233	38	64	102	28	46	15	16	31	12	....	1961-62	1971-72
ehoe, Rick	Tor., Pit.	14	906	371	396	767	120	39	4	17	21	4	....	1971-72	1984-85
ekalainen, Jarmo	Bos., Ott.	3	55	5	8	13	28	....	....	....	....	....	....	1989-90	1993-94
elleher, Chris	Bos.	1	1	0	0	0	0	....	....	....	....	....	....	2001-02	2001-02
eller, Ralph	NYR	1	3	1	0	1	6	....	....	....	....	....	....	1962-63	1962-63
ellgren, Christer	Col.	1	5	0	0	0	0	....	....	....	....	....	....	1981-82	1981-82
elly, Bob	Phi., Wsh.	12	837	154	208	362	1454	101	9	14	23	172	2	1970-71	1981-82
elly, Bob	St.L., Pit., Chi.	6	425	87	109	196	687	23	6	3	9	40	....	1973-74	1978-79
elly, Dave	Det.	1	16	2	0	2	4	....	....	....	....	....	....	1976-77	1976-77
elly, John Paul	L.A.	7	400	54	70	124	366	18	1	1	2	41	....	1979-80	1985-86
elly, Pep	Tor., Chi., Bro.	8	288	74	53	127	105	38	7	6	13	10	....	1934-35	1941-42
elly, Pete	St.L., Det., NYA, Bro.	7	177	21	38	59	68	19	3	1	4	2	2	1934-35	1941-42
elly, Red	Det., Tor.	20	1316	281	542	823	327	164	33	59	92	51	8	1947-48	1966-67
elly, Steve	Edm., T.B., N.J., L.A., Min.	9	149	9	12	21	83	25	0	0	0	8	1	1996-97	2007-08
emp, Kevin	Hfd.	1	3	0	0	0	4	....	....	....	....	....	....	1980-81	1980-81
emp, Stan	Tor.	1	1	0	0	0	2	....	....	....	....	....	....	1948-49	1948-49
enady, Chris	St.L., NYR	2	7	0	2	2	0	....	....	....	....	....	....	1997-98	1999-00
endall, Bill	Chi., Tor.	5	131	16	10	26	28	6	0	0	0	0	1	1933-34	1937-38
ennedy, Dean	L.A., NYR, Buf., Wpg., Edm.	12	717	26	108	134	1118	36	1	7	8	59	....	1982-83	1994-95
ennedy, Forbes	Chi., Det., Bos., Phi., Tor.	11	603	70	108	178	988	12	2	4	6	64	....	1956-57	1968-69
ennedy, Mike	Dal., Tor., NYI	5	145	16	36	52	112	5	0	0	0	9	....	1994-95	1998-99
ennedy, Sheldon	Det., Cgy., Bos.	8	310	49	58	107	233	24	6	4	10	20	....	1989-90	1996-97
ennedy, Ted	Tor.	14	696	231	329	560	432	78	29	31	60	32	5	1942-43	1956-57

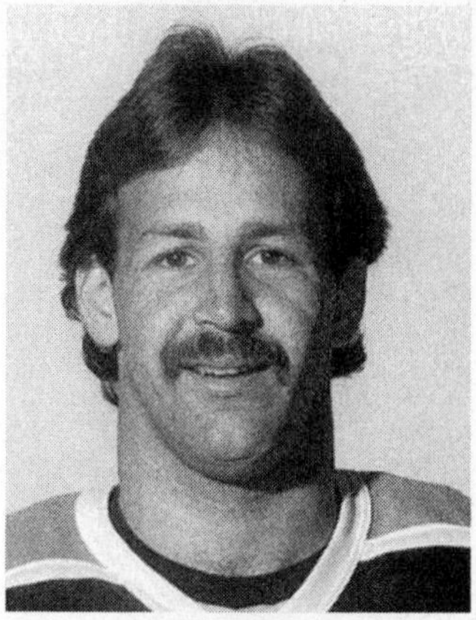
Claude Julien

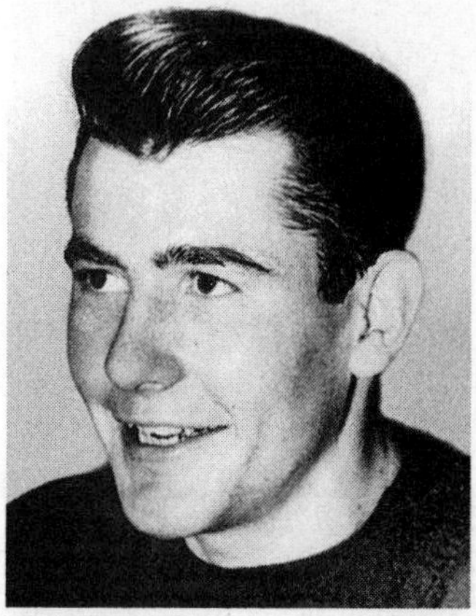
Francis Kane

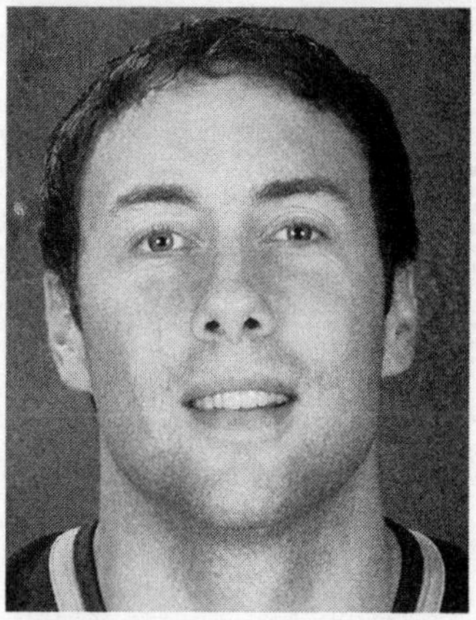
Steve Kelly

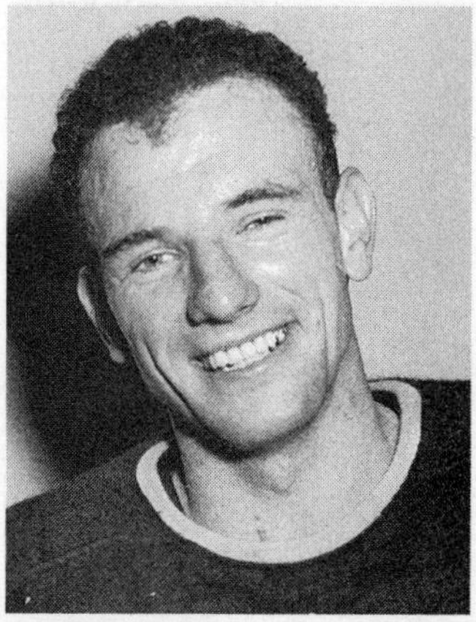
Ted Kennedy

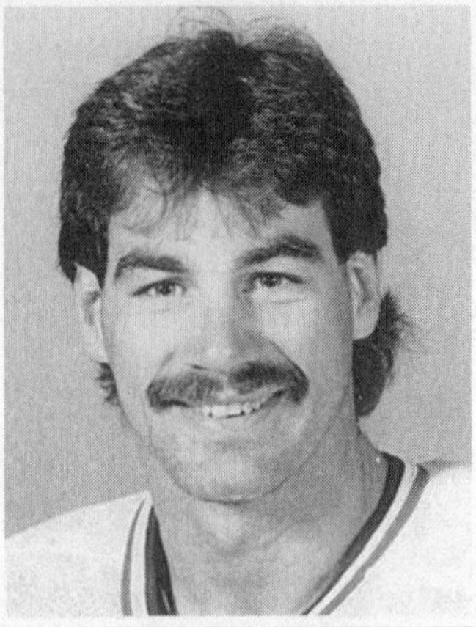

Scot Kleinendorst

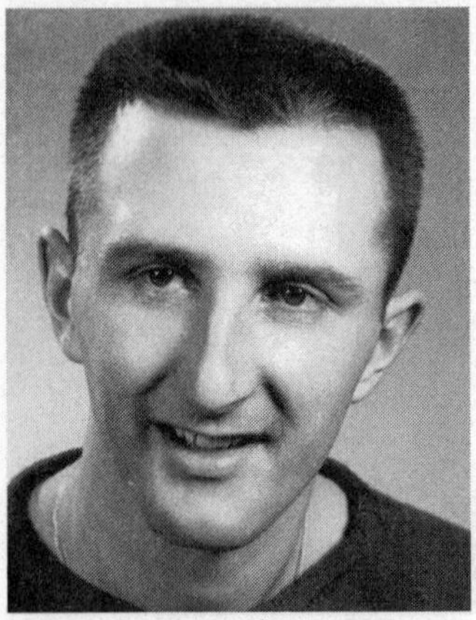

Aggie Kukulowicz

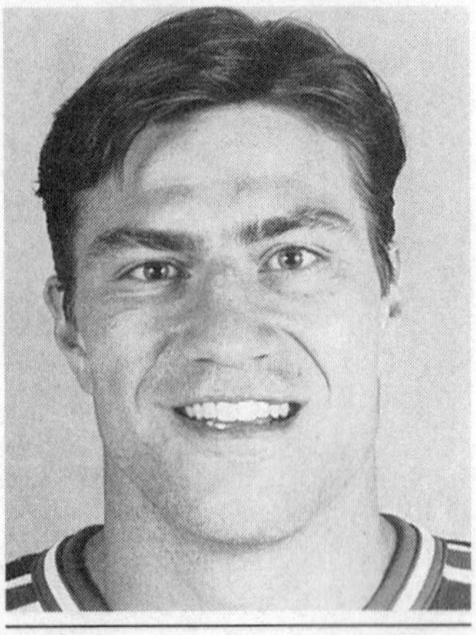

Nick Kypreos

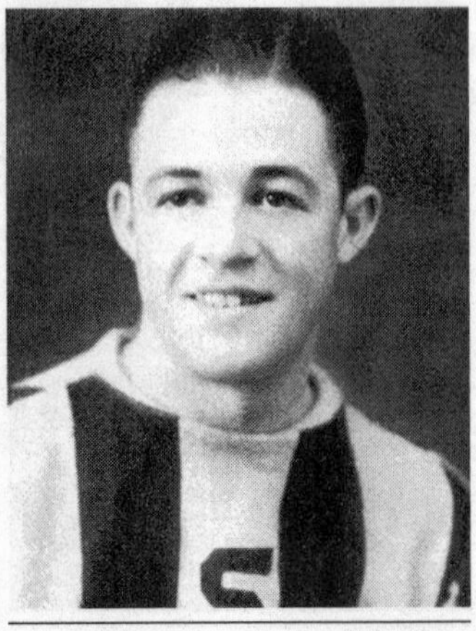

Adie Lafrance

			Regular Schedule					Playoffs							
Name	NHL Teams	NHL Seasons	GP	G	A	TP	PIM	GP	G	A	TP	PIM	NHL Cup Wins	First NHL Season	Last NHL Season
● Kenny, Ernest	NYR, Chi.	2	10	0	0	0	18	....	....	....	....	....	....	1930-31	1934-35
Keon, Dave	Tor., Hfd.	18	1296	396	590	986	117	92	32	36	68	6	4	1960-61	1981-82
Kerch, Alexander	Edm.	1	5	0	0	0	2	....	....	....	....	....	....	1993-94	1993-94
Kerr, Alan	NYI, Det., Wpg.	9	391	72	94	166	826	38	5	4	9	70	....	1984-85	1992-93
Kerr, Reg	Cle., Chi., Edm.	6	263	66	94	160	169	7	1	0	1	7	....	1977-78	1983-84
Kerr, Tim	Phi., NYR, Hfd.	13	655	370	304	674	596	81	40	31	71	58	....	1980-81	1992-93
Kesa, Dan	Van., Dal., Pit., T.B.	4	139	8	22	30	66	13	1	0	1	0	....	1993-94	1999-00
Kessell, Rick	Pit., Cal.	5	135	4	24	28	6	....	....	....	....	....	....	1969-70	1973-74
Ketola, Veli-Pekka	Col.	1	44	9	5	14	4	....	....	....	....	....	....	1981-82	1981-82
Ketter, Kerry	Atl.	1	41	0	2	2	58	....	....	....	....	....	....	1972-73	1972-73
Kharin, Sergei	Wpg.	1	7	2	3	5	2	....	....	....	....	....	....	1990-91	1990-91
‡ Kharitonov, Alexander	T.B., NYI	2	71	7	15	22	12	....	....	....	....	....	....	2000-01	2001-02
Khavanov, Alexander	St.L., Tor.	5	348	27	75	102	233	26	5	5	10	18	....	2000-01	2005-06
Khmylev, Yuri	Buf., St.L.	5	263	64	88	152	133	26	8	6	14	24	....	1992-93	1996-97
Khristich, Dmitri	Wsh., L.A., Bos., Tor.	12	811	259	337	596	422	75	15	25	40	41	....	1990-91	2001-02
Kidd, Ian	Van.	2	20	4	7	11	25	....	....	....	....	....	....	1987-88	1988-89
Kiessling, Udo	Min.	1	1	0	0	0	2	....	....	....	....	....	....	1981-82	1981-82
Kilger, Chad	Ana., Wpg., Phx., Chi., Edm., Mtl., Tor.	12	714	107	111	218	363	36	3	2	5	13	....	1995-96	2007-08
Kilrea, Brian	Det., L.A.	2	26	3	5	8	12	....	....	....	....	....	....	1957-58	1967-68
● Kilrea, Hec	Ott., Det., Tor.	15	633	167	129	296	438	48	8	7	15	18	3	1925-26	1939-40
● Kilrea, Ken	Det.	5	91	16	23	39	8	15	2	2	4	4	....	1938-39	1943-44
● Kilrea, Wally	Ott., Phi., NYA, Mtl.M., Det.	9	329	35	58	93	87	25	2	4	6	6	2	1929-30	1937-38
Kimble, Darin	Que., St.L., Bos., Chi.	7	311	23	20	43	1082	23	0	0	0	52	....	1988-89	1994-95
Kindrachuk, Orest	Phi., Pit., Wsh.	10	508	118	261	379	648	76	20	20	40	53	2	1972-73	1981-82
King, Derek	NYI, Hfd., Tor., St.L.	14	830	261	351	612	417	47	4	17	21	24	....	1986-87	1999-00
King, Frank	Mtl.	1	10	1	0	1	2	....	....	....	....	....	....	1950-51	1950-51
King, Kris	Det., NYR, Wpg., Phx., Tor., Chi.	14	849	66	85	151	2030	67	8	5	13	142	....	1987-88	2000-01
King, Steven	NYR, Ana.	3	67	17	8	25	75	....	....	....	....	....	....	1992-93	1995-96
King, Wayne	Cal.	3	73	5	18	23	34	....	....	....	....	....	....	1973-74	1975-76
Kinnear, Geordie	Atl.	1	4	0	0	0	13	....	....	....	....	....	....	1999-00	1999-00
Kinsella, Brian	Wsh.	2	10	0	1	1	0	....	....	....	....	....	....	1975-76	1976-77
● Kinsella, Ray	Ott.	1	14	0	0	0	0	....	....	....	....	....	....	1930-31	1930-31
‡ Kiprusoff, Marko	Mtl., NYI	2	51	0	10	10	12	....	....	....	....	....	....	1995-96	2001-02
● Kirk, Bobby	NYR	1	39	4	8	12	14	....	....	....	....	....	....	1937-38	1937-38
● Kirkpatrick, Bob	NYR	1	49	12	12	24	6	....	....	....	....	....	....	1942-43	1942-43
Kirton, Mark	Tor., Det., Van.	6	266	57	56	113	121	4	1	2	3	7	....	1979-80	1984-85
Kisio, Kelly	Det., NYR, S.J., Cgy.	13	761	229	429	658	768	39	6	15	21	52	....	1982-83	1994-95
Kitchen, Bill	Mtl., Tor.	4	41	1	4	5	40	3	0	1	1	0	....	1981-82	1984-85
● Kitchen, Hobie	Mtl.M., Det.	2	47	5	4	9	58	....	....	....	....	....	1	1925-26	1926-27
Kitchen, Mike	Col., N.J.	8	474	12	62	74	370	2	0	0	0	2	....	1976-77	1983-84
Kjellberg, Patric	Mtl., Nsh., Ana.	6	394	64	96	160	84	10	0	0	0	0	....	1992-93	2002-03
Klassen, Ralph	Cal., Cle., Col., St.L.	9	497	52	93	145	120	26	4	2	6	12	....	1975-76	1983-84
Klatt, Trent	Min., Dal., Phi., Van., L.A.	13	782	143	200	343	307	74	16	9	25	20	....	1991-92	2003-04
Klee, Ken	Wsh., Tor., N.J., Col., Atl., Ana., Phx.	14	934	55	140	195	880	51	2	2	4	50	....	1994-95	2008-09
● Klein, Lloyd	Bos., NYA	8	164	30	24	54	68	5	0	0	0	2	1	1928-29	1937-38
Kleinendorst, Scot	NYR, Hfd., Wsh.	8	281	12	46	58	452	26	2	7	9	40	....	1982-83	1989-90
‡ Klemm, Jon	Que., Col., Chi., Dal., L.A.	15	773	42	100	142	436	105	7	7	14	47	2	1991-92	2007-08
Klima, Petr	Det., Edm., T.B., L.A., Pit.	13	786	313	260	573	671	95	28	24	52	83	1	1985-86	1998-99
Klimovich, Sergei	Chi.	1	1	0	0	0	2	....	....	....	....	....	....	1996-97	1996-97
● Klingbeil, Ike	Chi.	1	5	1	2	3	2	....	....	....	....	....	....	1936-37	1936-37
‡ Kloucek, Tomas	NYR, Nsh., Atl.	5	141	2	8	10	250	....	....	....	....	....	....	2000-01	2005-06
● Klukay, Joe	Tor., Bos.	11	566	109	127	236	189	71	13	10	23	23	4	1942-43	1955-56
Kluzak, Gord	Bos.	7	299	25	98	123	543	46	6	13	19	129	....	1982-83	1990-91
● Knibbs, Bill	Bos.	1	53	7	10	17	4	....	....	....	....	....	....	1964-65	1964-65
Knipscheer, Fred	Bos., St.L.	3	28	6	3	9	18	16	2	1	3	6	....	1993-94	1995-96
● Knott, Nick	Bro.	1	14	3	1	4	9	....	....	....	....	....	....	1941-42	1941-42
Knox, Paul	Tor.	1	1	0	0	0	0	....	....	....	....	....	....	1954-55	1954-55
Knutsen, Espen	Ana., CBJ	5	207	30	81	111	105	....	....	....	....	....	....	1997-98	2003-04
Koalska, Matt	NYI	1	3	0	0	0	2	....	....	....	....	....	....	2005-06	2005-06
Kocur, Joe	Det., NYR, Van.	15	820	80	82	162	2519	118	10	12	22	231	3	1984-85	1998-99
Koehler, Greg	Car.	1	1	0	0	0	0	....	....	....	....	....	....	2000-01	2000-01
‡ Kohn, Ladislav	Cgy., Tor., Ana., Atl., Det.	7	186	14	28	42	125	2	0	0	0	5	....	1995-96	2002-03
‡ Koivisto, Tom	St.L.	1	22	2	4	6	10	....	....	....	....	....	....	2002-03	2002-03
‡ Kolarik, Pavel	Bos.	2	23	0	0	0	10	....	....	....	....	....	....	2000-01	2001-02
Kolesar, Mark	Tor.	2	28	2	2	4	14	3	1	0	1	2	....	1995-96	1996-97
‡ Kolnik, Juraj	NYI, Fla.	6	240	46	49	95	84	....	....	....	....	....	....	2000-01	2006-07
Kolstad, Dean	Min., S.J.	3	40	1	7	8	69	....	....	....	....	....	....	1988-89	1992-93
‡ Koltsov, Konstantin	Pit.	3	144	12	26	38	50	....	....	....	....	....	....	2002-03	2005-06
Komadoski, Neil	L.A., St.L.	8	502	16	76	92	632	23	0	2	2	47	....	1972-73	1979-80
Komarniski, Zenith	Van., CBJ	3	21	1	1	2	10	....	....	....	....	....	....	1999-00	2003-04
‡ Kondratiev, Maxim	Tor., NYR, Ana.	3	40	1	2	3	24	....	....	....	....	....	....	2003-04	2007-08
Konik, George	Pit.	1	52	7	8	15	26	....	....	....	....	....	....	1967-68	1967-68
Konowalchuk, Steve	Wsh., Col.	14	790	171	225	396	703	52	9	12	21	60	....	1991-92	2005-06
Konroyd, Steve	Cgy., NYI, Chi., Hfd., Det., Ott.	15	895	41	195	236	863	97	10	15	25	99	....	1980-81	1994-9
Konstantinov, Vladimir	Det.	6	446	47	128	175	838	82	5	14	19	107	1	1991-92	1996-97
Kontos, Chris	NYR, Pit., L.A., T.B.	8	230	54	69	123	103	20	11	0	11	12	....	1982-83	1992-9
● Kopak, Russ	Bos.	1	24	7	9	16	0	....	....	....	....	....	....	1943-44	1943-44
Korab, Jerry	Chi., Van., Buf., L.A.	15	975	114	341	455	1629	93	8	18	26	201	....	1970-71	1984-8
Kordic, Dan	Phi.	6	197	4	8	12	584	12	1	0	1	22	....	1991-92	1998-99
● Kordic, John	Mtl., Tor., Wsh., Que.	7	244	17	18	35	997	41	4	3	7	131	1	1985-86	1991-92
Korn, Jim	Det., Tor., Buf., N.J., Cgy.	10	597	66	122	188	1801	16	1	2	3	109	....	1979-80	1989-90
Korney, Mike	Det., NYR	4	77	9	10	19	59	....	....	....	....	....	....	1973-74	1978-79
Korolev, Evgeny	NYI	3	42	1	4	5	20	2	0	0	0	0	....	1999-00	2001-02
‡ Korolev, Igor	St.L., Wpg., Phx., Tor., Chi.	12	795	119	227	346	330	41	0	8	8	6	....	1992-93	2003-04
Koroll, Cliff	Chi.	11	814	208	254	462	376	85	19	29	48	67	....	1969-70	1979-80
‡ Korolyuk, Alexander	S.J.	6	296	62	80	142	140	34	6	8	14	18	....	1997-98	2003-04
Kortko, Roger	NYI	2	79	7	17	24	28	10	0	3	3	17	....	1984-85	1985-86
Kostynski, Doug	Bos.	2	15	3	1	4	4	....	....	....	....	....	....	1983-84	1984-85
Kotanen, Dick	NYR	1	1	0	0	0	0	....	....	....	....	....	....	1950-51	1950-51
Kotsopoulos, Chris	NYR, Hfd., Tor., Det.	10	479	44	109	153	827	31	1	3	4	91	....	1980-81	1989-90
‡ Kovalenko, Andrei	Que., Col., Mtl., Edm., Phi., Car., Bos.	9	620	173	206	379	389	33	5	6	11	20	....	1992-93	2000-01
Kowal, Joe	Buf.	2	22	0	5	5	13	2	0	0	0	0	....	1976-77	1977-78
Kozak, Don	L.A., Van.	7	437	96	86	182	480	29	7	2	9	69	....	1972-73	1978-79
Kozak, Les	Tor.	1	12	1	0	1	2	....	....	....	....	....	....	1961-62	1961-62
‡ Kraft, Milan	Pit.	4	207	41	41	82	52	8	0	0	0	2	....	2000-01	2003-04
Kraft, Ryan	S.J.	1	7	0	1	1	0	....	....	....	....	....	....	2002-03	2002-0
● Kraftcheck, Stephen	Bos., NYR, Tor.	4	157	11	18	29	83	6	0	0	0	7	....	1950-51	1958-5
Krake, Skip	Bos., L.A., Buf.	7	249	23	40	63	182	10	1	0	1	17	....	1963-64	1970-7
Kravchuk, Igor	Chi., Edm., St.L., Ott., Cgy., Fla.	12	699	64	210	274	251	51	6	15	21	18	....	1991-92	2002-0
Kravets, Mikhail	S.J.	2	2	0	0	0	0	....	....	....	....	....	....	1991-92	1992-9
Krentz, Dale	Det.	3	30	5	3	8	9	2	0	0	0	0	....	1986-87	1988-8
‡ Krestanovich, Jordan	Col.	2	22	0	2	2	6	....	....	....	....	....	....	2001-02	2003-0
‡ Kristek, Jaroslav	Buf.	1	6	0	0	0	4	....	....	....	....	....	....	2002-03	2002-0
‡ Krivokrasov, Sergei	Chi., Nsh., Cgy., Min., Ana.	10	450	86	109	195	288	21	2	0	2	14	....	1992-93	2001-0
● Krol, Joe	NYR, Bro.	3	26	10	4	14	8	....	....	....	....	....	....	1936-37	1941-4
Kromm, Richard	Cgy., NYI	9	372	70	103	173	138	36	2	6	8	22	....	1983-84	1992-9
Kron, Robert	Van., Hfd., Car., CBJ	12	771	144	194	338	119	16	3	2	5	2	....	1990-91	2001-0
Krook, Kevin	Col.	1	3	0	0	0	2	....	....	....	....	....	....	1978-79	1978-79
‡ Kroupa, Vlastimil	S.J., N.J.	5	105	4	19	23	66	20	1	2	3	25	....	1993-94	1997-98
Krulicki, Jim	NYR, Det.	1	41	0	3	3	6	....	....	....	....	....	....	1970-71	1970-7
Krupp, Uwe	Buf., NYI, Que., Col., Det., Atl.	15	729	69	212	281	660	81	6	23	29	86	1	1986-87	2002-0
Kruppke, Gord	Det.	3	23	0	0	0	32	....	....	....	....	....	....	1990-91	1993-9
Kruse, Paul	Cgy., NYI, Buf., S.J.	11	423	38	33	71	1074	28	5	2	7	36	....	1990-91	2000-0
Krushelnyski, Mike	Bos., Edm., L.A., Tor., Det.	14	897	241	328	569	699	139	29	43	72	106	3	1981-82	1994-9
Krutov, Vladimir	Van.	1	61	11	23	34	20	....	....	....	....	....	....	1989-90	1989-90
Krygier, Todd	Hfd., Wsh., Ana.	9	543	100	143	243	533	48	10	7	17	40	....	1989-90	1997-98
Kryskow, Dave	Chi., Wsh., Det., Atl.	4	231	33	56	89	174	12	2	0	2	4	....	1972-73	1975-7
● Kryzanowski, Ed	Bos., Chi.	5	237	15	22	37	65	18	0	1	1	4	....	1948-49	1952-5
Kucera, Frantisek	Chi., Hfd., Van., Phi., CBJ, Pit., Wsh.	9	465	24	95	119	251	12	0	1	1	0	....	1990-91	2001-0
‡ Kudashov, Alexei	Tor.	1	25	1	0	1	4	....	....	....	....	....	....	1993-94	1993-9
Kudelski, Bob	L.A., Ott., Fla.	9	442	139	102	241	218	22	4	4	8	4	....	1987-88	1995-9
‡ Kudroc, Kristian	T.B., Fla.	3	26	2	2	4	38	....	....	....	....	....	....	2000-01	2003-0
● Kuhn, Gord	NYA	1	12	1	1	2	4	....	....	....	....	....	....	1932-33	1932-3
● Kukulowicz, Aggie	NYR	2	4	1	0	1	0	....	....	....	....	....	....	1952-53	1953-5
Kulak, Stu	Van., Edm., NYR, Que., Wpg.	4	90	8	4	12	130	3	0	0	0	2	....	1982-83	1988-8
Kuleshov, Mikhail	Col.	1	3	0	0	0	0	....	....	....	....	....	....	2003-04	2003-0

Name	NHL Teams	NHL Seasons	Regular Schedule GP	G	A	TP	PIM	Playoffs GP	G	A	TP	PIM	NHL Cup Wins	First NHL Season	Last NHL Season
Kullman, Arnie	Bos.	2	13	0	1	1	11	....	....	....	....	....	....	1947-48	1949-50
Kullman, Eddie	NYR	6	343	56	70	126	298	6	1	0	1	2	....	1947-48	1953-54
Kultanen, Jarno	Bos.	3	102	2	11	13	59	....	....	....	....	....	....	2000-01	2002-03
Kumpel, Mark	Que., Det., Wpg.	6	288	38	46	84	113	39	6	4	10	14	....	1984-85	1990-91
Kuntz, Alan	NYR	2	45	10	12	22	12	6	1	0	1	2	....	1941-42	1945-46
Kuntz, Murray	St.L.	1	7	1	2	3	0	....	....	....	....	....	....	1974-75	1974-75
Kurka, Tomas	Car.	2	17	3	2	5	2	....	....	....	....	....	....	2002-03	2003-04
Kurri, Jari	Edm., L.A., NYR, Ana., Col.	17	1251	601	797	1398	545	200	106	127	233	123	5	1980-81	1997-98
Kurtenbach, Orland	NYR, Bos., Tor., Van.	13	639	119	213	332	628	19	2	4	6	70	....	1960-61	1973-74
Kurtz, Justin	Van.	1	27	3	5	8	14	....	....	....	....	....	....	2001-02	2001-02
Kurvers, Tom	Mtl., Buf., N.J., Tor., Van., NYI, Ana.	11	659	93	328	421	350	57	8	22	30	68	1	1984-85	1994-95
Kuryluk, Merv	Chi.	1	....	....	....	....	....	2	0	0	0	0	....	1961-62	1961-62
Kushner, Dale	NYI, Phi.	3	84	10	13	23	215	....	....	....	....	....	....	1989-90	1991-92
Kutlak, Zdenek	Bos.	3	16	1	2	3	4	....	....	....	....	....	....	2000-01	2003-04
Kuznetsov, Maxim	Det., L.A.	4	136	2	8	10	137	....	....	....	....	....	....	2000-01	2003-04
Kuznik, Greg	Car.	1	1	0	0	0	0	....	....	....	....	....	....	2000-01	2000-01
Kuzyk, Ken	Cle.	2	41	5	9	14	8	....	....	....	....	....	....	1976-77	1977-78
Kvartalnov, Dmitri	Bos.	2	112	42	49	91	26	4	0	0	0	0	....	1992-93	1993-94
Kvasha, Oleg	Fla., NYI, Phx.	7	493	81	136	217	335	21	1	2	3	8	....	1998-99	2005-06
Kwiatkowski, Joel	Ott., Wsh., Fla., Pit., Atl.	7	282	16	29	45	245	6	0	0	0	2	....	2000-01	2007-08
Kwong, Larry	NYR	1	1	0	0	0	0	....	....	....	....	....	....	1947-48	1947-48
Kyle, Bill	NYR	2	3	0	3	3	0	....	....	....	....	....	....	1949-50	1950-51
Kyle, Gus	NYR, Bos.	3	203	6	20	26	362	14	1	2	3	34	....	1949-50	1951-52
Kyllonen, Markku	Wpg.	1	9	0	2	2	2	....	....	....	....	....	....	1988-89	1988-89
Kypreos, Nick	Wsh., Hfd., NYR, Tor.	8	442	46	44	90	1210	34	1	3	4	65	1	1989-90	1996-97
Kyte, Jim	Wpg., Pit., Cgy., Ott., S.J.	13	598	17	49	66	1342	42	0	6	6	94	....	1982-83	1995-96
L															
Laaksonen, Antti	Bos., Min., Col.	8	483	81	87	168	152	25	1	5	6	6	....	1998-99	2006-07
Labadie, Mike	NYR	1	3	0	0	0	0	....	....	....	....	....	....	1952-53	1952-53
Labatte, Neil	St.L.	2	26	0	2	2	19	....	....	....	....	....	....	1978-79	1981-82
L'Abbe, Moe	Chi.	1	5	0	1	1	0	....	....	....	....	....	....	1972-73	1972-73
Labelle, Marc	Dal.	1	9	0	0	0	46	....	....	....	....	....	....	1996-97	1996-97
Labine, Leo	Bos., Det.	11	643	128	193	321	730	60	12	11	23	82	....	1951-52	1961-62
Labossiere, Gord	NYR, L.A., Min.	6	215	44	62	106	75	10	2	3	5	28	....	1963-64	1971-72
Labovitch, Max	NYR	1	5	0	0	0	4	....	....	....	....	....	....	1943-44	1943-44
Labraaten, Dan	Det., Cgy.	4	268	71	73	144	47	8	1	0	1	4	....	1978-79	1981-82
Labre, Yvon	Pit., Wsh.	9	371	14	87	101	788	....	....	....	....	....	....	1970-71	1980-81
Labrie, Guy	Bos., NYR	2	42	4	9	13	16	....	....	....	....	....	....	1943-44	1944-45
Lach, Elmer	Mtl.	14	664	215	408	623	478	76	19	45	64	36	3	1940-41	1953-54
Lachance, Michel	Col.	1	21	0	4	4	22	....	....	....	....	....	....	1978-79	1978-79
Lachance, Scott	NYI, Mtl., Van., CBJ	13	819	31	112	143	567	11	1	2	3	6	....	1991-92	2003-04
Lacombe, Francois	Oak., Buf., Que.	4	78	2	17	19	54	3	1	0	1	0	....	1968-69	1979-80
Lacombe, Normand	Buf., Edm., Phi.	7	319	53	62	115	196	26	5	1	6	49	1	1984-85	1990-91
Lacroix, Andre	Phi., Chi., Hfd.	6	325	79	119	198	44	16	2	5	7	0	....	1967-68	1979-80
Lacroix, Daniel	NYR, Bos., Phi., Edm., NYI	7	188	11	7	18	379	16	0	1	1	26	....	1993-94	1999-00
Lacroix, Eric	Tor., L.A., Col., NYR, Ott.	8	472	67	70	137	361	30	1	5	6	25	....	1993-94	2000-01
Lacroix, Pierre	Que., Hfd.	4	274	24	108	132	197	8	0	2	2	10	....	1979-80	1982-83
Ladouceur, Randy	Det., Hfd., Ana.	14	930	30	126	156	1322	40	5	8	13	59	....	1982-83	1995-96
LaFayette, Nathan	St.L., Van., NYR, L.A.	6	187	17	20	37	103	32	2	7	9	8	....	1993-94	1998-99
Laflamme, Christian	Chi., Edm., Mtl., St.L.	8	324	2	45	47	282	9	0	1	1	6	....	1996-97	2003-04
Lafleur, Guy	Mtl., NYR, Que.	17	1126	560	793	1353	399	128	58	76	134	67	5	1971-72	1990-91
Lafleur, Roland	Mtl.	1	1	0	0	0	0	....	....	....	....	....	....	1924-25	1924-25
LaFontaine, Pat	NYI, Buf., NYR	15	865	468	545	1013	552	69	26	36	62	36	....	1983-84	1997-98
Laforce, Ernie	Mtl.	1	1	0	0	0	0	....	....	....	....	....	....	1942-43	1942-43
LaForest, Bob	L.A.	1	5	1	0	1	2	....	....	....	....	....	....	1983-84	1983-84
Laforge, Claude	Mtl., Det., Phi.	8	193	24	33	57	82	5	1	2	3	15	....	1957-58	1968-69
Laforge, Marc	Hfd., Edm.	2	14	0	0	0	64	....	....	....	....	....	....	1989-90	1993-94
Laframboise, Pete	Cal., Wsh., Pit.	4	227	33	55	88	70	9	1	0	1	0	....	1971-72	1974-75
Lafrance, Adie	Mtl.	1	3	0	0	0	2	2	0	0	0	0	....	1933-34	1933-34
Lafrance, Leo	Mtl., Chi.	2	33	2	0	2	6	....	....	....	....	....	....	1926-27	1927-28
Lafreniere, Jason	Que., NYR, T.B.	5	146	34	53	87	22	15	1	5	6	19	....	1986-87	1993-94
Lafreniere, Roger	Det., St.L.	2	13	0	0	0	4	....	....	....	....	....	....	1962-63	1972-73
Lagace, Jean-Guy	Pit., Buf., K.C.	6	197	9	39	48	251	....	....	....	....	....	....	1968-69	1975-76
Laidlaw, Tom	NYR, L.A.	10	705	25	139	164	717	69	4	17	21	78	....	1980-81	1989-90
Laird, Robbie	Min.	1	1	0	0	0	0	....	....	....	....	....	....	1979-80	1979-80
Lajeunesse, Serge	Det., Phi.	5	103	1	4	5	103	....	....	....	....	....	....	1970-71	1974-75
Lakovic, Sasha	Cgy., N.J.	3	37	0	4	4	118	....	....	....	....	....	....	1996-97	1998-99
Lalande, Hec	Chi., Det.	4	151	21	39	60	120	....	....	....	....	....	....	1953-54	1957-58
Lalonde, Bobby	Van., Atl., Bos., Cgy.	11	641	124	210	334	298	16	4	2	6	6	....	1971-72	1981-82
Lalonde, Newsy	Mtl., NYA	6	99	125	41	166	183	7	15	4	19	32	....	1917-18	1926-27
Lalonde, Ron	Pit., Wsh.	7	397	45	78	123	106	....	....	....	....	....	....	1972-73	1978-79
Lalor, Mike	Mtl., St.L., Wsh., Wpg., S.J., Dal.	12	687	17	88	105	677	92	5	10	15	167	1	1985-86	1996-97
Lamb, Joe	Mtl.M., Ott., NYA, Bos., Mtl., St.L., Det.	11	443	108	101	209	601	18	1	1	2	51	....	1927-28	1937-38
Lamb, Mark	Cgy., Det., Edm., Ott., Phi., Mtl.	11	403	46	100	146	291	70	7	19	26	51	1	1985-86	1995-96
Lambert, Dan	Que.	2	29	6	9	15	22	....	....	....	....	....	....	1990-91	1991-92
Lambert, Denny	Ana., Ott., Nsh., Atl.	8	487	27	66	93	1391	17	0	1	1	28	....	1994-95	2001-02
Lambert, Lane	Det., NYR, Que.	6	283	58	66	124	521	17	2	4	6	40	....	1983-84	1988-89
Lambert, Yvon	Mtl., Buf.	10	683	206	273	479	340	90	27	22	49	67	4	1972-73	1981-82
Lamby, Dick	St.L.	3	22	0	5	5	22	....	....	....	....	....	....	1978-79	1980-81
Lamirande, Jean-Paul	NYR, Mtl.	4	49	5	5	10	26	8	0	0	0	4	....	1946-47	1954-55
Lammens, Hank	Ott.	1	27	1	2	3	22	....	....	....	....	....	....	1993-94	1993-94
Lamoureux, Leo	Mtl.	6	235	19	79	98	175	28	1	6	7	16	2	1941-42	1946-47
Lamoureux, Mitch	Pit., Phi.	3	73	11	9	20	59	....	....	....	....	....	....	1983-84	1987-88
Lampman, Mike	St.L., Van., Wsh.	4	96	17	20	37	34	....	....	....	....	....	....	1972-73	1976-77
Lancien, Jack	NYR	4	63	1	5	6	35	6	0	1	1	2	....	1946-47	1950-51
Landon, Larry	Mtl., Tor.	2	9	0	0	0	2	....	....	....	....	....	....	1983-84	1984-85
Landry, Eric	Cgy., Mtl.	4	68	5	9	14	47	....	....	....	....	....	....	1997-98	2001-02
Lane, Gord	Wsh., NYI	10	539	19	94	113	1228	75	3	14	17	214	4	1975-76	1984-85
Lane, Myles	NYR, Bos.	3	71	4	1	5	41	11	0	0	0	0	1	1928-29	1933-34
Langdon, Darren	NYR, Car., Van., Mtl., N.J.	11	521	16	23	39	1251	25	1	0	1	20	....	1994-95	2005-06
Langdon, Steve	Bos.	3	7	0	1	1	2	4	0	0	0	0	....	1974-75	1977-78
Langelle, Pete	Tor.	4	136	22	51	73	11	39	5	9	14	4	1	1938-39	1941-42
Langevin, Chris	Buf.	2	22	3	1	4	22	....	....	....	....	....	....	1983-84	1985-86
Langevin, Dave	NYI, Min., L.A.	8	513	12	107	119	530	87	2	17	19	106	4	1979-80	1986-87
Langfeld, Josh	Ott., S.J., Bos., Det., Nsh.	6	143	9	23	32	60	1	0	0	0	0	....	2001-02	2007-08
Langlais, Alain	Min.	2	25	4	4	8	10	....	....	....	....	....	....	1973-74	1974-75
Langlois, Albert	Mtl., NYR, Det., Bos.	9	497	21	91	112	488	53	1	5	6	50	3	1957-58	1965-66
Langlois, Charlie	Ham., NYA, Pit., Mtl.	4	151	22	5	27	189	2	0	0	0	0	....	1924-25	1927-28
Langway, Rod	Mtl., Wsh.	15	994	51	278	329	849	104	5	22	27	97	1	1978-79	1992-93
Lank, Jeff	Phi.	1	2	0	0	0	2	....	....	....	....	....	....	1999-00	1999-00
Lanthier, Jean-Marc	Van.	4	105	16	16	32	29	....	....	....	....	....	....	1983-84	1987-88
Lanyon, Ted	Pit.	1	5	0	0	0	4	....	....	....	....	....	....	1967-68	1967-68
Lanz, Rick	Van., Tor., Chi.	10	569	65	221	286	448	28	3	8	11	35	....	1980-81	1991-92
Laperriere, Daniel	St.L., Ott.	4	48	2	5	7	27	....	....	....	....	....	....	1992-93	1995-96
Laperriere, Jacques	Mtl.	12	691	40	242	282	674	88	9	22	31	101	6	1962-63	1973-74
Laplante, Darryl	Det.	3	35	0	6	6	10	....	....	....	....	....	....	1997-98	1999-00
Lapointe, Claude	Que., Col., Cgy., NYI, Phi.	14	879	127	178	305	721	34	4	7	11	44	....	1990-91	2003-04
Lapointe, Guy	Mtl., St.L., Bos.	16	884	171	451	622	893	123	26	44	70	138	6	1968-69	1983-84
Lapointe, Martin	Det., Bos., Chi., Ott.	16	991	181	200	381	1417	108	19	24	43	202	2	1991-92	2007-08
Lapointe, Rick	Det., Phi., St.L., Que., L.A.	11	664	44	176	220	831	46	2	7	9	64	....	1975-76	1985-86
Lappin, Peter	Min., S.J.	2	7	0	0	0	2	....	....	....	....	....	....	1989-90	1991-92
Laprade, Edgar	NYR	10	500	108	172	280	42	18	4	9	13	4	....	1945-46	1954-55
LaPrairie, Benjamin	Chi.	1	7	0	0	0	0	....	....	....	....	....	....	1936-37	1936-37
Larionov, Igor	Van., S.J., Det., Fla., N.J.	14	921	169	475	644	474	150	30	67	97	60	3	1989-90	2003-04
Lariviere, Garry	Que., Edm.	4	219	6	57	63	167	14	0	5	5	8	....	1979-80	1982-83
Larmer, Jeff	Col., N.J., Chi.	5	158	37	51	88	57	5	1	0	1	2	....	1981-82	1985-86
Larmer, Steve	Chi., NYR	15	1006	441	571	1012	532	140	56	75	131	89	1	1980-81	1994-95
Larochelle, Wildor	Mtl., Chi.	12	474	92	74	166	211	34	6	4	10	24	2	1925-26	1936-37
Larocque, Denis	L.A.	1	8	0	1	1	18	....	....	....	....	....	....	1987-88	1987-88
Larocque, Mario	T.B.	1	5	0	0	0	16	....	....	....	....	....	....	1998-99	1998-99
Larose, Bonner	Bos.	1	6	0	0	0	0	....	....	....	....	....	....	1925-26	1925-26
Larose, Claude	Mtl., Min., St.L.	16	943	226	257	483	887	97	14	18	32	143	5	1962-63	1977-78
Larose, Claude	NYR	2	25	4	7	11	2	2	0	0	0	0	....	1979-80	1981-82
Larose, Cory	NYR	1	7	0	1	1	4	....	....	....	....	....	....	2003-04	2003-04

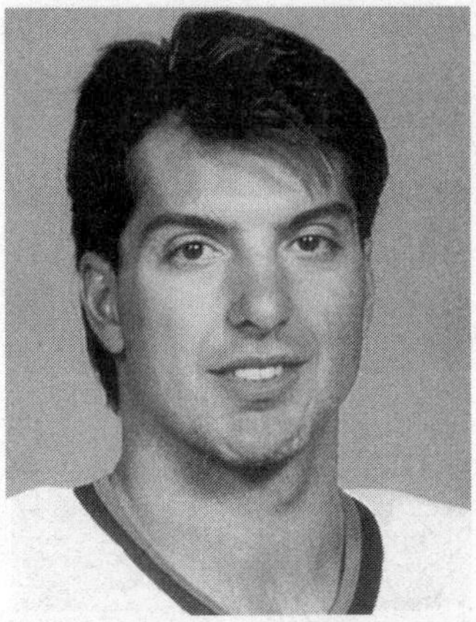

Brian Lawton

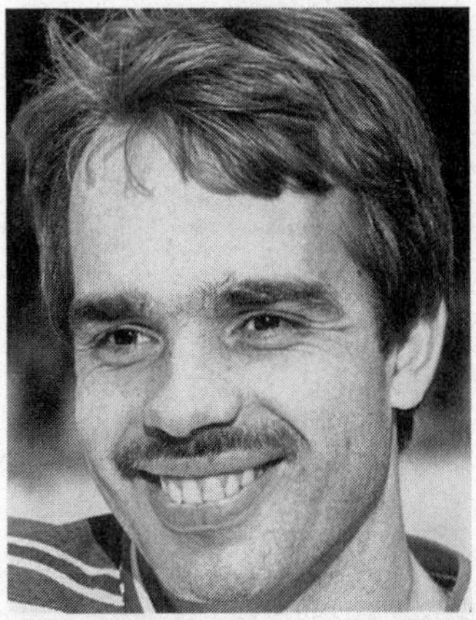

Mikko Leinonen

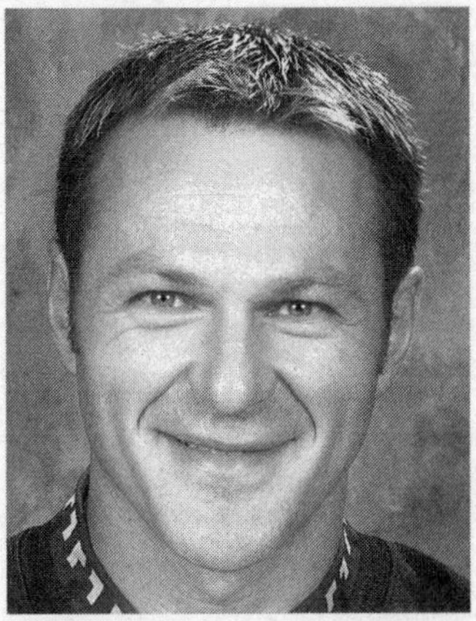

Claude Lemieux

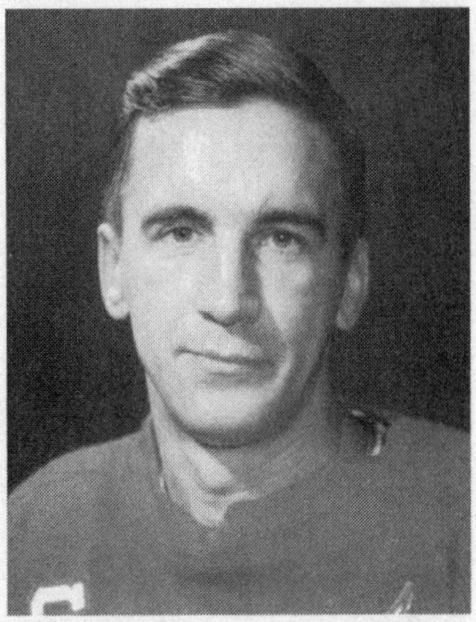

Ted Lindsay

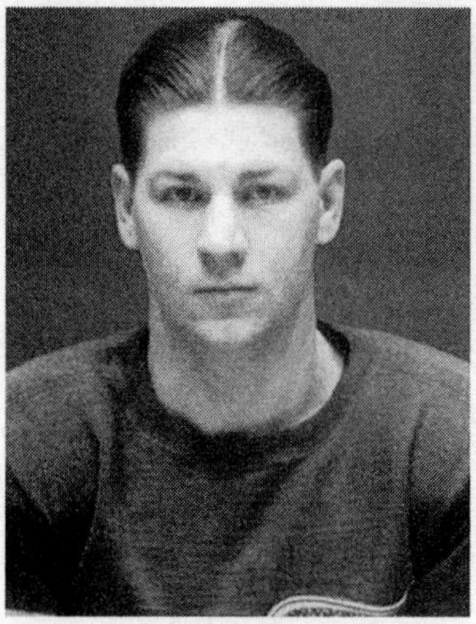

Carl Liscombe

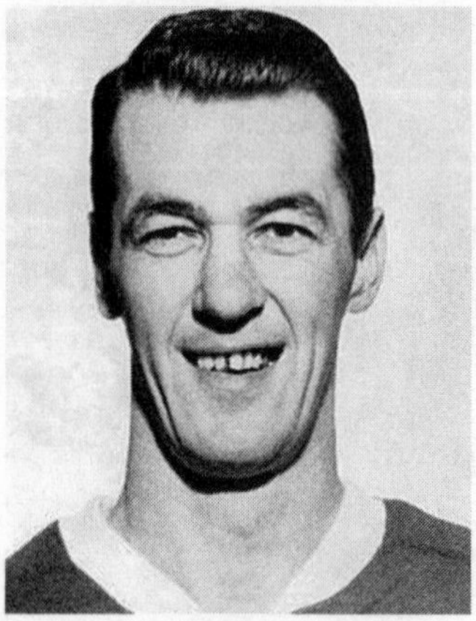

Ed Litzenberger

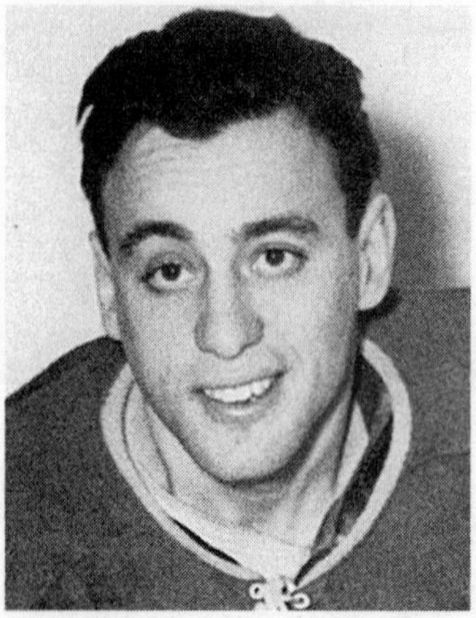

Jacques Locas

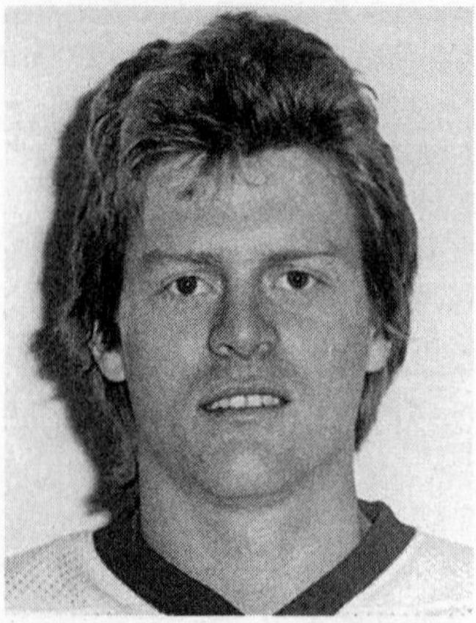

Danny Lucas

			Regular Schedule					Playoffs							
Name	NHL Teams	NHL Seasons	GP	G	A	TP	PIM	GP	G	A	TP	PIM	NHL Cup Wins	First NHL Season	Last NHL Season
Larose, Guy	Wpg., Tor., Cgy., Bos.	6	70	10	9	19	63	4	0	0	0	0	....	1988-89	1994-95
Larouche, Pierre	Pit., Mtl., Hfd., NYR	14	812	395	427	822	237	64	20	34	54	16	2	1974-75	1987-88
Larouche, Steve	Ott., NYR, L.A.	2	26	9	9	18	10	....	....	....	....	....	....	1994-95	1995-96
• Larson, Norm	NYA, Bro., NYR	3	89	25	18	43	12	....	....	....	....	....	....	1940-41	1946-47
Larson, Reed	Det., Bos., Edm., NYI, Min., Buf.	14	904	222	463	685	1391	32	4	7	11	63	....	1976-77	1989-90
Larter, Tyler	Wsh.	1	1	0	0	0	0	....	....	....	....	....	....	1989-90	1989-90
Latal, Jiri	Phi.	3	92	12	36	48	24	....	....	....	....	....	....	1989-90	1991-92
Latos, James	NYR	1	1	0	0	0	0	....	....	....	....	....	....	1988-89	1988-89
Latreille, Phil	NYR	1	4	0	0	0	2	....	....	....	....	....	....	1960-61	1960-61
Latta, David	Que.	4	36	4	8	12	4	....	....	....	....	....	....	1985-86	1990-91
• Lauder, Martin	Bos.	1	3	0	0	0	2	....	....	....	....	....	....	1927-28	1927-28
Lauen, Mike	Wpg.	1	4	0	1	1	0	....	....	....	....	....	....	1983-84	1983-84
Lauer, Brad	NYI, Chi., Ott., Pit.	9	323	44	67	111	218	34	7	5	12	24	....	1986-87	1995-96
Laughlin, Craig	Mtl., Wsh., L.A., Tor.	8	549	136	205	341	364	33	6	6	12	20	....	1981-82	1988-89
Laughton, Mike	Oak., Cal.	4	189	39	48	87	101	11	3	4	7	0	....	1967-68	1970-71
Laukkanen, Janne	Que., Col., Ott., Pit., T.B.	9	407	22	99	121	335	59	7	9	16	46	....	1994-95	2002-03
Laurence, Don	Atl., St.L.	2	79	15	22	37	14	....	....	....	....	....	....	1978-79	1979-80
Laus, Paul	Fla.	9	530	14	58	72	1702	30	2	7	9	74	....	1993-94	2001-02
LaVallee, Kevin	Cgy., L.A., St.L., Pit.	7	366	110	125	235	85	32	5	8	13	21	....	1980-81	1986-87
LaVarre, Mark	Chi.	3	78	9	16	25	58	1	0	0	0	2	....	1985-86	1987-88
Lavender, Brian	St.L., NYI, Det., Cal.	4	184	16	26	42	174	3	0	0	0	2	....	1971-72	1974-75
Lavigne, Eric	L.A.	1	1	0	0	0	0	....	....	....	....	....	....	1994-95	1994-95
• Laviolette, Jack	Mtl.	1	18	2	1	3	6	2	0	0	0	0	....	1917-18	1917-18
Laviolette, Peter	NYR	1	12	0	0	0	6	....	....	....	....	....	....	1988-89	1988-89
Lavoie, Dominic	St.L., Ott., Bos., L.A.	6	38	5	8	13	32	....	....	....	....	....	....	1988-89	1993-94
‡ Law, Kirby	Phi.	3	9	0	1	1	4	....	....	....	....	....	....	2000-01	2003-04
Lawless, Paul	Hfd., Phi., Van., Tor.	7	239	49	77	126	54	3	0	2	2	2	....	1982-83	1989-90
Lawrence, Mark	Dal., NYI	6	142	18	26	44	115	....	....	....	....	....	....	1994-95	2000-01
• Lawson, Danny	Det., Min., Buf.	5	219	28	29	57	61	16	0	1	1	2	....	1967-68	1971-72
Lawton, Brian	Min., NYR, Hfd., Que., Bos., S.J.	9	483	112	154	266	401	11	1	1	2	12	....	1983-84	1992-93
Laxdal, Derek	Tor., NYI	6	67	12	7	19	88	1	0	2	2	2	....	1984-85	1990-91
• Laycoe, Hal	NYR, Mtl., Bos.	11	531	25	77	102	292	40	2	5	7	39	....	1945-46	1955-56
Lazaro, Jeff	Bos., Ott.	3	102	14	23	37	114	28	3	3	6	32	....	1990-91	1992-93
Leach, Jamie	Pit., Hfd., Fla.	5	81	11	9	20	12	....	....	....	....	....	1	1989-90	1993-94
Leach, Larry	Bos.	3	126	13	29	42	91	7	1	1	2	8	....	1958-59	1961-62
Leach, Reggie	Bos., Cal., Phi., Det.	13	934	381	285	666	387	94	47	22	69	22	1	1970-71	1982-83
Leach, Stephen	Wsh., Bos., St.L., Car., Ott., Phx., Pit.	15	702	130	153	283	978	92	15	11	26	87	....	1985-86	1999-00
‡ Leahy, Patrick	Bos., Nsh.	3	50	4	4	8	19	....	....	....	....	....	....	2003-04	2006-07
Leavins, Jim	Det., NYR	2	41	2	12	14	30	....	....	....	....	....	....	1985-86	1986-87
Lebeau, Patrick	Mtl., Cgy., Fla., Pit.	4	15	3	2	5	6	....	....	....	....	....	....	1990-91	1998-99
Lebeau, Stephan	Mtl., Ana.	7	373	118	159	277	105	30	9	7	16	12	1	1988-89	1994-95
LeBlanc, Fern	Det.	3	34	5	6	11	0	....	....	....	....	....	....	1976-77	1978-79
LeBlanc, J.P.	Chi., Det.	5	153	14	30	44	87	2	0	0	0	0	....	1968-69	1978-79
LeBlanc, John	Van., Edm., Wpg.	7	83	26	13	39	28	1	0	0	0	0	....	1986-87	1994-95
LeBoutillier, Peter	Ana.	2	35	2	1	3	176	....	....	....	....	....	....	1996-97	1997-98
LeBrun, Al	NYR	2	6	0	2	2	4	....	....	....	....	....	....	1960-61	1965-66
Lecaine, Bill	Pit.	1	4	0	0	0	0	....	....	....	....	....	....	1968-69	1968-69
Leclair, Jackie	Mtl.	3	160	20	40	60	56	20	6	1	7	6	1	1954-55	1956-57
LeClair, John	Mtl., Phi., Pit.	16	967	406	413	819	501	154	42	47	89	94	1	1990-91	2006-07
Leclerc, Mike	Ana., Phx., Cgy.	9	341	64	94	158	288	26	2	9	11	14	....	1996-97	2005-06
Leclerc, Rene	Det.	2	87	10	11	21	105	....	....	....	....	....	....	1968-69	1970-71
Lecuyer, Doug	Chi., Wpg., Pit.	4	126	11	31	42	178	7	4	0	4	15	....	1978-79	1982-83
‡ Ledin, Per	Col.	1	3	0	0	0	2	....	....	....	....	....	....	2008-09	2008-09
Ledingham, Walt	Chi., NYI	3	15	0	2	2	4	....	....	....	....	....	....	1972-73	1976-77
• Leduc, Albert	Mtl., Ott., NYR	10	383	57	35	92	614	28	5	6	11	32	2	1925-26	1934-35
LeDuc, Rich	Bos., Que.	4	130	28	38	66	69	5	0	0	0	9	....	1972-73	1980-81
Ledyard, Grant	NYR, L.A., Wsh., Buf., Dal., Van., Bos., Ott., T.B.	18	1028	90	276	366	766	83	6	12	18	96	....	1984-85	2001-02
• Lee, Bobby	Mtl.	1	1	0	0	0	0	....	....	....	....	....	....	1942-43	1942-43
Lee, Edward	Que.	1	2	0	0	0	5	....	....	....	....	....	....	1984-85	1984-85
Lee, Peter	Pit.	6	431	114	131	245	257	19	0	8	8	4	....	1977-78	1982-83
‡ Leeb, Brad	Van., Tor.	3	5	0	0	0	2	....	....	....	....	....	....	1999-00	2003-04
‡ Leeb, Greg	Dal.	1	2	0	0	0	0	....	....	....	....	....	....	2000-01	2000-01
Leeman, Gary	Tor., Cgy., Mtl., Van., St.L.	14	667	199	267	466	531	36	8	16	24	36	1	1982-83	1996-97
Leetch, Brian	NYR, Tor., Bos.	18	1205	247	781	1028	571	95	28	69	97	36	1	1987-88	2005-06
‡ Lefebvre, Guillaume	Phi., Pit., Bos.	4	39	2	4	6	13	....	....	....	....	....	....	2001-02	2009-10
‡ Lefebvre, Patrice	Wsh.	1	3	0	0	0	2	....	....	....	....	....	....	1998-99	1998-99
Lefebvre, Sylvain	Mtl., Tor., Que., Col., NYR	14	945	30	154	184	674	129	4	14	18	101	1	1989-90	2002-03
• Lefley, Bryan	NYI, K.C., Col.	5	228	7	29	36	101	2	0	0	0	0	....	1972-73	1977-78
Lefley, Chuck	Mtl., St.L.	9	407	128	164	292	137	29	5	8	13	10	2	1970-71	1980-81
• Leger, Roger	NYR, Mtl.	5	187	18	53	71	71	20	0	7	7	14	....	1943-44	1949-50
Legge, Barry	Que., Wpg.	3	107	1	11	12	144	....	....	....	....	....	....	1979-80	1981-82
Legge, Randy	NYR	1	12	0	2	2	2	....	....	....	....	....	....	1972-73	1972-73
Lehman, Tommy	Bos., Edm.	3	36	5	5	10	16	....	....	....	....	....	....	1987-88	1989-90
Lehto, Petteri	Pit.	1	6	0	0	0	4	....	....	....	....	....	....	1984-85	1984-85
Lehtonen, Antero	Wsh.	1	65	9	12	21	14	....	....	....	....	....	....	1979-80	1979-80
‡ Lehtonen, Mikko	Nsh.	1	15	1	2	3	8	....	....	....	....	....	....	2006-07	2006-07
Lehvonen, Henry	K.C.	1	4	0	0	0	0	....	....	....	....	....	....	1974-75	1974-75
Leier, Edward	Chi.	2	16	2	1	3	2	....	....	....	....	....	....	1949-50	1950-51
Leinonen, Mikko	NYR, Wsh.	4	162	31	78	109	71	20	2	11	13	28	....	1981-82	1984-85
Leiter, Bobby	Bos., Pit., Atl.	10	447	98	126	224	144	8	3	0	3	2	....	1962-63	1975-76
Leiter, Ken	NYI, Min.	5	143	14	36	50	62	15	0	6	6	8	....	1984-85	1989-90
Lemaire, Jacques	Mtl.	12	853	366	469	835	217	145	61	78	139	63	8	1967-68	1978-79
Lemay, Moe	Van., Edm., Bos., Wpg.	8	317	72	94	166	442	28	6	3	9	55	1	1981-82	1988-89
Lemelin, Roger	K.C., Col.	4	36	1	2	3	27	....	....	....	....	....	....	1974-75	1977-78
Lemieux, Alain	St.L., Que., Pit.	6	119	28	44	72	38	19	4	6	10	0	....	1981-82	1986-87
Lemieux, Bob	Oak.	1	19	0	1	1	12	....	....	....	....	....	....	1967-68	1967-68
Lemieux, Claude	Mtl., N.J., Col., Phx., Dal., S.J.	21	1215	379	407	786	1777	234	80	78	158	529	4	1983-84	2008-09
Lemieux, Jacques	L.A.	3	19	0	4	4	8	1	0	0	0	0	....	1967-68	1969-70
Lemieux, Jean	Atl., Wsh.	5	204	23	63	86	39	3	1	1	2	0	....	1973-74	1977-78
Lemieux, Jocelyn	St.L., Mtl., Chi., Hfd., N.J., Cgy., Phx.	12	598	80	84	164	740	60	5	10	15	88	....	1986-87	1997-98
Lemieux, Mario	Pit.	18	915	690	1033	1723	834	107	76	96	172	87	2	1984-85	2005-06
• Lemieux, Real	Det., L.A., NYR, Buf.	8	456	51	104	155	262	18	2	4	6	10	....	1966-67	1973-74
Lemieux, Rich	Van., K.C., Atl.	5	274	39	82	121	132	2	0	0	0	0	....	1971-72	1975-76
Lenardon, Tim	N.J., Van.	2	15	2	1	3	4	....	....	....	....	....	....	1986-87	1989-90
• Lepine, Hec	Mtl.	1	33	5	2	7	2	....	....	....	....	....	....	1925-26	1925-26
• Lepine, Pit	Mtl.	13	526	143	98	241	392	41	7	5	12	26	2	1925-26	1937-38
Leroux, Francois	Edm., Ott., Pit., Col.	10	249	3	20	23	577	33	1	3	4	34	....	1988-89	1997-98
Leroux, Gaston	Mtl.	1	2	0	0	0	0	....	....	....	....	....	....	1935-36	1935-36
‡ Leroux, Jean-Yves	Chi.	5	220	16	22	38	146	....	....	....	....	....	....	1996-97	2000-01
Leschyshyn, Curtis	Que., Col., Wsh., Hfd., Car., Min., Ott.	16	1033	47	165	212	669	68	2	6	8	34	1	1988-89	2003-04
• Lesieur, Art	Mtl., Chi.	4	100	4	2	6	50	14	0	0	0	4	1	1928-29	1935-36
‡ Lessard, Junior	Dal., T.B.	3	27	3	1	4	23	....	....	....	....	....	....	2005-06	2007-08
Lessard, Rick	Cgy., S.J.	3	15	0	4	4	18	....	....	....	....	....	....	1988-89	1991-92
Lesuk, Bill	Bos., Phi., L.A., Wsh., Wpg.	8	388	44	63	107	368	9	1	0	1	12	1	1968-69	1979-80
• Leswick, Jack	Chi.	1	37	1	7	8	16	....	....	....	....	....	1	1933-34	1933-34
• Leswick, Pete	NYA, Bos.	2	3	1	0	1	0	....	....	....	....	....	....	1936-37	1944-45
• Leswick, Tony	NYR, Det., Chi.	12	740	165	159	324	900	59	13	10	23	91	3	1945-46	1957-58
‡ Letang, Alan	Dal., Cgy., NYI	3	14	0	0	0	2	....	....	....	....	....	....	1999-00	2002-03
• Levandoski, Joe	NYR	1	8	1	1	2	0	....	....	....	....	....	....	1946-47	1946-47
Leveille, Normand	Bos.	2	75	17	25	42	49	....	....	....	....	....	....	1981-82	1982-83
• Leveque, Guy	L.A.	2	17	2	2	4	21	....	....	....	....	....	....	1992-93	1993-94
Lever, Don	Van., Atl., Cgy., Col., N.J., Buf.	15	1020	313	367	680	593	30	7	10	17	26	....	1972-73	1986-87
Levie, Craig	Wpg., Min., St.L., Van.	6	183	22	53	75	177	16	2	3	5	32	....	1981-82	1986-87
Levins, Scott	Wpg., Fla., Ott., Phx.	5	124	13	20	33	316	....	....	....	....	....	....	1992-93	1997-98
• Levinsky, Alex	Tor., NYR, Chi.	9	367	19	49	68	307	37	2	1	3	26	2	1930-31	1938-39
Levo, Tapio	Col., N.J.	2	107	16	53	69	36	....	....	....	....	....	....	1981-82	1982-83
Lewicki, Danny	Tor., NYR, Chi.	9	461	105	135	240	177	28	0	4	4	8	1	1950-51	1958-59
Lewis, Dale	NYR	1	8	0	0	0	0	....	....	....	....	....	....	1975-76	1975-76
Lewis, Dave	NYI, L.A., N.J., Det.	15	1008	36	187	223	953	91	1	20	21	143	....	1973-74	1987-88
• Lewis, Doug	Mtl.	1	3	0	0	0	0	....	....	....	....	....	....	1946-47	1946-47
• Lewis, Herbie	Det.	11	483	148	161	309	248	38	13	10	23	6	2	1928-29	1938-39
Ley, Rick	Tor., Hfd.	6	310	12	72	84	528	14	0	2	2	20	....	1968-69	1980-81
Liba, Igor	NYR, L.A.	1	37	7	18	25	36	2	0	0	0	2	....	1988-89	1988-89
Libby, Jeff	NYI	1	1	0	0	0	0	....	....	....	....	....	....	1997-98	1997-98
Libett, Nick	Det., Pit.	14	982	237	268	505	472	16	6	2	8	2	....	1967-68	1980-81

			Regular Schedule					Playoffs							
ame	NHL Teams	NHL Seasons	GP	G	A	TP	PIM	GP	G	A	TP	PIM	NHL Cup Wins	First NHL Season	Last NHL Season
cari, Tony	Det.	1	9	0	1	1	0	....	....	....	....	....	....	1946-47	1946-47
ddington, Bob	Tor.	1	11	0	1	1	2	....	....	....	....	....	....	1970-71	1970-71
dster, Doug	Van., NYR, St.L., Dal.	16	897	75	268	343	679	80	6	15	21	64	1	1983-84	1998-99
lley, John	Ana.	3	23	3	8	11	13	....	....	....	....	....	....	1993-94	1995-96
nd, Juha	Dal., Mtl.	3	133	9	13	22	20	15	2	2	4	8	....	1997-98	2000-01
ndberg, Chris	Cgy., Que.	3	116	17	25	42	47	2	0	1	1	2	....	1991-92	1993-94
ndbom, Johan	NYR	1	38	1	3	4	28	....	....	....	....	....	....	1997-98	1997-98
nden, Jamie	Fla.	1	4	0	0	0	17	....	....	....	....	....	....	1994-95	1994-95
nden, Trevor	Van., NYI, Mtl., Wsh.	19	1382	375	492	867	895	124	34	65	99	104	....	1988-89	2007-08
ndgren, Lars	Van., Min.	6	394	25	113	138	325	40	5	6	11	20	....	1978-79	1983-84
ndgren, Mats	Edm., NYI, Van.	8	387	54	74	128	146	24	1	5	6	10	....	1996-97	2003-04
ndholm, Mikael	L.A.	1	18	2	2	4	2	....	....	....	....	....	....	1989-90	1989-90
ndros, Brett	NYI	2	51	2	5	7	147	....	....	....	....	....	....	1994-95	1995-96
ndros, Eric	Phi., NYR, Tor., Dal.	14	760	372	493	865	1398	53	24	33	57	122	....	1992-93	2006-07
ndsay, Bill	Que., Fla., Cgy., S.J., Mtl., Atl.	13	777	83	141	224	922	42	7	8	15	44	....	1991-92	2003-04
ndsay, Ted	Det., Chi.	17	1068	379	472	851	1808	133	47	49	96	194	4	1944-45	1964-65
ndstrom, Willy	Wpg., Edm., Pit.	8	582	161	162	323	200	57	14	18	32	24	2	1979-80	1986-87
ing, David	Mtl., CBJ	5	93	4	4	8	191	....	....	....	....	....	....	1996-97	2003-04
inseman, Ken	Phi., Edm., Bos., Tor.	14	860	256	551	807	1727	113	43	77	120	325	1	1978-79	1991-92
intner, Richard	Nsh., NYR, Pit.	3	112	8	12	20	54	....	....	....	....	....	....	1999-00	2002-03
ipuma, Chris	T.B., S.J.	5	72	0	9	9	146	....	....	....	....	....	....	1992-93	1996-97
iscombe, Carl	Det.	9	373	137	140	277	117	59	22	19	41	20	1	1937-38	1945-46
itzenberger, Ed	Mtl., Chi., Det., Tor.	12	618	178	238	416	283	40	5	13	18	34	4	1952-53	1963-64
oach, Lonnie	Ott., L.A., Ana.	2	56	10	13	23	29	1	0	0	0	0	....	1992-93	1993-94
ocas, Jacques	Mtl.	2	59	7	8	15	66	....	....	....	....	....	....	1947-48	1948-49
ochead, Bill	Det., Col., NYR	6	330	69	62	131	180	7	3	0	3	6	....	1974-75	1979-80
ocking, Norm	Chi.	2	48	2	6	8	26	....	....	....	....	....	....	1934-35	1935-36
oewen, Darcy	Buf., Ott.	5	135	4	8	12	211	....	....	....	....	....	....	1989-90	1993-94
ofthouse, Mark	Wsh., Det.	6	181	42	38	80	73	....	....	....	....	....	....	1977-78	1982-83
ogan, Dave	Chi., Van.	6	218	5	29	34	470	12	0	0	0	10	....	1975-76	1980-81
ogan, Robert	Buf., L.A.	3	42	10	5	15	0	....	....	....	....	....	....	1986-87	1988-89
oiselle, Claude	Det., N.J., Que., Tor., NYI	13	616	92	117	209	1149	41	4	11	15	58	....	1981-82	1993-94
omakin, Andrei	Phi., Fla.	4	215	42	62	104	92	....	....	....	....	....	....	1991-92	1994-95
oney, Brian	Van.	1	12	2	3	5	6	....	....	....	....	....	....	1995-96	1995-96
oney, Troy	Pit., Ana., NYI, NYR	12	624	87	110	197	1091	67	8	14	22	97	2	1983-84	1994-95
ong, Barry	L.A., Det., Wpg.	5	280	11	68	79	250	5	0	1	1	18	....	1972-73	1981-82
ong, Stan	Mtl.	1	....	....	....	....	....	3	0	0	0	0	....	1951-52	1951-52
onsberry, Ross	Bos., L.A., Phi., Pit.	15	968	256	310	566	806	100	21	25	46	87	2	1966-67	1980-81
oob, Hakan	Cgy.	6	450	193	236	429	189	73	26	28	54	16	1	1983-84	1988-89
oob, Peter	Que.	1	8	1	2	3	0	....	....	....	....	....	....	1984-85	1984-85
orentz, Jim	Bos., St.L., NYR, Buf.	10	659	161	238	399	208	54	12	10	22	30	1	1968-69	1977-78
orimer, Bob	NYI, Col., N.J.	10	529	22	90	112	431	49	3	10	13	83	2	1976-77	1985-86
orrain, Rod	Mtl.	6	179	28	39	67	30	11	0	3	3	0	....	1935-36	1941-42
oughlin, Clem	Det., Chi.	3	101	8	6	14	77	....	....	....	....	....	....	1926-27	1928-29
oughlin, Wilf	Tor.	1	14	0	0	0	2	....	....	....	....	....	....	1923-24	1923-24
ovsin, Ken	Wsh.	1	1	0	0	0	0	....	....	....	....	....	....	1990-91	1990-91
ow, Reed	St.L., Chi.	5	256	3	16	19	725	....	....	....	....	....	....	2000-01	2006-07
owdermilk, Dwayne	Wsh.	1	2	0	1	1	2	....	....	....	....	....	....	1980-81	1980-81
owe, Darren	Pit.	1	8	1	2	3	0	....	....	....	....	....	....	1983-84	1983-84
owe, Kevin	Edm., NYR	19	1254	84	347	431	1498	214	10	48	58	192	6	1979-80	1997-98
owe, Odie	NYR	1	4	1	1	2	0	....	....	....	....	....	....	1949-50	1949-50
owe, Ross	Bos., Mtl.	3	77	6	8	14	82	2	0	0	0	0	....	1949-50	1951-52
owrey, Ed	Ott., Ham.	3	27	2	2	4	6	....	....	....	....	....	....	1917-18	1920-21
owrey, Fred	Mtl.M., Pit.	2	53	1	1	2	10	2	0	0	0	6	....	1924-25	1925-26
owrey, Gerry	Tor., Pit., Phi., Chi., Ott.	6	211	48	48	96	148	2	1	0	1	2	....	1927-28	1932-33
owry, Dave	Van., St.L., Fla., S.J., Cgy.	19	1084	164	187	351	1191	111	16	20	36	181	....	1985-86	2003-04
oyns, Lynn	S.J., Cgy.	3	34	3	2	5	21	....	....	....	....	....	....	2002-03	2005-06
ucas, Danny	Phi.	1	6	1	0	1	0	....	....	....	....	....	....	1978-79	1978-79
ucas, Dave	Det.	1	1	0	0	0	0	....	....	....	....	....	....	1962-63	1962-63
uce, Don	NYR, Det., Buf., L.A., Tor.	13	894	225	329	554	364	71	17	22	39	52	....	1969-70	1981-82
udvig, Jan	N.J., Buf.	7	314	54	87	141	418	....	....	....	....	....	....	1982-83	1988-89
udwig, Craig	Mtl., NYI, Min., Dal.	17	1256	38	184	222	1437	177	4	25	29	244	2	1982-83	1998-99
udzik, Steve	Chi., Buf.	9	424	46	93	139	333	44	4	8	12	70	....	1981-82	1989-90
uhning, Warren	NYI, Dal.	3	29	0	1	1	21	....	....	....	....	....	....	1997-98	1999-00
ukowich, Bernie	Pit., St.L.	2	79	13	15	28	34	2	0	0	0	0	....	1973-74	1974-75
ukowich, Morris	Wpg., Bos., L.A.	8	582	199	219	418	584	11	0	2	2	24	....	1979-80	1986-87
uksa, Charlie	Hfd.	1	8	0	1	1	4	....	....	....	....	....	....	1979-80	1979-80
umley, Dave	Mtl., Edm., Hfd.	9	437	98	160	258	680	61	6	8	14	131	2	1978-79	1986-87
umme, Jyrki	Mtl., Van., Phx., Dal., Tor.	15	985	114	354	468	620	105	9	35	44	52	....	1988-89	2002-03
und, Pentti	Bos., NYR	7	259	44	55	99	40	19	7	5	12	0	....	1946-47	1952-53
undberg, Brian	Pit.	1	1	0	0	0	2	....	....	....	....	....	....	1982-83	1982-83
unde, Len	Det., Chi., Min., Van.	8	321	39	83	122	75	20	3	2	5	2	....	1958-59	1970-71
undholm, Bengt	Wpg.	5	275	48	95	143	72	14	3	4	7	14	....	1981-82	1985-86
undrigan, Joe	Tor., Wsh.	2	52	2	8	10	22	....	....	....	....	....	....	1972-73	1974-75
undstrom, Tord	Det.	1	11	1	1	2	0	....	....	....	....	....	....	1973-74	1973-74
undy, Pat	Det., Chi.	5	150	37	32	69	31	16	2	2	4	2	....	1945-46	1950-51
uoma, Mikko	Edm.	1	3	0	1	1	0	....	....	....	....	....	....	2003-04	2003-04
uongo, Chris	Det., Ott., NYI	5	218	8	23	31	176	....	....	....	....	....	....	1990-91	1995-96
upaschuk, Ross	Pit.	1	3	0	0	0	4	....	....	....	....	....	....	2002-03	2002-03
upien, Gilles	Mtl., Pit., Hfd.	5	226	5	25	30	416	25	0	0	0	21	2	1977-78	1981-82
upul, Gary	Van.	7	293	70	75	145	243	25	4	7	11	11	....	1979-80	1985-86
yashenko, Roman	Dal., NYR	4	139	14	9	23	55	17	2	1	3	0	....	1999-00	2002-03
yle, George	Det., Hfd.	4	99	24	38	62	51	....	....	....	....	....	....	1979-80	1982-83
ynch, Doug	Edm.	1	2	0	0	0	0	....	....	....	....	....	....	2003-04	2003-04
ynch, Jack	Pit., Det., Wsh.	7	382	24	106	130	336	....	....	....	....	....	....	1972-73	1978-79
ynn, Vic	NYR, Det., Mtl., Tor., Bos., Chi.	11	327	49	76	125	274	47	7	10	17	46	3	1942-43	1953-54
yon, Steve	Pit.	1	3	0	0	0	2	....	....	....	....	....	....	1976-77	1976-77
yons, Ron	Bos., Phi.	1	36	2	4	6	27	5	0	0	0	0	....	1930-31	1930-31
ysak, Brett	Car.	1	2	0	0	0	2	....	....	....	....	....	....	2003-04	2003-04
ysiak, Tom	Atl., Chi.	13	919	292	551	843	567	76	25	38	63	49	....	1973-74	1985-86

M

MacAdam, Al	Phi., Cal., Cle., Min., Van.	12	864	240	351	591	509	64	20	24	44	21	....	1973-74	1984-85
MacDermid, Paul	Hfd., Wpg., Wsh., Que.	14	690	116	142	258	1303	43	5	11	16	116	....	1981-82	1994-95
MacDonald, Blair	Edm., Van.	4	219	91	100	191	65	11	0	6	6	2	....	1979-80	1982-83
MacDonald, Brett	Van.	1	1	0	0	0	0	....	....	....	....	....	....	1987-88	1987-88
MacDonald, Doug	Buf.	3	11	1	0	1	2	....	....	....	....	....	....	1992-93	1994-95
MacDonald, Jason	NYR	1	4	0	0	0	19	....	....	....	....	....	....	2003-04	2003-04
MacDonald, Kevin	Ott.	1	1	0	0	0	2	....	....	....	....	....	....	1993-94	1993-94
MacDonald, Kilby	NYR	4	151	36	34	70	47	15	1	2	3	4	1	1939-40	1944-45
MacDonald, Lowell	Det., L.A., Pit.	13	506	180	210	390	92	30	11	11	22	12	....	1961-62	1977-78
MacDonald, Parker	Tor., NYR, Det., Bos., Min.	14	676	144	179	323	253	75	14	14	28	20	....	1952-53	1968-69
MacDougall, Kim	Min.	1	1	0	0	0	0	....	....	....	....	....	....	1974-75	1974-75
MacEachern, Shane	St.L.	1	1	0	0	0	0	....	....	....	....	....	....	1987-88	1987-88
Macey, Hub	NYR, Mtl.	3	30	6	9	15	0	8	0	0	0	0	....	1941-42	1946-47
MacGregor, Bruce	Det., NYR	14	893	213	257	470	217	107	19	28	47	44	....	1960-61	1973-74
MacGregor, Randy	Hfd.	1	2	1	1	2	2	....	....	....	....	....	....	1981-82	1981-82
MacGuigan, Garth	NYI	2	5	0	1	1	2	....	....	....	....	....	....	1979-80	1983-84
MacInnis, Al	Cgy., St.L.	23	1416	340	934	1274	1511	177	39	121	160	255	1	1981-82	2003-04
MacIntosh, Ian	NYR	1	4	0	0	0	4	....	....	....	....	....	....	1952-53	1952-53
MacIver, Don	Wpg.	1	6	0	0	0	2	....	....	....	....	....	....	1979-80	1979-80
Maciver, Norm	NYR, Hfd., Edm., Ott., Pit., Wpg., Phx.	12	500	55	230	285	350	56	3	11	14	32	....	1986-87	1997-98
MacKasey, Blair	Tor.	1	1	0	0	0	2	....	....	....	....	....	....	1976-77	1976-77
MacKay, Calum	Det., Mtl.	8	237	50	55	105	214	38	5	13	18	20	1	1946-47	1954-55
MacKay, Dave	Chi.	1	29	3	0	3	26	5	0	1	1	2	....	1940-41	1940-41
MacKay, Mickey	Chi., Pit., Bos.	4	147	44	19	63	79	11	0	0	0	6	1	1926-27	1929-30
MacKay, Murdo	Mtl.	4	19	0	3	3	0	15	1	2	3	0	....	1945-46	1948-49
MacKell, Fleming	Tor., Bos.	13	665	149	220	369	562	80	22	41	63	75	2	1947-48	1959-60
MacKell, Jack	Ott.	2	45	4	2	6	59	2	0	0	0	0	2	1919-20	1920-21
MacKenzie, Barry	Min.	1	6	0	1	1	6	....	....	....	....	....	....	1968-69	1968-69
MacKenzie, Bill	Chi., Mtl.M., NYR, Mtl.	7	264	15	14	29	145	21	1	1	2	11	1	1932-33	1939-40
Mackey, David	Chi., Min., St.L.	6	126	8	12	20	305	3	0	0	0	2	....	1987-88	1993-94
Mackey, Reg	NYR	1	34	0	0	0	16	1	0	0	0	0	....	1926-27	1926-27
Mackie, Howie	Det.	2	20	1	0	1	4	8	0	0	0	0	1	1936-37	1937-38
MacKinnon, Paul	Wsh.	5	147	5	23	28	91	....	....	....	....	....	....	1979-80	1983-84

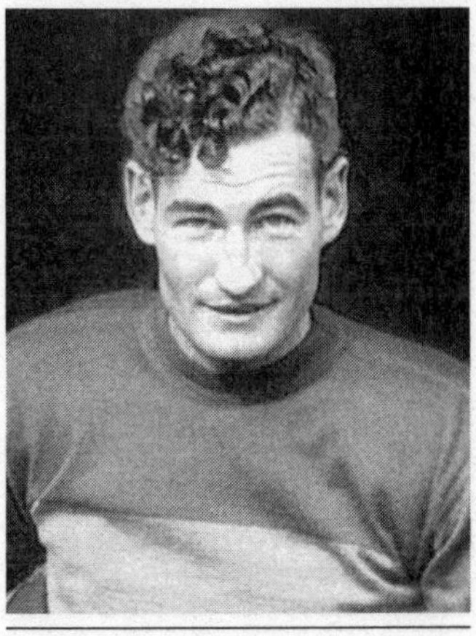
Ron Lyons

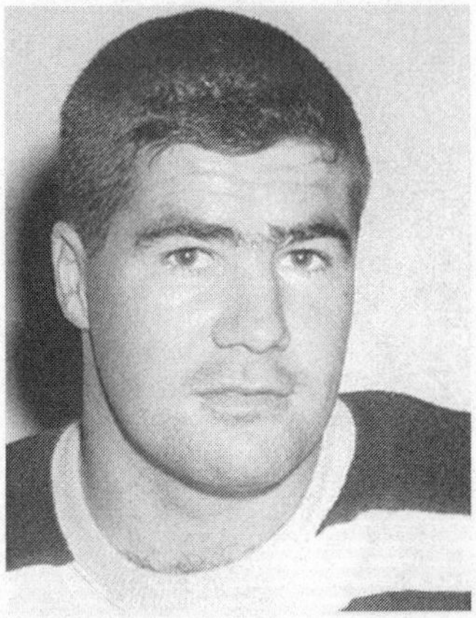
Fleming MacKell

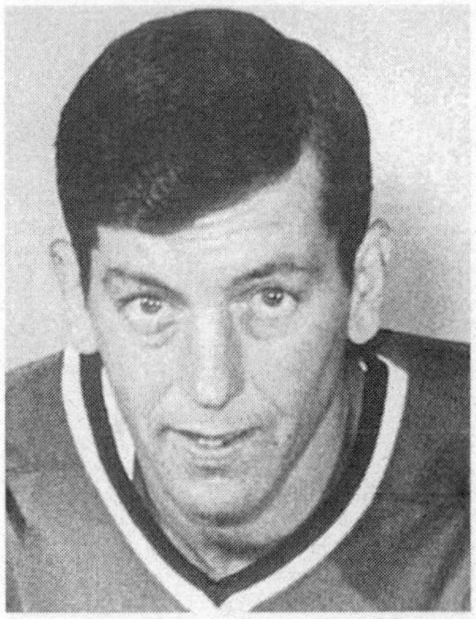
Chico Maki

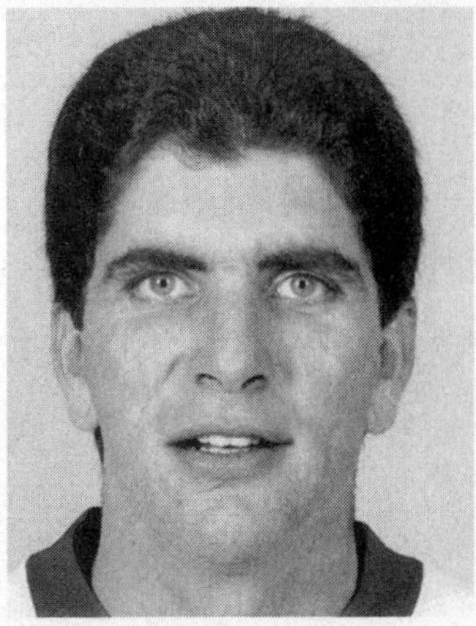
Bob Manno

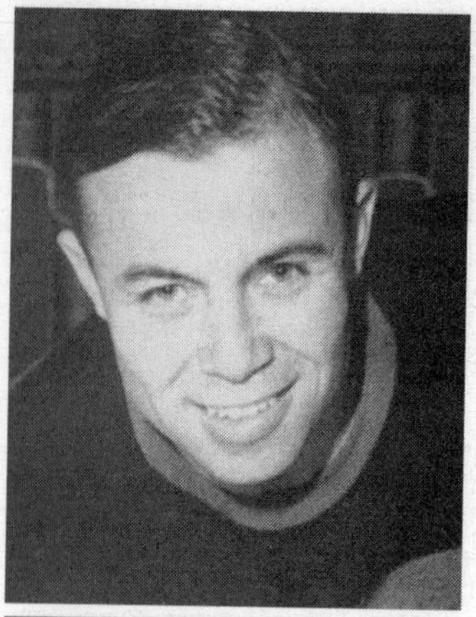

Mush March

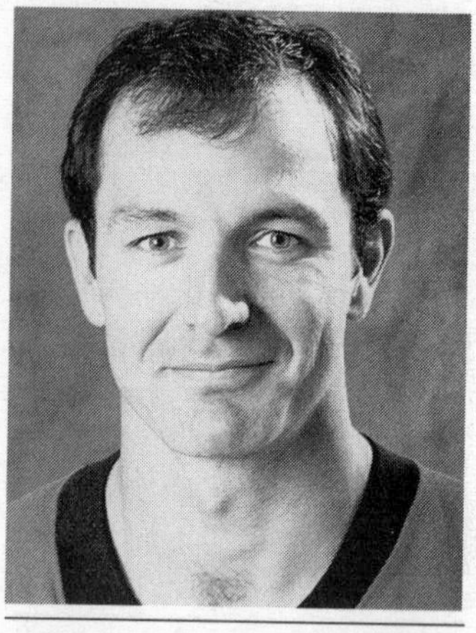

Stefan Matteau

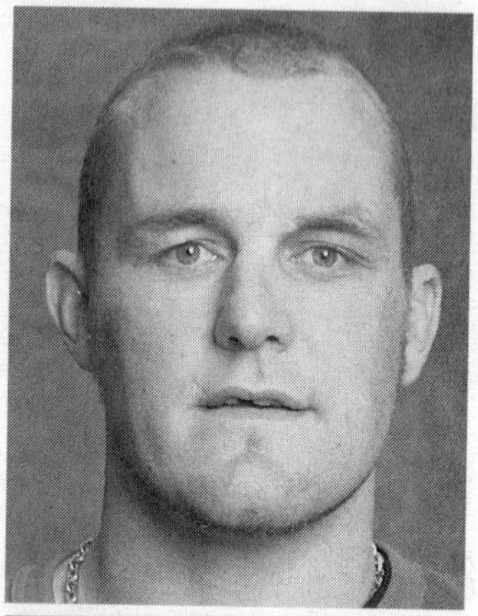

Darren McCarty

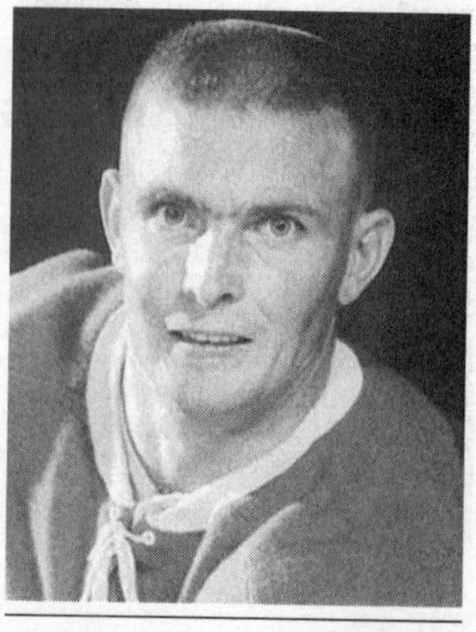

Bill McCreary Sr.

			Regular Schedule					Playoffs							
Name	NHL Teams	NHL Seasons	GP	G	A	TP	PIM	GP	G	A	TP	PIM	NHL Cup Wins	First NHL Season	Last NHL Season
‡ MacLean, Don	L.A., Tor., CBJ, Det., Phx.	6	41	8	5	13	6	3	0	0	0	0	....	1997-98	2006-0
MacLean, John	N.J., S.J., NYR, Dal.	18	1194	413	429	842	1328	104	35	48	83	152	1	1983-84	2001-0
MacLean, Paul	St.L., Wpg., Det.	11	719	324	349	673	968	53	21	14	35	110	....	1980-81	1990-9
MacLeish, Rick	Phi., Hfd., Pit., Det.	14	846	349	410	759	434	114	54	53	107	38	2	1970-71	1983-8
MacLellan, Brian	L.A., NYR, Min., Cgy., Det.	10	606	172	241	413	551	47	5	9	14	42	1	1982-83	1991-9
MacLeod, Pat	Min., S.J., Dal.	4	53	5	13	18	14	....	....	....	....	....	....	1990-91	1995-9
MacMillan, Billy	Tor., Atl., NYI	7	446	74	77	151	184	53	6	6	12	40	....	1970-71	1976-7
MacMillan, Bob	NYR, St.L., Atl., Cgy., Col., N.J., Chi.	11	753	228	349	577	260	31	8	11	19	16	....	1974-75	1984-8
MacMillan, Jeff	Dal.	1	4	0	0	0	0	....	....	....	....	....	....	2003-04	2003-0
MacMillan, John	Tor., Det.	5	104	5	10	15	32	12	0	1	1	2	2	1960-61	1964-6
MacNeil, Al	Tor., Mtl., Chi., NYR, Pit.	11	524	17	75	92	617	37	0	4	4	67	....	1955-56	1967-6
MacNeil, Bernie	St.L.	1	4	0	0	0	0	....	....	....	....	....	....	1973-74	1973-7
MacNeil, Ian	Phi.	1	2	0	0	0	0	....	....	....	....	....	....	2002-03	2002-0
Macoun, Jamie	Cgy., Tor., Det.	16	1128	76	282	358	1208	159	10	32	42	169	2	1982-83	1998-9
● MacPherson, Bud	Mtl.	7	259	5	33	38	233	29	0	3	3	21	1	1948-49	1956-5
● MacSweyn, Ralph	Phi.	5	47	0	5	5	10	8	0	0	0	6	....	1967-68	1971-7
MacTavish, Craig	Bos., Edm., NYR, Phi., St.L.	17	1093	213	267	480	891	193	20	38	58	218	4	1979-80	1996-9
MacWilliam, Mike	NYI	1	6	0	0	0	14	....	....	....	....	....	....	1995-96	1995-96
Madigan, Connie	St.L.	1	20	0	3	3	25	5	0	0	0	4	....	1972-73	1972-73
Madill, Jeff	N.J.	1	14	4	0	4	46	7	0	2	2	8	....	1990-91	1990-91
Magee, Dean	Min.	1	7	0	0	0	4	....	....	....	....	....	....	1977-78	1977-78
Maggs, Daryl	Chi., Cal., Tor.	3	135	14	19	33	54	4	0	0	0	0	....	1971-72	1979-80
Magnan, Marc	Tor.	1	4	0	1	1	5	....	....	....	....	....	....	1982-83	1982-83
● Magnuson, Keith	Chi.	11	589	14	125	139	1442	68	3	9	12	164	....	1969-70	1979-80
Maguire, Kevin	Tor., Buf., Phi.	6	260	29	30	59	782	11	0	0	0	86	....	1986-87	1991-92
Mahaffy, John	Mtl., NYR	3	37	11	25	36	4	1	0	1	1	0	....	1942-43	1944-45
Mahovlich, Frank	Tor., Det., Mtl.	18	1181	533	570	1103	1056	137	51	67	118	163	6	1956-57	1973-74
Mahovlich, Pete	Det., Mtl., Pit.	16	884	288	485	773	916	88	30	42	72	134	4	1965-66	1980-81
Mailhot, Jacques	Que.	1	5	0	0	0	33	....	....	....	....	....	....	1988-89	1988-89
● Mailley, Frank	Mtl.	1	1	0	0	0	0	....	....	....	....	....	....	1942-43	1942-43
Mair, Jim	Phi., NYI, Van.	5	76	4	15	19	49	3	1	2	3	4	....	1970-71	1974-75
● Majeau, Fern	Mtl.	2	56	22	24	46	43	1	0	0	0	0	1	1943-44	1944-45
‡ Majesky, Ivan	Fla., Atl., Wsh.	3	202	8	23	31	234	....	....	....	....	....	....	2002-03	2005-06
Major, Bruce	Que.	1	4	0	0	0	0	....	....	....	....	....	....	1990-91	1990-91
Major, Mark	Det.	1	2	0	0	0	5	....	....	....	....	....	....	1996-97	1996-97
Makarov, Sergei	Cgy., S.J., Dal.	7	424	134	250	384	317	34	12	11	23	8	....	1989-90	1996-97
Makela, Mikko	NYI, L.A., Buf., Bos.	7	423	118	147	265	139	18	3	8	11	14	....	1985-86	1994-95
Maki, Chico	Chi.	15	841	143	292	435	345	113	17	36	53	43	1	1960-61	1975-76
‡ Maki, Tomi	Cgy.	1	1	0	0	0	0	....	....	....	....	....	....	2006-07	2006-07
● Maki, Wayne	Chi., St.L., Van.	6	246	57	79	136	184	2	1	0	1	2	....	1967-68	1972-73
Makkonen, Kari	Edm.	1	9	2	2	4	0	....	....	....	....	....	....	1979-80	1979-80
Malakhov, Vladimir	NYI, Mtl., N.J., NYR, Phi.	13	712	86	260	346	697	75	8	19	27	64	1	1992-93	2005-06
‡ Malec, Tomas	Car., Ott.	4	46	0	2	2	47	....	....	....	....	....	....	2002-03	2006-07
Maley, David	Mtl., N.J., Edm., S.J., NYI	9	466	43	81	124	1043	46	5	5	10	111	1	1985-86	1993-94
Malgunas, Stewart	Phi., Wpg., Wsh., Cgy.	7	129	1	5	6	144	....	....	....	....	....	....	1993-94	1999-00
Malinowski, Merlin	Col., N.J., Hfd.	5	282	54	111	165	121	....	....	....	....	....	....	1978-79	1982-83
Malkoc, Dean	Van., Bos., NYI	4	116	1	3	4	299	....	....	....	....	....	....	1995-96	1998-99
Mallette, Troy	NYR, Edm., N.J., Ott., Bos., T.B.	9	456	51	68	119	1226	15	2	2	4	99	....	1989-90	1997-98
‡ Malmivaara, Olli	N.J.	1	2	0	0	0	0	....	....	....	....	....	....	2007-08	2007-08
● Malone, Cliff	Mtl.	1	3	0	0	0	0	....	....	....	....	....	....	1951-52	1951-52
Malone, Greg	Pit., Hfd., Que.	11	704	191	310	501	661	20	3	5	8	32	....	1976-77	1986-87
● Malone, Joe	Mtl., Que., Ham.	7	126	143	32	175	57	9	6	2	8	6	1	1917-18	1923-24
Maloney, Dan	Chi., L.A., Det., Tor.	11	737	192	259	451	1489	40	4	7	11	35	....	1970-71	1981-82
Maloney, Dave	NYR, Buf.	11	657	71	246	317	1154	49	7	17	24	91	....	1974-75	1984-85
Maloney, Don	NYR, Hfd., NYI	13	765	214	350	564	815	94	22	35	57	101	....	1978-79	1990-91
Maloney, Phil	Bos., Tor., Chi.	5	158	28	43	71	16	6	0	0	0	0	....	1949-50	1959-60
Maltais, Steve	Wsh., Min., T.B., Det., CBJ	6	120	9	18	27	53	1	0	0	0	0	....	1989-90	2000-01
Maluta, Ray	Bos.	2	25	2	3	5	6	2	0	0	0	0	....	1975-76	1976-77
Manastersky, Tom	Mtl.	1	6	0	0	0	11	....	....	....	....	....	....	1950-51	1950-51
● Mancuso, Gus	Mtl., NYR	4	42	7	9	16	17	....	....	....	....	....	....	1937-38	1942-43
Manderville, Kent	Tor., Edm., Hfd., Car., Phi., Pit.	12	646	37	67	104	348	67	3	3	6	44	....	1991-92	2002-03
Mandich, Dan	Min.	4	111	5	11	16	303	7	0	0	0	2	....	1982-83	1985-86
‡ Maneluk, Mike	Phi., Chi., NYR, CBJ	3	85	11	10	21	57	....	....	....	....	....	....	1998-99	2000-01
Manery, Kris	Cle., Min., Van., Wpg.	4	250	63	64	127	91	....	....	....	....	....	....	1977-78	1980-81
Manery, Randy	Det., Atl., L.A.	10	582	50	206	256	415	13	0	2	2	12	....	1970-71	1979-80
Manlow, Eric	Bos., NYI	4	37	2	4	6	8	....	....	....	....	....	....	2000-01	2003-04
‡ Mann, Cameron	Bos., Nsh.	5	93	14	10	24	40	1	0	0	0	0	....	1997-98	2002-03
Mann, Jack	NYR	2	9	3	4	7	0	....	....	....	....	....	....	1943-44	1944-45
Mann, Jimmy	Wpg., Que., Pit.	8	293	10	20	30	895	22	0	0	0	89	....	1979-80	1987-88
Mann, Ken	Det.	1	1	0	0	0	0	....	....	....	....	....	....	1975-76	1975-76
● Mann, Norm	Tor.	3	31	0	3	3	4	2	0	0	0	0	....	1935-36	1940-41
● Manners, Rennison	Pit., Phi.	2	37	3	2	5	14	....	....	....	....	....	....	1929-30	1930-31
‡ Manning, Paul	CBJ	1	8	0	0	0	2	....	....	....	....	....	....	2002-03	2002-03
Manno, Bob	Van., Tor., Det.	8	371	41	131	172	274	17	2	4	6	12	....	1976-77	1984-85
Manson, Dave	Chi., Edm., Wpg., Phx., Mtl., Dal., Tor.	16	1103	102	288	390	2792	112	7	24	31	343	....	1986-87	2001-02
Manson, Ray	Bos., NYR	2	2	0	1	1	0	....	....	....	....	....	....	1947-48	1948-49
● Mantha, Georges	Mtl.	13	488	89	102	191	148	36	6	2	8	24	2	1928-29	1940-41
Mantha, Moe	Wpg., Pit., Edm., Min., Phi.	12	656	81	289	370	501	17	5	10	15	18	....	1980-81	1991-92
● Mantha, Sylvio	Mtl., Bos.	14	542	63	78	141	671	39	5	5	10	64	3	1923-24	1936-37
‡ Mapletoft, Justin	NYI	2	38	3	6	9	8	2	0	0	0	0	....	2002-03	2003-04
● Maracle, Bud	NYR	1	11	1	3	4	4	4	0	0	0	0	....	1930-31	1930-31
Marcetta, Milan	Tor., Min.	3	54	7	15	22	10	17	7	7	14	4	1	1966-67	1968-69
● March, Mush	Chi.	17	759	153	230	383	540	45	12	15	27	41	2	1928-29	1944-45
Marchinko, Brian	Tor., NYI	4	47	2	6	8	0	....	....	....	....	....	....	1970-71	1973-74
Marchment, Bryan	Wpg., Chi., Hfd., Edm., T.B., S.J., Col., Tor., Cgy.	17	926	40	142	182	2307	83	4	3	7	102	....	1988-89	2005-06
Marcinyshyn, Dave	N.J., Que., NYR	3	16	0	1	1	49	....	....	....	....	....	....	1990-91	1992-93
Marcon, Lou	Det.	3	60	0	4	4	42	....	....	....	....	....	....	1958-59	1962-63
Marcotte, Don	Bos.	15	868	230	254	484	317	132	34	27	61	81	2	1965-66	1981-82
‡ Marha, Josef	Col., Ana., Chi.	6	159	21	32	53	32	....	....	....	....	....	....	1995-96	2000-01
Marini, Hector	NYI, N.J.	5	154	27	46	73	246	10	3	6	9	14	2	1978-79	1983-84
Marinucci, Chris	NYI, L.A.	2	13	1	4	5	2	....	....	....	....	....	....	1994-95	1996-97
● Mario, Frank	Bos.	2	53	9	19	28	24	....	....	....	....	....	....	1941-42	1944-45
● Mariucci, John	Chi.	5	223	11	34	45	308	12	0	3	3	26	....	1940-41	1947-48
‡ Marjamaki, Masi	NYI	1	1	0	0	0	0	....	....	....	....	....	....	2005-06	2005-06
Mark, Gordon	N.J., Edm.	4	85	3	10	13	187	....	....	....	....	....	....	1986-87	1994-95
Markell, John	Wpg., St.L., Min.	4	55	11	10	21	36	....	....	....	....	....	....	1979-80	1984-85
● Marker, Gus	Det., Mtl.M., Tor., Bro.	10	322	64	69	133	133	46	5	7	12	36	1	1932-33	1941-42
Markham, Ray	NYR	1	14	1	1	2	21	7	1	0	1	24	....	1979-80	1979-80
● Markle, Jack	Tor.	1	8	0	1	1	0	....	....	....	....	....	....	1935-36	1935-36
‡ Markov, Danny	Tor., Phx., Car., Phi., Nsh., Det.	9	538	29	118	147	456	81	2	12	14	84	....	1997-98	2006-07
● Marks, Jack	Mtl.W., Tor., Que.	2	7	0	0	0	4	....	....	....	....	....	1	1917-18	1919-20
Marks, John	Chi.	10	657	112	163	275	330	57	5	9	14	60	....	1972-73	1981-82
Markwart, Nevin	Bos., Cgy.	8	309	41	68	109	794	19	1	0	1	33	....	1983-84	1991-92
Marois, Daniel	Tor., NYI, Bos., Dal.	8	350	117	93	210	419	19	3	3	6	28	....	1987-88	1995-96
Marois, Mario	NYR, Van., Que., Wpg., St.L.	15	955	76	357	433	1746	100	4	34	38	182	....	1977-78	1991-92
● Marotte, Gilles	Bos., Chi., L.A., NYR, St.L.	12	808	56	265	321	919	29	3	3	6	26	....	1965-66	1976-77
Marquess, Mark	Bos.	1	27	5	4	9	6	4	0	0	0	0	....	1946-47	1946-47
Marsh, Brad	Atl., Cgy., Phi., Tor., Det., Ott.	15	1086	23	175	198	1241	97	6	18	24	124	....	1978-79	1992-93
Marsh, Gary	Det., Tor.	2	7	1	3	4	4	....	....	....	....	....	....	1967-68	1968-69
Marsh, Peter	Wpg., Chi.	5	278	48	71	119	224	26	1	5	6	33	....	1979-80	1983-84
Marshall, Bert	Det., Oak., Cal., NYR, NYI	14	868	17	181	198	926	72	4	22	26	99	....	1965-66	1978-79
Marshall, Don	Mtl., NYR, Buf., Tor.	19	1176	265	324	589	127	94	8	15	23	14	5	1951-52	1971-72
Marshall, Grant	Dal., CBJ, N.J.	11	700	92	147	239	793	90	6	11	17	95	2	1994-95	2005-06
Marshall, Jason	St.L., Ana., Wsh., Min., S.J.	12	526	16	51	67	1004	43	2	3	5	55	....	1991-92	2005-06
Marshall, Paul	Pit., Tor., Hfd.	4	95	15	18	33	17	1	0	0	0	0	....	1979-80	1982-83
Marshall, Willie	Tor.	4	33	1	5	6	2	....	....	....	....	....	....	1952-53	1958-59
Marson, Mike	Wsh., L.A.	6	196	24	24	48	233	....	....	....	....	....	....	1974-75	1979-80
‡ Martensson, Tony	Ana.	1	6	1	1	2	0	....	....	....	....	....	....	2003-04	2003-04
● Martin, Clare	Bos., Det., Chi., NYR	6	237	12	28	40	78	27	0	2	2	6	1	1941-42	1951-52
Martin, Craig	Wpg., Fla.	2	21	0	1	1	24	....	....	....	....	....	....	1994-95	1996-97
● Martin, Frank	Bos., Chi.	6	282	11	46	57	122	10	0	2	2	2	....	1952-53	1957-58
Martin, Grant	Van., Wsh.	4	44	0	4	4	55	1	1	0	1	2	....	1983-84	1986-87
Martin, Jack	Tor.	1	1	0	0	0	0	....	....	....	....	....	....	1960-61	1960-61
Martin, Matt	Tor.	4	76	0	5	5	71	....	....	....	....	....	....	1993-94	1996-97
● Martin, Pit	Det., Bos., Chi., Van.	17	1101	324	485	809	609	100	27	31	58	56	....	1961-62	1978-79

me	NHL Teams	NHL Seasons	Regular Schedule GP	G	A	TP	PIM	Playoffs GP	G	A	TP	PIM	NHL Cup Wins	First NHL Season	Last NHL Season
artin, Rick	Buf., L.A.	11	685	384	317	701	477	63	24	29	53	74	....	1971-72	1981-82
artin, Ron	NYA	2	94	13	16	29	36	....	....	....	....	....	....	1932-33	1933-34
artin, Terry	Buf., Que., Tor., Edm., Min.	10	479	104	101	205	202	21	4	2	6	26	....	1975-76	1984-85
artin, Tom	Tor.	1	3	1	0	1	0	....	....	....	....	....	....	1967-68	1967-68
artin, Tom	Wpg., Hfd., Min.	6	92	12	11	23	249	4	0	0	0	6	....	1984-85	1989-90
artineau, Don	Atl., Min., Det.	4	90	6	10	16	63	....	....	....	....	....	....	1973-74	1976-77
artini, Darcy	Edm.	1	2	0	0	0	0	....	....	....	....	....	....	1993-94	1993-94
artins, Steve	Hfd., Car., Ott., T.B., NYI, St.L.	10	267	21	25	46	142	5	0	1	1	0	....	1995-96	2005-06
artinson, Steve	Det., Mtl., Min.	4	49	2	1	3	244	1	0	0	0	10	....	1987-88	1991-92
aruk, Dennis	Cal., Cle., Min., Wsh.	14	888	356	522	878	761	34	14	22	36	26	....	1975-76	1988-89
asnick, Paul	Mtl., Chi., Tor.	6	232	18	41	59	139	33	4	5	9	27	1	1950-51	1957-58
ason, Charley	NYR, NYA, Det., Chi.	4	95	7	18	25	44	4	0	1	1	0	....	1934-35	1938-39
assecar, George	NYA	3	100	12	11	23	46	....	....	....	....	....	....	1929-30	1931-32
asters, Jamie	St.L.	3	33	1	13	14	2	2	0	0	0	0	....	1975-76	1978-79
asterton, Bill	Min.	1	38	4	8	12	4	....	....	....	....	....	....	1967-68	1967-68
athers, Frank	Tor.	3	23	1	3	4	4	....	....	....	....	....	....	1948-49	1951-52
athiasen, Dwight	Pit.	3	33	1	7	8	18	....	....	....	....	....	....	1985-86	1987-88
athieson, Jim	Wsh.	1	2	0	0	0	4	....	....	....	....	....	....	1989-90	1989-90
athieu, Marquis	Bos.	3	16	0	2	2	14	....	....	....	....	....	....	1998-99	2000-01
atte, Christian	Col., Min.	5	25	2	3	5	12	....	....	....	....	....	....	1996-97	2000-01
atte, Joe	Tor., Ham., Bos., Mtl.	4	68	17	15	32	54	....	....	....	....	....	....	1919-20	1925-26
atte, Joe	Det., Chi.	2	24	0	3	3	8	....	....	....	....	....	....	1929-30	1942-43
atteau, Stephane	Cgy., Chi., NYR, St.L., S.J., Fla.	13	848	144	172	316	742	109	12	22	34	80	1	1990-91	2002-03
atteucci, Mike	Min.	2	6	0	0	0	4	....	....	....	....	....	....	2000-01	2001-02
attiussi, Dick	Pit., Oak., Cal.	4	200	8	31	39	124	8	0	1	1	6	....	1967-68	1970-71
atvichuk, Richard	Min., Dal., N.J.	14	796	39	139	178	624	123	5	19	24	128	1	1992-93	2006-07
atz, Johnny	Mtl.	1	30	2	3	5	0	1	0	0	0	0	....	1924-25	1924-25
axner, Wayne	Bos.	2	62	8	9	17	48	....	....	....	....	....	....	1964-65	1965-66
axwell, Brad	Min., Que., Tor., Van., NYR	10	612	98	270	368	1292	79	12	49	61	178	....	1977-78	1986-87
axwell, Bryan	Min., St.L., Wpg., Pit.	8	331	18	77	95	745	15	1	1	2	86	....	1977-78	1984-85
axwell, Kevin	Min., Col., N.J.	3	66	6	15	21	61	16	3	4	7	24	....	1980-81	1983-84
axwell, Wally	Tor.	1	2	0	0	0	0	....	....	....	....	....	....	1952-53	1952-53
ay, Alan	Bos., Edm., Wsh., Dal., Cgy.	8	393	31	45	76	1348	40	1	2	3	80	....	1987-88	1994-95
ayer, Derek	Ott.	1	17	2	2	4	8	....	....	....	....	....	....	1993-94	1993-94
ayer, Jim	NYR	1	4	0	0	0	0	....	....	....	....	....	....	1979-80	1979-80
ayer, Pat	Pit.	1	1	0	0	0	4	....	....	....	....	....	....	1987-88	1987-88
ayer, Shep	Tor.	1	12	1	2	3	4	....	....	....	....	....	....	1942-43	1942-43
azur, Eddie	Mtl., Chi.	6	107	8	20	28	120	25	4	5	9	22	1	1950-51	1956-57
azur, Jay	Van.	4	47	11	7	18	20	6	0	1	1	8	....	1988-89	1991-92
cAdam, Gary	Buf., Pit., Det., Cgy., Wsh., N.J., Tor.	11	534	96	132	228	243	30	6	5	11	16	....	1975-76	1985-86
cAdam, Sam	NYR	1	5	0	0	0	0	....	....	....	....	....	....	1930-31	1930-31
cAllister, Chris	Van., Tor., Phi., Col., NYR	7	301	4	17	21	634	9	0	1	1	4	....	1997-98	2003-04
cAlpine, Chris	N.J., St.L., T.B., Atl., Chi., L.A.	8	289	6	24	30	245	28	0	1	1	18	1	1994-95	2002-03
cAndrew, Hazen	Bro.	1	7	0	1	1	6	....	....	....	....	....	....	1941-42	1941-42
cAneeley, Ted	Cal.	3	158	8	35	43	141	....	....	....	....	....	....	1972-73	1974-75
cAtee, Jud	Det.	3	46	15	13	28	6	14	2	1	3	0	....	1942-43	1944-45
cAtee, Norm	Bos.	1	13	0	1	1	0	....	....	....	....	....	....	1946-47	1946-47
cAvoy, George	Mtl.	1	....	....	....	....	....	4	0	0	0	0	....	1954-55	1954-55
cBain, Andrew	Wpg., Pit., Van., Ott.	11	608	129	172	301	633	24	5	7	12	39	....	1983-84	1993-94
cBain, Jason	Hfd.	2	9	0	0	0	0	....	....	....	....	....	....	1995-96	1996-97
cBain, Mike	T.B.	2	64	0	7	7	22	....	....	....	....	....	....	1997-98	1998-99
cBean, Wayne	L.A., NYI, Wpg.	6	211	10	39	49	168	2	1	1	2	0	....	1987-88	1993-94
cBride, Cliff	Mtl.M., Tor.	2	2	0	0	0	0	....	....	....	....	....	....	1928-29	1929-30
:Burney, Jim	Chi.	1	1	0	1	1	0	....	....	....	....	....	....	1952-53	1952-53
cCabe, Stan	Det., Mtl.M.	4	78	9	4	13	49	....	....	....	....	....	....	1929-30	1933-34
cCaffrey, Bert	Tor., Pit., Mtl.	7	260	43	30	73	202	8	2	1	3	10	1	1924-25	1930-31
cCahill, John	Col.	1	1	0	0	0	0	....	....	....	....	....	....	1977-78	1977-78
cCaig, Doug	Det., Chi.	7	263	8	21	29	255	7	0	1	1	10	....	1941-42	1950-51
cCallum, Dunc	NYR, Pit.	5	187	14	35	49	230	10	1	2	3	12	....	1965-66	1970-71
cCalmon, Eddie	Chi., Phi.	2	39	5	0	5	14	....	....	....	....	....	....	1927-28	1930-31
cCann, Rick	Det.	6	43	1	4	5	6	....	....	....	....	....	....	1967-68	1974-75
cCarthy, Dan	NYR	1	5	4	0	4	4	....	....	....	....	....	....	1980-81	1980-81
cCarthy, Kevin	Phi., Van., Pit.	10	537	67	191	258	527	21	2	3	5	20	....	1977-78	1986-87
cCarthy, Sandy	Cgy., T.B., Phi., Car., NYR, Bos.	11	736	72	76	148	1534	23	0	2	2	61	....	1993-94	2003-04
cCarthy, Thomas	Que., Ham.	2	35	22	7	29	10	....	....	....	....	....	....	1919-20	1920-21
cCarthy, Tom	Det., Bos.	4	60	8	9	17	8	....	....	....	....	....	....	1956-57	1960-61
cCarthy, Tom	Min., Bos.	9	460	178	221	399	330	68	12	26	38	67	....	1979-80	1987-88
cCartney, Walt	Mtl.	1	2	0	0	0	0	....	....	....	....	....	....	1932-33	1932-33
cCarty, Darren	Det., Cgy.	15	758	127	161	288	1477	174	23	26	49	228	4	1993-94	2008-09
cCaskill, Ted	Min.	1	4	0	2	2	0	....	....	....	....	....	....	1967-68	1967-68
cCauley, Alyn	Tor., S.J., L.A.	9	488	69	97	166	116	52	7	12	19	18	....	1997-98	2006-07
cClanahan, Rob	Buf., Hfd., NYR	5	224	38	63	101	126	34	4	12	16	31	....	1979-80	1983-84
cCleary, Trent	Ott., Bos., Mtl.	4	192	8	15	23	134	....	....	....	....	....	....	1995-96	1999-00
cClelland, Kevin	Pit., Edm., Det., Tor., Wpg.	12	588	68	112	180	1672	98	11	18	29	281	4	1981-82	1993-94
cCord, Bob	Bos., Det., Min., St.L.	7	316	10	58	68	262	14	2	5	7	10	....	1963-64	1972-73
cCord, Dennis	Van.	1	3	0	0	0	6	....	....	....	....	....	....	1973-74	1973-74
cCormack, John	Tor., Mtl., Chi.	8	311	25	49	74	35	22	1	1	2	0	2	1947-48	1954-55
cCosh, Shawn	L.A., NYR	2	9	1	0	1	6	....	....	....	....	....	....	1991-92	1994-95
cCourt, Dale	Det., Buf., Tor.	7	532	194	284	478	124	21	9	7	16	6	....	1977-78	1983-84
cCreary, Bill	NYR, Det., Mtl., St.L.	8	309	53	62	115	108	48	6	16	22	14	....	1953-54	1970-71
cCreary, Bill	Tor.	1	12	1	0	1	4	....	....	....	....	....	....	1980-81	1980-81
cCreary, Keith	Mtl., Pit., Atl.	10	532	131	112	243	294	16	0	4	4	6	....	1961-62	1974-75
cCreedy, John	Tor.	2	64	17	12	29	25	21	4	3	7	16	2	1941-42	1944-45
cCrimmon, Brad	Bos., Phi., Cgy., Det., Hfd., Phx.	18	1222	81	322	403	1416	116	11	18	29	176	1	1979-80	1996-97
cCrimmon, Jim	St.L.	1	2	0	0	0	0	....	....	....	....	....	....	1974-75	1974-75
cCulley, Bob	Mtl.	1	1	0	0	0	0	....	....	....	....	....	....	1934-35	1934-35
cCurry, Duke	Pit.	4	148	21	11	32	119	4	0	2	2	2	....	1925-26	1928-29
cCutcheon, Brian	Det.	3	37	3	1	4	7	....	....	....	....	....	....	1974-75	1976-77
cCutcheon, Darwin	Tor.	1	1	0	0	0	2	....	....	....	....	....	....	1981-82	1981-82
cDill, Jeff	Chi.	1	1	0	0	0	0	....	....	....	....	....	....	1976-77	1976-77
cDonagh, Bill	NYR	1	4	0	0	0	2	....	....	....	....	....	....	1949-50	1949-50
cDonald, Ab	Mtl., Chi., Bos., Det., Pit., St.L.	15	762	182	248	430	200	84	21	29	50	42	4	1957-58	1971-72
cDonald, Brian	Chi., Buf.	2	12	0	0	0	29	8	0	0	0	2	....	1967-68	1970-71
cDonald, Bucko	Det., Tor., NYR	11	446	35	88	123	206	50	6	1	7	24	3	1934-35	1944-45
cDonald, Butch	Det., Chi.	2	66	8	20	28	2	5	0	2	2	10	....	1939-40	1944-45
cDonald, Gerry	Hfd.	2	8	0	0	0	4	....	....	....	....	....	....	1981-82	1983-84
cDonald, Jack	Mtl.W., Mtl., Que., Tor.	5	69	26	14	40	30	7	1	3	4	3	....	1917-18	1921-22
cDonald, Jack	NYR	1	43	10	9	19	6	....	....	....	....	....	....	1943-44	1943-44
cDonald, Lanny	Tor., Col., Cgy.	16	1111	500	506	1006	899	117	44	40	84	120	1	1973-74	1988-89
cDonald, Robert	NYR	1	1	0	0	0	0	....	....	....	....	....	....	1943-44	1943-44
cDonald, Terry	K.C.	1	8	0	1	1	6	....	....	....	....	....	....	1975-76	1975-76
cDonell, Kent	CBJ	2	32	1	2	3	36	....	....	....	....	....	....	2002-03	2003-04
cDonnell, Joe	Van., Pit.	3	50	2	10	12	34	....	....	....	....	....	....	1981-82	1985-86
cDonnell, Moylan	Ham.	1	22	1	2	3	2	....	....	....	....	....	....	1920-21	1920-21
cDonough, Al	L.A., Pit., Atl., Det.	5	237	73	88	161	73	8	0	1	1	2	....	1970-71	1977-78
cDonough, Hubie	L.A., NYI, S.J.	5	195	40	26	66	67	5	1	0	1	4	....	1988-89	1992-93
cDougal, Mike	NYR, Hfd.	4	61	8	10	18	43	....	....	....	....	....	....	1978-79	1982-83
cDougall, Bill	Det., Edm., T.B.	3	28	5	5	10	12	1	0	0	0	0	....	1990-91	1993-94
cEachern, Shawn	Pit., L.A., Bos., Ott., Atl.	14	911	256	323	579	506	97	12	25	37	62	1	1991-92	2005-06
cElmury, Jim	Min., K.C., Col.	5	180	14	47	61	49	....	....	....	....	....	....	1972-73	1977-78
cEwen, Mike	NYR, Col., NYI, L.A., Wsh., Det., Hfd.	12	716	108	296	404	460	78	12	36	48	48	3	1976-77	1987-88
cFadden, Jim	Det., Chi.	8	412	100	126	226	89	49	10	9	19	30	1	1946-47	1953-54
cFadyen, Don	Chi.	4	179	12	33	45	77	11	2	2	4	5	1	1932-33	1935-36
cFall, Dan	Wpg.	2	9	0	1	1	0	....	....	....	....	....	....	1984-85	1985-86
cFarlane, Gord	Chi.	1	2	0	0	0	0	....	....	....	....	....	....	1926-27	1926-27
cGeough, Jim	Wsh., Pit.	4	57	7	10	17	32	....	....	....	....	....	....	1981-82	1986-87
cGibbon, Irv	Mtl.	1	1	0	0	0	2	....	....	....	....	....	....	1942-43	1942-43
cGill, Bob	Tor., Chi., S.J., Det., NYI, Hfd.	13	705	17	55	72	1766	49	0	0	0	88	....	1981-82	1993-94
cGill, Jack	Mtl.	3	134	27	10	37	71	3	2	0	2	0	....	1934-35	1936-37
cGill, Jack	Bos.	4	97	23	36	59	42	27	7	4	11	17	....	1941-42	1946-47
cGill, Ryan	Chi., Phi., Edm.	4	151	4	15	19	391	....	....	....	....	....	....	1991-92	1994-95
cGillis, Dan	Edm., Phi., S.J., Bos., N.J.	9	634	56	182	238	570	64	8	14	22	76	....	1996-97	2005-06
cGregor, Sandy	NYR	1	2	0	0	0	2	....	....	....	....	....	....	1963-64	1963-64
cGuire, Mickey	Pit.	2	36	3	0	3	6	....	....	....	....	....	....	1926-27	1927-28
cHugh, Mike	Min., S.J.	4	20	1	0	1	16	....	....	....	....	....	....	1988-89	1991-92
cIlhargey, Jack	Phi., Van., Hfd.	8	393	11	36	47	1102	27	0	3	3	68	....	1974-75	1981-82

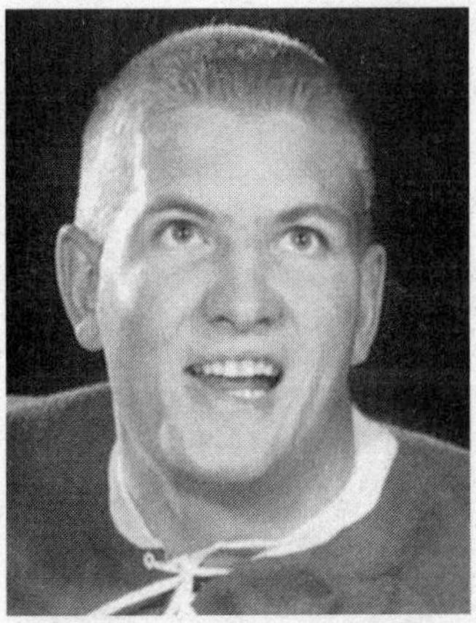
Keith McCreary

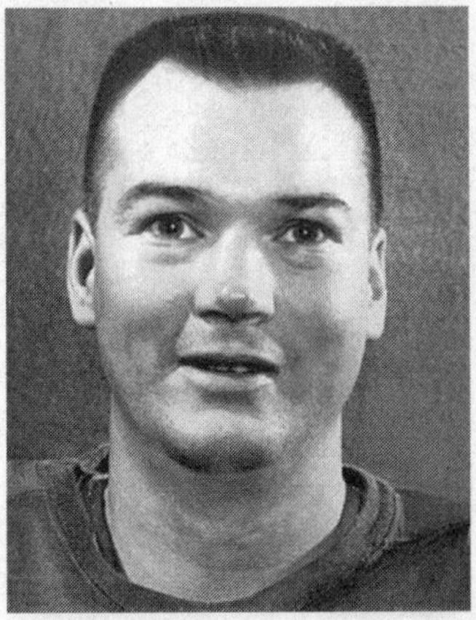
Ab McDonald

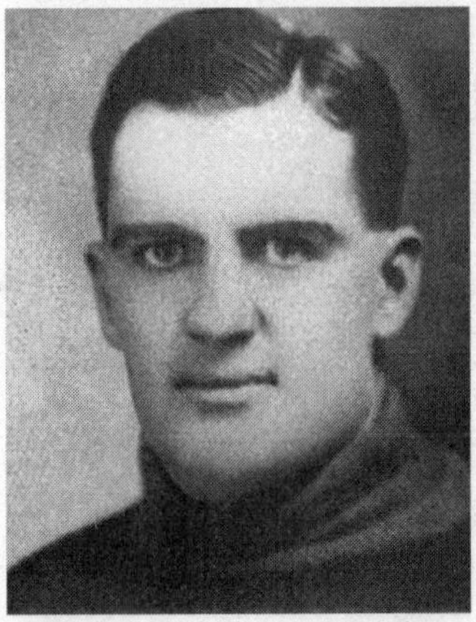
Howard McNamara

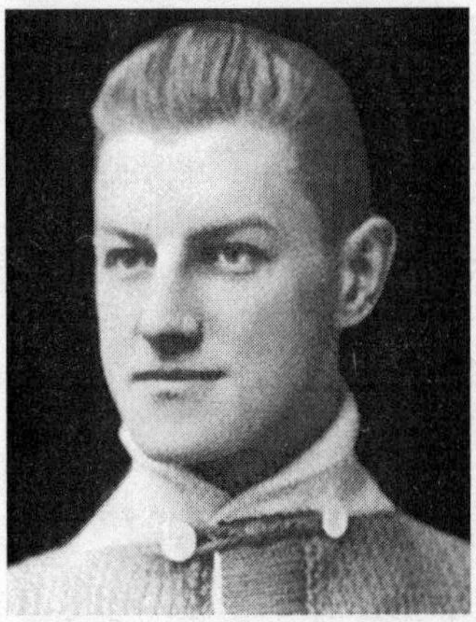
Harry Meeking

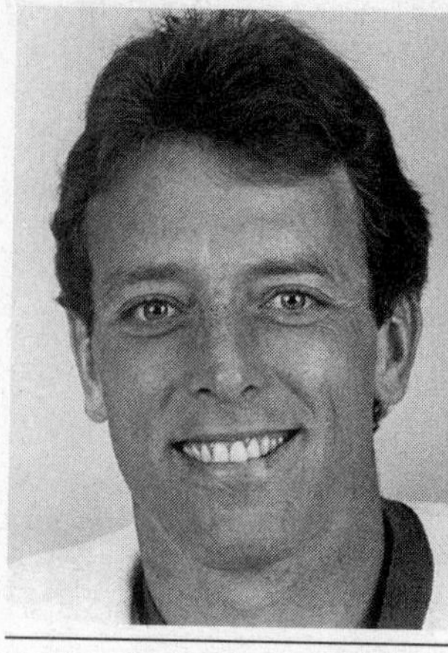
Wayne Merrick

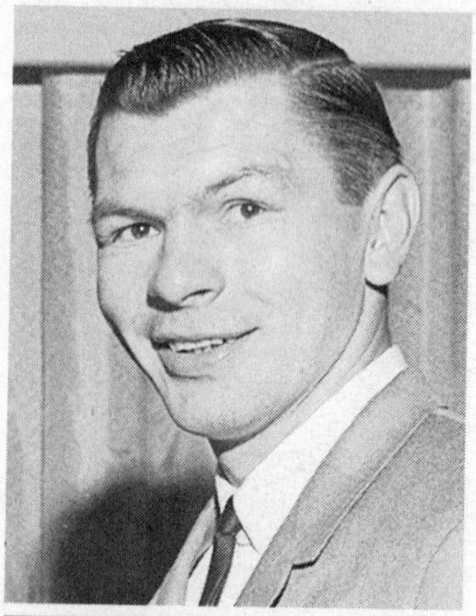
Stan Mikita

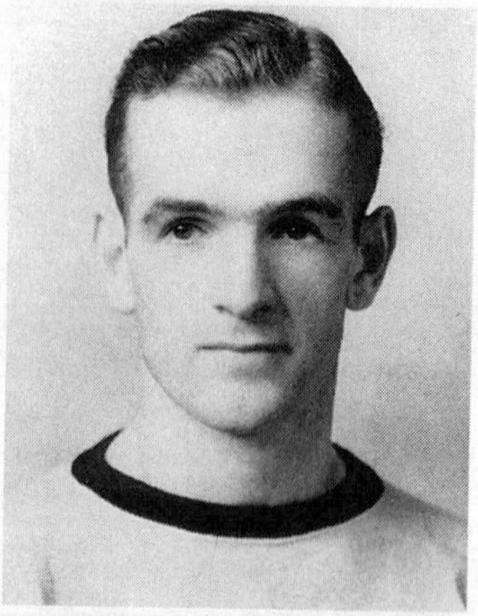
Bill Miller

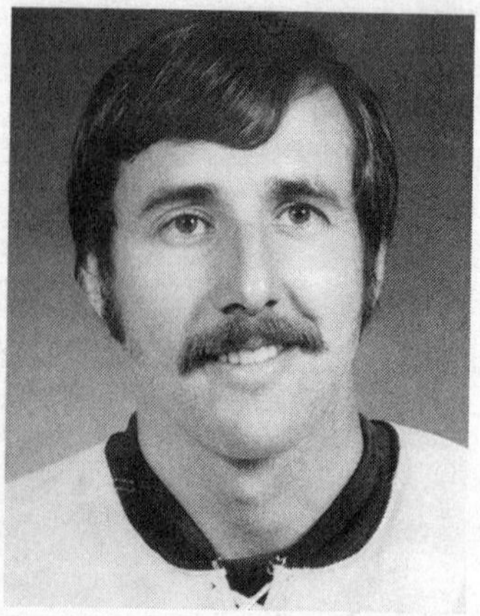
Tom Miller

Name	NHL Teams	NHL Seasons	Regular Schedule GP	G	A	TP	PIM	Playoffs GP	G	A	TP	PIM	NHL Cup Wins	First NHL Season	Last NHL Season
• McInenly, Bert	Det., NYA, Ott., Bos.	6	166	19	15	34	144	4	0	0	0	2	....	1930-31	1935-
McInnis, Marty	NYI, Cgy., Ana., Bos.	12	796	170	250	420	330	22	3	2	5	4	....	1991-92	2002-
McIntosh, Bruce	Min.	1	2	0	0	0	0	....	....	....	....	....	....	1972-73	1972-
McIntosh, Paul	Buf.	2	48	0	2	2	66	2	0	0	0	7	....	1974-75	1975-
• McIntyre, Jack	Bos., Chi., Det.	11	499	109	102	211	173	29	7	6	13	4	....	1949-50	1959-
McIntyre, John	Tor., L.A., NYR, Van.	6	351	24	54	78	516	44	0	6	6	54	....	1989-90	1994-
McIntyre, Larry	Tor.	2	41	0	3	3	26	....	....	....	....	....	....	1969-70	1972-
McKay, Doug	Det.	1	....	....	....	....	....	1	0	0	0	0	1	1949-50	1949-
McKay, Randy	Det., N.J., Dal., Mtl.	15	932	162	201	363	1731	123	20	23	43	123	2	1988-89	2002-0
McKay, Ray	Chi., Buf., Cal.	6	140	2	16	18	102	1	0	0	0	0	....	1968-69	1973-7
McKay, Scott	Ana.	1	1	0	0	0	0	....	....	....	....	....	....	1993-94	1993-
McKechnie, Walt	Min., Cal., Bos., Det., Wsh., Cle., Tor., Col.	16	955	214	392	606	469	15	7	5	12	7	....	1967-68	1982-8
McKee, Mike	Que.	1	48	3	12	15	41	....	....	....	....	....	....	1993-94	1993-
McKegney, Ian	Chi.	1	3	0	0	0	2	....	....	....	....	....	....	1976-77	1976-7
McKegney, Tony	Buf., Que., Min., NYR, St.L., Det., Chi.	13	912	320	319	639	517	79	24	23	47	56	....	1978-79	1990-9
McKendry, Alex	NYI, Cgy.	4	46	3	6	9	21	6	2	2	4	0	1	1977-78	1980-8
McKenna, Sean	Buf., L.A., Tor.	9	414	82	80	162	181	15	1	2	3	2	....	1981-82	1989-
‡ McKenna, Steve	L.A., Min., Pit., NYR	8	373	18	14	32	824	3	0	1	1	8	....	1996-97	2003-0
McKenney, Don	Bos., NYR, Tor., Det., St.L.	13	798	237	345	582	211	58	18	29	47	10	1	1954-55	1967-6
McKenny, Jim	Tor., Min.	14	604	82	247	329	294	37	7	9	16	10	....	1965-66	1978-7
McKenzie, Brian	Pit.	1	6	1	1	2	4	....	....	....	....	....	....	1971-72	1971-7
McKenzie, Jim	Hfd., Dal., Pit., Wpg., Phx., Ana., Wsh., N.J., Nsh.	15	880	48	52	100	1739	51	0	0	0	38	1	1989-90	2003-0
McKenzie, John	Chi., Det., NYR, Bos.	12	691	206	268	474	917	69	15	32	47	133	2	1958-59	1971-7
McKim, Andrew	Bos., Det.	3	38	1	4	5	6	....	....	....	....	....	....	1992-93	1994-9
• McKinnon, Alex	Ham., NYA, Chi.	5	193	19	11	30	237	....	....	....	....	....	....	1924-25	1928-2
• McKinnon, John	Mtl., Pit., Phi.	6	208	28	11	39	224	2	0	0	0	4	....	1925-26	1930-3
McLaren, Kyle	Bos., S.J.	12	719	46	161	207	671	70	1	13	14	78	....	1995-96	2007-0
McLaren, Steve	St.L.	1	6	0	0	0	25	....	....	....	....	....	....	2003-04	2003-0
McLean, Don	Wsh.	1	9	0	0	0	6	....	....	....	....	....	....	1975-76	1975-7
• McLean, Fred	Que., Ham.	2	8	0	0	0	2	....	....	....	....	....	....	1919-20	1920-2
• McLean, Jack	Tor.	3	67	14	24	38	76	13	2	2	4	8	1	1942-43	1944-4
• McLean, Jeff	S.J.	1	6	1	0	1	0	....	....	....	....	....	....	1993-94	1993-9
• McLellan, John	Tor.	1	2	0	0	0	0	....	....	....	....	....	....	1951-52	1951-5
McLellan, Scott	Bos.	1	2	0	0	0	0	....	....	....	....	....	....	1982-83	1982-8
McLellan, Todd	NYI	1	5	1	1	2	0	....	....	....	....	....	....	1987-88	1987-8
• McLenahan, Rollie	Det.	1	9	2	1	3	10	2	0	0	0	0	....	1945-46	1945-4
McLeod, Al	Det.	1	26	2	2	4	24	....	....	....	....	....	....	1973-74	1973-74
McLeod, Jackie	NYR	5	106	14	23	37	12	7	0	0	0	0	....	1949-50	1954-5
‡ McLlwain, Dave	Pit., Wpg., Buf., NYI, Tor., Ott.	10	501	100	107	207	292	20	0	2	2	2	....	1987-88	1996-9
• McMahon, Mike	Mtl., Bos.	3	57	7	18	25	102	13	1	2	3	30	1	1942-43	1945-4
McMahon, Mike	NYR, Min., Chi., Det., Pit., Buf.	8	224	15	68	83	171	14	3	7	10	4	....	1963-64	1971-72
McManama, Bob	Pit.	3	99	11	25	36	28	8	0	1	1	6	....	1973-74	1975-76
• McManus, Sammy	Mtl.M., Bos.	2	26	0	1	1	8	1	0	0	0	0	1	1934-35	1936-37
McMorrow, Sean	Buf.	1	1	0	0	0	0	....	....	....	....	....	....	2002-03	2002-03
McMurchy, Tom	Chi., Edm.	4	55	8	4	12	65	....	....	....	....	....	....	1983-84	1987-88
• McNab, Max	Det.	4	128	16	19	35	24	25	1	0	1	4	1	1947-48	1950-51
McNab, Peter	Buf., Bos., Van., N.J.	14	954	363	450	813	179	107	40	42	82	20	....	1973-74	1986-87
• McNabney, Sid	Mtl.	1	....	....	....	....	....	5	0	1	1	2	....	1950-51	1950-51
• McNamara, Howard	Mtl.	1	10	1	0	1	4	....	....	....	....	....	....	1919-20	1919-20
• McNaughton, George	Que.	1	1	0	0	0	0	....	....	....	....	....	....	1919-20	1919-20
• McNeill, Billy	Det.	6	257	21	46	67	142	4	1	1	2	4	....	1956-57	1963-64
‡ McNeill, Grant	Fla.	1	3	0	0	0	5	....	....	....	....	....	....	2003-04	2003-04
McNeill, Mike	Chi., Que.	2	63	5	11	16	18	....	....	....	....	....	....	1990-91	1991-92
McNeill, Stu	Det.	3	10	1	1	2	2	....	....	....	....	....	....	1957-58	1959-60
McPhee, George	NYR, N.J.	7	115	24	25	49	257	29	5	3	8	69	....	1982-83	1988-89
McPhee, Mike	Mtl., Min., Dal.	11	744	200	199	399	661	134	28	27	55	193	1	1983-84	1993-94
McRae, Basil	Que., Tor., Det., Min., T.B., St.L., Chi.	16	576	53	83	136	2457	78	8	4	12	349	....	1981-82	1996-97
McRae, Chris	Tor., Det.	3	21	1	0	1	122	....	....	....	....	....	....	1987-88	1989-90
McRae, Ken	Que., Tor.	7	137	14	21	35	364	6	0	0	0	4	....	1987-88	1993-94
• McReavy, Pat	Bos., Det.	4	55	5	10	15	4	22	3	3	6	9	1	1938-39	1941-42
McReynolds, Brian	Wpg., NYR, L.A.	3	30	1	5	6	8	....	....	....	....	....	....	1989-90	1993-94
McSheffrey, Bryan	Van., Buf.	3	90	13	7	20	44	....	....	....	....	....	....	1972-73	1974-75
McSorley, Marty	Pit., Edm., L.A., NYR, S.J., Bos.	17	961	108	251	359	3381	115	10	19	29	374	2	1983-84	1999-00
McSween, Don	Buf., Ana.	5	47	3	10	13	55	....	....	....	....	....	....	1987-88	1995-96
McTaggart, Jim	Wsh.	2	71	3	10	13	205	....	....	....	....	....	....	1980-81	1981-82
‡ McTavish, Dale	Cgy.	1	9	1	2	3	2	....	....	....	....	....	....	1996-97	1996-97
McTavish, Gord	St.L., Wpg.	2	11	1	3	4	2	....	....	....	....	....	....	1978-79	1979-80
• McVeigh, Charley	Chi., NYA	9	397	84	88	172	138	4	0	0	0	2	....	1926-27	1934-35
• McVicar, Jack	Mtl.M.	2	88	2	4	6	63	6	0	0	0	2	....	1930-31	1931-32
Meagher, Rick	Mtl., Hfd., N.J., St.L.	12	691	144	165	309	383	62	8	7	15	41	....	1979-80	1990-91
Meehan, Gerry	Tor., Phi., Buf., Van., Atl., Wsh.	10	670	180	243	423	111	10	0	1	1	0	....	1968-69	1978-79
Meeke, Brent	Cal., Cle.	5	75	9	22	31	8	....	....	....	....	....	....	1972-73	1976-77
Meeker, Howie	Tor.	8	346	83	102	185	329	42	6	9	15	50	4	1946-47	1953-54
Meeker, Mike	Pit.	1	4	0	0	0	5	....	....	....	....	....	....	1978-79	1978-79
• Meeking, Harry	Tor., Det., Bos.	3	64	18	12	30	66	9	3	0	3	6	....	1917-18	1926-27
Meger, Paul	Mtl.	6	212	39	52	91	118	35	3	8	11	16	1	1949-50	1954-55
Meighan, Ron	Min., Pit.	2	48	3	7	10	18	....	....	....	....	....	....	1981-82	1982-83
Meissner, Barrie	Min.	2	6	0	1	1	4	....	....	....	....	....	....	1967-68	1968-69
• Meissner, Dick	Bos., NYR	5	171	11	15	26	37	....	....	....	....	....	....	1959-60	1964-65
Melametsa, Anssi	Wpg.	1	27	0	3	3	2	....	....	....	....	....	....	1985-86	1985-86
Melanson, Dean	Buf., Wsh.	2	9	0	0	0	8	....	....	....	....	....	....	1994-95	2001-02
‡ Melin, Bjorn	Ana.	1	3	1	0	1	0	....	....	....	....	....	....	2006-07	2006-07
Melin, Roger	Min.	2	3	0	0	0	0	....	....	....	....	....	....	1980-81	1981-82
Mellanby, Scott	Phi., Edm., Fla., St.L., Atl.	21	1431	364	476	840	2479	136	24	29	53	220	....	1985-86	2006-07
Mellor, Tom	Det.	2	26	2	4	6	25	....	....	....	....	....	....	1973-74	1974-75
• Melnyk, Gerry	Det., Chi., St.L.	6	269	39	77	116	34	53	6	6	12	6	....	1955-56	1967-68
Melnyk, Larry	Bos., Edm., NYR, Van.	10	432	11	63	74	686	66	2	9	11	127	1	1980-81	1989-90
‡ Meloche, Eric	Pit., Phi.	4	74	9	11	20	36	....	....	....	....	....	....	2001-02	2006-07
Melrose, Barry	Wpg., Tor., Det.	6	300	10	23	33	728	7	0	2	2	38	....	1979-80	1985-86
Menard, Hillary	Chi.	1	1	0	0	0	0	....	....	....	....	....	....	1953-54	1953-54
Menard, Howie	Det., L.A., Chi., Oak.	4	151	23	42	65	87	19	3	7	10	36	....	1963-64	1969-70
Mercredi, Vic	Atl.	1	2	0	0	0	0	....	....	....	....	....	....	1974-75	1974-75
Meredith, Greg	Cgy.	2	38	6	4	10	8	5	3	1	4	4	....	1980-81	1982-83
Merkosky, Glenn	Hfd., N.J., Det.	5	66	5	12	17	22	....	....	....	....	....	....	1981-82	1989-90
• Meronek, Bill	Mtl.	2	19	5	8	13	0	1	0	0	0	0	....	1939-40	1942-43
Merrick, Wayne	St.L., Cal., Cle., NYI	12	774	191	265	456	303	102	19	30	49	30	4	1972-73	1983-84
• Merrill, Horace	Ott.	2	8	0	0	0	3	....	....	....	....	....	1	1917-18	1919-20
Mertzig, Jan	NYR	1	23	0	2	2	8	....	....	....	....	....	....	1998-99	1998-99
Messier, Eric	Col., Fla.	8	406	25	50	75	146	72	3	5	8	22	1	1996-97	2003-04
Messier, Joby	NYR	3	25	0	4	4	24	....	....	....	....	....	....	1992-93	1994-95
Messier, Mark	Edm., NYR, Van.	25	1756	694	1193	1887	1910	236	109	186	295	244	6	1979-80	2003-04
Messier, Mitch	Min.	4	20	0	2	2	11	....	....	....	....	....	....	1987-88	1990-91
Messier, Paul	Col.	1	9	0	0	0	4	....	....	....	....	....	....	1978-79	1978-79
Metcalfe, Scott	Edm., Buf.	3	19	1	2	3	18	....	....	....	....	....	....	1987-88	1989-90
• Metz, Don	Tor.	9	172	20	35	55	42	42	7	8	15	12	5	1938-39	1948-49
• Metz, Nick	Tor.	12	518	131	119	250	149	76	19	20	39	31	4	1934-35	1947-48
‡ Mezei, Branislav	NYI, Fla.	7	240	5	19	24	311	....	....	....	....	....	....	2000-01	2007-08
• Michaluk, Art	Chi.	1	5	0	0	0	0	....	....	....	....	....	....	1947-48	1947-48
Michaluk, John	Chi.	1	1	0	0	0	0	....	....	....	....	....	....	1950-51	1950-51
Michayluk, Dave	Phi., Pit.	3	14	2	6	8	8	7	1	1	2	0	1	1981-82	1991-92
Micheletti, Joe	St.L., Col.	3	158	11	60	71	114	11	1	11	12	10	....	1979-80	1981-82
Micheletti, Pat	Min.	1	12	2	0	2	8	....	....	....	....	....	....	1987-88	1987-88
• Mickey, Larry	Chi., NYR, Tor., Mtl., L.A., Phi., Buf.	11	292	39	53	92	160	9	1	0	1	10	....	1964-65	1974-75
• Mickoski, Nick	NYR, Chi., Det., Bos.	13	703	158	185	343	319	18	1	6	7	6	....	1947-48	1959-60
Middendorf, Max	Que., Edm.	4	13	2	4	6	6	....	....	....	....	....	....	1986-87	1990-91
Middleton, Rick	NYR, Bos.	14	1005	448	540	988	157	114	45	55	100	19	....	1974-75	1987-88
Miehm, Kevin	St.L.	2	22	1	4	5	8	2	0	1	1	0	....	1992-93	1993-94
Migay, Rudy	Tor.	10	418	59	92	151	293	15	1	0	1	20	....	1949-50	1959-60
Mika, Petr	NYI	1	3	0	0	0	0	....	....	....	....	....	....	1999-00	1999-00
‡ Mikhnov, Alexei	Edm.	1	2	0	0	0	0	....	....	....	....	....	....	2006-07	2006-07
Mikita, Stan	Chi.	22	1394	541	926	1467	1270	155	59	91	150	169	1	1958-59	1979-80
Mikkelson, Bill	L.A., NYI, Wsh.	4	147	4	18	22	105	....	....	....	....	....	....	1971-72	1976-77
Mikol, Jim	Tor., NYR	2	34	1	4	5	8	....	....	....	....	....	....	1962-63	1964-65
Mikulchik, Oleg	Wpg., Ana.	3	37	0	3	3	33	....	....	....	....	....	....	1993-94	1995-96

Name	NHL Teams	NHL Seasons	Regular Schedule					Playoffs					NHL Cup Wins	First NHL Season	Last NHL Season
			GP	G	A	TP	PIM	GP	G	A	TP	PIM			
Milbury, Mike	Bos.	12	754	49	189	238	1552	86	4	24	28	219	....	1975-76	1986-87
Milks, Hib	Pit., Phi., NYR, Ott.	8	317	87	41	128	179	11	0	0	0	2	....	1925-26	1932-33
Millar, Craig	Edm., Nsh., T.B.	5	114	8	14	22	73	....	....	....	....	....	....	1996-97	2000-01
Millar, Hugh	Det.	1	4	0	0	0	0	1	0	0	0	0	....	1946-47	1946-47
Millar, Mike	Hfd., Wsh., Bos., Tor.	5	78	18	18	36	12	....	....	....	....	....	....	1986-87	1990-91
Millen, Corey	NYR, L.A., N.J., Dal., Cgy.	8	335	90	119	209	236	47	5	7	12	22	....	1989-90	1996-97
Miller, Aaron	Que., Col., L.A., Van.	14	677	25	94	119	422	80	3	9	12	40	....	1993-94	2007-08
Miller, Bill	Mtl.M., Mtl.	3	95	7	3	10	16	12	0	0	0	0	1	1934-35	1936-37
Miller, Bob	Bos., Col., L.A.	6	404	75	119	194	220	36	4	7	11	27	....	1977-78	1984-85
Miller, Brad	Buf., Ott., Cgy.	6	82	1	5	6	321	....	....	....	....	....	....	1988-89	1993-94
Miller, Earl	Chi., Tor.	5	109	19	14	33	124	10	1	0	1	6	1	1927-28	1931-32
Miller, Jack	Chi.	2	17	0	0	0	4	....	....	....	....	....	....	1949-50	1950-51
Miller, Jason	N.J.	3	6	0	0	0	0	....	....	....	....	....	....	1990-91	1992-93
Miller, Jay	Bos., L.A.	7	446	40	44	84	1723	48	2	3	5	243	....	1985-86	1991-92
Miller, Kelly	NYR, Wsh.	15	1057	181	282	463	512	119	20	34	54	65	....	1984-85	1998-99
Miller, Kevin	NYR, Det., Wsh., St.L., S.J., Pit., Chi., NYI, Ott.	13	620	150	185	335	429	61	7	10	17	49	....	1988-89	2003-04
Miller, Kip	Que., Min., S.J., NYI, Chi., Pit., Ana., Wsh.	12	449	74	165	239	105	25	6	11	17	23	....	1990-91	2003-04
Miller, Paul	Col.	1	3	0	3	3	0	....	....	....	....	....	....	1981-82	1981-82
Miller, Perry	Det.	4	217	10	51	61	387	....	....	....	....	....	....	1977-78	1980-81
Miller, Tom	Det., NYI	4	118	16	25	41	34	....	....	....	....	....	....	1970-71	1974-75
Miller, Warren	NYR, Hfd.	4	262	40	50	90	137	6	1	0	1	0	....	1979-80	1982-83
Milley, Norm	Buf., T.B.	4	29	2	4	6	12	....	....	....	....	....	....	2001-02	2005-06
Mills, Craig	Wpg., Chi.	3	31	0	5	5	36	1	0	0	0	0	....	1995-96	1998-99
Miner, John	Edm.	1	14	2	3	5	16	....	....	....	....	....	....	1987-88	1987-88
Minor, Gerry	Van.	5	140	11	21	32	173	12	1	3	4	25	....	1979-80	1983-84
Mironov, Boris	Wpg., Edm., Chi., NYR	11	716	76	231	307	891	25	5	11	16	45	....	1993-94	2003-04
Mironov, Dmitri	Tor., Pit., Ana., Det., Wsh.	10	556	54	206	260	568	75	10	26	36	48	1	1991-92	2000-01
Miszuk, John	Det., Chi., Phi., Min.	6	237	7	39	46	232	19	0	3	3	19	....	1963-64	1969-70
Mitchell, Bill	Det.	1	1	0	0	0	0	....	....	....	....	....	....	1963-64	1963-64
Mitchell, Herb	Bos.	2	44	6	0	6	36	....	....	....	....	....	....	1924-25	1925-26
Mitchell, Jeff	Dal.	1	7	0	0	0	7	....	....	....	....	....	....	1997-98	1997-98
Mitchell, Red	Chi.	3	83	4	5	9	67	....	....	....	....	....	....	1941-42	1944-45
Mitchell, Roy	Min.	1	3	0	0	0	0	....	....	....	....	....	....	1992-93	1992-93
Modry, Jaroslav	N.J., Ott., L.A., Atl., Dal., Phi.	13	725	49	201	250	510	28	1	5	6	6	....	1993-94	2007-08
Moe, Bill	NYR	5	261	11	42	53	163	1	0	0	0	0	....	1944-45	1948-49
Moffat, Lyle	Tor., Wpg.	3	97	12	16	28	51	....	....	....	....	....	....	1972-73	1979-80
Moffat, Ron	Det.	3	37	1	1	2	8	7	0	0	0	0	....	1932-33	1934-35
Moger, Sandy	Bos., L.A.	5	236	41	38	79	212	5	2	2	4	12	....	1994-95	1998-99
Mogilny, Alexander	Buf., Van., N.J., Tor.	16	990	473	559	1032	432	124	39	47	86	58	1	1989-90	2005-06
Moher, Mike	N.J.	1	9	0	1	1	28	....	....	....	....	....	....	1982-83	1982-83
Mohns, Doug	Bos., Chi., Min., Atl., Wsh.	22	1390	248	462	710	1250	94	14	36	50	122	....	1953-54	1974-75
Mohns, Lloyd	NYR	1	1	0	0	0	0	....	....	....	....	....	....	1943-44	1943-44
Mokosak, Carl	Cgy., L.A., Phi., Pit., Bos.	6	83	11	15	26	170	1	0	0	0	0	....	1981-82	1988-89
Mokosak, John	Det.	2	41	0	2	2	96	....	....	....	....	....	....	1988-89	1989-90
Molin, Lars	Van.	3	172	33	65	98	37	19	2	9	11	7	....	1981-82	1983-84
Moller, Mike	Buf., Edm.	7	134	15	28	43	41	3	0	1	1	0	....	1980-81	1986-87
Moller, Randy	Que., NYR, Buf., Fla.	14	815	45	180	225	1692	78	6	16	22	197	....	1981-82	1994-95
Molloy, Mitch	Buf.	1	2	0	0	0	10	....	....	....	....	....	....	1989-90	1989-90
• Molyneaux, Larry	NYR	2	45	0	1	1	20	10	0	0	0	8	....	1937-38	1938-39
Momesso, Sergio	Mtl., St.L., Van., Tor., NYR	13	710	152	193	345	1557	119	18	26	44	311	....	1983-84	1996-97
Monahan, Garry	Mtl., Det., L.A., Tor., Van.	12	748	116	169	285	484	22	3	1	4	13	....	1967-68	1978-79
Monahan, Hartland	Cal., NYR, Wsh., Pit., L.A., St.L.	7	334	61	80	141	163	6	0	0	0	4	....	1973-74	1980-81
• Mondou, Armand	Mtl.	12	386	47	71	118	99	32	3	5	8	12	2	1928-29	1939-40
Mondou, Pierre	Mtl.	9	548	194	262	456	179	69	17	28	45	26	3	1976-77	1984-85
• Mongeau, Michel	St.L., T.B.	4	54	6	19	25	10	2	0	1	1	0	....	1989-90	1992-93
Mongrain, Bob	Buf., L.A.	6	81	13	14	27	14	11	1	2	3	2	....	1979-80	1985-86
Monteith, Hank	Det.	3	77	5	12	17	6	4	0	0	0	0	....	1968-69	1970-71
Montgomery, Jim	St.L., Mtl., Phi., S.J., Dal.	6	122	9	25	34	80	8	1	0	1	2	....	1993-94	2002-03
Moore, Barrie	Buf., Edm., Wsh.	3	39	2	6	8	18	....	....	....	....	....	....	1995-96	1999-00
Moore, Dickie	Mtl., Tor., St.L.	14	719	261	347	608	652	135	46	64	110	122	6	1951-52	1967-68
Moore, Steve	Col.	3	69	5	7	12	41	....	....	....	....	....	....	2001-02	2003-04
• Moran, Amby	Mtl., Chi.	2	35	1	1	2	24	....	....	....	....	....	....	1926-27	1927-28
‡ Moran, Ian	Pit., Bos., Ana.	12	489	21	50	71	321	66	1	7	8	24	....	1994-95	2006-07
‡ Moravec, David	Buf.	1	1	0	0	0	0	....	....	....	....	....	....	1999-00	1999-00
More, Jay	NYR, Min., S.J., Phx., Chi., Nsh.	10	406	18	54	72	702	31	0	6	6	45	....	1988-89	1998-99
• Morenz, Howie	Mtl., Chi., NYR	14	550	271	201	472	546	39	13	9	22	58	3	1923-24	1936-37
Moretto, Angelo	Cle.	1	5	1	2	3	2	....	....	....	....	....	....	1976-77	1976-77
Morgan, Gavin	Dal.	1	6	0	0	0	21	....	....	....	....	....	....	2003-04	2003-04
‡ Morgan, Jason	L.A., Cgy., Nsh., Chi., Min.	5	44	2	5	7	18	....	....	....	....	....	....	1996-97	2006-07
• Morin, Pete	Mtl.	1	31	10	12	22	7	1	0	0	0	0	....	1941-42	1941-42
• Morin, Stephane	Que., Van.	5	90	16	39	55	52	....	....	....	....	....	....	1989-90	1993-94
Morisset, Dave	Fla.	1	4	0	0	0	5	....	....	....	....	....	....	2001-02	2001-02
Morissette, Dave	Mtl.	2	11	0	0	0	57	....	....	....	....	....	....	1998-99	1999-00
Moro, Marc	Ana., Nsh., Tor.	4	30	0	0	0	77	....	....	....	....	....	....	1997-98	2001-02
‡ Morozov, Aleksey	Pit.	7	451	84	135	219	98	39	4	5	9	8	....	1997-98	2003-04
• Morris, Bernie	Bos.	1	6	1	0	1	0	....	....	....	....	....	....	1924-25	1924-25
Morris, Jon	N.J., S.J., Bos.	6	103	16	33	49	47	11	1	7	8	25	....	1988-89	1993-94
• Morris, Moe	Tor., NYR	4	135	13	29	42	58	18	4	2	6	16	1	1943-44	1948-49
Morrison, Dave	L.A., Van.	4	39	3	3	6	4	....	....	....	....	....	....	1980-81	1984-85
• Morrison, Don	Det., Chi.	3	112	18	28	46	12	3	0	1	1	0	....	1947-48	1950-51
Morrison, Doug	Bos.	4	23	7	3	10	15	....	....	....	....	....	....	1979-80	1984-85
Morrison, Gary	Phi.	3	43	1	15	16	70	5	0	1	1	2	....	1979-80	1981-82
• Morrison, George	St.L.	2	115	17	21	38	13	3	0	0	0	0	....	1970-71	1971-72
Morrison, Jim	Bos., Tor., Det., NYR, Pit.	12	704	40	160	200	542	36	0	12	12	38	....	1951-52	1970-71
• Morrison, John	NYA	1	18	0	0	0	0	....	....	....	....	....	....	1925-26	1925-26
Morrison, Kevin	Col.	1	41	4	11	15	23	....	....	....	....	....	....	1979-80	1979-80
Morrison, Lew	Phi., Atl., Wsh., Pit.	9	564	39	52	91	107	17	0	0	0	2	....	1969-70	1977-78
Morrison, Mark	NYR	2	10	1	1	2	0	....	....	....	....	....	....	1981-82	1983-84
• Morrison, Rod	Det.	1	34	8	7	15	4	3	0	0	0	0	....	1947-48	1947-48
Morrow, Ken	NYI	10	550	17	88	105	309	127	11	22	33	97	4	1979-80	1988-89
Morrow, Scott	Cgy.	1	4	0	0	0	0	....	....	....	....	....	....	1994-95	1994-95
Morton, Dean	Det.	1	1	1	0	1	2	....	....	....	....	....	....	1989-90	1989-90
Mortson, Gus	Tor., Chi., Det.	13	797	46	152	198	1380	54	5	8	13	68	4	1946-47	1958-59
• Mosdell, Ken	Bro., Mtl., Chi.	16	693	141	168	309	475	80	16	13	29	48	4	1941-42	1958-59
• Mosienko, Bill	Chi.	14	711	258	282	540	121	22	10	4	14	15	....	1941-42	1954-55
Mott, Morris	Cal.	3	199	18	32	50	49	....	....	....	....	....	....	1972-73	1974-75
• Motter, Alex	Bos., Det.	8	255	39	64	103	135	41	3	9	12	41	1	1934-35	1942-43
‡ Mowers, Mark	Nsh., Det., Bos., Ana.	7	278	18	44	62	70	3	0	0	0	0	....	1998-99	2007-08
Moxey, Jim	Cal., Cle., L.A.	3	127	22	27	49	59	....	....	....	....	....	....	1974-75	1976-77
Mrozik, Rick	Cgy.	1	2	0	0	0	0	....	....	....	....	....	....	2002-03	2002-03
Muckalt, Bill	Van., NYI, Ott., Min.	5	256	40	57	97	204	5	0	0	0	0	....	1998-99	2002-03
‡ Muir, Bryan	Edm., N.J., Chi., T.B., Col., L.A., Wsh.	11	279	16	37	53	281	29	0	0	0	6	1	1995-96	2006-07
Mulhern, Richard	Atl., L.A., Tor., Wpg.	6	303	27	93	120	217	7	0	3	3	5	....	1975-76	1980-81
Mulhern, Ryan	Wsh.	1	3	0	0	0	0	....	....	....	....	....	....	1997-98	1997-98
Mullen, Brian	Wpg., NYR, S.J., NYI	11	832	260	362	622	414	62	12	18	30	30	....	1982-83	1992-93
Mullen, Joe	St.L., Cgy., Pit., Bos.	17	1062	502	561	1063	241	143	60	46	106	42	3	1979-80	1996-97
Muller, Kirk	N.J., Mtl., NYI, Tor., Fla., Dal.	19	1349	357	602	959	1223	127	33	36	69	153	1	1984-85	2002-03
Muloin, Wayne	Det., Oak., Cal., Min.	3	147	3	21	24	93	11	0	0	0	2	....	1963-64	1970-71
Mulvenna, Glenn	Pit., Phi.	2	2	0	0	0	4	....	....	....	....	....	....	1991-92	1992-93
Mulvey, Grant	Chi., N.J.	10	586	149	135	284	816	42	10	5	15	70	....	1974-75	1983-84
Mulvey, Paul	Wsh., Pit., L.A.	4	225	30	51	81	613	....	....	....	....	....	....	1978-79	1981-82
• Mummery, Harry	Tor., Que., Mtl., Ham.	6	106	33	19	52	226	2	1	1	2	17	....	1917-18	1922-23
Muni, Craig	Tor., Edm., Chi., Buf., Wpg., Pit., Dal.	16	819	28	119	147	775	113	0	17	17	108	3	1981-82	1997-98
• Munro, Dunc	Mtl.M., Mtl.	8	239	28	18	46	172	21	2	2	4	18	1	1924-25	1931-32
• Munro, Gerry	Mtl.M., Tor.	2	34	1	0	1	37	....	....	....	....	....	....	1924-25	1925-26
Murdoch, Bob	Mtl., L.A., Atl., Cgy.	12	757	60	218	278	764	69	4	18	22	92	2	1970-71	1981-82
Murdoch, Bob	Cal., Cle., St.L.	4	260	72	85	157	127	....	....	....	....	....	....	1975-76	1978-79
Murdoch, Don	NYR, Edm., Det.	6	320	121	117	238	155	24	10	8	18	16	....	1976-77	1981-82
• Murdoch, Murray	NYR	11	508	84	108	192	197	55	9	12	21	28	2	1926-27	1936-37
‡ Murley, Matt	Pit., Phx.	3	62	2	7	9	38	....	....	....	....	....	....	2003-04	2007-08
Murphy, Brian	Det.	1	1	0	0	0	0	....	....	....	....	....	....	1974-75	1974-75
‡ Murphy, Curtis	Min.	1	1	0	0	0	0	....	....	....	....	....	....	2002-03	2002-03
Murphy, Gord	Phi., Bos., Fla., Atl.	14	862	85	238	323	668	53	3	16	19	35	....	1988-89	2001-02
Murphy, Joe	Det., Edm., Chi., St.L., S.J., Bos., Wsh.	15	779	233	295	528	810	120	34	43	77	185	1	1986-87	2000-01

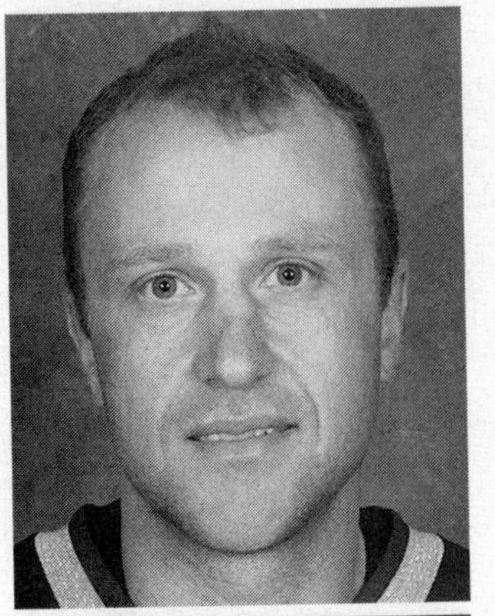

Jaroslav Modry

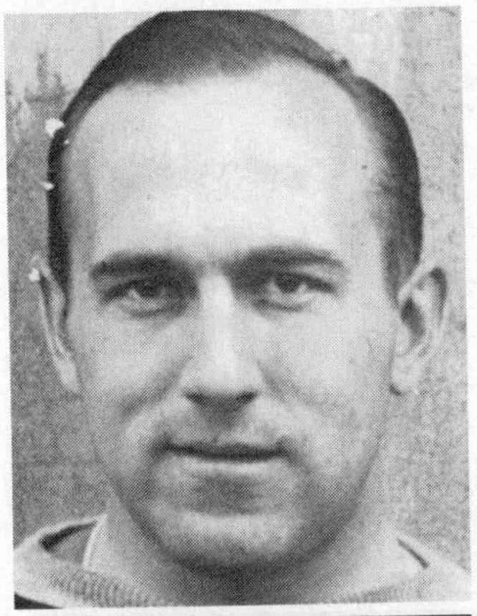

Howie Morenz

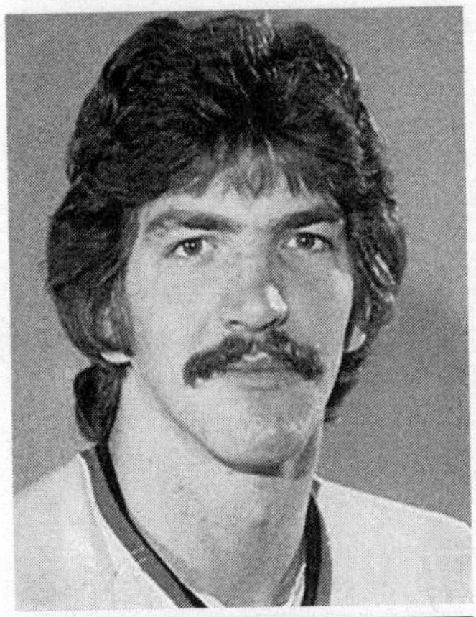

Grant Mulvey

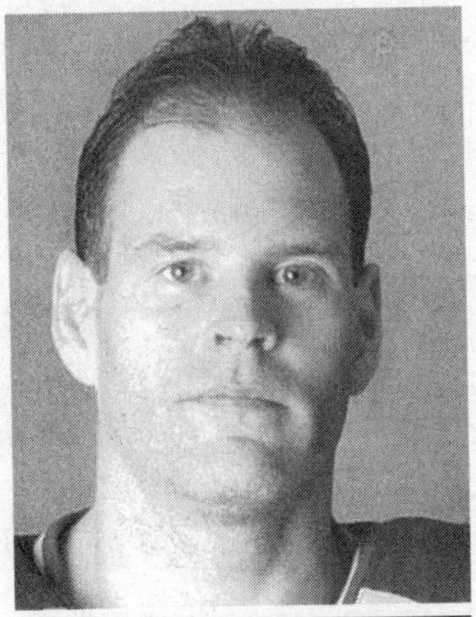

Troy Murray

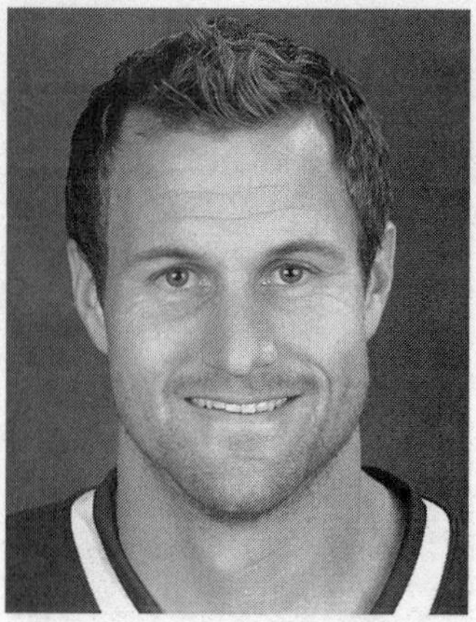

Markus Naslund

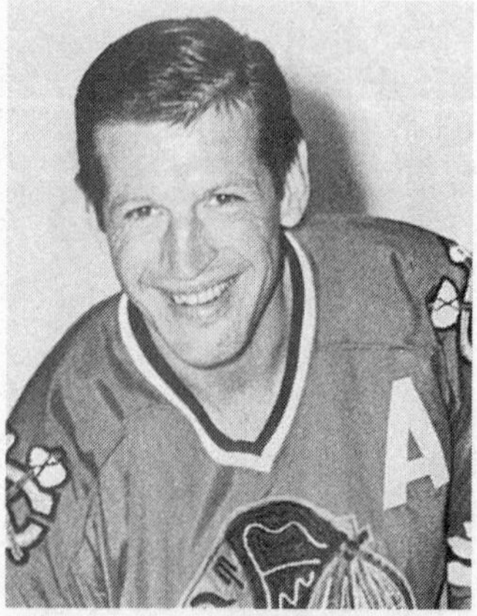

Eric Nesterenko

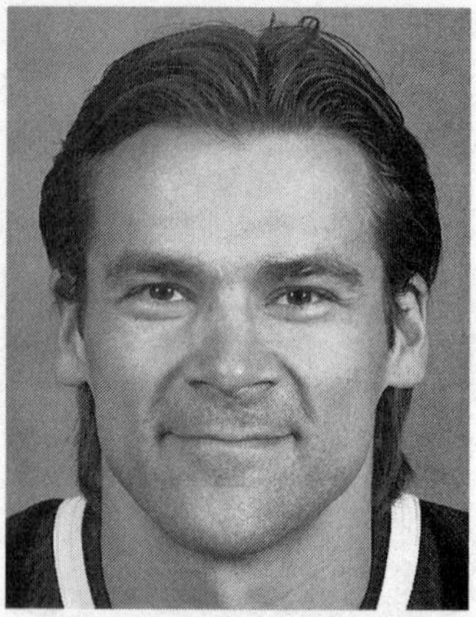

Teppo Numminen

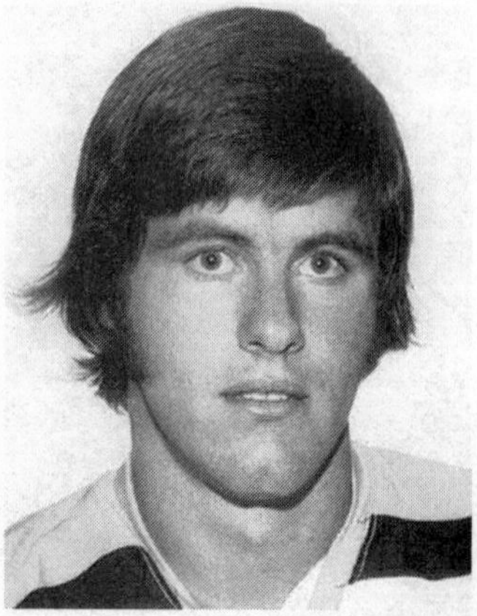

Chris Oddleifson

			Regular Schedule					Playoffs					NHL	First	Last
Name	NHL Teams	NHL Seasons	GP	G	A	TP	PIM	GP	G	A	TP	PIM	Cup Wins	NHL Season	NHL Season
Murphy, Larry	L.A., Wsh., Min., Pit., Tor., Det.	21	1615	287	929	1216	1084	215	37	115	152	201	4	1980-81	2000-01
Murphy, Mike	St.L., NYR, L.A.	12	831	238	318	556	514	66	13	23	36	54	....	1971-72	1982-83
Murphy, Rob	Van., Ott., L.A.	7	125	9	12	21	152	4	0	0	0	2	....	1987-88	1993-94
Murphy, Ron	NYR, Chi., Det., Bos.	18	889	205	274	479	460	53	7	8	15	26	2	1952-53	1969-70
• Murray, Allan	NYA	7	271	5	9	14	163	14	0	0	0	10	....	1933-34	1939-40
Murray, Bob	Atl., Van.	4	194	6	16	22	98	10	1	1	2	15	....	1973-74	1976-77
Murray, Bob	Chi.	15	1008	132	382	514	873	112	19	37	56	106	....	1975-76	1989-90
Murray, Chris	Mtl., Hfd., Car., Ott., Chi., Dal.	6	242	16	18	34	550	15	1	0	1	12	....	1994-95	1999-00
Murray, Glen	Bos., Pit., L.A.	16	1009	337	314	651	679	94	20	22	42	66	....	1991-92	2007-08
Murray, Jim	L.A.	1	30	0	2	2	14	....	....	....	....	....	....	1967-68	1967-68
Murray, Ken	Tor., NYI, Det., K.C.	5	106	1	10	11	135	....	....	....	....	....	....	1969-70	1975-76
• Murray, Leo	Mtl.	1	6	0	0	0	2	....	....	....	....	....	....	1932-33	1932-33
Murray, Mike	Phi.	1	1	0	0	0	0	....	....	....	....	....	....	1987-88	1987-88
Murray, Pat	Phi.	2	25	3	1	4	15	....	....	....	....	....	....	1990-91	1991-92
Murray, Randy	Tor.	1	3	0	0	0	2	....	....	....	....	....	....	1969-70	1969-70
‡ Murray, Rem	Edm., NYR, Nsh.	9	560	94	121	215	161	62	5	12	17	18	....	1996-97	2005-06
Murray, Rob	Wsh., Wpg., Phx.	8	107	4	15	19	111	9	0	0	0	18	....	1989-90	1998-99
Murray, Terry	Cal., Phi., Det., Wsh.	8	302	4	76	80	199	18	2	2	4	10	....	1972-73	1981-82
Murray, Troy	Chi., Wpg., Ott., Pit., Col.	15	915	230	354	584	875	113	17	26	43	145	1	1981-82	1995-96
Murzyn, Dana	Hfd., Cgy., Van.	14	838	52	152	204	1571	82	9	10	19	166	1	1985-86	1998-99
Musil, Frantisek	Min., Cgy., Ott., Edm.	15	797	34	106	140	1241	42	2	4	6	47	....	1986-87	2000-01
Myers, Hap	Buf.	1	13	0	0	0	6	....	....	....	....	....	....	1970-71	1970-71
Myhres, Brantt	T.B., Phi., S.J., Nsh., Wsh., Bos.	7	154	6	2	8	687	....	....	....	....	....	....	1994-95	2002-03
• Myles, Vic	NYR	1	45	6	9	15	57	....	....	....	....	....	....	1942-43	1942-43
‡ Myrvold, Anders	Col., Bos., NYI, Det.	4	33	0	5	5	12	....	....	....	....	....	....	1995-96	2003-04

N

Name	NHL Teams	NHL Seasons	GP	G	A	TP	PIM	GP	G	A	TP	PIM	Cup Wins	First NHL Season	Last NHL Season
‡ Nabokov, Dmitri	Chi., NYI	3	55	11	13	24	28	....	....	....	....	....	....	1997-98	1999-00
Nachbaur, Don	Hfd., Edm., Phi.	8	223	23	46	69	465	11	1	1	2	24	....	1980-81	1989-90
‡ Nagy, Ladislav	St.L., Phx., Dal., L.A.	8	435	115	196	311	358	18	2	2	4	23	....	1999-00	2007-08
Nahrgang, Jim	Det.	3	57	5	12	17	34	....	....	....	....	....	....	1974-75	1976-77
Namestnikov, John	Van., NYI, Nsh.	6	43	0	9	9	24	2	0	0	0	2	....	1993-94	1999-00
Nanne, Lou	Min.	11	635	68	157	225	356	32	4	10	14	8	....	1967-68	1977-78
Nantais, Rich	Min.	3	63	5	4	9	79	....	....	....	....	....	....	1974-75	1976-77
Napier, Mark	Mtl., Min., Edm., Buf.	11	767	235	306	541	157	82	18	24	42	11	2	1978-79	1988-89
Nash, Tyson	St.L., Phx.	7	374	27	37	64	673	23	3	2	5	52	....	1998-99	2005-06
‡ Naslund, Markus	Pit., Van., NYR	15	1117	395	474	869	736	52	14	22	36	56	....	1993-94	2008-09
Naslund, Mats	Mtl., Bos.	9	651	251	383	634	111	102	35	57	92	33	1	1982-83	1994-95
‡ Nasreddine, Alain	Chi., Mtl., NYI, Pit.	5	74	1	4	5	84	....	....	....	....	....	....	1998-99	2007-08
Nattrass, Ralph	Chi.	4	223	18	38	56	308	....	....	....	....	....	....	1946-47	1949-50
Nattress, Ric	Mtl., St.L., Cgy., Tor., Phi.	11	536	29	135	164	377	67	5	10	15	60	1	1982-83	1992-93
Natyshak, Mike	Que.	1	4	0	0	0	0	....	....	....	....	....	....	1987-88	1987-88
Nazarov, Andrei	S.J., T.B., Cgy., Ana., Bos., Phx., Min.	12	571	53	71	124	1409	9	0	0	0	11	....	1993-94	2005-06
Ndur, Rumun	Buf., NYR, Atl.	4	69	2	3	5	137	....	....	....	....	....	....	1996-97	1999-00
Neaton, Pat	Pit.	1	9	1	1	2	12	....	....	....	....	....	....	1993-94	1993-94
Nechayev, Viktor	L.A.	1	3	1	0	1	0	....	....	....	....	....	....	1982-83	1982-83
Neckar, Stan	Ott., NYR, Phx., T.B., Nsh.	10	510	12	41	53	316	29	0	3	3	8	1	1994-95	2003-04
Nedomansky, Vaclav	Det., NYR, St.L.	6	421	122	156	278	88	7	3	5	8	0	....	1977-78	1982-83
‡ Nedorost, Andrej	CBJ	3	28	2	3	5	12	....	....	....	....	....	....	2001-02	2003-04
‡ Nedorost, Vaclav	Col., Fla.	3	99	10	10	20	34	....	....	....	....	....	....	2001-02	2003-04
‡ Nedved, Petr	Van., St.L., NYR, Pit., Edm., Phx., Phi.	15	982	310	407	717	708	71	19	23	42	64	....	1990-91	2006-07
‡ Nedved, Zdenek	Tor.	3	31	4	6	10	14	....	....	....	....	....	....	1994-95	1996-97
Needham, Mike	Pit., Dal.	3	86	9	5	14	16	14	2	0	2	4	1	1991-92	1993-94
Neely, Bob	Tor., Col.	5	283	39	59	98	266	26	5	7	12	15	....	1973-74	1977-78
Neely, Cam	Van., Bos.	13	726	395	299	694	1241	93	57	32	89	168	....	1983-84	1995-96
Neilson, Jim	NYR, Cal., Cle.	16	1023	69	299	368	904	65	1	17	18	61	....	1962-63	1977-78
Nelson, Gordie	Tor.	1	3	0	0	0	11	....	....	....	....	....	....	1969-70	1969-70
Nelson, Jeff	Wsh., Nsh.	3	52	3	8	11	20	3	0	0	0	4	....	1994-95	1998-99
Nelson, Todd	Pit., Wsh.	2	3	1	0	1	2	4	0	0	0	0	....	1991-92	1993-94
Nemchinov, Sergei	NYR, Van., NYI, N.J.	11	761	152	193	345	251	105	11	20	31	24	2	1991-92	2001-02
Nemecek, Jan	L.A.	2	7	1	0	1	4	....	....	....	....	....	....	1998-99	1999-00
Nemeth, Steve	NYR	1	12	2	0	2	2	....	....	....	....	....	....	1987-88	1987-88
‡ Nemirovsky, David	Fla.	4	91	16	22	38	42	3	1	0	1	0	....	1995-96	1998-99
Nesterenko, Eric	Tor., Chi.	21	1219	250	324	574	1273	124	13	24	37	127	1	1951-52	1971-72
Nethery, Lance	NYR, Edm.	2	41	11	14	25	14	14	5	3	8	9	....	1980-81	1981-82
Neufeld, Ray	Hfd., Wpg., Bos.	11	595	157	200	357	816	28	8	6	14	55	....	1979-80	1989-90
• Neville, Mike	Tor., NYA	3	65	5	5	10	14	2	0	0	0	0	....	1924-25	1930-31
Nevin, Bob	Tor., NYR, Min., L.A.	18	1128	307	419	726	211	84	16	18	34	24	2	1957-58	1975-76
Newberry, John	Mtl., Hfd.	4	22	0	4	4	6	2	0	0	0	0	....	1982-83	1985-86
Newell, Rick	Det.	2	6	0	0	0	0	....	....	....	....	....	....	1972-73	1973-74
Newman, Dan	NYR, Mtl., Edm.	4	126	17	24	41	63	3	0	0	0	4	....	1976-77	1979-80
• Newman, John	Det.	1	8	1	1	2	0	....	....	....	....	....	....	1930-31	1930-31
Nicholls, Bernie	L.A., NYR, Edm., N.J., Chi., S.J.	18	1127	475	734	1209	1292	118	42	72	114	164	....	1981-82	1998-99
• Nicholson, Al	Bos.	2	19	0	1	1	4	....	....	....	....	....	....	1955-56	1956-57
• Nicholson, Ed	Det.	1	1	0	0	0	0	....	....	....	....	....	....	1947-48	1947-48
• Nicholson, Hickey	Chi.	1	2	1	0	1	0	....	....	....	....	....	....	1937-38	1937-38
Nicholson, Neil	Oak., NYI	4	39	3	1	4	23	2	0	0	0	0	....	1969-70	1977-78
Nicholson, Paul	Wsh.	3	62	4	8	12	18	....	....	....	....	....	....	1974-75	1976-77
‡ Nickulas, Eric	Bos., St.L., Chi.	6	118	15	23	38	82	1	0	0	0	2	....	1998-99	2005-06
Nicolson, Graeme	Bos., Col., NYR	3	52	2	7	9	60	....	....	....	....	....	....	1978-79	1982-83
Nieckar, Barry	Hfd., Cgy., Ana.	4	8	0	0	0	21	....	....	....	....	....	....	1992-93	1997-98
Niekamp, Jim	Det.	2	29	0	2	2	37	....	....	....	....	....	....	1970-71	1971-72
Nielsen, Chris	CBJ	2	52	6	8	14	8	....	....	....	....	....	....	2000-01	2001-02
Nielsen, Jeff	NYR, Ana., Min.	5	252	20	27	47	70	4	0	0	0	2	....	1996-97	2000-01
Nielsen, Kirk	Bos.	1	6	0	0	0	0	....	....	....	....	....	....	1997-98	1997-98
‡ Niemi, Antti-Jussi	Ana.	2	29	1	1	2	22	....	....	....	....	....	....	2000-01	2001-02
‡ Nieminen, Ville	Col., Pit., Chi., Cgy., NYR, S.J., St.L.	7	385	48	69	117	333	58	8	12	20	99	1	1999-00	2006-07
Nienhuis, Kraig	Bos.	3	87	20	16	36	39	2	0	0	0	14	....	1985-86	1987-88
Nieuwendyk, Joe	Cgy., Dal., N.J., Tor., Fla.	20	1257	564	562	1126	677	158	66	50	116	91	3	1986-87	2006-07
• Nighbor, Frank	Ott., Tor.	13	349	139	98	237	249	20	4	9	13	13	4	1917-18	1929-30
Nigro, Frank	Tor.	2	68	8	18	26	39	3	0	0	0	2	....	1982-83	1983-84
‡ Niinimaa, Janne	Phi., Edm., NYI, Dal., Mtl.	10	741	54	265	319	733	59	3	21	24	60	....	1996-97	2006-07
‡ Nikolishin, Andrei	Hfd., Wsh., Chi., Col.	10	628	93	187	280	270	43	1	17	18	22	....	1994-95	2003-04
Nikulin, Igor	Ana.	1	....	....	....	....	....	1	0	0	0	0	....	1996-97	1996-97
Nilan, Chris	Mtl., NYR, Bos.	13	688	110	115	225	3043	111	8	9	17	541	1	1979-80	1991-92
Nill, Jim	St.L., Van., Bos., Wpg., Det.	9	524	58	87	145	854	59	10	5	15	203	....	1981-82	1989-90
‡ Nilson, Marcus	Fla., Cgy.	9	521	67	101	168	270	34	4	7	11	14	....	1998-99	2007-08
Nilsson, Kent	Atl., Cgy., Min., Edm.	9	553	264	422	686	116	59	11	41	52	14	1	1979-80	1994-95
Nilsson, Ulf	NYR	4	170	57	112	169	85	25	8	14	22	27	....	1978-79	1982-83
‡ Niskala, Janne	T.B.	1	6	1	2	3	6	....	....	....	....	....	....	2008-09	2008-09
Nistico, Lou	Col.	1	3	0	0	0	0	....	....	....	....	....	....	1977-78	1977-78
• Noble, Reg	Tor., Mtl.M., Det.	16	510	168	106	274	916	18	2	2	4	33	3	1917-18	1932-33
Noel, Claude	Wsh.	1	7	0	0	0	0	....	....	....	....	....	....	1979-80	1979-80
Nolan, Brandon	Car.	1	6	0	1	1	0	....	....	....	....	....	....	2007-08	2007-08
• Nolan, Paddy	Tor.	1	2	0	0	0	0	....	....	....	....	....	....	1921-22	1921-22
Nolan, Ted	Det., Pit.	3	78	6	16	22	105	....	....	....	....	....	....	1981-82	1985-86
Nolet, Simon	Phi., K.C., Pit., Col.	10	562	150	182	332	187	34	6	3	9	8	1	1967-68	1976-77
Noonan, Brian	Chi., NYR, St.L., Van., Phx.	12	629	116	159	275	518	71	17	19	36	77	1	1987-88	1998-99
‡ Nordgren, Niklas	Car., Pit.	1	58	4	2	6	34	....	....	....	....	....	....	2005-06	2005-06
Nordmark, Robert	St.L., Van.	4	236	13	70	83	254	7	3	2	5	8	....	1987-88	1990-91
‡ Nordqvist, Jonas	Chi.	1	3	0	2	2	2	....	....	....	....	....	....	2006-07	2006-07
‡ Nordstrom, Peter	Bos.	1	2	0	0	0	0	....	....	....	....	....	....	1998-99	1998-99
Noris, Joe	Pit., St.L., Buf.	3	55	2	5	7	22	....	....	....	....	....	....	1971-72	1973-74
Norris, Dwayne	Que., Ana.	3	20	2	4	6	8	....	....	....	....	....	....	1993-94	1995-96
Norrish, Rod	Min.	2	21	3	3	6	2	....	....	....	....	....	....	1973-74	1974-75
Norstrom, Mattias	NYR, L.A., Dal.	14	903	18	147	165	661	56	2	5	7	54	....	1993-94	2007-08
• Northcott, Baldy	Mtl.M., Chi.	11	446	133	112	245	273	31	8	5	13	14	1	1928-29	1938-39
‡ Norton, Brad	Fla., L.A., Wsh., Ott., Det., S.J.	6	124	3	8	11	287	....	....	....	....	....	....	2001-02	2007-08
Norton, Jeff	NYI, S.J., St.L., Edm., T.B., Fla., Pit., Bos.	15	799	52	332	384	615	65	4	21	25	89	....	1987-88	2001-02
Norwich, Craig	Wpg., St.L., Col.	2	104	17	58	75	60	....	....	....	....	....	....	1979-80	1980-81
Norwood, Lee	Que., Wsh., St.L., Det., N.J., Hfd., Cgy.	12	503	58	153	211	1099	65	6	22	28	171	....	1980-81	1993-94
‡ Novak, Filip	Ott., CBJ	2	17	0	0	0	6	....	....	....	....	....	....	2005-06	2006-07
‡ Novoseltsev, Ivan	Fla., Phx.	5	234	31	44	75	112	....	....	....	....	....	....	1999-00	2003-04
Novy, Milan	Wsh.	1	73	18	30	48	16	2	0	0	0	0	....	1982-83	1982-83

ame	NHL Teams	NHL Seasons	Regular Schedule GP	G	A	TP	PIM	Playoffs GP	G	A	TP	PIM	NHL Cup Wins	First NHL Season	Last NHL Season
wak, Hank	Pit., Det., Bos.	4	180	26	29	55	161	13	1	0	1	8	....	1973-74	1976-77
mmelin, Petteri	CBJ, Min.	3	139	9	36	45	34	7	1	2	3	0	....	2000-01	2007-08
mminen, Teppo	Wpg., Phx., Dal., Buf.	20	1372	117	520	637	513	82	9	14	23	28	....	1988-89	2008-09
rminen, Kai	L.A., Min.	2	69	17	11	28	24	....	....	....	....	....	....	1996-97	2000-01
koluk, Mike	Tor.	1	32	3	1	4	20	....	....	....	....	....	....	1956-57	1956-57
lander, Michael	Hfd., Cgy., T.B., Chi., Wsh., Bos., NYR	15	920	209	470	679	468	47	12	22	34	14	....	1992-93	2008-09
lund, Gary	Tor., Chi., NYI	11	608	32	139	171	1235	24	0	6	6	63	....	1982-83	1992-93
rop, Bill	Mtl., Min.	4	207	12	51	63	101	35	1	7	8	22	3	1975-76	1981-82
strom, Bob	NYI	14	900	235	278	513	1248	157	39	44	83	236	4	1972-73	1985-86
)															
tes, Adam	Det., St.L., Bos., Wsh., Phi., Ana., Edm.	19	1337	341	1079	1420	415	163	42	114	156	66	....	1985-86	2003-04
tman, Russell	Det., Mtl.M., NYR	3	120	20	9	29	100	15	1	0	1	18	....	1926-27	1928-29
Brien, Dennis	Min., Col., Cle., Bos.	10	592	31	91	122	1017	34	1	2	3	101	....	1970-71	1979-80
Brien, Doug	T.B.	1	5	0	0	0	2	....	....	....	....	....	....	2005-06	2005-06
Brien, Ellard	Bos.	1	2	0	0	0	0	....	....	....	....	....	....	1955-56	1955-56
sut, Jaroslav	St.L., Col.	2	7	0	0	0	2	....	....	....	....	....	....	2000-01	2001-02
Callahan, Jack	Chi., N.J.	7	389	27	104	131	541	32	4	11	15	41	....	1982-83	1988-89
Connell, Mike	Chi., Bos., Det.	13	860	105	334	439	605	82	8	24	32	64	....	1977-78	1989-90
Connor, Buddy	Mtl., NYR	10	509	140	257	397	34	53	15	21	36	6	2	1941-42	1950-51
Connor, Myles	N.J., Ana.	4	43	3	4	7	69	....	....	....	....	....	....	1990-91	1993-94
dleifson, Chris	Bos., Van.	9	524	95	191	286	464	14	1	6	7	8	....	1972-73	1980-81
delein, Lyle	Mtl., N.J., Phx., CBJ, Chi., Dal., Fla., Pit.	16	1056	50	202	252	2316	86	5	13	18	209	1	1989-90	2005-06
delein, Selmar	Edm.	3	18	0	2	2	35	....	....	....	....	....	....	1985-86	1988-89
dgers, Jeff	S.J., Bos., Col., Atl.	12	821	75	70	145	2364	47	2	1	3	73	....	1991-92	2002-03
djick, Gino	Van., NYI, Phi., Mtl.	12	605	64	73	137	2567	44	4	1	5	142	....	1990-91	2001-02
Donnell, Fred	Bos.	2	115	15	11	26	98	5	0	1	1	5	....	1972-73	1973-74
Donoghue, Don	Oak., Cal.	3	125	18	17	35	35	3	0	0	0	0	....	1969-70	1971-72
drowski, Gerry	Det., Oak., St.L.	6	309	12	19	31	111	30	0	1	1	16	....	1960-61	1971-72
Dwyer, Bill	L.A., Bos.	5	120	9	13	22	108	10	0	0	0	2	....	1983-84	1989-90
Flaherty, Gerry	Tor., Van., Atl.	8	438	99	95	194	168	7	2	2	4	6	....	1971-72	1978-79
Flaherty, Peanuts	NYA, Bro.	2	21	5	1	6	0	....	....	....	....	....	....	1940-41	1941-42
gilvie, Brian	Chi., St.L.	6	90	15	21	36	29	....	....	....	....	....	....	1972-73	1978-79
Grady, George	Mtl.W.	1	4	0	0	0	0	....	....	....	....	....	....	1917-18	1917-18
grodnick, John	Det., Que., NYR	14	928	402	425	827	260	41	18	8	26	6	....	1979-80	1992-93
anen, Janne	N.J.	4	98	21	23	44	28	3	0	2	2	0	....	1988-89	1992-93
kerlund, Todd	NYI	1	4	0	0	0	2	....	....	....	....	....	....	1987-88	1987-88
ksiuta, Roman	Edm., Van., Ana., Pit.	4	153	46	41	87	100	10	2	3	5	0	....	1993-94	1996-97
ausson, Fredrik	Wpg., Edm., Ana., Pit., Det.	16	1022	147	434	581	450	71	6	23	29	28	1	1986-87	2002-03
czyk, Ed	Chi., Tor., Wpg., NYR, L.A., Pit.	16	1031	342	452	794	874	57	19	15	34	57	1	1984-85	1999-00
iver, David	Edm., NYR, Ott., Phx., Dal.	9	233	49	49	98	84	10	0	0	0	2	....	1994-95	2005-06
iver, Harry	Bos., NYA	11	463	127	85	212	147	35	10	6	16	24	1	1926-27	1936-37
iver, Murray	Det., Bos., Tor., Min.	17	1127	274	454	728	320	35	9	16	25	10	....	1957-58	1974-75
iwa, Krzysztof	N.J., CBJ, Pit., NYR, Bos., Cgy.	9	410	17	28	45	1447	32	2	0	2	47	1	1996-97	2005-06
mstead, Bert	Chi., Mtl., Tor.	14	848	181	421	602	884	115	16	43	59	101	5	1948-49	1961-62
sen, Darryl	Cgy.	1	1	0	0	0	0	....	....	....	....	....	....	1991-92	1991-92
son, Dennis	Det.	1	4	0	0	0	0	....	....	....	....	....	....	1957-58	1957-58
son, Josh	Fla.	1	5	1	0	1	0	....	....	....	....	....	....	2003-04	2003-04
sson, Christer	St.L., Ott.	2	56	4	12	16	24	3	0	0	0	0	....	1995-96	1996-97
vestad, Jimmie	T.B.	2	111	3	14	17	40	....	....	....	....	....	....	2001-02	2002-03
'Neil, Jim	Bos., Mtl.	6	156	6	30	36	109	9	1	1	2	13	....	1933-34	1941-42
'Neil, Paul	Van., Bos.	2	6	0	0	0	0	....	....	....	....	....	....	1973-74	1975-76
'Neill, Jeff	Hfd., Car., Tor.	11	821	237	259	496	670	34	9	8	17	37	....	1995-96	2006-07
'Neill, Tom	Tor.	2	66	10	12	22	53	4	0	0	0	6	1	1943-44	1944-45
rban, Bill	Chi., Min.	3	114	8	15	23	67	3	0	0	0	0	....	1967-68	1969-70
'Ree, Willie	Bos.	2	45	4	10	14	26	....	....	....	....	....	....	1957-58	1960-61
'Regan, Tom	Pit.	3	61	5	12	17	10	....	....	....	....	....	....	1983-84	1985-86
'Reilly, Terry	Bos.	14	891	204	402	606	2095	108	25	42	67	335	....	1971-72	1984-85
rlando, Gates	Buf.	3	98	18	26	44	51	5	0	4	4	14	....	1984-85	1986-87
rlando, Jimmy	Det.	6	199	6	25	31	375	36	0	9	9	105	1	1936-37	1942-43
rleski, Dave	Mtl.	2	2	0	0	0	0	....	....	....	....	....	....	1980-81	1981-82
rr, Bobby	Bos., Chi.	12	657	270	645	915	953	74	26	66	92	107	2	1966-67	1978-79
rszagh, Vladimir	NYI, Nsh., St.L.	7	289	54	65	119	194	6	2	0	2	4	....	1997-98	2005-06
sborne, Keith	St.L., T.B.	2	16	1	3	4	16	....	....	....	....	....	....	1989-90	1992-93
sborne, Mark	Det., NYR, Tor., Wpg.	14	919	212	319	531	1152	87	12	16	28	141	....	1981-82	1994-95
sburn, Randy	Tor., Phi.	2	27	0	2	2	0	....	....	....	....	....	....	1972-73	1974-75
'Shea, Danny	Min., Chi., St.L.	5	369	64	115	179	265	39	3	7	10	61	....	1968-69	1972-73
'Shea, Kevin	Buf., St.L.	3	134	13	18	31	85	12	2	1	3	10	....	1970-71	1972-73
siecki, Mark	Cgy., Ott., Wpg., Min.	2	93	3	11	14	43	....	....	....	....	....	....	1991-92	1992-93
'Sullivan, Chris	Cgy., Van., Ana.	5	62	2	17	19	16	....	....	....	....	....	....	1996-97	2002-03
tevrel, Jaroslav	S.J.	2	16	3	4	7	2	....	....	....	....	....	....	1992-93	1993-94
tto, Joel	Cgy., Phi.	14	943	195	313	508	1934	122	27	47	74	207	1	1984-85	1997-98
uellette, Eddie	Chi.	1	43	3	2	5	11	1	0	0	0	0	....	1935-36	1935-36
uellette, Gerry	Bos.	1	34	5	4	9	0	....	....	....	....	....	....	1960-61	1960-61
wchar, Dennis	Pit., Col.	6	288	30	85	115	200	10	1	1	2	8	....	1974-75	1979-80
wen, George	Bos.	5	183	44	33	77	151	21	2	5	7	25	1	1928-29	1932-33
zolinsh, Sandis	S.J., Col., Car., Fla., Ana., NYR	15	875	167	397	564	638	137	23	67	90	131	1	1992-93	2007-08
ɔ															
achal, Clayton	Bos., Col.	3	35	2	3	5	95	....	....	....	....	....	....	1976-77	1978-79
addock, John	Wsh., Phi., Que.	5	87	8	14	22	86	5	2	0	2	0	....	1975-76	1982-83
aek, Jim	Pit., L.A., Ott.	5	217	5	29	34	155	27	1	4	5	8	2	1990-91	1994-95
aiement, Rosaire	Phi., Van.	5	190	48	52	100	343	3	3	0	3	0	....	1967-68	1971-72
aiement, Wilf	K.C., Col., Tor., Que., NYR, Buf., Pit.	14	946	356	458	814	1757	69	18	17	35	185	....	1974-75	1987-88
alangio, Pete	Mtl., Det., Chi.	5	71	13	10	23	28	7	0	0	0	0	1	1926-27	1937-38
alazzari, Aldo	Bos., NYR	1	35	8	3	11	4	....	....	....	....	....	....	1943-44	1943-44
alazzari, Doug	St.L.	4	108	18	20	38	23	2	0	0	0	0	....	1974-75	1978-79
alffy, Ziggy	NYI, L.A., Pit.	12	684	329	384	713	322	24	9	10	19	8	....	1993-94	2005-06
almer, Brad	Min., Bos.	3	168	32	38	70	58	29	9	5	14	16	....	1980-81	1982-83
almer, Rob	Chi.	3	16	0	3	3	2	....	....	....	....	....	....	1973-74	1975-76
almer, Robert	L.A., N.J.	7	320	9	101	110	115	8	1	2	3	6	....	1977-78	1983-84
anagabko, Ed	Bos.	2	29	0	3	3	38	....	....	....	....	....	....	1955-56	1956-57
andolfo, Mike	CBJ	1	3	0	0	0	0	....	....	....	....	....	....	2003-04	2003-04
ankewicz, Greg	Ott., Cgy.	2	21	0	3	3	22	....	....	....	....	....	....	1993-94	1998-99
anteleev, Grigori	Bos., NYI	4	54	8	6	14	12	....	....	....	....	....	....	1992-93	1995-96
apike, Joe	Chi.	3	20	3	3	6	4	5	0	2	2	0	....	1940-41	1944-45
apineau, Justin	St.L., NYI	3	81	11	8	19	12	1	0	0	0	0	....	2001-02	2003-04
appin, Jim	Tor., Chi., Cal., Cle.	14	767	278	295	573	667	92	33	34	67	101	2	1963-64	1976-77
aradise, Bob	Min., Atl., Pit., Wsh.	8	368	8	54	62	393	12	0	1	1	19	....	1971-72	1978-79
argeter, George	Mtl.	1	4	0	0	0	0	....	....	....	....	....	....	1946-47	1946-47
arise, J.P.	Bos., Tor., Min., NYI, Cle.	14	890	238	356	594	706	86	27	31	58	87	....	1965-66	1978-79
arizeau, Michel	St.L., Phi.	1	58	3	14	17	18	....	....	....	....	....	....	1971-72	1971-72
ark, Brad	NYR, Bos., Det.	17	1113	213	683	896	1429	161	35	90	125	217	....	1968-69	1984-85
arker, Jeff	Buf., Hfd.	5	141	16	19	35	163	5	0	0	0	26	....	1986-87	1990-91
arker, Scott	Col., S.J.	8	308	7	14	21	699	5	0	0	0	4	1	1998-99	2007-08
arkes, Ernie	Mtl.M.	1	17	0	0	0	2	....	....	....	....	....	....	1924-25	1924-25
arks, Greg	NYI	3	23	1	2	3	6	2	0	0	0	0	....	1990-91	1992-93
arsons, George	Tor.	3	78	12	13	25	20	7	3	2	5	11	....	1936-37	1938-39
arssinen, Timo	Ana.	1	17	0	3	3	2	....	....	....	....	....	....	2001-02	2001-02
asek, Dusan	Min.	1	48	4	10	14	30	2	1	0	1	0	....	1988-89	1988-89
asin, Dave	Bos., L.A.	2	76	18	19	37	50	3	0	1	1	0	....	1985-86	1988-89
aslawski, Greg	Mtl., St.L., Wpg., Buf., Que., Phi., Cgy.	11	650	187	185	372	169	60	19	13	32	25	....	1983-84	1993-94
atera, Pavel	Dal., Min.	2	32	2	7	9	8	....	....	....	....	....	....	1999-00	2000-01
aterson, Joe	Det., Phi., L.A., NYR	9	291	19	37	56	829	22	3	4	7	77	....	1980-81	1988-89
aterson, Mark	Hfd.	4	29	3	3	6	33	....	....	....	....	....	....	1982-83	1985-86
aterson, Rick	Chi.	9	430	50	43	93	136	61	7	10	17	51	....	1978-79	1986-87
atey, Doug	Wsh.	3	45	4	2	6	8	....	....	....	....	....	....	1976-77	1978-79
atey, Larry	Cal., St.L., NYR	12	717	153	163	316	631	40	8	10	18	57	....	1973-74	1984-85
atrick, Craig	Cal., St.L., K.C., Wsh.	8	401	72	91	163	61	2	0	1	1	0	....	1971-72	1978-79
atrick, Glenn	St.L., Cal., Cle.	4	38	2	3	5	72	....	....	....	....	....	....	1973-74	1976-77
atrick, James	NYR, Hfd., Cgy., Buf.	21	1280	149	490	639	759	117	6	32	38	86	....	1983-84	2003-04
atrick, Lester	NYR	1	1	0	0	0	2	....	....	....	....	....	....	1926-27	1926-27
atrick, Lynn	NYR	10	455	145	190	335	240	44	10	6	16	22	1	1934-35	1945-46

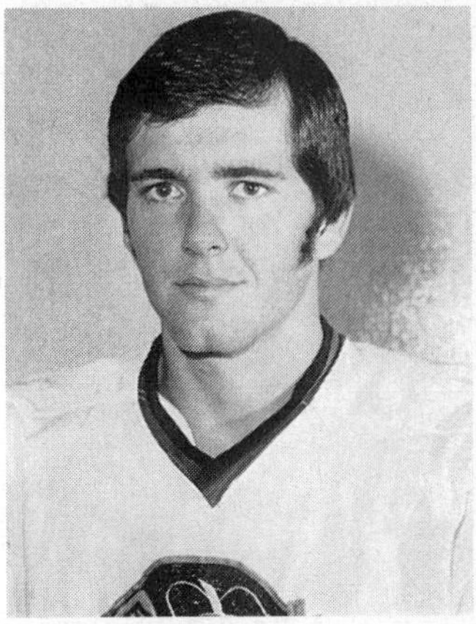

Brian Ogilvie

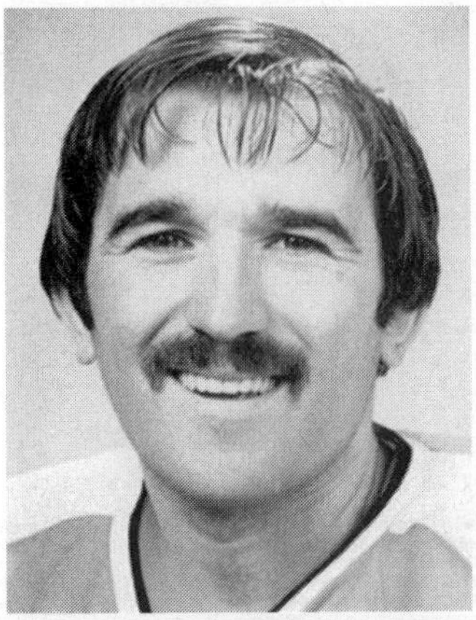

Dennis Patterson

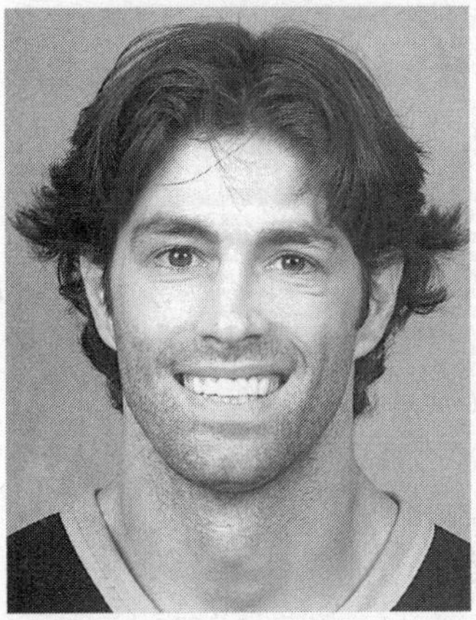

Michael Peca

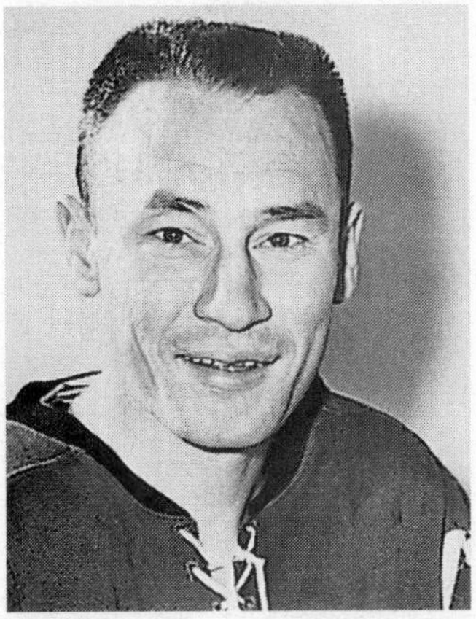

Pierre Pllote

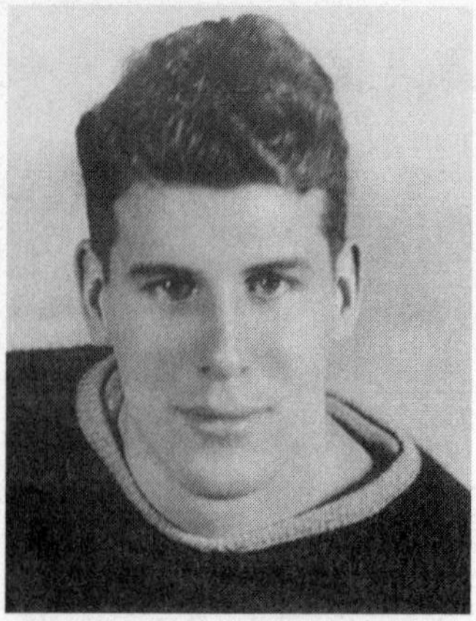

Jack Portland

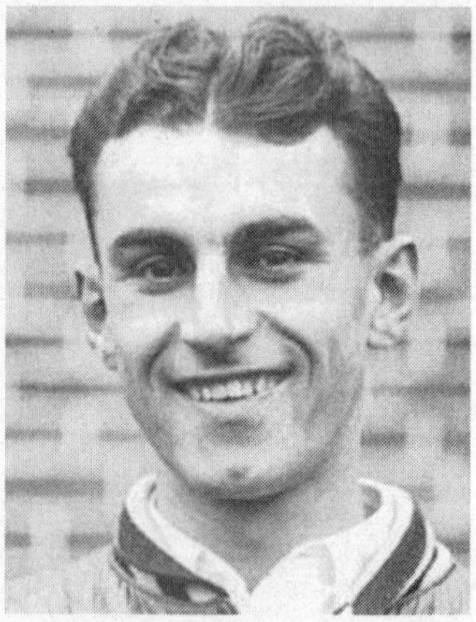

Joe Primeau

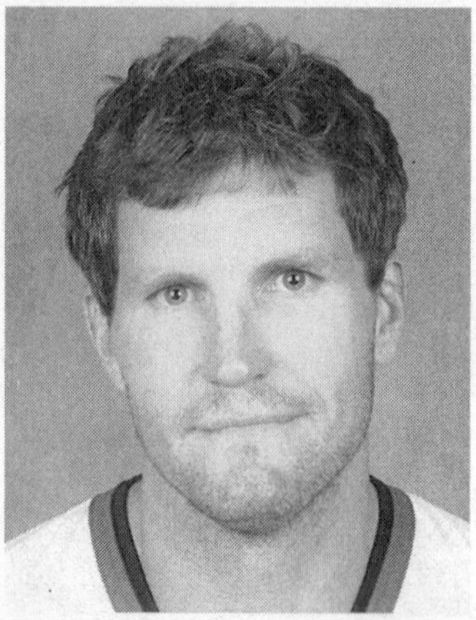

Bob Probert

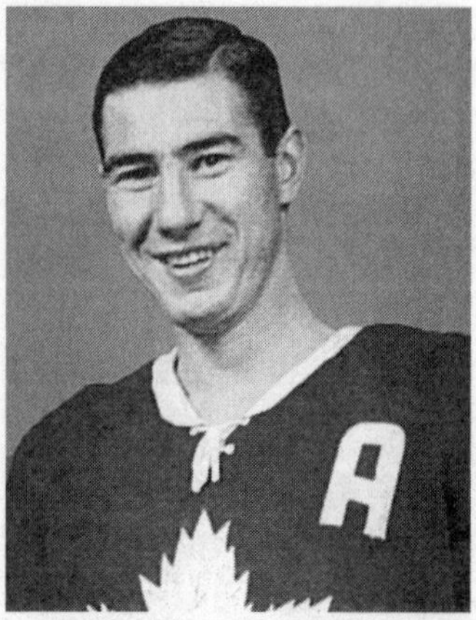

Bob Pulford

			Regular Schedule					Playoffs					NHL	First	Last
Name	NHL Teams	NHL Seasons	GP	G	A	TP	PIM	GP	G	A	TP	PIM	Cup Wins	NHL Season	NHL Seaso
• Patrick, Muzz	NYR	5	166	5	26	31	133	25	4	0	4	34	1	1937-38	1945-
Patrick, Steve	Buf., NYR, Que.	6	250	40	68	108	242	12	0	1	1	12	....	1980-81	1985-
Patterson, Colin	Cgy., Buf.	10	504	96	109	205	239	85	12	17	29	57	1	1983-84	1992-
Patterson, Dennis	K.C., Phi.	3	138	6	22	28	67	....	....	....	....	....	....	1974-75	1979-
Patterson, Ed	Pit.	3	68	3	3	6	56	....	....	....	....	....	....	1993-94	1996-
• Patterson, George	Tor., Mtl., NYA, Bos., Det., St.L.	9	284	51	27	78	218	3	0	0	0	2	....	1926-27	1934-
• Paul, Butch	Det.	1	3	0	0	0	0	....	....	....	....	....	....	1964-65	1964-
‡ Paul, Jeff	Col.	1	2	0	0	0	7	....	....	....	....	....	....	2002-03	2002-
• Paulhus, Rollie	Mtl.	1	33	0	0	0	0	....	....	....	....	....	....	1925-26	1925-
Pavelich, Mark	NYR, Min., S.J.	7	355	137	192	329	340	23	7	17	24	14	....	1981-82	1991-
Pavelich, Marty	Det.	10	634	93	159	252	454	91	13	15	28	74	4	1947-48	1956-
Pavese, Jim	St.L., NYR, Det., Hfd.	8	328	13	44	57	689	36	0	6	6	81	....	1981-82	1988-
• Payer, Evariste	Mtl.	1	1	0	0	0	0	....	....	....	....	....	....	1917-18	1917-
‡ Payer, Serge	Fla., Ott.	4	124	7	6	13	49	....	....	....	....	....	....	2000-01	2006-
Payne, Davis	Bos.	2	22	0	1	1	14	....	....	....	....	....	....	1995-96	1996-
Payne, Steve	Min.	10	613	228	238	466	435	71	35	35	70	60	....	1978-79	1987-
Paynter, Kent	Chi., Wsh., Wpg., Ott.	7	37	1	3	4	69	4	0	0	0	10	....	1987-88	1993-
Peake, Pat	Wsh.	5	134	28	41	69	105	13	2	2	4	20	....	1993-94	1997-
• Pearson, Mel	NYR, Pit.	5	38	2	6	8	25	....	....	....	....	....	....	1959-60	1967-
Pearson, Rob	Tor., Wsh., St.L.	6	269	56	54	110	645	33	4	2	6	94	....	1991-92	1996-
Pearson, Scott	Tor., Que., Edm., Buf., NYI	10	292	56	42	98	615	10	2	0	2	14	....	1988-89	1999-
Peat, Stephen	Wsh.	4	130	8	2	10	234	....	....	....	....	....	....	2001-02	2005-
Peca, Michael	Van., Buf., NYI, Edm., Tor., CBJ	14	864	176	289	465	798	97	15	19	34	80	....	1993-94	2008-
Pedersen, Allen	Bos., Min., Hfd.	8	428	5	36	41	487	64	0	0	0	91	....	1986-87	1993-
Pederson, Barry	Bos., Van., Pit., Hfd.	12	701	238	416	654	472	34	22	30	52	25	1	1980-81	1991-
‡ Pederson, Denis	N.J., Van., Phx., Nsh.	8	435	57	71	128	398	27	1	5	6	8	....	1995-96	2002-
Pederson, Mark	Mtl., Phi., S.J., Det.	5	169	35	50	85	77	2	0	0	0	0	....	1989-90	1993-
Pederson, Tom	S.J., Tor.	5	240	20	49	69	142	24	1	11	12	10	....	1992-93	1996-
• Peer, Bert	Det.	1	1	0	0	0	0	....	....	....	....	....	....	1939-40	1939-
Peirson, Johnny	Bos.	11	545	153	173	326	315	49	10	16	26	26	....	1946-47	1957-
Pelensky, Perry	Chi.	1	4	0	0	0	5	....	....	....	....	....	....	1983-84	1983-
Pellerin, Scott	N.J., St.L., Min., Car., Bos., Dal., Phx.	11	536	72	126	198	320	37	1	2	3	26	....	1992-93	2003-
Pelletier, Roger	Phi.	1	1	0	0	0	0	....	....	....	....	....	....	1967-68	1967-
Peloffy, Andre	Wsh.	1	9	0	0	0	0	....	....	....	....	....	....	1974-75	1974-
Peluso, Mike	Chi., Ott., N.J., St.L., Cgy.	9	458	38	52	90	1951	62	3	4	7	107	1	1989-90	1997-
Peluso, Mike	Chi., Phi.	2	38	4	2	6	19	....	....	....	....	....	....	2001-02	2003-
Pelyk, Mike	Tor.	9	441	26	88	114	566	40	0	3	3	41	....	1967-68	1977-
Penney, Chad	Ott.	1	3	0	0	0	2	....	....	....	....	....	....	1993-94	1993-
Pennington, Cliff	Mtl., Bos.	3	101	17	42	59	6	....	....	....	....	....	....	1960-61	1962-
Peplinski, Jim	Cgy.	11	711	161	263	424	1467	99	15	31	46	382	1	1980-81	1994-
Perlini, Fred	Tor.	2	8	2	3	5	0	....	....	....	....	....	....	1981-82	1983-
Perreault, Fern	NYR	2	3	0	0	0	0	....	....	....	....	....	....	1947-48	1949-
Perreault, Gilbert	Buf.	17	1191	512	814	1326	500	90	33	70	103	44	....	1970-71	1986-
Perreault, Yanic	Tor., L.A., Mtl., Nsh., Phx., Chi.	14	859	247	269	516	402	54	11	19	30	18	....	1993-94	2007-
‡ Perrott, Nathan	Nsh., Tor., Dal.	4	89	4	5	9	251	....	....	....	....	....	....	2001-02	2005-
Perry, Brian	Oak., Buf.	3	96	16	29	45	24	8	1	1	2	4	....	1968-69	1970-
Persson, Ricard	N.J., St.L., Ott.	7	229	10	44	54	262	26	1	3	4	59	....	1995-96	2001-
Persson, Stefan	NYI	9	622	52	317	369	574	102	7	50	57	69	4	1977-78	1985-
Pesut, George	Cal.	2	92	3	22	25	130	....	....	....	....	....	....	1974-75	1975-
• Peters, Frank	NYR	1	43	0	0	0	59	4	0	0	0	2	....	1930-31	1930-
Peters, Garry	Mtl., NYR, Phi., Bos.	8	311	34	34	68	261	9	2	2	4	31	1	1964-65	1971-
• Peters, Jimmy	Mtl., Bos., Det., Chi.	9	574	125	150	275	186	60	5	9	14	22	3	1945-46	1953-
Peters, Jimmy	Det., L.A.	9	309	37	36	73	48	11	0	2	2	2	....	1964-65	1974-
Peters, Steve	Col.	1	2	0	1	1	0	....	....	....	....	....	....	1979-80	1979-
Peterson, Brent	Det., Buf., Van., Hfd.	11	620	72	141	213	484	31	4	4	8	65	....	1978-79	1988-
Peterson, Brent	T.B.	3	56	9	1	10	6	....	....	....	....	....	....	1996-97	1998-
Petit, Michel	Van., NYR, Que., Tor., Cgy., L.A., T.B., Edm., Phi., Phx.	16	827	90	238	328	1839	19	0	2	2	61	....	1982-83	1997-
Petrenko, Sergei	Buf.	1	14	0	4	4	0	....	....	....	....	....	....	1993-94	1993-
‡ Petrov, Oleg	Mtl., Nsh.	8	382	72	115	187	101	20	1	6	7	2	....	1992-93	2002-
‡ Petrovicky, Robert	Hfd., Dal., St.L., T.B., NYI	8	208	27	38	65	118	2	0	0	0	0	....	1992-93	2000-
‡ Petrovicky, Ronald	Cgy., NYR, Atl., Pit.	6	342	41	51	92	429	3	0	0	0	2	....	2000-01	2006-
Pettersson, Jorgen	St.L., Hfd., Wsh.	6	435	174	192	366	117	44	15	12	27	4	....	1980-81	1985-
‡ Pettinen, Tomi	NYI	3	24	0	0	0	18	....	....	....	....	....	....	2002-03	2005-
• Pettinger, Eric	Bos., Tor., Ott.	3	98	7	12	19	83	4	1	0	1	8	....	1928-29	1930-
• Pettinger, Gord	NYR, Det., Bos.	8	292	42	74	116	77	47	4	5	9	11	4	1932-33	1939-
Phair, Lyle	L.A.	3	48	6	7	13	12	1	0	0	0	0	....	1985-86	1987-
Phillipoff, Harold	Atl., Chi.	3	141	26	57	83	267	6	0	2	2	9	....	1977-78	1979-
• Phillips, Bill	Mtl.M.	1	27	1	1	2	6	4	0	0	0	2	....	1929-30	1929-
• Phillips, Charlie	Mtl.	1	17	0	0	0	6	....	....	....	....	....	....	1942-43	1942-
• Phillips, Merlyn	Mtl.M., NYA	8	302	52	31	83	232	24	5	1	6	19	1	1925-26	1932-
Picard, Michel	Hfd., S.J., Ott., St.L., Edm., Phi.	9	166	28	42	70	103	5	0	0	0	2	....	1990-91	2000-
Picard, Noel	Mtl., St.L., Atl.	7	335	12	63	75	616	50	2	11	13	167	1	1964-65	1972-
Picard, Robert	Wsh., Tor., Mtl., Wpg., Que., Det.	13	899	104	319	423	1025	36	5	15	20	39	....	1977-78	1989-
Picard, Roger	St.L.	1	15	2	2	4	21	....	....	....	....	....	....	1967-68	1967-
Pichette, Dave	Que., St.L., N.J., NYR	7	322	41	140	181	348	28	3	7	10	54	....	1980-81	1987-
Picketts, Hal	NYA	1	48	3	1	4	32	....	....	....	....	....	....	1933-34	1933-
Pidhirny, Harry	Bos.	1	2	0	0	0	0	....	....	....	....	....	....	1957-58	1957-
Pierce, Randy	Col., N.J., Hfd.	8	277	62	76	138	223	2	0	0	0	0	....	1977-78	1984-
‡ Pihlman, Tuomas	N.J.	3	15	1	1	2	12	....	....	....	....	....	....	2003-04	2006-
• Pike, Alf	NYR	6	234	42	77	119	145	21	4	2	6	12	1	1939-40	1946-
‡ Pilar, Karel	Tor.	3	90	6	24	30	42	12	1	4	5	12	....	2001-02	2003-
Pilon, Rich	NYI, NYR, St.L.	14	631	8	69	77	1745	15	0	0	0	50	....	1988-89	2001-
Pilote, Pierre	Chi., Tor.	14	890	80	418	498	1251	86	8	53	61	102	1	1955-56	1968-
Pinder, Gerry	Chi., Cal.	3	223	55	69	124	135	17	0	4	4	6	....	1969-70	1971-
‡ Pirjeta, Lasse	CBJ, Pit.	3	146	23	27	50	50	....	....	....	....	....	....	2002-03	2005-
‡ Pirnes, Esa	L.A.	1	57	3	8	11	12	....	....	....	....	....	....	2003-04	2003-
‡ Piros, Kamil	Atl., Fla.	3	28	4	4	8	10	....	....	....	....	....	....	2001-02	2003-
Pirus, Alex	Min., Det.	4	159	30	28	58	94	2	0	1	1	2	....	1976-77	1979-
‡ Pisa, Ales	Edm., NYR	2	53	1	3	4	26	....	....	....	....	....	....	2001-02	2002-
Pitlick, Lance	Ott., Fla.	8	393	16	33	49	298	24	0	2	2	21	....	1994-95	2001-
• Pitre, Didier	Mtl.	6	127	64	33	97	87	9	2	4	6	19	....	1917-18	1922-
Pittis, Domenic	Pit., Buf., Edm., Nsh.	7	86	5	11	16	71	3	0	0	0	2	....	1996-97	2003-
‡ Pivko, Libor	Nsh.	1	1	0	0	0	0	....	....	....	....	....	....	2003-04	2003-
Pivonka, Michal	Wsh.	13	825	181	418	599	478	95	19	36	55	86	....	1986-87	1998-
• Plager, Barclay	St.L.	10	614	44	187	231	1115	68	3	20	23	182	....	1967-68	1976-
Plager, Bill	Min., St.L., Atl.	9	263	4	34	38	294	31	0	2	2	26	....	1967-68	1975-
Plager, Bob	NYR, St.L.	14	644	20	126	146	802	74	2	17	19	195	....	1964-65	1977-
Plamondon, Gerry	Mtl.	5	74	7	13	20	10	11	5	2	7	2	1	1945-46	1950-
Plante, Cam	Tor.	1	2	0	0	0	0	....	....	....	....	....	....	1984-85	1984-
Plante, Dan	NYI	4	159	9	14	23	135	1	1	0	1	2	....	1993-94	1997-
Plante, Derek	Buf., Dal., Chi., Phi.	8	450	96	152	248	138	41	6	10	16	18	1	1993-94	2000-
Plante, Pierre	Phi., St.L., Chi., NYR, Que.	9	599	125	172	297	599	33	2	6	8	51	....	1971-72	1979-
Plantery, Mark	Wpg.	1	25	1	5	6	14	....	....	....	....	....	....	1980-81	1980-
Plavsic, Adrien	St.L., Van., T.B., Ana.	8	214	16	56	72	161	13	1	7	8	4	....	1989-90	1996-
• Plaxton, Hugh	Mtl.M.	1	15	1	2	3	4	....	....	....	....	....	....	1932-33	1932-
Playfair, Jim	Edm., Chi.	3	21	2	4	6	51	....	....	....	....	....	....	1983-84	1988-
Playfair, Larry	Buf., L.A.	12	688	26	94	120	1812	43	0	6	6	111	....	1978-79	1989-
Pleau, Larry	Mtl.	3	94	9	15	24	27	4	0	0	0	0	....	1969-70	1971-
‡ Pletka, Vaclav	Phi.	1	1	0	0	0	0	....	....	....	....	....	....	2001-02	2001-
• Pletsch, Charles	Ham.	1	1	0	0	0	0	....	....	....	....	....	....	1920-21	1920-
Plett, Willi	Atl., Cgy., Min., Bos.	13	834	222	215	437	2572	83	24	22	46	466	....	1975-76	1987-
Plumb, Rob	Det.	2	14	3	2	5	2	....	....	....	....	....	....	1977-78	1978-
Plumb, Ron	Hfd.	1	26	3	4	7	14	....	....	....	....	....	....	1979-80	1979-
Poapst, Steve	Wsh., Chi., Pit., St.L.	7	307	8	28	36	173	11	0	0	0	0	....	1995-96	2005-
Pocza, Harvie	Wsh.	2	3	0	0	0	2	....	....	....	....	....	....	1979-80	1981-
• Poddubny, Walt	Edm., Tor., NYR, Que., N.J.	11	468	184	238	422	454	19	7	2	9	12	....	1981-82	1991-
Podein, Shjon	Edm., Phi., Col., St.L.	11	699	100	106	206	439	127	14	13	27	132	1	1992-93	2002-
‡ Podkonicky, Andrej	Fla., Wsh.	2	8	1	0	1	2	....	....	....	....	....	....	2000-01	2003-
Podloski, Ray	Bos.	1	8	0	1	1	17	....	....	....	....	....	....	1988-89	1988-
Podollan, Jason	Fla., Tor., L.A., NYI	4	41	1	5	6	19	....	....	....	....	....	....	1996-97	2001-
Podolsky, Nels	Det.	1	1	0	0	0	0	7	0	0	0	4	....	1948-49	1948-
Poeschek, Rudy	NYR, Wpg., T.B., St.L.	12	364	6	25	31	817	5	0	0	0	18	....	1987-88	1999-
• Poeta, Tony	Chi.	1	1	0	0	0	0	....	....	....	....	....	....	1951-52	1951-
• Poile, Bud	Tor., Chi., Det., NYR, Bos.	7	311	107	122	229	91	23	4	5	9	8	1	1942-43	1949-
Poile, Don	Det.	2	66	7	9	16	12	4	0	0	0	0	....	1954-55	1957-

ame	NHL Teams	NHL Seasons	Regular Schedule GP	G	A	TP	PIM	Playoffs GP	G	A	TP	PIM	NHL Cup Wins	First NHL Season	Last NHL Season
irier, Gordie	Mtl.	1	10	0	0	0	0	....	....	....	....	....	....	1939-40	1939-40
lanic, Tom	Min.	2	19	0	2	2	53	5	1	1	2	4	....	1969-70	1970-71
lich, John	NYR	2	3	0	1	1	0	....	....	....	....	....	....	1939-40	1940-41
lich, Mike	Mtl., Min.	5	226	24	29	53	57	23	2	1	3	2	1	1976-77	1980-81
lis, Greg	Pit., St.L., NYR, Wsh.	10	615	174	169	343	391	7	0	2	2	6	....	1970-71	1979-80
liziani, Dan	Bos.	1	1	0	0	0	0	3	0	0	0	0	....	1958-59	1958-59
llock, Jame	St.L.	1	9	0	0	0	6	....	....	....	....	....	....	2003-04	2003-04
lonich, Dennis	Det.	8	390	59	82	141	1242	7	1	0	1	19	....	1974-75	1982-83
oley, Paul	Wpg.	2	15	0	3	3	0	....	....	....	....	....	....	1984-85	1985-86
pein, Larry	NYR, Oak.	8	449	80	141	221	162	16	1	4	5	6	....	1954-55	1967-68
piel, Poul	Bos., L.A., Det., Van., Edm.	7	224	13	41	54	210	4	1	0	1	4	....	1965-66	1979-80
povic, Peter	Mtl., NYR, Pit., Bos.	8	485	10	63	73	291	35	1	4	5	18	....	1993-94	2000-01
rtland, Jack	Mtl., Bos., Chi.	10	381	15	56	71	323	33	1	3	4	25	1	1933-34	1942-43
rvari, Jukka	Col., N.J.	2	39	3	9	12	4	....	....	....	....	....	....	1981-82	1982-83
sa, Victor	Chi.	1	2	0	0	0	2	....	....	....	....	....	....	1985-86	1985-86
savad, Mike	St.L.	2	8	0	0	0	0	....	....	....	....	....	....	1985-86	1986-87
smyk, Marek	T.B.	2	19	1	2	3	20	....	....	....	....	....	....	1999-00	2000-01
tomski, Barry	L.A., S.J.	3	68	6	5	11	227	....	....	....	....	....	....	1995-96	1997-98
tvin, Denis	NYI	15	1060	310	742	1052	1356	185	56	108	164	253	4	1973-74	1987-88
tvin, Jean	L.A., Phi., NYI, Cle., Min.	11	613	63	224	287	478	39	2	9	11	17	2	1970-71	1980-81
tvin, Marc	Det., L.A., Hfd., Bos.	6	121	3	5	8	456	13	0	1	1	50	....	1990-91	1995-96
udrier, Daniel	Que.	3	25	1	5	6	10	....	....	....	....	....	....	1985-86	1987-88
ulin, Daniel	Min.	1	3	1	1	2	2	....	....	....	....	....	....	1981-82	1981-82
ulin, Dave	Phi., Bos., Wsh.	13	724	205	325	530	482	129	31	42	73	132	....	1982-83	1994-95
ulin, Patrick	Hfd., Chi., T.B., Mtl.	11	634	101	134	235	299	32	6	2	8	8	....	1991-92	2001-02
uzar, Jaroslav	Edm.	4	186	34	48	82	135	29	6	4	10	16	3	1982-83	1986-87
well, Ray	Chi.	1	31	7	15	22	2	....	....	....	....	....	....	1950-51	1950-51
wis, Geoff	Chi.	1	2	0	0	0	0	....	....	....	....	....	....	1967-68	1967-68
wis, Lynn	Chi., K.C.	2	130	19	33	52	25	1	0	0	0	0	....	1973-74	1974-75
ajsler, Petr	L.A., Bos.	4	46	3	10	13	51	4	0	0	0	0	....	1987-88	1991-92
att, Babe	NYR, Tor., Bos.	12	517	83	209	292	463	63	12	17	29	90	2	1935-36	1946-47
att, Jack	Bos.	2	37	2	0	2	42	4	0	0	0	0	....	1930-31	1931-32
att, Kelly	Pit.	1	22	0	6	6	15	....	....	....	....	....	....	1974-75	1974-75
att, Nolan	Hfd., Car., Col., T.B., Buf.	11	592	9	56	65	537	38	0	1	1	22	1	1996-97	2007-08
att, Tracy	Oak., Pit., Buf., Van., Col., Tor.	10	580	17	97	114	1026	25	0	1	1	62	....	1967-68	1976-77
entice, Dean	NYR, Bos., Det., Pit., Min.	22	1378	391	469	860	484	54	13	17	30	38	....	1952-53	1973-74
entice, Eric	Tor.	1	5	0	0	0	4	....	....	....	....	....	....	1943-44	1943-44
esley, Wayne	Chi., S.J., Buf., NYR, Tor.	12	684	155	147	302	953	83	26	17	43	142	....	1984-85	1995-96
eston, Rich	Chi., N.J.	8	580	127	164	291	348	47	4	18	22	56	....	1979-80	1986-87
eston, Yves	Phi.	2	28	7	3	10	4	....	....	....	....	....	....	1978-79	1980-81
iakin, Sergei	Cgy.	3	46	3	8	11	2	3	0	0	0	0	....	1988-89	1990-91
ice, Jack	Chi.	3	57	4	6	10	24	4	0	0	0	0	....	1951-52	1953-54
ice, Noel	Tor., NYR, Det., Mtl., Pit., L.A., Atl.	14	499	14	114	128	333	12	0	1	1	8	1	1957-58	1975-76
ice, Pat	NYI, Edm., Pit., Que., NYR, Min.	13	726	43	218	261	1456	74	2	10	12	195	....	1975-76	1987-88
ice, Tom	Cal., Cle., Pit.	5	29	0	2	2	12	....	....	....	....	....	....	1974-75	1978-79
iestlay, Ken	Buf., Pit.	6	168	27	34	61	63	14	0	0	0	21	1	1986-87	1991-92
imeau, Joe	Tor.	9	310	66	177	243	105	38	5	18	23	12	1	1927-28	1935-36
imeau, Keith	Det., Hfd., Car., Phi.	15	909	266	353	619	1541	128	18	39	57	213	....	1990-91	2005-06
imeau, Kevin	Van.	1	2	0	0	0	4	....	....	....	....	....	....	1980-81	1980-81
ingle, Ellie	NYA	1	6	0	0	0	0	....	....	....	....	....	....	1930-31	1930-31
intz, David	Phi.	2	13	0	0	0	4	....	....	....	....	....	....	2005-06	2006-07
obert, Bob	Det., Chi.	16	935	163	221	384	3300	81	16	32	48	274	....	1985-86	2001-02
ochazka, Martin	Tor., Atl.	2	32	2	5	7	8	....	....	....	....	....	....	1997-98	1999-00
odger, Goldie	Tor., Ham.	6	111	63	29	92	39	....	....	....	....	....	....	1919-20	1924-25
okhorov, Vitali	St.L.	3	83	19	11	30	35	4	0	0	0	0	....	1992-93	1994-95
okopec, Mike	Chi.	2	15	0	0	0	11	....	....	....	....	....	....	1995-96	1996-97
onger, Sean	Ana., Pit., NYR, L.A., Bos., CBJ, Van.	8	260	23	36	59	159	14	0	2	2	8	....	1995-96	2003-04
onovost, Andre	Mtl., Bos., Det., Min.	10	556	94	104	198	408	70	11	11	22	58	4	1956-57	1967-68
onovost, Jean	Pit., Atl., Wsh.	14	998	391	383	774	413	35	11	9	20	14	....	1968-69	1981-82
onovost, Marcel	Det., Tor.	21	1206	88	257	345	851	134	8	23	31	104	5	1949-50	1969-70
opp, Brian	Phi., Bos., Min., Hfd.	15	1016	425	579	1004	830	160	64	84	148	151	....	1979-80	1993-94
oulx, Christian	Mtl.	1	7	1	2	3	20	....	....	....	....	....	....	1993-94	1993-94
ovost, Claude	Mtl.	15	1005	254	335	589	469	126	25	38	63	86	9	1955-56	1969-70
pic, Joel	Bos., Col.	3	18	0	3	3	4	....	....	....	....	....	....	1997-98	2000-01
yor, Chris	Min., NYI	6	82	1	4	5	122	....	....	....	....	....	....	1984-85	1989-90
ystai, Metro	Chi., Det.	11	674	151	179	330	231	43	12	14	26	8	2	1947-48	1957-58
udas, Al	Tor.	1	4	0	0	0	0	....	....	....	....	....	....	1926-27	1926-27
ulford, Bob	Tor., L.A.	16	1079	281	362	643	792	89	25	26	51	126	4	1956-57	1971-72
ulkkinen, Dave	NYI	1	2	0	0	0	0	....	....	....	....	....	....	1972-73	1972-73
urinton, Dale	NYR	5	181	4	16	20	578	....	....	....	....	....	....	1999-00	2003-04
urpur, Fido	St.L., Chi., Det.	5	144	25	35	60	46	16	1	2	3	4	....	1934-35	1944-45
urves, John	Wsh.	1	7	1	0	1	0	....	....	....	....	....	....	1990-91	1990-91
ushor, Jamie	Det., Ana., Dal., CBJ, Pit., NYR	10	521	14	46	60	648	14	0	1	1	16	1	1995-96	2005-06
usie, Jean	Mtl., NYR, Bos.	5	61	1	4	5	28	7	0	0	0	0	1	1930-31	1935-36
yatt, Nelson	Det., Wsh., Col.	7	296	71	63	134	69	....	....	....	....	....	....	1973-74	1979-80

Q

ame	NHL Teams	NHL Seasons	Regular Schedule GP	G	A	TP	PIM	Playoffs GP	G	A	TP	PIM	NHL Cup Wins	First NHL Season	Last NHL Season
uackenbush, Bill	Det., Bos.	14	774	62	222	284	95	80	2	19	21	8	....	1942-43	1955-56
uackenbush, Max	Bos., Chi.	2	61	4	7	11	30	6	0	0	0	4	....	1950-51	1951-52
uenneville, Joel	Tor., Col., N.J., Hfd., Wsh.	13	803	54	136	190	705	32	0	8	8	22	....	1978-79	1990-91
uenneville, Leo	NYR	1	25	0	3	3	10	3	0	0	0	0	....	1929-30	1929-30
uilty, John	Mtl., Bos.	4	125	36	34	70	81	13	3	5	8	9	....	1940-41	1947-48
uinn, Dan	Cgy., Pit., Van., St.L., Phi., Min., Ott., L.A.	14	805	266	419	685	533	65	22	26	48	62	....	1983-84	1996-97
uinn, Pat	Tor., Van., Atl.	9	606	18	113	131	950	11	0	1	1	21	....	1968-69	1976-77
uinney, Ken	Que.	3	59	7	13	20	23	....	....	....	....	....	....	1986-87	1990-91
uint, Deron	Wpg., Phx., N.J., CBJ, Chi., NYI	10	463	46	97	143	166	7	0	2	2	0	....	1995-96	2006-07
uintal, Stephane	Bos., St.L., Wpg., Mtl., NYR, Chi.	16	1037	63	180	243	1320	52	2	10	12	51	....	1988-89	2003-04
uintin, Jean-Francois	S.J.	2	22	5	5	10	4	....	....	....	....	....	....	1991-92	1992-93

R

ame	NHL Teams	NHL Seasons	Regular Schedule GP	G	A	TP	PIM	Playoffs GP	G	A	TP	PIM	NHL Cup Wins	First NHL Season	Last NHL Season
achunek, Karel	Ott., NYR, N.J.	7	371	22	118	140	227	26	1	7	8	16	....	1999-00	2007-08
acine, Yves	Det., Phi., Mtl., S.J., Cgy., T.B.	9	508	37	194	231	439	25	5	4	9	37	....	1989-90	1997-98
adley, Yip	NYA, Mtl.M.	2	18	0	1	1	13	....	....	....	....	....	....	1930-31	1936-37
adulov, Igor	Chi.	2	43	9	7	16	22	....	....	....	....	....	....	2002-03	2003-04
aglan, Herb	St.L., Que., T.B., Ott.	9	343	33	56	89	775	32	3	6	9	50	....	1985-86	1993-94
aglan, Rags	Det., Chi.	3	100	4	9	13	52	3	0	0	0	0	....	1950-51	1952-53
agnarsson, Marcus	S.J., Phi.	9	632	37	140	177	482	68	2	13	15	60	....	1995-96	2003-04
aleigh, Don	NYR	10	535	101	219	320	96	18	6	5	11	6	....	1943-44	1955-56
alph, Brad	Phx.	1	1	0	0	0	0	....	....	....	....	....	....	2000-01	2000-01
amage, Rob	Col., St.L., Cgy., Tor., Min., T.B., Mtl., Phi.	15	1044	139	425	564	2226	84	8	42	50	218	2	1979-80	1993-94
amholt, Tim	Cgy.	1	1	0	0	0	0	....	....	....	....	....	....	2007-08	2007-08
amsay, Beattie	Tor.	1	43	0	2	2	10	....	....	....	....	....	....	1927-28	1927-28
amsay, Craig	Buf.	14	1070	252	420	672	201	89	17	31	48	27	....	1971-72	1984-85
amsay, Les	Chi.	1	11	2	2	4	2	....	....	....	....	....	....	1944-45	1944-45
amsey, Mike	Buf., Pit., Det.	18	1070	79	266	345	1012	115	8	29	37	176	....	1979-80	1996-97
amsey, Wayne	Buf.	1	2	0	0	0	0	....	....	....	....	....	....	1977-78	1977-78
andall, Ken	Tor., Ham., NYA	10	218	68	50	118	533	6	2	1	3	27	2	1917-18	1926-27
anheim, Paul	Cgy., Hfd., Car., Phi., Phx.	15	1013	161	199	360	288	36	3	8	11	6	....	1988-89	2002-03
anieri, George	Bos.	1	2	0	0	0	0	....	....	....	....	....	....	1956-57	1956-57
asmussen, Erik	Buf., L.A., N.J.	9	545	52	76	128	305	52	2	7	9	46	....	1997-98	2006-07
atchuk, Peter	Fla.	2	32	1	1	2	10	....	....	....	....	....	....	1998-99	2000-01
atelle, Jean	NYR, Bos.	21	1281	491	776	1267	276	123	32	66	98	24	....	1960-61	1980-81
athje, Mike	S.J., Phi.	13	768	30	150	180	491	77	9	14	23	51	....	1993-94	2006-07
athwell, Jake	Bos.	1	1	0	0	0	0	....	....	....	....	....	....	1974-75	1974-75
atushny, Dan	Van.	1	1	0	1	1	2	....	....	....	....	....	....	1992-93	1992-93
ausse, Errol	Wsh.	3	31	7	3	10	0	....	....	....	....	....	....	1979-80	1981-82
Rautakallio, Pekka	Atl., Cgy.	3	235	33	121	154	122	23	2	5	7	8	....	1979-80	1981-82
Ravlich, Matt	Bos., Chi., Det., L.A.	10	410	12	78	90	364	24	1	5	6	16	....	1962-63	1972-73
Ray, Rob	Buf., Ott.	15	900	41	50	91	3207	55	3	2	5	169	....	1989-90	2003-04
Raymond, Armand	Mtl.	2	22	0	2	2	10	....	....	....	....	....	....	1937-38	1939-40
Raymond, Paul	Mtl.	4	76	2	3	5	6	5	0	0	0	2	....	1932-33	1938-39
Read, Mel	NYR	1	1	0	0	0	0	....	....	....	....	....	....	1946-47	1946-47

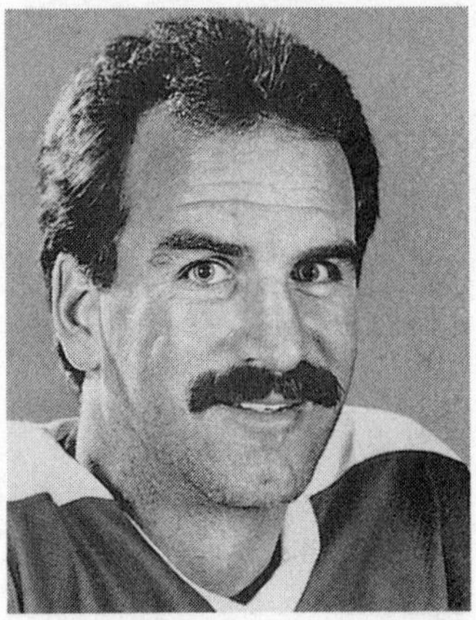
Joel Quenneville

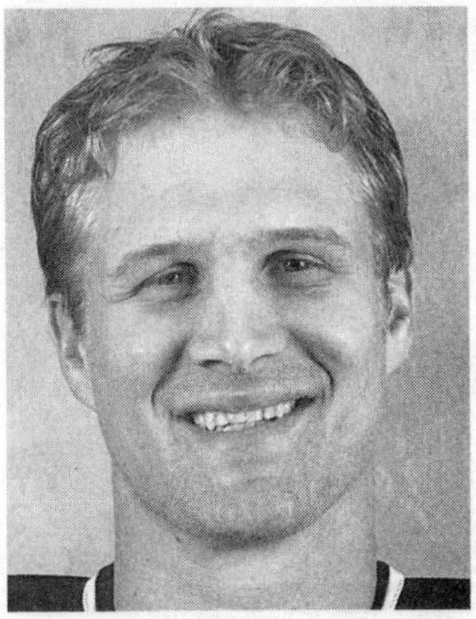
Erik Rasmussen

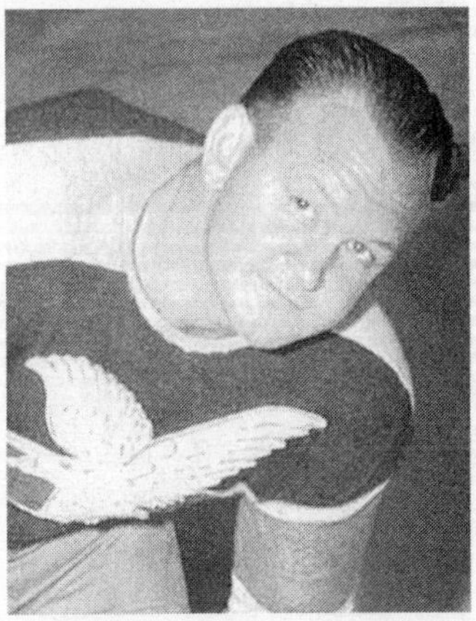
Gord Reid

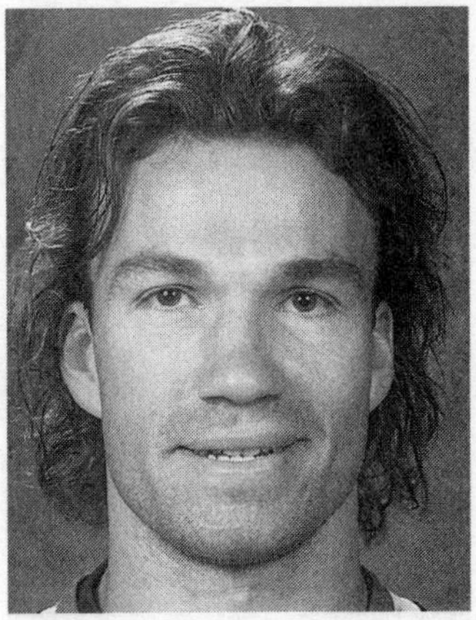
Luke Richardson

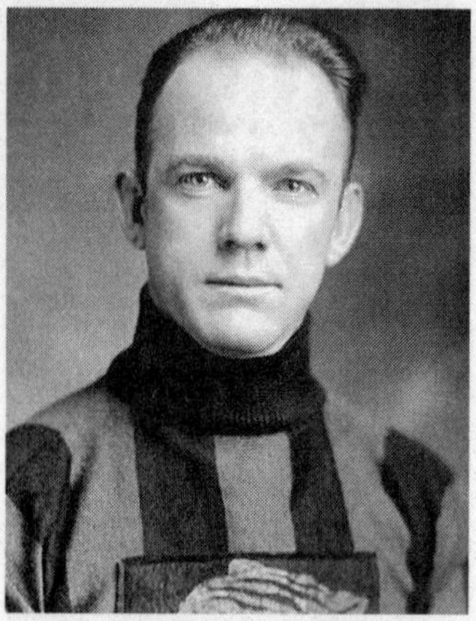

Mickey Roach

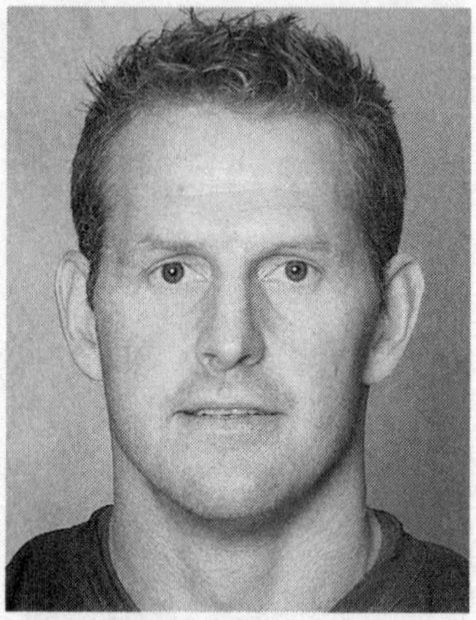

Gary Roberts

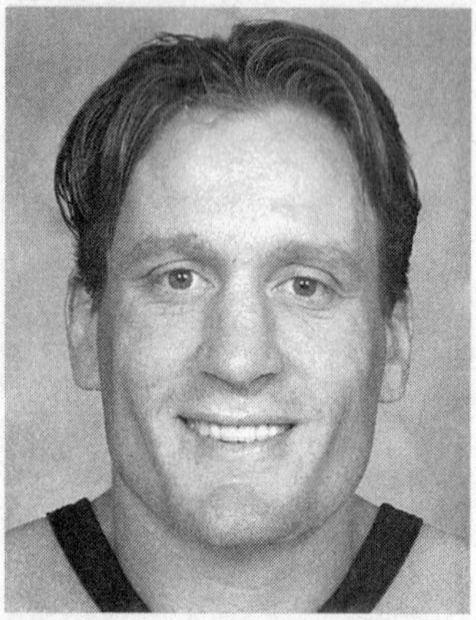

Jeremy Roenick

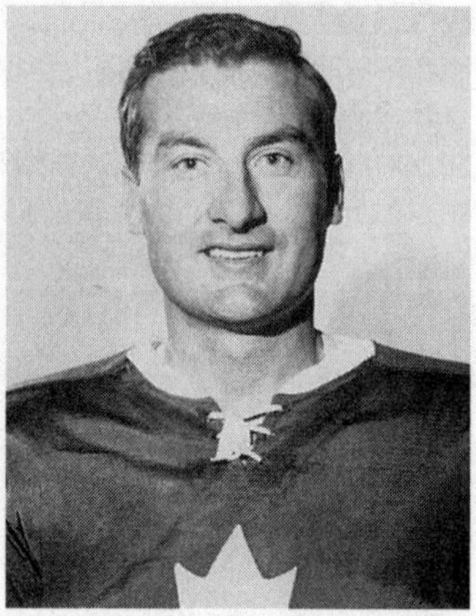

Duane Rupp

Name	NHL Teams	NHL Seasons	Regular Schedule GP	G	A	TP	PIM	Playoffs GP	G	A	TP	PIM	NHL Cup Wins	First NHL Season	Last NHL Seas
‡ Ready, Ryan	Phi.	1	7	0	1	1	0	....	....	....	....	....	....	2005-06	2005-0
• Reardon, Ken	Mtl.	7	341	26	96	122	604	31	2	5	7	62	1	1940-41	1949-5
• Reardon, Terry	Bos., Mtl.	7	193	47	53	100	73	30	8	10	18	12	1	1938-39	1946-4
Reaume, Marc	Tor., Det., Mtl., Van.	9	344	8	43	51	273	21	0	2	2	8	....	1954-55	1970-7
• Reay, Billy	Det., Mtl.	10	479	105	162	267	202	63	13	16	29	43	2	1943-44	1952-5
Redahl, Gord	Bos.	1	18	0	1	1	2	....	....	....	....	....	....	1958-59	1958-5
• Redding, George	Bos.	2	55	3	2	5	23	....	....	....	....	....	....	1924-25	1925-2
Redmond, Craig	L.A., Edm.	5	191	16	68	84	134	3	1	0	1	2	....	1984-85	1988-8
Redmond, Dick	Min., Cal., Chi., St.L., Atl., Bos.	13	771	133	312	445	504	66	9	22	31	27	....	1969-70	1981-8
Redmond, Keith	L.A.	1	12	1	0	1	20	....	....	....	....	....	....	1993-94	1993-9
Redmond, Mickey	Mtl., Det.	9	538	233	195	428	219	16	2	3	5	2	2	1967-68	1975-7
Reeds, Mark	St.L., Hfd.	8	365	45	114	159	135	53	8	9	17	23	....	1981-82	1988-8
Reekie, Joe	Buf., NYI, T.B., Wsh., Chi.	17	902	25	139	164	1326	51	3	4	7	63	....	1985-86	2001-0
• Regan, Bill	NYR, NYA	3	67	3	2	5	67	8	0	0	0	2	....	1929-30	1932-3
• Regan, Larry	Bos., Tor.	5	280	41	95	136	71	42	7	14	21	18	....	1956-57	1960-6
‡ Regehr, Richie	Cgy.	2	20	1	3	4	6	....	....	....	....	....	....	2005-06	2006-0
Regier, Darcy	Cle., NYI	3	26	0	2	2	35	....	....	....	....	....	....	1977-78	1983-8
• Reibel, Dutch	Det., Chi., Bos.	6	409	84	161	245	75	39	6	14	20	4	2	1953-54	1958-5
‡ Reichel, Robert	Cgy., NYI, Phx., Tor.	11	830	252	378	630	388	70	8	23	31	20	....	1990-91	2003-0
Reichert, Craig	Ana.	1	3	0	0	0	0	....	....	....	....	....	....	1996-97	1996-9
‡ Reid, Brandon	Van.	3	13	2	4	6	0	10	0	2	2	0	....	2002-03	2006-0
‡ Reid, Darren	T.B., Phi.	2	21	0	1	1	18	....	....	....	....	....	....	2005-06	2006-0
• Reid, Dave	Tor.	3	7	0	0	0	0	....	....	....	....	....	....	1952-53	1955-5
Reid, Dave	Bos., Tor., Dal., Col.	18	961	165	204	369	253	118	9	26	35	34	2	1983-84	2000-0
Reid, Gerry	Det.	1	....	....	....	....	....	2	0	0	0	2	....	1948-49	1948-4
Reid, Gord	NYA	1	1	0	0	0	2	....	....	....	....	....	....	1936-37	1936-3
• Reid, Reg	Tor.	2	39	1	0	1	4	2	0	0	0	0	....	1924-25	1925-2
Reid, Tom	Chi., Min.	11	701	17	113	130	654	42	1	13	14	49	....	1967-68	1977-7
Reierson, Dave	Cgy.	1	2	0	0	0	2	....	....	....	....	....	....	1988-89	1988-8
• Reigle, Ed	Bos.	1	17	0	2	2	25	....	....	....	....	....	....	1950-51	1950-5
Reinhart, Paul	Atl., Cgy., Van.	11	648	133	426	559	277	83	23	54	77	42	....	1979-80	1989-9
• Reinikka, Ollie	NYR	1	16	0	0	0	0	....	....	....	....	....	....	1926-27	1926-2
Reirden, Todd	Edm., St.L., Atl., Phx.	5	183	11	35	46	181	5	0	1	1	0	....	1998-99	2003-0
• Reise, Leo	Ham., NYA, NYR	8	223	36	29	65	181	6	0	0	0	16	....	1920-21	1929-3
Reise, Leo	Chi., Det., NYR	9	494	28	81	109	399	52	8	5	13	68	2	1945-46	1953-5
Renaud, Mark	Hfd., Buf.	5	152	6	50	56	86	....	....	....	....	....	....	1979-80	1983-8
‡ Renberg, Mikael	Phi., T.B., Phx., Tor.	10	661	190	274	464	372	67	16	22	38	42	....	1993-94	2003-0
Reynolds, Bobby	Tor.	1	7	1	1	2	0	....	....	....	....	....	....	1989-90	1989-9
‡ Rheaume, Pascal	N.J., St.L., Chi., Atl., NYR, Phx.	9	318	39	52	91	144	45	3	6	9	27	1	1996-97	2005-0
Ribble, Pat	Atl., Chi., Tor., Wsh., Cgy.	8	349	19	60	79	365	8	0	1	1	12	....	1975-76	1982-8
Ricci, Mike	Phi., Que., Col., S.J., Phx.	16	1099	243	362	605	974	110	23	43	66	77	1	1990-91	2006-0
Rice, Steven	NYR, Edm., Hfd., Car.	8	329	64	61	125	275	2	2	1	3	6	....	1990-91	1997-9
Richard, Henri	Mtl.	20	1256	358	688	1046	928	180	49	80	129	181	11	1955-56	1974-7
• Richard, Jacques	Atl., Buf., Que.	10	556	160	187	347	307	35	5	5	10	34	....	1972-73	1982-8
Richard, Jean-Marc	Que.	2	5	2	1	3	2	....	....	....	....	....	....	1987-88	1989-9
• Richard, Maurice	Mtl.	18	978	544	421	965	1285	133	82	44	126	188	8	1942-43	1959-6
‡ Richard, Mike	Wsh.	2	7	0	2	2	0	....	....	....	....	....	....	1987-88	1989-9
Richards, Todd	Hfd.	2	8	0	4	4	4	11	0	3	3	6	....	1990-91	1991-9
Richards, Travis	Dal.	2	3	0	0	0	2	....	....	....	....	....	....	1994-95	1995-9
Richardson, Dave	NYR, Chi., Det.	4	45	3	2	5	27	....	....	....	....	....	....	1963-64	1967-6
Richardson, Glen	Van.	1	24	3	6	9	19	....	....	....	....	....	....	1975-76	1975-7
Richardson, Ken	St.L.	3	49	8	13	21	16	....	....	....	....	....	....	1974-75	1978-7
Richardson, Luke	Tor., Edm., Phi., CBJ, T.B., Ott.	21	1417	35	166	201	2055	69	0	8	8	130	....	1987-88	2008-0
Richer, Bob	Buf.	1	3	0	0	0	0	....	....	....	....	....	....	1972-73	1972-7
Richer, Stephane	Mtl., N.J., T.B., St.L., Pit.	17	1054	421	398	819	614	134	53	45	98	61	2	1984-85	2001-0
Richer, Stephane	T.B., Bos., Fla.	3	27	1	5	6	20	3	0	0	0	0	....	1992-93	1994-9
Richmond, Steve	NYR, Det., N.J., L.A.	5	159	4	23	27	514	4	0	0	0	12	....	1983-84	1988-8
‡ Richter, Barry	NYR, Bos., NYI, Mtl.	5	151	11	34	45	76	....	....	....	....	....	....	1995-96	2000-0
Richter, Dave	Min., Phi., Van., St.L.	9	365	9	40	49	1030	22	1	0	1	80	....	1981-82	1989-9
Ridley, Mike	NYR, Wsh., Tor., Van.	12	866	292	466	758	424	104	28	50	78	70	....	1985-86	1996-9
‡ Riesen, Michel	Edm.	1	12	0	1	1	4	....	....	....	....	....	....	2000-01	2000-0
Riley, Bill	Wsh., Wpg.	5	139	31	30	61	320	....	....	....	....	....	....	1974-75	1979-8
• Riley, Jack	Det., Mtl., Bos.	4	104	10	22	32	8	4	0	3	3	0	....	1932-33	1935-3
• Riley, Jim	Chi., Det.	1	9	0	2	2	14	....	....	....	....	....	....	1926-27	1926-2
Riopelle, Rip	Mtl.	3	169	27	16	43	73	8	1	1	2	2	....	1947-48	1949-5
Rioux, Gerry	Wpg.	1	8	0	0	0	6	....	....	....	....	....	....	1979-80	1979-8
Rioux, Pierre	Cgy.	1	14	1	2	3	4	....	....	....	....	....	....	1982-83	1982-8
• Ripley, Vic	Chi., Bos., NYR, St.L.	7	278	51	49	100	173	20	4	1	5	10	....	1928-29	1934-3
Risebrough, Doug	Mtl., Cgy.	13	740	185	286	471	1542	124	21	37	58	238	4	1974-75	1986-8
Rissling, Gary	Wsh., Pit.	7	221	23	30	53	1008	5	0	1	1	4	....	1978-79	1984-8
‡ Rita, Jani	Edm., Pit.	4	66	9	5	14	10	....	....	....	....	....	....	2001-02	2005-0
Ritchie, Bob	Phi., Det.	2	29	8	4	12	10	....	....	....	....	....	....	1976-77	1977-7
‡ Ritchie, Byron	Car., Fla., Cgy., Van.	8	324	25	33	58	373	8	0	0	0	10	....	1998-99	2007-0
• Ritchie, Dave	Mtl.W., Ott., Tor., Que., Mtl.	6	58	15	6	21	50	1	0	0	0	0	....	1917-18	1925-2
Ritson, Alex	NYR	1	1	0	0	0	0	....	....	....	....	....	....	1944-45	1944-4
Rittinger, Alan	Bos.	1	19	3	7	10	0	....	....	....	....	....	....	1943-44	1943-4
Rivard, Bob	Pit.	1	27	5	12	17	4	....	....	....	....	....	....	1967-68	1967-6
• Rivers, Gus	Mtl.	3	88	4	5	9	12	16	2	0	2	2	2	1929-30	1931-3
Rivers, Shawn	T.B.	1	4	0	2	2	2	....	....	....	....	....	....	1992-93	1992-9
Rivers, Wayne	Det., Bos., St.L., NYR	7	108	15	30	45	94	....	....	....	....	....	....	1961-62	1968-6
Rizzuto, Garth	Van.	1	37	3	4	7	16	....	....	....	....	....	....	1970-71	1970-7
‡ Roach, Andy	St.L.	1	5	1	2	3	10	....	....	....	....	....	....	2005-06	2005-0
• Roach, Mickey	Tor., Ham., NYA	8	211	77	34	111	54	....	....	....	....	....	....	1919-20	1926-2
Roberge, Mario	Mtl.	5	112	7	7	14	314	15	0	0	0	24	1	1990-91	1994-9
Roberge, Serge	Que.	1	9	0	0	0	24	....	....	....	....	....	....	1990-91	1990-9
• Robert, Claude	Mtl.	1	23	1	0	1	9	....	....	....	....	....	....	1950-51	1950-5
Robert, Rene	Tor., Pit., Buf., Col.	12	744	284	418	702	597	50	22	19	41	73	....	1970-71	1981-8
Roberto, Phil	Mtl., St.L., Det., K.C., Col., Cle.	8	385	75	106	181	464	31	9	8	17	69	1	1969-70	1976-7
Roberts, David	St.L., Edm., Van.	5	125	20	33	53	85	9	0	0	0	16	....	1993-94	1997-9
Roberts, Doug	Det., Oak., Cal., Bos.	10	419	43	104	147	342	16	2	3	5	46	....	1965-66	1974-7
Roberts, Gary	Cgy., Car., Tor., Fla., Pit., T.B.	22	1224	438	472	910	2560	130	32	61	93	332	1	1986-87	2008-0
Roberts, Gordie	Hfd., Min., Phi., St.L., Pit., Bos.	15	1097	61	359	420	1582	153	10	47	57	273	2	1979-80	1993-9
Roberts, Jim	Min.	3	106	17	23	40	33	2	0	0	0	0	....	1976-77	1978-7
Roberts, Jimmy	Mtl., St.L.	15	1006	126	194	320	621	153	20	16	36	160	5	1963-64	1977-7
• Robertson, Fred	Tor., Det.	2	34	1	0	1	35	7	0	0	0	0	1	1931-32	1933-3
Robertson, Geordie	Buf.	1	5	1	2	3	7	....	....	....	....	....	....	1982-83	1982-8
• Robertson, George	Mtl.	2	31	2	5	7	6	....	....	....	....	....	....	1947-48	1948-4
Robertson, Torrie	Wsh., Hfd., Det.	10	442	49	99	148	1751	22	2	1	3	90	....	1980-81	1989-9
Robertsson, Bert	Van., Edm., NYR	4	123	4	10	14	75	5	0	0	0	0	....	1997-98	2000-0
Robidoux, Florent	Chi.	3	52	7	4	11	75	....	....	....	....	....	....	1980-81	1983-8
Robinson, Doug	Chi., NYR, L.A.	7	239	44	67	111	34	11	4	3	7	0	....	1963-64	1970-7
• Robinson, Earl	Mtl.M., Chi., Mtl.	11	417	83	98	181	133	25	5	4	9	0	1	1928-29	1939-4
Robinson, Larry	Mtl., L.A.	20	1384	208	750	958	793	227	28	116	144	211	6	1972-73	1991-9
Robinson, Moe	Mtl.	1	1	0	0	0	0	....	....	....	....	....	....	1979-80	1979-8
‡ Robinson, Nathan	Det., Bos.	2	7	0	0	0	2	....	....	....	....	....	....	2003-04	2005-0
Robinson, Rob	St.L.	1	22	0	1	1	8	....	....	....	....	....	....	1991-92	1991-9
Robinson, Scott	Min.	1	1	0	0	0	2	....	....	....	....	....	....	1989-90	1989-9
‡ Robitaille, Louis	Wsh.	1	2	0	0	0	5	....	....	....	....	....	....	2005-06	2005-0
Robitaille, Luc	L.A., Pit., NYR, Det.	19	1431	668	726	1394	1177	159	58	69	127	174	1	1986-87	2005-0
Robitaille, Mike	NYR, Det., Buf., Van.	8	382	23	105	128	280	13	0	1	1	4	....	1969-70	1976-7
‡ Robitaille, Randy	Bos., Nsh., L.A., Pit., NYI, Atl., Min., Phi., Ott.	11	531	84	172	256	201	13	1	4	5	8	....	1996-97	2007-0
Roche, Dave	Pit., Cgy., NYI	5	171	15	15	30	334	16	2	7	9	26	....	1995-96	2001-0
• Roche, Des	Mtl.M., Ott., St.L., Mtl., Det.	4	113	20	18	38	44	....	....	....	....	....	....	1930-31	1934-3
• Roche, Earl	Mtl.M., Bos., Ott., St.L., Det.	4	147	25	27	52	48	2	0	0	0	0	....	1930-31	1934-3
Roche, Ernie	Mtl.	1	4	0	0	0	2	....	....	....	....	....	....	1950-51	1950-5
‡ Roche, Travis	Min., Phx.	4	60	6	14	20	24	....	....	....	....	....	....	2000-01	2006-0
Rochefort, Dave	Det.	1	1	0	0	0	0	....	....	....	....	....	....	1966-67	1966-6
Rochefort, Leon	NYR, Mtl., Phi., L.A., Det., Atl., Van.	15	617	121	147	268	93	39	4	4	8	16	2	1960-61	1975-7
Rochefort, Normand	Que., NYR, T.B.	13	598	39	119	158	570	69	7	5	12	82	....	1980-81	1993-9
• Rockburn, Harvey	Det., Ott.	3	94	4	2	6	254	....	....	....	....	....	....	1929-30	1932-3
• Rodden, Eddie	Chi., Tor., Bos., NYR	4	97	6	14	20	60	2	0	1	1	0	....	1926-27	1930-3
Rodgers, Marc	Det.	1	21	1	1	2	10	....	....	....	....	....	....	1999-00	1999-0
Roenick, Jeremy	Chi., Phx., Phi., L.A., S.J.	20	1363	513	703	1216	1463	154	53	69	122	115	....	1988-89	2008-0
Roest, Stacy	Det., Min.	5	244	28	48	76	54	3	0	0	0	0	....	1998-99	2002-0
Rogers, John	Min.	2	14	2	4	6	0	....	....	....	....	....	....	1973-74	1974-7

ame	NHL Teams	NHL Seasons	Regular Schedule GP	G	A	TP	PIM	Playoffs GP	G	A	TP	PIM	NHL Cup Wins	First NHL Season	Last NHL Season
ogers, Mike	Hfd., NYR, Edm.	7	484	202	317	519	184	17	1	13	14	6	....	1979-80	1985-86
ohlicek, Jeff	Van.	2	9	0	0	0	8	....	....	....	....	....	....	1987-88	1988-89
ohlin, Leif	Van.	2	96	8	24	32	40	5	0	0	0	0	....	1995-96	1996-97
ohloff, Jon	Bos.	3	150	7	25	32	129	10	1	2	3	8	....	1994-95	1996-97
ohloff, Todd	Wsh., CBJ	2	75	0	6	6	40	....	....	....	....	....	....	2001-02	2003-04
olfe, Dale	Bos., L.A., Det., NYR	9	509	25	125	150	556	71	5	24	29	89	....	1959-60	1974-75
omanchych, Larry	Chi., Atl.	6	298	68	97	165	102	7	2	2	4	4	....	1970-71	1976-77
omaniuk, Russell	Wpg., Phi.	5	102	13	14	27	63	2	0	0	0	0	....	1991-92	1995-96
ombough, Doug	Buf., NYI, Min.	4	150	24	27	51	80	....	....	....	....	....	....	1972-73	1975-76
ominski, Dale	T.B.	1	3	0	1	1	2	....	....	....	....	....	....	1999-00	1999-00
omnes, Doc	Chi., Tor., NYA	10	360	68	136	204	42	43	7	18	25	4	2	1930-31	1939-40
onan, Ed	Mtl., Wpg., Buf.	6	182	13	23	36	101	27	4	3	7	16	1	1991-92	1996-97
onan, Skene	Ott.	1	11	0	0	0	6	....	....	....	....	....	....	1918-19	1918-19
onning, Cliff	St.L., Van., Phx., Nsh., L.A., Min., NYI	18	1137	306	563	869	453	126	29	57	86	72	....	1985-86	2003-04
Ronnqvist, Jonas	Ana.	1	38	0	4	4	14	....	....	....	....	....	....	2000-01	2000-01
Ronson, Len	NYR, Oak.	2	18	2	1	3	10	....	....	....	....	....	....	1960-61	1968-69
Ronty, Paul	Bos., NYR, Mtl.	8	488	101	211	312	103	21	1	7	8	6	....	1947-48	1954-55
Rooney, Steve	Mtl., Wpg., N.J.	5	154	15	13	28	496	25	3	2	5	86	1	1984-85	1988-89
Root, Bill	Mtl., Tor., St.L., Phi.	6	247	11	23	34	180	22	1	2	3	25	....	1982-83	1987-88
Rosa, Pavel	L.A.	4	36	5	13	18	6	....	....	....	....	....	....	1998-99	2003-04
Ross, Art	Mtl.W.	1	3	1	0	1	12	....	....	....	....	....	....	1917-18	1917-18
Ross, Jim	NYR	2	62	2	11	13	29	....	....	....	....	....	....	1951-52	1952-53
Rossignol, Roly	Det., Mtl.	3	14	3	5	8	6	1	0	0	0	2	....	1943-44	1945-46
Rossiter, Kyle	Fla., Atl.	3	11	0	1	1	9	....	....	....	....	....	....	2001-02	2003-04
Rota, Darcy	Chi., Atl., Van.	11	794	256	239	495	973	60	14	7	21	147	....	1973-74	1983-84
Rota, Randy	Mtl., L.A., K.C., Col.	5	212	38	39	77	60	5	0	1	1	0	....	1972-73	1976-77
Rothschild, Sam	Mtl.M., Pit., NYA	4	100	8	6	14	25	6	0	0	0	0	1	1924-25	1927-28
Roulston, Rolly	Det.	3	24	0	6	6	10	....	....	....	....	....	1	1935-36	1937-38
Roulston, Tom	Edm., Pit.	5	195	47	49	96	74	21	2	2	4	2	....	1980-81	1985-86
Roupe, Magnus	Phi.	2	40	3	5	8	42	....	....	....	....	....	....	1987-88	1988-89
Rourke, Allan	Car., NYI, Edm.	4	55	1	4	5	31	....	....	....	....	....	....	2003-04	2007-08
Rouse, Bob	Min., Wsh., Tor., Det., S.J.	17	1061	37	181	218	1559	136	7	21	28	198	2	1983-84	1999-00
Rousseau, Bobby	Mtl., Min., NYR	15	942	245	458	703	359	128	27	57	84	69	4	1960-61	1974-75
Rousseau, Guy	Mtl.	2	4	0	1	1	0	....	....	....	....	....	....	1954-55	1956-57
Rousseau, Roland	Mtl.	1	2	0	0	0	0	....	....	....	....	....	....	1952-53	1952-53
Routhier, Jean-Marc	Que.	1	8	0	0	0	9	....	....	....	....	....	....	1989-90	1989-90
Rowe, Bobby	Bos.	1	4	1	0	1	0	....	....	....	....	....	....	1924-25	1924-25
Rowe, Mike	Pit.	3	11	0	0	0	11	....	....	....	....	....	....	1984-85	1986-87
Rowe, Ron	NYR	1	5	1	0	1	0	....	....	....	....	....	....	1947-48	1947-48
Rowe, Tom	Wsh., Hfd., Det.	7	357	85	100	185	615	3	2	0	2	0	....	1976-77	1982-83
Roy, Andre	Bos., Ott., T.B., Pit., Cgy.	11	515	35	33	68	1169	41	1	3	4	98	1	1995-96	2008-09
Roy, Jean-Yves	NYR, Ott., Bos.	4	61	12	16	28	26	....	....	....	....	....	....	1994-95	1997-98
Roy, Stephane	Min.	1	12	1	0	1	0	....	....	....	....	....	....	1987-88	1987-88
Royer, Gaetan	T.B.	1	3	0	0	0	2	....	....	....	....	....	....	2001-02	2001-02
Royer, Remi	Chi.	1	18	0	0	0	67	....	....	....	....	....	....	1998-99	1998-99
Rozzini, Gino	Bos.	1	31	5	10	15	20	6	1	2	3	6	....	1944-45	1944-45
Rucchin, Steve	Ana., NYR, Atl.	12	735	171	318	489	164	37	9	8	17	12	....	1994-95	2006-07
Rucinski, Mike	Chi.	2	1	0	0	0	0	2	0	0	0	0	....	1987-88	1988-89
Rucinski, Mike	Car.	3	26	0	2	2	10	....	....	....	....	....	....	1997-98	2000-01
Rucinsky, Martin	Edm., Que., Col., Mtl., Dal., NYR, St.L., Van.	16	961	241	371	612	821	37	9	5	14	24	....	1991-92	2007-08
Ruelle, Bernie	Det.	1	2	1	0	1	0	....	....	....	....	....	....	1943-44	1943-44
Ruff, Jason	St.L., T.B.	2	14	3	3	6	10	....	....	....	....	....	....	1992-93	1993-94
Ruff, Lindy	Buf., NYR	12	691	105	195	300	1264	52	11	13	24	193	....	1979-80	1990-91
Ruhnke, Kent	Bos.	1	2	0	1	1	0	....	....	....	....	....	....	1975-76	1975-76
Rumble, Darren	Phi., Ott., St.L., T.B.	8	193	10	26	36	216	....	....	....	....	....	1	1990-91	2003-04
Rundqvist, Thomas	Mtl.	1	2	0	1	1	0	....	....	....	....	....	....	1984-85	1984-85
Runge, Paul	Bos., Mtl.M., Mtl.	7	140	18	22	40	57	7	0	0	0	6	....	1930-31	1937-38
Ruotsalainen, Reijo	NYR, Edm., N.J.	7	446	107	237	344	180	86	15	32	47	44	2	1981-82	1989-90
Rupp, Duane	NYR, Tor., Min., Pit.	10	374	24	93	117	220	10	2	2	4	8	....	1962-63	1972-73
Ruskowski, Terry	Chi., L.A., Pit., Min.	10	630	113	313	426	1354	21	1	6	7	86	....	1979-80	1988-89
Russell, Cam	Chi., Col.	10	396	9	21	30	872	44	0	5	5	16	....	1989-90	1998-99
Russell, Church	NYR	3	90	20	16	36	12	....	....	....	....	....	....	1945-46	1947-48
Russell, Phil	Chi., Atl., Cgy., N.J., Buf.	15	1016	99	325	424	2038	73	4	22	26	202	....	1972-73	1986-87
Ruuttu, Christian	Buf., Chi., Van.	9	621	134	298	432	714	42	4	9	13	49	....	1986-87	1994-95
Ruzicka, Vladimir	Edm., Bos., Ott.	5	233	82	85	167	129	30	4	14	18	2	....	1989-90	1993-94
Ryan, Matt	L.A.	1	12	0	1	1	2	....	....	....	....	....	....	2005-06	2005-06
Ryan, Prestin	Van.	1	1	0	0	0	2	....	....	....	....	....	....	2005-06	2005-06
Ryan, Terry	Mtl.	3	8	0	0	0	36	....	....	....	....	....	....	1996-97	1998-99
Rychel, Warren	Chi., L.A., Tor., Col., Ana.	9	406	38	39	77	1422	70	8	13	21	121	1	1988-89	1998-99
Rycroft, Mark	St.L., Col.	4	226	21	25	46	113	3	0	0	0	2	....	2001-02	2006-07
Rymsha, Andy	Que.	1	6	0	0	0	23	....	....	....	....	....	....	1991-92	1991-92
Ryznar, Jason	N.J.	1	8	0	0	0	2	....	....	....	....	....	....	2005-06	2005-06

S

Saarinen, Simo	NYR	1	8	0	0	0	0	....	....	....	....	....	....	1984-85	1984-85
Sabol, Shaun	Phi.	1	2	0	0	0	0	....	....	....	....	....	....	1989-90	1989-90
Sabourin, Bob	Tor.	1	1	0	0	0	2	....	....	....	....	....	....	1951-52	1951-52
Sabourin, Gary	St.L., Tor., Cal., Cle.	10	627	169	188	357	397	62	19	11	30	58	....	1967-68	1976-77
Sabourin, Ken	Cgy., Wsh.	4	74	2	8	10	201	12	0	0	0	34	....	1988-89	1991-92
Sacco, David	Tor., Ana.	3	35	5	13	18	22	....	....	....	....	....	....	1993-94	1995-96
Sacco, Joe	Tor., Ana., NYI, Wsh., Phi.	13	738	94	119	213	421	26	2	0	2	8	....	1990-91	2002-03
Sacharuk, Larry	NYR, St.L.	5	151	29	33	62	42	2	1	1	2	2	....	1972-73	1976-77
Safronov, Kirill	Phx., Atl.	2	35	2	2	4	16	....	....	....	....	....	....	2001-02	2002-03
Saganiuk, Rocky	Tor., Pit.	6	259	57	65	122	201	6	1	0	1	15	....	1978-79	1983-84
Sakic, Joe	Que., Col.	20	1378	625	1016	1641	614	172	84	104	188	78	2	1988-89	2008-09
Saleski, Don	Phi., Col.	9	543	128	125	253	629	82	13	17	30	131	2	1971-72	1979-80
Salmelainen, Tony	Edm., Chi.	2	70	6	12	18	30	....	....	....	....	....	....	2003-04	2006-07
Salming, Borje	Tor., Det.	17	1148	150	637	787	1344	81	12	37	49	91	....	1973-74	1989-90
Salomonsson, Andreas	N.J., Wsh.	2	71	5	9	14	36	4	0	1	1	0	....	2001-02	2002-03
Salovaara, Barry	Det.	2	90	2	13	15	70	....	....	....	....	....	....	1974-75	1975-76
Salvian, Dave	NYI	1	....	....	....	....	....	1	0	1	1	2	....	1976-77	1976-77
Samis, Phil	Tor.	2	2	0	0	0	0	5	0	1	1	2	1	1947-48	1949-50
Sampson, Gary	Wsh.	4	105	13	22	35	25	12	1	0	1	0	....	1983-84	1986-87
Samuelsson, Kjell	NYR, Phi., Pit., T.B.	14	813	48	138	186	1225	123	4	20	24	178	1	1985-86	1998-99
Samuelsson, Martin	Bos.	2	14	0	1	1	2	....	....	....	....	....	....	2002-03	2003-04
Samuelsson, Ulf	Hfd., Pit., NYR, Det., Phi.	16	1080	57	275	332	2453	132	7	27	34	272	2	1984-85	1999-00
Sandelin, Scott	Mtl., Phi., Min.	4	25	0	4	4	2	....	....	....	....	....	....	1986-87	1991-92
Sanderson, Derek	Bos., NYR, St.L., Van., Pit.	13	598	202	250	452	911	56	18	12	30	187	2	1965-66	1977-78
Sanderson, Geoff	Hfd., Car., Van., Buf., CBJ, Phx., Phi., Edm.	17	1104	355	345	700	511	55	9	10	19	32	....	1990-91	2007-08
Sandford, Ed	Bos., Det., Chi.	9	502	106	145	251	355	42	13	11	24	27	....	1947-48	1955-56
Sandlak, Jim	Van., Hfd.	11	549	110	119	229	821	33	7	10	17	30	....	1985-86	1995-96
• Sands, Charlie	Tor., Bos., Mtl., NYR	12	427	99	109	208	58	34	6	6	12	4	1	1932-33	1943-44
Sandstrom, Tomas	NYR, L.A., Pit., Det., Ana.	15	983	394	462	856	1193	139	32	49	81	183	1	1984-85	1998-99
Sandwith, Terran	Edm.	1	8	0	0	0	6	....	....	....	....	....	....	1997-98	1997-98
Sanipass, Everett	Chi., Que.	5	164	25	34	59	358	5	2	0	2	4	....	1986-87	1990-91
‡ Santala, Tommi	Atl., Van.	2	63	2	7	9	46	1	0	0	0	0	....	2003-04	2006-07
‡ Saprykin, Oleg	Cgy., Phx., Ott.	7	325	55	82	137	240	41	4	4	8	18	....	1999-00	2006-07
‡ Sarault, Yves	Mtl., Cgy., Col., Ott., Atl., Nsh.	8	106	10	10	20	51	5	0	0	0	2	....	1994-95	2001-02
Sargent, Gary	L.A., Min.	8	402	61	161	222	273	20	5	7	12	8	....	1975-76	1982-83
Sarner, Craig	Bos.	1	7	0	0	0	0	....	....	....	....	....	....	1974-75	1974-75
‡ Sarno, Peter	Edm., CBJ	2	7	1	0	1	2	....	....	....	....	....	....	2003-04	2005-06
Sarrazin, Dick	Phi.	3	100	20	35	55	22	4	0	0	0	0	....	1968-69	1971-72
Sasakamoose, Fred	Chi.	1	11	0	0	0	6	....	....	....	....	....	....	1953-54	1953-54
Sasser, Grant	Pit.	1	3	0	0	0	0	....	....	....	....	....	....	1983-84	1983-84
Sather, Glen	Bos., Pit., NYR, St.L., Mtl., Min.	10	658	80	113	193	724	72	1	5	6	86	....	1966-67	1975-76
Saunders, Bernie	Que.	2	10	0	1	1	8	....	....	....	....	....	....	1979-80	1980-81
Saunders, David	Van.	1	56	7	13	20	10	....	....	....	....	....	....	1987-88	1987-88
• Saunders, Ted	Ott.	1	18	1	3	4	4	....	....	....	....	....	....	1933-34	1933-34
Sauve, Jean-Francois	Buf., Que.	7	290	65	138	203	114	36	9	12	21	10	....	1980-81	1986-87
‡ Savage, Andre	Bos., Phi.	4	66	10	14	24	14	....	....	....	....	....	....	1998-99	2002-03
Savage, Brian	Mtl., Phx., St.L., Phi.	12	674	192	167	359	321	39	3	8	11	12	....	1993-94	2005-06
Savage, Joel	Buf.	1	3	0	1	1	0	....	....	....	....	....	....	1990-91	1990-91
Savage, Reggie	Wsh., Que.	3	34	5	7	12	28	....	....	....	....	....	....	1990-91	1993-94

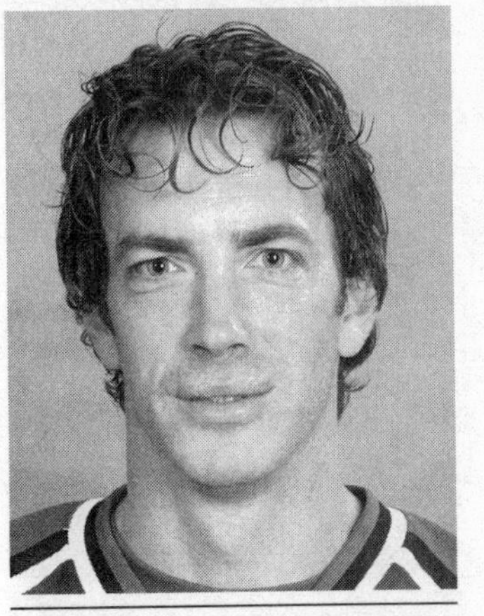
Joe Sakic

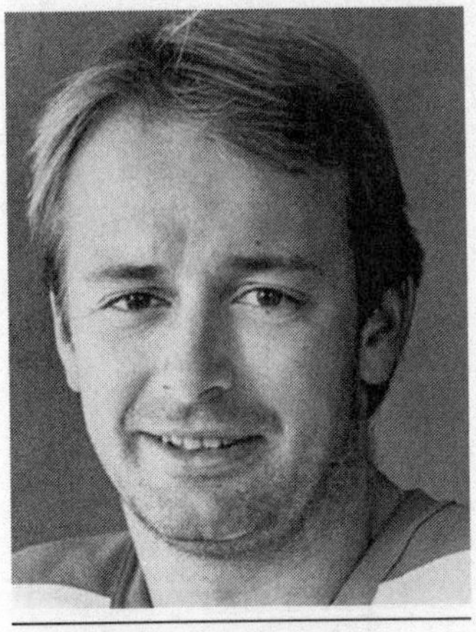
Gary Sampson

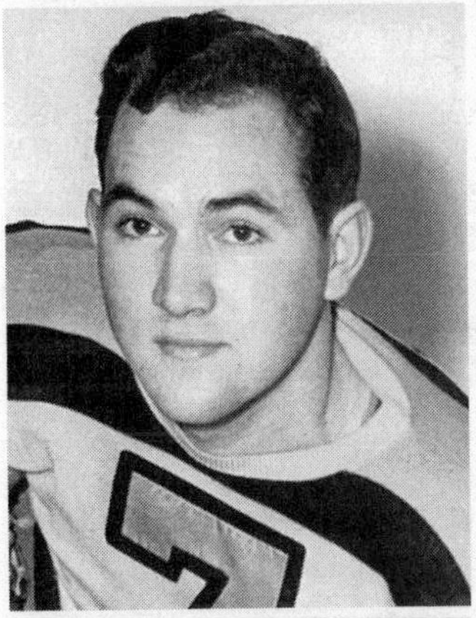
Jackie Schmidt

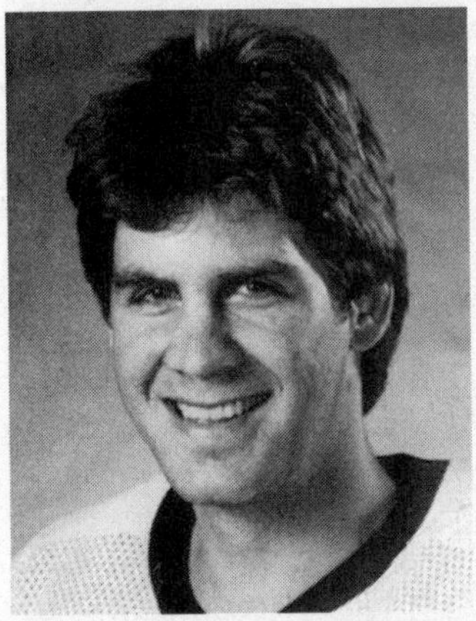
Norm Schmidt

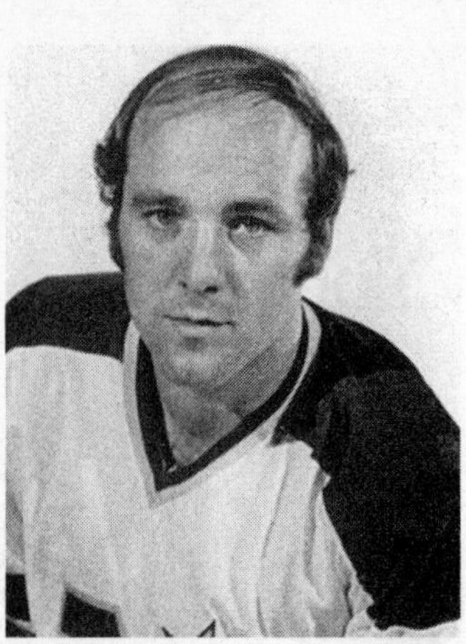

Dan Seguin

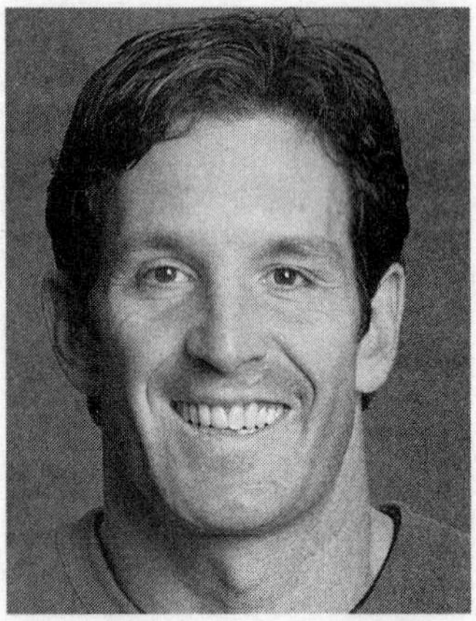

Brendan Shanahan

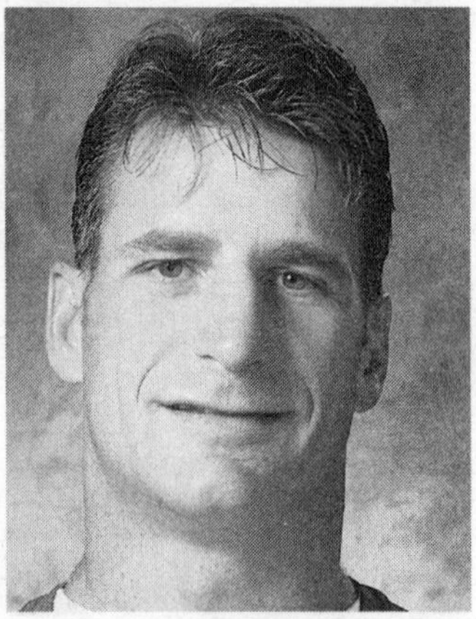

Mike Sillinger

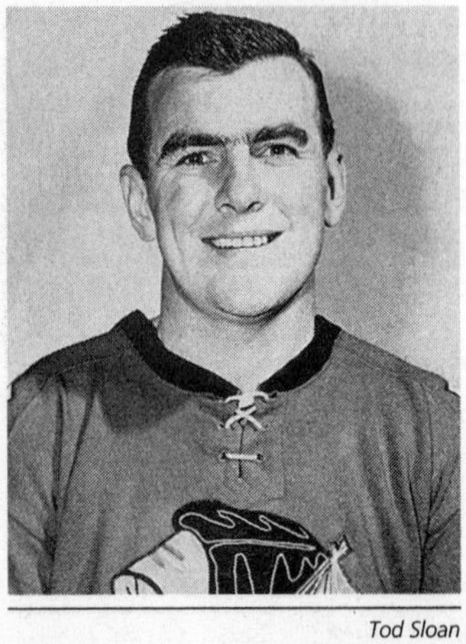

Tod Sloan

			Regular Schedule					Playoffs					NHL	First	Last
Name	NHL Teams	NHL Seasons	GP	G	A	TP	PIM	GP	G	A	TP	PIM	Cup Wins	NHL Season	NHL Seaso
• Savage, Tony	Bos., Mtl.	1	49	1	5	6	6	2	0	0	0	0	....	1934-35	1934-3
Savard, Andre	Bos., Buf., Que.	12	790	211	271	482	411	85	13	18	31	77	....	1973-74	1984-8
Savard, Denis	Chi., Mtl., T.B.	17	1196	473	865	1338	1336	169	66	109	175	256	1	1980-81	1996-9
Savard, Jean	Chi., Hfd.	3	43	7	12	19	29	....	....	....	....	....	....	1977-78	1979-8
Savard, Serge	Mtl., Wpg.	17	1040	106	333	439	592	130	19	49	68	88	8	1966-67	1982-8
‡ Savoia, Ryan	Pit.	1	3	0	0	0	0	....	....	....	....	....	....	1998-99	1998-9
Sawyer, Kevin	St.L., Bos., Phx., Ana.	6	110	3	3	6	403	....	....	....	....	....	....	1995-96	2002-0
Scamurra, Peter	Wsh.	4	132	8	25	33	59	....	....	....	....	....	....	1975-76	1979-8
Sceviour, Darin	Chi.	1	1	0	0	0	0	....	....	....	....	....	....	1986-87	1986-8
Schaefer, Peter	Van., Ott., Bos.	8	556	98	161	259	198	63	6	18	24	34	....	1998-99	2007-0
• Schaeffer, Butch	Chi.	1	5	0	0	0	6	....	....	....	....	....	....	1936-37	1936-3
Schamehorn, Kevin	Det., L.A.	3	10	0	0	0	17	....	....	....	....	....	....	1976-77	1980-8
‡ Schastlivy, Petr	Ott., Ana.	5	129	18	22	40	30	1	0	0	0	0	....	1999-00	2003-0
Schella, John	Van.	2	115	2	18	20	224	....	....	....	....	....	....	1970-71	1971-7
Scherza, Chuck	Bos., NYR	2	36	6	6	12	35	....	....	....	....	....	....	1943-44	1944-4
Schinkel, Ken	NYR, Pit.	12	636	127	198	325	163	19	7	2	9	4	....	1959-60	1972-7
Schlegel, Brad	Wsh., Cgy.	3	48	1	8	9	10	7	0	1	1	2	....	1991-92	1993-9
Schliebener, Andy	Van.	3	84	2	11	13	74	6	0	0	0	0	....	1981-82	1984-8
Schmautz, Bobby	Chi., Van., Bos., Edm., Col.	13	764	271	286	557	988	84	28	33	61	92	....	1967-68	1980-8
• Schmautz, Cliff	Buf., Phi.	1	56	13	19	32	33	....	....	....	....	....	....	1970-71	1970-7
‡ Schmidt, Chris	L.A.	1	10	0	2	2	5	....	....	....	....	....	....	2002-03	2002-0
• Schmidt, Clarence	Bos.	1	7	1	0	1	2	....	....	....	....	....	....	1943-44	1943-4
Schmidt, Jackie	Bos.	1	45	6	7	13	6	5	0	0	0	0	....	1942-43	1942-4
Schmidt, Milt	Bos.	16	776	229	346	575	466	86	24	25	49	60	2	1936-37	1954-5
Schmidt, Norm	Pit.	4	125	23	33	56	73	....	....	....	....	....	....	1983-84	1987-8
Schmidt, Otto	Bos.	1	2	0	0	0	0	....	....	....	....	....	....	1943-44	1943-4
‡ Schnabel, Robert	Nsh.	3	22	0	3	3	34	....	....	....	....	....	....	2001-02	2003-0
• Schnarr, Werner	Bos.	2	26	0	0	0	0	....	....	....	....	....	....	1924-25	1925-2
‡ Schneider, Andy	Ott.	1	10	0	0	0	15	....	....	....	....	....	....	1993-94	1993-9
Schock, Danny	Bos., Phi.	2	20	1	2	3	0	1	0	0	0	0	1	1969-70	1970-7
Schock, Ron	Bos., St.L., Pit., Buf.	15	909	166	351	517	260	55	4	16	20	29	....	1963-64	1977-7
Schoenfeld, Jim	Buf., Det., Bos.	13	719	51	204	255	1132	75	3	13	16	151	....	1972-73	1984-8
Schofield, Dwight	Det., Mtl., St.L., Wsh., Pit., Wpg.	7	211	8	22	30	631	9	0	0	0	55	....	1976-77	1987-8
Schreiber, Wally	Min.	2	41	8	10	18	12	....	....	....	....	....	....	1987-88	1988-8
• Schriner, Sweeney	NYA, Tor.	11	484	201	204	405	148	59	18	11	29	54	2	1934-35	1945-4
Schulte, Paxton	Que., Cgy.	2	2	0	0	0	4	....	....	....	....	....	....	1993-94	1996-9
Schultz, Dave	Phi., L.A., Pit., Buf.	9	535	79	121	200	2294	73	8	12	20	412	2	1971-72	1979-8
Schultz, Ray	NYI	6	45	0	4	4	155	2	0	0	0	2	....	1997-98	2002-0
Schurman, Maynard	Hfd.	1	7	0	0	0	0	....	....	....	....	....	....	1979-80	1979-8
Schutt, Rod	Mtl., Pit., Tor.	8	286	77	92	169	177	22	8	6	14	26	....	1977-78	1985-8
Scissons, Scott	NYI	3	2	0	0	0	0	1	0	0	0	0	....	1990-91	1993-9
Sclisizzi, Enio	Det., Chi.	6	81	12	11	23	26	13	0	0	0	6	1	1946-47	1952-5
• Scott, Ganton	Tor., Ham., Mtl.M.	3	57	1	1	2	0	....	....	....	....	....	....	1922-23	1924-2
• Scott, Laurie	NYA, NYR	2	62	6	3	9	28	....	....	....	....	....	....	1926-27	1927-2
Scott, Richard	NYR	2	10	0	0	0	28	....	....	....	....	....	....	2001-02	2003-0
Scoville, Darrel	Cgy., CBJ	3	16	0	1	1	12	....	....	....	....	....	....	1999-00	2003-0
Scremin, Claudio	S.J.	2	17	0	1	1	29	....	....	....	....	....	....	1991-92	1992-9
Scruton, Howard	L.A.	1	4	0	4	4	9	....	....	....	....	....	....	1982-83	1982-8
Seabrooke, Glen	Phi.	3	19	1	6	7	4	....	....	....	....	....	....	1986-87	1988-8
Secord, Al	Bos., Chi., Tor., Phi.	12	766	273	222	495	2093	102	21	34	55	382	....	1978-79	1989-9
Sedlbauer, Ron	Van., Chi., Tor.	7	430	143	86	229	210	19	1	3	4	27	....	1974-75	1980-8
Seftel, Steve	Wsh.	1	4	0	0	0	2	....	....	....	....	....	....	1990-91	1990-9
Seguin, Dan	Min., Van.	2	37	2	6	8	50	....	....	....	....	....	....	1970-71	1973-7
Seguin, Steve	L.A.	1	5	0	0	0	9	....	....	....	....	....	....	1984-85	1984-8
• Seibert, Earl	NYR, Chi., Det.	15	645	89	187	276	746	66	11	8	19	76	2	1931-32	1945-4
Seiling, Ric	Buf., Det.	10	738	179	208	387	573	62	14	14	28	36	....	1977-78	1986-8
Seiling, Rod	Tor., NYR, Wsh., St.L., Atl.	17	979	62	269	331	601	77	4	8	12	55	....	1962-63	1978-7
Sejba, Jiri	Buf.	1	11	0	2	2	8	....	....	....	....	....	....	1990-91	1990-9
‡ Sejna, Peter	St.L.	4	49	7	4	11	12	....	....	....	....	....	....	2002-03	2006-0
‡ Sekeras, Lubomir	Min., Dal.	4	213	18	53	71	122	15	1	1	2	6	....	2000-01	2003-0
Selby, Brit	Tor., Phi., St.L.	8	350	55	62	117	163	16	1	1	2	8	....	1964-65	1971-7
Self, Steve	Wsh.	1	3	0	0	0	0	....	....	....	....	....	....	1976-77	1976-7
‡ Selivanov, Alex	T.B., Edm., CBJ	7	459	121	114	235	379	13	2	3	5	16	....	1994-95	2000-0
‡ Sellars, Luke	Atl.	1	1	0	0	0	2	....	....	....	....	....	....	2001-02	2001-0
‡ Selmser, Sean	CBJ	1	1	0	0	0	5	....	....	....	....	....	....	2000-01	2000-0
Selwood, Brad	Tor., L.A.	3	163	7	40	47	153	6	0	0	0	4	....	1970-71	1979-8
Semak, Alexander	N.J., T.B., NYI, Van.	6	289	83	91	174	187	8	1	1	2	0	....	1991-92	1996-9
Semchuk, Brandy	L.A.	1	1	0	0	0	2	....	....	....	....	....	....	1992-93	1992-9
Semenko, Dave	Edm., Hfd., Tor.	9	575	65	88	153	1175	73	6	6	12	208	2	1979-80	1987-8
Semenov, Anatoli	Edm., T.B., Van., Ana., Phi., Buf.	8	362	68	126	194	122	49	9	13	22	12	....	1989-90	1996-9
• Senick, George	NYR	1	13	2	3	5	8	....	....	....	....	....	....	1952-53	1952-5
Seppa, Jyrki	Wpg.	1	13	0	2	2	6	....	....	....	....	....	....	1983-84	1983-8
Serafini, Ron	Cal.	1	2	0	0	0	2	....	....	....	....	....	....	1973-74	1973-7
Serowik, Jeff	Tor., Bos., Pit.	3	28	0	6	6	16	....	....	....	....	....	....	1990-91	1998-9
Servinis, George	Min.	1	5	0	0	0	0	....	....	....	....	....	....	1987-88	1987-8
Sevcik, Jaroslav	Que.	1	13	0	2	2	2	....	....	....	....	....	....	1989-90	1989-9
‡ Severson, Cam	Ana., CBJ	3	37	3	0	3	63	1	0	0	0	0	....	2002-03	2005-0
Severyn, Brent	Que., Fla., NYI, Col., Ana., Dal.	7	328	10	30	40	825	8	0	0	0	12	1	1989-90	1998-9
‡ Sevigny, Pierre	Mtl., NYR	4	78	4	5	9	64	3	0	1	1	0	....	1993-94	1997-9
Shack, Eddie	NYR, Tor., Bos., L.A., Buf., Pit.	17	1047	239	226	465	1437	74	6	7	13	151	4	1958-59	1974-7
• Shack, Joe	NYR	2	70	9	27	36	20	....	....	....	....	....	....	1942-43	1944-4
Shafranov, Konstantin	St.L.	1	5	2	1	3	0	....	....	....	....	....	....	1996-97	1996-9
Shakes, Paul	Cal.	1	21	0	4	4	12	....	....	....	....	....	....	1973-74	1973-7
Shaldybin, Yevgeny	Bos.	1	3	1	0	1	0	....	....	....	....	....	....	1996-97	1996-9
Shanahan, Brendan	N.J., St.L., Hfd., Det., NYR	21	1524	656	698	1354	2489	184	60	74	134	279	3	1987-88	2008-0
Shanahan, Sean	Mtl., Col., Bos.	3	40	1	3	4	47	....	....	....	....	....	....	1975-76	1977-7
Shand, Dave	Atl., Tor., Wsh.	8	421	19	84	103	544	26	1	2	3	83	....	1976-77	1984-8
Shank, Daniel	Det., Hfd.	3	77	13	14	27	175	5	0	0	0	22	....	1989-90	1991-9
• Shannon, Chuck	NYA	1	4	0	0	0	2	....	....	....	....	....	....	1939-40	1939-4
Shannon, Darrin	Buf., Wpg., Phx.	10	506	87	163	250	344	45	7	10	17	38	....	1988-89	1997-9
Shannon, Darryl	Tor., Wpg., Buf., Atl., Cgy., Mtl.	13	544	28	111	139	523	29	4	7	11	16	....	1988-89	2000-0
• Shannon, Gerry	Ott., St.L., Bos., Mtl.M.	5	180	23	29	52	80	9	0	1	1	2	....	1933-34	1937-3
Shantz, Jeff	Chi., Cgy., Col.	10	642	72	139	211	341	44	5	8	13	24	....	1993-94	2002-0
Sharifijanov, Vadim	N.J., Van.	3	92	16	21	37	50	4	0	0	0	0	....	1996-97	1999-0
Sharples, Jeff	Det.	3	105	14	35	49	70	7	0	3	3	6	....	1986-87	1988-8
Sharpley, Glen	Min., Chi.	6	389	117	161	278	199	27	7	11	18	24	....	1976-77	1981-8
Shaunessy, Scott	Que.	2	7	0	0	0	23	....	....	....	....	....	....	1986-87	1988-8
Shaw, Brad	Hfd., Ott., Wsh., St.L.	11	377	22	137	159	208	23	4	8	12	6	....	1985-86	1998-9
Shaw, David	Que., NYR, Edm., Min., Bos., T.B.	16	769	41	153	194	906	45	3	9	12	81	....	1982-83	1997-9
• Shay, Norm	Bos., Tor.	2	53	5	3	8	34	....	....	....	....	....	....	1924-25	1925-2
• Shea, Pat	Chi.	1	10	1	0	1	0	....	....	....	....	....	....	1931-32	1931-3
Shearer, Rob	Col.	1	2	0	0	0	0	....	....	....	....	....	....	2000-01	2000-0
Shedden, Doug	Pit., Det., Que., Tor.	8	416	139	186	325	176	....	....	....	....	....	....	1981-82	1990-9
Sheehan, Bobby	Mtl., Cal., Chi., Det., NYR, Col., L.A.	9	310	48	63	111	40	25	4	3	7	8	1	1969-70	1981-8
Sheehy, Neil	Cgy., Hfd., Wsh.	9	379	18	47	65	1311	54	0	3	3	241	....	1983-84	1991-9
Sheehy, Tim	Det., Hfd.	2	27	2	1	3	0	....	....	....	....	....	....	1977-78	1979-8
Shelton, Doug	Chi.	1	5	0	1	1	2	....	....	....	....	....	....	1967-68	1967-6
• Sheppard, Frank	Det.	1	8	1	1	2	0	....	....	....	....	....	....	1927-28	1927-2
Sheppard, Gregg	Bos., Pit.	10	657	205	293	498	243	82	32	40	72	31	....	1972-73	1981-8
• Sheppard, Johnny	Det., NYA, Bos., Chi.	8	308	68	58	126	224	10	0	0	0	0	1	1926-27	1933-3
Sheppard, Ray	Buf., NYR, Det., S.J., Fla., Car.	13	817	357	300	657	212	81	30	20	50	21	....	1987-88	1999-0
• Sherf, John	Det.	5	19	0	0	0	8	8	0	1	1	2	1	1935-36	1943-4
• Shero, Fred	NYR	3	145	6	14	20	137	13	0	2	2	8	....	1947-48	1949-5
• Sherritt, Gordon	Det.	1	8	0	0	0	12	....	....	....	....	....	....	1943-44	1943-4
Sherven, Gord	Edm., Min., Hfd.	5	97	13	22	35	33	3	0	0	0	0	....	1983-84	1987-8
Shevalier, Jeff	L.A., T.B.	3	32	5	9	14	8	....	....	....	....	....	....	1994-95	1999-0
• Shewchuk, Jack	Bos.	6	187	9	19	28	160	20	0	1	1	19	1	1938-39	1944-4
• Shibicky, Alex	NYR	8	324	110	91	201	161	39	12	12	24	12	1	1935-36	1945-4
• Shields, Al	Ott., Phi., NYA, Mtl.M., Bos.	11	459	42	46	88	637	17	0	1	1	14	1	1927-28	1937-3
• Shill, Bill	Bos.	3	79	21	13	34	18	7	1	2	3	2	....	1942-43	1946-4
• Shill, Jack	Tor., Bos., NYA, Chi.	6	160	15	20	35	70	25	1	6	7	23	1	1933-34	1938-3
Shinske, Rick	Cle., St.L.	3	63	5	16	21	10	....	....	....	....	....	....	1976-77	1978-7
Shires, Jim	Det., St.L., Pit.	3	56	3	6	9	32	....	....	....	....	....	....	1970-71	1972-7
‡ Shishkanov, Timofei	Nsh., St.L.	2	24	3	2	5	6	....	....	....	....	....	....	2003-04	2005-0
• Shmyr, Paul	Chi., Cal., Min., Hfd.	7	343	13	72	85	528	34	3	3	6	44	....	1968-69	1981-8
Shoebottom, Bruce	Bos.	4	35	1	4	5	53	14	1	2	3	77	....	1987-88	1990-9

			Regular Schedule					Playoffs							
lame	NHL Teams	NHL Seasons	GP	G	A	TP	PIM	GP	G	A	TP	PIM	NHL Cup Wins	First NHL Season	Last NHL Season
hore, Eddie	Bos., NYA	14	550	105	179	284	1047	55	7	12	19	181	2	1926-27	1939-40
hore, Hamby	Ott.	1	18	3	8	11	51	....	....	....	....	....	....	1917-18	1917-18
hort, Steve	L.A., Det.	2	6	0	0	0	2	....	....	....	....	....	....	1977-78	1978-79
huchuk, Gary	Det., L.A.	5	142	13	26	39	70	20	2	2	4	12	....	1990-91	1995-96
hudra, Ron	Edm.	1	10	0	5	5	6	....	....	....	....	....	....	1987-88	1987-88
hutt, Steve	Mtl., L.A.	13	930	424	393	817	410	99	50	48	98	65	5	1972-73	1984-85
hvidki, Denis	Fla.	4	76	11	14	25	30	....	....	....	....	....	....	2000-01	2003-04
iebert, Babe	Mtl.M., NYR, Bos., Mtl.	14	592	140	156	296	982	49	7	5	12	62	2	1925-26	1938-39
iklenka, Mike	Phi., NYR	2	2	0	0	0	0	....	....	....	....	....	....	2002-03	2003-04
ilk, Dave	NYR, Bos., Det., Wpg.	7	249	54	59	113	271	13	2	4	6	13	....	1979-80	1985-86
llinger, Mike	Det., Ana., Van., Phi., T.B., Fla., Ott., CBJ, Phx., St.L.	18	1049	240	308	548	644	43	11	7	18	28	....	1990-91	2003-04
ltala, Mike	Wsh., NYR	3	7	1	0	1	2	....	....	....	....	....	....	1981-82	1987-88
ltanen, Risto	Edm., Hfd., Que.	8	562	90	265	355	266	32	6	12	18	30	....	1979-80	1986-87
m, Trevor	Edm.	1	3	0	1	1	2	....	....	....	....	....	....	1989-90	1989-90
mard, Martin	Cgy., T.B.	3	44	1	5	6	183	....	....	....	....	....	....	1990-91	1992-93
micek, Roman	Pit., Min.	2	63	7	10	17	59	....	....	....	....	....	....	2000-01	2001-02
mmer, Charlie	Cal., Cle., L.A., Bos., Pit.	14	712	342	369	711	544	24	9	9	18	32	....	1974-75	1987-88
mmons, Al	Cal., Bos.	3	11	0	1	1	21	1	0	0	0	0	....	1971-72	1975-76
mon, Chris	Que., Col., Wsh., Chi., NYR, Cgy., NYI, Min.	15	782	144	161	305	1824	75	10	7	17	191	1	1992-93	2007-08
mon, Cully	Det., Chi.	3	130	4	11	15	121	14	1	0	1	6	1	1942-43	1944-45
mon, Jason	NYI, Phx.	2	5	0	0	0	34	....	....	....	....	....	....	1993-94	1996-97
mon, Thain	Det.	1	3	0	0	0	0	....	....	....	....	....	....	1946-47	1946-47
mon, Todd	Buf.	1	15	0	1	1	0	5	1	0	1	0	....	1993-94	1993-94
monetti, Frank	Bos.	4	115	5	8	13	76	12	0	1	1	8	....	1984-85	1987-88
mpson, Bobby	Atl., St.L., Pit.	5	175	35	29	64	98	6	0	1	1	2	....	1976-77	1982-83
mpson, Cliff	Det.	2	6	0	1	1	0	2	0	0	0	2	....	1946-47	1947-48
mpson, Craig	Pit., Edm., Buf.	10	634	247	250	497	659	67	36	32	68	56	2	1985-86	1994-95
mpson, Joe	NYA	6	228	21	19	40	156	2	0	0	0	0	....	1925-26	1930-31
mpson, Reid	Phi., Min., N.J., Chi., T.B., St.L., Mtl., Nsh., Pit.	12	301	18	18	36	838	10	0	0	0	31	....	1991-92	2003-04
mpson, Todd	Cgy., Fla., Phx., Ana., Ott., Chi., Mtl.	10	580	14	63	77	1357	9	0	2	2	10	....	1995-96	2005-06
ms, Al	Bos., Hfd., L.A.	10	475	49	116	165	286	41	0	2	2	14	....	1973-74	1982-83
nclair, Reg	NYR, Det.	3	208	49	43	92	139	3	1	0	1	0	....	1950-51	1952-53
ngbush, Alex	Mtl.	1	32	0	5	5	15	3	0	0	0	4	....	1940-41	1940-41
nisalo, Ilkka	Phi., Min., L.A.	11	582	204	222	426	208	68	21	11	32	6	....	1981-82	1991-92
ren, Ville	Pit., Min.	5	290	14	68	82	276	7	0	0	0	6	....	1985-86	1989-90
rois, Bob	Phi., Wsh.	6	286	92	120	212	42	....	....	....	....	....	....	1974-75	1979-80
ttler, Darryl	Tor., Phi., Det.	15	1096	484	637	1121	948	76	29	45	74	137	....	1970-71	1984-85
vek, Michal	Pit.	1	38	3	3	6	14	....	....	....	....	....	....	2002-03	2002-03
oberg, Lars-Erik	Wpg.	1	79	7	27	34	48	....	....	....	....	....	....	1979-80	1979-80
odin, Tommy	Min., Dal., Que.	2	106	8	40	48	52	....	....	....	....	....	....	1992-93	1993-94
kaare, Bjorn	Det.	1	1	0	0	0	0	....	....	....	....	....	....	1978-79	1978-79
kalde, Jarrod	N.J., Ana., Cgy., S.J., Chi., Dal., Atl., Phi.	9	115	13	21	34	62	....	....	....	....	....	....	1990-91	2001-02
karda, Randy	St.L.	2	26	0	5	5	11	....	....	....	....	....	....	1989-90	1991-92
kilton, Raymie	Mtl.W.	1	1	0	0	0	0	....	....	....	....	....	....	1917-18	1917-18
kinner, Alf	Tor., Bos., Mtl.M., Pit.	4	71	26	10	36	87	2	0	1	1	9	1	1917-18	1925-26
kinner, Larry	Col.	4	47	10	12	22	8	2	0	0	0	0	....	1976-77	1979-80
kolney, Wade	Phi.	1	1	0	0	0	2	....	....	....	....	....	....	2005-06	2005-06
kopintsev, Andrei	T.B., Atl.	3	40	2	4	6	32	....	....	....	....	....	....	1998-99	2000-01
kov, Glen	Det., Chi., Mtl.	12	650	106	136	242	413	53	7	7	14	48	3	1949-50	1960-61
krbek, Pavel	Pit., Nsh.	3	12	0	0	0	8	....	....	....	....	....	....	1998-99	2001-02
kriko, Petri	Van., Bos., Wpg., S.J.	9	541	183	222	405	246	28	5	9	14	4	....	1984-85	1992-93
krlac, Rob	N.J.	1	8	1	0	1	22	....	....	....	....	....	....	2003-04	2003-04
krudland, Brian	Mtl., Cgy., Fla., NYR, Dal.	15	881	124	219	343	1107	164	15	46	61	323	2	1985-86	1999-00
aney, John	Wsh., Col., L.A., Phx., Nsh., Pit., Phi.	9	268	22	69	91	99	14	2	1	3	4	....	1993-94	2003-04
eaver, John	Chi.	2	13	1	0	1	6	....	....	....	....	....	....	1953-54	1956-57
egr, Jiri	Van., Edm., Pit., Atl., Det., Bos.	11	622	56	193	249	838	42	4	14	18	39	1	1992-93	2005-06
eigher, Louis	Que., Bos.	6	194	46	53	99	146	17	1	1	2	64	....	1979-80	1985-86
oan, Blake	Dal., CBJ, Cgy.	6	290	11	32	43	162	35	0	2	2	20	1	1998-99	2003-04
oan, Tod	Tor., Chi.	13	745	220	262	482	831	47	9	12	21	47	2	1947-48	1960-61
obodian, Peter	NYA	1	41	3	2	5	54	....	....	....	....	....	....	1940-41	1940-41
owinski, Ed	NYR	6	291	58	74	132	63	16	2	6	8	6	....	1947-48	1952-53
y, Darryl	Tor., Min., Van.	4	79	1	2	3	20	....	....	....	....	....	....	1965-66	1970-71
nail, Doug	Wpg., Min., Que., Ott.	13	845	210	249	459	602	42	9	2	11	49	....	1980-81	1992-93
nart, Alex	Mtl.	1	8	5	2	7	0	....	....	....	....	....	....	1942-43	1942-43
nedsmo, Dale	Tor.	1	4	0	0	0	0	....	....	....	....	....	....	1972-73	1972-73
nehlik, Richard	Buf., Atl., N.J.	10	644	49	146	195	415	88	1	14	15	40	1	1992-93	2002-03
nillie, Don	Bos.	1	12	2	2	4	4	....	....	....	....	....	....	1933-34	1933-34
nirnov, Alexei	Ana.	2	52	3	3	6	20	4	0	0	0	2	....	2002-03	2003-04
nith, Alex	Ott., Det., Bos., NYA	11	443	41	50	91	645	19	0	2	2	26	1	1924-25	1934-35
nith, Art	Tor., Ott.	4	144	15	10	25	249	4	1	1	2	8	....	1927-28	1930-31
nith, Barry	Bos., Col.	3	114	7	7	14	10	....	....	....	....	....	....	1975-76	1980-81
nith, Bobby	Min., Mtl.	15	1077	357	679	1036	917	184	64	96	160	245	1	1978-79	1992-93
nith, Brad	Van., Atl., Cgy., Det., Tor.	9	222	28	34	62	591	20	3	3	6	49	....	1978-79	1986-87
nith, Brandon	Bos., NYI	4	33	3	4	7	10	....	....	....	....	....	....	1998-99	2002-03
nith, Brian	Det.	3	61	2	8	10	12	5	0	0	0	0	....	1957-58	1960-61
nith, Brian	L.A., Min.	2	67	10	10	20	33	7	0	0	0	0	....	1967-68	1968-69
nith, Carl	Det.	1	7	1	1	2	2	....	....	....	....	....	....	1943-44	1943-44
nith, Clint	NYR, Chi.	11	483	161	236	397	24	42	10	14	24	2	1	1936-37	1946-47
nith, D.J.	Tor., Col.	3	45	1	1	2	67	....	....	....	....	....	....	1996-97	2002-03
nith, Dallas	Bos., NYR	16	890	55	252	307	959	86	3	29	32	128	2	1959-60	1977-78
nith, Dan	Col., Edm.	3	22	0	0	0	16	....	....	....	....	....	....	1998-99	2005-06
nith, Dennis	Wsh., L.A.	2	8	0	0	0	4	....	....	....	....	....	....	1989-90	1990-91
nith, Derek	Buf., Det.	8	335	78	116	194	60	30	9	14	23	13	....	1975-76	1982-83
nith, Derrick	Phi., Min., Dal.	10	537	82	92	174	373	82	14	11	25	79	....	1984-85	1993-94
nith, Des	Mtl.M., Mtl., Chi., Bos.	5	196	22	25	47	236	25	1	4	5	18	1	1937-38	1941-42
nith, Don	Mtl.	1	12	1	0	1	6	....	....	....	....	....	....	1919-20	1919-20
nith, Don	NYR	1	11	1	1	2	0	1	0	0	0	0	....	1949-50	1949-50
nith, Doug	L.A., Buf., Edm., Van., Pit.	9	535	115	138	253	624	18	4	2	6	21	....	1981-82	1989-90
nith, Floyd	Bos., NYR, Det., Tor., Buf.	13	616	129	178	307	207	48	12	11	23	16	....	1954-55	1971-72
nith, Geoff	Edm., Fla., NYR	10	462	18	73	91	282	13	0	1	1	8	1	1989-90	1998-99
nith, Glen	Chi.	1	2	0	0	0	0	....	....	....	....	....	....	1950-51	1950-51
nith, Glenn	Tor.	1	9	0	0	0	0	....	....	....	....	....	....	1921-22	1921-22
nith, Gord	Wsh., Wpg.	6	299	9	30	39	284	....	....	....	....	....	....	1974-75	1979-80
nith, Greg	Cal., Cle., Min., Det., Wsh.	13	829	56	232	288	1110	63	4	7	11	106	....	1975-76	1987-88
nith, Hooley	Ott., Mtl.M., Bos., NYA	17	715	200	225	425	1013	54	11	8	19	109	2	1924-25	1940-41
nith, Jason	N.J., Tor., Edm., Phi., Ott.	15	1008	41	128	169	1099	68	1	10	11	60	....	1993-94	2008-09
nith, Ken	Bos.	7	331	78	93	171	49	30	8	13	21	6	....	1944-45	1950-51
nith, Mark	S.J., Cgy.	7	377	23	47	70	457	24	4	0	4	21	....	2000-01	2007-08
nith, Nakina	Det.	1	10	1	2	3	0	....	....	....	....	....	....	1943-44	1943-44
nith, Nick	Fla.	1	15	0	0	0	0	....	....	....	....	....	....	2001-02	2001-02
nith, Randy	Min.	2	3	0	0	0	0	....	....	....	....	....	....	1985-86	1986-87
nith, Rick	Bos., Cal., St.L., Det., Wsh.	11	687	52	167	219	560	78	3	23	26	73	1	1968-69	1980-81
nith, Rodger	Pit., Phi.	6	210	20	4	24	172	4	3	0	3	0	....	1925-26	1930-31
nith, Ron	NYI	1	11	1	1	2	14	....	....	....	....	....	....	1972-73	1972-73
nith, Sid	Tor.	12	601	186	183	369	94	44	17	10	27	2	3	1946-47	1957-58
nith, Stan	NYR	2	9	2	1	3	0	1	0	0	0	0	1	1939-40	1940-41
nith, Steve	Phi., Buf.	6	18	0	1	1	15	....	....	....	....	....	....	1981-82	1988-89
nith, Steve	Edm., Chi., Cgy.	16	804	72	303	375	2139	134	11	41	52	288	3	1984-85	2000-01
nith, Stu	Mtl.	2	4	2	2	4	2	1	0	0	0	0	....	1940-41	1941-42
nith, Stu	Hfd.	4	77	2	10	12	95	....	....	....	....	....	....	1979-80	1982-83
nith, Tommy	Que.	1	10	0	1	1	11	....	....	....	....	....	....	1919-20	1919-20
nith, Vern	NYI	1	1	0	0	0	0	....	....	....	....	....	....	1984-85	1984-85
nith, Wayne	Chi.	1	2	1	1	2	2	1	0	0	0	0	....	1966-67	1966-67
nolinski, Bryan	Bos., Pit., NYI, L.A., Ott., Chi., Van., Mtl.	15	1056	274	377	651	606	123	23	29	52	60	....	1992-93	2007-08
nrek, Peter	St.L., NYR	2	28	2	4	6	18	....	....	....	....	....	....	2000-01	2001-02
nrke, John	St.L., Que.	3	103	11	17	28	33	....	....	....	....	....	....	1977-78	1979-80
nrke, Stan	Mtl.	2	9	0	3	3	0	....	....	....	....	....	....	1956-57	1957-58
nyl, Stan	Van.	13	896	262	411	673	1556	41	16	17	33	64	....	1978-79	1990-91
nylie, Rod	Tor., Ott.	6	74	4	2	6	12	4	0	0	0	2	1	1920-21	1925-26
nyth, Brad	Fla., L.A., NYR, Nsh., Ott.	6	88	15	13	28	109	....	....	....	....	....	....	1995-96	2002-03
nyth, Greg	Phi., Que., Cgy., Fla., Tor., Chi.	10	229	4	16	20	783	12	0	0	0	40	....	1986-87	1996-97

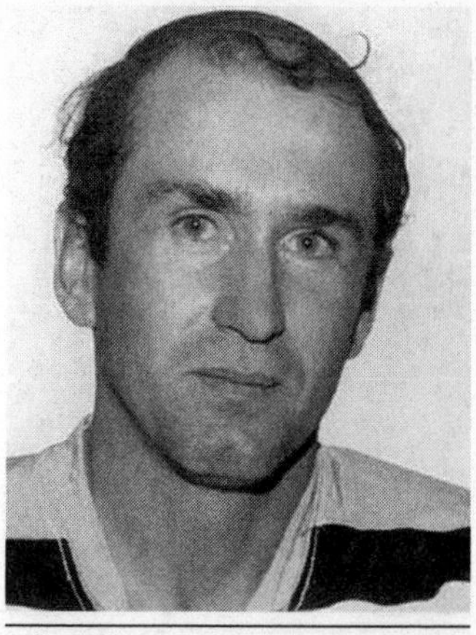

Dallas Smith

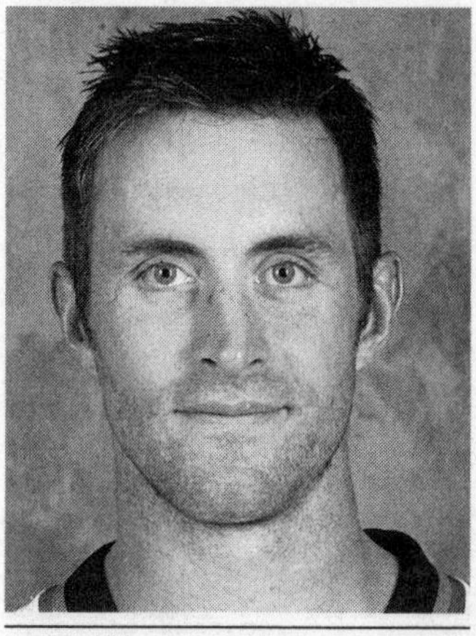

Jason Smith

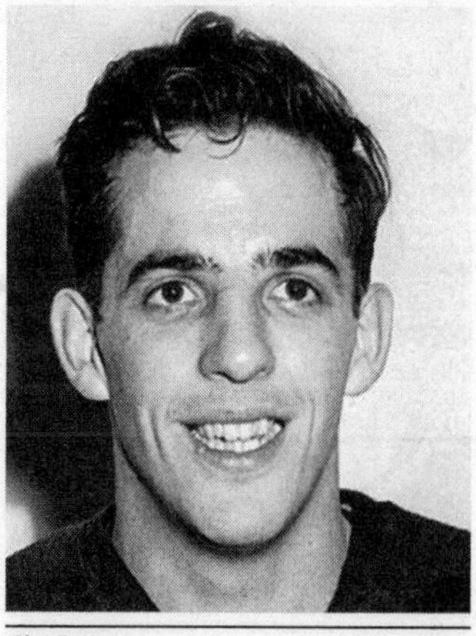

Glen Sonmor

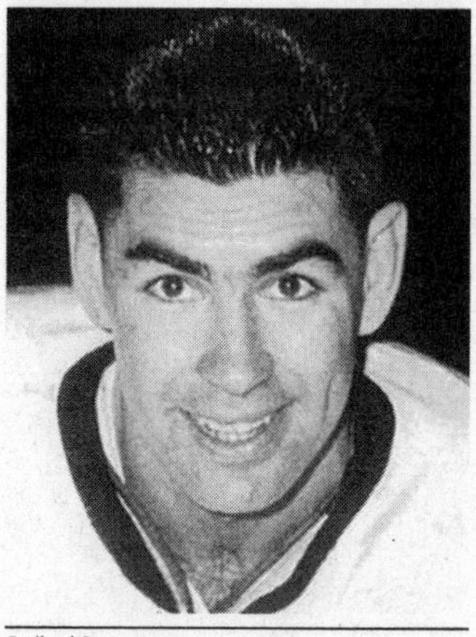

Dollard St. Laurent

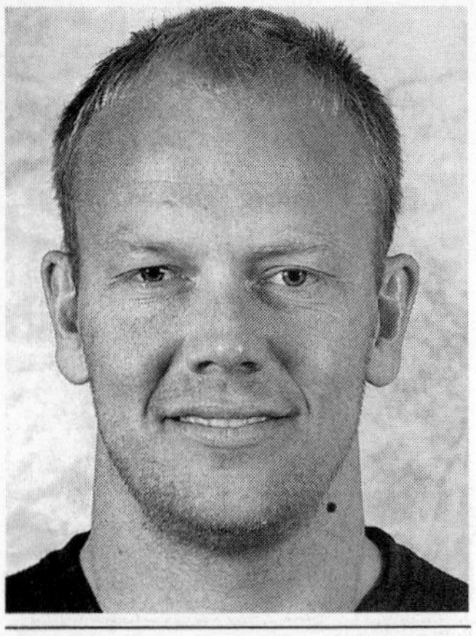

Mats Sundin

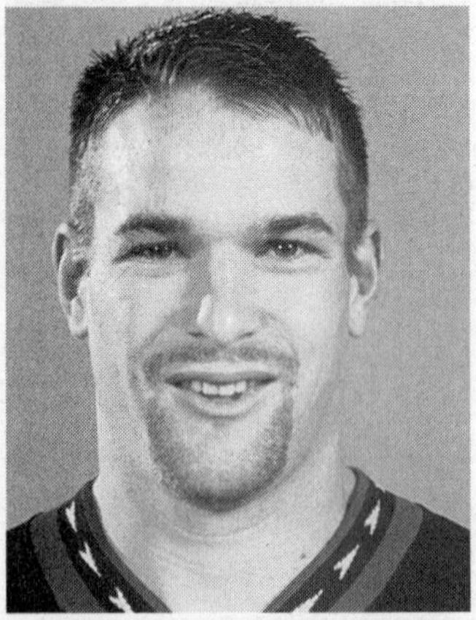

Dean Sylvester

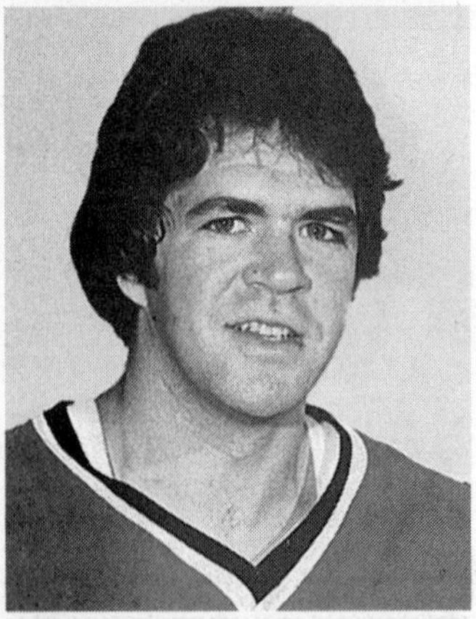

Dale Tallon

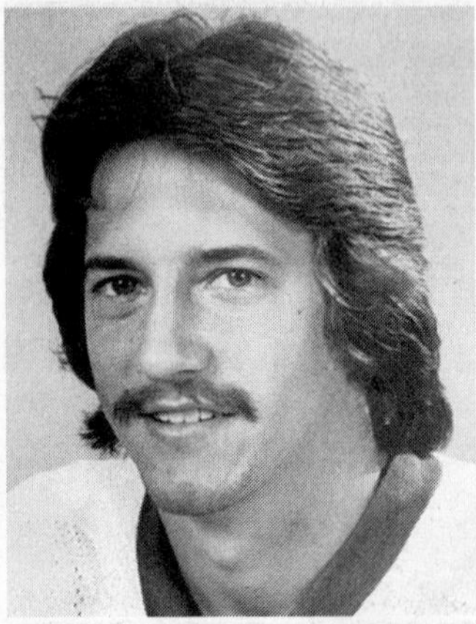

Steve Tambellini

Name	NHL Teams	NHL Seasons	Regular Schedule					Playoffs					NHL Cup Wins	First NHL Season	Last NHL Season
			GP	G	A	TP	PIM	GP	G	A	TP	PIM			
Smyth, Kevin	Hfd.	3	58	6	8	14	31	....	....	....	....	....	....	1993-94	1995-9
Snell, Chris	Tor., L.A.	2	34	2	7	9	24	....	....	....	....	....	....	1993-94	1994-9
Snell, Ron	Pit.	2	7	3	2	5	6	....	....	....	....	....	....	1968-69	1969-7
Snell, Ted	Pit., K.C., Det.	2	104	7	18	25	22	....	....	....	....	....	....	1973-74	1974-7
Snepsts, Harold	Van., Min., Det., St.L.	17	1033	38	195	233	2009	93	1	14	15	231	....	1974-75	1990-9
Snow, Sandy	Det.	1	3	0	0	0	2	....	....	....	....	....	....	1968-69	1968-6
Snuggerud, Dave	Buf., S.J., Phi.	4	265	30	54	84	127	12	1	3	4	6	....	1989-90	1992-9
• Snyder, Dan	Atl.	3	49	11	5	16	64	....	....	....	....	....	....	2000-01	2002-0
Sobchuk, Dennis	Det., Que.	2	35	5	6	11	2	....	....	....	....	....	....	1979-80	1982-8
Sobchuk, Gene	Van.	1	1	0	0	0	0	....	....	....	....	....	....	1973-74	1973-7
Solheim, Ken	Chi., Min., Det., Edm.	5	135	19	20	39	34	3	1	1	2	2	....	1980-81	1985-8
Solinger, Bob	Tor., Det.	5	99	10	11	21	19	....	....	....	....	....	....	1951-52	1959-6
• Somers, Art	Chi., NYR	6	222	33	56	89	189	30	1	5	6	20	1	1929-30	1934-3
‡ Somik, Radovan	Phi.	2	113	12	20	32	27	15	2	2	4	10	....	2002-03	2003-0
Sommer, Roy	Edm.	1	3	1	0	1	7	....	....	....	....	....	....	1980-81	1980-8
Songin, Tom	Bos.	3	43	5	5	10	22	....	....	....	....	....	....	1978-79	1980-8
Sonmor, Glen	NYR	2	28	2	0	2	21	....	....	....	....	....	....	1953-54	1954-5
‡ Sonnenberg, Martin	Pit., Cgy.	3	63	2	3	5	21	7	0	0	0	0	....	1998-99	2003-0
Sorochan, Lee	Cgy.	2	3	0	0	0	0	....	....	....	....	....	....	1998-99	1999-0
• Sorrell, John	Det., NYA	11	490	127	119	246	100	42	12	15	27	10	2	1930-31	1940-4
Spanhel, Martin	CBJ	2	10	2	0	2	4	....	....	....	....	....	....	2000-01	2001-0
• Sparrow, Emory	Bos.	1	8	0	0	0	4	....	....	....	....	....	....	1924-25	1924-2
Speck, Fred	Det., Van.	3	28	1	2	3	2	....	....	....	....	....	....	1968-69	1971-7
• Speer, Bill	Pit., Bos.	4	130	5	20	25	79	8	1	0	1	4	1	1967-68	1970-7
Speers, Ted	Det.	1	4	1	1	2	0	....	....	....	....	....	....	1985-86	1985-8
• Spence, Gordon	Tor.	1	3	0	0	0	0	....	....	....	....	....	....	1925-26	1925-2
• Spencer, Brian	Tor., NYI, Buf., Pit.	10	553	80	143	223	634	37	1	5	6	29	....	1969-70	1978-7
• Spencer, Irv	NYR, Bos., Det.	8	230	12	38	50	127	16	0	0	0	8	....	1959-60	1967-6
• Speyer, Chris	Tor., NYA	3	14	0	0	0	0	....	....	....	....	....	....	1923-24	1933-3
Spring, Corey	T.B.	2	16	1	1	2	12	....	....	....	....	....	....	1997-98	1998-9
Spring, Don	Wpg.	4	259	1	54	55	80	6	0	0	0	10	....	1980-81	1983-8
Spring, Frank	Bos., St.L., Cal., Cle.	5	61	14	20	34	12	....	....	....	....	....	....	1969-70	1976-7
• Spring, Jesse	Ham., Pit., Tor., NYA	6	133	11	4	15	74	2	0	2	2	2	....	1923-24	1929-3
Spruce, Andy	Van., Col.	3	172	31	42	73	111	2	0	2	2	0	....	1976-77	1978-7
Srsen, Tomas	Edm.	1	2	0	0	0	0	....	....	....	....	....	....	1990-91	1990-9
St. Amour, Martin	Ott.	1	1	0	0	0	2	....	....	....	....	....	....	1992-93	1992-9
‡ St. Jacques, Bruno	Phi., Car., Ana.	4	67	3	7	10	47	....	....	....	....	....	....	2001-02	2005-0
St. Laurent, Andre	NYI, Det., L.A., Pit.	11	644	129	187	316	749	59	8	12	20	48	....	1973-74	1983-8
St. Laurent, Dollard	Mtl., Chi.	12	652	29	133	162	496	92	2	22	24	87	5	1950-51	1961-6
St. Marseille, Frank	St.L., L.A.	10	707	140	285	425	242	88	20	25	45	18	....	1967-68	1976-7
St. Sauveur, Claude	Atl.	1	79	24	24	48	23	2	0	0	0	0	....	1975-76	1975-7
Stackhouse, Ron	Cal., Det., Pit.	12	889	87	372	459	824	32	5	8	13	38	....	1970-71	1981-8
• Stackhouse, Ted	Tor.	1	13	0	0	0	2	1	0	0	0	0	1	1921-22	1921-2
• Stahan, Butch	Mtl.	1	....	....	....	....	....	3	0	1	1	2	....	1944-45	1944-4
Stajduhar, Nick	Edm.	1	2	0	0	0	4	....	....	....	....	....	....	1995-96	1995-9
Staley, Al	NYR	1	1	0	1	1	0	....	....	....	....	....	....	1948-49	1948-4
Stamler, Lorne	L.A., Tor., Wpg.	4	116	14	11	25	16	....	....	....	....	....	....	1976-77	1979-8
Standing, George	Min.	1	2	0	0	0	0	....	....	....	....	....	....	1967-68	1967-6
Stanfield, Fred	Chi., Bos., Min., Buf.	14	914	211	405	616	134	106	21	35	56	10	2	1964-65	1977-7
Stanfield, Jack	Chi.	1	....	....	....	....	....	1	0	0	0	0	....	1965-66	1965-6
• Stanfield, Jim	L.A.	3	7	0	1	1	0	....	....	....	....	....	....	1969-70	1971-7
Stankiewicz, Ed	Det.	2	6	0	0	0	2	....	....	....	....	....	....	1953-54	1955-5
Stankiewicz, Myron	St.L., Phi.	1	35	0	7	7	36	1	0	0	0	0	....	1968-69	1968-6
Stanley, Allan	NYR, Chi., Bos., Tor., Phi.	21	1244	100	333	433	792	109	7	36	43	80	4	1948-49	1968-6
• Stanley, Barney	Chi.	1	1	0	0	0	0	....	....	....	....	....	....	1927-28	1927-2
Stanley, Daryl	Phi., Van.	6	189	8	17	25	408	17	0	0	0	30	....	1983-84	1989-9
Stanowski, Wally	Tor., NYR	10	428	23	88	111	160	60	3	14	17	13	4	1939-40	1950-5
Stanton, Paul	Pit., Bos., NYI	5	295	14	49	63	262	44	2	10	12	66	2	1990-91	1994-9
Stapleton, Brian	Wsh.	1	1	0	0	0	0	....	....	....	....	....	....	1975-76	1975-7
Stapleton, Mike	Chi., Pit., Edm., Wpg., Phx., Atl., NYI, Van.	14	697	71	111	182	342	34	1	0	1	39	....	1986-87	2000-0
Stapleton, Pat	Bos., Chi.	10	635	43	294	337	353	65	10	39	49	38	....	1961-62	1972-7
Starikov, Sergei	N.J.	1	16	0	1	1	8	....	....	....	....	....	....	1989-90	1989-9
• Starr, Harold	Ott., Mtl.M., Mtl., NYR	7	205	6	5	11	186	15	1	0	1	4	....	1929-30	1935-3
• Starr, Wilf	NYA, Det.	4	87	8	6	14	25	7	0	2	2	2	....	1932-33	1935-3
Stasiuk, Vic	Chi., Det., Bos.	14	745	183	254	437	669	69	16	18	34	40	2	1949-50	1962-6
Stastny, Anton	Que.	9	650	252	384	636	150	66	20	32	52	31	....	1980-81	1988-8
Stastny, Marian	Que., Tor.	5	322	121	173	294	110	32	5	17	22	7	....	1981-82	1985-8
Stastny, Peter	Que., N.J., St.L.	15	977	450	789	1239	824	93	33	72	105	123	....	1980-81	1994-9
Staszak, Ray	Det.	1	4	0	1	1	7	....	....	....	....	....	....	1985-86	1985-8
• Steele, Frank	Det.	1	1	0	0	0	0	....	....	....	....	....	....	1930-31	1930-3
Steen, Anders	Wpg.	1	42	5	11	16	22	....	....	....	....	....	....	1980-81	1980-8
Steen, Thomas	Wpg.	14	950	264	553	817	753	56	12	32	44	62	....	1981-82	1994-9
‡ Stefan, Patrik	Atl., Dal.	7	455	64	124	188	158	....	....	....	....	....	....	1999-00	2006-0
Stefaniw, Morris	Atl.	1	13	1	1	2	2	....	....	....	....	....	....	1972-73	1972-7
Stefanski, Bud	NYR	1	1	0	0	0	0	....	....	....	....	....	....	1977-78	1977-7
Stemkowski, Pete	Tor., Det., NYR, L.A.	15	967	206	349	555	866	83	25	29	54	136	1	1963-64	1977-7
Stenlund, Vern	Cle.	1	4	0	0	0	0	....	....	....	....	....	....	1976-77	1976-7
‡ Stephens, Charlie	Col.	2	8	0	2	2	4	....	....	....	....	....	....	2002-03	2003-0
Stephenson, Bob	Hfd., Tor.	1	18	2	3	5	4	....	....	....	....	....	....	1979-80	1979-8
‡ Stephenson, Shay	L.A.	1	2	0	0	0	0	....	....	....	....	....	....	2006-07	2006-0
Stern, Ron	Van., Cgy., S.J.	12	638	75	86	161	2077	43	7	7	14	119	....	1987-88	1999-0
Sterner, Ulf	NYR	1	4	0	0	0	0	....	....	....	....	....	....	1964-65	1964-6
Stevens, John	Phi., Hfd.	5	53	0	10	10	48	....	....	....	....	....	....	1986-87	1993-9
Stevens, Kevin	Pit., Bos., L.A., NYR, Phi.	15	874	329	397	726	1470	103	46	60	106	170	2	1987-88	2001-0
Stevens, Mike	Van., Bos., NYI, Tor.	4	23	1	4	5	29	....	....	....	....	....	....	1984-85	1989-9
• Stevens, Phil	Mtl.W., Mtl., Bos.	3	25	1	0	1	3	....	....	....	....	....	....	1917-18	1925-2
Stevens, Scott	Wsh., St.L., N.J.	22	1635	196	712	908	2785	233	26	92	118	402	3	1982-83	2003-0
‡ Stevenson, Jeremy	Ana., Nsh., Min., Dal.	9	207	19	19	38	451	21	0	5	5	20	....	1995-96	2005-0
Stevenson, Shayne	Bos., T.B.	3	27	0	2	2	35	....	....	....	....	....	....	1990-91	1992-9
Stevenson, Turner	Mtl., N.J., Phi.	13	644	75	115	190	969	67	6	12	18	66	1	1992-93	2005-0
Stewart, Allan	N.J., Bos.	6	64	6	4	10	243	....	....	....	....	....	....	1985-86	1991-9
Stewart, Bill	Buf., St.L., Tor., Min.	8	261	7	64	71	424	13	1	3	4	11	....	1977-78	1985-8
Stewart, Blair	Det., Wsh., Que.	7	229	34	44	78	326	....	....	....	....	....	....	1973-74	1979-8
Stewart, Bob	Bos., Cal., Cle., St.L., Pit.	9	575	27	101	128	809	5	1	1	2	2	....	1971-72	1979-8
Stewart, Cam	Bos., Fla., Min.	7	202	16	23	39	120	13	1	3	4	9	....	1993-94	2001-0
Stewart, Gaye	Tor., Chi., Det., NYR, Mtl.	11	502	185	159	344	274	25	2	9	11	16	2	1941-42	1953-5
• Stewart, Jack	Det., Chi.	12	565	31	84	115	765	80	5	14	19	143	2	1938-39	1951-5
Stewart, John	Pit., Atl., Cal.	5	258	58	60	118	158	4	0	0	0	10	....	1970-71	1974-7
Stewart, John	Que.	1	2	0	0	0	0	....	....	....	....	....	....	1979-80	1979-8
Stewart, Ken	Chi.	1	6	1	1	2	2	....	....	....	....	....	....	1941-42	1941-4
• Stewart, Nels	Mtl.M., Bos., NYA	15	650	324	191	515	953	50	9	12	21	47	1	1925-26	1939-4
Stewart, Paul	Que.	1	21	2	0	2	74	....	....	....	....	....	....	1979-80	1979-8
Stewart, Ralph	Van., NYI	7	252	57	73	130	28	19	4	4	8	2	....	1970-71	1977-7
Stewart, Ron	Tor., Bos., St.L., NYR, Van., NYI	21	1353	276	253	529	560	119	14	21	35	60	3	1952-53	1972-7
Stewart, Ryan	Wpg.	1	3	1	0	1	0	....	....	....	....	....	....	1985-86	1985-8
Stienburg, Trevor	Que.	4	71	8	4	12	161	1	0	0	0	0	....	1985-86	1988-8
Stiles, Tony	Cgy.	1	30	2	7	9	20	....	....	....	....	....	....	1983-84	1983-8
Stock, P.J.	NYR, Mtl., Phi., Bos.	7	235	5	21	26	523	8	1	0	1	19	....	1997-98	2003-0
Stoddard, Jack	NYR	2	80	16	15	31	31	....	....	....	....	....	....	1951-52	1952-5
Stojanov, Alek	Van., Pit.	3	107	2	5	7	222	14	0	0	0	21	....	1994-95	1996-9
Stoltz, Roland	Wsh.	1	14	2	2	4	14	....	....	....	....	....	....	1981-82	1981-8
Stone, Steve	Van.	1	2	0	0	0	0	....	....	....	....	....	....	1973-74	1973-7
Storm, Jim	Hfd., Dal.	3	84	7	15	22	44	....	....	....	....	....	....	1993-94	1995-9
Stothers, Mike	Phi., Tor.	4	30	0	2	2	65	5	0	0	0	11	....	1984-85	1987-8
Stoughton, Blaine	Pit., Tor., Hfd., NYR	8	526	258	191	449	204	8	4	2	6	2	....	1973-74	1983-8
Stoyanovich, Steve	Hfd.	1	23	3	5	8	11	....	....	....	....	....	....	1983-84	1983-8
• Strain, Neil	NYR	1	52	11	13	24	12	....	....	....	....	....	....	1952-53	1952-5
‡ Straka, Martin	Pit., Ott., NYI, Fla., L.A., NYR	15	954	257	460	717	360	106	26	44	70	52	....	1992-93	2007-0
Strate, Gord	Det.	3	61	0	0	0	34	....	....	....	....	....	....	1956-57	1958-5
Stratton, Art	NYR, Det., Chi., Pit., Phi.	4	95	18	33	51	24	5	0	0	0	0	....	1959-60	1967-6
‡ Strbak, Martin	L.A., Pit.	1	49	5	11	16	46	....	....	....	....	....	....	2003-04	2003-0
• Strobel, Art	NYR	1	7	0	0	0	0	....	....	....	....	....	....	1943-44	1943-4
Strong, Ken	Tor.	3	15	2	2	4	6	....	....	....	....	....	....	1982-83	1984-8
Stroshein, Garret	Wsh.	1	3	0	0	0	14	....	....	....	....	....	....	2003-04	2003-0
Struch, David	Cgy.	1	4	0	0	0	4	....	....	....	....	....	....	1993-94	1993-9

ame	NHL Teams	NHL Seasons	Regular Schedule GP	G	A	TP	PIM	Playoffs GP	G	A	TP	PIM	NHL Cup Wins	First NHL Season	Last NHL Season
ueby, Todd	Edm.	3	5	0	1	1	2	....	....	....	....	....	....	1981-82	1983-84
art, Billy	Tor., Bos.	7	195	30	20	50	151	12	1	1	2	6	1	1920-21	1926-27
art, Mike	St.L.	2	3	0	0	0	0	....	....	....	....	....	....	2003-04	2005-06
mpel, Jozef	Bos., L.A., Fla.	16	957	196	481	677	245	55	6	24	30	24	....	1991-92	2007-08
mpf, Bob	St.L., Pit.	1	10	1	1	2	20	....	....	....	....	....	....	1974-75	1974-75
rgeon, Peter	Col.	2	6	0	1	1	2	....	....	....	....	....	....	1979-80	1980-81
tzel, Mike	Phx.	1	9	0	0	0	0	....	....	....	....	....	....	2003-04	2003-04
chy, Radoslav	Phx., CBJ	6	451	13	58	71	104	10	1	1	2	0	....	1999-00	2005-06
globov, Alexander	N.J., Tor.	3	18	1	0	1	4	....	....	....	....	....	....	2003-04	2006-07
ikkanen, Kai	Buf.	2	2	0	0	0	0	....	....	....	....	....	....	1981-82	1982-83
lliman, Doug	NYR, Hfd., N.J., Phi.	11	631	160	168	328	175	16	1	3	4	2	....	1979-80	1989-90
llivan, Barry	Det.	1	1	0	0	0	0	....	....	....	....	....	....	1947-48	1947-48
llivan, Bob	Hfd.	1	62	18	19	37	18	....	....	....	....	....	....	1982-83	1982-83
llivan, Brian	N.J.	1	2	0	1	1	0	....	....	....	....	....	....	1992-93	1992-93
llivan, Frank	Tor., Chi.	4	8	0	0	0	2	....	....	....	....	....	....	1949-50	1955-56
llivan, Mike	S.J., Cgy., Bos., Phx.	11	709	54	82	136	203	34	4	8	12	14	....	1991-92	2001-02
llivan, Peter	Wpg.	2	126	28	54	82	40	....	....	....	....	....	....	1979-80	1980-81
llivan, Red	Bos., Chi., NYR	11	557	107	239	346	441	18	1	2	3	6	....	1949-50	1960-61
mmanen, Raimo	Edm., Van.	5	151	36	40	76	35	10	2	5	7	0	....	1983-84	1987-88
mmerhill, Bill	Mtl., Bro.	4	72	14	17	31	70	3	0	0	0	2	....	1937-38	1941-42
ndblad, Niklas	Cgy.	1	2	0	0	0	0	....	....	....	....	....	....	1995-96	1995-96
ndin, Mats	Que., Tor., Van.	18	1346	564	785	1349	1093	91	38	44	82	74	....	1990-91	2008-09
ndin, Ronnie	NYR	1	1	0	0	0	0	....	....	....	....	....	....	1997-98	1997-98
ndstrom, Niklas	NYR, S.J., Mtl.	10	750	117	232	349	256	59	6	22	28	22	....	1995-96	2005-06
ndstrom, Patrik	Van., N.J.	10	679	219	369	588	349	37	9	17	26	25	....	1982-83	1991-92
ndstrom, Peter	NYR, Wsh., N.J.	6	338	61	83	144	120	23	3	3	6	8	....	1983-84	1989-90
omi, Al	Chi.	1	5	0	0	0	0	....	....	....	....	....	....	1936-37	1936-37
rma, Damian	Car.	2	2	1	1	2	0	....	....	....	....	....	....	2002-03	2003-04
rovy, Tomas	Pit.	3	126	27	32	59	71	....	....	....	....	....	....	2002-03	2005-06
shinsky, Maxim	Min.	1	30	7	4	11	29	....	....	....	....	....	....	2000-01	2000-01
ter, Gary	Cgy., Chi., S.J.	17	1145	203	641	844	1349	108	17	56	73	120	1	1985-86	2001-02
therland, Bill	Mtl., Phi., Tor., St.L., Det.	6	250	70	58	128	99	14	2	4	6	0	....	1962-63	1971-72
therland, Max	Bos.	1	2	0	0	0	0	....	....	....	....	....	....	1931-32	1931-32
tter, Brent	NYI, Chi.	18	1111	363	466	829	1054	144	30	44	74	164	2	1980-81	1997-98
tter, Brian	St.L.	12	779	303	333	636	1786	65	21	21	42	249	....	1976-77	1987-88
tter, Darryl	Chi.	8	406	161	118	279	288	51	24	19	43	26	....	1979-80	1986-87
tter, Duane	NYI, Chi.	11	731	139	203	342	1333	161	26	32	58	405	4	1979-80	1989-90
tter, Rich	Pit., Phi., Van., St.L., Chi., T.B., Tor.	13	874	149	166	315	1411	78	13	5	18	133	....	1982-83	1994-95
tter, Ron	Phi., St.L., Que., NYI, Bos., S.J., Cgy.	19	1093	205	329	534	1352	104	8	32	40	193	....	1982-83	2000-01
tton, Ken	Buf., Edm., St.L., N.J., S.J., NYI	11	388	23	80	103	338	32	3	4	7	29	1	1990-91	2001-02
zor, Mark	Phi., Col.	2	64	4	16	20	60	....	....	....	....	....	....	1976-77	1977-78
artvadet, Per	Atl.	4	247	17	34	51	58	....	....	....	....	....	....	1999-00	2002-03
ehla, Robert	Fla., Tor.	9	655	68	267	335	649	38	1	14	15	42	....	1994-95	2002-03
ejkovsky, Jaroslav	Wsh., T.B.	4	113	23	19	42	56	1	0	0	0	2	....	1996-97	1999-00
ensson, Leif	Wsh.	2	121	6	40	46	49	....	....	....	....	....	....	1978-79	1979-80
ensson, Magnus	Fla.	2	46	4	14	18	31	....	....	....	....	....	....	1994-95	1995-96
tov, Alexander	T.B., CBJ	3	179	13	24	37	223	7	0	0	0	6	....	2002-03	2006-07
oboda, Jaroslav	Car., Dal.	4	134	12	17	29	62	25	1	4	5	30	....	2001-02	2005-06
oboda, Petr	Mtl., Buf., Phi., T.B.	17	1028	58	341	399	1605	127	4	45	49	140	1	1984-85	2000-01
oboda, Petr	Tor.	1	18	1	2	3	10	....	....	....	....	....	....	2000-01	2000-01
ain, Garry	Pit.	1	9	1	1	2	0	....	....	....	....	....	....	1968-69	1968-69
anson, Brian	Edm., Atl.	4	70	4	13	17	16	....	....	....	....	....	....	2000-01	2003-04
arbrick, George	Oak., Pit., Phi.	4	132	17	25	42	173	....	....	....	....	....	....	1967-68	1970-71
eeney, Bill	NYR	1	4	1	0	1	0	....	....	....	....	....	....	1959-60	1959-60
eeney, Bob	Bos., Buf., NYI, Cgy.	10	639	125	163	288	799	103	15	18	33	197	....	1986-87	1995-96
eeney, Don	Bos., Dal.	16	1115	52	221	273	681	108	9	10	19	81	....	1988-89	2003-04
eeney, Tim	Cgy., Bos., Ana., NYR	8	291	55	83	138	123	4	0	0	0	2	....	1990-91	1997-98
es, Bob	Tor.	1	2	0	0	0	0	....	....	....	....	....	....	1974-75	1974-75
es, Phil	L.A., Wpg.	10	456	79	85	164	519	26	0	3	3	29	....	1982-83	1991-92
ora, Michal	S.J., Chi., T.B., Phi.	7	267	15	54	69	185	7	0	1	1	0	....	1993-94	2000-01
ora, Petr	Nsh., Wsh.	2	12	2	2	4	6	....	....	....	....	....	....	1998-99	2005-06
vester, Dean	Buf., Atl.	3	96	21	16	37	32	4	0	0	0	0	....	1998-99	2000-01
ra, Joe	Oak.	2	90	10	15	25	30	7	2	3	5	2	....	1967-68	1968-69

t, John	Det.	1	15	0	2	2	4	....	....	....	....	....	....	1978-79	1978-79
glianetti, Peter	Wpg., Min., Pit., T.B.	11	451	18	74	92	1106	53	2	8	10	103	2	1984-85	1994-95
afous, Dean	Atl., Min., NYR	8	497	104	154	258	163	21	4	7	11	11	....	1974-75	1981-82
akoski, Ron	NYR	2	9	0	1	1	33	....	....	....	....	....	....	1986-87	1987-88
oot, Jean-Guy	Mtl., Min., Det., St.L., Buf.	17	1056	43	242	285	1006	150	4	26	30	142	7	1954-55	1970-71
on, Dale	Van., Chi., Pit.	10	642	98	238	336	568	33	2	10	12	45	....	1970-71	1979-80
nbellini, Steve	NYI, Col., N.J., Cgy., Van.	10	553	160	150	310	105	2	0	1	1	0	1	1978-79	1987-88
ner, Chris	Pit., NYR, Atl.	11	644	21	64	85	1183	37	0	8	8	52	....	1993-94	2003-04
abe, David	Car., Phx., Bos.	8	449	30	84	114	245	7	2	1	3	12	....	1999-00	2007-08
cill, Chris	Hfd., Det., Dal., S.J.	8	134	17	32	49	54	11	1	1	2	8	....	1990-91	1997-98
guay, Christian	Que.	1	2	0	0	0	0	....	....	....	....	....	....	1981-82	1981-82
nahill, Don	Van.	2	111	30	33	63	25	....	....	....	....	....	....	1972-73	1973-74
ti, Tony	Chi., Van., Pit., Buf.	11	697	287	273	560	661	30	3	12	15	27	....	1981-82	1991-92
per, Brad	Atl.	3	71	14	11	25	72	....	....	....	....	....	....	2000-01	2002-03
dif, Marc	Mtl., Que.	8	517	194	207	401	443	62	13	15	28	75	2	1969-70	1982-83
dif, Patrice	St.L., L.A.	2	65	7	11	18	78	....	....	....	....	....	....	1994-95	1995-96
nstrom, Dick	NYI, Pit., Edm., CBJ	5	306	35	105	140	254	17	0	2	2	12	....	2001-02	2007-08
arinov, Mikhail	Wsh., Que., Bos.	4	161	21	48	69	184	....	....	....	....	....	....	1990-91	1993-94
chell, Spence	NYR	1	1	0	0	0	0	....	....	....	....	....	....	1942-43	1942-43
icek, Petr	Fla.	1	3	0	0	0	0	....	....	....	....	....	....	2005-06	2005-06
lor, Billy	Tor., Det., Bos., NYR	7	323	87	180	267	120	33	6	18	24	13	1	1939-40	1947-48
lor, Billy	NYR	1	2	0	0	0	0	....	....	....	....	....	....	1964-65	1964-65
lor, Bob	Bos.	1	8	0	0	0	6	....	....	....	....	....	....	1929-30	1929-30
lor, Chris	NYI, Bos., Buf.	8	149	11	21	32	48	2	0	0	0	2	....	1994-95	2003-04
lor, Dave	L.A.	17	1111	431	638	1069	1589	92	26	33	59	145	....	1977-78	1993-94
lor, Harry	Tor., Chi.	3	66	5	10	15	30	1	0	0	0	0	1	1946-47	1951-52
lor, Mark	Phi., Pit., Wsh.	5	209	42	68	110	73	6	0	0	0	0	....	1981-82	1985-86
lor, Ralph	Chi., NYR	3	99	4	1	5	169	4	0	0	0	10	....	1927-28	1929-30
lor, Ted	NYR, Det., Min., Van.	6	166	23	35	58	181	....	....	....	....	....	....	1964-65	1971-72
lor, Tim	Det., Bos., NYR, T.B.	13	746	73	94	167	433	89	2	12	14	73	2	1993-94	2006-07
l, Jeff	Mtl.	1	6	0	1	1	0	....	....	....	....	....	....	1984-85	1984-85
l, Skip	Bos.	1	1	0	0	0	0	....	....	....	....	....	....	1954-55	1954-55
l, Vic	NYI	1	1	0	0	0	0	....	....	....	....	....	....	1973-74	1973-74
butt, Greg	Que., Pit.	2	26	0	3	3	35	....	....	....	....	....	....	1979-80	1983-84
krat, Petr	Ana., Nsh., Bos.	3	177	22	30	52	84	....	....	....	....	....	....	2000-01	2006-07
ute, Joey	Wsh.	1	1	0	0	0	0	....	....	....	....	....	....	2005-06	2005-06
per, Stephen	Chi.	1	1	0	0	0	0	....	....	....	....	....	....	1992-93	1992-93
oenche, Paul	Chi., Buf.	5	189	5	26	31	28	12	0	0	0	0	....	1967-68	1973-74
rion, Greg	L.A., Tor.	8	561	93	150	243	339	35	2	9	11	41	....	1980-81	1987-88
ry, Bill	Min.	1	5	0	0	0	0	....	....	....	....	....	....	1987-88	1987-88
tyshny, Dmitri	Phi.	1	62	2	8	10	30	1	0	0	0	0	....	1998-99	1998-99
sier, Orval	Mtl., Bos.	3	59	5	7	12	6	....	....	....	....	....	....	1954-55	1960-61
arenko, Joey	Fla., Ott., Car.	4	73	4	1	5	176	....	....	....	....	....	....	2000-01	2003-04
ikov, Alexei	Wsh., Van.	3	30	1	1	2	2	....	....	....	....	....	....	1998-99	2001-02
eberge, Greg	Wsh.	5	153	15	63	78	73	4	0	1	1	0	....	1979-80	1983-84
lin, Mats	Bos.	3	163	8	19	27	107	5	0	0	0	6	....	1984-85	1986-87
lven, Michael	Bos.	5	207	20	80	100	217	34	4	10	14	34	....	1985-86	1989-90
rien, Chris	Phi., Dal.	11	764	29	130	159	585	104	4	10	14	68	....	1994-95	2005-06
rrien, Gaston	Que.	3	22	0	8	8	12	9	0	1	1	4	....	1980-81	1982-83
baudeau, Gilles	Mtl., NYI, Tor.	5	119	25	37	62	40	8	3	3	6	2	....	1986-87	1990-91
beault, Lorrain	Det., Mtl.	2	5	0	2	2	2	....	....	....	....	....	....	1944-45	1945-46
ffault, Leo	Min.	1	....	....	....	....	....	5	0	0	0	0	....	1967-68	1967-68
mas, Cy	Chi., Tor.	1	14	2	2	4	12	....	....	....	....	....	....	1947-48	1947-48
mas, Reg	Que.	1	39	9	7	16	6	....	....	....	....	....	....	1979-80	1979-80
mas, Scott	Buf., L.A.	3	63	6	4	10	32	12	1	0	1	4	....	1992-93	2000-01
mas, Steve	Tor., Chi., NYI, N.J., Ana., Det.	20	1235	421	512	933	1306	174	54	53	107	187	....	1984-85	2003-04
mlinson, Dave	St.L., Bos., L.A.	5	42	1	3	4	50	9	3	1	4	4	....	1989-90	1994-95
mpson, Brent	L.A., Wpg., Phx.	6	121	1	10	11	352	4	0	0	0	4	....	1991-92	1996-97
mpson, Cliff	Bos.	2	13	0	1	1	2	....	....	....	....	....	....	1941-42	1948-49
mpson, Errol	Tor., Det., Pit.	10	599	208	185	393	184	34	7	5	12	11	....	1970-71	1980-81

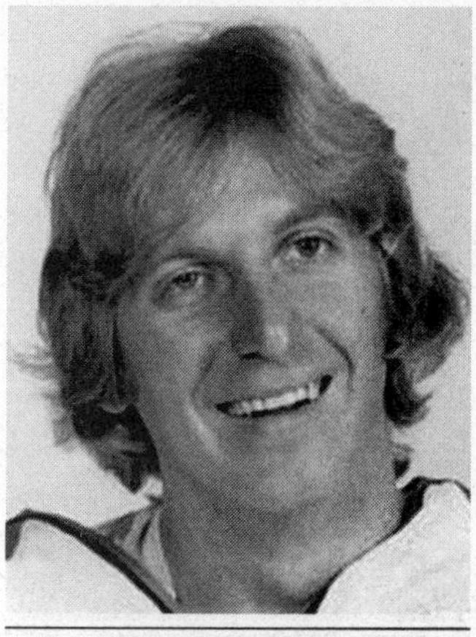

Vic Teal

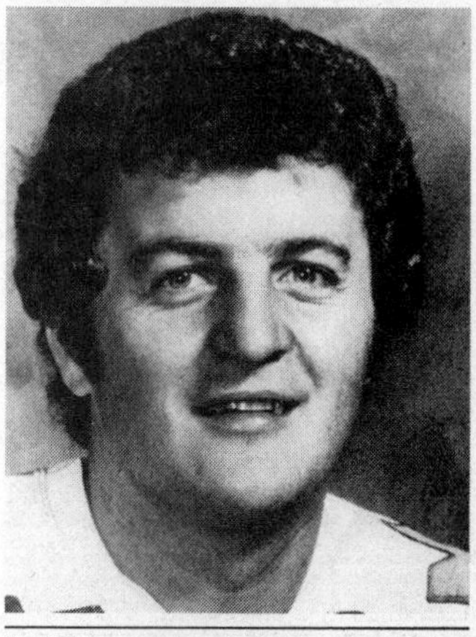

Errol Thompson

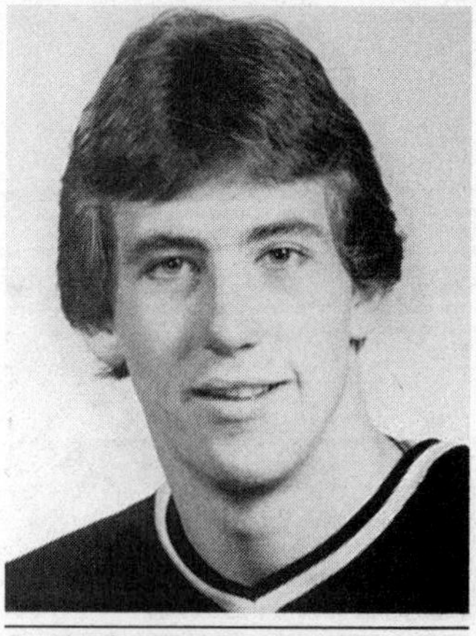

Tom Thornbury

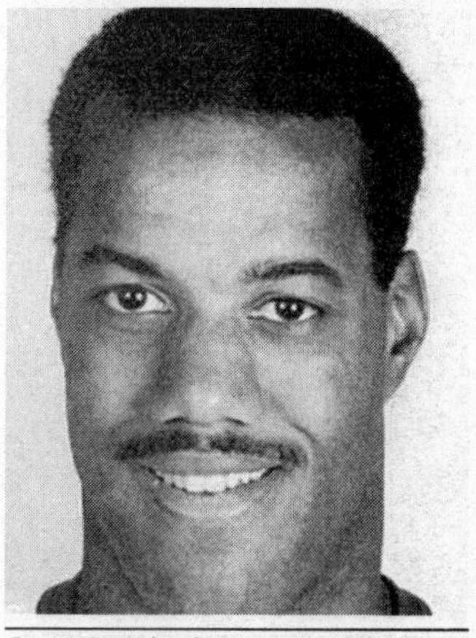

Graeme Townshend

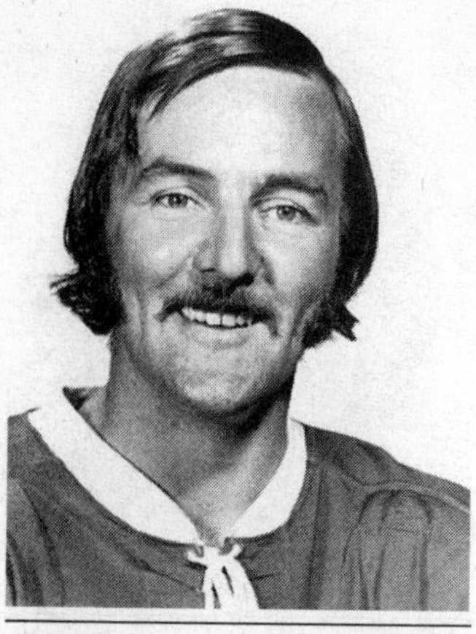
J.C. Tremblay

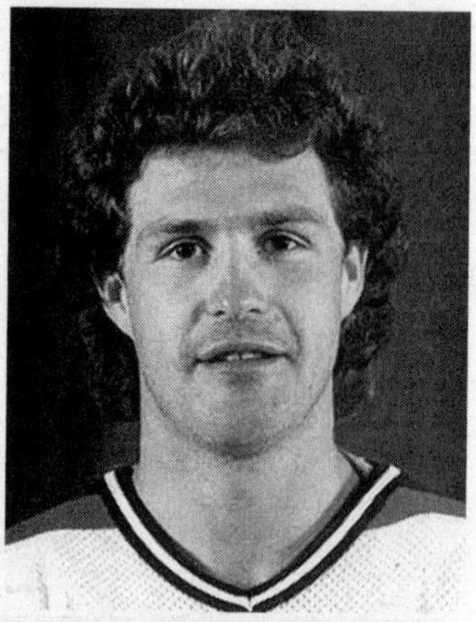
Perry Turnbull

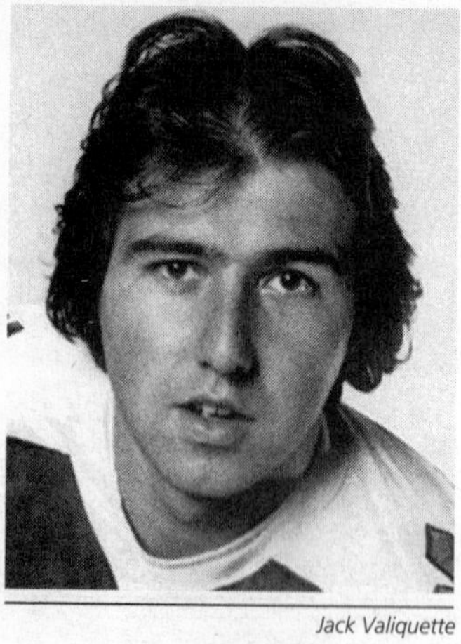
Jack Valiquette

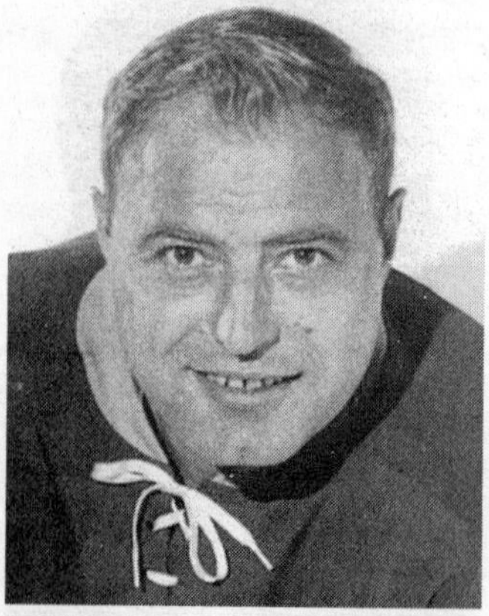
Moose Vasko

Name	NHL Teams	NHL Seasons	Regular Schedule GP	G	A	TP	PIM	Playoffs GP	G	A	TP	PIM	NHL Cup Wins	First NHL Season	Last NHL Season
• Thompson, Ken	Mtl.W.	1	1	0	0	0	0	....	....	....	....	....	....	1917-18	1917-
• Thompson, Paul	NYR, Chi.	13	582	153	179	332	336	48	11	11	22	54	3	1926-27	1938-
Thompson, Rocky	Cgy., Fla.	4	25	0	0	0	117	....	....	....	....	....	....	1997-98	2001-
• Thoms, Bill	Tor., Chi., Bos.	13	548	135	206	341	154	44	6	10	16	6	....	1932-33	1944-
• Thomson, Bill	Det.	2	9	2	2	4	0	2	0	0	0	0	....	1938-39	1943-
Thomson, Floyd	St.L.	8	411	56	97	153	341	10	0	2	2	6	....	1971-72	1979-
Thomson, Jim	Wsh., Hfd., N.J., L.A., Ott., Ana.	7	115	4	3	7	416	1	0	0	0	0	....	1986-87	1993-
• Thomson, Jimmy	Tor., Chi.	13	787	19	215	234	920	63	2	13	15	135	4	1945-46	1957-
• Thomson, Rhys	Mtl., Tor.	2	25	0	2	2	38	....	....	....	....	....	....	1939-40	1942-
Thornbury, Tom	Pit.	1	14	1	8	9	16	....	....	....	....	....	....	1983-84	1983-
Thornton, Scott	Tor., Edm., Mtl., Dal., S.J., L.A.	17	941	144	141	285	1459	79	13	14	27	82	....	1990-91	2007-
• Thorsteinson, Joe	NYA	1	4	0	0	0	0	....	....	....	....	....	....	1932-33	1932-
• Thurier, Fred	NYA, Bro., NYR	3	80	25	27	52	18	....	....	....	....	....	....	1940-41	1944-
Thurlby, Tom	Oak.	1	20	1	1	2	4	....	....	....	....	....	....	1967-68	1967-
Thyer, Mario	Min.	1	5	0	0	0	0	1	0	0	0	2	....	1989-90	1989-
Tibbetts, Billy	Pit., Phi., NYR	3	82	2	8	10	269	....	....	....	....	....	....	2000-01	2002-
Tichy, Milan	Chi., NYI	3	23	0	5	5	40	....	....	....	....	....	....	1992-93	1995-
Tidey, Alex	Buf., Edm.	3	9	0	0	0	8	2	0	0	0	0	....	1976-77	1979-
Tikkanen, Esa	Edm., NYR, St.L., N.J., Van., Fla., Wsh.	15	877	244	386	630	1077	186	72	60	132	275	5	1984-85	1998-
Tiley, Brad	Phx., Phi.	3	11	0	0	0	0	1	0	0	0	0	....	1997-98	2000-
Tilley, Tom	St.L.	4	174	4	38	42	89	14	1	3	4	19	....	1988-89	1993-
‡ Timander, Mattias	Bos., CBJ, NYI, Phi.	8	419	13	57	70	165	23	3	5	8	8	....	1996-97	2003-
• Timgren, Ray	Tor., Chi.	6	251	14	44	58	70	30	3	9	12	6	2	1948-49	1954-
‡ Timonen, Jussi	Phi.	1	14	0	4	4	6	....	....	....	....	....	....	2006-07	2006-
Tinordi, Mark	NYR, Min., Dal., Wsh.	12	663	52	148	200	1514	70	7	11	18	165	....	1987-88	1998-9
Tippett, Dave	Hfd., Wsh., Pit., Phi.	12	721	93	169	262	317	62	6	16	22	34	....	1983-84	1993-9
Titanic, Morris	Buf.	2	19	0	0	0	0	....	....	....	....	....	....	1974-75	1975-
Titov, German	Cgy., Pit., Edm., Ana.	9	624	157	220	377	311	34	11	12	23	18	....	1993-94	2001-0
‡ Tkaczuk, Daniel	Cgy.	1	19	4	7	11	14	....	....	....	....	....	....	2000-01	2000-0
Tkaczuk, Walt	NYR	14	945	227	451	678	556	93	19	32	51	119	....	1967-68	1980-8
Toal, Mike	Edm.	1	3	0	0	0	0	....	....	....	....	....	....	1979-80	1979-8
‡ Tobler, Ryan	T.B.	1	4	0	0	0	5	....	....	....	....	....	....	2001-02	2001-
Tocchet, Rick	Phi., Pit., L.A., Bos., Wsh., Phx.	18	1144	440	512	952	2972	145	52	60	112	471	1	1984-85	2001-
Todd, Kevin	N.J., Edm., Chi., L.A., Ana.	9	383	70	133	203	225	12	3	2	5	16	....	1988-89	1997-9
‡ Tolpeko, Denis	Phi.	1	26	1	5	6	24	....	....	....	....	....	....	2007-08	2007-0
Tomalty, Glenn	Wpg.	1	1	0	0	0	0	....	....	....	....	....	....	1979-80	1979-8
Tomlak, Mike	Hfd.	4	141	15	22	37	103	10	0	1	1	4	....	1989-90	1993-9
Tomlinson, Dave	Tor., Wpg., Fla.	4	42	1	3	4	28	....	....	....	....	....	....	1991-92	1994-9
Tomlinson, Kirk	Min.	1	1	0	0	0	0	....	....	....	....	....	....	1987-88	1987-8
‡ Toms, Jeff	T.B., Wsh., NYI, NYR, Pit., Fla.	8	236	22	33	55	59	1	0	0	0	0	....	1995-96	2002-0
• Tomson, Jack	NYA	3	15	1	1	2	0	2	0	0	0	0	....	1938-39	1940-4
Tonelli, John	NYI, Cgy., L.A., Chi., Que.	14	1028	325	511	836	911	172	40	75	115	200	4	1978-79	1991-9
Tookey, Tim	Wsh., Que., Pit., Phi., L.A.	7	106	22	36	58	71	10	1	3	4	2	....	1980-81	1988-8
Toomey, Sean	Min.	1	1	0	0	0	0	....	....	....	....	....	....	1986-87	1986-8
‡ Toporowski, Shayne	Tor.	1	3	0	0	0	7	....	....	....	....	....	....	1996-97	1996-9
Toppazzini, Jerry	Bos., Chi., Det.	12	783	163	244	407	436	40	13	9	22	13	....	1952-53	1963-6
• Toppazzini, Zellio	Bos., NYR, Chi.	5	123	21	22	43	49	2	0	0	0	0	....	1948-49	1956-5
Torgaev, Pavel	Cgy., T.B.	2	55	6	14	20	20	1	0	0	0	0	....	1995-96	1999-0
Torkki, Jari	Chi.	1	4	1	0	1	0	....	....	....	....	....	....	1988-89	1988-8
Tormanen, Antti	Ott.	1	50	7	8	15	28	....	....	....	....	....	....	1995-96	1995-9
• Touhey, Bill	Mtl.M., Ott., Bos.	7	280	65	40	105	107	2	1	0	1	0	....	1927-28	1933-3
• Toupin, Jacques	Chi.	1	8	1	2	3	0	4	0	0	0	0	....	1943-44	1943-4
• Townsend, Art	Chi.	1	5	0	0	0	0	....	....	....	....	....	....	1926-27	1926-2
Townshend, Graeme	Bos., NYI, Ott.	5	45	3	7	10	28	....	....	....	....	....	....	1989-90	1993-9
Trader, Larry	Det., St.L., Mtl.	4	91	5	13	18	74	3	0	0	0	0	....	1982-83	1987-8
• Trainor, Wes	NYR	1	17	1	2	3	6	....	....	....	....	....	....	1948-49	1948-4
• Trapp, Bob	Chi.	2	82	4	4	8	129	2	0	0	0	4	....	1926-27	1927-2
Trapp, Doug	Buf.	1	2	0	0	0	0	....	....	....	....	....	....	1986-87	1986-8
• Traub, Percy	Chi., Det.	3	130	3	3	6	217	4	0	0	0	6	....	1926-27	1928-2
‡ Traverse, Patrick	Ott., Ana., Bos., Mtl., Dal.	7	279	14	51	65	113	6	0	0	0	2	....	1995-96	2005-0
Trebil, Dan	Ana., Pit., St.L.	5	85	4	4	8	32	10	0	1	1	8	....	1996-97	2000-0
Tredway, Brock	L.A.	1	....	....	....	....	....	1	0	0	0	0	....	1981-82	1981-8
Tremblay, Brent	Wsh.	2	10	1	0	1	6	....	....	....	....	....	....	1978-79	1979-8
Tremblay, Gilles	Mtl.	9	509	168	162	330	161	48	9	14	23	4	4	1960-61	1968-6
• Tremblay, J.C.	Mtl.	13	794	57	306	363	204	108	14	51	65	58	5	1959-60	1971-7
• Tremblay, Marcel	Mtl.	1	10	0	2	2	0	....	....	....	....	....	....	1938-39	1938-3
Tremblay, Mario	Mtl.	12	852	258	326	584	1043	101	20	29	49	187	5	1974-75	1985-8
• Tremblay, Nils	Mtl.	2	3	0	1	1	0	2	0	0	0	0	....	1944-45	1945-4
Tremblay, Yannick	Tor., Atl., Van.	9	390	38	87	125	178	....	....	....	....	....	....	1996-97	2006-0
‡ Trepanier, Pascal	Col., Ana., Nsh.	6	229	12	22	34	252	2	0	0	0	0	....	1997-98	2002-0
Trimper, Tim	Chi., Wpg., Min.	6	190	30	36	66	153	2	0	0	0	2	....	1979-80	1984-8
‡ Tripp, John	NYR, L.A.	2	43	2	7	9	35	....	....	....	....	....	....	2002-03	2003-04
‡ Trnka, Pavel	Ana., Fla.	7	411	14	63	77	323	4	0	1	1	2	....	1997-98	2003-04
Trottier, Bryan	NYI, Pit.	18	1279	524	901	1425	912	221	71	113	184	277	6	1975-76	1993-94
• Trottier, Dave	Mtl.M., Det.	11	446	121	113	234	517	31	4	3	7	39	1	1928-29	1938-3
Trottier, Guy	NYR, Tor.	3	115	28	17	45	37	9	1	0	1	16	....	1968-69	1971-72
Trottier, Rocky	N.J.	2	38	6	4	10	2	....	....	....	....	....	....	1983-84	1984-8
‡ Trudel, Jean-Guy	Phx., Min.	3	5	0	0	0	4	....	....	....	....	....	....	1999-00	2002-0
• Trudel, Lou	Chi., Mtl.	8	306	49	69	118	122	24	1	3	4	4	2	1933-34	1940-41
• Trudell, Rene	NYR	3	129	24	28	52	72	5	0	0	0	2	....	1945-46	1947-48
Tselios, Nikos	Car.	1	2	0	0	0	6	....	....	....	....	....	....	2001-02	2001-02
‡ Tsulygin, Nikolai	Ana.	1	22	0	1	1	8	....	....	....	....	....	....	1996-97	1996-97
Tsygurov, Denis	Buf., L.A.	3	51	1	5	6	45	....	....	....	....	....	....	1993-94	1995-96
Tsyplakov, Vladimir	L.A., Buf.	6	331	69	101	170	90	18	1	2	3	16	....	1995-96	2000-01
Tucker, John	Buf., Wsh., NYI, T.B.	12	656	177	259	436	285	31	10	18	28	24	....	1983-84	1995-96
• Tudin, Connie	Mtl.	1	4	0	1	1	4	....	....	....	....	....	....	1941-42	1941-42
Tudor, Rob	Van., St.L.	3	28	4	4	8	19	3	0	0	0	0	....	1978-79	1982-83
Tuer, Allan	L.A., Min., Hfd.	4	57	1	1	2	208	....	....	....	....	....	....	1985-86	1989-90
‡ Tukonen, Lauri	L.A.	2	5	0	0	0	0	....	....	....	....	....	....	2006-07	2007-08
Tuomainen, Marko	Edm., L.A., NYI	4	79	9	9	18	84	1	0	0	0	0	....	1994-95	2001-02
Turcotte, Alfie	Mtl., Wpg., Wsh.	7	112	17	29	46	49	5	0	0	0	0	....	1983-84	1990-91
Turcotte, Darren	NYR, Hfd., Wpg., S.J., St.L., Nsh.	12	635	195	216	411	301	35	6	8	14	12	....	1988-89	1999-00
Turgeon, Pierre	Buf., NYI, Mtl., St.L., Dal., Col.	19	1294	515	812	1327	452	109	35	62	97	36	....	1987-88	2006-07
Turgeon, Sylvain	Hfd., N.J., Mtl., Ott.	12	669	269	226	495	691	36	4	7	11	22	....	1983-84	1994-95
Turlick, Gord	Bos.	1	2	0	0	0	2	....	....	....	....	....	....	1959-60	1959-60
Turnbull, Ian	Tor., L.A., Pit.	10	628	123	317	440	736	55	13	32	45	94	....	1973-74	1982-83
Turnbull, Perry	St.L., Mtl., Wpg.	9	608	188	163	351	1245	34	6	7	13	86	....	1979-80	1987-88
Turnbull, Randy	Cgy.	1	1	0	0	0	2	....	....	....	....	....	....	1981-82	1981-82
• Turner, Bob	Mtl., Chi.	8	478	19	51	70	307	68	1	4	5	44	5	1955-56	1962-63
Turner, Brad	NYI	1	3	0	0	0	0	....	....	....	....	....	....	1991-92	1991-92
Turner, Dean	NYR, Col., L.A.	4	35	1	0	1	59	....	....	....	....	....	....	1978-79	1982-83
• Tustin, Norm	NYR	1	18	2	4	6	0	....	....	....	....	....	....	1941-42	1941-42
• Tuten, Aud	Chi.	2	39	4	8	12	48	....	....	....	....	....	....	1941-42	1942-43
Tutt, Brian	Wsh.	1	7	1	0	1	2	....	....	....	....	....	....	1989-90	1989-90
Tuttle, Steve	St.L.	3	144	28	28	56	12	17	1	6	7	2	....	1988-89	1990-91
‡ Tuzzolino, Tony	Ana., NYR, Bos.	3	9	0	0	0	7	....	....	....	....	....	....	1997-98	2001-02
‡ Tverdovsky, Oleg	Ana., Wpg., Phx., N.J., Car., L.A.	11	713	77	240	317	291	45	0	14	14	6	2	1994-95	2006-07
‡ Tvrdon, Roman	Wsh.	1	9	0	1	1	2	....	....	....	....	....	....	2003-04	2003-04
Twist, Tony	St.L., Que.	10	445	10	18	28	1121	18	1	1	2	22	....	1989-90	1998-99

U V

Name	NHL Teams	NHL Seasons	Regular Schedule GP	G	A	TP	PIM	Playoffs GP	G	A	TP	PIM	NHL Cup Wins	First NHL Season	Last NHL Season
Ubriaco, Gene	Pit., Oak., Chi.	3	177	39	35	74	50	11	2	0	2	4	....	1967-68	1969-70
‡ Ulanov, Igor	Wpg., Wsh., Chi., T.B., Mtl., Edm., NYR, Fla.	14	739	27	135	162	1151	39	1	4	5	84	....	1991-92	2005-06
Ullman, Norm	Det., Tor.	20	1410	490	739	1229	712	106	30	53	83	67	....	1955-56	1974-75
‡ Ulmer, Jeff	NYR	1	21	3	0	3	8	....	....	....	....	....	....	2000-01	2000-01
‡ Ulmer, Layne	NYR	1	1	0	0	0	0	....	....	....	....	....	....	2003-04	2003-04
Unger, Garry	Tor., Det., St.L., Atl., L.A., Edm.	16	1105	413	391	804	1075	52	12	18	30	105	....	1967-68	1982-83
‡ Ustorf, Stefan	Wsh.	2	54	7	10	17	16	5	0	0	0	0	....	1995-96	1996-97
Vachon, Nick	NYI	1	1	0	0	0	0	....	....	....	....	....	....	1996-97	1996-97
Vadnais, Carol	Mtl., Oak., Cal., Bos., NYR, N.J.	17	1087	169	418	587	1813	106	10	40	50	185	2	1966-67	1982-83
‡ Vaic, Lubomir	Van.	2	9	1	1	2	2	....	....	....	....	....	....	1997-98	1999-00
Vail, Eric	Atl., Cgy., Det.	9	591	216	260	476	281	20	5	6	11	6	....	1973-74	1981-82
• Vail, Sparky	NYR	2	50	4	1	5	18	10	0	0	0	2	....	1928-29	1929-30
Vaive, Rick	Van., Tor., Chi., Buf.	13	876	441	347	788	1445	54	27	16	43	111	....	1979-80	1991-92

			Regular Schedule					Playoffs							
lame	NHL Teams	NHL Seasons	GP	G	A	TP	PIM	GP	G	A	TP	PIM	NHL Cup Wins	First NHL Season	Last NHL Season
alentine, Chris	Wsh.	3	105	43	52	95	127	2	0	0	0	4	....	1981-82	1983-84
alicevic, Rob	Nsh., L.A., Ana., Dal.	6	193	28	20	48	61	....	....	....	....	....	....	1998-99	2003-04
aliquette, Jack	Tor., Col.	7	350	84	134	218	79	23	3	6	9	4	....	1974-75	1980-81
alk, Garry	Van., Ana., Pit., Tor., Chi.	13	777	100	156	256	747	61	6	7	13	79	....	1990-91	2002-03
allis, Lindsay	Mtl.	1	1	0	0	0	0	....	....	....	....	....	....	1993-94	1993-94
an Allen, Shaun	Edm., Ana., Ott., Dal., Mtl.	13	794	84	185	269	481	61	1	7	8	45	....	1990-91	2003-04
an Boxmeer, John	Mtl., Col., Buf., Que.	11	588	84	274	358	465	38	5	15	20	37	....	1973-74	1983-84
an Dorp, Wayne	Edm., Pit., Chi., Que.	6	125	12	12	24	565	27	0	1	1	42	....	1986-87	1991-92
an Drunen, David	Ott.	1	1	0	0	0	0	....	....	....	....	....	....	1999-00	1999-00
an Impe, Darren	Ana., Bos., NYR, Fla., NYI, CBJ	9	411	25	90	115	397	33	3	9	12	28	....	1994-95	2002-03
an Impe, Ed	Chi., Phi., Pit.	11	700	27	126	153	1025	66	1	12	13	131	2	1966-67	1976-77
an Ryn, Mike	St.L., Fla., Tor.	8	353	30	99	129	260	9	0	0	0	0	....	2000-01	2008-09
andenBussche, Ryan	NYR, Chi., Pit.	9	310	10	10	20	702	1	0	0	0	0	....	1996-97	2005-06
arada, Vaclav	Buf., Ott.	10	493	58	125	183	410	87	11	19	30	82	....	1995-96	2005-06
aris, Petri	Chi.	1	1	0	0	0	0	....	....	....	....	....	....	1997-98	1997-98
arlamov, Sergei	Cgy., St.L.	4	63	8	7	15	26	1	0	0	0	2	....	1997-98	2002-03
arvio, Jarkko	Dal.	2	13	3	4	7	4	....	....	....	....	....	....	1993-94	1994-95
asicek, Josef	Car., Nsh., NYI	7	460	77	106	183	311	37	5	2	7	14	1	2000-01	2007-08
asilevski, Alexander	St.L.	2	4	0	0	0	2	....	....	....	....	....	....	1995-96	1996-97
asiliev, Alexei	NYR	1	1	0	0	0	2	....	....	....	....	....	....	1999-00	1999-00
asiljevs, Herbert	Fla., Atl., Van.	4	51	8	7	15	22	....	....	....	....	....	....	1998-99	2001-02
asilyev, Andrei	NYI, Phx.	4	16	2	5	7	6	....	....	....	....	....	....	1994-95	1998-99
aske, Dennis	NYI, Bos.	9	235	5	41	46	253	22	0	7	7	16	....	1990-91	1998-99
asko, Moose	Chi., Min.	13	786	34	166	200	719	78	2	7	9	73	1	1956-57	1969-70
asko, Rick	Det.	3	31	3	7	10	29	....	....	....	....	....	....	1977-78	1980-81
auclair, Julien	Ott.	1	1	0	0	0	2	....	....	....	....	....	....	2003-04	2003-04
autour, Yvon	NYI, Col., N.J., Que.	6	204	26	33	59	401	....	....	....	....	....	....	1979-80	1984-85
aydik, Greg	Chi.	1	5	0	0	0	0	....	....	....	....	....	....	1976-77	1976-77
eitch, Darren	Wsh., Det., Tor.	10	511	48	209	257	296	33	4	11	15	33	....	1980-81	1990-91
elischek, Randy	Min., N.J., Que.	10	509	21	76	97	401	44	2	5	7	32	....	1982-83	1991-92
ellucci, Mike	Hfd.	1	2	0	0	0	11	....	....	....	....	....	....	1987-88	1987-88
enasky, Vic	L.A.	7	430	61	101	162	66	21	1	5	6	12	....	1972-73	1978-79
eneruzzo, Gary	St.L.	2	7	1	1	2	0	9	0	2	2	2	....	1967-68	1971-72
erbeek, Pat	N.J., Hfd., NYR, Dal., Det.	20	1424	522	541	1063	2905	117	26	36	62	225	1	1982-83	2001-02
ermette, Mark	Que.	4	67	5	13	18	33	....	....	....	....	....	....	1988-89	1991-92
ernarsky, Kris	Bos.	2	17	1	0	1	2	....	....	....	....	....	....	2002-03	2003-04
erot, Darcy	Wsh.	1	37	0	2	2	135	....	....	....	....	....	....	2003-04	2003-04
erret, Claude	Buf.	2	14	2	5	7	2	....	....	....	....	....	....	1983-84	1984-85
erstraete, Leigh	Tor.	3	8	0	1	1	14	....	....	....	....	....	....	1982-83	1987-88
ervergaert, Dennis	Van., Phi., Wsh.	8	583	176	216	392	247	8	1	2	3	6	....	1973-74	1980-81
esey, Jim	St.L., Bos.	3	15	1	2	3	7	....	....	....	....	....	....	1988-89	1991-92
eysey, Sid	Van.	1	1	0	0	0	0	....	....	....	....	....	....	1977-78	1977-78
ial, Dennis	NYR, Det., Ott.	8	242	4	15	19	794	....	....	....	....	....	....	1990-91	1997-98
ickers, Steve	NYR	10	698	246	340	586	330	68	24	25	49	58	....	1972-73	1981-82
igier, J.P.	Atl.	6	213	23	23	46	97	....	....	....	....	....	....	2000-01	2006-07
igneault, Alain	St.L.	2	42	2	5	7	82	4	0	1	1	26	....	1981-82	1982-83
itakoski, Vesa	Cgy.	3	23	2	4	6	8	....	....	....	....	....	....	1993-94	1995-96
ilgrain, Claude	Van., N.J., Phi.	5	89	21	32	53	78	11	1	1	2	17	....	1987-88	1993-94
incelette, Dan	Chi., Que.	6	193	20	22	42	351	12	0	0	0	4	....	1986-87	1991-92
ipond, Pete	Cal.	1	3	0	0	0	0	....	....	....	....	....	....	1972-73	1972-73
irta, Hannu	Buf.	5	245	25	101	126	66	17	1	3	4	6	....	1981-82	1985-86
irta, Tony	Min.	1	8	2	3	5	0	....	....	....	....	....	....	2001-02	2001-02
irtue, Terry	Bos., NYR	2	5	0	0	0	0	....	....	....	....	....	....	1998-99	1999-00
isheau, Mark	Wpg., L.A.	2	29	1	3	4	107	....	....	....	....	....	....	1993-94	1998-99
ishnevski, Vitaly	Ana., Atl., Nsh., N.J.	8	552	16	52	68	494	40	0	5	5	18	....	1999-00	2007-08
itolinsh, Harijs	Wpg.	1	8	0	0	0	4	....	....	....	....	....	....	1993-94	1993-94
iveiros, Emanuel	Min.	3	29	1	11	12	6	....	....	....	....	....	....	1985-86	1987-88
lasak, Tomas	L.A.	1	10	1	3	4	2	....	....	....	....	....	....	2000-01	2000-01
okes, Ed	Chi.	1	5	0	0	0	0	....	....	....	....	....	....	1930-31	1930-31
olcan, Mickey	Hfd., Cgy.	4	162	8	33	41	146	....	....	....	....	....	....	1980-81	1983-84
olchkov, Alexandre	Wsh.	1	3	0	0	0	0	....	....	....	....	....	....	1999-00	1999-00
olek, David	NYI	6	396	95	154	249	201	15	5	5	10	2	....	1988-89	1993-94
olmar, Doug	Det., L.A.	4	62	13	8	21	26	2	1	0	1	0	....	1969-70	1972-73
on Arx, Reto	Chi.	1	19	3	1	4	4	....	....	....	....	....	....	2000-01	2000-01
on Stefenelli, Phil	Bos., Ott.	2	33	0	5	5	23	....	....	....	....	....	....	1995-96	1996-97
opat, Jan	L.A., Nsh.	5	126	11	20	31	70	2	0	1	1	2	....	1995-96	1999-00
opat, Roman	St.L., L.A., Chi., Phi.	4	133	6	14	20	253	....	....	....	....	....	....	1995-96	1998-99
orobiev, Pavel	Chi.	2	57	10	15	25	38	....	....	....	....	....	....	2003-04	2005-06
orobiev, Vladimir	NYR, Edm.	3	33	9	7	16	14	1	0	0	0	0	....	1996-97	1998-99
oss, Carl	Tor., NYR, Det., Ott., St.L., NYA, Mtl.M., Chi.	8	261	34	70	104	50	24	5	3	8	0	1	1926-27	1937-38
ujtek, Vladimir	Mtl., Edm., T.B., Atl., Pit.	6	110	7	30	37	38	....	....	....	....	....	....	1991-92	2002-03
ukota, Mick	NYI, T.B., Mtl.	11	574	17	29	46	2071	23	0	0	0	73	....	1987-88	1997-98
yazmikin, Igor	Edm.	1	4	1	0	1	0	....	....	....	....	....	....	1990-91	1990-91
yborny, David	CBJ	7	543	113	204	317	228	....	....	....	....	....	....	2000-01	2007-08
yshedkevich, Sergei	Atl.	2	30	2	5	7	16	....	....	....	....	....	....	1999-00	2000-01

W

addell, Don	L.A.	1	1	0	0	0	0	....	....	....	....	....	....	1980-81	1980-81
aite, Frank	NYR	1	17	1	3	4	4	....	....	....	....	....	....	1930-31	1930-31
alker, Gord	NYR, L.A.	4	31	3	4	7	23	....	....	....	....	....	....	1986-87	1989-90
alker, Howard	Wsh., Cgy.	3	83	2	13	15	133	....	....	....	....	....	....	1980-81	1982-83
alker, Jack	Det.	2	80	5	8	13	18	....	....	....	....	....	....	1926-27	1927-28
alker, Kurt	Tor.	3	71	4	5	9	142	16	0	0	0	34	....	1975-76	1977-78
alker, Russ	L.A.	2	17	1	0	1	41	....	....	....	....	....	....	1976-77	1977-78
all, Bob	Det., L.A., St.L.	8	322	30	55	85	155	22	0	3	3	2	....	1964-65	1971-72
allin, Jesse	Det.	4	49	0	2	2	34	....	....	....	....	....	....	1999-00	2002-03
allin, Peter	NYR	2	52	3	14	17	14	14	2	6	8	6	....	1980-81	1981-82
alser, Derrick	CBJ	4	91	8	21	29	56	....	....	....	....	....	....	2001-02	2006-07
alsh, Jim	Buf.	1	4	0	1	1	4	....	....	....	....	....	....	1981-82	1981-82
alsh, Mike	NYI	2	14	2	0	2	4	....	....	....	....	....	....	1987-88	1988-89
alter, Ryan	Wsh., Mtl., Van.	15	1003	264	382	646	946	113	16	35	51	62	1	1978-79	1992-93
alton, Bobby	Mtl.	1	4	0	0	0	0	....	....	....	....	....	....	1943-44	1943-44
alton, Mike	Tor., Bos., Van., St.L., Chi.	12	588	201	247	448	357	47	14	10	24	45	2	1965-66	1978-79
alz, Wes	Bos., Phi., Cgy., Det., Min.	13	607	109	151	260	343	32	10	7	17	20	....	1989-90	2007-08
anvig, Kyle	Min., T.B.	5	75	6	9	15	94	....	....	....	....	....	....	2002-03	2007-08
appel, Gord	Atl., Cgy.	3	20	1	1	2	10	2	0	0	0	4	....	1979-80	1981-82
ard, Dixon	Van., L.A., Tor., Buf., Bos., NYR	10	537	95	129	224	431	62	14	20	34	46	....	1992-93	2002-03
ard, Don	Chi., Bos.	2	34	0	1	1	16	....	....	....	....	....	....	1957-58	1959-60
ard, Ed	Que., Cgy., Atl., Ana., N.J.	8	278	23	26	49	354	....	....	....	....	....	....	1993-94	2000-01
ard, Jimmy	Mtl.M., Mtl.	12	527	147	127	274	455	36	4	4	8	26	1	1927-28	1938-39
ard, Joe	Col.	1	4	0	0	0	2	....	....	....	....	....	....	1980-81	1980-81
ard, Lance	Fla., Ana.	4	209	4	12	16	391	....	....	....	....	....	....	2000-01	2003-04
ard, Ron	Tor., Van.	2	89	2	5	7	6	....	....	....	....	....	....	1969-70	1971-72
are, Jeff	Tor., Fla.	3	21	0	1	1	12	....	....	....	....	....	....	1996-97	1998-99
are, Michael	Edm.	2	5	0	1	1	15	....	....	....	....	....	....	1988-89	1989-90
ares, Eddie	NYR, Det., Chi.	9	321	60	102	162	161	45	5	7	12	34	1	1936-37	1946-47
arner, Bob	Tor.	2	10	1	1	2	4	4	0	0	0	0	....	1975-76	1976-77
arner, Jim	Hfd.	1	32	0	3	3	10	....	....	....	....	....	....	1979-80	1979-80
arrener, Rhett	Fla., Buf., Cgy.	12	714	24	82	106	899	101	1	7	8	68	....	1995-96	2007-08
arriner, Todd	Tor., T.B., Phx., Van., Phi., Nsh.	9	453	65	89	154	249	21	2	1	3	6	....	1994-95	2002-03
arwick, Billy	NYR	2	14	3	3	6	16	....	....	....	....	....	....	1942-43	1943-44
arwick, Grant	NYR, Bos., Mtl.	9	395	147	142	289	220	16	2	4	6	6	....	1941-42	1949-50
ashburn, Steve	Fla., Van., Phi.	6	93	14	15	29	42	1	0	1	1	0	....	1995-96	2000-01
asnie, Nick	Chi., Mtl., NYA, Ott., St.L.	7	248	57	34	91	176	20	6	3	9	20	2	1927-28	1934-35
atson, Bill	Chi.	4	115	23	36	59	12	6	0	2	2	0	....	1985-86	1988-89
atson, Bryan	Mtl., Det., Oak., Pit., St.L., Wsh.	16	878	17	135	152	2212	32	2	0	2	70	1	1963-64	1978-79
atson, Dave	Col.	2	18	0	1	1	10	....	....	....	....	....	....	1979-80	1980-81
atson, Harry	Bro., Det., Tor., Chi.	14	809	236	207	443	150	62	16	9	25	27	5	1941-42	1956-57
atson, Jim	Det., Buf.	8	221	4	19	23	345	....	....	....	....	....	....	1963-64	1971-72
atson, Jimmy	Phi.	10	613	38	148	186	492	101	5	34	39	89	2	1972-73	1981-82
atson, Joe	Bos., Phi., Col.	14	835	38	178	216	447	84	3	12	15	82	2	1964-65	1978-79
atson, Phil	NYR, Mtl.	13	590	144	265	409	532	54	10	25	35	67	2	1935-36	1947-48
att, Mike	Edm., NYI, Nsh., Car.	5	157	15	26	41	41	....	....	....	....	....	....	1997-98	2002-03
atters, Tim	Wpg., L.A.	14	741	26	151	177	1289	82	1	5	6	115	....	1981-82	1994-95

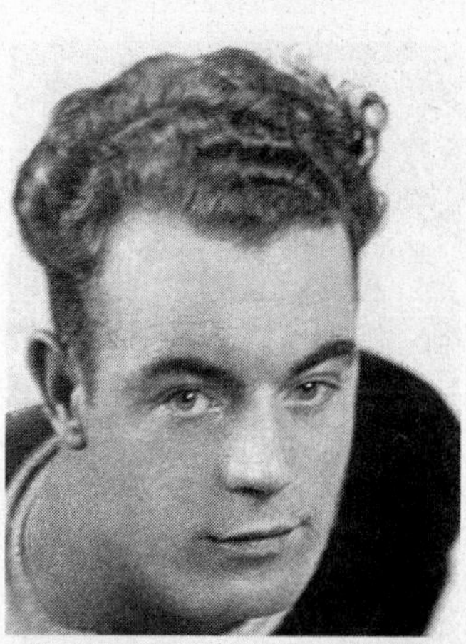
Jimmy Ward

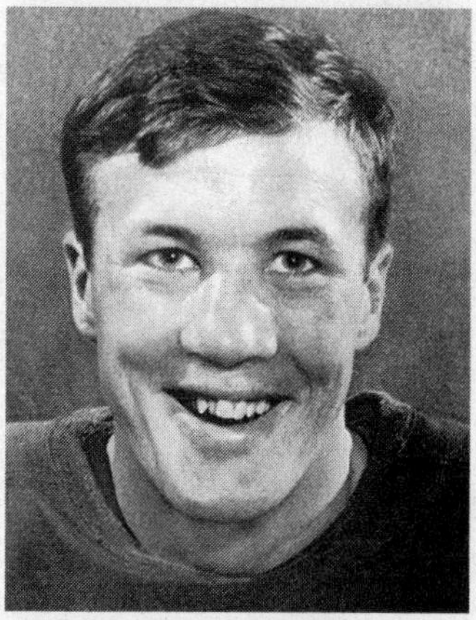
Bryan Watson

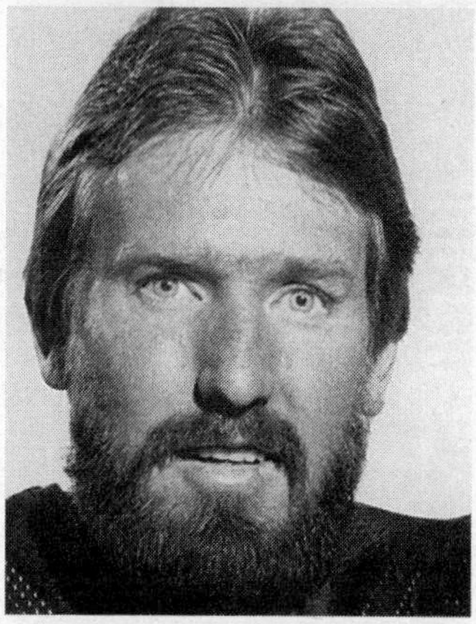
Stan Weir

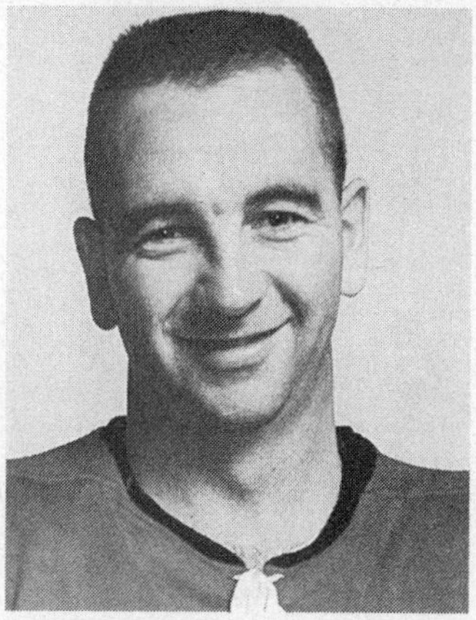
Kenny Wharram

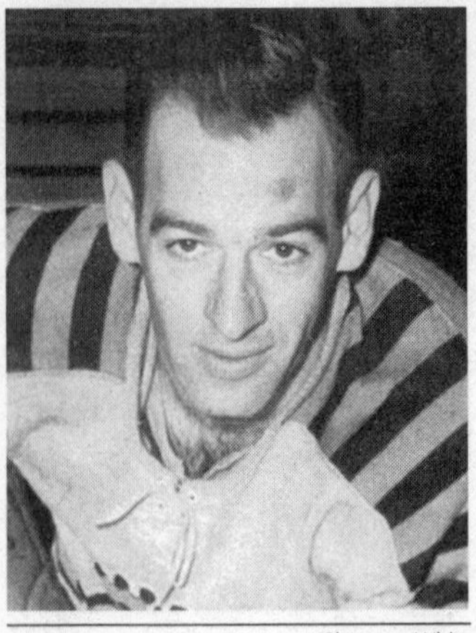

Sherman White

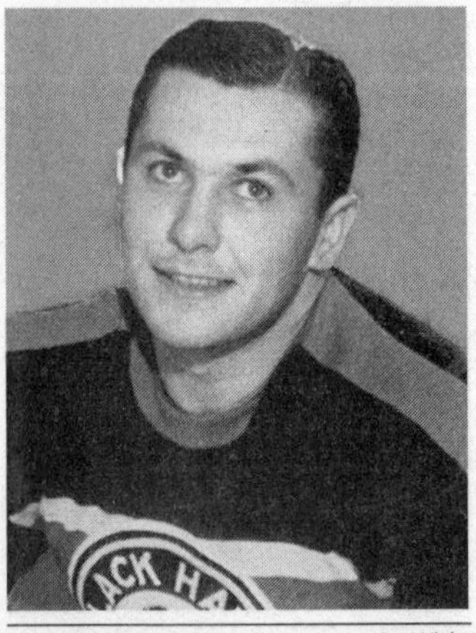

Art Wiebe

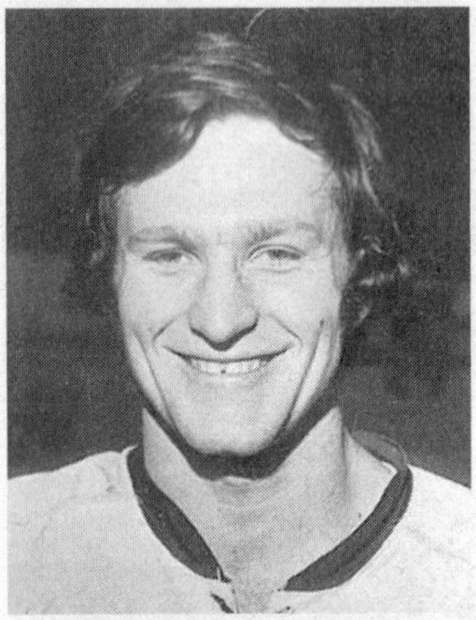

Ron Wilson

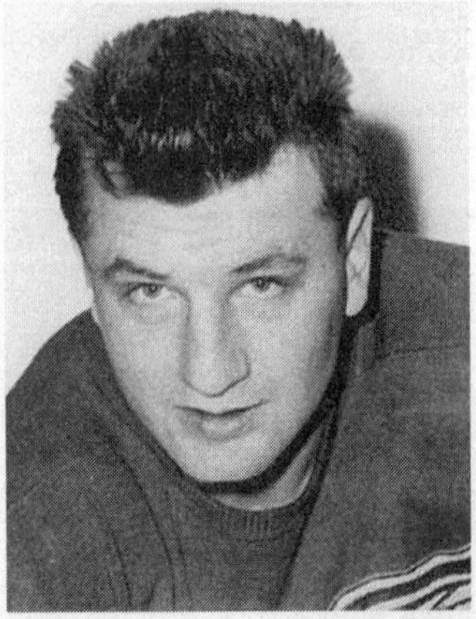

Benny Woit

Name	NHL Teams	NHL Seasons	Regular Schedule GP	G	A	TP	PIM	Playoffs GP	G	A	TP	PIM	NHL Cup Wins	First NHL Season	Last NHL Season
Watts, Brian	Det.	1	4	0	0	0	0	....	....	....	....	....	....	1975-76	1975-7
Webb, Steve	NYI, Pit.	8	321	5	13	18	532	14	0	0	0	28	....	1996-97	2003-0
● Webster, Aubrey	Phi., Mtl.M.	2	5	0	0	0	0	....	....	....	....	....	....	1930-31	1934-3
● Webster, Don	Tor.	1	27	7	6	13	28	5	0	0	0	12	....	1943-44	1943-4
Webster, John	NYR	1	14	0	0	0	4	....	....	....	....	....	....	1949-50	1949-5
Webster, Tom	Bos., Det., Cal.	5	102	33	42	75	61	1	0	0	0	0	....	1968-69	1979-8
● Weiland, Cooney	Bos., Ott., Det.	11	509	173	160	333	147	45	12	10	22	12	2	1928-29	1938-3
‡ Weinhandl, Mattias	NYI, Min.	4	182	19	37	56	70	5	0	0	0	2	....	2002-03	2006-0
Weinrich, Eric	N.J., Hfd., Chi., Mtl., Bos., Phi., St.L., Van.	17	1157	70	318	388	825	81	6	23	29	67	....	1988-89	2005-0
Weir, Stan	Cal., Tor., Edm., Col., Det.	10	642	139	207	346	183	37	6	5	11	4	....	1972-73	1982-8
Weir, Wally	Que., Hfd., Pit.	6	320	21	45	66	625	23	0	1	1	96	....	1979-80	1984-8
● Wellington, Alex	Que.	1	1	0	0	0	0	....	....	....	....	....	....	1919-20	1919-2
Wells, Chris	Pit., Fla.	5	195	9	20	29	193	3	0	0	0	0	....	1995-96	1999-0
Wells, Jay	L.A., Phi., Buf., NYR, St.L., T.B.	18	1098	47	216	263	2359	114	3	14	17	213	1	1979-80	1996-9
Wensink, John	St.L., Bos., Que., Col., N.J.	8	403	70	68	138	840	43	2	6	8	86	....	1973-74	1982-8
● Wentworth, Cy	Chi., Mtl.M., Mtl.	13	575	39	68	107	355	35	5	6	11	20	1	1927-28	1939-4
Werenka, Brad	Edm., Que., Chi., Pit., Cgy.	7	320	19	61	80	299	19	2	1	3	14	....	1992-93	2000-0
Wesenberg, Brian	Phi.	1	1	0	0	0	5	....	....	....	....	....	....	1998-99	1998-9
Wesley, Blake	Phi., Hfd., Que., Tor.	7	298	18	46	64	486	19	2	2	4	30	....	1979-80	1985-8
Wesley, Glen	Bos., Hfd., Car., Tor.	20	1457	128	409	537	1045	169	15	37	52	141	1	1987-88	2007-0
‡ Westcott, Duvie	CBJ	6	201	11	45	56	299	....	....	....	....	....	....	2001-02	2007-0
Westfall, Ed	Bos., NYI	18	1226	231	394	625	544	95	22	37	59	41	2	1961-62	1978-7
Westlund, Tommy	Car.	4	203	9	13	22	48	25	1	0	1	17	....	1999-00	2002-0
‡ Westrum, Erik	Phx., Min., Tor.	3	27	1	2	3	22	....	....	....	....	....	....	2003-04	2006-0
Wharram, Kenny	Chi.	14	766	252	281	533	222	80	16	27	43	38	1	1951-52	1968-6
● Wharton, Len	NYR	1	1	0	0	0	0	....	....	....	....	....	....	1944-45	1944-4
Wheeldon, Simon	NYR, Wpg.	3	15	0	2	2	10	....	....	....	....	....	....	1987-88	1990-9
● Wheldon, Don	St.L.	1	2	0	0	0	0	....	....	....	....	....	....	1974-75	1974-7
Whelton, Bill	Wpg.	1	2	0	0	0	0	....	....	....	....	....	....	1980-81	1980-8
Whistle, Rob	NYR, St.L.	2	51	7	5	12	16	4	0	0	0	2	....	1985-86	1987-8
White, Bill	L.A., Chi.	9	604	50	215	265	495	91	7	32	39	76	....	1967-68	1975-7
‡ White, Brian	Col.	1	2	0	0	0	0	....	....	....	....	....	....	1998-99	1998-9
White, Moe	Mtl.	1	4	0	1	1	2	....	....	....	....	....	....	1945-46	1945-4
White, Peter	Edm., Tor., Phi., Chi.	9	220	23	37	60	36	19	0	2	2	0	....	1993-94	2003-0
● White, Sherman	NYR	2	4	0	2	2	0	....	....	....	....	....	....	1946-47	1949-5
● White, Tex	Pit., NYA, Phi.	6	203	33	12	45	141	4	0	0	0	4	....	1925-26	1930-3
White, Tony	Wsh., Min.	5	164	37	28	65	104	....	....	....	....	....	....	1974-75	1979-8
Whitelaw, Bob	Det.	2	32	0	2	2	2	8	0	0	0	0	....	1940-41	1941-4
Whitlock, Bob	Min.	1	1	0	0	0	0	....	....	....	....	....	....	1969-70	1969-7
Whyte, Sean	L.A.	2	21	0	2	2	12	....	....	....	....	....	....	1991-92	1992-9
● Wickenheiser, Doug	Mtl., St.L., Van., NYR, Wsh.	10	556	111	165	276	286	41	4	7	11	18	....	1980-81	1989-9
● Widing, Juha	NYR, L.A., Cle.	8	575	144	226	370	208	8	1	2	3	2	....	1969-70	1976-7
Widmer, Jason	NYI, S.J.	3	7	0	1	1	7	....	....	....	....	....	....	1994-95	1996-9
● Wiebe, Art	Chi.	11	414	14	27	41	201	31	1	3	4	10	1	1932-33	1943-4
Wiemer, Jason	T.B., Cgy., Fla., NYI, Min., N.J.	11	726	90	112	202	1420	19	1	0	1	67	....	1994-95	2005-0
Wiemer, Jim	Buf., NYR, Edm., L.A., Bos.	11	325	29	72	101	378	62	5	8	13	63	....	1982-83	1993-9
● Wilcox, Archie	Mtl.M., Bos., St.L.	6	208	8	14	22	158	12	1	0	1	8	....	1929-30	1934-3
Wilcox, Barry	Van.	2	33	3	2	5	15	....	....	....	....	....	....	1972-73	1974-7
● Wilder, Arch	Det.	1	18	0	2	2	2	....	....	....	....	....	....	1940-41	1940-4
Wiley, Jim	Pit., Van.	5	63	4	10	14	8	....	....	....	....	....	....	1972-73	1976-7
Wilkie, Bob	Det., Phi.	2	18	2	5	7	10	....	....	....	....	....	....	1990-91	1993-9
Wilkie, David	Mtl., T.B., NYR	6	167	10	26	36	165	8	1	2	3	14	....	1994-95	2000-0
Wilkins, Barry	Bos., Van., Pit.	9	418	27	125	152	663	6	0	1	1	4	....	1966-67	1975-7
● Wilkinson, John	Bos.	1	9	0	0	0	6	....	....	....	....	....	....	1943-44	1943-4
Wilkinson, Neil	Min., S.J., Chi., Wpg., Pit.	10	460	16	67	83	813	53	3	6	9	41	....	1989-90	1998-9
Wilks, Brian	L.A.	4	48	4	8	12	27	....	....	....	....	....	....	1984-85	1988-8
Willard, Rod	Tor.	1	1	0	0	0	0	....	....	....	....	....	....	1982-83	1982-8
● Williams, Burr	Det., St.L., Bos.	3	19	0	1	1	28	7	0	0	0	8	....	1933-34	1936-3
Williams, Butch	St.L., Cal.	3	108	14	35	49	131	....	....	....	....	....	....	1973-74	1975-7
Williams, Darryl	L.A.	1	2	0	0	0	10	....	....	....	....	....	....	1992-93	1992-9
Williams, David	S.J., Ana.	4	173	11	53	64	157	....	....	....	....	....	....	1991-92	1994-9
Williams, Fred	Det.	1	44	2	5	7	10	....	....	....	....	....	....	1976-77	1976-7
Williams, Gord	Phi.	2	2	0	0	0	2	....	....	....	....	....	....	1981-82	1982-8
Williams, Sean	Chi.	1	2	0	0	0	4	....	....	....	....	....	....	1991-92	1991-9
Williams, Tiger	Tor., Van., Det., L.A., Hfd.	14	962	241	272	513	3966	83	12	23	35	455	....	1974-75	1987-8
Williams, Tom	NYR, L.A.	8	397	115	138	253	73	29	8	7	15	4	....	1971-72	1978-7
● Williams, Tommy	Bos., Min., Cal., Wsh.	13	663	161	269	430	177	10	2	5	7	2	....	1961-62	1975-7
‡ Willis, Shane	Car., T.B.	5	174	31	43	74	77	2	0	0	0	0	....	1998-99	2003-0
Willson, Don	Mtl.	2	22	2	7	9	0	3	0	0	0	0	....	1937-38	1938-3
‡ Wilm, Clarke	Cgy., Nsh., Tor.	7	455	37	60	97	336	5	0	1	1	2	....	1998-99	2005-0
Wilson, Behn	Phi., Chi.	9	601	98	260	358	1480	67	12	29	41	190	....	1978-79	1987-8
● Wilson, Bert	NYR, St.L., L.A., Cgy.	8	478	37	44	81	646	21	0	2	2	42	....	1973-74	1980-8
Wilson, Bob	Chi.	1	1	0	0	0	0	....	....	....	....	....	....	1953-54	1953-5
Wilson, Carey	Cgy., Hfd., NYR	10	552	169	258	427	314	52	11	13	24	14	....	1983-84	1992-9
● Wilson, Cully	Tor., Mtl., Ham., Chi.	5	127	59	28	87	243	2	1	0	1	6	....	1919-20	1926-2
Wilson, Doug	Chi., S.J.	16	1024	237	590	827	830	95	19	61	80	88	....	1977-78	1992-9
Wilson, Gord	Bos.	1	....	....	....	....	....	2	0	0	0	0	....	1954-55	1954-5
● Wilson, Hub	NYA	1	2	0	0	0	0	....	....	....	....	....	....	1931-32	1931-3
Wilson, Jerry	Mtl.	1	3	0	0	0	2	....	....	....	....	....	....	1956-57	1956-5
Wilson, Johnny	Det., Chi., Tor., NYR	13	688	161	171	332	190	66	14	13	27	11	4	1949-50	1961-6
● Wilson, Larry	Det., Chi.	6	152	21	48	69	75	4	0	0	0	0	1	1949-50	1955-5
Wilson, Mike	Buf., Fla., Pit., NYR	8	336	16	41	57	264	29	0	2	2	15	....	1995-96	2002-0
Wilson, Mitch	N.J., Pit.	2	26	2	3	5	104	....	....	....	....	....	....	1984-85	1986-8
Wilson, Murray	Mtl., L.A.	7	386	94	95	189	162	53	5	14	19	32	4	1972-73	1978-7
Wilson, Rick	Mtl., St.L., Det.	4	239	6	26	32	165	3	0	0	0	0	....	1973-74	1976-7
Wilson, Rik	St.L., Cgy., Chi.	6	251	25	65	90	220	22	0	4	4	23	....	1981-82	1987-8
Wilson, Roger	Chi.	1	7	0	2	2	6	....	....	....	....	....	....	1974-75	1974-7
Wilson, Ron	Tor., Min.	7	177	26	67	93	68	20	4	13	17	8	....	1977-78	1987-8
Wilson, Ron	Wpg., St.L., Mtl.	14	832	110	216	326	415	63	10	12	22	64	....	1979-80	1993-9
● Wilson, Wally	Bos.	1	53	11	8	19	18	1	0	0	0	0	....	1947-48	1947-4
Wing, Murray	Det.	1	1	0	1	1	0	....	....	....	....	....	....	1973-74	1973-7
Winnes, Chris	Bos., Phi.	4	33	1	6	7	6	1	0	0	0	0	....	1990-91	1993-9
Wiseman, Brian	Tor.	1	3	0	0	0	0	....	....	....	....	....	....	1996-97	1996-9
● Wiseman, Eddie	Det., NYA, Bos.	10	456	115	165	280	136	43	10	10	20	16	1	1932-33	1941-4
Wiste, Jim	Chi., Van.	3	52	1	10	11	8	....	....	....	....	....	....	1968-69	1970-7
Witehall, Johan	NYR, Mtl.	3	54	2	5	7	16	....	....	....	....	....	....	1998-99	2000-0
Witherspoon, Jim	L.A.	1	2	0	0	0	2	....	....	....	....	....	....	1975-76	1975-7
Witiuk, Steve	Chi.	1	33	3	8	11	14	....	....	....	....	....	....	1951-52	1951-5
Woit, Benny	Det., Chi.	7	334	7	26	33	170	41	2	6	8	18	3	1950-51	1956-5
Wojciechowski, Steve	Det.	2	54	19	20	39	17	6	0	1	1	0	....	1944-45	1946-4
Wolanin, Craig	N.J., Que., Col., T.B., Tor.	13	695	40	133	173	894	35	4	6	10	67	1	1985-86	1997-9
Wolf, Bennett	Pit.	3	30	0	1	1	133	....	....	....	....	....	....	1980-81	1982-8
Wong, Mike	Det.	1	22	1	1	2	12	....	....	....	....	....	....	1975-76	1975-7
Wood, Dody	S.J.	5	106	8	10	18	471	....	....	....	....	....	....	1992-93	1997-9
Wood, Randy	NYI, Buf., Tor., Dal.	11	741	175	159	334	603	51	8	9	17	40	....	1986-87	1996-9
● Wood, Robert	NYR	1	1	0	0	0	0	....	....	....	....	....	....	1950-51	1950-5
Woodley, Dan	Van.	1	5	2	0	2	17	....	....	....	....	....	....	1987-88	1987-8
Woods, Paul	Det.	7	501	72	124	196	276	7	0	5	5	4	....	1977-78	1983-8
Woolley, Jason	Wsh., Fla., Pit., Buf., Det.	14	718	68	246	314	430	79	11	36	47	44	....	1991-92	2005-0
Worrell, Peter	Fla., Col.	7	391	19	27	46	1554	4	1	0	1	8	....	1997-98	2003-0
Wortman, Kevin	Cgy.	1	5	0	0	0	2	....	....	....	....	....	....	1993-94	1993-9
‡ Wotton, Mark	Van., Dal.	4	43	3	6	9	25	5	0	0	0	4	....	1994-95	2000-0
● Woytowich, Bob	Bos., Min., Pit., L.A.	8	503	32	126	158	352	24	1	3	4	20	....	1964-65	1971-7
‡ Wren, Bob	Ana., Tor.	3	5	0	0	0	0	1	0	0	0	0	....	1997-98	2001-0
‡ Wright, Jamie	Dal., Cgy., Phi.	6	124	12	20	32	54	5	0	0	0	0	....	1997-98	2002-0
Wright, John	Van., St.L., K.C.	3	127	16	36	52	67	....	....	....	....	....	....	1972-73	1974-7
Wright, Keith	Phi.	1	1	0	0	0	0	....	....	....	....	....	....	1967-68	1967-6
Wright, Larry	Phi., Cal., Det.	5	106	4	8	12	19	....	....	....	....	....	....	1971-72	1977-7
Wright, Tyler	Edm., Pit., CBJ, Ana.	13	613	79	70	149	854	30	3	2	5	40	....	1992-93	2005-0
● Wycherley, Ralph	NYA, Bro.	2	28	4	7	11	6	....	....	....	....	....	....	1940-41	1941-4
● Wylie, Bill	NYR	1	1	0	0	0	0	....	....	....	....	....	....	1950-51	1950-5
Wylie, Duane	Chi.	2	14	3	3	6	2	....	....	....	....	....	....	1974-75	1976-7
Wyrozub, Randy	Buf.	4	100	8	10	18	10	....	....	....	....	....	....	1970-71	1973-7

ame	NHL Teams	NHL Seasons	GP	G	A	TP	PIM	GP	G	A	TP	PIM	NHL Cup Wins	First NHL Season	Last NHL Season
			Regular Schedule					Playoffs							

Y / Z

ame	NHL Teams	NHL Seasons	GP	G	A	TP	PIM	GP	G	A	TP	PIM	NHL Cup Wins	First NHL Season	Last NHL Season
achmenev, Vitali	L.A., Nsh.	8	487	83	133	216	88	....	....	....	....	....	....	1995-96	2002-03
ackel, Ken	Bos.	1	6	0	0	0	2	2	0	0	0	2	....	1958-59	1958-59
ake, Terry	Hfd., Ana., Tor., St.L., Wsh.	11	403	77	120	197	220	32	4	4	8	36	....	1988-89	2000-01
akubov, Mikhail	Chi., Fla.	2	53	2	10	12	20	....	....	....	....	....	....	2003-04	2005-06
akushin, Dmitri	Tor.	1	2	0	0	0	2	....	....	....	....	....	....	1999-00	1999-00
aremchuk, Gary	Tor.	4	34	1	4	5	28	....	....	....	....	....	....	1981-82	1984-85
aremchuk, Ken	Chi., Tor.	6	235	36	56	92	106	31	6	8	14	49	....	1983-84	1988-89
ashin, Alexei	Ott., NYI	12	850	337	444	781	401	48	11	16	27	24	....	1993-94	2006-07
ates, Ross	Hfd.	1	7	1	1	2	4	....	....	....	....	....	....	1983-84	1983-84
awney, Trent	Chi., Cgy., St.L.	12	593	27	102	129	783	60	9	17	26	81	....	1987-88	1998-99
egorov, Alexei	S.J.	2	11	3	3	6	2	....	....	....	....	....	....	1995-96	1996-97
onen, Juha	Phx., T.B., Ott.	6	341	26	76	102	90	15	0	7	7	4	....	1996-97	2001-02
ork, Harry	St.L., NYR, Pit., Van.	4	244	29	46	75	99	5	0	0	0	2	....	1996-97	1999-00
ork, Jason	Det., Ana., Ott., Nsh., Bos.	13	757	42	187	229	621	34	2	7	9	25	....	1992-93	2006-07
oung, B.J.	Det.	1	1	0	0	0	0	....	....	....	....	....	....	1999-00	1999-00
oung, Brian	Chi.	1	8	0	2	2	6	....	....	....	....	....	....	1980-81	1980-81
oung, C.J.	Cgy., Bos.	1	43	7	7	14	32	....	....	....	....	....	....	1992-93	1992-93
oung, Doug	Det., Mtl.	10	388	35	45	80	303	28	1	5	6	16	2	1931-32	1940-41
oung, Howie	Det., Chi., Van.	8	336	12	62	74	851	19	2	4	6	46	....	1960-61	1970-71
oung, Scott	Hfd., Pit., Que., Col., Ana., St.L., Dal.	17	1181	342	415	757	448	141	44	43	87	64	2	1987-88	2005-06
oung, Tim	Min., Wpg., Phi.	10	628	195	341	536	438	36	7	24	31	27	....	1975-76	1984-85
oung, Warren	Min., Pit., Det.	7	236	72	77	149	472	....	....	....	....	....	....	1981-82	1987-88
ounghans, Tom	Min., NYR	6	429	44	41	85	373	24	2	1	3	21	....	1976-77	1981-82
ebaert, Paul	N.J., Det., Wpg., Chi., T.B.	11	532	149	187	336	217	30	4	3	7	20	....	1988-89	1998-99
ushkevich, Dmitry	Phi., Tor., Fla., L.A.	11	786	43	182	225	659	72	4	19	23	52	....	1992-93	2002-03
terman, Steve	Det.	22	1514	692	1063	1755	924	196	70	115	185	84	3	1983-84	2005-06
abransky, Libor	St.L.	2	40	1	6	7	50	....	....	....	....	....	....	1996-97	1997-98
aharko, Miles	Atl., Chi.	4	129	5	32	37	84	3	0	0	0	0	....	1977-78	1981-82
aine, Rod	Pit., Buf.	2	61	10	6	16	25	....	....	....	....	....	....	1970-71	1971-72
alapski, Zarley	Pit., Hfd., Cgy., Mtl., Phi.	12	637	99	285	384	684	48	4	23	27	47	....	1987-88	1999-00
alesak, Miroslav	S.J.	2	12	1	2	3	0	....	....	....	....	....	....	2002-03	2003-04
amuner, Rob	NYR, T.B., Ott., Bos.	13	798	139	172	311	467	34	4	5	9	26	....	1991-92	2003-04
anussi, Joe	NYR, Bos., St.L.	3	87	1	13	14	46	4	0	1	1	2	....	1974-75	1976-77
anussi, Ron	Min., Tor.	5	299	52	83	135	373	17	0	4	4	17	....	1977-78	1981-82
avisha, Brad	Edm.	1	2	0	0	0	0	....	....	....	....	....	....	1993-94	1993-94
ehr, Jeff	Bos.	1	4	0	0	0	2	....	....	....	....	....	....	1999-00	1999-00
idel, Larry	Det., Chi., Phi.	5	158	3	16	19	198	12	0	1	1	12	1	1951-52	1968-69
elepukin, Valeri	N.J., Edm., Phi., Chi.	10	595	117	177	294	527	85	13	13	26	48	1	1991-92	2000-01
mlak, Richard	Que., Min., Pit., Cgy.	5	132	2	12	14	587	1	0	0	0	10	....	1986-87	1991-92
niuk, Ed	Det.	1	2	0	0	0	0	....	....	....	....	....	....	1954-55	1954-55
nt, Jason	Ott., Phi.	3	27	3	3	6	13	....	....	....	....	....	....	1996-97	1999-00
tterstrom, Lars	Van.	1	14	0	1	1	2	....	....	....	....	....	....	1978-79	1978-79
ttler, Rob	Min., S.J., Phi., Tor., Nsh., Wsh.	14	569	5	65	70	920	14	0	0	0	4	....	1988-89	2001-02
zel, Peter	Phi., St.L., Wsh., Tor., Dal., N.J., Van.	15	873	219	389	608	435	131	25	39	64	83	....	1984-85	1998-99
amnov, Alex	Wpg., Chi., Phi., Bos.	13	807	249	470	719	668	35	6	13	19	18	....	1992-93	2005-06
itnik, Alexei	L.A., Buf., NYI, Phi., Atl.	15	1085	96	375	471	1268	98	9	30	39	168	....	1992-93	2007-08
oltok, Sergei	Bos., Ott., Mtl., Edm., Min., Nsh.	10	588	111	147	258	166	45	4	14	18	0	....	1992-93	2003-04
egler, Thomas	T.B.	1	5	0	0	0	0	....	....	....	....	....	....	2000-01	2000-01
nger, Dwayne	Wsh.	1	7	0	1	1	9	....	....	....	....	....	....	2003-04	2003-04
novjev, Sergei	Bos.	1	10	0	1	1	2	....	....	....	....	....	....	2003-04	2003-04
rka, Tomas	L.A.	2	25	2	6	8	16	....	....	....	....	....	....	2002-03	2003-04
holek, Doug	S.J., Dal., L.A., Chi.	8	467	11	53	64	905	14	0	1	1	16	....	1992-93	1999-00
boborosky, Marty	Chi.	1	1	0	0	0	2	....	....	....	....	....	....	1944-45	1944-45
mbo, Rick	Det., St.L., Bos.	12	652	24	130	154	728	60	1	11	12	127	....	1984-85	1995-96
bov, Sergei	NYR, Pit., Dal.	16	1068	152	619	771	337	164	24	93	117	62	2	1992-93	2008-09
ke, Mike	St.L., Hfd.	8	455	86	196	282	220	26	6	6	12	12	....	1978-79	1985-86
nich, Rudy	Det.	1	2	0	0	0	0	....	....	....	....	....	....	1943-44	1943-44
uzin, Andrei	S.J., T.B., N.J., Min., Cgy., Chi.	10	496	38	82	120	446	29	2	1	3	30	....	1997-98	2007-08

Brian Young

Brad Zavisha

Retired Players, Goaltenders and Coaches Research Project

Throughout the Retired Players and Retired Goaltenders sections of this book, you will notice many players with a bullet (•) by their names. These players, according to our records, are deceased. The editors recognize that our information on the death dates of NHLers is incomplete. If you have documented information on the passing of any player not marked with a bullet (•) in this edition, we would like to hear from you. We also welcome information on deceased NHL head coaches. Please send this information to:

Retired Player Research Project
c/o NHL Publishing
194 Dovercourt Road
Toronto, Ontario
M6J 3C8   Canada
Fax: 416/531-3939

Many thanks to the following contributors . . .

Tim Bateman, Corey Bryant, Paul R. Carroll, Jr., Bob Duff, Peter Fillman, Ernie Fitzsimmons, Chris Gory, Calvin McLellan, Gary J. Pearce, Martin Schmid, Al Tario, Drew "Whitey" White.

Retired NHL Goaltender Index

Abbreviations: Teams/Cities: – **Ana**. – Anaheim; **Atl**. – Atlanta; **Bos**. – Boston; **Bro**. – Brooklyn; **Buf**. – Buffalo; **Cgy**. – Calgary; **Cal**. – California; **Car**. – Carolina; **Chi**. – Chicago; **Cle**. – Cleveland; **Col**. – Colorado; **CBJ** – Columbus; **Dal**. – Dallas; **Det**. – Detroit; **Edm**. – Edmonton; **Fla**. – Florida; **Ham**. – Hamilton; **Hfd**. – Hartford; **K.C.** – Kansas City; **L.A.** – Los Angeles; **Min**. – Minnesota; **Mtl**. – Montreal; **Mtl.M.** – Montreal Maroons; **Mtl.W.** – Montreal Wanderers; **Nsh**. – Nashville; **N.J.** – New Jersey; **NYA** – NY Americans; **NYI** – NY Islanders; **NYR** – New York Rangers; **Oak**. – Oakland; **Ott**. – Ottawa; **Phi**. – Philadelphia; **Phx**. – Phoenix; **Pit**. – Pittsburgh; **Que**. – Quebec; **St.L.** – St. Louis; **S.J.** – San Jose; **T.B.** – Tampa Bay; **Tor.** – Toronto; **Van.** – Vancouver; **Wsh.** – Washington; **Wpg.** – Winnipeg

Avg. – goals against per 60 minutes played; **GA** – goals agains; **GP** – games played; **Mins** – minutes played; **SO** – shutouts.
• – deceased. § – Forward, defenseman or coach who appeared in goal. For complete career, see Retired Player Index. ‡ – Remains active in other leagues.

NHL Seasons – A player or goaltender who does not play in a regular season but who does appear in that year's playoffs is credited with an NHL Season in this Index. Total seasons are rounded off to the nearest full season.

			Regular Schedule								Playoffs										
Name	NHL Teams	NHL Seasons	GP	W	L	T	Mins	GA	SO	Avg	GP	W	L	T	Mins	GA	SO	Avg	NHL Cup Wins	First NHL Season	Last NHL Season
Abbott, George	Bos.	1	1	0	1	0	60	7	0	7.00	....	....	....	....	....	....	....	....		1943-44	1943-4
Adams, John	Bos., Wsh.	3	22	9	10	1	1180	85	1	4.32	....	....	....	....	....	....	....	....	1	1969-70	1974-7
Aiken, Don	Mtl.	1	1	0	1	0	34	6	0	10.59	....	....	....	....	....	....	....	....		1957-58	1957-5
• Aitkenhead, Andy	NYR	3	106	47	43	16	6570	257	11	2.35	10	6	2	2	608	15	3	1.48	1	1932-33	1934-3
• Almas, Red	Det., Chi.	3	3	0	2	1	180	13	0	4.33	5	1	3	....	263	13	0	2.97		1946-47	1952-5
• Anderson, Lorne	NYR	1	3	1	2	0	180	18	0	6.00	....	....	....	....	....	....	....	....		1951-52	1951-5
Askey, Tom	Ana.	2	7	0	1	2	273	12	0	2.64	1	0	1	....	30	2	0	4.00		1997-98	1998-9
Astrom, Hardy	NYR, Col.	3	83	17	44	12	4456	278	0	3.74	....	....	....	....	....	....	....	....		1977-78	1980-8
Bach, Ryan	L.A.	1	3	0	3	0	108	8	0	4.44	....	....	....	....	....	....	....	....		1998-99	1998-9
Bailey, Scott	Bos.	2	19	6	6	2	965	55	0	3.42	....	....	....	....	....	....	....	....		1995-96	1996-9
Baker, Steve	NYR	4	57	20	20	11	3081	190	3	3.70	14	7	7	....	826	55	0	4.00		1979-80	1982-8
Bales, Mike	Bos., Ott.	4	23	2	15	1	1120	77	0	4.13	....	....	....	....	....	....	....	....		1992-93	1996-9
Bannerman, Murray	Van., Chi.	8	289	116	125	33	16470	1051	8	3.83	40	20	18	....	2322	165	0	4.26		1977-78	1986-8
Baron, Marco	Bos., L.A., Edm.	6	86	34	38	9	4822	292	1	3.63	1	0	1	....	20	3	0	9.00		1979-80	1984-8
Barrasso, Tom	Buf., Pit., Ott., Car., Tor., St.L.	19	777	369	277	86	44180	2385	38	3.24	119	61	54	....	6953	349	6	3.01	2	1983-84	2002-0
• Bassen, Hank	Chi., Det., Pit.	9	156	46	66	31	8759	434	5	2.97	5	1	3	....	274	11	0	2.41		1954-55	1967-6
• Bastien, Baz	Tor.	1	5	0	4	1	300	20	0	4.00	....	....	....	....	....	....	....	....		1945-46	1945-4
• Bauman, Garry	Mtl., Min.	3	35	5	16	6	1719	102	0	3.56	....	....	....	....	....	....	....	....		1966-67	1968-6
Beaupre, Don	Min., Wsh., Ott., Tor.	17	667	268	277	75	37396	2151	17	3.45	72	33	31	....	3943	220	3	3.35		1980-81	1996-9
Beauregard, Stephane	Wpg., Phi.	5	90	19	39	11	4402	268	2	3.65	4	1	3	....	238	12	0	3.03		1989-90	1993-9
Bedard, Jim	Wsh.	2	73	17	40	13	4232	278	1	3.94	....	....	....	....	....	....	....	....		1977-78	1978-7
Behrend, Marc	Wpg.	3	39	12	19	3	1991	160	1	4.82	7	1	3	....	312	19	0	3.65		1983-84	1985-8
Belanger, Yves	St.L., Atl., Bos.	6	78	29	33	6	4134	259	2	3.76	....	....	....	....	....	....	....	....		1974-75	1979-8
Belfour, Ed	Chi., S.J., Dal., Tor., Fla.	18	963	484	320	125	55695	2317	76	2.50	161	88	68	....	9945	359	14	2.17	1	1988-89	2006-0
Belhumeur, Michel	Phi., Wsh.	3	65	9	36	7	3306	254	0	4.61	1	0	0	....	10	1	0	6.00		1972-73	1975-7
• Bell, Gordie	Tor., NYR	2	8	3	5	0	480	31	0	3.88	2	1	1	....	120	9	0	4.50		1945-46	1955-5
• Benedict, Clint	Ott., Mtl.M.	13	362	190	143	28	22367	863	57	2.32	28	11	12	5	1707	53	9	1.86	4	1917-18	1929-3
• Bennett, Harvey	Bos.	1	25	10	12	2	1470	103	0	4.20	....	....	....	....	....	....	....	....		1944-45	1944-4
Bergeron, Jean-Claude	Mtl., T.B., L.A.	6	72	21	33	7	3772	232	1	3.69	....	....	....	....	....	....	....	....		1990-91	1996-9
Bernhardt, Tim	Cgy., Tor.	4	67	17	36	7	3748	267	0	4.27	....	....	....	....	....	....	....	....		1982-83	1986-8
Berthiaume, Daniel	Wpg., Min., L.A., Bos., Ott.	9	215	81	90	21	11662	714	5	3.67	14	5	9	....	807	50	0	3.72		1985-86	1993-9
Bester, Allan	Tor., Det., Dal.	10	219	73	99	17	11773	786	7	4.01	11	2	6	....	508	37	0	4.37		1983-84	1995-9
• Beveridge, Bill	Det., Ott., St.L., Mtl.M., NYR	9	297	87	166	42	18375	879	18	2.87	5	2	3	....	300	11	0	2.20		1929-30	1942-4
• Bibeault, Paul	Mtl., Tor., Bos., Chi.	7	214	81	107	25	12890	785	10	3.65	20	6	14	....	1237	71	2	3.44		1940-41	1946-4
Bierk, Zac	T.B., Min., Phx.	6	47	9	20	5	2135	113	1	3.18	....	....	....	....	....	....	....	....		1997-98	2003-0
Billington, Craig	N.J., Ott., Bos., Col., Wsh.	15	332	110	149	31	17097	1034	9	3.63	8	0	2	....	213	15	0	4.23		1985-86	2002-0
Binette, Andre	Mtl.	1	1	1	0	0	60	4	0	4.00	....	....	....	....	....	....	....	....		1954-55	1954-5
Binkley, Les	Pit.	5	196	58	94	34	11046	575	11	3.12	7	5	2	....	428	15	0	2.10		1967-68	1971-7
• Bittner, Richard	Bos.	1	1	0	0	1	60	3	0	3.00	....	....	....	....	....	....	....	....		1949-50	1949-5
Blackburn, Dan	NYR	2	63	20	32	4	3499	188	1	3.22	....	....	....	....	....	....	....	....		2001-02	2002-0
Blake, Mike	L.A.	3	40	13	15	5	2117	150	0	4.25	....	....	....	....	....	....	....	....		1981-82	1983-8
Blue, John	Bos., Buf.	3	46	16	18	7	2521	126	1	3.00	2	0	1	....	96	5	0	3.13		1992-93	1995-9
Boisvert, Gilles	Det.	1	3	0	3	0	180	9	0	3.00	....	....	....	....	....	....	....	....		1959-60	1959-6
Bouchard, Dan	Atl., Cgy., Que., Wpg.	14	655	286	232	113	37919	2061	27	3.26	43	13	30	....	2549	147	1	3.46		1972-73	1985-8
• Bourque, Claude	Mtl., Det.	2	62	16	38	8	3830	193	4	3.02	3	1	2	....	188	8	1	2.55		1938-39	1939-4
Boutin, Rollie	Wsh.	3	22	7	10	1	1137	75	0	3.96	....	....	....	....	....	....	....	....		1978-79	1980-8
• Bouvrette, Lionel	NYR	1	1	0	1	0	60	6	0	6.00	....	....	....	....	....	....	....	....		1942-43	1942-4
Bower, Johnny	NYR, Tor.	15	552	250	195	90	32016	1340	37	2.51	74	35	34	....	4378	180	5	2.47	4	1953-54	1969-7
§ • Branigan, Andy	NYA	1	1	0	0	0	7	0	0	0.00	....	....	....	....	....	....	....	....		1940-41	1940-4
‡ Brathwaite, Fred	Edm., Cgy., St.L., CBJ	9	254	81	99	37	13840	629	15	2.73	1	0	0	....	1	0	0	0.00		1993-94	2003-0
• Brimsek, Frank	Bos., Chi.	10	514	252	182	80	31210	1404	40	2.70	68	32	36	....	4395	186	2	2.54	2	1938-39	1949-5
Brochu, Martin	Wsh., Van., Pit.	3	9	0	5	0	369	22	0	3.58	....	....	....	....	....	....	....	....		1998-99	2003-0
• Broda, Turk	Tor.	14	629	302	224	101	38167	1609	62	2.53	101	60	39	....	6389	211	13	1.98	5	1936-37	1951-5
Broderick, Ken	Min., Bos.	3	27	11	12	1	1464	74	1	3.03	....	....	....	....	....	....	....	....		1969-70	1974-7
Broderick, Len	Mtl.	1	1	1	0	0	60	2	0	2.00	....	....	....	....	....	....	....	....		1957-58	1957-5
Brodeur, Richard	NYI, Van., Hfd.	9	385	131	175	62	21968	1410	6	3.85	33	13	20	....	2009	111	1	3.32		1979-80	1987-8
Bromley, Gary	Buf., Van.	6	136	54	44	28	7427	425	7	3.43	7	2	5	....	360	25	0	4.17		1973-74	1980-8
• Brooks, Art	Tor.	1	4	2	2	0	220	23	0	6.27	....	....	....	....	....	....	....	....		1917-18	1917-1
Brooks, Ross	Bos.	3	54	37	7	6	3047	134	4	2.64	1	0	0	....	20	3	0	9.00		1972-73	1974-7
• Brophy, Frank	Que.	1	21	3	18	0	1249	148	0	7.11	....	....	....	....	....	....	....	....		1919-20	1919-2
Brown, Andy	Det., Pit.	3	62	22	26	9	3373	213	1	3.79	....	....	....	....	....	....	....	....		1971-72	1973-
Brown, Ken	Chi.	1	1	0	0	0	18	1	0	3.33	....	....	....	....	....	....	....	....		1970-71	1970-
Brunetta, Mario	Que.	3	40	12	17	1	1967	128	0	3.90	....	....	....	....	....	....	....	....		1987-88	1989-9
Bullock, Bruce	Van.	3	16	3	9	3	927	74	0	4.79	....	....	....	....	....	....	....	....		1972-73	1976-
Burke, Sean	N.J., Hfd., Car., Van., Phi., Fla., Phx., T.B., L.A.	18	820	324	341	110	46442	2290	38	2.96	38	12	23	....	2151	119	1	3.32		1987-88	2006-
• Buzinski, Steve	NYR	1	9	2	6	1	560	55	0	5.89	....	....	....	....	....	....	....	....		1942-43	1942-
Caley, Don	St.L.	1	1	0	0	0	30	3	0	6.00	....	....	....	....	....	....	....	....		1967-68	1967-
Caprice, Frank	Van.	6	102	31	46	11	5589	391	1	4.20	....	....	....	....	....	....	....	....		1982-83	1987-
Carey, Jim	Wsh., Bos., St.L.	5	172	79	65	16	9668	416	16	2.58	10	2	5	....	455	35	0	4.62		1994-95	1998-
Caron, Jacques	L.A., St.L., Van.	5	72	24	29	11	3846	211	2	3.29	12	4	7	....	639	34	0	3.19		1967-68	1973-
Carter, Lyle	Cal.	1	15	4	7	0	721	50	0	4.16	....	....	....	....	....	....	....	....		1971-72	1971-
Casey, Jon	Min., Bos., St.L.	12	425	170	157	55	23255	1246	16	3.21	66	32	31	....	3743	192	3	3.08		1983-84	1996-
‡ Cassivi, Frederic	Atl., Wsh.	4	13	3	6	1	628	38	0	3.63	....	....	....	....	....	....	....	....		2001-02	2006-
Cechmanek, Roman	Phi., L.A.	4	212	110	64	28	12085	419	25	2.08	23	9	14	....	1441	56	3	2.33		2000-01	2003-
‡ Centomo, Sebastien	Tor.	1	1	0	0	0	40	3	0	4.50	....	....	....	....	....	....	....	....		2001-02	2001-
Chabot, Frederic	Mtl., Phi., L.A.	5	32	4	8	4	1262	62	0	2.95	....	....	....	....	....	....	....	....		1990-91	1998-
• Chabot, Lorne	NYR, Tor., Mtl., Chi., Mtl.M., NYA	11	412	201	147	62	25411	859	71	2.03	37	13	17	6	2498	64	5	1.54	2	1926-27	1936-
Chadwick, Ed	Tor., Bos.	6	184	57	92	35	11040	541	14	2.94	....	....	....	....	....	....	....	....		1955-56	1961-
Champoux, Bob	Det., Cal.	2	17	2	11	3	923	80	0	5.20	1	1	0	....	55	4	0	4.36		1963-64	1973-
Charpentier, Sebastien	Wsh.	3	26	6	14	1	1350	66	0	2.93	....	....	....	....	....	....	....	....		2001-02	2003-
Cheevers, Gerry	Tor., Bos.	13	418	230	102	74	24394	1174	26	2.89	88	53	34	....	5396	242	8	2.69	2	1961-62	1979-
Cheveldae, Tim	Det., Wpg., Bos.	9	340	149	136	37	19172	1116	10	3.49	25	9	15	....	1418	71	2	3.00		1988-89	1996-
Chevrier, Alain	N.J., Wpg., Chi., Pit., Det.	6	234	91	100	14	12202	845	2	4.16	16	9	7	....	1013	44	0	2.61		1985-86	1990-
‡ Chiodo, Andy	Pit.	1	8	3	4	1	486	28	0	3.46	....	....	....	....	....	....	....	....		2003-04	2003-
Chouinard, Mathieu	L.A.	1	1	0	0	0	3	0	0	0.00	....	....	....	....	....	....	....	....		2003-04	2003-
§ • Clancy, King	Ott., Tor.	2	2	0	0	0	3	1	0	20.00	....	....	....	....	....	....	....	....		1924-25	1931-
§ • Cleghorn, Odie	Pit.	1	1	1	0	0	60	2	0	2.00	....	....	....	....	....	....	....	....		1925-26	1925-
§ • Cleghorn, Sprague	Ott., Mtl.	2	2	0	0	0	5	0	0	0.00	....	....	....	....	....	....	....	....		1918-19	1921-
Clifford, Chris	Chi.	2	2	0	0	0	24	0	0	0.00	....	....	....	....	....	....	....	....		1984-85	1988-
‡ Cloutier, Dan	NYR, T.B., Van., L.A.	10	351	139	142	37	18927	874	15	2.77	25	10	13	....	1361	75	0	3.31		1997-98	2007-
Cloutier, Jacques	Buf., Chi., Que.	12	255	82	102	24	12826	778	3	3.64	8	1	5	....	413	18	1	2.62		1981-82	1993-
• Colvin, Les	Bos.	1	1	0	1	0	60	4	0	4.00	....	....	....	....	....	....	....	....		1948-49	1948-

Name	NHL Teams	NHL Seasons	Regular Schedule GP	W	L	T	Mins	GA	SO	Avg	Playoffs GP	W	L	T	Mins	GA	SO	Avg	NHL Cup Wins	First NHL Season	Last NHL Season
onacher, Charlie	Tor., Det.	3	4	0	0	0	10	0	0	0.00	....	....	....	....	....	....	....	....		1932-33	1938-39
onnell, Alec	Ott., Det., NYA, Mtl.M.	12	417	193	156	67	26050	830	81	1.91	21	8	5	8	1309	26	4	1.19	2	1924-25	1936-37
orsi, Jim	Edm.	1	26	8	14	3	1366	83	0	3.65	....	....	....	....	....	....	....	....		1979-80	1979-80
ourteau, Maurice	Bos.	1	6	2	4	0	360	33	0	5.50	....	....	....	....	....	....	....	....		1943-44	1943-44
ousineau, Marcel	Tor., NYI, L.A.	4	26	4	10	1	1047	51	1	2.92	....	....	....	....	....	....	....	....		1996-97	1999-00
owley, Wayne	Edm.	1	1	0	1	0	57	3	0	3.16	....	....	....	....	....	....	....	....		1993-94	1993-94
ox, Abbie	Mtl.M., NYA, Det., Mtl.	3	5	1	1	2	263	11	0	2.51	....	....	....	....	....	....	....	....		1929-30	1935-36
raig, Jim	Atl., Bos., Min.	3	30	11	10	7	1588	100	0	3.78	....	....	....	....	....	....	....	....		1979-80	1983-84
rha, Jiri	Tor.	2	69	28	27	11	3942	261	0	3.97	5	0	4	....	186	21	0	6.77		1979-80	1980-81
rozier, Roger	Det., Buf., Wsh.	14	518	206	197	70	28567	1446	30	3.04	32	14	16	....	1789	82	1	2.75		1963-64	1976-77
ude, Wilf	Phi., Bos., Chi., Mtl., Det.	10	282	100	132	49	17586	798	24	2.72	19	7	11	1	1257	51	1	2.43		1930-31	1940-41
utts, Don	Edm.	1	6	1	2	1	269	16	0	3.57	....	....	....	....	....	....	....	....		1979-80	1979-80
yr, Claude	Mtl.	1	1	0	0	0	20	1	0	3.00	....	....	....	....	....	....	....	....		1958-59	1958-59
adswell, Doug	Cgy.	2	27	8	8	3	1346	99	0	4.41	....	....	....	....	....	....	....	....		1986-87	1987-88
afoe, Byron	Wsh., L.A., Bos., Atl.	12	415	171	170	56	23478	1051	26	2.69	27	10	16	....	1686	65	3	2.31		1992-93	2003-04
Alessio, Corrie	Hfd.	1	1	0	0	0	11	0	0	0.00	....	....	....	....	....	....	....	....		1992-93	1992-93
aley, Joe	Pit., Buf., Det.	4	105	34	44	19	5836	326	3	3.35	....	....	....	....	....	....	....	....		1968-69	1971-72
amore, Nick	Bos.	1	1	1	0	0	60	3	0	3.00	....	....	....	....	....	....	....	....		1941-42	1941-42
Amour, Marc	Cgy., Phi.	2	16	2	4	2	579	32	0	3.32	....	....	....	....	....	....	....	....		1985-86	1988-89
amphousse, Jean-Fr.	N.J.	1	6	1	3	0	294	12	0	2.45	....	....	....	....	....	....	....	....		2001-02	2001-02
arragh, Jack	Ott.	1	1	0	0	0	2	0	0	0.00	....	....	....	....	....	....	....	....		1919-20	1919-20
askalakis, Cleon	Bos.	3	12	3	4	1	506	41	0	4.86	....	....	....	....	....	....	....	....		1984-85	1986-87
avidson, John	St.L., NYR	10	301	123	124	39	17109	1004	7	3.52	31	16	14	....	1862	77	1	2.48		1973-74	1982-83
ecourcy, Bob	NYR	1	1	0	1	0	29	6	0	12.41	....	....	....	....	....	....	....	....		1947-48	1947-48
efelice, Norm	Bos.	1	10	3	5	2	600	30	0	3.00	....	....	....	....	....	....	....	....		1956-57	1956-57
eJordy, Denis	Chi., L.A., Mtl., Det.	12	316	124	128	51	17798	929	15	3.13	18	6	9	....	946	55	0	3.49	1	1960-61	1973-74
elGuidice, Matt	Bos.	2	11	2	5	1	434	28	0	3.87	....	....	....	....	....	....	....	....		1990-91	1991-92
enis, Marc	Col., CBJ, T.B., Mtl.	11	349	112	179	31	19526	982	16	3.02	....	....	....	....	....	....	....	....		1996-97	2008-09
eRouville, Philippe	Pit.	2	3	1	2	0	171	9	0	3.16	....	....	....	....	....	....	....	....		1994-95	1996-97
esjardins, Gerry	L.A., Chi., NYI, Buf.	10	331	122	153	44	19014	1042	12	3.29	35	15	15	....	1874	108	0	3.46		1968-69	1977-78
esRochers, Patrick	Phx., Car.	2	11	2	6	1	540	33	0	3.67	....	....	....	....	....	....	....	....		2001-02	2002-03
ckie, Bill	Chi.	1	1	1	0	0	60	3	0	3.00	....	....	....	....	....	....	....	....		1941-42	1941-42
on, Connie	Det.	2	38	23	11	4	2280	119	1	3.13	5	1	4	....	300	17	0	3.40		1943-44	1944-45
on, Michel	Que., Wpg., Pit.	6	227	60	118	32	12695	898	2	4.24	5	2	3	....	304	22	0	4.34		1979-80	1984-85
vis, Reinhard	St.L.	4	28	6	9	3	1212	67	0	3.32	1	0	0	....	18	0	0	0.00		2001-02	2005-06
olson, Dolly	Det.	3	93	35	41	17	5820	192	16	1.98	2	0	2	0	120	7	0	3.50		1928-29	1930-31
opson, Rob	Pit.	1	2	0	0	0	45	3	0	4.00	....	....	....	....	....	....	....	....		1993-94	1993-94
owie, Bruce	Tor.	1	2	0	1	0	72	4	0	3.33	....	....	....	....	....	....	....	....		1983-84	1983-84
aper, Tom	Wpg., Buf., NYI	6	53	19	23	5	2807	173	1	3.70	7	3	4	....	433	19	1	2.63		1988-89	1995-96
yden, Dave	NYR, Chi., Buf., Edm.	9	203	66	76	31	10424	555	9	3.19	3	0	2	....	133	9	0	4.06		1961-62	1979-80
yden, Ken	Mtl.	8	397	258	57	74	23352	870	46	2.24	112	80	32	....	6846	274	10	2.40	6	1970-71	1978-79
uffus, Parris	Phx.	1	1	0	0	0	29	1	0	2.07	....	....	....	....	....	....	....	....		1996-97	1996-97
umas, Michel	Chi.	3	8	2	1	2	362	24	0	3.98	1	0	0	....	19	1	0	3.16		1974-75	1976-77
unham, Mike	N.J., Nsh., NYR, Atl., NYI	10	394	141	178	44	21653	989	19	2.74	....	....	....	....	....	....	....	....		1996-97	2006-07
upuis, Bob	Edm.	1	1	0	1	0	60	4	0	4.00	....	....	....	....	....	....	....	....		1979-80	1979-80
urnan, Bill	Mtl.	7	383	208	112	62	22945	901	34	2.36	45	27	18	....	2871	99	2	2.07	2	1943-44	1949-50
yck, Ed	Van.	3	49	8	28	5	2453	178	1	4.35	....	....	....	....	....	....	....	....		1971-72	1973-74
wards, Don	Buf., Cgy., Tor.	10	459	208	155	74	26181	1449	16	3.32	42	16	21	....	2302	132	1	3.44		1976-77	1985-86
wards, Gary	St.L., L.A., Cle., Min., Edm., Pit.	13	286	88	125	51	16002	973	10	3.65	11	5	4	....	537	34	0	3.80		1968-69	1981-82
wards, Marv	Pit., Tor., Cal.	4	61	15	34	7	3467	218	2	3.77	....	....	....	....	....	....	....	....		1968-69	1973-74
wards, Roy	Chi., Det., Pit.	8	236	97	88	38	13109	637	12	2.92	4	0	3	....	206	11	0	3.20	1	1960-61	1973-74
lund, Brian	T.B.	1	1	0	1	0	58	3	0	3.10	....	....	....	....	....	....	....	....		2005-06	2005-06
ot, Darren	L.A., Det., Buf.	5	89	25	41	12	4931	377	1	4.59	1	0	0	....	40	7	0	10.50		1984-85	1988-89
acott, Ken	Van.	1	12	2	3	4	555	41	0	4.43	....	....	....	....	....	....	....	....		1982-83	1982-83
ckson, Chad	N.J.	1	2	1	1	0	120	9	0	4.50	....	....	....	....	....	....	....	....		1991-92	1991-92
che, Robert	Phx., Phi.	8	186	78	64	22	10139	464	10	2.75	25	13	11	....	1405	64	1	2.73		1998-99	2006-07
posito, Tony	Mtl., Chi.	16	886	423	306	151	52585	2563	76	2.92	99	45	53	....	6017	308	6	3.07	1	1968-69	1983-84
sensa, Bob	Wpg., Det., Edm., Phx., Van., Buf.	12	446	173	176	47	24215	1270	18	3.15	16	4	9	....	864	51	0	3.54		1988-89	2001-02
ans, Claude	Mtl., Bos.	2	5	1	2	1	260	16	0	3.69	....	....	....	....	....	....	....	....		1954-55	1957-58
elby, Randy	Mtl., Edm.	2	2	0	1	0	63	5	0	4.76	....	....	....	....	....	....	....	....		1988-89	1989-90
nkhouser, Scott	Atl.	2	23	4	12	2	1180	65	0	3.31	....	....	....	....	....	....	....	....		1999-00	2000-01
rr, Rocky	Buf.	3	19	2	6	3	722	42	0	3.49	....	....	....	....	....	....	....	....		1972-73	1974-75
well, Doug	Phi., Tor., Col.	12	373	123	153	69	20771	1096	18	3.17	21	6	15	....	1270	66	1	3.12		1967-68	1978-79
rnandez, Manny	Dal., Min., Bos.	13	325	143	123	35	18580	775	15	2.50	11	3	4	....	571	19	0	2.00		1994-95	2008-09
haud, Eric	NYI, Nsh., Car., Mtl.	6	95	22	47	10	4799	251	2	3.14	....	....	....	....	....	....	....	....		1995-96	2000-01
ley, Brian	Nsh., Bos.	3	4	0	2	0	166	13	0	4.70	....	....	....	....	....	....	....	....		2002-03	2006-07
et, Stephane	Que., Col., L.A., Mtl.	13	390	164	153	44	21785	1114	16	3.07	14	1	7	....	563	37	0	3.94	1	1989-90	2001-02
zpatrick, Mark	L.A., NYI, Fla., T.B., Chi., Car.	12	329	113	136	49	18329	953	8	3.12	9	0	3	....	289	23	0	4.78		1988-89	1999-00
herty, Wade	S.J., NYI, T.B., Fla., Nsh.	11	120	27	56	9	5941	348	5	3.51	7	2	3	....	377	31	0	4.93		1991-92	2002-03
rbes, Jake	Tor., Ham., NYA, Phi.	13	210	85	114	11	12922	594	19	2.76	2	0	2	0	120	7	0	3.50		1919-20	1932-33
rd, Brian	Que., Pit.	2	11	3	7	0	580	61	0	6.31	....	....	....	....	....	....	....	....		1983-84	1984-85
ster, Norm	Bos., Edm.	2	13	7	4	0	623	34	0	3.27	....	....	....	....	....	....	....	....		1990-91	1991-92
untain, Mike	Van., Car., Ott.	4	11	2	6	0	483	28	1	3.48	....	....	....	....	....	....	....	....		1996-97	2000-01
wler, Hec	Bos.	1	7	1	6	0	409	42	0	6.16	....	....	....	....	....	....	....	....		1924-25	1924-25
ancis, Emile	Chi., NYR	6	95	31	52	11	5660	355	1	3.76	....	....	....	....	....	....	....	....		1946-47	1951-52
anks, Jimmy	Det., NYR, Bos.	4	42	12	23	7	2520	181	1	4.31	1	0	1	....	30	2	0	4.00	1	1936-37	1943-44
ederick, Ray	Chi.	1	5	0	4	1	300	22	0	4.40	....	....	....	....	....	....	....	....		1954-55	1954-55
esen, Karl	N.J.	1	4	0	2	1	130	16	0	7.38	....	....	....	....	....	....	....	....		1986-87	1986-87
oese, Bob	Phi., NYR	8	242	128	72	20	13451	694	13	3.10	18	3	9	....	830	55	0	3.98		1982-83	1989-90
hr, Grant	Edm., Tor., Buf., L.A., St.L., Cgy.	19	868	403	295	114	48945	2756	25	3.38	150	92	50	....	8834	430	6	2.92	5	1981-82	1999-00
kufuji, Yutaka	L.A.	1	4	0	3	0	96	7	0	4.38	....	....	....	....	....	....	....	....		2006-07	2006-07
ge, Joaquin	Edm.	3	23	4	12	1	1076	67	0	3.74	....	....	....	....	....	....	....	....		1994-95	2000-01
gnon, Dave	Det.	1	2	0	1	0	35	6	0	10.29	....	....	....	....	....	....	....	....		1990-91	1990-91
mble, Bruce	NYR, Bos., Tor., Phi.	10	327	110	150	46	18442	988	22	3.21	5	0	4	....	206	25	0	7.28		1958-59	1971-72
mble, Troy	Van.	4	72	22	29	9	3804	229	1	3.61	4	1	3	....	249	16	0	3.86		1986-87	1991-92
rdiner, Bert	NYR, Mtl., Chi., Bos.	6	144	49	68	27	8760	554	3	3.79	9	4	5	....	647	20	0	1.85		1935-36	1943-44
rdiner, Charlie	Chi.	7	316	112	152	52	19687	664	42	2.02	21	12	6	3	1472	35	5	1.43	1	1927-28	1933-34
rdner, George	Det., Van.	5	66	16	30	6	3313	207	0	3.75	....	....	....	....	....	....	....	....		1965-66	1971-72
rner, Tyrone	Cgy.	1	3	0	2	0	139	12	0	5.18	....	....	....	....	....	....	....	....		1998-99	1998-99
rnett, Michael	Atl.	1	24	10	7	4	1271	73	2	3.45	....	....	....	....	....	....	....	....		2005-06	2005-06
rrett, John	Hfd., Que., Van.	6	207	68	91	37	11763	837	1	4.27	9	4	3	....	461	33	0	4.30		1979-80	1984-85
therum, Dave	Det.	1	3	2	0	1	180	3	1	1.00	....	....	....	....	....	....	....	....	1	1953-54	1953-54
uthier, Paul	Mtl.	1	1	0	0	1	70	2	0	1.71	....	....	....	....	....	....	....	....		1937-38	1937-38
uthier, Sean	S.J.	1	1	0	0	0	3	0	0	0.00	....	....	....	....	....	....	....	....		1998-99	1998-99
lineau, Jack	Bos., Chi.	4	143	46	64	33	8580	447	7	3.13	4	1	2	....	260	7	1	1.62		1948-49	1953-54
acomin, Ed	NYR, Det.	13	609	289	209	96	35633	1672	54	2.82	65	29	35	....	3838	180	1	2.81		1965-66	1977-78
bert, Gilles	Min., Bos., Det.	14	416	192	143	60	23677	1290	18	3.27	32	17	15	....	1919	97	3	3.03		1969-70	1982-83
l, Andre	Bos.	1	5	3	2	0	270	13	1	2.89	....	....	....	....	....	....	....	....		1967-68	1967-68
odman, Paul	Chi.	3	52	23	20	9	3240	117	6	2.17	3	0	3	....	187	10	0	3.21	1	1937-38	1940-41
rdon, Scott	Que.	2	23	2	16	0	1082	101	0	5.60	....	....	....	....	....	....	....	....		1989-90	1990-91
sselin, Mario	Que., L.A., Hfd.	9	241	91	107	14	12857	801	6	3.74	32	16	15	....	1816	99	0	3.27		1983-84	1993-94
verde, David	L.A.	3	5	1	4	0	278	29	0	6.26	....	....	....	....	....	....	....	....		1991-92	1993-94
ahame, Ron	Bos., L.A., Que.	4	114	50	43	15	6472	409	5	3.79	4	2	1	....	202	7	0	2.08		1977-78	1980-81
ant, Benny	Tor., NYA, Bos.	6	52	17	27	4	3036	188	4	3.72	....	....	....	....	....	....	....	....		1928-29	1943-44
ant, Doug	Det., St.L.	7	77	27	34	8	4199	280	2	4.00	....	....	....	....	....	....	....	....		1973-74	1979-80
atton, Gilles	St.L., NYR	2	47	13	18	9	2299	154	0	4.02	....	....	....	....	....	....	....	....		1975-76	1976-77
ay, Gerry	Det., NYI	2	8	1	5	1	440	35	0	4.77	....	....	....	....	....	....	....	....		1970-71	1972-73
ay, Harrison	Det.	1	1	0	1	0	40	5	0	7.50	....	....	....	....	....	....	....	....		1963-64	1963-64

			Regular Schedule								Playoffs										
Name	NHL Teams	NHL Seasons	GP	W	L	T	Mins	GA	SO	Avg	GP	W	L	T	Mins	GA	SO	Avg	NHL Cup Wins	First NHL Season	Last NHL Season
Greenlay, Mike	Edm.	1	2	0	0	0	20	4	0	12.00	....	....	....	....	....	....	....	....		1989-90	1989-
Guenette, Steve	Pit., Cgy.	5	35	19	16	0	1958	122	1	3.74	....	....	....	....	....	....	....	....		1986-87	1990-
‡ Gustafson, Derek	Min.	2	5	1	3	0	265	10	0	2.26	....	....	....	....	....	....	....	....		2000-01	2001-
Hackett, Jeff	NYI, S.J., Chi., Mtl., Bos., Phi.	15	500	166	244	56	28125	1361	26	2.90	12	3	7	....	610	36	0	3.54		1988-89	2003-
• Hainsworth, George	Mtl., Tor.	11	465	246	145	74	29087	937	94	1.93	52	22	25	5	3486	112	8	1.93	2	1926-27	1936-
Hall, Glenn	Det., Chi., St.L.	19	906	407	326	163	53484	2222	84	2.49	115	49	65	....	6899	320	6	2.78	2	1951-52	1970-
Hamel, Pierre	Tor., Wpg.	4	69	13	41	7	3766	276	0	4.40	....	....	....	....	....	....	....	....		1974-75	1980-
Hanlon, Glen	Van., St.L., NYR, Det.	15	477	167	202	61	26037	1561	13	3.60	35	11	15	....	1756	92	4	3.14		1977-78	1990-
Harrison, Paul	Min., Tor., Pit., Buf.	7	109	28	59	9	5806	408	2	4.22	4	0	1	....	157	9	0	3.44		1975-76	1981-
‡ Hasek, Dominik	Chi., Buf., Det., Ott.	16	735	389	223	95	42837	1572	81	2.20	119	65	49	....	7318	246	14	2.02	2	1990-91	2007-
‡ Hauser, Adam	L.A.	1	1	0	0	0	51	6	0	7.06	....	....	....	....	....	....	....	....		2005-06	2005-
Hayward, Brian	Wpg., Mtl., Min., S.J.	11	357	143	156	37	20025	1242	8	3.72	37	11	18	....	1803	104	0	3.46		1982-83	1992-
Head, Don	Bos.	1	38	9	26	3	2280	158	2	4.16	....	....	....	....	....	....	....	....		1961-62	1961-
Healy, Glenn	L.A., NYI, NYR, Tor.	15	437	166	190	47	24256	1361	13	3.37	37	13	15	....	1930	108	0	3.36	1	1985-86	2000-
Hebert, Guy	St.L., Ana., NYR	10	491	191	222	56	27889	1307	28	2.81	14	4	7	....	744	33	1	2.66		1991-92	2000-
• Hebert, Sammy	Tor., Ott.	2	4	2	1	0	200	19	0	5.70	....	....	....	....	....	....	....	....	1	1917-18	1923-
Heinz, Rick	St.L., Van.	5	49	14	19	5	2356	159	2	4.05	1	0	0	....	8	1	0	7.50		1980-81	1984-
Henderson, John	Bos.	2	46	15	15	15	2688	113	5	2.52	2	0	2	....	120	8	0	4.00		1954-55	1955-
• Henry, Gord	Bos.	4	3	1	2	0	180	5	1	1.67	5	0	4	....	283	21	0	4.45		1948-49	1952-
• Henry, Jim	NYR, Chi., Bos.	9	406	161	173	70	24355	1166	28	2.87	29	11	18	....	1741	81	2	2.79		1941-42	1954-
Herron, Denis	Pit., K.C., Mtl.	14	462	146	203	76	25608	1579	10	3.70	15	5	10	....	901	50	0	3.33		1972-73	1985-
Hextall, Ron	Phi., Que., NYI	13	608	296	214	69	34750	1723	23	2.97	93	47	43	....	5456	276	2	3.04		1986-87	1998-
• Highton, Hec	Chi.	1	24	10	14	0	1440	108	0	4.50	....	....	....	....	....	....	....	....		1943-44	1943-
§ • Himes, Normie	NYA	2	2	0	1	0	79	3	0	2.28	....	....	....	....	....	....	....	....		1927-28	1928-
Hirsch, Corey	NYR, Van., Wsh., Dal.	7	108	34	45	14	5775	301	4	3.13	6	2	3	....	338	21	0	3.73		1992-93	2002-
‡ Hnilicka, Milan	NYR, Atl., L.A.	5	121	29	67	13	6509	359	5	3.31	....	....	....	....	....	....	....	....		1999-00	2003-
Hodge, Charlie	Mtl., Oak., Van.	14	358	150	125	61	20573	925	24	2.70	16	7	8	....	804	32	2	2.39	6	1954-55	1970-
Hodson, Kevin	Det., T.B.	6	71	17	18	10	2910	134	4	2.76	1	0	0	....	1	0	0	0.00	2	1995-96	2002-
Hoffort, Bruce	Phi.	2	9	4	0	3	368	22	0	3.59	....	....	....	....	....	....	....	....		1989-90	1990-
Hoganson, Paul	Pit.	1	2	0	1	0	57	7	0	7.37	....	....	....	....	....	....	....	....		1970-71	1970-
Hogosta, Goran	NYI, Que.	2	22	5	12	3	1208	83	1	4.12	....	....	....	....	....	....	....	....		1977-78	1979-
Holden, Mark	Mtl., Wpg.	4	8	2	2	1	372	25	0	4.03	....	....	....	....	....	....	....	....		1981-82	1984-
Holland, Ken	Hfd., Det.	2	4	0	2	1	206	17	0	4.95	....	....	....	....	....	....	....	....		1980-81	1983-
Holland, Rob	Pit.	2	44	11	22	9	2513	171	1	4.08	....	....	....	....	....	....	....	....		1979-80	1980-
• Holmes, Hap	Tor., Det.	4	103	39	54	10	6510	264	17	2.43	2	1	1	0	120	7	0	3.50	1	1917-18	1927-
§ • Horner, Red	Tor.	2	2	0	0	0	3	1	0	20.00	....	....	....	....	....	....	....	....		1928-29	1931-
‡ Houle, Martin	Phi.	1	1	0	0	0	2	1	0	30.00	....	....	....	....	....	....	....	....		2006-07	2006-
Hrivnak, Jim	Wsh., Wpg., St.L.	5	85	34	30	3	4217	262	0	3.73	....	....	....	....	....	....	....	....		1989-90	1993-
Hrudey, Kelly	NYI, L.A., S.J.	15	677	271	265	88	38084	2174	17	3.43	85	36	46	....	5163	283	0	3.29		1983-84	1997-
Hurme, Jani	Ott., Fla.	4	76	29	25	11	4041	176	6	2.61	....	....	....	....	....	....	....	....		1999-00	2002-
Ing, Peter	Tor., Edm., Det.	4	74	20	37	9	3941	266	1	4.05	....	....	....	....	....	....	....	....		1989-90	1993-
Inness, Gary	Pit., Phi., Wsh.	7	162	58	61	27	8710	494	2	3.40	9	5	4	....	540	24	0	2.67		1973-74	1980-
Irbe, Arturs	S.J., Dal., Van., Car.	13	568	218	236	79	32066	1513	33	2.83	51	23	27	....	2981	142	1	2.86		1991-92	2003-
Ireland, Randy	Buf.	1	2	0	0	0	30	3	0	6.00	....	....	....	....	....	....	....	....		1978-79	1978-
Irons, Robbie	St.L.	1	1	0	0	0	3	0	0	0.00	....	....	....	....	....	....	....	....		1968-69	1968-
• Ironstone, Joe	Ott., NYA, Tor.	3	2	0	0	1	110	3	1	1.64	....	....	....	....	....	....	....	....		1924-25	1927-
Jablonski, Pat	St.L., T.B., Mtl., Phx., Car.	8	128	28	62	18	6634	413	1	3.74	4	0	0	....	139	6	0	2.59		1989-90	1997-
Jackson, Doug	Chi.	1	6	2	3	1	360	42	0	7.00	....	....	....	....	....	....	....	....		1947-48	1947-
Jackson, Percy	Bos., NYA, NYR	4	7	1	3	1	392	26	0	3.98	....	....	....	....	....	....	....	....		1931-32	1935-
Jaks, Pauli	L.A.	1	1	0	0	0	40	2	0	3.00	....	....	....	....	....	....	....	....		1994-95	1994
Janaszak, Steve	Min., Col.	2	3	0	1	1	160	15	0	5.63	....	....	....	....	....	....	....	....		1979-80	1981
Janecyk, Bob	Chi., L.A.	6	110	43	47	13	6250	432	2	4.15	3	0	3	....	184	10	0	3.26		1983-84	1988
§ • Jenkins, Roger	NYA	1	1	0	1	0	30	7	0	14.00	....	....	....	....	....	....	....	....		1938-39	1938
Jensen, Al	Det., Wsh., L.A.	7	179	95	53	18	9974	557	8	3.35	12	5	5	....	598	32	0	3.21		1980-81	1986
Jensen, Darren	Phi.	2	30	15	10	1	1496	95	2	3.81	....	....	....	....	....	....	....	....		1984-85	1985
Johnson, Bob	St.L., Pit.	2	24	9	9	1	1059	66	0	3.74	....	....	....	....	....	....	....	....		1972-73	1974
Johnston, Eddie	Bos., Tor., St.L., Chi.	16	592	234	257	80	34216	1852	32	3.25	18	7	10	....	1023	57	1	3.34	2	1962-63	1977-
Joseph, Curtis	St.L., Edm., Tor., Det., Phx., Cgy.	19	943	454	352	96	54054	2516	51	2.79	133	63	66	....	8106	327	16	2.42		1989-90	2008
Junkin, Joe	Bos.	1	1	0	0	0	8	0	0	0.00	....	....	....	....	....	....	....	....		1968-69	1968
Kaarela, Jari	Col.	1	5	2	2	0	220	22	0	6.00	....	....	....	....	....	....	....	....		1980-81	1980
Kamppuri, Hannu	N.J.	1	13	1	10	1	645	54	0	5.02	....	....	....	....	....	....	....	....		1984-85	1984
• Karakas, Mike	Chi., Mtl.	8	336	114	169	53	20614	1002	28	2.92	23	11	12	0	1434	72	3	3.01	1	1935-36	1945
Keans, Doug	L.A., Bos.	9	210	96	64	26	11388	666	4	3.51	9	2	6	....	432	34	0	4.72		1979-80	1987-
• Keenan, Don	Bos.	1	1	0	1	0	60	4	0	4.00	....	....	....	....	....	....	....	....		1958-59	1958
• Kerr, Dave	Mtl.M., NYA, NYR	11	427	203	148	75	26639	954	51	2.15	40	18	19	3	2616	76	8	1.74	1	1930-31	1940
Kidd, Trevor	Cgy., Car., Fla., Tor.	12	387	140	162	52	21426	1014	19	2.84	10	3	5	....	550	36	1	3.93		1991-92	2003
King, Scott	Det.	2	2	0	0	0	61	3	0	2.95	....	....	....	....	....	....	....	....		1990-91	1991
Kleisinger, Terry	NYR	1	4	0	2	0	191	14	0	4.40	....	....	....	....	....	....	....	....		1985-86	1985
Klymkiw, Julian	NYR	1	1	0	0	0	19	2	0	6.32	....	....	....	....	....	....	....	....		1958-59	1958
Knickle, Rick	L.A.	2	14	7	6	0	706	44	0	3.74	....	....	....	....	....	....	....	....		1992-93	1993
Kochan, Dieter	T.B., Min.	4	21	1	11	1	849	56	0	3.96	....	....	....	....	....	....	....	....		1999-00	2002
‡ Kolesnik, Vitali	Col.	1	8	3	3	0	370	20	0	3.24	....	....	....	....	....	....	....	....		2005-06	2005
Kolzig, Olaf	Wsh., T.B.	17	719	303	297	87	41671	1885	35	2.71	45	20	24	....	2799	100	6	2.14		1989-90	2008
Konstantinov, Evgeny	T.B.	2	2	0	0	0	21	1	0	2.86	....	....	....	....	....	....	....	....		2000-01	2002
Kuntar, Les	Mtl.	1	6	2	2	0	302	16	0	3.18	....	....	....	....	....	....	....	....		1993-94	1993
Kurt, Gary	Cal.	1	16	1	7	5	838	60	0	4.30	....	....	....	....	....	....	....	....		1971-72	1971
Labbe, Jean-Francois	NYR, CBJ	3	15	3	6	0	628	36	0	3.44	....	....	....	....	....	....	....	....		1999-00	2002
Labrecque, Patrick	Mtl.	1	2	0	1	0	98	7	0	4.29	....	....	....	....	....	....	....	....		1995-96	1995
Lacher, Blaine	Bos.	2	47	22	16	4	2636	123	4	2.80	5	1	4	....	283	12	0	2.54		1994-95	1995
• Lacroix, Frenchy	Mtl.	2	5	1	4	0	280	16	0	3.43	....	....	....	....	....	....	....	....		1925-26	1926
LaFerriere, Rick	Col.	1	1	0	0	0	20	1	0	3.00	....	....	....	....	....	....	....	....		1981-82	1981
LaForest, Mark	Det., Phi., Tor., Ott.	6	103	25	54	4	5032	354	2	4.22	2	1	0	....	48	1	0	1.25		1985-86	1993
Lajeunesse, Simon	Ott.	1	1	0	0	0	24	0	0	0.00	....	....	....	....	....	....	....	....		2001-02	2001
Lamothe, Marc	Chi., Det.	2	4	2	1	1	241	13	0	3.24	....	....	....	....	....	....	....	....		1999-00	2003
‡ Langkow, Scott	Wpg., Phx., Atl.	4	20	3	12	1	943	68	0	4.33	....	....	....	....	....	....	....	....		1995-96	1999
• Larocque, Michel	Mtl., Tor., Phi., St.L.	11	312	160	89	45	17615	978	17	3.33	14	6	6	....	759	37	1	2.92	4	1973-74	1983
Larocque, Michel	Chi.	1	3	0	2	0	152	9	0	3.55	....	....	....	....	....	....	....	....		2000-01	2000
‡ Lasak, Jan	Nsh.	2	6	0	4	0	267	18	0	4.04	....	....	....	....	....	....	....	....		2001-02	2002
Laskoski, Gary	L.A.	2	59	19	27	5	2942	228	0	4.65	....	....	....	....	....	....	....	....		1982-83	1983
Laxton, Gord	Pit.	4	17	4	9	0	800	74	0	5.55	....	....	....	....	....	....	....	....		1975-76	1978
LeBlanc, Ray	Chi.	1	1	1	0	0	60	1	0	1.00	....	....	....	....	....	....	....	....		1991-92	1991
§ • Leduc, Albert	Mtl.	1	1	0	0	1	2	1	0	30.00	....	....	....	....	....	....	....	....		1931-32	1931
Legris, Claude	Det.	2	4	0	1	1	91	4	0	2.64	....	....	....	....	....	....	....	....		1980-81	1981
• Lehman, Hugh	Chi.	2	48	20	24	4	3047	136	6	2.68	2	0	1	1	120	10	0	5.00		1926-27	1927
Lemelin, Reggie	Atl., Cgy., Bos.	15	507	236	162	63	28006	1613	12	3.46	59	23	25	....	3119	186	2	3.58		1978-79	1992
Lenarduzzi, Mike	Hfd.	2	4	1	1	1	189	10	0	3.17	....	....	....	....	....	....	....	....		1992-93	1993
Lessard, Mario	L.A.	6	240	92	97	39	13529	843	9	3.74	20	6	12	....	1136	83	0	4.38		1978-79	1983
Levasseur, Jean-Louis	Min.	1	1	0	1	0	60	7	0	7.00	....	....	....	....	....	....	....	....		1979-80	1979
§ • Levinsky, Alex	Tor.	1	1	0	0	0	1	1	0	60.00	....	....	....	....	....	....	....	....		1931-32	1931
• Lindbergh, Pelle	Phi.	5	157	87	49	15	9150	503	7	3.30	23	12	10	....	1214	63	3	3.11		1981-82	1985
• Lindsay, Bert	Mtl.W., Tor.	2	20	6	14	0	1238	118	0	5.72	....	....	....	....	....	....	....	....		1917-18	1918
Little, Neil	Phi.	2	2	0	2	0	93	6	0	3.87	....	....	....	....	....	....	....	....		2001-02	2003
Littman, David	Buf., T.B.	3	3	0	2	0	141	14	0	5.96	....	....	....	....	....	....	....	....		1990-91	1992
Liut, Mike	St.L., Hfd., Wsh.	13	664	294	271	74	38215	2221	25	3.49	67	29	32	....	3814	215	2	3.38		1979-80	1991
Lockett, Ken	Van.	2	55	13	15	8	2348	131	2	3.35	1	0	1	....	60	6	0	6.00		1974-75	1975
• Lockhart, Howard	Tor., Que., Ham., Bos.	5	59	16	41	0	3413	287	1	5.05	....	....	....	....	....	....	....	....		1919-20	1924
LoPresti, Pete	Min., Edm.	6	175	43	102	20	9858	668	5	4.07	2	0	2	....	77	6	0	4.68		1974-75	1980
• LoPresti, Sam	Chi.	2	74	30	38	6	4530	236	4	3.13	8	3	5	....	530	17	1	1.92		1940-41	1941

Name	NHL Teams	NHL Seasons	Regular Schedule GP	W	L	T	Mins	GA	SO	Avg	Playoffs GP	W	L	T	Mins	GA	SO	Avg	NHL Cup Wins	First NHL Season	Last NHL Season
renz, Danny	NYI	3	8	1	5	0	357	25	0	4.20	....	....	....	....	....	....	....	....		1990-91	1992-93
ustel, Ron	Wpg.	1	1	0	1	0	60	10	0	10.00	....	....	....	....	....	....	....	....		1980-81	1980-81
w, Ron	Tor., Wsh., Det., Que., Edm., N.J.	11	382	102	203	38	20502	1463	4	4.28	7	1	6	....	452	29	0	3.85		1972-73	1984-85
zinski, Larry	Det.	1	30	6	11	7	1459	105	0	4.32	....	....	....	....	....	....	....	....		1980-81	1980-81
mley, Harry	Det., NYR, Chi., Tor., Bos.	16	803	330	329	142	48044	2206	71	2.75	76	29	47	....	4778	198	7	2.49	1	1943-44	1959-60
acKenzie, Shawn	N.J.	1	4	0	1	0	130	15	0	6.92	....	....	....	....	....	....	....	....		1982-83	1982-83
adeley, Darrin	Ott.	3	39	4	23	5	1928	140	0	4.36	....	....	....	....	....	....	....	....		1992-93	1994-95
alarchuk, Clint	Que., Wsh., Buf.	11	338	141	130	45	19030	1100	12	3.47	15	2	9	....	781	56	0	4.30		1981-82	1991-92
aneluk, George	NYI	1	4	1	1	0	140	15	0	6.43	....	....	....	....	....	....	....	....		1990-91	1990-91
aniago, Cesare	Tor., Mtl., NYR, Min., Van.	15	568	190	257	97	32569	1773	30	3.27	36	15	21	....	2247	100	3	2.67		1960-61	1977-78
aracle, Norm	Det., Atl.	5	66	14	33	8	3430	177	1	3.10	2	0	0	....	58	3	0	3.10		1997-98	2001-02
arkkanen, Jussi	Edm., NYR	5	128	43	47	15	6610	297	7	2.70	7	3	3	....	374	14	1	2.25		2001-02	2006-07
arois, Jean	Tor., Chi.	2	3	1	2	0	180	15	0	5.00	....	....	....	....	....	....	....	....		1943-44	1953-54
artin, Seth	St.L.	1	30	8	10	7	1552	67	1	2.59	2	0	0	....	73	5	0	4.11		1967-68	1967-68
ason, Bob	Wsh., Chi., Que., Van.	8	145	55	65	16	7988	500	1	3.76	5	2	3	....	369	12	1	1.95		1983-84	1990-91
attsson, Markus	Wpg., Min., L.A.	4	92	21	46	14	5007	343	6	4.11	....	....	....	....	....	....	....	....		1979-80	1983-84
ay, Darrell	St.L.	2	6	1	5	0	364	31	0	5.11	....	....	....	....	....	....	....	....		1985-86	1987-88
ayer, Gilles	Tor.	4	9	2	6	1	540	24	0	2.67	....	....	....	....	....	....	....	....		1949-50	1955-56
cAuley, Ken	NYR	2	96	17	64	15	5740	537	1	5.61	....	....	....	....	....	....	....	....		1943-44	1944-45
cCartan, Jack	NYR	2	12	2	7	3	680	42	1	3.71	....	....	....	....	....	....	....	....		1959-60	1960-61
cCool, Frank	Tor.	2	72	34	31	7	4320	242	4	3.36	13	8	5	....	807	30	4	2.23	1	1944-45	1945-46
cDuffe, Peter	St.L., NYR, K.C., Det.	5	57	11	36	6	3207	218	0	4.08	1	0	1	....	60	7	0	7.00		1971-72	1975-76
cGrattan, Tom	Det.	1	1	0	0	0	8	1	0	7.50	....	....	....	....	....	....	....	....		1947-48	1947-48
cKay, Ross	Hfd.	1	1	0	0	0	35	3	0	5.14	....	....	....	....	....	....	....	....		1990-91	1990-91
cKenzie, Bill	Det., K.C., Col.	6	91	18	49	13	4776	326	2	4.10	....	....	....	....	....	....	....	....		1973-74	1979-80
cKichan, Steve	Van.	1	1	0	0	0	20	2	0	6.00	....	....	....	....	....	....	....	....		1990-91	1990-91
cLachlan, Murray	Tor.	1	2	0	1	0	25	4	0	9.60	....	....	....	....	....	....	....	....		1970-71	1970-71
cLean, Kirk	N.J., Van., Car., Fla., NYR	16	612	245	262	72	35090	1904	22	3.26	68	34	34	....	4189	198	6	2.84		1985-86	2000-01
cLelland, Dave	Van.	1	2	1	1	0	120	10	0	5.00	....	....	....	....	....	....	....	....		1972-73	1972-73
cLennan, Jamie	NYI, St.L., Min., Cgy., NYR, Fla.	11	254	80	109	36	13834	617	13	2.68	5	0	2	....	134	7	0	3.13		1993-94	2006-07
cLeod, Don	Det., Phi.	2	18	3	10	1	879	74	0	5.05	....	....	....	....	....	....	....	....		1970-71	1971-72
cLeod, Jim	St.L.	1	16	6	6	4	880	44	0	3.00	....	....	....	....	....	....	....	....		1971-72	1971-72
cNamara, Gerry	Tor.	2	7	2	2	1	323	14	0	2.60	....	....	....	....	....	....	....	....		1960-61	1969-70
cNeil, Gerry	Mtl.	8	276	119	105	52	16535	649	28	2.36	35	17	18	....	2284	72	5	1.89	3	1947-48	1957-58
cRae, Gord	Tor.	5	71	30	22	10	3799	221	1	3.49	8	2	5	....	454	22	0	2.91		1972-73	1977-78
cVicar, Rob	Van.	1	1	0	0	0	3	0	0	0.00	....	....	....	....	....	....	....	....		2005-06	2005-06
elanson, Roland	NYI, Min., L.A., N.J., Mtl.	11	291	129	106	33	16452	995	6	3.63	23	4	9	....	801	59	0	4.42	3	1980-81	1991-92
eloche, Gilles	Chi., Cal., Cle., Min., Pit.	18	788	270	351	131	45401	2756	20	3.64	45	21	19	....	2464	143	2	3.48		1970-71	1987-88
calef, Corrado	Det.	5	113	26	59	15	5794	409	2	4.24	3	0	0	....	49	8	0	9.80		1981-82	1985-86
chaud, Alfie	Van.	1	2	0	1	0	69	5	0	4.35	....	....	....	....	....	....	....	....		1999-00	1999-00
chaud, Olivier	Mtl.	1	1	0	0	0	18	0	0	0.00	....	....	....	....	....	....	....	....		2001-02	2001-02
ddlebrook, Lindsay	Wpg., Min., N.J., Edm.	4	37	3	23	6	1845	152	0	4.94	....	....	....	....	....	....	....	....		1979-80	1982-83
llar, Al	Bos.	1	6	1	4	1	360	25	0	4.17	....	....	....	....	....	....	....	....		1957-58	1957-58
llen, Greg	Pit., Hfd., St.L., Que., Chi., Det.	14	604	215	284	89	35377	2281	17	3.87	59	27	29	....	3383	193	0	3.42		1978-79	1991-92
ller, Joe	NYA, NYR, Pit., Phi.	4	127	24	87	16	7871	383	16	2.92	3	2	1	0	180	3	1	1.00	1	1927-28	1930-31
nard, Mike	Edm.	1	1	1	0	0	60	3	0	3.00	....	....	....	....	....	....	....	....		1999-00	1999-00
o, Eddie	Edm., NYR, Det.	7	192	64	73	30	10428	705	4	4.06	17	9	7	....	986	63	0	3.83		1979-80	1985-86
tchell, Mike	Tor.	3	22	10	9	0	1190	88	0	4.44	....	....	....	....	....	....	....	....	1	1919-20	1921-22
ffat, Mike	Bos.	3	19	7	7	2	979	70	0	4.29	11	6	5	....	663	38	0	3.44		1981-82	1983-84
og, Andy	Edm., Bos., Dal., Mtl.	18	713	372	209	88	40151	2097	28	3.13	132	68	57	....	7452	377	4	3.04	3	1980-81	1997-98
ore, Alfie	NYA, Chi., Det.	4	21	7	14	0	1290	81	1	3.77	3	1	2	....	180	7	0	2.33	1	1936-37	1939-40
ore, Robbie	Phi., Wsh.	2	6	3	1	1	257	8	2	1.87	5	3	2	....	268	18	0	4.03		1978-79	1982-83
rissette, Jean-Guy	Mtl.	1	1	0	1	0	36	4	0	6.67	....	....	....	....	....	....	....	....		1963-64	1963-64
rrison, Mike	Edm., Ott., Phx.	2	29	11	7	3	1226	67	0	3.28	....	....	....	....	....	....	....	....		2005-06	2006-07
ss, Tyler	Cgy., Car., Van.	4	30	6	16	1	1496	81	0	3.25	....	....	....	....	....	....	....	....		1997-98	2002-03
wers, Johnny	Det.	4	152	65	61	26	9350	399	15	2.56	32	19	13	....	2000	85	2	2.55	1	1940-41	1946-47
azek, Jerome	Phi.	1	1	0	0	0	6	1	0	10.00	....	....	....	....	....	....	....	....		1975-76	1975-76
mmery, Harry	Que., Ham.	2	4	2	1	0	192	20	0	6.25	....	....	....	....	....	....	....	....		1919-20	1921-22
nro, Dunc	Mtl.M.	1	1	0	0	0	2	0	0	0.00	....	....	....	....	....	....	....	....		1924-25	1924-25
rphy, Hal	Mtl.	1	1	1	0	0	60	4	0	4.00	....	....	....	....	....	....	....	....		1952-53	1952-53
rray, Mickey	Mtl.	1	1	0	1	0	60	4	0	4.00	....	....	....	....	....	....	....	....		1929-30	1929-30
zzatti, Jason	Cgy., Hfd., NYR, S.J.	5	62	13	25	10	3014	167	1	3.32	....	....	....	....	....	....	....	....		1993-94	1997-98
llys, Jarmo	Min., S.J.	4	39	4	27	1	1846	161	0	5.23	....	....	....	....	....	....	....	....		1988-89	1991-92
lnikov, Sergei	Que.	1	10	1	7	2	568	47	0	4.96	....	....	....	....	....	....	....	....		1989-90	1989-90
re, Phil	Mtl., Atl., St.L., Phi., Col., Buf.	14	439	149	198	76	25220	1482	14	3.53	12	6	5	....	747	41	1	3.29		1969-70	1982-83
umenko, Gregg	Ana.	1	2	0	1	0	70	7	0	6.00	....	....	....	....	....	....	....	....		2000-01	2000-01
wton, Cam	Pit.	2	16	4	7	1	814	51	0	3.76	....	....	....	....	....	....	....	....		1970-71	1972-73
onen, Mika	Buf., Van.	5	71	23	32	6	3652	163	3	2.68	....	....	....	....	....	....	....	....		2000-01	2005-06
rena, Fredrik	CBJ	3	100	35	45	11	5235	243	5	2.79	....	....	....	....	....	....	....	....		2006-07	2008-09
ris, Jack	Bos., Chi., L.A.	4	58	20	25	4	3119	202	2	3.89	....	....	....	....	....	....	....	....		1964-65	1970-71
minen, Pasi	Atl.	3	125	48	54	12	7059	338	5	2.87	....	....	....	....	....	....	....	....		2001-02	2003-04
schuk, Bill	K.C., Col.	4	55	7	28	10	2835	188	1	3.98	....	....	....	....	....	....	....	....		1975-76	1979-80
sevich, Dan	NYR	1	1	0	0	1	29	2	0	4.14	....	....	....	....	....	....	....	....		1961-62	1961-62
eill, Mike	Wpg., Ana.	4	21	0	9	2	855	61	0	4.28	....	....	....	....	....	....	....	....		1991-92	1996-97
ellet, Maxime	Phi., Wsh., Van.	3	12	2	6	2	663	34	1	3.08	....	....	....	....	....	....	....	....		2000-01	2005-06
met, Ted	St.L.	1	1	0	1	0	60	2	0	2.00	....	....	....	....	....	....	....	....		1968-69	1968-69
geau, Paul	L.A.	1	1	0	1	0	60	8	0	8.00	....	....	....	....	....	....	....	....		1980-81	1980-81
le, Marcel	NYR	7	107	32	52	22	6342	362	2	3.42	....	....	....	....	....	....	....	....		1957-58	1964-65
mateer, Mike	Tor., Wsh.	8	356	149	138	52	20131	1183	17	3.53	29	12	17	....	1765	89	2	3.03		1976-77	1983-84
g, Darren	Chi.	3	81	27	35	7	4252	287	0	4.05	6	1	3	....	250	18	0	4.32		1984-85	1988-89
ent, Bernie	Bos., Phi., Tor.	13	608	271	198	121	35136	1493	54	2.55	71	38	33	....	4302	174	6	2.43	2	1965-66	1978-79
ent, Bob	Tor.	2	3	0	2	0	160	15	0	5.63	....	....	....	....	....	....	....	....		1981-82	1982-83
ent, Rich	St.L., T.B., Pit.	4	32	7	11	5	1561	82	1	3.15	....	....	....	....	....	....	....	....		1997-98	2000-01
o, Dave	Wsh.	4	77	21	36	10	4015	274	2	4.09	....	....	....	....	....	....	....	....		1980-81	1983-84
smore, Steve	Edm., Chi., L.A.	6	93	23	44	12	5045	235	2	2.79	3	0	2	....	138	6	0	2.61		1998-99	2003-04
ick, Lester	NYR	1	....	....	....	....	....	....	....	....	1	1	0	0	46	1	0	1.30	1	1927-28	1927-28
zold, Dimitri	S.J.	1	3	0	0	0	44	4	0	5.45	....	....	....	....	....	....	....	....		2007-08	2007-08
ters, Pete	Phi., Bos., Wsh.	13	489	246	155	51	27699	1424	21	3.08	71	35	35	....	4200	232	2	3.31		1978-79	1990-91
etier, Jean-Marc	Phi., Phx.	3	7	1	4	0	354	23	0	3.90	....	....	....	....	....	....	....	....		1998-99	2003-04
etier, Marcel	Chi., NYR	2	8	1	6	0	395	32	0	4.86	....	....	....	....	....	....	....	....		1950-51	1962-63
ney, Steve	Mtl., Wpg.	5	91	35	38	12	5194	313	1	3.62	27	15	12	....	1604	72	4	2.69		1983-84	1987-88
reault, Bob	Mtl., Det., Bos.	3	31	8	16	7	1827	103	3	3.38	....	....	....	....	....	....	....	....		1955-56	1962-63
tie, Jim	Bos.	3	21	9	7	2	1157	71	1	3.68	....	....	....	....	....	....	....	....		1976-77	1978-79
rangelo, Frank	Pit., Hfd.	7	141	46	59	6	7141	490	1	4.12	12	7	5	....	713	34	1	2.86	1	1987-88	1993-94
nte, Jacques	Mtl., NYR, St.L., Tor., Bos.	18	837	437	246	145	49533	1964	82	2.38	112	71	36	....	6651	237	14	2.14	6	1952-53	1972-73
sse, Michel	St.L., Mtl., K.C., Pit., Col., Que.	11	299	92	136	54	16760	1058	2	3.79	4	1	2	....	195	9	1	2.77	1	1970-71	1981-82
ton, Hugh	Mtl.M.	1	1	0	1	0	57	5	0	5.26	....	....	....	....	....	....	....	....		1932-33	1932-33
perle, Tomas	CBJ	1	2	0	0	0	45	1	0	1.33	....	....	....	....	....	....	....	....		2006-07	2006-07
vin, Felix	Tor., NYI, Van., L.A., Bos.	13	635	266	260	85	36765	1694	32	2.76	72	35	37	....	4435	195	8	2.64		1991-92	2003-04
novost, Claude	Bos., Mtl.	2	3	1	1	0	120	7	1	3.50	....	....	....	....	....	....	....	....		1955-56	1958-59
sek, Martin	Ott., CBJ	4	57	31	12	4	2898	114	3	2.36	1	0	0	....	40	1	0	1.50		2001-02	2005-06
pa, Daren	Buf., Tor., T.B.	15	429	179	161	54	23819	1204	19	3.03	16	4	9	....	786	51	0	3.89		1985-86	1999-00
ey, Chris	Det.	1	1	0	0	0	40	3	0	4.50	....	....	....	....	....	....	....	....		1985-86	1985-86
icot, Andre	Mtl.	5	68	26	23	8	3357	196	2	3.50	4	0	1	....	31	4	0	7.74	1	1989-90	1993-94
ne, Bruce	St.L.	1	11	0	3	0	230	12	0	3.13	1	0	0	....	1	0	0	0.00		1995-96	1995-96
, Jamie	NYR	1	1	0	0	0	27	0	0	0.00	....	....	....	....	....	....	....	....		1995-96	1995-96
ford, Bill	Bos., Edm., Wsh., T.B., Det.	15	647	240	279	76	35936	2042	15	3.41	53	28	25	....	3110	159	4	3.07	2	1985-86	1999-00
mond, Alain	Wsh.	1	1	0	1	0	40	2	0	3.00	....	....	....	....	....	....	....	....		1987-88	1987-88

Name	NHL Teams	NHL Seasons	Regular Schedule GP	W	L	T	Mins	GA	SO	Avg	Playoffs GP	W	L	T	Mins	GA	SO	Avg	NHL Cup Wins	First NHL Season	Last NHL Season
• Rayner, Chuck	NYA, Bro., NYR	10	424	138	208	77	25491	1294	25	3.05	18	9	9	....	1135	46	1	2.43		1940-41	1952-5
Reaugh, Daryl	Edm., Hfd.	3	27	8	9	1	1246	72	1	3.47	....	....	....	....	....	....	....	....		1984-85	1990-9
Reddick, Pokey	Wpg., Edm., Fla.	6	132	46	58	16	7162	443	0	3.71	4	0	2	....	168	10	0	3.57	1	1986-87	1993-9
§ • Redding, George	Bos.	1	1	0	0	0	11	1	0	5.45	....	....	....	....	....	....	....	....		1924-25	1924-2
Redquest, Greg	Pit.	1	1	0	0	0	13	3	0	13.85	....	....	....	....	....	....	....	....		1977-78	1977-7
Reece, Dave	Bos.	1	14	7	5	2	777	43	2	3.32	....	....	....	....	....	....	....	....		1975-76	1975-7
Reese, Jeff	Tor., Cgy., Hfd., T.B., N.J.	11	174	53	65	17	8667	529	5	3.66	11	3	5	....	515	35	0	4.08		1987-88	1998-9
Resch, Glenn	NYI, Col., N.J., Phi.	14	571	231	224	82	32279	1761	26	3.27	41	17	17	....	2044	85	2	2.50	1	1973-74	1986-8
• Rheaume, Herb	Mtl.	1	31	10	20	1	1889	92	0	2.92	....	....	....	....	....	....	....	....		1925-26	1925-2
Rhodes, Damian	Tor., Ott., Atl.	10	309	99	140	48	17339	820	12	2.84	13	5	7	....	741	27	0	2.19		1990-91	2001-0
Ricci, Nick	Pit.	4	19	7	12	0	1087	79	0	4.36	....	....	....	....	....	....	....	....		1979-80	1982-8
Richardson, Terry	Det., St.L.	5	20	3	11	0	906	85	0	5.63	....	....	....	....	....	....	....	....		1973-74	1978-7
Richter, Mike	NYR	15	666	301	258	73	38183	1840	24	2.89	76	41	33	....	4514	202	9	2.68	1	1988-89	2002-0
Ridley, Curt	NYR, Van., Tor.	6	104	27	47	16	5498	355	1	3.87	2	0	2	....	120	8	0	4.00		1974-75	1980-8
Riendeau, Vincent	Mtl., St.L., Det., Bos.	8	184	85	65	20	10423	573	5	3.30	25	11	12	....	1277	71	1	3.34		1987-88	1994-9
Riggin, Dennis	Det.	2	18	6	10	2	999	52	1	3.12	....	....	....	....	....	....	....	....		1959-60	1962-6
Riggin, Pat	Atl., Cgy., Wsh., Bos., Pit.	9	350	153	120	52	19872	1135	11	3.43	25	8	13	....	1336	72	0	3.23		1979-80	1987-8
Ring, Bob	Bos.	1	1	0	0	0	33	4	0	7.27	....	....	....	....	....	....	....	....		1965-66	1965-6
Rivard, Fern	Min.	4	55	9	27	11	2865	190	2	3.98	....	....	....	....	....	....	....	....		1968-69	1974-7
• Roach, John Ross	Tor., NYR, Det.	14	492	219	204	68	30444	1246	58	2.46	29	12	14	3	1901	60	7	1.89	1	1921-22	1934-3
• Roberts, Moe	Bos., NYA, Chi.	4	10	3	5	0	501	31	0	3.71	....	....	....	....	....	....	....	....		1925-26	1951-5
• Robertson, Earl	Det., NYA, Bro.	6	190	60	95	34	11820	575	16	2.92	15	7	7	....	995	29	2	1.75	1	1936-37	1941-4
• Rollins, Al	Tor., Chi., NYR	9	430	141	205	83	25723	1192	28	2.78	13	6	7	....	755	30	0	2.38	1	1949-50	1959-6
Romano, Roberto	Pit., Bos.	6	126	46	63	8	7111	471	4	3.97	....	....	....	....	....	....	....	....		1982-83	1993-9
Rosati, Mike	Wsh.	1	1	1	0	0	28	0	0	0.00	....	....	....	....	....	....	....	....		1998-99	1998-9
Roussel, Dominic	Phi., Wpg., Ana., Edm.	8	205	77	70	23	10665	555	7	3.12	1	0	0	....	23	0	0	0.00		1991-92	2000-0
Roy, Patrick	Mtl., Col.	19	1029	551	315	131	60235	2546	66	2.54	247	151	94	....	15209	584	23	2.30	4	1984-85	2002-0
‡ Rudkowsky, Cody	St.L.	1	1	0	0	0	30	0	0	0.00	....	....	....	....	....	....	....	....		2002-03	2002-0
• Rupp, Pat	Det.	1	1	0	1	0	60	4	0	4.00	....	....	....	....	....	....	....	....		1963-64	1963-6
Rutherford, Jim	Det., Pit., Tor., L.A.	13	457	151	227	59	25895	1576	14	3.65	8	2	5	....	440	28	0	3.82		1970-71	1982-8
• Rutledge, Wayne	L.A.	3	82	28	37	9	4325	241	2	3.34	8	2	4	....	378	20	0	3.17		1967-68	1969-
St. Croix, Rick	Phi., Tor.	8	130	49	54	18	7295	451	2	3.71	11	4	6	....	562	29	1	3.10		1977-78	1984-
St. Laurent, Sam	N.J., Det.	5	34	7	12	4	1572	92	1	3.51	1	0	0	....	10	1	0	6.00		1985-86	1989-
Salo, Tommy	NYI, Edm., Col.	10	526	210	225	73	30436	1296	37	2.55	22	5	16	....	1369	58	0	2.54		1994-95	2003-
§ • Sands, Charlie	Mtl.	1	1	0	0	0	25	5	0	12.00	....	....	....	....	....	....	....	....		1939-40	1939-
Sands, Mike	Min.	2	6	0	5	0	302	26	0	5.17	....	....	....	....	....	....	....	....		1984-85	1986-
Sarjeant, Geoff	St.L., S.J.	2	8	1	2	1	291	20	0	4.12	....	....	....	....	....	....	....	....		1994-95	1995-
Sauve, Bob	Buf., Det., Chi., N.J.	13	420	182	154	54	23711	1377	8	3.48	34	15	16	....	1850	95	4	3.08		1976-77	1988-
Sauve, Philippe	Col., Cgy., Phx., Bos.	3	32	10	14	3	1616	93	0	3.45	....	....	....	....	....	....	....	....		2003-04	2006-
• Sawchuk, Terry	Det., Bos., Tor., L.A., NYR	21	971	447	330	172	57194	2389	103	2.51	106	54	48	....	6290	266	12	2.54	4	1949-50	1969-
• Schaefer, Joe	NYR	2	2	0	2	0	86	8	0	5.58	....	....	....	....	....	....	....	....		1959-60	1960-
Schafer, Paxton	Bos.	1	3	0	0	0	77	6	0	4.68	....	....	....	....	....	....	....	....		1996-97	1996-
Schwab, Corey	N.J., T.B., Van., Tor.	8	147	42	63	13	7476	360	6	2.89	3	0	0	....	40	0	0	0.00	1	1995-96	2003-
Scott, Ron	NYR, L.A.	5	28	8	13	4	1450	91	0	3.77	1	0	0	....	32	4	0	7.50		1983-84	1989-
‡ Scott, Travis	L.A.	1	1	0	0	0	25	3	0	7.20	....	....	....	....	....	....	....	....		2000-01	2000-
Sevigny, Richard	Mtl., Que.	9	176	80	54	20	9485	507	5	3.21	4	0	3	....	208	13	0	3.75	1	1978-79	1986-
Sharples, Scott	Cgy.	1	1	0	0	1	65	4	0	3.69	....	....	....	....	....	....	....	....		1991-92	1991-
§ • Shields, Al	NYA	1	2	0	0	0	41	9	0	13.17	....	....	....	....	....	....	....	....		1931-32	1931-
Shields, Steve	Buf., S.J., Ana., Bos., Fla., Atl.	10	246	80	104	40	13630	606	10	2.67	25	9	16	....	1445	74	1	3.07		1995-96	2005-
Shtalenkov, Mikhail	Ana., Edm., Phx., Fla.	7	190	62	82	19	9966	480	8	2.89	4	0	3	....	211	10	0	2.84		1993-94	1999-
Shulmistra, Richard	N.J., Fla.	2	2	1	1	0	122	3	0	1.48	....	....	....	....	....	....	....	....		1997-98	1999-
Sidorkiewicz, Peter	Hfd., Ott., N.J.	8	246	79	128	27	13884	832	8	3.60	15	5	10	....	912	55	0	3.62		1987-88	1997-
Sigalet, Jordan	Bos.	1	1	0	0	0	1	0	0	0.00	....	....	....	....	....	....	....	....		2005-06	2005-
Simmons, Don	Bos., Tor., NYR	11	249	101	101	41	14555	701	20	2.89	24	13	11	....	1436	62	3	2.59	3	1956-57	1968-
Simmons, Gary	Cal., Cle., L.A.	4	107	30	57	15	6162	366	5	3.56	1	0	0	....	20	1	0	3.00		1974-75	1977-
Skidmore, Paul	St.L.	1	2	1	1	0	120	6	0	3.00	....	....	....	....	....	....	....	....		1981-82	1981-
Skorodenski, Warren	Chi., Edm.	5	35	12	11	4	1732	100	2	3.46	2	0	0	....	33	6	0	10.91		1981-82	1987-
Skudra, Peter	Pit., Buf., Bos., Van.	6	146	51	47	20	7162	326	6	2.73	3	0	1	....	116	6	0	3.10		1997-98	2002-
• Smith, Al	Tor., Pit., Det., Buf., Hfd., Col.	10	233	74	99	36	12752	735	10	3.46	6	1	4	....	317	21	0	3.97		1965-66	1980-
Smith, Billy	L.A., NYI	18	680	305	233	105	38431	2031	22	3.17	132	88	36	....	7645	348	5	2.73	4	1971-72	1988-
Smith, Gary	Tor., Oak., Cal., Chi., Van., Min., Wsh., Wpg.	14	532	173	261	74	29619	1675	26	3.39	20	5	13	....	1153	62	1	3.23		1965-66	1979-
• Smith, Normie	Mtl.M., Det.	8	199	81	83	35	12357	479	17	2.33	12	9	2	0	820	18	3	1.32	2	1931-32	1944-
Sneddon, Bob	Cal.	1	5	0	2	0	225	21	0	5.60	....	....	....	....	....	....	....	....		1970-71	1970-
Snow, Garth	Que., Phi., Van., Pit., NYI	12	368	135	147	44	19837	925	16	2.80	20	9	8	....	1040	48	1	2.77		1993-94	2005-
Soderstrom, Tommy	Phi., NYI	5	156	45	69	19	8189	496	10	3.63	....	....	....	....	....	....	....	....		1992-93	1996-
Soetaert, Doug	NYR, Wpg., Mtl.	12	284	110	104	42	15583	1030	6	3.97	5	1	2	....	180	14	0	4.67	1	1975-76	1986-
Soucy, Christian	Chi.	1	1	0	0	0	3	0	0	0.00	....	....	....	....	....	....	....	....		1993-94	1993-
• Spooner, Red	Pit.	1	1	0	1	0	60	6	0	6.00	....	....	....	....	....	....	....	....		1929-30	1929-
§ • Spring, Jesse	Ham.	1	1	0	0	0	2	0	0	0.00	....	....	....	....	....	....	....	....		1924-25	1924-
‡ Stana, Rastislav	Wsh.	1	6	1	2	0	211	11	0	3.13	....	....	....	....	....	....	....	....		2003-04	2003-
Staniowski, Ed	St.L., Wpg., Hfd.	10	219	67	104	21	12075	818	2	4.06	8	1	6	....	428	28	0	3.93		1975-76	1984-
§ • Starr, Harold	Mtl.M.	1	1	0	0	0	3	0	0	0.00	....	....	....	....	....	....	....	....		1931-32	1931-
Stauber, Robb	L.A., Buf.	4	62	21	23	9	3295	209	1	3.81	4	3	1	....	240	16	0	4.00		1989-90	1994-
Stefan, Greg	Det.	9	299	115	127	30	16333	1068	5	3.92	30	12	17	....	1681	99	1	3.53		1981-82	1989-
• Stein, Phil	Tor.	1	1	0	0	1	70	2	0	1.71	....	....	....	....	....	....	....	....		1939-40	1939-
• Stephenson, Wayne	St.L., Phi., Wsh.	10	328	146	103	49	18343	937	14	3.06	26	11	12	....	1522	79	2	3.11	1	1971-72	1980-
• Stevenson, Doug	NYR, Chi.	3	8	2	6	0	480	39	0	4.88	....	....	....	....	....	....	....	....		1944-45	1945-
• Stewart, Charles	Bos.	3	77	30	41	5	4742	194	10	2.45	....	....	....	....	....	....	....	....		1924-25	1926
Stewart, Jim	Bos.	1	1	0	1	0	20	5	0	15.00	....	....	....	....	....	....	....	....		1979-80	1979
‡ Storr, Jamie	L.A., Car.	10	219	85	86	23	11512	488	16	2.54	5	0	3	....	182	11	0	3.63		1994-95	2003-
• Stuart, Herb	Det.	1	3	1	2	0	180	5	0	1.67	....	....	....	....	....	....	....	....		1926-27	1926-
Sylvestri, Don	Bos.	1	3	0	0	2	102	6	0	3.53	....	....	....	....	....	....	....	....		1984-85	1984-
Tabaracci, Rick	Pit., Wpg., Wsh., Cgy., T.B., Atl., Col.	11	286	93	125	30	15255	760	15	2.99	17	4	12	....	1025	53	0	3.10		1988-89	1999-
Takko, Kari	Min., Edm.	6	142	37	71	14	7317	475	1	3.90	4	0	1	....	109	7	0	3.85		1985-86	1990-
Tallas, Robbie	Bos., Chi.	6	99	28	42	10	5069	246	3	2.91	....	....	....	....	....	....	....	....		1995-96	2000-
Tanner, John	Que.	3	21	2	11	5	1084	65	1	3.60	....	....	....	....	....	....	....	....		1989-90	1991-
Tataryn, Dave	NYR	1	2	1	1	0	80	10	0	7.50	....	....	....	....	....	....	....	....		1976-77	1976
Taylor, Bobby	Phi., Pit.	5	46	15	17	6	2268	155	0	4.10	....	....	....	....	....	....	....	....	1	1971-72	1975
• Teno, Harvey	Det.	1	5	2	3	0	300	15	0	3.00	....	....	....	....	....	....	....	....		1938-39	1938
Terreri, Chris	N.J., S.J., Chi., NYI	14	406	151	172	43	22369	1143	9	3.07	29	12	12	....	1523	86	0	3.39	2	1986-87	2000
Thibault, Jocelyn	Que., Col., Mtl., Chi., Pit., Buf.	14	586	238	238	75	32892	1508	39	2.75	18	4	11	....	848	50	0	3.54		1993-94	2007
Thomas, Wayne	Mtl., Tor., NYR	9	243	103	93	34	13768	766	10	3.34	15	6	8	....	849	50	1	3.53		1972-73	1980
• Thompson, Tiny	Bos., Det.	12	553	284	194	75	34175	1183	81	2.08	44	20	24	0	2974	93	7	1.88	1	1928-29	1939
§ Toppazzini, Jerry	Bos.	1	1	0	0	0	1	0	0	0.00	....	....	....	....	....	....	....	....		1960-61	1960
Torchia, Mike	Dal.	1	6	3	2	1	327	18	0	3.30	....	....	....	....	....	....	....	....		1994-95	1994
Trefilov, Andrei	Cgy., Buf., Chi.	7	54	12	25	4	2663	153	2	3.45	1	0	0	....	5	0	0	0.00		1992-93	1998
Tremblay, Vincent	Tor., Pit.	5	58	12	26	8	2785	223	1	4.80	....	....	....	....	....	....	....	....		1979-80	1983
Tucker, Ted	Cal.	1	5	1	1	1	177	10	0	3.39	....	....	....	....	....	....	....	....		1973-74	1973
Tugnutt, Ron	Que., Edm., Ana., Mtl., Ott., Pit., CBJ, Dal.	16	537	186	239	62	29486	1497	26	3.05	25	9	13	....	1482	56	3	2.27		1987-88	2003
‡ Turek, Roman	Dal., St.L., Cgy.	8	328	159	115	43	19095	734	27	2.31	22	12	9	....	1342	50	0	2.24	1	1996-97	2003
• Turner, Joe	Det.	1	1	0	0	1	70	3	0	2.57	....	....	....	....	....	....	....	....		1941-42	1941
Underhill, Matt	Chi.	1	1	0	1	0	61	4	0	3.93	....	....	....	....	....	....	....	....		2003-04	2003
Vachon, Rogie	Mtl., L.A., Det., Bos.	16	795	355	291	127	46298	2310	51	2.99	48	23	23	....	2876	133	2	2.77	3	1966-67	1981
Vanbiesbrouck, John	NYR, Fla., Phi., NYI, N.J.	20	882	374	346	119	50475	2503	40	2.98	71	28	38	....	3969	177	5	2.68		1981-82	2001
Veisor, Mike	Chi., Hfd., Wpg.	10	139	41	62	26	7806	532	5	4.09	4	0	2	....	180	15	0	5.00		1973-74	1983
Vernon, Mike	Cgy., Det., S.J., Fla.	19	781	385	273	92	44449	2206	27	2.98	138	77	56	....	8214	367	6	2.68	2	1982-83	2001

Name	NHL Teams	NHL Seasons	Regular Schedule								Playoffs								NHL Cup Wins	First NHL Season	Last NHL Season
			GP	W	L	T	Mins	GA	SO	Avg	GP	W	L	T	Mins	GA	SO	Avg			
Vezina, Georges	Mtl.	9	190	103	81	5	11592	633	13	3.28	13	10	3	0	780	35	2	2.69	1	1917-18	1925-26
Villemure, Gilles	NYR, Chi.	10	205	100	64	29	11581	542	13	2.81	14	5	5	....	656	32	0	2.93		1963-64	1976-77
Waite, Jimmy	Chi., S.J., Phx.	11	106	28	41	12	5253	293	4	3.35	6	0	3	....	211	14	0	3.98		1988-89	1998-99
Wakaluk, Darcy	Buf., Min., Dal., Phx.	8	191	67	75	21	9756	524	9	3.22	8	4	2	....	364	18	0	2.97		1988-89	1996-97
Wakely, Ernie	Mtl., St.L.	7	113	41	42	17	6244	290	8	2.79	10	2	6	....	509	37	1	4.36	2	1962-63	1971-72
Wall, Michael	Ana.	1	4	2	2	0	202	10	0	2.97	....									2006-07	2006-07
Walsh, Flat	Mtl.M., NYA	7	108	48	43	16	6641	256	12	2.31	8	2	4	2	570	16	2	1.68		1926-27	1932-33
Wamsley, Rick	Mtl., St.L., Cgy., Tor.	13	407	204	131	46	23123	1287	12	3.34	27	7	18	....	1397	81	0	3.48	1	1980-81	1992-93
Watt, Jim	St.L.	1	1	0	0	0	20	2	0	6.00	....									1973-74	1973-74
Weekes, Kevin	Fla., Van., NYI, T.B., Car., NYR, N.J.	11	348	105	163	39	18837	903	19	2.88	9	3	3	....	468	15	2	1.92		1997-98	2008-09
Weeks, Steve	NYR, Hfd., Van., NYI, L.A., Ott.	18	290	111	119	33	15879	989	5	3.74	12	3	5	....	486	27	0	3.33		1980-81	1992-93
Wetzel, Carl	Det., Min.	2	7	1	4	1	301	22	0	4.39	....									1964-65	1967-68
Whitmore, Kay	Hfd., Van., Bos., Cgy.	9	155	60	64	16	8596	508	4	3.55	4	0	2	....	174	13	0	4.48		1988-89	2001-02
Wilkinson, Derek	T.B.	4	22	3	12	3	933	57	0	3.67	....									1995-96	1998-99
Willis, Jordan	Dal.	1	1	0	1	0	19	1	0	3.16	....									1995-96	1995-96
Wilson, Dunc	Phi., Van., Tor., NYR, Pit.	10	287	80	150	33	15851	988	8	3.74	....									1969-70	1978-79
Wilson, Lefty	Det., Tor., Bos.	3	3	0	0	1	81	1	0	0.74	....									1953-54	1957-58
Winkler, Hal	NYR, Bos.	2	75	35	26	14	4739	126	21	1.60	10	2	3	5	640	18	2	1.69		1926-27	1927-28
Wolfe, Bernie	Wsh.	4	120	20	61	21	6104	424	1	4.17	....									1975-76	1978-79
Wood, Alex	NYA	1	1	0	1	0	70	3	0	2.57	....									1936-37	1936-37
Worsley, Gump	NYR, Mtl., Min.	21	861	335	352	150	50183	2407	43	2.88	70	40	26	....	4084	189	5	2.78	4	1952-53	1973-74
Worters, Roy	Pit., NYA, Mtl.	12	484	171	229	83	30175	1143	67	2.27	11	3	6	2	690	24	3	2.09		1925-26	1936-37
Worthy, Chris	Oak., Cal.	3	26	5	10	4	1326	98	0	4.43	....									1968-69	1970-71
Wregget, Ken	Tor., Phi., Pit., Cgy., Det.	17	575	225	248	53	31663	1917	9	3.63	56	28	25	....	3341	160	3	2.87	1	1983-84	1999-00
Yeats, Matthew	Wsh.	1	5	1	3	0	258	13	0	3.02	....									2003-04	2003-04
Yeremeyev, Vitali	NYR	1	4	0	4	0	212	16	0	4.53	....									2000-01	2000-01
Young, Doug	Det.	1	1	0	0	0	21	1	0	2.86	....									1933-34	1933-34
Young, Wendell	Van., Phi., Pit., T.B.	10	187	59	86	12	9410	618	2	3.94	2	0	1	....	99	6	0	3.64	2	1985-86	1994-95
Zanier, Mike	Edm.	1	3	1	1	1	185	12	0	3.89	....									1984-85	1984-85

Turk Broda

Curtis Joseph

Corrado Micalef

Georges Vezina

Connie Dion

Olaf Kolzig

Vincent Riendeau

Kevin Weekes

2009-10
NHL Player of the Week/Month Award Winners

Player of the Week/Month

Period Ending	First Star	Second Star	Third Star
Oct. 5	Alex Ovechkin, Wsh	Craig Anderson, Col	Keith Tkachuk, StL
Oct. 12	Dany Heatley, SJ	Jonathan Quick, LA	Henrik Sedin, Van
Oct. 19	Ilya Bryzgalov, Phx	Craig Anderson, Col	Alex Ovechkin, Wsh
Oct. 26	Anze Kopitar, LA	Michael Cammalleri, Mtl	Patrick Marleau, SJ
October	**Craig Anderson, Col**	Alex Ovechkin, Wsh	Ilya Bryzgalov, Phx
Nov. 2	Tomas Kaberle, Tor	Pekka Rinne, Nsh	Evgeni Nabokov, SJ
Nov. 9	Jarome Iginla, Cgy	Evgeni Nabokov, SJ	Chris Pronger, Phi
Nov. 16	Henrik Zetterberg, Det	Ilya Kovalchuk, Atl	Ryan Miller, Buf
Nov. 23	Joe Thornton, SJ	Carey Price, Mtl	Mike Fisher, Ott
Nov. 30	Sidney Crosby, Pit	Martin Brodeur, NJ	Niklas Hagman, Tor
November	**Jarome Iginla, Cgy**	Joe Thornton, SJ	Marian Gaborik, NYR
Dec. 7	Nicklas Backstrom, Wsh	Stephen Weiss, Fla	Matt Duchene, Col
Dec. 14	Jonathan Quick, LA	Daniel Sedin, Van	Ilya Bryzgalov, Phx
Dec. 21	Cristobal Huet, Chi	Marc-Andre Fleury, Pit	Patric Hornqvist, Nsh
Dec. 28	Jaroslav Halak, Mtl	Patrick Kane, Chi	Roberto Luongo, Van
December	**Henrik Sedin, Van**	Ilya Bryzgalov, Phx	Patrick Kane, Chi
Jan. 4	Jamie Langenbrunner, NJ	Mike Smith, TB	Loui Eriksson, Dal
Jan. 11	Alex Burrows, Van	Jonas Hiller, Ana	Mathieu Garon, CBJ
Jan. 18	Alex Ovechkin, Wsh	Chris Mason, StL	G. Latendresse, Min
Jan. 25	Brian Elliott, Ott	Craig Anderson, Col	Sidney Crosby, Pit
January	**Alex Ovechkin, Wsh**	Henrik Sedin, Van	Tomas Vokoun, Fla
Feb. 1	Shane Doan, Phx	Brian Elliott, Ott	Nicklas Backstrom, Wsh
Feb. 8	Alex Ovechkin, Wsh	J.S. Giguere, Ana	Nicklas Backstrom, Wsh
Feb. 15	Steven Stamkos, TB	Michael Leighton, Phi	Marty Turco, Dal
Feb. 22	none (Olympic break)		
February	**none (Olympic break)**		
Mar. 1	none (Olympic break)		
Mar. 8	Chris Stewart, Col	Steven Stamkos, TB	Bryan McCabe, Fla
Mar. 15	Mikael Samuelsson, Van	Lee Stempniak, Phx	Pekka Rinne, Nsh
Mar. 22	Pekka Rinne, Nsh	John Tavares, NYI	Teemu Selanne, Ana
Mar. 29	Brian Elliott, Ott	Jimmy Howard, Det	Ilya Kovalchuk, NJ
March	**Lee Stempniak, Phx**	Jimmy Howard, Det	Henrik Sedin, Van
Apr. 5	Jaroslav Halak, Mtl	Saku Koivu, Ana	Tuukka Rask, Bos
Apr. 12	Sidney Crosby, Pit	Eric Staal, Car	Nicklas Backstrom, Wsh

Rookie of the Month

Month	Player
October	Michael Del Zotto, NYR
November	James van Riemsdyk, Phi
December	Matt Duchene, Col
January	Tyler Myers, Buf
February	none (Olympic break)
March	Jimmy Howard, Det

Nicklas Backstrom (above) of the Washington Capitals was the NHL's first star of the week for December 7, 2009. Backstrom had four goals and five assists as the Capitals won three straight games to take over first place in the Eastern Conference standings. He was later named third star of the week twice in February and then again for the final week of the 2009-10 season.

Ilya Kovalchuk (right) was the only player to win a weekly honor with two different teams, being named second star for the week ending November 16, 2009 with Atlanta and third star for the week ending March 29, 2010 with New Jersey.

Craig Anderson (far right) got off to a hot start for Colorado, earning two weekly honors in October and then being named player of the month. Anderson gave the Avalanche an early confidence boost by posting a record of 10-2-2 with a 2.04 average and .939 save percentage in the season's opening month.

Dino Ciccarelli

Cammi Granato

Angela James

Jim Devellano

Daryl "Doc" Seaman

2010
Hockey Hall of Fame Inductees

TWO OF THE GREATEST PLAYERS IN WOMEN'S HOCKEY, *Cammi Granato and Angela James, are among the inductees as the Hockey Hall of Fame welcomes five new members in 2010. They are the first women ever inducted.*

*Undrafted out of junior hockey despite big scoring numbers because he had suffered a badly broken leg, **Dino Ciccarelli** went on to set rookie scoring records in the 1981 playoffs and collect 55 goals in his first full NHL season in 1981-82. A gritty player who was willing to go to the front of the net, Ciccarelli scored 35 goals or more 11 times in his 19-year career and topped 100 points twice. He finished his career with 1,200 points on 608 goals and 592 assists in 1,232 games.*

***Cammi Granato** was born into a hockey family as the youngest of five children including brother Tony who grew up to play in the NHL. Granato played with boys from age five to 16 and would later star on the women's team at Providence College and at Concordia University in Montreal. A founding member of the United States Women's National Team, Granato played at the first official IIIHF Women's World Championship in 1990 and captained the U.S. team to a gold medal at the 1998 Winter Olympics.*

*Dubbed "The Wayne Gretzky of Women's Hockey," **Angela James** began playing in the Ontario Women's Hockey Association in the late 1970s and was a dominant player. She was the leading scorer in eight seasons and most valuable player six times while leading her team to numerous Ontario Women's Hockey Association league and provincial championships. Internationally, James led Canada to Women's World Championship titles in 1990, 1992, 1994 and 1997.*

*Though he never played professional hockey, **Jim Devellano** rose through the ranks in his native Toronto. He entered the NHL as a scout with the St. Louis Blues when the league expanded in 1967, then joined the New York Islanders in 1972 and contributed to the four consecutive Stanley Cup titles the Islanders won from 1980 to 1983. Devellano was the first person hired by owners Mike and Marian Ilitch after purchasing the Detroit Red Wings in 1982. He has won the Stanley Cup four more times in Detroit and continues to work in the club's front office.*

*The late **Daryl "Doc" Seaman** was a successful oilman and industrialist who was among the original Calgary Flames owners that brought the team to the city in 1980 and built them into Stanley Cup champions in 1989. He was also a key player in building the Saddledome and bringing the 1988 Winter Olympics to Calgary. Seaman was a strong supporter of Hockey Canada's grass roots development programs.*

Also honored are Ron Weber, winner of the Foster Hewitt Memorial Award for excellence in hockey broadcasting, and Marc de Foy, winner of the Elmer Ferguson Memorial Award for excellence in hockey journalism.

Free Agent Signing Register, 2010

SIGNING DATE		POS.	PLAYER	SIGNED BY	PREVIOUS ORGANIZATION
July 1	–	C	Derek MacKenzie	Columbus	Columbus
	–	C	Colin Fraser	Edmonton	Chicago
	–	LW	Ray Whitney	Phoenix	Carolina
	–	C	Jeremy Reich	Boston	NY Islanders
	–	G	Andrew Raycroft	Dallas	Vancouver
	–	RW	Adam Burish	Dallas	Chicago
	–	LW	Eric Nystrom	Minnesota	Calgary
	–	C	Matt Cullen	Minnesota	Ottawa
	–	C	Dustin Boyd	Montreal	Montreal
	–	G	Curtis Sanford	Montreal	Montreal
	–	D	Dan Hamhuis	Vancouver	Nashville
	–	G	Johan Hedberg	New Jersey	Atlanta
	–	C	Vinny Prospal	NY Rangers	NY Rangers
	–	C	Olli Jokinen	Calgary	NY Rangers
	–	D	Anton Volchenkov	New Jersey	Ottawa
	–	D	Henrik Tallinder	New Jersey	Buffalo
	–	G	Dan Ellis	Tampa Bay	Nashville
	–	C	Saku Koivu	Anaheim	Anaheim
	–	LW	Jeff Tambellini	Vancouver	NY Islanders
	–	D	Jordan Leopold	Buffalo	Pittsburgh
	–	RW	Colby Armstrong	Toronto	Atlanta
	–	D	Paul Martin	Pittsburgh	New Jersey
	–	G	Chris Mason	Atlanta	St. Louis
	–	LW	Jonathan Matsumoto	Carolina	Philadelphia
	–	LW	Mitch Fritz	Tampa Bay	Tampa Bay
	–	LW	Derek Boogaard	NY Rangers	Minnesota
	–	D	Kurtis Foster	Edmonton	Tampa Bay
	–	D	Toni Lydman	Anaheim	Buffalo
	–	D	Derek Morris	Phoenix	Phoenix
	–	C	Vladimir Sobotka	St. Louis	Boston
	–	C	Alex Steen	St. Louis	St. Louis
	–	LW	Jody Shelley	Philadelphia	NY Rangers
	–	C	Joel Perrault	Vancouver	Phoenix
	–	LW	Daniel Paille	Boston	Boston
	–	D	Sean O'Donnell	Philadelphia	Los Angeles
	–	C	Manny Malhotra	Vancouver	San Jose
	–	C	Jesse Winchester	Ottawa	Ottawa
	–	G	Antero Niittymaki	San Jose	Tampa Bay
	–	D	Zbynek Michalek	Pittsburgh	Phoenix
	–	G	Alex Auld	Montreal	NY Rangers
	–	D	Sergei Gonchar	Ottawa	Pittsburgh
	–	D	Braydon Coburn	Philadelphia	Philadelphia
	–	LW	Guillaume Latendresse	Minnesota	Minnesota
	–	LW	Alex Tanguay	Calgary	Tampa Bay
	–	G	Martin Biron	NY Rangers	NY Islanders
	–	C	Erik Christensen	NY Rangers	NY Rangers
July 2	–	LW	Nikolai Kulemin	Toronto	Toronto
	–	LW	Daniel Winnik	Colorado	Colorado
	–	D	Kyle Quincey	Colorado	Colorado
	–	C	Trevor Smith	Anaheim	NY Islanders
	–	C	Andrew Ebbett	Phoenix	Minnesota
	–	LW	Brandon Prust	NY Rangers	NY Rangers
	–	C	Warren Peters	Minnesota	Dallas
	–	D	Drew Bagnall	Minnesota	Los Angeles
	–	C	Zenon Konopka	NY Islanders	Tampa Bay
	–	LW	P.A. Parenteau	NY Islanders	NY Rangers
	–	LW	Brad Winchester	St. Louis	St. Louis
	–	C	Cody McCormick	Buffalo	Buffalo
	–	D	Milan Jurcina	NY Islanders	Washington
	–	D	Mark Eaton	NY Islanders	Pittsburgh
	–	D	John Scott	Chicago	Minnesota
	–	LW	Chris Higgins	Florida	Calgary
	–	D	Pavel Kubina	Tampa Bay	Atlanta
	–	D	Jason Strudwick	Edmonton	Edmonton
	–	C	Kyle Wilson	Columbus	Washington
	–	C	Trevor Frischmon	Columbus	Columbus
	–	D	Nathan Guenin	Columbus	Pittsburgh
	–	G	Nathan Lawson	NY Islanders	NY Islanders
	–	LW	Raitis Ivanans	Calgary	Los Angeles
	–	RW	Tim Jackman	Calgary	NY Islanders
	–	G	Dany Sabourin	Washington	Boston
	–	LW	Steve MacIntyre	Edmonton	Edmonton
	–	LW	Triston Grant	Florida	Nashville
	–	C	Ryan Craig	Pittsburgh	Tampa Bay
	–	C	Matthew Lombardi	Nashville	Phoenix
July 3	–	LW	Brett Sterling	Pittsburgh	San Jose
	–	G	Matt Climie	Phoenix	Dallas
	–	D	Nolan Yonkman	Phoenix	Nashville
	–	D	Garrett Stafford	Phoenix	Dallas
	–	LW	Alexandre Giroux	Edmonton	Washington
July 5	–	D	Brett Clark	Tampa Bay	Colorado
	–	G	Justin Peters	Carolina	Carolina
	–	D	Nathan McIver	Boston	Vancouver
	–	C	John Mitchell	Toronto	Toronto
July 6	–	D	Jamie Fraser	Minnesota	Minnesota
	–	RW	Jon DiSalvatore	Minnesota	Minnesota
	–	LW	Sergei Kostitsyn	Nashville	Montreal
	–	D	Carlo Colaiacovo	St. Louis	St. Louis
	–	C/W	Boyd Gordon	Washington	Washington
	–	LW	Drew Miller	Detroit	Detroit
	–	D	Mike Lundin	Tampa Bay	Tampa Bay
	–	RW	Teddy Purcell	Tampa Bay	Tampa Bay
	–	RW	Cam Janssen	St. Louis	St. Louis
	–	G	Jaroslav Halak	St. Louis	Montreal
	–	G	Joey MacDonald	Detroit	Anaheim
	–	C	Jamie Johnson	Detroit	Edmonton
	–	LW	Chris Minard	Detroit	Edmonton
July 7	–	D	Mike Weber	Buffalo	Buffalo
	–	C	Nicolas Blanchard	Carolina	Carolina
	–	D	Casey Borer	Carolina	Carolina
	–	D	Nathan Paetsch	Florida	Columbus
	–	D	Jason Garrison	Florida	Florida
	–	D	Brett Lebda	Toronto	Detroit
	–	D	Jay Leach	San Jose	San Jose
	–	G	Patrick Lalime	Buffalo	Buffalo
	–	LW	Eric Boulton	Atlanta	Atlanta
	–	LW	Brandon Yip	Colorado	Colorado
	–	LW	Kyle Greentree	Washington	Chicago
	–	D	Brian Fahey	Washington	Colorado
	–	D	Joe Corvo	Carolina	Washington
	–	C	Corey Locke	Ottawa	NY Rangers
	–	D	Andrew Hutchinson	Pittsburgh	Dallas
	–	RW	Patrick Eaves	Detroit	Detroit
	–	C	Rob Niedermayer	Buffalo	New Jersey
	–	D	Jeff Schultz	Washington	Washington
	–	C	Jared Ross	Atlanta	Philadelphia
	–	D	Jaime Sifers	Atlanta	Minnesota
	–	C	Ryan Stone	Calgary	Edmonton
July 8	–	RW	Eric Fehr	Washington	Washington
	–	LW	Robbie Earl	Minnesota	Minnesota
July 9	–	RW	Ben Ondrus	Edmonton	Toronto
	–	D	Dan Girardi	NY Rangers	NY Rangers
	–	D	Mark Stuart	Boston	Boston
	–	D	Brett Palin	Nashville	Calgary
July 12	–	D	Niklas Hjalmarsson	Chicago	Chicago
	–	C	Nick Dodge	Carolina	Carolina
	–	RW	Jeremy Williams	NY Rangers	Detroit
	–	C	Aaron Gagnon	Dallas	Dallas
	–	D	Brennan Evans	St. Louis	Anaheim
	–	D	Shane O'Brien	Vancouver	Vancouver
	–	LW	Tanner Glass	Vancouver	Vancouver
	–	C	Alexandre Bolduc	Vancouver	Vancouver
	–	G	Tyler Weiman	Vancouver	Colorado
July 13	–	G	Devan Dubnyk	Edmonton	Edmonton
	–	D	Shawn Belle	Edmonton	Montreal
	–	LW	Daniel Carcillo	Philadelphia	Philadelphia
	–	RW	Jared Boll	Columbus	Columbus
	–	D	Derek Smith	Ottawa	Ottawa
	–	C	Maxim Lapierre	Montreal	Montreal
	–	D	Mathieu Carle	Montreal	Montreal
	–	RW	James Wyman	Montreal	Montreal
	–	RW	Chris Conner	Pittsburgh	Pittsburgh

SIGNING DATE		POS.	PLAYER	SIGNED BY	PREVIOUS ORGANIZATION
July 14	–	LW	J.F. Jacques	Edmonton	Edmonton
	–	G	Josh Harding	Minnesota	Minnesota
	–	RW	Brian Willsie	Washington	Colorado
	–	C	Brodie Dupont	NY Rangers	NY Rangers
	–	LW	Derek Whitmore	Buffalo	Buffalo
	–	G	Tyler Plante	Florida	Florida
	–	LW	Kenndal McArdle	Florida	Florida
	–	D	Brendan Mikkelson	Anaheim	Anaheim
	–	C	Jay Beagle	Washington	Washington
	–	D	Zach Miskovic	Washington	Washington
	–	D	Patrick McNeill	Washington	Washington
	–	RW	Andrew Gordon	Washington	Washington
	–	D	Bryan Rodney	Carolina	Carolina
July 15	–	D	Michael Sauer	NY Rangers	NY Rangers
	–	G	Anton Khudobin	Minnesota	Minnesota
	–	D	Dustin Kohn	NY Islanders	NY Islanders
	–	C	Robbie Schremp	NY Islanders	NY Islanders
	–	D	Adam McQuaid	Boston	Boston
	–	C	Gregory Campbell	Boston	Boston
	–	C	Blair Jones	Tampa Bay	Tampa Bay
	–	G	Justin Pogge	Carolina	Carolina
	–	D	Sean Sullivan	San Jose	Phoenix
	–	LW	T.J. Trevelyan	San Jose	San Jose
	–	D	Theo Peckham	Edmonton	Edmonton
	–	D	Derek Meech	Detroit	Detroit
	–	D	Danny Richmond	Toronto	Chicago
	–	RW	Joey Crabb	Toronto	Chicago
	–	G	Matt Keetley	Calgary	Calgary
	–	C	David Desharnais	Montreal	Montreal
	–	D	Tyson Strachan	St. Louis	St. Louis
	–	LW	Tom Sestito	Columbus	Columbus
July 16	–	C	Nate Thompson	Tampa Bay	Tampa Bay
	–	C	Ryan O'Marra	Edmonton	Edmonton
	–	C	Chad Kolarik	Columbus	Columbus
	–	RW	Raymond Sawada	Dallas	Dallas
	–	C	Paul Szczechura	Tampa Bay	Tampa Bay
	–	C	Jamie Lundmark	Nashville	NY Rangers
	–	D	Corey Potter	Pittsburgh	NY Rangers
	–	D	Sergei Kolosov	Detroit	Detroit
	–	C	T.J. Hensick	St. Louis	St. Louis
	–	LW	Gregory Stewart	Edmonton	Montreal
	–	D	Trevor Ludwig	Dallas	Dallas
	–	D	Maxime Fortunus	Dallas	Dallas
	–	D	Brad Lukowich	Dallas	Vancouver
	–	RW	Tim Conboy	Buffalo	Carolina
July 17	–	C	Brad Richardson	Los Angeles	Los Angeles
	–	D	Gord Baldwin	Calgary	Calgary
	–	RW	Kris Chucko	Calgary	Calgary
July 18	–	D	Matt Pelech	Calgary	Calgary
	–	LW	Rich Clune	Los Angeles	Los Angeles
	–	C	Trevor Lewis	Los Angeles	Los Angeles
	–	C	Corey Elkins	Los Angeles	Los Angeles
	–	C	Marc-Andre Cliche	Los Angeles	Los Angeles
July 19	–	RW	Ryan Reaves	St. Louis	St. Louis
July 20	–	LW	Stefan Meyer	Calgary	Phoenix
	–	C	Ryan Russell	Montreal	Montreal
	–	G	Cedrick Desjardins	Montreal	Montreal
	–	LW	Brett Sutter	Calgary	Calgary
	–	D	Brett Carson	Carolina	Carolina
July 21	–	RW	Jeremy Yablonski	NY Islanders	Ottawa
	–	RW	Patrick Kaleta	Buffalo	Buffalo
	–	LW	Nick Foligno	Ottawa	Ottawa
	–	LW	David Perron	St. Louis	St. Louis
	–	D	Danny Syvret	Anaheim	Philadelphia
July 22	–	RW	Jannik Hansen	Vancouver	Vancouver
	–	G	J.P. Lamoureux	Calgary	Buffalo
	–	D	Grant Clitsome	Columbus	Columbus
	–	D	Dan Jancevski	Philadelphia	Dallas
	–	LW	Matthew Clackson	Philadelphia	Philadelphia
	–	RW	David Laliberte	Philadelphia	Philadelphia
	–	C	Darroll Powe	Philadelphia	Philadelphia
	–	C	Cody Bass	Ottawa	Ottawa

SIGNING DATE		POS.	PLAYER	SIGNED BY	PREVIOUS ORGANIZATION
	–	G	Ondrej Pavelec	Atlanta	Atlanta
July 23	–	C	Marc-Antoine Pouliot	Tampa Bay	Edmonton
	–	LW	Fabian Brunnstrom	Dallas	Dallas
July 25	–	LW	Chris Durno	Tampa Bay	Colorado
July 26	–	LW	Alexandre Picard	Phoenix	Phoenix
	–	D	Ryan Parent	Nashville	Philadelphia
	–	LW	Mason Raymond	Vancouver	Vancouver
July 27	–	LW	Tomas Fleischmann	Washington	Washington
	–	C	Gilbert Brule	Edmonton	Edmonton
	–	LW	Alexei Ponikarovsky	Los Angeles	Pittsburgh
	–	LW	Alexander Frolov	NY Rangers	Los Angeles
	–	LW	Matt Moulson	NY Islanders	NY Islanders
July 28	–	LW	Ben Eager	Atlanta	Chicago
	–	LW	Bryan Bickell	Chicago	Chicago
	–	RW	Jack Skille	Chicago	Chicago
	–	D	Anton Stralman	Columbus	Columbus
	–	D	Mark Fraser	New Jersey	New Jersey
July 29	–	C	Peter Regin	Ottawa	Ottawa
	–	G	Peter Mannino	Atlanta	Atlanta
	–	LW	Tim Kennedy	Buffalo	Buffalo
	–	LW	Andrew Ladd	Atlanta	Chicago
	–	D	Mike Vernace	Tampa Bay	Atlanta
	–	D	Mathieu Roy	Tampa Bay	Columbus
	–	D	Vladimir Mihalik	Tampa Bay	Tampa Bay
July 30	–	D	Chris Campoli	Ottawa	Ottawa
	–	D	Alex Henry	Montreal	Montreal
	–	C	Dominic Moore	Tampa Bay	Montreal
	–	D	Ian White	Calgary	Calgary
	–	RW	Blake Wheeler	Boston	Boston
July 31	–	G	Jeff Deslauriers	Edmonton	Edmonton
	–	D	Alexandre Picard	Montreal	Carolina
	–	RW	Devin Setoguchi	San Jose	San Jose
Aug. 2	–	D	Shaone Morrisonn	Buffalo	Washington
	–	D	Andy Sutton	Anaheim	Ottawa
	–	G	Marty Turco	Chicago	Dallas
	–	D	Erik Johnson	St. Louis	St. Louis
Aug. 3	–	D	Mike Weaver	Florida	St. Louis
	–	C	Michael Angelidis	Tampa Bay	Carolina
	–	LW	Jon Sim	NY Islanders	NY Islanders
Aug. 4	–	RW	Jamal Mayers	San Jose	Calgary
	–	C	Darren Helm	Detroit	Detroit
	–	D	David Hale	Ottawa	Tampa Bay
	–	RW	Francis Lessard	Ottawa	Phoenix
	–	C	Dave Scatchard	St. Louis	Nashville
	–	G	Hannu Toivonen	Chicago	Chicago
	–	D	Jassen Cullimore	Chicago	Chicago
	–	RW	Hugh Jessiman	Chicago	Nashville
	–	C	Nathan Davis	Chicago	Chicago
	–	C	Evan Brophey	Chicago	Chicago
Aug. 5	–	D	Derek Joslin	San Jose	San Jose
	–	D	Marc-Andre Gragnani	Buffalo	Buffalo
	–	C	Mike Modano	Detroit	Dallas
	–	D	Geoff Kinrade	Ottawa	Ottawa
Aug. 6	–	C	John Madden	Minnesota	Chicago
Aug. 9	–	RW	Teemu Selanne	Anaheim	Anaheim
	–	D	Ruslan Salei	Detroit	Colorado
	–	LW	Liam Reddox	Edmonton	Edmonton
Aug. 10	–	RW	Michael Blunden	Columbus	Columbus
Aug. 11	–	C	Craig Conroy	Calgary	Calgary
	–	D	Dean Arsene	St. Louis	Edmonton
	–	RW	Mark Mancari	Buffalo	Buffalo
	–	LW	Juraj Simek	Tampa Bay	Tampa Bay
	–	D	Jordan Henry	Chicago	Chicago

Trade Register, 2009-10

Aug. 2009

13—Anaheim traded LW **Drew Miller** to Tampa Bay for RW **Evgeny Artyukhin**.

28—San Jose traded D **Daniel Rahimi** and D **Patrick White** to Vancouver for D **Christian Ehrhoff** and D **Brad Lukowich**.

31—Carolina traded C **Bobby Hughes** to NY Islanders for C **Rob Hennigar**.

September 2009

4—Anaheim traded RW **Jason Bailey** to Ottawa for LW **Shawn Weller**.

12—Ottawa traded LW **Dany Heatley** and Ottawa's 5th round choice (D **Isaac MacLeod**) in 2010 Entry Draft to San Jose for RW **Jonathan Cheechoo**, LW **Milan Michalek** and San Jose's 2nd round choice (later traded to NY Islanders, later traded to Chicago – Chicago selected C **Kent Simpson**) in 2010 Entry Draft.

18—Philadelphia traded D **Patrik Hersley** to Nashville for future considerations.

—Boston traded C **Phil Kessel** to Toronto for Toronto's 1st (C **Tyler Seguin**) and 2nd (C **Jared Knight**) round choices in 2010 Entry Draft and a 1st round choice in 2011 Entry Draft.

24—Anaheim traded D **Steve McCarthy** to Atlanta for future considerations.

28—Calgary traded D **Anton Stralman** to Columbus for Columbus' 3rd round choice (C **Max Reinhart**) in 2010 Entry Draft.

October 2009

7—Chicago traded D **Aaron Johnson** to Calgary for LW **Kyle Greentree**.

8—Atlanta traded LW **Jordan LaVallee** to Columbus for future considerations.

18—Boston traded RW **Chuck Kobasew** to Minnesota for RW **Craig Weller**, RW **Alexander Fallstrom** and Minnesota's 2nd round choice in 2011 Entry Draft.

20—Columbus traded RW **Stefan Legein** to Philadelphia for D **Michael Ratchuk**.

—Buffalo traded LW **Daniel Paille** to Boston for Boston's 3rd round choice (C **Kevin Sundher**) in 2010 Entry Draft and future considerations.

November 2009

23—Minnesota traded LW **Benoit Pouliot** to Montreal for LW **Guillaume Latendresse**.

December 2009

1—Montreal traded C **Kyle Chipchura** to Anaheim for a 4th round choice in 2011 Entry Draft.

3—Toronto traded C **Jiri Tlusty** to Carolina for C **Phillipe Paradis**.

8—St. Louis traded D **Brendan Bell** and C **Tomas Kana** to Columbus for LW **Pascal Pelletier**.

28—Columbus traded LW **Jason Chimera** to Washington for RW **Chris Clark** and D **Milan Jurcina**.

January 2010

31—Calgary traded D **Dion Phaneuf**, LW **Fredrik Sjostrom** and D **Keith Aulie** to Toronto for LW **Niklas Hagman**, RW **Jamal Mayers**, C **Matt Stajan** and D **Ian White**.

—Anaheim traded G **Jean-Sebastien Giguere** to Toronto for LW **Jason Blake** and G **Vesa Toskala**.

February 2010

2—NY Rangers traded LW **Christopher Higgins** and RW **Ales Kotalik** to Calgary for D **Olli Jokinen** and LW **Brandon Prust**.

4—Atlanta traded LW **Ilya Kovalchuk**, D **Anssi Salmela** and Atlanta's 2nd round choice (D **Jonathon Merrill**) in 2010 Entry Draft to New Jersey for D **Johnny Oduya**, RW **Niclas Bergfors**, C **Patrice Cormier** and New Jersey's 1st (later traded to Chicago – Chicago selected RW **Kevin Hayes**) and 2nd (later traded to Chicago – Chicago selected D **Justin Holl**) round choices in 2010 Entry Draft.

6—Detroit traded LW **Ville Leino** to Philadelphia for D **Ole-Kristian Tollefsen** and a 5th round choice in 2011 Entry Draft.

7—Carolina traded D **Niclas Wallin** and Carolina's 5th round choice (C **Cody Ferriero**) in 2010 Entry Draft to San Jose for Buffalo's 2nd round choice (previously acquired, Carolina selected D **Mark Alt**) in 2010 Entry Draft.

9—Atlanta traded G **Kari Lehtonen** to Dallas for D **Ivan Vishnevskiy** and Dallas' 4th round choice (LW **Ivan Telegin**) in 2010 Entry Draft.

11—Pittsburgh traded D **Nate Guenin** to St. Louis for D **Steve Wagner**.

—Florida traded C **Dominic Moore** to Montreal for Montreal's 2nd round choice in 2011 Entry Draft.

12—Carolina traded C **Matt Cullen** to Ottawa for D **Alexandre Picard** and Ottawa's 2nd round choice (later traded to Edmonton – Edmonton selected D **Martin Marincin**) in 2010 Entry Draft.

—San Jose traded LW **Jody Shelley** to NY Rangers for future considerations.

—Chicago traded D **Cam Barker** to Minnesota for D **Kim Johnsson** and D **Nick Leddy**.

March 2010

1—Florida traded D **Jordan Leopold** to Pittsburgh for Pittsburgh's 2nd round choice (C **Connor Brickley**) in 2010 Entry Draft.

—Chicago traded G **Joe Fallon** to Pittsburgh for G **Hannu Toivonen** and D **Danny Richmond**.

—Anaheim traded RW **Evgeny Artyukhin** to Atlanta for D **Nathan Oystrick** and future considerations.

—Columbus traded D **Dylan Reese** to NY Islanders for C **Greg Moore**.

—Edmonton traded D **Dennis Grebeshkov** to Nashville for Nashville's 2nd round choice (LW **Curtis Hamilton**) in 2010 Entry Draft.

2—Anaheim traded D **Nick Boynton** to Chicago for future considerations.

—Anaheim traded D **Steven Kampfer** to Boston for future considerations.

—Boston traded D **Cody Wild** to Edmonton for LW **Matt Marquardt**.

—NY Islanders traded D **Andy Sutton** to Ottawa for San Jose's 2nd round choice (previously acquired, later traded to Chicago – Chicago selected G **Kent Simpson**) in 2010 Entry Draft.

3—Anaheim traded D **Ryan Whitney** and Anaheim's 6th round choice (D **Brandon Davidson**) in 2010 Entry Draft to Edmonton for D **Lubomir Visnovsky**.

—Anaheim traded G **Justin Pogge** and future considerations to Carolina for D **Aaron Ward**.

—Anaheim traded G **Vesa Toskala** to Calgary for G **Curtis McElhinney**.

—Anaheim traded C **Petteri Nokelainen** to Phoenix for Phoenix's 6th round choice in 2011 Entry Draft.

—Boston traded D **Derek Morris** to Phoenix for future considerations.

—Boston traded RW **Byron Bitz**, RW **Craig Weller** and Tampa Bay's 2nd round choice (previously acquired, Florida selected D **Alex Petrovic**) in 2010 Entry Draft to Florida for D **Dennis Seidenberg** and D **Matt Bartkowski**.

—Buffalo traded D **Nathan Paetsch** and Vancouver's 2nd round choice (previously acquired, Columbus selected RW **Petr Straka**) in 2010 Entry Draft to Columbus for LW **Raffi Torres**.

—Buffalo traded LW **Clarke MacArthur** to Atlanta for Atlanta's 3rd (D **Jerome Gauthier Leduc**) and 4th (C **Steven Shipley**) round choices in 2010 Entry Draft.

—Calgary traded D **Aaron Johnson** and Calgary's 3rd round choice in 2011 Entry Draft to Edmonton for D **Steve Staios**.

—Calgary traded C **Dustin Boyd** to Nashville for Nashville's 4th round choice (C **Bill Arnold**) in 2010 Entry Draft.

—Calgary traded C **Riley Armstrong** to Detroit for D **Andy Delmore**.

—Carolina traded D **Joe Corvo** to Washington for D **Brian Pothier**, LW **Oskar Oskala** and Washington's 2nd round choice in 2011 Entry draft.

—Carolina traded F **Scott Walker** to Washington for Washington's 7th round choice (later traded to Philadelphia – Philadelphia selected D **Ricard Blidstrand**) in 2010 Entry Draft.

—Carolina traded C **Stephane Yelle** and RW **Harrison Reed** to Colorado for C **Cedric Lalonde-McNicoll** and Colorado's 6th round choice (D **Tyler Stahl**) in 2010 Entry Draft.

—Carolina traded D **Andrew Alberts** to Vancouver for Vancouver's 3rd round choice (D **Austin Levi**) in 2010 Entry Draft.

—Colorado traded LW **Wojtek Wolski** to Phoenix for C **Peter Mueller** and C **Kevin Porter**.

—Columbus traded D **Mila Jurcina** to Washington for future considerations.

—Columbus traded D **Mathieu Roy** to Florida for C **Matt Rust**.

—Columbus traded LW **Fredrik Modin** to Los Angeles for future considerations.

—Columbus traded LW **Alexandre Picard** to Phoenix for C **Chad Kolarik**.

—Detroit traded C **Kris Newbury** to NY Rangers for LW **Jordan Owens**.

—Los Angeles traded LW **Teddy Purcell** and Florida's 3rd round choice (previously acquired, Florida selected D **Brock Beukeboom**) in 2010 Entry Draft to Tampa Bay for C **Jeff Halpern**.

—Minnesota traded C **Eric Belanger** to Washington for Washington's 2nd round choice (LW **Johan Larsson**) in 2010 Entry Draft.

—Montreal traded RW **Matt D'Agostini** to St. Louis for RW **Aaron Palushaj**.

—NY Rangers traded G **Miika Wiikman** and NY Rangers' 7th round choice in 2011 Entry Draft to Phoenix for D **Anders Eriksson**.

—Phoenix traded D **Matt Jones** and Phoenix's 4th (later traded to Washington – Washington selected G **Phillip Grubauer**) and 7th (later traded to Edmonton – Edmonton selected F **Kellen Jones**) round choices in 2010 Entry Draft to Toronto for RW **Lee Stempniak**.

- Pittsburgh traded D **Chris Peluso** to Toronto for Toronto's 6th round choice (D **Joe Rogalski**) in 2010 Entry Draft.
- St. Louis traded C **Yan Stastny** to Vancouver for LW **Pierre-Cedric Labrie**.
- Toronto traded D **Martin Skoula** to New Jersey for New Jersey's 5th round choice (C **Sam Carrick**) in 2010 Entry Draft.
- Toronto traded G **Joey MacDonald** to Anaheim for Anaheim's 7th round choice in 2011 Entry Draft.
- Vancouver traded D **Mathieu Schneider** to Phoenix for D **Sean Zimmerman** and future considerations.

May 2010

13 – Phoenix traded RW **Jared Staal** to Carolina for Nashville's 5th round choice (previously acquired, Phoenix selected G **Louis Domingue**) in 2010 Entry Draft.
25 – NY Islanders traded D **Jyri Niemi** to NY Rangers for NY Rangers 6th round choice (later traded to Atlanta – Atlanta selected C **Tanner Lane**) in 2010 Entry Draft.
28 – Anaheim traded G **Mattias Modig** to Pittsburgh for Montreal's 6th round choice (previously acquired, Anaheim selected D **Kevin Lind**) in 2010 Entry Draft.

June 2010

17 – Montreal traded G **Jaroslav Halak** to St. Louis for C **Lars Eller** and RW **Ian Schultz**.
- Colorado traded C **Julian Talbot** to St. Louis for C **T.J. Hensick**.
19 – Nashville traded C **Jason Arnott** to New Jersey for RW **Matt Halischuk** and New Jersey's 2nd round choice in 2011 Entry Draft.
- Nashville traded D **Dan Hamhuis** to Philadelphia for D **Ryan Parent** and future considerations.
21 – San Jose traded RW **Brad Staubitz** to Minnesota for Minnesota's 5th round choice (C **Freddie Hamilton**) in 2010 Entry Draft.
22 – Florida traded C **Nathan Horton** and LW **Gregory Campbell** to Boston for D **Dennis Wideman**, Boston's 1st round choice (later traded to Los Angeles – Los Angeles selected D **Derek Forbort**) in 2010 Entry Draft and Boston's 3rd round choice in 2011 Entry Draft.
23 – Atlanta traded D **Michael Vernace**, LW **Brett Sterling** and Atlanta's 7th round choice (**Lee Moffie**) in 2010 Entry Draft to San Jose for future considerations.
24 – Chicago traded LW **Dustin Byfuglien**, C **Ben Eager**, D **Brent Sopel** and RW **Akim Aliu** to Atlanta for C **Marty Reasoner**, LW **Jeremy Morin**, RW **Joey Crabb** and New Jersey's 1st (previously acquired, Chicago selected RW **Kevin Hayes**) and 2nd (D **Justin Holl**) round choices in 2010 Entry Draft.
- Chicago traded C **Colin Fraser** to Edmonton for Edmonton's 6th round choice (C **Mirko Hofflin**) in 2010 Entry Draft.
25 – Los Angeles traded its 1st round choice (C **Nick Bjugstad**) and Philadelphia's 2nd round choice (previously acquired, later traded to Minnesota – Minnesota selected LW **Jason Zucker**) in 2010 Entry Draft to Florida for Boston's 1st round choice (previously acquired, Los Angeles selected D **Derek Forbort**) in 2010 Entry Draft.
- NY Islanders traded their 2nd round choice (LW **Ludvig Rensfeldt**) and San Jose's 2nd round choice (previously acquired, Chicago selected G **Kent Simpson**) in 2010 Entry Draft to NY Islanders for Chicago's 1st round choice (C **Brock Nelson**) in 2010 Entry Draft.
- St. Louis traded D **David Rundblad** to Ottawa for Ottawa's 1st round choice (RW **Vladimir Tarasenko**) in 2010 Entry Draft.
- Vancouver traded RW **Michael Grabner**, RW **Steve Bernier** and its 1st round choice (C **Quinton Howden**) in 2010 Entry Draft to Florida for D **Keith Ballard** and RW **Victor Oreskovich**.
- Montreal traded its 1st (G **Mark Visentin**) and 2nd (C **Oscar Lindberg**) round choices in 2010 Entry Draft to Phoenix for Phoenix's 1st round choice (D **Jared Tinordi**) and Buffalo's 4th round choice (previously acquired, Montreal selected **Mark MacMillan**) in 2010 Entry Draft.
- Philadelphia traded the rights to D **Dan Hamhuis** to Pittsburgh for a 3rd round choice in 2011 Entry Draft.
- Florida traded Boston's 1st round choice (previously acquired, Los Angeles selected D **Derek Forbort**) in 2010 Entry Draft to Los Angeles for Los Angeles' 1st round choice (C **Nick Bjugstad**) and Philadelphia's 2nd round choice (previously acquired, later traded to Minnesota – Minnesota selected LW **Jason Zucker**) in 2010 Entry Draft.
26 – NY Rangers traded D **Bobby Sanguinetti** to Carolina for Carolina's 6th round choice (RW **Jesper Fasth**) in 2010 Entry Draft and Washington's 2nd round choice (previously acquired) in 2011 Entry Draft.
- Anaheim traded RW **Mike Brown** to Toronto for Toronto's 5th round choice (RW **Chris Wagner**) in 2010 Entry Draft.
- Edmonton traded C **Riley Nash** to Carolina for Ottawa's 2nd round choice (previously acquired, Edmonton selected **Martin Marincin**) in 2010 Entry Draft.

- Toronto traded C **Jimmy Hayes** to Chicago for Calgary's 2nd round choice (previously acquired, Toronto selected LW **Brad Ross**) in 2010 Entry Draft.
- San Jose traded G **Henrik Karlsson** to Calgary for Calgary's 6th round choice (D **Konrad Abeltshauser**) in 2010 Entry Draft.
- Philadelphia traded C **Jonathan Matsumoto** to Carolina for Washington's 7th round choice (previously acquired, Philadelphia selected D **Ricard Blidstrand**) in 2010 Entry Draft.
- Colorado traded its 2nd round choice (C **Tyler Toffoli**) in 2010 Entry Draft to Los Angeles for Los Angeles' 2nd (G **Calvin Pickard**) and 4th (later traded to Dallas – Dallas selected D **Alex Theriau**) round choices in 2010 Entry Draft.
- Florida traded Philadelphia's 2nd round choice (previously acquired, Minnesota selected LW **Jason Zucker**) in 2010 Entry Draft to Minnesota for Minnesota's 3rd (RW **Joe Basaraba**) and 4th (RW **Joonas Donskoi**) round choices in 2010 Entry Draft.
- Dallas traded its 3rd round choice (LW **Michael Bournival**) in 2010 Entry Draft to Colorado for Colorado's 3rd round choice (LW **Alexander Guptill**) and Los Angeles' 4th (previously acquired, Dallas selected D **Alex Theriau**) in 2010 Entry Draft.
- Los Angeles traded its 3rd round choice (C **Sondre Olden**) in 2010 Entry Draft to Toronto for Toronto's 3rd round choice in 2012 Entry Draft.
- Toronto traded Phoenix's 4th round choice (previously acquired, Washington selected C **Caleb Herbert**) in 2010 Entry Draft to Washington for Washington's 4th (LW **Daniel Brodin**) and 5th (later traded back to Washington – Washington selected D **Samuel Carrier**) round choices in 2010 Entry Draft.
- NY Islanders traded their 6th round choice (D **Kendall McFaull**) and NY Rangers' 6th round choice (previously acquired, Atlanta selected C **Tanner Lane**) in 2010 Entry Draft to Atlanta for Atlanta's 5th round choice in 2011 Entry Draft.
- Atlanta traded its 6th round choice (LW **Maxim Kitsyn**) in 2010 Entry Draft to Los Angeles for Los Angeles' 6th (D **Sebastian Owuya**) and 7th (D **Peter Stoykewych**) round choices in 2010 Entry Draft.
- Toronto traded Phoenix's 7th round choice (previously acquired, Edmonton selected F **Kellen Jones**) in 2010 Entry Draft to Edmonton for Edmonton's 6th round choice in 2011 Entry Draft.
- Chicago traded its 7th round choice (D **Zach Trotman**) in 2010 Entry Draft to Boston for Boston's 7th round choice in 2011 Entry Draft.
- Pittsburgh traded its 7th round choice (RW **Chris Crane**) in 2010 Entry Draft to San Jose for San Jose's 7th round choice in 2011 Entry Draft.
28 – Phoenix traded C **Daniel Winnik** to Colorado for a 4th round choice in 2012 Entry Draft.
29 – Montreal traded LW **Sergei Kostitsyn** to Nashville for G **Dan Ellis** and C **Dustin Boyd**.
30 – Phoenix traded C **Jim Vandermeer** to Edmonton for C **Patrick O'Sullivan**.
- Calgary traded RW **Jason Jaffray** to Anaheim for C **Logan MacMillan**.
- Chicago traded LW **Kris Versteeg** and LW **Bill Sweatt** to Toronto for LW **Viktor Stalberg**, C **Phillipe Paradis** and C **Christopher DiDomenico**.

July 2010

1 – Tampa Bay traded D **Andrej Meszaros** to Philadelphia for a 2nd round choice in 2012 entry Draft.
- Atlanta traded D **Ivan Vishnevskiy** and a 2nd round choice in 2011 Entry Draft to Chicago for LW **Andrew Ladd**.
9 – NY Rangers traded F **Aaron Voros** and F **Ryan Hillier** to Anaheim for D **Steve Eminger**.
19 – Anaheim traded D **Matt McCue** to NY Rangers for LW **Tomas Zaborsky**.
- Philadelphia traded LW **Simon Gagne** to Tampa Bay for D **Matt Walker** and a 4th round choice in 2011 Entry Draft.
22 – Chicago traded C **Marty Reasoner** to Florida for C **Jeff Taffe**.
28 – St. Louis traded LW **D.J. King** to Washington for LW **Stefan Della Rovere**.
30 – Anaheim traded D **James Wisniewski** to Anaheim for an optional 3rd round choice in 2011 Entry Draft.

August 2010

2 – Atlanta traded C **Todd White** to NY Rangers for LW **Donald Brashear** and LW **Patrick Rissmiller**.
3 – St. Louis traded D **T.J. Fast** to Florida for LW **Graham Mink**.
5 – Nashville traded F **Mike Santorelli** to Florida for a conditional 5th round choice in 2011 Entry Draft.

Trades and free agent signings after Aug. 14, 2010 are listed on page 609.

League Abbreviations

AHA ....Alberta Amateur Hockey Association
AAHL ....Alaska Amateur Hockey League
AASHA............Alaska All-Stars Hockey Association
ACHA ....American Collegiate Hockey Association
ACHL ....Atlantic Coast Hockey League
AFHL ....American Frontier Hockey League
AH ....Atlantic Hockey
AHL ....American Hockey League
AJHL ....Alberta Junior Hockey League
ALIH ....Asia League Ice Hockey
Alpenliga ....Alpenliga (Austria, Italy, Slovenia 1994-1999)
AMHA............Alberta Minor Hockey Association
AMBHL ....Alberta Major Bantam Hockey League
AMHL ....Alberta Midget AAA Hockey League
AUAA.............Atlantic University Athletic Association
AtJHL ....Atlantic Junior Hockey League
AWHL ....American West Hockey League
AYHL.............Atlantic Youth Hockey League
BCAHA ....British Columbia Amateur Hockey Association
BCHL ....British Columbia (Junior) Hockey League (also BCJHL)
BCMML ....British Columbia Major Midget League
CABHL...........Central Alberta Bantam Hockey League
CBHL ....Calgary Bantam Hockey League
CCHA ....Central Collegiate Hockey Association
CEGEP ....Quebec College Prep
CHA...............College Hockey America
CHL ....Central Hockey League
CIS.................Commonwealth of Independent States
CIS.................Canadian Interuniversity Sport
CJHL ....Central Junior A Hockey League
CMHA............Calgary Minor Hockey Association
ColHL.............Colonial Hockey League
CSHL ....Central States Hockey League
CSJHL ....Central States Junior Hockey League
CWUAA ....Canadian Western University Athletic Association
ECAC ....Eastern College Athletic Conference
ECACHL ....ECAC Hockey League
ECHL..............East Coast Hockey League
EEHL..............Eastern European Hockey League
EJHL..............Eastern Junior Hockey League
EMHA ....Edmonton Minor Hockey Association
EmJHL ....Empire Junior B Hockey League
EuroHL...........European Hockey League
Exhib. ....Exhibition Games, Series or Season
GLHL..............Great Lakes Hockey League
GNML ....Greater North Midget League
GPAC ....Great Plains Athletic Conference
GTHL ....Greater Toronto Hockey League
H-East.............Hockey East
HJHL ....Heritage Junior Hockey League
High-XX ....High School (state/province)
IEHL...............Internationale Eishockey Liga
IHL.................International Hockey League
KIJHL ....Kootenay International Junior B Hockey League
LCJHL.............Little Caesar's Junior Hockey League
MAAC............Metro Atlantic Athletic Conference
MAHA............Manitoba Amateur Hockey Association
MAHL ....Mid America Hockey League
MBAHL ....Metropolitan Boston Amateur Hockey League
MBHL ....Metropolitan Boston Hockey League
MEHL.............Midwest Elite Hockey League
Metro-HL ....Metro Hockey League
MIAC ....Minnesota Intercollegiate Athletic Conference
Minor-XX ....Minor/Youth hockey (state/province)
MJHL ....Manitoba Junior Hockey League
MJrHL ....Maritime Junior A Hockey League
MMBHL ....Manitoba Major Bantam Hockey League
MMHL ....Manitoba Midget AAA Hockey League
MMHL ....Michigan Minor Hockey League
MMMHL ....Manitoba Minor Midget Hockey League
MNHL ....Michigan National Hockey League
MtJHL ....Metropolitan Junior Hockey League (New York)
MTJHL............Metropolitan Toronto Junior Hockey League
MTHL.............Metro Toronto Hockey League

MWEHL ....Midwest Elite Hockey League
NAHL ....North American Hockey League (Tier I Junior)
NAJHL............North American Junior Hockey League
Nat-Team ....National Team (also Nt.-Team)
NBAHA ....New Brunswick Amateur Hockey Association
NBMHL..........New Brunswick Midget Hockey League
NBPEI ....New Brunswick Prince Edward Island Midget Hockey League
NCAA ....National Collegiate Athletic Association
NCHA ....Northern Collegiate Hockey Association
NEJHL ....New England Junior Hockey League
NFAHA ....Newfoundland Amateur Hockey Association
NHL ....National Hockey League
NJCAA ....National Junior Collegiate Athletic Association
NOBHL...........Northern Ontario Bantam Hockey League
NOHA ....Northern Ontario Hockey Association
NOJHA ....Northern Ontario Junior Hockey Association
NOJHL ....Northern Ontario Junior Hockey League
NSBHL ....Nova Scotia Bantam Hockey League
NSMHL ....Nova Scotia Midget AAA Hockey League
NTHL ....North Texas Hockey League
NWJHL ....Northwest Junior B Hockey League
NYJHL............New York Junior Hockey League
OCJHL............Ontario Central Junior A Hockey League
OHA ....Ontario Hockey Association
OHL ....Ontario Hockey League
OJHL-B...........Ontario Junior B Hockey Leagues
OMJHL...........Ontario Major Junior Hockey League
OPJHL ....Ontario Provincial Junior A Hockey League
OUAA ....Ontario Universities Athletic Association
PAHA ....Pennsylvania Amateur Hockey Association
PCJHL ....Pacific Coast Junior Hockey League
PEIHA ....Prince Edward Island Hockey Association
PIJHL..............Pacific International Junior Hockey League
QAA ....Quebec Junior AA
QAAA ....Quebec Midget AAA Hockey League
QAHA ....Quebec Amateur Hockey Association
QJHL ....Quebec Junior Hockey League
QMJHL...........Quebec Major Junior Hockey League
QNAHL ....(Quebec) North American Hockey League
Q-RHL............(Quebec) Richelieu Elite Hockey League
QSPHL ....Quebec Semi-Pro Hockey League
RAMHL ....Rural Alberta Midget Hockey League
RMJHL ....Rocky Mountain Junior Hockey League
SAHA.............Saskatchewan Amateur Hockey Association
SAMHL ....Southern Alberta Midget Hockey League
SBHL ....Saskatchewan Bantam Hockey League
SCAHA...........Southern California Amateur Hockey Association
SIJHL ....Superior International Junior Hockey League
SJHL...............Saskatchewan Junior Hockey League
SMBHL...........Saskatchewan Major Bantam Hockey League
SMHL.............Saskatchewan Midget AAA Hockey League
SMMHL..........Saskatchewan Minor Midget Hockey League
SPHL..............Southern Professional Hockey League
SSJHL.............South Saskatchewan Junior B Hockey League
SSMHL ....South Saskatchewan Minor Hockey League
SunHL ....Sunshine Hockey League
T1EHL............Tier 1 Elite Hockey League
TBAHA...........Thunder Bay Amateur Hockey Association
TBJHL.............Thunder Bay Junior Hockey League
TBMHL...........Thunder Bay Midget Hockey League
U-17 ....Under 17
U-18 ....Under 18
UHL ....United Hockey League
UMEHL ....Upper Midwest Elite Hockey League
UMHSEL ....Upper Midwest High School Elite League
USAHA ....United States Amateur Hockey Association
USHL ....United States (Junior A) Hockey League
VIJHL ....Vancouver Island Junior Hockey League
WCHA ....Western Collegiate Hockey Association
WCHL ....West Coast Hockey League
WHL ....Western Hockey League
WNYHA ....Western New York Hockey Association
WPHL ....Western Professional Hockey League
WSJHL ....Western States Junior Hockey League

Contributors

The NHL Official Guide & Record Book is produced with the help of many.
Special thanks to: Manny Almela, Tom Annelin, Terry Bangen, Jim Barhydt, John Batchelor, Jacob Bestebroer, Bill Bestwick, Wes Bolin, Bob Borgen, Minako Borgen, Andre Brin (Hockey Canada), Mark Calandra, Craig Campbell, Hugh Campbell, Paul Capizzano, Jason Chaimovitch (AHL), Michael Chraba, Des Christopher, Terry Cowie, John Craig, Brad Curle, Bill Currie, Brian Day, Michael Delay, Denis Demers (QMJHL), Chris Denardo, Jeff Dubois, Kari-Ann Faubion, Dave Fischer (USA Hockey), Ernie Fitzsimmons, Cory Flett (WHL), Peter Flynn, Marguerite Focht, Jeremy Friesen, Paul Friesen, Vernon Frizzell, Rob Gagnon, Stu Hackel, Sandi Henning, Dale "Duner" Hladun, Hockey Hall of Fame, www.hockey-reference.com, Nancy Hughes, Mark Hunter, Peter Jagla, Christy Jeffries (USA Hockey), Paul Jones, Edward Krajewski (ECAC), Igor Kuperman, Bob Lekun, Paul Lewicki, Jeff Lundquist, Jim McKellar, Roberta McLain, Dave McNaught, Len McNeely, Kathy Merkel, Molly Merrell (ECHL), Bruce Moar, Herb Morell (OHL), Dan Mulhausen, Jeff Nash (Hockey Canada), NCAA Conference and School Sports Information Departments, NHL Broadcasters' Association, NHL Central Registry, NHL Officiating, NHL Players' Association, Frank Nelson, Blair Noel, Jim O'Neill, Chris Peters (U.S. National Team Development Program), Fred Pletsch (CCHA), Steven Poapst, www.pointstreak.com, Tammy Prasad, Rick Prasad, Dan Price, Phil Pritchard, Mary Beth Proctor, Garry Punchard, Pearl Rajwanth, Marnel Rasmussen, Alex Riazanov, David Rourke (AH), Danna Rudniski, Paul Santi, Frank Scarpaci, Martin Schmid, Chris Smith (CHA), Susan Snow, SIHR, Peter Souris (Hockey East), Doug Spencer (WCHA), Brian Urlick, Tom Vannelli, Tom Ward, Jesse Watts (WHL), Paul Wilkinson (OPJHL), Jason Wilson, Jim Wright, Jack Zahr.

Photo Credits

Hockey Hall of Fame: Various Collections. Getty Images: Graig Abel, Justin K. Aller, Scott Audette, Brian Babineau, Steve Babineau, Brian Bahr, Bruce Bennett, Scott Cunningham, Jonathan Daniel, Melchior DiGiacomo, Andy Devlin, Greg Flume, Gregg Forwerck, Noah Graham, Jeff Gross, Harry How, Jed Jacobsohn, Glenn James, Jimmy Jeong, Robert Laberge, Francois Lacasse, Rich Lam, Mitchell Layton, Phillip MacCallum, Andy Marlin, Michael Martin, Jim McIsaac, Donald Miralle, Doug Pensinger, Scott Pilling, Len Redkoles, Dave Reginek, Mike Ridewood, Andre Ringuette, Debora Robinson, John Russell, Jamie Sabau, Eliot J. Schechter, Harry Scull Jr., Gregory Shamus, Bill Smith, Dave Sandford, Mike Stobe, Gerry Thomas, Jeff Vinnick, Bill Wippert. Additional NHL team photographers: Doug Benc, Andrew D. Bernstein, Mark Buckner, Andy Devlin, Bob Fisher, Norm Hall, Bruce Kluckhon, Juan Ocampo, Don Smith, Rebecca Taylor, Rocky Widner.

Special thanks to Paul Michinard, Getty Images.

Researchers and historians: contact the Society for International Hockey Research www.sihrhockey.org

THREE STAR SELECTION...

NHL OFFICIAL GUIDE IS PLEASED TO OFFER...

NHL PUBLICATIONS
ORDER FORM

2010-11 editions available now

2011-12 editions available Sept. 2011

Please send...

☐ ☐ copies of the NHL Guide & Record Book

☐ ☐ copies of the NHL Yearbook magazine

☐ ☐ copies of the NHL Rule Book

PRICES:	CANADA	USA	OVERSEAS	
GUIDE & RECORD BOOK	$ 29.95	$ 27.95	$ 27.95	U.S.$
Handling (per copy)	$ 11.00	$ 18.00	$ 30.00	U.S.$
13% HST	$ 5.32	—	—	
Total (per copy)	**$ 46.27**	**$ 45.95**	**$ 57.95**	**U.S.$**
Add Extra for air/express	$ 10.00	$ 13.00	$22.00	U.S.$
YEARBOOK	$ 9.99	$ 9.99	$ 9.99	U.S.$
Handling (per copy)	$ 9.00	$ 12.00	$ 16.00	U.S.$
13% HST	$ 2.47	—	—	
Total (per copy)	**$ 21.46**	**$ 21.99**	**$ 25.99**	**U.S.$**
Add Extra for air/express	$ 4.00	$ 5.00	$ 10.00	U.S.$
RULE BOOK	$ 15.95	$ 14.95	$ 14.95	U.S.$
Handling (per copy)	$ 6.00	$ 8.50	$ 12.00	U.S.$
13% HST	$ 2.85	—	—	
Total (per copy)	**$ 24.80**	**$ 23.45**	**$ 26.95**	**U.S.$**
Add Extra for air/express	$ 3.30	$ 4.00	$8.00	U.S.$

Charge my   ☐ Visa   ☐ MasterCard/EuroCard   ☐ Am Ex

Credit Card Account Number   Expiry Date (important)

_____

Signature

☐ Enclosed is my cheque/check or money order.

A note to U.S. and overseas buyers paying by money order: Please send an International Money Order that can be cashed in Canada.

Name

_____

Address

_____

_____

Province/State   Postal/Zip Code

IN CANADA
Mail completed form to:
NHL Official Guide
194 Dovercourt Rd.
Toronto, Ontario
M6J 3C8

IN USA
Mail completed form to:
NHL Official Guide
194 Dovercourt Rd.
Toronto, Ontario
CANADA M6J 3C8
Remit in U.S. funds

OVERSEAS
Mail completed form to:
NHL Official Guide
194 Dovercourt Rd.
Toronto, Ontario
CANADA M6J 3C8
**Money order or
credit card only.
No cheques please.**

DELIVERY: Canada & USA – up to three weeks. Overseas – up to five weeks.
Make cheque/check payable to NHL Publications

1. THE NHL OFFICIAL GUIDE & RECORD BOOK

The NHL's authoritative information source. 79th year in print. 664 pages. The "Bible of Hockey". Read worldwide. This is the book issued to reporters, broadcasters, scouts and general managers.

2. THE NHL YEARBOOK

200-page, full-color magazine with features on each club. Award winners, All-Stars and special statistics.

3. THE NHL RULE BOOK

Larger format for 2010-11. Coil bound, new diagrams and tables. Combines complete playing rules, with the NHL officiating casebook. Plus rink dimensions and officials' signals.

Free Book List with each order.

SECURE ONLINE ORDERING and many more hockey books available at www.nhlofficialguide.com

3 Ways to Order with your Credit Card :
ONLINE, by FAX or by E-MAIL
ONLINE   www.nhlofficialguide.com
FAX   **416/531-3939** or
(OVERSEAS CUSTOMERS: USE INTERNATIONAL DIALING CODE FOR CANADA)
E-MAIL   **dda.nhl@sympatico.ca**
24 HOURS
PLEASE INCLUDE YOUR CARD'S EXPIRY DATE